Peterson's

How to Get Money for College

Financing Your Future Beyond Federal Aid

2012

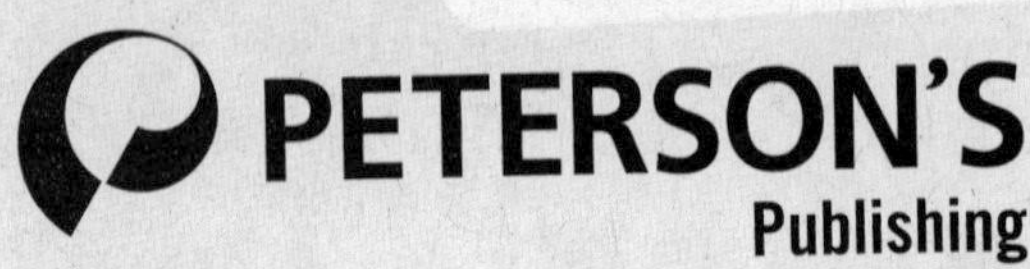

About Peterson's Publishing
Peterson's Publishing provides the accurate, dependable, high-quality education content and guidance you need to succeed. No matter where you are on your academic or professional path, you can rely on Peterson's print and digital publications for the most up-to-date education exploration data, expert test-p0rep tools, and top-notch career success resources—everything you need to achieve your goals.

Visit us online at **www.petersonspublishing.com** and let Peterson's help you achieve your goals.

For more information, contact Peterson's, 2000 Lenox Drive, Lawrenceville, NJ 08648; 800-338-3282 Ext. 54229.

Previous editions published as *Peterson's How to Get Money for College* © 2009, 2010; *Peterson's College Money Handbook* © 1983, 1984, 1985, 1986, 1987, 1988, 1989, 1990, 1991, 1997, 1998, 1999, 2000, 2001 2002, 2003, 2004, 2005, 2006, 2007, 2008 and as *Paying Less for College* © 1992, 1993, 1994, 1995, 1996

Bernadette Webster, Director of Publishing; Jill C. Schwartz, Editor; Ken Britschge, Research Project Manager; Nicole Gallo, Research Associate; Phyllis Johnson, Software Engineer; Ray Golaszewski, Publishing Operations Manager; Linda M. Williams, Composition Manager

ISSN 1089-831X
ISBN-13: 978-0-7689-3295-9
ISBN-10: 0-7689-3295-5

Printed in the United States of America

10 9 8 7 6 5 4 3 2 1 13 12 11

Twenty-ninth Edition

By producing this book on recycled paper (40% post-consumer waste) 184 trees were saved.

Certified Chain of Custody

60% Certified Fiber Sourcing and 40% Post-Consumer Recycled

www.sfiprogram.org

*This label applies to the text stock.

Sustainability—Its Importance to Peterson's Publishing

What does sustainability mean to Peterson's? As a leading publisher, we are aware that our business has a direct impact on vital resources—most especially the trees that are used to make our books. Peterson's Publishing is proud that its products are certified by the Sustainable Forestry Initiative (SFI) and that all of its books are printed on paper that is 40% post-consumer waste using vegetable-based ink.

Being a part of the Sustainable Forestry Initiative (SFI) means that all of our vendors—from paper suppliers to printers—have undergone rigorous audits to demonstrate that they are maintaining a sustainable environment.

Peterson's Publishing continuously strives to find new ways to incorporate sustainability throughout all aspects of its business.

Other Recommended Titles

Peterson's Best Scholarships for the Best Students
Peterson's Scholarships, Grants & Prizes

Contents

A Note from the Peterson's Editors

The news media seem to constantly remind us that a college education is expensive. It certainly appears to be beyond the means of many Americans. The sticker price for four years at state-supported colleges can be more than $45,000, and private colleges and universities can cost more than $150,000. And these numbers continue to rise.

But there is good news. The system operates to provide the needed money so that most families and students are able to afford a college education while making only a reasonable financial sacrifice. However, because the college financial aid system is complex, finding the money is often easier said than done. That is why the process demands study, planning, calculation, flexibility, filling out forms, and meeting deadlines. Fortunately, for most people, it can produce positive results. There are many ways to manage college costs and many channels through which you can receive help. Be sure to take full advantage of the opportunities that have been opened up to students and their families by the many organizations, foundations, and businesses that have organized to help you with the burden of college expenses.

For nearly forty years, Peterson's has given students and parents the most comprehensive, up-to-date information on how to get their fair share of the financial aid pie. *Peterson's How to Get Money for College* is both a quick reference and a comprehensive resource that puts valuable information about college costs and financial aid opportunities at your fingertips.

- **The ABCs of Paying for College** provides insight into federal financial aid programs that are available, offers an overview of the financial aid landscape, walks you through the process of filing for aid, and provides proven tips on how to successfully navigate the financial aid process to obtain the federal, state, and institutional aid you deserve.
- The **Quick-Reference Chart** offers a snapshot comparison of the financial aid programs available at more than 2,400 four-year institutions across the country.
- The **Profiles of College Financial Aid Programs** provide unbiased financial aid data for each of the more than 2,400 four-year institutions listed.
- The **Appendix** lists the state scholarship and grant programs offered by all fifty states and the District of Columbia.
- The six **Indexes** included in the back of the book allow you to search for specific award programs based on a variety of criteria, including merit-based awards, athletic grants, ROTC programs, and much more.
- The **Special Advertising Section** features ads placed by Peterson's preferred clients. Their financial support helps make it possible for Peterson's Publishing to continue to provide you with the highest-quality educational exploration, test-prep, and career-preparation resources you need to succeed on your educational journey.

Join the Peterson's financial aid conversation on Facebook® at www.facebook.com/pay4college. Peterson's resources are available to help you find your slice of the financial aid pie.

Peterson's publishes a full line of books—financial aid, education exploration, test prep, and career preparation. Peterson's publications can be found at high school guidance offices, college libraries and career centers, and your local bookstore and library. Peterson's books are now also available as eBooks.

We welcome any comments or suggestions you may have about this publication. Your feedback will help us make educational dreams possible for you—and others like you.

The ABCs of Paying for College

A Guide to Financing Your Child's College Education

Don Betterton

Given the lifelong benefit of a college degree (college graduates are projected to earn in a lifetime $1 million more than those with only a high school diploma), higher education is a worthwhile investment. However, it is also an expensive one made even more difficult to manage by cost increases that have outpaced both inflation and gains in family income. This reality of higher education economics is that paying for a child's college education is a dilemma that shows no sign of getting easier.

Because of the high cost involved (even the most inexpensive four-year education at a public institution costs about $10,000 a year), good information about college budgets and strategies for reducing the "sticker price" is essential. You have made a good start by taking the time to read *Peterson's How to Get Money for College*. In the pages that follow, you will find valuable information about the four main sources of aid—federal, state, institutional, and private. Before you learn about the various programs, however, it will be helpful if you have an overview of how the college financial aid system operates and what long-range financing strategies are available.

Financial Aid

Financial aid refers to money that is awarded to a student, usually in a "package" that consists of gift aid (commonly called a scholarship or grant), a student loan, and a campus job.

College Costs

The starting point for organizing a plan to pay for your child's college education is to make a good estimate of the yearly cost of attendance. You can use the **College Cost Worksheet** on the next page to do this.

To estimate your college costs for 2012–13, refer to the tuition and fees and room and board figures shown in the **College Costs At-a-Glance** chart. If your child will commute from your home, use $2500 instead of the college's room and board charges and $900 for transportation. We have used $800 for books and $1500 for personal expenses. Finally, estimate the cost of two round trips if your home is more than a few hundred miles from the college. Add the items to calculate the total budget. You should now have a reasonably good estimate of college costs for 2012–13. (To determine the costs for later years, adding 4 percent per year will probably give you a fairly accurate estimate.)

Do You Qualify for Need-Based Aid?

The next step is to evaluate whether or not you are likely to qualify for financial aid based on need. This step is critical, since more than 90 percent of the yearly total of $128 billion in student aid is awarded only after a determination is made that the family lacks sufficient financial resources to pay the full cost of college on its own. To judge your chance of receiving need-based aid, it is necessary to estimate an Expected Family Contribution (EFC) according to a government formula known as the Federal Methodology (FM). You can estimate how much you will be expected to contribute by referring to the EFC Calculator at http://www.finaid.org/calculators/quickefc.phtml.

Applying for Need-Based Aid

Because the federal government provides about 67 percent of all aid awarded, the application and need evaluation process is controlled by Congress and the U.S. Department of Education. The application is the Free Application for Federal Student Aid, or FAFSA. In addition, nearly every state that offers student assistance uses the federal government's system to award its own aid. Furthermore, in addition to arranging for the payment of federal and state aid, many colleges use the FAFSA to award their own funds to eligible students. (Note: In addition to the FAFSA, some colleges also ask the family to complete the CSS/Financial Aid PROFILE® application.)

The FAFSA is your "passport" to receiving your share of the billions of dollars awarded annually in need-based aid. Even if you're uncertain as to whether or not you qualify for need-based aid, everyone who might need assistance in financing an

College Cost Worksheet

	College 1	College 2	College 3	Commuter College
Tuition and Fees	______	______	______	______
Room and Board	______	______	______	$2,500
Books	$ 800	$ 800	$ 800	$ 750
Personal Expenses	$1,500	$1,500	$1,500	$1,500
Travel	______	______	______	$ 900
Total Budget	______	______	______	______

education should pick up a FAFSA from the high school guidance office after mid-November 2011. This form will ask for 2011 financial data, and it should be filed after January 1, 2012, in time to meet the earliest college or state scholarship deadline. Within two to four weeks after you submit the form, you will receive a summary of the FAFSA information, called the Student Aid Report, or SAR. The SAR will give you the EFC and also allow you to make corrections to the data you submitted.

You can also apply for federal student aid via the Internet using FAFSA on the Web. FAFSA on the Web can be accessed at www.fafsa.ed.gov. Both the student and at least one parent should apply for a federal PIN number at www.pin.ed.gov. The PIN number serves as your electronic signature when applying for aid on the Web. (Note: Many colleges provide the option to apply for early decision or early action admission. If you apply for this before January 1, 2012, which is prior to when the FAFSA can be used, follow the college's instructions. Many colleges use either PROFILE or their own application form for early admission candidates.)

Awarding Aid

About the same time you receive the SAR, the colleges you list will receive your FAFSA information so they can calculate a financial aid award in a package that typically includes aid from at least one of the major sources—federal, state, college, or private. In addition, the award will probably consist of a combination of a scholarship or a grant, a loan, and a campus job. These last two pieces—loan and job—are called self-help aid because they require effort on your child's part (that is, the aid must be either earned through work or paid back later). Scholarships or grants are outright gifts that have no such obligation.

How Need Is Calculated and Aid Is Awarded

	College 1	College 2
Total Cost of Attendance	$10,000	$ 24,000
– Expected Family Contribution	– 5,500	– 5,500
= Financial Need	$ 4,500	$ 18,500
– Grant Aid Awarded	– 675	–14,575
– Campus Job (Work-Study) Awarded	– 1,400	– 1,300
+ Student Loan Awarded	– 2,425	– 2,625
= Unmet Need	0	0

Note: Sometimes an institution is unable to meet all need. The amount of unmet need is called "the gap."

Comparing Financial Aid Awards and Family Contribution Worksheet

	College 1	College 2	College 3
Cost of Attendance	______	______	______
Aid Awarded	______	______	______
Grant/Scholarship	______	______	______
Loan	______	______	______
Job	______	______	______
Total Aid	______	______	______
Expected Family Contribution	______	______	______
Student Contribution	______	______	______
Parent Contribution	______	______	______

It is important that you understand each part of the package. You'll want to know, for example, how much does gift aid provide, the interest rate and repayment terms of the student loan, and how many hours per week the campus job requires. There should be an enclosure with the award letter that answers these questions. If not, make a list of your questions and call or visit the financial aid office.

Once you understand the terms of each item in the award letter, you should turn your attention to the "bottom line"—how much you will have to pay at each college where your child was accepted. In addition to understanding the aid award, this means having a good estimate of the college budget so you can accurately calculate how much you and your child will have to contribute. (Often, an aid package does not cover the entire need.) Colleges differ in how much detail they include in their award notifications. Many colleges provide full information—types and amounts of aid, yearly costs, and the EFC for the parent and student shares. If these important items are missing or incomplete, you can do the work on your own. (See the **Comparing Financial Aid Awards and Family Contribution Worksheet**.) For example, if only the college's direct charges for tuition, room, and board are shown on the award letter, make your own estimate of indirect costs like books, personal expenses, and travel. Then subtract the total aid awarded from the yearly cost to get the EFC. A portion of that amount may be your child's contribution (35 percent of student assets and 50 percent of student earnings over $2200) and the remainder is the parental share. If you can afford this amount at your child's first-choice college, the financial aid system has worked well for you, and your child's college enrollment plans can go forward.

But if you think your EFC is too high, you should contact the college's financial aid office and ask whether additional aid is available. Many colleges, private high-cost colleges in particular, are enrollment-oriented—they are willing to work with families to help make attendance at their institutions possible. Most colleges also allow applicants to appeal their financial aid awards, the budget used for you, or any of the elements used to determine the family contribution, especially if there are extenuating circumstances or if the information has changed since the application was submitted. Some colleges may also reconsider an award based on a "competitive appeal," the submission of a more favorable award letter from another college.

If your appeal is unsuccessful and there is still a gap between the expected family contribution and what you feel you can pay from income and savings, you are left with two choices. One option is for your child to attend a college where paying your share of the bill will not be a problem. (This assumes that an affordable option was included on your child's original list of colleges, a wise admission application strategy.) The second is to look into alternate methods of financing. At this stage, parental loans and tuition payment plans are the best financing options. A parental loan can bring the yearly cost down to a manageable level by spreading payments over a number of years. This is the type of financing that families use when purchasing a home or automobile. A tuition payment plan is essentially a short-term loan and allows you to pay the costs over ten to twelve months. It is an option for families who have the resources available but need help with managing their cash flow.

Non-Need-Based Aid

Regardless of whether you might qualify for a need-based award, it is always worthwhile to look into merit, or non-need, scholarships from sources such as foundations, agencies, religious groups, and service organizations. For a family that isn't eligible for need-based aid, merit scholarships are the only form of gift aid available. If your child later qualifies for a need-based award, a merit scholarship can be quite helpful in providing additional resources if the aid does not fully cover the costs. Even if the college meets 100 percent of need, a merit scholarship reduces the self-help (loan and job) portion of an award.

In searching for merit-based scholarships, keep in mind that there are relatively few awards (compared to those that are need-based), and most of them are highly competitive. Use the following checklist when investigating merit scholarships.

- Take advantage of any scholarships for which your child is automatically eligible based on parents' employer benefits, military service, association or church membership, other affiliations, or student or parent attributes (ethnic background, nationality, etc.). Company or union tuition remissions are the most common examples of these awards.
- Look for other awards for which your child might be eligible based on the previous characteristics and affiliations but where there is a selection process and an application is required. Free computerized searches are available on the Internet. (You should not pay a fee for a scholarship search.) Peterson's free scholarship search can be accessed by logging on to www.petersons.com/finaid. Scholarship directories, such as *Peterson's Scholarships, Grants & Prizes*, which details more than 4,000 scholarship programs, and *Peterson's Best Scholarships for Best Students* are useful resources and can be found in bookstores, high school guidance offices, or public libraries and are also available as eBooks.
- See if your state has a merit scholarship program.
- Look into national scholarship competitions. High school guidance counselors usually know about these scholarships. Examples of these awards are the National Merit® Scholarship Program, the Coca-Cola Scholarship, Gates Millennium Scholars, Intel Science Talent Search, and the U.S. Senate Youth Program.
- ROTC (Reserve Officers' Training Corps) scholarships are offered by the Army, Navy, Air Force, and Marine Corps. A full ROTC scholarship covers tuition, fees, textbook costs and, in some cases, a stipend. Acceptance of an ROTC scholarship entails a commitment to take military science courses and to serve for a specific number of years as an officer in the sponsoring branch of the service. Competition is heavy, and preference may be given to students in certain fields of study, such as engineering, languages, science, and health professions. Application procedures vary by service. Contact an armed services recruiter or high school guidance counselor for further information.
- Investigate community scholarships. High school guidance counselors usually have a list of these awards, and announcements are published in local newspapers. Most common are awards given by service organizations like the American Legion, Rotary International, and the local women's club.
- If your child is strong academically (for example, a National Merit Commended Student or better) or is very talented in fields such as athletics or performing/creative arts, you may want to consider colleges that offer their own merit awards to gifted students they wish to enroll. Refer to the Non-Need Scholarships for Undergraduates index.

In addition to merit scholarships, there are loan and job opportunities for students who do not qualify for need-based aid. Some

Note

A point of clarification about whether to put college savings in your name or your child's: If you are certain that your child will not be a candidate for need-based aid, there may be a tax advantage to accumulating money in his or her name. However, when it comes to maximizing aid eligibility, it is important to understand that student assets are assessed at a 20 percent rate and parental assets at about 5 percent. Therefore, if your college savings are in your child's name, it may be wise to reestablish title to these funds before applying for financial aid. You should contact your financial planner or accountant before making any modifications to your asset structure.

What Is CSS/Financial Aid PROFILE®?

There are many complexities in the financial aid process: knowing which aid is merit-based and which aid is need-based; understanding the difference between grants, loans, and work-study; and determining whether funds are from federal, state, institutional, or private sources.

In addition, the aid application process itself can be confusing. It can involve more than the Free Application for Federal Student Aid (FAFSA) and the Federal Methodology (FM). Many colleges feel that the federal aid system (FAFSA and FM) does not collect or evaluate information thoroughly enough for them to award their own institutional funds. These colleges have made an arrangement with the College Scholarship Service, a branch of the College Board, to establish a separate application system.

The application is called the CSS/Financial Aid PROFILE®, and the need-analysis formula is referred to as the Institutional Methodology (IM). If you apply for financial aid at one of the colleges that uses the PROFILE, the admission material will state that the PROFILE is required in addition to the FAFSA. You should read the information carefully and file the PROFILE to meet the earliest college deadline. Before you can receive the PROFILE, however, you must register, either by phone or through the Web (https://profileonline.collegeboard.com/index.jsp), providing enough basic information so the PROFILE package can be designed specifically for you. The FAFSA is free, but there is a charge for the PROFILE. As with the FAFSA, the PROFILE can be submitted online.

In addition to the requirement by certain colleges that you submit both the FAFSA and PROFILE (when used, the PROFILE is always in addition to the FAFSA; it does not replace it), you should understand that each system has its own method for analyzing a family's ability to pay for college. The main differences between the PROFILE's Institutional Methodology and the FAFSA's Federal Methodology are:

- PROFILE includes equity in the family home as an asset; the FAFSA doesn't.
- PROFILE takes a broader look at assets not included on the FAFSA.
- PROFILE expects a minimum student contribution, usually in the form of summer earnings; the FAFSA has no such minimum.
- PROFILE may collect information on the noncustodial parent; the FAFSA does not.
- PROFILE allows for more professional judgment than the FAFSA. Medical expenses, private secondary school costs, and a variety of special circumstances are considered under PROFILE, subject to the discretion of the aid counselor on campus.
- PROFILE includes information on assets not reported on the FAFSA, including life insurance, annuities, retirement plans, etc.

To summarize: The PROFILE's Institutional Methodology tends to be both more complete in its data collection and more rigorous in its analysis than the FAFSA's Federal Methodology. When IM results are compared to FM results for thousands of applicants, IM will usually come up with a somewhat higher expected parental contribution than FM.

Creditworthiness

If you will be borrowing to pay for your child's college education, making sure you qualify for a loan is critical. For the most part, that means your credit record must be free of default or delinquency. You can check your credit history with one or more of the following three major credit bureaus and clean up any adverse information that appears. The numbers below will offer specific information on what you need to provide to obtain a report. All of the credit bureaus accept credit report requests over their Web sites. You will usually be asked to provide your full name, phone number, social security number, birth date, and addresses for the last five years. You are entitled to a free report from each bureau.

Equifax Credit Information
P.O. Box 740241
Atlanta, GA 30374
800-685-1111
http://www.equifax.com

Trans Union
800-888-4213
http://www.transunion.com

Experian
888-397-3742
http://www.experian.com

of the organizations that sponsor scholarships—for example, the Air Force Aid Society—also provide loans.

Work opportunities during the academic year are another type of assistance that is not restricted to aid recipients. Many colleges will, after assigning jobs to students on aid, open campus positions to all students looking for work. In addition, there are usually off-campus employment opportunities available to everyone.

Financing Your Child's College Education

"Financing" means putting together resources to pay the balance due the college over and above payments from the primary sources of aid—grants, scholarships, student loans, and jobs. Financing strategies are important because the high cost of a college education today often requires a family, whether or not it receives aid, to think about stretching its college payment beyond the four-year period of enrollment. For high-cost colleges, it is not unreasonable to think about a 10-4-10 plan: ten years of saving; four years of paying college bills out of current income, savings, and borrowing; and ten years to repay a parental loan.

Savings

Although saving for college is always a good idea, many families are unclear about its advantages. Some families do not save because after normal living expenses have been covered, they do not have much money to set aside. An affordable but regular savings plan through a payroll deduction is usually the answer to the problem of spending your entire paycheck every month.

The second reason why saving for college is not a high priority is the belief that the financial aid system penalizes a family by lowering aid eligibility. The Federal Methodology of need determination is very kind to families that save. In fact, savings are ignored completely for most families that earn less than $50,000. Savings in the form of home equity, retirement plans, and most annuities are excluded from the calculation. And even when savings are counted, a maximum of 5 percent of the total is expected each year. In other words, if a family has $40,000 in savings after an asset protection allowance is considered, the contribution is no greater than $2000. Given the impact of compound interest, it is easy to see that a long-term savings plan can make paying for college much easier.

A sensible savings plan is important because of the financial advantage of saving compared to borrowing. The amount of money students borrow for college is now greater than the amount they receive in grants and scholarships. With loans becoming so widespread, savings should be carefully considered as an alternative to borrowing. Your incentive for saving is that a dollar saved is a dollar not borrowed.

Borrowing

Once you've calculated your "bottom-line" parental contribution and determined that the amount is not affordable out of your current income and assets, the most likely alternative is borrowing. As of July 1, 2010, as a result of the Health Care and Education Reconciliation Act, federal student loans are no longer made by private lenders under the Federal Family Education Loan (FFEL) Program. Instead, all new federal student loans come directly from the U.S. Department of Education under the Direct Loan Program, which offers subsidized and unsubsidized (Stafford) loans for students, PLUS loans for parents and graduate/professional students, and consolidation loans for both students and parents. For additional information, go online to https://studentloans.gov/myDirectLoan/index.action or call 800-4-FED-AID (toll-free).

For the Direct PLUS Loan, parents must complete a Direct PLUS Loan application and promissory note, contained in a single form that can be obtained from a school's financial aid office. The yearly limit on a PLUS Loan is equal to the student's cost of attendance minus any other financial aid the student receives. For example, if your cost of attendance is $6000, and you receive $4500 in other financial aid, your parents can borrow up to $1500. PLUS loans carry fixed rates fro loans made on or after July 1, 2006. The fixed interest rate for FFEL PLUS loans is 8.5%, and the fixed interest rate for Direct PLUS loans is 7.9%. Interest is charged on a PLUS Loan from the date of the first disbursement until the loan is paid in full. A PLUS Loan made to the parent cannot be transferred to the student. The parent is responsible for repaying the PLUS Loan. For more details about PLUS Loans, visit www.direct.ed.gov/about.html.

Make Financial Aid Work for You

If you are like millions of families that benefit from financial aid, it is likely that your child's college plans can go forward without undue worry about the costs involved. The key is to understand the financial aid system and to follow the best path for your family. The result of good information and good planning should be that you will receive your fair share of the billions of dollars available each year and that the cost of college will not prevent your child from attending.

Don Betterton is a former Director of Undergraduate Financial Aid at Princeton University and a Certified College Planner (CCP).

Federal Financial Aid Programs

There are a number of sources of financial aid available to students: federal and state governments, private agencies, and the colleges themselves. In addition, there are three different forms of aid: grants, earnings, and loans.

The federal government is the single largest source of financial aid for students. In recent years, the U.S. Department of Education's student financial aid programs made more than $80 billion available in loans, grants, and other aid to 14 million students. At present, the available federal grant programs are the Federal Pell Grant and the Federal Supplemental Educational Opportunity Grant (FSEOG). There are two federal loan programs: Federal Perkins Loan Program and the Direct Loan Program. The federal government also has a job program, Federal Work-Study Program (FWS), which helps colleges provide employment for students. In addition to the student aid programs, there are also tuition tax credits and deductions. They are the American Opportunity Credit for freshmen and sophomores, the Lifetime Learning Credit for undergraduate students after their second year, the Tuition and Fees Tax Deduction, and the Student Loan Interest Tax Deduction. Also, there is AmeriCorps. AmeriCorps will pay the interest that is accrued on qualified student loans for members who complete the service program.

The majority of federal higher education loans are made in the Direct Loan Program, which makes available two kinds of loans: loans to students and PLUS loans to parents or to graduate or professional students. These loans are either subsidized or unsubsidized. Subsidized loans are made on the basis of demonstrated student need, and the interest is paid by the government during the time the student is in school. For the unsubsidized (non-need-based) loans and PLUS loans, interest begins to accrue as funds are disbursed.

As a result of the Health Care and Education Reconciliation Act, beginning July 1, 2010, federal student loans will no longer be made by private lenders under the Federal Family Education Loan (FFEL) Program. Instead, all new federal student loans will come directly from the U.S. Department of Education under the Direct Loan Program. This change does not impact the process of applying for federal grants, loans, and work-study opportunities or the amount of federal aid that students are eligible to receive. Students interested in receiving federal student aid should continue to complete a Free Application for Federal Student Aid (FAFSASM) for each school year that they wish to be considered for aid. For more information about applying for federal student aid, call 800-4-FED-AID (toll-free).

Federal Pell Grant

The Federal Pell Grant is the largest grant program; more than 6 million students receive Pell Grants annually. This grant is intended to be the starting point of assistance for lower-income families. Eligibility for a Pell Grant is based on the Expected Family Contribution. The amount you receive will depend on your EFC and the cost of education at the college you will attend. The highest award depends on how much funding the program receives from the government. The maximum for 2010–11 is $5550.

To give you some idea of your possible eligibility for a Pell Grant, the following table may be helpful. The amounts shown are based on a family of four, with one student in college, no emergency expenses, no contribution from student income or assets, and college costs of at least $4050 per year. Pell Grants range from $555 to $5550.

Federal Supplemental Educational Opportunity Grant (FSEOG)

As its name implies, Federal Supplemental Educational Opportunity Grants provide additional need-based federal grant money to supplement the Federal Pell Grant Program. Each participating college is given funds to award to especially needy students. The maximum award is $4000 per year, but the amount you receive depends on the college's awarding policy, the availability of FSEOG funds, the total cost of education, and the amount of other aid awarded.

Federal Financial Aid Programs

Name of Program	Type of Program	Maximum Award Per Year
Federal Pell Grant	need-based grant	$5550
Federal Supplemental Educational Opportunity Grant (FSEOG)	need-based grant	$4000
Federal Work-Study Program (FWS)	need-based part-time job	no maximum
Federal Perkins Loan Program	need-based loan	$5500
Subsidized Federal Direct Loan	need-based student loan	$3500 (first year)
Unsubsidized Federal Direct Loan	non-need-based student loan	$5500 (first year, dependent student)

Federal Work-Study Program (FWS)

This program provides jobs for students who demonstrate need. Salaries are paid by funds from the federal government as well as the college. Students work on an hourly basis on or off campus and must be paid at least the federal minimum wage. Students may earn only up to the amount awarded in the financial aid package.

Federal Perkins Loan Program

This is a low-interest (5%) loan for students with exceptional financial need. Perkins Loans are made through the college's financial aid office with the college as the lender. Students can borrow a maximum of $5500 per year for up to five years of undergraduate study. Borrowers may take up to ten years to repay the loan, beginning nine months after they graduate, leave school, or drop below half-time status. No interest accrues while they are in school, and, under certain conditions (e.g., they teach in low-income areas, work in law enforcement, are full-time nurses or medical technicians, serve as Peace Corps or VISTA volunteers, etc.), some or all of the loan can be cancelled. In addition, payments can be deferred under certain conditions such as unemployment.

Federal Direct Loans

A Direct Loan is borrowed directly from the U.S. Department of Education through the college's financial aid office.

The unsubsidized Direct Loan Program carries a fixed 6.8 percent interest rate. The interest rate for subsidized Federal Direct Loans first dispursed between July 1, 2010, and June 30, 2011, is 4.5 percent. If a student qualifies for a need-based subsidized Federal Direct Loan, the interest is paid by the federal government while he or she is enrolled in college, during grace, and during periods of deferment. Over a four-year period beginning July 1, 2008, the fixed interest rate on subsidized Direct Student Loans made to undergraduate students who purchased a loan made before July 1, 2006, will be reduced in phases. For loans first disbursed on or after

- July 1, 2010, and before July 1, 2011, the interest rate is fixed at 4.50 percent;
- July 1, 2011, and before July 1, 2012, the interest rate will be fixed at 3.40 percent.

The maximum amount dependent students may borrow in any one year is $5500 for freshmen, $6500 for sophomores, and $7500 for juniors and seniors, with a maximum of $31,000 for the total undergraduate program (of which not more than $23,000 can be subsidized). The maximum amount independent students can borrow is $9500 for freshmen (of which no more than $3500 can be subsidized), $10,500 for sophomores (of which no more than $4500 can be subsidized), and $12,500 for juniors and seniors (of which no more than $5500 can be subsidized). Independent students can borrow up to $57,500 (of which no more than $23,000 can be subsidized) for the total undergraduate program. Borrowers may be charged a small origination fee, which is deducted from the loan proceeds.

To apply for a Federal Student Loan, you must first complete the FAFSA to determine eligibility for a subsidized loan and then complete a separate loan application that is submitted to the Department of Education. The Department of Education will send a master promissory for completion. The proceeds of the loan, less the origination fee, will be sent to the college to be either credited to your account or released to you directly. Direct Loans are processed by the financial aid office as part of the overall financial aid package.

Once the repayment period starts, borrowers of both subsidized and unsubsidized Federal Direct Loans have to pay a combination of interest and principal monthly for up to a ten-year period. There are a number of repayment options as well as opportunities to consolidate federal loans. There are also provisions for extended repayments, deferments, and repayment forbearance, if needed.

Direct PLUS Loans

PLUS loans are for parents of dependent students to help families with the cost of education. There is no needs test to qualify. A Direct PLUS Loan has a fixed interest rate of 7.9 percent. There is no yearly limit; you can borrow up to the cost of your child's education, less other financial aid received. Repayment begins sixty days after the funds are disbursed. The origination fee is 4 percent and may be subtracted from the proceeds. Parent borrowers must generally have a good credit record to qualify.

American Opportunity Credit and Lifetime Learning Credit

Tuition tax credits allow families to reduce their tax bill by the out-of-pocket college tuition expense. Unlike a tax deduction, which is modified according to your tax bracket, a tax credit is a dollar-for-dollar reduction in taxes paid.

There are two programs: the American Opportunity Credit and the Lifetime Learning Credit. As is true of many federal programs, there are numerous rules and restrictions that apply. You should check with your tax preparer, financial adviser, or IRS Publication 970 for information about your own particular situation.

American Opportunity Credit

The American Opportunity Credit (formerly the Hope Credit) can be claimed for expenses for the first four years of postsecondary education. This is a change from the previous Hope Credit. The American Opportunity Credit is also different from the Hope Credit in that it includes expenses for course-related books, supplies, and equipment. It is a tax credit of up to $2500 of the cost of qualifying tuition and expenses, and up to 40% of the credit is refundable (up to $1000).

Eligibility also difers from the former Hope Credit. A taxpayer who pays qualified tuition and related expenses and whose federal income tax return has a modified adjusted gross income of $80,000 or less ($160,000 or less for joint filers) is eligible for the credit. The credit is reduced ratably if a taxpayer's modified adjusted gross income exceeds those amounts. A taxpayer whose modified adjusted gross income is greater than $90,000 ($180,000 for joint filers) cannot benefit from this credit.

For more information about the new American Opportunity Credit, go online to http://www.irs.gov/newsroom/article/0,,id=211309,00.html.

Lifetime Learning Credit

The Lifetime Learning Credit is the counterpart of the American Opportunity Credit; it is for college juniors, seniors, graduate students, and part-time students pursuing lifelong learning to improve or upgrade their job skills. The qualifying taxpayer can claim an annual tax credit of up to $2000—20 percent of the first $10,000 of tuition. The credit is available for net tuition and fees, less grant aid. The total credit available is limited to $2000 per year per taxpayer (or joint-filing couple), and is phased out at the same income levels as the American Opportunity Credit. (The income figures are subject to change and can be found in each year's IRS Publication 970.)

Tuition and Fees Tax Deduction

The Tuition and Fees Tax Deduction could reduce taxable income by as much as $4000. This deduction is taken as an adjustment to income, which means you can claim this deduction even if you do not itemize deductions on Schedule A of Form 1040. This deduction may benefit taxpayers who do not qualify for either the American Opportunity Credit or Lifetime Learning Credit.

Up to $4000 may be deducted for tuition and fees required for enrollment or attendance at an eligible postsecondary institution. Personal living and family expenses, including room and board, insurance, medical, and transportation, are not deductible expenses.

The exact amount of the Tuition and Fees Tax Deduction depends on the amount of qualified tuition and related expenses paid for one's self, spouse, or dependents, and your Adjusted Gross Income. Consult the IRS or your tax preparer for more information.

Student Loan Interest Tax Deduction

If you made student loan interest payments in 2011, you may be able to reduce your taxable income by up to $2500. You should check with your lender with regards to the amount of interest you paid if you did not receive an IRS Form 1098-E and your tax preparer or IRS Publication 970 for additional information.

AmeriCorps

AmeriCorps is a national umbrella group of service programs for students. Participants work in a public or private nonprofit agency and provide service to the community in one of four priority areas: education, human services, the environment, and public safety. In exchange, they earn a stipend (for living expenses), health insurance coverage, and $4725 per year for up to two years to apply toward college expenses. Many student-loan lenders will postpone the repayment of student loans during service in AmeriCorps, and AmeriCorps will pay the interest that is accrued on qualified student loans for members who complete the service program. Participants can work before, during, or after college and can use the funds to either pay current educational expenses or repay federal student loans. For more information, visit www.americorps.org.

Analyzing Financial Aid Award Letters

Richard Woodland

You have just received the financial aid award letters. Now what? This is the time to do a detailed analysis of each college's offer to help you pay for your child's education. Remember, accepting financial aid is a family matter. More often than not, parents need to borrow money to send their dependent children to college. You need to clearly understand the types of aid you and your child are being offered. How much is "free" money in the form of grants and/or scholarships that does not have to be repaid? If your financial aid award package includes loans, what are the terms and conditions for these loans? A good tool to have with you is the federal government's most recent issue of *Funding Education Beyond High School: The Guide to Federal Student Aid,* available from the school's financial aid office or at http://studentaid.ed.gov/students/publications/student_guide/index.html. This publication is very helpful in explaining the federal grant and loan programs that are usually a part of the aid package.

Let's take a minute to explain what is meant by "financial aid award package." A college will offer an aid applicant a combination of aid types, "packaged" in the form of grants and scholarships, loans, and a work-study job, based on the information provided on the FAFSA and/or another application. Many schools use a priority filing date, which guarantees that all applications received by this date will be considered for the full range of institutional aid programs available. Late applicants (by even one day!) often are only awarded the basic aid programs from state and federal sources. *It is important to apply on time.*

Evaluate Each Letter

As each award letter comes in, read it through carefully. The following are some critical points to consider:

- **Does the Cost of Attendance (COA) include all projected costs?** Each award letter should state the school's academic year COA. Tuition, fees, room, board, books, transportation, and personal expenses are what normally make up the COA. Does the award letter itemize all these components? Or does it omit some? This is crucial because this is what you will need to budget for. If you need additional information, be sure to contact the financial aid office. They will be glad to provide you with information or answer any questions you may have about their costs.
- **What is your Expected Family Contribution (EFC)?** Is the school's—not just the federal government's—EFC listed on the award letter? Some schools may require a higher EFC than you expected. Be aware that the EFC may increase or decrease each year depending on the information you provide on the renewal FAFSA or other financial aid application.
- **Is there unmet need?** Does the aid package cover the difference between the COA and the EFC? Not every school can cover your full need. If the aid package does not cover your full need, does the information with the award letter provide you with alternative loan options? If not, contact the financial aid office for more information.
- **Is the scholarship renewable for four years?** If your child is awarded a scholarship based on scholastic achievement or talent, you need to ask these questions: Is there a minimum grade point average he has to maintain? Can he switch majors but keep the scholarship? Does he need to participate in an "honors college" program to maintain the scholarship? If he needs to change to part-time status, will the award amount be prorated, or does he need to maintain full-time status? If it is an athletic or "special talent" scholarship, will he continue to receive the award if for some reason he cannot continue with the specific program? Renewal of scholarship funds is often the biggest misunderstanding between families and colleges. Be sure you clearly understand the terms and conditions of all grants and scholarships.
- **What will the college do to your child's award if she receives outside, noninstitutional scholarships?** Will the award be used to cover unmet need or reduce her student loans? Will the college reduce her institutional grants or scholarships? Or will they reduce her work-study award? (This is a good time to compare each school's policy on this matter.) Remember, your overall aid cannot total more than the COA, and many programs cannot exceed your financial need.
- **What are the interest rates of the loans that are offered?** Did another school offer you more than one loan and why? *Do not* sign the award letter until you understand your loan obligations.

Analyzing Financial Aid Award Letters

Again, *Funding Education Beyond High School: The Guide to Federal Student Aid* can be very helpful with this part of the analysis.

- **Is the school likely to cover the same expenses every year?** In particular, ask if grant or scholarship funds are normally reduced or increased after the freshman year, even if family income and EFC remain the same. Some colleges will *increase* the self-help (loan, job) percentage every year but not necessarily the free money.
- **If work-study was awarded, how many hours a week will your child be expected to work?** If you feel working that many hours will have a negative impact on your child's academic performance, you may want to request that the awarded job funds be changed to a loan. You must ask immediately because funds are limited. Many schools are flexible with these funds early in the process.
- **What happens if (or more likely, when) tuition increases?** Check with the financial aid office to find out what its policy is for renewing an aid package. If, for example, tuition increases by 5 percent each of the next three years and your EFC remains the same, what will happen to your scholarships, grants, and loans?

You can always appeal your award letter if you feel that your needs are not being met, if your family situation has changed, or if you have received a better award from a competitive school. You have the right to ask for a reconsideration of your award. (Do not use the word *negotiate*.) When asking for reconsideration, be sure to provide the aid officer with all relevant information.

Compare Letters

After you have received and reviewed all the award letters from the schools your child is considering, the next step is to compare them and determine which schools are offering the best aid packages. Following are three sample award letters and a sample spreadsheet that shows you how to analyze and compare each school's awards.

(Note: These award letters are simply for discussion purposes. They should not be considered to be representative award letters with an EFC of $9550.)

UNIVERSITY A
FINANCIAL AID AWARD LETTER
2011–2012

Date: 4/21/11
ID#: 000000009

Dear Jane Smith,

We are pleased to inform you that you are eligible to receive the financial assistance indicated in the area labeled "Your Financial Aid." We estimated your budget based on the following assumptions:

In-state resident and living on campus.

	FALL	**SPRING**	**TOTAL**
Tuition and Fees	$3849	$3849	$ 7698
Room & Board	3769	3770	7539
Books	420	420	840
Transportation	973	974	1947
Personal Expenses	369	369	738
Estimated Cost of Attendance	**$9380**	**$9382**	**$18,762**

Your Financial Aid

	FALL	**SPRING**	**TOTAL**
Federal Pell Grant	$1950	$1950	$ 3900
Federal Direct Subsidized Loan	1750	1750	3500
State Grant	432	432	864
Total Financial Aid	**$4132**	**$4132**	**$ 8264**
Unmet Need	**$5248**	**$5250**	**$10,498**

What to Do Next:

- Verify that accurate assumptions have been used to determine your awards.
- Carefully review and follow the instructions on the Data Changes Form.
- To reduce or decline all or part of your loans, you must complete and return the Data Changes Form.
- We will assume you fully accept the awards above unless you submit changes to us immediately.
- Return corrections and required documents promptly.
- Retain this letter for your records.

UNIVERSITY B

FINANCIAL AID AWARD LETTER

2011–2012

Date: 4/21/11
ID#: 000000009

Dear Jane Smith,

We are pleased to inform you that you are eligible to receive the financial assistance indicated in the area labeled "Your Financial Aid." We estimated your budget based on the following assumptions:

Nonresident and living on campus.

	FALL	SPRING	TOTAL
Tuition and Fees	$ 9085	$ 9085	$18,170
Room & Board	2835	2835	5670
Books	410	410	820
Transportation	875	875	1750
Personal Expenses	378	377	755
Estimated Cost of Attendance	**$13,583**	**$13,582**	**$27,165**

Your Financial Aid

	FALL	SPRING	TOTAL
Federal Pell Grant	$ 1950	$ 1950	$ 3900
Federal SEOG Grant	225	225	450
Academic Excellence Scholarship	500	500	1000
Federal Work-Study Program	1050	1050	2100
Federal Perkins Loan Program	1250	1250	2500
Subsidized Federal Stafford Student Loan	1750	1750	3500
University Student Loan	2000	2000	4000
Total Financial Aid	**$ 8725**	**$ 8725**	**$17,450**
Unmet Need	**$ 4858**	**$ 4857**	**$ 9715**

What to Do Next:

- Verify that accurate assumptions have been used to determine your awards.
- Carefully review and follow the instructions on the Data Changes Form.
- To reduce or decline all or part of your loans, you must complete and return the Data Changes Form.
- We will assume you fully accept the awards above unless you submit changes to us immediately.
- Return corrections and required documents promptly.
- Retain this letter for your records.

UNIVERSITY C
FINANCIAL AID AWARD LETTER
2011–2012

Date: 4/21/11
ID#: 000000009

Dear Jane Smith,

We are pleased to inform you that you are eligible to receive the financial assistance indicated in the area labeled "Your Financial Aid." We estimated your budget based on the following assumptions:

Living on campus.

	FALL	**SPRING**	**TOTAL**
Tuition and Fees	$14,955	$14,955	$29,910
Room & Board	4194	4193	8387
Books	450	450	900
Transportation	350	350	700
Personal Expenses	1295	1293	2588
Estimated Cost of Attendance	**$21,244**	**$21,241**	**$42,485**

Your Financial Aid

	FALL	**SPRING**	**TOTAL**
Institutional Grant	$10,805	$10,805	$21,610
Federal Pell Grant	1950	1950	3900
Federal SEOG Grant	2000	2000	4000
Federal Work-Study Program	1713	1712	3425
Total Financial Aid	**$16,468**	**$16,467**	**$32,935**
Unmet Need	**$ 4776**	**$ 4774**	**$ 9550**

What to Do Next:

- Verify that accurate assumptions have been used to determine your awards.
- Carefully review and follow the instructions on the Data Changes Form.
- To reduce or decline all or part of your loans, you must complete and return the Data Changes Form.
- We will assume you fully accept the awards above unless you submit changes to us immediately.
- Return corrections and required documents promptly.
- Retain this letter for your records.

Comparison Grid

	University A (State University)	University B (Nonresident State University)	University C (Private College)
Cost of Attendance	**$18,762**	**$27,165**	**$42,485**
Tuition and Fees	7698	18,170	29,910
Room & Board	7539	5670	8367
Books	840	820	900
Transportation	1947	1750	700
Personal Expenses	738	755	2558
Grants and Scholarships	**4764**	**5350**	**29,510**
Loans	**3500**	**10,000**	**0**
Work-Study	**0**	**2100**	**3425**
Expected Family Contribution	**9550**	**9550**	**9550**
Balance	**$ 948**	**$ 165**	**$ 0**

Some things to notice:

- At all schools, the Federal Pell Grant remains the same.
- The loan amounts varied greatly among these schools.
- Even though University C (a private college) has the highest "sticker price," the net cost is less than the state schools.
- University B is a state university, but you are classified as an out-of-state resident (or nonresident). Many students in this situation find that the higher out-of-state costs combined with lower grant aid make this a costly decision.
- All schools assume that you will be residing in on-campus housing. But if you choose to commute to University A, you would save a substantial amount because you would not have the $7539 room and board cost.

Once you have entered all the information into a spreadsheet of your own and come up with the balances, here are some things to consider for each school:

- **How much is the balance?** Ideally, your balance should be $0, but look to see which school has the lowest balance amount.
- **What part of the aid package comes in the form of grants and scholarships?** It is important to note this because these awards (gift aid) do not have to be paid back.
- **Look at the loans.** Usually, the best financial deal contains more money in scholarships and less in loan dollars. Based on expected freshman-year borrowing, determine the debt burden at each school once your child graduates. You have to multiply the amount of your loan by four or five years, depending on how long it will take for your child to graduate. And remember that the loan amounts will probably increase each year. You also should take into consideration that you will have to borrow even more as the COA increases each year. To determine the best loan deal, consider:
  - —What are the terms of the loans?
  - —What are interest rates?
  - —Do you pay the yearly interest rate during enrollment or is the interest subsidized or paid by the government?
  - —Is any money due during enrollment or is it deferred until after graduation? Figuring out how much you will owe at each school at graduation will give you a clear picture of what your financial situation will be *after* graduation.

However, unless cost is your only concern, you shouldn't simply choose the school offering the lowest loan amounts.

Many other factors need to be considered, such as academic and social environment. And you should never reject a school based solely on insufficient financial aid. Consult with an aid administrator to discuss possible alternatives.

Finally, if the college that costs the most is still the one your child wants to attend, there are a number of ways to find money to cover the gap between the aid package and your actual cost, including paying more than the EFC figure, increasing student borrowing, working more hours, and taking out a PLUS loan.

Richard Woodland is the former Director of Financial Aid at Rutgers University–Camden and the current Associate Dean of Student Services at the Curtis Institute of Music in Philadelphia, Pennsylvania.

Online Filing of FAFSA and CSS/Financial Aid PROFILE® Applications

Richard Woodland

Over the past few years, there have been major advancements in the way students apply both for admission to college and for financial aid. The two primary financial aid applications, the Free Application for Federal Student Aid (FAFSA) and the CSS/Financial Aid PROFILE® application from the College Scholarship Service offer direct, online applications. FAFSA on the Web and PROFILE are available in both English and Spanish.

Why File Online?

There are two reasons why it is a good idea to file online. First, the online environment prevents you from making many mistakes. For example, if there is a question that is required of all applicants, you cannot inadvertently skip it. If the application software thinks your answer may not be accurate, it will prompt you to check it before proceeding. The financial aid process can be complicated, and applying online greatly reduces the chance for error. The second reason is turnaround time. The online applications are processed in a matter of days, not weeks. Since time is an important factor when applying for financial aid, it is prudent to have your application processed as quickly as possible.

Some Common Concerns About Online Filing

Both the FASFA and PROFILE online applications have become much more user-friendly. You do not have to be a computer expert to use these programs. Both applications allow you to save your completed data and return later if you are interrupted or need to gather additional information. Both systems use secure encryption technology to protect your privacy. FASFA information is shared with other federal agencies as required as part of the application process, online or paper. FAFSA information is also sent to your state of legal residence for state aid purposes and to any college or program your child lists on the application. The information on the application is highly personal, and every precaution is taken to safeguard your privacy.

Now, let's discuss some specific issues related to each application.

The FAFSA

The FAFSA is the universal application for all federal financial aid programs. It is the primary application used for most state and college financial aid programs. Before using the FAFSA online application, you need to secure an electronic signature, or Personal Identification Number (PIN). This is similar to the access codes used at ATM machines, online banking, etc. It is easy to obtain a PIN number. Simply go to www.pin.ed.gov and apply online. You will receive a reply via e-mail in about 48 hours. If your child is under 24 years of age, he or she and one parent will need a PIN number. If there is more than one child in college, a parent only needs one PIN number. However, each college applicant will need to have his or her own PIN.

The FASFA online application is not presented in the same format as the paper FAFSA. Although all of the questions are exactly the same, the order of some of the items on the online application has been rearranged to make it easier to complete and allow for some built-in skip-logic. You can easily obtain a copy of the electronic FAFSA by logging on to www.fafsa.ed.gov. Just click on "FAFSA on the Web Worksheet." Completing this first will make the online entry that much easier. There are a number of other worksheets available that can also make the process easier. You should print them out and decide which are applicable to your situation. Everyone should review Worksheets A, B, and C. If you have not completed your federal tax return, the Income Estimator worksheets are easy to use and can reduce much of the guesswork.

After completing the online FASFA, be sure to print a copy of the pages at the end of the process so that you have a copy of your answers and the confirmation number. Although lost applications are extremely rare, having this information will give you peace of mind. You can go online as often as you wish to check the status of your application.

The CSS/Financial Aid PROFILE®

The CSS/Financial Aid PROFILE® is a more comprehensive financial aid application that is used primarily at private, higher-cost colleges and universities to award nonfederal student aid funds. Many private scholarship programs also use the PROFILE. A complete list of colleges and programs that use the PROFILE can be found at https://profileonline.collegeboard.com/index.jsp.

The PROFILE application fee is $25 for the application and initial school report and $16 for each additional school report. You must have a credit card, debit card, or checking account to use this service. (Note: A limited number of fee waivers are available for families with incomes below the poverty line. See the high school guidance officer for more information on the fee waiver program.)

Complete information on the online PROFILE application is available at www.collegeboard.com/profile. Although the customized PROFILE application is processed in about one week, you should allow for enough processing time (usually two to three weeks) to meet the earliest deadline established by the school or program.

What Happens Next?

Both the FAFSA and PROFILE processors want more applicants to use the online environment. Not only is the process easier for them, but it is faster and more accurate. Once you decide to apply online, the processors will only respond to you electronically. You will not receive any paper acknowledgments—all confirmations will be sent via e-mail. When it is time to reapply for aid in subsequent years (usually quite easy as most of the data are carried over from the previous application), all reminders will be sent to the e-mail address that is on file, so it is important to report any changes in your e-mail address.

It is easy to update the FAFSA following your initial application. For example, if you used estimated income information and now you have your federal tax return completed, you can simply return to www.fafsa.ed.gov and change your income figures. But be sure to go through the entire process and print out the updated confirmation page. In general, the PROFILE is a one-time application, filed well before tax season. Any updates are usually done directly through the schools.

Both processors offer helpful information, both in print and online. Check with your high school guidance office or local college financial aid office for additional assistance. If you need to call the FAFSA processor, the phone number is 800-4-FED-AID (toll-free). You can contact PROFILE customer service via e-mail at help@cssprofile.org or by phone at 305-829-9793 or 800-915-9990 (toll-free).

Richard Woodland is the former Director of Financial Aid at Rutgers University–Camden and the current Associate Dean of Student Services at the Curtis Institute of Music in Philadelphia, Pennsylvania.

Middle-Income Families: Making the Financial Aid Process Work

Richard Woodland

A report from the U.S. Department of Education's National Center for Education Statistics took a close look at how middle-income families finance a college education. The report, *Middle Income Undergraduates: Where They Enroll and How They Pay for Their Education,* was one of the first detailed studies of these families. Even though 31 percent of middle-income families have the entire cost of attendance covered by financial aid, there is widespread angst among middle-income families that, while they earn too much to qualify for grant assistance, they are financially unable to pay the spiraling costs of higher education.

First, we have to agree on what constitutes a "middle-income" family. For the purposes of the federal study, middle income is defined as those families with incomes between $35,000 and $70,000. The good news is that 52 percent of these families received grants, while the balance received loans. Other sources of aid, including work-study, also helped close the gap.

So how do these families do it? Is there a magic key that will open the door to significant amounts of grants and scholarships?

The report found some interesting trends. One way families can make college more affordable is by choosing a less expensive college. In fact, in this income group, 29 percent choose to enroll in low- to moderate-cost schools. These include schools where the total cost is less than $8500 per year. In this sector, we find the community colleges and lower-priced state colleges and universities. But almost half of these middle-income families choose schools in the upper-level tier, with costs ranging from $8500 to $16,000. The remaining 23 percent enrolled at the highest-tier schools, with costs above $16,000. Clearly, while cost is a factor, middle-income families are not limiting their choices based on costs alone.

The report shows that families pay these higher costs with a combination of family assets, current income, and long-term borrowing. This is often referred to as the "past-present-future" model of financing. In fact, just by looking at the Expected Family Contributions, it is clear that there is a significant gap in what families need and what the financial aid process can provide. Families are closing this gap by making the financial sacrifices necessary to pay the price at higher-cost schools, especially if they think their child is academically strong. The report concludes that parents are more likely to pay for a higher-priced education if their child scores high on the SAT.

The best place for middle-income families to start is with the high school guidance office. This office has information on financial aid and valuable leads on local scholarships. Most guidance officers report that there are far fewer applicants for these locally based scholarships than one would expect. So read the information they send home and check on the application process. A few of those $500–$1000 scholarships can add up!

Plan to attend a financial aid awareness program. If your school does not offer one, contact your local college financial aid office and see when and where they will be speaking. You can get a lot of "inside" information on how the financial aid process works.

Next, be sure to file the correct applications for aid. Remember, each school can have a different set of requirements. For example, many higher-cost private colleges will require the CSS/Financial Aid PROFILE® application, filed in September or October of the senior year. Other schools may have their own institutional aid application. All schools will require the Free Application for Federal Student Aid (FAFSA). Watch the deadlines! It is imperative that you meet the school's published application deadline. Generally, schools are not flexible about this, so be sure to double-check the due date of all applications.

Finally, become a smart educational consumer. Peterson's has a wide range of resources available to help you understand the process. Be sure to also check your local library, bookstore, and of course, the Internet. Two great Web sites to check are www.petersons.com and www.finaid.org.

Once admitted to the various colleges and universities, you will receive an award notice outlining the aid you are eligible to receive. If you feel the offer is not sufficient, or if you have some unique financial circumstances, call the school's financial aid office to see if you can have your application reviewed again. The financial aid office is your best source for putting the pieces together and finding financial solutions.

The financial aid office will help you determine the "net price." This is the actual out-of-pocket cost that you will need to cover. Through a combination of student and parent loans, most families are able to meet these expenses with other forms of financial aid and family resources.

Many students help meet their educational expenses by working while in school. While this works for many students, research shows that too many hours spent away from your studies will negatively impact your academic success. Most experts feel that working 10 to 15 hours a week is optimal.

An overlooked source of aid is the tax credits given to middle-income families. Rather than extending eligibility for traditional sources of grant assistance to middle-income families, the federal tax system has built in a number of significant tax benefits, known as the American Opportunity Tax Credit (AOTC) and Lifetime Learning Tax Credit, for middle-income families. The AOTC was enacted in 2009 for 2009 and 2010. It was extended for two years as part of the Tax Relief, Unemployment Insurance Reauthorization, and Job Creation Act of 2010 and expires on December 31, 2012. The maximum AOTC tax credit is $2500 per student. This is real money in your pocket. You do not need to itemize your deductions to qualify for this tax credit.

A tool to help families get a handle on the ever-rising costs of college is to assume that you can pay one third of the "net charges" from savings, another third from available (non-retirement) assets, and the rest from parent borrowing. If any one of these "thirds" is not available, shift that amount to one of the other resources. However, if it looks like you will be financing most or all of the costs from future income (borrowing), it may be wise to consider a lower-cost college.

Millions of middle-income families send their children to colleges and universities every year. Only 8 percent attend the lowest-priced schools. By using the concept of past-present-future financing, institutional assistance, federal and state aid, meaningful targeted tax relief, and student earnings, you can afford even the highest-cost schools.

Richard Woodland is the former Director of Financial Aid at Rutgers University–Camden and the current Associate Dean of Student Services at the Curtis Institute of Music in Philadelphia, Pennsylvania.

Parents' and Students' Common Questions Answered

Q ***Are a student's chances of being admitted to a college reduced if the student applies for financial aid?***

A Generally no. Nearly all colleges have a policy of "need-blind" admissions, which means that a student's financial need is not taken into account in the admission decision. There are a few selective colleges, however, that do consider ability to pay before deciding whether or not to admit a student. Some colleges will mention this in their literature; others may not. The best advice is to apply for financial aid if the student needs assistance to attend college.

Q ***Are parents penalized for saving money for college?***

A No. As a matter of fact, families that have made a concerted effort to save money for college are in a much better position than those who have not. For example, a student from a family that has saved money may not have to borrow as much. Furthermore, the "taxing rate" on savings is quite low—only about 5 percent of the parents' assets are assessed and neither the home equity nor retirement savings are included. For example, a single 40-year-old parent who saved $40,000 for college expenses will have about $1900 counted as part of the parental contribution. Two parents, if the older one is 40 years old (a parent's age factors into the formulation), would have about $300 counted. (Note: The "taxing rate" for student assets is much higher—20 percent—compared to 5 percent for parents.)

Q ***How does the financial aid system work in cases of divorce or separation? How are stepparents treated?***

A In cases of divorce or separation, the financial aid application(s) should be completed by the parent with whom the student lived for the longest period of time in the past twelve months (custodial parent). If the custodial parent has remarried, the stepparent is considered a family member and must complete the application along with the biological parent. If your family has any special circumstances, you should discuss these directly with the financial aid office. (Note: Colleges that award their own aid may ask the noncustodial biological parent to complete a separate aid application and a contribution will be calculated.)

Q ***When are students considered independent of parental support in applying for financial aid?***

A The student must be at least 24 years of age in order to be considered independent. If younger than 24, the student must be married, be a graduate or professional student, have legal dependents other than a spouse, be an orphan or ward of the court, or be a veteran of the armed forces or on active military duty. However, in very unusual situations, students who can clearly document estrangement from their parents can appeal to the financial aid office for additional consideration.

Q ***What can a family do if a job loss occurs?***

A Financial aid eligibility is based on the previous year's income. So the family's 2011 income would be reported to determine eligibility for the 2012–13 academic year. In that way, the family's income can be verified with an income tax return. But the previous year's income may not accurately reflect the current financial situation, particularly if a parent lost a job or retired. In these instances, the projected income for the coming year can be used instead. Families should discuss the situation directly with the financial aid office and be prepared to provide appropriate documentation.

Q ***When my daughter first went to college, we applied for financial aid and were denied because our Expected Family Contribution was too high. Now, my***

son is a high school senior, and we will soon have two in college. Will we get the same results?

A The results will definitely be different. Both your son and your daughter should apply. As described earlier, need-based financial aid is based on your Expected Family Contribution, or EFC. When you have two children in college, this amount is divided in half for each child.

Q *I've heard about the "middle-income squeeze" in regard to financial aid. What is it?*

A The so-called "middle-income squeeze" is the idea that low-income families qualify for aid, high-income families have adequate resources to pay for education, and those in the middle are not eligible for aid but do not have the ability to pay full college costs. There is no provision in the Federal Methodology that treats middle-income students differently than others (such as an income cutoff for eligibility). The Expected Family Contribution rises proportionately as income and assets increase. If a middle-income family does not qualify for aid, it is because the need analysis formula yields a contribution that exceeds college costs. But keep in mind that if a $65,000-income family does not qualify for grant aid at a public university with a $16,000 cost, the same family will likely be eligible for aid at a private college with a cost of $25,000 or more. Also, there are loan programs available to parents and students that are not based on need. Middle-income families should realize, however, that many of the grant programs funded by federal and state governments are directed at lower-income families. It is therefore likely that a larger share of an aid package for a middle-income student will consist of loans rather than grants.

Q *Given our financial condition, my daughter will be receiving financial aid. We will help out as much as we can, and, in fact, we ourselves will be borrowing. But I am concerned that she will have to take on a lot of loans in order to go to the college of her choice. Does she have any options?*

A She does. If offered a loan, she can decline all or part of it. One option is for her to ask in the financial aid office to have some of the loan changed to a work-study job. If this is not possible, she can find her own part-time work. Often there is an employment office on campus that can help her locate a job. In most cases, the more she works, the less she has to borrow. It is important to remember that the education loans offered to students have very attractive terms and conditions, with flexible repayment options. Students should look upon these loans as a long-term investment that will reap significant rewards.

Q *What are some easy ways to improve my chances of receiving aid?*

A When filling out your scholarship or financial aid application, it's important to remember that the smallest mistake could hurt your chances for landing free money, or even worse, it could disqualify you completely from an awards contest. Grants and scholarships are highly competitive, so it's a good idea to make a list of what's needed and make sure you have everything before submitting your application. If you are submitting an essay, have another pair of eyes look at it for any spelling and grammar errors. Keep a file on everything you're applying for so that you don't miss any elements of an application. Make sure you're using reputable sites to conduct your free scholarship searches. If you have to pay to apply for an award or look for scholarships, chances are you're being scammed. In a nutshell, the best advice is to follow all directions, and make sure that you meet all deadlines.

In addition, when filling out the FAFSA, it's important to pay close attention to the details, since any errors may delay the application process. These days, it's preferable to fill out the FAFSA online, since mailed forms can take weeks to process. If you're confused or concerned about something on the application, contact the Federal Student Aid Information Center at 1-800-4-FED-AID; questions can also be asked through the FAFSA Web site. Your college's financial aid office should also be able to assist you. The FAFSA is available each year starting Jan. 1, and it's essential that you don't miss the deadline to apply. The sooner you apply, the sooner you'll know the kind of funding package you are likely to receive, and this will help you determine if you need to apply for any additional aid.

Q *Is it possible to change your financial aid package?*

A Yes. Most colleges have an appeal process. A request to change a need-based loan to a work-study job is usually approved if funds are available. A request to consider special financial circumstances may also be granted. At most colleges, a request for more grant money is rarely approved unless it is based on a change in the information reported. Applicants should speak with the financial aid office if they have concerns about their financial package. Some colleges may even respond to a competitive appeal, that is, a request to match another college's offer.

Q *The cost of attending college seems to be going up so much faster than the Consumer Price Index. Why is that, and how can I plan for my child's four years?*

A The cost of higher education cannot be compared to the Consumer Price Index (CPI). The CPI does not take into account most of the costs faced by colleges. For example, the dollars that universities spend on grants and scholarships have risen rapidly. Many universities have increased enrollment of students from less affluent families, further increasing the need for institutional financial aid. Colleges are expected to be on the cutting edge of technology, not only in research but also in the classroom and in the library. Many colleges have deferred needed maintenance and repairs that can now no longer be put off. In addition, there is market pressure to provide many expensive lifestyle amenities that were not expected ten years ago. In general, you can expect that college costs will rise at least 2 to 3 percent faster than inflation.

Q ***I'm struggling with the idea that all students should apply to the college of their choice, regardless of cost, because financial aid will level the playing field. I feel I will be penalized because I have saved for college. My son has been required to save half of his allowance since age six for his college education. Will that count against him when he applies for financial aid? It's difficult to explain to him that his college choices may be limited because of the responsible choices and sacrifices we have made as a family. What can we do to make the most of our situation?***

A In general, it is always better to have planned ahead for college by saving. Families that have put away sufficient funds to pay for college will quickly realize that they have made the burden easier for themselves and their children. In today's college financing world, schools assume that paying for the cost of attendance is a ten-year commitment. So by saving when your child is young, you reap significant advantages from compound interest on the assets and reduce the need to borrow as much while in school. This should reduce the number of years after college that you will be burdened with loans. Families should spend the student's assets first, since the financial aid formulas count these more heavily than parental assets. Then, after the first year, you can explain to the college how you spent these assets, and why you might now need assistance. When looking at parental information, the income of the family is by far the most important component. Contrary to popular belief, parental assets play a minor role in the calculation of need. With this strategy, you have done the right thing, and in the long run, it should prove to be a wise financial plan.

Picking the right college also involves other factors. Students should select the colleges to which they are going to apply in two ways. First, and most important, is to look at colleges that meet your son's academic and lifestyle interests. Most experts will tell him to pick a few "reach" schools (i.e., schools where he is not sure he has the grades and scores required) and at least one or two academically "safe" schools. He should also select one or two financially "safe" schools that you are sure you can afford with either moderate or little financial aid. Most students do not get into all of their first-choice schools, and not everyone can afford the schools to which they are admitted. By working closely with the guidance office in high school and the admissions and financial aid offices at the college, you can maximize your options.

Q ***My son was awarded a $2500 scholarship. This can be split and used for two years. When filling out the FAFSA, do we have to claim the full amount, or just the $1250 he plans to use the first year?***

A Congratulations to your son on the scholarship. Nowhere on the FAFSA should you report this scholarship. It is not considered income or an asset. However, once you choose a school to attend, you must notify the financial aid office for its advice on how to take the funds. But remember, do NOT report it on the FAFSA.

Q ***I will be receiving a scholarship from my local high school. How will this scholarship be treated in my financial aid award?***

A Federal student aid regulations specify that all forms of aid must be included within the defined level of need. This means that additional aid, such as outside scholarships, must be combined with any need-based aid you receive; it may not be kept separate and used to reduce your family's contribution. If the college has not filled 100 percent of your need, it will usually allow outside scholarships to close the gap. Once your total need has been met, the college must reduce other aid and replace it with the outside award. Most colleges will allow you to use some, if not all, of an outside scholarship to replace self-help aid (loans and Federal Work-Study Program awards) rather than grant aid.

Q ***I know we're supposed to apply for financial aid as soon as possible after January 1. What if I don't have my W-2s yet and my tax return isn't done?***

A The first financial aid application deadlines usually fall in early February. Most colleges use either March 1 or March 15 as their "priority filing date." Chances are you'll have your W-2 forms by then, but you won't have a completed tax return. If that is the case, complete the financial aid application using your best estimates. Then, when you receive the Student Aid Report (SAR), you can use your tax return to make corrections. Just be sure to check with each college for its deadline.

Q ***Is there enough aid available to make it worthwhile for me to consider colleges that are more expensive than I can afford?***

A Definitely. More than $100 billion in aid is awarded to undergraduates every year. With more than half of all enrolled students qualifying for some type of assistance, this totals more than $5500 per student. You should view financial aid as a large, national system of tuition discounts, some given according to a student's ability and talent, others based on what a student's family can afford to pay. If you qualify for need-based financial aid, you will essentially pay only your calculated family contribution, regardless of the cost of the college. You will not pay the "sticker price" (the cost of attendance listed in the college catalog) but a lower rate that is reduced by the amount of aid you receive. No college should be ruled out until after financial aid is considered. In addition, when deciding which college to attend, consider that the short-term cost of a college education is only one criterion. If the college meets your educational needs and you are convinced it can launch you on an exciting career, a significant up-front investment may turn out to be a bargain over the long run.

Q ***If I don't qualify for need-based aid, what options are available?***

A You should try to put together your own aid package to help reduce your parents' share. There are three sources to look into. First, search for merit scholarships. Second, seek employment, during both the summer and the academic year. The student employment office should be able to help you find a campus job. Third, look into borrowing. Even if you don't qualify for the need-based loan programs, the unsubsidized Federal Direct Loan is available to all students. The terms and conditions are the same as the subsidized loan programs except that interest accrues while you are in college.

After you have contributed what you can through scholarships, employment, and loans, your parents will be faced with their share of the college bill. Many colleges have monthly payment plans that allow families to spread their payments over the academic year. If these monthly payments turn out to be more than your parents can afford, they can take out a parent loan. By borrowing from the college itself, from a commercial agency or lender, or through PLUS, your parents can extend the payments over a ten-year period or longer. Borrowing reduces the monthly obligation to its lowest level, but the total amount paid will be the highest due to principal and interest payments. Before making a decision on where to borrow parental loan funds, be sure to first check with the financial aid office to determine what is the best source of alternative funds.

How to Use This Guide

Quick-Reference Chart

The amount of aid available at colleges can vary greatly. "College Costs At-a-Glance" lists the percent of freshmen who applied for and received need-based gift aid and the percent of those whose need was fully met. Also listed are the average freshman financial aid package, the average cost after aid, and the average indebtedness upon graduation.

Profiles of College Financial Aid Programs

After the federal government, colleges provide the largest amount of financial aid to students. In addition, they control most of the money channeled to students from the federal government. The amount and makeup of your financial aid package will depend on the institution's particular circumstances and its decisions concerning your application. The main section of this book shows you the pattern and extent of each college's current awards. The profiles present detailed factual and statistical data for each school in a uniform format to enable easy, quick references and comparisons. Items that could not be collected in time for publication for specific institutions do not appear in those institutions' profiles. Colleges that supplied no data are listed by name and address only so that you do not overlook them in your search for colleges.

There is much anecdotal evidence that students and their families fail to apply for financial aid under the misconception that student aid goes only to poor families. Financial need in the context of college expenses is not the same as being needy in the broad social context. Middle-class families typically qualify for need-based financial aid; at expensive schools, even upper-middle-income families can qualify for need-based financial aid. We encourage you to apply for financial aid whether or not you think that you will qualify.

To help you understand the definition and significance of each item, the following outline of the profile format explains what is covered in each section. The term college or colleges is frequently used throughout to refer to any institution of higher education, regardless of its official definition.

The College

The name of the college is the official name as it appears on the institution's charter. The city and state listed are the official location of the school. The subhead line shows tuition and required fees, as they were charged to the majority of full-time undergraduate students in the 2010–11 academic year. Any exceptions to the 2010–11 academic year are so noted. For a public institution, the tuition and fees shown are for state residents, and this is noted. If a college's annual expenses are expressed as a comprehensive fee (including full-time tuition, mandatory fees, and college room and board), this is noted, as are any unusual definitions, such as tuition only. The average undergraduate aid package is the average total package of grant, loan, and work-study aid that was awarded to meet the officially defined financial need of full-time undergraduates enrolled in fall 2010 (or fall 2009) who applied for financial aid, were determined to have need, and then actually received financial aid. This information appears in more detail in each profile.

About the Institution

This paragraph gives the reader a brief introduction to a college. It contains the following elements:

Institutional Control

Private institutions are designated as *independent* (nonprofit), *independent/religious* (sponsored by or affiliated with a religious group or having a nondenominational or interdenominational religious orientation), or *proprietary* (profit-making). Public institutions are designated by their primary source of support, such as *federal*, *state*, *commonwealth* (Puerto Rico), *territory* (U.S. territories), *county, district* (an administrative unit of public education, often having boundaries different from those of units of local government), *state- and locally-supported* ("locally" refers to county, district, or city), *state-supported* (funded by the state), or *state-related* (funded primarily by the state but administered autonomously).

Type of Student Body

The categories are *men* (100 percent of student body), *coed-primarily men*, *women* (100 percent of student body), *coed-primarily women*, and *coed*. A few schools are designated as *undergraduate: women only, graduate: coed* or *undergraduate: men only, graduate: coed.*

Degrees Awarded

Associate, bachelor's (baccalaureate), *master's, doctoral* (doctorate), and *first professional* (in such fields as law and medicine). There are no institutions in this book that award the associate degree only. Many award the bachelor's as their highest degree.

Number of Undergraduate Majors

This shows the number of academic fields in which the institution offers associate and/or bachelor's degrees. The purpose of this is to give you an indication of the range of subjects available.

Enrollment

These figures are based on the actual number of full-time and part-time students enrolled in degree programs as of fall 2010. In most instances, they are designated as *total enrollment* (for the specific college or university) and *freshmen*. If the institution is a university and its total enrollment figure includes graduate students, a separate figure for *undergraduates* may be provided. If the profiled institution is a subunit of a university, the figures may be designated *total university enrollment* for the entire university and *total unit enrollment* for the specific subunit.

Methodology Used for Determining Need

Private colleges usually have larger financial aid programs, but public colleges usually have lower sticker prices, especially for in-state or local students. At a public college, your financial need will be less, and you will receive a smaller financial aid package. This note on whether a college uses federal (FAFSA) or institutional methodology (usually CSS/Financial Aid PROFILE®) will let you know whether you will have to complete one or two kinds of financial aid application forms. Federal Methodology is the needs-analysis formula used by the U.S. Department of Education to determine the Expected Family Contribution (EFC), which, when subtracted from the cost of attendance at an institution, determines the financial need of a student. There is no relative advantage or disadvantage to using one methodology over the other.

Undergraduate Expenses

If provided by the institution, the one-time application fee is listed. Costs are given for the 2011–12 academic year or for the 2010–11 academic year if 2011–12 figures were not yet available. (Peterson's collects information for freshmen specifically.) Annual expenses may be expressed as a comprehensive fee (including full-time tuition, mandatory fees, and college room and board) or may be given as separate figures for full-time tuition, fees, room and board, or room only. For public institutions where tuition differs according to state residence, separate figures are given for area or state residents and for nonresidents. Part-time tuition is expressed in terms of a per-unit rate (per credit, per semester hour, etc.), as specified by the institution.

The tuition structure at some institutions is complex. Freshmen and sophomores may be charged a different rate from that charged juniors and seniors, a professional or vocational division may have a different fee structure from the liberal arts division of the same institution, or part-time tuition may be prorated on a sliding scale according to the number of credit hours taken. Tuition and fees may vary according to academic program, campus/location, class time (day, evening, weekend), course/credit load, course level, degree level, reciprocity agreements, and student level. If tuition and fees differ for international students, the rate charged is listed.

Room and board charges are reported as a double occupancy and nineteen meals per week plan or the equivalent and may vary according to board plan selected, campus/location, gender, type of housing facility, or student level. If no college-owned or -operated housing facilities are offered, the phrase *college housing not available* will appear.

If a college offers a *guaranteed tuition* plan, it promises that the tuition rate of an entering student will not increase for the entire term of enrollment, from entrance to graduation. Other payment plans might include *tuition prepayment*, which allows an entering student to lock in the current tuition rate for the entire term of enrollment by paying the full amount in advance rather than year by year, and *installment* and *deferred payment* plans, which allow students to delay the payment of the full tuition.

Guaranteed tuition and tuition prepayment help you to plan the total cost of education and can save you from the financial distress sometimes caused by tuition hikes. Colleges that offer such plans may also help you to arrange financing, which in the long run can cost less than the total of four years of increasing tuition rates. Deferred payment or installment payments may better fit your personal financial situation, especially if you do not qualify for financial aid and, due to other financial commitments, find that obtaining the entire amount due is burdensome. Carefully investigate these plans, however, to see what premium you may pay at the end to allow you to defer immediate payment.

Freshman Financial Aid

Usually, these are actual figures for the 2009–10 term, beginning in fall 2009; figures may also be estimated for the 2010–11 term. The particular term for which these data apply is indicated. The figures are for degree-seeking full-time freshman students. The first figure is the number of freshmen who applied for any kind of financial aid. The next figure is the percentage of those freshmen financial aid applicants who were determined to have financial need—that is, through the formal needs-assessment process, had a calculated expected family contribution that was less than the total college cost. The next figure is the percentage of this group of eligible freshmen who received any financial aid. The next figure is the percentage of this preceding group of eligible aid recipients whose need was fully met by financial aid. The *Average percent of need met* is the average percentage of financial need met for freshmen who received any need-based aid. The *Average financial aid package* is the average dollar amount awarded (need-based or non-need-based) to freshmen who applied for aid, were deemed eligible, and received any aid; awards used to reduce the expected family contribution are excluded from this average. The final line in most profiles is the percentage of freshmen who had no financial need but who received non-need-based aid other than athletic scholarships or special-group tuition benefits.

What do these data mean to you? If financial aid is important in your comparison of colleges, the relative percentage of students who received any aid, whose need was fully met, and the average percentage of need met have the most weight. These figures reflect the relative abundance of student aid available to the average eligible applicant. The average dollar amount of the aid package has real meaning, but only in relation to the college's expense; you will be especially interested in the difference between this figure and the costs figure, which is what the average student (in any given statistical group, there actually may be no average individual) will have to pay. Of course, if the financial aid package is largely loans rather than grants, you will have to pay this amount eventually. Relative differences in the figures of the number of students who apply for aid and who are deemed eligible can hinge on any number of factors: the relative sticker price of the college, the relative level of wealth of the students' families, the proportion of only children in college and students with siblings in college (families with two or more children in college are more likely to apply for aid and be considered eligible), or the relative sophistication in financial aid matters (or quality of college counseling they may have received) of the students and their families. While these may be interesting, they will not mean too much to most students and families. If you are among the unlucky (or, perhaps, lucky) families who do not qualify for need-based financial aid, the final sentence of this paragraph in the profile will be of interest because it reveals the relative policies that the college has in distributing merit-based aid to students who cannot demonstrate need.

Undergraduate Financial Aid

This is the parallel paragraph to the Freshman Financial Aid paragraph. The same definitions apply, except that the group being considered is degree-seeking full-time undergraduate students (including freshmen).

There are cases of students who chose a particular college because they received a really generous financial aid package in their freshman year and then had to scramble to pay the tuition bill in their later years. If a financial aid package is a key factor in the decision to attend a particular college, you want to be certain that the package offered to all undergraduates is not too far from that offered to freshmen. The key figures are those for the percentage of students who received any aid, the percentage of financial aid recipients whose need was fully met, the average percentage of need met, and the dollar figure of the average financial aid package. Generally, colleges assume that after the freshman year, students develop study habits and time-management skills that will allow them to take on part-time and summer employment without hurting their academic performance. So, the proportion of self-help aid (work-study and student loans) in the financial aid package tends to increase after the freshman year. This pattern, which is true of most colleges, can be verified in the freshman-undergraduate figures in the paragraph on Gift Aid (Need-Based).

Gift Aid (Need-Based)

Total amount is the total dollar figure in 2010–11 (estimated) or 2009–10 (actual) of need-based scholarships and grant (gift) aid awarded to degree-seeking full-time and part-time students that was used to meet financial need. The percentages of this aid from federal, state, institutional (college or university), and external (e.g., foundations, civic organizations, etc.) sources are shown. *Receiving aid* shows the percentages (and number, in parentheses) of freshmen and of all undergraduates who applied for aid, were considered eligible, and received any need-based gift aid. *Average award* is the average dollar amount of awards to freshmen and all undergraduates who applied for aid, were considered eligible, and received any need-based gift aid. *Scholarships, grants, and awards* cites major categories of need-based gift aid provided by the college; these include Federal Pell Grants, Federal Supplemental Educational Opportunity Grants (FSEOG), state scholarships, private scholarships, college/university gift aid from institutional funds, United Negro College Fund aid, Federal Nursing Scholarships, and others.

Scholarships and grants are gifts awarded to students that do not need to be repaid. These are preferable to loans, which have to be repaid, or work-study wages, which may take time away from studies and personal pursuits. The total amount of need-based gift aid has to be placed into the context of the total number of undergraduate students (shown in the About the Institution paragraph) and the relative expense of the institution. Filing the FAFSA automatically puts you in line to receive any available federal grants for which you may qualify. However, if the college being considered has a higher than usual proportion of gift aid coming from state, institutional, or external sources, be sure to check with the financial aid office to find out what these sources may be and how to apply for them. For almost all colleges, the percentage of freshmen receiving need-based gift aid will be higher than the percentage of all undergraduates receiving need-based gift aid. However, if you are dependent on need-based gift aid and the particular college under consideration shows a sharper drop from the freshman to undergraduate years than other colleges of a similar type, you might want to think about how this change will affect your ability to pay for later years at this college.

Gift Aid (Non-Need-Based)

Total amount is the total dollar figure in 2010–11 (estimated) or 2009–10 (actual) of non-need-based scholarships and grant (gift) aid awarded to degree-seeking full-time and part-time students. Non-need-based aid that was used to meet financial need is not included in this total. The percentages of this aid from federal, state, institutional (college or university), and external (e.g., National Merit Scholarships, civic, religious, fraternal organizations, etc.) sources are shown. *Receiving aid* shows the percentages (and number, in parentheses) of freshmen and of all undergraduates who were determined to have need and received non-need-based gift aid. *Average award* is the average dollar amount of awards to freshmen and all undergraduates determined to have no need but received non-need-based awards. *Scholarships, grants, and awards by category* cites the major categories in which non-need-based awards are available and the number of awards made in that category (in parentheses, the total dollar value of these awards). The categories listed are *Academic interests/achievement*, *Creative arts/performance*, *Special achievements/activities*, and *Special characteristics*. *Tuition waivers* indicate special categories of students (minority students, children of alumni, college employees or children of employees, adult students, and senior citizens) who may qualify for a full or partial waiver of tuition. *ROTC* indicates Army, Naval, and Air Force ROTC programs that are offered on campus; a program offered by arrangement on another campus is indicated by the word *cooperative*.

This section covers college-administered scholarships awarded to undergraduates on the basis of merit or personal attributes without regard to need. If you do not qualify for financial aid but nevertheless lack the resources to pay for college, non-need-based awards will be of special interest to you. Some personal characteristics are completely beyond an individual's control, and talents and achievements take a number of years to develop or attain. However, certain criteria for these awards, such as religious involvement, community service, and special academic interests can be attained in a relatively brief period of time. ROTC programs offer such benefits as tuition, the cost of textbooks, and living allowances. In return, you must fulfill a service obligation after graduating from college. Because they can be a significant help in paying for college, these programs have become quite competitive. Certain subject areas, such as nursing, health care, or the technical fields, are in stronger demand than others. Among the obligations to consider about ROTC are that you must spend a regular portion of your available time in military training programs and that ROTC entails a multiyear commitment after your graduation to serve as an officer in the armed services branch sponsoring the program.

Loans

The figures here represent loans that are part of the financial aid award package. *Student loans* represents the total dollar amount of loans from all sources to full-time and part-time degree-seeking undergraduates or their parents. *Average need-based loan* represents the percentage of these loans that goes to meet financial need, and the percentage that goes to pay the non-need portion (the expected family contribution) are indicated. The percentage of a past graduating class who borrowed through any loan program (except parent loans) while enrolled at the college is shown, as is the average dollar figure per-borrower of cumulative undergraduate indebtedness (this does not include loans from other institutions). *Parent loans* shows the total amount borrowed through parent loan programs as well as the percentages that were applied to the need-based and non-need-based portions of financial need. *Programs* indicates the major loan programs available to undergraduates. These include Direct and Federal Stafford Student Loans (subsidized and unsubsidized and PLUS), Perkins Loans, Federal Nursing Loans, state loans, college/university loans, and other types.

Note: As a result of the Health Care and Education Reconciliation Act, as of July 1, 2010, federal student loans are no longer made by private lenders under the Federal Family Education Loan (FFEL) Program. Instead, all new federal student loans come directly from the U.S. Department of Education under the Direct Loan Program. Any FFEL loans noted in this section of an institution's profile are no longer available.

Loans are forms of aid that must be repaid with interest. Most people will borrow money to pay college costs. The loans available through financial aid programs are offered at very favorable interest rates. Student loans are preferable to parent loans because the payoff is deferred. In comparing colleges, the dollar amount of total indebtedness of the last class is a factor to be considered. Typically, this amount would increase proportionate to the tuition. However, if it does not, this could mean that the college provides relatively generous grant or work-study aid rather than loans in its financial aid package.

Work-Study

The total dollar amounts, number, and average dollar amount of *Federal work-study* (FWS) jobs appear first. The total dollar figure of *State or other work-study/employment*, if available, is shown, as is the percentage of those dollars that go to meet financial need. The number of part-time jobs available on campus to undergraduates, other than work-study, is shown last.

FWS is a federally funded program that enables students with demonstrated need to earn money by working on or off campus, usually in a nonprofit organization. FWS jobs are a special category of jobs that are open to students only through the financial aid office. Other kinds of part-time jobs are routinely available at most colleges and may vary widely. In comparing colleges, you may find characteristic differences in how the "self-help" amounts (loans and work-study) are apportioned.

Athletic Awards

The total dollar amount of athletic scholarships given by the college to undergraduate students, including percentages that are need-based and non-need-based, is indicated.

Applying for Financial Aid

Required financial aid forms include the FAFSA (Free Application for Federal Student Aid), the institution's own form, CSS/Financial Aid PROFILE, a state aid form, a noncustodial (divorced/separated) parent's statement, a business/farm supplement, and others. The college's financial aid application deadline is noted as the *Financial aid deadline* and is shown in one of three ways: as a specific date if it is an absolute deadline; noted as *continuous*, which means processing goes on without a deadline or until all available aid has been awarded; or as a date with the note *(priority)*, meaning that you are encouraged to apply before that date in order to have the best chance of obtaining aid. *Notification date* is listed as either a specific date or *continuous*. The date by which a reply to the college with the decision to accept or decline its financial aid package is listed as either a specific date or as a number of weeks from the date of notification.

Be prepared to check early with the colleges as to exactly which forms will be required. All colleges require the FAFSA for students applying for federal aid. In most cases, colleges have a limited amount of funds set aside to use as financial aid. It is possible that the first eligible students will get a larger share of what is available.

Contact

The name, title, address, telephone and fax numbers, and e-mail address of the person to contact for further information (student financial aid contact) are given at the end of the profile. You should feel free to write or call for any materials you need or if you have questions.

Appendix

This section lists more than 400 state-specific grants and loans. Award amounts, number of awards, eligibility requirements, application requirements, and deadlines are given for all programs.

Indexes

Six indexes in the back of the book allow you to search for particular award programs based on the following criteria:

Non-Need Scholarships for Undergraduates

This index lists the colleges that report that they offer scholarships based on academic interests, abilities, achievements, or personal characteristics other than financial need. Specific categories appear in alphabetical order under the following broad groups:

- Academic Interests/Achievements
- Creative Arts/Performance
- Special Achievements/Activities
- Special Characteristics

See the index for specific categories in each group.

Athletic Grants for Undergraduates

This index lists the colleges that report offering scholarships on the basis of athletic abilities.

Co-op Programs

This index lists colleges that report offering cooperative education programs. These are formal arrangements with off-campus employers that are designed to allow students to combine study and work, often in a position related to the student's field of study. Salaries typically are set at regular marketplace levels, and academic credit is often given.

ROTC Programs

This index lists colleges that offer Reserve Officers' Training Corps programs. The index is arranged by the branch of service that sponsors the program.

Tuition Waivers

This index lists colleges that report offering full or partial tuition waivers for certain categories of students. A majority of colleges offer tuition waivers to employees or children of employees.

Because this benefit is so common and the affected employees usually are aware of it, no separate index of schools offering this option is provided. However, this information is included in the individual college profiles.

Tuition Payment Alternatives

This index lists colleges that report offering tuition payment alternatives. These payment alternatives include deferred payment plans, guaranteed tuition plans, installment payment plans, and prepayment plans.

Data Collection Procedures

The data contained in the college chart, profiles, and indexes were collected in winter and spring 2011 through *Peterson's Annual Survey of Undergraduate Financial Aid* and *Peterson's Annual Survey of Undergraduate Institutions*. Questionnaires were sent to the more than 2,100 institutions of higher education that are accredited in the U.S. and U.S. territories and offer full four- or five-year baccalaureate degrees via full-time on-campus programs of study. Officials at the colleges—usually financial aid or admission officers but sometimes registrars or institutional research staff members—completed and returned the forms. Peterson's has every reason to believe that the data presented in this book are accurate. However, students should always confirm costs and other facts with a specific school at the time of application, since colleges can and do change policies and fees whenever necessary.

The state aid data presented in *Peterson's How to Get Money for College* was submitted by state officials (usually the director of the state scholarship commission) to Peterson's in spring 2011. Because regulations for any government-sponsored program may be changed at any time, you should request written descriptive materials from the office administering a program in which you are interested.

Criteria for Inclusion in This Book

To be included in this guide, an institution must have full accreditation or be a candidate for accreditation (preaccreditation) status by an institutional or specialized accrediting body recognized by the U.S. Department of Education or the Council for Higher Education Accreditation (CHEA). Institutional accrediting bodies, which review each institution as a whole, include the six regional associations of schools and colleges (Middle States, New England, North Central, Northwest, Southern, and Western), each of which is responsible for a specified portion of the United States and its territories. Other institutional accrediting bodies are national in scope and accredit specific kinds of institutions (e.g., Bible colleges, independent colleges, and rabbinical and Talmudic schools). Program registration by the New York State Board of Regents is considered to be the equivalent of institutional accreditation, since the board requires that all programs offered by an institution meet its standards before recognition is granted. There are recognized specialized or professional accrediting bodies in more than forty different fields, each of which is authorized to accredit institutions or specific programs in its particular field. For specialized institutions that offer programs in one field only, we designate this to be the equivalent of institutional accreditation. A full explanation of the accrediting process and complete information on recognized, institutional (regional and national) and specialized accrediting bodies can be found online at www.chea.org or at www.ed.gov/admins/finaid/accred/index.html.

Quick-Reference Chart

College Costs At-a-Glance

Michael Steidel

To help shed some light on the typical patterns of financial aid offered by colleges, we have prepared the following chart. This chart can help you to better understand financial aid practices in general, form realistic expectations about the amounts of aid that might be provided by specific colleges or universities, and prepare for meaningful discussions with the financial aid officers at colleges being considered. The data appearing in the chart have been supplied by the schools themselves and are also shown in the individual college profiles.

Tuition and fees are based on the total of full-time tuition and mandatory fees for the 2011–12 academic year or for the 2010–11 academic year if 2011–12 figures are not available. More information about these costs, as well as the costs of room and board and the year for which they are current, can be found in the individual college profiles. For institutions that have two or more tuition rates for different categories of students or types of programs, the lowest rate is used in figuring the cost.

The colleges are listed alphabetically by state. An "NR" in any individual column indicates that the applicable data element was "Not Reported."

The chart is divided into eight columns of information for each college:

1. Institutional Control
Whether the school is independent (ind.), including independent, independent–religious, and proprietary, or public (pub.), including federal, state, commonwealth, territory, county, district, city, state, local, and state-related.

2. Tuition and Fees
Based on the total of full-time tuition and mandatory fees. An asterisk indicates that the school includes room and board in their mandatory fees.

3. Room and Board
If a school has room and board costs that vary according to the type of accommodation and meal plan, either the lowest figures are represented or the figures are for the most common room arrangement and a full meal plan. If a school has only housing arrangements, a dagger appears to the right of the number. An "NA" will appear in this column if no college-owned or -operated housing facilities are offered.

4. Percent of Eligible Freshmen Receiving Need-Based Gift Awards
Calculated by dividing the number of freshman students determined to have need who received need-based gift aid by the number of full-time freshmen.

5. Percent of Freshmen Whose Need Was Fully Met
Calculated by dividing the number of freshman students whose financial need was fully met by the number of freshmen with need.

6. Average Financial Aid Package for Freshmen
The average dollar amount from all sources, including *gift aid* (scholarships and grants) and *self-help* (jobs and loans), awarded to freshmen receiving aid. Note that this aid package may exceed tuition and fees if the average aid package included coverage of room and board expenses.

7. Average Net Cost After Aid
Average aid package subtracted from published costs (tuition, fees, room, and board) to produce what the average student will have to pay.

8. Average Indebtedness Upon Graduation
Average per-student indebtedness of graduating seniors.

Because personal situations vary widely, it is very important to note that an individual's aid package can be quite different from the averages. Moreover, the data shown for each school can fluctuate widely from year to year, depending on the number of applicants, the amount of need to be met, and the financial resources and policies of the college. Peterson's intent in presenting this chart is to provide you with useful facts and figures that can serve as general guidelines in the pursuit of financial aid. We caution you to use the data only as a jumping-off point for further investigation and analysis, not as a means to rank or select colleges.

After you have narrowed down the choice of colleges based on academic and personal criteria, we recommend that you carefully study this chart. From it, you can develop a list of questions for financial aid officers at the colleges under serious consideration. Here are just a few questions you might want to ask:

- What are the specific types and sources of aid provided to freshmen at this school?

- What factors does this college consider in determining whether a financial aid applicant is qualified for its need-based aid programs?
- How does the college determine the combination of types of aid that make up an individual's package?
- How are non-need-based awards treated: as a part of the aid package or as a part of the parental/family contribution?
- Does this school "guarantee" financial aid and, if so, how is its policy implemented? Guaranteed aid means that, by policy, 100 percent of need is met for all students judged to have need. Implementation determines *how* need is met and varies widely from school to school. For example, grade point average may determine the apportioning of scholarship, loan, and work-study aid. Rules for freshmen may be different from those for upperclass students.
- To what degree is the admission process "need-blind"? Need-blind means that admission decisions are made without regard to the student's need for financial aid.
- What are the norms and practices for upperclass students? Peterson's chart presents information on *freshmen* financial aid only; however, the financial aid office should be able and willing to provide you with comparable figures for upperclass students. A college might offer a wonderful package for the freshman year, then leave students mostly on their own to fund the remaining three years. Or the school may provide a higher proportion of scholarship money for freshmen, then rebalance its aid packages to contain more self-help aid (loans and work-study) in upperclass years. There is an assumption that, all other factors being equal, students who have settled into the pattern of college time management can handle more work-study hours than freshmen. Grade point average, tuition increases, changes in parental financial circumstances, and other factors may also affect the redistribution.

Michael Steidel is Director of Admission at Carnegie Mellon University.

College Costs At-a-Glance

	Institutional Control ind.=independent; pub.=public	Tuition and Fees	Room and Board	Percent of Eligible Freshmen Receiving Need-Based Gift Awards	Percent of Freshmen Whose Need Was Fully Met	Average Financial Aid Package for Freshmen	Average Net Cost After Aid	Average Indebtedness Upon Graduation
Alabama								
Alabama Agricultural and Mechanical University	pub.	$ 5800	$ 6200	86%	12%	$ 9896	$ 2104	$31,863
Alabama State University	pub.	$ 7164	$ 4800	89%	59%	$15,174	—	$29,795
Amridge University	ind.	$ 8420	NA	NR	NR	NR	NR	$18,000
Athens State University	pub.	$ 4860	NA	NR	NR	$10,198	—	NR
Auburn University	pub.	$ 7900	$ 9630	83%	28%	$11,218	$ 6312	$23,491
Auburn University Montgomery	pub.	$ 7280	$ 3820†	74%	75%	NR	NR	NR
Birmingham-Southern College	ind.	$27,890	$ 9320	79%	27%	$27,723	$ 9487	$28,157
Faulkner University	ind.	$14,810	$ 6570	74%	9%	$ 5000	$16,380	$19,300
Huntingdon College	ind.	$20,990	$ 8000	100%	18%	$16,646	$12,344	$17,993
Samford University	ind.	$23,932	$ 8158	99%	26%	$16,801	$15,289	$20,328
Spring Hill College	ind.	$26,730	$10,250	100%	16%	$31,152	$ 5828	$26,325
Troy University	pub.	$ 7200	$ 6570	71%	NR	$ 3910	$ 9860	NR
Tuskegee University	ind.	$16,750	$ 7570	85%	68%	$19,250	$ 5070	$28,575
The University of Alabama	pub.	$ 7900	$ 8214	77%	20%	$10,090	$ 6024	$26,701
The University of Alabama at Birmingham	pub.	$ 6256	$ 8810	66%	14%	$ 9408	$ 5658	$24,936
The University of Alabama in Huntsville	pub.	$ 7492	$ 7540	89%	20%	$10,202	$ 4830	$19,852
University of Mobile	ind.	$16,120	$ 7780	100%	NR	$15,525	$ 8375	$16,660
University of Montevallo	pub.	$ 8520	$ 5192	92%	24%	$ 9785	$ 3927	$12,712
University of North Alabama	pub.	$ 6668	$ 5012	79%	47%	$ 6254	$ 5426	$29,200
University of South Alabama	pub.	$ 6810	$ 5608	86%	16%	$ 8756	$ 3662	NR
The University of West Alabama	pub.	$ 5530	$ 4466	NR	NR	NR	NR	NR
Alaska								
Alaska Pacific University	ind.	$26,360	$ 9300	80%	17%	$23,105	$12,555	$31,000
University of Alaska Anchorage	pub.	$ 5096	NR	78%	15%	$ 9147	—	$21,148
University of Alaska Fairbanks	pub.	$ 6075	$ 6960	76%	34%	$ 9574	$ 3461	$29,534
University of Alaska Southeast	pub.	$ 5139	$ 8165	66%	16%	$ 7295	$ 6009	$ 2611
Arizona								
Arizona Christian University	ind.	$15,854	$ 6780	100%	NR	$13,085	$ 9549	$21,801
Arizona State University	pub.	$ 8132	$ 9706	93%	24%	$12,473	$ 5365	$18,542
Embry-Riddle Aeronautical University–Prescott	ind.	$29,672	$ 8900	97%	NR	$14,674	$23,898	NR
Northern Arizona University	pub.	$ 7667	$ 8072	69%	11%	$ 9713	$ 6026	$18,764
Prescott College	ind.	$27,265	$ 3810†	100%	6%	$18,954	$12,121	$15,182
University of Advancing Technology	ind.	$19,500	$10,926	NR	NR	NR	NR	NR
The University of Arizona	pub.	$ 8860	$ 9024	95%	15%	$11,058	$ 6826	$20,074
Arkansas								
Arkansas State University	pub.	$ 6640	$ 6544	98%	38%	$11,400	$ 1784	$19,000
Arkansas Tech University	pub.	$ 5908	$ 5270	89%	20%	$ 8860	$ 2318	$16,363
Harding University	ind.	$14,040	$ 5922	97%	30%	$11,884	$ 8078	$33,989
Hendrix College	ind.	$34,230	$ 9714	100%	53%	$25,383	$18,561	$21,170
John Brown University	ind.	$20,766	$ 7562	94%	45%	NR	NR	$19,500
Lyon College	ind.	$22,906	$ 7340	100%	16%	$21,830	$ 8416	$18,180
Ouachita Baptist University	ind.	$20,630	$ 6040	99%	54%	$17,618	$ 9052	$15,970

NA = not applicable; NR = not reported; * = includes room and board; † = room only; — = not available.

College Costs At-a-Glance	Institutional Control ind.=independent; pub.=public	Tuition and Fees	Room and Board	Percent of Eligible Freshmen Receiving Need-Based Gift Awards	Percent of Freshmen Whose Need Was Fully Met	Average Financial Aid Package for Freshmen	Average Net Cost After Aid	Average Indebtedness Upon Graduation
Arkansas—*continued*								
University of Arkansas	pub.	$ 6768	$ 8042	90%	30%	$10,349	$ 4461	$21,562
University of Arkansas at Little Rock	pub.	$ 6643	$ 3255†	NR	NR	NR	NR	NR
University of the Ozarks	ind.	$22,050	$ 6500	99%	26%	$22,655	$ 5895	$21,520
Williams Baptist College	ind.	$12,020	$ 5400	82%	NR	$12,541	$ 4879	$18,338
California								
Alliant International University	ind.	$16,570	$ 7404	NR	NR	NR	NR	NR
American Jewish University	ind.	$25,688	$12,364	86%	79%	$24,000	$14,052	$28,000
Azusa Pacific University	ind.	$28,800	$ 7082	80%	34%	$26,061	$ 9821	NR
Bethesda Christian University	ind.	$ 7050	NR	100%	56%	$ 4000	$ 3050	$ 2500
Biola University	ind.	$28,897	$ 8000	84%	100%	$33,285	$ 3612	$29,075
California Christian College	ind.	$ 7610	$ 4150	100%	NR	$10,450	$ 1310	$26,237
California College of the Arts	ind.	$35,222	$ 7000†	92%	6%	$22,810	$19,412	$24,677
California Institute of Integral Studies	ind.	$15,060	NA	NR	NR	NR	NR	$29,000
California Institute of Technology	ind.	$37,704	$11,676	100%	100%	$33,494	$15,886	$10,760
California Institute of the Arts	ind.	$38,260	$ 9626	95%	5%	$30,584	$17,302	$50,017
California Lutheran University	ind.	$31,000	$10,580	100%	20%	$23,625	$17,955	$23,900
California Polytechnic State University, San Luis Obispo	pub.	$ 6480	$ 9992	74%	7%	$ 9113	$ 7359	NR
California State Polytechnic University, Pomona	pub.	$ 4806	$10,011	84%	9%	$10,280	$ 4537	$16,736
California State University, Bakersfield	pub.	$ 5314	$ 7041	100%	2%	$ 3720	$ 8635	$ 6730
California State University, Chico	pub.	$ 5620	$11,138	70%	15%	$13,033	$ 3725	NR
California State University, Dominguez Hills	pub.	$ 4849	$10,085	85%	1%	$ 4705	$10,229	$12,786
California State University, East Bay	pub.	$ 4872	$10,029	85%	2%	$11,240	$ 3661	$15,958
California State University, Fresno	pub.	$ 4230	$10,200	85%	12%	$10,329	$ 4101	$12,670
California State University, Fullerton	pub.	$ 4971	$ 9632	84%	89%	$ 9417	$ 5186	$14,989
California State University, Long Beach	pub.	$ 5464	$11,294	86%	71%	$12,074	$ 4684	$10,787
California State University, Monterey Bay	pub.	$ 4721	$ 8440	79%	30%	$10,312	$ 2849	$14,365
California State University, Northridge	pub.	$ 5076	$12,414	81%	NR	$10,656	$ 6834	$15,582
California State University, Sacramento	pub.	$ 5194	$ 9512	75%	13%	$ 5049	$ 9657	$14,679
California State University, San Bernardino	pub.	$ 5189	NR	88%	12%	$11,374	—	$23,791
California State University, Stanislaus	pub.	$ 5994	$ 8250	82%	7%	$ 1652	$12,592	$13,400
Claremont McKenna College	ind.	$42,480	$13,120	100%	100%	$35,591	$20,009	$10,280
Cogswell Polytechnical College	ind.	$18,924	$ 8200†	NR	NR	NR	NR	NR
The Colburn School Conservatory of Music	ind.	$ 0	$ 0	NR	NR	NR	NR	NR
Concordia University	ind.	$27,300	$ 8590	100%	22%	$22,232	$13,658	$23,465
Dominican University of California	ind.	$37,350	$14,460	99%	11%	$24,916	$26,894	$32,314
Fresno Pacific University	ind.	$23,904	$ 6300	84%	10%	$21,525	$ 8679	$16,898
Golden Gate University	ind.	$15,390	NA	NR	NR	NR	NR	NR
Harvey Mudd College	ind.	$40,390	$13,198	95%	100%	$34,282	$19,306	$21,806
Hope International University	ind.	$24,235	$ 7800	100%	NR	$17,152	$14,883	$27,000
Humboldt State University	pub.	$ 6496	$10,486	79%	1%	$11,392	$ 5590	$17,444
The King's College and Seminary	ind.	$ 7755	NA	NR	NR	NR	NR	NR
Loyola Marymount University	ind.	$36,404	$13,930	95%	18%	$24,069	$26,265	$29,906

NA = not applicable; NR = not reported; * = includes room and board; † = room only; — = not available.

College Costs At-a-Glance

	Institutional Control ind.=independent; pub.=public	Tuition and Fees	Room and Board	Percent of Eligible Freshmen Receiving Need-Based Gift Awards	Percent of Freshmen Whose Need Was Fully Met	Average Financial Aid Package for Freshmen	Average Net Cost After Aid	Average Indebtedness Upon Graduation
California—*continued*								
The Master's College and Seminary	ind.	$26,880	$ 8400	100%	15%	$19,544	$15,736	$12,842
Menlo College	ind.	$34,900	$11,300	100%	5%	$28,339	$17,861	$28,333
Mills College	ind.	$37,605	$11,644	100%	50%	$35,446	$13,803	$28,914
Mount St. Mary's College	ind.	$31,626	$10,125	99%	11%	$29,000	$12,751	$26,500
National University	ind.	$11,148	NA	63%	1%	$ 3625	$ 7523	NR
Notre Dame de Namur University	ind.	$29,980	$11,680	100%	8%	$24,149	$17,511	$25,843
Occidental College	ind.	$40,939	$11,360	100%	100%	$38,423	$13,876	$25,549
Otis College of Art and Design	ind.	$35,354	NR	100%	1%	$17,935	$17,419	$10,963
Pacific Union College	ind.	$25,965	$ 7275	100%	3%	$21,700	$11,540	$21,000
Pepperdine University (Malibu)	ind.	$39,080	$11,390	93%	23%	$34,994	$15,476	$35,747
Pitzer College	ind.	$41,130	$11,950	95%	100%	$39,076	$14,004	$20,089
Point Loma Nazarene University	ind.	$27,100	$ 9000	94%	13%	$17,462	$18,638	$25,607
Pomona College	ind.	$39,883	$13,227	100%	100%	$38,352	$14,758	$ 9700
Saint Mary's College of California	ind.	$35,430	$12,350	87%	7%	$29,365	$18,415	$36,745
San Diego Christian College	ind.	$23,824	$ 8322	59%	17%	$15,867	$16,279	$20,921
San Diego State University	pub.	$ 5206	$11,485	80%	5%	$ 9300	$ 7391	$15,500
San Francisco State University	pub.	$ 5668	$11,408	69%	7%	$ 9958	$ 7118	$17,706
San Jose State University	pub.	$ 5475	$10,733	71%	51%	$11,420	$ 4788	$ 9483
Santa Clara University	ind.	$37,368	$11,742	78%	42%	$26,456	$22,654	$23,909
Scripps College	ind.	$40,450	$12,450	97%	100%	$36,915	$15,985	$ 9435
Shasta Bible College	ind.	$ 9600	$ 2400†	100%	NR	$ 2500	$ 9500	NR
Simpson University	ind.	$21,600	$ 7300	100%	12%	$18,990	$ 9910	$22,831
Soka University of America	ind.	$26,202	$ 9640	68%	75%	$23,665	$12,177	$24,000
Sonoma State University	pub.	$ 5508	$10,522	62%	8%	$ 9740	$ 6290	$18,201
Stanford University	ind.	$41,006	$12,291	99%	91%	$40,298	$12,999	$14,058
Thomas Aquinas College	ind.	$22,850	$ 7550	91%	100%	$19,825	$10,575	$16,311
TUI University	ind.	$ 9440	NA	62%	86%	$ 4305	$ 5135	$38,298
University of California, Berkeley	pub.	$12,462	$15,308	97%	18%	$20,619	$ 7151	$16,056
University of California, Davis	pub.	$11,984	$12,498	97%	15%	$19,310	$ 5172	$16,659
University of California, Irvine	pub.	$11,927	$11,400	95%	41%	$18,782	$ 4545	$16,878
University of California, Los Angeles	pub.	$11,868	$13,734	96%	23%	$19,561	$ 6041	$18,203
University of California, Merced	pub.	$10,130	$12,801	98%	37%	$20,781	$ 2150	$15,913
University of California, Riverside	pub.	$11,029	$11,600	96%	45%	$21,402	$ 1227	$18,094
University of California, San Diego	pub.	$12,176	$11,719	96%	18%	$21,196	$ 2699	$18,757
University of California, Santa Barbara	pub.	$11,686	$13,109	93%	43%	$20,393	$ 4402	$17,596
University of California, Santa Cruz	pub.	$12,447	$14,610	95%	33%	$22,015	$ 5042	$17,546
University of La Verne	ind.	$31,300	$11,280	66%	11%	$27,624	$14,956	$31,112
University of Redlands	ind.	$35,540	$10,832	99%	18%	$32,497	$13,875	$20,364
University of San Diego	ind.	$38,578	$11,752	96%	15%	$29,920	$20,410	$29,928
University of Southern California	ind.	$41,022	$11,580	89%	93%	$36,291	$16,311	$30,090
University of the Pacific	ind.	$34,100	$11,142	97%	19%	$28,223	$17,019	NR
Vanguard University of Southern California	ind.	$26,342	$ 8274	82%	15%	$21,454	$13,162	$28,256
Westmont College	ind.	$34,460	$10,960	100%	18%	$26,289	$19,131	$27,690

NA = not applicable; NR = not reported; * = includes room and board; † = room only; — = not available.

College Costs At-a-Glance

	Institutional Control ind.=independent; pub.=public	Tuition and Fees	Room and Board	Percent of Eligible Freshmen Receiving Need-Based Gift Awards	Percent of Freshmen Whose Need Was Fully Met	Average Financial Aid Package for Freshmen	Average Net Cost After Aid	Average Indebtedness Upon Graduation
California—*continued*								
Whittier College	ind.	$35,742	$10,026	89%	14%	$32,204	$13,564	$24,687
William Jessup University	ind.	$21,800	$ 8640	100%	12%	$21,540	$ 8900	$23,160
Woodbury University	ind.	$28,855	$ 9293	100%	1%	$21,369	$16,779	$44,579
Colorado								
Adams State College	pub.	$ 4971	$ 7060	93%	1%	$ 9636	$ 2395	$22,915
The Colorado College	ind.	$38,948	$ 9416	97%	85%	$35,263	$13,101	$18,349
Colorado School of Mines	pub.	$13,425	$ 8596	66%	21%	$12,139	$ 9882	$28,126
Colorado State University	pub.	$ 6985	$ 8744	81%	46%	$10,856	$ 4873	$21,224
Colorado State University–Pueblo	pub.	$ 5615	$ 8660	86%	5%	$ 8132	$ 6143	$20,141
Fort Lewis College	pub.	$ 4924	$ 7840	100%	35%	$ 7326	$ 5438	$17,371
Johnson & Wales University	ind.	$25,407	$ 9261	90%	13%	$16,685	$17,983	NR
Jones International University	ind.	$12,480	NA	79%	NR	$ 5630	$ 6850	NR
Mesa State College	pub.	$ 6248	$ 8298	83%	29%	$10,437	$ 4109	$18,966
Metropolitan State College of Denver	pub.	$ 4093	NA	80%	4%	$ 6489	—	$25,774
Naropa University	ind.	$26,360	$ 8712	84%	NR	$29,185	$ 5887	$24,958
Nazarene Bible College	ind.	$ 9045	NA	25%	NR	$ 6171	$ 2874	$31,211
Regis University	ind.	$23,882	$ 9100	96%	52%	$21,325	$11,657	$29,590
Rocky Mountain College of Art + Design	ind.	$26,832	NA	43%	10%	$18,237	$ 8595	$26,247
University of Colorado at Colorado Springs	pub.	$ 7416	$ 6778†	82%	10%	$ 7391	$ 6803	$21,551
University of Colorado Boulder	pub.	$ 8511	$10,792	90%	64%	$13,160	$ 6143	$19,758
University of Colorado Denver	pub.	$ 7214	$ 9956	82%	8%	$ 8509	$ 8661	$17,823
University of Denver	ind.	$37,833	$10,184	99%	27%	$29,352	$18,665	$25,578
University of Northern Colorado	pub.	$ 5997	$ 8920	66%	58%	$14,646	$ 271	NR
Western State College of Colorado	pub.	$ 4775	$ 8518	50%	15%	$ 7500	$ 5793	$18,600
Connecticut								
Central Connecticut State University	pub.	$ 7861	$ 9576	92%	8%	$ 8799	$ 8638	$19,086
Connecticut College	ind.	$43,990	$ 9120	90%	100%	$30,502	$22,608	$22,038
Eastern Connecticut State University	pub.	$ 8350	$10,048	70%	8%	$ 8152	$10,246	$24,427
Fairfield University	ind.	$39,040	$11,740	82%	25%	$29,154	$21,626	$37,015
Lyme Academy College of Fine Arts	ind.	$26,784	$ 8550	NR	NR	$18,405	$16,929	$24,578
Post University	ind.	$25,050	$ 9700	NR	NR	NR	NR	NR
Quinnipiac University	ind.	$36,130	$13,430	98%	14%	$21,596	$27,964	$38,953
Sacred Heart University	ind.	$31,440	$12,340	98%	7%	$16,366	$27,414	$40,865
Southern Connecticut State University	pub.	$ 8050	$ 9983	78%	41%	$13,965	$ 4068	$21,096
Trinity College	ind.	$42,370	$10,960	90%	100%	$37,881	$15,449	$21,671
University of Bridgeport	ind.	$26,495	$11,400	100%	NR	$23,900	$13,995	NR
University of Connecticut	pub.	$10,670	$11,050	81%	18%	$13,731	$ 7989	$23,237
University of Hartford	ind.	$30,754	$11,920	45%	30%	$ 5509	$37,165	$14,855
Wesleyan University	ind.	$42,084	$11,592	93%	100%	$35,985	$17,691	$29,227
Western Connecticut State University	pub.	$ 7909	$ 5698†	87%	5%	$ 8199	$ 5408	$23,487
Yale University	ind.	$38,300	$11,500	100%	100%	$40,900	$ 8900	$ 9254

NA = not applicable; NR = not reported; * = includes room and board; † = room only; — = not available.

College Costs At-a-Glance

	Institutional Control ind.=independent; pub.=public	Tuition and Fees	Room and Board	Percent of Eligible Freshmen Receiving Need-Based Gift Awards	Percent of Freshmen Whose Need Was Fully Met	Average Financial Aid Package for Freshmen	Average Net Cost After Aid	Average Indebtedness Upon Graduation
Delaware								
Delaware State University	pub.	$ 7561	NR	92%	36%	$10,384	—	$36,410
Goldey-Beacom College	ind.	$19,860	$ 5172†	100%	21%	$13,111	$11,921	$26,045
University of Delaware	pub.	$10,208	$ 9636	80%	50%	$12,790	$ 7054	$17,200
District of Columbia								
American University	ind.	$36,697	$13,468	52%	22%	$31,635	$18,530	$36,206
The Catholic University of America	ind.	$33,780	$12,742	98%	48%	$31,487	$15,035	NR
Corcoran College of Art and Design	ind.	$30,140	$12,470	93%	NR	$20,160	$22,450	$35,562
Gallaudet University	ind.	$11,226	$ 9660	100%	43%	$18,319	$ 2567	$14,066
Georgetown University	ind.	$40,203	$12,240	99%	100%	$33,108	$19,335	$25,315
The George Washington University	ind.	$42,905	$10,120	98%	92%	$38,579	$14,446	$32,547
Howard University	ind.	$17,905	$ 8498	54%	10%	$12,103	$14,300	$ 9863
University of the District of Columbia	pub.	$ 7000	$ 6660	86%	31%	$ 5250	$ 8410	NR
Florida								
The Baptist College of Florida	ind.	$ 8800	$ 4066	98%	3%	$ 6872	$ 5994	$ 7988
Bethune-Cookman University	ind.	$13,572	$ 7980	97%	5%	$12,396	$ 9156	$27,645
Eckerd College	ind.	$34,546	$ 9652	100%	18%	$28,491	$15,707	$30,881
Embry-Riddle Aeronautical University–Daytona	ind.	$29,852	$ 9750	99%	NR	$15,505	$24,097	NR
Embry-Riddle Aeronautical University–Worldwide	ind.	$ 5580	NA	100%	NR	$ 5113	$ 467	NR
Flagler College	ind.	$13,860	$ 7590	86%	18%	$11,676	$ 9774	$20,895
Florida Agricultural and Mechanical University	pub.	$ 4248	$ 7856	82%	26%	$13,324	—	$28,144
Florida Atlantic University	pub.	$ 4797	$ 9690	92%	19%	$ 9941	$ 4546	$18,342
Florida College	ind.	$12,350	$ 7040	61%	6%	$10,802	$ 8588	NR
Florida Gulf Coast University	pub.	$ 6728	$ 8150	63%	9%	$ 6705	$ 8173	$22,328
Florida Hospital College of Health Sciences	ind.	$ 9580	NR	NR	NR	NR	NR	NR
Florida Institute of Technology	ind.	$32,294	$11,210	100%	23%	$29,176	$14,328	$41,565
Florida International University	pub.	$ 5091	$11,440	58%	13%	$ 7139	$ 9392	$16,026
Florida National College	ind.	$13,170	NA	99%	NR	NR	NR	$ 8750
Florida Southern College	ind.	$26,112	$ 8808	78%	14%	$23,529	$11,391	$28,294
Florida State University	pub.	$ 5235	$ 9180	61%	79%	$10,422	$ 3993	$20,993
Hodges University	ind.	$16,940	NA	88%	23%	$ 8250	$ 8690	$18,900
Jacksonville University	ind.	$26,600	$ 9320	85%	18%	$20,758	$15,162	NR
Johnson & Wales University	ind.	$25,407	$ 9261	92%	12%	$19,114	$15,554	NR
Lynn University	ind.	$30,900	$11,950	81%	100%	$18,256	$24,594	$37,698
New College of Florida	pub.	$ 6032	$ 8472	100%	42%	$13,221	$ 1283	$11,458
Palm Beach Atlantic University	ind.	$23,400	$ 8220	100%	21%	$18,504	$13,116	$22,150
Ringling College of Art and Design	ind.	$30,730	$10,890	92%	3%	$14,715	$26,905	NR
Rollins College	ind.	$37,640	$11,760	100%	17%	$36,999	$12,401	$25,294
Saint Leo University	ind.	$18,870	$ 9120	100%	26%	$19,648	$ 8342	$26,780
St. Thomas University	ind.	$22,770	$ 6842	75%	4%	NR	NR	NR
Southeastern University	ind.	$16,430	$ 7900	99%	14%	$11,723	$12,607	$25,006
Stetson University	ind.	$35,081	$10,255	99%	23%	$31,956	$13,380	$33,817
University of Central Florida	pub.	$ 5020	$ 8765	47%	20%	$ 7595	$ 6190	$18,966

NA = not applicable; NR = not reported; * = includes room and board; † = room only; — = not available.

College Costs At-a-Glance

	Institutional Control ind.=independent; pub.=public	Tuition and Fees	Room and Board	Percent of Eligible Freshmen Receiving Need-Based Gift Awards	Percent of Freshmen Whose Need Was Fully Met	Average Financial Aid Package for Freshmen	Average Net Cost After Aid	Average Indebtedness Upon Graduation
Florida—*continued*								
University of Florida	pub.	$ 5044	$ 8640	64%	29%	$12,470	$ 1214	$16,013
University of Miami	ind.	$37,836	$11,062	96%	39%	$32,310	$16,588	$26,438
University of North Florida	pub.	$ 5449	$ 8452	73%	19%	$ 9150	$ 4751	$15,300
University of South Florida	pub.	$ 5198	$ 5380†	61%	8%	$ 9860	$ 718	$21,679
The University of Tampa	ind.	$23,218	$ 8590	92%	20%	$15,860	$15,948	$29,264
University of West Florida	pub.	$ 4794	$ 7856	NR	NR	NR	NR	NR
Webber International University	ind.	$18,742	$ 7252	100%	4%	$19,143	$ 6851	$28,655
Georgia								
Abraham Baldwin Agricultural College	pub.	$ 3496	$ 7220	NR	NR	NR	NR	NR
Agnes Scott College	ind.	$31,283	$ 9850	100%	35%	$31,320	$ 9813	$26,493
Armstrong Atlantic State University	pub.	$ 4510	$ 8440	80%	82%	$ 6500	$ 6450	$19,000
Augusta State University	pub.	$ 5184	$ 5250†	77%	7%	$ 3376	$ 7058	$ 7735
Berry College	ind.	$24,620	$ 8724	100%	30%	$21,069	$12,275	$12,412
Brenau University	ind.	$21,124	$10,366	100%	23%	$20,230	$11,260	$20,634
Columbus State University	pub.	$ 5896	$ 7296	71%	25%	$ 8575	$ 4617	$21,486
Covenant College	ind.	$26,226	$ 7450	98%	29%	$20,128	$13,548	$20,519
Dalton State College	pub.	$ 2536	$ 6750	79%	20%	$ 6566	$ 2720	$11,953
Emmanuel College	ind.	$14,550	$ 6100	100%	12%	$12,375	$ 8275	$28,298
Emory University	ind.	$39,158	$11,198	96%	96%	$34,871	$15,485	$26,311
Fort Valley State University	pub.	$ 5562	$ 7326	NR	NR	NR	NR	NR
Georgia College & State University	pub.	$ 7852	$ 8414	38%	NR	$ 8634	$ 7632	$17,141
Georgia Health Sciences University	pub.	$ 8182	NR	NR	NR	NR	NR	NR
Georgia Institute of Technology	pub.	$ 8716	$ 8746	97%	47%	$12,892	$ 4570	$21,838
Georgia Southern University	pub.	$ 6240	$ 8414	87%	15%	$ 9157	$ 5497	$19,418
Georgia State University	pub.	$ 8698	$ 9325	67%	16%	$10,842	$ 7181	$20,336
Kennesaw State University	pub.	$ 5942	$ 7298	80%	14%	$ 8210	$ 5030	$ 947
Life University	ind.	$ 9369	$12,480	74%	1%	$10,250	$11,599	$28,000
Luther Rice University	ind.	$ 5376	NA	75%	75%	$ 5546	—	$50,400
Mercer University	ind.	$30,560	$10,088	100%	43%	$32,893	$ 7755	$30,460
Morehouse College	ind.	$22,444	$11,494	64%	8%	$11,250	$22,688	NR
North Georgia College & State University	pub.	$ 6094	$ 6166	92%	9%	$ 8087	$ 4173	$10,021
Oglethorpe University	ind.	$27,950	$ 9990	100%	14%	$26,950	$10,990	NR
Piedmont College	ind.	$19,000	$ 7500	99%	20%	$18,887	$ 7613	$18,402
Reinhardt University	ind.	$17,840	$ 6580	100%	10%	$11,178	$13,242	$18,329
Savannah College of Art and Design	ind.	$31,010	$12,255	71%	10%	$21,816	$21,449	$39,066
Savannah State University	pub.	$ 5624	$ 6288	NR	NR	NR	NR	NR
Shorter University	ind.	$17,070	$ 8200	100%	20%	$16,632	$ 8638	$30,890
Southern Polytechnic State University	pub.	$ 6176	$ 6604	41%	46%	$ 3239	$ 9541	$24,360
Spelman College	ind.	$22,010	$10,464	88%	33%	$15,696	$16,778	$14,070
Thomas University	ind.	$12,720	$ 3150†	NR	NR	NR	NR	NR
University of Georgia	pub.	$ 8736	$ 8460	97%	37%	$11,993	$ 5203	$15,938
University of West Georgia	pub.	$ 6182	$ 6754	90%	24%	$ 8914	$ 4022	$15,365

NA = not applicable; NR = not reported; * = includes room and board; † = room only; — = not available.

College Costs At-a-Glance

	Institutional Control ind.=independent; pub.=public	Tuition and Fees	Room and Board	Percent of Eligible Freshmen Receiving Need-Based Gift Awards	Percent of Freshmen Whose Need Was Fully Met	Average Financial Aid Package for Freshmen	Average Net Cost After Aid	Average Indebtedness Upon Graduation
Georgia—*continued*								
Valdosta State University	pub.	$ 4972	$ 6520	84%	13%	$ 9180	$ 2312	$19,592
Wesleyan College	ind.	$18,000	$ 8100	100%	37%	$15,947	$10,153	$20,896
Young Harris College	ind.	$21,970	$ 7480	99%	23%	$15,430	$14,020	NR
Hawaii								
Hawai'i Pacific University	ind.	$15,820	$11,648	47%	28%	$17,742	$ 9726	$32,172
University of Hawaii at Hilo	pub.	$ 5416	$ 7134	78%	25%	$ 8692	$ 3858	$11,944
University of Hawaii at Manoa	pub.	$ 8911	$ 9410	81%	21%	$ 8283	$10,038	$16,528
University of Hawaii–West Oahu	pub.	$ 5141	NA	75%	NR	$ 2779	$ 2362	NR
Idaho								
Boise State University	pub.	$ 5300	$ 5610	79%	23%	$ 8380	$ 2530	$23,594
Lewis-Clark State College	pub.	$ 6230	NR	70%	7%	$ 6882	—	NR
New Saint Andrews College	ind.	$10,400	NA	NR	NR	NR	NR	NR
Northwest Nazarene University	ind.	$24,030	$ 6220	68%	21%	$16,828	$13,422	$26,752
University of Idaho	pub.	$ 5402	$ 7194	62%	20%	$12,148	$ 448	$24,396
Illinois								
Augustana College	ind.	$33,363	$ 8466	98%	26%	$22,493	$19,336	$28,198
Aurora University	ind.	$18,700	$ 8800	78%	28%	$18,208	$ 9292	$24,083
Benedictine University	ind.	$23,750	$ 7500	64%	NR	$20,094	$11,156	$28,100
Bradley University	ind.	$25,424	$ 7950	99%	14%	$16,833	$16,541	NR
Concordia University Chicago	ind.	$25,631	$ 8250	100%	31%	$21,607	$12,274	$31,945
DePaul University	ind.	$28,858	$10,955	87%	12%	$22,241	$17,572	$26,190
Dominican University	ind.	$25,710	$ 8000	100%	12%	$20,008	$13,702	$22,605
East-West University	ind.	$15,750	NA	100%	NR	$13,818	$ 1932	$ 3500
Elmhurst College	ind.	$30,054	$ 8524	100%	26%	$22,386	$16,192	$23,912
Eureka College	ind.	$18,080	$ 7500	100%	3%	$14,997	$10,583	$22,720
Governors State University	pub.	$ 8746	NA	NR	NR	NR	NR	$ 2828
Greenville College	ind.	$21,658	$ 7338	100%	7%	$18,058	$10,938	$24,002
Illinois College	ind.	$22,800	$ 7900	100%	24%	$22,745	$ 7955	$24,401
Illinois Institute of Technology	ind.	$34,880	$10,338	100%	28%	$30,905	$14,313	NR
Illinois State University	pub.	$11,417	$ 8436	61%	39%	$12,461	$ 7392	$22,847
Illinois Wesleyan University	ind.	$35,256	$ 8106	100%	31%	$25,400	$17,962	$31,904
Judson University	ind.	$24,780	$ 8500	NR	NR	NR	NR	NR
Knox College	ind.	$34,464	$ 7488	100%	27%	$28,521	$13,431	$26,506
Lake Forest College	ind.	$35,525	$ 8327	100%	25%	$30,020	$13,832	$31,790
Lakeview College of Nursing	ind.	$13,760	NA	NR	NR	NR	NR	$25,000
Loyola University Chicago	ind.	$33,294	$11,570	99%	13%	$28,805	$16,059	NR
McKendree University	ind.	$25,090	$ 8500	100%	23%	$22,166	$11,424	$23,025
Millikin University	ind.	$27,425	$ 8291	97%	43%	$22,854	$12,862	$28,475
Monmouth College	ind.	$28,650	$ 7300	100%	17%	$26,653	$ 9297	$25,909
National-Louis University	ind.	$18,435	NA	100%	NR	$ 3123	$15,312	$29,637
North Central College	ind.	$28,224	$ 8463	100%	26%	$22,348	$14,339	$29,137
Northeastern Illinois University	pub.	$ 9003	NA	96%	NR	$ 8365	$ 638	$10,976

NA = not applicable; NR = not reported; * = includes room and board; † = room only; — = not available.

College Costs At-a-Glance

	Institutional Control ind.=independent; pub.=public	Tuition and Fees	Room and Board	Percent of Eligible Freshmen Receiving Need-Based Gift Awards	Percent of Freshmen Whose Need Was Fully Met	Average Financial Aid Package for Freshmen	Average Net Cost After Aid	Average Indebtedness Upon Graduation
Illinois—*continued*								
Northern Illinois University	pub.	$ 9854	$10,366	71%	10%	$11,719	$ 8501	$27,101
Principia College	ind.	$25,640	$ 9500	78%	88%	$23,837	$11,303	$14,963
Quincy University	ind.	$24,140	$ 9420	100%	27%	$23,967	$ 9593	$23,711
Robert Morris University Illinois	ind.	$21,600	$10,326	97%	4%	$13,499	$18,427	$28,103
Rockford College	ind.	$24,750	$ 6950	98%	12%	$18,425	$13,275	$28,343
Saint Francis Medical Center College of Nursing	ind.	$14,956	$ 2400†	NR	NR	NR	NR	NR
Saint Xavier University	ind.	$25,520	$ 8692	100%	18%	$23,380	$10,832	$29,326
School of the Art Institute of Chicago	ind.	$35,950	$ 9800†	99%	3%	$29,919	$15,831	$39,306
Shimer College	ind.	$27,810	$12,850	94%	6%	$14,687	$25,973	$37,500
Southern Illinois University Carbondale	pub.	$11,038	$ 8648	75%	88%	$11,811	$ 7875	$21,359
Southern Illinois University Edwardsville	pub.	$ 8401	$ 7821	65%	33%	$16,880	—	$21,633
Trinity Christian College	ind.	$21,508	$ 7964	100%	16%	$15,829	$13,643	$25,794
Trinity College of Nursing and Health Sciences	ind.	$12,656	NA	100%	NR	NR	NR	$ 9500
University of Chicago	ind.	$43,780	$12,633	NR	100%	$38,991	$17,422	$22,359
University of Illinois at Chicago	pub.	$12,056	$ 9994	82%	10%	$13,888	$ 8162	$18,526
University of Illinois at Springfield	pub.	$10,367	$ 9400	95%	12%	$12,474	$ 7293	$17,335
University of Illinois at Urbana–Champaign	pub.	$14,414	$10,080	82%	37%	$13,766	$10,728	$21,543
University of St. Francis	ind.	$24,742	$ 8176	68%	57%	$22,066	$10,852	$27,088
Western Illinois University	pub.	$ 9490	$ 8138	73%	35%	$ 9580	$ 8048	$22,007
Wheaton College	ind.	$27,580	$ 8050	98%	14%	$22,763	$12,867	$21,241
Indiana								
Ball State University	pub.	$ 8214	$ 8208	60%	20%	$10,039	$ 6383	$24,121
Bethel College	ind.	$23,030	$ 7070	71%	17%	$20,528	$ 9572	$26,173
Butler University	ind.	$30,558	$10,130	99%	12%	$23,432	$17,256	$30,581
Calumet College of Saint Joseph	ind.	$14,200	NA	78%	20%	$11,594	$ 2606	$28,434
Crossroads Bible College	ind.	$ 9850	$ 3400†	NR	NR	NR	NR	NR
DePauw University	ind.	$34,905	$ 9180	100%	29%	$28,960	$15,125	$23,778
Earlham College	ind.	$36,694	$ 7400	90%	31%	$32,423	$11,671	$17,573
Franklin College	ind.	$24,655	$ 7295	100%	17%	$18,894	$13,056	$29,387
Goshen College	ind.	$24,500	$ 8300	100%	19%	$21,517	$11,283	$19,819
Grace College	ind.	$21,700	$ 7074	100%	NR	$13,722	$15,052	NR
Hanover College	ind.	$28,850	$ 8650	100%	23%	$24,114	$13,386	$26,714
Huntington University	ind.	$23,210	$ 7680	95%	11%	$18,480	$12,410	$30,885
Indiana State University	pub.	$ 7714	$ 7752	67%	10%	$ 8557	$ 6909	$22,124
Indiana University Bloomington	pub.	$ 9028	$ 7918	83%	20%	$10,834	$ 6112	$27,752
Indiana University East	pub.	$ 6069	NA	89%	11%	$ 7322	—	$27,069
Indiana University Kokomo	pub.	$ 6109	NA	77%	6%	$ 6688	—	$23,454
Indiana University Northwest	pub.	$ 6193	NA	81%	4%	$ 7063	—	$27,356
Indiana University–Purdue University Fort Wayne	pub.	$ 6545	$ 5900†	64%	NR	$ 8804	$ 3641	$23,607
Indiana University–Purdue University Indianapolis	pub.	$ 7885	$ 7944	81%	6%	$ 9196	$ 6633	$29,112
Indiana University South Bend	pub.	$ 6290	$ 5382†	82%	3%	$ 6920	$ 4752	$25,373
Indiana University Southeast	pub.	$ 6163	$ 5686†	83%	5%	$ 6883	$ 4966	$21,456

NA = not applicable; NR = not reported; * = includes room and board; † = room only; — = not available.

College Costs At-a-Glance

	Institutional Control ind.=independent; pub.=public	Tuition and Fees	Room and Board	Percent of Eligible Freshmen Receiving Need-Based Gift Awards	Percent of Freshmen Whose Need Was Fully Met	Average Financial Aid Package for Freshmen	Average Net Cost After Aid	Average Indebtedness Upon Graduation
Indiana—*continued*								
Indiana Wesleyan University	ind.	$21,956	$ 7148	99%	37%	$20,735	$ 8369	$28,657
Manchester College	ind.	$24,920	$ 8860	100%	17%	$24,144	$ 9636	$21,305
Purdue University	pub.	$ 9069	$ 9120	73%	55%	$11,144	$ 7045	$26,360
Purdue University Calumet	pub.	$ 6654	$ 6924	68%	17%	$ 4210	$ 9368	$22,106
Purdue University North Central	pub.	$ 6704	NA	73%	15%	$ 7309	—	$22,137
Rose-Hulman Institute of Technology	ind.	$36,270	$ 9957	100%	20%	$26,078	$20,149	$40,619
Saint Joseph's College	ind.	$26,330	$ 7980	98%	26%	$21,563	$12,747	$28,135
Saint Mary-of-the-Woods College	ind.	$24,500	$ 8890	100%	41%	$18,820	$14,570	$35,223
Saint Mary's College	ind.	$31,020	$ 9480	95%	21%	$25,037	$15,463	$28,838
Taylor University	ind.	$27,438	$ 7218	94%	21%	$17,984	$16,672	$21,302
Trine University	ind.	$26,730	$ 8800	87%	78%	$23,520	$12,010	$26,050
University of Evansville	ind.	$28,076	$ 9110	96%	27%	$24,631	$12,555	$26,389
University of Indianapolis	ind.	$22,240	$ 8440	75%	20%	$18,127	$12,553	$27,070
University of Notre Dame	ind.	$41,417	$11,388	97%	98%	$35,326	$17,479	$30,341
University of Southern Indiana	pub.	$ 5740	$ 6920	80%	13%	$ 8528	$ 4132	NR
Valparaiso University	ind.	$31,040	$ 8756	99%	20%	$22,795	$17,001	$33,024
Wabash College	ind.	$31,050	$ 8300	96%	86%	$28,538	$10,812	$29,897
Iowa								
Allen College	ind.	$14,995	$ 7157	100%	NR	$17,363	$ 4789	$27,792
Buena Vista University	ind.	$26,306	$ 7582	73%	46%	$26,518	$ 7370	$37,502
Central College	ind.	$26,242	$ 8702	100%	17%	$24,262	$10,682	$34,237
Clarke University	ind.	$24,610	$ 7340	99%	21%	$20,713	$11,237	$38,847
Coe College	ind.	$30,860	$ 7290	100%	28%	$25,654	$12,496	$33,260
Cornell College	ind.	$32,920	$ 7730	100%	48%	$28,076	$12,574	$22,455
Dordt College	ind.	$23,180	$ 6520	100%	17%	$22,605	$ 7095	$21,881
Drake University	ind.	$28,382	$ 8410	98%	29%	$21,464	$15,328	$35,027
Graceland University	ind.	$20,980	$ 7040	100%	18%	$20,812	$ 7208	$31,404
Grand View University	ind.	$20,292	$ 6732	94%	24%	$18,380	$ 8644	$33,222
Grinnell College	ind.	$39,810	$ 9334	98%	100%	$36,233	$12,911	$18,578
Iowa State University of Science and Technology	pub.	$ 6997	$ 7472	100%	42%	$11,209	$ 3260	$30,062
Iowa Wesleyan College	ind.	$22,050	$ 7106	NR	NR	NR	NR	NR
Loras College	ind.	$26,088	$ 7306	75%	43%	$20,965	$12,429	$30,790
Luther College	ind.	$34,885	$ 5850	100%	36%	$27,463	$13,272	$33,492
Morningside College	ind.	$23,984	$ 7364	81%	29%	$21,170	$10,178	$38,411
Mount Mercy University	ind.	$24,360	$ 7470	99%	19%	$18,428	$13,402	$23,373
St. Ambrose University	ind.	$24,920	$ 8885	100%	10%	$ 6344	$27,461	$32,530
Simpson College	ind.	$28,123	$ 7963	100%	39%	$27,683	$ 8403	$34,214
University of Dubuque	ind.	$21,590	$ 7370	100%	29%	$19,471	$ 9489	$41,399
The University of Iowa	pub.	$ 7765	$ 8750	68%	35%	$11,589	$ 4926	$27,391
University of Northern Iowa	pub.	$ 7008	$ 7140	53%	24%	$ 7472	$ 6676	$25,735
Upper Iowa University	ind.	$23,356	$ 7070	100%	NR	$16,671	$13,755	$22,666
Waldorf College	ind.	$18,760	$ 5954	98%	11%	$13,262	$11,452	$26,262

NA = not applicable; NR = not reported; * = includes room and board; † = room only; — = not available.

College Costs At-a-Glance

	Institutional Control ind.=independent; pub.=public	Tuition and Fees	Room and Board	Percent of Eligible Freshmen Receiving Need-Based Gift Awards	Percent of Freshmen Whose Need Was Fully Met	Average Financial Aid Package for Freshmen	Average Net Cost After Aid	Average Indebtedness Upon Graduation
Iowa—*continued*								
Wartburg College	ind.	$30,960	$8150	100%	37%	$23,483	$15,627	$29,867
Kansas								
Benedictine College	ind.	$20,475	$7375	58%	12%	NR	NR	$28,887
Bethel College	ind.	$20,700	$6980	73%	58%	$22,259	$ 5421	$24,860
Emporia State University	pub.	$ 4636	$6230	94%	11%	$ 5444	$ 5422	$23,498
Kansas State University	pub.	$ 7376	$6954	67%	25%	$10,734	$ 3596	$22,633
Manhattan Christian College	ind.	$12,288	$6054	93%	51%	$16,727	$ 1615	$16,572
McPherson College	ind.	$19,625	$7325	91%	35%	$24,222	$ 2728	$30,889
Southwestern College	ind.	$21,680	$6322	100%	18%	$18,749	$ 9253	$30,794
Tabor College	ind.	$20,630	$7160	84%	19%	$19,990	$ 7800	$27,380
The University of Kansas	pub.	$ 8733	$6982	72%	22%	$10,346	$ 5369	$23,319
Washburn University	pub.	$ 6296	$5982	68%	12%	$ 8689	$ 3589	$17,017
Wichita State University	pub.	$ 5890	$6200	66%	82%	$ 7134	$ 4956	$15,847
Kentucky								
Asbury University	ind.	$24,229	$5634	100%	32%	$19,430	$10,433	$29,411
Bellarmine University	ind.	$30,310	$8820	100%	21%	$26,601	$12,529	$23,925
Berea College	ind.	$ 910	$5574	100%	NR	$31,261	—	$ 5836
Campbellsville University	ind.	$20,740	$6980	100%	13%	$18,796	$ 8924	$18,132
Centre College	ind.	*$42,500	NR	100%	34%	$26,787	$15,713	$19,820
Clear Creek Baptist Bible College	ind.	$ 8700	NR	100%	NR	$ 7134	$ 1566	NR
Eastern Kentucky University	pub.	$ 6624	$6714	69%	4%	$ 8530	$ 4808	$10,152
Georgetown College	ind.	$27,640	$7320	100%	32%	$27,444	$ 7516	$23,612
Kentucky State University	pub.	$ 6210	$6480	81%	11%	$10,765	$ 1925	$33,320
Kentucky Wesleyan College	ind.	$19,390	$6920	100%	22%	$15,311	$10,999	$19,516
Lindsey Wilson College	ind.	$18,950	$7645	100%	20%	NR	NR	$21,637
Mid-Continent University	ind.	$13,300	$6600	96%	4%	$ 7968	$11,932	$11,005
Morehead State University	pub.	$ 6492	$6582	66%	26%	$ 9490	$ 3584	$25,182
Murray State University	pub.	$ 6264	$6860	82%	94%	$ 6425	$ 6699	$26,100
Northern Kentucky University	pub.	$ 7128	$6260	53%	17%	$ 8373	$ 5015	$21,535
Pikeville College	ind.	$15,250	$6300	100%	66%	$17,255	$ 4295	$21,250
Thomas More College	ind.	$24,720	$6790	100%	23%	$18,847	$12,663	$32,720
Transylvania University	ind.	$26,740	$8090	100%	27%	$22,458	$12,372	$22,432
Union College	ind.	$20,004	$6200	100%	12%	$17,976	$ 8228	$15,272
University of Kentucky	pub.	$ 8610	$9439	44%	23%	$ 9457	$ 8592	$19,812
University of Louisville	pub.	$ 8424	$6602	97%	25%	$11,172	$ 3854	$18,713
University of the Cumberlands	ind.	$18,000	$6826	100%	19%	$17,890	$ 6936	$15,221
Western Kentucky University	pub.	$ 7560	$6600	72%	32%	$11,991	$ 2169	$19,347
Louisiana								
Centenary College of Louisiana	ind.	$23,280	$7940	100%	27%	$21,762	$ 9458	$22,920
Louisiana College	ind.	$12,980	$4448	100%	29%	$ 7210	$10,218	NR
Louisiana State University and Agricultural and Mechanical College	pub.	$ 5764	$8210	97%	28%	$11,686	$ 2288	$19,242
Louisiana Tech University	pub.	$ 5643	$5160	95%	25%	$ 9451	$ 1352	$14,039

NA = not applicable; NR = not reported; * = includes room and board; † = room only; — = not available.

College Costs At-a-Glance

	Institutional Control ind.=independent; pub.=public	Tuition and Fees	Room and Board	Percent of Eligible Freshmen Receiving Need-Based Gift Awards	Percent of Freshmen Whose Need Was Fully Met	Average Financial Aid Package for Freshmen	Average Net Cost After Aid	Average Indebtedness Upon Graduation
Louisiana—*continued*								
Loyola University New Orleans	ind.	$33,302	$10,990	100%	18%	$25,739	$18,553	$22,319
Nicholls State University	pub.	$ 4292	$ 7808	93%	78%	$ 8204	$ 3896	$20,589
Northwestern State University of Louisiana	pub.	$ 4384	$ 7070	72%	49%	$ 6543	$ 4911	$23,710
Our Lady of Holy Cross College	ind.	$ 8604	NA	89%	17%	$ 8213	$ 391	$36,863
Southeastern Louisiana University	pub.	$ 4000	$ 6640	NR	NR	NR	NR	$36,560
Tulane University	ind.	$41,884	$ 9824	98%	71%	$34,341	$17,367	$27,510
University of Louisiana at Lafayette	pub.	$ 4426	$ 4758	94%	17%	$ 7422	$ 1762	NR
University of New Orleans	pub.	$ 4811	$ 8127	74%	12%	$ 8613	$ 4325	$16,427
Xavier University of Louisiana	ind.	$17,100	$ 7200	73%	NR	$16,230	$ 8070	$45,916
Maine								
Bates College	ind.	*$53,300	NR	98%	95%	$36,476	$16,824	$18,699
Bowdoin College	ind.	$41,565	$11,315	100%	100%	$41,086	$11,794	$18,229
Colby College	ind.	*$51,990	NR	100%	100%	$38,072	$13,918	$24,600
College of the Atlantic	ind.	$36,063	$ 8820	99%	44%	$32,877	$12,006	$20,125
Husson University	ind.	$13,960	$ 7520	97%	3%	$ 9944	$11,536	$23,613
Maine College of Art	ind.	$28,645	$ 9995	NR	NR	NR	NR	NR
Maine Maritime Academy	pub.	$10,525	$ 8870	80%	9%	$ 9017	$10,378	$40,375
New England School of Communications	ind.	$11,930	$ 7240	13%	2%	NR	NR	$33,000
Unity College	ind.	$22,500	$ 8220	100%	3%	$17,693	$13,027	NR
University of Maine	pub.	$10,168	$ 8766	88%	30%	$11,818	$ 7116	$29,143
University of Maine at Fort Kent	pub.	$ 7163	$ 7500	54%	86%	$ 6000	$ 8663	NR
University of Maine at Presque Isle	pub.	$ 7235	$ 7046	92%	30%	$10,195	$ 4086	$18,272
University of Southern Maine	pub.	$ 8538	$ 9394	77%	8%	$ 9496	$ 8436	$38,899
Maryland								
Bowie State University	pub.	$ 6154	$ 8570	70%	59%	$ 7868	$ 6856	$19,003
Capitol College	ind.	$19,890	NR	80%	8%	$16,423	$ 3467	$16,814
College of Notre Dame of Maryland	ind.	$28,350	$ 9500	100%	17%	$23,263	$14,587	$30,801
Coppin State University	pub.	$ 5545	$ 8108	79%	16%	$ 8549	$ 5104	$ 8559
Frostburg State University	pub.	$ 6904	$ 7378	66%	20%	$ 8526	$ 5756	$20,970
Garrett College	pub.	$ 3110	$ 6474	92%	NR	$ 3911	$ 5673	NR
Goucher College	ind.	$36,553	$10,569	96%	15%	$25,618	$21,504	$20,900
Hood College	ind.	$29,860	$ 9901	100%	23%	$23,471	$16,290	$17,144
The Johns Hopkins University	ind.	$40,680	$12,510	86%	98%	$33,193	$19,997	$24,307
Loyola University Maryland	ind.	$39,350	$11,730	88%	100%	$25,500	$25,580	$26,740
McDaniel College	ind.	$33,280	$ 7060	98%	24%	$28,967	$11,373	$30,825
Mount St. Mary's University	ind.	$31,536	$10,544	100%	19%	$22,008	$20,072	$29,637
Peabody Conservatory of The Johns Hopkins University	ind.	$37,425	$12,200	86%	17%	$16,458	$33,167	$38,034
St. John's College	ind.	$42,192	$ 9984	93%	97%	$36,260	$15,916	$29,869
St. Mary's College of Maryland	pub.	$13,630	$10,250	98%	3%	$11,675	$12,205	$17,505
Towson University	pub.	$ 7656	$ 9614	59%	14%	$ 8266	$ 9004	$19,069
University of Maryland, Baltimore County	pub.	$ 9171	$ 9620	82%	20%	$10,901	$ 7890	$19,594
University of Maryland, College Park	pub.	$ 8416	$ 9599	56%	15%	$10,396	$ 7619	$22,696

NA = not applicable; NR = not reported; * = includes room and board; † = room only; — = not available.

College Costs At-a-Glance

	Institutional Control ind.=independent; pub.=public	Tuition and Fees	Room and Board	Percent of Eligible Freshmen Receiving Need-Based Gift Awards	Percent of Freshmen Whose Need Was Fully Met	Average Financial Aid Package for Freshmen	Average Net Cost After Aid	Average Indebtedness Upon Graduation
Maryland—*continued*								
University of Maryland University College	pub.	$ 6000	NA	84%	NR	$ 6313	—	NR
Washington Adventist University	ind.	$20,180	$ 7530	NR	NR	NR	NR	NR
Washington College	ind.	$36,738	$ 7834	100%	42%	$26,989	$17,583	$35,831
Massachusetts								
Amherst College	ind.	$40,862	$10,660	98%	100%	$40,441	$11,081	$12,843
Assumption College	ind.	$31,305	$10,260	100%	22%	$22,394	$19,171	$32,416
Babson College	ind.	$39,040	$12,876	92%	24%	$31,375	$20,541	$30,357
Bard College at Simon's Rock	ind.	$41,982	$11,450	79%	17%	$33,336	$20,096	$44,910
Bentley University	ind.	$38,328	$12,520	82%	45%	$30,818	$20,030	$32,710
Berklee College of Music	ind.	$32,520	$15,830	54%	5%	$16,188	$32,162	NR
Boston Architectural College	ind.	$16,148	NR	59%	7%	$ 9137	$ 7011	$31,385
Boston College	ind.	$40,542	$12,082	90%	100%	$31,597	$21,027	$19,514
Boston University	ind.	$39,864	$12,260	91%	57%	$34,533	$17,591	$31,809
Brandeis University	ind.	$40,274	$11,214	99%	28%	$33,646	$17,842	$21,351
Cambridge College	ind.	$13,280	NA	81%	NR	$ 7494	$ 5786	NR
Clark University	ind.	$37,350	$ 7100	100%	60%	$28,165	$16,285	$24,000
College of the Holy Cross	ind.	$41,488	$11,270	81%	100%	$31,178	$21,580	$23,662
Curry College	ind.	$32,210	$12,285	97%	2%	$18,399	$26,096	$36,874
Eastern Nazarene College	ind.	$23,772	$ 8000	99%	35%	$26,469	$ 5303	$51,336
Emerson College	ind.	$31,272	$12,881	89%	74%	$18,674	$25,479	$17,459
Emmanuel College	ind.	$30,890	$12,300	94%	45%	$25,857	$17,333	NR
Endicott College	ind.	$26,248	$12,388	82%	9%	$18,786	$19,850	$39,168
Fisher College	ind.	$25,778	$13,786	75%	NR	NR	NR	NR
Fitchburg State University	pub.	$ 7800	$ 8106	82%	93%	$ 8942	$ 6964	$19,902
Framingham State University	pub.	$ 7065	$ 7100	79%	44%	$ 6800	$ 7365	$19,300
Franklin W. Olin College of Engineering	ind.	$39,450	$14,000	62%	100%	$26,986	$26,464	$13,200
Gordon College	ind.	$30,606	$ 8434	100%	14%	$18,990	$20,050	$37,154
Hampshire College	ind.	$42,900	$11,180	100%	54%	$36,740	$17,340	$21,673
Harvard University	ind.	$38,415	$12,308	100%	100%	$42,801	$ 7922	$10,102
Hebrew College	ind.	$22,700	NA	NR	NR	NR	NR	$ 8300
Lasell College	ind.	$27,500	$12,300	100%	13%	$21,189	$18,611	$36,720
Lesley University	ind.	$29,400	$12,800	73%	19%	$20,496	$21,704	$18,000
Massachusetts College of Art and Design	pub.	$ 9000	$11,750	80%	NR	$ 9399	$11,351	$21,759
Massachusetts College of Liberal Arts	pub.	$ 7575	$ 8246	83%	NR	$13,144	$ 2677	$23,587
Massachusetts Institute of Technology	ind.	$39,212	$11,234	98%	100%	$37,874	$12,572	$15,228
Massachusetts Maritime Academy	pub.	$11,922	$ 9204	NR	NR	NR	NR	$32,553
Merrimack College	ind.	$31,380	$10,700	99%	29%	$18,857	$23,223	$27,000
Mount Holyoke College	ind.	$40,256	$11,780	100%	100%	$37,362	$14,674	$22,499
New England Conservatory of Music	ind.	$34,950	$12,100	100%	13%	$24,914	$22,136	$26,373
Nichols College	ind.	$28,870	$ 9330	98%	10%	$23,581	$14,619	$27,715
Northeastern University	ind.	$36,792	$12,760	98%	18%	$22,783	$26,769	NR
Simmons College	ind.	$32,230	$12,470	100%	11%	$22,688	$22,012	NR

NA = not applicable; NR = not reported; * = includes room and board; † = room only; — = not available.

College Costs At-a-Glance

	Institutional Control ind.=independent; pub.=public	Tuition and Fees	Room and Board	Percent of Eligible Freshmen Receiving Need-Based Gift Awards	Percent of Freshmen Whose Need Was Fully Met	Average Financial Aid Package for Freshmen	Average Net Cost After Aid	Average Indebtedness Upon Graduation
Massachusetts—*continued*								
Smith College	ind.	$38,898	$13,000	95%	100%	$34,718	$17,180	$20,989
Springfield College	ind.	$30,660	NR	99%	6%	$20,607	$10,053	$33,697
Stonehill College	ind.	$32,620	$12,610	96%	52%	$22,970	$22,260	$30,435
Suffolk University	ind.	$28,526	$14,624	95%	7%	$21,387	$21,763	NR
Tufts University	ind.	$42,532	$11,268	93%	100%	$32,483	$21,317	$27,443
University of Massachusetts Amherst	pub.	$11,732	$ 9339	93%	24%	$13,844	$ 7227	$25,420
University of Massachusetts Boston	pub.	$10,611	NA	97%	62%	$12,185	—	$22,387
University of Massachusetts Dartmouth	pub.	$10,358	$ 9134	88%	38%	$14,027	$ 5465	$34,369
University of Massachusetts Lowell	pub.	$10,506	$ 9067	99%	70%	$12,351	$ 7222	$24,087
Wellesley College	ind.	$39,666	$12,284	98%	100%	$38,024	$13,926	$12,495
Wentworth Institute of Technology	ind.	$24,000	NR	50%	2%	$19,786	$ 4214	$20,208
Western New England University	ind.	$29,812	$11,336	100%	23%	$21,682	$19,466	NR
Westfield State University	pub.	$ 7431	$ 8525	67%	10%	$ 7405	$ 8551	$21,182
Wheaton College	ind.	$41,084	$10,180	93%	54%	$33,056	$18,208	$27,546
Williams College	ind.	$41,434	$10,906	100%	100%	$41,400	$10,940	$ 8065
Worcester Polytechnic Institute	ind.	$40,030	$11,934	99%	47%	$29,755	$22,209	NR
Worcester State University	pub.	$ 7155	$ 9658	88%	43%	$10,532	$ 6281	$20,851
Michigan								
Adrian College	ind.	$25,900	$ 7900	100%	8%	$23,488	$10,312	$17,160
Alma College	ind.	$29,230	$ 8840	100%	23%	$25,202	$12,868	$28,734
Andrews University	ind.	$22,242	$ 7140	74%	20%	$23,091	$ 6291	$34,200
Calvin College	ind.	$24,870	$ 8525	100%	17%	$18,234	$15,161	$27,700
Central Michigan University	pub.	$10,380	$ 8092	87%	53%	$12,040	$ 6432	$28,142
Cleary University	ind.	$16,560	NA	85%	9%	$13,595	$ 2965	$20,830
College for Creative Studies	ind.	$32,785	NR	NR	NR	NR	NR	$47,604
Concordia University	ind.	$20,982	$ 7828	100%	33%	$16,098	$12,712	$16,011
Cornerstone University	ind.	$21,178	$ 6786	85%	14%	$20,739	$ 7225	$29,510
Davenport University (Grand Rapids)	ind.	$11,794	$ 8412	NR	NR	NR	NR	NR
Eastern Michigan University	pub.	$ 8378	$ 7785	81%	10%	$ 9665	$ 6498	$23,669
Ferris State University	pub.	$ 9930	$ 9180	73%	20%	$16,536	$ 2574	$35,468
Finlandia University	ind.	$18,974	$ 6154	NR	NR	NR	NR	NR
Grace Bible College	ind.	$14,850	$ 6250	98%	NR	$12,513	$ 8587	$ 7957
Grand Valley State University	pub.	$ 9088	$ 7624	83%	14%	$ 9716	$ 6996	$25,279
Hillsdale College	ind.	$20,500	$ 7990	62%	38%	$12,610	$15,880	$16,500
Hope College	ind.	$27,020	$ 8260	83%	33%	$23,271	$12,009	$28,500
Kalamazoo College	ind.	$34,317	$ 7893	94%	48%	$27,734	$14,476	NR
Kettering University	ind.	$29,116	$ 6440	100%	13%	$20,810	$14,746	$45,570
Kuyper College	ind.	$16,416	$ 6280	100%	NR	$14,772	$ 7924	$18,709
Lake Superior State University	pub.	$ 8764	$ 8081	49%	64%	$13,469	$ 3376	$24,672
Lawrence Technological University	ind.	$24,633	$ 9147	98%	11%	$18,237	$15,543	$38,303
Michigan State University	pub.	$11,153	$ 7770	58%	21%	$ 7882	$11,041	$21,818
Michigan Technological University	pub.	$12,017	$ 8462	84%	18%	$12,590	$ 7889	$33,310

NA = not applicable; NR = not reported; * = includes room and board; † = room only; — = not available.

College Costs At-a-Glance	Institutional Control ind.=independent; pub.=public	Tuition and Fees	Room and Board	Percent of Eligible Freshmen Receiving Need-Based Gift Awards	Percent of Freshmen Whose Need Was Fully Met	Average Financial Aid Package for Freshmen	Average Net Cost After Aid	Average Indebtedness Upon Graduation
Michigan—*continued*								
Northern Michigan University	pub.	$ 8416	$ 8026	61%	16%	$ 8231	$ 8211	$27,091
Oakland University	pub.	$ 9285	$ 7644	75%	15%	$12,018	$ 4911	$20,663
Olivet College	ind.	$20,500	$ 7000	100%	30%	$15,477	$12,023	$25,500
Sacred Heart Major Seminary	ind.	$15,270	$ 8268	NR	NR	NR	NR	NR
Saginaw Valley State University	pub.	$ 7308	$ 7768	62%	22%	$ 7136	$ 7940	$23,555
Spring Arbor University	ind.	$20,536	$ 7254	99%	18%	$20,082	$ 7708	$28,212
University of Michigan	pub.	$12,779	$ 9192	65%	90%	$10,432	$11,539	$27,828
University of Michigan–Dearborn	pub.	$ 9456	NA	80%	49%	$ 9916	—	$19,463
University of Michigan–Flint	pub.	$ 8601	$ 7212	74%	5%	$10,272	$ 5541	$25,945
Walsh College of Accountancy and Business Administration	ind.	$11,770	NA	NR	NR	NR	NR	$13,100
Wayne State University	pub.	$ 9026	$ 7500	82%	77%	$20,586	—	$20,250
Western Michigan University	pub.	$ 9006	$ 8095	59%	19%	$10,000	$ 7101	$20,000
Minnesota								
Augsburg College	ind.	$30,418	$ 8072	99%	16%	$24,860	$13,630	$24,311
Bemidji State University	pub.	$ 7513	$ 6480	66%	17%	$ 8037	$ 5956	$26,799
Bethany Lutheran College	ind.	$20,950	$ 6500	100%	28%	$18,324	$ 9126	$26,519
Bethel University	ind.	$29,460	$ 8530	100%	16%	$22,783	$15,207	$32,698
Carleton College	ind.	$42,942	$11,238	100%	100%	$33,708	$20,472	$19,436
College of Saint Benedict	ind.	$32,246	$ 8652	100%	48%	$26,424	$14,474	NR
The College of St. Scholastica	ind.	$29,506	$ 7716	86%	21%	$22,206	$15,016	$40,816
College of Visual Arts	ind.	$23,988	NA	100%	3%	$15,906	$ 8082	$38,402
Concordia College	ind.	$29,360	$ 6790	99%	21%	$21,188	$14,962	$32,271
Concordia University, St. Paul	ind.	$28,500	$ 7500	92%	2%	$22,625	$13,375	$36,295
Crown College	ind.	$21,470	$ 7380	59%	11%	$12,610	$16,240	$38,042
Gustavus Adolphus College	ind.	$33,400	$ 8400	90%	47%	$30,375	$11,425	$25,694
Hamline University	ind.	$31,802	$ 8504	100%	14%	$26,663	$13,643	$36,339
Macalester College	ind.	$42,021	$ 9396	99%	100%	$33,891	$17,526	NR
Martin Luther College	ind.	$11,320	$ 4390	98%	12%	$ 9336	$ 6374	$21,799
McNally Smith College of Music	ind.	$26,120	NR	NR	NR	NR	NR	NR
Metropolitan State University	pub.	$ 5923	NA	NR	NR	NR	NR	NR
Minneapolis College of Art and Design	ind.	$30,585	$ 4540†	96%	10%	$17,128	$17,997	$46,293
Minnesota State University Mankato	pub.	$ 6725	$ 6730	79%	25%	$ 8292	$ 5163	$27,086
Minnesota State University Moorhead	pub.	$ 6923	$ 6468	63%	NR	$ 5465	$ 7926	$29,410
Northwestern College	ind.	$25,700	$ 8000	100%	6%	$19,464	$14,236	$25,707
St. Catherine University	ind.	$30,168	$ 7658	90%	17%	$29,300	$ 8526	$33,610
Saint John's University	ind.	$31,576	$ 8044	98%	50%	$23,906	$15,714	NR
Saint Mary's University of Minnesota	ind.	$27,250	$ 7150	99%	20%	$22,436	$11,964	$30,237
St. Olaf College	ind.	$36,800	$ 8500	100%	100%	$29,494	$15,806	$26,115
Southwest Minnesota State University	pub.	$ 7244	$ 6637	67%	18%	$ 8858	$ 5023	$18,909
University of Minnesota, Crookston	pub.	$10,623	$ 6568	98%	32%	$12,540	$ 4651	$25,852
University of Minnesota, Duluth	pub.	$11,807	$ 6422	99%	18%	$10,478	$ 7751	$30,098
University of Minnesota, Morris	pub.	$11,532	$ 7050	99%	49%	$15,622	$ 2960	$22,952

NA = not applicable; NR = not reported; * = includes room and board; † = room only; — = not available.

College Costs At-a-Glance

	Institutional Control ind.=independent; pub.=public	Tuition and Fees	Room and Board	Percent of Eligible Freshmen Receiving Need-Based Gift Awards	Percent of Freshmen Whose Need Was Fully Met	Average Financial Aid Package for Freshmen	Average Net Cost After Aid	Average Indebtedness Upon Graduation
Minnesota—*continued*								
University of Minnesota, Twin Cities Campus	pub.	$12,203	$ 7774	98%	35%	$12,440	$ 7537	$ 27,578
University of St. Thomas	ind.	$30,493	$ 8320	99%	22%	$22,656	$16,157	$ 32,705
Walden University	ind.	$ 9465	NR	87%	NR	$ 8355	$ 1110	NR
Winona State University	pub.	$ 8200	$ 7330	50%	13%	$ 6559	$ 8971	$ 29,123
Mississippi								
Alcorn State University	pub.	$ 4858	$ 7348	92%	7%	$10,304	$ 1902	$ 19,838
Delta State University	pub.	$ 4852	$ 6166	80%	NR	$ 7436	$ 3582	$ 16,633
Jackson State University	pub.	$ 5050	$ 6244	85%	2%	$11,359	—	NR
Millsaps College	ind.	$29,482	$10,312	99%	39%	$26,118	$13,676	$ 28,745
Mississippi State University	pub.	$ 5461	$ 7729	97%	25%	$10,854	$ 2336	$ 25,261
Mississippi University for Women	pub.	$ 4644	$ 5482	77%	50%	$ 9132	$ 994	$ 18,363
University of Mississippi	pub.	$ 5708	NR	90%	15%	$ 9333	—	$ 23,637
University of Southern Mississippi	pub.	$ 5452	$ 6634	80%	24%	$ 9916	$ 2170	$ 19,854
Missouri								
Calvary Bible College and Theological Seminary	ind.	$10,048	$ 8800	NR	NR	NR	NR	NR
Central Methodist University	ind.	$19,390	$ 6240	88%	10%	$22,251	$ 3379	$ 18,390
College of the Ozarks	ind.	$ 430	$ 5600	100%	20%	$14,732	—	$ 5389
Columbia College	ind.	$16,532	$ 6254	61%	NR	$13,498	$ 9288	$ 14,989
Cox College	ind.	$11,340	NR	NR	NR	NR	NR	NR
Culver-Stockton College	ind.	$22,550	$ 7600	100%	16%	$20,158	$ 9992	$ 31,200
Drury University	ind.	$21,043	$ 7466	88%	72%	$ 7750	$20,759	$ 20,500
Evangel University	ind.	$16,990	$ 6000	97%	10%	$12,677	$10,313	$ 30,449
Lincoln University	pub.	$ 6175	$ 5144	88%	7%	$ 9091	$ 2228	$ 25,950
Lindenwood University	ind.	$13,600	$ 7210	84%	90%	$ 9389	$11,421	NR
Maryville University of Saint Louis	ind.	$21,910	$ 8500	99%	20%	$18,956	$11,454	$ 22,636
Missouri Baptist University	ind.	$18,700	$ 7440	61%	NR	$15,262	$10,878	NR
Missouri Southern State University	pub.	$ 4816	$ 5500	85%	13%	$ 7124	$ 3192	$ 16,772
Missouri State University	pub.	$ 6276	$ 6394	87%	17%	$ 8048	$ 4622	$ 21,359
Missouri University of Science and Technology	pub.	$ 8528	$ 8290	100%	62%	$11,459	$ 5359	$ 21,700
Northwest Missouri State University	pub.	$ 7047	$ 7962	89%	71%	$ 9117	$ 5892	$ 21,230
Research College of Nursing	ind.	$27,190	$ 7890	NR	NR	NR	NR	NR
Rockhurst University	ind.	$27,390	$ 7490	78%	44%	$27,394	$ 7486	$ 24,841
St. Louis Christian College	ind.	$16,180	$ 8900	NR	NR	$14,102	$10,978	$ 11,654
St. Louis College of Pharmacy	ind.	$23,770	$ 8755	100%	12%	$13,292	$19,233	$107,649
Saint Louis University	ind.	$32,656	$ 9170	97%	19%	$23,873	$17,953	$ 33,734
Southeast Missouri State University	pub.	$ 6255	$ 7342	94%	23%	$ 8656	$ 4941	$ 22,400
Southwest Baptist University	ind.	$17,280	$ 5720	86%	21%	$16,155	$ 6845	NR
Truman State University	pub.	$ 6692	$ 7097	98%	75%	$10,920	$ 2869	$ 19,118
University of Central Missouri	pub.	$ 7311	$ 6320	53%	19%	$ 9803	$ 3828	$ 20,282
University of Missouri	pub.	$ 8501	$ 8607	88%	15%	$13,836	$ 3272	$ 22,145
University of Missouri–Kansas City	pub.	$ 8602	$10,131	87%	6%	$ 9350	$ 9383	$ 25,374
University of Missouri–St. Louis	pub.	$ 9038	$ 8404	95%	10%	$ 8890	$ 8552	$ 27,334

NA = not applicable; NR = not reported; * = includes room and board; † = room only; — = not available.

College Costs At-a-Glance

	Institutional Control ind.=independent; pub.=public	Tuition and Fees	Room and Board	Percent of Eligible Freshmen Receiving Need-Based Gift Awards	Percent of Freshmen Whose Need Was Fully Met	Average Financial Aid Package for Freshmen	Average Net Cost After Aid	Average Indebtedness Upon Graduation
Missouri—*continued*								
Washington University in St. Louis	ind.	$41,992	$13,119	94%	100%	$30,603	$24,508	NR
Westminster College	ind.	$19,740	$ 7610	100%	78%	$18,346	$ 9004	$21,964
William Jewell College	ind.	$29,900	$ 7560	100%	12%	$20,554	$16,906	$23,210
Montana								
Carroll College	ind.	$23,594	$ 7518	98%	20%	$20,152	$10,960	$29,122
Montana State University	pub.	$ 6168	$ 7900	75%	6%	$11,242	$ 2826	$24,420
Montana State University Billings	pub.	$ 5242	$ 5620	84%	3%	$ 8587	$ 2275	$24,026
Montana State University–Northern	pub.	$ 4476	$ 6461	92%	5%	$ 8985	$ 1952	$18,604
Montana Tech of The University of Montana	pub.	$ 6162	$ 6924	92%	25%	$ 8007	$ 5079	$23,000
Rocky Mountain College	ind.	$22,134	$ 6896	100%	18%	$19,443	$ 9587	$20,122
University of Great Falls	ind.	$18,856	$ 6712	92%	2%	$15,684	$ 9884	NR
The University of Montana	pub.	$ 5685	$ 6860	68%	16%	$ 7871	$ 4674	$20,223
Nebraska								
College of Saint Mary	ind.	$24,350	$ 6700	100%	9%	$20,513	$10,537	$30,325
Concordia University, Nebraska	ind.	$23,060	$ 6110	100%	22%	$17,894	$11,276	$22,586
Creighton University	ind.	$30,578	$ 9164	100%	37%	$25,985	$13,757	$32,152
Doane College	ind.	$22,170	$ 6460	100%	36%	$18,543	$10,087	$20,748
Grace University	ind.	$15,728	$ 5546	100%	22%	$12,027	$ 9247	$21,586
Nebraska Methodist College	ind.	$11,770	$ 5770†	94%	26%	$ 9287	$ 8253	$29,132
Nebraska Wesleyan University	ind.	$23,474	$ 6300	100%	21%	$17,117	$12,657	$24,873
Union College	ind.	$18,780	$ 6020	NR	NR	NR	NR	NR
University of Nebraska at Omaha	pub.	$ 6626	$ 7750	66%	NR	$ 2341	$12,035	$20,000
University of Nebraska–Lincoln	pub.	$ 7224	$ 7660	87%	12%	$11,572	$ 3312	$16,664
Wayne State College	pub.	$ 5071	$ 5540	77%	29%	$ 7593	$ 3018	NR
York College	ind.	$14,998	$ 5680	100%	16%	$13,434	$ 7244	$26,679
Nevada								
Sierra Nevada College	ind.	$25,235	$ 9750	100%	27%	$18,500	$16,485	$11,187
University of Nevada, Las Vegas	pub.	$ 5689	$10,454	83%	17%	$ 8804	$ 7339	$17,165
University of Nevada, Reno	pub.	$ 4841	$ 9518	85%	17%	$ 6336	$ 8023	$15,814
New Hampshire								
Dartmouth College	ind.	$40,437	$11,838	98%	100%	$39,399	$12,876	$18,712
Keene State College	pub.	$10,140	$ 8670	69%	16%	$ 9867	$ 8943	$28,986
New England College	ind.	$30,495	$10,668	97%	10%	$25,178	$15,985	$36,203
Plymouth State University	pub.	$ 9906	$ 8840	65%	16%	$ 9847	$ 8899	$30,925
Rivier College	ind.	$25,020	$ 9522	100%	7%	$16,672	$17,870	$43,189
Saint Anselm College	ind.	$31,555	$11,650	100%	16%	$23,844	$19,361	$38,858
Thomas More College of Liberal Arts	ind.	$16,100	$ 9100	85%	15%	$16,100	$ 9100	$28,194
University of New Hampshire	pub.	$13,672	$ 9053	71%	23%	$20,987	$ 1738	$32,323
University of New Hampshire at Manchester	pub.	$11,226	NA	40%	10%	$10,639	$ 587	$23,685
New Jersey								
Bloomfield College	ind.	$22,400	$10,600	97%	10%	$24,442	$ 8558	$30,515
Caldwell College	ind.	$25,602	$ 8990	100%	19%	$20,863	$13,729	$18,369

NA = not applicable; NR = not reported; * = includes room and board; † = room only; — = not available.

College Costs At-a-Glance

	Institutional Control ind.=independent; pub.=public	Tuition and Fees	Room and Board	Percent of Eligible Freshmen Receiving Need-Based Gift Awards	Percent of Freshmen Whose Need Was Fully Met	Average Financial Aid Package for Freshmen	Average Net Cost After Aid	Average Indebtedness Upon Graduation
New Jersey—*continued*								
The College of New Jersey	pub.	$13,273	$10,358	41%	16%	$ 9816	$13,815	$27,057
College of Saint Elizabeth	ind.	$26,887	$11,340	75%	10%	$25,717	$12,510	NR
Drew University	ind.	$39,550	$10,772	100%	18%	$29,574	$20,748	$19,634
Felician College	ind.	$27,925	$10,750	87%	10%	NR	NR	$22,963
Georgian Court University	ind.	$26,176	$ 9856	100%	32%	$26,339	$ 9693	$35,632
Kean University	pub.	$ 9815	$12,950	100%	6%	$ 8719	$14,046	$20,668
Monmouth University	ind.	$28,000	$10,680	41%	3%	$19,500	$19,180	$29,921
Montclair State University	pub.	$ 7324	$10,712	46%	18%	$ 7835	$10,201	$18,805
New Jersey City University	pub.	$ 9348	$ 9364	82%	7%	$10,229	$ 8483	$17,699
New Jersey Institute of Technology	pub.	$13,370	$10,122	88%	13%	$13,040	$10,452	$34,760
Princeton University	ind.	$37,000	$12,069	100%	100%	$36,912	$12,157	$ 5225
Ramapo College of New Jersey	pub.	$11,874	$10,250	43%	18%	$11,691	$10,433	$26,187
The Richard Stockton College of New Jersey	pub.	$11,393	$10,281	53%	28%	$15,813	$ 5861	$30,843
Rider University	ind.	$30,470	$11,200	99%	21%	$22,253	$19,417	$35,404
Rowan University	pub.	$11,676	$10,348	49%	29%	$ 9276	$12,748	$29,073
Rutgers, The State University of New Jersey, Camden	pub.	$12,364	$10,362	82%	21%	$11,831	$10,895	$21,330
Rutgers, The State University of New Jersey, Newark	pub.	$12,069	$11,653	82%	6%	$13,420	$10,302	$17,373
Rutgers, The State University of New Jersey, New Brunswick	pub.	$12,582	$11,216	65%	3%	$13,413	$10,385	$16,766
Thomas Edison State College	pub.	$ 4883	NA	NR	NR	NR	NR	NR
William Paterson University of New Jersey	pub.	$11,238	$10,380	59%	33%	$ 9908	$11,710	$28,537
New Mexico								
New Mexico Institute of Mining and Technology	pub.	$ 4942	$ 5874	81%	30%	$11,777	—	$15,974
New Mexico State University	pub.	$ 5400	$ 6526	95%	8%	$ 7927	$ 3999	$16,619
University of the Southwest	ind.	$11,689	$ 6530	93%	19%	$12,681	$ 5538	$19,645
New York								
Adelphi University	ind.	$26,915	$11,000	78%	2%	$18,475	$19,440	$31,096
Alfred University	ind.	$25,976	$11,364	100%	18%	$24,925	$12,415	$19,474
Bard College	ind.	$41,670	$11,810	96%	60%	$36,952	$16,528	$24,311
Barnard College	ind.	$40,546	$12,950	97%	100%	$39,578	$13,918	$14,617
Brooklyn College of the City University of New York	pub.	$ 5284	NR	93%	98%	$ 7550	—	$16,500
Buffalo State College, State University of New York	pub.	$ 6053	$ 9748	76%	57%	$11,430	$ 4371	$22,565
Canisius College	ind.	$30,077	$10,980	99%	29%	$20,489	$20,568	$33,918
Cazenovia College	ind.	$26,736	$11,470	100%	9%	$21,690	$16,516	NR
City College of the City University of New York	pub.	$ 4830	NR	91%	97%	$ 8343	—	$15,900
Clarkson University	ind.	$36,780	$12,050	99%	20%	$33,671	$15,159	$36,142
Colgate University	ind.	$41,870	$10,190	99%	100%	$39,896	$12,164	$18,629
The College at Brockport, State University of New York	pub.	$ 6176	$ 9780	83%	16%	$ 9981	$ 5975	$25,733
The College of New Rochelle	ind.	$28,010	$10,176	85%	3%	$24,301	$13,885	$28,462
The College of Saint Rose	ind.	$25,464	$10,534	94%	1%	$14,129	$21,869	$30,281
College of Staten Island of the City University of New York	pub.	$ 4978	NR	NR	NR	$10,993	—	$ 7423
Columbia University	ind.	$41,160	$10,570	97%	100%	$40,259	$11,471	NR
Columbia University, School of General Studies	ind.	$39,900	$12,960	NR	NR	NR	NR	NR

NA = not applicable; NR = not reported; * = includes room and board; † = room only; — = not available.

College Costs At-a-Glance

	Institutional Control ind.=independent; pub.=public	Tuition and Fees	Room and Board	Percent of Eligible Freshmen Receiving Need-Based Gift Awards	Percent of Freshmen Whose Need Was Fully Met	Average Financial Aid Package for Freshmen	Average Net Cost After Aid	Average Indebtedness Upon Graduation
New York—*continued*								
Cooper Union for the Advancement of Science and Art	ind.	$39,150	$13,700	100%	60%	$35,000	$17,850	$10,390
Cornell University	ind.	$39,666	$12,650	98%	100%	$37,846	$14,470	$20,648
Daemen College	ind.	$21,460	$ 9850	92%	33%	$16,606	$14,704	$27,444
Dominican College	ind.	$21,990	$10,560	93%	12%	$18,118	$14,432	$18,398
Dowling College	ind.	$24,630	$10,770	97%	83%	$18,368	$17,032	$22,177
D'Youville College	ind.	$21,060	$ 9800	99%	16%	$15,914	$14,946	$42,042
Elmira College	ind.	$35,900	$11,150	100%	21%	$27,850	$19,200	$25,438
Eugene Lang College The New School for Liberal Arts	ind.	$36,090	$15,260	97%	14%	$33,675	$17,675	$30,830
Fashion Institute of Technology	pub.	$ 5668	$11,700	71%	18%	$10,169	$ 7199	$24,143
Fordham University	ind.	$38,277	$12,890	98%	31%	$27,288	$23,879	$33,365
Hamilton College	ind.	$41,280	$10,480	100%	100%	$38,222	$13,538	$16,982
Hartwick College	ind.	$34,630	$ 9345	100%	15%	$29,167	$14,808	$32,327
Hobart and William Smith Colleges	ind.	$41,710	$10,548	100%	97%	$31,015	$21,243	$29,932
Hofstra University	ind.	$31,800	$11,710	94%	17%	$23,000	$20,510	NR
Houghton College	ind.	$25,460	$ 7330	100%	17%	$23,416	$ 9374	$23,010
Hunter College of the City University of New York	pub.	$ 5229	$ 5500†	98%	27%	$ 5241	$ 5488	$ 7500
Iona College	ind.	$30,192	$12,154	82%	18%	$19,922	$22,424	$19,958
Ithaca College	ind.	$33,630	$12,314	97%	55%	$27,803	$18,141	NR
John Jay College of Criminal Justice of the City University of New York	pub.	$ 4930	NA	85%	NR	$10,150	—	$47,250
The Juilliard School	ind.	$32,180	$12,280	89%	31%	$26,303	$18,157	$20,382
Keuka College	ind.	$23,770	$ 9500	100%	8%	$19,160	$14,110	$13,874
The King's College	ind.	$29,240	$11,050†	100%	11%	$18,746	$21,544	$16,102
Lehman College of the City University of New York	pub.	$ 5208	NR	83%	2%	$ 3864	$ 1344	$13,700
Le Moyne College	ind.	$28,380	$10,890	100%	30%	$20,132	$19,138	$25,587
Long Island University, C.W. Post Campus	ind.	$30,210	$10,980	79%	18%	$14,045	$27,145	NR
Manhattan College	ind.	$29,800	$11,420	92%	17%	$19,365	$21,855	$31,912
Manhattan School of Music	ind.	$35,140	$13,810	74%	18%	$16,328	$32,622	$23,508
Manhattanville College	ind.	$34,350	$13,920	96%	10%	$29,687	$18,583	NR
Mannes College The New School for Music	ind.	$35,100	$15,260	56%	11%	$20,975	$29,385	$33,060
Marist College	ind.	$27,650	$12,350	69%	23%	$19,397	$20,603	$25,135
Medaille College	ind.	$20,580	$ 9750	100%	3%	$15,800	$14,530	$22,000
Medgar Evers College of the City University of New York	pub.	$ 5132	NA	97%	NR	$ 3866	$ 1266	NR
Mercy College	ind.	$17,010	$11,140	93%	2%	$13,701	$14,449	$23,307
Molloy College	ind.	$22,130	NA	98%	16%	$14,879	$ 7251	$29,823
Mount Saint Mary College	ind.	$24,410	$12,320	100%	17%	$16,295	$20,435	$37,273
Nazareth College of Rochester	ind.	$26,184	$10,716	100%	19%	$20,112	$16,788	$38,545
The New School for General Studies	ind.	$25,320	$15,260	NR	NR	NR	NR	NR
The New School for Jazz and Contemporary Music	ind.	$35,100	$15,260	91%	39%	$27,383	$22,977	$25,735
New York City College of Technology of the City University of New York	pub.	$ 4939	NA	99%	2%	$ 7751	—	NR
New York Institute of Technology	ind.	$25,470	$11,100	72%	NR	$15,703	$20,867	NR
New York School of Interior Design	ind.	$23,856	$15,200†	79%	11%	$ 9134	$29,922	$13,327

NA = not applicable; NR = not reported; * = includes room and board; † = room only; — = not available.

College Costs At-a-Glance

	Institutional Control ind.=independent; pub.=public	Tuition and Fees	Room and Board	Percent of Eligible Freshmen Receiving Need-Based Gift Awards	Percent of Freshmen Whose Need Was Fully Met	Average Financial Aid Package for Freshmen	Average Net Cost After Aid	Average Indebtedness Upon Graduation
New York—*continued*								
New York University	ind.	$40,082	$13,510	98%	NR	$27,501	$26,091	$41,300
Niagara University	ind.	$25,650	$10,650	98%	52%	$21,997	$14,303	$27,813
Nyack College	ind.	$21,500	$ 8250	100%	9%	$18,140	$11,610	$35,879
Pace University	ind.	$33,702	$13,800	100%	10%	$29,952	$17,550	$38,035
Parsons The New School for Design	ind.	$37,610	$15,260	99%	11%	$32,019	$20,851	$38,290
Paul Smith's College	ind.	$20,695	$ 9390	100%	3%	$18,034	$12,051	$22,036
Polytechnic Institute of NYU	ind.	$36,284	$10,080	92%	77%	$30,099	$16,265	$31,035
Pratt Institute	ind.	$39,310	$10,210	70%	NR	$17,800	$31,720	NR
Purchase College, State University of New York	pub.	$ 6504	$10,646	77%	4%	$ 8542	$ 8608	$33,125
Queens College of the City University of New York	pub.	$ 5047	$11,125	79%	63%	$ 8000	$ 8172	$17,700
Rensselaer Polytechnic Institute	ind.	$40,680	$11,465	100%	37%	$34,430	$17,715	$30,125
Roberts Wesleyan College	ind.	$24,360	$ 8826	100%	12%	$21,558	$11,628	$36,486
Rochester Institute of Technology	ind.	$30,717	$10,044	NR	NR	NR	NR	NR
Russell Sage College	ind.	$27,850	$10,150	100%	63%	$34,400	$ 3600	$28,300
Sage College of Albany	ind.	$27,850	$10,950	94%	75%	$34,054	$ 4746	$26,400
St. Bonaventure University	ind.	$26,895	$ 9071	100%	11%	$24,786	$11,180	$36,940
St. John Fisher College	ind.	$25,270	$10,290	100%	27%	$20,472	$15,088	$32,975
St. John's University	ind.	$31,980	$13,900	92%	7%	$26,591	$19,289	$32,886
St. Joseph's College, Long Island Campus	ind.	$17,565	NR	71%	23%	$12,518	$ 5047	$23,031
St. Joseph's College, New York	ind.	$17,565	NR	100%	15%	$15,268	$ 2297	$22,825
St. Lawrence University	ind.	$41,155	$10,615	100%	39%	$37,509	$14,261	$29,489
St. Thomas Aquinas College	ind.	$22,410	$10,300	NR	NR	NR	NR	NR
Sarah Lawrence College	ind.	$45,212	$13,504	96%	60%	$34,056	$24,660	$21,590
School of Visual Arts	ind.	$28,140	$15,500	66%	2%	$12,371	$31,269	$41,495
Siena College	ind.	$28,985	$11,434	100%	19%	$18,600	$21,819	$29,700
Skidmore College	ind.	$41,184	$10,986	99%	100%	$34,915	$17,255	$19,850
State University of New York at Binghamton	pub.	$ 6881	$11,244	79%	6%	$ 9543	$ 8582	$21,110
State University of New York at Fredonia	pub.	$ 6333	$10,110	77%	13%	$ 9280	$ 7163	$27,110
State University of New York at New Paltz	pub.	$ 6135	$ 9786	50%	10%	$ 9178	$ 6743	$25,732
State University of New York at Oswego	pub.	$ 6186	$11,610	91%	19%	$ 7332	$10,464	$25,931
State University of New York at Plattsburgh	pub.	$ 6143	$ 9000	91%	30%	$11,242	$ 3901	$25,326
State University of New York College at Cortland	pub.	$ 6215	$10,490	76%	16%	$12,010	$ 4695	NR
State University of New York College at Geneseo	pub.	$ 6401	$10,042	45%	70%	$ 3321	$13,122	$21,200
State University of New York College at Old Westbury	pub.	$ 5966	$ 9700	100%	100%	$ 6204	$ 9462	$16,371
State University of New York College at Oneonta	pub.	$ 6250	$ 9284	95%	46%	$14,422	$ 1112	$17,564
State University of New York College at Potsdam	pub.	$ 6183	$ 9630	90%	74%	$13,413	$ 2400	$21,427
State University of New York College of Environmental Science and Forestry	pub.	$ 5941	$14,032	97%	95%	$12,500	$ 7473	$27,000
State University of New York College of Technology at Delhi	pub.	$ 6445	$ 9720	92%	NR	NR	NR	NR
State University of New York Maritime College	pub.	$ 6157	$10,090	98%	8%	$ 9071	$ 7176	NR
Stony Brook University, State University of New York	pub.	$ 6580	$10,142	89%	13%	$11,324	$ 5398	$19,807
Syracuse University	ind.	$36,302	$12,850	93%	82%	$31,675	$17,477	$30,813
Union College	ind.	*$52,329	NR	97%	99%	$34,706	$17,623	$25,621

NA = not applicable; NR = not reported; * = includes room and board; † = room only; — = not available.

College Costs At-a-Glance

	Institutional Control ind.=independent; pub.=public	Tuition and Fees	Room and Board	Percent of Eligible Freshmen Receiving Need-Based Gift Awards	Percent of Freshmen Whose Need Was Fully Met	Average Financial Aid Package for Freshmen	Average Net Cost After Aid	Average Indebtedness Upon Graduation
New York—*continued*								
University at Albany, State University of New York	pub.	$ 6830	$10,633	86%	8%	$10,028	$ 7435	$24,146
University at Buffalo, the State University of New York	pub.	$ 7136	$10,028	90%	49%	$10,086	$ 7078	$17,425
University of Rochester	ind.	$40,282	$11,640	99%	100%	$64,176	—	$28,100
Utica College	ind.	$28,620	$11,590	100%	8%	$24,163	$16,047	$39,371
Vassar College	ind.	$43,190	$ 9900	100%	100%	$41,054	$12,036	$18,153
Villa Maria College of Buffalo	ind.	$15,919	NA	83%	NR	$ 5335	$10,584	$26,304
Wagner College	ind.	$35,820	$10,680	99%	23%	$23,327	$23,173	$36,988
Wells College	ind.	$32,180	$11,000	100%	13%	$27,315	$15,865	$26,207
Yeshiva University	ind.	$32,094	$10,380	98%	26%	$28,296	$14,178	$21,654
North Carolina								
Appalachian State University	pub.	$ 5175	$ 6600	88%	41%	$ 8509	$ 3266	$16,130
Belmont Abbey College	ind.	$24,584	$10,272	100%	18%	$18,620	$16,236	$21,000
Brevard College	ind.	$22,175	$ 7850	100%	26%	$19,400	$10,625	$20,770
Campbell University	ind.	$22,520	$ 7600	100%	76%	$37,703	—	$38,696
Carolina Christian College	ind.	$ 7200	NA	13%	NR	NR	NR	NR
Catawba College	ind.	$25,160	$ 8700	81%	20%	$21,098	$12,762	$27,907
Chowan University	ind.	$19,750	$ 7410	100%	18%	$16,172	$10,988	$29,180
Davidson College	ind.	$38,866	$10,857	93%	100%	$29,491	$20,232	$23,233
Duke University	ind.	$40,243	$11,622	97%	100%	$38,340	$13,525	$21,884
East Carolina University	pub.	$ 4797	$ 7700	82%	9%	$ 9069	$ 3428	$17,243
Elizabeth City State University	pub.	$ 2204	$ 5639	93%	NR	NR	NR	$ 3846
Elon University	ind.	$27,881	$ 9090	87%	NR	$17,312	$19,659	$27,163
Fayetteville State University	pub.	$ 3756	$ 5812	97%	27%	$10,426	—	NR
Gardner-Webb University	ind.	$22,410	$ 7220	93%	18%	$20,821	$ 8809	NR
High Point University	ind.	*$35,900	NR	87%	14%	$12,602	$23,298	$ 9117
Johnson & Wales University—Charlotte Campus	ind.	$25,407	$10,314	92%	15%	$18,846	$16,875	NR
Johnson C. Smith University	ind.	$16,542	$ 6439	95%	6%	$13,928	$ 9053	$29,218
Laurel University	ind.	$10,730	$ 2344†	100%	NR	$ 8186	$ 4888	NR
Lenoir-Rhyne University	ind.	$25,290	$ 8930	100%	25%	$22,571	$11,649	$24,358
Mars Hill College	ind.	$21,997	$ 7632	100%	14%	$17,572	$12,057	$27,775
Meredith College	ind.	$26,200	$ 7500	100%	21%	$20,517	$13,183	$33,691
Methodist University	ind.	$24,220	$ 8900	88%	47%	$26,575	$ 6545	$30,786
Mid-Atlantic Christian University	ind.	$11,600	$ 7200	100%	3%	$ 8825	$ 9975	$32,413
Montreat College	ind.	$23,164	$ 7346	100%	12%	$19,268	$11,242	NR
Mount Olive College	ind.	$15,500	$ 6200	99%	13%	$13,035	$ 8665	$19,091
New Life Theological Seminary	ind.	$ 7020	NA	73%	100%	$ 8648	—	$36,498
North Carolina Agricultural and Technical State University	pub.	$ 4416	$ 6029	78%	18%	$12,853	—	$21,644
North Carolina Central University	pub.	$ 5280	$ 9509	83%	8%	$ 2562	$12,227	NR
North Carolina State University	pub.	$ 6529	$ 8154	97%	34%	$11,787	$ 2896	$19,988
St. Andrews Presbyterian College	ind.	$21,614	$ 8938	100%	21%	$18,891	$11,661	$22,599
Saint Augustine's College	ind.	$17,160	$ 7126	96%	3%	$ 2228	$22,058	$12,614
Salem College	ind.	$21,965	$11,520	95%	100%	$24,045	$ 9440	$19,000

NA = not applicable; NR = not reported; * = includes room and board; † = room only; — = not available.

College Costs At-a-Glance

	Institutional Control ind.=independent; pub.=public	Tuition and Fees	Room and Board	Percent of Eligible Freshmen Receiving Need-Based Gift Awards	Percent of Freshmen Whose Need Was Fully Met	Average Financial Aid Package for Freshmen	Average Net Cost After Aid	Average Indebtedness Upon Graduation
North Carolina—*continued*								
The University of North Carolina at Asheville	pub.	$ 4772	$ 7040	97%	42%	$10,313	$ 1499	$15,443
The University of North Carolina at Chapel Hill	pub.	$ 6666	$ 9036	100%	98%	$13,449	$ 2253	NR
The University of North Carolina at Charlotte	pub.	$ 5138	$ 7260	94%	23%	$ 8970	$ 3428	$17,472
The University of North Carolina at Greensboro	pub.	$ 4520	$ 3855†	58%	25%	$ 9844	—	$23,772
The University of North Carolina at Pembroke	pub.	$ 4140	$ 5990	95%	20%	$10,216	—	NR
The University of North Carolina Wilmington	pub.	$ 5416	$ 7608	88%	46%	$ 8896	$ 4128	$19,277
Wake Forest University	ind.	$41,576	$11,410	98%	89%	$34,652	$18,334	$32,237
Warren Wilson College	ind.	$25,944	$ 8028	92%	12%	$19,314	$14,658	$20,018
Western Carolina University	pub.	$ 5367	$ 6980	98%	22%	$ 9400	$ 2947	NR
Wingate University	ind.	$22,180	$ 8770	100%	37%	$20,238	$10,712	$25,504
North Dakota								
Dickinson State University	pub.	$ 6337	$ 4262	92%	99%	$ 7360	$ 3239	$18,837
Jamestown College	ind.	$17,270	$ 5700	100%	28%	$13,174	$ 9796	$25,899
Mayville State University	pub.	$ 5937	$ 4454	94%	100%	$ 7935	$ 2456	$19,986
Medcenter One College of Nursing	ind.	$10,851	NA	NR	NR	NR	NR	NR
Minot State University	pub.	$ 5638	$ 4530	93%	100%	$ 7208	$ 2960	$20,272
University of Mary	ind.	$13,126	$ 5180	65%	30%	$11,787	$ 6519	$25,287
University of North Dakota	pub.	$ 6934	$ 5950	78%	99%	$ 9429	$ 3455	$45,369
Valley City State University	pub.	$ 6270	$ 5218	98%	100%	$ 9539	$ 1949	$22,428
Ohio								
Antioch University Midwest	ind.	$21,080	NA	NR	NR	NR	NR	$23,000
Ashland University	ind.	$28,580	$ 9352	100%	NR	$25,572	$12,360	$39,399
Baldwin-Wallace College	ind.	$25,260	$ 8300	100%	31%	$22,073	$11,487	$30,096
Bluffton University	ind.	$26,154	$ 8757	100%	48%	$24,480	$10,431	$31,457
Bowling Green State University	pub.	$ 9704	$ 7800	92%	10%	$15,114	$ 2390	$31,515
Capital University	ind.	$29,310	$ 7864	90%	30%	$25,135	$12,039	NR
Case Western Reserve University	ind.	$37,648	$11,400	98%	80%	$32,739	$16,309	$39,236
Cedarville University	ind.	$23,500	$ 5086	80%	20%	$14,754	$13,832	$29,177
Cincinnati Christian University	ind.	$13,780	$ 6710	90%	10%	$ 9521	$10,969	$34,040
The Cleveland Institute of Art	ind.	$33,882	$11,366	100%	8%	$23,672	$21,576	$55,231
Cleveland Institute of Music	ind.	$38,890	$ 9504	100%	32%	$23,132	$25,262	$26,995
Cleveland State University	pub.	$ 8466	$10,285	88%	5%	$ 9453	$ 9298	$19,537
College of Mount St. Joseph	ind.	$23,550	$ 7392	100%	19%	$17,513	$13,429	$35,569
The College of Wooster	ind.	$38,290	$ 9310	99%	66%	$30,477	$17,123	$25,252
Columbus College of Art & Design	ind.	$25,824	$ 9410	100%	10%	$20,218	$15,016	$37,355
Defiance College	ind.	$25,890	$ 8450	86%	9%	$21,653	$12,687	$31,410
Denison University	ind.	$40,210	$ 9960	99%	49%	$34,352	$15,818	NR
Heidelberg University	ind.	$22,780	$ 8636	100%	9%	$20,526	$10,890	$35,885
John Carroll University	ind.	$31,710	$ 9150	99%	22%	$25,865	$14,995	$28,830
Kent State University	pub.	$ 9030	$ 8376	83%	44%	$ 9067	$ 8339	$28,186
Kent State University at Stark	pub.	$ 5110	NA	77%	44%	$ 6768	—	NR
Kenyon College	ind.	$42,630	$10,020	93%	55%	$30,623	$22,027	$20,492

NA = not applicable; NR = not reported; * = includes room and board; † = room only; — = not available.

College Costs At-a-Glance	Institutional Control ind.=independent; pub.=public	Tuition and Fees	Room and Board	Percent of Eligible Freshmen Receiving Need-Based Gift Awards	Percent of Freshmen Whose Need Was Fully Met	Average Financial Aid Package for Freshmen	Average Net Cost After Aid	Average Indebtedness Upon Graduation
Ohio—*continued*								
Lourdes College	ind.	$15,870	$ 7800	81%	NR	$11,526	$12,144	NR
Malone University	ind.	$23,420	$ 8088	100%	12%	$21,248	$10,260	$32,306
Marietta College	ind.	$28,340	$ 8440	98%	36%	$25,310	$11,470	$34,152
Mercy College of Northwest Ohio	ind.	$10,624	NR	61%	3%	$ 7698	$ 2926	$25,560
Miami University	pub.	$12,786	$ 9786	52%	16%	$11,532	$11,040	$27,315
Mount Carmel College of Nursing	ind.	$15,644	$ 4500†	24%	9%	$ 7500	$12,644	$ 8675
Mount Vernon Nazarene University	ind.	$22,280	$ 6430	99%	12%	$18,422	$10,288	$31,609
Muskingum University	ind.	$20,616	$ 8170	100%	19%	$21,125	$ 7661	$34,207
Oberlin College	ind.	$41,577	$11,010	100%	100%	$30,901	$21,686	$17,085
Ohio Northern University	ind.	$33,099	$ 9072	100%	18%	$27,281	$14,890	$48,886
Ohio University	pub.	$ 9603	$ 9621	90%	13%	$ 8407	$10,817	$25,330
Ohio University–Chillicothe	pub.	$ 3060	NA	99%	6%	$ 8025	—	$25,330
Ohio University–Eastern	pub.	$ 4461	NA	99%	19%	$ 6098	—	$25,330
Ohio University–Lancaster	pub.	$ 3060	NA	97%	12%	$ 7101	—	$25,330
Ohio University–Southern Campus	pub.	$ 1487	NA	98%	8%	$ 7603	—	$25,330
Ohio University–Zanesville	pub.	$ 4662	NR	94%	22%	$ 7793	—	$25,330
Ohio Wesleyan University	ind.	$36,390	$ 9700	100%	31%	$30,401	$15,689	$30,920
Tiffin University	ind.	$19,124	$ 8750	97%	9%	$13,990	$13,884	$29,130
The University of Akron	pub.	$ 9247	$ 9160	63%	21%	$ 7656	$10,751	$28,421
University of Cincinnati	pub.	$10,068	$ 9702	44%	5%	$ 8305	$11,465	$26,462
University of Dayton	ind.	$29,930	$ 9400	99%	36%	$24,211	$15,119	$35,421
The University of Findlay	ind.	$26,798	$ 8810	100%	1%	$22,854	$12,754	$32,822
University of Mount Union	ind.	$24,800	$ 7780	99%	6%	$20,103	$12,477	$25,804
University of Rio Grande	ind.	$18,808	$ 7828	79%	75%	$10,238	$16,398	$18,689
The University of Toledo	pub.	$ 8491	$ 9708	99%	14%	$11,006	$ 7193	$27,378
Ursuline College	ind.	$23,940	$ 7970	100%	14%	$18,673	$13,237	$25,242
Walsh University	ind.	$22,280	$ 8360	92%	48%	$16,848	$13,792	$24,753
Wittenberg University	ind.	$36,434	$ 9294	100%	31%	$31,018	$14,710	$29,506
Wright State University	pub.	$ 7797	$ 8125	83%	9%	$ 9140	$ 6782	$26,542
Xavier University	ind.	$29,970	$ 9900	97%	21%	$18,711	$21,159	$25,881
Youngstown State University	pub.	$ 7199	$ 7600	79%	7%	$ 7890	$ 6909	NR
Oklahoma								
Cameron University	pub.	$ 4336	$ 3668	94%	83%	$12,200	—	$ 7200
Hillsdale Free Will Baptist College	ind.	$10,020	$ 5500	73%	13%	$ 8510	$ 7010	$23,822
Northeastern State University	pub.	$ 4385	$ 5020	80%	69%	$ 8769	$ 636	$23,155
Northwestern Oklahoma State University	pub.	$ 4336	$ 3640	88%	NR	NR	NR	$14,281
Oklahoma Baptist University	ind.	$18,670	$ 5630	83%	30%	$21,291	$ 3009	$23,039
Oklahoma Christian University	ind.	$18,456	$ 5900	55%	20%	$15,647	$ 8709	$22,333
Oklahoma City University	ind.	$25,760	$ 7500	97%	66%	$17,463	$15,797	$37,023
Oklahoma Panhandle State University	pub.	$ 5344	$ 3652	NR	NR	NR	NR	NR
Oklahoma State University	pub.	$ 6779	$ 6680	78%	18%	$11,788	$ 1671	$19,934
Oklahoma Wesleyan University	ind.	$20,160	$ 6874	90%	NR	$ 8723	$18,311	$21,276

NA = not applicable; NR = not reported; * = includes room and board; † = room only; — = not available.

College Costs At-a-Glance

	Institutional Control ind.=independent; pub.=public	Tuition and Fees	Room and Board	Percent of Eligible Freshmen Receiving Need-Based Gift Awards	Percent of Freshmen Whose Need Was Fully Met	Average Financial Aid Package for Freshmen	Average Net Cost After Aid	Average Indebtedness Upon Graduation
Oklahoma—*continued*								
Rogers State University	pub.	$ 4513	$ 5990†	68%	11%	$ 6915	$ 3588	$15,962
Southeastern Oklahoma State University	pub.	$ 4552	$ 4520	76%	19%	$10,321	—	$13,828
Southwestern Oklahoma State University	pub.	$ 4335	$ 4100	86%	29%	$ 4986	$ 3449	NR
University of Central Oklahoma	pub.	$ 4456	$ 8005	97%	14%	$ 7348	$ 5113	$19,820
University of Oklahoma	pub.	$ 5477	$ 7826	59%	83%	$11,997	$ 1306	$21,517
University of Science and Arts of Oklahoma	pub.	$ 4680	$ 4990	99%	17%	$ 8938	$ 732	$15,339
University of Tulsa	ind.	$28,310	$ 9018	45%	49%	$28,014	$ 9314	NR
Oregon								
Corban University	ind.	$25,445	$ 7980	100%	12%	$19,022	$14,403	$27,071
Eastern Oregon University	pub.	$ 6639	$ 8000	65%	53%	$ 8475	$ 6164	NR
George Fox University	ind.	$27,970	$ 8630	97%	42%	$26,306	$10,294	$18,428
Lewis & Clark College	ind.	$36,632	$ 9648	97%	87%	$27,142	$19,138	$22,148
Linfield College	ind.	$30,604	$ 8650	89%	39%	$23,350	$15,904	$31,135
Marylhurst University	ind.	$17,730	NA	67%	NR	$11,349	$ 6381	$10,278
New Hope Christian College	ind.	$13,190	$ 6260	NR	NR	NR	NR	NR
Northwest Christian University	ind.	$23,600	$ 7400	100%	9%	$20,999	$10,001	$22,818
Oregon College of Art & Craft	ind.	$21,860	$ 6210	100%	NR	$14,176	$13,894	$37,000
Oregon Health & Science University	pub.	$18,996	NA	NR	NR	NR	NR	NR
Oregon Institute of Technology	pub.	$ 7260	$ 8145	53%	31%	$ 5553	$ 9852	$21,733
Oregon State University	pub.	$ 7115	NR	81%	17%	$ 9502	—	NR
Pacific University	ind.	$33,612	$ 9208	98%	16%	$26,939	$15,881	$31,306
Portland State University	pub.	$ 7130	$10,065	74%	13%	$11,174	$ 6021	$26,287
Reed College	ind.	$41,200	$10,650	87%	100%	$34,856	$16,994	$16,910
Southern Oregon University	pub.	$ 6729	$ 8508	93%	16%	$10,614	$ 4623	$24,132
University of Oregon	pub.	$ 8190	$ 9429	51%	12%	$ 8786	$ 8833	$20,928
University of Portland	ind.	$33,538	$ 9760	73%	9%	$22,186	$21,112	$26,831
Warner Pacific College	ind.	$17,604	$ 6980	90%	9%	$14,287	$10,297	$30,559
Western Oregon University	pub.	$ 8055	$ 8439	85%	11%	$ 8890	$ 7604	$24,131
Willamette University	ind.	$37,361	$ 8900	99%	46%	$31,883	$14,378	$23,248
Pennsylvania								
Allegheny College	ind.	$36,190	$ 9160	100%	36%	$29,710	$15,640	NR
Alvernia University	ind.	$26,630	$ 9487	99%	13%	$16,253	$19,864	$27,327
Arcadia University	ind.	$34,150	$11,640	99%	11%	$23,393	$22,397	$33,765
Baptist Bible College of Pennsylvania	ind.	$18,240	$ 6650	62%	9%	$11,293	$13,597	$19,176
Bloomsburg University of Pennsylvania	pub.	$ 7456	$ 6890	52%	90%	$12,677	$ 1669	$23,882
Bryn Mawr College	ind.	$39,360	$12,420	100%	100%	$35,291	$16,489	$23,509
Bucknell University	ind.	$43,866	$10,374	100%	95%	$27,000	$27,240	$18,900
Cabrini College	ind.	$32,084	$11,400	82%	11%	$24,533	$18,951	$30,637
Carnegie Mellon University	ind.	$41,940	$10,750	95%	30%	$29,849	$22,841	$30,744
Cedar Crest College	ind.	$28,967	$ 9540	100%	13%	$25,150	$13,357	$32,225
Chestnut Hill College	ind.	$29,100	$ 9340	100%	18%	$20,552	$17,888	NR
Clarion University of Pennsylvania	pub.	$ 8164	$ 7000	79%	12%	$ 8362	$ 6802	NR

NA = not applicable; NR = not reported; * = includes room and board; † = room only; — = not available.

College Costs At-a-Glance	Institutional Control ind.=independent; pub.=public	Tuition and Fees	Room and Board	Percent of Eligible Freshmen Receiving Need-Based Gift Awards	Percent of Freshmen Whose Need Was Fully Met	Average Financial Aid Package for Freshmen	Average Net Cost After Aid	Average Indebtedness Upon Graduation
Pennsylvania—*continued*								
Delaware Valley College	ind.	$30,646	$10,842	100%	14%	$20,080	$21,408	$28,896
DeSales University	ind.	$28,000	$10,140	100%	21%	$22,207	$15,933	$33,835
Dickinson College	ind.	$41,520	$10,430	97%	84%	$34,695	$17,255	$22,451
Duquesne University	ind.	$27,502	$ 9476	99%	24%	$21,517	$15,461	NR
Edinboro University of Pennsylvania	pub.	$ 7740	$ 7820	93%	16%	$ 9228	$ 6332	$18,726
Elizabethtown College	ind.	$34,830	$ 8800	100%	18%	$24,254	$19,376	NR
Franklin & Marshall College	ind.	$41,150	$10,920	97%	100%	$35,253	$16,817	$28,451
Gannon University	ind.	$24,582	$ 9720	99%	14%	$21,030	$13,272	$34,830
Geneva College	ind.	$22,236	$ 8000	100%	18%	$19,428	$10,808	$24,000
Gettysburg College	ind.	$41,070	$ 9810	97%	97%	$33,937	$16,943	$24,981
Grove City College	ind.	$13,088	$ 7132	100%	11%	$ 6149	$14,071	$25,773
Gwynedd-Mercy College	ind.	$25,660	$ 9760	85%	11%	$17,864	$17,556	$34,520
Harrisburg University of Science and Technology	ind.	$19,500	NA	100%	6%	$13,701	$ 5799	$21,298
Haverford College	ind.	$40,624	$12,346	98%	100%	$36,749	$16,221	$16,238
Indiana University of Pennsylvania	pub.	$ 7571	$ 9300	69%	12%	$10,032	$ 6839	$25,224
Juniata College	ind.	$34,090	$ 9330	100%	24%	$25,564	$17,856	$23,637
Keystone College	ind.	$19,620	$ 9200	98%	29%	$23,718	$ 5102	$24,750
King's College	ind.	$26,644	$10,068	99%	16%	$20,688	$16,024	$31,113
Kutztown University of Pennsylvania	pub.	$ 7732	$ 8094	72%	47%	$ 7260	$ 8566	$22,670
Lafayette College	ind.	$39,115	$11,959	96%	80%	$33,866	$17,208	$20,687
Lancaster Bible College & Graduate School	ind.	$16,560	$ 7110	98%	3%	$13,603	$10,067	$18,605
La Roche College	ind.	$22,476	$ 8916	98%	37%	$26,958	$ 4434	$18,719
Lebanon Valley College	ind.	$33,200	$ 8800	99%	21%	$23,719	$18,281	$32,428
Lehigh University	ind.	$39,780	$10,520	97%	84%	$30,132	$20,168	$31,922
Lock Haven University of Pennsylvania	pub.	$ 7540	$ 6695	66%	45%	$ 8256	$ 5979	$22,883
Lycoming College	ind.	$30,800	$ 8542	100%	19%	$26,221	$13,121	$27,273
Marywood University	ind.	$27,150	$12,172	99%	21%	$24,514	$14,808	$27,736
Mercyhurst College	ind.	$26,346	$ 9195	100%	49%	$24,616	$10,925	$25,357
Messiah College	ind.	$28,356	$ 8420	100%	24%	$19,985	$16,791	$34,132
Millersville University of Pennsylvania	pub.	$ 7700	$ 8298	76%	15%	$ 8278	$ 7720	$25,876
Misericordia University	ind.	$24,990	$10,410	100%	21%	$18,843	$16,557	$36,742
Moravian College	ind.	$32,177	$ 9164	100%	18%	$24,203	$17,138	NR
Mount Aloysius College	ind.	$18,000	$ 7660	100%	NR	$13,945	$11,715	$32,312
Muhlenberg College	ind.	$38,380	$ 8735	98%	94%	$23,768	$23,347	$23,004
Peirce College	ind.	$15,900	NA	73%	NR	$11,827	$ 4073	$18,721
Penn State Abington	pub.	$12,730	NA	84%	3%	$ 9768	$ 2962	$31,135
Penn State Altoona	pub.	$13,250	$ 8370	63%	4%	$ 8356	$13,264	$31,135
Penn State Berks	pub.	$13,250	$ 9160	65%	3%	$ 8501	$13,909	$31,135
Penn State Erie, The Behrend College	pub.	$13,250	$ 8370	68%	4%	$ 8641	$12,979	$31,135
Penn State Harrisburg	pub.	$13,240	$ 9580	60%	6%	$ 8943	$13,877	$31,135
Penn State University Park	pub.	$15,250	$ 8370	50%	8%	$ 9529	$14,091	$31,135
Pennsylvania College of Technology	pub.	$13,080	$ 9500	100%	NR	NR	NR	NR
Philadelphia Biblical University	ind.	$20,888	$ 8275	98%	8%	$15,215	$13,948	$25,971

NA = not applicable; NR = not reported; * = includes room and board; † = room only; — = not available.

College Costs At-a-Glance

	Institutional Control ind.=independent; pub.=public	Tuition and Fees	Room and Board	Percent of Eligible Freshmen Receiving Need-Based Gift Awards	Percent of Freshmen Whose Need Was Fully Met	Average Financial Aid Package for Freshmen	Average Net Cost After Aid	Average Indebtedness Upon Graduation
Pennsylvania—*continued*								
Philadelphia University	ind.	$28,890	$ 9502	100%	11%	$25,826	$12,566	$32,337
Point Park University	ind.	$22,500	$ 9480	100%	14%	$19,711	$12,269	$26,687
Robert Morris University	ind.	$21,550	$10,660	100%	14%	$19,334	$12,876	$37,523
Rosemont College	ind.	$29,050	$11,440	100%	10%	$24,310	$16,180	$21,490
St. Charles Borromeo Seminary, Overbrook	ind.	$18,228	$11,472	50%	50%	$19,500	$10,200	$19,000
Saint Francis University	ind.	$26,534	$ 9066	NR	NR	NR	NR	NR
Saint Joseph's University	ind.	$35,230	$11,925	98%	25%	$20,876	$26,279	$45,530
Saint Vincent College	ind.	$27,190	$ 9048	100%	26%	$23,489	$12,749	NR
Seton Hill University	ind.	$27,548	$ 8810	100%	21%	$22,752	$13,606	$30,997
Shippensburg University of Pennsylvania	pub.	$ 8056	$ 7400	76%	5%	$ 7307	$ 8149	$24,165
Slippery Rock University of Pennsylvania	pub.	$ 7666	$ 8884	65%	32%	$ 7858	$ 8692	$26,452
Swarthmore College	ind.	$39,600	$11,900	100%	100%	$36,825	$14,675	$18,739
Temple University	pub.	$12,424	$ 9550	100%	33%	$15,802	$ 6172	$31,123
Thiel College	ind.	$24,856	$ 9652	100%	6%	$18,614	$15,894	$34,606
University of Pennsylvania	ind.	$42,098	$11,878	97%	100%	$35,264	$18,712	$17,013
University of Pittsburgh	pub.	$14,936	$ 9230	75%	41%	$10,310	$13,856	$26,612
University of Pittsburgh at Bradford	pub.	$12,046	$ 7650	65%	98%	$13,642	$ 6054	$21,695
University of Pittsburgh at Greensburg	pub.	$12,176	$ 8110	70%	9%	$12,192	$ 8094	$26,163
University of Pittsburgh at Johnstown	pub.	$12,078	$ 7826	76%	9%	$10,174	$ 9730	$21,220
The University of Scranton	ind.	$36,042	$12,432	98%	28%	$23,096	$25,378	$47,251
University of the Sciences in Philadelphia	ind.	$30,794	$12,034	80%	56%	$33,328	$ 9500	$12,005
Ursinus College	ind.	$40,120	$ 9750	100%	24%	$31,250	$18,620	$26,780
Valley Forge Christian College	ind.	$16,250	$ 7556	95%	8%	$10,439	$13,367	$32,581
Villanova University	ind.	$39,665	$10,640	89%	21%	$28,626	$21,679	$37,267
Washington & Jefferson College	ind.	$34,610	$ 9280	82%	14%	$25,444	$18,446	$30,000
Waynesburg University	ind.	$18,410	$ 7580	100%	20%	$15,209	$10,781	$25,000
West Chester University of Pennsylvania	pub.	$ 7680	$ 7188	69%	34%	$ 6997	$ 7871	$25,159
Westminster College	ind.	$29,150	$ 8840	100%	14%	$23,791	$14,199	$28,637
Widener University	ind.	$33,270	$11,720	82%	15%	$26,423	$18,567	$40,386
Wilkes University	ind.	$27,178	$11,470	100%	13%	$20,706	$17,942	$35,244
Wilson College	ind.	$29,340	$ 9711	100%	17%	$22,961	$16,090	$36,021
York College of Pennsylvania	ind.	$15,880	$ 8920	72%	26%	$11,149	$13,651	$28,851
Puerto Rico								
Carlos Albizu University	ind.	$ 6939	NA	NR	NR	NR	NR	NR
EDP College of Puerto Rico–San Sebastian	ind.	$ 6120	NR	59%	NR	$ 5550	$ 570	$ 2500
Inter American University of Puerto Rico, Bayamón Campus	ind.	$ 5616	NR	94%	NR	$ 207	$ 5409	NR
Inter American University of Puerto Rico, Guayama Campus	ind.	$ 4558	NA	73%	NR	$ 315	$ 4243	NR
Inter American University of Puerto Rico, San Germán Campus	ind.	$ 5616	$ 2500	96%	NR	$ 339	$ 7777	NR
National University College	ind.	$ 6315	NR	100%	NR	$ 1659	$ 4656	NR
Pontifical Catholic University of Puerto Rico	ind.	$ 5468	$ 1300†	100%	4%	$ 7138	—	$12,707
Universidad Teológica del Caribe	ind.	$ 3880	$ 2400	100%	NR	NR	NR	NR
University of Puerto Rico at Bayamón	pub.	$ 2076	NA	NR	NR	NR	NR	NR

NA = not applicable; NR = not reported; * = includes room and board; † = room only; — = not available.

College Costs At-a-Glance	Institutional Control ind.=independent; pub.=public	Tuition and Fees	Room and Board	Percent of Eligible Freshmen Receiving Need-Based Gift Awards	Percent of Freshmen Whose Need Was Fully Met	Average Financial Aid Package for Freshmen	Average Net Cost After Aid	Average Indebtedness Upon Graduation
Rhode Island								
Brown University	ind.	$42,230	$10,906	98%	100%	$37,355	$15,781	$22,468
Bryant University	ind.	$34,624	$12,829	81%	50%	$20,646	$26,807	$39,490
Johnson & Wales University	ind.	$24,141	NR	89%	14%	$17,455	$ 6686	NR
Providence College	ind.	$39,435	$11,690	95%	44%	$27,100	$24,025	$32,850
Rhode Island College	pub.	$ 6986	$ 9256	88%	31%	$ 9929	$ 6313	$18,939
Salve Regina University	ind.	$31,450	$11,300	99%	13%	$22,332	$20,418	$35,737
University of Rhode Island	pub.	$ 9014	$10,854	90%	99%	$12,470	$ 7398	$22,750
South Carolina								
Anderson University	ind.	$22,570	$ 7825	100%	31%	$18,498	$11,897	NR
Bob Jones University	ind.	$12,120	$ 5100	87%	1%	$ 8900	$ 8320	$28,000
The Citadel, The Military College of South Carolina	pub.	$11,020	$ 5889	82%	19%	$12,365	$ 4544	$33,998
Clemson University	pub.	$12,346	NR	35%	20%	$14,547	—	$18,463
Coastal Carolina University	pub.	$ 9390	$ 7350	47%	10%	$ 8848	$ 7892	$31,907
Coker College	ind.	$20,818	$ 6590	96%	30%	$21,357	$ 6051	$25,593
College of Charleston	pub.	$10,314	$ 9843	72%	29%	$12,690	$ 7467	$19,875
Columbia International University	ind.	$17,395	$ 6410	66%	5%	$16,088	$ 7717	$21,057
Converse College	ind.	$26,138	$ 8032	100%	21%	$24,379	$ 9791	$24,187
Erskine College	ind.	$26,475	$ 8775	100%	47%	$22,681	$12,569	$24,450
Francis Marion University	pub.	$ 8480	$ 6380	85%	NR	NR	NR	$26,453
Furman University	ind.	$38,088	$ 9572	100%	39%	$29,378	$18,282	$26,202
Limestone College	ind.	$20,000	$ 7500	100%	15%	$13,936	$13,564	$28,939
Presbyterian College	ind.	$30,180	$ 8670	100%	43%	$31,483	$ 7367	$24,067
University of South Carolina	pub.	$ 9786	$ 7764	47%	26%	$11,934	$ 5616	$21,811
University of South Carolina Aiken	pub.	$ 8424	$ 6450	95%	16%	$10,094	$ 4780	$19,369
Winthrop University	pub.	$12,176	$ 6922	99%	14%	$12,423	$ 6675	$26,066
Wofford College	ind.	$31,710	$ 8870	91%	45%	$29,916	$10,664	$23,103
South Dakota								
Augustana College	ind.	$25,104	$ 6260	100%	25%	$21,983	$ 9381	$31,520
Black Hills State University	pub.	$ 6951	$ 5729	NR	NR	NR	NR	$25,628
Dakota State University	pub.	$ 7171	$ 5004	65%	8%	$ 7754	$ 4421	$21,811
Dakota Wesleyan University	ind.	$19,850	$ 5930	100%	19%	$16,900	$ 8880	$32,400
Mount Marty College	ind.	$19,932	$ 5636	100%	47%	$23,275	$ 2293	$34,983
Northern State University	pub.	$ 6351	$ 5068	97%	21%	$ 7843	$ 3576	NR
South Dakota School of Mines and Technology	pub.	$ 7130	$ 5610	75%	47%	$12,376	$ 364	$16,045
South Dakota State University	pub.	$ 6444	$ 5899	62%	79%	$ 8748	$ 3595	$20,733
The University of South Dakota	pub.	$ 6762	$ 6123	57%	70%	$ 6243	$ 6642	$22,954
Tennessee								
Aquinas College	ind.	$18,330	NA	NR	NR	NR	NR	NR
Austin Peay State University	pub.	$ 6048	$ 6450	62%	NR	$ 9201	$ 3297	$19,149
Belmont University	ind.	$23,680	$11,680	66%	33%	$13,060	$22,300	$29,058
Bryan College	ind.	$18,740	$ 5454	96%	61%	$39,484	—	$15,637
Carson-Newman College	ind.	$21,778	$ 6246	99%	21%	$18,063	$ 9961	$20,528

NA = not applicable; NR = not reported; * = includes room and board; † = room only; — = not available.

College Costs At-a-Glance	Institutional Control ind.=independent; pub.=public	Tuition and Fees	Room and Board	Percent of Eligible Freshmen Receiving Need-Based Gift Awards	Percent of Freshmen Whose Need Was Fully Met	Average Financial Aid Package for Freshmen	Average Net Cost After Aid	Average Indebtedness Upon Graduation
Tennessee—*continued*								
Christian Brothers University	ind.	$24,870	$ 6410	65%	30%	$24,188	$ 7092	$29,207
East Tennessee State University	pub.	$ 5823	$ 5783	87%	35%	$ 7998	$ 3608	$20,984
Freed-Hardeman University	ind.	$15,922	$ 7216	100%	21%	$15,475	$ 7663	$34,533
Free Will Baptist Bible College	ind.	$14,306	$ 6042	33%	NR	$ 4973	$15,375	$19,455
Johnson Bible College	ind.	$ 9100	$ 5100	99%	9%	$ 9856	$ 4344	$18,494
King College	ind.	$22,908	$ 7790	99%	20%	$18,137	$12,561	$13,484
Lane College	ind.	$ 8220	$ 5800	21%	52%	$ 3341	$10,679	$ 8754
Lee University	ind.	$12,680	$ 6010	94%	30%	$11,359	$ 7331	$28,911
LeMoyne-Owen College	ind.	$10,318	$ 4852	96%	2%	$ 9613	$ 5557	NR
Lincoln Memorial University	ind.	$16,200	$ 5780	99%	21%	$18,761	$ 3219	$21,749
Lipscomb University	ind.	$23,494	$ 8790	53%	16%	$17,363	$14,921	$21,034
Maryville College	ind.	$29,924	$ 9234	100%	23%	$30,091	$ 9067	$21,343
Middle Tennessee State University	pub.	$ 6298	$ 7132	66%	87%	$10,062	$ 3368	$14,822
Milligan College	ind.	$25,260	$ 5650	100%	31%	$18,061	$12,849	$22,360
Rhodes College	ind.	$34,580	$ 8480	100%	43%	$32,280	$10,780	$24,946
Sewanee: The University of the South	ind.	$32,292	$ 9226	100%	72%	$34,988	$ 6530	$19,337
Southern Adventist University	ind.	$18,324	$ 5786	100%	88%	$15,674	$ 8436	$27,121
Tennessee Technological University	pub.	$ 5828	$ 7158	61%	31%	$ 9997	$ 2989	$ 9510
Tennessee Wesleyan College	ind.	$19,100	$ 6350	100%	19%	$13,794	$11,656	$17,919
Trevecca Nazarene University	ind.	$18,518	$ 7734	NR	NR	NR	NR	NR
Union University	ind.	$22,390	$ 7460	84%	19%	$19,433	$10,417	$22,017
University of Memphis	pub.	$ 6990	$ 6190	82%	10%	$ 9873	$ 3307	$20,856
The University of Tennessee	pub.	$ 7382	$ 7800	97%	28%	$11,621	$ 3561	$19,987
The University of Tennessee at Chattanooga	pub.	$ 6062	$ 8210	58%	17%	$ 7106	$ 7166	$13,845
The University of Tennessee at Martin	pub.	$ 6190	$ 5104	72%	39%	$12,846	—	$19,048
Vanderbilt University	ind.	$39,930	$13,058	88%	100%	$42,397	$10,591	$18,605
Victory University	ind.	$10,620	NA	88%	100%	$ 7325	$ 3295	$27,625
Texas								
Abilene Christian University	ind.	$22,760	$ 7884	100%	21%	$15,191	$15,453	$38,634
Angelo State University	pub.	$ 6692	$ 6666	95%	20%	$10,796	$ 2562	$10,712
Austin College	ind.	$31,270	$10,078	100%	100%	$28,858	$12,490	NR
Austin Graduate School of Theology	ind.	$ 7230	NA	NR	NR	NR	NR	NR
Baptist University of the Americas	ind.	$ 4560	NR	NR	NR	NR	NR	NR
Baylor University	ind.	$29,754	$ 8331	99%	15%	$22,971	$15,114	NR
Dallas Baptist University	ind.	$18,690	$ 5868	68%	54%	$17,029	$ 7529	$18,629
East Texas Baptist University	ind.	$20,500	$ 5666	77%	22%	$15,658	$10,508	$25,284
Hardin-Simmons University	ind.	$22,460	$ 6804	73%	21%	$24,292	$ 4972	$37,383
Houston Baptist University	ind.	$23,180	$ 6975	86%	35%	$27,186	$ 2969	NR
Howard Payne University	ind.	$19,950	$ 5692	100%	25%	$16,992	$ 8650	$30,690
Huston-Tillotson University	ind.	$12,430	$ 6946	56%	30%	$15,162	$ 4214	NR
Jarvis Christian College	ind.	$11,146	$ 7788	99%	21%	$11,549	$ 7385	$18,500
Lamar University	pub.	$ 6934	$ 7010	87%	NR	$ 5187	$ 8757	$ 8234

NA = not applicable; NR = not reported; * = includes room and board; † = room only; — = not available.

College Costs At-a-Glance

	Institutional Control ind.=independent; pub.=public	Tuition and Fees	Room and Board	Percent of Eligible Freshmen Receiving Need-Based Gift Awards	Percent of Freshmen Whose Need Was Fully Met	Average Financial Aid Package for Freshmen	Average Net Cost After Aid	Average Indebtedness Upon Graduation
Texas—*continued*								
LeTourneau University	ind.	$21,980	$ 8390	100%	12%	$18,639	$11,731	NR
Lubbock Christian University	ind.	$16,180	$ 6368	99%	9%	$13,126	$ 9422	$26,440
McMurry University	ind.	$20,680	$ 6976	97%	16%	$19,895	$ 7761	$33,212
Midwestern State University	pub.	$ 6720	$ 5940	94%	29%	$ 9994	$ 2666	$16,620
Northwood University, Texas Campus	ind.	$19,272	$ 8117	87%	14%	$18,128	$ 9261	$23,182
Our Lady of the Lake University of San Antonio	ind.	$21,900	$ 6838	99%	20%	$26,729	$ 2009	$32,356
Prairie View A&M University	pub.	$ 6855	$ 7064	NR	NR	NR	NR	NR
Rice University	ind.	$35,551	$12,270	100%	100%	$31,457	$16,364	$13,944
St. Edward's University	ind.	$28,700	$ 9784	90%	10%	$21,910	$16,574	$32,515
Schreiner University	ind.	$20,354	$ 9676	100%	16%	$14,490	$15,540	$28,967
Southern Methodist University	ind.	$39,430	NR	77%	45%	$35,099	$ 4331	$24,569
Southwestern University	ind.	$31,630	$ 9770	100%	44%	$28,629	$12,771	$29,548
Stephen F. Austin State University	pub.	$ 6998	$ 7670	78%	65%	$ 9746	$ 4922	$20,483
Sul Ross State University	pub.	$ 2928	$ 6370	91%	70%	$ 9784	—	NR
Tarleton State University	pub.	$ 6199	$ 6591	76%	66%	$ 6502	$ 6288	$14,879
Texas A&M International University	pub.	$ 6153	$ 6918	97%	9%	$10,392	$ 2679	$19,400
Texas A&M University	pub.	$ 8387	$ 8008	97%	61%	$16,562	—	$22,243
Texas A&M University–Commerce	pub.	$ 5998	$ 7090	96%	52%	$12,642	$ 446	$26,090
Texas A&M University–Corpus Christi	pub.	$ 6514	$ 9528	84%	14%	$10,243	$ 5799	$18,314
Texas A&M University–Texarkana	pub.	$ 4946	NA	90%	NR	$ 2650	$ 2296	NR
Texas Christian University	ind.	$32,490	$10,600	96%	25%	$18,496	$24,594	$36,546
Texas College	ind.	$ 9490	$ 6600	98%	5%	$ 8905	$ 7185	$27,158
Texas Lutheran University	ind.	$22,890	$ 6740	99%	24%	$20,600	$ 9030	$34,410
Texas Southern University	pub.	$ 7462	$11,880	100%	30%	$15,140	$ 4202	$ 7883
Texas State University–San Marcos	pub.	$ 7838	$ 6810	79%	11%	$14,630	$ 18	$21,667
Texas Tech University	pub.	$ 8260	$ 7800	80%	13%	$ 9627	$ 6433	$21,500
Texas Wesleyan University	ind.	$18,710	$ 6910	100%	9%	$12,000	$13,620	NR
Texas Woman's University	pub.	$ 6960	$ 6210	84%	15%	$11,507	$ 1663	$21,194
Trinity University	ind.	$30,012	$10,312	100%	29%	$25,928	$14,396	NR
University of Dallas	ind.	$29,325	$ 9326	100%	21%	$22,944	$15,707	$28,020
University of Houston	pub.	$ 9000	$ 7300	93%	40%	$12,816	$ 3484	$14,922
University of Houston–Clear Lake	pub.	$ 6188	$10,340†	NR	NR	NR	NR	$ 8061
University of Houston–Downtown	pub.	$ 5492	NA	98%	5%	$ 9585	—	$15,484
University of Mary Hardin-Baylor	ind.	$23,050	$ 6221	100%	11%	$13,918	$15,353	$17,500
University of North Texas	pub.	$ 7960	$ 6716	85%	40%	$12,147	$ 2529	NR
University of St. Thomas	ind.	$23,500	$ 7900	98%	13%	$16,860	$14,540	$29,245
The University of Texas at Arlington	pub.	$ 8500	$ 6224	80%	30%	$11,870	$ 2854	$18,749
The University of Texas at Austin	pub.	$ 9794	NR	90%	35%	$13,526	—	$24,667
The University of Texas at Brownsville	pub.	$ 4766	$ 5782	93%	NR	$ 8634	$ 1914	NR
The University of Texas at Dallas	pub.	$10,744	$ 8210	93%	39%	$12,793	$ 6161	$17,384
The University of Texas at El Paso	pub.	$ 6535	NR	85%	35%	$14,717	—	$18,773
The University of Texas at San Antonio	pub.	$ 8283	$ 8696	87%	24%	$ 9944	$ 7035	$24,017
The University of Texas at Tyler	pub.	$ 6322	$ 8106	89%	20%	$ 9062	$ 5366	$18,605

NA = not applicable; NR = not reported; * = includes room and board; † = room only; — = not available.

College Costs At-a-Glance

	Institutional Control ind.=independent; pub.=public	Tuition and Fees	Room and Board	Percent of Eligible Freshmen Receiving Need-Based Gift Awards	Percent of Freshmen Whose Need Was Fully Met	Average Financial Aid Package for Freshmen	Average Net Cost After Aid	Average Indebtedness Upon Graduation
Texas—*continued*								
The University of Texas Medical Branch	pub.	$ 5740	NR	NR	NR	NR	NR	NR
The University of Texas of the Permian Basin	pub.	$ 5599	$ 6964	80%	15%	$ 6284	$ 6279	$13,420
The University of Texas–Pan American	pub.	$ 4560	$ 5298	98%	8%	$10,269	—	$13,480
University of the Incarnate Word	ind.	$22,790	$ 9658	99%	33%	$18,192	$14,256	NR
Wayland Baptist University	ind.	$13,340	$ 4084	100%	14%	$12,924	$ 4500	$26,959
West Texas A&M University	pub.	$ 6236	$ 6000	72%	100%	$ 8788	$ 3448	$13,678
Utah								
Brigham Young University	ind.	$ 4560	$ 7120	50%	3%	$ 6176	$ 5504	$13,354
Dixie State College of Utah	pub.	$ 3490	$ 4100	97%	3%	$ 6597	$ 993	$15,564
Southern Utah University	pub.	$ 4736	$ 2086†	99%	15%	$ 6900	—	$11,170
University of Utah	pub.	$ 6274	$ 6240	82%	20%	$11,068	$ 1446	$17,343
Utah State University	pub.	$ 5150	$ 5070	63%	18%	$ 9145	$ 1075	$15,194
Utah Valley University	pub.	$ 4288	$ 8904	79%	4%	$17,947	—	$15,593
Westminster College	ind.	$27,182	$ 7584	100%	33%	$21,969	$12,797	$20,002
Vermont								
Bennington College	ind.	$41,350	$11,550	97%	8%	$34,719	$18,181	$26,224
Burlington College	ind.	$21,465	$ 7100†	88%	NR	$13,756	$14,809	$21,670
Champlain College	ind.	$28,400	$12,520	92%	8%	$18,995	$21,925	$34,658
College of St. Joseph	ind.	$19,465	$ 9200	100%	10%	$18,493	$10,172	$25,848
Green Mountain College	ind.	$27,945	$10,142	100%	14%	$19,884	$18,203	$39,983
Marlboro College	ind.	$36,560	$ 9640	100%	NR	$20,250	$25,950	$22,456
Middlebury College	ind.	*$52,500	NR	100%	100%	$35,640	$16,860	$21,520
Saint Michael's College	ind.	$36,240	$ 9030	98%	29%	$25,540	$19,730	$29,410
Sterling College	ind.	$27,152	$ 8090	100%	17%	$18,753	$16,489	$19,751
University of Vermont	pub.	$14,036	$ 9382	83%	18%	$20,894	$ 2524	$27,696
Vermont Technical College	pub.	$11,555	$ 8445	83%	21%	$ 9234	$10,766	$24,000
Virginia								
Averett University	ind.	$22,956	$ 8274	100%	20%	$17,296	$13,934	$39,110
Bluefield College	ind.	$18,800	$ 7350	100%	17%	$13,683	$12,467	$18,661
Bridgewater College	ind.	$25,500	$10,350	100%	23%	$23,299	$12,551	$29,036
Christendom College	ind.	$20,434	$ 7656	100%	94%	$13,340	$14,750	$26,614
Christopher Newport University	pub.	$13,220	$ 9540	76%	15%	$ 7720	$15,040	$21,572
The College of William and Mary	pub.	$12,188	$ 8684	100%	22%	$14,950	$ 5922	$21,367
Emory & Henry College	ind.	$26,000	$ 8570	90%	22%	$24,775	$ 9795	$23,049
Ferrum College	ind.	$24,945	$ 8080	98%	NR	$21,207	$11,818	$30,460
George Mason University	pub.	$ 8684	$ 8220	84%	9%	$12,807	$ 4097	$22,219
Hampden-Sydney College	ind.	$32,364	$10,126	100%	29%	$24,392	$18,098	$25,426
Hampton University	ind.	$18,074	$ 8048	98%	56%	$ 4204	$21,918	$11,334
Hollins University	ind.	$29,485	$10,200	96%	16%	$24,002	$15,683	$19,982
James Madison University	pub.	$ 8448	$ 8340	58%	94%	$10,524	$ 6264	$20,417
Jefferson College of Health Sciences	ind.	$18,810	$ 4700†	100%	4%	$ 8466	$15,044	$18,133
Liberty University	ind.	$19,154	$ 6680	98%	11%	$ 9948	$15,886	$32,936

NA = not applicable; NR = not reported; * = includes room and board; † = room only; — = not available.

College Costs At-a-Glance	Institutional Control ind.=independent; pub.=public	Tuition and Fees	Room and Board	Percent of Eligible Freshmen Receiving Need-Based Gift Awards	Percent of Freshmen Whose Need Was Fully Met	Average Financial Aid Package for Freshmen	Average Net Cost After Aid	Average Indebtedness Upon Graduation
Virginia—*continued*								
Longwood University	pub.	$ 9855	$ 8114	96%	44%	$11,371	$ 6598	$23,379
Lynchburg College	ind.	$30,805	$ 8210	100%	25%	$21,304	$17,711	$32,130
Mary Baldwin College	ind.	$25,555	$ 7420	100%	11%	$21,619	$11,356	$29,245
Marymount University	ind.	$23,974	$10,580	63%	19%	$18,529	$16,025	$23,945
Norfolk State University	pub.	$ 9162	$ 7719	NR	NR	NR	NR	NR
Old Dominion University	pub.	$ 8144	$ 8796	54%	53%	$ 8479	$ 8461	$17,250
Patrick Henry College	ind.	$21,520	$ 8530	100%	NR	$10,530	$19,520	NR
Radford University	pub.	$ 8104	$ 7302	62%	29%	$ 9080	$ 6326	$20,678
Randolph College	ind.	$29,254	$ 9995	100%	25%	$23,693	$15,556	$22,000
Randolph-Macon College	ind.	$30,608	$ 9326	100%	20%	$24,773	$15,161	$31,603
Regent University	ind.	$15,308	$ 5900†	90%	19%	$10,858	$10,350	$40,942
Roanoke College	ind.	$32,900	$10,772	100%	22%	$25,188	$18,484	$27,984
Shenandoah University	ind.	$25,080	$ 8870	100%	19%	$19,000	$14,950	$27,000
Sweet Briar College	ind.	$30,195	$10,780	76%	61%	$20,476	$20,499	$27,712
University of Mary Washington	pub.	$ 8800	$ 8900	55%	12%	$ 8370	$ 9330	$16,000
University of Richmond	ind.	$43,170	$ 9250	100%	95%	$38,477	$13,943	$23,070
University of Virginia	pub.	$10,628	$ 8652	86%	100%	$21,218	—	$19,384
The University of Virginia's College at Wise	pub.	$ 7721	$ 8890	86%	82%	$11,181	$ 5430	$14,801
Virginia Commonwealth University	pub.	$ 8717	$ 8526	81%	8%	$ 9652	$ 7591	$25,151
Virginia Military Institute	pub.	$12,328	$ 7132	96%	44%	$19,200	$ 260	$18,063
Virginia Polytechnic Institute and State University	pub.	$ 9458	$ 6290	68%	16%	$10,990	$ 4758	$23,100
Virginia State University	pub.	$ 6570	$ 8152	80%	34%	$ 8800	$ 5922	$28,250
Virginia Wesleyan College	ind.	$29,680	$ 7988	100%	8%	$20,941	$16,727	$29,679
Washington and Lee University	ind.	$40,387	$10,243	100%	100%	$42,427	$ 8203	$23,807
Washington								
Central Washington University	pub.	$ 7113	$ 8901	86%	60%	$ 8578	$ 7436	$16,507
Cornish College of the Arts	ind.	$29,237	$ 8300	100%	7%	$15,214	$22,323	$36,567
Eastern Washington University	pub.	$ 6604	$ 7470	77%	30%	$11,156	$ 2918	$20,114
The Evergreen State College	pub.	$ 6679	$ 8460	90%	19%	$ 9749	$ 5390	$16,700
Gonzaga University	ind.	$30,925	$ 8300	100%	29%	$21,867	$17,358	$27,136
Northwest University	ind.	$23,400	$ 6884	100%	21%	$16,548	$13,736	$29,160
Pacific Lutheran University	ind.	$30,950	$ 9250	100%	42%	$29,895	$10,305	$28,640
Saint Martin's University	ind.	$27,621	$ 8960	100%	29%	$20,642	$15,939	$22,966
Seattle Pacific University	ind.	$30,339	$ 9081	100%	9%	$25,568	$13,852	$30,073
Seattle University	ind.	$30,825	$ 9315	91%	8%	$26,578	$13,562	$26,607
University of Puget Sound	ind.	$38,720	$10,020	100%	24%	$28,061	$20,679	$28,660
University of Washington, Tacoma	pub.	$ 8689	$ 8949†	77%	23%	$11,200	$ 6438	$17,900
Walla Walla University	ind.	$23,454	$ 5331	79%	25%	$19,219	$ 9566	$32,697
Washington State University	pub.	$ 9489	$ 9644	65%	27%	$12,302	$ 6831	NR
Western Washington University	pub.	$ 6858	$ 8749	81%	26%	$12,469	$ 3138	$17,652
Whitman College	ind.	$40,496	$10,160	79%	54%	$29,357	$21,299	$14,285
Whitworth University	ind.	$29,890	NR	100%	20%	$27,360	$ 2530	$22,540

NA = not applicable; NR = not reported; * = includes room and board; † = room only; — = not available.

College Costs At-a-Glance

	Institutional Control ind.=independent; pub.=public	Tuition and Fees	Room and Board	Percent of Eligible Freshmen Receiving Need-Based Gift Awards	Percent of Freshmen Whose Need Was Fully Met	Average Financial Aid Package for Freshmen	Average Net Cost After Aid	Average Indebtedness Upon Graduation
West Virginia								
Alderson-Broaddus College	ind.	$22,204	$ 7222	100%	35%	$22,926	$ 6500	$31,751
Appalachian Bible College	ind.	$10,934	$ 5790	98%	6%	$ 7665	$ 9059	$10,585
Bethany College	ind.	$22,596	$ 9300	97%	NR	NR	NR	NR
Bluefield State College	pub.	$ 4596	NA	100%	57%	$ 6800	—	$22,000
Concord University	pub.	$ 4974	$ 6962	84%	27%	$11,959	—	$14,700
Glenville State College	pub.	$ 4888	$ 7350	82%	18%	$11,227	$ 1011	$25,145
Marshall University	pub.	$ 5285	$ 7858	74%	30%	$ 9713	$ 3430	$21,156
Mountain State University	ind.	$ 7680	$ 8865	78%	8%	$ 8258	$ 8287	$34,088
Ohio Valley University	ind.	$14,050	$ 6446	98%	15%	$13,591	$ 6905	$21,735
Shepherd University	pub.	$ 5234	$ 7720	64%	27%	$10,639	$ 2315	$20,429
University of Charleston	ind.	$25,000	$ 8800	59%	26%	$22,093	$11,707	$24,000
West Liberty University	pub.	$ 4880	$ 7310	83%	46%	$ 8955	$ 3235	$19,200
West Virginia University	pub.	$ 5406	$ 8120	73%	30%	$ 6664	$ 6862	NR
West Virginia University Institute of Technology	pub.	$ 5164	$ 8130	71%	14%	$ 9601	$ 3693	$18,319
West Virginia Wesleyan College	ind.	$23,980	$ 7140	100%	26%	$22,686	$ 8434	$25,240
Wheeling Jesuit University	ind.	$25,010	$ 8874	75%	33%	$23,921	$ 9963	$32,927
Wisconsin								
Alverno College	ind.	$21,063	$ 6966	100%	NR	$16,425	$11,604	$33,220
Bellin College	ind.	$10,167	NA	NR	NR	NR	NR	$39,584
Beloit College	ind.	$35,038	$ 7164	100%	64%	$32,422	$ 9780	$19,930
Carroll University	ind.	$25,248	$ 7736	100%	42%	$18,397	$14,587	$28,777
Concordia University Wisconsin	ind.	$22,150	$ 8310	99%	36%	$21,409	$ 9051	$28,247
Edgewood College	ind.	$21,988	$ 7384	100%	16%	$17,619	$11,753	$29,745
Lawrence University	ind.	$38,481	$ 7890	97%	53%	$28,672	$17,699	$30,224
Maranatha Baptist Bible College	ind.	$11,550	$ 6290	55%	6%	$ 7462	$10,378	$19,191
Marian University	ind.	$21,490	$ 5700	100%	36%	$19,400	$ 7790	$22,125
Marquette University	ind.	$31,822	$10,370	99%	25%	$21,818	$20,374	$32,824
Milwaukee School of Engineering	ind.	$30,990	$ 7794	100%	15%	$20,349	$18,435	$35,236
Mount Mary College	ind.	$22,118	$ 7498	100%	4%	$20,334	$ 9282	$24,614
Northland College	ind.	$26,566	$ 7210	NR	NR	NR	NR	NR
Ripon College	ind.	$28,689	$ 8270	100%	23%	$24,893	$12,066	$30,694
St. Norbert College	ind.	$28,043	$ 7349	97%	41%	$20,583	$14,809	$29,836
Silver Lake College	ind.	$21,820	$ 8500	100%	9%	$22,771	$ 7549	$19,386
University of Wisconsin–Eau Claire	pub.	$ 7364	$ 5830	73%	54%	$ 8663	$ 4531	$21,185
University of Wisconsin–Green Bay	pub.	$ 6973	$ 7290	66%	40%	$10,281	$ 3982	$22,399
University of Wisconsin–La Crosse	pub.	$ 7911	$ 5630	43%	14%	$ 6431	$ 7110	$21,420
University of Wisconsin–Madison	pub.	$ 8987	$ 7690	57%	20%	$10,995	$ 5682	$22,872
University of Wisconsin–Milwaukee	pub.	$ 9075	$ 4310†	51%	23%	$ 7317	$ 6068	$25,312
University of Wisconsin–Parkside	pub.	$ 6623	$ 6828	72%	NR	NR	NR	NR
University of Wisconsin–River Falls	pub.	$ 6893	$ 5730	49%	NR	$ 2613	$10,010	$14,800
University of Wisconsin–Stevens Point	pub.	$ 6849	$ 5760	51%	68%	$ 6681	$ 5928	$22,370
University of Wisconsin–Stout	pub.	$ 8099	$ 5560	54%	40%	$ 9200	$ 4459	$25,855

NA = not applicable; NR = not reported; * = includes room and board; † = room only; — = not available.

College Costs At-a-Glance

	Institutional Control ind.=independent; pub.=public	Tuition and Fees	Room and Board	Percent of Eligible Freshmen Receiving Need-Based Gift Awards	Percent of Freshmen Whose Need Was Fully Met	Average Financial Aid Package for Freshmen	Average Net Cost After Aid	Average Indebtedness Upon Graduation
Wisconsin—*continued*								
University of Wisconsin–Superior	pub.	$7169	$5730	61%	22%	NR	NR	$23,466
Wyoming								
University of Wyoming	pub.	$3927	$8360	65%	23%	$8353	$3934	$20,571

NA = not applicable; NR = not reported; * = includes room and board; † = room only; — = not available.

Profiles of College Financial Aid Programs

ABILENE CHRISTIAN UNIVERSITY

Abilene, TX

Tuition & fees: $22,760 **Average undergraduate aid package: $15,102**

ABOUT THE INSTITUTION Independent religious, coed. 73 undergraduate majors. Federal methodology is used as a basis for awarding need-based institutional aid.

UNDERGRADUATE EXPENSES for 2010–11 ***Comprehensive fee:*** $30,644 includes full-time tuition ($21,510), mandatory fees ($1250), and room and board ($7884). ***College room only:*** $3460. Full-time tuition and fees vary according to course load. Room and board charges vary according to board plan and student level. ***Part-time tuition:*** $717 per semester hour. ***Part-time fees:*** $61.50 per semester hour; $10 per term. Part-time tuition and fees vary according to course load. ***Payment plans:*** Tuition prepayment, installment.

FRESHMAN FINANCIAL AID (Fall 2010, est.) 837 applied for aid; of those 81% were deemed to have need. 100% of freshmen with need received aid; of those 21% had need fully met. ***Average percent of need met:*** 68% (excluding resources awarded to replace EFC). ***Average financial aid package:*** $15,191 (excluding resources awarded to replace EFC). 14% of all full-time freshmen had no need and received non-need-based gift aid.

UNDERGRADUATE FINANCIAL AID (Fall 2010, est.) 2,824 applied for aid; of those 84% were deemed to have need. 100% of undergraduates with need received aid; of those 22% had need fully met. ***Average percent of need met:*** 66% (excluding resources awarded to replace EFC). ***Average financial aid package:*** $15,102 (excluding resources awarded to replace EFC). 11% of all full-time undergraduates had no need and received non-need-based gift aid.

GIFT AID (NEED-BASED) ***Total amount:*** $23,788,738 (18% federal, 15% state, 62% institutional, 5% external sources). ***Receiving aid:*** Freshmen: 69% (680); all full-time undergraduates: 64% (2,331). ***Average award:*** Freshmen: $11,948; Undergraduates: $11,289. ***Scholarships, grants, and awards:*** Federal Pell, FSEOG, state, private, college/university gift aid from institutional funds, United Negro College Fund.

GIFT AID (NON-NEED-BASED) ***Total amount:*** $7,843,212 (1% state, 94% institutional, 5% external sources). ***Receiving aid:*** Freshmen: 63% (617). Undergraduates: 58% (2,085). ***Average award:*** Freshmen: $8589. Undergraduates: $7272. ***Scholarships, grants, and awards by category:*** *Academic interests/achievement:* agriculture, biological sciences, business, communication, education, English, foreign languages, general academic interests/achievements, mathematics, physical sciences, religion/biblical studies, social sciences. *Creative arts/performance:* art/fine arts, debating, journalism/publications, music, theater/drama. *Special achievements/activities:* cheerleading/drum major, leadership. *Special characteristics:* children of faculty/staff, ethnic background, first-generation college students, local/state students, members of minority groups, out-of-state students, previous college experience, relatives of clergy, religious affiliation. ***Tuition waivers:*** Full or partial for employees or children of employees.

LOANS ***Student loans:*** $24,694,244 (31% need-based, 69% non-need-based). 70% of past graduating class borrowed through all loan programs. *Average indebtedness per student:* $38,634. ***Average need-based loan:*** Freshmen: $3426. Undergraduates: $4358. ***Parent loans:*** $4,821,919 (100% non-need-based). ***Programs:*** Perkins, state, college/university.

WORK-STUDY ***Federal work-study:*** Total amount: $597,468; 244 jobs averaging $1632. ***State or other work-study/employment:*** Total amount: $1,201,243 (9% need-based, 91% non-need-based). 14 part-time jobs averaging $5348.

ATHLETIC AWARDS Total amount: $3,519,659 (53% need-based, 47% non-need-based).

APPLYING FOR FINANCIAL AID ***Required financial aid forms:*** FAFSA, institution's own form. ***Financial aid deadline (priority):*** 3/1. ***Notification date:*** Continuous beginning 4/1. Students must reply within 3 weeks of notification.

CONTACT Ed Kerestly, Director of Student Financial Services, Abilene Christian University, ACU Box 29007, Abilene, TX 79699-9007, 325-674-2130. *E-mail:* thedepot@acu.edu.

ABRAHAM BALDWIN AGRICULTURAL COLLEGE

Tifton, GA

Tuition & fees (GA res): $3496 **Average undergraduate aid package: N/A**

ABOUT THE INSTITUTION State-supported, coed. 48 undergraduate majors. Federal methodology is used as a basis for awarding need-based institutional aid.

UNDERGRADUATE EXPENSES for 2010–11 ***Tuition, state resident:*** full-time $2694. ***Tuition, nonresident:*** full-time $10,176. ***Required fees:*** full-time $802. Part-time tuition and fees vary according to course load. ***College room and board:*** $7220; ***Room only:*** $4920. Room and board charges vary according to board plan and housing facility. ***Payment plan:*** Guaranteed tuition.

GIFT AID (NEED-BASED) ***Scholarships, grants, and awards:*** Federal Pell, FSEOG, state, private, college/university gift aid from institutional funds, HOPE Scholarships.

GIFT AID (NON-NEED-BASED) ***Tuition waivers:*** Full or partial for employees or children of employees, senior citizens.

LOANS ***Programs:*** Perkins, state.

WORK-STUDY Federal work-study jobs available.

APPLYING FOR FINANCIAL AID ***Required financial aid forms:*** FAFSA, institution's own form. ***Financial aid deadline:*** 7/15. ***Notification date:*** Continuous beginning 5/15.

CONTACT Traci K. Bryan, Interim Director of Financial Aid, Abraham Baldwin Agricultural College, 2802 Moore Highway, ABAC 23, Tifton, GA 31793-2601, 229-391-4910 or toll-free 800-733-3653. *Fax:* 229-391-4911. *E-mail:* finaid@abac.edu.

ACADEMY COLLEGE

Minneapolis, MN

CONTACT Financial Aid Office, Academy College, 1101 East 78th Street, Suite 100, Minneapolis, MN 55420, 952-851-0066 or toll-free 800-292-9149.

ACADEMY OF ART UNIVERSITY

San Francisco, CA

ABOUT THE INSTITUTION Proprietary, coed. 19 undergraduate majors.

GIFT AID (NEED-BASED) ***Scholarships, grants, and awards:*** Federal Pell, FSEOG, state, private.

LOANS ***Programs:*** Federal Direct (Subsidized and Unsubsidized Stafford, PLUS), alternative loans.

WORK-STUDY ***Federal work-study:*** Total amount: $285,310; 105 jobs averaging $2717.

APPLYING FOR FINANCIAL AID ***Required financial aid forms:*** FAFSA, institution's own form.

CONTACT Mr. Joe Vollaro, Executive Vice President of Financial Aid and Compliance, Academy of Art University, 79 New Montgomery Street, San Francisco, CA 94105-3410, 415-618-6528 or toll-free 800-544-ARTS. *Fax:* 415-618-6273. *E-mail:* jvollaro@academyart.edu.

ADAMS STATE COLLEGE

Alamosa, CO

Tuition & fees (CO res): $4971 **Average undergraduate aid package: $9453**

ABOUT THE INSTITUTION State-supported, coed. 78 undergraduate majors. Federal methodology is used as a basis for awarding need-based institutional aid.

UNDERGRADUATE EXPENSES for 2010–11 ***Tuition, state resident:*** full-time $2952; part-time $123 per credit hour. ***Tuition, nonresident:*** full-time $12,912; part-time $538 per credit hour. ***Required fees:*** full-time $2019; $84 per credit hour. Full-time tuition and fees vary according to course load. Part-time tuition and fees vary according to course load. ***College room and board:*** $7060; ***Room only:*** $3300. Room and board charges vary according to board plan and housing facility. ***Payment plans:*** Installment, deferred payment.

FRESHMAN FINANCIAL AID (Fall 2009) 512 applied for aid; of those 85% were deemed to have need. 99% of freshmen with need received aid; of those 1% had need fully met. ***Average percent of need met:*** 54% (excluding resources awarded to replace EFC). ***Average financial aid package:*** $9636 (excluding resources awarded to replace EFC). 5% of all full-time freshmen had no need and received non-need-based gift aid.

UNDERGRADUATE FINANCIAL AID (Fall 2009) 1,816 applied for aid; of those 87% were deemed to have need. 99% of undergraduates with need received aid; of those 1% had need fully met. ***Average percent of need met:*** 51% (excluding resources awarded to replace EFC). ***Average financial aid package:*** $9453 (excluding resources awarded to replace EFC). 4% of all full-time undergraduates had no need and received non-need-based gift aid.

GIFT AID (NEED-BASED) ***Total amount:*** $8,271,986 (77% federal, 20% state, 1% institutional, 2% external sources). ***Receiving aid:*** Freshmen: 75% (397); all full-time undergraduates: 75% (1,426). ***Average award:*** Freshmen: $5313; Undergraduates: $5313. ***Scholarships, grants, and awards:*** Federal Pell, FSEOG, state, private, college/university gift aid from institutional funds.

GIFT AID (NON-NEED-BASED) ***Total amount:*** $2,487,509 (1% federal, 74% institutional, 25% external sources). ***Receiving aid:*** Freshmen: 51% (271). Undergraduates: 40% (770). ***Average award:*** Freshmen: $2579. Undergraduates: $2323. ***Tuition waivers:*** Full or partial for employees or children of employees, senior citizens.

LOANS ***Student loans:*** $9,536,358 (49% need-based, 51% non-need-based). 72% of past graduating class borrowed through all loan programs. *Average indebtedness per student:* $22,915. ***Average need-based loan:*** Freshmen: $2981. Undergraduates: $3588. ***Parent loans:*** $549,769 (100% non-need-based). ***Programs:*** Federal Direct (Subsidized and Unsubsidized Stafford, PLUS), Perkins, alternative loans.

WORK-STUDY ***Federal work-study:*** Total amount: $340,503; 279 jobs averaging $1220. ***State or other work-study/employment:*** Total amount: $374,768 (63% need-based, 37% non-need-based). 333 part-time jobs averaging $1125.

ATHLETIC AWARDS Total amount: $1,119,832 (12% need-based, 88% non-need-based).

APPLYING FOR FINANCIAL AID ***Required financial aid form:*** FAFSA. ***Financial aid deadline:*** Continuous. ***Notification date:*** Continuous beginning 3/1.

CONTACT Phil Schroeder, Student Financial Aid Director, Adams State College, 208 Edgemont Boulevard, Alamosa, CO 81102, 719-587-7306 or toll-free 800-824-6494. *Fax:* 719-587-7366.

ADELPHI UNIVERSITY

Garden City, NY

Tuition & fees: $26,915 **Average undergraduate aid package: $18,475**

ABOUT THE INSTITUTION Independent, coed. 45 undergraduate majors. Federal methodology is used as a basis for awarding need-based institutional aid.

UNDERGRADUATE EXPENSES for 2010–11 ***Comprehensive fee:*** $37,915 includes full-time tuition ($25,465), mandatory fees ($1450), and room and board ($11,000). Full-time tuition and fees vary according to course level, location, and program. Room and board charges vary according to board plan and housing facility. ***Part-time tuition:*** $820 per credit hour. ***Part-time fees:*** $365 per term. Part-time tuition and fees vary according to course level, location, and program. ***Payment plans:*** Installment, deferred payment.

FRESHMAN FINANCIAL AID (Fall 2010, est.) 786 applied for aid; of those 85% were deemed to have need. 97% of freshmen with need received aid; of those 2% had need fully met. ***Average percent of need met:*** 42% (excluding resources awarded to replace EFC). ***Average financial aid package:*** $18,475 (excluding resources awarded to replace EFC). 17% of all full-time freshmen had no need and received non-need-based gift aid.

UNDERGRADUATE FINANCIAL AID (Fall 2010, est.) 3,536 applied for aid; of those 88% were deemed to have need. 92% of undergraduates with need received aid; of those 2% had need fully met. ***Average percent of need met:*** 37% (excluding resources awarded to replace EFC). ***Average financial aid package:*** $18,475 (excluding resources awarded to replace EFC). 18% of all full-time undergraduates had no need and received non-need-based gift aid.

GIFT AID (NEED-BASED) ***Total amount:*** $32,059,765 (19% federal, 15% state, 66% institutional). ***Receiving aid:*** Freshmen: 56% (506); all full-time undergraduates: 51% (2,190). ***Average award:*** Freshmen: $7632; Undergraduates: $6722. ***Scholarships, grants, and awards:*** Federal Pell, FSEOG, state, private, college/university gift aid from institutional funds, United Negro College Fund, endowed-donor scholarships.

GIFT AID (NON-NEED-BASED) ***Total amount:*** $9,792,755 (93% institutional, 7% external sources). ***Receiving aid:*** Freshmen: 45% (405). Undergraduates: 45% (1,955). ***Average award:*** Freshmen: $11,549. Undergraduates: $10,351. ***Scholarships, grants, and awards by category:*** *Academic interests/achievement:* 2,607 awards ($23,331,884 total): communication, foreign languages, general academic interests/achievements. *Creative arts/performance:* 127 awards ($905,438 total): art/fine arts, dance, music, performing arts, theater/drama. *Special achievements/activities:* 871 awards ($722,406 total): community service, general special achievements/activities, memberships. *Special characteristics:* 374 awards ($2,728,150 total): children and siblings of alumni, children of faculty/staff. ***Tuition waivers:*** Full or partial for employees or children of employees.

LOANS ***Student loans:*** $30,095,051 (56% need-based, 44% non-need-based). 67% of past graduating class borrowed through all loan programs. *Average indebtedness per student:* $31,096. ***Average need-based loan:*** Freshmen: $4805. Undergraduates: $4679. ***Parent loans:*** $8,064,374 (84% need-based, 16% non-need-based). ***Programs:*** Federal Direct (Subsidized and Unsubsidized Stafford, PLUS), Perkins, Federal Nursing, New York HELP Program, private loans.

WORK-STUDY ***Federal work-study:*** Total amount: $2,560,766; jobs available. ***State or other work-study/employment:*** Total amount: $1,648,938 (100% non-need-based). Part-time jobs available.

ATHLETIC AWARDS Total amount: $3,139,474 (57% need-based, 43% non-need-based).

APPLYING FOR FINANCIAL AID ***Required financial aid forms:*** FAFSA, state aid form. ***Financial aid deadline (priority):*** 3/1. ***Notification date:*** Continuous beginning 3/1.

CONTACT Ms. Sheryl Mihopulos, Director of Student Financial Services, Adelphi University, 1 South Avenue, PO Box 701, Garden City, NY 11530, 516-877-3365 or toll-free 800-ADELPHI. *Fax:* 516-877-3380. *E-mail:* mihopulos@adelphi.edu.

ADRIAN COLLEGE

Adrian, MI

Tuition & fees: $25,900 **Average undergraduate aid package: $22,648**

ABOUT THE INSTITUTION Independent religious, coed. ***Awards:*** associate and bachelor's degrees. 46 undergraduate majors. ***Total enrollment:*** 1,469. Undergraduates: 1,469. Freshmen: 500. Both federal and institutional methodology are used as a basis for awarding need-based institutional aid.

UNDERGRADUATE EXPENSES for 2010–11 ***Comprehensive fee:*** $33,800 includes full-time tuition ($25,560), mandatory fees ($340), and room and board ($7900). ***College room only:*** $3820. Room and board charges vary according to board plan and housing facility. ***Payment plan:*** Installment.

FRESHMAN FINANCIAL AID (Fall 2010, est.) 450 applied for aid; of those 93% were deemed to have need. 100% of freshmen with need received aid; of those 8% had need fully met. ***Average percent of need met:*** 82% (excluding resources awarded to replace EFC). ***Average financial aid package:*** $23,488 (excluding resources awarded to replace EFC). 18% of all full-time freshmen had no need and received non-need-based gift aid.

UNDERGRADUATE FINANCIAL AID (Fall 2010, est.) 1,448 applied for aid; of those 95% were deemed to have need. 100% of undergraduates with need received aid; of those 8% had need fully met. ***Average percent of need met:*** 80% (excluding resources awarded to replace EFC). ***Average financial aid package:*** $22,648 (excluding resources awarded to replace EFC). 16% of all full-time undergraduates had no need and received non-need-based gift aid.

GIFT AID (NEED-BASED) ***Total amount:*** $24,069,232 (13% federal, 6% state, 80% institutional, 1% external sources). ***Receiving aid:*** Freshmen: 80% (417); all full-time undergraduates: 82% (1,369). ***Average award:*** Freshmen: $19,305; Undergraduates: $17,550. ***Scholarships, grants, and awards:*** Federal Pell, FSEOG, state, private, college/university gift aid from institutional funds.

GIFT AID (NON-NEED-BASED) ***Total amount:*** $3,618,631 (93% institutional, 7% external sources). ***Receiving aid:*** Freshmen: 5% (27). Undergraduates: 6% (92). ***Average award:*** Freshmen: $11,075. Undergraduates: $10,648. ***Scholarships, grants, and awards by category:*** *Academic interests/achievement:* 1,004 awards ($8,554,453 total): business, general academic interests/achievements. *Creative arts/performance:* 998 awards ($1,588,147 total): art/fine arts, music, theater/drama. *Special achievements/activities:* 70 awards ($94,122 total): religious involvement. *Special characteristics:* 189 awards ($1,337,142 total): children and siblings of alumni, children of faculty/staff, children of union members/company employees, ethnic background, general special characteristics, international students, religious affiliation. ***Tuition waivers:*** Full or partial for children of alumni, employees or children of employees.

LOANS ***Student loans:*** $12,062,645 (77% need-based, 23% non-need-based). 81% of past graduating class borrowed through all loan programs. *Average indebtedness per student:* $17,160. ***Average need-based loan:*** Freshmen: $3298. Undergraduates: $4288. ***Parent loans:*** $2,783,126 (37% need-based, 63% non-need-based). ***Programs:*** Federal Direct (Subsidized and Unsubsidized Stafford, PLUS), Perkins.

WORK-STUDY ***Federal work-study:*** Total amount: $1,594,522; 1,158 jobs averaging $1800. ***State or other work-study/employment:*** Total amount: $121,262 (100% non-need-based). 76 part-time jobs averaging $1800.

APPLYING FOR FINANCIAL AID ***Required financial aid form:*** FAFSA. ***Financial aid deadline (priority):*** 3/1. ***Notification date:*** Continuous beginning 3/15. Students must reply by 5/1 or within 2 weeks of notification.

CONTACT Mr. Andrew Spohn, Director of Financial Aid, Adrian College, 110 South Madison Street, Adrian, MI 49221-2575, 517-265-5161 Ext. 4306 or toll-free 800-877-2246. *Fax:* 517-264-3394. *E-mail:* aspohn@adrian.edu.

AGNES SCOTT COLLEGE

Decatur, GA

Tuition & fees: $31,283 **Average undergraduate aid package: $31,243**

ABOUT THE INSTITUTION Independent religious, undergraduate: women only; graduate: coed. 34 undergraduate majors. Both federal and institutional methodology are used as a basis for awarding need-based institutional aid.

UNDERGRADUATE EXPENSES for 2010–11 ***Comprehensive fee:*** $41,133 includes full-time tuition ($31,068), mandatory fees ($215), and room and board ($9850). ***College room only:*** $4925. Full-time tuition and fees vary according to course load. Room and board charges vary according to board plan and housing facility. ***Part-time tuition:*** $1294 per hour. Part-time tuition and fees vary according to course load. ***Payment plan:*** Installment.

FRESHMAN FINANCIAL AID (Fall 2010, est.) 220 applied for aid; of those 90% were deemed to have need. 100% of freshmen with need received aid; of those 35% had need fully met. ***Average percent of need met:*** 93% (excluding resources awarded to replace EFC). ***Average financial aid package:*** $31,320 (excluding resources awarded to replace EFC). 25% of all full-time freshmen had no need and received non-need-based gift aid.

UNDERGRADUATE FINANCIAL AID (Fall 2010, est.) 660 applied for aid; of those 91% were deemed to have need. 100% of undergraduates with need received aid; of those 35% had need fully met. ***Average percent of need met:*** 92% (excluding resources awarded to replace EFC). ***Average financial aid package:*** $31,243 (excluding resources awarded to replace EFC). 27% of all full-time undergraduates had no need and received non-need-based gift aid.

GIFT AID (NEED-BASED) ***Total amount:*** $14,523,703 (14% federal, 7% state, 78% institutional, 1% external sources). ***Receiving aid:*** Freshmen: 75% (198); all full-time undergraduates: 73% (598). ***Average award:*** Freshmen: $25,131; Undergraduates: $24,148. ***Scholarships, grants, and awards:*** Federal Pell, FSEOG, state, private, college/university gift aid from institutional funds.

GIFT AID (NON-NEED-BASED) ***Total amount:*** $4,752,305 (10% state, 88% institutional, 2% external sources). ***Receiving aid:*** Freshmen: 25% (66). Undergraduates: 20% (161). ***Average award:*** Freshmen: $19,727. Undergraduates: $17,628. ***Scholarships, grants, and awards by category:*** *Academic interests/achievement:* general academic interests/achievements. *Creative arts/performance:* music. *Special achievements/activities:* community service, leadership. *Special characteristics:* adult students, children of educators, children of faculty/staff, international students, local/state students, religious affiliation, veterans, veterans' children. ***Tuition waivers:*** Full or partial for employees or children of employees.

LOANS ***Student loans:*** $4,597,228 (49% need-based, 51% non-need-based). 69% of past graduating class borrowed through all loan programs. *Average indebtedness per student:* $26,493. ***Average need-based loan:*** Freshmen: $2797. Undergraduates: $3763. ***Parent loans:*** $1,214,428 (24% need-based, 76% non-need-based). ***Programs:*** Federal Direct (Subsidized and Unsubsidized Stafford, PLUS).

WORK-STUDY ***Federal work-study:*** Total amount: $1,136,130; 498 jobs averaging $2300. ***State or other work-study/employment:*** Total amount: $260,071 (2% need-based, 98% non-need-based). 116 part-time jobs averaging $2300.

APPLYING FOR FINANCIAL AID ***Required financial aid forms:*** FAFSA, copy of previous year's tax returns. ***Financial aid deadline:*** 5/1 (priority: 2/15). ***Notification date:*** Continuous beginning 3/1. Students must reply within 2 weeks of notification.

CONTACT Patrick Bonones, Director of Financial Aid, Agnes Scott College, 141 East College Avenue, Decatur, GA 30030-3797, 404-471-6395 or toll-free 800-868-8602. *Fax:* 404-471-6159. *E-mail:* finaid@agnesscott.edu.

AIB COLLEGE OF BUSINESS

Des Moines, IA

CONTACT Financial Aid Office, AIB College of Business, 2500 Fleur Drive, Des Moines, IA 50321-1799, 515-244-4221 or toll-free 800-444-1921.

AIBT INTERNATIONAL INSTITUTE OF THE AMERICAS

Phoenix, AZ

See Brookline College.

ALABAMA AGRICULTURAL AND MECHANICAL UNIVERSITY

Huntsville, AL

Tuition & fees (AL res): $5800 **Average undergraduate aid package: $10,342**

ABOUT THE INSTITUTION State-supported, coed. 36 undergraduate majors. Federal methodology is used as a basis for awarding need-based institutional aid.

UNDERGRADUATE EXPENSES for 2011–12 ***Tuition, state resident:*** full-time $4872; part-time $203 per credit. ***Tuition, nonresident:*** full-time $9744; part-time $406 per credit. ***Required fees:*** full-time $928. Full-time tuition and fees vary according to course load. Part-time tuition and fees vary according to course load. ***College room and board:*** $6200; ***Room only:*** $3090. Room and board charges vary according to board plan, housing facility, and location. ***Payment plan:*** Installment.

FRESHMAN FINANCIAL AID (Fall 2010, est.) 1,005 applied for aid; of those 85% were deemed to have need. 99% of freshmen with need received aid; of those 12% had need fully met. ***Average percent of need met:*** 13% (excluding resources awarded to replace EFC). ***Average financial aid package:*** $9896 (excluding resources awarded to replace EFC). 6% of all full-time freshmen had no need and received non-need-based gift aid.

UNDERGRADUATE FINANCIAL AID (Fall 2010, est.) 3,784 applied for aid; of those 87% were deemed to have need. 98% of undergraduates with need received aid; of those 12% had need fully met. ***Average percent of need met:*** 12% (excluding resources awarded to replace EFC). ***Average financial aid package:*** $10,342 (excluding resources awarded to replace EFC). 6% of all full-time undergraduates had no need and received non-need-based gift aid.

GIFT AID (NEED-BASED) ***Total amount:*** $20,235,416 (76% federal, 1% state, 20% institutional, 3% external sources). ***Receiving aid:*** Freshmen: 70% (728); all full-time undergraduates: 66% (2,734). ***Average award:*** Freshmen: $7400; Undergraduates: $7405. ***Scholarships, grants, and awards:*** Federal Pell, FSEOG, state, private, college/university gift aid from institutional funds.

GIFT AID (NON-NEED-BASED) ***Total amount:*** $3,470,913 (1% state, 90% institutional, 9% external sources). ***Receiving aid:*** Freshmen: 5% (50). Undergraduates: 4% (157). ***Average award:*** Freshmen: $9086. Undergraduates: $8605. ***Scholarships, grants, and awards by category:*** *Academic interests/achievement:* general academic interests/achievements. *Creative arts/performance:* art/fine arts, music. *Special characteristics:* parents of current students. ***Tuition waivers:*** Full or partial for employees or children of employees.

LOANS ***Student loans:*** $27,973,759 (86% need-based, 14% non-need-based). 78% of past graduating class borrowed through all loan programs. *Average indebtedness per student:* $31,863. ***Average need-based loan:*** Freshmen: $3452. ***Parent loans:*** $5,222,271 (58% need-based, 42% non-need-based). ***Programs:*** Perkins.

WORK-STUDY ***Federal work-study:*** Total amount: $380,297; jobs available.

ATHLETIC AWARDS Total amount: $1,975,632 (57% need-based, 43% non-need-based).

APPLYING FOR FINANCIAL AID ***Required financial aid form:*** FAFSA. ***Financial aid deadline (priority):*** 3/1. ***Notification date:*** Continuous beginning 4/15. Students must reply within 2 weeks of notification.

CONTACT Ms. Deborah Gordon, Financial Aid Officer, Alabama Agricultural and Mechanical University, 4900 Meridian Street, Normal, AL 35762, 256-372-5853 or toll-free 800-553-0816. *Fax:* 256-372-8162. *E-mail:* deborah.gordon@aamu.edu.

ALABAMA STATE UNIVERSITY

Montgomery, AL

Tuition & fees (AL res): $7164 **Average undergraduate aid package: $17,220**

ABOUT THE INSTITUTION State-supported, coed. 31 undergraduate majors. Federal methodology is used as a basis for awarding need-based institutional aid.

UNDERGRADUATE EXPENSES for 2010–11 ***One-time required fee:*** $150. ***Tuition, state resident:*** full-time $6312; part-time $263 per credit hour. ***Tuition, nonresident:*** full-time $12,624; part-time $526 per credit hour. ***Required fees:*** full-time $852; $213 per term. ***College room and board:*** $4800; ***Room only:*** $2460. Room and board charges vary according to board plan and housing facility. ***Payment plan:*** Deferred payment.

FRESHMAN FINANCIAL AID (Fall 2010, est.) 905 applied for aid; of those 100% were deemed to have need. 98% of freshmen with need received aid; of those 59% had need fully met. ***Average percent of need met:*** 83% (excluding resources awarded to replace EFC). ***Average financial aid package:*** $15,174 (excluding resources awarded to replace EFC). 1% of all full-time freshmen had no need and received non-need-based gift aid.

UNDERGRADUATE FINANCIAL AID (Fall 2010, est.) 4,404 applied for aid; of those 97% were deemed to have need. 100% of undergraduates with need received aid; of those 62% had need fully met. ***Average percent of need met:*** 87% (excluding resources awarded to replace EFC). ***Average financial aid package:*** $17,220 (excluding resources awarded to replace EFC). 1% of all full-time undergraduates had no need and received non-need-based gift aid.

GIFT AID (NEED-BASED) ***Total amount:*** $25,405,184 (77% federal, 1% state, 22% institutional). ***Receiving aid:*** Freshmen: 72% (787); all full-time undergraduates: 80% (3,590). ***Average award:*** Freshmen: $5476; Undergraduates: $5141. ***Scholarships, grants, and awards:*** Federal Pell, FSEOG, state, private, college/university gift aid from institutional funds, United Negro College Fund.

GIFT AID (NON-NEED-BASED) ***Total amount:*** $4,299,236 (7% federal, 54% state, 28% institutional, 11% external sources). ***Receiving aid:*** Freshmen: 21% (236). Undergraduates: 27% (1,222). ***Average award:*** Freshmen: $8918. Undergraduates: $8832. ***Scholarships, grants, and awards by category:*** *Academic interests/achievement:* general academic interests/achievements. *Creative arts/performance:* general creative arts/performance, music, theater/drama. *Special achievements/activities:* leadership. *Special characteristics:* general special characteristics, members of minority groups. ***Tuition waivers:*** Full or partial for employees or children of employees.

LOANS ***Student loans:*** $31,474,374 (47% need-based, 53% non-need-based). 79% of past graduating class borrowed through all loan programs. *Average indebtedness per student:* $29,795. ***Average need-based loan:*** Freshmen: $3351. Undergraduates: $3748. ***Parent loans:*** $7,927,649 (75% need-based, 25% non-need-based). ***Programs:*** Federal Direct (Subsidized and Unsubsidized Stafford, PLUS), Perkins.

WORK-STUDY ***Federal work-study:*** Total amount: $1,505,000; jobs available. ***State or other work-study/employment:*** Total amount: $522,827 (100% non-need-based). Part-time jobs available.

ATHLETIC AWARDS Total amount: $2,970,048 (81% need-based, 19% non-need-based).

APPLYING FOR FINANCIAL AID ***Required financial aid form:*** FAFSA. ***Financial aid deadline (priority):*** 4/1. ***Notification date:*** Continuous beginning 5/1.

CONTACT Mrs. Dorenda A. Adams, Director of Financial Aid, Alabama State University, PO Box 271, Montgomery, AL 36101-0271, 334-229-4323 or toll-free 800-253-5037. *Fax:* 334-299-4924. *E-mail:* dadams@alasu.edu.

ALASKA BIBLE COLLEGE

Glennallen, AK

ABOUT THE INSTITUTION Independent nondenominational, coed. 1 undergraduate major.

GIFT AID (NEED-BASED) ***Scholarships, grants, and awards:*** private, college/university gift aid from institutional funds.

GIFT AID (NON-NEED-BASED) ***Scholarships, grants, and awards by category:*** *Academic interests/achievement:* general academic interests/achievements, religion/biblical studies. *Creative arts/performance:* music. *Special achievements/activities:* religious involvement. *Special characteristics:* children of faculty/staff, local/state students, married students, religious affiliation, spouses of current students.

LOANS ***Programs:*** state.

WORK-STUDY ***State or other work-study/employment:*** Total amount: $17,128 (100% need-based). 20 part-time jobs averaging $842.

APPLYING FOR FINANCIAL AID ***Required financial aid form:*** institution's own form.

CONTACT Jared Palmer, Financial Aid Officer, Alaska Bible College, PO Box 289, Glennallen, AK 99588-0289, 907-822-3201 Ext. 225 or toll-free 800-478-7884. *Fax:* 907-822-5027. *E-mail:* jpalmer@akbible.edu.

ALASKA PACIFIC UNIVERSITY

Anchorage, AK

Tuition & fees: $26,360 **Average undergraduate aid package: $17,990**

ABOUT THE INSTITUTION Independent, coed. 16 undergraduate majors. Federal methodology is used as a basis for awarding need-based institutional aid.

UNDERGRADUATE EXPENSES for 2010–11 ***Comprehensive fee:*** $35,660 includes full-time tuition ($26,250), mandatory fees ($110), and room and board ($9300). ***College room only:*** $4400. Full-time tuition and fees vary according to class time, course load, degree level, location, program, and reciprocity agreements. Room and board charges vary according to board plan and housing facility. ***Part-time tuition:*** $1100 per semester hour. ***Part-time fees:*** $55 per term. Part-time tuition and fees vary according to class time, course load, degree level, location, and program. ***Payment plans:*** Guaranteed tuition, installment, deferred payment.

FRESHMAN FINANCIAL AID (Fall 2010, est.) 42 applied for aid; of those 83% were deemed to have need. 100% of freshmen with need received aid; of those 17% had need fully met. ***Average percent of need met:*** 89% (excluding resources awarded to replace EFC). ***Average financial aid package:*** $23,105 (excluding resources awarded to replace EFC). 13% of all full-time freshmen had no need and received non-need-based gift aid.

UNDERGRADUATE FINANCIAL AID (Fall 2010, est.) 301 applied for aid; of those 81% were deemed to have need. 92% of undergraduates with need received aid; of those 9% had need fully met. ***Average percent of need met:*** 92% (excluding resources awarded to replace EFC). ***Average financial aid package:*** $17,990 (excluding resources awarded to replace EFC). 5% of all full-time undergraduates had no need and received non-need-based gift aid.

GIFT AID (NEED-BASED) ***Total amount:*** $1,095,236 (60% federal, 2% state, 17% institutional, 21% external sources). ***Receiving aid:*** Freshmen: 62% (28); all full-time undergraduates: 27% (108). ***Average award:*** Freshmen: $14,578; Undergraduates: $8400. ***Scholarships, grants, and awards:*** Federal Pell, FSEOG, state, private, college/university gift aid from institutional funds, Bureau of Indian Affairs Grants, Yellow Ribbon Program.

GIFT AID (NON-NEED-BASED) ***Total amount:*** $3,341,781 (95% institutional, 5% external sources). ***Receiving aid:*** Freshmen: 76% (34). Undergraduates: 46% (184). ***Average award:*** Freshmen: $21,012. Undergraduates: $19,600. ***Scholarships, grants, and awards by category:*** *Academic interests/achievement:* biological sciences, business, education, general academic interests/achievements, humanities, physical sciences, social sciences. *Creative arts/performance:* art/fine arts, music, theater/drama. *Special achievements/activities:* community service, general special achievements/activities, leadership, religious involvement. *Special characteristics:* children and siblings of alumni, children of faculty/staff, ethnic background, general special characteristics, international students, local/state students, members of minority groups, out-of-state students, religious affiliation. ***Tuition waivers:*** Full or partial for employees or children of employees, adult students.

LOANS ***Student loans:*** $4,834,213 (42% need-based, 58% non-need-based). 55% of past graduating class borrowed through all loan programs. *Average indebtedness per student:* $31,000. ***Average need-based loan:*** Freshmen: $3339. Undergraduates: $4590. ***Parent loans:*** $639,200 (100% non-need-based). ***Programs:*** Federal Direct (Subsidized and Unsubsidized Stafford, PLUS), state, alternative loans.

WORK-STUDY ***Federal work-study:*** Total amount: $47,660; jobs available. ***State or other work-study/employment:*** Total amount: $152,223 (100% non-need-based). Part-time jobs available.

APPLYING FOR FINANCIAL AID ***Required financial aid form:*** FAFSA. ***Financial aid deadline (priority):*** 4/15. ***Notification date:*** Continuous beginning 2/1. Students must reply by 2/1 or within 4 weeks of notification.

CONTACT Jo Holland, Director of Student Financial Services, Alaska Pacific University, 4101 University Drive, Anchorage, AK 99508-4672, 907-564-8342 or toll-free 800-252-7528. *Fax:* 907-564-8372. *E-mail:* sfs@alaskapacific.edu.

ALBANY COLLEGE OF PHARMACY AND HEALTH SCIENCES

Albany, NY

CONTACT Tiffany M. Gutierrez, Director of Financial Aid, Albany College of Pharmacy and Health Sciences, 106 New Scotland Avenue, Albany, NY 12208-3425, 518-445-7256 or toll-free 888-203-8010. *Fax:* 518-445-7322. *E-mail:* gutierrt@mail.acp.edu.

ALBANY STATE UNIVERSITY

Albany, GA

CONTACT Ms. Kathleen J. Caldwell, Director of Financial Aid, Albany State University, 504 College Drive, Albany, GA 31705-2717, 912-430-4650 or toll-free 800-822-RAMS (in-state). *Fax:* 912-430-3936. *E-mail:* finaid@asurams.edu.

ALBERTUS MAGNUS COLLEGE

New Haven, CT

CONTACT Andrew Foster, Director of Financial Aid, Albertus Magnus College, 700 Prospect Street, New Haven, CT 06511-1189, 203-773-8508 or toll-free 800-578-9160. *Fax:* 203-773-8972. *E-mail:* financial_aid@albertus.edu.

ALBION COLLEGE

Albion, MI

Tuition & fees: N/R **Average undergraduate aid package: $24,898**

ABOUT THE INSTITUTION Independent Methodist, coed. 37 undergraduate majors. Federal methodology is used as a basis for awarding need-based institutional aid.

FRESHMAN FINANCIAL AID (Fall 2010, est.) 339 applied for aid; of those 83% were deemed to have need. 100% of freshmen with need received aid; of those 28% had need fully met. ***Average percent of need met:*** 86% (excluding resources awarded to replace EFC). ***Average financial aid package:*** $25,276 (excluding resources awarded to replace EFC). 25% of all full-time freshmen had no need and received non-need-based gift aid.

UNDERGRADUATE FINANCIAL AID (Fall 2010, est.) 1,206 applied for aid; of those 89% were deemed to have need. 100% of undergraduates with need received aid; of those 24% had need fully met. ***Average percent of need met:*** 84% (excluding resources awarded to replace EFC). ***Average financial aid package:*** $24,898 (excluding resources awarded to replace EFC). 31% of all full-time undergraduates had no need and received non-need-based gift aid.

GIFT AID (NEED-BASED) ***Total amount:*** $21,564,821 (10% federal, 6% state, 83% institutional, 1% external sources). ***Receiving aid:*** Freshmen: 74% (283); all full-time undergraduates: 68% (1,075). ***Average award:*** Freshmen: $21,084; Undergraduates: $19,847. ***Scholarships, grants, and awards:*** Federal Pell, FSEOG, state, private, college/university gift aid from institutional funds.

GIFT AID (NON-NEED-BASED) ***Total amount:*** $6,852,156 (99% institutional, 1% external sources). ***Receiving aid:*** Freshmen: 70% (269). Undergraduates: 63% (995). ***Average award:*** Freshmen: $15,963. Undergraduates: $14,004. ***Scholarships, grants, and awards by category:*** *Academic interests/achievement:* 1,021 awards ($13,582,464 total): business, communication, general academic interests/achievements, mathematics. *Creative arts/performance:* 108 awards ($103,750 total): art/fine arts, dance, music, performing arts, theater/drama. *Special characteristics:* 156 awards ($237,450 total): children and siblings of alumni, relatives of clergy.

LOANS ***Student loans:*** $10,363,413 (44% need-based, 56% non-need-based). 50% of past graduating class borrowed through all loan programs. *Average indebtedness per student:* $34,282. ***Average need-based loan:*** Freshmen: $4121. Undergraduates: $5202. ***Parent loans:*** $2,581,938 (100% non-need-based). ***Programs:*** Federal Direct (Subsidized and Unsubsidized Stafford, PLUS), Perkins.

WORK-STUDY ***Federal work-study:*** Total amount: $610,947; 492 jobs averaging $1242.

APPLYING FOR FINANCIAL AID ***Required financial aid form:*** FAFSA. ***Financial aid deadline (priority):*** 3/1. ***Notification date:*** Continuous beginning 3/15.

CONTACT Ms. Ann Whitmer, Director of Financial Aid, Albion College, Kellogg Center Box 4670, Albion, MI 49224-1831, 517-629-0440 or toll-free 800-858-6770. *Fax:* 517-629-0581. *E-mail:* awhitmer@albion.edu.

ALBRIGHT COLLEGE

Reading, PA

Tuition & fees: $32,740 **Average undergraduate aid package: N/A**

ABOUT THE INSTITUTION Independent religious, coed. 44 undergraduate majors. Federal methodology is used as a basis for awarding need-based institutional aid.

UNDERGRADUATE EXPENSES for 2010–11 ***Comprehensive fee:*** $41,598 includes full-time tuition ($31,940), mandatory fees ($800), and room and board ($8858). ***College room only:*** $4919. Full-time tuition and fees vary according to course load. Room and board charges vary according to board plan and housing facility. ***Part-time tuition:*** $3993 per course. Part-time tuition and fees vary according to course load. ***Payment plan:*** Installment.

GIFT AID (NEED-BASED) ***Scholarships, grants, and awards:*** Federal Pell, FSEOG, state, private, college/university gift aid from institutional funds, Academic Competitiveness Grants, National SMART Grants.

GIFT AID (NON-NEED-BASED) ***Scholarships, grants, and awards by category:*** *Creative arts/performance:* art/fine arts, journalism/publications, music, theater/drama. *Special achievements/activities:* general special achievements/activities, leadership, memberships, religious involvement. *Special characteristics:* children and siblings of alumni, ethnic background, siblings of current students. ***Tuition waivers:*** Full or partial for children of alumni, employees or children of employees, adult students, senior citizens.

LOANS ***Programs:*** Federal Direct (Subsidized and Unsubsidized Stafford, PLUS), Perkins, private loans.

APPLYING FOR FINANCIAL AID ***Required financial aid form:*** FAFSA. ***Financial aid deadline:*** Continuous. ***Notification date:*** Continuous beginning 2/15. Students must reply by 5/1 or within 2 weeks of notification.

CONTACT Mary Ellen Duffy, Director of Financial Aid, Albright College, PO Box 15234, Reading, PA 19612-5234, 610-921-7515 or toll-free 800-252-1856. *Fax:* 610-921-7729. *E-mail:* mduffy@alb.edu.

ALCORN STATE UNIVERSITY

Alcorn State, MS

Tuition & fees (MS res): $4858 **Average undergraduate aid package: $9873**

ABOUT THE INSTITUTION State-supported, coed. 25 undergraduate majors. Both federal and institutional methodology are used as a basis for awarding need-based institutional aid.

UNDERGRADUATE EXPENSES for 2010–11 ***Tuition, state resident:*** full-time $4858; part-time $202 per credit hour. ***Tuition, nonresident:*** full-time $11,950; part-time $498 per credit hour. Full-time tuition and fees vary according to course load. Part-time tuition and fees vary according to course load. ***College room and board:*** $7348. ***Payment plan:*** Deferred payment.

FRESHMAN FINANCIAL AID (Fall 2010, est.) 522 applied for aid; of those 97% were deemed to have need. 100% of freshmen with need received aid; of those 7% had need fully met. ***Average percent of need met:*** 57% (excluding resources awarded to replace EFC). ***Average financial aid package:*** $10,304 (excluding resources awarded to replace EFC). 31% of all full-time freshmen had no need and received non-need-based gift aid.

UNDERGRADUATE FINANCIAL AID (Fall 2010, est.) 1,324 applied for aid; of those 97% were deemed to have need. 100% of undergraduates with need received aid; of those 9% had need fully met. ***Average percent of need met:*** 40% (excluding resources awarded to replace EFC). ***Average financial aid package:*** $9873 (excluding resources awarded to replace EFC). 19% of all full-time undergraduates had no need and received non-need-based gift aid.

GIFT AID (NEED-BASED) ***Total amount:*** $16,346,084 (77% federal, 1% state, 22% institutional). ***Receiving aid:*** Freshmen: 79% (466); all full-time undergraduates: 43% (1,179). ***Average award:*** Freshmen: $5570; Undergraduates: $5356. ***Scholarships, grants, and awards:*** Federal Pell, FSEOG, state, private, college/university gift aid from institutional funds.

GIFT AID (NON-NEED-BASED) ***Receiving aid:*** Freshmen: 30% (175). Undergraduates: 11% (310). ***Average award:*** Freshmen: $5627. Undergraduates: $5493. ***Scholarships, grants, and awards by category:*** *Academic interests/achievement:*

general academic interests/achievements. *Creative arts/performance:* music. *Special characteristics:* children of faculty/staff, local/state students, members of minority groups. ***Tuition waivers:*** Full or partial for employees or children of employees.

LOANS ***Student loans:*** $25,277,512 (48% need-based, 52% non-need-based). *Average indebtedness per student:* $19,838. ***Average need-based loan:*** Freshmen: $3329. Undergraduates: $3773. ***Parent loans:*** $1,099,208 (100% non-need-based). ***Programs:*** Federal Direct (Subsidized and Unsubsidized Stafford, PLUS).

WORK-STUDY ***Federal work-study:*** Total amount: $271,296; 213 jobs averaging $964.

ATHLETIC AWARDS Total amount: $1,673,382 (100% non-need-based).

APPLYING FOR FINANCIAL AID ***Required financial aid forms:*** FAFSA, institution's own form. ***Financial aid deadline (priority):*** 3/15. ***Notification date:*** Continuous beginning 4/1. Students must reply within 4 weeks of notification.

CONTACT Mrs. Juanita M. Russell, Director of Financial Aid, Alcorn State University, 1000 ASU Drive #28, Alcorn State, MS 39096-7500, 601-877-6190 or toll-free 800-222-6790. *Fax:* 601-877-6110. *E-mail:* juanita@alcorn.edu.

ALDERSON-BROADDUS COLLEGE

Philippi, WV

Tuition & fees: $22,204 **Average undergraduate aid package: $21,596**

ABOUT THE INSTITUTION Independent religious, coed. 41 undergraduate majors. Federal methodology is used as a basis for awarding need-based institutional aid.

UNDERGRADUATE EXPENSES for 2010–11 ***Comprehensive fee:*** $29,426 includes full-time tuition ($21,994), mandatory fees ($210), and room and board ($7222). ***College room only:*** $3556. Full-time tuition and fees vary according to program and student level. Room and board charges vary according to housing facility. ***Part-time tuition:*** $733 per credit hour. ***Part-time fees:*** $52.50 per term. Part-time tuition and fees vary according to program and student level. ***Payment plan:*** Installment.

FRESHMAN FINANCIAL AID (Fall 2010, est.) 130 applied for aid; of those 95% were deemed to have need. 100% of freshmen with need received aid; of those 35% had need fully met. ***Average percent of need met:*** 87% (excluding resources awarded to replace EFC). ***Average financial aid package:*** $22,926 (excluding resources awarded to replace EFC). 5% of all full-time freshmen had no need and received non-need-based gift aid.

UNDERGRADUATE FINANCIAL AID (Fall 2010, est.) 520 applied for aid; of those 95% were deemed to have need. 100% of undergraduates with need received aid; of those 26% had need fully met. ***Average percent of need met:*** 81% (excluding resources awarded to replace EFC). ***Average financial aid package:*** $21,596 (excluding resources awarded to replace EFC). 6% of all full-time undergraduates had no need and received non-need-based gift aid.

GIFT AID (NEED-BASED) ***Total amount:*** $6,983,021 (20% federal, 14% state, 62% institutional, 4% external sources). ***Receiving aid:*** Freshmen: 94% (124); all full-time undergraduates: 93% (489). ***Average award:*** Freshmen: $19,068; Undergraduates: $17,655. ***Scholarships, grants, and awards:*** Federal Pell, FSEOG, state, private, college/university gift aid from institutional funds, Federal Nursing, Scholarships for Disadvantaged Students (SDS), National Health Service Corps Scholarships.

GIFT AID (NON-NEED-BASED) ***Total amount:*** $482,220 (9% state, 91% institutional). ***Receiving aid:*** Freshmen: 21% (28). Undergraduates: 13% (68). ***Average award:*** Freshmen: $13,001. Undergraduates: $8942. ***Scholarships, grants, and awards by category:*** *Academic interests/achievement:* 455 awards ($3,447,557 total): biological sciences, business, communication, computer science, education, general academic interests/achievements, health fields, humanities, mathematics, physical sciences, premedicine, religion/biblical studies, social sciences. *Creative arts/performance:* 62 awards ($705,957 total): art/fine arts, creative writing, debating, journalism/publications, music, performing arts, theater/drama. *Special achievements/activities:* general special achievements/activities, leadership. *Special characteristics:* 16 awards ($234,518 total): children of faculty/staff, ethnic background, general special characteristics, international students, religious affiliation. ***Tuition waivers:*** Full or partial for employees or children of employees.

LOANS ***Student loans:*** $4,787,159 (89% need-based, 11% non-need-based). 88% of past graduating class borrowed through all loan programs. *Average indebtedness per student:* $31,751. ***Average need-based loan:*** Freshmen: $4296. Undergraduates: $4838. ***Parent loans:*** $532,529 (91% need-based, 9% non-need-based). ***Programs:*** Federal Direct (Subsidized and Unsubsidized Stafford, PLUS), Perkins, Federal Nursing.

WORK-STUDY ***Federal work-study:*** Total amount: $259,876; 189 jobs averaging $1390. ***State or other work-study/employment:*** Total amount: $199,230 (100% non-need-based). 90 part-time jobs averaging $2198.

ATHLETIC AWARDS Total amount: $1,238,577 (73% need-based, 27% non-need-based).

APPLYING FOR FINANCIAL AID ***Required financial aid form:*** FAFSA. ***Financial aid deadline (priority):*** 3/1. ***Notification date:*** Continuous beginning 3/1. Students must reply within 2 weeks of notification.

CONTACT Brian Weingart, Director of Financial Aid, Alderson-Broaddus College, College Hill Road, Philippi, WV 26416, 304-457-6354 or toll-free 800-263-1549. *Fax:* 304-457-6391.

ALFRED UNIVERSITY

Alfred, NY

Tuition & fees: $25,976 **Average undergraduate aid package: $23,100**

ABOUT THE INSTITUTION Independent, coed. 44 undergraduate majors. Both federal and institutional methodology are used as a basis for awarding need-based institutional aid.

UNDERGRADUATE EXPENSES for 2010–11 ***Comprehensive fee:*** $37,340 includes full-time tuition ($25,096), mandatory fees ($880), and room and board ($11,364). ***College room only:*** $5766. Full-time tuition and fees vary according to program. Room and board charges vary according to board plan and housing facility. ***Part-time tuition:*** $814 per credit hour. ***Part-time fees:*** $72 per term. Part-time tuition and fees vary according to course load. ***Payment plans:*** Tuition prepayment, installment, deferred payment.

FRESHMAN FINANCIAL AID (Fall 2010, est.) 493 applied for aid; of those 89% were deemed to have need. 100% of freshmen with need received aid; of those 18% had need fully met. ***Average percent of need met:*** 87% (excluding resources awarded to replace EFC). ***Average financial aid package:*** $24,925 (excluding resources awarded to replace EFC). 5% of all full-time freshmen had no need and received non-need-based gift aid.

UNDERGRADUATE FINANCIAL AID (Fall 2010, est.) 1,653 applied for aid; of those 91% were deemed to have need. 100% of undergraduates with need received aid; of those 16% had need fully met. ***Average percent of need met:*** 84% (excluding resources awarded to replace EFC). ***Average financial aid package:*** $23,100 (excluding resources awarded to replace EFC). 6% of all full-time undergraduates had no need and received non-need-based gift aid.

GIFT AID (NEED-BASED) ***Total amount:*** $25,713,272 (16% federal, 9% state, 75% institutional). ***Receiving aid:*** Freshmen: 83% (440); all full-time undergraduates: 80% (1,482). ***Average award:*** Freshmen: $18,939; Undergraduates: $16,763. ***Scholarships, grants, and awards:*** Federal Pell, FSEOG, state, private, college/university gift aid from institutional funds.

GIFT AID (NON-NEED-BASED) ***Total amount:*** $2,282,194 (3% federal, 4% state, 74% institutional, 19% external sources). ***Receiving aid:*** Freshmen: 45% (239). Undergraduates: 44% (805). ***Average award:*** Freshmen: $9088. Undergraduates: $9378. ***Scholarships, grants, and awards by category:*** *Academic interests/achievement:* biological sciences, business, communication, education, engineering/technologies, English, foreign languages, general academic interests/achievements, humanities, international studies, mathematics, military science, physical sciences, premedicine, social sciences. *Creative arts/performance:* art/fine arts, general creative arts/performance, performing arts. *Special achievements/activities:* leadership. *Special characteristics:* children of educators, children of faculty/staff, international students. ***Tuition waivers:*** Full or partial for employees or children of employees.

LOANS ***Student loans:*** $13,947,870 (54% need-based, 46% non-need-based). 50% of past graduating class borrowed through all loan programs. *Average indebtedness per student:* $19,474. ***Average need-based loan:*** Freshmen: $5055. Undergraduates: $5623. ***Parent loans:*** $3,170,290 (100% non-need-based). ***Programs:*** Federal Direct (Subsidized and Unsubsidized Stafford, PLUS), Perkins, college/university, alternative loans.

WORK-STUDY ***Federal work-study:*** Total amount: $1,825,286; jobs available.

APPLYING FOR FINANCIAL AID ***Required financial aid forms:*** FAFSA, institution's own form, state aid form, noncustodial (divorced/separated) parent's statement, business/farm supplement. ***Financial aid deadline:*** 3/15. ***Notification date:*** Continuous beginning 2/15. Students must reply by 5/1 or within 2 weeks of notification.

CONTACT Mr. Earl Pierce, Director of Student Financial Aid, Alfred University, Alumni Hall, One Saxon Drive, Alfred, NY 14802-1205, 607-871-2159 or toll-free 800-541-9229. *Fax:* 607-871-2252. *E-mail:* pierce@alfred.edu.

ALICE LLOYD COLLEGE

Pippa Passes, KY

ABOUT THE INSTITUTION Independent, coed. ***Awards:*** bachelor's degrees. 17 undergraduate majors. ***Total enrollment:*** 609. Undergraduates: 609. Freshmen: 187.

GIFT AID (NEED-BASED) ***Scholarships, grants, and awards:*** Federal Pell, FSEOG, state, private, college/university gift aid from institutional funds.

GIFT AID (NON-NEED-BASED) ***Scholarships, grants, and awards by category:*** *Special achievements/activities:* general special achievements/activities. *Special characteristics:* members of minority groups.

LOANS ***Programs:*** Federal Direct (Subsidized and Unsubsidized Stafford, PLUS), college/university, Bagby Loans (for freshmen).

WORK-STUDY ***Federal work-study:*** Total amount: $814,350; 359 jobs averaging $2320. ***State or other work-study/employment:*** Total amount: $557,581 (100% non-need-based). 250 part-time jobs averaging $2320.

APPLYING FOR FINANCIAL AID ***Required financial aid form:*** FAFSA.

CONTACT Ms. Jacqueline Stewart, Director of Financial Aid, Alice Lloyd College, 100 Purpose Road, Pippa Passes, KY 41844, 606-368-6058. *E-mail:* jacquelinestewart@alc.edu.

ALLEGHENY COLLEGE

Meadville, PA

Tuition & fees: $36,190 **Average undergraduate aid package: $28,033**

ABOUT THE INSTITUTION Independent, coed. 47 undergraduate majors. Federal methodology is used as a basis for awarding need-based institutional aid.

UNDERGRADUATE EXPENSES for 2011–12 ***Comprehensive fee:*** $45,350 includes full-time tuition ($35,850), mandatory fees ($340), and room and board ($9160). ***College room only:*** $4820. Room and board charges vary according to board plan and housing facility. ***Part-time tuition:*** $1494 per credit hour. ***Part-time fees:*** $170 per term. Part-time tuition and fees vary according to course load. ***Payment plans:*** Tuition prepayment, installment.

FRESHMAN FINANCIAL AID (Fall 2010, est.) 519 applied for aid; of those 84% were deemed to have need. 100% of freshmen with need received aid; of those 36% had need fully met. ***Average percent of need met:*** 91% (excluding resources awarded to replace EFC). ***Average financial aid package:*** $29,710 (excluding resources awarded to replace EFC). 25% of all full-time freshmen had no need and received non-need-based gift aid.

UNDERGRADUATE FINANCIAL AID (Fall 2010, est.) 1,668 applied for aid; of those 89% were deemed to have need. 100% of undergraduates with need received aid; of those 34% had need fully met. ***Average percent of need met:*** 89% (excluding resources awarded to replace EFC). ***Average financial aid package:*** $28,033 (excluding resources awarded to replace EFC). 27% of all full-time undergraduates had no need and received non-need-based gift aid.

GIFT AID (NEED-BASED) ***Total amount:*** $30,936,226 (11% federal, 5% state, 81% institutional, 3% external sources). ***Receiving aid:*** Freshmen: 73% (438); all full-time undergraduates: 70% (1,486). ***Average award:*** Freshmen: $23,168; Undergraduates: $21,202. ***Scholarships, grants, and awards:*** Federal Pell, FSEOG, state, private, college/university gift aid from institutional funds, Academic Competitiveness Grants, National SMART Grants, Yellow Ribbon, Veterans Educational Benefit.

GIFT AID (NON-NEED-BASED) ***Total amount:*** $8,474,358 (95% institutional, 5% external sources). ***Receiving aid:*** Freshmen: 13% (80). Undergraduates: 11% (233). ***Average award:*** Freshmen: $13,931. Undergraduates: $12,460. ***Scholarships, grants, and awards by category:*** *Academic interests/achievement:* 1,765 awards ($22,125,910 total): general academic interests/achievements. *Special characteristics:* 89 awards ($2,167,133 total): adult students, children of educators, children of faculty/staff, international students. ***Tuition waivers:*** Full or partial for employees or children of employees.

LOANS ***Student loans:*** $12,546,835 (46% need-based, 54% non-need-based). ***Average need-based loan:*** Freshmen: $4349. Undergraduates: $4789. ***Parent loans:*** $4,345,336 (100% non-need-based). ***Programs:*** Federal Direct (Subsidized and Unsubsidized Stafford, PLUS), Perkins, private loans.

WORK-STUDY ***Federal work-study:*** Total amount: $2,535,414; 1,222 jobs averaging $2075. ***State or other work-study/employment:*** Total amount: $419,380 (100% non-need-based). 95 part-time jobs averaging $4415.

APPLYING FOR FINANCIAL AID ***Required financial aid form:*** FAFSA. ***Financial aid deadline (priority):*** 2/15. ***Notification date:*** Continuous beginning 3/1. Students must reply by 5/1 or within 4 weeks of notification.

CONTACT Ms. Sheryle Proper, Director of Financial Aid, Allegheny College, 520 North Main Street, Meadville, PA 16335, 800-835-7780 or toll-free 800-521-5293. *Fax:* 814-332-2349. *E-mail:* fao@allegheny.edu.

ALLEGHENY WESLEYAN COLLEGE

Salem, OH

ABOUT THE INSTITUTION Independent religious, coed. ***Awards:*** bachelor's degrees. 2 undergraduate majors. ***Total enrollment:*** 54. Undergraduates: 54.

CONTACT Esther Phelps, Financial Aid Director, Allegheny Wesleyan College, 2161 Woodsdale Road, Salem, OH 44460, 330-337-6403 Ext. 15 or toll-free 800-292-3153. *Fax:* 330-337-6255.

ALLEN COLLEGE

Waterloo, IA

Tuition & fees: $14,995 **Average undergraduate aid package: $9118**

ABOUT THE INSTITUTION Independent, coed, primarily women. 4 undergraduate majors. Federal methodology is used as a basis for awarding need-based institutional aid.

UNDERGRADUATE EXPENSES for 2010–11 ***Comprehensive fee:*** $22,152 includes full-time tuition ($13,458), mandatory fees ($1537), and room and board ($7157). ***College room only:*** $3578. Full-time tuition and fees vary according to course load and program. Room and board charges vary according to housing facility. ***Part-time tuition:*** $500 per credit hour. ***Part-time fees:*** $68 per credit hour. Part-time tuition and fees vary according to course load and program. ***Payment plan:*** Deferred payment.

FRESHMAN FINANCIAL AID (Fall 2009) 3 applied for aid; of those 100% were deemed to have need. 100% of freshmen with need received aid. ***Average percent of need met:*** 55% (excluding resources awarded to replace EFC). ***Average financial aid package:*** $17,363 (excluding resources awarded to replace EFC).

UNDERGRADUATE FINANCIAL AID (Fall 2009) 285 applied for aid; of those 89% were deemed to have need. 100% of undergraduates with need received aid; of those 4% had need fully met. ***Average percent of need met:*** 49% (excluding resources awarded to replace EFC). ***Average financial aid package:*** $9118 (excluding resources awarded to replace EFC). 3% of all full-time undergraduates had no need and received non-need-based gift aid.

GIFT AID (NEED-BASED) ***Total amount:*** $1,388,052 (34% federal, 49% state, 14% institutional, 3% external sources). ***Receiving aid:*** Freshmen: 100% (3); all full-time undergraduates: 74% (212). ***Average award:*** Freshmen: $13,863; Undergraduates: $5997. ***Scholarships, grants, and awards:*** Federal Pell, FSEOG, state, private, college/university gift aid from institutional funds, Federal Nursing, Scholarships for Disadvantaged Students (SDS).

GIFT AID (NON-NEED-BASED) ***Total amount:*** $129,328 (2% federal, 1% state, 81% institutional, 16% external sources). ***Receiving aid:*** Freshmen: 100% (3). Undergraduates: 3% (8). ***Average award:*** Undergraduates: $1559. ***Scholarships, grants, and awards by category:*** *Academic interests/achievement:* 7 awards ($3437 total): health fields. *Special achievements/activities:* community service, general special achievements/activities, leadership. *Special characteristics:* 22 awards ($112,972 total): children of faculty/staff, general special characteristics, local/state students, members of minority groups, out-of-state students. ***Tuition waivers:*** Full or partial for employees or children of employees.

LOANS ***Student loans:*** $2,712,585 (78% need-based, 22% non-need-based). 100% of past graduating class borrowed through all loan programs. *Average indebtedness per student:* $27,792. ***Average need-based loan:*** Freshmen: $3500. Undergraduates: $4398. ***Parent loans:*** $639,806 (39% need-based, 61% non-need-based). ***Programs:*** Federal Direct (Subsidized and Unsubsidized Stafford, PLUS), Perkins, Federal Nursing, state, college/university.

WORK-STUDY ***Federal work-study:*** Total amount: $39,949; 15 jobs averaging $2663.

APPLYING FOR FINANCIAL AID ***Required financial aid forms:*** FAFSA, institution's own form. ***Financial aid deadline:*** Continuous. ***Notification date:*** Continuous beginning 4/1. Students must reply within 2 weeks of notification.

CONTACT Kathie S. Walters, Financial Aid Coordinator, Allen College, Barrett Forum, 1825 Logan Avenue, Waterloo, IA 50703-1990, 319-226-2003. *Fax:* 319-226-2051. *E-mail:* walterks@ihs.org.

ALLEN UNIVERSITY

Columbia, SC

CONTACT Ms. Donna Foster, Director of Financial Aid, Allen University, 1530 Harden Street, Columbia, SC 29204-1085, 803-376-5736 or toll-free 877-625-5368 (in-state). *E-mail:* donnaf@allenuniversity.edu.

ALLIANT INTERNATIONAL UNIVERSITY

San Diego, CA

Tuition & fees: $16,570 **Average undergraduate aid package: $13,550**

ABOUT THE INSTITUTION Independent, coed. 9 undergraduate majors. Federal methodology is used as a basis for awarding need-based institutional aid.

UNDERGRADUATE EXPENSES for 2010–11 ***Comprehensive fee:*** $23,974 includes full-time tuition ($16,350), mandatory fees ($220), and room and board ($7404). Full-time tuition and fees vary according to course load. Room and board charges vary according to board plan. ***Part-time tuition:*** $600 per semester hour. Part-time tuition and fees vary according to course load. ***Payment plan:*** Installment.

UNDERGRADUATE FINANCIAL AID (Fall 2010, est.) 101 applied for aid; of those 100% were deemed to have need. 100% of undergraduates with need received aid. ***Average percent of need met:*** 62% (excluding resources awarded to replace EFC). ***Average financial aid package:*** $13,550 (excluding resources awarded to replace EFC). 20% of all full-time undergraduates had no need and received non-need-based gift aid.

GIFT AID (NEED-BASED) ***Total amount:*** $573,248 (85% federal, 15% state). ***Receiving aid:*** All full-time undergraduates: 41% (64). ***Average award:*** Undergraduates: $6750. ***Scholarships, grants, and awards:*** Federal Pell, FSEOG, state, private, college/university gift aid from institutional funds.

GIFT AID (NON-NEED-BASED) ***Total amount:*** $141,599 (100% institutional). ***Receiving aid:*** Undergraduates: 40% (62). ***Average award:*** Undergraduates: $1700. ***Scholarships, grants, and awards by category:*** *Academic interests/achievement:* business, communication, computer science, education, English, foreign languages, general academic interests/achievements, humanities, international studies, social sciences. *Special achievements/activities:* community service, general special achievements/activities, leadership. *Special characteristics:* children and siblings of alumni, children of current students, children of faculty/staff, ethnic background, international students, local/state students, members of minority groups, veterans. ***Tuition waivers:*** Full or partial for children of alumni, employees or children of employees.

LOANS ***Student loans:*** $979,534 (46% need-based, 54% non-need-based). ***Average need-based loan:*** Undergraduates: $5500. ***Parent loans:*** $78,117 (100% non-need-based). ***Programs:*** Federal Direct (Subsidized and Unsubsidized Stafford, PLUS), Perkins, alternative loans.

WORK-STUDY ***Federal work-study:*** Total amount: $23,216; 12 jobs averaging $2000. ***State or other work-study/employment:*** Total amount: $15,000 (100% non-need-based). 5 part-time jobs averaging $3000.

APPLYING FOR FINANCIAL AID ***Required financial aid form:*** FAFSA. ***Financial aid deadline (priority):*** 3/2. ***Notification date:*** Continuous beginning 3/15. Students must reply within 3 weeks of notification.

CONTACT Deborah Spindler, Director of Financial Aid, Alliant International University, 10455 Pomerado Road, San Diego, CA 92131-1799, 858-635-4559 Ext. 4700 or toll-free 866-825-5426. *Fax:* 858-635-4848.

ALLIED AMERICAN UNIVERSITY

Laguna Hills, CA

CONTACT Financial Aid Office, Allied American University, 22952 Alcade Drive, Laguna Hills, CA 92653, 888-384-0849.

ALMA COLLEGE

Alma, MI

Tuition & fees: $29,230 **Average undergraduate aid package: $23,877**

ABOUT THE INSTITUTION Independent Presbyterian, coed. 69 undergraduate majors. Federal methodology is used as a basis for awarding need-based institutional aid.

UNDERGRADUATE EXPENSES for 2011–12 ***Comprehensive fee:*** $38,070 includes full-time tuition ($28,980), mandatory fees ($250), and room and board ($8840). ***College room only:*** $4420. Room and board charges vary according to board plan and housing facility. ***Part-time tuition:*** $1000 per credit hour. Part-time tuition and fees vary according to course load. ***Payment plans:*** Installment, deferred payment.

FRESHMAN FINANCIAL AID (Fall 2010, est.) 344 applied for aid; of those 93% were deemed to have need. 100% of freshmen with need received aid; of those 23% had need fully met. ***Average percent of need met:*** 83% (excluding resources awarded to replace EFC). ***Average financial aid package:*** $25,202 (excluding resources awarded to replace EFC). 15% of all full-time freshmen had no need and received non-need-based gift aid.

UNDERGRADUATE FINANCIAL AID (Fall 2010, est.) 1,275 applied for aid; of those 89% were deemed to have need. 100% of undergraduates with need received aid; of those 19% had need fully met. ***Average percent of need met:*** 81% (excluding resources awarded to replace EFC). ***Average financial aid package:*** $23,877 (excluding resources awarded to replace EFC). 17% of all full-time undergraduates had no need and received non-need-based gift aid.

GIFT AID (NEED-BASED) ***Total amount:*** $20,709,935 (11% federal, 7% state, 81% institutional, 1% external sources). ***Receiving aid:*** Freshmen: 90% (320); all full-time undergraduates: 83% (1,139). ***Average award:*** Freshmen: $22,104; Undergraduates: $17,025. ***Scholarships, grants, and awards:*** Federal Pell, FSEOG, state, private, college/university gift aid from institutional funds.

GIFT AID (NON-NEED-BASED) ***Total amount:*** $4,229,596 (97% institutional, 3% external sources). ***Receiving aid:*** Freshmen: 16% (58). Undergraduates: 11% (156). ***Average award:*** Freshmen: $15,198. Undergraduates: $13,913. ***Scholarships, grants, and awards by category:*** *Academic interests/achievement:* 1,331 awards ($14,671,073 total): general academic interests/achievements. *Creative arts/performance:* 306 awards ($345,742 total): art/fine arts, dance, music, performing arts, theater/drama. *Special achievements/activities:* 11 awards ($10,750 total): religious involvement. *Special characteristics:* 198 awards ($186,351 total): children and siblings of alumni, children of current students. ***Tuition waivers:*** Full or partial for employees or children of employees.

LOANS ***Student loans:*** $7,329,537 (97% need-based, 3% non-need-based). 70% of past graduating class borrowed through all loan programs. *Average indebtedness per student:* $28,734. ***Average need-based loan:*** Freshmen: $3968. Undergraduates: $4905. ***Parent loans:*** $3,398,012 (30% need-based, 70% non-need-based). ***Programs:*** Federal Direct (Subsidized and Unsubsidized Stafford, PLUS), Perkins, state, college/university, alternative loans.

WORK-STUDY ***Federal work-study:*** Total amount: $165,238; 174 jobs averaging $950. ***State or other work-study/employment:*** Part-time jobs available.

APPLYING FOR FINANCIAL AID ***Required financial aid form:*** FAFSA. ***Financial aid deadline (priority):*** 3/1. ***Notification date:*** Continuous beginning 3/1. Students must reply within 3 weeks of notification.

CONTACT Mr. Christopher A. Brown, Director of Student Financial Assistance, Alma College, 614 West Superior Street, Alma, MI 48801-1599, 989-463-7347 or toll-free 800-321-ALMA. *Fax:* 989-463-7993. *E-mail:* cabrown@alma.edu.

ALVERNIA UNIVERSITY

Reading, PA

Tuition & fees: $26,630 **Average undergraduate aid package: $15,576**

ABOUT THE INSTITUTION Independent Roman Catholic, coed. 43 undergraduate majors. Federal methodology is used as a basis for awarding need-based institutional aid.

UNDERGRADUATE EXPENSES for 2011–12 ***Comprehensive fee:*** $36,117 includes full-time tuition ($26,100), mandatory fees ($530), and room and board ($9487). ***College room only:*** $4657. Full-time tuition and fees vary according to class time and reciprocity agreements. Room and board charges vary according to board plan and housing facility. ***Part-time tuition:*** $720 per credit hour. Part-time tuition and fees vary according to class time and course load. ***Payment plan:*** Installment.

FRESHMAN FINANCIAL AID (Fall 2009) 340 applied for aid; of those 89% were deemed to have need. 100% of freshmen with need received aid; of those 13% had need fully met. ***Average percent of need met:*** 65% (excluding resources awarded to replace EFC). ***Average financial aid package:*** $16,253 (excluding resources awarded to replace EFC). 11% of all full-time freshmen had no need and received non-need-based gift aid.

UNDERGRADUATE FINANCIAL AID (Fall 2009) 1,636 applied for aid; of those 94% were deemed to have need. 99% of undergraduates with need received aid; of those 9% had need fully met. ***Average percent of need met:*** 63% (excluding resources awarded to replace EFC). ***Average financial aid package:*** $15,576 (excluding resources awarded to replace EFC). 7% of all full-time undergraduates had no need and received non-need-based gift aid.

GIFT AID (NEED-BASED) ***Total amount:*** $15,690,008 (21% federal, 16% state, 55% institutional, 8% external sources). ***Receiving aid:*** Freshmen: 78% (299); all full-time undergraduates: 82% (1,460). ***Average award:*** Freshmen: $12,240; Undergraduates: $10,668. ***Scholarships, grants, and awards:*** Federal Pell, FSEOG, state, private, college/university gift aid from institutional funds.

GIFT AID (NON-NEED-BASED) ***Total amount:*** $1,506,022 (1% state, 61% institutional, 38% external sources). ***Receiving aid:*** Freshmen: 6% (24). Undergraduates: 5% (89). ***Average award:*** Freshmen: $6861. Undergraduates: $5875. ***Scholarships, grants, and awards by category:*** *Academic interests/achievement:* 484 awards ($3,125,230 total): general academic interests/achievements. *Special achievements/activities:* 214 awards ($557,196 total): community service, leadership, memberships, religious involvement. *Special characteristics:* 529 awards ($1,529,090 total): children and siblings of alumni, children of faculty/staff, general special characteristics, local/state students, siblings of current students. ***Tuition waivers:*** Full or partial for employees or children of employees, senior citizens.

LOANS ***Student loans:*** $16,302,598 (80% need-based, 20% non-need-based). 87% of past graduating class borrowed through all loan programs. *Average indebtedness per student:* $27,327. ***Average need-based loan:*** Freshmen: $4383. Undergraduates: $5699. ***Parent loans:*** $3,186,633 (44% need-based, 56% non-need-based). ***Programs:*** Federal Direct (Subsidized and Unsubsidized Stafford, PLUS), Perkins.

WORK-STUDY ***Federal work-study:*** Total amount: $118,395; 205 jobs averaging $1076. ***State or other work-study/employment:*** Total amount: $110,232 (72% need-based, 28% non-need-based). 17 part-time jobs averaging $1541.

APPLYING FOR FINANCIAL AID ***Required financial aid forms:*** FAFSA, state aid form. ***Financial aid deadline (priority):*** 5/1. ***Notification date:*** Continuous beginning 2/10. Students must reply by 5/1 or within 2 weeks of notification.

CONTACT Ms. Christine Saadi, Director of Student Financial Planning, Alvernia University, 400 Saint Bernardine Street, Reading, PA 19607-1799, 610-796-8213 or toll-free 888-ALVERNIA (in-state). *Fax:* 610-796-8336. *E-mail:* christine.saadi@alvernia.edu.

ALVERNO COLLEGE

Milwaukee, WI

Tuition & fees: $21,063 | **Average undergraduate aid package: $15,269**

ABOUT THE INSTITUTION Independent Roman Catholic, undergraduate: women only; graduate: coed. 42 undergraduate majors. Federal methodology is used as a basis for awarding need-based institutional aid.

UNDERGRADUATE EXPENSES for 2011–12 ***Comprehensive fee:*** $28,029 includes full-time tuition ($20,538), mandatory fees ($525), and room and board ($6966). Full-time tuition and fees vary according to program. Room and board charges vary according to board plan and housing facility. Part-time tuition and fees vary according to program. ***Payment plans:*** Installment, deferred payment.

FRESHMAN FINANCIAL AID (Fall 2010, est.) 240 applied for aid; of those 96% were deemed to have need. 100% of freshmen with need received aid. ***Average financial aid package:*** $16,425 (excluding resources awarded to replace EFC). 8% of all full-time freshmen had no need and received non-need-based gift aid.

UNDERGRADUATE FINANCIAL AID (Fall 2010, est.) 1,548 applied for aid; of those 93% were deemed to have need. 100% of undergraduates with need received aid. ***Average financial aid package:*** $15,269 (excluding resources awarded to replace EFC). 10% of all full-time undergraduates had no need and received non-need-based gift aid.

GIFT AID (NEED-BASED) ***Total amount:*** $17,216,922 (36% federal, 19% state, 45% institutional). ***Receiving aid:*** Freshmen: 92% (230); all full-time undergraduates: 87% (1,431). ***Average award:*** Freshmen: $14,132; Undergraduates: $11,209. ***Scholarships, grants, and awards:*** Federal Pell, FSEOG, state, private, college/university gift aid from institutional funds, Federal Nursing.

GIFT AID (NON-NEED-BASED) ***Total amount:*** $1,339,044 (76% institutional, 24% external sources). ***Receiving aid:*** Freshmen: 83% (207). Undergraduates: 72% (1,180). ***Average award:*** Freshmen: $6305. Undergraduates: $6159. ***Scholarships, grants, and awards by category:*** *Academic interests/achievement:* 1,483 awards ($6,297,133 total): general academic interests/achievements. *Creative arts/performance:* 10 awards ($20,063 total): art/fine arts, music. *Special achievements/activities:* 4 awards ($55,625 total): community service. *Special characteristics:* 29 awards ($254,976 total): children of faculty/staff, international students. ***Tuition waivers:*** Full or partial for employees or children of employees.

LOANS ***Student loans:*** $18,448,047 (48% need-based, 52% non-need-based). 100% of past graduating class borrowed through all loan programs. *Average indebtedness per student:* $33,220. ***Average need-based loan:*** Freshmen: $2923. Undergraduates: $4058. ***Parent loans:*** $778,479 (100% non-need-based). ***Programs:*** Federal Direct (Subsidized and Unsubsidized Stafford, PLUS), Perkins, state.

WORK-STUDY ***Federal work-study:*** Total amount: $213,252; 183 jobs averaging $2324. ***State or other work-study/employment:*** Total amount: $475,434 (100% non-need-based). Part-time jobs available.

APPLYING FOR FINANCIAL AID ***Required financial aid forms:*** FAFSA, institution's own form. ***Financial aid deadline (priority):*** 3/15. ***Notification date:*** Continuous beginning 3/15. Students must reply within 2 weeks of notification.

CONTACT Dan Goyette, Director of Financial Aid, Alverno College, 3400 South 43rd Street, PO Box 343922, Milwaukee, WI 53234-3922, 414-382-6046 or toll-free 800-933-3401. *Fax:* 414-382-6354. *E-mail:* dan.goyette@alverno.edu.

AMERICAN ACADEMY OF ART

Chicago, IL

CONTACT Ms. Ione Fitzgerald, Director of Financial Aid, American Academy of Art, 332 South Michigan Avenue, Suite 300, Chicago, IL 60604, 312-461-0600. *Fax:* 312-294-9570.

AMERICAN BAPTIST COLLEGE OF AMERICAN BAPTIST THEOLOGICAL SEMINARY

Nashville, TN

ABOUT THE INSTITUTION Independent Baptist, coed. 1 undergraduate major.

GIFT AID (NEED-BASED) ***Scholarships, grants, and awards:*** Federal Pell, FSEOG, state.

GIFT AID (NON-NEED-BASED) ***Scholarships, grants, and awards by category:*** *Academic interests/achievement:* religion/biblical studies. *Special characteristics:* religious affiliation.

WORK-STUDY ***Federal work-study:*** Total amount: $6741; 1 job averaging $6741.

APPLYING FOR FINANCIAL AID ***Required financial aid form:*** FAFSA.

CONTACT Marcella Lockhart, Director of Enrollment Management, American Baptist College of American Baptist Theological Seminary, 1800 Baptist World Center Drive, Nashville, TN 37207, 615-687-6896 Ext. 6896. *Fax:* 615-226-7855. *E-mail:* mlockhart@abcnash.edu.

AMERICAN INDIAN COLLEGE OF THE ASSEMBLIES OF GOD, INC.

Phoenix, AZ

CONTACT Nadine Waldrop, Office of Student Financial Aid, American Indian College of the Assemblies of God, Inc., 10020 North Fifteenth Avenue, Phoenix, AZ 85021-2199, 602-944-3335 or toll-free 800-933-3828. *Fax:* 602-944-1952. *E-mail:* financialaid@aicag.edu.

AMERICAN INTERCONTINENTAL UNIVERSITY ATLANTA

Atlanta, GA

CONTACT Financial Aid Office, American InterContinental University Atlanta, 6600 Peachtree-Dunwoody Road, 500 Embassy Row, Atlanta, GA 30328, 404-965-6500 or toll-free 800-353-1744.

AMERICAN INTERCONTINENTAL UNIVERSITY HOUSTON

Houston, TX

CONTACT Financial Aid Office, American InterContinental University Houston, 9999 Richmond Avenue, Houston, TX 77042, 832-242-5788 or toll-free 888-607-9888.

AMERICAN INTERCONTINENTAL UNIVERSITY ONLINE

Hoffman Estates, IL

CONTACT Financial Aid Office, American InterContinental University Online, 5550 Prairie Stone Parkway, Suite 400, Hoffman Estates, IL 60192, 847-851-5000 or toll-free 877-701-3800.

AMERICAN INTERCONTINENTAL UNIVERSITY SOUTH FLORIDA

Weston, FL

CONTACT Financial Aid Office, American InterContinental University South Florida, 2250 North Commerce Parkway, Suite 100, Weston, FL 33326, 954-446-6100 or toll-free 888-603-4888.

AMERICAN INTERNATIONAL COLLEGE

Springfield, MA

ABOUT THE INSTITUTION Independent, coed. 42 undergraduate majors.

GIFT AID (NEED-BASED) ***Scholarships, grants, and awards:*** Federal Pell, FSEOG, state, private, college/university gift aid from institutional funds, Federal Nursing.

GIFT AID (NON-NEED-BASED) ***Scholarships, grants, and awards by category:*** *Academic interests/achievement:* general academic interests/achievements. *Special achievements/activities:* general special achievements/activities. *Special characteristics:* children and siblings of alumni, children of faculty/staff, children of public servants, first-generation college students, previous college experience.

LOANS ***Programs:*** Perkins, college/university, alternative loans.

WORK-STUDY ***Federal work-study:*** Total amount: $532,723; jobs available.

APPLYING FOR FINANCIAL AID ***Required financial aid forms:*** FAFSA, state aid form.

CONTACT Mr. Douglas E. Fish, Associate Vice President for Financial Services, American International College, 1000 State Street, Springfield, MA 01109-3189, 413-205-3259. *Fax:* 413-205-3912. *E-mail:* douglas.fish@aic.edu.

AMERICAN JEWISH UNIVERSITY

Bel Air, CA

Tuition & fees: $25,688 **Average undergraduate aid package: $24,500**

ABOUT THE INSTITUTION Independent Jewish, coed. 10 undergraduate majors. Both federal and institutional methodology are used as a basis for awarding need-based institutional aid.

UNDERGRADUATE EXPENSES for 2011–12 ***One-time required fee:*** $200. ***Comprehensive fee:*** $38,052 includes full-time tuition ($24,744), mandatory fees ($944), and room and board ($12,364). Full-time tuition and fees vary according to course load and degree level. Room and board charges vary according to board plan and housing facility. ***Part-time tuition:*** $1031 per unit. Part-time tuition and fees vary according to course load and degree level. ***Payment plan:*** Installment.

FRESHMAN FINANCIAL AID (Fall 2010, est.) 28 applied for aid; of those 100% were deemed to have need. 100% of freshmen with need received aid; of those 79% had need fully met. ***Average percent of need met:*** 100% (excluding resources awarded to replace EFC). ***Average financial aid package:*** $24,000 (excluding resources awarded to replace EFC). 55% of all full-time freshmen had no need and received non-need-based gift aid.

UNDERGRADUATE FINANCIAL AID (Fall 2010, est.) 136 applied for aid; of those 100% were deemed to have need. 100% of undergraduates with need received aid; of those 88% had need fully met. ***Average percent of need met:*** 96% (excluding resources awarded to replace EFC). ***Average financial aid package:*** $24,500 (excluding resources awarded to replace EFC). 32% of all full-time undergraduates had no need and received non-need-based gift aid.

GIFT AID (NEED-BASED) ***Total amount:*** $674,873 (28% federal, 21% state, 51% institutional). ***Receiving aid:*** Freshmen: 83% (24); all full-time undergraduates: 40% (70). ***Average award:*** Freshmen: $10,007; Undergraduates: $9238. ***Scholarships, grants, and awards:*** Federal Pell, FSEOG, state, private, college/university gift aid from institutional funds.

GIFT AID (NON-NEED-BASED) ***Total amount:*** $919,100 (100% institutional). ***Receiving aid:*** Freshmen: 41% (12). Undergraduates: 30% (53). ***Average award:*** Freshmen: $2000. Undergraduates: $2000. ***Scholarships, grants, and awards by category:*** *Academic interests/achievement:* 36 awards ($234,750 total): general academic interests/achievements, premedicine. *Special achievements/activities:* 53 awards ($220,250 total): leadership. ***Tuition waivers:*** Full or partial for employees or children of employees.

LOANS ***Student loans:*** $509,500 (49% need-based, 51% non-need-based). 75% of past graduating class borrowed through all loan programs. *Average indebtedness per student:* $28,000. ***Average need-based loan:*** Freshmen: $5500. Undergraduates: $6500. ***Parent loans:*** $234,912 (100% non-need-based). ***Programs:*** Federal Direct (Subsidized and Unsubsidized Stafford, PLUS), alternative loans.

WORK-STUDY ***Federal work-study:*** Total amount: $34,886; 35 jobs averaging $929.

APPLYING FOR FINANCIAL AID ***Required financial aid forms:*** FAFSA, institution's own form, federal income tax returns (student and parent). ***Financial aid deadline (priority):*** 3/2. ***Notification date:*** Continuous beginning 3/15. Students must reply within 3 weeks of notification.

CONTACT Larisa Zadoyen, Director of Financial Aid, American Jewish University, 15600 Mulholland Drive, Bel Air, CA 90077-1599, 310-476-9777 Ext. 252 or toll-free 888-853-6763. *Fax:* 310-476-4613. *E-mail:* lzadoyen@ajula.edu.

AMERICAN MUSICAL AND DRAMATIC ACADEMY, LOS ANGELES

Los Angeles, CA

CONTACT Financial Aid Office, American Musical and Dramatic Academy, Los Angeles, 6305 Yucca Street, Los Angeles, CA 90028, 323-469-3300 or toll-free 866-374-5300.

AMERICAN SENTINEL UNIVERSITY

Aurora, CO

CONTACT Financial Aid Office, American Sentinel University, 2260 South Xanadu Way, Suite 310, Aurora, CO 80014, toll-free 800-729-2427 (out-of-state).

AMERICAN UNIVERSITY

Washington, DC

Tuition & fees: $36,697 **Average undergraduate aid package: $29,620**

ABOUT THE INSTITUTION Independent Methodist, coed. 75 undergraduate majors. Institutional methodology is used as a basis for awarding need-based institutional aid.

UNDERGRADUATE EXPENSES for 2010–11 ***Comprehensive fee:*** $50,165 includes full-time tuition ($36,180), mandatory fees ($517), and room and board ($13,468). ***College room only:*** $9018. Full-time tuition and fees vary according to degree level. Room and board charges vary according to board plan, housing facility, and location. ***Part-time tuition:*** $1205 per credit hour. Part-time tuition and fees vary according to course load. ***Payment plan:*** Installment.

FRESHMAN FINANCIAL AID (Fall 2010, est.) 1,129 applied for aid; of those 80% were deemed to have need. 100% of freshmen with need received aid; of those 22% had need fully met. ***Average percent of need met:*** 85% (excluding resources awarded to replace EFC). ***Average financial aid package:*** $31,635 (excluding resources awarded to replace EFC). 17% of all full-time freshmen had no need and received non-need-based gift aid.

UNDERGRADUATE FINANCIAL AID (Fall 2010, est.) 3,967 applied for aid; of those 85% were deemed to have need. 99% of undergraduates with need received aid; of those 20% had need fully met. ***Average percent of need met:*** 76% (excluding resources awarded to replace EFC). ***Average financial aid package:*** $29,620 (excluding resources awarded to replace EFC). 17% of all full-time undergraduates had no need and received non-need-based gift aid.

GIFT AID (NEED-BASED) ***Total amount:*** $30,848,471 (16% federal, 1% state, 76% institutional, 7% external sources). ***Receiving aid:*** Freshmen: 32% (474); all full-time undergraduates: 25% (1,592). ***Average award:*** Freshmen: $15,448; Undergraduates: $14,487. ***Scholarships, grants, and awards:*** Federal Pell, FSEOG, state, private, college/university gift aid from institutional funds.

GIFT AID (NON-NEED-BASED) ***Total amount:*** $45,450,361 (100% institutional). ***Receiving aid:*** Freshmen: 28% (418). Undergraduates: 22% (1,446). ***Average award:*** Freshmen: $19,686. Undergraduates: $18,780. ***Scholarships, grants, and awards by category:*** *Academic interests/achievement:* general academic interests/achievements. *Creative arts/performance:* general creative arts/performance. *Special achievements/activities:* general special achievements/activities, leadership, memberships. *Special characteristics:* adult students, children and siblings of alumni, children of faculty/staff, ethnic background, first-generation college students, local/state students, members of minority groups, previous college experience, relatives of clergy, spouses of current students.

LOANS ***Student loans:*** $14,716,593 (93% need-based, 7% non-need-based). 60% of past graduating class borrowed through all loan programs. *Average indebtedness per student:* $36,206. ***Average need-based loan:*** Freshmen: $4109. Undergraduates: $5043. ***Parent loans:*** $17,934,120 (100% non-need-based). ***Programs:*** Federal Direct (Subsidized and Unsubsidized Stafford, PLUS), Perkins, college/university.

WORK-STUDY ***Federal work-study:*** Total amount: $3,835,721; jobs available.

ATHLETIC AWARDS Total amount: $4,010,521 (100% non-need-based).

APPLYING FOR FINANCIAL AID ***Required financial aid forms:*** FAFSA, institution's own form. ***Financial aid deadline:*** 2/15. ***Notification date:*** 4/1. Students must reply by 5/1 or within 4 weeks of notification.

CONTACT Brian Lee Sang, Director of Financial Aid, American University, 4400 Massachusetts Avenue, NW, Washington, DC 20016-8001, 202-885-6100. *Fax:* 202-885-1129. *E-mail:* financialaid@american.edu.

AMERICAN UNIVERSITY OF PUERTO RICO

Bayamón, PR

CONTACT Mr. Yahaira Melendez, Financial Aid Director, American University of Puerto Rico, PO Box 2037, Bayamón, PR 00960-2037, 787-620-2040 Ext. 2031. *Fax:* 787-785-7377. *E-mail:* melendezy@aupr.edu.

AMHERST COLLEGE

Amherst, MA

Tuition & fees: $40,862 **Average undergraduate aid package: $40,087**

ABOUT THE INSTITUTION Independent, coed. 38 undergraduate majors. Institutional methodology is used as a basis for awarding need-based institutional aid.

UNDERGRADUATE EXPENSES for 2011–12 ***Comprehensive fee:*** $51,522 includes full-time tuition ($40,160), mandatory fees ($702), and room and board ($10,660). ***College room only:*** $5780. ***Payment plans:*** Installment, deferred payment.

FRESHMAN FINANCIAL AID (Fall 2010, est.) 343 applied for aid; of those 87% were deemed to have need. 100% of freshmen with need received aid; of those 100% had need fully met. ***Average percent of need met:*** 100% (excluding resources awarded to replace EFC). ***Average financial aid package:*** $40,441 (excluding resources awarded to replace EFC).

UNDERGRADUATE FINANCIAL AID (Fall 2010, est.) 1,202 applied for aid; of those 90% were deemed to have need. 100% of undergraduates with need received aid; of those 100% had need fully met. ***Average percent of need met:*** 100% (excluding resources awarded to replace EFC). ***Average financial aid package:*** $40,087 (excluding resources awarded to replace EFC).

GIFT AID (NEED-BASED) ***Total amount:*** $41,453,662 (5% federal, 94% institutional, 1% external sources). ***Receiving aid:*** Freshmen: 60% (292); all full-time undergraduates: 58% (1,048). ***Average award:*** Freshmen: $39,962; Undergraduates: $39,675. ***Scholarships, grants, and awards:*** Federal Pell, FSEOG, state, private, college/university gift aid from institutional funds.

GIFT AID (NON-NEED-BASED) ***Total amount:*** $328,934 (13% federal, 87% external sources).

LOANS ***Student loans:*** $2,148,109 (30% need-based, 70% non-need-based). 42% of past graduating class borrowed through all loan programs. *Average indebtedness per student:* $12,843. ***Average need-based loan:*** Freshmen: $2459. Undergraduates: $2977. ***Parent loans:*** $2,684,965 (100% non-need-based). ***Programs:*** Federal Direct (Subsidized and Unsubsidized Stafford, PLUS), Perkins, college/university.

WORK-STUDY ***Federal work-study:*** Total amount: $986,934; 590 jobs averaging $1609. ***State or other work-study/employment:*** Total amount: $446,663 (100% need-based). 262 part-time jobs averaging $1580.

APPLYING FOR FINANCIAL AID ***Required financial aid forms:*** FAFSA, CSS Financial Aid PROFILE, federal income tax form(s), W-2 forms. ***Financial aid deadline (priority):*** 2/15. ***Notification date:*** 4/1. Students must reply by 5/1.

CONTACT Joe Paul Case, Dean of Financial Aid, Amherst College, B-5 Converse Hall, PO Box 5000, Amherst, MA 01002-5000, 413-542-2296. *Fax:* 413-542-2628. *E-mail:* finaid@amherst.edu.

AMRIDGE UNIVERSITY

Montgomery, AL

Tuition & fees: $8420 **Average undergraduate aid package: $8500**

ABOUT THE INSTITUTION Independent religious, coed. 12 undergraduate majors. Federal methodology is used as a basis for awarding need-based institutional aid.

UNDERGRADUATE EXPENSES for 2011–12 ***Tuition:*** full-time $7620; part-time $330 per semester hour. ***Required fees:*** full-time $800; $400 per term. Full-time tuition and fees vary according to course load. Part-time tuition and fees vary according to course load.

UNDERGRADUATE FINANCIAL AID (Fall 2010, est.) 370 applied for aid; of those 92% were deemed to have need. 100% of undergraduates with need received aid; of those 88% had need fully met. ***Average percent of need met:*** 85% (excluding resources awarded to replace EFC). ***Average financial aid package:*** $8500 (excluding resources awarded to replace EFC). 5% of all full-time undergraduates had no need and received non-need-based gift aid.

GIFT AID (NEED-BASED) ***Total amount:*** $1,450,000 (93% federal, 1% state, 3% institutional, 3% external sources). ***Receiving aid:*** All full-time undergraduates: 83% (310). ***Average award:*** Undergraduates: $6500. ***Scholarships, grants, and awards:*** Federal Pell, FSEOG, state, private, college/university gift aid from institutional funds.

GIFT AID (NON-NEED-BASED) ***Total amount:*** $750,000 (100% institutional). ***Receiving aid:*** Undergraduates: 13% (50). ***Average award:*** Undergraduates: $4000. ***Scholarships, grants, and awards by category:*** *Special achievements/activities:* religious involvement. *Special characteristics:* children of faculty/staff, veterans. ***Tuition waivers:*** Full or partial for employees or children of employees.

LOANS ***Student loans:*** $3,625,000 (43% need-based, 57% non-need-based). 85% of past graduating class borrowed through all loan programs. *Average indebtedness per student:* $18,000. ***Average need-based loan:*** Undergraduates: $5500. ***Parent loans:*** $7000 (100% need-based). ***Programs:*** Federal Direct (Subsidized and Unsubsidized Stafford, PLUS).

WORK-STUDY Federal work-study jobs available.

APPLYING FOR FINANCIAL AID ***Required financial aid forms:*** FAFSA, institution's own form. ***Financial aid deadline:*** Continuous. ***Notification date:*** 8/31. Students must reply within 2 weeks of notification.

CONTACT Louise Hicks, Director of Financial Aid, Amridge University, 1200 Taylor Road, Montgomery, AL 36117, 334-387-3877 Ext. 7525 or toll-free 800-351-4040 Ext. 213. *Fax:* 334-387-3878. *E-mail:* financialaid@amridgeuniversity.edu.

ANDERSON UNIVERSITY

Anderson, IN

ABOUT THE INSTITUTION Independent religious, coed. 63 undergraduate majors.

GIFT AID (NEED-BASED) ***Scholarships, grants, and awards:*** Federal Pell, FSEOG, state, private, college/university gift aid from institutional funds.

GIFT AID (NON-NEED-BASED) ***Scholarships, grants, and awards by category:*** *Academic interests/achievement:* general academic interests/achievements. *Creative arts/performance:* art/fine arts, music. *Special achievements/activities:* leadership. *Special characteristics:* adult students, children of faculty/staff, international students, relatives of clergy.

LOANS ***Programs:*** Perkins.

WORK-STUDY ***Federal work-study:*** Total amount: $510,516; 1,500 jobs averaging $2200. ***State or other work-study/employment:*** Total amount: $854,501 (26% need-based, 74% non-need-based). Part-time jobs available.

APPLYING FOR FINANCIAL AID ***Required financial aid form:*** FAFSA.

CONTACT Mr. Kenneth Nieman, Director of Student Financial Services, Anderson University, 1100 East Fifth Street, Anderson, IN 46012-3495, 765-641-4180 or toll-free 800-421-3014 (in-state), 800-428-6414 (out-of-state). *Fax:* 765-641-3831. *E-mail:* kfnieman@anderson.edu.

ANDERSON UNIVERSITY

Anderson, SC

Tuition & fees: $22,570 **Average undergraduate aid package: $15,597**

ABOUT THE INSTITUTION Independent Baptist, coed. 32 undergraduate majors. Federal methodology is used as a basis for awarding need-based institutional aid.

UNDERGRADUATE EXPENSES for 2011–12 ***Comprehensive fee:*** $30,395 includes full-time tuition ($20,910), mandatory fees ($1660), and room and board ($7825). ***College room only:*** $3950. Full-time tuition and fees vary according to course load and program. Room and board charges vary according to board plan and housing facility. ***Part-time tuition:*** $480 per credit hour. Part-time tuition and fees vary according to program. ***Payment plan:*** Installment.

FRESHMAN FINANCIAL AID (Fall 2010, est.) 478 applied for aid; of those 90% were deemed to have need. 100% of freshmen with need received aid; of those 31% had need fully met. ***Average percent of need met:*** 78% (excluding resources awarded to replace EFC). ***Average financial aid package:*** $18,498 (excluding resources awarded to replace EFC). 14% of all full-time freshmen had no need and received non-need-based gift aid.

UNDERGRADUATE FINANCIAL AID (Fall 2010, est.) 1,718 applied for aid; of those 91% were deemed to have need. 100% of undergraduates with need received aid; of those 23% had need fully met. ***Average percent of need met:*** 70% (excluding resources awarded to replace EFC). ***Average financial aid package:*** $15,597 (excluding resources awarded to replace EFC). 13% of all full-time undergraduates had no need and received non-need-based gift aid.

GIFT AID (NEED-BASED) ***Total amount:*** $18,690,814 (22% federal, 27% state, 50% institutional, 1% external sources). ***Receiving aid:*** Freshmen: 84% (429); all full-time undergraduates: 84% (1,551). ***Average award:*** Freshmen: $16,318; Undergraduates: $12,468. ***Scholarships, grants, and awards:*** Federal Pell, FSEOG, state, private, college/university gift aid from institutional funds.

GIFT AID (NON-NEED-BASED) ***Total amount:*** $4,746,193 (38% state, 60% institutional, 2% external sources). ***Receiving aid:*** Freshmen: 22% (111). Undergraduates: 16% (296). ***Average award:*** Freshmen: $10,294. Undergraduates: $8911. ***Scholarships, grants, and awards by category:*** *Academic interests/achievement:* 1,368 awards ($8,388,586 total): business, education, general academic interests/achievements, religion/biblical studies. *Creative arts/performance:* 163 awards ($332,263 total): art/fine arts, music, performing arts, theater/drama. *Special characteristics:* 879 awards ($1,353,103 total): children and siblings of alumni, children of faculty/staff, international students, members of minority groups, out-of-state students, relatives of clergy, religious affiliation, siblings of current students, spouses of current students. ***Tuition waivers:*** Full or partial for employees or children of employees.

LOANS ***Student loans:*** $11,430,262 (77% need-based, 23% non-need-based). 60% of past graduating class borrowed through all loan programs. ***Average need-based loan:*** Freshmen: $3602. Undergraduates: $4466. ***Parent loans:*** $1,712,450 (54% need-based, 46% non-need-based). ***Programs:*** Federal Direct (Subsidized and Unsubsidized Stafford, PLUS), Perkins, state, private loans.

WORK-STUDY ***Federal work-study:*** Total amount: $146,504; 133 jobs averaging $1317. ***State or other work-study/employment:*** Part-time jobs available.

ATHLETIC AWARDS Total amount: $1,345,614 (48% need-based, 52% non-need-based).

APPLYING FOR FINANCIAL AID ***Required financial aid form:*** FAFSA. ***Financial aid deadline:*** 7/30 (priority: 3/1). ***Notification date:*** Continuous beginning 3/15. Students must reply within 2 weeks of notification.

CONTACT Rebekah Burdick, Director of Financial Aid, Anderson University, 316 Boulevard, Anderson, SC 29621-4035, 864-231-2070 or toll-free 800-542-3594. *Fax:* 864-231-2008. *E-mail:* bpressley@andersonuniversity.edu.

ANDREWS UNIVERSITY

Berrien Springs, MI

Tuition & fees: $22,242 **Average undergraduate aid package: $25,030**

ABOUT THE INSTITUTION Independent Seventh-day Adventist, coed. 64 undergraduate majors. Federal methodology is used as a basis for awarding need-based institutional aid.

UNDERGRADUATE EXPENSES for 2010–11 ***Comprehensive fee:*** $29,382 includes full-time tuition ($21,550), mandatory fees ($692), and room and board ($7140). ***College room only:*** $3670. Full-time tuition and fees vary according to course load. Room and board charges vary according to board plan. ***Part-time tuition:*** $900 per credit hour. Part-time tuition and fees vary according to course load. ***Payment plan:*** Installment.

FRESHMAN FINANCIAL AID (Fall 2010, est.) 275 applied for aid; of those 83% were deemed to have need. 100% of freshmen with need received aid; of those 20% had need fully met. ***Average percent of need met:*** 85% (excluding resources awarded to replace EFC). ***Average financial aid package:*** $23,091 (excluding resources awarded to replace EFC). 36% of all full-time freshmen had no need and received non-need-based gift aid.

UNDERGRADUATE FINANCIAL AID (Fall 2010, est.) 1,271 applied for aid; of those 91% were deemed to have need. 100% of undergraduates with need received aid; of those 11% had need fully met. ***Average percent of need met:*** 85% (excluding resources awarded to replace EFC). ***Average financial aid package:*** $25,030 (excluding resources awarded to replace EFC). 32% of all full-time undergraduates had no need and received non-need-based gift aid.

GIFT AID (NEED-BASED) ***Total amount:*** $21,460,081 (17% federal, 1% state, 67% institutional, 15% external sources). ***Receiving aid:*** Freshmen: 47% (170); all full-time undergraduates: 52% (917). ***Average award:*** Freshmen: $6709; Undergraduates: $8686. ***Scholarships, grants, and awards:*** Federal Pell, FSEOG, state, private, college/university gift aid from institutional funds.

GIFT AID (NON-NEED-BASED) ***Receiving aid:*** Freshmen: 63% (228). Undergraduates: 63% (1,104). ***Average award:*** Freshmen: $8530. Undergraduates: $6861. ***Scholarships, grants, and awards by category:*** *Academic interests/achievement:* 1,696 awards ($8,835,556 total): general academic interests/achievements. *Creative arts/performance:* 58 awards ($56,488 total): music. *Special achievements/activities:* 221 awards ($286,470 total): leadership, religious involvement. *Special characteristics:* 115 awards ($1,106,232 total): children of faculty/staff, general special characteristics, international students. ***Tuition waivers:*** Full or partial for employees or children of employees, senior citizens.

LOANS ***Student loans:*** $18,975,252 (29% need-based, 71% non-need-based). 75% of past graduating class borrowed through all loan programs. *Average indebtedness per student:* $34,200. ***Average need-based loan:*** Freshmen: $3399. Undergraduates: $4681. ***Parent loans:*** $3,900,932 (100% non-need-based). ***Programs:*** Federal Direct (Subsidized and Unsubsidized Stafford, PLUS).

WORK-STUDY ***Federal work-study:*** Total amount: $569,829; 632 jobs averaging $902. ***State or other work-study/employment:*** Total amount: $247,595 (100% need-based). 272 part-time jobs averaging $910.

APPLYING FOR FINANCIAL AID ***Required financial aid forms:*** FAFSA, institution's own form. ***Financial aid deadline:*** Continuous.

CONTACT Cynthia Gammon, Assistant Director of Student Financial Services, Andrews University, Student Financial Services Administration Building, Berrien Springs, MI 49104, 800-253-2874. *Fax:* 269-471-3228. *E-mail:* sfs@andrews.edu.

ANGELO STATE UNIVERSITY

San Angelo, TX

Tuition & fees (TX res): $6692 **Average undergraduate aid package: $10,780**

ABOUT THE INSTITUTION State-supported, coed. 43 undergraduate majors. Federal methodology is used as a basis for awarding need-based institutional aid.

UNDERGRADUATE EXPENSES for 2011–12 ***Tuition, state resident:*** full-time $4560; part-time $152 per hour. ***Tuition, nonresident:*** full-time $13,860; part-time $462 per hour. ***Required fees:*** full-time $2132; $39 per hour or $572 per term. ***College room and board:*** $6666; ***Room only:*** $4066. Room and board charges vary according to board plan and housing facility. ***Payment plan:*** Installment.

FRESHMAN FINANCIAL AID (Fall 2010, est.) 1,079 applied for aid; of those 83% were deemed to have need. 98% of freshmen with need received aid; of those 20% had need fully met. ***Average percent of need met:*** 87% (excluding resources awarded to replace EFC). ***Average financial aid package:*** $10,796 (excluding resources awarded to replace EFC). 7% of all full-time freshmen had no need and received non-need-based gift aid.

UNDERGRADUATE FINANCIAL AID (Fall 2010, est.) 2,616 applied for aid; of those 84% were deemed to have need. 99% of undergraduates with need received aid; of those 20% had need fully met. ***Average percent of need met:*** 85% (excluding resources awarded to replace EFC). ***Average financial aid package:*** $10,780 (excluding resources awarded to replace EFC). 4% of all full-time undergraduates had no need and received non-need-based gift aid.

GIFT AID (NEED-BASED) ***Total amount:*** $47,038,462 (61% federal, 35% state, 4% institutional). ***Receiving aid:*** Freshmen: 57% (827); all full-time undergraduates: 35% (1,815). ***Average award:*** Freshmen: $3258; Undergraduates: $2986. ***Scholarships, grants, and awards:*** Federal Pell, FSEOG, state, private, college/university gift aid from institutional funds, Federal Nursing, Carr academic scholarships.

GIFT AID (NON-NEED-BASED) ***Total amount:*** $42,742,143 (62% federal, 30% institutional, 8% external sources). ***Receiving aid:*** Freshmen: 54% (774). Undergraduates: 36% (1,886). ***Average award:*** Freshmen: $2400. Undergraduates: $2815. ***Scholarships, grants, and awards by category:*** *Academic interests/achievement:* agriculture, biological sciences, business, communication, computer science, education, English, foreign languages, general academic interests/achievements, international studies, mathematics, military science, physical sciences, premedicine, social sciences. *Creative arts/performance:* art/fine arts, dance, journalism/publications, music, performing arts, theater/drama. *Special achievements/activities:* cheerleading/drum major, general special achievements/activities, hobbies/interests, leadership, memberships, rodeo. *Special characteristics:* first-generation college students, local/state students. ***Tuition waivers:*** Full or partial for employees or children of employees, senior citizens.

LOANS ***Student loans:*** $63,664,880 (48% need-based, 52% non-need-based). 43% of past graduating class borrowed through all loan programs. *Average indebtedness per student:* $10,712. ***Average need-based loan:*** Freshmen: $3079. Undergraduates: $3603. ***Parent loans:*** $19,775,248 (100% non-need-based). ***Programs:*** Perkins, Federal Nursing, state, college/university, alternative loans.

WORK-STUDY ***Federal work-study:*** Total amount: $13,523,336; jobs available. ***State or other work-study/employment:*** Total amount: $135,204 (100% need-based). Part-time jobs available.

ATHLETIC AWARDS Total amount: $2,595,481 (100% non-need-based).

APPLYING FOR FINANCIAL AID ***Required financial aid forms:*** FAFSA, institution's own form. ***Financial aid deadline (priority):*** 4/1. ***Notification date:*** Continuous.

CONTACT Ms. Michelle Bennett, Director of Financial Aid, Angelo State University, ASU Station #11015, San Angelo, TX 76909-1015, 325-942-2246 or toll-free 800-946-8627 (in-state). *Fax:* 325-942-2082. *E-mail:* michelle.bennett@angelo.edu.

ANNA MARIA COLLEGE

Paxton, MA

Tuition & fees: N/R **Average undergraduate aid package: $28,535**

ABOUT THE INSTITUTION Independent Roman Catholic, coed. 57 undergraduate majors. Federal methodology is used as a basis for awarding need-based institutional aid.

UNDERGRADUATE EXPENSES for 2011–12 ***Tuition:*** part-time $318 per credit hour. ***Required fees:*** $100 per credit hour. Full-time tuition and fees vary according to course load and program. Part-time tuition and fees vary according to class time, course load, and program. Room and board charges vary according to board plan and housing facility. ***Payment plan:*** Installment.

FRESHMAN FINANCIAL AID (Fall 2009) 251 applied for aid; of those 92% were deemed to have need. 100% of freshmen with need received aid; of those 18% had need fully met. ***Average percent of need met:*** 92% (excluding resources awarded to replace EFC). ***Average financial aid package:*** $28,791 (excluding resources awarded to replace EFC). 23% of all full-time freshmen had no need and received non-need-based gift aid.

UNDERGRADUATE FINANCIAL AID (Fall 2009) 1,001 applied for aid; of those 93% were deemed to have need. 100% of undergraduates with need received aid; of those 11% had need fully met. ***Average percent of need met:*** 92% (excluding resources awarded to replace EFC). ***Average financial aid package:*** $28,535 (excluding resources awarded to replace EFC). 5% of all full-time undergraduates had no need and received non-need-based gift aid.

GIFT AID (NEED-BASED) ***Total amount:*** $5,149,386 (35% federal, 12% state, 53% institutional). ***Receiving aid:*** Freshmen: 57% (157); all full-time undergraduates: 19% (213). ***Average award:*** Freshmen: $5588; Undergraduates: $5862. ***Scholarships, grants, and awards:*** Federal Pell, FSEOG, state, private, college/university gift aid from institutional funds.

GIFT AID (NON-NEED-BASED) ***Total amount:*** $4,970,530 (2% state, 98% institutional). ***Receiving aid:*** Freshmen: 52% (143). Undergraduates: 34% (390). ***Average award:*** Freshmen: $7450. Undergraduates: $7300. ***Scholarships, grants, and awards by category:*** *Academic interests/achievement:* $4,852,765 total: general academic interests/achievements. *Creative arts/performance:* $32,500 total: music. *Special achievements/activities:* $1,980,050 total: religious involvement. *Special characteristics:* $2,830,861 total: children and siblings of alumni, children of faculty/staff, children with a deceased or disabled parent, general special characteristics, local/state students, previous college experience, siblings of current students. ***Tuition waivers:*** Full or partial for employees or children of employees, senior citizens.

LOANS ***Student loans:*** $7,470,105 (50% need-based, 50% non-need-based). 77% of past graduating class borrowed through all loan programs. *Average indebtedness per student:* $36,200. ***Average need-based loan:*** Freshmen: $4598. Undergraduates: $4744. ***Parent loans:*** $1,996,632 (100% non-need-based). ***Programs:*** Federal Direct (Subsidized and Unsubsidized Stafford, PLUS), Perkins.

WORK-STUDY ***Federal work-study:*** Total amount: $111,328; 215 jobs averaging $454.

APPLYING FOR FINANCIAL AID ***Required financial aid form:*** FAFSA. ***Financial aid deadline (priority):*** 3/1. ***Notification date:*** Continuous beginning 4/1. Students must reply within 4 weeks of notification.

CONTACT Sandra J. Pereira, Director of Financial Aid, Anna Maria College, 50 Sunset Lane, Paxton, MA 01612-1198, 508-849-3363 or toll-free 800-344-4586 Ext. 360. *Fax:* 508-849-3229. *E-mail:* spereira@annamaria.edu.

ANTIOCH UNIVERSITY MIDWEST

Yellow Springs, OH

Tuition & fees: $21,080 **Average undergraduate aid package: $3263**

ABOUT THE INSTITUTION Independent, coed. 11 undergraduate majors. Federal methodology is used as a basis for awarding need-based institutional aid.

UNDERGRADUATE EXPENSES for 2010–11 ***Tuition:*** full-time $20,480; part-time $320 per credit hour. ***Required fees:*** full-time $600; $150 per term.

UNDERGRADUATE FINANCIAL AID (Fall 2010, est.) 52 applied for aid; of those 98% were deemed to have need. 100% of undergraduates with need received aid. ***Average percent of need met:*** 30% (excluding resources awarded to replace EFC). ***Average financial aid package:*** $3263 (excluding resources awarded to replace EFC).

GIFT AID (NEED-BASED) ***Total amount:*** $179,859 (81% federal, 19% state). ***Receiving aid:*** All full-time undergraduates: 75% (39). ***Average award:*** Undergraduates: $2300. ***Scholarships, grants, and awards:*** Federal Pell, FSEOG, state.

GIFT AID (NON-NEED-BASED) ***Total amount:*** $19,750 (91% federal, 9% external sources). ***Receiving aid:*** Undergraduates: 12% (6). ***Tuition waivers:*** Full or partial for employees or children of employees.

LOANS ***Student loans:*** $146,732 (43% need-based, 57% non-need-based). 88% of past graduating class borrowed through all loan programs. *Average* *indebtedness per student:* $23,000. ***Average need-based loan:*** Undergraduates: $5667. ***Programs:*** Federal Direct (Subsidized and Unsubsidized Stafford, PLUS), Perkins.

WORK-STUDY ***Federal work-study:*** Total amount: $58,032; 9 jobs averaging $2450.

APPLYING FOR FINANCIAL AID ***Required financial aid forms:*** FAFSA, institution's own form. ***Financial aid deadline:*** Continuous. ***Notification date:*** Continuous beginning 4/1.

CONTACT Diana Tomas, Financial Aid Coordinator, Antioch University Midwest, 900 Dayton Street, Yellow Springs, OH 45387, 937-769-1841. *Fax:* 937-769-1804. *E-mail:* kjohn@antioch.edu.

ANTIOCH UNIVERSITY SANTA BARBARA

Santa Barbara, CA

CONTACT Cecilia Schneider, Financial Aid Director, Antioch University Santa Barbara, 801 Garden Street, Santa Barbara, CA 93101-1580, 805-962-8179 Ext. 108. *Fax:* 805-962-4786.

ANTIOCH UNIVERSITY SEATTLE

Seattle, WA

CONTACT Katy Stahl, Director of Financial Aid, Antioch University Seattle, 2326 Sixth Avenue, Seattle, WA 98121-1814, 206-268-4004. *Fax:* 206-268-4242. *E-mail:* kstahl@antiochseattle.edu.

APEX SCHOOL OF THEOLOGY

Durham, NC

CONTACT Financial Aid Office, Apex School of Theology, 2945 South Miami Boulevard, Suite 114, Durham, NC 27703, 919-572-1625.

APPALACHIAN BIBLE COLLEGE

Bradley, WV

Tuition & fees: $10,934 **Average undergraduate aid package: $8477**

ABOUT THE INSTITUTION Independent nondenominational, coed. 2 undergraduate majors. Both federal and institutional methodology are used as a basis for awarding need-based institutional aid.

UNDERGRADUATE EXPENSES for 2010–11 ***Comprehensive fee:*** $16,724 includes full-time tuition ($9384), mandatory fees ($1550), and room and board ($5790). Full-time tuition and fees vary according to program. Room and board charges vary according to housing facility. ***Part-time fees:*** $391 per credit hour. Part-time tuition and fees vary according to program. ***Payment plans:*** Tuition prepayment, installment.

FRESHMAN FINANCIAL AID (Fall 2010, est.) 67 applied for aid; of those 93% were deemed to have need. 100% of freshmen with need received aid; of those 6% had need fully met. ***Average percent of need met:*** 53% (excluding resources awarded to replace EFC). ***Average financial aid package:*** $7665 (excluding resources awarded to replace EFC). 11% of all full-time freshmen had no need and received non-need-based gift aid.

UNDERGRADUATE FINANCIAL AID (Fall 2010, est.) 211 applied for aid; of those 92% were deemed to have need. 98% of undergraduates with need received aid; of those 6% had need fully met. ***Average percent of need met:*** 53% (excluding resources awarded to replace EFC). ***Average financial aid package:*** $8477 (excluding resources awarded to replace EFC). 7% of all full-time undergraduates had no need and received non-need-based gift aid.

GIFT AID (NEED-BASED) ***Total amount:*** $1,310,000 (47% federal, 12% state, 29% institutional, 12% external sources). ***Receiving aid:*** Freshmen: 85% (61); all full-time undergraduates: 83% (189). ***Average award:*** Freshmen: $6463; Undergraduates: $6867. ***Scholarships, grants, and awards:*** Federal Pell, FSEOG, state, private, college/university gift aid from institutional funds.

GIFT AID (NON-NEED-BASED) ***Total amount:*** $100,025 (26% state, 54% institutional, 20% external sources). ***Receiving aid:*** Freshmen: 6% (4). Undergraduates: 5% (11). ***Average award:*** Freshmen: $1028. Undergraduates: $1982. ***Scholarships, grants, and awards by category:*** *Academic interests/achievement:* 42 awards ($60,000 total): general academic interests/achievements, religion/biblical studies. *Special achievements/activities:* 1 award ($1000 total): general special achievements/activities, religious involvement. *Special characteristics:* 44 awards ($61,592 total): children and siblings of alumni, children of educators, children of faculty/staff, general special characteristics, international students, married students, relatives of clergy, religious affiliation, spouses of current students, veterans. ***Tuition waivers:*** Full or partial for children of alumni, employees or children of employees, adult students, senior citizens.

LOANS ***Student loans:*** $451,821 (94% need-based, 6% non-need-based). 56% of past graduating class borrowed through all loan programs. *Average indebtedness per student:* $10,585. ***Average need-based loan:*** Freshmen: $3375. Undergraduates: $3079. ***Parent loans:*** $33,600 (88% need-based, 12% non-need-based). ***Programs:*** Federal Direct (Subsidized and Unsubsidized Stafford, PLUS).

WORK-STUDY ***Federal work-study:*** Total amount: $16,508; 29 jobs averaging $569. ***State or other work-study/employment:*** Part-time jobs available.

APPLYING FOR FINANCIAL AID ***Required financial aid forms:*** FAFSA, institution's own form. ***Financial aid deadline:*** 6/15 (priority: 3/1). ***Notification date:*** Continuous. Students must reply by 7/30 or within 4 weeks of notification.

CONTACT Cindi Turner, Director of Financial Aid, Appalachian Bible College, 161 College Drive, Mount Hope, WV 25880, 304-877-6428 Ext. 3247 or toll-free 800-678-9ABC Ext. 3213. *Fax:* 304-877-5082. *E-mail:* cindi.turner@abc.edu.

APPALACHIAN STATE UNIVERSITY

Boone, NC

Tuition & fees (NC res): $5175 **Average undergraduate aid package: $9127**

ABOUT THE INSTITUTION State-supported, coed. 88 undergraduate majors. Federal methodology is used as a basis for awarding need-based institutional aid.

UNDERGRADUATE EXPENSES for 2011–12 ***Tuition, state resident:*** full-time $2961; part-time $100 per semester hour. ***Tuition, nonresident:*** full-time $14,273; part-time $482 per semester hour. ***Required fees:*** full-time $2214; $12.25 per semester hour. Part-time tuition and fees vary according to course load. ***College room and board:*** $6600; ***Room only:*** $3700. Room and board charges vary according to board plan and housing facility. ***Payment plan:*** Installment.

FRESHMAN FINANCIAL AID (Fall 2010, est.) 1,335 applied for aid; of those 99% were deemed to have need. 94% of freshmen with need received aid; of those 41% had need fully met. ***Average percent of need met:*** 78% (excluding resources awarded to replace EFC). ***Average financial aid package:*** $8509 (excluding resources awarded to replace EFC). 3% of all full-time freshmen had no need and received non-need-based gift aid.

UNDERGRADUATE FINANCIAL AID (Fall 2010, est.) 6,948 applied for aid; of those 98% were deemed to have need. 96% of undergraduates with need received aid; of those 42% had need fully met. ***Average percent of need met:*** 79% (excluding resources awarded to replace EFC). ***Average financial aid package:*** $9127 (excluding resources awarded to replace EFC). 3% of all full-time undergraduates had no need and received non-need-based gift aid.

GIFT AID (NEED-BASED) ***Total amount:*** $40,273,528 (41% federal, 40% state, 15% institutional, 4% external sources). ***Receiving aid:*** Freshmen: 39% (1,100); all full-time undergraduates: 41% (5,790). ***Average award:*** Freshmen: $7178; Undergraduates: $6935. ***Scholarships, grants, and awards:*** Federal Pell, FSEOG, state, private, college/university gift aid from institutional funds.

GIFT AID (NON-NEED-BASED) ***Total amount:*** $2,538,527 (2% federal, 17% state, 43% institutional, 38% external sources). ***Receiving aid:*** Freshmen: 24% (670). Undergraduates: 25% (3,618). ***Average award:*** Freshmen: $3067. Undergraduates: $2352. ***Scholarships, grants, and awards by category:*** *Academic interests/achievement:* 1,376 awards ($1,948,165 total): general academic interests/achievements. *Creative arts/performance:* general creative arts/performance. *Special achievements/activities:* general special achievements/activities. *Special characteristics:* first-generation college students, general special characteristics, handicapped students, members of minority groups, out-of-state students, veterans, veterans' children. ***Tuition waivers:*** Full or partial for employees or children of employees.

LOANS ***Student loans:*** $42,761,230 (74% need-based, 26% non-need-based). 55% of past graduating class borrowed through all loan programs. *Average indebtedness per student:* $16,130. ***Average need-based loan:*** Freshmen: $3116. Undergraduates: $4001. ***Parent loans:*** $18,847,342 (56% need-based, 44% non-need-based). ***Programs:*** Federal Direct (Subsidized and Unsubsidized Stafford, PLUS), Perkins.

WORK-STUDY ***Federal work-study:*** Total amount: $476,880; 289 jobs averaging $1619.

ATHLETIC AWARDS Total amount: $3,452,675 (42% need-based, 58% non-need-based).

APPLYING FOR FINANCIAL AID ***Required financial aid form:*** FAFSA. ***Financial aid deadline:*** Continuous. ***Notification date:*** Continuous beginning 4/1. Students must reply within 3 weeks of notification.

CONTACT Esther Manogin, Director of Student Financial Aid, Appalachian State University, John E. Thomas Hall, ASU Box 32059, Boone, NC 28608-2059, 828-262-2190. *Fax:* 828-262-2585. *E-mail:* manoginem@appstate.edu.

AQUINAS COLLEGE

Grand Rapids, MI

CONTACT David J. Steffee, Director, Financial Aid, Aquinas College, 1607 Robinson Road, Grand Rapids, MI 49506-1799, 616-459-8281 Ext. 5127 or toll-free 800-678-9593. *Fax:* 616-732-4547. *E-mail:* steffdav@aquinas.edu.

AQUINAS COLLEGE

Nashville, TN

Tuition & fees: $18,330 **Average undergraduate aid package: N/A**

ABOUT THE INSTITUTION Independent Roman Catholic, coed. 8 undergraduate majors. Federal methodology is used as a basis for awarding need-based institutional aid.

UNDERGRADUATE EXPENSES for 2010–11 ***Tuition:*** full-time $17,730; part-time $591 per credit hour. ***Required fees:*** full-time $600; $300 per term. Full-time tuition and fees vary according to course load and program. Part-time tuition and fees vary according to course load and program. ***Payment plan:*** Installment.

GIFT AID (NEED-BASED) ***Total amount:*** $1,128,506 (73% federal, 23% state, 4% institutional). ***Scholarships, grants, and awards:*** Federal Pell, FSEOG, state, private, college/university gift aid from institutional funds.

GIFT AID (NON-NEED-BASED) ***Total amount:*** $671,057 (36% state, 47% institutional, 17% external sources). ***Scholarships, grants, and awards by category:*** *Academic interests/achievement:* business, education, general academic interests/achievements, health fields. *Special achievements/activities:* leadership. *Special characteristics:* general special characteristics. ***Tuition waivers:*** Full or partial for employees or children of employees.

LOANS ***Student loans:*** $4,096,648 (40% need-based, 60% non-need-based). ***Parent loans:*** $225,559 (100% non-need-based). ***Programs:*** state, alternative loans.

WORK-STUDY ***Federal work-study:*** Total amount: $83,549; jobs available.

APPLYING FOR FINANCIAL AID ***Required financial aid form:*** FAFSA. ***Financial aid deadline (priority):*** 2/15. ***Notification date:*** Continuous beginning 3/1. Students must reply within 2 weeks of notification.

CONTACT Mrs. Kylie Pruitt, Director of Financial Aid, Aquinas College, 4210 Harding Road, Nashville, TN 37205-2005, 615-297-7545 Ext. 431 or toll-free 800-649-9956. *Fax:* 615-279-3891. *E-mail:* pruittk@aquinascollege.edu.

ARCADIA UNIVERSITY

Glenside, PA

Tuition & fees: $34,150 **Average undergraduate aid package: $22,693**

ABOUT THE INSTITUTION Independent religious, coed. 66 undergraduate majors. Federal methodology is used as a basis for awarding need-based institutional aid.

UNDERGRADUATE EXPENSES for 2011–12 ***Comprehensive fee:*** $45,790 includes full-time tuition ($33,490), mandatory fees ($660), and room and board ($11,640). Full-time tuition and fees vary according to course load, degree level, and program. Room and board charges vary according to board plan. ***Payment plans:*** Installment, deferred payment.

FRESHMAN FINANCIAL AID (Fall 2010, est.) 534 applied for aid; of those 92% were deemed to have need. 100% of freshmen with need received aid; of those 11% had need fully met. ***Average percent of need met:*** 55% (excluding resources awarded to replace EFC). ***Average financial aid package:*** $23,393 (excluding resources awarded to replace EFC). 12% of all full-time freshmen had no need and received non-need-based gift aid.

UNDERGRADUATE FINANCIAL AID (Fall 2010, est.) 1,868 applied for aid; of those 93% were deemed to have need. 100% of undergraduates with need received aid; of those 15% had need fully met. ***Average percent of need met:*** 63% (excluding resources awarded to replace EFC). ***Average financial aid package:*** $22,693 (excluding resources awarded to replace EFC). 12% of all full-time undergraduates had no need and received non-need-based gift aid.

GIFT AID (NEED-BASED) ***Total amount:*** $32,012,479 (12% federal, 5% state, 81% institutional, 2% external sources). ***Receiving aid:*** Freshmen: 88% (487); all full-time undergraduates: 78% (1,735). ***Average award:*** Freshmen: $20,027; Undergraduates: $18,407. ***Scholarships, grants, and awards:*** Federal Pell, FSEOG, state, private, college/university gift aid from institutional funds, Academic Competitiveness Grants, National SMART Grants, TEACH Grants.

GIFT AID (NON-NEED-BASED) ***Total amount:*** $5,308,832 (97% institutional, 3% external sources). ***Receiving aid:*** Freshmen: 7% (37). Undergraduates: 9% (197). ***Average award:*** Freshmen: $14,391. Undergraduates: $14,100. ***Scholarships, grants, and awards by category:*** *Academic interests/achievement:* 1,700 awards ($19,469,688 total): general academic interests/achievements. *Creative arts/performance:* 29 awards ($22,200 total): applied art and design, art/fine arts, theater/drama. *Special achievements/activities:* 755 awards ($6,591,540 total): community service, general special achievements/activities, leadership, memberships. *Special characteristics:* 21 awards ($61,500 total): children and siblings of alumni, relatives of clergy, religious affiliation. ***Tuition waivers:*** Full or partial for children of alumni, employees or children of employees.

LOANS ***Student loans:*** $19,076,272 (73% need-based, 27% non-need-based). 76% of past graduating class borrowed through all loan programs. *Average indebtedness per student:* $33,765. ***Average need-based loan:*** Freshmen: $3166. Undergraduates: $4137. ***Parent loans:*** $5,422,050 (50% need-based, 50% non-need-based). ***Programs:*** Federal Direct (Subsidized and Unsubsidized Stafford, PLUS), Perkins.

WORK-STUDY ***Federal work-study:*** Total amount: $1,951,512; 1,185 jobs averaging $1626. ***State or other work-study/employment:*** Total amount: $260,824 (100% non-need-based). 176 part-time jobs averaging $1575.

APPLYING FOR FINANCIAL AID ***Required financial aid forms:*** FAFSA, institution's own form. ***Financial aid deadline (priority):*** 3/1. ***Notification date:*** Continuous beginning 3/1. Students must reply by 5/1.

CONTACT Holly Kirkpatrick, Director of Financial Aid, Arcadia University, 450 South Easton Road, Glenside, PA 19038, 215-572-4475 or toll-free 877-ARCADIA. *Fax:* 215-572-4049. *E-mail:* kirkpath@arcadia.edu.

ARGOSY UNIVERSITY, ATLANTA

Atlanta, GA

UNDERGRADUATE EXPENSES Tuition varies by program. Students should contact Argosy University for tuition information.

CONTACT Financial Aid Office, Argosy University, Atlanta, 980 Hammond Drive, Suite 100, Atlanta, GA 30328, 770-671-1200 or toll-free 888-671-4777.

ARGOSY UNIVERSITY, CHICAGO

Chicago, IL

UNDERGRADUATE EXPENSES Tuition varies by program. Students should contact Argosy University for tuition information.

CONTACT Financial Aid Office, Argosy University, Chicago, 225 North Michigan Avenue, Suite 1300, Chicago, IL 60601, 312-777-7600 or toll-free 800-626-4123.

ARGOSY UNIVERSITY, DALLAS

Farmers Branch, TX

UNDERGRADUATE EXPENSES Tuition varies by program. Students should contact Argosy University for tuition information.

CONTACT Financial Aid Office, Argosy University, Dallas, 5001 Lyndon B. Johnson Freeway, Heritage Square, Farmers Branch, TX 75244, 214-890-9900 or toll-free 866-954-9900.

ARGOSY UNIVERSITY, DENVER

Denver, CO

UNDERGRADUATE EXPENSES Tuition varies by program. Students should contact Argosy University for tuition information.

CONTACT Financial Aid Office, Argosy University, Denver, 7600 East Eastman Avenue, Denver, CO 80231, 303-923-4110 or toll-free 866-431-5981.

ARGOSY UNIVERSITY, HAWAI'I

Honolulu, HI

UNDERGRADUATE EXPENSES Tuition varies by program. Students should contact Argosy University for tuition information.

CONTACT Financial Aid Office, Argosy University, Hawai'i, 400 ASB Tower, 1001 Bishop Street, Honolulu, HI 96813, 808-536-5555 or toll-free 888-323-2777.

ARGOSY UNIVERSITY, INLAND EMPIRE

San Bernardino, CA

UNDERGRADUATE EXPENSES Tuition varies by program. Students should contact Argosy University for tuition information.

CONTACT Financial Aid Office, Argosy University, Inland Empire, 636 East Brier Drive, Suite 120, San Bernardino, CA 92408, 909-915-3800 or toll-free 866-217-9075.

ARGOSY UNIVERSITY, NASHVILLE

Nashville, TN

UNDERGRADUATE EXPENSES Tuition varies by program. Students should contact Argosy University for tuition information.

CONTACT Financial Aid Office, Argosy University, Nashville, 100 Centerview Drive, Suite 225, Nashville, TN 37214, 615-525-2800 or toll-free 866-833-6598 (out-of-state).

ARGOSY UNIVERSITY, ORANGE COUNTY

Orange, CA

UNDERGRADUATE EXPENSES Tuition varies by program. Students should contact Argosy University for tuition information.

CONTACT Financial Aid Office, Argosy University, Orange County, 601 South Lewis Street, Orange, CA 92868, 714-338-6200 or toll-free 800-716-9598.

ARGOSY UNIVERSITY, PHOENIX

Phoenix, AZ

UNDERGRADUATE EXPENSES Tuition varies by program. Students should contact Argosy University for tuition information.

CONTACT Financial Aid Office, Argosy University, Phoenix, 2233 West Dunlap Avenue, Phoenix, AZ 85021, 602-216-2600 or toll-free 866-216-2777.

ARGOSY UNIVERSITY, SALT LAKE CITY

Draper, UT

UNDERGRADUATE EXPENSES Tuition varies by program. Students should contact Argosy University for tuition information.

CONTACT Financial Aid Office, Argosy University, Salt Lake City, 121 West Election Road, Suite 300, Draper, UT 84020, toll-free 888-639-4756.

ARGOSY UNIVERSITY, SAN DIEGO

San Diego, CA

UNDERGRADUATE EXPENSES Tuition varies by program. Students should contact Argosy University for tuition information.

CONTACT Financial Aid Office, Argosy University, San Diego, 1615 Murray Canyon Road, Suite 100, San Diego, CA 92108, 619-321-3000 or toll-free 866-505-0333.

ARGOSY UNIVERSITY, SAN FRANCISCO BAY AREA

Alameda, CA

UNDERGRADUATE EXPENSES Tuition varies by program. Students should contact Argosy University for tuition information.

CONTACT Financial Aid Office, Argosy University, San Francisco Bay Area, 1005 Atlantic Avenue, Alameda, CA 94501, 510-217-4700 or toll-free 866-215-2777.

ARGOSY UNIVERSITY, SARASOTA

Sarasota, FL

UNDERGRADUATE EXPENSES Tuition varies by program. Students should contact Argosy University for tuition information.

CONTACT Financial Aid Office, Argosy University, Sarasota, 5250 17th Street, Sarasota, FL 34235, 941-379-0404 or toll-free 800-331-5995.

ARGOSY UNIVERSITY, SCHAUMBURG

Schaumburg, IL

UNDERGRADUATE EXPENSES Tuition varies by program. Students should contact Argosy University for tuition information.

CONTACT Financial Aid Office, Argosy University, Schaumburg, 999 North Plaza Drive, Suite 111, Schaumburg, IL 60173-5403, 847-969-4900 or toll-free 866-290-2777.

ARGOSY UNIVERSITY, SEATTLE

Seattle, WA

UNDERGRADUATE EXPENSES Tuition varies by program. Students should contact Argosy University for tuition information.

CONTACT Financial Aid Office, Argosy University, Seattle, 2601-A Elliott Avenue, Seattle, WA 98121, 206-283-4500 or toll-free 866-283-2777.

ARGOSY UNIVERSITY, TAMPA

Tampa, FL

UNDERGRADUATE EXPENSES Tuition varies by program. Students should contact Argosy University for tuition information.

CONTACT Financial Aid Office, Argosy University, Tampa, 1403 North Howard Avenue, Tampa, FL 33607, 813-393-5290 or toll-free 800-850-6488.

ARGOSY UNIVERSITY, TWIN CITIES

Eagan, MN

UNDERGRADUATE EXPENSES Tuition varies by program. Students should contact Argosy University for tuition information.

CONTACT Financial Aid Office, Argosy University, Twin Cities, 1515 Central Parkway, Eagan, MN 55121, 651-846-2882 or toll-free 888-844-2004.

ARGOSY UNIVERSITY, WASHINGTON DC

Arlington, VA

UNDERGRADUATE EXPENSES Tuition varies by program. Students should contact Argosy University for tuition information.

CONTACT Financial Aid Office, Argosy University, Washington DC, 1550 Wilson Boulevard, Suite 600, Arlington, VA 22209, 703-526-5800 or toll-free 866-703-2777.

ARIZONA CHRISTIAN UNIVERSITY

Phoenix, AZ

Tuition & fees: $15,854 **Average undergraduate aid package: $10,878**

ABOUT THE INSTITUTION Independent Conservative Baptist, coed. ***Awards:*** associate and bachelor's degrees. 7 undergraduate majors. ***Total enrollment:*** 361. Undergraduates: 361. Federal methodology is used as a basis for awarding need-based institutional aid.

UNDERGRADUATE EXPENSES for 2010–11 ***Application fee:*** $30. ***Comprehensive fee:*** $22,634 includes full-time tuition ($15,264), mandatory fees ($590), and room and board ($6780). ***College room only:*** $4444. Full-time tuition and fees vary according to course load and program. Room and board charges vary according to board plan and student level. Part-time tuition and fees vary according to course load and program. ***Payment plan:*** Installment.

FRESHMAN FINANCIAL AID (Fall 2009) 84 applied for aid; of those 100% were deemed to have need. 100% of freshmen with need received aid. ***Average financial aid package:*** $13,085 (excluding resources awarded to replace EFC).
UNDERGRADUATE FINANCIAL AID (Fall 2009) 377 applied for aid; of those 100% were deemed to have need. 100% of undergraduates with need received aid. ***Average financial aid package:*** $10,878 (excluding resources awarded to replace EFC).
GIFT AID (NEED-BASED) ***Total amount:*** $1,266,337 (48% federal, 40% state, 12% external sources). ***Receiving aid:*** Freshmen: 100% (84); all full-time undergraduates: 95% (377). ***Average award:*** Freshmen: $10,440; Undergraduates: $8327. ***Scholarships, grants, and awards:*** Federal Pell, FSEOG, state, private, college/university gift aid from institutional funds.
GIFT AID (NON-NEED-BASED) ***Total amount:*** $1,961,633 (5% federal, 95% institutional). ***Receiving aid:*** Freshmen: 99% (83). Undergraduates: 90% (356). ***Scholarships, grants, and awards by category:*** *Academic interests/achievement:* 235 awards ($827,550 total): general academic interests/achievements, religion/biblical studies. *Creative arts/performance:* 40 awards ($92,950 total): music. *Special achievements/activities:* 38 awards ($375,000 total): community service, general special achievements/activities, leadership, religious involvement. *Special characteristics:* 145 awards ($241,400 total): adult students, children and siblings of alumni, children of educators, children of faculty/staff, ethnic background, international students, members of minority groups, previous college experience, relatives of clergy, siblings of current students, spouses of current students, twins, veterans, veterans' children. ***Tuition waivers:*** Full or partial for employees or children of employees. ***ROTC:*** Air Force cooperative.
LOANS ***Student loans:*** $2,365,577 (41% need-based, 59% non-need-based). 65% of past graduating class borrowed through all loan programs. *Average indebtedness per student:* $21,801. ***Average need-based loan:*** Freshmen: $3258. Undergraduates: $4013. ***Parent loans:*** $236,783 (100% need-based). ***Programs:*** Federal Direct (Subsidized and Unsubsidized Stafford, PLUS).
WORK-STUDY ***Federal work-study:*** Total amount: $42,653; 32 jobs averaging $1333.
ATHLETIC AWARDS Total amount: $163,800 (100% need-based).
APPLYING FOR FINANCIAL AID ***Required financial aid forms:*** FAFSA, institution's own form. ***Financial aid deadline (priority):*** 3/1. ***Notification date:*** Continuous beginning 4/15. Students must reply by 6/1 or within 2 weeks of notification.
CONTACT Ms. Jill Golike, Director of Financial Aid, Arizona Christian University, 2625 East Cactus Road, Phoenix, AZ 85032-7097, 602-489-5300 Ext. 115 or toll-free 800-247-2697. *Fax:* 800-971-3688. *E-mail:* jill.golike@arizonachristian.edu.

ARIZONA STATE UNIVERSITY

Tempe, AZ

Tuition & fees (AZ res): $8132 **Average undergraduate aid package: $11,482**

ABOUT THE INSTITUTION State-supported, coed. 126 undergraduate majors. Federal methodology is used as a basis for awarding need-based institutional aid.
UNDERGRADUATE EXPENSES for 2010–11 ***Tuition, state resident:*** full-time $7793; part-time $557 per credit hour. ***Tuition, nonresident:*** full-time $20,257; part-time $844 per credit hour. ***Required fees:*** full-time $339; $110 per term. Full-time tuition and fees vary according to program. Part-time tuition and fees vary according to program. ***College room and board:*** $9706; ***Room only:*** $5640. Room and board charges vary according to board plan, housing facility, and location. ***Payment plan:*** Installment.
FRESHMAN FINANCIAL AID (Fall 2009) 6,088 applied for aid; of those 79% were deemed to have need. 100% of freshmen with need received aid; of those 24% had need fully met. ***Average percent of need met:*** 70% (excluding resources awarded to replace EFC). ***Average financial aid package:*** $12,473 (excluding resources awarded to replace EFC). 18% of all full-time freshmen had no need and received non-need-based gift aid.
UNDERGRADUATE FINANCIAL AID (Fall 2009) 26,685 applied for aid; of those 86% were deemed to have need. 100% of undergraduates with need received aid; of those 17% had need fully met. ***Average percent of need met:*** 60% (excluding resources awarded to replace EFC). ***Average financial aid package:*** $11,482 (excluding resources awarded to replace EFC). 13% of all full-time undergraduates had no need and received non-need-based gift aid.
GIFT AID (NEED-BASED) ***Total amount:*** $181,384,352 (43% federal, 1% state, 49% institutional, 7% external sources). ***Receiving aid:*** Freshmen: 54% (4,474); all full-time undergraduates: 44% (20,084). ***Average award:*** Freshmen: $9898; Undergraduates: $8016. ***Scholarships, grants, and awards:*** Federal Pell, FSEOG, state, private, college/university gift aid from institutional funds, Federal Nursing.
GIFT AID (NON-NEED-BASED) ***Total amount:*** $62,359,833 (2% federal, 85% institutional, 13% external sources). ***Receiving aid:*** Freshmen: 9% (721). Undergraduates: 4% (1,698). ***Average award:*** Freshmen: $7923. Undergraduates: $7722. ***Scholarships, grants, and awards by category:*** *Academic interests/achievement:* architecture, area/ethnic studies, biological sciences, business, communication, computer science, education, engineering/technologies, English, foreign languages, general academic interests/achievements, health fields, humanities, mathematics, military science, physical sciences, premedicine, social sciences. *Creative arts/performance:* applied art and design, art/fine arts, cinema/film/broadcasting, creative writing, dance, debating, general creative arts/performance, journalism/publications, music, performing arts, theater/drama. *Special achievements/activities:* general special achievements/activities. ***Tuition waivers:*** Full or partial for employees or children of employees.
LOANS ***Student loans:*** $184,850,683 (76% need-based, 24% non-need-based). 46% of past graduating class borrowed through all loan programs. *Average indebtedness per student:* $18,542. ***Average need-based loan:*** Freshmen: $2771. Undergraduates: $3969. ***Parent loans:*** $61,138,656 (39% need-based, 61% non-need-based). ***Programs:*** Federal Direct (Subsidized and Unsubsidized Stafford, PLUS), Perkins, Federal Nursing, state.
WORK-STUDY ***Federal work-study:*** Total amount: $1,990,729; 954 jobs averaging $2087. ***State or other work-study/employment:*** Total amount: $20,814,052 (30% need-based, 70% non-need-based). 6,235 part-time jobs averaging $3338.
ATHLETIC AWARDS Total amount: $6,017,562 (37% need-based, 63% non-need-based).
APPLYING FOR FINANCIAL AID ***Required financial aid form:*** FAFSA. ***Financial aid deadline (priority):*** 3/1. ***Notification date:*** Continuous.
CONTACT Craig Fennell, Director of Student Financial Assistance, Arizona State University, Box 870412, Tempe, AZ 85287-0412, 480-965-3355. *Fax:* 480-965-9484. *E-mail:* financialaid@asu.edu.

ARKANSAS BAPTIST COLLEGE

Little Rock, AR

CONTACT Office of Financial Aid, Arkansas Baptist College, 1600 Bishop Street, Little Rock, AR 72202-6067, 501-374-7856.

ARKANSAS STATE UNIVERSITY

Jonesboro, AR

Tuition & fees (AR res): $6640 **Average undergraduate aid package: $12,100**

ABOUT THE INSTITUTION State-supported, coed. 71 undergraduate majors. Both federal and institutional methodology are used as a basis for awarding need-based institutional aid.
UNDERGRADUATE EXPENSES for 2010–11 ***Tuition, state resident:*** full-time $5100; part-time $170 per credit hour. ***Tuition, nonresident:*** full-time $13,320; part-time $444 per credit hour. ***Required fees:*** full-time $1540; $49 per credit hour or $25 per term. Full-time tuition and fees vary according to course load, location, and program. Part-time tuition and fees vary according to course load, location, and program. ***College room and board:*** $6544. Room and board charges vary according to board plan, housing facility, and student level. ***Payment plan:*** Installment.
FRESHMAN FINANCIAL AID (Fall 2010, est.) 1,527 applied for aid; of those 85% were deemed to have need. 100% of freshmen with need received aid; of those 38% had need fully met. ***Average percent of need met:*** 61% (excluding resources awarded to replace EFC). ***Average financial aid package:*** $11,400 (excluding resources awarded to replace EFC). 12% of all full-time freshmen had no need and received non-need-based gift aid.
UNDERGRADUATE FINANCIAL AID (Fall 2010, est.) 7,468 applied for aid; of those 80% were deemed to have need. 97% of undergraduates with need received aid; of those 26% had need fully met. ***Average percent of need met:*** 50% (excluding resources awarded to replace EFC). ***Average financial aid package:*** $12,100 (excluding resources awarded to replace EFC). 7% of all full-time undergraduates had no need and received non-need-based gift aid.
GIFT AID (NEED-BASED) ***Total amount:*** $46,725,000 (45% federal, 18% state, 29% institutional, 8% external sources). ***Receiving aid:*** Freshmen: 75% (1,280); all full-time undergraduates: 52% (4,947). ***Average award:*** Freshmen: $6950;

Undergraduates: $6000. ***Scholarships, grants, and awards:*** Federal Pell, FSEOG, state, private, college/university gift aid from institutional funds.

GIFT AID (NON-NEED-BASED) ***Receiving aid:*** Freshmen: 34% (589). Undergraduates: 27% (2,516). ***Average award:*** Freshmen: $5500. Undergraduates: $6500. ***Scholarships, grants, and awards by category:*** *Academic interests/achievement:* 1,655 awards ($10,376,037 total): agriculture, area/ethnic studies, biological sciences, business, communication, computer science, education, engineering/technologies, English, general academic interests/achievements, health fields, humanities, library science, mathematics, military science, physical sciences, premedicine, social sciences. *Creative arts/performance:* 320 awards ($779,072 total): art/fine arts, cinema/film/broadcasting, debating, journalism/publications, music, performing arts, theater/drama. *Special achievements/activities:* 98 awards ($141,228 total): cheerleading/drum major, community service, general special achievements/activities, leadership. *Special characteristics:* 120 awards ($419,991 total): adult students, children and siblings of alumni, children of faculty/staff, ethnic background, first-generation college students, general special characteristics, handicapped students, local/state students, members of minority groups, out-of-state students, veterans, veterans' children. ***Tuition waivers:*** Full or partial for employees or children of employees, senior citizens.

LOANS ***Student loans:*** $45,800,000 (67% need-based, 33% non-need-based). 68% of past graduating class borrowed through all loan programs. *Average indebtedness per student:* $19,000. ***Average need-based loan:*** Freshmen: $5800. Undergraduates: $8600. ***Programs:*** Federal Direct (Subsidized and Unsubsidized Stafford, PLUS), Perkins.

WORK-STUDY ***Federal work-study:*** Total amount: $800,000; 200 jobs averaging $3000. ***State or other work-study/employment:*** Total amount: $2,500,000 (100% non-need-based). 300 part-time jobs averaging $3500.

ATHLETIC AWARDS Total amount: $3,850,000 (74% need-based, 26% non-need-based).

APPLYING FOR FINANCIAL AID ***Required financial aid forms:*** FAFSA, institution's own form. ***Financial aid deadline:*** 7/1 (priority: 2/15). ***Notification date:*** Continuous beginning 6/1. Students must reply within 2 weeks of notification.

CONTACT Mr. Terry Finney, Director of Financial Aid, Arkansas State University, PO Box 1620, State University, AR 72467, 870-972-2310 or toll-free 800-382-3030 (in-state). *Fax:* 870-972-2794. *E-mail:* finaid@astate.edu.

ARKANSAS TECH UNIVERSITY

Russellville, AR

Tuition & fees (AR res): $5908   Average undergraduate aid package: $8635

ABOUT THE INSTITUTION State-supported, coed. 60 undergraduate majors. Federal methodology is used as a basis for awarding need-based institutional aid.

UNDERGRADUATE EXPENSES for 2010–11 ***Tuition, state resident:*** full-time $5100; part-time $170 per credit hour. ***Tuition, nonresident:*** full-time $10,200; part-time $340 per credit hour. ***Required fees:*** full-time $808; $14 per credit hour or $388 per term. Full-time tuition and fees vary according to course load and location. Part-time tuition and fees vary according to course load and location. ***College room and board:*** $5270; ***Room only:*** $3144. Room and board charges vary according to board plan, housing facility, and location. ***Payment plans:*** Installment, deferred payment.

FRESHMAN FINANCIAL AID (Fall 2009) 1,469 applied for aid; of those 77% were deemed to have need. 98% of freshmen with need received aid; of those 20% had need fully met. ***Average percent of need met:*** 72% (excluding resources awarded to replace EFC). ***Average financial aid package:*** $8860 (excluding resources awarded to replace EFC). 24% of all full-time freshmen had no need and received non-need-based gift aid.

UNDERGRADUATE FINANCIAL AID (Fall 2009) 4,943 applied for aid; of those 83% were deemed to have need. 98% of undergraduates with need received aid; of those 20% had need fully met. ***Average percent of need met:*** 72% (excluding resources awarded to replace EFC). ***Average financial aid package:*** $8635 (excluding resources awarded to replace EFC). 16% of all full-time undergraduates had no need and received non-need-based gift aid.

GIFT AID (NEED-BASED) ***Total amount:*** $19,572,314 (87% federal, 13% state). ***Receiving aid:*** Freshmen: 57% (988); all full-time undergraduates: 53% (3,375). ***Average award:*** Freshmen: $4619; Undergraduates: $4884. ***Scholarships, grants, and awards:*** Federal Pell, FSEOG, state, private.

GIFT AID (NON-NEED-BASED) ***Total amount:*** $16,113,350 (9% state, 83% institutional, 8% external sources). ***Receiving aid:*** Freshmen: 35% (604). Undergraduates: 20% (1,271). ***Average award:*** Freshmen: $6695. Undergraduates: $7183. ***Scholarships, grants, and awards by category:*** *Academic interests/achievement:* agriculture, biological sciences, business, computer science, education, English, general academic interests/achievements, health fields, mathematics, military science, physical sciences, social sciences. *Creative arts/performance:* art/fine arts, cinema/film/broadcasting, creative writing, music. *Special achievements/activities:* cheerleading/drum major, community service, general special achievements/activities, hobbies/interests, leadership. ***Tuition waivers:*** Full or partial for employees or children of employees, senior citizens.

LOANS ***Student loans:*** $29,285,963 (48% need-based, 52% non-need-based). 57% of past graduating class borrowed through all loan programs. *Average indebtedness per student:* $16,363. ***Average need-based loan:*** Freshmen: $2871. Undergraduates: $3756. ***Parent loans:*** $881,531 (100% non-need-based). ***Programs:*** Federal Direct (Subsidized and Unsubsidized Stafford, PLUS), Perkins.

WORK-STUDY ***Federal work-study:*** Total amount: $341,521; jobs available. ***State or other work-study/employment:*** Total amount: $423,313 (27% need-based, 73% non-need-based). Part-time jobs available.

ATHLETIC AWARDS Total amount: $1,018,904 (100% non-need-based).

APPLYING FOR FINANCIAL AID ***Required financial aid forms:*** FAFSA, institution's own form. ***Financial aid deadline (priority):*** 4/15. ***Notification date:*** Continuous beginning 5/1. Students must reply within 2 weeks of notification.

CONTACT Financial Aid Office, Arkansas Tech University, 1605 Coliseum Drive, Suite 117, Russellville, AR 72801, 479-968-0399 or toll-free 800-582-6953. *Fax:* 479-964-0857. *E-mail:* fa.help@atu.edu.

ARLINGTON BAPTIST COLLEGE

Arlington, TX

CONTACT Mr. David B. Clogston Jr., Business Manager, Arlington Baptist College, 3001 West Division Street, Arlington, TX 76012-3425, 817-461-8741 Ext. 110. *Fax:* 817-274-1138.

ARMSTRONG ATLANTIC STATE UNIVERSITY

Savannah, GA

Tuition & fees (GA res): $4510   Average undergraduate aid package: $7750

ABOUT THE INSTITUTION State-supported, coed. 33 undergraduate majors. Federal methodology is used as a basis for awarding need-based institutional aid.

UNDERGRADUATE EXPENSES for 2010–11 ***Tuition, state resident:*** full-time $3432; part-time $143 per credit hour. ***Tuition, nonresident:*** full-time $12,720; part-time $530 per credit hour. ***Required fees:*** full-time $1078; $539 per term. Full-time tuition and fees vary according to location and program. Part-time tuition and fees vary according to location and program. ***College room and board:*** $8440; ***Room only:*** $5590. Room and board charges vary according to board plan and housing facility.

FRESHMAN FINANCIAL AID (Fall 2009) 872 applied for aid; of those 75% were deemed to have need. 75% of freshmen with need received aid; of those 82% had need fully met. ***Average percent of need met:*** 82% (excluding resources awarded to replace EFC). ***Average financial aid package:*** $6500 (excluding resources awarded to replace EFC). 20% of all full-time freshmen had no need and received non-need-based gift aid.

UNDERGRADUATE FINANCIAL AID (Fall 2009) 4,275 applied for aid; of those 66% were deemed to have need. 75% of undergraduates with need received aid; of those 82% had need fully met. ***Average percent of need met:*** 82% (excluding resources awarded to replace EFC). ***Average financial aid package:*** $7750 (excluding resources awarded to replace EFC). 17% of all full-time undergraduates had no need and received non-need-based gift aid.

GIFT AID (NEED-BASED) ***Total amount:*** $12,164,819 (100% federal). ***Receiving aid:*** Freshmen: 40% (392); all full-time undergraduates: 32% (1,700). ***Average award:*** Freshmen: $4000; Undergraduates: $4000. ***Scholarships, grants, and awards:*** Federal Pell, FSEOG, state, private, college/university gift aid from institutional funds, Federal Nursing.

GIFT AID (NON-NEED-BASED) ***Total amount:*** $8,405,081 (84% state, 2% institutional, 14% external sources). ***Receiving aid:*** Freshmen: 49% (474). Undergraduates: 40% (2,092). ***Average award:*** Freshmen: $3000. Undergraduates: $3000. ***Scholarships, grants, and awards by category:*** *Academic interests/achievement:* biological sciences, computer science, education, engineering/technologies, English, foreign languages, general academic interests/

achievements, health fields, humanities, international studies, mathematics, military science, physical sciences. *Creative arts/performance:* art/fine arts, general creative arts/performance, music. *Special achievements/activities:* community service. *Special characteristics:* ethnic background, international students, religious affiliation. ***Tuition waivers:*** Full or partial for employees or children of employees, senior citizens.

LOANS ***Student loans:*** $30,676,584 (54% need-based, 46% non-need-based). 47% of past graduating class borrowed through all loan programs. *Average indebtedness per student:* $19,000. ***Average need-based loan:*** Freshmen: $4500. Undergraduates: $4500. ***Parent loans:*** $802,620 (100% non-need-based). ***Programs:*** Federal Direct (Subsidized and Unsubsidized Stafford, PLUS), college/university, alternative loans.

WORK-STUDY ***Federal work-study:*** Total amount: $317,059; jobs available. ***State or other work-study/employment:*** Total amount: $84,990 (100% non-need-based). Part-time jobs available.

ATHLETIC AWARDS Total amount: $1,023,280 (100% non-need-based).

APPLYING FOR FINANCIAL AID ***Required financial aid forms:*** FAFSA, scholarship application form. ***Financial aid deadline (priority):*** 3/15. ***Notification date:*** Continuous beginning 2/1. Students must reply by 4/15 or within 6 weeks of notification.

CONTACT Lee Ann Kirkland, Director of Financial Aid, Armstrong Atlantic State University, 11935 Abercorn Street, Savannah, GA 31419-1997, 912-344-2614 or toll-free 800-633-2349. *Fax:* 912-344-3448. *E-mail:* finaid@armstrong.edu.

ART ACADEMY OF CINCINNATI

Cincinnati, OH

CONTACT Ms. Karen Geiger, Director of Financial Aid, Art Academy of Cincinnati, 1212 Jackson Street, Cincinnati, OH 45202, 513-562-8773 or toll-free 800-323-5692 (in-state). *Fax:* 513-562-8778. *E-mail:* financialaid@artacademy.edu.

ART CENTER COLLEGE OF DESIGN

Pasadena, CA

CONTACT Clema McKenzie, Director of Financial Aid, Art Center College of Design, 1700 Lida Street, Pasadena, CA 91103-1999, 626-396-2215. *Fax:* 626-683-8684.

THE ART CENTER DESIGN COLLEGE

Tucson, AZ

CONTACT Financial Aid Office, The Art Center Design College, 2525 North Country Club Road, Tucson, AZ 85716-2505, 520-325-0123 or toll-free 800-825-8753.

THE ART INSTITUTE OF ATLANTA

Atlanta, GA

UNDERGRADUATE EXPENSES Tuition cost varies by program. Prospective students should contact the school for current tuition costs. Other charges include a starting kit for all first-quarter students. Kits vary in price, depending on the program of study.

CONTACT Financial Aid Office, The Art Institute of Atlanta, 6600 Peachtree Dunwoody Road, NE, 100 Embassy Row, Atlanta, GA 30328, 770-394-8300 or toll-free 800-275-4242.

THE ART INSTITUTE OF ATLANTA–DECATUR

Decatur, GA

UNDERGRADUATE EXPENSES Tuition cost varies by program. Prospective students should contact the school for current tuition costs. Other charges include a starting kit for all first-quarter students. Kits vary in price, depending on the program of study.

CONTACT Financial Aid Office, The Art Institute of Atlanta–Decatur, One West Court Square, Suite 110, Decatur, GA 30030, toll-free 866-856-6203.

THE ART INSTITUTE OF AUSTIN

Austin, TX

UNDERGRADUATE EXPENSES Tuition cost varies by program. Prospective students should contact the school for current tuition costs. Other charges include a starting kit for all first-quarter students. Kits vary in price, depending on the program of study.

CONTACT Financial Aid Office, The Art Institute of Austin, 101 W. Louis Henna Boulevard, Suite 100, Austin, TX 78728, 512-691-1707 or toll-free 866-583-7952.

THE ART INSTITUTE OF CALIFORNIA–HOLLYWOOD

North Hollywood, CA

UNDERGRADUATE EXPENSES Tuition cost varies by program. Prospective students should contact the school for current tuition costs. Other charges include a starting kit for all first-quarter students. Kits vary in price, depending on the program of study.

CONTACT Financial Aid Office, The Art Institute of California–Hollywood, 3440 Wilshire Boulevard, Seventh Floor, Los Angeles, CA 90010, 213-251-3636 Ext. 209 or toll-free 877-468-6232. *Fax:* 213-385-3545. *E-mail:* jason@cdc.edu.

THE ART INSTITUTE OF CALIFORNIA–INLAND EMPIRE

San Bernardino, CA

UNDERGRADUATE EXPENSES Tuition cost varies by program. Prospective students should contact the school for current tuition costs. Other charges include a starting kit for all first-quarter students. Kits vary in price, depending on the program of study.

CONTACT Financial Aid Office, The Art Institute of California–Inland Empire, 674 East Brier Drive, San Bernardino, CA 92408, 909-915-2100 or toll-free 800-353-0812.

THE ART INSTITUTE OF CALIFORNIA–LOS ANGELES

Santa Monica, CA

UNDERGRADUATE EXPENSES Tuition cost varies by program. Prospective students should contact the school for current tuition costs. Other charges include a starting kit for all first-quarter students. Kits vary in price, depending on the program of study.

CONTACT Financial Aid Office, The Art Institute of California–Los Angeles, 2900 31st Street, Santa Monica, CA 90405-3035, 310-752-4700 or toll-free 888-646-4610.

THE ART INSTITUTE OF CALIFORNIA–ORANGE COUNTY

Santa Ana, CA

UNDERGRADUATE EXPENSES Tuition cost varies by program. Prospective students should contact the school for current tuition costs. Other charges include a starting kit for all first-quarter students. Kits vary in price, depending on the program of study.

CONTACT Financial Aid Office, The Art Institute of California–Orange County, 3601 West Sunflower Avenue, Santa Ana, CA 92704, 714-830-0200 or toll-free 888-549-3055.

THE ART INSTITUTE OF CALIFORNIA–SACRAMENTO

Sacramento, CA

UNDERGRADUATE EXPENSES Tuition cost varies by program. Prospective students should contact the school for current tuition costs. Other charges include a starting kit for all first-quarter students. Kits vary in price, depending on the program of study.

CONTACT Financial Aid Office, The Art Institute of California–Sacramento, 2850 Gateway Oaks Drive, Suite 100, Sacramento, CA 95833, toll-free 800-477-1957.

THE ART INSTITUTE OF CALIFORNIA–SAN DIEGO

San Diego, CA

UNDERGRADUATE EXPENSES Tuition cost varies by program. Prospective students should contact the school for current tuition costs. Other charges include a starting kit for all first-quarter students. Kits vary in price, depending on the program of study.

CONTACT Financial Aid Office, The Art Institute of California–San Diego, 10025 Mesa Rim Road, San Diego, CA 92121, 619-546-0602 or toll-free 866-275-2422.

THE ART INSTITUTE OF CALIFORNIA–SAN FRANCISCO

San Francisco, CA

UNDERGRADUATE EXPENSES Tuition cost varies by program. Prospective students should contact the school for current tuition costs. Other charges include a starting kit for all first-quarter students. Kits vary in price, depending on the program of study.

CONTACT Financial Aid Office, The Art Institute of California–San Francisco, 1170 Market Street, San Francisco, CA 94102-4908, 415-865-0198 or toll-free 888-493-3261. *Fax:* 415-863-5831.

THE ART INSTITUTE OF CALIFORNIA–SUNNYVALE

Sunnyvale, CA

UNDERGRADUATE EXPENSES Tuition cost varies by program. Prospective students should contact the school for current tuition costs. Other charges include a starting kit for all first-quarter students. Kits vary in price, depending on the program of study.

CONTACT Financial Aid Office, The Art Institute of California–Sunnyvale, 1120 Kifer Road, Sunnyvale, CA 94086, 408-962-6400 or toll-free 866-583-7961.

THE ART INSTITUTE OF CHARLESTON

Charleston, SC

UNDERGRADUATE EXPENSES Tuition cost varies by program. Prospective students should contact the school for current tuition costs. Other charges include a starting kit for all first-quarter students. Kits vary in price, depending on the program of study.

CONTACT Financial Aid Office, The Art Institute of Charleston, 24 North Market Street, Charleston, SC 29401, 843-727-3500 or toll-free 866-211-0107.

THE ART INSTITUTE OF CHARLOTTE

Charlotte, NC

UNDERGRADUATE EXPENSES Tuition cost varies by program. Prospective students should contact the school for current tuition costs. Other charges include a starting kit for all first-quarter students. Kits vary in price, depending on the program of study.

CONTACT Financial Aid Office, The Art Institute of Charlotte, Three LakePointe Plaza, 2110 Water Ridge Parkway, Charlotte, NC 28217, 704-357-8020 or toll-free 800-872-4417.

THE ART INSTITUTE OF COLORADO

Denver, CO

UNDERGRADUATE EXPENSES Tuition cost varies by program. Prospective students should contact the school for current tuition costs. Other charges include a starting kit for all first-quarter students. Kits vary in price, depending on the program of study.

CONTACT Financial Aid Office, The Art Institute of Colorado, 1200 Lincoln Street, Denver, CO 80203, 303-837-0825 or toll-free 800-275-2420.

THE ART INSTITUTE OF DALLAS

Dallas, TX

UNDERGRADUATE EXPENSES Tuition cost varies by program. Prospective students should contact the school for current tuition costs. Other charges include a starting kit for all first-quarter students. Kits vary in price, depending on the program of study.

CONTACT Financial Aid Office, The Art Institute of Dallas, 8080 Park Lane, Suite 100, Dallas, TX 75231-5993, 214-692-8080 or toll-free 800-275-4243.

THE ART INSTITUTE OF FORT LAUDERDALE

Fort Lauderdale, FL

UNDERGRADUATE EXPENSES Tuition cost varies by program. Prospective students should contact the school for current tuition costs. Other charges include a starting kit for all first-quarter students. Kits vary in price, depending on the program of study.

CONTACT Financial Aid Office, The Art Institute of Fort Lauderdale, 1799 Southeast 17th Street Causeway, Fort Lauderdale, FL 33316-3000, 954-527-1799 or toll-free 800-275-7603.

THE ART INSTITUTE OF FORT WORTH

Fort Worth, TX

UNDERGRADUATE EXPENSES Tuition cost varies by program. Prospective students should contact the school for current tuition costs. Other charges include a starting kit for all first-quarter students. Kits vary in price, depending on the program of study.

CONTACT Financial Aid Office, The Art Institute of Fort Worth, 7000 Calmont Avenue, Suite 150, Fort Worth, TX 76116, 817-210-0808 or toll-free 888-422-9686.

THE ART INSTITUTE OF HOUSTON

Houston, TX

UNDERGRADUATE EXPENSES Tuition cost varies by program. Prospective students should contact the school for current tuition costs. Other charges include a starting kit for all first-quarter students. Kits vary in price, depending on the program of study.

CONTACT Financial Aid Office, The Art Institute of Houston, 1900 Yorktown, Houston, TX 77056, 713-623-2040 Ext. 780 or toll-free 800-275-4244. *Fax:* 713-966-2700. *E-mail:* bensons@aii.edu.

THE ART INSTITUTE OF HOUSTON—NORTH

Houston, TX

UNDERGRADUATE EXPENSES Tuition cost varies by program. Prospective students should contact the school for current tuition costs. Other charges include a starting kit for all first-quarter students. Kits vary in price, depending on the program of study.

CONTACT Financial Aid Office, The Art Institute of Houston—North, 10740 North Gessner Drive, Suite 190, Houston, TX 77064, toll-free 866-830-4450.

THE ART INSTITUTE OF INDIANAPOLIS

Indianapolis, IN

UNDERGRADUATE EXPENSES Tuition cost varies by program. Prospective students should contact the school for current tuition costs. Other charges include a starting kit for all first-quarter students. Kits vary in price, depending on the program of study.

CONTACT Financial Aid Office, The Art Institute of Indianapolis, 3500 Depauw Boulevard, Suite 1010, Indianapolis, IN 46268, 317-613-4800 or toll-free 866-441-9031.

THE ART INSTITUTE OF JACKSONVILLE

Jacksonville, FL

UNDERGRADUATE EXPENSES Tuition cost varies by program. Prospective students should contact the school for current tuition costs. Other charges include a starting kit for all first-quarter students. Kits vary in price, depending on the program of study.

CONTACT Financial Aid Office, The Art Institute of Jacksonville, 8775 Baypine Road, Jacksonville, FL 32256, 904-732-9393 or toll-free 800-924-1589.

THE ART INSTITUTE OF LAS VEGAS

Henderson, NV

UNDERGRADUATE EXPENSES Tuition cost varies by program. Prospective students should contact the school for current tuition costs. Other charges include a starting kit for all first-quarter students. Kits vary in price, depending on the program of study.

CONTACT Financial Aid Office, The Art Institute of Las Vegas, 2350 Corporate Circle Drive, Henderson, NV 89074, 702-369-9944 or toll-free 800-833-2678.

THE ART INSTITUTE OF MICHIGAN

Novi, MI

UNDERGRADUATE EXPENSES Tuition cost varies by program. Prospective students should contact the school for current tuition costs. Other charges include a starting kit for all first-quarter students. Kits vary in price, depending on the program of study.

CONTACT Financial Aid Office, The Art Institute of Michigan, 28125 Cabot Drive, Suite 120, Novi, MI 48377, 248-675-3800 or toll-free 800-479-0087.

THE ART INSTITUTE OF PHILADELPHIA

Philadelphia, PA

UNDERGRADUATE EXPENSES Tuition cost varies by program. Prospective students should contact the school for current tuition costs. Other charges include a starting kit for all first-quarter students. Kits vary in price, depending on the program of study.

CONTACT Financial Aid Office, The Art Institute of Philadelphia, 1622 Chestnut Street, Philadelphia, PA 19103-5198, 215-246-3311 or toll-free 800-275-2474. *Fax:* 215-246-3339.

THE ART INSTITUTE OF PHOENIX

Phoenix, AZ

UNDERGRADUATE EXPENSES Tuition cost varies by program. Prospective students should contact the school for current tuition costs. Other charges include a starting kit for all first-quarter students. Kits vary in price, depending on the program of study.

CONTACT Financial Aid Office, The Art Institute of Phoenix, 2233 West Dunlap Avenue, Phoenix, AZ 85021-2859, 602-331-7500 or toll-free 800-474-2479.

THE ART INSTITUTE OF PITTSBURGH

Pittsburgh, PA

UNDERGRADUATE EXPENSES Tuition cost varies by program. Prospective students should contact the school for current tuition costs. Other charges include a starting kit for all first-quarter students. Kits vary in price, depending on the program of study.

CONTACT Financial Aid Office, The Art Institute of Pittsburgh, 526 Penn Avenue, Pittsburgh, PA 15222-3269, 412-263-6600 or toll-free 800-275-2470.

THE ART INSTITUTE OF PORTLAND

Portland, OR

UNDERGRADUATE EXPENSES Tuition cost varies by program. Prospective students should contact the school for current tuition costs. Other charges include a starting kit for all first-quarter students. Kits vary in price, depending on the program of study.

CONTACT Financial Aid Office, The Art Institute of Portland, 1122 NW Davis Street, Portland, OR 97209, 503-228-6528 or toll-free 888-228-6528.

THE ART INSTITUTE OF RALEIGH-DURHAM

Durham, NC

UNDERGRADUATE EXPENSES Tuition cost varies by program. Prospective students should contact the school for current tuition costs. Other charges include a starting kit for all first-quarter students. Kits vary in price, depending on the program of study.

CONTACT Financial Aid Office, The Art Institute of Raleigh-Durham, 410 Blackwell Street, Suite 200, Durham, NC 27701, toll-free 888-245-9593.

THE ART INSTITUTE OF SALT LAKE CITY

Draper, UT

UNDERGRADUATE EXPENSES Tuition cost varies by program. Prospective students should contact the school for current tuition costs. Other charges include a starting kit for all first-quarter students. Kits vary in price, depending on the program of study.

CONTACT Financial Aid Office, The Art Institute of Salt Lake City, 121 West Election Road, Suite 100, Draper, UT 84020-9492, toll-free 800-978-0096.

THE ART INSTITUTE OF SAN ANTONIO

San Antonio, TX

UNDERGRADUATE EXPENSES Tuition cost varies by program. Prospective students should contact the school for current tuition costs. Other charges include a starting kit for all first-quarter students. Kits vary in price, depending on the program of study.

CONTACT Financial Aid Office, The Art Institute of San Antonio, 1000 IH-10 West, Suite 200, San Antonio, TX 78230, 210-338-7320 or toll-free 888-222-0040.

THE ART INSTITUTE OF TAMPA

Tampa, FL

UNDERGRADUATE EXPENSES Tuition cost varies by program. Prospective students should contact the school for current tuition costs. Other charges include a starting kit for all first-quarter students. Kits vary in price, depending on the program of study.

CONTACT Financial Aid Office, The Art Institute of Tampa, Parkside at Tampa Bay Park, 4401 North Himes Avenue, Suite 150, Tampa, FL 33614, 813-873-2112 or toll-free 866-703-3277.

THE ART INSTITUTE OF TENNESSEE–NASHVILLE

Nashville, TN

UNDERGRADUATE EXPENSES Tuition cost varies by program. Prospective students should contact the school for current tuition costs. Other charges include a starting kit for all first-quarter students. Kits vary in price, depending on the program of study.

CONTACT Financial Aid Office, The Art Institute of Tennessee–Nashville, 100 Centerview Drive, Suite 250, Nashville, TN 37214, 615-874-1067 or toll-free 866-747-5770.

THE ART INSTITUTE OF TUCSON

Tucson, AZ

UNDERGRADUATE EXPENSES Tuition cost varies by program. Prospective students should contact the school for current tuition costs. Other charges include a starting kit for all first-quarter students. Kits vary in price, depending on the program of study.

CONTACT Financial Aid Office, The Art Institute of Tucson, 5099 East Grant Road, Suite 100, Tucson, AZ 85712, 520-881-2900 or toll-free 866-690-8850.

THE ART INSTITUTE OF VIRGINIA BEACH

Virginia Beach, VA

UNDERGRADUATE EXPENSES Tuition cost varies by program. Prospective students should contact the school for current tuition costs. Other charges include a starting kit for all first-quarter students. Kits vary in price, depending on the program of study.

CONTACT Financial Aid Office, The Art Institute of Virginia Beach, Two Columbus Center, 4500 Main Street, Suite 100, Virginia Beach, VA 23462, 757-493-6700 or toll-free 877-437-4428.

THE ART INSTITUTE OF WASHINGTON

Arlington, VA

UNDERGRADUATE EXPENSES Tuition cost varies by program. Prospective students should contact the school for current tuition costs. Other charges include a starting kit for all first-quarter students. Kits vary in price, depending on the program of study.

CONTACT Financial Aid Office, The Art Institute of Washington, 1820 North Fort Myer Drive, Arlington, VA 22209, 703-247-6849 or toll-free 877-303-3771. *Fax:* 703-247-6829.

THE ART INSTITUTE OF WASHINGTON–NORTHERN VIRGINIA

Sterling, VA

UNDERGRADUATE EXPENSES Tuition cost varies by program. Prospective students should contact the school for current tuition costs. Other charges include a starting kit for all first-quarter students. Kits vary in price, depending on the program of study.

CONTACT Financial Aid Office, The Art Institute of Washington–Northern Virginia, The Corporate Office Park at Dulles Town Center, 21000 Atlantic Boulevard, Suite 100, Sterling, VA 20166, 571-449-4400 or toll-free 888-627-5008.

THE ART INSTITUTE OF WISCONSIN

Milwaukee, WI

UNDERGRADUATE EXPENSES Tuition cost varies by program. Prospective students should contact the school for current tuition costs.

CONTACT Financial Aid Office, The Art Institute of Wisconsin, 320 East Buffalo Street, Suite 600, Milwaukee, WI 53202, 414-978-5000 or toll-free 877-285-4234.

THE ART INSTITUTES INTERNATIONAL–KANSAS CITY

Lenexa, KS

UNDERGRADUATE EXPENSES Tuition cost varies by program. Prospective students should contact the school for current tuition costs. Other charges include a starting kit for all first-quarter students. Kits vary in price, depending on the program of study.

CONTACT Financial Aid Office, The Art Institutes International–Kansas City, 8208 Melrose Drive, Lenexa, KS 66214, toll-free 866-530-8508.

THE ART INSTITUTES INTERNATIONAL MINNESOTA

Minneapolis, MN

UNDERGRADUATE EXPENSES Tuition cost varies by program. Prospective students should contact the school for current tuition costs. Other charges include a starting kit for all first-quarter students. Kits vary in price, depending on the program of study.

CONTACT Financial Aid Office, The Art Institutes International Minnesota, 825 2nd Avenue South, Minneapolis, MN 55402, 612-332-3361 Ext. 110 or toll-free 800-777-3643. *Fax:* 612-332-3934. *E-mail:* robbt@aii.edu.

ASBURY UNIVERSITY

Wilmore, KY

Tuition & fees: $24,229 **Average undergraduate aid package: $17,754**

ABOUT THE INSTITUTION Independent nondenominational, coed. 47 undergraduate majors. Federal methodology is used as a basis for awarding need-based institutional aid.

UNDERGRADUATE EXPENSES for 2011–12 ***Comprehensive fee:*** $29,863 includes full-time tuition ($24,058), mandatory fees ($171), and room and board ($5634). ***College room only:*** $3270. Full-time tuition and fees vary according to course load and program. Room and board charges vary according to board plan, housing facility, and location. ***Part-time tuition:*** $925 per credit hour. Part-time tuition and fees vary according to course load and program. ***Payment plan:*** Installment.

FRESHMAN FINANCIAL AID (Fall 2009) 290 applied for aid; of those 84% were deemed to have need. 99% of freshmen with need received aid; of those 32% had need fully met. ***Average percent of need met:*** 87% (excluding resources awarded to replace EFC). ***Average financial aid package:*** $19,430 (excluding resources awarded to replace EFC). 14% of all full-time freshmen had no need and received non-need-based gift aid.

UNDERGRADUATE FINANCIAL AID (Fall 2009) 1,061 applied for aid; of those 86% were deemed to have need. 100% of undergraduates with need received aid; of those 26% had need fully met. ***Average percent of need met:*** 80% (excluding resources awarded to replace EFC). ***Average financial aid package:*** $17,754 (excluding resources awarded to replace EFC). 11% of all full-time undergraduates had no need and received non-need-based gift aid.

GIFT AID (NEED-BASED) ***Total amount:*** $10,414,641 (19% federal, 17% state, 62% institutional, 2% external sources). ***Receiving aid:*** Freshmen: 77% (243); all full-time undergraduates: 73% (901). ***Average award:*** Freshmen: $13,353; Undergraduates: $11,667. ***Scholarships, grants, and awards:*** Federal Pell, FSEOG, state, private, college/university gift aid from institutional funds.

GIFT AID (NON-NEED-BASED) ***Total amount:*** $2,391,988 (8% state, 89% institutional, 3% external sources). ***Receiving aid:*** Freshmen: 29% (90). Undergraduates: 23% (285). ***Average award:*** Freshmen: $10,868. Undergraduates: $10,252. ***Scholarships, grants, and awards by category:*** *Academic interests/achievement:* general academic interests/achievements. *Creative arts/performance:* music. *Special achievements/activities:* leadership. *Special characteristics:* children and siblings of alumni, children of faculty/staff, ethnic background, international students, siblings of current students. ***Tuition waivers:*** Full or partial for employees or children of employees, senior citizens.

LOANS ***Student loans:*** $8,602,387 (85% need-based, 15% non-need-based). 75% of past graduating class borrowed through all loan programs. *Average indebtedness per student:* $29,411. ***Average need-based loan:*** Freshmen: $3183. Undergraduates: $3897. ***Parent loans:*** $1,442,249 (86% need-based, 14% non-need-based). ***Programs:*** Federal Direct (Subsidized and Unsubsidized Stafford, PLUS), Perkins, college/university, private loans.

WORK-STUDY ***Federal work-study:*** Total amount: $819,295; jobs available.

ATHLETIC AWARDS Total amount: $963,145 (74% need-based, 26% non-need-based).

APPLYING FOR FINANCIAL AID ***Required financial aid forms:*** FAFSA, institution's own form. ***Financial aid deadline (priority):*** 3/1. ***Notification date:*** Continuous. Students must reply within 4 weeks of notification.

CONTACT Mr. Ronald Anderson, Director of Financial Aid, Asbury University, One Macklem Drive, Wilmore, KY 40390, 859-858-3511 Ext. 2195 or toll-free 800-888-1818. *Fax:* 859-858-3921. *E-mail:* ron.anderson@asbury.edu.

ASHFORD UNIVERSITY

Clinton, IA

CONTACT Lisa Kramer, Director of Financial Aid, Ashford University, 400 North Bluff Boulevard, PO Box 2967, Clinton, IA 52733-2967, 563-242-4023 Ext. 1243 or toll-free 800-242-4153. *Fax:* 563-242-8684.

ASHLAND UNIVERSITY

Ashland, OH

Tuition & fees: $28,580 **Average undergraduate aid package: $23,953**

ABOUT THE INSTITUTION Independent religious, coed. 67 undergraduate majors. Federal methodology is used as a basis for awarding need-based institutional aid.

UNDERGRADUATE EXPENSES for 2011–12 ***Comprehensive fee:*** $37,932 includes full-time tuition ($27,654), mandatory fees ($926), and room and board ($9352). ***College room only:*** $5022. Full-time tuition and fees vary according to degree level, location, and reciprocity agreements. Room and board charges vary according to board plan and housing facility. ***Part-time tuition:*** $848 per semester hour. ***Part-time fees:*** $18 per semester hour. Part-time tuition and fees vary according to course load, degree level, location, and program. ***Payment plan:*** Installment.

FRESHMAN FINANCIAL AID (Fall 2010, est.) 620 applied for aid; of those 88% were deemed to have need. 100% of freshmen with need received aid. ***Average percent of need met:*** 90% (excluding resources awarded to replace EFC). ***Average financial aid package:*** $25,572 (excluding resources awarded to replace EFC). 7% of all full-time freshmen had no need and received non-need-based gift aid.

UNDERGRADUATE FINANCIAL AID (Fall 2010, est.) 2,221 applied for aid; of those 83% were deemed to have need. 100% of undergraduates with need received aid. ***Average percent of need met:*** 90% (excluding resources awarded to replace EFC). ***Average financial aid package:*** $23,953 (excluding resources awarded to replace EFC). 10% of all full-time undergraduates had no need and received non-need-based gift aid.

GIFT AID (NEED-BASED) ***Total amount:*** $27,543,116 (18% federal, 4% state, 77% institutional, 1% external sources). ***Receiving aid:*** Freshmen: 88% (545); all full-time undergraduates: 83% (1,840). ***Average award:*** Freshmen: $18,627; Undergraduates: $16,975. ***Scholarships, grants, and awards:*** Federal Pell, FSEOG, state, private, college/university gift aid from institutional funds.

GIFT AID (NON-NEED-BASED) ***Total amount:*** $2,796,861 (1% federal, 98% institutional, 1% external sources). ***Receiving aid:*** Freshmen: 82% (507). Undergraduates: 77% (1,706). ***Average award:*** Freshmen: $10,240. Undergraduates: $8994. ***Scholarships, grants, and awards by category:*** *Academic interests/achievement:* general academic interests/achievements, mathematics, physical sciences, social sciences. *Creative arts/performance:* art/fine arts, music, theater/drama. *Special achievements/activities:* cheerleading/drum major. *Special characteristics:* children and siblings of alumni, children of faculty/staff, international students, relatives of clergy, religious affiliation. ***Tuition waivers:*** Full or partial for children of alumni, employees or children of employees, senior citizens.

LOANS ***Student loans:*** $13,610,486 (92% need-based, 8% non-need-based). 79% of past graduating class borrowed through all loan programs. *Average indebtedness per student:* $39,399. ***Average need-based loan:*** Freshmen: $3829. Undergraduates: $4580. ***Parent loans:*** $6,215,916 (95% need-based, 5% non-need-based). ***Programs:*** Federal Direct (Subsidized and Unsubsidized Stafford, PLUS), Perkins, college/university.

WORK-STUDY ***Federal work-study:*** Total amount: $3,605,473; jobs available.

ATHLETIC AWARDS Total amount: $4,506,961 (78% need-based, 22% non-need-based).

APPLYING FOR FINANCIAL AID ***Required financial aid form:*** FAFSA. ***Financial aid deadline (priority):*** 3/15. ***Notification date:*** Continuous beginning 3/15. Students must reply within 3 weeks of notification.

CONTACT Mr. Stephen C. Howell, Director of Financial Aid, Ashland University, 401 College Avenue, Ashland, OH 44805-3702, 419-289-5944 or toll-free 800-882-1548. *Fax:* 419-289-5976. *E-mail:* showell@ashland.edu.

ASHWORTH COLLEGE

Norcross, GA

CONTACT Financial Aid Office, Ashworth College, 6625 The Corners Parkway, Suite 500, Norcross, GA 30092, 770-729-8400 or toll-free 800-957-5412.

ASPEN UNIVERSITY

Denver, CO

CONTACT Jennifer Quinn, Director of Financial Aid, Aspen University, 720 South Colorado Bouleavrd #1150N, Denver, CO 80246, 800-441-4746. *Fax:* 303-336-1144. *E-mail:* jquinn@aspen.edu.

ASSUMPTION COLLEGE

Worcester, MA

Tuition & fees: $31,305 **Average undergraduate aid package: $22,125**

ABOUT THE INSTITUTION Independent Roman Catholic, coed. 43 undergraduate majors. Federal methodology is used as a basis for awarding need-based institutional aid.

UNDERGRADUATE EXPENSES for 2010–11 ***Comprehensive fee:*** $41,565 includes full-time tuition ($30,940), mandatory fees ($365), and room and board ($10,260). ***College room only:*** $6530. Full-time tuition and fees vary according to course load and reciprocity agreements. Room and board charges vary according to housing facility. ***Part-time tuition:*** $1031.33 per credit hour. ***Part-time fees:*** $365 per year. Part-time tuition and fees vary according to course load.

FRESHMAN FINANCIAL AID (Fall 2010, est.) 536 applied for aid; of those 89% were deemed to have need. 100% of freshmen with need received aid; of those 22% had need fully met. ***Average percent of need met:*** 74% (excluding resources awarded to replace EFC). ***Average financial aid package:*** $22,394 (excluding resources awarded to replace EFC). 14% of all full-time freshmen had no need and received non-need-based gift aid.

UNDERGRADUATE FINANCIAL AID (Fall 2010, est.) 1,717 applied for aid; of those 90% were deemed to have need. 100% of undergraduates with need received aid; of those 20% had need fully met. ***Average percent of need met:*** 73% (excluding resources awarded to replace EFC). ***Average financial aid package:*** $22,125 (excluding resources awarded to replace EFC). 16% of all full-time undergraduates had no need and received non-need-based gift aid.

GIFT AID (NEED-BASED) ***Total amount:*** $24,472,328 (9% federal, 3% state, 85% institutional, 3% external sources). ***Receiving aid:*** Freshmen: 81% (475); all full-time undergraduates: 76% (1,539). ***Average award:*** Freshmen: $18,327; Undergraduates: $169,812. ***Scholarships, grants, and awards:*** Federal Pell, FSEOG, state, private, college/university gift aid from institutional funds.

GIFT AID (NON-NEED-BASED) ***Total amount:*** $4,016,586 (91% institutional, 9% external sources). ***Receiving aid:*** Freshmen: 11% (63). Undergraduates: 9% (180). ***Average award:*** Freshmen: $10,509. Undergraduates: $9954. ***Scholarships, grants, and awards by category:*** *Academic interests/achievement:* 1,387 awards ($13,691,176 total): general academic interests/achievements. *Special characteristics:* members of minority groups. ***Tuition waivers:*** Full or partial for employees or children of employees.

LOANS ***Student loans:*** $16,188,619 (63% need-based, 37% non-need-based). 80% of past graduating class borrowed through all loan programs. *Average indebtedness per student:* $32,416. ***Average need-based loan:*** Freshmen: $3604. Undergraduates: $4880. ***Parent loans:*** $5,776,598 (25% need-based, 75% non-need-based). ***Programs:*** Perkins, state, college/university.

WORK-STUDY ***Federal work-study:*** Total amount: $704,548; 410 jobs averaging $1718.

ATHLETIC AWARDS Total amount: $1,528,859 (29% need-based, 71% non-need-based).

APPLYING FOR FINANCIAL AID ***Required financial aid form:*** FAFSA. ***Financial aid deadline:*** 2/15. ***Notification date:*** Continuous beginning 2/16. Students must reply by 5/1.

CONTACT Linda Mularczyk, Director of Financial Aid, Assumption College, 500 Salisbury Street, Worcester, MA 01609-1296, 508-767-7157 or toll-free 888-882-7786. *Fax:* 508-767-7376. *E-mail:* fa@assumption.edu.

ATHENS STATE UNIVERSITY

Athens, AL

Tuition & fees (AL res): $4860 **Average undergraduate aid package: N/A**

ABOUT THE INSTITUTION State-supported, coed. 29 undergraduate majors. Federal methodology is used as a basis for awarding need-based institutional aid.

UNDERGRADUATE EXPENSES for 2010–11 ***Tuition, state resident:*** full-time $4110; part-time $137 per credit hour. ***Tuition, nonresident:*** full-time $8220; part-time $274 per credit hour. ***Required fees:*** full-time $750; $25 per credit hour.

UNDERGRADUATE FINANCIAL AID (Fall 2010, est.) 1,049 applied for aid.

GIFT AID (NEED-BASED) ***Total amount:*** $4,905,696 (99% federal, 1% state). ***Scholarships, grants, and awards:*** Federal Pell, FSEOG, state, private, college/university gift aid from institutional funds.

GIFT AID (NON-NEED-BASED) ***Total amount:*** $238,211 (85% federal, 5% institutional, 10% external sources). ***Tuition waivers:*** Full or partial for employees or children of employees, senior citizens.

LOANS ***Student loans:*** $13,855,603 (100% non-need-based). ***Programs:*** Federal Direct (Subsidized and Unsubsidized Stafford, PLUS), college/university.

WORK-STUDY ***Federal work-study:*** Total amount: $79,090; jobs available.

APPLYING FOR FINANCIAL AID ***Required financial aid form:*** FAFSA. ***Financial aid deadline:*** Continuous. ***Notification date:*** Continuous beginning 5/1. Students must reply within 2 weeks of notification.

CONTACT Renee Stanford, Financial Aid Officer, Athens State University, 300 North Beaty Street, Athens, AL 35611, 256-233-8122 or toll-free 800-522-0272. *Fax:* 256-233-8178. *E-mail:* finaid@athens.edu.

ATLANTA CHRISTIAN COLLEGE

East Point, GA

CONTACT Blair Walker, Director of Financial Aid, Atlanta Christian College, 2605 Ben Hill Road, East Point, GA 30344, 404-761-8861 or toll-free 800-776-1ACC. *Fax:* 404-669-2024. *E-mail:* blairw@acc.edu.

ATLANTIC COLLEGE

Guaynabo, PR

CONTACT Mrs. Velma Aponte, Financial Aid Coordinator, Atlantic College, Calle Colton #9, Guaynabo, PR 00970, 787-720-1092. *E-mail:* atlaneco@coqui.net.

ATLANTIC UNION COLLEGE

South Lancaster, MA

ABOUT THE INSTITUTION Independent Seventh-day Adventist, coed. 21 undergraduate majors.

GIFT AID (NEED-BASED) ***Scholarships, grants, and awards:*** Federal Pell, FSEOG, state, private, college/university gift aid from institutional funds.

GIFT AID (NON-NEED-BASED) ***Scholarships, grants, and awards by category:*** *Academic interests/achievement:* business, computer science, education, English, general academic interests/achievements, health fields, mathematics, premedicine, religion/biblical studies. *Creative arts/performance:* music. *Special achievements/activities:* leadership. *Special characteristics:* adult students, children of faculty/staff, international students, siblings of current students.

LOANS ***Programs:*** Perkins, TERI Loans, Signature Loans, Campus Door Loans.

WORK-STUDY ***Federal work-study:*** Total amount: $149,416; 221 jobs averaging $686. ***State or other work-study/employment:*** Total amount: $497,406 (100% need-based). 240 part-time jobs averaging $1989.

APPLYING FOR FINANCIAL AID ***Required financial aid forms:*** FAFSA, institution's own form.

CONTACT Sandra Pereira, Director of Financial Aid, Atlantic Union College, PO Box 1000, South Lancaster, MA 01561-1000, 978-368-2284 or toll-free 800-282-2030. *Fax:* 978-368-2283. *E-mail:* sandra.pereira@auc.edu.

AUBURN UNIVERSITY

Auburn University, AL

Tuition & fees (AL res): $7900 **Average undergraduate aid package: $9832**

ABOUT THE INSTITUTION State-supported, coed. 137 undergraduate majors. Federal methodology is used as a basis for awarding need-based institutional aid.

UNDERGRADUATE EXPENSES for 2010–11 ***Tuition, state resident:*** full-time $7008; part-time $292 per semester hour. ***Tuition, nonresident:*** full-time $21,024; part-time $876 per semester hour. ***Required fees:*** full-time $892; $446 per term. Full-time tuition and fees vary according to program and reciprocity agreements. Part-time tuition and fees vary according to course load, program, and reciprocity agreements. ***College room and board:*** $9630; ***Room only:*** $4780. Room and board charges vary according to board plan and housing facility. ***Payment plan:*** Installment.

FRESHMAN FINANCIAL AID (Fall 2009) 2,222 applied for aid; of those 55% were deemed to have need. 100% of freshmen with need received aid; of those 28% had need fully met. ***Average percent of need met:*** 62% (excluding resources awarded to replace EFC). ***Average financial aid package:*** $11,218 (excluding resources awarded to replace EFC). 25% of all full-time freshmen had no need and received non-need-based gift aid.

UNDERGRADUATE FINANCIAL AID (Fall 2009) 10,513 applied for aid; of those 58% were deemed to have need. 100% of undergraduates with need received aid; of those 16% had need fully met. ***Average percent of need met:*** 54% (excluding resources awarded to replace EFC). ***Average financial aid package:*** $9832 (excluding resources awarded to replace EFC). 14% of all full-time undergraduates had no need and received non-need-based gift aid.

GIFT AID (NEED-BASED) ***Total amount:*** $27,566,965 (55% federal, 3% state, 34% institutional, 8% external sources). ***Receiving aid:*** Freshmen: 26% (1,013); all full-time undergraduates: 23% (4,262). ***Average award:*** Freshmen: $7048; Undergraduates: $6167. ***Scholarships, grants, and awards:*** Federal Pell, FSEOG, state, private, college/university gift aid from institutional funds.

GIFT AID (NON-NEED-BASED) ***Total amount:*** $34,737,106 (6% state, 59% institutional, 35% external sources). ***Receiving aid:*** Freshmen: 6% (251). Undergraduates: 3% (557). ***Average award:*** Freshmen: $5023. Undergraduates: $4974. ***Scholarships, grants, and awards by category:*** *Academic interests/achievement:* agriculture, architecture, biological sciences, business, communication, computer science, education, engineering/technologies, English, foreign languages, general academic interests/achievements, health fields, home economics, humanities, mathematics, physical sciences, premedicine, social sciences. *Creative arts/performance:* applied art and design, art/fine arts, cinema/film/broadcasting, creative writing, journalism/publications, music, performing arts, theater/drama. *Special achievements/activities:* cheerleading/drum major, leadership, memberships. *Special characteristics:* children and siblings of alumni, children of faculty/staff, children of union members/company employees, ethnic background, local/state students, married students, out-of-state students. ***Tuition waivers:*** Full or partial for employees or children of employees.

LOANS ***Student loans:*** $60,126,330 (67% need-based, 33% non-need-based). 46% of past graduating class borrowed through all loan programs. *Average indebtedness per student:* $23,491. ***Average need-based loan:*** Freshmen: $3395. Undergraduates: $4606. ***Parent loans:*** $20,548,108 (36% need-based, 64% non-need-based). ***Programs:*** Federal Direct (Subsidized and Unsubsidized Stafford, PLUS), Perkins, Federal Nursing, college/university.

WORK-STUDY ***Federal work-study:*** Total amount: $1,192,653; 259 jobs averaging $3812.

ATHLETIC AWARDS Total amount: $9,085,455 (2% need-based, 98% non-need-based).

APPLYING FOR FINANCIAL AID ***Required financial aid form:*** FAFSA. ***Financial aid deadline (priority):*** 3/1. ***Notification date:*** Continuous beginning 10/2. Students must reply by 5/1.

CONTACT Mr. Mike Reynolds, Director of Student Financial Services, Auburn University, 203 Mary Martin Hall, Auburn University, AL 36849, 334-844-4634 or toll-free 800-AUBURN9 (in-state). *Fax:* 334-844-6085. *E-mail:* finaid7@auburn.edu.

AUBURN UNIVERSITY MONTGOMERY

Montgomery, AL

Tuition & fees (AL res): $7280 **Average undergraduate aid package: N/A**

ABOUT THE INSTITUTION State-supported, coed. 24 undergraduate majors. Federal methodology is used as a basis for awarding need-based institutional aid.

UNDERGRADUATE EXPENSES for 2010–11 ***Tuition, state resident:*** full-time $6730; part-time $206 per credit hour. ***Tuition, nonresident:*** full-time $18,286; part-time $618 per credit hour. ***Required fees:*** full-time $550; $8 per semester hour or $155 per term. Full-time tuition and fees vary according to course load. Part-time tuition and fees vary according to course load. ***College room and board: Room only:*** $3820. Room and board charges vary according to housing facility.

FRESHMAN FINANCIAL AID (Fall 2010, est.) 534 applied for aid; of those 96% were deemed to have need. 96% of freshmen with need received aid; of those 75% had need fully met.

UNDERGRADUATE FINANCIAL AID (Fall 2010, est.) 2,284 applied for aid; of those 96% were deemed to have need. 96% of undergraduates with need received aid; of those 77% had need fully met.

GIFT AID (NEED-BASED) ***Total amount:*** $9,952,365 (98% federal, 1% state, 1% institutional). ***Receiving aid:*** Freshmen: 49% (361); all full-time undergraduates: 41% (1,453). ***Average award:*** Freshmen: $5054; Undergraduates: $4693. ***Scholarships, grants, and awards:*** Federal Pell, FSEOG, state, college/university gift aid from institutional funds.

GIFT AID (NON-NEED-BASED) ***Total amount:*** $1,947,440 (100% institutional). ***Scholarships, grants, and awards by category:*** *Academic interests/achievement:* general academic interests/achievements. ***Tuition waivers:*** Full or partial for employees or children of employees.

LOANS ***Student loans:*** $33,489,609 (46% need-based, 54% non-need-based). ***Average need-based loan:*** Freshmen: $3320. Undergraduates: $3958. ***Parent loans:*** $401,832 (100% non-need-based). ***Programs:*** Federal Direct (Subsidized and Unsubsidized Stafford, PLUS), Perkins.

WORK-STUDY ***Federal work-study:*** Total amount: $181,831; 46 jobs averaging $3888.

APPLYING FOR FINANCIAL AID ***Required financial aid form:*** FAFSA. ***Financial aid deadline (priority):*** 3/1. ***Notification date:*** 6/1. Students must reply within 2 weeks of notification.

CONTACT Anthony Richey, Senior Director of Financial Aid, Auburn University Montgomery, PO Box 244023, Montgomery, AL 36124-4023, 334-244-3571 or toll-free 800-227-2649 (in-state). *Fax:* 334-244-3913. *E-mail:* arichey@aum.edu.

AUGSBURG COLLEGE

Minneapolis, MN

Tuition & fees: $30,418 **Average undergraduate aid package: $20,143**

ABOUT THE INSTITUTION Independent Lutheran, coed. 64 undergraduate majors. Federal methodology is used as a basis for awarding need-based institutional aid.

UNDERGRADUATE EXPENSES for 2011–12 ***Comprehensive fee:*** $38,490 includes full-time tuition ($29,794), mandatory fees ($624), and room and board ($8072). ***College room only:*** $4116. Full-time tuition and fees vary according to location. Room and board charges vary according to board plan and housing facility. ***Part-time tuition:*** $3599 per course. Part-time tuition and fees vary according to course load and location. ***Payment plan:*** Installment.

FRESHMAN FINANCIAL AID (Fall 2010, est.) 409 applied for aid; of those 86% were deemed to have need. 100% of freshmen with need received aid; of those 16% had need fully met. ***Average percent of need met:*** 78% (excluding resources awarded to replace EFC). ***Average financial aid package:*** $24,860 (excluding resources awarded to replace EFC). 13% of all full-time freshmen had no need and received non-need-based gift aid.

UNDERGRADUATE FINANCIAL AID (Fall 2010, est.) 2,338 applied for aid; of those 87% were deemed to have need. 100% of undergraduates with need received aid; of those 11% had need fully met. ***Average percent of need met:*** 67% (excluding resources awarded to replace EFC). ***Average financial aid package:*** $20,143 (excluding resources awarded to replace EFC). 10% of all full-time undergraduates had no need and received non-need-based gift aid.

GIFT AID (NEED-BASED) ***Total amount:*** $30,232,599 (20% federal, 10% state, 64% institutional, 6% external sources). ***Receiving aid:*** Freshmen: 83% (348); all full-time undergraduates: 61% (1,852). ***Average award:*** Freshmen: $19,929; Undergraduates: $16,115. ***Scholarships, grants, and awards:*** Federal Pell, FSEOG, state, private, college/university gift aid from institutional funds, Federal Nursing.

GIFT AID (NON-NEED-BASED) ***Total amount:*** $3,507,897 (1% state, 85% institutional, 14% external sources). ***Receiving aid:*** Freshmen: 16% (66). Undergraduates: 12% (348). ***Average award:*** Freshmen: $10,973. Undergraduates: $8739. ***Scholarships, grants, and awards by category:*** *Academic interests/achievement:* biological sciences, business, communication, computer science, education, English, foreign languages, general academic interests/achievements, health fields, international studies, mathematics, physical sciences, religion/biblical studies, social sciences. *Creative arts/performance:* art/fine arts, music, performing arts, theater/drama. *Special achievements/activities:* community service, general special achievements/activities, junior miss, leadership, religious involvement. *Special characteristics:* children and siblings of alumni, international students, members of minority groups, relatives of clergy, siblings of current students. ***Tuition waivers:*** Full or partial for children of alumni, employees or children of employees, senior citizens.

LOANS ***Student loans:*** $21,121,479 (90% need-based, 10% non-need-based). 83% of past graduating class borrowed through all loan programs. *Average indebtedness per student:* $24,311. ***Average need-based loan:*** Freshmen: $4219. Undergraduates: $4902. ***Parent loans:*** $2,617,311 (66% need-based, 34% non-need-based). ***Programs:*** Federal Direct (Subsidized and Unsubsidized Stafford, PLUS), Perkins, Federal Nursing, state.

WORK-STUDY ***Federal work-study:*** Total amount: $1,069,387; 363 jobs averaging $2850. ***State or other work-study/employment:*** Total amount: $2,338,804 (95% need-based, 5% non-need-based). 818 part-time jobs averaging $2843.

APPLYING FOR FINANCIAL AID ***Required financial aid form:*** FAFSA. ***Financial aid deadline:*** 8/15 (priority: 5/1). ***Notification date:*** Continuous beginning 3/1. Students must reply within 3 weeks of notification.

CONTACT Mr. Paul L. Terrio, Director of Student Financial Services, Augsburg College, 2211 Riverside Avenue, Minneapolis, MN 55454-1351, 612-330-1049 or toll-free 800-788-5678. *Fax:* 612-330-1308. *E-mail:* terriop@augsburg.edu.

AUGUSTANA COLLEGE

Rock Island, IL

Tuition & fees: $33,363 **Average undergraduate aid package: $21,093**

ABOUT THE INSTITUTION Independent religious, coed. 58 undergraduate majors. Federal methodology is used as a basis for awarding need-based institutional aid.

UNDERGRADUATE EXPENSES for 2011–12 ***Comprehensive fee:*** $41,829 includes full-time tuition ($33,363) and room and board ($8466). Full-time tuition and fees vary according to student level. Room and board charges vary according to board plan and housing facility. Part-time tuition and fees vary according to course load. ***Payment plans:*** Tuition prepayment, installment.

FRESHMAN FINANCIAL AID (Fall 2009) 556 applied for aid; of those 80% were deemed to have need. 100% of freshmen with need received aid; of those 26% had need fully met. ***Average percent of need met:*** 85% (excluding resources awarded to replace EFC). ***Average financial aid package:*** $22,493 (excluding resources awarded to replace EFC). 28% of all full-time freshmen had no need and received non-need-based gift aid.

UNDERGRADUATE FINANCIAL AID (Fall 2009) 2,006 applied for aid; of those 84% were deemed to have need. 100% of undergraduates with need received aid; of those 24% had need fully met. ***Average percent of need met:*** 85% (excluding resources awarded to replace EFC). ***Average financial aid package:*** $21,093 (excluding resources awarded to replace EFC). 29% of all full-time undergraduates had no need and received non-need-based gift aid.

GIFT AID (NEED-BASED) ***Total amount:*** $25,958,574 (8% federal, 10% state, 80% institutional, 2% external sources). ***Receiving aid:*** Freshmen: 71% (436); all full-time undergraduates: 68% (1,661). ***Average award:*** Freshmen: $17,615; Undergraduates: $15,619. ***Scholarships, grants, and awards:*** Federal Pell, FSEOG, state, private, college/university gift aid from institutional funds.

GIFT AID (NON-NEED-BASED) ***Total amount:*** $10,132,300 (98% institutional, 2% external sources). ***Receiving aid:*** Freshmen: 13% (82). Undergraduates: 10% (243). ***Average award:*** Freshmen: $12,543. Undergraduates: $11,815. ***Scholarships, grants, and awards by category:*** *Academic interests/achievement:* 1,905 awards ($21,590,069 total): biological sciences, business, communication, computer science, education, English, foreign languages, general academic interests/achievements, humanities, mathematics, physical sciences, religion/biblical studies, social sciences. *Creative arts/performance:* 418 awards ($909,885 total): art/fine arts, creative writing, debating, music, theater/drama. *Special characteristics:* 423 awards ($1,829,339 total): children and siblings of alumni, children of faculty/staff, ethnic background, international students, members of minority groups, religious affiliation, siblings of current students. ***Tuition waivers:*** Full or partial for employees or children of employees.

LOANS ***Student loans:*** $14,963,567 (64% need-based, 36% non-need-based). 80% of past graduating class borrowed through all loan programs. *Average indebtedness per student:* $28,198. ***Average need-based loan:*** Freshmen: $3692. Undergraduates: $4601. ***Parent loans:*** $5,214,471 (27% need-based, 73% non-need-based). ***Programs:*** Federal Direct (Subsidized and Unsubsidized Stafford, PLUS), Perkins.

WORK-STUDY ***Federal work-study:*** Total amount: $2,333,624; 1,142 jobs averaging $2043.

APPLYING FOR FINANCIAL AID ***Required financial aid forms:*** FAFSA, institution's own form. ***Financial aid deadline (priority):*** 4/1. ***Notification date:*** Continuous. Students must reply by 5/1.

CONTACT Sue Standley, Director of Financial Aid, Augustana College, 639 38th Street, Rock Island, IL 61201-2296, 309-794-7207 or toll-free 800-798-8100. *Fax:* 309-794-7174. *E-mail:* suestandley@augustana.edu.

AUGUSTANA COLLEGE

Sioux Falls, SD

Tuition & fees: $25,104 **Average undergraduate aid package: $20,828**

ABOUT THE INSTITUTION Independent religious, coed. 57 undergraduate majors. Federal methodology is used as a basis for awarding need-based institutional aid.

UNDERGRADUATE EXPENSES for 2010–11 ***Comprehensive fee:*** $31,364 includes full-time tuition ($24,790), mandatory fees ($314), and room and board ($6260). ***College room only:*** $3048. Full-time tuition and fees vary according to course load and degree level. Room and board charges vary according to board plan and housing facility. ***Part-time tuition:*** $375 per credit hour. Part-time tuition and fees vary according to course load and degree level. ***Payment plan:*** Installment.

FRESHMAN FINANCIAL AID (Fall 2010, est.) 365 applied for aid; of those 85% were deemed to have need. 100% of freshmen with need received aid; of those 25% had need fully met. ***Average percent of need met:*** 94% (excluding resources awarded to replace EFC). ***Average financial aid package:*** $21,983 (excluding resources awarded to replace EFC). 25% of all full-time freshmen had no need and received non-need-based gift aid.

UNDERGRADUATE FINANCIAL AID (Fall 2010, est.) 1,362 applied for aid; of those 86% were deemed to have need. 100% of undergraduates with need received aid; of those 22% had need fully met. ***Average percent of need met:*** 88% (excluding resources awarded to replace EFC). ***Average financial aid package:*** $20,828 (excluding resources awarded to replace EFC). 29% of all full-time undergraduates had no need and received non-need-based gift aid.

GIFT AID (NEED-BASED) ***Total amount:*** $15,960,796 (16% federal, 79% institutional, 5% external sources). ***Receiving aid:*** Freshmen: 74% (309); all full-time undergraduates: 69% (1,173). ***Average award:*** Freshmen: $17,703; Undergraduates: $15,916. ***Scholarships, grants, and awards:*** Federal Pell, FSEOG, state, private, college/university gift aid from institutional funds, need-linked special talent scholarships, minority scholarships.

GIFT AID (NON-NEED-BASED) ***Total amount:*** $6,301,460 (2% federal, 5% state, 90% institutional, 3% external sources). ***Receiving aid:*** Freshmen: 73% (305). Undergraduates: 68% (1,154). ***Average award:*** Freshmen: $12,849. Undergraduates: $10,754. ***Scholarships, grants, and awards by category:*** *Academic interests/achievement:* biological sciences, business, communication, computer science, education, English, foreign languages, general academic interests/achievements, health fields, humanities, international studies, mathematics, physical sciences, premedicine, religion/biblical studies, social sciences. *Creative arts/performance:* art/fine arts, creative writing, music, performing arts, theater/drama. *Special achievements/activities:* general special achievements/activities, leadership. *Special characteristics:* children and siblings of alumni, children of current students, children of faculty/staff, ethnic background, international students, local/state students, members of minority groups, religious affiliation, siblings of current students, spouses of current students, veterans. ***Tuition waivers:*** Full or partial for employees or children of employees.

LOANS ***Student loans:*** $11,458,096 (64% need-based, 36% non-need-based). 76% of past graduating class borrowed through all loan programs. *Average indebtedness per student:* $31,520. ***Average need-based loan:*** Freshmen: $4898. Undergraduates: $5440. ***Parent loans:*** $1,018,604 (23% need-based, 77% non-need-based). ***Programs:*** Federal Direct (Subsidized and Unsubsidized Stafford, PLUS), Perkins, Federal Nursing, college/university, private loans, Minnesota SELF Loans.

WORK-STUDY ***Federal work-study:*** Total amount: $608,931; 349 jobs averaging $1643. ***State or other work-study/employment:*** Total amount: $213,353 (14% need-based, 86% non-need-based). 187 part-time jobs averaging $1159.

ATHLETIC AWARDS Total amount: $2,427,902 (46% need-based, 54% non-need-based).

APPLYING FOR FINANCIAL AID ***Required financial aid form:*** FAFSA. ***Financial aid deadline (priority):*** 3/1. ***Notification date:*** Continuous beginning 4/1. Students must reply by 5/1 or within 3 weeks of notification.

CONTACT Ms. Brenda L. Murtha, Director of Financial Aid, Augustana College, 2001 South Summit Avenue, Sioux Falls, SD 57197, 605-274-5216 or toll-free 800-727-2844 Ext. 5516 (in-state), 800-727-2844 (out-of-state). *Fax:* 605-274-5295. *E-mail:* brenda.murtha@augie.edu.

AUGUSTA STATE UNIVERSITY

Augusta, GA

Tuition & fees (GA res): $5184 **Average undergraduate aid package: $3866**

ABOUT THE INSTITUTION State-supported, coed. 32 undergraduate majors. Federal methodology is used as a basis for awarding need-based institutional aid.

UNDERGRADUATE EXPENSES for 2010–11 ***Tuition, state resident:*** full-time $4274; part-time $143 per credit hour. ***Tuition, nonresident:*** full-time $15,888; part-time $530 per credit hour. ***Required fees:*** full-time $910; $455 per term. ***College room and board: Room only:*** $5250.

FRESHMAN FINANCIAL AID (Fall 2009) 680 applied for aid; of those 81% were deemed to have need. 94% of freshmen with need received aid; of those 7% had need fully met. ***Average financial aid package:*** $3376 (excluding resources awarded to replace EFC). 1% of all full-time freshmen had no need and received non-need-based gift aid.

UNDERGRADUATE FINANCIAL AID (Fall 2009) 3,236 applied for aid; of those 76% were deemed to have need. 95% of undergraduates with need received aid; of those 11% had need fully met. ***Average financial aid package:*** $3866 (excluding resources awarded to replace EFC). 1% of all full-time undergraduates had no need and received non-need-based gift aid.

GIFT AID (NEED-BASED) ***Total amount:*** $11,326,787 (100% federal). ***Receiving aid:*** Freshmen: 50% (394); all full-time undergraduates: 41% (1,726). ***Average award:*** Freshmen: $2331; Undergraduates: $2356. ***Scholarships, grants, and awards:*** Federal Pell, FSEOG, state, private, college/university gift aid from institutional funds.

GIFT AID (NON-NEED-BASED) ***Total amount:*** $6,599,767 (85% state, 2% institutional, 13% external sources). ***Receiving aid:*** Freshmen: 15% (117). Undergraduates: 15% (638). ***Average award:*** Freshmen: $250. Undergraduates: $843. ***Scholarships, grants, and awards by category:*** *Academic interests/achievement:* biological sciences, business, communication, computer science, education, English, general academic interests/achievements, health fields, mathematics, military science, physical sciences, social sciences. *Creative arts/performance:* art/fine arts, cinema/film/broadcasting, creative writing, general creative arts/performance, journalism/publications, music, performing arts, theater/drama. *Special achievements/activities:* community service, general special achievements/activities, hobbies/interests, leadership, memberships. *Special characteristics:* general special characteristics, handicapped students, international students, local/state students, veterans, veterans' children. ***Tuition waivers:*** Full or partial for employees or children of employees, senior citizens.

LOANS ***Student loans:*** $29,072,386 (46% need-based, 54% non-need-based). 38% of past graduating class borrowed through all loan programs. *Average indebtedness per student:* $7735. ***Average need-based loan:*** Freshmen: $1578. Undergraduates: $2012. ***Parent loans:*** $201,207 (100% non-need-based). ***Programs:*** Federal Direct (Subsidized and Unsubsidized Stafford, PLUS), Perkins, state.

WORK-STUDY ***Federal work-study:*** Total amount: $235,008; jobs available. ***State or other work-study/employment:*** Part-time jobs available.

ATHLETIC AWARDS Total amount: $506,933 (100% non-need-based).

APPLYING FOR FINANCIAL AID ***Required financial aid form:*** FAFSA. ***Financial aid deadline:*** 4/1. ***Notification date:*** Continuous beginning 4/1.

CONTACT Ms. Roxanne Padgett, Assistant Director of Financial Aid, Augusta State University, 2500 Walton Way, Augusta, GA 30904-2200, 706-737-1431 or toll-free 800-341-4373. *Fax:* 706-737-1777. *E-mail:* bpadgett@aug.edu.

AURORA UNIVERSITY

Aurora, IL

Tuition & fees: $18,700 **Average undergraduate aid package: $17,080**

ABOUT THE INSTITUTION Independent, coed. 28 undergraduate majors. Federal methodology is used as a basis for awarding need-based institutional aid.

UNDERGRADUATE EXPENSES for 2010–11 ***Comprehensive fee:*** $27,500 includes full-time tuition ($18,600), mandatory fees ($100), and room and board ($8800). Full-time tuition and fees vary according to location. Room and board charges vary according to board plan, housing facility, and location. ***Part-time tuition:*** $550 per semester hour. Part-time tuition and fees vary according to course load, location, and program. ***Payment plans:*** Installment, deferred payment.

FRESHMAN FINANCIAL AID (Fall 2010, est.) 476 applied for aid; of those 91% were deemed to have need. 100% of freshmen with need received aid; of those 28% had need fully met. ***Average percent of need met:*** 86% (excluding resources awarded to replace EFC). ***Average financial aid package:*** $18,208 (excluding resources awarded to replace EFC). 13% of all full-time freshmen had no need and received non-need-based gift aid.

UNDERGRADUATE FINANCIAL AID (Fall 2010, est.) 2,040 applied for aid; of those 90% were deemed to have need. 99% of undergraduates with need received aid; of those 31% had need fully met. ***Average percent of need met:*** 86% (excluding resources awarded to replace EFC). ***Average financial aid package:*** $17,080 (excluding resources awarded to replace EFC). 17% of all full-time undergraduates had no need and received non-need-based gift aid.

GIFT AID (NEED-BASED) ***Total amount:*** $10,884,057 (42% federal, 42% state, 16% institutional). ***Receiving aid:*** Freshmen: 67% (335); all full-time undergraduates: 65% (1,492). ***Average award:*** Freshmen: $7628; Undergraduates: $7033. ***Scholarships, grants, and awards:*** Federal Pell, FSEOG, state, private, college/university gift aid from institutional funds.

GIFT AID (NON-NEED-BASED) ***Total amount:*** $15,719,837 (1% federal, 97% institutional, 2% external sources). ***Receiving aid:*** Freshmen: 86% (429). Undergraduates: 74% (1,720). ***Average award:*** Freshmen: $9138. Undergraduates: $7375. ***Scholarships, grants, and awards by category:*** *Academic interests/achievement:* 2,103 awards ($14,394,501 total): education, general academic interests/achievements, mathematics. *Creative arts/performance:* 45 awards ($58,250 total): music, theater/drama. *Special achievements/activities:* 169 awards ($348,377 total): general special achievements/activities, religious involvement. *Special characteristics:* 315 awards ($744,271 total): children and siblings of alumni, children of educators, children of faculty/staff, members of minority groups, out-of-state students, parents of current students, religious affiliation, siblings of current students, spouses of current students, veterans, veterans' children. ***Tuition waivers:*** Full or partial for employees or children of employees, senior citizens.

LOANS ***Student loans:*** $14,570,942 (46% need-based, 54% non-need-based). 80% of past graduating class borrowed through all loan programs. *Average indebtedness per student:* $24,083. ***Average need-based loan:*** Freshmen: $3357. Undergraduates: $4395. ***Parent loans:*** $1,639,469 (100% non-need-based). ***Programs:*** Federal Direct (Subsidized and Unsubsidized Stafford, PLUS), Perkins, college/university.

WORK-STUDY ***Federal work-study:*** Total amount: $1,677,899; 1,032 jobs averaging $1724. ***State or other work-study/employment:*** Total amount: $235,410 (100% non-need-based). Part-time jobs available.

APPLYING FOR FINANCIAL AID ***Required financial aid form:*** FAFSA. ***Financial aid deadline (priority):*** 1/1. ***Notification date:*** Continuous beginning 3/1. Students must reply by 5/1 or within 3 weeks of notification.

CONTACT Mrs. Heather McKane, Dean of Student Financial Services, Aurora University, 347 South Gladstone Avenue, Aurora, IL 60506-4892, 630-844-6190 or toll-free 800-742-5281. *Fax:* 630-844-6191. *E-mail:* finaid@aurora.edu.

AUSTIN COLLEGE

Sherman, TX

Tuition & fees: $31,270 **Average undergraduate aid package: $28,120**

ABOUT THE INSTITUTION Independent Presbyterian, coed. 27 undergraduate majors. Federal methodology is used as a basis for awarding need-based institutional aid.

UNDERGRADUATE EXPENSES for 2011–12 ***One-time required fee:*** $25. ***Comprehensive fee:*** $41,348 includes full-time tuition ($31,110), mandatory fees ($160), and room and board ($10,078). Full-time tuition and fees vary according to student level. Room and board charges vary according to board plan. ***Part-time tuition:*** $4424 per course. ***Payment plan:*** Installment.

FRESHMAN FINANCIAL AID (Fall 2010, est.) 268 applied for aid; of those 85% were deemed to have need. 100% of freshmen with need received aid; of those 100% had need fully met. ***Average percent of need met:*** 99% (excluding resources awarded to replace EFC). ***Average financial aid package:*** $28,858 (excluding resources awarded to replace EFC). 24% of all full-time freshmen had no need and received non-need-based gift aid.

UNDERGRADUATE FINANCIAL AID (Fall 2010, est.) 996 applied for aid; of those 84% were deemed to have need. 100% of undergraduates with need received aid; of those 100% had need fully met. ***Average percent of need met:*** 99% (excluding resources awarded to replace EFC). ***Average financial aid package:*** $28,120 (excluding resources awarded to replace EFC). 23% of all full-time undergraduates had no need and received non-need-based gift aid.

GIFT AID (NEED-BASED) ***Total amount:*** $16,750,886 (12% federal, 10% state, 76% institutional, 2% external sources). ***Receiving aid:*** Freshmen: 72% (229); all full-time undergraduates: 65% (838). ***Average award:*** Freshmen: $21,318; Undergraduates: $20,189. ***Scholarships, grants, and awards:*** Federal Pell, FSEOG, state, private, college/university gift aid from institutional funds.

GIFT AID (NON-NEED-BASED) ***Total amount:*** $6,697,347 (97% institutional, 3% external sources). ***Receiving aid:*** Freshmen: 28% (88). Undergraduates: 25% (322). ***Average award:*** Freshmen: $10,919. Undergraduates: $10,884. ***Scholarships, grants, and awards by category:*** *Academic interests/achievement:* biological sciences, business, communication, education, engineering/technologies, English, foreign languages, general academic interests/achievements, health fields, humanities, international studies, physical sciences, premedicine, religion/biblical studies, social sciences. *Creative arts/performance:* art/fine arts, music, theater/drama. *Special achievements/activities:* community service, general special achievements/activities, leadership, religious involvement. *Special characteristics:* children of faculty/staff, ethnic background, first-generation college students, handicapped students, international students, local/state students, relatives of clergy. ***Tuition waivers:*** Full or partial for employees or children of employees.

LOANS ***Student loans:*** $10,428,199 (55% need-based, 45% non-need-based). ***Average need-based loan:*** Freshmen: $3871. Undergraduates: $5469. ***Parent loans:*** $9,442,556 (13% need-based, 87% non-need-based). ***Programs:*** Federal Direct (Subsidized and Unsubsidized Stafford, PLUS), Perkins, state, college/university, alternative loans.

WORK-STUDY ***Federal work-study:*** Total amount: $547,428; jobs available. ***State or other work-study/employment:*** Total amount: $258,060 (13% need-based, 87% non-need-based). Part-time jobs available.

APPLYING FOR FINANCIAL AID ***Required financial aid form:*** FAFSA. ***Financial aid deadline (priority):*** 4/1. ***Notification date:*** Continuous beginning 3/1. Students must reply by 5/1.

CONTACT Mrs. Laurie Coulter, Assistant Vice President for Institutional Enrollment and Executive Director of Financial Aid, Austin College, 900 North Grand Avenue, Sherman, TX 75090, 903-813-2900 or toll-free 800-442-5363. *Fax:* 903-813-3198. *E-mail:* finaid@austincollege.edu.

AUSTIN GRADUATE SCHOOL OF THEOLOGY

Austin, TX

Tuition & fees: $7230 **Average undergraduate aid package: N/A**

ABOUT THE INSTITUTION Independent religious, coed. 1 undergraduate major. Both federal and institutional methodology are used as a basis for awarding need-based institutional aid.

UNDERGRADUATE EXPENSES for 2010–11 ***Tuition:*** full-time $7080; part-time $295 per semester hour. ***Required fees:*** full-time $150; $75 per term. Full-time tuition and fees vary according to course load. Part-time tuition and fees vary according to course load. ***Payment plan:*** Installment.

GIFT AID (NEED-BASED) ***Total amount:*** $71,944 (78% federal, 22% institutional). ***Scholarships, grants, and awards:*** Federal Pell, FSEOG, college/university gift aid from institutional funds.

GIFT AID (NON-NEED-BASED) ***Scholarships, grants, and awards by category:*** *Academic interests/achievement:* religion/biblical studies. *Special achievements/activities:* religious involvement. ***Tuition waivers:*** Full or partial for employees or children of employees.

LOANS ***Student loans:*** $113,800 (53% need-based, 47% non-need-based). ***Programs:*** Federal Direct (Subsidized and Unsubsidized Stafford, PLUS).

WORK-STUDY ***Federal work-study:*** Total amount: $4325; 5 jobs averaging $860.

APPLYING FOR FINANCIAL AID ***Required financial aid forms:*** FAFSA, institution's own form. ***Financial aid deadline:*** Continuous.

CONTACT David Arthur, Director of Financial Aid, Austin Graduate School of Theology, 7640 Guadalupe Street, Austin, TX 78752, 512-476-2772 Ext. 105 or toll-free 866-AUS-GRAD. *Fax:* 512-476-3919. *E-mail:* darthur@austingrad.edu.

AUSTIN PEAY STATE UNIVERSITY

Clarksville, TN

Tuition & fees (TN res): $6048 **Average undergraduate aid package: $8902**

ABOUT THE INSTITUTION State-supported, coed. 33 undergraduate majors. Federal methodology is used as a basis for awarding need-based institutional aid.

UNDERGRADUATE EXPENSES for 2010–11 ***Tuition, state resident:*** full-time $4824; part-time $201 per credit hour. ***Tuition, nonresident:*** full-time $17,352; part-time $723 per credit hour. ***Required fees:*** full-time $1224; $61.20 per credit hour. Full-time tuition and fees vary according to location and program. Part-time tuition and fees vary according to location and program. ***College room and board:*** $6450; ***Room only:*** $3960. Room and board charges vary according to board plan and housing facility. ***Payment plan:*** Installment.

FRESHMAN FINANCIAL AID (Fall 2009) 1,406 applied for aid; of those 81% were deemed to have need. 100% of freshmen with need received aid. ***Average financial aid package:*** $9201 (excluding resources awarded to replace EFC). 15% of all full-time freshmen had no need and received non-need-based gift aid.

UNDERGRADUATE FINANCIAL AID (Fall 2009) 6,216 applied for aid; of those 85% were deemed to have need. 99% of undergraduates with need received aid. ***Average financial aid package:*** $8902 (excluding resources awarded to replace EFC). 9% of all full-time undergraduates had no need and received non-need-based gift aid.

GIFT AID (NEED-BASED) ***Total amount:*** $21,856,289 (85% federal, 15% state). ***Receiving aid:*** Freshmen: 48% (696); all full-time undergraduates: 49% (3,429). ***Average award:*** Freshmen: $5545; Undergraduates: $5158. ***Scholarships, grants, and awards:*** Federal Pell, FSEOG, state, private, college/university gift aid from institutional funds.

GIFT AID (NON-NEED-BASED) ***Total amount:*** $16,876,391 (51% state, 11% institutional, 38% external sources). ***Receiving aid:*** Freshmen: 56% (819). Undergraduates: 35% (2,445). ***Average award:*** Freshmen: $4579. Undergraduates: $4315. ***Scholarships, grants, and awards by category:*** *Academic interests/achievement:* 383 awards ($1,062,093 total): agriculture, biological sciences, business, communication, computer science, education, English, foreign languages, general academic interests/achievements, health fields, humanities, international studies, mathematics, military science, physical sciences, social sciences. *Creative arts/performance:* 389 awards ($394,298 total): art/fine arts, creative writing, debating, journalism/publications, music, performing arts, theater/drama. *Special achievements/activities:* 198 awards ($138,144 total): general special achievements/activities, leadership, memberships. *Special characteristics:* 85 awards ($148,050 total): children of educators, children of faculty/staff, ethnic background, general special characteristics, members of minority groups, veterans. ***Tuition waivers:*** Full or partial for employees or children of employees, senior citizens.

LOANS ***Student loans:*** $38,637,890 (44% need-based, 56% non-need-based). 55% of past graduating class borrowed through all loan programs. *Average indebtedness per student:* $19,149. ***Average need-based loan:*** Freshmen: $3116. Undergraduates: $3811. ***Parent loans:*** $1,917,611 (100% non-need-based). ***Programs:*** Perkins.

WORK-STUDY ***Federal work-study:*** Total amount: $726,074; 177 jobs averaging $1946. ***State or other work-study/employment:*** Total amount: $646,298 (100% non-need-based). 409 part-time jobs averaging $1580.

ATHLETIC AWARDS Total amount: $2,242,430 (100% non-need-based).

APPLYING FOR FINANCIAL AID ***Required financial aid form:*** FAFSA. ***Financial aid deadline (priority):*** 4/1. ***Notification date:*** Continuous beginning 5/1.

CONTACT Donna Price, Director of Student Financial Aid, Austin Peay State University, PO Box 4546, Clarksville, TN 37044, 931-221-7907 or toll-free 800-844-2778 (out-of-state). *Fax:* 931-221-6329. *E-mail:* priced@apsu.edu.

AVE MARIA UNIVERSITY

Ave Maria, FL

ABOUT THE INSTITUTION Independent Roman Catholic, coed. ***Awards:*** bachelor's and master's degrees. 13 undergraduate majors. ***Total enrollment:*** 672. Undergraduates: 532. Freshmen: 228.

GIFT AID (NEED-BASED) ***Scholarships, grants, and awards:*** Federal Pell, state, private, college/university gift aid from institutional funds.

GIFT AID (NON-NEED-BASED) ***Scholarships, grants, and awards by category:*** *Special achievements/activities:* leadership.

LOANS ***Programs:*** college/university.

WORK-STUDY ***Federal work-study:*** Total amount: $93,454; jobs available. ***State or other work-study/employment:*** Part-time jobs available.

APPLYING FOR FINANCIAL AID ***Required financial aid forms:*** FAFSA, state aid form.

CONTACT Anne Hart, Financial Aid Director, Ave Maria University, 5050 Ave Maria Boulevard, Ave Maria, FL 34142, 239-280-1669 or toll-free 877-283-8648. *Fax:* 239-280-2566. *E-mail:* amufinancialaid@avemaria.edu.

AVERETT UNIVERSITY

Danville, VA

Tuition & fees: $22,956 **Average undergraduate aid package: $17,442**

ABOUT THE INSTITUTION Independent religious, coed. 54 undergraduate majors. Federal methodology is used as a basis for awarding need-based institutional aid.

UNDERGRADUATE EXPENSES for 2010–11 ***Comprehensive fee:*** $31,230 includes full-time tuition ($21,956), mandatory fees ($1000), and room and board ($8274). ***College room only:*** $5492. Full-time tuition and fees vary according to course load, degree level, location, and program. Room and board charges vary according to board plan and housing facility. ***Part-time tuition:*** $375 per credit hour. Part-time tuition and fees vary according to course load, degree level, location, and program. ***Payment plan:*** Installment.

FRESHMAN FINANCIAL AID (Fall 2009) 231 applied for aid; of those 90% were deemed to have need. 100% of freshmen with need received aid; of those 20% had need fully met. ***Average percent of need met:*** 72% (excluding resources awarded to replace EFC). ***Average financial aid package:*** $17,296 (excluding resources awarded to replace EFC). 22% of all full-time freshmen had no need and received non-need-based gift aid.

UNDERGRADUATE FINANCIAL AID (Fall 2009) 775 applied for aid; of those 91% were deemed to have need. 100% of undergraduates with need received aid; of those 21% had need fully met. ***Average percent of need met:*** 74% (excluding resources awarded to replace EFC). ***Average financial aid package:*** $17,442 (excluding resources awarded to replace EFC). 20% of all full-time undergraduates had no need and received non-need-based gift aid.

GIFT AID (NEED-BASED) ***Total amount:*** $9,789,056 (22% federal, 12% state, 60% institutional, 6% external sources). ***Receiving aid:*** Freshmen: 78% (207); all full-time undergraduates: 78% (697). ***Average award:*** Freshmen: $14,371; Undergraduates: $13,971. ***Scholarships, grants, and awards:*** Federal Pell, FSEOG, state, private, college/university gift aid from institutional funds.

GIFT AID (NON-NEED-BASED) ***Total amount:*** $2,239,433 (16% state, 75% institutional, 9% external sources). ***Receiving aid:*** Freshmen: 12% (33). Undergraduates: 11% (102). ***Average award:*** Freshmen: $10,032. Undergraduates: $8525. ***Scholarships, grants, and awards by category:*** *Academic interests/achievement:* 118 awards ($231,599 total): biological sciences, business, education, engineering/technologies, English, foreign languages, general academic interests/achievements, health fields, home economics, humanities, mathematics, physical sciences, premedicine, religion/biblical studies. *Creative arts/performance:* 8 awards ($8839 total): art/fine arts, journalism/publications, music, theater/drama. *Special achievements/activities:* 12 awards ($43,688 total): general special achievements/activities, leadership, memberships, religious involvement. *Special characteristics:* 127 awards ($187,783 total): adult students, children and siblings of alumni, children of union members/company employees, first-generation college students, general special characteristics, international students, local/state students, out-of-state students, relatives of clergy, religious affiliation. ***Tuition waivers:*** Full or partial for employees or children of employees, senior citizens.

LOANS ***Student loans:*** $5,291,224 (79% need-based, 21% non-need-based). 75% of past graduating class borrowed through all loan programs. *Average indebtedness per student:* $39,110. ***Average need-based loan:*** Freshmen: $3332. Undergraduates: $4114. ***Parent loans:*** $2,315,359 (40% need-based, 60% non-need-based). ***Programs:*** Federal Direct (Subsidized and Unsubsidized Stafford, PLUS), Perkins, alternative loans.

WORK-STUDY ***Federal work-study:*** Total amount: $107,154; 164 jobs averaging $938. ***State or other work-study/employment:*** Total amount: $5,398,378 (79% need-based, 21% non-need-based). Part-time jobs available.

APPLYING FOR FINANCIAL AID ***Required financial aid forms:*** FAFSA, state aid form. ***Financial aid deadline (priority):*** 4/1. ***Notification date:*** Continuous. Students must reply within 2 weeks of notification.

CONTACT Carl Bradsher, Dean of Financial Assistance, Averett University, 420 West Main Street, Danville, VA 24541-3692, 434-791-5646 or toll-free 800-AVERETT. *Fax:* 434-791-5647. *E-mail:* carl.bradsher@averett.edu.

AVILA UNIVERSITY

Kansas City, MO

CONTACT Nancy Merz, Director of Financial Aid, Avila University, 11901 Wornall Road, Kansas City, MO 64145, 816-501-3782 or toll-free 800-GO-AVILA. *Fax:* 816-501-2462. *E-mail:* nancy.merz@avila.edu.

AZUSA PACIFIC UNIVERSITY

Azusa, CA

Tuition & fees: $28,800 **Average undergraduate aid package: $25,999**

ABOUT THE INSTITUTION Independent nondenominational, coed. 36 undergraduate majors. Federal methodology is used as a basis for awarding need-based institutional aid.

UNDERGRADUATE EXPENSES for 2010–11 ***Comprehensive fee:*** $35,882 includes full-time tuition ($28,000), mandatory fees ($800), and room and board ($7082). ***College room only:*** $4076.

FRESHMAN FINANCIAL AID (Fall 2009) 820 applied for aid; of those 82% were deemed to have need. 100% of freshmen with need received aid; of those 34% had need fully met. ***Average percent of need met:*** 74% (excluding resources awarded to replace EFC). ***Average financial aid package:*** $26,061 (excluding resources awarded to replace EFC). 26% of all full-time freshmen had no need and received non-need-based gift aid.

UNDERGRADUATE FINANCIAL AID (Fall 2009) 2,970 applied for aid; of those 86% were deemed to have need. 99% of undergraduates with need received aid; of those 35% had need fully met. ***Average percent of need met:*** 71% (excluding resources awarded to replace EFC). ***Average financial aid package:*** $25,999 (excluding resources awarded to replace EFC). 28% of all full-time undergraduates had no need and received non-need-based gift aid.

GIFT AID (NEED-BASED) ***Total amount:*** $33,877,430 (17% federal, 22% state, 58% institutional, 3% external sources). ***Receiving aid:*** Freshmen: 53% (533); all full-time undergraduates: 53% (2,192). ***Average award:*** Freshmen: $5588; Undergraduates: $5470. ***Scholarships, grants, and awards:*** Federal Pell, FSEOG, state, private, college/university gift aid from institutional funds, Federal Nursing.

GIFT AID (NON-NEED-BASED) ***Total amount:*** $10,081,102 (85% institutional, 15% external sources). ***Receiving aid:*** Freshmen: 66% (666). Undergraduates: 60% (2,509). ***Average award:*** Freshmen: $7981. Undergraduates: $6696. ***Scholarships, grants, and awards by category:*** *Academic interests/achievement:* general academic interests/achievements. *Creative arts/performance:* general creative arts/performance. *Special achievements/activities:* leadership. *Special characteristics:* members of minority groups, religious affiliation.

LOANS ***Student loans:*** $37,820,969 (77% need-based, 23% non-need-based). ***Average need-based loan:*** Freshmen: $3497. Undergraduates: $4492. ***Parent loans:*** $13,136,047 (43% need-based, 57% non-need-based). ***Programs:*** Perkins, Federal Nursing.

WORK-STUDY ***Federal work-study:*** Total amount: $1,175,831; jobs available.

ATHLETIC AWARDS Total amount: $3,045,501 (52% need-based, 48% non-need-based).

APPLYING FOR FINANCIAL AID ***Required financial aid forms:*** FAFSA, institution's own form. ***Financial aid deadline:*** 7/1 (priority: 3/2). ***Notification date:*** Continuous beginning 3/1. Students must reply within 3 weeks of notification.

CONTACT Todd Ross, Interim Director of Student Financial Services, Azusa Pacific University, 901 East Alosta Avenue, PO Box 7000, Azusa, CA 91702-7000, 626-812-3009 or toll-free 800-TALK-APU. *E-mail:* tross@apu.edu.

BABSON COLLEGE

Wellesley, MA

Tuition & fees: $39,040 **Average undergraduate aid package: $32,105**

ABOUT THE INSTITUTION Independent, coed. 24 undergraduate majors. Both federal and institutional methodology are used as a basis for awarding need-based institutional aid.

UNDERGRADUATE EXPENSES for 2010–11 ***Comprehensive fee:*** $51,916 includes full-time tuition ($39,040) and room and board ($12,876). ***College room only:*** $8308. Room and board charges vary according to board plan and housing facility. ***Payment plan:*** Installment.

FRESHMAN FINANCIAL AID (Fall 2010, est.) 269 applied for aid; of those 83% were deemed to have need. 100% of freshmen with need received aid; of those 24% had need fully met. ***Average percent of need met:*** 92% (excluding resources awarded to replace EFC). ***Average financial aid package:*** $31,375 (excluding resources awarded to replace EFC). 7% of all full-time freshmen had no need and received non-need-based gift aid.

UNDERGRADUATE FINANCIAL AID (Fall 2010, est.) 946 applied for aid; of those 93% were deemed to have need. 100% of undergraduates with need received aid; of those 45% had need fully met. ***Average percent of need met:*** 94% (excluding resources awarded to replace EFC). ***Average financial aid package:*** $32,105 (excluding resources awarded to replace EFC). 5% of all full-time undergraduates had no need and received non-need-based gift aid.

GIFT AID (NEED-BASED) ***Total amount:*** $23,851,000 (9% federal, 1% state, 90% institutional). ***Receiving aid:*** Freshmen: 42% (204); all full-time undergraduates: 42% (826). ***Average award:*** Freshmen: $28,454; Undergraduates: $27,950. ***Scholarships, grants, and awards:*** Federal Pell, FSEOG, state, college/university gift aid from institutional funds.

GIFT AID (NON-NEED-BASED) ***Total amount:*** $2,526,000 (81% institutional, 19% external sources). ***Receiving aid:*** Freshmen: 8% (37). Undergraduates: 7% (128). ***Average award:*** Freshmen: $22,390. Undergraduates: $20,000. ***Scholarships, grants, and awards by category:*** *Academic interests/achievement:* 82 awards ($1,459,000 total): general academic interests/achievements. *Special achievements/activities:* 160 awards ($3,481,000 total): leadership. *Special characteristics:* 1 award ($5000 total): veterans. ***Tuition waivers:*** Full or partial for employees or children of employees.

LOANS ***Student loans:*** $7,423,000 (47% need-based, 53% non-need-based). 47% of past graduating class borrowed through all loan programs. *Average indebtedness per student:* $30,357. ***Average need-based loan:*** Freshmen: $2811. Undergraduates: $3948. ***Parent loans:*** $3,660,000 (100% non-need-based). ***Programs:*** Federal Direct (Subsidized and Unsubsidized Stafford, PLUS), Perkins, state.

WORK-STUDY ***Federal work-study:*** Total amount: $1,421,000; 697 jobs averaging $1982. ***State or other work-study/employment:*** Total amount: $839,000 (100% non-need-based). 8 part-time jobs averaging $2200.

APPLYING FOR FINANCIAL AID ***Required financial aid forms:*** FAFSA, CSS Financial Aid PROFILE, noncustodial (divorced/separated) parent's statement, business/farm supplement, federal income tax form(s), W-2 forms, verification worksheet. ***Financial aid deadline:*** 2/15. ***Notification date:*** 4/1. Students must reply by 5/1.

CONTACT Ms. Melissa Shaak, Director of Financial Aid, Babson College, Hollister Hall, Third Floor, Babson Park, MA 02457-0310, 781-239-4219 or toll-free 800-488-3696. *Fax:* 781-239-5510. *E-mail:* shaak@babson.edu.

BACONE COLLEGE

Muskogee, OK

ABOUT THE INSTITUTION Independent religious, coed. ***Awards:*** associate and bachelor's degrees. 26 undergraduate majors. ***Total enrollment:*** 884. Undergraduates: 884.

GIFT AID (NEED-BASED) ***Scholarships, grants, and awards:*** Federal Pell, FSEOG, state, private, college/university gift aid from institutional funds.

WORK-STUDY Federal work-study jobs available.

APPLYING FOR FINANCIAL AID ***Required financial aid forms:*** FAFSA, institution's own form.

CONTACT Mrs. Kathye Watson, Office of Financial Aid, Bacone College, 2299 Old Bacone Road, Muskogee, OK 74403-1597, 918-781-7294 or toll-free 888-682-5514 Ext. 7340. *Fax:* 918-781-7416. *E-mail:* financialaid@bacone.edu.

BAIS BINYOMIN ACADEMY

Stamford, CT

CONTACT Financial Aid Office, Bais Binyomin Academy, 132 Prospect Street, Stamford, CT 06901-1202, 203-325-4351.

BAKER COLLEGE OF ALLEN PARK

Allen Park, MI

CONTACT Financial Aid Office, Baker College of Allen Park, 4500 Enterprise Drive, Allen Park, MI 48101, 313-425-3700 or toll-free 800-767-4120 (in-state).

BAKER COLLEGE OF AUBURN HILLS

Auburn Hills, MI

CONTACT Financial Aid Office, Baker College of Auburn Hills, 1500 University Drive, Auburn Hills, MI 48326-1586, 248-340-0600 or toll-free 888-429-0410 (in-state).

BAKER COLLEGE OF CADILLAC

Cadillac, MI

CONTACT Financial Aid Office, Baker College of Cadillac, 9600 East 13th Street, Cadillac, MI 49601, 231-876-3100 or toll-free 888-313-3463 (in-state).

BAKER COLLEGE OF CLINTON TOWNSHIP

Clinton Township, MI

CONTACT Financial Aid Office, Baker College of Clinton Township, 34950 Little Mack Avenue, Clinton Township, MI 48035-4701, 586-791-6610 or toll-free 888-272-2842.

BAKER COLLEGE OF FLINT

Flint, MI

CONTACT Financial Aid Office, Baker College of Flint, 1050 West Bristol Road, Flint, MI 48507-5508, 810-767-7600 or toll-free 800-964-4299.

BAKER COLLEGE OF JACKSON

Jackson, MI

CONTACT Financial Aid Office, Baker College of Jackson, 2800 Springport Road, Jackson, MI 49202, 517-789-6123 or toll-free 888-343-3683.

BAKER COLLEGE OF MUSKEGON

Muskegon, MI

CONTACT Financial Aid Office, Baker College of Muskegon, 1903 Marquette Avenue, Muskegon, MI 49442-3497, 231-777-5200 or toll-free 800-937-0337 (in-state).

BAKER COLLEGE OF OWOSSO

Owosso, MI

CONTACT Financial Aid Office, Baker College of Owosso, 1020 South Washington Street, Owosso, MI 48867-4400, 989-729-3300 or toll-free 800-879-3797.

BAKER COLLEGE OF PORT HURON

Port Huron, MI

CONTACT Financial Aid Office, Baker College of Port Huron, 3403 Lapeer Road, Port Huron, MI 48060-2597, 810-985-7000 or toll-free 888-262-2442.

BAKER UNIVERSITY

Baldwin City, KS

CONTACT Mrs. Jeanne Mott, Financial Aid Director, Baker University, Box 65, Baldwin City, KS 66006-0065, 785-594-4595 or toll-free 800-873-4282. *Fax:* 785-594-8358.

BALDWIN-WALLACE COLLEGE

Berea, OH

Tuition & fees: $25,260 **Average undergraduate aid package: $20,739**

ABOUT THE INSTITUTION Independent Methodist, coed. 66 undergraduate majors. Federal methodology is used as a basis for awarding need-based institutional aid.

UNDERGRADUATE EXPENSES for 2010–11 ***Comprehensive fee:*** $33,560 includes full-time tuition ($25,260) and room and board ($8300). ***College room only:*** $4056. Full-time tuition and fees vary according to class time and course load. ***Part-time tuition:*** $785 per semester hour. Part-time tuition and fees vary according to class time and course load. ***Payment plans:*** Installment, deferred payment.

FRESHMAN FINANCIAL AID (Fall 2010, est.) 666 applied for aid; of those 91% were deemed to have need. 100% of freshmen with need received aid; of those 31% had need fully met. ***Average percent of need met:*** 88% (excluding resources awarded to replace EFC). ***Average financial aid package:*** $22,073 (excluding resources awarded to replace EFC). 14% of all full-time freshmen had no need and received non-need-based gift aid.

UNDERGRADUATE FINANCIAL AID (Fall 2010, est.) 2,702 applied for aid; of those 90% were deemed to have need. 100% of undergraduates with need received aid; of those 36% had need fully met. ***Average percent of need met:*** 86% (excluding resources awarded to replace EFC). ***Average financial aid package:*** $20,739 (excluding resources awarded to replace EFC). 15% of all full-time undergraduates had no need and received non-need-based gift aid.

GIFT AID (NEED-BASED) ***Total amount:*** $31,595,859 (19% federal, 5% state, 74% institutional, 2% external sources). ***Receiving aid:*** Freshmen: 85% (603); all full-time undergraduates: 77% (2,424). ***Average award:*** Freshmen: $15,463; Undergraduates: $15,052. ***Scholarships, grants, and awards:*** Federal Pell, FSEOG, state, private, college/university gift aid from institutional funds.

GIFT AID (NON-NEED-BASED) ***Total amount:*** $7,762,979 (1% state, 97% institutional, 2% external sources). ***Receiving aid:*** Freshmen: 27% (188). Undergraduates: 28% (872). ***Average award:*** Freshmen: $10,633. Undergraduates: $8923. ***Scholarships, grants, and awards by category:*** *Academic interests/achievement:* 2,080 awards ($17,274,816 total): general academic interests/achievements. *Creative arts/performance:* 229 awards ($655,550 total): music. *Special achievements/activities:* 52 awards ($104,765 total): leadership. *Special characteristics:* 1,065 awards ($2,730,999 total): children and siblings of alumni, members of minority groups, religious affiliation, siblings of current students. ***Tuition waivers:*** Full or partial for children of alumni, employees or children of employees.

LOANS ***Student loans:*** $24,281,000 (77% need-based, 23% non-need-based). 78% of past graduating class borrowed through all loan programs. *Average indebtedness per student:* $30,096. ***Average need-based loan:*** Freshmen: $3991. Undergraduates: $4564. ***Parent loans:*** $7,851,000 (26% need-based, 74% non-need-based). *Programs:* Federal Direct (Subsidized and Unsubsidized Stafford, PLUS), Perkins, college/university.

WORK-STUDY ***Federal work-study:*** Total amount: $466,000; 909 jobs averaging $710. ***State or other work-study/employment:*** Total amount: $1,502,000 (50% need-based, 50% non-need-based). 411 part-time jobs averaging $506.

APPLYING FOR FINANCIAL AID ***Required financial aid form:*** FAFSA. ***Financial aid deadline:*** 9/1 (priority: 5/1). ***Notification date:*** Continuous beginning 2/14.

CONTACT Dr. George L. Rolleston, Director of Financial Aid, Baldwin-Wallace College, 275 Eastland Road, Berea, OH 44017-2088, 440-826-2108 or toll-free 877-BWAPPLY (in-state). *Fax:* 440-826-8048. *E-mail:* grollest@bw.edu.

BALL STATE UNIVERSITY

Muncie, IN

Tuition & fees (IN res): $8214 **Average undergraduate aid package: $9849**

ABOUT THE INSTITUTION State-supported, coed. 85 undergraduate majors. Federal methodology is used as a basis for awarding need-based institutional aid.

UNDERGRADUATE EXPENSES for 2010–11 ***Tuition, state resident:*** full-time $7508; part-time $289 per credit hour. ***Tuition, nonresident:*** full-time $20,960; part-time $771 per credit hour. ***Required fees:*** full-time $706. Full-time tuition and fees vary according to course level, program, and reciprocity agreements. Part-time tuition and fees vary according to course level, course load, and reciprocity agreements. ***College room and board:*** $8208. Room and board charges vary according to board plan and housing facility. ***Payment plan:*** Installment.

FRESHMAN FINANCIAL AID (Fall 2010, est.) 3,534 applied for aid; of those 79% were deemed to have need. 99% of freshmen with need received aid; of those 20% had need fully met. ***Average percent of need met:*** 51% (excluding resources awarded to replace EFC). ***Average financial aid package:*** $10,039 (excluding resources awarded to replace EFC). 7% of all full-time freshmen had no need and received non-need-based gift aid.

UNDERGRADUATE FINANCIAL AID (Fall 2010, est.) 13,860 applied for aid; of those 81% were deemed to have need. 99% of undergraduates with need received aid; of those 20% had need fully met. ***Average percent of need met:*** 56% (excluding resources awarded to replace EFC). ***Average financial aid package:*** $9849 (excluding resources awarded to replace EFC). 6% of all full-time undergraduates had no need and received non-need-based gift aid.

GIFT AID (NEED-BASED) ***Total amount:*** $44,879,908 (58% federal, 34% state, 8% institutional). ***Receiving aid:*** Freshmen: 43% (1,650); all full-time undergraduates: 41% (6,838). ***Average award:*** Freshmen: $6834; Undergraduates: $6130. ***Scholarships, grants, and awards:*** Federal Pell, FSEOG, state, private, college/university gift aid from institutional funds.

GIFT AID (NON-NEED-BASED) ***Total amount:*** $33,522,424 (8% federal, 23% state, 55% institutional, 14% external sources). ***Receiving aid:*** Freshmen: 35% (1,348). Undergraduates: 23% (3,920). ***Average award:*** Freshmen: $6048. Undergraduates: $6525. ***Scholarships, grants, and awards by category:*** *Academic interests/achievement:* 2,533 awards ($15,316,240 total): architecture, biological sciences, business, communication, education, engineering/technologies, English, foreign languages, general academic interests/achievements, health fields, humanities, international studies, mathematics, military science, physical sciences, social sciences. *Creative arts/performance:* 149 awards ($168,078 total): art/fine arts, cinema/film/broadcasting, dance, debating, general creative arts/performance, journalism/publications, music, performing arts, theater/drama. *Special achievements/activities:* 178 awards ($1,325,043 total): community service, general special achievements/activities, leadership. *Special characteristics:* 785 awards ($8,382,262 total): adult students, children and siblings of alumni, children of faculty/staff, general special characteristics, international students, local/state students, members of minority groups, out-of-state students, veterans, veterans' children. ***Tuition waivers:*** Full or partial for employees or children of employees, senior citizens.

LOANS ***Student loans:*** $95,746,520 (43% need-based, 57% non-need-based). 66% of past graduating class borrowed through all loan programs. *Average indebtedness per student:* $24,121. ***Average need-based loan:*** Freshmen: $3408. Undergraduates: $4203. ***Parent loans:*** $101,649,047 (100% non-need-based). ***Programs:*** Federal Direct (Subsidized and Unsubsidized Stafford, PLUS), Perkins.

WORK-STUDY ***Federal work-study:*** Total amount: $1,982,800; 794 jobs averaging $2235. ***State or other work-study/employment:*** Total amount: $9,078,170 (8% need-based, 92% non-need-based). Part-time jobs available.

ATHLETIC AWARDS Total amount: $5,396,755 (100% non-need-based).

APPLYING FOR FINANCIAL AID ***Required financial aid form:*** FAFSA. ***Financial aid deadline (priority):*** 3/10. ***Notification date:*** Continuous beginning 4/1.

CONTACT John McPherson, Director of Scholarships and Financial Aid, Ball State University, Lucina Hall, Muncie, IN 47306-1099, 800-227-4017 or toll-free 800-482-4BSU. *Fax:* 765-285-4247. *E-mail:* finaid@bsu.edu.

BALTIMORE INTERNATIONAL COLLEGE

Baltimore, MD

CONTACT Kim Wittler, Director, Student Financial Planning, Baltimore International College, 17 Commerce Street, Baltimore, MD 21202, 410-752-0490 or toll-free 800-624-9926 Ext. 120 (out-of-state). *Fax:* 410-752-3730.

BAPTIST BIBLE COLLEGE

Springfield, MO

CONTACT Bob Kotulski, Director of Financial Aid, Baptist Bible College, 628 East Kearney, Springfield, MO 65803-3498, 417-268-6036. *Fax:* 417-268-6694.

BAPTIST BIBLE COLLEGE OF PENNSYLVANIA

Clarks Summit, PA

Tuition & fees: $18,240 **Average undergraduate aid package: $11,820**

ABOUT THE INSTITUTION Independent Baptist, coed. 28 undergraduate majors. Federal methodology is used as a basis for awarding need-based institutional aid.

UNDERGRADUATE EXPENSES for 2011–12 ***Comprehensive fee:*** $24,890 includes full-time tuition ($17,040), mandatory fees ($1200), and room and board ($6650). ***College room only:*** $2400. Room and board charges vary according to board plan. ***Part-time tuition:*** $598 per credit. ***Part-time fees:*** $40 per credit. Part-time tuition and fees vary according to course load. ***Payment plan:*** Installment.

FRESHMAN FINANCIAL AID (Fall 2009) 111 applied for aid; of those 92% were deemed to have need. 99% of freshmen with need received aid; of those 9% had need fully met. ***Average percent of need met:*** 61% (excluding resources awarded to replace EFC). ***Average financial aid package:*** $11,293 (excluding resources awarded to replace EFC). 6% of all full-time freshmen had no need and received non-need-based gift aid.

UNDERGRADUATE FINANCIAL AID (Fall 2009) 538 applied for aid; of those 91% were deemed to have need. 100% of undergraduates with need received aid; of those 9% had need fully met. ***Average percent of need met:*** 62% (excluding resources awarded to replace EFC). ***Average financial aid package:*** $11,820 (excluding resources awarded to replace EFC). 6% of all full-time undergraduates had no need and received non-need-based gift aid.

GIFT AID (NEED-BASED) ***Total amount:*** $1,678,948 (69% federal, 26% state, 5% institutional). ***Receiving aid:*** Freshmen: 55% (63); all full-time undergraduates: 53% (320). ***Average award:*** Freshmen: $5241; Undergraduates: $5050. ***Scholarships, grants, and awards:*** Federal Pell, FSEOG, state, private, college/university gift aid from institutional funds.

GIFT AID (NON-NEED-BASED) ***Total amount:*** $2,412,860 (97% institutional, 3% external sources). ***Receiving aid:*** Freshmen: 85% (98). Undergraduates: 72% (432). ***Average award:*** Freshmen: $6257. Undergraduates: $5189. ***Scholarships, grants, and awards by category:*** *Academic interests/achievement:* 427 awards ($1,539,526 total): education, general academic interests/achievements, religion/biblical studies. *Creative arts/performance:* 15 awards ($20,441 total): general creative arts/performance, music. *Special achievements/activities:* 141 awards ($240,782 total): general special achievements/activities, leadership, religious involvement. *Special characteristics:* 197 awards ($474,568 total): children and siblings of alumni, children of faculty/staff, general special characteristics, married students, previous college experience, relatives of clergy, siblings of current students. ***Tuition waivers:*** Full or partial for employees or children of employees.

LOANS ***Student loans:*** $3,208,727 (49% need-based, 51% non-need-based). 82% of past graduating class borrowed through all loan programs. *Average indebtedness per student:* $19,176. ***Average need-based loan:*** Freshmen: $3443. Undergraduates: $4306. ***Parent loans:*** $623,999 (100% non-need-based). ***Programs:*** Federal Direct (Subsidized and Unsubsidized Stafford, PLUS), alternative loans.

WORK-STUDY ***Federal work-study:*** Total amount: $80,616; 59 jobs averaging $1366. ***State or other work-study/employment:*** Total amount: $415,612 (100% non-need-based). 206 part-time jobs averaging $2018.

APPLYING FOR FINANCIAL AID ***Required financial aid form:*** FAFSA. ***Financial aid deadline (priority):*** 5/1. ***Notification date:*** Continuous beginning 2/1.

CONTACT Mr. Steven E. Brown, Director of Student Financial Services, Baptist Bible College of Pennsylvania, 538 Venard Road, Clarks Summit, PA 18411, 570-586-2400 Ext. 9206 or toll-free 800-451-7664. *Fax:* 570-587-8045. *E-mail:* sbrown@bbc.edu.

THE BAPTIST COLLEGE OF FLORIDA

Graceville, FL

Tuition & fees: $8800 **Average undergraduate aid package: $7348**

ABOUT THE INSTITUTION Independent Southern Baptist, coed. 8 undergraduate majors. Federal methodology is used as a basis for awarding need-based institutional aid.

UNDERGRADUATE EXPENSES for 2010–11 ***Comprehensive fee:*** $12,866 includes full-time tuition ($8400), mandatory fees ($400), and room and board ($4066). Full-time tuition and fees vary according to course load and location. Room and board charges vary according to board plan and housing facility. ***Part-time tuition:*** $280 per semester hour. Part-time tuition and fees vary according to course load and location. ***Payment plan:*** Installment.

FRESHMAN FINANCIAL AID (Fall 2010, est.) 94 applied for aid; of those 87% were deemed to have need. 77% of freshmen with need received aid; of those 3% had need fully met. ***Average percent of need met:*** 41% (excluding resources awarded to replace EFC). ***Average financial aid package:*** $6872 (excluding resources awarded to replace EFC). 3% of all full-time freshmen had no need and received non-need-based gift aid.

UNDERGRADUATE FINANCIAL AID (Fall 2010, est.) 496 applied for aid; of those 89% were deemed to have need. 88% of undergraduates with need received aid; of those 6% had need fully met. ***Average percent of need met:*** 45% (excluding resources awarded to replace EFC). ***Average financial aid package:*** $7348 (excluding resources awarded to replace EFC). 2% of all full-time undergraduates had no need and received non-need-based gift aid.

GIFT AID (NEED-BASED) ***Total amount:*** $2,047,462 (62% federal, 21% state, 2% institutional, 15% external sources). ***Receiving aid:*** Freshmen: 58% (62); all full-time undergraduates: 61% (374). ***Average award:*** Freshmen: $5186; Undergraduates: $5145. ***Scholarships, grants, and awards:*** Federal Pell, FSEOG, state, private, college/university gift aid from institutional funds.

GIFT AID (NON-NEED-BASED) ***Total amount:*** $251,704 (1% federal, 44% state, 8% institutional, 47% external sources). ***Receiving aid:*** Freshmen: 1% (1). Undergraduates: 2% (12). ***Average award:*** Freshmen: $1500. Undergraduates: $1428. ***Scholarships, grants, and awards by category:*** *Academic interests/achievement:* 242 awards ($206,376 total): education, religion/biblical studies. *Creative arts/performance:* 7 awards ($2487 total): music. *Special characteristics:* 246 awards ($214,878 total): children with a deceased or disabled parent, religious affiliation, spouses of current students. ***Tuition waivers:*** Full or partial for employees or children of employees.

LOANS ***Student loans:*** $1,865,491 (83% need-based, 17% non-need-based). 65% of past graduating class borrowed through all loan programs. *Average indebtedness per student:* $7988. ***Average need-based loan:*** Freshmen: $2641. Undergraduates: $3325. ***Parent loans:*** $71,050 (40% need-based, 60% non-need-based). ***Programs:*** Federal Direct (Subsidized and Unsubsidized Stafford, PLUS).

WORK-STUDY ***Federal work-study:*** Total amount: $46,171; 24 jobs averaging $2035.

APPLYING FOR FINANCIAL AID ***Required financial aid forms:*** FAFSA, institution's own form, state aid form, business/farm supplement, student authorization form. ***Financial aid deadline:*** 4/15 (priority: 4/1). ***Notification date:*** Continuous beginning 6/15. Students must reply within 4 weeks of notification.

CONTACT Angela Rathel, Director of Financial Aid, The Baptist College of Florida, 5400 College Drive, Graceville, FL 32440-3306, 850-263-3261 Ext. 461 or toll-free 800-328-2660 Ext. 460. *Fax:* 850-263-2141. *E-mail:* finaid@baptistcollege.edu.

BAPTIST COLLEGE OF HEALTH SCIENCES

Memphis, TN

CONTACT Leanne Smith, Financial Aid Officer, Baptist College of Health Sciences, 1003 Monroe Avenue, Memphis, TN 38104, 901-227-6805 or toll-free 866-575-2247. *Fax:* 901-227-4311. *E-mail:* leanne.smith@bchs.edu.

BAPTIST MISSIONARY ASSOCIATION THEOLOGICAL SEMINARY

Jacksonville, TX

CONTACT Dr. Philip Attebery, Dean/Registrar, Baptist Missionary Association Theological Seminary, 1530 East Pine Street, Jacksonville, TX 75766-5407, 903-586-2501. *Fax:* 903-586-0378. *E-mail:* bmatsem@bmats.edu.

BAPTIST UNIVERSITY OF THE AMERICAS

San Antonio, TX

Tuition & fees: $4560 **Average undergraduate aid package: N/A**

ABOUT THE INSTITUTION Independent Baptist, coed. 4 undergraduate majors. Both federal and institutional methodology are used as a basis for awarding need-based institutional aid.

UNDERGRADUATE EXPENSES for 2010–11 ***Tuition:*** full-time $4080; part-time $170 per hour.

GIFT AID (NEED-BASED) ***Scholarships, grants, and awards:*** Federal Pell, FSEOG, private, college/university gift aid from institutional funds.

GIFT AID (NON-NEED-BASED) ***Scholarships, grants, and awards by category:*** *Academic interests/achievement:* business, humanities, religion/biblical studies.

LOANS ***Programs:*** Federal Direct (Subsidized and Unsubsidized Stafford).

WORK-STUDY Federal work-study jobs available. ***State or other work-study/employment:*** Part-time jobs available.

APPLYING FOR FINANCIAL AID ***Required financial aid form:*** FAFSA.

CONTACT Mrs. Araceli G. Acosta, Financial Aid Administrator, Baptist University of the Americas, 8019 South Pan Am Expressway, San Antonio, TX 78224, 210-924-4338 Ext. 214 or toll-free 800-721-1396. *Fax:* 210-924-2701. *E-mail:* araceli.acosta@bua.edu.

BARCLAY COLLEGE

Haviland, KS

CONTACT Christina Foster, Financial Aid Coordinator, Barclay College, 607 North Kingman, Haviland, KS 67059, 800-862-0226. *Fax:* 620-862-5403. *E-mail:* financialaid@barclaycollege.edu.

BARD COLLEGE

Annandale-on-Hudson, NY

Tuition & fees: $41,670 **Average undergraduate aid package: $38,530**

ABOUT THE INSTITUTION Independent, coed. 78 undergraduate majors. Both federal and institutional methodology are used as a basis for awarding need-based institutional aid.

UNDERGRADUATE EXPENSES for 2010–11 ***One-time required fee:*** $800. ***Comprehensive fee:*** $53,480 includes full-time tuition ($40,840), mandatory fees ($830), and room and board ($11,810). Room and board charges vary according to housing facility. ***Part-time tuition:*** $1277 per credit. ***Payment plans:*** Tuition prepayment, installment.

FRESHMAN FINANCIAL AID (Fall 2010, est.) 357 applied for aid; of those 92% were deemed to have need. 100% of freshmen with need received aid; of those 60% had need fully met. ***Average percent of need met:*** 91% (excluding resources awarded to replace EFC). ***Average financial aid package:*** $36,952 (excluding resources awarded to replace EFC). 2% of all full-time freshmen had no need and received non-need-based gift aid.

UNDERGRADUATE FINANCIAL AID (Fall 2010, est.) 1,277 applied for aid; of those 94% were deemed to have need. 100% of undergraduates with need received aid; of those 51% had need fully met. ***Average percent of need met:*** 94% (excluding resources awarded to replace EFC). ***Average financial aid package:*** $38,530 (excluding resources awarded to replace EFC). 2% of all full-time undergraduates had no need and received non-need-based gift aid.

GIFT AID (NEED-BASED) ***Total amount:*** $34,137,381 (6% federal, 2% state, 91% institutional, 1% external sources). ***Receiving aid:*** Freshmen: 64% (317); all full-time undergraduates: 59% (1,142). ***Average award:*** Freshmen: $33,329; Undergraduates: $31,136. ***Scholarships, grants, and awards:*** Federal Pell, FSEOG, state, private, college/university gift aid from institutional funds.

GIFT AID (NON-NEED-BASED) ***Total amount:*** $548,876 (1% state, 98% institutional, 1% external sources). ***Average award:*** Freshmen: $20,199. Undergraduates: $17,841. ***Scholarships, grants, and awards by category:*** *Academic interests/achievement:* 2 awards ($10,000 total): biological sciences, computer science, mathematics, physical sciences. *Special achievements/activities:* leadership. *Special characteristics:* 5 awards ($204,200 total): children of educators, children of faculty/staff. ***Tuition waivers:*** Full or partial for employees or children of employees.

LOANS ***Student loans:*** $6,783,428 (80% need-based, 20% non-need-based). 49% of past graduating class borrowed through all loan programs. *Average indebtedness per student:* $24,311. ***Average need-based loan:*** Freshmen: $4435. Undergraduates: $4942. ***Parent loans:*** $4,531,574 (74% need-based, 26% non-need-based). ***Programs:*** Federal Direct (Subsidized and Unsubsidized Stafford, PLUS), Perkins, college/university loans from institutional funds (international students only).

WORK-STUDY ***Federal work-study:*** Total amount: $1,142,535; 716 jobs averaging $1595. ***State or other work-study/employment:*** Total amount: $146,025 (100% need-based). 88 part-time jobs averaging $1660.

APPLYING FOR FINANCIAL AID ***Required financial aid forms:*** FAFSA, CSS Financial Aid PROFILE, state aid form, noncustodial (divorced/separated) parent's statement, business/farm supplement. ***Financial aid deadline:*** 2/15 (priority: 2/1). ***Notification date:*** 4/1. Students must reply by 5/1 or within 2 weeks of notification.

CONTACT Denise Ann Ackerman, Director of Financial Aid, Bard College, Annandale Road, Annandale-on-Hudson, NY 12504, 845-758-7525. *Fax:* 845-758-7336. *E-mail:* finaid@bard.edu.

BARD COLLEGE AT SIMON'S ROCK

Great Barrington, MA

Tuition & fees: $41,982 **Average undergraduate aid package: $32,525**

ABOUT THE INSTITUTION Independent, coed. 44 undergraduate majors. Both federal and institutional methodology are used as a basis for awarding need-based institutional aid.

UNDERGRADUATE EXPENSES for 2010–11 ***One-time required fee:*** $550. ***Comprehensive fee:*** $53,432 includes full-time tuition ($41,160), mandatory fees ($822), and room and board ($11,450). Full-time tuition and fees vary according to course load. Part-time tuition and fees vary according to course load. ***Payment plan:*** Installment.

FRESHMAN FINANCIAL AID (Fall 2010, est.) 113 applied for aid; of those 88% were deemed to have need. 100% of freshmen with need received aid; of those 17% had need fully met. ***Average percent of need met:*** 65% (excluding resources awarded to replace EFC). ***Average financial aid package:*** $33,336 (excluding resources awarded to replace EFC). 17% of all full-time freshmen had no need and received non-need-based gift aid.

UNDERGRADUATE FINANCIAL AID (Fall 2010, est.) 301 applied for aid; of those 94% were deemed to have need. 98% of undergraduates with need received aid; of those 19% had need fully met. ***Average percent of need met:*** 64% (excluding resources awarded to replace EFC). ***Average financial aid package:*** $32,525 (excluding resources awarded to replace EFC). 17% of all full-time undergraduates had no need and received non-need-based gift aid.

GIFT AID (NEED-BASED) ***Total amount:*** $4,091,798 (14% federal, 1% state, 85% institutional). ***Receiving aid:*** Freshmen: 57% (78); all full-time undergraduates: 57% (228). ***Average award:*** Freshmen: $18,915; Undergraduates: $17,947. ***Scholarships, grants, and awards:*** Federal Pell, FSEOG, state, private, college/university gift aid from institutional funds.

GIFT AID (NON-NEED-BASED) ***Total amount:*** $4,534,801 (97% institutional, 3% external sources). ***Receiving aid:*** Freshmen: 51% (69). Undergraduates: 51% (204). ***Average award:*** Freshmen: $20,074. Undergraduates: $16,190. ***Scholarships, grants, and awards by category:*** *Academic interests/achievement:* 175 awards ($3,017,405 total): general academic interests/achievements. *Special characteristics:* 198 awards ($2,166,910 total): children and siblings of alumni, children of faculty/staff, local/state students, members of minority groups. ***Tuition waivers:*** Full or partial for employees or children of employees.

LOANS ***Student loans:*** $2,120,750 (100% need-based). 44% of past graduating class borrowed through all loan programs. *Average indebtedness per student:* $44,910. ***Average need-based loan:*** Freshmen: $4228. Undergraduates: $4729. ***Parent loans:*** $1,114,676 (100% need-based). ***Programs:*** Federal Direct (Subsidized and Unsubsidized Stafford, PLUS), Perkins.

WORK-STUDY ***Federal work-study:*** Total amount: $165,000; 165 jobs averaging $1000.

APPLYING FOR FINANCIAL AID ***Required financial aid forms:*** FAFSA, CSS Financial Aid PROFILE, noncustodial (divorced/separated) parent's statement. ***Financial aid deadline (priority):*** 3/15. ***Notification date:*** Continuous beginning 3/15. Students must reply within 2 weeks of notification.

CONTACT Ms. Ann Murtagh Gitto, Director of Financial Aid, Bard College at Simon's Rock, 84 Alford Road, Great Barrington, MA 01230-9702, 413-528-7297 or toll-free 800-235-7186. *Fax:* 413-528-7339. *E-mail:* agitto@simons-rock.edu.

BARNARD COLLEGE

New York, NY

Tuition & fees: $40,546 **Average undergraduate aid package: $38,073**

ABOUT THE INSTITUTION Independent, women only. 48 undergraduate majors. Both federal and institutional methodology are used as a basis for awarding need-based institutional aid.

UNDERGRADUATE EXPENSES for 2010–11 ***Comprehensive fee:*** $53,496 includes full-time tuition ($38,868), mandatory fees ($1678), and room and board ($12,950). ***College room only:*** $7750. Room and board charges vary according to board plan and housing facility. ***Part-time tuition:*** $1295 per credit. ***Payment plans:*** Tuition prepayment, installment, deferred payment.

FRESHMAN FINANCIAL AID (Fall 2010, est.) 314 applied for aid; of those 77% were deemed to have need. 100% of freshmen with need received aid; of those 100% had need fully met. ***Average percent of need met:*** 100% (excluding resources awarded to replace EFC). ***Average financial aid package:*** $39,578 (excluding resources awarded to replace EFC).

UNDERGRADUATE FINANCIAL AID (Fall 2010, est.) 1,167 applied for aid; of those 85% were deemed to have need. 100% of undergraduates with need received aid; of those 100% had need fully met. ***Average percent of need met:*** 100% (excluding resources awarded to replace EFC). ***Average financial aid package:*** $38,073 (excluding resources awarded to replace EFC).

GIFT AID (NEED-BASED) ***Total amount:*** $32,234,319 (9% federal, 4% state, 84% institutional, 3% external sources). ***Receiving aid:*** Freshmen: 41% (235); all full-time undergraduates: 40% (956). ***Average award:*** Freshmen: $36,670; Undergraduates: $33,617. ***Scholarships, grants, and awards:*** Federal Pell, FSEOG, state, private, college/university gift aid from institutional funds, Academic Competitiveness Grants, National SMART Grants.

GIFT AID (NON-NEED-BASED) ***Total amount:*** $705,405 (5% state, 95% external sources). ***Tuition waivers:*** Full or partial for employees or children of employees.

LOANS ***Student loans:*** $5,278,866 (69% need-based, 31% non-need-based). 48% of past graduating class borrowed through all loan programs. *Average indebtedness per student:* $14,617. ***Average need-based loan:*** Freshmen: $3330. Undergraduates: $4647. ***Parent loans:*** $5,194,015 (100% non-need-based). ***Programs:*** Federal Direct (Subsidized and Unsubsidized Stafford, PLUS), Perkins, state, college/university, alternative loans.

WORK-STUDY ***Federal work-study:*** Total amount: $697,807; 390 jobs averaging $1789. ***State or other work-study/employment:*** Total amount: $808,507 (72% need-based, 28% non-need-based). 321 part-time jobs averaging $1811.

APPLYING FOR FINANCIAL AID ***Required financial aid forms:*** FAFSA, institution's own form, CSS Financial Aid PROFILE, state aid form, noncustodial (divorced/separated) parent's statement, business/farm supplement, federal income tax return(s). ***Financial aid deadline:*** 2/1. ***Notification date:*** 3/31. Students must reply by 5/1.

CONTACT Nanette DiLauro, Director of Financial Aid, Barnard College, 3009 Broadway, New York, NY 10027-6598, 212-854-2154. *Fax:* 212-854-2902. *E-mail:* finaid@barnard.edu.

BARRY UNIVERSITY

Miami Shores, FL

Tuition & fees: N/R **Average undergraduate aid package: $20,365**

ABOUT THE INSTITUTION Independent Roman Catholic, coed. 58 undergraduate majors. Federal methodology is used as a basis for awarding need-based institutional aid.

UNDERGRADUATE EXPENSES for 2011–12 ***Tuition:*** part-time $845 per credit. Full-time tuition and fees vary according to program. Part-time tuition and fees vary according to course load. Room and board charges vary according to board plan. ***Payment plans:*** Tuition prepayment, installment, deferred payment.

FRESHMAN FINANCIAL AID (Fall 2009) 558 applied for aid; of those 93% were deemed to have need. 100% of freshmen with need received aid; of those 6% had need fully met. ***Average percent of need met:*** 71% (excluding resources awarded to replace EFC). ***Average financial aid package:*** $26,371 (excluding resources awarded to replace EFC). 13% of all full-time freshmen had no need and received non-need-based gift aid.

UNDERGRADUATE FINANCIAL AID (Fall 2009) 3,482 applied for aid; of those 97% were deemed to have need. 100% of undergraduates with need received aid; of those 4% had need fully met. ***Average percent of need met:*** 53%

(excluding resources awarded to replace EFC). *Average financial aid package:* $20,365 (excluding resources awarded to replace EFC). 10% of all full-time undergraduates had no need and received non-need-based gift aid.

GIFT AID (NEED-BASED) *Total amount:* $20,411,947 (64% federal, 7% state, 29% institutional). *Receiving aid:* Freshmen: 71% (444); all full-time undergraduates: 64% (2,616). *Average award:* Freshmen: $11,183; Undergraduates: $8596. *Scholarships, grants, and awards:* Federal Pell, FSEOG, state, private, college/university gift aid from institutional funds, Federal Nursing.

GIFT AID (NON-NEED-BASED) *Total amount:* $31,039,834 (21% state, 76% institutional, 3% external sources). *Receiving aid:* Freshmen: 83% (519). Undergraduates: 81% (3,302). *Average award:* Freshmen: $8590. Undergraduates: $6786. *Tuition waivers:* Full or partial for employees or children of employees.

LOANS *Student loans:* $36,900,249 (42% need-based, 58% non-need-based). 66% of past graduating class borrowed through all loan programs. *Average indebtedness per student:* $35,880. *Average need-based loan:* Freshmen: $3479. Undergraduates: $5212. *Parent loans:* $3,487,138 (100% non-need-based). *Programs:* Perkins, Federal Nursing, college/university, alternative loans.

WORK-STUDY *Federal work-study:* Total amount: $1,416,502; jobs available. *State or other work-study/employment:* Total amount: $373,192 (100% non-need-based). Part-time jobs available.

ATHLETIC AWARDS Total amount: $2,352,102 (100% non-need-based).

APPLYING FOR FINANCIAL AID *Required financial aid form:* FAFSA. *Financial aid deadline:* Continuous. *Notification date:* Continuous beginning 1/25.

CONTACT Mr. Dart Humeston, Assistant Dean of Enrollment Services and Director of Financial Aid, Barry University, 11300 Northeast Second Avenue, Miami Shores, FL 33161-6695, 305-899-3673 or toll-free 800-695-2279. *E-mail:* finaid@mail.barry.edu.

BARTON COLLEGE

Wilson, NC

ABOUT THE INSTITUTION Independent religious, coed. 33 undergraduate majors.

GIFT AID (NEED-BASED) *Scholarships, grants, and awards:* Federal Pell, FSEOG, state, private, college/university gift aid from institutional funds.

GIFT AID (NON-NEED-BASED) *Scholarships, grants, and awards by category:* *Academic interests/achievement:* biological sciences, business, communication, computer science, education, English, general academic interests/achievements, health fields, humanities, international studies, mathematics, physical sciences, religion/biblical studies, social sciences. *Creative arts/performance:* art/fine arts, music, theater/drama. *Special achievements/activities:* general special achievements/activities, leadership, religious involvement. *Special characteristics:* adult students, children and siblings of alumni, children of faculty/staff, international students, local/state students, relatives of clergy, religious affiliation, siblings of current students, veterans.

LOANS *Programs:* Perkins, alternative loans.

WORK-STUDY *Federal work-study:* Total amount: $492,600; jobs available.

APPLYING FOR FINANCIAL AID *Required financial aid form:* FAFSA.

CONTACT Mrs. Bridget Ellis, Director of Financial Aid, Barton College, Box 5000, Wilson, NC 27893, 252-399-6371 or toll-free 800-345-4973. *Fax:* 252-399-6572. *E-mail:* aid@barton.edu.

BASTYR UNIVERSITY

Kenmore, WA

ABOUT THE INSTITUTION Independent, coed. 6 undergraduate majors.

GIFT AID (NEED-BASED) *Scholarships, grants, and awards:* Federal Pell, FSEOG, state, private, college/university gift aid from institutional funds.

GIFT AID (NON-NEED-BASED) *Scholarships, grants, and awards by category:* *Academic interests/achievement:* health fields.

LOANS *Programs:* Perkins.

WORK-STUDY *Federal work-study:* Total amount: $67,321; 40 jobs averaging $3000. *State or other work-study/employment:* Total amount: $40,017 (100% need-based). 31 part-time jobs averaging $3000.

APPLYING FOR FINANCIAL AID *Required financial aid forms:* FAFSA, institution's own form.

CONTACT Sheila Arisa, Financial Aid Advisor, Bastyr University, 14500 Juanita Drive NE, Kenmore, WA 98028-4966, 425-602-3407. *Fax:* 425-602-3094. *E-mail:* finaid@bastyr.edu.

BATES COLLEGE

Lewiston, ME

Comprehensive fee: $53,300 **Average undergraduate aid package: $35,741**

ABOUT THE INSTITUTION Independent, coed. 34 undergraduate majors. Institutional methodology is used as a basis for awarding need-based institutional aid.

UNDERGRADUATE EXPENSES for 2010–11 *Comprehensive fee:* $53,300. *Payment plans:* Tuition prepayment, installment.

FRESHMAN FINANCIAL AID (Fall 2010, est.) 259 applied for aid; of those 86% were deemed to have need. 95% of freshmen with need received aid; of those 95% had need fully met. *Average percent of need met:* 100% (excluding resources awarded to replace EFC). *Average financial aid package:* $36,476 (excluding resources awarded to replace EFC).

UNDERGRADUATE FINANCIAL AID (Fall 2010, est.) 870 applied for aid; of those 92% were deemed to have need. 95% of undergraduates with need received aid; of those 94% had need fully met. *Average percent of need met:* 100% (excluding resources awarded to replace EFC). *Average financial aid package:* $35,741 (excluding resources awarded to replace EFC).

GIFT AID (NEED-BASED) *Total amount:* $24,057,554 (5% federal, 93% institutional, 2% external sources). *Receiving aid:* Freshmen: 41% (205); all full-time undergraduates: 43% (731). *Average award:* Freshmen: $33,878; Undergraduates: $32,910. *Scholarships, grants, and awards:* Federal Pell, FSEOG, state, private, college/university gift aid from institutional funds.

GIFT AID (NON-NEED-BASED) *Total amount:* $50,670 (100% external sources). *Tuition waivers:* Full or partial for employees or children of employees.

LOANS *Student loans:* $3,902,033 (52% need-based, 48% non-need-based). 36% of past graduating class borrowed through all loan programs. *Average indebtedness per student:* $18,699. *Average need-based loan:* Freshmen: $3684. Undergraduates: $4347. *Parent loans:* $2,412,560 (100% non-need-based). *Programs:* Federal Direct (Subsidized and Unsubsidized Stafford, PLUS), Perkins, state.

WORK-STUDY *Federal work-study:* Total amount: $1,017,111; 606 jobs averaging $1678. *State or other work-study/employment:* Total amount: $174,500 (100% need-based). 101 part-time jobs averaging $1728.

APPLYING FOR FINANCIAL AID *Required financial aid forms:* FAFSA, CSS Financial Aid PROFILE, noncustodial (divorced/separated) parent's statement. *Financial aid deadline:* 2/1. *Notification date:* 4/1. Students must reply by 5/1.

CONTACT Ms. Wendy G. Glass, Director of Student Financial Services, Bates College, 44 Mountain Avenue, Lewiston, ME 04240, 207-786-6096. *Fax:* 207-786-8350. *E-mail:* wglass@bates.edu.

BAUDER COLLEGE

Atlanta, GA

CONTACT Financial Aid Office, Bauder College, 384 Northyards Boulevard NW, Suites 190 and 400, Atlanta, GA 30313, 404-237-7573 or toll-free 800-241-3797.

BAYAMÓN CENTRAL UNIVERSITY

Bayamón, PR

CONTACT Financial Aid Director, Bayamón Central University, PO Box 1725, Bayamón, PR 00960-1725, 787-786-3030 Ext. 2115. *Fax:* 787-785-4365.

BAYLOR UNIVERSITY

Waco, TX

Tuition & fees: $29,754 **Average undergraduate aid package: $21,568**

ABOUT THE INSTITUTION Independent Baptist, coed. 126 undergraduate majors. Federal methodology is used as a basis for awarding need-based institutional aid.

UNDERGRADUATE EXPENSES for 2010–11 *Comprehensive fee:* $38,085 includes full-time tuition ($26,996), mandatory fees ($2758), and room and board ($8331). *College room only:* $4494. Room and board charges vary according to board plan and housing facility. *Part-time tuition:* $1124 per semester hour. *Payment plan:* Installment.

FRESHMAN FINANCIAL AID (Fall 2010, est.) 2,501 applied for aid; of those 82% were deemed to have need. 100% of freshmen with need received aid; of those 15% had need fully met. ***Average percent of need met:*** 68% (excluding resources awarded to replace EFC). ***Average financial aid package:*** $22,971 (excluding resources awarded to replace EFC). 33% of all full-time freshmen had no need and received non-need-based gift aid.

UNDERGRADUATE FINANCIAL AID (Fall 2010, est.) 8,053 applied for aid; of those 87% were deemed to have need. 100% of undergraduates with need received aid; of those 15% had need fully met. ***Average percent of need met:*** 66% (excluding resources awarded to replace EFC). ***Average financial aid package:*** $21,568 (excluding resources awarded to replace EFC). 30% of all full-time undergraduates had no need and received non-need-based gift aid.

GIFT AID (NEED-BASED) ***Total amount:*** $104,544,304 (13% federal, 10% state, 73% institutional, 4% external sources). ***Receiving aid:*** Freshmen: 62% (2,021); all full-time undergraduates: 55% (6,658). ***Average award:*** Freshmen: $17,679; Undergraduates: $16,079. ***Scholarships, grants, and awards:*** Federal Pell, FSEOG, state, college/university gift aid from institutional funds.

GIFT AID (NON-NEED-BASED) ***Total amount:*** $39,847,013 (96% institutional, 4% external sources). ***Receiving aid:*** Freshmen: 60% (1,963). Undergraduates: 50% (6,051). ***Average award:*** Freshmen: $11,949. Undergraduates: $9913. ***Scholarships, grants, and awards by category:*** *Academic interests/achievement:* 11,055 awards ($79,643,885 total): business, communication, computer science, education, engineering/technologies, English, foreign languages, general academic interests/achievements, health fields, home economics, humanities, international studies, mathematics, military science, physical sciences, premedicine, religion/biblical studies, social sciences. *Creative arts/performance:* 495 awards ($2,357,106 total): art/fine arts, cinema/film/broadcasting, debating, journalism/publications, music, theater/drama. *Special achievements/activities:* 310 awards ($536,263 total): community service, leadership, religious involvement. *Special characteristics:* 233 awards ($4,642,871 total): children of faculty/staff. ***Tuition waivers:*** Full or partial for employees or children of employees.

LOANS ***Student loans:*** $65,617,611 (74% need-based, 26% non-need-based). ***Average need-based loan:*** Freshmen: $4726. Undergraduates: $4870. ***Parent loans:*** $22,494,935 (42% need-based, 58% non-need-based). ***Programs:*** Federal Direct (Subsidized and Unsubsidized Stafford, PLUS), Perkins, Federal Nursing, state, private loans.

WORK-STUDY ***Federal work-study:*** Total amount: $13,749,448; 4,864 jobs averaging $2827. ***State or other work-study/employment:*** Part-time jobs available.

ATHLETIC AWARDS Total amount: $66,436,086 (5% need-based, 95% non-need-based).

APPLYING FOR FINANCIAL AID ***Required financial aid forms:*** FAFSA, state residency affirmation (TX residents only). ***Financial aid deadline (priority):*** 3/1. ***Notification date:*** Continuous beginning 3/15. Students must reply by 5/1 or within 2 weeks of notification.

CONTACT Office of Admission Services, Baylor University, PO Box 97056, Waco, TX 76798-7056, 254-710-3435 or toll-free 800-BAYLORU. *Fax:* 254-710-3436. *E-mail:* admissions@baylor.edu.

BAY PATH COLLEGE

Longmeadow, MA

CONTACT Phyllis Brand, Financial Aid Assistant, Bay Path College, 588 Longmeadow Street, Longmeadow, MA 01106-2292, 413-565-1261 or toll-free 800-782-7284 Ext. 1331. *Fax:* 413-565-1101. *E-mail:* pbrand@baypath.edu.

BEACON COLLEGE

Leesburg, FL

CONTACT Financial Aid Office, Beacon College, 105 East Main Street, Leesburg, FL 34748, 352-787-7660.

BECKER COLLEGE

Worcester, MA

ABOUT THE INSTITUTION Independent, coed. ***Awards:*** associate and bachelor's degrees (also includes Leicester, MA small town campus). 27 undergraduate majors. ***Total enrollment:*** 1,752. Undergraduates: 1,752. Freshmen: 347.

GIFT AID (NEED-BASED) ***Scholarships, grants, and awards:*** Federal Pell, FSEOG, state, private, college/university gift aid from institutional funds.

GIFT AID (NON-NEED-BASED) ***Scholarships, grants, and awards by category:*** *Academic interests/achievement:* general academic interests/achievements. *Special achievements/activities:* general special achievements/activities, leadership. *Special characteristics:* children of faculty/staff, siblings of current students, twins.

LOANS ***Programs:*** Federal Direct (Subsidized and Unsubsidized Stafford, PLUS), state, alternative loans.

WORK-STUDY ***Federal work-study:*** Total amount: $474,560; 338 jobs averaging $1404.

APPLYING FOR FINANCIAL AID ***Required financial aid form:*** FAFSA.

CONTACT Mr. Russ Romandini, Director of Student Administrative Services, Becker College, 61 Sever Street, Worcester, MA 01615-0071, 508-373-9440 or toll-free 877-5BECKER Ext. 245. *Fax:* 508-890-1511. *E-mail:* financialaid@becker.edu.

BEIS MEDRASH HEICHAL DOVID

Far Rockaway, NY

CONTACT Financial Aid Office, Beis Medrash Heichal Dovid, 257 Beach 17th Street, Far Rockaway, NY 11691, 718-868-2300.

BELHAVEN UNIVERSITY

Jackson, MS

ABOUT THE INSTITUTION Independent Presbyterian, coed. 29 undergraduate majors.

GIFT AID (NEED-BASED) ***Scholarships, grants, and awards:*** Federal Pell, FSEOG, state, private, college/university gift aid from institutional funds.

GIFT AID (NON-NEED-BASED) ***Scholarships, grants, and awards by category:*** *Academic interests/achievement:* biological sciences, business, communication, education, English, foreign languages, general academic interests/achievements, humanities, international studies, mathematics, premedicine, religion/biblical studies, social sciences. *Creative arts/performance:* applied art and design, art/fine arts, creative writing, dance, journalism/publications, music, performing arts, theater/drama. *Special achievements/activities:* cheerleading/drum major, general special achievements/activities, junior miss, leadership. *Special characteristics:* children of faculty/staff, general special characteristics, international students, local/state students.

LOANS ***Programs:*** Federal Direct (Subsidized and Unsubsidized Stafford, PLUS), Perkins.

WORK-STUDY ***Federal work-study:*** Total amount: $278,193; 148 jobs averaging $1743.

APPLYING FOR FINANCIAL AID ***Required financial aid form:*** FAFSA.

CONTACT Ms. Linda Phillips, Assistant Vice President for Institutional Advancement, Belhaven University, 1500 Peachtree Street, Jackson, MS 39202-1789, 601-968-5933 or toll-free 800-960-5940. *Fax:* 601-353-0701. *E-mail:* lphillips@belhaven.edu.

BELLARMINE UNIVERSITY

Louisville, KY

Tuition & fees: $30,310 **Average undergraduate aid package: $22,192**

ABOUT THE INSTITUTION Independent Roman Catholic, coed. 38 undergraduate majors. Both federal and institutional methodology are used as a basis for awarding need-based institutional aid.

UNDERGRADUATE EXPENSES for 2010–11 ***One-time required fee:*** $300. ***Comprehensive fee:*** $39,130 includes full-time tuition ($29,160), mandatory fees ($1150), and room and board ($8820). ***College room only:*** $5200. Room and board charges vary according to board plan and housing facility. ***Part-time tuition:*** $690 per credit hour. ***Part-time fees:*** $45 per course. ***Payment plan:*** Installment.

FRESHMAN FINANCIAL AID (Fall 2010, est.) 518 applied for aid; of those 92% were deemed to have need. 100% of freshmen with need received aid; of those 21% had need fully met. ***Average percent of need met:*** 77% (excluding resources awarded to replace EFC). ***Average financial aid package:*** $26,601 (excluding resources awarded to replace EFC). 17% of all full-time freshmen had no need and received non-need-based gift aid.

UNDERGRADUATE FINANCIAL AID (Fall 2010, est.) 1,828 applied for aid; of those 93% were deemed to have need. 97% of undergraduates with need

received aid; of those 14% had need fully met. ***Average percent of need met:*** 63% (excluding resources awarded to replace EFC). ***Average financial aid package:*** $22,192 (excluding resources awarded to replace EFC). 21% of all full-time undergraduates had no need and received non-need-based gift aid.

GIFT AID (NEED-BASED) ***Total amount:*** $33,503,863 (9% federal, 13% state, 76% institutional, 2% external sources). ***Receiving aid:*** Freshmen: 83% (479); all full-time undergraduates: 75% (1,649). ***Average award:*** Freshmen: $17,560; Undergraduates: $16,878. ***Scholarships, grants, and awards:*** Federal Pell, FSEOG, state, private, college/university gift aid from institutional funds.

GIFT AID (NON-NEED-BASED) ***Total amount:*** $9,678,015 (7% state, 88% institutional, 5% external sources). ***Receiving aid:*** Freshmen: 27% (157). Undergraduates: 23% (513). ***Average award:*** Freshmen: $19,735. Undergraduates: $17,265. ***Scholarships, grants, and awards by category:*** *Academic interests/achievement:* biological sciences, business, education, general academic interests/achievements, health fields. *Creative arts/performance:* art/fine arts, music. *Special achievements/activities:* cheerleading/drum major, community service, general special achievements/activities, leadership, religious involvement. *Special characteristics:* adult students, children and siblings of alumni, children of faculty/staff, ethnic background, international students, local/state students, members of minority groups, out-of-state students, previous college experience, religious affiliation. ***Tuition waivers:*** Full or partial for employees or children of employees, senior citizens.

LOANS ***Student loans:*** $12,098,951 (76% need-based, 24% non-need-based). 67% of past graduating class borrowed through all loan programs. *Average indebtedness per student:* $23,925. ***Average need-based loan:*** Freshmen: $3611. Undergraduates: $3428. ***Parent loans:*** $2,279,228 (49% need-based, 51% non-need-based). ***Programs:*** Federal Direct (Subsidized and Unsubsidized Stafford, PLUS), Perkins, college/university.

WORK-STUDY ***Federal work-study:*** Total amount: $491,089; 241 jobs averaging $1661. ***State or other work-study/employment:*** Total amount: $44,582 (100% non-need-based). Part-time jobs available.

ATHLETIC AWARDS Total amount: $2,455,122 (49% need-based, 51% non-need-based).

APPLYING FOR FINANCIAL AID ***Required financial aid form:*** FAFSA. ***Financial aid deadline (priority):*** 3/1. ***Notification date:*** Continuous beginning 3/15. Students must reply by 5/1.

CONTACT Ms. Heather Boutell, Director of Financial Aid, Bellarmine University, 2001 Newburg Road, Louisville, KY 40205-0671, 502-452-8124 or toll-free 800-274-4723 Ext. 8131. *Fax:* 502-452-8002. *E-mail:* hboutell@bellarmine.edu.

BELLEVUE UNIVERSITY

Bellevue, NE

CONTACT Mr. Jon Dotterer, Director of Financial Aid, Bellevue University, 1000 Galvin Road South, Bellevue, NE 68005, 402-293-3762 or toll-free 800-756-7920. *Fax:* 402-293-2062.

BELLIN COLLEGE

Green Bay, WI

Tuition & fees: $10,167 **Average undergraduate aid package: $13,656**

ABOUT THE INSTITUTION Independent, coed, primarily women. ***Awards:*** bachelor's and master's degrees. 1 undergraduate major. ***Total enrollment:*** 304. Undergraduates: 259. Federal methodology is used as a basis for awarding need-based institutional aid.

UNDERGRADUATE EXPENSES for 2010–11 ***Application fee:*** $30. ***Tuition:*** full-time $9778. Full-time tuition and fees vary according to course level. Part-time tuition and fees vary according to course load. ***Payment plan:*** Installment.

UNDERGRADUATE FINANCIAL AID (Fall 2009) 152 applied for aid; of those 93% were deemed to have need. 100% of undergraduates with need received aid; of those 4% had need fully met. ***Average percent of need met:*** 78% (excluding resources awarded to replace EFC). ***Average financial aid package:*** $13,656 (excluding resources awarded to replace EFC). 1% of all full-time undergraduates had no need and received non-need-based gift aid.

GIFT AID (NEED-BASED) ***Total amount:*** $800,902 (25% federal, 17% state, 45% institutional, 13% external sources). ***Receiving aid:*** All full-time undergraduates: 61% (137). ***Average award:*** Undergraduates: $5332. ***Scholarships, grants, and awards:*** Federal Pell, FSEOG, state, private, college/university gift aid from institutional funds.

GIFT AID (NON-NEED-BASED) ***Total amount:*** $24,176 (65% institutional, 35% external sources). ***Receiving aid:*** Undergraduates: 1% (3). ***Average award:*** Undergraduates: $4285. ***Scholarships, grants, and awards by category:*** *Academic interests/achievement:* 41 awards ($78,931 total): general academic interests/achievements. ***ROTC:*** Army cooperative.

LOANS ***Student loans:*** $3,136,614 (80% need-based, 20% non-need-based). 91% of past graduating class borrowed through all loan programs. *Average indebtedness per student:* $39,584. ***Average need-based loan:*** Undergraduates: $4832. ***Parent loans:*** $191,212 (36% need-based, 64% non-need-based). ***Programs:*** Federal Direct (Subsidized and Unsubsidized Stafford, PLUS), state, Private Lender Educational Loans.

WORK-STUDY ***Federal work-study:*** Total amount: $3000; 2 jobs averaging $1500.

APPLYING FOR FINANCIAL AID ***Required financial aid form:*** FAFSA. ***Financial aid deadline (priority):*** 3/1. ***Notification date:*** 4/1. Students must reply within 2 weeks of notification.

CONTACT Mrs. Lena C. Goodman, Director of Financial Aid, Bellin College, 3201 Eaton Road, Green Bay, WI 54311, 920-433-6638 or toll-free 800-236-8707. *Fax:* 920-433-1922. *E-mail:* lena.goodman@bellincollege.edu.

BELMONT ABBEY COLLEGE

Belmont, NC

Tuition & fees: $24,584 **Average undergraduate aid package: $14,188**

ABOUT THE INSTITUTION Independent Roman Catholic, coed. 15 undergraduate majors. Federal methodology is used as a basis for awarding need-based institutional aid.

UNDERGRADUATE EXPENSES for 2010–11 ***One-time required fee:*** $400. ***Comprehensive fee:*** $34,856 includes full-time tuition ($24,584) and room and board ($10,272). ***College room only:*** $6006. Full-time tuition and fees vary according to class time, course load, location, program, and reciprocity agreements. Room and board charges vary according to board plan, housing facility, and location. ***Part-time tuition:*** $819 per credit hour. ***Part-time fees:*** $45 per credit hour. Part-time tuition and fees vary according to class time, course load, location, and reciprocity agreements. ***Payment plans:*** Installment, deferred payment.

FRESHMAN FINANCIAL AID (Fall 2010, est.) 281 applied for aid; of those 88% were deemed to have need. 100% of freshmen with need received aid; of those 18% had need fully met. ***Average percent of need met:*** 72% (excluding resources awarded to replace EFC). ***Average financial aid package:*** $18,620 (excluding resources awarded to replace EFC). 24% of all full-time freshmen had no need and received non-need-based gift aid.

UNDERGRADUATE FINANCIAL AID (Fall 2010, est.) 1,546 applied for aid; of those 91% were deemed to have need. 99% of undergraduates with need received aid; of those 11% had need fully met. ***Average percent of need met:*** 58% (excluding resources awarded to replace EFC). ***Average financial aid package:*** $14,188 (excluding resources awarded to replace EFC). 16% of all full-time undergraduates had no need and received non-need-based gift aid.

GIFT AID (NEED-BASED) ***Total amount:*** $13,811,250 (28% federal, 23% state, 45% institutional, 4% external sources). ***Receiving aid:*** Freshmen: 74% (245); all full-time undergraduates: 79% (1,383). ***Average award:*** Freshmen: $15,711; Undergraduates: $10,312. ***Scholarships, grants, and awards:*** Federal Pell, FSEOG, state, private, college/university gift aid from institutional funds.

GIFT AID (NON-NEED-BASED) ***Total amount:*** $3,788,253 (6% state, 90% institutional, 4% external sources). ***Receiving aid:*** Freshmen: 9% (29). Undergraduates: 5% (87). ***Average award:*** Freshmen: $11,116. Undergraduates: $10,608. ***Scholarships, grants, and awards by category:*** *Academic interests/achievement:* 808 awards ($7,752,365 total): general academic interests/achievements. *Creative arts/performance:* 23 awards ($44,000 total): theater/drama. *Special achievements/activities:* 26 awards ($290,600 total): religious involvement. *Special characteristics:* 21 awards ($230,857 total): children of faculty/staff. ***Tuition waivers:*** Full or partial for employees or children of employees, senior citizens.

LOANS ***Student loans:*** $10,567,449 (83% need-based, 17% non-need-based). 75% of past graduating class borrowed through all loan programs. *Average indebtedness per student:* $21,000. ***Average need-based loan:*** Freshmen: $3112. Undergraduates: $4084. ***Parent loans:*** $7,425,190 (31% need-based, 69% non-need-based). ***Programs:*** Federal Direct (Subsidized and Unsubsidized Stafford, PLUS), Perkins.

WORK-STUDY ***Federal work-study:*** Total amount: $113,948; 95 jobs averaging $1200.

ATHLETIC AWARDS Total amount: $1,464,990 (48% need-based, 52% non-need-based).

APPLYING FOR FINANCIAL AID ***Required financial aid form:*** FAFSA. ***Financial aid deadline (priority):*** 4/1. ***Notification date:*** Continuous beginning 3/1. Students must reply within 2 weeks of notification.

CONTACT Ms. Julie Hodge, Associate Director of Financial Aid, Belmont Abbey College, 100 Belmont Mt. Holly Road, Belmont, NC 28012-1802, 704-461-6718 or toll-free 888-BAC-0110. *Fax:* 704-461-6882. *E-mail:* juliehodge@bac.edu.

BELMONT UNIVERSITY

Nashville, TN

Tuition & fees: $23,680 **Average undergraduate aid package: $12,214**

ABOUT THE INSTITUTION Independent Christian, coed. 66 undergraduate majors. Federal methodology is used as a basis for awarding need-based institutional aid.

UNDERGRADUATE EXPENSES for 2010–11 ***Comprehensive fee:*** $35,360 includes full-time tuition ($22,530), mandatory fees ($1150), and room and board ($11,680). ***College room only:*** $7650. Full-time tuition and fees vary according to class time and course load. Room and board charges vary according to board plan, housing facility, and location. ***Part-time tuition:*** $865 per credit hour. ***Part-time fees:*** $410 per term. Part-time tuition and fees vary according to course load. ***Payment plans:*** Installment, deferred payment.

FRESHMAN FINANCIAL AID (Fall 2010, est.) 976 applied for aid; of those 62% were deemed to have need. 96% of freshmen with need received aid; of those 33% had need fully met. ***Average percent of need met:*** 84% (excluding resources awarded to replace EFC). ***Average financial aid package:*** $13,060 (excluding resources awarded to replace EFC). 14% of all full-time freshmen had no need and received non-need-based gift aid.

UNDERGRADUATE FINANCIAL AID (Fall 2010, est.) 4,001 applied for aid; of those 65% were deemed to have need. 91% of undergraduates with need received aid; of those 27% had need fully met. ***Average percent of need met:*** 79% (excluding resources awarded to replace EFC). ***Average financial aid package:*** $12,214 (excluding resources awarded to replace EFC). 12% of all full-time undergraduates had no need and received non-need-based gift aid.

GIFT AID (NEED-BASED) ***Total amount:*** $12,456,183 (29% federal, 4% state, 58% institutional, 9% external sources). ***Receiving aid:*** Freshmen: 38% (383); all full-time undergraduates: 34% (1,465). ***Average award:*** Freshmen: $7137; Undergraduates: $6896. ***Scholarships, grants, and awards:*** Federal Pell, FSEOG, state, private, college/university gift aid from institutional funds.

GIFT AID (NON-NEED-BASED) ***Total amount:*** $13,870,329 (31% state, 69% institutional). ***Receiving aid:*** Freshmen: 38% (381). Undergraduates: 29% (1,231). ***Average award:*** Freshmen: $7333. Undergraduates: $6851. ***Scholarships, grants, and awards by category:*** *Academic interests/achievement:* 1,753 awards ($7,692,052 total): general academic interests/achievements, religion/biblical studies. *Creative arts/performance:* 230 awards ($501,640 total): music. *Special characteristics:* 27 awards ($302,262 total): children of faculty/staff. ***Tuition waivers:*** Full or partial for employees or children of employees, senior citizens.

LOANS ***Student loans:*** $21,110,920 (65% need-based, 35% non-need-based). 54% of past graduating class borrowed through all loan programs. *Average indebtedness per student:* $29,058. ***Average need-based loan:*** Freshmen: $3439. Undergraduates: $4434. ***Parent loans:*** $17,469,969 (100% non-need-based). ***Programs:*** Federal Direct (PLUS), Perkins, college/university.

WORK-STUDY ***Federal work-study:*** Total amount: $239,103; 534 jobs averaging $6297.

ATHLETIC AWARDS Total amount: $3,512,201 (100% non-need-based).

APPLYING FOR FINANCIAL AID ***Required financial aid form:*** FAFSA. ***Financial aid deadline (priority):*** 3/1. ***Notification date:*** Continuous beginning 3/15. Students must reply by 5/1 or within 2 weeks of notification.

CONTACT Mrs. Pat Smedley, Director of Student Financial Services, Belmont University, 1900 Belmont Boulevard, Nashville, TN 37212-3757, 615-460-6403 or toll-free 800-56E-NROL. *E-mail:* pat.smedley@belmont.edu.

BELOIT COLLEGE

Beloit, WI

Tuition & fees: $35,038 **Average undergraduate aid package: $32,229**

ABOUT THE INSTITUTION Independent, coed. 54 undergraduate majors. Both federal and institutional methodology are used as a basis for awarding need-based institutional aid.

UNDERGRADUATE EXPENSES for 2010–11 ***Comprehensive fee:*** $42,202 includes full-time tuition ($34,808), mandatory fees ($230), and room and board ($7164). ***College room only:*** $3512. Room and board charges vary according to board plan. ***Part-time tuition:*** $4351 per course. ***Payment plan:*** Installment.

FRESHMAN FINANCIAL AID (Fall 2010, est.) 273 applied for aid; of those 85% were deemed to have need. 100% of freshmen with need received aid; of those 64% had need fully met. ***Average percent of need met:*** 96% (excluding resources awarded to replace EFC). ***Average financial aid package:*** $32,422 (excluding resources awarded to replace EFC). 28% of all full-time freshmen had no need and received non-need-based gift aid.

UNDERGRADUATE FINANCIAL AID (Fall 2010, est.) 1,004 applied for aid; of those 86% were deemed to have need. 100% of undergraduates with need received aid; of those 66% had need fully met. ***Average percent of need met:*** 96% (excluding resources awarded to replace EFC). ***Average financial aid package:*** $32,229 (excluding resources awarded to replace EFC). 25% of all full-time undergraduates had no need and received non-need-based gift aid.

GIFT AID (NEED-BASED) ***Total amount:*** $19,412,907 (9% federal, 2% state, 86% institutional, 3% external sources). ***Receiving aid:*** Freshmen: 70% (233); all full-time undergraduates: 66% (860). ***Average award:*** Freshmen: $24,212; Undergraduates: $22,612. ***Scholarships, grants, and awards:*** Federal Pell, FSEOG, state, private, college/university gift aid from institutional funds.

GIFT AID (NON-NEED-BASED) ***Total amount:*** $5,075,495 (94% institutional, 6% external sources). ***Average award:*** Freshmen: $14,969. Undergraduates: $14,169. ***Scholarships, grants, and awards by category:*** *Academic interests/achievement:* 525 awards ($6,206,445 total): general academic interests/achievements. *Creative arts/performance:* 43 awards ($177,000 total): music. *Special achievements/activities:* 37 awards ($157,000 total): community service, general special achievements/activities. *Special characteristics:* 89 awards ($1,510,539 total): members of minority groups, siblings of current students. ***Tuition waivers:*** Full or partial for employees or children of employees.

LOANS ***Student loans:*** $8,442,570 (89% need-based, 11% non-need-based). 78% of past graduating class borrowed through all loan programs. *Average indebtedness per student:* $19,930. ***Average need-based loan:*** Freshmen: $6277. Undergraduates: $7236. ***Parent loans:*** $1,412,693 (79% need-based, 21% non-need-based). ***Programs:*** Federal Direct (Subsidized and Unsubsidized Stafford, PLUS), Perkins, college/university.

WORK-STUDY ***Federal work-study:*** Total amount: $1,099,667; 629 jobs averaging $1741. ***State or other work-study/employment:*** Total amount: $524,416 (43% need-based, 57% non-need-based). 419 part-time jobs averaging $1253.

APPLYING FOR FINANCIAL AID ***Required financial aid forms:*** FAFSA, institution's own form, state aid form. ***Financial aid deadline (priority):*** 3/1. ***Notification date:*** Continuous beginning 4/1. Students must reply by 5/1 or within 2 weeks of notification.

CONTACT Mr. Jon Urish, Senior Associate Director of Admissions and Financial Aid, Beloit College, 700 College Street, Beloit, WI 53511-5596, 800-356-0751 or toll-free 800-9-BELOIT. *Fax:* 608-363-2075. *E-mail:* urishj@beloit.edu.

BEMIDJI STATE UNIVERSITY

Bemidji, MN

Tuition & fees (MN res): $7513 **Average undergraduate aid package: $8995**

ABOUT THE INSTITUTION State-supported, coed. 70 undergraduate majors. Federal methodology is used as a basis for awarding need-based institutional aid.

UNDERGRADUATE EXPENSES for 2011–12 ***Tuition, state resident:*** full-time $6577; part-time $230 per credit. ***Tuition, nonresident:*** full-time $6577; part-time $230 per credit. ***Required fees:*** full-time $936; $92.54 per credit. Full-time tuition and fees vary according to course load, location, program, and reciprocity agreements. Part-time tuition and fees vary according to course load, location, program, and reciprocity agreements. ***College room and board:*** $6480. Room and board charges vary according to board plan and housing facility. ***Payment plan:*** Installment.

FRESHMAN FINANCIAL AID (Fall 2010, est.) 755 applied for aid; of those 74% were deemed to have need. 99% of freshmen with need received aid; of those 17% had need fully met. ***Average percent of need met:*** 68% (excluding resources awarded to replace EFC). ***Average financial aid package:*** $8037 (excluding resources awarded to replace EFC). 19% of all full-time freshmen had no need and received non-need-based gift aid.

UNDERGRADUATE FINANCIAL AID (Fall 2010, est.) 3,053 applied for aid; of those 80% were deemed to have need. 99% of undergraduates with need received aid; of those 19% had need fully met. ***Average percent of need met:*** 68% (excluding resources awarded to replace EFC). ***Average financial aid package:*** $8995 (excluding resources awarded to replace EFC). 16% of all full-time undergraduates had no need and received non-need-based gift aid.

GIFT AID (NEED-BASED) ***Total amount:*** $10,846,981 (75% federal, 23% state, 2% external sources). ***Receiving aid:*** Freshmen: 43% (369); all full-time undergraduates: 47% (1,773). ***Average award:*** Freshmen: $5519; Undergraduates: $5403. ***Scholarships, grants, and awards:*** Federal Pell, FSEOG, state, private, college/university gift aid from institutional funds.

GIFT AID (NON-NEED-BASED) ***Total amount:*** $4,758,747 (9% federal, 17% state, 55% institutional, 19% external sources). ***Receiving aid:*** Freshmen: 48% (410). Undergraduates: 49% (1,837). ***Average award:*** Freshmen: $8729. Undergraduates: $9246. ***Scholarships, grants, and awards by category:*** *Academic interests/achievement:* 691 awards ($750,038 total): general academic interests/achievements. *Creative arts/performance:* 46 awards ($84,098 total): general creative arts/performance. *Special characteristics:* 177 awards ($476,612 total): children and siblings of alumni, children of faculty/staff, international students, out-of-state students. ***Tuition waivers:*** Full or partial for employees or children of employees, senior citizens.

LOANS ***Student loans:*** $25,470,520 (40% need-based, 60% non-need-based). 89% of past graduating class borrowed through all loan programs. *Average indebtedness per student:* $26,799. ***Average need-based loan:*** Freshmen: $3394. Undergraduates: $4020. ***Parent loans:*** $573,836 (100% non-need-based). ***Programs:*** Federal Direct (Subsidized and Unsubsidized Stafford, PLUS), Perkins, state.

WORK-STUDY ***Federal work-study:*** Total amount: $360,112; 280 jobs averaging $1286. ***State or other work-study/employment:*** Total amount: $187,242 (100% need-based). 158 part-time jobs averaging $1185.

ATHLETIC AWARDS Total amount: $1,058,567 (100% non-need-based).

APPLYING FOR FINANCIAL AID ***Required financial aid forms:*** FAFSA, institution's own form. ***Financial aid deadline (priority):*** 4/15. ***Notification date:*** Continuous beginning 6/15.

CONTACT Financial Aid Office, Bemidji State University, 1500 Birchmont Drive NE #14, Bemidji, MN 56601-2699, 218-755-2034 or toll-free 800-475-2001 (in-state), 800-652-9747 (out-of-state). *Fax:* 218-755-4361. *E-mail:* financialaid@bemidjistate.edu.

BENEDICT COLLEGE

Columbia, SC

ABOUT THE INSTITUTION Independent Baptist, coed. ***Awards:*** bachelor's degrees. 32 undergraduate majors. ***Total enrollment:*** 2,641. Undergraduates: 2,641.

GIFT AID (NEED-BASED) ***Scholarships, grants, and awards:*** Federal Pell, FSEOG, state, private.

GIFT AID (NON-NEED-BASED) ***Scholarships, grants, and awards by category:*** *Academic interests/achievement:* general academic interests/achievements. *Creative arts/performance:* general creative arts/performance, music.

LOANS ***Programs:*** Federal Direct (Subsidized and Unsubsidized Stafford, PLUS), Perkins, state, college/university.

WORK-STUDY Federal work-study jobs available.

APPLYING FOR FINANCIAL AID ***Required financial aid form:*** FAFSA.

CONTACT Mrs. Bichevia Green, Associate Director of Financial Aid, Benedict College, 1600 Harden Street, Columbia, SC 29204, 803-705-4418 or toll-free 800-868-6598 (in-state). *Fax:* 803-705-6629. *E-mail:* greenb@benedict.edu.

BENEDICTINE COLLEGE

Atchison, KS

Tuition & fees: $20,475 **Average undergraduate aid package: $24,117**

ABOUT THE INSTITUTION Independent Roman Catholic, coed. 34 undergraduate majors. Federal methodology is used as a basis for awarding need-based institutional aid.

UNDERGRADUATE EXPENSES for 2010–11 ***Comprehensive fee:*** $27,850 includes full-time tuition ($20,475) and room and board ($7375). ***College room only:*** $4125. Full-time tuition and fees vary according to course load and degree level. Room and board charges vary according to board plan and housing facility. ***Part-time tuition:*** $600 per credit hour. Part-time tuition and fees vary according to course load and degree level. ***Payment plan:*** Installment.

FRESHMAN FINANCIAL AID (Fall 2010, est.) 345 applied for aid; of those 91% were deemed to have need. 100% of freshmen with need received aid; of those 12% had need fully met. ***Average percent of need met:*** 66% (excluding resources awarded to replace EFC). 13% of all full-time freshmen had no need and received non-need-based gift aid.

UNDERGRADUATE FINANCIAL AID (Fall 2010, est.) 1,257 applied for aid; of those 90% were deemed to have need. 100% of undergraduates with need received aid; of those 15% had need fully met. ***Average percent of need met:*** 66% (excluding resources awarded to replace EFC). ***Average financial aid package:*** $24,117 (excluding resources awarded to replace EFC). 17% of all full-time undergraduates had no need and received non-need-based gift aid.

GIFT AID (NEED-BASED) ***Total amount:*** $10,288,982 (21% federal, 5% state, 71% institutional, 3% external sources). ***Receiving aid:*** Freshmen: 47% (182); all full-time undergraduates: 43% (637). ***Average award:*** Freshmen: $4251; Undergraduates: $4168. ***Scholarships, grants, and awards:*** Federal Pell, FSEOG, state, private, college/university gift aid from institutional funds.

GIFT AID (NON-NEED-BASED) ***Total amount:*** $2,436,915 (96% institutional, 4% external sources). ***Receiving aid:*** Freshmen: 81% (313). Undergraduates: 70% (1,036). ***Average award:*** Freshmen: $9024. Undergraduates: $8608. ***Scholarships, grants, and awards by category:*** *Academic interests/achievement:* general academic interests/achievements. *Creative arts/performance:* music, theater/drama. *Special achievements/activities:* general special achievements/activities. *Special characteristics:* children of educators, ethnic background, general special characteristics, international students, local/state students, members of minority groups, out-of-state students, religious affiliation, veterans' children. ***Tuition waivers:*** Full or partial for employees or children of employees, senior citizens.

LOANS ***Student loans:*** $8,620,617 (81% need-based, 19% non-need-based). 82% of past graduating class borrowed through all loan programs. *Average indebtedness per student:* $28,887. ***Average need-based loan:*** Freshmen: $3791. Undergraduates: $4650. ***Parent loans:*** $2,784,596 (55% need-based, 45% non-need-based). ***Programs:*** Perkins, alternative loans.

WORK-STUDY ***Federal work-study:*** Total amount: $657,162; jobs available. ***State or other work-study/employment:*** Total amount: $137,743 (45% need-based, 55% non-need-based). Part-time jobs available.

ATHLETIC AWARDS Total amount: $5,803,258 (71% need-based, 29% non-need-based).

APPLYING FOR FINANCIAL AID ***Required financial aid form:*** FAFSA. ***Financial aid deadline (priority):*** 3/15. ***Notification date:*** Continuous. Students must reply within 2 weeks of notification.

CONTACT Mr. Tony Tanking, Director of Financial Aid, Benedictine College, 1020 North Second Street, Atchison, KS 66002-1499, 913-360-7484 or toll-free 800-467-5340. *Fax:* 913-367-5462. *E-mail:* ttanking@benedictine.edu.

BENEDICTINE UNIVERSITY

Lisle, IL

Tuition & fees: $23,750 **Average undergraduate aid package: $17,967**

ABOUT THE INSTITUTION Independent Roman Catholic, coed. 44 undergraduate majors. Federal methodology is used as a basis for awarding need-based institutional aid.

UNDERGRADUATE EXPENSES for 2011–12 ***Comprehensive fee:*** $31,250 includes full-time tuition ($22,950), mandatory fees ($800), and room and board ($7500). Full-time tuition and fees vary according to class time, degree level, and location. Room and board charges vary according to board plan, housing facility, and location. Part-time tuition and fees vary according to class time and degree level. ***Payment plans:*** Installment, deferred payment.

FRESHMAN FINANCIAL AID (Fall 2010, est.) 403 applied for aid; of those 91% were deemed to have need. 100% of freshmen with need received aid. ***Average financial aid package:*** $20,094 (excluding resources awarded to replace EFC). 10% of all full-time freshmen had no need and received non-need-based gift aid.

UNDERGRADUATE FINANCIAL AID (Fall 2010, est.) 1,850 applied for aid; of those 92% were deemed to have need. 98% of undergraduates with need received aid. ***Average financial aid package:*** $17,967 (excluding resources awarded to replace EFC). 12% of all full-time undergraduates had no need and received non-need-based gift aid.

GIFT AID (NEED-BASED) ***Total amount:*** $9,176,855 (49% federal, 46% state, 5% institutional). ***Receiving aid:*** Freshmen: 53% (236); all full-time undergraduates: 49% (1,131). ***Average award:*** Freshmen: $8240; Undergraduates: $7921. ***Scholarships, grants, and awards:*** Federal Pell, FSEOG, state, private, college/university gift aid from institutional funds.

GIFT AID (NON-NEED-BASED) ***Total amount:*** $15,536,380 (98% institutional, 2% external sources). ***Receiving aid:*** Freshmen: 81% (365). Undergraduates: 61% (1,412). ***Average award:*** Freshmen: $10,079. Undergraduates: $8783. ***Scholarships, grants, and awards by category:*** *Academic interests/achievement:* 1,745 awards ($12,755,422 total): general academic interests/achievements. *Creative arts/performance:* 16 awards ($39,469 total): music. *Special achievements/activities:* 376 awards ($913,500 total): community service, leadership, memberships. *Special characteristics:* 788 awards ($2,149,593 total): children and siblings of alumni, international students, out-of-state students, relatives of clergy, siblings of current students, veterans, veterans' children. ***Tuition waivers:*** Full or partial for employees or children of employees.

LOANS ***Student loans:*** $14,054,184 (45% need-based, 55% non-need-based). 80% of past graduating class borrowed through all loan programs. *Average indebtedness per student:* $28,100. ***Average need-based loan:*** Freshmen: $2663. Undergraduates: $3426. ***Parent loans:*** $2,957,065 (100% non-need-based). ***Programs:*** Federal Direct (Subsidized and Unsubsidized Stafford, PLUS), Perkins, alternative loans.

WORK-STUDY ***Federal work-study:*** Total amount: $227,926; 184 jobs averaging $1239. ***State or other work-study/employment:*** Total amount: $501,216 (100% non-need-based). 283 part-time jobs averaging $1771.

APPLYING FOR FINANCIAL AID ***Required financial aid form:*** FAFSA. ***Financial aid deadline:*** Continuous. ***Notification date:*** Continuous beginning 2/15. Students must reply within 2 weeks of notification.

CONTACT Diane Battistella, Senior Associate Dean of Financial Aid, Benedictine University, 5700 College Road, Lisle, IL 60532, 630-829-6415 or toll-free 888-829-6363 (out-of-state). *Fax:* 630-829-6101. *E-mail:* dbattistella@ben.edu.

BENNETT COLLEGE FOR WOMEN

Greensboro, NC

CONTACT Monty K. Hickman, Financial Aid Director, Bennett College for Women, 900 East Washington Street, Greensboro, NC 27401, 336-370-8677. *Fax:* 336-517-2204. *E-mail:* mhickman@bennett.edu.

BENNINGTON COLLEGE

Bennington, VT

Tuition & fees: $41,350 **Average undergraduate aid package: $34,170**

ABOUT THE INSTITUTION Independent, coed. 98 undergraduate majors. Both federal and institutional methodology are used as a basis for awarding need-based institutional aid.

UNDERGRADUATE EXPENSES for 2010–11 ***Comprehensive fee:*** $52,900 includes full-time tuition ($40,280), mandatory fees ($1070), and room and board ($11,550). ***College room only:*** $6190. ***Part-time tuition:*** $1340 per credit hour. ***Payment plan:*** Installment.

FRESHMAN FINANCIAL AID (Fall 2010, est.) 121 applied for aid; of those 80% were deemed to have need. 100% of freshmen with need received aid; of those 8% had need fully met. ***Average percent of need met:*** 81% (excluding resources awarded to replace EFC). ***Average financial aid package:*** $34,719 (excluding resources awarded to replace EFC). 25% of all full-time freshmen had no need and received non-need-based gift aid.

UNDERGRADUATE FINANCIAL AID (Fall 2010, est.) 486 applied for aid; of those 87% were deemed to have need. 100% of undergraduates with need received aid; of those 8% had need fully met. ***Average percent of need met:*** 82% (excluding resources awarded to replace EFC). ***Average financial aid package:*** $34,170 (excluding resources awarded to replace EFC). 18% of all full-time undergraduates had no need and received non-need-based gift aid.

GIFT AID (NEED-BASED) ***Total amount:*** $12,043,377 (9% federal, 89% institutional, 2% external sources). ***Receiving aid:*** Freshmen: 56% (94); all full-time undergraduates: 62% (410). ***Average award:*** Freshmen: $31,113; Undergraduates: $29,493. ***Scholarships, grants, and awards:*** Federal Pell, FSEOG, state, private, college/university gift aid from institutional funds.

GIFT AID (NON-NEED-BASED) ***Total amount:*** $2,633,030 (93% institutional, 7% external sources). ***Receiving aid:*** Freshmen: 2% (4). Undergraduates: 4% (25). ***Average award:*** Freshmen: $17,436. Undergraduates: $19,633. ***Scholarships, grants, and awards by category:*** *Academic interests/achievement:* 322 awards ($3,900,776 total): general academic interests/achievements. *Special characteristics:* 7 awards ($195,000 total): children of educators, children of faculty/staff. ***Tuition waivers:*** Full or partial for employees or children of employees.

LOANS ***Student loans:*** $3,074,399 (78% need-based, 22% non-need-based). 74% of past graduating class borrowed through all loan programs. *Average indebtedness per student:* $26,224. ***Average need-based loan:*** Freshmen: $3130. Undergraduates: $4098. ***Parent loans:*** $1,779,831 (29% need-based, 71% non-need-based). ***Programs:*** Federal Direct (Subsidized and Unsubsidized Stafford, PLUS), college/university.

WORK-STUDY ***Federal work-study:*** Total amount: $679,822; 367 jobs averaging $2200. ***State or other work-study/employment:*** Total amount: $78,100 (100% non-need-based). 36 part-time jobs averaging $2200.

APPLYING FOR FINANCIAL AID ***Required financial aid forms:*** FAFSA, institution's own form, CSS Financial Aid PROFILE, noncustodial (divorced/separated) parent's statement, student and parent federal tax returns and W-2 forms. ***Financial aid deadline:*** 2/15 (priority: 2/1). ***Notification date:*** 4/1. Students must reply by 5/1 or within 2 weeks of notification.

CONTACT Meg Woolmington, Director of Financial Aid, Bennington College, One College Drive, Bennington, VT 05201, 802-440-4325 or toll-free 800-833-6845. *Fax:* 802-440-4880. *E-mail:* finaid@bennington.edu.

BENTLEY UNIVERSITY

Waltham, MA

Tuition & fees: $38,328 **Average undergraduate aid package: $30,391**

ABOUT THE INSTITUTION Independent, coed. 17 undergraduate majors. Both federal and institutional methodology are used as a basis for awarding need-based institutional aid.

UNDERGRADUATE EXPENSES for 2011–12 ***Comprehensive fee:*** $50,848 includes full-time tuition ($36,840), mandatory fees ($1488), and room and board ($12,520). ***College room only:*** $7530. Room and board charges vary according to board plan and housing facility. ***Part-time tuition:*** $1866 per course. ***Part-time fees:*** $45 per term. Part-time tuition and fees vary according to class time and course load. ***Payment plan:*** Installment.

FRESHMAN FINANCIAL AID (Fall 2009) 701 applied for aid; of those 69% were deemed to have need. 99% of freshmen with need received aid; of those 45% had need fully met. ***Average percent of need met:*** 95% (excluding resources awarded to replace EFC). ***Average financial aid package:*** $30,818 (excluding resources awarded to replace EFC). 18% of all full-time freshmen had no need and received non-need-based gift aid.

UNDERGRADUATE FINANCIAL AID (Fall 2009) 2,619 applied for aid; of those 78% were deemed to have need. 99% of undergraduates with need received aid; of those 43% had need fully met. ***Average percent of need met:*** 93% (excluding resources awarded to replace EFC). ***Average financial aid package:*** $30,391 (excluding resources awarded to replace EFC). 14% of all full-time undergraduates had no need and received non-need-based gift aid.

GIFT AID (NEED-BASED) ***Total amount:*** $36,896,605 (10% federal, 3% state, 87% institutional). ***Receiving aid:*** Freshmen: 41% (394); all full-time undergraduates: 40% (1,687). ***Average award:*** Freshmen: $24,930; Undergraduates: $23,502. ***Scholarships, grants, and awards:*** Federal Pell, FSEOG, state, private, college/university gift aid from institutional funds.

GIFT AID (NON-NEED-BASED) ***Total amount:*** $18,233,718 (94% institutional, 6% external sources). ***Receiving aid:*** Freshmen: 16% (160). Undergraduates: 15% (612). ***Average award:*** Freshmen: $13,492. Undergraduates: $15,176.

Scholarships, grants, and awards by category: Academic interests/achievement: 1,017 awards ($15,382,903 total): general academic interests/achievements. *Special achievements/activities:* 20 awards ($182,000 total): community service. *Special characteristics:* 60 awards ($942,760 total): international students, members of minority groups. ***Tuition waivers:*** Full or partial for employees or children of employees.

LOANS ***Student loans:*** $21,208,192 (48% need-based, 52% non-need-based). 64% of past graduating class borrowed through all loan programs. *Average indebtedness per student:* $32,710. ***Average need-based loan:*** Freshmen: $4732. Undergraduates: $5330. ***Parent loans:*** $9,791,954 (100% non-need-based). ***Programs:*** Federal Direct (Subsidized and Unsubsidized Stafford, PLUS), Perkins, state.

WORK-STUDY ***Federal work-study:*** Total amount: $1,734,213; 1,177 jobs averaging $1458. ***State or other work-study/employment:*** Total amount: $864,761 (100% non-need-based). 738 part-time jobs averaging $1918.

ATHLETIC AWARDS Total amount: $2,166,077 (41% need-based, 59% non-need-based).

APPLYING FOR FINANCIAL AID ***Required financial aid forms:*** FAFSA, CSS Financial Aid PROFILE, noncustodial (divorced/separated) parent's statement, business/farm supplement, federal income tax returns, including all schedules for parents and student. ***Financial aid deadline:*** 2/1. ***Notification date:*** 3/25.

CONTACT Ms. Donna Kendall, Executive Director of Financial Assistance, Bentley University, 175 Forest Street, Waltham, MA 02452-4705, 781-891-3441 or toll-free 800-523-2354. *Fax:* 781-891-2448. *E-mail:* finaid@bentley.edu.

BEREA COLLEGE

Berea, KY

Tuition & fees: $910 — **Average undergraduate aid package: $30,672**

ABOUT THE INSTITUTION Independent, coed. 38 undergraduate majors. Federal methodology is used as a basis for awarding need-based institutional aid.

UNDERGRADUATE EXPENSES for 2010–11 includes mandatory fees ($910) and room and board ($5574). financial aid is provided to all students for tuition costs.

FRESHMAN FINANCIAL AID (Fall 2010, est.) 429 applied for aid; of those 100% were deemed to have need. 100% of freshmen with need received aid. ***Average percent of need met:*** 95% (excluding resources awarded to replace EFC). ***Average financial aid package:*** $31,261 (excluding resources awarded to replace EFC).

UNDERGRADUATE FINANCIAL AID (Fall 2010, est.) 1,551 applied for aid; of those 100% were deemed to have need. 100% of undergraduates with need received aid. ***Average percent of need met:*** 93% (excluding resources awarded to replace EFC). ***Average financial aid package:*** $30,672 (excluding resources awarded to replace EFC).

GIFT AID (NEED-BASED) ***Total amount:*** $44,686,813 (17% federal, 6% state, 77% institutional). ***Receiving aid:*** Freshmen: 100% (429); all full-time undergraduates: 100% (1,551). ***Average award:*** Freshmen: $29,682; Undergraduates: $28,663. ***Scholarships, grants, and awards:*** Federal Pell, FSEOG, state, private, college/university gift aid from institutional funds.

LOANS ***Student loans:*** $701,132 (31% need-based, 69% non-need-based). 73% of past graduating class borrowed through all loan programs. *Average indebtedness per student:* $5836. ***Average need-based loan:*** Freshmen: $574. Undergraduates: $874. ***Programs:*** Federal Direct (Subsidized and Unsubsidized Stafford, PLUS), Perkins, college/university.

WORK-STUDY ***Federal work-study:*** Total amount: $2,564,626; jobs available. ***State or other work-study/employment:*** Total amount: $348,900 (100% need-based). Part-time jobs available.

APPLYING FOR FINANCIAL AID ***Required financial aid form:*** FAFSA. ***Financial aid deadline:*** 5/1 (priority: 2/1). ***Notification date:*** Continuous beginning 4/15.

CONTACT Nancy Melton, Director of Student Financial Aid Services, Berea College, CPO 2172, Berea, KY 40404, 859-985-3313 or toll-free 800-326-5948. *Fax:* 859-985-3914. *E-mail:* nancy_melton@berea.edu.

BERKLEE COLLEGE OF MUSIC

Boston, MA

Tuition & fees: $32,520 — **Average undergraduate aid package: $15,824**

ABOUT THE INSTITUTION Independent, coed. 13 undergraduate majors. Federal methodology is used as a basis for awarding need-based institutional aid.

UNDERGRADUATE EXPENSES for 2010–11 ***Comprehensive fee:*** $48,350 includes full-time tuition ($31,300), mandatory fees ($1220), and room and board ($15,830). ***Part-time tuition:*** $1100 per credit hour. ***Payment plans:*** Tuition prepayment, deferred payment.

FRESHMAN FINANCIAL AID (Fall 2010, est.) 475 applied for aid; of those 89% were deemed to have need. 100% of freshmen with need received aid; of those 5% had need fully met. ***Average percent of need met:*** 37% (excluding resources awarded to replace EFC). ***Average financial aid package:*** $16,188 (excluding resources awarded to replace EFC). 25% of all full-time freshmen had no need and received non-need-based gift aid.

UNDERGRADUATE FINANCIAL AID (Fall 2010, est.) 2,050 applied for aid; of those 90% were deemed to have need. 99% of undergraduates with need received aid; of those 4% had need fully met. ***Average percent of need met:*** 37% (excluding resources awarded to replace EFC). ***Average financial aid package:*** $15,824 (excluding resources awarded to replace EFC). 25% of all full-time undergraduates had no need and received non-need-based gift aid.

GIFT AID (NEED-BASED) ***Total amount:*** $19,872,841 (23% federal, 2% state, 75% institutional). ***Receiving aid:*** Freshmen: 28% (225); all full-time undergraduates: 25% (984). ***Average award:*** Freshmen: $8881; Undergraduates: $8513. ***Scholarships, grants, and awards:*** Federal Pell, FSEOG, state, private, college/university gift aid from institutional funds, Academic Competitiveness Grants.

GIFT AID (NON-NEED-BASED) ***Total amount:*** $12,189,187 (92% institutional, 8% external sources). ***Receiving aid:*** Freshmen: 29% (233). Undergraduates: 23% (883). ***Average award:*** Freshmen: $13,460. Undergraduates: $13,020. ***Scholarships, grants, and awards by category:*** *Academic interests/achievement:* education, engineering/technologies, general academic interests/achievements. *Creative arts/performance:* music. *Special characteristics:* children of faculty/staff. ***Tuition waivers:*** Full or partial for employees or children of employees.

LOANS ***Student loans:*** $24,879,185 (37% need-based, 63% non-need-based). ***Average need-based loan:*** Freshmen: $4484. Undergraduates: $5070. ***Parent loans:*** $18,163,734 (100% non-need-based). ***Programs:*** Federal Direct (Subsidized and Unsubsidized Stafford, PLUS), Perkins, state.

WORK-STUDY ***Federal work-study:*** Total amount: $366,485; jobs available. ***State or other work-study/employment:*** Total amount: $3,150,253 (100% non-need-based). Part-time jobs available.

APPLYING FOR FINANCIAL AID ***Required financial aid form:*** FAFSA. ***Financial aid deadline:*** 5/1. ***Notification date:*** Continuous. Students must reply within 2 weeks of notification.

CONTACT Frank Mullen, Director of Financial Aid, Berklee College of Music, 1140 Boylston Street, Boston, MA 02215-3693, 617-747-2274 or toll-free 800-BERKLEE. *Fax:* 617-747-2073. *E-mail:* financialaid@berklee.edu.

BERNARD M. BARUCH COLLEGE OF THE CITY UNIVERSITY OF NEW YORK

New York, NY

ABOUT THE INSTITUTION State and locally supported, coed. 41 undergraduate majors.

GIFT AID (NEED-BASED) ***Scholarships, grants, and awards:*** Federal Pell, FSEOG, state, college/university gift aid from institutional funds.

GIFT AID (NON-NEED-BASED) ***Scholarships, grants, and awards by category:*** *Academic interests/achievement:* general academic interests/achievements.

LOANS ***Programs:*** Federal Direct (Subsidized and Unsubsidized Stafford, PLUS), Perkins.

WORK-STUDY ***Federal work-study:*** Total amount: $475,126; 675 jobs averaging $800. ***State or other work-study/employment:*** Total amount: $325,900 (100% need-based). 755 part-time jobs averaging $1200.

APPLYING FOR FINANCIAL AID ***Required financial aid forms:*** FAFSA, state aid form.

CONTACT Financial Aid Office, Bernard M. Baruch College of the City University of New York, 151 East 25th Street, Room 720, New York, NY 10010-5585, 646-312-1360. *Fax:* 646-312-1361. *E-mail:* financial_aid@baruch.cuny.edu.

BERRY COLLEGE

Mount Berry, GA

Tuition & fees: $24,620 **Average undergraduate aid package: $20,845**

ABOUT THE INSTITUTION Independent interdenominational, coed. 36 undergraduate majors. Federal methodology is used as a basis for awarding need-based institutional aid.

UNDERGRADUATE EXPENSES for 2010–11 ***Comprehensive fee:*** $33,344 includes full-time tuition ($24,420), mandatory fees ($200), and room and board ($8724). ***College room only:*** $4894. Room and board charges vary according to board plan and housing facility. ***Part-time tuition:*** $814 per credit hour. ***Payment plan:*** Installment.

FRESHMAN FINANCIAL AID (Fall 2010, est.) 607 applied for aid; of those 79% were deemed to have need. 100% of freshmen with need received aid; of those 30% had need fully met. ***Average percent of need met:*** 81% (excluding resources awarded to replace EFC). ***Average financial aid package:*** $21,069 (excluding resources awarded to replace EFC). 27% of all full-time freshmen had no need and received non-need-based gift aid.

UNDERGRADUATE FINANCIAL AID (Fall 2010, est.) 1,622 applied for aid; of those 82% were deemed to have need. 100% of undergraduates with need received aid; of those 26% had need fully met. ***Average percent of need met:*** 78% (excluding resources awarded to replace EFC). ***Average financial aid package:*** $20,845 (excluding resources awarded to replace EFC). 27% of all full-time undergraduates had no need and received non-need-based gift aid.

GIFT AID (NEED-BASED) ***Total amount:*** $21,709,130 (12% federal, 15% state, 71% institutional, 2% external sources). ***Receiving aid:*** Freshmen: 73% (477); all full-time undergraduates: 70% (1,318). ***Average award:*** Freshmen: $17,540; Undergraduates: $16,699. ***Scholarships, grants, and awards:*** Federal Pell, FSEOG, state, private, college/university gift aid from institutional funds.

GIFT AID (NON-NEED-BASED) ***Total amount:*** $8,501,287 (23% state, 73% institutional, 4% external sources). ***Receiving aid:*** Freshmen: 16% (105). Undergraduates: 13% (248). ***Average award:*** Freshmen: $11,167. Undergraduates: $10,596. ***Scholarships, grants, and awards by category:*** *Academic interests/achievement:* agriculture, business, communication, education, English, general academic interests/achievements, humanities, religion/biblical studies. *Creative arts/performance:* art/fine arts, debating, journalism/publications, music, theater/drama. *Special achievements/activities:* community service, leadership, religious involvement. *Special characteristics:* adult students, children of faculty/staff, ethnic background, first-generation college students, international students, local/state students, members of minority groups, out-of-state students, veterans, veterans' children. ***Tuition waivers:*** Full or partial for employees or children of employees, senior citizens.

LOANS ***Student loans:*** $10,592,221 (63% need-based, 37% non-need-based). 50% of past graduating class borrowed through all loan programs. *Average indebtedness per student:* $12,412. ***Average need-based loan:*** Freshmen: $3476. Undergraduates: $4351. ***Parent loans:*** $3,219,757 (33% need-based, 67% non-need-based). ***Programs:*** Federal Direct (Subsidized and Unsubsidized Stafford, PLUS), Perkins, college/university.

WORK-STUDY ***Federal work-study:*** Total amount: $935,600; 241 jobs averaging $3880. ***State or other work-study/employment:*** Total amount: $7,022,974 (5% need-based, 95% non-need-based). 1,670 part-time jobs averaging $3840.

APPLYING FOR FINANCIAL AID ***Required financial aid forms:*** FAFSA, state aid form. ***Financial aid deadline (priority):*** 4/1. ***Notification date:*** Continuous beginning 2/15.

CONTACT Mrs. Marcia McConnell, Director of Financial Aid, Berry College, 2277 Martha Berry Highway, NW, Mount Berry, GA 30149-5007, 706-236-1714 or toll-free 800-237-7942. *Fax:* 706-290-2160. *E-mail:* financialaid@berry.edu.

BETHANY COLLEGE

Lindsborg, KS

ABOUT THE INSTITUTION Independent Lutheran, coed. 45 undergraduate majors.

GIFT AID (NEED-BASED) ***Scholarships, grants, and awards:*** Federal Pell, FSEOG, state, private, college/university gift aid from institutional funds, Academic Competitiveness Grants, National SMART Grants, TEACH Grants.

GIFT AID (NON-NEED-BASED) ***Scholarships, grants, and awards by category:*** *Academic interests/achievement:* general academic interests/achievements. *Creative arts/performance:* art/fine arts, music, theater/drama. *Special achievements/activities:* cheerleading/drum major. *Special characteristics:* children and siblings of alumni, international students, relatives of clergy, religious affiliation.

LOANS ***Programs:*** Perkins, college/university.

WORK-STUDY ***Federal work-study:*** Total amount: $419,008; 97 jobs averaging $1500. ***State or other work-study/employment:*** Part-time jobs available.

APPLYING FOR FINANCIAL AID ***Required financial aid form:*** FAFSA.

CONTACT Ms. Amber Maneth, Director of Financial Aid, Bethany College, 335 East Swensson, Lindsborg, KS 67456-1897, 785-227-3311 Ext. 8248 or toll-free 800-826-2281. *Fax:* 785-227-2004. *E-mail:* meagherb@bethanylb.edu.

BETHANY COLLEGE

Bethany, WV

Tuition & fees: $22,596 **Average undergraduate aid package: N/A**

ABOUT THE INSTITUTION Independent religious, coed. 30 undergraduate majors. Institutional methodology is used as a basis for awarding need-based institutional aid.

UNDERGRADUATE EXPENSES for 2010–11 ***Comprehensive fee:*** $31,896 includes full-time tuition ($21,696), mandatory fees ($900), and room and board ($9300). Room and board charges vary according to housing facility. ***Part-time tuition:*** $650 per credit hour. ***Payment plan:*** Installment.

FRESHMAN FINANCIAL AID (Fall 2009) 274 applied for aid; of those 92% were deemed to have need. 100% of freshmen with need received aid. ***Average percent of need met:*** 51% (excluding resources awarded to replace EFC). 8% of all full-time freshmen had no need and received non-need-based gift aid.

UNDERGRADUATE FINANCIAL AID (Fall 2009) 777 applied for aid; of those 90% were deemed to have need. 100% of undergraduates with need received aid. ***Average percent of need met:*** 49% (excluding resources awarded to replace EFC). 7% of all full-time undergraduates had no need and received non-need-based gift aid.

GIFT AID (NEED-BASED) ***Total amount:*** $7,811,046 (29% federal, 7% state, 60% institutional, 4% external sources). ***Receiving aid:*** Freshmen: 86% (243); all full-time undergraduates: 77% (628). ***Average award:*** Freshmen: $10,988; Undergraduates: $9824. ***Scholarships, grants, and awards:*** Federal Pell, FSEOG, state, private, college/university gift aid from institutional funds.

GIFT AID (NON-NEED-BASED) ***Average award:*** Freshmen: $8886. Undergraduates: $7189. ***Scholarships, grants, and awards by category:*** *Academic interests/achievement:* general academic interests/achievements. *Creative arts/performance:* music. *Special achievements/activities:* leadership. *Special characteristics:* children and siblings of alumni, children of faculty/staff, international students, relatives of clergy, religious affiliation. ***Tuition waivers:*** Full or partial for children of alumni, employees or children of employees.

LOANS ***Student loans:*** $6,867,796 (100% need-based). ***Average need-based loan:*** Freshmen: $4342. Undergraduates: $7258. ***Parent loans:*** $5,111,346 (100% need-based). ***Programs:*** Federal Direct (Subsidized and Unsubsidized Stafford, PLUS), Perkins, alternative loans.

WORK-STUDY ***Federal work-study:*** Total amount: $831,854; jobs available. ***State or other work-study/employment:*** Total amount: $282,623 (100% need-based). Part-time jobs available.

APPLYING FOR FINANCIAL AID ***Required financial aid forms:*** FAFSA, state aid form, Master Promissory Notes and Entrance Counseling (for federal loans). ***Financial aid deadline:*** Continuous. ***Notification date:*** Continuous. Students must reply within 2 weeks of notification.

CONTACT Sheila Nelson-Hensley, Director of Financial Aid, Bethany College, PO Box 488, Bethany, WV 26032, 304-829-7141 or toll-free 800-922-7611 (out-of-state). *Fax:* 304-829-7142. *E-mail:* admission@bethanywv.edu.

BETHANY LUTHERAN COLLEGE

Mankato, MN

Tuition & fees: $20,950 **Average undergraduate aid package: $16,769**

ABOUT THE INSTITUTION Independent Lutheran, coed. 19 undergraduate majors. Federal methodology is used as a basis for awarding need-based institutional aid.

UNDERGRADUATE EXPENSES for 2010–11 ***One-time required fee:*** $130. ***Comprehensive fee:*** $27,450 includes full-time tuition ($20,650), mandatory fees ($300), and room and board ($6500). ***College room only:*** $2890. Room and board charges vary according to board plan and housing facility. ***Part-time tuition:*** $870 per credit hour. ***Part-time fees:*** $150 per term. ***Payment plan:*** Installment.

FRESHMAN FINANCIAL AID (Fall 2009) 158 applied for aid; of those 89% were deemed to have need. 100% of freshmen with need received aid; of those 28% had need fully met. ***Average percent of need met:*** 86% (excluding resources awarded to replace EFC). ***Average financial aid package:*** $18,324 (excluding resources awarded to replace EFC). 11% of all full-time freshmen had no need and received non-need-based gift aid.

UNDERGRADUATE FINANCIAL AID (Fall 2009) 583 applied for aid; of those 91% were deemed to have need. 100% of undergraduates with need received aid; of those 27% had need fully met. ***Average percent of need met:*** 85% (excluding resources awarded to replace EFC). ***Average financial aid package:*** $16,769 (excluding resources awarded to replace EFC). 13% of all full-time undergraduates had no need and received non-need-based gift aid.

GIFT AID (NEED-BASED) ***Total amount:*** $6,114,605 (18% federal, 17% state, 63% institutional, 2% external sources). ***Receiving aid:*** Freshmen: 85% (141); all full-time undergraduates: 84% (530). ***Average award:*** Freshmen: $14,872; Undergraduates: $12,414. ***Scholarships, grants, and awards:*** Federal Pell, FSEOG, state, private, college/university gift aid from institutional funds.

GIFT AID (NON-NEED-BASED) ***Total amount:*** $567,814 (1% state, 91% institutional, 8% external sources). ***Receiving aid:*** Freshmen: 6% (10). Undergraduates: 7% (47). ***Average award:*** Freshmen: $5282. Undergraduates: $5487. ***Scholarships, grants, and awards by category:*** *Creative arts/performance:* 72 awards ($138,000 total): art/fine arts, debating, journalism/publications, music, theater/drama. *Special characteristics:* 20 awards ($308,017 total): children of faculty/staff. ***Tuition waivers:*** Full or partial for employees or children of employees.

LOANS ***Student loans:*** $4,092,808 (67% need-based, 33% non-need-based). 81% of past graduating class borrowed through all loan programs. *Average indebtedness per student:* $26,519. ***Average need-based loan:*** Freshmen: $3770. Undergraduates: $4778. ***Parent loans:*** $430,642 (24% need-based, 76% non-need-based). ***Programs:*** Federal Direct (Subsidized and Unsubsidized Stafford, PLUS), Perkins, state, alternative loans.

WORK-STUDY ***Federal work-study:*** Total amount: $40,168; 33 jobs averaging $1217. ***State or other work-study/employment:*** Total amount: $189,025 (53% need-based, 47% non-need-based). 256 part-time jobs averaging $738.

APPLYING FOR FINANCIAL AID ***Required financial aid forms:*** FAFSA, institution's own form, business/farm supplement, federal income tax form(s), W-2 forms. ***Financial aid deadline (priority):*** 4/15. ***Notification date:*** Continuous beginning 3/1. Students must reply within 4 weeks of notification.

CONTACT Financial Aid Office, Bethany Lutheran College, 700 Luther Drive, Mankato, MN 56001-6163, 507-344-7328 or toll-free 800-944-3066 Ext. 331. *Fax:* 507-344-7376. *E-mail:* finaid@blc.edu.

BETHANY UNIVERSITY
Scotts Valley, CA

CONTACT Deborah Snow, Financial Aid Director, Bethany University, 800 Bethany Drive, Scotts Valley, CA 95066-2820, 831-438-3800 Ext. 1477 or toll-free 800-843-9410. *Fax:* 831-461-1533.

BETHEL COLLEGE
Mishawaka, IN

Tuition & fees: $23,030 **Average undergraduate aid package: $17,095**

ABOUT THE INSTITUTION Independent religious, coed. 52 undergraduate majors. Federal methodology is used as a basis for awarding need-based institutional aid.

UNDERGRADUATE EXPENSES for 2011–12 ***One-time required fee:*** $600. ***Comprehensive fee:*** $30,100 includes full-time tuition ($23,030) and room and board ($7070). ***College room only:*** $3560. Full-time tuition and fees vary according to program. Room and board charges vary according to board plan and housing facility. ***Part-time tuition:*** $730 per hour. Part-time tuition and fees vary according to course load and program. ***Payment plan:*** Installment.

FRESHMAN FINANCIAL AID (Fall 2010, est.) 261 applied for aid; of those 91% were deemed to have need. 100% of freshmen with need received aid; of those 17% had need fully met. ***Average percent of need met:*** 72% (excluding resources awarded to replace EFC). ***Average financial aid package:*** $20,528 (excluding resources awarded to replace EFC). 11% of all full-time freshmen had no need and received non-need-based gift aid.

UNDERGRADUATE FINANCIAL AID (Fall 2010, est.) 1,378 applied for aid; of those 91% were deemed to have need. 99% of undergraduates with need received aid; of those 17% had need fully met. ***Average percent of need met:*** 70% (excluding resources awarded to replace EFC). ***Average financial aid package:*** $17,095 (excluding resources awarded to replace EFC). 11% of all full-time undergraduates had no need and received non-need-based gift aid.

GIFT AID (NEED-BASED) ***Total amount:*** $6,530,700 (64% federal, 36% state). ***Receiving aid:*** Freshmen: 62% (168); all full-time undergraduates: 57% (865). ***Average award:*** Freshmen: $8615; Undergraduates: $7687. ***Scholarships, grants, and awards:*** Federal Pell, FSEOG, state, private, college/university gift aid from institutional funds, Federal Nursing.

GIFT AID (NON-NEED-BASED) ***Total amount:*** $7,428,800 (91% institutional, 9% external sources). ***Receiving aid:*** Freshmen: 84% (227). Undergraduates: 64% (968). ***Average award:*** Freshmen: $6300. Undergraduates: $6279. ***Scholarships, grants, and awards by category:*** *Academic interests/achievement:* 770 awards ($3,870,000 total): biological sciences, business, communication, education, English, general academic interests/achievements, health fields, mathematics, physical sciences, premedicine, religion/biblical studies, social sciences. *Creative arts/performance:* 65 awards ($150,000 total): art/fine arts, journalism/publications, music, theater/drama. *Special achievements/activities:* 82 awards ($125,000 total): cheerleading/drum major, general special achievements/activities, leadership, religious involvement. *Special characteristics:* 587 awards ($1,619,000 total): adult students, children of faculty/staff, international students, members of minority groups, relatives of clergy, religious affiliation, siblings of current students, spouses of current students. ***Tuition waivers:*** Full or partial for employees or children of employees.

LOANS ***Student loans:*** $14,762,500 (87% need-based, 13% non-need-based). 78% of past graduating class borrowed through all loan programs. *Average indebtedness per student:* $26,173. ***Average need-based loan:*** Freshmen: $3644. Undergraduates: $4393. ***Parent loans:*** $6,805,900 (100% non-need-based). ***Programs:*** Federal Direct (Subsidized and Unsubsidized Stafford, PLUS), Perkins, Federal Nursing, college/university, GATE loans.

WORK-STUDY ***Federal work-study:*** Total amount: $1,453,900; 718 jobs averaging $2400. ***State or other work-study/employment:*** Total amount: $669,100 (100% non-need-based). 271 part-time jobs averaging $2440.

ATHLETIC AWARDS Total amount: $1,661,100 (100% non-need-based).

APPLYING FOR FINANCIAL AID ***Required financial aid forms:*** FAFSA, institution's own form. ***Financial aid deadline (priority):*** 3/1. ***Notification date:*** Continuous beginning 4/1.

CONTACT Mr. Guy A. Fisher, Director of Financial Aid, Bethel College, 1001 Bethel Circle, Mishawaka, IN 46545-5591, 574-257-3316 or toll-free 800-422-4101. *Fax:* 574-807-7122. *E-mail:* fisherg@bethelcollege.edu.

BETHEL COLLEGE
North Newton, KS

Tuition & fees: $20,700 **Average undergraduate aid package: $21,698**

ABOUT THE INSTITUTION Independent religious, coed. 17 undergraduate majors. Federal methodology is used as a basis for awarding need-based institutional aid.

UNDERGRADUATE EXPENSES for 2010–11 ***Comprehensive fee:*** $27,680 includes full-time tuition ($20,700) and room and board ($6980). ***College room only:*** $3730. Full-time tuition and fees vary according to course load. Room and board charges vary according to board plan and housing facility. ***Part-time tuition:*** $745 per semester hour. Part-time tuition and fees vary according to course load. ***Payment plans:*** Installment, deferred payment.

FRESHMAN FINANCIAL AID (Fall 2009) 86 applied for aid; of those 100% were deemed to have need. 100% of freshmen with need received aid; of those 58% had need fully met. ***Average percent of need met:*** 100% (excluding resources awarded to replace EFC). ***Average financial aid package:*** $22,259 (excluding resources awarded to replace EFC). 5% of all full-time freshmen had no need and received non-need-based gift aid.

UNDERGRADUATE FINANCIAL AID (Fall 2009) 357 applied for aid; of those 95% were deemed to have need. 100% of undergraduates with need received aid; of those 47% had need fully met. ***Average percent of need met:*** 94% (excluding resources awarded to replace EFC). ***Average financial aid package:***

$21,698 (excluding resources awarded to replace EFC). 19% of all full-time undergraduates had no need and received non-need-based gift aid.

GIFT AID (NEED-BASED) ***Total amount:*** $1,204,024 (60% federal, 36% state, 4% institutional). ***Receiving aid:*** Freshmen: 69% (63); all full-time undergraduates: 56% (237). ***Average award:*** Freshmen: $5240; Undergraduates: $5359. ***Scholarships, grants, and awards:*** Federal Pell, FSEOG, state, college/university gift aid from institutional funds.

GIFT AID (NON-NEED-BASED) ***Total amount:*** $3,288,912 (96% institutional, 4% external sources). ***Receiving aid:*** Freshmen: 90% (82). Undergraduates: 76% (319). ***Average award:*** Freshmen: $6975. Undergraduates: $8932. ***Scholarships, grants, and awards by category:*** *Academic interests/achievement:* $1,248,460 total: biological sciences, general academic interests/achievements. *Creative arts/performance:* $510,015 total: art/fine arts, debating, music, theater/drama. *Special characteristics:* $760,774 total: children and siblings of alumni, children of current students, children of faculty/staff, ethnic background, general special characteristics, international students, local/state students, previous college experience, relatives of clergy, religious affiliation, siblings of current students, spouses of current students. ***Tuition waivers:*** Full or partial for children of alumni, employees or children of employees, senior citizens.

LOANS ***Student loans:*** $2,627,555 (67% need-based, 33% non-need-based). 78% of past graduating class borrowed through all loan programs. *Average indebtedness per student:* $24,860. ***Average need-based loan:*** Freshmen: $6563. Undergraduates: $6764. ***Parent loans:*** $224,995 (100% non-need-based). ***Programs:*** Federal Direct (Subsidized and Unsubsidized Stafford, PLUS), Perkins.

WORK-STUDY ***Federal work-study:*** Total amount: $328,925; 194 jobs averaging $1711. ***State or other work-study/employment:*** Total amount: $230,684 (100% non-need-based). 193 part-time jobs averaging $1195.

ATHLETIC AWARDS Total amount: $589,573 (100% non-need-based).

APPLYING FOR FINANCIAL AID ***Required financial aid form:*** FAFSA. ***Financial aid deadline (priority):*** 4/1. ***Notification date:*** Continuous beginning 2/1. Students must reply by 5/1 or within 2 weeks of notification.

CONTACT Mr. Tony Graber, Financial Aid Director, Bethel College, 300 East 27th Street, North Newton, KS 67117, 316-284-5232 or toll-free 800-522-1887 Ext. 230. *Fax:* 316-284-5845. *E-mail:* tgraber@bethelks.edu.

BETHEL UNIVERSITY

St. Paul, MN

Tuition & fees: $29,460 **Average undergraduate aid package: $20,930**

ABOUT THE INSTITUTION Independent religious, coed. 55 undergraduate majors. Federal methodology is used as a basis for awarding need-based institutional aid.

UNDERGRADUATE EXPENSES for 2011–12 ***Comprehensive fee:*** $37,990 includes full-time tuition ($29,320), mandatory fees ($140), and room and board ($8530). ***College room only:*** $4900. Room and board charges vary according to board plan. ***Part-time tuition:*** $1225 per credit. Part-time tuition and fees vary according to course load. ***Payment plans:*** Tuition prepayment, installment.

FRESHMAN FINANCIAL AID (Fall 2010, est.) 511 applied for aid; of those 87% were deemed to have need. 100% of freshmen with need received aid; of those 16% had need fully met. ***Average percent of need met:*** 81% (excluding resources awarded to replace EFC). ***Average financial aid package:*** $22,783 (excluding resources awarded to replace EFC). 19% of all full-time freshmen had no need and received non-need-based gift aid.

UNDERGRADUATE FINANCIAL AID (Fall 2010, est.) 2,247 applied for aid; of those 88% were deemed to have need. 100% of undergraduates with need received aid; of those 16% had need fully met. ***Average percent of need met:*** 76% (excluding resources awarded to replace EFC). ***Average financial aid package:*** $20,930 (excluding resources awarded to replace EFC). 21% of all full-time undergraduates had no need and received non-need-based gift aid.

GIFT AID (NEED-BASED) ***Total amount:*** $28,605,000 (16% federal, 8% state, 73% institutional, 3% external sources). ***Receiving aid:*** Freshmen: 80% (447); all full-time undergraduates: 75% (1,970). ***Average award:*** Freshmen: $17,200; Undergraduates: $14,941. ***Scholarships, grants, and awards:*** Federal Pell, FSEOG, state, private, college/university gift aid from institutional funds.

GIFT AID (NON-NEED-BASED) ***Total amount:*** $4,417,000 (7% federal, 87% institutional, 6% external sources). ***Receiving aid:*** Freshmen: 8% (47). Undergraduates: 7% (179). ***Average award:*** Freshmen: $8575. Undergraduates: $6877. ***Scholarships, grants, and awards by category:*** *Academic interests/achievement:* 1,756 awards ($8,754,000 total): general academic interests/achievements. *Creative arts/performance:* 115 awards ($277,000 total): art/fine arts, debating, music, theater/drama. *Special achievements/activities:* community service, junior miss, leadership, religious involvement. *Special characteristics:* children and siblings of alumni, children of faculty/staff, ethnic background, international students, members of minority groups, out-of-state students, relatives of clergy, religious affiliation. ***Tuition waivers:*** Full or partial for employees or children of employees.

LOANS ***Student loans:*** $20,209,000 (74% need-based, 26% non-need-based). 78% of past graduating class borrowed through all loan programs. *Average indebtedness per student:* $32,698. ***Average need-based loan:*** Freshmen: $4114. Undergraduates: $4655. ***Parent loans:*** $4,330,000 (40% need-based, 60% non-need-based). ***Programs:*** Federal Direct (Subsidized and Unsubsidized Stafford, PLUS), Perkins, state, alternative loans.

WORK-STUDY ***Federal work-study:*** Total amount: $824,000; 375 jobs averaging $2200. ***State or other work-study/employment:*** Total amount: $2,397,000 (61% need-based, 39% non-need-based). 1,200 part-time jobs averaging $2000.

APPLYING FOR FINANCIAL AID ***Required financial aid forms:*** FAFSA, institution's own form. ***Financial aid deadline (priority):*** 4/15. ***Notification date:*** Continuous beginning 2/1.

CONTACT Mr. Jeffrey D. Olson, Director of Financial Aid, Bethel University, 3900 Bethel Drive, St. Paul, MN 55112-6999, 651-638-6241 or toll-free 800-255-8706 Ext. 6242. *Fax:* 651-635-1491. *E-mail:* finaid@bethel.edu.

BETHEL UNIVERSITY

McKenzie, TN

CONTACT Laura Bateman, Office of Financial Aid, Bethel University, 325 Cherry Avenue, McKenzie, TN 38201, 901-352-4007. *Fax:* 901-352-4069.

BETHESDA CHRISTIAN UNIVERSITY

Anaheim, CA

Tuition & fees: $7050 **Average undergraduate aid package: $5000**

ABOUT THE INSTITUTION Independent religious, coed. ***Awards:*** bachelor's and master's degrees. 10 undergraduate majors. ***Total enrollment:*** 345. Undergraduates: 232. Federal methodology is used as a basis for awarding need-based institutional aid.

UNDERGRADUATE EXPENSES for 2010–11 ***Application fee:*** $35. ***Tuition:*** full-time $6930; part-time $231 per semester hour. ***Required fees:*** full-time $120; $60 per term. Room and board charges vary according to housing facility. ***Payment plans:*** Installment, deferred payment.

FRESHMAN FINANCIAL AID (Fall 2010, est.) 18 applied for aid; of those 100% were deemed to have need. 100% of freshmen with need received aid; of those 56% had need fully met. ***Average percent of need met:*** 80% (excluding resources awarded to replace EFC). ***Average financial aid package:*** $4000 (excluding resources awarded to replace EFC). 28% of all full-time freshmen had no need and received non-need-based gift aid.

UNDERGRADUATE FINANCIAL AID (Fall 2010, est.) 50 applied for aid; of those 90% were deemed to have need. 100% of undergraduates with need received aid; of those 67% had need fully met. ***Average percent of need met:*** 80% (excluding resources awarded to replace EFC). ***Average financial aid package:*** $5000 (excluding resources awarded to replace EFC). 15% of all full-time undergraduates had no need and received non-need-based gift aid.

GIFT AID (NEED-BASED) ***Total amount:*** $77,000 (87% federal, 13% institutional). ***Receiving aid:*** Freshmen: 100% (18); all full-time undergraduates: 30% (40). ***Average award:*** Freshmen: $4000; Undergraduates: $4000. ***Scholarships, grants, and awards:*** Federal Pell, college/university gift aid from institutional funds.

GIFT AID (NON-NEED-BASED) ***Receiving aid:*** Freshmen: 22% (4). Undergraduates: 11% (15). ***Average award:*** Freshmen: $500. Undergraduates: $500. ***Scholarships, grants, and awards by category:*** *Academic interests/achievement:* education, religion/biblical studies. *Creative arts/performance:* applied art and design, music. *Special achievements/activities:* religious involvement. *Special characteristics:* children of current students, children of educators, children of faculty/staff, married students, relatives of clergy, siblings of current students, spouses of current students.

LOANS ***Student loans:*** $44,500 (55% need-based, 45% non-need-based). 25% of past graduating class borrowed through all loan programs. *Average indebted-*

ness per student: $2500. ***Average need-based loan:*** Freshmen: $3000. Undergraduates: $4000. ***Programs:*** Federal Direct (Subsidized and Unsubsidized Stafford).

ATHLETIC AWARDS Total amount: $25,000 (100% non-need-based).

APPLYING FOR FINANCIAL AID ***Required financial aid forms:*** FAFSA, institution's own form. ***Financial aid deadline:*** Continuous. ***Notification date:*** Continuous beginning 8/1. Students must reply within 2 weeks of notification.

CONTACT Ms. Grace Choi, Financial Aid Administrator, Bethesda Christian University, 730 North Euclid Street, Anaheim, CA 92801, 714-683-1413. *Fax:* 714-517-1948. *E-mail:* financialaid@bcu.edu.

BETH HAMEDRASH SHAAREI YOSHER INSTITUTE

Brooklyn, NY

CONTACT Financial Aid Office, Beth HaMedrash Shaarei Yosher Institute, 4102-10 16th Avenue, Brooklyn, NY 11204, 718-854-2290.

BETH HATALMUD RABBINICAL COLLEGE

Brooklyn, NY

CONTACT Financial Aid Office, Beth Hatalmud Rabbinical College, 2127 82nd Street, Brooklyn, NY 11204, 718-259-2525.

BETH MEDRASH GOVOHA

Lakewood, NJ

CONTACT Financial Aid Office, Beth Medrash Govoha, 617 Sixth Street, Lakewood, NJ 08701-2797, 732-367-1060.

BETHUNE-COOKMAN UNIVERSITY

Daytona Beach, FL

Tuition & fees: $13,572 **Average undergraduate aid package: $13,186**

ABOUT THE INSTITUTION Independent Methodist, coed. 38 undergraduate majors. Federal methodology is used as a basis for awarding need-based institutional aid.

UNDERGRADUATE EXPENSES for 2010–11 ***Comprehensive fee:*** $21,552 includes full-time tuition ($13,572) and room and board ($7980). Full-time tuition and fees vary according to course load. ***Part-time tuition:*** $560 per credit hour. Part-time tuition and fees vary according to course load. ***Payment plan:*** Installment.

FRESHMAN FINANCIAL AID (Fall 2010, est.) 993 applied for aid; of those 97% were deemed to have need. 100% of freshmen with need received aid; of those 5% had need fully met. ***Average percent of need met:*** 50% (excluding resources awarded to replace EFC). ***Average financial aid package:*** $12,396 (excluding resources awarded to replace EFC). 1% of all full-time freshmen had no need and received non-need-based gift aid.

UNDERGRADUATE FINANCIAL AID (Fall 2010, est.) 3,352 applied for aid; of those 97% were deemed to have need. 100% of undergraduates with need received aid; of those 6% had need fully met. ***Average percent of need met:*** 52% (excluding resources awarded to replace EFC). ***Average financial aid package:*** $13,186 (excluding resources awarded to replace EFC). 1% of all full-time undergraduates had no need and received non-need-based gift aid.

GIFT AID (NEED-BASED) ***Total amount:*** $26,164,119 (53% federal, 25% state, 19% institutional, 3% external sources). ***Receiving aid:*** Freshmen: 94% (936); all full-time undergraduates: 93% (3,134). ***Average award:*** Freshmen: $9829; Undergraduates: $9161. ***Scholarships, grants, and awards:*** Federal Pell, FSEOG, state, private, college/university gift aid from institutional funds, United Negro College Fund.

GIFT AID (NON-NEED-BASED) ***Total amount:*** $756,109 (1% federal, 33% state, 64% institutional, 2% external sources). ***Receiving aid:*** Freshmen: 3% (28). Undergraduates: 3% (111). ***Average award:*** Freshmen: $8908. Undergraduates: $8611. ***Scholarships, grants, and awards by category:*** *Academic interests/achievement:* 265 awards ($1,817,000 total): general academic interests/achievements. ***Tuition waivers:*** Full or partial for employees or children of employees.

LOANS ***Student loans:*** $26,767,928 (94% need-based, 6% non-need-based). 96% of past graduating class borrowed through all loan programs. *Average indebtedness per student:* $27,645. ***Average need-based loan:*** Freshmen: $3597. Undergraduates: $4609. ***Parent loans:*** $8,747,663 (84% need-based, 16% non-need-based). ***Programs:*** Federal Direct (Subsidized and Unsubsidized Stafford, PLUS).

WORK-STUDY ***Federal work-study:*** Total amount: $457,150; 261 jobs averaging $2000. ***State or other work-study/employment:*** 130 part-time jobs averaging $2100.

ATHLETIC AWARDS Total amount: $3,211,744 (83% need-based, 17% non-need-based).

APPLYING FOR FINANCIAL AID ***Required financial aid form:*** FAFSA. ***Financial aid deadline (priority):*** 4/1. ***Notification date:*** Continuous beginning 4/1. Students must reply within 3 weeks of notification.

CONTACT Mr. Joseph Coleman, Director of Financial Aid, Bethune-Cookman University, 640 Mary McLeod Bethune Boulevard, Daytona Beach, FL 32114-3099, 386-481-2626 or toll-free 800-448-0228. *Fax:* 386-481-2621. *E-mail:* colemanj@cookman.edu.

BEULAH HEIGHTS UNIVERSITY

Atlanta, GA

Tuition & fees: N/R **Average undergraduate aid package: $5619**

ABOUT THE INSTITUTION Independent Pentecostal, coed. 2 undergraduate majors. Federal methodology is used as a basis for awarding need-based institutional aid.

UNDERGRADUATE EXPENSES for 2011–12 ***Tuition:*** part-time $230 per credit. ***Required fees:*** $100 per term. Full-time tuition and fees vary according to course load. Room and board charges vary according to housing facility. ***Payment plans:*** Installment, deferred payment.

FRESHMAN FINANCIAL AID (Fall 2009) 13 applied for aid; of those 100% were deemed to have need. 100% of freshmen with need received aid. ***Average percent of need met:*** 75% (excluding resources awarded to replace EFC). ***Average financial aid package:*** $4625 (excluding resources awarded to replace EFC).

UNDERGRADUATE FINANCIAL AID (Fall 2009) 113 applied for aid; of those 100% were deemed to have need. 100% of undergraduates with need received aid. ***Average percent of need met:*** 75% (excluding resources awarded to replace EFC). ***Average financial aid package:*** $5619 (excluding resources awarded to replace EFC).

GIFT AID (NEED-BASED) ***Total amount:*** $1,893,302 (90% federal, 10% institutional). ***Receiving aid:*** Freshmen: 34% (13); all full-time undergraduates: 32% (110). ***Average award:*** Freshmen: $2900; Undergraduates: $3500. ***Scholarships, grants, and awards:*** Federal Pell, FSEOG, private, college/university gift aid from institutional funds.

GIFT AID (NON-NEED-BASED) ***Scholarships, grants, and awards by category:*** *Academic interests/achievement:* religion/biblical studies. *Special characteristics:* 33 awards ($142,017 total): children of faculty/staff, general special characteristics, international students, married students, religious affiliation, spouses of current students. ***Tuition waivers:*** Full or partial for employees or children of employees.

LOANS ***Student loans:*** $6,512,004 (39% need-based, 61% non-need-based). 78% of past graduating class borrowed through all loan programs. *Average indebtedness per student:* $40,000. ***Average need-based loan:*** Freshmen: $1750. Undergraduates: $2250. ***Parent loans:*** $14,360 (100% non-need-based). ***Programs:*** Federal Direct (Subsidized and Unsubsidized Stafford, PLUS).

WORK-STUDY ***Federal work-study:*** Total amount: $56,359; 13 jobs averaging $4335.

APPLYING FOR FINANCIAL AID ***Required financial aid forms:*** FAFSA, institution's own form. ***Financial aid deadline (priority):*** 5/15. ***Notification date:*** 7/30. Students must reply by 7/1 or within 2 weeks of notification.

CONTACT Ms. Patricia Banks, Director of Financial Aid, Beulah Heights University, 892 Berne Street, SE, Atlanta, GA 30316, 404-627-2681 or toll-free 888-777-BHBC. *Fax:* 404-627-0702. *E-mail:* pat.banks@beulah.org.

BIOLA UNIVERSITY

La Mirada, CA

Tuition & fees: $28,897 **Average undergraduate aid package: $33,123**

ABOUT THE INSTITUTION Independent interdenominational, coed. 78 undergraduate majors. Both federal and institutional methodology are used as a basis for awarding need-based institutional aid.

UNDERGRADUATE EXPENSES for 2010–11 ***Comprehensive fee:*** $36,897 includes full-time tuition ($28,852), mandatory fees ($45), and room and board ($8000). ***College room only:*** $4500. Full-time tuition and fees vary according to course load. Room and board charges vary according to board plan, housing facility, and location. Part-time tuition and fees vary according to course load. ***Payment plan:*** Installment.

FRESHMAN FINANCIAL AID (Fall 2010, est.) 618 applied for aid; of those 82% were deemed to have need. 100% of freshmen with need received aid; of those 100% had need fully met. ***Average percent of need met:*** 69% (excluding resources awarded to replace EFC). ***Average financial aid package:*** $33,285 (excluding resources awarded to replace EFC). 13% of all full-time freshmen had no need and received non-need-based gift aid.

UNDERGRADUATE FINANCIAL AID (Fall 2010, est.) 2,688 applied for aid; of those 88% were deemed to have need. 100% of undergraduates with need received aid; of those 100% had need fully met. ***Average percent of need met:*** 70% (excluding resources awarded to replace EFC). ***Average financial aid package:*** $33,123 (excluding resources awarded to replace EFC). 10% of all full-time undergraduates had no need and received non-need-based gift aid.

GIFT AID (NEED-BASED) ***Total amount:*** $51,857,168 (12% federal, 13% state, 70% institutional, 5% external sources). ***Receiving aid:*** Freshmen: 47% (425); all full-time undergraduates: 55% (1,949). ***Average award:*** Freshmen: $13,812; Undergraduates: $12,955. ***Scholarships, grants, and awards:*** Federal Pell, FSEOG, state, private, college/university gift aid from institutional funds.

GIFT AID (NON-NEED-BASED) ***Receiving aid:*** Freshmen: 45% (412). Undergraduates: 51% (1,815). ***Average award:*** Freshmen: $13,251. Undergraduates: $14,829. ***Scholarships, grants, and awards by category:*** *Academic interests/achievement:* 1,402 awards ($791,823 total): biological sciences, communication, general academic interests/achievements. *Creative arts/performance:* 272 awards ($864,185 total): art/fine arts, cinema/film/broadcasting, journalism/publications, music, theater/drama. *Special achievements/activities:* 321 awards ($971,186 total): community service, leadership. *Special characteristics:* 937 awards ($4,765,518 total): adult students, children and siblings of alumni, children of faculty/staff, ethnic background, international students, relatives of clergy.

LOANS ***Student loans:*** $31,390,641 (31% need-based, 69% non-need-based). 75% of past graduating class borrowed through all loan programs. *Average indebtedness per student:* $29,075. ***Average need-based loan:*** Freshmen: $1281. Undergraduates: $1339. ***Parent loans:*** $7,785,514 (100% non-need-based). ***Programs:*** Federal Direct (Subsidized and Unsubsidized Stafford, PLUS), Perkins, Federal Nursing, college/university, alternative loans.

WORK-STUDY ***Federal work-study:*** Total amount: $1,603,282; 642 jobs averaging $1390. ***State or other work-study/employment:*** Part-time jobs available.

ATHLETIC AWARDS Total amount: $1,653,165 (100% non-need-based).

APPLYING FOR FINANCIAL AID ***Required financial aid forms:*** FAFSA, state aid form. ***Financial aid deadline:*** Continuous. ***Notification date:*** Continuous beginning 3/1.

CONTACT Jonathan Choy, Financial Aid Office, Biola University, 13800 Biola Avenue, La Mirada, CA 90639-0001, 562-903-4742 or toll-free 800-652-4652. *Fax:* 562-906-4541. *E-mail:* finaid@biola.edu.

BIRMINGHAM-SOUTHERN COLLEGE

Birmingham, AL

Tuition & fees: $27,890 **Average undergraduate aid package: $27,468**

ABOUT THE INSTITUTION Independent Methodist, coed. 47 undergraduate majors. Federal methodology is used as a basis for awarding need-based institutional aid.

UNDERGRADUATE EXPENSES for 2010–11 ***One-time required fee:*** $200. ***Comprehensive fee:*** $37,210 includes full-time tuition ($26,900), mandatory fees ($990), and room and board ($9320). ***College room only:*** $5450. Full-time tuition and fees vary according to program and reciprocity agreements. Room and board charges vary according to board plan, housing facility, and location. ***Part-time tuition:*** $4483 per course. ***Part-time fees:*** $495 per term. Part-time tuition and fees vary according to course load, program, and reciprocity agreements. ***Payment plan:*** Installment.

FRESHMAN FINANCIAL AID (Fall 2010, est.) 269 applied for aid; of those 84% were deemed to have need. 100% of freshmen with need received aid; of those 27% had need fully met. ***Average percent of need met:*** 83% (excluding resources awarded to replace EFC). ***Average financial aid package:*** $27,723 (excluding resources awarded to replace EFC). 35% of all full-time freshmen had no need and received non-need-based gift aid.

UNDERGRADUATE FINANCIAL AID (Fall 2010, est.) 994 applied for aid; of those 85% were deemed to have need. 100% of undergraduates with need received aid; of those 27% had need fully met. ***Average percent of need met:*** 82% (excluding resources awarded to replace EFC). ***Average financial aid package:*** $27,468 (excluding resources awarded to replace EFC). 40% of all full-time undergraduates had no need and received non-need-based gift aid.

GIFT AID (NEED-BASED) ***Total amount:*** $5,754,447 (28% federal, 1% state, 71% institutional). ***Receiving aid:*** Freshmen: 49% (179); all full-time undergraduates: 46% (698). ***Average award:*** Freshmen: $3889; Undergraduates: $5341. ***Scholarships, grants, and awards:*** Federal Pell, FSEOG, state, private, college/university gift aid from institutional funds, United Negro College Fund.

GIFT AID (NON-NEED-BASED) ***Total amount:*** $20,282,816 (2% state, 91% institutional, 7% external sources). ***Receiving aid:*** Freshmen: 60% (222). Undergraduates: 55% (825). ***Average award:*** Freshmen: $10,554. Undergraduates: $9987. ***Scholarships, grants, and awards by category:*** *Academic interests/achievement:* area/ethnic studies, biological sciences, business, communication, computer science, education, engineering/technologies, English, foreign languages, general academic interests/achievements, health fields, humanities, international studies, mathematics, physical sciences, premedicine, religion/biblical studies, social sciences. *Creative arts/performance:* art/fine arts, dance, music, performing arts, theater/drama. *Special achievements/activities:* junior miss, memberships, religious involvement. *Special characteristics:* adult students, children and siblings of alumni, children of faculty/staff, ethnic background, first-generation college students, previous college experience, relatives of clergy, religious affiliation. ***Tuition waivers:*** Full or partial for employees or children of employees.

LOANS ***Student loans:*** $3,191,599 (86% need-based, 14% non-need-based). 30% of past graduating class borrowed through all loan programs. *Average indebtedness per student:* $28,157. ***Average need-based loan:*** Freshmen: $3416. Undergraduates: $3935. ***Parent loans:*** $2,431,014 (100% non-need-based). ***Programs:*** Federal Direct (Subsidized and Unsubsidized Stafford, PLUS), Perkins, college/university.

WORK-STUDY ***Federal work-study:*** Total amount: $167,000; 178 jobs averaging $1351. ***State or other work-study/employment:*** Total amount: $412,000 (100% non-need-based). 281 part-time jobs averaging $1213.

APPLYING FOR FINANCIAL AID ***Required financial aid forms:*** FAFSA, state aid form. ***Financial aid deadline (priority):*** 3/1. ***Notification date:*** Continuous beginning 3/1. Students must reply by 5/30 or within 2 weeks of notification.

CONTACT Financial Aid Office, Birmingham-Southern College, 900 Arkadelphia Road, Birmingham, AL 35254, 205-226-4688 or toll-free 800-523-5793. *Fax:* 205-226-3082. *E-mail:* finaid@bsc.edu.

BIRTHINGWAY COLLEGE OF MIDWIFERY

Portland, OR

CONTACT Financial Aid Office, Birthingway College of Midwifery, 12113 SE Foster Road, Portland, OR 97299, 503-760-3131.

BLACKBURN COLLEGE

Carlinville, IL

ABOUT THE INSTITUTION Independent Presbyterian, coed. 41 undergraduate majors.

GIFT AID (NEED-BASED) ***Scholarships, grants, and awards:*** Federal Pell, FSEOG, state, private, college/university gift aid from institutional funds.

GIFT AID (NON-NEED-BASED) ***Scholarships, grants, and awards by category:*** *Academic interests/achievement:* general academic interests/achievements. *Special achievements/activities:* general special achievements/activities. *Special characteristics:* siblings of current students.

LOANS ***Programs:*** Federal Direct (Subsidized and Unsubsidized Stafford, PLUS).

WORK-STUDY ***Federal work-study:*** Total amount: $1,029,554; 388 jobs averaging $2653. ***State or other work-study/employment:*** Total amount: $264,106 (100% non-need-based). 113 part-time jobs averaging $2337.

APPLYING FOR FINANCIAL AID ***Required financial aid form:*** FAFSA.

CONTACT Mrs. Jane Kelsey, Financial Aid Administrator, Blackburn College, 700 College Avenue, Carlinville, IL 62626-1498, 217-854-3231 Ext. 4227 or toll-free 800-233-3550. *Fax:* 217-854-3731.

BLACK HILLS STATE UNIVERSITY

Spearfish, SD

Tuition & fees (SD res): $6951 **Average undergraduate aid package: N/A**

ABOUT THE INSTITUTION State-supported, coed. 47 undergraduate majors. Federal methodology is used as a basis for awarding need-based institutional aid.

UNDERGRADUATE EXPENSES for 2010–11 ***Tuition, state resident:*** full-time $3194; part-time $99.80 per credit hour. ***Tuition, nonresident:*** full-time $4790; part-time $149.70 per credit hour. ***Required fees:*** full-time $3757; $117.40 per credit hour. Full-time tuition and fees vary according to course load and reciprocity agreements. Part-time tuition and fees vary according to course load and reciprocity agreements. ***College room and board:*** $5729; ***Room only:*** $2738. Room and board charges vary according to board plan and housing facility. ***Payment plans:*** Installment, deferred payment.

GIFT AID (NEED-BASED) ***Total amount:*** $6,301,225 (97% federal, 3% external sources). ***Scholarships, grants, and awards:*** Federal Pell, FSEOG, state, private, college/university gift aid from institutional funds, Academic Competitiveness Grants, National SMART Grants, TEACH Grants.

GIFT AID (NON-NEED-BASED) ***Total amount:*** $1,152,703 (5% federal, 17% state, 37% institutional, 41% external sources). ***Scholarships, grants, and awards by category:*** *Academic interests/achievement:* biological sciences, business, communication, computer science, education, English, foreign languages, general academic interests/achievements, health fields, humanities, mathematics, military science, physical sciences, social sciences. *Creative arts/performance:* art/fine arts, music, theater/drama. ***Tuition waivers:*** Full or partial for employees or children of employees, senior citizens.

LOANS ***Student loans:*** $17,197,663 (45% need-based, 55% non-need-based). *Average indebtedness per student:* $25,628. ***Parent loans:*** $552,254 (100% non-need-based). ***Programs:*** Perkins.

WORK-STUDY ***Federal work-study:*** Total amount: $409,756; 239 jobs averaging $1714. ***State or other work-study/employment:*** Total amount: $1,746,009 (100% non-need-based). 414 part-time jobs averaging $4217.

ATHLETIC AWARDS Total amount: $416,100 (100% non-need-based).

APPLYING FOR FINANCIAL AID ***Required financial aid form:*** FAFSA. ***Financial aid deadline (priority):*** 3/1. ***Notification date:*** Continuous beginning 5/1. Students must reply within 3 weeks of notification.

CONTACT Ms. Deb Henriksen, Director of Financial Aid, Black Hills State University, 1200 University Street, Spearfish, SD 57799-9670, 605-642-6581 or toll-free 800-255-2478. *Fax:* 605-642-6913. *E-mail:* deb.henriksen@bhsu.edu.

BLESSING-RIEMAN COLLEGE OF NURSING

Quincy, IL

ABOUT THE INSTITUTION Independent, coed, primarily women. 1 undergraduate major.

GIFT AID (NEED-BASED) ***Scholarships, grants, and awards:*** Federal Pell, state, private, college/university gift aid from institutional funds.

GIFT AID (NON-NEED-BASED) ***Scholarships, grants, and awards by category:*** *Academic interests/achievement:* general academic interests/achievements.

LOANS ***Programs:*** Federal Direct (Subsidized and Unsubsidized Stafford, PLUS), Federal Nursing, college/university.

APPLYING FOR FINANCIAL AID ***Required financial aid form:*** FAFSA.

CONTACT Mrs. Misty McBee, Financial Aid Coordinator, Blessing-Rieman College of Nursing, Broadway at 11th Street, PO Box 7005, Quincy, IL 62301, 217-223-8400 Ext. 6993 or toll-free 800-877-9140 Ext. 6964. *Fax:* 217-223-1781. *E-mail:* mmcbee@brcn.edu.

BLOOMFIELD COLLEGE

Bloomfield, NJ

Tuition & fees: $22,400 **Average undergraduate aid package: $23,758**

ABOUT THE INSTITUTION Independent religious, coed. 22 undergraduate majors. Federal methodology is used as a basis for awarding need-based institutional aid.

UNDERGRADUATE EXPENSES for 2010–11 ***Comprehensive fee:*** $33,000 includes full-time tuition ($21,200), mandatory fees ($1200), and room and board ($10,600). ***College room only:*** $5300. Room and board charges vary according to housing facility. ***Part-time tuition:*** $2230 per course. Part-time tuition and fees vary according to course load. ***Payment plans:*** Installment, deferred payment.

FRESHMAN FINANCIAL AID (Fall 2010, est.) 397 applied for aid; of those 96% were deemed to have need. 100% of freshmen with need received aid; of those 10% had need fully met. ***Average percent of need met:*** 75% (excluding resources awarded to replace EFC). ***Average financial aid package:*** $24,442 (excluding resources awarded to replace EFC). 2% of all full-time freshmen had no need and received non-need-based gift aid.

UNDERGRADUATE FINANCIAL AID (Fall 2010, est.) 1,693 applied for aid; of those 93% were deemed to have need. 100% of undergraduates with need received aid; of those 11% had need fully met. ***Average percent of need met:*** 74% (excluding resources awarded to replace EFC). ***Average financial aid package:*** $23,758 (excluding resources awarded to replace EFC). 5% of all full-time undergraduates had no need and received non-need-based gift aid.

GIFT AID (NEED-BASED) ***Total amount:*** $23,288,293 (27% federal, 38% state, 35% institutional). ***Receiving aid:*** Freshmen: 93% (373); all full-time undergraduates: 87% (1,492). ***Average award:*** Freshmen: $15,272; Undergraduates: $14,334. ***Scholarships, grants, and awards:*** Federal Pell, FSEOG, state, private, college/university gift aid from institutional funds.

GIFT AID (NON-NEED-BASED) ***Total amount:*** $3,530,723 (6% federal, 1% state, 90% institutional, 3% external sources). ***Receiving aid:*** Freshmen: 62% (251). Undergraduates: 41% (702). ***Average award:*** Freshmen: $10,288. Undergraduates: $12,986. ***Scholarships, grants, and awards by category:*** *Academic interests/achievement:* 281 awards ($1,690,440 total): biological sciences, business, computer science, education, English, general academic interests/achievements, health fields, humanities, mathematics, physical sciences, religion/biblical studies, social sciences. *Creative arts/performance:* 3 awards ($2500 total): applied art and design, art/fine arts, cinema/film/broadcasting, general creative arts/performance, performing arts, theater/drama. *Special achievements/activities:* 304 awards ($2,417,586 total): community service, general special achievements/activities, leadership. *Special characteristics:* 103 awards ($772,585 total): adult students, children and siblings of alumni, children of current students, general special characteristics, international students, out-of-state students, siblings of current students, spouses of current students. ***Tuition waivers:*** Full or partial for employees or children of employees, senior citizens.

LOANS ***Student loans:*** $12,428,404 (49% need-based, 51% non-need-based). 90% of past graduating class borrowed through all loan programs. *Average indebtedness per student:* $30,515. ***Average need-based loan:*** Freshmen: $3293. Undergraduates: $4044. ***Parent loans:*** $1,750,257 (100% non-need-based). ***Programs:*** Federal Direct (Subsidized and Unsubsidized Stafford, PLUS).

WORK-STUDY ***Federal work-study:*** Total amount: $1,056,771; 478 jobs averaging $2211. ***State or other work-study/employment:*** Part-time jobs available.

ATHLETIC AWARDS Total amount: $1,553,060 (100% non-need-based).

APPLYING FOR FINANCIAL AID ***Required financial aid form:*** FAFSA. ***Financial aid deadline:*** 6/1 (priority: 3/15). ***Notification date:*** Continuous beginning 3/15. Students must reply within 2 weeks of notification.

CONTACT Ms. Stacy Salinas, Director of Financial Aid, Bloomfield College, 467 Franklin Street, Bloomfield, NJ 07003-9981, 973-748-9000 Ext. 213 or toll-free 800-848-4555 Ext. 230. *Fax:* 973-748-9735. *E-mail:* stacy_salinas@bloomfield.edu.

BLOOMSBURG UNIVERSITY OF PENNSYLVANIA

Bloomsburg, PA

Tuition & fees (PA res): $7456 **Average undergraduate aid package: $12,317**

ABOUT THE INSTITUTION State-supported, coed. 40 undergraduate majors. Federal methodology is used as a basis for awarding need-based institutional aid.

UNDERGRADUATE EXPENSES for 2010–11 ***Tuition, state resident:*** full-time $5804; part-time $242 per credit. ***Tuition, nonresident:*** full-time $14,510; part-time $605 per credit. ***Required fees:*** full-time $1652; $46 per credit or $123 per term. Full-time tuition and fees vary according to course load. Part-time tuition and fees vary according to course load. ***College room and board:*** $6890; ***Room only:*** $4232. Room and board charges vary according to board plan and housing facility. ***Payment plan:*** Installment.

FRESHMAN FINANCIAL AID (Fall 2010, est.) 1,937 applied for aid; of those 95% were deemed to have need. 92% of freshmen with need received aid; of those 90% had need fully met. ***Average percent of need met:*** 71% (excluding resources awarded to replace EFC). ***Average financial aid package:*** $12,677 (excluding resources awarded to replace EFC). 2% of all full-time freshmen had no need and received non-need-based gift aid.

UNDERGRADUATE FINANCIAL AID (Fall 2010, est.) 7,419 applied for aid; of those 95% were deemed to have need. 96% of undergraduates with need received aid; of those 90% had need fully met. ***Average percent of need met:*** 71% (excluding resources awarded to replace EFC). ***Average financial aid package:*** $12,317 (excluding resources awarded to replace EFC). 2% of all full-time undergraduates had no need and received non-need-based gift aid.

GIFT AID (NEED-BASED) ***Total amount:*** $20,667,893 (65% federal, 33% state, 1% institutional, 1% external sources). ***Receiving aid:*** Freshmen: 42% (887); all full-time undergraduates: 42% (3,584). ***Average award:*** Freshmen: $6167; Undergraduates: $5655. ***Scholarships, grants, and awards:*** Federal Pell, FSEOG, state, private, college/university gift aid from institutional funds, Academic Competitiveness Grants, National SMART Grants.

GIFT AID (NON-NEED-BASED) ***Total amount:*** $2,622,329 (1% federal, 11% state, 45% institutional, 43% external sources). ***Receiving aid:*** Freshmen: 16% (342). Undergraduates: 13% (1,114). ***Average award:*** Freshmen: $1915. Undergraduates: $1941. ***Scholarships, grants, and awards by category:*** *Academic interests/achievement:* 450 awards ($620,033 total): biological sciences, business, communication, computer science, education, English, foreign languages, general academic interests/achievements, health fields, humanities, international studies, mathematics, physical sciences, religion/biblical studies, social sciences. *Special characteristics:* 233 awards ($978,175 total): children of faculty/staff, international students. ***Tuition waivers:*** Full or partial for minority students, employees or children of employees, senior citizens.

LOANS ***Student loans:*** $40,803,843 (43% need-based, 57% non-need-based). 73% of past graduating class borrowed through all loan programs. *Average indebtedness per student:* $23,882. ***Average need-based loan:*** Freshmen: $3407. Undergraduates: $4192. ***Parent loans:*** $10,440,007 (100% non-need-based). ***Programs:*** Federal Direct (Subsidized and Unsubsidized Stafford, PLUS), Perkins, state, alternative loans.

WORK-STUDY ***Federal work-study:*** Total amount: $3,967,500; 1,063 jobs averaging $3732. ***State or other work-study/employment:*** Total amount: $3,872,411 (100% non-need-based). 942 part-time jobs averaging $4111.

ATHLETIC AWARDS Total amount: $538,995 (100% non-need-based).

APPLYING FOR FINANCIAL AID ***Required financial aid form:*** FAFSA. ***Financial aid deadline (priority):*** 3/15. ***Notification date:*** Continuous beginning 4/1.

CONTACT Mr. John J. Bieryla, Interim Director of Financial Aid, Bloomsburg University of Pennsylvania, 119 Warren Student Services Center, 400 East 2nd Street, Bloomsburg, PA 17815-1301, 570-389-4279. *Fax:* 570-389-4795. *E-mail:* stfinaid@bloomu.edu.

BLUEFIELD COLLEGE

Bluefield, VA

Tuition & fees: $18,800 **Average undergraduate aid package: $14,035**

ABOUT THE INSTITUTION Independent Southern Baptist, coed. 42 undergraduate majors. Federal methodology is used as a basis for awarding need-based institutional aid.

UNDERGRADUATE EXPENSES for 2010–11 ***Comprehensive fee:*** $26,150 includes full-time tuition ($17,990), mandatory fees ($810), and room and board ($7350). Full-time tuition and fees vary according to program. Room and board charges vary according to housing facility. ***Part-time tuition:*** $750 per credit hour. ***Part-time fees:*** $300 per term. Part-time tuition and fees vary according to program. ***Payment plan:*** Installment.

FRESHMAN FINANCIAL AID (Fall 2010, est.) 99 applied for aid; of those 89% were deemed to have need. 100% of freshmen with need received aid; of those 17% had need fully met. ***Average percent of need met:*** 68% (excluding resources awarded to replace EFC). ***Average financial aid package:*** $13,683 (excluding resources awarded to replace EFC). 13% of all full-time freshmen had no need and received non-need-based gift aid.

UNDERGRADUATE FINANCIAL AID (Fall 2010, est.) 545 applied for aid; of those 91% were deemed to have need. 100% of undergraduates with need received aid; of those 14% had need fully met. ***Average percent of need met:*** 62% (excluding resources awarded to replace EFC). ***Average financial aid package:*** $14,035 (excluding resources awarded to replace EFC). 12% of all full-time undergraduates had no need and received non-need-based gift aid.

GIFT AID (NEED-BASED) ***Total amount:*** $4,080,392 (31% federal, 20% state, 37% institutional, 12% external sources). ***Receiving aid:*** Freshmen: 85% (88); all full-time undergraduates: 82% (485). ***Average award:*** Freshmen: $10,873; Undergraduates: $9827. ***Scholarships, grants, and awards:*** Federal Pell, FSEOG, state, private, college/university gift aid from institutional funds.

GIFT AID (NON-NEED-BASED) ***Total amount:*** $697,088 (27% state, 66% institutional, 7% external sources). ***Receiving aid:*** Freshmen: 14% (15). Undergraduates: 8% (46). ***Average award:*** Freshmen: $5935. Undergraduates: $5345. ***Scholarships, grants, and awards by category:*** *Creative arts/performance:* 63 awards ($124,875 total): art/fine arts, music, performing arts, theater/drama. *Special achievements/activities:* 13 awards ($9750 total): cheerleading/drum major. *Special characteristics:* children of faculty/staff, ethnic background, first-generation college students, general special characteristics, members of minority groups, out-of-state students, religious affiliation, veterans. ***Tuition waivers:*** Full or partial for employees or children of employees, senior citizens.

LOANS ***Student loans:*** $4,230,689 (84% need-based, 16% non-need-based). 98% of past graduating class borrowed through all loan programs. *Average indebtedness per student:* $18,661. ***Average need-based loan:*** Freshmen: $3362. Undergraduates: $4960. ***Parent loans:*** $996,461 (39% need-based, 61% non-need-based). ***Programs:*** Federal Direct (Subsidized and Unsubsidized Stafford, PLUS), alternative loans.

WORK-STUDY ***Federal work-study:*** Total amount: $74,945; 65 jobs averaging $1125.

ATHLETIC AWARDS Total amount: $995,913 (69% need-based, 31% non-need-based).

APPLYING FOR FINANCIAL AID ***Required financial aid forms:*** FAFSA, state aid form. ***Financial aid deadline (priority):*** 6/1. ***Notification date:*** Continuous. Students must reply by 8/24.

CONTACT Ms. Carly Jean Kestner, Assistant Director of Financial Aid, Bluefield College, 3000 College Drive, Bluefield, VA 24605, 276-326-4215 or toll-free 800-872-0175. *Fax:* 276-326-4356. *E-mail:* ckestner@bluefield.edu.

BLUEFIELD STATE COLLEGE

Bluefield, WV

Tuition & fees (WV res): $4596 **Average undergraduate aid package: $6800**

ABOUT THE INSTITUTION State-supported, coed. 17 undergraduate majors. Federal methodology is used as a basis for awarding need-based institutional aid.

UNDERGRADUATE EXPENSES for 2010–11 ***Tuition, state resident:*** full-time $4596; part-time $192 per credit hour. ***Tuition, nonresident:*** full-time $9288; part-time $387 per credit hour. ***Payment plan:*** Installment.

FRESHMAN FINANCIAL AID (Fall 2010, est.) 265 applied for aid; of those 87% were deemed to have need. 100% of freshmen with need received aid; of those 57% had need fully met. ***Average percent of need met:*** 70% (excluding resources awarded to replace EFC). ***Average financial aid package:*** $6800 (excluding resources awarded to replace EFC). 18% of all full-time freshmen had no need and received non-need-based gift aid.

UNDERGRADUATE FINANCIAL AID (Fall 2010, est.) 1,310 applied for aid; of those 85% were deemed to have need. 100% of undergraduates with need received aid; of those 39% had need fully met. ***Average percent of need met:*** 70% (excluding resources awarded to replace EFC). ***Average financial aid package:*** $6800 (excluding resources awarded to replace EFC). 23% of all full-time undergraduates had no need and received non-need-based gift aid.

GIFT AID (NEED-BASED) ***Total amount:*** $6,940,000 (79% federal, 21% state). ***Receiving aid:*** Freshmen: 73% (230); all full-time undergraduates: 64% (1,120). ***Average award:*** Freshmen: $3500; Undergraduates: $3500. ***Scholarships, grants, and awards:*** Federal Pell, FSEOG, state.

GIFT AID (NON-NEED-BASED) ***Total amount:*** $1,337,000 (42% state, 17% institutional, 41% external sources). ***Receiving aid:*** Freshmen: 27% (85). Undergraduates: 3% (45). ***Average award:*** Freshmen: $1500. Undergraduates: $1500. ***Scholarships, grants, and awards by category:*** *Academic interests/achievement:* 258 awards ($218,889 total): engineering/technologies, general academic interests/achievements. *Special achievements/activities:* 6 awards ($5100 total): cheerleading/drum major, general special achievements/activities, junior miss, leadership. *Special characteristics:* 1 award ($900 total): general special characteristics. ***Tuition waivers:*** Full or partial for adult students, senior citizens.

LOANS ***Student loans:*** $8,400,000 (48% need-based, 52% non-need-based). 70% of past graduating class borrowed through all loan programs. *Average indebtedness per student:* $22,000. ***Average need-based loan:*** Freshmen: $3600. Undergraduates: $3600. ***Parent loans:*** $37,100 (100% non-need-based). ***Programs:*** Federal Direct (Subsidized and Unsubsidized Stafford, PLUS), Perkins.

WORK-STUDY ***Federal work-study:*** Total amount: $115,000; 42 jobs averaging $2750. ***State or other work-study/employment:*** Total amount: $350,000 (100% non-need-based). 110 part-time jobs averaging $3100.

ATHLETIC AWARDS Total amount: $252,000 (100% non-need-based).

APPLYING FOR FINANCIAL AID ***Required financial aid forms:*** FAFSA, institution's own form. ***Financial aid deadline (priority):*** 3/1. ***Notification date:*** 6/1.

CONTACT Mr. Tom Ilse, Director of Financial Aid, Bluefield State College, 219 Rock Street, Bluefield, WV 24701-2198, 304-327-4020 or toll-free 800-344-8892 Ext. 4065 (in-state), 800-654-7798 Ext. 4065 (out-of-state). *Fax:* 304-325-7747. *E-mail:* tilse@bluefieldstate.edu.

BLUE MOUNTAIN COLLEGE

Blue Mountain, MS

ABOUT THE INSTITUTION Independent Southern Baptist, coed. 23 undergraduate majors.

GIFT AID (NEED-BASED) ***Scholarships, grants, and awards:*** Federal Pell, FSEOG, state, private, college/university gift aid from institutional funds.

GIFT AID (NON-NEED-BASED) ***Scholarships, grants, and awards by category:*** *Academic interests/achievement:* biological sciences, business, education, English, general academic interests/achievements, health fields, humanities, library science, mathematics, physical sciences, premedicine, religion/biblical studies, social sciences. *Creative arts/performance:* art/fine arts, music, theater/drama. *Special achievements/activities:* general special achievements/activities, leadership, memberships, religious involvement. *Special characteristics:* children and siblings of alumni, children of current students, children of faculty/staff, married students, parents of current students, religious affiliation, siblings of current students, spouses of current students, twins.

LOANS ***Programs:*** Federal Direct (Subsidized and Unsubsidized Stafford, PLUS), Perkins.

WORK-STUDY Federal work-study jobs available (averaging $1200). ***State or other work-study/employment:*** Part-time jobs available (averaging $1200).

APPLYING FOR FINANCIAL AID ***Required financial aid forms:*** FAFSA, state aid form.

CONTACT Mrs. Michelle L. Hall, Financial Aid Director, Blue Mountain College, PO Box 160, Blue Mountain, MS 38610-0160, 662-685-4771 Ext. 141 or toll-free 800-235-0136. *Fax:* 662-685-4776. *E-mail:* financialaid@bmc.edu.

BLUFFTON UNIVERSITY

Bluffton, OH

Tuition & fees: $26,154 **Average undergraduate aid package: $23,924**

ABOUT THE INSTITUTION Independent Mennonite, coed. 39 undergraduate majors. Both federal and institutional methodology are used as a basis for awarding need-based institutional aid.

UNDERGRADUATE EXPENSES for 2011–12 ***Comprehensive fee:*** $34,911 includes full-time tuition ($25,704), mandatory fees ($450), and room and board ($8757). ***College room only:*** $4302. Full-time tuition and fees vary according to course load. Room and board charges vary according to board plan and housing facility. ***Part-time tuition:*** $1071 per credit hour. ***Part-time fees:*** $113 per term. Part-time tuition and fees vary according to course load. ***Payment plan:*** Installment.

FRESHMAN FINANCIAL AID (Fall 2010, est.) 212 applied for aid; of those 96% were deemed to have need. 100% of freshmen with need received aid; of those 48% had need fully met. ***Average percent of need met:*** 90% (excluding resources awarded to replace EFC). ***Average financial aid package:*** $24,480 (excluding resources awarded to replace EFC). 7% of all full-time freshmen had no need and received non-need-based gift aid.

UNDERGRADUATE FINANCIAL AID (Fall 2010, est.) 726 applied for aid; of those 96% were deemed to have need. 100% of undergraduates with need received aid; of those 48% had need fully met. ***Average percent of need met:*** 91% (excluding resources awarded to replace EFC). ***Average financial aid package:*** $23,924 (excluding resources awarded to replace EFC). 8% of all full-time undergraduates had no need and received non-need-based gift aid.

GIFT AID (NEED-BASED) ***Total amount:*** $11,763,139 (17% federal, 4% state, 74% institutional, 5% external sources). ***Receiving aid:*** Freshmen: 93% (203); all full-time undergraduates: 80% (695). ***Average award:*** Freshmen: $18,348; Undergraduates: $16,937. ***Scholarships, grants, and awards:*** Federal Pell, FSEOG, state, private, college/university gift aid from institutional funds.

GIFT AID (NON-NEED-BASED) ***Total amount:*** $1,661,548 (1% federal, 88% institutional, 11% external sources). ***Receiving aid:*** Freshmen: 4% (8). Undergraduates: 4% (36). ***Average award:*** Freshmen: $12,319. Undergraduates: $10,997. ***Scholarships, grants, and awards by category:*** *Academic interests/achievement:* 443 awards ($3,857,940 total): general academic interests/achievements. *Creative arts/performance:* 31 awards ($35,600 total): art/fine arts, music. *Special achievements/activities:* 71 awards ($276,388 total): leadership. *Special characteristics:* 317 awards ($1,264,430 total): children of faculty/staff, international students, members of minority groups, out-of-state students, relatives of clergy, religious affiliation. ***Tuition waivers:*** Full or partial for employees or children of employees.

LOANS ***Student loans:*** $7,690,251 (95% need-based, 5% non-need-based). 88% of past graduating class borrowed through all loan programs. *Average indebtedness per student:* $31,457. ***Average need-based loan:*** Freshmen: $4446. Undergraduates: $4971. ***Parent loans:*** $1,911,167 (80% need-based, 20% non-need-based). ***Programs:*** Federal Direct (Subsidized and Unsubsidized Stafford, PLUS), Perkins, alternative loans.

WORK-STUDY ***Federal work-study:*** Total amount: $1,366,805; 590 jobs averaging $2297. ***State or other work-study/employment:*** Total amount: $442,250 (55% need-based, 45% non-need-based). 178 part-time jobs averaging $2470.

APPLYING FOR FINANCIAL AID ***Required financial aid form:*** FAFSA. ***Financial aid deadline:*** 10/1 (priority: 5/1). ***Notification date:*** Continuous beginning 3/1. Students must reply within 3 weeks of notification.

CONTACT Lawrence Matthews, Director of Financial Aid, Bluffton University, 1 University Drive, Bluffton, OH 45817-2104, 419-358-3266 or toll-free 800-488-3257. *Fax:* 419-358-3073. *E-mail:* matthewsl@bluffton.edu.

BOB JONES UNIVERSITY

Greenville, SC

Tuition & fees: $12,120 **Average undergraduate aid package: $9400**

ABOUT THE INSTITUTION Independent religious, coed. 75 undergraduate majors. Both federal and institutional methodology are used as a basis for awarding need-based institutional aid.

UNDERGRADUATE EXPENSES for 2011–12 ***One-time required fee:*** $610. ***Comprehensive fee:*** $17,220 includes full-time tuition ($12,120) and room and board ($5100). ***Part-time tuition:*** $576 per unit. ***Payment plan:*** Installment.

FRESHMAN FINANCIAL AID (Fall 2010, est.) 484 applied for aid; of those 94% were deemed to have need. 98% of freshmen with need received aid; of those 1% had need fully met. ***Average financial aid package:*** $8900 (excluding resources awarded to replace EFC).

UNDERGRADUATE FINANCIAL AID (Fall 2010, est.) 2,425 applied for aid; of those 93% were deemed to have need. 100% of undergraduates with need received aid; of those 3% had need fully met. ***Average financial aid package:*** $9400 (excluding resources awarded to replace EFC).

GIFT AID (NEED-BASED) ***Total amount:*** $11,210,000 (51% federal, 13% state, 32% institutional, 4% external sources). ***Receiving aid:*** Freshmen: 60% (386); all full-time undergraduates: 55% (1,962). ***Average award:*** Freshmen: $7000; Undergraduates: $7000. ***Scholarships, grants, and awards:*** Federal Pell, FSEOG, state, private, college/university gift aid from institutional funds.

GIFT AID (NON-NEED-BASED) ***Total amount:*** $3,019,200 (80% state, 20% external sources). ***Receiving aid:*** Freshmen: 14% (87). Undergraduates: 12% (415). ***Tuition waivers:*** Full or partial for employees or children of employees, senior citizens.

LOANS ***Student loans:*** $8,613,000 (62% need-based, 38% non-need-based). 60% of past graduating class borrowed through all loan programs. *Average indebtedness per student:* $28,000. ***Average need-based loan:*** Freshmen: $2985. Undergraduates: $3930. ***Parent loans:*** $1,313,000 (100% non-need-based). ***Programs:*** Federal Direct (Subsidized and Unsubsidized Stafford, PLUS), college/university.

WORK-STUDY ***Federal work-study:*** Total amount: $160,000; jobs available. ***State or other work-study/employment:*** Total amount: $6,000,000 (100% non-need-based). Part-time jobs available.

APPLYING FOR FINANCIAL AID ***Required financial aid forms:*** FAFSA, state aid form. ***Financial aid deadline:*** Continuous. ***Notification date:*** Continuous.

CONTACT Mr. Chris Baker, Director of Financial Aid, Bob Jones University, 1700 Wade Hampton Boulevard, Greenville, SC 29614, 864-242-5100 Ext. 3040 or toll-free 800-BJANDME. *E-mail:* finaid@bju.edu.

BOISE BIBLE COLLEGE

Boise, ID

CONTACT Beth Turner, Financial Aid Counselor, Boise Bible College, 8695 West Marigold Street, Boise, ID 83714-1220, 208-376-7731 Ext. 12 or toll-free 800-893-7755. *Fax:* 208-376-7743. *E-mail:* betht@boisebible.edu.

BOISE STATE UNIVERSITY

Boise, ID

Tuition & fees (ID res): $5300 **Average undergraduate aid package: $8959**

ABOUT THE INSTITUTION State-supported, coed. 77 undergraduate majors. Federal methodology is used as a basis for awarding need-based institutional aid.

UNDERGRADUATE EXPENSES for 2010–11 ***One-time required fee:*** $75. ***Tuition, state resident:*** full-time $3555; part-time $148.72 per credit hour. ***Tuition, nonresident:*** full-time $13,011; part-time $232.72 per credit hour. ***Required fees:*** full-time $1745; $83.28 per credit hour. Full-time tuition and fees vary according to reciprocity agreements. ***College room and board:*** $5610; ***Room only:*** $2642. Room and board charges vary according to board plan and housing facility. ***Payment plan:*** Installment.

FRESHMAN FINANCIAL AID (Fall 2010, est.) 1,950 applied for aid; of those 100% were deemed to have need. 100% of freshmen with need received aid; of those 23% had need fully met. ***Average percent of need met:*** 17% (excluding resources awarded to replace EFC). ***Average financial aid package:*** $8380 (excluding resources awarded to replace EFC). 15% of all full-time freshmen had no need and received non-need-based gift aid.

UNDERGRADUATE FINANCIAL AID (Fall 2010, est.) 9,673 applied for aid; of those 100% were deemed to have need. 100% of undergraduates with need received aid; of those 16% had need fully met. ***Average percent of need met:*** 21% (excluding resources awarded to replace EFC). ***Average financial aid package:*** $8959 (excluding resources awarded to replace EFC). 5% of all full-time undergraduates had no need and received non-need-based gift aid.

GIFT AID (NEED-BASED) ***Total amount:*** $39,420,899 (85% federal, 3% state, 9% institutional, 3% external sources). ***Receiving aid:*** Freshmen: 67% (1,543); all full-time undergraduates: 59% (7,434). ***Average award:*** Freshmen: $4414; Undergraduates: $4664. ***Scholarships, grants, and awards:*** Federal Pell, FSEOG, state, private, college/university gift aid from institutional funds, Leveraging Educational Assistance Program (LEAP).

GIFT AID (NON-NEED-BASED) ***Total amount:*** $1,105,424 (8% federal, 17% state, 57% institutional, 18% external sources). ***Receiving aid:*** Freshmen: 8% (195). Undergraduates: 3% (437). ***Average award:*** Freshmen: $1022. Undergraduates: $1172. ***Scholarships, grants, and awards by category:*** *Academic interests/achievement:* 1,972 awards ($3,758,294 total): biological sciences, business, communication, computer science, education, engineering/technologies, English, foreign languages, general academic interests/achievements, health fields, humanities, international studies, mathematics, military science, physical sciences, premedicine, social sciences. *Creative arts/performance:* 267 awards ($348,814 total): art/fine arts, dance, debating, general creative arts/performance, journalism/publications, music, performing arts, theater/drama. *Special achievements/activities:* 53 awards ($173,867 total): cheerleading/drum major, community service, leadership, rodeo. *Special characteristics:* 2,065 awards ($2,024,808 total): ethnic background, first-generation college students, general special characteristics, handicapped students, international students, local/state students, members of minority groups, out-of-state students, previous college experience, spouses of current students, veterans, veterans' children. ***Tuition waivers:*** Full or partial for employees or children of employees, senior citizens.

LOANS ***Student loans:*** $83,043,520 (83% need-based, 17% non-need-based). 66% of past graduating class borrowed through all loan programs. *Average indebtedness per student:* $23,594. ***Average need-based loan:*** Freshmen: $5282. Undergraduates: $6987. ***Parent loans:*** $2,476,374 (38% need-based, 62% non-need-based). ***Programs:*** Federal Direct (Subsidized and Unsubsidized Stafford, PLUS), Perkins, state, college/university, Alaska Loans.

WORK-STUDY ***Federal work-study:*** Total amount: $2,977,415; 754 jobs averaging $3793. ***State or other work-study/employment:*** Total amount: $2,824,295 (100% need-based). 691 part-time jobs averaging $3776.

ATHLETIC AWARDS Total amount: $5,050,000 (91% need-based, 9% non-need-based).

APPLYING FOR FINANCIAL AID ***Required financial aid form:*** FAFSA. ***Financial aid deadline:*** 6/1 (priority: 2/18). ***Notification date:*** Continuous beginning 3/16. Students must reply by 6/1 or within 4 weeks of notification.

CONTACT Office of Financial Aid and Scholarships, Boise State University, Administration Building, Room 123, Boise, ID 83725-1315, 208-426-1664 or toll-free 800-632-6586 (in-state), 800-824-7017 (out-of-state). *Fax:* 208-426-1305. *E-mail:* faquest@boisestate.edu.

BORICUA COLLEGE

New York, NY

CONTACT Ms. Rosalia Cruz, Financial Aid Administrator, Boricua College, 3755 Broadway, New York, NY 10032-1560, 212-694-1000 Ext. 611. *Fax:* 212-694-1015. *E-mail:* rcruz@boricuacollege.edu.

BOSTON ARCHITECTURAL COLLEGE

Boston, MA

Tuition & fees: $16,148 **Average undergraduate aid package: $9124**

ABOUT THE INSTITUTION Independent, coed. 4 undergraduate majors. Federal methodology is used as a basis for awarding need-based institutional aid.

UNDERGRADUATE EXPENSES for 2010–11 ***Tuition:*** full-time $16,128; part-time $1344 per credit hour. ***Required fees:*** full-time $20; $10 per term. Full-time tuition and fees vary according to course load, degree level, program, and reciprocity agreements. Part-time tuition and fees vary according to course load, degree level, program, and reciprocity agreements. ***Payment plan:*** Installment.

FRESHMAN FINANCIAL AID (Fall 2010, est.) 31 applied for aid; of those 97% were deemed to have need. 97% of freshmen with need received aid; of those 7% had need fully met. ***Average percent of need met:*** 28% (excluding resources awarded to replace EFC). ***Average financial aid package:*** $9137 (excluding resources awarded to replace EFC).

UNDERGRADUATE FINANCIAL AID (Fall 2010, est.) 864 applied for aid; of those 92% were deemed to have need. 66% of undergraduates with need received aid; of those 3% had need fully met. ***Average percent of need met:*** 26% (excluding resources awarded to replace EFC). ***Average financial aid package:*** $9124 (excluding resources awarded to replace EFC). 3% of all full-time undergraduates had no need and received non-need-based gift aid.

GIFT AID (NEED-BASED) ***Total amount:*** $2,449,315 (34% federal, 1% state, 60% institutional, 5% external sources). ***Receiving aid:*** Freshmen: 52% (17); all full-time undergraduates: 56% (484). ***Average award:*** Freshmen: $5885; Undergraduates: $5201. ***Scholarships, grants, and awards:*** Federal Pell, FSEOG, state, college/university gift aid from institutional funds.

GIFT AID (NON-NEED-BASED) ***Total amount:*** $111,917 (89% institutional, 11% external sources). ***Receiving aid:*** Undergraduates: 1% (12). ***Average award:*** Undergraduates: $3198. ***Scholarships, grants, and awards by category:*** *Academic interests/achievement:* architecture. *Creative arts/performance:* general creative arts/performance. ***Tuition waivers:*** Full or partial for employees or children of employees.

LOANS ***Student loans:*** $4,537,307 (91% need-based, 9% non-need-based). 66% of past graduating class borrowed through all loan programs. *Average indebtedness per student:* $31,385. ***Average need-based loan:*** Freshmen: $5135. Undergraduates: $4580. ***Parent loans:*** $1,060,600 (75% need-based, 25% non-need-based). ***Programs:*** Federal Direct (Subsidized and Unsubsidized Stafford, PLUS), state.

WORK-STUDY ***Federal work-study:*** Total amount: $100,500; 45 jobs averaging $3066.

APPLYING FOR FINANCIAL AID ***Required financial aid form:*** FAFSA. ***Financial aid deadline (priority):*** 4/15. ***Notification date:*** Continuous beginning 4/1. Students must reply within 2 weeks of notification.

CONTACT Mr. James Ryan, Director of Financial Aid Operations, Boston Architectural College, 320 Newbury Street, Boston, MA 02115, 617-585-0125 or toll-free 877-585-0100. *Fax:* 617-585-0131. *E-mail:* james.ryan@the-bac.edu.

BOSTON BAPTIST COLLEGE
Boston, MA

CONTACT Financial Aid Office, Boston Baptist College, 950 Metropolitan Avenue, Boston, MA 02136, 617-364-3510 or toll-free 888-235-2014 (out-of-state).

BOSTON COLLEGE
Chestnut Hill, MA

Tuition & fees: $40,542 **Average undergraduate aid package: $30,979**

ABOUT THE INSTITUTION Independent Roman Catholic (Jesuit), coed. 49 undergraduate majors. Institutional methodology is used as a basis for awarding need-based institutional aid.

UNDERGRADUATE EXPENSES for 2010–11 ***One-time required fee:*** $430. ***Comprehensive fee:*** $52,624 includes full-time tuition ($39,880), mandatory fees ($662), and room and board ($12,082). ***College room only:*** $7450. Room and board charges vary according to housing facility. ***Payment plan:*** Installment.

FRESHMAN FINANCIAL AID (Fall 2009) 1,091 applied for aid; of those 85% were deemed to have need. 100% of freshmen with need received aid; of those 100% had need fully met. ***Average percent of need met:*** 100% (excluding resources awarded to replace EFC). ***Average financial aid package:*** $31,597 (excluding resources awarded to replace EFC). 1% of all full-time freshmen had no need and received non-need-based gift aid.

UNDERGRADUATE FINANCIAL AID (Fall 2009) 4,421 applied for aid; of those 88% were deemed to have need. 100% of undergraduates with need received aid; of those 100% had need fully met. ***Average percent of need met:*** 100% (excluding resources awarded to replace EFC). ***Average financial aid package:*** $30,979 (excluding resources awarded to replace EFC). 2% of all full-time undergraduates had no need and received non-need-based gift aid.

GIFT AID (NEED-BASED) ***Total amount:*** $89,441,295 (8% federal, 1% state, 87% institutional, 4% external sources). ***Receiving aid:*** Freshmen: 39% (842); all full-time undergraduates: 37% (3,368). ***Average award:*** Freshmen: $27,621; Undergraduates: $26,556. ***Scholarships, grants, and awards:*** Federal Pell, FSEOG, state, private, college/university gift aid from institutional funds.

GIFT AID (NON-NEED-BASED) ***Total amount:*** $6,135,952 (26% federal, 55% institutional, 19% external sources). ***Receiving aid:*** Freshmen: 1% (28). Undergraduates: 1% (65). ***Average award:*** Freshmen: $10,656. Undergraduates: $16,443. ***Scholarships, grants, and awards by category:*** *Academic interests/achievement:* 99 awards ($2,617,790 total): general academic interests/achievements, military science. ***Tuition waivers:*** Full or partial for employees or children of employees.

LOANS ***Student loans:*** $20,993,613 (78% need-based, 22% non-need-based). 49% of past graduating class borrowed through all loan programs. *Average indebtedness per student:* $19,514. ***Average need-based loan:*** Freshmen: $3402. Undergraduates: $4623. ***Parent loans:*** $40,479,677 (100% non-need-based). ***Programs:*** Perkins, Federal Nursing, state.

WORK-STUDY ***Federal work-study:*** Total amount: $6,761,385; 3,156 jobs averaging $2143.

ATHLETIC AWARDS Total amount: $13,373,175 (11% need-based, 89% non-need-based).

APPLYING FOR FINANCIAL AID ***Required financial aid forms:*** FAFSA, CSS Financial Aid PROFILE, business/farm supplement, federal income tax form(s), W-2 forms. ***Financial aid deadline (priority):*** 2/1. ***Notification date:*** 4/1. Students must reply by 5/1.

CONTACT Office of Student Services, Boston College, Lyons Hall, 140 Commonwealth Avenue, Chestnut Hill, MA 02467, 617-552-3300 or toll-free 800-360-2522. *Fax:* 617-552-4889. *E-mail:* studentservices@bc.edu.

THE BOSTON CONSERVATORY
Boston, MA

CONTACT Jessica Raine, Financial Aid Assistant, The Boston Conservatory, 8 The Fenway, Boston, MA 02215, 617-912-9147. *Fax:* 617-536-1496. *E-mail:* jraine@bostonconservatory.edu.

BOSTON UNIVERSITY
Boston, MA

Tuition & fees: $39,864 **Average undergraduate aid package: $35,198**

ABOUT THE INSTITUTION Independent, coed. 132 undergraduate majors. Both federal and institutional methodology are used as a basis for awarding need-based institutional aid.

UNDERGRADUATE EXPENSES for 2010–11 ***Comprehensive fee:*** $52,124 includes full-time tuition ($39,314), mandatory fees ($550), and room and board ($12,260). ***College room only:*** $7980. Full-time tuition and fees vary according to class time and degree level. Room and board charges vary according to board plan and housing facility. ***Part-time tuition:*** $1228 per credit. ***Part-time fees:*** $40 per term. Part-time tuition and fees vary according to class time, course load, and degree level. ***Payment plans:*** Tuition prepayment, installment.

FRESHMAN FINANCIAL AID (Fall 2010, est.) 2,685 applied for aid; of those 83% were deemed to have need. 100% of freshmen with need received aid; of those 57% had need fully met. ***Average percent of need met:*** 90% (excluding resources awarded to replace EFC). ***Average financial aid package:*** $34,533 (excluding resources awarded to replace EFC). 7% of all full-time freshmen had no need and received non-need-based gift aid.

UNDERGRADUATE FINANCIAL AID (Fall 2010, est.) 8,200 applied for aid; of those 91% were deemed to have need. 100% of undergraduates with need received aid; of those 48% had need fully met. ***Average percent of need met:*** 89% (excluding resources awarded to replace EFC). ***Average financial aid package:*** $35,198 (excluding resources awarded to replace EFC). 8% of all full-time undergraduates had no need and received non-need-based gift aid.

GIFT AID (NEED-BASED) ***Total amount:*** $187,552,745 (10% federal, 1% state, 85% institutional, 4% external sources). ***Receiving aid:*** Freshmen: 46% (2,018); all full-time undergraduates: 44% (7,063). ***Average award:*** Freshmen: $23,413; Undergraduates: $23,454. ***Scholarships, grants, and awards:*** Federal Pell, FSEOG, state, private, college/university gift aid from institutional funds, Academic Competitiveness Grants, National SMART Grants.

GIFT AID (NON-NEED-BASED) ***Total amount:*** $26,100,264 (12% federal, 70% institutional, 18% external sources). ***Receiving aid:*** Freshmen: 18% (793). Undergraduates: 11% (1,793). ***Average award:*** Freshmen: $19,620. Undergraduates: $19,843. ***Scholarships, grants, and awards by category:*** *Academic interests/achievement:* 1,698 awards ($24,850,542 total): education, engineering/technologies, foreign languages, general academic interests/achievements. *Creative arts/performance:* 200 awards ($1,726,492 total): art/fine arts, music, theater/drama. *Special achievements/activities:* 70 awards ($1,639,540 total): general special achievements/activities, leadership, memberships. *Special characteristics:* 624 awards ($6,958,640 total): children and siblings of alumni, local/state students, relatives of clergy, religious affiliation. ***Tuition waivers:*** Full or partial for employees or children of employees, senior citizens.

LOANS ***Student loans:*** $88,667,619 (70% need-based, 30% non-need-based). 54% of past graduating class borrowed through all loan programs. *Average indebtedness per student:* $31,809. ***Average need-based loan:*** Freshmen: $6226. Undergraduates: $7185. ***Parent loans:*** $42,593,290 (38% need-based, 62% non-need-based). ***Programs:*** Federal Direct (Subsidized and Unsubsidized Stafford, PLUS), Perkins, state, alternative loans.

WORK-STUDY ***Federal work-study:*** Total amount: $7,390,767; 3,483 jobs averaging $2122. ***State or other work-study/employment:*** Total amount: $2,400,388 (54% need-based, 46% non-need-based). 115 part-time jobs averaging $11,339.

ATHLETIC AWARDS Total amount: $11,967,514 (24% need-based, 76% non-need-based).

APPLYING FOR FINANCIAL AID ***Required financial aid forms:*** FAFSA, CSS Financial Aid PROFILE. ***Financial aid deadline:*** 2/15. ***Notification date:*** Continuous beginning 3/15. Students must reply by 5/1 or within 2 weeks of notification.

CONTACT Julie Wickstrom, Director of Financial Assistance, Boston University, 881 Commonwealth Avenue, Boston, MA 02215, 617-353-4176. *Fax:* 617-353-8200. *E-mail:* finaid@bu.edu.

BOWDOIN COLLEGE
Brunswick, ME

Tuition & fees: $41,565 **Average undergraduate aid package: $39,484**

ABOUT THE INSTITUTION Independent, coed. 43 undergraduate majors. Institutional methodology is used as a basis for awarding need-based institutional aid.

UNDERGRADUATE EXPENSES for 2010–11 ***Comprehensive fee:*** $52,880 includes full-time tuition ($41,150), mandatory fees ($415), and room and board ($11,315). ***College room only:*** $5295. Room and board charges vary according to board plan. ***Payment plans:*** Installment, deferred payment.

FRESHMAN FINANCIAL AID (Fall 2010, est.) 298 applied for aid; of those 80% were deemed to have need. 100% of freshmen with need received aid; of those 100% had need fully met. ***Average percent of need met:*** 100% (excluding resources awarded to replace EFC). ***Average financial aid package:*** $41,086 (excluding resources awarded to replace EFC). 6% of all full-time freshmen had no need and received non-need-based gift aid.

UNDERGRADUATE FINANCIAL AID (Fall 2010, est.) 969 applied for aid; of those 83% were deemed to have need. 100% of undergraduates with need received aid; of those 100% had need fully met. ***Average percent of need met:*** 100% (excluding resources awarded to replace EFC). ***Average financial aid package:*** $39,484 (excluding resources awarded to replace EFC). 5% of all full-time undergraduates had no need and received non-need-based gift aid.

GIFT AID (NEED-BASED) ***Total amount:*** $28,730,039 (6% federal, 91% institutional, 3% external sources). ***Receiving aid:*** Freshmen: 47% (238); all full-time undergraduates: 46% (800). ***Average award:*** Freshmen: $37,640; Undergraduates: $35,590. ***Scholarships, grants, and awards:*** Federal Pell, FSEOG, state, private, college/university gift aid from institutional funds.

GIFT AID (NON-NEED-BASED) ***Total amount:*** $1,004,902 (9% institutional, 91% external sources). ***Average award:*** Freshmen: $1000. Undergraduates: $1000. ***Scholarships, grants, and awards by category:*** *Academic interests/achievement:* 91 awards ($91,000 total): general academic interests/achievements. *Special achievements/activities:* leadership. *Special characteristics:* children of faculty/staff. ***Tuition waivers:*** Full or partial for employees or children of employees.

LOANS ***Student loans:*** 43% of past graduating class borrowed through all loan programs. *Average indebtedness per student:* $18,229. ***Programs:*** Federal Direct (Subsidized and Unsubsidized Stafford), Perkins, state.

WORK-STUDY ***Federal work-study:*** Total amount: $479,843; 279 jobs averaging $1720. ***State or other work-study/employment:*** Total amount: $641,339 (100% need-based). 369 part-time jobs averaging $1738.

APPLYING FOR FINANCIAL AID ***Required financial aid forms:*** FAFSA, CSS Financial Aid PROFILE, noncustodial (divorced/separated) parent's statement, business/farm supplement. ***Financial aid deadline:*** 2/15. ***Notification date:*** 4/5. Students must reply by 5/1 or within 1 week of notification.

CONTACT Mr. Stephen H. Joyce, Director of Student Aid, Bowdoin College, 5300 College Station, Brunswick, ME 04011-8444, 207-725-3273. *Fax:* 207-725-3864. *E-mail:* sjoyce@bowdoin.edu.

BOWIE STATE UNIVERSITY

Bowie, MD

Tuition & fees (MD res): $6154 **Average undergraduate aid package: $8376**

ABOUT THE INSTITUTION State-supported, coed. 29 undergraduate majors. Both federal and institutional methodology are used as a basis for awarding need-based institutional aid.

UNDERGRADUATE EXPENSES for 2010–11 ***Tuition, state resident:*** full-time $4415; part-time $195 per credit hour. ***Tuition, nonresident:*** full-time $14,939; part-time $629 per credit hour. ***Required fees:*** full-time $1739; $87.38 per credit hour. Part-time tuition and fees vary according to course load. ***College room and board:*** $8570. Room and board charges vary according to board plan and housing facility. ***Payment plans:*** Installment, deferred payment.

FRESHMAN FINANCIAL AID (Fall 2010, est.) 499 applied for aid; of those 99% were deemed to have need. 100% of freshmen with need received aid; of those 59% had need fully met. ***Average percent of need met:*** 48% (excluding resources awarded to replace EFC). ***Average financial aid package:*** $7868 (excluding resources awarded to replace EFC). 3% of all full-time freshmen had no need and received non-need-based gift aid.

UNDERGRADUATE FINANCIAL AID (Fall 2010, est.) 2,664 applied for aid; of those 100% were deemed to have need. 100% of undergraduates with need received aid; of those 48% had need fully met. ***Average percent of need met:*** 49% (excluding resources awarded to replace EFC). ***Average financial aid package:*** $8376 (excluding resources awarded to replace EFC). 2% of all full-time undergraduates had no need and received non-need-based gift aid.

GIFT AID (NEED-BASED) ***Total amount:*** $16,925,259 (55% federal, 25% state, 19% institutional, 1% external sources). ***Receiving aid:*** Freshmen: 56% (349); all full-time undergraduates: 61% (2,007). ***Average award:*** Freshmen: $7135; Undergraduates: $6466. ***Scholarships, grants, and awards:*** Federal Pell, FSEOG, state, private, college/university gift aid from institutional funds, United Negro College Fund, Federal Nursing.

GIFT AID (NON-NEED-BASED) ***Total amount:*** $741,631 (1% federal, 14% state, 80% institutional, 5% external sources). ***Receiving aid:*** Freshmen: 67% (414). Undergraduates: 64% (2,089). ***Average award:*** Freshmen: $262. Undergraduates: $138. ***Scholarships, grants, and awards by category:*** *Academic interests/achievement:* 4 awards ($8830 total): biological sciences, business, communication, computer science, engineering/technologies, mathematics, military science. *Creative arts/performance:* 87 awards ($215,794 total): applied art and design, art/fine arts, general creative arts/performance, music. *Special achievements/activities:* 306 awards ($1,707,317 total). *Special characteristics:* first-generation college students. ***Tuition waivers:*** Full or partial for employees or children of employees, senior citizens.

LOANS ***Student loans:*** $22,133,735 (80% need-based, 20% non-need-based). 73% of past graduating class borrowed through all loan programs. *Average indebtedness per student:* $19,003. ***Average need-based loan:*** Freshmen: $3309. Undergraduates: $4110. ***Parent loans:*** $4,616,327 (40% need-based, 60% non-need-based). ***Programs:*** Federal Direct (Subsidized and Unsubsidized Stafford, PLUS), Perkins, Federal Nursing, state, college/university.

WORK-STUDY ***Federal work-study:*** Total amount: $170,772; 65 jobs averaging $2627.

ATHLETIC AWARDS Total amount: $794,762 (68% need-based, 32% non-need-based).

APPLYING FOR FINANCIAL AID ***Required financial aid forms:*** FAFSA, institution's own form. ***Financial aid deadline (priority):*** 3/1. ***Notification date:*** Continuous beginning 4/1. Students must reply within 2 weeks of notification.

CONTACT Deborah Stanley, Financial Aid Director, Bowie State University, 14000 Jericho Park Road, Bowie, MD 20715, 301-860-3543 or toll-free 877-772-6943 (out-of-state). *Fax:* 301-860-3549. *E-mail:* dstanley@bowiestate.edu.

BOWLING GREEN STATE UNIVERSITY

Bowling Green, OH

Tuition & fees (OH res): $9704 **Average undergraduate aid package: $15,306**

ABOUT THE INSTITUTION State-supported, coed. 113 undergraduate majors. Federal methodology is used as a basis for awarding need-based institutional aid.

UNDERGRADUATE EXPENSES for 2010–11 ***Tuition, state resident:*** full-time $8322; part-time $347 per credit hour. ***Tuition, nonresident:*** full-time $15,630; part-time $652 per credit hour. ***Required fees:*** full-time $1382; $57 per credit hour. Full-time tuition and fees vary according to course load and location. Part-time tuition and fees vary according to course load and location. ***College room and board:*** $7800. Room and board charges vary according to board plan and housing facility. ***Payment plan:*** Installment.

FRESHMAN FINANCIAL AID (Fall 2010, est.) 3,404 applied for aid; of those 86% were deemed to have need. 100% of freshmen with need received aid; of those 10% had need fully met. ***Average percent of need met:*** 83% (excluding resources awarded to replace EFC). ***Average financial aid package:*** $15,114 (excluding resources awarded to replace EFC). 18% of all full-time freshmen had no need and received non-need-based gift aid.

UNDERGRADUATE FINANCIAL AID (Fall 2010, est.) 11,557 applied for aid; of those 89% were deemed to have need. 100% of undergraduates with need received aid; of those 9% had need fully met. ***Average percent of need met:*** 81% (excluding resources awarded to replace EFC). ***Average financial aid package:*** $15,306 (excluding resources awarded to replace EFC). 13% of all full-time undergraduates had no need and received non-need-based gift aid.

GIFT AID (NEED-BASED) ***Total amount:*** $54,444,992 (49% federal, 7% state, 41% institutional, 3% external sources). ***Receiving aid:*** Freshmen: 70% (2,687); all full-time undergraduates: 57% (8,331). ***Average award:*** Freshmen: $6551; Undergraduates: $6369. ***Scholarships, grants, and awards:*** Federal Pell, FSEOG, state, private, college/university gift aid from institutional funds.

GIFT AID (NON-NEED-BASED) ***Total amount:*** $9,825,614 (4% state, 91% institutional, 5% external sources). ***Receiving aid:*** Freshmen: 5% (178). Undergraduates: 3% (459). ***Average award:*** Freshmen: $3549. Undergraduates: $3943. ***Scholarships, grants, and awards by category:*** *Academic interests/achievement:* biological sciences, business, communication, computer science, education, engineering/technologies, English, foreign languages, general academic interests/achievements, health fields, home economics, humanities, international studies, mathematics, military science, physical sciences, social sciences. *Creative arts/performance:* art/fine arts, cinema/film/broadcasting, creative writing, dance, debating, journalism/publications, music, performing arts, theater/drama. *Special achievements/activities:* general special achievements/activities, leadership. *Special characteristics:* children and siblings of alumni, children of faculty/staff, general special characteristics, international students, members of minority groups. ***Tuition waivers:*** Full or partial for employees or children of employees, senior citizens.

LOANS ***Student loans:*** $88,407,379 (81% need-based, 19% non-need-based). 76% of past graduating class borrowed through all loan programs. *Average indebtedness per student:* $31,515. ***Average need-based loan:*** Freshmen: $6319. Undergraduates: $7503. ***Parent loans:*** $71,956,302 (44% need-based, 56% non-need-based). ***Programs:*** Federal Direct (Subsidized and Unsubsidized Stafford, PLUS), Perkins, Federal Nursing, state, college/university, alternative loans.

WORK-STUDY ***Federal work-study:*** Total amount: $321,104; 322 jobs averaging $997.

ATHLETIC AWARDS Total amount: $5,620,312 (36% need-based, 64% non-need-based).

APPLYING FOR FINANCIAL AID ***Required financial aid form:*** FAFSA. ***Financial aid deadline:*** Continuous. ***Notification date:*** Continuous beginning 4/15. Students must reply within 3 weeks of notification.

CONTACT Eric Bucks, Associate Director of Student Financial Aid, Bowling Green State University, 231 Administration Building, Bowling Green, OH 43403, 419-372-2651. *Fax:* 419-372-0404.

BRADLEY UNIVERSITY

Peoria, IL

Tuition & fees: $25,424 **Average undergraduate aid package: $16,725**

ABOUT THE INSTITUTION Independent, coed. 102 undergraduate majors. Federal methodology is used as a basis for awarding need-based institutional aid.

UNDERGRADUATE EXPENSES for 2010–11 ***Comprehensive fee:*** $33,374 includes full-time tuition ($25,150), mandatory fees ($274), and room and board ($7950). Full-time tuition and fees vary according to course load and program. Room and board charges vary according to board plan. ***Part-time tuition:*** $630 per credit hour. Part-time tuition and fees vary according to course load and program. ***Payment plan:*** Installment.

FRESHMAN FINANCIAL AID (Fall 2010, est.) 1,093 applied for aid; of those 89% were deemed to have need. 98% of freshmen with need received aid; of those 14% had need fully met. ***Average percent of need met:*** 67% (excluding resources awarded to replace EFC). ***Average financial aid package:*** $16,833 (excluding resources awarded to replace EFC). 15% of all full-time freshmen had no need and received non-need-based gift aid.

UNDERGRADUATE FINANCIAL AID (Fall 2010, est.) 4,171 applied for aid; of those 89% were deemed to have need. 98% of undergraduates with need received aid; of those 14% had need fully met. ***Average percent of need met:*** 62% (excluding resources awarded to replace EFC). ***Average financial aid package:*** $16,725 (excluding resources awarded to replace EFC). 20% of all full-time undergraduates had no need and received non-need-based gift aid.

GIFT AID (NEED-BASED) ***Total amount:*** $50,367,543 (13% federal, 14% state, 70% institutional, 3% external sources). ***Receiving aid:*** Freshmen: 83% (948); all full-time undergraduates: 73% (3,518). ***Average award:*** Freshmen: $14,317; Undergraduates: $12,988. ***Scholarships, grants, and awards:*** Federal Pell, FSEOG, state, private, college/university gift aid from institutional funds.

GIFT AID (NON-NEED-BASED) ***Total amount:*** $6,301,240 (1% state, 93% institutional, 6% external sources). ***Receiving aid:*** Freshmen: 9% (100). Undergraduates: 6% (305). ***Average award:*** Freshmen: $8494. Undergraduates: $6718. ***Scholarships, grants, and awards by category:*** *Academic interests/achievement:* general academic interests/achievements. *Creative arts/performance:* art/fine arts, music, theater/drama. *Special achievements/activities:* community service, leadership. *Special characteristics:* children and siblings of alumni, children of faculty/staff. ***Tuition waivers:*** Full or partial for children of alumni, employees or children of employees, senior citizens.

LOANS ***Student loans:*** $28,748,612 (67% need-based, 33% non-need-based). ***Average need-based loan:*** Freshmen: $4232. Undergraduates: $5376. ***Programs:*** Federal Direct (Subsidized and Unsubsidized Stafford, PLUS), Perkins, Federal Nursing.

WORK-STUDY ***Federal work-study:*** Total amount: $749,151; jobs available.

APPLYING FOR FINANCIAL AID ***Required financial aid form:*** FAFSA. ***Financial aid deadline (priority):*** 3/1. ***Notification date:*** Continuous beginning 3/1.

CONTACT Mr. David L. Pardieck, Director of Financial Assistance, Bradley University, 1501 West Bradley Avenue, Peoria, IL 61625-0002, 309-677-3089 or toll-free 800-447-6460. *E-mail:* dlp@bradley.edu.

BRANDEIS UNIVERSITY

Waltham, MA

Tuition & fees: $40,274 **Average undergraduate aid package: $32,260**

ABOUT THE INSTITUTION Independent, coed. 43 undergraduate majors. Institutional methodology is used as a basis for awarding need-based institutional aid.

UNDERGRADUATE EXPENSES for 2010–11 ***Comprehensive fee:*** $51,488 includes full-time tuition ($38,994), mandatory fees ($1280), and room and board ($11,214). Room and board charges vary according to board plan and housing facility. Part-time tuition and fees vary according to course load. ***Payment plans:*** Tuition prepayment, installment.

FRESHMAN FINANCIAL AID (Fall 2010, est.) 517 applied for aid; of those 79% were deemed to have need. 99% of freshmen with need received aid; of those 28% had need fully met. ***Average percent of need met:*** 94% (excluding resources awarded to replace EFC). ***Average financial aid package:*** $33,646 (excluding resources awarded to replace EFC). 5% of all full-time freshmen had no need and received non-need-based gift aid.

UNDERGRADUATE FINANCIAL AID (Fall 2010, est.) 1,686 applied for aid; of those 89% were deemed to have need. 100% of undergraduates with need received aid; of those 27% had need fully met. ***Average percent of need met:*** 92% (excluding resources awarded to replace EFC). ***Average financial aid package:*** $32,260 (excluding resources awarded to replace EFC). 14% of all full-time undergraduates had no need and received non-need-based gift aid.

GIFT AID (NEED-BASED) ***Total amount:*** $41,099,812 (9% federal, 1% state, 88% institutional, 2% external sources). ***Receiving aid:*** Freshmen: 58% (400); all full-time undergraduates: 45% (1,480). ***Average award:*** Freshmen: $30,543; Undergraduates: $27,772. ***Scholarships, grants, and awards:*** Federal Pell, FSEOG, state, private, college/university gift aid from institutional funds.

GIFT AID (NON-NEED-BASED) ***Total amount:*** $13,025,436 (4% federal, 1% state, 83% institutional, 12% external sources). ***Receiving aid:*** Freshmen: 6% (41). Undergraduates: 3% (111). ***Average award:*** Freshmen: $11,853. Undergraduates: $23,117. ***Tuition waivers:*** Full or partial for employees or children of employees.

LOANS ***Student loans:*** $13,949,783 (55% need-based, 45% non-need-based). 70% of past graduating class borrowed through all loan programs. *Average indebtedness per student:* $21,351. ***Average need-based loan:*** Freshmen: $3185. Undergraduates: $4338. ***Parent loans:*** $11,129,033 (53% need-based, 47% non-need-based). ***Programs:*** Federal Direct (Subsidized and Unsubsidized Stafford, PLUS), Perkins, state, college/university.

WORK-STUDY ***Federal work-study:*** Total amount: $906,632; jobs available. ***State or other work-study/employment:*** Total amount: $695,570 (19% need-based, 81% non-need-based). Part-time jobs available.

APPLYING FOR FINANCIAL AID ***Required financial aid forms:*** CSS Financial Aid PROFILE, noncustodial (divorced/separated) parent's statement. ***Financial aid deadline:*** 2/1.

CONTACT Peter Giumette, Student Financial Services, Brandeis University, 415 South Street, Usdan Student Center, Waltham, MA 02454-9110, 781-736-3700 or toll-free 800-622-0622 (out-of-state). *Fax:* 781-736-3719. *E-mail:* sfs@brandeis.edu.

BRENAU UNIVERSITY

Gainesville, GA

Tuition & fees: $21,124 **Average undergraduate aid package: $18,714**

ABOUT THE INSTITUTION Independent, women only. 33 undergraduate majors. Federal methodology is used as a basis for awarding need-based institutional aid.

UNDERGRADUATE EXPENSES for 2011–12 ***Comprehensive fee:*** $31,490 includes full-time tuition ($20,864), mandatory fees ($260), and room and board ($10,366). Full-time tuition and fees vary according to location and program. ***Part-time tuition:*** $695 per credit hour. ***Part-time fees:*** $130 per term. Part-time tuition and fees vary according to course load, location, and program. ***Payment plan:*** Installment.

FRESHMAN FINANCIAL AID (Fall 2010, est.) 162 applied for aid; of those 92% were deemed to have need. 100% of freshmen with need received aid; of those 23% had need fully met. ***Average percent of need met:*** 76% (excluding resources awarded to replace EFC). ***Average financial aid package:*** $20,230 (excluding resources awarded to replace EFC). 15% of all full-time freshmen had no need and received non-need-based gift aid.

UNDERGRADUATE FINANCIAL AID (Fall 2010, est.) 634 applied for aid; of those 93% were deemed to have need. 100% of undergraduates with need received aid; of those 19% had need fully met. ***Average percent of need met:*** 70% (excluding resources awarded to replace EFC). ***Average financial aid package:*** $18,714 (excluding resources awarded to replace EFC). 19% of all full-time undergraduates had no need and received non-need-based gift aid.

GIFT AID (NEED-BASED) ***Total amount:*** $8,271,632 (23% federal, 18% state, 58% institutional, 1% external sources). ***Receiving aid:*** Freshmen: 85% (149); all full-time undergraduates: 79% (588). ***Average award:*** Freshmen: $26,952; Undergraduates: $14,609. ***Scholarships, grants, and awards:*** Federal Pell, FSEOG, state, private, college/university gift aid from institutional funds, Academic Competitiveness Grants, National SMART Grants.

GIFT AID (NON-NEED-BASED) ***Total amount:*** $2,258,099 (17% state, 83% institutional). ***Receiving aid:*** Freshmen: 14% (25). Undergraduates: 10% (74). ***Average award:*** Freshmen: $14,055. Undergraduates: $12,542. ***Scholarships, grants, and awards by category:*** *Academic interests/achievement:* 685 awards ($4,827,901 total): biological sciences, business, communication, education, general academic interests/achievements, health fields, humanities. *Creative arts/performance:* 103 awards ($339,864 total): applied art and design, art/fine arts, cinema/film/broadcasting, creative writing, dance, journalism/publications, music, performing arts, theater/drama. *Special achievements/activities:* 14 awards ($6500 total): general special achievements/activities, leadership. *Special characteristics:* 36 awards ($466,541 total): children of faculty/staff, first-generation college students, general special characteristics, international students. ***Tuition waivers:*** Full or partial for employees or children of employees.

LOANS ***Student loans:*** $4,394,011 (83% need-based, 17% non-need-based). 80% of past graduating class borrowed through all loan programs. *Average indebtedness per student:* $20,634. ***Average need-based loan:*** Freshmen: $3199. Undergraduates: $4206. ***Parent loans:*** $504,071 (52% need-based, 48% non-need-based). ***Programs:*** Federal Direct (Subsidized and Unsubsidized Stafford, PLUS), Perkins, state.

WORK-STUDY ***Federal work-study:*** Total amount: $210,003; 108 jobs averaging $1944.

ATHLETIC AWARDS Total amount: $1,115,382 (35% need-based, 65% non-need-based).

APPLYING FOR FINANCIAL AID ***Required financial aid forms:*** FAFSA, state aid form. ***Financial aid deadline (priority):*** 3/15. ***Notification date:*** Continuous beginning 2/1.

CONTACT Pam Barrett, Associate Vice President and Director of Financial Aid, Brenau University, 500 Washington Street, SE, Gainesville, GA 30501-3697, 770-534-6176 or toll-free 800-252-5119. *Fax:* 770-538-4306. *E-mail:* pbarrett@brenau.edu.

BRESCIA UNIVERSITY

Owensboro, KY

ABOUT THE INSTITUTION Independent Roman Catholic, coed. 32 undergraduate majors.

GIFT AID (NEED-BASED) ***Scholarships, grants, and awards:*** Federal Pell, FSEOG, state, private, college/university gift aid from institutional funds.

GIFT AID (NON-NEED-BASED) ***Scholarships, grants, and awards by category:*** *Academic interests/achievement:* biological sciences, business, education, English, general academic interests/achievements, health fields, physical sciences, premedicine, religion/biblical studies, social sciences. *Creative arts/performance:* art/fine arts, creative writing, music. *Special achievements/activities:* leadership. *Special characteristics:* children and siblings of alumni, children of faculty/staff, ethnic background, international students, members of minority groups.

LOANS ***Programs:*** Federal Direct (Subsidized and Unsubsidized Stafford, PLUS), Perkins, college/university.

WORK-STUDY ***Federal work-study:*** Total amount: $64,426; 64 jobs averaging $1200. ***State or other work-study/employment:*** Total amount: $71,236 (100% non-need-based). 15 part-time jobs averaging $2500.

APPLYING FOR FINANCIAL AID ***Required financial aid form:*** FAFSA.

CONTACT Mr. Britton Hibbitt, Administrative Assistant to Financial Aid, Brescia University, 717 Frederica Street, Owensboro, KY 42301-3023, 270-686-4253 or toll-free 877-273-7242. *Fax:* 270-686-4253. *E-mail:* financial.aid@brescia.edu.

BREVARD COLLEGE

Brevard, NC

Tuition & fees: $22,175 **Average undergraduate aid package: $20,500**

ABOUT THE INSTITUTION Independent United Methodist, coed. 17 undergraduate majors. Federal methodology is used as a basis for awarding need-based institutional aid.

UNDERGRADUATE EXPENSES for 2010–11 ***Comprehensive fee:*** $30,025 includes full-time tuition ($22,100), mandatory fees ($75), and room and board ($7850). Full-time tuition and fees vary according to course load. Room and board charges vary according to board plan and housing facility. ***Part-time tuition:*** $815 per credit hour. Part-time tuition and fees vary according to course load. ***Payment plan:*** Installment.

FRESHMAN FINANCIAL AID (Fall 2009) 150 applied for aid; of those 89% were deemed to have need. 100% of freshmen with need received aid; of those 26% had need fully met. ***Average percent of need met:*** 81% (excluding resources awarded to replace EFC). ***Average financial aid package:*** $19,400 (excluding resources awarded to replace EFC). 18% of all full-time freshmen had no need and received non-need-based gift aid.

UNDERGRADUATE FINANCIAL AID (Fall 2009) 512 applied for aid; of those 90% were deemed to have need. 100% of undergraduates with need received aid; of those 28% had need fully met. ***Average percent of need met:*** 83% (excluding resources awarded to replace EFC). ***Average financial aid package:*** $20,500 (excluding resources awarded to replace EFC). 20% of all full-time undergraduates had no need and received non-need-based gift aid.

GIFT AID (NEED-BASED) ***Total amount:*** $5,437,876 (20% federal, 19% state, 57% institutional, 4% external sources). ***Receiving aid:*** Freshmen: 70% (134); all full-time undergraduates: 72% (460). ***Average award:*** Freshmen: $13,500; Undergraduates: $14,200. ***Scholarships, grants, and awards:*** Federal Pell, FSEOG, state, private, college/university gift aid from institutional funds.

GIFT AID (NON-NEED-BASED) ***Total amount:*** $1,005,838 (8% state, 85% institutional, 7% external sources). ***Receiving aid:*** Freshmen: 9% (18). Undergraduates: 9% (55). ***Average award:*** Freshmen: $3500. Undergraduates: $2600. ***Scholarships, grants, and awards by category:*** *Academic interests/achievement:* $1,750,000 total: biological sciences, business, education, English, general academic interests/achievements, health fields, mathematics, physical sciences, premedicine, religion/biblical studies, social sciences. *Creative arts/performance:* $235,000 total: art/fine arts, journalism/publications, music, theater/drama. *Special achievements/activities:* $450,000 total: cheerleading/drum major, community service, general special achievements/activities, hobbies/interests, leadership. *Special characteristics:* $2,125,000 total: children of faculty/staff, international students, local/state students, previous college experience, relatives of clergy, religious affiliation, siblings of current students, veterans' children. ***Tuition waivers:*** Full or partial for employees or children of employees, senior citizens.

LOANS ***Student loans:*** $4,097,712 (79% need-based, 21% non-need-based). 59% of past graduating class borrowed through all loan programs. *Average indebtedness per student:* $20,770. ***Average need-based loan:*** Freshmen: $3850. Undergraduates: $4260. ***Parent loans:*** $644,065 (59% need-based, 41% non-need-based). ***Programs:*** Perkins, state.

WORK-STUDY ***Federal work-study:*** Total amount: $43,705; 51 jobs averaging $897. ***State or other work-study/employment:*** Part-time jobs available.

ATHLETIC AWARDS Total amount: $1,904,944 (64% need-based, 36% non-need-based).

APPLYING FOR FINANCIAL AID ***Required financial aid forms:*** FAFSA, state aid form. ***Financial aid deadline (priority):*** 4/15. ***Notification date:*** Continuous beginning 2/1. Students must reply within 4 weeks of notification.

CONTACT Ms. Beth Pocock, Director of Financial Aid, Brevard College, 1 Brevard College Drive, Brevard, NC 28712, 828-884-8287 or toll-free 800-527-9090. *Fax:* 828-884-3790. *E-mail:* finaid@brevard.edu.

BREWTON-PARKER COLLEGE

Mt. Vernon, GA

ABOUT THE INSTITUTION Independent Southern Baptist, coed. 25 undergraduate majors.

GIFT AID (NEED-BASED) ***Scholarships, grants, and awards:*** Federal Pell, FSEOG, state, private, college/university gift aid from institutional funds, United Negro College Fund.

GIFT AID (NON-NEED-BASED) ***Scholarships, grants, and awards by category:*** *Academic interests/achievement:* general academic interests/achievements. *Creative arts/performance:* music. *Special achievements/activities:* cheerleading/drum major, religious involvement. *Special characteristics:* children of faculty/staff, international students, out-of-state students, relatives of clergy, religious affiliation.

LOANS ***Programs:*** Perkins, state, college/university.

WORK-STUDY ***Federal work-study:*** Total amount: $92,982; 170 jobs averaging $676. ***State or other work-study/employment:*** Total amount: $54,786 (17% need-based, 83% non-need-based). 114 part-time jobs averaging $466.

APPLYING FOR FINANCIAL AID ***Required financial aid forms:*** FAFSA, state aid form, individual grant forms.

CONTACT Mrs. Shannon Mullins, Executive Director of Financial Aid, Brewton-Parker College, PO Box 197, Mt. Vernon, GA 30445-0197, 800-342-1087 Ext. 213 or toll-free 800-342-1087 Ext. 245. *Fax:* 912-583-3598. *E-mail:* smullins@bpc.edu.

BRIARCLIFFE COLLEGE

Bethpage, NY

CONTACT Johanna Kelly, Financial Aid Director, Briarcliffe College, 1055 Stewart Avenue, Bethpage, NY 11714, 516-918-3600 or toll-free 888-349-4999 (in-state).

BRIAR CLIFF UNIVERSITY

Sioux City, IA

ABOUT THE INSTITUTION Independent Roman Catholic, coed. 29 undergraduate majors.

GIFT AID (NEED-BASED) ***Scholarships, grants, and awards:*** Federal Pell, FSEOG, state, private, college/university gift aid from institutional funds.

GIFT AID (NON-NEED-BASED) ***Scholarships, grants, and awards by category:*** *Academic interests/achievement:* biological sciences, business, communication, computer science, education, English, foreign languages, general academic interests/achievements, health fields, humanities, mathematics, physical sciences, religion/biblical studies, social sciences. *Creative arts/performance:* art/fine arts, music, theater/drama. *Special achievements/activities:* leadership, religious involvement. *Special characteristics:* children and siblings of alumni, international students, members of minority groups.

LOANS ***Programs:*** Federal Direct (Subsidized and Unsubsidized Stafford, PLUS), Perkins, alternative loans, partnership loans, Minnesota SELF Loans.

WORK-STUDY ***Federal work-study:*** Total amount: $225,391; 240 jobs averaging $1500. ***State or other work-study/employment:*** Total amount: $345,000 (100% non-need-based). 115 part-time jobs averaging $1500.

APPLYING FOR FINANCIAL AID ***Required financial aid forms:*** FAFSA, income tax form(s).

CONTACT Financial Aid Office, Briar Cliff University, 3303 Rebecca Street, PO Box 2100, Sioux City, IA 51104-2100, 712-279-5239 or toll-free 800-662-3303 Ext. 5200. *Fax:* 712-279-1632.

BRIDGEWATER COLLEGE

Bridgewater, VA

Tuition & fees: $25,500 **Average undergraduate aid package: $21,692**

ABOUT THE INSTITUTION Independent religious, coed. 44 undergraduate majors. Federal methodology is used as a basis for awarding need-based institutional aid.

UNDERGRADUATE EXPENSES for 2010–11 ***Comprehensive fee:*** $35,850 includes full-time tuition ($25,500) and room and board ($10,350). ***College room only:*** $5260. Room and board charges vary according to board plan and housing facility. ***Part-time tuition:*** $850 per credit hour. ***Part-time fees:*** $30 per term. ***Payment plan:*** Installment.

FRESHMAN FINANCIAL AID (Fall 2010, est.) 523 applied for aid; of those 90% were deemed to have need. 100% of freshmen with need received aid; of those 23% had need fully met. ***Average percent of need met:*** 82% (excluding resources awarded to replace EFC). ***Average financial aid package:*** $23,299 (excluding resources awarded to replace EFC). 15% of all full-time freshmen had no need and received non-need-based gift aid.

UNDERGRADUATE FINANCIAL AID (Fall 2010, est.) 1,457 applied for aid; of those 92% were deemed to have need. 100% of undergraduates with need received aid; of those 21% had need fully met. ***Average percent of need met:*** 79% (excluding resources awarded to replace EFC). ***Average financial aid package:*** $21,692 (excluding resources awarded to replace EFC). 20% of all full-time undergraduates had no need and received non-need-based gift aid.

GIFT AID (NEED-BASED) ***Total amount:*** $19,510,704 (11% federal, 12% state, 75% institutional, 2% external sources). ***Receiving aid:*** Freshmen: 85% (470); all full-time undergraduates: 80% (1,333). ***Average award:*** Freshmen: $20,025; Undergraduates: $17,954. ***Scholarships, grants, and awards:*** Federal Pell, FSEOG, state, private, college/university gift aid from institutional funds.

GIFT AID (NON-NEED-BASED) ***Total amount:*** $8,960,720 (11% state, 87% institutional, 2% external sources). ***Receiving aid:*** Freshmen: 84% (462). Undergraduates: 77% (1,281). ***Average award:*** Freshmen: $13,164. Undergraduates: $10,737. ***Scholarships, grants, and awards by category:*** *Academic interests/achievement:* general academic interests/achievements. *Creative arts/performance:* music. *Special characteristics:* international students, religious affiliation, siblings of current students. ***Tuition waivers:*** Full or partial for employees or children of employees, senior citizens.

LOANS ***Student loans:*** $10,460,403 (75% need-based, 25% non-need-based). 73% of past graduating class borrowed through all loan programs. *Average indebtedness per student:* $29,036. ***Average need-based loan:*** Freshmen: $4057. Undergraduates: $4618. ***Parent loans:*** $4,116,954 (62% need-based, 38% non-need-based). ***Programs:*** Federal Direct (Subsidized and Unsubsidized Stafford, PLUS), Perkins.

WORK-STUDY ***Federal work-study:*** Total amount: $307,779; jobs available.

APPLYING FOR FINANCIAL AID ***Required financial aid forms:*** FAFSA, state aid form. ***Financial aid deadline (priority):*** 3/1. ***Notification date:*** Continuous beginning 3/16. Students must reply within 2 weeks of notification.

CONTACT Mr. Scott Morrison, Director of Financial Aid, Bridgewater College, 402 East College Street, Bridgewater, VA 22812-1599, 540-828-5376 or toll-free 800-759-8328. *Fax:* 540-828-5671. *E-mail:* smorriso@bridgewater.edu.

BRIDGEWATER STATE UNIVERSITY

Bridgewater, MA

ABOUT THE INSTITUTION State-supported, coed. 75 undergraduate majors.

GIFT AID (NEED-BASED) ***Scholarships, grants, and awards:*** Federal Pell, FSEOG, state, private, college/university gift aid from institutional funds.

GIFT AID (NON-NEED-BASED) ***Scholarships, grants, and awards by category:*** *Academic interests/achievement:* general academic interests/achievements. *Special achievements/activities:* leadership. *Special characteristics:* local/state students, members of minority groups.

LOANS ***Programs:*** Federal Direct (Subsidized and Unsubsidized Stafford, PLUS), Perkins, state.

WORK-STUDY ***Federal work-study:*** Total amount: $700,876; jobs available.

APPLYING FOR FINANCIAL AID ***Required financial aid form:*** FAFSA.

CONTACT Office of Financial Aid, Bridgewater State University, Tillinghast Hall, Room 100, 45 School Street, Bridgewater, MA 02325-0001, 508-531-1341. *Fax:* 508-531-1728. *E-mail:* finaid@bridgew.edu.

BRIGHAM YOUNG UNIVERSITY

Provo, UT

Tuition & fees: $4560 **Average undergraduate aid package: $7405**

ABOUT THE INSTITUTION Independent religious, coed. 102 undergraduate majors. Both federal and institutional methodology are used as a basis for awarding need-based institutional aid.

UNDERGRADUATE EXPENSES for 2010–11 ***Comprehensive fee:*** $11,680 includes full-time tuition ($4560) and room and board ($7120). Room and board charges vary according to board plan, housing facility, and location. ***Part-time tuition:*** $234 per credit hour. Part-time tuition and fees vary according to course load. Latter Day Saints full-time student $4,560 per year, non-LDS full-time student $9,120.

FRESHMAN FINANCIAL AID (Fall 2009) 2,244 applied for aid; of those 66% were deemed to have need. 89% of freshmen with need received aid; of those 3% had need fully met. ***Average percent of need met:*** 31% (excluding resources awarded to replace EFC). ***Average financial aid package:*** $6176 (excluding resources awarded to replace EFC). 37% of all full-time freshmen had no need and received non-need-based gift aid.

UNDERGRADUATE FINANCIAL AID (Fall 2009) 15,850 applied for aid; of those 85% were deemed to have need. 93% of undergraduates with need received aid; of those 4% had need fully met. ***Average percent of need met:*** 40% (excluding resources awarded to replace EFC). ***Average financial aid package:*** $7405 (excluding resources awarded to replace EFC). 24% of all full-time undergraduates had no need and received non-need-based gift aid.

GIFT AID (NEED-BASED) ***Total amount:*** $61,131,184 (88% federal, 12% institutional). ***Receiving aid:*** Freshmen: 13% (667); all full-time undergraduates: 33% (9,972). ***Average award:*** Freshmen: $4817; Undergraduates: $5491. ***Scholarships, grants, and awards:*** Federal Pell, state, private, college/university gift aid from institutional funds.

GIFT AID (NON-NEED-BASED) ***Total amount:*** $47,505,612 (80% institutional, 20% external sources). ***Receiving aid:*** Freshmen: 19% (954). Undergraduates: 18% (5,507). ***Average award:*** Freshmen: $3498. Undergraduates: $3436. ***Scholarships, grants, and awards by category:*** *Academic interests/achievement:* general academic interests/achievements. *Creative arts/performance:* art/fine arts, music, theater/drama. *Special achievements/activities:* religious involvement. *Special characteristics:* members of minority groups. ***Tuition waivers:*** Full or partial for employees or children of employees.

LOANS ***Student loans:*** $37,919,176 (58% need-based, 42% non-need-based). 31% of past graduating class borrowed through all loan programs. *Average indebtedness per student:* $13,354. ***Average need-based loan:*** Freshmen: $3161. Undergraduates: $4274. ***Parent loans:*** $3,866,492 (100% non-need-based). ***Programs:*** Federal Direct (Subsidized and Unsubsidized Stafford, PLUS).

WORK-STUDY ***State or other work-study/employment:*** Part-time jobs available.

ATHLETIC AWARDS Total amount: $4,248,263 (100% non-need-based).

APPLYING FOR FINANCIAL AID ***Required financial aid forms:*** FAFSA, institution's own form. ***Financial aid deadline (priority):*** 4/15. ***Notification date:*** Continuous beginning 5/1.

CONTACT Paul R. Conrad, Director of Financial Aid, Brigham Young University, A-41 ASB, Provo, UT 84602, 801-422-7355. *Fax:* 801-422-0234. *E-mail:* paul_conrad@byu.edu.

BRIGHAM YOUNG UNIVERSITY–HAWAII

Laie, HI

CONTACT Mr. Wes Duke, Director of Financial Aid, Brigham Young University–Hawaii, BYUH #1980, 55-220 Kulanui Street, Laie, HI 96762, 808-293-3530. *Fax:* 808-293-3349. *E-mail:* duekw@byuh.edu.

BRIGHAM YOUNG UNIVERSITY–IDAHO

Rexburg, ID

CONTACT Financial Aid Office, Brigham Young University–Idaho, Rexburg, ID 83460, 208-496-2011.

BROADVIEW UNIVERSITY

West Jordan, UT

CONTACT Financial Aid Office, Broadview University, 1902 West 7800 South, West Jordan, UT 84088, 801-304-4224 or toll-free 866-304-4224.

BROADVIEW UNIVERSITY-BOISE

Meridian, ID

CONTACT Financial Aid Office, Broadview University-Boise, 2750 East Gala Court, Meridian, ID 83642, 208-577-2900 or toll-free 877-572-5757.

BROADVIEW UNIVERSITY-LAYTON

Layton, UT

CONTACT Financial Aid Office, Broadview University-Layton, 869 West Hill Field Road, Layton, UT 84041, 801-660-6000 or toll-free 866-253-7744.

BROADVIEW UNIVERSITY-OREM

Orem, UT

CONTACT Financial Aid Office, Broadview University-Orem, 898 North 1200 West, Orem, UT 84057, 801-822-5800 or toll-free 877-822-5838.

BROADVIEW UNIVERSITY-SALT LAKE CITY

Salt Lake City, UT

CONTACT Financial Aid Office, Broadview University-Salt Lake City, 240 East Morris Avenue, Salt Lake City, UT 84115, 801-300-4300 or toll-free 877-801-8889.

BROOKLINE COLLEGE

Phoenix, AZ

CONTACT Financial Aid Office, Brookline College, 2445 West Dunlap Avenue, Suite 100, Phoenix, AZ 85021, 602-242-6265 or toll-free 800-793-2428.

BROOKLINE COLLEGE

Tempe, AZ

CONTACT Financial Aid Office, Brookline College, 1140-1150 South Priest Drive, Tempe, AZ 85281, 480-545-8755 or toll-free 888-886-2428.

BROOKLINE COLLEGE

Tucson, AZ

CONTACT Financial Aid Office, Brookline College, 5441 East 22nd Street, Suite 125, Tucson, AZ 85711, 520-748-9799 or toll-free 888-292-2428.

BROOKLINE COLLEGE

Albuquerque, NM

CONTACT Financial Aid Office, Brookline College, 4201 Central Avenue NW, Suite J, Albuquerque, NM 87105-1649, 505-880-2877 or toll-free 888-660-2428.

BROOKLYN COLLEGE OF THE CITY UNIVERSITY OF NEW YORK

Brooklyn, NY

Tuition & fees (NY res): $5284 **Average undergraduate aid package: $7550**

ABOUT THE INSTITUTION State and locally supported, coed. 76 undergraduate majors. Federal methodology is used as a basis for awarding need-based institutional aid.

UNDERGRADUATE EXPENSES for 2010–11 ***Tuition, state resident:*** full-time $4830; part-time $205 per credit. ***Tuition, nonresident:*** full-time $13,050; part-time $435 per credit. ***Required fees:*** full-time $454; $177.05 per term. ***Payment plan:*** Installment.

FRESHMAN FINANCIAL AID (Fall 2010, est.) 1,176 applied for aid; of those 93% were deemed to have need. 97% of freshmen with need received aid; of those 98% had need fully met. ***Average percent of need met:*** 99% (excluding resources awarded to replace EFC). ***Average financial aid package:*** $7550 (excluding resources awarded to replace EFC). 14% of all full-time freshmen had no need and received non-need-based gift aid.

UNDERGRADUATE FINANCIAL AID (Fall 2010, est.) 7,131 applied for aid; of those 95% were deemed to have need. 100% of undergraduates with need received aid; of those 100% had need fully met. ***Average percent of need met:*** 99% (excluding resources awarded to replace EFC). ***Average financial aid***

package: $7550 (excluding resources awarded to replace EFC). 11% of all full-time undergraduates had no need and received non-need-based gift aid.

GIFT AID (NEED-BASED) ***Total amount:*** $43,821,012 (57% federal, 43% state). ***Receiving aid:*** Freshmen: 71% (991); all full-time undergraduates: 66% (6,018). ***Average award:*** Freshmen: $3300; Undergraduates: $3300. ***Scholarships, grants, and awards:*** Federal Pell, FSEOG, state, private, college/university gift aid from institutional funds.

GIFT AID (NON-NEED-BASED) ***Total amount:*** $836,081 (8% federal, 60% state, 22% institutional, 10% external sources). ***Receiving aid:*** Freshmen: 24% (329). Undergraduates: 18% (1,650). ***Average award:*** Freshmen: $4000. Undergraduates: $4000. ***Scholarships, grants, and awards by category:*** *Academic interests/achievement:* 180 awards ($500,000 total): general academic interests/achievements. *Creative arts/performance:* 20 awards ($40,000 total): general creative arts/performance. ***Tuition waivers:*** Full or partial for employees or children of employees, senior citizens.

LOANS ***Student loans:*** $27,798,581 (98% need-based, 2% non-need-based). 48% of past graduating class borrowed through all loan programs. *Average indebtedness per student:* $16,500. ***Average need-based loan:*** Freshmen: $2720. Undergraduates: $2720. ***Parent loans:*** $402,491 (100% need-based). ***Programs:*** Federal Direct (Subsidized and Unsubsidized Stafford, PLUS), Perkins.

WORK-STUDY ***Federal work-study:*** Total amount: $680,000; 1,570 jobs averaging $1250.

APPLYING FOR FINANCIAL AID ***Required financial aid forms:*** FAFSA, state aid form. ***Financial aid deadline:*** 5/1. ***Notification date:*** Continuous beginning 5/15.

CONTACT Mr. Ahad Farhang, Director of Financial Aid, Brooklyn College of the City University of New York, 2900 Bedford Avenue, Brooklyn, NY 11210-2889, 718-951-5669. *Fax:* 718-951-4778. *E-mail:* AFarhang@Brooklyn.cuny.edu.

BROOKS INSTITUTE

Santa Barbara, CA

Tuition & fees: N/R **Average undergraduate aid package: N/A**

ABOUT THE INSTITUTION Proprietary, coed. 4 undergraduate majors. Federal methodology is used as a basis for awarding need-based institutional aid.

GIFT AID (NEED-BASED) ***Scholarships, grants, and awards:*** Federal Pell, FSEOG, state, private, college/university gift aid from institutional funds.

GIFT AID (NON-NEED-BASED) ***Scholarships, grants, and awards by category:*** *Creative arts/performance:* applied art and design, art/fine arts, cinema/film/broadcasting, journalism/publications. *Special achievements/activities:* general special achievements/activities.

LOANS ***Programs:*** Federal Direct (Subsidized and Unsubsidized Stafford, PLUS), alternative loans.

WORK-STUDY Federal work-study jobs available.

APPLYING FOR FINANCIAL AID ***Required financial aid forms:*** FAFSA, institution's own form. ***Financial aid deadline:*** Continuous. ***Notification date:*** Continuous. Students must reply within 4 weeks of notification.

CONTACT Stacey Eymann, Director of Financial Aid, Brooks Institute, 27 East Cota Street, Santa Barbara, CA 93101, 888-304-3456 or toll-free 888-276-4999 (out-of-state). *Fax:* 805-966-2909. *E-mail:* seymann@brooks.edu.

BROWN UNIVERSITY

Providence, RI

Tuition & fees: $42,230 **Average undergraduate aid package: $36,815**

ABOUT THE INSTITUTION Independent, coed. 76 undergraduate majors. Both federal and institutional methodology are used as a basis for awarding need-based institutional aid.

UNDERGRADUATE EXPENSES for 2011–12 ***Comprehensive fee:*** $53,136 includes full-time tuition ($41,328), mandatory fees ($902), and room and board ($10,906). ***College room only:*** $6748. Room and board charges vary according to board plan. ***Payment plan:*** Installment.

FRESHMAN FINANCIAL AID (Fall 2010, est.) 812 applied for aid; of those 91% were deemed to have need. 100% of freshmen with need received aid; of those 100% had need fully met. ***Average percent of need met:*** 100% (excluding resources awarded to replace EFC). ***Average financial aid package:*** $37,355 (excluding resources awarded to replace EFC).

UNDERGRADUATE FINANCIAL AID (Fall 2010, est.) 2,970 applied for aid; of those 93% were deemed to have need. 100% of undergraduates with need received aid; of those 100% had need fully met. ***Average percent of need met:*** 100% (excluding resources awarded to replace EFC). ***Average financial aid package:*** $36,815 (excluding resources awarded to replace EFC). 1% of all full-time undergraduates had no need and received non-need-based gift aid.

GIFT AID (NEED-BASED) ***Total amount:*** $89,473,465 (7% federal, 89% institutional, 4% external sources). ***Receiving aid:*** Freshmen: 48% (718); all full-time undergraduates: 43% (2,643). ***Average award:*** Freshmen: $34,611; Undergraduates: $33,861. ***Scholarships, grants, and awards:*** Federal Pell, FSEOG, state, private, college/university gift aid from institutional funds.

GIFT AID (NON-NEED-BASED) ***Total amount:*** $3,915,726 (10% federal, 1% institutional, 89% external sources). ***Average award:*** Undergraduates: $11,600. ***Scholarships, grants, and awards by category:*** *Special characteristics:* 5 awards ($58,000 total): veterans, veterans' children. ***Tuition waivers:*** Full or partial for employees or children of employees.

LOANS ***Student loans:*** $12,302,213 (66% need-based, 34% non-need-based). 41% of past graduating class borrowed through all loan programs. *Average indebtedness per student:* $22,468. ***Average need-based loan:*** Freshmen: $4876. Undergraduates: $5320. ***Parent loans:*** $9,132,338 (3% need-based, 97% non-need-based). ***Programs:*** Federal Direct (Subsidized and Unsubsidized Stafford, PLUS), Perkins, college/university.

WORK-STUDY ***Federal work-study:*** Total amount: $3,372,478; 1,479 jobs averaging $2280. ***State or other work-study/employment:*** Total amount: $739,144 (100% need-based). 316 part-time jobs averaging $2339.

APPLYING FOR FINANCIAL AID ***Required financial aid forms:*** FAFSA, CSS Financial Aid PROFILE, noncustodial (divorced/separated) parent's statement. ***Financial aid deadline:*** 2/1. ***Notification date:*** 4/1. Students must reply by 5/1.

CONTACT Office of Financial Aid, Brown University, PO Box 1827, Providence, RI 02912, 401-863-2721. *Fax:* 401-863-7575. *E-mail:* financial_aid@brown.edu.

BRYAN COLLEGE

Dayton, TN

Tuition & fees: $18,740 **Average undergraduate aid package: $31,573**

ABOUT THE INSTITUTION Independent interdenominational, coed. 28 undergraduate majors. Both federal and institutional methodology are used as a basis for awarding need-based institutional aid.

UNDERGRADUATE EXPENSES for 2011–12 ***Comprehensive fee:*** $24,194 includes full-time tuition ($18,620), mandatory fees ($120), and room and board ($5454). Full-time tuition and fees vary according to course load. Room and board charges vary according to board plan and housing facility. ***Part-time tuition:*** $775 per credit. Part-time tuition and fees vary according to course load. ***Payment plan:*** Installment.

FRESHMAN FINANCIAL AID (Fall 2010, est.) 221 applied for aid; of those 87% were deemed to have need. 97% of freshmen with need received aid; of those 61% had need fully met. ***Average percent of need met:*** 98% (excluding resources awarded to replace EFC). ***Average financial aid package:*** $39,484 (excluding resources awarded to replace EFC). 12% of all full-time freshmen had no need and received non-need-based gift aid.

UNDERGRADUATE FINANCIAL AID (Fall 2010, est.) 918 applied for aid; of those 86% were deemed to have need. 99% of undergraduates with need received aid; of those 99% had need fully met. ***Average percent of need met:*** 92% (excluding resources awarded to replace EFC). ***Average financial aid package:*** $31,573 (excluding resources awarded to replace EFC). 10% of all full-time undergraduates had no need and received non-need-based gift aid.

GIFT AID (NEED-BASED) ***Total amount:*** $6,552,099 (33% federal, 24% state, 40% institutional, 3% external sources). ***Receiving aid:*** Freshmen: 77% (179); all full-time undergraduates: 67% (683). ***Average award:*** Freshmen: $24,635; Undergraduates: $18,160. ***Scholarships, grants, and awards:*** Federal Pell, FSEOG, state, private, college/university gift aid from institutional funds.

GIFT AID (NON-NEED-BASED) ***Total amount:*** $583,881 (30% state, 66% institutional, 4% external sources). ***Receiving aid:*** Freshmen: 79% (183). Undergraduates: 55% (567). ***Average award:*** Freshmen: $8751. Undergraduates: $8448. ***Scholarships, grants, and awards by category:*** *Academic interests/achievement:* biological sciences, business, communication, computer science, education, English, foreign languages, general academic interests/achievements, humanities, mathematics, physical sciences, premedicine, religion/biblical studies, social sciences. *Creative arts/performance:* journalism/publications, music, performing arts, theater/drama. *Special achievements/activities:* community service, general special achievements/activities, leadership, religious involvement. *Special characteristics:* children and siblings of alumni, children of current students, children of educators, children of faculty/staff, general special characteristics, handicapped students, international students, local/state students, members of minority groups, relatives of clergy, spouses of current students. ***Tuition waivers:*** Full or partial for employees or children of employees.

LOANS *Student loans:* $5,586,372 (92% need-based, 8% non-need-based). 74% of past graduating class borrowed through all loan programs. *Average indebtedness per student:* $15,637. ***Average need-based loan:*** Freshmen: $6629. Undergraduates: $7073. ***Parent loans:*** $798,482 (79% need-based, 21% non-need-based). ***Programs:*** Federal Direct (Subsidized and Unsubsidized Stafford, PLUS), Perkins, college/university.

WORK-STUDY *Federal work-study:* Total amount: $714,732; jobs available.

ATHLETIC AWARDS Total amount: $1,598,850 (78% need-based, 22% non-need-based).

APPLYING FOR FINANCIAL AID *Required financial aid form:* FAFSA. ***Financial aid deadline (priority):*** 2/15. ***Notification date:*** Continuous beginning 2/15.

CONTACT Rick Taphorn, Director of Financial Aid, Bryan College, PO Box 7000, Dayton, TN 37321-7000, 423-775-7339 or toll-free 800-277-9522. *Fax:* 423-775-7300. *E-mail:* finaid@bryan.edu.

BRYANT & STRATTON COLLEGE

Cleveland, OH

CONTACT Bill Davenport, Financial Aid Supervisor, Bryant & Stratton College, 1700 East 13th Street, Cleveland, OH 44114-3203, 216-771-1700. *Fax:* 216-771-7787.

BRYANT & STRATTON COLLEGE—WAUWATOSA CAMPUS

Wauwatosa, WI

CONTACT Financial Aid Office, Bryant & Stratton College—Wauwatosa Campus, 10950 W. Potter Road, Wauwatosa, WI 53226, 414-302-7000.

BRYANT UNIVERSITY

Smithfield, RI

Tuition & fees: $34,624 **Average undergraduate aid package: $21,206**

ABOUT THE INSTITUTION Independent, coed. 26 undergraduate majors. Federal methodology is used as a basis for awarding need-based institutional aid.

UNDERGRADUATE EXPENSES for 2011–12 *Comprehensive fee:* $47,453 includes full-time tuition ($34,288), mandatory fees ($336), and room and board ($12,829). ***College room only:*** $7530. Room and board charges vary according to board plan and housing facility. ***Part-time tuition:*** $1998 per course. Part-time tuition and fees vary according to course load. ***Payment plan:*** Installment.

FRESHMAN FINANCIAL AID (Fall 2010, est.) 612 applied for aid; of those 90% were deemed to have need. 100% of freshmen with need received aid; of those 50% had need fully met. ***Average percent of need met:*** 50% (excluding resources awarded to replace EFC). ***Average financial aid package:*** $20,646 (excluding resources awarded to replace EFC). 15% of all full-time freshmen had no need and received non-need-based gift aid.

UNDERGRADUATE FINANCIAL AID (Fall 2010, est.) 2,465 applied for aid; of those 89% were deemed to have need. 100% of undergraduates with need received aid; of those 50% had need fully met. ***Average percent of need met:*** 51% (excluding resources awarded to replace EFC). ***Average financial aid package:*** $21,206 (excluding resources awarded to replace EFC). 12% of all full-time undergraduates had no need and received non-need-based gift aid.

GIFT AID (NEED-BASED) *Total amount:* $23,776,254 (12% federal, 1% state, 85% institutional, 2% external sources). ***Receiving aid:*** Freshmen: 54% (448); all full-time undergraduates: 57% (1,837). ***Average award:*** Freshmen: $11,152; Undergraduates: $11,553. ***Scholarships, grants, and awards:*** Federal Pell, FSEOG, state, private, college/university gift aid from institutional funds.

GIFT AID (NON-NEED-BASED) *Total amount:* $15,114,853 (97% institutional, 3% external sources). ***Receiving aid:*** Freshmen: 30% (253). Undergraduates: 25% (809). ***Average award:*** Freshmen: $13,204. Undergraduates: $13,225. ***Scholarships, grants, and awards by category:*** *Academic interests/achievement:* 922 awards ($11,628,611 total): general academic interests/achievements. *Special characteristics:* 245 awards ($4,544,704 total): international students, members of minority groups, siblings of current students. ***Tuition waivers:*** Full or partial for employees or children of employees.

LOANS *Student loans:* $24,561,121 (38% need-based, 62% non-need-based). 65% of past graduating class borrowed through all loan programs. *Average indebtedness per student:* $39,490. ***Average need-based loan:*** Freshmen: $3612. Undergraduates: $4899. ***Parent loans:*** $9,606,863 (15% need-based, 85% non-need-based). ***Programs:*** Federal Direct (Subsidized and Unsubsidized Stafford, PLUS), Perkins, private loans.

WORK-STUDY *Federal work-study:* Total amount: $428,334; jobs available. ***State or other work-study/employment:*** Total amount: $894,685 (41% need-based, 59% non-need-based). Part-time jobs available.

ATHLETIC AWARDS Total amount: $4,249,481 (30% need-based, 70% non-need-based).

APPLYING FOR FINANCIAL AID *Required financial aid form:* FAFSA. ***Financial aid deadline (priority):*** 2/15. ***Notification date:*** 3/24. Students must reply by 5/1.

CONTACT Mr. John B. Canning, Director of Financial Aid, Bryant University, 1150 Douglas Pike, Smithfield, RI 02917-1284, 401-232-6020 or toll-free 800-622-7001. *Fax:* 401-232-6293. *E-mail:* jcanning@bryant.edu.

BRYN ATHYN COLLEGE OF THE NEW CHURCH

Bryn Athyn, PA

CONTACT Wendy Cooper, Associate Director of Financial Aid, Bryn Athyn College of the New Church, Box 717, Bryn Athyn, PA 19009, 267-502-2630. *Fax:* 267-502-4866. *E-mail:* financialaid@brynathyn.edu.

BRYN MAWR COLLEGE

Bryn Mawr, PA

Tuition & fees: $39,360 **Average undergraduate aid package: $36,789**

ABOUT THE INSTITUTION Independent, undergraduate: women only; graduate: coed. 33 undergraduate majors. Institutional methodology is used as a basis for awarding need-based institutional aid.

UNDERGRADUATE EXPENSES for 2010–11 *Comprehensive fee:* $51,780 includes full-time tuition ($38,420), mandatory fees ($940), and room and board ($12,420). ***College room only:*** $7100. ***Part-time tuition:*** $4800 per course. ***Payment plans:*** Tuition prepayment, installment.

FRESHMAN FINANCIAL AID (Fall 2010, est.) 268 applied for aid; of those 90% were deemed to have need. 100% of freshmen with need received aid; of those 100% had need fully met. ***Average percent of need met:*** 100% (excluding resources awarded to replace EFC). ***Average financial aid package:*** $35,291 (excluding resources awarded to replace EFC). 6% of all full-time freshmen had no need and received non-need-based gift aid.

UNDERGRADUATE FINANCIAL AID (Fall 2010, est.) 823 applied for aid; of those 92% were deemed to have need. 100% of undergraduates with need received aid; of those 100% had need fully met. ***Average percent of need met:*** 100% (excluding resources awarded to replace EFC). ***Average financial aid package:*** $36,789 (excluding resources awarded to replace EFC). 2% of all full-time undergraduates had no need and received non-need-based gift aid.

GIFT AID (NEED-BASED) *Total amount:* $23,900,947 (7% federal, 92% institutional, 1% external sources). ***Receiving aid:*** Freshmen: 65% (241); all full-time undergraduates: 59% (755). ***Average award:*** Freshmen: $29,807; Undergraduates: $31,543. ***Scholarships, grants, and awards:*** Federal Pell, FSEOG, state, college/university gift aid from institutional funds.

GIFT AID (NON-NEED-BASED) *Total amount:* $816,187 (1% state, 76% institutional, 23% external sources). ***Receiving aid:*** Freshmen: 3% (11). Undergraduates: 3% (34). ***Average award:*** Freshmen: $15,000. Undergraduates: $15,851.

LOANS *Student loans:* $4,719,004 (57% need-based, 43% non-need-based). 59% of past graduating class borrowed through all loan programs. *Average indebtedness per student:* $23,509. ***Average need-based loan:*** Freshmen: $4520. Undergraduates: $4546. ***Parent loans:*** $2,193,075 (100% non-need-based). ***Programs:*** Federal Direct (Subsidized and Unsubsidized Stafford, PLUS), Perkins.

WORK-STUDY ***Federal work-study:*** Total amount: $1,112,254; 567 jobs averaging $1958. ***State or other work-study/employment:*** Total amount: $275,200 (100% need-based). 135 part-time jobs averaging $2039.

APPLYING FOR FINANCIAL AID ***Required financial aid forms:*** FAFSA, CSS Financial Aid PROFILE, business/farm supplement. ***Financial aid deadline:*** 3/1. ***Notification date:*** 3/23. Students must reply by 5/1.

CONTACT Ethel M. Desmarais, Director of Financial Aid, Bryn Mawr College, 101 North Merion Avenue, Bryn Mawr, PA 19010-2899, 610-526-7922 or toll-free 800-BMC-1885 (out-of-state). *Fax:* 610-526-5249. *E-mail:* edesmara@brynmawr.edu.

BUCKNELL UNIVERSITY

Lewisburg, PA

Tuition & fees: $43,866 **Average undergraduate aid package: $25,600**

ABOUT THE INSTITUTION Independent, coed. 60 undergraduate majors. Both federal and institutional methodology are used as a basis for awarding need-based institutional aid.

UNDERGRADUATE EXPENSES for 2011–12 ***Comprehensive fee:*** $54,240 includes full-time tuition ($43,628), mandatory fees ($238), and room and board ($10,374). ***College room only:*** $6048. Room and board charges vary according to board plan and housing facility. ***Payment plans:*** Tuition prepayment, installment.

FRESHMAN FINANCIAL AID (Fall 2010, est.) 541 applied for aid; of those 78% were deemed to have need. 100% of freshmen with need received aid; of those 95% had need fully met. ***Average percent of need met:*** 95% (excluding resources awarded to replace EFC). ***Average financial aid package:*** $27,000 (excluding resources awarded to replace EFC). 5% of all full-time freshmen had no need and received non-need-based gift aid.

UNDERGRADUATE FINANCIAL AID (Fall 2010, est.) 1,857 applied for aid; of those 86% were deemed to have need. 100% of undergraduates with need received aid; of those 95% had need fully met. ***Average percent of need met:*** 95% (excluding resources awarded to replace EFC). ***Average financial aid package:*** $25,600 (excluding resources awarded to replace EFC). 4% of all full-time undergraduates had no need and received non-need-based gift aid.

GIFT AID (NEED-BASED) ***Total amount:*** $44,113,017 (5% federal, 1% state, 91% institutional, 3% external sources). ***Receiving aid:*** Freshmen: 45% (421); all full-time undergraduates: 43% (1,503). ***Average award:*** Freshmen: $23,500; Undergraduates: $22,300. ***Scholarships, grants, and awards:*** Federal Pell, FSEOG, state, private, college/university gift aid from institutional funds, Academic Competitiveness Grants, National SMART Grants.

GIFT AID (NON-NEED-BASED) ***Total amount:*** $2,234,686 (100% institutional). ***Receiving aid:*** Freshmen: 6% (52). Undergraduates: 6% (195). ***Average award:*** Freshmen: $9323. Undergraduates: $11,641. ***Scholarships, grants, and awards by category:*** *Academic interests/achievement:* 68 awards ($792,500 total): business, engineering/technologies, general academic interests/achievements, mathematics, physical sciences. *Creative arts/performance:* 124 awards ($741,000 total): art/fine arts, creative writing, dance, music, performing arts, theater/drama. *Special achievements/activities:* 91 awards ($3,839,119 total): general special achievements/activities, leadership. ***Tuition waivers:*** Full or partial for employees or children of employees.

LOANS ***Student loans:*** $10,779,203 (100% need-based). 61% of past graduating class borrowed through all loan programs. *Average indebtedness per student:* $18,900. ***Average need-based loan:*** Freshmen: $4400. Undergraduates: $5400. ***Parent loans:*** $8,002,037 (100% non-need-based). ***Programs:*** Federal Direct (Subsidized and Unsubsidized Stafford, PLUS), Perkins.

WORK-STUDY ***Federal work-study:*** Total amount: $700,000; 700 jobs averaging $1500. ***State or other work-study/employment:*** Total amount: $50,000 (100% need-based). 50 part-time jobs averaging $1500.

ATHLETIC AWARDS Total amount: $563,080 (100% non-need-based).

APPLYING FOR FINANCIAL AID ***Required financial aid forms:*** FAFSA, CSS Financial Aid PROFILE, noncustodial (divorced/separated) parent's statement. ***Financial aid deadline:*** 1/15. ***Notification date:*** 4/1. Students must reply by 5/1.

CONTACT Andrea Leithner Stauffer, Director of Financial Aid, Bucknell University, Bucknell University, 621 St. George Street, Lewisburg, PA 17837, 570-577-1331. *Fax:* 570-577-1481. *E-mail:* finaid@bucknell.edu.

BUENA VISTA UNIVERSITY

Storm Lake, IA

Tuition & fees: $26,306 **Average undergraduate aid package: $25,343**

ABOUT THE INSTITUTION Independent religious, coed. 60 undergraduate majors. Federal methodology is used as a basis for awarding need-based institutional aid.

UNDERGRADUATE EXPENSES for 2010–11 ***Comprehensive fee:*** $33,888 includes full-time tuition ($26,306) and room and board ($7582). Full-time tuition and fees vary according to location. Room and board charges vary according to board plan. ***Part-time tuition:*** $884 per credit hour. Part-time tuition and fees vary according to location. ***Payment plans:*** Guaranteed tuition, installment.

FRESHMAN FINANCIAL AID (Fall 2010, est.) 250 applied for aid; of those 94% were deemed to have need. 100% of freshmen with need received aid; of those 46% had need fully met. ***Average percent of need met:*** 37% (excluding resources awarded to replace EFC). ***Average financial aid package:*** $26,518 (excluding resources awarded to replace EFC). 9% of all full-time freshmen had no need and received non-need-based gift aid.

UNDERGRADUATE FINANCIAL AID (Fall 2010, est.) 871 applied for aid; of those 95% were deemed to have need. 100% of undergraduates with need received aid; of those 46% had need fully met. ***Average percent of need met:*** 43% (excluding resources awarded to replace EFC). ***Average financial aid package:*** $25,343 (excluding resources awarded to replace EFC). 7% of all full-time undergraduates had no need and received non-need-based gift aid.

GIFT AID (NEED-BASED) ***Total amount:*** $5,487,822 (45% federal, 33% state, 22% institutional). ***Receiving aid:*** Freshmen: 65% (172); all full-time undergraduates: 69% (655). ***Average award:*** Freshmen: $7817; Undergraduates: $8230. ***Scholarships, grants, and awards:*** Federal Pell, FSEOG, state, private, college/university gift aid from institutional funds.

GIFT AID (NON-NEED-BASED) ***Total amount:*** $11,876,940 (97% institutional, 3% external sources). ***Receiving aid:*** Freshmen: 87% (230). Undergraduates: 86% (818). ***Average award:*** Freshmen: $17,858. Undergraduates: $14,341. ***Scholarships, grants, and awards by category:*** *Academic interests/achievement:* biological sciences, business, computer science, education, general academic interests/achievements, humanities, international studies, mathematics. *Creative arts/performance:* art/fine arts, music, theater/drama. *Special achievements/activities:* general special achievements/activities, leadership. *Special characteristics:* children of faculty/staff, ethnic background, international students, out-of-state students, religious affiliation, siblings of current students. ***Tuition waivers:*** Full or partial for employees or children of employees.

LOANS ***Student loans:*** $6,562,989 (55% need-based, 45% non-need-based). 96% of past graduating class borrowed through all loan programs. *Average indebtedness per student:* $37,502. ***Average need-based loan:*** Freshmen: $4462. Undergraduates: $4939. ***Parent loans:*** $1,012,072 (100% non-need-based). ***Programs:*** Federal Direct (Subsidized and Unsubsidized Stafford, PLUS), Perkins, college/university.

WORK-STUDY ***Federal work-study:*** Total amount: $538,350; jobs available. ***State or other work-study/employment:*** Total amount: $137,600 (100% non-need-based). Part-time jobs available.

APPLYING FOR FINANCIAL AID ***Required financial aid form:*** FAFSA. ***Financial aid deadline (priority):*** 6/1. ***Notification date:*** Continuous beginning 2/1.

CONTACT Mrs. Leanne Valentine, Director of Financial Assistance, Buena Vista University, 610 West Fourth Street, Storm Lake, IA 50588, 712-749-2164 or toll-free 800-383-9600. *Fax:* 712-749-1451. *E-mail:* valentinel@bvu.edu.

BUFFALO STATE COLLEGE, STATE UNIVERSITY OF NEW YORK

Buffalo, NY

Tuition & fees (NY res): $6053 **Average undergraduate aid package: $12,248**

ABOUT THE INSTITUTION State-supported, coed. 79 undergraduate majors. Federal methodology is used as a basis for awarding need-based institutional aid.

UNDERGRADUATE EXPENSES for 2010–11 ***Tuition, state resident:*** full-time $4970; part-time $207 per credit hour. ***Tuition, nonresident:*** full-time $13,380; part-time $558 per credit hour. ***Required fees:*** full-time $1083; $45.15 per credit hour. Part-time tuition and fees vary according to course load. ***College***

room and board: $9748; ***Room only:*** $5770. Room and board charges vary according to board plan, housing facility, and student level. ***Payment plan:*** Installment.

FRESHMAN FINANCIAL AID (Fall 2009) 1,334 applied for aid; of those 100% were deemed to have need. 100% of freshmen with need received aid; of those 57% had need fully met. ***Average percent of need met:*** 69% (excluding resources awarded to replace EFC). ***Average financial aid package:*** $11,430 (excluding resources awarded to replace EFC). 10% of all full-time freshmen had no need and received non-need-based gift aid.

UNDERGRADUATE FINANCIAL AID (Fall 2009) 7,805 applied for aid; of those 100% were deemed to have need. 100% of undergraduates with need received aid; of those 57% had need fully met. ***Average percent of need met:*** 67% (excluding resources awarded to replace EFC). ***Average financial aid package:*** $12,248 (excluding resources awarded to replace EFC). 4% of all full-time undergraduates had no need and received non-need-based gift aid.

GIFT AID (NEED-BASED) ***Total amount:*** $33,294,116 (57% federal, 43% state). ***Receiving aid:*** Freshmen: 70% (1,015); all full-time undergraduates: 71% (6,238). ***Average award:*** Freshmen: $6604; Undergraduates: $5760. ***Scholarships, grants, and awards:*** Federal Pell, FSEOG, state.

GIFT AID (NON-NEED-BASED) ***Total amount:*** $4,455,374 (34% federal, 1% state, 35% institutional, 30% external sources). ***Receiving aid:*** Freshmen: 9% (133). Undergraduates: 4% (381). ***Average award:*** Freshmen: $2578. Undergraduates: $2074. ***Scholarships, grants, and awards by category:*** *Academic interests/achievement:* general academic interests/achievements. *Creative arts/performance:* general creative arts/performance. *Special achievements/activities:* general special achievements/activities. ***Tuition waivers:*** Full or partial for employees or children of employees.

LOANS ***Student loans:*** $59,559,363 (49% need-based, 51% non-need-based). *Average indebtedness per student:* $22,565. ***Average need-based loan:*** Freshmen: $3646. Undergraduates: $4592. ***Parent loans:*** $2,118,422 (2% need-based, 98% non-need-based). ***Programs:*** Perkins.

WORK-STUDY ***Federal work-study:*** Total amount: $1,452,035; jobs available. ***State or other work-study/employment:*** Part-time jobs available.

APPLYING FOR FINANCIAL AID ***Required financial aid form:*** FAFSA. ***Financial aid deadline:*** 5/1 (priority: 3/15). ***Notification date:*** Continuous beginning 5/1.

CONTACT Connie F. Cooke, Director of Financial Aid, Buffalo State College, State University of New York, 1300 Elmwood Avenue, Buffalo, NY 14222-1095, 716-878-4902. *Fax:* 716-878-4903. *E-mail:* finaid@buffalostate.edu.

BURLINGTON COLLEGE

Burlington, VT

Tuition & fees: $21,465 **Average undergraduate aid package: $12,710**

ABOUT THE INSTITUTION Independent, coed. 15 undergraduate majors. Federal methodology is used as a basis for awarding need-based institutional aid.

UNDERGRADUATE EXPENSES for 2010–11 ***Tuition:*** full-time $21,340; part-time $705 per credit hour. Full-time tuition and fees vary according to course load, program, and reciprocity agreements. Part-time tuition and fees vary according to course load, program, and reciprocity agreements. Room and board charges vary according to housing facility. Resident students should expect to spend $2,700 per year for meals as the college does not offer a dining service. ***Payment plan:*** Installment.

FRESHMAN FINANCIAL AID (Fall 2010, est.) 26 applied for aid; of those 96% were deemed to have need. 100% of freshmen with need received aid. ***Average percent of need met:*** 49% (excluding resources awarded to replace EFC). ***Average financial aid package:*** $13,756 (excluding resources awarded to replace EFC). 7% of all full-time freshmen had no need and received non-need-based gift aid.

UNDERGRADUATE FINANCIAL AID (Fall 2010, est.) 115 applied for aid; of those 95% were deemed to have need. 99% of undergraduates with need received aid; of those 3% had need fully met. ***Average percent of need met:*** 46% (excluding resources awarded to replace EFC). ***Average financial aid package:*** $12,710 (excluding resources awarded to replace EFC). 2% of all full-time undergraduates had no need and received non-need-based gift aid.

GIFT AID (NEED-BASED) ***Total amount:*** $893,602 (45% federal, 25% state, 25% institutional, 5% external sources). ***Receiving aid:*** Freshmen: 73% (22); all full-time undergraduates: 67% (95). ***Average award:*** Freshmen: $9127; Undergraduates: $8011. ***Scholarships, grants, and awards:*** Federal Pell, FSEOG, state, private, college/university gift aid from institutional funds.

GIFT AID (NON-NEED-BASED) ***Total amount:*** $8000 (69% institutional, 31% external sources). ***Receiving aid:*** Freshmen: 27% (8). Undergraduates: 6% (8). ***Average award:*** Freshmen: $2500. Undergraduates: $1833. ***Scholarships, grants, and awards by category:*** *Special achievements/activities:* community service, general special achievements/activities, leadership. ***Tuition waivers:*** Full or partial for employees or children of employees.

LOANS ***Student loans:*** $1,199,143 (89% need-based, 11% non-need-based). 42% of past graduating class borrowed through all loan programs. *Average indebtedness per student:* $21,670. ***Average need-based loan:*** Freshmen: $5154. Undergraduates: $5255. ***Parent loans:*** $473,029 (58% need-based, 42% non-need-based). ***Programs:*** Federal Direct (Subsidized and Unsubsidized Stafford, PLUS), Perkins, college/university.

WORK-STUDY ***Federal work-study:*** Total amount: $66,998; jobs available.

APPLYING FOR FINANCIAL AID ***Required financial aid form:*** FAFSA. ***Financial aid deadline:*** Continuous. ***Notification date:*** Continuous beginning 2/15. Students must reply within 4 weeks of notification.

CONTACT Ms. Lindy Walsh, Director of Financial Aid, Burlington College, 95 North Avenue, Burlington, VT 05401, 802-862-9616 or toll-free 800-862-9616. *Fax:* 802-846-3072. *E-mail:* lwalsh@burlington.edu.

BUTLER UNIVERSITY

Indianapolis, IN

Tuition & fees: $30,558 **Average undergraduate aid package: $21,971**

ABOUT THE INSTITUTION Independent, coed. 55 undergraduate majors. Federal methodology is used as a basis for awarding need-based institutional aid.

UNDERGRADUATE EXPENSES for 2010–11 ***Comprehensive fee:*** $40,688 includes full-time tuition ($29,740), mandatory fees ($818), and room and board ($10,130). ***College room only:*** $4960. Full-time tuition and fees vary according to course load, degree level, and program. Room and board charges vary according to housing facility. ***Part-time tuition:*** $1250 per credit hour. Part-time tuition and fees vary according to course load, degree level, and program. ***Payment plan:*** Installment.

FRESHMAN FINANCIAL AID (Fall 2010, est.) 986 applied for aid; of those 75% were deemed to have need. 100% of freshmen with need received aid; of those 12% had need fully met. ***Average percent of need met:*** 78% (excluding resources awarded to replace EFC). ***Average financial aid package:*** $23,432 (excluding resources awarded to replace EFC). 20% of all full-time freshmen had no need and received non-need-based gift aid.

UNDERGRADUATE FINANCIAL AID (Fall 2010, est.) 3,696 applied for aid; of those 75% were deemed to have need. 100% of undergraduates with need received aid; of those 13% had need fully met. ***Average percent of need met:*** 74% (excluding resources awarded to replace EFC). ***Average financial aid package:*** $21,971 (excluding resources awarded to replace EFC). 21% of all full-time undergraduates had no need and received non-need-based gift aid.

GIFT AID (NEED-BASED) ***Total amount:*** $43,382,812 (8% federal, 6% state, 76% institutional, 10% external sources). ***Receiving aid:*** Freshmen: 70% (735); all full-time undergraduates: 65% (2,638). ***Average award:*** Freshmen: $18,270; Undergraduates: $16,943. ***Scholarships, grants, and awards:*** Federal Pell, FSEOG, state, private, college/university gift aid from institutional funds.

GIFT AID (NON-NEED-BASED) ***Total amount:*** $11,546,949 (81% institutional, 19% external sources). ***Receiving aid:*** Freshmen: 9% (98). Undergraduates: 8% (339). ***Average award:*** Freshmen: $10,864. Undergraduates: $11,452. ***Scholarships, grants, and awards by category:*** *Academic interests/achievement:* biological sciences, business, communication, computer science, education, engineering/technologies, English, foreign languages, general academic interests/achievements, humanities, international studies, mathematics, physical sciences, social sciences. *Creative arts/performance:* art/fine arts, cinema/film/broadcasting, dance, music, theater/drama. ***Tuition waivers:*** Full or partial for employees or children of employees.

LOANS ***Student loans:*** $30,055,964 (73% need-based, 27% non-need-based). 67% of past graduating class borrowed through all loan programs. *Average indebtedness per student:* $30,581. ***Average need-based loan:*** Freshmen: $4751. Undergraduates: $5411. ***Parent loans:*** $5,616,717 (28% need-based, 72% non-need-based). ***Programs:*** Federal Direct (Subsidized and Unsubsidized Stafford, PLUS), Perkins.

WORK-STUDY ***Federal work-study:*** Total amount: $518,000; 331 jobs averaging $759. ***State or other work-study/employment:*** Part-time jobs available.

ATHLETIC AWARDS Total amount: $3,799,299 (37% need-based, 63% non-need-based).

APPLYING FOR FINANCIAL AID ***Required financial aid form:*** FAFSA. ***Financial aid deadline (priority):*** 3/1. ***Notification date:*** 3/15. Students must reply within 3 weeks of notification.

CONTACT Ms. Kristine Butz, Associate Director of Financial Aid, Butler University, 4600 Sunset Avenue, Indianapolis, IN 46208-3485, 317-940-8200 or toll-free 888-940-8100. *Fax:* 317-940-8250. *E-mail:* kbutz@butler.edu.

CABARRUS COLLEGE OF HEALTH SCIENCES

Concord, NC

CONTACT Valerie Richard, Director of Financial Aid, Cabarrus College of Health Sciences, 401 Medical Park Drive, Concord, NC 28025, 704-403-3507. *Fax:* 704-403-2077. *E-mail:* valerie.richard@carolinashealthcare.org.

CABRINI COLLEGE

Radnor, PA

Tuition & fees: $32,084 **Average undergraduate aid package: $22,385**

ABOUT THE INSTITUTION Independent Roman Catholic, coed. 35 undergraduate majors. Federal methodology is used as a basis for awarding need-based institutional aid.

UNDERGRADUATE EXPENSES for 2010–11 ***Comprehensive fee:*** $43,484 includes full-time tuition ($31,174), mandatory fees ($910), and room and board ($11,400). Room and board charges vary according to board plan and housing facility. ***Part-time tuition:*** $475 per credit hour. ***Part-time fees:*** $45 per term. Part-time tuition and fees vary according to course load. ***Payment plan:*** Installment.

FRESHMAN FINANCIAL AID (Fall 2010, est.) 306 applied for aid; of those 94% were deemed to have need. 100% of freshmen with need received aid; of those 11% had need fully met. ***Average percent of need met:*** 70% (excluding resources awarded to replace EFC). ***Average financial aid package:*** $24,533 (excluding resources awarded to replace EFC). 15% of all full-time freshmen had no need and received non-need-based gift aid.

UNDERGRADUATE FINANCIAL AID (Fall 2010, est.) 1,078 applied for aid; of those 93% were deemed to have need. 100% of undergraduates with need received aid; of those 12% had need fully met. ***Average percent of need met:*** 66% (excluding resources awarded to replace EFC). ***Average financial aid package:*** $22,385 (excluding resources awarded to replace EFC). 20% of all full-time undergraduates had no need and received non-need-based gift aid.

GIFT AID (NEED-BASED) ***Total amount:*** $17,716,597 (10% federal, 5% state, 83% institutional, 2% external sources). ***Receiving aid:*** Freshmen: 70% (236); all full-time undergraduates: 61% (793). ***Average award:*** Freshmen: $10,739; Undergraduates: $9106. ***Scholarships, grants, and awards:*** Federal Pell, FSEOG, state, private, college/university gift aid from institutional funds.

GIFT AID (NON-NEED-BASED) ***Total amount:*** $3,520,244 (97% institutional, 3% external sources). ***Receiving aid:*** Freshmen: 83% (280). Undergraduates: 72% (949). ***Average award:*** Freshmen: $11,759. Undergraduates: $11,494. ***Scholarships, grants, and awards by category:*** *Academic interests/achievement:* 1,215 awards ($13,527,492 total): general academic interests/achievements. *Special characteristics:* 65 awards ($67,750 total): children and siblings of alumni, siblings of current students. ***Tuition waivers:*** Full or partial for children of alumni, employees or children of employees, senior citizens.

LOANS ***Student loans:*** $10,899,516 (71% need-based, 29% non-need-based). 78% of past graduating class borrowed through all loan programs. *Average indebtedness per student:* $30,637. ***Average need-based loan:*** Freshmen: $3613. Undergraduates: $4467. ***Parent loans:*** $3,379,735 (44% need-based, 56% non-need-based). ***Programs:*** Federal Direct (Subsidized and Unsubsidized Stafford, PLUS), Perkins.

WORK-STUDY ***Federal work-study:*** Total amount: $214,186; 166 jobs averaging $1047.

APPLYING FOR FINANCIAL AID ***Required financial aid form:*** FAFSA. ***Financial aid deadline:*** Continuous. ***Notification date:*** Continuous beginning 3/1.

CONTACT Mike Colahan, Director of Financial Aid, Cabrini College, 610 King of Prussia Road, Grace Hall, First Floor, Radnor, PA 19087-3698, 610-902-8420 or toll-free 800-848-1003. *Fax:* 610-902-8426.

CALDWELL COLLEGE

Caldwell, NJ

Tuition & fees: $25,602 **Average undergraduate aid package: $19,198**

ABOUT THE INSTITUTION Independent Roman Catholic, coed. 23 undergraduate majors. Both federal and institutional methodology are used as a basis for awarding need-based institutional aid.

UNDERGRADUATE EXPENSES for 2010–11 ***Comprehensive fee:*** $34,592 includes full-time tuition ($24,752), mandatory fees ($850), and room and board ($8990). ***College room only:*** $4935. Room and board charges vary according to board plan and housing facility. Part-time tuition and fees vary according to course load. ***Payment plan:*** Installment.

FRESHMAN FINANCIAL AID (Fall 2010, est.) 257 applied for aid; of those 89% were deemed to have need. 100% of freshmen with need received aid; of those 19% had need fully met. ***Average percent of need met:*** 77% (excluding resources awarded to replace EFC). ***Average financial aid package:*** $20,863 (excluding resources awarded to replace EFC). 14% of all full-time freshmen had no need and received non-need-based gift aid.

UNDERGRADUATE FINANCIAL AID (Fall 2010, est.) 994 applied for aid; of those 91% were deemed to have need. 100% of undergraduates with need received aid; of those 14% had need fully met. ***Average percent of need met:*** 74% (excluding resources awarded to replace EFC). ***Average financial aid package:*** $19,198 (excluding resources awarded to replace EFC). 18% of all full-time undergraduates had no need and received non-need-based gift aid.

GIFT AID (NEED-BASED) ***Total amount:*** $8,804,956 (29% federal, 40% state, 31% institutional). ***Receiving aid:*** Freshmen: 81% (228); all full-time undergraduates: 75% (882). ***Average award:*** Freshmen: $17,992; Undergraduates: $15,719. ***Scholarships, grants, and awards:*** Federal Pell, FSEOG, state, private, college/university gift aid from institutional funds.

GIFT AID (NON-NEED-BASED) ***Total amount:*** $7,813,651 (99% institutional, 1% external sources). ***Receiving aid:*** Freshmen: 12% (35). Undergraduates: 9% (102). ***Average award:*** Freshmen: $13,864. Undergraduates: $12,641. ***Scholarships, grants, and awards by category:*** *Academic interests/achievement:* 597 awards ($6,989,126 total): biological sciences, general academic interests/achievements, health fields. *Creative arts/performance:* 30 awards ($63,400 total): art/fine arts, music. *Special achievements/activities:* 242 awards ($530,002 total): community service, general special achievements/activities, religious involvement. *Special characteristics:* 40 awards ($115,591 total): children of current students, general special characteristics, parents of current students, public servants, relatives of clergy, religious affiliation, siblings of current students, veterans. ***Tuition waivers:*** Full or partial for children of alumni, employees or children of employees, senior citizens.

LOANS ***Student loans:*** $6,915,193 (42% need-based, 58% non-need-based). 85% of past graduating class borrowed through all loan programs. *Average indebtedness per student:* $18,369. ***Average need-based loan:*** Freshmen: $3356. Undergraduates: $4238. ***Parent loans:*** $2,445,636 (100% non-need-based). ***Programs:*** Federal Direct (Subsidized and Unsubsidized Stafford, PLUS), state.

WORK-STUDY ***Federal work-study:*** Total amount: $116,262; 119 jobs averaging $977. ***State or other work-study/employment:*** Total amount: $517,210 (100% non-need-based). 230 part-time jobs averaging $2250.

ATHLETIC AWARDS Total amount: $829,400 (100% non-need-based).

APPLYING FOR FINANCIAL AID ***Required financial aid forms:*** FAFSA, state aid form. ***Financial aid deadline:*** Continuous. ***Notification date:*** Continuous beginning 2/15. Students must reply within 4 weeks of notification.

CONTACT Mr. Vincent Zelizo, Financial Aid Counselor, Caldwell College, 120 Bloomfield Avenue, Caldwell, NJ 07006, 973-618-3261. *Fax:* 973-618-3650. *E-mail:* financialaid@caldwell.edu.

CALIFORNIA BAPTIST UNIVERSITY

Riverside, CA

ABOUT THE INSTITUTION Independent Southern Baptist, coed. 56 undergraduate majors.

GIFT AID (NEED-BASED) ***Scholarships, grants, and awards:*** Federal Pell, FSEOG, state, private, college/university gift aid from institutional funds.

GIFT AID (NON-NEED-BASED) ***Scholarships, grants, and awards by category:*** *Academic interests/achievement:* general academic interests/achievements, religion/biblical studies. *Creative arts/performance:* art/fine arts, music, theater/drama. *Special achievements/activities:* cheerleading/drum major. *Special* *characteristics:* adult students, children and siblings of alumni, children of faculty/staff, international students, relatives of clergy, siblings of current students, veterans.

LOANS ***Programs:*** Perkins, alternative loans.

WORK-STUDY ***Federal work-study:*** Total amount: $142,195; 178 jobs averaging $888.

APPLYING FOR FINANCIAL AID ***Required financial aid forms:*** FAFSA, state aid form.

CONTACT Ms. Rebecca Sanchez, Financial Aid Director, California Baptist University, 8432 Magnolia Avenue, Riverside, CA 92504-3297, 951-343-4236 or toll-free 877-228-8866. *Fax:* 951-343-4518. *E-mail:* rsanchez@calbaptist.edu.

CALIFORNIA CHRISTIAN COLLEGE

Fresno, CA

Tuition & fees: $7610 **Average undergraduate aid package: $11,676**

ABOUT THE INSTITUTION Independent religious, coed. 1 undergraduate major. Federal methodology is used as a basis for awarding need-based institutional aid.

UNDERGRADUATE EXPENSES for 2011–12 ***Comprehensive fee:*** $11,760 includes full-time tuition ($7080), mandatory fees ($530), and room and board ($4150). ***Payment plan:*** Installment.

FRESHMAN FINANCIAL AID (Fall 2009) 6 applied for aid; of those 83% were deemed to have need. 100% of freshmen with need received aid. ***Average percent of need met:*** 63% (excluding resources awarded to replace EFC). ***Average financial aid package:*** $10,450 (excluding resources awarded to replace EFC).

UNDERGRADUATE FINANCIAL AID (Fall 2009) 25 applied for aid; of those 92% were deemed to have need. 100% of undergraduates with need received aid; of those 4% had need fully met. ***Average percent of need met:*** 67% (excluding resources awarded to replace EFC). ***Average financial aid package:*** $11,676 (excluding resources awarded to replace EFC).

GIFT AID (NEED-BASED) ***Total amount:*** $133,244 (67% federal, 33% state). ***Receiving aid:*** Freshmen: 62% (5); all full-time undergraduates: 65% (17). ***Average award:*** Freshmen: $5350; Undergraduates: $2625. ***Scholarships, grants, and awards:*** Federal Pell, FSEOG, state, private, college/university gift aid from institutional funds.

GIFT AID (NON-NEED-BASED) ***Receiving aid:*** Undergraduates: 4% (1).

LOANS ***Student loans:*** $153,184 (90% need-based, 10% non-need-based). 66% of past graduating class borrowed through all loan programs. *Average indebtedness per student:* $26,237. ***Average need-based loan:*** Freshmen: $3625. Undergraduates: $4138. ***Parent loans:*** $8219 (100% need-based). ***Programs:*** Federal Direct (Subsidized and Unsubsidized Stafford, PLUS).

WORK-STUDY ***Federal work-study:*** Total amount: $7314; 4 jobs averaging $1829.

APPLYING FOR FINANCIAL AID ***Required financial aid forms:*** FAFSA, institution's own form, GPA verification form (for CA residents). ***Financial aid deadline (priority):*** 3/2. ***Notification date:*** 8/15.

CONTACT Mindy Scroggins, Financial Aid Coordinator, California Christian College, 4881 East University Avenue, Fresno, CA 93703, 559-251-4215 Ext. 5580. *Fax:* 559-251-4231. *E-mail:* cccfindir@sbcglobal.net.

CALIFORNIA COAST UNIVERSITY

Santa Ana, CA

CONTACT Financial Aid Office, California Coast University, 925 North Spurgeon Street, Santa Ana, CA 92701, 714-547-9625 or toll-free 888-CCU-UNIV (out-of-state).

CALIFORNIA COLLEGE

San Diego, CA

CONTACT Financial Aid Office, California College, 2820 Camino del Rio South, Suite 300, San Diego, CA 92108, 619-295-5785 or toll-free 800-622-3188 (out-of-state).

CALIFORNIA COLLEGE OF THE ARTS

San Francisco, CA

Tuition & fees: $35,222 **Average undergraduate aid package: $22,923**

ABOUT THE INSTITUTION Independent, coed. 22 undergraduate majors. Federal methodology is used as a basis for awarding need-based institutional aid.

UNDERGRADUATE EXPENSES for 2011–12 ***Tuition:*** full-time $34,872; part-time $1453 per unit. Full-time tuition and fees vary according to degree level. Part-time tuition and fees vary according to course load and degree level. Room and board charges vary according to housing facility. ***Payment plan:*** Installment.

FRESHMAN FINANCIAL AID (Fall 2010, est.) 168 applied for aid; of those 92% were deemed to have need. 100% of freshmen with need received aid; of those 6% had need fully met. ***Average percent of need met:*** 62% (excluding resources awarded to replace EFC). ***Average financial aid package:*** $22,810 (excluding resources awarded to replace EFC). 19% of all full-time freshmen had no need and received non-need-based gift aid.

UNDERGRADUATE FINANCIAL AID (Fall 2010, est.) 943 applied for aid; of those 94% were deemed to have need. 100% of undergraduates with need received aid; of those 4% had need fully met. ***Average percent of need met:*** 56% (excluding resources awarded to replace EFC). ***Average financial aid package:*** $22,923 (excluding resources awarded to replace EFC). 13% of all full-time undergraduates had no need and received non-need-based gift aid.

GIFT AID (NEED-BASED) ***Total amount:*** $15,925,737 (17% federal, 9% state, 73% institutional, 1% external sources). ***Receiving aid:*** Freshmen: 62% (143); all full-time undergraduates: 65% (841). ***Average award:*** Freshmen: $19,788; Undergraduates: $18,202. ***Scholarships, grants, and awards:*** Federal Pell, FSEOG, state, private, college/university gift aid from institutional funds.

GIFT AID (NON-NEED-BASED) ***Total amount:*** $1,556,935 (98% institutional, 2% external sources). ***Receiving aid:*** Freshmen: 53% (122). Undergraduates: 35% (453). ***Average award:*** Freshmen: $9151. Undergraduates: $7905. ***Scholarships, grants, and awards by category:*** *Academic interests/achievement:* general academic interests/achievements. ***Tuition waivers:*** Full or partial for employees or children of employees.

LOANS ***Student loans:*** $8,637,847 (93% need-based, 7% non-need-based). 75% of past graduating class borrowed through all loan programs. *Average indebtedness per student:* $24,677. ***Average need-based loan:*** Freshmen: $3537. Undergraduates: $4772. ***Parent loans:*** $2,901,425 (60% need-based, 40% non-need-based). ***Programs:*** Federal Direct (Subsidized and Unsubsidized Stafford, PLUS), Perkins, private loans.

WORK-STUDY ***Federal work-study:*** Total amount: $448,267; 845 jobs averaging $2926. ***State or other work-study/employment:*** Total amount: $275,000 (100% non-need-based). 71 part-time jobs averaging $3238.

APPLYING FOR FINANCIAL AID ***Required financial aid form:*** FAFSA. ***Financial aid deadline (priority):*** 3/1. ***Notification date:*** Continuous beginning 4/1. Students must reply by 5/1 or within 3 weeks of notification.

CONTACT Financial Aid Office, California College of the Arts, 1111 Eighth Street, San Francisco, CA 94107, 415-703-9528 or toll-free 800-447-1ART. *Fax:* 415-551-9261. *E-mail:* finaid@cca.edu.

CALIFORNIA INSTITUTE OF INTEGRAL STUDIES

San Francisco, CA

Tuition & fees: $15,060 **Average undergraduate aid package: $11,500**

ABOUT THE INSTITUTION Independent, coed. 1 undergraduate major. Federal methodology is used as a basis for awarding need-based institutional aid.

UNDERGRADUATE EXPENSES for 2010–11 ***Tuition:*** full-time $14,760; part-time $620 per unit.

UNDERGRADUATE FINANCIAL AID (Fall 2010, est.) 74 applied for aid; of those 81% were deemed to have need. 100% of undergraduates with need received aid. ***Average percent of need met:*** 20% (excluding resources awarded to replace EFC). ***Average financial aid package:*** $11,500 (excluding resources awarded to replace EFC).

GIFT AID (NEED-BASED) ***Total amount:*** $345,000 (63% federal, 9% state, 25% institutional, 3% external sources). ***Receiving aid:*** All full-time undergraduates:

81% (60). ***Average award:*** Undergraduates: $4000. ***Scholarships, grants, and awards:*** Federal Pell, FSEOG, state, private, college/university gift aid from institutional funds.

GIFT AID (NON-NEED-BASED) ***Total amount:*** $10,000 (100% institutional). ***Receiving aid:*** Undergraduates: 27% (20). ***Scholarships, grants, and awards by category:*** *Academic interests/achievement:* general academic interests/achievements, humanities, social sciences. *Special achievements/activities:* community service, general special achievements/activities, leadership.

LOANS ***Student loans:*** $455,000 (47% need-based, 53% non-need-based). 100% of past graduating class borrowed through all loan programs. *Average indebtedness per student:* $29,000. ***Average need-based loan:*** Undergraduates: $5000. ***Parent loans:*** $10,000 (100% non-need-based). ***Programs:*** Federal Direct (Subsidized and Unsubsidized Stafford, PLUS), college/university.

WORK-STUDY ***Federal work-study:*** Total amount: $24,000; 3 jobs averaging $6000.

APPLYING FOR FINANCIAL AID ***Required financial aid form:*** FAFSA. ***Financial aid deadline (priority):*** 4/15. ***Notification date:*** Students must reply within 4 weeks of notification.

CONTACT Financial Aid Office, California Institute of Integral Studies, 1453 Mission Street, San Francisco, CA 94103, 415-575-6122. *Fax:* 415-575-1268. *E-mail:* finaid@ciis.edu.

CALIFORNIA INSTITUTE OF TECHNOLOGY

Pasadena, CA

Tuition & fees: $37,704 **Average undergraduate aid package: $34,928**

ABOUT THE INSTITUTION Independent, coed. 25 undergraduate majors. Federal methodology is used as a basis for awarding need-based institutional aid.

UNDERGRADUATE EXPENSES for 2011–12 ***One-time required fee:*** $500. ***Comprehensive fee:*** $49,380 includes full-time tuition ($36,387), mandatory fees ($1317), and room and board ($11,676). ***College room only:*** $6570. ***Payment plans:*** Installment, deferred payment.

FRESHMAN FINANCIAL AID (Fall 2010, est.) 181 applied for aid; of those 65% were deemed to have need. 100% of freshmen with need received aid; of those 100% had need fully met. ***Average percent of need met:*** 100% (excluding resources awarded to replace EFC). ***Average financial aid package:*** $33,494 (excluding resources awarded to replace EFC).

UNDERGRADUATE FINANCIAL AID (Fall 2010, est.) 602 applied for aid; of those 85% were deemed to have need. 100% of undergraduates with need received aid; of those 100% had need fully met. ***Average percent of need met:*** 100% (excluding resources awarded to replace EFC). ***Average financial aid package:*** $34,928 (excluding resources awarded to replace EFC). 2% of all full-time undergraduates had no need and received non-need-based gift aid.

GIFT AID (NEED-BASED) ***Total amount:*** $15,664,151 (5% federal, 2% state, 91% institutional, 2% external sources). ***Receiving aid:*** Freshmen: 53% (118); all full-time undergraduates: 53% (513). ***Average award:*** Freshmen: $31,302; Undergraduates: $31,030. ***Scholarships, grants, and awards:*** Federal Pell, FSEOG, state, private, college/university gift aid from institutional funds.

GIFT AID (NON-NEED-BASED) ***Total amount:*** $1,392,339 (1% state, 68% institutional, 31% external sources). ***Receiving aid:*** Undergraduates: 3% (28). ***Average award:*** Undergraduates: $40,888. ***Scholarships, grants, and awards by category:*** *Academic interests/achievement:* 23 awards ($940,424 total): general academic interests/achievements. ***Tuition waivers:*** Full or partial for employees or children of employees.

LOANS ***Student loans:*** $1,275,063 (85% need-based, 15% non-need-based). 43% of past graduating class borrowed through all loan programs. *Average indebtedness per student:* $10,760. ***Average need-based loan:*** Freshmen: $3131. Undergraduates: $3442. ***Parent loans:*** $466,821 (10% need-based, 90% non-need-based). ***Programs:*** Federal Direct (Subsidized and Unsubsidized Stafford, PLUS), Perkins, college/university.

WORK-STUDY ***Federal work-study:*** Total amount: $883,114; 325 jobs averaging $2763. ***State or other work-study/employment:*** Total amount: $190,150 (93% need-based, 7% non-need-based). 76 part-time jobs averaging $2502.

APPLYING FOR FINANCIAL AID ***Required financial aid forms:*** FAFSA, CSS Financial Aid PROFILE, state aid form, noncustodial (divorced/separated) parent's statement, business/farm supplement. ***Financial aid deadline (priority):*** 2/1. ***Notification date:*** Continuous beginning 3/20. Students must reply by 5/1 or within 2 weeks of notification.

CONTACT Don Crewell, Director of Financial Aid, California Institute of Technology, 1200 East California Boulevard, MC 110-87, Pasadena, CA 91125-8700, 626-395-6280. *Fax:* 626-564-8136. *E-mail:* dcrewell@caltech.edu.

CALIFORNIA INSTITUTE OF THE ARTS

Valencia, CA

Tuition & fees: $38,260 **Average undergraduate aid package: $30,448**

ABOUT THE INSTITUTION Independent, coed. 10 undergraduate majors. Federal methodology is used as a basis for awarding need-based institutional aid.

UNDERGRADUATE EXPENSES for 2011–12 ***Comprehensive fee:*** $47,886 includes full-time tuition ($37,684), mandatory fees ($576), and room and board ($9626). ***College room only:*** $5450. Room and board charges vary according to board plan, housing facility, and location. Part-time tuition and fees vary according to course load. ***Payment plan:*** Installment.

FRESHMAN FINANCIAL AID (Fall 2010, est.) 128 applied for aid; of those 89% were deemed to have need. 97% of freshmen with need received aid; of those 5% had need fully met. ***Average percent of need met:*** 75% (excluding resources awarded to replace EFC). ***Average financial aid package:*** $30,584 (excluding resources awarded to replace EFC). 8% of all full-time freshmen had no need and received non-need-based gift aid.

UNDERGRADUATE FINANCIAL AID (Fall 2010, est.) 734 applied for aid; of those 89% were deemed to have need. 98% of undergraduates with need received aid; of those 6% had need fully met. ***Average percent of need met:*** 74% (excluding resources awarded to replace EFC). ***Average financial aid package:*** $30,448 (excluding resources awarded to replace EFC). 7% of all full-time undergraduates had no need and received non-need-based gift aid.

GIFT AID (NEED-BASED) ***Total amount:*** $10,032,624 (19% federal, 10% state, 69% institutional, 2% external sources). ***Receiving aid:*** Freshmen: 70% (105); all full-time undergraduates: 69% (610). ***Average award:*** Freshmen: $16,642; Undergraduates: $16,573. ***Scholarships, grants, and awards:*** Federal Pell, FSEOG, state, private, college/university gift aid from institutional funds.

GIFT AID (NON-NEED-BASED) ***Total amount:*** $415,530 (92% institutional, 8% external sources). ***Average award:*** Freshmen: $6654. Undergraduates: $7043. ***Scholarships, grants, and awards by category:*** *Creative arts/performance:* 58 awards ($381,580 total): applied art and design, art/fine arts, cinema/film/broadcasting, creative writing, dance, music, performing arts, theater/drama. ***Tuition waivers:*** Full or partial for employees or children of employees.

LOANS ***Student loans:*** $7,394,938 (95% need-based, 5% non-need-based). 61% of past graduating class borrowed through all loan programs. *Average indebtedness per student:* $50,017. ***Average need-based loan:*** Freshmen: $7672. Undergraduates: $9445. ***Parent loans:*** $2,507,694 (78% need-based, 22% non-need-based). ***Programs:*** Federal Direct (Subsidized and Unsubsidized Stafford, PLUS), Perkins, college/university, private loans.

WORK-STUDY ***Federal work-study:*** Total amount: $593,517; 236 jobs averaging $2515. ***State or other work-study/employment:*** Total amount: $6000 (100% need-based). 4 part-time jobs averaging $1500.

APPLYING FOR FINANCIAL AID ***Required financial aid form:*** FAFSA. ***Financial aid deadline (priority):*** 3/2. ***Notification date:*** Continuous beginning 4/1. Students must reply by 5/1 or within 3 weeks of notification.

CONTACT Ms. Bobbi Heuer, Director of Financial Aid, California Institute of the Arts, 24700 McBean Parkway, Valencia, CA 91355-2340, 661-253-7869 or toll-free 800-545-2787. *Fax:* 661-287-3816. *E-mail:* bheuer@calarts.edu.

CALIFORNIA INTERCONTINENTAL UNIVERSITY

Diamond Bar, CA

CONTACT Financial Aid Office, California Intercontinental University, 1470 Valley Vista Drive, Suite 150, Diamond Bar, CA 91765, 909-396-6090 or toll-free 866-687-2258.

CALIFORNIA LUTHERAN UNIVERSITY

Thousand Oaks, CA

Tuition & fees: $31,000 **Average undergraduate aid package: $22,580**

ABOUT THE INSTITUTION Independent Lutheran, coed. 55 undergraduate majors. Both federal and institutional methodology are used as a basis for awarding need-based institutional aid.

UNDERGRADUATE EXPENSES for 2010–11 ***Comprehensive fee:*** $41,580 includes full-time tuition ($30,750), mandatory fees ($250), and room and board ($10,580). ***College room only:*** $5690. Room and board charges vary according to board plan. ***Part-time tuition:*** $990 per unit. ***Part-time fees:*** $250 per year. ***Payment plan:*** Installment.

FRESHMAN FINANCIAL AID (Fall 2010, est.) 494 applied for aid; of those 83% were deemed to have need. 100% of freshmen with need received aid; of those 20% had need fully met. ***Average percent of need met:*** 74% (excluding resources awarded to replace EFC). ***Average financial aid package:*** $23,625 (excluding resources awarded to replace EFC). 26% of all full-time freshmen had no need and received non-need-based gift aid.

UNDERGRADUATE FINANCIAL AID (Fall 2010, est.) 1,809 applied for aid; of those 88% were deemed to have need. 100% of undergraduates with need received aid; of those 17% had need fully met. ***Average percent of need met:*** 70% (excluding resources awarded to replace EFC). ***Average financial aid package:*** $22,580 (excluding resources awarded to replace EFC). 32% of all full-time undergraduates had no need and received non-need-based gift aid.

GIFT AID (NEED-BASED) ***Total amount:*** $28,552,789 (11% federal, 14% state, 73% institutional, 2% external sources). ***Receiving aid:*** Freshmen: 74% (411); all full-time undergraduates: 67% (1,559). ***Average award:*** Freshmen: $19,400; Undergraduates: $18,150. ***Scholarships, grants, and awards:*** Federal Pell, FSEOG, state, private, college/university gift aid from institutional funds.

GIFT AID (NON-NEED-BASED) ***Total amount:*** $6,776,661 (99% institutional, 1% external sources). ***Receiving aid:*** Freshmen: 8% (47). Undergraduates: 5% (127). ***Average award:*** Freshmen: $12,020. Undergraduates: $11,400. ***Scholarships, grants, and awards by category:*** *Academic interests/achievement:* 1,732 awards ($19,254,800 total): biological sciences, business, communication, computer science, education, English, foreign languages, general academic interests/achievements, humanities, international studies, mathematics, physical sciences, religion/biblical studies, social sciences. *Creative arts/performance:* 120 awards ($393,460 total): art/fine arts, creative writing, journalism/publications, music, performing arts, theater/drama. *Special achievements/activities:* 363 awards ($393,460 total): community service, general special achievements/activities, leadership, religious involvement. *Special characteristics:* 266 awards ($1,078,980 total): adult students, children and siblings of alumni, children of faculty/staff, international students, relatives of clergy, religious affiliation, veterans, veterans' children. ***Tuition waivers:*** Full or partial for employees or children of employees.

LOANS ***Student loans:*** $13,828,097 (91% need-based, 9% non-need-based). 68% of past graduating class borrowed through all loan programs. *Average indebtedness per student:* $23,900. ***Average need-based loan:*** Freshmen: $3450. Undergraduates: $4430. ***Parent loans:*** $8,276,979 (84% need-based, 16% non-need-based). ***Programs:*** Federal Direct (Subsidized and Unsubsidized Stafford, PLUS), Perkins.

WORK-STUDY ***Federal work-study:*** Total amount: $454,555; 189 jobs averaging $2500. ***State or other work-study/employment:*** Total amount: $1,047,867 (100% need-based). 440 part-time jobs averaging $2500.

APPLYING FOR FINANCIAL AID ***Required financial aid forms:*** FAFSA, GPA Verification Form for Cal Grants (CA residents only). ***Financial aid deadline (priority):*** 3/1. ***Notification date:*** Continuous beginning 3/15. Students must reply by 5/1 or within 2 weeks of notification.

CONTACT Rebecca Kennan, Associate Director of Financial Aid and Scholarships, California Lutheran University, 60 West Olsen Road, Thousand Oaks, CA 91360-2787, 805-493-3115 or toll-free 877-258-3678. *Fax:* 805-493-3114. *E-mail:* rkeenan@callutheran.edu.

CALIFORNIA MARITIME ACADEMY

Vallejo, CA

ABOUT THE INSTITUTION State-supported, coed. 4 undergraduate majors.

GIFT AID (NEED-BASED) ***Scholarships, grants, and awards:*** Federal Pell, FSEOG, state, private, college/university gift aid from institutional funds.

GIFT AID (NON-NEED-BASED) ***Scholarships, grants, and awards by category:*** *Academic interests/achievement:* general academic interests/achievements. *Special achievements/activities:* community service, leadership. *Special characteristics:* first-generation college students, general special characteristics, local/state students, out-of-state students.

LOANS ***Programs:*** Perkins.

WORK-STUDY ***Federal work-study:*** Total amount: $57,724; jobs available.

APPLYING FOR FINANCIAL AID ***Required financial aid form:*** FAFSA.

CONTACT Ken Walsh, Director of Financial Aid, California Maritime Academy, 200 Maritime Academy Drive, Vallejo, CA 94590-0644, 707-654-1275 or toll-free 800-561-1945. *Fax:* 707-654-1007. *E-mail:* finaid@csum.edu.

CALIFORNIA MIRAMAR UNIVERSITY

San Diego, CA

CONTACT Financial Aid Office, California Miramar University, 9750 Miramar Road, Suite 180, San Diego, CA 92126, 858-653-3000 or toll-free 877-570-5678 (out-of-state).

CALIFORNIA NATIONAL UNIVERSITY FOR ADVANCED STUDIES

Northridge, CA

CONTACT Office of Academic Affairs, California National University for Advanced Studies, 16909 Parthenia Street, North Hills, CA 91343, 800-782-2422 or toll-free 800-744-2822 (in-state).

CALIFORNIA POLYTECHNIC STATE UNIVERSITY, SAN LUIS OBISPO

San Luis Obispo, CA

Tuition & fees (CA res): $6480 **Average undergraduate aid package: $9396**

ABOUT THE INSTITUTION State-supported, coed. 65 undergraduate majors. Federal methodology is used as a basis for awarding need-based institutional aid.

UNDERGRADUATE EXPENSES for 2010–11 ***Tuition, state resident:*** full-time $0. ***Tuition, nonresident:*** full-time $11,160; part-time $248 per unit. ***Required fees:*** full-time $6480; $1432 per term. Full-time tuition and fees vary according to course load, degree level, and program. Part-time tuition and fees vary according to course load, degree level, and program. ***College room and board:*** $9992; ***Room only:*** $5653. Room and board charges vary according to board plan and housing facility. ***Payment plan:*** Installment.

FRESHMAN FINANCIAL AID (Fall 2009) 2,912 applied for aid; of those 51% were deemed to have need. 86% of freshmen with need received aid; of those 7% had need fully met. ***Average percent of need met:*** 60% (excluding resources awarded to replace EFC). ***Average financial aid package:*** $9113 (excluding resources awarded to replace EFC). 4% of all full-time freshmen had no need and received non-need-based gift aid.

UNDERGRADUATE FINANCIAL AID (Fall 2009) 9,764 applied for aid; of those 68% were deemed to have need. 91% of undergraduates with need received aid; of those 7% had need fully met. ***Average percent of need met:*** 59% (excluding resources awarded to replace EFC). ***Average financial aid package:*** $9396 (excluding resources awarded to replace EFC). 3% of all full-time undergraduates had no need and received non-need-based gift aid.

GIFT AID (NEED-BASED) ***Total amount:*** $36,340,005 (42% federal, 44% state, 8% institutional, 6% external sources). ***Receiving aid:*** Freshmen: 24% (948); all full-time undergraduates: 25% (4,383). ***Average award:*** Freshmen: $2394; Undergraduates: $2824. ***Scholarships, grants, and awards:*** Federal Pell, FSEOG, state, private, college/university gift aid from institutional funds, TEACH Grants.

GIFT AID (NON-NEED-BASED) ***Total amount:*** $3,351,525 (44% institutional, 56% external sources). ***Receiving aid:*** Freshmen: 1% (37). Undergraduates: 1% (89). ***Average award:*** Freshmen: $1785. Undergraduates: $2126. ***Scholarships, grants, and awards by category:*** *Academic interests/achievement:* agriculture, architecture, biological sciences, business, communication, computer science, education, engineering/technologies, English, foreign languages, general academic interests/achievements, health fields, home economics, humanities, international studies, library science, mathematics, military science, physical sciences, social sciences. *Creative arts/performance:* applied art and design, art/fine arts, cinema/film/broadcasting, creative writing, dance, debating, general creative arts/performance, journalism/publications, music, performing arts, theater/drama. *Special achievements/activities:* community service, leadership, rodeo. *Special characteristics:* children and siblings of alumni, general special characteristics, local/state students. ***Tuition waivers:*** Full or partial for employees or children of employees.

LOANS ***Student loans:*** $39,470,897 (64% need-based, 36% non-need-based). ***Average need-based loan:*** Freshmen: $2947. Undergraduates: $3593. ***Parent loans:*** $22,259,579 (23% need-based, 77% non-need-based). ***Programs:*** Federal Direct (Subsidized and Unsubsidized Stafford, PLUS), Perkins, college/university, alternative loans.

WORK-STUDY ***Federal work-study:*** Total amount: $695,693; jobs available.

ATHLETIC AWARDS Total amount: $3,229,278 (32% need-based, 68% non-need-based).

APPLYING FOR FINANCIAL AID ***Required financial aid form:*** FAFSA. ***Financial aid deadline (priority):*** 3/2. ***Notification date:*** Continuous beginning 4/1.

CONTACT Lois Kelly, Director of Financial Aid, California Polytechnic State University, San Luis Obispo, Administration Building, Room 212, San Luis Obispo, CA 93407, 805-756-5893. *Fax:* 805-756-7243. *E-mail:* lkelly@calpoly.edu.

CALIFORNIA STATE POLYTECHNIC UNIVERSITY, POMONA

Pomona, CA

Tuition & fees (CA res): $4806 Average undergraduate aid package: $11,309

ABOUT THE INSTITUTION State-supported, coed. 53 undergraduate majors. Federal methodology is used as a basis for awarding need-based institutional aid.

UNDERGRADUATE EXPENSES for 2011–12 ***Tuition, state resident:*** full-time $0. ***Tuition, nonresident:*** full-time $11,160; part-time $248 per unit. ***Required fees:*** full-time $4806; $3301 per year. Full-time tuition and fees vary according to degree level and program. Part-time tuition and fees vary according to course load, degree level, and program. ***College room and board:*** $10,011; ***Room only:*** $6327. Room and board charges vary according to board plan and housing facility. ***Payment plans:*** Installment, deferred payment.

FRESHMAN FINANCIAL AID (Fall 2010, est.) 1,586 applied for aid; of those 76% were deemed to have need. 96% of freshmen with need received aid; of those 9% had need fully met. ***Average percent of need met:*** 77% (excluding resources awarded to replace EFC). ***Average financial aid package:*** $10,280 (excluding resources awarded to replace EFC). 1% of all full-time freshmen had no need and received non-need-based gift aid.

UNDERGRADUATE FINANCIAL AID (Fall 2010, est.) 11,142 applied for aid; of those 87% were deemed to have need. 97% of undergraduates with need received aid; of those 16% had need fully met. ***Average percent of need met:*** 72% (excluding resources awarded to replace EFC). ***Average financial aid package:*** $11,309 (excluding resources awarded to replace EFC). 1% of all full-time undergraduates had no need and received non-need-based gift aid.

GIFT AID (NEED-BASED) ***Total amount:*** $78,692,265 (51% federal, 49% state). ***Receiving aid:*** Freshmen: 50% (965); all full-time undergraduates: 49% (7,751). ***Average award:*** Freshmen: $9029; Undergraduates: $8982. ***Scholarships, grants, and awards:*** Federal Pell, FSEOG, state, private, college/university gift aid from institutional funds.

GIFT AID (NON-NEED-BASED) ***Total amount:*** $1,704,653 (10% state, 18% institutional, 72% external sources). ***Receiving aid:*** Freshmen: 7% (138). Undergraduates: 4% (559). ***Average award:*** Freshmen: $4918. Undergraduates: $3516. ***Scholarships, grants, and awards by category:*** *Academic interests/achievement:* agriculture, architecture, biological sciences, business, computer science, education, engineering/technologies, general academic interests/achievements, humanities, mathematics, physical sciences, social sciences. *Special achievements/activities:* hobbies/interests, leadership. *Special characteristics:* children and siblings of alumni, children of current students, members of minority groups. ***Tuition waivers:*** Full or partial for employees or children of employees.

LOANS ***Student loans:*** $78,074,790 (53% need-based, 47% non-need-based). 35% of past graduating class borrowed through all loan programs. *Average indebtedness per student:* $16,736. ***Average need-based loan:*** Freshmen: $3048. Undergraduates: $4058. ***Parent loans:*** $1,622,976 (100% non-need-based). ***Programs:*** Perkins, college/university, alternative loans.

WORK-STUDY ***Federal work-study:*** Total amount: $592,148; 231 jobs averaging $2564.

ATHLETIC AWARDS Total amount: $499,438 (100% non-need-based).

APPLYING FOR FINANCIAL AID ***Required financial aid form:*** FAFSA. ***Financial aid deadline:*** Continuous. ***Notification date:*** Continuous beginning 4/1. Students must reply within 6 weeks of notification.

CONTACT Diana Minor, Director of Financial Aid and Scholarships, California State Polytechnic University, Pomona, 3801 West Temple Avenue, Pomona, CA 91768-2557, 909-869-3704. *Fax:* 909-869-4757. *E-mail:* dyminor@csupomona.edu.

CALIFORNIA STATE UNIVERSITY, BAKERSFIELD

Bakersfield, CA

Tuition & fees (CA res): $5314 Average undergraduate aid package: $3890

ABOUT THE INSTITUTION State-supported, coed. 30 undergraduate majors. Federal methodology is used as a basis for awarding need-based institutional aid.

UNDERGRADUATE EXPENSES for 2010–11 ***Tuition, state resident:*** full-time $0. ***Tuition, nonresident:*** full-time $11,160; part-time $248 per unit. ***Required fees:*** full-time $5314; $3538 per year. Full-time tuition and fees vary according to course load, degree level, and reciprocity agreements. Part-time tuition and fees vary according to course load, degree level, and reciprocity agreements. ***College room and board:*** $7041; ***Room only:*** $3500. Room and board charges vary according to board plan. ***Payment plan:*** Installment.

FRESHMAN FINANCIAL AID (Fall 2010, est.) 878 applied for aid; of those 76% were deemed to have need. 99% of freshmen with need received aid; of those 2% had need fully met. ***Average percent of need met:*** 2% (excluding resources awarded to replace EFC). ***Average financial aid package:*** $3720 (excluding resources awarded to replace EFC).

UNDERGRADUATE FINANCIAL AID (Fall 2010, est.) 4,366 applied for aid; of those 79% were deemed to have need. 99% of undergraduates with need received aid; of those 3% had need fully met. ***Average percent of need met:*** 3% (excluding resources awarded to replace EFC). ***Average financial aid package:*** $3890 (excluding resources awarded to replace EFC).

GIFT AID (NEED-BASED) ***Total amount:*** $35,066,320 (51% federal, 46% state, 1% institutional, 2% external sources). ***Receiving aid:*** Freshmen: 69% (661); all full-time undergraduates: 71% (3,418). ***Average award:*** Freshmen: $3238; Undergraduates: $3099. ***Scholarships, grants, and awards:*** Federal Pell, FSEOG, state, private, college/university gift aid from institutional funds, Federal Nursing.

GIFT AID (NON-NEED-BASED) ***Receiving aid:*** Freshmen: 6% (60). Undergraduates: 5% (239). ***Scholarships, grants, and awards by category:*** *Academic interests/achievement:* agriculture, architecture, biological sciences, business, communication, education, foreign languages, general academic interests/achievements, health fields, humanities, mathematics, physical sciences, premedicine, religion/biblical studies, social sciences. *Creative arts/performance:* art/fine arts, dance, music, theater/drama. *Special achievements/activities:* community service, general special achievements/activities. *Special characteristics:* children of faculty/staff, children of union members/company employees, ethnic background, first-generation college students, veterans. ***Tuition waivers:*** Full or partial for employees or children of employees, senior citizens.

LOANS ***Student loans:*** $38,736,045 (100% need-based). 72% of past graduating class borrowed through all loan programs. *Average indebtedness per student:* $6730. ***Average need-based loan:*** Freshmen: $1148. Undergraduates: $1480. ***Parent loans:*** $326,343 (100% need-based). ***Programs:*** Federal Direct (Subsidized and Unsubsidized Stafford, PLUS), Perkins, Federal Nursing, college/university.

WORK-STUDY ***Federal work-study:*** Total amount: $293,490; jobs available.

ATHLETIC AWARDS Total amount: $1,658,839 (100% need-based).

APPLYING FOR FINANCIAL AID ***Required financial aid forms:*** FAFSA, state aid form. ***Financial aid deadline:*** Continuous. ***Notification date:*** Continuous beginning 5/1. Students must reply within 3 weeks of notification.

CONTACT Mr. Ron Radney, Interim Director of Financial Aid, California State University, Bakersfield, 9001 Stockdale Highway, Bakersfield, CA 93311-1099, 661-654-3271 or toll-free 800-788-2782 (in-state). *Fax:* 661-654-6800. *E-mail:* rradney@csub.edu.

CALIFORNIA STATE UNIVERSITY CHANNEL ISLANDS

Camarillo, CA

CONTACT Financial Aid Office, California State University Channel Islands, One University Drive, Camarillo, CA 93012, 805-437-8400.

CALIFORNIA STATE UNIVERSITY, CHICO

Chico, CA

Tuition & fees (CA res): $5620 **Average undergraduate aid package: $11,706**

ABOUT THE INSTITUTION State-supported, coed. 114 undergraduate majors. Federal methodology is used as a basis for awarding need-based institutional aid.

UNDERGRADUATE EXPENSES for 2011–12 ***Tuition, state resident:*** full-time $0. ***Tuition, nonresident:*** full-time $11,160; part-time $372 per unit. ***Required fees:*** full-time $5620; $1922 per term. Full-time tuition and fees vary according to degree level. Part-time tuition and fees vary according to course load and degree level. ***College room and board:*** $11,138; ***Room only:*** $6746. Room and board charges vary according to board plan and housing facility. ***Payment plans:*** Installment, deferred payment.

FRESHMAN FINANCIAL AID (Fall 2009) 1,398 applied for aid; of those 85% were deemed to have need. 93% of freshmen with need received aid; of those 15% had need fully met. ***Average percent of need met:*** 89% (excluding resources awarded to replace EFC). ***Average financial aid package:*** $13,033 (excluding resources awarded to replace EFC). 4% of all full-time freshmen had no need and received non-need-based gift aid.

UNDERGRADUATE FINANCIAL AID (Fall 2009) 8,947 applied for aid; of those 81% were deemed to have need. 96% of undergraduates with need received aid; of those 16% had need fully met. ***Average percent of need met:*** 89% (excluding resources awarded to replace EFC). ***Average financial aid package:*** $11,706 (excluding resources awarded to replace EFC). 4% of all full-time undergraduates had no need and received non-need-based gift aid.

GIFT AID (NEED-BASED) ***Total amount:*** $45,742,911 (52% federal, 48% state). ***Receiving aid:*** Freshmen: 31% (778); all full-time undergraduates: 37% (5,343). ***Average award:*** Freshmen: $10,043; Undergraduates: $8982. ***Scholarships, grants, and awards:*** Federal Pell, FSEOG, state, private, college/university gift aid from institutional funds, United Negro College Fund.

GIFT AID (NON-NEED-BASED) ***Total amount:*** $1,587,432 (1% federal, 2% state, 8% institutional, 89% external sources). ***Receiving aid:*** Freshmen: 12% (301). Undergraduates: 8% (1,161). ***Average award:*** Freshmen: $1467. Undergraduates: $1978. ***Scholarships, grants, and awards by category:*** *Academic interests/achievement:* agriculture, area/ethnic studies, biological sciences, business, communication, computer science, education, engineering/technologies, English, foreign languages, general academic interests/achievements, health fields, humanities, international studies, mathematics, physical sciences, social sciences. *Creative arts/performance:* applied art and design, art/fine arts, cinema/film/broadcasting, creative writing, dance, debating, general creative arts/performance, journalism/publications, music, performing arts, theater/drama. *Special achievements/activities:* community service, general special achievements/activities, hobbies/interests, leadership, memberships. *Special characteristics:* adult students, children of faculty/staff, ethnic background, first-generation college students, handicapped students, international students, local/state students, married students, members of minority groups, out-of-state students. ***Tuition waivers:*** Full or partial for employees or children of employees, senior citizens.

LOANS ***Student loans:*** $34,888,115 (64% need-based, 36% non-need-based). ***Average need-based loan:*** Freshmen: $3420. Undergraduates: $4475. ***Parent loans:*** $3,963,091 (100% non-need-based). ***Programs:*** Federal Direct (Subsidized and Unsubsidized Stafford, PLUS), Perkins, college/university.

WORK-STUDY ***Federal work-study:*** Total amount: $8,283,295; jobs available.

ATHLETIC AWARDS Total amount: $635,736 (65% need-based, 35% non-need-based).

APPLYING FOR FINANCIAL AID ***Required financial aid forms:*** FAFSA, institution's own form. ***Financial aid deadline:*** Continuous. ***Notification date:*** Continuous beginning 3/2.

CONTACT Dan Reed, Director of Financial Aid and Scholarships, California State University, Chico, 400 West First Street, Student Services Center, Room 250, Chico, CA 95929-0705, 530-898-6451 or toll-free 800-542-4426. *Fax:* 530-898-6883. *E-mail:* finaid@csuchico.edu.

CALIFORNIA STATE UNIVERSITY, DOMINGUEZ HILLS

Carson, CA

Tuition & fees (CA res): $4849 **Average undergraduate aid package: $5457**

ABOUT THE INSTITUTION State-supported, coed. 67 undergraduate majors. Federal methodology is used as a basis for awarding need-based institutional aid.

UNDERGRADUATE EXPENSES for 2010–11 ***Tuition, state resident:*** full-time $0. ***Tuition, nonresident:*** full-time $11,160; part-time $372 per unit. ***Required fees:*** full-time $4849; $1539 per term. ***College room and board:*** $10,085; ***Room only:*** $5693. Room and board charges vary according to housing facility. ***Payment plan:*** Installment.

FRESHMAN FINANCIAL AID (Fall 2009) 984 applied for aid; of those 92% were deemed to have need. 96% of freshmen with need received aid; of those 1% had need fully met. ***Average percent of need met:*** 34% (excluding resources awarded to replace EFC). ***Average financial aid package:*** $4705 (excluding resources awarded to replace EFC). 4% of all full-time freshmen had no need and received non-need-based gift aid.

UNDERGRADUATE FINANCIAL AID (Fall 2009) 4,684 applied for aid; of those 95% were deemed to have need. 96% of undergraduates with need received aid; of those 2% had need fully met. ***Average percent of need met:*** 34% (excluding resources awarded to replace EFC). ***Average financial aid package:*** $5457 (excluding resources awarded to replace EFC). 2% of all full-time undergraduates had no need and received non-need-based gift aid.

GIFT AID (NEED-BASED) ***Total amount:*** $22,339,397 (49% federal, 49% state, 1% institutional, 1% external sources). ***Receiving aid:*** Freshmen: 69% (741); all full-time undergraduates: 52% (3,494). ***Average award:*** Freshmen: $4454; Undergraduates: $4310. ***Scholarships, grants, and awards:*** Federal Pell, FSEOG, state, private, college/university gift aid from institutional funds.

GIFT AID (NON-NEED-BASED) ***Total amount:*** $25,338 (8% state, 82% institutional, 10% external sources). ***Receiving aid:*** Freshmen: 12% (126). Undergraduates: 14% (953). ***Average award:*** Freshmen: $2629. Undergraduates: $3165. ***Tuition waivers:*** Full or partial for employees or children of employees, senior citizens.

LOANS ***Student loans:*** $10,916,378 (92% need-based, 8% non-need-based). 54% of past graduating class borrowed through all loan programs. *Average indebtedness per student:* $12,786. ***Average need-based loan:*** Freshmen: $1637. Undergraduates: $2401. ***Parent loans:*** $70,221 (34% need-based, 66% non-need-based). ***Programs:*** Federal Direct (Subsidized and Unsubsidized Stafford, PLUS), Perkins, college/university.

WORK-STUDY ***Federal work-study:*** Total amount: $362,804; 189 jobs averaging $1920.

ATHLETIC AWARDS Total amount: $205,695 (92% need-based, 8% non-need-based).

APPLYING FOR FINANCIAL AID ***Required financial aid form:*** FAFSA. ***Financial aid deadline (priority):*** 3/2. ***Notification date:*** Continuous beginning 3/15. Students must reply within 2 weeks of notification.

CONTACT Mrs. Delores S. Lee, Director of Financial Aid, California State University, Dominguez Hills, 1000 East Victoria Street, Carson, CA 90747-0001, 310-243-3189. *Fax:* 310-516-4498. *E-mail:* dslee@csudh.edu.

CALIFORNIA STATE UNIVERSITY, EAST BAY

Hayward, CA

Tuition & fees (CA res): $4872 **Average undergraduate aid package: $10,823**

ABOUT THE INSTITUTION State-supported, coed. 90 undergraduate majors. Federal methodology is used as a basis for awarding need-based institutional aid.

UNDERGRADUATE EXPENSES for 2010–11 ***Tuition, state resident:*** full-time $0. ***Tuition, nonresident:*** full-time $13,800. ***Required fees:*** full-time $4872. ***College room and board:*** $10,029. ***Payment plan:*** Installment.

FRESHMAN FINANCIAL AID (Fall 2010, est.) 777 applied for aid; of those 93% were deemed to have need. 98% of freshmen with need received aid; of those

2% had need fully met. ***Average percent of need met:*** 61% (excluding resources awarded to replace EFC). ***Average financial aid package:*** $11,240 (excluding resources awarded to replace EFC).

UNDERGRADUATE FINANCIAL AID (Fall 2010, est.) 4,842 applied for aid; of those 97% were deemed to have need. 98% of undergraduates with need received aid; of those 1% had need fully met. ***Average percent of need met:*** 55% (excluding resources awarded to replace EFC). ***Average financial aid package:*** $10,823 (excluding resources awarded to replace EFC).

GIFT AID (NEED-BASED) ***Total amount:*** $38,269,187 (52% federal, 44% state, 2% institutional, 2% external sources). ***Receiving aid:*** Freshmen: 50% (604); all full-time undergraduates: 45% (3,879). ***Average award:*** Freshmen: $10,151; Undergraduates: $9027. ***Scholarships, grants, and awards:*** Federal Pell, FSEOG, state, private, college/university gift aid from institutional funds.

GIFT AID (NON-NEED-BASED) ***Scholarships, grants, and awards by category:*** *Academic interests/achievement:* general academic interests/achievements. *Creative arts/performance:* music. ***Tuition waivers:*** Full or partial for employees or children of employees, senior citizens.

LOANS ***Student loans:*** $24,934,193 (88% need-based, 12% non-need-based). 40% of past graduating class borrowed through all loan programs. *Average indebtedness per student:* $15,958. ***Average need-based loan:*** Freshmen: $5138. Undergraduates: $7097. ***Parent loans:*** $3,287,999 (38% need-based, 62% non-need-based). ***Programs:*** Federal Direct (Subsidized and Unsubsidized Stafford, PLUS), Perkins, college/university.

WORK-STUDY ***Federal work-study:*** Total amount: $1,436,593; 699 jobs averaging $2400.

APPLYING FOR FINANCIAL AID ***Required financial aid form:*** FAFSA. ***Financial aid deadline (priority):*** 3/2. ***Notification date:*** Continuous beginning 3/31. Students must reply within 4 weeks of notification.

CONTACT Office of Financial Aid, California State University, East Bay, 25800 Carlos Bee Boulevard, Hayward, CA 94542-3028, 510-885-2784. *Fax:* 510-885-2161. *E-mail:* finaid@csueastbay.edu.

CALIFORNIA STATE UNIVERSITY, FRESNO

Fresno, CA

Tuition & fees (CA res): $4230 **Average undergraduate aid package: $11,251**

ABOUT THE INSTITUTION State-supported, coed. 87 undergraduate majors. Federal methodology is used as a basis for awarding need-based institutional aid.

UNDERGRADUATE EXPENSES for 2010–11 ***Tuition, state resident:*** full-time $0. ***Tuition, nonresident:*** full-time $11,160. ***Required fees:*** full-time $4230. ***College room and board:*** $10,200. Room and board charges vary according to board plan. ***Payment plan:*** Installment.

FRESHMAN FINANCIAL AID (Fall 2010, est.) 2,173 applied for aid; of those 87% were deemed to have need. 97% of freshmen with need received aid; of those 12% had need fully met. ***Average percent of need met:*** 70% (excluding resources awarded to replace EFC). ***Average financial aid package:*** $10,329 (excluding resources awarded to replace EFC). 2% of all full-time freshmen had no need and received non-need-based gift aid.

UNDERGRADUATE FINANCIAL AID (Fall 2010, est.) 11,721 applied for aid; of those 92% were deemed to have need. 97% of undergraduates with need received aid; of those 13% had need fully met. ***Average percent of need met:*** 71% (excluding resources awarded to replace EFC). ***Average financial aid package:*** $11,251 (excluding resources awarded to replace EFC). 1% of all full-time undergraduates had no need and received non-need-based gift aid.

GIFT AID (NEED-BASED) ***Total amount:*** $89,509,654 (52% federal, 48% state). ***Receiving aid:*** Freshmen: 60% (1,559); all full-time undergraduates: 56% (8,762). ***Average award:*** Freshmen: $9541; Undergraduates: $9380. ***Scholarships, grants, and awards:*** Federal Pell, FSEOG, state, private, college/university gift aid from institutional funds.

GIFT AID (NON-NEED-BASED) ***Total amount:*** $4,846,615 (54% institutional, 46% external sources). ***Receiving aid:*** Freshmen: 12% (311). Undergraduates: 7% (1,063). ***Average award:*** Freshmen: $2417. Undergraduates: $2843. ***Scholarships, grants, and awards by category:*** *Academic interests/achievement:* 1,013 awards ($2,470,802 total): agriculture, area/ethnic studies, biological sciences, business, communication, education, engineering/technologies, English, foreign languages, general academic interests/achievements, health fields, humanities, mathematics, physical sciences, social sciences. *Creative arts/performance:* 229 awards ($189,082 total): art/fine arts, journalism/publications, music, theater/drama. *Special achievements/activities:* 27 awards ($38,250 total): community service, leadership. *Special characteristics:* 2 awards ($1699 total): handicapped students, local/state students.

LOANS ***Student loans:*** $53,888,586 (44% need-based, 56% non-need-based). 60% of past graduating class borrowed through all loan programs. *Average indebtedness per student:* $12,670. ***Average need-based loan:*** Freshmen: $2979. Undergraduates: $4058. ***Parent loans:*** $1,930,211 (100% non-need-based). ***Programs:*** Perkins, Federal Nursing, college/university, alternative loans.

WORK-STUDY ***Federal work-study:*** Total amount: $976,773; 320 jobs averaging $3197.

ATHLETIC AWARDS Total amount: $1,944,354 (100% non-need-based).

APPLYING FOR FINANCIAL AID ***Required financial aid form:*** FAFSA. ***Financial aid deadline (priority):*** 3/2. ***Notification date:*** Continuous beginning 4/1. Students must reply within 3 weeks of notification.

CONTACT Maria Hernandez, Director of Financial Aid, California State University, Fresno, 5150 North Maple Avenue, Fresno, CA 93740, 559-278-2182. *Fax:* 559-278-4833. *E-mail:* mariah@csufresno.edu.

CALIFORNIA STATE UNIVERSITY, FULLERTON

Fullerton, CA

Tuition & fees (CA res): $4971 **Average undergraduate aid package: $10,023**

ABOUT THE INSTITUTION State-supported, coed. 74 undergraduate majors. Federal methodology is used as a basis for awarding need-based institutional aid.

UNDERGRADUATE EXPENSES for 2011–12 ***Tuition, state resident:*** full-time $0. ***Tuition, nonresident:*** full-time $11,160; part-time $3837 per term. ***Required fees:*** full-time $4971; $1605 per term. Full-time tuition and fees vary according to course load. Part-time tuition and fees vary according to course load. ***College room and board:*** $9632; ***Room only:*** $6122. ***Payment plans:*** Installment, deferred payment.

FRESHMAN FINANCIAL AID (Fall 2010, est.) 3,070 applied for aid; of those 67% were deemed to have need. 100% of freshmen with need received aid; of those 89% had need fully met. ***Average percent of need met:*** 63% (excluding resources awarded to replace EFC). ***Average financial aid package:*** $9417 (excluding resources awarded to replace EFC). 8% of all full-time freshmen had no need and received non-need-based gift aid.

UNDERGRADUATE FINANCIAL AID (Fall 2010, est.) 15,531 applied for aid; of those 78% were deemed to have need. 100% of undergraduates with need received aid; of those 89% had need fully met. ***Average percent of need met:*** 53% (excluding resources awarded to replace EFC). ***Average financial aid package:*** $10,023 (excluding resources awarded to replace EFC). 5% of all full-time undergraduates had no need and received non-need-based gift aid.

GIFT AID (NEED-BASED) ***Total amount:*** $96,085,600 (48% federal, 51% state, 1% external sources). ***Receiving aid:*** Freshmen: 46% (1,732); all full-time undergraduates: 44% (9,924). ***Average award:*** Freshmen: $8595; Undergraduates: $8412. ***Scholarships, grants, and awards:*** Federal Pell, FSEOG, state, private, college/university gift aid from institutional funds, Federal Nursing.

GIFT AID (NON-NEED-BASED) ***Total amount:*** $2,194,461 (48% institutional, 52% external sources). ***Receiving aid:*** Freshmen: 1% (41). Undergraduates: 73. ***Average award:*** Freshmen: $6240. Undergraduates: $7024. ***Scholarships, grants, and awards by category:*** *Academic interests/achievement:* 1,798 awards ($2,997,653 total): business, communication, engineering/technologies, general academic interests/achievements, humanities, mathematics, military science, social sciences. *Creative arts/performance:* 85 awards ($52,275 total): art/fine arts, dance, music, performing arts, theater/drama. *Special achievements/activities:* 60 awards ($202,918 total): general special achievements/activities, leadership. *Special characteristics:* 40 awards ($224,715 total): general special characteristics. ***Tuition waivers:*** Full or partial for employees or children of employees, senior citizens.

LOANS ***Student loans:*** $46,032,541 (98% need-based, 2% non-need-based). 41% of past graduating class borrowed through all loan programs. *Average indebtedness per student:* $14,989. ***Average need-based loan:*** Freshmen: $4826. Undergraduates: $6522. ***Parent loans:*** $1,350,930 (59% need-based, 41% non-need-based). ***Programs:*** Federal Direct (Subsidized and Unsubsidized Stafford, PLUS), Perkins, college/university, private loans.

WORK-STUDY ***Federal work-study:*** Total amount: $1,330,942; 456 jobs averaging $2577.

ATHLETIC AWARDS Total amount: $1,777,584 (96% need-based, 4% non-need-based).

APPLYING FOR FINANCIAL AID ***Required financial aid form:*** FAFSA. ***Financial aid deadline (priority):*** 3/2. ***Notification date:*** Continuous beginning 4/22. Students must reply within 4 weeks of notification.

CONTACT Ms. Cecilia Schouwe, Director of Financial Aid, California State University, Fullerton, 800 North State College Boulevard, Fullerton, CA 92831-3599, 657-278-3128. *Fax:* 657-278-7090. *E-mail:* cschouwe@fullerton.edu.

CALIFORNIA STATE UNIVERSITY, LONG BEACH

Long Beach, CA

Tuition & fees (CA res): $5464 **Average undergraduate aid package: $12,981**

ABOUT THE INSTITUTION State-supported, coed. 148 undergraduate majors. Federal methodology is used as a basis for awarding need-based institutional aid.

UNDERGRADUATE EXPENSES for 2011–12 ***Tuition, state resident:*** full-time $0. ***Tuition, nonresident:*** full-time $11,160. ***Required fees:*** full-time $5464. Full-time tuition and fees vary according to program. Part-time tuition and fees vary according to course load and program. ***College room and board:*** $11,294. Room and board charges vary according to board plan. ***Payment plan:*** Installment.

FRESHMAN FINANCIAL AID (Fall 2010, est.) 3,284 applied for aid; of those 82% were deemed to have need. 91% of freshmen with need received aid; of those 71% had need fully met. ***Average percent of need met:*** 80% (excluding resources awarded to replace EFC). ***Average financial aid package:*** $12,074 (excluding resources awarded to replace EFC). 2% of all full-time freshmen had no need and received non-need-based gift aid.

UNDERGRADUATE FINANCIAL AID (Fall 2010, est.) 17,032 applied for aid; of those 95% were deemed to have need. 87% of undergraduates with need received aid; of those 57% had need fully met. ***Average percent of need met:*** 83% (excluding resources awarded to replace EFC). ***Average financial aid package:*** $12,981 (excluding resources awarded to replace EFC). 5% of all full-time undergraduates had no need and received non-need-based gift aid.

GIFT AID (NEED-BASED) ***Total amount:*** $116,506,719 (47% federal, 50% state, 2% institutional, 1% external sources). ***Receiving aid:*** Freshmen: 54% (2,101); all full-time undergraduates: 52% (11,166). ***Average award:*** Freshmen: $5729; Undergraduates: $5444. ***Scholarships, grants, and awards:*** Federal Pell, FSEOG, state, private, college/university gift aid from institutional funds.

GIFT AID (NON-NEED-BASED) ***Total amount:*** $32,928 (54% federal, 46% state). ***Receiving aid:*** Freshmen: 8% (299). Undergraduates: 10% (2,120). ***Average award:*** Freshmen: $2623. Undergraduates: $2478. ***Tuition waivers:*** Full or partial for employees or children of employees, senior citizens.

LOANS ***Student loans:*** $84,507,644 (56% need-based, 44% non-need-based). 38% of past graduating class borrowed through all loan programs. *Average indebtedness per student:* $10,787. ***Average need-based loan:*** Freshmen: $2663. Undergraduates: $3436. ***Parent loans:*** $2,575,000 (100% non-need-based). ***Programs:*** Federal Direct (Subsidized and Unsubsidized Stafford, PLUS), Perkins, college/university.

WORK-STUDY ***Federal work-study:*** Total amount: $1,372,894; jobs available.

ATHLETIC AWARDS Total amount: $2,010,496 (100% non-need-based).

APPLYING FOR FINANCIAL AID ***Required financial aid form:*** FAFSA. ***Financial aid deadline (priority):*** 3/2. ***Notification date:*** Continuous beginning 3/30. Students must reply within 3 weeks of notification.

CONTACT Nicolas Valdivia, Office of Financial Aid, California State University, Long Beach, 1250 Bellflower Boulevard, Long Beach, CA 90840, 562-985-8403.

CALIFORNIA STATE UNIVERSITY, LOS ANGELES

Los Angeles, CA

CONTACT Tamie L. Nguyen, Director of Financial Aid, California State University, Los Angeles, 5151 State University Drive, Los Angeles, CA 90032, 323-343-6260. *Fax:* 323-343-3166. *E-mail:* tnguyen10@cslanet.calstatela.edu.

CALIFORNIA STATE UNIVERSITY, MONTEREY BAY

Seaside, CA

Tuition & fees (CA res): $4721 **Average undergraduate aid package: $9744**

ABOUT THE INSTITUTION State-supported, coed. 20 undergraduate majors. Federal methodology is used as a basis for awarding need-based institutional aid.

UNDERGRADUATE EXPENSES for 2010–11 ***Tuition, state resident:*** full-time $0. ***Tuition, nonresident:*** full-time $11,160; part-time $372 per unit. ***Required fees:*** full-time $4721; $1472 per term. Full-time tuition and fees vary according to degree level. Part-time tuition and fees vary according to degree level. ***College room and board:*** $8440; ***Room only:*** $5440. Room and board charges vary according to board plan and housing facility. ***Payment plans:*** Guaranteed tuition, installment.

FRESHMAN FINANCIAL AID (Fall 2010, est.) 713 applied for aid; of those 77% were deemed to have need. 93% of freshmen with need received aid; of those 30% had need fully met. ***Average percent of need met:*** 76% (excluding resources awarded to replace EFC). ***Average financial aid package:*** $10,312 (excluding resources awarded to replace EFC).

UNDERGRADUATE FINANCIAL AID (Fall 2010, est.) 3,014 applied for aid; of those 84% were deemed to have need. 93% of undergraduates with need received aid; of those 36% had need fully met. ***Average percent of need met:*** 74% (excluding resources awarded to replace EFC). ***Average financial aid package:*** $9744 (excluding resources awarded to replace EFC).

GIFT AID (NEED-BASED) ***Total amount:*** $16,090,705 (53% federal, 46% state, 1% institutional). ***Receiving aid:*** Freshmen: 50% (408); all full-time undergraduates: 46% (1,872). ***Average award:*** Freshmen: $9643; Undergraduates: $8234. ***Scholarships, grants, and awards:*** Federal Pell, FSEOG, state, private, college/university gift aid from institutional funds.

GIFT AID (NON-NEED-BASED) ***Total amount:*** $194,952 (100% external sources). ***Receiving aid:*** Freshmen: 7% (58). Undergraduates: 4% (153). ***Scholarships, grants, and awards by category:*** *Academic interests/achievement:* business, general academic interests/achievements. *Special achievements/activities:* leadership. *Special characteristics:* children and siblings of alumni, general special characteristics, local/state students. ***Tuition waivers:*** Full or partial for employees or children of employees, senior citizens.

LOANS ***Student loans:*** $13,701,298 (53% need-based, 47% non-need-based). 68% of past graduating class borrowed through all loan programs. *Average indebtedness per student:* $14,365. ***Average need-based loan:*** Freshmen: $3324. Undergraduates: $4211. ***Parent loans:*** $2,200,384 (100% non-need-based). ***Programs:*** Federal Direct (Subsidized and Unsubsidized Stafford, PLUS), Perkins.

WORK-STUDY ***Federal work-study:*** Total amount: $122,770; jobs available. ***State or other work-study/employment:*** Part-time jobs available.

ATHLETIC AWARDS Total amount: $311,650 (100% non-need-based).

APPLYING FOR FINANCIAL AID ***Required financial aid forms:*** FAFSA, state aid form. ***Financial aid deadline (priority):*** 3/2.

CONTACT Office of Financial Aid, California State University, Monterey Bay, 100 Campus Center, Building 47, Seaside, CA 93955-8001, 831-582-5100. *Fax:* 831-582-3782.

CALIFORNIA STATE UNIVERSITY, NORTHRIDGE

Northridge, CA

Tuition & fees (CA res): $5076 **Average undergraduate aid package: $15,296**

ABOUT THE INSTITUTION State-supported, coed. 59 undergraduate majors. Federal methodology is used as a basis for awarding need-based institutional aid.

UNDERGRADUATE EXPENSES for 2010–11 ***Tuition, state resident:*** full-time $0. ***Tuition, nonresident:*** full-time $11,160. ***Required fees:*** full-time $5076. ***College room and board:*** $12,414. Room and board charges vary according to board plan and housing facility. ***Payment plan:*** Installment.

FRESHMAN FINANCIAL AID (Fall 2009) 3,280 applied for aid; of those 89% were deemed to have need. 100% of freshmen with need received aid. ***Average financial aid package:*** $10,656 (excluding resources awarded to replace EFC). 2% of all full-time freshmen had no need and received non-need-based gift aid.

UNDERGRADUATE FINANCIAL AID (Fall 2009) 15,251 applied for aid; of those 92% were deemed to have need. 100% of undergraduates with need received aid. ***Average financial aid package:*** $15,296 (excluding resources awarded to replace EFC). 4% of all full-time undergraduates had no need and received non-need-based gift aid.

GIFT AID (NEED-BASED) ***Total amount:*** $113,068,870 (51% federal, 49% state). ***Receiving aid:*** Freshmen: 58% (2,360); all full-time undergraduates: 52% (11,373). ***Average award:*** Freshmen: $10,017; Undergraduates: $12,948. ***Scholarships, grants, and awards:*** Federal Pell, FSEOG, state, private, college/university gift aid from institutional funds.

GIFT AID (NON-NEED-BASED) ***Total amount:*** $1,906,337 (48% institutional, 52% external sources). ***Receiving aid:*** Freshmen: 2% (74). Undergraduates: 4% (911). ***Average award:*** Freshmen: $1310. Undergraduates: $1479. ***Scholarships, grants, and awards by category:*** *Academic interests/achievement:* business, communication, computer science, education, engineering/technologies, English, general academic interests/achievements, mathematics, social sciences. *Creative arts/performance:* journalism/publications, music. *Special achievements/activities:* leadership. ***Tuition waivers:*** Full or partial for employees or children of employees, senior citizens.

LOANS ***Student loans:*** $65,075,744 (56% need-based, 44% non-need-based). 40% of past graduating class borrowed through all loan programs. *Average indebtedness per student:* $15,582. ***Average need-based loan:*** Freshmen: $4918. Undergraduates: $6020. ***Parent loans:*** $1,934,519 (100% non-need-based). ***Programs:*** Federal Direct (Subsidized and Unsubsidized Stafford, PLUS), Perkins.

WORK-STUDY ***Federal work-study:*** Total amount: $1,661,426; jobs available.

ATHLETIC AWARDS Total amount: $1,709,153 (100% non-need-based).

APPLYING FOR FINANCIAL AID ***Required financial aid forms:*** FAFSA, state aid form. ***Financial aid deadline (priority):*** 3/2. ***Notification date:*** Continuous beginning 4/1.

CONTACT Lili Vidal, Director of Financial Aid and Scholarships, California State University, Northridge, 18111 Nordhoff Street, Northridge, CA 91330-8307, 818-677-4085. *Fax:* 818-677-3047. *E-mail:* financial.aid@csun.edu.

CALIFORNIA STATE UNIVERSITY, SACRAMENTO

Sacramento, CA

Tuition & fees (CA res): $5194 **Average undergraduate aid package: $6818**

ABOUT THE INSTITUTION State-supported, coed. 55 undergraduate majors. Federal methodology is used as a basis for awarding need-based institutional aid.

UNDERGRADUATE EXPENSES for 2010–11 ***Tuition, state resident:*** full-time $0. ***Tuition, nonresident:*** full-time $11,160; part-time $372 per unit. ***Required fees:*** full-time $5194; $1709 per term. Full-time tuition and fees vary according to degree level. Part-time tuition and fees vary according to degree level. ***College room and board:*** $9512. Room and board charges vary according to board plan and housing facility. ***Payment plan:*** Installment.

FRESHMAN FINANCIAL AID (Fall 2009) 1,133 applied for aid; of those 85% were deemed to have need. 96% of freshmen with need received aid; of those 13% had need fully met. ***Average percent of need met:*** 59% (excluding resources awarded to replace EFC). ***Average financial aid package:*** $5049 (excluding resources awarded to replace EFC).

UNDERGRADUATE FINANCIAL AID (Fall 2009) 10,252 applied for aid; of those 94% were deemed to have need. 98% of undergraduates with need received aid; of those 19% had need fully met. ***Average percent of need met:*** 80% (excluding resources awarded to replace EFC). ***Average financial aid package:*** $6818 (excluding resources awarded to replace EFC). 1% of all full-time undergraduates had no need and received non-need-based gift aid.

GIFT AID (NEED-BASED) ***Total amount:*** $1,609,035 (29% institutional, 71% external sources). ***Receiving aid:*** Freshmen: 58% (689); all full-time undergraduates: 61% (6,866). ***Average award:*** Freshmen: $3550; Undergraduates: $5862. ***Scholarships, grants, and awards:*** Federal Pell, FSEOG, state, private, college/university gift aid from institutional funds, Federal Nursing.

GIFT AID (NON-NEED-BASED) ***Receiving aid:*** Freshmen: 13% (151). Undergraduates: 7% (761). ***Average award:*** Undergraduates: $1538. ***Tuition waivers:*** Full or partial for employees or children of employees, senior citizens.

LOANS ***Student loans:*** $46,344,561 (54% need-based, 46% non-need-based). 41% of past graduating class borrowed through all loan programs. *Average indebtedness per student:* $14,679. ***Average need-based loan:*** Freshmen: $1650. Undergraduates: $4051. ***Parent loans:*** $6,011,049 (100% non-need-based). ***Programs:*** Perkins, Federal Nursing.

WORK-STUDY ***Federal work-study:*** Total amount: $806,058; jobs available. ***State or other work-study/employment:*** Total amount: $171,727 (100% need-based). Part-time jobs available.

ATHLETIC AWARDS Total amount: $2,295,717 (100% need-based).

APPLYING FOR FINANCIAL AID ***Required financial aid form:*** FAFSA. ***Financial aid deadline:*** Continuous. ***Notification date:*** Continuous.

CONTACT Judith Hawthorne, Assistant Director of Financial Aid, California State University, Sacramento, Lassen Hall 1006, 6000 J Street, Sacramento, CA 95819-6044, 916-278-6554. *Fax:* 916-278-6082.

CALIFORNIA STATE UNIVERSITY, SAN BERNARDINO

San Bernardino, CA

Tuition & fees (CA res): $5189 **Average undergraduate aid package: $10,958**

ABOUT THE INSTITUTION State-supported, coed. 52 undergraduate majors. Federal methodology is used as a basis for awarding need-based institutional aid.

UNDERGRADUATE EXPENSES for 2011–12 ***Tuition, state resident:*** full-time $0. ***Tuition, nonresident:*** full-time $11,160. ***Required fees:*** full-time $5189. Part-time tuition and fees vary according to course load. Room and board charges vary according to board plan and housing facility.

FRESHMAN FINANCIAL AID (Fall 2010, est.) 1,256 applied for aid; of those 90% were deemed to have need. 98% of freshmen with need received aid; of those 12% had need fully met. ***Average percent of need met:*** 72% (excluding resources awarded to replace EFC). ***Average financial aid package:*** $11,374 (excluding resources awarded to replace EFC). 1% of all full-time freshmen had no need and received non-need-based gift aid.

UNDERGRADUATE FINANCIAL AID (Fall 2010, est.) 9,715 applied for aid; of those 93% were deemed to have need. 98% of undergraduates with need received aid; of those 11% had need fully met. ***Average percent of need met:*** 68% (excluding resources awarded to replace EFC). ***Average financial aid package:*** $10,958 (excluding resources awarded to replace EFC). 1% of all full-time undergraduates had no need and received non-need-based gift aid.

GIFT AID (NEED-BASED) ***Total amount:*** $67,514,067 (53% federal, 44% state, 1% institutional, 2% external sources). ***Receiving aid:*** Freshmen: 65% (973); all full-time undergraduates: 64% (7,561). ***Average award:*** Freshmen: $9571; Undergraduates: $8235. ***Scholarships, grants, and awards:*** Federal Pell, FSEOG, state, private, college/university gift aid from institutional funds, Academic Competitiveness Grants, National SMART Grants.

GIFT AID (NON-NEED-BASED) ***Total amount:*** $312,079 (100% institutional). ***Receiving aid:*** Freshmen: 8% (126). Undergraduates: 6% (715). ***Average award:*** Freshmen: $2684. Undergraduates: $3728. ***Scholarships, grants, and awards by category:*** *Academic interests/achievement:* 129 awards ($1,263,138 total): biological sciences, business, computer science, education, foreign languages, general academic interests/achievements, health fields, mathematics, physical sciences, social sciences. *Creative arts/performance:* 18 awards ($20,310 total): art/fine arts, general creative arts/performance, journalism/publications, music, theater/drama. *Special achievements/activities:* community service, general special achievements/activities, hobbies/interests, memberships. *Special characteristics:* children of public servants, children with a deceased or disabled parent, first-generation college students, handicapped students. ***Tuition waivers:*** Full or partial for employees or children of employees.

LOANS ***Student loans:*** $38,276,329 (90% need-based, 10% non-need-based). 69% of past graduating class borrowed through all loan programs. *Average indebtedness per student:* $23,791. ***Average need-based loan:*** Freshmen: $2614. Undergraduates: $3499. ***Parent loans:*** $31,326,458 (100% non-need-based). ***Programs:*** Federal Direct (Subsidized and Unsubsidized Stafford, PLUS), Perkins.

WORK-STUDY ***Federal work-study:*** Total amount: $1,346,585; 345 jobs averaging $3911.

ATHLETIC AWARDS Total amount: $532,971 (100% non-need-based).

APPLYING FOR FINANCIAL AID ***Required financial aid forms:*** FAFSA, state aid form. ***Financial aid deadline (priority):*** 3/2. ***Notification date:*** Continuous beginning 4/1.

CONTACT Ms. Roseanna Ruiz, Director of Financial Aid, California State University, San Bernardino, 5500 University Parkway, San Bernardino, CA 92407-2397, 909-537-5227. *Fax:* 909-537-4024.

CALIFORNIA STATE UNIVERSITY, SAN MARCOS

San Marcos, CA

CONTACT Addalou Davis, Director of Financial Aid, California State University, San Marcos, 333 South Twin Oaks Valley Road, San Marcos, CA 92096-0001, 760-750-4852. *Fax:* 760-750-3047. *E-mail:* finaid@csusm.edu.

CALIFORNIA STATE UNIVERSITY, STANISLAUS

Turlock, CA

Tuition & fees (CA res): $5994 **Average undergraduate aid package: $8717**

ABOUT THE INSTITUTION State-supported, coed. 38 undergraduate majors. Federal methodology is used as a basis for awarding need-based institutional aid.

UNDERGRADUATE EXPENSES for 2011–12 ***Tuition, state resident:*** full-time $0. ***Tuition, nonresident:*** full-time $11,160; part-time $372 per unit. ***Required fees:*** full-time $5994. Full-time tuition and fees vary according to course load, degree level, reciprocity agreements, and student level. Part-time tuition and fees vary according to course load, degree level, reciprocity agreements, and student level. ***College room and board:*** $8250; ***Room only:*** $7450. Room and board charges vary according to board plan and housing facility. ***Payment plans:*** Installment, deferred payment.

FRESHMAN FINANCIAL AID (Fall 2010, est.) 617 applied for aid; of those 86% were deemed to have need. 99% of freshmen with need received aid; of those 7% had need fully met. ***Average percent of need met:*** 63% (excluding resources awarded to replace EFC). ***Average financial aid package:*** $1652 (excluding resources awarded to replace EFC). 1% of all full-time freshmen had no need and received non-need-based gift aid.

UNDERGRADUATE FINANCIAL AID (Fall 2010, est.) 4,446 applied for aid; of those 95% were deemed to have need. 98% of undergraduates with need received aid; of those 3% had need fully met. ***Average percent of need met:*** 57% (excluding resources awarded to replace EFC). ***Average financial aid package:*** $8717 (excluding resources awarded to replace EFC). 1% of all full-time undergraduates had no need and received non-need-based gift aid.

GIFT AID (NEED-BASED) ***Total amount:*** $32,515,748 (54% federal, 23% state, 23% institutional). ***Receiving aid:*** Freshmen: 43% (432); all full-time undergraduates: 63% (3,476). ***Average award:*** Freshmen: $6152; Undergraduates: $7381. ***Scholarships, grants, and awards:*** Federal Pell, FSEOG, state, private, college/university gift aid from institutional funds.

GIFT AID (NON-NEED-BASED) ***Total amount:*** $1,161,757 (1% federal, 55% institutional, 44% external sources). ***Receiving aid:*** Freshmen: 2% (23). Undergraduates: 4% (198). ***Average award:*** Freshmen: $1250. Undergraduates: $2766. ***Scholarships, grants, and awards by category:*** *Academic interests/achievement:* 140 awards ($207,073 total): agriculture, area/ethnic studies, biological sciences, business, communication, computer science, education, English, foreign languages, general academic interests/achievements, health fields, humanities, international studies, mathematics, physical sciences, premedicine, social sciences. *Creative arts/performance:* 52 awards ($66,056 total): art/fine arts, music. *Special achievements/activities:* 105 awards ($494,150 total): community service, general special achievements/activities, leadership, memberships. *Special characteristics:* 66 awards ($140,088 total): children of faculty/staff, first-generation college students, general special characteristics, local/state students. ***Tuition waivers:*** Full or partial for employees or children of employees, adult students, senior citizens.

LOANS ***Student loans:*** $9,830,995 (83% need-based, 17% non-need-based). 48% of past graduating class borrowed through all loan programs. *Average indebtedness per student:* $13,400. ***Average need-based loan:*** Freshmen: $4500. Undergraduates: $6537. ***Parent loans:*** $1,756,105 (100% non-need-based). ***Programs:*** Federal Direct (Subsidized and Unsubsidized Stafford, PLUS), Perkins, private loans.

WORK-STUDY ***Federal work-study:*** Total amount: $594,446; 176 jobs averaging $3377. ***State or other work-study/employment:*** Part-time jobs available.

ATHLETIC AWARDS Total amount: $477,050 (100% non-need-based).

APPLYING FOR FINANCIAL AID ***Required financial aid forms:*** FAFSA, state aid form. ***Financial aid deadline (priority):*** 3/2. ***Notification date:*** Continuous beginning 3/15. Students must reply within 3 weeks of notification.

CONTACT Ms. Noelia Gonzalez, Director of Financial Aid and Scholarships, California State University, Stanislaus, One University Circle, Turlock, CA 95382, 209-667-3337 or toll-free 800-300-7420 (in-state). *Fax:* 209-664-7064. *E-mail:* ngonzalez4@csustan.edu.

CALIFORNIA UNIVERSITY OF PENNSYLVANIA

California, PA

CONTACT Financial Aid Office, California University of Pennsylvania, 250 University Avenue, California, PA 15419-1394, 724-938-4415 or toll-free 888-412-0479 (in-state).

CALUMET COLLEGE OF SAINT JOSEPH

Whiting, IN

Tuition & fees: $14,200 **Average undergraduate aid package: $12,391**

ABOUT THE INSTITUTION Independent Roman Catholic, coed. 28 undergraduate majors. Federal methodology is used as a basis for awarding need-based institutional aid.

UNDERGRADUATE EXPENSES for 2010–11 ***Tuition:*** full-time $14,000; part-time $440 per credit hour. ***Required fees:*** full-time $200; $100 per term. Full-time tuition and fees vary according to course load, degree level, and program. Part-time tuition and fees vary according to course load, degree level, and program. ***Payment plan:*** Installment.

FRESHMAN FINANCIAL AID (Fall 2010, est.) 132 applied for aid; of those 92% were deemed to have need. 89% of freshmen with need received aid; of those 20% had need fully met. ***Average percent of need met:*** 62% (excluding resources awarded to replace EFC). ***Average financial aid package:*** $11,594 (excluding resources awarded to replace EFC). 4% of all full-time freshmen had no need and received non-need-based gift aid.

UNDERGRADUATE FINANCIAL AID (Fall 2010, est.) 529 applied for aid; of those 92% were deemed to have need. 92% of undergraduates with need received aid; of those 19% had need fully met. ***Average percent of need met:*** 63% (excluding resources awarded to replace EFC). ***Average financial aid package:*** $12,391 (excluding resources awarded to replace EFC). 3% of all full-time undergraduates had no need and received non-need-based gift aid.

GIFT AID (NEED-BASED) ***Total amount:*** $4,247,086 (56% federal, 25% state, 17% institutional, 2% external sources). ***Receiving aid:*** Freshmen: 62% (85); all full-time undergraduates: 59% (326). ***Average award:*** Freshmen: $8873; Undergraduates: $9480. ***Scholarships, grants, and awards:*** Federal Pell, FSEOG, state, private, college/university gift aid from institutional funds, United Negro College Fund.

GIFT AID (NON-NEED-BASED) ***Total amount:*** $430,412 (20% federal, 74% institutional, 6% external sources). ***Receiving aid:*** Freshmen: 30% (41). Undergraduates: 26% (146). ***Average award:*** Freshmen: $5722. Undergraduates: $4294. ***Scholarships, grants, and awards by category:*** *Academic interests/achievement:* 41 awards ($121,742 total): general academic interests/achievements. *Creative arts/performance:* 2 awards ($8000 total): art/fine arts, theater/drama. *Special achievements/activities:* 30 awards ($41,450 total): leadership. *Special characteristics:* 61 awards ($216,954 total): children and siblings of alumni, children of faculty/staff, general special characteristics, previous college experience. ***Tuition waivers:*** Full or partial for children of alumni, employees or children of employees, senior citizens.

LOANS ***Student loans:*** $5,447,310 (69% need-based, 31% non-need-based). 77% of past graduating class borrowed through all loan programs. *Average indebtedness per student:* $28,434. ***Average need-based loan:*** Freshmen: $2947. Undergraduates: $3588. ***Parent loans:*** $126,875 (54% need-based, 46% non-need-based). ***Programs:*** Federal Direct (Subsidized and Unsubsidized Stafford, PLUS).

WORK-STUDY ***Federal work-study:*** Total amount: $61,599; 32 jobs averaging $1925. ***State or other work-study/employment:*** Part-time jobs available.

ATHLETIC AWARDS Total amount: $1,072,088 (80% need-based, 20% non-need-based).

APPLYING FOR FINANCIAL AID ***Required financial aid form:*** FAFSA. ***Financial aid deadline (priority):*** 3/1. ***Notification date:*** Continuous.

CONTACT Gina Pirtle, Director of Financial Aid and Business Office Operations, Calumet College of Saint Joseph, 2400 New York Avenue, Whiting, IN 46394, 219-473-4379 or toll-free 877-700-9100. *E-mail:* gpirtle@ccsj.edu.

CALVARY BIBLE COLLEGE AND THEOLOGICAL SEMINARY

Kansas City, MO

Tuition & fees: $10,048 **Average undergraduate aid package: N/A**

ABOUT THE INSTITUTION Independent nondenominational, coed. 20 undergraduate majors. Both federal and institutional methodology are used as a basis for awarding need-based institutional aid.

UNDERGRADUATE EXPENSES for 2011–12 ***Comprehensive fee:*** $18,848 includes full-time tuition ($9280), mandatory fees ($768), and room and board ($8800). Room and board charges vary according to housing facility. ***Payment plans:*** Guaranteed tuition, installment.

GIFT AID (NEED-BASED) ***Scholarships, grants, and awards:*** Federal Pell, FSEOG, private, college/university gift aid from institutional funds.

GIFT AID (NON-NEED-BASED) ***Scholarships, grants, and awards by category:*** *Academic interests/achievement:* general academic interests/achievements. *Creative arts/performance:* general creative arts/performance. *Special achievements/activities:* general special achievements/activities, religious involvement. *Special characteristics:* children and siblings of alumni, children of educators, children of faculty/staff, relatives of clergy, religious affiliation, siblings of current students, spouses of current students. ***Tuition waivers:*** Full or partial for employees or children of employees.

LOANS ***Programs:*** Federal Direct (Subsidized and Unsubsidized Stafford, PLUS).

APPLYING FOR FINANCIAL AID ***Required financial aid forms:*** FAFSA, institution's own form. ***Financial aid deadline:*** 4/1 (priority: 3/1). ***Notification date:*** Continuous beginning 5/1.

CONTACT Office of Financial Aid, Calvary Bible College and Theological Seminary, 15800 Calvary Road, Kansas City, MO 64147-1341, 816-322-0110 Ext. 1323 or toll-free 800-326-3960. *Fax:* 816-331-4474. *E-mail:* finaid@calvary.edu.

CALVIN COLLEGE

Grand Rapids, MI

Tuition & fees: $24,870 **Average undergraduate aid package: $18,019**

ABOUT THE INSTITUTION Independent Christian Reformed, coed. 95 undergraduate majors. Both federal and institutional methodology are used as a basis for awarding need-based institutional aid.

UNDERGRADUATE EXPENSES for 2010–11 ***Comprehensive fee:*** $33,395 includes full-time tuition ($24,645), mandatory fees ($225), and room and board ($8525). Full-time tuition and fees vary according to degree level and program. Room and board charges vary according to board plan. ***Part-time tuition:*** $590 per credit hour. Part-time tuition and fees vary according to course load and degree level. ***Payment plans:*** Tuition prepayment, installment.

FRESHMAN FINANCIAL AID (Fall 2010, est.) 830 applied for aid; of those 79% were deemed to have need. 100% of freshmen with need received aid; of those 17% had need fully met. ***Average percent of need met:*** 71% (excluding resources awarded to replace EFC). ***Average financial aid package:*** $18,234 (excluding resources awarded to replace EFC). 27% of all full-time freshmen had no need and received non-need-based gift aid.

UNDERGRADUATE FINANCIAL AID (Fall 2010, est.) 3,081 applied for aid; of those 81% were deemed to have need. 100% of undergraduates with need received aid; of those 15% had need fully met. ***Average percent of need met:*** 70% (excluding resources awarded to replace EFC). ***Average financial aid package:*** $18,019 (excluding resources awarded to replace EFC). 29% of all full-time undergraduates had no need and received non-need-based gift aid.

GIFT AID (NEED-BASED) ***Total amount:*** $29,750,267 (17% federal, 6% state, 74% institutional, 3% external sources). ***Receiving aid:*** Freshmen: 70% (654); all full-time undergraduates: 65% (2,473). ***Average award:*** Freshmen: $13,103; Undergraduates: $11,775. ***Scholarships, grants, and awards:*** Federal Pell, FSEOG, state, private, college/university gift aid from institutional funds.

GIFT AID (NON-NEED-BASED) ***Total amount:*** $8,624,962 (96% institutional, 4% external sources). ***Receiving aid:*** Freshmen: 7% (63). Undergraduates: 5% (188). ***Average award:*** Freshmen: $5949. Undergraduates: $4888. ***Scholarships, grants, and awards by category:*** *Academic interests/achievement:* $9,500,000 total: biological sciences, business, communication, computer science, education, engineering/technologies, English, foreign languages, general academic interests/achievements, health fields, humanities, international studies, mathematics, physical sciences, premedicine, religion/biblical studies, social sciences. *Creative arts/performance:* $200,000 total: art/fine arts, music, performing arts, theater/drama. *Special achievements/activities:* $50,000 total: community service, religious involvement. *Special characteristics:* $6,300,000 total: adult students, children and siblings of alumni, children of faculty/staff, children of union members/company employees, ethnic background, first-generation college students, handicapped students, international students, members of minority groups, religious affiliation, twins. ***Tuition waivers:*** Full or partial for employees or children of employees.

LOANS ***Student loans:*** $23,522,911 (75% need-based, 25% non-need-based). 66% of past graduating class borrowed through all loan programs. *Average indebtedness per student:* $27,700. ***Average need-based loan:*** Freshmen: $3894. Undergraduates: $6275. ***Parent loans:*** $3,133,058 (46% need-based, 54% non-need-based). ***Programs:*** Federal Direct (Subsidized and Unsubsidized Stafford, PLUS), Perkins, state, college/university, alternative loans.

WORK-STUDY ***Federal work-study:*** Total amount: $1,679,625; 1,190 jobs averaging $1411. ***State or other work-study/employment:*** Total amount: $1,380,071 (4% need-based, 96% non-need-based). 963 part-time jobs averaging $1433.

APPLYING FOR FINANCIAL AID ***Required financial aid form:*** FAFSA. ***Financial aid deadline (priority):*** 2/15. ***Notification date:*** Continuous beginning 3/15.

CONTACT Mr. Craig Heerema, Financial Aid Administrator, Calvin College, Spoelhof Center 263, Grand Rapids, MI 49546, 616-526-6134 or toll-free 800-688-0122. *Fax:* 616-526-6883. *E-mail:* cheerema@calvin.edu.

CAMBRIDGE COLLEGE

Cambridge, MA

Tuition & fees: $13,280 **Average undergraduate aid package: $8198**

ABOUT THE INSTITUTION Independent, coed. 4 undergraduate majors. Federal methodology is used as a basis for awarding need-based institutional aid.

UNDERGRADUATE EXPENSES for 2010–11 ***Tuition:*** full-time $13,140; part-time $365 per credit hour. ***Payment plan:*** Installment.

FRESHMAN FINANCIAL AID (Fall 2009) 31 applied for aid; of those 100% were deemed to have need. 100% of freshmen with need received aid. ***Average percent of need met:*** 26% (excluding resources awarded to replace EFC). ***Average financial aid package:*** $7494 (excluding resources awarded to replace EFC).

UNDERGRADUATE FINANCIAL AID (Fall 2009) 232 applied for aid; of those 96% were deemed to have need. 100% of undergraduates with need received aid. ***Average percent of need met:*** 31% (excluding resources awarded to replace EFC). ***Average financial aid package:*** $8198 (excluding resources awarded to replace EFC).

GIFT AID (NEED-BASED) ***Total amount:*** $2,977,303 (77% federal, 15% state, 5% institutional, 3% external sources). ***Receiving aid:*** Freshmen: 48% (25); all full-time undergraduates: 54% (167). ***Average award:*** Freshmen: $5037; Undergraduates: $5653. ***Scholarships, grants, and awards:*** Federal Pell, FSEOG, state, private, college/university gift aid from institutional funds.

GIFT AID (NON-NEED-BASED) ***Scholarships, grants, and awards by category:*** *Academic interests/achievement:* education. ***Tuition waivers:*** Full or partial for employees or children of employees.

LOANS ***Student loans:*** $8,813,469 (100% need-based). ***Average need-based loan:*** Freshmen: $3389. Undergraduates: $4313. ***Parent loans:*** $6000 (100% need-based). ***Programs:*** Federal Direct (Subsidized and Unsubsidized Stafford, PLUS), Perkins.

WORK-STUDY ***Federal work-study:*** Total amount: $81,406; jobs available.

APPLYING FOR FINANCIAL AID ***Required financial aid forms:*** FAFSA, institution's own form. ***Financial aid deadline (priority):*** 9/1. ***Notification date:*** Continuous beginning 6/1.

CONTACT Dr. Frank Lauder, Director of Financial Aid, Cambridge College, 1000 Massachusetts Avenue, Cambridge, MA 02138, 617-868-1000 Ext. 1440 or toll-free 800-877-4723. *Fax:* 617-349-3561. *E-mail:* francis.lauder@cambridgecollege.edu.

CAMERON UNIVERSITY

Lawton, OK

Tuition & fees (OK res): $4336 **Average undergraduate aid package: $12,200**

ABOUT THE INSTITUTION State-supported, coed. 46 undergraduate majors. Federal methodology is used as a basis for awarding need-based institutional aid.

UNDERGRADUATE EXPENSES for 2010–11 ***Tuition, state resident:*** full-time $2963; part-time $98.75 per credit hour. ***Tuition, nonresident:*** full-time $9180; part-time $306 per credit hour. ***Required fees:*** full-time $1373; $45.75 per credit hour. Full-time tuition and fees vary according to course load, location, and program. Part-time tuition and fees vary according to course load, location, and program. ***College room and board:*** $3668. Room and board charges vary according to board plan and housing facility. ***Payment plan:*** Installment.

FRESHMAN FINANCIAL AID (Fall 2009) 880 applied for aid; of those 86% were deemed to have need. 88% of freshmen with need received aid; of those 83% had need fully met. ***Average percent of need met:*** 92% (excluding resources awarded to replace EFC). ***Average financial aid package:*** $12,200 (excluding resources awarded to replace EFC). 37% of all full-time freshmen had no need and received non-need-based gift aid.

UNDERGRADUATE FINANCIAL AID (Fall 2009) 2,516 applied for aid; of those 85% were deemed to have need. 93% of undergraduates with need received aid; of those 91% had need fully met. ***Average percent of need met:*** 88% (excluding resources awarded to replace EFC). ***Average financial aid package:*** $12,200 (excluding resources awarded to replace EFC). 42% of all full-time undergraduates had no need and received non-need-based gift aid.

GIFT AID (NEED-BASED) ***Total amount:*** $13,860,371 (75% federal, 16% state, 3% institutional, 6% external sources). ***Receiving aid:*** Freshmen: 52% (626); all full-time undergraduates: 50% (1,888). ***Average award:*** Freshmen: $4200; Undergraduates: $4000. ***Scholarships, grants, and awards:*** Federal Pell, FSEOG, state, private, college/university gift aid from institutional funds.

GIFT AID (NON-NEED-BASED) ***Total amount:*** $2,030,394 (8% state, 14% institutional, 78% external sources). ***Receiving aid:*** Freshmen: 48% (573). Undergraduates: 31% (1,146). ***Average award:*** Freshmen: $750. Undergraduates: $500. ***Scholarships, grants, and awards by category:*** *Academic interests/achievement:* agriculture, biological sciences, business, communication, computer science, education, engineering/technologies, English, foreign languages, general academic interests/achievements, mathematics, military science, physical sciences, social sciences. *Creative arts/performance:* art/fine arts, cinema/film/broadcasting, creative writing, debating, journalism/publications, music, performing arts, theater/drama. *Special achievements/activities:* cheerleading/drum major, general special achievements/activities, leadership. *Special characteristics:* members of minority groups. ***Tuition waivers:*** Full or partial for employees or children of employees.

LOANS ***Student loans:*** $11,008,483 (60% need-based, 40% non-need-based). 32% of past graduating class borrowed through all loan programs. *Average indebtedness per student:* $7200. ***Average need-based loan:*** Freshmen: $1200. Undergraduates: $5000. ***Parent loans:*** $104,896 (100% non-need-based). ***Programs:*** Federal Direct (Subsidized and Unsubsidized Stafford, PLUS).

WORK-STUDY ***Federal work-study:*** Total amount: $174,284; jobs available. ***State or other work-study/employment:*** Total amount: $969,836 (100% non-need-based). Part-time jobs available.

ATHLETIC AWARDS Total amount: $583,891 (100% non-need-based).

APPLYING FOR FINANCIAL AID ***Required financial aid form:*** FAFSA. ***Financial aid deadline:*** Continuous. ***Notification date:*** Continuous beginning 4/1. Students must reply by 8/1 or within 2 weeks of notification.

CONTACT Donald Hall, Director of Financial Aid, Cameron University, 2800 West Gore Boulevard, Lawton, OK 73505-6377, 580-581-2293 or toll-free 888-454-7600. *Fax:* 580-581-2556. *E-mail:* dhall@cameron.edu.

CAMPBELLSVILLE UNIVERSITY

Campbellsville, KY

Tuition & fees: $20,740 **Average undergraduate aid package: $17,039**

ABOUT THE INSTITUTION Independent religious, coed. 55 undergraduate majors. Federal methodology is used as a basis for awarding need-based institutional aid.

UNDERGRADUATE EXPENSES for 2011–12 ***Comprehensive fee:*** $27,720 includes full-time tuition ($20,290), mandatory fees ($450), and room and board ($6980). Room and board charges vary according to housing facility. ***Part-time tuition:*** $846 per credit. ***Payment plan:*** Installment.

FRESHMAN FINANCIAL AID (Fall 2010, est.) 465 applied for aid; of those 95% were deemed to have need. 100% of freshmen with need received aid; of those 13% had need fully met. ***Average percent of need met:*** 78% (excluding resources awarded to replace EFC). ***Average financial aid package:*** $18,796 (excluding resources awarded to replace EFC). 10% of all full-time freshmen had no need and received non-need-based gift aid.

UNDERGRADUATE FINANCIAL AID (Fall 2010, est.) 1,630 applied for aid; of those 94% were deemed to have need. 100% of undergraduates with need received aid; of those 12% had need fully met. ***Average percent of need met:*** 73% (excluding resources awarded to replace EFC). ***Average financial aid package:*** $17,039 (excluding resources awarded to replace EFC). 7% of all full-time undergraduates had no need and received non-need-based gift aid.

GIFT AID (NEED-BASED) ***Total amount:*** $19,622,366 (25% federal, 25% state, 45% institutional, 5% external sources). ***Receiving aid:*** Freshmen: 87% (441); all full-time undergraduates: 83% (1,515). ***Average award:*** Freshmen: $15,851; Undergraduates: $13,891. ***Scholarships, grants, and awards:*** Federal Pell, FSEOG, state, college/university gift aid from institutional funds.

GIFT AID (NON-NEED-BASED) ***Total amount:*** $1,524,294 (1% federal, 18% state, 67% institutional, 14% external sources). ***Receiving aid:*** Freshmen: 9% (44). Undergraduates: 7% (128). ***Average award:*** Freshmen: $6247. Undergraduates: $6527. ***Scholarships, grants, and awards by category:*** *Academic interests/achievement:* 515 awards ($2,906,418 total): biological sciences, business, communication, computer science, education, English, general academic interests/achievements, health fields, humanities, mathematics, physical sciences, premedicine, religion/biblical studies, social sciences. *Creative arts/performance:* 165 awards ($492,720 total): art/fine arts, journalism/publications, music, theater/drama. *Special achievements/activities:* 280 awards ($642,135 total): cheerleading/drum major, junior miss, leadership, religious involvement. *Special characteristics:* 152 awards ($795,215 total): adult students, children of educators, children of faculty/staff, international students, relatives of clergy, religious affiliation, veterans. ***Tuition waivers:*** Full or partial for employees or children of employees, adult students, senior citizens.

LOANS ***Student loans:*** $8,752,317 (88% need-based, 12% non-need-based). 90% of past graduating class borrowed through all loan programs. *Average indebtedness per student:* $18,132. ***Average need-based loan:*** Freshmen: $2912. Undergraduates: $3745. ***Parent loans:*** $1,142,629 (56% need-based, 44% non-need-based). ***Programs:*** Federal Direct (Subsidized and Unsubsidized Stafford, PLUS), Perkins, college/university.

WORK-STUDY ***Federal work-study:*** Total amount: $605,096; 365 jobs averaging $1690. ***State or other work-study/employment:*** Total amount: $44,300 (56% need-based, 44% non-need-based). 30 part-time jobs averaging $1650.

ATHLETIC AWARDS Total amount: $2,612,569 (55% need-based, 45% non-need-based).

APPLYING FOR FINANCIAL AID ***Required financial aid form:*** FAFSA. ***Financial aid deadline (priority):*** 3/1. ***Notification date:*** Continuous beginning 3/15. Students must reply within 3 weeks of notification.

CONTACT Mr. Aaron Gabehart, Financial Aid Counselor, Campbellsville University, 1 University Drive, Campbellsville, KY 42718, 270-789-5305 or toll-free 800-264-6014. *Fax:* 270-789-5060. *E-mail:* finaid@campbellsville.edu.

CAMPBELL UNIVERSITY

Buies Creek, NC

Tuition & fees: $22,520 **Average undergraduate aid package: $35,929**

ABOUT THE INSTITUTION Independent religious, coed. ***Awards:*** associate, bachelor's, and master's degrees. 85 undergraduate majors. ***Total enrollment:*** 4,743. Undergraduates: 2,934. Freshmen: 899. Federal methodology is used as a basis for awarding need-based institutional aid.

UNDERGRADUATE EXPENSES for 2010–11 ***Application fee:*** $35. ***Comprehensive fee:*** $30,120 includes full-time tuition ($21,740), mandatory fees ($780), and room and board ($7600). ***College room only:*** $3600. Full-time tuition and fees vary according to course load, location, and program. Room and board charges vary according to board plan and housing facility. ***Part-time tuition:*** $360 per credit hour. Part-time tuition and fees vary according to course load, location, and program. ***Payment plan:*** Installment.

FRESHMAN FINANCIAL AID (Fall 2009) 726 applied for aid; of those 80% were deemed to have need. 100% of freshmen with need received aid; of those 76% had need fully met. ***Average percent of need met:*** 80% (excluding resources awarded to replace EFC). ***Average financial aid package:*** $37,703 (excluding resources awarded to replace EFC). 19% of all full-time freshmen had no need and received non-need-based gift aid.

UNDERGRADUATE FINANCIAL AID (Fall 2009) 3,751 applied for aid; of those 68% were deemed to have need. 100% of undergraduates with need received aid; of those 45% had need fully met. ***Average percent of need met:*** 80% (excluding resources awarded to replace EFC). ***Average financial aid package:*** $35,929 (excluding resources awarded to replace EFC). 13% of all full-time undergraduates had no need and received non-need-based gift aid.

GIFT AID (NEED-BASED) ***Total amount:*** $30,080,892 (20% federal, 27% state, 47% institutional, 6% external sources). ***Receiving aid:*** Freshmen: 80% (584); all full-time undergraduates: 54% (2,292). ***Average award:*** Freshmen: $32,708; Undergraduates: $25,239. ***Scholarships, grants, and awards:*** Federal Pell, FSEOG, state, private, college/university gift aid from institutional funds.

GIFT AID (NON-NEED-BASED) ***Total amount:*** $6,796,813 (11% federal, 17% state, 66% institutional, 6% external sources). ***Receiving aid:*** Freshmen: 79% (577). Undergraduates: 47% (1,968). ***Average award:*** Freshmen: $23,348. Undergraduates: $14,848. ***Scholarships, grants, and awards by category:*** *Academic interests/achievement:* 1,747 awards ($13,977,560 total): general academic interests/achievements. *Creative arts/performance:* 76 awards ($75,000 total): art/fine arts, creative writing, journalism/publications, music, theater/drama. *Special achievements/activities:* 27 awards ($85,000 total): cheerleading/drum major, religious involvement. *Special characteristics:* 84 awards ($859,947 total): children of faculty/staff. ***Tuition waivers:*** Full or partial for employees or children of employees. ***ROTC:*** Army.

LOANS ***Student loans:*** $26,428,451 (92% need-based, 8% non-need-based). 66% of past graduating class borrowed through all loan programs. *Average indebtedness per student:* $38,696. ***Average need-based loan:*** Freshmen: $2880. Undergraduates: $3980. ***Parent loans:*** $21,480,770 (85% need-based, 15% non-need-based). ***Programs:*** Federal Direct (Subsidized and Unsubsidized Stafford, PLUS), Perkins, state.

WORK-STUDY ***Federal work-study:*** Total amount: $732,380; 1,186 jobs averaging $619. ***State or other work-study/employment:*** Total amount: $618,861 (100% non-need-based). 604 part-time jobs averaging $773.

ATHLETIC AWARDS Total amount: $3,315,866 (46% need-based, 54% non-need-based).

APPLYING FOR FINANCIAL AID ***Required financial aid form:*** FAFSA. ***Financial aid deadline (priority):*** 2/15. ***Notification date:*** Continuous. Students must reply within 2 weeks of notification.

CONTACT Financial Aid Office, Campbell University, PO Box 36, Buies Creek, NC 27506, 910-893-1310 or toll-free 800-334-4111. *Fax:* 910-814-5788.

CANISIUS COLLEGE

Buffalo, NY

Tuition & fees: $30,077 **Average undergraduate aid package: $25,536**

ABOUT THE INSTITUTION Independent Roman Catholic (Jesuit), coed. 54 undergraduate majors. Federal methodology is used as a basis for awarding need-based institutional aid.

UNDERGRADUATE EXPENSES for 2010–11 ***Comprehensive fee:*** $41,057 includes full-time tuition ($29,020), mandatory fees ($1057), and room and board ($10,980). ***College room only:*** $6480. Full-time tuition and fees vary according to course load. Room and board charges vary according to board plan and housing facility. ***Part-time tuition:*** $828 per credit hour. ***Part-time fees:*** $20.50 per credit hour; $33 per term. Part-time tuition and fees vary according to course load. ***Payment plans:*** Installment, deferred payment.

FRESHMAN FINANCIAL AID (Fall 2010, est.) 637 applied for aid; of those 93% were deemed to have need. 100% of freshmen with need received aid; of those 29% had need fully met. ***Average percent of need met:*** 87% (excluding resources awarded to replace EFC). ***Average financial aid package:*** $20,489 (excluding resources awarded to replace EFC). 13% of all full-time freshmen had no need and received non-need-based gift aid.

UNDERGRADUATE FINANCIAL AID (Fall 2010, est.) 2,501 applied for aid; of those 94% were deemed to have need. 100% of undergraduates with need received aid; of those 23% had need fully met. ***Average percent of need met:*** 81% (excluding resources awarded to replace EFC). ***Average financial aid package:*** $25,536 (excluding resources awarded to replace EFC). 18% of all full-time undergraduates had no need and received non-need-based gift aid.

GIFT AID (NEED-BASED) ***Total amount:*** $43,897,865 (12% federal, 9% state, 78% institutional, 1% external sources). ***Receiving aid:*** Freshmen: 83% (589); all full-time undergraduates: 77% (2,328). ***Average award:*** Freshmen: $21,710; Undergraduates: $19,366. ***Scholarships, grants, and awards:*** Federal Pell, FSEOG, state, private, college/university gift aid from institutional funds.

GIFT AID (NON-NEED-BASED) ***Total amount:*** $3,535,716 (1% state, 98% institutional, 1% external sources). ***Receiving aid:*** Freshmen: 17% (123). Undergraduates: 15% (440). ***Average award:*** Freshmen: $14,618. Undergraduates: $14,220. ***Scholarships, grants, and awards by category:*** *Academic interests/achievement:* 2,324 awards ($26,403,971 total): general academic interests/achievements. *Creative arts/performance:* 71 awards ($136,000 total): art/fine arts, music. *Special achievements/activities:* 5 awards ($11,741 total): religious involvement. *Special characteristics:* 464 awards ($3,657,435 total): children and siblings of alumni, children of educators, children of faculty/staff, international students, religious affiliation. ***Tuition waivers:*** Full or partial for employees or children of employees.

LOANS ***Student loans:*** $18,318,858 (73% need-based, 27% non-need-based). 75% of past graduating class borrowed through all loan programs. *Average indebtedness per student:* $33,918. ***Average need-based loan:*** Freshmen: $4790. Undergraduates: $4297. ***Parent loans:*** $6,563,766 (25% need-based, 75% non-need-based). ***Programs:*** Federal Direct (Subsidized and Unsubsidized Stafford, PLUS), Perkins, college/university.

WORK-STUDY ***Federal work-study:*** Total amount: $984,336; 556 jobs averaging $1739. ***State or other work-study/employment:*** Total amount: $50,980 (81% need-based, 19% non-need-based). Part-time jobs available.

ATHLETIC AWARDS Total amount: $1,141,118 (75% need-based, 25% non-need-based).

APPLYING FOR FINANCIAL AID ***Required financial aid forms:*** FAFSA, state aid form. ***Financial aid deadline (priority):*** 2/15. ***Notification date:*** Continuous beginning 3/1. Students must reply by 5/1.

CONTACT Mr. Curtis Gaume, Director of Student Financial Aid, Canisius College, 2001 Main Street, Buffalo, NY 14208-1098, 716-888-2300 or toll-free 800-843-1517. *Fax:* 716-888-2377. *E-mail:* gaume@canisius.edu.

CAPELLA UNIVERSITY

Minneapolis, MN

CONTACT University Services, Capella University, 222 South Ninth Street, Minneapolis, MN 55402, 888-227-3552 or toll-free 888-CAPELLA.

CAPITAL UNIVERSITY

Columbus, OH

Tuition & fees: $29,310 **Average undergraduate aid package: $22,556**

ABOUT THE INSTITUTION Independent religious, coed. 60 undergraduate majors. Federal methodology is used as a basis for awarding need-based institutional aid.

UNDERGRADUATE EXPENSES for 2010–11 ***Comprehensive fee:*** $37,174 includes full-time tuition ($29,310) and room and board ($7864). Full-time tuition and fees vary according to course load. Room and board charges vary according to board plan and housing facility. ***Part-time tuition:*** $977 per credit hour. Part-time tuition and fees vary according to course load. ***Payment plan:*** Installment.

FRESHMAN FINANCIAL AID (Fall 2010, est.) 669 applied for aid; of those 93% were deemed to have need. 100% of freshmen with need received aid; of those 30% had need fully met. ***Average percent of need met:*** 34% (excluding resources awarded to replace EFC). ***Average financial aid package:*** $25,135 (excluding resources awarded to replace EFC). 7% of all full-time freshmen had no need and received non-need-based gift aid.

UNDERGRADUATE FINANCIAL AID (Fall 2010, est.) 2,083 applied for aid; of those 93% were deemed to have need. 100% of undergraduates with need received aid; of those 28% had need fully met. ***Average percent of need met:*** 26% (excluding resources awarded to replace EFC). ***Average financial aid package:*** $22,556 (excluding resources awarded to replace EFC). 12% of all full-time undergraduates had no need and received non-need-based gift aid.

GIFT AID (NEED-BASED) ***Total amount:*** $36,994,339 (11% federal, 2% state, 84% institutional, 3% external sources). ***Receiving aid:*** Freshmen: 77% (557);

all full-time undergraduates: 73% (1,737). ***Average award:*** Freshmen: $17,644; Undergraduates: $17,075. ***Scholarships, grants, and awards:*** Federal Pell, FSEOG, state, private, college/university gift aid from institutional funds, Federal Nursing.

GIFT AID (NON-NEED-BASED) ***Total amount:*** $1,184,627 (2% state, 30% institutional, 68% external sources). ***Receiving aid:*** Freshmen: 86% (622). Undergraduates: 81% (1,940). ***Average award:*** Freshmen: $16,012. Undergraduates: $12,748. ***Scholarships, grants, and awards by category:*** *Academic interests/achievement:* general academic interests/achievements. *Creative arts/performance:* music, performing arts. *Special achievements/activities:* hobbies/interests, leadership, religious involvement. *Special characteristics:* children and siblings of alumni, children of faculty/staff, ethnic background, international students, members of minority groups, relatives of clergy, religious affiliation, siblings of current students. ***Tuition waivers:*** Full or partial for employees or children of employees, senior citizens.

LOANS ***Student loans:*** $8,707,698 (99% need-based, 1% non-need-based). ***Average need-based loan:*** Freshmen: $3207. Undergraduates: $3646. ***Parent loans:*** $16,578,596 (100% need-based). ***Programs:*** Federal Direct (Subsidized and Unsubsidized Stafford, PLUS), Perkins, Federal Nursing, state, college/university, alternative loans.

WORK-STUDY ***Federal work-study:*** Total amount: $2,408,174; jobs available. ***State or other work-study/employment:*** Part-time jobs available.

APPLYING FOR FINANCIAL AID ***Required financial aid form:*** FAFSA. ***Financial aid deadline (priority):*** 2/28. ***Notification date:*** Continuous beginning 3/1. Students must reply by 5/1.

CONTACT Ms. Pamela Varda, Office of Financial Aid, Capital University, 1 College and Main Street, Columbus, OH 43209-2394, 614-236-6511 or toll-free 800-289-6289. *Fax:* 614-236-6926. *E-mail:* finaid@capital.edu.

CAPITOL COLLEGE

Laurel, MD

Tuition & fees: $19,890 **Average undergraduate aid package: $12,766**

ABOUT THE INSTITUTION Independent, coed. ***Awards:*** associate, bachelor's, and master's degrees and post-bachelor's certificates. 13 undergraduate majors. ***Total enrollment:*** 699. Undergraduates: 309. Federal methodology is used as a basis for awarding need-based institutional aid.

UNDERGRADUATE EXPENSES for 2010–11 ***Application fee:*** $25. ***Tuition:*** full-time $19,890; part-time $638 per credit. Room and board charges vary according to housing facility. ***Payment plans:*** Installment, deferred payment.

FRESHMAN FINANCIAL AID (Fall 2010, est.) 50 applied for aid; of those 80% were deemed to have need. 100% of freshmen with need received aid; of those 8% had need fully met. ***Average financial aid package:*** $16,423 (excluding resources awarded to replace EFC). 35% of all full-time freshmen had no need and received non-need-based gift aid.

UNDERGRADUATE FINANCIAL AID (Fall 2010, est.) 238 applied for aid; of those 74% were deemed to have need. 100% of undergraduates with need received aid; of those 3% had need fully met. ***Average financial aid package:*** $12,766 (excluding resources awarded to replace EFC). 16% of all full-time undergraduates had no need and received non-need-based gift aid.

GIFT AID (NEED-BASED) ***Total amount:*** $2,238,833 (83% federal, 12% state, 3% institutional, 2% external sources). ***Receiving aid:*** Freshmen: 58% (32); all full-time undergraduates: 44% (151). ***Average award:*** Freshmen: $6030; Undergraduates: $6642. ***Scholarships, grants, and awards:*** Federal Pell, FSEOG, state, private, college/university gift aid from institutional funds.

GIFT AID (NON-NEED-BASED) ***Total amount:*** $1,578,848 (100% institutional). ***Receiving aid:*** Freshmen: 73% (40). Undergraduates: 42% (146). ***Average award:*** Freshmen: $15,314. Undergraduates: $11,547. ***Scholarships, grants, and awards by category:*** *Academic interests/achievement:* general academic interests/achievements. ***Tuition waivers:*** Full or partial for employees or children of employees. ***ROTC:*** Army cooperative.

LOANS ***Student loans:*** $1,471,184 (100% need-based). 80% of past graduating class borrowed through all loan programs. *Average indebtedness per student:* $16,814. ***Average need-based loan:*** Freshmen: $3192. Undergraduates: $3958. ***Parent loans:*** $227,942 (100% need-based). ***Programs:*** Federal Direct (Subsidized and Unsubsidized Stafford, PLUS), Perkins.

WORK-STUDY ***Federal work-study:*** Total amount: $64,458; jobs available.

APPLYING FOR FINANCIAL AID ***Required financial aid form:*** FAFSA. ***Financial aid deadline:*** Continuous. ***Notification date:*** Continuous. Students must reply within 3 weeks of notification.

CONTACT Suzanne Thompson, Director of Financial Aid, Capitol College, 11301 Springfield Road, Laurel, MD 20708-9759, 301-369-2800 Ext. 3037 or toll-free 800-950-1992. *Fax:* 301-369-2328. *E-mail:* sthompson@capitol-college.edu.

CARDINAL STRITCH UNIVERSITY

Milwaukee, WI

CONTACT Financial Aid Director, Cardinal Stritch University, 6801 North Yates Road, Milwaukee, WI 53217-3985, 414-410-4000 or toll-free 800-347-8822 Ext. 4040.

CARIBBEAN UNIVERSITY

Bayamón, PR

CONTACT Financial Aid Office, Caribbean University, Box 493, Bayamón, PR 00960-0493, 787-780-0070.

CARLETON COLLEGE

Northfield, MN

Tuition & fees: $42,942 **Average undergraduate aid package: $35,456**

ABOUT THE INSTITUTION Independent, coed. 39 undergraduate majors. Both federal and institutional methodology are used as a basis for awarding need-based institutional aid.

UNDERGRADUATE EXPENSES for 2011–12 ***Comprehensive fee:*** $54,180 includes full-time tuition ($42,690), mandatory fees ($252), and room and board ($11,238). ***College room only:*** $5904. Room and board charges vary according to board plan. ***Payment plans:*** Tuition prepayment, installment.

FRESHMAN FINANCIAL AID (Fall 2009) 317 applied for aid; of those 84% were deemed to have need. 100% of freshmen with need received aid; of those 100% had need fully met. ***Average percent of need met:*** 100% (excluding resources awarded to replace EFC). ***Average financial aid package:*** $33,708 (excluding resources awarded to replace EFC). 5% of all full-time freshmen had no need and received non-need-based gift aid.

UNDERGRADUATE FINANCIAL AID (Fall 2009) 1,714 applied for aid; of those 64% were deemed to have need. 100% of undergraduates with need received aid; of those 100% had need fully met. ***Average percent of need met:*** 100% (excluding resources awarded to replace EFC). ***Average financial aid package:*** $35,456 (excluding resources awarded to replace EFC). 6% of all full-time undergraduates had no need and received non-need-based gift aid.

GIFT AID (NEED-BASED) ***Total amount:*** $30,648,462 (5% federal, 1% state, 90% institutional, 4% external sources). ***Receiving aid:*** Freshmen: 52% (266); all full-time undergraduates: 55% (1,103). ***Average award:*** Freshmen: $30,179; Undergraduates: $29,471. ***Scholarships, grants, and awards:*** Federal Pell, FSEOG, state, private, college/university gift aid from institutional funds.

GIFT AID (NON-NEED-BASED) ***Total amount:*** $1,106,873 (3% federal, 31% institutional, 66% external sources). ***Receiving aid:*** Freshmen: 5% (27). Undergraduates: 10% (199). ***Average award:*** Freshmen: $3368. Undergraduates: $2440. ***Scholarships, grants, and awards by category:*** *Academic interests/achievement:* 235 awards ($311,566 total): general academic interests/achievements. *Creative arts/performance:* 4 awards ($1530 total): music. ***Tuition waivers:*** Full or partial for employees or children of employees.

LOANS ***Student loans:*** $5,363,103 (95% need-based, 5% non-need-based). 44% of past graduating class borrowed through all loan programs. *Average indebtedness per student:* $19,436. ***Average need-based loan:*** Freshmen: $3916. Undergraduates: $4452. ***Parent loans:*** $951,148 (75% need-based, 25% non-need-based). ***Programs:*** Federal Direct (Subsidized and Unsubsidized Stafford, PLUS), Perkins, state, college/university.

WORK-STUDY ***Federal work-study:*** Total amount: $898,122; 364 jobs averaging $2467. ***State or other work-study/employment:*** Total amount: $3,309,335 (56% need-based, 44% non-need-based). 1,306 part-time jobs averaging $2533.

APPLYING FOR FINANCIAL AID ***Required financial aid forms:*** FAFSA, CSS Financial Aid PROFILE, noncustodial (divorced/separated) parent's statement. ***Financial aid deadline:*** 2/15. ***Notification date:*** 4/1. Students must reply by 5/1 or within 2 weeks of notification.

CONTACT Mr. Rodney M. Oto, Director of Student Financial Services, Carleton College, One North College Street, Northfield, MN 55057-4001, 507-222-4138 or toll-free 800-995-2275. *Fax:* 507-222-4269.

CARLOS ALBIZU UNIVERSITY

San Juan, PR

Tuition & fees: $6939 **Average undergraduate aid package: $6548**

ABOUT THE INSTITUTION Independent, coed, primarily women. 2 undergraduate majors. Federal methodology is used as a basis for awarding need-based institutional aid.

UNDERGRADUATE EXPENSES for 2010–11 ***Tuition:*** full-time $5940; part-time $165 per credit. ***Required fees:*** full-time $999; $333 per term.

UNDERGRADUATE FINANCIAL AID (Fall 2010, est.) 55 applied for aid; of those 100% were deemed to have need. 100% of undergraduates with need received aid. ***Average percent of need met:*** 30% (excluding resources awarded to replace EFC). ***Average financial aid package:*** $6548 (excluding resources awarded to replace EFC).

GIFT AID (NEED-BASED) ***Total amount:*** $184,085 (91% federal, 5% state, 4% external sources). ***Receiving aid:*** All full-time undergraduates: 59% (44). ***Average award:*** Undergraduates: $3789. ***Scholarships, grants, and awards:*** Federal Pell, FSEOG, state, college/university gift aid from institutional funds.

GIFT AID (NON-NEED-BASED) ***Scholarships, grants, and awards by category:*** *Academic interests/achievement:* social sciences. ***Tuition waivers:*** Full or partial for employees or children of employees.

LOANS ***Student loans:*** $175,850 (71% need-based, 29% non-need-based). ***Average need-based loan:*** Undergraduates: $5450. ***Programs:*** Federal Direct (Subsidized and Unsubsidized Stafford, PLUS).

WORK-STUDY ***Federal work-study:*** Total amount: $6712; 6 jobs averaging $1118.

CONTACT Mrs. Doris J. Quero, Director, Carlos Albizu University, PO Box 9023711, San Juan, PR 00901, 787-725-6500 Ext. 1529. *Fax:* 787-721-4008. *E-mail:* dquero@albizu.edu.

CARLOS ALBIZU UNIVERSITY, MIAMI CAMPUS

Miami, FL

CONTACT Maria V. Chavez, Senior Financial Aid Officer, Carlos Albizu University, Miami Campus, 2173 Northwest 99th Avenue, Miami, FL 33172, 305-593-1223 Ext. 153 or toll-free 888-672-3246. *Fax:* 305-593-8902. *E-mail:* mchavez@albizu.edu.

CARLOW UNIVERSITY

Pittsburgh, PA

CONTACT Ms. Natalie Wilson, Director of Financial Aid, Carlow University, 3333 Fifth Avenue, Pittsburgh, PA 15213-3165, 412-578-6171 or toll-free 800-333-CARLOW.

CARNEGIE MELLON UNIVERSITY

Pittsburgh, PA

Tuition & fees: $41,940 **Average undergraduate aid package: $29,315**

ABOUT THE INSTITUTION Independent, coed. 79 undergraduate majors. Both federal and institutional methodology are used as a basis for awarding need-based institutional aid.

UNDERGRADUATE EXPENSES for 2010–11 ***One-time required fee:*** $192. ***Comprehensive fee:*** $52,690 includes full-time tuition ($41,500), mandatory fees ($440), and room and board ($10,750). ***College room only:*** $6300. Full-time tuition and fees vary according to student level. Room and board charges vary according to board plan and housing facility. Part-time tuition and fees vary according to student level. ***Payment plan:*** Installment.

FRESHMAN FINANCIAL AID (Fall 2010, est.) 1,065 applied for aid; of those 76% were deemed to have need. 99% of freshmen with need received aid; of those 30% had need fully met. ***Average percent of need met:*** 82% (excluding resources awarded to replace EFC). ***Average financial aid package:*** $29,849 (excluding resources awarded to replace EFC). 8% of all full-time freshmen had no need and received non-need-based gift aid.

UNDERGRADUATE FINANCIAL AID (Fall 2010, est.) 3,428 applied for aid; of those 86% were deemed to have need. 99% of undergraduates with need received aid; of those 32% had need fully met. ***Average percent of need met:*** 81% (excluding resources awarded to replace EFC). ***Average financial aid package:*** $29,315 (excluding resources awarded to replace EFC). 7% of all full-time undergraduates had no need and received non-need-based gift aid.

GIFT AID (NEED-BASED) ***Total amount:*** $68,193,537 (9% federal, 1% state, 86% institutional, 4% external sources). ***Receiving aid:*** Freshmen: 51% (765); all full-time undergraduates: 47% (2,799). ***Average award:*** Freshmen: $24,680; Undergraduates: $24,819. ***Scholarships, grants, and awards:*** Federal Pell, FSEOG, state, private, college/university gift aid from institutional funds.

GIFT AID (NON-NEED-BASED) ***Total amount:*** $13,044,016 (85% institutional, 15% external sources). ***Receiving aid:*** Freshmen: 21% (312). Undergraduates: 19% (1,125). ***Average award:*** Freshmen: $8422. Undergraduates: $11,851. ***Scholarships, grants, and awards by category:*** *Academic interests/achievement:* general academic interests/achievements. *Creative arts/performance:* art/fine arts, music. *Special achievements/activities:* leadership. *Special characteristics:* members of minority groups, out-of-state students. ***Tuition waivers:*** Full or partial for employees or children of employees.

LOANS ***Student loans:*** $20,991,328 (88% need-based, 12% non-need-based). 47% of past graduating class borrowed through all loan programs. *Average indebtedness per student:* $30,744. ***Average need-based loan:*** Freshmen: $3637. Undergraduates: $4668. ***Parent loans:*** $8,955,829 (23% need-based, 77% non-need-based). ***Programs:*** Perkins.

WORK-STUDY ***Federal work-study:*** Total amount: $5,294,766; jobs available. ***State or other work-study/employment:*** Total amount: $5584 (100% need-based). Part-time jobs available.

APPLYING FOR FINANCIAL AID ***Required financial aid forms:*** FAFSA, institution's own form, parent and student federal tax returns and parent W-2 forms. ***Financial aid deadline:*** 5/1 (priority: 2/15). ***Notification date:*** 3/15.

CONTACT Linda M. Anderson, Director of Enrollment Services, Carnegie Mellon University, 5000 Forbes Avenue, Pittsburgh, PA 15213-3890, 412-268-8186. *Fax:* 412-268-8084. *E-mail:* thehub@andrew.cmu.edu.

CAROLINA CHRISTIAN COLLEGE

Winston-Salem, NC

Tuition & fees: $7200 **Average undergraduate aid package: N/A**

ABOUT THE INSTITUTION Independent nondenominational, coed. 1 undergraduate major. Federal methodology is used as a basis for awarding need-based institutional aid.

UNDERGRADUATE EXPENSES for 2011–12 ***Tuition:*** full-time $7000; part-time $875 per course. ***Payment plan:*** Installment.

FRESHMAN FINANCIAL AID (Fall 2009) 45 applied for aid; of those 100% were deemed to have need. 100% of freshmen with need received aid.

GIFT AID (NEED-BASED) ***Total amount:*** $5000 (100% federal). ***Receiving aid:*** Freshmen: 13% (6). ***Average award:*** Freshmen: $1500. ***Scholarships, grants, and awards:*** Federal Pell, FSEOG.

LOANS ***Student loans:*** $245,000 (100% need-based). ***Programs:*** Federal Direct (Subsidized and Unsubsidized Stafford).

APPLYING FOR FINANCIAL AID ***Required financial aid form:*** FAFSA. ***Financial aid deadline:*** Continuous.

CONTACT LaTanya V. Lucas, Academic Dean, Carolina Christian College, 4209 Indiana Avenue, Winston Salem, NC 27105, 336-744-0900 Ext. 106. *E-mail:* latanya@carolina.edu.

CARROLL COLLEGE

Helena, MT

Tuition & fees: $23,594 **Average undergraduate aid package: $19,272**

ABOUT THE INSTITUTION Independent Roman Catholic, coed. ***Awards:*** associate and bachelor's degrees. 43 undergraduate majors. ***Total enrollment:*** 1,409. Undergraduates: 1,409. Freshmen: 345. Federal methodology is used as a basis for awarding need-based institutional aid.

UNDERGRADUATE EXPENSES for 2010–11 ***Application fee:*** $35. ***Comprehensive fee:*** $31,112 includes full-time tuition ($23,144), mandatory fees ($450), and room and board ($7518). Full-time tuition and fees vary according to course load. Room and board charges vary according to board plan and housing facility. Part-time tuition and fees vary according to course load. ***Payment plan:*** Installment.

FRESHMAN FINANCIAL AID (Fall 2010, est.) 292 applied for aid; of those 85% were deemed to have need. 100% of freshmen with need received aid; of those 20% had need fully met. ***Average percent of need met:*** 79% (excluding resources awarded to replace EFC). ***Average financial aid package:*** $20,152 (excluding resources awarded to replace EFC). 26% of all full-time freshmen had no need and received non-need-based gift aid.

UNDERGRADUATE FINANCIAL AID (Fall 2010, est.) 990 applied for aid; of those 87% were deemed to have need. 100% of undergraduates with need received aid; of those 19% had need fully met. ***Average percent of need met:*** 76% (excluding resources awarded to replace EFC). ***Average financial aid package:*** $19,272 (excluding resources awarded to replace EFC). 30% of all full-time undergraduates had no need and received non-need-based gift aid.

GIFT AID (NEED-BASED) ***Total amount:*** $11,466,650 (17% federal, 1% state, 74% institutional, 8% external sources). ***Receiving aid:*** Freshmen: 72% (242); all full-time undergraduates: 66% (852). ***Average award:*** Freshmen: $14,099; Undergraduates: $13,059. ***Scholarships, grants, and awards:*** Federal Pell, FSEOG, state, private, college/university gift aid from institutional funds.

GIFT AID (NON-NEED-BASED) ***Total amount:*** $4,955,045 (12% federal, 75% institutional, 13% external sources). ***Receiving aid:*** Freshmen: 12% (39). Undergraduates: 9% (113). ***Average award:*** Freshmen: $9811. Undergraduates: $8558. ***Scholarships, grants, and awards by category:*** *Academic interests/achievement:* 1,186 awards ($10,264,545 total): general academic interests/achievements. *Creative arts/performance:* 19 awards ($38,025 total): debating, theater/drama. *Special achievements/activities:* 31 awards ($93,090 total): cheerleading/drum major, general special achievements/activities, leadership, religious involvement. *Special characteristics:* 86 awards ($1,120,954 total): children of faculty/staff, children of union members/company employees, international students, siblings of current students, spouses of current students, veterans. ***Tuition waivers:*** Full or partial for employees or children of employees, senior citizens. ***ROTC:*** Army.

LOANS ***Student loans:*** $6,734,089 (73% need-based, 27% non-need-based). 74% of past graduating class borrowed through all loan programs. *Average indebtedness per student:* $29,122. ***Average need-based loan:*** Freshmen: $3966. Undergraduates: $4338. ***Parent loans:*** $1,971,242 (37% need-based, 63% non-need-based). ***Programs:*** Perkins, private loans.

WORK-STUDY ***Federal work-study:*** Total amount: $508,016; 242 jobs averaging $2094. ***State or other work-study/employment:*** Part-time jobs available.

ATHLETIC AWARDS Total amount: $1,698,304 (49% need-based, 51% non-need-based).

APPLYING FOR FINANCIAL AID ***Required financial aid form:*** FAFSA. ***Financial aid deadline (priority):*** 3/1. ***Notification date:*** Continuous beginning 3/1. Students must reply by 5/1 or within 2 weeks of notification.

CONTACT Ms. Janet Riis, Director of Financial Aid, Carroll College, 1601 North Benton Avenue, Helena, MT 59625-0002, 406-447-5423 or toll-free 800-992-3648. *Fax:* 406-447-4533. *E-mail:* jriis@carroll.edu.

CARROLL UNIVERSITY

Waukesha, WI

Tuition & fees: $25,248 **Average undergraduate aid package: $19,499**

ABOUT THE INSTITUTION Independent Presbyterian, coed. 77 undergraduate majors. Federal methodology is used as a basis for awarding need-based institutional aid.

UNDERGRADUATE EXPENSES for 2011–12 ***Comprehensive fee:*** $32,984 includes full-time tuition ($24,749), mandatory fees ($499), and room and board ($7736). ***College room only:*** $4222. Full-time tuition and fees vary according to program. Room and board charges vary according to board plan and housing facility. ***Part-time tuition:*** $310 per credit. Part-time tuition and fees vary according to course load and program. ***Payment plan:*** Installment.

FRESHMAN FINANCIAL AID (Fall 2010, est.) 710 applied for aid; of those 88% were deemed to have need. 100% of freshmen with need received aid; of those 42% had need fully met. ***Average percent of need met:*** 100% (excluding resources awarded to replace EFC). ***Average financial aid package:*** $18,397 (excluding resources awarded to replace EFC). 17% of all full-time freshmen had no need and received non-need-based gift aid.

UNDERGRADUATE FINANCIAL AID (Fall 2010, est.) 2,399 applied for aid; of those 89% were deemed to have need. 100% of undergraduates with need received aid; of those 39% had need fully met. ***Average percent of need met:*** 100% (excluding resources awarded to replace EFC). ***Average financial aid package:*** $19,499 (excluding resources awarded to replace EFC). 20% of all full-time undergraduates had no need and received non-need-based gift aid.

GIFT AID (NEED-BASED) ***Total amount:*** $25,178,398 (16% federal, 10% state, 74% institutional). ***Receiving aid:*** Freshmen: 83% (628); all full-time undergraduates: 80% (2,136). ***Average award:*** Freshmen: $14,445; Undergraduates: $13,117. ***Scholarships, grants, and awards:*** Federal Pell, FSEOG, state, private, college/university gift aid from institutional funds.

GIFT AID (NON-NEED-BASED) ***Total amount:*** $5,586,382 (1% state, 83% institutional, 16% external sources). ***Receiving aid:*** Freshmen: 77% (580). Undergraduates: 74% (1,953). ***Average award:*** Freshmen: $12,162. Undergraduates: $10,437. ***Scholarships, grants, and awards by category:*** *Academic interests/achievement:* 2,156 awards ($19,795,868 total): biological sciences, business, computer science, education, general academic interests/achievements, health fields, humanities, international studies, mathematics, physical sciences, premedicine, social sciences. *Creative arts/performance:* 97 awards ($161,250 total): art/fine arts, journalism/publications, music, performing arts, theater/drama. *Special achievements/activities:* 930 awards ($484,091 total): general special achievements/activities, junior miss, leadership, memberships, religious involvement. *Special characteristics:* 1,445 awards ($1,472,902 total): adult students, children and siblings of alumni, children of current students, children of faculty/staff, general special characteristics, international students, siblings of current students, spouses of current students. ***Tuition waivers:*** Full or partial for employees or children of employees.

LOANS ***Student loans:*** $21,122,066 (45% need-based, 55% non-need-based). 78% of past graduating class borrowed through all loan programs. *Average indebtedness per student:* $28,777. ***Average need-based loan:*** Freshmen: $3507. Undergraduates: $4549. ***Parent loans:*** $2,753,603 (75% need-based, 25% non-need-based). ***Programs:*** Federal Direct (Subsidized and Unsubsidized Stafford, PLUS), Perkins, state, college/university.

WORK-STUDY ***Federal work-study:*** Total amount: $1,962,075; 897 jobs averaging $2187. ***State or other work-study/employment:*** Total amount: $1,628,270 (100% non-need-based). 782 part-time jobs averaging $2082.

APPLYING FOR FINANCIAL AID ***Required financial aid form:*** FAFSA. ***Financial aid deadline:*** Continuous. ***Notification date:*** Continuous beginning 2/15. Students must reply by 5/1 or within 2 weeks of notification.

CONTACT Dawn Scott, Director of Financial Aid, Carroll University, 100 North East Avenue, Waukesha, WI 53186-5593, 262-524-7297 or toll-free 800-CARROLL. *Fax:* 262-951-3037. *E-mail:* dscott@carrollu.edu.

CARSON-NEWMAN COLLEGE

Jefferson City, TN

Tuition & fees: $21,778 **Average undergraduate aid package: $16,621**

ABOUT THE INSTITUTION Independent Southern Baptist, coed. 71 undergraduate majors. Federal methodology is used as a basis for awarding need-based institutional aid.

UNDERGRADUATE EXPENSES for 2011–12 ***Comprehensive fee:*** $28,024 includes full-time tuition ($20,786), mandatory fees ($992), and room and board ($6246). Full-time tuition and fees vary according to class time and course load. Room and board charges vary according to board plan, gender, and housing facility. ***Part-time tuition:*** $818 per semester hour. ***Payment plans:*** Installment, deferred payment.

FRESHMAN FINANCIAL AID (Fall 2010, est.) 418 applied for aid; of those 89% were deemed to have need. 100% of freshmen with need received aid; of those 21% had need fully met. ***Average percent of need met:*** 75% (excluding resources awarded to replace EFC). ***Average financial aid package:*** $18,063 (excluding resources awarded to replace EFC). 12% of all full-time freshmen had no need and received non-need-based gift aid.

UNDERGRADUATE FINANCIAL AID (Fall 2010, est.) 1,556 applied for aid; of those 88% were deemed to have need. 100% of undergraduates with need received aid; of those 21% had need fully met. ***Average percent of need met:*** 70% (excluding resources awarded to replace EFC). ***Average financial aid***

package: $16,621 (excluding resources awarded to replace EFC). 15% of all full-time undergraduates had no need and received non-need-based gift aid.

GIFT AID (NEED-BASED) ***Total amount:*** $16,586,007 (20% federal, 23% state, 54% institutional, 3% external sources). ***Receiving aid:*** Freshmen: 86% (367); all full-time undergraduates: 79% (1,344). ***Average award:*** Freshmen: $14,493; Undergraduates: $12,279. ***Scholarships, grants, and awards:*** Federal Pell, FSEOG, state, private, college/university gift aid from institutional funds.

GIFT AID (NON-NEED-BASED) ***Total amount:*** $2,127,651 (23% state, 73% institutional, 4% external sources). ***Receiving aid:*** Freshmen: 85% (362). Undergraduates: 77% (1,306). ***Average award:*** Freshmen: $10,122. Undergraduates: $7864. ***Scholarships, grants, and awards by category:*** *Academic interests/achievement:* biological sciences, business, education, general academic interests/achievements, home economics, mathematics, military science, religion/biblical studies. *Creative arts/performance:* art/fine arts, debating, journalism/publications, music. *Special achievements/activities:* leadership, memberships. *Special characteristics:* children and siblings of alumni, members of minority groups, relatives of clergy, siblings of current students. ***Tuition waivers:*** Full or partial for employees or children of employees, senior citizens.

LOANS ***Student loans:*** $8,178,775 (95% need-based, 5% non-need-based). 69% of past graduating class borrowed through all loan programs. *Average indebtedness per student:* $20,528. ***Average need-based loan:*** Freshmen: $2765. Undergraduates: $3693. ***Parent loans:*** $1,815,354 (92% need-based, 8% non-need-based). ***Programs:*** Perkins, state, college/university, alternative loans.

WORK-STUDY ***Federal work-study:*** Total amount: $189,968; 119 jobs averaging $1596. ***State or other work-study/employment:*** Total amount: $11,400 (87% need-based, 13% non-need-based). 14 part-time jobs averaging $814.

ATHLETIC AWARDS Total amount: $1,866,060 (73% need-based, 27% non-need-based).

APPLYING FOR FINANCIAL AID ***Required financial aid forms:*** FAFSA, institution's own form. ***Financial aid deadline (priority):*** 4/1. ***Notification date:*** Continuous. Students must reply within 2 weeks of notification.

CONTACT Danette Seale, Director of Financial Aid, Carson-Newman College, 1646 Russell Avenue, Jefferson City, TN 37760, 865-471-3247 or toll-free 800-678-9061. *Fax:* 865-471-3502. *E-mail:* dseale@cn.edu.

CARTHAGE COLLEGE

Kenosha, WI

ABOUT THE INSTITUTION Independent religious, coed. ***Awards:*** bachelor's and master's degrees. 50 undergraduate majors. ***Total enrollment:*** 2,778. Undergraduates: 2,660. Freshmen: 686.

GIFT AID (NEED-BASED) ***Scholarships, grants, and awards:*** Federal Pell, FSEOG, state, private, college/university gift aid from institutional funds.

GIFT AID (NON-NEED-BASED) ***Scholarships, grants, and awards by category:*** *Academic interests/achievement:* biological sciences, business, computer science, engineering/technologies, foreign languages, general academic interests/achievements, health fields, mathematics, physical sciences, premedicine, religion/biblical studies. *Creative arts/performance:* applied art and design, art/fine arts, music, theater/drama. *Special achievements/activities:* general special achievements/activities, leadership, religious involvement. *Special characteristics:* children and siblings of alumni, children of educators, children of faculty/staff, children of public servants, local/state students, members of minority groups, previous college experience, relatives of clergy, religious affiliation, siblings of current students.

LOANS ***Programs:*** Federal Direct (Subsidized and Unsubsidized Stafford, PLUS), Perkins, state, college/university.

WORK-STUDY ***Federal work-study:*** Total amount: $358,859; 843 jobs averaging $4000. ***State or other work-study/employment:*** Total amount: $7000 (100% non-need-based). Part-time jobs available.

APPLYING FOR FINANCIAL AID ***Required financial aid form:*** FAFSA.

CONTACT Vatistas Vatistas, Director of Financial Aid, Carthage College, 2001 Alford Park Drive, Kenosha, WI 53140, 262-551-6001 or toll-free 800-351-4058. *Fax:* 262-551-5762. *E-mail:* vvatistas@carthage.edu.

CASE WESTERN RESERVE UNIVERSITY

Cleveland, OH

Tuition & fees: $37,648 **Average undergraduate aid package: $33,130**

ABOUT THE INSTITUTION Independent, coed. 66 undergraduate majors. Federal methodology is used as a basis for awarding need-based institutional aid.

UNDERGRADUATE EXPENSES for 2010–11 ***One-time required fee:*** $380. ***Comprehensive fee:*** $49,048 includes full-time tuition ($37,300), mandatory fees ($348), and room and board ($11,400). ***College room only:*** $6550. Room and board charges vary according to board plan, housing facility, and student level. ***Part-time tuition:*** $1554 per credit hour. Part-time tuition and fees vary according to course load. ***Payment plan:*** Installment.

FRESHMAN FINANCIAL AID (Fall 2010, est.) 802 applied for aid; of those 84% were deemed to have need. 100% of freshmen with need received aid; of those 80% had need fully met. ***Average percent of need met:*** 92% (excluding resources awarded to replace EFC). ***Average financial aid package:*** $32,739 (excluding resources awarded to replace EFC). 21% of all full-time freshmen had no need and received non-need-based gift aid.

UNDERGRADUATE FINANCIAL AID (Fall 2010, est.) 2,889 applied for aid; of those 91% were deemed to have need. 100% of undergraduates with need received aid; of those 86% had need fully met. ***Average percent of need met:*** 83% (excluding resources awarded to replace EFC). ***Average financial aid package:*** $33,130 (excluding resources awarded to replace EFC). 20% of all full-time undergraduates had no need and received non-need-based gift aid.

GIFT AID (NEED-BASED) ***Total amount:*** $64,428,989 (10% federal, 2% state, 83% institutional, 5% external sources). ***Receiving aid:*** Freshmen: 65% (661); all full-time undergraduates: 62% (2,542). ***Average award:*** Freshmen: $25,342; Undergraduates: $23,585. ***Scholarships, grants, and awards:*** Federal Pell, FSEOG, state, private, college/university gift aid from institutional funds.

GIFT AID (NON-NEED-BASED) ***Total amount:*** $16,281,519 (1% state, 95% institutional, 4% external sources). ***Receiving aid:*** Freshmen: 64% (651). Undergraduates: 61% (2,511). ***Average award:*** Freshmen: $20,462. Undergraduates: $19,476. ***Scholarships, grants, and awards by category:*** *Academic interests/achievement:* 2,331 awards ($42,818,584 total): biological sciences, business, communication, computer science, education, engineering/technologies, English, foreign languages, general academic interests/achievements, health fields, humanities, international studies, mathematics, physical sciences, premedicine, religion/biblical studies, social sciences. *Creative arts/performance:* 35 awards ($490,400 total): art/fine arts, creative writing, dance, general creative arts/performance, music, performing arts, theater/drama. *Special achievements/activities:* 49 awards ($134,375 total): leadership. *Special characteristics:* 210 awards ($6,474,830 total): children of faculty/staff. ***Tuition waivers:*** Full or partial for employees or children of employees.

LOANS ***Student loans:*** $35,283,783 (60% need-based, 40% non-need-based). 60% of past graduating class borrowed through all loan programs. *Average indebtedness per student:* $39,236. ***Average need-based loan:*** Freshmen: $6183. Undergraduates: $7430. ***Parent loans:*** $9,104,628 (95% need-based, 5% non-need-based). ***Programs:*** Perkins, Federal Nursing, state, college/university, alternative loans.

WORK-STUDY ***Federal work-study:*** Total amount: $5,756,343; 1,871 jobs averaging $3058.

APPLYING FOR FINANCIAL AID ***Required financial aid forms:*** FAFSA, institution's own form. ***Financial aid deadline (priority):*** 2/15. ***Notification date:*** Continuous beginning 3/15. Students must reply by 5/1 or within 2 weeks of notification.

CONTACT Mrs. Venus M. Puliafico, Director of University Financial Aid, Case Western Reserve University, 2049 Martin Luther King Jr. Drive, Cleveland, OH 44106-7049, 216-368-4530. *Fax:* 216-368-5054. *E-mail:* vxp4@case.edu.

CASTLETON STATE COLLEGE

Castleton, VT

CONTACT Kathleen O'Meara, Director of Financial Aid, Castleton State College, Castleton, VT 05735, 802-468-1292 or toll-free 800-639-8521. *Fax:* 802-468-5237. *E-mail:* kathy.omeara@castleton.edu.

CATAWBA COLLEGE

Salisbury, NC

Tuition & fees: $25,160 **Average undergraduate aid package: $19,968**

ABOUT THE INSTITUTION Independent religious, coed. 42 undergraduate majors. Federal methodology is used as a basis for awarding need-based institutional aid.

UNDERGRADUATE EXPENSES for 2010–11 ***Comprehensive fee:*** $33,860 includes full-time tuition ($25,160) and room and board ($8700). ***Part-time tuition:*** $655 per credit hour. ***Payment plan:*** Installment.

FRESHMAN FINANCIAL AID (Fall 2010, est.) 236 applied for aid; of those 91% were deemed to have need. 100% of freshmen with need received aid; of those 20% had need fully met. ***Average percent of need met:*** 83% (excluding resources awarded to replace EFC). ***Average financial aid package:*** $21,098 (excluding resources awarded to replace EFC). 6% of all full-time freshmen had no need and received non-need-based gift aid.

UNDERGRADUATE FINANCIAL AID (Fall 2010, est.) 1,038 applied for aid; of those 94% were deemed to have need. 100% of undergraduates with need received aid; of those 20% had need fully met. ***Average percent of need met:*** 80% (excluding resources awarded to replace EFC). ***Average financial aid package:*** $19,968 (excluding resources awarded to replace EFC). 6% of all full-time undergraduates had no need and received non-need-based gift aid.

GIFT AID (NEED-BASED) ***Total amount:*** $4,283,748 (64% federal, 36% state). ***Receiving aid:*** Freshmen: 69% (175); all full-time undergraduates: 57% (699). ***Average award:*** Freshmen: $6032; Undergraduates: $5727. ***Scholarships, grants, and awards:*** Federal Pell, FSEOG, state, private, college/university gift aid from institutional funds.

GIFT AID (NON-NEED-BASED) ***Total amount:*** $11,298,760 (16% state, 82% institutional, 2% external sources). ***Receiving aid:*** Freshmen: 85% (215). Undergraduates: 78% (967). ***Average award:*** Freshmen: $12,345. Undergraduates: $11,053. ***Scholarships, grants, and awards by category:*** *Academic interests/achievement:* education, general academic interests/achievements. *Creative arts/performance:* music, theater/drama. *Special achievements/activities:* general special achievements/activities. ***Tuition waivers:*** Full or partial for employees or children of employees.

LOANS ***Student loans:*** $6,532,175 (50% need-based, 50% non-need-based). 74% of past graduating class borrowed through all loan programs. *Average indebtedness per student:* $27,907. ***Average need-based loan:*** Freshmen: $3134. Undergraduates: $4053. ***Parent loans:*** $1,880,823 (100% non-need-based). ***Programs:*** Federal Direct (Subsidized and Unsubsidized Stafford, PLUS), TERI Loans, Nellie Mae Loans, Advantage Loans, alternative loans, CitiAssist Loans.

WORK-STUDY ***Federal work-study:*** Total amount: $356,641; 195 jobs averaging $1633. ***State or other work-study/employment:*** Total amount: $369,658 (100% non-need-based). Part-time jobs available.

ATHLETIC AWARDS Total amount: $2,723,890 (100% non-need-based).

APPLYING FOR FINANCIAL AID ***Required financial aid forms:*** FAFSA, state aid form. ***Financial aid deadline (priority):*** 3/15. ***Notification date:*** Continuous beginning 2/15. Students must reply within 2 weeks of notification.

CONTACT Mrs. Melanie McCulloh, Director of Scholarships and Financial Aid, Catawba College, 2300 West Innes Street, Salisbury, NC 28144-2488, 704-637-4416 or toll-free 800-CATAWBA. *Fax:* 704-637-4252. *E-mail:* mcmccull@catawba.edu.

THE CATHOLIC UNIVERSITY OF AMERICA

Washington, DC

Tuition & fees: $33,780 **Average undergraduate aid package: $30,654**

ABOUT THE INSTITUTION Independent religious, coed. 60 undergraduate majors. Federal methodology is used as a basis for awarding need-based institutional aid.

UNDERGRADUATE EXPENSES for 2010–11 ***One-time required fee:*** $425. ***Comprehensive fee:*** $46,522 includes full-time tuition ($33,580), mandatory fees ($200), and room and board ($12,742). ***College room only:*** $7744. Full-time tuition and fees vary according to program. Room and board charges vary according to board plan and housing facility. ***Part-time tuition:*** $1315 per credit hour. ***Part-time fees:*** $100 per year. Part-time tuition and fees vary according to course load. ***Payment plan:*** Installment.

FRESHMAN FINANCIAL AID (Fall 2010, est.) 769 applied for aid; of those 83% were deemed to have need. 100% of freshmen with need received aid; of those 48% had need fully met. ***Average percent of need met:*** 80% (excluding resources awarded to replace EFC). ***Average financial aid package:*** $31,487 (excluding resources awarded to replace EFC). 29% of all full-time freshmen had no need and received non-need-based gift aid.

UNDERGRADUATE FINANCIAL AID (Fall 2010, est.) 2,292 applied for aid; of those 86% were deemed to have need. 100% of undergraduates with need received aid; of those 43% had need fully met. ***Average percent of need met:*** 77% (excluding resources awarded to replace EFC). ***Average financial aid package:*** $30,654 (excluding resources awarded to replace EFC). 29% of all full-time undergraduates had no need and received non-need-based gift aid.

GIFT AID (NEED-BASED) ***Total amount:*** $31,103,917 (6% federal, 92% institutional, 2% external sources). ***Receiving aid:*** Freshmen: 63% (621); all full-time undergraduates: 57% (1,912). ***Average award:*** Freshmen: $17,324; Undergraduates: $16,212. ***Scholarships, grants, and awards:*** Federal Pell, FSEOG, state, private, college/university gift aid from institutional funds.

GIFT AID (NON-NEED-BASED) ***Total amount:*** $11,342,022 (99% institutional, 1% external sources). ***Average award:*** Freshmen: $13,091. Undergraduates: $11,578. ***Scholarships, grants, and awards by category:*** *Academic interests/achievement:* general academic interests/achievements. *Creative arts/performance:* music, theater/drama. *Special characteristics:* children and siblings of alumni, children of faculty/staff, religious affiliation, siblings of current students, twins, veterans, veterans' children. ***Tuition waivers:*** Full or partial for employees or children of employees.

LOANS ***Student loans:*** $19,044,764 (89% need-based, 11% non-need-based). ***Average need-based loan:*** Freshmen: $3433. Undergraduates: $4364. ***Parent loans:*** $12,764,579 (86% need-based, 14% non-need-based). ***Programs:*** Federal Direct (Subsidized and Unsubsidized Stafford, PLUS), Federal Nursing, alternative loans.

WORK-STUDY ***Federal work-study:*** Total amount: $1,301,601; 509 jobs averaging $2557.

APPLYING FOR FINANCIAL AID ***Required financial aid forms:*** FAFSA, alumni and parish scholarship application (if appropriate). ***Financial aid deadline:*** 4/10 (priority: 2/15). ***Notification date:*** Continuous beginning 4/1. Students must reply by 5/1 or within 2 weeks of notification.

CONTACT Mr. Donald Bosse, Director of Financial Aid, The Catholic University of America, 620 Michigan Avenue, NE, Washington, DC 20064, 202-319-5307 or toll-free 800-673-2772 (out-of-state). *Fax:* 202-319-5573. *E-mail:* bosse@cua.edu.

CAZENOVIA COLLEGE

Cazenovia, NY

Tuition & fees: $26,736 **Average undergraduate aid package: $21,982**

ABOUT THE INSTITUTION Independent, coed. 21 undergraduate majors. Federal methodology is used as a basis for awarding need-based institutional aid.

UNDERGRADUATE EXPENSES for 2011–12 ***Comprehensive fee:*** $38,206 includes full-time tuition ($26,288), mandatory fees ($448), and room and board ($11,470). Full-time tuition and fees vary according to class time, course load, and program. Room and board charges vary according to board plan and housing facility. ***Part-time tuition:*** $558 per credit hour. Part-time tuition and fees vary according to class time and course load. ***Payment plan:*** Installment.

FRESHMAN FINANCIAL AID (Fall 2010, est.) 231 applied for aid; of those 94% were deemed to have need. 100% of freshmen with need received aid; of those 9% had need fully met. ***Average percent of need met:*** 76% (excluding resources awarded to replace EFC). ***Average financial aid package:*** $21,690 (excluding resources awarded to replace EFC). 9% of all full-time freshmen had no need and received non-need-based gift aid.

UNDERGRADUATE FINANCIAL AID (Fall 2010, est.) 881 applied for aid; of those 94% were deemed to have need. 100% of undergraduates with need received aid; of those 17% had need fully met. ***Average percent of need met:*** 75% (excluding resources awarded to replace EFC). ***Average financial aid package:*** $21,982 (excluding resources awarded to replace EFC). 10% of all full-time undergraduates had no need and received non-need-based gift aid.

GIFT AID (NEED-BASED) ***Total amount:*** $15,511,741 (16% federal, 10% state, 73% institutional, 1% external sources). ***Receiving aid:*** Freshmen: 88% (216); all full-time undergraduates: 87% (829). ***Average award:*** Freshmen: $14,608; Undergraduates: $16,350. ***Scholarships, grants, and awards:*** Federal Pell, FSEOG, state, private, college/university gift aid from institutional funds.

GIFT AID (NON-NEED-BASED) ***Total amount:*** $1,740,182 (1% state, 98% institutional, 1% external sources). ***Receiving aid:*** Freshmen: 7% (16). Undergraduates: 9% (82). ***Average award:*** Freshmen: $8099. Undergraduates: $12,359. ***Scholarships, grants, and awards by category:*** *Academic interests/achievement:* general academic interests/achievements. ***Tuition waivers:*** Full or partial for employees or children of employees.

LOANS ***Student loans:*** $7,430,874 (75% need-based, 25% non-need-based). 86% of past graduating class borrowed through all loan programs. ***Average***

need-based loan: Freshmen: $3454. Undergraduates: $4405. **Parent loans:** $2,720,766 (45% need-based, 55% non-need-based). **Programs:** Federal Direct (Subsidized and Unsubsidized Stafford, PLUS).

WORK-STUDY **Federal work-study:** Total amount: $333,000; jobs available.

APPLYING FOR FINANCIAL AID **Required financial aid forms:** FAFSA, state aid form. **Financial aid deadline (priority):** 3/1. **Notification date:** Continuous. Students must reply by 5/1 or within 2 weeks of notification.

CONTACT Christine L. Mandel, Director of Financial Aid, Cazenovia College, 3 Sullivan Street, Cazenovia, NY 13035, 315-655-7887 or toll-free 800-654-3210. *Fax:* 315-655-7219. *E-mail:* finaid@cazenovia.edu.

CEDAR CREST COLLEGE

Allentown, PA

Tuition & fees: $28,967 **Average undergraduate aid package: $22,826**

ABOUT THE INSTITUTION Independent religious, coed, primarily women. 35 undergraduate majors. Federal methodology is used as a basis for awarding need-based institutional aid.

UNDERGRADUATE EXPENSES for 2010–11 **Comprehensive fee:** $38,507 includes full-time tuition ($28,567), mandatory fees ($400), and room and board ($9540). **College room only:** $5010. Full-time tuition and fees vary according to class time, course load, and program. Room and board charges vary according to board plan and housing facility. **Part-time tuition:** $795 per credit hour. **Part-time fees:** $75 per term. Part-time tuition and fees vary according to class time, course load, and program. **Payment plans:** Installment, deferred payment.

FRESHMAN FINANCIAL AID (Fall 2010, est.) 85 applied for aid; of those 92% were deemed to have need. 100% of freshmen with need received aid; of those 13% had need fully met. **Average percent of need met:** 81% (excluding resources awarded to replace EFC). **Average financial aid package:** $25,150 (excluding resources awarded to replace EFC). 11% of all full-time freshmen had no need and received non-need-based gift aid.

UNDERGRADUATE FINANCIAL AID (Fall 2010, est.) 659 applied for aid; of those 93% were deemed to have need. 100% of undergraduates with need received aid; of those 12% had need fully met. **Average percent of need met:** 76% (excluding resources awarded to replace EFC). **Average financial aid package:** $22,826 (excluding resources awarded to replace EFC). 9% of all full-time undergraduates had no need and received non-need-based gift aid.

GIFT AID (NEED-BASED) **Total amount:** $11,295,359 (15% federal, 8% state, 72% institutional, 5% external sources). **Receiving aid:** Freshmen: 86% (78); all full-time undergraduates: 88% (613). **Average award:** Freshmen: $21,709; Undergraduates: $18,215. **Scholarships, grants, and awards:** Federal Pell, FSEOG, state, private, college/university gift aid from institutional funds, Federal Nursing.

GIFT AID (NON-NEED-BASED) **Total amount:** $868,356 (86% institutional, 14% external sources). **Receiving aid:** Freshmen: 5% (5). Undergraduates: 6% (43). **Average award:** Freshmen: $10,656. Undergraduates: $8719. **Scholarships, grants, and awards by category:** *Academic interests/achievement:* 265 awards ($2,724,614 total): business, communication, English, general academic interests/achievements. *Creative arts/performance:* 78 awards ($111,999 total): art/fine arts, dance, performing arts, theater/drama. *Special achievements/activities:* 80 awards ($132,150 total): community service, general special achievements/activities, junior miss, leadership, memberships, religious involvement. *Special characteristics:* 200 awards ($526,464 total): adult students, children and siblings of alumni, general special characteristics, previous college experience, relatives of clergy, religious affiliation, siblings of current students. **Tuition waivers:** Full or partial for children of alumni, employees or children of employees.

LOANS **Student loans:** $6,196,526 (77% need-based, 23% non-need-based). 90% of past graduating class borrowed through all loan programs. *Average indebtedness per student:* $32,225. **Average need-based loan:** Freshmen: $3315. Undergraduates: $4675. **Parent loans:** $2,157,722 (38% need-based, 62% non-need-based). **Programs:** Federal Direct (Subsidized and Unsubsidized Stafford, PLUS), Perkins, Federal Nursing.

WORK-STUDY **Federal work-study:** Total amount: $159,858; 104 jobs averaging $1500. **State or other work-study/employment:** Total amount: $117,230 (81% need-based, 19% non-need-based). Part-time jobs available.

APPLYING FOR FINANCIAL AID **Required financial aid forms:** FAFSA, state aid form. **Financial aid deadline:** 5/1 (priority: 3/15). **Notification date:** Continuous beginning 2/15. Students must reply by 5/15.

CONTACT Mr. Stephen C. Cassel, Director of Financial Aid, Cedar Crest College, Cedar Crest College, 100 College Drive, Allentown, PA 18104-6196, 610-606-4602 or toll-free 800-360-1222. *Fax:* 610-606-4653. *E-mail:* financialservices@cedarcrest.edu.

CEDARVILLE UNIVERSITY

Cedarville, OH

Tuition & fees: $23,500 **Average undergraduate aid package: $14,544**

ABOUT THE INSTITUTION Independent Baptist, coed. 88 undergraduate majors. Federal methodology is used as a basis for awarding need-based institutional aid.

UNDERGRADUATE EXPENSES for 2011–12 **One-time required fee:** $130. **Comprehensive fee:** $28,586 includes full-time tuition ($23,500) and room and board ($5086). **College room only:** $2820. Room and board charges vary according to board plan. **Part-time tuition:** $870 per credit. Part-time tuition and fees vary according to course load. **Payment plan:** Installment.

FRESHMAN FINANCIAL AID (Fall 2010, est.) 692 applied for aid; of those 82% were deemed to have need. 100% of freshmen with need received aid; of those 20% had need fully met. **Average percent of need met:** 33% (excluding resources awarded to replace EFC). **Average financial aid package:** $14,754 (excluding resources awarded to replace EFC). 23% of all full-time freshmen had no need and received non-need-based gift aid.

UNDERGRADUATE FINANCIAL AID (Fall 2010, est.) 2,184 applied for aid; of those 86% were deemed to have need. 100% of undergraduates with need received aid; of those 20% had need fully met. **Average percent of need met:** 42% (excluding resources awarded to replace EFC). **Average financial aid package:** $14,544 (excluding resources awarded to replace EFC). 21% of all full-time undergraduates had no need and received non-need-based gift aid.

GIFT AID (NEED-BASED) **Total amount:** $8,886,198 (38% federal, 5% state, 56% institutional, 1% external sources). **Receiving aid:** Freshmen: 57% (457); all full-time undergraduates: 54% (1,507). **Average award:** Freshmen: $3850; Undergraduates: $4426. **Scholarships, grants, and awards:** Federal Pell, FSEOG, state, private, college/university gift aid from institutional funds.

GIFT AID (NON-NEED-BASED) **Total amount:** $15,361,118 (1% federal, 1% state, 74% institutional, 24% external sources). **Receiving aid:** Freshmen: 62% (498). Undergraduates: 53% (1,502). **Average award:** Freshmen: $15,499. Undergraduates: $14,213. **Scholarships, grants, and awards by category:** *Academic interests/achievement:* 1,446 awards ($4,782,390 total): general academic interests/achievements. *Creative arts/performance:* 58 awards ($150,260 total): debating, music. *Special achievements/activities:* 514 awards ($1,188,575 total): leadership. *Special characteristics:* 199 awards ($2,680,008 total): children and siblings of alumni, children of faculty/staff, ethnic background, general special characteristics, religious affiliation, veterans. **Tuition waivers:** Full or partial for employees or children of employees, senior citizens.

LOANS **Student loans:** $10,910,759 (70% need-based, 30% non-need-based). 67% of past graduating class borrowed through all loan programs. *Average indebtedness per student:* $29,177. **Average need-based loan:** Freshmen: $4971. Undergraduates: $6312. **Parent loans:** $14,655,568 (100% non-need-based). **Programs:** Perkins, Federal Nursing, college/university.

WORK-STUDY **Federal work-study:** Total amount: $324,238; 272 jobs averaging $1192. **State or other work-study/employment:** Total amount: $1,680,147 (100% non-need-based). 1,461 part-time jobs averaging $1150.

ATHLETIC AWARDS Total amount: $860,177 (100% non-need-based).

APPLYING FOR FINANCIAL AID **Required financial aid form:** FAFSA. **Financial aid deadline (priority):** 3/1. **Notification date:** Continuous beginning 3/1. Students must reply within 4 weeks of notification.

CONTACT Mr. Roscoe Smith, Associate Vice President Enrollment Management and Marketing, Cedarville University, 251 North Main Street, Cedarville, OH 45314-0601, 937-766-7474 or toll-free 800-CEDARVILLE. *E-mail:* smithr@cedarville.edu.

CENTENARY COLLEGE

Hackettstown, NJ

ABOUT THE INSTITUTION Independent religious, coed. 27 undergraduate majors.

GIFT AID (NEED-BASED) **Scholarships, grants, and awards:** Federal Pell, FSEOG, state, private, college/university gift aid from institutional funds.

GIFT AID (NON-NEED-BASED) ***Scholarships, grants, and awards by category:*** *Academic interests/achievement:* general academic interests/achievements. *Special achievements/activities:* leadership. *Special characteristics:* children and siblings of alumni, children of faculty/staff, ethnic background, general special characteristics, local/state students, out-of-state students, previous college experience, religious affiliation, siblings of current students.

LOANS ***Programs:*** Perkins, state, NJ Class Loans.

WORK-STUDY ***Federal work-study:*** Total amount: $154,269; 239 jobs averaging $645. ***State or other work-study/employment:*** Total amount: $261,796 (100% non-need-based). 276 part-time jobs averaging $480.

APPLYING FOR FINANCIAL AID ***Required financial aid form:*** FAFSA.

CONTACT Michelle Burwell, Associate Director of Financial Aid, Centenary College, 400 Jefferson Street, Hackettstown, NJ 07840-2100, 908-852-1400 Ext. 2207 or toll-free 800-236-8679. *Fax:* 908-813-2632. *E-mail:* burwellm@centenarycollege.edu.

CENTENARY COLLEGE OF LOUISIANA

Shreveport, LA

Tuition & fees: $23,280 **Average undergraduate aid package: $21,547**

ABOUT THE INSTITUTION Independent United Methodist, coed. 29 undergraduate majors. Federal methodology is used as a basis for awarding need-based institutional aid.

UNDERGRADUATE EXPENSES for 2010–11 ***Comprehensive fee:*** $31,220 includes full-time tuition ($22,080), mandatory fees ($1200), and room and board ($7940). ***College room only:*** $4020. Room and board charges vary according to board plan and housing facility. Part-time tuition and fees vary according to course load and program. ***Payment plans:*** Installment, deferred payment.

FRESHMAN FINANCIAL AID (Fall 2010, est.) 186 applied for aid; of those 87% were deemed to have need. 100% of freshmen with need received aid; of those 27% had need fully met. ***Average percent of need met:*** 78% (excluding resources awarded to replace EFC). ***Average financial aid package:*** $21,762 (excluding resources awarded to replace EFC). 15% of all full-time freshmen had no need and received non-need-based gift aid.

UNDERGRADUATE FINANCIAL AID (Fall 2010, est.) 654 applied for aid; of those 83% were deemed to have need. 100% of undergraduates with need received aid; of those 26% had need fully met. ***Average percent of need met:*** 83% (excluding resources awarded to replace EFC). ***Average financial aid package:*** $21,547 (excluding resources awarded to replace EFC). 27% of all full-time undergraduates had no need and received non-need-based gift aid.

GIFT AID (NEED-BASED) ***Total amount:*** $9,136,155 (14% federal, 11% state, 74% institutional, 1% external sources). ***Receiving aid:*** Freshmen: 84% (161); all full-time undergraduates: 69% (542). ***Average award:*** Freshmen: $18,754; Undergraduates: $18,453. ***Scholarships, grants, and awards:*** Federal Pell, FSEOG, state, private, college/university gift aid from institutional funds.

GIFT AID (NON-NEED-BASED) ***Total amount:*** $3,069,334 (10% state, 89% institutional, 1% external sources). ***Receiving aid:*** Freshmen: 20% (39). Undergraduates: 13% (103). ***Average award:*** Freshmen: $11,345. Undergraduates: $9767. ***Scholarships, grants, and awards by category:*** *Academic interests/achievement:* 755 awards ($5,898,398 total): biological sciences, business, communication, education, engineering/technologies, English, foreign languages, general academic interests/achievements, health fields, humanities, mathematics, physical sciences, premedicine, religion/biblical studies, social sciences. *Creative arts/performance:* 194 awards ($646,870 total): art/fine arts, dance, general creative arts/performance, music, performing arts, theater/drama. *Special achievements/activities:* 83 awards ($123,810 total): community service, general special achievements/activities, hobbies/interests, religious involvement. *Special characteristics:* 119 awards ($597,670 total): children and siblings of alumni, children of educators, children of faculty/staff, ethnic background, general special characteristics, international students, local/state students, members of minority groups, out-of-state students, relatives of clergy, religious affiliation, siblings of current students. ***Tuition waivers:*** Full or partial for employees or children of employees.

LOANS ***Student loans:*** $2,708,289 (49% need-based, 51% non-need-based). 46% of past graduating class borrowed through all loan programs. *Average indebtedness per student:* $22,920. ***Average need-based loan:*** Freshmen: $3311. Undergraduates: $3959. ***Parent loans:*** $1,746,946 (68% need-based, 32% non-need-based). ***Programs:*** Federal Direct (Subsidized and Unsubsidized Stafford, PLUS), Perkins.

WORK-STUDY ***Federal work-study:*** Total amount: $383,800; 190 jobs averaging $2020. ***State or other work-study/employment:*** Total amount: $76,650 (100% non-need-based). 51 part-time jobs averaging $1503.

ATHLETIC AWARDS Total amount: $1,615,895 (51% need-based, 49% non-need-based).

APPLYING FOR FINANCIAL AID ***Required financial aid form:*** FAFSA. ***Financial aid deadline (priority):*** 2/15. ***Notification date:*** 3/15. Students must reply by 5/1.

CONTACT Ms. Mary Sue Rix, Director of Financial Aid, Centenary College of Louisiana, PO Box 41188, Shreveport, LA 71134-1188, 318-869-5137 or toll-free 800-234-4448. *Fax:* 318-841-7266. *E-mail:* msrix@centenary.edu.

CENTRAL BAPTIST COLLEGE

Conway, AR

CONTACT Christi Bell, Financial Aid Director, Central Baptist College, 1501 College Avenue, Conway, AR 72032-6470, 800-205-6872 Ext. 185 or toll-free 800-205-6872. *Fax:* 501-329-2941. *E-mail:* financialaid@cbc.edu.

CENTRAL BIBLE COLLEGE

Springfield, MO

CONTACT Rick Woolverton, Director of Financial Aid, Central Bible College, 3000 North Grant, Springfield, MO 65803-1096, 417-833-2551 or toll-free 800-831-4222 Ext. 1184. *Fax:* 417-833-2168.

CENTRAL CHRISTIAN COLLEGE OF KANSAS

McPherson, KS

CONTACT Mike Reimer, Financial Aid Director, Central Christian College of Kansas, 1200 South Main, PO Box 1403, McPherson, KS 67460, 620-241-0723 Ext. 333 or toll-free 800-835-0078 Ext. 337. *Fax:* 620-241-6032. *E-mail:* miker@centralchristian.edu.

CENTRAL CHRISTIAN COLLEGE OF THE BIBLE

Moberly, MO

CONTACT Rhonda J. Dunham, Financial Aid Director, Central Christian College of the Bible, 911 East Urbandale Drive, Moberly, MO 65270-1997, 660-263-3900 Ext. 121 or toll-free 888-263-3900 (in-state). *Fax:* 660-263-3936. *E-mail:* rdunham@cccb.edu.

CENTRAL COLLEGE

Pella, IA

Tuition & fees: $26,242 **Average undergraduate aid package: $22,661**

ABOUT THE INSTITUTION Independent religious, coed. 37 undergraduate majors. Federal methodology is used as a basis for awarding need-based institutional aid.

UNDERGRADUATE EXPENSES for 2010–11 ***Comprehensive fee:*** $34,944 includes full-time tuition ($25,862), mandatory fees ($380), and room and board ($8702). ***College room only:*** $4268. Room and board charges vary according to board plan. ***Part-time tuition:*** $898 per semester hour. Part-time tuition and fees vary according to course load. ***Payment plan:*** Installment.

FRESHMAN FINANCIAL AID (Fall 2010, est.) 387 applied for aid; of those 89% were deemed to have need. 100% of freshmen with need received aid; of those 17% had need fully met. ***Average percent of need met:*** 83% (excluding resources awarded to replace EFC). ***Average financial aid package:*** $24,262 (excluding resources awarded to replace EFC). 14% of all full-time freshmen had no need and received non-need-based gift aid.

UNDERGRADUATE FINANCIAL AID (Fall 2010, est.) 1,375 applied for aid; of those 91% were deemed to have need. 100% of undergraduates with need received aid; of those 16% had need fully met. ***Average percent of need met:*** 80% (excluding resources awarded to replace EFC). ***Average financial aid***

package: $22,661 (excluding resources awarded to replace EFC). 17% of all full-time undergraduates had no need and received non-need-based gift aid.

GIFT AID (NEED-BASED) ***Total amount:*** $21,384,963 (14% federal, 13% state, 71% institutional, 2% external sources). ***Receiving aid:*** Freshmen: 86% (345); all full-time undergraduates: 83% (1,254). ***Average award:*** Freshmen: $19,076; Undergraduates: $17,464. ***Scholarships, grants, and awards:*** Federal Pell, FSEOG, state, private, college/university gift aid from institutional funds.

GIFT AID (NON-NEED-BASED) ***Total amount:*** $3,487,541 (2% federal, 97% institutional, 1% external sources). ***Receiving aid:*** Freshmen: 7% (28). Undergraduates: 9% (129). ***Average award:*** Freshmen: $12,463. Undergraduates: $11,313. ***Scholarships, grants, and awards by category:*** *Academic interests/achievement:* biological sciences, business, communication, computer science, education, foreign languages, general academic interests/achievements, health fields, humanities, international studies, mathematics, physical sciences, premedicine, religion/biblical studies, social sciences. *Creative arts/performance:* art/fine arts, creative writing, music, theater/drama. *Special achievements/activities:* community service, religious involvement. *Special characteristics:* children and siblings of alumni, children of current students, children of faculty/staff, general special characteristics, handicapped students, international students, local/state students, members of minority groups, out-of-state students, previous college experience, religious affiliation, siblings of current students, twins, veterans, veterans' children. ***Tuition waivers:*** Full or partial for employees or children of employees.

LOANS ***Student loans:*** $10,643,023 (74% need-based, 26% non-need-based). 85% of past graduating class borrowed through all loan programs. *Average indebtedness per student:* $34,237. ***Average need-based loan:*** Freshmen: $3706. Undergraduates: $4144. ***Parent loans:*** $3,105,822 (37% need-based, 63% non-need-based). ***Programs:*** Federal Direct (Subsidized and Unsubsidized Stafford, PLUS), Perkins, college/university, alternative loans.

WORK-STUDY ***Federal work-study:*** Total amount: $1,254,970; jobs available. ***State or other work-study/employment:*** Total amount: $448,541 (37% need-based, 63% non-need-based). Part-time jobs available.

APPLYING FOR FINANCIAL AID ***Required financial aid form:*** FAFSA. ***Financial aid deadline (priority):*** 3/15. ***Notification date:*** Continuous beginning 3/15. Students must reply by 5/1 or within 2 weeks of notification.

CONTACT Wayne Dille, Director of Financial Aid, Central College, 812 University Street, Campus Box 5800, Pella, IA 50219-1999, 641-628-5336 or toll-free 877-462-3687 (in-state), 877-462-3689 (out-of-state). *Fax:* 641-628-7199. *E-mail:* dillew@central.edu.

CENTRAL CONNECTICUT STATE UNIVERSITY

New Britain, CT

Tuition & fees (CT res): $7861 **Average undergraduate aid package: $7759**

ABOUT THE INSTITUTION State-supported, coed. 52 undergraduate majors. Federal methodology is used as a basis for awarding need-based institutional aid.

UNDERGRADUATE EXPENSES for 2010–11 ***Tuition, state resident:*** full-time $4023; part-time $168 per credit. ***Tuition, nonresident:*** full-time $13,020; part-time $171 per credit. ***Required fees:*** full-time $3838; $207 per credit or $55 per term. Full-time tuition and fees vary according to course level, course load, program, and reciprocity agreements. Part-time tuition and fees vary according to course level, course load, and program. ***College room and board:*** $9576; ***Room only:*** $5572. Room and board charges vary according to board plan. ***Payment plan:*** Installment.

FRESHMAN FINANCIAL AID (Fall 2010, est.) 1,281 applied for aid; of those 72% were deemed to have need. 92% of freshmen with need received aid; of those 8% had need fully met. ***Average percent of need met:*** 65% (excluding resources awarded to replace EFC). ***Average financial aid package:*** $8799 (excluding resources awarded to replace EFC). 3% of all full-time freshmen had no need and received non-need-based gift aid.

UNDERGRADUATE FINANCIAL AID (Fall 2010, est.) 6,898 applied for aid; of those 77% were deemed to have need. 92% of undergraduates with need received aid; of those 10% had need fully met. ***Average percent of need met:*** 62% (excluding resources awarded to replace EFC). ***Average financial aid package:*** $7759 (excluding resources awarded to replace EFC). 2% of all full-time undergraduates had no need and received non-need-based gift aid.

GIFT AID (NEED-BASED) ***Total amount:*** $21,576,015 (56% federal, 19% state, 25% institutional). ***Receiving aid:*** Freshmen: 60% (780); all full-time undergraduates: 51% (4,288). ***Average award:*** Freshmen: $4709; Undergraduates: $4007. ***Scholarships, grants, and awards:*** Federal Pell, FSEOG, state, private, college/university gift aid from institutional funds.

GIFT AID (NON-NEED-BASED) ***Total amount:*** $2,052,945 (58% institutional, 42% external sources). ***Receiving aid:*** Freshmen: 11% (147). Undergraduates: 11% (917). ***Average award:*** Freshmen: $2998. Undergraduates: $3615. ***Scholarships, grants, and awards by category:*** *Academic interests/achievement:* general academic interests/achievements. *Special characteristics:* members of minority groups. ***Tuition waivers:*** Full or partial for employees or children of employees, senior citizens.

LOANS ***Student loans:*** $55,336,022 (46% need-based, 54% non-need-based). 48% of past graduating class borrowed through all loan programs. *Average indebtedness per student:* $19,086. ***Average need-based loan:*** Freshmen: $3466. Undergraduates: $4181. ***Parent loans:*** $4,097,595 (100% non-need-based). ***Programs:*** Federal Direct (Subsidized and Unsubsidized Stafford, PLUS), Perkins.

WORK-STUDY ***Federal work-study:*** Total amount: $378,862; jobs available. ***State or other work-study/employment:*** Part-time jobs available.

ATHLETIC AWARDS Total amount: $2,946,786 (100% non-need-based).

APPLYING FOR FINANCIAL AID ***Required financial aid forms:*** FAFSA, institution's own form. ***Financial aid deadline (priority):*** 3/1. ***Notification date:*** Continuous. Students must reply within 3 weeks of notification.

CONTACT Mr. Dennis Williams, Associate Director of Financial Aid, Central Connecticut State University, Memorial Hall, Room 103, New Britain, CT 06050-4010, 860-832-2200 or toll-free 888-733-2278 (in-state). *Fax:* 860-832-1105. *E-mail:* lupachinok@ccsu.edu.

CENTRAL METHODIST UNIVERSITY

Fayette, MO

Tuition & fees: $19,390 **Average undergraduate aid package: $17,331**

ABOUT THE INSTITUTION Independent Methodist, coed. ***Awards:*** associate, bachelor's, and master's degrees. 47 undergraduate majors. ***Total enrollment:*** 1,031. Undergraduates: 1,031. Freshmen: 300. Federal methodology is used as a basis for awarding need-based institutional aid.

UNDERGRADUATE EXPENSES for 2010–11 ***Application fee:*** $20. ***One-time required fee:*** $100. ***Comprehensive fee:*** $25,630 includes full-time tuition ($18,660), mandatory fees ($730), and room and board ($6240). ***College room only:*** $3080. Full-time tuition and fees vary according to location. Room and board charges vary according to board plan and housing facility. ***Part-time tuition:*** $185 per semester hour. ***Part-time fees:*** $32.25 per credit hour. Part-time tuition and fees vary according to course load and location. ***Payment plan:*** Installment.

FRESHMAN FINANCIAL AID (Fall 2010, est.) 296 applied for aid; of those 75% were deemed to have need. 100% of freshmen with need received aid; of those 10% had need fully met. ***Average percent of need met:*** 74% (excluding resources awarded to replace EFC). ***Average financial aid package:*** $22,251 (excluding resources awarded to replace EFC). 29% of all full-time freshmen had no need and received non-need-based gift aid.

UNDERGRADUATE FINANCIAL AID (Fall 2010, est.) 1,119 applied for aid; of those 72% were deemed to have need. 100% of undergraduates with need received aid; of those 10% had need fully met. ***Average percent of need met:*** 58% (excluding resources awarded to replace EFC). ***Average financial aid package:*** $17,331 (excluding resources awarded to replace EFC). 28% of all full-time undergraduates had no need and received non-need-based gift aid.

GIFT AID (NEED-BASED) ***Total amount:*** $3,619,425 (71% federal, 28% state, 1% institutional). ***Receiving aid:*** Freshmen: 62% (196); all full-time undergraduates: 58% (655). ***Average award:*** Freshmen: $4791; Undergraduates: $3952. ***Scholarships, grants, and awards:*** Federal Pell, FSEOG, state, private, college/university gift aid from institutional funds.

GIFT AID (NON-NEED-BASED) ***Total amount:*** $9,398,365 (1% state, 95% institutional, 4% external sources). ***Receiving aid:*** Freshmen: 71% (223). Undergraduates: 72% (808). ***Average award:*** Freshmen: $7457. Undergraduates: $7316. ***Scholarships, grants, and awards by category:*** *Academic interests/achievement:* 863 awards ($5,938,913 total): biological sciences, business, communication, computer science, education, English, foreign languages, general academic interests/achievements, health fields, humanities, mathematics, physical sciences, premedicine, religion/biblical studies, social sciences. *Creative arts/performance:* 115 awards ($355,562 total): music, theater/drama. *Special* *achievements/activities:* 196 awards ($1,358,082 total): cheerleading/drum major, leadership, religious involvement. *Special characteristics:* 259 awards ($1,394,470 total): children and siblings of alumni, children of faculty/staff, general special characteristics, international students, relatives of clergy, religious affiliation, siblings of current students, spouses of current students. ***Tuition waivers:*** Full or partial for employees or children of employees. ***ROTC:*** Army cooperative, Air Force cooperative.

LOANS ***Student loans:*** $5,623,497 (56% need-based, 44% non-need-based). 75% of past graduating class borrowed through all loan programs. *Average indebtedness per student:* $18,390. ***Average need-based loan:*** Freshmen: $3200. Undergraduates: $3494. ***Parent loans:*** $1,255,722 (100% non-need-based). ***Programs:*** Federal Direct (Subsidized and Unsubsidized Stafford, PLUS), Perkins, college/university.

WORK-STUDY ***Federal work-study:*** Total amount: $183,438; 164 jobs averaging $1118. ***State or other work-study/employment:*** Total amount: $103,918 (100% non-need-based). 98 part-time jobs averaging $1060.

ATHLETIC AWARDS Total amount: $2,131,200 (100% non-need-based).

APPLYING FOR FINANCIAL AID ***Required financial aid form:*** FAFSA. ***Financial aid deadline (priority):*** 3/15. ***Notification date:*** Continuous. Students must reply within 2 weeks of notification.

CONTACT Linda Mackey, Director of Financial Assistance, Central Methodist University, 411 Central Methodist Square, Fayette, MO 65248-1198, 660-248-6244 or toll-free 888-CMU-1854 (in-state). *Fax:* 660-248-6288. *E-mail:* lmackey@centralmethodist.edu.

CENTRAL MICHIGAN UNIVERSITY

Mount Pleasant, MI

Tuition & fees (MI res): $10,380 Average undergraduate aid package: $11,764

ABOUT THE INSTITUTION State-supported, coed. 136 undergraduate majors. Federal methodology is used as a basis for awarding need-based institutional aid.

UNDERGRADUATE EXPENSES for 2010–11 ***Tuition, state resident:*** full-time $10,380; part-time $346 per credit hour. ***Tuition, nonresident:*** full-time $23,670; part-time $789 per credit hour. Full-time tuition and fees vary according to location and student level. Part-time tuition and fees vary according to location and student level. ***College room and board:*** $8092; ***Room only:*** $4046. Room and board charges vary according to board plan, housing facility, location, and student level. ***Payment plan:*** Installment.

FRESHMAN FINANCIAL AID (Fall 2009) 3,215 applied for aid; of those 73% were deemed to have need. 98% of freshmen with need received aid; of those 53% had need fully met. ***Average percent of need met:*** 83% (excluding resources awarded to replace EFC). ***Average financial aid package:*** $12,040 (excluding resources awarded to replace EFC). 13% of all full-time freshmen had no need and received non-need-based gift aid.

UNDERGRADUATE FINANCIAL AID (Fall 2009) 14,260 applied for aid; of those 75% were deemed to have need. 98% of undergraduates with need received aid; of those 56% had need fully met. ***Average percent of need met:*** 84% (excluding resources awarded to replace EFC). ***Average financial aid package:*** $11,764 (excluding resources awarded to replace EFC). 8% of all full-time undergraduates had no need and received non-need-based gift aid.

GIFT AID (NEED-BASED) ***Total amount:*** $43,365,584 (63% federal, 3% state, 31% institutional, 3% external sources). ***Receiving aid:*** Freshmen: 54% (1,978); all full-time undergraduates: 44% (7,990). ***Average award:*** Freshmen: $6454; Undergraduates: $5344. ***Scholarships, grants, and awards:*** Federal Pell, FSEOG, state, private, college/university gift aid from institutional funds, United Negro College Fund.

GIFT AID (NON-NEED-BASED) ***Total amount:*** $7,957,637 (1% state, 80% institutional, 19% external sources). ***Receiving aid:*** Freshmen: 5% (168). Undergraduates: 2% (428). ***Average award:*** Freshmen: $4404. Undergraduates: $3930. ***Scholarships, grants, and awards by category:*** *Academic interests/achievement:* 3,747 awards ($11,863,242 total): biological sciences, business, communication, computer science, education, engineering/technologies, English, foreign languages, general academic interests/achievements, health fields, home economics, humanities, international studies, mathematics, military science, physical sciences, premedicine, religion/biblical studies, social sciences. *Creative arts/performance:* 158 awards ($236,800 total): applied art and design, art/fine arts, cinema/film/broadcasting, creative writing, dance, general creative arts/performance, journalism/publications, music, performing arts, theater/drama. *Special achievements/activities:* 646 awards ($5,489,819 total): general special achievements/activities, leadership. *Special characteristics:* 416 awards ($2,783,326 total): children and siblings of alumni, children of faculty/staff, ethnic background, international students, local/state students, out-of-state students. ***Tuition waivers:*** Full or partial for children of alumni, employees or children of employees, senior citizens.

LOANS ***Student loans:*** $112,263,649 (65% need-based, 35% non-need-based). 74% of past graduating class borrowed through all loan programs. *Average indebtedness per student:* $28,142. ***Average need-based loan:*** Freshmen: $5564. Undergraduates: $6696. ***Parent loans:*** $26,079,739 (26% need-based, 74% non-need-based). ***Programs:*** Federal Direct (Subsidized and Unsubsidized Stafford, PLUS), Perkins, alternative loans.

WORK-STUDY ***Federal work-study:*** Total amount: $1,434,597; 829 jobs averaging $1731. ***State or other work-study/employment:*** Total amount: $9,077,929 (24% need-based, 76% non-need-based). 4,001 part-time jobs averaging $2269.

ATHLETIC AWARDS Total amount: $4,443,491 (35% need-based, 65% non-need-based).

APPLYING FOR FINANCIAL AID ***Required financial aid form:*** FAFSA. ***Financial aid deadline (priority):*** 3/1. ***Notification date:*** Continuous beginning 4/1.

CONTACT Financial Aid Office, Central Michigan University, Mount Pleasant, MI 48859, 989-774-3674 or toll-free 888-292-5366. *Fax:* 989-774-3634. *E-mail:* cmuadmit@cmich.edu.

CENTRAL PENNSYLVANIA COLLEGE

Summerdale, PA

CONTACT Kathy Shepard, Financial Aid Director, Central Pennsylvania College, College Hill and Valley Roads, Summerdale, PA 17093, 717-728-2261 or toll-free 800-759-2727 Ext. 2201. *Fax:* 717-728-2350. *E-mail:* financial-aid@centralpenn.edu.

CENTRAL STATE UNIVERSITY

Wilberforce, OH

CONTACT Jean Hurst, Interim Director of Student Financial Aid, Central State University, PO Box 1004, Wilberforce, OH 45384, 937-376-6579 or toll-free 800-388-CSU1 (in-state). *Fax:* 937-376-6519. *E-mail:* jhurst@centralstate.edu.

CENTRAL WASHINGTON UNIVERSITY

Ellensburg, WA

Tuition & fees (WA res): $7113 Average undergraduate aid package: $8993

ABOUT THE INSTITUTION State-supported, coed. ***Awards:*** bachelor's and master's degrees and post-bachelor's certificates. 73 undergraduate majors. ***Total enrollment:*** 10,662. Undergraduates: 10,181. Freshmen: 1,570. Federal methodology is used as a basis for awarding need-based institutional aid.

UNDERGRADUATE EXPENSES for 2010–11 ***Application fee:*** $50. ***Tuition, state resident:*** full-time $6201; part-time $201.70 per credit hour. ***Tuition, nonresident:*** full-time $16,842; part-time $561.40 per credit hour. ***Required fees:*** full-time $912. Part-time tuition and fees vary according to course load. ***College room and board:*** $8901. Room and board charges vary according to board plan and housing facility. ***Payment plan:*** Installment.

FRESHMAN FINANCIAL AID (Fall 2009) 1,169 applied for aid; of those 67% were deemed to have need. 96% of freshmen with need received aid; of those 60% had need fully met. ***Average percent of need met:*** 71% (excluding resources awarded to replace EFC). ***Average financial aid package:*** $8578 (excluding resources awarded to replace EFC). 1% of all full-time freshmen had no need and received non-need-based gift aid.

UNDERGRADUATE FINANCIAL AID (Fall 2009) 5,997 applied for aid; of those 78% were deemed to have need. 97% of undergraduates with need received aid; of those 55% had need fully met. ***Average percent of need met:*** 70% (excluding resources awarded to replace EFC). ***Average financial aid package:*** $8993 (excluding resources awarded to replace EFC). 1% of all full-time undergraduates had no need and received non-need-based gift aid.

GIFT AID (NEED-BASED) ***Total amount:*** $24,826,064 (36% federal, 45% state, 9% institutional, 10% external sources). ***Receiving aid:*** Freshmen: 42% (653); all full-time undergraduates: 44% (3,859). ***Average award:*** Freshmen: $6149; Undergraduates: $6201. ***Scholarships, grants, and awards:*** Federal Pell, FSEOG, state, private, college/university gift aid from institutional funds.

GIFT AID (NON-NEED-BASED) ***Total amount:*** $1,331,721 (12% state, 5% institutional, 83% external sources). ***Receiving aid:*** Freshmen: 8% (130). Undergraduates: 2% (216). ***Average award:*** Freshmen: $710. Undergraduates: $710. ***Scholarships, grants, and awards by category:*** *Academic interests/achievement:* general academic interests/achievements. *Creative arts/performance:* art/fine arts, general creative arts/performance. *Special achievements/activities:* leadership. *Special characteristics:* children and siblings of alumni, local/state students, members of minority groups, religious affiliation. ***Tuition waivers:*** Full or partial for employees or children of employees, senior citizens. ***ROTC:*** Army, Air Force.

LOANS ***Student loans:*** $37,293,501 (75% need-based, 25% non-need-based). 55% of past graduating class borrowed through all loan programs. *Average indebtedness per student:* $16,507. ***Average need-based loan:*** Freshmen: $3511. Undergraduates: $4052. ***Parent loans:*** $13,974,237 (55% need-based, 45% non-need-based). ***Programs:*** Federal Direct (Subsidized and Unsubsidized Stafford, PLUS), Perkins, college/university.

WORK-STUDY ***Federal work-study:*** Total amount: $523,381; jobs available. ***State or other work-study/employment:*** Total amount: $824,016 (100% need-based). Part-time jobs available.

ATHLETIC AWARDS Total amount: $654,151 (50% need-based, 50% non-need-based).

APPLYING FOR FINANCIAL AID ***Required financial aid form:*** FAFSA. ***Financial aid deadline (priority):*** 3/1. ***Notification date:*** Continuous beginning 5/15. Students must reply within 4 weeks of notification.

CONTACT Ms. Agnes Canedo, Director of Financial Aid, Central Washington University, 400 East University Way, Ellensburg, WA 98926-7495, 509-963-3049 or toll-free 866-298-4968. *Fax:* 509-963-1788. *E-mail:* canedoa@cwu.edu.

CENTRAL YESHIVA TOMCHEI TMIMIM-LUBAVITCH

Brooklyn, NY

CONTACT Rabbi Moshe M. Gluckowsky, Director of Financial Aid, Central Yeshiva Tomchei Tmimim-Lubavitch, 841-853 Ocean Parkway, Brooklyn, NY 11230, 718-859-2277.

CENTRE COLLEGE

Danville, KY

Comprehensive fee: $42,500 **Average undergraduate aid package: $25,713**

ABOUT THE INSTITUTION Independent religious, coed. 27 undergraduate majors. Institutional methodology is used as a basis for awarding need-based institutional aid.

UNDERGRADUATE EXPENSES for 2011–12 ***Comprehensive fee:*** $42,500. ***Payment plan:*** Installment.

FRESHMAN FINANCIAL AID (Fall 2010, est.) 313 applied for aid; of those 77% were deemed to have need. 100% of freshmen with need received aid; of those 34% had need fully met. ***Average percent of need met:*** 89% (excluding resources awarded to replace EFC). ***Average financial aid package:*** $26,787 (excluding resources awarded to replace EFC). 30% of all full-time freshmen had no need and received non-need-based gift aid.

UNDERGRADUATE FINANCIAL AID (Fall 2010, est.) 908 applied for aid; of those 84% were deemed to have need. 100% of undergraduates with need received aid; of those 31% had need fully met. ***Average percent of need met:*** 85% (excluding resources awarded to replace EFC). ***Average financial aid package:*** $25,713 (excluding resources awarded to replace EFC). 35% of all full-time undergraduates had no need and received non-need-based gift aid.

GIFT AID (NEED-BASED) ***Total amount:*** $17,219,433 (7% federal, 13% state, 77% institutional, 3% external sources). ***Receiving aid:*** Freshmen: 67% (240); all full-time undergraduates: 62% (764). ***Average award:*** Freshmen: $24,295; Undergraduates: $22,538. ***Scholarships, grants, and awards:*** Federal Pell, FSEOG, state, private, college/university gift aid from institutional funds.

GIFT AID (NON-NEED-BASED) ***Total amount:*** $6,696,142 (1% federal, 7% state, 88% institutional, 4% external sources). ***Average award:*** Freshmen: $15,347. Undergraduates: $15,287. ***Scholarships, grants, and awards by category:*** *Academic interests/achievement:* 945 awards ($12,172,130 total): foreign languages, general academic interests/achievements. *Creative arts/performance:* 112 awards ($435,000 total): music, theater/drama. *Special achievements/activities:* 21 awards ($47,500 total): community service. *Special characteristics:* 192 awards ($1,741,812 total): children and siblings of alumni, children of faculty/staff, ethnic background, first-generation college students. ***Tuition waivers:*** Full or partial for employees or children of employees.

LOANS ***Student loans:*** $3,780,747 (55% need-based, 45% non-need-based). 59% of past graduating class borrowed through all loan programs. *Average indebtedness per student:* $19,820. ***Average need-based loan:*** Freshmen: $3461. Undergraduates: $4436. ***Parent loans:*** $1,934,090 (100% non-need-based). ***Programs:*** Federal Direct (Subsidized and Unsubsidized Stafford, PLUS), Perkins, college/university.

WORK-STUDY ***Federal work-study:*** Total amount: $535,485; 331 jobs averaging $1577. ***State or other work-study/employment:*** Total amount: $8260 (100% non-need-based). 5 part-time jobs averaging $1652.

APPLYING FOR FINANCIAL AID ***Required financial aid forms:*** FAFSA, institution's own form. ***Financial aid deadline:*** 3/1. ***Notification date:*** 4/1. Students must reply by 5/1.

CONTACT Ms. Elaine Larson, Director of Student Financial Planning, Centre College, 600 West Walnut Street, Danville, KY 40422-1394, 859-238-5365 or toll-free 800-423-6236. *Fax:* 859-238-8719. *E-mail:* finaid@centre.edu.

CHADRON STATE COLLEGE

Chadron, NE

CONTACT Ms. Sherry Douglas, Director of Financial Aid, Chadron State College, 1000 Main Street, Chadron, NE 69337, 308-432-6230 or toll-free 800-242-3766 (in-state). *Fax:* 308-432-6229. *E-mail:* finaid@csc.edu.

CHAMBERLAIN COLLEGE OF NURSING

St. Louis, MO

ABOUT THE INSTITUTION Proprietary, coed. 1 undergraduate major.

GIFT AID (NEED-BASED) ***Scholarships, grants, and awards:*** Federal Pell, FSEOG, private, college/university gift aid from institutional funds.

GIFT AID (NON-NEED-BASED) ***Scholarships, grants, and awards by category:*** *Academic interests/achievement:* general academic interests/achievements, health fields. *Special achievements/activities:* leadership.

LOANS ***Programs:*** state.

APPLYING FOR FINANCIAL AID ***Required financial aid forms:*** FAFSA, institution's own form.

CONTACT Financial Aid Counselor, Chamberlain College of Nursing, 6150 Oakland Avenue, St. Louis, MO 63139-3215, 314-768-5604 or toll-free 800-942-4310.

CHAMINADE UNIVERSITY OF HONOLULU

Honolulu, HI

Tuition & fees: $17,740 **Average undergraduate aid package: N/A**

ABOUT THE INSTITUTION Independent Roman Catholic, coed. 22 undergraduate majors. Federal methodology is used as a basis for awarding need-based institutional aid.

UNDERGRADUATE EXPENSES for 2010–11 ***Comprehensive fee:*** $28,160 includes full-time tuition ($17,600), mandatory fees ($140), and room and board ($10,420). ***College room only:*** $5170. Full-time tuition and fees vary according to course load. Room and board charges vary according to board plan and housing facility. ***Part-time tuition:*** $587 per credit hour. Part-time tuition and fees vary according to course load. ***Payment plan:*** Installment.

GIFT AID (NEED-BASED) ***Scholarships, grants, and awards:*** Federal Pell, FSEOG, state, private, college/university gift aid from institutional funds.

GIFT AID (NON-NEED-BASED) ***Scholarships, grants, and awards by category:*** *Academic interests/achievement:* general academic interests/achievements.

LOANS ***Programs:*** Perkins, alternative loans.

APPLYING FOR FINANCIAL AID ***Required financial aid form:*** FAFSA. ***Financial aid deadline (priority):*** 3/1. ***Notification date:*** Continuous beginning 3/1. Students must reply within 4 weeks of notification.

CONTACT Amy Takiguchi, Director of Financial Aid, Chaminade University of Honolulu, 3140 Waialae Avenue, Honolulu, HI 96816-1578, 808-735-4780 or toll-free 800-735-3733 (out-of-state). *Fax:* 808-739-8362. *E-mail:* finaid@chaminade.edu.

CHAMPLAIN COLLEGE

Burlington, VT

Tuition & fees: $28,400 **Average undergraduate aid package: $16,489**

ABOUT THE INSTITUTION Independent, coed. 45 undergraduate majors. Federal methodology is used as a basis for awarding need-based institutional aid.

UNDERGRADUATE EXPENSES for 2011–12 ***Comprehensive fee:*** $40,920 includes full-time tuition ($28,350), mandatory fees ($50), and room and board ($12,520). ***College room only:*** $7620. Full-time tuition and fees vary according to course load. Room and board charges vary according to housing facility. ***Part-time tuition:*** $1180 per credit. Part-time tuition and fees vary according to course load. ***Payment plan:*** Installment.

FRESHMAN FINANCIAL AID (Fall 2010, est.) 553 applied for aid; of those 83% were deemed to have need. 100% of freshmen with need received aid; of those 8% had need fully met. ***Average percent of need met:*** 71% (excluding resources awarded to replace EFC). ***Average financial aid package:*** $18,995 (excluding resources awarded to replace EFC). 12% of all full-time freshmen had no need and received non-need-based gift aid.

UNDERGRADUATE FINANCIAL AID (Fall 2010, est.) 1,590 applied for aid; of those 86% were deemed to have need. 99% of undergraduates with need received aid; of those 6% had need fully met. ***Average percent of need met:*** 64% (excluding resources awarded to replace EFC). ***Average financial aid package:*** $16,489 (excluding resources awarded to replace EFC). 10% of all full-time undergraduates had no need and received non-need-based gift aid.

GIFT AID (NEED-BASED) ***Total amount:*** $11,226,131 (22% federal, 13% state, 61% institutional, 4% external sources). ***Receiving aid:*** Freshmen: 64% (422); all full-time undergraduates: 59% (1,196). ***Average award:*** Freshmen: $9351; Undergraduates: $9093. ***Scholarships, grants, and awards:*** Federal Pell, FSEOG, state, private, college/university gift aid from institutional funds.

GIFT AID (NON-NEED-BASED) ***Total amount:*** $3,317,265 (100% institutional). ***Receiving aid:*** Freshmen: 30% (199). Undergraduates: 30% (615). ***Average award:*** Freshmen: $5135. Undergraduates: $3917. ***Scholarships, grants, and awards by category:*** *Academic interests/achievement:* 720 awards ($2,968,265 total): business, communication, computer science, education, engineering/technologies, general academic interests/achievements, health fields, social sciences. ***Tuition waivers:*** Full or partial for employees or children of employees.

LOANS ***Student loans:*** $10,019,503 (100% need-based). 85% of past graduating class borrowed through all loan programs. *Average indebtedness per student:* $34,658. ***Average need-based loan:*** Freshmen: $6299. Undergraduates: $6880. ***Parent loans:*** $2,256,951 (100% need-based). ***Programs:*** Federal Direct (Subsidized and Unsubsidized Stafford), Perkins.

WORK-STUDY ***Federal work-study:*** Total amount: $2,782,414; 1,086 jobs averaging $2484.

APPLYING FOR FINANCIAL AID ***Required financial aid form:*** FAFSA. ***Financial aid deadline (priority):*** 3/1. ***Notification date:*** Continuous beginning 3/20. Students must reply by 5/1.

CONTACT Kristi Jovell, Director of Financial Aid, Champlain College, 163 South Willard Street, Burlington, VT 05401, 802-860-2730 or toll-free 800-570-5858. *Fax:* 802-860-2775. *E-mail:* veladotam@champlain.edu.

CHANCELLOR UNIVERSITY

Cleveland, OH

CONTACT Eric Damon, Director of Financial Aid, Chancellor University, 3921 Chester Avenue, Cleveland, OH 44114, 216-361-2734 or toll-free 877-366-9377. *Fax:* 216-361-9096.

CHAPMAN UNIVERSITY

Orange, CA

ABOUT THE INSTITUTION Independent religious, coed. 49 undergraduate majors.

GIFT AID (NEED-BASED) ***Scholarships, grants, and awards:*** Federal Pell, FSEOG, state, private, college/university gift aid from institutional funds.

GIFT AID (NON-NEED-BASED) ***Scholarships, grants, and awards by category:*** *Academic interests/achievement:* biological sciences, general academic interests/achievements, physical sciences. *Creative arts/performance:* art/fine arts, cinema/film/broadcasting, creative writing, dance, music, performing arts, theater/drama. *Special characteristics:* children and siblings of alumni.

LOANS ***Programs:*** Federal Direct (Subsidized and Unsubsidized Stafford), Perkins.

WORK-STUDY ***Federal work-study:*** Total amount: $1,856,517; 828 jobs averaging $2186.

APPLYING FOR FINANCIAL AID ***Required financial aid forms:*** FAFSA, state aid form.

CONTACT Mr. Gregory L. Ball, Director of Financial Aid, Chapman University, One University Drive, Orange, CA 92866, 714-997-6740 or toll-free 888-CUAPPLY. *Fax:* 714-997-6743. *E-mail:* gball@chapman.edu.

CHARLES DREW UNIVERSITY OF MEDICINE AND SCIENCE

Los Angeles, CA

CONTACT Financial Aid Office, Charles Drew University of Medicine and Science, 1731 East 120th Street, Los Angeles, CA 90059, 323-563-4824. *Fax:* 323-569-0597.

CHARLESTON SOUTHERN UNIVERSITY

Charleston, SC

CONTACT Mr. Jim Rhoden, Director of Admissions, Charleston Southern University, PO Box 118087, 9200 University Boulevard, Charleston, SC 29423-8087, 843-863-7050 or toll-free 800-947-7474. *Fax:* 843-863-7070.

CHARTER OAK STATE COLLEGE

New Britain, CT

CONTACT Velma Walters, Director, Financial Aid, Charter Oak State College, 55 Paul J. Manafort Drive, New Britain, CT 06053-2142, 860-832-3872. *Fax:* 860-832-3999. *E-mail:* sfa@charteroak.edu.

CHATHAM UNIVERSITY

Pittsburgh, PA

ABOUT THE INSTITUTION Independent, undergraduate: women only; graduate: coed. 43 undergraduate majors.

GIFT AID (NEED-BASED) ***Scholarships, grants, and awards:*** Federal Pell, FSEOG, state, private, college/university gift aid from institutional funds, United Negro College Fund.

GIFT AID (NON-NEED-BASED) ***Scholarships, grants, and awards by category:*** *Academic interests/achievement:* biological sciences, business, communication, education, English, general academic interests/achievements, international studies, mathematics, physical sciences, premedicine, social sciences. *Creative arts/performance:* theater/drama. *Special characteristics:* children and siblings of alumni, children of faculty/staff, siblings of current students.

LOANS ***Programs:*** Perkins.

WORK-STUDY ***Federal work-study:*** Total amount: $443,558; jobs available. ***State or other work-study/employment:*** Part-time jobs available.

APPLYING FOR FINANCIAL AID ***Required financial aid form:*** FAFSA.

CONTACT Jennifer Burns, Director of Financial Aid, Chatham University, Woodland Road, Pittsburgh, PA 15232-2826, 412-365-1849 or toll-free 800-837-1290. *Fax:* 412-365-1643. *E-mail:* jburns@chatham.edu.

CHESTER COLLEGE OF NEW ENGLAND

Chester, NH

CONTACT Jason Graves, Director of Financial Aid, Chester College of New England, 40 Chester Street, Chester, NH 03036-4331, 603-887-4401 Ext. 7404 or toll-free 800-974-6372. *Fax:* 603-887-1777. *E-mail:* financialaid@chestercollege.edu.

CHESTNUT HILL COLLEGE

Philadelphia, PA

Tuition & fees: $29,100 **Average undergraduate aid package: $21,066**

ABOUT THE INSTITUTION Independent Roman Catholic, coed. 37 undergraduate majors. Federal methodology is used as a basis for awarding need-based institutional aid.

UNDERGRADUATE EXPENSES for 2011–12 ***Comprehensive fee:*** $38,440 includes full-time tuition ($29,100) and room and board ($9340). ***Part-time tuition:*** $620 per credit.

FRESHMAN FINANCIAL AID (Fall 2010, est.) 208 applied for aid; of those 87% were deemed to have need. 99% of freshmen with need received aid; of those 18% had need fully met. ***Average percent of need met:*** 73% (excluding resources awarded to replace EFC). ***Average financial aid package:*** $20,552 (excluding resources awarded to replace EFC). 2% of all full-time freshmen had no need and received non-need-based gift aid.

UNDERGRADUATE FINANCIAL AID (Fall 2010, est.) 778 applied for aid; of those 91% were deemed to have need. 99% of undergraduates with need received aid; of those 17% had need fully met. ***Average percent of need met:*** 73% (excluding resources awarded to replace EFC). ***Average financial aid package:*** $21,066 (excluding resources awarded to replace EFC). 1% of all full-time undergraduates had no need and received non-need-based gift aid.

GIFT AID (NEED-BASED) ***Total amount:*** $15,492,121 (18% federal, 10% state, 71% institutional, 1% external sources). ***Receiving aid:*** Freshmen: 82% (180); all full-time undergraduates: 56% (695). ***Average award:*** Freshmen: $16,673; Undergraduates: $16,548. ***Scholarships, grants, and awards:*** Federal Pell, FSEOG, state, private, college/university gift aid from institutional funds.

GIFT AID (NON-NEED-BASED) ***Total amount:*** $2,119,243 (98% institutional, 2% external sources). ***Receiving aid:*** Freshmen: 12% (26). Undergraduates: 7% (83). ***Average award:*** Freshmen: $3470. Undergraduates: $3307. ***Scholarships, grants, and awards by category:*** *Academic interests/achievement:* 854 awards ($13,143,491 total): general academic interests/achievements. *Creative arts/performance:* 1 award ($500 total): music. *Special characteristics:* 23 awards ($513,250 total): children and siblings of alumni, children of faculty/staff, international students.

LOANS ***Student loans:*** $6,897,702 (69% need-based, 31% non-need-based). ***Average need-based loan:*** Freshmen: $3929. Undergraduates: $4680. ***Parent loans:*** $1,911,462 (41% need-based, 59% non-need-based). ***Programs:*** Federal Direct (Subsidized and Unsubsidized Stafford, PLUS), Perkins.

WORK-STUDY ***Federal work-study:*** Total amount: $150,555; jobs available. ***State or other work-study/employment:*** Part-time jobs available.

ATHLETIC AWARDS Total amount: $784,870 (58% need-based, 42% non-need-based).

APPLYING FOR FINANCIAL AID ***Required financial aid form:*** FAFSA. ***Financial aid deadline:*** Continuous. ***Notification date:*** Continuous beginning 2/15.

CONTACT Mr. Nicholas Flocco, Director of Financial Aid, Chestnut Hill College, 9601 Germantown Avenue, Philadelphia, PA 19118-2693, 215-248-7192 or toll-free 800-248-0052 (out-of-state). *Fax:* 215-248-7217. *E-mail:* nfloccon@chc.edu.

CHEYNEY UNIVERSITY OF PENNSYLVANIA

Cheyney, PA

CONTACT Mr. James Brown, Director of Financial Aid, Cheyney University of Pennsylvania, 1837 University Circle, Cheyney, PA 19319, 610-399-2302 or toll-free 800-CHEYNEY. *Fax:* 610-399-2411. *E-mail:* jbrown@cheyney.edu.

CHICAGO STATE UNIVERSITY

Chicago, IL

Tuition & fees: N/R **Average undergraduate aid package: $4850**

ABOUT THE INSTITUTION State-supported, coed. ***Awards:*** bachelor's and master's degrees and post-bachelor's certificates. 33 undergraduate majors. ***Total enrollment:*** 6,810. Undergraduates: 5,217. Freshmen: 448. Both federal and institutional methodology are used as a basis for awarding need-based institutional aid.

FRESHMAN FINANCIAL AID (Fall 2010, est.) 505 applied for aid; of those 100% were deemed to have need. 100% of freshmen with need received aid. ***Average percent of need met:*** 53% (excluding resources awarded to replace EFC). ***Average financial aid package:*** $5390 (excluding resources awarded to replace EFC).

UNDERGRADUATE FINANCIAL AID (Fall 2010, est.) 3,699 applied for aid; of those 100% were deemed to have need. 100% of undergraduates with need received aid. ***Average percent of need met:*** 48% (excluding resources awarded to replace EFC). ***Average financial aid package:*** $4850 (excluding resources awarded to replace EFC).

GIFT AID (NEED-BASED) ***Total amount:*** $45,215,378 (80% federal, 19% state, 1% institutional). ***Receiving aid:*** Freshmen: 91% (466); all full-time undergraduates: 87% (3,326). ***Average award:*** Freshmen: $4350; Undergraduates: $3850. ***Scholarships, grants, and awards:*** Federal Pell, FSEOG, state, private, college/university gift aid from institutional funds, Federal Nursing.

GIFT AID (NON-NEED-BASED) ***Receiving aid:*** Freshmen: 2% (10). Undergraduates: 3% (116). ***Scholarships, grants, and awards by category:*** *Academic interests/achievement:* general academic interests/achievements, physical sciences. *Creative arts/performance:* art/fine arts, journalism/publications, music. *Special achievements/activities:* leadership. ***ROTC:*** Army, Naval cooperative, Air Force cooperative.

LOANS ***Student loans:*** $36,558,403 (99% need-based, 1% non-need-based). 82% of past graduating class borrowed through all loan programs. *Average indebtedness per student:* $27,322. ***Average need-based loan:*** Freshmen: $1020. Undergraduates: $980. ***Parent loans:*** $2,667,844 (50% need-based, 50% non-need-based). ***Programs:*** Federal Direct (Subsidized and Unsubsidized Stafford, PLUS), Perkins, Federal Nursing.

WORK-STUDY ***Federal work-study:*** Total amount: $417,603; 252 jobs averaging $1682. ***State or other work-study/employment:*** 234 part-time jobs averaging $1567.

ATHLETIC AWARDS Total amount: $979,741 (100% non-need-based).

APPLYING FOR FINANCIAL AID ***Required financial aid form:*** FAFSA. ***Financial aid deadline:*** 6/30 (priority: 1/15). ***Notification date:*** Continuous beginning 4/1. Students must reply within 16 weeks of notification.

CONTACT Office of Student Financial Aid, Chicago State University, 9501 South Martin Luther King Drive, Chicago, IL 60628, 773-995-2304.

CHOWAN UNIVERSITY

Murfreesboro, NC

Tuition & fees: $19,750 **Average undergraduate aid package: $16,365**

ABOUT THE INSTITUTION Independent Baptist, coed. 50 undergraduate majors. Federal methodology is used as a basis for awarding need-based institutional aid.

UNDERGRADUATE EXPENSES for 2010–11 ***One-time required fee:*** $145. ***Comprehensive fee:*** $27,160 includes full-time tuition ($19,750) and room and board ($7410). ***College room only:*** $3560. Room and board charges vary according to board plan. ***Payment plans:*** Installment, deferred payment.

FRESHMAN FINANCIAL AID (Fall 2010, est.) 499 applied for aid; of those 94% were deemed to have need. 100% of freshmen with need received aid; of those 18% had need fully met. ***Average percent of need met:*** 81% (excluding resources awarded to replace EFC). ***Average financial aid package:*** $16,172 (excluding resources awarded to replace EFC). 3% of all full-time freshmen had no need and received non-need-based gift aid.

UNDERGRADUATE FINANCIAL AID (Fall 2010, est.) 1,172 applied for aid; of those 95% were deemed to have need. 100% of undergraduates with need received aid; of those 12% had need fully met. ***Average percent of need met:*** 76% (excluding resources awarded to replace EFC). ***Average financial aid package:*** $16,365 (excluding resources awarded to replace EFC). 4% of all full-time undergraduates had no need and received non-need-based gift aid.

GIFT AID (NEED-BASED) ***Total amount:*** $11,999,303 (33% federal, 7% state, 53% institutional, 7% external sources). ***Receiving aid:*** Freshmen: 90% (465); all full-time undergraduates: 86% (1,083). ***Average award:*** Freshmen: $16,242; Undergraduates: $13,396. ***Scholarships, grants, and awards:*** Federal Pell, FSEOG, state, private, college/university gift aid from institutional funds.

GIFT AID (NON-NEED-BASED) ***Total amount:*** $1,224,772 (10% state, 84% institutional, 6% external sources). ***Receiving aid:*** Freshmen: 9% (46). Undergraduates: 9% (111). ***Average award:*** Freshmen: $10,823. Undergraduates: $6201. ***Scholarships, grants, and awards by category:*** *Academic interests/achievement:* 1,207 awards ($6,447,317 total): general academic interests/achievements. *Creative arts/performance:* 29 awards ($50,828 total): music. *Special achievements/activities:* 323 awards ($841,214 total): leadership. *Special characteristics:* 244 awards ($420,726 total): children of educators, children of faculty/staff, first-generation college students, international students, local/state students, relatives of clergy, religious affiliation. ***Tuition waivers:*** Full or partial for employees or children of employees, senior citizens.

LOANS ***Student loans:*** $8,122,043 (78% need-based, 22% non-need-based). 94% of past graduating class borrowed through all loan programs. *Average indebtedness per student:* $29,180. ***Average need-based loan:*** Freshmen: $3276. Undergraduates: $3226. ***Parent loans:*** $3,592,020 (20% need-based, 80% non-need-based). ***Programs:*** Perkins, state, alternative loans.

WORK-STUDY ***Federal work-study:*** Total amount: $359,534; 287 jobs averaging $1252. ***State or other work-study/employment:*** Total amount: $191,798 (100% non-need-based). 165 part-time jobs averaging $1162.

ATHLETIC AWARDS Total amount: $882,738 (58% need-based, 42% non-need-based).

APPLYING FOR FINANCIAL AID ***Required financial aid form:*** FAFSA. ***Financial aid deadline (priority):*** 5/1. ***Notification date:*** Continuous. Students must reply within 2 weeks of notification.

CONTACT Mrs. Sharon W. Rose, Director of Financial Aid, Chowan University, One University Place, Murfreesboro, NC 27855, 252-398-1229 or toll-free 888-4-Chowan. *Fax:* 252-398-6513. *E-mail:* roses1@chowan.edu.

CHRISTENDOM COLLEGE

Front Royal, VA

Tuition & fees: $20,434 **Average undergraduate aid package: $13,440**

ABOUT THE INSTITUTION Independent Roman Catholic, coed. 7 undergraduate majors. Institutional methodology is used as a basis for awarding need-based institutional aid.

UNDERGRADUATE EXPENSES for 2011–12 ***Comprehensive fee:*** $28,090 includes full-time tuition ($19,884), mandatory fees ($550), and room and board ($7656). ***Payment plan:*** Installment.

FRESHMAN FINANCIAL AID (Fall 2010, est.) 70 applied for aid; of those 91% were deemed to have need. 100% of freshmen with need received aid; of those 94% had need fully met. ***Average percent of need met:*** 90% (excluding resources awarded to replace EFC). ***Average financial aid package:*** $13,340 (excluding resources awarded to replace EFC). 22% of all full-time freshmen had no need and received non-need-based gift aid.

UNDERGRADUATE FINANCIAL AID (Fall 2010, est.) 230 applied for aid; of those 93% were deemed to have need. 100% of undergraduates with need received aid; of those 100% had need fully met. ***Average percent of need met:*** 90% (excluding resources awarded to replace EFC). ***Average financial aid package:*** $13,440 (excluding resources awarded to replace EFC). 21% of all full-time undergraduates had no need and received non-need-based gift aid.

GIFT AID (NEED-BASED) ***Total amount:*** $1,546,208 (100% institutional). ***Receiving aid:*** Freshmen: 57% (64); all full-time undergraduates: 52% (211). ***Average award:*** Freshmen: $6815; Undergraduates: $7325. ***Scholarships, grants, and awards:*** private, college/university gift aid from institutional funds.

GIFT AID (NON-NEED-BASED) ***Total amount:*** $668,376 (97% institutional, 3% external sources). ***Receiving aid:*** Freshmen: 25% (28). Undergraduates: 18% (73). ***Average award:*** Freshmen: $7750. Undergraduates: $7700. ***Scholarships, grants, and awards by category:*** *Academic interests/achievement:* 160 awards ($945,000 total): general academic interests/achievements. ***Tuition waivers:*** Full or partial for employees or children of employees.

LOANS ***Student loans:*** $1,829,028 (72% need-based, 28% non-need-based). 61% of past graduating class borrowed through all loan programs. *Average indebtedness per student:* $26,614. ***Average need-based loan:*** Freshmen: $6700. Undergraduates: $6360. ***Programs:*** college/university.

WORK-STUDY ***State or other work-study/employment:*** Total amount: $287,100 (100% need-based). 145 part-time jobs averaging $1980.

APPLYING FOR FINANCIAL AID ***Required financial aid form:*** institution's own form. ***Financial aid deadline (priority):*** 4/1. ***Notification date:*** Continuous beginning 3/1. Students must reply within 4 weeks of notification.

CONTACT Mrs. Alisa Polk, Financial Aid Officer, Christendom College, 134 Christendom Drive, Front Royal, VA 22630-5103, 800-877-5456 Ext. 1214 or toll-free 800-877-5456 Ext. 290. *Fax:* 540-636-1655. *E-mail:* apolk@christendom.edu.

CHRISTIAN BROTHERS UNIVERSITY

Memphis, TN

Tuition & fees: $24,870 **Average undergraduate aid package: $20,985**

ABOUT THE INSTITUTION Independent Roman Catholic, coed. 35 undergraduate majors. Federal methodology is used as a basis for awarding need-based institutional aid.

UNDERGRADUATE EXPENSES for 2010–11 ***Comprehensive fee:*** $31,280 includes full-time tuition ($24,320), mandatory fees ($550), and room and board ($6410). ***College room only:*** $3000. Full-time tuition and fees vary according to class time and course load. Room and board charges vary according to board plan and housing facility. ***Part-time tuition:*** $870 per credit hour. Part-time tuition and fees vary according to class time. ***Payment plans:*** Installment, deferred payment.

FRESHMAN FINANCIAL AID (Fall 2010, est.) 271 applied for aid; of those 86% were deemed to have need. 100% of freshmen with need received aid; of those 30% had need fully met. ***Average percent of need met:*** 90% (excluding resources awarded to replace EFC). ***Average financial aid package:*** $24,188 (excluding resources awarded to replace EFC). 15% of all full-time freshmen had no need and received non-need-based gift aid.

UNDERGRADUATE FINANCIAL AID (Fall 2010, est.) 1,080 applied for aid; of those 85% were deemed to have need. 100% of undergraduates with need received aid; of those 24% had need fully met. ***Average percent of need met:*** 81% (excluding resources awarded to replace EFC). ***Average financial aid package:*** $20,985 (excluding resources awarded to replace EFC). 16% of all full-time undergraduates had no need and received non-need-based gift aid.

GIFT AID (NEED-BASED) ***Total amount:*** $4,158,515 (70% federal, 30% state). ***Receiving aid:*** Freshmen: 53% (152); all full-time undergraduates: 47% (571). ***Average award:*** Freshmen: $6507; Undergraduates: $6590. ***Scholarships, grants, and awards:*** Federal Pell, FSEOG, state, private, college/university gift aid from institutional funds.

GIFT AID (NON-NEED-BASED) ***Total amount:*** $14,810,367 (15% state, 82% institutional, 3% external sources). ***Receiving aid:*** Freshmen: 81% (233). Undergraduates: 67% (810). ***Average award:*** Freshmen: $10,572. Undergraduates: $9265. ***Scholarships, grants, and awards by category:*** *Academic interests/achievement:* 898 awards ($9,823,299 total): engineering/technologies, general academic interests/achievements. *Creative arts/performance:* 17 awards ($17,500 total): general creative arts/performance. *Special achievements/activities:* 110 awards ($571,290 total): general special achievements/activities, leadership. *Special characteristics:* 540 awards ($1,662,622 total): children and siblings of alumni, general special characteristics, religious affiliation. ***Tuition waivers:*** Full or partial for children of alumni, employees or children of employees.

LOANS ***Student loans:*** $6,782,809 (43% need-based, 57% non-need-based). 69% of past graduating class borrowed through all loan programs. *Average indebtedness per student:* $29,207. ***Average need-based loan:*** Freshmen: $3423. Undergraduates: $4413. ***Parent loans:*** $651,288 (100% non-need-based). ***Programs:*** Perkins, college/university, alternative loans.

WORK-STUDY ***Federal work-study:*** Total amount: $155,140; 157 jobs averaging $988. ***State or other work-study/employment:*** Total amount: $181,900 (100% non-need-based). 186 part-time jobs averaging $978.

ATHLETIC AWARDS Total amount: $1,282,970 (100% non-need-based).

APPLYING FOR FINANCIAL AID ***Required financial aid form:*** FAFSA. ***Financial aid deadline (priority):*** 2/15. ***Notification date:*** Continuous beginning 2/28. Students must reply by 5/1 or within 2 weeks of notification.

CONTACT Mr. Jim Shannon, Dean of Student Financial Assistance, Christian Brothers University, 650 East Parkway South, Memphis, TN 38104, 901-321-3305 or toll-free 800-288-7576. *Fax:* 901-321-3327. *E-mail:* jshannon@cbu.edu.

CHRISTIAN LIFE COLLEGE

Mount Prospect, IL

CONTACT Jeanna Wilson, Office of Financial Aid, Christian Life College, 400 East Gregory Street, Mt. Prospect, IL 60056, 847-259-1840. *Fax:* 847-259-3888.

CHRISTOPHER NEWPORT UNIVERSITY

Newport News, VA

Tuition & fees (VA res): $13,220 **Average undergraduate aid package: $8099**

ABOUT THE INSTITUTION State-supported, coed. 37 undergraduate majors. Federal methodology is used as a basis for awarding need-based institutional aid.

UNDERGRADUATE EXPENSES for 2010–11 ***Tuition, state resident:*** full-time $9250; part-time $385 per semester hour. ***Tuition, nonresident:*** full-time $17,992; part-time $665 per semester hour. ***Required fees:*** full-time $3970; $165 per semester hour. Full-time tuition and fees vary according to course load. Part-time tuition and fees vary according to course load. ***College room and board:*** $9540; ***Room only:*** $6420. Room and board charges vary according to board plan and housing facility. ***Payment plan:*** Installment.

FRESHMAN FINANCIAL AID (Fall 2010, est.) 896 applied for aid; of those 63% were deemed to have need. 96% of freshmen with need received aid; of those 15% had need fully met. ***Average percent of need met:*** 69% (excluding resources awarded to replace EFC). ***Average financial aid package:*** $7720 (excluding resources awarded to replace EFC). 17% of all full-time freshmen had no need and received non-need-based gift aid.

UNDERGRADUATE FINANCIAL AID (Fall 2010, est.) 3,047 applied for aid; of those 71% were deemed to have need. 96% of undergraduates with need received aid; of those 16% had need fully met. ***Average percent of need met:*** 69% (excluding resources awarded to replace EFC). ***Average financial aid package:*** $8099 (excluding resources awarded to replace EFC). 10% of all full-time undergraduates had no need and received non-need-based gift aid.

GIFT AID (NEED-BASED) ***Total amount:*** $8,196,795 (43% federal, 49% state, 8% institutional). ***Receiving aid:*** Freshmen: 36% (418); all full-time undergraduates: 34% (1,576). ***Average award:*** Freshmen: $5085; Undergraduates: $5087. ***Scholarships, grants, and awards:*** Federal Pell, FSEOG, state, private, college/university gift aid from institutional funds.

GIFT AID (NON-NEED-BASED) ***Total amount:*** $2,455,765 (2% state, 58% institutional, 40% external sources). ***Receiving aid:*** Freshmen: 22% (253). Undergraduates: 12% (546). ***Average award:*** Freshmen: $1606. Undergraduates: $1772. ***Scholarships, grants, and awards by category:*** *Academic interests/achievement:* 101 awards ($126,200 total): biological sciences, business, communication, computer science, education, engineering/technologies, English, foreign languages, general academic interests/achievements, humanities, mathematics, military science, religion/biblical studies. *Creative arts/performance:* 56 awards ($48,225 total): art/fine arts, music, theater/drama. *Special achievements/activities:* 667 awards ($1,243,000 total): general special achievements/activities, leadership. ***Tuition waivers:*** Full or partial for employees or children of employees, senior citizens.

LOANS ***Student loans:*** $19,482,718 (40% need-based, 60% non-need-based). 51% of past graduating class borrowed through all loan programs. *Average indebtedness per student:* $21,572. ***Average need-based loan:*** Freshmen: $3154. Undergraduates: $4033. ***Parent loans:*** $5,814,396 (100% non-need-based). ***Programs:*** Federal Direct (Subsidized and Unsubsidized Stafford, PLUS), state, college/university, alternative loans.

WORK-STUDY ***Federal work-study:*** Total amount: $97,429; 117 jobs averaging $833. ***State or other work-study/employment:*** Total amount: $2,074,304 (100% non-need-based). 1,762 part-time jobs averaging $1177.

APPLYING FOR FINANCIAL AID ***Required financial aid form:*** FAFSA. ***Financial aid deadline (priority):*** 3/1. ***Notification date:*** Continuous beginning 2/10. Students must reply within 3 weeks of notification.

CONTACT Mary L. Wigginton, Director of Financial Aid, Christopher Newport University, 1 University Place, Newport News, VA 23606, 757-594-7170 or toll-free 800-333-4268. *Fax:* 757-594-7113. *E-mail:* finaid@cnu.edu.

CINCINNATI CHRISTIAN UNIVERSITY

Cincinnati, OH

Tuition & fees: $13,780 **Average undergraduate aid package: $9556**

ABOUT THE INSTITUTION Independent religious, coed. 12 undergraduate majors. Federal methodology is used as a basis for awarding need-based institutional aid.

UNDERGRADUATE EXPENSES for 2010–11 ***Comprehensive fee:*** $20,490 includes full-time tuition ($13,280), mandatory fees ($500), and room and board ($6710). ***College room only:*** $3210. Full-time tuition and fees vary according to course load and student level. Room and board charges vary according to board plan, housing facility, and student level. ***Part-time tuition:*** $425 per credit hour. Part-time tuition and fees vary according to course load and student level. ***Payment plan:*** Installment.

FRESHMAN FINANCIAL AID (Fall 2009) 113 applied for aid; of those 93% were deemed to have need. 100% of freshmen with need received aid; of those 10% had need fully met. ***Average percent of need met:*** 58% (excluding resources awarded to replace EFC). ***Average financial aid package:*** $9521 (excluding resources awarded to replace EFC). 8% of all full-time freshmen had no need and received non-need-based gift aid.

UNDERGRADUATE FINANCIAL AID (Fall 2009) 446 applied for aid; of those 91% were deemed to have need. 100% of undergraduates with need received aid; of those 10% had need fully met. ***Average percent of need met:*** 55% (excluding resources awarded to replace EFC). ***Average financial aid package:*** $9556 (excluding resources awarded to replace EFC). 10% of all full-time undergraduates had no need and received non-need-based gift aid.

GIFT AID (NEED-BASED) ***Total amount:*** $2,136,558 (39% federal, 9% state, 42% institutional, 10% external sources). ***Receiving aid:*** Freshmen: 66% (95); all full-time undergraduates: 50% (354). ***Average award:*** Freshmen: $7266; Undergraduates: $6743. ***Scholarships, grants, and awards:*** Federal Pell, FSEOG, state, private, college/university gift aid from institutional funds.

GIFT AID (NON-NEED-BASED) ***Total amount:*** $524,949 (1% state, 77% institutional, 22% external sources). ***Receiving aid:*** Freshmen: 8% (11). Undergraduates: 5% (38). ***Average award:*** Freshmen: $4903. Undergraduates: $5280. ***Scholarships, grants, and awards by category:*** *Academic interests/achievement:* general academic interests/achievements, religion/biblical studies. *Creative arts/performance:* music, theater/drama. *Special achievements/activities:* general special achievements/activities, leadership, religious involvement. *Special characteristics:* children of current students, children of faculty/staff, international students, married students, members of minority groups, parents of current students, siblings of current students, spouses of current students, twins. ***Tuition waivers:*** Full or partial for employees or children of employees.

LOANS ***Student loans:*** $3,482,558 (76% need-based, 24% non-need-based). 91% of past graduating class borrowed through all loan programs. *Average indebtedness per student:* $34,040. ***Average need-based loan:*** Freshmen: $2953. Undergraduates: $3706. ***Parent loans:*** $754,887 (49% need-based, 51% non-need-based). ***Programs:*** Federal Direct (Subsidized and Unsubsidized Stafford, PLUS), college/university.

WORK-STUDY ***Federal work-study:*** Total amount: $118,421; jobs available.

ATHLETIC AWARDS Total amount: $394,793 (82% need-based, 18% non-need-based).

APPLYING FOR FINANCIAL AID ***Required financial aid form:*** FAFSA. ***Financial aid deadline (priority):*** 3/15. ***Notification date:*** Continuous beginning 4/1. Students must reply within 8 weeks of notification.

CONTACT Michael R. Gibboney Jr., Director of Financial Aid, Cincinnati Christian University, 2700 Glenway Avenue, Cincinnati, OH 45204-1799, 513-244-8450 or toll-free 800-949-4228 (in-state). *Fax:* 513-244-8140. *E-mail:* financialaid@ccuniversity.edu.

CINCINNATI COLLEGE OF MORTUARY SCIENCE

Cincinnati, OH

CONTACT Ms. Pat Leon, Financial Aid Officer, Cincinnati College of Mortuary Science, 645 West North Bend Road, Cincinnati, OH 45224-1428, 513-761-2020.

THE CITADEL, THE MILITARY COLLEGE OF SOUTH CAROLINA

Charleston, SC

Tuition & fees (SC res): $11,020 **Average undergraduate aid package: $14,267**

ABOUT THE INSTITUTION State-supported, coed, primarily men. 16 undergraduate majors. Federal methodology is used as a basis for awarding need-based institutional aid.

UNDERGRADUATE EXPENSES for 2010–11 ***Tuition, state resident:*** full-time $9871; part-time $365 per credit. ***Tuition, nonresident:*** full-time $24,800; part-time $640 per credit. ***Required fees:*** full-time $1149. ***College room and board:*** $5889.

FRESHMAN FINANCIAL AID (Fall 2010, est.) 540 applied for aid; of those 79% were deemed to have need. 97% of freshmen with need received aid; of those 19% had need fully met. ***Average percent of need met:*** 56% (excluding resources awarded to replace EFC). ***Average financial aid package:*** $12,365 (excluding resources awarded to replace EFC). 15% of all full-time freshmen had no need and received non-need-based gift aid.

UNDERGRADUATE FINANCIAL AID (Fall 2010, est.) 1,654 applied for aid; of those 79% were deemed to have need. 98% of undergraduates with need received aid; of those 29% had need fully met. ***Average percent of need met:*** 66% (excluding resources awarded to replace EFC). ***Average financial aid package:*** $14,267 (excluding resources awarded to replace EFC). 21% of all full-time undergraduates had no need and received non-need-based gift aid.

GIFT AID (NEED-BASED) ***Total amount:*** $11,835,861 (22% federal, 14% state, 21% institutional, 43% external sources). ***Receiving aid:*** Freshmen: 54% (340); all full-time undergraduates: 45% (1,027). ***Average award:*** Freshmen: $11,886; Undergraduates: $13,593. ***Scholarships, grants, and awards:*** Federal Pell, FSEOG, state, private, college/university gift aid from institutional funds.

GIFT AID (NON-NEED-BASED) ***Total amount:*** $7,473,053 (16% state, 27% institutional, 57% external sources). ***Receiving aid:*** Freshmen: 9% (59). Undergraduates: 10% (226). ***Average award:*** Freshmen: $10,538. Undergraduates: $15,106. ***Scholarships, grants, and awards by category:*** *Academic interests/achievement:* biological sciences, business, engineering/technologies, general academic interests/achievements, humanities, military science, religion/biblical studies. *Creative arts/performance:* journalism/publications, music. *Special achievements/activities:* community service, leadership, religious involvement. *Special characteristics:* children and siblings of alumni, children with a deceased or disabled parent, local/state students, out-of-state students. ***Tuition waivers:*** Full or partial for employees or children of employees, senior citizens.

LOANS ***Student loans:*** $10,520,447 (81% need-based, 19% non-need-based). 41% of past graduating class borrowed through all loan programs. *Average indebtedness per student:* $33,998. ***Average need-based loan:*** Freshmen: $3322. Undergraduates: $4158. ***Parent loans:*** $10,985,493 (79% need-based, 21% non-need-based). ***Programs:*** Federal Direct (Subsidized and Unsubsidized Stafford, PLUS), Perkins, state.

WORK-STUDY ***Federal work-study:*** Total amount: $55,486; jobs available.

ATHLETIC AWARDS Total amount: $4,519,224 (45% need-based, 55% non-need-based).

APPLYING FOR FINANCIAL AID ***Required financial aid form:*** FAFSA. ***Financial aid deadline (priority):*** 2/28. ***Notification date:*** 3/15. Students must reply within 2 weeks of notification.

CONTACT Lt. Col. Hank M. Fuller, Director of Financial Aid and Scholarships, The Citadel, The Military College of South Carolina, 171 Moultrie Street, Charleston, SC 29409, 843-953-5187 or toll-free 800-868-1842. *Fax:* 843-953-6759. *E-mail:* hank.fuller@citadel.edu.

CITY COLLEGE OF THE CITY UNIVERSITY OF NEW YORK

New York, NY

Tuition & fees (NY res): $4830 **Average undergraduate aid package: $9002**

ABOUT THE INSTITUTION State and locally supported, coed. 67 undergraduate majors. Federal methodology is used as a basis for awarding need-based institutional aid.

UNDERGRADUATE EXPENSES for 2011–12 ***Tuition, state resident:*** full-time $4830; part-time $205 per credit hour. ***Tuition, nonresident:*** full-time $10,440; part-time $435 per credit hour. Full-time tuition and fees vary according to course load and program. Part-time tuition and fees vary according to course load and program. Room and board charges vary according to housing facility. ***Payment plan:*** Deferred payment.

FRESHMAN FINANCIAL AID (Fall 2010, est.) 1,075 applied for aid; of those 95% were deemed to have need. 96% of freshmen with need received aid; of those 97% had need fully met. ***Average percent of need met:*** 79% (excluding resources awarded to replace EFC). ***Average financial aid package:*** $8343 (excluding resources awarded to replace EFC). 15% of all full-time freshmen had no need and received non-need-based gift aid.

UNDERGRADUATE FINANCIAL AID (Fall 2010, est.) 8,932 applied for aid; of those 97% were deemed to have need. 99% of undergraduates with need received aid; of those 80% had need fully met. ***Average percent of need met:*** 80% (excluding resources awarded to replace EFC). ***Average financial aid package:*** $9002 (excluding resources awarded to replace EFC). 11% of all full-time undergraduates had no need and received non-need-based gift aid.

GIFT AID (NEED-BASED) ***Total amount:*** $49,649,000 (57% federal, 40% state, 3% institutional). ***Receiving aid:*** Freshmen: 65% (890); all full-time undergraduates: 89% (8,259). ***Average award:*** Freshmen: $6001; Undergraduates: $6725. ***Scholarships, grants, and awards:*** Federal Pell, FSEOG, state, private, college/university gift aid from institutional funds, United Negro College Fund.

GIFT AID (NON-NEED-BASED) ***Total amount:*** $3,050,000 (12% state, 80% institutional, 8% external sources). ***Receiving aid:*** Freshmen: 34% (465). Undergraduates: 9% (850). ***Average award:*** Freshmen: $2140. Undergraduates: $2524. ***Scholarships, grants, and awards by category:*** *Academic interests/achievement:* architecture, area/ethnic studies, biological sciences, communication, computer science, education, engineering/technologies, English, foreign languages, general academic interests/achievements, humanities, international studies, mathematics, premedicine, social sciences. *Creative arts/performance:* applied art and design, art/fine arts, cinema/film/broadcasting, creative writing, general creative arts/performance, music, performing arts. *Special achievements/activities:* community service, general special achievements/activities, leadership. ***Tuition waivers:*** Full or partial for senior citizens.

LOANS ***Student loans:*** $13,333,000 (91% need-based, 9% non-need-based). 21% of past graduating class borrowed through all loan programs. *Average indebtedness per student:* $15,900. ***Average need-based loan:*** Freshmen: $1870. Undergraduates: $3907. ***Parent loans:*** $230,000 (100% non-need-based). ***Programs:*** Federal Direct (Subsidized and Unsubsidized Stafford, PLUS), Perkins.

WORK-STUDY ***Federal work-study:*** Total amount: $3,356,000; jobs available. ***State or other work-study/employment:*** Part-time jobs available.

APPLYING FOR FINANCIAL AID ***Required financial aid forms:*** FAFSA, state aid form. ***Financial aid deadline (priority):*** 3/15. ***Notification date:*** Continuous beginning 4/1.

CONTACT Thelma Mason, Director of Financial Aid, City College of the City University of New York, 160 Convent Avenue, Administration Building, Room 104, New York, NY 10031, 212-650-5816. *Fax:* 212-650-5829. *E-mail:* tmason@ccny.cuny.edu.

CITY UNIVERSITY OF SEATTLE

Bellevue, WA

CONTACT Ms. Jean L. Roberts, Director of Student Financial Services, City University of Seattle, 11900 Northeast 1st Street, Bellevue, WA 98005, 425-709-5251 or toll-free 888-42-CITYU. *Fax:* 425-709-5263. *E-mail:* jroberts@cityu.edu.

CITY VISION COLLEGE

Kansas City, MO

CONTACT Financial Aid Office, City Vision College, PO Box 413188, Kansas City, MO 64141-3188, 816-960-2008.

CLAFLIN UNIVERSITY

Orangeburg, SC

CONTACT Ms. Yolanda Frazier, Interim Director of Financial Aid, Claflin University, Tingly Hall, Suite 12, 400 Magnolia Street, Orangeburg, SC 29115, 803-535-5720 or toll-free 800-922-1276 (in-state). *Fax:* 803-535-5383. *E-mail:* yfrazier@claflin.edu.

CLAREMONT McKENNA COLLEGE

Claremont, CA

Tuition & fees: $42,480 **Average undergraduate aid package: $35,781**

ABOUT THE INSTITUTION Independent, coed. 75 undergraduate majors. Both federal and institutional methodology are used as a basis for awarding need-based institutional aid.

UNDERGRADUATE EXPENSES for 2011–12 ***Comprehensive fee:*** $55,600 includes full-time tuition ($42,245), mandatory fees ($235), and room and board ($13,120). ***College room only:*** $7166. Full-time tuition and fees vary according to reciprocity agreements. Room and board charges vary according to board plan and housing facility. ***Part-time tuition:*** $6666 per course. Part-time tuition and fees vary according to course load and reciprocity agreements. ***Payment plan:*** Installment.

FRESHMAN FINANCIAL AID (Fall 2010, est.) 195 applied for aid; of those 85% were deemed to have need. 100% of freshmen with need received aid; of those 100% had need fully met. ***Average percent of need met:*** 100% (excluding

resources awarded to replace EFC). ***Average financial aid package:*** $35,591 (excluding resources awarded to replace EFC). 4% of all full-time freshmen had no need and received non-need-based gift aid.

UNDERGRADUATE FINANCIAL AID (Fall 2010, est.) 630 applied for aid; of those 90% were deemed to have need. 100% of undergraduates with need received aid; of those 100% had need fully met. ***Average percent of need met:*** 100% (excluding resources awarded to replace EFC). ***Average financial aid package:*** $35,781 (excluding resources awarded to replace EFC). 7% of all full-time undergraduates had no need and received non-need-based gift aid.

GIFT AID (NEED-BASED) ***Total amount:*** $19,717,237 (5% federal, 5% state, 88% institutional, 2% external sources). ***Receiving aid:*** Freshmen: 53% (165); all full-time undergraduates: 45% (567). ***Average award:*** Freshmen: $31,156; Undergraduates: $30,891. ***Scholarships, grants, and awards:*** Federal Pell, FSEOG, state, private, college/university gift aid from institutional funds, United Negro College Fund.

GIFT AID (NON-NEED-BASED) ***Total amount:*** $1,222,132 (1% state, 89% institutional, 10% external sources). ***Receiving aid:*** Freshmen: 6% (18). Undergraduates: 4% (55). ***Average award:*** Freshmen: $14,499. Undergraduates: $13,266. ***Scholarships, grants, and awards by category:*** *Academic interests/achievement:* general academic interests/achievements. *Special achievements/activities:* 86 awards ($1,082,827 total): leadership. ***Tuition waivers:*** Full or partial for employees or children of employees.

LOANS ***Student loans:*** $400,064 (100% non-need-based). 35% of past graduating class borrowed through all loan programs. *Average indebtedness per student:* $10,280. ***Parent loans:*** $20,639,828 (100% non-need-based). ***Programs:*** Federal Direct (Subsidized and Unsubsidized Stafford, PLUS), Perkins, college/university.

WORK-STUDY ***Federal work-study:*** Total amount: $240,000; 280 jobs averaging $1850. ***State or other work-study/employment:*** Part-time jobs available.

APPLYING FOR FINANCIAL AID ***Required financial aid forms:*** FAFSA, CSS Financial Aid PROFILE, noncustodial (divorced/separated) parent's statement, business/farm supplement. ***Financial aid deadline:*** 2/1 (priority: 2/1). ***Notification date:*** 4/1. Students must reply by 5/1.

CONTACT Ms. Georgette R. DeVeres, Associate Vice President of Admission and Director of Financial Aid, Claremont McKenna College, 890 Columbia Avenue, Claremont, CA 91711, 909-621-8356. *Fax:* 909-607-0661. *E-mail:* gdeveres@cmc.edu.

CLARION UNIVERSITY OF PENNSYLVANIA

Clarion, PA

Tuition & fees (PA res): $8164 **Average undergraduate aid package: $8384**

ABOUT THE INSTITUTION State-supported, coed. 53 undergraduate majors. Federal methodology is used as a basis for awarding need-based institutional aid.

UNDERGRADUATE EXPENSES for 2011–12 ***One-time required fee:*** $30. ***Tuition, state resident:*** full-time $6066; part-time $252 per credit hour. ***Tuition, nonresident:*** full-time $12,130; part-time $505 per credit hour. ***Required fees:*** full-time $2098; $57 per credit. Full-time tuition and fees vary according to course load. Part-time tuition and fees vary according to course load. ***College room and board:*** $7000; ***Room only:*** $4725. Room and board charges vary according to board plan, housing facility, and location. ***Payment plan:*** Installment.

FRESHMAN FINANCIAL AID (Fall 2010, est.) 1,299 applied for aid; of those 82% were deemed to have need. 99% of freshmen with need received aid; of those 12% had need fully met. ***Average percent of need met:*** 62% (excluding resources awarded to replace EFC). ***Average financial aid package:*** $8362 (excluding resources awarded to replace EFC). 7% of all full-time freshmen had no need and received non-need-based gift aid.

UNDERGRADUATE FINANCIAL AID (Fall 2010, est.) 4,610 applied for aid; of those 85% were deemed to have need. 97% of undergraduates with need received aid; of those 13% had need fully met. ***Average percent of need met:*** 74% (excluding resources awarded to replace EFC). ***Average financial aid package:*** $8384 (excluding resources awarded to replace EFC). 5% of all full-time undergraduates had no need and received non-need-based gift aid.

GIFT AID (NEED-BASED) ***Total amount:*** $17,476,796 (54% federal, 33% state, 5% institutional, 8% external sources). ***Receiving aid:*** Freshmen: 59% (826); all full-time undergraduates: 55% (2,882). ***Average award:*** Freshmen: $6584; Undergraduates: $6010. ***Scholarships, grants, and awards:*** Federal Pell, FSEOG, state, private, college/university gift aid from institutional funds, Federal Nursing.

GIFT AID (NON-NEED-BASED) ***Receiving aid:*** Freshmen: 20% (279). Undergraduates: 17% (917). ***Average award:*** Freshmen: $2389. Undergraduates: $3029. ***Tuition waivers:*** Full or partial for employees or children of employees, senior citizens.

LOANS ***Student loans:*** $26,005,573 (51% need-based, 49% non-need-based). ***Average need-based loan:*** Freshmen: $3200. Undergraduates: $3937. ***Parent loans:*** $5,642,373 (100% non-need-based). ***Programs:*** Federal Direct (Subsidized and Unsubsidized Stafford, PLUS), Perkins.

WORK-STUDY ***Federal work-study:*** Total amount: $415,949; jobs available. ***State or other work-study/employment:*** Total amount: $963,381 (100% non-need-based). Part-time jobs available.

ATHLETIC AWARDS Total amount: $575,022 (100% need-based).

APPLYING FOR FINANCIAL AID ***Required financial aid form:*** FAFSA. ***Financial aid deadline:*** 4/15. ***Notification date:*** Continuous.

CONTACT Dr. Kenneth Grugel, Director of Financial Aid, Clarion University of Pennsylvania, 104 Egbert Hall, Clarion, PA 16214, 814-393-2315 or toll-free 800-672-7171. *Fax:* 814-393-2520. *E-mail:* aidoffice@clarion.edu.

CLARK ATLANTA UNIVERSITY

Atlanta, GA

CONTACT Office of Financial Aid, Clark Atlanta University, 223 James P. Brawley Drive, Atlanta, GA 30314, 404-880-8992 or toll-free 800-688-3228. *Fax:* 404-880-8070. *E-mail:* studentfinancialaid@cau.edu.

CLARKE UNIVERSITY

Dubuque, IA

Tuition & fees: $24,610 **Average undergraduate aid package: $19,896**

ABOUT THE INSTITUTION Independent Roman Catholic, coed. 29 undergraduate majors. Federal methodology is used as a basis for awarding need-based institutional aid.

UNDERGRADUATE EXPENSES for 2010–11 ***Comprehensive fee:*** $31,950 includes full-time tuition ($23,800), mandatory fees ($810), and room and board ($7340). ***College room only:*** $3600. Room and board charges vary according to housing facility. ***Part-time tuition:*** $600 per credit hour. ***Payment plans:*** Installment, deferred payment.

FRESHMAN FINANCIAL AID (Fall 2010, est.) 173 applied for aid; of those 92% were deemed to have need. 100% of freshmen with need received aid; of those 21% had need fully met. ***Average percent of need met:*** 71% (excluding resources awarded to replace EFC). ***Average financial aid package:*** $20,713 (excluding resources awarded to replace EFC). 10% of all full-time freshmen had no need and received non-need-based gift aid.

UNDERGRADUATE FINANCIAL AID (Fall 2010, est.) 772 applied for aid; of those 92% were deemed to have need. 100% of undergraduates with need received aid; of those 20% had need fully met. ***Average percent of need met:*** 72% (excluding resources awarded to replace EFC). ***Average financial aid package:*** $19,896 (excluding resources awarded to replace EFC). 10% of all full-time undergraduates had no need and received non-need-based gift aid.

GIFT AID (NEED-BASED) ***Total amount:*** $8,988,634 (20% federal, 15% state, 64% institutional, 1% external sources). ***Receiving aid:*** Freshmen: 90% (158); all full-time undergraduates: 88% (705). ***Average award:*** Freshmen: $17,474; Undergraduates: $15,907. ***Scholarships, grants, and awards:*** Federal Pell, FSEOG, state, private, college/university gift aid from institutional funds.

GIFT AID (NON-NEED-BASED) ***Total amount:*** $605,147 (98% institutional, 2% external sources). ***Receiving aid:*** Freshmen: 88% (154). Undergraduates: 80% (643). ***Average award:*** Freshmen: $17,575. Undergraduates: $15,929. ***Scholarships, grants, and awards by category:*** *Academic interests/achievement:* 550 awards ($3,270,378 total): computer science, foreign languages, general academic interests/achievements. *Creative arts/performance:* 57 awards ($193,900 total): art/fine arts, music, theater/drama. *Special achievements/activities:* 57 awards ($73,200 total): leadership. *Special characteristics:* 472 awards ($997,575 total): children and siblings of alumni, children of faculty/staff, local/state students, members of minority groups, relatives of clergy, religious affiliation, siblings of current students, spouses of current students. ***Tuition waivers:*** Full or partial for children of alumni, employees or children of employees, adult students, senior citizens.

LOANS ***Student loans:*** $7,959,272 (41% need-based, 59% non-need-based). 88% of past graduating class borrowed through all loan programs. *Average*

indebtedness per student: $38,847. ***Average need-based loan:*** Freshmen: $3353. Undergraduates: $4539. ***Parent loans:*** $1,027,405 (91% need-based, 9% non-need-based). ***Programs:*** Federal Direct (Subsidized and Unsubsidized Stafford, PLUS), Perkins, Federal Nursing, college/university, private loans.

WORK-STUDY ***Federal work-study:*** Total amount: $202,154; 152 jobs averaging $1300.

ATHLETIC AWARDS Total amount: $1,484,725 (100% non-need-based).

APPLYING FOR FINANCIAL AID ***Financial aid deadline (priority):*** 4/15. ***Notification date:*** Continuous beginning 3/1. Students must reply by 5/1 or within 2 weeks of notification.

CONTACT Amy Norton, Director of Financial Aid, Clarke University, 1550 Clarke Drive, Dubuque, IA 52001-3198, 563-588-6327 or toll-free 800-383-2345. *Fax:* 563-584-8605. *E-mail:* amy.norton@clarke.edu.

CLARKSON COLLEGE

Omaha, NE

CONTACT Pam Shelton, Director of Financial Aid, Clarkson College, 101 South 42nd Street, Omaha, NE 68131-2739, 402-552-2749 or toll-free 800-647-5500. *Fax:* 402-552-6165. *E-mail:* shelton@clarksoncollege.edu.

CLARKSON UNIVERSITY

Potsdam, NY

Tuition & fees: $36,780 | **Average undergraduate aid package: $32,857**

ABOUT THE INSTITUTION Independent, coed. 36 undergraduate majors. Federal methodology is used as a basis for awarding need-based institutional aid.

UNDERGRADUATE EXPENSES for 2011–12 ***Comprehensive fee:*** $48,830 includes full-time tuition ($35,940), mandatory fees ($840), and room and board ($12,050). ***College room only:*** $6384. Full-time tuition and fees vary according to course load. Room and board charges vary according to board plan and housing facility. ***Part-time tuition:*** $1198 per credit. Part-time tuition and fees vary according to course load. ***Payment plans:*** Tuition prepayment, installment.

FRESHMAN FINANCIAL AID (Fall 2010, est.) 659 applied for aid; of those 94% were deemed to have need. 100% of freshmen with need received aid; of those 20% had need fully met. ***Average percent of need met:*** 90% (excluding resources awarded to replace EFC). ***Average financial aid package:*** $33,671 (excluding resources awarded to replace EFC). 11% of all full-time freshmen had no need and received non-need-based gift aid.

UNDERGRADUATE FINANCIAL AID (Fall 2010, est.) 2,492 applied for aid; of those 95% were deemed to have need. 100% of undergraduates with need received aid; of those 18% had need fully met. ***Average percent of need met:*** 88% (excluding resources awarded to replace EFC). ***Average financial aid package:*** $32,857 (excluding resources awarded to replace EFC). 14% of all full-time undergraduates had no need and received non-need-based gift aid.

GIFT AID (NEED-BASED) ***Total amount:*** $53,975,863 (10% federal, 5% state, 83% institutional, 2% external sources). ***Receiving aid:*** Freshmen: 86% (614); all full-time undergraduates: 84% (2,339). ***Average award:*** Freshmen: $25,626; Undergraduates: $23,124. ***Scholarships, grants, and awards:*** Federal Pell, FSEOG, state, private, college/university gift aid from institutional funds, Higher Education Opportunity Program (HEOP).

GIFT AID (NON-NEED-BASED) ***Total amount:*** $8,481,948 (14% federal, 1% state, 81% institutional, 4% external sources). ***Receiving aid:*** Freshmen: 11% (78). Undergraduates: 10% (267). ***Average award:*** Freshmen: $13,142. Undergraduates: $13,981. ***Scholarships, grants, and awards by category:*** *Academic interests/achievement:* 1,864 awards ($13,886,637 total): biological sciences, business, communication, computer science, engineering/technologies, general academic interests/achievements, humanities, mathematics, military science, physical sciences, social sciences. *Special achievements/activities:* 920 awards ($6,726,250 total): general special achievements/activities, leadership. *Special characteristics:* 780 awards ($2,479,925 total): children and siblings of alumni, children of faculty/staff, general special characteristics, international students, local/state students, members of minority groups, veterans. ***Tuition waivers:*** Full or partial for employees or children of employees.

LOANS ***Student loans:*** $20,047,315 (76% need-based, 24% non-need-based). 84% of past graduating class borrowed through all loan programs. *Average indebtedness per student:* $36,142. ***Average need-based loan:*** Freshmen: $3345. Undergraduates: $4417. ***Parent loans:*** $7,626,641 (46% need-based, 54% non-need-based). ***Programs:*** Federal Direct (Subsidized and Unsubsidized Stafford, PLUS), Perkins, college/university, alternative loans.

WORK-STUDY ***Federal work-study:*** Total amount: $567,465; jobs available. ***State or other work-study/employment:*** Total amount: $199,483 (78% need-based, 22% non-need-based). Part-time jobs available.

ATHLETIC AWARDS Total amount: $1,638,137 (7% need-based, 93% non-need-based).

APPLYING FOR FINANCIAL AID ***Required financial aid forms:*** FAFSA, state aid form. ***Financial aid deadline:*** 3/1 (priority: 2/15). ***Notification date:*** Continuous beginning 3/19. Students must reply by 5/1 or within 2 weeks of notification.

CONTACT Mrs. Pamela A. Nichols, Director of Financial Aid, Clarkson University, Clarkson University, PO Box 5615, Potsdam, NY 13699, 315-268-6413 or toll-free 800-527-6577. *Fax:* 315-268-3899. *E-mail:* pnichols@clarkson.edu.

CLARK UNIVERSITY

Worcester, MA

Tuition & fees: $37,350 | **Average undergraduate aid package: $28,165**

ABOUT THE INSTITUTION Independent, coed. 48 undergraduate majors. Institutional methodology is used as a basis for awarding need-based institutional aid.

UNDERGRADUATE EXPENSES for 2011–12 ***Comprehensive fee:*** $44,450 includes full-time tuition ($37,000), mandatory fees ($350), and room and board ($7100). ***College room only:*** $4000. Room and board charges vary according to board plan and housing facility. ***Part-time tuition:*** $1156.25 per course. ***Payment plans:*** Tuition prepayment, installment.

FRESHMAN FINANCIAL AID (Fall 2010, est.) 461 applied for aid; of those 78% were deemed to have need. 99% of freshmen with need received aid; of those 60% had need fully met. ***Average percent of need met:*** 94% (excluding resources awarded to replace EFC). ***Average financial aid package:*** $28,165 (excluding resources awarded to replace EFC). 27% of all full-time freshmen had no need and received non-need-based gift aid.

UNDERGRADUATE FINANCIAL AID (Fall 2010, est.) 1,772 applied for aid; of those 78% were deemed to have need. 99% of undergraduates with need received aid; of those 60% had need fully met. ***Average percent of need met:*** 94% (excluding resources awarded to replace EFC). ***Average financial aid package:*** $28,165 (excluding resources awarded to replace EFC). 27% of all full-time undergraduates had no need and received non-need-based gift aid.

GIFT AID (NEED-BASED) ***Total amount:*** $27,945,297 (10% federal, 2% state, 86% institutional, 2% external sources). ***Receiving aid:*** Freshmen: 62% (356); all full-time undergraduates: 62% (1,368). ***Average award:*** Freshmen: $23,789; Undergraduates: $23,789. ***Scholarships, grants, and awards:*** Federal Pell, FSEOG, state, college/university gift aid from institutional funds.

GIFT AID (NON-NEED-BASED) ***Total amount:*** $8,147,770 (100% institutional). ***Receiving aid:*** Freshmen: 28% (163). Undergraduates: 28% (626). ***Average award:*** Freshmen: $13,763. Undergraduates: $13,763. ***Scholarships, grants, and awards by category:*** *Academic interests/achievement:* general academic interests/achievements. *Special achievements/activities:* community service, general special achievements/activities. ***Tuition waivers:*** Full or partial for employees or children of employees.

LOANS ***Student loans:*** $10,355,234 (60% need-based, 40% non-need-based). 92% of past graduating class borrowed through all loan programs. *Average indebtedness per student:* $24,000. ***Average need-based loan:*** Freshmen: $3225. Undergraduates: $3225. ***Parent loans:*** $3,692,891 (7% need-based, 93% non-need-based). ***Programs:*** Federal Direct (Subsidized and Unsubsidized Stafford, PLUS), Perkins, state.

WORK-STUDY ***Federal work-study:*** Total amount: $1,654,281; 1,000 jobs averaging $2000.

APPLYING FOR FINANCIAL AID ***Required financial aid forms:*** FAFSA, CSS Financial Aid PROFILE, noncustodial (divorced/separated) parent's statement. ***Financial aid deadline:*** 2/1. ***Notification date:*** 3/31. Students must reply by 5/1.

CONTACT Ms. Mary Ellen Severance, Director of Financial Assistance, Clark University, 950 Main Street, Worcester, MA 01610-1477, 508-793-7478 or toll-free 800-GO-CLARK. *Fax:* 508-793-8802. *E-mail:* finaid@clarku.edu.

CLAYTON STATE UNIVERSITY

Morrow, GA

CONTACT Patricia Barton, Director of Financial Aid, Clayton State University, 2000 Clayton State Boulevard, Morrow, GA 30260, 678-466-4185. *Fax:* 678-466-4189. *E-mail:* financialaid@mail.clayton.edu.

CLEAR CREEK BAPTIST BIBLE COLLEGE

Pineville, KY

Tuition & fees: $8700 **Average undergraduate aid package: $6949**

ABOUT THE INSTITUTION Independent Southern Baptist, coed, primarily men. 2 undergraduate majors. Institutional methodology is used as a basis for awarding need-based institutional aid.

UNDERGRADUATE EXPENSES for 2010–11 ***Tuition:*** full-time $8700; part-time $238 per credit hour. Room and board charges vary according to housing facility. ***Payment plan:*** Installment.

FRESHMAN FINANCIAL AID (Fall 2010, est.) 20 applied for aid; of those 80% were deemed to have need. 100% of freshmen with need received aid. ***Average percent of need met:*** 71% (excluding resources awarded to replace EFC). ***Average financial aid package:*** $7134 (excluding resources awarded to replace EFC). 19% of all full-time freshmen had no need and received non-need-based gift aid.

UNDERGRADUATE FINANCIAL AID (Fall 2010, est.) 121 applied for aid; of those 88% were deemed to have need. 100% of undergraduates with need received aid; of those 7% had need fully met. ***Average percent of need met:*** 69% (excluding resources awarded to replace EFC). ***Average financial aid package:*** $6949 (excluding resources awarded to replace EFC). 10% of all full-time undergraduates had no need and received non-need-based gift aid.

GIFT AID (NEED-BASED) ***Total amount:*** $847,351 (70% federal, 2% state, 21% institutional, 7% external sources). ***Receiving aid:*** Freshmen: 76% (16); all full-time undergraduates: 82% (107). ***Average award:*** Freshmen: $7134; Undergraduates: $6949. ***Scholarships, grants, and awards:*** Federal Pell, FSEOG, state, private, college/university gift aid from institutional funds.

GIFT AID (NON-NEED-BASED) ***Total amount:*** $71,316 (78% federal, 22% institutional). ***Receiving aid:*** Freshmen: 67% (14). Undergraduates: 22% (29). ***Average award:*** Freshmen: $300. Undergraduates: $407. ***Scholarships, grants, and awards by category:*** *Academic interests/achievement:* 3 awards ($1800 total): general academic interests/achievements. *Creative arts/performance:* 6 awards ($1200 total): music. *Special characteristics:* 2 awards ($1792 total): handicapped students, international students.

LOANS ***Student loans:*** $30,700 (100% non-need-based).

WORK-STUDY ***Federal work-study:*** Total amount: $38,082; 23 jobs averaging $1656.

APPLYING FOR FINANCIAL AID ***Required financial aid forms:*** FAFSA, institution's own form. ***Financial aid deadline (priority):*** 6/30. ***Notification date:*** 7/1.

CONTACT Mr. Sam Risner, Director of Financial Aid, Clear Creek Baptist Bible College, 300 Clear Creek Road, Pineville, KY 40977-9754, 606-337-3196 Ext. 142. *Fax:* 606-337-1631. *E-mail:* srisner@ccbbc.edu.

CLEARWATER CHRISTIAN COLLEGE

Clearwater, FL

ABOUT THE INSTITUTION Independent nondenominational, coed. 24 undergraduate majors.

GIFT AID (NEED-BASED) ***Scholarships, grants, and awards:*** Federal Pell, FSEOG, state, private, college/university gift aid from institutional funds.

GIFT AID (NON-NEED-BASED) ***Scholarships, grants, and awards by category:*** *Academic interests/achievement:* business, education, general academic interests/achievements, premedicine, religion/biblical studies. *Creative arts/performance:* music. *Special achievements/activities:* leadership. *Special characteristics:* children and siblings of alumni, ethnic background, religious affiliation, siblings of current students.

LOANS ***Programs:*** state, alternative loans.

WORK-STUDY ***Federal work-study:*** Total amount: $27,000; 50 jobs averaging $670. ***State or other work-study/employment:*** Total amount: $15,000 (100% need-based). 20 part-time jobs averaging $612.

APPLYING FOR FINANCIAL AID ***Required financial aid forms:*** FAFSA, institution's own form, state aid form.

CONTACT Mrs. Ruth Strum, Director of Financial Aid, Clearwater Christian College, 3400 Gulf-to-Bay Boulevard, Clearwater, FL 33759-4595, 727-726-1153 Ext. 214 or toll-free 800-348-4463. *Fax:* 727-791-1347. *E-mail:* ruthstrum@clearwater.edu.

CLEARY UNIVERSITY

Ann Arbor, MI

Tuition & fees: $16,560 **Average undergraduate aid package: $12,759**

ABOUT THE INSTITUTION Independent, coed. 14 undergraduate majors. Federal methodology is used as a basis for awarding need-based institutional aid.

UNDERGRADUATE EXPENSES for 2010–11 ***Tuition:*** full-time $16,560; part-time $345 per credit hour. Full-time tuition and fees vary according to degree level. ***Payment plans:*** Guaranteed tuition, installment, deferred payment.

FRESHMAN FINANCIAL AID (Fall 2009) 55 applied for aid; of those 100% were deemed to have need. 100% of freshmen with need received aid; of those 9% had need fully met. ***Average percent of need met:*** 44% (excluding resources awarded to replace EFC). ***Average financial aid package:*** $13,595 (excluding resources awarded to replace EFC). 18% of all full-time freshmen had no need and received non-need-based gift aid.

UNDERGRADUATE FINANCIAL AID (Fall 2009) 391 applied for aid; of those 100% were deemed to have need. 100% of undergraduates with need received aid; of those 3% had need fully met. ***Average percent of need met:*** 42% (excluding resources awarded to replace EFC). ***Average financial aid package:*** $12,759 (excluding resources awarded to replace EFC). 11% of all full-time undergraduates had no need and received non-need-based gift aid.

GIFT AID (NEED-BASED) ***Total amount:*** $1,339,872 (70% federal, 24% state, 5% institutional, 1% external sources). ***Receiving aid:*** Freshmen: 59% (47); all full-time undergraduates: 60% (315). ***Average award:*** Freshmen: $1296; Undergraduates: $1265. ***Scholarships, grants, and awards:*** Federal Pell, FSEOG, state, private, college/university gift aid from institutional funds.

GIFT AID (NON-NEED-BASED) ***Total amount:*** $138,590 (100% institutional). ***Receiving aid:*** Freshmen: 20% (16). Undergraduates: 13% (68). ***Average award:*** Freshmen: $1738. Undergraduates: $2258. ***Scholarships, grants, and awards by category:*** *Academic interests/achievement:* business, computer science, general academic interests/achievements. *Special characteristics:* children of faculty/staff, veterans. ***Tuition waivers:*** Full or partial for children of alumni, employees or children of employees, senior citizens.

LOANS ***Student loans:*** $3,771,925 (57% need-based, 43% non-need-based). 82% of past graduating class borrowed through all loan programs. *Average indebtedness per student:* $20,830. ***Average need-based loan:*** Freshmen: $1107. Undergraduates: $1193. ***Parent loans:*** $24,417 (100% non-need-based). ***Programs:*** Federal Direct (Subsidized and Unsubsidized Stafford, PLUS).

WORK-STUDY ***Federal work-study:*** Total amount: $70,982; jobs available. ***State or other work-study/employment:*** Part-time jobs available.

APPLYING FOR FINANCIAL AID ***Required financial aid form:*** FAFSA. ***Financial aid deadline:*** 7/1 (priority: 4/1). ***Notification date:*** Continuous beginning 4/1. Students must reply by 7/1 or within 2 weeks of notification.

CONTACT Vesta Smith-Campbell, Director of Financial Aid, Cleary University, 3750 Cleary Drive, Howell, MI 48843, 800-589-1979 Ext. 2234 or toll-free 888-5-CLEARY Ext. 2249. *Fax:* 517-552-8022. *E-mail:* vscampbell@cleary.edu.

CLEMSON UNIVERSITY

Clemson, SC

Tuition & fees (SC res): $12,346 **Average undergraduate aid package: $11,253**

ABOUT THE INSTITUTION State-supported, coed. 76 undergraduate majors. Federal methodology is used as a basis for awarding need-based institutional aid.

UNDERGRADUATE EXPENSES for 2010–11 ***One-time required fee:*** $1300. ***Tuition, state resident:*** full-time $12,346; part-time $499 per credit hour. ***Tuition, nonresident:*** full-time $27,858; part-time $1171 per credit hour. ***Required fees:*** $9 per credit hour or $4 per term. Full-time tuition and fees vary according to course load, location, and program. Part-time tuition and fees vary according to program. Room and board charges vary according to board plan, housing facility, and location. ***Payment plan:*** Installment.

FRESHMAN FINANCIAL AID (Fall 2010, est.) 2,208 applied for aid; of those 72% were deemed to have need. 96% of freshmen with need received aid; of those 20% had need fully met. ***Average percent of need met:*** 69% (excluding resources awarded to replace EFC). ***Average financial aid package:*** $14,547 (excluding resources awarded to replace EFC). 19% of all full-time freshmen had no need and received non-need-based gift aid.

UNDERGRADUATE FINANCIAL AID (Fall 2010, est.) 8,608 applied for aid; of those 78% were deemed to have need. 96% of undergraduates with need received aid; of those 22% had need fully met. ***Average percent of need met:*** 57% (excluding resources awarded to replace EFC). ***Average financial aid package:*** $11,253 (excluding resources awarded to replace EFC). 19% of all full-time undergraduates had no need and received non-need-based gift aid.

GIFT AID (NEED-BASED) ***Total amount:*** $19,102,050 (68% federal, 11% state, 11% institutional, 10% external sources). ***Receiving aid:*** Freshmen: 18% (535); all full-time undergraduates: 21% (2,897). ***Average award:*** Freshmen: $4762; Undergraduates: $4778. ***Scholarships, grants, and awards:*** Federal Pell, FSEOG, state, private, college/university gift aid from institutional funds.

GIFT AID (NON-NEED-BASED) ***Total amount:*** $57,312,840 (73% state, 17% institutional, 10% external sources). ***Receiving aid:*** Freshmen: 43% (1,272). Undergraduates: 31% (4,247). ***Average award:*** Freshmen: $2342. Undergraduates: $2360. ***Scholarships, grants, and awards by category:*** *Academic interests/achievement:* agriculture, architecture, biological sciences, business, communication, computer science, education, engineering/technologies, English, foreign languages, general academic interests/achievements, health fields, humanities, international studies, mathematics, military science, physical sciences, premedicine, social sciences. *Creative arts/performance:* applied art and design, art/fine arts, performing arts, theater/drama. *Special achievements/activities:* community service, general special achievements/activities, leadership. *Special characteristics:* children of faculty/staff, ethnic background, local/state students, members of minority groups, veterans. ***Tuition waivers:*** Full or partial for senior citizens.

LOANS ***Student loans:*** $59,930,523 (36% need-based, 64% non-need-based). 49% of past graduating class borrowed through all loan programs. *Average indebtedness per student:* $18,463. ***Average need-based loan:*** Freshmen: $3530. Undergraduates: $4285. ***Parent loans:*** $15,493,377 (100% non-need-based). ***Programs:*** Federal Direct (Subsidized and Unsubsidized Stafford, PLUS), Perkins, state, college/university, private loans.

WORK-STUDY ***Federal work-study:*** Total amount: $1,456,190; 589 jobs averaging $2346. ***State or other work-study/employment:*** Total amount: $8,000,000 (100% non-need-based). 3,700 part-time jobs averaging $2100.

ATHLETIC AWARDS Total amount: $5,374,368 (100% non-need-based).

APPLYING FOR FINANCIAL AID ***Required financial aid form:*** FAFSA. ***Financial aid deadline (priority):*** 4/1. ***Notification date:*** Continuous beginning 4/16. Students must reply within 3 weeks of notification.

CONTACT Mr. Chuck Knepfle, Director of Financial Aid, Clemson University, G01 Sikes Hall, Clemson, SC 29634-5123, 864-656-2280. *Fax:* 864-656-1831. *E-mail:* finaid@clemson.edu.

THE CLEVELAND INSTITUTE OF ART

Cleveland, OH

Tuition & fees: $33,882 **Average undergraduate aid package: $23,052**

ABOUT THE INSTITUTION Independent, coed. 19 undergraduate majors. Federal methodology is used as a basis for awarding need-based institutional aid.

UNDERGRADUATE EXPENSES for 2011–12 ***Comprehensive fee:*** $45,248 includes full-time tuition ($31,760), mandatory fees ($2122), and room and board ($11,366). ***College room only:*** $6516. Full-time tuition and fees vary according to program, reciprocity agreements, and student level. Room and board charges vary according to board plan. ***Part-time tuition:*** $1325 per credit hour. ***Part-time fees:*** $142 per credit hour; $105 per term. Part-time tuition and fees vary according to course load, program, reciprocity agreements, and student level. ***Payment plan:*** Installment.

FRESHMAN FINANCIAL AID (Fall 2010, est.) 139 applied for aid; of those 92% were deemed to have need. 100% of freshmen with need received aid; of those 8% had need fully met. ***Average percent of need met:*** 59% (excluding resources awarded to replace EFC). ***Average financial aid package:*** $23,672 (excluding resources awarded to replace EFC). 17% of all full-time freshmen had no need and received non-need-based gift aid.

UNDERGRADUATE FINANCIAL AID (Fall 2010, est.) 477 applied for aid; of those 95% were deemed to have need. 100% of undergraduates with need received aid; of those 8% had need fully met. ***Average percent of need met:*** 59% (excluding resources awarded to replace EFC). ***Average financial aid package:*** $23,052 (excluding resources awarded to replace EFC). 12% of all full-time undergraduates had no need and received non-need-based gift aid.

GIFT AID (NEED-BASED) ***Total amount:*** $7,892,706 (14% federal, 3% state, 81% institutional, 2% external sources). ***Receiving aid:*** Freshmen: 82% (128); all full-time undergraduates: 87% (451). ***Average award:*** Freshmen: $18,335; Undergraduates: $17,220. ***Scholarships, grants, and awards:*** Federal Pell, FSEOG, state, private, college/university gift aid from institutional funds.

GIFT AID (NON-NEED-BASED) ***Total amount:*** $711,194 (100% institutional). ***Receiving aid:*** Freshmen: 6% (9). Undergraduates: 6% (29). ***Average award:*** Freshmen: $10,584. Undergraduates: $9873. ***Scholarships, grants, and awards by category:*** *Creative arts/performance:* 519 awards ($7,111,940 total): art/fine arts. ***Tuition waivers:*** Full or partial for employees or children of employees.

LOANS ***Student loans:*** $4,691,239 (71% need-based, 29% non-need-based). 82% of past graduating class borrowed through all loan programs. *Average indebtedness per student:* $55,231. ***Average need-based loan:*** Freshmen: $4060. Undergraduates: $4538. ***Parent loans:*** $2,370,298 (100% non-need-based). ***Programs:*** Federal Direct (Subsidized and Unsubsidized Stafford, PLUS), Perkins.

WORK-STUDY ***Federal work-study:*** Total amount: $217,908; 356 jobs averaging $2353.

APPLYING FOR FINANCIAL AID ***Required financial aid forms:*** FAFSA, institution's own form. ***Financial aid deadline (priority):*** 3/15. ***Notification date:*** Continuous beginning 3/1. Students must reply by 5/1 or within 3 weeks of notification.

CONTACT Mr. Martin Joseph Carney Jr., Director of Financial Aid, The Cleveland Institute of Art, 11141 East Boulevard, Cleveland, OH 44106-1700, 216-421-7425 or toll-free 800-223-4700. *Fax:* 216-754-3634. *E-mail:* financialaid@cia.edu.

CLEVELAND INSTITUTE OF MUSIC

Cleveland, OH

Tuition & fees: $38,890 **Average undergraduate aid package: $24,221**

ABOUT THE INSTITUTION Independent, coed. 3 undergraduate majors. Federal methodology is used as a basis for awarding need-based institutional aid.

UNDERGRADUATE EXPENSES for 2010–11 ***Comprehensive fee:*** $48,394 includes full-time tuition ($36,000), mandatory fees ($2890), and room and board ($9504). ***College room only:*** $6584. Room and board charges vary according to board plan. ***Part-time tuition:*** $1500 per credit hour. ***Payment plan:*** Installment.

FRESHMAN FINANCIAL AID (Fall 2010, est.) 47 applied for aid; of those 85% were deemed to have need. 100% of freshmen with need received aid; of those 32% had need fully met. ***Average percent of need met:*** 72% (excluding resources awarded to replace EFC). ***Average financial aid package:*** $23,132 (excluding resources awarded to replace EFC). 31% of all full-time freshmen had no need and received non-need-based gift aid.

UNDERGRADUATE FINANCIAL AID (Fall 2010, est.) 184 applied for aid; of those 82% were deemed to have need. 100% of undergraduates with need received aid; of those 23% had need fully met. ***Average percent of need met:*** 71% (excluding resources awarded to replace EFC). ***Average financial aid package:*** $24,221 (excluding resources awarded to replace EFC). 37% of all full-time undergraduates had no need and received non-need-based gift aid.

GIFT AID (NEED-BASED) ***Total amount:*** $3,047,874 (7% federal, 1% state, 90% institutional, 2% external sources). ***Receiving aid:*** Freshmen: 60% (40); all full-time undergraduates: 57% (150). ***Average award:*** Freshmen: $20,546; Undergraduates: $20,463. ***Scholarships, grants, and awards:*** Federal Pell, FSEOG, state, private, college/university gift aid from institutional funds.

GIFT AID (NON-NEED-BASED) ***Total amount:*** $1,958,359 (95% institutional, 5% external sources). ***Receiving aid:*** Freshmen: 19% (13). Undergraduates: 11% (28). ***Average award:*** Freshmen: $16,133. Undergraduates: $16,823. ***Scholarships, grants, and awards by category:*** *Creative arts/performance:* 230 awards ($4,297,710 total): music. *Special characteristics:* 1 award ($21,600 total): children of faculty/staff. ***Tuition waivers:*** Full or partial for employees or children of employees.

LOANS ***Student loans:*** $1,032,331 (71% need-based, 29% non-need-based). 64% of past graduating class borrowed through all loan programs. *Average indebtedness per student:* $26,995. ***Average need-based loan:*** Freshmen: $3380. Undergraduates: $4215. ***Parent loans:*** $1,173,279 (42% need-based, 58% non-need-based). ***Programs:*** Federal Direct (Subsidized and Unsubsidized Stafford, PLUS), Perkins, college/university, private loans.

WORK-STUDY ***Federal work-study:*** Total amount: $91,586; 77 jobs averaging $1189. ***State or other work-study/employment:*** Total amount: $21,686 (100% non-need-based). 15 part-time jobs averaging $1446.

APPLYING FOR FINANCIAL AID ***Required financial aid forms:*** FAFSA, CSS Financial Aid PROFILE. ***Financial aid deadline (priority):*** 2/15. ***Notification date:*** 4/1. Students must reply by 5/1.

CONTACT Ms. Kristie Gripp, Director of Financial Aid, Cleveland Institute of Music, 11021 East Boulevard, Cleveland, OH 44106-1776, 216-795-3192. *Fax:* 216-707-4519. *E-mail:* kxg26@case.edu.

CLEVELAND STATE UNIVERSITY

Cleveland, OH

Tuition & fees (OH res): $8466 **Average undergraduate aid package: $8950**

ABOUT THE INSTITUTION State-supported, coed. 70 undergraduate majors. Federal methodology is used as a basis for awarding need-based institutional aid.

UNDERGRADUATE EXPENSES for 2011–12 ***Tuition, state resident:*** full-time $8466; part-time $353 per credit hour. ***Tuition, nonresident:*** full-time $11,387; part-time $474 per credit hour. Full-time tuition and fees vary according to course load, degree level, and program. Part-time tuition and fees vary according to course load, degree level, and program. ***College room and board:*** $10,285; ***Room only:*** $6985. Room and board charges vary according to board plan and housing facility. ***Payment plan:*** Installment.

FRESHMAN FINANCIAL AID (Fall 2010, est.) 918 applied for aid; of those 91% were deemed to have need. 99% of freshmen with need received aid; of those 5% had need fully met. ***Average percent of need met:*** 51% (excluding resources awarded to replace EFC). ***Average financial aid package:*** $9453 (excluding resources awarded to replace EFC). 5% of all full-time freshmen had no need and received non-need-based gift aid.

UNDERGRADUATE FINANCIAL AID (Fall 2010, est.) 7,186 applied for aid; of those 93% were deemed to have need. 98% of undergraduates with need received aid; of those 6% had need fully met. ***Average percent of need met:*** 48% (excluding resources awarded to replace EFC). ***Average financial aid package:*** $8950 (excluding resources awarded to replace EFC). 4% of all full-time undergraduates had no need and received non-need-based gift aid.

GIFT AID (NEED-BASED) ***Total amount:*** $33,190,921 (76% federal, 11% state, 9% institutional, 4% external sources). ***Receiving aid:*** Freshmen: 63% (731); all full-time undergraduates: 63% (5,086). ***Average award:*** Freshmen: $6717; Undergraduates: $6188. ***Scholarships, grants, and awards:*** Federal Pell, FSEOG, state, private, college/university gift aid from institutional funds.

GIFT AID (NON-NEED-BASED) ***Total amount:*** $2,146,643 (1% federal, 6% state, 82% institutional, 11% external sources). ***Receiving aid:*** Freshmen: 1% (16). Undergraduates: 2% (128). ***Average award:*** Freshmen: $3238. Undergraduates: $4786. ***Scholarships, grants, and awards by category:*** *Academic interests/achievement:* biological sciences, business, communication, computer science, education, engineering/technologies, English, general academic interests/achievements, health fields, humanities, mathematics, physical sciences, premedicine, social sciences. *Creative arts/performance:* art/fine arts, creative writing, dance, journalism/publications, music, performing arts, theater/drama. *Special achievements/activities:* cheerleading/drum major. *Special characteristics:* children of faculty/staff, general special characteristics, out-of-state students. ***Tuition waivers:*** Full or partial for employees or children of employees, senior citizens.

LOANS ***Student loans:*** $64,495,731 (90% need-based, 10% non-need-based). 55% of past graduating class borrowed through all loan programs. *Average indebtedness per student:* $19,537. ***Average need-based loan:*** Freshmen: $3311. Undergraduates: $4262. ***Parent loans:*** $2,513,716 (57% need-based, 43% non-need-based). ***Programs:*** Federal Direct (Subsidized and Unsubsidized Stafford, PLUS), Perkins, state, alternative loans.

WORK-STUDY ***Federal work-study:*** Total amount: $2,416,194; 703 jobs averaging $3437. ***State or other work-study/employment:*** Part-time jobs available.

ATHLETIC AWARDS Total amount: $2,523,061 (40% need-based, 60% non-need-based).

APPLYING FOR FINANCIAL AID ***Required financial aid forms:*** FAFSA, Tax forms (for base year), if selected for verification. ***Financial aid deadline (priority):*** 2/15. ***Notification date:*** Continuous beginning 3/15. Students must reply within 4 weeks of notification.

CONTACT Financial Aid Office, Cleveland State University, 1621 Euclid Avenue, Cleveland, OH 44115, 216-687-5594 or toll-free 888-CSU-OHIO. *E-mail:* campus411@csuohio.edu.

COASTAL CAROLINA UNIVERSITY

Conway, SC

Tuition & fees (SC res): $9390 **Average undergraduate aid package: $8886**

ABOUT THE INSTITUTION State-supported, coed. 37 undergraduate majors. Federal methodology is used as a basis for awarding need-based institutional aid.

UNDERGRADUATE EXPENSES for 2010–11 ***Tuition, state resident:*** full-time $9310; part-time $382 per credit hour. ***Tuition, nonresident:*** full-time $20,190; part-time $830 per credit hour. ***Required fees:*** full-time $80. Full-time tuition and fees vary according to course load and degree level. Part-time tuition and fees vary according to course load and degree level. ***College room and board:*** $7350; ***Room only:*** $4750. Room and board charges vary according to board plan and housing facility. ***Payment plan:*** Installment.

FRESHMAN FINANCIAL AID (Fall 2009) 1,580 applied for aid; of those 77% were deemed to have need. 98% of freshmen with need received aid; of those 10% had need fully met. ***Average percent of need met:*** 51% (excluding resources awarded to replace EFC). ***Average financial aid package:*** $8848 (excluding resources awarded to replace EFC). 17% of all full-time freshmen had no need and received non-need-based gift aid.

UNDERGRADUATE FINANCIAL AID (Fall 2009) 5,816 applied for aid; of those 80% were deemed to have need. 98% of undergraduates with need received aid; of those 11% had need fully met. ***Average percent of need met:*** 48% (excluding resources awarded to replace EFC). ***Average financial aid package:*** $8886 (excluding resources awarded to replace EFC). 17% of all full-time undergraduates had no need and received non-need-based gift aid.

GIFT AID (NEED-BASED) ***Total amount:*** $12,537,756 (91% federal, 9% state). ***Receiving aid:*** Freshmen: 32% (566); all full-time undergraduates: 32% (2,266). ***Average award:*** Freshmen: $5679; Undergraduates: $5309. ***Scholarships, grants, and awards:*** Federal Pell, FSEOG, state, private, college/university gift aid from institutional funds, Academic Competitiveness Grants, National SMART Grants.

GIFT AID (NON-NEED-BASED) ***Total amount:*** $10,515,005 (71% state, 18% institutional, 11% external sources). ***Receiving aid:*** Freshmen: 31% (549). Undergraduates: 17% (1,228). ***Average award:*** Freshmen: $11,033. Undergraduates: $11,090. ***Scholarships, grants, and awards by category:*** *Academic interests/achievement:* 1,562 awards ($3,172,810 total): biological sciences, business, education, general academic interests/achievements, humanities, mathematics. *Creative arts/performance:* 50 awards ($36,438 total): art/fine arts, music, theater/drama. *Special achievements/activities:* 33 awards ($32,500 total): cheerleading/drum major. *Special characteristics:* 1,169 awards ($3,201,469 total): general special characteristics, international students, local/state students, out-of-state students, veterans' children. ***Tuition waivers:*** Full or partial for employees or children of employees, senior citizens.

LOANS ***Student loans:*** $46,042,882 (35% need-based, 65% non-need-based). 69% of past graduating class borrowed through all loan programs. *Average indebtedness per student:* $31,907. ***Average need-based loan:*** Freshmen: $7727. Undergraduates: $8051. ***Parent loans:*** $10,206,889 (100% non-need-based). ***Programs:*** Federal Direct (Subsidized and Unsubsidized Stafford, PLUS), Perkins, state.

WORK-STUDY ***Federal work-study:*** Total amount: $285,740; 103 jobs averaging $939. ***State or other work-study/employment:*** Total amount: $2,281,183 (1% need-based, 99% non-need-based). 985 part-time jobs averaging $2220.

ATHLETIC AWARDS Total amount: $3,241,248 (100% non-need-based).

APPLYING FOR FINANCIAL AID ***Required financial aid form:*** FAFSA. ***Financial aid deadline (priority):*** 3/1. ***Notification date:*** Continuous beginning 3/1. Students must reply by 5/15.

CONTACT Mr. Gregory Thornburg, Director of Financial Aid, Coastal Carolina University, PO Box 261954, Conway, SC 29528-6054, 843-349-2474 or toll-free 800-277-7000. *Fax:* 843-349-2347. *E-mail:* gthornbu@coastal.edu.

COE COLLEGE

Cedar Rapids, IA

Tuition & fees: $30,860 **Average undergraduate aid package: $24,287**

ABOUT THE INSTITUTION Independent religious, coed. ***Awards:*** bachelor's and master's degrees. 63 undergraduate majors. ***Total enrollment:*** 1,326. Undergraduates: 1,310. Freshmen: 342. Federal methodology is used as a basis for awarding need-based institutional aid.

UNDERGRADUATE EXPENSES for 2010–11 ***Application fee:*** $30. ***Comprehensive fee:*** $38,150 includes full-time tuition ($30,540), mandatory fees ($320), and room and board ($7290). ***College room only:*** $3270. Room and board charges vary according to board plan and housing facility. ***Part-time tuition:*** $3690 per course. ***Payment plan:*** Installment.

FRESHMAN FINANCIAL AID (Fall 2010, est.) 324 applied for aid; of those 90% were deemed to have need. 100% of freshmen with need received aid; of those 28% had need fully met. ***Average percent of need met:*** 88% (excluding resources awarded to replace EFC). ***Average financial aid package:*** $25,654 (excluding resources awarded to replace EFC). 18% of all full-time freshmen had no need and received non-need-based gift aid.

UNDERGRADUATE FINANCIAL AID (Fall 2010, est.) 1,112 applied for aid; of those 92% were deemed to have need. 100% of undergraduates with need received aid; of those 23% had need fully met. ***Average percent of need met:*** 81% (excluding resources awarded to replace EFC). ***Average financial aid package:*** $24,287 (excluding resources awarded to replace EFC). 20% of all full-time undergraduates had no need and received non-need-based gift aid.

GIFT AID (NEED-BASED) ***Total amount:*** $19,834,762 (11% federal, 8% state, 77% institutional, 4% external sources). ***Receiving aid:*** Freshmen: 82% (293); all full-time undergraduates: 79% (1,017). ***Average award:*** Freshmen: $21,753; Undergraduates: $19,817. ***Scholarships, grants, and awards:*** Federal Pell, FSEOG, state, private, college/university gift aid from institutional funds, Federal Nursing, ROTC scholarships.

GIFT AID (NON-NEED-BASED) ***Total amount:*** $5,746,017 (3% federal, 94% institutional, 3% external sources). ***Receiving aid:*** Freshmen: 17% (60). Undergraduates: 13% (170). ***Average award:*** Freshmen: $16,430. Undergraduates: $17,011. ***Scholarships, grants, and awards by category:*** *Academic interests/achievement:* 1,193 awards ($14,342,043 total): biological sciences, business, English, foreign languages, general academic interests/achievements, mathematics, physical sciences, premedicine. *Creative arts/performance:* 116 awards ($461,720 total): art/fine arts, creative writing, music, performing arts, theater/drama. *Special achievements/activities:* 4 awards ($2000 total): community service. *Special characteristics:* 430 awards ($2,648,815 total): adult students, children and siblings of alumni, children of educators, children of faculty/staff, international students, members of minority groups, siblings of current students, veterans, veterans' children. ***Tuition waivers:*** Full or partial for children of alumni, employees or children of employees, adult students, senior citizens. ***ROTC:*** Army cooperative, Air Force cooperative.

LOANS ***Student loans:*** $8,115,330 (75% need-based, 25% non-need-based). 79% of past graduating class borrowed through all loan programs. *Average indebtedness per student:* $33,260. ***Average need-based loan:*** Freshmen: $4349. Undergraduates: $5064. ***Parent loans:*** $2,501,004 (30% need-based, 70% non-need-based). ***Programs:*** Federal Direct (Subsidized and Unsubsidized Stafford, PLUS), Perkins, college/university.

WORK-STUDY ***Federal work-study:*** Total amount: $526,406; 417 jobs averaging $1400. ***State or other work-study/employment:*** Total amount: $271,950 (8% need-based, 92% non-need-based). 192 part-time jobs averaging $1300.

APPLYING FOR FINANCIAL AID ***Required financial aid form:*** FAFSA. ***Financial aid deadline (priority):*** 3/1. ***Notification date:*** Continuous beginning 3/15. Students must reply by 5/1 or within 2 weeks of notification.

CONTACT Ms. Barbara Hoffman, Director of Financial Aid, Coe College, 1220 First Avenue, NE, Cedar Rapids, IA 52402-5070, 319-399-8540 or toll-free 877-225-5263. *Fax:* 319-399-8886.

COGSWELL POLYTECHNICAL COLLEGE

Sunnyvale, CA

Tuition & fees: $18,924 **Average undergraduate aid package: N/A**

ABOUT THE INSTITUTION Independent, coed, primarily men. 6 undergraduate majors. Federal methodology is used as a basis for awarding need-based institutional aid.

UNDERGRADUATE EXPENSES for 2011–12 ***Tuition:*** full-time $18,744; part-time $781 per credit hour. Full-time tuition and fees vary according to course load. Part-time tuition and fees vary according to course load. Room and board charges vary according to housing facility. ***Payment plan:*** Deferred payment.

GIFT AID (NEED-BASED) ***Scholarships, grants, and awards:*** Federal Pell, FSEOG, state, private, college/university gift aid from institutional funds.

GIFT AID (NON-NEED-BASED) ***Tuition waivers:*** Full or partial for employees or children of employees.

WORK-STUDY Federal work-study jobs available.

APPLYING FOR FINANCIAL AID ***Required financial aid forms:*** FAFSA, state aid form. ***Financial aid deadline (priority):*** 3/1. ***Notification date:*** Continuous. Students must reply by 5/1 or within 2 weeks of notification.

CONTACT Lisa Mandy, Director of Financial Aid, Cogswell Polytechnical College, 1175 Bordeaux Drive, Sunnyvale, CA 94089, 408-541-0100 Ext. 107 or toll-free 800-264-7955. *Fax:* 408-747-0765. *E-mail:* lmandy@cogswell.edu.

COKER COLLEGE

Hartsville, SC

Tuition & fees: $20,818 **Average undergraduate aid package: $20,486**

ABOUT THE INSTITUTION Independent, coed. 46 undergraduate majors. Both federal and institutional methodology are used as a basis for awarding need-based institutional aid.

UNDERGRADUATE EXPENSES for 2010–11 ***Comprehensive fee:*** $27,408 includes full-time tuition ($20,328), mandatory fees ($490), and room and board ($6590). ***College room only:*** $3220. ***Part-time tuition:*** $847 per semester hour.

FRESHMAN FINANCIAL AID (Fall 2010, est.) 175 applied for aid; of those 92% were deemed to have need. 100% of freshmen with need received aid; of those 30% had need fully met. ***Average percent of need met:*** 88% (excluding resources awarded to replace EFC). ***Average financial aid package:*** $21,357 (excluding resources awarded to replace EFC). 9% of all full-time freshmen had no need and received non-need-based gift aid.

UNDERGRADUATE FINANCIAL AID (Fall 2010, est.) 605 applied for aid; of those 93% were deemed to have need. 100% of undergraduates with need received aid; of those 29% had need fully met. ***Average percent of need met:*** 85% (excluding resources awarded to replace EFC). ***Average financial aid package:*** $20,486 (excluding resources awarded to replace EFC). 8% of all full-time undergraduates had no need and received non-need-based gift aid.

GIFT AID (NEED-BASED) ***Total amount:*** $4,215,413 (46% federal, 27% state, 24% institutional, 3% external sources). ***Receiving aid:*** Freshmen: 83% (155); all full-time undergraduates: 83% (541). ***Average award:*** Freshmen: $7050; Undergraduates: $7456. ***Scholarships, grants, and awards:*** Federal Pell, FSEOG, state, private, college/university gift aid from institutional funds.

GIFT AID (NON-NEED-BASED) ***Total amount:*** $6,473,613 (3% federal, 20% state, 75% institutional, 2% external sources). ***Receiving aid:*** Freshmen: 86% (161). Undergraduates: 80% (524). ***Average award:*** Freshmen: $7608. Undergraduates: $7196. ***Scholarships, grants, and awards by category:*** *Academic interests/achievement:* general academic interests/achievements. *Creative arts/performance:* art/fine arts, creative writing, dance, general creative arts/performance, music, theater/drama. *Special characteristics:* children and siblings of alumni, children of faculty/staff, international students, previous college experience. ***Tuition waivers:*** Full or partial for employees or children of employees.

LOANS ***Student loans:*** $4,592,150 (45% need-based, 55% non-need-based). 81% of past graduating class borrowed through all loan programs. *Average indebtedness per student:* $25,593. ***Average need-based loan:*** Freshmen: $3639. Undergraduates: $4527. ***Parent loans:*** $558,644 (100% non-need-based). ***Programs:*** Federal Direct (Subsidized and Unsubsidized Stafford, PLUS), Perkins, state, private loans.

WORK-STUDY ***Federal work-study:*** Total amount: $95,493; 98 jobs averaging $974. ***State or other work-study/employment:*** Total amount: $1000 (100% need-based). Part-time jobs available.

ATHLETIC AWARDS Total amount: $644,631 (100% non-need-based).

APPLYING FOR FINANCIAL AID ***Required financial aid form:*** FAFSA. ***Financial aid deadline:*** 6/1 (priority: 4/1). ***Notification date:*** Continuous beginning 3/1. Students must reply by 5/1 or within 3 weeks of notification.

CONTACT Betty Williams, Director of Financial Aid, Coker College, 300 East College Avenue, Hartsville, SC 29550, 843-383-8055 or toll-free 800-950-1908. *Fax:* 843-383-8056. *E-mail:* bwilliams@coker.edu.

THE COLBURN SCHOOL CONSERVATORY OF MUSIC

Los Angeles, CA

Tuition & fees: **Average undergraduate aid package: N/A**

ABOUT THE INSTITUTION Independent, coed. 5 undergraduate majors. Institutional methodology is used as a basis for awarding need-based institutional aid.

UNDERGRADUATE EXPENSES for 2011–12 ***One-time required fee:*** $500. . The Colburn School does not charge its Conservatory students for tuition, room or board.

GIFT AID (NON-NEED-BASED) ***Scholarships, grants, and awards by category:*** *Creative arts/performance:* music.

APPLYING FOR FINANCIAL AID ***Financial aid deadline:*** Continuous.

CONTACT Ms. Kathleen Tesar, Associate Dean, The Colburn School Conservatory of Music, 200 South Grand Avenue, Los Angeles, CA 90012, 213-621-4534. *Fax:* 213-625-0371. *E-mail:* admissions@colburnschool.edu.

COLBY COLLEGE

Waterville, ME

Comprehensive fee: $51,990 **Average undergraduate aid package: $33,838**

ABOUT THE INSTITUTION Independent, coed. 41 undergraduate majors. Both federal and institutional methodology are used as a basis for awarding need-based institutional aid.

UNDERGRADUATE EXPENSES for 2010–11 ***Comprehensive fee:*** $51,990. Full-time tuition and fees vary according to course load. Room and board charges vary according to housing facility. Part-time tuition and fees vary according to course load. ***Payment plan:*** Installment.

FRESHMAN FINANCIAL AID (Fall 2010, est.) 260 applied for aid; of those 74% were deemed to have need. 100% of freshmen with need received aid; of those 100% had need fully met. ***Average percent of need met:*** 100% (excluding resources awarded to replace EFC). ***Average financial aid package:*** $38,072 (excluding resources awarded to replace EFC). 1% of all full-time freshmen had no need and received non-need-based gift aid.

UNDERGRADUATE FINANCIAL AID (Fall 2010, est.) 900 applied for aid; of those 85% were deemed to have need. 100% of undergraduates with need received aid; of those 100% had need fully met. ***Average percent of need met:*** 100% (excluding resources awarded to replace EFC). ***Average financial aid package:*** $33,838 (excluding resources awarded to replace EFC). 2% of all full-time undergraduates had no need and received non-need-based gift aid.

GIFT AID (NEED-BASED) ***Total amount:*** $24,783,673 (7% federal, 91% institutional, 2% external sources). ***Receiving aid:*** Freshmen: 40% (192); all full-time undergraduates: 42% (760). ***Average award:*** Freshmen: $34,449; Undergraduates: $32,609. ***Scholarships, grants, and awards:*** Federal Pell, FSEOG, state, private, college/university gift aid from institutional funds, Academic Competitiveness Grants, National SMART Grants, Colby National Merit Scholarships.

GIFT AID (NON-NEED-BASED) ***Total amount:*** $895,158 (1% federal, 38% institutional, 61% external sources). ***Receiving aid:*** Freshmen: 1% (3). Undergraduates: 1% (19). ***Average award:*** Freshmen: $16,148. Undergraduates: $2970. ***Scholarships, grants, and awards by category:*** *Academic interests/achievement:* 39 awards ($13,900 total): general academic interests/achievements. *Special characteristics:* 18 awards ($328,370 total): general special characteristics. ***Tuition waivers:*** Full or partial for employees or children of employees.

LOANS ***Student loans:*** $3,898,826 (100% non-need-based). 37% of past graduating class borrowed through all loan programs. *Average indebtedness per student:* $24,600. ***Average need-based loan:*** Undergraduates: $1535. ***Parent loans:*** $2,322,705 (100% non-need-based). ***Programs:*** Federal Direct (Subsidized and Unsubsidized Stafford, PLUS), Perkins, state, alternative loans.

WORK-STUDY ***Federal work-study:*** Total amount: $742,704; 447 jobs averaging $1636. ***State or other work-study/employment:*** Total amount: $257,795 (100% need-based). 152 part-time jobs averaging $1683.

APPLYING FOR FINANCIAL AID ***Required financial aid forms:*** FAFSA, CSS Financial Aid PROFILE, federal income tax returns for student and parents. ***Financial aid deadline:*** 2/1. ***Notification date:*** 4/1. Students must reply by 5/1.

CONTACT Ms. Lucia Whittelsey, Director of Financial Aid, Colby College, 4850 Mayflower Hill, Waterville, ME 04901-8848, 207-859-4832 or toll-free 800-723-3032. *Fax:* 207-859-4828. *E-mail:* finaid@colby.edu.

COLBY-SAWYER COLLEGE

New London, NH

CONTACT Office of Financial Aid, Colby-Sawyer College, 541 Main Street, New London, NH 03257-7835, 603-526-3717 or toll-free 800-272-1015. *Fax:* 603-526-3452. *E-mail:* cscfinaid@colby-sawyer.edu.

COLEGIO PENTECOSTAL MIZPA

Río Piedras, PR

CONTACT Financial Aid Office, Colegio Pentecostal Mizpa, Bo Caimito Road 199, Apartado 20966, Río Piedras, PR 00928-0966, 787-720-4476.

COLEMAN UNIVERSITY

San Diego, CA

ABOUT THE INSTITUTION Independent, coed. ***Awards:*** associate, bachelor's, and master's degrees. 4 undergraduate majors. ***Total enrollment:*** 488. Undergraduates: 477.

GIFT AID (NEED-BASED) ***Scholarships, grants, and awards:*** Federal Pell, FSEOG, state.

GIFT AID (NON-NEED-BASED) ***Scholarships, grants, and awards by category:*** *Academic interests/achievement:* general academic interests/achievements. *Special characteristics:* children and siblings of alumni.

LOANS ***Programs:*** Federal Direct (Subsidized and Unsubsidized Stafford, PLUS).

WORK-STUDY Federal work-study jobs available.

APPLYING FOR FINANCIAL AID ***Required financial aid forms:*** FAFSA, institution's own form, state aid form.

CONTACT Financial Aid Office, Coleman University, 8888 Balboa Avenue, San Diego, CA 92123, 858-499-0202. *Fax:* 858-499-0233. *E-mail:* faoffice@coleman.edu.

COLGATE UNIVERSITY

Hamilton, NY

Tuition & fees: $41,870 **Average undergraduate aid package: $38,568**

ABOUT THE INSTITUTION Independent, coed. 51 undergraduate majors. Institutional methodology is used as a basis for awarding need-based institutional aid.

UNDERGRADUATE EXPENSES for 2010–11 ***One-time required fee:*** $50. ***Comprehensive fee:*** $52,060 includes full-time tuition ($41,585), mandatory fees ($285), and room and board ($10,190). ***College room only:*** $4920. Full-time tuition and fees vary according to course load. Room and board charges vary according to board plan and housing facility. ***Part-time tuition:*** $5198.12 per course. Part-time tuition and fees vary according to course load. ***Payment plans:*** Tuition prepayment, installment, deferred payment.

FRESHMAN FINANCIAL AID (Fall 2010, est.) 327 applied for aid; of those 85% were deemed to have need. 100% of freshmen with need received aid; of those 100% had need fully met. ***Average percent of need met:*** 100% (excluding resources awarded to replace EFC). ***Average financial aid package:*** $39,896 (excluding resources awarded to replace EFC).

UNDERGRADUATE FINANCIAL AID (Fall 2010, est.) 1,047 applied for aid; of those 94% were deemed to have need. 100% of undergraduates with need received aid; of those 100% had need fully met. ***Average percent of need met:*** 100% (excluding resources awarded to replace EFC). ***Average financial aid package:*** $38,568 (excluding resources awarded to replace EFC).

GIFT AID (NEED-BASED) ***Total amount:*** $34,094,832 (5% federal, 2% state, 92% institutional, 1% external sources). ***Receiving aid:*** Freshmen: 32% (275); all full-time undergraduates: 33% (958). ***Average award:*** Freshmen: $37,204; Undergraduates: $35,264. ***Scholarships, grants, and awards:*** Federal Pell, FSEOG, state, college/university gift aid from institutional funds.

GIFT AID (NON-NEED-BASED) ***Total amount:*** $365,386 (100% external sources). ***Tuition waivers:*** Full or partial for employees or children of employees.

LOANS ***Student loans:*** $4,005,829 (59% need-based, 41% non-need-based). 33% of past graduating class borrowed through all loan programs. *Average indebtedness per student:* $18,629. ***Average need-based loan:*** Freshmen: $1610. Undergraduates: $3123. ***Parent loans:*** $5,045,832 (100% non-need-based). ***Programs:*** Federal Direct (Subsidized and Unsubsidized Stafford, PLUS), Perkins.

WORK-STUDY ***Federal work-study:*** Total amount: $1,040,781; 489 jobs averaging $2066. ***State or other work-study/employment:*** Total amount: $574,622 (100% need-based). 307 part-time jobs averaging $1961.

ATHLETIC AWARDS Total amount: $6,168,588 (100% non-need-based).

APPLYING FOR FINANCIAL AID ***Required financial aid forms:*** CSS Financial Aid PROFILE, noncustodial (divorced/separated) parent's statement. ***Financial aid deadline:*** 1/15. ***Notification date:*** 4/1. Students must reply by 5/1 or within 2 weeks of notification.

CONTACT Office of Financial Aid, Colgate University, 13 Oak Drive, Hamilton, NY 13346, 315-228-7431. *Fax:* 315-228-7050. *E-mail:* financialaid@colgate.edu.

THE COLLEGE AT BROCKPORT, STATE UNIVERSITY OF NEW YORK

Brockport, NY

Tuition & fees (NY res): $6176 **Average undergraduate aid package: $9529**

ABOUT THE INSTITUTION State-supported, coed. 107 undergraduate majors. Federal methodology is used as a basis for awarding need-based institutional aid.

UNDERGRADUATE EXPENSES for 2011–12 ***Tuition, state resident:*** full-time $4970. ***Tuition, nonresident:*** full-time $13,380. ***Required fees:*** full-time $1206. Part-time tuition and fees vary according to course load. ***College room and board:*** $9780; ***Room only:*** $6400. Room and board charges vary according to board plan and housing facility. ***Payment plans:*** Installment, deferred payment.

FRESHMAN FINANCIAL AID (Fall 2010, est.) 901 applied for aid; of those 77% were deemed to have need. 100% of freshmen with need received aid; of those 16% had need fully met. ***Average percent of need met:*** 75% (excluding resources awarded to replace EFC). ***Average financial aid package:*** $9981 (excluding resources awarded to replace EFC). 8% of all full-time freshmen had no need and received non-need-based gift aid.

UNDERGRADUATE FINANCIAL AID (Fall 2010, est.) 4,958 applied for aid; of those 82% were deemed to have need. 99% of undergraduates with need received aid; of those 15% had need fully met. ***Average percent of need met:*** 71% (excluding resources awarded to replace EFC). ***Average financial aid package:*** $9529 (excluding resources awarded to replace EFC). 3% of all full-time undergraduates had no need and received non-need-based gift aid.

GIFT AID (NEED-BASED) ***Total amount:*** $21,207,426 (63% federal, 37% state). ***Receiving aid:*** Freshmen: 59% (574); all full-time undergraduates: 62% (3,440). ***Average award:*** Freshmen: $5866; Undergraduates: $5275. ***Scholarships, grants, and awards:*** Federal Pell, FSEOG, state, private, college/university gift aid from institutional funds.

GIFT AID (NON-NEED-BASED) ***Total amount:*** $4,971,028 (11% federal, 9% state, 59% institutional, 21% external sources). ***Receiving aid:*** Freshmen: 25% (245). Undergraduates: 15% (838). ***Average award:*** Freshmen: $3195. Undergraduates: $3891. ***Scholarships, grants, and awards by category:*** *Academic interests/achievement:* 935 awards ($2,892,044 total): biological sciences, business, communication, computer science, education, English, foreign languages, general academic interests/achievements, health fields, humanities, international studies, mathematics, military science, physical sciences, premedicine, social sciences. *Creative arts/performance:* 30 awards ($31,225 total): art/fine arts, cinema/film/broadcasting, creative writing, dance, general creative arts/performance, journalism/publications, music, performing arts, theater/drama. *Special achievements/activities:* 30 awards ($31,150 total): community service, general special achievements/activities, hobbies/interests, leadership, religious involvement. *Special characteristics:* 47 awards ($44,750 total): children and siblings of alumni, ethnic background, first-generation college students, general special characteristics, international students, local/state students, married students, members of minority groups, out-of-state students, previous college experience, religious affiliation, veterans. ***Tuition waivers:*** Full or partial for employees or children of employees, senior citizens.

LOANS ***Student loans:*** $42,028,727 (48% need-based, 52% non-need-based). 80% of past graduating class borrowed through all loan programs. *Average indebtedness per student:* $25,733. ***Average need-based loan:*** Freshmen: $4201. Undergraduates: $4705. ***Parent loans:*** $4,552,902 (100% non-need-based). ***Programs:*** Federal Direct (Subsidized and Unsubsidized Stafford, PLUS), Perkins, Federal Nursing, alternative loans.

WORK-STUDY ***Federal work-study:*** Total amount: $1,103,937; 654 jobs averaging $1799. ***State or other work-study/employment:*** Total amount: $2,256,321 (100% non-need-based). 1,664 part-time jobs averaging $1356.

APPLYING FOR FINANCIAL AID ***Required financial aid forms:*** FAFSA, state aid form. ***Financial aid deadline (priority):*** 2/15. ***Notification date:*** Continuous beginning 3/1. Students must reply by 5/1.

CONTACT Mr. J. Scott Atkinson, Interim Assistant Vice President for Enrollment Management, The College at Brockport, State University of New York, 350 New Campus Drive, Brockport, NY 14420-2937, 585-395-2501. *Fax:* 585-395-5445. *E-mail:* satkinso@brockport.edu.

COLLEGE FOR CREATIVE STUDIES

Detroit, MI

Tuition & fees: $32,785 **Average undergraduate aid package: N/A**

ABOUT THE INSTITUTION Independent, coed. 10 undergraduate majors. Federal methodology is used as a basis for awarding need-based institutional aid.

UNDERGRADUATE EXPENSES for 2011–12 ***Tuition:*** full-time $31,440; part-time $1048 per credit hour. Full-time tuition and fees vary according to course load. Part-time tuition and fees vary according to course load. Room and board charges vary according to board plan and location. ***Payment plans:*** Installment, deferred payment.

GIFT AID (NEED-BASED) ***Total amount:*** $4,115,999 (37% federal, 28% state, 34% institutional, 1% external sources). ***Scholarships, grants, and awards:*** Federal Pell, FSEOG, state, private, college/university gift aid from institutional funds.

GIFT AID (NON-NEED-BASED) ***Total amount:*** $7,299,007 (2% state, 95% institutional, 3% external sources). ***Scholarships, grants, and awards by category:*** *Academic interests/achievement:* general academic interests/achievements. *Creative arts/performance:* applied art and design, art/fine arts. ***Tuition waivers:*** Full or partial for employees or children of employees.

LOANS ***Student loans:*** $12,466,214 (30% need-based, 70% non-need-based). 79% of past graduating class borrowed through all loan programs. *Average indebtedness per student:* $47,604. ***Parent loans:*** $1,943,656 (100% non-need-based). ***Programs:*** Federal Direct (Subsidized and Unsubsidized Stafford, PLUS), private loans.

WORK-STUDY ***Federal work-study:*** Total amount: $101,391; jobs available. ***State or other work-study/employment:*** Total amount: $197,428 (14% need-based, 86% non-need-based). Part-time jobs available.

APPLYING FOR FINANCIAL AID ***Required financial aid form:*** FAFSA. ***Financial aid deadline:*** Continuous. ***Notification date:*** Continuous beginning 3/1. Students must reply within 3 weeks of notification.

CONTACT Office of Financial Aid, College for Creative Studies, 201 East Kirby, Detroit, MI 48202-4034, 313-664-7495 or toll-free 800-872-2739. *Fax:* 313-872-1521. *E-mail:* finaid@collegeforcreativestudies.edu.

COLLEGE OF BIBLICAL STUDIES–HOUSTON

Houston, TX

CONTACT Financial Aid Office, College of Biblical Studies–Houston, 7000 Regency Square Boulevard, Houston, TX 77036, 713-785-5995.

COLLEGE OF CHARLESTON

Charleston, SC

Tuition & fees (SC res): $10,314 **Average undergraduate aid package: $12,882**

ABOUT THE INSTITUTION State-supported, coed. 46 undergraduate majors. Federal methodology is used as a basis for awarding need-based institutional aid.

UNDERGRADUATE EXPENSES for 2010–11 ***Tuition, state resident:*** full-time $10,314; part-time $430 per semester hour. ***Tuition, nonresident:*** full-time $23,172; part-time $965 per semester hour. Full-time tuition and fees vary according to degree level. Part-time tuition and fees vary according to course load and degree level. ***College room and board:*** $9843; ***Room only:*** $6743. Room and board charges vary according to board plan and housing facility. ***Payment plan:*** Installment.

FRESHMAN FINANCIAL AID (Fall 2009) 1,449 applied for aid; of those 66% were deemed to have need. 96% of freshmen with need received aid; of those 29% had need fully met. ***Average percent of need met:*** 64% (excluding resources awarded to replace EFC). ***Average financial aid package:*** $12,690 (excluding resources awarded to replace EFC). 13% of all full-time freshmen had no need and received non-need-based gift aid.

UNDERGRADUATE FINANCIAL AID (Fall 2009) 5,407 applied for aid; of those 75% were deemed to have need. 96% of undergraduates with need received aid; of those 27% had need fully met. ***Average percent of need met:*** 63% (excluding resources awarded to replace EFC). ***Average financial aid package:*** $12,882 (excluding resources awarded to replace EFC). 12% of all full-time undergraduates had no need and received non-need-based gift aid.

GIFT AID (NEED-BASED) ***Total amount:*** $20,574,311 (42% federal, 34% state, 18% institutional, 6% external sources). ***Receiving aid:*** Freshmen: 31% (669); all full-time undergraduates: 28% (2,578). ***Average award:*** Freshmen: $3073; Undergraduates: $3173. ***Scholarships, grants, and awards:*** Federal Pell, FSEOG, state, private, college/university gift aid from institutional funds.

GIFT AID (NON-NEED-BASED) ***Total amount:*** $20,006,664 (55% state, 33% institutional, 12% external sources). ***Receiving aid:*** Freshmen: 33% (701). Undergraduates: 19% (1,753). ***Average award:*** Freshmen: $11,412. Undergraduates: $11,423. ***Scholarships, grants, and awards by category:*** *Academic interests/achievement:* biological sciences, business, communication, computer science, education, engineering/technologies, English, foreign languages, general academic interests/achievements, health fields, humanities, mathematics, physical sciences, premedicine, social sciences. *Creative arts/performance:* art/fine arts, music, performing arts, theater/drama. *Special characteristics:* general special characteristics. ***Tuition waivers:*** Full or partial for senior citizens.

LOANS ***Student loans:*** $31,798,211 (64% need-based, 36% non-need-based). 46% of past graduating class borrowed through all loan programs. *Average indebtedness per student:* $19,875. ***Average need-based loan:*** Freshmen: $3199. Undergraduates: $4008. ***Parent loans:*** $22,648,232 (53% need-based, 47% non-need-based). ***Programs:*** Federal Direct (Subsidized and Unsubsidized Stafford, PLUS), Perkins.

WORK-STUDY ***Federal work-study:*** Total amount: $291,211; jobs available. ***State or other work-study/employment:*** Total amount: $13,200 (18% need-based, 82% non-need-based). Part-time jobs available.

ATHLETIC AWARDS Total amount: $3,272,212 (31% need-based, 69% non-need-based).

APPLYING FOR FINANCIAL AID ***Required financial aid form:*** FAFSA. ***Financial aid deadline (priority):*** 4/15. ***Notification date:*** Continuous beginning 4/10. Students must reply within 8 weeks of notification.

CONTACT Mr. Don Griggs, Financial Aid Director, College of Charleston, 66 George Street, Charleston, SC 29424, 843-953-5540 or toll-free 843-953-5670 (in-state). *Fax:* 843-953-7192.

COLLEGE OF COASTAL GEORGIA

Brunswick, GA

CONTACT Financial Aid Office, College of Coastal Georgia, 3700 Altama Avenue, Brunswick, GA 31520, 912-264-7235 or toll-free 800-675-7235.

THE COLLEGE OF IDAHO

Caldwell, ID

CONTACT Juanitta M. Pearson, Director of Financial Aid Services, The College of Idaho, 2112 Cleveland Boulevard, Caldwell, ID 83605, 208-459-5307 or toll-free 800-244-3246. *Fax:* 208-459-5844. *E-mail:* jpearson@collegeofidaho.edu.

COLLEGE OF MOUNT ST. JOSEPH

Cincinnati, OH

Tuition & fees: $23,550 **Average undergraduate aid package: $16,827**

ABOUT THE INSTITUTION Independent Roman Catholic, coed. 35 undergraduate majors. Federal methodology is used as a basis for awarding need-based institutional aid.

UNDERGRADUATE EXPENSES for 2010–11 ***One-time required fee:*** $150. ***Comprehensive fee:*** $30,942 includes full-time tuition ($22,750), mandatory fees ($800), and room and board ($7392). ***College room only:*** $3646. Full-time tuition and fees vary according to course load and reciprocity agreements. Room and board charges vary according to board plan and housing facility. ***Part-time tuition:*** $475 per credit hour. ***Part-time fees:*** $400 per year. Part-time tuition and fees vary according to course load and reciprocity agreements. ***Payment plans:*** Installment, deferred payment.

FRESHMAN FINANCIAL AID (Fall 2010, est.) 358 applied for aid; of those 92% were deemed to have need. 100% of freshmen with need received aid; of those 19% had need fully met. ***Average percent of need met:*** 80% (excluding resources awarded to replace EFC). ***Average financial aid package:*** $17,513 (excluding resources awarded to replace EFC). 13% of all full-time freshmen had no need and received non-need-based gift aid.

UNDERGRADUATE FINANCIAL AID (Fall 2010, est.) 1,241 applied for aid; of those 92% were deemed to have need. 100% of undergraduates with need received aid; of those 17% had need fully met. ***Average percent of need met:*** 73% (excluding resources awarded to replace EFC). ***Average financial aid package:*** $16,827 (excluding resources awarded to replace EFC). 13% of all full-time undergraduates had no need and received non-need-based gift aid.

GIFT AID (NEED-BASED) ***Total amount:*** $15,415,464 (25% federal, 6% state, 67% institutional, 2% external sources). ***Receiving aid:*** Freshmen: 86% (330); all full-time undergraduates: 80% (1,110). ***Average award:*** Freshmen: $13,529; Undergraduates: $12,764. ***Scholarships, grants, and awards:*** Federal Pell, FSEOG, state, private, college/university gift aid from institutional funds.

GIFT AID (NON-NEED-BASED) ***Total amount:*** $1,965,833 (24% federal, 75% institutional, 1% external sources). ***Receiving aid:*** Freshmen: 10% (38). Undergraduates: 7% (104). ***Average award:*** Freshmen: $10,849. Undergraduates: $10,429. ***Scholarships, grants, and awards by category:*** *Academic interests/achievement:* 939 awards ($7,793,014 total): general academic interests/achievements. *Creative arts/performance:* 63 awards ($125,400 total): art/fine arts, music. *Special achievements/activities:* 20 awards ($51,840 total): community service, leadership. *Special characteristics:* 37 awards ($731,011 total): adult students, children and siblings of alumni, children of faculty/staff. ***Tuition waivers:*** Full or partial for employees or children of employees, senior citizens.

LOANS ***Student loans:*** $13,201,333 (93% need-based, 7% non-need-based). 74% of past graduating class borrowed through all loan programs. *Average indebtedness per student:* $35,569. ***Average need-based loan:*** Freshmen: $3918. Undergraduates: $4507. ***Parent loans:*** $2,341,786 (93% need-based, 7% non-need-based). ***Programs:*** Perkins, Federal Nursing, state.

WORK-STUDY ***Federal work-study:*** Total amount: $353,375; 240 jobs averaging $1472. ***State or other work-study/employment:*** Total amount: $187,450 (96% need-based, 4% non-need-based). 131 part-time jobs averaging $1431.

APPLYING FOR FINANCIAL AID ***Required financial aid form:*** FAFSA. ***Financial aid deadline (priority):*** 3/1. ***Notification date:*** Continuous beginning 1/31. Students must reply by 5/1 or within 4 weeks of notification.

CONTACT Ms. Kathryn Kelly, Director of Student Administrative Services, College of Mount St. Joseph, 5701 Delhi Road, Cincinnati, OH 45233-1670, 513-244-4418 or toll-free 800-654-9314. *Fax:* 513-244-4201. *E-mail:* kathy_kelly@mail.msj.edu.

COLLEGE OF MOUNT SAINT VINCENT

Riverdale, NY

CONTACT Ms. Monica Simotas, Director of Financial Aid, College of Mount Saint Vincent, 6301 Riverdale Avenue, Riverdale, NY 10471, 718-405-3290 or toll-free 800-665-CMSV. *Fax:* 718-405-3490. *E-mail:* msimotas@mountsaintvincent.edu.

THE COLLEGE OF NEW JERSEY

Ewing, NJ

Tuition & fees (NJ res): $13,273 **Average undergraduate aid package: $9775**

ABOUT THE INSTITUTION State-supported, coed. 48 undergraduate majors. Federal methodology is used as a basis for awarding need-based institutional aid.

UNDERGRADUATE EXPENSES for 2010–11 ***Tuition, state resident:*** full-time $9340; part-time $331 per credit hour. ***Tuition, nonresident:*** full-time $18,726; part-time $662.80 per credit hour. ***Required fees:*** full-time $3933; $157.35 per credit hour. Part-time tuition and fees vary according to course load. ***College room and board:*** $10,358; ***Room only:*** $7510. Room and board charges vary according to board plan. ***Payment plan:*** Installment.

FRESHMAN FINANCIAL AID (Fall 2010, est.) 1,227 applied for aid; of those 64% were deemed to have need. 98% of freshmen with need received aid; of those 16% had need fully met. ***Average percent of need met:*** 45% (excluding resources awarded to replace EFC). ***Average financial aid package:*** $9816 (excluding resources awarded to replace EFC). 22% of all full-time freshmen had no need and received non-need-based gift aid.

UNDERGRADUATE FINANCIAL AID (Fall 2010, est.) 4,544 applied for aid; of those 70% were deemed to have need. 98% of undergraduates with need received aid; of those 16% had need fully met. ***Average percent of need met:*** 49% (excluding resources awarded to replace EFC). ***Average financial aid package:*** $9775 (excluding resources awarded to replace EFC). 12% of all full-time undergraduates had no need and received non-need-based gift aid.

GIFT AID (NEED-BASED) ***Total amount:*** $19,283,576 (25% federal, 31% state, 37% institutional, 7% external sources). ***Receiving aid:*** Freshmen: 23% (320); all full-time undergraduates: 20% (1,258). ***Average award:*** Freshmen: $10,883; Undergraduates: $9690. ***Scholarships, grants, and awards:*** Federal Pell, FSEOG, state, private, college/university gift aid from institutional funds.

GIFT AID (NON-NEED-BASED) ***Total amount:*** $6,185,788 (8% state, 79% institutional, 13% external sources). ***Receiving aid:*** Freshmen: 38% (531). Undergraduates: 22% (1,377). ***Average award:*** Freshmen: $3812. Undergraduates: $4242. ***Scholarships, grants, and awards by category:*** *Academic interests/achievement:* general academic interests/achievements. *Creative arts/performance:* music. *Special characteristics:* children with a deceased or disabled parent, members of minority groups. ***Tuition waivers:*** Full or partial for employees or children of employees, senior citizens.

LOANS ***Student loans:*** $35,116,270 (77% need-based, 23% non-need-based). 56% of past graduating class borrowed through all loan programs. *Average indebtedness per student:* $27,057. ***Average need-based loan:*** Freshmen: $3458. Undergraduates: $4520. ***Parent loans:*** $3,823,306 (72% need-based, 28% non-need-based). ***Programs:*** Federal Direct (Subsidized and Unsubsidized Stafford, PLUS), Perkins, Federal Nursing.

WORK-STUDY ***Federal work-study:*** Total amount: $255,804; 182 jobs averaging $1426.

APPLYING FOR FINANCIAL AID ***Required financial aid form:*** FAFSA. ***Financial aid deadline (priority):*** 3/1. ***Notification date:*** Continuous beginning 6/1. Students must reply within 2 weeks of notification.

CONTACT Mr. Joseph DiMartile, Interim Director of Student Financial Services, The College of New Jersey, PO Box 7718, Ewing, NJ 08628, 609-771-3098 or toll-free 800-624-0967. *Fax:* 609-637-5154. *E-mail:* dimartij@tcnj.edu.

THE COLLEGE OF NEW ROCHELLE

New Rochelle, NY

Tuition & fees: $28,010 **Average undergraduate aid package: $20,339**

ABOUT THE INSTITUTION Independent, coed, primarily women. 36 undergraduate majors. Federal methodology is used as a basis for awarding need-based institutional aid.

UNDERGRADUATE EXPENSES for 2010–11 ***Comprehensive fee:*** $38,186 includes full-time tuition ($27,110), mandatory fees ($900), and room and board ($10,176). Full-time tuition and fees vary according to course load and program. Room and board charges vary according to housing facility. ***Part-time tuition:*** $861 per credit. ***Part-time fees:*** $250 per term. Part-time tuition and fees vary according to course load and program. ***Payment plan:*** Installment.

FRESHMAN FINANCIAL AID (Fall 2009) 78 applied for aid; of those 95% were deemed to have need. 100% of freshmen with need received aid; of those 3% had need fully met. ***Average percent of need met:*** 70% (excluding resources awarded to replace EFC). ***Average financial aid package:*** $24,301 (excluding resources awarded to replace EFC). 6% of all full-time freshmen had no need and received non-need-based gift aid.

UNDERGRADUATE FINANCIAL AID (Fall 2009) 495 applied for aid; of those 96% were deemed to have need. 100% of undergraduates with need received aid; of those 3% had need fully met. ***Average percent of need met:*** 57% (excluding resources awarded to replace EFC). ***Average financial aid package:*** $20,339 (excluding resources awarded to replace EFC). 6% of all full-time undergraduates had no need and received non-need-based gift aid.

GIFT AID (NEED-BASED) ***Total amount:*** $7,902,243 (25% federal, 12% state, 63% institutional). ***Receiving aid:*** Freshmen: 80% (63); all full-time undergraduates: 72% (393). ***Average award:*** Freshmen: $9594; Undergraduates: $11,070. ***Scholarships, grants, and awards:*** Federal Pell, FSEOG, state, private, college/university gift aid from institutional funds.

GIFT AID (NON-NEED-BASED) ***Total amount:*** $364,532 (100% institutional). ***Receiving aid:*** Freshmen: 94% (74). Undergraduates: 53% (288). ***Average award:*** Freshmen: $8400. Undergraduates: $11,888. ***Scholarships, grants, and awards by category:*** *Academic interests/achievement:* 265 awards ($3,105,000 total): area/ethnic studies, biological sciences, business, communication, education, English, foreign languages, general academic interests/achievements, health fields, humanities, mathematics, physical sciences, premedicine, religion/biblical studies, social sciences. *Creative arts/performance:* 48 awards ($365,000 total): applied art and design, art/fine arts, cinema/film/broadcasting, creative writing, dance, debating, general creative arts/performance, journalism/publications, music, performing arts, theater/drama. *Special achievements/activities:* 90 awards ($987,650 total): community service, general special achievements/activities, hobbies/interests, junior miss, leadership, memberships, religious involvement. *Special characteristics:* 62 awards ($278,000 total): children of current students, children of faculty/staff, general special characteristics, out-of-state students, parents of current students, previous college experience, siblings of current students, spouses of current students. ***Tuition waivers:*** Full or partial for employees or children of employees, senior citizens.

LOANS ***Student loans:*** $6,396,806 (45% need-based, 55% non-need-based). 88% of past graduating class borrowed through all loan programs. *Average indebtedness per student:* $28,462. ***Average need-based loan:*** Freshmen: $4780. Undergraduates: $5470. ***Parent loans:*** $525,577 (91% need-based, 9% non-need-based). ***Programs:*** Federal Direct (Subsidized and Unsubsidized Stafford, PLUS), Perkins, Federal Nursing.

WORK-STUDY ***Federal work-study:*** Total amount: $1,056,455; 383 jobs averaging $2758. ***State or other work-study/employment:*** Part-time jobs available.

APPLYING FOR FINANCIAL AID ***Required financial aid forms:*** FAFSA, institution's own form, federal income tax form(s). ***Financial aid deadline:*** Continuous. ***Notification date:*** Continuous beginning 1/1. Students must reply within 2 weeks of notification.

CONTACT Anne Pelak, Director of Financial Aid, The College of New Rochelle, 29 Castle Place, New Rochelle, NY 10805-2339, 914-654-5225 or toll-free 800-933-5923. *Fax:* 914-654-5420. *E-mail:* apelak@cnr.edu.

COLLEGE OF NOTRE DAME OF MARYLAND

Baltimore, MD

Tuition & fees: $28,350 **Average undergraduate aid package: $20,927**

ABOUT THE INSTITUTION Independent Roman Catholic, coed, primarily women. 38 undergraduate majors. Federal methodology is used as a basis for awarding need-based institutional aid.

UNDERGRADUATE EXPENSES for 2010–11 ***Comprehensive fee:*** $37,850 includes full-time tuition ($27,600), mandatory fees ($750), and room and board ($9500). Room and board charges vary according to board plan. ***Part-time tuition:*** $425 per credit hour.

FRESHMAN FINANCIAL AID (Fall 2010, est.) 112 applied for aid; of those 96% were deemed to have need. 100% of freshmen with need received aid; of those 17% had need fully met. ***Average percent of need met:*** 73% (excluding resources awarded to replace EFC). ***Average financial aid package:*** $23,263 (excluding resources awarded to replace EFC). 9% of all full-time freshmen had no need and received non-need-based gift aid.

UNDERGRADUATE FINANCIAL AID (Fall 2010, est.) 456 applied for aid; of those 92% were deemed to have need. 100% of undergraduates with need received aid; of those 27% had need fully met. ***Average percent of need met:*** 68% (excluding resources awarded to replace EFC). ***Average financial aid package:*** $20,927 (excluding resources awarded to replace EFC). 10% of all full-time undergraduates had no need and received non-need-based gift aid.

GIFT AID (NEED-BASED) ***Total amount:*** $7,253,920 (20% federal, 12% state, 66% institutional, 2% external sources). ***Receiving aid:*** Freshmen: 90% (107); all full-time undergraduates: 81% (406). ***Average award:*** Freshmen: $18,962; Undergraduates: $17,012. ***Scholarships, grants, and awards:*** Federal Pell, FSEOG, state, private, college/university gift aid from institutional funds, Academic Competitiveness Grants, National SMART Grants, TEACH Grants.

GIFT AID (NON-NEED-BASED) ***Total amount:*** $949,022 (97% institutional, 3% external sources). ***Receiving aid:*** Freshmen: 14% (17). Undergraduates: 9% (44). ***Average award:*** Freshmen: $11,977. Undergraduates: $12,711. ***Scholarships, grants, and awards by category:*** *Academic interests/achievement:* 208

awards ($2,227,365 total): general academic interests/achievements. *Creative arts/performance:* 26 awards ($141,250 total): art/fine arts, general creative arts/performance. *Special achievements/activities:* 261 awards ($1,657,511 total): community service, general special achievements/activities, leadership, memberships, religious involvement. *Special characteristics:* 54 awards ($57,000 total): general special characteristics, international students, siblings of current students.

LOANS ***Student loans:*** $6,843,595 (77% need-based, 23% non-need-based). 75% of past graduating class borrowed through all loan programs. *Average indebtedness per student:* $30,801. ***Average need-based loan:*** Freshmen: $3570. Undergraduates: $3569. ***Parent loans:*** $1,641,735 (70% need-based, 30% non-need-based). ***Programs:*** Federal Direct (Subsidized and Unsubsidized Stafford, PLUS), Perkins.

WORK-STUDY ***Federal work-study:*** Total amount: $88,500; 92 jobs averaging $962.

APPLYING FOR FINANCIAL AID ***Required financial aid form:*** FAFSA. ***Financial aid deadline (priority):*** 2/15. ***Notification date:*** Continuous beginning 3/1. Students must reply by 5/1.

CONTACT Zhanna Goltser, Director of Financial Aid, College of Notre Dame of Maryland, 4701 North Charles Street, Baltimore, MD 21210-2404, 410-532-5369 or toll-free 800-435-0200 (in-state), 800-435-0300 (out-of-state). *Fax:* 410-532-6287. *E-mail:* finaid@ndm.edu.

COLLEGE OF SAINT BENEDICT

Saint Joseph, MN

Tuition & fees: $32,246 **Average undergraduate aid package: $25,413**

ABOUT THE INSTITUTION Independent Roman Catholic, women only. 51 undergraduate majors. Federal methodology is used as a basis for awarding need-based institutional aid.

UNDERGRADUATE EXPENSES for 2010–11 ***Comprehensive fee:*** $40,898 includes full-time tuition ($31,416), mandatory fees ($830), and room and board ($8652). ***College room only:*** $4166. Room and board charges vary according to board plan and housing facility. ***Part-time tuition:*** $1309 per credit hour. Part-time tuition and fees vary according to course load. ***Payment plan:*** Installment.

FRESHMAN FINANCIAL AID (Fall 2010, est.) 458 applied for aid; of those 85% were deemed to have need. 100% of freshmen with need received aid; of those 48% had need fully met. ***Average percent of need met:*** 90% (excluding resources awarded to replace EFC). ***Average financial aid package:*** $26,424 (excluding resources awarded to replace EFC). 23% of all full-time freshmen had no need and received non-need-based gift aid.

UNDERGRADUATE FINANCIAL AID (Fall 2010, est.) 1,568 applied for aid; of those 89% were deemed to have need. 100% of undergraduates with need received aid; of those 40% had need fully met. ***Average percent of need met:*** 86% (excluding resources awarded to replace EFC). ***Average financial aid package:*** $25,413 (excluding resources awarded to replace EFC). 26% of all full-time undergraduates had no need and received non-need-based gift aid.

GIFT AID (NEED-BASED) ***Total amount:*** $26,842,528 (10% federal, 6% state, 81% institutional, 3% external sources). ***Receiving aid:*** Freshmen: 72% (388); all full-time undergraduates: 68% (1,373). ***Average award:*** Freshmen: $20,037; Undergraduates: $18,606. ***Scholarships, grants, and awards:*** Federal Pell, FSEOG, state, private, college/university gift aid from institutional funds.

GIFT AID (NON-NEED-BASED) ***Total amount:*** $8,521,108 (94% institutional, 6% external sources). ***Receiving aid:*** Freshmen: 66% (352). Undergraduates: 62% (1,258). ***Average award:*** Freshmen: $12,860. Undergraduates: $11,724. ***Scholarships, grants, and awards by category:*** *Academic interests/achievement:* general academic interests/achievements, military science. *Creative arts/performance:* art/fine arts, music, theater/drama. *Special achievements/activities:* junior miss. *Special characteristics:* international students.

LOANS ***Student loans:*** $15,177,227 (91% need-based, 9% non-need-based). ***Average need-based loan:*** Freshmen: $3965. Undergraduates: $4453. ***Parent loans:*** $1,281,853 (88% need-based, 12% non-need-based). ***Programs:*** Federal Direct (Subsidized and Unsubsidized Stafford, PLUS), Perkins, state, private loans.

WORK-STUDY ***Federal work-study:*** Total amount: $1,279,328; jobs available. ***State or other work-study/employment:*** Total amount: $1,917,450 (70% need-based, 30% non-need-based). Part-time jobs available.

APPLYING FOR FINANCIAL AID ***Required financial aid forms:*** FAFSA, institution's own form. ***Financial aid deadline (priority):*** 3/15. ***Notification date:*** Continuous beginning 3/1. Students must reply by 5/1.

CONTACT Ms. Jane Haugen, Executive Director of Financial Aid, College of Saint Benedict, 37 South College Avenue, Saint Joseph, MN 56374-2099, 320-363-5388 or toll-free 800-544-1489. *Fax:* 320-363-6099. *E-mail:* jhaugen@csbsju.edu.

COLLEGE OF SAINT ELIZABETH

Morristown, NJ

Tuition & fees: $26,887 **Average undergraduate aid package: $21,992**

ABOUT THE INSTITUTION Independent Roman Catholic, coed, primarily women. 28 undergraduate majors. Both federal and institutional methodology are used as a basis for awarding need-based institutional aid.

UNDERGRADUATE EXPENSES for 2010–11 ***Comprehensive fee:*** $38,227 includes full-time tuition ($25,180), mandatory fees ($1707), and room and board ($11,340). Full-time tuition and fees vary according to degree level. ***Part-time tuition:*** $670 per credit hour. ***Part-time fees:*** $70 per credit hour. Part-time tuition and fees vary according to course load, degree level, location, and reciprocity agreements. ***Payment plan:*** Installment.

FRESHMAN FINANCIAL AID (Fall 2009) 167 applied for aid; of those 100% were deemed to have need. 100% of freshmen with need received aid; of those 10% had need fully met. ***Average percent of need met:*** 80% (excluding resources awarded to replace EFC). ***Average financial aid package:*** $25,717 (excluding resources awarded to replace EFC). 3% of all full-time freshmen had no need and received non-need-based gift aid.

UNDERGRADUATE FINANCIAL AID (Fall 2009) 576 applied for aid; of those 100% were deemed to have need. 100% of undergraduates with need received aid; of those 12% had need fully met. ***Average percent of need met:*** 73% (excluding resources awarded to replace EFC). ***Average financial aid package:*** $21,992 (excluding resources awarded to replace EFC). 4% of all full-time undergraduates had no need and received non-need-based gift aid.

GIFT AID (NEED-BASED) ***Total amount:*** $6,943,455 (23% federal, 42% state, 35% institutional). ***Receiving aid:*** Freshmen: 70% (125); all full-time undergraduates: 61% (413). ***Average award:*** Freshmen: $19,627; Undergraduates: $16,489. ***Scholarships, grants, and awards:*** Federal Pell, FSEOG, state, private, college/university gift aid from institutional funds.

GIFT AID (NON-NEED-BASED) ***Total amount:*** $4,363,659 (1% state, 99% institutional). ***Receiving aid:*** Freshmen: 62% (110). Undergraduates: 49% (330). ***Average award:*** Freshmen: $12,607. Undergraduates: $9942. ***Scholarships, grants, and awards by category:*** *Academic interests/achievement:* general academic interests/achievements. *Special achievements/activities:* community service, leadership. *Special characteristics:* adult students, children and siblings of alumni. ***Tuition waivers:*** Full or partial for children of alumni, employees or children of employees, senior citizens.

LOANS ***Student loans:*** $5,055,204 (45% need-based, 55% non-need-based). ***Average need-based loan:*** Freshmen: $4040. Undergraduates: $5005. ***Programs:*** Perkins.

WORK-STUDY ***Federal work-study:*** Total amount: $113,847; 120 jobs averaging $949.

APPLYING FOR FINANCIAL AID ***Required financial aid form:*** FAFSA. ***Financial aid deadline:*** Continuous. ***Notification date:*** Continuous beginning 11/15. Students must reply by 5/1 or within 2 weeks of notification.

CONTACT Debra Wulff, Director of Financial Aid, College of Saint Elizabeth, 2 Convent Road, Morristown, NJ 07960-6989, 973-290-4492 or toll-free 800-210-7900. *E-mail:* dwulff@cse.edu.

COLLEGE OF ST. JOSEPH

Rutland, VT

Tuition & fees: $19,465 **Average undergraduate aid package: $19,062**

ABOUT THE INSTITUTION Independent Roman Catholic, coed. 13 undergraduate majors. Federal methodology is used as a basis for awarding need-based institutional aid.

UNDERGRADUATE EXPENSES for 2011–12 ***Comprehensive fee:*** $28,665 includes full-time tuition ($18,990), mandatory fees ($475), and room and board ($9200). Full-time tuition and fees vary according to course load, degree level, and program. Room and board charges vary according to housing facility.

Part-time tuition: $260 per credit. Part-time tuition and fees vary according to course load, degree level, and program. ***Payment plans:*** Guaranteed tuition, installment.

FRESHMAN FINANCIAL AID (Fall 2009) 43 applied for aid; of those 95% were deemed to have need. 100% of freshmen with need received aid; of those 10% had need fully met. ***Average percent of need met:*** 86% (excluding resources awarded to replace EFC). ***Average financial aid package:*** $18,493 (excluding resources awarded to replace EFC). 5% of all full-time freshmen had no need and received non-need-based gift aid.

UNDERGRADUATE FINANCIAL AID (Fall 2009) 166 applied for aid; of those 95% were deemed to have need. 100% of undergraduates with need received aid; of those 8% had need fully met. ***Average percent of need met:*** 87% (excluding resources awarded to replace EFC). ***Average financial aid package:*** $19,062 (excluding resources awarded to replace EFC). 5% of all full-time undergraduates had no need and received non-need-based gift aid.

GIFT AID (NEED-BASED) ***Total amount:*** $1,561,401 (34% federal, 25% state, 34% institutional, 7% external sources). ***Receiving aid:*** Freshmen: 95% (41); all full-time undergraduates: 89% (148). ***Average award:*** Freshmen: $12,014; Undergraduates: $10,133. ***Scholarships, grants, and awards:*** Federal Pell, FSEOG, state, private, college/university gift aid from institutional funds.

GIFT AID (NON-NEED-BASED) ***Total amount:*** $29,971 (89% institutional, 11% external sources). ***Receiving aid:*** Freshmen: 9% (4). Undergraduates: 8% (13). ***Average award:*** Freshmen: $3250. Undergraduates: $2843. ***Scholarships, grants, and awards by category:*** *Academic interests/achievement:* 37 awards ($126,450 total): general academic interests/achievements. *Creative arts/performance:* 1 award ($250 total): music. *Special achievements/activities:* leadership. *Special characteristics:* 46 awards ($78,400 total): general special characteristics, local/state students, previous college experience, religious affiliation. ***Tuition waivers:*** Full or partial for employees or children of employees, senior citizens.

LOANS ***Student loans:*** $1,517,222 (86% need-based, 14% non-need-based). 77% of past graduating class borrowed through all loan programs. *Average indebtedness per student:* $25,848. ***Average need-based loan:*** Freshmen: $6558. Undergraduates: $8905. ***Parent loans:*** $208,510 (35% need-based, 65% non-need-based). ***Programs:*** Federal Direct (Subsidized and Unsubsidized Stafford, PLUS), Perkins.

WORK-STUDY ***Federal work-study:*** Total amount: $28,354; 32 jobs averaging $886. ***State or other work-study/employment:*** Total amount: $24,099 (88% need-based, 12% non-need-based). 37 part-time jobs averaging $651.

APPLYING FOR FINANCIAL AID ***Required financial aid forms:*** FAFSA, institution's own form. ***Financial aid deadline:*** Continuous. ***Notification date:*** Continuous beginning 3/15. Students must reply within 2 weeks of notification.

CONTACT Julie Rosmus, Director of Financial Aid, College of St. Joseph, 71 Clement Road, Rutland, VT 05701-3899, 802-773-5900 Ext. 3274 or toll-free 877-270-9998 (in-state). *Fax:* 802-776-5275. *E-mail:* jrosmus@csj.edu.

COLLEGE OF SAINT MARY

Omaha, NE

Tuition & fees: $24,350 **Average undergraduate aid package: $16,517**

ABOUT THE INSTITUTION Independent Roman Catholic, women only. 24 undergraduate majors. Federal methodology is used as a basis for awarding need-based institutional aid.

UNDERGRADUATE EXPENSES for 2011–12 ***Comprehensive fee:*** $31,050 includes full-time tuition ($23,870), mandatory fees ($480), and room and board ($6700). Full-time tuition and fees vary according to location and program. ***Part-time tuition:*** $785 per credit. ***Part-time fees:*** $16 per credit. Part-time tuition and fees vary according to class time, course load, location, and program. ***Payment plans:*** Installment, deferred payment.

FRESHMAN FINANCIAL AID (Fall 2010, est.) 92 applied for aid; of those 97% were deemed to have need. 100% of freshmen with need received aid; of those 9% had need fully met. ***Average percent of need met:*** 72% (excluding resources awarded to replace EFC). ***Average financial aid package:*** $20,513 (excluding resources awarded to replace EFC). 3% of all full-time freshmen had no need and received non-need-based gift aid.

UNDERGRADUATE FINANCIAL AID (Fall 2010, est.) 710 applied for aid; of those 96% were deemed to have need. 100% of undergraduates with need received aid; of those 7% had need fully met. ***Average percent of need met:*** 61% (excluding resources awarded to replace EFC). ***Average financial aid package:*** $16,517 (excluding resources awarded to replace EFC). 3% of all full-time undergraduates had no need and received non-need-based gift aid.

GIFT AID (NEED-BASED) ***Total amount:*** $7,302,232 (30% federal, 4% state, 59% institutional, 7% external sources). ***Receiving aid:*** Freshmen: 97% (89); all full-time undergraduates: 91% (648). ***Average award:*** Freshmen: $16,660; Undergraduates: $11,538. ***Scholarships, grants, and awards:*** Federal Pell, FSEOG, state, college/university gift aid from institutional funds.

GIFT AID (NON-NEED-BASED) ***Total amount:*** $227,742 (1% federal, 80% institutional, 19% external sources). ***Receiving aid:*** Freshmen: 7% (6). Undergraduates: 4% (27). ***Average award:*** Freshmen: $9505. Undergraduates: $5596. ***Scholarships, grants, and awards by category:*** *Academic interests/achievement:* 493 awards ($2,145,791 total): biological sciences, education, general academic interests/achievements, mathematics. *Creative arts/performance:* 5 awards ($6500 total): art/fine arts, music. *Special achievements/activities:* 218 awards ($251,750 total): community service, general special achievements/activities, leadership, religious involvement. *Special characteristics:* 101 awards ($99,500 total): children of faculty/staff, first-generation college students, general special characteristics, international students. ***Tuition waivers:*** Full or partial for employees or children of employees, senior citizens.

LOANS ***Student loans:*** $7,180,365 (87% need-based, 13% non-need-based). 79% of past graduating class borrowed through all loan programs. *Average indebtedness per student:* $30,325. ***Average need-based loan:*** Freshmen: $3356. Undergraduates: $5305. ***Parent loans:*** $1,160,101 (53% need-based, 47% non-need-based). ***Programs:*** Federal Direct (Subsidized and Unsubsidized Stafford, PLUS), Perkins, Federal Nursing.

WORK-STUDY ***Federal work-study:*** Total amount: $195,367; 178 jobs averaging $1200. ***State or other work-study/employment:*** Total amount: $67,200 (100% need-based). 11 part-time jobs averaging $6400.

ATHLETIC AWARDS Total amount: $466,861 (86% need-based, 14% non-need-based).

APPLYING FOR FINANCIAL AID ***Required financial aid form:*** FAFSA. ***Financial aid deadline (priority):*** 3/15. ***Notification date:*** Continuous beginning 3/15. Students must reply within 2 weeks of notification.

CONTACT Beth Sisk, Director of Financial Aid, College of Saint Mary, 7000 Mercy Road, Omaha, NE 68106, 402-399-2415 or toll-free 800-926-5534. *Fax:* 402-399-2480. *E-mail:* bsisk@csm.edu.

THE COLLEGE OF SAINT ROSE

Albany, NY

Tuition & fees: $25,464 **Average undergraduate aid package: $11,279**

ABOUT THE INSTITUTION Independent, coed. 53 undergraduate majors. Federal methodology is used as a basis for awarding need-based institutional aid.

UNDERGRADUATE EXPENSES for 2011–12 ***Comprehensive fee:*** $35,998 includes full-time tuition ($24,614), mandatory fees ($850), and room and board ($10,534). Full-time tuition and fees vary according to class time and course load. Room and board charges vary according to board plan and housing facility. ***Part-time tuition:*** $819 per credit. ***Part-time fees:*** $25 per credit; $68 per year. Part-time tuition and fees vary according to class time and course load. ***Payment plan:*** Installment.

FRESHMAN FINANCIAL AID (Fall 2009) 567 applied for aid; of those 97% were deemed to have need. 100% of freshmen with need received aid; of those 1% had need fully met. ***Average percent of need met:*** 28% (excluding resources awarded to replace EFC). ***Average financial aid package:*** $14,129 (excluding resources awarded to replace EFC). 4% of all full-time freshmen had no need and received non-need-based gift aid.

UNDERGRADUATE FINANCIAL AID (Fall 2009) 2,581 applied for aid; of those 98% were deemed to have need. 99% of undergraduates with need received aid; of those 1% had need fully met. ***Average percent of need met:*** 22% (excluding resources awarded to replace EFC). ***Average financial aid package:*** $11,279 (excluding resources awarded to replace EFC). 7% of all full-time undergraduates had no need and received non-need-based gift aid.

GIFT AID (NEED-BASED) ***Total amount:*** $27,737,565 (16% federal, 13% state, 70% institutional, 1% external sources). ***Receiving aid:*** Freshmen: 88% (514); all full-time undergraduates: 80% (2,271). ***Average award:*** Freshmen: $9326; Undergraduates: $7340. ***Scholarships, grants, and awards:*** Federal Pell, FSEOG, state, private, college/university gift aid from institutional funds.

GIFT AID (NON-NEED-BASED) ***Total amount:*** $2,222,414 (1% federal, 2% state, 96% institutional, 1% external sources). ***Average award:*** Freshmen: $11,866. Undergraduates: $11,193. ***Scholarships, grants, and awards by category:*** *Academic interests/achievement:* business, education, engineering/technologies, English, foreign languages, general academic interests/

achievements, mathematics, premedicine, social sciences. *Creative arts/performance:* art/fine arts, music. *Special achievements/activities:* community service. *Special characteristics:* adult students, children and siblings of alumni, children of faculty/staff, children of union members/company employees, ethnic background, general special characteristics, members of minority groups, out-of-state students, siblings of current students, twins. ***Tuition waivers:*** Full or partial for employees or children of employees.

LOANS ***Student loans:*** $11,581,355 (99% need-based, 1% non-need-based). 86% of past graduating class borrowed through all loan programs. *Average indebtedness per student:* $30,281. ***Average need-based loan:*** Freshmen: $3266. Undergraduates: $4262. ***Parent loans:*** $5,232,668 (98% need-based, 2% non-need-based). ***Programs:*** Federal Direct (Subsidized and Unsubsidized Stafford, PLUS), Perkins.

WORK-STUDY ***Federal work-study:*** Total amount: $381,196; jobs available. ***State or other work-study/employment:*** Total amount: $289,749 (91% need-based, 9% non-need-based). Part-time jobs available.

ATHLETIC AWARDS Total amount: $1,961,706 (77% need-based, 23% non-need-based).

APPLYING FOR FINANCIAL AID ***Required financial aid forms:*** FAFSA, state aid form. ***Financial aid deadline (priority):*** 3/1. ***Notification date:*** 3/15. Students must reply by 5/1 or within 2 weeks of notification.

CONTACT Steven Dwire, Director of Financial Aid, The College of Saint Rose, 432 Western Avenue, Albertus Hall, Room 206, Albany, NY 12203-1419, 518-458-4915 or toll-free 800-637-8556. *Fax:* 518-454-2802. *E-mail:* finaid@strose.edu.

THE COLLEGE OF ST. SCHOLASTICA

Duluth, MN

Tuition & fees: $29,506 **Average undergraduate aid package: $19,807**

ABOUT THE INSTITUTION Independent religious, coed. 36 undergraduate majors. Federal methodology is used as a basis for awarding need-based institutional aid.

UNDERGRADUATE EXPENSES for 2011–12 ***Comprehensive fee:*** $37,222 includes full-time tuition ($29,328), mandatory fees ($178), and room and board ($7716). ***College room only:*** $4376. Full-time tuition and fees vary according to class time. Room and board charges vary according to board plan and housing facility. Part-time tuition and fees vary according to class time and course load. ***Payment plan:*** Installment.

FRESHMAN FINANCIAL AID (Fall 2010, est.) 516 applied for aid; of those 90% were deemed to have need. 100% of freshmen with need received aid; of those 21% had need fully met. ***Average percent of need met:*** 75% (excluding resources awarded to replace EFC). ***Average financial aid package:*** $22,206 (excluding resources awarded to replace EFC). 9% of all full-time freshmen had no need and received non-need-based gift aid.

UNDERGRADUATE FINANCIAL AID (Fall 2010, est.) 2,233 applied for aid; of those 92% were deemed to have need. 99% of undergraduates with need received aid; of those 20% had need fully met. ***Average percent of need met:*** 71% (excluding resources awarded to replace EFC). ***Average financial aid package:*** $19,807 (excluding resources awarded to replace EFC). 6% of all full-time undergraduates had no need and received non-need-based gift aid.

GIFT AID (NEED-BASED) ***Total amount:*** $11,422,849 (42% federal, 23% state, 35% institutional). ***Receiving aid:*** Freshmen: 69% (396); all full-time undergraduates: 66% (1,672). ***Average award:*** Freshmen: $7170; Undergraduates: $6640. ***Scholarships, grants, and awards:*** Federal Pell, FSEOG, state, private, college/university gift aid from institutional funds.

GIFT AID (NON-NEED-BASED) ***Total amount:*** $24,516,049 (1% federal, 95% institutional, 4% external sources). ***Receiving aid:*** Freshmen: 75% (433). Undergraduates: 64% (1,643). ***Average award:*** Freshmen: $10,743. Undergraduates: $10,918. ***Scholarships, grants, and awards by category:*** *Academic interests/achievement:* general academic interests/achievements. *Creative arts/performance:* music. *Special characteristics:* children and siblings of alumni, children of faculty/staff, ethnic background, handicapped students, international students, members of minority groups, previous college experience, religious affiliation, siblings of current students, spouses of current students. ***Tuition waivers:*** Full or partial for employees or children of employees, senior citizens.

LOANS ***Student loans:*** $26,673,361 (30% need-based, 70% non-need-based). 81% of past graduating class borrowed through all loan programs. *Average indebtedness per student:* $40,816. ***Average need-based loan:*** Freshmen: $3706. Undergraduates: $4488. ***Parent loans:*** $2,803,015 (100% non-need-based). ***Programs:*** Federal Direct (Subsidized and Unsubsidized Stafford, PLUS), Perkins, Federal Nursing, state, private loans.

WORK-STUDY ***Federal work-study:*** Total amount: $412,148; jobs available. ***State or other work-study/employment:*** Total amount: $1,401,197 (20% need-based, 80% non-need-based). Part-time jobs available.

APPLYING FOR FINANCIAL AID ***Required financial aid form:*** FAFSA. ***Financial aid deadline (priority):*** 3/1. ***Notification date:*** Continuous beginning 5/1. Students must reply by 5/1 or within 2 weeks of notification.

CONTACT Mr. Jon P. Erickson, Director of Financial Aid, The College of St. Scholastica, 1200 Kenwood Avenue, Duluth, MN 55811-4199, 218-723-6725 or toll-free 800-249-6412. *Fax:* 218-733-2229. *E-mail:* jerickso@css.edu.

THE COLLEGE OF SAINT THOMAS MORE

Fort Worth, TX

ABOUT THE INSTITUTION Independent religious, coed. 1 undergraduate major.

GIFT AID (NEED-BASED) ***Scholarships, grants, and awards:*** Federal Pell, state, private, college/university gift aid from institutional funds.

GIFT AID (NON-NEED-BASED) ***Scholarships, grants, and awards by category:*** *Academic interests/achievement:* general academic interests/achievements.

WORK-STUDY ***State or other work-study/employment:*** Total amount: $2000 (100% need-based). 5 part-time jobs averaging $625.

APPLYING FOR FINANCIAL AID ***Required financial aid form:*** FAFSA.

CONTACT Mrs. Mary E. Swanson, Director of Financial Aid, The College of Saint Thomas More, 1463 Beechwood Lane, Abilene, TX 79603, 325-673-1934 or toll-free 800-583-6489 (out-of-state). *Fax:* 325-673-1934. *E-mail:* corkyswanson@suddenlink.net.

COLLEGE OF STATEN ISLAND OF THE CITY UNIVERSITY OF NEW YORK

Staten Island, NY

Tuition & fees (NY res): $4978 **Average undergraduate aid package: $11,735**

ABOUT THE INSTITUTION State and locally supported, coed. 33 undergraduate majors. Federal methodology is used as a basis for awarding need-based institutional aid.

UNDERGRADUATE EXPENSES for 2010–11 ***Tuition, state resident:*** full-time $4600; part-time $195 per credit. ***Tuition, nonresident:*** full-time $9960; part-time $415 per credit. ***Required fees:*** full-time $378; $113 per term. Full-time tuition and fees vary according to course load. Part-time tuition and fees vary according to course load. ***Payment plan:*** Installment.

FRESHMAN FINANCIAL AID (Fall 2010, est.) ***Average percent of need met:*** 60% (excluding resources awarded to replace EFC). ***Average financial aid package:*** $10,993 (excluding resources awarded to replace EFC). 10% of all full-time freshmen had no need and received non-need-based gift aid.

UNDERGRADUATE FINANCIAL AID (Fall 2010, est.) ***Average percent of need met:*** 58% (excluding resources awarded to replace EFC). ***Average financial aid package:*** $11,735 (excluding resources awarded to replace EFC). 5% of all full-time undergraduates had no need and received non-need-based gift aid.

GIFT AID (NEED-BASED) ***Total amount:*** $41,220,947 (61% federal, 36% state, 3% external sources). ***Average award:*** Freshmen: $6643; Undergraduates: $6800. ***Scholarships, grants, and awards:*** Federal Pell, FSEOG, state, private, college/university gift aid from institutional funds.

GIFT AID (NON-NEED-BASED) ***Total amount:*** $1,297,046 (11% federal, 37% state, 52% external sources). ***Receiving aid:*** Freshmen: 22% (501). Undergraduates: 9% (869). ***Average award:*** Freshmen: $995. Undergraduates: $450. ***Scholarships, grants, and awards by category:*** *Academic interests/achievement:* biological sciences, business, computer science, education, engineering/technologies, general academic interests/achievements, health fields, humanities, international studies, mathematics, physical sciences, premedicine, social sciences. *Creative arts/performance:* art/fine arts, music, theater/drama. *Special achievements/activities:* community service, general special achievements/activities. *Special characteristics:* children of public servants, children with a deceased or disabled parent, general special characteristics, handicapped students, international students, members of minority groups, public servants, spouses of deceased or disabled public servants, veterans' children. ***Tuition waivers:*** Full or partial for employees or children of employees, senior citizens.

LOANS ***Student loans:*** $8,667,968 (99% need-based, 1% non-need-based). 23% of past graduating class borrowed through all loan programs. *Average indebtedness per student:* $7423. ***Average need-based loan:*** Freshmen: $2959. Undergraduates: $4345. ***Programs:*** Federal Direct (Subsidized and Unsubsidized Stafford, PLUS), Perkins.

WORK-STUDY ***Federal work-study:*** Total amount: $1,028,962; 740 jobs averaging $1400. ***State or other work-study/employment:*** Total amount: $6750 (100% non-need-based). Part-time jobs available.

APPLYING FOR FINANCIAL AID ***Required financial aid forms:*** FAFSA, state aid form. ***Financial aid deadline (priority):*** 3/30. ***Notification date:*** Continuous beginning 4/1.

CONTACT Mr. Philippe Marius, Director of Financial Aid, College of Staten Island of the City University of New York, 2800 Victory Boulevard, 2A-401A, Staten Island, NY 10314-6600, 718-982-2030. *Fax:* 718-982-2037. *E-mail:* philippe.marius@csi.cuny.edu.

COLLEGE OF THE ATLANTIC

Bar Harbor, ME

Tuition & fees: $36,063 **Average undergraduate aid package: $31,981**

ABOUT THE INSTITUTION Independent, coed. 42 undergraduate majors. Both federal and institutional methodology are used as a basis for awarding need-based institutional aid.

UNDERGRADUATE EXPENSES for 2011–12 ***Comprehensive fee:*** $44,883 includes full-time tuition ($35,532), mandatory fees ($531), and room and board ($8820). ***College room only:*** $5670. Room and board charges vary according to board plan. ***Part-time tuition:*** $3948 per credit. ***Part-time fees:*** $177 per term. ***Payment plan:*** Installment.

FRESHMAN FINANCIAL AID (Fall 2010, est.) 77 applied for aid; of those 97% were deemed to have need. 100% of freshmen with need received aid; of those 44% had need fully met. ***Average percent of need met:*** 96% (excluding resources awarded to replace EFC). ***Average financial aid package:*** $32,877 (excluding resources awarded to replace EFC).

UNDERGRADUATE FINANCIAL AID (Fall 2010, est.) 296 applied for aid; of those 98% were deemed to have need. 100% of undergraduates with need received aid; of those 50% had need fully met. ***Average percent of need met:*** 96% (excluding resources awarded to replace EFC). ***Average financial aid package:*** $31,981 (excluding resources awarded to replace EFC).

GIFT AID (NEED-BASED) ***Total amount:*** $7,955,499 (7% federal, 1% state, 90% institutional, 2% external sources). ***Receiving aid:*** Freshmen: 87% (74); all full-time undergraduates: 84% (282). ***Average award:*** Freshmen: $28,135; Undergraduates: $27,548. ***Scholarships, grants, and awards:*** Federal Pell, FSEOG, state, private, college/university gift aid from institutional funds.

GIFT AID (NON-NEED-BASED) ***Tuition waivers:*** Full or partial for employees or children of employees.

LOANS ***Student loans:*** $1,402,291 (66% need-based, 34% non-need-based). 66% of past graduating class borrowed through all loan programs. *Average indebtedness per student:* $20,125. ***Average need-based loan:*** Freshmen: $3932. Undergraduates: $4489. ***Parent loans:*** $247,947 (100% non-need-based). ***Programs:*** Perkins.

WORK-STUDY ***Federal work-study:*** Total amount: $518,279; 220 jobs averaging $2356. ***State or other work-study/employment:*** Total amount: $106,200 (100% need-based). 58 part-time jobs averaging $1831.

APPLYING FOR FINANCIAL AID ***Required financial aid forms:*** FAFSA, institution's own form, noncustodial (divorced/separated) parent's statement. ***Financial aid deadline (priority):*** 2/15. ***Notification date:*** 4/1. Students must reply by 5/1 or within 2 weeks of notification.

CONTACT Bruce Hazam, Director of Financial Aid, College of the Atlantic, 105 Eden Street, Bar Harbor, ME 04609-1198, 207-801-5645 or toll-free 800-528-0025. *Fax:* 207-288-4126. *E-mail:* bhazam@coa.edu.

COLLEGE OF THE HOLY CROSS

Worcester, MA

Tuition & fees: $41,488 **Average undergraduate aid package: $29,917**

ABOUT THE INSTITUTION Independent Roman Catholic (Jesuit), coed. 35 undergraduate majors. Both federal and institutional methodology are used as a basis for awarding need-based institutional aid.

UNDERGRADUATE EXPENSES for 2011–12 ***Comprehensive fee:*** $52,758 includes full-time tuition ($40,910), mandatory fees ($578), and room and board ($11,270). ***College room only:*** $5970. Room and board charges vary according to board plan and housing facility. ***Payment plans:*** Tuition prepayment, installment.

FRESHMAN FINANCIAL AID (Fall 2010, est.) 504 applied for aid; of those 89% were deemed to have need. 94% of freshmen with need received aid; of those 100% had need fully met. ***Average percent of need met:*** 100% (excluding resources awarded to replace EFC). ***Average financial aid package:*** $31,178 (excluding resources awarded to replace EFC). 1% of all full-time freshmen had no need and received non-need-based gift aid.

UNDERGRADUATE FINANCIAL AID (Fall 2010, est.) 1,814 applied for aid; of those 92% were deemed to have need. 95% of undergraduates with need received aid; of those 100% had need fully met. ***Average percent of need met:*** 100% (excluding resources awarded to replace EFC). ***Average financial aid package:*** $29,917 (excluding resources awarded to replace EFC). 1% of all full-time undergraduates had no need and received non-need-based gift aid.

GIFT AID (NEED-BASED) ***Total amount:*** $32,964,427 (9% federal, 3% state, 83% institutional, 5% external sources). ***Receiving aid:*** Freshmen: 47% (339); all full-time undergraduates: 44% (1,248). ***Average award:*** Freshmen: $29,590; Undergraduates: $28,077. ***Scholarships, grants, and awards:*** Federal Pell, FSEOG, state, private, college/university gift aid from institutional funds.

GIFT AID (NON-NEED-BASED) ***Total amount:*** $1,446,419 (100% institutional). ***Receiving aid:*** Freshmen: 1% (5). Undergraduates: 2% (49). ***Average award:*** Freshmen: $29,665. Undergraduates: $31,389. ***Scholarships, grants, and awards by category:*** *Academic interests/achievement:* 28 awards ($834,510 total): general academic interests/achievements, humanities, military science. *Creative arts/performance:* 5 awards ($196,650 total): music. *Special characteristics:* 32 awards ($1,238,895 total): children of faculty/staff. ***Tuition waivers:*** Full or partial for employees or children of employees.

LOANS ***Student loans:*** $11,802,294 (84% need-based, 16% non-need-based). 58% of past graduating class borrowed through all loan programs. *Average indebtedness per student:* $23,662. ***Average need-based loan:*** Freshmen: $4840. Undergraduates: $5313. ***Parent loans:*** $10,120,748 (100% non-need-based). ***Programs:*** Federal Direct (Subsidized and Unsubsidized Stafford, PLUS), Perkins, MEFA Loans.

WORK-STUDY ***Federal work-study:*** Total amount: $1,645,928; 1,035 jobs averaging $1588.

ATHLETIC AWARDS Total amount: $7,111,324 (68% need-based, 32% non-need-based).

APPLYING FOR FINANCIAL AID ***Required financial aid forms:*** FAFSA, CSS Financial Aid PROFILE, noncustodial (divorced/separated) parent's statement, business/farm supplement, parent and student federal income tax forms. ***Financial aid deadline:*** 2/1. ***Notification date:*** 4/1. Students must reply by 5/1.

CONTACT Ms. Lynne Myers, Director of Financial Aid, College of the Holy Cross, One College Street, Worcester, MA 01610-2395, 508-793-2265 or toll-free 800-442-2421. *Fax:* 508-793-2527.

COLLEGE OF THE OZARKS

Point Lookout, MO

Tuition & fees: $430 **Average undergraduate aid package: $16,351**

ABOUT THE INSTITUTION Independent Presbyterian, coed. 62 undergraduate majors. Federal methodology is used as a basis for awarding need-based institutional aid.

UNDERGRADUATE EXPENSES for 2011–12 includes mandatory fees ($430) and room and board ($5600). ***College room only:*** $2750. ***Part-time tuition:*** $295 per credit hour. Part-time tuition and fees vary according to course load. The college guarantees to meet all of the tuition cost for each full-time student by using earnings from its endowment, operation of its own mandatory student work program, accepting student aid grants, gifts and other sources. In effect, each full-time student's Cost of Education (tuition) is met 100 percent by participating in the work program and a combination of private, institutional and federal/state student aid. ***Payment plan:*** Installment.

FRESHMAN FINANCIAL AID (Fall 2009) 340 applied for aid; of those 96% were deemed to have need. 100% of freshmen with need received aid; of those 20% had need fully met. ***Average percent of need met:*** 81% (excluding resources awarded to replace EFC). ***Average financial aid package:*** $14,732 (excluding resources awarded to replace EFC). 14% of all full-time freshmen had no need and received non-need-based gift aid.

UNDERGRADUATE FINANCIAL AID (Fall 2009) 1,445 applied for aid; of those 95% were deemed to have need. 100% of undergraduates with need received aid; of those 31% had need fully met. ***Average percent of need met:*** 85% (excluding resources awarded to replace EFC). ***Average financial aid package:*** $16,351 (excluding resources awarded to replace EFC). 7% of all full-time undergraduates had no need and received non-need-based gift aid.

GIFT AID (NEED-BASED) ***Total amount:*** $18,952,797 (20% federal, 9% state, 69% institutional, 2% external sources). ***Receiving aid:*** Freshmen: 86% (326); all full-time undergraduates: 92% (1,376). ***Average award:*** Freshmen: $11,423; Undergraduates: $12,869. ***Scholarships, grants, and awards:*** Federal Pell, FSEOG, state, private, college/university gift aid from institutional funds.

GIFT AID (NON-NEED-BASED) ***Total amount:*** $2,229,252 (3% federal, 94% institutional, 3% external sources). ***Receiving aid:*** Freshmen: 8% (30). Undergraduates: 13% (193). ***Average award:*** Freshmen: $13,400. Undergraduates: $12,347.

LOANS ***Student loans:*** $395,425 (75% need-based, 25% non-need-based). 11% of past graduating class borrowed through all loan programs. *Average indebtedness per student:* $5389. ***Programs:*** alternative loans.

WORK-STUDY ***Federal work-study:*** Total amount: $3,663,154; 837 jobs averaging $4376. ***State or other work-study/employment:*** Total amount: $1,834,840 (90% need-based, 10% non-need-based). 819 part-time jobs averaging $2240.

ATHLETIC AWARDS Total amount: $237,925 (43% need-based, 57% non-need-based).

APPLYING FOR FINANCIAL AID ***Required financial aid form:*** FAFSA. ***Financial aid deadline (priority):*** 2/15. ***Notification date:*** 7/1.

CONTACT Mrs. Kyla R. McCarty, Director of Financial Aid, College of the Ozarks, PO Box 17, Point Lookout, MO 65726, 417-690-3290 or toll-free 800-222-0525. *Fax:* 417-690-3286.

COLLEGE OF VISUAL ARTS

St. Paul, MN

Tuition & fees: $23,988 **Average undergraduate aid package: $14,826**

ABOUT THE INSTITUTION Independent, coed. 7 undergraduate majors. Federal methodology is used as a basis for awarding need-based institutional aid.

UNDERGRADUATE EXPENSES for 2010–11 ***Tuition:*** full-time $23,488; part-time $1174 per credit. ***Required fees:*** full-time $500; $50 per course. Full-time tuition and fees vary according to course load. Part-time tuition and fees vary according to course load. ***Payment plan:*** Installment.

FRESHMAN FINANCIAL AID (Fall 2009) 36 applied for aid; of those 94% were deemed to have need. 100% of freshmen with need received aid; of those 3% had need fully met. ***Average percent of need met:*** 58% (excluding resources awarded to replace EFC). ***Average financial aid package:*** $15,906 (excluding resources awarded to replace EFC). 6% of all full-time freshmen had no need and received non-need-based gift aid.

UNDERGRADUATE FINANCIAL AID (Fall 2009) 166 applied for aid; of those 92% were deemed to have need. 100% of undergraduates with need received aid; of those 2% had need fully met. ***Average percent of need met:*** 53% (excluding resources awarded to replace EFC). ***Average financial aid package:*** $14,826 (excluding resources awarded to replace EFC). 7% of all full-time undergraduates had no need and received non-need-based gift aid.

GIFT AID (NEED-BASED) ***Total amount:*** $1,511,129 (19% federal, 27% state, 54% institutional). ***Receiving aid:*** Freshmen: 94% (34); all full-time undergraduates: 87% (153). ***Average award:*** Freshmen: $12,507; Undergraduates: $9863. ***Scholarships, grants, and awards:*** Federal Pell, FSEOG, state, private, college/university gift aid from institutional funds.

GIFT AID (NON-NEED-BASED) ***Total amount:*** $141,772 (25% institutional, 75% external sources). ***Receiving aid:*** Freshmen: 8% (3). Undergraduates: 16% (29). ***Average award:*** Freshmen: $5000. Undergraduates: $2431. ***Scholarships, grants, and awards by category:*** *Academic interests/achievement:* general academic interests/achievements. *Creative arts/performance:* art/fine arts. *Special characteristics:* children of faculty/staff. ***Tuition waivers:*** Full or partial for employees or children of employees.

LOANS ***Student loans:*** $1,707,848 (63% need-based, 37% non-need-based). 29% of past graduating class borrowed through all loan programs. *Average indebtedness per student:* $38,402. ***Average need-based loan:*** Freshmen: $3328. Undergraduates: $4488. ***Parent loans:*** $173,798 (72% need-based, 28% non-need-based). ***Programs:*** Federal Direct (Subsidized and Unsubsidized Stafford, PLUS), state, alternative loans.

WORK-STUDY ***Federal work-study:*** Total amount: $27,096; 22 jobs averaging $2000. ***State or other work-study/employment:*** Total amount: $73,679 (86% need-based, 14% non-need-based). 65 part-time jobs averaging $2000.

APPLYING FOR FINANCIAL AID ***Required financial aid forms:*** FAFSA, institution's own form. ***Financial aid deadline:*** 6/1 (priority: 4/1). ***Notification date:*** Continuous beginning 2/15. Students must reply within 4 weeks of notification.

CONTACT David Woodward, Director of Financial Aid, College of Visual Arts, 344 Summit Avenue, St. Paul, MN 55102-2124, 651-757-4021 or toll-free 800-224-1536. *Fax:* 651-757-4010. *E-mail:* dwoodward@cva.edu.

THE COLLEGE OF WILLIAM AND MARY

Williamsburg, VA

Tuition & fees (VA res): $12,188 **Average undergraduate aid package: $15,606**

ABOUT THE INSTITUTION State-supported, coed. 41 undergraduate majors. Federal methodology is used as a basis for awarding need-based institutional aid.

UNDERGRADUATE EXPENSES for 2010–11 ***One-time required fee:*** $157. ***Tuition, state resident:*** full-time $7523; part-time $260 per credit hour. ***Tuition, nonresident:*** full-time $28,547; part-time $920 per credit hour. ***Required fees:*** full-time $4665. ***College room and board:*** $8684; ***Room only:*** $5232. Room and board charges vary according to board plan and housing facility. ***Payment plan:*** Installment.

FRESHMAN FINANCIAL AID (Fall 2009) 906 applied for aid; of those 49% were deemed to have need. 73% of freshmen with need received aid; of those 22% had need fully met. ***Average percent of need met:*** 76% (excluding resources awarded to replace EFC). ***Average financial aid package:*** $14,950 (excluding resources awarded to replace EFC). 2% of all full-time freshmen had no need and received non-need-based gift aid.

UNDERGRADUATE FINANCIAL AID (Fall 2009) 3,005 applied for aid; of those 63% were deemed to have need. 76% of undergraduates with need received aid; of those 23% had need fully met. ***Average percent of need met:*** 79% (excluding resources awarded to replace EFC). ***Average financial aid package:*** $15,606 (excluding resources awarded to replace EFC). 5% of all full-time undergraduates had no need and received non-need-based gift aid.

GIFT AID (NEED-BASED) ***Total amount:*** $15,904,359 (21% federal, 17% state, 62% institutional). ***Receiving aid:*** Freshmen: 23% (325); all full-time undergraduates: 25% (1,443). ***Average award:*** Freshmen: $11,843; Undergraduates: $11,555. ***Scholarships, grants, and awards:*** Federal Pell, FSEOG, state, private, college/university gift aid from institutional funds.

GIFT AID (NON-NEED-BASED) ***Total amount:*** $5,851,239 (8% federal, 58% institutional, 34% external sources). ***Receiving aid:*** Freshmen: 14% (194). Undergraduates: 12% (680). ***Average award:*** Freshmen: $7796. Undergraduates: $5977. ***Scholarships, grants, and awards by category:*** *Academic interests/achievement:* 17 awards ($328,134 total): general academic interests/achievements. *Creative arts/performance:* 58 awards ($51,792 total): music, theater/drama. *Special characteristics:* 161 awards ($1,686,602 total): general special characteristics. ***Tuition waivers:*** Full or partial for senior citizens.

LOANS ***Student loans:*** $14,599,520 (37% need-based, 63% non-need-based). 38% of past graduating class borrowed through all loan programs. *Average indebtedness per student:* $21,367. ***Average need-based loan:*** Freshmen: $3975. Undergraduates: $4467. ***Parent loans:*** $6,056,879 (100% non-need-based). ***Programs:*** Federal Direct (Subsidized and Unsubsidized Stafford, PLUS), Perkins.

WORK-STUDY ***Federal work-study:*** Total amount: $92,665; 98 jobs averaging $960.

ATHLETIC AWARDS Total amount: $5,855,862 (17% need-based, 83% non-need-based).

APPLYING FOR FINANCIAL AID ***Required financial aid form:*** FAFSA. ***Financial aid deadline (priority):*** 3/15. ***Notification date:*** Continuous beginning 3/15. Students must reply by 5/1 or within 2 weeks of notification.

CONTACT Mr. Edward P. Irish, Director of Financial Aid, The College of William and Mary, PO Box 8795, Williamsburg, VA 23187, 757-221-2425. *Fax:* 757-221-2515. *E-mail:* epiris@wm.edu.

THE COLLEGE OF WOOSTER

Wooster, OH

Tuition & fees: $38,290 **Average undergraduate aid package: $29,025**

ABOUT THE INSTITUTION Independent religious, coed. 45 undergraduate majors. Both federal and institutional methodology are used as a basis for awarding need-based institutional aid.

UNDERGRADUATE EXPENSES for 2011–12 ***Comprehensive fee:*** $47,600 includes full-time tuition ($38,000), mandatory fees ($290), and room and board ($9310). ***College room only:*** $4275. Full-time tuition and fees vary according to course load. Room and board charges vary according to board plan and housing facility. Part-time tuition and fees vary according to course load. ***Payment plan:*** Installment.

FRESHMAN FINANCIAL AID (Fall 2010, est.) 461 applied for aid; of those 82% were deemed to have need. 100% of freshmen with need received aid; of those 66% had need fully met. ***Average percent of need met:*** 90% (excluding resources awarded to replace EFC). ***Average financial aid package:*** $30,477 (excluding resources awarded to replace EFC). 38% of all full-time freshmen had no need and received non-need-based gift aid.

UNDERGRADUATE FINANCIAL AID (Fall 2010, est.) 1,368 applied for aid; of those 85% were deemed to have need. 100% of undergraduates with need received aid; of those 54% had need fully met. ***Average percent of need met:*** 86% (excluding resources awarded to replace EFC). ***Average financial aid package:*** $29,025 (excluding resources awarded to replace EFC). 38% of all full-time undergraduates had no need and received non-need-based gift aid.

GIFT AID (NEED-BASED) ***Total amount:*** $26,690,378 (7% federal, 1% state, 90% institutional, 2% external sources). ***Receiving aid:*** Freshmen: 60% (375); all full-time undergraduates: 58% (1,134). ***Average award:*** Freshmen: $24,670; Undergraduates: $23,088. ***Scholarships, grants, and awards:*** Federal Pell, FSEOG, state, private, college/university gift aid from institutional funds.

GIFT AID (NON-NEED-BASED) ***Total amount:*** $13,641,464 (97% institutional, 3% external sources). ***Receiving aid:*** Freshmen: 11% (68). Undergraduates: 8% (163). ***Average award:*** Freshmen: $20,220. Undergraduates: $18,000. ***Scholarships, grants, and awards by category:*** *Academic interests/achievement:* 1,443 awards ($22,439,601 total): general academic interests/achievements. *Creative arts/performance:* 90 awards ($371,000 total): dance, music, theater/drama. *Special achievements/activities:* 200 awards ($1,217,940 total): community service, religious involvement. *Special characteristics:* 97 awards ($2,830,220 total): children of educators, children of faculty/staff, members of minority groups, veterans. ***Tuition waivers:*** Full or partial for employees or children of employees.

LOANS ***Student loans:*** $7,204,591 (69% need-based, 31% non-need-based). 58% of past graduating class borrowed through all loan programs. *Average indebtedness per student:* $25,252. ***Average need-based loan:*** Freshmen: $3315. Undergraduates: $3700. ***Parent loans:*** $4,544,318 (27% need-based, 73% non-need-based). ***Programs:*** Federal Direct (Subsidized and Unsubsidized Stafford, PLUS), Perkins, college/university.

WORK-STUDY ***Federal work-study:*** Total amount: $1,024,924; 727 jobs averaging $1366. ***State or other work-study/employment:*** Total amount: $130,920 (3% need-based, 97% non-need-based). 67 part-time jobs averaging $1954.

APPLYING FOR FINANCIAL AID ***Required financial aid forms:*** FAFSA, institution's own form. ***Financial aid deadline:*** 9/1 (priority: 2/15). ***Notification date:*** Continuous beginning 2/15. Students must reply by 5/1.

CONTACT Dr. David Miller, Director of Financial Aid, The College of Wooster, Flo K. Gault Library, Ground Floor, 1140 Beall Avenue, Wooster, OH 44691, 800-877-3688 or toll-free 800-877-9905. *Fax:* 330-263-2634. *E-mail:* financialaid@wooster.edu.

COLLINS COLLEGE

Tempe, AZ

CONTACT Kari Yearwood, Director of Financial Aid, Collins College, 4750 South 44th Place, Phoenix, AZ 85040, 800-876-7070. *Fax:* 866-553-6597. *E-mail:* fa@collinscollege.edu.

COLORADO CHRISTIAN UNIVERSITY

Lakewood, CO

CONTACT Mr. Steve Woodburn, Director of Financial Aid, Colorado Christian University, 180 South Garrison Street, Lakewood, CO 80226-7499, 303-963-3230 or toll-free 800-44-FAITH. *Fax:* 303-963-3231. *E-mail:* sfs@ccu.edu.

THE COLORADO COLLEGE

Colorado Springs, CO

Tuition & fees: $38,948 **Average undergraduate aid package: $33,298**

ABOUT THE INSTITUTION Independent, coed. 46 undergraduate majors. Both federal and institutional methodology are used as a basis for awarding need-based institutional aid.

UNDERGRADUATE EXPENSES for 2010–11 ***One-time required fee:*** $150. ***Comprehensive fee:*** $48,364 includes full-time tuition ($38,748), mandatory fees ($200), and room and board ($9416). ***College room only:*** $5184. Room and board charges vary according to board plan and housing facility. ***Part-time tuition:*** $6458 per course. Part-time tuition and fees vary according to course load. ***Payment plan:*** Installment.

FRESHMAN FINANCIAL AID (Fall 2010, est.) 235 applied for aid; of those 83% were deemed to have need. 100% of freshmen with need received aid; of those 85% had need fully met. ***Average percent of need met:*** 97% (excluding resources awarded to replace EFC). ***Average financial aid package:*** $35,263 (excluding resources awarded to replace EFC). 7% of all full-time freshmen had no need and received non-need-based gift aid.

UNDERGRADUATE FINANCIAL AID (Fall 2010, est.) 888 applied for aid; of those 84% were deemed to have need. 99% of undergraduates with need received aid; of those 63% had need fully met. ***Average percent of need met:*** 92% (excluding resources awarded to replace EFC). ***Average financial aid package:*** $33,298 (excluding resources awarded to replace EFC). 8% of all full-time undergraduates had no need and received non-need-based gift aid.

GIFT AID (NEED-BASED) ***Total amount:*** $23,752,484 (5% federal, 1% state, 91% institutional, 3% external sources). ***Receiving aid:*** Freshmen: 35% (189); all full-time undergraduates: 35% (722). ***Average award:*** Freshmen: $32,450; Undergraduates: $30,672. ***Scholarships, grants, and awards:*** Federal Pell, FSEOG, state, private, college/university gift aid from institutional funds.

GIFT AID (NON-NEED-BASED) ***Total amount:*** $2,922,220 (65% institutional, 35% external sources). ***Receiving aid:*** Freshmen: 10% (51). Undergraduates: 8% (159). ***Average award:*** Freshmen: $10,416. Undergraduates: $13,573. ***Scholarships, grants, and awards by category:*** *Academic interests/achievement:* 183 awards ($1,900,000 total): biological sciences, general academic interests/achievements, mathematics, physical sciences. ***Tuition waivers:*** Full or partial for employees or children of employees.

LOANS ***Student loans:*** $4,089,372 (55% need-based, 45% non-need-based). 33% of past graduating class borrowed through all loan programs. *Average indebtedness per student:* $18,349. ***Average need-based loan:*** Freshmen: $3163. Undergraduates: $4355. ***Parent loans:*** $2,390,775 (14% need-based, 86% non-need-based). ***Programs:*** Federal Direct (Subsidized and Unsubsidized Stafford, PLUS), Perkins.

WORK-STUDY ***Federal work-study:*** Total amount: $398,820; 225 jobs averaging $1750. ***State or other work-study/employment:*** Total amount: $279,744 (76% need-based, 24% non-need-based). 128 part-time jobs averaging $1664.

ATHLETIC AWARDS Total amount: $1,514,714 (100% non-need-based).

APPLYING FOR FINANCIAL AID ***Required financial aid forms:*** FAFSA, CSS Financial Aid PROFILE, noncustodial (divorced/separated) parent's statement, federal income tax form(s) for parents and student. ***Financial aid deadline:*** 2/15. ***Notification date:*** 3/20. Students must reply by 5/1.

CONTACT Mr. James M. Swanson, Director of Financial Aid, The Colorado College, 14 East Cache La Poudre Street, Colorado Springs, CO 80903-3294, 719-389-6651 or toll-free 800-542-7214. *Fax:* 719-389-6173. *E-mail:* financialaid@coloradocollege.edu.

COLORADO HEIGHTS UNIVERSITY

Denver, CO

CONTACT Financial Aid Office, Colorado Heights University, 3001 South Federal Boulevard, Denver, CO 80236, 303-936-4200.

COLORADO SCHOOL OF MINES

Golden, CO

Tuition & fees (CO res): $13,425 **Average undergraduate aid package: $9004**

ABOUT THE INSTITUTION State-supported, coed. 12 undergraduate majors. Federal methodology is used as a basis for awarding need-based institutional aid.

UNDERGRADUATE EXPENSES for 2010–11 ***Tuition, state resident:*** full-time $11,550; part-time $385 per credit hour. ***Tuition, nonresident:*** full-time $25,980; part-time $866 per credit hour. ***Required fees:*** full-time $1875. Part-time tuition and fees vary according to course load. ***College room and board:*** $8596. Room and board charges vary according to board plan and housing facility. ***Payment plan:*** Installment.

FRESHMAN FINANCIAL AID (Fall 2009) 707 applied for aid; of those 64% were deemed to have need. 100% of freshmen with need received aid; of those 21% had need fully met. ***Average percent of need met:*** 75% (excluding resources awarded to replace EFC). ***Average financial aid package:*** $12,139 (excluding resources awarded to replace EFC). 21% of all full-time freshmen had no need and received non-need-based gift aid.

UNDERGRADUATE FINANCIAL AID (Fall 2009) 2,342 applied for aid; of those 73% were deemed to have need. 99% of undergraduates with need received aid; of those 29% had need fully met. ***Average percent of need met:*** 53% (excluding resources awarded to replace EFC). ***Average financial aid package:*** $9004 (excluding resources awarded to replace EFC). 19% of all full-time undergraduates had no need and received non-need-based gift aid.

GIFT AID (NEED-BASED) ***Total amount:*** $14,474,854 (23% federal, 8% state, 59% institutional, 10% external sources). ***Receiving aid:*** Freshmen: 34% (298); all full-time undergraduates: 35% (1,203). ***Average award:*** Freshmen: $8692; Undergraduates: $7677. ***Scholarships, grants, and awards:*** Federal Pell, FSEOG, state, private, college/university gift aid from institutional funds.

GIFT AID (NON-NEED-BASED) ***Total amount:*** $3,789,221 (79% institutional, 21% external sources). ***Receiving aid:*** Freshmen: 24% (213). Undergraduates: 23% (798). ***Average award:*** Freshmen: $6004. Undergraduates: $4411. ***Scholarships, grants, and awards by category:*** *Academic interests/achievement:* business, computer science, engineering/technologies, general academic interests/achievements, mathematics, military science, physical sciences. ***Tuition waivers:*** Full or partial for employees or children of employees.

LOANS ***Student loans:*** $21,425,480 (73% need-based, 27% non-need-based). 58% of past graduating class borrowed through all loan programs. *Average indebtedness per student:* $28,126. ***Average need-based loan:*** Freshmen: $4329. Undergraduates: $5490. ***Parent loans:*** $4,107,052 (62% need-based, 38% non-need-based). ***Programs:*** Federal Direct (Subsidized and Unsubsidized Stafford, PLUS), Perkins, college/university.

WORK-STUDY ***Federal work-study:*** Total amount: $387,038; jobs available. ***State or other work-study/employment:*** Total amount: $2,221,450 (56% need-based, 44% non-need-based). Part-time jobs available.

ATHLETIC AWARDS Total amount: $1,919,025 (47% need-based, 53% non-need-based).

APPLYING FOR FINANCIAL AID ***Required financial aid forms:*** FAFSA, institution's own form. ***Financial aid deadline (priority):*** 3/1. ***Notification date:*** Continuous beginning 3/1.

CONTACT Jill Robertson, Director of Financial Aid, Colorado School of Mines, 1600 Maple Street, Golden, CO 80401-1887, 303-273-3220 or toll-free 800-446-9488 Ext. 3220 (out-of-state). *Fax:* 303-384-2252. *E-mail:* finaid@mines.edu.

COLORADO STATE UNIVERSITY

Fort Collins, CO

Tuition & fees (CO res): $6985 **Average undergraduate aid package: $11,085**

ABOUT THE INSTITUTION State-supported, coed. 119 undergraduate majors. Federal methodology is used as a basis for awarding need-based institutional aid.

UNDERGRADUATE EXPENSES for 2010–11 ***Tuition, state resident:*** full-time $5256; part-time $262.80 per credit hour. ***Tuition, nonresident:*** full-time $21,366; part-time $1068 per credit hour. ***Required fees:*** full-time $1729; $29.60 per credit hour or $148 per term. Full-time tuition and fees vary according to course load. Part-time tuition and fees vary according to course load. ***College room and board:*** $8744; ***Room only:*** $4322. Room and board charges vary according to board plan and housing facility.

FRESHMAN FINANCIAL AID (Fall 2009) 3,340 applied for aid; of those 58% were deemed to have need. 100% of freshmen with need received aid; of those 46% had need fully met. ***Average percent of need met:*** 78% (excluding resources awarded to replace EFC). ***Average financial aid package:*** $10,856 (excluding resources awarded to replace EFC). 14% of all full-time freshmen had no need and received non-need-based gift aid.

UNDERGRADUATE FINANCIAL AID (Fall 2009) 13,383 applied for aid; of those 68% were deemed to have need. 100% of undergraduates with need received aid; of those 44% had need fully met. ***Average percent of need met:*** 77% (excluding resources awarded to replace EFC). ***Average financial aid package:*** $11,085 (excluding resources awarded to replace EFC). 10% of all full-time undergraduates had no need and received non-need-based gift aid.

GIFT AID (NEED-BASED) ***Total amount:*** $46,329,863 (44% federal, 15% state, 33% institutional, 8% external sources). ***Receiving aid:*** Freshmen: 37% (1,555); all full-time undergraduates: 36% (7,015). ***Average award:*** Freshmen: $8313; Undergraduates: $6626. ***Scholarships, grants, and awards:*** Federal Pell, FSEOG, state, private, college/university gift aid from institutional funds.

GIFT AID (NON-NEED-BASED) ***Total amount:*** $9,410,891 (2% federal, 1% state, 72% institutional, 25% external sources). ***Average award:*** Freshmen: $3994. Undergraduates: $3539. ***Scholarships, grants, and awards by category:*** *Academic interests/achievement:* 11,921 awards ($19,356,947 total): general academic interests/achievements. *Creative arts/performance:* 454 awards ($448,600 total): art/fine arts, creative writing, dance, music, theater/drama. *Special achievements/activities:* 208 awards ($538,426 total): general special achievements/activities. *Special characteristics:* 385 awards ($925,498 total): children of faculty/staff, first-generation college students. ***Tuition waivers:*** Full or partial for employees or children of employees.

LOANS ***Student loans:*** $74,848,165 (73% need-based, 27% non-need-based). 60% of past graduating class borrowed through all loan programs. *Average indebtedness per student:* $21,224. ***Average need-based loan:*** Freshmen: $5303. Undergraduates: $6906. ***Parent loans:*** $33,933,370 (57% need-based, 43% non-need-based). ***Programs:*** Federal Direct (Subsidized and Unsubsidized Stafford, PLUS), Perkins, alternative loans.

WORK-STUDY ***Federal work-study:*** Total amount: $817,404; 419 jobs averaging $2063. ***State or other work-study/employment:*** Total amount: $2,402,087 (75% need-based, 25% non-need-based). 997 part-time jobs averaging $1823.

ATHLETIC AWARDS Total amount: $5,834,450 (24% need-based, 76% non-need-based).

APPLYING FOR FINANCIAL AID ***Required financial aid form:*** FAFSA. ***Financial aid deadline (priority):*** 3/1. ***Notification date:*** Continuous beginning 3/1.

CONTACT Office of Student Financial Services, Colorado State University, Room 103, Centennial Hall, Fort Collins, CO 80523-8024, 970-491-6321. *E-mail:* sfs@colostate.edu.

COLORADO STATE UNIVERSITY–PUEBLO

Pueblo, CO

Tuition & fees (CO res): $5615 **Average undergraduate aid package: $8828**

ABOUT THE INSTITUTION State-supported, coed. 26 undergraduate majors. Federal methodology is used as a basis for awarding need-based institutional aid.

UNDERGRADUATE EXPENSES for 2010–11 ***Tuition, state resident:*** full-time $4068; part-time $161.65 per credit hour. ***Tuition, nonresident:*** full-time $14,141; part-time $565 per credit hour. ***Required fees:*** full-time $1547; $51.55 per credit hour. Full-time tuition and fees vary according to course load. Part-time tuition and fees vary according to course load. ***College room and board:*** $8660; ***Room only:*** $5000. Room and board charges vary according to board plan. ***Payment plans:*** Installment, deferred payment.

FRESHMAN FINANCIAL AID (Fall 2010, est.) 748 applied for aid; of those 80% were deemed to have need. 99% of freshmen with need received aid; of those 5% had need fully met. ***Average percent of need met:*** 56% (excluding resources awarded to replace EFC). ***Average financial aid package:*** $8132 (excluding resources awarded to replace EFC). 6% of all full-time freshmen had no need and received non-need-based gift aid.

UNDERGRADUATE FINANCIAL AID (Fall 2010, est.) 3,223 applied for aid; of those 85% were deemed to have need. 99% of undergraduates with need received aid; of those 5% had need fully met. ***Average percent of need met:*** 56% (excluding resources awarded to replace EFC). ***Average financial aid package:*** $8828 (excluding resources awarded to replace EFC). 5% of all full-time undergraduates had no need and received non-need-based gift aid.

GIFT AID (NEED-BASED) ***Total amount:*** $15,233,678 (69% federal, 15% state, 11% institutional, 5% external sources). ***Receiving aid:*** Freshmen: 63% (512); all full-time undergraduates: 63% (2,346). ***Average award:*** Freshmen: $6426; Undergraduates: $6344. ***Scholarships, grants, and awards:*** Federal Pell, FSEOG, state, private, college/university gift aid from institutional funds, Academic Competitiveness Grants, National SMART Grants, TEACH Grants.

GIFT AID (NON-NEED-BASED) ***Total amount:*** $926,581 (1% federal, 3% state, 63% institutional, 33% external sources). ***Receiving aid:*** Freshmen: 2% (16). Undergraduates: 2% (68). ***Average award:*** Freshmen: $2553. Undergraduates: $2482. ***Scholarships, grants, and awards by category:*** *Academic interests/achievement:* 311 awards ($746,107 total): biological sciences, business, communication, computer science, education, engineering/technologies, English, foreign languages, general academic interests/achievements, health fields, mathematics, physical sciences, premedicine, social sciences. *Creative arts/performance:* 49 awards ($83,095 total): applied art and design, art/fine arts, cinema/film/broadcasting, journalism/publications, music. *Special achievements/activities:* 63 awards ($56,150 total): community service, general special achievements/activities, leadership. *Special characteristics:* 599 awards ($1,571,934 total): children and siblings of alumni, children of faculty/staff, ethnic background, first-generation college students, general special characteristics, handicapped students, international students, out-of-state students. ***Tuition waivers:*** Full or partial for employees or children of employees, senior citizens.

LOANS ***Student loans:*** $20,315,098 (79% need-based, 21% non-need-based). 64% of past graduating class borrowed through all loan programs. *Average indebtedness per student:* $20,141. ***Average need-based loan:*** Freshmen: $2982. Undergraduates: $3555. ***Parent loans:*** $1,878,252 (37% need-based, 63% non-need-based). ***Programs:*** Federal Direct (Subsidized and Unsubsidized Stafford, PLUS), Perkins, Federal Nursing.

WORK-STUDY ***Federal work-study:*** Total amount: $443,039; 215 jobs averaging $2061. ***State or other work-study/employment:*** Total amount: $769,279 (67% need-based, 33% non-need-based). 281 part-time jobs averaging $2738.

ATHLETIC AWARDS Total amount: $1,126,439 (61% need-based, 39% non-need-based).

APPLYING FOR FINANCIAL AID ***Required financial aid forms:*** FAFSA, institution's own form. ***Financial aid deadline (priority):*** 3/1. ***Notification date:*** Continuous beginning 3/10. Students must reply within 3 weeks of notification.

CONTACT Sean McGivney, Director of Student Financial Services, Colorado State University–Pueblo, 2200 Bonforte Boulevard, Pueblo, CO 81001-4901, 719-549-2753. *Fax:* 719-549-2088.

COLORADO TECHNICAL UNIVERSITY COLORADO SPRINGS

Colorado Springs, CO

CONTACT Jacqueline Harris, Senior Director of Student Finance Services, Colorado Technical University Colorado Springs, 4435 North Chestnut Street, Colorado Springs, CO 80907-3896, 719-598-0200. *Fax:* 719-598-3740.

COLORADO TECHNICAL UNIVERSITY DENVER

Greenwood Village, CO

CONTACT Ms. Natalie Dietsch, Financial Aid Manager, Colorado Technical University Denver, 5775 Denver Tech Center Boulevard, Suite 100, Greenwood Village, CO 80111, 303-694-6600. *Fax:* 303-694-6673.

COLORADO TECHNICAL UNIVERSITY NORTH KANSAS CITY

North Kansas City, MO

CONTACT Financial Aid Office, Colorado Technical University North Kansas City, 520 East 19th Avenue, North Kansas City, MO 64116, 816-472-7400.

COLORADO TECHNICAL UNIVERSITY SIOUX FALLS

Sioux Falls, SD

CONTACT Vikki Van Hull, Financial Aid Officer, Colorado Technical University Sioux Falls, 3901 West 59th Street, Sioux Falls, SD 57108, 605-361-0200 Ext. 140. *Fax:* 605-361-5954. *E-mail:* vvanhull@sf.coloradotech.edu.

COLUMBIA CENTRO UNIVERSITARIO

Yauco, PR

CONTACT Financial Aid Office, Columbia Centro Universitario, Calle Betances #3, Box 3062, Yauco, PR 00698, 787-856-0945.

COLUMBIA COLLEGE

Columbia, MO

Tuition & fees: $16,532 **Average undergraduate aid package: $13,965**

ABOUT THE INSTITUTION Independent religious, coed. 38 undergraduate majors. Federal methodology is used as a basis for awarding need-based institutional aid.

UNDERGRADUATE EXPENSES for 2011–12 ***Comprehensive fee:*** $22,786 includes full-time tuition ($16,532) and room and board ($6254). ***College room only:*** $3892. Full-time tuition and fees vary according to class time and course load. Room and board charges vary according to board plan. ***Part-time tuition:*** $411 per credit hour. Part-time tuition and fees vary according to class time, course load, and location. ***Payment plans:*** Installment, deferred payment.

FRESHMAN FINANCIAL AID (Fall 2009) 136 applied for aid; of those 88% were deemed to have need. 99% of freshmen with need received aid. ***Average percent of need met:*** 27% (excluding resources awarded to replace EFC). ***Average financial aid package:*** $13,498 (excluding resources awarded to replace EFC). 22% of all full-time freshmen had no need and received non-need-based gift aid.

UNDERGRADUATE FINANCIAL AID (Fall 2009) 617 applied for aid; of those 89% were deemed to have need. 98% of undergraduates with need received aid. ***Average percent of need met:*** 31% (excluding resources awarded to replace EFC). ***Average financial aid package:*** $13,965 (excluding resources awarded to replace EFC). 21% of all full-time undergraduates had no need and received non-need-based gift aid.

GIFT AID (NEED-BASED) ***Total amount:*** $2,553,589 (63% federal, 34% state, 3% institutional). ***Receiving aid:*** Freshmen: 44% (72); all full-time undergraduates: 43% (368). ***Average award:*** Freshmen: $4358; Undergraduates: $4609. ***Scholarships, grants, and awards:*** Federal Pell, FSEOG, state, private.

GIFT AID (NON-NEED-BASED) ***Total amount:*** $3,267,761 (1% state, 90% institutional, 9% external sources). ***Receiving aid:*** Freshmen: 59% (97). Undergraduates: 42% (352). ***Average award:*** Freshmen: $9068. Undergraduates: $10,145. ***Scholarships, grants, and awards by category:*** *Academic interests/achievement:* 451 awards ($3,935,772 total): biological sciences, business, education, English, general academic interests/achievements, humanities, mathematics, physical sciences, religion/biblical studies, social sciences. *Creative arts/performance:* 16 awards ($11,850 total): art/fine arts, creative writing, music. *Special achievements/activities:* 46 awards ($43,500 total): leadership. *Special characteristics:* 162 awards ($701,651 total): children and siblings of alumni, children of current students, children of educators, children of faculty/staff, first-generation college students, international students, local/state students, parents of current students, previous college experience, religious affiliation, siblings of current students, spouses of current students, veterans. ***Tuition waivers:*** Full or partial for children of alumni, employees or children of employees, senior citizens.

LOANS ***Student loans:*** $4,200,923 (45% need-based, 55% non-need-based). 63% of past graduating class borrowed through all loan programs. *Average indebtedness per student:* $14,989. ***Average need-based loan:*** Freshmen: $3024. Undergraduates: $3981. ***Parent loans:*** $614,814 (100% non-need-based). ***Programs:*** Federal Direct (Subsidized and Unsubsidized Stafford, PLUS).

WORK-STUDY ***Federal work-study:*** Total amount: $243,627; 139 jobs averaging $1753. ***State or other work-study/employment:*** Total amount: $294,600 (100% non-need-based). 218 part-time jobs averaging $1351.

ATHLETIC AWARDS Total amount: $1,062,483 (100% non-need-based).

APPLYING FOR FINANCIAL AID ***Required financial aid form:*** FAFSA. ***Financial aid deadline (priority):*** 3/1. ***Notification date:*** Continuous beginning 3/1.

CONTACT Sharon Abernathy, Director of Financial Aid, Columbia College, 1001 Rogers Street, Columbia, MO 65216-0002, 573-875-7390 or toll-free 800-231-2391 Ext. 7366. *Fax:* 573-875-7452. *E-mail:* saabernathy@ccis.edu.

COLUMBIA COLLEGE
Caguas, PR

ABOUT THE INSTITUTION Proprietary, coed. 7 undergraduate majors.

GIFT AID (NEED-BASED) ***Scholarships, grants, and awards:*** Federal Pell, FSEOG, state, college/university gift aid from institutional funds.

GIFT AID (NON-NEED-BASED) ***Scholarships, grants, and awards by category:*** *Academic interests/achievement:* general academic interests/achievements.

WORK-STUDY ***Federal work-study:*** Total amount: $59,906; 61 jobs averaging $982.

APPLYING FOR FINANCIAL AID ***Required financial aid forms:*** FAFSA, institution's own form.

CONTACT Financial Aid Officer, Columbia College, Carr 183, Km 1.7, PO Box 8517, Caguas, PR 00726, 787-743-4041 Ext. 244 or toll-free 800-981-4877 Ext. 239 (in-state). *Fax:* 787-744-7031.

COLUMBIA COLLEGE
Columbia, SC

CONTACT Anita Kaminer Elliott, Director of Financial Aid, Columbia College, 1301 Columbia College Drive, Columbia, SC 29203-5998, 803-786-3612 or toll-free 800-277-1301. *Fax:* 803-786-3560.

COLUMBIA COLLEGE CHICAGO
Chicago, IL

ABOUT THE INSTITUTION Independent, coed. 40 undergraduate majors.

GIFT AID (NEED-BASED) ***Scholarships, grants, and awards:*** Federal Pell, FSEOG, state, private, college/university gift aid from institutional funds.

GIFT AID (NON-NEED-BASED) ***Scholarships, grants, and awards by category:*** *Academic interests/achievement:* business, communication, education, general academic interests/achievements. *Creative arts/performance:* applied art and design, art/fine arts, cinema/film/broadcasting, creative writing, dance, journalism/publications, music, performing arts, theater/drama. *Special achievements/activities:* leadership. *Special characteristics:* children of faculty/staff, handicapped students.

LOANS ***Programs:*** Federal Direct (Subsidized and Unsubsidized Stafford, PLUS).

WORK-STUDY Federal work-study jobs available. ***State or other work-study/employment:*** Part-time jobs available.

APPLYING FOR FINANCIAL AID ***Required financial aid forms:*** FAFSA, institution's own form.

CONTACT Ms. Jennifer Waters, Executive Director of Student Financial Services, Columbia College Chicago, 600 South Michigan Avenue, Chicago, IL 60605-1996, 312-369-7831. *Fax:* 312-986-7008. *E-mail:* jwaters@colum.edu.

COLUMBIA COLLEGE HOLLYWOOD
Tarzana, CA

ABOUT THE INSTITUTION Independent, coed. ***Awards:*** associate and bachelor's degrees. 5 undergraduate majors. ***Total enrollment:*** 301. Undergraduates: 301.

GIFT AID (NEED-BASED) ***Scholarships, grants, and awards:*** Federal Pell, FSEOG, state, private.

LOANS ***Programs:*** Federal Direct (Subsidized and Unsubsidized Stafford, PLUS), private loans.

WORK-STUDY ***Federal work-study:*** Total amount: $20,000; 10 jobs averaging $2000.

APPLYING FOR FINANCIAL AID ***Required financial aid forms:*** FAFSA, institution's own form.

CONTACT Mr. Jan Hastings, Financial Aid Administrator, Columbia College Hollywood, 18618 Oxnard Street, Tarzana, CA 91356, 818-401-1030 or toll-free 800-785-0585 (in-state). *Fax:* 818-345-8660. *E-mail:* finaid@columbiacollege.edu.

COLUMBIA INTERNATIONAL UNIVERSITY
Columbia, SC

Tuition & fees: $17,395 **Average undergraduate aid package: $16,042**

ABOUT THE INSTITUTION Independent nondenominational, coed. 15 undergraduate majors. Federal methodology is used as a basis for awarding need-based institutional aid.

UNDERGRADUATE EXPENSES for 2010–11 ***Comprehensive fee:*** $23,805 includes full-time tuition ($16,850), mandatory fees ($545), and room and board ($6410). Full-time tuition and fees vary according to course load. Room and board charges vary according to board plan. ***Part-time tuition:*** $695 per credit. ***Part-time fees:*** $272.50 per term. Part-time tuition and fees vary according to course load. ***Payment plan:*** Installment.

FRESHMAN FINANCIAL AID (Fall 2009) 99 applied for aid; of those 100% were deemed to have need. 100% of freshmen with need received aid; of those 5% had need fully met. ***Average percent of need met:*** 100% (excluding resources awarded to replace EFC). ***Average financial aid package:*** $16,088 (excluding resources awarded to replace EFC). 24% of all full-time freshmen had no need and received non-need-based gift aid.

UNDERGRADUATE FINANCIAL AID (Fall 2009) 433 applied for aid; of those 95% were deemed to have need. 100% of undergraduates with need received aid; of those 6% had need fully met. ***Average percent of need met:*** 72% (excluding resources awarded to replace EFC). ***Average financial aid package:*** $16,042 (excluding resources awarded to replace EFC). 12% of all full-time undergraduates had no need and received non-need-based gift aid.

GIFT AID (NEED-BASED) ***Total amount:*** $1,916,852 (58% federal, 27% state, 15% institutional). ***Receiving aid:*** Freshmen: 64% (65); all full-time undergraduates: 63% (317). ***Scholarships, grants, and awards:*** Federal Pell, FSEOG, state, private, college/university gift aid from institutional funds.

GIFT AID (NON-NEED-BASED) ***Total amount:*** $3,162,850 (16% state, 78% institutional, 6% external sources). ***Receiving aid:*** Undergraduates: 80% (404). ***Average award:*** Freshmen: $6242. ***Scholarships, grants, and awards by category:*** *Academic interests/achievement:* 318 awards ($1,389,452 total): business, communication, education, English, general academic interests/achievements, international studies, religion/biblical studies. *Creative arts/performance:* 1 award ($3000 total): music, performing arts. *Special achievements/activities:* 74 awards ($109,619 total): general special achievements/activities, leadership. *Special characteristics:* 229 awards ($212,695 total): children and siblings of alumni, ethnic background, international students, married students, relatives of clergy, religious affiliation, spouses of current students, veterans, veterans' children. ***Tuition waivers:*** Full or partial for employees or children of employees.

LOANS ***Student loans:*** $2,607,209 (46% need-based, 54% non-need-based). 55% of past graduating class borrowed through all loan programs. *Average indebtedness per student:* $21,057. ***Average need-based loan:*** Freshmen: $1182. Undergraduates: $3966. ***Parent loans:*** $388,174 (100% non-need-based). ***Programs:*** Federal Direct (Subsidized and Unsubsidized Stafford, PLUS).

WORK-STUDY ***Federal work-study:*** Total amount: $102,455; 67 jobs averaging $2000. ***State or other work-study/employment:*** Total amount: $434,850 (100% non-need-based). 274 part-time jobs averaging $2000.

APPLYING FOR FINANCIAL AID ***Required financial aid forms:*** FAFSA, institution's own form, state aid form. ***Financial aid deadline (priority):*** 2/25. ***Notification date:*** Continuous beginning 3/1. Students must reply by 5/1.

CONTACT Mrs. Melissa Chambers, Financial Aid Office Manager, Columbia International University, 7435 Monticello Road, Columbia, SC 29203, 800-777-2227 Ext. 5036 or toll-free 800-777-2227 Ext. 3024. *Fax:* 803-223-2505. *E-mail:* mchambers@ciu.edu.

COLUMBIA JUNIOR COLLEGE
Columbia, SC

See South University.

COLUMBIA UNIVERSITY
New York, NY

Tuition & fees: $41,160 **Average undergraduate aid package: $40,937**

ABOUT THE INSTITUTION Independent, coed. 78 undergraduate majors. Both federal and institutional methodology are used as a basis for awarding need-based institutional aid.

UNDERGRADUATE EXPENSES for 2010–11 ***Comprehensive fee:*** $51,730 includes full-time tuition ($41,160) and room and board ($10,570).

FRESHMAN FINANCIAL AID (Fall 2010, est.) 909 applied for aid; of those 82% were deemed to have need. 100% of freshmen with need received aid; of those 100% had need fully met. ***Average percent of need met:*** 100% (excluding resources awarded to replace EFC). ***Average financial aid package:*** $40,259 (excluding resources awarded to replace EFC).

UNDERGRADUATE FINANCIAL AID (Fall 2010, est.) 3,367 applied for aid; of those 90% were deemed to have need. 100% of undergraduates with need received aid; of those 100% had need fully met. ***Average percent of need met:*** 100% (excluding resources awarded to replace EFC). ***Average financial aid package:*** $40,937 (excluding resources awarded to replace EFC).

GIFT AID (NEED-BASED) ***Total amount:*** $113,744,963 (7% federal, 1% state, 91% institutional, 1% external sources). ***Receiving aid:*** Freshmen: 52% (726); all full-time undergraduates: 50% (2,961). ***Average award:*** Freshmen: $38,544; Undergraduates: $38,356. ***Scholarships, grants, and awards:*** Federal Pell, FSEOG, state, private, college/university gift aid from institutional funds.

GIFT AID (NON-NEED-BASED) ***Total amount:*** $212,159 (35% federal, 15% state, 50% external sources). ***Receiving aid:*** Freshmen: 1% (20). Undergraduates: 1% (87).

LOANS ***Student loans:*** $4,523,006 (44% need-based, 56% non-need-based). ***Average need-based loan:*** Freshmen: $801. Undergraduates: $796. ***Parent loans:*** $5,771,722 (3% need-based, 97% non-need-based). ***Programs:*** Perkins, alternative loans.

WORK-STUDY ***Federal work-study:*** Total amount: $4,299,004; jobs available. ***State or other work-study/employment:*** Total amount: $2,470,503 (29% need-based, 71% non-need-based). Part-time jobs available.

APPLYING FOR FINANCIAL AID ***Required financial aid forms:*** FAFSA, CSS Financial Aid PROFILE, noncustodial (divorced/separated) parent's statement, federal income tax forms (student and parent). ***Financial aid deadline:*** 3/1. ***Notification date:*** 4/1. Students must reply by 5/1.

CONTACT Kathryn Tuman, Director of Financial Aid, Columbia University, 100 Hamilton Hall, MC 2802, 1130 Amsterdam Avenue, New York, NY 10027, 212-854-3711. *Fax:* 212-854-5353. *E-mail:* kat56@columbia.edu.

COLUMBIA UNIVERSITY, SCHOOL OF GENERAL STUDIES

New York, NY

Tuition & fees: $39,900 **Average undergraduate aid package: N/A**

ABOUT THE INSTITUTION Independent, coed. 77 undergraduate majors. Both federal and institutional methodology are used as a basis for awarding need-based institutional aid.

UNDERGRADUATE EXPENSES for 2010–11 ***One-time required fee:*** $230. ***Comprehensive fee:*** $52,860 includes full-time tuition ($39,900) and room and board ($12,960). ***College room only:*** $8775. Full-time tuition and fees vary according to course load, program, and student level. Room and board charges vary according to board plan and housing facility. ***Part-time tuition:*** $1330 per credit hour. Part-time tuition and fees vary according to course load, program, and student level. ***Payment plans:*** Tuition prepayment, installment.

GIFT AID (NEED-BASED) ***Total amount:*** $13,725,033 (30% federal, 2% state, 67% institutional, 1% external sources). ***Scholarships, grants, and awards:*** Federal Pell, FSEOG, state, private, college/university gift aid from institutional funds.

GIFT AID (NON-NEED-BASED) ***Total amount:*** $2,162,485 (7% federal, 92% institutional, 1% external sources). ***Scholarships, grants, and awards by category:*** *Academic interests/achievement:* general academic interests/achievements. ***Tuition waivers:*** Full or partial for employees or children of employees.

LOANS ***Student loans:*** $17,701,870 (94% need-based, 6% non-need-based). ***Parent loans:*** $822,624 (79% need-based, 21% non-need-based). ***Programs:*** Perkins, college/university.

WORK-STUDY ***Federal work-study:*** Total amount: $601,972; jobs available.

APPLYING FOR FINANCIAL AID ***Required financial aid forms:*** FAFSA, institution's own form. ***Financial aid deadline:*** 6/1 (priority: 6/1). ***Notification date:*** Continuous. Students must reply within 3 weeks of notification.

CONTACT Mr. Skip Bailey, Director of Educational Financing, Columbia University, School of General Studies, 408 Lewisohn Hall, 2970 Broadway, New York, NY 10027, 212-854-2772 or toll-free 800-895-1169 (out-of-state). *Fax:* 212-854-6316. *E-mail:* gs_financial_aid@columbia.edu.

COLUMBUS COLLEGE OF ART & DESIGN

Columbus, OH

Tuition & fees: $25,824 **Average undergraduate aid package: $17,684**

ABOUT THE INSTITUTION Independent, coed. 7 undergraduate majors. Federal methodology is used as a basis for awarding need-based institutional aid.

UNDERGRADUATE EXPENSES for 2010–11 ***Comprehensive fee:*** $35,234 includes full-time tuition ($24,864), mandatory fees ($960), and room and board ($9410). Full-time tuition and fees vary according to course load. Room and board charges vary according to housing facility and student level. ***Part-time tuition:*** $1036 per credit hour. ***Part-time fees:*** $180 per term. Part-time tuition and fees vary according to course load. ***Payment plans:*** Installment, deferred payment.

FRESHMAN FINANCIAL AID (Fall 2010, est.) 298 applied for aid; of those 94% were deemed to have need. 100% of freshmen with need received aid; of those 10% had need fully met. ***Average percent of need met:*** 65% (excluding resources awarded to replace EFC). ***Average financial aid package:*** $20,218 (excluding resources awarded to replace EFC). 14% of all full-time freshmen had no need and received non-need-based gift aid.

UNDERGRADUATE FINANCIAL AID (Fall 2010, est.) 1,217 applied for aid; of those 91% were deemed to have need. 100% of undergraduates with need received aid; of those 11% had need fully met. ***Average percent of need met:*** 60% (excluding resources awarded to replace EFC). ***Average financial aid package:*** $17,684 (excluding resources awarded to replace EFC). 13% of all full-time undergraduates had no need and received non-need-based gift aid.

GIFT AID (NEED-BASED) ***Total amount:*** $13,961,239 (19% federal, 4% state, 75% institutional, 2% external sources). ***Receiving aid:*** Freshmen: 84% (278); all full-time undergraduates: 81% (1,100). ***Average award:*** Freshmen: $16,542; Undergraduates: $12,565. ***Scholarships, grants, and awards:*** Federal Pell, FSEOG, state, private, college/university gift aid from institutional funds.

GIFT AID (NON-NEED-BASED) ***Total amount:*** $1,945,152 (97% institutional, 3% external sources). ***Receiving aid:*** Freshmen: 5% (16). Undergraduates: 4% (54). ***Average award:*** Freshmen: $10,506. Undergraduates: $8908. ***Scholarships, grants, and awards by category:*** *Creative arts/performance:* art/fine arts. *Special characteristics:* children of educators, children of faculty/staff, local/state students. ***Tuition waivers:*** Full or partial for employees or children of employees.

LOANS ***Student loans:*** $9,497,644 (79% need-based, 21% non-need-based). 75% of past graduating class borrowed through all loan programs. *Average indebtedness per student:* $37,355. ***Average need-based loan:*** Freshmen: $4188. Undergraduates: $5395. ***Parent loans:*** $5,249,969 (76% need-based, 24% non-need-based). ***Programs:*** Federal Direct (Subsidized and Unsubsidized Stafford, PLUS), Perkins, state.

WORK-STUDY ***Federal work-study:*** Total amount: $598,203; 157 jobs averaging $3150. ***State or other work-study/employment:*** 340 part-time jobs averaging $3075.

APPLYING FOR FINANCIAL AID ***Required financial aid forms:*** FAFSA, institution's own form, federal income tax form(s), verification statement. ***Financial aid deadline (priority):*** 3/1. ***Notification date:*** 3/15. Students must reply within 2 weeks of notification.

CONTACT Mrs. Anna Marie Schofield, Director of Financial Aid, Columbus College of Art & Design, 60 Cleveland Avenue, Columbus, OH 43215-1758, 614-224-9101 Ext. 3274 or toll-free 877-997-2223. *Fax:* 614-222-4034. *E-mail:* aschofield@ccad.edu.

COLUMBUS STATE UNIVERSITY

Columbus, GA

Tuition & fees (GA res): $5896 **Average undergraduate aid package: $8501**

ABOUT THE INSTITUTION State-supported, coed. 40 undergraduate majors. Federal methodology is used as a basis for awarding need-based institutional aid.

UNDERGRADUATE EXPENSES for 2010–11 ***Tuition, state resident:*** full-time $4596; part-time $154 per semester hour. ***Tuition, nonresident:*** full-time $16,572; part-time $553 per credit hour. ***Required fees:*** full-time $1300. ***College room and board:*** $7296. Room and board charges vary according to board plan.

FRESHMAN FINANCIAL AID (Fall 2010, est.) 961 applied for aid; of those 78% were deemed to have need. 99% of freshmen with need received aid; of those

25% had need fully met. ***Average percent of need met:*** 78% (excluding resources awarded to replace EFC). ***Average financial aid package:*** $8575 (excluding resources awarded to replace EFC). 3% of all full-time freshmen had no need and received non-need-based gift aid.

UNDERGRADUATE FINANCIAL AID (Fall 2010, est.) 4,019 applied for aid; of those 80% were deemed to have need. 98% of undergraduates with need received aid; of those 30% had need fully met. ***Average percent of need met:*** 78% (excluding resources awarded to replace EFC). ***Average financial aid package:*** $8501 (excluding resources awarded to replace EFC). 3% of all full-time undergraduates had no need and received non-need-based gift aid.

GIFT AID (NEED-BASED) ***Total amount:*** $14,352,488 (100% federal). ***Receiving aid:*** Freshmen: 49% (528); all full-time undergraduates: 47% (2,340). ***Average award:*** Freshmen: $4850; Undergraduates: $4862. ***Scholarships, grants, and awards:*** Federal Pell, FSEOG, state, private, college/university gift aid from institutional funds.

GIFT AID (NON-NEED-BASED) ***Total amount:*** $11,743,226 (91% state, 5% institutional, 4% external sources). ***Receiving aid:*** Freshmen: 35% (377). Undergraduates: 22% (1,079). ***Average award:*** Freshmen: $1593. Undergraduates: $1681. ***Scholarships, grants, and awards by category:*** *Academic interests/achievement:* 59 awards ($89,767 total): biological sciences, business, communication, computer science, education, English, general academic interests/achievements, health fields, humanities, international studies, mathematics, military science, physical sciences. *Creative arts/performance:* 145 awards ($289,933 total): art/fine arts, dance, music, performing arts, theater/drama. *Special achievements/activities:* 98 awards ($120,348 total): cheerleading/drum major, community service, general special achievements/activities, leadership. ***Tuition waivers:*** Full or partial for employees or children of employees, senior citizens.

LOANS ***Student loans:*** $27,576,666 (43% need-based, 57% non-need-based). 63% of past graduating class borrowed through all loan programs. *Average indebtedness per student:* $21,486. ***Average need-based loan:*** Freshmen: $3267. Undergraduates: $3912. ***Parent loans:*** $1,088,240 (100% non-need-based). ***Programs:*** Federal Direct (Subsidized and Unsubsidized Stafford, PLUS), Perkins, Federal Nursing, state, college/university.

WORK-STUDY ***Federal work-study:*** Total amount: $254,118; 73 jobs averaging $1953.

ATHLETIC AWARDS Total amount: $1,003,299 (100% non-need-based).

APPLYING FOR FINANCIAL AID ***Required financial aid form:*** FAFSA. ***Financial aid deadline (priority):*** 5/1. ***Notification date:*** Continuous beginning 5/1.

CONTACT Ms. Janis Bowles, Director of Financial Aid, Columbus State University, 4225 University Avenue, Columbus, GA 31907-5645, 706-507-8800 or toll-free 866-264-2035. *Fax:* 706-568-2230. *E-mail:* bowles_janis@colstate.edu.

CONCEPTION SEMINARY COLLEGE

Conception, MO

CONTACT Br. Justin Hernandez, PhD, Financial Aid Director, Conception Seminary College, PO Box 502, Conception, MO 64433-0502, 660-944-2851. *Fax:* 660-944-2829. *E-mail:* justin@conception.edu.

CONCORDIA COLLEGE

Selma, AL

CONTACT Mrs. T. H. Bridges, Financial Aid Office, Concordia College, 1804 Green Street, Selma, AL 36701, 334-874-5700. *Fax:* 334-874-3728. *E-mail:* tbridges@concordiaselma.edu.

CONCORDIA COLLEGE

Moorhead, MN

Tuition & fees: $29,360 **Average undergraduate aid package: $21,679**

ABOUT THE INSTITUTION Independent religious, coed. 74 undergraduate majors. Federal methodology is used as a basis for awarding need-based institutional aid.

UNDERGRADUATE EXPENSES for 2011–12 ***Comprehensive fee:*** $36,150 includes full-time tuition ($29,150), mandatory fees ($210), and room and board ($6790). ***College room only:*** $3000. Full-time tuition and fees vary according to course load and degree level. Room and board charges vary according to board plan and housing facility. ***Part-time tuition:*** $1145 per credit hour. Part-time tuition and fees vary according to course load and degree level. ***Payment plan:*** Installment.

FRESHMAN FINANCIAL AID (Fall 2009) 653 applied for aid; of those 82% were deemed to have need. 100% of freshmen with need received aid; of those 21% had need fully met. ***Average percent of need met:*** 92% (excluding resources awarded to replace EFC). ***Average financial aid package:*** $21,188 (excluding resources awarded to replace EFC). 25% of all full-time freshmen had no need and received non-need-based gift aid.

UNDERGRADUATE FINANCIAL AID (Fall 2009) 2,270 applied for aid; of those 86% were deemed to have need. 100% of undergraduates with need received aid; of those 15% had need fully met. ***Average percent of need met:*** 89% (excluding resources awarded to replace EFC). ***Average financial aid package:*** $21,679 (excluding resources awarded to replace EFC). 25% of all full-time undergraduates had no need and received non-need-based gift aid.

GIFT AID (NEED-BASED) ***Total amount:*** $27,368,364 (14% federal, 11% state, 72% institutional, 3% external sources). ***Receiving aid:*** Freshmen: 73% (530); all full-time undergraduates: 70% (1,908). ***Average award:*** Freshmen: $15,858; Undergraduates: $14,314. ***Scholarships, grants, and awards:*** Federal Pell, FSEOG, state, private, college/university gift aid from institutional funds.

GIFT AID (NON-NEED-BASED) ***Total amount:*** $7,959,272 (3% federal, 1% state, 89% institutional, 7% external sources). ***Receiving aid:*** Freshmen: 12% (88). Undergraduates: 8% (216). ***Average award:*** Freshmen: $10,424. Undergraduates: $9324. ***Scholarships, grants, and awards by category:*** *Academic interests/achievement:* 2,342 awards ($18,346,722 total): general academic interests/achievements. *Creative arts/performance:* 254 awards ($572,581 total): art/fine arts, debating, music, theater/drama. *Special characteristics:* 206 awards ($3,384,347 total): children of faculty/staff, international students. ***Tuition waivers:*** Full or partial for employees or children of employees.

LOANS ***Student loans:*** $20,317,571 (61% need-based, 39% non-need-based). 79% of past graduating class borrowed through all loan programs. *Average indebtedness per student:* $32,271. ***Average need-based loan:*** Freshmen: $5836. Undergraduates: $7655. ***Parent loans:*** $3,200,947 (23% need-based, 77% non-need-based). ***Programs:*** Federal Direct (Subsidized and Unsubsidized Stafford, PLUS), Perkins, state, college/university, private loans.

WORK-STUDY ***Federal work-study:*** Total amount: $1,168,550; 695 jobs averaging $1695. ***State or other work-study/employment:*** Total amount: $3,492,720 (28% need-based, 72% non-need-based). 1,840 part-time jobs averaging $1755.

APPLYING FOR FINANCIAL AID ***Required financial aid form:*** FAFSA. ***Financial aid deadline:*** Continuous. ***Notification date:*** Continuous beginning 3/1.

CONTACT Mrs. Jane Williams, Financial Aid Director, Concordia College, 901 South 8th Street, Moorhead, MN 56562, 218-299-3010 or toll-free 800-699-9897. *Fax:* 218-299-3025. *E-mail:* jwilliam@cord.edu.

CONCORDIA COLLEGE–NEW YORK

Bronxville, NY

CONTACT Janice Spikereit, Director of Financial Aid, Concordia College–New York, 171 White Plains Road, Bronxville, NY 10708, 914-337-9300 Ext. 2146 or toll-free 800-YES-COLLEGE. *Fax:* 914-395-4500. *E-mail:* financialaid@concordia-ny.edu.

CONCORDIA UNIVERSITY

Irvine, CA

Tuition & fees: $27,300 **Average undergraduate aid package: $21,699**

ABOUT THE INSTITUTION Independent religious, coed. 22 undergraduate majors. Federal methodology is used as a basis for awarding need-based institutional aid.

UNDERGRADUATE EXPENSES for 2011–12 ***Comprehensive fee:*** $35,890 includes full-time tuition ($26,700), mandatory fees ($600), and room and board ($8590). ***College room only:*** $4900. Full-time tuition and fees vary according to course load. Room and board charges vary according to board plan and housing facility. ***Part-time tuition:*** $815 per unit. ***Part-time fees:*** $300 per term. Part-time tuition and fees vary according to course load. ***Payment plan:*** Installment.

FRESHMAN FINANCIAL AID (Fall 2010, est.) 290 applied for aid; of those 83% were deemed to have need. 100% of freshmen with need received aid; of those 22% had need fully met. ***Average percent of need met:*** 75% (excluding

resources awarded to replace EFC). ***Average financial aid package:*** $22,232 (excluding resources awarded to replace EFC). 19% of all full-time freshmen had no need and received non-need-based gift aid.

UNDERGRADUATE FINANCIAL AID (Fall 2010, est.) 1,214 applied for aid; of those 85% were deemed to have need. 99% of undergraduates with need received aid; of those 24% had need fully met. ***Average percent of need met:*** 74% (excluding resources awarded to replace EFC). ***Average financial aid package:*** $21,699 (excluding resources awarded to replace EFC). 19% of all full-time undergraduates had no need and received non-need-based gift aid.

GIFT AID (NEED-BASED) ***Total amount:*** $11,567,470 (18% federal, 22% state, 60% institutional). ***Receiving aid:*** Freshmen: 78% (240); all full-time undergraduates: 64% (940). ***Average award:*** Freshmen: $15,789; Undergraduates: $14,237. ***Scholarships, grants, and awards:*** Federal Pell, FSEOG, state, private, college/university gift aid from institutional funds.

GIFT AID (NON-NEED-BASED) ***Total amount:*** $2,210,753 (100% institutional). ***Receiving aid:*** Freshmen: 6% (19). Undergraduates: 5% (76). ***Average award:*** Freshmen: $6492. Undergraduates: $6699. ***Scholarships, grants, and awards by category:*** *Academic interests/achievement:* 960 awards ($5,151,616 total): general academic interests/achievements. *Creative arts/performance:* 171 awards ($463,875 total): applied art and design, debating, music, theater/drama. *Special characteristics:* 253 awards ($1,271,530 total): children of faculty/staff, first-generation college students, religious affiliation, siblings of current students. ***Tuition waivers:*** Full or partial for employees or children of employees.

LOANS ***Student loans:*** $9,577,122 (38% need-based, 62% non-need-based). 73% of past graduating class borrowed through all loan programs. *Average indebtedness per student:* $23,465. ***Average need-based loan:*** Freshmen: $3251. Undergraduates: $4302. ***Parent loans:*** $3,650,499 (100% non-need-based). ***Programs:*** Federal Direct (Subsidized and Unsubsidized Stafford, PLUS), private loans.

WORK-STUDY ***Federal work-study:*** Total amount: $84,501; 39 jobs averaging $2199. ***State or other work-study/employment:*** Total amount: $30,500 (100% need-based). 18 part-time jobs averaging $1750.

ATHLETIC AWARDS Total amount: $3,176,350 (60% need-based, 40% non-need-based).

APPLYING FOR FINANCIAL AID ***Required financial aid forms:*** FAFSA, state aid form, department scholarship form. ***Financial aid deadline:*** 3/2 (priority: 3/2). ***Notification date:*** Continuous beginning 3/15. Students must reply within 4 weeks of notification.

CONTACT Lori McDonald, Director of Financial Aid, Concordia University, 1530 Concordia West, Irvine, CA 92612-3299, 949-214-3074 or toll-free 800-229-1200. *Fax:* 949-214-3500. *E-mail:* lori.mcdonald@cui.edu.

CONCORDIA UNIVERSITY
Ann Arbor, MI

Tuition & fees: $20,982 **Average undergraduate aid package: $15,602**

ABOUT THE INSTITUTION Independent religious, coed. ***Awards:*** associate, bachelor's, and master's degrees and post-bachelor's certificates. 47 undergraduate majors. ***Total enrollment:*** 1,075. Undergraduates: 521. Freshmen: 94. Federal methodology is used as a basis for awarding need-based institutional aid.

UNDERGRADUATE EXPENSES for 2010–11 ***Application fee:*** $25. ***Comprehensive fee:*** $28,810 includes full-time tuition ($20,982) and room and board ($7828). Full-time tuition and fees vary according to location and program. Room and board charges vary according to housing facility. ***Part-time tuition:*** $693 per credit hour. Part-time tuition and fees vary according to course load, location, and program. ***Payment plan:*** Installment.

FRESHMAN FINANCIAL AID (Fall 2009) 86 applied for aid; of those 81% were deemed to have need. 100% of freshmen with need received aid; of those 33% had need fully met. ***Average percent of need met:*** 80% (excluding resources awarded to replace EFC). ***Average financial aid package:*** $16,098 (excluding resources awarded to replace EFC). 19% of all full-time freshmen had no need and received non-need-based gift aid.

UNDERGRADUATE FINANCIAL AID (Fall 2009) 379 applied for aid; of those 87% were deemed to have need. 100% of undergraduates with need received aid; of those 23% had need fully met. ***Average percent of need met:*** 77% (excluding resources awarded to replace EFC). ***Average financial aid package:*** $15,602 (excluding resources awarded to replace EFC). 16% of all full-time undergraduates had no need and received non-need-based gift aid.

GIFT AID (NEED-BASED) ***Total amount:*** $3,195,031 (21% federal, 10% state, 63% institutional, 6% external sources). ***Receiving aid:*** Freshmen: 67% (70); all full-time undergraduates: 78% (328). ***Average award:*** Freshmen: $12,848; Undergraduates: $11,713. ***Scholarships, grants, and awards:*** Federal Pell, FSEOG, state, private, college/university gift aid from institutional funds.

GIFT AID (NON-NEED-BASED) ***Total amount:*** $748,549 (81% institutional, 19% external sources). ***Receiving aid:*** Freshmen: 17% (18). Undergraduates: 13% (54). ***Average award:*** Freshmen: $7981. Undergraduates: $6734. ***Scholarships, grants, and awards by category:*** *Academic interests/achievement:* 448 awards ($1,440,042 total): business, education, general academic interests/achievements, religion/biblical studies. *Creative arts/performance:* 74 awards ($223,700 total): art/fine arts, music, performing arts, theater/drama. *Special characteristics:* 284 awards ($659,371 total): children and siblings of alumni, children of faculty/staff, ethnic background, general special characteristics, out-of-state students, religious affiliation, siblings of current students. ***Tuition waivers:*** Full or partial for employees or children of employees. ***ROTC:*** Army cooperative, Air Force cooperative.

LOANS ***Student loans:*** $2,739,383 (69% need-based, 31% non-need-based). 97% of past graduating class borrowed through all loan programs. *Average indebtedness per student:* $16,011. ***Average need-based loan:*** Freshmen: $4104. Undergraduates: $4571. ***Parent loans:*** $750,954 (28% need-based, 72% non-need-based). ***Programs:*** Federal Direct (Subsidized and Unsubsidized Stafford, PLUS), Perkins.

WORK-STUDY ***Federal work-study:*** Total amount: $75,038; 109 jobs averaging $827. ***State or other work-study/employment:*** Total amount: $97,305 (22% need-based, 78% non-need-based). 72 part-time jobs averaging $1320.

ATHLETIC AWARDS Total amount: $883,865 (60% need-based, 40% non-need-based).

APPLYING FOR FINANCIAL AID ***Required financial aid form:*** FAFSA. ***Financial aid deadline:*** Continuous. ***Notification date:*** Continuous beginning 3/1. Students must reply by 5/1 or within 4 weeks of notification.

CONTACT Mrs. Karen E. Neuendorf, Financial Aid Office, Concordia University, 4090 Geddes Road, Ann Arbor, MI 48105-2797, 734-995-7439 or toll-free 800-253-0680. *Fax:* 734-995-4610. *E-mail:* neuenke@cuaa.edu.

CONCORDIA UNIVERSITY
Portland, OR

CONTACT Mr. James W. Cullen, Director of Financial Aid, Concordia University, 2811 Northeast Holman Street, Portland, OR 97211-6099, 503-493-6508 or toll-free 800-321-9371. *Fax:* 503-280-8661. *E-mail:* jcullen@cu-portland.edu.

CONCORDIA UNIVERSITY CHICAGO
River Forest, IL

Tuition & fees: $25,631 **Average undergraduate aid package: $21,388**

ABOUT THE INSTITUTION Independent religious, coed. 61 undergraduate majors. Federal methodology is used as a basis for awarding need-based institutional aid.

UNDERGRADUATE EXPENSES for 2011–12 ***Comprehensive fee:*** $33,881 includes full-time tuition ($24,944), mandatory fees ($687), and room and board ($8250). Full-time tuition and fees vary according to program. ***Part-time tuition:*** $779 per semester hour. Part-time tuition and fees vary according to program. ***Payment plan:*** Installment.

FRESHMAN FINANCIAL AID (Fall 2009) 348 applied for aid; of those 90% were deemed to have need. 100% of freshmen with need received aid; of those 31% had need fully met. ***Average percent of need met:*** 84% (excluding resources awarded to replace EFC). ***Average financial aid package:*** $21,607 (excluding resources awarded to replace EFC). 13% of all full-time freshmen had no need and received non-need-based gift aid.

UNDERGRADUATE FINANCIAL AID (Fall 2009) 1,110 applied for aid; of those 89% were deemed to have need. 100% of undergraduates with need received aid; of those 39% had need fully met. ***Average percent of need met:*** 86% (excluding resources awarded to replace EFC). ***Average financial aid package:*** $21,388 (excluding resources awarded to replace EFC). 14% of all full-time undergraduates had no need and received non-need-based gift aid.

GIFT AID (NEED-BASED) ***Total amount:*** $12,272,869 (16% federal, 13% state, 71% institutional). ***Receiving aid:*** Freshmen: 87% (314); all full-time undergradu-

ates: 82% (969). ***Average award:*** Freshmen: $14,227; Undergraduates: $12,571. ***Scholarships, grants, and awards:*** Federal Pell, FSEOG, state, private, college/university gift aid from institutional funds.

GIFT AID (NON-NEED-BASED) ***Total amount:*** $3,055,945 (81% institutional, 19% external sources). ***Receiving aid:*** Freshmen: 13% (47). Undergraduates: 15% (180). ***Average award:*** Freshmen: $9903. Undergraduates: $9667. ***Scholarships, grants, and awards by category:*** *Academic interests/achievement:* biological sciences, business, communication, computer science, education, English, foreign languages, general academic interests/achievements, mathematics, religion/biblical studies. *Creative arts/performance:* art/fine arts, music. *Special characteristics:* children and siblings of alumni, children of faculty/staff, international students, religious affiliation. ***Tuition waivers:*** Full or partial for minority students, children of alumni, employees or children of employees, senior citizens.

LOANS ***Student loans:*** $7,885,127 (41% need-based, 59% non-need-based). 81% of past graduating class borrowed through all loan programs. *Average indebtedness per student:* $31,945. ***Average need-based loan:*** Freshmen: $3228. Undergraduates: $4076. ***Parent loans:*** $1,176,847 (100% non-need-based). ***Programs:*** Federal Direct (Subsidized and Unsubsidized Stafford, PLUS), Perkins.

WORK-STUDY ***Federal work-study:*** Total amount: $204,345; 116 jobs averaging $1797. ***State or other work-study/employment:*** Total amount: $670,082 (100% non-need-based). 321 part-time jobs averaging $2012.

APPLYING FOR FINANCIAL AID ***Required financial aid form:*** FAFSA. ***Financial aid deadline:*** 8/15 (priority: 4/1). ***Notification date:*** Continuous beginning 3/1. Students must reply within 4 weeks of notification.

CONTACT Aida Asencio-Pinto, Director of Student Financial Planning, Concordia University Chicago, 7400 Augusta Street, River Forest, IL 60305-1499, 708-209-3113 or toll-free 800-285-2668. *Fax:* 708-488-4102. *E-mail:* aida.asencio-pinto@cuchicago.edu.

CONCORDIA UNIVERSITY, NEBRASKA

Seward, NE

Tuition & fees: $23,060 **Average undergraduate aid package: $17,502**

ABOUT THE INSTITUTION Independent religious, coed. 73 undergraduate majors. Federal methodology is used as a basis for awarding need-based institutional aid.

UNDERGRADUATE EXPENSES for 2011–12 ***Comprehensive fee:*** $29,170 includes full-time tuition ($22,860), mandatory fees ($200), and room and board ($6110). ***College room only:*** $2590. Room and board charges vary according to board plan and housing facility. ***Part-time tuition:*** $715 per credit hour. ***Part-time fees:*** $75 per term. ***Payment plan:*** Installment.

FRESHMAN FINANCIAL AID (Fall 2010, est.) 253 applied for aid; of those 87% were deemed to have need. 100% of freshmen with need received aid; of those 22% had need fully met. ***Average percent of need met:*** 76% (excluding resources awarded to replace EFC). ***Average financial aid package:*** $17,894 (excluding resources awarded to replace EFC). 10% of all full-time freshmen had no need and received non-need-based gift aid.

UNDERGRADUATE FINANCIAL AID (Fall 2010, est.) 984 applied for aid; of those 88% were deemed to have need. 100% of undergraduates with need received aid; of those 26% had need fully met. ***Average percent of need met:*** 78% (excluding resources awarded to replace EFC). ***Average financial aid package:*** $17,502 (excluding resources awarded to replace EFC). 11% of all full-time undergraduates had no need and received non-need-based gift aid.

GIFT AID (NEED-BASED) ***Total amount:*** $10,139,555 (18% federal, 1% state, 68% institutional, 13% external sources). ***Receiving aid:*** Freshmen: 80% (221); all full-time undergraduates: 77% (856). ***Average award:*** Freshmen: $14,309; Undergraduates: $13,518. ***Scholarships, grants, and awards:*** Federal Pell, FSEOG, state, private, college/university gift aid from institutional funds.

GIFT AID (NON-NEED-BASED) ***Total amount:*** $2,739,024 (100% institutional). ***Receiving aid:*** Freshmen: 14% (39). Undergraduates: 13% (141). ***Average award:*** Freshmen: $12,104. Undergraduates: $10,575. ***Scholarships, grants, and awards by category:*** *Academic interests/achievement:* biological sciences, business, communication, computer science, education, English, general academic interests/achievements, health fields, humanities, mathematics, physical sciences, premedicine, religion/biblical studies, social sciences. *Creative arts/performance:* applied art and design, art/fine arts, dance, debating, music, theater/drama. *Special characteristics:* children and siblings of alumni, children of educators, children of faculty/staff, international students, local/state students, members of minority groups, religious affiliation, veterans, veterans' children. ***Tuition waivers:*** Full or partial for employees or children of employees.

LOANS ***Student loans:*** $5,761,889 (47% need-based, 53% non-need-based). 78% of past graduating class borrowed through all loan programs. *Average indebtedness per student:* $22,586. ***Average need-based loan:*** Freshmen: $3657. Undergraduates: $4420. ***Parent loans:*** $2,329,105 (100% non-need-based). ***Programs:*** Federal Direct (Subsidized and Unsubsidized Stafford, PLUS), Perkins.

WORK-STUDY ***Federal work-study:*** Total amount: $101,788; 111 jobs averaging $917.

ATHLETIC AWARDS Total amount: $2,197,565 (75% need-based, 25% non-need-based).

APPLYING FOR FINANCIAL AID ***Required financial aid form:*** FAFSA. ***Financial aid deadline (priority):*** 3/1. ***Notification date:*** Continuous beginning 3/1. Students must reply within 4 weeks of notification.

CONTACT Mr. Aaron W. Roberts, Director of Undergraduate Recruitment, Concordia University, Nebraska, 800 North Columbia Avenue, Seward, NE 68434-1556, 800-535-5494. *Fax:* 402-643-4073. *E-mail:* admiss@cune.edu.

CONCORDIA UNIVERSITY, ST. PAUL

St. Paul, MN

Tuition & fees: $28,500 **Average undergraduate aid package: $18,771**

ABOUT THE INSTITUTION Independent religious, coed. 41 undergraduate majors. Federal methodology is used as a basis for awarding need-based institutional aid.

UNDERGRADUATE EXPENSES for 2011–12 ***Comprehensive fee:*** $36,000 includes full-time tuition ($28,500) and room and board ($7500). Full-time tuition and fees vary according to program. Room and board charges vary according to housing facility. ***Part-time tuition:*** $600 per credit. Part-time tuition and fees vary according to course load and program. ***Payment plan:*** Installment.

FRESHMAN FINANCIAL AID (Fall 2010, est.) 208 applied for aid; of those 79% were deemed to have need. 100% of freshmen with need received aid; of those 2% had need fully met. ***Average percent of need met:*** 77% (excluding resources awarded to replace EFC). ***Average financial aid package:*** $22,625 (excluding resources awarded to replace EFC). 12% of all full-time freshmen had no need and received non-need-based gift aid.

UNDERGRADUATE FINANCIAL AID (Fall 2010, est.) 1,175 applied for aid; of those 80% were deemed to have need. 97% of undergraduates with need received aid; of those 2% had need fully met. ***Average percent of need met:*** 63% (excluding resources awarded to replace EFC). ***Average financial aid package:*** $18,771 (excluding resources awarded to replace EFC). 12% of all full-time undergraduates had no need and received non-need-based gift aid.

GIFT AID (NEED-BASED) ***Total amount:*** $17,076,720 (26% federal, 12% state, 61% institutional, 1% external sources). ***Receiving aid:*** Freshmen: 70% (151); all full-time undergraduates: 55% (735). ***Average award:*** Freshmen: $8320; Undergraduates: $7099. ***Scholarships, grants, and awards:*** Federal Pell, FSEOG, state, private, college/university gift aid from institutional funds.

GIFT AID (NON-NEED-BASED) ***Total amount:*** $5,828,510 (1% federal, 98% institutional, 1% external sources). ***Receiving aid:*** Freshmen: 76% (165). Undergraduates: 61% (813). ***Average award:*** Freshmen: $15,420. Undergraduates: $8357. ***Scholarships, grants, and awards by category:*** *Academic interests/achievement:* 1,014 awards ($6,757,884 total): general academic interests/achievements, mathematics, physical sciences, religion/biblical studies. *Creative arts/performance:* 101 awards ($120,000 total): art/fine arts, music, theater/drama. *Special characteristics:* 347 awards ($771,346 total): children of faculty/staff, religious affiliation, veterans, veterans' children. ***Tuition waivers:*** Full or partial for employees or children of employees.

LOANS ***Student loans:*** $16,484,544 (87% need-based, 13% non-need-based). 93% of past graduating class borrowed through all loan programs. *Average indebtedness per student:* $36,295. ***Average need-based loan:*** Freshmen: $3363. Undergraduates: $4467. ***Parent loans:*** $2,927,549 (72% need-based, 28% non-need-based). ***Programs:*** Federal Direct (Subsidized and Unsubsidized Stafford, PLUS), Perkins, state, private loans.

WORK-STUDY ***Federal work-study:*** Total amount: $209,508; jobs available. ***State or other work-study/employment:*** Total amount: $25,498 (100% need-based). Part-time jobs available.

ATHLETIC AWARDS Total amount: $3,634,464 (50% need-based, 50% non-need-based).

APPLYING FOR FINANCIAL AID ***Required financial aid forms:*** FAFSA, institution's own form. ***Financial aid deadline (priority):*** 5/1. ***Notification date:*** Continuous beginning 3/1. Students must reply within 3 weeks of notification.

CONTACT Jeanie Peck, Financial Aid Director, Concordia University, St. Paul, 275 North Syndicate Street, St. Paul, MN 55104-5494, 651-603-6300 or toll-free 800-333-4705. *Fax:* 651-603-6298. *E-mail:* finaid@csp.edu.

CONCORDIA UNIVERSITY TEXAS

Austin, TX

ABOUT THE INSTITUTION Independent religious, coed. 21 undergraduate majors.

GIFT AID (NEED-BASED) ***Scholarships, grants, and awards:*** Federal Pell, FSEOG, state, private, college/university gift aid from institutional funds.

GIFT AID (NON-NEED-BASED) ***Scholarships, grants, and awards by category:*** *Academic interests/achievement:* biological sciences, business, computer science, education, foreign languages, general academic interests/achievements, health fields, international studies, mathematics, physical sciences, religion/biblical studies, social sciences. *Creative arts/performance:* music. *Special achievements/activities:* junior miss, leadership, religious involvement. *Special characteristics:* adult students, children and siblings of alumni, children of faculty/staff, religious affiliation, veterans, veterans' children.

LOANS ***Programs:*** Federal Direct (Subsidized and Unsubsidized Stafford, PLUS), state.

WORK-STUDY ***Federal work-study:*** Total amount: $102,067; 77 jobs averaging $1326. ***State or other work-study/employment:*** Total amount: $12,655 (100% need-based). 4 part-time jobs averaging $3164.

APPLYING FOR FINANCIAL AID ***Required financial aid forms:*** FAFSA, institution's own form.

CONTACT Mrs. Cathy L. Schryer, Director of Student Financial Services, Concordia University Texas, 11400 Concordia University Drive, Austin, TX 78726, 512-313-4671 or toll-free 800-865-4282. *Fax:* 888-828-5120. *E-mail:* cathy.schryer@concordia.edu.

CONCORDIA UNIVERSITY WISCONSIN

Mequon, WI

Tuition & fees: $22,150 **Average undergraduate aid package: $20,585**

ABOUT THE INSTITUTION Independent religious, coed. 73 undergraduate majors. Federal methodology is used as a basis for awarding need-based institutional aid.

UNDERGRADUATE EXPENSES for 2010–11 ***Comprehensive fee:*** $30,460 includes full-time tuition ($21,940), mandatory fees ($210), and room and board ($8310). Full-time tuition and fees vary according to program. Room and board charges vary according to board plan. ***Part-time tuition:*** $915 per credit hour. Part-time tuition and fees vary according to program. ***Payment plans:*** Guaranteed tuition, installment, deferred payment.

FRESHMAN FINANCIAL AID (Fall 2010, est.) 498 applied for aid; of those 90% were deemed to have need. 100% of freshmen with need received aid; of those 36% had need fully met. ***Average percent of need met:*** 83% (excluding resources awarded to replace EFC). ***Average financial aid package:*** $21,409 (excluding resources awarded to replace EFC). 13% of all full-time freshmen had no need and received non-need-based gift aid.

UNDERGRADUATE FINANCIAL AID (Fall 2010, est.) 2,023 applied for aid; of those 90% were deemed to have need. 100% of undergraduates with need received aid; of those 32% had need fully met. ***Average percent of need met:*** 81% (excluding resources awarded to replace EFC). ***Average financial aid package:*** $20,585 (excluding resources awarded to replace EFC). 13% of all full-time undergraduates had no need and received non-need-based gift aid.

GIFT AID (NEED-BASED) ***Total amount:*** $24,211,065 (27% federal, 8% state, 60% institutional, 5% external sources). ***Receiving aid:*** Freshmen: 85% (443); all full-time undergraduates: 79% (1,718). ***Average award:*** Freshmen: $14,066; Undergraduates: $12,024. ***Scholarships, grants, and awards:*** Federal Pell, FSEOG, state, private, college/university gift aid from institutional funds.

GIFT AID (NON-NEED-BASED) ***Total amount:*** $4,201,285 (2% federal, 98% institutional). ***Receiving aid:*** Freshmen: 19% (100). Undergraduates: 14% (308). ***Average award:*** Freshmen: $9885. Undergraduates: $8772. ***Scholarships, grants, and awards by category:*** *Academic interests/achievement:* 352 awards ($4,365,253 total): religion/biblical studies. *Creative arts/performance:* 78 awards ($129,224 total): music. *Special characteristics:* 212 awards ($352,587 total): out-of-state students. ***Tuition waivers:*** Full or partial for employees or children of employees.

LOANS ***Student loans:*** $25,394,464 (52% need-based, 48% non-need-based). 79% of past graduating class borrowed through all loan programs. *Average indebtedness per student:* $28,247. ***Average need-based loan:*** Freshmen: $4996. Undergraduates: $5944. ***Parent loans:*** $2,706,038 (100% non-need-based). ***Programs:*** Federal Direct (Subsidized and Unsubsidized Stafford, PLUS), state.

WORK-STUDY ***Federal work-study:*** Total amount: $635,189; 250 jobs averaging $1621.

APPLYING FOR FINANCIAL AID ***Required financial aid form:*** FAFSA. ***Financial aid deadline (priority):*** 3/15. ***Notification date:*** Continuous beginning 1/21. Students must reply within 3 weeks of notification.

CONTACT Mr. Steven P. Taylor, Director of Financial Aid, Concordia University Wisconsin, 12800 North Lake Shore Drive, Mequon, WI 53097-2402, 262-243-4392 or toll-free 888-628-9472. *Fax:* 262-243-2992. *E-mail:* steve.taylor@cuw.edu.

CONCORD UNIVERSITY

Athens, WV

Tuition & fees (WV res): $4974 **Average undergraduate aid package: $11,726**

ABOUT THE INSTITUTION State-supported, coed. 38 undergraduate majors. Federal methodology is used as a basis for awarding need-based institutional aid.

UNDERGRADUATE EXPENSES for 2011–12 ***Tuition, state resident:*** full-time $4974; part-time $207 per credit. ***Tuition, nonresident:*** full-time $11,050; part-time $460 per credit. Full-time tuition and fees vary according to course load. Part-time tuition and fees vary according to course load. ***College room and board:*** $6962; ***Room only:*** $3546. ***Payment plan:*** Installment.

FRESHMAN FINANCIAL AID (Fall 2010, est.) 525 applied for aid; of those 79% were deemed to have need. 100% of freshmen with need received aid; of those 27% had need fully met. ***Average percent of need met:*** 100% (excluding resources awarded to replace EFC). ***Average financial aid package:*** $11,959 (excluding resources awarded to replace EFC). 15% of all full-time freshmen had no need and received non-need-based gift aid.

UNDERGRADUATE FINANCIAL AID (Fall 2010, est.) 2,092 applied for aid; of those 81% were deemed to have need. 99% of undergraduates with need received aid; of those 32% had need fully met. ***Average percent of need met:*** 93% (excluding resources awarded to replace EFC). ***Average financial aid package:*** $11,726 (excluding resources awarded to replace EFC). 7% of all full-time undergraduates had no need and received non-need-based gift aid.

GIFT AID (NEED-BASED) ***Total amount:*** $7,470,868 (79% federal, 21% state). ***Receiving aid:*** Freshmen: 61% (348); all full-time undergraduates: 59% (1,411). ***Average award:*** Freshmen: $4989; Undergraduates: $5292. ***Scholarships, grants, and awards:*** Federal Pell, FSEOG, state, private, college/university gift aid from institutional funds.

GIFT AID (NON-NEED-BASED) ***Total amount:*** $4,393,754 (46% state, 43% institutional, 11% external sources). ***Receiving aid:*** Freshmen: 38% (214). Undergraduates: 25% (604). ***Average award:*** Freshmen: $2048. Undergraduates: $2760. ***Scholarships, grants, and awards by category:*** *Academic interests/achievement:* 621 awards ($1,114,734 total): business, communication, education, English, general academic interests/achievements, social sciences. *Creative arts/performance:* 27 awards ($51,588 total): art/fine arts, journalism/publications, music, theater/drama. *Special achievements/activities:* 272 awards ($80,375 total): community service, general special achievements/activities, leadership. *Special characteristics:* 21 awards ($99,328 total): children of faculty/staff, veterans, veterans' children. ***Tuition waivers:*** Full or partial for employees or children of employees, adult students, senior citizens.

LOANS ***Student loans:*** $9,657,761 (98% need-based, 2% non-need-based). 88% of past graduating class borrowed through all loan programs. *Average indebtedness per student:* $14,700. ***Average need-based loan:*** Freshmen: $5639. Undergraduates: $6642. ***Parent loans:*** $695,313 (100% non-need-based). ***Programs:*** Federal Direct (Subsidized and Unsubsidized Stafford, PLUS), Perkins.

WORK-STUDY ***Federal work-study:*** Total amount: $304,006; 248 jobs averaging $1205. ***State or other work-study/employment:*** Total amount: $487,848 (100% non-need-based). 385 part-time jobs averaging $1191.

ATHLETIC AWARDS Total amount: $1,230,642 (100% non-need-based).

APPLYING FOR FINANCIAL AID ***Required financial aid forms:*** FAFSA, institution's own form, verification worksheet. ***Financial aid deadline (priority):*** 4/15. ***Notification date:*** Continuous beginning 5/15. Students must reply within 2 weeks of notification.

CONTACT Debra Turner, Financial Aid Director, Concord University, PO Box 1000, Athens, WV 24712-1000, 304-384-6069 or toll-free 888-384-5249. *Fax:* 304-384-3084. *E-mail:* turner@concord.edu.

CONNECTICUT COLLEGE

New London, CT

Tuition & fees: $43,990 **Average undergraduate aid package: $31,101**

ABOUT THE INSTITUTION Independent, coed. 48 undergraduate majors. Both federal and institutional methodology are used as a basis for awarding need-based institutional aid.

UNDERGRADUATE EXPENSES for 2010–11 ***Comprehensive fee:*** $53,110 includes full-time tuition ($43,780), mandatory fees ($210), and room and board ($9120). ***College room only:*** $4080. ***Part-time tuition:*** $1232 per credit hour. ***Payment plan:*** Installment.

FRESHMAN FINANCIAL AID (Fall 2009) 300 applied for aid; of those 80% were deemed to have need. 100% of freshmen with need received aid; of those 100% had need fully met. ***Average percent of need met:*** 100% (excluding resources awarded to replace EFC). ***Average financial aid package:*** $30,502 (excluding resources awarded to replace EFC).

UNDERGRADUATE FINANCIAL AID (Fall 2009) 997 applied for aid; of those 86% were deemed to have need. 100% of undergraduates with need received aid; of those 100% had need fully met. ***Average percent of need met:*** 100% (excluding resources awarded to replace EFC). ***Average financial aid package:*** $31,101 (excluding resources awarded to replace EFC).

GIFT AID (NEED-BASED) ***Total amount:*** $23,440,332 (5% federal, 2% state, 89% institutional, 4% external sources). ***Receiving aid:*** Freshmen: 42% (214); all full-time undergraduates: 41% (777). ***Average award:*** Freshmen: $30,739; Undergraduates: $29,616. ***Scholarships, grants, and awards:*** Federal Pell, FSEOG, state, college/university gift aid from institutional funds.

GIFT AID (NON-NEED-BASED) ***Total amount:*** $441,790 (2% institutional, 98% external sources). ***Tuition waivers:*** Full or partial for employees or children of employees, senior citizens.

LOANS ***Student loans:*** $6,792,297 (46% need-based, 54% non-need-based). 34% of past graduating class borrowed through all loan programs. *Average indebtedness per student:* $22,038. ***Average need-based loan:*** Freshmen: $3022. Undergraduates: $4389. ***Parent loans:*** $4,269,219 (100% non-need-based). ***Programs:*** Federal Direct (Subsidized and Unsubsidized Stafford, PLUS), Perkins, college/university.

WORK-STUDY ***Federal work-study:*** Total amount: $984,468; 719 jobs averaging $1386. ***State or other work-study/employment:*** Total amount: $17,703 (100% need-based). 18 part-time jobs averaging $992.

APPLYING FOR FINANCIAL AID ***Required financial aid forms:*** FAFSA, CSS Financial Aid PROFILE, noncustodial (divorced/separated) parent's statement, business/farm supplement. ***Financial aid deadline:*** 2/1. ***Notification date:*** 4/1. Students must reply by 5/1 or within 2 weeks of notification.

CONTACT Ms. Elaine Solinga, Director of Financial Aid Services, Connecticut College, 270 Mohegan Avenue, New London, CT 06320-4196, 860-439-2058. *Fax:* 860-439-2159. *E-mail:* finaid@conncoll.edu.

CONSERVATORY OF MUSIC OF PUERTO RICO

San Juan, PR

CONTACT Mr. Jorge Medina, Director of Financial Aid, Conservatory of Music of Puerto Rico, 350 Rafael Lamar Street at FDR Avenue, San Juan, PR 00918, 787-751-0160 Ext. 230. *Fax:* 787-758-8268. *E-mail:* jmedina@cmpr.gobierno.pr.

CONVERSE COLLEGE

Spartanburg, SC

Tuition & fees: $26,138 **Average undergraduate aid package: $22,546**

ABOUT THE INSTITUTION Independent, undergraduate: women only; graduate: coed. 45 undergraduate majors. Federal methodology is used as a basis for awarding need-based institutional aid.

UNDERGRADUATE EXPENSES for 2010–11 ***One-time required fee:*** $100. ***Comprehensive fee:*** $34,170 includes full-time tuition ($26,138) and room and board ($8032). Full-time tuition and fees vary according to program and reciprocity agreements. Room and board charges vary according to housing facility. ***Part-time tuition:*** $825 per credit hour. Part-time tuition and fees vary according to program. ***Payment plan:*** Installment.

FRESHMAN FINANCIAL AID (Fall 2010, est.) 164 applied for aid; of those 88% were deemed to have need. 100% of freshmen with need received aid; of those 21% had need fully met. ***Average percent of need met:*** 80% (excluding resources awarded to replace EFC). ***Average financial aid package:*** $24,379 (excluding resources awarded to replace EFC). 17% of all full-time freshmen had no need and received non-need-based gift aid.

UNDERGRADUATE FINANCIAL AID (Fall 2010, est.) 570 applied for aid; of those 94% were deemed to have need. 100% of undergraduates with need received aid; of those 24% had need fully met. ***Average percent of need met:*** 78% (excluding resources awarded to replace EFC). ***Average financial aid package:*** $22,546 (excluding resources awarded to replace EFC). 13% of all full-time undergraduates had no need and received non-need-based gift aid.

GIFT AID (NEED-BASED) ***Total amount:*** $9,602,349 (18% federal, 19% state, 62% institutional, 1% external sources). ***Receiving aid:*** Freshmen: 86% (144); all full-time undergraduates: 86% (530). ***Average award:*** Freshmen: $21,170; Undergraduates: $18,918. ***Scholarships, grants, and awards:*** Federal Pell, FSEOG, state, private, college/university gift aid from institutional funds.

GIFT AID (NON-NEED-BASED) ***Total amount:*** $1,897,382 (30% state, 68% institutional, 2% external sources). ***Receiving aid:*** Freshmen: 15% (26). Undergraduates: 14% (89). ***Average award:*** Freshmen: $11,823. Undergraduates: $13,341. ***Scholarships, grants, and awards by category:*** *Academic interests/achievement:* 517 awards ($5,100,139 total): general academic interests/achievements. *Creative arts/performance:* 271 awards ($1,014,317 total): applied art and design, general creative arts/performance, music, theater/drama. *Special achievements/activities:* 14 awards ($65,988 total): leadership. *Special characteristics:* 57 awards ($156,116 total): children and siblings of alumni, children of faculty/staff. ***Tuition waivers:*** Full or partial for employees or children of employees, adult students.

LOANS ***Student loans:*** $4,385,821 (84% need-based, 16% non-need-based). 66% of past graduating class borrowed through all loan programs. *Average indebtedness per student:* $24,187. ***Average need-based loan:*** Freshmen: $3845. Undergraduates: $4717. ***Parent loans:*** $1,078,226 (45% need-based, 55% non-need-based). ***Programs:*** Federal Direct (Subsidized and Unsubsidized Stafford, PLUS), Perkins, state.

WORK-STUDY ***Federal work-study:*** Total amount: $130,226; 107 jobs averaging $1595. ***State or other work-study/employment:*** 60 part-time jobs averaging $1000.

ATHLETIC AWARDS Total amount: $784,070 (60% need-based, 40% non-need-based).

APPLYING FOR FINANCIAL AID ***Required financial aid form:*** FAFSA. ***Financial aid deadline (priority):*** 3/15. ***Notification date:*** Continuous beginning 3/15. Students must reply by 5/1 or within 2 weeks of notification.

CONTACT Ms. Margaret P. Collins, Director of Financial Assistance, Converse College, 580 East Main Street, Spartanburg, SC 29302-0006, 864-596-9019 or toll-free 800-766-1125. *Fax:* 864-596-9749. *E-mail:* peggy.collins@converse.edu.

COOPER UNION FOR THE ADVANCEMENT OF SCIENCE AND ART

New York, NY

Tuition & fees: $39,150 **Average undergraduate aid package: $35,000**

ABOUT THE INSTITUTION Independent, coed. 8 undergraduate majors. Both federal and institutional methodology are used as a basis for awarding need-based institutional aid.

UNDERGRADUATE EXPENSES for 2010–11 ***Comprehensive fee:*** $52,850 includes full-time tuition ($37,500), mandatory fees ($1650), and room and board ($13,700). ***College room only:*** $9700. Room and board charges vary according to board plan and housing facility.

FRESHMAN FINANCIAL AID (Fall 2009) 91 applied for aid; of those 58% were deemed to have need. 100% of freshmen with need received aid; of those 60% had need fully met. ***Average percent of need met:*** 92% (excluding resources awarded to replace EFC). ***Average financial aid package:*** $35,000 (excluding resources awarded to replace EFC). 75% of all full-time freshmen had no need and received non-need-based gift aid.

UNDERGRADUATE FINANCIAL AID (Fall 2009) 407 applied for aid; of those 69% were deemed to have need. 100% of undergraduates with need received aid; of those 47% had need fully met. ***Average percent of need met:*** 93% (excluding resources awarded to replace EFC). ***Average financial aid package:*** $35,000 (excluding resources awarded to replace EFC). 69% of all full-time undergraduates had no need and received non-need-based gift aid.

GIFT AID (NEED-BASED) ***Total amount:*** $1,917,514 (41% federal, 19% state, 26% institutional, 14% external sources). ***Receiving aid:*** Freshmen: 25% (53); all full-time undergraduates: 27% (244). ***Average award:*** Freshmen: $3755; Undergraduates: $5034. ***Scholarships, grants, and awards:*** Federal Pell, FSEOG, state, private, college/university gift aid from institutional funds.

GIFT AID (NON-NEED-BASED) ***Total amount:*** $30,074,149 (100% institutional). ***Receiving aid:*** Freshmen: 25% (53). Undergraduates: 31% (280). ***Average award:*** Freshmen: $35,000. Undergraduates: $35,000. ***Scholarships, grants, and awards by category:*** *Academic interests/achievement:* 616 awards ($21,560,000 total): architecture, engineering/technologies. *Creative arts/performance:* 275 awards ($9,625,000 total): art/fine arts.

LOANS ***Student loans:*** $933,160 (95% need-based, 5% non-need-based). 27% of past graduating class borrowed through all loan programs. *Average indebtedness per student:* $10,390. ***Average need-based loan:*** Freshmen: $2858. Undergraduates: $3164. ***Parent loans:*** $58,300 (60% need-based, 40% non-need-based). ***Programs:*** Federal Direct (Subsidized and Unsubsidized Stafford, PLUS), Perkins, college/university.

WORK-STUDY ***Federal work-study:*** Total amount: $36,625; 46 jobs averaging $796. ***State or other work-study/employment:*** Total amount: $803,947 (22% need-based, 78% non-need-based). 529 part-time jobs averaging $1248.

APPLYING FOR FINANCIAL AID ***Required financial aid forms:*** FAFSA, CSS Financial Aid PROFILE. ***Financial aid deadline:*** 6/1 (priority: 4/15). ***Notification date:*** 6/1. Students must reply by 6/30 or within 2 weeks of notification.

CONTACT Ms. Mary Ruokonen, Director of Financial Aid, Cooper Union for the Advancement of Science and Art, 30 Cooper Square, New York, NY 10003-7120, 212-353-4130. *Fax:* 212-353-4343. *E-mail:* ruokon@cooper.edu.

COPPIN STATE UNIVERSITY

Baltimore, MD

Tuition & fees (MD res): $5545 **Average undergraduate aid package: $8873**

ABOUT THE INSTITUTION State-supported, coed. 20 undergraduate majors. Federal methodology is used as a basis for awarding need-based institutional aid.

UNDERGRADUATE EXPENSES for 2010–11 ***Tuition, state resident:*** full-time $3633; part-time $156 per credit hour. ***Tuition, nonresident:*** full-time $12,833; part-time $441 per credit hour. ***Required fees:*** full-time $1912; $339 per semester hour. Full-time tuition and fees vary according to course load. Part-time tuition and fees vary according to course load. ***College room and board:*** $8108; ***Room only:*** $4920. Room and board charges vary according to board plan. ***Payment plan:*** Deferred payment.

FRESHMAN FINANCIAL AID (Fall 2010, est.) 476 applied for aid; of those 93% were deemed to have need. 100% of freshmen with need received aid; of those 16% had need fully met. ***Average percent of need met:*** 63% (excluding resources awarded to replace EFC). ***Average financial aid package:*** $8549 (excluding resources awarded to replace EFC). 1% of all full-time freshmen had no need and received non-need-based gift aid.

UNDERGRADUATE FINANCIAL AID (Fall 2010, est.) 2,303 applied for aid; of those 95% were deemed to have need. 100% of undergraduates with need received aid; of those 19% had need fully met. ***Average percent of need met:*** 74% (excluding resources awarded to replace EFC). ***Average financial aid package:*** $8873 (excluding resources awarded to replace EFC). 1% of all full-time undergraduates had no need and received non-need-based gift aid.

GIFT AID (NEED-BASED) ***Total amount:*** $34,185,819 (90% federal, 4% state, 6% institutional). ***Receiving aid:*** Freshmen: 69% (347); all full-time undergraduates: 71% (1,790). ***Average award:*** Freshmen: $6132; Undergraduates: $5887. ***Scholarships, grants, and awards:*** Federal Pell, FSEOG, state, private, college/university gift aid from institutional funds, Federal Nursing.

GIFT AID (NON-NEED-BASED) ***Total amount:*** $3,544,983 (2% federal, 38% state, 52% institutional, 8% external sources). ***Receiving aid:*** Freshmen: 13% (66). Undergraduates: 11% (277). ***Average award:*** Freshmen: $1000. Undergraduates: $1056. ***Scholarships, grants, and awards by category:*** *Academic interests/achievement:* general academic interests/achievements. ***Tuition waivers:*** Full or partial for minority students, children of alumni, employees or children of employees, adult students, senior citizens.

LOANS ***Student loans:*** $30,028,040 (70% need-based, 30% non-need-based). 97% of past graduating class borrowed through all loan programs. *Average indebtedness per student:* $8559. ***Average need-based loan:*** Freshmen: $3306. Undergraduates: $4036. ***Parent loans:*** $1,580,240 (100% non-need-based). ***Programs:*** Federal Direct (Subsidized and Unsubsidized Stafford, PLUS), Perkins, alternative loans.

WORK-STUDY ***Federal work-study:*** Total amount: $2,139,857; 165 jobs averaging $3212.

ATHLETIC AWARDS Total amount: $1,298,351 (100% non-need-based).

APPLYING FOR FINANCIAL AID ***Required financial aid form:*** FAFSA. ***Financial aid deadline (priority):*** 3/1. ***Notification date:*** 4/15. Students must reply within 4 weeks of notification.

CONTACT Mr. Mose Cartier, Director of Financial Aid, Coppin State University, 2500 West North Avenue, Baltimore, MD 21216-3698, 410-951-3647 or toll-free 800-635-3674. *Fax:* 410-951-3637. *E-mail:* ftayree@coppin.edu.

CORBAN UNIVERSITY

Salem, OR

Tuition & fees: $25,445 **Average undergraduate aid package: $18,182**

ABOUT THE INSTITUTION Independent religious, coed. 49 undergraduate majors. Federal methodology is used as a basis for awarding need-based institutional aid.

UNDERGRADUATE EXPENSES for 2011–12 ***One-time required fee:*** $100. ***Comprehensive fee:*** $33,425 includes full-time tuition ($24,975), mandatory fees ($470), and room and board ($7980). Full-time tuition and fees vary according to program and reciprocity agreements. Room and board charges vary according to board plan. ***Part-time tuition:*** $1041 per credit hour. Part-time tuition and fees vary according to course load, program, and reciprocity agreements. ***Payment plan:*** Installment.

FRESHMAN FINANCIAL AID (Fall 2010, est.) 193 applied for aid; of those 90% were deemed to have need. 100% of freshmen with need received aid; of those 12% had need fully met. ***Average percent of need met:*** 66% (excluding resources awarded to replace EFC). ***Average financial aid package:*** $19,022 (excluding resources awarded to replace EFC). 14% of all full-time freshmen had no need and received non-need-based gift aid.

UNDERGRADUATE FINANCIAL AID (Fall 2010, est.) 679 applied for aid; of those 90% were deemed to have need. 100% of undergraduates with need received aid; of those 12% had need fully met. ***Average percent of need met:*** 64% (excluding resources awarded to replace EFC). ***Average financial aid package:*** $18,182 (excluding resources awarded to replace EFC). 15% of all full-time undergraduates had no need and received non-need-based gift aid.

GIFT AID (NEED-BASED) ***Total amount:*** $7,316,769 (22% federal, 2% state, 70% institutional, 6% external sources). ***Receiving aid:*** Freshmen: 85% (173); all full-time undergraduates: 83% (610). ***Average award:*** Freshmen: $15,912; Undergraduates: $14,827. ***Scholarships, grants, and awards:*** Federal Pell, FSEOG, state, private, college/university gift aid from institutional funds.

GIFT AID (NON-NEED-BASED) ***Total amount:*** $937,562 (6% federal, 84% institutional, 10% external sources). ***Receiving aid:*** Freshmen: 6% (13). Undergraduates: 6% (46). ***Average award:*** Freshmen: $7418. Undergraduates: $6389. ***Scholarships, grants, and awards by category:*** *Academic interests/achievement:* general academic interests/achievements. *Creative arts/performance:* music, performing arts. *Special achievements/activities:* general special achievements/activities, hobbies/interests, leadership, memberships, religious involvement. *Special characteristics:* children of faculty/staff, international students, relatives of clergy, siblings of current students. ***Tuition waivers:*** Full or partial for employees or children of employees, senior citizens.

LOANS ***Student loans:*** $4,152,238 (80% need-based, 20% non-need-based). 85% of past graduating class borrowed through all loan programs. *Average indebtedness per student:* $27,071. ***Average need-based loan:*** Freshmen: $3789. Undergraduates: $4420. ***Parent loans:*** $956,066 (70% need-based, 30% non-need-based). ***Programs:*** Federal Direct (Subsidized and Unsubsidized Stafford, PLUS), Perkins, state.

WORK-STUDY ***Federal work-study:*** Total amount: $69,711; 100 jobs averaging $697.

ATHLETIC AWARDS Total amount: $1,286,199 (74% need-based, 26% non-need-based).

APPLYING FOR FINANCIAL AID ***Required financial aid form:*** FAFSA. ***Financial aid deadline (priority):*** 2/15. ***Notification date:*** Continuous beginning 3/1.

CONTACT Nathan Warthan, Director of Financial Aid, Corban University, 5000 Deer Park Drive, SE, Salem, OR 97301-9392, 503-375-7006 or toll-free 800-845-3005 (out-of-state). *Fax:* 503-585-4316. *E-mail:* financialaid@corban.edu.

CORCORAN COLLEGE OF ART AND DESIGN

Washington, DC

Tuition & fees: $30,140 **Average undergraduate aid package: $19,972**

ABOUT THE INSTITUTION Independent, coed. 8 undergraduate majors. Federal methodology is used as a basis for awarding need-based institutional aid.

UNDERGRADUATE EXPENSES for 2011–12 ***Comprehensive fee:*** $42,610 includes full-time tuition ($29,940), mandatory fees ($200), and room and board ($12,470). ***College room only:*** $9970. ***Part-time tuition:*** $998 per credit hour. ***Part-time fees:*** $998 per credit hour; $200 per year. Part-time tuition and fees vary according to course load and degree level. ***Payment plan:*** Installment.

FRESHMAN FINANCIAL AID (Fall 2010, est.) 72 applied for aid; of those 100% were deemed to have need. 100% of freshmen with need received aid. ***Average percent of need met:*** 27% (excluding resources awarded to replace EFC). ***Average financial aid package:*** $20,160 (excluding resources awarded to replace EFC). 5% of all full-time freshmen had no need and received non-need-based gift aid.

UNDERGRADUATE FINANCIAL AID (Fall 2010, est.) 248 applied for aid; of those 100% were deemed to have need. 100% of undergraduates with need received aid. ***Average percent of need met:*** 28% (excluding resources awarded to replace EFC). ***Average financial aid package:*** $19,972 (excluding resources awarded to replace EFC). 20% of all full-time undergraduates had no need and received non-need-based gift aid.

GIFT AID (NEED-BASED) ***Total amount:*** $702,847 (80% federal, 1% state, 19% institutional). ***Receiving aid:*** Freshmen: 77% (67); all full-time undergraduates: 63% (228). ***Average award:*** Freshmen: $9887; Undergraduates: $9234. ***Scholarships, grants, and awards:*** Federal Pell, FSEOG, state, college/university gift aid from institutional funds.

GIFT AID (NON-NEED-BASED) ***Total amount:*** $701,240 (1% state, 95% institutional, 4% external sources). ***Receiving aid:*** Freshmen: 75% (65). Undergraduates: 59% (214). ***Average award:*** Freshmen: $7000. Undergraduates: $6507. ***Scholarships, grants, and awards by category:*** *Academic interests/achievement:* general academic interests/achievements. *Creative arts/performance:* applied art and design. ***Tuition waivers:*** Full or partial for employees or children of employees.

LOANS ***Student loans:*** $2,439,557 (42% need-based, 58% non-need-based). 79% of past graduating class borrowed through all loan programs. *Average indebtedness per student:* $35,562. ***Average need-based loan:*** Freshmen: $2981. Undergraduates: $4090. ***Parent loans:*** $1,460,306 (100% non-need-based). ***Programs:*** Federal Direct (Subsidized and Unsubsidized Stafford, PLUS), Perkins.

WORK-STUDY ***Federal work-study:*** Total amount: $89,139; 48 jobs averaging $1857.

APPLYING FOR FINANCIAL AID ***Required financial aid forms:*** FAFSA, institution's own form. ***Financial aid deadline (priority):*** 3/1. ***Notification date:*** Continuous beginning 4/1. Students must reply within 2 weeks of notification.

CONTACT Diane Morris, Financial Aid Director, Corcoran College of Art and Design, 500 17th Street, NW, Washington, DC 20006-4804, 202-639-1816 or toll-free 888-CORCORAN (out-of-state). *Fax:* 202-737-6921. *E-mail:* dmorris@corcoran.org.

CORNELL COLLEGE

Mount Vernon, IA

Tuition & fees: $32,920 **Average undergraduate aid package: $31,400**

ABOUT THE INSTITUTION Independent Methodist, coed. 49 undergraduate majors. Both federal and institutional methodology are used as a basis for awarding need-based institutional aid.

UNDERGRADUATE EXPENSES for 2011–12 ***Comprehensive fee:*** $40,650 includes full-time tuition ($32,720), mandatory fees ($200), and room and board ($7730). Room and board charges vary according to board plan and housing facility. ***Part-time tuition:*** $1022 per semester hour. Part-time tuition and fees vary according to course load and reciprocity agreements. ***Payment plan:*** Installment.

FRESHMAN FINANCIAL AID (Fall 2010, est.) 295 applied for aid; of those 88% were deemed to have need. 100% of freshmen with need received aid; of those 48% had need fully met. ***Average percent of need met:*** 95% (excluding resources awarded to replace EFC). ***Average financial aid package:*** $28,076 (excluding resources awarded to replace EFC). 21% of all full-time freshmen had no need and received non-need-based gift aid.

UNDERGRADUATE FINANCIAL AID (Fall 2010, est.) 978 applied for aid; of those 90% were deemed to have need. 100% of undergraduates with need received aid; of those 35% had need fully met. ***Average percent of need met:*** 92% (excluding resources awarded to replace EFC). ***Average financial aid package:*** $31,400 (excluding resources awarded to replace EFC). 21% of all full-time undergraduates had no need and received non-need-based gift aid.

GIFT AID (NEED-BASED) ***Total amount:*** $19,226,901 (11% federal, 3% state, 84% institutional, 2% external sources). ***Receiving aid:*** Freshmen: 75% (259); all full-time undergraduates: 74% (881). ***Average award:*** Freshmen: $24,700; Undergraduates: $22,045. ***Scholarships, grants, and awards:*** Federal Pell, FSEOG, state, private, college/university gift aid from institutional funds, TEACH Grants.

GIFT AID (NON-NEED-BASED) ***Total amount:*** $3,614,854 (98% institutional, 2% external sources). ***Receiving aid:*** Freshmen: 67% (229). Undergraduates: 63% (741). ***Average award:*** Freshmen: $12,050. Undergraduates: $12,565. ***Scholarships, grants, and awards by category:*** *Academic interests/achievement:* 405 awards ($5,258,063 total): general academic interests/achievements. *Creative arts/performance:* 125 awards ($630,875 total): art/fine arts, music, performing arts, theater/drama. *Special achievements/activities:* 303 awards ($1,891,408 total): community service, leadership, religious involvement. *Special characteristics:* 240 awards ($2,353,477 total): children of educators, children of faculty/staff, ethnic background, international students, local/state students, members of minority groups, relatives of clergy, religious affiliation. ***Tuition waivers:*** Full or partial for employees or children of employees.

LOANS ***Student loans:*** $6,186,556 (71% need-based, 29% non-need-based). 73% of past graduating class borrowed through all loan programs. *Average indebtedness per student:* $22,455. ***Average need-based loan:*** Freshmen: $3275. Undergraduates: $4443. ***Parent loans:*** $1,938,654 (100% non-need-based). ***Programs:*** Federal Direct (Subsidized and Unsubsidized Stafford, PLUS), Perkins, state, college/university, United Methodist Loan Programs.

WORK-STUDY ***Federal work-study:*** Total amount: $788,262; 618 jobs averaging $1275. ***State or other work-study/employment:*** Part-time jobs available.

APPLYING FOR FINANCIAL AID ***Required financial aid forms:*** FAFSA, institution's own form, noncustodial (divorced/separated) parent's statement. ***Financial aid deadline:*** 3/1. ***Notification date:*** Continuous beginning 3/1. Students must reply by 5/1 or within 2 weeks of notification.

CONTACT Ms. Cindi P. Reints, Director of Financial Assistance, Cornell College, Peter Paul Luce Admission Center, 600 First Street West, Mount Vernon, IA 52314-1098, 319-895-4216 or toll-free 800-747-1112. *Fax:* 319-895-4106. *E-mail:* creints@cornellcollege.edu.

CORNELL UNIVERSITY

Ithaca, NY

Tuition & fees: $39,666 **Average undergraduate aid package: $37,425**

ABOUT THE INSTITUTION Independent, coed. 81 undergraduate majors. Institutional methodology is used as a basis for awarding need-based institutional aid.

UNDERGRADUATE EXPENSES for 2010–11 ***Comprehensive fee:*** $52,316 includes full-time tuition ($39,450), mandatory fees ($216), and room and board ($12,650). ***College room only:*** $7500. Full-time tuition and fees vary according to degree level. Room and board charges vary according to board plan and housing facility. ***Payment plan:*** Installment.

FRESHMAN FINANCIAL AID (Fall 2010, est.) 1,938 applied for aid; of those 84% were deemed to have need. 100% of freshmen with need received aid; of those 100% had need fully met. ***Average percent of need met:*** 100% (excluding resources awarded to replace EFC). ***Average financial aid package:*** $37,846 (excluding resources awarded to replace EFC).

UNDERGRADUATE FINANCIAL AID (Fall 2010, est.) 7,824 applied for aid; of those 88% were deemed to have need. 100% of undergraduates with need received aid; of those 100% had need fully met. ***Average percent of need met:*** 100% (excluding resources awarded to replace EFC). ***Average financial aid package:*** $37,425 (excluding resources awarded to replace EFC).

GIFT AID (NEED-BASED) ***Total amount:*** $219,221,696 (7% federal, 2% state, 88% institutional, 3% external sources). ***Receiving aid:*** Freshmen: 50% (1,600); all full-time undergraduates: 49% (6,742). ***Average award:*** Freshmen: $33,653; Undergraduates: $32,511. ***Scholarships, grants, and awards:*** Federal Pell, FSEOG, state, private, college/university gift aid from institutional funds.

GIFT AID (NON-NEED-BASED) ***Tuition waivers:*** Full or partial for employees or children of employees.

LOANS ***Student loans:*** $23,649,523 (100% need-based). 52% of past graduating class borrowed through all loan programs. *Average indebtedness per student:* $20,648. ***Average need-based loan:*** Freshmen: $2735. Undergraduates: $3378. ***Parent loans:*** $9,272,799 (100% need-based). ***Programs:*** Federal Direct (Subsidized and Unsubsidized Stafford, PLUS), Perkins, college/university.

WORK-STUDY ***Federal work-study:*** Total amount: $8,386,616; 4,852 jobs averaging $1728. ***State or other work-study/employment:*** Total amount: $2,057,199 (100% need-based). 1,357 part-time jobs averaging $1516.

APPLYING FOR FINANCIAL AID ***Required financial aid forms:*** FAFSA, institution's own form, CSS Financial Aid PROFILE, noncustodial (divorced/separated) parent's statement, business/farm supplement, prior years' federal income tax form(s). ***Financial aid deadline:*** 1/2. ***Notification date:*** 4/1. Students must reply by 5/1.

CONTACT Mr. Thomas Keane, Director of Financial Aid and Student Employment, Cornell University, 203 Day Hall, Ithaca, NY 14853-2488, 607-255-5145.

CORNERSTONE UNIVERSITY

Grand Rapids, MI

Tuition & fees: $21,178 **Average undergraduate aid package: $19,772**

ABOUT THE INSTITUTION Independent nondenominational, coed. 39 undergraduate majors. Federal methodology is used as a basis for awarding need-based institutional aid.

UNDERGRADUATE EXPENSES for 2010–11 ***Comprehensive fee:*** $27,964 includes full-time tuition ($20,808), mandatory fees ($370), and room and board ($6786). Full-time tuition and fees vary according to course load and reciprocity agreements. Room and board charges vary according to board plan. ***Part-time tuition:*** $798 per semester hour. Part-time tuition and fees vary according to course load. ***Payment plan:*** Installment.

FRESHMAN FINANCIAL AID (Fall 2010, est.) 300 applied for aid; of those 91% were deemed to have need. 100% of freshmen with need received aid; of those 14% had need fully met. ***Average percent of need met:*** 84% (excluding resources awarded to replace EFC). ***Average financial aid package:*** $20,739 (excluding resources awarded to replace EFC). 14% of all full-time freshmen had no need and received non-need-based gift aid.

UNDERGRADUATE FINANCIAL AID (Fall 2010, est.) 1,002 applied for aid; of those 91% were deemed to have need. 100% of undergraduates with need received aid; of those 14% had need fully met. ***Average percent of need met:*** 83% (excluding resources awarded to replace EFC). ***Average financial aid package:*** $19,772 (excluding resources awarded to replace EFC). 16% of all full-time undergraduates had no need and received non-need-based gift aid.

GIFT AID (NEED-BASED) ***Total amount:*** $10,474,002 (20% federal, 8% state, 69% institutional, 3% external sources). ***Receiving aid:*** Freshmen: 72% (232); all full-time undergraduates: 69% (758). ***Average award:*** Freshmen: $14,563; Undergraduates: $12,708. ***Scholarships, grants, and awards:*** Federal Pell, FSEOG, state, private, college/university gift aid from institutional funds.

GIFT AID (NON-NEED-BASED) ***Total amount:*** $1,270,747 (98% institutional, 2% external sources). ***Receiving aid:*** Freshmen: 72% (232). Undergraduates: 69% (758). ***Average award:*** Freshmen: $7996. Undergraduates: $6742. ***Scholarships, grants, and awards by category:*** *Academic interests/achievement:* 1,088 awards ($5,146,201 total): business, communication, computer science, education, English, foreign languages, general academic interests/achievements, humanities, mathematics, physical sciences, religion/biblical studies, social sciences. *Creative arts/performance:* 61 awards ($137,838 total): music. *Special achievements/activities:* 17 awards ($15,100 total): leadership. *Special characteristics:* 55 awards ($752,946 total): children of faculty/staff. ***Tuition waivers:*** Full or partial for employees or children of employees.

LOANS ***Student loans:*** $6,727,498 (92% need-based, 8% non-need-based). 85% of past graduating class borrowed through all loan programs. *Average indebtedness per student:* $29,510. ***Average need-based loan:*** Freshmen: $3661. Undergraduates: $4365. ***Parent loans:*** $828,400 (80% need-based, 20% non-need-based). ***Programs:*** Federal Direct (Subsidized and Unsubsidized Stafford, PLUS), Perkins.

WORK-STUDY ***Federal work-study:*** Total amount: $172,838; 237 jobs averaging $825.

ATHLETIC AWARDS Total amount: $890,791 (72% need-based, 28% non-need-based).

APPLYING FOR FINANCIAL AID ***Required financial aid form:*** FAFSA. ***Financial aid deadline:*** Continuous. ***Notification date:*** Continuous beginning 3/1. Students must reply within 4 weeks of notification.

CONTACT Mr. Scott W. Stewart, Director of Student Financial Services, Cornerstone University, 1001 East Beltline Avenue, NE, Grand Rapids, MI 49525-5897, 616-222-1424 or toll-free 800-787-9778. *Fax:* 616-222-1400. *E-mail:* scott.stewart@cornerstone.edu.

CORNISH COLLEGE OF THE ARTS

Seattle, WA

Tuition & fees: $29,237 **Average undergraduate aid package: $16,134**

ABOUT THE INSTITUTION Independent, coed. 16 undergraduate majors. Federal methodology is used as a basis for awarding need-based institutional aid.

UNDERGRADUATE EXPENSES for 2010–11 ***Comprehensive fee:*** $37,537 includes full-time tuition ($28,750), mandatory fees ($487), and room and board ($8300). ***College room only:*** $5900. Room and board charges vary according to board plan. ***Part-time tuition:*** $1200 per credit. ***Payment plan:*** Installment.

FRESHMAN FINANCIAL AID (Fall 2010, est.) 171 applied for aid; of those 90% were deemed to have need. 100% of freshmen with need received aid; of those 7% had need fully met. ***Average percent of need met:*** 48% (excluding resources awarded to replace EFC). ***Average financial aid package:*** $15,214 (excluding resources awarded to replace EFC). 15% of all full-time freshmen had no need and received non-need-based gift aid.

UNDERGRADUATE FINANCIAL AID (Fall 2010, est.) 736 applied for aid; of those 89% were deemed to have need. 100% of undergraduates with need received aid; of those 9% had need fully met. ***Average percent of need met:*** 52% (excluding resources awarded to replace EFC). ***Average financial aid package:*** $16,134 (excluding resources awarded to replace EFC). 14% of all full-time undergraduates had no need and received non-need-based gift aid.

GIFT AID (NEED-BASED) ***Total amount:*** $6,528,069 (23% federal, 14% state, 54% institutional, 9% external sources). ***Receiving aid:*** Freshmen: 85% (154); all full-time undergraduates: 81% (628). ***Average award:*** Freshmen: $10,259; Undergraduates: $10,296. ***Scholarships, grants, and awards:*** Federal Pell, FSEOG, state, private, college/university gift aid from institutional funds.

GIFT AID (NON-NEED-BASED) ***Total amount:*** $652,972 (93% institutional, 7% external sources). ***Receiving aid:*** Freshmen: 4% (8). Undergraduates: 4% (30). ***Average award:*** Freshmen: $5046. Undergraduates: $4736. ***Scholarships, grants, and awards by category:*** *Academic interests/achievement:* general academic interests/achievements. *Creative arts/performance:* art/fine arts, dance, music, theater/drama. ***Tuition waivers:*** Full or partial for employees or children of employees.

LOANS ***Student loans:*** $7,142,859 (82% need-based, 18% non-need-based). 95% of past graduating class borrowed through all loan programs. *Average indebtedness per student:* $36,567. ***Average need-based loan:*** Freshmen: $3377. Undergraduates: $4494. ***Parent loans:*** $5,402,736 (57% need-based, 43% non-need-based). ***Programs:*** Federal Direct (Subsidized and Unsubsidized Stafford, PLUS).

WORK-STUDY ***Federal work-study:*** Total amount: $480,470; jobs available. ***State or other work-study/employment:*** Total amount: $809,665 (100% need-based). Part-time jobs available.

APPLYING FOR FINANCIAL AID ***Required financial aid form:*** FAFSA. ***Financial aid deadline (priority):*** 3/1. ***Notification date:*** 4/15. Students must reply by 5/1 or within 2 weeks of notification.

CONTACT Sharron Starling, Office of Admissions, Cornish College of the Arts, 1000 Lenora Street, Seattle, WA 98121, 206-726-5017 or toll-free 800-726-ARTS. *Fax:* 206-720-1011. *E-mail:* admissions@cornish.edu.

COVENANT COLLEGE

Lookout Mountain, GA

Tuition & fees: $26,226 **Average undergraduate aid package: $18,953**

ABOUT THE INSTITUTION Independent religious, coed. 27 undergraduate majors. Federal methodology is used as a basis for awarding need-based institutional aid.

UNDERGRADUATE EXPENSES for 2011–12 ***Comprehensive fee:*** $33,676 includes full-time tuition ($25,476), mandatory fees ($750), and room and board ($7450). Full-time tuition and fees vary according to course load. Part-time tuition and fees vary according to course load. ***Payment plan:*** Installment.

FRESHMAN FINANCIAL AID (Fall 2009) 211 applied for aid; of those 86% were deemed to have need. 100% of freshmen with need received aid; of those 29% had need fully met. ***Average percent of need met:*** 79% (excluding resources awarded to replace EFC). ***Average financial aid package:*** $20,128 (excluding resources awarded to replace EFC). 22% of all full-time freshmen had no need and received non-need-based gift aid.

UNDERGRADUATE FINANCIAL AID (Fall 2009) 689 applied for aid; of those 85% were deemed to have need. 100% of undergraduates with need received aid; of those 29% had need fully met. ***Average percent of need met:*** 77% (excluding resources awarded to replace EFC). ***Average financial aid package:*** $18,953 (excluding resources awarded to replace EFC). 22% of all full-time undergraduates had no need and received non-need-based gift aid.

GIFT AID (NEED-BASED) ***Total amount:*** $9,598,719 (15% federal, 5% state, 75% institutional, 5% external sources). ***Receiving aid:*** Freshmen: 64% (178); all full-time undergraduates: 59% (573). ***Average award:*** Freshmen: $16,795; Undergraduates: $14,127. ***Scholarships, grants, and awards:*** Federal Pell, FSEOG, state, private, college/university gift aid from institutional funds.

GIFT AID (NON-NEED-BASED) ***Total amount:*** $2,585,521 (9% state, 78% institutional, 13% external sources). ***Average award:*** Freshmen: $10,307. Undergraduates: $8392. ***Scholarships, grants, and awards by category:*** *Academic interests/achievement:* general academic interests/achievements. *Creative arts/performance:* music. *Special achievements/activities:* leadership. *Special characteristics:* children of faculty/staff, international students, members of minority groups, religious affiliation. ***Tuition waivers:*** Full or partial for employees or children of employees, senior citizens.

LOANS ***Student loans:*** $3,774,889 (90% need-based, 10% non-need-based). 64% of past graduating class borrowed through all loan programs. *Average indebtedness per student:* $20,519. ***Average need-based loan:*** Freshmen: $3635. Undergraduates: $4331. ***Parent loans:*** $1,159,568 (74% need-based, 26% non-need-based). ***Programs:*** Perkins, state, college/university.

WORK-STUDY ***Federal work-study:*** Total amount: $304,655; jobs available. ***State or other work-study/employment:*** Total amount: $763,014 (89% need-based, 11% non-need-based). Part-time jobs available.

APPLYING FOR FINANCIAL AID ***Required financial aid forms:*** FAFSA, state aid form. ***Financial aid deadline:*** Continuous. ***Notification date:*** Continuous beginning 2/1. Students must reply within 3 weeks of notification.

CONTACT Mrs. Margaret Stewart, Assistant Director of Student Financial Planning, Covenant College, 14049 Scenic Highway, Lookout Mountain, GA 30750, 706-419-1152 or toll-free 888-451-2683. *Fax:* 706-820-2820. *E-mail:* margaret.stewart@covenant.edu.

COX COLLEGE

Springfield, MO

Tuition & fees: $11,340 **Average undergraduate aid package: N/A**

ABOUT THE INSTITUTION Independent, coed, primarily women. 1 undergraduate major. Federal methodology is used as a basis for awarding need-based institutional aid.

UNDERGRADUATE EXPENSES for 2010–11 ***Tuition:*** full-time $10,140; part-time $338 per credit hour.

GIFT AID (NEED-BASED) ***Total amount:*** $1,878,453 (60% federal, 23% state, 16% institutional, 1% external sources). ***Scholarships, grants, and awards:*** Federal Pell, FSEOG, state, private, college/university gift aid from institutional funds, United Negro College Fund, Federal Nursing.

LOANS ***Student loans:*** $3,978,383 (100% need-based). ***Parent loans:*** $86,980 (100% need-based). ***Programs:*** Federal Direct (Subsidized and Unsubsidized Stafford, PLUS).

WORK-STUDY ***Federal work-study:*** Total amount: $71,929; 30 jobs averaging $2398.

APPLYING FOR FINANCIAL AID ***Required financial aid forms:*** FAFSA, institution's own form. ***Financial aid deadline (priority):*** 4/1.

CONTACT Leesa Taylor, Financial Aid Counselor, Cox College, 1423 North Jefferson Avenue, Springfield, MO 65802, 417-269-3160 or toll-free 866-898-5355 (in-state). *Fax:* 417-269-3586. *E-mail:* ltaylo@coxcollege.edu.

CREIGHTON UNIVERSITY

Omaha, NE

Tuition & fees: $30,578 **Average undergraduate aid package: $25,122**

ABOUT THE INSTITUTION Independent Roman Catholic (Jesuit), coed. 48 undergraduate majors. Federal methodology is used as a basis for awarding need-based institutional aid.

UNDERGRADUATE EXPENSES for 2010–11 ***Comprehensive fee:*** $39,742 includes full-time tuition ($29,226), mandatory fees ($1352), and room and board ($9164). ***College room only:*** $5220. Full-time tuition and fees vary according to degree level. Room and board charges vary according to board plan and housing facility. ***Part-time tuition:*** $913 per credit hour. Part-time tuition and fees vary according to degree level. ***Payment plan:*** Installment.

FRESHMAN FINANCIAL AID (Fall 2010, est.) 834 applied for aid; of those 82% were deemed to have need. 100% of freshmen with need received aid; of those 37% had need fully met. ***Average percent of need met:*** 89% (excluding resources awarded to replace EFC). ***Average financial aid package:*** $25,985 (excluding resources awarded to replace EFC). 28% of all full-time freshmen had no need and received non-need-based gift aid.

UNDERGRADUATE FINANCIAL AID (Fall 2010, est.) 2,761 applied for aid; of those 85% were deemed to have need. 99% of undergraduates with need received aid; of those 45% had need fully met. ***Average percent of need met:*** 90% (excluding resources awarded to replace EFC). ***Average financial aid package:*** $25,122 (excluding resources awarded to replace EFC). 31% of all full-time undergraduates had no need and received non-need-based gift aid.

GIFT AID (NEED-BASED) ***Total amount:*** $38,439,083 (11% federal, 1% state, 83% institutional, 5% external sources). ***Receiving aid:*** Freshmen: 67% (682); all full-time undergraduates: 51% (2,022). ***Average award:*** Freshmen: $21,035; Undergraduates: $19,622. ***Scholarships, grants, and awards:*** Federal Pell, FSEOG, state, private, college/university gift aid from institutional funds, Federal Nursing.

GIFT AID (NON-NEED-BASED) ***Total amount:*** $17,513,429 (98% institutional, 2% external sources). ***Receiving aid:*** Freshmen: 66% (664). Undergraduates: 56% (2,200). ***Average award:*** Freshmen: $12,081. Undergraduates: $12,524. ***Scholarships, grants, and awards by category:*** *Academic interests/achievement:* business, education, general academic interests/achievements, military science. *Creative arts/performance:* art/fine arts, creative writing, dance, debating, journalism/publications, music, performing arts, theater/drama. *Special achievements/activities:* leadership. *Special characteristics:* children of faculty/staff, first-generation college students, local/state students, members of minority groups, religious affiliation, siblings of current students. ***Tuition waivers:*** Full or partial for employees or children of employees, adult students.

LOANS ***Student loans:*** $26,199,482 (42% need-based, 58% non-need-based). 67% of past graduating class borrowed through all loan programs. *Average indebtedness per student:* $32,152. ***Average need-based loan:*** Freshmen: $4856. Undergraduates: $5902. ***Parent loans:*** $4,745,763 (100% non-need-based). ***Programs:*** Federal Direct (Subsidized and Unsubsidized Stafford, PLUS), Perkins, Federal Nursing, college/university.

WORK-STUDY ***Federal work-study:*** Total amount: $1,935,278; 954 jobs averaging $2022.

ATHLETIC AWARDS Total amount: $3,724,895 (35% need-based, 65% non-need-based).

APPLYING FOR FINANCIAL AID ***Required financial aid forms:*** FAFSA, institution's own form. ***Financial aid deadline (priority):*** 3/1. ***Notification date:*** Continuous beginning 3/15. Students must reply by 5/1 or within 4 weeks of notification.

CONTACT Sarah Sell, Assistant Director of Financial Aid, Creighton University, 2500 California Plaza, Omaha, NE 68178, 402-280-2731 or toll-free 800-282-5835. *Fax:* 402-280-2895. *E-mail:* sarahsell@creighton.edu.

THE CRISWELL COLLEGE
Dallas, TX

CONTACT Ester Waggoner, Financial Aid Director, The Criswell College, 4010 Gaston Avenue, Dallas, TX 75246, 800-899-0012. *Fax:* 214-818-1310. *E-mail:* ewaggoner@criswell.edu.

CROSSROADS BIBLE COLLEGE
Indianapolis, IN

Tuition & fees: $9850 **Average undergraduate aid package: N/A**

ABOUT THE INSTITUTION Independent Baptist, coed. 7 undergraduate majors. Institutional methodology is used as a basis for awarding need-based institutional aid.

UNDERGRADUATE EXPENSES for 2011–12 ***Tuition:*** full-time $9480. ***Payment plan:*** Installment.

GIFT AID (NEED-BASED) ***Scholarships, grants, and awards:*** Federal Pell, FSEOG, state, college/university gift aid from institutional funds.

GIFT AID (NON-NEED-BASED) ***Scholarships, grants, and awards by category:*** *Special characteristics:* children of faculty/staff, married students, siblings of current students, spouses of current students. ***Tuition waivers:*** Full or partial for employees or children of employees.

LOANS ***Programs:*** Federal Direct (Subsidized and Unsubsidized Stafford, PLUS).

WORK-STUDY Federal work-study jobs available. ***State or other work-study/employment:*** Part-time jobs available.

APPLYING FOR FINANCIAL AID ***Required financial aid forms:*** FAFSA, institution's own form. ***Financial aid deadline:*** 6/30 (priority: 5/31). ***Notification date:*** 7/31. Students must reply within 2 weeks of notification.

CONTACT Mrs. Phyllis Dodson, Senior Director of Financial Aid, Crossroads Bible College, 601 North Shortridge Road, Indianapolis, IN 46219, 317-352-8736 Ext. 228 or toll-free 800-273-2224 Ext. 230. *Fax:* 317-352-9145.

CROSSROADS COLLEGE
Rochester, MN

ABOUT THE INSTITUTION Independent religious, coed. ***Awards:*** associate and bachelor's degrees. 13 undergraduate majors. ***Total enrollment:*** 160. Undergraduates: 160. Freshmen: 24.

GIFT AID (NEED-BASED) ***Scholarships, grants, and awards:*** Federal Pell, FSEOG, state, private, college/university gift aid from institutional funds.

GIFT AID (NON-NEED-BASED) ***Scholarships, grants, and awards by category:*** *Academic interests/achievement:* general academic interests/achievements, religion/biblical studies. *Creative arts/performance:* music. *Special achievements/activities:* general special achievements/activities, religious involvement. *Special characteristics:* children of faculty/staff, general special characteristics, international students, parents of current students, religious affiliation, siblings of current students, spouses of current students.

LOANS ***Programs:*** state, college/university, alternative loans.

WORK-STUDY Federal work-study jobs available. ***State or other work-study/employment:*** Part-time jobs available.

APPLYING FOR FINANCIAL AID ***Required financial aid forms:*** FAFSA, institution's own form.

CONTACT Polly Kellogg-Bradley, Director of Financial Aid, Crossroads College, 920 Mayowood Road SW, Rochester, MN 55902, 507-288-4563 or toll-free 800-456-7651. *Fax:* 507-288-9046. *E-mail:* financialaid@crossroadscollege.edu.

CROWN COLLEGE
St. Bonifacius, MN

Tuition & fees: $21,470 **Average undergraduate aid package: $15,563**

ABOUT THE INSTITUTION Independent religious, coed. 36 undergraduate majors. Both federal and institutional methodology are used as a basis for awarding need-based institutional aid.

UNDERGRADUATE EXPENSES for 2011–12 ***Comprehensive fee:*** $28,850 includes full-time tuition ($21,470) and room and board ($7380). ***College room only:*** $3790. Room and board charges vary according to board plan and housing facility. ***Part-time tuition:*** $895 per credit. ***Payment plan:*** Installment.

FRESHMAN FINANCIAL AID (Fall 2010, est.) 137 applied for aid; of those 92% were deemed to have need. 100% of freshmen with need received aid; of those 11% had need fully met. ***Average percent of need met:*** 68% (excluding resources awarded to replace EFC). ***Average financial aid package:*** $12,610 (excluding resources awarded to replace EFC). 15% of all full-time freshmen had no need and received non-need-based gift aid.

UNDERGRADUATE FINANCIAL AID (Fall 2010, est.) 546 applied for aid; of those 93% were deemed to have need. 100% of undergraduates with need received aid; of those 9% had need fully met. ***Average percent of need met:*** 62% (excluding resources awarded to replace EFC). ***Average financial aid package:*** $15,563 (excluding resources awarded to replace EFC). 6% of all full-time undergraduates had no need and received non-need-based gift aid.

GIFT AID (NEED-BASED) ***Total amount:*** $2,430,934 (53% federal, 21% state, 26% institutional). ***Receiving aid:*** Freshmen: 50% (74); all full-time undergraduates: 69% (404). ***Average award:*** Freshmen: $6034; Undergraduates: $6017. ***Scholarships, grants, and awards:*** Federal Pell, FSEOG, state, private, college/university gift aid from institutional funds.

GIFT AID (NON-NEED-BASED) ***Total amount:*** $3,669,220 (96% institutional, 4% external sources). ***Receiving aid:*** Freshmen: 76% (113). Undergraduates: 88% (510). ***Average award:*** Freshmen: $11,621. Undergraduates: $7675. ***Scholarships, grants, and awards by category:*** *Academic interests/achievement:* 507 awards ($1,770,951 total): general academic interests/achievements. *Creative arts/performance:* 10 awards ($17,300 total): music. *Special achievements/activities:* 165 awards ($691,845 total): leadership. *Special characteristics:* 301 awards ($909,189 total): children and siblings of alumni, children of faculty/staff, international students, members of minority groups, relatives of clergy, siblings of current students. ***Tuition waivers:*** Full or partial for minority students, children of alumni, employees or children of employees.

LOANS ***Student loans:*** $4,304,186 (45% need-based, 55% non-need-based). 79% of past graduating class borrowed through all loan programs. *Average indebtedness per student:* $38,042. ***Average need-based loan:*** Freshmen: $3571. Undergraduates: $4640. ***Parent loans:*** $826,883 (100% non-need-based). ***Programs:*** Federal Direct (Subsidized and Unsubsidized Stafford, PLUS), Perkins, state, SELF Loans, CitiAssist Loans, Sallie Mae Signature loans, alternative loans.

WORK-STUDY ***Federal work-study:*** Total amount: $299,148; 98 jobs averaging $1881. ***State or other work-study/employment:*** Total amount: $41,419 (100% need-based). 61 part-time jobs averaging $679.

APPLYING FOR FINANCIAL AID ***Required financial aid form:*** FAFSA. ***Financial aid deadline:*** 8/1 (priority: 4/15). ***Notification date:*** Continuous. Students must reply by 4/1 or within 3 weeks of notification.

CONTACT Mrs. Marla Rupp, Director of Financial Aid, Crown College, 8700 College View Drive, St. Bonifacius, MN 55375-9001, 952-446-4175 or toll-free 800-68-CROWN. *Fax:* 952-446-4178. *E-mail:* finaid@crown.edu.

THE CULINARY INSTITUTE OF AMERICA
Hyde Park, NY

CONTACT Patricia A. Arcuri, Director of Financial Aid, The Culinary Institute of America, 1946 Campus Drive, Hyde Park, NY 12538-1499, 845-451-1243 or toll-free 800-CULINARY. *Fax:* 845-905-4030. *E-mail:* p_arcuri@culinary.edu.

CULINARY INSTITUTE OF VIRGINIA
Norfolk, VA

CONTACT Ms. Lynn Robinson, Director of Financial Aid, Culinary Institute of Virginia, 8 Abbott Park Place, Providence, RI 02903, 401-598-4648 or toll-free 866-619-CHEF. *Fax:* 401-598-1040. *E-mail:* fp@jwu.edu.

CULVER-STOCKTON COLLEGE
Canton, MO

Tuition & fees: $22,550 **Average undergraduate aid package: $20,090**

ABOUT THE INSTITUTION Independent religious, coed. 31 undergraduate majors. Federal methodology is used as a basis for awarding need-based institutional aid.

UNDERGRADUATE EXPENSES for 2011–12 ***One-time required fee:*** $200. ***Comprehensive fee:*** $30,150 includes full-time tuition ($22,250), mandatory fees ($300), and room and board ($7600). ***College room only:*** $3400. Room and board charges vary according to board plan. ***Part-time tuition:*** $515 per credit hour. ***Part-time fees:*** $12.50 per credit hour. ***Payment plan:*** Installment.

FRESHMAN FINANCIAL AID (Fall 2010, est.) 200 applied for aid; of those 94% were deemed to have need. 100% of freshmen with need received aid; of those 16% had need fully met. ***Average percent of need met:*** 77% (excluding resources awarded to replace EFC). ***Average financial aid package:*** $20,158 (excluding resources awarded to replace EFC). 12% of all full-time freshmen had no need and received non-need-based gift aid.

UNDERGRADUATE FINANCIAL AID (Fall 2010, est.) 647 applied for aid; of those 94% were deemed to have need. 100% of undergraduates with need received aid; of those 18% had need fully met. ***Average percent of need met:*** 77% (excluding resources awarded to replace EFC). ***Average financial aid package:*** $20,090 (excluding resources awarded to replace EFC). 12% of all full-time undergraduates had no need and received non-need-based gift aid.

GIFT AID (NEED-BASED) ***Total amount:*** $8,785,152 (22% federal, 5% state, 71% institutional, 2% external sources). ***Receiving aid:*** Freshmen: 88% (187); all full-time undergraduates: 88% (608). ***Average award:*** Freshmen: $16,297; Undergraduates: $15,772. ***Scholarships, grants, and awards:*** Federal Pell, FSEOG, state, private, college/university gift aid from institutional funds.

GIFT AID (NON-NEED-BASED) ***Total amount:*** $1,392,881 (1% federal, 1% state, 95% institutional, 3% external sources). ***Receiving aid:*** Freshmen: 11% (24). Undergraduates: 12% (85). ***Average award:*** Freshmen: $11,900. Undergraduates: $11,564. ***Scholarships, grants, and awards by category:*** *Academic interests/achievement:* 690 awards ($6,200,652 total): general academic interests/achievements. *Creative arts/performance:* 103 awards ($238,988 total): art/fine arts, debating, music, theater/drama. *Special achievements/activities:* 18 awards ($30,653 total): cheerleading/drum major, general special achievements/ activities, leadership. *Special characteristics:* 229 awards ($470,559 total): children and siblings of alumni, children of faculty/staff, international students, local/ state students, religious affiliation, veterans, veterans' children. ***Tuition waivers:*** Full or partial for employees or children of employees, senior citizens.

LOANS ***Student loans:*** $5,583,306 (78% need-based, 22% non-need-based). 93% of past graduating class borrowed through all loan programs. *Average indebtedness per student:* $31,200. ***Average need-based loan:*** Freshmen: $4090. Undergraduates: $4814. ***Parent loans:*** $1,442,911 (40% need-based, 60% non-need-based). ***Programs:*** Federal Direct (Subsidized and Unsubsidized Stafford, PLUS), Perkins, Federal Nursing, state, college/university.

WORK-STUDY ***Federal work-study:*** Total amount: $73,601; 63 jobs averaging $1168. ***State or other work-study/employment:*** Total amount: $329,947 (55% need-based, 45% non-need-based). 320 part-time jobs averaging $1031.

ATHLETIC AWARDS Total amount: $1,187,079 (77% need-based, 23% non-need-based).

APPLYING FOR FINANCIAL AID ***Required financial aid form:*** FAFSA. ***Financial aid deadline:*** 6/1 (priority: 3/1). ***Notification date:*** Continuous. Students must reply within 2 weeks of notification.

CONTACT Ms. Tina M. Wiseman, Director of Financial Aid, Culver-Stockton College, One College Hill, Canton, MO 63435, 573-288-6307 Ext. 6306 or toll-free 800-537-1883. *Fax:* 573-288-6308. *E-mail:* twiseman@culver.edu.

CUMBERLAND UNIVERSITY

Lebanon, TN

CONTACT Ms. Beatrice LaChance, Director of Student Financial Services, Cumberland University, One Cumberland Square, Lebanon, TN 37087-3554, 615-444-2562 Ext. 1244 or toll-free 800-467-0562. *Fax:* 615-443-8424. *E-mail:* lvaughan@cumberland.edu.

CURRY COLLEGE

Milton, MA

Tuition & fees: $21,210 **Average undergraduate aid package: $17,600**

ABOUT THE INSTITUTION Independent, coed. 28 undergraduate majors. Federal methodology is used as a basis for awarding need-based institutional aid.

UNDERGRADUATE EXPENSES for 2011–12 ***One-time required fee:*** $280. ***Comprehensive fee:*** $44,495 includes full-time tuition ($30,700), mandatory fees ($1510), and room and board ($12,285). ***College room only:*** $6895. Room and board charges vary according to board plan and housing facility. ***Part-time tuition:*** $1023 per credit. Part-time tuition and fees vary according to course load. ***Payment plan:*** Installment.

FRESHMAN FINANCIAL AID (Fall 2010, est.) 438 applied for aid; of those 100% were deemed to have need. 100% of freshmen with need received aid; of those 2% had need fully met. ***Average percent of need met:*** 58% (excluding resources awarded to replace EFC). ***Average financial aid package:*** $18,399 (excluding resources awarded to replace EFC). 6% of all full-time freshmen had no need and received non-need-based gift aid.

UNDERGRADUATE FINANCIAL AID (Fall 2010, est.) 1,407 applied for aid; of those 100% were deemed to have need. 100% of undergraduates with need received aid; of those 2% had need fully met. ***Average percent of need met:*** 59% (excluding resources awarded to replace EFC). ***Average financial aid package:*** $17,600 (excluding resources awarded to replace EFC). 5% of all full-time undergraduates had no need and received non-need-based gift aid.

GIFT AID (NEED-BASED) ***Total amount:*** $19,170,636 (14% federal, 3% state, 80% institutional, 3% external sources). ***Receiving aid:*** Freshmen: 74% (423); all full-time undergraduates: 65% (1,301). ***Average award:*** Freshmen: $12,315; Undergraduates: $11,349. ***Scholarships, grants, and awards:*** Federal Pell, FSEOG, state, private, college/university gift aid from institutional funds.

GIFT AID (NON-NEED-BASED) ***Total amount:*** $808,131 (6% federal, 83% institutional, 11% external sources). ***Receiving aid:*** Freshmen: 1% (4). Undergraduates: 1% (11). ***Average award:*** Freshmen: $5271. Undergraduates: $5858. ***Scholarships, grants, and awards by category:*** *Academic interests/ achievement:* 339 awards ($2,014,763 total): general academic interests/ achievements. ***Tuition waivers:*** Full or partial for children of alumni, employees or children of employees.

LOANS ***Student loans:*** $16,833,860 (36% need-based, 64% non-need-based). 78% of past graduating class borrowed through all loan programs. *Average indebtedness per student:* $36,874. ***Average need-based loan:*** Freshmen: $3450. Undergraduates: $4263. ***Parent loans:*** $9,779,870 (100% non-need-based). ***Programs:*** Federal Direct (Subsidized and Unsubsidized Stafford, PLUS), Perkins, state.

WORK-STUDY ***Federal work-study:*** Total amount: $1,498,273; 835 jobs averaging $1848.

APPLYING FOR FINANCIAL AID ***Required financial aid form:*** FAFSA. ***Financial aid deadline (priority):*** 3/1. ***Notification date:*** Continuous beginning 3/1.

CONTACT Dyan Teehan, Director of Financial Aid, Curry College, 1071 Blue Hill Avenue, Milton, MA 02186-2395, 617-333-2354 or toll-free 800-669-0686. *Fax:* 617-333-2915. *E-mail:* dteehan0107@curry.edu.

CURTIS INSTITUTE OF MUSIC

Philadelphia, PA

CONTACT Richard Woodland, Director of Student Financial Assistance, Curtis Institute of Music, 1726 Locust Street, Philadelphia, PA 19103-6107, 215-717-3143. *E-mail:* richard.woodland@curtis.edu.

DAEMEN COLLEGE

Amherst, NY

Tuition & fees: $21,460 **Average undergraduate aid package: $16,217**

ABOUT THE INSTITUTION Independent, coed. 31 undergraduate majors. Federal methodology is used as a basis for awarding need-based institutional aid.

UNDERGRADUATE EXPENSES for 2010–11 ***Comprehensive fee:*** $31,310 includes full-time tuition ($20,950), mandatory fees ($510), and room and board ($9850). Full-time tuition and fees vary according to course load and reciprocity agreements. Room and board charges vary according to board plan and housing facility. ***Part-time tuition:*** $695 per credit hour. ***Part-time fees:*** $6 per credit hour; $70 per term. Part-time tuition and fees vary according to course load and reciprocity agreements. ***Payment plans:*** Installment, deferred payment.

FRESHMAN FINANCIAL AID (Fall 2009) 390 applied for aid; of those 88% were deemed to have need. 100% of freshmen with need received aid; of those 33% had need fully met. ***Average percent of need met:*** 81% (excluding resources awarded to replace EFC). ***Average financial aid package:*** $16,606 (excluding resources awarded to replace EFC). 15% of all full-time freshmen had no need and received non-need-based gift aid.

UNDERGRADUATE FINANCIAL AID (Fall 2009) 1,380 applied for aid; of those 87% were deemed to have need. 100% of undergraduates with need received aid; of those 35% had need fully met. ***Average percent of need met:*** 80% (excluding resources awarded to replace EFC). ***Average financial aid package:*** $16,217 (excluding resources awarded to replace EFC). 16% of all full-time undergraduates had no need and received non-need-based gift aid.

GIFT AID (NEED-BASED) ***Total amount:*** $7,733,495 (36% federal, 28% state, 36% institutional). ***Receiving aid:*** Freshmen: 79% (315); all full-time undergraduates: 75% (1,132). ***Average award:*** Freshmen: $17,080; Undergraduates: $16,528. ***Scholarships, grants, and awards:*** Federal Pell, FSEOG, state, private, college/university gift aid from institutional funds.

GIFT AID (NON-NEED-BASED) ***Total amount:*** $10,066,122 (2% federal, 2% state, 96% institutional). ***Receiving aid:*** Freshmen: 82% (329). Undergraduates: 77% (1,157). ***Average award:*** Freshmen: $9064. Undergraduates: $9388. ***Scholarships, grants, and awards by category:*** *Academic interests/achievement:* 1,319 awards ($7,349,104 total): general academic interests/achievements. *Creative arts/performance:* 11 awards ($38,500 total): art/fine arts. *Special achievements/activities:* 6 awards ($7000 total): leadership. *Special characteristics:* children and siblings of alumni, children of faculty/staff, general special characteristics, siblings of current students. ***Tuition waivers:*** Full or partial for employees or children of employees, senior citizens.

LOANS ***Student loans:*** $15,815,594 (46% need-based, 54% non-need-based). 87% of past graduating class borrowed through all loan programs. *Average indebtedness per student:* $27,444. ***Average need-based loan:*** Freshmen: $3057. Undergraduates: $4837. ***Parent loans:*** $887,568 (100% non-need-based). ***Programs:*** Perkins, college/university, alternative loans.

WORK-STUDY ***Federal work-study:*** Total amount: $385,866; 265 jobs averaging $1456. ***State or other work-study/employment:*** Total amount: $460,815 (61% need-based, 39% non-need-based). 327 part-time jobs averaging $1464.

ATHLETIC AWARDS Total amount: $616,761 (100% non-need-based).

APPLYING FOR FINANCIAL AID ***Required financial aid forms:*** FAFSA, state aid form. ***Financial aid deadline (priority):*** 2/15. ***Notification date:*** Continuous. Students must reply within 2 weeks of notification.

CONTACT Mr. Jeffrey Pagano, Director of Financial Aid, Daemen College, 4380 Main Street, Amherst, NY 14226-3592, 716-839-8254 or toll-free 800-462-7652. *Fax:* 716-839-8378. *E-mail:* jpagano@daemen.edu.

DAKOTA STATE UNIVERSITY

Madison, SD

Tuition & fees (SD res): $7171 **Average undergraduate aid package: $7897**

ABOUT THE INSTITUTION State-supported, coed. 30 undergraduate majors. Federal methodology is used as a basis for awarding need-based institutional aid.

UNDERGRADUATE EXPENSES for 2010–11 ***Tuition, state resident:*** full-time $2994; part-time $99.80 per credit hour. ***Tuition, nonresident:*** full-time $4491; part-time $149.70 per credit hour. ***Required fees:*** full-time $4177; $115.35 per credit hour. Full-time tuition and fees vary according to location and reciprocity agreements. Part-time tuition and fees vary according to location and reciprocity agreements. ***College room and board:*** $5004; ***Room only:*** $2676. Room and board charges vary according to board plan and housing facility. ***Payment plans:*** Installment, deferred payment.

FRESHMAN FINANCIAL AID (Fall 2009) 265 applied for aid; of those 79% were deemed to have need. 100% of freshmen with need received aid; of those 8% had need fully met. ***Average percent of need met:*** 84% (excluding resources awarded to replace EFC). ***Average financial aid package:*** $7754 (excluding resources awarded to replace EFC). 13% of all full-time freshmen had no need and received non-need-based gift aid.

UNDERGRADUATE FINANCIAL AID (Fall 2009) 985 applied for aid; of those 78% were deemed to have need. 100% of undergraduates with need received aid; of those 16% had need fully met. ***Average percent of need met:*** 84% (excluding resources awarded to replace EFC). ***Average financial aid package:*** $7897 (excluding resources awarded to replace EFC). 9% of all full-time undergraduates had no need and received non-need-based gift aid.

GIFT AID (NEED-BASED) ***Total amount:*** $3,205,432 (77% federal, 3% state, 9% institutional, 11% external sources). ***Receiving aid:*** Freshmen: 47% (136); all full-time undergraduates: 40% (453). ***Average award:*** Freshmen: $4505; Undergraduates: $4756. ***Scholarships, grants, and awards:*** Federal Pell, FSEOG, state, private, college/university gift aid from institutional funds, Agency Assistance (Veteran Benefits/Department of Labor).

GIFT AID (NON-NEED-BASED) ***Total amount:*** $328,786 (9% federal, 12% state, 37% institutional, 42% external sources). ***Receiving aid:*** Freshmen: 48% (138). Undergraduates: 28% (320). ***Average award:*** Freshmen: $2942. Undergraduates: $3454. ***Scholarships, grants, and awards by category:*** *Academic interests/achievement:* 272 awards ($364,074 total): business, communication, computer science, education, English, general academic interests/achievements, mathematics. *Creative arts/performance:* 5 awards ($1550 total): music. ***Tuition waivers:*** Full or partial for employees or children of employees, senior citizens.

LOANS ***Student loans:*** $8,568,799 (71% need-based, 29% non-need-based). 78% of past graduating class borrowed through all loan programs. *Average indebtedness per student:* $21,811. ***Average need-based loan:*** Freshmen: $3259. Undergraduates: $3868. ***Parent loans:*** $667,839 (71% need-based, 29% non-need-based). ***Programs:*** Federal Direct (Subsidized and Unsubsidized Stafford, PLUS), Perkins, alternative loans.

WORK-STUDY ***Federal work-study:*** Total amount: $262,040; 110 jobs averaging $2382. ***State or other work-study/employment:*** Total amount: $103,849 (100% non-need-based). 18 part-time jobs averaging $5749.

ATHLETIC AWARDS Total amount: $235,050 (71% need-based, 29% non-need-based).

APPLYING FOR FINANCIAL AID ***Required financial aid forms:*** FAFSA, institution's own scholarship application. ***Financial aid deadline (priority):*** 3/1. ***Notification date:*** Continuous beginning 4/1. Students must reply within 2 weeks of notification.

CONTACT Denise Grayson, Financial Aid Director, Dakota State University, 103 Heston Hall, 820 North Washington Avenue, Madison, SD 57042-1799, 605-256-5158 or toll-free 888-DSU-9988. *Fax:* 605-256-5020. *E-mail:* fa@dsu.edu.

DAKOTA WESLEYAN UNIVERSITY

Mitchell, SD

Tuition & fees: $19,850 **Average undergraduate aid package: $17,000**

ABOUT THE INSTITUTION Independent United Methodist, coed. 46 undergraduate majors. Federal methodology is used as a basis for awarding need-based institutional aid.

UNDERGRADUATE EXPENSES for 2010–11 ***Comprehensive fee:*** $25,780 includes full-time tuition ($19,850) and room and board ($5930). ***College room only:*** $2400. Room and board charges vary according to board plan and housing facility. ***Part-time tuition:*** $430 per credit hour.

FRESHMAN FINANCIAL AID (Fall 2010, est.) 164 applied for aid; of those 90% were deemed to have need. 100% of freshmen with need received aid; of those 19% had need fully met. ***Average percent of need met:*** 73% (excluding resources awarded to replace EFC). ***Average financial aid package:*** $16,900 (excluding resources awarded to replace EFC). 14% of all full-time freshmen had no need and received non-need-based gift aid.

UNDERGRADUATE FINANCIAL AID (Fall 2010, est.) 613 applied for aid; of those 93% were deemed to have need. 100% of undergraduates with need received aid; of those 19% had need fully met. ***Average percent of need met:*** 70% (excluding resources awarded to replace EFC). ***Average financial aid package:*** $17,000 (excluding resources awarded to replace EFC). 13% of all full-time undergraduates had no need and received non-need-based gift aid.

GIFT AID (NEED-BASED) ***Total amount:*** $6,437,886 (29% federal, 1% state, 67% institutional, 3% external sources). ***Receiving aid:*** Freshmen: 86% (148); all full-time undergraduates: 86% (567). ***Average award:*** Freshmen: $10,800; Undergraduates: $12,700. ***Scholarships, grants, and awards:*** Federal Pell, FSEOG, state, college/university gift aid from institutional funds.

GIFT AID (NON-NEED-BASED) ***Total amount:*** $916,460 (1% federal, 3% state, 89% institutional, 7% external sources). ***Receiving aid:*** Freshmen: 12% (21). Undergraduates: 10% (66). ***Average award:*** Freshmen: $8100. Undergraduates: $8100. ***Tuition waivers:*** Full or partial for senior citizens.

LOANS ***Student loans:*** $5,496,239 (79% need-based, 21% non-need-based). 87% of past graduating class borrowed through all loan programs. *Average indebtedness per student:* $32,400. ***Average need-based loan:*** Freshmen: $3500. Undergraduates: $4400. ***Parent loans:*** $523,479 (38% need-based, 62% non-need-based). ***Programs:*** Federal Direct (Subsidized and Unsubsidized Stafford, PLUS), Perkins, private loans, United Methodist Student Loans (for members of Methodist Church).

WORK-STUDY ***Federal work-study:*** Total amount: $104,099; 100 jobs averaging $1400. ***State or other work-study/employment:*** Total amount: $2400 (100% non-need-based). 3 part-time jobs averaging $1200.

ATHLETIC AWARDS Total amount: $1,315,975 (72% need-based, 28% non-need-based).

APPLYING FOR FINANCIAL AID ***Financial aid deadline (priority):*** 4/1. ***Notification date:*** Continuous beginning 3/1. Students must reply within 2 weeks of notification.

CONTACT Kristy O'Kief, Director of Financial Aid, Dakota Wesleyan University, 1200 West University Avenue, Mitchell, SD 57301, 605-995-2656 or toll-free 800-333-8506. *Fax:* 605-995-2638. *E-mail:* krokief@dwu.edu.

DALLAS BAPTIST UNIVERSITY

Dallas, TX

Tuition & fees: $18,690 **Average undergraduate aid package: $14,769**

ABOUT THE INSTITUTION Independent religious, coed. 43 undergraduate majors. Federal methodology is used as a basis for awarding need-based institutional aid.

UNDERGRADUATE EXPENSES for 2010–11 ***Comprehensive fee:*** $24,558 includes full-time tuition ($18,690) and room and board ($5868). ***College room only:*** $2326. Room and board charges vary according to board plan and housing facility. ***Part-time tuition:*** $623 per credit hour. ***Payment plans:*** Installment, deferred payment.

FRESHMAN FINANCIAL AID (Fall 2010, est.) 361 applied for aid; of those 73% were deemed to have need. 99% of freshmen with need received aid; of those 54% had need fully met. ***Average percent of need met:*** 81% (excluding resources awarded to replace EFC). ***Average financial aid package:*** $17,029 (excluding resources awarded to replace EFC). 21% of all full-time freshmen had no need and received non-need-based gift aid.

UNDERGRADUATE FINANCIAL AID (Fall 2010, est.) 2,017 applied for aid; of those 75% were deemed to have need. 95% of undergraduates with need received aid; of those 39% had need fully met. ***Average percent of need met:*** 65% (excluding resources awarded to replace EFC). ***Average financial aid package:*** $14,769 (excluding resources awarded to replace EFC). 16% of all full-time undergraduates had no need and received non-need-based gift aid.

GIFT AID (NEED-BASED) ***Total amount:*** $7,123,672 (54% federal, 45% state, 1% institutional). ***Receiving aid:*** Freshmen: 47% (175); all full-time undergraduates: 44% (1,009). ***Average award:*** Freshmen: $3254; Undergraduates: $3515. ***Scholarships, grants, and awards:*** Federal Pell, FSEOG, state, private, college/university gift aid from institutional funds.

GIFT AID (NON-NEED-BASED) ***Total amount:*** $12,184,839 (86% institutional, 14% external sources). ***Receiving aid:*** Freshmen: 69% (259). Undergraduates: 52% (1,192). ***Average award:*** Freshmen: $7791. Undergraduates: $7469. ***Scholarships, grants, and awards by category:*** *Academic interests/achievement:* 1,297 awards ($2,872,780 total): business, communication, computer science, education, general academic interests/achievements, humanities, mathematics, premedicine, religion/biblical studies. *Creative arts/performance:* 93 awards ($253,401 total): music. *Special achievements/activities:* 1,372 awards ($5,175,370 total): community service, general special achievements/activities, leadership, memberships, religious involvement. *Special characteristics:* 191 awards ($809,344 total): children of faculty/staff, general special characteristics, relatives of clergy, religious affiliation. ***Tuition waivers:*** Full or partial for employees or children of employees.

LOANS ***Student loans:*** $17,818,695 (38% need-based, 62% non-need-based). 81% of past graduating class borrowed through all loan programs. *Average indebtedness per student:* $18,629. ***Average need-based loan:*** Freshmen: $3109. Undergraduates: $4094. ***Parent loans:*** $2,666,848 (100% non-need-based). ***Programs:*** Federal Direct (Unsubsidized Stafford, PLUS), Perkins, state, college/university.

WORK-STUDY ***Federal work-study:*** Total amount: $381,682; 130 jobs averaging $2575. ***State or other work-study/employment:*** Total amount: $6020 (100% need-based). 56 part-time jobs averaging $663.

ATHLETIC AWARDS Total amount: $1,549,724 (100% non-need-based).

APPLYING FOR FINANCIAL AID ***Required financial aid forms:*** FAFSA, institution's own form. ***Financial aid deadline:*** Continuous. ***Notification date:*** Continuous beginning 2/1.

CONTACT Mr. Lee Ferguson, Director of Financial Aid, Dallas Baptist University, 3000 Mountain Creek Parkway, Dallas, TX 75211-9299, 214-333-5363 or toll-free 800-460-1328. *Fax:* 214-333-5586. *E-mail:* lee@dbu.edu.

DALLAS CHRISTIAN COLLEGE

Dallas, TX

CONTACT Robin L. Walker, Director of Student Financial Aid, Dallas Christian College, 2700 Christian Parkway, Dallas, TX 75234-7299, 972-241-3371 Ext. 105. *Fax:* 972-241-8021. *E-mail:* finaid@dallas.edu.

DALTON STATE COLLEGE

Dalton, GA

Tuition & fees (GA res): $2536 **Average undergraduate aid package: $8985**

ABOUT THE INSTITUTION State-supported, coed. 63 undergraduate majors. Federal methodology is used as a basis for awarding need-based institutional aid.

UNDERGRADUATE EXPENSES for 2010–11 ***One-time required fee:*** $300. ***Tuition, state resident:*** full-time $2160; part-time $90 per credit hour. ***Tuition, nonresident:*** full-time $8160; part-time $340 per credit hour. ***Required fees:*** full-time $376; $7.33 per credit hour or $165 per term. ***College room and board:*** $6750.

FRESHMAN FINANCIAL AID (Fall 2009) 764 applied for aid; of those 71% were deemed to have need. 95% of freshmen with need received aid; of those 20% had need fully met. ***Average percent of need met:*** 70% (excluding resources awarded to replace EFC). ***Average financial aid package:*** $6566 (excluding resources awarded to replace EFC). 1% of all full-time freshmen had no need and received non-need-based gift aid.

UNDERGRADUATE FINANCIAL AID (Fall 2009) 2,749 applied for aid; of those 74% were deemed to have need. 95% of undergraduates with need received aid; of those 49% had need fully met. ***Average percent of need met:*** 77% (excluding resources awarded to replace EFC). ***Average financial aid package:*** $8985 (excluding resources awarded to replace EFC). 1% of all full-time undergraduates had no need and received non-need-based gift aid.

GIFT AID (NEED-BASED) ***Total amount:*** $13,409,383 (98% federal, 2% external sources). ***Receiving aid:*** Freshmen: 40% (407); all full-time undergraduates: 46% (1,565). ***Average award:*** Freshmen: $3568; Undergraduates: $3636. ***Scholarships, grants, and awards:*** Federal Pell, FSEOG, state, private.

GIFT AID (NON-NEED-BASED) ***Total amount:*** $4,258,879 (90% state, 4% institutional, 6% external sources). ***Receiving aid:*** Freshmen: 38% (392). Undergraduates: 53% (1,795). ***Average award:*** Freshmen: $1000. Undergraduates: $1295. ***Scholarships, grants, and awards by category:*** *Academic interests/achievement:* biological sciences, business, computer science, education, engineering/technologies, English, general academic interests/achievements, health fields, humanities, social sciences. *Special achievements/activities:* community service, hobbies/interests, leadership, memberships. *Special characteristics:* adult students, children of faculty/staff, local/state students, members of minority groups, out-of-state students. ***Tuition waivers:*** Full or partial for senior citizens.

LOANS ***Student loans:*** $6,623,981 (60% need-based, 40% non-need-based). 44% of past graduating class borrowed through all loan programs. *Average indebtedness per student:* $11,953. ***Average need-based loan:*** Freshmen: $2650. Undergraduates: $3476. ***Parent loans:*** $31,604 (100% non-need-based). ***Programs:*** state.

WORK-STUDY ***Federal work-study:*** Total amount: $155,925; jobs available. ***State or other work-study/employment:*** Total amount: $259,044 (100% non-need-based). Part-time jobs available.

APPLYING FOR FINANCIAL AID ***Required financial aid form:*** FAFSA. ***Financial aid deadline:*** 7/1 (priority: 6/1). ***Notification date:*** Continuous beginning 4/1.

CONTACT Holly Woods, Assistant Director of Student Financial Aid, Dalton State College, 650 College Drive, Dalton, GA 30720, 706-272-4545 or toll-free 800-829-4436. *Fax:* 706-272-2458. *E-mail:* finaid@daltonstate.edu.

DANIEL WEBSTER COLLEGE

Nashua, NH

CONTACT Office of Financial Aid, Daniel Webster College, 20 University Drive, Nashua, NH 03063-1300, 603-577-6590 or toll-free 800-325-6876. *Fax:* 603-577-6593.

DANIEL WEBSTER COLLEGE–PORTSMOUTH CAMPUS

Portsmouth, NH

CONTACT Financial Aid Office, Daniel Webster College–Portsmouth Campus, 119 International Drive, Pease International Tradeport, Portsmouth, NH 03801, 603-430-4077 or toll-free 800-794-6188.

DARKEI NOAM RABBINICAL COLLEGE

Brooklyn, NY

CONTACT Ms. Rivi Horowitz, Director of Financial Aid, Darkei Noam Rabbinical College, 2822 Avenue J, Brooklyn, NY 11219, 718-338-6464.

DARTMOUTH COLLEGE

Hanover, NH

Tuition & fees: $40,437 **Average undergraduate aid package: $39,203**

ABOUT THE INSTITUTION Independent, coed. 60 undergraduate majors. Both federal and institutional methodology are used as a basis for awarding need-based institutional aid.

UNDERGRADUATE EXPENSES for 2010–11 ***Comprehensive fee:*** $52,275 includes full-time tuition ($39,978), mandatory fees ($459), and room and board ($11,838). ***College room only:*** $7077. Room and board charges vary according to board plan. ***Payment plans:*** Tuition prepayment, installment.

FRESHMAN FINANCIAL AID (Fall 2010, est.) 647 applied for aid; of those 83% were deemed to have need. 100% of freshmen with need received aid; of those 100% had need fully met. ***Average percent of need met:*** 100% (excluding resources awarded to replace EFC). ***Average financial aid package:*** $39,399 (excluding resources awarded to replace EFC).

UNDERGRADUATE FINANCIAL AID (Fall 2010, est.) 2,599 applied for aid; of those 88% were deemed to have need. 100% of undergraduates with need received aid; of those 100% had need fully met. ***Average percent of need met:*** 100% (excluding resources awarded to replace EFC). ***Average financial aid package:*** $39,203 (excluding resources awarded to replace EFC).

GIFT AID (NEED-BASED) ***Total amount:*** $79,817,373 (7% federal, 90% institutional, 3% external sources). ***Receiving aid:*** Freshmen: 46% (524); all full-time undergraduates: 52% (2,197). ***Average award:*** Freshmen: $37,014; Undergraduates: $36,373. ***Scholarships, grants, and awards:*** Federal Pell, FSEOG, state, private, college/university gift aid from institutional funds.

GIFT AID (NON-NEED-BASED) ***Total amount:*** $876,809 (34% federal, 66% external sources).

LOANS ***Student loans:*** $9,613,867 (57% need-based, 43% non-need-based). 51% of past graduating class borrowed through all loan programs. *Average indebtedness per student:* $18,712. ***Average need-based loan:*** Freshmen: $3102. Undergraduates: $3537. ***Parent loans:*** $5,223,517 (100% non-need-based). ***Programs:*** Perkins, college/university.

WORK-STUDY ***Federal work-study:*** Total amount: $3,043,470; 1,386 jobs averaging $2196. ***State or other work-study/employment:*** Total amount: $834,562 (100% need-based). 475 part-time jobs averaging $1760.

APPLYING FOR FINANCIAL AID ***Required financial aid forms:*** FAFSA, CSS Financial Aid PROFILE, noncustodial (divorced/separated) parent's statement, business/farm supplement, federal income tax form(s), W-2 forms. ***Financial aid deadline:*** 2/1. ***Notification date:*** 3/31. Students must reply by 5/1.

CONTACT Ms. Virginia S. Hazen, Director of Financial Aid, Dartmouth College, 6024 McNutt Hall, Hanover, NH 03755, 603-646-2451. *Fax:* 603-646-1414. *E-mail:* virginia.s.hazen@dartmouth.edu.

DAVENPORT UNIVERSITY

Grand Rapids, MI

Tuition & fees: $11,794 **Average undergraduate aid package: N/A**

ABOUT THE INSTITUTION Independent, coed. 21 undergraduate majors. Federal methodology is used as a basis for awarding need-based institutional aid.

UNDERGRADUATE EXPENSES for 2010–11 ***Comprehensive fee:*** $20,206 includes full-time tuition ($11,544), mandatory fees ($250), and room and board ($8412). Full-time tuition and fees vary according to location and program. Room and board charges vary according to board plan and housing facility. ***Part-time tuition:*** $481 per credit hour. Part-time tuition and fees vary according to location and program. ***Payment plan:*** Installment.

GIFT AID (NEED-BASED) ***Total amount:*** $28,279,048 (89% federal, 11% state). ***Scholarships, grants, and awards:*** Federal Pell, FSEOG, state, private, college/university gift aid from institutional funds.

GIFT AID (NON-NEED-BASED) ***Total amount:*** $11,575,374 (2% state, 98% institutional). ***Scholarships, grants, and awards by category:*** *Academic interests/achievement:* general academic interests/achievements. *Special achievements/activities:* memberships. ***Tuition waivers:*** Full or partial for employees or children of employees.

LOANS ***Student loans:*** $141,369,192 (100% need-based). ***Parent loans:*** $2,515,219 (100% need-based). ***Programs:*** private loans.

WORK-STUDY ***Federal work-study:*** Total amount: $1,405,606; jobs available. ***State or other work-study/employment:*** Part-time jobs available.

APPLYING FOR FINANCIAL AID ***Required financial aid form:*** FAFSA. ***Financial aid deadline (priority):*** 3/1. ***Notification date:*** 3/1.

CONTACT David DeBoer, Executive Director of Financial Aid, Davenport University, 6191 Kraft Avenue SE, Grand Rapids, MI 49512, 616-732-1132 or toll-free 800-632-9569. *Fax:* 616-732-1167. *E-mail:* david.debore@davenport.edu.

DAVIDSON COLLEGE

Davidson, NC

Tuition & fees: $38,866 **Average undergraduate aid package: $27,634**

ABOUT THE INSTITUTION Independent Presbyterian, coed. 22 undergraduate majors. Both federal and institutional methodology are used as a basis for awarding need-based institutional aid.

UNDERGRADUATE EXPENSES for 2011–12 ***Comprehensive fee:*** $49,723 includes full-time tuition ($38,481), mandatory fees ($385), and room and board ($10,857). ***College room only:*** $5733. Room and board charges vary according to board plan.

FRESHMAN FINANCIAL AID (Fall 2009) 309 applied for aid; of those 72% were deemed to have need. 100% of freshmen with need received aid; of those 100% had need fully met. ***Average percent of need met:*** 100% (excluding resources awarded to replace EFC). ***Average financial aid package:*** $29,491 (excluding resources awarded to replace EFC). 4% of all full-time freshmen had no need and received non-need-based gift aid.

UNDERGRADUATE FINANCIAL AID (Fall 2009) 851 applied for aid; of those 87% were deemed to have need. 100% of undergraduates with need received aid; of those 100% had need fully met. ***Average percent of need met:*** 100% (excluding resources awarded to replace EFC). ***Average financial aid package:*** $27,634 (excluding resources awarded to replace EFC). 11% of all full-time undergraduates had no need and received non-need-based gift aid.

GIFT AID (NEED-BASED) ***Total amount:*** $17,684,628 (5% federal, 3% state, 92% institutional). ***Receiving aid:*** Freshmen: 42% (207); all full-time undergraduates: 12% (211). ***Average award:*** Freshmen: $27,125; Undergraduates: $24,873. ***Scholarships, grants, and awards:*** Federal Pell, FSEOG, state, private, college/university gift aid from institutional funds, need-linked special talent scholarships.

GIFT AID (NON-NEED-BASED) ***Total amount:*** $7,902,785 (5% federal, 9% state, 72% institutional, 14% external sources). ***Receiving aid:*** Freshmen: 18% (86). Undergraduates: 17% (301). ***Average award:*** Freshmen: $24,259. Undergraduates: $18,503. ***Scholarships, grants, and awards by category:*** *Academic interests/achievement:* 104 awards ($2,490,761 total): biological sciences, business, education, foreign languages, general academic interests/achievements, international studies, mathematics, physical sciences, premedicine, religion/biblical studies, social sciences. *Creative arts/performance:* 28 awards ($267,273 total): art/fine arts, creative writing, music, performing arts, theater/drama. *Special achievements/activities:* 76 awards ($1,546,774 total): community service, general special achievements/activities, leadership, religious involvement. *Special characteristics:* 93 awards ($1,381,862 total): first-generation college students, general special characteristics, local/state students, out-of-state students, relatives of clergy. ***Tuition waivers:*** Full or partial for employees or children of employees.

LOANS ***Student loans:*** $3,254,999 (19% need-based, 81% non-need-based). 32% of past graduating class borrowed through all loan programs. *Average indebtedness per student:* $23,233. ***Average need-based loan:*** Freshmen: $2623. Undergraduates: $3121. ***Parent loans:*** $2,196,896 (100% non-need-based). ***Programs:*** Federal Direct (Subsidized and Unsubsidized Stafford, PLUS), alternative loans.

WORK-STUDY ***Federal work-study:*** Total amount: $353,545; 244 jobs averaging $1425. ***State or other work-study/employment:*** Total amount: $188,719 (90% need-based, 10% non-need-based). 116 part-time jobs averaging $1473.

APPLYING FOR FINANCIAL AID ***Required financial aid forms:*** FAFSA, CSS Financial Aid PROFILE, noncustodial (divorced/separated) parent's statement, business/farm supplement, parent and student tax returns and W-2 forms, corporate tax returns (if applicable). ***Financial aid deadline:*** 2/15. ***Notification date:*** 4/5. Students must reply by 5/1.

CONTACT Mr. David R. Gelinas, Director of Financial Aid, Davidson College, 413 North Main Street, PO Box 7157, Davidson, NC 28035-7157, 704-894-2232 or toll-free 800-768-0380. *Fax:* 704-894-2845. *E-mail:* dagelinas@davidson.edu.

DAVIS & ELKINS COLLEGE

Elkins, WV

CONTACT Susan M. George, Director of Financial Planning, Davis & Elkins College, 100 Campus Drive, Elkins, WV 26241-3996, 304-637-1373 or toll-free 800-624-3157 Ext. 1230. *Fax:* 304-637-1986. *E-mail:* ssw@davisandelkins.edu.

DAVIS COLLEGE

Johnson City, NY

CONTACT Stephanie D. Baker, Financial Aid Director, Davis College, 400 Riverside Drive, Johnson City, NY 13790, 607-729-1581 Ext. 401 or toll-free 800-331-4137 Ext. 406. *Fax:* 607-770-6886. *E-mail:* financialaid@davisny.edu.

DAYMAR INSTITUTE

Clarksville, TN

CONTACT Financial Aid Office, Daymar Institute, 1860 Wilma Rudolph Boulevard, Clarksville, TN 37040, 931-552-7600.

DEACONESS COLLEGE OF NURSING

St. Louis, MO

See Chamberlain College of Nursing.

DEFIANCE COLLEGE

Defiance, OH

Tuition & fees: $25,890 **Average undergraduate aid package: $20,818**

ABOUT THE INSTITUTION Independent religious, coed. 32 undergraduate majors. Federal methodology is used as a basis for awarding need-based institutional aid.

UNDERGRADUATE EXPENSES for 2011–12 ***One-time required fee:*** $75. ***Comprehensive fee:*** $34,340 includes full-time tuition ($25,300), mandatory fees ($590), and room and board ($8450). ***College room only:*** $4680. Full-time tuition and fees vary according to program. Room and board charges vary according to board plan and housing facility. Part-time tuition and fees vary according to course load. ***Payment plan:*** Installment.

FRESHMAN FINANCIAL AID (Fall 2010, est.) 257 applied for aid; of those 96% were deemed to have need. 100% of freshmen with need received aid; of those 9% had need fully met. ***Average percent of need met:*** 72% (excluding resources awarded to replace EFC). ***Average financial aid package:*** $21,653 (excluding resources awarded to replace EFC). 6% of all full-time freshmen had no need and received non-need-based gift aid.

UNDERGRADUATE FINANCIAL AID (Fall 2010, est.) 729 applied for aid; of those 96% were deemed to have need. 100% of undergraduates with need received aid; of those 10% had need fully met. ***Average percent of need met:*** 71% (excluding resources awarded to replace EFC). ***Average financial aid package:*** $20,818 (excluding resources awarded to replace EFC). 8% of all full-time undergraduates had no need and received non-need-based gift aid.

GIFT AID (NEED-BASED) ***Total amount:*** $8,829,929 (25% federal, 5% state, 68% institutional, 2% external sources). ***Receiving aid:*** Freshmen: 81% (211); all full-time undergraduates: 76% (582). ***Average award:*** Freshmen: $7465; Undergraduates: $6970. ***Scholarships, grants, and awards:*** Federal Pell, FSEOG, state, private, college/university gift aid from institutional funds.

GIFT AID (NON-NEED-BASED) ***Total amount:*** $2,156,368 (92% institutional, 8% external sources). ***Receiving aid:*** Freshmen: 94% (245). Undergraduates: 89% (684). ***Average award:*** Freshmen: $8667. Undergraduates: $8826. ***Scholarships, grants, and awards by category:*** *Academic interests/achievement:* biological sciences, business, communication, computer science, education, English, general academic interests/achievements, health fields, humanities, international studies, mathematics, physical sciences, premedicine, religion/biblical studies, social sciences. *Creative arts/performance:* music. *Special achievements/activities:* community service, general special achievements/activities, leadership, religious involvement. *Special characteristics:* children of faculty/staff, international students, members of minority groups, out-of-state students, previous college experience, religious affiliation, veterans, veterans' children. ***Tuition waivers:*** Full or partial for employees or children of employees, senior citizens.

LOANS ***Student loans:*** $7,648,865 (62% need-based, 38% non-need-based). 90% of past graduating class borrowed through all loan programs. *Average indebtedness per student:* $31,410. ***Average need-based loan:*** Freshmen: $3546. Undergraduates: $4523. ***Parent loans:*** $1,451,796 (38% need-based, 62% non-need-based). ***Programs:*** Federal Direct (Subsidized and Unsubsidized Stafford, PLUS), Perkins, alternative loans.

WORK-STUDY ***Federal work-study:*** Total amount: $1,304,098; 535 jobs averaging $2438. ***State or other work-study/employment:*** Total amount: $73,270 (100% non-need-based). 30 part-time jobs averaging $2527.

APPLYING FOR FINANCIAL AID ***Required financial aid form:*** FAFSA. ***Financial aid deadline (priority):*** 4/1. ***Notification date:*** Continuous beginning 2/1. Students must reply by 5/1 or within 2 weeks of notification.

CONTACT Amy Francis, Director of Financial Aid, Defiance College, 701 North Clinton Street, Defiance, OH 43512-1610, 419-783-2376 or toll-free 800-520-4632 Ext. 2359. *Fax:* 419-783-2579. *E-mail:* afrancis@defiance.edu.

DELAWARE STATE UNIVERSITY

Dover, DE

Tuition & fees (DE res): $7561 **Average undergraduate aid package: $11,274**

ABOUT THE INSTITUTION State-supported, coed. 137 undergraduate majors. Federal methodology is used as a basis for awarding need-based institutional aid.

UNDERGRADUATE EXPENSES for 2010–11 ***Tuition, state resident:*** full-time $6731; part-time $246 per credit hour. ***Tuition, nonresident:*** full-time $14,310; part-time $562 per credit hour. ***Required fees:*** full-time $830; $50 per term. Full-time tuition and fees vary according to reciprocity agreements. Part-time tuition and fees vary according to reciprocity agreements. Room and board charges vary according to board plan and housing facility. ***Payment plan:*** Deferred payment.

FRESHMAN FINANCIAL AID (Fall 2010, est.) 855 applied for aid; of those 93% were deemed to have need. 99% of freshmen with need received aid; of those 36% had need fully met. ***Average percent of need met:*** 45% (excluding resources awarded to replace EFC). ***Average financial aid package:*** $10,384 (excluding resources awarded to replace EFC). 9% of all full-time freshmen had no need and received non-need-based gift aid.

UNDERGRADUATE FINANCIAL AID (Fall 2010, est.) 2,817 applied for aid; of those 92% were deemed to have need. 99% of undergraduates with need received aid; of those 34% had need fully met. ***Average percent of need met:*** 48% (excluding resources awarded to replace EFC). ***Average financial aid package:*** $11,274 (excluding resources awarded to replace EFC). 13% of all full-time undergraduates had no need and received non-need-based gift aid.

GIFT AID (NEED-BASED) ***Total amount:*** $19,129,496 (47% federal, 14% state, 37% institutional, 2% external sources). ***Receiving aid:*** Freshmen: 82% (729); all full-time undergraduates: 72% (2,221). ***Average award:*** Freshmen: $10,384; Undergraduates: $11,274. ***Scholarships, grants, and awards:*** Federal Pell, FSEOG, state, Federal Nursing.

GIFT AID (NON-NEED-BASED) ***Receiving aid:*** Freshmen: 62% (549). Undergraduates: 37% (1,148). ***Average award:*** Freshmen: $10,514. Undergraduates: $7131. ***Scholarships, grants, and awards by category:*** *Academic interests/achievement:* general academic interests/achievements. *Creative arts/performance:* music. *Special achievements/activities:* general special achievements/activities. *Special characteristics:* out-of-state students. ***Tuition waivers:*** Full or partial for minority students, employees or children of employees, senior citizens.

LOANS ***Student loans:*** $20,060,679 (100% need-based). 91% of past graduating class borrowed through all loan programs. *Average indebtedness per student:*

$36,410. ***Average need-based loan:*** Freshmen: $2813. Undergraduates: $3481. ***Parent loans:*** $13,406,041 (100% need-based). ***Programs:*** Perkins, Federal Nursing.

WORK-STUDY ***Federal work-study:*** Total amount: $187,426; jobs available. ***State or other work-study/employment:*** Total amount: $574,238 (100% non-need-based). Part-time jobs available.

ATHLETIC AWARDS Total amount: $4,148,131 (100% need-based).

APPLYING FOR FINANCIAL AID ***Required financial aid form:*** FAFSA.

CONTACT Janet Lynn Iocono, Executive Director of Student Financial Services, Delaware State University, 1200 North DuPont Highway, Dover, DE 19901-2277, 302-857-6250 or toll-free 800-845-2544.

DELAWARE VALLEY COLLEGE

Doylestown, PA

Tuition & fees: $30,646 **Average undergraduate aid package: $19,784**

ABOUT THE INSTITUTION Independent, coed. 29 undergraduate majors. Federal methodology is used as a basis for awarding need-based institutional aid.

UNDERGRADUATE EXPENSES for 2011–12 ***Comprehensive fee:*** $41,488 includes full-time tuition ($28,596), mandatory fees ($2050), and room and board ($10,842). ***College room only:*** $4916. ***Part-time tuition:*** $788 per credit.

FRESHMAN FINANCIAL AID (Fall 2010, est.) 460 applied for aid; of those 90% were deemed to have need. 99% of freshmen with need received aid; of those 14% had need fully met. ***Average percent of need met:*** 76% (excluding resources awarded to replace EFC). ***Average financial aid package:*** $20,080 (excluding resources awarded to replace EFC). 14% of all full-time freshmen had no need and received non-need-based gift aid.

UNDERGRADUATE FINANCIAL AID (Fall 2010, est.) 1,479 applied for aid; of those 92% were deemed to have need. 99% of undergraduates with need received aid; of those 14% had need fully met. ***Average percent of need met:*** 67% (excluding resources awarded to replace EFC). ***Average financial aid package:*** $19,784 (excluding resources awarded to replace EFC). 19% of all full-time undergraduates had no need and received non-need-based gift aid.

GIFT AID (NEED-BASED) ***Total amount:*** $18,845,340 (15% federal, 7% state, 77% institutional, 1% external sources). ***Receiving aid:*** Freshmen: 83% (411); all full-time undergraduates: 79% (1,341). ***Average award:*** Freshmen: $17,668; Undergraduates: $15,465. ***Scholarships, grants, and awards:*** Federal Pell, FSEOG, state, private, college/university gift aid from institutional funds.

GIFT AID (NON-NEED-BASED) ***Total amount:*** $4,666,860 (99% institutional, 1% external sources). ***Receiving aid:*** Freshmen: 8% (39). Undergraduates: 7% (113). ***Average award:*** Freshmen: $13,028. Undergraduates: $14,238. ***Scholarships, grants, and awards by category:*** *Academic interests/achievement:* general academic interests/achievements. *Creative arts/performance:* general creative arts/performance. *Special characteristics:* children and siblings of alumni.

LOANS ***Student loans:*** $15,138,560 (61% need-based, 39% non-need-based). 73% of past graduating class borrowed through all loan programs. *Average indebtedness per student:* $28,896. ***Average need-based loan:*** Freshmen: $3531. Undergraduates: $5200. ***Parent loans:*** $6,571,251 (31% need-based, 69% non-need-based). ***Programs:*** Federal Direct (Subsidized and Unsubsidized Stafford, PLUS), Perkins, alternative loans.

WORK-STUDY ***Federal work-study:*** Total amount: $167,971; jobs available. ***State or other work-study/employment:*** Part-time jobs available.

APPLYING FOR FINANCIAL AID ***Required financial aid forms:*** FAFSA, state aid form. ***Financial aid deadline:*** 4/1. ***Notification date:*** Continuous beginning 2/1. Students must reply by 5/1 or within 2 weeks of notification.

CONTACT Ms. Joan Hock, Acting Director of Student Financial Aid, Delaware Valley College, 700 East Butler Avenue, Doylestown, PA 18901-2697, 215-489-2975 or toll-free 800-2DELVAL (in-state). *E-mail:* finaid@devalcol.edu.

DELTA STATE UNIVERSITY

Cleveland, MS

Tuition & fees (MS res): $4852 **Average undergraduate aid package: $8395**

ABOUT THE INSTITUTION State-supported, coed. 37 undergraduate majors. Federal methodology is used as a basis for awarding need-based institutional aid.

UNDERGRADUATE EXPENSES for 2010–11 ***Tuition, state resident:*** full-time $4852; part-time $202 per credit hour. ***Tuition, nonresident:*** full-time $12,558; part-time $523 per credit hour. Part-time tuition and fees vary according to course load. ***College room and board:*** $6166. Room and board charges vary according to housing facility. ***Payment plan:*** Installment.

FRESHMAN FINANCIAL AID (Fall 2009) 328 applied for aid; of those 78% were deemed to have need. 99% of freshmen with need received aid. ***Average financial aid package:*** $7436 (excluding resources awarded to replace EFC).

UNDERGRADUATE FINANCIAL AID (Fall 2009) 2,088 applied for aid; of those 86% were deemed to have need. 99% of undergraduates with need received aid. ***Average financial aid package:*** $8395 (excluding resources awarded to replace EFC).

GIFT AID (NEED-BASED) ***Total amount:*** $7,072,469 (100% federal). ***Receiving aid:*** Freshmen: 55% (202); all full-time undergraduates: 56% (1,394). ***Average award:*** Freshmen: $4565; Undergraduates: $4475. ***Scholarships, grants, and awards:*** Federal Pell, FSEOG, state, private, college/university gift aid from institutional funds.

GIFT AID (NON-NEED-BASED) ***Total amount:*** $5,532,964 (15% state, 44% institutional, 41% external sources). ***Scholarships, grants, and awards by category:*** *Academic interests/achievement:* 249 awards ($526,051 total): biological sciences, business, computer science, education, English, foreign languages, general academic interests/achievements, health fields, humanities, mathematics, physical sciences, premedicine, social sciences. *Creative arts/performance:* 142 awards ($359,546 total): art/fine arts, creative writing, journalism/publications, music, performing arts. *Special achievements/activities:* 447 awards ($515,870 total): cheerleading/drum major, general special achievements/activities, leadership, memberships. *Special characteristics:* 372 awards ($1,866,763 total): children and siblings of alumni, children of faculty/staff, general special characteristics, out-of-state students. ***Tuition waivers:*** Full or partial for children of alumni, employees or children of employees, senior citizens.

LOANS ***Student loans:*** $17,489,000 (52% need-based, 48% non-need-based). 50% of past graduating class borrowed through all loan programs. *Average indebtedness per student:* $16,633. ***Parent loans:*** $308,000 (100% non-need-based). ***Programs:*** Federal Direct (Subsidized and Unsubsidized Stafford, PLUS), Perkins.

WORK-STUDY ***Federal work-study:*** Total amount: $422,458; 274 jobs averaging $1850. ***State or other work-study/employment:*** Total amount: $210,000 (100% non-need-based). 145 part-time jobs averaging $1108.

ATHLETIC AWARDS Total amount: $1,669,000 (100% non-need-based).

APPLYING FOR FINANCIAL AID ***Required financial aid forms:*** FAFSA, institution's own form. ***Financial aid deadline (priority):*** 3/1. ***Notification date:*** Continuous beginning 5/1.

CONTACT Ms. Ann Margaret Mullins, Director of Student Financial Assistance, Delta State University, Kent Wyatt Hall 144, Highway 8 West, Cleveland, MS 38733-0001, 662-846-4670 or toll-free 800-468-6378. *Fax:* 662-846-4683. *E-mail:* amullins@deltastate.edu.

DENISON UNIVERSITY

Granville, OH

Tuition & fees: $40,210 **Average undergraduate aid package: $33,286**

ABOUT THE INSTITUTION Independent, coed. 38 undergraduate majors. Federal methodology is used as a basis for awarding need-based institutional aid.

UNDERGRADUATE EXPENSES for 2011–12 ***Comprehensive fee:*** $50,170 includes full-time tuition ($39,330), mandatory fees ($880), and room and board ($9960). ***College room only:*** $5480. Room and board charges vary according to board plan and housing facility. ***Part-time tuition:*** $1229 per semester hour. ***Part-time fees:*** $440 per term. Part-time tuition and fees vary according to course load. ***Payment plan:*** Installment.

FRESHMAN FINANCIAL AID (Fall 2010, est.) 421 applied for aid; of those 79% were deemed to have need. 100% of freshmen with need received aid; of those 49% had need fully met. ***Average percent of need met:*** 97% (excluding resources awarded to replace EFC). ***Average financial aid package:*** $34,352 (excluding resources awarded to replace EFC). 43% of all full-time freshmen had no need and received non-need-based gift aid.

UNDERGRADUATE FINANCIAL AID (Fall 2010, est.) 1,306 applied for aid; of those 85% were deemed to have need. 100% of undergraduates with need received aid; of those 36% had need fully met. ***Average percent of need met:*** 97% (excluding resources awarded to replace EFC). ***Average financial aid package:*** $33,286 (excluding resources awarded to replace EFC). 45% of all full-time undergraduates had no need and received non-need-based gift aid.

GIFT AID (NEED-BASED) ***Total amount:*** $16,971,109 (12% federal, 1% state, 83% institutional, 4% external sources). ***Receiving aid:*** Freshmen: 53% (328); all full-time undergraduates: 49% (1,098). ***Average award:*** Freshmen: $28,299; Undergraduates: $27,112. ***Scholarships, grants, and awards:*** Federal Pell, FSEOG, state, private, college/university gift aid from institutional funds.

GIFT AID (NON-NEED-BASED) ***Total amount:*** $29,744,514 (100% institutional). ***Receiving aid:*** Freshmen: 48% (301). Undergraduates: 43% (976). ***Average award:*** Freshmen: $15,723. Undergraduates: $15,552. ***Tuition waivers:*** Full or partial for employees or children of employees.

LOANS ***Student loans:*** $7,336,291 (100% need-based). ***Average need-based loan:*** Freshmen: $4198. Undergraduates: $4631. ***Parent loans:*** $3,881,331 (100% non-need-based). ***Programs:*** Federal Direct (Subsidized and Unsubsidized Stafford, PLUS), Perkins, college/university.

WORK-STUDY ***Federal work-study:*** Total amount: $1,154,589; jobs available. ***State or other work-study/employment:*** Total amount: $3,173,534 (100% non-need-based). Part-time jobs available.

APPLYING FOR FINANCIAL AID ***Required financial aid form:*** FAFSA. ***Financial aid deadline (priority):*** 3/15. ***Notification date:*** 3/28. Students must reply within 2 weeks of notification.

CONTACT Ms. Nancy Hoover, Director of Financial Aid, Denison University, PO Box M, Granville, OH 43023-0613, 740-587-6279 or toll-free 800-DENISON. *Fax:* 740-587-5706. *E-mail:* hoover@denison.edu.

DENVER TECHNICAL COLLEGE AT COLORADO SPRINGS

Westminster, CO

See DeVry University.

DePAUL UNIVERSITY

Chicago, IL

Tuition & fees: $28,858 **Average undergraduate aid package: $20,113**

ABOUT THE INSTITUTION Independent Roman Catholic, coed. 102 undergraduate majors. Federal methodology is used as a basis for awarding need-based institutional aid.

UNDERGRADUATE EXPENSES for 2011–12 ***Comprehensive fee:*** $39,813 includes full-time tuition ($28,240), mandatory fees ($618), and room and board ($10,955). ***College room only:*** $8015. Full-time tuition and fees vary according to program. Room and board charges vary according to board plan, housing facility, and location. ***Part-time tuition:*** $490 per quarter hour. Part-time tuition and fees vary according to program. ***Payment plans:*** Installment, deferred payment.

FRESHMAN FINANCIAL AID (Fall 2010, est.) 2,078 applied for aid; of those 81% were deemed to have need. 99% of freshmen with need received aid; of those 12% had need fully met. ***Average percent of need met:*** 66% (excluding resources awarded to replace EFC). ***Average financial aid package:*** $22,241 (excluding resources awarded to replace EFC). 7% of all full-time freshmen had no need and received non-need-based gift aid.

UNDERGRADUATE FINANCIAL AID (Fall 2010, est.) 11,105 applied for aid; of those 83% were deemed to have need. 97% of undergraduates with need received aid; of those 8% had need fully met. ***Average percent of need met:*** 62% (excluding resources awarded to replace EFC). ***Average financial aid package:*** $20,113 (excluding resources awarded to replace EFC). 3% of all full-time undergraduates had no need and received non-need-based gift aid.

GIFT AID (NEED-BASED) ***Total amount:*** $127,900,000 (19% federal, 16% state, 65% institutional). ***Receiving aid:*** Freshmen: 64% (1,437); all full-time undergraduates: 56% (7,423). ***Average award:*** Freshmen: $14,166; Undergraduates: $14,448. ***Scholarships, grants, and awards:*** Federal Pell, FSEOG, state, private, college/university gift aid from institutional funds, Academic Competitiveness Grants, National SMART Grants, TEACH Grants.

GIFT AID (NON-NEED-BASED) ***Total amount:*** $21,600,000 (93% institutional, 7% external sources). ***Receiving aid:*** Freshmen: 45% (1,018). Undergraduates: 27% (3,520). ***Average award:*** Freshmen: $10,720. Undergraduates: $9850. ***Scholarships, grants, and awards by category:*** *Academic interests/achievement:* general academic interests/achievements. *Creative arts/performance:* art/fine arts, debating, music, performing arts, theater/drama. *Special achievements/activities:* community service, leadership. *Special characteristics:* children of faculty/staff, local/state students. ***Tuition waivers:*** Full or partial for employees or children of employees.

LOANS ***Student loans:*** $136,100,000 (72% need-based, 28% non-need-based). 65% of past graduating class borrowed through all loan programs. *Average indebtedness per student:* $26,190. ***Average need-based loan:*** Freshmen: $3496. Undergraduates: $4695. ***Parent loans:*** $48,000,000 (100% non-need-based). ***Programs:*** Federal Direct (Subsidized and Unsubsidized Stafford, PLUS), Perkins, private loans.

WORK-STUDY ***Federal work-study:*** Total amount: $2,100,000; jobs available. ***State or other work-study/employment:*** Total amount: $6,800,000 (35% need-based, 65% non-need-based). Part-time jobs available.

ATHLETIC AWARDS Total amount: $4,300,000 (100% non-need-based).

APPLYING FOR FINANCIAL AID ***Required financial aid form:*** FAFSA. ***Financial aid deadline (priority):*** 3/1. ***Notification date:*** Continuous beginning 3/15. Students must reply by 5/1 or within 4 weeks of notification.

CONTACT Christopher Rone, Associate Director of Financial Aid, DePaul University, 1 East Jackson Boulevard, Chicago, IL 60604-2287, 773-325-7815. *Fax:* 773-325-7746.

DePAUW UNIVERSITY

Greencastle, IN

Tuition & fees: $34,905 **Average undergraduate aid package: $28,549**

ABOUT THE INSTITUTION Independent religious, coed. 45 undergraduate majors. Both federal and institutional methodology are used as a basis for awarding need-based institutional aid.

UNDERGRADUATE EXPENSES for 2011–12 ***Comprehensive fee:*** $44,085 includes full-time tuition ($34,440), mandatory fees ($465), and room and board ($9180). Room and board charges vary according to board plan. ***Part-time tuition:*** $1076.25 per credit hour. ***Payment plan:*** Installment.

FRESHMAN FINANCIAL AID (Fall 2010, est.) 474 applied for aid; of those 81% were deemed to have need. 100% of freshmen with need received aid; of those 29% had need fully met. ***Average percent of need met:*** 86% (excluding resources awarded to replace EFC). ***Average financial aid package:*** $28,960 (excluding resources awarded to replace EFC). 36% of all full-time freshmen had no need and received non-need-based gift aid.

UNDERGRADUATE FINANCIAL AID (Fall 2010, est.) 1,541 applied for aid; of those 87% were deemed to have need. 100% of undergraduates with need received aid; of those 27% had need fully met. ***Average percent of need met:*** 87% (excluding resources awarded to replace EFC). ***Average financial aid package:*** $28,549 (excluding resources awarded to replace EFC). 41% of all full-time undergraduates had no need and received non-need-based gift aid.

GIFT AID (NEED-BASED) ***Total amount:*** $33,181,061 (7% federal, 3% state, 82% institutional, 8% external sources). ***Receiving aid:*** Freshmen: 63% (385); all full-time undergraduates: 57% (1,345). ***Average award:*** Freshmen: $25,824; Undergraduates: $24,625. ***Scholarships, grants, and awards:*** Federal Pell, FSEOG, state, private, college/university gift aid from institutional funds, United Negro College Fund.

GIFT AID (NON-NEED-BASED) ***Total amount:*** $18,813,746 (92% institutional, 8% external sources). ***Receiving aid:*** Freshmen: 14% (86). Undergraduates: 12% (272). ***Average award:*** Freshmen: $15,602. Undergraduates: $15,592. ***Scholarships, grants, and awards by category:*** *Academic interests/achievement:* biological sciences, business, communication, computer science, English, foreign languages, general academic interests/achievements, health fields, international studies, mathematics, physical sciences. *Creative arts/performance:* art/fine arts, journalism/publications, music, performing arts. *Special achievements/activities:* community service, leadership. *Special characteristics:* children and siblings of alumni, children of faculty/staff, first-generation college students, international students, local/state students, members of minority groups, relatives of clergy, religious affiliation. ***Tuition waivers:*** Full or partial for employees or children of employees.

LOANS ***Student loans:*** $10,892,958 (58% need-based, 42% non-need-based). 53% of past graduating class borrowed through all loan programs. *Average indebtedness per student:* $23,778. ***Average need-based loan:*** Freshmen: $3410. Undergraduates: $4043. ***Parent loans:*** $4,003,922 (25% need-based, 75% non-need-based). ***Programs:*** Federal Direct (Subsidized and Unsubsidized Stafford, PLUS), Perkins, college/university.

WORK-STUDY ***Federal work-study:*** Total amount: $908,788; jobs available. ***State or other work-study/employment:*** Total amount: $718,400 (45% need-based, 55% non-need-based). Part-time jobs available.

APPLYING FOR FINANCIAL AID ***Required financial aid forms:*** FAFSA, institution's own form. ***Financial aid deadline:*** Continuous. ***Notification date:*** 4/1. Students must reply by 5/1.

CONTACT Craig Slaughter, Financial Aid Director, DePauw University, PO Box 37, Greencastle, IN 46135-0037, 765-658-4030 or toll-free 800-447-2495. *Fax:* 765-658-4137. *E-mail:* craigslaughter@depauw.edu.

DeSALES UNIVERSITY

Center Valley, PA

Tuition & fees: $28,000 **Average undergraduate aid package: $19,432**

ABOUT THE INSTITUTION Independent Roman Catholic, coed. 32 undergraduate majors. Federal methodology is used as a basis for awarding need-based institutional aid.

UNDERGRADUATE EXPENSES for 2011–12 ***Comprehensive fee:*** $38,140 includes full-time tuition ($27,000), mandatory fees ($1000), and room and board ($10,140). Full-time tuition and fees vary according to class time. Room and board charges vary according to board plan. ***Part-time tuition:*** $1125 per credit hour. Part-time tuition and fees vary according to class time. ***Payment plan:*** Installment.

FRESHMAN FINANCIAL AID (Fall 2010, est.) 399 applied for aid; of those 89% were deemed to have need. 99% of freshmen with need received aid; of those 21% had need fully met. ***Average percent of need met:*** 67% (excluding resources awarded to replace EFC). ***Average financial aid package:*** $22,207 (excluding resources awarded to replace EFC). 16% of all full-time freshmen had no need and received non-need-based gift aid.

UNDERGRADUATE FINANCIAL AID (Fall 2010, est.) 1,542 applied for aid; of those 89% were deemed to have need. 99% of undergraduates with need received aid; of those 18% had need fully met. ***Average percent of need met:*** 61% (excluding resources awarded to replace EFC). ***Average financial aid package:*** $19,432 (excluding resources awarded to replace EFC). 17% of all full-time undergraduates had no need and received non-need-based gift aid.

GIFT AID (NEED-BASED) ***Total amount:*** $19,313,838 (13% federal, 8% state, 77% institutional, 2% external sources). ***Receiving aid:*** Freshmen: 83% (353); all full-time undergraduates: 73% (1,281). ***Average award:*** Freshmen: $18,007; Undergraduates: $14,648. ***Scholarships, grants, and awards:*** Federal Pell, FSEOG, state, private, college/university gift aid from institutional funds.

GIFT AID (NON-NEED-BASED) ***Total amount:*** $2,601,652 (3% federal, 96% institutional, 1% external sources). ***Receiving aid:*** Freshmen: 69% (293). Undergraduates: 49% (870). ***Average award:*** Freshmen: $10,627. Undergraduates: $9224. ***Scholarships, grants, and awards by category:*** *Academic interests/achievement:* 184 awards ($130,300 total): biological sciences, business, communication, computer science, education, English, foreign languages, general academic interests/achievements, health fields, humanities, mathematics, physical sciences, premedicine, religion/biblical studies, social sciences. *Creative arts/performance:* 23 awards ($38,000 total): cinema/film/broadcasting, dance, performing arts, theater/drama. ***Tuition waivers:*** Full or partial for employees or children of employees, senior citizens.

LOANS ***Student loans:*** $16,248,814 (88% need-based, 12% non-need-based). *Average indebtedness per student:* $33,835. ***Average need-based loan:*** Freshmen: $3350. Undergraduates: $4617. ***Parent loans:*** $3,668,392 (92% need-based, 8% non-need-based). ***Programs:*** Federal Direct (Subsidized and Unsubsidized Stafford, PLUS), Perkins, Federal Nursing.

WORK-STUDY ***Federal work-study:*** Total amount: $791,975; 103 jobs averaging $2426. ***State or other work-study/employment:*** Total amount: $490,102 (54% need-based, 46% non-need-based). 91 part-time jobs averaging $2501.

APPLYING FOR FINANCIAL AID ***Required financial aid forms:*** FAFSA, state aid form, PHEAA form for PA residents. ***Financial aid deadline:*** 5/1 (priority: 2/15). ***Notification date:*** Continuous beginning 2/15. Students must reply by 5/1 or within 2 weeks of notification.

CONTACT Mrs. Joyce Farmer, Director of Financial Aid, DeSales University, 2755 Station Avenue, Center Valley, PA 18034-9568, 610-282-1100 Ext. 1208 or toll-free 877-4DESALES. *Fax:* 610-282-0131. *E-mail:* joyce.farmer@desales.edu.

DESIGN INSTITUTE OF SAN DIEGO

San Diego, CA

CONTACT Financial Aid Office, Design Institute of San Diego, 8555 Commerce Avenue, San Diego, CA 92121, 858-566-1200 or toll-free 800-619-4337.

DeVRY COLLEGE OF NEW YORK

Long Island City, NY

CONTACT Elvira Senese, Dean of Student Finance, DeVry College of New York, 30-20 Thomson Avenue, Long Island City, NY 11101, 718-472-2728. *Fax:* 718-269-4284.

DeVRY UNIVERSITY

Mesa, AZ

CONTACT Financial Aid Office, DeVry University, 1201 South Alma School Road, Mesa, AZ 85210-2011, 480-827-1511.

DeVRY UNIVERSITY

Phoenix, AZ

CONTACT Kathy Wyse, Dean of Student Finance, DeVry University, 2149 West Dunlap Avenue, Phoenix, AZ 85021-2995, 602-870-9222. *Fax:* 602-870-1209.

DeVRY UNIVERSITY

Alhambra, CA

CONTACT Financial Aid Office, DeVry University, Unit 100, Building A-11, First Floor, 1000 South Fremont Avenue, Alhambra, CA 91803, 626-293-4300.

DeVRY UNIVERSITY

Anaheim, CA

CONTACT Financial Aid Office, DeVry University, 1900 South State College Boulevard, Suite 150, Anaheim, CA 92806-6136, 714-935-3200.

DeVRY UNIVERSITY

Bakersfield, CA

CONTACT Financial Aid Office, DeVry University, 3000 Ming Avenue, Bakersfield, CA 93304-4136, 661-833-7120.

DeVRY UNIVERSITY

Daly City, CA

CONTACT Financial Aid Office, DeVry University, 2001 Junipero Serra Boulevard, Suite 161, Daly City, CA 94014-3899, 650-991-3520.

DeVRY UNIVERSITY

Elk Grove, CA

CONTACT Financial Aid Office, DeVry University, Sacramento Center, 2216 Kausen Drive, Elk Grove, CA 95758, 916-478-2847 or toll-free 866-573-3879.

DeVRY UNIVERSITY

Fremont, CA

CONTACT Kim Kane, Director of Student Finance, DeVry University, 6600 Dumbarton Circle, Fremont, CA 94555, 510-574-1100. *Fax:* 510-742-0868.

DeVRY UNIVERSITY

Irvine, CA

CONTACT Financial Aid Office, DeVry University, 430 Exchange, Suite 250, Irvine, CA 92602-1303, 949-752-5631.

DeVRY UNIVERSITY
Long Beach, CA

CONTACT Kathy Odom, Director of Financial Aid, DeVry University, 3880 Kilroy Airport Way, Long Beach, CA 90806, 562-427-0861. *Fax:* 562-989-1578.

DeVRY UNIVERSITY
Oakland, CA

CONTACT Financial Aid Office, DeVry University, 505 14th Street, Oakland, CA 94612, 866-473-3879.

DeVRY UNIVERSITY
Palmdale, CA

CONTACT Ann Logan, Dean of Student Finance, DeVry University, 22801 Roscoe Boulevard, West Hills, CA 91304, 818-932-3001 or toll-free 866-986-9388. *Fax:* 818-932-3131.

DeVRY UNIVERSITY
Pomona, CA

CONTACT Kathy Odom, Director of Financial Aid, DeVry University, 901 Corporate Center Drive, Pomona, CA 91768-2642, 909-622-8866. *Fax:* 909-623-5666.

DeVRY UNIVERSITY
San Diego, CA

CONTACT Financial Aid Office, DeVry University, 2655 Camino Del Rio North, Suite 201, San Diego, CA 92108-1633, 619-683-2446.

DeVRY UNIVERSITY
Sherman Oaks, CA

CONTACT Financial Aid Office, DeVry University, 15301 Ventura Boulevard, D-100, Sherman Oaks, CA 91403, 888-610-0800.

DeVRY UNIVERSITY
Colorado Springs, CO

CONTACT Carol Oppman, Director of Financial Aid, DeVry University, 225 South Union Boulevard, Colorado Springs, CO 80910, 719-632-3000 or toll-free 866-338-7934. *Fax:* 719-632-1909.

DeVRY UNIVERSITY
Westminster, CO

CONTACT Office of Financial Aid, DeVry University, 1870 West 122nd Avenue, Westminster, CO 80234-2010, 303-280-7400.

DeVRY UNIVERSITY
Jacksonville, FL

CONTACT Financial Aid Office, DeVry University, 5200 Belfort Road, Jacksonville, FL 32256-6040.

DeVRY UNIVERSITY
Miami, FL

CONTACT Financial Aid Office, DeVry University, 8700 West Flagler Street, Suite 100, Miami, FL 33174-2535, 305-229-4833.

DeVRY UNIVERSITY
Miramar, FL

CONTACT Office of Financial Aid, DeVry University, 2300 Southwest 145th Avenue, Miramar, FL 33027, 954-499-9700.

DeVRY UNIVERSITY
Orlando, FL

CONTACT Estrella Velazquez-Domenech, Director of Student Finance, DeVry University, 4000 Millenia Boulevard, Orlando, FL 32839, 407-345-2816. *Fax:* 407-355-4855.

DeVRY UNIVERSITY
Tampa, FL

CONTACT Financial Aid Office, DeVry University, 3030 North Rocky Point Drive West, Suite 100, Tampa, FL 33607-5901, 813-288-8994.

DeVRY UNIVERSITY
Alpharetta, GA

CONTACT David Pickett, Assistant Director of Financial Aid, DeVry University, 2555 Northwinds Parkway, Alpharetta, GA 30004, 770-521-4900 or toll-free 800-346-5420. *Fax:* 770-664-8024.

DeVRY UNIVERSITY
Decatur, GA

CONTACT Robin Winston, Director of Financial Aid, DeVry University, 250 North Arcadia Avenue, Decatur, GA 30030-2198, 404-292-7900. *Fax:* 404-292-2321.

DeVRY UNIVERSITY
Duluth, GA

CONTACT Financial Aid Office, DeVry University, 3505 Koger Boulevard, Suite 170, Duluth, GA 30096-7671, 678-380-9780.

DeVRY UNIVERSITY
Addison, IL

CONTACT Sejal Amin, Director of Student Finance, DeVry University, 1221 North Swift Road, Addison, IL 60101-6106, 630-953-1300 or toll-free 800-346-5420.

DeVRY UNIVERSITY
Chicago, IL

CONTACT Milena Dobrina, Director of Financial Aid, DeVry University, 3300 North Campbell Avenue, Chicago, IL 60618-5994, 773-929-8500. *Fax:* 773-348-1780.

DeVRY UNIVERSITY
Downers Grove, IL

CONTACT Financial Aid Office, DeVry University, 3005 Highland Parkway, Downers Grove, IL 60515, 630-515-3000.

DeVRY UNIVERSITY
Elgin, IL

CONTACT Financial Aid Office, DeVry University, Randall Point, 2250 Point Boulevard, Suite 250, Elgin, IL 60123, 847-649-3980.

DeVRY UNIVERSITY
Gurnee, IL

CONTACT Financial Aid Office, DeVry University, 1075 Tri-State Parkway, Suite 800, Gurnee, IL 60031-9126, 847-855-2649 or toll-free 866-563-3879.

DeVry University
Naperville, IL

CONTACT Financial Aid Office, DeVry University, 2056 Westings Avenue, Suite 40, Naperville, IL 60563-2361, 630-428-9086 or toll-free 877-496-9050.

DeVry University
Tinley Park, IL

CONTACT Director of Student Finance, DeVry University, 18624 West Creek Drive, Tinley Park, IL 60477, 708-342-3300. *Fax:* 708-342-3120.

DeVry University
Indianapolis, IN

CONTACT Financial Aid Office, DeVry University, 9100 Keystone Crossing, Suite 350, Indianapolis, IN 46240-2158, 317-581-8854.

DeVry University
Merrillville, IN

CONTACT Financial Aid Office, DeVry University, Twin Towers, 1000 East 80th Place, Suite 222 Mall, Merrillville, IN 46410-5673, 219-736-7440.

DeVry University
Louisville, KY

CONTACT Financial Aid Office, DeVry University, 10172 Linn Station Road, Suite 300, Louisville, KY 40223, toll-free 866-906-9388.

DeVry University
Bethesda, MD

CONTACT Financial Aid Office, DeVry University, 4550 Montgomery Avenue, Suite 100 North, Bethesda, MD 20814-3304, 301-652-8477.

DeVry University
Southfield, MI

CONTACT Mr. Stephen Haworth, Regulatory Compliance Specialist, DeVry University, 26999 Central Park Boulevard, Suite 125, Southfield, MI 48076, 630-706-3172. *Fax:* 630-574-1991. *E-mail:* shaworth@devry.com.

DeVry University
Edina, MN

CONTACT Financial Aid Office, DeVry University, 7700 France Avenue South, Suite 575, Edina, MN 55435, 952-838-1860.

DeVry University
Kansas City, MO

CONTACT Maureen Kelly, Senior Associate Director of Financial Aid, DeVry University, 11224 Holmes Street, Kansas City, MO 64131-3698, 816-941-0430.

DeVry University
Kansas City, MO

CONTACT Financial Aid Office, DeVry University, City Center Square, 1100 Main Street, Suite 118, Kansas City, MO 64105-2112, 816-221-1300.

DeVry University
St. Louis, MO

CONTACT Financial Aid Office, DeVry University, 1801 Park 270 Drive, Suite 260, St. Louis, MO 63146-4020, 314-542-4222.

DeVry University
Henderson, NV

CONTACT Financial Aid Office, DeVry University, 2490 Paseo Verde Parkway, Henderson, NV 89074-7120, 702-933-9700.

DeVry University
North Brunswick, NJ

CONTACT Albert Cama, Director of Financial Aid, DeVry University, 630 US Highway 1, North Brunswick, NJ 08902, 732-435-4880. *Fax:* 732-435-4867.

DeVry University
Paramus, NJ

CONTACT Financial Aid Office, DeVry University, 35 Plaza, 81 East State Route 4, Suite 102, Paramus, NJ 07652, 201-556-2840.

DeVry University
Charlotte, NC

CONTACT Financial Aid Office, DeVry University, 2015 Ayrsley Town Boulevard, Suite 109, Charlotte, NC 28273-4068, 704-362-2345.

DeVry University
Columbus, OH

CONTACT Cynthia Price, Director of Financial Aid, DeVry University, 1350 Alum Creek Drive, Columbus, OH 43209-2705, 614-253-7291. *Fax:* 614-252-4108.

DeVry University
Columbus, OH

CONTACT Financial Aid Office, DeVry University, 8800 Lyra Drive, Columbus, OH 43240, 614-854-7500.

DeVry University
Seven Hills, OH

CONTACT Financial Aid Office, DeVry University, The Genesis Building, 6000 Lombardo Center, Suite 200, Seven Hills, OH 44131, 216-328-8754 or toll-free 866-453-3879.

DeVry University
Oklahoma City, OK

CONTACT Financial Aid Office, DeVry University, Lakepointe Towers, 4013 Northwest Expressway Street, Suite 100, Oklahoma City, OK 73116, 405-767-9516.

DeVry University
Portland, OR

CONTACT Financial Aid Office, DeVry University, 9755 Southwest Barnes Road, Suite 150, Portland, OR 97225-6651, 503-296-7468.

DeVry University
Fort Washington, PA

CONTACT Financial Aid Office, DeVry University, 1140 Virginia Drive, Fort Washington, PA 19034, 215-591-5700.

DeVry University
King of Prussia, PA

CONTACT Financial Aid Office, DeVry University, 150 Allendale Road, Buillding 3, Suite 3201, King of Prussia, PA 19406-2926, 610-205-3130.

DeVry University
Philadelphia, PA

CONTACT Financial Aid Office, DeVry University, Philadelphia Downtown Center, 1800 JFK Boulevard, Suite 104, Philadelphia, PA 19103-7421.

DeVry University
Pittsburgh, PA

CONTACT Financial Aid Office, DeVry University, FreeMarkets Center, 210 Sixth Avenue, Suite 200, Pittsburgh, PA 15222-2606, 412-642-9072 or toll-free 866-77DEVRY.

DeVry University
Memphis, TN

CONTACT Financial Aid Office, DeVry University, 6401 Poplar Avenue, Suite 600, Memphis, TN 38119, 901-537-2560 or toll-free 888-563-3879.

DeVry University
Nashville, TN

CONTACT Financial Aid Office, DeVry University, 3343 Perimeter Hill Drive, Suite 200, Nashville, TN 37211-4147, 615-445-3456.

DeVry University
Houston, TX

CONTACT Financial Aid Office, DeVry University, 11125 Equity Drive, Houston, TX 77041, 713-850-0888 or toll-free 866-703-3879.

DeVry University
Irving, TX

CONTACT Tommy Sims, Financial Aid Officer, DeVry University, 4800 Regent Boulevard, Irving, TX 75063-2440, 972-929-6777.

DeVry University
Richardson, TX

CONTACT Financial Aid Office, DeVry University, Richardson Center, 2201 North Central Expressway, Richardson, TX 75080, 972-792-7450.

DeVry University
Sandy, UT

CONTACT Financial Aid Office, DeVry University, 9350 South 150 E, Suite 420, Sandy, UT 84070, 801-565-5110.

DeVry University
Arlington, VA

CONTACT Roberta McDevitt, Director of Student Finance, DeVry University, 2341 Jefferson Davis Highway, Arlington, VA 22202, 866-338-7932. *Fax:* 703-414-4040.

DeVry University
Chesapeake, VA

CONTACT Financial Aid Office, DeVry University, 1317 Executive Boulevard, Suite 100, Chesapeake, VA 23320-3671, 757-382-5680.

DeVry University
Manassas, VA

CONTACT Financial Aid Office, DeVry University, 10432 Balls Ford Road, Suite 130, Manassas, VA 20109-3173, 703-396-6611.

DeVry University
Bellevue, WA

CONTACT Financial Aid Office, DeVry University, 600 108th Avenue NE, Suite 230, Bellevue, WA 98004-5110, 425-455-2242.

DeVry University
Federal Way, WA

CONTACT Diane Rooney, Assistant Director of Student Finance, DeVry University, 3600 South 344th Way, Federal Way, WA 98001, 253-943-2800. *Fax:* 253-943-5503.

DeVry University
Milwaukee, WI

CONTACT Financial Aid Office, DeVry University, 411 East Wisconsin Avenue, Suite 300, Milwaukee, WI 53202, 414-278-7677.

DeVry University
Waukesha, WI

CONTACT Financial Aid Office, DeVry University, N14 W23833 Stone Ridge Drive, Suite 450, Waukesha, WI 53188-1157, 262-347-2911.

DeVry University Online
Addison, IL

CONTACT Financial Aid Office, DeVry University Online, 1221 North Swift Road, Addison, IL 60101-6106, 877-496-9050.

Dickinson College
Carlisle, PA

Tuition & fees: $41,520 **Average undergraduate aid package: $34,687**

ABOUT THE INSTITUTION Independent, coed. 42 undergraduate majors. Both federal and institutional methodology are used as a basis for awarding need-based institutional aid.

UNDERGRADUATE EXPENSES for 2010–11 ***One-time required fee:*** $25. ***Comprehensive fee:*** $51,950 includes full-time tuition ($41,170), mandatory fees ($350), and room and board ($10,430). ***College room only:*** $5380. Room and board charges vary according to board plan and housing facility. ***Part-time tuition:*** $5145 per course. ***Part-time fees:*** $44 per course. ***Payment plan:*** Installment.

FRESHMAN FINANCIAL AID (Fall 2010, est.) 446 applied for aid; of those 87% were deemed to have need. 99% of freshmen with need received aid; of those 84% had need fully met. ***Average percent of need met:*** 99% (excluding resources awarded to replace EFC). ***Average financial aid package:*** $34,695 (excluding resources awarded to replace EFC). 13% of all full-time freshmen had no need and received non-need-based gift aid.

UNDERGRADUATE FINANCIAL AID (Fall 2010, est.) 1,430 applied for aid; of those 90% were deemed to have need. 100% of undergraduates with need received aid; of those 73% had need fully met. ***Average percent of need met:*** 96% (excluding resources awarded to replace EFC). ***Average financial aid package:*** $34,687 (excluding resources awarded to replace EFC). 9% of all full-time undergraduates had no need and received non-need-based gift aid.

GIFT AID (NEED-BASED) ***Total amount:*** $35,947,079 (7% federal, 1% state, 91% institutional, 1% external sources). ***Receiving aid:*** Freshmen: 57% (375); all full-time undergraduates: 52% (1,238). ***Average award:*** Freshmen: $29,628; Undergraduates: $28,994. ***Scholarships, grants, and awards:*** Federal Pell, FSEOG, state, private, college/university gift aid from institutional funds.

GIFT AID (NON-NEED-BASED) ***Total amount:*** $4,272,178 (27% federal, 65% institutional, 8% external sources). ***Receiving aid:*** Freshmen: 6% (37). Undergraduates: 3% (82). ***Average award:*** Freshmen: $10,746. Undergraduates: $11,160. ***Scholarships, grants, and awards by category:*** *Academic interests/achievement:* 552 awards ($6,608,595 total): general academic interests/achievements, military science. *Special characteristics:* 23 awards ($708,390 total): children and siblings of alumni, children of faculty/staff. ***Tuition waivers:*** Full or partial for employees or children of employees, senior citizens.

LOANS ***Student loans:*** $8,794,908 (66% need-based, 34% non-need-based). 51% of past graduating class borrowed through all loan programs. *Average indebtedness per student:* $22,451. ***Average need-based loan:*** Freshmen: $4191. Undergraduates: $5055. ***Parent loans:*** $4,726,525 (18% need-based, 82% non-need-based). ***Programs:*** Federal Direct (Subsidized and Unsubsidized Stafford, PLUS), Perkins, college/university.

WORK-STUDY ***Federal work-study:*** Total amount: $2,085,446; 934 jobs averaging $2231. ***State or other work-study/employment:*** Total amount: $660,350 (68% need-based, 32% non-need-based). 195 part-time jobs averaging $3386.

APPLYING FOR FINANCIAL AID ***Required financial aid forms:*** FAFSA, CSS Financial Aid PROFILE, state aid form, noncustodial (divorced/separated) parent's statement. ***Financial aid deadline:*** 2/1 (priority: 11/15). ***Notification date:*** 3/20. Students must reply by 5/1 or within 2 weeks of notification.

CONTACT Rick A. Heckman, Director of Financial Aid, Dickinson College, PO Box 1773, Carlisle, PA 17013-2896, 717-245-1308 or toll-free 800-644-1773. *Fax:* 717-245-1972. *E-mail:* finaid@dickinson.edu.

DICKINSON STATE UNIVERSITY

Dickinson, ND

Tuition & fees (ND res): $6337 **Average undergraduate aid package: $7577**

ABOUT THE INSTITUTION State-supported, coed. 43 undergraduate majors. Federal methodology is used as a basis for awarding need-based institutional aid.

UNDERGRADUATE EXPENSES for 2010–11 ***Tuition, state resident:*** full-time $5248. ***Tuition, nonresident:*** full-time $12,195. ***Required fees:*** full-time $1089. ***College room and board:*** $4262; ***Room only:*** $1610. Room and board charges vary according to board plan. ***Payment plan:*** Installment.

FRESHMAN FINANCIAL AID (Fall 2010, est.) 239 applied for aid; of those 80% were deemed to have need. 100% of freshmen with need received aid; of those 99% had need fully met. ***Average percent of need met:*** 45% (excluding resources awarded to replace EFC). ***Average financial aid package:*** $7360 (excluding resources awarded to replace EFC). 44% of all full-time freshmen had no need and received non-need-based gift aid.

UNDERGRADUATE FINANCIAL AID (Fall 2010, est.) 1,147 applied for aid; of those 79% were deemed to have need. 98% of undergraduates with need received aid; of those 99% had need fully met. ***Average percent of need met:*** 35% (excluding resources awarded to replace EFC). ***Average financial aid package:*** $7577 (excluding resources awarded to replace EFC). 30% of all full-time undergraduates had no need and received non-need-based gift aid.

GIFT AID (NEED-BASED) ***Total amount:*** $3,416,500 (73% federal, 12% state, 11% institutional, 4% external sources). ***Receiving aid:*** Freshmen: 56% (175); all full-time undergraduates: 45% (755). ***Average award:*** Freshmen: $4263; Undergraduates: $4020. ***Scholarships, grants, and awards:*** Federal Pell, FSEOG, state, college/university gift aid from institutional funds, National Guard tuition waivers, staff waivers.

GIFT AID (NON-NEED-BASED) ***Total amount:*** $30,426 (4% state, 51% institutional, 45% external sources). ***Receiving aid:*** Freshmen: 2% (5). Undergraduates: 1% (9). ***Average award:*** Freshmen: $1396. Undergraduates: $1491. ***Scholarships, grants, and awards by category:*** *Academic interests/achievement:* agriculture, biological sciences, business, communication, computer science, education, English, foreign languages, general academic interests/achievements, health fields, humanities, mathematics, physical sciences, premedicine, social sciences. *Creative arts/performance:* art/fine arts, creative writing, journalism/publications, music, theater/drama. *Special achievements/activities:* cheerleading/drum major, leadership, rodeo. *Special characteristics:* children of faculty/staff, children with a deceased or disabled parent, ethnic background, general special characteristics, international students, members of minority groups, veterans, veterans' children. ***Tuition waivers:*** Full or partial for minority students, children of alumni, employees or children of employees, adult students, senior citizens.

LOANS ***Student loans:*** $5,495,571 (78% need-based, 22% non-need-based). 75% of past graduating class borrowed through all loan programs. *Average indebtedness per student:* $18,837. ***Average need-based loan:*** Freshmen: $3076. Undergraduates: $3799. ***Parent loans:*** $72,699 (40% need-based, 60% non-need-based). ***Programs:*** Perkins, Federal Nursing, state, college/university, Alaska Loans, alternative loans.

WORK-STUDY ***Federal work-study:*** Total amount: $183,135; jobs available. ***State or other work-study/employment:*** Part-time jobs available.

ATHLETIC AWARDS Total amount: $102,407 (75% need-based, 25% non-need-based).

APPLYING FOR FINANCIAL AID ***Required financial aid form:*** FAFSA. ***Financial aid deadline (priority):*** 3/15. ***Notification date:*** Continuous beginning 6/15. Students must reply by 7/31 or within 4 weeks of notification.

CONTACT Ms. Sandy Klein, Director of Financial Aid, Dickinson State University, 291 Campus Drive, Dickinson, ND 58601-4896, 701-483-2371 or toll-free 800-279-4295. *Fax:* 701-483-2720. *E-mail:* sandy.klein@dickinsonstate.edu.

DIGIPEN INSTITUTE OF TECHNOLOGY

Redmond, WA

Tuition & fees: $25,160 **Average undergraduate aid package: N/A**

ABOUT THE INSTITUTION Proprietary, coed. 4 undergraduate majors. Federal methodology is used as a basis for awarding need-based institutional aid.

UNDERGRADUATE EXPENSES for 2011–12 ***One-time required fee:*** $150. ***Tuition:*** full-time $25,000; part-time $618 per semester hour. ***Required fees:*** full-time $160; $80 per term. Full-time tuition and fees vary according to course load and program. Part-time tuition and fees vary according to course load and program. Room and board charges vary according to housing facility. ***Payment plan:*** Installment.

GIFT AID (NEED-BASED) ***Scholarships, grants, and awards:*** Federal Pell, state, private, college/university gift aid from institutional funds.

GIFT AID (NON-NEED-BASED) ***Scholarships, grants, and awards by category:*** *Special achievements/activities:* community service, general special achievements/activities. *Special characteristics:* ethnic background, local/state students, members of minority groups, spouses of current students, veterans, veterans' children. ***Tuition waivers:*** Full or partial for employees or children of employees.

LOANS ***Programs:*** Federal Direct (Subsidized and Unsubsidized Stafford, PLUS).

APPLYING FOR FINANCIAL AID ***Required financial aid forms:*** FAFSA, institution's own form. ***Financial aid deadline:*** Continuous. ***Notification date:*** Continuous beginning 1/1. Students must reply within 2 weeks of notification.

CONTACT Mrs. Kimberly King, Director of Financial Aid, DigiPen Institute of Technology, 5001 150th Avenue, NE, Suite 210, Redmond, WA 98052, 425-895-4446. *Fax:* 425-558-0378. *E-mail:* kimking@digipen.edu.

DILLARD UNIVERSITY

New Orleans, LA

Tuition & fees: N/R **Average undergraduate aid package: $18,745**

ABOUT THE INSTITUTION Independent interdenominational, coed. 23 undergraduate majors. Federal methodology is used as a basis for awarding need-based institutional aid.

UNDERGRADUATE EXPENSES for 2011–12 ***Tuition:*** part-time $542 per credit hour. Part-time tuition and fees vary according to course load. Room and board charges vary according to housing facility. ***Payment plan:*** Installment.

FRESHMAN FINANCIAL AID (Fall 2010, est.) 433 applied for aid; of those 97% were deemed to have need. 100% of freshmen with need received aid; of those 25% had need fully met. ***Average percent of need met:*** 73% (excluding resources awarded to replace EFC). ***Average financial aid package:*** $19,051 (excluding resources awarded to replace EFC).

UNDERGRADUATE FINANCIAL AID (Fall 2010, est.) 1,177 applied for aid; of those 96% were deemed to have need. 99% of undergraduates with need received aid; of those 25% had need fully met. ***Average percent of need met:*** 69% (excluding resources awarded to replace EFC). ***Average financial aid package:*** $18,745 (excluding resources awarded to replace EFC).

GIFT AID (NEED-BASED) ***Total amount:*** $9,941,500 (47% federal, 6% state, 45% institutional, 2% external sources). ***Receiving aid:*** Freshmen: 93% (414); all full-time undergraduates: 90% (1,069). ***Average award:*** Freshmen: $11,041; Undergraduates: $9469. ***Scholarships, grants, and awards:*** Federal Pell, FSEOG, state, private, college/university gift aid from institutional funds, United Negro College Fund, Federal Nursing.

GIFT AID (NON-NEED-BASED) ***Total amount:*** $86,928 (100% institutional). ***Receiving aid:*** Freshmen: 1% (4). Undergraduates: 1% (8). ***Scholarships, grants, and awards by category:*** *Academic interests/achievement:* general academic interests/achievements. *Creative arts/performance:* art/fine arts, music, theater/drama. *Special characteristics:* children of faculty/staff, religious affiliation. ***Tuition waivers:*** Full or partial for employees or children of employees.

LOANS ***Student loans:*** $8,270,782 (49% need-based, 51% non-need-based). *Average indebtedness per student:* $26,250. ***Average need-based loan:*** Freshmen: $3102. Undergraduates: $3563. ***Parent loans:*** $1,670,958 (100% non-need-based). ***Programs:*** Federal Direct (Subsidized and Unsubsidized Stafford, PLUS), Perkins, Federal Nursing, alternative loans.

WORK-STUDY ***Federal work-study:*** Total amount: $461,676; 291 jobs averaging $1565. ***State or other work-study/employment:*** Part-time jobs available.

ATHLETIC AWARDS Total amount: $400,151 (100% need-based).

APPLYING FOR FINANCIAL AID ***Required financial aid forms:*** FAFSA, institution's own form. ***Financial aid deadline (priority):*** 3/1. ***Notification date:*** Continuous. Students must reply within 2 weeks of notification.

CONTACT Mrs. Shannon Neal, Interim Director, Dillard University, 2601 Gentilly Boulevard, New Orleans, LA 70122-3097, 504-816-4677 or toll-free 800-716-8353 (in-state), 800-216-6637 (out-of-state). *Fax:* 504-816-5456. *E-mail:* sneal@dillard.edu.

DIXIE STATE COLLEGE OF UTAH

St. George, UT

Tuition & fees (UT res): $3490 **Average undergraduate aid package: $7614**

ABOUT THE INSTITUTION State-supported, coed. 30 undergraduate majors. Federal methodology is used as a basis for awarding need-based institutional aid.

UNDERGRADUATE EXPENSES for 2010–11 ***Tuition, state resident:*** full-time $2940; part-time $123 per credit hour. ***Tuition, nonresident:*** full-time $11,568; part-time $482 per credit hour. ***Required fees:*** full-time $550. Full-time tuition and fees vary according to course load and program. Part-time tuition and fees vary according to course load and program. ***College room and board:*** $4100; ***Room only:*** $1450. Room and board charges vary according to board plan and housing facility. ***Payment plan:*** Installment.

FRESHMAN FINANCIAL AID (Fall 2009) 973 applied for aid; of those 90% were deemed to have need. 98% of freshmen with need received aid; of those 3% had need fully met. ***Average percent of need met:*** 36% (excluding resources awarded to replace EFC). ***Average financial aid package:*** $6597 (excluding resources awarded to replace EFC). 23% of all full-time freshmen had no need and received non-need-based gift aid.

UNDERGRADUATE FINANCIAL AID (Fall 2009) 3,221 applied for aid; of those 87% were deemed to have need. 98% of undergraduates with need received aid; of those 2% had need fully met. ***Average percent of need met:*** 37% (excluding resources awarded to replace EFC). ***Average financial aid package:*** $7614 (excluding resources awarded to replace EFC). 21% of all full-time undergraduates had no need and received non-need-based gift aid.

GIFT AID (NEED-BASED) ***Total amount:*** $15,866,075 (81% federal, 7% state, 8% institutional, 4% external sources). ***Receiving aid:*** Freshmen: 60% (837); all full-time undergraduates: 61% (2,691). ***Average award:*** Freshmen: $5415; Undergraduates: $5917. ***Scholarships, grants, and awards:*** Federal Pell, FSEOG, state, private, college/university gift aid from institutional funds.

GIFT AID (NON-NEED-BASED) ***Receiving aid:*** Freshmen: 25% (353). Undergraduates: 22% (984). ***Average award:*** Freshmen: $2500. Undergraduates: $3241. ***Tuition waivers:*** Full or partial for children of alumni, employees or children of employees, senior citizens.

LOANS ***Student loans:*** $18,375,199 (51% need-based, 49% non-need-based). 40% of past graduating class borrowed through all loan programs. *Average indebtedness per student:* $15,564. ***Average need-based loan:*** Freshmen: $3126. Undergraduates: $3826. ***Parent loans:*** $305,005 (100% non-need-based). ***Programs:*** Federal Direct (Subsidized and Unsubsidized Stafford, PLUS), Perkins.

WORK-STUDY ***Federal work-study:*** Total amount: $200,555; jobs available. ***State or other work-study/employment:*** Total amount: $121,629 (100% need-based). Part-time jobs available.

ATHLETIC AWARDS Total amount: $1,110,384 (100% need-based).

APPLYING FOR FINANCIAL AID ***Required financial aid forms:*** FAFSA, institution's own form. ***Financial aid deadline:*** 5/1 (priority: 3/1). ***Notification date:*** Continuous beginning 2/1. Students must reply within 2 weeks of notification.

CONTACT J.D. Robertson, Director, Dixie State College of Utah, 225 South 700 East, St. George, UT 84770, 435-652-7575 or toll-free 888-GO2DIXIE. *Fax:* 435-656-4087. *E-mail:* finaid@dixie.edu.

DOANE COLLEGE

Crete, NE

Tuition & fees: $22,170 **Average undergraduate aid package: $18,025**

ABOUT THE INSTITUTION Independent religious, coed. 41 undergraduate majors. Both federal and institutional methodology are used as a basis for awarding need-based institutional aid.

UNDERGRADUATE EXPENSES for 2010–11 ***Comprehensive fee:*** $28,630 includes full-time tuition ($21,570), mandatory fees ($600), and room and board ($6460). ***College room only:*** $2650. Full-time tuition and fees vary according to location. Room and board charges vary according to board plan, housing facility, and location. ***Part-time tuition:*** $720 per credit hour. Part-time tuition and fees vary according to course load and location. ***Payment plan:*** Installment.

FRESHMAN FINANCIAL AID (Fall 2010, est.) 314 applied for aid; of those 87% were deemed to have need. 100% of freshmen with need received aid; of those 36% had need fully met. ***Average percent of need met:*** 89% (excluding resources awarded to replace EFC). ***Average financial aid package:*** $18,543 (excluding resources awarded to replace EFC). 7% of all full-time freshmen had no need and received non-need-based gift aid.

UNDERGRADUATE FINANCIAL AID (Fall 2010, est.) 947 applied for aid; of those 88% were deemed to have need. 100% of undergraduates with need received aid; of those 34% had need fully met. ***Average percent of need met:*** 86% (excluding resources awarded to replace EFC). ***Average financial aid package:*** $18,025 (excluding resources awarded to replace EFC). 7% of all full-time undergraduates had no need and received non-need-based gift aid.

GIFT AID (NEED-BASED) ***Total amount:*** $5,731,427 (35% federal, 6% state, 50% institutional, 9% external sources). ***Receiving aid:*** Freshmen: 83% (272); all full-time undergraduates: 79% (825). ***Average award:*** Freshmen: $14,708; Undergraduates: $13,741. ***Scholarships, grants, and awards:*** Federal Pell, FSEOG, state, private, college/university gift aid from institutional funds.

GIFT AID (NON-NEED-BASED) ***Total amount:*** $4,363,566 (1% federal, 99% institutional). ***Receiving aid:*** Undergraduates: 1% (8). ***Average award:*** Freshmen: $10,233. Undergraduates: $11,016. ***Scholarships, grants, and awards by category:*** *Academic interests/achievement:* general academic interests/achievements. *Creative arts/performance:* art/fine arts, debating, music, performing arts, theater/drama. *Special characteristics:* children and siblings of alumni, children of faculty/staff, religious affiliation, siblings of current students. ***Tuition waivers:*** Full or partial for employees or children of employees, senior citizens.

LOANS ***Student loans:*** $5,949,323 (50% need-based, 50% non-need-based). 77% of past graduating class borrowed through all loan programs. *Average indebtedness per student:* $20,748. ***Average need-based loan:*** Freshmen: $3995. Undergraduates: $4375. ***Parent loans:*** $2,815,251 (100% non-need-based). ***Programs:*** Federal Direct (Subsidized and Unsubsidized Stafford, PLUS), Perkins.

WORK-STUDY ***Federal work-study:*** Total amount: $552,380; jobs available. ***State or other work-study/employment:*** Total amount: $350,835 (100% non-need-based). Part-time jobs available.

ATHLETIC AWARDS Total amount: $3,480,901 (61% need-based, 39% non-need-based).

APPLYING FOR FINANCIAL AID ***Required financial aid form:*** FAFSA. ***Financial aid deadline:*** Continuous. ***Notification date:*** Continuous beginning 3/1. Students must reply within 2 weeks of notification.

CONTACT Peggy Tvrdy, Director of Financial Aid, Doane College, 1014 Boswell Avenue, Crete, NE 68333-2430, 402-826-8260 or toll-free 800-333-6263. *Fax:* 402-826-8600. *E-mail:* peggy.tvrdy@doane.edu.

DOMINICAN COLLEGE

Orangeburg, NY

Tuition & fees: $21,990 **Average undergraduate aid package: $15,385**

ABOUT THE INSTITUTION Independent, coed. 36 undergraduate majors. Federal methodology is used as a basis for awarding need-based institutional aid.

UNDERGRADUATE EXPENSES for 2010–11 ***One-time required fee:*** $35. ***Comprehensive fee:*** $32,550 includes full-time tuition ($21,250), mandatory fees ($740), and room and board ($10,560). Full-time tuition and fees vary according to degree level. Room and board charges vary according to board plan and housing facility. ***Part-time tuition:*** $640 per credit hour. Part-time tuition and fees vary according to degree level and program. ***Payment plans:*** Installment, deferred payment.

FRESHMAN FINANCIAL AID (Fall 2009) 304 applied for aid; of those 99% were deemed to have need. 100% of freshmen with need received aid; of those 12% had need fully met. ***Average percent of need met:*** 65% (excluding resources awarded to replace EFC). ***Average financial aid package:*** $18,118 (excluding resources awarded to replace EFC). 8% of all full-time freshmen had no need and received non-need-based gift aid.

UNDERGRADUATE FINANCIAL AID (Fall 2009) 1,343 applied for aid; of those 92% were deemed to have need. 99% of undergraduates with need received aid; of those 11% had need fully met. ***Average percent of need met:*** 59% (excluding resources awarded to replace EFC). ***Average financial aid package:*** $15,385 (excluding resources awarded to replace EFC). 8% of all full-time undergraduates had no need and received non-need-based gift aid.

GIFT AID (NEED-BASED) ***Total amount:*** $13,842,898 (23% federal, 13% state, 63% institutional, 1% external sources). ***Receiving aid:*** Freshmen: 86% (278); all full-time undergraduates: 86% (1,167). ***Average award:*** Freshmen: $14,876; Undergraduates: $12,101. ***Scholarships, grants, and awards:*** Federal Pell, FSEOG, state, private, college/university gift aid from institutional funds.

GIFT AID (NON-NEED-BASED) ***Total amount:*** $974,203 (7% state, 92% institutional, 1% external sources). ***Receiving aid:*** Freshmen: 8% (25). Undergraduates: 6% (83). ***Average award:*** Freshmen: $8692. Undergraduates: $6662. ***Scholarships, grants, and awards by category:*** *Academic interests/achievement:* education, general academic interests/achievements, health fields. *Special characteristics:* 8 awards ($85,000 total): children of faculty/staff, general special characteristics, relatives of clergy. ***Tuition waivers:*** Full or partial for employees or children of employees, senior citizens.

LOANS ***Student loans:*** $15,868,027 (92% need-based, 8% non-need-based). 97% of past graduating class borrowed through all loan programs. *Average indebtedness per student:* $18,398. ***Average need-based loan:*** Freshmen: $3390. Undergraduates: $4270. ***Parent loans:*** $3,842,137 (63% need-based, 37% non-need-based). ***Programs:*** Perkins, Federal Nursing.

WORK-STUDY ***Federal work-study:*** Total amount: $272,292; 217 jobs averaging $1200. ***State or other work-study/employment:*** Total amount: $342,398 (82% need-based, 18% non-need-based). 73 part-time jobs averaging $3000.

ATHLETIC AWARDS Total amount: $2,114,497 (77% need-based, 23% non-need-based).

APPLYING FOR FINANCIAL AID ***Required financial aid forms:*** FAFSA, state aid form. ***Financial aid deadline (priority):*** 2/15. ***Notification date:*** Continuous beginning 2/15. Students must reply within 4 weeks of notification.

CONTACT Dr. Daniel Shields, Director of Financial Aid, Dominican College, 470 Western Highway, Orangeburg, NY 10962-1210, 845-848-7818 or toll-free 866-432-4636. *Fax:* 845-359-4317. *E-mail:* daniel.shields@dc.edu.

DOMINICAN UNIVERSITY

River Forest, IL

Tuition & fees: $25,710 **Average undergraduate aid package: $18,162**

ABOUT THE INSTITUTION Independent Roman Catholic, coed. 50 undergraduate majors. Federal methodology is used as a basis for awarding need-based institutional aid.

UNDERGRADUATE EXPENSES for 2010–11 ***One-time required fee:*** $150. ***Comprehensive fee:*** $33,710 includes full-time tuition ($25,560), mandatory fees ($150), and room and board ($8000). Full-time tuition and fees vary according to course load. Room and board charges vary according to board plan and housing facility. ***Part-time tuition:*** $852 per semester hour. ***Part-time fees:*** $15 per course. Part-time tuition and fees vary according to course load. ***Payment plan:*** Installment.

FRESHMAN FINANCIAL AID (Fall 2010, est.) 382 applied for aid; of those 91% were deemed to have need. 100% of freshmen with need received aid; of those 12% had need fully met. ***Average percent of need met:*** 79% (excluding resources awarded to replace EFC). ***Average financial aid package:*** $20,008 (excluding resources awarded to replace EFC). 30% of all full-time freshmen had no need and received non-need-based gift aid.

UNDERGRADUATE FINANCIAL AID (Fall 2010, est.) 1,521 applied for aid; of those 92% were deemed to have need. 100% of undergraduates with need received aid; of those 14% had need fully met. ***Average percent of need met:*** 73% (excluding resources awarded to replace EFC). ***Average financial aid package:*** $18,162 (excluding resources awarded to replace EFC). 11% of all full-time undergraduates had no need and received non-need-based gift aid.

GIFT AID (NEED-BASED) ***Total amount:*** $17,372,398 (18% federal, 20% state, 61% institutional, 1% external sources). ***Receiving aid:*** Freshmen: 82% (349); all full-time undergraduates: 81% (1,369). ***Average award:*** Freshmen: $16,261; Undergraduates: $14,312. ***Scholarships, grants, and awards:*** Federal Pell, FSEOG, state, private, college/university gift aid from institutional funds.

GIFT AID (NON-NEED-BASED) ***Total amount:*** $1,890,613 (96% institutional, 4% external sources). ***Receiving aid:*** Freshmen: 9% (37). Undergraduates: 8% (129). ***Average award:*** Freshmen: $8878. Undergraduates: $8039. ***Scholarships, grants, and awards by category:*** *Academic interests/achievement:* 1,642 awards ($17,211,046 total): general academic interests/achievements, physical sciences. *Creative arts/performance:* 6 awards ($45,000 total): applied art and design, art/fine arts. *Special characteristics:* 278 awards ($926,187 total): children and siblings of alumni, children of educators, children of faculty/staff, siblings of current students. ***Tuition waivers:*** Full or partial for children of alumni, employees or children of employees.

LOANS ***Student loans:*** $11,418,998 (76% need-based, 24% non-need-based). 91% of past graduating class borrowed through all loan programs. *Average indebtedness per student:* $22,605. ***Average need-based loan:*** Freshmen: $2919. Undergraduates: $4125. ***Parent loans:*** $1,392,560 (24% need-based, 76% non-need-based). ***Programs:*** Federal Direct (Subsidized and Unsubsidized Stafford, PLUS), Perkins.

WORK-STUDY ***Federal work-study:*** Total amount: $839,844; 393 jobs averaging $2270. ***State or other work-study/employment:*** Total amount: $317,615 (100% non-need-based). 125 part-time jobs averaging $2421.

APPLYING FOR FINANCIAL AID ***Required financial aid form:*** FAFSA. ***Financial aid deadline (priority):*** 4/15. ***Notification date:*** Continuous. Students must reply within 2 weeks of notification.

CONTACT Marie von Ebers, Director of Financial Aid, Dominican University, 7900 West Division Street, River Forest, IL 60305-1099, 708-524-6809 or toll-free 800-828-8475. *Fax:* 708-366-6478. *E-mail:* vonebers@dom.edu.

DOMINICAN UNIVERSITY OF CALIFORNIA

San Rafael, CA

Tuition & fees: $37,350 **Average undergraduate aid package: $22,418**

ABOUT THE INSTITUTION Independent religious, coed. 25 undergraduate majors. Federal methodology is used as a basis for awarding need-based institutional aid.

UNDERGRADUATE EXPENSES for 2011–12 ***Comprehensive fee:*** $51,810 includes full-time tuition ($36,900), mandatory fees ($450), and room and board ($14,460). ***College room only:*** $8400. Full-time tuition and fees vary according to course load, degree level, and program. Room and board charges vary according to board plan. ***Part-time tuition:*** $1560 per unit. Part-time tuition and fees vary according to degree level and program. ***Payment plan:*** Installment.

FRESHMAN FINANCIAL AID (Fall 2009) 261 applied for aid; of those 90% were deemed to have need. 99% of freshmen with need received aid; of those 11% had need fully met. ***Average percent of need met:*** 64% (excluding resources awarded to replace EFC). ***Average financial aid package:*** $24,916 (excluding resources awarded to replace EFC). 9% of all full-time freshmen had no need and received non-need-based gift aid.

UNDERGRADUATE FINANCIAL AID (Fall 2009) 934 applied for aid; of those 92% were deemed to have need. 99% of undergraduates with need received aid; of those 8% had need fully met. ***Average percent of need met:*** 55% (excluding resources awarded to replace EFC). ***Average financial aid package:*** $22,418 (excluding resources awarded to replace EFC). 6% of all full-time undergraduates had no need and received non-need-based gift aid.

GIFT AID (NEED-BASED) ***Total amount:*** $17,034,770 (12% federal, 13% state, 71% institutional, 4% external sources). ***Receiving aid:*** Freshmen: 81% (231); all full-time undergraduates: 76% (854). ***Average award:*** Freshmen: $22,100; Undergraduates: $18,314. ***Scholarships, grants, and awards:*** Federal Pell, FSEOG, state, private, college/university gift aid from institutional funds, Scholarships for Disadvantaged Students (SDS).

GIFT AID (NON-NEED-BASED) ***Total amount:*** $1,378,799 (100% institutional). ***Receiving aid:*** Freshmen: 25% (72). Undergraduates: 17% (197). ***Average award:*** Freshmen: $12,600. Undergraduates: $10,528. ***Scholarships, grants, and awards by category:*** *Academic interests/achievement:* 1,059 awards ($10,732,393 total): general academic interests/achievements. *Creative arts/*

performance: 6 awards ($10,500 total): music. *Special achievements/activities:* 5 awards ($3750 total): community service, leadership. *Special characteristics:* 113 awards ($321,847 total): adult students, children and siblings of alumni, children of faculty/staff, international students, religious affiliation, veterans, veterans' children. ***Tuition waivers:*** Full or partial for employees or children of employees, senior citizens.

LOANS ***Student loans:*** $11,760,154 (80% need-based, 20% non-need-based). 80% of past graduating class borrowed through all loan programs. *Average indebtedness per student:* $32,314. ***Average need-based loan:*** Freshmen: $3370. Undergraduates: $4458. ***Parent loans:*** $3,060,062 (54% need-based, 46% non-need-based). ***Programs:*** Federal Direct (Subsidized and Unsubsidized Stafford, PLUS), Perkins, college/university, private loans.

WORK-STUDY ***Federal work-study:*** Total amount: $357,794; 200 jobs averaging $1778. ***State or other work-study/employment:*** Total amount: $151,560 (68% need-based, 32% non-need-based). 46 part-time jobs averaging $5412.

ATHLETIC AWARDS Total amount: $542,541 (89% need-based, 11% non-need-based).

APPLYING FOR FINANCIAL AID ***Required financial aid forms:*** FAFSA, institution's own form. ***Financial aid deadline (priority):*** 3/2. ***Notification date:*** Continuous beginning 3/15. Students must reply within 2 weeks of notification.

CONTACT Ms. Shanon Little, Director of Financial Aid, Dominican University of California, 50 Acacia Avenue, San Rafael, CA 94901-2298, 415-257-1302 or toll-free 888-323-6763. *Fax:* 415-485-3294. *E-mail:* shanon.little@dominican.edu.

DORDT COLLEGE

Sioux Center, IA

Tuition & fees: $23,180 **Average undergraduate aid package: $21,200**

ABOUT THE INSTITUTION Independent Christian Reformed, coed. 84 undergraduate majors. Federal methodology is used as a basis for awarding need-based institutional aid.

UNDERGRADUATE EXPENSES for 2010–11 ***Comprehensive fee:*** $29,700 includes full-time tuition ($22,800), mandatory fees ($380), and room and board ($6520). ***College room only:*** $3330. Full-time tuition and fees vary according to course load. Room and board charges vary according to board plan and housing facility. ***Part-time tuition:*** $930 per semester hour. ***Part-time fees:*** $190 per term. ***Payment plan:*** Installment.

FRESHMAN FINANCIAL AID (Fall 2010, est.) 319 applied for aid; of those 86% were deemed to have need. 100% of freshmen with need received aid; of those 17% had need fully met. ***Average percent of need met:*** 85% (excluding resources awarded to replace EFC). ***Average financial aid package:*** $22,605 (excluding resources awarded to replace EFC). 17% of all full-time freshmen had no need and received non-need-based gift aid.

UNDERGRADUATE FINANCIAL AID (Fall 2010, est.) 1,113 applied for aid; of those 88% were deemed to have need. 100% of undergraduates with need received aid; of those 16% had need fully met. ***Average percent of need met:*** 84% (excluding resources awarded to replace EFC). ***Average financial aid package:*** $21,200 (excluding resources awarded to replace EFC). 18% of all full-time undergraduates had no need and received non-need-based gift aid.

GIFT AID (NEED-BASED) ***Total amount:*** $13,423,151 (14% federal, 8% state, 70% institutional, 8% external sources). ***Receiving aid:*** Freshmen: 74% (273); all full-time undergraduates: 73% (980). ***Average award:*** Freshmen: $13,400; Undergraduates: $11,807. ***Scholarships, grants, and awards:*** Federal Pell, FSEOG, state, private, college/university gift aid from institutional funds.

GIFT AID (NON-NEED-BASED) ***Total amount:*** $1,637,518 (91% institutional, 9% external sources). ***Average award:*** Freshmen: $13,787. Undergraduates: $12,119. ***Scholarships, grants, and awards by category:*** *Academic interests/achievement:* agriculture, biological sciences, business, communication, computer science, education, engineering/technologies, English, foreign languages, general academic interests/achievements, humanities, mathematics, physical sciences, premedicine, religion/biblical studies, social sciences. *Creative arts/performance:* journalism/publications, music, theater/drama. *Special achievements/activities:* general special achievements/activities, leadership. *Special characteristics:* children and siblings of alumni, children of faculty/staff, general special characteristics, handicapped students, international students, local/state students, members of minority groups, out-of-state students, religious affiliation. ***Tuition waivers:*** Full or partial for employees or children of employees, senior citizens.

LOANS ***Student loans:*** $9,555,225 (91% need-based, 9% non-need-based). 85% of past graduating class borrowed through all loan programs. *Average indebtedness per student:* $21,881. ***Average need-based loan:*** Freshmen: $5283. Undergraduates: $5475. ***Parent loans:*** $4,694,183 (90% need-based, 10% non-need-based). ***Programs:*** Federal Direct (Subsidized and Unsubsidized Stafford, PLUS), Perkins, state, college/university, alternative loans.

WORK-STUDY ***Federal work-study:*** Total amount: $808,740; 500 jobs averaging $1500. ***State or other work-study/employment:*** Total amount: $1,060,200 (75% need-based, 25% non-need-based). 600 part-time jobs averaging $1500.

ATHLETIC AWARDS Total amount: $1,652,750 (81% need-based, 19% non-need-based).

APPLYING FOR FINANCIAL AID ***Required financial aid forms:*** FAFSA, institution's own form. ***Financial aid deadline (priority):*** 4/1. ***Notification date:*** Continuous beginning 3/1. Students must reply within 3 weeks of notification.

CONTACT Michael Epema, Director of Financial Aid, Dordt College, 498 4th Avenue NE, Sioux Center, IA 51250-1697, 712-722-6087 Ext. 6082 or toll-free 800-343-6738. *Fax:* 712-722-6035. *E-mail:* epema@dordt.edu.

DOWLING COLLEGE

Oakdale, NY

Tuition & fees: $24,630 **Average undergraduate aid package: $15,570**

ABOUT THE INSTITUTION Independent, coed. 47 undergraduate majors. Federal methodology is used as a basis for awarding need-based institutional aid.

UNDERGRADUATE EXPENSES for 2010–11 ***Comprehensive fee:*** $35,400 includes full-time tuition ($22,860), mandatory fees ($1770), and room and board ($10,770). Full-time tuition and fees vary according to course load, degree level, and program. Room and board charges vary according to housing facility and location. ***Part-time tuition:*** $767 per credit. ***Part-time fees:*** $566 per term. Part-time tuition and fees vary according to course load, degree level, and program. ***Payment plans:*** Installment, deferred payment.

FRESHMAN FINANCIAL AID (Fall 2009) 367 applied for aid; of those 98% were deemed to have need. 100% of freshmen with need received aid; of those 83% had need fully met. ***Average percent of need met:*** 95% (excluding resources awarded to replace EFC). ***Average financial aid package:*** $18,368 (excluding resources awarded to replace EFC). 9% of all full-time freshmen had no need and received non-need-based gift aid.

UNDERGRADUATE FINANCIAL AID (Fall 2009) 1,543 applied for aid; of those 100% were deemed to have need. 100% of undergraduates with need received aid; of those 11% had need fully met. ***Average percent of need met:*** 94% (excluding resources awarded to replace EFC). ***Average financial aid package:*** $15,570 (excluding resources awarded to replace EFC). 11% of all full-time undergraduates had no need and received non-need-based gift aid.

GIFT AID (NEED-BASED) ***Total amount:*** $11,662,797 (32% federal, 25% state, 43% institutional). ***Receiving aid:*** Freshmen: 66% (348); all full-time undergraduates: 69% (1,469). ***Average award:*** Freshmen: $3185; Undergraduates: $8270. ***Scholarships, grants, and awards:*** Federal Pell, FSEOG, state, private, college/university gift aid from institutional funds.

GIFT AID (NON-NEED-BASED) ***Total amount:*** $7,939,957 (3% federal, 1% state, 92% institutional, 4% external sources). ***Receiving aid:*** Freshmen: 58% (305). Undergraduates: 43% (907). ***Average award:*** Freshmen: $10,360. Undergraduates: $5770. ***Scholarships, grants, and awards by category:*** *Academic interests/achievement:* 719 awards ($3,612,428 total): business, education, general academic interests/achievements, mathematics, social sciences. *Special achievements/activities:* 212 awards ($2,338,347 total): general special achievements/activities. *Special characteristics:* 431 awards ($2,584,194 total): adult students, children and siblings of alumni, children of educators, children of faculty/staff, children of public servants, children of union members/company employees, children of workers in trades, ethnic background, first-generation college students, general special characteristics, local/state students, members of minority groups, previous college experience, public servants, siblings of current students, twins, veterans. ***Tuition waivers:*** Full or partial for minority students, children of alumni, employees or children of employees, adult students, senior citizens.

LOANS ***Student loans:*** $6,203,994 (100% need-based). 69% of past graduating class borrowed through all loan programs. *Average indebtedness per student:* $22,177. ***Average need-based loan:*** Freshmen: $3185. Undergraduates: $4200. ***Parent loans:*** $4,652,997 (100% non-need-based). ***Programs:*** Federal Direct (Subsidized and Unsubsidized Stafford, PLUS), Perkins, state, private loans.

WORK-STUDY ***Federal work-study:*** Total amount: $409,890; 311 jobs averaging $1674. ***State or other work-study/employment:*** Total amount: $201,455 (100% need-based). 131 part-time jobs averaging $2076.

ATHLETIC AWARDS Total amount: $2,360,478 (100% non-need-based).

APPLYING FOR FINANCIAL AID ***Required financial aid forms:*** FAFSA, state aid form. ***Financial aid deadline (priority):*** 3/1. ***Notification date:*** Continuous beginning 3/15.

CONTACT Ms. Denise Scalzo, Director of Student Financial Services, Dowling College, 150 Idle Hour Boulevard, Oakdale, NY 11769-1999, 631-244-3159 or toll-free 800-DOWLING. *E-mail:* scalzod@dowling.edu.

DRAKE UNIVERSITY

Des Moines, IA

Tuition & fees: $28,382 **Average undergraduate aid package: $21,212**

ABOUT THE INSTITUTION Independent, coed. 66 undergraduate majors. Federal methodology is used as a basis for awarding need-based institutional aid.

UNDERGRADUATE EXPENSES for 2011–12 ***Comprehensive fee:*** $36,792 includes full-time tuition ($28,250), mandatory fees ($132), and room and board ($8410). ***College room only:*** $4420. Full-time tuition and fees vary according to course load, program, and student level. Room and board charges vary according to board plan. ***Part-time tuition:*** $573 per hour. Part-time tuition and fees vary according to class time and program. ***Payment plan:*** Installment.

FRESHMAN FINANCIAL AID (Fall 2010, est.) 759 applied for aid; of those 78% were deemed to have need. 100% of freshmen with need received aid; of those 29% had need fully met. ***Average percent of need met:*** 80% (excluding resources awarded to replace EFC). ***Average financial aid package:*** $21,464 (excluding resources awarded to replace EFC). 27% of all full-time freshmen had no need and received non-need-based gift aid.

UNDERGRADUATE FINANCIAL AID (Fall 2010, est.) 2,425 applied for aid; of those 81% were deemed to have need. 100% of undergraduates with need received aid; of those 28% had need fully met. ***Average percent of need met:*** 78% (excluding resources awarded to replace EFC). ***Average financial aid package:*** $21,212 (excluding resources awarded to replace EFC). 34% of all full-time undergraduates had no need and received non-need-based gift aid.

GIFT AID (NEED-BASED) ***Total amount:*** $28,772,422 (13% federal, 7% state, 78% institutional, 2% external sources). ***Receiving aid:*** Freshmen: 68% (585); all full-time undergraduates: 59% (1,937). ***Average award:*** Freshmen: $15,587; Undergraduates: $14,579. ***Scholarships, grants, and awards:*** Federal Pell, FSEOG, state, private, college/university gift aid from institutional funds.

GIFT AID (NON-NEED-BASED) ***Total amount:*** $15,375,941 (2% federal, 95% institutional, 3% external sources). ***Receiving aid:*** Freshmen: 15% (131). Undergraduates: 11% (357). ***Average award:*** Freshmen: $12,478. Undergraduates: $11,072. ***Scholarships, grants, and awards by category:*** *Academic interests/achievement:* 2,571 awards ($27,129,806 total): general academic interests/achievements. *Creative arts/performance:* 306 awards ($1,383,847 total): art/fine arts, music, theater/drama. *Special characteristics:* 256 awards ($376,875 total): children and siblings of alumni, international students. ***Tuition waivers:*** Full or partial for children of alumni, employees or children of employees, senior citizens.

LOANS ***Student loans:*** $27,440,594 (47% need-based, 53% non-need-based). 66% of past graduating class borrowed through all loan programs. *Average indebtedness per student:* $35,027. ***Average need-based loan:*** Freshmen: $3250. Undergraduates: $4352. ***Parent loans:*** $36,599,375 (20% need-based, 80% non-need-based). ***Programs:*** Federal Direct (Subsidized and Unsubsidized Stafford, PLUS), Perkins, college/university.

WORK-STUDY ***Federal work-study:*** Total amount: $3,213,682; 1,676 jobs averaging $1917.

ATHLETIC AWARDS Total amount: $3,473,205 (30% need-based, 70% non-need-based).

APPLYING FOR FINANCIAL AID ***Required financial aid form:*** FAFSA. ***Financial aid deadline (priority):*** 3/1. ***Notification date:*** Continuous beginning 3/1. Students must reply by 5/1 or within 3 weeks of notification.

CONTACT Office of Student Financial Planning, Drake University, 2507 University Avenue, Des Moines, IA 50311-4516, 800-443-7253 Ext. 2905 or toll-free 800-44DRAKE Ext. 3181. *Fax:* 515-271-4042.

DRAUGHONS JUNIOR COLLEGE

Montgomery, AL

See South University.

DREW UNIVERSITY

Madison, NJ

Tuition & fees: $39,550 **Average undergraduate aid package: $30,018**

ABOUT THE INSTITUTION Independent religious, coed. 30 undergraduate majors. Institutional methodology is used as a basis for awarding need-based institutional aid.

UNDERGRADUATE EXPENSES for 2010–11 ***One-time required fee:*** $325. ***Comprehensive fee:*** $50,322 includes full-time tuition ($38,765), mandatory fees ($785), and room and board ($10,772). ***College room only:*** $6964. Full-time tuition and fees vary according to course load. Room and board charges vary according to board plan and housing facility. Part-time tuition and fees vary according to course load. ***Payment plans:*** Tuition prepayment, installment, deferred payment.

FRESHMAN FINANCIAL AID (Fall 2009) 404 applied for aid; of those 78% were deemed to have need. 100% of freshmen with need received aid; of those 18% had need fully met. ***Average percent of need met:*** 77% (excluding resources awarded to replace EFC). ***Average financial aid package:*** $29,574 (excluding resources awarded to replace EFC). 33% of all full-time freshmen had no need and received non-need-based gift aid.

UNDERGRADUATE FINANCIAL AID (Fall 2009) 1,186 applied for aid; of those 82% were deemed to have need. 100% of undergraduates with need received aid; of those 22% had need fully met. ***Average percent of need met:*** 79% (excluding resources awarded to replace EFC). ***Average financial aid package:*** $30,018 (excluding resources awarded to replace EFC). 36% of all full-time undergraduates had no need and received non-need-based gift aid.

GIFT AID (NEED-BASED) ***Total amount:*** $23,608,016 (9% federal, 12% state, 77% institutional, 2% external sources). ***Receiving aid:*** Freshmen: 62% (314); all full-time undergraduates: 58% (969). ***Average award:*** Freshmen: $24,969; Undergraduates: $24,363. ***Scholarships, grants, and awards:*** Federal Pell, FSEOG, state, private, college/university gift aid from institutional funds.

GIFT AID (NON-NEED-BASED) ***Total amount:*** $8,593,241 (1% state, 94% institutional, 5% external sources). ***Receiving aid:*** Freshmen: 8% (39). Undergraduates: 8% (129). ***Average award:*** Freshmen: $10,914. Undergraduates: $11,578. ***Scholarships, grants, and awards by category:*** *Academic interests/achievement:* general academic interests/achievements. *Creative arts/performance:* general creative arts/performance. *Special characteristics:* members of minority groups. ***Tuition waivers:*** Full or partial for employees or children of employees, senior citizens.

LOANS ***Student loans:*** $6,852,441 (56% need-based, 44% non-need-based). 62% of past graduating class borrowed through all loan programs. *Average indebtedness per student:* $19,634. ***Average need-based loan:*** Freshmen: $4041. Undergraduates: $5007. ***Parent loans:*** $8,400,694 (34% need-based, 66% non-need-based). ***Programs:*** Federal Direct (Subsidized and Unsubsidized Stafford, PLUS), Perkins, state.

WORK-STUDY ***Federal work-study:*** Total amount: $363,246; 288 jobs averaging $1261. ***State or other work-study/employment:*** Total amount: $413,853 (75% need-based, 25% non-need-based). 42 part-time jobs averaging $9854.

APPLYING FOR FINANCIAL AID ***Required financial aid forms:*** FAFSA, CSS Financial Aid PROFILE. ***Financial aid deadline:*** 2/15. ***Notification date:*** 3/30. Students must reply by 5/1.

CONTACT Renee Volak, Director of Financial Assistance, Drew University, 36 Madison Avenue, Madison, NJ 07940-1493, 973-408-3112. *Fax:* 973-408-3188. *E-mail:* finaid@drew.edu.

DREXEL UNIVERSITY

Philadelphia, PA

CONTACT Helen Gourousis, Director of Financial Aid, Drexel University, 3141 Chestnut Street, Philadelphia, PA 19104-2875, 215-895-5928 or toll-free 800-2-DREXEL. *Fax:* 215-895-6903. *E-mail:* gouroush@drexel.edu.

DRURY UNIVERSITY

Springfield, MO

Tuition & fees: $21,043 **Average undergraduate aid package: $7890**

ABOUT THE INSTITUTION Independent, coed. 61 undergraduate majors. Federal methodology is used as a basis for awarding need-based institutional aid.

UNDERGRADUATE EXPENSES for 2011–12 ***One-time required fee:*** $145. ***Comprehensive fee:*** $28,509 includes full-time tuition ($20,500), mandatory fees ($543), and room and board ($7466). Full-time tuition and fees vary according to class time. Room and board charges vary according to board plan and housing facility. Part-time tuition and fees vary according to class time. ***Payment plans:*** Tuition prepayment, installment, deferred payment.

FRESHMAN FINANCIAL AID (Fall 2010, est.) 384 applied for aid; of those 91% were deemed to have need. 100% of freshmen with need received aid; of those 72% had need fully met. ***Average percent of need met:*** 84% (excluding resources awarded to replace EFC). ***Average financial aid package:*** $7750 (excluding resources awarded to replace EFC). 9% of all full-time freshmen had no need and received non-need-based gift aid.

UNDERGRADUATE FINANCIAL AID (Fall 2010, est.) 1,579 applied for aid; of those 98% were deemed to have need. 100% of undergraduates with need received aid; of those 84% had need fully met. ***Average percent of need met:*** 86% (excluding resources awarded to replace EFC). ***Average financial aid package:*** $7890 (excluding resources awarded to replace EFC). 4% of all full-time undergraduates had no need and received non-need-based gift aid.

GIFT AID (NEED-BASED) ***Total amount:*** $11,938,158 (12% federal, 15% state, 66% institutional, 7% external sources). ***Receiving aid:*** Freshmen: 76% (308); all full-time undergraduates: 91% (1,483). ***Average award:*** Freshmen: $5850; Undergraduates: $6885. ***Scholarships, grants, and awards:*** Federal Pell, FSEOG, state, private, college/university gift aid from institutional funds.

GIFT AID (NON-NEED-BASED) ***Total amount:*** $3,390,848 (7% state, 89% institutional, 4% external sources). ***Receiving aid:*** Freshmen: 81% (327). Undergraduates: 93% (1,520). ***Average award:*** Freshmen: $3550. Undergraduates: $415. ***Scholarships, grants, and awards by category:*** *Academic interests/achievement:* 1,463 awards ($2,774,880 total): architecture, biological sciences, business, communication, computer science, education, English, foreign languages, general academic interests/achievements, health fields, humanities, mathematics, physical sciences, premedicine, social sciences. *Creative arts/performance:* 209 awards ($439,110 total): art/fine arts, creative writing, debating, music, theater/drama. *Special achievements/activities:* 276 awards ($133,850 total): cheerleading/drum major, leadership, religious involvement. *Special characteristics:* 240 awards ($738,128 total): children and siblings of alumni, children of faculty/staff, relatives of clergy, religious affiliation. ***Tuition waivers:*** Full or partial for minority students, children of alumni, employees or children of employees.

LOANS ***Student loans:*** $25,530,854 (93% need-based, 7% non-need-based). 67% of past graduating class borrowed through all loan programs. *Average indebtedness per student:* $20,500. ***Average need-based loan:*** Freshmen: $4500. Undergraduates: $6500. ***Parent loans:*** $1,695,481 (100% need-based). ***Programs:*** Federal Direct (Subsidized and Unsubsidized Stafford, PLUS), Perkins.

WORK-STUDY ***Federal work-study:*** Total amount: $329,500; jobs available. ***State or other work-study/employment:*** Total amount: $182,690 (100% non-need-based). Part-time jobs available.

ATHLETIC AWARDS Total amount: $2,860,424 (17% need-based, 83% non-need-based).

APPLYING FOR FINANCIAL AID ***Required financial aid forms:*** FAFSA, institution's own form. ***Financial aid deadline (priority):*** 2/15. ***Notification date:*** Continuous beginning 3/1. Students must reply by 3/1 or within 2 weeks of notification.

CONTACT Ms. Annette Avery, Director of Financial Aid, Drury University, 900 North Benton Avenue, Springfield, MO 65802-3791, 417-873-7312 or toll-free 800-922-2274. *Fax:* 417-873-6906. *E-mail:* aavery@drury.edu.

DUKE UNIVERSITY

Durham, NC

Tuition & fees: $40,243 **Average undergraduate aid package: $39,186**

ABOUT THE INSTITUTION Independent religious, coed. 45 undergraduate majors. Both federal and institutional methodology are used as a basis for awarding need-based institutional aid.

UNDERGRADUATE EXPENSES for 2010–11 ***Comprehensive fee:*** $51,865 includes full-time tuition ($38,985), mandatory fees ($1258), and room and board ($11,622). ***College room only:*** $6502. Room and board charges vary according to board plan and housing facility. ***Part-time tuition:*** $4872 per course. Part-time tuition and fees vary according to course load. ***Payment plans:*** Tuition prepayment, installment, deferred payment.

FRESHMAN FINANCIAL AID (Fall 2010, est.) 939 applied for aid; of those 88% were deemed to have need. 100% of freshmen with need received aid; of those 100% had need fully met. ***Average percent of need met:*** 100% (excluding resources awarded to replace EFC). ***Average financial aid package:*** $38,340 (excluding resources awarded to replace EFC). 3% of all full-time freshmen had no need and received non-need-based gift aid.

UNDERGRADUATE FINANCIAL AID (Fall 2010, est.) 3,233 applied for aid; of those 93% were deemed to have need. 100% of undergraduates with need received aid; of those 100% had need fully met. ***Average percent of need met:*** 100% (excluding resources awarded to replace EFC). ***Average financial aid package:*** $39,186 (excluding resources awarded to replace EFC). 7% of all full-time undergraduates had no need and received non-need-based gift aid.

GIFT AID (NEED-BASED) ***Total amount:*** $99,905,094 (6% federal, 2% state, 85% institutional, 7% external sources). ***Receiving aid:*** Freshmen: 46% (796); all full-time undergraduates: 43% (2,888). ***Average award:*** Freshmen: $35,394; Undergraduates: $35,578. ***Scholarships, grants, and awards:*** Federal Pell, FSEOG, state, private, college/university gift aid from institutional funds.

GIFT AID (NON-NEED-BASED) ***Total amount:*** $16,610,798 (4% state, 56% institutional, 40% external sources). ***Receiving aid:*** Freshmen: 5% (86). Undergraduates: 4% (242). ***Average award:*** Freshmen: $24,985. Undergraduates: $21,158. ***Scholarships, grants, and awards by category:*** *Academic interests/achievement:* general academic interests/achievements, mathematics. *Creative arts/performance:* creative writing. *Special achievements/activities:* general special achievements/activities, leadership. *Special characteristics:* children and siblings of alumni, ethnic background, local/state students. ***Tuition waivers:*** Full or partial for employees or children of employees.

LOANS ***Student loans:*** $11,629,427 (81% need-based, 19% non-need-based). 39% of past graduating class borrowed through all loan programs. *Average indebtedness per student:* $21,884. ***Average need-based loan:*** Freshmen: $2296. Undergraduates: $2585. ***Parent loans:*** $7,444,133 (73% need-based, 27% non-need-based). ***Programs:*** Federal Direct (Subsidized and Unsubsidized Stafford, PLUS), Perkins, college/university, alternative loans.

WORK-STUDY ***Federal work-study:*** Total amount: $3,108,614; 1,650 jobs averaging $1884. ***State or other work-study/employment:*** Total amount: $967,617 (82% need-based, 18% non-need-based). 581 part-time jobs averaging $1665.

ATHLETIC AWARDS Total amount: $13,432,858 (22% need-based, 78% non-need-based).

APPLYING FOR FINANCIAL AID ***Required financial aid forms:*** FAFSA, CSS Financial Aid PROFILE, noncustodial (divorced/separated) parent's statement, business/farm supplement, federal income tax form(s), W-2 forms. ***Financial aid deadline:*** 3/1. ***Notification date:*** 4/1. Students must reply by 5/1.

CONTACT Alison Rabil, Director, Duke University, 2127 Campus Drive Annex, Box 90397, Durham, NC 27708-0397, 919-684-6225. *Fax:* 919-660-9811. *E-mail:* finaid@duke.edu.

DUNLAP-STONE UNIVERSITY

Phoenix, AZ

CONTACT Financial Aid Office, Dunlap-Stone University, 11225 North 28th Drive, Suite B-201, Phoenix, AZ 85029, 602-648-5750 or toll-free 800-474-8013.

DUQUESNE UNIVERSITY

Pittsburgh, PA

Tuition & fees: $27,502 **Average undergraduate aid package: $21,312**

ABOUT THE INSTITUTION Independent Roman Catholic, coed. 69 undergraduate majors. Federal methodology is used as a basis for awarding need-based institutional aid.

UNDERGRADUATE EXPENSES for 2010–11 ***Comprehensive fee:*** $36,978 includes full-time tuition ($25,336), mandatory fees ($2166), and room and board ($9476). ***College room only:*** $5168. Full-time tuition and fees vary according to program. Room and board charges vary according to board plan and housing facility. ***Part-time tuition:*** $826 per credit. ***Part-time fees:*** $84 per credit. Part-time tuition and fees vary according to program. ***Payment plans:*** Installment, deferred payment.

FRESHMAN FINANCIAL AID (Fall 2009) 1,294 applied for aid; of those 81% were deemed to have need. 100% of freshmen with need received aid; of those 24% had need fully met. ***Average percent of need met:*** 89% (excluding

resources awarded to replace EFC). ***Average financial aid package:*** $21,517 (excluding resources awarded to replace EFC). 25% of all full-time freshmen had no need and received non-need-based gift aid.

UNDERGRADUATE FINANCIAL AID (Fall 2009) 4,612 applied for aid; of those 84% were deemed to have need. 100% of undergraduates with need received aid; of those 25% had need fully met. ***Average percent of need met:*** 79% (excluding resources awarded to replace EFC). ***Average financial aid package:*** $21,312 (excluding resources awarded to replace EFC). 25% of all full-time undergraduates had no need and received non-need-based gift aid.

GIFT AID (NEED-BASED) ***Total amount:*** $50,159,428 (11% federal, 11% state, 71% institutional, 7% external sources). ***Receiving aid:*** Freshmen: 73% (1,042); all full-time undergraduates: 68% (3,788). ***Average award:*** Freshmen: $14,567; Undergraduates: $13,231. ***Scholarships, grants, and awards:*** Federal Pell, FSEOG, state, private, college/university gift aid from institutional funds, United Negro College Fund.

GIFT AID (NON-NEED-BASED) ***Total amount:*** $11,441,620 (1% state, 93% institutional, 6% external sources). ***Receiving aid:*** Freshmen: 72% (1,026). Undergraduates: 63% (3,467). ***Average award:*** Freshmen: $8664. Undergraduates: $7800. ***Scholarships, grants, and awards by category:*** *Academic interests/achievement:* 4,530 awards ($30,937,109 total): general academic interests/achievements. *Creative arts/performance:* 202 awards ($1,515,735 total): dance, music. *Special characteristics:* 981 awards ($8,749,163 total): children and siblings of alumni, children of faculty/staff, ethnic background, general special characteristics, international students, members of minority groups, relatives of clergy, religious affiliation. ***Tuition waivers:*** Full or partial for employees or children of employees, senior citizens.

LOANS ***Student loans:*** $49,596,530 (88% need-based, 12% non-need-based). ***Average need-based loan:*** Freshmen: $3785. Undergraduates: $4402. ***Parent loans:*** $11,877,752 (84% need-based, 16% non-need-based). ***Programs:*** Federal Direct (Subsidized and Unsubsidized Stafford, PLUS), Perkins, Federal Nursing, private loans.

WORK-STUDY ***Federal work-study:*** Total amount: $8,985,459; 2,939 jobs averaging $3057.

ATHLETIC AWARDS Total amount: $5,442,963 (56% need-based, 44% non-need-based).

APPLYING FOR FINANCIAL AID ***Required financial aid forms:*** FAFSA, institution's own form. ***Financial aid deadline:*** 5/1. ***Notification date:*** Continuous beginning 3/1. Students must reply by 5/1 or within 3 weeks of notification.

CONTACT Mr. Richard C. Esposito, Director of Financial Aid, Duquesne University, 600 Forbes Avenue, Pittsburgh, PA 15282-0299, 412-396-6607 or toll-free 800-456-0590. *Fax:* 412-396-5284. *E-mail:* esposito@duq.edu.

D'YOUVILLE COLLEGE

Buffalo, NY

Tuition & fees: $21,060 **Average undergraduate aid package: $13,908**

ABOUT THE INSTITUTION Independent, coed. 24 undergraduate majors. Federal methodology is used as a basis for awarding need-based institutional aid.

UNDERGRADUATE EXPENSES for 2010–11 ***Comprehensive fee:*** $30,860 includes full-time tuition ($20,800), mandatory fees ($260), and room and board ($9800). Full-time tuition and fees vary according to course load, degree level, and program. Room and board charges vary according to board plan and housing facility. ***Part-time tuition:*** $640 per credit hour. ***Part-time fees:*** $2 per credit hour; $40 per term. Part-time tuition and fees vary according to course load, degree level, and program. ***Payment plans:*** Guaranteed tuition, installment, deferred payment.

FRESHMAN FINANCIAL AID (Fall 2010, est.) 244 applied for aid; of those 93% were deemed to have need. 100% of freshmen with need received aid; of those 16% had need fully met. ***Average percent of need met:*** 72% (excluding resources awarded to replace EFC). ***Average financial aid package:*** $15,914 (excluding resources awarded to replace EFC). 7% of all full-time freshmen had no need and received non-need-based gift aid.

UNDERGRADUATE FINANCIAL AID (Fall 2010, est.) 1,529 applied for aid; of those 90% were deemed to have need. 99% of undergraduates with need received aid; of those 13% had need fully met. ***Average percent of need met:*** 57% (excluding resources awarded to replace EFC). ***Average financial aid package:*** $13,908 (excluding resources awarded to replace EFC). 9% of all full-time undergraduates had no need and received non-need-based gift aid.

GIFT AID (NEED-BASED) ***Total amount:*** $13,557,245 (28% federal, 14% state, 53% institutional, 5% external sources). ***Receiving aid:*** Freshmen: 84% (224); all full-time undergraduates: 82% (1,317). ***Average award:*** Freshmen: $12,934; Undergraduates: $10,256. ***Scholarships, grants, and awards:*** Federal Pell, FSEOG, state, private, college/university gift aid from institutional funds.

GIFT AID (NON-NEED-BASED) ***Total amount:*** $1,092,712 (2% state, 93% institutional, 5% external sources). ***Receiving aid:*** Freshmen: 7% (20). Undergraduates: 5% (80). ***Average award:*** Freshmen: $8055. Undergraduates: $5823. ***Scholarships, grants, and awards by category:*** *Academic interests/achievement:* 1,366 awards ($6,490,247 total): biological sciences, business, education, English, general academic interests/achievements, health fields, humanities, international studies, mathematics, premedicine, social sciences. *Special characteristics:* 111 awards ($977,481 total): children and siblings of alumni, children of faculty/staff, veterans. ***Tuition waivers:*** Full or partial for children of alumni, employees or children of employees, senior citizens.

LOANS ***Student loans:*** $17,252,268 (82% need-based, 18% non-need-based). 90% of past graduating class borrowed through all loan programs. *Average indebtedness per student:* $42,042. ***Average need-based loan:*** Freshmen: $3339. Undergraduates: $4351. ***Parent loans:*** $1,870,122 (63% need-based, 37% non-need-based). ***Programs:*** Federal Direct (Subsidized and Unsubsidized Stafford, PLUS), Perkins, Federal Nursing, college/university.

WORK-STUDY ***Federal work-study:*** Total amount: $254,461; 182 jobs averaging $1301. ***State or other work-study/employment:*** Total amount: $108,391 (100% non-need-based). 125 part-time jobs averaging $867.

APPLYING FOR FINANCIAL AID ***Required financial aid forms:*** FAFSA, state aid form. ***Financial aid deadline (priority):*** 2/15. ***Notification date:*** Continuous beginning 3/15. Students must reply within 2 weeks of notification.

CONTACT Ms. Lorraine A. Metz, Director of Financial Aid, D'Youville College, 320 Porter Avenue, Buffalo, NY 14201-1084, 716-829-7500 or toll-free 800-777-3921. *Fax:* 716-829-7779. *E-mail:* metzla@dyc.edu.

EARLHAM COLLEGE

Richmond, IN

Tuition & fees: $36,694 **Average undergraduate aid package: $30,359**

ABOUT THE INSTITUTION Independent religious, coed. 36 undergraduate majors. Federal methodology is used as a basis for awarding need-based institutional aid.

UNDERGRADUATE EXPENSES for 2010–11 ***Comprehensive fee:*** $44,094 includes full-time tuition ($35,920), mandatory fees ($774), and room and board ($7400). ***College room only:*** $3750. Room and board charges vary according to board plan. ***Part-time tuition:*** $1197 per credit. ***Payment plans:*** Tuition prepayment, installment, deferred payment.

FRESHMAN FINANCIAL AID (Fall 2009) 200 applied for aid; of those 88% were deemed to have need. 100% of freshmen with need received aid; of those 31% had need fully met. ***Average percent of need met:*** 86% (excluding resources awarded to replace EFC). ***Average financial aid package:*** $32,423 (excluding resources awarded to replace EFC). 14% of all full-time freshmen had no need and received non-need-based gift aid.

UNDERGRADUATE FINANCIAL AID (Fall 2009) 719 applied for aid; of those 91% were deemed to have need. 100% of undergraduates with need received aid; of those 31% had need fully met. ***Average percent of need met:*** 86% (excluding resources awarded to replace EFC). ***Average financial aid package:*** $30,359 (excluding resources awarded to replace EFC). 17% of all full-time undergraduates had no need and received non-need-based gift aid.

GIFT AID (NEED-BASED) ***Total amount:*** $17,080,857 (9% federal, 3% state, 88% institutional). ***Receiving aid:*** Freshmen: 54% (157); all full-time undergraduates: 50% (565). ***Average award:*** Freshmen: $21,432; Undergraduates: $19,965. ***Scholarships, grants, and awards:*** Federal Pell, FSEOG, state, private, college/university gift aid from institutional funds.

GIFT AID (NON-NEED-BASED) ***Total amount:*** $4,675,713 (91% institutional, 9% external sources). ***Receiving aid:*** Freshmen: 33% (96). Undergraduates: 31% (344). ***Average award:*** Freshmen: $8526. Undergraduates: $7555. ***Scholarships, grants, and awards by category:*** *Academic interests/achievement:* 430 awards ($3,826,750 total): general academic interests/achievements. *Special achievements/activities:* 97 awards ($277,500 total): religious involvement. *Special characteristics:* 59 awards ($538,500 total): ethnic background. ***Tuition waivers:*** Full or partial for employees or children of employees.

LOANS ***Student loans:*** $5,145,442 (63% need-based, 37% non-need-based). 55% of past graduating class borrowed through all loan programs. *Average indebtedness per student:* $17,573. ***Average need-based loan:*** Freshmen: $3734.

Undergraduates: $4871. ***Parent loans:*** $1,559,874 (100% non-need-based). ***Programs:*** Federal Direct (Subsidized and Unsubsidized Stafford, PLUS), Perkins, college/university.

WORK-STUDY ***Federal work-study:*** Total amount: $426,350; 494 jobs averaging $2034. ***State or other work-study/employment:*** Total amount: $385,618 (52% need-based, 48% non-need-based). 158 part-time jobs averaging $2176.

APPLYING FOR FINANCIAL AID ***Required financial aid form:*** FAFSA. ***Financial aid deadline:*** 3/1. ***Notification date:*** Continuous beginning 2/15. Students must reply by 5/1 or within 3 weeks of notification.

CONTACT Mr. Robert W. Arnold, Director of Financial Aid, Earlham College, National Road West, Richmond, IN 47374-4095, 765-983-1217 or toll-free 800-327-5426. *Fax:* 765-983-1299. *E-mail:* boba@earlham.edu.

EAST CAROLINA UNIVERSITY

Greenville, NC

Tuition & fees (NC res): $4797 **Average undergraduate aid package: $9557**

ABOUT THE INSTITUTION State-supported, coed. 86 undergraduate majors. Federal methodology is used as a basis for awarding need-based institutional aid.

UNDERGRADUATE EXPENSES for 2010–11 ***Tuition, state resident:*** full-time $2881. ***Tuition, nonresident:*** full-time $14,955. ***Required fees:*** full-time $1916. Part-time tuition and fees vary according to course load. ***College room and board:*** $7700; ***Room only:*** $4450. Room and board charges vary according to board plan and housing facility. ***Payment plans:*** Installment, deferred payment.

FRESHMAN FINANCIAL AID (Fall 2010, est.) 3,260 applied for aid; of those 74% were deemed to have need. 97% of freshmen with need received aid; of those 9% had need fully met. ***Average percent of need met:*** 70% (excluding resources awarded to replace EFC). ***Average financial aid package:*** $9069 (excluding resources awarded to replace EFC). 2% of all full-time freshmen had no need and received non-need-based gift aid.

UNDERGRADUATE FINANCIAL AID (Fall 2010, est.) 12,940 applied for aid; of those 80% were deemed to have need. 97% of undergraduates with need received aid; of those 11% had need fully met. ***Average percent of need met:*** 72% (excluding resources awarded to replace EFC). ***Average financial aid package:*** $9557 (excluding resources awarded to replace EFC). 3% of all full-time undergraduates had no need and received non-need-based gift aid.

GIFT AID (NEED-BASED) ***Total amount:*** $63,139,030 (51% federal, 35% state, 13% institutional, 1% external sources). ***Receiving aid:*** Freshmen: 47% (1,931); all full-time undergraduates: 46% (8,310). ***Average award:*** Freshmen: $7038; Undergraduates: $6634. ***Scholarships, grants, and awards:*** Federal Pell, FSEOG, state, private, college/university gift aid from institutional funds, Federal Nursing.

GIFT AID (NON-NEED-BASED) ***Total amount:*** $5,539,296 (18% state, 16% institutional, 66% external sources). ***Receiving aid:*** Freshmen: 4% (179). Undergraduates: 5% (913). ***Average award:*** Freshmen: $2062. Undergraduates: $1844. ***Scholarships, grants, and awards by category:*** *Academic interests/achievement:* biological sciences, business, communication, education, engineering/technologies, English, foreign languages, general academic interests/achievements, health fields, home economics, humanities, international studies, mathematics, military science, physical sciences. *Creative arts/performance:* applied art and design, art/fine arts, dance, music, performing arts. *Special characteristics:* adult students, children and siblings of alumni, children of faculty/staff, ethnic background, general special characteristics, handicapped students. ***Tuition waivers:*** Full or partial for employees or children of employees, senior citizens.

LOANS ***Student loans:*** $90,384,050 (96% need-based, 4% non-need-based). 57% of past graduating class borrowed through all loan programs. *Average indebtedness per student:* $17,243. ***Average need-based loan:*** Freshmen: $3311. Undergraduates: $4126. ***Parent loans:*** $14,455,197 (100% need-based). ***Programs:*** Federal Direct (Subsidized and Unsubsidized Stafford, PLUS), Perkins, Federal Nursing, state.

WORK-STUDY ***Federal work-study:*** Total amount: $1,268,576; 400 jobs averaging $2800. ***State or other work-study/employment:*** 1,600 part-time jobs averaging $2000.

ATHLETIC AWARDS Total amount: $4,515,612 (42% need-based, 58% non-need-based).

APPLYING FOR FINANCIAL AID ***Required financial aid form:*** FAFSA. ***Financial aid deadline (priority):*** 3/1. ***Notification date:*** 4/1. Students must reply within 3 weeks of notification.

CONTACT Ms. Julie Poorman, Director of Financial Aid, East Carolina University, East 5th Street, Greenville, NC 27858-4353, 252-328-6610. *Fax:* 252-328-4347. *E-mail:* poormanj@ecu.edu.

EAST CENTRAL UNIVERSITY

Ada, OK

CONTACT Marcia Carter, Director of Financial Aid, East Central University, 1100 East 14th, Ada, OK 74820-6899, 580-332-8000 Ext. 242. *Fax:* 580-436-5612.

EASTERN CONNECTICUT STATE UNIVERSITY

Willimantic, CT

Tuition & fees (CT res): $8350 **Average undergraduate aid package: $8018**

ABOUT THE INSTITUTION State-supported, coed. 29 undergraduate majors. Federal methodology is used as a basis for awarding need-based institutional aid.

UNDERGRADUATE EXPENSES for 2010–11 ***Tuition, state resident:*** full-time $4023; part-time $400 per credit hour. ***Tuition, nonresident:*** full-time $13,020; part-time $400 per credit hour. ***Required fees:*** full-time $4327. Full-time tuition and fees vary according to reciprocity agreements. ***College room and board:*** $10,048; ***Room only:*** $5674. Room and board charges vary according to board plan. ***Payment plan:*** Installment.

FRESHMAN FINANCIAL AID (Fall 2009) 827 applied for aid; of those 71% were deemed to have need. 97% of freshmen with need received aid; of those 8% had need fully met. ***Average percent of need met:*** 57% (excluding resources awarded to replace EFC). ***Average financial aid package:*** $8152 (excluding resources awarded to replace EFC). 1% of all full-time freshmen had no need and received non-need-based gift aid.

UNDERGRADUATE FINANCIAL AID (Fall 2009) 3,327 applied for aid; of those 77% were deemed to have need. 97% of undergraduates with need received aid; of those 8% had need fully met. ***Average percent of need met:*** 56% (excluding resources awarded to replace EFC). ***Average financial aid package:*** $8018 (excluding resources awarded to replace EFC). 1% of all full-time undergraduates had no need and received non-need-based gift aid.

GIFT AID (NEED-BASED) ***Total amount:*** $11,059,340 (42% federal, 19% state, 36% institutional, 3% external sources). ***Receiving aid:*** Freshmen: 43% (402); all full-time undergraduates: 39% (1,694). ***Average award:*** Freshmen: $7275; Undergraduates: $6226. ***Scholarships, grants, and awards:*** Federal Pell, FSEOG, state, private, college/university gift aid from institutional funds.

GIFT AID (NON-NEED-BASED) ***Total amount:*** $378,556 (76% institutional, 24% external sources). ***Receiving aid:*** Freshmen: 2% (22). Undergraduates: 1% (22). ***Average award:*** Freshmen: $2520. Undergraduates: $2520. ***Scholarships, grants, and awards by category:*** *Academic interests/achievement:* area/ethnic studies, biological sciences, business, communication, computer science, education, English, foreign languages, general academic interests/achievements, humanities, mathematics, physical sciences, social sciences. *Special achievements/activities:* community service, general special achievements/activities, leadership, memberships. *Special characteristics:* children of faculty/staff, children of union members/company employees, general special characteristics, international students, local/state students, members of minority groups, previous college experience, veterans. ***Tuition waivers:*** Full or partial for employees or children of employees.

LOANS ***Student loans:*** $23,745,601 (73% need-based, 27% non-need-based). 74% of past graduating class borrowed through all loan programs. *Average indebtedness per student:* $24,427. ***Average need-based loan:*** Freshmen: $3257. Undergraduates: $4116. ***Parent loans:*** $3,725,511 (75% need-based, 25% non-need-based). ***Programs:*** Federal Direct (Subsidized and Unsubsidized Stafford, PLUS), Perkins, alternative loans.

WORK-STUDY ***Federal work-study:*** Total amount: $117,850; 61 jobs averaging $1932. ***State or other work-study/employment:*** Total amount: $110,462 (100% need-based). 44 part-time jobs averaging $2421.

APPLYING FOR FINANCIAL AID ***Required financial aid form:*** FAFSA. ***Financial aid deadline (priority):*** 3/15. ***Notification date:*** Continuous. Students must reply within 2 weeks of notification.

CONTACT Financial Aid Office, Eastern Connecticut State University, 83 Windham Street, Willimantic, CT 06226-2295, 860-465-5205 or toll-free 877-353-3278. *Fax:* 860-465-2811. *E-mail:* financialaid@easternct.edu.

EASTERN ILLINOIS UNIVERSITY

Charleston, IL

CONTACT Tracy L. Hall, Assistant Director of Financial Aid, Eastern Illinois University, 600 Lincoln Avenue, Charleston, IL 61920-3099, 217-581-7511 or toll-free 800-252-5711. *Fax:* 217-581-6422. *E-mail:* tlhall@eiu.edu.

EASTERN KENTUCKY UNIVERSITY

Richmond, KY

Tuition & fees (KY res): $6624 Average undergraduate aid package: $8963

ABOUT THE INSTITUTION State-supported, coed. ***Awards:*** associate, bachelor's, and master's degrees and post-bachelor's and post-master's certificates. 111 undergraduate majors. ***Total enrollment:*** 15,839. Undergraduates: 13,659. Freshmen: 2,493. Federal methodology is used as a basis for awarding need-based institutional aid.

UNDERGRADUATE EXPENSES for 2010–11 ***Application fee:*** $30. ***Tuition, state resident:*** full-time $6624; part-time $276 per credit hour. ***Tuition, nonresident:*** full-time $18,144; part-time $756 per credit hour. Part-time tuition and fees vary according to course load. ***College room and board:*** $6714; ***Room only:*** $3550. Room and board charges vary according to board plan and housing facility. ***Payment plan:*** Deferred payment.

FRESHMAN FINANCIAL AID (Fall 2010, est.) 2,322 applied for aid; of those 82% were deemed to have need. 99% of freshmen with need received aid; of those 4% had need fully met. ***Average percent of need met:*** 81% (excluding resources awarded to replace EFC). ***Average financial aid package:*** $8530 (excluding resources awarded to replace EFC). 9% of all full-time freshmen had no need and received non-need-based gift aid.

UNDERGRADUATE FINANCIAL AID (Fall 2010, est.) 9,701 applied for aid; of those 85% were deemed to have need. 97% of undergraduates with need received aid; of those 7% had need fully met. ***Average percent of need met:*** 82% (excluding resources awarded to replace EFC). ***Average financial aid package:*** $8963 (excluding resources awarded to replace EFC). 10% of all full-time undergraduates had no need and received non-need-based gift aid.

GIFT AID (NEED-BASED) ***Total amount:*** $40,944,558 (65% federal, 22% state, 11% institutional, 2% external sources). ***Receiving aid:*** Freshmen: 49% (1,295); all full-time undergraduates: 47% (5,579). ***Average award:*** Freshmen: $5706; Undergraduates: $5401. ***Scholarships, grants, and awards:*** Federal Pell, FSEOG, state, private, college/university gift aid from institutional funds.

GIFT AID (NON-NEED-BASED) ***Total amount:*** $5,763,840 (1% federal, 51% state, 38% institutional, 10% external sources). ***Receiving aid:*** Freshmen: 59% (1,542). Undergraduates: 35% (4,205). ***Average award:*** Freshmen: $5753. Undergraduates: $5619. ***Scholarships, grants, and awards by category:*** *Academic interests/achievement:* 1,625 awards ($8,613,758 total): general academic interests/achievements. *Creative arts/performance:* 150 awards ($346,653 total): music. *Special achievements/activities:* 26 awards ($20,650 total): cheerleading/drum major. *Special characteristics:* 478 awards ($1,640,319 total): children and siblings of alumni, children of faculty/staff, members of minority groups. ***Tuition waivers:*** Full or partial for employees or children of employees, senior citizens. ***ROTC:*** Army, Air Force cooperative.

LOANS ***Student loans:*** $76,895,446 (87% need-based, 13% non-need-based). 71% of past graduating class borrowed through all loan programs. *Average indebtedness per student:* $10,152. ***Average need-based loan:*** Freshmen: $2916. Undergraduates: $3729. ***Parent loans:*** $19,296,539 (71% need-based, 29% non-need-based). ***Programs:*** Federal Direct (Subsidized and Unsubsidized Stafford, PLUS), Perkins, college/university.

WORK-STUDY ***Federal work-study:*** Total amount: $4,275,946; 1,000 jobs averaging $1800. ***State or other work-study/employment:*** Total amount: $3,512,015 (100% non-need-based). 1,000 part-time jobs averaging $1800.

ATHLETIC AWARDS Total amount: $3,853,960 (45% need-based, 55% non-need-based).

APPLYING FOR FINANCIAL AID ***Required financial aid form:*** FAFSA. ***Financial aid deadline (priority):*** 2/15. ***Notification date:*** Continuous beginning 4/1.

CONTACT Financial Aid Office, Eastern Kentucky University, 521 Lancaster Avenue, SSB CPO 59, Richmond, KY 40475-3102, 859-622-2361 or toll-free 800-465-9191 (in-state). *Fax:* 859-622-2019. *E-mail:* finaid@eku.edu.

EASTERN MENNONITE UNIVERSITY

Harrisonburg, VA

CONTACT Ms. Renee Leap, Assistant Director of Financial Assistance, Eastern Mennonite University, 1200 Park Road, Harrisonburg, VA 22802-2462, 540-432-4138 or toll-free 800-368-2665. *Fax:* 540-432-4081. *E-mail:* leapr@emu.edu.

EASTERN MICHIGAN UNIVERSITY

Ypsilanti, MI

Tuition & fees (MI res): $8378 Average undergraduate aid package: $8767

ABOUT THE INSTITUTION State-supported, coed. 129 undergraduate majors. Federal methodology is used as a basis for awarding need-based institutional aid.

UNDERGRADUATE EXPENSES for 2011–12 ***One-time required fee:*** $300. ***Tuition, state resident:*** full-time $7148; part-time $238.25 per credit hour. ***Tuition, nonresident:*** full-time $21,053; part-time $701.75 per credit hour. ***Required fees:*** full-time $1230; $38 per credit hour or $44.75 per term. Full-time tuition and fees vary according to course level and reciprocity agreements. Part-time tuition and fees vary according to course level and reciprocity agreements. ***College room and board:*** $7785; ***Room only:*** $3656. Room and board charges vary according to board plan, housing facility, and location. ***Payment plan:*** Installment.

FRESHMAN FINANCIAL AID (Fall 2009) 1,929 applied for aid; of those 82% were deemed to have need. 99% of freshmen with need received aid; of those 10% had need fully met. ***Average percent of need met:*** 61% (excluding resources awarded to replace EFC). ***Average financial aid package:*** $9665 (excluding resources awarded to replace EFC). 14% of all full-time freshmen had no need and received non-need-based gift aid.

UNDERGRADUATE FINANCIAL AID (Fall 2009) 7,976 applied for aid; of those 86% were deemed to have need. 98% of undergraduates with need received aid; of those 1% had need fully met. ***Average percent of need met:*** 54% (excluding resources awarded to replace EFC). ***Average financial aid package:*** $8767 (excluding resources awarded to replace EFC). 9% of all full-time undergraduates had no need and received non-need-based gift aid.

GIFT AID (NEED-BASED) ***Total amount:*** $36,021,636 (88% federal, 1% state, 11% institutional). ***Receiving aid:*** Freshmen: 57% (1,281); all full-time undergraduates: 37% (4,698). ***Average award:*** Freshmen: $4954; Undergraduates: $4960. ***Scholarships, grants, and awards:*** Federal Pell, FSEOG, state, private, college/university gift aid from institutional funds.

GIFT AID (NON-NEED-BASED) ***Total amount:*** $16,528,569 (2% state, 92% institutional, 6% external sources). ***Receiving aid:*** Freshmen: 37% (826). Undergraduates: 15% (1,905). ***Average award:*** Freshmen: $4465. Undergraduates: $4183. ***Scholarships, grants, and awards by category:*** *Academic interests/achievement:* 2,161 awards ($5,568,579 total): agriculture, architecture, biological sciences, business, communication, computer science, education, engineering/technologies, English, foreign languages, general academic interests/achievements, health fields, home economics, humanities, mathematics, physical sciences, religion/biblical studies, social sciences. *Creative arts/performance:* 134 awards ($115,425 total): applied art and design, art/fine arts, cinema/film/broadcasting, creative writing, dance, debating, general creative arts/performance, music, performing arts, theater/drama. *Special achievements/activities:* 195 awards ($216,310 total): general special achievements/activities, leadership, memberships, religious involvement. *Special characteristics:* 323 awards ($3,279,564 total): children and siblings of alumni, ethnic background, international students, members of minority groups, out-of-state students, previous college experience, religious affiliation. ***Tuition waivers:*** Full or partial for employees or children of employees.

LOANS ***Student loans:*** $139,690,251 (42% need-based, 58% non-need-based). 63% of past graduating class borrowed through all loan programs. *Average indebtedness per student:* $23,669. ***Average need-based loan:*** Freshmen: $3675. Undergraduates: $4437. ***Parent loans:*** $12,337,296 (100% non-need-based). ***Programs:*** Federal Direct (Subsidized and Unsubsidized Stafford), Perkins, college/university, private loans.

WORK-STUDY ***Federal work-study:*** Total amount: $1,464,002; 908 jobs averaging $1486. ***State or other work-study/employment:*** Part-time jobs available.

ATHLETIC AWARDS Total amount: $6,378,541 (100% non-need-based).

APPLYING FOR FINANCIAL AID ***Required financial aid form:*** FAFSA. ***Financial aid deadline:*** Continuous. ***Notification date:*** Continuous beginning 3/1.

CONTACT Cynthia Van Pelt, Director, Eastern Michigan University, 403 Pierce Hall, Ypsilanti, MI 48197, 734-487-1048 or toll-free 800-GO TO EMU. *Fax:* 734-487-0174. *E-mail:* cvanpelt@emich.edu.

EASTERN NAZARENE COLLEGE

Quincy, MA

Tuition & fees: $23,772 **Average undergraduate aid package: $22,758**

ABOUT THE INSTITUTION Independent religious, coed. 107 undergraduate majors. Federal methodology is used as a basis for awarding need-based institutional aid.

UNDERGRADUATE EXPENSES for 2010–11 ***Comprehensive fee:*** $31,772 includes full-time tuition ($22,982), mandatory fees ($790), and room and board ($8000). Full-time tuition and fees vary according to course load, degree level, program, reciprocity agreements, and student level. Room and board charges vary according to board plan and housing facility. ***Part-time tuition:*** $901 per credit hour. ***Part-time fees:*** $102 per term. Part-time tuition and fees vary according to degree level, program, reciprocity agreements, and student level. ***Payment plan:*** Installment.

FRESHMAN FINANCIAL AID (Fall 2009) 178 applied for aid; of those 94% were deemed to have need. 100% of freshmen with need received aid; of those 35% had need fully met. ***Average percent of need met:*** 81% (excluding resources awarded to replace EFC). ***Average financial aid package:*** $26,469 (excluding resources awarded to replace EFC). 7% of all full-time freshmen had no need and received non-need-based gift aid.

UNDERGRADUATE FINANCIAL AID (Fall 2009) 514 applied for aid; of those 84% were deemed to have need. 100% of undergraduates with need received aid; of those 31% had need fully met. ***Average percent of need met:*** 71% (excluding resources awarded to replace EFC). ***Average financial aid package:*** $22,758 (excluding resources awarded to replace EFC). 9% of all full-time undergraduates had no need and received non-need-based gift aid.

GIFT AID (NEED-BASED) ***Total amount:*** $6,771,571 (24% federal, 3% state, 71% institutional, 2% external sources). ***Receiving aid:*** Freshmen: 91% (166); all full-time undergraduates: 61% (391). ***Average award:*** Freshmen: $15,330; Undergraduates: $10,391. ***Scholarships, grants, and awards:*** Federal Pell, FSEOG, state, private, college/university gift aid from institutional funds, United Negro College Fund.

GIFT AID (NON-NEED-BASED) ***Total amount:*** $926,722 (1% federal, 90% institutional, 9% external sources). ***Receiving aid:*** Freshmen: 9% (16). Undergraduates: 4% (29). ***Average award:*** Freshmen: $16,636. Undergraduates: $9116. ***Scholarships, grants, and awards by category:*** *Academic interests/achievement:* general academic interests/achievements. *Special achievements/activities:* hobbies/interests, leadership. *Special characteristics:* children and siblings of alumni, religious affiliation. ***Tuition waivers:*** Full or partial for children of alumni, employees or children of employees.

LOANS ***Student loans:*** $5,177,175 (81% need-based, 19% non-need-based). 87% of past graduating class borrowed through all loan programs. *Average indebtedness per student:* $51,336. ***Average need-based loan:*** Freshmen: $6314. Undergraduates: $8559. ***Parent loans:*** $2,306,441 (75% need-based, 25% non-need-based). ***Programs:*** Federal Direct (Subsidized and Unsubsidized Stafford, PLUS), Perkins, state, alternative loans.

WORK-STUDY ***Federal work-study:*** Total amount: $68,930; jobs available. ***State or other work-study/employment:*** Part-time jobs available.

APPLYING FOR FINANCIAL AID ***Required financial aid forms:*** FAFSA, institution's own form. ***Financial aid deadline (priority):*** 7/1. ***Notification date:*** Continuous beginning 3/15. Students must reply within 2 weeks of notification.

CONTACT Lerick Fanfanx, Director of Financial Aid and Retention, Eastern Nazarene College, 23 East Elm Avenue, Quincy, MA 02170, 617-745-3869 or toll-free 800-88-ENC88. *Fax:* 617-745-3992. *E-mail:* financialaid@enc.edu.

EASTERN NEW MEXICO UNIVERSITY

Portales, NM

ABOUT THE INSTITUTION State-supported, coed. 52 undergraduate majors.

GIFT AID (NEED-BASED) ***Scholarships, grants, and awards:*** Federal Pell, FSEOG, state, private, college/university gift aid from institutional funds.

GIFT AID (NON-NEED-BASED) ***Scholarships, grants, and awards by category:*** *Academic interests/achievement:* agriculture, biological sciences, business, communication, computer science, education, engineering/technologies, English, foreign languages, general academic interests/achievements, health fields, home economics, humanities, mathematics, military science, physical sciences, premedicine, religion/biblical studies, social sciences. *Creative arts/performance:* applied art and design, art/fine arts, cinema/film/broadcasting, creative writing, dance, debating, general creative arts/performance, journalism/publications, music, performing arts, theater/drama. *Special achievements/activities:* community service, general special achievements/activities, hobbies/interests, leadership, memberships, rodeo. *Special characteristics:* children and siblings of alumni, ethnic background, first-generation college students, general special characteristics, international students, members of minority groups, out-of-state students, veterans.

LOANS ***Programs:*** Federal Direct (Subsidized and Unsubsidized Stafford, PLUS), Perkins, state, college/university.

WORK-STUDY ***Federal work-study:*** Total amount: $1,585,910; jobs available. ***State or other work-study/employment:*** Total amount: $370,345 (100% need-based). Part-time jobs available.

APPLYING FOR FINANCIAL AID ***Required financial aid form:*** FAFSA.

CONTACT Mr. Brent Small, Director of Financial Aid, Eastern New Mexico University, Station 20, 1500 S. Ave K, Portales, NM 88130, 575-562-2194 or toll-free 800-367-3668. *Fax:* 575-562-2198. *E-mail:* brent.small@enmu.edu.

EASTERN OREGON UNIVERSITY

La Grande, OR

Tuition & fees (OR res): $6639 **Average undergraduate aid package: $9242**

ABOUT THE INSTITUTION State-supported, coed. 22 undergraduate majors. Federal methodology is used as a basis for awarding need-based institutional aid.

UNDERGRADUATE EXPENSES for 2010–11 ***Tuition, state resident:*** full-time $5244; part-time $118 per credit hour. ***Tuition, nonresident:*** full-time $5244; part-time $118 per credit hour. ***Required fees:*** full-time $1395. Full-time tuition and fees vary according to course load. Part-time tuition and fees vary according to course load. ***College room and board:*** $8000; ***Room only:*** $4335. Room and board charges vary according to board plan and housing facility. ***Payment plan:*** Installment.

FRESHMAN FINANCIAL AID (Fall 2010, est.) 409 applied for aid; of those 81% were deemed to have need. 100% of freshmen with need received aid; of those 53% had need fully met. ***Average percent of need met:*** 47% (excluding resources awarded to replace EFC). ***Average financial aid package:*** $8475 (excluding resources awarded to replace EFC). 2% of all full-time freshmen had no need and received non-need-based gift aid.

UNDERGRADUATE FINANCIAL AID (Fall 2010, est.) 1,988 applied for aid; of those 90% were deemed to have need. 98% of undergraduates with need received aid; of those 40% had need fully met. ***Average percent of need met:*** 50% (excluding resources awarded to replace EFC). ***Average financial aid package:*** $9242 (excluding resources awarded to replace EFC). 1% of all full-time undergraduates had no need and received non-need-based gift aid.

GIFT AID (NEED-BASED) ***Total amount:*** $9,460,043 (98% federal, 2% state). ***Receiving aid:*** Freshmen: 50% (217); all full-time undergraduates: 58% (1,329). ***Average award:*** Freshmen: $4935; Undergraduates: $5308. ***Scholarships, grants, and awards:*** Federal Pell, FSEOG, state, private, college/university gift aid from institutional funds.

GIFT AID (NON-NEED-BASED) ***Total amount:*** $754,555 (34% institutional, 66% external sources). ***Receiving aid:*** Freshmen: 42% (186). Undergraduates: 21% (484). ***Average award:*** Freshmen: $734. Undergraduates: $1204. ***Scholarships, grants, and awards by category:*** *Academic interests/achievement:* general academic interests/achievements. *Creative arts/performance:* general creative arts/performance. *Special achievements/activities:* leadership. *Special characteristics:* local/state students, members of minority groups. ***Tuition waivers:*** Full or partial for employees or children of employees, senior citizens.

LOANS ***Student loans:*** $21,868,884 (44% need-based, 56% non-need-based). ***Average need-based loan:*** Freshmen: $2908. Undergraduates: $3693. ***Parent loans:*** $4,926,885 (100% non-need-based). ***Programs:*** Perkins.

WORK-STUDY ***Federal work-study:*** Total amount: $238,032; jobs available.

APPLYING FOR FINANCIAL AID ***Required financial aid form:*** FAFSA. ***Financial aid deadline (priority):*** 3/1. ***Notification date:*** Continuous beginning 4/1. Students must reply within 4 weeks of notification.

CONTACT Mr. Sam Collie, Interim Director of Financial Aid, Eastern Oregon University, One University Boulevard, La Grande, OR 97850-2899, 541-962-3456 or toll-free 800-452-8639 (in-state), 800-452-3393 (out-of-state). *Fax:* 541-962-3661. *E-mail:* scollie@eou.edu.

EASTERN UNIVERSITY

St. Davids, PA

CONTACT Financial Aid Office, Eastern University, 1300 Eagle Road, St. Davids, PA 19087-3696, 610-341-5842 or toll-free 800-452-0996. *Fax:* 610-341-1492. *E-mail:* finaid@eastern.edu.

EASTERN WASHINGTON UNIVERSITY

Cheney, WA

Tuition & fees (WA res): $6604 **Average undergraduate aid package: $11,827**

ABOUT THE INSTITUTION State-supported, coed. 94 undergraduate majors. Federal methodology is used as a basis for awarding need-based institutional aid.

UNDERGRADUATE EXPENSES for 2011–12 ***Tuition, state resident:*** full-time $6063; part-time $202.10 per credit. ***Tuition, nonresident:*** full-time $14,781; part-time $492.70 per credit. ***Required fees:*** full-time $541; $541 per year. Full-time tuition and fees vary according to course load and program. Part-time tuition and fees vary according to course load and program. ***College room and board:*** $7470; ***Room only:*** $3960. Room and board charges vary according to board plan and housing facility. ***Payment plan:*** Installment.

FRESHMAN FINANCIAL AID (Fall 2009) 1,232 applied for aid; of those 74% were deemed to have need. 98% of freshmen with need received aid; of those 30% had need fully met. ***Average percent of need met:*** 91% (excluding resources awarded to replace EFC). ***Average financial aid package:*** $11,156 (excluding resources awarded to replace EFC). 12% of all full-time freshmen had no need and received non-need-based gift aid.

UNDERGRADUATE FINANCIAL AID (Fall 2009) 6,490 applied for aid; of those 81% were deemed to have need. 97% of undergraduates with need received aid; of those 28% had need fully met. ***Average percent of need met:*** 71% (excluding resources awarded to replace EFC). ***Average financial aid package:*** $11,827 (excluding resources awarded to replace EFC). 5% of all full-time undergraduates had no need and received non-need-based gift aid.

GIFT AID (NEED-BASED) ***Total amount:*** $31,768,110 (50% federal, 37% state, 6% institutional, 7% external sources). ***Receiving aid:*** Freshmen: 47% (690); all full-time undergraduates: 45% (3,881). ***Average award:*** Freshmen: $6936; Undergraduates: $7281. ***Scholarships, grants, and awards:*** Federal Pell, FSEOG, state, private, college/university gift aid from institutional funds.

GIFT AID (NON-NEED-BASED) ***Total amount:*** $634,963 (19% institutional, 81% external sources). ***Receiving aid:*** Freshmen: 21% (316). Undergraduates: 10% (848). ***Average award:*** Freshmen: $2763. Undergraduates: $2945. ***Scholarships, grants, and awards by category:*** *Academic interests/achievement:* 475 awards ($650,000 total): area/ethnic studies, biological sciences, business, communication, computer science, education, engineering/technologies, English, foreign languages, general academic interests/achievements, health fields, mathematics, military science, physical sciences, social sciences. *Creative arts/performance:* 60 awards ($75,000 total): art/fine arts, cinema/film/broadcasting, creative writing, journalism/publications, music, theater/drama. *Special characteristics:* 325 awards ($705,500 total): children of union members/company employees, ethnic background, first-generation college students, handicapped students, local/state students, spouses of deceased or disabled public servants, veterans, veterans' children.

LOANS ***Student loans:*** $34,467,538 (82% need-based, 18% non-need-based). 49% of past graduating class borrowed through all loan programs. *Average indebtedness per student:* $20,114. ***Average need-based loan:*** Freshmen: $2191. Undergraduates: $2958. ***Parent loans:*** $5,772,648 (56% need-based, 44% non-need-based). ***Programs:*** Federal Direct (Subsidized and Unsubsidized Stafford, PLUS), Perkins.

WORK-STUDY ***Federal work-study:*** Total amount: $534,207; 230 jobs averaging $2322. ***State or other work-study/employment:*** Total amount: $898,731 (100% need-based). 335 part-time jobs averaging $2683.

ATHLETIC AWARDS Total amount: $1,713,388 (46% need-based, 54% non-need-based).

APPLYING FOR FINANCIAL AID ***Required financial aid form:*** FAFSA. ***Financial aid deadline (priority):*** 2/15. ***Notification date:*** Continuous beginning 4/1. Students must reply within 4 weeks of notification.

CONTACT Mr. Bruce DeFrates, Director of Financial Aid and Scholarships, Eastern Washington University, 102 Sutton Hall, Cheney, WA 99004-2447, 509-359-2314. *Fax:* 509-359-4330. *E-mail:* bdefrates@ewu.edu.

EAST STROUDSBURG UNIVERSITY OF PENNSYLVANIA

East Stroudsburg, PA

ABOUT THE INSTITUTION State-supported, coed. 49 undergraduate majors.

GIFT AID (NEED-BASED) ***Scholarships, grants, and awards:*** Federal Pell, FSEOG, state, private, college/university gift aid from institutional funds.

GIFT AID (NON-NEED-BASED) ***Scholarships, grants, and awards by category:*** *Academic interests/achievement:* biological sciences, business, communication, computer science, education, English, foreign languages, general academic interests/achievements, health fields, mathematics, physical sciences, social sciences. *Creative arts/performance:* applied art and design, music, theater/drama. *Special achievements/activities:* general special achievements/activities, leadership. *Special characteristics:* adult students, children and siblings of alumni, handicapped students, international students, local/state students, members of minority groups, religious affiliation.

LOANS ***Programs:*** Perkins.

WORK-STUDY ***Federal work-study:*** Total amount: $367,832; jobs available. ***State or other work-study/employment:*** Total amount: $1,226,790 (100% non-need-based). Part-time jobs available.

APPLYING FOR FINANCIAL AID ***Required financial aid form:*** FAFSA.

CONTACT Kizzy Morris, Registrar/Director of Enrollment Services, East Stroudsburg University of Pennsylvania, 200 Prospect Street, East Stroudsburg, PA 18301-2999, 570-422-2820 or toll-free 877-230-5547. *Fax:* 570-422-2849.

EAST TENNESSEE STATE UNIVERSITY

Johnson City, TN

Tuition & fees (TN res): $5823 **Average undergraduate aid package: $5079**

ABOUT THE INSTITUTION State-supported, coed. 49 undergraduate majors. Federal methodology is used as a basis for awarding need-based institutional aid.

UNDERGRADUATE EXPENSES for 2010–11 ***Tuition, state resident:*** full-time $4824; part-time $201 per credit hour. ***Tuition, nonresident:*** full-time $17,352; part-time $723 per credit hour. ***Required fees:*** full-time $999; $64 per credit hour. Full-time tuition and fees vary according to course load and program. Part-time tuition and fees vary according to course load and program. ***College room and board:*** $5783; ***Room only:*** $2930. Room and board charges vary according to board plan and housing facility. ***Payment plans:*** Installment, deferred payment.

FRESHMAN FINANCIAL AID (Fall 2010, est.) 1,666 applied for aid; of those 75% were deemed to have need. 97% of freshmen with need received aid; of those 35% had need fully met. ***Average percent of need met:*** 82% (excluding resources awarded to replace EFC). ***Average financial aid package:*** $7998 (excluding resources awarded to replace EFC). 9% of all full-time freshmen had no need and received non-need-based gift aid.

UNDERGRADUATE FINANCIAL AID (Fall 2010, est.) 8,339 applied for aid; of those 73% were deemed to have need. 97% of undergraduates with need received aid; of those 47% had need fully met. ***Average percent of need met:*** 81% (excluding resources awarded to replace EFC). ***Average financial aid package:*** $5079 (excluding resources awarded to replace EFC). 12% of all full-time undergraduates had no need and received non-need-based gift aid.

GIFT AID (NEED-BASED) ***Total amount:*** $55,657,846 (43% federal, 39% state, 16% institutional, 2% external sources). ***Receiving aid:*** Freshmen: 51% (1,057); all full-time undergraduates: 44% (4,535). ***Average award:*** Freshmen: $4936; Undergraduates: $3560. ***Scholarships, grants, and awards:*** Federal Pell, FSEOG, state, private, college/university gift aid from institutional funds, Federal Nursing.

GIFT AID (NON-NEED-BASED) ***Receiving aid:*** Freshmen: 19% (392). Undergraduates: 17% (1,737). ***Average award:*** Freshmen: $3667. Undergraduates: $3826. ***Scholarships, grants, and awards by category:*** *Academic interests/achievement:* biological sciences, business, computer science, education, engineering/technologies, English, general academic interests/achievements, health fields, mathematics, military science, social sciences. *Creative arts/performance:* art/fine arts, journalism/publications, music, theater/drama. *Special achievements/activities:* leadership, memberships. *Special characteristics:* children of union members/company employees, members of minority groups. ***Tuition waivers:*** Full or partial for employees or children of employees, senior citizens.

LOANS ***Student loans:*** $58,899,997 (51% need-based, 49% non-need-based). 80% of past graduating class borrowed through all loan programs. *Average indebtedness per student:* $20,984. ***Average need-based loan:*** Freshmen: $1268. Undergraduates: $3408. ***Parent loans:*** $6,270,381 (100% non-need-based). ***Programs:*** Federal Direct (Subsidized and Unsubsidized Stafford, PLUS), Perkins, Federal Nursing, state, college/university.

WORK-STUDY ***Federal work-study:*** Total amount: $606,728; 595 jobs averaging $1117.

APPLYING FOR FINANCIAL AID ***Required financial aid form:*** FAFSA. ***Financial aid deadline (priority):*** 4/15. ***Notification date:*** Continuous beginning 3/1. Students must reply within 3 weeks of notification.

CONTACT Margaret L. Miller, Director of Financial Aid, East Tennessee State University, PO Box 70722, Johnson City, TN 37614, 423-439-4300 or toll-free 800-462-3878. *Fax:* 423-439-5855. *E-mail:* finaid@etsu.edu.

EAST TEXAS BAPTIST UNIVERSITY

Marshall, TX

Tuition & fees: $20,500 **Average undergraduate aid package: $14,472**

ABOUT THE INSTITUTION Independent Baptist, coed. 41 undergraduate majors. Federal methodology is used as a basis for awarding need-based institutional aid.

UNDERGRADUATE EXPENSES for 2011–12 ***Comprehensive fee:*** $26,166 includes full-time tuition ($19,680), mandatory fees ($820), and room and board ($5666). ***College room only:*** $2400. Room and board charges vary according to board plan and housing facility. ***Part-time tuition:*** $656 per credit hour. ***Payment plan:*** Installment.

FRESHMAN FINANCIAL AID (Fall 2009) 268 applied for aid; of those 89% were deemed to have need. 100% of freshmen with need received aid; of those 22% had need fully met. ***Average percent of need met:*** 41% (excluding resources awarded to replace EFC). ***Average financial aid package:*** $15,658 (excluding resources awarded to replace EFC). 14% of all full-time freshmen had no need and received non-need-based gift aid.

UNDERGRADUATE FINANCIAL AID (Fall 2009) 1,024 applied for aid; of those 87% were deemed to have need. 100% of undergraduates with need received aid; of those 20% had need fully met. ***Average percent of need met:*** 48% (excluding resources awarded to replace EFC). ***Average financial aid package:*** $14,472 (excluding resources awarded to replace EFC). 17% of all full-time undergraduates had no need and received non-need-based gift aid.

GIFT AID (NEED-BASED) ***Total amount:*** $3,823,196 (56% federal, 44% state). ***Receiving aid:*** Freshmen: 66% (183); all full-time undergraduates: 65% (702). ***Average award:*** Freshmen: $6665; Undergraduates: $6273. ***Scholarships, grants, and awards:*** Federal Pell, FSEOG, state, private, college/university gift aid from institutional funds, Federal Nursing.

GIFT AID (NON-NEED-BASED) ***Total amount:*** $7,719,920 (1% state, 95% institutional, 4% external sources). ***Receiving aid:*** Freshmen: 86% (239). Undergraduates: 78% (843). ***Average award:*** Freshmen: $6956. Undergraduates: $6700. ***Scholarships, grants, and awards by category:*** *Academic interests/achievement:* 598 awards ($2,432,929 total): biological sciences, business, communication, education, English, general academic interests/achievements, health fields, humanities, mathematics, physical sciences, religion/biblical studies, social sciences. *Creative arts/performance:* 78 awards ($209,575 total): music, theater/drama. *Special achievements/activities:* 604 awards ($1,450,162 total): cheerleading/drum major, general special achievements/activities, leadership, religious involvement. *Special characteristics:* 205 awards ($845,900 total): children and siblings of alumni, children of educators, children of faculty/staff, general special characteristics, international students, local/state students, previous college experience, religious affiliation, siblings of current students, twins. ***Tuition waivers:*** Full or partial for employees or children of employees.

LOANS ***Student loans:*** $6,173,958 (41% need-based, 59% non-need-based). 75% of past graduating class borrowed through all loan programs. *Average indebtedness per student:* $25,284. ***Average need-based loan:*** Freshmen: $2930. Undergraduates: $3703. ***Parent loans:*** $457,231 (100% non-need-based). ***Programs:*** Federal Direct (Subsidized and Unsubsidized Stafford, PLUS), Perkins, state.

WORK-STUDY ***Federal work-study:*** Total amount: $129,305; 87 jobs averaging $1437. ***State or other work-study/employment:*** Total amount: $332,108 (5% need-based, 95% non-need-based). 217 part-time jobs averaging $1461.

APPLYING FOR FINANCIAL AID ***Required financial aid forms:*** FAFSA, institution's own form. ***Financial aid deadline (priority):*** 6/1. ***Notification date:*** Continuous.

CONTACT Tommy Young, Director of Financial Aid, East Texas Baptist University, 1209 North Grove, Marshall, TX 75670-1498, 903-923-2137 or toll-free 800-804-ETBU. *Fax:* 903-934-8120. *E-mail:* tyoung@etbu.edu.

EAST-WEST UNIVERSITY

Chicago, IL

Tuition & fees: $15,750 **Average undergraduate aid package: N/A**

ABOUT THE INSTITUTION Independent, coed. 7 undergraduate majors. Federal methodology is used as a basis for awarding need-based institutional aid.

UNDERGRADUATE EXPENSES for 2010–11 ***One-time required fee:*** $45. ***Tuition:*** full-time $15,000; part-time $500 per credit hour. Full-time tuition and fees vary according to degree level and program. ***Payment plan:*** Installment.

FRESHMAN FINANCIAL AID (Fall 2010, est.) 531 applied for aid; of those 100% were deemed to have need. 100% of freshmen with need received aid. ***Average financial aid package:*** $13,818 (excluding resources awarded to replace EFC).

GIFT AID (NEED-BASED) ***Total amount:*** $5,988,204 (58% federal, 39% state, 3% institutional). ***Receiving aid:*** Freshmen: 100% (531). ***Average award:*** Freshmen: $4500. ***Scholarships, grants, and awards:*** Federal Pell, FSEOG, state, college/university gift aid from institutional funds.

GIFT AID (NON-NEED-BASED) ***Scholarships, grants, and awards by category:*** *Academic interests/achievement:* general academic interests/achievements. ***Tuition waivers:*** Full or partial for employees or children of employees.

LOANS ***Student loans:*** $2,897,345 (100% need-based). 45% of past graduating class borrowed through all loan programs. *Average indebtedness per student:* $3500. ***Parent loans:*** $11,000 (100% need-based). ***Programs:*** Federal Direct (Subsidized and Unsubsidized Stafford, PLUS).

WORK-STUDY ***Federal work-study:*** Total amount: $135,805; 53 jobs averaging $4500.

APPLYING FOR FINANCIAL AID ***Required financial aid form:*** FAFSA. ***Financial aid deadline (priority):*** 3/30. ***Notification date:*** Continuous beginning 1/31. Students must reply by 5/28 or within 4 weeks of notification.

CONTACT Elizabeth Guzman, Financial Aid Office, East-West University, 816 South Michigan Avenue, Chicago, IL 60605-2103, 312-939-0111 Ext. 1801. *Fax:* 312-939-0083. *E-mail:* elizabth@eastwest.edu.

ECCLESIA COLLEGE

Springdale, AR

CONTACT Financial Aid Office, Ecclesia College, 9653 Nations Drive, Springdale, AR 72762, 479-248-7236 or toll-free 800-735-9926 (out-of-state).

ECKERD COLLEGE

St. Petersburg, FL

Tuition & fees: $34,546 **Average undergraduate aid package: $28,769**

ABOUT THE INSTITUTION Independent Presbyterian, coed. 36 undergraduate majors. Federal methodology is used as a basis for awarding need-based institutional aid.

UNDERGRADUATE EXPENSES for 2011–12 ***Comprehensive fee:*** $44,198 includes full-time tuition ($34,250), mandatory fees ($296), and room and board ($9652). ***College room only:*** $4858. Room and board charges vary according to board plan and housing facility. ***Part-time tuition:*** $4110 per course. ***Payment plan:*** Installment.

FRESHMAN FINANCIAL AID (Fall 2010, est.) 365 applied for aid; of those 82% were deemed to have need. 100% of freshmen with need received aid; of those 18% had need fully met. ***Average percent of need met:*** 87% (excluding resources awarded to replace EFC). ***Average financial aid package:*** $28,491 (excluding resources awarded to replace EFC). 34% of all full-time freshmen had no need and received non-need-based gift aid.

UNDERGRADUATE FINANCIAL AID (Fall 2010, est.) 1,235 applied for aid; of those 85% were deemed to have need. 100% of undergraduates with need received aid; of those 18% had need fully met. ***Average percent of need met:*** 88% (excluding resources awarded to replace EFC). ***Average financial aid package:*** $28,769 (excluding resources awarded to replace EFC). 35% of all full-time undergraduates had no need and received non-need-based gift aid.

GIFT AID (NEED-BASED) ***Total amount:*** $18,612,238 (11% federal, 7% state, 82% institutional). ***Receiving aid:*** Freshmen: 60% (299); all full-time undergraduates: 59% (1,043). ***Average award:*** Freshmen: $19,462; Undergraduates: $18,717. ***Scholarships, grants, and awards:*** Federal Pell, FSEOG, state, college/university gift aid from institutional funds.

GIFT AID (NON-NEED-BASED) ***Total amount:*** $8,167,919 (8% state, 92% institutional). ***Average award:*** Freshmen: $13,874. Undergraduates: $12,342. ***Scholarships, grants, and awards by category:*** *Academic interests/achievement:* general academic interests/achievements. *Creative arts/performance:* art/fine arts, creative writing, music, theater/drama. *Special achievements/activities:* community service, leadership. *Special characteristics:* children of faculty/staff, international students, local/state students, religious affiliation. ***Tuition waivers:*** Full or partial for employees or children of employees.

LOANS ***Student loans:*** $10,618,762 (68% need-based, 32% non-need-based). 66% of past graduating class borrowed through all loan programs. *Average indebtedness per student:* $30,881. ***Average need-based loan:*** Freshmen: $4034. Undergraduates: $4758. ***Parent loans:*** $4,402,568 (42% need-based, 58% non-need-based). ***Programs:*** Federal Direct (Subsidized and Unsubsidized Stafford, PLUS), Perkins, college/university.

WORK-STUDY ***Federal work-study:*** Total amount: $1,641,927; jobs available. ***State or other work-study/employment:*** Total amount: $58,500 (100% non-need-based). Part-time jobs available.

ATHLETIC AWARDS Total amount: $1,243,574 (37% need-based, 63% non-need-based).

APPLYING FOR FINANCIAL AID ***Required financial aid form:*** FAFSA. ***Financial aid deadline (priority):*** 3/1. ***Notification date:*** Continuous. Students must reply by 5/1.

CONTACT Dr. Pat Garrett Watkins, Director of Financial Aid, Eckerd College, 4200 54th Avenue, South, St. Petersburg, FL 33711, 727-864-8334 or toll-free 800-456-9009. *Fax:* 727-866-2304. *E-mail:* watkinpe@eckerd.edu.

ECPI COLLEGE OF TECHNOLOGY

Raleigh, NC

CONTACT Financial Aid Office, ECPI College of Technology, 4101 Doie Cope Road, Raleigh, NC 27613, 919-571-0057 or toll-free 800-986-1200.

ECPI COLLEGE OF TECHNOLOGY

Glen Allen, VA

CONTACT Financial Aid Office, ECPI College of Technology, 4305 Cox Road, Glen Allen, VA 23060, 804-934-0100 or toll-free 800-986-1200.

ECPI COLLEGE OF TECHNOLOGY

Manassas, VA

CONTACT Financial Aid Office, ECPI College of Technology, 10021 Balls Ford Road, Manassas, VA 20109, 703-330-5300 or toll-free 866-708-6172.

ECPI COLLEGE OF TECHNOLOGY

Newport News, VA

CONTACT Financial Aid Office, ECPI College of Technology, 1001 Omni Boulevard, #100, Newport News, VA 23606, 757-838-9191 or toll-free 866-499-0335.

ECPI COLLEGE OF TECHNOLOGY

Virginia Beach, VA

Tuition & fees: N/R **Average undergraduate aid package: N/A**

ABOUT THE INSTITUTION Proprietary, coed. 28 undergraduate majors. Federal methodology is used as a basis for awarding need-based institutional aid.

FRESHMAN FINANCIAL AID (Fall 2010, est.) 1,775 applied for aid.

UNDERGRADUATE FINANCIAL AID (Fall 2010, est.) 8,500 applied for aid.

GIFT AID (NEED-BASED) ***Total amount:*** $56,000,000 (89% federal, 1% state, 10% institutional). ***Scholarships, grants, and awards:*** Federal Pell, FSEOG, state, private, college/university gift aid from institutional funds.

GIFT AID (NON-NEED-BASED) ***Total amount:*** $17,010,000 (82% federal, 15% institutional, 3% external sources). ***Scholarships, grants, and awards by category:*** *Academic interests/achievement:* business, computer science, engineering/technologies, health fields. *Special achievements/activities:* community service, general special achievements/activities. *Special characteristics:* adult students, children and siblings of alumni, children of current students, children of faculty/staff, general special characteristics, parents of current students, veterans, veterans' children.

LOANS ***Student loans:*** $106,000,000 (94% need-based, 6% non-need-based). 93% of past graduating class borrowed through all loan programs. ***Parent loans:*** $15,000,000 (67% need-based, 33% non-need-based). ***Programs:*** Federal Direct (Subsidized and Unsubsidized Stafford, PLUS), Perkins, college/university, private loans.

WORK-STUDY ***Federal work-study:*** Total amount: $400,000; jobs available. ***State or other work-study/employment:*** Part-time jobs available.

APPLYING FOR FINANCIAL AID ***Required financial aid forms:*** FAFSA, institution's own form. ***Financial aid deadline:*** Continuous. ***Notification date:*** Continuous beginning 3/1. Students must reply within 12 weeks of notification.

CONTACT Mrs. Kathi Turner, Director of Financial Aid, ECPI College of Technology, 5555 Greenwich Road, Suite 300, Virginia Beach, VA 23462, 757-490-9090 or toll-free 866-499-0336. *Fax:* 757-671-8661. *E-mail:* kturner@ecpi.edu.

EDGEWOOD COLLEGE

Madison, WI

Tuition & fees: $21,988 **Average undergraduate aid package: $15,719**

ABOUT THE INSTITUTION Independent Roman Catholic, coed, primarily women. 48 undergraduate majors. Federal methodology is used as a basis for awarding need-based institutional aid.

UNDERGRADUATE EXPENSES for 2010–11 ***Comprehensive fee:*** $29,372 includes full-time tuition ($21,988) and room and board ($7384). ***College room only:*** $3750. Full-time tuition and fees vary according to degree level. Room and board charges vary according to housing facility. ***Part-time tuition:*** $692 per credit. Part-time tuition and fees vary according to course load and degree level. ***Payment plan:*** Installment.

FRESHMAN FINANCIAL AID (Fall 2009) 252 applied for aid; of those 90% were deemed to have need. 100% of freshmen with need received aid; of those 16% had need fully met. ***Average percent of need met:*** 80% (excluding resources awarded to replace EFC). ***Average financial aid package:*** $17,619 (excluding resources awarded to replace EFC). 16% of all full-time freshmen had no need and received non-need-based gift aid.

UNDERGRADUATE FINANCIAL AID (Fall 2009) 1,321 applied for aid; of those 96% were deemed to have need. 93% of undergraduates with need received aid; of those 13% had need fully met. ***Average percent of need met:*** 71% (excluding resources awarded to replace EFC). ***Average financial aid package:*** $15,719 (excluding resources awarded to replace EFC). 15% of all full-time undergraduates had no need and received non-need-based gift aid.

GIFT AID (NEED-BASED) ***Total amount:*** $11,732,979 (21% federal, 13% state, 56% institutional, 10% external sources). ***Receiving aid:*** Freshmen: 79% (225); all full-time undergraduates: 70% (1,090). ***Average award:*** Freshmen: $13,297; Undergraduates: $10,446. ***Scholarships, grants, and awards:*** Federal Pell, FSEOG, state, private, college/university gift aid from institutional funds.

GIFT AID (NON-NEED-BASED) ***Total amount:*** $1,623,449 (2% federal, 64% institutional, 34% external sources). ***Receiving aid:*** Freshmen: 8% (22). Undergraduates: 4% (59). ***Average award:*** Freshmen: $5772. Undergraduates: $3922. ***Scholarships, grants, and awards by category:*** *Academic interests/achievement:* foreign languages, general academic interests/achievements. *Creative arts/performance:* art/fine arts, creative writing, music, performing arts, theater/drama. *Special achievements/activities:* community service. *Special characteristics:* children of faculty/staff, local/state students. ***Tuition waivers:*** Full or partial for employees or children of employees.

LOANS ***Student loans:*** $13,507,192 (72% need-based, 28% non-need-based). 76% of past graduating class borrowed through all loan programs. *Average indebtedness per student:* $29,745. ***Average need-based loan:*** Freshmen: $3619.

Undergraduates: $5106. ***Parent loans:*** $1,788,373 (37% need-based, 63% non-need-based). ***Programs:*** Federal Direct (Subsidized and Unsubsidized Stafford, PLUS), Perkins, state.

WORK-STUDY ***Federal work-study:*** Total amount: $714,348; jobs available. ***State or other work-study/employment:*** Total amount: $1,875,072 (46% need-based, 54% non-need-based). Part-time jobs available.

APPLYING FOR FINANCIAL AID ***Required financial aid forms:*** FAFSA, institution's own form. ***Financial aid deadline (priority):*** 3/1. ***Notification date:*** Continuous beginning 3/15.

CONTACT Ms. Kari Gribble, Director for Financial Aid, Edgewood College, 1000 Edgewood College Drive, Madison, WI 53711-1997, 608-663-4300 or toll-free 800-444-4861 Ext. 2294. *E-mail:* ecentral@edgewood.edu.

EDINBORO UNIVERSITY OF PENNSYLVANIA

Edinboro, PA

Tuition & fees (PA res): $7740 **Average undergraduate aid package: $9012**

ABOUT THE INSTITUTION State-supported, coed. 53 undergraduate majors. Federal methodology is used as a basis for awarding need-based institutional aid.

UNDERGRADUATE EXPENSES for 2010–11 ***Tuition, state resident:*** full-time $5814; part-time $242 per credit hour. ***Tuition, nonresident:*** full-time $8706; part-time $363 per credit hour. ***Required fees:*** full-time $1926; $76.57 per credit hour or $68 per term. Part-time tuition and fees vary according to course load. ***College room and board:*** $7820; ***Room only:*** $4980. Room and board charges vary according to board plan. ***Payment plan:*** Installment.

FRESHMAN FINANCIAL AID (Fall 2009) 1,401 applied for aid; of those 87% were deemed to have need. 97% of freshmen with need received aid; of those 16% had need fully met. ***Average percent of need met:*** 61% (excluding resources awarded to replace EFC). ***Average financial aid package:*** $9228 (excluding resources awarded to replace EFC). 4% of all full-time freshmen had no need and received non-need-based gift aid.

UNDERGRADUATE FINANCIAL AID (Fall 2009) 5,343 applied for aid; of those 87% were deemed to have need. 98% of undergraduates with need received aid; of those 8% had need fully met. ***Average percent of need met:*** 61% (excluding resources awarded to replace EFC). ***Average financial aid package:*** $9012 (excluding resources awarded to replace EFC). 5% of all full-time undergraduates had no need and received non-need-based gift aid.

GIFT AID (NEED-BASED) ***Total amount:*** $20,215,601 (64% federal, 35% state, 1% institutional). ***Receiving aid:*** Freshmen: 71% (1,103); all full-time undergraduates: 66% (4,342). ***Average award:*** Freshmen: $2569; Undergraduates: $2864. ***Scholarships, grants, and awards:*** Federal Pell, FSEOG, state, private, college/university gift aid from institutional funds.

GIFT AID (NON-NEED-BASED) ***Total amount:*** $2,431,259 (6% federal, 11% state, 52% institutional, 31% external sources). ***Receiving aid:*** Freshmen: 71% (1,100). Undergraduates: 63% (4,153). ***Average award:*** Freshmen: $3000. Undergraduates: $2200. ***Scholarships, grants, and awards by category:*** *Academic interests/achievement:* biological sciences, business, communication, computer science, education, engineering/technologies, English, foreign languages, general academic interests/achievements, health fields, humanities, mathematics, military science, physical sciences, premedicine, religion/biblical studies, social sciences. *Creative arts/performance:* art/fine arts, cinema/film/broadcasting, journalism/publications, music. *Special achievements/activities:* general special achievements/activities. *Special characteristics:* adult students, children and siblings of alumni, children of faculty/staff, children of union members/company employees, children with a deceased or disabled parent, first-generation college students, general special characteristics, handicapped students, international students, local/state students, members of minority groups, out-of-state students, religious affiliation, veterans, veterans' children. ***Tuition waivers:*** Full or partial for minority students, employees or children of employees, senior citizens.

LOANS ***Student loans:*** $36,790,092 (39% need-based, 61% non-need-based). 48% of past graduating class borrowed through all loan programs. *Average indebtedness per student:* $18,726. ***Average need-based loan:*** Freshmen: $3579. Undergraduates: $3751. ***Parent loans:*** $4,076,274 (100% non-need-based). ***Programs:*** Federal Direct (Subsidized and Unsubsidized Stafford, PLUS), Perkins, Federal Nursing, college/university.

WORK-STUDY ***Federal work-study:*** Total amount: $622,868; jobs available. ***State or other work-study/employment:*** Total amount: $962,863 (7% need-based, 93% non-need-based). Part-time jobs available.

ATHLETIC AWARDS Total amount: $865,046 (100% non-need-based).

APPLYING FOR FINANCIAL AID ***Required financial aid form:*** FAFSA. ***Financial aid deadline (priority):*** 3/15. ***Notification date:*** 3/31. Students must reply within 2 weeks of notification.

CONTACT Ms. Judith Viveralli, Associate Director of Financial Aid, Edinboro University of Pennsylvania, Hamilton Hall, Edinboro, PA 16444, 814-732-5555 Ext. 474 or toll-free 888-846-2676 (in-state), 800-626-2203 (out-of-state). *Fax:* 814-732-2129. *E-mail:* finaid@edinboro.edu.

EDP COLLEGE OF PUERTO RICO, INC.

Hato Rey, PR

Tuition & fees: $6120 **Average undergraduate aid package: N/A**

ABOUT THE INSTITUTION Proprietary, coed. 12 undergraduate majors. Federal methodology is used as a basis for awarding need-based institutional aid.

UNDERGRADUATE EXPENSES for 2010–11 ***Tuition:*** full-time $5400; part-time $156 per credit. ***Required fees:*** full-time $720; $156 per credit or $360 per term. Full-time tuition and fees vary according to course load and program. Part-time tuition and fees vary according to course load and program. ***Payment plan:*** Installment.

GIFT AID (NEED-BASED) ***Scholarships, grants, and awards:*** Federal Pell, FSEOG, state.

GIFT AID (NON-NEED-BASED) ***Scholarships, grants, and awards by category:*** *Special characteristics:* veterans, veterans' children. ***Tuition waivers:*** Full or partial for employees or children of employees.

APPLYING FOR FINANCIAL AID ***Required financial aid form:*** FAFSA. ***Financial aid deadline:*** Continuous. ***Notification date:*** Continuous beginning 8/15.

CONTACT Marie Luz Pastrana Muriel, Associate Dean of Financial Aid, EDP College of Puerto Rico, Inc., PO Box 192303, San Juan, PR 00919-2303, 787-765-3560 Ext. 249. *Fax:* 787-765-2650. *E-mail:* marieuz@edpcollege.edu.

EDP COLLEGE OF PUERTO RICO–SAN SEBASTIAN

San Sebastian, PR

Tuition & fees: $6120 **Average undergraduate aid package: $6000**

ABOUT THE INSTITUTION Proprietary, coed. 7 undergraduate majors. Federal methodology is used as a basis for awarding need-based institutional aid.

UNDERGRADUATE EXPENSES for 2010–11 ***Tuition:*** full-time $5400; part-time $156 per credit hour. ***Required fees:*** full-time $720; $156 per credit hour or $360 per term. Full-time tuition and fees vary according to course load and program. Part-time tuition and fees vary according to course load and program. ***Payment plan:*** Installment.

FRESHMAN FINANCIAL AID (Fall 2009) 452 applied for aid; of those 72% were deemed to have need. 100% of freshmen with need received aid. ***Average percent of need met:*** 75% (excluding resources awarded to replace EFC). ***Average financial aid package:*** $5550 (excluding resources awarded to replace EFC).

UNDERGRADUATE FINANCIAL AID (Fall 2009) 1,348 applied for aid; of those 99% were deemed to have need. 100% of undergraduates with need received aid. ***Average percent of need met:*** 77% (excluding resources awarded to replace EFC). ***Average financial aid package:*** $6000 (excluding resources awarded to replace EFC).

GIFT AID (NEED-BASED) ***Total amount:*** $10,862,561 (97% federal, 2% state, 1% external sources). ***Receiving aid:*** Freshmen: 35% (192); all full-time undergraduates: 43% (690). ***Average award:*** Freshmen: $250; Undergraduates: $250. ***Scholarships, grants, and awards:*** Federal Pell, FSEOG.

GIFT AID (NON-NEED-BASED) ***Scholarships, grants, and awards by category:*** *Academic interests/achievement:* health fields. *Special characteristics:* veterans, veterans' children. ***Tuition waivers:*** Full or partial for employees or children of employees.

LOANS ***Student loans:*** $1,195,554 (100% need-based). 1% of past graduating class borrowed through all loan programs. *Average indebtedness per student:*

$2500. ***Average need-based loan:*** Freshmen: $2500. Undergraduates: $2500. ***Programs:*** Federal Direct (Subsidized and Unsubsidized Stafford, PLUS).

WORK-STUDY ***Federal work-study:*** Total amount: $187,341; 81 jobs averaging $2500.

APPLYING FOR FINANCIAL AID ***Required financial aid form:*** FAFSA. ***Financial aid deadline:*** Continuous. ***Notification date:*** Continuous beginning 8/15.

CONTACT Mrs. Yaitzaenid Gonzalez, Financial Aid Administrator, EDP College of Puerto Rico–San Sebastian, PO Box 192303, San Juan, PR 00919, 787-765-3560 Ext. 253. *Fax:* 787-777-0025. *E-mail:* ygonzalez@edpcollege.edu.

EDWARD WATERS COLLEGE

Jacksonville, FL

CONTACT Gabriel Mbomeh, Director of Financial Aid, Edward Waters College, 1658 Kings Road, Jacksonville, FL 32209-6199, 904-366-2528 or toll-free 888-898-3191.

ELIZABETH CITY STATE UNIVERSITY

Elizabeth City, NC

Tuition & fees (NC res): $2204 **Average undergraduate aid package: N/A**

ABOUT THE INSTITUTION State-supported, coed. 35 undergraduate majors. Federal methodology is used as a basis for awarding need-based institutional aid.

UNDERGRADUATE EXPENSES for 2010–11 ***Tuition, state resident:*** full-time $2204. ***Tuition, nonresident:*** full-time $11,841. ***College room and board:*** $5639; ***Room only:*** $3267.

FRESHMAN FINANCIAL AID (Fall 2009) 639 applied for aid; of those 100% were deemed to have need. 100% of freshmen with need received aid.

UNDERGRADUATE FINANCIAL AID (Fall 2009) 2,711 applied for aid; of those 100% were deemed to have need. 100% of undergraduates with need received aid.

GIFT AID (NEED-BASED) ***Total amount:*** $16,188,109 (64% federal, 32% state, 3% institutional, 1% external sources). ***Receiving aid:*** Freshmen: 89% (593); all full-time undergraduates: 93% (2,653). ***Average award:*** Undergraduates: $6482. ***Scholarships, grants, and awards:*** Federal Pell, FSEOG, state, private, college/university gift aid from institutional funds, United Negro College Fund.

GIFT AID (NON-NEED-BASED) ***Total amount:*** $575,456 (100% institutional). ***Receiving aid:*** Freshmen: 6% (37). Undergraduates: 7% (211). ***Scholarships, grants, and awards by category:*** *Academic interests/achievement:* computer science, education, general academic interests/achievements, mathematics, military science. *Creative arts/performance:* music, performing arts. *Special characteristics:* ethnic background, handicapped students, international students, members of minority groups, veterans, veterans' children.

LOANS ***Student loans:*** $8,636,945 (100% need-based). 44% of past graduating class borrowed through all loan programs. *Average indebtedness per student:* $3846. ***Average need-based loan:*** Undergraduates: $5036. ***Programs:*** Federal Direct (Subsidized and Unsubsidized Stafford, PLUS), Perkins.

WORK-STUDY ***Federal work-study:*** Total amount: $182,412; jobs available.

ATHLETIC AWARDS Total amount: $104,325 (100% need-based).

APPLYING FOR FINANCIAL AID ***Required financial aid form:*** FAFSA. ***Financial aid deadline (priority):*** 3/15. ***Notification date:*** Continuous beginning 4/1.

CONTACT LaTonya M. Gregory, Assistant Director of Financial Aid, Elizabeth City State University, 1704 Weeksville Road, Campus Box 914, Elizabeth City, NC 27909-7806, 252-335-3285 or toll-free 800-347-3278. *Fax:* 252-335-3716.

ELIZABETHTOWN COLLEGE

Elizabethtown, PA

Tuition & fees: $34,830 **Average undergraduate aid package: $23,281**

ABOUT THE INSTITUTION Independent religious, coed. 50 undergraduate majors. Both federal and institutional methodology are used as a basis for awarding need-based institutional aid.

UNDERGRADUATE EXPENSES for 2011–12 ***Comprehensive fee:*** $43,630 includes full-time tuition ($34,830) and room and board ($8800). ***College room only:*** $4400. Full-time tuition and fees vary according to course load. Room and board charges vary according to board plan and housing facility. ***Part-time tuition:*** $845 per credit hour. Part-time tuition and fees vary according to class time and course load. ***Payment plan:*** Installment.

FRESHMAN FINANCIAL AID (Fall 2010, est.) 423 applied for aid; of those 87% were deemed to have need. 100% of freshmen with need received aid; of those 18% had need fully met. ***Average percent of need met:*** 81% (excluding resources awarded to replace EFC). ***Average financial aid package:*** $24,254 (excluding resources awarded to replace EFC). 25% of all full-time freshmen had no need and received non-need-based gift aid.

UNDERGRADUATE FINANCIAL AID (Fall 2010, est.) 1,568 applied for aid; of those 90% were deemed to have need. 100% of undergraduates with need received aid; of those 17% had need fully met. ***Average percent of need met:*** 80% (excluding resources awarded to replace EFC). ***Average financial aid package:*** $23,281 (excluding resources awarded to replace EFC). 21% of all full-time undergraduates had no need and received non-need-based gift aid.

GIFT AID (NEED-BASED) ***Total amount:*** $26,810,911 (9% federal, 6% state, 77% institutional, 8% external sources). ***Receiving aid:*** Freshmen: 74% (366); all full-time undergraduates: 75% (1,405). ***Average award:*** Freshmen: $20,216; Undergraduates: $18,578. ***Scholarships, grants, and awards:*** Federal Pell, FSEOG, state, private, college/university gift aid from institutional funds.

GIFT AID (NON-NEED-BASED) ***Total amount:*** $7,520,051 (79% institutional, 21% external sources). ***Receiving aid:*** Freshmen: 11% (56). Undergraduates: 10% (185). ***Average award:*** Freshmen: $15,463. Undergraduates: $13,405. ***Scholarships, grants, and awards by category:*** *Academic interests/achievement:* biological sciences, business, communication, computer science, education, engineering/technologies, English, foreign languages, general academic interests/achievements, health fields, humanities, international studies, mathematics, physical sciences, premedicine, religion/biblical studies, social sciences. *Creative arts/performance:* art/fine arts, music, performing arts, theater/drama. *Special achievements/activities:* religious involvement. *Special characteristics:* children of faculty/staff, international students, local/state students, members of minority groups, religious affiliation, siblings of current students. ***Tuition waivers:*** Full or partial for employees or children of employees.

LOANS ***Student loans:*** $14,667,176 (66% need-based, 34% non-need-based). ***Average need-based loan:*** Freshmen: $3597. Undergraduates: $4547. ***Parent loans:*** $6,214,995 (29% need-based, 71% non-need-based). ***Programs:*** Federal Direct (Subsidized and Unsubsidized Stafford, PLUS), Perkins, state.

WORK-STUDY ***Federal work-study:*** Total amount: $1,291,621; 968 jobs averaging $1351.

APPLYING FOR FINANCIAL AID ***Required financial aid forms:*** FAFSA, institution's own form, state aid form, federal income tax form(s), W-2 forms. ***Financial aid deadline (priority):*** 3/15. ***Notification date:*** Continuous beginning 3/15. Students must reply by 5/1 or within 2 weeks of notification.

CONTACT Ms. Elizabeth K. McCloud, Director of Financial Aid, Elizabethtown College, 1 Alpha Drive, Elizabethtown, PA 17022-2298, 717-361-1404. *Fax:* 717-361-1514. *E-mail:* mcclouek@etown.edu.

ELLIS UNIVERSITY

Chicago, IL

CONTACT Financial Aid Office, Ellis University, 111 North Canal Street, Suite 380, Chicago, IL 60606-7204, toll-free 877-355-4762 (out-of-state).

ELMHURST COLLEGE

Elmhurst, IL

Tuition & fees: $30,054 **Average undergraduate aid package: $20,180**

ABOUT THE INSTITUTION Independent religious, coed. 68 undergraduate majors. Federal methodology is used as a basis for awarding need-based institutional aid.

UNDERGRADUATE EXPENSES for 2011–12 ***Comprehensive fee:*** $38,578 includes full-time tuition ($29,994), mandatory fees ($60), and room and board ($8524). ***College room only:*** $5154. Room and board charges vary according to board plan and housing facility. ***Part-time tuition:*** $854 per semester hour. Part-time tuition and fees vary according to course load. ***Payment plan:*** Installment.

FRESHMAN FINANCIAL AID (Fall 2010, est.) 485 applied for aid; of those 89% were deemed to have need. 100% of freshmen with need received aid; of those 26% had need fully met. ***Average percent of need met:*** 74% (excluding

resources awarded to replace EFC). ***Average financial aid package:*** $22,386 (excluding resources awarded to replace EFC). 12% of all full-time freshmen had no need and received non-need-based gift aid.

UNDERGRADUATE FINANCIAL AID (Fall 2010, est.) 2,330 applied for aid; of those 92% were deemed to have need. 100% of undergraduates with need received aid; of those 27% had need fully met. ***Average percent of need met:*** 69% (excluding resources awarded to replace EFC). ***Average financial aid package:*** $20,180 (excluding resources awarded to replace EFC). 19% of all full-time undergraduates had no need and received non-need-based gift aid.

GIFT AID (NEED-BASED) ***Total amount:*** $37,920,067 (12% federal, 11% state, 76% institutional, 1% external sources). ***Receiving aid:*** Freshmen: 81% (434); all full-time undergraduates: 74% (2,147). ***Average award:*** Freshmen: $18,139; Undergraduates: $17,988. ***Scholarships, grants, and awards:*** Federal Pell, FSEOG, state, private, college/university gift aid from institutional funds.

GIFT AID (NON-NEED-BASED) ***Total amount:*** $7,024,566 (2% state, 97% institutional, 1% external sources). ***Receiving aid:*** Freshmen: 15% (82). Undergraduates: 19% (562). ***Average award:*** Freshmen: $12,002. Undergraduates: $11,386. ***Scholarships, grants, and awards by category:*** *Academic interests/achievement:* 1,905 awards ($20,797,164 total): biological sciences, business, communication, computer science, education, English, foreign languages, general academic interests/achievements, health fields, humanities, international studies, mathematics, physical sciences, premedicine, religion/biblical studies, social sciences. *Creative arts/performance:* 199 awards ($1,506,729 total): art/fine arts, music, theater/drama. *Special characteristics:* 688 awards ($2,622,021 total): children and siblings of alumni, children of current students, children with a deceased or disabled parent, ethnic background, members of minority groups, religious affiliation, siblings of current students, spouses of current students, veterans, veterans' children. ***Tuition waivers:*** Full or partial for employees or children of employees, senior citizens.

LOANS ***Student loans:*** $16,352,546 (51% need-based, 49% non-need-based). 73% of past graduating class borrowed through all loan programs. *Average indebtedness per student:* $23,912. ***Average need-based loan:*** Freshmen: $3418. Undergraduates: $4439. ***Parent loans:*** $5,198,051 (5% need-based, 95% non-need-based). ***Programs:*** Federal Direct (Subsidized and Unsubsidized Stafford, PLUS), Perkins, alternative loans.

WORK-STUDY ***Federal work-study:*** Total amount: $479,534; 409 jobs averaging $1172. ***State or other work-study/employment:*** Total amount: $517,418 (100% non-need-based). 302 part-time jobs averaging $1713.

APPLYING FOR FINANCIAL AID ***Required financial aid form:*** FAFSA. ***Financial aid deadline (priority):*** 4/15. ***Notification date:*** Continuous beginning 2/20. Students must reply within 3 weeks of notification.

CONTACT Ruth A. Pusich, Director of Financial Aid, Elmhurst College, Goebel Hall 106A, 190 Prospect Avenue, Elmhurst, IL 60126-3296, 630-617-3080 or toll-free 800-697-1871 (out-of-state). *Fax:* 630-617-5188. *E-mail:* ruthp@elmhurst.edu.

ELMIRA COLLEGE

Elmira, NY

Tuition & fees: $35,900 **Average undergraduate aid package: $26,953**

ABOUT THE INSTITUTION Independent, coed. 61 undergraduate majors. Federal methodology is used as a basis for awarding need-based institutional aid.

UNDERGRADUATE EXPENSES for 2010–11 ***Comprehensive fee:*** $47,050 includes full-time tuition ($34,500), mandatory fees ($1400), and room and board ($11,150). Room and board charges vary according to housing facility. ***Part-time tuition:*** $305 per credit hour. Part-time tuition and fees vary according to course load and degree level. ***Payment plans:*** Tuition prepayment, installment.

FRESHMAN FINANCIAL AID (Fall 2010, est.) 354 applied for aid; of those 91% were deemed to have need. 100% of freshmen with need received aid; of those 21% had need fully met. ***Average percent of need met:*** 80% (excluding resources awarded to replace EFC). ***Average financial aid package:*** $27,850 (excluding resources awarded to replace EFC). 19% of all full-time freshmen had no need and received non-need-based gift aid.

UNDERGRADUATE FINANCIAL AID (Fall 2010, est.) 1,035 applied for aid; of those 93% were deemed to have need. 100% of undergraduates with need received aid; of those 17% had need fully met. ***Average percent of need met:*** 80% (excluding resources awarded to replace EFC). ***Average financial aid package:*** $26,953 (excluding resources awarded to replace EFC). 19% of all full-time undergraduates had no need and received non-need-based gift aid.

GIFT AID (NEED-BASED) ***Total amount:*** $21,555,870 (9% federal, 4% state, 84% institutional, 3% external sources). ***Receiving aid:*** Freshmen: 79% (321); all full-time undergraduates: 78% (962). ***Average award:*** Freshmen: $24,862; Undergraduates: $23,024. ***Scholarships, grants, and awards:*** Federal Pell, FSEOG, state, private, college/university gift aid from institutional funds.

GIFT AID (NON-NEED-BASED) ***Total amount:*** $6,199,640 (1% state, 87% institutional, 12% external sources). ***Receiving aid:*** Freshmen: 12% (47). Undergraduates: 10% (117). ***Average award:*** Freshmen: $21,461. Undergraduates: $19,232. ***Scholarships, grants, and awards by category:*** *Academic interests/achievement:* 775 awards ($13,765,759 total): general academic interests/achievements. *Special achievements/activities:* 112 awards ($842,600 total): leadership. *Special characteristics:* 387 awards ($2,337,289 total): children of faculty/staff, international students, local/state students, out-of-state students, previous college experience, siblings of current students, veterans. ***Tuition waivers:*** Full or partial for employees or children of employees.

LOANS ***Student loans:*** $8,660,034 (73% need-based, 27% non-need-based). 79% of past graduating class borrowed through all loan programs. *Average indebtedness per student:* $25,438. ***Average need-based loan:*** Freshmen: $3094. Undergraduates: $4148. ***Parent loans:*** $4,390,970 (45% need-based, 55% non-need-based). ***Programs:*** Federal Direct (Subsidized and Unsubsidized Stafford, PLUS), Perkins, college/university.

WORK-STUDY ***Federal work-study:*** Total amount: $383,742; 376 jobs averaging $1000. ***State or other work-study/employment:*** Total amount: $283,300 (29% need-based, 71% non-need-based). 220 part-time jobs averaging $1300.

APPLYING FOR FINANCIAL AID ***Required financial aid forms:*** FAFSA, state aid form. ***Financial aid deadline (priority):*** 2/1. ***Notification date:*** Continuous beginning 2/1. Students must reply by 5/1 or within 3 weeks of notification.

CONTACT Kathleen L. Cohen, Dean of Financial Aid, Elmira College, One Park Place, Elmira, NY 14901-2099, 607-735-1728 or toll-free 800-935-6472. *Fax:* 607-735-1718. *E-mail:* kcohen@elmira.edu.

ELMS COLLEGE

Chicopee, MA

CONTACT Ms. April Arcouette, Assistant Director of Student Financial Aid Services, Elms College, 291 Springfield Street, Chicopee, MA 01013-2839, 413-265-2249 or toll-free 800-255-ELMS. *Fax:* 413-265-2671. *E-mail:* arcouettea@elms.edu.

ELON UNIVERSITY

Elon, NC

Tuition & fees: $27,881 **Average undergraduate aid package: $17,388**

ABOUT THE INSTITUTION Independent religious, coed. 49 undergraduate majors. Institutional methodology is used as a basis for awarding need-based institutional aid.

UNDERGRADUATE EXPENSES for 2011–12 ***Comprehensive fee:*** $36,971 includes full-time tuition ($27,534), mandatory fees ($347), and room and board ($9090). ***College room only:*** $4440. Room and board charges vary according to board plan and housing facility. Part-time tuition and fees vary according to course load. ***Payment plan:*** Installment.

FRESHMAN FINANCIAL AID (Fall 2010, est.) 794 applied for aid; of those 66% were deemed to have need. 99% of freshmen with need received aid. ***Average percent of need met:*** 71% (excluding resources awarded to replace EFC). ***Average financial aid package:*** $17,312 (excluding resources awarded to replace EFC). 18% of all full-time freshmen had no need and received non-need-based gift aid.

UNDERGRADUATE FINANCIAL AID (Fall 2010, est.) 2,392 applied for aid; of those 75% were deemed to have need. 100% of undergraduates with need received aid. ***Average percent of need met:*** 71% (excluding resources awarded to replace EFC). ***Average financial aid package:*** $17,388 (excluding resources awarded to replace EFC). 20% of all full-time undergraduates had no need and received non-need-based gift aid.

GIFT AID (NEED-BASED) ***Total amount:*** $16,949,809 (15% federal, 19% state, 64% institutional, 2% external sources). ***Receiving aid:*** Freshmen: 33% (449); all full-time undergraduates: 33% (1,586). ***Average award:*** Freshmen: $11,331; Undergraduates: $10,846. ***Scholarships, grants, and awards:*** Federal Pell, FSEOG, state, private, college/university gift aid from institutional funds.

GIFT AID (NON-NEED-BASED) ***Total amount:*** $8,164,583 (19% state, 78% institutional, 3% external sources). ***Receiving aid:*** Freshmen: 3% (36). Undergraduates: 3% (141). ***Average award:*** Freshmen: $5323. Undergraduates: $5565. ***Scholarships, grants, and awards by category:*** *Academic interests/achievement:* 1,535 awards ($8,054,789 total): biological sciences, business, communication, computer science, education, engineering/technologies, general academic interests/achievements, mathematics, military science, physical sciences, premedicine, religion/biblical studies, social sciences. *Creative arts/performance:* 67 awards ($170,700 total): art/fine arts, journalism/publications, music, performing arts, theater/drama. *Special achievements/activities:* 31 awards ($51,150 total): community service, general special achievements/activities, leadership, religious involvement. *Special characteristics:* 73 awards ($986,008 total): adult students, children of faculty/staff, ethnic background, first-generation college students, international students, members of minority groups, relatives of clergy. ***Tuition waivers:*** Full or partial for employees or children of employees.

LOANS ***Student loans:*** $14,858,479 (43% need-based, 57% non-need-based). 46% of past graduating class borrowed through all loan programs. *Average indebtedness per student:* $27,163. ***Average need-based loan:*** Freshmen: $3933. Undergraduates: $5087. ***Parent loans:*** $9,958,376 (35% need-based, 65% non-need-based). ***Programs:*** Federal Direct (Subsidized and Unsubsidized Stafford, PLUS), Perkins, state, college/university, alternative loans.

WORK-STUDY ***Federal work-study:*** Total amount: $2,917,481; 1,204 jobs averaging $2344.

ATHLETIC AWARDS Total amount: $6,524,860 (45% need-based, 55% non-need-based).

APPLYING FOR FINANCIAL AID ***Required financial aid forms:*** FAFSA, institution's own form, CSS Financial Aid PROFILE. ***Financial aid deadline (priority):*** 3/15. ***Notification date:*** 3/30.

CONTACT Patrick Murphy, Director of Financial Planning, Elon University, 2725 Campus Box, Elon, NC 27244, 336-278-7640 or toll-free 800-334-8448. *Fax:* 336-278-7639. *E-mail:* finaid@elon.edu.

EMBRY-RIDDLE AERONAUTICAL UNIVERSITY–DAYTONA

Daytona Beach, FL

Tuition & fees: $29,852 **Average undergraduate aid package: $15,667**

ABOUT THE INSTITUTION Independent, coed. 24 undergraduate majors. Federal methodology is used as a basis for awarding need-based institutional aid.

UNDERGRADUATE EXPENSES for 2011–12 ***Comprehensive fee:*** $39,602 includes full-time tuition ($28,680), mandatory fees ($1172), and room and board ($9750). ***College room only:*** $5350. Room and board charges vary according to board plan and housing facility. ***Part-time tuition:*** $1195 per credit hour. ***Payment plans:*** Installment, deferred payment.

FRESHMAN FINANCIAL AID (Fall 2010, est.) 775 applied for aid; of those 88% were deemed to have need. 100% of freshmen with need received aid. ***Average financial aid package:*** $15,505 (excluding resources awarded to replace EFC).

UNDERGRADUATE FINANCIAL AID (Fall 2010, est.) 3,048 applied for aid; of those 90% were deemed to have need. 99% of undergraduates with need received aid. ***Average financial aid package:*** $15,667 (excluding resources awarded to replace EFC).

GIFT AID (NEED-BASED) ***Total amount:*** $40,096,702 (16% federal, 7% state, 53% institutional, 24% external sources). ***Receiving aid:*** Freshmen: 71% (671); all full-time undergraduates: 61% (2,597). ***Average award:*** Freshmen: $10,380; Undergraduates: $9466. ***Scholarships, grants, and awards:*** Federal Pell, FSEOG, state, private, college/university gift aid from institutional funds.

GIFT AID (NON-NEED-BASED) ***Scholarships, grants, and awards by category:*** *Academic interests/achievement:* 2,184 awards ($10,662,813 total): general academic interests/achievements. *Special achievements/activities:* 81 awards ($221,112 total): leadership. *Special characteristics:* 114 awards ($1,788,526 total): children of faculty/staff. ***Tuition waivers:*** Full or partial for employees or children of employees.

LOANS ***Student loans:*** $31,485,339 (100% need-based). 71% of past graduating class borrowed through all loan programs. ***Average need-based loan:*** Freshmen: $3432. Undergraduates: $4739. ***Parent loans:*** $22,873,247 (100% need-based). ***Programs:*** Federal Direct (Subsidized and Unsubsidized Stafford, PLUS), Perkins, college/university.

WORK-STUDY ***Federal work-study:*** Total amount: $300,923; 140 jobs averaging $1888. ***State or other work-study/employment:*** Total amount: $4,076,762 (100% need-based). 1,096 part-time jobs averaging $1935.

ATHLETIC AWARDS Total amount: $2,124,456 (100% need-based).

APPLYING FOR FINANCIAL AID ***Required financial aid form:*** FAFSA. ***Financial aid deadline (priority):*** 3/1. ***Notification date:*** Continuous beginning 3/1. Students must reply within 4 weeks of notification.

CONTACT Barbara Dryden, Director of Financial Aid, Embry-Riddle Aeronautical University–Daytona, 600 South Clyde Morris Boulevard, Daytona Beach, FL 32114-3900, 800-943-6279 or toll-free 800-862-2416. *Fax:* 386-226-6307. *E-mail:* dbfinaid@erau.edu.

EMBRY-RIDDLE AERONAUTICAL UNIVERSITY–PRESCOTT

Prescott, AZ

Tuition & fees: $29,672 **Average undergraduate aid package: $18,696**

ABOUT THE INSTITUTION Independent, coed. 14 undergraduate majors. Federal methodology is used as a basis for awarding need-based institutional aid.

UNDERGRADUATE EXPENSES for 2011–12 ***Comprehensive fee:*** $38,572 includes full-time tuition ($28,860), mandatory fees ($812), and room and board ($8900). ***College room only:*** $5000. Room and board charges vary according to board plan and housing facility. ***Part-time tuition:*** $1195 per credit hour. ***Payment plans:*** Installment, deferred payment.

FRESHMAN FINANCIAL AID (Fall 2010, est.) 312 applied for aid; of those 87% were deemed to have need. 100% of freshmen with need received aid. ***Average financial aid package:*** $14,674 (excluding resources awarded to replace EFC).

UNDERGRADUATE FINANCIAL AID (Fall 2010, est.) 1,541 applied for aid; of those 78% were deemed to have need. 90% of undergraduates with need received aid. ***Average financial aid package:*** $18,696 (excluding resources awarded to replace EFC).

GIFT AID (NEED-BASED) ***Total amount:*** $20,166,319 (14% federal, 60% institutional, 26% external sources). ***Receiving aid:*** Freshmen: 75% (264); all full-time undergraduates: 67% (1,039). ***Average award:*** Freshmen: $10,285; Undergraduates: $11,020. ***Scholarships, grants, and awards:*** Federal Pell, FSEOG, state, private, college/university gift aid from institutional funds.

GIFT AID (NON-NEED-BASED) ***Scholarships, grants, and awards by category:*** *Academic interests/achievement:* 1,019 awards ($7,725,451 total): general academic interests/achievements. *Special achievements/activities:* 21 awards ($111,800 total): leadership. *Special characteristics:* 50 awards ($563,520 total): children and siblings of alumni, children of faculty/staff. ***Tuition waivers:*** Full or partial for employees or children of employees.

LOANS ***Student loans:*** $12,242,289 (100% need-based). 75% of past graduating class borrowed through all loan programs. ***Average need-based loan:*** Freshmen: $3396. Undergraduates: $4989. ***Parent loans:*** $8,156,406 (100% need-based). ***Programs:*** Federal Direct (Subsidized and Unsubsidized Stafford, PLUS), Perkins, college/university.

WORK-STUDY ***Federal work-study:*** Total amount: $85,958; 50 jobs averaging $1657. ***State or other work-study/employment:*** Total amount: $873,400 (100% need-based). 496 part-time jobs averaging $1383.

ATHLETIC AWARDS Total amount: $757,871 (100% need-based).

APPLYING FOR FINANCIAL AID ***Required financial aid form:*** FAFSA. ***Financial aid deadline (priority):*** 3/1. ***Notification date:*** Continuous beginning 3/1. Students must reply within 4 weeks of notification.

CONTACT Mr. Dan Lupin, Director of Financial Aid, Embry-Riddle Aeronautical University–Prescott, 3700 Willow Creek Road, Prescott, AZ 86301-3720, 800-888-3728. *Fax:* 928-777-3893. *E-mail:* prfinaid@erau.edu.

EMBRY-RIDDLE AERONAUTICAL UNIVERSITY–WORLDWIDE

Daytona Beach, FL

Tuition & fees: $5580 **Average undergraduate aid package: $7005**

ABOUT THE INSTITUTION Independent, coed. 4 undergraduate majors. Federal methodology is used as a basis for awarding need-based institutional aid.

UNDERGRADUATE EXPENSES for 2011–12 ***Tuition:*** full-time $5580; part-time $290 per credit hour. Full-time tuition and fees vary according to program. Part-time tuition and fees vary according to program. ***Payment plan:*** Deferred payment.

FRESHMAN FINANCIAL AID (Fall 2009) 11 applied for aid; of those 73% were deemed to have need. 88% of freshmen with need received aid. ***Average financial aid package:*** $5113 (excluding resources awarded to replace EFC).

UNDERGRADUATE FINANCIAL AID (Fall 2009) 726 applied for aid; of those 92% were deemed to have need. 96% of undergraduates with need received aid. ***Average financial aid package:*** $7005 (excluding resources awarded to replace EFC).

GIFT AID (NEED-BASED) ***Total amount:*** $5,200,940 (82% federal, 13% state, 4% institutional, 1% external sources). ***Receiving aid:*** Freshmen: 12% (7); all full-time undergraduates: 20% (486). ***Average award:*** Freshmen: $4480; Undergraduates: $4457. ***Scholarships, grants, and awards:*** Federal Pell, state, private, college/university gift aid from institutional funds.

GIFT AID (NON-NEED-BASED) ***Scholarships, grants, and awards by category:*** *Academic interests/achievement:* general academic interests/achievements. *Special achievements/activities:* 5 awards ($487 total): leadership. *Special characteristics:* 9 awards ($68,250 total): children of faculty/staff. ***Tuition waivers:*** Full or partial for employees or children of employees.

LOANS ***Student loans:*** $14,414,175 (100% need-based). 16% of past graduating class borrowed through all loan programs. ***Average need-based loan:*** Freshmen: $4500. Undergraduates: $4570. ***Parent loans:*** $24,759 (100% need-based).

APPLYING FOR FINANCIAL AID ***Required financial aid form:*** FAFSA. ***Financial aid deadline:*** Continuous. ***Notification date:*** Continuous beginning 3/1. Students must reply within 4 weeks of notification.

CONTACT Frederic Ndiaye, Director of Financial Aid, Embry-Riddle Aeronautical University–Worldwide, 600 South Clyde Morris Boulevard, Daytona Beach, FL 32114-3900, 866-567-7202 or toll-free 800-522-6787. *Fax:* 386-226-6915. *E-mail:* wwfinaid@erau.edu.

EMERSON COLLEGE

Boston, MA

Tuition & fees: $31,272 **Average undergraduate aid package: $17,981**

ABOUT THE INSTITUTION Independent, coed. 28 undergraduate majors. Institutional methodology is used as a basis for awarding need-based institutional aid.

UNDERGRADUATE EXPENSES for 2010–11 ***Comprehensive fee:*** $44,153 includes full-time tuition ($30,752), mandatory fees ($520), and room and board ($12,881). Room and board charges vary according to board plan. ***Part-time tuition:*** $961 per credit hour. ***Payment plan:*** Installment.

FRESHMAN FINANCIAL AID (Fall 2010, est.) 569 applied for aid; of those 80% were deemed to have need. 100% of freshmen with need received aid; of those 74% had need fully met. ***Average percent of need met:*** 74% (excluding resources awarded to replace EFC). ***Average financial aid package:*** $18,674 (excluding resources awarded to replace EFC). 10% of all full-time freshmen had no need and received non-need-based gift aid.

UNDERGRADUATE FINANCIAL AID (Fall 2010, est.) 2,286 applied for aid; of those 86% were deemed to have need. 100% of undergraduates with need received aid; of those 48% had need fully met. ***Average percent of need met:*** 70% (excluding resources awarded to replace EFC). ***Average financial aid package:*** $17,981 (excluding resources awarded to replace EFC). 6% of all full-time undergraduates had no need and received non-need-based gift aid.

GIFT AID (NEED-BASED) ***Total amount:*** $25,775,976 (11% federal, 2% state, 81% institutional, 6% external sources). ***Receiving aid:*** Freshmen: 49% (408); all full-time undergraduates: 49% (1,677). ***Average award:*** Freshmen: $16,854; Undergraduates: $15,444. ***Scholarships, grants, and awards:*** Federal Pell, FSEOG, state, private, college/university gift aid from institutional funds.

GIFT AID (NON-NEED-BASED) ***Total amount:*** $3,144,832 (93% institutional, 7% external sources). ***Receiving aid:*** Freshmen: 3% (27). Undergraduates: 2% (64). ***Average award:*** Freshmen: $13,396. Undergraduates: $12,713. ***Scholarships, grants, and awards by category:*** *Academic interests/achievement:* 249 awards ($5,317,513 total): general academic interests/achievements. *Creative arts/performance:* 29 awards ($218,000 total): performing arts. *Special achievements/activities:* 12 awards ($70,105 total): leadership. *Special characteristics:* 138 awards ($655,316 total): general special characteristics. ***Tuition waivers:*** Full or partial for employees or children of employees.

LOANS ***Student loans:*** $24,095,775 (68% need-based, 32% non-need-based). 64% of past graduating class borrowed through all loan programs. *Average indebtedness per student:* $17,459. ***Average need-based loan:*** Freshmen: $3508. Undergraduates: $4490. ***Parent loans:*** $11,505,875 (40% need-based, 60% non-need-based). ***Programs:*** Perkins, state.

WORK-STUDY ***Federal work-study:*** Total amount: $617,699; 427 jobs averaging $2000. ***State or other work-study/employment:*** Total amount: $725,773 (46% need-based, 54% non-need-based). 60 part-time jobs averaging $12,071.

APPLYING FOR FINANCIAL AID ***Required financial aid forms:*** FAFSA, CSS Financial Aid PROFILE, noncustodial (divorced/separated) parent's statement, business/farm supplement. ***Financial aid deadline (priority):*** 3/1. ***Notification date:*** 4/1. Students must reply by 5/1 or within 3 weeks of notification.

CONTACT Michelle Smith, Director of Student Financial Services, Emerson College, 120 Boylston Street, Boston, MA 02116-4624, 617-824-8655. *Fax:* 617-824-8619. *E-mail:* finaid@emerson.edu.

EMMANUEL COLLEGE

Franklin Springs, GA

Tuition & fees: $14,550 **Average undergraduate aid package: $12,455**

ABOUT THE INSTITUTION Independent religious, coed. 23 undergraduate majors. Federal methodology is used as a basis for awarding need-based institutional aid.

UNDERGRADUATE EXPENSES for 2011–12 ***Comprehensive fee:*** $20,650 includes full-time tuition ($14,550) and room and board ($6100). ***Part-time tuition:*** $600 per credit hour. ***Payment plan:*** Installment.

FRESHMAN FINANCIAL AID (Fall 2010, est.) 181 applied for aid; of those 91% were deemed to have need. 100% of freshmen with need received aid; of those 12% had need fully met. ***Average percent of need met:*** 70% (excluding resources awarded to replace EFC). ***Average financial aid package:*** $12,375 (excluding resources awarded to replace EFC). 11% of all full-time freshmen had no need and received non-need-based gift aid.

UNDERGRADUATE FINANCIAL AID (Fall 2010, est.) 634 applied for aid; of those 93% were deemed to have need. 100% of undergraduates with need received aid; of those 9% had need fully met. ***Average percent of need met:*** 66% (excluding resources awarded to replace EFC). ***Average financial aid package:*** $12,455 (excluding resources awarded to replace EFC). 10% of all full-time undergraduates had no need and received non-need-based gift aid.

GIFT AID (NEED-BASED) ***Total amount:*** $4,701,904 (41% federal, 20% state, 36% institutional, 3% external sources). ***Receiving aid:*** Freshmen: 86% (165); all full-time undergraduates: 86% (586). ***Average award:*** Freshmen: $9372; Undergraduates: $8768. ***Scholarships, grants, and awards:*** Federal Pell, FSEOG, state, college/university gift aid from institutional funds.

GIFT AID (NON-NEED-BASED) ***Total amount:*** $616,851 (28% state, 62% institutional, 10% external sources). ***Receiving aid:*** Freshmen: 5% (10). Undergraduates: 6% (38). ***Average award:*** Freshmen: $5423. Undergraduates: $4658. ***Scholarships, grants, and awards by category:*** *Academic interests/achievement:* 226 awards ($427,327 total): business, communication, education, English, general academic interests/achievements, health fields, religion/biblical studies. *Creative arts/performance:* 109 awards ($137,496 total): applied art and design, art/fine arts, creative writing, dance, general creative arts/performance, music, performing arts, theater/drama. *Special achievements/activities:* 6 awards ($48,445 total): general special achievements/activities, leadership, memberships, religious involvement. *Special characteristics:* 391 awards ($682,160 total): adult students, children of current students, children of faculty/staff, first-generation college students, general special characteristics, international students, married students, parents of current students, relatives of clergy, religious affiliation, siblings of current students, spouses of current students, twins. ***Tuition waivers:*** Full or partial for employees or children of employees, senior citizens.

LOANS ***Student loans:*** $3,774,218 (88% need-based, 12% non-need-based). 80% of past graduating class borrowed through all loan programs. *Average indebtedness per student:* $28,298. ***Average need-based loan:*** Freshmen: $2910. Undergraduates: $3512. ***Parent loans:*** $828,910 (46% need-based, 54% non-need-based). ***Programs:*** Federal Direct (Subsidized and Unsubsidized Stafford, PLUS).

WORK-STUDY ***Federal work-study:*** Total amount: $410,195; 286 jobs averaging $1871. ***State or other work-study/employment:*** Total amount: $315,859 (100% non-need-based). Part-time jobs available.

ATHLETIC AWARDS Total amount: $603,449 (68% need-based, 32% non-need-based).

APPLYING FOR FINANCIAL AID ***Required financial aid forms:*** FAFSA, institution's own form, state aid form. ***Financial aid deadline:*** 6/15 (priority: 5/1). ***Notification date:*** Continuous beginning 3/1. Students must reply within 2 weeks of notification.

CONTACT Mr. Vince Welch, Director of Financial Aid, Emmanuel College, PO Box 129, Franklin Springs, GA 30639-0129, 706-245-2871 or toll-free 800-860-8800 (in-state). *Fax:* 706-245-2846. *E-mail:* vwelch@ec.edu.

EMMANUEL COLLEGE

Boston, MA

Tuition & fees: $30,890 **Average undergraduate aid package: $22,286**

ABOUT THE INSTITUTION Independent Roman Catholic, coed. 36 undergraduate majors. Federal methodology is used as a basis for awarding need-based institutional aid.

UNDERGRADUATE EXPENSES for 2010–11 ***Comprehensive fee:*** $43,190 includes full-time tuition ($30,600), mandatory fees ($290), and room and board ($12,300). Full-time tuition and fees vary according to course load, degree level, and program. Room and board charges vary according to housing facility. Part-time tuition and fees vary according to program. ***Payment plan:*** Installment.

FRESHMAN FINANCIAL AID (Fall 2010, est.) 486 applied for aid; of those 92% were deemed to have need. 100% of freshmen with need received aid; of those 45% had need fully met. ***Average percent of need met:*** 85% (excluding resources awarded to replace EFC). ***Average financial aid package:*** $25,857 (excluding resources awarded to replace EFC).

UNDERGRADUATE FINANCIAL AID (Fall 2010, est.) 1,642 applied for aid; of those 90% were deemed to have need. 97% of undergraduates with need received aid; of those 54% had need fully met. ***Average percent of need met:*** 72% (excluding resources awarded to replace EFC). ***Average financial aid package:*** $22,286 (excluding resources awarded to replace EFC).

GIFT AID (NEED-BASED) ***Total amount:*** $25,284,264 (13% federal, 3% state, 82% institutional, 2% external sources). ***Receiving aid:*** Freshmen: 80% (420); all full-time undergraduates: 72% (1,363). ***Average award:*** Freshmen: $10,100; Undergraduates: $11,179. ***Scholarships, grants, and awards:*** Federal Pell, FSEOG, state, private, college/university gift aid from institutional funds.

GIFT AID (NON-NEED-BASED) ***Total amount:*** $2,565,054 (11% federal, 88% institutional, 1% external sources). ***Receiving aid:*** Freshmen: 84% (444). Undergraduates: 72% (1,376). ***Scholarships, grants, and awards by category:*** *Academic interests/achievement:* biological sciences, education, engineering/technologies, foreign languages, general academic interests/achievements, health fields, humanities, mathematics, physical sciences, religion/biblical studies, social sciences. *Creative arts/performance:* general creative arts/performance. *Special achievements/activities:* community service, leadership. *Special characteristics:* children and siblings of alumni, children of educators, children of faculty/staff, children of union members/company employees, ethnic background, general special characteristics, handicapped students, international students, local/state students, religious affiliation, siblings of current students. ***Tuition waivers:*** Full or partial for employees or children of employees.

LOANS ***Student loans:*** $15,020,184 (94% need-based, 6% non-need-based). ***Average need-based loan:*** Freshmen: $3704. Undergraduates: $4835. ***Parent loans:*** $7,774,656 (100% non-need-based). ***Programs:*** Federal Direct (Subsidized and Unsubsidized Stafford, PLUS), Perkins, state, alternative loans.

WORK-STUDY ***Federal work-study:*** Total amount: $1,517,353; jobs available. ***State or other work-study/employment:*** Total amount: $350,000 (100% non-need-based). Part-time jobs available.

APPLYING FOR FINANCIAL AID ***Required financial aid forms:*** FAFSA, institution's own form. ***Financial aid deadline (priority):*** 4/1. ***Notification date:*** Continuous beginning 3/15.

CONTACT Jennifer Porter, Associate Vice President for Student Financial Services, Emmanuel College, 400 The Fenway, Boston, MA 02115, 617-735-9938. *Fax:* 617-735-9939. *E-mail:* financialservices@emmanuel.edu.

EMMAUS BIBLE COLLEGE

Dubuque, IA

CONTACT Steve Seeman, Financial Aid Director, Emmaus Bible College, 2570 Asbury Road, Dubuque, IA 52001-3097, 800-397-2425 Ext. 1309 or toll-free 800-397-2425. *Fax:* 563-588-1216. *E-mail:* financialaid@emmaus.edu.

EMORY & HENRY COLLEGE

Emory, VA

Tuition & fees: $26,000 **Average undergraduate aid package: $24,225**

ABOUT THE INSTITUTION Independent United Methodist, coed. 37 undergraduate majors. Federal methodology is used as a basis for awarding need-based institutional aid.

UNDERGRADUATE EXPENSES for 2010–11 ***Comprehensive fee:*** $34,570 includes full-time tuition ($26,000) and room and board ($8570). ***College room only:*** $4140. Full-time tuition and fees vary according to course load and degree level. Room and board charges vary according to board plan. ***Part-time tuition:*** $1040 per credit hour. Part-time tuition and fees vary according to course load and degree level. ***Payment plan:*** Installment.

FRESHMAN FINANCIAL AID (Fall 2010, est.) 235 applied for aid; of those 92% were deemed to have need. 100% of freshmen with need received aid; of those 22% had need fully met. ***Average percent of need met:*** 89% (excluding resources awarded to replace EFC). ***Average financial aid package:*** $24,775 (excluding resources awarded to replace EFC). 13% of all full-time freshmen had no need and received non-need-based gift aid.

UNDERGRADUATE FINANCIAL AID (Fall 2010, est.) 774 applied for aid; of those 93% were deemed to have need. 100% of undergraduates with need received aid; of those 15% had need fully met. ***Average percent of need met:*** 87% (excluding resources awarded to replace EFC). ***Average financial aid package:*** $24,225 (excluding resources awarded to replace EFC). 17% of all full-time undergraduates had no need and received non-need-based gift aid.

GIFT AID (NEED-BASED) ***Total amount:*** $14,370,315 (15% federal, 9% state, 75% institutional, 1% external sources). ***Receiving aid:*** Freshmen: 79% (195); all full-time undergraduates: 75% (650). ***Average award:*** Freshmen: $22,123; Undergraduates: $20,940. ***Scholarships, grants, and awards:*** Federal Pell, FSEOG, state, private, college/university gift aid from institutional funds.

GIFT AID (NON-NEED-BASED) ***Total amount:*** $2,044,910 (16% state, 81% institutional, 3% external sources). ***Receiving aid:*** Freshmen: 8% (21). Undergraduates: 8% (67). ***Average award:*** Freshmen: $12,169. Undergraduates: $12,173. ***Scholarships, grants, and awards by category:*** *Academic interests/achievement:* 823 awards ($8,085,861 total): general academic interests/achievements, premedicine, religion/biblical studies. *Creative arts/performance:* 27 awards ($38,954 total): art/fine arts, journalism/publications, music, theater/drama. *Special characteristics:* 298 awards ($779,551 total): children of educators, children of faculty/staff, out-of-state students. ***Tuition waivers:*** Full or partial for employees or children of employees.

LOANS ***Student loans:*** $4,551,877 (84% need-based, 16% non-need-based). 58% of past graduating class borrowed through all loan programs. *Average indebtedness per student:* $23,049. ***Average need-based loan:*** Freshmen: $3380. Undergraduates: $4334. ***Parent loans:*** $2,911,020 (60% need-based, 40% non-need-based). ***Programs:*** Federal Direct (Subsidized and Unsubsidized Stafford, PLUS), Perkins.

WORK-STUDY ***Federal work-study:*** Total amount: $229,282; 231 jobs averaging $1071.

APPLYING FOR FINANCIAL AID ***Required financial aid forms:*** FAFSA, state aid form. ***Financial aid deadline (priority):*** 4/1. ***Notification date:*** Continuous beginning 3/1. Students must reply within 2 weeks of notification.

CONTACT Ms. Margaret L. Murphy, Director of Student Financial Planning, Emory & Henry College, PO Box 947, Emory, VA 24327-0010, 276-944-6115 or toll-free 800-848-5493. *Fax:* 276-944-6884. *E-mail:* mmurphy@ehc.edu.

EMORY UNIVERSITY

Atlanta, GA

Tuition & fees: $39,158 **Average undergraduate aid package: $34,853**

ABOUT THE INSTITUTION Independent Methodist, coed. 58 undergraduate majors. Both federal and institutional methodology are used as a basis for awarding need-based institutional aid.

UNDERGRADUATE EXPENSES for 2010–11 ***Comprehensive fee:*** $50,356 includes full-time tuition ($38,600), mandatory fees ($558), and room and board ($11,198). ***College room only:*** $6800. Full-time tuition and fees vary according to degree level and location. Room and board charges vary according to board plan, housing facility, location, and student level. ***Part-time tuition:*** $1608 per credit hour. ***Part-time fees:*** $24 per credit hour. ***Payment plan:*** Installment.

FRESHMAN FINANCIAL AID (Fall 2010, est.) 1,044 applied for aid; of those 85% were deemed to have need. 100% of freshmen with need received aid; of those 96% had need fully met. ***Average percent of need met:*** 100% (excluding resources awarded to replace EFC). ***Average financial aid package:*** $34,871 (excluding resources awarded to replace EFC). 7% of all full-time freshmen had no need and received non-need-based gift aid.

UNDERGRADUATE FINANCIAL AID (Fall 2010, est.) 3,680 applied for aid; of those 90% were deemed to have need. 100% of undergraduates with need received aid; of those 96% had need fully met. ***Average percent of need met:*** 100% (excluding resources awarded to replace EFC). ***Average financial aid package:*** $34,853 (excluding resources awarded to replace EFC). 7% of all full-time undergraduates had no need and received non-need-based gift aid.

GIFT AID (NEED-BASED) ***Total amount:*** $101,828,979 (8% federal, 4% state, 86% institutional, 2% external sources). ***Receiving aid:*** Freshmen: 45% (851); all full-time undergraduates: 45% (3,199). ***Average award:*** Freshmen: $32,425; Undergraduates: $31,710. ***Scholarships, grants, and awards:*** Federal Pell, FSEOG, private, college/university gift aid from institutional funds.

GIFT AID (NON-NEED-BASED) ***Total amount:*** $14,546,050 (15% state, 79% institutional, 6% external sources). ***Receiving aid:*** Freshmen: 5% (95). Undergraduates: 4% (263). ***Average award:*** Freshmen: $15,756. Undergraduates: $20,859. ***Scholarships, grants, and awards by category:*** *Academic interests/achievement:* general academic interests/achievements. *Creative arts/performance:* art/fine arts, music, theater/drama. *Special achievements/activities:* leadership. *Special characteristics:* local/state students, religious affiliation. ***Tuition waivers:*** Full or partial for employees or children of employees.

LOANS ***Student loans:*** $19,720,618 (45% need-based, 55% non-need-based). 43% of past graduating class borrowed through all loan programs. *Average indebtedness per student:* $26,311. ***Average need-based loan:*** Freshmen: $3219. Undergraduates: $4147. ***Parent loans:*** $7,111,035 (100% non-need-based). ***Programs:*** Federal Direct (Subsidized and Unsubsidized Stafford, PLUS), Perkins, Federal Nursing, college/university.

WORK-STUDY ***Federal work-study:*** Total amount: $5,103,985; jobs available. ***State or other work-study/employment:*** Total amount: $749,414 (69% need-based, 31% non-need-based). Part-time jobs available.

APPLYING FOR FINANCIAL AID ***Required financial aid forms:*** FAFSA, CSS Financial Aid PROFILE, noncustodial (divorced/separated) parent's statement. ***Financial aid deadline:*** 3/1 (priority: 2/15). ***Notification date:*** 4/1. Students must reply by 5/1.

CONTACT Dean Bentley, Director of Financial Aid, Emory University, 200 Dowman Drive, Atlanta, GA 30322-1960, 404-727-6039 or toll-free 800-727-6036. *Fax:* 404-727-6709. *E-mail:* finaid1@emory.edu.

EMPORIA STATE UNIVERSITY

Emporia, KS

Tuition & fees (KS res): $4636 **Average undergraduate aid package: $5297**

ABOUT THE INSTITUTION State-supported, coed. 36 undergraduate majors. Federal methodology is used as a basis for awarding need-based institutional aid.

UNDERGRADUATE EXPENSES for 2010–11 ***Tuition, state resident:*** full-time $3614; part-time $120 per credit hour. ***Tuition, nonresident:*** full-time $13,324; part-time $444 per credit hour. ***Required fees:*** full-time $1022; $62 per credit hour. Full-time tuition and fees vary according to course load, degree level, and location. Part-time tuition and fees vary according to course load, degree level, and location. ***College room and board:*** $6230; ***Room only:*** $3180. Room and board charges vary according to board plan and housing facility. ***Payment plans:*** Installment, deferred payment.

FRESHMAN FINANCIAL AID (Fall 2010, est.) 536 applied for aid; of those 75% were deemed to have need. 100% of freshmen with need received aid; of those 11% had need fully met. ***Average percent of need met:*** 69% (excluding resources awarded to replace EFC). ***Average financial aid package:*** $5444 (excluding resources awarded to replace EFC). 21% of all full-time freshmen had no need and received non-need-based gift aid.

UNDERGRADUATE FINANCIAL AID (Fall 2010, est.) 2,760 applied for aid; of those 82% were deemed to have need. 100% of undergraduates with need received aid; of those 11% had need fully met. ***Average percent of need met:*** 72% (excluding resources awarded to replace EFC). ***Average financial aid package:*** $5297 (excluding resources awarded to replace EFC). 14% of all full-time undergraduates had no need and received non-need-based gift aid.

GIFT AID (NEED-BASED) ***Total amount:*** $10,445,471 (73% federal, 7% state, 11% institutional, 9% external sources). ***Receiving aid:*** Freshmen: 61% (377); all full-time undergraduates: 56% (1,976). ***Average award:*** Freshmen: $5112; Undergraduates: $5344. ***Scholarships, grants, and awards:*** Federal Pell, FSEOG, state, private, college/university gift aid from institutional funds, Jones Foundation Grants.

GIFT AID (NON-NEED-BASED) ***Total amount:*** $2,066,340 (1% federal, 3% state, 35% institutional, 61% external sources). ***Receiving aid:*** Freshmen: 4% (24). Undergraduates: 2% (88). ***Average award:*** Freshmen: $1649. Undergraduates: $1351. ***Scholarships, grants, and awards by category:*** *Academic interests/achievement:* 1,687 awards ($1,580,634 total): biological sciences, business, communication, computer science, education, engineering/technologies, English, foreign languages, general academic interests/achievements, health fields, humanities, library science, mathematics, physical sciences, premedicine, social sciences. *Creative arts/performance:* 109 awards ($93,650 total): art/fine arts, creative writing, debating, music, theater/drama. *Special achievements/activities:* memberships. *Special characteristics:* 34 awards ($11,150 total): children and siblings of alumni, children of faculty/staff, children of union members/company employees, handicapped students, international students, members of minority groups, religious affiliation, veterans, veterans' children. ***Tuition waivers:*** Full or partial for employees or children of employees, senior citizens.

LOANS ***Student loans:*** $17,780,566 (70% need-based, 30% non-need-based). 73% of past graduating class borrowed through all loan programs. *Average indebtedness per student:* $23,498. ***Average need-based loan:*** Freshmen: $4096. Undergraduates: $5143. ***Parent loans:*** $4,588,719 (16% need-based, 84% non-need-based). ***Programs:*** Perkins, Alaska Loans, alternative loans.

WORK-STUDY ***Federal work-study:*** Total amount: $453,583; 125 jobs averaging $1922. ***State or other work-study/employment:*** Total amount: $24,625 (15% need-based, 85% non-need-based). 15 part-time jobs averaging $1642.

ATHLETIC AWARDS Total amount: $1,127,539 (45% need-based, 55% non-need-based).

APPLYING FOR FINANCIAL AID ***Required financial aid forms:*** FAFSA, state aid form. ***Financial aid deadline (priority):*** 3/15. ***Notification date:*** Continuous. Students must reply within 2 weeks of notification.

CONTACT Elaine Henrie, Director of Financial Aid, Emporia State University, 1200 Commercial Street, Emporia, KS 66801-5087, 620-341-5457 or toll-free 877-GOTOESU (in-state), 877-468-6378 (out-of-state). *Fax:* 620-341-6088. *E-mail:* ehenrie@emporia.edu.

ENDICOTT COLLEGE

Beverly, MA

Tuition & fees: $26,248 **Average undergraduate aid package: $17,981**

ABOUT THE INSTITUTION Independent, coed. 27 undergraduate majors. Federal methodology is used as a basis for awarding need-based institutional aid.

UNDERGRADUATE EXPENSES for 2010–11 ***Comprehensive fee:*** $38,636 includes full-time tuition ($25,848), mandatory fees ($400), and room and board ($12,388). ***College room only:*** $8578. Room and board charges vary according to board plan and housing facility. ***Part-time tuition:*** $793 per credit hour. ***Part-time fees:*** $150 per term. ***Payment plan:*** Installment.

FRESHMAN FINANCIAL AID (Fall 2010, est.) 578 applied for aid; of those 76% were deemed to have need. 100% of freshmen with need received aid; of those 9% had need fully met. ***Average percent of need met:*** 63% (excluding resources awarded to replace EFC). ***Average financial aid package:*** $18,786 (excluding resources awarded to replace EFC). 16% of all full-time freshmen had no need and received non-need-based gift aid.

UNDERGRADUATE FINANCIAL AID (Fall 2010, est.) 1,852 applied for aid; of those 73% were deemed to have need. 100% of undergraduates with need received aid; of those 12% had need fully met. ***Average percent of need met:*** 62% (excluding resources awarded to replace EFC). ***Average financial aid***

package: $17,981 (excluding resources awarded to replace EFC). 18% of all full-time undergraduates had no need and received non-need-based gift aid.

GIFT AID (NEED-BASED) ***Total amount:*** $15,055,552 (13% federal, 2% state, 85% institutional). ***Receiving aid:*** Freshmen: 59% (361); all full-time undergraduates: 49% (1,066). ***Average award:*** Freshmen: $10,687; Undergraduates: $9901. ***Scholarships, grants, and awards:*** Federal Pell, FSEOG, state, private, college/university gift aid from institutional funds.

GIFT AID (NON-NEED-BASED) ***Total amount:*** $3,406,904 (87% institutional, 13% external sources). ***Receiving aid:*** Freshmen: 47% (288). Undergraduates: 36% (773). ***Average award:*** Freshmen: $7720. Undergraduates: $7512. ***Scholarships, grants, and awards by category:*** *Academic interests/achievement:* 976 awards ($6,887,157 total): business, education, general academic interests/achievements, health fields. *Creative arts/performance:* 1 award ($1000 total): art/fine arts, music, performing arts. *Special achievements/activities:* 7 awards ($10,250 total): community service, general special achievements/activities, leadership, religious involvement. *Special characteristics:* 126 awards ($550,333 total): children and siblings of alumni, children of educators, general special characteristics, international students, local/state students, religious affiliation. ***Tuition waivers:*** Full or partial for employees or children of employees.

LOANS ***Student loans:*** $15,862,541 (36% need-based, 64% non-need-based). 78% of past graduating class borrowed through all loan programs. *Average indebtedness per student:* $39,168. ***Average need-based loan:*** Freshmen: $3860. Undergraduates: $4541. ***Parent loans:*** $4,686,269 (100% non-need-based). ***Programs:*** Federal Direct (Subsidized and Unsubsidized Stafford, PLUS), Perkins.

WORK-STUDY ***Federal work-study:*** Total amount: $891,775; 461 jobs averaging $2000.

APPLYING FOR FINANCIAL AID ***Required financial aid forms:*** FAFSA, institution's own form. ***Financial aid deadline (priority):*** 3/15. ***Notification date:*** Continuous beginning 3/15. Students must reply within 2 weeks of notification.

CONTACT Ms. Marcia Toomey, Director of Financial Aid, Endicott College, 376 Hale Street, Beverly, MA 01915-2096, 978-232-2060 or toll-free 800-325-1114 (out-of-state). *Fax:* 978-232-2085. *E-mail:* mtoomey@endicott.edu.

EPIC BIBLE COLLEGE

Sacramento, CA

CONTACT Financial Aid Office, Epic Bible College, 5225 Hillsdale Boulevard, Sacramento, CA 95842, 916-348-4689.

ERSKINE COLLEGE

Due West, SC

Tuition & fees: $26,475 **Average undergraduate aid package: $21,093**

ABOUT THE INSTITUTION Independent religious, coed. 23 undergraduate majors. Federal methodology is used as a basis for awarding need-based institutional aid.

UNDERGRADUATE EXPENSES for 2010–11 ***Comprehensive fee:*** $35,250 includes full-time tuition ($24,750), mandatory fees ($1725), and room and board ($8775). ***Part-time tuition:*** $917 per semester hour. ***Payment plan:*** Installment.

FRESHMAN FINANCIAL AID (Fall 2009) 162 applied for aid; of those 80% were deemed to have need. 100% of freshmen with need received aid; of those 47% had need fully met. ***Average percent of need met:*** 86% (excluding resources awarded to replace EFC). ***Average financial aid package:*** $22,681 (excluding resources awarded to replace EFC). 22% of all full-time freshmen had no need and received non-need-based gift aid.

UNDERGRADUATE FINANCIAL AID (Fall 2009) 498 applied for aid; of those 80% were deemed to have need. 100% of undergraduates with need received aid; of those 39% had need fully met. ***Average percent of need met:*** 86% (excluding resources awarded to replace EFC). ***Average financial aid package:*** $21,093 (excluding resources awarded to replace EFC). 21% of all full-time undergraduates had no need and received non-need-based gift aid.

GIFT AID (NEED-BASED) ***Total amount:*** $6,769,016 (13% federal, 14% state, 73% institutional). ***Receiving aid:*** Freshmen: 69% (130); all full-time undergraduates: 69% (400). ***Average award:*** Freshmen: $16,524; Undergraduates: $16,222. ***Scholarships, grants, and awards:*** Federal Pell, FSEOG, state, private, college/university gift aid from institutional funds, TEACH Grants.

GIFT AID (NON-NEED-BASED) ***Total amount:*** $4,052,648 (42% state, 53% institutional, 5% external sources). ***Receiving aid:*** Freshmen: 69% (130). Undergraduates: 69% (400). ***Average award:*** Freshmen: $10,621. Undergraduates: $10,725. ***Scholarships, grants, and awards by category:*** *Academic interests/achievement:* biological sciences, business, education, English, foreign languages, general academic interests/achievements, mathematics, premedicine, religion/biblical studies, social sciences. *Creative arts/performance:* music, theater/drama. *Special achievements/activities:* general special achievements/activities, leadership, memberships. *Special characteristics:* children and siblings of alumni, children of faculty/staff, children with a deceased or disabled parent, ethnic background, first-generation college students, members of minority groups, out-of-state students, relatives of clergy, religious affiliation, siblings of current students. ***Tuition waivers:*** Full or partial for children of alumni, employees or children of employees.

LOANS ***Student loans:*** $2,463,627 (47% need-based, 53% non-need-based). 72% of past graduating class borrowed through all loan programs. *Average indebtedness per student:* $24,450. ***Average need-based loan:*** Freshmen: $3768. Undergraduates: $4750. ***Parent loans:*** $343,375 (100% non-need-based). ***Programs:*** Federal Direct (Subsidized and Unsubsidized Stafford, PLUS), Perkins, state, college/university, alternative loans.

WORK-STUDY ***Federal work-study:*** Total amount: $101,400; jobs available. ***State or other work-study/employment:*** Total amount: $30,500 (100% non-need-based). Part-time jobs available.

ATHLETIC AWARDS Total amount: $1,258,807 (100% non-need-based).

APPLYING FOR FINANCIAL AID ***Required financial aid forms:*** FAFSA, institution's own form, state aid form. ***Financial aid deadline (priority):*** 4/1. ***Notification date:*** Continuous beginning 11/1. Students must reply within 2 weeks of notification.

CONTACT Mrs. Becky Pressley, Director of Financial Aid, Erskine College, PO Box 337, Due West, SC 29639, 864-379-8832 or toll-free 800-241-8721. *Fax:* 864-379-2172. *E-mail:* pressley@erskine.edu.

ESCUELA DE ARTES PLASTICAS DE PUERTO RICO

San Juan, PR

CONTACT Mr. Alfred Diaz Melendez, Financial Aid Administrator, Escuela de Artes Plasticas de Puerto Rico, PO Box 9021112, San Juan, PR 00902-1112, 787-725-8120 Ext. 317. *Fax:* 787-725-3798. *E-mail:* adiaz@eap.edu.

EUGENE LANG COLLEGE THE NEW SCHOOL FOR LIBERAL ARTS

New York, NY

Tuition & fees: $36,090 **Average undergraduate aid package: $34,210**

ABOUT THE INSTITUTION Independent, coed. 23 undergraduate majors. Federal methodology is used as a basis for awarding need-based institutional aid.

UNDERGRADUATE EXPENSES for 2010–11 ***Comprehensive fee:*** $51,350 includes full-time tuition ($35,330), mandatory fees ($760), and room and board ($15,260). ***College room only:*** $12,260. Room and board charges vary according to board plan and housing facility. ***Part-time tuition:*** $1200 per credit. Part-time tuition and fees vary according to course load. ***Payment plan:*** Installment.

FRESHMAN FINANCIAL AID (Fall 2010, est.) 223 applied for aid; of those 93% were deemed to have need. 98% of freshmen with need received aid; of those 14% had need fully met. ***Average percent of need met:*** 78% (excluding resources awarded to replace EFC). ***Average financial aid package:*** $33,675 (excluding resources awarded to replace EFC). 2% of all full-time freshmen had no need and received non-need-based gift aid.

UNDERGRADUATE FINANCIAL AID (Fall 2010, est.) 1,061 applied for aid; of those 79% were deemed to have need. 96% of undergraduates with need received aid; of those 15% had need fully met. ***Average percent of need met:*** 80% (excluding resources awarded to replace EFC). ***Average financial aid package:*** $34,210 (excluding resources awarded to replace EFC). 3% of all full-time undergraduates had no need and received non-need-based gift aid.

GIFT AID (NEED-BASED) ***Total amount:*** $20,283,505 (11% federal, 3% state, 84% institutional, 2% external sources). ***Receiving aid:*** Freshmen: 66% (197); all full-time undergraduates: 55% (787). ***Average award:*** Freshmen: $22,350; Undergraduates: $22,555. ***Scholarships, grants, and awards:*** Federal Pell, FSEOG, state, private, college/university gift aid from institutional funds.

GIFT AID (NON-NEED-BASED) ***Total amount:*** $351,745 (70% institutional, 30% external sources). ***Receiving aid:*** Freshmen: 5% (15). Undergraduates: 1% (14). ***Average award:*** Freshmen: $3977. Undergraduates: $2925. ***Scholarships, grants, and awards by category:*** *Academic interests/achievement:* general academic interests/achievements. *Special achievements/activities:* general special achievements/activities, leadership. ***Tuition waivers:*** Full or partial for employees or children of employees.

LOANS ***Student loans:*** $7,814,668 (91% need-based, 9% non-need-based). 67% of past graduating class borrowed through all loan programs. *Average indebtedness per student:* $30,830. ***Average need-based loan:*** Freshmen: $8300. Undergraduates: $8390. ***Parent loans:*** $4,012,486 (86% need-based, 14% non-need-based). ***Programs:*** Federal Direct (Subsidized and Unsubsidized Stafford, PLUS), Perkins.

WORK-STUDY ***Federal work-study:*** Total amount: $667,880; jobs available. ***State or other work-study/employment:*** Part-time jobs available.

APPLYING FOR FINANCIAL AID ***Required financial aid form:*** FAFSA. ***Financial aid deadline:*** Continuous. ***Notification date:*** 3/1. Students must reply within 4 weeks of notification.

CONTACT Office of Student Financial Services, Eugene Lang College The New School for Liberal Arts, 65 West 11th Street, New York, NY 10011, 212-229-5665 or toll-free 877-528-3321. *E-mail:* sfs@newschool.edu.

EUREKA COLLEGE

Eureka, IL

Tuition & fees: $18,080 **Average undergraduate aid package: $12,682**

ABOUT THE INSTITUTION Independent religious, coed. ***Awards:*** bachelor's degrees. 35 undergraduate majors. ***Total enrollment:*** 672. Undergraduates: 672. Both federal and institutional methodology are used as a basis for awarding need-based institutional aid.

UNDERGRADUATE EXPENSES for 2010–11 ***Comprehensive fee:*** $25,580 includes full-time tuition ($17,680), mandatory fees ($400), and room and board ($7500). ***College room only:*** $3615. Full-time tuition and fees vary according to course load and program. Room and board charges vary according to board plan and housing facility. ***Part-time tuition:*** $425 per credit hour. Part-time tuition and fees vary according to course load and program. ***Payment plan:*** Installment.

FRESHMAN FINANCIAL AID (Fall 2010, est.) 172 applied for aid; of those 93% were deemed to have need. 100% of freshmen with need received aid; of those 3% had need fully met. ***Average percent of need met:*** 67% (excluding resources awarded to replace EFC). ***Average financial aid package:*** $14,997 (excluding resources awarded to replace EFC). 8% of all full-time freshmen had no need and received non-need-based gift aid.

UNDERGRADUATE FINANCIAL AID (Fall 2010, est.) 701 applied for aid; of those 89% were deemed to have need. 100% of undergraduates with need received aid; of those 4% had need fully met. ***Average percent of need met:*** 65% (excluding resources awarded to replace EFC). ***Average financial aid package:*** $12,682 (excluding resources awarded to replace EFC). 20% of all full-time undergraduates had no need and received non-need-based gift aid.

GIFT AID (NEED-BASED) ***Total amount:*** $4,813,999 (29% federal, 32% state, 38% institutional, 1% external sources). ***Receiving aid:*** Freshmen: 92% (160); all full-time undergraduates: 80% (626). ***Average award:*** Freshmen: $10,993; Undergraduates: $9144. ***Scholarships, grants, and awards:*** Federal Pell, FSEOG, state, private, college/university gift aid from institutional funds.

GIFT AID (NON-NEED-BASED) ***Total amount:*** $999,934 (100% institutional). ***Average award:*** Freshmen: $4143. Undergraduates: $3548. ***Scholarships, grants, and awards by category:*** *Academic interests/achievement:* 643 awards ($2,848,384 total): general academic interests/achievements. *Creative arts/performance:* 107 awards ($96,047 total): art/fine arts, music, performing arts, theater/drama. *Special achievements/activities:* 22 awards ($325,833 total): leadership. *Special characteristics:* 112 awards ($364,346 total): children and siblings of alumni, children of faculty/staff, religious affiliation, siblings of current students. ***Tuition waivers:*** Full or partial for children of alumni, employees or children of employees, adult students, senior citizens.

LOANS ***Student loans:*** $4,383,991 (51% need-based, 49% non-need-based). 92% of past graduating class borrowed through all loan programs. *Average indebtedness per student:* $22,720. ***Average need-based loan:*** Freshmen: $3147. Undergraduates: $4013. ***Parent loans:*** $1,218,905 (100% non-need-based). ***Programs:*** Federal Direct (Subsidized and Unsubsidized Stafford, PLUS), Perkins, college/university, alternative loans.

WORK-STUDY ***Federal work-study:*** Total amount: $73,907; 91 jobs averaging $760. ***State or other work-study/employment:*** Total amount: $202,018 (100% non-need-based). 140 part-time jobs averaging $1120.

APPLYING FOR FINANCIAL AID ***Required financial aid form:*** FAFSA. ***Financial aid deadline (priority):*** 3/1. ***Notification date:*** 5/1. Students must reply within 2 weeks of notification.

CONTACT Ms. Ellen Rigsby, Assistant Dean and Director of Financial Aid, Eureka College, 300 East College Avenue, Eureka, IL 61530, 309-467-6311 or toll-free 888-4-EUREKA. *Fax:* 309-467-6897. *E-mail:* eraid@eureka.edu.

EVANGEL UNIVERSITY

Springfield, MO

Tuition & fees: $16,990 **Average undergraduate aid package: $9851**

ABOUT THE INSTITUTION Independent religious, coed. 48 undergraduate majors. Federal methodology is used as a basis for awarding need-based institutional aid.

UNDERGRADUATE EXPENSES for 2010–11 ***Comprehensive fee:*** $22,990 includes full-time tuition ($15,950), mandatory fees ($1040), and room and board ($6000). ***College room only:*** $3100. Full-time tuition and fees vary according to course load. Room and board charges vary according to board plan. ***Part-time tuition:*** $622 per credit hour. ***Payment plan:*** Installment.

FRESHMAN FINANCIAL AID (Fall 2009) 449 applied for aid; of those 89% were deemed to have need. 100% of freshmen with need received aid; of those 10% had need fully met. ***Average percent of need met:*** 59% (excluding resources awarded to replace EFC). ***Average financial aid package:*** $12,677 (excluding resources awarded to replace EFC). 8% of all full-time freshmen had no need and received non-need-based gift aid.

UNDERGRADUATE FINANCIAL AID (Fall 2009) 1,572 applied for aid; of those 89% were deemed to have need. 100% of undergraduates with need received aid; of those 9% had need fully met. ***Average percent of need met:*** 47% (excluding resources awarded to replace EFC). ***Average financial aid package:*** $9851 (excluding resources awarded to replace EFC). 9% of all full-time undergraduates had no need and received non-need-based gift aid.

GIFT AID (NEED-BASED) ***Total amount:*** $7,126,303 (46% federal, 1% state, 43% institutional, 10% external sources). ***Receiving aid:*** Freshmen: 83% (387); all full-time undergraduates: 73% (1,269). ***Average award:*** Freshmen: $8902; Undergraduates: $6201. ***Scholarships, grants, and awards:*** Federal Pell, FSEOG, state, private, college/university gift aid from institutional funds.

GIFT AID (NON-NEED-BASED) ***Total amount:*** $888,933 (1% state, 72% institutional, 27% external sources). ***Receiving aid:*** Freshmen: 7% (33). Undergraduates: 5% (89). ***Average award:*** Freshmen: $4615. Undergraduates: $2549. ***Scholarships, grants, and awards by category:*** *Academic interests/achievement:* 908 awards ($2,413,840 total): business, communication, computer science, education, engineering/technologies, English, foreign languages, general academic interests/achievements, humanities, mathematics, physical sciences, religion/biblical studies, social sciences. *Creative arts/performance:* 168 awards ($346,046 total): art/fine arts, debating, music, theater/drama. *Special achievements/activities:* 279 awards ($242,602 total): cheerleading/drum major, general special achievements/activities, leadership, religious involvement. *Special characteristics:* 464 awards ($2,285,280 total): adult students, children and siblings of alumni, children of educators, children of faculty/staff, general special characteristics, relatives of clergy, religious affiliation. ***Tuition waivers:*** Full or partial for employees or children of employees.

LOANS ***Student loans:*** $14,165,670 (80% need-based, 20% non-need-based). 95% of past graduating class borrowed through all loan programs. *Average indebtedness per student:* $30,449. ***Average need-based loan:*** Freshmen: $3451. Undergraduates: $4131. ***Parent loans:*** $2,053,149 (55% need-based, 45% non-need-based). ***Programs:*** Federal Direct (Subsidized and Unsubsidized Stafford, PLUS), Perkins, college/university.

WORK-STUDY ***Federal work-study:*** Total amount: $1,718,358; 1,151 jobs averaging $1493. ***State or other work-study/employment:*** Total amount: $193,334 (100% need-based). 124 part-time jobs averaging $1564.

ATHLETIC AWARDS Total amount: $1,945,992 (76% need-based, 24% non-need-based).

APPLYING FOR FINANCIAL AID ***Required financial aid form:*** FAFSA. ***Financial aid deadline:*** Continuous. ***Notification date:*** Continuous beginning 3/1. Students must reply within 4 weeks of notification.

CONTACT Mrs. Dorynda Carpenter, Director of Student Financial Services, Evangel University, 1111 North Glenstone Avenue, Springfield, MO 65802-2191, 417-865-2811 Ext. 7302 or toll-free 800-382-6435 (in-state). *Fax:* 417-575-5478. *E-mail:* carpenterd@evangel.edu.

EVEREST UNIVERSITY
Clearwater, FL

CONTACT Mr. Will Scott, Director of Student Finance, Everest University, 1199 East Bay Drive, Largo, FL 33770, 727-725-2688 Ext. 166 or toll-free 800-353-FMUS. *Fax:* 727-373-4408. *E-mail:* wscott@cci.edu.

EVEREST UNIVERSITY
Jacksonville, FL

CONTACT Financial Aid Office, Everest University, 8226 Phillips Highway, Jacksonville, FL 32256, 904-731-4949 or toll-free 888-741-4270.

EVEREST UNIVERSITY
Lakeland, FL

CONTACT Brian Jones, Senior Finance Officer, Everest University, Office of Financial Aid, 995 East Memorial Boulevard, Lakeland, FL 33801, 863-686-1444 Ext. 118 or toll-free 877-225-0014 (in-state). *Fax:* 863-682-1077.

EVEREST UNIVERSITY
Melbourne, FL

ABOUT THE INSTITUTION Proprietary, coed. ***Awards:*** associate, bachelor's, and master's degrees. 10 undergraduate majors. ***Total enrollment:*** 291. Undergraduates: 287.

GIFT AID (NEED-BASED) ***Scholarships, grants, and awards:*** Federal Pell, FSEOG, state, private, college/university gift aid from institutional funds.

GIFT AID (NON-NEED-BASED) ***Scholarships, grants, and awards by category:*** *Academic interests/achievement:* business, computer science, health fields. *Creative arts/performance:* cinema/film/broadcasting. *Special characteristics:* children of faculty/staff, children of union members/company employees.

LOANS ***Programs:*** Federal Direct (Subsidized and Unsubsidized Stafford, PLUS), college/university.

WORK-STUDY Federal work-study jobs available.

APPLYING FOR FINANCIAL AID ***Required financial aid form:*** FAFSA.

CONTACT Ida C. Liska, Director of Student Finance, Everest University, 2401 North Harbor City Boulevard, Melbourne, FL 32935-6657, 321-253-2929 Ext. 142. *E-mail:* iliska@cci.edu.

EVEREST UNIVERSITY
Orlando, FL

CONTACT Ms. Linda Kaisrlik, Director of Student Finance, Everest University, 5421 Diplomat Circle, Orlando, FL 32810-5674, 407-628-5870 Ext. 118 or toll-free 800-628-5870.

EVEREST UNIVERSITY
Orlando, FL

CONTACT Sherri Williams, Director of Financial Aid, Everest University, 2411 Sand Lake Road, Orlando, FL 32809, 407-851-2525 or toll-free 888-471-4270 (out-of-state).

EVEREST UNIVERSITY
Pompano Beach, FL

CONTACT Sharon Scheible, Director of Student Financial Aid, Everest University, 1040 Bayview Drive, Fort Lauderdale, FL 33304-2522, 954-568-1600 Ext. 52. *Fax:* 954-564-5283. *E-mail:* scheible@cci.edu.

EVEREST UNIVERSITY
Tampa, FL

CONTACT Mr. Rod Kirkwood, Financial Aid Director, Everest University, 3319 West Hillsborough Avenue, Tampa, FL 33614, 813-879-6000 Ext. 145. *Fax:* 813-871-2483. *E-mail:* rkirkwoo@cci.edu.

EVEREST UNIVERSITY
Tampa, FL

CONTACT Ms. Ginger Waymire, Director of Financial Aid, Everest University, 3924 Coconut Palm Drive, Tampa, FL 33619, 813-621-0041 Ext. 118 or toll-free 877-338-0068. *Fax:* 813-621-6283. *E-mail:* gwaymire@cci.edu.

EVERGLADES UNIVERSITY
Altamonte Springs, FL

CONTACT Financial Aid Office, Everglades University, 887 East Altamonte Drive, Altamonte Springs, FL 32701, 407-277-0311 or toll-free 866-289-1078 (out-of-state).

EVERGLADES UNIVERSITY
Boca Raton, FL

CONTACT Seeta Singh Moonilal, Financial Aid Director, Everglades University, 5002 T Rex Avenue, Suite 100, Boca Raton, FL 33431, 561-912-1211 or toll-free 888-772-6077 (out-of-state). *Fax:* 561-912-1191. *E-mail:* seetasm@evergladesuniversity.edu.

EVERGLADES UNIVERSITY
Sarasota, FL

CONTACT Financial Aid Office, Everglades University, 6001 Lake Osprey Drive #110, Sarasota, FL 34240, 941-907-2262 or toll-free 866-907-2262.

THE EVERGREEN STATE COLLEGE
Olympia, WA

Tuition & fees (WA res): $6679 **Average undergraduate aid package: $11,459**

ABOUT THE INSTITUTION State-supported, coed. 41 undergraduate majors. Federal methodology is used as a basis for awarding need-based institutional aid.

UNDERGRADUATE EXPENSES for 2010–11 ***Tuition, state resident:*** full-time $6108; part-time $203.60 per credit hour. ***Tuition, nonresident:*** full-time $17,235; part-time $574.50 per credit hour. ***Required fees:*** full-time $571; $7.85 per credit hour or $69 per term. Full-time tuition and fees vary according to course load and location. Part-time tuition and fees vary according to course load and location. ***College room and board:*** $8460; ***Room only:*** $5730. Room and board charges vary according to board plan, housing facility, location, and student level. ***Payment plan:*** Installment.

FRESHMAN FINANCIAL AID (Fall 2010, est.) 473 applied for aid; of those 79% were deemed to have need. 97% of freshmen with need received aid; of those 19% had need fully met. ***Average percent of need met:*** 61% (excluding resources awarded to replace EFC). ***Average financial aid package:*** $9749 (excluding resources awarded to replace EFC). 17% of all full-time freshmen had no need and received non-need-based gift aid.

UNDERGRADUATE FINANCIAL AID (Fall 2010, est.) 2,936 applied for aid; of those 88% were deemed to have need. 97% of undergraduates with need received aid; of those 18% had need fully met. ***Average percent of need met:*** 67% (excluding resources awarded to replace EFC). ***Average financial aid package:*** $11,459 (excluding resources awarded to replace EFC). 7% of all full-time undergraduates had no need and received non-need-based gift aid.

GIFT AID (NEED-BASED) ***Total amount:*** $15,745,379 (53% federal, 38% state, 8% institutional, 1% external sources). ***Receiving aid:*** Freshmen: 54% (328); all full-time undergraduates: 56% (2,260). ***Average award:*** Freshmen: $7686; Undergraduates: $8596. ***Scholarships, grants, and awards:*** Federal Pell, FSEOG, state, private, college/university gift aid from institutional funds.

GIFT AID (NON-NEED-BASED) ***Total amount:*** $1,748,045 (1% state, 15% institutional, 84% external sources). ***Receiving aid:*** Freshmen: 37% (225). Undergraduates: 12% (481). ***Average award:*** Freshmen: $2373. Undergraduates: $2460. ***Scholarships, grants, and awards by category:*** *Academic interests/achievement:* general academic interests/achievements. *Creative arts/performance:* applied art and design, art/fine arts, creative writing. *Special achievements/activities:* community service, general special achievements/activities. *Special characteristics:* adult students, first-generation college students, members of minority groups, veterans, veterans' children. ***Tuition waivers:*** Full or partial for employees or children of employees, senior citizens.

LOANS ***Student loans:*** $13,509,694 (59% need-based, 41% non-need-based). 49% of past graduating class borrowed through all loan programs. *Average indebtedness per student:* $16,700. ***Average need-based loan:*** Freshmen: $3304. Undergraduates: $4298. ***Parent loans:*** $4,013,983 (72% need-based, 28% non-need-based). ***Programs:*** Federal Direct (Subsidized and Unsubsidized Stafford, PLUS), Perkins, college/university.

WORK-STUDY ***Federal work-study:*** Total amount: $327,578; 125 jobs averaging $3357. ***State or other work-study/employment:*** Total amount: $735,321 (100% need-based). 263 part-time jobs averaging $3300.

ATHLETIC AWARDS Total amount: $119,519 (100% non-need-based).

APPLYING FOR FINANCIAL AID ***Required financial aid form:*** FAFSA. ***Financial aid deadline (priority):*** 3/15. ***Notification date:*** Continuous beginning 4/1. Students must reply within 6 weeks of notification.

CONTACT Financial Aid Office, The Evergreen State College, 2700 Evergreen Parkway NW, Olympia, WA 98505, 360-867-6205. *Fax:* 360-866-6576. *E-mail:* financialaid@evergreen.edu.

EXCELSIOR COLLEGE

Albany, NY

Tuition & fees: N/R **Average undergraduate aid package: N/A**

ABOUT THE INSTITUTION Independent, coed. 40 undergraduate majors. Federal methodology is used as a basis for awarding need-based institutional aid.

UNDERGRADUATE EXPENSES for 2010–11 ***Tuition:*** part-time $335 per credit hour. ***Required fees:*** $440 per year. ***Payment plan:*** Installment.

GIFT AID (NEED-BASED) ***Total amount:*** $12,208,805 (92% federal, 4% state, 4% institutional). ***Scholarships, grants, and awards:*** Federal Pell, FSEOG, state, private, college/university gift aid from institutional funds.

GIFT AID (NON-NEED-BASED) ***Tuition waivers:*** Full or partial for employees or children of employees.

LOANS ***Student loans:*** $7,869,368 (100% need-based). ***Programs:*** Federal Direct (Subsidized and Unsubsidized Stafford, PLUS), Federal Nursing, college/university, private loans.

CONTACT Donna L. Cooper, Director of Financial Aid, Excelsior College, 7 Columbia Circle, Albany, NY 12203-5159, 518-464-8500 or toll-free 888-647-2388. *Fax:* 518-464-8777.

EX'PRESSION COLLEGE FOR DIGITAL ARTS

Emeryville, CA

CONTACT Financial Aid Office, Ex'pression College for Digital Arts, 6601 Shellmound Street, Emeryville, CA 94608, 510-654-2934 or toll-free 877-833-8800.

FAIRFIELD UNIVERSITY

Fairfield, CT

Tuition & fees: $39,040 **Average undergraduate aid package: $28,923**

ABOUT THE INSTITUTION Independent Roman Catholic (Jesuit), coed. 45 undergraduate majors. Both federal and institutional methodology are used as a basis for awarding need-based institutional aid.

UNDERGRADUATE EXPENSES for 2010–11 ***One-time required fee:*** $60. ***Comprehensive fee:*** $50,780 includes full-time tuition ($38,450), mandatory fees ($590), and room and board ($11,740). ***College room only:*** $7010. Room and board charges vary according to board plan and housing facility. ***Part-time tuition:*** $525 per credit hour. ***Part-time fees:*** $25 per term. Part-time tuition and fees vary according to course load. ***Payment plan:*** Installment.

FRESHMAN FINANCIAL AID (Fall 2010, est.) 662 applied for aid; of those 88% were deemed to have need. 98% of freshmen with need received aid; of those 25% had need fully met. ***Average percent of need met:*** 88% (excluding resources awarded to replace EFC). ***Average financial aid package:*** $29,154 (excluding resources awarded to replace EFC). 11% of all full-time freshmen had no need and received non-need-based gift aid.

UNDERGRADUATE FINANCIAL AID (Fall 2010, est.) 2,179 applied for aid; of those 88% were deemed to have need. 98% of undergraduates with need received aid; of those 21% had need fully met. ***Average percent of need met:*** 85% (excluding resources awarded to replace EFC). ***Average financial aid package:*** $28,923 (excluding resources awarded to replace EFC). 9% of all full-time undergraduates had no need and received non-need-based gift aid.

GIFT AID (NEED-BASED) ***Total amount:*** $37,476,375 (9% federal, 6% state, 85% institutional). ***Receiving aid:*** Freshmen: 50% (465); all full-time undergraduates: 49% (1,632). ***Average award:*** Freshmen: $22,916; Undergraduates: $22,147. ***Scholarships, grants, and awards:*** Federal Pell, FSEOG, state, private, college/university gift aid from institutional funds, United Negro College Fund, Federal Nursing, Academic Competitiveness Grants, National SMART Grants, TEACH Grants.

GIFT AID (NON-NEED-BASED) ***Total amount:*** $9,753,288 (91% institutional, 9% external sources). ***Receiving aid:*** Freshmen: 29% (263). Undergraduates: 20% (647). ***Average award:*** Freshmen: $18,700. Undergraduates: $19,733. ***Scholarships, grants, and awards by category:*** *Academic interests/achievement:* 614 awards ($8,424,785 total): general academic interests/achievements. *Creative arts/performance:* 15 awards ($22,100 total): general creative arts/performance. *Special achievements/activities:* 18 awards ($113,730 total): general special achievements/activities. *Special characteristics:* 60 awards ($2,032,900 total): children and siblings of alumni, children of faculty/staff, ethnic background, first-generation college students, parents of current students, veterans. ***Tuition waivers:*** Full or partial for employees or children of employees.

LOANS ***Student loans:*** $23,505,549 (45% need-based, 55% non-need-based). 65% of past graduating class borrowed through all loan programs. *Average indebtedness per student:* $37,015. ***Average need-based loan:*** Freshmen: $3892. Undergraduates: $4600. ***Parent loans:*** $6,770,356 (100% non-need-based). ***Programs:*** Federal Direct (Subsidized and Unsubsidized Stafford, PLUS), Perkins, Federal Nursing, alternative loans.

WORK-STUDY ***Federal work-study:*** Total amount: $1,504,688; 598 jobs averaging $1251.

ATHLETIC AWARDS Total amount: $5,391,099 (100% non-need-based).

APPLYING FOR FINANCIAL AID ***Required financial aid forms:*** FAFSA, CSS Financial Aid PROFILE, noncustodial (divorced/separated) parent's statement, business/farm supplement. ***Financial aid deadline:*** 2/15. ***Notification date:*** 4/1. Students must reply by 5/1.

CONTACT Mr. Erin Chiaro, Director of Financial Aid, Fairfield University, 1073 North Benson Road, Fairfield, CT 06824-5195, 203-254-4125. *Fax:* 203-254-4008. *E-mail:* echiaro@fairfield.edu.

FAIRLEIGH DICKINSON UNIVERSITY, COLLEGE AT FLORHAM

Madison, NJ

CONTACT Financial Aid Office, Fairleigh Dickinson University, College at Florham, 285 Madison Avenue, Madison, NJ 07940-1099, 973-443-8700 or toll-free 800-338-8803.

FAIRLEIGH DICKINSON UNIVERSITY, METROPOLITAN CAMPUS

Teaneck, NJ

CONTACT Financial Aid Office, Fairleigh Dickinson University, Metropolitan Campus, 100 River Road, Teaneck, NJ 07666-1914, 201-692-2363 or toll-free 800-338-8803.

FAIRMONT STATE UNIVERSITY

Fairmont, WV

ABOUT THE INSTITUTION State-supported, coed. 42 undergraduate majors.

GIFT AID (NEED-BASED) ***Scholarships, grants, and awards:*** Federal Pell, FSEOG, state, private, college/university gift aid from institutional funds, Academic Competitiveness Grants, National SMART Grants.

LOANS ***Programs:*** Federal Direct (Subsidized and Unsubsidized Stafford, PLUS), Perkins.

WORK-STUDY ***Federal work-study:*** Total amount: $295,356; jobs available. ***State or other work-study/employment:*** Part-time jobs available.

APPLYING FOR FINANCIAL AID ***Required financial aid form:*** FAFSA.

CONTACT Cynthia K. Hudok, Director of Financial Aid and Scholarships, Fairmont State University, 1201 Locust Avenue, Fairmont, WV 26554, 304-367-4213 or toll-free 800-641-5678. *Fax:* 304-367-4584. *E-mail:* financialaid@fairmontstate.edu.

FAITH BAPTIST BIBLE COLLEGE AND THEOLOGICAL SEMINARY

Ankeny, IA

CONTACT Mr. Breck Appell, Director of Financial Assistance, Faith Baptist Bible College and Theological Seminary, 1900 Northwest 4th Street, Ankeny, IA 50021-2152, 515-964-0601 or toll-free 888-FAITH 4U. *Fax:* 515-964-1638.

FAITH THEOLOGICAL SEMINARY

Baltimore, MD

CONTACT Financial Aid Office, Faith Theological Seminary, 529 Walker Avenue, Baltimore, MD 21212, 410-323-6211.

FARMINGDALE STATE COLLEGE

Farmingdale, NY

CONTACT Dionne Walker-Belgrave, Assistant Director of Financial Aid, Farmingdale State College, 2350 Broadhollow Road, Route 110, Farmingdale, NY 11735, 631-420-2328 or toll-free 877-4-FARMINGDALE. *Fax:* 631-420-3662.

FASHION INSTITUTE OF TECHNOLOGY

New York, NY

Tuition & fees (NY res): $5668 **Average undergraduate aid package: $11,305**

ABOUT THE INSTITUTION State and locally supported, coed, primarily women. 20 undergraduate majors. Federal methodology is used as a basis for awarding need-based institutional aid.

UNDERGRADUATE EXPENSES for 2010–11 ***Tuition, state resident:*** full-time $5168; part-time $215 per credit hour. ***Tuition, nonresident:*** full-time $13,550; part-time $564 per credit hour. ***Required fees:*** full-time $500. Full-time tuition and fees vary according to degree level. Part-time tuition and fees vary according to degree level. ***College room and board:*** $11,700. Room and board charges vary according to board plan and housing facility. ***Payment plan:*** Installment.

FRESHMAN FINANCIAL AID (Fall 2009) 828 applied for aid; of those 68% were deemed to have need. 99% of freshmen with need received aid; of those 18% had need fully met. ***Average percent of need met:*** 68% (excluding resources awarded to replace EFC). ***Average financial aid package:*** $10,169 (excluding resources awarded to replace EFC). 5% of all full-time freshmen had no need and received non-need-based gift aid.

UNDERGRADUATE FINANCIAL AID (Fall 2009) 4,507 applied for aid; of those 78% were deemed to have need. 99% of undergraduates with need received aid; of those 13% had need fully met. ***Average percent of need met:*** 63% (excluding resources awarded to replace EFC). ***Average financial aid package:*** $11,305 (excluding resources awarded to replace EFC). 2% of all full-time undergraduates had no need and received non-need-based gift aid.

GIFT AID (NEED-BASED) ***Total amount:*** $16,040,317 (68% federal, 28% state, 4% institutional). ***Receiving aid:*** Freshmen: 35% (393); all full-time undergraduates: 33% (2,534). ***Average award:*** Freshmen: $5398; Undergraduates: $5355. ***Scholarships, grants, and awards:*** Federal Pell, FSEOG, state, private, college/university gift aid from institutional funds.

GIFT AID (NON-NEED-BASED) ***Total amount:*** $1,234,107 (5% institutional, 95% external sources). ***Receiving aid:*** Freshmen: 13% (143). Undergraduates: 5% (360). ***Average award:*** Freshmen: $1314. Undergraduates: $1676. ***Scholarships, grants, and awards by category:*** *Creative arts/performance:* 160 awards ($77,500 total): applied art and design. ***Tuition waivers:*** Full or partial for employees or children of employees.

LOANS ***Student loans:*** $32,115,989 (37% need-based, 63% non-need-based). 50% of past graduating class borrowed through all loan programs. *Average indebtedness per student:* $24,143. ***Average need-based loan:*** Freshmen: $3384. Undergraduates: $4298. ***Parent loans:*** $6,716,753 (100% need-based). ***Programs:*** Federal Direct (Subsidized and Unsubsidized Stafford, PLUS), Perkins, alternative loans.

WORK-STUDY ***Federal work-study:*** Total amount: $815,816; 553 jobs averaging $1479.

APPLYING FOR FINANCIAL AID ***Required financial aid forms:*** FAFSA, state aid form. ***Financial aid deadline (priority):*** 2/15. ***Notification date:*** Continuous beginning 4/15. Students must reply within 2 weeks of notification.

CONTACT Financial Aid Office, Fashion Institute of Technology, Seventh Avenue at 27th Street, New York, NY 10001-5992, 212-217-3560 or toll-free 800-GOTOFIT (out-of-state).

FAULKNER UNIVERSITY

Montgomery, AL

Tuition & fees: $14,810 **Average undergraduate aid package: $7400**

ABOUT THE INSTITUTION Independent religious, coed. 30 undergraduate majors. Federal methodology is used as a basis for awarding need-based institutional aid.

UNDERGRADUATE EXPENSES for 2010–11 ***Comprehensive fee:*** $21,380 includes full-time tuition ($13,740), mandatory fees ($1070), and room and board ($6570). Full-time tuition and fees vary according to location and program. Room and board charges vary according to board plan and housing facility. ***Part-time tuition:*** $480 per semester hour. ***Part-time fees:*** $270 per semester hour; $60 per term. Part-time tuition and fees vary according to location. ***Payment plan:*** Installment.

FRESHMAN FINANCIAL AID (Fall 2010, est.) 184 applied for aid; of those 78% were deemed to have need. 100% of freshmen with need received aid; of those 9% had need fully met. ***Average percent of need met:*** 60% (excluding resources awarded to replace EFC). ***Average financial aid package:*** $5000 (excluding resources awarded to replace EFC). 3% of all full-time freshmen had no need and received non-need-based gift aid.

UNDERGRADUATE FINANCIAL AID (Fall 2010, est.) 1,851 applied for aid; of those 78% were deemed to have need. 100% of undergraduates with need received aid; of those 9% had need fully met. ***Average percent of need met:*** 62% (excluding resources awarded to replace EFC). ***Average financial aid package:*** $7400 (excluding resources awarded to replace EFC). 3% of all full-time undergraduates had no need and received non-need-based gift aid.

GIFT AID (NEED-BASED) ***Total amount:*** $9,600,000 (100% federal). ***Receiving aid:*** Freshmen: 53% (106); all full-time undergraduates: 53% (1,066). ***Average award:*** Freshmen: $2650; Undergraduates: $4000. ***Scholarships, grants, and awards:*** Federal Pell, FSEOG, state, private, college/university gift aid from institutional funds.

GIFT AID (NON-NEED-BASED) ***Total amount:*** $2,033,000 (30% state, 64% institutional, 6% external sources). ***Receiving aid:*** Freshmen: 42% (84). Undergraduates: 42% (845). ***Average award:*** Freshmen: $2600. Undergraduates: $4300. ***Scholarships, grants, and awards by category:*** *Academic interests/achievement:* 186 awards ($802,000 total): general academic interests/achievements, religion/biblical studies. *Creative arts/performance:* 46 awards ($56,500 total): journalism/publications, music, theater/drama. *Special achievements/activities:* 38 awards ($119,600 total): cheerleading/drum major, leadership, religious involvement. *Special characteristics:* 241 awards ($257,800 total): adult students, children and siblings of alumni, children of faculty/staff, local/state students, out-of-state students, relatives of clergy, religious affiliation, siblings of current students. ***Tuition waivers:*** Full or partial for employees or children of employees, adult students, senior citizens.

LOANS ***Student loans:*** $29,300,000 (48% need-based, 52% non-need-based). 90% of past graduating class borrowed through all loan programs. *Average indebtedness per student:* $19,300. ***Average need-based loan:*** Freshmen: $3500. Undergraduates: $5200. ***Parent loans:*** $1,300,000 (100% non-need-based). ***Programs:*** Federal Direct (Subsidized and Unsubsidized Stafford, PLUS), Perkins.

WORK-STUDY ***Federal work-study:*** Total amount: $260,000; 154 jobs averaging $1688. ***State or other work-study/employment:*** Total amount: $1100 (100% non-need-based). 3 part-time jobs averaging $366.

ATHLETIC AWARDS Total amount: $2,425,000 (100% non-need-based).

APPLYING FOR FINANCIAL AID ***Required financial aid forms:*** FAFSA, institution's own form, state aid form. ***Financial aid deadline (priority):*** 5/1. ***Notification date:*** 4/1. Students must reply by 8/1.

CONTACT Mr. William G. Jackson II, Director of Financial Aid, Faulkner University, 5345 Atlanta Highway, Montgomery, AL 36109-3398, 334-386-7195 or toll-free 800-879-9816. *Fax:* 334-386-7201. *E-mail:* faid@faulkner.edu.

FAYETTEVILLE STATE UNIVERSITY

Fayetteville, NC

Tuition & fees (NC res): $3756 **Average undergraduate aid package: $9586**

ABOUT THE INSTITUTION State-supported, coed. 39 undergraduate majors. Federal methodology is used as a basis for awarding need-based institutional aid.

UNDERGRADUATE EXPENSES for 2010–11 ***Tuition, state resident:*** full-time $2129. ***Tuition, nonresident:*** full-time $12,593. ***Required fees:*** full-time $1627. Full-time tuition and fees vary according to course level, course load, degree level, location, and program. Part-time tuition and fees vary according to course level, course load, degree level, location, and program. ***College room and board:*** $5812; ***Room only:*** $3071. Room and board charges vary according to board plan and housing facility. ***Payment plan:*** Installment.

FRESHMAN FINANCIAL AID (Fall 2010, est.) 739 applied for aid; of those 92% were deemed to have need. 99% of freshmen with need received aid; of those 27% had need fully met. ***Average percent of need met:*** 88% (excluding resources awarded to replace EFC). ***Average financial aid package:*** $10,426 (excluding resources awarded to replace EFC). 6% of all full-time freshmen had no need and received non-need-based gift aid.

UNDERGRADUATE FINANCIAL AID (Fall 2010, est.) 4,022 applied for aid; of those 92% were deemed to have need. 98% of undergraduates with need received aid; of those 21% had need fully met. ***Average percent of need met:*** 80% (excluding resources awarded to replace EFC). ***Average financial aid package:*** $9586 (excluding resources awarded to replace EFC). 3% of all full-time undergraduates had no need and received non-need-based gift aid.

GIFT AID (NEED-BASED) ***Total amount:*** $26,710,131 (63% federal, 25% state, 9% institutional, 3% external sources). ***Receiving aid:*** Freshmen: 87% (651); all full-time undergraduates: 78% (3,367). ***Average award:*** Freshmen: $8094; Undergraduates: $6380. ***Scholarships, grants, and awards:*** Federal Pell, FSEOG, state, private, college/university gift aid from institutional funds, United Negro College Fund, Federal Nursing.

GIFT AID (NON-NEED-BASED) ***Total amount:*** $183,960 (16% state, 49% institutional, 35% external sources). ***Receiving aid:*** Freshmen: 46% (345). Undergraduates: 43% (1,867). ***Average award:*** Freshmen: $656. Undergraduates: $495. ***Scholarships, grants, and awards by category:*** *Academic interests/achievement:* general academic interests/achievements. *Creative arts/performance:* music. *Special characteristics:* local/state students. ***Tuition waivers:*** Full or partial for employees or children of employees, senior citizens.

LOANS ***Student loans:*** $27,417,622 (93% need-based, 7% non-need-based). ***Average need-based loan:*** Freshmen: $2585. Undergraduates: $3824. ***Parent loans:*** $370,643 (79% need-based, 21% non-need-based). ***Programs:*** Federal Direct (Subsidized and Unsubsidized Stafford, PLUS), Perkins.

WORK-STUDY ***Federal work-study:*** Total amount: $240,953; jobs available. ***State or other work-study/employment:*** Part-time jobs available.

ATHLETIC AWARDS Total amount: $448,070 (79% need-based, 21% non-need-based).

APPLYING FOR FINANCIAL AID ***Required financial aid forms:*** FAFSA, federal income tax return(s) and W-2 forms. ***Financial aid deadline:*** 3/1. ***Notification date:*** Continuous beginning 4/1.

CONTACT Tony Browne, Administrative Support Associate, Fayetteville State University, 1200 Murchison Road, Fayetteville, NC 28301-4298, 910-672-1325 or toll-free 800-222-2594. *Fax:* 910-672-1423. *E-mail:* lmckoy@uncfsu.edu.

FELICIAN COLLEGE

Lodi, NJ

Tuition & fees: $27,925 **Average undergraduate aid package: N/A**

ABOUT THE INSTITUTION Independent Roman Catholic, coed. 31 undergraduate majors. Federal methodology is used as a basis for awarding need-based institutional aid.

UNDERGRADUATE EXPENSES for 2011–12 ***Comprehensive fee:*** $38,675 includes full-time tuition ($26,350), mandatory fees ($1575), and room and board ($10,750). Room and board charges vary according to housing facility. ***Part-time tuition:*** $865 per credit hour. ***Payment plan:*** Installment.

FRESHMAN FINANCIAL AID (Fall 2010, est.) 227 applied for aid; of those 82% were deemed to have need. 100% of freshmen with need received aid; of those 10% had need fully met. 6% of all full-time freshmen had no need and received non-need-based gift aid.

UNDERGRADUATE FINANCIAL AID (Fall 2010, est.) 1,169 applied for aid; of those 84% were deemed to have need. 100% of undergraduates with need received aid; of those 9% had need fully met. 5% of all full-time undergraduates had no need and received non-need-based gift aid.

GIFT AID (NEED-BASED) ***Total amount:*** $9,220,041 (35% federal, 58% state, 7% institutional). ***Receiving aid:*** Freshmen: 65% (163); all full-time undergraduates: 54% (722). ***Average award:*** Freshmen: $13,784; Undergraduates: $12,249. ***Scholarships, grants, and awards:*** Federal Pell, FSEOG, state, private, college/university gift aid from institutional funds.

GIFT AID (NON-NEED-BASED) ***Total amount:*** $5,965,975 (5% federal, 94% institutional, 1% external sources). ***Receiving aid:*** Freshmen: 50% (125). Undergraduates: 34% (465). ***Average award:*** Freshmen: $20,060. Undergraduates: $18,968. ***Scholarships, grants, and awards by category:*** *Academic interests/achievement:* 554 awards ($5,475,064 total): business, education, English, general academic interests/achievements, health fields, religion/biblical studies. *Special characteristics:* 10 awards ($197,208 total): children of faculty/staff, siblings of current students.

LOANS ***Student loans:*** $13,135,381 (33% need-based, 67% non-need-based). 66% of past graduating class borrowed through all loan programs. *Average indebtedness per student:* $22,963. ***Average need-based loan:*** Freshmen: $4427. Undergraduates: $5217. ***Parent loans:*** $2,364,327 (100% non-need-based). ***Programs:*** state.

WORK-STUDY ***Federal work-study:*** Total amount: $121,711; 88 jobs averaging $1352. ***State or other work-study/employment:*** 90 part-time jobs averaging $2652.

ATHLETIC AWARDS Total amount: $1,593,417 (100% non-need-based).

APPLYING FOR FINANCIAL AID ***Required financial aid form:*** FAFSA. ***Financial aid deadline:*** Continuous. ***Notification date:*** Continuous beginning 4/1.

CONTACT Janet Mariano Merli, Financial Aid Director, Felician College, 262 South Main Street, Lodi, NJ 07644, 201-559-6040. *Fax:* 201-559-6025. *E-mail:* merlij@felician.edu.

FERRIS STATE UNIVERSITY

Big Rapids, MI

Tuition & fees (MI res): $9930 **Average undergraduate aid package: $15,925**

ABOUT THE INSTITUTION State-supported, coed. 131 undergraduate majors. Federal methodology is used as a basis for awarding need-based institutional aid.

UNDERGRADUATE EXPENSES for 2010–11 ***One-time required fee:*** $162. ***Tuition, state resident:*** full-time $9930; part-time $331 per credit hour. ***Tuition, nonresident:*** full-time $15,900; part-time $530 per credit hour. Full-time tuition and fees vary according to location and program. Part-time tuition and fees vary according to location. ***College room and board:*** $9180. Room and board charges vary according to board plan and housing facility. ***Payment plan:*** Deferred payment.

FRESHMAN FINANCIAL AID (Fall 2010, est.) 1,519 applied for aid; of those 84% were deemed to have need. 99% of freshmen with need received aid; of those 20% had need fully met. ***Average percent of need met:*** 91% (excluding resources awarded to replace EFC). ***Average financial aid package:*** $16,536 (excluding resources awarded to replace EFC). 15% of all full-time freshmen had no need and received non-need-based gift aid.

UNDERGRADUATE FINANCIAL AID (Fall 2010, est.) 6,538 applied for aid; of those 82% were deemed to have need. 99% of undergraduates with need received aid; of those 15% had need fully met. ***Average percent of need met:*** 87% (excluding resources awarded to replace EFC). ***Average financial aid package:*** $15,925 (excluding resources awarded to replace EFC). 9% of all full-time undergraduates had no need and received non-need-based gift aid.

GIFT AID (NEED-BASED) ***Total amount:*** $33,504,758 (80% federal, 2% state, 17% institutional, 1% external sources). ***Receiving aid:*** Freshmen: 56% (920); all full-time undergraduates: 54% (3,826). ***Average award:*** Freshmen: $5623; Undergraduates: $5379. ***Scholarships, grants, and awards:*** Federal Pell, FSEOG, state, private, college/university gift aid from institutional funds.

GIFT AID (NON-NEED-BASED) ***Total amount:*** $15,812,848 (33% state, 60% institutional, 7% external sources). ***Receiving aid:*** Freshmen: 56% (916). Undergraduates: 36% (2,586). ***Average award:*** Freshmen: $4214. Undergraduates: $4318. ***Scholarships, grants, and awards by category:*** *Academic interests/achievement:* 3,402 awards ($8,542,438 total): agriculture, architecture, biological sciences, business, communication, computer science, education, engineering/technologies, general academic interests/achievements, health fields, mathematics. *Creative arts/performance:* 631 awards ($1,833,793 total): applied art and design, art/fine arts, debating, general creative arts/performance, journalism/publications, music, theater/drama. *Special achievements/activities:* 161 awards ($38,171 total): general special achievements/activities, memberships. *Special characteristics:* 179 awards ($160,611 total): adult students, children and siblings of alumni, ethnic background, general special characteristics, international students, local/state students, members of minority groups, previous college experience, veterans. ***Tuition waivers:*** Full or partial for employees or children of employees.

LOANS ***Student loans:*** $78,064,572 (44% need-based, 56% non-need-based). 76% of past graduating class borrowed through all loan programs. *Average indebtedness per student:* $35,468. ***Average need-based loan:*** Freshmen: $3289. Undergraduates: $4266. ***Parent loans:*** $11,465,348 (100% non-need-based). ***Programs:*** Federal Direct (Subsidized and Unsubsidized Stafford, PLUS), Perkins, Federal Nursing, college/university, alternative loans.

WORK-STUDY ***Federal work-study:*** Total amount: $1,361,242; 616 jobs averaging $2150. ***State or other work-study/employment:*** Part-time jobs available.

ATHLETIC AWARDS Total amount: $1,936,624 (100% non-need-based).

APPLYING FOR FINANCIAL AID ***Required financial aid form:*** FAFSA. ***Financial aid deadline (priority):*** 3/1. ***Notification date:*** Continuous beginning 4/1. Students must reply within 3 weeks of notification.

CONTACT Nancy Wencl, Coordinator of Federal Aid Programs, Ferris State University, 1201 South State Street, Big Rapids, MI 49307-2020, 231-591-2100 or toll-free 800-433-7747. *Fax:* 231-591-2950. *E-mail:* wencln@ferris.edu.

FERRUM COLLEGE
Ferrum, VA

Tuition & fees: $24,945 **Average undergraduate aid package: $19,984**

ABOUT THE INSTITUTION Independent United Methodist, coed. 31 undergraduate majors. Both federal and institutional methodology are used as a basis for awarding need-based institutional aid.

UNDERGRADUATE EXPENSES for 2010–11 ***Comprehensive fee:*** $33,025 includes full-time tuition ($24,900), mandatory fees ($45), and room and board ($8080). Full-time tuition and fees vary according to course load. Room and board charges vary according to board plan and housing facility. ***Part-time tuition:*** $500 per credit hour. Part-time tuition and fees vary according to course load. ***Payment plan:*** Installment.

FRESHMAN FINANCIAL AID (Fall 2010, est.) 582 applied for aid; of those 90% were deemed to have need. 100% of freshmen with need received aid. ***Average percent of need met:*** 70% (excluding resources awarded to replace EFC). ***Average financial aid package:*** $21,207 (excluding resources awarded to replace EFC). 11% of all full-time freshmen had no need and received non-need-based gift aid.

UNDERGRADUATE FINANCIAL AID (Fall 2010, est.) 1,455 applied for aid; of those 93% were deemed to have need. 100% of undergraduates with need received aid. ***Average percent of need met:*** 64% (excluding resources awarded to replace EFC). ***Average financial aid package:*** $19,984 (excluding resources awarded to replace EFC). 9% of all full-time undergraduates had no need and received non-need-based gift aid.

GIFT AID (NEED-BASED) ***Total amount:*** $20,444,399 (18% federal, 13% state, 66% institutional, 3% external sources). ***Receiving aid:*** Freshmen: 85% (514); all full-time undergraduates: 87% (1,312). ***Average award:*** Freshmen: $8277; Undergraduates: $7438. ***Scholarships, grants, and awards:*** Federal Pell, FSEOG, state, private, college/university gift aid from institutional funds.

GIFT AID (NON-NEED-BASED) ***Total amount:*** $1,393,280 (21% state, 73% institutional, 6% external sources). ***Receiving aid:*** Freshmen: 86% (520). Undergraduates: 88% (1,332). ***Average award:*** Freshmen: $7352. Undergraduates: $6899. ***Scholarships, grants, and awards by category:*** *Academic interests/achievement:* $6,438,017 total: general academic interests/achievements. *Special achievements/activities:* 14 awards ($64,400 total): general special achievements/activities, religious involvement. *Special characteristics:* $4,164,688 total: children of faculty/staff, international students, local/state students, relatives of clergy, religious affiliation. ***Tuition waivers:*** Full or partial for employees or children of employees.

LOANS ***Student loans:*** $9,201,077 (96% need-based, 4% non-need-based). 78% of past graduating class borrowed through all loan programs. *Average indebtedness per student:* $30,460. ***Average need-based loan:*** Freshmen: $3160. Undergraduates: $3824. ***Parent loans:*** $5,599,250 (91% need-based, 9% non-need-based). ***Programs:*** Federal Direct (Subsidized and Unsubsidized Stafford, PLUS), Perkins.

WORK-STUDY ***Federal work-study:*** Total amount: $1,799,485; 834 jobs averaging $2042. ***State or other work-study/employment:*** 83 part-time jobs averaging $1778.

APPLYING FOR FINANCIAL AID ***Required financial aid forms:*** FAFSA, state aid form. ***Financial aid deadline (priority):*** 3/1. ***Notification date:*** Continuous beginning 1/15.

CONTACT Heather Hollandsworth, Director of Financial Aid, Ferrum College, PO Box 1000, Ferrum, VA 24088-9001, 540-365-4282 or toll-free 800-868-9797. *Fax:* 540-365-4266. *E-mail:* hhollandsworth@ferrum.edu.

FINLANDIA UNIVERSITY
Hancock, MI

Tuition & fees: $18,974 **Average undergraduate aid package: N/A**

ABOUT THE INSTITUTION Independent religious, coed. ***Awards:*** associate and bachelor's degrees. 15 undergraduate majors. ***Total enrollment:*** 545. Undergraduates: 545. Freshmen: 82. Federal methodology is used as a basis for awarding need-based institutional aid.

UNDERGRADUATE EXPENSES for 2010–11 ***Application fee:*** $30. ***Comprehensive fee:*** $25,128 includes full-time tuition ($18,474), mandatory fees ($500), and room and board ($6154). Full-time tuition and fees vary according to program. Room and board charges vary according to housing facility. ***Part-time tuition:*** $616 per credit hour. Part-time tuition and fees vary according to course load and program. ***Payment plan:*** Installment.

GIFT AID (NEED-BASED) ***Total amount:*** $2,951,966 (80% federal, 20% state). ***Scholarships, grants, and awards:*** Federal Pell, FSEOG, state, private, college/university gift aid from institutional funds.

GIFT AID (NON-NEED-BASED) ***Total amount:*** $312,246 (71% state, 29% external sources). ***Scholarships, grants, and awards by category:*** *Academic interests/achievement:* general academic interests/achievements. *Creative arts/performance:* art/fine arts, general creative arts/performance. *Special achievements/activities:* community service, general special achievements/activities, leadership, religious involvement. *Special characteristics:* children of current students, children of faculty/staff, first-generation college students, international students, religious affiliation, siblings of current students, spouses of current students, twins. ***Tuition waivers:*** Full or partial for employees or children of employees. ***ROTC:*** Army cooperative, Air Force cooperative.

LOANS ***Student loans:*** $4,460,564 (54% need-based, 46% non-need-based). ***Parent loans:*** $611,227 (100% non-need-based). ***Programs:*** Federal Direct (Subsidized and Unsubsidized Stafford, PLUS), private loans.

WORK-STUDY ***Federal work-study:*** Total amount: $283,133; jobs available.

APPLYING FOR FINANCIAL AID ***Required financial aid form:*** FAFSA. ***Financial aid deadline (priority):*** 3/1. ***Notification date:*** Continuous beginning 3/1. Students must reply within 3 weeks of notification.

CONTACT Sandra Turnquist, Director of Financial Aid, Finlandia University, 601 Quincy Street, Hancock, MI 49930, 906-487-7240 or toll-free 877-202-5491. *Fax:* 906-487-7383. *E-mail:* sandy.turnquist@finlandia.edu.

FISHER COLLEGE
Boston, MA

Tuition & fees: $25,778 **Average undergraduate aid package: N/A**

ABOUT THE INSTITUTION Independent, coed. 26 undergraduate majors. Federal methodology is used as a basis for awarding need-based institutional aid.

UNDERGRADUATE EXPENSES for 2011–12 ***Comprehensive fee:*** $39,564 includes full-time tuition ($24,783), mandatory fees ($995), and room and board ($13,786). Full-time tuition and fees vary according to class time, course level, course load, degree level, location, program, reciprocity agreements, and student level. ***Part-time tuition:*** $266.66 per credit. Part-time tuition and fees vary according to class time, course level, course load, degree level, location, program, reciprocity agreements, and student level. ***Payment plan:*** Installment.

FRESHMAN FINANCIAL AID (Fall 2010, est.) 307 applied for aid; of those 96% were deemed to have need. 100% of freshmen with need received aid.

UNDERGRADUATE FINANCIAL AID (Fall 2010, est.) 828 applied for aid; of those 77% were deemed to have need. 100% of undergraduates with need received aid.

GIFT AID (NEED-BASED) ***Total amount:*** $12,925,813 (59% federal, 2% state, 39% institutional). ***Receiving aid:*** Freshmen: 70% (222); all full-time undergraduates: 49% (515). ***Scholarships, grants, and awards:*** FSEOG, state, private, college/university gift aid from institutional funds.

GIFT AID (NON-NEED-BASED) ***Total amount:*** $3,460,902 (60% federal, 39% institutional, 1% external sources). ***Receiving aid:*** Freshmen: 72% (227). Undergraduates: 31% (327). ***Scholarships, grants, and awards by category:*** *Academic interests/achievement:* general academic interests/achievements.

LOANS ***Student loans:*** $5,221,257 (48% need-based, 52% non-need-based). 67% of past graduating class borrowed through all loan programs. ***Parent loans:*** $2,051,810 (100% non-need-based). ***Programs:*** Federal Direct (Subsidized and Unsubsidized Stafford, PLUS), Perkins, state.

WORK-STUDY ***Federal work-study:*** Total amount: $63,000; jobs available.

APPLYING FOR FINANCIAL AID ***Required financial aid form:*** FAFSA. ***Financial aid deadline:*** Continuous. ***Notification date:*** Continuous.

CONTACT Anne Sylvain, Director of Financial Aid, Fisher College, 1 Arlington Street, Third Floor, Boston, MA 02116, 617-236-5470 or toll-free 800-821-3050 (in-state), 800-446-1226 (out-of-state). *E-mail:* asylvain@fisher.edu.

FISK UNIVERSITY

Nashville, TN

ABOUT THE INSTITUTION Independent religious, coed. 20 undergraduate majors.

GIFT AID (NEED-BASED) ***Scholarships, grants, and awards:*** Federal Pell, FSEOG, state, private, college/university gift aid from institutional funds, United Negro College Fund.

LOANS ***Programs:*** Federal Direct (Subsidized and Unsubsidized Stafford, PLUS), Perkins.

WORK-STUDY ***Federal work-study:*** Total amount: $282,902; 181 jobs averaging $1573.

APPLYING FOR FINANCIAL AID ***Required financial aid form:*** FAFSA.

CONTACT Russelle Keese, Director of Financial Aid, Fisk University, 1000 17th Avenue North, Nashville, TN 37208-3051, 615-329-8735 or toll-free 800-443-FISK. *E-mail:* finaid@fisk.edu.

FITCHBURG STATE UNIVERSITY

Fitchburg, MA

Tuition & fees (MA res): $7800 **Average undergraduate aid package: $8645**

ABOUT THE INSTITUTION State-supported, coed. 55 undergraduate majors. Federal methodology is used as a basis for awarding need-based institutional aid.

UNDERGRADUATE EXPENSES for 2010–11 ***Tuition, state resident:*** full-time $970; part-time $40.42 per credit. ***Tuition, nonresident:*** full-time $7050; part-time $293.75 per credit. ***Required fees:*** full-time $6830; $284.58 per credit. Full-time tuition and fees vary according to class time and reciprocity agreements. Part-time tuition and fees vary according to class time and reciprocity agreements. ***College room and board:*** $8106. Room and board charges vary according to board plan and housing facility. ***Payment plan:*** Installment.

FRESHMAN FINANCIAL AID (Fall 2009) 915 applied for aid; of those 62% were deemed to have need. 99% of freshmen with need received aid; of those 93% had need fully met. ***Average percent of need met:*** 93% (excluding resources awarded to replace EFC). ***Average financial aid package:*** $8942 (excluding resources awarded to replace EFC). 7% of all full-time freshmen had no need and received non-need-based gift aid.

UNDERGRADUATE FINANCIAL AID (Fall 2009) 3,132 applied for aid; of those 62% were deemed to have need. 97% of undergraduates with need received aid; of those 93% had need fully met. ***Average percent of need met:*** 93% (excluding resources awarded to replace EFC). ***Average financial aid package:*** $8645 (excluding resources awarded to replace EFC). 2% of all full-time undergraduates had no need and received non-need-based gift aid.

GIFT AID (NEED-BASED) ***Total amount:*** $8,422,556 (53% federal, 18% state, 29% institutional). ***Receiving aid:*** Freshmen: 48% (460); all full-time undergraduates: 40% (1,404). ***Average award:*** Freshmen: $4337; Undergraduates: $4336. ***Scholarships, grants, and awards:*** Federal Pell, FSEOG, state, private, college/university gift aid from institutional funds.

GIFT AID (NON-NEED-BASED) ***Total amount:*** $1,092,715 (16% state, 44% institutional, 40% external sources). ***Receiving aid:*** Freshmen: 9% (91). Undergraduates: 5% (157). ***Average award:*** Freshmen: $1098. Undergraduates: $1292. ***Scholarships, grants, and awards by category:*** *Academic interests/achievement:* 218 awards ($270,499 total): biological sciences, business, communication, computer science, education, engineering/technologies, English, foreign languages, general academic interests/achievements, health fields, mathematics, social sciences. *Special achievements/activities:* 134 awards ($171,540 total): general special achievements/activities, leadership. *Special characteristics:* 31 awards ($29,023 total): adult students, children and siblings of alumni, ethnic background, local/state students, members of minority groups, out-of-state students, previous college experience, veterans. ***Tuition waivers:*** Full or partial for employees or children of employees, senior citizens.

LOANS ***Student loans:*** $17,345,147 (40% need-based, 60% non-need-based). 67% of past graduating class borrowed through all loan programs. *Average indebtedness per student:* $19,902. ***Average need-based loan:*** Freshmen: $2884. Undergraduates: $3679. ***Parent loans:*** $1,269,318 (100% non-need-based). ***Programs:*** Federal Direct (Subsidized and Unsubsidized Stafford, PLUS), Perkins, Federal Nursing, state.

WORK-STUDY ***Federal work-study:*** Total amount: $375,000; 248 jobs averaging $1076.

APPLYING FOR FINANCIAL AID ***Required financial aid form:*** FAFSA. ***Financial aid deadline (priority):*** 3/1. ***Notification date:*** Continuous beginning 3/15. Students must reply within 2 weeks of notification.

CONTACT Office of Financial Aid, Fitchburg State University, 160 Pearl Street, Fitchburg, MA 01420, 978-665-3454 or toll-free 800-705-9692. *Fax:* 978-665-3556. *E-mail:* finaid@fitchburgstate.edu.

FIVE TOWNS COLLEGE

Dix Hills, NY

ABOUT THE INSTITUTION Independent, coed. 18 undergraduate majors.

GIFT AID (NEED-BASED) ***Scholarships, grants, and awards:*** Federal Pell, FSEOG, state, private, college/university gift aid from institutional funds.

GIFT AID (NON-NEED-BASED) ***Scholarships, grants, and awards by category:*** *Academic interests/achievement:* business, education, general academic interests/achievements. *Creative arts/performance:* cinema/film/broadcasting, music, theater/drama. *Special characteristics:* siblings of current students.

LOANS ***Programs:*** Federal Direct (Subsidized and Unsubsidized Stafford, PLUS).

WORK-STUDY ***Federal work-study:*** Total amount: $131,758; 95 jobs averaging $1387. ***State or other work-study/employment:*** Total amount: $80,000 (100% non-need-based). Part-time jobs available.

APPLYING FOR FINANCIAL AID ***Required financial aid forms:*** FAFSA, institution's own form, state aid form.

CONTACT Ms. Mary Venezia, Financial Aid Director, Five Towns College, 305 North Service Road, Dix Hills, NY 11746-6055, 631-656-2113. *Fax:* 631-656-2191. *E-mail:* mvenezia@ftc.edu.

FLAGLER COLLEGE

St. Augustine, FL

Tuition & fees: $13,860 **Average undergraduate aid package: $13,820**

ABOUT THE INSTITUTION Independent, coed. 24 undergraduate majors. Federal methodology is used as a basis for awarding need-based institutional aid.

UNDERGRADUATE EXPENSES for 2010–11 ***Comprehensive fee:*** $21,450 includes full-time tuition ($13,860) and room and board ($7590). Room and board charges vary according to board plan. ***Part-time tuition:*** $465 per credit hour.

FRESHMAN FINANCIAL AID (Fall 2010, est.) 505 applied for aid; of those 73% were deemed to have need. 99% of freshmen with need received aid; of those

18% had need fully met. ***Average percent of need met:*** 93% (excluding resources awarded to replace EFC). ***Average financial aid package:*** $11,676 (excluding resources awarded to replace EFC). 1% of all full-time freshmen had no need and received non-need-based gift aid.

UNDERGRADUATE FINANCIAL AID (Fall 2010, est.) 1,957 applied for aid; of those 79% were deemed to have need. 100% of undergraduates with need received aid; of those 18% had need fully met. ***Average percent of need met:*** 90% (excluding resources awarded to replace EFC). ***Average financial aid package:*** $13,820 (excluding resources awarded to replace EFC). 4% of all full-time undergraduates had no need and received non-need-based gift aid.

GIFT AID (NEED-BASED) ***Total amount:*** $10,202,198 (34% federal, 42% state, 22% institutional, 2% external sources). ***Receiving aid:*** Freshmen: 52% (318); all full-time undergraduates: 44% (1,178). ***Average award:*** Freshmen: $5667; Undergraduates: $5072. ***Scholarships, grants, and awards:*** Federal Pell, FSEOG, state, private, college/university gift aid from institutional funds.

GIFT AID (NON-NEED-BASED) ***Total amount:*** $2,924,866 (1% federal, 85% state, 10% institutional, 4% external sources). ***Receiving aid:*** Freshmen: 41% (254). Undergraduates: 41% (1,099). ***Average award:*** Freshmen: $1675. Undergraduates: $2073. ***Scholarships, grants, and awards by category:*** *Academic interests/achievement:* 42 awards ($81,200 total): business, communication, education, English, foreign languages, general academic interests/achievements, humanities, religion/biblical studies, social sciences. *Creative arts/performance:* 6 awards ($33,800 total): applied art and design, art/fine arts, cinema/film/broadcasting, performing arts, theater/drama. *Special achievements/activities:* 24 awards ($21,653 total): general special achievements/activities, leadership, memberships, religious involvement. *Special characteristics:* 242 awards ($623,302 total): children of educators, children of faculty/staff, ethnic background, first-generation college students, general special characteristics, local/state students, members of minority groups, out-of-state students. ***Tuition waivers:*** Full or partial for employees or children of employees.

LOANS ***Student loans:*** $11,401,128 (81% need-based, 19% non-need-based). 60% of past graduating class borrowed through all loan programs. *Average indebtedness per student:* $20,895. ***Average need-based loan:*** Freshmen: $2706. Undergraduates: $3583. ***Parent loans:*** $2,344,823 (67% need-based, 33% non-need-based). ***Programs:*** Federal Direct (Subsidized and Unsubsidized Stafford, PLUS), Perkins.

WORK-STUDY ***Federal work-study:*** Total amount: $230,375; 240 jobs averaging $1223. ***State or other work-study/employment:*** Total amount: $51,200 (15% need-based, 85% non-need-based). 65 part-time jobs averaging $1141.

ATHLETIC AWARDS Total amount: $1,088,150 (44% need-based, 56% non-need-based).

APPLYING FOR FINANCIAL AID ***Required financial aid forms:*** FAFSA, institution's own form. ***Financial aid deadline (priority):*** 4/1. ***Notification date:*** Continuous beginning 2/15. Students must reply within 2 weeks of notification.

CONTACT Ms. Sheia Pleasant, Assistant Director of Financial Aid, Flagler College, PO Box 1027, St. Augustine, FL 32085-1027, 904-819-6225 or toll-free 800-304-4208. *Fax:* 904-819-6453. *E-mail:* spleasant@flagler.edu.

FLORIDA AGRICULTURAL AND MECHANICAL UNIVERSITY

Tallahassee, FL

Tuition & fees (FL res): $4248 **Average undergraduate aid package: $13,514**

ABOUT THE INSTITUTION State-supported, coed. 67 undergraduate majors. Federal methodology is used as a basis for awarding need-based institutional aid.

UNDERGRADUATE EXPENSES for 2010–11 ***Tuition, state resident:*** full-time $3990; part-time $133.11 per credit hour. ***Tuition, nonresident:*** full-time $15,933; part-time $531.13 per credit hour. ***Required fees:*** full-time $258; $129 per term. ***College room and board:*** $7856; ***Room only:*** $4212. Room and board charges vary according to board plan and housing facility.

FRESHMAN FINANCIAL AID (Fall 2009) 1,801 applied for aid; of those 99% were deemed to have need. 99% of freshmen with need received aid; of those 26% had need fully met. ***Average percent of need met:*** 78% (excluding resources awarded to replace EFC). ***Average financial aid package:*** $13,324 (excluding resources awarded to replace EFC). 3% of all full-time freshmen had no need and received non-need-based gift aid.

UNDERGRADUATE FINANCIAL AID (Fall 2009) 7,329 applied for aid; of those 98% were deemed to have need. 99% of undergraduates with need received aid; of those 37% had need fully met. ***Average percent of need met:*** 87% (excluding resources awarded to replace EFC). ***Average financial aid package:*** $13,514 (excluding resources awarded to replace EFC). 2% of all full-time undergraduates had no need and received non-need-based gift aid.

GIFT AID (NEED-BASED) ***Total amount:*** $38,492,231 (89% federal, 10% state, 1% institutional). ***Receiving aid:*** Freshmen: 60% (1,447); all full-time undergraduates: 62% (5,696). ***Average award:*** Freshmen: $4916; Undergraduates: $4527. ***Scholarships, grants, and awards:*** Federal Pell, FSEOG, state, private, college/university gift aid from institutional funds, United Negro College Fund.

GIFT AID (NON-NEED-BASED) ***Total amount:*** $17,594,349 (31% state, 46% institutional, 23% external sources). ***Receiving aid:*** Freshmen: 35% (841). Undergraduates: 25% (2,321). ***Average award:*** Freshmen: $7935. Undergraduates: $8107. ***Scholarships, grants, and awards by category:*** *Academic interests/achievement:* agriculture, architecture, area/ethnic studies, biological sciences, business, communication, computer science, education, engineering/technologies, English, foreign languages, general academic interests/achievements, health fields, humanities, mathematics, military science, physical sciences, premedicine, social sciences. *Creative arts/performance:* applied art and design, art/fine arts, cinema/film/broadcasting, creative writing, dance, journalism/publications, music, performing arts, theater/drama. *Special achievements/activities:* cheerleading/drum major, community service, general special achievements/activities, leadership. *Special characteristics:* ethnic background, first-generation college students, general special characteristics, local/state students, out-of-state students. ***Tuition waivers:*** Full or partial for employees or children of employees, senior citizens.

LOANS ***Student loans:*** $51,641,904 (49% need-based, 51% non-need-based). 86% of past graduating class borrowed through all loan programs. *Average indebtedness per student:* $28,144. ***Average need-based loan:*** Freshmen: $3161. Undergraduates: $3982. ***Parent loans:*** $6,152,812 (100% non-need-based). ***Programs:*** Federal Direct (Subsidized and Unsubsidized Stafford, PLUS), Perkins, private loans.

WORK-STUDY ***Federal work-study:*** Total amount: $433,451; 250 jobs averaging $1734.

ATHLETIC AWARDS Total amount: $1,752,231 (100% non-need-based).

APPLYING FOR FINANCIAL AID ***Required financial aid form:*** FAFSA. ***Financial aid deadline:*** Continuous. ***Notification date:*** Continuous beginning 4/15.

CONTACT Ms. Marcia M. Conliffe, Director of Student Financial Aid, Florida Agricultural and Mechanical University, 101 Foote-Hilyer Administration Center, Tallahassee, FL 32307, 850-599-3730. *E-mail:* marcia.conliffe@famu.edu.

FLORIDA ATLANTIC UNIVERSITY

Boca Raton, FL

Tuition & fees (FL res): $4797 **Average undergraduate aid package: $10,337**

ABOUT THE INSTITUTION State-supported, coed. 65 undergraduate majors. Federal methodology is used as a basis for awarding need-based institutional aid.

UNDERGRADUATE EXPENSES for 2010–11 ***Tuition, state resident:*** full-time $4797; part-time $159.81 per credit hour. ***Tuition, nonresident:*** full-time $18,132; part-time $604.39 per credit hour. Full-time tuition and fees vary according to course load. Part-time tuition and fees vary according to course load. ***College room and board:*** $9690. Room and board charges vary according to board plan and housing facility. ***Payment plans:*** Tuition prepayment, installment, deferred payment.

FRESHMAN FINANCIAL AID (Fall 2010, est.) 2,010 applied for aid; of those 75% were deemed to have need. 99% of freshmen with need received aid; of those 19% had need fully met. ***Average percent of need met:*** 72% (excluding resources awarded to replace EFC). ***Average financial aid package:*** $9941 (excluding resources awarded to replace EFC). 3% of all full-time freshmen had no need and received non-need-based gift aid.

UNDERGRADUATE FINANCIAL AID (Fall 2010, est.) 9,606 applied for aid; of those 84% were deemed to have need. 98% of undergraduates with need received aid; of those 17% had need fully met. ***Average percent of need met:*** 70% (excluding resources awarded to replace EFC). ***Average financial aid package:*** $10,337 (excluding resources awarded to replace EFC). 1% of all full-time undergraduates had no need and received non-need-based gift aid.

GIFT AID (NEED-BASED) ***Total amount:*** $58,375,656 (65% federal, 20% state, 13% institutional, 2% external sources). ***Receiving aid:*** Freshmen: 53% (1,379); all full-time undergraduates: 49% (6,913). ***Average award:*** Freshmen: $7255;

Undergraduates: $6487. ***Scholarships, grants, and awards:*** Federal Pell, FSEOG, state, private, college/university gift aid from institutional funds, Federal Nursing.

GIFT AID (NON-NEED-BASED) ***Total amount:*** $9,872,375 (79% state, 12% institutional, 9% external sources). ***Receiving aid:*** Freshmen: 6% (156). Undergraduates: 3% (469). ***Average award:*** Freshmen: $2547. Undergraduates: $2557. ***Scholarships, grants, and awards by category:*** *Academic interests/achievement:* business, engineering/technologies, general academic interests/achievements, physical sciences, social sciences. *Creative arts/performance:* music, performing arts. ***Tuition waivers:*** Full or partial for employees or children of employees, senior citizens.

LOANS ***Student loans:*** $71,115,532 (75% need-based, 25% non-need-based). 46% of past graduating class borrowed through all loan programs. *Average indebtedness per student:* $18,342. ***Average need-based loan:*** Freshmen: $4263. Undergraduates: $5976. ***Parent loans:*** $2,225,059 (38% need-based, 62% non-need-based). ***Programs:*** Perkins, college/university.

WORK-STUDY ***Federal work-study:*** Total amount: $515,535; 182 jobs averaging $3210. ***State or other work-study/employment:*** Total amount: $12,400 (100% need-based). 5 part-time jobs averaging $3000.

ATHLETIC AWARDS Total amount: $2,551,955 (37% need-based, 63% non-need-based).

APPLYING FOR FINANCIAL AID ***Required financial aid form:*** FAFSA. ***Financial aid deadline (priority):*** 3/1. ***Notification date:*** Continuous beginning 5/1. Students must reply within 3 weeks of notification.

CONTACT Carole Pfeilsticker, Director of Student Financial Aid, Florida Atlantic University, 777 Glades Road, Boca Raton, FL 33431-0991, 561-297-3528 or toll-free 800-299-4FAU. *E-mail:* pfeilsti@fau.edu.

FLORIDA CHRISTIAN COLLEGE

Kissimmee, FL

CONTACT Ms. Sandra Peppard, Director of Student Financial Aid, Florida Christian College, 1011 Bill Beck Boulevard, Kissimmee, FL 34744-5301, 407-847-8966 Ext. 365 or toll-free 888-GO-TO-FCC (in-state). *Fax:* 407-847-3925. *E-mail:* sandi.peppard@fcc.edu.

FLORIDA COLLEGE

Temple Terrace, FL

Tuition & fees: $12,350 **Average undergraduate aid package: $12,478**

ABOUT THE INSTITUTION Independent, coed. 5 undergraduate majors. Both federal and institutional methodology are used as a basis for awarding need-based institutional aid.

UNDERGRADUATE EXPENSES for 2010–11 ***One-time required fee:*** $150. ***Comprehensive fee:*** $19,390 includes full-time tuition ($11,600), mandatory fees ($750), and room and board ($7040). ***College room only:*** $3650. Room and board charges vary according to board plan and housing facility. ***Part-time tuition:*** $485 per credit hour. ***Part-time fees:*** $300 per term. Part-time tuition and fees vary according to course load. ***Payment plan:*** Installment.

FRESHMAN FINANCIAL AID (Fall 2009) 154 applied for aid; of those 82% were deemed to have need. 98% of freshmen with need received aid; of those 6% had need fully met. ***Average percent of need met:*** 52% (excluding resources awarded to replace EFC). ***Average financial aid package:*** $10,802 (excluding resources awarded to replace EFC). 23% of all full-time freshmen had no need and received non-need-based gift aid.

UNDERGRADUATE FINANCIAL AID (Fall 2009) 354 applied for aid; of those 79% were deemed to have need. 99% of undergraduates with need received aid; of those 12% had need fully met. ***Average percent of need met:*** 57% (excluding resources awarded to replace EFC). ***Average financial aid package:*** $12,478 (excluding resources awarded to replace EFC). 24% of all full-time undergraduates had no need and received non-need-based gift aid.

GIFT AID (NEED-BASED) ***Total amount:*** $1,108,809 (40% federal, 3% state, 55% institutional, 2% external sources). ***Receiving aid:*** Freshmen: 40% (76); all full-time undergraduates: 41% (182). ***Average award:*** Freshmen: $5880; Undergraduates: $5859. ***Scholarships, grants, and awards:*** Federal Pell, FSEOG, state, private, college/university gift aid from institutional funds.

GIFT AID (NON-NEED-BASED) ***Total amount:*** $1,570,108 (34% state, 40% institutional, 26% external sources). ***Receiving aid:*** Freshmen: 45% (85). Undergraduates: 45% (204). ***Average award:*** Freshmen: $1280. Undergraduates: $1907. ***Scholarships, grants, and awards by category:*** *Academic interests/achievement:* general academic interests/achievements. *Creative arts/performance:* debating, journalism/publications, music, theater/drama. *Special characteristics:* children of educators, children of faculty/staff. ***Tuition waivers:*** Full or partial for employees or children of employees.

LOANS ***Student loans:*** $1,921,819 (45% need-based, 55% non-need-based). ***Average need-based loan:*** Freshmen: $3440. Undergraduates: $3973. ***Parent loans:*** $710,948 (100% non-need-based). ***Programs:*** Federal Direct (Subsidized and Unsubsidized Stafford, PLUS), Perkins.

WORK-STUDY ***Federal work-study:*** Total amount: $22,616; jobs available. ***State or other work-study/employment:*** Part-time jobs available.

ATHLETIC AWARDS Total amount: $144,250 (100% non-need-based).

APPLYING FOR FINANCIAL AID ***Required financial aid form:*** FAFSA. ***Financial aid deadline (priority):*** 4/1. ***Notification date:*** Continuous beginning 3/1. Students must reply by 8/1.

CONTACT Lisa McClister, Director of Financial Aid, Florida College, 119 North Glen Arven Avenue, Temple Terrace, FL 33617, 813-849-6720 or toll-free 800-326-7655. *Fax:* 813-899-6772. *E-mail:* mcclisterl@floridacollege.edu.

FLORIDA GULF COAST UNIVERSITY

Fort Myers, FL

Tuition & fees (FL res): $6728 **Average undergraduate aid package: $7519**

ABOUT THE INSTITUTION State-supported, coed. 44 undergraduate majors. Federal methodology is used as a basis for awarding need-based institutional aid.

UNDERGRADUATE EXPENSES for 2010–11 ***Tuition, state resident:*** full-time $4991. ***Tuition, nonresident:*** full-time $21,318. ***Required fees:*** full-time $1737. Full-time tuition and fees vary according to course load. Part-time tuition and fees vary according to course load. ***College room and board:*** $8150. Room and board charges vary according to board plan.

FRESHMAN FINANCIAL AID (Fall 2009) 1,697 applied for aid; of those 43% were deemed to have need. 100% of freshmen with need received aid; of those 9% had need fully met. ***Average percent of need met:*** 58% (excluding resources awarded to replace EFC). ***Average financial aid package:*** $6705 (excluding resources awarded to replace EFC). 4% of all full-time freshmen had no need and received non-need-based gift aid.

UNDERGRADUATE FINANCIAL AID (Fall 2009) 6,150 applied for aid; of those 46% were deemed to have need. 100% of undergraduates with need received aid; of those 8% had need fully met. ***Average percent of need met:*** 60% (excluding resources awarded to replace EFC). ***Average financial aid package:*** $7519 (excluding resources awarded to replace EFC). 4% of all full-time undergraduates had no need and received non-need-based gift aid.

GIFT AID (NEED-BASED) ***Total amount:*** $15,457,912 (53% federal, 30% state, 13% institutional, 4% external sources). ***Receiving aid:*** Freshmen: 24% (463); all full-time undergraduates: 24% (1,851). ***Average award:*** Freshmen: $4470; Undergraduates: $5035. ***Scholarships, grants, and awards:*** Federal Pell, FSEOG, state, private, college/university gift aid from institutional funds.

GIFT AID (NON-NEED-BASED) ***Total amount:*** $8,032,195 (80% state, 14% institutional, 6% external sources). ***Receiving aid:*** Freshmen: 29% (578). Undergraduates: 35% (2,721). ***Average award:*** Freshmen: $3015. Undergraduates: $3399. ***Scholarships, grants, and awards by category:*** *Academic interests/achievement:* biological sciences, business, education, engineering/technologies, general academic interests/achievements, health fields, humanities, mathematics, physical sciences, religion/biblical studies, social sciences. *Creative arts/performance:* art/fine arts, music. *Special achievements/activities:* community service, leadership. *Special characteristics:* adult students, ethnic background, handicapped students, international students, local/state students, members of minority groups, out-of-state students. ***Tuition waivers:*** Full or partial for employees or children of employees, senior citizens.

LOANS ***Student loans:*** $22,739,056 (68% need-based, 32% non-need-based). 36% of past graduating class borrowed through all loan programs. *Average indebtedness per student:* $22,328. ***Average need-based loan:*** Freshmen: $4492. Undergraduates: $5699.

WORK-STUDY ***Federal work-study:*** Total amount: $262,266; jobs available. ***State or other work-study/employment:*** Total amount: $1,737,472 (100% need-based). Part-time jobs available.

ATHLETIC AWARDS Total amount: $502,794 (100% non-need-based).

APPLYING FOR FINANCIAL AID ***Required financial aid form:*** FAFSA. ***Financial aid deadline:*** 6/30 (priority: 3/1). ***Notification date:*** Continuous.

CONTACT Jorge Lopez-Rosado, Director of Student Financial Services, Florida Gulf Coast University, 10501 FGCU Boulevard South, Fort Myers, FL 33965, 239-590-1210 or toll-free 888-889-1095. *Fax:* 239-590-7923. *E-mail:* faso@fgcu.edu.

FLORIDA HOSPITAL COLLEGE OF HEALTH SCIENCES

Orlando, FL

Tuition & fees: $9580 **Average undergraduate aid package: N/A**

ABOUT THE INSTITUTION Independent, coed. ***Awards:*** associate, bachelor's, and master's degrees. 6 undergraduate majors. ***Total enrollment:*** 2,207. Undergraduates: 2,207. Federal methodology is used as a basis for awarding need-based institutional aid.

UNDERGRADUATE EXPENSES for 2010–11 ***Application fee:*** $20. ***Tuition:*** full-time $9000; part-time $300 per credit. ***Required fees:*** full-time $580; $290 per term. Full-time tuition and fees vary according to course load and program. Part-time tuition and fees vary according to course load and program. ***Payment plans:*** Installment, deferred payment.

GIFT AID (NEED-BASED) ***Total amount:*** $2,365,448 (88% federal, 9% state, 3% institutional). ***Scholarships, grants, and awards:*** Federal Pell, FSEOG, state, private, college/university gift aid from institutional funds.

GIFT AID (NON-NEED-BASED) ***Total amount:*** $2,159,642 (70% state, 11% institutional, 19% external sources). ***Tuition waivers:*** Full or partial for employees or children of employees. ***ROTC:*** Air Force cooperative.

LOANS ***Student loans:*** $13,390,262 (31% need-based, 69% non-need-based). ***Parent loans:*** $377,618 (100% non-need-based). ***Programs:*** Federal Direct (Subsidized and Unsubsidized Stafford, PLUS), private loans.

APPLYING FOR FINANCIAL AID ***Required financial aid forms:*** FAFSA, institution's own form. ***Financial aid deadline:*** 7/22 (priority: 4/10). ***Notification date:*** Continuous. Students must reply within 2 weeks of notification.

CONTACT Starr Bender, Director of Financial Aid, Florida Hospital College of Health Sciences, 671 Winyah Drive, Orlando, FL 32803, 407-303-6963 or toll-free 800-500-7747 (out-of-state). *Fax:* 407-303-7680. *E-mail:* starr.bender@fhchs.edu.

FLORIDA INSTITUTE OF TECHNOLOGY

Melbourne, FL

Tuition & fees: $32,294 **Average undergraduate aid package: $28,521**

ABOUT THE INSTITUTION Independent, coed. 64 undergraduate majors. Federal methodology is used as a basis for awarding need-based institutional aid.

UNDERGRADUATE EXPENSES for 2010–11 ***Comprehensive fee:*** $43,504 includes full-time tuition ($31,734), mandatory fees ($560), and room and board ($11,210). ***College room only:*** $6670. Full-time tuition and fees vary according to course load and program. Room and board charges vary according to board plan and housing facility. ***Part-time tuition:*** $950 per credit hour. ***Payment plan:*** Installment.

FRESHMAN FINANCIAL AID (Fall 2010, est.) 378 applied for aid; of those 90% were deemed to have need. 100% of freshmen with need received aid; of those 23% had need fully met. ***Average percent of need met:*** 82% (excluding resources awarded to replace EFC). ***Average financial aid package:*** $29,176 (excluding resources awarded to replace EFC). 26% of all full-time freshmen had no need and received non-need-based gift aid.

UNDERGRADUATE FINANCIAL AID (Fall 2010, est.) 1,613 applied for aid; of those 91% were deemed to have need. 100% of undergraduates with need received aid; of those 21% had need fully met. ***Average percent of need met:*** 79% (excluding resources awarded to replace EFC). ***Average financial aid package:*** $28,521 (excluding resources awarded to replace EFC). 23% of all full-time undergraduates had no need and received non-need-based gift aid.

GIFT AID (NEED-BASED) ***Total amount:*** $28,232,987 (19% federal, 11% state, 68% institutional, 2% external sources). ***Receiving aid:*** Freshmen: 70% (340); all full-time undergraduates: 63% (1,455). ***Average award:*** Freshmen: $20,493; Undergraduates: $19,809. ***Scholarships, grants, and awards:*** Federal Pell, FSEOG, state, private, college/university gift aid from institutional funds.

GIFT AID (NON-NEED-BASED) ***Total amount:*** $7,653,688 (14% federal, 6% state, 79% institutional, 1% external sources). ***Receiving aid:*** Freshmen: 70% (340). Undergraduates: 60% (1,396). ***Average award:*** Freshmen: $11,258. Undergraduates: $10,298. ***Scholarships, grants, and awards by category:*** *Academic interests/achievement:* 1,445 awards ($12,967,258 total): general academic interests/achievements, military science. *Creative arts/performance:* 21 awards ($20,500 total): music. *Special achievements/activities:* 136 awards ($1,221,498 total): cheerleading/drum major, hobbies/interests, memberships. *Special characteristics:* 1,345 awards ($2,877,503 total): children and siblings of alumni, children of faculty/staff, general special characteristics, international students, previous college experience, siblings of current students. ***Tuition waivers:*** Full or partial for employees or children of employees, senior citizens.

LOANS ***Student loans:*** $17,313,537 (95% need-based, 5% non-need-based). 65% of past graduating class borrowed through all loan programs. *Average indebtedness per student:* $41,565. ***Average need-based loan:*** Freshmen: $3547. Undergraduates: $4813. ***Parent loans:*** $4,574,704 (96% need-based, 4% non-need-based). ***Programs:*** Perkins.

WORK-STUDY ***Federal work-study:*** Total amount: $968,173; 755 jobs averaging $1282. ***State or other work-study/employment:*** Total amount: $33,266 (100% need-based). 10 part-time jobs averaging $3327.

ATHLETIC AWARDS Total amount: $2,784,180 (59% need-based, 41% non-need-based).

APPLYING FOR FINANCIAL AID ***Required financial aid forms:*** FAFSA, state aid form. ***Financial aid deadline (priority):*** 3/1. ***Notification date:*** Continuous beginning 2/15. Students must reply by 5/1 or within 4 weeks of notification.

CONTACT Office of Financial Aid, Florida Institute of Technology, 150 West University Boulevard, Melbourne, FL 32901-6975, 321-674-8070 or toll-free 800-888-4348. *Fax:* 321-724-2778. *E-mail:* finaid@fit.edu.

FLORIDA INTERNATIONAL UNIVERSITY

Miami, FL

Tuition & fees (FL res): $5091 **Average undergraduate aid package: $8514**

ABOUT THE INSTITUTION State-supported, coed. 59 undergraduate majors. Federal methodology is used as a basis for awarding need-based institutional aid.

UNDERGRADUATE EXPENSES for 2010–11 ***Tuition, state resident:*** full-time $4743; part-time $158.10 per credit hour. ***Tuition, nonresident:*** full-time $17,142; part-time $571.40 per credit hour. ***Required fees:*** full-time $348; $174 per term. Full-time tuition and fees vary according to course load. Part-time tuition and fees vary according to course load. ***College room and board:*** $11,440. Room and board charges vary according to housing facility. ***Payment plan:*** Installment.

FRESHMAN FINANCIAL AID (Fall 2010, est.) 2,303 applied for aid; of those 99% were deemed to have need. 98% of freshmen with need received aid; of those 13% had need fully met. ***Average percent of need met:*** 26% (excluding resources awarded to replace EFC). ***Average financial aid package:*** $7139 (excluding resources awarded to replace EFC). 39% of all full-time freshmen had no need and received non-need-based gift aid.

UNDERGRADUATE FINANCIAL AID (Fall 2010, est.) 12,444 applied for aid; of those 98% were deemed to have need. 98% of undergraduates with need received aid; of those 17% had need fully met. ***Average percent of need met:*** 24% (excluding resources awarded to replace EFC). ***Average financial aid package:*** $8514 (excluding resources awarded to replace EFC). 6% of all full-time undergraduates had no need and received non-need-based gift aid.

GIFT AID (NEED-BASED) ***Total amount:*** $81,462,589 (75% federal, 9% state, 16% institutional). ***Receiving aid:*** Freshmen: 48% (1,296); all full-time undergraduates: 45% (8,593). ***Average award:*** Freshmen: $6665; Undergraduates: $6452. ***Scholarships, grants, and awards:*** Federal Pell, FSEOG, state, private, college/university gift aid from institutional funds.

GIFT AID (NON-NEED-BASED) ***Total amount:*** $35,999,516 (9% federal, 61% state, 23% institutional, 7% external sources). ***Receiving aid:*** Freshmen: 70% (1,910). Undergraduates: 31% (5,851). ***Average award:*** Freshmen: $708. Undergraduates: $606. ***Scholarships, grants, and awards by category:*** *Academic interests/achievement:* 1,997 awards ($3,024,938 total): biological sciences, business, communication, computer science, education, engineering/technologies, English, foreign languages, general academic interests/achievements, health fields, humanities, mathematics, physical sciences, social sciences. *Creative arts/performance:* 35 awards ($55,550 total): dance, journalism/publications, music, performing arts, theater/drama. *Special characteristics:* children and siblings of alumni, members of minority groups. ***Tuition waivers:*** Full or partial for employees or children of employees, senior citizens.

LOANS ***Student loans:*** $184,569,413 (46% need-based, 54% non-need-based). 45% of past graduating class borrowed through all loan programs. *Average indebtedness per student:* $16,026. ***Average need-based loan:*** Freshmen: $7847. Undergraduates: $9151. ***Parent loans:*** $1,840,724 (100% non-need-based). ***Programs:*** Federal Direct (Subsidized and Unsubsidized Stafford, PLUS), Perkins, college/university.

WORK-STUDY ***Federal work-study:*** Total amount: $1,731,386; 529 jobs averaging $2249. ***State or other work-study/employment:*** Total amount: $73,189 (100% need-based). 9 part-time jobs averaging $5008.

ATHLETIC AWARDS Total amount: $4,530,397 (1% need-based, 99% non-need-based).

APPLYING FOR FINANCIAL AID ***Required financial aid form:*** FAFSA. ***Financial aid deadline:*** 5/15 (priority: 3/1). ***Notification date:*** Continuous beginning 2/15. Students must reply within 4 weeks of notification.

CONTACT Francisco Valines, Director of Financial Aid, Florida International University, 12200 SW 8th Street, PC 125, Miami, FL 33199, 305-348-7272. *Fax:* 305-348-2346. *E-mail:* finaid@fiu.edu.

FLORIDA MEMORIAL UNIVERSITY

Miami-Dade, FL

CONTACT Brian Phillip, Director of Financial Aid, Florida Memorial University, 15800 Northwest 42nd Avenue, Miami, FL 33054, 305-626-3745 or toll-free 800-822-1362. *Fax:* 305-626-3106.

FLORIDA METROPOLITAN UNIVERSITY–BRANDON CAMPUS

Tampa, FL

See Everest University.

FLORIDA METROPOLITAN UNIVERSITY–JACKSONVILLE CAMPUS

Jacksonville, FL

See Everest University.

FLORIDA METROPOLITAN UNIVERSITY–LAKELAND CAMPUS

Lakeland, FL

See Everest University.

FLORIDA METROPOLITAN UNIVERSITY–MELBOURNE CAMPUS

Melbourne, FL

See Everest University.

FLORIDA METROPOLITAN UNIVERSITY–NORTH ORLANDO CAMPUS

Orlando, FL

See Everest University.

FLORIDA METROPOLITAN UNIVERSITY–PINELLAS CAMPUS

Clearwater, FL

See Everest University.

FLORIDA METROPOLITAN UNIVERSITY–POMPANO BEACH CAMPUS

Pompano Beach, FL

See Everest University.

FLORIDA METROPOLITAN UNIVERSITY–SOUTH ORLANDO CAMPUS

Orlando, FL

See Everest University.

FLORIDA METROPOLITAN UNIVERSITY–TAMPA CAMPUS

Tampa, FL

See Everest University.

FLORIDA NATIONAL COLLEGE

Hialeah, FL

Tuition & fees: $13,170 **Average undergraduate aid package: N/A**

ABOUT THE INSTITUTION Proprietary, coed. 43 undergraduate majors. Federal methodology is used as a basis for awarding need-based institutional aid.

UNDERGRADUATE EXPENSES for 2011–12 ***Tuition:*** full-time $12,600; part-time $525 per credit. ***Payment plans:*** Guaranteed tuition, tuition prepayment, installment.

FRESHMAN FINANCIAL AID (Fall 2009) 554 applied for aid; of those 99% were deemed to have need. 100% of freshmen with need received aid.

UNDERGRADUATE FINANCIAL AID (Fall 2009) 1,344 applied for aid; of those 99% were deemed to have need. 100% of undergraduates with need received aid.

GIFT AID (NEED-BASED) ***Total amount:*** $13,897,211 (98% federal, 2% state). ***Receiving aid:*** Freshmen: 93% (543); all full-time undergraduates: 93% (1,316). ***Average award:*** Freshmen: $4650; Undergraduates: $4650. ***Scholarships, grants, and awards:*** Federal Pell, FSEOG, state.

GIFT AID (NON-NEED-BASED) ***Receiving aid:*** Freshmen: 93% (543). Undergraduates: 93% (1,316). ***Tuition waivers:*** Full or partial for employees or children of employees.

LOANS ***Student loans:*** $18,718,849 (100% need-based). 95% of past graduating class borrowed through all loan programs. *Average indebtedness per student:* $8750. ***Parent loans:*** $645,174 (100% need-based). ***Programs:*** Federal Direct (Subsidized and Unsubsidized Stafford, PLUS), Perkins.

WORK-STUDY ***Federal work-study:*** Total amount: $101,544; 14 jobs averaging $7253. ***State or other work-study/employment:*** Part-time jobs available.

APPLYING FOR FINANCIAL AID ***Required financial aid form:*** FAFSA. ***Financial aid deadline:*** Continuous.

CONTACT Mr. Omar Sanchez, Director of Financial Aid, Florida National College, 4425 West 20th Avenue, Hialeah, FL 33012, 305-821-3333 Ext. 1003. *Fax:* 305-362-0595. *E-mail:* omarsnc@mm.fnc.edu.

FLORIDA SOUTHERN COLLEGE

Lakeland, FL

Tuition & fees: $26,112 **Average undergraduate aid package: $21,825**

ABOUT THE INSTITUTION Independent religious, coed. 53 undergraduate majors. Federal methodology is used as a basis for awarding need-based institutional aid.

UNDERGRADUATE EXPENSES for 2011–12 ***Comprehensive fee:*** $34,920 includes full-time tuition ($25,529), mandatory fees ($583), and room and board ($8808). ***College room only:*** $4982. Full-time tuition and fees vary according to student level. Room and board charges vary according to board plan and housing facility. ***Part-time tuition:*** $750 per semester hour. Part-time tuition and fees vary according to class time. ***Payment plan:*** Installment.

FRESHMAN FINANCIAL AID (Fall 2010, est.) 544 applied for aid; of those 95% were deemed to have need. 100% of freshmen with need received aid; of those 14% had need fully met. ***Average percent of need met:*** 72% (excluding resources awarded to replace EFC). ***Average financial aid package:*** $23,529 (excluding resources awarded to replace EFC). 11% of all full-time freshmen had no need and received non-need-based gift aid.

UNDERGRADUATE FINANCIAL AID (Fall 2010, est.) 1,531 applied for aid; of those 91% were deemed to have need. 100% of undergraduates with need received aid; of those 21% had need fully met. ***Average percent of need met:*** 76% (excluding resources awarded to replace EFC). ***Average financial aid package:*** $21,825 (excluding resources awarded to replace EFC). 11% of all full-time undergraduates had no need and received non-need-based gift aid.

GIFT AID (NEED-BASED) ***Total amount:*** $25,185,018 (13% federal, 20% state, 53% institutional, 14% external sources). ***Receiving aid:*** Freshmen: 66% (401); all full-time undergraduates: 58% (1,130). ***Average award:*** Freshmen: $9191; Undergraduates: $9236. ***Scholarships, grants, and awards:*** Federal Pell, FSEOG, state, private, college/university gift aid from institutional funds.

GIFT AID (NON-NEED-BASED) ***Total amount:*** $2,149,808 (22% state, 65% institutional, 13% external sources). ***Receiving aid:*** Freshmen: 85% (515). Undergraduates: 72% (1,390). ***Average award:*** Freshmen: $9748. Undergraduates: $9656. ***Scholarships, grants, and awards by category:*** *Academic interests/achievement:* agriculture, biological sciences, business, communication, education, general academic interests/achievements, health fields, physical sciences, religion/biblical studies, social sciences. *Creative arts/performance:* art/fine arts, music, theater/drama. *Special achievements/activities:* community service, general special achievements/activities, leadership. *Special characteristics:* children and siblings of alumni, children of faculty/staff, general special characteristics, local/state students, out-of-state students, relatives of clergy, siblings of current students. ***Tuition waivers:*** Full or partial for children of alumni, employees or children of employees.

LOANS ***Student loans:*** $10,832,064 (93% need-based, 7% non-need-based). 64% of past graduating class borrowed through all loan programs. *Average indebtedness per student:* $28,294. ***Average need-based loan:*** Freshmen: $3377. Undergraduates: $4213. ***Parent loans:*** $4,589,149 (90% need-based, 10% non-need-based). ***Programs:*** Federal Direct (Subsidized and Unsubsidized Stafford, PLUS), Perkins.

WORK-STUDY ***Federal work-study:*** Total amount: $498,968; 244 jobs averaging $1500. ***State or other work-study/employment:*** Total amount: $561,380 (88% need-based, 12% non-need-based). 501 part-time jobs averaging $1500.

ATHLETIC AWARDS Total amount: $2,496,316 (87% need-based, 13% non-need-based).

APPLYING FOR FINANCIAL AID ***Required financial aid forms:*** FAFSA, institution's own form. ***Financial aid deadline:*** 7/1 (priority: 3/1). ***Notification date:*** Continuous beginning 3/1. Students must reply within 3 weeks of notification.

CONTACT William L. Healy, Financial Aid Director, Florida Southern College, 111 Lake Hollingsworth Drive, Lakeland, FL 33801-5698, 863-680-4140 or toll-free 800-274-4131. *Fax:* 863-680-4567. *E-mail:* whealy@flsouthern.edu.

FLORIDA STATE UNIVERSITY

Tallahassee, FL

Tuition & fees (FL res): $5235 **Average undergraduate aid package: $10,709**

ABOUT THE INSTITUTION State-supported, coed. 56 undergraduate majors. Federal methodology is used as a basis for awarding need-based institutional aid.

UNDERGRADUATE EXPENSES for 2010–11 ***Tuition, state resident:*** full-time $3153; part-time $105.21 per credit hour. ***Tuition, nonresident:*** full-time $17,691; part-time $586.69 per credit hour. ***Required fees:*** full-time $2082; $68.05 per credit hour or $20 per term. Full-time tuition and fees vary according to course load, degree level, and location. Part-time tuition and fees vary according to course load, degree level, and location. ***College room and board:*** $9180; ***Room only:*** $5280. Room and board charges vary according to board plan and housing facility. ***Payment plans:*** Tuition prepayment, installment.

FRESHMAN FINANCIAL AID (Fall 2010, est.) 4,595 applied for aid; of those 47% were deemed to have need. 100% of freshmen with need received aid; of those 79% had need fully met. ***Average percent of need met:*** 72% (excluding resources awarded to replace EFC). ***Average financial aid package:*** $10,422 (excluding resources awarded to replace EFC). 7% of all full-time freshmen had no need and received non-need-based gift aid.

UNDERGRADUATE FINANCIAL AID (Fall 2010, est.) 18,080 applied for aid; of those 53% were deemed to have need. 100% of undergraduates with need received aid; of those 76% had need fully met. ***Average percent of need met:*** 75% (excluding resources awarded to replace EFC). ***Average financial aid package:*** $10,709 (excluding resources awarded to replace EFC). 5% of all full-time undergraduates had no need and received non-need-based gift aid.

GIFT AID (NEED-BASED) ***Total amount:*** $84,211,910 (53% federal, 29% state, 16% institutional, 2% external sources). ***Receiving aid:*** Freshmen: 23% (1,334); all full-time undergraduates: 23% (5,826). ***Average award:*** Freshmen: $4402; Undergraduates: $4390. ***Scholarships, grants, and awards:*** Federal Pell, FSEOG, state, private, college/university gift aid from institutional funds, Academic Competitiveness Grants, National SMART Grants.

GIFT AID (NON-NEED-BASED) ***Total amount:*** $50,815,785 (78% state, 17% institutional, 5% external sources). ***Receiving aid:*** Freshmen: 36% (2,047). Undergraduates: 17% (4,265). ***Average award:*** Freshmen: $2331. Undergraduates: $2302. ***Scholarships, grants, and awards by category:*** *Academic interests/achievement:* general academic interests/achievements. *Creative arts/performance:* cinema/film/broadcasting, dance, music, theater/drama. *Special characteristics:* local/state students. ***Tuition waivers:*** Full or partial for employees or children of employees, senior citizens.

LOANS ***Student loans:*** $93,791,251 (57% need-based, 43% non-need-based). 48% of past graduating class borrowed through all loan programs. *Average indebtedness per student:* $20,993. ***Average need-based loan:*** Freshmen: $2998. Undergraduates: $3703. ***Parent loans:*** $7,296,523 (25% need-based, 75% non-need-based). ***Programs:*** Federal Direct (Subsidized and Unsubsidized Stafford, PLUS), Perkins, college/university.

WORK-STUDY ***Federal work-study:*** Total amount: $1,419,681; 697 jobs averaging $1100. ***State or other work-study/employment:*** Total amount: $56,183 (100% need-based). 26 part-time jobs averaging $1100.

ATHLETIC AWARDS Total amount: $2,598,511 (3% need-based, 97% non-need-based).

APPLYING FOR FINANCIAL AID ***Required financial aid form:*** FAFSA. ***Financial aid deadline:*** Continuous. ***Notification date:*** Continuous beginning 3/1.

CONTACT Darryl Marshall, Director of Financial Aid, Florida State University, University Center A4400, Tallahassee, FL 32306-2430, 850-644-5716. *Fax:* 850-644-6404. *E-mail:* ofacs@admin.fsu.edu.

FONTBONNE UNIVERSITY

St. Louis, MO

CONTACT Financial Aid Office, Fontbonne University, 6800 Wydown Boulevard, St. Louis, MO 63105-3098, 314-889-1414. *Fax:* 314-889-1451.

FORDHAM UNIVERSITY

New York, NY

Tuition & fees: $38,277 **Average undergraduate aid package: $26,057**

ABOUT THE INSTITUTION Independent Roman Catholic (Jesuit), coed. 93 undergraduate majors. Both federal and institutional methodology are used as a basis for awarding need-based institutional aid.

UNDERGRADUATE EXPENSES for 2010–11 ***Comprehensive fee:*** $51,167 includes full-time tuition ($37,545), mandatory fees ($732), and room and board ($12,890). ***College room only:*** $7245. Full-time tuition and fees vary according to student level. Room and board charges vary according to board plan and location. ***Part-time tuition:*** $1250 per credit. Part-time tuition and fees vary according to course load. ***Payment plan:*** Installment.

FRESHMAN FINANCIAL AID (Fall 2009) 1,620 applied for aid; of those 74% were deemed to have need. 100% of freshmen with need received aid; of those 31% had need fully met. ***Average percent of need met:*** 80% (excluding resources awarded to replace EFC). ***Average financial aid package:*** $27,288 (excluding resources awarded to replace EFC). 22% of all full-time freshmen had no need and received non-need-based gift aid.

UNDERGRADUATE FINANCIAL AID (Fall 2009) 6,253 applied for aid; of those 76% were deemed to have need. 100% of undergraduates with need received aid; of those 26% had need fully met. ***Average percent of need met:*** 75% (excluding resources awarded to replace EFC). ***Average financial aid package:*** $26,057 (excluding resources awarded to replace EFC). 18% of all full-time undergraduates had no need and received non-need-based gift aid.

GIFT AID (NEED-BASED) ***Total amount:*** $78,832,323 (12% federal, 8% state, 75% institutional, 5% external sources). ***Receiving aid:*** Freshmen: 65% (1,170); all full-time undergraduates: 62% (4,572). ***Average award:*** Freshmen: $20,044; Undergraduates: $18,140. ***Scholarships, grants, and awards:*** Federal Pell, FSEOG, state, private, college/university gift aid from institutional funds.

GIFT AID (NON-NEED-BASED) ***Total amount:*** $19,355,396 (2% state, 87% institutional, 11% external sources). ***Receiving aid:*** Freshmen: 12% (213). Undergraduates: 9% (654). ***Average award:*** Freshmen: $11,627. Undergraduates: $10,264. ***Scholarships, grants, and awards by category:*** *Academic interests/achievement:* biological sciences, business, communication, foreign languages, general academic interests/achievements. *Creative arts/performance:* dance, music. *Special achievements/activities:* general special achievements/activities. *Special characteristics:* adult students, children and siblings of alumni, children of faculty/staff, children with a deceased or disabled parent, handicapped students.

LOANS ***Student loans:*** $53,146,358 (65% need-based, 35% non-need-based). 65% of past graduating class borrowed through all loan programs. *Average indebtedness per student:* $33,365. ***Average need-based loan:*** Freshmen: $5159. Undergraduates: $8964. ***Parent loans:*** $17,481,888 (40% need-based, 60% non-need-based). ***Programs:*** Perkins.

WORK-STUDY ***Federal work-study:*** Total amount: $3,271,576; 1,189 jobs averaging $2752. ***State or other work-study/employment:*** Total amount: $2762 (100% need-based). Part-time jobs available.

ATHLETIC AWARDS Total amount: $9,070,574 (76% need-based, 24% non-need-based).

APPLYING FOR FINANCIAL AID ***Required financial aid forms:*** FAFSA, CSS Financial Aid PROFILE, noncustodial (divorced/separated) parent's statement, business/farm supplement. ***Financial aid deadline:*** 2/1. ***Notification date:*** Continuous beginning 4/1. Students must reply by 5/1 or within 2 weeks of notification.

CONTACT Angela Van Dekker, Assistant Vice President of Student Financial Services, Fordham University, 441 East Fordham Road, Thebaud Hall, Room 208, New York, NY 10458, 718-817-3804 or toll-free 800-FORDHAM. *Fax:* 718-817-3817. *E-mail:* avandekker@fordham.edu.

FORT HAYS STATE UNIVERSITY

Hays, KS

CONTACT Craig Karlin, Director of Financial Assistance, Fort Hays State University, Custer Hall, Room 306, 600 Park Street, Hays, KS 67601, 785-628-4408 or toll-free 800-628-FHSU. *Fax:* 785-628-4014. *E-mail:* finaid@fhsu.edu.

FORT LEWIS COLLEGE

Durango, CO

Tuition & fees (CO res): $4924 **Average undergraduate aid package: $7927**

ABOUT THE INSTITUTION State-supported, coed. 62 undergraduate majors. Federal methodology is used as a basis for awarding need-based institutional aid.

UNDERGRADUATE EXPENSES for 2011–12 ***Tuition, state resident:*** full-time $3380; part-time $169 per credit hour. ***Tuition, nonresident:*** full-time $16,072; part-time $803 per credit hour. ***Required fees:*** full-time $1544. Full-time tuition and fees vary according to course load and reciprocity agreements. Part-time tuition and fees vary according to course load and reciprocity agreements. ***College room and board:*** $7840; ***Room only:*** $3940. Room and board charges vary according to board plan and housing facility. ***Payment plan:*** Installment.

FRESHMAN FINANCIAL AID (Fall 2009) 717 applied for aid; of those 69% were deemed to have need. 100% of freshmen with need received aid; of those 35% had need fully met. ***Average percent of need met:*** 68% (excluding resources awarded to replace EFC). ***Average financial aid package:*** $7326 (excluding resources awarded to replace EFC). 33% of all full-time freshmen had no need and received non-need-based gift aid.

UNDERGRADUATE FINANCIAL AID (Fall 2009) 2,624 applied for aid; of those 79% were deemed to have need. 100% of undergraduates with need received aid; of those 30% had need fully met. ***Average percent of need met:*** 71% (excluding resources awarded to replace EFC). ***Average financial aid package:*** $7927 (excluding resources awarded to replace EFC). 18% of all full-time undergraduates had no need and received non-need-based gift aid.

GIFT AID (NEED-BASED) ***Total amount:*** $8,406,760 (69% federal, 9% state, 15% institutional, 7% external sources). ***Receiving aid:*** Freshmen: 60% (494); all full-time undergraduates: 61% (2,072). ***Average award:*** Freshmen: $3315; Undergraduates: $3670. ***Scholarships, grants, and awards:*** Federal Pell, FSEOG, state, private, college/university gift aid from institutional funds.

GIFT AID (NON-NEED-BASED) ***Total amount:*** $2,084,489 (1% federal, 26% state, 41% institutional, 32% external sources). ***Receiving aid:*** Freshmen: 37% (303). Undergraduates: 29% (1,002). ***Average award:*** Freshmen: $1210. Undergraduates: $1573. ***Scholarships, grants, and awards by category:*** *Academic interests/achievement:* agriculture, area/ethnic studies, biological sciences, business, communication, computer science, education, English, general academic interests/achievements, humanities, mathematics, physical sciences, social sciences. *Creative arts/performance:* art/fine arts, music, performing arts, theater/drama. *Special achievements/activities:* general special achievements/activities, leadership. *Special characteristics:* children and siblings of alumni, children of faculty/staff, ethnic background, first-generation college students, general special characteristics, handicapped students, international students, local/state students, members of minority groups, out-of-state students, veterans' children. ***Tuition waivers:*** Full or partial for minority students, employees or children of employees.

LOANS ***Student loans:*** $11,243,078 (74% need-based, 26% non-need-based). 61% of past graduating class borrowed through all loan programs. *Average indebtedness per student:* $17,371. ***Average need-based loan:*** Freshmen: $3473. Undergraduates: $3990. ***Parent loans:*** $2,374,547 (60% need-based, 40% non-need-based). ***Programs:*** Federal Direct (Subsidized and Unsubsidized Stafford, PLUS), Perkins.

WORK-STUDY ***Federal work-study:*** Total amount: $240,034; jobs available. ***State or other work-study/employment:*** Total amount: $1,076,583 (84% need-based, 16% non-need-based). Part-time jobs available.

ATHLETIC AWARDS Total amount: $1,532,800 (37% need-based, 63% non-need-based).

APPLYING FOR FINANCIAL AID ***Required financial aid form:*** FAFSA. ***Financial aid deadline (priority):*** 2/15. ***Notification date:*** Continuous beginning 3/15.

CONTACT Ms. Elaine Redwine, Director of Financial Aid, Fort Lewis College, 1000 Rim Drive, 101 Miller Student Services Building, Durango, CO 81301, 800-352-7512. *Fax:* 970-247-7108. *E-mail:* finaid_off@fortlewis.edu.

FORT VALLEY STATE UNIVERSITY

Fort Valley, GA

Tuition & fees (GA res): $5562 **Average undergraduate aid package: N/A**

ABOUT THE INSTITUTION State-supported, coed. 35 undergraduate majors. Federal methodology is used as a basis for awarding need-based institutional aid.

UNDERGRADUATE EXPENSES for 2010–11 ***Tuition, state resident:*** full-time $4274; part-time $143 per credit hour. ***Tuition, nonresident:*** full-time $15,888; part-time $530 per credit hour. ***Required fees:*** full-time $1288. Full-time tuition and fees vary according to course load, degree level, and student level. Part-time tuition and fees vary according to course load, degree level, and student level. ***College room and board:*** $7326; ***Room only:*** $4456. Room and board charges vary according to board plan, housing facility, and student level.

GIFT AID (NEED-BASED) ***Total amount:*** $14,281,037 (100% federal). ***Scholarships, grants, and awards:*** Federal Pell, FSEOG, state, private, college/university gift aid from institutional funds.

GIFT AID (NON-NEED-BASED) ***Total amount:*** $4,615,385 (13% federal, 61% state, 24% institutional, 2% external sources). ***Scholarships, grants, and awards by category:*** *Academic interests/achievement:* agriculture, business, general academic interests/achievements, home economics, military science, premedicine, social sciences. *Creative arts/performance:* journalism/publications, music. *Special achievements/activities:* general special achievements/activities. *Special characteristics:* handicapped students, international students, out-of-state students. ***Tuition waivers:*** Full or partial for employees or children of employees, senior citizens.

LOANS ***Student loans:*** $25,677,899 (49% need-based, 51% non-need-based). ***Parent loans:*** $8,087,526 (100% need-based). ***Programs:*** Federal Direct (Subsidized and Unsubsidized Stafford, PLUS), Perkins.

WORK-STUDY ***Federal work-study:*** Total amount: $400,683; jobs available.

ATHLETIC AWARDS Total amount: $664,585 (100% non-need-based).

APPLYING FOR FINANCIAL AID ***Required financial aid form:*** FAFSA. ***Financial aid deadline (priority):*** 3/1. ***Notification date:*** Continuous beginning 4/15. Students must reply by 8/15.

CONTACT Office of Financial Aid, Fort Valley State University, 1005 State University Drive, Fort Valley, GA 31030, 478-825-6182 or toll-free 877-462-3878. *Fax:* 478-825-6976.

FRAMINGHAM STATE UNIVERSITY

Framingham, MA

Tuition & fees (MA res): $7065 **Average undergraduate aid package: $6880**

ABOUT THE INSTITUTION State-supported, coed. 23 undergraduate majors. Federal methodology is used as a basis for awarding need-based institutional aid.

UNDERGRADUATE EXPENSES for 2010–11 ***Tuition, state resident:*** full-time $970; part-time $162 per course. ***Tuition, nonresident:*** full-time $7050; part-time $1175 per course. ***Required fees:*** full-time $6095; $1080 per course. Full-time tuition and fees vary according to class time. Part-time tuition and fees vary according to class time and course load. ***College room and board:*** $7100; ***Room only:*** $5600. Room and board charges vary according to board plan and housing facility. ***Payment plans:*** Tuition prepayment, installment.

FRESHMAN FINANCIAL AID (Fall 2009) 647 applied for aid; of those 66% were deemed to have need. 100% of freshmen with need received aid; of those 44% had need fully met. ***Average percent of need met:*** 75% (excluding resources awarded to replace EFC). ***Average financial aid package:*** $6800 (excluding resources awarded to replace EFC). 4% of all full-time freshmen had no need and received non-need-based gift aid.

UNDERGRADUATE FINANCIAL AID (Fall 2009) 2,362 applied for aid; of those 69% were deemed to have need. 100% of undergraduates with need received aid; of those 55% had need fully met. ***Average percent of need met:*** 76% (excluding resources awarded to replace EFC). ***Average financial aid package:*** $6880 (excluding resources awarded to replace EFC). 2% of all full-time undergraduates had no need and received non-need-based gift aid.

GIFT AID (NEED-BASED) ***Total amount:*** $5,686,538 (57% federal, 22% state, 18% institutional, 3% external sources). ***Receiving aid:*** Freshmen: 47% (341); all full-time undergraduates: 42% (1,305). ***Average award:*** Freshmen: $4010; Undergraduates: $4090. ***Scholarships, grants, and awards:*** Federal Pell, FSEOG, state, private, college/university gift aid from institutional funds.

GIFT AID (NON-NEED-BASED) ***Total amount:*** $276,921 (1% federal, 13% state, 66% institutional, 20% external sources). ***Receiving aid:*** Freshmen: 1% (5). Undergraduates: 6% (190). ***Average award:*** Freshmen: $2010. Undergraduates: $2208. ***Scholarships, grants, and awards by category:*** *Academic interests/achievement:* biological sciences, education, general academic interests/achievements, home economics, physical sciences. *Special characteristics:* children of faculty/staff, children of public servants, children of union members/company employees, veterans. ***Tuition waivers:*** Full or partial for employees or children of employees, senior citizens.

LOANS ***Student loans:*** $15,450,606 (71% need-based, 29% non-need-based). 68% of past graduating class borrowed through all loan programs. *Average indebtedness per student:* $19,300. ***Average need-based loan:*** Freshmen: $4620. Undergraduates: $4950. ***Parent loans:*** $1,086,631 (100% need-based). ***Programs:*** Federal Direct (Subsidized and Unsubsidized Stafford, PLUS), Perkins, state.

WORK-STUDY ***Federal work-study:*** Total amount: $130,000; jobs available. ***State or other work-study/employment:*** Total amount: $119,548 (100% need-based). Part-time jobs available.

APPLYING FOR FINANCIAL AID ***Required financial aid form:*** FAFSA. ***Financial aid deadline (priority):*** 3/1. ***Notification date:*** Continuous beginning 4/15. Students must reply by 5/1 or within 2 weeks of notification.

CONTACT Office of Financial Aid, Framingham State University, 100 State Street, PO Box 9101, Framingham, MA 01701-9101, 508-626-4534. *Fax:* 508-626-4598.

FRANCISCAN UNIVERSITY OF STEUBENVILLE

Steubenville, OH

ABOUT THE INSTITUTION Independent Roman Catholic, coed. 32 undergraduate majors.

GIFT AID (NEED-BASED) ***Scholarships, grants, and awards:*** Federal Pell, FSEOG, state, private, college/university gift aid from institutional funds.

GIFT AID (NON-NEED-BASED) ***Scholarships, grants, and awards by category:*** *Academic interests/achievement:* general academic interests/achievements. *Special achievements/activities:* religious involvement. *Special characteristics:* children of faculty/staff, international students, local/state students, religious affiliation, siblings of current students.

LOANS ***Programs:*** Perkins, Federal Nursing.

WORK-STUDY ***Federal work-study:*** Total amount: $143,290; jobs available. ***State or other work-study/employment:*** Total amount: $971,486 (85% need-based, 15% non-need-based). Part-time jobs available.

APPLYING FOR FINANCIAL AID ***Required financial aid form:*** FAFSA.

CONTACT John Herrmann, Director of Student Financial Services, Franciscan University of Steubenville, 1235 University Boulevard, Steubenville, OH 43952-1763, 740-284-5215 or toll-free 800-783-6220. *Fax:* 740-284-5469. *E-mail:* jherrmann@franciscan.edu.

FRANCIS MARION UNIVERSITY

Florence, SC

Tuition & fees (SC res): $8480 **Average undergraduate aid package: N/A**

ABOUT THE INSTITUTION State-supported, coed. 31 undergraduate majors. Federal methodology is used as a basis for awarding need-based institutional aid.

UNDERGRADUATE EXPENSES for 2010–11 ***Tuition, state resident:*** full-time $8145; part-time $407.25 per credit hour. ***Tuition, nonresident:*** full-time $16,290; part-time $814.50 per credit hour. ***Required fees:*** full-time $335; $12.25 per credit hour or $30 per term. Part-time tuition and fees vary according to course load. ***College room and board:*** $6380; ***Room only:*** $3600. Room and board charges vary according to board plan and housing facility. ***Payment plan:*** Installment.

FRESHMAN FINANCIAL AID (Fall 2010, est.) 660 applied for aid; of those 92% were deemed to have need. 100% of freshmen with need received aid. 1% of all full-time freshmen had no need and received non-need-based gift aid.

UNDERGRADUATE FINANCIAL AID (Fall 2010, est.) 2,960 applied for aid; of those 92% were deemed to have need. 100% of undergraduates with need received aid. 1% of all full-time undergraduates had no need and received non-need-based gift aid.

GIFT AID (NEED-BASED) ***Total amount:*** $12,120,000 (91% federal, 9% state). ***Receiving aid:*** Freshmen: 70% (517); all full-time undergraduates: 69% (2,287). ***Scholarships, grants, and awards:*** Federal Pell, FSEOG, state, private, Academic Competitiveness Grants, National SMART Grants.

GIFT AID (NON-NEED-BASED) ***Total amount:*** $6,535,000 (81% state, 12% institutional, 7% external sources). ***Average award:*** Freshmen: $2812. Undergraduates: $2367. ***Scholarships, grants, and awards by category:*** *Academic interests/achievement:* biological sciences, business, computer science, education, English, general academic interests/achievements, health fields, humanities, mathematics, premedicine, social sciences. *Creative arts/performance:* art/fine arts, music, theater/drama. *Special achievements/activities:* cheerleading/drum major. *Special characteristics:* adult students, children and siblings of alumni, children of faculty/staff, children of union members/company employees, handicapped students, international students, out-of-state students, spouses of deceased or disabled public servants, veterans, veterans' children. ***Tuition waivers:*** Full or partial for employees or children of employees, senior citizens.

LOANS ***Student loans:*** $29,000,000 (48% need-based, 52% non-need-based). 76% of past graduating class borrowed through all loan programs. *Average indebtedness per student:* $26,453. ***Parent loans:*** $1,600,000 (100% non-need-based). ***Programs:*** Federal Direct (Subsidized and Unsubsidized Stafford, PLUS), Perkins, state.

WORK-STUDY ***Federal work-study:*** Total amount: $159,000; jobs available. ***State or other work-study/employment:*** Total amount: $350,000 (100% non-need-based). Part-time jobs available.

ATHLETIC AWARDS Total amount: $710,000 (100% non-need-based).

APPLYING FOR FINANCIAL AID ***Required financial aid form:*** FAFSA. ***Financial aid deadline (priority):*** 3/1. ***Notification date:*** Continuous beginning 1/30.

CONTACT Miss Kim Ellisor, Director of Financial Assistance, Francis Marion University, PO Box 100547, Florence, SC 29502-0547, 843-661-1190 or toll-free 800-368-7551.

FRANKLIN & MARSHALL COLLEGE

Lancaster, PA

Tuition & fees: $41,150 **Average undergraduate aid package: $32,018**

ABOUT THE INSTITUTION Independent, coed. 38 undergraduate majors. Both federal and institutional methodology are used as a basis for awarding need-based institutional aid.

UNDERGRADUATE EXPENSES for 2010–11 ***One-time required fee:*** $200. ***Comprehensive fee:*** $52,070 includes full-time tuition ($41,090), mandatory fees ($60), and room and board ($10,920). ***College room only:*** $6940. Room and board charges vary according to board plan and housing facility. ***Part-time tuition:*** $5136 per course. ***Payment plans:*** Installment, deferred payment.

FRESHMAN FINANCIAL AID (Fall 2010, est.) 398 applied for aid; of those 76% were deemed to have need. 100% of freshmen with need received aid; of those 100% had need fully met. ***Average percent of need met:*** 100% (excluding resources awarded to replace EFC). ***Average financial aid package:*** $35,253 (excluding resources awarded to replace EFC). 3% of all full-time freshmen had no need and received non-need-based gift aid.

UNDERGRADUATE FINANCIAL AID (Fall 2010, est.) 1,300 applied for aid; of those 82% were deemed to have need. 100% of undergraduates with need received aid; of those 70% had need fully met. ***Average percent of need met:*** 95% (excluding resources awarded to replace EFC). ***Average financial aid package:*** $32,018 (excluding resources awarded to replace EFC). 10% of all full-time undergraduates had no need and received non-need-based gift aid.

GIFT AID (NEED-BASED) ***Total amount:*** $27,732,160 (5% federal, 2% state, 90% institutional, 3% external sources). ***Receiving aid:*** Freshmen: 46% (291); all full-time undergraduates: 41% (991). ***Average award:*** Freshmen: $31,296; Undergraduates: $27,913. ***Scholarships, grants, and awards:*** Federal Pell, FSEOG, state, private, college/university gift aid from institutional funds.

GIFT AID (NON-NEED-BASED) ***Total amount:*** $2,822,770 (1% federal, 70% institutional, 29% external sources). ***Receiving aid:*** Freshmen: 1% (8). Undergraduates: 1% (32). ***Average award:*** Freshmen: $12,576. Undergraduates: $11,291. ***Scholarships, grants, and awards by category:*** *Creative arts/performance:* music. ***Tuition waivers:*** Full or partial for employees or children of employees.

LOANS ***Student loans:*** $10,017,997 (66% need-based, 34% non-need-based). 52% of past graduating class borrowed through all loan programs. *Average indebtedness per student:* $28,451. ***Average need-based loan:*** Freshmen: $3360. Undergraduates: $4339. ***Parent loans:*** $4,962,291 (19% need-based, 81% non-need-based). ***Programs:*** Federal Direct (Subsidized and Unsubsidized Stafford, PLUS), Perkins, college/university.

WORK-STUDY ***Federal work-study:*** Total amount: $1,671,090; jobs available. ***State or other work-study/employment:*** Total amount: $350,075 (100% need-based). Part-time jobs available.

APPLYING FOR FINANCIAL AID ***Required financial aid forms:*** FAFSA, CSS Financial Aid PROFILE, noncustodial (divorced/separated) parent's statement, business/farm supplement, federal income tax form(s), W-2 forms. ***Financial aid deadline:*** 2/15. ***Notification date:*** 4/1. Students must reply by 5/1.

CONTACT Mr. Clarke Paine, Director of Financial Aid, Franklin & Marshall College, PO Box 3003, Lancaster, PA 17604-3003, 717-291-3991. *Fax:* 717-291-4462. *E-mail:* clarke.paine@fandm.edu.

FRANKLIN COLLEGE

Franklin, IN

Tuition & fees: $24,655 **Average undergraduate aid package: $18,496**

ABOUT THE INSTITUTION Independent religious, coed. 32 undergraduate majors. Federal methodology is used as a basis for awarding need-based institutional aid.

UNDERGRADUATE EXPENSES for 2010–11 ***Comprehensive fee:*** $31,950 includes full-time tuition ($24,470), mandatory fees ($185), and room and board ($7295). ***College room only:*** $4330. Room and board charges vary according to board plan and housing facility. ***Part-time tuition:*** $345 per credit hour. Part-time tuition and fees vary according to course load. ***Payment plan:*** Installment.

FRESHMAN FINANCIAL AID (Fall 2009) 308 applied for aid; of those 90% were deemed to have need. 100% of freshmen with need received aid; of those 17% had need fully met. ***Average percent of need met:*** 80% (excluding resources awarded to replace EFC). ***Average financial aid package:*** $18,894 (excluding resources awarded to replace EFC). 11% of all full-time freshmen had no need and received non-need-based gift aid.

UNDERGRADUATE FINANCIAL AID (Fall 2009) 1,034 applied for aid; of those 88% were deemed to have need. 100% of undergraduates with need received aid; of those 16% had need fully met. ***Average percent of need met:*** 81% (excluding resources awarded to replace EFC). ***Average financial aid package:*** $18,496 (excluding resources awarded to replace EFC). 15% of all full-time undergraduates had no need and received non-need-based gift aid.

GIFT AID (NEED-BASED) ***Total amount:*** $12,604,174 (14% federal, 18% state, 64% institutional, 4% external sources). ***Receiving aid:*** Freshmen: 88% (277); all full-time undergraduates: 84% (909). ***Average award:*** Freshmen: $15,712; Undergraduates: $14,213. ***Scholarships, grants, and awards:*** Federal Pell, FSEOG, state, private, college/university gift aid from institutional funds.

GIFT AID (NON-NEED-BASED) ***Total amount:*** $1,994,781 (2% state, 86% institutional, 12% external sources). ***Receiving aid:*** Freshmen: 13% (42). Undergraduates: 12% (124). ***Average award:*** Freshmen: $8066. Undergraduates: $8197. ***Scholarships, grants, and awards by category:*** *Academic interests/achievement:* 1,085 awards ($9,540,712 total): general academic interests/achievements. *Creative arts/performance:* 35 awards ($165,591 total): art/fine arts, journalism/publications, music, performing arts, theater/drama. *Special characteristics:* 231 awards ($658,718 total): children and siblings of alumni, children of faculty/staff, ethnic background, members of minority groups, out-of-state students, religious affiliation, siblings of current students. ***Tuition waivers:*** Full or partial for employees or children of employees, senior citizens.

LOANS ***Student loans:*** $8,195,909 (70% need-based, 30% non-need-based). 86% of past graduating class borrowed through all loan programs. *Average indebtedness per student:* $29,387. ***Average need-based loan:*** Freshmen: $3821. Undergraduates: $5051. ***Parent loans:*** $1,506,207 (23% need-based, 77% non-need-based). ***Programs:*** Federal Direct (Subsidized and Unsubsidized Stafford, PLUS), Perkins, college/university.

WORK-STUDY ***Federal work-study:*** Total amount: $201,748; 328 jobs averaging $863. ***State or other work-study/employment:*** Total amount: $19,732 (22% need-based, 78% non-need-based). 31 part-time jobs averaging $637.

APPLYING FOR FINANCIAL AID ***Required financial aid forms:*** FAFSA, institution's own form. ***Financial aid deadline (priority):*** 3/10. ***Notification date:*** Continuous beginning 3/1. Students must reply by 5/1 or within 4 weeks of notification.

CONTACT Elizabeth Sappenfield, Director of Financial Aid, Franklin College, 101 Branigin Boulevard, Franklin, IN 46131-2598, 317-738-8075 or toll-free 800-852-0232. *Fax:* 317-738-8072. *E-mail:* finaid@franklincollege.edu.

FRANKLIN PIERCE UNIVERSITY

Rindge, NH

CONTACT Kenneth Ferreira, Executive Director of Student Financial Services, Franklin Pierce University, 20 College Road, Rindge, NH 03461-0060, 603-899-4180 or toll-free 800-437-0048. *Fax:* 603-899-4372. *E-mail:* ferreirak@fpc.edu.

FRANKLIN UNIVERSITY

Columbus, OH

CONTACT Ms. Marlowe Collier, Financial Aid Assistant, Franklin University, 201 South Grant Avenue, Columbus, OH 43215-5399, 614-797-4700 or toll-free 877-341-6300. *Fax:* 614-220-8931. *E-mail:* finaid@franklin.edu.

FRANKLIN W. OLIN COLLEGE OF ENGINEERING

Needham, MA

Tuition & fees: $39,450 **Average undergraduate aid package: $34,439**

ABOUT THE INSTITUTION Independent, coed. 3 undergraduate majors. Federal methodology is used as a basis for awarding need-based institutional aid.

UNDERGRADUATE EXPENSES for 2011–12 ***Comprehensive fee:*** $53,450 includes full-time tuition ($39,000), mandatory fees ($450), and room and board ($14,000). ***College room only:*** $8800. ***Payment plan:*** Installment.

FRESHMAN FINANCIAL AID (Fall 2010, est.) 71 applied for aid; of those 85% were deemed to have need. 100% of freshmen with need received aid; of those 100% had need fully met. ***Average percent of need met:*** 100% (excluding

resources awarded to replace EFC). ***Average financial aid package:*** $26,986 (excluding resources awarded to replace EFC). 35% of all full-time freshmen had no need and received non-need-based gift aid.

UNDERGRADUATE FINANCIAL AID (Fall 2010, est.) 130 applied for aid; of those 88% were deemed to have need. 100% of undergraduates with need received aid; of those 100% had need fully met. ***Average percent of need met:*** 100% (excluding resources awarded to replace EFC). ***Average financial aid package:*** $34,439 (excluding resources awarded to replace EFC). 67% of all full-time undergraduates had no need and received non-need-based gift aid.

GIFT AID (NEED-BASED) ***Total amount:*** $1,240,208 (16% federal, 4% state, 69% institutional, 11% external sources). ***Receiving aid:*** Freshmen: 40% (37); all full-time undergraduates: 18% (63). ***Average award:*** Freshmen: $19,560; Undergraduates: $13,754. ***Scholarships, grants, and awards:*** Federal Pell, FSEOG, state, private, college/university gift aid from institutional funds, Academic Competitiveness Grants, National SMART Grants, National Merit Scholarships.

GIFT AID (NON-NEED-BASED) ***Total amount:*** $11,116,000 (100% institutional). ***Receiving aid:*** Freshmen: 65% (60). Undergraduates: 34% (115). ***Average award:*** Freshmen: $19,000. Undergraduates: $35,310. ***Scholarships, grants, and awards by category:*** *Academic interests/achievement:* general academic interests/achievements.

LOANS ***Student loans:*** $348,648 (32% need-based, 68% non-need-based). 17% of past graduating class borrowed through all loan programs. *Average indebtedness per student:* $13,200. ***Average need-based loan:*** Freshmen: $2650. Undergraduates: $2805. ***Parent loans:*** $84,113 (100% non-need-based). ***Programs:*** Federal Direct (Subsidized and Unsubsidized Stafford, PLUS).

APPLYING FOR FINANCIAL AID ***Required financial aid form:*** FAFSA. ***Financial aid deadline:*** 2/15. ***Notification date:*** Continuous beginning 3/31. Students must reply by 5/1.

CONTACT Ms. Jean Ricker, Manager of Financial Aid, Franklin W. Olin College of Engineering, Campus Center 300, Needham, MA 02492, 781-292-2343. *E-mail:* jean.ricker@olin.edu.

FREED-HARDEMAN UNIVERSITY

Henderson, TN

Tuition & fees: $15,922 **Average undergraduate aid package: $14,853**

ABOUT THE INSTITUTION Independent religious, coed. 54 undergraduate majors. Federal methodology is used as a basis for awarding need-based institutional aid.

UNDERGRADUATE EXPENSES for 2010–11 ***Comprehensive fee:*** $23,138 includes full-time tuition ($12,840), mandatory fees ($3082), and room and board ($7216). ***College room only:*** $3980. Full-time tuition and fees vary according to course load and degree level. Room and board charges vary according to board plan and housing facility. ***Part-time tuition:*** $428 per semester hour. Part-time tuition and fees vary according to course load and degree level. ***Payment plan:*** Installment.

FRESHMAN FINANCIAL AID (Fall 2010, est.) 336 applied for aid; of those 88% were deemed to have need. 100% of freshmen with need received aid; of those 21% had need fully met. ***Average percent of need met:*** 70% (excluding resources awarded to replace EFC). ***Average financial aid package:*** $15,475 (excluding resources awarded to replace EFC). 17% of all full-time freshmen had no need and received non-need-based gift aid.

UNDERGRADUATE FINANCIAL AID (Fall 2010, est.) 1,328 applied for aid; of those 88% were deemed to have need. 100% of undergraduates with need received aid; of those 20% had need fully met. ***Average percent of need met:*** 65% (excluding resources awarded to replace EFC). ***Average financial aid package:*** $14,853 (excluding resources awarded to replace EFC). 14% of all full-time undergraduates had no need and received non-need-based gift aid.

GIFT AID (NEED-BASED) ***Total amount:*** $11,669,177 (26% federal, 17% state, 53% institutional, 4% external sources). ***Receiving aid:*** Freshmen: 79% (294); all full-time undergraduates: 81% (1,136). ***Average award:*** Freshmen: $12,473; Undergraduates: $11,230. ***Scholarships, grants, and awards:*** Federal Pell, FSEOG, state, private, college/university gift aid from institutional funds.

GIFT AID (NON-NEED-BASED) ***Total amount:*** $2,520,855 (4% federal, 23% state, 65% institutional, 8% external sources). ***Receiving aid:*** Freshmen: 11% (40). Undergraduates: 12% (166). ***Average award:*** Freshmen: $6493. Undergraduates: $6437. ***Tuition waivers:*** Full or partial for employees or children of employees, senior citizens.

LOANS ***Student loans:*** $9,323,710 (77% need-based, 23% non-need-based). 72% of past graduating class borrowed through all loan programs. *Average indebtedness per student:* $34,533. ***Average need-based loan:*** Freshmen: $2790. Undergraduates: $3790. ***Parent loans:*** $3,728,344 (43% need-based, 57% non-need-based). ***Programs:*** Perkins, alternative loans.

WORK-STUDY ***Federal work-study:*** Total amount: $956,032; jobs available. ***State or other work-study/employment:*** Total amount: $1300 (100% need-based). Part-time jobs available.

ATHLETIC AWARDS Total amount: $1,453,909 (53% need-based, 47% non-need-based).

APPLYING FOR FINANCIAL AID ***Required financial aid form:*** FAFSA. ***Financial aid deadline (priority):*** 8/1. ***Notification date:*** Continuous beginning 3/1. Students must reply within 4 weeks of notification.

CONTACT Ms. Molly Risley, Director of Financial Aid, Freed-Hardeman University, 158 East Main Street, Henderson, TN 38340-2399, 731-989-6662 or toll-free 800-630-3480. *Fax:* 731-989-6775. *E-mail:* mrisley@fhu.edu.

FREE WILL BAPTIST BIBLE COLLEGE

Nashville, TN

Tuition & fees: $14,306 **Average undergraduate aid package: $5295**

ABOUT THE INSTITUTION Independent Free Will Baptist, coed. 30 undergraduate majors. Federal methodology is used as a basis for awarding need-based institutional aid.

UNDERGRADUATE EXPENSES for 2011–12 ***Comprehensive fee:*** $20,348 includes full-time tuition ($13,410), mandatory fees ($896), and room and board ($6042). Room and board charges vary according to board plan. ***Part-time tuition:*** $447 per credit. ***Payment plans:*** Installment, deferred payment.

FRESHMAN FINANCIAL AID (Fall 2010, est.) 44 applied for aid; of those 98% were deemed to have need. 100% of freshmen with need received aid. ***Average financial aid package:*** $4973 (excluding resources awarded to replace EFC). 72% of all full-time freshmen had no need and received non-need-based gift aid.

UNDERGRADUATE FINANCIAL AID (Fall 2010, est.) 188 applied for aid; of those 98% were deemed to have need. 100% of undergraduates with need received aid. ***Average financial aid package:*** $5295 (excluding resources awarded to replace EFC). 56% of all full-time undergraduates had no need and received non-need-based gift aid.

GIFT AID (NEED-BASED) ***Total amount:*** $730,830 (69% federal, 4% state, 27% institutional). ***Receiving aid:*** Freshmen: 28% (14); all full-time undergraduates: 40% (77). ***Average award:*** Freshmen: $2411; Undergraduates: $2294. ***Scholarships, grants, and awards:*** Federal Pell, FSEOG, state, private, college/university gift aid from institutional funds.

GIFT AID (NON-NEED-BASED) ***Total amount:*** $886,739 (17% state, 74% institutional, 9% external sources). ***Average award:*** Freshmen: $3709. Undergraduates: $5289. ***Scholarships, grants, and awards by category:*** *Special characteristics:* 29 awards ($100,596 total): children of faculty/staff, international students, married students, relatives of clergy, veterans, veterans' children. ***Tuition waivers:*** Full or partial for employees or children of employees.

LOANS ***Student loans:*** $1,278,837 (51% need-based, 49% non-need-based). 77% of past graduating class borrowed through all loan programs. *Average indebtedness per student:* $19,455. ***Average need-based loan:*** Freshmen: $4973. Undergraduates: $5295. ***Parent loans:*** $263,500 (100% non-need-based). ***Programs:*** Federal Direct (Subsidized and Unsubsidized Stafford, PLUS), alternative loans.

WORK-STUDY ***Federal work-study:*** Total amount: $16,381; 9 jobs averaging $1820. ***State or other work-study/employment:*** 103 part-time jobs averaging $1548.

APPLYING FOR FINANCIAL AID ***Required financial aid forms:*** FAFSA, institution's own form. ***Financial aid deadline (priority):*** 4/15. ***Notification date:*** Continuous beginning 4/1.

CONTACT Angie Edgmon, Financial Aid Coordinator, Free Will Baptist Bible College, 3606 West End Avenue, Nashville, TN 37205, 615-844-5000 or toll-free 800-763-9222. *Fax:* 615-269-6028. *E-mail:* finaid@fwbbc.edu.

FRESNO PACIFIC UNIVERSITY

Fresno, CA

Tuition & fees: $23,904 **Average undergraduate aid package: $15,202**

ABOUT THE INSTITUTION Independent religious, coed. ***Awards:*** associate, bachelor's, and master's degrees. 42 undergraduate majors. ***Total enrollment:*** 2,353. Undergraduates: 1,539. Freshmen: 170. Federal methodology is used as a basis for awarding need-based institutional aid.

UNDERGRADUATE EXPENSES for 2010–11 ***Application fee:*** $40. ***Comprehensive fee:*** $30,204 includes full-time tuition ($23,640), mandatory fees ($264), and room and board ($6300). ***College room only:*** $3960. Full-time tuition and fees vary according to degree level and program. Room and board charges vary according to board plan and housing facility. ***Part-time tuition:*** $845 per unit. ***Part-time fees:*** $132 per term. Part-time tuition and fees vary according to degree level and program. ***Payment plan:*** Installment.

FRESHMAN FINANCIAL AID (Fall 2009) 157 applied for aid; of those 92% were deemed to have need. 99% of freshmen with need received aid; of those 10% had need fully met. ***Average percent of need met:*** 72% (excluding resources awarded to replace EFC). ***Average financial aid package:*** $21,525 (excluding resources awarded to replace EFC). 8% of all full-time freshmen had no need and received non-need-based gift aid.

UNDERGRADUATE FINANCIAL AID (Fall 2009) 1,380 applied for aid; of those 93% were deemed to have need. 99% of undergraduates with need received aid; of those 8% had need fully met. ***Average percent of need met:*** 58% (excluding resources awarded to replace EFC). ***Average financial aid package:*** $15,202 (excluding resources awarded to replace EFC). 10% of all full-time undergraduates had no need and received non-need-based gift aid.

GIFT AID (NEED-BASED) ***Total amount:*** $8,870,430 (41% federal, 47% state, 12% institutional). ***Receiving aid:*** Freshmen: 69% (119); all full-time undergraduates: 62% (962). ***Average award:*** Freshmen: $12,621; Undergraduates: $8745. ***Scholarships, grants, and awards:*** Federal Pell, FSEOG, state, private, college/university gift aid from institutional funds.

GIFT AID (NON-NEED-BASED) ***Total amount:*** $6,371,379 (96% institutional, 4% external sources). ***Receiving aid:*** Freshmen: 81% (139). Undergraduates: 42% (653). ***Average award:*** Freshmen: $8332. Undergraduates: $9805. ***Scholarships, grants, and awards by category:*** *Academic interests/achievement:* business, general academic interests/achievements, humanities, social sciences. *Creative arts/performance:* music, performing arts, theater/drama. *Special characteristics:* children of faculty/staff, members of minority groups, relatives of clergy, religious affiliation, spouses of current students. ***Tuition waivers:*** Full or partial for employees or children of employees, senior citizens.

LOANS ***Student loans:*** $10,625,961 (100% need-based). 76% of past graduating class borrowed through all loan programs. *Average indebtedness per student:* $16,898. ***Average need-based loan:*** Freshmen: $5571. Undergraduates: $4644. ***Parent loans:*** $648,403 (100% need-based). ***Programs:*** Federal Direct (Subsidized and Unsubsidized Stafford, PLUS), Perkins.

WORK-STUDY ***Federal work-study:*** Total amount: $804,370; jobs available.

ATHLETIC AWARDS Total amount: $1,995,499 (100% non-need-based).

APPLYING FOR FINANCIAL AID ***Required financial aid forms:*** FAFSA, institution's own form. ***Financial aid deadline (priority):*** 3/2. ***Notification date:*** Continuous beginning 3/2. Students must reply by 7/30 or within 3 weeks of notification.

CONTACT April Powell, Director of Financial Aid, Fresno Pacific University, 1717 South Chestnut Avenue, #2004, Fresno, CA 93702, 559-453-2041 or toll-free 800-660-6089 (in-state). *Fax:* 559-453-5595. *E-mail:* sfs@fresno.edu.

FRIENDS UNIVERSITY
Wichita, KS

CONTACT Brandon Pierce, Director of Financial Aid, Friends University, 2100 University Street, Wichita, KS 67213, 316-295-5658 or toll-free 800-577-2233. *Fax:* 316-295-5703. *E-mail:* piercb@friends.edu.

FROSTBURG STATE UNIVERSITY
Frostburg, MD

Tuition & fees (MD res): $6904 **Average undergraduate aid package: $8888**

ABOUT THE INSTITUTION State-supported, coed. 56 undergraduate majors. Federal methodology is used as a basis for awarding need-based institutional aid.

UNDERGRADUATE EXPENSES for 2010–11 ***Tuition, state resident:*** full-time $5150; part-time $213 per credit hour. ***Tuition, nonresident:*** full-time $15,196; part-time $427 per credit hour. ***Required fees:*** full-time $1754; $86 per credit hour or $12 per term. Full-time tuition and fees vary according to location. Part-time tuition and fees vary according to course load and location. ***College room and board:*** $7378; ***Room only:*** $3510. Room and board charges vary according to board plan and housing facility. ***Payment plans:*** Installment, deferred payment.

FRESHMAN FINANCIAL AID (Fall 2010, est.) 901 applied for aid; of those 73% were deemed to have need. 100% of freshmen with need received aid; of those 20% had need fully met. ***Average percent of need met:*** 66% (excluding resources awarded to replace EFC). ***Average financial aid package:*** $8526 (excluding resources awarded to replace EFC). 9% of all full-time freshmen had no need and received non-need-based gift aid.

UNDERGRADUATE FINANCIAL AID (Fall 2010, est.) 3,763 applied for aid; of those 74% were deemed to have need. 100% of undergraduates with need received aid; of those 19% had need fully met. ***Average percent of need met:*** 67% (excluding resources awarded to replace EFC). ***Average financial aid package:*** $8888 (excluding resources awarded to replace EFC). 7% of all full-time undergraduates had no need and received non-need-based gift aid.

GIFT AID (NEED-BASED) ***Total amount:*** $13,399,301 (58% federal, 27% state, 11% institutional, 4% external sources). ***Receiving aid:*** Freshmen: 41% (429); all full-time undergraduates: 41% (1,958). ***Average award:*** Freshmen: $7453; Undergraduates: $6419. ***Scholarships, grants, and awards:*** Federal Pell, FSEOG, state, private, college/university gift aid from institutional funds.

GIFT AID (NON-NEED-BASED) ***Total amount:*** $3,307,665 (16% state, 74% institutional, 10% external sources). ***Receiving aid:*** Freshmen: 18% (188). Undergraduates: 15% (703). ***Average award:*** Freshmen: $2608. Undergraduates: $3081. ***Scholarships, grants, and awards by category:*** *Academic interests/achievement:* biological sciences, business, communication, computer science, education, engineering/technologies, English, foreign languages, general academic interests/achievements, health fields, humanities, international studies, mathematics, physical sciences, premedicine, social sciences. *Creative arts/performance:* art/fine arts, creative writing, journalism/publications, music, performing arts, theater/drama. *Special achievements/activities:* community service, leadership. *Special characteristics:* adult students, children of union members/company employees, international students, local/state students, out-of-state students, veterans, veterans' children. ***Tuition waivers:*** Full or partial for employees or children of employees, senior citizens.

LOANS ***Student loans:*** $25,561,358 (42% need-based, 58% non-need-based). 69% of past graduating class borrowed through all loan programs. *Average indebtedness per student:* $20,970. ***Average need-based loan:*** Freshmen: $3042. Undergraduates: $3848. ***Parent loans:*** $3,930,298 (100% non-need-based). ***Programs:*** Federal Direct (Subsidized and Unsubsidized Stafford, PLUS), Perkins.

WORK-STUDY ***Federal work-study:*** Total amount: $92,560; 145 jobs averaging $614. ***State or other work-study/employment:*** Part-time jobs available.

APPLYING FOR FINANCIAL AID ***Required financial aid form:*** FAFSA. ***Financial aid deadline (priority):*** 3/1. ***Notification date:*** Continuous beginning 3/15. Students must reply within 3 weeks of notification.

CONTACT Mrs. Angela Hovatter, Director of Financial Aid, Frostburg State University, 114 Pullen Hall, Frostburg, MD 21532-1099, 301-687-4301. *Fax:* 301-687-7074. *E-mail:* ahovatter@frostburg.edu.

FULL SAIL UNIVERSITY
Winter Park, FL

ABOUT THE INSTITUTION Proprietary, coed, primarily men. 20 undergraduate majors.

GIFT AID (NEED-BASED) ***Scholarships, grants, and awards:*** Federal Pell, FSEOG, state, college/university gift aid from institutional funds, Office of Vocational Rehabilitation Awards.

LOANS ***Programs:*** Federal Direct (Subsidized and Unsubsidized Stafford, PLUS).

WORK-STUDY ***Federal work-study:*** Total amount: $655,500; 475 jobs averaging $1380.

APPLYING FOR FINANCIAL AID ***Required financial aid form:*** FAFSA.

CONTACT Financial Aid Office, Full Sail University, 3300 University Boulevard, Winter Park, FL 32792, 800-575-1142 or toll-free 800-226-7625.

FURMAN UNIVERSITY
Greenville, SC

Tuition & fees: $38,088 **Average undergraduate aid package: $29,184**

ABOUT THE INSTITUTION Independent, coed. 48 undergraduate majors. Both federal and institutional methodology are used as a basis for awarding need-based institutional aid.

UNDERGRADUATE EXPENSES for 2010–11 ***Comprehensive fee:*** $47,660 includes full-time tuition ($37,728), mandatory fees ($360), and room and board ($9572). ***College room only:*** $5198. Room and board charges vary according to board plan and housing facility. ***Part-time tuition:*** $1179 per credit. Part-time tuition and fees vary according to course load. ***Payment plan:*** Installment.

FRESHMAN FINANCIAL AID (Fall 2010, est.) 472 applied for aid; of those 70% were deemed to have need. 100% of freshmen with need received aid; of those 39% had need fully met. ***Average percent of need met:*** 86% (excluding resources awarded to replace EFC). ***Average financial aid package:*** $29,378 (excluding resources awarded to replace EFC). 36% of all full-time freshmen had no need and received non-need-based gift aid.

UNDERGRADUATE FINANCIAL AID (Fall 2010, est.) 1,487 applied for aid; of those 84% were deemed to have need. 100% of undergraduates with need received aid; of those 36% had need fully met. ***Average percent of need met:*** 81% (excluding resources awarded to replace EFC). ***Average financial aid package:*** $29,184 (excluding resources awarded to replace EFC). 31% of all full-time undergraduates had no need and received non-need-based gift aid.

GIFT AID (NEED-BASED) ***Total amount:*** $24,614,906 (11% federal, 5% state, 78% institutional, 6% external sources). ***Receiving aid:*** Freshmen: 48% (332); all full-time undergraduates: 48% (1,235). ***Average award:*** Freshmen: $24,506; Undergraduates: $23,124. ***Scholarships, grants, and awards:*** Federal Pell, FSEOG, state, private, college/university gift aid from institutional funds.

GIFT AID (NON-NEED-BASED) ***Total amount:*** $22,876,893 (19% state, 74% institutional, 7% external sources). ***Receiving aid:*** Freshmen: 48% (332). Undergraduates: 48% (1,235). ***Average award:*** Freshmen: $18,012. Undergraduates: $18,924. ***Scholarships, grants, and awards by category:*** *Academic interests/achievement:* area/ethnic studies, biological sciences, business, communication, computer science, education, engineering/technologies, English, foreign languages, general academic interests/achievements, health fields, humanities, international studies, mathematics, military science, physical sciences, premedicine, religion/biblical studies, social sciences. *Creative arts/performance:* art/fine arts, creative writing, music, theater/drama. *Special achievements/activities:* community service, leadership, religious involvement. *Special characteristics:* children of faculty/staff, ethnic background, international students, local/state students, relatives of clergy, religious affiliation, veterans. ***Tuition waivers:*** Full or partial for employees or children of employees.

LOANS ***Student loans:*** $7,945,005 (59% need-based, 41% non-need-based). 43% of past graduating class borrowed through all loan programs. *Average indebtedness per student:* $26,202. ***Average need-based loan:*** Freshmen: $3348. Undergraduates: $4600. ***Parent loans:*** $4,277,099 (67% need-based, 33% non-need-based). ***Programs:*** Perkins, state, alternative loans.

WORK-STUDY ***Federal work-study:*** Total amount: $988,874; 680 jobs averaging $1446.

ATHLETIC AWARDS Total amount: $7,183,049 (44% need-based, 56% non-need-based).

APPLYING FOR FINANCIAL AID ***Required financial aid forms:*** FAFSA, CSS Financial Aid PROFILE, state aid form. ***Financial aid deadline:*** 1/15. ***Notification date:*** 3/15. Students must reply by 5/1.

CONTACT Mr. Forrest Stuart, Director of Financial Aid, Furman University, 3300 Poinsett Highway, Greenville, SC 29613, 864-294-2204. *Fax:* 864-294-3127. *E-mail:* forrest.stuart@furman.edu.

GALLAUDET UNIVERSITY

Washington, DC

Tuition & fees: $11,226 **Average undergraduate aid package: $18,139**

ABOUT THE INSTITUTION Independent, coed. 23 undergraduate majors. Federal methodology is used as a basis for awarding need-based institutional aid.

UNDERGRADUATE EXPENSES for 2010–11 ***Comprehensive fee:*** $20,886 includes full-time tuition ($10,850), mandatory fees ($376), and room and board ($9660). ***College room only:*** $5460. Full-time tuition and fees vary according to degree level. Room and board charges vary according to board plan. ***Part-time tuition:*** $542.50 per credit hour. Part-time tuition and fees vary according to degree level.

FRESHMAN FINANCIAL AID (Fall 2009) 176 applied for aid; of those 89% were deemed to have need. 99% of freshmen with need received aid; of those 43% had need fully met. ***Average percent of need met:*** 90% (excluding resources awarded to replace EFC). ***Average financial aid package:*** $18,319 (excluding resources awarded to replace EFC). 12% of all full-time freshmen had no need and received non-need-based gift aid.

UNDERGRADUATE FINANCIAL AID (Fall 2009) 916 applied for aid; of those 90% were deemed to have need. 98% of undergraduates with need received aid; of those 35% had need fully met. ***Average percent of need met:*** 84% (excluding resources awarded to replace EFC). ***Average financial aid package:*** $18,139 (excluding resources awarded to replace EFC). 5% of all full-time undergraduates had no need and received non-need-based gift aid.

GIFT AID (NEED-BASED) ***Total amount:*** $13,469,023 (18% federal, 57% state, 24% institutional, 1% external sources). ***Receiving aid:*** Freshmen: 79% (154); all full-time undergraduates: 74% (808). ***Average award:*** Freshmen: $17,358; Undergraduates: $16,537. ***Scholarships, grants, and awards:*** Federal Pell, FSEOG, state, private, college/university gift aid from institutional funds.

GIFT AID (NON-NEED-BASED) ***Total amount:*** $1,590,364 (73% state, 26% institutional, 1% external sources). ***Receiving aid:*** Freshmen: 41% (80). Undergraduates: 30% (326). ***Average award:*** Freshmen: $7192. Undergraduates: $7142. ***Scholarships, grants, and awards by category:*** *Academic interests/achievement:* general academic interests/achievements. *Special achievements/activities:* leadership. *Special characteristics:* members of minority groups. ***Tuition waivers:*** Full or partial for employees or children of employees.

LOANS ***Student loans:*** $2,658,657 (91% need-based, 9% non-need-based). 62% of past graduating class borrowed through all loan programs. *Average indebtedness per student:* $14,066. ***Average need-based loan:*** Freshmen: $2879. Undergraduates: $3846. ***Parent loans:*** $448,063 (72% need-based, 28% non-need-based). ***Programs:*** Perkins.

WORK-STUDY ***Federal work-study:*** Total amount: $81,659; 67 jobs averaging $1218.

APPLYING FOR FINANCIAL AID ***Required financial aid forms:*** FAFSA, institution's own form. ***Financial aid deadline:*** Continuous. ***Notification date:*** Continuous beginning 3/1.

CONTACT Janel Grossinger, Director of Financial Aid, Gallaudet University, Chapel Hall, Room G-02, 800 Florida Avenue, NE, Washington, DC 20002, 202-651-5290 or toll-free 800-995-0550 (out-of-state). *Fax:* 202-651-5740. *E-mail:* financial.aid@gallaudet.edu.

GANNON UNIVERSITY

Erie, PA

Tuition & fees: $24,582 **Average undergraduate aid package: $20,647**

ABOUT THE INSTITUTION Independent Roman Catholic, coed. 63 undergraduate majors. Federal methodology is used as a basis for awarding need-based institutional aid.

UNDERGRADUATE EXPENSES for 2010–11 ***Comprehensive fee:*** $34,302 includes full-time tuition ($24,040), mandatory fees ($542), and room and board ($9720). ***College room only:*** $5050. Full-time tuition and fees vary according to class time, course load, and program. Room and board charges vary according to board plan and housing facility. ***Part-time tuition:*** $745 per credit hour. ***Part-time fees:*** $18 per credit hour. Part-time tuition and fees vary according to class time, course load, and program. ***Payment plans:*** Installment, deferred payment.

FRESHMAN FINANCIAL AID (Fall 2010, est.) 587 applied for aid; of those 93% were deemed to have need. 100% of freshmen with need received aid; of those 14% had need fully met. ***Average percent of need met:*** 72% (excluding resources awarded to replace EFC). ***Average financial aid package:*** $21,030 (excluding resources awarded to replace EFC). 11% of all full-time freshmen had no need and received non-need-based gift aid.

UNDERGRADUATE FINANCIAL AID (Fall 2010, est.) 2,275 applied for aid; of those 94% were deemed to have need. 100% of undergraduates with need received aid; of those 22% had need fully met. ***Average percent of need met:*** 76% (excluding resources awarded to replace EFC). ***Average financial aid package:*** $20,647 (excluding resources awarded to replace EFC). 14% of all full-time undergraduates had no need and received non-need-based gift aid.

GIFT AID (NEED-BASED) ***Total amount:*** $31,009,168 (17% federal, 9% state, 69% institutional, 5% external sources). ***Receiving aid:*** Freshmen: 87% (541); all full-time undergraduates: 85% (2,092). ***Average award:*** Freshmen: $17,340; Undergraduates: $16,035. ***Scholarships, grants, and awards:*** Federal Pell, FSEOG, state, private, college/university gift aid from institutional funds.

GIFT AID (NON-NEED-BASED) ***Total amount:*** $3,119,467 (94% institutional, 6% external sources). ***Receiving aid:*** Freshmen: 9% (53). Undergraduates: 11% (271). ***Average award:*** Freshmen: $10,857. Undergraduates: $9623. ***Scholarships, grants, and awards by category:*** *Academic interests/achievement:* 1,352 awards ($10,392,608 total): biological sciences, business, education, engineering/technologies, English, foreign languages, general academic interests/achievements, humanities, international studies, mathematics, premedicine, religion/biblical studies, social sciences. *Creative arts/performance:* 78 awards ($128,750 total): music, performing arts, theater/drama. *Special achievements/activities:* 1,466 awards ($2,403,434 total): community service, leadership. *Special characteristics:* 931 awards ($1,620,862 total): adult students, ethnic background, international students, members of minority groups, religious affiliation, veterans. ***Tuition waivers:*** Full or partial for employees or children of employees, senior citizens.

LOANS ***Student loans:*** $20,012,087 (68% need-based, 32% non-need-based). 82% of past graduating class borrowed through all loan programs. *Average indebtedness per student:* $34,830. ***Average need-based loan:*** Freshmen: $3408. Undergraduates: $4251. ***Parent loans:*** $4,135,294 (94% need-based, 6% non-need-based). ***Programs:*** Federal Direct (Subsidized and Unsubsidized Stafford, PLUS), Perkins, Federal Nursing.

WORK-STUDY ***Federal work-study:*** Total amount: $859,645; 598 jobs averaging $2300. ***State or other work-study/employment:*** Total amount: $254,632 (100% non-need-based). 149 part-time jobs averaging $2300.

ATHLETIC AWARDS Total amount: $3,118,458 (71% need-based, 29% non-need-based).

APPLYING FOR FINANCIAL AID ***Required financial aid form:*** FAFSA. ***Financial aid deadline (priority):*** 3/15. ***Notification date:*** Continuous beginning 11/1.

CONTACT Ms. Sharon Krahe, Director of Financial Aid, Gannon University, 109 University Square, Erie, PA 16541, 814-871-7670 or toll-free 800-GANNONU. *Fax:* 814-871-5826. *E-mail:* krahe001@gannon.edu.

GARDNER-WEBB UNIVERSITY

Boiling Springs, NC

Tuition & fees: $22,410 **Average undergraduate aid package: $20,710**

ABOUT THE INSTITUTION Independent Baptist, coed. 65 undergraduate majors. Federal methodology is used as a basis for awarding need-based institutional aid.

UNDERGRADUATE EXPENSES for 2010–11 ***One-time required fee:*** $100. ***Comprehensive fee:*** $29,630 includes full-time tuition ($22,020), mandatory fees ($390), and room and board ($7220). ***College room only:*** $3700. Full-time tuition and fees vary according to degree level and program. Room and board charges vary according to board plan and housing facility. ***Part-time tuition:*** $357 per credit hour. Part-time tuition and fees vary according to course load. ***Payment plan:*** Installment.

FRESHMAN FINANCIAL AID (Fall 2010, est.) 434 applied for aid; of those 89% were deemed to have need. 100% of freshmen with need received aid; of those 18% had need fully met. ***Average percent of need met:*** 87% (excluding resources awarded to replace EFC). ***Average financial aid package:*** $20,821 (excluding resources awarded to replace EFC). 14% of all full-time freshmen had no need and received non-need-based gift aid.

UNDERGRADUATE FINANCIAL AID (Fall 2010, est.) 1,379 applied for aid; of those 91% were deemed to have need. 100% of undergraduates with need received aid; of those 15% had need fully met. ***Average percent of need met:*** 87% (excluding resources awarded to replace EFC). ***Average financial aid package:*** $20,710 (excluding resources awarded to replace EFC). 11% of all full-time undergraduates had no need and received non-need-based gift aid.

GIFT AID (NEED-BASED) ***Total amount:*** $17,081,321 (18% federal, 26% state, 53% institutional, 3% external sources). ***Receiving aid:*** Freshmen: 76% (359); all full-time undergraduates: 46% (1,109). ***Average award:*** Freshmen: $10,141; Undergraduates: $8728. ***Scholarships, grants, and awards:*** Federal Pell, FSEOG, state, private, college/university gift aid from institutional funds.

GIFT AID (NON-NEED-BASED) ***Total amount:*** $2,607,461 (11% state, 86% institutional, 3% external sources). ***Receiving aid:*** Freshmen: 61% (289). Undergraduates: 37% (889). ***Average award:*** Freshmen: $7396. Undergraduates: $7371. ***Scholarships, grants, and awards by category:*** *Academic interests/achievement:* biological sciences, business, communication, computer science, education, English, foreign languages, general academic interests/achievements, health fields, humanities, mathematics, physical sciences, premedicine, religion/biblical studies, social sciences. *Creative arts/performance:* art/fine arts, music, theater/drama. *Special achievements/activities:* cheerleading/drum major, religious involvement. *Special characteristics:* children of faculty/staff, handicapped students, local/state students, members of minority groups, out-of-state students, previous college experience, relatives of clergy. ***Tuition waivers:*** Full or partial for employees or children of employees.

LOANS ***Student loans:*** $8,483,357 (95% need-based, 5% non-need-based). ***Average need-based loan:*** Freshmen: $3210. Undergraduates: $4122. ***Parent loans:*** $3,572,494 (95% need-based, 5% non-need-based). ***Programs:*** Federal Direct (Subsidized and Unsubsidized Stafford, PLUS), Perkins, state, alternative loans.

WORK-STUDY ***Federal work-study:*** Total amount: $243,646; jobs available. ***State or other work-study/employment:*** Total amount: $26,896 (63% need-based, 37% non-need-based). Part-time jobs available.

ATHLETIC AWARDS Total amount: $5,430,824 (58% need-based, 42% non-need-based).

APPLYING FOR FINANCIAL AID ***Required financial aid forms:*** FAFSA, state aid form. ***Financial aid deadline (priority):*** 3/15. ***Notification date:*** 3/1. Students must reply within 2 weeks of notification.

CONTACT Summer Nance, Assistant Vice President of Financial Planning, Gardner-Webb University, PO Box 955, Boiling Springs, NC 28017, 704-406-4243 or toll-free 800-253-6472. *Fax:* 704-406-4102.

GARRETT COLLEGE

McHenry, MD

Tuition & fees (area res): $3110 **Average undergraduate aid package: $5782**

ABOUT THE INSTITUTION State and locally supported, coed. 12 undergraduate majors. Federal methodology is used as a basis for awarding need-based institutional aid.

UNDERGRADUATE EXPENSES for 2011–12 ***One-time required fee:*** $15. ***Tuition, area resident:*** full-time $2520; part-time $90 per credit hour. ***Tuition, state resident:*** full-time $6048; part-time $216 per credit hour. ***Tuition, nonresident:*** full-time $7140; part-time $255 per credit hour. ***Required fees:*** full-time $590; $20 per credit hour or $15 per term. Full-time tuition and fees vary according to location and reciprocity agreements. Part-time tuition and fees vary according to location and reciprocity agreements. ***College room and board:*** $6474; ***Room only:*** $4346. Room and board charges vary according to board plan and housing facility. ***Payment plans:*** Installment, deferred payment.

FRESHMAN FINANCIAL AID (Fall 2010, est.) 242 applied for aid; of those 88% were deemed to have need. 100% of freshmen with need received aid. ***Average percent of need met:*** 26% (excluding resources awarded to replace EFC). ***Average financial aid package:*** $3911 (excluding resources awarded to replace EFC). 12% of all full-time freshmen had no need and received non-need-based gift aid.

UNDERGRADUATE FINANCIAL AID (Fall 2010, est.) 504 applied for aid; of those 90% were deemed to have need. 100% of undergraduates with need received aid; of those 1% had need fully met. ***Average percent of need met:*** 40% (excluding resources awarded to replace EFC). ***Average financial aid package:*** $5782 (excluding resources awarded to replace EFC). 14% of all full-time undergraduates had no need and received non-need-based gift aid.

GIFT AID (NEED-BASED) ***Total amount:*** $2,915,394 (69% federal, 18% state, 12% institutional, 1% external sources). ***Receiving aid:*** Freshmen: 77% (196); all full-time undergraduates: 79% (441). ***Average award:*** Freshmen: $4916; Undergraduates: $5612. ***Scholarships, grants, and awards:*** Federal Pell, FSEOG, state, private, college/university gift aid from institutional funds.

GIFT AID (NON-NEED-BASED) ***Receiving aid:*** Freshmen: 26% (66). Undergraduates: 24% (137). ***Average award:*** Freshmen: $1611. Undergraduates: $1445. ***Tuition waivers:*** Full or partial for employees or children of employees, senior citizens.

LOANS ***Student loans:*** $1,662,508 (57% need-based, 43% non-need-based). ***Average need-based loan:*** Freshmen: $1732. Undergraduates: $1789. ***Parent loans:*** $234,694 (100% need-based). ***Programs:*** Federal Direct (Subsidized and Unsubsidized Stafford, PLUS), college/university.

WORK-STUDY ***Federal work-study:*** Total amount: $52,000; jobs available. ***State or other work-study/employment:*** Total amount: $10,000 (100% need-based). Part-time jobs available.

ATHLETIC AWARDS Total amount: $25,850 (100% need-based).

APPLYING FOR FINANCIAL AID ***Required financial aid form:*** FAFSA. ***Financial aid deadline (priority):*** 3/1. ***Notification date:*** Continuous beginning 6/1. Students must reply within 2 weeks of notification.

CONTACT Ms. Kathy Fauber, Counselor, Garrett College, 687 Mosser Road, McHenry, MD 21541, 301-387-3057. *Fax:* 301-387-3038. *E-mail:* kathy.fauber@garrettcollege.edu.

GENEVA COLLEGE

Beaver Falls, PA

Tuition & fees: $22,236 **Average undergraduate aid package: $18,433**

ABOUT THE INSTITUTION Independent religious, coed. 32 undergraduate majors. Federal methodology is used as a basis for awarding need-based institutional aid.

UNDERGRADUATE EXPENSES for 2010–11 ***Comprehensive fee:*** $30,236 includes full-time tuition ($22,236) and room and board ($8000). Full-time tuition and fees vary according to course load. Room and board charges vary according to board plan. ***Part-time tuition:*** $745 per credit. Part-time tuition and fees vary according to course load. ***Payment plan:*** Installment.

FRESHMAN FINANCIAL AID (Fall 2010, est.) 380 applied for aid; of those 92% were deemed to have need. 100% of freshmen with need received aid; of those 18% had need fully met. ***Average percent of need met:*** 80% (excluding resources awarded to replace EFC). ***Average financial aid package:*** $19,428 (excluding resources awarded to replace EFC). 13% of all full-time freshmen had no need and received non-need-based gift aid.

UNDERGRADUATE FINANCIAL AID (Fall 2010, est.) 1,367 applied for aid; of those 92% were deemed to have need. 99% of undergraduates with need received aid; of those 17% had need fully met. ***Average percent of need met:*** 78% (excluding resources awarded to replace EFC). ***Average financial aid package:*** $18,433 (excluding resources awarded to replace EFC). 13% of all full-time undergraduates had no need and received non-need-based gift aid.

GIFT AID (NEED-BASED) ***Total amount:*** $16,478,508 (18% federal, 12% state, 66% institutional, 4% external sources). ***Receiving aid:*** Freshmen: 85% (349); all full-time undergraduates: 82% (1,234). ***Average award:*** Freshmen: $15,511; Undergraduates: $14,096. ***Scholarships, grants, and awards:*** Federal Pell, FSEOG, state, private, college/university gift aid from institutional funds.

GIFT AID (NON-NEED-BASED) ***Total amount:*** $2,174,666 (1% state, 94% institutional, 5% external sources). ***Receiving aid:*** Freshmen: 11% (45). Undergraduates: 9% (128). ***Average award:*** Freshmen: $10,639. Undergraduates: $8179. ***Scholarships, grants, and awards by category:*** *Academic interests/achievement:* engineering/technologies, general academic interests/achievements, religion/biblical studies. *Creative arts/performance:* music. *Special characteristics:* children of faculty/staff, religious affiliation. ***Tuition waivers:*** Full or partial for minority students, employees or children of employees.

LOANS ***Student loans:*** $8,762,806 (78% need-based, 22% non-need-based). 95% of past graduating class borrowed through all loan programs. *Average indebtedness per student:* $24,000. ***Average need-based loan:*** Freshmen: $3805. Undergraduates: $4192. ***Parent loans:*** $1,947,709 (35% need-based, 65% non-need-based). ***Programs:*** Federal Direct (Subsidized and Unsubsidized Stafford, PLUS), Perkins.

WORK-STUDY ***Federal work-study:*** Total amount: $238,000; 250 jobs averaging $2000.

APPLYING FOR FINANCIAL AID ***Required financial aid form:*** FAFSA. ***Financial aid deadline (priority):*** 3/15. ***Notification date:*** Continuous beginning 3/1. Students must reply within 4 weeks of notification.

CONTACT Mr. Steven Bell, Director of Financial Aid, Geneva College, 3200 College Avenue, Beaver Falls, PA 15010-3599, 800-847-8255. *Fax:* 724-847-6776. *E-mail:* financialaid@geneva.edu.

GEORGE FOX UNIVERSITY

Newberg, OR

Tuition & fees: $27,970 **Average undergraduate aid package: $25,387**

ABOUT THE INSTITUTION Independent Friends, coed. 46 undergraduate majors. Both federal and institutional methodology are used as a basis for awarding need-based institutional aid.

UNDERGRADUATE EXPENSES for 2010–11 ***Comprehensive fee:*** $36,600 includes full-time tuition ($27,640), mandatory fees ($330), and room and board ($8630). ***College room only:*** $4880. Room and board charges vary according to board plan. ***Part-time tuition:*** $840 per semester hour. Part-time tuition and fees vary according to course load. ***Payment plan:*** Installment.

FRESHMAN FINANCIAL AID (Fall 2010, est.) 454 applied for aid; of those 87% were deemed to have need. 100% of freshmen with need received aid; of those 42% had need fully met. ***Average percent of need met:*** 89% (excluding resources awarded to replace EFC). ***Average financial aid package:*** $26,306 (excluding resources awarded to replace EFC). 9% of all full-time freshmen had no need and received non-need-based gift aid.

UNDERGRADUATE FINANCIAL AID (Fall 2010, est.) 1,552 applied for aid; of those 91% were deemed to have need. 100% of undergraduates with need received aid; of those 38% had need fully met. ***Average percent of need met:*** 87% (excluding resources awarded to replace EFC). ***Average financial aid package:*** $25,387 (excluding resources awarded to replace EFC). 6% of all full-time undergraduates had no need and received non-need-based gift aid.

GIFT AID (NEED-BASED) ***Total amount:*** $23,103,327 (12% federal, 1% state, 83% institutional, 4% external sources). ***Receiving aid:*** Freshmen: 78% (385); all full-time undergraduates: 73% (1,322). ***Average award:*** Freshmen: $10,365; Undergraduates: $15,040. ***Scholarships, grants, and awards:*** Federal Pell, FSEOG, state, private, college/university gift aid from institutional funds, Academic Competitiveness Grants, National SMART Grants, TEACH Grants.

GIFT AID (NON-NEED-BASED) ***Total amount:*** $1,484,718 (92% institutional, 8% external sources). ***Receiving aid:*** Freshmen: 68% (335). Undergraduates: 63% (1,147). ***Average award:*** Freshmen: $7763. Undergraduates: $7016. ***Scholarships, grants, and awards by category:*** *Academic interests/achievement:* biological sciences, computer science, education, engineering/technologies, general academic interests/achievements, mathematics, physical sciences, religion/biblical studies. *Creative arts/performance:* art/fine arts, debating, music, theater/drama. *Special achievements/activities:* leadership, religious involvement. *Special characteristics:* children and siblings of alumni, children of faculty/staff, ethnic background, international students, members of minority groups, out-of-state students, relatives of clergy, religious affiliation. ***Tuition waivers:*** Full or partial for employees or children of employees, senior citizens.

LOANS ***Student loans:*** $10,615,193 (86% need-based, 14% non-need-based). 85% of past graduating class borrowed through all loan programs. *Average indebtedness per student:* $18,428. ***Average need-based loan:*** Freshmen: $3003. Undergraduates: $3602. ***Parent loans:*** $1,041,343 (45% need-based, 55% non-need-based). ***Programs:*** Federal Direct (Subsidized and Unsubsidized Stafford, PLUS), Perkins, alternative loans.

WORK-STUDY ***Federal work-study:*** Total amount: $379,000; jobs available. ***State or other work-study/employment:*** Total amount: $2,056,832 (91% need-based, 9% non-need-based). Part-time jobs available.

APPLYING FOR FINANCIAL AID ***Required financial aid forms:*** FAFSA, state aid form. ***Financial aid deadline (priority):*** 2/1. ***Notification date:*** Continuous beginning 3/1. Students must reply by 5/1 or within 6 weeks of notification.

CONTACT James Oshiro, Associate Director of Financial Services, George Fox University, 414 North Meridian Street, Newberg, OR 97132-2697, 503-554-2290 or toll-free 800-765-4369. *Fax:* 503-554-3880. *E-mail:* sfs@georgefox.edu.

GEORGE MASON UNIVERSITY

Fairfax, VA

Tuition & fees (VA res): $8684 **Average undergraduate aid package: $11,715**

ABOUT THE INSTITUTION State-supported, coed. 56 undergraduate majors. Federal methodology is used as a basis for awarding need-based institutional aid.

UNDERGRADUATE EXPENSES for 2010–11 ***Tuition, state resident:*** full-time $6320; part-time $263 per credit hour. ***Tuition, nonresident:*** full-time $23,084; part-time $962 per credit hour. ***Required fees:*** full-time $2364; $98.50 per credit hour. Full-time tuition and fees vary according to course load. Part-time tuition and fees vary according to course load. ***College room and board:*** $8220; ***Room only:*** $4720. Room and board charges vary according to board plan and housing facility. ***Payment plans:*** Installment, deferred payment.

FRESHMAN FINANCIAL AID (Fall 2010, est.) 2,001 applied for aid; of those 65% were deemed to have need. 94% of freshmen with need received aid; of those 9% had need fully met. ***Average percent of need met:*** 73% (excluding resources awarded to replace EFC). ***Average financial aid package:*** $12,807 (excluding resources awarded to replace EFC). 4% of all full-time freshmen had no need and received non-need-based gift aid.

UNDERGRADUATE FINANCIAL AID (Fall 2010, est.) 9,912 applied for aid; of those 78% were deemed to have need. 96% of undergraduates with need received aid; of those 9% had need fully met. ***Average percent of need met:*** 67% (excluding resources awarded to replace EFC). ***Average financial aid package:*** $11,715 (excluding resources awarded to replace EFC). 3% of all full-time undergraduates had no need and received non-need-based gift aid.

GIFT AID (NEED-BASED) ***Total amount:*** $43,273,829 (56% federal, 36% state, 8% institutional). ***Receiving aid:*** Freshmen: 40% (1,028); all full-time undergraduates: 36% (5,679). ***Average award:*** Freshmen: $7239; Undergraduates: $6909. ***Scholarships, grants, and awards:*** Federal Pell, FSEOG, state, private, college/university gift aid from institutional funds.

GIFT AID (NON-NEED-BASED) ***Total amount:*** $7,510,779 (72% institutional, 28% external sources). ***Receiving aid:*** Freshmen: 14% (370). Undergraduates: 7% (1,158). ***Average award:*** Freshmen: $8921. Undergraduates: $5987. ***Scholarships, grants, and awards by category:*** *Academic interests/achievement:* 1,306 awards ($5,526,010 total): general academic interests/achievements. *Creative arts/performance:* general creative arts/performance. *Special characteristics:* general special characteristics. ***Tuition waivers:*** Full or partial for employees or children of employees, senior citizens.

LOANS ***Student loans:*** $70,088,761 (71% need-based, 29% non-need-based). 54% of past graduating class borrowed through all loan programs. *Average indebtedness per student:* $22,219. ***Average need-based loan:*** Freshmen: $3339. Undergraduates: $4350. ***Parent loans:*** $16,304,753 (39% need-based, 61% non-need-based). ***Programs:*** Federal Direct (Subsidized and Unsubsidized Stafford, PLUS), Perkins, Federal Nursing.

WORK-STUDY ***Federal work-study:*** Total amount: $575,652; 275 jobs averaging $1394.

ATHLETIC AWARDS Total amount: $4,077,185 (100% non-need-based).

APPLYING FOR FINANCIAL AID ***Required financial aid form:*** FAFSA. ***Financial aid deadline (priority):*** 3/1. ***Notification date:*** Continuous beginning 4/1. Students must reply within 3 weeks of notification.

CONTACT Office of Student Financial Aid, George Mason University, Mail Stop 3B5, Fairfax, VA 22030-4444, 703-993-2353. *Fax:* 703-993-2350. *E-mail:* finaid@gmu.edu.

GEORGETOWN COLLEGE

Georgetown, KY

Tuition & fees: $27,640 — **Average undergraduate aid package: $25,683**

ABOUT THE INSTITUTION Independent religious, coed. 35 undergraduate majors. Federal methodology is used as a basis for awarding need-based institutional aid.

UNDERGRADUATE EXPENSES for 2010–11 ***Comprehensive fee:*** $34,960 includes full-time tuition ($27,640) and room and board ($7320). ***College room only:*** $3530. Full-time tuition and fees vary according to course load and degree level. Room and board charges vary according to board plan and housing facility. ***Part-time tuition:*** $1140 per credit hour. Part-time tuition and fees vary according to degree level. ***Payment plan:*** Installment.

FRESHMAN FINANCIAL AID (Fall 2010, est.) 309 applied for aid; of those 94% were deemed to have need. 100% of freshmen with need received aid; of those 32% had need fully met. ***Average percent of need met:*** 88% (excluding resources awarded to replace EFC). ***Average financial aid package:*** $27,444 (excluding resources awarded to replace EFC). 10% of all full-time freshmen had no need and received non-need-based gift aid.

UNDERGRADUATE FINANCIAL AID (Fall 2010, est.) 1,031 applied for aid; of those 94% were deemed to have need. 100% of undergraduates with need received aid; of those 29% had need fully met. ***Average percent of need met:*** 84% (excluding resources awarded to replace EFC). ***Average financial aid package:*** $25,683 (excluding resources awarded to replace EFC). 16% of all full-time undergraduates had no need and received non-need-based gift aid.

GIFT AID (NEED-BASED) ***Total amount:*** $19,147,736 (12% federal, 12% state, 73% institutional, 3% external sources). ***Receiving aid:*** Freshmen: 86% (289); all full-time undergraduates: 78% (969). ***Average award:*** Freshmen: $23,946; Undergraduates: $21,654. ***Scholarships, grants, and awards:*** Federal Pell, FSEOG, state, private, college/university gift aid from institutional funds.

GIFT AID (NON-NEED-BASED) ***Total amount:*** $5,836,794 (2% federal, 28% state, 69% institutional, 1% external sources). ***Receiving aid:*** Freshmen: 14% (48). Undergraduates: 11% (138). ***Average award:*** Freshmen: $15,509. Undergraduates: $14,123. ***Scholarships, grants, and awards by category:*** *Academic interests/achievement:* 690 awards ($7,694,983 total): general academic interests/achievements. *Creative arts/performance:* 139 awards ($293,114 total): art/fine arts, music, performing arts, theater/drama. *Special achievements/activities:* 213 awards ($254,250 total): junior miss, leadership, religious involvement. *Special characteristics:* 503 awards ($1,277,293 total): children and siblings of alumni, children of faculty/staff, local/state students, out-of-state students, relatives of clergy, religious affiliation. ***Tuition waivers:*** Full or partial for employees or children of employees, senior citizens.

LOANS ***Student loans:*** $6,402,298 (51% need-based, 49% non-need-based). 65% of past graduating class borrowed through all loan programs. *Average indebtedness per student:* $23,612. ***Average need-based loan:*** Freshmen: $3657. Undergraduates: $4629. ***Parent loans:*** $2,037,064 (100% non-need-based). ***Programs:*** Federal Direct (Subsidized and Unsubsidized Stafford, PLUS), Perkins, college/university.

WORK-STUDY ***Federal work-study:*** Total amount: $681,067; 589 jobs averaging $1108.

ATHLETIC AWARDS Total amount: $2,420,062 (72% need-based, 28% non-need-based).

APPLYING FOR FINANCIAL AID ***Required financial aid forms:*** FAFSA, institution's own form. ***Financial aid deadline:*** 3/15 (priority: 2/1). ***Notification date:*** 3/1. Students must reply by 5/1.

CONTACT Tiffany Hornberger, Director of Student Financial Planning, Georgetown College, 400 East College Street, Georgetown, KY 40324-1696, 502-863-8027 or toll-free 800-788-9985. *Fax:* 502-868-7733. *E-mail:* financialaid@georgetowncollege.edu.

GEORGETOWN UNIVERSITY

Washington, DC

Tuition & fees: $40,203 — **Average undergraduate aid package: $33,784**

ABOUT THE INSTITUTION Independent Roman Catholic (Jesuit), coed. 48 undergraduate majors. Both federal and institutional methodology are used as a basis for awarding need-based institutional aid.

UNDERGRADUATE EXPENSES for 2010–11 ***Comprehensive fee:*** $52,443 includes full-time tuition ($39,768), mandatory fees ($435), and room and board ($12,240). ***College room only:*** $8770. Full-time tuition and fees vary according to course load and program. Room and board charges vary according to board plan and housing facility. ***Part-time tuition:*** $1657 per credit hour. ***Part-time fees:*** $435 per year. Part-time tuition and fees vary according to course load and program. ***Payment plan:*** Installment.

FRESHMAN FINANCIAL AID (Fall 2010, est.) 944 applied for aid; of those 74% were deemed to have need. 100% of freshmen with need received aid; of those 100% had need fully met. ***Average percent of need met:*** 100% (excluding resources awarded to replace EFC). ***Average financial aid package:*** $33,108 (excluding resources awarded to replace EFC).

UNDERGRADUATE FINANCIAL AID (Fall 2010, est.) 3,525 applied for aid; of those 87% were deemed to have need. 100% of undergraduates with need received aid; of those 100% had need fully met. ***Average percent of need met:*** 100% (excluding resources awarded to replace EFC). ***Average financial aid package:*** $33,784 (excluding resources awarded to replace EFC).

GIFT AID (NEED-BASED) ***Total amount:*** $91,005,000 (7% federal, 89% institutional, 4% external sources). ***Receiving aid:*** Freshmen: 45% (699); all full-time undergraduates: 39% (2,779). ***Average award:*** Freshmen: $29,961; Undergraduates: $30,715. ***Scholarships, grants, and awards:*** Federal Pell, FSEOG, state, private, college/university gift aid from institutional funds.

GIFT AID (NON-NEED-BASED) ***Total amount:*** $3,700,000 (41% federal, 5% institutional, 54% external sources). ***Receiving aid:*** Freshmen: 16% (250). Undergraduates: 11% (800). ***Scholarships, grants, and awards by category:*** *Special characteristics:* 130 awards ($3,000,000 total): children of faculty/staff.

LOANS ***Student loans:*** $20,500,000 (51% need-based, 49% non-need-based). 39% of past graduating class borrowed through all loan programs. *Average indebtedness per student:* $25,315. ***Average need-based loan:*** Freshmen: $3492. Undergraduates: $4716. ***Parent loans:*** $9,000,000 (100% non-need-based). ***Programs:*** Perkins, Federal Nursing, alternative loans.

WORK-STUDY ***Federal work-study:*** Total amount: $5,400,000; 1,925 jobs averaging $2800.

ATHLETIC AWARDS Total amount: $6,775,000 (25% need-based, 75% non-need-based).

APPLYING FOR FINANCIAL AID ***Required financial aid forms:*** FAFSA, CSS Financial Aid PROFILE, business/farm supplement. ***Financial aid deadline:*** 2/1. ***Notification date:*** 4/1. Students must reply by 5/1 or within 2 weeks of notification.

CONTACT Ms. Patricia A. McWade, Dean of Student Financial Services, Georgetown University, 37th and O Street, NW, Box 1252, Washington, DC 20057, 202-687-4547. *Fax:* 202-687-6542. *E-mail:* mcwadep@georgetown.edu.

THE GEORGE WASHINGTON UNIVERSITY

Washington, DC

Tuition & fees: $42,905 **Average undergraduate aid package: $39,572**

ABOUT THE INSTITUTION Independent, coed. 81 undergraduate majors. Federal methodology is used as a basis for awarding need-based institutional aid.

UNDERGRADUATE EXPENSES for 2010–11 ***Comprehensive fee:*** $53,025 includes full-time tuition ($42,860), mandatory fees ($45), and room and board ($10,120). ***College room only:*** $6720. Full-time tuition and fees vary according to student level. Room and board charges vary according to housing facility. ***Part-time tuition:*** $1192 per credit hour. ***Part-time fees:*** $1.50 per credit hour; $22.50 per term. Part-time tuition and fees vary according to course load. ***Payment plans:*** Guaranteed tuition, installment.

FRESHMAN FINANCIAL AID (Fall 2009) 1,665 applied for aid; of those 74% were deemed to have need. 96% of freshmen with need received aid; of those 92% had need fully met. ***Average percent of need met:*** 95% (excluding resources awarded to replace EFC). ***Average financial aid package:*** $38,579 (excluding resources awarded to replace EFC). 10% of all full-time freshmen had no need and received non-need-based gift aid.

UNDERGRADUATE FINANCIAL AID (Fall 2009) 5,104 applied for aid; of those 84% were deemed to have need. 97% of undergraduates with need received aid; of those 87% had need fully met. ***Average percent of need met:*** 93% (excluding resources awarded to replace EFC). ***Average financial aid package:*** $39,572 (excluding resources awarded to replace EFC). 12% of all full-time undergraduates had no need and received non-need-based gift aid.

GIFT AID (NEED-BASED) ***Total amount:*** $127,635,271 (6% federal, 94% institutional). ***Receiving aid:*** Freshmen: 45% (1,158); all full-time undergraduates: 42% (3,998). ***Average award:*** Freshmen: $28,704; Undergraduates: $27,633. ***Scholarships, grants, and awards:*** Federal Pell, FSEOG, state, college/university gift aid from institutional funds.

GIFT AID (NON-NEED-BASED) ***Total amount:*** $16,538,528 (100% institutional). ***Receiving aid:*** Freshmen: 5% (127). Undergraduates: 8% (760). ***Average award:*** Freshmen: $14,530. Undergraduates: $13,050. ***Scholarships, grants, and awards by category:*** *Academic interests/achievement:* general academic interests/achievements. *Creative arts/performance:* general creative arts/performance. ***Tuition waivers:*** Full or partial for employees or children of employees.

LOANS ***Student loans:*** $31,423,778 (80% need-based, 20% non-need-based). 47% of past graduating class borrowed through all loan programs. *Average indebtedness per student:* $32,547. ***Average need-based loan:*** Freshmen: $3553. Undergraduates: $5229. ***Parent loans:*** $23,064,187 (16% need-based, 84% non-need-based). ***Programs:*** Perkins.

WORK-STUDY ***Federal work-study:*** Total amount: $6,103,106; jobs available.

ATHLETIC AWARDS Total amount: $5,841,453 (22% need-based, 78% non-need-based).

APPLYING FOR FINANCIAL AID ***Required financial aid forms:*** FAFSA, CSS Financial Aid PROFILE. ***Financial aid deadline:*** 2/1. ***Notification date:*** Continuous beginning 3/24. Students must reply by 5/1.

CONTACT Dan Small, Executive Director of Student Financial Assistance, The George Washington University, 2121 I Street, NW, Rice Hall, Suite 301, Washington, DC 21044, 202-994-6620 or toll-free 800-447-3765 (in-state). *Fax:* 202-994-0906. *E-mail:* finaid@gwu.edu.

GEORGIA COLLEGE & STATE UNIVERSITY

Milledgeville, GA

Tuition & fees (GA res): $7852 **Average undergraduate aid package: $7988**

ABOUT THE INSTITUTION State-supported, coed. 38 undergraduate majors. Federal methodology is used as a basis for awarding need-based institutional aid.

UNDERGRADUATE EXPENSES for 2010–11 ***Tuition, state resident:*** full-time $6284. ***Tuition, nonresident:*** full-time $23,322. ***Required fees:*** full-time $1568; $784 per term. Full-time tuition and fees vary according to course load and location. Part-time tuition and fees vary according to course load and location. ***College room and board:*** $8414; ***Room only:*** $4918. Room and board charges vary according to board plan and housing facility. ***Payment plan:*** Installment.

FRESHMAN FINANCIAL AID (Fall 2010, est.) 1,036 applied for aid; of those 51% were deemed to have need. 99% of freshmen with need received aid. ***Average financial aid package:*** $8634 (excluding resources awarded to replace EFC). 1% of all full-time freshmen had no need and received non-need-based gift aid.

UNDERGRADUATE FINANCIAL AID (Fall 2010, est.) 4,816 applied for aid; of those 53% were deemed to have need. 98% of undergraduates with need received aid. ***Average financial aid package:*** $7988 (excluding resources awarded to replace EFC). 1% of all full-time undergraduates had no need and received non-need-based gift aid.

GIFT AID (NEED-BASED) ***Total amount:*** $5,309,161 (100% federal). ***Receiving aid:*** Freshmen: 18% (195); all full-time undergraduates: 22% (1,135). ***Average award:*** Freshmen: $3901; Undergraduates: $3936. ***Scholarships, grants, and awards:*** Federal Pell, FSEOG, state, college/university gift aid from institutional funds.

GIFT AID (NON-NEED-BASED) ***Total amount:*** $22,134,415 (95% state, 3% institutional, 2% external sources). ***Receiving aid:*** Freshmen: 46% (491). Undergraduates: 35% (1,790). ***Average award:*** Freshmen: $2203. Undergraduates: $2494. ***Scholarships, grants, and awards by category:*** *Academic interests/achievement:* business, computer science, education, English, foreign languages, general academic interests/achievements, health fields, humanities, international studies, mathematics, physical sciences, social sciences. *Creative arts/performance:* applied art and design, art/fine arts, creative writing, journalism/publications, music, performing arts, theater/drama. *Special achievements/activities:* community service, general special achievements/activities, leadership. *Special characteristics:* adult students, children of faculty/staff, children with a deceased or disabled parent, handicapped students, international students, local/state students, members of minority groups, out-of-state students, religious affiliation. ***Tuition waivers:*** Full or partial for employees or children of employees, senior citizens.

LOANS ***Student loans:*** $20,557,995 (52% need-based, 48% non-need-based). 55% of past graduating class borrowed through all loan programs. *Average indebtedness per student:* $17,141. ***Average need-based loan:*** Freshmen: $3122. Undergraduates: $3135. ***Parent loans:*** $2,590,765 (100% non-need-based). ***Programs:*** Federal Direct (PLUS), Perkins, state, college/university.

WORK-STUDY ***Federal work-study:*** Total amount: $200,000; 68 jobs averaging $2941.

ATHLETIC AWARDS Total amount: $663,084 (100% non-need-based).

APPLYING FOR FINANCIAL AID ***Required financial aid form:*** FAFSA. ***Financial aid deadline (priority):*** 3/1. ***Notification date:*** Continuous beginning 3/1. Students must reply within 2 weeks of notification.

CONTACT Ms. Cathy Crawley, Director of Financial Aid, Georgia College & State University, Campus Box 30, Milledgeville, GA 31061, 478-445-5149 or toll-free 800-342-0471 (in-state). *Fax:* 478-445-0729. *E-mail:* cathy.crawley@gcsu.edu.

GEORGIA GWINNETT COLLEGE

Lawrenceville, GA

CONTACT Financial Aid Office, Georgia Gwinnett College, 1000 University Center Lane, Lawrenceville, GA 60043, 678-407-5000.

GEORGIA HEALTH SCIENCES UNIVERSITY

Augusta, GA

Tuition & fees (GA res): $8182 **Average undergraduate aid package: $8594**

ABOUT THE INSTITUTION State-supported, coed. 8 undergraduate majors. Federal methodology is used as a basis for awarding need-based institutional aid.

UNDERGRADUATE EXPENSES for 2010–11 ***Tuition, state resident:*** full-time $7070; part-time $236 per credit hour. ***Tuition, nonresident:*** full-time $25,280; part-time $843 per credit hour. ***Required fees:*** full-time $1112. Full-time tuition and fees vary according to course load, location, program, and reciprocity agreements. Part-time tuition and fees vary according to course load, location, program, and reciprocity agreements. Room and board charges vary according to housing facility and location.

UNDERGRADUATE FINANCIAL AID (Fall 2010, est.) 403 applied for aid; of those 100% were deemed to have need. 100% of undergraduates with need received aid. ***Average financial aid package:*** $8594 (excluding resources awarded to replace EFC).

GIFT AID (NEED-BASED) ***Total amount:*** $751,095 (83% federal, 2% institutional, 15% external sources). ***Receiving aid:*** All full-time undergraduates: 55% (260). ***Average award:*** Undergraduates: $1897. ***Scholarships, grants, and awards:*** Federal Pell, FSEOG, state, private, college/university gift aid from institutional funds, Federal Nursing.

GIFT AID (NON-NEED-BASED) ***Total amount:*** $1,440,106 (1% federal, 99% state). ***Receiving aid:*** Undergraduates: 51% (242). ***Scholarships, grants, and awards by category:*** *Academic interests/achievement:* 45 awards ($164,500 total): health fields. *Special characteristics:* 44 awards ($90,540 total): religious affiliation. ***Tuition waivers:*** Full or partial for employees or children of employees.

LOANS ***Student loans:*** $2,146,657 (50% need-based, 50% non-need-based). ***Average need-based loan:*** Undergraduates: $3747. ***Parent loans:*** $65,632 (100% need-based). ***Programs:*** Federal Direct (Subsidized and Unsubsidized Stafford, PLUS), Perkins, Federal Nursing, state, college/university.

WORK-STUDY ***Federal work-study:*** Total amount: $34,350; 22 jobs averaging $1561.

APPLYING FOR FINANCIAL AID ***Required financial aid forms:*** FAFSA, institution's own form, state aid form. ***Financial aid deadline:*** Continuous. ***Notification date:*** Continuous beginning 6/10. Students must reply within 2 weeks of notification.

CONTACT Dr. Beverly Boggs, Executive Director of Student Financial Aid, Georgia Health Sciences University, 2013 Administration Building, Augusta, GA 30912-7320, 706-721-4901 or toll-free 800-519-3388 (in-state). *Fax:* 706-721-9407. *E-mail:* osfa@georgiahealth.edu.

GEORGIA INSTITUTE OF TECHNOLOGY

Atlanta, GA

Tuition & fees (GA res): $8716 **Average undergraduate aid package: $11,005**

ABOUT THE INSTITUTION State-supported, coed. 35 undergraduate majors. Federal methodology is used as a basis for awarding need-based institutional aid.

UNDERGRADUATE EXPENSES for 2010–11 ***Tuition, state resident:*** full-time $7070; part-time $350 per credit hour. ***Tuition, nonresident:*** full-time $25,280; part-time $1250 per credit hour. ***Required fees:*** full-time $1646; $373 per course or $823 per term. Full-time tuition and fees vary according to reciprocity agreements. Part-time tuition and fees vary according to course load and reciprocity agreements. ***College room and board:*** $8746; ***Room only:*** $5332. Room and board charges vary according to board plan and housing facility.

FRESHMAN FINANCIAL AID (Fall 2009) 1,978 applied for aid; of those 51% were deemed to have need. 97% of freshmen with need received aid; of those 47% had need fully met. ***Average percent of need met:*** 72% (excluding resources awarded to replace EFC). ***Average financial aid package:*** $12,892 (excluding resources awarded to replace EFC). 11% of all full-time freshmen had no need and received non-need-based gift aid.

UNDERGRADUATE FINANCIAL AID (Fall 2009) 7,646 applied for aid; of those 62% were deemed to have need. 97% of undergraduates with need received aid; of those 34% had need fully met. ***Average percent of need met:*** 62% (excluding resources awarded to replace EFC). ***Average financial aid package:*** $11,005 (excluding resources awarded to replace EFC). 8% of all full-time undergraduates had no need and received non-need-based gift aid.

GIFT AID (NEED-BASED) ***Total amount:*** $35,965,903 (34% federal, 36% state, 27% institutional, 3% external sources). ***Receiving aid:*** Freshmen: 36% (952); all full-time undergraduates: 32% (3,928). ***Average award:*** Freshmen: $11,350; Undergraduates: $9422. ***Scholarships, grants, and awards:*** Federal Pell, FSEOG, state, private, college/university gift aid from institutional funds, Wayne Clough Georgia Tech Promise Program.

GIFT AID (NON-NEED-BASED) ***Total amount:*** $24,585,649 (81% state, 14% institutional, 5% external sources). ***Receiving aid:*** Freshmen: 25% (677). Undergraduates: 19% (2,337). ***Average award:*** Freshmen: $3077. Undergraduates: $3067. ***Scholarships, grants, and awards by category:*** *Academic interests/achievement:* 2,564 awards ($9,040,463 total): architecture, biological sciences, computer science, engineering/technologies, general academic interests/achievements, physical sciences. *Special achievements/activities:* 376 awards ($560,800 total): cheerleading/drum major, general special achievements/activities, leadership. *Special characteristics:* 4,902 awards ($32,292,921 total): local/state students, members of minority groups. ***Tuition waivers:*** Full or partial for employees or children of employees.

LOANS ***Student loans:*** $36,919,410 (74% need-based, 26% non-need-based). 51% of past graduating class borrowed through all loan programs. *Average indebtedness per student:* $21,838. ***Average need-based loan:*** Freshmen: $3740. Undergraduates: $3587. ***Parent loans:*** $18,022,514 (68% need-based, 32% non-need-based). ***Programs:*** Federal Direct (Subsidized and Unsubsidized Stafford, PLUS), Perkins, college/university.

WORK-STUDY ***Federal work-study:*** Total amount: $672,434; 274 jobs averaging $2345.

ATHLETIC AWARDS Total amount: $5,329,949 (42% need-based, 58% non-need-based).

APPLYING FOR FINANCIAL AID ***Required financial aid forms:*** FAFSA, institution's own form. ***Financial aid deadline:*** 3/1. ***Notification date:*** 4/1. Students must reply by 5/1.

CONTACT Ms. Marie Mons, Director of Student Financial Planning and Services, Georgia Institute of Technology, 225 North Avenue, NW, Atlanta, GA 30332-0460, 404-894-4160. *Fax:* 404-894-7412. *E-mail:* marie.mons@finaid.gatech.edu.

GEORGIAN COURT UNIVERSITY

Lakewood, NJ

Tuition & fees: $26,176 **Average undergraduate aid package: $21,915**

ABOUT THE INSTITUTION Independent Roman Catholic, coed, primarily women. 30 undergraduate majors. Federal methodology is used as a basis for awarding need-based institutional aid.

UNDERGRADUATE EXPENSES for 2010–11 ***Comprehensive fee:*** $36,032 includes full-time tuition ($24,932), mandatory fees ($1244), and room and board ($9856). ***Part-time tuition:*** $570 per credit hour. ***Part-time fees:*** $622 per year. Part-time tuition and fees vary according to location. ***Payment plan:*** Installment.

FRESHMAN FINANCIAL AID (Fall 2010, est.) 214 applied for aid; of those 90% were deemed to have need. 100% of freshmen with need received aid; of those 32% had need fully met. ***Average percent of need met:*** 86% (excluding resources awarded to replace EFC). ***Average financial aid package:*** $26,339 (excluding resources awarded to replace EFC). 9% of all full-time freshmen had no need and received non-need-based gift aid.

UNDERGRADUATE FINANCIAL AID (Fall 2010, est.) 1,345 applied for aid; of those 90% were deemed to have need. 100% of undergraduates with need received aid; of those 33% had need fully met. ***Average percent of need met:*** 86% (excluding resources awarded to replace EFC). ***Average financial aid package:*** $21,915 (excluding resources awarded to replace EFC). 8% of all full-time undergraduates had no need and received non-need-based gift aid.

GIFT AID (NEED-BASED) ***Total amount:*** $16,580,154 (21% federal, 27% state, 52% institutional). ***Receiving aid:*** Freshmen: 87% (193); all full-time undergraduates: 79% (1,160). ***Average award:*** Freshmen: $18,104; Undergraduates: $13,565. ***Scholarships, grants, and awards:*** Federal Pell, FSEOG, state, private, college/university gift aid from institutional funds.

GIFT AID (NON-NEED-BASED) ***Total amount:*** $1,223,828 (99% institutional, 1% external sources). ***Receiving aid:*** Freshmen: 7% (15). Undergraduates: 4% (64). ***Average award:*** Freshmen: $9461. Undergraduates: $7132. ***Scholarships, grants, and awards by category:*** *Academic interests/achievement:* biological sciences, business, English, foreign languages, general academic interests/achievements, mathematics, physical sciences. *Creative arts/performance:* art/fine arts, creative writing, music. *Special achievements/activities:* general special achievements/activities. *Special characteristics:* children of faculty/staff, religious affiliation, spouses of current students, veterans. ***Tuition waivers:*** Full or partial for employees or children of employees.

LOANS ***Student loans:*** $12,711,902 (73% need-based, 27% non-need-based). 91% of past graduating class borrowed through all loan programs. *Average indebtedness per student:* $35,632. ***Average need-based loan:*** Freshmen: $6214. Undergraduates: $7133. ***Parent loans:*** $859,298 (46% need-based, 54% non-need-based). ***Programs:*** state.

WORK-STUDY ***Federal work-study:*** Total amount: $295,538; 199 jobs averaging $1478. ***State or other work-study/employment:*** Total amount: $44,250 (19% need-based, 81% non-need-based). 30 part-time jobs averaging $1425.

ATHLETIC AWARDS Total amount: $858,284 (73% need-based, 27% non-need-based).

APPLYING FOR FINANCIAL AID ***Required financial aid form:*** FAFSA. ***Financial aid deadline:*** 8/1 (priority: 4/15). ***Notification date:*** Continuous beginning 2/1. Students must reply within 2 weeks of notification.

CONTACT Judith Schneider, Interim Director of Financial Aid, Georgian Court University, 900 Lakewood Avenue, Lakewood, NJ 08701-2697, 732-987-2258 or toll-free 800-458-8422. *Fax:* 732-987-2023. *E-mail:* financialaid@georgian.edu.

GEORGIA SOUTHERN UNIVERSITY

Statesboro, GA

Tuition & fees (GA res): $6240 **Average undergraduate aid package: $8944**

ABOUT THE INSTITUTION State-supported, coed. 80 undergraduate majors. Federal methodology is used as a basis for awarding need-based institutional aid.

UNDERGRADUATE EXPENSES for 2010–11 ***Tuition, state resident:*** full-time $4596; part-time $154 per credit hour. ***Tuition, nonresident:*** full-time $16,572; part-time $553 per credit hour. ***Required fees:*** full-time $1644; $822 per term. Full-time tuition and fees vary according to degree level, location, and program. Part-time tuition and fees vary according to course load, degree level, location, and program. ***College room and board:*** $8414; ***Room only:*** $5364. Room and board charges vary according to board plan and housing facility.

FRESHMAN FINANCIAL AID (Fall 2009) 3,214 applied for aid; of those 62% were deemed to have need. 97% of freshmen with need received aid; of those 15% had need fully met. ***Average percent of need met:*** 60% (excluding resources awarded to replace EFC). ***Average financial aid package:*** $9157 (excluding resources awarded to replace EFC). 4% of all full-time freshmen had no need and received non-need-based gift aid.

UNDERGRADUATE FINANCIAL AID (Fall 2009) 12,869 applied for aid; of those 69% were deemed to have need. 98% of undergraduates with need received aid; of those 10% had need fully met. ***Average percent of need met:*** 55% (excluding resources awarded to replace EFC). ***Average financial aid package:*** $8944 (excluding resources awarded to replace EFC). 2% of all full-time undergraduates had no need and received non-need-based gift aid.

GIFT AID (NEED-BASED) ***Total amount:*** $48,556,793 (60% federal, 37% state, 1% institutional, 2% external sources). ***Receiving aid:*** Freshmen: 49% (1,699); all full-time undergraduates: 47% (6,956). ***Average award:*** Freshmen: $7757; Undergraduates: $6921. ***Scholarships, grants, and awards:*** Federal Pell, FSEOG, state, private, college/university gift aid from institutional funds, Academic Competitiveness Grants, National SMART Grants, TEACH Grants, Hope Scholarships.

GIFT AID (NON-NEED-BASED) ***Total amount:*** $13,486,434 (91% state, 6% institutional, 3% external sources). ***Receiving aid:*** Freshmen: 4% (157). Undergraduates: 3% (443). ***Average award:*** Freshmen: $1949. Undergraduates: $1837. ***Scholarships, grants, and awards by category:*** *Academic interests/achievement:* 747 awards ($1,201,069 total): biological sciences, business, communication, computer science, education, engineering/technologies, English, foreign languages, general academic interests/achievements, health fields, humanities, international studies, mathematics, military science, social sciences. *Creative arts/performance:* 54 awards ($63,700 total): art/fine arts, cinema/film/broadcasting, general creative arts/performance, music, theater/drama. *Special achievements/activities:* 187 awards ($196,050 total): cheerleading/drum major, community service, junior miss, leadership, memberships, religious involvement. *Special characteristics:* 29 awards ($95,117 total): adult students, children and siblings of alumni, children of public servants, first-generation college students, handicapped students, married students, members of minority groups. ***Tuition waivers:*** Full or partial for employees or children of employees, senior citizens.

LOANS ***Student loans:*** $56,555,814 (78% need-based, 22% non-need-based). 66% of past graduating class borrowed through all loan programs. *Average indebtedness per student:* $19,418. ***Average need-based loan:*** Freshmen: $3222. Undergraduates: $4075. ***Parent loans:*** $10,111,240 (65% need-based, 35% non-need-based). ***Programs:*** Federal Direct (Subsidized and Unsubsidized Stafford, PLUS), Perkins, state, private loans, Service-Cancelable State Direct Student Loans.

WORK-STUDY ***Federal work-study:*** Total amount: $415,679; 245 jobs averaging $1697.

ATHLETIC AWARDS Total amount: $2,300,058 (51% need-based, 49% non-need-based).

APPLYING FOR FINANCIAL AID ***Required financial aid form:*** FAFSA. ***Financial aid deadline (priority):*** 4/20. ***Notification date:*** Continuous beginning 4/20.

CONTACT Mrs. Elise Boyett, Associate Director of Financial Aid, Georgia Southern University, PO Box 8065, Statesboro, GA 30460-8065, 912-478-5413. *Fax:* 912-478-0573. *E-mail:* eboyett@georgiasouthern.edu.

GEORGIA SOUTHWESTERN STATE UNIVERSITY

Americus, GA

ABOUT THE INSTITUTION State-supported, coed. ***Awards:*** bachelor's and master's degrees and post-bachelor's and post-master's certificates. 29 undergraduate majors. ***Total enrollment:*** 2,405. Undergraduates: 2,221. Freshmen: 426.

GIFT AID (NEED-BASED) ***Scholarships, grants, and awards:*** Federal Pell, FSEOG, state, private, college/university gift aid from institutional funds.

GIFT AID (NON-NEED-BASED) ***Scholarships, grants, and awards by category:*** *Academic interests/achievement:* general academic interests/achievements. *Creative arts/performance:* art/fine arts, music. *Special achievements/activities:* leadership.

LOANS ***Programs:*** Perkins, state, college/university.

WORK-STUDY ***Federal work-study:*** Total amount: $86,607; 58 jobs averaging $1493. ***State or other work-study/employment:*** Part-time jobs available.

APPLYING FOR FINANCIAL AID ***Required financial aid forms:*** FAFSA, institution's own form.

CONTACT Angela Bryant, Director of Financial Aid, Georgia Southwestern State University, 800 Georgia Southwestern State University Drive, Americus, GA 31709-4693, 229-928-1378 or toll-free 800-338-0082. *Fax:* 229-931-2061.

GEORGIA STATE UNIVERSITY

Atlanta, GA

Tuition & fees (GA res): $8698 **Average undergraduate aid package: $9480**

ABOUT THE INSTITUTION State-supported, coed. 50 undergraduate majors. Federal methodology is used as a basis for awarding need-based institutional aid.

UNDERGRADUATE EXPENSES for 2010–11 ***Tuition, state resident:*** full-time $7070; part-time $236 per credit hour. ***Tuition, nonresident:*** full-time $25,280; part-time $843 per credit hour. ***Required fees:*** full-time $1628; $107.66 per credit hour. Part-time tuition and fees vary according to course load. ***College room and board:*** $9325; ***Room only:*** $7660. Room and board charges vary according to housing facility.

FRESHMAN FINANCIAL AID (Fall 2010, est.) 2,724 applied for aid; of those 79% were deemed to have need. 99% of freshmen with need received aid; of those 16% had need fully met. ***Average percent of need met:*** 28% (excluding resources awarded to replace EFC). ***Average financial aid package:*** $10,842 (excluding resources awarded to replace EFC). 20% of all full-time freshmen had no need and received non-need-based gift aid.

UNDERGRADUATE FINANCIAL AID (Fall 2010, est.) 15,687 applied for aid; of those 84% were deemed to have need. 98% of undergraduates with need received aid; of those 12% had need fully met. ***Average percent of need met:*** 30% (excluding resources awarded to replace EFC). ***Average financial aid package:*** $9480 (excluding resources awarded to replace EFC). 14% of all full-time undergraduates had no need and received non-need-based gift aid.

GIFT AID (NEED-BASED) ***Total amount:*** $68,177,243 (100% federal). ***Receiving aid:*** Freshmen: 47% (1,428); all full-time undergraduates: 44% (8,804). ***Average award:*** Freshmen: $2902; Undergraduates: $3520. ***Scholarships, grants, and awards:*** Federal Pell, FSEOG, state, private, college/university gift aid from institutional funds, United Negro College Fund.

GIFT AID (NON-NEED-BASED) ***Total amount:*** $44,382,353 (95% state, 2% institutional, 3% external sources). ***Receiving aid:*** Freshmen: 68% (2,076). Undergraduates: 60% (11,989). ***Average award:*** Freshmen: $3407. Undergraduates: $3077. ***Tuition waivers:*** Full or partial for employees or children of employees, senior citizens.

LOANS ***Student loans:*** $96,698,344 (46% need-based, 54% non-need-based). 57% of past graduating class borrowed through all loan programs. *Average indebtedness per student:* $20,336. ***Average need-based loan:*** Freshmen: $2966. Undergraduates: $3637. ***Parent loans:*** $6,868,361 (100% non-need-based). ***Programs:*** Federal Direct (Subsidized and Unsubsidized Stafford, PLUS), Perkins.

WORK-STUDY ***Federal work-study:*** Total amount: $498,845; 214 jobs averaging $2369.

ATHLETIC AWARDS Total amount: $4,315,688 (100% non-need-based).

APPLYING FOR FINANCIAL AID ***Required financial aid form:*** FAFSA. ***Financial aid deadline:*** 11/1 (priority: 4/1). ***Notification date:*** Continuous beginning 3/30.

CONTACT Louis Scott, Financial Aid Office, Georgia State University, PO Box 4040, Atlanta, GA 30302, 404-413-2600. *Fax:* 404-413-2102. *E-mail:* onestopshop@gsu.edu.

GETTYSBURG COLLEGE

Gettysburg, PA

Tuition & fees: $41,070 **Average undergraduate aid package: $32,938**

ABOUT THE INSTITUTION Independent religious, coed. 81 undergraduate majors. Both federal and institutional methodology are used as a basis for awarding need-based institutional aid.

UNDERGRADUATE EXPENSES for 2010–11 ***Comprehensive fee:*** $50,880 includes full-time tuition ($41,070) and room and board ($9810). ***College room only:*** $5260. Full-time tuition and fees vary according to program. Room and board charges vary according to board plan and housing facility. Part-time tuition and fees vary according to program. ***Payment plans:*** Tuition prepayment, installment.

FRESHMAN FINANCIAL AID (Fall 2010, est.) 568 applied for aid; of those 73% were deemed to have need. 99% of freshmen with need received aid; of those 97% had need fully met. ***Average percent of need met:*** 100% (excluding resources awarded to replace EFC). ***Average financial aid package:*** $33,937 (excluding resources awarded to replace EFC). 15% of all full-time freshmen had no need and received non-need-based gift aid.

UNDERGRADUATE FINANCIAL AID (Fall 2010, est.) 1,791 applied for aid; of those 83% were deemed to have need. 98% of undergraduates with need received aid; of those 97% had need fully met. ***Average percent of need met:*** 100% (excluding resources awarded to replace EFC). ***Average financial aid package:*** $32,938 (excluding resources awarded to replace EFC). 13% of all full-time undergraduates had no need and received non-need-based gift aid.

GIFT AID (NEED-BASED) ***Total amount:*** $39,841,300 (5% federal, 1% state, 92% institutional, 2% external sources). ***Receiving aid:*** Freshmen: 55% (398); all full-time undergraduates: 53% (1,425). ***Average award:*** Freshmen: $28,444; Undergraduates: $25,548. ***Scholarships, grants, and awards:*** Federal Pell, FSEOG, state, private, college/university gift aid from institutional funds, Academic Competitiveness Grants, National SMART Grants.

GIFT AID (NON-NEED-BASED) ***Total amount:*** $4,875,624 (93% institutional, 7% external sources). ***Receiving aid:*** Freshmen: 31% (223). Undergraduates: 27% (717). ***Average award:*** Freshmen: $12,436. Undergraduates: $11,498. ***Scholarships, grants, and awards by category:*** *Academic interests/achievement:* 1,000 awards ($11,409,075 total): general academic interests/achievements. *Creative arts/performance:* 35 awards ($335,500 total): music. ***Tuition waivers:*** Full or partial for employees or children of employees.

LOANS ***Student loans:*** $10,181,268 (60% need-based, 40% non-need-based). 60% of past graduating class borrowed through all loan programs. *Average indebtedness per student:* $24,981. ***Average need-based loan:*** Freshmen: $5183. Undergraduates: $7139. ***Parent loans:*** $7,022,499 (100% non-need-based). ***Programs:*** Federal Direct (Subsidized and Unsubsidized Stafford, PLUS), Perkins, college/university.

WORK-STUDY ***Federal work-study:*** Total amount: $680,790; 740 jobs averaging $919. ***State or other work-study/employment:*** Total amount: $981,914 (100% non-need-based). 650 part-time jobs averaging $1250.

APPLYING FOR FINANCIAL AID ***Required financial aid forms:*** FAFSA, CSS Financial Aid PROFILE, business/farm supplement, federal income tax form(s), verification worksheet. ***Financial aid deadline:*** 2/15. ***Notification date:*** 3/27. Students must reply by 5/1.

CONTACT Christina Gormley, Director of Financial Aid, Gettysburg College, 300 North Washington Street, Gettysburg, PA 17325, 717-337-6620 or toll-free 800-431-0803. *Fax:* 717-337-8555. *E-mail:* finaid@gettysburg.edu.

GLENVILLE STATE COLLEGE

Glenville, WV

Tuition & fees (WV res): $4888 **Average undergraduate aid package: $11,686**

ABOUT THE INSTITUTION State-supported, coed. 32 undergraduate majors. Federal methodology is used as a basis for awarding need-based institutional aid.

UNDERGRADUATE EXPENSES for 2010–11 ***Tuition, state resident:*** full-time $4888; part-time $203.67 per credit hour. ***Tuition, nonresident:*** full-time $12,000; part-time $500 per credit hour. ***Required fees:*** $203.67 per credit hour. Full-time tuition and fees vary according to course load. ***College room and board:*** $7350; ***Room only:*** $4000. Room and board charges vary according to board plan and housing facility. ***Payment plan:*** Installment.

FRESHMAN FINANCIAL AID (Fall 2010, est.) 296 applied for aid; of those 89% were deemed to have need. 99% of freshmen with need received aid; of those 18% had need fully met. ***Average percent of need met:*** 71% (excluding resources awarded to replace EFC). ***Average financial aid package:*** $11,227 (excluding resources awarded to replace EFC). 4% of all full-time freshmen had no need and received non-need-based gift aid.

UNDERGRADUATE FINANCIAL AID (Fall 2010, est.) 1,114 applied for aid; of those 92% were deemed to have need. 99% of undergraduates with need received aid; of those 22% had need fully met. ***Average percent of need met:*** 73% (excluding resources awarded to replace EFC). ***Average financial aid package:*** $11,686 (excluding resources awarded to replace EFC). 4% of all full-time undergraduates had no need and received non-need-based gift aid.

GIFT AID (NEED-BASED) ***Total amount:*** $4,784,379 (78% federal, 22% state). ***Receiving aid:*** Freshmen: 68% (214); all full-time undergraduates: 65% (827). ***Average award:*** Freshmen: $5666; Undergraduates: $5299. ***Scholarships, grants, and awards:*** Federal Pell, FSEOG, state, private, college/university gift aid from institutional funds.

GIFT AID (NON-NEED-BASED) ***Total amount:*** $1,365,900 (60% state, 20% institutional, 20% external sources). ***Receiving aid:*** Freshmen: 51% (159). Undergraduates: 39% (497). ***Average award:*** Freshmen: $1508. Undergraduates: $2077. ***Scholarships, grants, and awards by category:*** *Academic interests/achievement:* 233 awards ($265,210 total): biological sciences, business, education, English, general academic interests/achievements, mathematics, social sciences. *Creative arts/performance:* 31 awards ($35,416 total): journalism/publications, music. *Special achievements/activities:* 4 awards ($2000 total): cheerleading/drum major. *Special characteristics:* 79 awards ($70,812 total): first-generation college students, veterans' children. ***Tuition waivers:*** Full or partial for senior citizens.

LOANS ***Student loans:*** $6,642,950 (47% need-based, 53% non-need-based). 80% of past graduating class borrowed through all loan programs. *Average indebtedness per student:* $25,145. ***Average need-based loan:*** Freshmen: $3058. Undergraduates: $3727. ***Parent loans:*** $389,217 (100% non-need-based). ***Programs:*** Federal Direct (Subsidized and Unsubsidized Stafford, PLUS), alternative loans.

WORK-STUDY ***Federal work-study:*** Total amount: $141,000; 94 jobs averaging $1500. ***State or other work-study/employment:*** Total amount: $450,000 (100% non-need-based). 255 part-time jobs averaging $2200.

ATHLETIC AWARDS Total amount: $817,440 (100% non-need-based).

APPLYING FOR FINANCIAL AID ***Required financial aid form:*** FAFSA. ***Financial aid deadline (priority):*** 2/1. ***Notification date:*** Continuous beginning 3/1. Students must reply within 3 weeks of notification.

CONTACT Ms. Karen Lay, Director of Financial Aid, Glenville State College, 200 High Street, Glenville, WV 26351-1200, 304-462-4103 Ext. 5 or toll-free 800-924-2010 (in-state). *Fax:* 304-462-4407. *E-mail:* karen.lay@glenville.edu.

GLOBAL COLLEGE OF LONG ISLAND UNIVERSITY

Brooklyn, NY

CONTACT Financial Aid Office, Global College of Long Island University, 9 Hanover Place, 4th Floor, Brooklyn, NY 11201, 631-287-8474.

GLOBE INSTITUTE OF TECHNOLOGY
New York, NY

CONTACT Office of Admissions, Globe Institute of Technology, 291 Broadway, 2nd Floor, New York, NY 10007, 212-349-4330 or toll-free 877-394-5623. *Fax:* 212-227-5920. *E-mail:* admission@globe.edu.

GLOBE UNIVERSITY
Woodbury, MN

CONTACT Financial Aid Office, Globe University, 8089 Globe Drive, Woodbury, MN 55125, 651-730-5100 or toll-free 800-231-0660.

GLOBE UNIVERSITY
Sioux Falls, SD

CONTACT Financial Aid Office, Globe University, 5101 South Broadband Lane, Sioux Falls, SD 57108-2208, 605-977-0705 or toll-free 866-437-0705 (out-of-state).

GODDARD COLLEGE
Plainfield, VT

CONTACT Beverly Jene, Director of Financial Aid, Goddard College, 123 Pitkin Road, Plainfield, VT 05667, 802-454-8311 Ext. 324 or toll-free 800-906-8312. *Fax:* 802-454-1029. *E-mail:* beverly.jene@goddard.edu.

GOD'S BIBLE SCHOOL AND COLLEGE
Cincinnati, OH

ABOUT THE INSTITUTION Independent interdenominational, coed. 10 undergraduate majors.

GIFT AID (NEED-BASED) ***Scholarships, grants, and awards:*** Federal Pell, state, college/university gift aid from institutional funds.

GIFT AID (NON-NEED-BASED) ***Scholarships, grants, and awards by category:*** *Academic interests/achievement:* general academic interests/achievements. *Creative arts/performance:* music. *Special characteristics:* international students.

LOANS ***Programs:*** Federal Direct (Subsidized and Unsubsidized Stafford, PLUS).

APPLYING FOR FINANCIAL AID ***Required financial aid form:*** FAFSA.

CONTACT Mrs. Lori Waggoner, Financial Aid Director, God's Bible School and College, 1810 Young Street, Cincinnati, OH 45202-6899, 513-721-7944 Ext. 205 or toll-free 800-486-4637. *Fax:* 513-721-1357. *E-mail:* lwaggoner@gbs.edu.

GOLDEN GATE UNIVERSITY
San Francisco, CA

Tuition & fees: $15,390 **Average undergraduate aid package: $8200**

ABOUT THE INSTITUTION Independent, coed. ***Awards:*** bachelor's and master's degrees and post-bachelor's certificates. 8 undergraduate majors. ***Total enrollment:*** 3,528. Undergraduates: 414. Federal methodology is used as a basis for awarding need-based institutional aid.

UNDERGRADUATE EXPENSES for 2010–11 ***Application fee:*** $55. ***Tuition:*** full-time $15,390; part-time $1710 per course. Full-time tuition and fees vary according to course load, degree level, and program. Part-time tuition and fees vary according to course load and program. ***Payment plans:*** Installment, deferred payment.

UNDERGRADUATE FINANCIAL AID (Fall 2009) ***Average financial aid package:*** $8200 (excluding resources awarded to replace EFC).

GIFT AID (NEED-BASED) ***Total amount:*** $580,306 (79% federal, 4% state, 17% institutional). ***Average award:*** Undergraduates: $3700. ***Scholarships, grants, and awards:*** Federal Pell, FSEOG, state, private, college/university gift aid from institutional funds.

GIFT AID (NON-NEED-BASED) ***Total amount:*** $470,605 (94% institutional, 6% external sources). ***Average award:*** Undergraduates: $3700. ***Scholarships, grants, and awards by category:*** *Academic interests/achievement:* business, computer science, general academic interests/achievements. *Special achievements/activities:* 15 awards ($48,500 total): community service, leadership. *Special characteristics:* adult students, general special characteristics, members of minority groups, previous college experience. ***Tuition waivers:*** Full or partial for employees or children of employees.

LOANS ***Student loans:*** $4,782,727 (40% need-based, 60% non-need-based). ***Average need-based loan:*** Undergraduates: $5500. ***Programs:*** Federal Direct (Subsidized and Unsubsidized Stafford, PLUS), Perkins.

WORK-STUDY ***Federal work-study:*** Total amount: $12,500; 1 job averaging $4000.

APPLYING FOR FINANCIAL AID ***Required financial aid forms:*** FAFSA, institution's own form. ***Financial aid deadline:*** Continuous. ***Notification date:*** Continuous beginning 4/1. Students must reply within 3 weeks of notification.

CONTACT Kathleen Kelly, Associate Director of Financial Services, Golden Gate University, 536 Mission Street, San Francisco, CA 94105-2968, 415-442-7297 or toll-free 800-448-3381. *Fax:* 415-442-7819. *E-mail:* kwalsh@ggu.edu.

GOLDEY-BEACOM COLLEGE
Wilmington, DE

Tuition & fees: $19,860 **Average undergraduate aid package: $14,174**

ABOUT THE INSTITUTION Independent, coed. 18 undergraduate majors. Federal methodology is used as a basis for awarding need-based institutional aid.

UNDERGRADUATE EXPENSES for 2011–12 ***Tuition:*** full-time $19,560; part-time $623 per credit hour. ***Required fees:*** full-time $300; $10 per credit hour. Full-time tuition and fees vary according to course load. Part-time tuition and fees vary according to course load. Room and board charges vary according to housing facility. ***Payment plans:*** Installment, deferred payment.

FRESHMAN FINANCIAL AID (Fall 2009) 52 applied for aid; of those 92% were deemed to have need. 100% of freshmen with need received aid; of those 21% had need fully met. ***Average percent of need met:*** 61% (excluding resources awarded to replace EFC). ***Average financial aid package:*** $13,111 (excluding resources awarded to replace EFC). 43% of all full-time freshmen had no need and received non-need-based gift aid.

UNDERGRADUATE FINANCIAL AID (Fall 2009) 358 applied for aid; of those 90% were deemed to have need. 97% of undergraduates with need received aid; of those 16% had need fully met. ***Average percent of need met:*** 60% (excluding resources awarded to replace EFC). ***Average financial aid package:*** $14,174 (excluding resources awarded to replace EFC). 33% of all full-time undergraduates had no need and received non-need-based gift aid.

GIFT AID (NEED-BASED) ***Total amount:*** $3,366,140 (25% federal, 67% institutional, 8% external sources). ***Receiving aid:*** Freshmen: 55% (48); all full-time undergraduates: 62% (306). ***Average award:*** Freshmen: $10,309; Undergraduates: $10,285. ***Scholarships, grants, and awards:*** Federal Pell, FSEOG, state, private, college/university gift aid from institutional funds.

GIFT AID (NON-NEED-BASED) ***Total amount:*** $1,201,473 (85% institutional, 15% external sources). ***Receiving aid:*** Freshmen: 11% (10). Undergraduates: 10% (48). ***Average award:*** Freshmen: $3384. Undergraduates: $4857. ***Scholarships, grants, and awards by category:*** *Academic interests/achievement:* business. ***Tuition waivers:*** Full or partial for employees or children of employees.

LOANS ***Student loans:*** $2,470,013 (82% need-based, 18% non-need-based). 70% of past graduating class borrowed through all loan programs. *Average indebtedness per student:* $26,045. ***Average need-based loan:*** Freshmen: $3741. Undergraduates: $4597. ***Parent loans:*** $156,811 (50% need-based, 50% non-need-based). ***Programs:*** Federal Direct (Subsidized and Unsubsidized Stafford, PLUS), Perkins.

WORK-STUDY ***Federal work-study:*** Total amount: $58,618; jobs available.

APPLYING FOR FINANCIAL AID ***Required financial aid form:*** FAFSA. ***Financial aid deadline (priority):*** 4/1. ***Notification date:*** Continuous beginning 10/1. Students must reply within 2 weeks of notification.

CONTACT Jane H. Lysle, Dean of Enrollment Management, Goldey-Beacom College, 4701 Limestone Road, Wilmington, DE 19808-1999, 302-225-6274 or toll-free 800-833-4877. *Fax:* 302-998-8631. *E-mail:* lyslej@goldey.gbc.edu.

GOLDFARB SCHOOL OF NURSING AT BARNES-JEWISH COLLEGE
St. Louis, MO

CONTACT Regina Blackshear, Chief Financial Aid Officer, Goldfarb School of Nursing at Barnes-Jewish College, 306 South Kingshighway, St. Louis, MO 63110-1091, 314-454-7770 or toll-free 800-832-9009 (in-state).

GONZAGA UNIVERSITY

Spokane, WA

Tuition & fees: $30,925 **Average undergraduate aid package: $20,412**

ABOUT THE INSTITUTION Independent Roman Catholic, coed. 51 undergraduate majors. Federal methodology is used as a basis for awarding need-based institutional aid.

UNDERGRADUATE EXPENSES for 2010–11 ***Comprehensive fee:*** $39,225 includes full-time tuition ($30,440), mandatory fees ($485), and room and board ($8300). ***College room only:*** $4240. Full-time tuition and fees vary according to course load, location, program, reciprocity agreements, and student level. Room and board charges vary according to board plan and housing facility. ***Part-time fees:*** $850 per credit hour. Part-time tuition and fees vary according to course load, location, program, reciprocity agreements, and student level. ***Payment plans:*** Installment, deferred payment.

FRESHMAN FINANCIAL AID (Fall 2010, est.) 923 applied for aid; of those 73% were deemed to have need. 100% of freshmen with need received aid; of those 29% had need fully met. ***Average percent of need met:*** 79% (excluding resources awarded to replace EFC). ***Average financial aid package:*** $21,867 (excluding resources awarded to replace EFC). 35% of all full-time freshmen had no need and received non-need-based gift aid.

UNDERGRADUATE FINANCIAL AID (Fall 2010, est.) 3,364 applied for aid; of those 79% were deemed to have need. 100% of undergraduates with need received aid; of those 20% had need fully met. ***Average percent of need met:*** 71% (excluding resources awarded to replace EFC). ***Average financial aid package:*** $20,412 (excluding resources awarded to replace EFC). 37% of all full-time undergraduates had no need and received non-need-based gift aid.

GIFT AID (NEED-BASED) ***Total amount:*** $39,438,321 (12% federal, 6% state, 79% institutional, 3% external sources). ***Receiving aid:*** Freshmen: 61% (678); all full-time undergraduates: 57% (2,635). ***Average award:*** Freshmen: $18,092; Undergraduates: $17,477. ***Scholarships, grants, and awards:*** Federal Pell, FSEOG, state, private, college/university gift aid from institutional funds, United Negro College Fund, Federal Nursing, Academic Competitiveness Grants, National SMART Grants, TEACH Grants.

GIFT AID (NON-NEED-BASED) ***Total amount:*** $28,487,090 (93% institutional, 7% external sources). ***Receiving aid:*** Freshmen: 17% (186). Undergraduates: 11% (505). ***Average award:*** Freshmen: $11,363. Undergraduates: $10,673. ***Scholarships, grants, and awards by category:*** *Academic interests/achievement:* 200 awards ($536,689 total): business, engineering/technologies, military science. *Creative arts/performance:* 77 awards ($156,756 total): debating, music. *Special achievements/activities:* 134 awards ($447,250 total): leadership, memberships. *Special characteristics:* 396 awards ($3,520,906 total): children and siblings of alumni, children of faculty/staff, international students, members of minority groups, siblings of current students. ***Tuition waivers:*** Full or partial for employees or children of employees.

LOANS ***Student loans:*** $26,898,110 (78% need-based, 22% non-need-based). 68% of past graduating class borrowed through all loan programs. *Average indebtedness per student:* $27,136. ***Average need-based loan:*** Freshmen: $4374. Undergraduates: $5225. ***Parent loans:*** $5,681,462 (70% need-based, 30% non-need-based). ***Programs:*** Federal Direct (Subsidized and Unsubsidized Stafford, PLUS), Perkins, Federal Nursing, state, college/university.

WORK-STUDY ***Federal work-study:*** Total amount: $1,228,261; 443 jobs averaging $2935. ***State or other work-study/employment:*** Total amount: $1,968,366 (100% need-based). 412 part-time jobs averaging $4308.

ATHLETIC AWARDS Total amount: $3,288,095 (17% need-based, 83% non-need-based).

APPLYING FOR FINANCIAL AID ***Required financial aid form:*** FAFSA. ***Financial aid deadline (priority):*** 2/1. ***Notification date:*** Continuous beginning 3/1. Students must reply by 5/1 or within 3 weeks of notification.

CONTACT James White, Director of Operations for Financial Aid, Gonzaga University, 502 East Boone Avenue, Spokane, WA 99258-0072, 509-313-6568 or toll-free 800-322-2584 Ext. 6572. *Fax:* 509-313-5816. *E-mail:* whitej@gonzaga.edu.

GORDON COLLEGE

Wenham, MA

Tuition & fees: $30,606 **Average undergraduate aid package: $18,370**

ABOUT THE INSTITUTION Independent nondenominational, coed. 33 undergraduate majors. Both federal and institutional methodology are used as a basis for awarding need-based institutional aid.

UNDERGRADUATE EXPENSES for 2011–12 ***Comprehensive fee:*** $39,040 includes full-time tuition ($29,310), mandatory fees ($1296), and room and board ($8434). ***College room only:*** $5628. Full-time tuition and fees vary according to course load. Room and board charges vary according to board plan and housing facility. ***Part-time tuition:*** $1035 per credit. Part-time tuition and fees vary according to course load. ***Payment plan:*** Installment.

FRESHMAN FINANCIAL AID (Fall 2010, est.) 298 applied for aid; of those 87% were deemed to have need. 100% of freshmen with need received aid; of those 14% had need fully met. ***Average percent of need met:*** 68% (excluding resources awarded to replace EFC). ***Average financial aid package:*** $18,990 (excluding resources awarded to replace EFC). 22% of all full-time freshmen had no need and received non-need-based gift aid.

UNDERGRADUATE FINANCIAL AID (Fall 2010, est.) 1,192 applied for aid; of those 87% were deemed to have need. 100% of undergraduates with need received aid; of those 14% had need fully met. ***Average percent of need met:*** 67% (excluding resources awarded to replace EFC). ***Average financial aid package:*** $18,370 (excluding resources awarded to replace EFC). 24% of all full-time undergraduates had no need and received non-need-based gift aid.

GIFT AID (NEED-BASED) ***Total amount:*** $14,317,793 (12% federal, 2% state, 73% institutional, 13% external sources). ***Receiving aid:*** Freshmen: 74% (260); all full-time undergraduates: 69% (1,034). ***Average award:*** Freshmen: $15,218; Undergraduates: $13,765. ***Scholarships, grants, and awards:*** Federal Pell, FSEOG, state, private, college/university gift aid from institutional funds.

GIFT AID (NON-NEED-BASED) ***Total amount:*** $4,712,596 (1% federal, 84% institutional, 15% external sources). ***Receiving aid:*** Freshmen: 7% (24). Undergraduates: 61% (912). ***Average award:*** Freshmen: $10,786. Undergraduates: $10,018. ***Scholarships, grants, and awards by category:*** *Academic interests/achievement:* 845 awards ($6,754,556 total): general academic interests/achievements. *Creative arts/performance:* 90 awards ($197,292 total): art/fine arts, music, theater/drama. *Special achievements/activities:* 269 awards ($1,631,590 total): leadership. *Special characteristics:* 213 awards ($152,809 total): children and siblings of alumni, relatives of clergy. ***Tuition waivers:*** Full or partial for employees or children of employees.

LOANS ***Student loans:*** $11,396,408 (70% need-based, 30% non-need-based). 82% of past graduating class borrowed through all loan programs. *Average indebtedness per student:* $37,154. ***Average need-based loan:*** Freshmen: $3407. Undergraduates: $4540. ***Parent loans:*** $2,822,220 (52% need-based, 48% non-need-based). ***Programs:*** Federal Direct (Subsidized and Unsubsidized Stafford, PLUS), Perkins, state.

WORK-STUDY ***Federal work-study:*** Total amount: $759,642; 760 jobs averaging $1468.

APPLYING FOR FINANCIAL AID ***Required financial aid form:*** FAFSA. ***Financial aid deadline (priority):*** 3/1. ***Notification date:*** Continuous beginning 3/1. Students must reply by 5/1 or within 2 weeks of notification.

CONTACT Daniel O'Connell, Director of Student Financial Services, Gordon College, 255 Grapevine Road, Wenham, MA 01984-1899, 978-867-4246 or toll-free 866-464-6736. *Fax:* 978-867-4657. *E-mail:* daniel.oconnell@gordon.edu.

GOSHEN COLLEGE

Goshen, IN

Tuition & fees: $24,500 **Average undergraduate aid package: $19,304**

ABOUT THE INSTITUTION Independent Mennonite, coed. 29 undergraduate majors. Federal methodology is used as a basis for awarding need-based institutional aid.

UNDERGRADUATE EXPENSES for 2010–11 ***Comprehensive fee:*** $32,800 includes full-time tuition ($24,500) and room and board ($8300). ***College room only:*** $4350. Full-time tuition and fees vary according to degree level. Room and board charges vary according to board plan and housing facility. ***Part-time tuition:*** $1020 per credit hour. Part-time tuition and fees vary according to course load and degree level.

FRESHMAN FINANCIAL AID (Fall 2010, est.) 159 applied for aid; of those 91% were deemed to have need. 100% of freshmen with need received aid; of those 19% had need fully met. ***Average percent of need met:*** 85% (excluding

resources awarded to replace EFC). ***Average financial aid package:*** $21,517 (excluding resources awarded to replace EFC). 26% of all full-time freshmen had no need and received non-need-based gift aid.

UNDERGRADUATE FINANCIAL AID (Fall 2010, est.) 744 applied for aid; of those 91% were deemed to have need. 100% of undergraduates with need received aid; of those 16% had need fully met. ***Average percent of need met:*** 81% (excluding resources awarded to replace EFC). ***Average financial aid package:*** $19,304 (excluding resources awarded to replace EFC). 22% of all full-time undergraduates had no need and received non-need-based gift aid.

GIFT AID (NEED-BASED) ***Total amount:*** $16,759,202 (9% federal, 50% state, 32% institutional, 9% external sources). ***Receiving aid:*** Freshmen: 73% (144); all full-time undergraduates: 73% (663). ***Average award:*** Freshmen: $18,190; Undergraduates: $15,731. ***Scholarships, grants, and awards:*** Federal Pell, FSEOG, state, private, college/university gift aid from institutional funds.

GIFT AID (NON-NEED-BASED) ***Total amount:*** $2,954,105 (73% institutional, 27% external sources). ***Receiving aid:*** Freshmen: 12% (24). Undergraduates: 7% (65). ***Average award:*** Freshmen: $11,676. Undergraduates: $9879. ***Scholarships, grants, and awards by category:*** *Academic interests/achievement:* 555 awards ($3,615,625 total): business, communication, education, general academic interests/achievements. *Creative arts/performance:* 52 awards ($102,000 total): music, theater/drama. *Special achievements/activities:* 1 award ($2625 total): junior miss. *Special characteristics:* 193 awards ($1,830,952 total): children of educators, children of faculty/staff, international students, members of minority groups. ***Tuition waivers:*** Full or partial for employees or children of employees.

LOANS ***Student loans:*** $4,521,685 (74% need-based, 26% non-need-based). 66% of past graduating class borrowed through all loan programs. *Average indebtedness per student:* $19,819. ***Average need-based loan:*** Freshmen: $3493. Undergraduates: $4423. ***Parent loans:*** $635,802 (28% need-based, 72% non-need-based). ***Programs:*** Federal Direct (Subsidized and Unsubsidized Stafford, PLUS), Perkins, Federal Nursing.

WORK-STUDY ***Federal work-study:*** Total amount: $169,000; 250 jobs averaging $800. ***State or other work-study/employment:*** Total amount: $40,000 (100% need-based). 50 part-time jobs averaging $1000.

ATHLETIC AWARDS Total amount: $935,470 (71% need-based, 29% non-need-based).

APPLYING FOR FINANCIAL AID ***Required financial aid forms:*** FAFSA, institution's own form. ***Financial aid deadline (priority):*** 3/15. ***Notification date:*** Continuous beginning 3/1. Students must reply by 5/1 or within 2 weeks of notification.

CONTACT Mrs. Judy S. Moore, Director of Enrollment, Goshen College, 1700 South Main Street, Goshen, IN 46526-4794, 574-535-7525 or toll-free 800-348-7422. *Fax:* 574-535-7654. *E-mail:* judysm@goshen.edu.

GOUCHER COLLEGE

Baltimore, MD

Tuition & fees: $36,553 **Average undergraduate aid package: $26,377**

ABOUT THE INSTITUTION Independent, coed. 32 undergraduate majors. Both federal and institutional methodology are used as a basis for awarding need-based institutional aid.

UNDERGRADUATE EXPENSES for 2011–12 ***Comprehensive fee:*** $47,122 includes full-time tuition ($36,011), mandatory fees ($542), and room and board ($10,569). ***College room only:*** $6404. Room and board charges vary according to board plan and housing facility. ***Payment plans:*** Tuition prepayment, installment.

FRESHMAN FINANCIAL AID (Fall 2010, est.) 385 applied for aid; of those 61% were deemed to have need. 100% of freshmen with need received aid; of those 15% had need fully met. ***Average percent of need met:*** 74% (excluding resources awarded to replace EFC). ***Average financial aid package:*** $25,618 (excluding resources awarded to replace EFC). 19% of all full-time freshmen had no need and received non-need-based gift aid.

UNDERGRADUATE FINANCIAL AID (Fall 2010, est.) 983 applied for aid; of those 88% were deemed to have need. 100% of undergraduates with need received aid; of those 17% had need fully met. ***Average percent of need met:*** 77% (excluding resources awarded to replace EFC). ***Average financial aid package:*** $26,377 (excluding resources awarded to replace EFC). 20% of all full-time undergraduates had no need and received non-need-based gift aid.

GIFT AID (NEED-BASED) ***Total amount:*** $19,149,901 (7% federal, 4% state, 85% institutional, 4% external sources). ***Receiving aid:*** Freshmen: 57% (224); all full-time undergraduates: 57% (834). ***Average award:*** Freshmen: $23,157; Undergraduates: $22,921. ***Scholarships, grants, and awards:*** Federal Pell, FSEOG, state, private, college/university gift aid from institutional funds.

GIFT AID (NON-NEED-BASED) ***Total amount:*** $4,548,392 (86% institutional, 14% external sources). ***Receiving aid:*** Freshmen: 5% (19). Undergraduates: 4% (62). ***Average award:*** Freshmen: $11,313. Undergraduates: $11,942. ***Scholarships, grants, and awards by category:*** *Creative arts/performance:* 19 awards ($112,500 total): art/fine arts, dance, music, performing arts, theater/drama. ***Tuition waivers:*** Full or partial for employees or children of employees, adult students, senior citizens.

LOANS ***Student loans:*** $7,212,445 (72% need-based, 28% non-need-based). 82% of past graduating class borrowed through all loan programs. *Average indebtedness per student:* $20,900. ***Average need-based loan:*** Freshmen: $3180. Undergraduates: $4128. ***Parent loans:*** $2,915,337 (55% need-based, 45% non-need-based). ***Programs:*** Federal Direct (Subsidized and Unsubsidized Stafford, PLUS), Perkins, college/university.

WORK-STUDY ***Federal work-study:*** Total amount: $449,993; 358 jobs averaging $1075. ***State or other work-study/employment:*** Part-time jobs available.

APPLYING FOR FINANCIAL AID ***Required financial aid forms:*** FAFSA, CSS Financial Aid PROFILE. ***Financial aid deadline (priority):*** 2/1. ***Notification date:*** 4/1. Students must reply by 5/1 or within 2 weeks of notification.

CONTACT Ellen Ostendorf, Director of Student Financial Aid, Goucher College, 1021 Dulaney Valley Road, Baltimore, MD 21204-2794, 410-337-6141 or toll-free 800-468-2437. *Fax:* 410-337-6504.

GOVERNORS STATE UNIVERSITY

University Park, IL

Tuition & fees (IL res): $8746 **Average undergraduate aid package: $4795**

ABOUT THE INSTITUTION State-supported, coed. 37 undergraduate majors. Federal methodology is used as a basis for awarding need-based institutional aid.

UNDERGRADUATE EXPENSES for 2010–11 ***Tuition, state resident:*** full-time $7110; part-time $237 per credit hour. ***Tuition, nonresident:*** full-time $14,220; part-time $474 per credit hour. ***Required fees:*** full-time $1636; $63 per credit hour or $126 per term. Full-time tuition and fees vary according to reciprocity agreements and student level. Part-time tuition and fees vary according to reciprocity agreements and student level. ***Payment plans:*** Guaranteed tuition, installment, deferred payment.

UNDERGRADUATE FINANCIAL AID (Fall 2010, est.) 859 applied for aid; of those 94% were deemed to have need. 100% of undergraduates with need received aid; of those 15% had need fully met. ***Average percent of need met:*** 65% (excluding resources awarded to replace EFC). ***Average financial aid package:*** $4795 (excluding resources awarded to replace EFC). 4% of all full-time undergraduates had no need and received non-need-based gift aid.

GIFT AID (NEED-BASED) ***Total amount:*** $4,170,026 (66% federal, 30% state, 2% institutional, 2% external sources). ***Receiving aid:*** All full-time undergraduates: 62% (705). ***Average award:*** Undergraduates: $3087. ***Scholarships, grants, and awards:*** Federal Pell, FSEOG, state, college/university gift aid from institutional funds.

GIFT AID (NON-NEED-BASED) ***Total amount:*** $3,294,652 (84% federal, 15% state, 1% external sources). ***Receiving aid:*** Undergraduates: 9% (102). ***Average award:*** Undergraduates: $2055. ***Scholarships, grants, and awards by category:*** *Academic interests/achievement:* biological sciences, business, communication, education, English, general academic interests/achievements, health fields, mathematics, physical sciences, social sciences. *Creative arts/performance:* general creative arts/performance. *Special achievements/activities:* general special achievements/activities. *Special characteristics:* children of educators, children of public servants, members of minority groups, veterans. ***Tuition waivers:*** Full or partial for employees or children of employees, senior citizens.

LOANS ***Student loans:*** $7,681,163 (62% need-based, 38% non-need-based). 53% of past graduating class borrowed through all loan programs. *Average indebtedness per student:* $2828. ***Average need-based loan:*** Undergraduates: $2227. ***Parent loans:*** $15,787 (85% need-based, 15% non-need-based). ***Programs:*** Federal Direct (Subsidized and Unsubsidized Stafford, PLUS), Perkins.

WORK-STUDY ***Federal work-study:*** Total amount: $112,570; jobs available. ***State or other work-study/employment:*** Total amount: $115,815 (100% non-need-based). Part-time jobs available.

APPLYING FOR FINANCIAL AID ***Required financial aid form:*** FAFSA. ***Financial aid deadline (priority):*** 5/1. ***Notification date:*** Continuous.

CONTACT Brenda Moore, Financial Aid Counselor, Governors State University, One University Parkway, University Park, IL 60466-0975, 708-534-4480. *E-mail:* bmoore@govst.edu.

GRACE BIBLE COLLEGE

Grand Rapids, MI

Tuition & fees: $14,850 **Average undergraduate aid package: $10,108**

ABOUT THE INSTITUTION Independent religious, coed. 18 undergraduate majors. Federal methodology is used as a basis for awarding need-based institutional aid.

UNDERGRADUATE EXPENSES for 2011–12 ***Comprehensive fee:*** $21,100 includes full-time tuition ($14,850) and room and board ($6250). ***College room only:*** $3150. Room and board charges vary according to board plan and housing facility. ***Part-time tuition:*** $495 per credit. Part-time tuition and fees vary according to course load. ***Payment plan:*** Installment.

FRESHMAN FINANCIAL AID (Fall 2009) 44 applied for aid; of those 91% were deemed to have need. 100% of freshmen with need received aid. ***Average percent of need met:*** 64% (excluding resources awarded to replace EFC). ***Average financial aid package:*** $12,513 (excluding resources awarded to replace EFC). 15% of all full-time freshmen had no need and received non-need-based gift aid.

UNDERGRADUATE FINANCIAL AID (Fall 2009) 165 applied for aid; of those 95% were deemed to have need. 100% of undergraduates with need received aid; of those 3% had need fully met. ***Average percent of need met:*** 58% (excluding resources awarded to replace EFC). ***Average financial aid package:*** $10,108 (excluding resources awarded to replace EFC). 11% of all full-time undergraduates had no need and received non-need-based gift aid.

GIFT AID (NEED-BASED) ***Total amount:*** $621,903 (70% federal, 30% state). ***Receiving aid:*** Freshmen: 83% (39); all full-time undergraduates: 82% (149). ***Average award:*** Freshmen: $5685; Undergraduates: $4442. ***Scholarships, grants, and awards:*** Federal Pell, FSEOG, state, private, college/university gift aid from institutional funds.

GIFT AID (NON-NEED-BASED) ***Total amount:*** $519,627 (1% federal, 90% institutional, 9% external sources). ***Receiving aid:*** Freshmen: 83% (39). Undergraduates: 71% (129). ***Average award:*** Freshmen: $2564. Undergraduates: $2255. ***Scholarships, grants, and awards by category:*** *Academic interests/achievement:* 136 awards ($272,000 total): general academic interests/achievements. *Creative arts/performance:* 15 awards ($13,250 total): music. *Special characteristics:* 45 awards ($160,266 total): children of faculty/staff, general special characteristics, relatives of clergy. ***Tuition waivers:*** Full or partial for employees or children of employees.

LOANS ***Student loans:*** $1,110,287 (48% need-based, 52% non-need-based). 66% of past graduating class borrowed through all loan programs. *Average indebtedness per student:* $7957. ***Average need-based loan:*** Freshmen: $3228. Undergraduates: $4093. ***Parent loans:*** $154,541 (100% non-need-based). ***Programs:*** Federal Direct (Subsidized and Unsubsidized Stafford, PLUS).

WORK-STUDY ***Federal work-study:*** Total amount: $24,581; 45 jobs averaging $497. ***State or other work-study/employment:*** Part-time jobs available.

APPLYING FOR FINANCIAL AID ***Required financial aid form:*** FAFSA. ***Financial aid deadline (priority):*** 2/28. ***Notification date:*** Continuous beginning 5/15. Students must reply within 2 weeks of notification.

CONTACT Mr. Kurt Postma, Director of Financial Aid, Grace Bible College, 1011 Aldon Street, SW, Grand Rapids, MI 49509-1921, 616-538-2330 or toll-free 800-968-1887. *Fax:* 616-538-0599. *E-mail:* kpostma@gbcol.edu.

GRACE COLLEGE

Winona Lake, IN

Tuition & fees: $21,700 **Average undergraduate aid package: $11,338**

ABOUT THE INSTITUTION Independent religious, coed. 46 undergraduate majors. Federal methodology is used as a basis for awarding need-based institutional aid.

UNDERGRADUATE EXPENSES for 2010–11 ***Comprehensive fee:*** $28,774 includes full-time tuition ($21,700) and room and board ($7074). ***College room only:*** $3700. Full-time tuition and fees vary according to course load, degree level, and program. Room and board charges vary according to board plan and housing facility. ***Part-time tuition:*** $480 per credit hour. Part-time tuition and fees vary according to course load, degree level, and program. ***Payment plan:*** Installment.

FRESHMAN FINANCIAL AID (Fall 2009) 225 applied for aid; of those 100% were deemed to have need. 100% of freshmen with need received aid. ***Average financial aid package:*** $13,722 (excluding resources awarded to replace EFC).

UNDERGRADUATE FINANCIAL AID (Fall 2009) 1,276 applied for aid; of those 100% were deemed to have need. 100% of undergraduates with need received aid. ***Average financial aid package:*** $11,338 (excluding resources awarded to replace EFC).

GIFT AID (NEED-BASED) ***Total amount:*** $9,515,745 (18% federal, 27% state, 53% institutional, 2% external sources). ***Receiving aid:*** Freshmen: 99% (224); all full-time undergraduates: 93% (1,214). ***Scholarships, grants, and awards:*** Federal Pell, FSEOG, state, private, college/university gift aid from institutional funds.

GIFT AID (NON-NEED-BASED) ***Total amount:*** $7,837,216 (55% institutional, 45% external sources). ***Scholarships, grants, and awards by category:*** *Academic interests/achievement:* biological sciences, business, education, English, premedicine. *Creative arts/performance:* applied art and design, art/fine arts, journalism/publications, theater/drama. *Special characteristics:* children of faculty/staff, members of minority groups, relatives of clergy, religious affiliation. ***Tuition waivers:*** Full or partial for employees or children of employees, senior citizens.

LOANS ***Student loans:*** $13,255,886 (27% need-based, 73% non-need-based). ***Parent loans:*** $171,891 (100% need-based). ***Programs:*** Federal Direct (Subsidized and Unsubsidized Stafford, PLUS), Perkins.

WORK-STUDY ***Federal work-study:*** Total amount: $460,000; jobs available.

ATHLETIC AWARDS Total amount: $681,452 (100% need-based).

APPLYING FOR FINANCIAL AID ***Required financial aid form:*** FAFSA. ***Financial aid deadline (priority):*** 3/10. ***Notification date:*** Continuous.

CONTACT Charlette Sauders, Director of Financial Aid, Grace College, 200 Seminary Drive, Winona Lake, IN 46590-1294, 574-372-5100 Ext. 6161 or toll-free 800-54-GRACE Ext. 6412 (in-state), 800-54 GRACE Ext. 6412 (out-of-state). *Fax:* 574-372-5144. *E-mail:* charlette.sauders@grace.edu.

GRACELAND UNIVERSITY

Lamoni, IA

Tuition & fees: $20,980 **Average undergraduate aid package: $18,364**

ABOUT THE INSTITUTION Independent Community of Christ, coed. 45 undergraduate majors. Federal methodology is used as a basis for awarding need-based institutional aid.

UNDERGRADUATE EXPENSES for 2011–12 ***Comprehensive fee:*** $28,020 includes full-time tuition ($20,680), mandatory fees ($300), and room and board ($7040). ***College room only:*** $2810. Full-time tuition and fees vary according to course load. Room and board charges vary according to board plan, housing facility, and location. ***Part-time tuition:*** $650 per semester hour. ***Payment plan:*** Installment.

FRESHMAN FINANCIAL AID (Fall 2010, est.) 198 applied for aid; of those 92% were deemed to have need. 95% of freshmen with need received aid; of those 18% had need fully met. ***Average percent of need met:*** 79% (excluding resources awarded to replace EFC). ***Average financial aid package:*** $20,812 (excluding resources awarded to replace EFC). 20% of all full-time freshmen had no need and received non-need-based gift aid.

UNDERGRADUATE FINANCIAL AID (Fall 2010, est.) 1,022 applied for aid; of those 92% were deemed to have need. 97% of undergraduates with need received aid; of those 15% had need fully met. ***Average percent of need met:*** 73% (excluding resources awarded to replace EFC). ***Average financial aid package:*** $18,364 (excluding resources awarded to replace EFC). 18% of all full-time undergraduates had no need and received non-need-based gift aid.

GIFT AID (NEED-BASED) ***Total amount:*** $9,755,011 (30% federal, 6% state, 61% institutional, 3% external sources). ***Receiving aid:*** Freshmen: 75% (174); all full-time undergraduates: 69% (857). ***Average award:*** Freshmen: $16,981; Undergraduates: $14,183. ***Scholarships, grants, and awards:*** Federal Pell, FSEOG, state, private, college/university gift aid from institutional funds.

GIFT AID (NON-NEED-BASED) ***Total amount:*** $2,379,143 (4% federal, 85% institutional, 11% external sources). ***Receiving aid:*** Freshmen: 29% (68). Undergraduates: 23% (285). ***Average award:*** Freshmen: $11,595. Undergraduates: $10,059. ***Scholarships, grants, and awards by category:*** *Academic* *interests/achievement:* 489 awards ($2,193,641 total): computer science, engineering/technologies, English, general academic interests/achievements, physical sciences. *Creative arts/performance:* 149 awards ($241,999 total): applied art and design, creative writing, dance, music, theater/drama. *Special achievements/activities:* 113 awards ($169,748 total): cheerleading/drum major, general special achievements/activities, leadership, religious involvement. *Special characteristics:* 1,430 awards ($5,038,709 total): children and siblings of alumni, children of faculty/staff, first-generation college students, general special characteristics, international students, local/state students, members of minority groups, religious affiliation. ***Tuition waivers:*** Full or partial for employees or children of employees, senior citizens.

LOANS ***Student loans:*** $8,899,584 (82% need-based, 18% non-need-based). 91% of past graduating class borrowed through all loan programs. *Average indebtedness per student:* $31,404. ***Average need-based loan:*** Freshmen: $4264. Undergraduates: $5164. ***Parent loans:*** $1,307,250 (47% need-based, 53% non-need-based). ***Programs:*** Federal Direct (Subsidized and Unsubsidized Stafford, PLUS), Perkins, state, college/university.

WORK-STUDY ***Federal work-study:*** Total amount: $384,245; 252 jobs averaging $1390. ***State or other work-study/employment:*** Total amount: $472,107 (12% need-based, 88% non-need-based). 273 part-time jobs averaging $1631.

ATHLETIC AWARDS Total amount: $2,804,765 (63% need-based, 37% non-need-based).

APPLYING FOR FINANCIAL AID ***Required financial aid form:*** FAFSA. ***Financial aid deadline:*** Continuous. ***Notification date:*** Continuous beginning 2/1. Students must reply within 2 weeks of notification.

CONTACT Mr. James D. Wesenberg, Director of Financial Aid, Graceland University, 1 University Place, Lamoni, IA 50140, 641-784-5136 or toll-free 866-GRACELAND. *Fax:* 641-784-5020. *E-mail:* financialaidservices@graceland.edu.

GRACE UNIVERSITY

Omaha, NE

Tuition & fees: $15,728 **Average undergraduate aid package: $12,607**

ABOUT THE INSTITUTION Independent interdenominational, coed. ***Awards:*** associate, bachelor's, and master's degrees. 34 undergraduate majors. ***Total enrollment:*** 434. Undergraduates: 366. Freshmen: 97. Federal methodology is used as a basis for awarding need-based institutional aid.

UNDERGRADUATE EXPENSES for 2010–11 ***Application fee:*** $20. ***Comprehensive fee:*** $21,274 includes full-time tuition ($15,268), mandatory fees ($460), and room and board ($5546). ***College room only:*** $2600. Room and board charges vary according to board plan and student level. Part-time tuition and fees vary according to course load. ***Payment plan:*** Installment.

FRESHMAN FINANCIAL AID (Fall 2009) 61 applied for aid; of those 84% were deemed to have need. 100% of freshmen with need received aid; of those 22% had need fully met. ***Average percent of need met:*** 74% (excluding resources awarded to replace EFC). ***Average financial aid package:*** $12,027 (excluding resources awarded to replace EFC). 24% of all full-time freshmen had no need and received non-need-based gift aid.

UNDERGRADUATE FINANCIAL AID (Fall 2009) 247 applied for aid; of those 85% were deemed to have need. 100% of undergraduates with need received aid; of those 16% had need fully met. ***Average percent of need met:*** 72% (excluding resources awarded to replace EFC). ***Average financial aid package:*** $12,607 (excluding resources awarded to replace EFC). 20% of all full-time undergraduates had no need and received non-need-based gift aid.

GIFT AID (NEED-BASED) ***Total amount:*** $2,098,585 (28% federal, 3% state, 60% institutional, 9% external sources). ***Receiving aid:*** Freshmen: 67% (51); all full-time undergraduates: 73% (208). ***Average award:*** Freshmen: $9186; Undergraduates: $8841. ***Scholarships, grants, and awards:*** Federal Pell, FSEOG, state, private, college/university gift aid from institutional funds, Academic Competitiveness Grants, TEACH Grants.

GIFT AID (NON-NEED-BASED) ***Total amount:*** $565,031 (3% federal, 1% state, 78% institutional, 18% external sources). ***Receiving aid:*** Freshmen: 14% (11). Undergraduates: 9% (27). ***Average award:*** Freshmen: $6783. Undergraduates: $5924. ***Scholarships, grants, and awards by category:*** *Academic interests/achievement:* 239 awards ($1,540,898 total): business, education, general academic interests/achievements, health fields, international studies, religion/biblical studies. *Creative arts/performance:* 13 awards ($18,000 total): cinema/film/broadcasting, music. *Special achievements/activities:* 56 awards ($62,511 total): general special achievements/activities, leadership, religious involvement. *Special characteristics:* 103 awards ($224,476 total): adult students, children and siblings of alumni, children of current students, children of faculty/staff, ethnic background, general special characteristics, handicapped students, international students, local/state students, married students, members of minority groups, out-of-state students, parents of current students, previous college experience, relatives of clergy, siblings of current students, spouses of current students, veterans, veterans' children. ***Tuition waivers:*** Full or partial for children of alumni, employees or children of employees, senior citizens. ***ROTC:*** Army cooperative, Air Force cooperative.

LOANS ***Student loans:*** $2,331,166 (80% need-based, 20% non-need-based). 92% of past graduating class borrowed through all loan programs. *Average indebtedness per student:* $21,586. ***Average need-based loan:*** Freshmen: $3274. Undergraduates: $4089. ***Parent loans:*** $1,139,637 (34% need-based, 66% non-need-based). ***Programs:*** Federal Direct (Subsidized and Unsubsidized Stafford, PLUS).

WORK-STUDY ***Federal work-study:*** Total amount: $37,000; 37 jobs averaging $1103. ***State or other work-study/employment:*** Total amount: $50,200 (36% need-based, 64% non-need-based). 45 part-time jobs averaging $1101.

APPLYING FOR FINANCIAL AID ***Required financial aid form:*** FAFSA. ***Financial aid deadline (priority):*** 4/1. ***Notification date:*** Continuous. Students must reply within 3 weeks of notification.

CONTACT Marcy Pierce, Director of Financial Aid, Grace University, 1311 South Ninth Street, Omaha, NE 68108-3629, 402-449-2810 or toll-free 800-383-1422. *Fax:* 402-449-2921. *E-mail:* gufinaid@graceu.edu.

GRAMBLING STATE UNIVERSITY

Grambling, LA

CONTACT Assistant Director of Student Financial Aid and Scholarships, Grambling State University, PO Box 629, Grambling, LA 71245, 318-274-6415. *Fax:* 318-274-3358.

GRAND CANYON UNIVERSITY

Phoenix, AZ

CONTACT Director of Financial Aid, Grand Canyon University, 3300 West Camelback Road, PO Box 11097, Phoenix, AZ 85017-3030, 800-800-9776 Ext. 2885 or toll-free 800-800-9776 (in-state). *Fax:* 602-589-2044.

GRAND VALLEY STATE UNIVERSITY

Allendale, MI

Tuition & fees (MI res): $9088 **Average undergraduate aid package: $8760**

ABOUT THE INSTITUTION State-supported, coed. 105 undergraduate majors. Federal methodology is used as a basis for awarding need-based institutional aid.

UNDERGRADUATE EXPENSES for 2010–11 ***Tuition, state resident:*** full-time $9088; part-time $395 per credit hour. ***Tuition, nonresident:*** full-time $13,402; part-time $571 per credit hour. Full-time tuition and fees vary according to degree level, program, and student level. Part-time tuition and fees vary according to course load, degree level, program, and student level. ***College room and board:*** $7624; ***Room only:*** $5344. Room and board charges vary according to board plan, housing facility, and location. ***Payment plans:*** Installment, deferred payment.

FRESHMAN FINANCIAL AID (Fall 2010, est.) 3,014 applied for aid; of those 76% were deemed to have need. 99% of freshmen with need received aid; of those 14% had need fully met. ***Average percent of need met:*** 70% (excluding resources awarded to replace EFC). ***Average financial aid package:*** $9716 (excluding resources awarded to replace EFC). 10% of all full-time freshmen had no need and received non-need-based gift aid.

UNDERGRADUATE FINANCIAL AID (Fall 2010, est.) 14,860 applied for aid; of those 81% were deemed to have need. 98% of undergraduates with need received aid; of those 13% had need fully met. ***Average percent of need met:*** 61% (excluding resources awarded to replace EFC). ***Average financial aid package:*** $8760 (excluding resources awarded to replace EFC). 7% of all full-time undergraduates had no need and received non-need-based gift aid.

GIFT AID (NEED-BASED) ***Total amount:*** $52,847,392 (65% federal, 32% institutional, 3% external sources). ***Receiving aid:*** Freshmen: 55% (1,887); all full-time undergraduates: 47% (8,589). ***Average award:*** Freshmen: $6986;

Undergraduates: $6042. ***Scholarships, grants, and awards:*** Federal Pell, FSEOG, state, private, college/university gift aid from institutional funds.

GIFT AID (NON-NEED-BASED) ***Total amount:*** $5,941,822 (6% federal, 83% institutional, 11% external sources). ***Receiving aid:*** Freshmen: 2% (69). Undergraduates: 1% (241). ***Average award:*** Freshmen: $3320. Undergraduates: $3608. ***Scholarships, grants, and awards by category:*** *Academic interests/achievement:* business, communication, computer science, education, engineering/technologies, English, foreign languages, general academic interests/achievements, health fields, humanities, international studies, mathematics, physical sciences, premedicine, social sciences. *Creative arts/performance:* applied art and design, art/fine arts, cinema/film/broadcasting, dance, journalism/publications, music, theater/drama. *Special characteristics:* adult students, children and siblings of alumni, children of faculty/staff, children of union members/company employees, children of workers in trades, general special characteristics, handicapped students, international students, local/state students, out-of-state students, public servants, spouses of deceased or disabled public servants, veterans, veterans' children. ***Tuition waivers:*** Full or partial for employees or children of employees.

LOANS ***Student loans:*** $117,188,455 (45% need-based, 55% non-need-based). 70% of past graduating class borrowed through all loan programs. *Average indebtedness per student:* $25,279. ***Average need-based loan:*** Freshmen: $3830. Undergraduates: $4572. ***Parent loans:*** $54,574,168 (100% non-need-based). ***Programs:*** Federal Direct (Subsidized and Unsubsidized Stafford, PLUS), Perkins, Federal Nursing.

WORK-STUDY ***Federal work-study:*** Total amount: $3,746,394; 1,259 jobs averaging $2689. ***State or other work-study/employment:*** Part-time jobs available.

ATHLETIC AWARDS Total amount: $2,438,941 (51% need-based, 49% non-need-based).

APPLYING FOR FINANCIAL AID ***Required financial aid form:*** FAFSA. ***Financial aid deadline (priority):*** 3/1. ***Notification date:*** 3/10. Students must reply by 5/1 or within 4 weeks of notification.

CONTACT Michelle Rhodes, Office of Financial Aid, Grand Valley State University, 100 Student Services Building, Allendale, MI 49401, 616-331-3234 or toll-free 800-748-0246. *Fax:* 616-331-3180. *E-mail:* rhodesmi@gvsu.edu.

GRAND VIEW UNIVERSITY

Des Moines, IA

Tuition & fees: $20,292 **Average undergraduate aid package: $15,224**

ABOUT THE INSTITUTION Independent religious, coed. 30 undergraduate majors. Federal methodology is used as a basis for awarding need-based institutional aid.

UNDERGRADUATE EXPENSES for 2010–11 ***Comprehensive fee:*** $27,024 includes full-time tuition ($19,872), mandatory fees ($420), and room and board ($6732). Full-time tuition and fees vary according to class time and course load. Room and board charges vary according to board plan and housing facility. ***Part-time tuition:*** $495 per credit hour. Part-time tuition and fees vary according to class time and course load. ***Payment plan:*** Installment.

FRESHMAN FINANCIAL AID (Fall 2010, est.) 289 applied for aid; of those 91% were deemed to have need. 100% of freshmen with need received aid; of those 24% had need fully met. ***Average percent of need met:*** 80% (excluding resources awarded to replace EFC). ***Average financial aid package:*** $18,380 (excluding resources awarded to replace EFC). 12% of all full-time freshmen had no need and received non-need-based gift aid.

UNDERGRADUATE FINANCIAL AID (Fall 2010, est.) 1,541 applied for aid; of those 91% were deemed to have need. 100% of undergraduates with need received aid; of those 19% had need fully met. ***Average percent of need met:*** 73% (excluding resources awarded to replace EFC). ***Average financial aid package:*** $15,224 (excluding resources awarded to replace EFC). 14% of all full-time undergraduates had no need and received non-need-based gift aid.

GIFT AID (NEED-BASED) ***Total amount:*** $14,756,425 (25% federal, 27% state, 46% institutional, 2% external sources). ***Receiving aid:*** Freshmen: 83% (246); all full-time undergraduates: 78% (1,314). ***Average award:*** Freshmen: $15,142; Undergraduates: $12,016. ***Scholarships, grants, and awards:*** Federal Pell, FSEOG, state, private, college/university gift aid from institutional funds.

GIFT AID (NON-NEED-BASED) ***Total amount:*** $1,486,280 (1% federal, 2% state, 87% institutional, 10% external sources). ***Receiving aid:*** Freshmen: 9% (27). Undergraduates: 6% (97). ***Average award:*** Freshmen: $6920. Undergraduates: $5379. ***Scholarships, grants, and awards by category:*** *Academic interests/achievement:* 1,631 awards ($6,776,638 total): general academic interests/achievements. *Creative arts/performance:* 84 awards ($88,200 total): art/fine arts, music, theater/drama. *Special achievements/activities:* 7 awards ($8750 total): junior miss, religious involvement. *Special characteristics:* 114 awards ($539,953 total): children and siblings of alumni, children of educators, children of faculty/staff. ***Tuition waivers:*** Full or partial for children of alumni, employees or children of employees, senior citizens.

LOANS ***Student loans:*** $16,993,509 (70% need-based, 30% non-need-based). 85% of past graduating class borrowed through all loan programs. *Average indebtedness per student:* $33,222. ***Average need-based loan:*** Freshmen: $3462. Undergraduates: $4299. ***Parent loans:*** $1,908,319 (14% need-based, 86% non-need-based). ***Programs:*** Federal Direct (Subsidized and Unsubsidized Stafford, PLUS), Perkins.

WORK-STUDY ***Federal work-study:*** Total amount: $567,736; 396 jobs averaging $1347. ***State or other work-study/employment:*** Part-time jobs available.

ATHLETIC AWARDS Total amount: $2,127,927 (66% need-based, 34% non-need-based).

APPLYING FOR FINANCIAL AID ***Required financial aid form:*** FAFSA. ***Financial aid deadline (priority):*** 3/1. ***Notification date:*** Continuous beginning 3/10. Students must reply by 5/1 or within 3 weeks of notification.

CONTACT Michele Dunne, Director of Financial Aid, Grand View University, 1200 Grandview Avenue, Des Moines, IA 50316-1599, 515-263-2820 or toll-free 800-444-6083 Ext. 2810. *Fax:* 515-263-6191. *E-mail:* mdunne@grandview.edu.

GRATZ COLLEGE

Melrose Park, PA

CONTACT Karen West, Student Financial Services Adviser, Gratz College, 7605 Old York Road, Melrose Park, PA 19027, 215-635-7300 Ext. 163 or toll-free 800-475-4635 (out-of-state). *Fax:* 215-635-7320.

GREAT LAKES CHRISTIAN COLLEGE

Lansing, MI

CONTACT Financial Aid Officer, Great Lakes Christian College, 6211 West Willow Highway, Lansing, MI 48917-1299, 517-321-0242 or toll-free 800-YES-GLCC.

GREEN MOUNTAIN COLLEGE

Poultney, VT

Tuition & fees: $27,945 **Average undergraduate aid package: $19,432**

ABOUT THE INSTITUTION Independent, coed. 20 undergraduate majors. Federal methodology is used as a basis for awarding need-based institutional aid.

UNDERGRADUATE EXPENSES for 2010–11 ***One-time required fee:*** $250. ***Comprehensive fee:*** $38,087 includes full-time tuition ($26,920), mandatory fees ($1025), and room and board ($10,142). ***College room only:*** $6022. Full-time tuition and fees vary according to course load, location, and program. Room and board charges vary according to housing facility. ***Part-time tuition:*** $898 per credit hour. Part-time tuition and fees vary according to course load, location, and program. ***Payment plan:*** Installment.

FRESHMAN FINANCIAL AID (Fall 2010, est.) 161 applied for aid; of those 91% were deemed to have need. 100% of freshmen with need received aid; of those 14% had need fully met. ***Average percent of need met:*** 66% (excluding resources awarded to replace EFC). ***Average financial aid package:*** $19,884 (excluding resources awarded to replace EFC). 17% of all full-time freshmen had no need and received non-need-based gift aid.

UNDERGRADUATE FINANCIAL AID (Fall 2010, est.) 607 applied for aid; of those 91% were deemed to have need. 99% of undergraduates with need received aid; of those 12% had need fully met. ***Average percent of need met:*** 65% (excluding resources awarded to replace EFC). ***Average financial aid package:*** $19,432 (excluding resources awarded to replace EFC). 15% of all full-time undergraduates had no need and received non-need-based gift aid.

GIFT AID (NEED-BASED) ***Total amount:*** $8,103,419 (21% federal, 3% state, 74% institutional, 2% external sources). ***Receiving aid:*** Freshmen: 84% (146); all full-time undergraduates: 71% (542). ***Average award:*** Freshmen: $16,518; Undergraduates: $15,462. ***Scholarships, grants, and awards:*** Federal Pell, FSEOG, state, private, college/university gift aid from institutional funds.

GIFT AID (NON-NEED-BASED) ***Total amount:*** $1,680,742 (96% institutional, 4% external sources). ***Receiving aid:*** Freshmen: 10% (18). Undergraduates:

6% (44). ***Average award:*** Freshmen: $11,256. Undergraduates: $12,669. ***Scholarships, grants, and awards by category:*** *Academic interests/achievement:* 117 awards ($379,625 total): biological sciences, physical sciences. *Creative arts/performance:* 55 awards ($110,500 total): art/fine arts, creative writing, music, performing arts, theater/drama. *Special achievements/activities:* 338 awards ($1,483,625 total): community service, leadership, religious involvement. *Special characteristics:* 22 awards ($116,190 total): children and siblings of alumni, children of current students, international students, parents of current students, relatives of clergy, religious affiliation, siblings of current students. ***Tuition waivers:*** Full or partial for employees or children of employees.

LOANS ***Student loans:*** $5,378,387 (76% need-based, 24% non-need-based). 79% of past graduating class borrowed through all loan programs. *Average indebtedness per student:* $39,983. ***Average need-based loan:*** Freshmen: $3413. Undergraduates: $4162. ***Parent loans:*** $1,534,942 (46% need-based, 54% non-need-based). ***Programs:*** Federal Direct (Subsidized and Unsubsidized Stafford, PLUS), private loans.

WORK-STUDY ***Federal work-study:*** Total amount: $235,927; 213 jobs averaging $1700. ***State or other work-study/employment:*** Total amount: $129,514 (51% need-based, 49% non-need-based). 104 part-time jobs averaging $1700.

APPLYING FOR FINANCIAL AID ***Required financial aid form:*** FAFSA. ***Financial aid deadline (priority):*** 3/1. ***Notification date:*** Continuous. Students must reply by 5/1 or within 4 weeks of notification.

CONTACT Wendy J. Ellis, Director of Student Financial Services, Green Mountain College, One Brennan Circle, Poultney, VT 05764-1199, 800-776-6675 Ext. 8209 or toll-free 800-776-6675 (out-of-state). *Fax:* 802-287-8096. *E-mail:* ellisw@greenmtn.edu.

GREENSBORO COLLEGE

Greensboro, NC

CONTACT Dawn VanArsdale Young, Director of Financial Aid, Greensboro College, 815 West Market Street, Greensboro, NC 27401-1875, 336-272-7102 Ext. 408 or toll-free 800-346-8226. *Fax:* 336-271-6634. *E-mail:* dvanarsdale@reensgborocollege.edu.

GREENVILLE COLLEGE

Greenville, IL

Tuition & fees: $21,658 **Average undergraduate aid package: $17,718**

ABOUT THE INSTITUTION Independent Free Methodist, coed. 54 undergraduate majors. Federal methodology is used as a basis for awarding need-based institutional aid.

UNDERGRADUATE EXPENSES for 2011–12 ***Comprehensive fee:*** $28,996 includes full-time tuition ($21,494), mandatory fees ($164), and room and board ($7338). ***College room only:*** $3550. Room and board charges vary according to housing facility. ***Part-time tuition:*** $452 per credit hour. Part-time tuition and fees vary according to course load.

FRESHMAN FINANCIAL AID (Fall 2010, est.) 281 applied for aid; of those 93% were deemed to have need. 100% of freshmen with need received aid; of those 7% had need fully met. ***Average percent of need met:*** 72% (excluding resources awarded to replace EFC). ***Average financial aid package:*** $18,058 (excluding resources awarded to replace EFC). 15% of all full-time freshmen had no need and received non-need-based gift aid.

UNDERGRADUATE FINANCIAL AID (Fall 2010, est.) 1,014 applied for aid; of those 93% were deemed to have need. 100% of undergraduates with need received aid; of those 9% had need fully met. ***Average percent of need met:*** 71% (excluding resources awarded to replace EFC). ***Average financial aid package:*** $17,718 (excluding resources awarded to replace EFC). 14% of all full-time undergraduates had no need and received non-need-based gift aid.

GIFT AID (NEED-BASED) ***Total amount:*** $12,707,193 (18% federal, 14% state, 64% institutional, 4% external sources). ***Receiving aid:*** Freshmen: 83% (260); all full-time undergraduates: 85% (931). ***Average award:*** Freshmen: $14,697; Undergraduates: $13,564. ***Scholarships, grants, and awards:*** Federal Pell, FSEOG, state, private, college/university gift aid from institutional funds.

GIFT AID (NON-NEED-BASED) ***Total amount:*** $1,289,778 (90% institutional, 10% external sources). ***Receiving aid:*** Freshmen: 4% (11). Undergraduates: 5% (51). ***Average award:*** Freshmen: $5981. Undergraduates: $6747. ***Scholarships, grants, and awards by category:*** *Academic interests/achievement:* biological sciences, business, education, engineering/technologies, general academic interests/achievements, mathematics, physical sciences, religion/biblical studies. *Creative arts/performance:* applied art and design, art/fine arts, music, performing arts. *Special achievements/activities:* leadership, memberships, religious involvement. *Special characteristics:* children and siblings of alumni, children of faculty/staff, international students, local/state students, out-of-state students, relatives of clergy, religious affiliation, siblings of current students. ***Tuition waivers:*** Full or partial for employees or children of employees, senior citizens.

LOANS ***Student loans:*** $7,235,970 (83% need-based, 17% non-need-based). 95% of past graduating class borrowed through all loan programs. *Average indebtedness per student:* $24,002. ***Average need-based loan:*** Freshmen: $3272. Undergraduates: $4138. ***Parent loans:*** $1,754,782 (38% need-based, 62% non-need-based). ***Programs:*** Federal Direct (Subsidized and Unsubsidized Stafford, PLUS), Perkins, college/university.

WORK-STUDY ***Federal work-study:*** Total amount: $141,945; jobs available. ***State or other work-study/employment:*** Total amount: $3000 (100% non-need-based). Part-time jobs available.

APPLYING FOR FINANCIAL AID ***Required financial aid form:*** FAFSA. ***Financial aid deadline (priority):*** 4/1. ***Notification date:*** Continuous beginning 3/1. Students must reply within 3 weeks of notification.

CONTACT Marilae Latham, Director of Financial Aid, Greenville College, 315 East College Avenue, Greenville, IL 62246-0159, 618-664-7110 or toll-free 800-345-4440. *Fax:* 618-664-7198. *E-mail:* marilae.latham@greenville.edu.

GRINNELL COLLEGE

Grinnell, IA

Tuition & fees: $39,810 **Average undergraduate aid package: $35,139**

ABOUT THE INSTITUTION Independent, coed. 27 undergraduate majors. Both federal and institutional methodology are used as a basis for awarding need-based institutional aid.

UNDERGRADUATE EXPENSES for 2011–12 ***Comprehensive fee:*** $49,144 includes full-time tuition ($39,250), mandatory fees ($560), and room and board ($9334). ***College room only:*** $4372. Room and board charges vary according to board plan and housing facility. ***Part-time tuition:*** $1227 per credit. ***Payment plan:*** Installment.

FRESHMAN FINANCIAL AID (Fall 2010, est.) 350 applied for aid; of those 87% were deemed to have need. 100% of freshmen with need received aid; of those 100% had need fully met. ***Average percent of need met:*** 100% (excluding resources awarded to replace EFC). ***Average financial aid package:*** $36,233 (excluding resources awarded to replace EFC). 14% of all full-time freshmen had no need and received non-need-based gift aid.

UNDERGRADUATE FINANCIAL AID (Fall 2010, est.) 1,185 applied for aid; of those 91% were deemed to have need. 100% of undergraduates with need received aid; of those 100% had need fully met. ***Average percent of need met:*** 100% (excluding resources awarded to replace EFC). ***Average financial aid package:*** $35,139 (excluding resources awarded to replace EFC). 19% of all full-time undergraduates had no need and received non-need-based gift aid.

GIFT AID (NEED-BASED) ***Total amount:*** $32,250,856 (5% federal, 1% state, 92% institutional, 2% external sources). ***Receiving aid:*** Freshmen: 72% (300); all full-time undergraduates: 67% (1,072). ***Average award:*** Freshmen: $30,577; Undergraduates: $30,085. ***Scholarships, grants, and awards:*** Federal Pell, FSEOG, state, private, college/university gift aid from institutional funds.

GIFT AID (NON-NEED-BASED) ***Total amount:*** $4,317,983 (85% institutional, 15% external sources). ***Receiving aid:*** Freshmen: 8% (35). Undergraduates: 5% (74). ***Average award:*** Freshmen: $10,145. Undergraduates: $10,957. ***Scholarships, grants, and awards by category:*** *Academic interests/achievement:* general academic interests/achievements. ***Tuition waivers:*** Full or partial for employees or children of employees.

LOANS ***Student loans:*** $3,057,997 (81% need-based, 19% non-need-based). 53% of past graduating class borrowed through all loan programs. *Average indebtedness per student:* $18,578. ***Average need-based loan:*** Freshmen: $3037. Undergraduates: $3246. ***Programs:*** Federal Direct (Subsidized and Unsubsidized Stafford, PLUS), Perkins, college/university.

WORK-STUDY ***Federal work-study:*** Total amount: $1,218,661; 619 jobs averaging $1969. ***State or other work-study/employment:*** Total amount: $778,832 (43% need-based, 57% non-need-based). 372 part-time jobs averaging $2094.

APPLYING FOR FINANCIAL AID ***Required financial aid forms:*** FAFSA, institution's own form, noncustodial (divorced/separated) parent's statement. ***Financial aid deadline:*** 2/1. ***Notification date:*** 4/1. Students must reply by 5/1.

CONTACT Mr. Arnold Woods, Director of Student Financial Aid, Grinnell College, 1103 Park Street, Grinnell, IA 50112-1690, 641-269-3250 or toll-free 800-247-0113. *Fax:* 641-269-4937. *E-mail:* woods@grinnell.edu.

GROVE CITY COLLEGE

Grove City, PA

Tuition & fees: $13,088 **Average undergraduate aid package: $5820**

ABOUT THE INSTITUTION Independent Presbyterian, coed. 44 undergraduate majors. Institutional methodology is used as a basis for awarding need-based institutional aid.

UNDERGRADUATE EXPENSES for 2010–11 ***Comprehensive fee:*** $20,220 includes full-time tuition ($13,088) and room and board ($7132). Full-time tuition and fees vary according to course load. Room and board charges vary according to housing facility. ***Part-time tuition:*** $410 per credit hour. ***Payment plan:*** Installment.

FRESHMAN FINANCIAL AID (Fall 2010, est.) 375 applied for aid; of those 69% were deemed to have need. 100% of freshmen with need received aid; of those 11% had need fully met. ***Average percent of need met:*** 52% (excluding resources awarded to replace EFC). ***Average financial aid package:*** $6149 (excluding resources awarded to replace EFC). 6% of all full-time freshmen had no need and received non-need-based gift aid.

UNDERGRADUATE FINANCIAL AID (Fall 2010, est.) 1,235 applied for aid; of those 81% were deemed to have need. 98% of undergraduates with need received aid; of those 8% had need fully met. ***Average percent of need met:*** 49% (excluding resources awarded to replace EFC). ***Average financial aid package:*** $5820 (excluding resources awarded to replace EFC). 11% of all full-time undergraduates had no need and received non-need-based gift aid.

GIFT AID (NEED-BASED) ***Total amount:*** $5,744,720 (13% state, 78% institutional, 9% external sources). ***Receiving aid:*** Freshmen: 40% (257); all full-time undergraduates: 38% (947). ***Average award:*** Freshmen: $6149; Undergraduates: $5820. ***Scholarships, grants, and awards:*** state, private, college/university gift aid from institutional funds.

GIFT AID (NON-NEED-BASED) ***Total amount:*** $1,368,744 (49% institutional, 51% external sources). ***Receiving aid:*** Freshmen: 4% (29). Undergraduates: 3% (77). ***Average award:*** Freshmen: $2671. Undergraduates: $2298. ***Scholarships, grants, and awards by category:*** *Academic interests/achievement:* 444 awards ($836,756 total): biological sciences, business, communication, education, engineering/technologies; English, foreign languages, general academic interests/achievements, physical sciences, religion/biblical studies, social sciences. *Creative arts/performance:* 8 awards ($9500 total): creative writing, music. *Special achievements/activities:* 19 awards ($54,150 total): general special achievements/activities, leadership, memberships, religious involvement. *Special characteristics:* 16 awards ($56,400 total): ethnic background, general special characteristics, members of minority groups. ***Tuition waivers:*** Full or partial for employees or children of employees.

LOANS ***Student loans:*** $10,092,655 (37% need-based, 63% non-need-based). 58% of past graduating class borrowed through all loan programs. *Average indebtedness per student:* $25,773. ***Programs:*** alternative loans.

APPLYING FOR FINANCIAL AID ***Required financial aid forms:*** institution's own form, state aid form. ***Financial aid deadline:*** 4/15. ***Notification date:*** Continuous beginning 3/18. Students must reply by 5/1.

CONTACT Thomas G. Ball, Director of Financial Aid, Grove City College, 100 Campus Drive, Grove City, PA 16127-2104, 724-458-3300. *Fax:* 724-450-4040. *E-mail:* financialaid@gcc.edu.

GUILFORD COLLEGE

Greensboro, NC

ABOUT THE INSTITUTION Independent religious, coed. 37 undergraduate majors.

GIFT AID (NEED-BASED) ***Scholarships, grants, and awards:*** Federal Pell, FSEOG, state, private, college/university gift aid from institutional funds.

GIFT AID (NON-NEED-BASED) ***Scholarships, grants, and awards by category:*** *Academic interests/achievement:* biological sciences, general academic interests/achievements. *Creative arts/performance:* music, theater/drama. *Special achievements/activities:* religious involvement. *Special characteristics:* children of faculty/staff, first-generation college students, local/state students.

LOANS ***Programs:*** Perkins, college/university.

WORK-STUDY ***Federal work-study:*** Total amount: $426,250; 213 jobs averaging $1993. ***State or other work-study/employment:*** Total amount: $241,308 (80% need-based, 20% non-need-based). 121 part-time jobs averaging $1588.

APPLYING FOR FINANCIAL AID ***Required financial aid forms:*** FAFSA, noncustodial (divorced/separated) parent's statement, business/farm supplement.

CONTACT Mr. Paul J. Coscia, Director of Student Financial Services, Guilford College, 5800 West Friendly Avenue, Greensboro, NC 27410, 336-316-2395 or toll-free 800-992-7759. *Fax:* 336-316-2942. *E-mail:* pcoscia@guilford.edu.

GUSTAVUS ADOLPHUS COLLEGE

St. Peter, MN

Tuition & fees: $33,400 **Average undergraduate aid package: $26,967**

ABOUT THE INSTITUTION Independent religious, coed. 67 undergraduate majors. Both federal and institutional methodology are used as a basis for awarding need-based institutional aid.

UNDERGRADUATE EXPENSES for 2010–11 ***One-time required fee:*** $400. ***Comprehensive fee:*** $41,800 includes full-time tuition ($33,100), mandatory fees ($300), and room and board ($8400). ***College room only:*** $5400.

FRESHMAN FINANCIAL AID (Fall 2010, est.) 563 applied for aid; of those 82% were deemed to have need. 100% of freshmen with need received aid; of those 47% had need fully met. ***Average percent of need met:*** 94% (excluding resources awarded to replace EFC). ***Average financial aid package:*** $30,375 (excluding resources awarded to replace EFC). 29% of all full-time freshmen had no need and received non-need-based gift aid.

UNDERGRADUATE FINANCIAL AID (Fall 2010, est.) 1,947 applied for aid; of those 92% were deemed to have need. 99% of undergraduates with need received aid; of those 55% had need fully met. ***Average percent of need met:*** 93% (excluding resources awarded to replace EFC). ***Average financial aid package:*** $26,967 (excluding resources awarded to replace EFC). 28% of all full-time undergraduates had no need and received non-need-based gift aid.

GIFT AID (NEED-BASED) ***Total amount:*** $11,383,702 (9% federal, 6% state, 82% institutional, 3% external sources). ***Receiving aid:*** Freshmen: 62% (415); all full-time undergraduates: 72% (1,770). ***Average award:*** Freshmen: $25,862; Undergraduates: $21,786. ***Scholarships, grants, and awards:*** Federal Pell, FSEOG, state, private, college/university gift aid from institutional funds.

GIFT AID (NON-NEED-BASED) ***Total amount:*** $2,945,834 (92% institutional, 8% external sources). ***Receiving aid:*** Freshmen: 32% (214). Undergraduates: 27% (665). ***Average award:*** Freshmen: $13,743. Undergraduates: $10,229. ***Scholarships, grants, and awards by category:*** *Academic interests/achievement:* general academic interests/achievements. *Creative arts/performance:* art/fine arts, dance, debating, music, theater/drama. *Special achievements/activities:* junior miss. *Special characteristics:* children and siblings of alumni, ethnic background, first-generation college students, international students, members of minority groups, out-of-state students, siblings of current students.

LOANS ***Student loans:*** $3,714,137 (44% need-based, 56% non-need-based). 71% of past graduating class borrowed through all loan programs. *Average indebtedness per student:* $25,694. ***Average need-based loan:*** Freshmen: $3981. Undergraduates: $3758. ***Parent loans:*** $741,558 (100% non-need-based). ***Programs:*** Federal Direct (Subsidized and Unsubsidized Stafford, PLUS), Perkins, state.

WORK-STUDY ***Federal work-study:*** Total amount: $572,841; jobs available. ***State or other work-study/employment:*** Total amount: $253,204 (56% need-based, 44% non-need-based). Part-time jobs available.

APPLYING FOR FINANCIAL AID ***Required financial aid form:*** FAFSA. ***Financial aid deadline:*** 4/15 (priority: 2/15). ***Notification date:*** Continuous beginning 1/20. Students must reply by 5/1 or within 2 weeks of notification.

CONTACT Doug Minter, Director of Financial Aid, Gustavus Adolphus College, 800 West College Avenue, St. Peter, MN 56082-1498, 507-933-7527 or toll-free 800-GUSTAVU(S). *Fax:* 507-933-7727. *E-mail:* finaid@gustavus.edu.

GUTENBERG COLLEGE

Eugene, OR

CONTACT Financial Aid Office, Gutenberg College, 1883 University Street, Eugene, OR 97403, 541-683-5141.

GWYNEDD-MERCY COLLEGE

Gwynedd Valley, PA

Tuition & fees: $25,660 **Average undergraduate aid package: $17,616**

ABOUT THE INSTITUTION Independent Roman Catholic, coed. 32 undergraduate majors. Federal methodology is used as a basis for awarding need-based institutional aid.

UNDERGRADUATE EXPENSES for 2010–11 ***Comprehensive fee:*** $35,420 includes full-time tuition ($25,160), mandatory fees ($500), and room and board ($9760). Full-time tuition and fees vary according to program. Room and board charges vary according to board plan and housing facility. ***Part-time tuition:*** $515 per credit hour. ***Part-time fees:*** $10 per credit. Part-time tuition and fees vary according to program. ***Payment plan:*** Installment.

FRESHMAN FINANCIAL AID (Fall 2010, est.) 243 applied for aid; of those 88% were deemed to have need. 100% of freshmen with need received aid; of those 11% had need fully met. ***Average percent of need met:*** 72% (excluding resources awarded to replace EFC). ***Average financial aid package:*** $17,864 (excluding resources awarded to replace EFC). 17% of all full-time freshmen had no need and received non-need-based gift aid.

UNDERGRADUATE FINANCIAL AID (Fall 2010, est.) 1,308 applied for aid; of those 89% were deemed to have need. 100% of undergraduates with need received aid; of those 11% had need fully met. ***Average percent of need met:*** 71% (excluding resources awarded to replace EFC). ***Average financial aid package:*** $17,616 (excluding resources awarded to replace EFC). 13% of all full-time undergraduates had no need and received non-need-based gift aid.

GIFT AID (NEED-BASED) ***Total amount:*** $16,481,320 (12% federal, 10% state, 74% institutional, 4% external sources). ***Receiving aid:*** Freshmen: 63% (181); all full-time undergraduates: 86% (1,154). ***Average award:*** Freshmen: $14,688; Undergraduates: $14,042. ***Scholarships, grants, and awards:*** Federal Pell, FSEOG, state, private, college/university gift aid from institutional funds.

GIFT AID (NON-NEED-BASED) ***Total amount:*** $2,229,881 (92% institutional, 8% external sources). ***Receiving aid:*** Freshmen: 50% (143). Undergraduates: 49% (661). ***Average award:*** Freshmen: $8049. Undergraduates: $8925. ***Scholarships, grants, and awards by category:*** *Academic interests/achievement:* 663 awards ($5,249,120 total): general academic interests/achievements. *Special achievements/activities:* 331 awards ($1,616,500 total): general special achievements/activities. *Special characteristics:* 77 awards ($145,000 total): children and siblings of alumni, siblings of current students. ***Tuition waivers:*** Full or partial for employees or children of employees.

LOANS ***Student loans:*** $12,731,477 (63% need-based, 37% non-need-based). 94% of past graduating class borrowed through all loan programs. *Average indebtedness per student:* $34,520. ***Average need-based loan:*** Freshmen: $3246. Undergraduates: $4050. ***Parent loans:*** $2,052,364 (35% need-based, 65% non-need-based). ***Programs:*** Federal Direct (Subsidized and Unsubsidized Stafford, PLUS), Perkins, Federal Nursing, alternative loans.

WORK-STUDY ***Federal work-study:*** Total amount: $180,566; 194 jobs averaging $928. ***State or other work-study/employment:*** Part-time jobs available.

APPLYING FOR FINANCIAL AID ***Required financial aid forms:*** FAFSA, institution's own form, verification form and copies of student's and parents' 1040 tax returns if requested. ***Financial aid deadline (priority):*** 3/15. ***Notification date:*** Continuous beginning 3/1. Students must reply by 5/1 or within 2 weeks of notification.

CONTACT Sr. Barbara A. Kaufmann, Director of Student Financial Aid, Gwynedd-Mercy College, PO Box 901, Gwynedd Valley, PA 19437-0901, 215-641-5570 or toll-free 800-DIAL-GMC (in-state). *Fax:* 215-641-5556.

HAMILTON COLLEGE

Clinton, NY

Tuition & fees: $41,280 **Average undergraduate aid package: $37,737**

ABOUT THE INSTITUTION Independent, coed. 44 undergraduate majors. Both federal and institutional methodology are used as a basis for awarding need-based institutional aid.

UNDERGRADUATE EXPENSES for 2010–11 ***Comprehensive fee:*** $51,760 includes full-time tuition ($40,870), mandatory fees ($410), and room and board ($10,480). ***College room only:*** $5730. Room and board charges vary according to board plan. ***Part-time tuition:*** $5109 per course. ***Payment plan:*** Installment.

FRESHMAN FINANCIAL AID (Fall 2010, est.) 284 applied for aid; of those 83% were deemed to have need. 100% of freshmen with need received aid; of those 100% had need fully met. ***Average percent of need met:*** 100% (excluding resources awarded to replace EFC). ***Average financial aid package:*** $38,222 (excluding resources awarded to replace EFC). 1% of all full-time freshmen had no need and received non-need-based gift aid.

UNDERGRADUATE FINANCIAL AID (Fall 2010, est.) 897 applied for aid; of those 87% were deemed to have need. 100% of undergraduates with need received aid; of those 100% had need fully met. ***Average percent of need met:*** 100% (excluding resources awarded to replace EFC). ***Average financial aid package:*** $37,737 (excluding resources awarded to replace EFC). 2% of all full-time undergraduates had no need and received non-need-based gift aid.

GIFT AID (NEED-BASED) ***Total amount:*** $25,649,043 (5% federal, 3% state, 90% institutional, 2% external sources). ***Receiving aid:*** Freshmen: 51% (236); all full-time undergraduates: 42% (778). ***Average award:*** Freshmen: $34,682; Undergraduates: $33,381. ***Scholarships, grants, and awards:*** Federal Pell, FSEOG, state, private, college/university gift aid from institutional funds.

GIFT AID (NON-NEED-BASED) ***Total amount:*** $1,438,570 (5% state, 70% institutional, 25% external sources). ***Average award:*** Freshmen: $40,870. Undergraduates: $31,497. ***Tuition waivers:*** Full or partial for employees or children of employees.

LOANS ***Student loans:*** $2,456,646 (100% need-based). 41% of past graduating class borrowed through all loan programs. *Average indebtedness per student:* $16,982. ***Average need-based loan:*** Freshmen: $2781. Undergraduates: $3880. ***Programs:*** Federal Direct (Subsidized and Unsubsidized Stafford, PLUS), Perkins, college/university.

WORK-STUDY ***Federal work-study:*** Total amount: $815,365; 509 jobs averaging $1602. ***State or other work-study/employment:*** Total amount: $116,665 (100% need-based). 62 part-time jobs averaging $1882.

APPLYING FOR FINANCIAL AID ***Required financial aid forms:*** FAFSA, institution's own form, CSS Financial Aid PROFILE, state aid form, noncustodial (divorced/separated) parent's statement, business/farm supplement. ***Financial aid deadline:*** 2/8 (priority: 2/8). ***Notification date:*** 4/1. Students must reply by 5/1.

CONTACT Office of Financial Aid, Hamilton College, 198 College Hill Road, Clinton, NY 13323, 315-859-4434 or toll-free 800-843-2655. *Fax:* 315-859-4962. *E-mail:* finaid@hamilton.edu.

HAMILTON TECHNICAL COLLEGE

Davenport, IA

CONTACT Ms. Lisa Boyd, Executive Vice President/Director of Financial Aid, Hamilton Technical College, 1011 East 53rd Street, Davenport, IA 52807-2653, 563-386-3570 Ext. 33. *Fax:* 563-386-6756.

HAMLINE UNIVERSITY

St. Paul, MN

Tuition & fees: $31,802 **Average undergraduate aid package: $23,853**

ABOUT THE INSTITUTION Independent religious, coed. 52 undergraduate majors. Federal methodology is used as a basis for awarding need-based institutional aid.

UNDERGRADUATE EXPENSES for 2011–12 ***Comprehensive fee:*** $40,306 includes full-time tuition ($31,652), mandatory fees ($150), and room and board ($8504). ***College room only:*** $4230. Full-time tuition and fees vary according to program. Room and board charges vary according to board plan and housing facility. ***Part-time tuition:*** $990 per credit hour. Part-time tuition and fees vary according to course load and program. ***Payment plan:*** Installment.

FRESHMAN FINANCIAL AID (Fall 2010, est.) 408 applied for aid; of those 90% were deemed to have need. 100% of freshmen with need received aid; of those 14% had need fully met. ***Average percent of need met:*** 84% (excluding resources awarded to replace EFC). ***Average financial aid package:*** $26,663 (excluding resources awarded to replace EFC). 12% of all full-time freshmen had no need and received non-need-based gift aid.

UNDERGRADUATE FINANCIAL AID (Fall 2010, est.) 1,606 applied for aid; of those 92% were deemed to have need. 100% of undergraduates with need received aid; of those 16% had need fully met. ***Average percent of need met:*** 78% (excluding resources awarded to replace EFC). ***Average financial aid package:*** $23,853 (excluding resources awarded to replace EFC). 14% of all full-time undergraduates had no need and received non-need-based gift aid.

GIFT AID (NEED-BASED) ***Total amount:*** $24,533,695 (14% federal, 8% state, 76% institutional, 2% external sources). ***Receiving aid:*** Freshmen: 84% (369); all full-time undergraduates: 81% (1,467). ***Average award:*** Freshmen: $20,547; Undergraduates: $17,325. ***Scholarships, grants, and awards:*** Federal Pell, FSEOG, state, private, college/university gift aid from institutional funds, Academic Competitiveness Grants, National SMART Grants, TEACH Grants, United Methodist scholarships.

GIFT AID (NON-NEED-BASED) ***Total amount:*** $3,370,345 (1% federal, 95% institutional, 4% external sources). ***Receiving aid:*** Freshmen: 6% (28). Undergraduates: 7% (132). ***Average award:*** Freshmen: $11,419. Undergraduates: $10,337. ***Scholarships, grants, and awards by category:*** *Academic interests/achievement:* 985 awards ($9,960,814 total): biological sciences, business, communication, education, English, foreign languages, general academic interests/achievements, health fields, humanities, international studies, mathematics, physical sciences, premedicine, religion/biblical studies, social sciences. *Creative arts/performance:* 48 awards ($152,921 total): art/fine arts, creative writing, general creative arts/performance, journalism/publications, music, performing arts, theater/drama. *Special achievements/activities:* 103 awards ($236,435 total): community service, leadership, memberships. *Special characteristics:* 198 awards ($1,010,367 total): children and siblings of alumni, ethnic background, general special characteristics, handicapped students, international students, local/state students, members of minority groups, previous college experience, relatives of clergy, religious affiliation, veterans. ***Tuition waivers:*** Full or partial for employees or children of employees.

LOANS ***Student loans:*** $13,208,675 (43% need-based, 57% non-need-based). 78% of past graduating class borrowed through all loan programs. *Average indebtedness per student:* $36,339. ***Average need-based loan:*** Freshmen: $4037. Undergraduates: $4874. ***Parent loans:*** $3,983,092 (100% non-need-based). ***Programs:*** Federal Direct (Subsidized and Unsubsidized Stafford, PLUS), Perkins, state, alternative loans, United Methodist Student Loans.

WORK-STUDY ***Federal work-study:*** Total amount: $1,199,442; 522 jobs averaging $2322. ***State or other work-study/employment:*** Total amount: $2,317,287 (69% need-based, 31% non-need-based). 1,016 part-time jobs averaging $2311.

APPLYING FOR FINANCIAL AID ***Required financial aid form:*** FAFSA. ***Financial aid deadline (priority):*** 3/15. ***Notification date:*** Continuous beginning 3/15. Students must reply by 5/1 or within 2 weeks of notification.

CONTACT Ms. Lynette Wahl, Office of Financial Aid, Hamline University, 1536 Hewitt Avenue, MS C1915, St. Paul, MN 55104, 651-523-3000 or toll-free 800-753-9753. *Fax:* 651-523-2585. *E-mail:* sasmail@hamline.edu.

HAMPDEN-SYDNEY COLLEGE

Hampden-Sydney, VA

Tuition & fees: $32,364 **Average undergraduate aid package: $25,250**

ABOUT THE INSTITUTION Independent religious, men only. 28 undergraduate majors. Both federal and institutional methodology are used as a basis for awarding need-based institutional aid.

UNDERGRADUATE EXPENSES for 2010–11 ***Comprehensive fee:*** $42,490 includes full-time tuition ($30,994), mandatory fees ($1370), and room and board ($10,126). Room and board charges vary according to board plan and housing facility. ***Payment plan:*** Installment.

FRESHMAN FINANCIAL AID (Fall 2010, est.) 245 applied for aid; of those 78% were deemed to have need. 100% of freshmen with need received aid; of those 29% had need fully met. ***Average percent of need met:*** 80% (excluding resources awarded to replace EFC). ***Average financial aid package:*** $24,392 (excluding resources awarded to replace EFC). 39% of all full-time freshmen had no need and received non-need-based gift aid.

UNDERGRADUATE FINANCIAL AID (Fall 2010, est.) 695 applied for aid; of those 85% were deemed to have need. 100% of undergraduates with need received aid; of those 27% had need fully met. ***Average percent of need met:*** 81% (excluding resources awarded to replace EFC). ***Average financial aid package:*** $25,250 (excluding resources awarded to replace EFC). 41% of all full-time undergraduates had no need and received non-need-based gift aid.

GIFT AID (NEED-BASED) ***Total amount:*** $11,832,434 (10% federal, 9% state, 78% institutional, 3% external sources). ***Receiving aid:*** Freshmen: 60% (190); all full-time undergraduates: 56% (589). ***Average award:*** Freshmen: $20,133; Undergraduates: $20,089. ***Scholarships, grants, and awards:*** Federal Pell, FSEOG, state, private, college/university gift aid from institutional funds.

GIFT AID (NON-NEED-BASED) ***Total amount:*** $7,065,494 (13% state, 73% institutional, 14% external sources). ***Receiving aid:*** Freshmen: 12% (39). Undergraduates: 10% (106). ***Average award:*** Freshmen: $13,886. Undergraduates: $10,815. ***Scholarships, grants, and awards by category:*** *Academic interests/achievement:* 414 awards ($5,406,350 total): biological sciences, education, general academic interests/achievements, health fields, international studies, premedicine, religion/biblical studies. *Creative arts/performance:* music. *Special achievements/activities:* 448 awards ($2,046,023 total): general special achievements/activities, leadership. *Special characteristics:* 94 awards ($1,310,940 total): children of educators, children of faculty/staff, ethnic background, international students, members of minority groups, out-of-state students, religious affiliation, veterans, veterans' children. ***Tuition waivers:*** Full or partial for employees or children of employees.

LOANS ***Student loans:*** $5,064,613 (61% need-based, 39% non-need-based). 49% of past graduating class borrowed through all loan programs. *Average indebtedness per student:* $25,426. ***Average need-based loan:*** Freshmen: $3879. Undergraduates: $4892. ***Parent loans:*** $9,586,650 (23% need-based, 77% non-need-based). ***Programs:*** Federal Direct (Subsidized and Unsubsidized Stafford, PLUS), Perkins, college/university.

WORK-STUDY ***Federal work-study:*** Total amount: $681,703; 356 jobs averaging $1699.

APPLYING FOR FINANCIAL AID ***Required financial aid forms:*** FAFSA, state aid form. ***Financial aid deadline (priority):*** 3/1. ***Notification date:*** 3/15. Students must reply by 5/1 or within 2 weeks of notification.

CONTACT Mrs. Zita Marie Barree, Director of Financial Aid, Hampden-Sydney College, PO Box 726, Hampden-Sydney, VA 23943-0726, 434-223-6119 or toll-free 800-755-0733. *Fax:* 434-223-6075. *E-mail:* hsfinaid@hsc.edu.

HAMPSHIRE COLLEGE

Amherst, MA

Tuition & fees: $42,900 **Average undergraduate aid package: $37,165**

ABOUT THE INSTITUTION Independent, coed. 57 undergraduate majors. Institutional methodology is used as a basis for awarding need-based institutional aid.

UNDERGRADUATE EXPENSES for 2011–12 ***One-time required fee:*** $110. ***Comprehensive fee:*** $54,080 includes full-time tuition ($41,900), mandatory fees ($1000), and room and board ($11,180). ***College room only:*** $7130. Room and board charges vary according to board plan. ***Payment plan:*** Installment.

FRESHMAN FINANCIAL AID (Fall 2010, est.) 317 applied for aid; of those 84% were deemed to have need. 100% of freshmen with need received aid; of those 54% had need fully met. ***Average percent of need met:*** 91% (excluding resources awarded to replace EFC). ***Average financial aid package:*** $36,740 (excluding resources awarded to replace EFC). 23% of all full-time freshmen had no need and received non-need-based gift aid.

UNDERGRADUATE FINANCIAL AID (Fall 2010, est.) 1,047 applied for aid; of those 88% were deemed to have need. 100% of undergraduates with need received aid; of those 72% had need fully met. ***Average percent of need met:*** 95% (excluding resources awarded to replace EFC). ***Average financial aid package:*** $37,165 (excluding resources awarded to replace EFC). 18% of all full-time undergraduates had no need and received non-need-based gift aid.

GIFT AID (NEED-BASED) ***Total amount:*** $27,834,700 (7% federal, 92% institutional, 1% external sources). ***Receiving aid:*** Freshmen: 62% (265); all full-time undergraduates: 61% (919). ***Average award:*** Freshmen: $31,140; Undergraduates: $29,940. ***Scholarships, grants, and awards:*** Federal Pell, FSEOG, state, private, college/university gift aid from institutional funds.

GIFT AID (NON-NEED-BASED) ***Total amount:*** $2,677,935 (2% federal, 81% institutional, 17% external sources). ***Receiving aid:*** Freshmen: 49% (210). Undergraduates: 37% (560). ***Average award:*** Freshmen: $7245. Undergraduates: $6880. ***Scholarships, grants, and awards by category:*** *Academic interests/achievement:* general academic interests/achievements, international studies, physical sciences, social sciences. *Creative arts/performance:* creative writing. *Special achievements/activities:* community service, leadership. *Special characteristics:* children of faculty/staff. ***Tuition waivers:*** Full or partial for employees or children of employees.

LOANS ***Student loans:*** $4,466,150 (91% need-based, 9% non-need-based). 58% of past graduating class borrowed through all loan programs. *Average indebtedness per student:* $21,673. ***Average need-based loan:*** Freshmen: $3500. Undergraduates: $4750. ***Parent loans:*** $3,822,440 (71% need-based, 29% non-need-based). ***Programs:*** Federal Direct (Subsidized and Unsubsidized Stafford, PLUS), Perkins.

WORK-STUDY ***Federal work-study:*** Total amount: $1,536,480; jobs available. ***State or other work-study/employment:*** Total amount: $682,190 (81% need-based, 19% non-need-based). Part-time jobs available.

APPLYING FOR FINANCIAL AID ***Required financial aid forms:*** FAFSA, CSS Financial Aid PROFILE, noncustodial (divorced/separated) parent's statement. ***Financial aid deadline (priority):*** 2/1. ***Notification date:*** 4/1. Students must reply by 5/1 or within 2 weeks of notification.

CONTACT Ms. Jennifer Garratt Lawton, Director of Financial Aid, Hampshire College, 893 West Street, Amherst, MA 01002, 413-559-5484 or toll-free 877-937-4267 (out-of-state). *Fax:* 413-559-5585. *E-mail:* financialaid@hampshire.edu.

HAMPTON UNIVERSITY

Hampton, VA

Tuition & fees: $18,074 **Average undergraduate aid package: $4563**

ABOUT THE INSTITUTION Independent, coed. 82 undergraduate majors. Federal methodology is used as a basis for awarding need-based institutional aid.

UNDERGRADUATE EXPENSES for 2010–11 ***Comprehensive fee:*** $26,122 includes full-time tuition ($16,238), mandatory fees ($1836), and room and board ($8048). ***College room only:*** $4186. Full-time tuition and fees vary according to course load, degree level, and program. Room and board charges vary according to board plan and housing facility. ***Part-time tuition:*** $410 per credit hour. ***Payment plan:*** Deferred payment.

FRESHMAN FINANCIAL AID (Fall 2010, est.) 666 applied for aid; of those 89% were deemed to have need. 91% of freshmen with need received aid; of those 56% had need fully met. ***Average percent of need met:*** 56% (excluding resources awarded to replace EFC). ***Average financial aid package:*** $4204 (excluding resources awarded to replace EFC). 4% of all full-time freshmen had no need and received non-need-based gift aid.

UNDERGRADUATE FINANCIAL AID (Fall 2010, est.) 2,524 applied for aid; of those 88% were deemed to have need. 93% of undergraduates with need received aid; of those 51% had need fully met. ***Average percent of need met:*** 51% (excluding resources awarded to replace EFC). ***Average financial aid package:*** $4563 (excluding resources awarded to replace EFC). 3% of all full-time undergraduates had no need and received non-need-based gift aid.

GIFT AID (NEED-BASED) ***Total amount:*** $9,143,817 (78% federal, 17% state, 3% institutional, 2% external sources). ***Receiving aid:*** Freshmen: 57% (529); all full-time undergraduates: 52% (2,033). ***Average award:*** Freshmen: $3929; Undergraduates: $4035. ***Scholarships, grants, and awards:*** Federal Pell, FSEOG, state, private, college/university gift aid from institutional funds, Federal Nursing.

GIFT AID (NON-NEED-BASED) ***Total amount:*** $11,056,362 (5% state, 67% institutional, 28% external sources). ***Receiving aid:*** Freshmen: 17% (157). Undergraduates: 14% (556). ***Average award:*** Freshmen: $11,298. Undergraduates: $12,587. ***Scholarships, grants, and awards by category:*** *Academic interests/achievement:* 336 awards ($8,048,312 total): architecture, biological sciences, business, communication, computer science, education, engineering/technologies, general academic interests/achievements, health fields, physical sciences. *Creative arts/performance:* 9 awards ($31,000 total): music. *Special achievements/activities:* 99 awards ($247,500 total): leadership. *Special characteristics:* 494 awards ($1,302,862 total): adult students, children of faculty/staff, international students, members of minority groups, veterans, veterans' children. ***Tuition waivers:*** Full or partial for employees or children of employees.

LOANS ***Student loans:*** $24,525,365 (91% need-based, 9% non-need-based). 88% of past graduating class borrowed through all loan programs. *Average indebtedness per student:* $11,334. ***Average need-based loan:*** Freshmen: $2750. Undergraduates: $3450. ***Parent loans:*** $26,858,708 (83% need-based, 17% non-need-based). ***Programs:*** Federal Direct (Subsidized and Unsubsidized Stafford, PLUS), Perkins, Federal Nursing, college/university, private loans.

WORK-STUDY ***Federal work-study:*** Total amount: $119,330; 127 jobs averaging $1127. ***State or other work-study/employment:*** 18 part-time jobs averaging $1179.

ATHLETIC AWARDS Total amount: $3,003,945 (91% need-based, 9% non-need-based).

APPLYING FOR FINANCIAL AID ***Required financial aid forms:*** FAFSA, Virginia Tuition Assistance Grant forms (VA residents only). ***Financial aid deadline:*** 4/15 (priority: 2/15). ***Notification date:*** Continuous beginning 4/15. Students must reply within 2 weeks of notification.

CONTACT Martin Miles, Director of Financial Aid, Hampton University, Hampton University, 2nd Floor, Whipple Barn, Hampton, VA 23668, 757-727-5332 or toll-free 800-624-3328. *Fax:* 757-728-6567. *E-mail:* martin.miles@hamptonu.edu.

HANNIBAL-LAGRANGE UNIVERSITY

Hannibal, MO

Tuition & fees: $16,890 **Average undergraduate aid package: N/A**

ABOUT THE INSTITUTION Independent Southern Baptist, coed. 40 undergraduate majors. Federal methodology is used as a basis for awarding need-based institutional aid.

UNDERGRADUATE EXPENSES for 2011–12 ***Comprehensive fee:*** $23,090 includes full-time tuition ($16,170), mandatory fees ($720), and room and board ($6200). Full-time tuition and fees vary according to course load, degree level, program, and reciprocity agreements. Room and board charges vary according to housing facility. ***Part-time tuition:*** $539 per credit. Part-time tuition and fees vary according to course load, degree level, program, and reciprocity agreements. ***Payment plan:*** Installment.

GIFT AID (NEED-BASED) ***Scholarships, grants, and awards:*** Federal Pell, FSEOG, state, private, college/university gift aid from institutional funds.

GIFT AID (NON-NEED-BASED) ***Scholarships, grants, and awards by category:*** *Academic interests/achievement:* general academic interests/achievements, religion/biblical studies. *Creative arts/performance:* art/fine arts, journalism/publications, music, performing arts, theater/drama. *Special characteristics:* children of faculty/staff, public servants, relatives of clergy, religious affiliation. ***Tuition waivers:*** Full or partial for employees or children of employees.

LOANS ***Programs:*** Federal Direct (Subsidized and Unsubsidized Stafford, PLUS), Perkins.

APPLYING FOR FINANCIAL AID ***Required financial aid forms:*** FAFSA, institution's own form. ***Financial aid deadline:*** Continuous.

CONTACT Brice Baumgardner, Director of Financial Aid, Hannibal-LaGrange University, 2800 Palmyra Road, Hannibal, MO 63401-1940, 573-629-3279 Ext. 3279 or toll-free 800-HLG-1119. *Fax:* 573-248-0954. *E-mail:* bbaumgardner@hlg.edu.

HANOVER COLLEGE

Hanover, IN

Tuition & fees: $28,850 **Average undergraduate aid package: $25,098**

ABOUT THE INSTITUTION Independent Presbyterian, coed. 29 undergraduate majors. Federal methodology is used as a basis for awarding need-based institutional aid.

UNDERGRADUATE EXPENSES for 2011–12 ***One-time required fee:*** $250. ***Comprehensive fee:*** $37,500 includes full-time tuition ($28,250), mandatory fees ($600), and room and board ($8650). ***College room only:*** $4300. Full-time tuition and fees vary according to reciprocity agreements. Room and board charges vary according to housing facility and location. ***Part-time tuition:*** $3150 per unit. Part-time tuition and fees vary according to course load and reciprocity agreements. ***Payment plan:*** Installment.

FRESHMAN FINANCIAL AID (Fall 2010, est.) 304 applied for aid; of those 91% were deemed to have need. 100% of freshmen with need received aid; of those 23% had need fully met. ***Average percent of need met:*** 84% (excluding resources awarded to replace EFC). ***Average financial aid package:*** $24,114 (excluding resources awarded to replace EFC). 14% of all full-time freshmen had no need and received non-need-based gift aid.

UNDERGRADUATE FINANCIAL AID (Fall 2010, est.) 896 applied for aid; of those 93% were deemed to have need. 100% of undergraduates with need received aid; of those 25% had need fully met. ***Average percent of need met:*** 86% (excluding resources awarded to replace EFC). ***Average financial aid package:*** $25,098 (excluding resources awarded to replace EFC). 18% of all full-time undergraduates had no need and received non-need-based gift aid.

GIFT AID (NEED-BASED) ***Total amount:*** $16,952,002 (9% federal, 7% state, 75% institutional, 9% external sources). ***Receiving aid:*** Freshmen: 86% (277); all full-time undergraduates: 83% (831). ***Average award:*** Freshmen: $19,555; Undergraduates: $20,399. ***Scholarships, grants, and awards:*** Federal Pell, FSEOG, state, private, college/university gift aid from institutional funds.

GIFT AID (NON-NEED-BASED) ***Total amount:*** $3,233,193 (82% institutional, 18% external sources). ***Receiving aid:*** Freshmen: 8% (27). Undergraduates: 9% (87). ***Average award:*** Freshmen: $14,110. Undergraduates: $13,064. ***Scholarships, grants, and awards by category:*** *Academic interests/achievement:* general academic interests/achievements. *Creative arts/performance:* art/fine arts, music, theater/drama. *Special characteristics:* children and siblings of alumni, children of faculty/staff, international students, members of minority groups, out-of-state students, religious affiliation, siblings of current students. ***Tuition waivers:*** Full or partial for employees or children of employees, senior citizens.

LOANS ***Student loans:*** $7,102,742 (70% need-based, 30% non-need-based). 77% of past graduating class borrowed through all loan programs. *Average indebtedness per student:* $26,714. ***Average need-based loan:*** Freshmen: $4362. Undergraduates: $4885. ***Parent loans:*** $2,639,234 (28% need-based, 72% non-need-based). ***Programs:*** Federal Direct (Subsidized and Unsubsidized Stafford, PLUS), college/university.

WORK-STUDY ***Federal work-study:*** Total amount: $171,464; 331 jobs averaging $996. ***State or other work-study/employment:*** Part-time jobs available.

APPLYING FOR FINANCIAL AID ***Required financial aid form:*** FAFSA. ***Financial aid deadline (priority):*** 3/1. ***Notification date:*** Continuous beginning 3/1. Students must reply by 5/1.

CONTACT Richard A. Nash, Director of Financial Assistance, Hanover College, PO Box 108, Hanover, IN 47243-0108, 800-213-2178 Ext. 7029 or toll-free 800-213-2178. *Fax:* 812-866-7284. *E-mail:* finaid@hanover.edu.

HARDING UNIVERSITY

Searcy, AR

Tuition & fees: $14,040 **Average undergraduate aid package: $12,219**

ABOUT THE INSTITUTION Independent religious, coed. 85 undergraduate majors. Federal methodology is used as a basis for awarding need-based institutional aid.

UNDERGRADUATE EXPENSES for 2010–11 ***Comprehensive fee:*** $19,962 includes full-time tuition ($13,590), mandatory fees ($450), and room and board ($5922). ***College room only:*** $2934. Full-time tuition and fees vary according to course load. Room and board charges vary according to board plan and housing facility. ***Part-time tuition:*** $453 per credit hour. ***Part-time fees:*** $22.50 per credit hour. Part-time tuition and fees vary according to course load. ***Payment plans:*** Tuition prepayment, installment.

FRESHMAN FINANCIAL AID (Fall 2009) 772 applied for aid; of those 74% were deemed to have need. 99% of freshmen with need received aid; of those 30% had need fully met. ***Average percent of need met:*** 77% (excluding resources awarded to replace EFC). ***Average financial aid package:*** $11,884 (excluding resources awarded to replace EFC). 19% of all full-time freshmen had no need and received non-need-based gift aid.

UNDERGRADUATE FINANCIAL AID (Fall 2009) 2,800 applied for aid; of those 80% were deemed to have need. 99% of undergraduates with need received aid; of those 25% had need fully met. ***Average percent of need met:*** 70% (excluding resources awarded to replace EFC). ***Average financial aid package:*** $12,219 (excluding resources awarded to replace EFC). 11% of all full-time undergraduates had no need and received non-need-based gift aid.

GIFT AID (NEED-BASED) ***Total amount:*** $14,252,731 (37% federal, 4% state, 56% institutional, 3% external sources). ***Receiving aid:*** Freshmen: 58% (553); all full-time undergraduates: 52% (2,003). ***Average award:*** Freshmen: $7971; Undergraduates: $7457. ***Scholarships, grants, and awards:*** Federal Pell, FSEOG, state, private, college/university gift aid from institutional funds.

GIFT AID (NON-NEED-BASED) ***Total amount:*** $10,555,304 (6% state, 89% institutional, 5% external sources). ***Receiving aid:*** Freshmen: 13% (126). Undergraduates: 9% (345). ***Average award:*** Freshmen: $6032. Undergraduates: $5443. ***Scholarships, grants, and awards by category:*** *Academic interests/achievement:* 3,412 awards ($13,985,592 total): communication, computer science, engineering/technologies, English, general academic interests/achievements, health fields, religion/biblical studies. *Creative arts/performance:* 254 awards ($190,894 total): art/fine arts, cinema/film/broadcasting, debating, journalism/publications, music. *Special achievements/activities:* 107 awards ($82,911 total): cheerleading/drum major, leadership, religious involvement. *Special characteristics:* 533 awards ($2,743,570 total): children of faculty/staff, children with a deceased or disabled parent, international students, relatives of clergy, siblings of current students. ***Tuition waivers:*** Full or partial for employees or children of employees, senior citizens.

LOANS ***Student loans:*** $22,171,159 (65% need-based, 35% non-need-based). 68% of past graduating class borrowed through all loan programs. *Average indebtedness per student:* $33,989. ***Average need-based loan:*** Freshmen: $4014. Undergraduates: $5106. ***Parent loans:*** $4,151,313 (27% need-based, 73% non-need-based). ***Programs:*** Perkins, Federal Nursing, state, college/university.

WORK-STUDY ***Federal work-study:*** Total amount: $407,147; 439 jobs averaging $935. ***State or other work-study/employment:*** Total amount: $2,037,588 (23% need-based, 77% non-need-based). 1,327 part-time jobs averaging $1556.

ATHLETIC AWARDS Total amount: $1,827,883 (28% need-based, 72% non-need-based).

APPLYING FOR FINANCIAL AID ***Required financial aid form:*** FAFSA. ***Financial aid deadline (priority):*** 4/15. ***Notification date:*** Continuous. Students must reply within 2 weeks of notification.

CONTACT Dr. Jonathan C. Roberts, Director of Student Financial Services, Harding University, Box 12282, Searcy, AR 72149-2282, 501-279-4257 or toll-free 800-477-4407. *Fax:* 501-279-4129. *E-mail:* jroberts@harding.edu.

HARDIN-SIMMONS UNIVERSITY

Abilene, TX

Tuition & fees: $22,460 **Average undergraduate aid package: $23,956**

ABOUT THE INSTITUTION Independent Baptist, coed. 72 undergraduate majors. Federal methodology is used as a basis for awarding need-based institutional aid.

UNDERGRADUATE EXPENSES for 2011–12 ***Comprehensive fee:*** $29,264 includes full-time tuition ($21,450), mandatory fees ($1010), and room and board ($6804). ***College room only:*** $3384. Full-time tuition and fees vary according to program. Room and board charges vary according to board plan and housing facility. ***Part-time tuition:*** $715 per credit hour. ***Part-time fees:*** $150 per term. Part-time tuition and fees vary according to course load and program. ***Payment plans:*** Guaranteed tuition, installment.

FRESHMAN FINANCIAL AID (Fall 2010, est.) 402 applied for aid; of those 78% were deemed to have need. 100% of freshmen with need received aid; of those 21% had need fully met. ***Average percent of need met:*** 71% (excluding resources awarded to replace EFC). ***Average financial aid package:*** $24,292 (excluding resources awarded to replace EFC). 22% of all full-time freshmen had no need and received non-need-based gift aid.

UNDERGRADUATE FINANCIAL AID (Fall 2010, est.) 1,682 applied for aid; of those 76% were deemed to have need. 100% of undergraduates with need received aid; of those 19% had need fully met. ***Average percent of need met:*** 68% (excluding resources awarded to replace EFC). ***Average financial aid package:*** $23,956 (excluding resources awarded to replace EFC). 21% of all full-time undergraduates had no need and received non-need-based gift aid.

GIFT AID (NEED-BASED) ***Total amount:*** $5,834,905 (55% federal, 45% state). ***Receiving aid:*** Freshmen: 57% (228); all full-time undergraduates: 53% (912). ***Average award:*** Freshmen: $7902; Undergraduates: $7520. ***Scholarships, grants, and awards:*** Federal Pell, FSEOG, state, private, college/university gift aid from institutional funds, Academic Competitiveness Grants, National SMART Grants.

GIFT AID (NON-NEED-BASED) ***Total amount:*** $11,575,162 (93% institutional, 7% external sources). ***Receiving aid:*** Freshmen: 71% (288). Undergraduates: 66% (1,125). ***Average award:*** Freshmen: $7554. Undergraduates: $8214. ***Scholarships, grants, and awards by category:*** *Academic interests/achievement:* 1,631 awards ($8,347,611 total): biological sciences, business, communication, computer science, education, English, foreign languages, general academic interests/achievements, health fields, humanities, mathematics, physical sciences, premedicine, religion/biblical studies, social sciences. *Creative arts/performance:* 118 awards ($165,067 total): applied art and design, art/fine arts, creative writing, journalism/publications, music, performing arts, theater/drama. *Special achievements/activities:* 37 awards ($62,178 total): general special achievements/activities, leadership. *Special characteristics:* 323 awards ($1,046,954 total): children of educators, children of faculty/staff, ethnic background, general special characteristics, handicapped students, local/state students, members of minority groups, out-of-state students, public servants, relatives of clergy, religious affiliation, siblings of current students. ***Tuition waivers:*** Full or partial for employees or children of employees.

LOANS ***Student loans:*** $15,608,289 (39% need-based, 61% non-need-based). 67% of past graduating class borrowed through all loan programs. *Average indebtedness per student:* $37,383. ***Average need-based loan:*** Freshmen: $3080.

Undergraduates: $4203. ***Parent loans:*** $3,873,610 (100% non-need-based). ***Programs:*** Federal Direct (Subsidized and Unsubsidized Stafford, PLUS), Perkins, state, college/university.

WORK-STUDY ***Federal work-study:*** Total amount: $304,428; 119 jobs averaging $1900. ***State or other work-study/employment:*** Total amount: $24,593 (100% need-based). 221 part-time jobs averaging $1900.

APPLYING FOR FINANCIAL AID ***Required financial aid form:*** FAFSA. ***Financial aid deadline (priority):*** 3/15. ***Notification date:*** Continuous beginning 2/1.

CONTACT Mrs. Bridget Moore, Director of Financial Aid, Hardin-Simmons University, PO Box 16050, Abilene, TX 79698-6050, 325-670-1482 or toll-free 877-464-7889. *Fax:* 325-670-5822. *E-mail:* bnmoore@hsutx.edu.

HARRINGTON COLLEGE OF DESIGN

Chicago, IL

CONTACT Ms. Renee Darosky, Director of Financial Aid, Harrington College of Design, 410 South Michigan Avenue, Chicago, IL 60605-1496, 312-939-4975 or toll-free 877-939-4975. *Fax:* 312-697-8058. *E-mail:* financialaid@interiordesign.edu.

HARRISBURG UNIVERSITY OF SCIENCE AND TECHNOLOGY

Harrisburg, PA

Tuition & fees: $19,500 **Average undergraduate aid package: $12,990**

ABOUT THE INSTITUTION Independent, coed. 5 undergraduate majors. Federal methodology is used as a basis for awarding need-based institutional aid.

UNDERGRADUATE EXPENSES for 2010–11 ***Tuition:*** full-time $19,500; part-time $850 per semester hour. Part-time tuition and fees vary according to course load. ***Payment plans:*** Installment, deferred payment.

FRESHMAN FINANCIAL AID (Fall 2009) 73 applied for aid; of those 92% were deemed to have need. 99% of freshmen with need received aid; of those 6% had need fully met. ***Average percent of need met:*** 54% (excluding resources awarded to replace EFC). ***Average financial aid package:*** $13,701 (excluding resources awarded to replace EFC). 5% of all full-time freshmen had no need and received non-need-based gift aid.

UNDERGRADUATE FINANCIAL AID (Fall 2009) 183 applied for aid; of those 94% were deemed to have need. 99% of undergraduates with need received aid; of those 5% had need fully met. ***Average percent of need met:*** 52% (excluding resources awarded to replace EFC). ***Average financial aid package:*** $12,990 (excluding resources awarded to replace EFC). 5% of all full-time undergraduates had no need and received non-need-based gift aid.

GIFT AID (NEED-BASED) ***Total amount:*** $1,761,168 (32% federal, 19% state, 37% institutional, 12% external sources). ***Receiving aid:*** Freshmen: 72% (66); all full-time undergraduates: 84% (170). ***Average award:*** Freshmen: $11,016; Undergraduates: $9889. ***Scholarships, grants, and awards:*** Federal Pell, FSEOG, state, private, college/university gift aid from institutional funds.

GIFT AID (NON-NEED-BASED) ***Total amount:*** $93,553 (89% institutional, 11% external sources). ***Receiving aid:*** Freshmen: 4% (4). Undergraduates: 3% (7). ***Average award:*** Freshmen: $8700. Undergraduates: $5363. ***Scholarships, grants, and awards by category:*** *Academic interests/achievement:* biological sciences, business, computer science, physical sciences.

LOANS ***Student loans:*** $1,172,787 (89% need-based, 11% non-need-based). 100% of past graduating class borrowed through all loan programs. *Average indebtedness per student:* $21,298. ***Average need-based loan:*** Freshmen: $3221. Undergraduates: $3741. ***Parent loans:*** $244,774 (53% need-based, 47% non-need-based). ***Programs:*** Federal Direct (Subsidized and Unsubsidized Stafford, PLUS).

WORK-STUDY ***Federal work-study:*** Total amount: $11,000; 6 jobs averaging $1500.

APPLYING FOR FINANCIAL AID ***Required financial aid form:*** FAFSA. ***Financial aid deadline:*** Continuous. ***Notification date:*** Continuous. Students must reply within 2 weeks of notification.

CONTACT Mr. Vince P. Frank, Director of Financial Aid Services, Harrisburg University of Science and Technology, 326 Market Street, Harrisburg, PA 17101-2208, 717-901-5115 or toll-free 866-HBG-UNIV. *Fax:* 717-901-3115. *E-mail:* vfrank@harrisburgu.edu.

HARRIS-STOWE STATE UNIVERSITY

St. Louis, MO

CONTACT Regina Blackshear, Director of Financial Aid, Harris-Stowe State University, 3026 Laclede Avenue, St. Louis, MO 63103-2136, 314-340-3502. *Fax:* 314-340-3503.

HARTWICK COLLEGE

Oneonta, NY

Tuition & fees: $34,630 **Average undergraduate aid package: $26,713**

ABOUT THE INSTITUTION Independent, coed. 33 undergraduate majors. Federal methodology is used as a basis for awarding need-based institutional aid.

UNDERGRADUATE EXPENSES for 2010–11 ***One-time required fee:*** $300. ***Comprehensive fee:*** $43,975 includes full-time tuition ($33,850), mandatory fees ($780), and room and board ($9345). ***College room only:*** $4840. Room and board charges vary according to board plan and housing facility. ***Part-time tuition:*** $1070 per credit hour. ***Payment plan:*** Installment.

FRESHMAN FINANCIAL AID (Fall 2010, est.) 445 applied for aid; of those 91% were deemed to have need. 100% of freshmen with need received aid; of those 15% had need fully met. ***Average percent of need met:*** 83% (excluding resources awarded to replace EFC). ***Average financial aid package:*** $29,167 (excluding resources awarded to replace EFC). 15% of all full-time freshmen had no need and received non-need-based gift aid.

UNDERGRADUATE FINANCIAL AID (Fall 2010, est.) 1,256 applied for aid; of those 93% were deemed to have need. 100% of undergraduates with need received aid; of those 14% had need fully met. ***Average percent of need met:*** 79% (excluding resources awarded to replace EFC). ***Average financial aid package:*** $26,713 (excluding resources awarded to replace EFC). 18% of all full-time undergraduates had no need and received non-need-based gift aid.

GIFT AID (NEED-BASED) ***Total amount:*** $22,625,013 (11% federal, 7% state, 79% institutional, 3% external sources). ***Receiving aid:*** Freshmen: 83% (406); all full-time undergraduates: 79% (1,169). ***Average award:*** Freshmen: $23,645; Undergraduates: $21,372. ***Scholarships, grants, and awards:*** Federal Pell, FSEOG, state, private, college/university gift aid from institutional funds.

GIFT AID (NON-NEED-BASED) ***Total amount:*** $4,536,932 (92% institutional, 8% external sources). ***Receiving aid:*** Freshmen: 11% (56). Undergraduates: 9% (131). ***Average award:*** Freshmen: $15,048. Undergraduates: $12,063. ***Scholarships, grants, and awards by category:*** *Special characteristics:* children and siblings of alumni, children of faculty/staff, international students, siblings of current students. ***Tuition waivers:*** Full or partial for employees or children of employees.

LOANS ***Student loans:*** $11,728,832 (75% need-based, 25% non-need-based). 70% of past graduating class borrowed through all loan programs. *Average indebtedness per student:* $32,327. ***Average need-based loan:*** Freshmen: $4528. Undergraduates: $4755. ***Parent loans:*** $16,000,235 (91% need-based, 9% non-need-based). ***Programs:*** Federal Direct (Subsidized and Unsubsidized Stafford, PLUS), Perkins, Federal Nursing, college/university, alternative loans.

WORK-STUDY ***Federal work-study:*** Total amount: $1,391,205; jobs available.

ATHLETIC AWARDS Total amount: $645,469 (17% need-based, 83% non-need-based).

APPLYING FOR FINANCIAL AID ***Required financial aid form:*** FAFSA. ***Financial aid deadline:*** Continuous. ***Notification date:*** Continuous beginning 10/15. Students must reply by 5/1 or within 2 weeks of notification.

CONTACT Melissa Allen, Director of Financial Aid, Hartwick College, One Hartwick Drive, Oneonta, NY 13820, 607-431-4130 or toll-free 888-HARTWICK (out-of-state). *Fax:* 607-431-4006. *E-mail:* allenm@hartwick.edu.

HARVARD UNIVERSITY

Cambridge, MA

Tuition & fees: $38,415 **Average undergraduate aid package: $41,648**

ABOUT THE INSTITUTION Independent, coed. 45 undergraduate majors. Institutional methodology is used as a basis for awarding need-based institutional aid.

UNDERGRADUATE EXPENSES for 2010–11 ***Comprehensive fee:*** $50,723 includes full-time tuition ($34,976), mandatory fees ($3439), and room and board ($12,308). ***College room only:*** $7525. ***Payment plans:*** Tuition prepayment, installment.

FRESHMAN FINANCIAL AID (Fall 2010, est.) 1,182 applied for aid; of those 89% were deemed to have need. 100% of freshmen with need received aid; of those 100% had need fully met. ***Average percent of need met:*** 100% (excluding resources awarded to replace EFC). ***Average financial aid package:*** $42,801 (excluding resources awarded to replace EFC).

UNDERGRADUATE FINANCIAL AID (Fall 2010, est.) 4,439 applied for aid; of those 93% were deemed to have need. 100% of undergraduates with need received aid; of those 100% had need fully met. ***Average percent of need met:*** 100% (excluding resources awarded to replace EFC). ***Average financial aid package:*** $41,648 (excluding resources awarded to replace EFC).

GIFT AID (NEED-BASED) ***Total amount:*** $161,231,000 (5% federal, 91% institutional, 4% external sources). ***Receiving aid:*** Freshmen: 63% (1,048); all full-time undergraduates: 61% (4,137). ***Average award:*** Freshmen: $41,476; Undergraduates: $39,156. ***Scholarships, grants, and awards:*** Federal Pell, FSEOG, state, private, college/university gift aid from institutional funds.

GIFT AID (NON-NEED-BASED) ***Total amount:*** $4,606,600 (18% federal, 3% institutional, 79% external sources).

LOANS ***Student loans:*** $4,822,000 (85% need-based, 15% non-need-based). 34% of past graduating class borrowed through all loan programs. *Average indebtedness per student:* $10,102. ***Average need-based loan:*** Freshmen: $3107. Undergraduates: $3956. ***Parent loans:*** $8,000,000 (100% non-need-based). ***Programs:*** Federal Direct (Subsidized and Unsubsidized Stafford, PLUS), Perkins, state, college/university.

WORK-STUDY ***Federal work-study:*** Total amount: $2,400,000; 937 jobs averaging $2553. ***State or other work-study/employment:*** Total amount: $5,450,000 (90% need-based, 10% non-need-based). 1,890 part-time jobs averaging $2602.

APPLYING FOR FINANCIAL AID ***Required financial aid forms:*** FAFSA, CSS Financial Aid PROFILE, noncustodial (divorced/separated) parent's statement, business/farm supplement, federal income tax form(s). ***Financial aid deadline (priority):*** 2/1. ***Notification date:*** 4/1. Students must reply by 5/1 or within 2 weeks of notification.

CONTACT Financial Aid Office, Harvard University, 86 Brattle Street, Cambridge, MA 02138, 617-495-1581. *Fax:* 617-496-0256.

HARVEY MUDD COLLEGE

Claremont, CA

Tuition & fees: $40,390 — **Average undergraduate aid package: $33,470**

ABOUT THE INSTITUTION Independent, coed. 6 undergraduate majors. Both federal and institutional methodology are used as a basis for awarding need-based institutional aid.

UNDERGRADUATE EXPENSES for 2010–11 ***Comprehensive fee:*** $53,588 includes full-time tuition ($40,133), mandatory fees ($257), and room and board ($13,198). ***College room only:*** $6935. Room and board charges vary according to board plan. ***Part-time tuition:*** $1194 per credit hour. ***Payment plan:*** Installment.

FRESHMAN FINANCIAL AID (Fall 2010, est.) 134 applied for aid; of those 75% were deemed to have need. 100% of freshmen with need received aid; of those 100% had need fully met. ***Average percent of need met:*** 100% (excluding resources awarded to replace EFC). ***Average financial aid package:*** $34,282 (excluding resources awarded to replace EFC). 18% of all full-time freshmen had no need and received non-need-based gift aid.

UNDERGRADUATE FINANCIAL AID (Fall 2010, est.) 478 applied for aid; of those 87% were deemed to have need. 100% of undergraduates with need received aid; of those 100% had need fully met. ***Average percent of need met:*** 100% (excluding resources awarded to replace EFC). ***Average financial aid package:*** $33,470 (excluding resources awarded to replace EFC). 24% of all full-time undergraduates had no need and received non-need-based gift aid.

GIFT AID (NEED-BASED) ***Total amount:*** $11,928,109 (6% federal, 4% state, 87% institutional, 3% external sources). ***Receiving aid:*** Freshmen: 49% (96); all full-time undergraduates: 52% (405). ***Average award:*** Freshmen: $32,248; Undergraduates: $29,588. ***Scholarships, grants, and awards:*** Federal Pell, FSEOG, state, private, college/university gift aid from institutional funds, Academic Competitiveness Grants, National SMART Grants.

GIFT AID (NON-NEED-BASED) ***Total amount:*** $2,514,301 (87% institutional, 13% external sources). ***Receiving aid:*** Freshmen: 25% (48). Undergraduates: 27% (206). ***Average award:*** Freshmen: $7702. Undergraduates: $10,452. ***Scholarships, grants, and awards by category:*** *Academic interests/achievement:* 374 awards ($4,094,267 total): general academic interests/achievements. *Special characteristics:* 6 awards ($243,500 total): international students. ***Tuition waivers:*** Full or partial for employees or children of employees.

LOANS ***Student loans:*** $2,675,731 (86% need-based, 14% non-need-based). 58% of past graduating class borrowed through all loan programs. *Average indebtedness per student:* $21,806. ***Average need-based loan:*** Freshmen: $3415. Undergraduates: $4895. ***Parent loans:*** $1,310,411 (72% need-based, 28% non-need-based). ***Programs:*** Federal Direct (Subsidized and Unsubsidized Stafford, PLUS), Perkins, college/university, alternative loans.

WORK-STUDY ***Federal work-study:*** Total amount: $522,991; 238 jobs averaging $2197. ***State or other work-study/employment:*** Total amount: $109,985 (83% need-based, 17% non-need-based). 17 part-time jobs averaging $6470.

APPLYING FOR FINANCIAL AID ***Required financial aid forms:*** FAFSA, CSS Financial Aid PROFILE, state aid form, noncustodial (divorced/separated) parent's statement, business/farm supplement. ***Financial aid deadline:*** 2/1. ***Notification date:*** 4/1. Students must reply by 5/1 or within 2 weeks of notification.

CONTACT Mrs. Gilma Lopez, Office of Financial Aid, Harvey Mudd College, 301 Platt Boulevard, Claremont, CA 91711-5994, 909-621-8055. *Fax:* 909-607-7046. *E-mail:* financial_aid@hmc.edu.

HASKELL INDIAN NATIONS UNIVERSITY

Lawrence, KS

CONTACT Reta Brewer, Director of Financial Aid, Haskell Indian Nations University, 155 Indian Avenue, Box 5027, Lawrence, KS 66046-4800, 785-749-8468. *Fax:* 785-832-6617.

HASTINGS COLLEGE

Hastings, NE

Tuition & fees: N/R — **Average undergraduate aid package: $16,021**

ABOUT THE INSTITUTION Independent Presbyterian, coed. ***Awards:*** bachelor's and master's degrees. 81 undergraduate majors. ***Total enrollment:*** 1,138. Undergraduates: 1,091. Freshmen: 304. Federal methodology is used as a basis for awarding need-based institutional aid.

FRESHMAN FINANCIAL AID (Fall 2009) 265 applied for aid; of those 86% were deemed to have need. 100% of freshmen with need received aid; of those 19% had need fully met. ***Average percent of need met:*** 75% (excluding resources awarded to replace EFC). ***Average financial aid package:*** $16,350 (excluding resources awarded to replace EFC). 18% of all full-time freshmen had no need and received non-need-based gift aid.

UNDERGRADUATE FINANCIAL AID (Fall 2009) 915 applied for aid; of those 89% were deemed to have need. 100% of undergraduates with need received aid; of those 23% had need fully met. ***Average percent of need met:*** 75% (excluding resources awarded to replace EFC). ***Average financial aid package:*** $16,021 (excluding resources awarded to replace EFC). 23% of all full-time undergraduates had no need and received non-need-based gift aid.

GIFT AID (NEED-BASED) ***Total amount:*** $7,908,763 (20% federal, 3% state, 68% institutional, 9% external sources). ***Receiving aid:*** Freshmen: 78% (229); all full-time undergraduates: 72% (797). ***Average award:*** Freshmen: $13,310; Undergraduates: $12,412. ***Scholarships, grants, and awards:*** Federal Pell, FSEOG, state, private, college/university gift aid from institutional funds.

GIFT AID (NON-NEED-BASED) ***Total amount:*** $2,820,844 (85% institutional, 15% external sources). ***Receiving aid:*** Freshmen: 12% (34). Undergraduates: 10% (113). ***Average award:*** Freshmen: $9492. Undergraduates: $8292. ***Scholarships, grants, and awards by category:*** *Academic interests/achievement:* communication, general academic interests/achievements, religion/biblical studies. *Creative arts/performance:* art/fine arts, dance, debating, journalism/publications, music, performing arts, theater/drama. *Special achievements/activities:* cheerleading/drum major, rodeo. *Special characteristics:* adult students, children of educators, children of faculty/staff, relatives of clergy, religious affiliation, siblings of current students. ***Tuition waivers:*** Full or partial for adult students.

LOANS ***Student loans:*** $6,045,053 (71% need-based, 29% non-need-based). 84% of past graduating class borrowed through all loan programs. *Average indebtedness per student:* $22,923. ***Average need-based loan:*** Freshmen: $3924.

Undergraduates: $4554. ***Parent loans:*** $1,784,535 (36% need-based, 64% non-need-based). ***Programs:*** Federal Direct (Subsidized and Unsubsidized Stafford, PLUS), Perkins, college/university.

WORK-STUDY ***Federal work-study:*** Total amount: $54,468; jobs available (averaging $690). ***State or other work-study/employment:*** Total amount: $306,778 (27% need-based, 73% non-need-based). Part-time jobs available.

ATHLETIC AWARDS Total amount: $2,952,292 (68% need-based, 32% non-need-based).

APPLYING FOR FINANCIAL AID ***Required financial aid forms:*** FAFSA, institution's own form. ***Financial aid deadline:*** 9/1 (priority: 5/1). ***Notification date:*** Continuous beginning 2/15. Students must reply within 2 weeks of notification.

CONTACT Ms. Terri Lynn Graham, Director of Student Financial Aid, Hastings College, 710 North Turner Avenue, Hastings, NE 68901, 402-461-7431 or toll-free 800-532-7642. *Fax:* 402-461-7714. *E-mail:* tgraham@hastings.edu.

HAVERFORD COLLEGE

Haverford, PA

Tuition & fees: $40,624 **Average undergraduate aid package: $37,509**

ABOUT THE INSTITUTION Independent, coed. 44 undergraduate majors. Institutional methodology is used as a basis for awarding need-based institutional aid.

UNDERGRADUATE EXPENSES for 2010–11 ***One-time required fee:*** $200. ***Comprehensive fee:*** $52,970 includes full-time tuition ($40,260), mandatory fees ($364), and room and board ($12,346). ***College room only:*** $7026. ***Payment plans:*** Tuition prepayment, installment.

FRESHMAN FINANCIAL AID (Fall 2010, est.) 196 applied for aid; of those 86% were deemed to have need. 100% of freshmen with need received aid; of those 100% had need fully met. ***Average percent of need met:*** 100% (excluding resources awarded to replace EFC). ***Average financial aid package:*** $36,749 (excluding resources awarded to replace EFC).

UNDERGRADUATE FINANCIAL AID (Fall 2010, est.) 674 applied for aid; of those 91% were deemed to have need. 100% of undergraduates with need received aid; of those 100% had need fully met. ***Average percent of need met:*** 100% (excluding resources awarded to replace EFC). ***Average financial aid package:*** $37,509 (excluding resources awarded to replace EFC).

GIFT AID (NEED-BASED) ***Total amount:*** $20,684,125 (5% federal, 1% state, 92% institutional, 2% external sources). ***Receiving aid:*** Freshmen: 51% (165); all full-time undergraduates: 50% (586). ***Average award:*** Freshmen: $34,673; Undergraduates: $35,416. ***Scholarships, grants, and awards:*** Federal Pell, FSEOG, state, college/university gift aid from institutional funds.

GIFT AID (NON-NEED-BASED) ***Tuition waivers:*** Full or partial for employees or children of employees.

LOANS ***Student loans:*** $1,444,730 (49% need-based, 51% non-need-based). 34% of past graduating class borrowed through all loan programs. *Average indebtedness per student:* $16,238. ***Average need-based loan:*** Freshmen: $788. Undergraduates: $1274. ***Parent loans:*** $1,793,618 (100% non-need-based). ***Programs:*** Federal Direct (Subsidized and Unsubsidized Stafford, PLUS), Perkins.

WORK-STUDY ***Federal work-study:*** Total amount: $284,412; jobs available. ***State or other work-study/employment:*** Total amount: $617,518 (27% need-based, 73% non-need-based). Part-time jobs available.

APPLYING FOR FINANCIAL AID ***Required financial aid forms:*** FAFSA, CSS Financial Aid PROFILE, noncustodial (divorced/separated) parent's statement, business/farm supplement. ***Financial aid deadline:*** 2/1. ***Notification date:*** 4/1. Students must reply by 5/1.

CONTACT Mr. David J. Hoy, Director of Financial Aid, Haverford College, 370 Lancaster Avenue, Haverford, PA 19041-1392, 610-896-1350. *Fax:* 610-896-1338. *E-mail:* finaid@haverford.edu.

HAWAI'I PACIFIC UNIVERSITY

Honolulu, HI

Tuition & fees: $15,820 **Average undergraduate aid package: $17,448**

ABOUT THE INSTITUTION Independent, coed. 66 undergraduate majors. Federal methodology is used as a basis for awarding need-based institutional aid.

UNDERGRADUATE EXPENSES for 2010–11 ***Comprehensive fee:*** $27,468 includes full-time tuition ($15,720), mandatory fees ($100), and room and board ($11,648). Full-time tuition and fees vary according to course level, course load, program, and student level. Room and board charges vary according to housing facility. ***Part-time tuition:*** $330 per credit hour. Part-time tuition and fees vary according to course level, course load, program, and student level. ***Payment plan:*** Installment.

FRESHMAN FINANCIAL AID (Fall 2010, est.) 605 applied for aid; of those 67% were deemed to have need. 100% of freshmen with need received aid; of those 28% had need fully met. ***Average percent of need met:*** 86% (excluding resources awarded to replace EFC). ***Average financial aid package:*** $17,742 (excluding resources awarded to replace EFC). 8% of all full-time freshmen had no need and received non-need-based gift aid.

UNDERGRADUATE FINANCIAL AID (Fall 2010, est.) 3,031 applied for aid; of those 64% were deemed to have need. 99% of undergraduates with need received aid; of those 24% had need fully met. ***Average percent of need met:*** 78% (excluding resources awarded to replace EFC). ***Average financial aid package:*** $17,448 (excluding resources awarded to replace EFC). 5% of all full-time undergraduates had no need and received non-need-based gift aid.

GIFT AID (NEED-BASED) ***Total amount:*** $6,374,624 (92% federal, 3% state, 5% institutional). ***Receiving aid:*** Freshmen: 30% (190); all full-time undergraduates: 28% (1,092). ***Average award:*** Freshmen: $1891; Undergraduates: $2031. ***Scholarships, grants, and awards:*** Federal Pell, FSEOG, state, private, college/university gift aid from institutional funds, Federal Nursing.

GIFT AID (NON-NEED-BASED) ***Total amount:*** $11,810,777 (87% institutional, 13% external sources). ***Receiving aid:*** Freshmen: 5% (34). Undergraduates: 6% (233). ***Average award:*** Freshmen: $3200. Undergraduates: $2153. ***Scholarships, grants, and awards by category:*** *Academic interests/achievement:* biological sciences, business, communication, general academic interests/achievements, health fields, social sciences. *Creative arts/performance:* dance, journalism/publications, music. *Special achievements/activities:* cheerleading/drum major, community service, hobbies/interests, junior miss, leadership, memberships, religious involvement. *Special characteristics:* ethnic background, international students, local/state students, out-of-state students, previous college experience, relatives of clergy, religious affiliation. ***Tuition waivers:*** Full or partial for employees or children of employees.

LOANS ***Student loans:*** $29,961,998 (100% need-based). *Average indebtedness per student:* $32,172. ***Average need-based loan:*** Freshmen: $4552. Undergraduates: $6159. ***Parent loans:*** $6,876,181 (100% need-based). ***Programs:*** Federal Direct (Subsidized and Unsubsidized Stafford, PLUS), Perkins, Federal Nursing.

WORK-STUDY ***Federal work-study:*** Total amount: $327,360; 157 jobs averaging $3000.

ATHLETIC AWARDS Total amount: $1,962,635 (100% non-need-based).

APPLYING FOR FINANCIAL AID ***Required financial aid form:*** FAFSA. ***Financial aid deadline (priority):*** 3/1. ***Notification date:*** Continuous beginning 3/15. Students must reply within 3 weeks of notification.

CONTACT Adam Hatch, Director of Financial Aid, Hawai'i Pacific University, 1164 Bishop Street, Suite 201, Honolulu, HI 96813-2785, 808-544-0253 or toll-free 866-225-5478 (out-of-state). *Fax:* 808-544-0884. *E-mail:* financialaid@hpu.edu.

HEBREW COLLEGE

Newton Centre, MA

Tuition & fees: $22,700 **Average undergraduate aid package: $2900**

ABOUT THE INSTITUTION Independent Jewish, coed. 5 undergraduate majors. Both federal and institutional methodology are used as a basis for awarding need-based institutional aid.

UNDERGRADUATE EXPENSES for 2010–11 ***Tuition:*** full-time $22,500. Full-time tuition and fees vary according to program. Part-time tuition and fees vary according to course load and program. ***Payment plan:*** Installment.

UNDERGRADUATE FINANCIAL AID (Fall 2010, est.) 2 applied for aid; of those 100% were deemed to have need. 100% of undergraduates with need received aid. ***Average percent of need met:*** 40% (excluding resources awarded to replace EFC). ***Average financial aid package:*** $2900 (excluding resources awarded to replace EFC). 100% of all full-time undergraduates had no need and received non-need-based gift aid.

GIFT AID (NEED-BASED) ***Total amount:*** $9099 (48% federal, 52% institutional). ***Receiving aid:*** All full-time undergraduates: 100% (2). ***Average award:*** Undergraduates: $2900. ***Scholarships, grants, and awards:*** Federal Pell, state, private, college/university gift aid from institutional funds.

GIFT AID (NON-NEED-BASED) ***Total amount:*** $3600 (100% institutional). ***Average award:*** Undergraduates: $1200. ***Scholarships, grants, and awards by category:*** *Academic interests/achievement:* education, religion/biblical studies. ***Tuition waivers:*** Full or partial for employees or children of employees.

LOANS ***Student loans:*** $16,700 (100% need-based). 33% of past graduating class borrowed through all loan programs. *Average indebtedness per student:* $8300. ***Programs:*** Federal Direct (Subsidized and Unsubsidized Stafford, PLUS).

CONTACT Marilyn Jaye, Registrar, Hebrew College, 160 Herrick Road, Newton Centre, MA 02459, 617-559-8642 or toll-free 800-866-4814 Ext. 8619. *Fax:* 617-559-8825. *E-mail:* mjaye@hebrewcollege.edu.

HEBREW THEOLOGICAL COLLEGE

Skokie, IL

CONTACT Ms. Rhoda Morris, Financial Aid Administrator, Hebrew Theological College, 7135 Carpenter Road, Skokie, IL 60077-3263, 847-982-2500. *Fax:* 847-674-6381.

HEIDELBERG UNIVERSITY

Tiffin, OH

Tuition & fees: $22,780 **Average undergraduate aid package: $19,020**

ABOUT THE INSTITUTION Independent religious, coed. 48 undergraduate majors. Federal methodology is used as a basis for awarding need-based institutional aid.

UNDERGRADUATE EXPENSES for 2010–11 ***Comprehensive fee:*** $31,416 includes full-time tuition ($22,242), mandatory fees ($538), and room and board ($8636). ***College room only:*** $4088. Full-time tuition and fees vary according to course load, degree level, and location. Room and board charges vary according to housing facility and location. ***Part-time tuition:*** $612 per credit hour. ***Part-time fees:*** $269 per term. Part-time tuition and fees vary according to course load, degree level, and location. ***Payment plan:*** Installment.

FRESHMAN FINANCIAL AID (Fall 2010, est.) 326 applied for aid; of those 92% were deemed to have need. 100% of freshmen with need received aid; of those 9% had need fully met. ***Average percent of need met:*** 78% (excluding resources awarded to replace EFC). ***Average financial aid package:*** $20,526 (excluding resources awarded to replace EFC). 10% of all full-time freshmen had no need and received non-need-based gift aid.

UNDERGRADUATE FINANCIAL AID (Fall 2010, est.) 1,086 applied for aid; of those 92% were deemed to have need. 100% of undergraduates with need received aid; of those 14% had need fully met. ***Average percent of need met:*** 77% (excluding resources awarded to replace EFC). ***Average financial aid package:*** $19,020 (excluding resources awarded to replace EFC). 11% of all full-time undergraduates had no need and received non-need-based gift aid.

GIFT AID (NEED-BASED) ***Total amount:*** $13,390,356 (19% federal, 4% state, 74% institutional, 3% external sources). ***Receiving aid:*** Freshmen: 91% (301); all full-time undergraduates: 85% (996). ***Average award:*** Freshmen: $15,338; Undergraduates: $13,650. ***Scholarships, grants, and awards:*** Federal Pell, FSEOG, state, private, college/university gift aid from institutional funds.

GIFT AID (NON-NEED-BASED) ***Total amount:*** $948,790 (98% institutional, 2% external sources). ***Receiving aid:*** Freshmen: 81% (269). Undergraduates: 70% (818). ***Average award:*** Freshmen: $11,121. Undergraduates: $9200. ***Scholarships, grants, and awards by category:*** *Academic interests/achievement:* 790 awards ($6,552,531 total): general academic interests/achievements. *Creative arts/performance:* 63 awards ($125,700 total): music, performing arts. *Special characteristics:* 248 awards ($1,012,512 total): children of faculty/staff, international students, out-of-state students, relatives of clergy, religious affiliation. ***Tuition waivers:*** Full or partial for employees or children of employees.

LOANS ***Student loans:*** $7,390,056 (96% need-based, 4% non-need-based). 94% of past graduating class borrowed through all loan programs. *Average indebtedness per student:* $35,885. ***Average need-based loan:*** Freshmen: $4244. Undergraduates: $4694. ***Parent loans:*** $2,136,796 (91% need-based, 9% non-need-based). ***Programs:*** Federal Direct (Subsidized and Unsubsidized Stafford, PLUS), Perkins.

WORK-STUDY ***Federal work-study:*** Total amount: $1,226,200; 649 jobs averaging $1870. ***State or other work-study/employment:*** Total amount: $148,029 (70% need-based, 30% non-need-based). 96 part-time jobs averaging $1575.

APPLYING FOR FINANCIAL AID ***Required financial aid form:*** FAFSA. ***Financial aid deadline (priority):*** 3/1. ***Notification date:*** Continuous beginning 3/1. Students must reply by 5/1.

CONTACT Ms. Juli L. Weininger, Director of Financial Aid, Heidelberg University, 310 East Market Street, Tiffin, OH 44883-2462, 419-448-2293 or toll-free 800-434-3352. *Fax:* 419-448-2296.

HELLENIC COLLEGE

Brookline, MA

CONTACT Gregory Floor, Director of Admissions/Financial Aid, Hellenic College, 50 Goddard Avenue, Brookline, MA 02146-7496, 617-731-3500 Ext. 1285 or toll-free 866-424-2338. *Fax:* 617-850-1465. *E-mail:* gfloor@hchc.edu.

HENDERSON STATE UNIVERSITY

Arkadelphia, AR

ABOUT THE INSTITUTION State-supported, coed. 35 undergraduate majors.

GIFT AID (NEED-BASED) ***Scholarships, grants, and awards:*** Federal Pell, FSEOG, state, private, college/university gift aid from institutional funds.

GIFT AID (NON-NEED-BASED) ***Scholarships, grants, and awards by category:*** *Academic interests/achievement:* biological sciences, education, general academic interests/achievements, international studies, mathematics. *Creative arts/performance:* art/fine arts, cinema/film/broadcasting, dance, debating, journalism/publications, music, performing arts, theater/drama. *Special achievements/activities:* cheerleading/drum major, general special achievements/activities, leadership. *Special characteristics:* children and siblings of alumni, children of faculty/staff, international students, out-of-state students.

LOANS ***Programs:*** Perkins.

WORK-STUDY ***Federal work-study:*** Total amount: $159,111; jobs available. ***State or other work-study/employment:*** Total amount: $148,188 (100% non-need-based). Part-time jobs available.

APPLYING FOR FINANCIAL AID ***Required financial aid form:*** FAFSA.

CONTACT Ms. Vicki Taylor, Director of Financial Aid, Henderson State University, 1100 Henderson Street, HSU Box 7812, Arkadelphia, AR 71999-0001, 870-230-5138 or toll-free 800-228-7333. *Fax:* 870-230-5481. *E-mail:* taylorv@hsu.edu.

HENDRIX COLLEGE

Conway, AR

Tuition & fees: $34,230 **Average undergraduate aid package: $24,445**

ABOUT THE INSTITUTION Independent United Methodist, coed. 31 undergraduate majors. Federal methodology is used as a basis for awarding need-based institutional aid.

UNDERGRADUATE EXPENSES for 2011–12 ***Comprehensive fee:*** $43,944 includes full-time tuition ($33,930), mandatory fees ($300), and room and board ($9714). ***College room only:*** $4968. Full-time tuition and fees vary according to course load. Room and board charges vary according to board plan and housing facility. ***Part-time tuition:*** $4279 per course. Part-time tuition and fees vary according to course load. ***Payment plan:*** Installment.

FRESHMAN FINANCIAL AID (Fall 2010, est.) 353 applied for aid; of those 75% were deemed to have need. 100% of freshmen with need received aid; of those 53% had need fully met. ***Average percent of need met:*** 89% (excluding resources awarded to replace EFC). ***Average financial aid package:*** $25,383 (excluding resources awarded to replace EFC). 34% of all full-time freshmen had no need and received non-need-based gift aid.

UNDERGRADUATE FINANCIAL AID (Fall 2010, est.) 1,222 applied for aid; of those 77% were deemed to have need. 100% of undergraduates with need received aid; of those 42% had need fully met. ***Average percent of need met:*** 84% (excluding resources awarded to replace EFC). ***Average financial aid package:*** $24,445 (excluding resources awarded to replace EFC). 35% of all full-time undergraduates had no need and received non-need-based gift aid.

GIFT AID (NEED-BASED) ***Total amount:*** $18,613,458 (8% federal, 9% state, 81% institutional, 2% external sources). ***Receiving aid:*** Freshmen: 66% (266); all full-time undergraduates: 64% (939). ***Average award:*** Freshmen: $22,229; Undergraduates: $20,473. ***Scholarships, grants, and awards:*** Federal Pell, FSEOG, state, private, college/university gift aid from institutional funds.

GIFT AID (NON-NEED-BASED) ***Total amount:*** $12,703,517 (14% state, 84% institutional, 2% external sources). ***Receiving aid:*** Freshmen: 29% (119).

Undergraduates: 20% (298). ***Average award:*** Freshmen: $19,297. Undergraduates: $17,095. ***Scholarships, grants, and awards by category:*** *Academic interests/achievement:* $14,697,183 total: general academic interests/achievements. *Creative arts/performance:* $217,400 total: art/fine arts, dance, music, theater/drama. *Special achievements/activities:* $4,400,875 total: community service, general special achievements/activities, leadership, religious involvement. *Special characteristics:* $1,421,005 total: children of educators, children of faculty/staff, international students, previous college experience, relatives of clergy. ***Tuition waivers:*** Full or partial for employees or children of employees.

LOANS ***Student loans:*** $6,730,964 (55% need-based, 45% non-need-based). 89% of past graduating class borrowed through all loan programs. *Average indebtedness per student:* $21,170. ***Average need-based loan:*** Freshmen: $4332. Undergraduates: $4633. ***Parent loans:*** $3,236,153 (31% need-based, 69% non-need-based). ***Programs:*** Federal Direct (Subsidized and Unsubsidized Stafford, PLUS), Perkins, United Methodist Student Loans.

WORK-STUDY ***Federal work-study:*** Total amount: $804,542; 556 jobs averaging $1400. ***State or other work-study/employment:*** Total amount: $280,115 (11% need-based, 89% non-need-based). 263 part-time jobs averaging $1298.

APPLYING FOR FINANCIAL AID ***Required financial aid forms:*** FAFSA, state aid form. ***Financial aid deadline (priority):*** 2/15. ***Notification date:*** Continuous beginning 2/15. Students must reply by 5/1.

CONTACT Ms. Kristina Burford, Director of Financial Aid, Hendrix College, 1600 Washington Avenue, Conway, AR 72032, 501-450-1368 or toll-free 800-277-9017. *Fax:* 501-450-3871. *E-mail:* burford@hendrix.edu.

HENLEY-PUTNAM UNIVERSITY

San Jose, CA

CONTACT Financial Aid Office, Henley-Putnam University, 25 Metro Drive, Suite 500, San Jose, CA 95110, 408-453-9900 or toll-free 888-852-8746 (out-of-state).

HERITAGE BIBLE COLLEGE

Dunn, NC

CONTACT Mrs. Laurie Minard, Director of Financial Aid, Heritage Bible College, Box 1628, Dunn, NC 28335, 800-297-6351 Ext. 226 or toll-free 800-297-6351 Ext. 230. *Fax:* 910-892-1809. *E-mail:* lminard@heritagebiblecollege.edu.

HERITAGE CHRISTIAN UNIVERSITY

Florence, AL

ABOUT THE INSTITUTION Independent religious, coed, primarily men. 1 undergraduate major.

GIFT AID (NEED-BASED) ***Scholarships, grants, and awards:*** Federal Pell, FSEOG, college/university gift aid from institutional funds.

GIFT AID (NON-NEED-BASED) ***Scholarships, grants, and awards by category:*** *Academic interests/achievement:* general academic interests/achievements. *Special characteristics:* children and siblings of alumni, children of educators, children of faculty/staff, spouses of current students.

WORK-STUDY Federal work-study jobs available.

APPLYING FOR FINANCIAL AID ***Required financial aid forms:*** FAFSA, federal income tax form(s).

CONTACT Mechelle Thompson, Financial Aid Administrator, Heritage Christian University, PO Box HCU, Florence, AL 35630, 800-367-3565 Ext. 224 or toll-free 800-367-3565. *Fax:* 256-766-9289. *E-mail:* mthompson@hcu.edu.

HERITAGE UNIVERSITY

Toppenish, WA

CONTACT Mr. Norberto Espindola, Director of Enrollment Management Services, Heritage University, 3240 Fort Road, Toppenish, WA 98948-9599, 509-865-8500 or toll-free 888-272-6190 (in-state). *Fax:* 509-865-8659. *E-mail:* financial_aid@heritage.edu.

HERZING UNIVERSITY

Birmingham, AL

CONTACT Financial Aid Office, Herzing University, 280 West Valley Avenue, Birmingham, AL 35209, 205-916-2800.

HERZING UNIVERSITY

Winter Park, FL

CONTACT Financial Aid Office, Herzing University, 1595 South Semoran Boulevard, Winter Park, FL 32792, 407-478-0500.

HERZING UNIVERSITY

Atlanta, GA

CONTACT Financial Aid Office, Herzing University, 3393 Peachtree Road, Suite 1003, Atlanta, GA 30326, 404-816-4533 or toll-free 800-573-4533.

HERZING UNIVERSITY

Kenner, LA

CONTACT Financial Aid Office, Herzing University, 2500 Williams Boulevard, Kenner, LA 70062, 504-733-0074.

HERZING UNIVERSITY

Brookfield, WI

CONTACT Financial Aid Office, Herzing University, 555 South Executive Drive, Brookfield, WI 53005, 262-649-1710.

HERZING UNIVERSITY

Kenosha, WI

CONTACT Financial Aid Office, Herzing University, 4006 Washington Road, Kenosha, WI 53144, 866—724-9144.

HERZING UNIVERSITY

Madison, WI

CONTACT Financial Aid Office, Herzing University, 5218 East Terrace Drive, Madison, WI 53718, 608-249-6611 or toll-free 800-582-1227.

HERZING UNIVERSITY ONLINE

Milwaukee, WI

CONTACT Financial Aid Office, Herzing University Online, 525 North 6th Street, Milwaukee, WI 53203, 866-508-0748.

HICKEY COLLEGE

St. Louis, MO

CONTACT Financial Aid Office, Hickey College, 940 West Port Plaza, Suite 101, St. Louis, MO 63146, 314-434-2212 or toll-free 800-777-1544.

HIGH POINT UNIVERSITY

High Point, NC

Comprehensive fee: $35,900 **Average undergraduate aid package: $12,167**

ABOUT THE INSTITUTION Independent United Methodist, coed. 49 undergraduate majors. Institutional methodology is used as a basis for awarding need-based institutional aid.

UNDERGRADUATE EXPENSES for 2010–11 ***Comprehensive fee:*** $35,900. Full-time tuition and fees vary according to class time, course load, and reciprocity agreements. Room and board charges vary according to board plan, housing facility, and location. ***Part-time tuition:*** $700 per credit hour. Part-time tuition and fees vary according to class time, course load, and reciprocity agreements. ***Payment plan:*** Installment.

FRESHMAN FINANCIAL AID (Fall 2010, est.) 836 applied for aid; of those 76% were deemed to have need. 100% of freshmen with need received aid; of those 14% had need fully met. ***Average percent of need met:*** 51% (excluding resources awarded to replace EFC). ***Average financial aid package:*** $12,602 (excluding resources awarded to replace EFC). 17% of all full-time freshmen had no need and received non-need-based gift aid.

UNDERGRADUATE FINANCIAL AID (Fall 2010, est.) 2,640 applied for aid; of those 84% were deemed to have need. 94% of undergraduates with need received aid; of those 9% had need fully met. ***Average percent of need met:*** 44% (excluding resources awarded to replace EFC). ***Average financial aid package:*** $12,167 (excluding resources awarded to replace EFC). 5% of all full-time undergraduates had no need and received non-need-based gift aid.

GIFT AID (NEED-BASED) ***Total amount:*** $7,905,429 (45% federal, 21% state, 34% institutional). ***Receiving aid:*** Freshmen: 45% (548); all full-time undergraduates: 48% (1,729). ***Average award:*** Freshmen: $4404; Undergraduates: $4568. ***Scholarships, grants, and awards:*** Federal Pell, FSEOG, state, private, college/university gift aid from institutional funds.

GIFT AID (NON-NEED-BASED) ***Total amount:*** $13,899,761 (5% federal, 13% state, 63% institutional, 19% external sources). ***Receiving aid:*** Freshmen: 39% (476). Undergraduates: 45% (1,626). ***Average award:*** Freshmen: $3122. Undergraduates: $6131. ***Scholarships, grants, and awards by category:*** *Academic interests/achievement:* biological sciences, business, education, English, foreign languages, general academic interests/achievements, humanities, international studies, mathematics, physical sciences, premedicine, religion/biblical studies. *Creative arts/performance:* art/fine arts, music. *Special achievements/activities:* general special achievements/activities. *Special characteristics:* relatives of clergy. ***Tuition waivers:*** Full or partial for employees or children of employees.

LOANS ***Student loans:*** $20,117,471 (37% need-based, 63% non-need-based). 67% of past graduating class borrowed through all loan programs. *Average indebtedness per student:* $9117. ***Average need-based loan:*** Freshmen: $2923. Undergraduates: $3454. ***Parent loans:*** $11,180,142 (100% non-need-based). ***Programs:*** Federal Direct (Subsidized and Unsubsidized Stafford, PLUS), Perkins.

WORK-STUDY ***Federal work-study:*** Total amount: $721,150; 534 jobs averaging $1350. ***State or other work-study/employment:*** Part-time jobs available.

ATHLETIC AWARDS Total amount: $3,115,605 (100% non-need-based).

APPLYING FOR FINANCIAL AID ***Required financial aid forms:*** FAFSA, state aid form. ***Financial aid deadline (priority):*** 3/1. ***Notification date:*** Continuous. Students must reply within 3 weeks of notification.

CONTACT Ms. Kay Stroud, Director of Student Financial Planning, High Point University, Box 3232, University Station, 833 Montlieu Avenue, High Point, NC 27262, 336-841-9128 or toll-free 800-345-6993. *Fax:* 336-884-0221. *E-mail:* kstroud@highpoint.edu.

HILBERT COLLEGE

Hamburg, NY

CONTACT Beverly Chudy, Director of Financial Aid, Hilbert College, 5200 South Park Avenue, Hamburg, NY 14075-1597, 716-649-7900 Ext. 207. *Fax:* 716-649-1152. *E-mail:* bchudy@hilbert.edu.

HILLSDALE COLLEGE

Hillsdale, MI

Tuition & fees: $20,500 **Average undergraduate aid package: $16,760**

ABOUT THE INSTITUTION Independent, coed. 42 undergraduate majors. Both federal and institutional methodology are used as a basis for awarding need-based institutional aid.

UNDERGRADUATE EXPENSES for 2011–12 ***Comprehensive fee:*** $28,490 includes full-time tuition ($19,960), mandatory fees ($540), and room and board ($7990). ***College room only:*** $3970. Room and board charges vary according to board plan. ***Part-time tuition:*** $785 per credit. ***Payment plans:*** Tuition prepayment, installment.

FRESHMAN FINANCIAL AID (Fall 2009) 221 applied for aid; of those 89% were deemed to have need. 92% of freshmen with need received aid; of those 38% had need fully met. ***Average percent of need met:*** 62% (excluding resources awarded to replace EFC). ***Average financial aid package:*** $12,610 (excluding resources awarded to replace EFC). 47% of all full-time freshmen had no need and received non-need-based gift aid.

UNDERGRADUATE FINANCIAL AID (Fall 2009) 672 applied for aid; of those 89% were deemed to have need. 93% of undergraduates with need received aid; of those 42% had need fully met. ***Average percent of need met:*** 72% (excluding resources awarded to replace EFC). ***Average financial aid package:*** $16,760 (excluding resources awarded to replace EFC). 47% of all full-time undergraduates had no need and received non-need-based gift aid.

GIFT AID (NEED-BASED) ***Total amount:*** $2,968,620 (100% institutional). ***Receiving aid:*** Freshmen: 27% (113); all full-time undergraduates: 28% (379). ***Average award:*** Freshmen: $7290; Undergraduates: $7350. ***Scholarships, grants, and awards:*** private, college/university gift aid from institutional funds.

GIFT AID (NON-NEED-BASED) ***Total amount:*** $10,606,692 (93% institutional, 7% external sources). ***Receiving aid:*** Freshmen: 35% (144). Undergraduates: 36% (495). ***Average award:*** Freshmen: $8680. Undergraduates: $9740. ***Scholarships, grants, and awards by category:*** *Academic interests/achievement:* 641 awards ($297,000 total): biological sciences, business, education, English, foreign languages, general academic interests/achievements, health fields, humanities, international studies, mathematics, physical sciences, premedicine, religion/biblical studies, social sciences. *Creative arts/performance:* 50 awards ($120,000 total): art/fine arts, debating, journalism/publications, music, theater/drama. *Special achievements/activities:* 230 awards ($1,500,000 total): community service, general special achievements/activities, leadership. *Special characteristics:* 65 awards ($890,000 total): children of faculty/staff, international students. ***Tuition waivers:*** Full or partial for children of alumni, employees or children of employees.

LOANS ***Student loans:*** $5,272,951 (39% need-based, 61% non-need-based). 65% of past graduating class borrowed through all loan programs. *Average indebtedness per student:* $16,500. ***Average need-based loan:*** Freshmen: $5300. Undergraduates: $5900. ***Programs:*** college/university, alternative loans.

ATHLETIC AWARDS Total amount: $2,482,495 (100% non-need-based).

APPLYING FOR FINANCIAL AID ***Required financial aid forms:*** institution's own form, noncustodial (divorced/separated) parent's statement, business/farm supplement. ***Financial aid deadline:*** 4/1 (priority: 2/1). ***Notification date:*** Continuous beginning 1/20. Students must reply by 5/1 or within 3 weeks of notification.

CONTACT Mr. Rich Moeggengberg, Director of Student Financial Aid, Hillsdale College, 33 East College Street, Hillsdale, MI 49242-1298, 517-607-2550. *Fax:* 517-607-2298. *E-mail:* rich.moeggenbeng@hillsdale.edu.

HILLSDALE FREE WILL BAPTIST COLLEGE

Moore, OK

Tuition & fees: $10,020 **Average undergraduate aid package: $9253**

ABOUT THE INSTITUTION Independent Free Will Baptist, coed. 22 undergraduate majors. Both federal and institutional methodology are used as a basis for awarding need-based institutional aid.

UNDERGRADUATE EXPENSES for 2010–11 ***One-time required fee:*** $150. ***Comprehensive fee:*** $15,520 includes full-time tuition ($8400), mandatory fees ($1620), and room and board ($5500). ***College room only:*** $2300. Full-time tuition and fees vary according to course load. Room and board charges vary according to board plan and housing facility. ***Part-time tuition:*** $350 per credit hour. ***Part-time fees:*** $26 per credit hour; $220 per term. Part-time tuition and fees vary according to course load. ***Payment plan:*** Installment.

FRESHMAN FINANCIAL AID (Fall 2009) 67 applied for aid; of those 85% were deemed to have need. 96% of freshmen with need received aid; of those 13% had need fully met. ***Average percent of need met:*** 40% (excluding resources awarded to replace EFC). ***Average financial aid package:*** $8510 (excluding resources awarded to replace EFC). 29% of all full-time freshmen had no need and received non-need-based gift aid.

UNDERGRADUATE FINANCIAL AID (Fall 2009) 172 applied for aid; of those 83% were deemed to have need. 99% of undergraduates with need received aid; of those 13% had need fully met. ***Average percent of need met:*** 49% (excluding resources awarded to replace EFC). ***Average financial aid package:*** $9253 (excluding resources awarded to replace EFC). 33% of all full-time undergraduates had no need and received non-need-based gift aid.

GIFT AID (NEED-BASED) ***Total amount:*** $480,981 (63% federal, 27% state, 10% institutional). ***Receiving aid:*** Freshmen: 50% (40); all full-time undergraduates: 51% (109). ***Average award:*** Freshmen: $3257; Undergraduates: $3821. ***Scholarships, grants, and awards:*** Federal Pell, state, private, college/university gift aid from institutional funds, Bureau of Indian Affairs Grants.

GIFT AID (NON-NEED-BASED) ***Total amount:*** $503,530 (2% federal, 11% state, 65% institutional, 22% external sources). ***Receiving aid:*** Freshmen: 56% (45). Undergraduates: 49% (105). ***Average award:*** Freshmen: $3119. Undergraduates: $3113. ***Scholarships, grants, and awards by category:*** *Academic interests/achievement:* 86 awards ($226,050 total): business, education, English, general academic interests/achievements, mathematics, religion/biblical studies. *Creative arts/performance:* 1 award ($1000 total): music, performing arts, theater/drama. *Special achievements/activities:* 13 awards ($8150 total): community service, religious involvement. *Special characteristics:* 95 awards ($80,744 total): adult students, children and siblings of alumni, children of educators, children of faculty/staff, general special characteristics, relatives of clergy, religious affiliation, siblings of current students, spouses of current students. ***Tuition waivers:*** Full or partial for children of alumni, employees or children of employees, senior citizens.

LOANS ***Student loans:*** $1,003,027 (47% need-based, 53% non-need-based). 85% of past graduating class borrowed through all loan programs. *Average indebtedness per student:* $23,822. ***Average need-based loan:*** Freshmen: $2949. Undergraduates: $3017. ***Parent loans:*** $16,700 (100% non-need-based). ***Programs:*** Federal Direct (Subsidized and Unsubsidized Stafford, PLUS), Perkins.

WORK-STUDY ***Federal work-study:*** Total amount: $47,713; 48 jobs averaging $994.

APPLYING FOR FINANCIAL AID ***Required financial aid forms:*** FAFSA, institution's own form. ***Financial aid deadline (priority):*** 6/30. ***Notification date:*** Continuous beginning 4/1. Students must reply within 2 weeks of notification.

CONTACT Denise Conklin, Director of Financial Aid, Hillsdale Free Will Baptist College, PO Box 7208, Moore, OK 73153-1208, 405-912-9012. *Fax:* 405-912-9050. *E-mail:* dconklin@hc.edu.

HIRAM COLLEGE

Hiram, OH

CONTACT Ann Marie Gruber, Associate Director of Financial Aid, Hiram College, Box 67, Hiram, OH 44234-0067, 330-569-5107 or toll-free 800-362-5280. *Fax:* 330-569-5499.

HOBART AND WILLIAM SMITH COLLEGES

Geneva, NY

Tuition & fees: $41,710 **Average undergraduate aid package: $29,446**

ABOUT THE INSTITUTION Independent, coed. 47 undergraduate majors. Both federal and institutional methodology are used as a basis for awarding need-based institutional aid.

UNDERGRADUATE EXPENSES for 2010–11 ***Comprehensive fee:*** $52,258 includes full-time tuition ($40,592), mandatory fees ($1118), and room and board ($10,548). Room and board charges vary according to board plan. ***Payment plans:*** Tuition prepayment, installment.

FRESHMAN FINANCIAL AID (Fall 2009) 435 applied for aid; of those 81% were deemed to have need. 99% of freshmen with need received aid; of those 97% had need fully met. ***Average percent of need met:*** 87% (excluding resources awarded to replace EFC). ***Average financial aid package:*** $31,015 (excluding resources awarded to replace EFC). 24% of all full-time freshmen had no need and received non-need-based gift aid.

UNDERGRADUATE FINANCIAL AID (Fall 2009) 1,581 applied for aid; of those 84% were deemed to have need. 98% of undergraduates with need received aid; of those 85% had need fully met. ***Average percent of need met:*** 78% (excluding resources awarded to replace EFC). ***Average financial aid package:*** $29,446 (excluding resources awarded to replace EFC). 22% of all full-time undergraduates had no need and received non-need-based gift aid.

GIFT AID (NEED-BASED) ***Total amount:*** $32,376,565 (7% federal, 5% state, 83% institutional, 5% external sources). ***Receiving aid:*** Freshmen: 73% (348); all full-time undergraduates: 72% (1,295). ***Average award:*** Freshmen: $27,412; Undergraduates: $25,001. ***Scholarships, grants, and awards:*** Federal Pell, FSEOG, state, private, college/university gift aid from institutional funds, Academic Competitiveness Grants, National SMART Grants.

GIFT AID (NON-NEED-BASED) ***Total amount:*** $7,512,309 (89% institutional, 11% external sources). ***Receiving aid:*** Freshmen: 10% (48). Undergraduates: 10% (181). ***Average award:*** Freshmen: $15,029. Undergraduates: $14,182. ***Scholarships, grants, and awards by category:*** *Academic interests/achievement:* 114 awards ($1,687,340 total): general academic interests/achievements. *Creative arts/performance:* 11 awards ($97,000 total): art/fine arts, creative writing, dance, music, performing arts. *Special achievements/activities:* 47 awards ($534,000 total): leadership. ***Tuition waivers:*** Full or partial for employees or children of employees.

LOANS ***Student loans:*** $11,082,248 (65% need-based, 35% non-need-based). 82% of past graduating class borrowed through all loan programs. *Average indebtedness per student:* $29,932. ***Average need-based loan:*** Freshmen: $3355. Undergraduates: $4211. ***Parent loans:*** $4,966,614 (33% need-based, 67% non-need-based). ***Programs:*** Federal Direct (Subsidized and Unsubsidized Stafford, PLUS), Perkins.

WORK-STUDY ***Federal work-study:*** Total amount: $1,136,317; 901 jobs averaging $1752. ***State or other work-study/employment:*** Total amount: $1,059,155 (14% need-based, 86% non-need-based). 423 part-time jobs averaging $1896.

APPLYING FOR FINANCIAL AID ***Required financial aid forms:*** FAFSA, CSS Financial Aid PROFILE, state aid form, noncustodial (divorced/separated) parent's statement, federal income tax form(s). ***Financial aid deadline:*** 3/15 (priority: 2/15). ***Notification date:*** 4/1. Students must reply by 5/1.

CONTACT Beth Nepa, Director of Financial Aid, Hobart and William Smith Colleges, Demarest Hall, 300 Pulteney Street, Geneva, NY 14456-3397, 315-781-3315 or toll-free 800-245-0100. *Fax:* 315-781-4048. *E-mail:* finaid@hws.edu.

HOBE SOUND BIBLE COLLEGE

Hobe Sound, FL

CONTACT Director of Financial Aid, Hobe Sound Bible College, PO Box 1065, Hobe Sound, FL 33475-1065, 561-546-5534 or toll-free 800-930-4722. *Fax:* 561-545-1422.

HODGES UNIVERSITY

Naples, FL

Tuition & fees: $16,940 **Average undergraduate aid package: $9275**

ABOUT THE INSTITUTION Independent, coed. 8 undergraduate majors. Federal methodology is used as a basis for awarding need-based institutional aid.

UNDERGRADUATE EXPENSES for 2010–11 ***Tuition:*** full-time $16,560; part-time $460 per semester hour. ***Payment plan:*** Installment.

FRESHMAN FINANCIAL AID (Fall 2010, est.) 170 applied for aid; of those 89% were deemed to have need. 100% of freshmen with need received aid; of those 23% had need fully met. ***Average percent of need met:*** 67% (excluding resources awarded to replace EFC). ***Average financial aid package:*** $8250 (excluding resources awarded to replace EFC). 18% of all full-time freshmen had no need and received non-need-based gift aid.

UNDERGRADUATE FINANCIAL AID (Fall 2010, est.) 1,558 applied for aid; of those 90% were deemed to have need. 100% of undergraduates with need received aid; of those 20% had need fully met. ***Average percent of need met:*** 76% (excluding resources awarded to replace EFC). ***Average financial aid package:*** $9275 (excluding resources awarded to replace EFC). 4% of all full-time undergraduates had no need and received non-need-based gift aid.

GIFT AID (NEED-BASED) ***Total amount:*** $11,810,672 (98% federal, 2% state). ***Receiving aid:*** Freshmen: 73% (133); all full-time undergraduates: 76% (1,306). ***Average award:*** Freshmen: $2750; Undergraduates: $4625. ***Scholarships, grants, and awards:*** Federal Pell, FSEOG, state, private, college/university gift aid from institutional funds.

GIFT AID (NON-NEED-BASED) ***Total amount:*** $6,051,378 (63% state, 36% institutional, 1% external sources). ***Receiving aid:*** Freshmen: 35% (64). Undergraduates: 55% (949). ***Average award:*** Freshmen: $365. Undergraduates: $220. ***Scholarships, grants, and awards by category:*** *Special achievements/activities:* general special achievements/activities. ***Tuition waivers:*** Full or partial for employees or children of employees.

LOANS ***Student loans:*** $19,800,000 (50% need-based, 50% non-need-based). 83% of past graduating class borrowed through all loan programs. *Average indebtedness per student:* $18,900. ***Average need-based loan:*** Freshmen: $2775. Undergraduates: $4310. ***Parent loans:*** $136,451 (100% need-based).

WORK-STUDY ***Federal work-study:*** Total amount: $196,549; 50 jobs averaging $3931.

APPLYING FOR FINANCIAL AID ***Required financial aid form:*** FAFSA. ***Financial aid deadline:*** Continuous. ***Notification date:*** Continuous.

CONTACT Mr. Joe Gilchrist, Vice President of Student Financial Assistance, Hodges University, 2655 Northbrooke Drive, Naples, FL 34119, 239-598-6116 or toll-free 800-466-8017. *Fax:* 239-598-6257. *E-mail:* jgilchrist@hodges.edu.

HOFSTRA UNIVERSITY

Hempstead, NY

Tuition & fees: $31,800 **Average undergraduate aid package: $20,000**

ABOUT THE INSTITUTION Independent, coed. 124 undergraduate majors. Federal methodology is used as a basis for awarding need-based institutional aid.

UNDERGRADUATE EXPENSES for 2010–11 ***Comprehensive fee:*** $43,510 includes full-time tuition ($30,750), mandatory fees ($1050), and room and board ($11,710). ***College room only:*** $7830. Full-time tuition and fees vary according to course load and program. Room and board charges vary according to board plan and housing facility. ***Part-time tuition:*** $940 per term. ***Part-time fees:*** $155 per term. Part-time tuition and fees vary according to course load and program. ***Payment plans:*** Installment, deferred payment.

FRESHMAN FINANCIAL AID (Fall 2010, est.) 1,232 applied for aid; of those 82% were deemed to have need. 100% of freshmen with need received aid; of those 17% had need fully met. ***Average percent of need met:*** 64% (excluding resources awarded to replace EFC). ***Average financial aid package:*** $23,000 (excluding resources awarded to replace EFC). 22% of all full-time freshmen had no need and received non-need-based gift aid.

UNDERGRADUATE FINANCIAL AID (Fall 2010, est.) 5,150 applied for aid; of those 84% were deemed to have need. 99% of undergraduates with need received aid; of those 18% had need fully met. ***Average percent of need met:*** 58% (excluding resources awarded to replace EFC). ***Average financial aid package:*** $20,000 (excluding resources awarded to replace EFC). 20% of all full-time undergraduates had no need and received non-need-based gift aid.

GIFT AID (NEED-BASED) ***Total amount:*** $47,650,000 (17% federal, 9% state, 72% institutional, 2% external sources). ***Receiving aid:*** Freshmen: 65% (947); all full-time undergraduates: 56% (3,797). ***Average award:*** Freshmen: $16,000; Undergraduates: $12,000. ***Scholarships, grants, and awards:*** Federal Pell, FSEOG, state, private, college/university gift aid from institutional funds, Academic Competitiveness Grants, National SMART Grants.

GIFT AID (NON-NEED-BASED) ***Total amount:*** $17,020,000 (2% federal, 1% state, 94% institutional, 3% external sources). ***Receiving aid:*** Freshmen: 6% (89). Undergraduates: 5% (341). ***Average award:*** Freshmen: $9000. Undergraduates: $10,000. ***Scholarships, grants, and awards by category:*** *Academic interests/achievement:* 5,255 awards ($40,680,973 total): communication, general academic interests/achievements. *Creative arts/performance:* 251 awards ($551,293 total): art/fine arts, cinema/film/broadcasting, dance, journalism/publications, music, theater/drama. *Special achievements/activities:* 241 awards ($6,818,635 total): general special achievements/activities, leadership. *Special characteristics:* 363 awards ($6,680,604 total): children and siblings of alumni, children of union members/company employees, general special characteristics, handicapped students, public servants, veterans. ***Tuition waivers:*** Full or partial for employees or children of employees, senior citizens.

LOANS ***Student loans:*** $52,500,000 (70% need-based, 30% non-need-based). 68% of past graduating class borrowed through all loan programs. ***Average need-based loan:*** Freshmen: $3000. Undergraduates: $5000. ***Parent loans:*** $34,000,000 (46% need-based, 54% non-need-based). ***Programs:*** Federal Direct (Subsidized and Unsubsidized Stafford, PLUS), Perkins, state, college/university.

WORK-STUDY ***Federal work-study:*** Total amount: $3,300,000; 1,095 jobs averaging $3009. ***State or other work-study/employment:*** Total amount: $4,700,000 (30% need-based, 70% non-need-based). 1,641 part-time jobs averaging $2840.

ATHLETIC AWARDS Total amount: $6,800,000 (56% need-based, 44% non-need-based).

APPLYING FOR FINANCIAL AID ***Required financial aid forms:*** FAFSA, state aid form. ***Financial aid deadline (priority):*** 2/15. ***Notification date:*** Continuous beginning 3/1. Students must reply by 5/1 or within 2 weeks of notification.

CONTACT Sandra Filbry, Director of Financial Aid Operations and Compliance, Hofstra University, 126 Hofstra University, Hempstead, NY 11549, 516-463-4335 or toll-free 800-HOFSTRA. *Fax:* 516-463-4936. *E-mail:* sandra.a.filbry@hofstra.edu.

HOLLINS UNIVERSITY

Roanoke, VA

Tuition & fees: $29,485 **Average undergraduate aid package: $22,803**

ABOUT THE INSTITUTION Independent, undergraduate: women only; graduate: coed. 27 undergraduate majors. Federal methodology is used as a basis for awarding need-based institutional aid.

UNDERGRADUATE EXPENSES for 2010–11 ***Comprehensive fee:*** $39,685 includes full-time tuition ($28,910), mandatory fees ($575), and room and board ($10,200). ***College room only:*** $6050. ***Part-time tuition:*** $903 per credit hour. ***Part-time fees:*** $146.25 per term. ***Payment plans:*** Tuition prepayment, installment.

FRESHMAN FINANCIAL AID (Fall 2010, est.) 176 applied for aid; of those 91% were deemed to have need. 100% of freshmen with need received aid; of those 16% had need fully met. ***Average percent of need met:*** 85% (excluding resources awarded to replace EFC). ***Average financial aid package:*** $24,002 (excluding resources awarded to replace EFC). 17% of all full-time freshmen had no need and received non-need-based gift aid.

UNDERGRADUATE FINANCIAL AID (Fall 2010, est.) 662 applied for aid; of those 92% were deemed to have need. 100% of undergraduates with need received aid; of those 14% had need fully met. ***Average percent of need met:*** 81% (excluding resources awarded to replace EFC). ***Average financial aid package:*** $22,803 (excluding resources awarded to replace EFC). 16% of all full-time undergraduates had no need and received non-need-based gift aid.

GIFT AID (NEED-BASED) ***Total amount:*** $9,333,218 (17% federal, 8% state, 74% institutional, 1% external sources). ***Receiving aid:*** Freshmen: 77% (153); all full-time undergraduates: 80% (590). ***Average award:*** Freshmen: $19,644; Undergraduates: $17,890. ***Scholarships, grants, and awards:*** Federal Pell, FSEOG, state, private, college/university gift aid from institutional funds.

GIFT AID (NON-NEED-BASED) ***Total amount:*** $3,690,237 (6% state, 93% institutional, 1% external sources). ***Receiving aid:*** Freshmen: 67% (134). Undergraduates: 40% (292). ***Average award:*** Freshmen: $16,445. Undergraduates: $15,435. ***Scholarships, grants, and awards by category:*** *Academic interests/achievement:* 352 awards ($4,368,353 total): general academic interests/achievements. *Creative arts/performance:* 194 awards ($932,261 total): art/fine arts, creative writing, dance, music. *Special achievements/activities:* 78 awards ($441,622 total): community service, general special achievements/activities, hobbies/interests, leadership. *Special characteristics:* 310 awards ($1,386,150 total): adult students, children and siblings of alumni, children of faculty/staff, international students, local/state students, out-of-state students, previous college experience, veterans. ***Tuition waivers:*** Full or partial for employees or children of employees.

LOANS ***Student loans:*** $4,869,129 (89% need-based, 11% non-need-based). 80% of past graduating class borrowed through all loan programs. *Average indebtedness per student:* $19,982. ***Average need-based loan:*** Freshmen: $4654. Undergraduates: $5164. ***Parent loans:*** $1,885,901 (78% need-based, 22% non-need-based). ***Programs:*** Federal Direct (Subsidized and Unsubsidized Stafford, PLUS), Perkins, college/university, alternative loans.

WORK-STUDY ***Federal work-study:*** Total amount: $852,380; 327 jobs averaging $2347. ***State or other work-study/employment:*** Total amount: $239,200 (24% need-based, 76% non-need-based). 96 part-time jobs averaging $2421.

APPLYING FOR FINANCIAL AID ***Required financial aid forms:*** FAFSA, state aid form. ***Financial aid deadline:*** 2/15 (priority: 2/1). ***Notification date:*** Continuous beginning 3/1. Students must reply by 5/1.

CONTACT Ms. MaryJean Corriss, Director of Scholarships and Financial Assistance, Hollins University, PO Box 9718, Roanoke, VA 24020-1688, 540-362-6332 or toll-free 800-456-9595. *Fax:* 540-362-6093. *E-mail:* corrissmj@hollins.edu.

HOLY CROSS COLLEGE

Notre Dame, IN

ABOUT THE INSTITUTION Independent Roman Catholic, coed. 16 undergraduate majors.

GIFT AID (NEED-BASED) ***Scholarships, grants, and awards:*** Federal Pell, FSEOG, state, private, college/university gift aid from institutional funds.

LOANS ***Programs:*** Perkins, alternative loans.

APPLYING FOR FINANCIAL AID ***Required financial aid form:*** FAFSA.

CONTACT Robert Benjamin, Director of Financial Aid, Holy Cross College, PO Box 308, Notre Dame, IN 46556, 574-239-8362. *E-mail:* rbenjamin@hcc-nd.edu.

HOLY FAMILY UNIVERSITY

Philadelphia, PA

ABOUT THE INSTITUTION Independent Roman Catholic, coed. 43 undergraduate majors.

GIFT AID (NEED-BASED) ***Scholarships, grants, and awards:*** Federal Pell, FSEOG, state, private, college/university gift aid from institutional funds.

GIFT AID (NON-NEED-BASED) ***Scholarships, grants, and awards by category:*** *Academic interests/achievement:* general academic interests/achievements.

LOANS ***Programs:*** Perkins, Federal Nursing.

WORK-STUDY ***Federal work-study:*** Total amount: $492,125; 324 jobs averaging $1518.

APPLYING FOR FINANCIAL AID ***Required financial aid form:*** FAFSA.

CONTACT Financial Aid Office, Holy Family University, 9801 Frankford Avenue, Philadelphia, PA 19114-2094, 215-637-7700 Ext. 3233 or toll-free 800-637-1191. *Fax:* 215-599-1694. *E-mail:* finaid@holyfamily.edu.

HOLY NAMES UNIVERSITY

Oakland, CA

CONTACT Christina Miller, Director of Financial Aid, Holy Names University, 3500 Mountain Boulevard, Oakland, CA 94619-1699, 510-436-1327 or toll-free 800-430-1321. *Fax:* 510-436-1199. *E-mail:* miller@hnu.edu.

HOOD COLLEGE

Frederick, MD

Tuition & fees: $29,860 **Average undergraduate aid package: $23,553**

ABOUT THE INSTITUTION Independent, coed. 31 undergraduate majors. Federal methodology is used as a basis for awarding need-based institutional aid.

UNDERGRADUATE EXPENSES for 2010–11 ***Comprehensive fee:*** $39,761 includes full-time tuition ($29,440), mandatory fees ($420), and room and board ($9901). ***College room only:*** $5171. Room and board charges vary according to board plan. ***Part-time tuition:*** $850 per credit hour. ***Part-time fees:*** $140 per term. ***Payment plan:*** Installment.

FRESHMAN FINANCIAL AID (Fall 2010, est.) 312 applied for aid; of those 92% were deemed to have need. 100% of freshmen with need received aid; of those 23% had need fully met. ***Average percent of need met:*** 69% (excluding resources awarded to replace EFC). ***Average financial aid package:*** $23,471 (excluding resources awarded to replace EFC). 11% of all full-time freshmen had no need and received non-need-based gift aid.

UNDERGRADUATE FINANCIAL AID (Fall 2010, est.) 1,272 applied for aid; of those 93% were deemed to have need. 99% of undergraduates with need received aid; of those 19% had need fully met. ***Average percent of need met:*** 76% (excluding resources awarded to replace EFC). ***Average financial aid package:*** $23,553 (excluding resources awarded to replace EFC). 10% of all full-time undergraduates had no need and received non-need-based gift aid.

GIFT AID (NEED-BASED) ***Total amount:*** $23,304,668 (12% federal, 6% state, 78% institutional, 4% external sources). ***Receiving aid:*** Freshmen: 87% (286); all full-time undergraduates: 89% (1,173). ***Average award:*** Freshmen: $21,283; Undergraduates: $20,186. ***Scholarships, grants, and awards:*** Federal Pell, FSEOG, state, private, college/university gift aid from institutional funds.

GIFT AID (NON-NEED-BASED) ***Total amount:*** $3,265,970 (3% federal, 1% state, 79% institutional, 17% external sources). ***Receiving aid:*** Freshmen: 15% (50). Undergraduates: 12% (157). ***Average award:*** Freshmen: $15,180. Undergraduates: $13,967. ***Scholarships, grants, and awards by category:*** *Academic interests/achievement:* general academic interests/achievements. *Creative arts/performance:* creative writing. *Special characteristics:* children and siblings of alumni, children of faculty/staff, international students, siblings of current students. ***Tuition waivers:*** Full or partial for employees or children of employees, senior citizens.

LOANS ***Student loans:*** $8,314,434 (75% need-based, 25% non-need-based). 67% of past graduating class borrowed through all loan programs. *Average indebtedness per student:* $17,144. ***Average need-based loan:*** Freshmen: $3144. Undergraduates: $4195. ***Parent loans:*** $3,088,572 (30% need-based, 70% non-need-based). ***Programs:*** Federal Direct (Subsidized and Unsubsidized Stafford, PLUS), Perkins.

WORK-STUDY ***Federal work-study:*** Total amount: $358,968; jobs available. ***State or other work-study/employment:*** Total amount: $108,800 (7% need-based, 93% non-need-based). Part-time jobs available.

APPLYING FOR FINANCIAL AID ***Required financial aid form:*** FAFSA. ***Financial aid deadline (priority):*** 2/15. ***Notification date:*** Continuous beginning 3/1. Students must reply by 5/1 or within 3 weeks of notification.

CONTACT Ms. Carol A. Schroyer, Director of Financial Aid, Hood College, 401 Rosemont Avenue, Frederick, MD 21701-8575, 301-696-3411 or toll-free 800-922-1599. *Fax:* 301-696-3812. *E-mail:* schroyer@hood.edu.

HOPE COLLEGE

Holland, MI

Tuition & fees: $27,020 **Average undergraduate aid package: $22,917**

ABOUT THE INSTITUTION Independent religious, coed. 61 undergraduate majors. Federal methodology is used as a basis for awarding need-based institutional aid.

UNDERGRADUATE EXPENSES for 2011–12 ***Comprehensive fee:*** $35,280 includes full-time tuition ($26,860), mandatory fees ($160), and room and board ($8260). ***College room only:*** $3780. Room and board charges vary according to board plan. Part-time tuition and fees vary according to course load. ***Payment plan:*** Installment.

FRESHMAN FINANCIAL AID (Fall 2010, est.) 650 applied for aid; of those 76% were deemed to have need. 99% of freshmen with need received aid; of those 33% had need fully met. ***Average percent of need met:*** 82% (excluding resources awarded to replace EFC). ***Average financial aid package:*** $23,271 (excluding resources awarded to replace EFC). 27% of all full-time freshmen had no need and received non-need-based gift aid.

UNDERGRADUATE FINANCIAL AID (Fall 2010, est.) 2,273 applied for aid; of those 83% were deemed to have need. 99% of undergraduates with need received aid; of those 32% had need fully met. ***Average percent of need met:*** 82% (excluding resources awarded to replace EFC). ***Average financial aid package:*** $22,917 (excluding resources awarded to replace EFC). 25% of all full-time undergraduates had no need and received non-need-based gift aid.

GIFT AID (NEED-BASED) ***Total amount:*** $24,606,191 (13% federal, 8% state, 79% institutional). ***Receiving aid:*** Freshmen: 53% (408); all full-time undergraduates: 54% (1,614). ***Average award:*** Freshmen: $18,542; Undergraduates: $17,436. ***Scholarships, grants, and awards:*** Federal Pell, FSEOG, state, private, college/university gift aid from institutional funds.

GIFT AID (NON-NEED-BASED) ***Total amount:*** $9,676,415 (6% federal, 83% institutional, 11% external sources). ***Receiving aid:*** Freshmen: 49% (373). Undergraduates: 41% (1,245). ***Average award:*** Freshmen: $7009. Undergraduates: $7664. ***Scholarships, grants, and awards by category:*** *Academic interests/achievement:* 1,917 awards ($12,285,907 total): general academic interests/achievements. *Creative arts/performance:* 163 awards ($434,302 total): art/fine arts, creative writing, dance, music, theater/drama. *Special characteristics:* 87 awards ($1,548,860 total): ethnic background. ***Tuition waivers:*** Full or partial for employees or children of employees.

LOANS ***Student loans:*** $14,744,651 (48% need-based, 52% non-need-based). 65% of past graduating class borrowed through all loan programs. *Average indebtedness per student:* $28,500. ***Average need-based loan:*** Freshmen: $3813. Undergraduates: $4765. ***Parent loans:*** $4,050,171 (100% non-need-based). ***Programs:*** Federal Direct (Subsidized and Unsubsidized Stafford, PLUS), Perkins.

WORK-STUDY ***Federal work-study:*** Total amount: $331,094; 352 jobs averaging $1246. ***State or other work-study/employment:*** Total amount: $1,950,047 (60% need-based, 40% non-need-based). 356 part-time jobs averaging $441.

APPLYING FOR FINANCIAL AID ***Required financial aid forms:*** FAFSA, institution's own form. ***Financial aid deadline (priority):*** 3/1. ***Notification date:*** Continuous beginning 3/25. Students must reply within 2 weeks of notification.

CONTACT Ms. Phyllis Hooyman, Director of Financial Aid, Hope College, 141 East 12th Street, Holland, MI 49422-9000, 616-395-7765 or toll-free 800-968-7850. *Fax:* 616-395-7160. *E-mail:* hooyman@hope.edu.

HOPE INTERNATIONAL UNIVERSITY

Fullerton, CA

Tuition & fees: $24,235 **Average undergraduate aid package: $14,597**

ABOUT THE INSTITUTION Independent religious, coed. ***Awards:*** associate, bachelor's, and master's degrees and post-bachelor's and post-master's certificates. 19 undergraduate majors. ***Total enrollment:*** 1,059. Undergraduates: 794. Freshmen: 87. Federal methodology is used as a basis for awarding need-based institutional aid.

UNDERGRADUATE EXPENSES for 2010–11 ***Application fee:*** $40. ***One-time required fee:*** $300. ***Comprehensive fee:*** $32,035 includes full-time tuition ($22,890), mandatory fees ($1345), and room and board ($7800). ***College room only:*** $4300. Full-time tuition and fees vary according to course load, location, and program. Room and board charges vary according to board plan and student level. ***Part-time tuition:*** $850 per unit. ***Part-time fees:*** $850 per credit. Part-time tuition and fees vary according to course load, location, and program. ***Payment plan:*** Installment.

FRESHMAN FINANCIAL AID (Fall 2010, est.) 68 applied for aid; of those 46% were deemed to have need. 100% of freshmen with need received aid. ***Average percent of need met:*** 50% (excluding resources awarded to replace EFC). ***Average financial aid package:*** $17,152 (excluding resources awarded to replace EFC).

UNDERGRADUATE FINANCIAL AID (Fall 2010, est.) 321 applied for aid; of those 45% were deemed to have need. 100% of undergraduates with need received aid; of those 6% had need fully met. ***Average percent of need met:*** 43% (excluding resources awarded to replace EFC). ***Average financial aid package:*** $14,597 (excluding resources awarded to replace EFC). 2% of all full-time undergraduates had no need and received non-need-based gift aid.

GIFT AID (NEED-BASED) ***Total amount:*** $1,607,473 (44% federal, 41% state, 15% institutional). ***Receiving aid:*** Freshmen: 39% (31); all full-time undergraduates: 37% (144). ***Average award:*** Freshmen: $10,327; Undergraduates: $9339. ***Scholarships, grants, and awards:*** Federal Pell, FSEOG, state, private, college/university gift aid from institutional funds.

GIFT AID (NON-NEED-BASED) ***Total amount:*** $1,919,537 (97% institutional, 3% external sources). ***Receiving aid:*** Freshmen: 25% (20). Undergraduates: 25% (98). ***Average award:*** Undergraduates: $5400. ***Scholarships, grants, and awards by category:*** *Academic interests/achievement:* general academic interests/achievements. *Special achievements/activities:* leadership. *Special characteristics:* 77 awards ($504,376 total): children of faculty/staff, international students, relatives of clergy, religious affiliation, spouses of current students. ***Tuition waivers:*** Full or partial for employees or children of employees.

LOANS ***Student loans:*** $2,743,143 (44% need-based, 56% non-need-based). 97% of past graduating class borrowed through all loan programs. *Average indebtedness per student:* $27,000. ***Average need-based loan:*** Freshmen: $3583. Undergraduates: $4688. ***Parent loans:*** $586,287 (100% non-need-based). ***Programs:*** Federal Direct (Subsidized and Unsubsidized Stafford, PLUS), Perkins.

WORK-STUDY ***Federal work-study:*** Total amount: $75,653; 50 jobs averaging $1500. ***State or other work-study/employment:*** Part-time jobs available.

ATHLETIC AWARDS Total amount: $1,670,672 (100% non-need-based).

APPLYING FOR FINANCIAL AID ***Required financial aid forms:*** FAFSA, institution's own form. ***Financial aid deadline (priority):*** 3/2. ***Notification date:*** Continuous beginning 4/1. Students must reply within 2 weeks of notification.

CONTACT Mrs. Shannon O'Shields, Director of Financial Aid, Hope International University, 2500 East Nutwood Avenue, Fullerton, CA 92831, 714-879-3901 or toll-free 800-762-1294. *Fax:* 714-681-7421. *E-mail:* soshields@hiu.edu.

HOUGHTON COLLEGE

Houghton, NY

Tuition & fees: $25,460 **Average undergraduate aid package: $21,540**

ABOUT THE INSTITUTION Independent Wesleyan, coed. 60 undergraduate majors. Federal methodology is used as a basis for awarding need-based institutional aid.

UNDERGRADUATE EXPENSES for 2010–11 ***Comprehensive fee:*** $32,790 includes full-time tuition ($25,360), mandatory fees ($100), and room and board ($7330). ***College room only:*** $3932. Room and board charges vary according to board plan and housing facility. ***Part-time tuition:*** $1065 per credit hour. ***Payment plan:*** Installment.

FRESHMAN FINANCIAL AID (Fall 2010, est.) 234 applied for aid; of those 94% were deemed to have need. 100% of freshmen with need received aid; of those 17% had need fully met. ***Average percent of need met:*** 82% (excluding resources awarded to replace EFC). ***Average financial aid package:*** $23,416 (excluding resources awarded to replace EFC). 13% of all full-time freshmen had no need and received non-need-based gift aid.

UNDERGRADUATE FINANCIAL AID (Fall 2010, est.) 1,054 applied for aid; of those 94% were deemed to have need. 99% of undergraduates with need received aid; of those 18% had need fully met. ***Average percent of need met:*** 79% (excluding resources awarded to replace EFC). ***Average financial aid package:*** $21,540 (excluding resources awarded to replace EFC). 14% of all full-time undergraduates had no need and received non-need-based gift aid.

GIFT AID (NEED-BASED) ***Total amount:*** $13,342,258 (19% federal, 8% state, 68% institutional, 5% external sources). ***Receiving aid:*** Freshmen: 86% (219); all full-time undergraduates: 82% (976). ***Average award:*** Freshmen: $17,668; Undergraduates: $15,315. ***Scholarships, grants, and awards:*** Federal Pell, FSEOG, state, private, college/university gift aid from institutional funds, United Negro College Fund.

GIFT AID (NON-NEED-BASED) ***Total amount:*** $2,195,715 (1% federal, 2% state, 85% institutional, 12% external sources). ***Receiving aid:*** Freshmen: 13% (32). Undergraduates: 10% (115). ***Average award:*** Freshmen: $11,883. Undergraduates: $9743. ***Scholarships, grants, and awards by category:*** *Academic interests/achievement:* 586 awards ($3,694,428 total): general academic interests/achievements. *Creative arts/performance:* 93 awards ($311,500 total): art/fine arts, music. *Special achievements/activities:* 286 awards ($210,880 total): religious involvement. *Special characteristics:* 445 awards ($1,576,404 total): children and siblings of alumni, children of faculty/staff, international students, local/state students, relatives of clergy, religious affiliation, siblings of current students. ***Tuition waivers:*** Full or partial for employees or children of employees.

LOANS ***Student loans:*** $8,536,408 (77% need-based, 23% non-need-based). 94% of past graduating class borrowed through all loan programs. *Average indebtedness per student:* $23,010. ***Average need-based loan:*** Freshmen: $4421. Undergraduates: $5350. ***Parent loans:*** $1,499,955 (49% need-based, 51% non-need-based). ***Programs:*** Federal Direct (Subsidized and Unsubsidized Stafford, PLUS), Perkins, college/university, alternative loans.

WORK-STUDY ***Federal work-study:*** Total amount: $1,582,412; 744 jobs averaging $2127. ***State or other work-study/employment:*** Total amount: $2250 (100% non-need-based). 1 part-time job averaging $2250.

ATHLETIC AWARDS Total amount: $504,000 (80% need-based, 20% non-need-based).

APPLYING FOR FINANCIAL AID ***Required financial aid forms:*** FAFSA, state aid form. ***Financial aid deadline (priority):*** 3/1. ***Notification date:*** Continuous beginning 3/15. Students must reply by 5/1 or within 4 weeks of notification.

CONTACT Mr. Troy Martin, Director of Financial Aid, Houghton College, One Willard Avenue, Houghton, NY 14744, 585-567-9328 or toll-free 800-777-2556. *Fax:* 585-567-9610. *E-mail:* troy.martin@houghton.edu.

HOUSTON BAPTIST UNIVERSITY

Houston, TX

Tuition & fees: $23,180 **Average undergraduate aid package: $19,578**

ABOUT THE INSTITUTION Independent Baptist, coed. 65 undergraduate majors. Federal methodology is used as a basis for awarding need-based institutional aid.

UNDERGRADUATE EXPENSES for 2010–11 ***Comprehensive fee:*** $30,155 includes full-time tuition ($21,970), mandatory fees ($1210), and room and board ($6975). Room and board charges vary according to board plan and housing facility. ***Part-time tuition:*** $750 per semester hour. Part-time tuition and fees vary according to course load. ***Payment plan:*** Installment.

FRESHMAN FINANCIAL AID (Fall 2010, est.) 437 applied for aid; of those 90% were deemed to have need. 100% of freshmen with need received aid; of those 35% had need fully met. ***Average percent of need met:*** 87% (excluding resources awarded to replace EFC). ***Average financial aid package:*** $27,186 (excluding resources awarded to replace EFC). 12% of all full-time freshmen had no need and received non-need-based gift aid.

UNDERGRADUATE FINANCIAL AID (Fall 2010, est.) 1,496 applied for aid; of those 92% were deemed to have need. 100% of undergraduates with need received aid; of those 31% had need fully met. ***Average percent of need met:*** 88% (excluding resources awarded to replace EFC). ***Average financial aid***

package: $19,578 (excluding resources awarded to replace EFC). 6% of all full-time undergraduates had no need and received non-need-based gift aid.

GIFT AID (NEED-BASED) ***Total amount:*** $19,722,622 (29% federal, 13% state, 56% institutional, 2% external sources). ***Receiving aid:*** Freshmen: 67% (339); all full-time undergraduates: 59% (1,179). ***Average award:*** Freshmen: $6674; Undergraduates: $6259. ***Scholarships, grants, and awards:*** Federal Pell, FSEOG, state, private, college/university gift aid from institutional funds.

GIFT AID (NON-NEED-BASED) ***Total amount:*** $611,338 (98% institutional, 2% external sources). ***Receiving aid:*** Freshmen: 72% (366). Undergraduates: 64% (1,278). ***Average award:*** Freshmen: $4595. Undergraduates: $4348. ***Scholarships, grants, and awards by category:*** *Academic interests/achievement:* 1,723 awards ($9,748,985 total): general academic interests/achievements, health fields, religion/biblical studies. *Creative arts/performance:* 88 awards ($66,255 total): art/fine arts, debating, music. *Special achievements/activities:* 261 awards ($254,641 total): cheerleading/drum major, community service, leadership, religious involvement. *Special characteristics:* 132 awards ($222,480 total): children of faculty/staff, relatives of clergy. ***Tuition waivers:*** Full or partial for employees or children of employees.

LOANS ***Student loans:*** $10,556,677 (95% need-based, 5% non-need-based). ***Average need-based loan:*** Freshmen: $8835. Undergraduates: $3873. ***Parent loans:*** $6,554,096 (85% need-based, 15% non-need-based). ***Programs:*** Federal Direct (Subsidized and Unsubsidized Stafford, PLUS).

WORK-STUDY ***Federal work-study:*** Total amount: $2,928,614; 988 jobs available. ***State or other work-study/employment:*** Part-time jobs available.

ATHLETIC AWARDS Total amount: $4,717,633 (99% need-based, 1% non-need-based).

APPLYING FOR FINANCIAL AID ***Required financial aid form:*** FAFSA. ***Financial aid deadline:*** 4/15 (priority: 3/1). ***Notification date:*** Continuous beginning 3/10.

CONTACT Sherry Byrd, Director of Student Aid Programs, Houston Baptist University, 7502 Fondren Road, Houston, TX 77074-3298, 281-649-3389 or toll-free 800-696-3210. *Fax:* 281-649-3298. *E-mail:* financialaid@hbu.edu.

HOWARD PAYNE UNIVERSITY

Brownwood, TX

Tuition & fees: $19,950 | **Average undergraduate aid package: $16,145**

ABOUT THE INSTITUTION Independent religious, coed. 65 undergraduate majors. Federal methodology is used as a basis for awarding need-based institutional aid.

UNDERGRADUATE EXPENSES for 2010–11 ***Comprehensive fee:*** $25,642 includes full-time tuition ($18,850), mandatory fees ($1100), and room and board ($5692). ***College room only:*** $2400. Full-time tuition and fees vary according to course load, location, and program. Room and board charges vary according to board plan and housing facility. ***Part-time tuition:*** $575 per credit hour. Part-time tuition and fees vary according to location and program. ***Payment plan:*** Installment.

FRESHMAN FINANCIAL AID (Fall 2010, est.) 304 applied for aid; of those 93% were deemed to have need. 100% of freshmen with need received aid; of those 25% had need fully met. ***Average percent of need met:*** 84% (excluding resources awarded to replace EFC). ***Average financial aid package:*** $16,992 (excluding resources awarded to replace EFC). 13% of all full-time freshmen had no need and received non-need-based gift aid.

UNDERGRADUATE FINANCIAL AID (Fall 2010, est.) 904 applied for aid; of those 91% were deemed to have need. 100% of undergraduates with need received aid; of those 28% had need fully met. ***Average percent of need met:*** 82% (excluding resources awarded to replace EFC). ***Average financial aid package:*** $16,145 (excluding resources awarded to replace EFC). 15% of all full-time undergraduates had no need and received non-need-based gift aid.

GIFT AID (NEED-BASED) ***Total amount:*** $8,173,837 (29% federal, 16% state, 51% institutional, 4% external sources). ***Receiving aid:*** Freshmen: 88% (281); all full-time undergraduates: 81% (816). ***Average award:*** Freshmen: $12,904; Undergraduates: $11,420. ***Scholarships, grants, and awards:*** Federal Pell, FSEOG, state, private, college/university gift aid from institutional funds.

GIFT AID (NON-NEED-BASED) ***Total amount:*** $2,693,917 (95% institutional, 5% external sources). ***Receiving aid:*** Freshmen: 13% (42). Undergraduates: 10% (99). ***Average award:*** Freshmen: $6548. Undergraduates: $6968. ***Scholarships, grants, and awards by category:*** *Academic interests/achievement:* biological sciences, business, communication, education, English, general academic interests/achievements, mathematics, physical sciences, premedicine, religion/biblical studies, social sciences. *Creative arts/performance:* art/fine arts, music, theater/drama. *Special achievements/activities:* community service, leadership, religious involvement. *Special characteristics:* children and siblings of alumni, children of faculty/staff, local/state students, relatives of clergy, religious affiliation. ***Tuition waivers:*** Full or partial for employees or children of employees.

LOANS ***Student loans:*** $6,167,813 (62% need-based, 38% non-need-based). 76% of past graduating class borrowed through all loan programs. *Average indebtedness per student:* $30,690. ***Average need-based loan:*** Freshmen: $3252. Undergraduates: $3937. ***Parent loans:*** $1,503,672 (41% need-based, 59% non-need-based). ***Programs:*** Federal Direct (Subsidized and Unsubsidized Stafford, PLUS), Perkins, state.

WORK-STUDY ***Federal work-study:*** Total amount: $130,359; 103 jobs averaging $1300. ***State or other work-study/employment:*** Total amount: $9700 (100% need-based). 9 part-time jobs averaging $9700.

APPLYING FOR FINANCIAL AID ***Required financial aid forms:*** FAFSA, institution's own form. ***Financial aid deadline (priority):*** 3/15. ***Notification date:*** Continuous beginning 2/1. Students must reply within 2 weeks of notification.

CONTACT Glenda Huff, Director of Financial Aid, Howard Payne University, 1000 Fisk Avenue, Brownwood, TX 76801, 325-649-8014 or toll-free 800-880-4478. *Fax:* 325-649-8973. *E-mail:* ghuff@hputx.edu.

HOWARD UNIVERSITY

Washington, DC

Tuition & fees: $17,905 | **Average undergraduate aid package: $11,531**

ABOUT THE INSTITUTION Independent, coed. ***Awards:*** bachelor's and master's degrees and post-master's certificates. 64 undergraduate majors. ***Total enrollment:*** 10,288. Undergraduates: 6,969. Federal methodology is used as a basis for awarding need-based institutional aid.

UNDERGRADUATE EXPENSES for 2010–11 ***Application fee:*** $45. ***Comprehensive fee:*** $26,403 includes full-time tuition ($17,100), mandatory fees ($805), and room and board ($8498). ***College room only:*** $5094. Full-time tuition and fees vary according to course load. Room and board charges vary according to board plan and housing facility. ***Part-time tuition:*** $713 per credit hour. ***Part-time fees:*** $805 per year. Part-time tuition and fees vary according to course load. ***Payment plans:*** Installment, deferred payment.

FRESHMAN FINANCIAL AID (Fall 2010, est.) 1,381 applied for aid; of those 89% were deemed to have need. 97% of freshmen with need received aid; of those 10% had need fully met. ***Average percent of need met:*** 74% (excluding resources awarded to replace EFC). ***Average financial aid package:*** $12,103 (excluding resources awarded to replace EFC). 5% of all full-time freshmen had no need and received non-need-based gift aid.

UNDERGRADUATE FINANCIAL AID (Fall 2010, est.) 6,068 applied for aid; of those 91% were deemed to have need. 98% of undergraduates with need received aid; of those 11% had need fully met. ***Average percent of need met:*** 77% (excluding resources awarded to replace EFC). ***Average financial aid package:*** $11,531 (excluding resources awarded to replace EFC). 5% of all full-time undergraduates had no need and received non-need-based gift aid.

GIFT AID (NEED-BASED) ***Total amount:*** $26,193,811 (58% federal, 1% state, 41% institutional). ***Receiving aid:*** Freshmen: 46% (647); all full-time undergraduates: 48% (3,033). ***Average award:*** Freshmen: $2506; Undergraduates: $2493. ***Scholarships, grants, and awards:*** Federal Pell, FSEOG, state, private, college/university gift aid from institutional funds, Federal Nursing.

GIFT AID (NON-NEED-BASED) ***Total amount:*** $30,323,051 (4% federal, 94% institutional, 2% external sources). ***Receiving aid:*** Freshmen: 1% (10). Undergraduates: 1% (58). ***Average award:*** Freshmen: $9776. Undergraduates: $8786. ***Scholarships, grants, and awards by category:*** *Creative arts/performance:* art/fine arts, dance, music. ***Tuition waivers:*** Full or partial for employees or children of employees. ***ROTC:*** Army, Air Force.

LOANS ***Student loans:*** $48,501,852 (43% need-based, 57% non-need-based). 63% of past graduating class borrowed through all loan programs. *Average indebtedness per student:* $9863. ***Average need-based loan:*** Freshmen: $1749. Undergraduates: $2261. ***Parent loans:*** $33,975,089 (100% non-need-based). ***Programs:*** Federal Direct (Subsidized and Unsubsidized Stafford, PLUS), Perkins, Federal Nursing, district, college/university.

WORK-STUDY ***Federal work-study:*** Total amount: $1,095,168; 444 jobs averaging $2467. ***State or other work-study/employment:*** Total amount: $447,466 (100% non-need-based). 169 part-time jobs averaging $2648.

ATHLETIC AWARDS Total amount: $5,564,776 (100% non-need-based).

APPLYING FOR FINANCIAL AID ***Required financial aid form:*** FAFSA. ***Financial aid deadline:*** 8/15 (priority: 2/15). ***Notification date:*** Continuous beginning 4/1. Students must reply by 6/1 or within 1 week of notification.

CONTACT Derek Kindle, Director of Financial Aid and Scholarships, Howard University, 2400 Sixth Street, NW, Washington, DC 20059-0002, 202-806-2850 or toll-free 800-HOWARD-U. *Fax:* 202-806-2818. *E-mail:* dkindle@howard.edu.

HUMBOLDT STATE UNIVERSITY

Arcata, CA

Tuition & fees (CA res): $6496 **Average undergraduate aid package: $11,206**

ABOUT THE INSTITUTION State-supported, coed. 71 undergraduate majors. Federal methodology is used as a basis for awarding need-based institutional aid.

UNDERGRADUATE EXPENSES for 2011–12 ***Tuition, state resident:*** full-time $0. ***Tuition, nonresident:*** full-time $17,656; part-time $372 per unit. ***Required fees:*** full-time $6496; $2048 per term. Full-time tuition and fees vary according to degree level. Part-time tuition and fees vary according to course load and degree level. ***College room and board:*** $10,486; ***Room only:*** $5302. Room and board charges vary according to board plan and housing facility. ***Payment plan:*** Installment.

FRESHMAN FINANCIAL AID (Fall 2010, est.) 1,084 applied for aid; of those 81% were deemed to have need. 93% of freshmen with need received aid; of those 1% had need fully met. ***Average percent of need met:*** 66% (excluding resources awarded to replace EFC). ***Average financial aid package:*** $11,392 (excluding resources awarded to replace EFC). 3% of all full-time freshmen had no need and received non-need-based gift aid.

UNDERGRADUATE FINANCIAL AID (Fall 2010, est.) 4,966 applied for aid; of those 87% were deemed to have need. 96% of undergraduates with need received aid; of those 1% had need fully met. ***Average percent of need met:*** 66% (excluding resources awarded to replace EFC). ***Average financial aid package:*** $11,206 (excluding resources awarded to replace EFC). 1% of all full-time undergraduates had no need and received non-need-based gift aid.

GIFT AID (NEED-BASED) ***Total amount:*** $24,823,692 (67% federal, 14% state, 16% institutional, 3% external sources). ***Receiving aid:*** Freshmen: 50% (647); all full-time undergraduates: 52% (3,419). ***Average award:*** Freshmen: $9728; Undergraduates: $8793. ***Scholarships, grants, and awards:*** Federal Pell, FSEOG, state, private, college/university gift aid from institutional funds.

GIFT AID (NON-NEED-BASED) ***Total amount:*** $105,184 (3% state, 17% institutional, 80% external sources). ***Receiving aid:*** Freshmen: 12% (150). Undergraduates: 4% (270). ***Average award:*** Freshmen: $1465. Undergraduates: $1558. ***Scholarships, grants, and awards by category:*** *Academic interests/achievement:* general academic interests/achievements. ***Tuition waivers:*** Full or partial for employees or children of employees.

LOANS ***Student loans:*** $30,864,603 (90% need-based, 10% non-need-based). 49% of past graduating class borrowed through all loan programs. *Average indebtedness per student:* $17,444. ***Average need-based loan:*** Freshmen: $3391. Undergraduates: $4201. ***Parent loans:*** $685,738 (84% need-based, 16% non-need-based). ***Programs:*** Federal Direct (Subsidized and Unsubsidized Stafford, PLUS), Perkins.

WORK-STUDY ***Federal work-study:*** Total amount: $888,856; 325 jobs averaging $2600.

ATHLETIC AWARDS Total amount: $545,797 (81% need-based, 19% non-need-based).

APPLYING FOR FINANCIAL AID ***Required financial aid form:*** FAFSA. ***Financial aid deadline (priority):*** 3/2. ***Notification date:*** Continuous beginning 4/1. Students must reply within 4 weeks of notification.

CONTACT Kim Coughlin-Lamphear, Director of Financial Aid, Humboldt State University, 1 Harpst Street, Arcata, CA 95521-8299, 707-826-4321. *E-mail:* coughlin@humboldt.edu.

HUMPHREYS COLLEGE

Stockton, CA

ABOUT THE INSTITUTION Independent, coed. ***Awards:*** associate, bachelor's, and master's degrees. 11 undergraduate majors. ***Total enrollment:*** 756. Undergraduates: 669.

GIFT AID (NEED-BASED) ***Scholarships, grants, and awards:*** Federal Pell, FSEOG, state.

GIFT AID (NON-NEED-BASED) ***Scholarships, grants, and awards by category:*** *Academic interests/achievement:* business, computer science, general academic interests/achievements. *Special achievements/activities:* community service. *Special characteristics:* ethnic background, members of minority groups.

WORK-STUDY Federal work-study jobs available.

APPLYING FOR FINANCIAL AID ***Required financial aid form:*** FAFSA.

CONTACT Rita Franco, Director of Financial Aid, Humphreys College, 6650 Inglewood Avenue, Stockton, CA 95207-3896, 209-478-0800. *Fax:* 209-235-2983.

HUNTER COLLEGE OF THE CITY UNIVERSITY OF NEW YORK

New York, NY

Tuition & fees (NY res): $5229 **Average undergraduate aid package: $5092**

ABOUT THE INSTITUTION State and locally supported, coed. 63 undergraduate majors. Federal methodology is used as a basis for awarding need-based institutional aid.

UNDERGRADUATE EXPENSES for 2011–12 ***Tuition, state resident:*** full-time $4830; part-time $205 per term. ***Tuition, nonresident:*** full-time $13,050; part-time $435 per term. ***Required fees:*** full-time $399; $183.50 per term. Full-time tuition and fees vary according to degree level and program. Part-time tuition and fees vary according to degree level and program. ***College room and board: Room only:*** $5500. ***Payment plan:*** Installment.

FRESHMAN FINANCIAL AID (Fall 2009) 1,571 applied for aid; of those 72% were deemed to have need. 92% of freshmen with need received aid; of those 27% had need fully met. ***Average percent of need met:*** 77% (excluding resources awarded to replace EFC). ***Average financial aid package:*** $5241 (excluding resources awarded to replace EFC). 16% of all full-time freshmen had no need and received non-need-based gift aid.

UNDERGRADUATE FINANCIAL AID (Fall 2009) 7,634 applied for aid; of those 82% were deemed to have need. 97% of undergraduates with need received aid; of those 17% had need fully met. ***Average percent of need met:*** 78% (excluding resources awarded to replace EFC). ***Average financial aid package:*** $5092 (excluding resources awarded to replace EFC). 7% of all full-time undergraduates had no need and received non-need-based gift aid.

GIFT AID (NEED-BASED) ***Total amount:*** $33,637,114 (50% federal, 47% state, 3% institutional). ***Receiving aid:*** Freshmen: 52% (1,022); all full-time undergraduates: 54% (6,013). ***Average award:*** Freshmen: $5599; Undergraduates: $4141. ***Scholarships, grants, and awards:*** Federal Pell, FSEOG, state, private, college/university gift aid from institutional funds.

GIFT AID (NON-NEED-BASED) ***Total amount:*** $1,382,266 (100% institutional). ***Receiving aid:*** Freshmen: 43% (846). Undergraduates: 20% (2,218). ***Average award:*** Freshmen: $2110. Undergraduates: $2368. ***Scholarships, grants, and awards by category:*** *Academic interests/achievement:* general academic interests/achievements.

LOANS ***Student loans:*** $4,500,667 (26% need-based, 74% non-need-based). 53% of past graduating class borrowed through all loan programs. *Average indebtedness per student:* $7500. ***Average need-based loan:*** Freshmen: $2746. Undergraduates: $3179. ***Parent loans:*** $3,053,210 (100% need-based). ***Programs:*** Federal Direct (Subsidized and Unsubsidized Stafford, PLUS), Perkins.

WORK-STUDY ***Federal work-study:*** Total amount: $1,383,803; jobs available.

APPLYING FOR FINANCIAL AID ***Required financial aid forms:*** FAFSA, state aid form. ***Financial aid deadline (priority):*** 4/1. ***Notification date:*** Continuous beginning 5/15.

CONTACT Aristalia Cortorreal Diaz, Director of Financial Aid, Hunter College of the City University of New York, 695 Park Avenue, New York, NY 10065-5085, 212-772-4400. *Fax:* 212-650-3666. *E-mail:* aristalia@hunter.cuny.edu.

HUNTINGDON COLLEGE

Montgomery, AL

Tuition & fees: $20,990 **Average undergraduate aid package: $15,853**

ABOUT THE INSTITUTION Independent United Methodist, coed. 28 undergraduate majors. Both federal and institutional methodology are used as a basis for awarding need-based institutional aid.

UNDERGRADUATE EXPENSES for 2010–11 ***Comprehensive fee:*** $28,990 includes full-time tuition ($19,990), mandatory fees ($1000), and room and board ($8000). Full-time tuition and fees vary according to course load, program, and student level. Room and board charges vary according to housing facility. ***Part-time tuition:*** $830 per credit hour. Part-time tuition and fees vary according to course load and program. ***Payment plans:*** Guaranteed tuition, deferred payment.

FRESHMAN FINANCIAL AID (Fall 2010, est.) 241 applied for aid; of those 88% were deemed to have need. 100% of freshmen with need received aid; of those 18% had need fully met. ***Average percent of need met:*** 72% (excluding resources awarded to replace EFC). ***Average financial aid package:*** $16,646 (excluding resources awarded to replace EFC). 23% of all full-time freshmen had no need and received non-need-based gift aid.

UNDERGRADUATE FINANCIAL AID (Fall 2010, est.) 716 applied for aid; of those 90% were deemed to have need. 100% of undergraduates with need received aid; of those 20% had need fully met. ***Average percent of need met:*** 74% (excluding resources awarded to replace EFC). ***Average financial aid package:*** $15,853 (excluding resources awarded to replace EFC). 25% of all full-time undergraduates had no need and received non-need-based gift aid.

GIFT AID (NEED-BASED) ***Total amount:*** $8,290,259 (24% federal, 2% state, 71% institutional, 3% external sources). ***Receiving aid:*** Freshmen: 77% (211); all full-time undergraduates: 71% (635). ***Average award:*** Freshmen: $13,701; Undergraduates: $12,556. ***Scholarships, grants, and awards:*** Federal Pell, FSEOG, state, private, college/university gift aid from institutional funds.

GIFT AID (NON-NEED-BASED) ***Total amount:*** $2,848,057 (1% state, 88% institutional, 11% external sources). ***Receiving aid:*** Freshmen: 8% (22). Undergraduates: 8% (71). ***Average award:*** Freshmen: $10,052. Undergraduates: $9652. ***Scholarships, grants, and awards by category:*** *Academic interests/achievement:* 79 awards ($724,988 total): biological sciences, computer science, general academic interests/achievements, mathematics. *Creative arts/performance:* 11 awards ($40,605 total): music, performing arts. *Special achievements/activities:* 11 awards ($83,812 total): cheerleading/drum major, community service, junior miss. *Special characteristics:* 444 awards ($2,586,431 total): children and siblings of alumni, children of faculty/staff, children of workers in trades, international students, local/state students, religious affiliation, spouses of current students, veterans, veterans' children. ***Tuition waivers:*** Full or partial for children of alumni, employees or children of employees.

LOANS ***Student loans:*** $5,795,109 (75% need-based, 25% non-need-based). 66% of past graduating class borrowed through all loan programs. *Average indebtedness per student:* $17,993. ***Average need-based loan:*** Freshmen: $3505. Undergraduates: $4164. ***Parent loans:*** $1,257,917 (35% need-based, 65% non-need-based). ***Programs:*** Federal Direct (Subsidized and Unsubsidized Stafford, PLUS), Perkins.

WORK-STUDY ***Federal work-study:*** Total amount: $96,000; 99 jobs averaging $970.

APPLYING FOR FINANCIAL AID ***Required financial aid form:*** FAFSA. ***Financial aid deadline (priority):*** 3/15. ***Notification date:*** Continuous beginning 3/1. Students must reply by 5/1 or within 2 weeks of notification.

CONTACT Ms. Belinda Goris Duett, Director of Financial Aid, Huntingdon College, 1500 East Fairview Avenue, Montgomery, AL 36106-2148, 334-833-4519 or toll-free 800-763-0313. *Fax:* 334-833-4235. *E-mail:* bduett@huntingdon.edu.

HUNTINGTON UNIVERSITY

Huntington, IN

Tuition & fees: $23,210 **Average undergraduate aid package: $16,111**

ABOUT THE INSTITUTION Independent religious, coed. 72 undergraduate majors. Both federal and institutional methodology are used as a basis for awarding need-based institutional aid.

UNDERGRADUATE EXPENSES for 2011–12 ***Comprehensive fee:*** $30,890 includes full-time tuition ($22,710), mandatory fees ($500), and room and board ($7680). Full-time tuition and fees vary according to course load, degree level, and program. Room and board charges vary according to board plan. Part-time tuition and fees vary according to course load, degree level, and program. ***Payment plan:*** Installment.

FRESHMAN FINANCIAL AID (Fall 2010, est.) 236 applied for aid; of those 92% were deemed to have need. 100% of freshmen with need received aid; of those 11% had need fully met. ***Average percent of need met:*** 74% (excluding resources awarded to replace EFC). ***Average financial aid package:*** $18,480 (excluding resources awarded to replace EFC). 14% of all full-time freshmen had no need and received non-need-based gift aid.

UNDERGRADUATE FINANCIAL AID (Fall 2010, est.) 936 applied for aid; of those 91% were deemed to have need. 100% of undergraduates with need received aid; of those 6% had need fully met. ***Average percent of need met:*** 68% (excluding resources awarded to replace EFC). ***Average financial aid package:*** $16,111 (excluding resources awarded to replace EFC). 15% of all full-time undergraduates had no need and received non-need-based gift aid.

GIFT AID (NEED-BASED) ***Total amount:*** $9,483,984 (19% federal, 13% state, 65% institutional, 3% external sources). ***Receiving aid:*** Freshmen: 79% (205); all full-time undergraduates: 72% (776). ***Average award:*** Freshmen: $12,201; Undergraduates: $13,243. ***Scholarships, grants, and awards:*** Federal Pell, FSEOG, state, private, college/university gift aid from institutional funds.

GIFT AID (NON-NEED-BASED) ***Total amount:*** $581,184 (88% institutional, 12% external sources). ***Receiving aid:*** Freshmen: 19% (49). Undergraduates: 20% (213). ***Average award:*** Freshmen: $7482. Undergraduates: $8716. ***Scholarships, grants, and awards by category:*** *Academic interests/achievement:* biological sciences, business, communication, computer science, education, general academic interests/achievements, mathematics. *Creative arts/performance:* applied art and design, art/fine arts, cinema/film/broadcasting, creative writing, journalism/publications, music, theater/drama. *Special achievements/activities:* cheerleading/drum major, religious involvement. *Special characteristics:* children and siblings of alumni, children of current students, children of faculty/staff, ethnic background, international students, local/state students, parents of current students, previous college experience, relatives of clergy, religious affiliation, siblings of current students, spouses of current students, veterans, veterans' children. ***Tuition waivers:*** Full or partial for employees or children of employees.

LOANS ***Student loans:*** $6,970,010 (81% need-based, 19% non-need-based). 48% of past graduating class borrowed through all loan programs. *Average indebtedness per student:* $30,885. ***Average need-based loan:*** Freshmen: $3690. Undergraduates: $4556. ***Parent loans:*** $1,372,770 (46% need-based, 54% non-need-based). ***Programs:*** Federal Direct (Subsidized and Unsubsidized Stafford, PLUS), Perkins.

WORK-STUDY ***Federal work-study:*** Total amount: $236,650; 138 jobs averaging $2106.

ATHLETIC AWARDS Total amount: $960,690 (55% need-based, 45% non-need-based).

APPLYING FOR FINANCIAL AID ***Required financial aid form:*** FAFSA. ***Financial aid deadline (priority):*** 3/1. ***Notification date:*** Continuous beginning 2/1. Students must reply by 5/1 or within 2 weeks of notification.

CONTACT Mrs. Sharon Woods, Director of Financial Aid, Huntington University, 2303 College Avenue, Huntington, IN 46750, 260-359-4014 or toll-free 800-642-6493. *Fax:* 260-358-3699. *E-mail:* finaid@huntington.edu.

HUSSON UNIVERSITY

Bangor, ME

Tuition & fees: $13,960 **Average undergraduate aid package: $9986**

ABOUT THE INSTITUTION Independent, coed. 33 undergraduate majors. Federal methodology is used as a basis for awarding need-based institutional aid.

UNDERGRADUATE EXPENSES for 2011–12 ***Comprehensive fee:*** $21,480 includes full-time tuition ($13,650), mandatory fees ($310), and room and board ($7520). Full-time tuition and fees vary according to class time. ***Part-time tuition:*** $455 per credit. Part-time tuition and fees vary according to class time and course load. ***Payment plans:*** Tuition prepayment, installment.

FRESHMAN FINANCIAL AID (Fall 2010, est.) 1,406 applied for aid; of those 59% were deemed to have need. 88% of freshmen with need received aid; of those 3% had need fully met. ***Average percent of need met:*** 62% (excluding resources awarded to replace EFC). ***Average financial aid package:*** $9944 (excluding resources awarded to replace EFC). 3% of all full-time freshmen had no need and received non-need-based gift aid.

UNDERGRADUATE FINANCIAL AID (Fall 2010, est.) 3,446 applied for aid; of those 71% were deemed to have need. 90% of undergraduates with need received aid; of those 5% had need fully met. ***Average percent of need met:*** 57% (excluding resources awarded to replace EFC). ***Average financial aid package:*** $9986 (excluding resources awarded to replace EFC). 3% of all full-time undergraduates had no need and received non-need-based gift aid.

GIFT AID (NEED-BASED) ***Total amount:*** $14,629,961 (54% federal, 8% state, 34% institutional, 4% external sources). ***Receiving aid:*** Freshmen: 49% (697);

all full-time undergraduates: 58% (2,014). ***Average award:*** Freshmen: $7781; Undergraduates: $7024. ***Scholarships, grants, and awards:*** Federal Pell, FSEOG, state, private, college/university gift aid from institutional funds.

GIFT AID (NON-NEED-BASED) ***Total amount:*** $572,001 (1% federal, 84% institutional, 15% external sources). ***Receiving aid:*** Freshmen: 1% (11). Undergraduates: 1% (35). ***Average award:*** Freshmen: $4269. Undergraduates: $3406. ***Scholarships, grants, and awards by category:*** *Academic interests/achievement:* business, computer science, education, general academic interests/achievements, health fields. *Special achievements/activities:* general special achievements/activities, leadership. *Special characteristics:* children of union members/company employees. ***Tuition waivers:*** Full or partial for employees or children of employees, senior citizens.

LOANS ***Student loans:*** $16,387,635 (79% need-based, 21% non-need-based). 86% of past graduating class borrowed through all loan programs. *Average indebtedness per student:* $23,613. ***Average need-based loan:*** Freshmen: $3098. Undergraduates: $4075. ***Parent loans:*** $1,449,304 (39% need-based, 61% non-need-based). ***Programs:*** Federal Direct (Subsidized and Unsubsidized Stafford, PLUS), Perkins, state, alternative loans.

WORK-STUDY ***Federal work-study:*** Total amount: $1,307,270; 1,001 jobs averaging $1300.

APPLYING FOR FINANCIAL AID ***Required financial aid form:*** FAFSA. ***Financial aid deadline (priority):*** 4/15. ***Notification date:*** Continuous. Students must reply by 5/1 or within 2 weeks of notification.

CONTACT Linda B. Hill, Director of Financial Aid, Husson University, One College Circle, Bangor, ME 04401, 207-941-7156 or toll-free 800-4-HUSSON. *Fax:* 207-973-1038. *E-mail:* conantl@husson.edu.

HUSTON-TILLOTSON UNIVERSITY

Austin, TX

Tuition & fees: $12,430 **Average undergraduate aid package: $14,885**

ABOUT THE INSTITUTION Independent interdenominational, coed. 20 undergraduate majors. Federal methodology is used as a basis for awarding need-based institutional aid.

UNDERGRADUATE EXPENSES for 2010–11 ***Comprehensive fee:*** $19,376 includes full-time tuition ($10,396), mandatory fees ($2034), and room and board ($6946). ***College room only:*** $3020. Full-time tuition and fees vary according to course load. Room and board charges vary according to housing facility. ***Part-time tuition:*** $347 per credit hour. ***Part-time fees:*** $138 per credit hour. Part-time tuition and fees vary according to course load. ***Payment plan:*** Deferred payment.

FRESHMAN FINANCIAL AID (Fall 2009) 229 applied for aid; of those 91% were deemed to have need. 100% of freshmen with need received aid; of those 30% had need fully met. ***Average percent of need met:*** 82% (excluding resources awarded to replace EFC). ***Average financial aid package:*** $15,162 (excluding resources awarded to replace EFC).

UNDERGRADUATE FINANCIAL AID (Fall 2009) 775 applied for aid; of those 99% were deemed to have need. 100% of undergraduates with need received aid; of those 21% had need fully met. ***Average percent of need met:*** 78% (excluding resources awarded to replace EFC). ***Average financial aid package:*** $14,885 (excluding resources awarded to replace EFC). 1% of all full-time undergraduates had no need and received non-need-based gift aid.

GIFT AID (NEED-BASED) ***Total amount:*** $4,222,542 (71% federal, 28% state, 1% institutional). ***Receiving aid:*** Freshmen: 45% (117); all full-time undergraduates: 52% (460). ***Average award:*** Freshmen: $10,025; Undergraduates: $9772. ***Scholarships, grants, and awards:*** Federal Pell, FSEOG, state, private, college/university gift aid from institutional funds.

GIFT AID (NON-NEED-BASED) ***Total amount:*** $408,000 (100% external sources). ***Receiving aid:*** Freshmen: 27% (71). Undergraduates: 20% (175). ***Scholarships, grants, and awards by category:*** *Academic interests/achievement:* general academic interests/achievements. *Creative arts/performance:* music. *Special characteristics:* general special characteristics. ***Tuition waivers:*** Full or partial for employees or children of employees.

LOANS ***Student loans:*** $5,848,730 (45% need-based, 55% non-need-based). ***Average need-based loan:*** Freshmen: $3331. Undergraduates: $4875. ***Parent loans:*** $249,076 (100% non-need-based). ***Programs:*** alternative loans.

WORK-STUDY ***Federal work-study:*** Total amount: $122,312; jobs available. ***State or other work-study/employment:*** Total amount: $6411 (100% need-based). Part-time jobs available.

ATHLETIC AWARDS Total amount: $600,000 (100% non-need-based).

APPLYING FOR FINANCIAL AID ***Required financial aid forms:*** FAFSA, institution's own form. ***Financial aid deadline (priority):*** 3/15. ***Notification date:*** Continuous. Students must reply within 2 weeks of notification.

CONTACT Antonio Holloway, Director of Financial Aid, Huston-Tillotson University, 900 Chicon Street, Austin, TX 78702, 512-505-3031. *Fax:* 512-505-3192. *E-mail:* aholloway@htu.edu.

IDAHO STATE UNIVERSITY

Pocatello, ID

ABOUT THE INSTITUTION State-supported, coed. 104 undergraduate majors.

GIFT AID (NEED-BASED) ***Scholarships, grants, and awards:*** Federal Pell, FSEOG, state, private, college/university gift aid from institutional funds, Federal Nursing.

GIFT AID (NON-NEED-BASED) ***Scholarships, grants, and awards by category:*** *Academic interests/achievement:* biological sciences, business, communication, computer science, education, engineering/technologies, English, foreign languages, general academic interests/achievements, health fields, home economics, humanities, international studies, mathematics, military science, physical sciences, premedicine, religion/biblical studies, social sciences. *Creative arts/performance:* art/fine arts, dance, debating, music, performing arts, theater/drama. *Special achievements/activities:* cheerleading/drum major, general special achievements/activities, junior miss, leadership, memberships, rodeo. *Special characteristics:* children and siblings of alumni, children of faculty/staff, ethnic background, first-generation college students, general special characteristics, handicapped students, international students, local/state students, members of minority groups, out-of-state students, previous college experience.

LOANS ***Programs:*** Federal Direct (Subsidized and Unsubsidized Stafford, PLUS), Perkins, Federal Nursing.

WORK-STUDY Federal work-study jobs available. ***State or other work-study/employment:*** Part-time jobs available.

APPLYING FOR FINANCIAL AID ***Required financial aid forms:*** FAFSA, university application for admission.

CONTACT Mr. Kent Larson, Director of Financial Aid, Idaho State University, 921 South 8th Avenue, Stop 8077, Pocatello, ID 83209, 208-282-2981. *Fax:* 208-282-4755. *E-mail:* larskent@isu.edu.

ILLINOIS COLLEGE

Jacksonville, IL

Tuition & fees: $22,800 **Average undergraduate aid package: $20,096**

ABOUT THE INSTITUTION Independent interdenominational, coed. 44 undergraduate majors. Federal methodology is used as a basis for awarding need-based institutional aid.

UNDERGRADUATE EXPENSES for 2010–11 ***Comprehensive fee:*** $30,700 includes full-time tuition ($22,350), mandatory fees ($450), and room and board ($7900). ***College room only:*** $4100. Room and board charges vary according to board plan and housing facility. ***Part-time tuition:*** $700 per semester hour. ***Part-time fees:*** $225 per year. ***Payment plan:*** Installment.

FRESHMAN FINANCIAL AID (Fall 2010, est.) 199 applied for aid; of those 91% were deemed to have need. 100% of freshmen with need received aid; of those 24% had need fully met. ***Average percent of need met:*** 90% (excluding resources awarded to replace EFC). ***Average financial aid package:*** $22,745 (excluding resources awarded to replace EFC). 17% of all full-time freshmen had no need and received non-need-based gift aid.

UNDERGRADUATE FINANCIAL AID (Fall 2010, est.) 778 applied for aid; of those 91% were deemed to have need. 100% of undergraduates with need received aid; of those 25% had need fully met. ***Average percent of need met:*** 89% (excluding resources awarded to replace EFC). ***Average financial aid package:*** $20,096 (excluding resources awarded to replace EFC). 15% of all full-time undergraduates had no need and received non-need-based gift aid.

GIFT AID (NEED-BASED) ***Total amount:*** $10,930,181 (13% federal, 15% state, 71% institutional, 1% external sources). ***Receiving aid:*** Freshmen: 83% (182); all full-time undergraduates: 84% (709). ***Average award:*** Freshmen: $18,575; Undergraduates: $15,409. ***Scholarships, grants, and awards:*** Federal Pell, FSEOG, state, private, college/university gift aid from institutional funds.

GIFT AID (NON-NEED-BASED) ***Total amount:*** $1,980,069 (95% institutional, 5% external sources). ***Receiving aid:*** Freshmen: 9% (20). Undergraduates:

12% (98). ***Average award:*** Freshmen: $15,302. Undergraduates: $10,944. ***Scholarships, grants, and awards by category:*** *Academic interests/achievement:* general academic interests/achievements. *Creative arts/performance:* music, theater/drama. *Special characteristics:* children of faculty/staff, international students, previous college experience. ***Tuition waivers:*** Full or partial for employees or children of employees.

LOANS ***Student loans:*** $5,719,364 (67% need-based, 33% non-need-based). 81% of past graduating class borrowed through all loan programs. *Average indebtedness per student:* $24,401. ***Average need-based loan:*** Freshmen: $3799. Undergraduates: $4580. ***Parent loans:*** $1,183,148 (23% need-based, 77% non-need-based). ***Programs:*** Federal Direct (Subsidized and Unsubsidized Stafford, PLUS), Perkins.

WORK-STUDY ***Federal work-study:*** Total amount: $602,425; jobs available. ***State or other work-study/employment:*** Part-time jobs available.

APPLYING FOR FINANCIAL AID ***Required financial aid form:*** FAFSA. ***Financial aid deadline (priority):*** 3/1. ***Notification date:*** Continuous beginning 3/7. Students must reply within 2 weeks of notification.

CONTACT Kate Taylor, Director of Financial Aid, Illinois College, 1101 West College Avenue, Jacksonville, IL 62650-2299, 217-245-3035 or toll-free 866-464-5265. *Fax:* 217-245-3274. *E-mail:* finaid@hilltop.ic.edu.

THE ILLINOIS INSTITUTE OF ART–CHICAGO

Chicago, IL

UNDERGRADUATE EXPENSES Tuition cost varies by program. Prospective students should contact the school for current tuition costs. Other charges include a starting kit for all first-quarter students. Kits vary in price, depending on the program of study.

CONTACT Financial Aid Office, The Illinois Institute of Art–Chicago, 350 North Orleans Street, Suite 136, Chicago, IL 60654-1593, 800-351-3450.

THE ILLINOIS INSTITUTE OF ART–SCHAUMBURG

Schaumburg, IL

UNDERGRADUATE EXPENSES Tuition cost varies by program. Prospective students should contact the school for current tuition costs. Other charges include a starting kit for all first-quarter students. Kits vary in price, depending on the program of study.

CONTACT Financial Aid Office, The Illinois Institute of Art–Schaumburg, 1000 North Plaza Drive, Suite 100, Schaumburg, IL 60173, 847-619-3450 or toll-free 800-314-3450.

ILLINOIS INSTITUTE OF TECHNOLOGY

Chicago, IL

Tuition & fees: $34,880 **Average undergraduate aid package: $27,639**

ABOUT THE INSTITUTION Independent, coed. 28 undergraduate majors. Federal methodology is used as a basis for awarding need-based institutional aid.

UNDERGRADUATE EXPENSES for 2011–12 ***One-time required fee:*** $165. ***Comprehensive fee:*** $45,218 includes full-time tuition ($33,800), mandatory fees ($1080), and room and board ($10,338). ***College room only:*** $5384. Full-time tuition and fees vary according to student level. Room and board charges vary according to board plan and housing facility. ***Part-time tuition:*** $1032 per credit hour. ***Part-time fees:*** $25 per course; $75 per term. Part-time tuition and fees vary according to course load and student level. ***Payment plan:*** Installment.

FRESHMAN FINANCIAL AID (Fall 2010, est.) 291 applied for aid; of those 90% were deemed to have need. 100% of freshmen with need received aid; of those 28% had need fully met. ***Average percent of need met:*** 87% (excluding resources awarded to replace EFC). ***Average financial aid package:*** $30,905 (excluding resources awarded to replace EFC). 32% of all full-time freshmen had no need and received non-need-based gift aid.

UNDERGRADUATE FINANCIAL AID (Fall 2010, est.) 1,576 applied for aid; of those 94% were deemed to have need. 100% of undergraduates with need received aid; of those 15% had need fully met. ***Average percent of need met:*** 77% (excluding resources awarded to replace EFC). ***Average financial aid package:*** $27,639 (excluding resources awarded to replace EFC). 35% of all full-time undergraduates had no need and received non-need-based gift aid.

GIFT AID (NEED-BASED) ***Total amount:*** $32,928,079 (16% federal, 8% state, 75% institutional, 1% external sources). ***Receiving aid:*** Freshmen: 66% (263); all full-time undergraduates: 61% (1,481). ***Average award:*** Freshmen: $25,628; Undergraduates: $22,054. ***Scholarships, grants, and awards:*** Federal Pell, FSEOG, state, private, college/university gift aid from institutional funds.

GIFT AID (NON-NEED-BASED) ***Total amount:*** $15,087,566 (3% federal, 96% institutional, 1% external sources). ***Receiving aid:*** Freshmen: 12% (48). Undergraduates: 6% (143). ***Average award:*** Freshmen: $19,275. Undergraduates: $14,481. ***Scholarships, grants, and awards by category:*** *Academic interests/achievement:* 1,605 awards ($22,048,176 total): architecture, business, engineering/technologies, foreign languages, general academic interests/achievements, health fields. *Special achievements/activities:* 431 awards ($3,890,234 total): community service, general special achievements/activities, hobbies/interests, leadership, memberships. *Special characteristics:* 891 awards ($7,012,378 total): children and siblings of alumni, children of faculty/staff, children of public servants, ethnic background, general special characteristics, international students, local/state students, members of minority groups, previous college experience, veterans, veterans' children. ***Tuition waivers:*** Full or partial for employees or children of employees.

LOANS ***Student loans:*** $11,195,841 (81% need-based, 19% non-need-based). ***Average need-based loan:*** Freshmen: $3476. Undergraduates: $4829. ***Parent loans:*** $4,398,691 (49% need-based, 51% non-need-based). ***Programs:*** Perkins, college/university.

WORK-STUDY ***Federal work-study:*** Total amount: $1,798,197; 741 jobs averaging $2415. ***State or other work-study/employment:*** Total amount: $12,994,037 (84% need-based, 16% non-need-based). Part-time jobs available.

ATHLETIC AWARDS Total amount: $911,633 (26% need-based, 74% non-need-based).

APPLYING FOR FINANCIAL AID ***Required financial aid form:*** FAFSA. ***Financial aid deadline (priority):*** 4/15. ***Notification date:*** Continuous beginning 3/5.

CONTACT Nareth Phin, Assistant Director of Financial Aid, Illinois Institute of Technology, 3300 South Federal Street, Chicago, IL 60616, 312-567-5730 or toll-free 800-448-2329 (out-of-state). *Fax:* 312-567-3982. *E-mail:* finaid@iit.edu.

ILLINOIS STATE UNIVERSITY

Normal, IL

Tuition & fees (IL res): $11,417 **Average undergraduate aid package: $12,512**

ABOUT THE INSTITUTION State-supported, coed. 65 undergraduate majors. Federal methodology is used as a basis for awarding need-based institutional aid.

UNDERGRADUATE EXPENSES for 2010–11 ***Tuition, state resident:*** full-time $9030; part-time $301 per credit hour. ***Tuition, nonresident:*** full-time $15,570; part-time $519 per credit hour. ***Required fees:*** full-time $2387; $68.23 per credit hour. Full-time tuition and fees vary according to course load and degree level. Part-time tuition and fees vary according to course load and degree level. ***College room and board:*** $8436; ***Room only:*** $4326. Room and board charges vary according to board plan, housing facility, and location. ***Payment plans:*** Guaranteed tuition, installment.

FRESHMAN FINANCIAL AID (Fall 2010, est.) 2,648 applied for aid; of those 77% were deemed to have need. 90% of freshmen with need received aid; of those 39% had need fully met. ***Average percent of need met:*** 75% (excluding resources awarded to replace EFC). ***Average financial aid package:*** $12,461 (excluding resources awarded to replace EFC). 1% of all full-time freshmen had no need and received non-need-based gift aid.

UNDERGRADUATE FINANCIAL AID (Fall 2010, est.) 12,609 applied for aid; of those 82% were deemed to have need. 93% of undergraduates with need received aid; of those 37% had need fully met. ***Average percent of need met:*** 78% (excluding resources awarded to replace EFC). ***Average financial aid package:*** $12,512 (excluding resources awarded to replace EFC). 1% of all full-time undergraduates had no need and received non-need-based gift aid.

GIFT AID (NEED-BASED) ***Total amount:*** $53,639,232 (39% federal, 41% state, 18% institutional, 2% external sources). ***Receiving aid:*** Freshmen: 35% (1,103); all full-time undergraduates: 33% (5,677). ***Average award:*** Freshmen: $9658; Undergraduates: $9501. ***Scholarships, grants, and awards:*** Federal Pell, FSEOG, state, private, college/university gift aid from institutional funds, Federal Nursing.

GIFT AID (NON-NEED-BASED) ***Total amount:*** $6,436,791 (4% federal, 66% state, 20% institutional, 10% external sources). ***Receiving aid:*** Freshmen: 29% (924). Undergraduates: 17% (2,868). ***Average award:*** Freshmen: $1949. Undergraduates: $4024. ***Scholarships, grants, and awards by category:*** *Academic interests/achievement:* 310 awards ($1,245,159 total): agriculture, biological sciences, business, communication, computer science, education, engineering/technologies, English, foreign languages, general academic interests/achievements, health fields, home economics, humanities, international studies, library science, mathematics, military science, physical sciences, premedicine, social sciences. *Creative arts/performance:* 183 awards ($358,292 total): applied art and design, art/fine arts, cinema/film/broadcasting, creative writing, debating, general creative arts/performance, music, performing arts, theater/drama. *Special achievements/activities:* 1 award ($1500 total): community service, leadership. *Special characteristics:* 317 awards ($1,717,673 total): children of faculty/staff, children of union members/company employees, children with a deceased or disabled parent, first-generation college students, general special characteristics, members of minority groups, previous college experience. ***Tuition waivers:*** Full or partial for minority students, employees or children of employees, senior citizens.

LOANS ***Student loans:*** $85,249,950 (68% need-based, 32% non-need-based). 65% of past graduating class borrowed through all loan programs. *Average indebtedness per student:* $22,847. ***Average need-based loan:*** Freshmen: $7327. Undergraduates: $7556. ***Parent loans:*** $28,709,124 (30% need-based, 70% non-need-based). ***Programs:*** Federal Direct (Subsidized and Unsubsidized Stafford, PLUS), Perkins, Federal Nursing.

WORK-STUDY ***Federal work-study:*** Total amount: $1,588,406; 431 jobs averaging $2480. ***State or other work-study/employment:*** Total amount: $86,959 (47% need-based, 53% non-need-based). 54 part-time jobs averaging $2046.

ATHLETIC AWARDS Total amount: $2,413,818 (33% need-based, 67% non-need-based).

APPLYING FOR FINANCIAL AID ***Required financial aid form:*** FAFSA. ***Financial aid deadline (priority):*** 3/1. ***Notification date:*** Continuous beginning 4/1.

CONTACT Mr. David Krueger, Assistant Director of Financial Aid, Illinois State University, Campus Box 2320, Normal, IL 61790-2320, 309-438-2231 or toll-free 800-366-2478 (in-state). *Fax:* 309-438-3755. *E-mail:* financialaid@illinoisitate.edu.

ILLINOIS WESLEYAN UNIVERSITY

Bloomington, IL

Tuition & fees: $35,256 **Average undergraduate aid package: $25,017**

ABOUT THE INSTITUTION Independent, coed. 48 undergraduate majors. Both federal and institutional methodology are used as a basis for awarding need-based institutional aid.

UNDERGRADUATE EXPENSES for 2010–11 ***Comprehensive fee:*** $43,362 includes full-time tuition ($35,076), mandatory fees ($180), and room and board ($8106). ***College room only:*** $5040. Room and board charges vary according to board plan and housing facility. ***Part-time tuition:*** $1096 per credit hour.

FRESHMAN FINANCIAL AID (Fall 2010, est.) 502 applied for aid; of those 83% were deemed to have need. 100% of freshmen with need received aid; of those 31% had need fully met. ***Average percent of need met:*** 91% (excluding resources awarded to replace EFC). ***Average financial aid package:*** $25,400 (excluding resources awarded to replace EFC). 26% of all full-time freshmen had no need and received non-need-based gift aid.

UNDERGRADUATE FINANCIAL AID (Fall 2010, est.) 1,593 applied for aid; of those 89% were deemed to have need. 100% of undergraduates with need received aid; of those 47% had need fully met. ***Average percent of need met:*** 97% (excluding resources awarded to replace EFC). ***Average financial aid package:*** $25,017 (excluding resources awarded to replace EFC). 26% of all full-time undergraduates had no need and received non-need-based gift aid.

GIFT AID (NEED-BASED) ***Total amount:*** $25,279,600 (9% federal, 9% state, 80% institutional, 2% external sources). ***Receiving aid:*** Freshmen: 71% (417); all full-time undergraduates: 68% (1,415). ***Average award:*** Freshmen: $19,432; Undergraduates: $19,513. ***Scholarships, grants, and awards:*** Federal Pell, FSEOG, state, private, college/university gift aid from institutional funds.

GIFT AID (NON-NEED-BASED) ***Total amount:*** $8,765,129 (100% institutional). ***Receiving aid:*** Freshmen: 10% (56). Undergraduates: 9% (192). ***Average award:*** Freshmen: $12,617. Undergraduates: $12,369. ***Scholarships, grants, and awards by category:*** *Academic interests/achievement:* general academic interests/achievements. *Creative arts/performance:* general creative arts/performance, music, theater/drama. *Special characteristics:* children of faculty/staff, general special characteristics, international students.

LOANS ***Student loans:*** $11,471,816 (51% need-based, 49% non-need-based). 68% of past graduating class borrowed through all loan programs. *Average indebtedness per student:* $31,904. ***Average need-based loan:*** Freshmen: $3947. Undergraduates: $5016. ***Parent loans:*** $3,980,929 (100% non-need-based). ***Programs:*** Federal Direct (Subsidized and Unsubsidized Stafford, PLUS), Perkins, Federal Nursing, college/university.

WORK-STUDY ***Federal work-study:*** Total amount: $361,586; jobs available. ***State or other work-study/employment:*** Total amount: $1,735,100 (81% need-based, 19% non-need-based). Part-time jobs available.

APPLYING FOR FINANCIAL AID ***Required financial aid form:*** FAFSA, institution's own financial aid form or CSS/Financial Aid PROFILE. ***Financial aid deadline:*** 3/1. ***Notification date:*** Continuous beginning 2/15. Students must reply by 5/1.

CONTACT Mr. Scott Seibring, Director of Financial Aid, Illinois Wesleyan University, 1312 North Park Street, PO Box 2900, Bloomington, IL 61702-2900, 309-556-3393 or toll-free 800-332-2498. *Fax:* 309-556-3833. *E-mail:* seibring@iwu.edu.

IMMACULATA UNIVERSITY

Immaculata, PA

CONTACT Mr. Peter Lysionek, Director of Student Financial Aid, Immaculata University, 1145 King Road, Box 500, Immaculata, PA 19345, 610-647-4400 Ext. 3026 or toll-free 877-428-6329. *Fax:* 610-640-0836. *E-mail:* plysionek@immaculata.edu.

INDEPENDENCE UNIVERSITY

Salt Lake City, UT

CONTACT Financial Aid Director, Independence University, 2423 Hoover Avenue, National City, CA 91950-6605, 619-477-4800 or toll-free 800-791-7353. *Fax:* 619-477-5202.

INDIANA STATE UNIVERSITY

Terre Haute, IN

Tuition & fees (IN res): $7714 **Average undergraduate aid package: $9054**

ABOUT THE INSTITUTION State-supported, coed. 65 undergraduate majors. Federal methodology is used as a basis for awarding need-based institutional aid.

UNDERGRADUATE EXPENSES for 2010–11 ***Tuition, state resident:*** full-time $7514; part-time $272 per credit hour. ***Tuition, nonresident:*** full-time $16,426; part-time $580 per credit hour. ***Required fees:*** full-time $200; $100 per term. Full-time tuition and fees vary according to reciprocity agreements. Part-time tuition and fees vary according to course load and reciprocity agreements. ***College room and board:*** $7752; ***Room only:*** $4488. Room and board charges vary according to board plan, housing facility, and student level. ***Payment plans:*** Installment, deferred payment.

FRESHMAN FINANCIAL AID (Fall 2009) 1,828 applied for aid; of those 82% were deemed to have need. 96% of freshmen with need received aid; of those 10% had need fully met. ***Average percent of need met:*** 75% (excluding resources awarded to replace EFC). ***Average financial aid package:*** $8557 (excluding resources awarded to replace EFC). 12% of all full-time freshmen had no need and received non-need-based gift aid.

UNDERGRADUATE FINANCIAL AID (Fall 2009) 6,167 applied for aid; of those 82% were deemed to have need. 96% of undergraduates with need received aid; of those 11% had need fully met. ***Average percent of need met:*** 77% (excluding resources awarded to replace EFC). ***Average financial aid package:*** $9054 (excluding resources awarded to replace EFC). 10% of all full-time undergraduates had no need and received non-need-based gift aid.

GIFT AID (NEED-BASED) ***Total amount:*** $21,004,300 (64% federal, 31% state, 3% institutional, 2% external sources). ***Receiving aid:*** Freshmen: 49% (968); all full-time undergraduates: 44% (3,208). ***Average award:*** Freshmen: $6388; Undergraduates: $6211. ***Scholarships, grants, and awards:*** Federal Pell, FSEOG, state, private, college/university gift aid from institutional funds.

GIFT AID (NON-NEED-BASED) ***Total amount:*** $13,915,952 (32% state, 53% institutional, 15% external sources). ***Receiving aid:*** Freshmen: 43% (848). Undergraduates: 29% (2,115). ***Average award:*** Freshmen: $3884. Undergraduates: $4782. ***Scholarships, grants, and awards by category:*** *Academic interests/achievement:* 1,865 awards ($4,025,841 total): general academic interests/achievements, premedicine. *Creative arts/performance:* 91 awards ($224,000 total): art/fine arts, performing arts. *Special characteristics:* 342 awards ($960,226 total): children and siblings of alumni, children of faculty/staff, members of minority groups, previous college experience, veterans. ***Tuition waivers:*** Full or partial for employees or children of employees, senior citizens.

LOANS ***Student loans:*** $33,386,859 (42% need-based, 58% non-need-based). 66% of past graduating class borrowed through all loan programs. *Average indebtedness per student:* $22,124. ***Average need-based loan:*** Freshmen: $3039. Undergraduates: $3814. ***Parent loans:*** $6,552,804 (100% non-need-based). ***Programs:*** Federal Direct (Subsidized and Unsubsidized Stafford, PLUS), Perkins, alternative loans.

WORK-STUDY ***Federal work-study:*** Total amount: $605,871; 426 jobs averaging $1387. ***State or other work-study/employment:*** Part-time jobs available.

ATHLETIC AWARDS Total amount: $3,248,275 (100% non-need-based).

APPLYING FOR FINANCIAL AID ***Required financial aid form:*** FAFSA. ***Financial aid deadline (priority):*** 3/1. ***Notification date:*** Continuous beginning 4/1.

CONTACT Kim Donat, Director of Student Financial Aid, Indiana State University, 150 Tirey Hall, Terre Haute, IN 47809-1401, 812-237-2215 or toll-free 800-742-0891. *Fax:* 812-237-4330. *E-mail:* finaid@indstate.edu.

INDIANA TECH

Fort Wayne, IN

CONTACT Financial Aid Office, Indiana Tech, 1600 East Washington Boulevard, Fort Wayne, IN 46803-1297, 800-937-2448 or toll-free 888-666-TECH (out-of-state). *Fax:* 219-422-1578.

INDIANA UNIVERSITY BLOOMINGTON

Bloomington, IN

Tuition & fees (IN res): $9028 **Average undergraduate aid package: $10,480**

ABOUT THE INSTITUTION State-supported, coed. 122 undergraduate majors. Federal methodology is used as a basis for awarding need-based institutional aid.

UNDERGRADUATE EXPENSES for 2010–11 ***Tuition, state resident:*** full-time $8124; part-time $253.70 per credit hour. ***Tuition, nonresident:*** full-time $26,785; part-time $837.20 per credit hour. ***Required fees:*** full-time $904. Full-time tuition and fees vary according to location and program. Part-time tuition and fees vary according to course load, location, and program. ***College room and board:*** $7918; ***Room only:*** $5018. Room and board charges vary according to board plan and housing facility. ***Payment plan:*** Deferred payment.

FRESHMAN FINANCIAL AID (Fall 2009) 5,277 applied for aid; of those 64% were deemed to have need. 97% of freshmen with need received aid; of those 20% had need fully met. ***Average percent of need met:*** 91% (excluding resources awarded to replace EFC). ***Average financial aid package:*** $10,834 (excluding resources awarded to replace EFC). 24% of all full-time freshmen had no need and received non-need-based gift aid.

UNDERGRADUATE FINANCIAL AID (Fall 2009) 18,782 applied for aid; of those 71% were deemed to have need. 97% of undergraduates with need received aid; of those 15% had need fully met. ***Average percent of need met:*** 89% (excluding resources awarded to replace EFC). ***Average financial aid package:*** $10,480 (excluding resources awarded to replace EFC). 22% of all full-time undergraduates had no need and received non-need-based gift aid.

GIFT AID (NEED-BASED) ***Total amount:*** $84,877,764 (31% federal, 26% state, 37% institutional, 6% external sources). ***Receiving aid:*** Freshmen: 37% (2,738); all full-time undergraduates: 32% (10,011). ***Average award:*** Freshmen: $9724; Undergraduates: $8655. ***Scholarships, grants, and awards:*** Federal Pell, FSEOG, state, private, college/university gift aid from institutional funds.

GIFT AID (NON-NEED-BASED) ***Total amount:*** $53,292,227 (1% federal, 3% state, 81% institutional, 15% external sources). ***Receiving aid:*** Freshmen: 7% (513). Undergraduates: 4% (1,346). ***Average award:*** Freshmen: $6646. Undergraduates: $5699. ***Tuition waivers:*** Full or partial for employees or children of employees.

LOANS ***Student loans:*** $120,274,261 (55% need-based, 45% non-need-based). 55% of past graduating class borrowed through all loan programs. *Average indebtedness per student:* $27,752. ***Average need-based loan:*** Freshmen: $3103. Undergraduates: $4318. ***Parent loans:*** $40,114,319 (29% need-based, 71% non-need-based). ***Programs:*** Federal Direct (Subsidized and Unsubsidized Stafford, PLUS), Perkins, college/university.

WORK-STUDY ***Federal work-study:*** Total amount: $951,273; jobs available. ***State or other work-study/employment:*** Total amount: $32,479 (46% need-based, 54% non-need-based). Part-time jobs available.

ATHLETIC AWARDS Total amount: $9,084,262 (29% need-based, 71% non-need-based).

APPLYING FOR FINANCIAL AID ***Required financial aid form:*** FAFSA. ***Financial aid deadline (priority):*** 3/1. ***Notification date:*** Continuous beginning 4/1.

CONTACT Susan Pugh, Director of Student Financial Assistance, Indiana University Bloomington, Franklin Hall 208, Bloomington, IN 47405, 812-855-0321. *Fax:* 812-855-7615. *E-mail:* rsvposfa@indiana.edu.

INDIANA UNIVERSITY EAST

Richmond, IN

Tuition & fees (IN res): $6069 **Average undergraduate aid package: $8044**

ABOUT THE INSTITUTION State-supported, coed. 29 undergraduate majors. Federal methodology is used as a basis for awarding need-based institutional aid.

UNDERGRADUATE EXPENSES for 2010–11 ***Tuition, state resident:*** full-time $5676; part-time $189.21 per credit hour. ***Tuition, nonresident:*** full-time $15,912; part-time $530.41 per credit hour. ***Required fees:*** full-time $393. Full-time tuition and fees vary according to course load, location, program, and reciprocity agreements. Part-time tuition and fees vary according to course load, location, program, and reciprocity agreements. ***Payment plan:*** Deferred payment.

FRESHMAN FINANCIAL AID (Fall 2009) 340 applied for aid; of those 87% were deemed to have need. 98% of freshmen with need received aid; of those 11% had need fully met. ***Average percent of need met:*** 97% (excluding resources awarded to replace EFC). ***Average financial aid package:*** $7322 (excluding resources awarded to replace EFC). 4% of all full-time freshmen had no need and received non-need-based gift aid.

UNDERGRADUATE FINANCIAL AID (Fall 2009) 1,382 applied for aid; of those 89% were deemed to have need. 98% of undergraduates with need received aid; of those 5% had need fully met. ***Average percent of need met:*** 96% (excluding resources awarded to replace EFC). ***Average financial aid package:*** $8044 (excluding resources awarded to replace EFC). 4% of all full-time undergraduates had no need and received non-need-based gift aid.

GIFT AID (NEED-BASED) ***Total amount:*** $7,348,663 (66% federal, 26% state, 4% institutional, 4% external sources). ***Receiving aid:*** Freshmen: 72% (257); all full-time undergraduates: 69% (1,040). ***Average award:*** Freshmen: $6101; Undergraduates: $5786. ***Scholarships, grants, and awards:*** Federal Pell, FSEOG, state, private, college/university gift aid from institutional funds.

GIFT AID (NON-NEED-BASED) ***Total amount:*** $255,406 (9% federal, 12% state, 39% institutional, 40% external sources). ***Receiving aid:*** Freshmen: 6% (22). Undergraduates: 2% (35). ***Average award:*** Freshmen: $1702. Undergraduates: $1412. ***Tuition waivers:*** Full or partial for employees or children of employees.

LOANS ***Student loans:*** $11,296,483 (82% need-based, 18% non-need-based). 78% of past graduating class borrowed through all loan programs. *Average indebtedness per student:* $27,069. ***Average need-based loan:*** Freshmen: $2791. Undergraduates: $3684. ***Parent loans:*** $72,304 (29% need-based, 71% non-need-based). ***Programs:*** Federal Direct (Subsidized and Unsubsidized Stafford, PLUS), Perkins, college/university.

WORK-STUDY ***Federal work-study:*** Total amount: $107,214; jobs available.

ATHLETIC AWARDS Total amount: $60,750 (100% need-based).

APPLYING FOR FINANCIAL AID ***Required financial aid forms:*** FAFSA, institution's own form. ***Financial aid deadline (priority):*** 3/1. ***Notification date:*** Continuous beginning 5/1. Students must reply within 2 weeks of notification.

CONTACT Sarah Soper, Associate Director of Financial Aid and Scholarships, Indiana University East, 2325 Chester Boulevard, Whitewater Hall 112, Richmond, IN 47374-1289, 765-973-8206 or toll-free 800-959-EAST. *Fax:* 765-973-8288. *E-mail:* eaosfa@iue.edu.

INDIANA UNIVERSITY KOKOMO

Kokomo, IN

Tuition & fees (IN res): $6109 **Average undergraduate aid package: $7744**

ABOUT THE INSTITUTION State-supported, coed. 29 undergraduate majors. Federal methodology is used as a basis for awarding need-based institutional aid.

UNDERGRADUATE EXPENSES for 2010–11 ***Tuition, state resident:*** full-time $5663; part-time $188.75 per credit hour. ***Tuition, nonresident:*** full-time $14,928; part-time $497.61 per credit hour. ***Required fees:*** full-time $446. Full-time tuition and fees vary according to course load, location, and program. Part-time tuition and fees vary according to course load, location, and program. Room and board charges vary according to board plan, housing facility, and location. ***Payment plan:*** Deferred payment.

FRESHMAN FINANCIAL AID (Fall 2009) 372 applied for aid; of those 74% were deemed to have need. 95% of freshmen with need received aid; of those 6% had need fully met. ***Average percent of need met:*** 92% (excluding resources awarded to replace EFC). ***Average financial aid package:*** $6688 (excluding resources awarded to replace EFC). 6% of all full-time freshmen had no need and received non-need-based gift aid.

UNDERGRADUATE FINANCIAL AID (Fall 2009) 1,351 applied for aid; of those 81% were deemed to have need. 96% of undergraduates with need received aid; of those 4% had need fully met. ***Average percent of need met:*** 92% (excluding resources awarded to replace EFC). ***Average financial aid package:*** $7744 (excluding resources awarded to replace EFC). 3% of all full-time undergraduates had no need and received non-need-based gift aid.

GIFT AID (NEED-BASED) ***Total amount:*** $6,290,888 (57% federal, 33% state, 6% institutional, 4% external sources). ***Receiving aid:*** Freshmen: 50% (201); all full-time undergraduates: 53% (820). ***Average award:*** Freshmen: $6347; Undergraduates: $6212. ***Scholarships, grants, and awards:*** Federal Pell, FSEOG, state, private, college/university gift aid from institutional funds.

GIFT AID (NON-NEED-BASED) ***Total amount:*** $562,408 (6% federal, 23% state, 17% institutional, 54% external sources). ***Receiving aid:*** Freshmen: 3% (11). Undergraduates: 2% (29). ***Average award:*** Freshmen: $1475. Undergraduates: $1501. ***Tuition waivers:*** Full or partial for employees or children of employees.

LOANS ***Student loans:*** $9,611,676 (73% need-based, 27% non-need-based). 71% of past graduating class borrowed through all loan programs. *Average indebtedness per student:* $23,454. ***Average need-based loan:*** Freshmen: $2853. Undergraduates: $3669. ***Parent loans:*** $65,654 (13% need-based, 87% non-need-based). ***Programs:*** Federal Direct (Subsidized and Unsubsidized Stafford, PLUS), Perkins, Federal Nursing, college/university.

WORK-STUDY ***Federal work-study:*** Total amount: $54,176; jobs available. ***State or other work-study/employment:*** Total amount: $3363 (35% need-based, 65% non-need-based). Part-time jobs available.

APPLYING FOR FINANCIAL AID ***Required financial aid forms:*** FAFSA, institution's own form. ***Financial aid deadline:*** 3/1. ***Notification date:*** Continuous beginning 5/1. Students must reply within 4 weeks of notification.

CONTACT Karen Gallatin, Associate Director of Financial Aid, Indiana University Kokomo, 2300 South Washington Street, Kelley Student Center, Room 230, Kokomo, IN 46904-9003, 765-455-9216 or toll-free 888-875-4485. *Fax:* 765-455-9537. *E-mail:* finaidko@iuk.edu.

INDIANA UNIVERSITY NORTHWEST

Gary, IN

Tuition & fees (IN res): $6193 **Average undergraduate aid package: $8070**

ABOUT THE INSTITUTION State-supported, coed. 41 undergraduate majors. Federal methodology is used as a basis for awarding need-based institutional aid.

UNDERGRADUATE EXPENSES for 2010–11 ***Tuition, state resident:*** full-time $5752; part-time $191.74 per credit hour. ***Tuition, nonresident:*** full-time $15,940; part-time $531.32 per credit hour. ***Required fees:*** full-time $441. Full-time tuition and fees vary according to course load, location, and program. Part-time tuition and fees vary according to course load, location, and program. ***Payment plans:*** Installment, deferred payment.

FRESHMAN FINANCIAL AID (Fall 2009) 644 applied for aid; of those 81% were deemed to have need. 94% of freshmen with need received aid; of those 4% had need fully met. ***Average percent of need met:*** 92% (excluding resources awarded to replace EFC). ***Average financial aid package:*** $7063 (excluding resources awarded to replace EFC). 6% of all full-time freshmen had no need and received non-need-based gift aid.

UNDERGRADUATE FINANCIAL AID (Fall 2009) 2,535 applied for aid; of those 84% were deemed to have need. 96% of undergraduates with need received aid; of those 3% had need fully met. ***Average percent of need met:*** 91% (excluding resources awarded to replace EFC). ***Average financial aid package:*** $8070 (excluding resources awarded to replace EFC). 4% of all full-time undergraduates had no need and received non-need-based gift aid.

GIFT AID (NEED-BASED) ***Total amount:*** $12,387,283 (65% federal, 29% state, 3% institutional, 3% external sources). ***Receiving aid:*** Freshmen: 52% (401); all full-time undergraduates: 53% (1,632). ***Average award:*** Freshmen: $5954; Undergraduates: $6247. ***Scholarships, grants, and awards:*** Federal Pell, FSEOG, state, private, college/university gift aid from institutional funds, Federal Nursing.

GIFT AID (NON-NEED-BASED) ***Total amount:*** $868,653 (10% federal, 9% state, 63% institutional, 18% external sources). ***Receiving aid:*** Freshmen: 2% (14). Undergraduates: 1% (27). ***Average award:*** Freshmen: $3223. Undergraduates: $3739. ***Tuition waivers:*** Full or partial for employees or children of employees.

LOANS ***Student loans:*** $20,732,693 (79% need-based, 21% non-need-based). 74% of past graduating class borrowed through all loan programs. *Average indebtedness per student:* $27,356. ***Average need-based loan:*** Freshmen: $3136. Undergraduates: $3743. ***Parent loans:*** $169,224 (26% need-based, 74% non-need-based). ***Programs:*** Federal Direct (Subsidized and Unsubsidized Stafford, PLUS), Perkins, college/university.

WORK-STUDY ***Federal work-study:*** Total amount: $242,702; jobs available.

ATHLETIC AWARDS Total amount: $41,700 (54% need-based, 46% non-need-based).

APPLYING FOR FINANCIAL AID ***Required financial aid forms:*** FAFSA, institution's own form. ***Financial aid deadline (priority):*** 3/1. ***Notification date:*** Continuous beginning 5/1. Students must reply within 2 weeks of notification.

CONTACT Harold Burtley, Director of Scholarships and Financial Aid, Indiana University Northwest, 3400 Broadway, Hawthorn Hall, Room 111, Gary, IN 46408, 219-980-6778 or toll-free 800-968-7486. *Fax:* 219-981-5622. *E-mail:* finaidnw@iun.edu.

INDIANA UNIVERSITY OF PENNSYLVANIA

Indiana, PA

Tuition & fees (PA res): $7571 **Average undergraduate aid package: $8991**

ABOUT THE INSTITUTION State-supported, coed. 70 undergraduate majors. Federal methodology is used as a basis for awarding need-based institutional aid.

UNDERGRADUATE EXPENSES for 2010–11 ***Tuition, state resident:*** full-time $5804; part-time $242 per credit hour. ***Tuition, nonresident:*** full-time $14,510; part-time $605 per credit hour. ***Required fees:*** full-time $1767; $24.20 per credit hour or $261.50 per term. Full-time tuition and fees vary according to course load and reciprocity agreements. Part-time tuition and fees vary according to course load and reciprocity agreements. ***College room and board:*** $9300; ***Room only:*** $6840. Room and board charges vary according to board plan, housing facility, and location. ***Payment plans:*** Installment, deferred payment.

FRESHMAN FINANCIAL AID (Fall 2009) 2,787 applied for aid; of those 75% were deemed to have need. 99% of freshmen with need received aid; of those 12% had need fully met. ***Average percent of need met:*** 77% (excluding resources awarded to replace EFC). ***Average financial aid package:*** $10,032 (excluding resources awarded to replace EFC). 5% of all full-time freshmen had no need and received non-need-based gift aid.

UNDERGRADUATE FINANCIAL AID (Fall 2009) 9,293 applied for aid; of those 79% were deemed to have need. 99% of undergraduates with need received aid; of those 10% had need fully met. ***Average percent of need met:*** 70% (excluding resources awarded to replace EFC). ***Average financial aid package:*** $8991 (excluding resources awarded to replace EFC). 3% of all full-time undergraduates had no need and received non-need-based gift aid.

GIFT AID (NEED-BASED) ***Total amount:*** $26,068,563 (56% federal, 44% state). ***Receiving aid:*** Freshmen: 47% (1,433); all full-time undergraduates: 46% (5,029). ***Average award:*** Freshmen: $5387; Undergraduates: $5035. ***Scholarships, grants, and awards:*** Federal Pell, FSEOG, state, private, college/university gift aid from institutional funds, United Negro College Fund.

GIFT AID (NON-NEED-BASED) ***Total amount:*** $5,633,503 (53% institutional, 47% external sources). ***Receiving aid:*** Freshmen: 25% (766). Undergraduates: 15% (1,680). ***Average award:*** Freshmen: $2346. Undergraduates: $2705. ***Scholarships, grants, and awards by category:*** *Academic interests/achievement:* 1,158 awards ($2,510,567 total): area/ethnic studies, biological sciences, business, communication, computer science, education, engineering/technologies, English, foreign languages, general academic interests/achievements, health fields, home economics, humanities, international studies, mathematics, physical sciences, premedicine, social sciences. *Creative arts/performance:* applied art and design, art/fine arts, dance, general creative arts/performance, journalism/publications, music, performing arts, theater/drama. *Special achievements/activities:* community service, general special achievements/activities, hobbies/interests, leadership. *Special characteristics:* 2,016 awards ($10,503,441 total): adult students, children of faculty/staff, ethnic background, international students. ***Tuition waivers:*** Full or partial for employees or children of employees, senior citizens.

LOANS *Student loans:* $66,222,332 (42% need-based, 58% non-need-based). 84% of past graduating class borrowed through all loan programs. *Average indebtedness per student:* $25,224. ***Average need-based loan:*** Freshmen: $3650. Undergraduates: $4093. ***Parent loans:*** $6,219,320 (100% non-need-based). ***Programs:*** Perkins, private loans.

WORK-STUDY *Federal work-study:* Total amount: $7,256,912; 1,158 jobs averaging $1827. ***State or other work-study/employment:*** 1,767 part-time jobs averaging $2550.

ATHLETIC AWARDS Total amount: $833,814 (100% non-need-based).

APPLYING FOR FINANCIAL AID *Required financial aid form:* FAFSA. ***Financial aid deadline:*** 4/15. ***Notification date:*** Continuous.

CONTACT Mrs. Patricia C. McCarthy, Director of Financial Aid, Indiana University of Pennsylvania, 213 Clark Hall, Indiana, PA 15705, 724-357-2218 or toll-free 800-442-6830. *Fax:* 724-357-2094. *E-mail:* mccarthy@iup.edu.

INDIANA UNIVERSITY–PURDUE UNIVERSITY FORT WAYNE

Fort Wayne, IN

Tuition & fees (IN res): $6545 **Average undergraduate aid package: $9513**

ABOUT THE INSTITUTION State-supported, coed. 101 undergraduate majors. Federal methodology is used as a basis for awarding need-based institutional aid.

UNDERGRADUATE EXPENSES for 2010–11 *Tuition, state resident:* full-time $5712; part-time $211.55 per credit hour. ***Tuition, nonresident:*** full-time $14,886; part-time $551.35 per credit hour. ***Required fees:*** full-time $833; $30.85 per credit hour. Full-time tuition and fees vary according to course load. Part-time tuition and fees vary according to course load. ***College room and board: Room only:*** $5900. Room and board charges vary according to housing facility. ***Payment plans:*** Installment, deferred payment.

FRESHMAN FINANCIAL AID (Fall 2009) 1,796 applied for aid; of those 82% were deemed to have need. 95% of freshmen with need received aid; of those .4% had need fully met. ***Average percent of need met:*** 52% (excluding resources awarded to replace EFC). ***Average financial aid package:*** $8804 (excluding resources awarded to replace EFC). 1% of all full-time freshmen had no need and received non-need-based gift aid.

UNDERGRADUATE FINANCIAL AID (Fall 2009) 7,146 applied for aid; of those 84% were deemed to have need. 96% of undergraduates with need received aid; of those .1% had need fully met. ***Average percent of need met:*** 52% (excluding resources awarded to replace EFC). ***Average financial aid package:*** $9513 (excluding resources awarded to replace EFC). 1% of all full-time undergraduates had no need and received non-need-based gift aid.

GIFT AID (NEED-BASED) *Total amount:* $30,323,294 (62% federal, 33% state, 2% institutional, 3% external sources). ***Receiving aid:*** Freshmen: 45% (905); all full-time undergraduates: 45% (3,758). ***Average award:*** Freshmen: $6397; Undergraduates: $6170. ***Scholarships, grants, and awards:*** Federal Pell, FSEOG, state, private, college/university gift aid from institutional funds.

GIFT AID (NON-NEED-BASED) *Total amount:* $1,181,801 (29% state, 33% institutional, 38% external sources). ***Receiving aid:*** Freshmen: 25% (501). Undergraduates: 16% (1,303). ***Average award:*** Freshmen: $1770. Undergraduates: $1946. ***Scholarships, grants, and awards by category:*** *Academic interests/achievement:* general academic interests/achievements. *Creative arts/performance:* art/fine arts, music, theater/drama. *Special achievements/activities:* leadership. *Special characteristics:* children and siblings of alumni, local/state students. ***Tuition waivers:*** Full or partial for employees or children of employees, senior citizens.

LOANS *Student loans:* $49,312,262 (98% need-based, 2% non-need-based). 25% of past graduating class borrowed through all loan programs. *Average indebtedness per student:* $23,607. ***Average need-based loan:*** Freshmen: $3018. Undergraduates: $3768. ***Parent loans:*** $1,474,688 (97% need-based, 3% non-need-based). ***Programs:*** Federal Direct (Subsidized and Unsubsidized Stafford, PLUS), Perkins.

WORK-STUDY *Federal work-study:* Total amount: $434,484; jobs available.

ATHLETIC AWARDS Total amount: $1,760,407 (28% need-based, 72% non-need-based).

APPLYING FOR FINANCIAL AID *Required financial aid form:* FAFSA. ***Financial aid deadline (priority):*** 3/10. ***Notification date:*** Continuous beginning 5/15. Students must reply within 3 weeks of notification.

CONTACT Ms. Judith Cramer, Director of Financial Aid, Indiana University–Purdue University Fort Wayne, 2101 East Coliseum Boulevard, Fort Wayne, IN 46805-1499, 260-481-6130 or toll-free 800-324-4739 (in-state). *E-mail:* finaid@ipfw.edu.

INDIANA UNIVERSITY–PURDUE UNIVERSITY INDIANAPOLIS

Indianapolis, IN

Tuition & fees (IN res): $7885 **Average undergraduate aid package: $9094**

ABOUT THE INSTITUTION State-supported, coed. 90 undergraduate majors. Federal methodology is used as a basis for awarding need-based institutional aid.

UNDERGRADUATE EXPENSES for 2010–11 *Tuition, state resident:* full-time $7255; part-time $241.84 per credit hour. ***Tuition, nonresident:*** full-time $23,798; part-time $793.25 per credit hour. ***Required fees:*** full-time $630. Full-time tuition and fees vary according to course load, location, and program. Part-time tuition and fees vary according to course load, location, and program. ***College room and board:*** $7944. Room and board charges vary according to housing facility. ***Payment plans:*** Installment, deferred payment.

FRESHMAN FINANCIAL AID (Fall 2009) 2,462 applied for aid; of those 79% were deemed to have need. 97% of freshmen with need received aid; of those 6% had need fully met. ***Average percent of need met:*** 90% (excluding resources awarded to replace EFC). ***Average financial aid package:*** $9196 (excluding resources awarded to replace EFC). 7% of all full-time freshmen had no need and received non-need-based gift aid.

UNDERGRADUATE FINANCIAL AID (Fall 2009) 12,522 applied for aid; of those 84% were deemed to have need. 97% of undergraduates with need received aid; of those 5% had need fully met. ***Average percent of need met:*** 89% (excluding resources awarded to replace EFC). ***Average financial aid package:*** $9094 (excluding resources awarded to replace EFC). 7% of all full-time undergraduates had no need and received non-need-based gift aid.

GIFT AID (NEED-BASED) *Total amount:* $60,059,499 (50% federal, 32% state, 13% institutional, 5% external sources). ***Receiving aid:*** Freshmen: 55% (1,528); all full-time undergraduates: 51% (7,837). ***Average award:*** Freshmen: $8106; Undergraduates: $7059. ***Scholarships, grants, and awards:*** Federal Pell, FSEOG, state, private, college/university gift aid from institutional funds.

GIFT AID (NON-NEED-BASED) *Total amount:* $12,406,105 (5% federal, 9% state, 38% institutional, 48% external sources). ***Receiving aid:*** Freshmen: 4% (100). Undergraduates: 2% (364). ***Average award:*** Freshmen: $4997. Undergraduates: $3770. ***Tuition waivers:*** Full or partial for employees or children of employees.

LOANS *Student loans:* $100,750,844 (77% need-based, 23% non-need-based). 73% of past graduating class borrowed through all loan programs. *Average indebtedness per student:* $29,112. ***Average need-based loan:*** Freshmen: $3228. Undergraduates: $4124. ***Parent loans:*** $5,098,785 (29% need-based, 71% non-need-based). ***Programs:*** Federal Direct (Subsidized and Unsubsidized Stafford, PLUS), Perkins, Federal Nursing, college/university.

WORK-STUDY *Federal work-study:* Total amount: $1,728,260; jobs available. ***State or other work-study/employment:*** Total amount: $43,078 (65% need-based, 35% non-need-based). Part-time jobs available.

ATHLETIC AWARDS Total amount: $1,660,556 (47% need-based, 53% non-need-based).

APPLYING FOR FINANCIAL AID *Required financial aid form:* FAFSA. ***Financial aid deadline (priority):*** 3/1. ***Notification date:*** Continuous beginning 4/1.

CONTACT Kathy Purvis, Director of Financial Aid Services, Indiana University–Purdue University Indianapolis, 420 University Boulevard, CE 250, Indianapolis, IN 46202-5145, 317-274-4162. *Fax:* 317-274-3664. *E-mail:* finaid@iupui.edu.

INDIANA UNIVERSITY SOUTH BEND

South Bend, IN

Tuition & fees (IN res): $6290 **Average undergraduate aid package: $7859**

ABOUT THE INSTITUTION State-supported, coed. 64 undergraduate majors. Federal methodology is used as a basis for awarding need-based institutional aid.

UNDERGRADUATE EXPENSES for 2010–11 ***Tuition, state resident:*** full-time $5843; part-time $194.75 per credit hour. ***Tuition, nonresident:*** full-time $16,170; part-time $539 per credit hour. ***Required fees:*** full-time $447. Full-time tuition and fees vary according to course load, location, and program. Part-time tuition and fees vary according to course load, location, and program. ***College room and board: Room only:*** $5382. Room and board charges vary according to board plan, housing facility, and location. ***Payment plan:*** Deferred payment.

FRESHMAN FINANCIAL AID (Fall 2009) 944 applied for aid; of those 82% were deemed to have need. 94% of freshmen with need received aid; of those 3% had need fully met. ***Average percent of need met:*** 91% (excluding resources awarded to replace EFC). ***Average financial aid package:*** $6920 (excluding resources awarded to replace EFC). 2% of all full-time freshmen had no need and received non-need-based gift aid.

UNDERGRADUATE FINANCIAL AID (Fall 2009) 3,622 applied for aid; of those 84% were deemed to have need. 96% of undergraduates with need received aid; of those 3% had need fully met. ***Average percent of need met:*** 93% (excluding resources awarded to replace EFC). ***Average financial aid package:*** $7859 (excluding resources awarded to replace EFC). 3% of all full-time undergraduates had no need and received non-need-based gift aid.

GIFT AID (NEED-BASED) ***Total amount:*** $17,381,562 (61% federal, 29% state, 6% institutional, 4% external sources). ***Receiving aid:*** Freshmen: 58% (602); all full-time undergraduates: 56% (2,391). ***Average award:*** Freshmen: $6069; Undergraduates: $6186. ***Scholarships, grants, and awards:*** Federal Pell, FSEOG, state, private, college/university gift aid from institutional funds.

GIFT AID (NON-NEED-BASED) ***Total amount:*** $1,721,795 (7% federal, 8% state, 36% institutional, 49% external sources). ***Receiving aid:*** Freshmen: 1% (11). Undergraduates: 1% (56). ***Average award:*** Freshmen: $2980. Undergraduates: $4454. ***Tuition waivers:*** Full or partial for employees or children of employees.

LOANS ***Student loans:*** $24,487,160 (78% need-based, 22% non-need-based). 74% of past graduating class borrowed through all loan programs. *Average indebtedness per student:* $25,373. ***Average need-based loan:*** Freshmen: $2820. Undergraduates: $3629. ***Parent loans:*** $571,552 (21% need-based, 79% non-need-based). ***Programs:*** Federal Direct (Subsidized and Unsubsidized Stafford, PLUS), Perkins, college/university.

WORK-STUDY ***Federal work-study:*** Total amount: $161,762; jobs available. ***State or other work-study/employment:*** Total amount: $16,702 (82% need-based, 18% non-need-based). Part-time jobs available.

ATHLETIC AWARDS Total amount: $166,484 (66% need-based, 34% non-need-based).

APPLYING FOR FINANCIAL AID ***Required financial aid forms:*** FAFSA, institution's own form. ***Financial aid deadline:*** 3/1. ***Notification date:*** Continuous beginning 5/1.

CONTACT Cynthia A. Lang, Associate Director of Financial Aid and Scholarships, Indiana University South Bend, 1700 Mishawaka Avenue, Financial Aid Administration Building 157, South Bend, IN 46634-7111, 574-520-4357 or toll-free 877-GO-2-IUSB. *Fax:* 574-520-5561. *E-mail:* sbfinaid@iusb.edu.

INDIANA UNIVERSITY SOUTHEAST

New Albany, IN

Tuition & fees (IN res): $6163 **Average undergraduate aid package: $7667**

ABOUT THE INSTITUTION State-supported, coed. 49 undergraduate majors. Federal methodology is used as a basis for awarding need-based institutional aid.

UNDERGRADUATE EXPENSES for 2010–11 ***Tuition, state resident:*** full-time $5672; part-time $189.07 per credit hour. ***Tuition, nonresident:*** full-time $14,937; part-time $497.89 per credit hour. ***Required fees:*** full-time $491. Full-time tuition and fees vary according to course load, location, program, and reciprocity agreements. Part-time tuition and fees vary according to course load, location, program, and reciprocity agreements. ***College room and board: Room only:*** $5686. Room and board charges vary according to board plan and housing facility. ***Payment plan:*** Deferred payment.

FRESHMAN FINANCIAL AID (Fall 2009) 865 applied for aid; of those 78% were deemed to have need. 95% of freshmen with need received aid; of those 5% had need fully met. ***Average percent of need met:*** 93% (excluding resources awarded to replace EFC). ***Average financial aid package:*** $6883 (excluding resources awarded to replace EFC). 4% of all full-time freshmen had no need and received non-need-based gift aid.

UNDERGRADUATE FINANCIAL AID (Fall 2009) 3,133 applied for aid; of those 80% were deemed to have need. 97% of undergraduates with need received aid; of those 5% had need fully met. ***Average percent of need met:*** 93% (excluding resources awarded to replace EFC). ***Average financial aid package:*** $7667 (excluding resources awarded to replace EFC). 4% of all full-time undergraduates had no need and received non-need-based gift aid.

GIFT AID (NEED-BASED) ***Total amount:*** $13,641,611 (61% federal, 28% state, 6% institutional, 5% external sources). ***Receiving aid:*** Freshmen: 53% (531); all full-time undergraduates: 51% (1,984). ***Average award:*** Freshmen: $5865; Undergraduates: $5948. ***Scholarships, grants, and awards:*** Federal Pell, FSEOG, state, private, college/university gift aid from institutional funds.

GIFT AID (NON-NEED-BASED) ***Total amount:*** $1,176,445 (1% federal, 16% state, 26% institutional, 57% external sources). ***Receiving aid:*** Freshmen: 3% (25). Undergraduates: 2% (67). ***Average award:*** Freshmen: $1736. Undergraduates: $1855. ***Tuition waivers:*** Full or partial for employees or children of employees.

LOANS ***Student loans:*** $19,677,854 (74% need-based, 26% non-need-based). 66% of past graduating class borrowed through all loan programs. *Average indebtedness per student:* $21,456. ***Average need-based loan:*** Freshmen: $3106. Undergraduates: $3783. ***Parent loans:*** $503,970 (30% need-based, 70% non-need-based). ***Programs:*** Federal Direct (Subsidized and Unsubsidized Stafford, PLUS), Perkins, Federal Nursing, college/university.

WORK-STUDY ***Federal work-study:*** Total amount: $345,881; jobs available. ***State or other work-study/employment:*** Total amount: $4588 (100% non-need-based). Part-time jobs available.

ATHLETIC AWARDS Total amount: $90,963 (66% need-based, 34% non-need-based).

APPLYING FOR FINANCIAL AID ***Required financial aid form:*** FAFSA. ***Financial aid deadline (priority):*** 3/1. ***Notification date:*** Continuous beginning 5/1. Students must reply within 3 weeks of notification.

CONTACT Brittany Hubbard, Director of Financial Aid, Indiana University Southeast, University Center, South Room 105, New Albany, IN 47150, 812-941-2246 or toll-free 800-852-8835 (in-state). *Fax:* 812-941-2546. *E-mail:* financialaid@ius.edu.

INDIANA WESLEYAN UNIVERSITY

Marion, IN

Tuition & fees: $21,956 **Average undergraduate aid package: $21,291**

ABOUT THE INSTITUTION Independent Wesleyan, coed. 86 undergraduate majors. Federal methodology is used as a basis for awarding need-based institutional aid.

UNDERGRADUATE EXPENSES for 2011–12 ***Comprehensive fee:*** $29,104 includes full-time tuition ($21,956) and room and board ($7148). ***College room only:*** $3458. Full-time tuition and fees vary according to course load. Room and board charges vary according to board plan. ***Part-time tuition:*** $785 per credit. Part-time tuition and fees vary according to course load. ***Payment plan:*** Installment.

FRESHMAN FINANCIAL AID (Fall 2009) 729 applied for aid; of those 76% were deemed to have need. 100% of freshmen with need received aid; of those 37% had need fully met. ***Average percent of need met:*** 85% (excluding resources awarded to replace EFC). ***Average financial aid package:*** $20,735 (excluding resources awarded to replace EFC). 22% of all full-time freshmen had no need and received non-need-based gift aid.

UNDERGRADUATE FINANCIAL AID (Fall 2009) 2,833 applied for aid; of those 75% were deemed to have need. 100% of undergraduates with need received aid; of those 42% had need fully met. ***Average percent of need met:*** 87% (excluding resources awarded to replace EFC). ***Average financial aid package:*** $21,291 (excluding resources awarded to replace EFC). 21% of all full-time undergraduates had no need and received non-need-based gift aid.

GIFT AID (NEED-BASED) ***Total amount:*** $22,570,223 (17% federal, 9% state, 68% institutional, 6% external sources). ***Receiving aid:*** Freshmen: 72% (545); all full-time undergraduates: 70% (2,084). ***Average award:*** Freshmen: $13,574; Undergraduates: $12,723. ***Scholarships, grants, and awards:*** Federal Pell, FSEOG, state, private, college/university gift aid from institutional funds.

GIFT AID (NON-NEED-BASED) ***Total amount:*** $4,926,962 (8% federal, 4% state, 71% institutional, 17% external sources). ***Receiving aid:*** Freshmen: 9% (68). Undergraduates: 8% (246). ***Average award:*** Freshmen: $6936. Undergraduates: $7388. ***Scholarships, grants, and awards by category:*** *Academic interests/achievement:* general academic interests/achievements. *Creative arts/performance:* art/fine arts, music, theater/drama. *Special achievements/activities:* 15 awards ($18,549 total): cheerleading/drum major. *Special characteristics:* children and siblings of alumni, children of faculty/staff, relatives of clergy, religious affiliation, siblings of current students, veterans. ***Tuition waivers:*** Full or partial for employees or children of employees.

LOANS ***Student loans:*** $18,541,033 (64% need-based, 36% non-need-based). 70% of past graduating class borrowed through all loan programs. *Average indebtedness per student:* $28,657. ***Average need-based loan:*** Freshmen: $7282. Undergraduates: $8904. ***Parent loans:*** $2,768,407 (20% need-based, 80% non-need-based). ***Programs:*** Federal Direct (Subsidized and Unsubsidized Stafford, PLUS), Perkins, college/university.

WORK-STUDY ***Federal work-study:*** Total amount: $872,988; 1,325 jobs averaging $617.

ATHLETIC AWARDS Total amount: $1,313,746 (55% need-based, 45% non-need-based).

APPLYING FOR FINANCIAL AID ***Required financial aid form:*** FAFSA. ***Financial aid deadline (priority):*** 3/10. ***Notification date:*** Continuous beginning 2/15.

CONTACT Undergraduate Traditional Financial Aid Office, Indiana Wesleyan University, 4201 South Washington Street, Marion, IN 46953-4999, 765-677-2116 or toll-free 800-332-6901. *Fax:* 765-677-2809. *E-mail:* finaid@indwes.edu.

INSTE BIBLE COLLEGE

Ankeny, IA

CONTACT Financial Aid Office, INSTE Bible College, 2302 SW 3rd Street, Ankeny, IA 50023, 515-289-9200.

INTER AMERICAN UNIVERSITY OF PUERTO RICO, AGUADILLA CAMPUS

Aguadilla, PR

CONTACT Mr. Juan Gonzalez, Director of Financial Aid, Inter American University of Puerto Rico, Aguadilla Campus, PO Box 20000, Aguadilla, PR 00605, 787-891-0925 Ext. 2108. *Fax:* 787-882-3020.

INTER AMERICAN UNIVERSITY OF PUERTO RICO, ARECIBO CAMPUS

Arecibo, PR

CONTACT Ramón O. de Jesús, Financial Aid Director, Inter American University of Puerto Rico, Arecibo Campus, PO Box 4050, Arecibo, PR 00614-4050, 787-878-5475 Ext. 2275. *Fax:* 787-880-1624.

INTER AMERICAN UNIVERSITY OF PUERTO RICO, BARRANQUITAS CAMPUS

Barranquitas, PR

ABOUT THE INSTITUTION Independent, coed. ***Awards:*** associate, bachelor's, and master's degrees and post-bachelor's certificates. 21 undergraduate majors. ***Total enrollment:*** 2,418. Undergraduates: 2,247.

GIFT AID (NEED-BASED) ***Scholarships, grants, and awards:*** Federal Pell, FSEOG, state, private, college/university gift aid from institutional funds.

GIFT AID (NON-NEED-BASED) ***Scholarships, grants, and awards by category:*** *Special characteristics:* adult students, veterans.

LOANS ***Programs:*** Federal Direct (Subsidized Stafford), Perkins.

APPLYING FOR FINANCIAL AID ***Required financial aid forms:*** FAFSA, institution's own form.

CONTACT Mr. Eduardo Fontanez Colon, Financial Aid Officer, Inter American University of Puerto Rico, Barranquitas Campus, Box 517, Barranquitas, PR 00794, 787-857-3600 Ext. 2049. *Fax:* 787-857-2244.

INTER AMERICAN UNIVERSITY OF PUERTO RICO, BAYAMÓN CAMPUS

Bayamón, PR

Tuition & fees: $5616 **Average undergraduate aid package: $983**

ABOUT THE INSTITUTION Independent, coed. 45 undergraduate majors. Federal methodology is used as a basis for awarding need-based institutional aid.

UNDERGRADUATE EXPENSES for 2011–12 ***Tuition:*** full-time $5100; part-time $258 per semester hour. Full-time tuition and fees vary according to course load and program. Part-time tuition and fees vary according to course load and program. ***Payment plan:*** Deferred payment.

FRESHMAN FINANCIAL AID (Fall 2010, est.) 1,203 applied for aid; of those 98% were deemed to have need. 71% of freshmen with need received aid; of those .4% had need fully met. ***Average percent of need met:*** 1% (excluding resources awarded to replace EFC). ***Average financial aid package:*** $207 (excluding resources awarded to replace EFC).

UNDERGRADUATE FINANCIAL AID (Fall 2010, est.) 2,985 applied for aid; of those 99% were deemed to have need. 73% of undergraduates with need received aid; of those .2% had need fully met. ***Average percent of need met:*** 8% (excluding resources awarded to replace EFC). ***Average financial aid package:*** $983 (excluding resources awarded to replace EFC).

GIFT AID (NEED-BASED) ***Total amount:*** $1,409,186 (42% federal, 7% state, 51% institutional). ***Receiving aid:*** Freshmen: 64% (786); all full-time undergraduates: 59% (1,822). ***Average award:*** Freshmen: $179; Undergraduates: $387. ***Scholarships, grants, and awards:*** Federal Pell, state, college/university gift aid from institutional funds.

GIFT AID (NON-NEED-BASED) ***Receiving aid:*** Undergraduates: 3.

LOANS ***Student loans:*** $186,276 (100% need-based). ***Average need-based loan:*** Freshmen: $120. Undergraduates: $1580. ***Programs:*** Perkins.

WORK-STUDY ***Federal work-study:*** Total amount: $188,381; jobs available.

ATHLETIC AWARDS Total amount: $33,300 (100% need-based).

APPLYING FOR FINANCIAL AID ***Required financial aid form:*** FAFSA.

CONTACT Mr. Carlos N. Alicea, Students Services Director, Inter American University of Puerto Rico, Bayamón Campus, 500 Dr. John Will Harris Road, Bayamon, PR 00957, 787-279-1912 Ext. 2017. *E-mail:* calicea@bc.inter.edu.

INTER AMERICAN UNIVERSITY OF PUERTO RICO, FAJARDO CAMPUS

Fajardo, PR

CONTACT Financial Aid Director, Inter American University of Puerto Rico, Fajardo Campus, Call Box 700003, Fajardo, PR 00738-7003, 787-863-2390 Ext. 2208.

INTER AMERICAN UNIVERSITY OF PUERTO RICO, GUAYAMA CAMPUS

Guayama, PR

Tuition & fees: $4558 **Average undergraduate aid package: $2821**

ABOUT THE INSTITUTION Independent, coed. 14 undergraduate majors. Federal methodology is used as a basis for awarding need-based institutional aid.

UNDERGRADUATE EXPENSES for 2011–12 ***Tuition:*** full-time $4080. ***Payment plan:*** Deferred payment.

FRESHMAN FINANCIAL AID (Fall 2010, est.) 252 applied for aid; of those 100% were deemed to have need. 83% of freshmen with need received aid. ***Average percent of need met:*** 2% (excluding resources awarded to replace EFC). ***Average financial aid package:*** $315 (excluding resources awarded to replace EFC).

UNDERGRADUATE FINANCIAL AID (Fall 2010, est.) 1,607 applied for aid; of those 100% were deemed to have need. 87% of undergraduates with need

received aid. ***Average percent of need met:*** 16% (excluding resources awarded to replace EFC). ***Average financial aid package:*** $2821 (excluding resources awarded to replace EFC).

GIFT AID (NEED-BASED) ***Total amount:*** $493,476 (57% federal, 26% state, 17% institutional). ***Receiving aid:*** Freshmen: 59% (152); all full-time undergraduates: 54% (865). ***Average award:*** Freshmen: $63; Undergraduates: $528. ***Scholarships, grants, and awards:*** Federal Pell, FSEOG, state, college/university gift aid from institutional funds, Federal Nursing.

GIFT AID (NON-NEED-BASED) ***Receiving aid:*** Freshmen: 2% (4). Undergraduates: 3% (56). ***Tuition waivers:*** Full or partial for employees or children of employees.

LOANS ***Average need-based loan:*** Freshmen: $367. Undergraduates: $3281. ***Programs:*** Federal Direct (Subsidized and Unsubsidized Stafford, PLUS), Perkins, Federal Nursing.

WORK-STUDY Federal work-study jobs available. ***State or other work-study/employment:*** Part-time jobs available.

APPLYING FOR FINANCIAL AID ***Required financial aid form:*** FAFSA. ***Financial aid deadline:*** Continuous. ***Notification date:*** Continuous beginning 7/1. Students must reply within 5 weeks of notification.

CONTACT Senor Jose A. Vechini, Director of Financial Aid Office, Inter American University of Puerto Rico, Guayama Campus, Call Box 10004, Guyama, PR 00785, 787-864-2222 Ext. 2206 or toll-free 787-864-2222 Ext. 2243 (in-state). *Fax:* 787-864-8232. *E-mail:* javechi@inter.edu.

INTER AMERICAN UNIVERSITY OF PUERTO RICO, METROPOLITAN CAMPUS

San Juan, PR

CONTACT Mrs. Luz M. Medina, Acting Director of Financial Aid, Inter American University of Puerto Rico, Metropolitan Campus, PO Box 191293, San Juan, PR 00919-1293, 787-758-2891. *Fax:* 787-250-0782.

INTER AMERICAN UNIVERSITY OF PUERTO RICO, PONCE CAMPUS

Mercedita, PR

ABOUT THE INSTITUTION Independent, coed. 37 undergraduate majors.

GIFT AID (NEED-BASED) ***Scholarships, grants, and awards:*** Federal Pell, FSEOG, state, college/university gift aid from institutional funds, Federal Nursing.

LOANS ***Programs:*** Federal Direct (Subsidized and Unsubsidized Stafford, PLUS), Perkins.

WORK-STUDY ***Federal work-study:*** Total amount: $526,896; jobs available.

APPLYING FOR FINANCIAL AID ***Required financial aid form:*** FAFSA.

CONTACT Juan Portalatin, Financial Aid Officer, Inter American University of Puerto Rico, Ponce Campus, 104 Turpeaux Industrial Park, Mercedita, PR 00715-2201, 787-284-1912 Ext. 2161. *Fax:* 787-841-0103. *E-mail:* japortal@ponce.inter.edu.

INTER AMERICAN UNIVERSITY OF PUERTO RICO, SAN GERMÁN CAMPUS

San Germán, PR

Tuition & fees: $5616 **Average undergraduate aid package: $2009**

ABOUT THE INSTITUTION Independent, coed. 81 undergraduate majors. Both federal and institutional methodology are used as a basis for awarding need-based institutional aid.

UNDERGRADUATE EXPENSES for 2011–12 ***Comprehensive fee:*** $8116 includes full-time tuition ($5100), mandatory fees ($516), and room and board ($2500). ***College room only:*** $1000. Room and board charges vary according to board plan and housing facility. ***Part-time tuition:*** $170 per credit. ***Part-time fees:*** $170 per credit; $258 per term. ***Payment plan:*** Installment.

FRESHMAN FINANCIAL AID (Fall 2009) 1,103 applied for aid; of those 98% were deemed to have need. 80% of freshmen with need received aid; of those .1% had need fully met. ***Average percent of need met:*** 2% (excluding resources awarded to replace EFC). ***Average financial aid package:*** $339 (excluding resources awarded to replace EFC).

UNDERGRADUATE FINANCIAL AID (Fall 2009) 2,797 applied for aid; of those 98% were deemed to have need. 84% of undergraduates with need received aid; of those .2% had need fully met. ***Average percent of need met:*** 12% (excluding resources awarded to replace EFC). ***Average financial aid package:*** $2009 (excluding resources awarded to replace EFC).

GIFT AID (NEED-BASED) ***Total amount:*** $22,641,477 (90% federal, 6% state, 4% institutional). ***Receiving aid:*** Freshmen: 74% (834); all full-time undergraduates: 69% (2,005). ***Average award:*** Freshmen: $278; Undergraduates: $642. ***Scholarships, grants, and awards:*** Federal Pell, FSEOG, state, college/university gift aid from institutional funds.

GIFT AID (NON-NEED-BASED) ***Receiving aid:*** Freshmen: 1% (11). Undergraduates: 11. ***Scholarships, grants, and awards by category:*** *Academic interests/achievement:* general academic interests/achievements. ***Tuition waivers:*** Full or partial for employees or children of employees.

LOANS ***Student loans:*** $9,989,460 (100% need-based). ***Average need-based loan:*** Freshmen: $231. Undergraduates: $3080. ***Parent loans:*** $122,491 (100% need-based). ***Programs:*** Federal Direct (Subsidized and Unsubsidized Stafford, PLUS), Perkins.

WORK-STUDY ***Federal work-study:*** Total amount: $341,255; jobs available.

ATHLETIC AWARDS Total amount: $664,434 (100% need-based).

APPLYING FOR FINANCIAL AID ***Required financial aid forms:*** FAFSA, institution's own form. ***Financial aid deadline (priority):*** 4/26. ***Notification date:*** Continuous beginning 6/15.

CONTACT Ms. Maria I. Lugo, Financial Aid Director, Inter American University of Puerto Rico, San Germán Campus, PO Box 5100, San German, PR 00683-5008, 787-264-1912 Ext. 7252. *Fax:* 787-892-6350.

INTERIOR DESIGNERS INSTITUTE

Newport Beach, CA

CONTACT Office of Financial Aid, Interior Designers Institute, 1061 Camelback Road, Newport Beach, CA 92660, 949-675-4451.

INTERNATIONAL ACADEMY OF DESIGN & TECHNOLOGY

Tampa, FL

CONTACT Financial Aid Office, International Academy of Design & Technology, 5225 Memorial Highway, Tampa, FL 33634-7350, 813-881-0007 or toll-free 800-ACADEMY. *Fax:* 813-881-3440.

INTERNATIONAL ACADEMY OF DESIGN & TECHNOLOGY

Chicago, IL

CONTACT Barbara Williams, Financial Aid Director, International Academy of Design & Technology, 1 North State Street, Suite 400, Chicago, IL 60602, 312-980-9200 or toll-free 877-ACADEMY (out-of-state). *Fax:* 312-541-3929.

INTERNATIONAL BAPTIST COLLEGE

Chandler, AZ

CONTACT Financial Aid Office, International Baptist College, 2211 West Germann Road, Chandler, AZ 85286, 480-838-7070 Ext. 268 or toll-free 800-422-4858. *Fax:* 480-838-5432. *E-mail:* financialaid@ibconline.edu.

INTERNATIONAL BUSINESS COLLEGE

Fort Wayne, IN

CONTACT Financial Aid Office, International Business College, 5699 Coventry Lane, Fort Wayne, IN 46804, 219-459-4500 or toll-free 800-589-6363.

IONA COLLEGE

New Rochelle, NY

Tuition & fees: $30,192 **Average undergraduate aid package: $18,313**

ABOUT THE INSTITUTION Independent religious, coed. 58 undergraduate majors. Federal methodology is used as a basis for awarding need-based institutional aid.

UNDERGRADUATE EXPENSES for 2011–12 ***Comprehensive fee:*** $42,346 includes full-time tuition ($28,192), mandatory fees ($2000), and room and board ($12,154). Full-time tuition and fees vary according to class time. Room and board charges vary according to housing facility. ***Part-time tuition:*** $937 per credit. ***Part-time fees:*** $500 per term. Part-time tuition and fees vary according to class time and course load. ***Payment plans:*** Installment, deferred payment.

FRESHMAN FINANCIAL AID (Fall 2010, est.) 864 applied for aid; of those 85% were deemed to have need. 100% of freshmen with need received aid; of those 18% had need fully met. ***Average percent of need met:*** 29% (excluding resources awarded to replace EFC). ***Average financial aid package:*** $19,922 (excluding resources awarded to replace EFC). 14% of all full-time freshmen had no need and received non-need-based gift aid.

UNDERGRADUATE FINANCIAL AID (Fall 2010, est.) 3,086 applied for aid; of those 82% were deemed to have need. 100% of undergraduates with need received aid; of those 19% had need fully met. ***Average percent of need met:*** 28% (excluding resources awarded to replace EFC). ***Average financial aid package:*** $18,313 (excluding resources awarded to replace EFC). 16% of all full-time undergraduates had no need and received non-need-based gift aid.

GIFT AID (NEED-BASED) ***Total amount:*** $12,828,787 (31% federal, 25% state, 43% institutional, 1% external sources). ***Receiving aid:*** Freshmen: 69% (605); all full-time undergraduates: 53% (1,669). ***Average award:*** Freshmen: $6338; Undergraduates: $5721. ***Scholarships, grants, and awards:*** Federal Pell, FSEOG, state, private, college/university gift aid from institutional funds.

GIFT AID (NON-NEED-BASED) ***Total amount:*** $26,687,859 (97% institutional, 3% external sources). ***Receiving aid:*** Freshmen: 83% (722). Undergraduates: 77% (2,424). ***Average award:*** Freshmen: $12,020. Undergraduates: $11,494. ***Scholarships, grants, and awards by category:*** *Academic interests/achievement:* 3,145 awards ($24,993,755 total): general academic interests/achievements. *Creative arts/performance:* 30 awards ($83,500 total): music. *Special characteristics:* 391 awards ($1,517,444 total): children and siblings of alumni, children of faculty/staff, religious affiliation, siblings of current students. ***Tuition waivers:*** Full or partial for employees or children of employees, senior citizens.

LOANS ***Student loans:*** $18,111,638 (40% need-based, 60% non-need-based). 71% of past graduating class borrowed through all loan programs. *Average indebtedness per student:* $19,958. ***Average need-based loan:*** Freshmen: $1750. Undergraduates: $2857. ***Parent loans:*** $9,762,536 (100% non-need-based). ***Programs:*** Perkins, alternative loans.

WORK-STUDY ***Federal work-study:*** Total amount: $558,952; 503 jobs averaging $1008. ***State or other work-study/employment:*** Total amount: $300,000 (100% non-need-based). 222 part-time jobs averaging $853.

ATHLETIC AWARDS Total amount: $3,395,886 (100% non-need-based).

APPLYING FOR FINANCIAL AID ***Required financial aid forms:*** FAFSA, institution's own form, state aid form. ***Financial aid deadline:*** 4/15 (priority: 2/15). ***Notification date:*** Continuous. Students must reply by 5/1 or within 2 weeks of notification.

CONTACT Mary Grant, Director of Financial Aid, Iona College, 715 North Avenue, New Rochelle, NY 10801-1890, 914-633-2676 or toll-free 800-231-IONA (in-state). *Fax:* 914-633-2486.

IOWA STATE UNIVERSITY OF SCIENCE AND TECHNOLOGY

Ames, IA

Tuition & fees (IA res): $6997 **Average undergraduate aid package: $11,509**

ABOUT THE INSTITUTION State-supported, coed. 116 undergraduate majors. Federal methodology is used as a basis for awarding need-based institutional aid.

UNDERGRADUATE EXPENSES for 2010–11 ***Tuition, state resident:*** full-time $6102; part-time $255 per semester hour. ***Tuition, nonresident:*** full-time $17,668; part-time $736 per semester hour. ***Required fees:*** full-time $895. Full-time tuition and fees vary according to class time, degree level, and program. Part-time tuition and fees vary according to class time, course load, degree level, and program. ***College room and board:*** $7472; ***Room only:*** $3882. Room and board charges vary according to board plan and housing facility. ***Payment plans:*** Installment, deferred payment.

FRESHMAN FINANCIAL AID (Fall 2010, est.) 3,655 applied for aid; of those 66% were deemed to have need. 98% of freshmen with need received aid; of those 42% had need fully met. ***Average percent of need met:*** 83% (excluding resources awarded to replace EFC). ***Average financial aid package:*** $11,209 (excluding resources awarded to replace EFC). 33% of all full-time freshmen had no need and received non-need-based gift aid.

UNDERGRADUATE FINANCIAL AID (Fall 2010, est.) 16,056 applied for aid; of those 72% were deemed to have need. 99% of undergraduates with need received aid; of those 39% had need fully met. ***Average percent of need met:*** 81% (excluding resources awarded to replace EFC). ***Average financial aid package:*** $11,509 (excluding resources awarded to replace EFC). 30% of all full-time undergraduates had no need and received non-need-based gift aid.

GIFT AID (NEED-BASED) ***Total amount:*** $65,106,747 (41% federal, 4% state, 50% institutional, 5% external sources). ***Receiving aid:*** Freshmen: 54% (2,363); all full-time undergraduates: 54% (11,372). ***Average award:*** Freshmen: $7443; Undergraduates: $6413. ***Scholarships, grants, and awards:*** Federal Pell, FSEOG, state, college/university gift aid from institutional funds.

GIFT AID (NON-NEED-BASED) ***Total amount:*** $22,045,324 (7% federal, 2% state, 76% institutional, 15% external sources). ***Receiving aid:*** Freshmen: 27% (1,169). Undergraduates: 26% (5,407). ***Average award:*** Freshmen: $3063. Undergraduates: $2429. ***Scholarships, grants, and awards by category:*** *Academic interests/achievement:* agriculture, architecture, area/ethnic studies, biological sciences, business, communication, computer science, education, engineering/technologies, English, foreign languages, general academic interests/achievements, health fields, home economics, humanities, international studies, library science, mathematics, military science, physical sciences, premedicine, social sciences. *Creative arts/performance:* applied art and design, art/fine arts, journalism/publications, music, theater/drama. *Special achievements/activities:* community service, general special achievements/activities, leadership, rodeo. *Special characteristics:* adult students, children and siblings of alumni, ethnic background, first-generation college students, general special characteristics, international students, local/state students, members of minority groups, out-of-state students, religious affiliation.

LOANS ***Student loans:*** $111,710,072 (60% need-based, 40% non-need-based). 69% of past graduating class borrowed through all loan programs. *Average indebtedness per student:* $30,062. ***Average need-based loan:*** Freshmen: $3136. Undergraduates: $4341. ***Parent loans:*** $22,405,548 (22% need-based, 78% non-need-based). ***Programs:*** Federal Direct (Subsidized and Unsubsidized Stafford, PLUS), Perkins, state, college/university, private loans.

WORK-STUDY ***Federal work-study:*** Total amount: $1,600,089; jobs available. ***State or other work-study/employment:*** Total amount: $633,588 (100% need-based). Part-time jobs available.

ATHLETIC AWARDS Total amount: $5,903,392 (43% need-based, 57% non-need-based).

APPLYING FOR FINANCIAL AID ***Required financial aid form:*** FAFSA. ***Financial aid deadline (priority):*** 3/1. ***Notification date:*** Continuous beginning 4/1. Students must reply by 5/1.

CONTACT Roberta Johnson, Director of Financial Aid, Iowa State University of Science and Technology, 0210 Beardshear Hall, Ames, IA 50011, 515-294-2223 or toll-free 800-262-3810. *Fax:* 515-294-3622. *E-mail:* rljohns@iastate.edu.

IOWA WESLEYAN COLLEGE

Mount Pleasant, IA

Tuition & fees: $22,050 **Average undergraduate aid package: N/A**

ABOUT THE INSTITUTION Independent United Methodist, coed. 54 undergraduate majors. Federal methodology is used as a basis for awarding need-based institutional aid.

UNDERGRADUATE EXPENSES for 2010–11 ***Comprehensive fee:*** $29,156 includes full-time tuition ($22,050) and room and board ($7106). ***College room only:*** $2846. Room and board charges vary according to board plan and housing facility. ***Part-time tuition:*** $550 per credit hour. Part-time tuition and fees vary according to class time, course load, and location. ***Payment plans:*** Installment, deferred payment.

GIFT AID (NEED-BASED) ***Total amount:*** $3,188,865 (58% federal, 27% state, 15% institutional). ***Scholarships, grants, and awards:*** Federal Pell, FSEOG, state, private, college/university gift aid from institutional funds.

GIFT AID (NON-NEED-BASED) ***Total amount:*** $4,049,897 (97% institutional, 3% external sources). ***Scholarships, grants, and awards by category:*** *Academic interests/achievement:* general academic interests/achievements. *Creative arts/*

performance: art/fine arts, music. *Special characteristics:* children of faculty/staff, international students, religious affiliation. ***Tuition waivers:*** Full or partial for employees or children of employees.

LOANS ***Student loans:*** $5,399,641 (43% need-based, 57% non-need-based). ***Parent loans:*** $397,869 (100% non-need-based). ***Programs:*** Federal Direct (Subsidized and Unsubsidized Stafford, PLUS), Perkins, alternative loans.

WORK-STUDY ***Federal work-study:*** Total amount: $137,816; jobs available.

ATHLETIC AWARDS Total amount: $1,566,496 (100% non-need-based).

APPLYING FOR FINANCIAL AID ***Required financial aid form:*** FAFSA.

CONTACT Renae Armentrout, Director of Financial Aid, Iowa Wesleyan College, 601 North Main Street, Mount Pleasant, IA 52641-1398, 319-385-6242 or toll-free 800-582-2383 Ext. 6231. *Fax:* 319-385-6203. *E-mail:* rarmentrout@iwc.edu.

ITHACA COLLEGE

Ithaca, NY

Tuition & fees: $33,630 **Average undergraduate aid package: $28,737**

ABOUT THE INSTITUTION Independent, coed. 107 undergraduate majors. Institutional methodology is used as a basis for awarding need-based institutional aid.

UNDERGRADUATE EXPENSES for 2010–11 ***Comprehensive fee:*** $45,944 includes full-time tuition ($33,630) and room and board ($12,314). ***College room only:*** $6550. Room and board charges vary according to board plan and housing facility. ***Part-time tuition:*** $1121 per credit hour. ***Payment plan:*** Installment.

FRESHMAN FINANCIAL AID (Fall 2010, est.) 1,381 applied for aid; of those 84% were deemed to have need. 100% of freshmen with need received aid; of those 55% had need fully met. ***Average percent of need met:*** 89% (excluding resources awarded to replace EFC). ***Average financial aid package:*** $27,803 (excluding resources awarded to replace EFC). 18% of all full-time freshmen had no need and received non-need-based gift aid.

UNDERGRADUATE FINANCIAL AID (Fall 2010, est.) 4,954 applied for aid; of those 88% were deemed to have need. 100% of undergraduates with need received aid; of those 49% had need fully met. ***Average percent of need met:*** 88% (excluding resources awarded to replace EFC). ***Average financial aid package:*** $28,737 (excluding resources awarded to replace EFC). 19% of all full-time undergraduates had no need and received non-need-based gift aid.

GIFT AID (NEED-BASED) ***Total amount:*** $82,053,509 (9% federal, 4% state, 84% institutional, 3% external sources). ***Receiving aid:*** Freshmen: 69% (1,120); all full-time undergraduates: 67% (4,260). ***Average award:*** Freshmen: $18,707; Undergraduates: $19,199. ***Scholarships, grants, and awards:*** Federal Pell, FSEOG, state, private, college/university gift aid from institutional funds.

GIFT AID (NON-NEED-BASED) ***Total amount:*** $16,682,886 (3% federal, 1% state, 88% institutional, 8% external sources). ***Receiving aid:*** Freshmen: 19% (315). Undergraduates: 16% (981). ***Average award:*** Freshmen: $8480. Undergraduates: $9716. ***Scholarships, grants, and awards by category:*** *Academic interests/achievement:* 2,402 awards ($26,401,848 total): communication, general academic interests/achievements. *Creative arts/performance:* 75 awards ($456,865 total): cinema/film/broadcasting, dance, journalism/publications, music, performing arts, theater/drama. *Special achievements/activities:* 266 awards ($1,500,000 total): leadership. *Special characteristics:* 2,169 awards ($12,647,164 total): children and siblings of alumni, children of faculty/staff, general special characteristics, members of minority groups, siblings of current students. ***Tuition waivers:*** Full or partial for children of alumni, employees or children of employees.

LOANS ***Student loans:*** $33,156,693 (76% need-based, 24% non-need-based). ***Average need-based loan:*** Freshmen: $5432. Undergraduates: $6299. ***Parent loans:*** $29,790,193 (30% need-based, 70% non-need-based). ***Programs:*** Federal Direct (Subsidized and Unsubsidized Stafford, PLUS), Perkins, alternative loans.

WORK-STUDY ***Federal work-study:*** Total amount: $1,500,000; 3,317 jobs averaging $2400. ***State or other work-study/employment:*** Total amount: $10,103,780 (68% need-based, 32% non-need-based). 1,646 part-time jobs averaging $2400.

APPLYING FOR FINANCIAL AID ***Required financial aid forms:*** FAFSA, CSS Financial Aid PROFILE. ***Financial aid deadline (priority):*** 2/1. ***Notification date:*** Continuous beginning 2/15.

CONTACT Ms. Lisa Hoskey, Director of Financial Aid, Ithaca College, 953 Danby Road, Ithaca, NY 14850-7002, 800-429-4275 or toll-free 800-429-4274. *Fax:* 607-274-1895. *E-mail:* finaid@ithaca.edu.

ITT TECHNICAL INSTITUTE

Tempe, AZ

CONTACT Financial Aid Office, ITT Technical Institute, 5005 S. Wendler Drive, Tempe, AZ 85282, 602-437-7500 or toll-free 800-879-4881.

ITT TECHNICAL INSTITUTE

Clovis, CA

CONTACT Financial Aid Office, ITT Technical Institute, 362 N. Clovis Avenue, Clovis, CA 93612, 559-325-5400 or toll-free 800-564-9771 (in-state).

ITT TECHNICAL INSTITUTE

Concord, CA

CONTACT Financial Aid Office, ITT Technical Institute, 1140 Galaxy Way, Suite 400, Concord, CA 94520, 925-674-8200 or toll-free 800-211-7062.

ITT TECHNICAL INSTITUTE

Corona, CA

CONTACT Financial Aid Office, ITT Technical Institute, 4160 Temescal Canyon Road, Suite 100, Corona, CA 92883, 951-277-5400 or toll-free 877-764-9661 (out-of-state).

ITT TECHNICAL INSTITUTE

South Bend, IN

CONTACT Financial Aid Office, ITT Technical Institute, 17390 Dugdale Drive, Suite 100, South Bend, IN 46635, 574-247-8300 or toll-free 877-474-1926.

ITT TECHNICAL INSTITUTE

Wichita, KS

CONTACT Financial Aid Office, ITT Technical Institute, 8111 E. 32nd Street North, Suite 103, Wichita, KS 67208, 316-681-8400 or toll-free 877-207-1047.

ITT TECHNICAL INSTITUTE

Lexington, KY

CONTACT Financial Aid Office, ITT Technical Institute, 2473 Fortune Drive, Suite 180, Lexington, KY 40509, 859-246-3300 or toll-free 800-519-8151.

ITT TECHNICAL INSTITUTE

Madison, MS

CONTACT Financial Aid Office, ITT Technical Institute, 382 Galleria Parkway, Suite 100, Madison, MS 39110, 601-607-4500 or toll-free 800-209-2521.

ITT TECHNICAL INSTITUTE

Springfield, MO

CONTACT Financial Aid Office, ITT Technical Institute, 3216 South National Avenue, Springfield, MO 65807, 417-877-4800 or toll-free 877-219-4387.

ITT TECHNICAL INSTITUTE

Charlotte, NC

CONTACT Financial Aid Office, ITT Technical Institute, 10926 David Taylor Drive, Suite 100, Charlotte, NC 28262, 704-548-2300 or toll-free 877-243-7685.

ITT TECHNICAL INSTITUTE

Oklahoma City, OK

CONTACT Financial Aid Office, ITT Technical Institute, 50 Penn Place Office Tower, 1900 Northwest Expressway, Suite 305R, Oklahoma City, OK 73118, 405-810-4100 or toll-free 800-518-1612.

JACKSON STATE UNIVERSITY
Jackson, MS

Tuition & fees (MS res): $5050 **Average undergraduate aid package: $11,117**

ABOUT THE INSTITUTION State-supported, coed. 42 undergraduate majors. Federal methodology is used as a basis for awarding need-based institutional aid.

UNDERGRADUATE EXPENSES for 2010–11 ***Tuition, state resident:*** full-time $5050; part-time $211 per credit hour. ***Tuition, nonresident:*** full-time $12,380; part-time $517 per credit hour. Full-time tuition and fees vary according to course load. Part-time tuition and fees vary according to course load. ***College room and board:*** $6244; ***Room only:*** $3820. Room and board charges vary according to board plan and housing facility. ***Payment plan:*** Installment.

FRESHMAN FINANCIAL AID (Fall 2010, est.) 680 applied for aid; of those 97% were deemed to have need. 100% of freshmen with need received aid; of those 2% had need fully met. ***Average percent of need met:*** 27% (excluding resources awarded to replace EFC). ***Average financial aid package:*** $11,359 (excluding resources awarded to replace EFC).

UNDERGRADUATE FINANCIAL AID (Fall 2010, est.) 5,196 applied for aid; of those 97% were deemed to have need. 100% of undergraduates with need received aid; of those 1% had need fully met. ***Average percent of need met:*** 27% (excluding resources awarded to replace EFC). ***Average financial aid package:*** $11,117 (excluding resources awarded to replace EFC).

GIFT AID (NEED-BASED) ***Total amount:*** $29,695,366 (100% federal). ***Receiving aid:*** Freshmen: 63% (556); all full-time undergraduates: 78% (4,401). ***Average award:*** Freshmen: $5731; Undergraduates: $5768. ***Scholarships, grants, and awards:*** Federal Pell, FSEOG, state, private, college/university gift aid from institutional funds.

GIFT AID (NON-NEED-BASED) ***Total amount:*** $15,940,686 (1% federal, 77% state, 9% institutional, 13% external sources). ***Receiving aid:*** Freshmen: 36% (316). Undergraduates: 30% (1,699). ***Scholarships, grants, and awards by category:*** *Academic interests/achievement:* general academic interests/achievements. *Creative arts/performance:* music. *Special achievements/activities:* leadership. *Special characteristics:* children of faculty/staff. ***Tuition waivers:*** Full or partial for children of alumni, employees or children of employees.

LOANS ***Student loans:*** $74,841,190 (45% need-based, 55% non-need-based). ***Average need-based loan:*** Freshmen: $3303. Undergraduates: $4198. ***Parent loans:*** $4,371,208 (100% non-need-based). ***Programs:*** Federal Direct (Subsidized and Unsubsidized Stafford, PLUS), Perkins.

WORK-STUDY ***Federal work-study:*** Total amount: $2,084,094; jobs available.

APPLYING FOR FINANCIAL AID ***Required financial aid forms:*** FAFSA, institution's own form, state aid form. ***Financial aid deadline (priority):*** 4/15. ***Notification date:*** Continuous beginning 5/1.

CONTACT Mrs. B. J. Moncure, Director of Financial Aid, Jackson State University, 1400 J.R. Lynch Street, PO Box 17065, Jackson, MS 39217, 601-979-2227 or toll-free 800-682-5390 (in-state), 800-848-6817 (out-of-state). *Fax:* 601-979-2237.

JACKSONVILLE STATE UNIVERSITY
Jacksonville, AL

ABOUT THE INSTITUTION State-supported, coed. 58 undergraduate majors.

GIFT AID (NEED-BASED) ***Scholarships, grants, and awards:*** Federal Pell, FSEOG, state, private, college/university gift aid from institutional funds.

GIFT AID (NON-NEED-BASED) ***Scholarships, grants, and awards by category:*** *Academic interests/achievement:* biological sciences, business, communication, computer science, education, English, health fields, home economics, humanities, mathematics, military science, physical sciences, social sciences. *Creative arts/performance:* art/fine arts, journalism/publications, music, theater/drama. *Special achievements/activities:* general special achievements/activities.

LOANS ***Programs:*** Federal Direct (Subsidized and Unsubsidized Stafford, PLUS), state, college/university.

WORK-STUDY ***Federal work-study:*** Total amount: $562,989; 224 jobs averaging $1302. ***State or other work-study/employment:*** Total amount: $1,266,552 (100% non-need-based). Part-time jobs available.

APPLYING FOR FINANCIAL AID ***Required financial aid forms:*** FAFSA, institution's own form.

CONTACT Ms. Vickie Adams, Director of Financial Aid, Jacksonville State University, 700 Pelham Road North, Jacksonville, AL 36265-9982, 256-782-5006 Ext. 8399 or toll-free 800-231-5291. *Fax:* 256-782-5476. *E-mail:* finaid@jsu.edu.

JACKSONVILLE UNIVERSITY
Jacksonville, FL

Tuition & fees: $26,600 **Average undergraduate aid package: $19,750**

ABOUT THE INSTITUTION Independent, coed. 58 undergraduate majors. Federal methodology is used as a basis for awarding need-based institutional aid.

UNDERGRADUATE EXPENSES for 2010–11 ***Comprehensive fee:*** $35,920 includes full-time tuition ($26,600) and room and board ($9320). ***College room only:*** $5560. Room and board charges vary according to board plan and housing facility. ***Part-time tuition:*** $883 per credit hour.

FRESHMAN FINANCIAL AID (Fall 2010, est.) 583 applied for aid; of those 79% were deemed to have need. 100% of freshmen with need received aid; of those 18% had need fully met. ***Average percent of need met:*** 62% (excluding resources awarded to replace EFC). ***Average financial aid package:*** $20,758 (excluding resources awarded to replace EFC). 19% of all full-time freshmen had no need and received non-need-based gift aid.

UNDERGRADUATE FINANCIAL AID (Fall 2010, est.) 2,260 applied for aid; of those 77% were deemed to have need. 100% of undergraduates with need received aid; of those 15% had need fully met. ***Average percent of need met:*** 57% (excluding resources awarded to replace EFC). ***Average financial aid package:*** $19,750 (excluding resources awarded to replace EFC). 21% of all full-time undergraduates had no need and received non-need-based gift aid.

GIFT AID (NEED-BASED) ***Total amount:*** $25,807,481 (22% federal, 16% state, 61% institutional, 1% external sources). ***Receiving aid:*** Freshmen: 63% (395); all full-time undergraduates: 62% (1,435). ***Average award:*** Freshmen: $17,387; Undergraduates: $16,333. ***Scholarships, grants, and awards:*** Federal Pell, FSEOG, state, private, college/university gift aid from institutional funds, Academic Competitiveness Grants, National SMART Grants.

GIFT AID (NON-NEED-BASED) ***Total amount:*** $6,328,016 (19% federal, 11% state, 69% institutional, 1% external sources). ***Receiving aid:*** Freshmen: 15% (96). Undergraduates: 23% (520). ***Average award:*** Freshmen: $12,959. Undergraduates: $12,269. ***Scholarships, grants, and awards by category:*** *Academic interests/achievement:* business, general academic interests/achievements. *Creative arts/performance:* general creative arts/performance. *Special achievements/activities:* general special achievements/activities, leadership. *Special characteristics:* children of educators, children of faculty/staff, international students.

LOANS ***Student loans:*** $14,305,151 (89% need-based, 11% non-need-based). ***Average need-based loan:*** Freshmen: $3173. Undergraduates: $4284. ***Parent loans:*** $4,601,305 (93% need-based, 7% non-need-based). ***Programs:*** Federal Direct (Subsidized and Unsubsidized Stafford, PLUS), Perkins, college/university, private loans.

WORK-STUDY ***Federal work-study:*** Total amount: $328,968; jobs available. ***State or other work-study/employment:*** Total amount: $2573 (100% need-based). Part-time jobs available.

ATHLETIC AWARDS Total amount: $3,875,521 (50% need-based, 50% non-need-based).

APPLYING FOR FINANCIAL AID ***Required financial aid forms:*** FAFSA, institution's own form, state aid form. ***Financial aid deadline (priority):*** 3/1. ***Notification date:*** Continuous beginning 2/15.

CONTACT Mrs. Catherine Huntress, Director of Financial Aid, Jacksonville University, 2800 University Boulevard North, Jacksonville, FL 32211, 904-256-7060 or toll-free 800-225-2027. *Fax:* 904-256-7148. *E-mail:* chuntres@ju.edu.

JAMES MADISON UNIVERSITY
Harrisonburg, VA

Tuition & fees (VA res): $8448 **Average undergraduate aid package: $7967**

ABOUT THE INSTITUTION State-supported, coed. 48 undergraduate majors. Federal methodology is used as a basis for awarding need-based institutional aid.

UNDERGRADUATE EXPENSES for 2011–12 ***Tuition, state resident:*** full-time $4642; part-time $139 per credit hour. ***Tuition, nonresident:*** full-time $17,932; part-time $547 per credit hour. ***Required fees:*** full-time $3806. ***College room and board:*** $8340; ***Room only:*** $4184.

FRESHMAN FINANCIAL AID (Fall 2010, est.) 3,195 applied for aid; of those 56% were deemed to have need. 85% of freshmen with need received aid; of those 94% had need fully met. ***Average percent of need met:*** 43% (excluding resources awarded to replace EFC). ***Average financial aid package:*** $10,524 (excluding resources awarded to replace EFC). 1% of all full-time freshmen had no need and received non-need-based gift aid.

UNDERGRADUATE FINANCIAL AID (Fall 2010, est.) 15,833 applied for aid; of those 46% were deemed to have need. 85% of undergraduates with need received aid; of those 74% had need fully met. ***Average percent of need met:*** 48% (excluding resources awarded to replace EFC). ***Average financial aid package:*** $7967 (excluding resources awarded to replace EFC). 1% of all full-time undergraduates had no need and received non-need-based gift aid.

GIFT AID (NEED-BASED) ***Total amount:*** $24,219,012 (42% federal, 27% state, 22% institutional, 9% external sources). ***Receiving aid:*** Freshmen: 22% (873); all full-time undergraduates: 18% (3,040). ***Average award:*** Freshmen: $7048; Undergraduates: $6680. ***Scholarships, grants, and awards:*** Federal Pell, FSEOG, state, private, college/university gift aid from institutional funds.

GIFT AID (NON-NEED-BASED) ***Total amount:*** $3,018,174 (6% state, 76% institutional, 18% external sources). ***Receiving aid:*** Freshmen: 4% (148). Undergraduates: 27% (4,565). ***Average award:*** Freshmen: $3313. Undergraduates: $3120. ***Scholarships, grants, and awards by category:*** *Academic interests/achievement:* 615 awards ($1,369,156 total): architecture, biological sciences, business, computer science, education, engineering/technologies, English, general academic interests/achievements, health fields, humanities, international studies, mathematics, military science, physical sciences, premedicine, religion/biblical studies, social sciences. *Creative arts/performance:* 152 awards ($129,850 total): art/fine arts, cinema/film/broadcasting, dance, journalism/publications, music, theater/drama. *Special achievements/activities:* 30 awards ($38,753 total): cheerleading/drum major, general special achievements/activities, leadership. *Special characteristics:* 90 awards ($107,750 total): children and siblings of alumni, children of faculty/staff, handicapped students, international students, local/state students, members of minority groups, out-of-state students, siblings of current students.

LOANS ***Student loans:*** $50,995,448 (42% need-based, 58% non-need-based). 50% of past graduating class borrowed through all loan programs. *Average indebtedness per student:* $20,417. ***Average need-based loan:*** Freshmen: $3570. Undergraduates: $4224. ***Parent loans:*** $35,275,287 (100% non-need-based). ***Programs:*** Federal Direct (Subsidized and Unsubsidized Stafford, PLUS), Perkins, Federal Nursing.

WORK-STUDY ***Federal work-study:*** Total amount: $436,250; 275 jobs averaging $1998. ***State or other work-study/employment:*** Total amount: $5,400,000 (100% non-need-based). 2,448 part-time jobs averaging $2206.

ATHLETIC AWARDS Total amount: $5,577,804 (100% non-need-based).

APPLYING FOR FINANCIAL AID ***Required financial aid form:*** FAFSA. ***Financial aid deadline (priority):*** 3/1. ***Notification date:*** Continuous beginning 4/1. Students must reply within 4 weeks of notification.

CONTACT Lisa L. Tumer, Director of Financial Aid and Scholarships, James Madison University, 800 South Main Street, MSC 3519, Harrisonburg, VA 22807, 540-568-7820. *Fax:* 540-568-7994. *E-mail:* fin_aid@jmu.edu.

JAMESTOWN COLLEGE

Jamestown, ND

Tuition & fees: $17,270 — **Average undergraduate aid package: $12,532**

ABOUT THE INSTITUTION Independent Presbyterian, coed. 43 undergraduate majors. Both federal and institutional methodology are used as a basis for awarding need-based institutional aid.

UNDERGRADUATE EXPENSES for 2011–12 ***Comprehensive fee:*** $22,970 includes full-time tuition ($16,850), mandatory fees ($420), and room and board ($5700). ***College room only:*** $2530. Room and board charges vary according to board plan. Part-time tuition and fees vary according to course load. ***Payment plan:*** Installment.

FRESHMAN FINANCIAL AID (Fall 2010, est.) 212 applied for aid; of those 67% were deemed to have need. 100% of freshmen with need received aid; of those 28% had need fully met. ***Average percent of need met:*** 79% (excluding resources awarded to replace EFC). ***Average financial aid package:*** $13,174 (excluding resources awarded to replace EFC). 30% of all full-time freshmen had no need and received non-need-based gift aid.

UNDERGRADUATE FINANCIAL AID (Fall 2010, est.) 921 applied for aid; of those 70% were deemed to have need. 100% of undergraduates with need received aid; of those 21% had need fully met. ***Average percent of need met:*** 76% (excluding resources awarded to replace EFC). ***Average financial aid package:*** $12,532 (excluding resources awarded to replace EFC). 27% of all full-time undergraduates had no need and received non-need-based gift aid.

GIFT AID (NEED-BASED) ***Total amount:*** $4,667,718 (30% federal, 6% state, 59% institutional, 5% external sources). ***Receiving aid:*** Freshmen: 67% (143); all full-time undergraduates: 68% (633). ***Average award:*** Freshmen: $10,457; Undergraduates: $8993. ***Scholarships, grants, and awards:*** Federal Pell, FSEOG, state, private, college/university gift aid from institutional funds, Federal Nursing, Academic Competitiveness Grants, National SMART Grants.

GIFT AID (NON-NEED-BASED) ***Total amount:*** $1,659,146 (3% state, 90% institutional, 7% external sources). ***Receiving aid:*** Freshmen: 16% (34). Undergraduates: 11% (100). ***Average award:*** Freshmen: $5965. Undergraduates: $5070. ***Scholarships, grants, and awards by category:*** *Academic interests/achievement:* 788 awards ($3,290,975 total): general academic interests/achievements, physical sciences. *Creative arts/performance:* 102 awards ($190,575 total): art/fine arts, music, theater/drama. *Special achievements/activities:* 572 awards ($551,122 total): community service, leadership. *Special characteristics:* 259 awards ($447,505 total): children of faculty/staff, general special characteristics, international students, relatives of clergy, religious affiliation, siblings of current students, spouses of current students, veterans. ***Tuition waivers:*** Full or partial for employees or children of employees.

LOANS ***Student loans:*** $5,684,458 (60% need-based, 40% non-need-based). 82% of past graduating class borrowed through all loan programs. *Average indebtedness per student:* $25,899. ***Average need-based loan:*** Freshmen: $3532. Undergraduates: $4277. ***Parent loans:*** $299,833 (37% need-based, 63% non-need-based). ***Programs:*** Federal Direct (Subsidized and Unsubsidized Stafford, PLUS), Perkins, alternative loans.

WORK-STUDY ***Federal work-study:*** Total amount: $237,794; 230 jobs averaging $1035. ***State or other work-study/employment:*** Total amount: $53,171 (100% non-need-based). 59 part-time jobs averaging $901.

ATHLETIC AWARDS Total amount: $1,531,964 (65% need-based, 35% non-need-based).

APPLYING FOR FINANCIAL AID ***Required financial aid form:*** FAFSA. ***Financial aid deadline (priority):*** 3/15. ***Notification date:*** Continuous beginning 1/15. Students must reply within 3 weeks of notification.

CONTACT Margery Michael, Director of Financial Aid, Jamestown College, 6085 College Lane, Jamestown, ND 58405, 701-252-3467 Ext. 5568 or toll-free 800-336-2554. *Fax:* 701-253-4318. *E-mail:* mmichael@jc.edu.

JARVIS CHRISTIAN COLLEGE

Hawkins, TX

Tuition & fees: $11,146 — **Average undergraduate aid package: $11,535**

ABOUT THE INSTITUTION Independent religious, coed. 15 undergraduate majors. Federal methodology is used as a basis for awarding need-based institutional aid.

UNDERGRADUATE EXPENSES for 2011–12 ***Comprehensive fee:*** $18,934 includes full-time tuition ($9892), mandatory fees ($1254), and room and board ($7788). ***College room only:*** $4312. Room and board charges vary according to board plan and housing facility. ***Part-time tuition:*** $412 per semester hour. ***Part-time fees:*** $412 per semester hour; $627 per term. ***Payment plan:*** Installment.

FRESHMAN FINANCIAL AID (Fall 2010, est.) 148 applied for aid; of those 100% were deemed to have need. 100% of freshmen with need received aid; of those 21% had need fully met. ***Average percent of need met:*** 83% (excluding resources awarded to replace EFC). ***Average financial aid package:*** $11,549 (excluding resources awarded to replace EFC). 1% of all full-time freshmen had no need and received non-need-based gift aid.

UNDERGRADUATE FINANCIAL AID (Fall 2010, est.) 535 applied for aid; of those 100% were deemed to have need. 100% of undergraduates with need received aid; of those 4% had need fully met. ***Average percent of need met:*** 82% (excluding resources awarded to replace EFC). ***Average financial aid package:*** $11,535 (excluding resources awarded to replace EFC).

GIFT AID (NEED-BASED) ***Total amount:*** $3,306,022 (69% federal, 29% state, 2% external sources). ***Receiving aid:*** Freshmen: 99% (146); all full-time undergraduates: 92% (490). ***Average award:*** Freshmen: $7879; Undergraduates: $9730. ***Scholarships, grants, and awards:*** Federal Pell, FSEOG, state, private, college/university gift aid from institutional funds, United Negro College Fund.

GIFT AID (NON-NEED-BASED) ***Total amount:*** $476,875 (54% institutional, 46% external sources). ***Receiving aid:*** Freshmen: 27% (40). Undergraduates: 27% (144). ***Average award:*** Freshmen: $3500. ***Scholarships, grants, and awards by category:*** *Academic interests/achievement:* 82 awards ($357,925 total): education, general academic interests/achievements. *Special characteristics:* 6 awards ($77,938 total): religious affiliation.

LOANS ***Student loans:*** $3,572,570 (48% need-based, 52% non-need-based). 83% of past graduating class borrowed through all loan programs. *Average indebtedness per student:* $18,500. ***Average need-based loan:*** Freshmen: $2976. Undergraduates: $3551. ***Parent loans:*** $1,027,968 (100% non-need-based). ***Programs:*** Federal Direct (Subsidized and Unsubsidized Stafford, PLUS), Perkins.

WORK-STUDY ***Federal work-study:*** Total amount: $220,000; 152 jobs averaging $1475. ***State or other work-study/employment:*** Total amount: $5000 (100% need-based). 2 part-time jobs averaging $2745.

ATHLETIC AWARDS Total amount: $357,851 (100% non-need-based).

APPLYING FOR FINANCIAL AID ***Required financial aid form:*** FAFSA. ***Financial aid deadline (priority):*** 4/15. ***Notification date:*** Continuous beginning 5/1. Students must reply within 2 weeks of notification.

CONTACT MaEsther Francis, Director of Financial Aid, Jarvis Christian College, PO Box 1470, Hawkins, TX 75765, 903-769-5740. *Fax:* 903-769-1282. *E-mail:* alice.copeland@jarvis.edu.

JEFFERSON COLLEGE OF HEALTH SCIENCES

Roanoke, VA

Tuition & fees: $18,810 **Average undergraduate aid package: $11,113**

ABOUT THE INSTITUTION Independent, coed. 11 undergraduate majors. Federal methodology is used as a basis for awarding need-based institutional aid.

UNDERGRADUATE EXPENSES for 2010–11 ***Tuition:*** full-time $18,810; part-time $545 per credit hour. ***Payment plan:*** Installment.

FRESHMAN FINANCIAL AID (Fall 2010, est.) 305 applied for aid; of those 76% were deemed to have need. 73% of freshmen with need received aid; of those 4% had need fully met. ***Average percent of need met:*** 40% (excluding resources awarded to replace EFC). ***Average financial aid package:*** $8466 (excluding resources awarded to replace EFC). 1% of all full-time freshmen had no need and received non-need-based gift aid.

UNDERGRADUATE FINANCIAL AID (Fall 2010, est.) 1,436 applied for aid; of those 86% were deemed to have need. 79% of undergraduates with need received aid; of those 5% had need fully met. ***Average percent of need met:*** 43% (excluding resources awarded to replace EFC). ***Average financial aid package:*** $11,113 (excluding resources awarded to replace EFC). 2% of all full-time undergraduates had no need and received non-need-based gift aid.

GIFT AID (NEED-BASED) ***Total amount:*** $8,247,833 (38% federal, 17% state, 29% institutional, 16% external sources). ***Receiving aid:*** Freshmen: 13% (171); all full-time undergraduates: 36% (957). ***Average award:*** Freshmen: $6963; Undergraduates: $8103. ***Scholarships, grants, and awards:*** Federal Pell, FSEOG, state, private, college/university gift aid from institutional funds.

GIFT AID (NON-NEED-BASED) ***Total amount:*** $1,037,581 (13% state, 17% institutional, 70% external sources). ***Receiving aid:*** Freshmen: 3. Undergraduates: 1% (18). ***Average award:*** Freshmen: $3500. Undergraduates: $2909. ***Scholarships, grants, and awards by category:*** *Academic interests/achievement:* 598 awards ($1,363,804 total): biological sciences, health fields. *Special characteristics:* 593 awards ($1,363,804 total): local/state students. ***Tuition waivers:*** Full or partial for employees or children of employees.

LOANS ***Student loans:*** $6,073,958 (89% need-based, 11% non-need-based). 61% of past graduating class borrowed through all loan programs. *Average indebtedness per student:* $18,133. ***Average need-based loan:*** Freshmen: $4475. Undergraduates: $4931. ***Parent loans:*** $995,113 (61% need-based, 39% non-need-based). ***Programs:*** alternative loans.

WORK-STUDY ***Federal work-study:*** Total amount: $73,317; 91 jobs averaging $952. ***State or other work-study/employment:*** Total amount: $157,602 (89% need-based, 11% non-need-based). 115 part-time jobs averaging $1513.

APPLYING FOR FINANCIAL AID ***Required financial aid forms:*** FAFSA, state aid form. ***Financial aid deadline (priority):*** 5/1. ***Notification date:*** Continuous beginning 5/1.

CONTACT Debra A. Johnson, Director of Financial Aid, Jefferson College of Health Sciences, 101 Elm Avenue SE, Roanoke, VA 24013-2222, 540-985-8492 or toll-free 888-985-8483. *Fax:* 540-224-6916. *E-mail:* djohnson@jchs.edu.

THE JEWISH THEOLOGICAL SEMINARY

New York, NY

CONTACT Linda Levine, Registrar/Director of Financial Aid, The Jewish Theological Seminary, 3080 Broadway, New York, NY 10027-4649, 212-678-8007. *Fax:* 212-678-8947. *E-mail:* financialaid@jtsa.edu.

JOHN BROWN UNIVERSITY

Siloam Springs, AR

Tuition & fees: $20,766 **Average undergraduate aid package: $18,376**

ABOUT THE INSTITUTION Independent interdenominational, coed. 90 undergraduate majors. Federal methodology is used as a basis for awarding need-based institutional aid.

UNDERGRADUATE EXPENSES for 2011–12 ***Comprehensive fee:*** $28,328 includes full-time tuition ($19,834), mandatory fees ($932), and room and board ($7562). Full-time tuition and fees vary according to course load. Room and board charges vary according to board plan and housing facility. ***Part-time tuition:*** $628 per credit. Part-time tuition and fees vary according to course load. ***Payment plan:*** Installment.

FRESHMAN FINANCIAL AID (Fall 2010, est.) 280 applied for aid; of those 86% were deemed to have need. 100% of freshmen with need received aid; of those 45% had need fully met. ***Average percent of need met:*** 1% (excluding resources awarded to replace EFC). 84% of all full-time freshmen had no need and received non-need-based gift aid.

UNDERGRADUATE FINANCIAL AID (Fall 2010, est.) 1,161 applied for aid; of those 89% were deemed to have need. 100% of undergraduates with need received aid; of those 31% had need fully met. ***Average percent of need met:*** 1% (excluding resources awarded to replace EFC). ***Average financial aid package:*** $18,376 (excluding resources awarded to replace EFC). 12% of all full-time undergraduates had no need and received non-need-based gift aid.

GIFT AID (NEED-BASED) ***Total amount:*** $10,716,260 (25% federal, 11% state, 60% institutional, 4% external sources). ***Receiving aid:*** Freshmen: 70% (226); all full-time undergraduates: 59% (875). ***Average award:*** Freshmen: $10,197; Undergraduates: $12,620. ***Scholarships, grants, and awards:*** Federal Pell, FSEOG, state, private, college/university gift aid from institutional funds.

GIFT AID (NON-NEED-BASED) ***Total amount:*** $2,198,784 (13% state, 78% institutional, 9% external sources). ***Receiving aid:*** Freshmen: 55% (178). Undergraduates: 40% (594). ***Average award:*** Freshmen: $6756. Undergraduates: $6700. ***Scholarships, grants, and awards by category:*** *Academic interests/achievement:* general academic interests/achievements. *Creative arts/performance:* art/fine arts, journalism/publications, music, theater/drama. *Special achievements/activities:* cheerleading/drum major, leadership. *Special characteristics:* children and siblings of alumni, children of educators, children of faculty/staff, ethnic background, international students, members of minority groups, relatives of clergy, siblings of current students. ***Tuition waivers:*** Full or partial for employees or children of employees.

LOANS ***Student loans:*** $6,590,480 (94% need-based, 6% non-need-based). 60% of past graduating class borrowed through all loan programs. *Average indebtedness per student:* $19,500. ***Average need-based loan:*** Freshmen: $3241. Undergraduates: $9177. ***Parent loans:*** $1,128,011 (85% need-based, 15% non-need-based). ***Programs:*** Federal Direct (Subsidized and Unsubsidized Stafford, PLUS), Perkins, college/university.

WORK-STUDY ***Federal work-study:*** Total amount: $630,700; jobs available. ***State or other work-study/employment:*** Total amount: $363,010 (68% need-based, 32% non-need-based). Part-time jobs available.

ATHLETIC AWARDS Total amount: $1,341,090 (45% need-based, 55% non-need-based).

APPLYING FOR FINANCIAL AID ***Required financial aid form:*** FAFSA. ***Financial aid deadline (priority):*** 3/1. ***Notification date:*** Continuous beginning 3/1. Students must reply by 6/1 or within 4 weeks of notification.

CONTACT Mr. Kim Eldridge, Director of Student Financial Aid, John Brown University, 2000 West University Street, Siloam Springs, AR 72761-2121, 479-524-7424 or toll-free 877-JBU-INFO. *Fax:* 479-524-7405. *E-mail:* keldridg@jbu.edu.

JOHN CARROLL UNIVERSITY

University Heights, OH

Tuition & fees: $31,710 **Average undergraduate aid package: $24,519**

ABOUT THE INSTITUTION Independent Roman Catholic (Jesuit), coed. 51 undergraduate majors. Federal methodology is used as a basis for awarding need-based institutional aid.

UNDERGRADUATE EXPENSES for 2011–12 ***One-time required fee:*** $325. ***Comprehensive fee:*** $40,860 includes full-time tuition ($30,660), mandatory fees ($1050), and room and board ($9150). ***College room only:*** $4850. Room and board charges vary according to board plan and housing facility. ***Part-time tuition:*** $935 per credit hour. Part-time tuition and fees vary according to course load. ***Payment plans:*** Installment, deferred payment.

FRESHMAN FINANCIAL AID (Fall 2010, est.) 646 applied for aid; of those 89% were deemed to have need. 100% of freshmen with need received aid; of those 22% had need fully met. ***Average percent of need met:*** 85% (excluding resources awarded to replace EFC). ***Average financial aid package:*** $25,865 (excluding resources awarded to replace EFC). 16% of all full-time freshmen had no need and received non-need-based gift aid.

UNDERGRADUATE FINANCIAL AID (Fall 2010, est.) 2,486 applied for aid; of those 90% were deemed to have need. 100% of undergraduates with need received aid; of those 18% had need fully met. ***Average percent of need met:*** 81% (excluding resources awarded to replace EFC). ***Average financial aid package:*** $24,519 (excluding resources awarded to replace EFC). 18% of all full-time undergraduates had no need and received non-need-based gift aid.

GIFT AID (NEED-BASED) ***Total amount:*** $25,377,454 (19% federal, 5% state, 74% institutional, 2% external sources). ***Receiving aid:*** Freshmen: 81% (569); all full-time undergraduates: 75% (2,191). ***Average award:*** Freshmen: $21,641; Undergraduates: $19,440. ***Scholarships, grants, and awards:*** Federal Pell, FSEOG, state, private, college/university gift aid from institutional funds.

GIFT AID (NON-NEED-BASED) ***Total amount:*** $22,948,073 (97% institutional, 3% external sources). ***Receiving aid:*** Freshmen: 82% (575). Undergraduates: 75% (2,204). ***Average award:*** Freshmen: $12,812. Undergraduates: $10,152. ***Scholarships, grants, and awards by category:*** *Academic interests/achievement:* biological sciences, business, communication, computer science, education, English, foreign languages, health fields, mathematics, military science, physical sciences, premedicine, religion/biblical studies, social sciences. *Special achievements/activities:* community service, leadership. *Special characteristics:* children and siblings of alumni, children of educators, children of faculty/staff, ethnic background, first-generation college students, local/state students, members of minority groups, veterans, veterans' children. ***Tuition waivers:*** Full or partial for employees or children of employees, senior citizens.

LOANS ***Student loans:*** $14,866,992 (88% need-based, 12% non-need-based). 82% of past graduating class borrowed through all loan programs. *Average indebtedness per student:* $28,830. ***Average need-based loan:*** Freshmen: $2879. Undergraduates: $4016. ***Parent loans:*** $5,727,524 (100% need-based). ***Programs:*** Federal Direct (Subsidized and Unsubsidized Stafford, PLUS), Perkins.

WORK-STUDY ***Federal work-study:*** Total amount: $1,097,620; 524 jobs averaging $2200.

APPLYING FOR FINANCIAL AID ***Required financial aid form:*** FAFSA. ***Financial aid deadline:*** 3/15 (priority: 2/15). ***Notification date:*** 2/1. Students must reply by 5/1 or within 4 weeks of notification.

CONTACT Ms. Claudia A. Wenzel, Director of Financial Aid, John Carroll University, 20700 North Park Boulevard, University Heights, OH 44118-4581, 216-397-4248. *Fax:* 216-397-3098. *E-mail:* jcuofa@jcu.edu.

JOHN F. KENNEDY UNIVERSITY

Pleasant Hill, CA

CONTACT Mindy Bergeron, Director of Financial Aid, John F. Kennedy University, 100 Ellinwood Way, Pleasant Hill, CA 94523, 925-969-3385 or toll-free 800-696-JFKU. *Fax:* 925-969-3390. *E-mail:* bergeron@jfku.edu.

JOHN JAY COLLEGE OF CRIMINAL JUSTICE OF THE CITY UNIVERSITY OF NEW YORK

New York, NY

Tuition & fees (NY res): $4930 **Average undergraduate aid package: $10,150**

ABOUT THE INSTITUTION State and locally supported, coed. 17 undergraduate majors. Federal methodology is used as a basis for awarding need-based institutional aid.

UNDERGRADUATE EXPENSES for 2010–11 ***Tuition, state resident:*** full-time $4600; part-time $195 per credit. ***Tuition, nonresident:*** full-time $12,450; part-time $415 per credit. ***Required fees:*** full-time $330; $139.85 per course. Full-time tuition and fees vary according to course load and program. Part-time tuition and fees vary according to course load and program. ***Payment plan:*** Installment.

FRESHMAN FINANCIAL AID (Fall 2009) 2,515 applied for aid; of those 87% were deemed to have need. 86% of freshmen with need received aid. ***Average percent of need met:*** 85% (excluding resources awarded to replace EFC). ***Average financial aid package:*** $10,150 (excluding resources awarded to replace EFC).

UNDERGRADUATE FINANCIAL AID (Fall 2009) 9,114 applied for aid; of those 94% were deemed to have need. 93% of undergraduates with need received aid. ***Average percent of need met:*** 85% (excluding resources awarded to replace EFC). ***Average financial aid package:*** $10,150 (excluding resources awarded to replace EFC).

GIFT AID (NEED-BASED) ***Total amount:*** $531,850,164 (61% federal, 39% state). ***Receiving aid:*** Freshmen: 57% (1,609); all full-time undergraduates: 71% (7,394). ***Average award:*** Freshmen: $3175; Undergraduates: $3175. ***Scholarships, grants, and awards:*** Federal Pell, FSEOG, state, college/university gift aid from institutional funds.

GIFT AID (NON-NEED-BASED) ***Receiving aid:*** Freshmen: 6% (170). Undergraduates: 3% (300). ***Scholarships, grants, and awards by category:*** *Academic interests/achievement:* general academic interests/achievements. ***Tuition waivers:*** Full or partial for senior citizens.

LOANS ***Student loans:*** $20,083,028 (100% need-based). 47% of past graduating class borrowed through all loan programs. *Average indebtedness per student:* $47,250. ***Average need-based loan:*** Freshmen: $3500. Undergraduates: $3500. ***Parent loans:*** $489,888 (100% need-based). ***Programs:*** Federal Direct (Subsidized and Unsubsidized Stafford, PLUS), Perkins.

WORK-STUDY ***Federal work-study:*** Total amount: $296,359; jobs available. ***State or other work-study/employment:*** Total amount: $55,668 (100% need-based). Part-time jobs available.

APPLYING FOR FINANCIAL AID ***Required financial aid forms:*** FAFSA, state aid form. ***Financial aid deadline:*** Continuous. ***Notification date:*** 4/1. Students must reply within 2 weeks of notification.

CONTACT Sylvia Lopez-Crespo, Director of Financial Aid, John Jay College of Criminal Justice of the City University of New York, 445 West 59th Street, New York, NY 10019-1093, 212-237-8897 or toll-free 877-JOHNJAY. *Fax:* 212-237-8936. *E-mail:* slopez@jjay.cuny.edu.

THE JOHNS HOPKINS UNIVERSITY

Baltimore, MD

Tuition & fees: $40,680 **Average undergraduate aid package: $33,142**

ABOUT THE INSTITUTION Independent, coed. 59 undergraduate majors. Institutional methodology is used as a basis for awarding need-based institutional aid.

UNDERGRADUATE EXPENSES for 2010–11 ***One-time required fee:*** $500. ***Comprehensive fee:*** $53,190 includes full-time tuition ($40,680) and room and board ($12,510). ***College room only:*** $7150. Room and board charges vary according to board plan and housing facility. ***Part-time tuition:*** $1355 per credit hour. ***Payment plan:*** Installment.

FRESHMAN FINANCIAL AID (Fall 2010, est.) 802 applied for aid; of those 80% were deemed to have need. 100% of freshmen with need received aid; of those 98% had need fully met. ***Average percent of need met:*** 99% (excluding resources awarded to replace EFC). ***Average financial aid package:*** $33,193 (excluding resources awarded to replace EFC). 1% of all full-time freshmen had no need and received non-need-based gift aid.

UNDERGRADUATE FINANCIAL AID (Fall 2010, est.) 2,895 applied for aid; of those 81% were deemed to have need. 100% of undergraduates with need received aid; of those 99% had need fully met. ***Average percent of need met:*** 99% (excluding resources awarded to replace EFC). ***Average financial aid package:*** $33,142 (excluding resources awarded to replace EFC). 1% of all full-time undergraduates had no need and received non-need-based gift aid.

GIFT AID (NEED-BASED) ***Total amount:*** $64,189,000 (7% federal, 1% state, 89% institutional, 3% external sources). ***Receiving aid:*** Freshmen: 44% (551); all full-time undergraduates: 41% (2,051). ***Average award:*** Freshmen: $30,791; Undergraduates: $25,595. ***Scholarships, grants, and awards:*** Federal Pell, FSEOG, state, private, college/university gift aid from institutional funds.

GIFT AID (NON-NEED-BASED) ***Total amount:*** $4,459,069 (21% federal, 4% state, 59% institutional, 16% external sources). ***Receiving aid:*** Freshmen: 6% (78). Undergraduates: 5% (259). ***Average award:*** Freshmen: $26,318. Undergraduates: $27,491. ***Scholarships, grants, and awards by category:*** *Academic interests/achievement:* 80 awards ($2,098,360 total): engineering/technologies, general academic interests/achievements. *Special characteristics:* 108 awards ($3,535,240 total): children of faculty/staff, local/state students. ***Tuition waivers:*** Full or partial for employees or children of employees.

LOANS ***Student loans:*** $13,200,083 (67% need-based, 33% non-need-based). 49% of past graduating class borrowed through all loan programs. *Average indebtedness per student:* $24,307. ***Average need-based loan:*** Freshmen: $3353. Undergraduates: $4486. ***Parent loans:*** $9,718,950 (12% need-based, 88% non-need-based). ***Programs:*** Federal Direct (Subsidized and Unsubsidized Stafford, PLUS), Perkins, college/university.

WORK-STUDY ***Federal work-study:*** Total amount: $4,273,295; 1,840 jobs averaging $2322.

ATHLETIC AWARDS Total amount: $1,356,231 (22% need-based, 78% non-need-based).

APPLYING FOR FINANCIAL AID ***Required financial aid forms:*** FAFSA, CSS Financial Aid PROFILE, noncustodial (divorced/separated) parent's statement, business/farm supplement, federal income tax form(s). ***Financial aid deadline:*** 3/1. ***Notification date:*** 4/1. Students must reply by 5/1 or within 2 weeks of notification.

CONTACT Mr. Vincent Amoroso, Director of Student Financial Services, The Johns Hopkins University, 146 Garland Hall, Baltimore, MD 21218, 410-516-8028. *Fax:* 410-516-6015. *E-mail:* vamoros1@jhu.edu.

JOHNSON & WALES UNIVERSITY

Denver, CO

Tuition & fees: $25,407 **Average undergraduate aid package: $16,423**

ABOUT THE INSTITUTION Independent, coed. 16 undergraduate majors. Federal methodology is used as a basis for awarding need-based institutional aid.

UNDERGRADUATE EXPENSES for 2011–12 ***Comprehensive fee:*** $34,668 includes full-time tuition ($23,955), mandatory fees ($1452), and room and board ($9261). Room and board charges vary according to board plan, housing facility, and location. ***Part-time tuition:*** $164 per credit hour. ***Payment plan:*** Installment.

FRESHMAN FINANCIAL AID (Fall 2010, est.) 357 applied for aid; of those 87% were deemed to have need. 100% of freshmen with need received aid; of those 13% had need fully met. ***Average percent of need met:*** 63% (excluding resources awarded to replace EFC). ***Average financial aid package:*** $16,685 (excluding resources awarded to replace EFC). 18% of all full-time freshmen had no need and received non-need-based gift aid.

UNDERGRADUATE FINANCIAL AID (Fall 2010, est.) 1,279 applied for aid; of those 86% were deemed to have need. 99% of undergraduates with need received aid; of those 14% had need fully met. ***Average percent of need met:*** 67% (excluding resources awarded to replace EFC). ***Average financial aid package:*** $16,423 (excluding resources awarded to replace EFC). 18% of all full-time undergraduates had no need and received non-need-based gift aid.

GIFT AID (NEED-BASED) ***Total amount:*** $6,275,238 (41% federal, 59% institutional). ***Receiving aid:*** Freshmen: 74% (282); all full-time undergraduates: 66% (959). ***Average award:*** Freshmen: $6277; Undergraduates: $6325. ***Scholarships, grants, and awards:*** Federal Pell, FSEOG, state, private, college/university gift aid from institutional funds.

GIFT AID (NON-NEED-BASED) ***Total amount:*** $8,240,159 (85% institutional, 15% external sources). ***Receiving aid:*** Freshmen: 78% (298). Undergraduates: 65% (949). ***Average award:*** Freshmen: $6022. Undergraduates: $6332. ***Scholarships, grants, and awards by category:*** *Academic interests/achievement:* general academic interests/achievements. *Special achievements/activities:* leadership, memberships. *Special characteristics:* children and siblings of alumni, children of faculty/staff, local/state students. ***Tuition waivers:*** Full or partial for employees or children of employees.

LOANS ***Student loans:*** $11,485,467 (81% need-based, 19% non-need-based). ***Average need-based loan:*** Freshmen: $3527. Undergraduates: $5006. ***Parent loans:*** $3,377,973 (100% non-need-based). ***Programs:*** Federal Direct (Subsidized and Unsubsidized Stafford, PLUS), Perkins, state.

WORK-STUDY ***Federal work-study:*** Total amount: $783,933; jobs available.

APPLYING FOR FINANCIAL AID ***Required financial aid form:*** FAFSA. ***Financial aid deadline (priority):*** 3/1. ***Notification date:*** Continuous beginning 3/15. Students must reply within 2 weeks of notification.

CONTACT Ms. Lynn Robinson, Executive Director of Student Financial Services, Johnson & Wales University, 8 Abbott Park Place, Providence, RI 02903, 401-598-4648 or toll-free 877-598-3368. *Fax:* 401-598-1040. *E-mail:* fp@jwu.edu.

JOHNSON & WALES UNIVERSITY

North Miami, FL

Tuition & fees: $25,407 **Average undergraduate aid package: $18,719**

ABOUT THE INSTITUTION Independent, coed. 14 undergraduate majors. Federal methodology is used as a basis for awarding need-based institutional aid.

UNDERGRADUATE EXPENSES for 2011–12 ***Comprehensive fee:*** $34,668 includes full-time tuition ($23,955), mandatory fees ($1452), and room and board ($9261). Room and board charges vary according to board plan and housing facility. ***Payment plan:*** Installment.

FRESHMAN FINANCIAL AID (Fall 2010, est.) 533 applied for aid; of those 95% were deemed to have need. 99% of freshmen with need received aid; of those 12% had need fully met. ***Average percent of need met:*** 67% (excluding resources awarded to replace EFC). ***Average financial aid package:*** $19,114 (excluding resources awarded to replace EFC). 9% of all full-time freshmen had no need and received non-need-based gift aid.

UNDERGRADUATE FINANCIAL AID (Fall 2010, est.) 1,776 applied for aid; of those 92% were deemed to have need. 99% of undergraduates with need received aid; of those 11% had need fully met. ***Average percent of need met:*** 68% (excluding resources awarded to replace EFC). ***Average financial aid package:*** $18,719 (excluding resources awarded to replace EFC). 12% of all full-time undergraduates had no need and received non-need-based gift aid.

GIFT AID (NEED-BASED) ***Total amount:*** $13,456,587 (44% federal, 4% state, 52% institutional). ***Receiving aid:*** Freshmen: 80% (466); all full-time undergraduates: 75% (1,498). ***Average award:*** Freshmen: $9112; Undergraduates: $8710. ***Scholarships, grants, and awards:*** Federal Pell, FSEOG, state, private, college/university gift aid from institutional funds.

GIFT AID (NON-NEED-BASED) ***Total amount:*** $9,614,912 (5% state, 87% institutional, 8% external sources). ***Receiving aid:*** Freshmen: 79% (457). Undergraduates: 63% (1,263). ***Average award:*** Freshmen: $6456. Undergraduates: $5454. ***Scholarships, grants, and awards by category:*** *Academic interests/achievement:* general academic interests/achievements. *Special achievements/activities:* leadership, memberships. *Special characteristics:* children and siblings of alumni, children of faculty/staff, local/state students. ***Tuition waivers:*** Full or partial for employees or children of employees.

LOANS ***Student loans:*** $15,775,722 (90% need-based, 10% non-need-based). ***Average need-based loan:*** Freshmen: $3416. Undergraduates: $5150. ***Parent loans:*** $5,059,134 (100% non-need-based). ***Programs:*** Federal Direct (Subsidized and Unsubsidized Stafford, PLUS), Perkins.

WORK-STUDY ***Federal work-study:*** Total amount: $1,174,251; jobs available. ***State or other work-study/employment:*** Part-time jobs available.

APPLYING FOR FINANCIAL AID ***Required financial aid form:*** FAFSA. ***Financial aid deadline (priority):*** 3/1. ***Notification date:*** Continuous beginning 3/15. Students must reply within 2 weeks of notification.

CONTACT Ms. Lynn Robinson, Executive Director of Student Financial Services, Johnson & Wales University, 8 Abbott Park Place, Providence, RI 02903, 401-598-4648 or toll-free 800-232-2433. *Fax:* 401-598-1040. *E-mail:* fp@jwu.edu.

JOHNSON & WALES UNIVERSITY

Providence, RI

Tuition & fees: $24,141 **Average undergraduate aid package: $16,400**

ABOUT THE INSTITUTION Independent, coed. 38 undergraduate majors. Federal methodology is used as a basis for awarding need-based institutional aid.

UNDERGRADUATE EXPENSES for 2010–11 ***One-time required fee:*** $288. ***Tuition:*** full-time $23,034. Room and board charges vary according to board plan, housing facility, and location. ***Payment plan:*** Installment.

FRESHMAN FINANCIAL AID (Fall 2010, est.) 1,892 applied for aid; of those 90% were deemed to have need. 100% of freshmen with need received aid; of those 14% had need fully met. ***Average percent of need met:*** 67% (excluding resources awarded to replace EFC). ***Average financial aid package:*** $17,455 (excluding resources awarded to replace EFC). 15% of all full-time freshmen had no need and received non-need-based gift aid.

UNDERGRADUATE FINANCIAL AID (Fall 2010, est.) 6,987 applied for aid; of those 90% were deemed to have need. 99% of undergraduates with need received aid; of those 13% had need fully met. ***Average percent of need met:*** 69% (excluding resources awarded to replace EFC). ***Average financial aid package:*** $16,400 (excluding resources awarded to replace EFC). 17% of all full-time undergraduates had no need and received non-need-based gift aid.

GIFT AID (NEED-BASED) ***Total amount:*** $42,133,086 (34% federal, 2% state, 64% institutional). ***Receiving aid:*** Freshmen: 69% (1,521); all full-time undergraduates: 61% (5,426). ***Average award:*** Freshmen: $8092; Undergraduates: $7514. ***Scholarships, grants, and awards:*** Federal Pell, FSEOG, state, private, college/university gift aid from institutional funds.

GIFT AID (NON-NEED-BASED) ***Total amount:*** $35,401,187 (94% institutional, 6% external sources). ***Receiving aid:*** Freshmen: 69% (1,513). Undergraduates: 54% (4,777). ***Average award:*** Freshmen: $5712. Undergraduates: $4962. ***Scholarships, grants, and awards by category:*** *Academic interests/achievement:* general academic interests/achievements. *Special achievements/activities:* leadership, memberships. *Special characteristics:* children and siblings of alumni, children of faculty/staff, local/state students. ***Tuition waivers:*** Full or partial for employees or children of employees.

LOANS ***Student loans:*** $66,115,097 (80% need-based, 20% non-need-based). ***Average need-based loan:*** Freshmen: $3587. Undergraduates: $5096. ***Parent loans:*** $22,554,156 (100% non-need-based). ***Programs:*** Federal Direct (Subsidized and Unsubsidized Stafford, PLUS), Perkins.

WORK-STUDY ***Federal work-study:*** Total amount: $3,752,001; jobs available.

APPLYING FOR FINANCIAL AID ***Required financial aid form:*** FAFSA. ***Financial aid deadline (priority):*** 3/1. ***Notification date:*** Continuous beginning 3/15.

CONTACT Ms. Lynn Robinson, Executive Director of Student Financial Services, Johnson & Wales University, 8 Abbott Park Place, Providence, RI 02903, 401-598-4648 or toll-free 800-598-1000 (in-state), 800-342-5598 (out-of-state). *Fax:* 401-598-1040. *E-mail:* fp@jwu.edu.

JOHNSON & WALES UNIVERSITY—CHARLOTTE CAMPUS

Charlotte, NC

Tuition & fees: $25,407 **Average undergraduate aid package: $18,403**

ABOUT THE INSTITUTION Independent, coed. 13 undergraduate majors. Federal methodology is used as a basis for awarding need-based institutional aid.

UNDERGRADUATE EXPENSES for 2011–12 ***Comprehensive fee:*** $35,721 includes full-time tuition ($23,955), mandatory fees ($1452), and room and board ($10,314). Room and board charges vary according to board plan, housing facility, and location. ***Payment plan:*** Installment.

FRESHMAN FINANCIAL AID (Fall 2010, est.) 684 applied for aid; of those 94% were deemed to have need. 100% of freshmen with need received aid; of those 15% had need fully met. ***Average percent of need met:*** 68% (excluding resources awarded to replace EFC). ***Average financial aid package:*** $18,846 (excluding resources awarded to replace EFC). 9% of all full-time freshmen had no need and received non-need-based gift aid.

UNDERGRADUATE FINANCIAL AID (Fall 2010, est.) 2,294 applied for aid; of those 92% were deemed to have need. 99% of undergraduates with need received aid; of those 16% had need fully met. ***Average percent of need met:*** 72% (excluding resources awarded to replace EFC). ***Average financial aid package:*** $18,403 (excluding resources awarded to replace EFC). 12% of all full-time undergraduates had no need and received non-need-based gift aid.

GIFT AID (NEED-BASED) ***Total amount:*** $15,762,240 (39% federal, 6% state, 55% institutional). ***Receiving aid:*** Freshmen: 81% (586); all full-time undergraduates: 75% (1,904). ***Average award:*** Freshmen: $8670; Undergraduates: $8161. ***Scholarships, grants, and awards:*** Federal Pell, FSEOG, state, private, college/university gift aid from institutional funds.

GIFT AID (NON-NEED-BASED) ***Total amount:*** $14,020,999 (9% state, 75% institutional, 16% external sources). ***Receiving aid:*** Freshmen: 82% (596). Undergraduates: 73% (1,842). ***Average award:*** Freshmen: $5571. Undergraduates: $5457. ***Scholarships, grants, and awards by category:*** *Academic interests/achievement:* general academic interests/achievements. *Special achievements/activities:* leadership, memberships. *Special characteristics:* children and siblings of alumni, children of faculty/staff, local/state students. ***Tuition waivers:*** Full or partial for employees or children of employees.

LOANS ***Student loans:*** $20,344,037 (87% need-based, 13% non-need-based). ***Average need-based loan:*** Freshmen: $3643. Undergraduates: $5089. ***Parent loans:*** $7,397,124 (100% non-need-based). ***Programs:*** Federal Direct (Subsidized and Unsubsidized Stafford, PLUS), Perkins.

WORK-STUDY ***Federal work-study:*** Total amount: $1,090,623; jobs available.

APPLYING FOR FINANCIAL AID ***Required financial aid form:*** FAFSA. ***Financial aid deadline (priority):*** 3/1. ***Notification date:*** Continuous beginning 3/15. Students must reply within 2 weeks of notification.

CONTACT Ms. Lynn Robinson, Executive Director of Student Financial Services, Johnson & Wales University—Charlotte Campus, 8 Abbott Park Place, Providence, RI 02903, 401-598-1648 or toll-free 866-598-2427. *Fax:* 401-598-4751. *E-mail:* fp@jwu.edu.

JOHNSON BIBLE COLLEGE

Knoxville, TN

Tuition & fees: $9100 **Average undergraduate aid package: $11,642**

ABOUT THE INSTITUTION Independent religious, coed. 6 undergraduate majors. Institutional methodology is used as a basis for awarding need-based institutional aid.

UNDERGRADUATE EXPENSES for 2010–11 ***Comprehensive fee:*** $14,200 includes full-time tuition ($8300), mandatory fees ($800), and room and board ($5100). ***College room only:*** $2400. Room and board charges vary according to board plan and housing facility. ***Part-time tuition:*** $332 per credit hour. ***Part-time fees:*** $35 per credit hour. Part-time tuition and fees vary according to course load. ***Payment plan:*** Installment.

FRESHMAN FINANCIAL AID (Fall 2010, est.) 158 applied for aid; of those 95% were deemed to have need. 99% of freshmen with need received aid; of those 9% had need fully met. ***Average percent of need met:*** 63% (excluding resources awarded to replace EFC). ***Average financial aid package:*** $9856 (excluding resources awarded to replace EFC).

UNDERGRADUATE FINANCIAL AID (Fall 2010, est.) 649 applied for aid; of those 84% were deemed to have need. 100% of undergraduates with need received aid; of those 9% had need fully met. ***Average percent of need met:*** 63% (excluding resources awarded to replace EFC). ***Average financial aid package:*** $11,642 (excluding resources awarded to replace EFC).

GIFT AID (NEED-BASED) ***Total amount:*** $3,429,762 (45% federal, 18% state, 37% institutional). ***Receiving aid:*** Freshmen: 93% (147); all full-time undergraduates: 82% (530). ***Average award:*** Freshmen: $5890; Undergraduates: $6471. ***Scholarships, grants, and awards:*** Federal Pell, FSEOG, state, private, college/university gift aid from institutional funds, Academic Competitiveness Grants.

GIFT AID (NON-NEED-BASED) ***Total amount:*** $815,706 (3% federal, 25% institutional, 72% external sources). ***Receiving aid:*** Freshmen: 38% (60). Undergraduates: 33% (211). ***Scholarships, grants, and awards by category:*** *Academic interests/achievement:* $692,321 total: business, communication, education, general academic interests/achievements, religion/biblical studies. *Creative arts/performance:* $1500 total: art/fine arts, general creative arts/performance, music. *Special achievements/activities:* $63,833 total: community service, general special achievements/activities, leadership, religious involvement. *Special characteristics:* $296,008 total: children of current students, children of educators, children of faculty/staff, ethnic background, general special characteristics, international students, married students, members of minority groups, parents of current students, relatives of clergy, religious affiliation, siblings of current students, spouses of current students. ***Tuition waivers:*** Full or partial for employees or children of employees.

LOANS ***Student loans:*** $2,792,955 (51% need-based, 49% non-need-based). 76% of past graduating class borrowed through all loan programs. *Average indebtedness per student:* $18,494. ***Average need-based loan:*** Freshmen: $3183. Undergraduates: $3414. ***Parent loans:*** $479,107 (100% non-need-based). ***Programs:*** Federal Direct (Subsidized and Unsubsidized Stafford, PLUS), college/university, alternative loans.

WORK-STUDY ***Federal work-study:*** Total amount: $103,483; 64 jobs averaging $1602. ***State or other work-study/employment:*** Total amount: $538,893 (27% need-based, 73% non-need-based). 335 part-time jobs averaging $1611.

APPLYING FOR FINANCIAL AID ***Required financial aid forms:*** FAFSA, institution's own form. ***Financial aid deadline (priority):*** 3/1. ***Notification date:*** Continuous beginning 4/1. Students must reply within 2 weeks of notification.

CONTACT Mr. Lawrence Rector, CPA, Financial Aid Director, Johnson Bible College, 7900 Johnson Drive, Knoxville, TN 37998, 865-251-2303 Ext. 2316 or toll-free 800-827-2122. *Fax:* 865-251-2337. *E-mail:* lrector@jbc.edu.

JOHNSON C. SMITH UNIVERSITY

Charlotte, NC

Tuition & fees: $16,542 **Average undergraduate aid package: $13,562**

ABOUT THE INSTITUTION Independent, coed. 28 undergraduate majors. Federal methodology is used as a basis for awarding need-based institutional aid.

UNDERGRADUATE EXPENSES for 2010–11 ***Comprehensive fee:*** $22,981 includes full-time tuition ($14,029), mandatory fees ($2513), and room and board ($6439). ***College room only:*** $3706. Full-time tuition and fees vary according to course load. Room and board charges vary according to board plan and housing facility. ***Part-time tuition:*** $379 per credit hour. ***Part-time fees:*** $345.50 per term. Part-time tuition and fees vary according to course load. ***Payment plan:*** Installment.

FRESHMAN FINANCIAL AID (Fall 2010, est.) 204 applied for aid; of those 96% were deemed to have need. 99% of freshmen with need received aid; of those 6% had need fully met. ***Average percent of need met:*** 54% (excluding resources awarded to replace EFC). ***Average financial aid package:*** $13,928 (excluding resources awarded to replace EFC). 11% of all full-time freshmen had no need and received non-need-based gift aid.

UNDERGRADUATE FINANCIAL AID (Fall 2010, est.) 1,228 applied for aid; of those 95% were deemed to have need. 100% of undergraduates with need received aid; of those 4% had need fully met. ***Average percent of need met:*** 52% (excluding resources awarded to replace EFC). ***Average financial aid package:*** $13,562 (excluding resources awarded to replace EFC). 3% of all full-time undergraduates had no need and received non-need-based gift aid.

GIFT AID (NEED-BASED) ***Total amount:*** $9,000,458 (58% federal, 15% state, 23% institutional, 4% external sources). ***Receiving aid:*** Freshmen: 83% (184); all full-time undergraduates: 82% (1,058). ***Average award:*** Freshmen: $11,036; Undergraduates: $9219. ***Scholarships, grants, and awards:*** Federal Pell, FSEOG, state, private, college/university gift aid from institutional funds, United Negro College Fund.

GIFT AID (NON-NEED-BASED) ***Total amount:*** $818,377 (4% federal, 4% state, 88% institutional, 4% external sources). ***Receiving aid:*** Freshmen: 5% (12). Undergraduates: 3% (43). ***Average award:*** Freshmen: $21,542. Undergraduates: $18,311. ***Scholarships, grants, and awards by category:*** *Academic interests/achievement:* general academic interests/achievements. *Creative arts/performance:* music. *Special achievements/activities:* general special achievements/activities. *Special characteristics:* children of faculty/staff, ethnic background, siblings of current students. ***Tuition waivers:*** Full or partial for children of alumni, employees or children of employees.

LOANS ***Student loans:*** $10,914,697 (93% need-based, 7% non-need-based). 98% of past graduating class borrowed through all loan programs. *Average indebtedness per student:* $29,218. ***Average need-based loan:*** Freshmen: $3764. Undergraduates: $4968. ***Parent loans:*** $4,717,473 (74% need-based, 26% non-need-based). ***Programs:*** Perkins, alternative loans.

WORK-STUDY ***Federal work-study:*** Total amount: $376,946; jobs available. ***State or other work-study/employment:*** Total amount: $252,332 (83% need-based, 17% non-need-based). Part-time jobs available.

ATHLETIC AWARDS Total amount: $1,455,769 (75% need-based, 25% non-need-based).

APPLYING FOR FINANCIAL AID ***Required financial aid forms:*** FAFSA, state aid form. ***Financial aid deadline (priority):*** 3/1. ***Notification date:*** Continuous beginning 3/1. Students must reply within 2 weeks of notification.

CONTACT Mrs. Terry Jeffries, Director of Financial Aid, Johnson C. Smith University, 100 Beatties Ford Road, Charlotte, NC 28216, 704-378-1498 or toll-free 800-782-7303. *Fax:* 704-378-1292. *E-mail:* tjeffries@jcsu.edu.

JOHNSON STATE COLLEGE

Johnson, VT

CONTACT Ms. Kimberly Goodell, Financial Aid Officer, Johnson State College, 337 College Hill, Johnson, VT 05656-9405, 802-635-2356 or toll-free 800-635-2356. *Fax:* 802-635-1463. *E-mail:* goodellk@badger.jsc.vsc.edu.

JONES COLLEGE

Jacksonville, FL

CONTACT Mrs. Becky Davis, Director of Financial Assistance, Jones College, 5353 Arlington Expressway, Jacksonville, FL 32211-5540, 904-743-1122. *Fax:* 904-743-4446.

JONES INTERNATIONAL UNIVERSITY

Centennial, CO

Tuition & fees: $12,480 **Average undergraduate aid package: $7020**

ABOUT THE INSTITUTION Proprietary, coed. 2 undergraduate majors. Federal methodology is used as a basis for awarding need-based institutional aid.

UNDERGRADUATE EXPENSES for 2011–12 ***Tuition:*** full-time $12,480; part-time $520 per credit hour. Full-time tuition and fees vary according to course level, course load, degree level, and program. Part-time tuition and fees vary according to course level, course load, degree level, and program. ***Payment plan:*** Installment.

FRESHMAN FINANCIAL AID (Fall 2009) 194 applied for aid; of those 77% were deemed to have need. 100% of freshmen with need received aid. ***Average percent of need met:*** 80% (excluding resources awarded to replace EFC). ***Average financial aid package:*** $5630 (excluding resources awarded to replace EFC).

UNDERGRADUATE FINANCIAL AID (Fall 2009) 469 applied for aid; of those 78% were deemed to have need. 100% of undergraduates with need received aid. ***Average percent of need met:*** 80% (excluding resources awarded to replace EFC). ***Average financial aid package:*** $7020 (excluding resources awarded to replace EFC).

GIFT AID (NEED-BASED) ***Total amount:*** $4,242,543 (100% federal). ***Receiving aid:*** Freshmen: 61% (118); all full-time undergraduates: 53% (248). ***Average award:*** Freshmen: $3160; Undergraduates: $3570. ***Scholarships, grants, and awards:*** Federal Pell, FSEOG, private.

GIFT AID (NON-NEED-BASED) ***Tuition waivers:*** Full or partial for employees or children of employees.

LOANS ***Student loans:*** $12,205,967 (40% need-based, 60% non-need-based). ***Average need-based loan:*** Freshmen: $2470. Undergraduates: $3450. ***Parent loans:*** $151,129 (100% non-need-based). ***Programs:*** Federal Direct (Subsidized and Unsubsidized Stafford, PLUS).

APPLYING FOR FINANCIAL AID ***Required financial aid forms:*** FAFSA, Master Promissory Note. ***Financial aid deadline:*** Continuous. ***Notification date:*** Continuous.

CONTACT Mr. Tim Lehmann, Financial Aid Director, Jones International University, 9697 East Mineral Avenue, Centennial, CO 80112, 800-811-5663. *E-mail:* financialaid@international.edu.

JUDSON COLLEGE

Marion, AL

ABOUT THE INSTITUTION Independent Baptist, coed, primarily women. 22 undergraduate majors.

GIFT AID (NEED-BASED) ***Scholarships, grants, and awards:*** Federal Pell, FSEOG, state, private, college/university gift aid from institutional funds, Academic Competitiveness Grants, National SMART Grants, TEACH Grants.

GIFT AID (NON-NEED-BASED) ***Scholarships, grants, and awards by category:*** *Academic interests/achievement:* biological sciences, general academic interests/achievements, premedicine. *Creative arts/performance:* art/fine arts, music. *Special* *achievements/activities:* general special achievements/activities. *Special characteristics:* children of educators, children of faculty/staff, relatives of clergy, religious affiliation.

LOANS ***Programs:*** Perkins, college/university.

WORK-STUDY ***Federal work-study:*** Total amount: $117,547; jobs available. ***State or other work-study/employment:*** Total amount: $47,360 (79% need-based, 21% non-need-based). Part-time jobs available.

APPLYING FOR FINANCIAL AID ***Required financial aid forms:*** FAFSA, institution's own form, state aid form.

CONTACT Mrs. Doris A. Wilson, Director of Financial Aid, Judson College, 302 Bibb Street, Marion, AL 36756, 334-683-5157 or toll-free 800-447-9472. *Fax:* 334-683-5282. *E-mail:* dwilson@judson.edu.

JUDSON UNIVERSITY

Elgin, IL

Tuition & fees: $24,780 **Average undergraduate aid package: N/A**

ABOUT THE INSTITUTION Independent Baptist, coed. 21 undergraduate majors. Federal methodology is used as a basis for awarding need-based institutional aid.

UNDERGRADUATE EXPENSES for 2010–11 ***Comprehensive fee:*** $33,280 includes full-time tuition ($24,150), mandatory fees ($630), and room and board ($8500). Room and board charges vary according to board plan. ***Part-time tuition:*** $925 per credit hour. Part-time tuition and fees vary according to course load. ***Payment plan:*** Installment.

GIFT AID (NEED-BASED) ***Scholarships, grants, and awards:*** Federal Pell, FSEOG, state, private, college/university gift aid from institutional funds.

GIFT AID (NON-NEED-BASED) ***Scholarships, grants, and awards by category:*** *Academic interests/achievement:* general academic interests/achievements. *Creative arts/performance:* art/fine arts, music. *Special achievements/activities:* leadership. ***Tuition waivers:*** Full or partial for employees or children of employees, senior citizens.

LOANS ***Programs:*** Federal Direct (Subsidized and Unsubsidized Stafford, PLUS), Perkins.

WORK-STUDY Federal work-study jobs available. ***State or other work-study/employment:*** Part-time jobs available.

APPLYING FOR FINANCIAL AID ***Required financial aid form:*** FAFSA. ***Financial aid deadline:*** Continuous. ***Notification date:*** Continuous. Students must reply within 4 weeks of notification.

CONTACT Roberto Santizo, Director of Financial Aid, Judson University, 1151 North State Street, Elgin, IL 60123-1498, 847-628-2532 or toll-free 800-879-5376. *Fax:* 847-628-2533. *E-mail:* rsantizo@judsonu.edu.

THE JUILLIARD SCHOOL

New York, NY

Tuition & fees: $32,180 **Average undergraduate aid package: $28,300**

ABOUT THE INSTITUTION Independent, coed. 4 undergraduate majors. Federal methodology is used as a basis for awarding need-based institutional aid.

UNDERGRADUATE EXPENSES for 2010–11 ***Comprehensive fee:*** $44,460 includes full-time tuition ($32,180) and room and board ($12,280). Room and board charges vary according to housing facility. ***Payment plan:*** Installment.

FRESHMAN FINANCIAL AID (Fall 2010, est.) 125 applied for aid; of those 78% were deemed to have need. 100% of freshmen with need received aid; of those 31% had need fully met. ***Average percent of need met:*** 76% (excluding resources awarded to replace EFC). ***Average financial aid package:*** $26,303 (excluding resources awarded to replace EFC). 7% of all full-time freshmen had no need and received non-need-based gift aid.

UNDERGRADUATE FINANCIAL AID (Fall 2010, est.) 461 applied for aid; of those 87% were deemed to have need. 100% of undergraduates with need received aid; of those 21% had need fully met. ***Average percent of need met:*** 75% (excluding resources awarded to replace EFC). ***Average financial aid package:*** $28,300 (excluding resources awarded to replace EFC). 6% of all full-time undergraduates had no need and received non-need-based gift aid.

GIFT AID (NEED-BASED) ***Total amount:*** $9,217,293 (6% federal, 1% state, 90% institutional, 3% external sources). ***Receiving aid:*** Freshmen: 66% (87); all full-time undergraduates: 74% (379). ***Average award:*** Freshmen: $24,513; Undergraduates: $24,303. ***Scholarships, grants, and awards:*** Federal Pell, FSEOG, state, private, college/university gift aid from institutional funds.

GIFT AID (NON-NEED-BASED) ***Total amount:*** $454,450 (1% state, 96% institutional, 3% external sources). ***Average award:*** Freshmen: $14,280. Undergraduates: $14,280. ***Scholarships, grants, and awards by category:*** *Creative arts/performance:* dance, music, performing arts, theater/drama. ***Tuition waivers:*** Full or partial for employees or children of employees.

LOANS ***Student loans:*** $2,134,800 (95% need-based, 5% non-need-based). 68% of past graduating class borrowed through all loan programs. *Average indebtedness per student:* $20,382. ***Average need-based loan:*** Freshmen: $3508. Undergraduates: $4977. ***Parent loans:*** $873,824 (94% need-based, 6% non-need-based). ***Programs:*** Federal Direct (Subsidized and Unsubsidized Stafford, PLUS), Perkins.

WORK-STUDY ***Federal work-study:*** Total amount: $606,847; jobs available. ***State or other work-study/employment:*** Total amount: $719,592 (74% need-based, 26% non-need-based). Part-time jobs available.

APPLYING FOR FINANCIAL AID ***Required financial aid forms:*** FAFSA, institution's own form, federal income tax return(s) or salary documentation. ***Financial aid deadline:*** 3/1. ***Notification date:*** 4/1. Students must reply by 5/1.

CONTACT Tina Gonzalez, Director of Financial Aid, The Juilliard School, 60 Lincoln Center Plaza, New York, NY 10023, 212-799-5000 Ext. 211. *Fax:* 212-769-6420. *E-mail:* financialaid@juilliard.edu.

JUNIATA COLLEGE

Huntingdon, PA

Tuition & fees: $34,090 **Average undergraduate aid package: $24,962**

ABOUT THE INSTITUTION Independent religious, coed. 88 undergraduate majors. Federal methodology is used as a basis for awarding need-based institutional aid.

UNDERGRADUATE EXPENSES for 2011–12 ***Comprehensive fee:*** $43,420 includes full-time tuition ($33,370), mandatory fees ($720), and room and board ($9330). ***College room only:*** $4920. Room and board charges vary according to board plan. ***Part-time tuition:*** $1385 per credit hour. ***Payment plan:*** Installment.

FRESHMAN FINANCIAL AID (Fall 2010, est.) 356 applied for aid; of those 88% were deemed to have need. 100% of freshmen with need received aid; of those 24% had need fully met. ***Average percent of need met:*** 85% (excluding resources awarded to replace EFC). ***Average financial aid package:*** $25,564 (excluding resources awarded to replace EFC). 25% of all full-time freshmen had no need and received non-need-based gift aid.

UNDERGRADUATE FINANCIAL AID (Fall 2010, est.) 1,199 applied for aid; of those 90% were deemed to have need. 100% of undergraduates with need received aid; of those 22% had need fully met. ***Average percent of need met:*** 82% (excluding resources awarded to replace EFC). ***Average financial aid package:*** $24,962 (excluding resources awarded to replace EFC). 27% of all full-time undergraduates had no need and received non-need-based gift aid.

GIFT AID (NEED-BASED) ***Total amount:*** $21,198,098 (8% federal, 6% state, 84% institutional, 2% external sources). ***Receiving aid:*** Freshmen: 74% (312); all full-time undergraduates: 72% (1,070). ***Average award:*** Freshmen: $21,298; Undergraduates: $19,811. ***Scholarships, grants, and awards:*** Federal Pell, FSEOG, state, private, college/university gift aid from institutional funds.

GIFT AID (NON-NEED-BASED) ***Total amount:*** $7,030,963 (1% state, 97% institutional, 2% external sources). ***Receiving aid:*** Freshmen: 14% (58). Undergraduates: 11% (161). ***Average award:*** Freshmen: $14,515. Undergraduates: $14,471. ***Scholarships, grants, and awards by category:*** *Academic interests/achievement:* biological sciences, business, communication, computer science, education, English, foreign languages, general academic interests/achievements, health fields, humanities, international studies, mathematics, physical sciences, premedicine, social sciences. *Creative arts/performance:* art/fine arts, music, performing arts. *Special achievements/activities:* community service, general special achievements/activities, leadership. *Special characteristics:* adult students, children of faculty/staff, ethnic background, international students, local/state students. ***Tuition waivers:*** Full or partial for employees or children of employees, adult students, senior citizens.

LOANS ***Student loans:*** $8,525,893 (65% need-based, 35% non-need-based). 87% of past graduating class borrowed through all loan programs. *Average indebtedness per student:* $23,637. ***Average need-based loan:*** Freshmen: $3825.

Undergraduates: $4745. ***Parent loans:*** $2,962,771 (39% need-based, 61% non-need-based). ***Programs:*** Federal Direct (Subsidized and Unsubsidized Stafford, PLUS), Perkins, college/university.

WORK-STUDY ***Federal work-study:*** Total amount: $1,107,619; 352 jobs averaging $644. ***State or other work-study/employment:*** Total amount: $1,065,650 (11% need-based, 89% non-need-based). 365 part-time jobs averaging $1022.

APPLYING FOR FINANCIAL AID ***Required financial aid form:*** FAFSA. ***Financial aid deadline:*** 3/1. ***Notification date:*** Continuous. Students must reply by 5/1 or within 2 weeks of notification.

CONTACT Valerie Rennell, Director of Student Financial Planning, Juniata College, 1700 Moore Street, Huntingdon, PA 16652-2119, 814-641-3141 or toll-free 877-JUNIATA. *Fax:* 814-641-5311. *E-mail:* rennelv@juniata.edu.

KALAMAZOO COLLEGE

Kalamazoo, MI

Tuition & fees: $34,317 **Average undergraduate aid package: N/A**

ABOUT THE INSTITUTION Independent religious, coed. 23 undergraduate majors. Both federal and institutional methodology are used as a basis for awarding need-based institutional aid.

UNDERGRADUATE EXPENSES for 2010–11 ***One-time required fee:*** $100. ***Comprehensive fee:*** $42,210 includes full-time tuition ($34,017), mandatory fees ($300), and room and board ($7893). ***College room only:*** $3849. Room and board charges vary according to board plan. ***Payment plan:*** Installment.

FRESHMAN FINANCIAL AID (Fall 2010, est.) 276 applied for aid; of those 83% were deemed to have need. 100% of freshmen with need received aid; of those 48% had need fully met. ***Average percent of need met:*** 87% (excluding resources awarded to replace EFC). ***Average financial aid package:*** $27,734 (excluding resources awarded to replace EFC). 28% of all full-time freshmen had no need and received non-need-based gift aid.

UNDERGRADUATE FINANCIAL AID (Fall 2010, est.) 931 applied for aid; of those 88% were deemed to have need. 100% of undergraduates with need received aid; of those 44% had need fully met.

GIFT AID (NEED-BASED) ***Total amount:*** $15,955,915 (8% federal, 4% state, 87% institutional, 1% external sources). ***Receiving aid:*** Freshmen: 63% (214); all full-time undergraduates: 58% (774). ***Average award:*** Freshmen: $23,055. ***Scholarships, grants, and awards:*** Federal Pell, FSEOG, state, private, college/university gift aid from institutional funds.

GIFT AID (NON-NEED-BASED) ***Total amount:*** $7,770,744 (82% institutional, 18% external sources). ***Receiving aid:*** Freshmen: 65% (222). Undergraduates: 52% (694). ***Average award:*** Freshmen: $13,097. ***Scholarships, grants, and awards by category:*** *Academic interests/achievement:* general academic interests/achievements. *Special characteristics:* children and siblings of alumni. ***Tuition waivers:*** Full or partial for employees or children of employees.

LOANS ***Student loans:*** $4,489,761 (49% need-based, 51% non-need-based). ***Average need-based loan:*** Freshmen: $3984. ***Parent loans:*** $2,670,500 (100% non-need-based). ***Programs:*** Federal Direct (Subsidized and Unsubsidized Stafford, PLUS), Perkins.

WORK-STUDY ***Federal work-study:*** Total amount: $312,000; jobs available. ***State or other work-study/employment:*** Total amount: $78,000 (100% non-need-based). Part-time jobs available.

APPLYING FOR FINANCIAL AID ***Required financial aid forms:*** FAFSA, institution's own form. ***Financial aid deadline (priority):*** 2/15. ***Notification date:*** Continuous beginning 3/21. Students must reply by 5/1.

CONTACT Marian Stowers, Director of Financial Aid, Kalamazoo College, 1200 Academy Street, Kalamazoo, MI 49006-3295, 269-337-7192 or toll-free 800-253-3602. *Fax:* 269-337-7390.

KANSAS CITY ART INSTITUTE

Kansas City, MO

ABOUT THE INSTITUTION Independent, coed. ***Awards:*** bachelor's degrees. 12 undergraduate majors. ***Total enrollment:*** 676. Undergraduates: 676. Freshmen: 152.

GIFT AID (NEED-BASED) ***Scholarships, grants, and awards:*** Federal Pell, FSEOG, state, private, college/university gift aid from institutional funds.

GIFT AID (NON-NEED-BASED) ***Scholarships, grants, and awards by category:*** *Creative arts/performance:* art/fine arts.

LOANS ***Programs:*** Perkins, alternative loans.

WORK-STUDY ***Federal work-study:*** Total amount: $140,768; 124 jobs averaging $997. ***State or other work-study/employment:*** Total amount: $70,967 (100% non-need-based). 30 part-time jobs averaging $1000.

APPLYING FOR FINANCIAL AID ***Required financial aid form:*** FAFSA.

CONTACT Ms. Kimberly Warren, Director of Financial Aid, Kansas City Art Institute, 4415 Warwick Boulevard, Kansas City, MO 64111-1874, 816-802-3448 or toll-free 800-522-5224. *Fax:* 816-802-3453. *E-mail:* kwarren@kcai.edu.

KANSAS STATE UNIVERSITY

Manhattan, KS

Tuition & fees (KS res): $7376 **Average undergraduate aid package: $10,607**

ABOUT THE INSTITUTION State-supported, coed. 81 undergraduate majors. Federal methodology is used as a basis for awarding need-based institutional aid.

UNDERGRADUATE EXPENSES for 2010–11 ***Tuition, state resident:*** full-time $6672. ***Tuition, nonresident:*** full-time $17,700. ***Required fees:*** full-time $704. Full-time tuition and fees vary according to course load, degree level, location, program, and reciprocity agreements. Part-time tuition and fees vary according to course load, degree level, location, program, and reciprocity agreements. ***College room and board:*** $6954. Room and board charges vary according to board plan, housing facility, and location. ***Payment plans:*** Installment, deferred payment.

FRESHMAN FINANCIAL AID (Fall 2009) 2,600 applied for aid; of those 66% were deemed to have need. 99% of freshmen with need received aid; of those 25% had need fully met. ***Average percent of need met:*** 86% (excluding resources awarded to replace EFC). ***Average financial aid package:*** $10,734 (excluding resources awarded to replace EFC). 18% of all full-time freshmen had no need and received non-need-based gift aid.

UNDERGRADUATE FINANCIAL AID (Fall 2009) 11,299 applied for aid; of those 74% were deemed to have need. 98% of undergraduates with need received aid; of those 20% had need fully met. ***Average percent of need met:*** 83% (excluding resources awarded to replace EFC). ***Average financial aid package:*** $10,607 (excluding resources awarded to replace EFC). 7% of all full-time undergraduates had no need and received non-need-based gift aid.

GIFT AID (NEED-BASED) ***Total amount:*** $38,843,638 (48% federal, 8% state, 36% institutional, 8% external sources). ***Receiving aid:*** Freshmen: 33% (1,143); all full-time undergraduates: 31% (5,114). ***Average award:*** Freshmen: $4357; Undergraduates: $4179. ***Scholarships, grants, and awards:*** Federal Pell, FSEOG, state, private, college/university gift aid from institutional funds.

GIFT AID (NON-NEED-BASED) ***Total amount:*** $4,459,435 (2% state, 95% institutional, 3% external sources). ***Receiving aid:*** Freshmen: 37% (1,252). Undergraduates: 24% (3,865). ***Average award:*** Freshmen: $3463. Undergraduates: $3014. ***Tuition waivers:*** Full or partial for employees or children of employees.

LOANS ***Student loans:*** $70,931,176 (68% need-based, 32% non-need-based). 54% of past graduating class borrowed through all loan programs. *Average indebtedness per student:* $22,633. ***Average need-based loan:*** Freshmen: $3315. Undergraduates: $4185. ***Parent loans:*** $21,963,875 (21% need-based, 79% non-need-based). ***Programs:*** Federal Direct (Subsidized and Unsubsidized Stafford, PLUS), Perkins, college/university.

WORK-STUDY ***Federal work-study:*** Total amount: $1,928,868; jobs available. ***State or other work-study/employment:*** Total amount: $89,052 (75% need-based, 25% non-need-based). Part-time jobs available.

ATHLETIC AWARDS Total amount: $4,341,332 (90% need-based, 10% non-need-based).

APPLYING FOR FINANCIAL AID ***Required financial aid form:*** FAFSA. ***Financial aid deadline (priority):*** 3/1. ***Notification date:*** Continuous beginning 4/1. Students must reply within 2 weeks of notification.

CONTACT Mr. Larry Moeder, Director of Admissions and Student Financial Assistance, Kansas State University, 104 Fairchild Hall, Manhattan, KS 66506, 785-532-6420 or toll-free 800-432-8270 (in-state). *E-mail:* larrym@ksu.edu.

KANSAS WESLEYAN UNIVERSITY

Salina, KS

CONTACT Mrs. Glenna Alexander, Director of Financial Assistance, Kansas Wesleyan University, 100 East Claflin, Salina, KS 67401-6196, 785-827-5541 Ext. 1130 or toll-free 800-874-1154 Ext. 1285. *Fax:* 785-827-0927. *E-mail:* kglennaa@acck.edu.

KAPLAN UNIVERSITY, DAVENPORT CAMPUS

Davenport, IA

CONTACT Financial Aid Office, Kaplan University, Davenport Campus, 1801 East Kimberly Road, Suite 1, Davenport, IA 52807-2095, 563-355-3500 or toll-free 800-747-1035 (in-state).

KAPLAN UNIVERSITY, MASON CITY CAMPUS

Mason City, IA

CONTACT Financial Aid Office, Kaplan University, Mason City Campus, 2570 4th Street, SW, Mason City, IA 50401, 641-423-2530.

KEAN UNIVERSITY

Union, NJ

Tuition & fees (NJ res): $9815 **Average undergraduate aid package: $9431**

ABOUT THE INSTITUTION State-supported, coed. 47 undergraduate majors. Federal methodology is used as a basis for awarding need-based institutional aid.

UNDERGRADUATE EXPENSES for 2010–11 ***Tuition, state resident:*** full-time $6411; part-time $230 per credit hour. ***Tuition, nonresident:*** full-time $12,000; part-time $400 per credit hour. ***Required fees:*** full-time $3404; $125 per credit hour. Part-time tuition and fees vary according to course load. ***College room and board:*** $12,950; ***Room only:*** $10,000. Room and board charges vary according to board plan and housing facility. ***Payment plan:*** Installment.

FRESHMAN FINANCIAL AID (Fall 2010, est.) 1,532 applied for aid; of those 85% were deemed to have need. 87% of freshmen with need received aid; of those 6% had need fully met. ***Average percent of need met:*** 56% (excluding resources awarded to replace EFC). ***Average financial aid package:*** $8719 (excluding resources awarded to replace EFC). 1% of all full-time freshmen had no need and received non-need-based gift aid.

UNDERGRADUATE FINANCIAL AID (Fall 2010, est.) 8,056 applied for aid; of those 86% were deemed to have need. 94% of undergraduates with need received aid; of those 11% had need fully met. ***Average percent of need met:*** 58% (excluding resources awarded to replace EFC). ***Average financial aid package:*** $9431 (excluding resources awarded to replace EFC). 1% of all full-time undergraduates had no need and received non-need-based gift aid.

GIFT AID (NEED-BASED) ***Total amount:*** $34,682,563 (63% federal, 32% state, 4% institutional, 1% external sources). ***Receiving aid:*** Freshmen: 65% (1,123); all full-time undergraduates: 64% (6,468). ***Average award:*** Freshmen: $7300; Undergraduates: $7044. ***Scholarships, grants, and awards:*** Federal Pell, FSEOG, state, private, college/university gift aid from institutional funds.

GIFT AID (NON-NEED-BASED) ***Total amount:*** $630,740 (18% state, 82% institutional). ***Receiving aid:*** Freshmen: 8% (142). Undergraduates: 8% (853). ***Average award:*** Freshmen: $6119. Undergraduates: $3808. ***Scholarships, grants, and awards by category:*** *Academic interests/achievement:* 880 awards ($1,460,242 total): area/ethnic studies, biological sciences, business, communication, computer science, education, English, foreign languages, general academic interests/achievements, health fields, humanities, international studies, mathematics, physical sciences, social sciences. *Creative arts/performance:* 11 awards ($87,288 total): applied art and design, art/fine arts, cinema/film/broadcasting, general creative arts/performance, music, performing arts, theater/drama. *Special achievements/activities:* 24 awards ($259,904 total): community service, leadership. *Special characteristics:* 113 awards ($718,032 total): general special characteristics. ***Tuition waivers:*** Full or partial for employees or children of employees, senior citizens.

LOANS ***Student loans:*** $65,108,619 (43% need-based, 57% non-need-based). 69% of past graduating class borrowed through all loan programs. *Average indebtedness per student:* $20,668. ***Average need-based loan:*** Freshmen: $3475. Undergraduates: $4436. ***Parent loans:*** $4,895,339 (100% non-need-based). ***Programs:*** Federal Direct (Subsidized and Unsubsidized Stafford, PLUS), Perkins.

WORK-STUDY ***Federal work-study:*** Total amount: $716,237; 334 jobs averaging $2154.

APPLYING FOR FINANCIAL AID ***Required financial aid form:*** FAFSA. ***Financial aid deadline (priority):*** 3/15. ***Notification date:*** Continuous beginning 3/15. Students must reply by 5/1.

CONTACT Ms. Sharon Audet, Associate Director of Financial Aid, Kean University, 1000 Morris Avenue, Union, NJ 07083, 908-737-3190. *Fax:* 908-737-3200. *E-mail:* finaid@kean.edu.

KEENE STATE COLLEGE

Keene, NH

Tuition & fees (NH res): $10,140 **Average undergraduate aid package: $9656**

ABOUT THE INSTITUTION State-supported, coed. 69 undergraduate majors. Federal methodology is used as a basis for awarding need-based institutional aid.

UNDERGRADUATE EXPENSES for 2010–11 ***Tuition, state resident:*** full-time $7650; part-time $320 per credit. ***Tuition, nonresident:*** full-time $15,820; part-time $660 per credit. ***Required fees:*** full-time $2490; $99 per credit. Part-time tuition and fees vary according to course load. ***College room and board:*** $8670; ***Room only:*** $5630. Room and board charges vary according to board plan and housing facility. ***Payment plan:*** Installment.

FRESHMAN FINANCIAL AID (Fall 2009) 1,064 applied for aid; of those 70% were deemed to have need. 99% of freshmen with need received aid; of those 16% had need fully met. ***Average percent of need met:*** 68% (excluding resources awarded to replace EFC). ***Average financial aid package:*** $9867 (excluding resources awarded to replace EFC). 5% of all full-time freshmen had no need and received non-need-based gift aid.

UNDERGRADUATE FINANCIAL AID (Fall 2009) 3,882 applied for aid; of those 73% were deemed to have need. 99% of undergraduates with need received aid; of those 19% had need fully met. ***Average percent of need met:*** 70% (excluding resources awarded to replace EFC). ***Average financial aid package:*** $9656 (excluding resources awarded to replace EFC). 6% of all full-time undergraduates had no need and received non-need-based gift aid.

GIFT AID (NEED-BASED) ***Total amount:*** $11,202,328 (39% federal, 7% state, 46% institutional, 8% external sources). ***Receiving aid:*** Freshmen: 42% (503); all full-time undergraduates: 37% (1,798). ***Average award:*** Freshmen: $6605; Undergraduates: $6025. ***Scholarships, grants, and awards:*** Federal Pell, FSEOG, state, private, college/university gift aid from institutional funds.

GIFT AID (NON-NEED-BASED) ***Total amount:*** $3,263,478 (78% institutional, 22% external sources). ***Receiving aid:*** Freshmen: 16% (193). Undergraduates: 14% (685). ***Average award:*** Freshmen: $2391. Undergraduates: $2818. ***Scholarships, grants, and awards by category:*** *Academic interests/achievement:* 546 awards ($1,230,250 total): general academic interests/achievements. *Creative arts/performance:* 25 awards ($70,875 total): applied art and design, art/fine arts, cinema/film/broadcasting, dance, general creative arts/performance, music, theater/drama. *Special achievements/activities:* 17 awards ($39,750 total): general special achievements/activities, leadership. ***Tuition waivers:*** Full or partial for employees or children of employees, senior citizens.

LOANS ***Student loans:*** $31,729,390 (34% need-based, 66% non-need-based). 78% of past graduating class borrowed through all loan programs. *Average indebtedness per student:* $28,986. ***Average need-based loan:*** Freshmen: $3649. Undergraduates: $4201. ***Parent loans:*** $8,182,096 (100% non-need-based). ***Programs:*** Perkins, college/university.

WORK-STUDY ***Federal work-study:*** Total amount: $3,332,400; 784 jobs averaging $1004. ***State or other work-study/employment:*** Total amount: $684,493 (100% non-need-based). 644 part-time jobs averaging $1063.

APPLYING FOR FINANCIAL AID ***Required financial aid form:*** FAFSA. ***Financial aid deadline:*** 3/1. ***Notification date:*** Continuous. Students must reply within 4 weeks of notification.

CONTACT Ms. Patricia Blodgett, Director of Student Financial Management, Keene State College, 229 Main Street, Keene, NH 03435-2606, 603-358-2280 or toll-free 800-KSC-1909. *Fax:* 603-358-2794. *E-mail:* pblodget@keene.edu.

KEHILATH YAKOV RABBINICAL SEMINARY

Ossining, NY

CONTACT Financial Aid Office, Kehilath Yakov Rabbinical Seminary, 206 Wilson Street, Brooklyn, NY 11211-7207, 718-963-1212.

KEISER UNIVERSITY

Fort Lauderdale, FL

CONTACT Judy Martin, Financial Aid Director, Keiser University, 1500 NW 49 Street, Fort Lauderdale, FL 33309, 954-776-4456 or toll-free 888-KEISER-9 (out-of-state). *Fax:* 954-749-4456. *E-mail:* judym@keiseruniversity.edu.

KENDALL COLLEGE

Chicago, IL

CONTACT Chris Miller, Director of Financial Aid, Kendall College, 900 N North Branch Street, Chicago, IL 60622, 312-752-2428 or toll-free 866-667-3344 (in-state), 877-588-8860 (out-of-state). *Fax:* 312-752-2267.

KENNESAW STATE UNIVERSITY

Kennesaw, GA

Tuition & fees (GA res): $5942 **Average undergraduate aid package: $7579**

ABOUT THE INSTITUTION State-supported, coed. 49 undergraduate majors. Federal methodology is used as a basis for awarding need-based institutional aid.

UNDERGRADUATE EXPENSES for 2010–11 ***Tuition, state resident:*** full-time $4596; part-time $154 per credit hour. ***Tuition, nonresident:*** full-time $16,572; part-time $553 per credit hour. ***Required fees:*** full-time $1346. Part-time tuition and fees vary according to course load. ***College room and board:*** $7298. Room and board charges vary according to board plan and housing facility. ***Payment plan:*** Deferred payment.

FRESHMAN FINANCIAL AID (Fall 2010, est.) 2,509 applied for aid; of those 76% were deemed to have need. 96% of freshmen with need received aid; of those 14% had need fully met. ***Average percent of need met:*** 92% (excluding resources awarded to replace EFC). ***Average financial aid package:*** $8210 (excluding resources awarded to replace EFC). 1% of all full-time freshmen had no need and received non-need-based gift aid.

UNDERGRADUATE FINANCIAL AID (Fall 2010, est.) 12,806 applied for aid; of those 82% were deemed to have need. 96% of undergraduates with need received aid; of those 19% had need fully met. ***Average percent of need met:*** 73% (excluding resources awarded to replace EFC). ***Average financial aid package:*** $7579 (excluding resources awarded to replace EFC). 1% of all full-time undergraduates had no need and received non-need-based gift aid.

GIFT AID (NEED-BASED) ***Total amount:*** $23,232,973 (98% federal, 2% state). ***Receiving aid:*** Freshmen: 51% (1,465); all full-time undergraduates: 54% (8,787). ***Average award:*** Freshmen: $5045; Undergraduates: $5989. ***Scholarships, grants, and awards:*** Federal Pell, FSEOG, state, private, college/university gift aid from institutional funds.

GIFT AID (NON-NEED-BASED) ***Total amount:*** $28,857,350 (97% state, 1% institutional, 2% external sources). ***Receiving aid:*** Freshmen: 51% (1,473). Undergraduates: 29% (4,814). ***Average award:*** Freshmen: $988. Undergraduates: $1116. ***Scholarships, grants, and awards by category:*** *Academic interests/achievement:* biological sciences, business, communication, computer science, education, English, foreign languages, general academic interests/achievements, health fields, humanities, international studies, mathematics, physical sciences, premedicine, social sciences. *Creative arts/performance:* music, performing arts, theater/drama. *Special achievements/activities:* community service, leadership, memberships. *Special characteristics:* children and siblings of alumni, children of union members/company employees, children of workers in trades, ethnic background, general special characteristics, handicapped students, international students, local/state students, members of minority groups, religious affiliation, veterans' children. ***Tuition waivers:*** Full or partial for employees or children of employees, senior citizens.

LOANS ***Student loans:*** $55,968,471 (42% need-based, 58% non-need-based). 48% of past graduating class borrowed through all loan programs. *Average indebtedness per student:* $947. ***Average need-based loan:*** Freshmen: $1742. Undergraduates: $3507. ***Parent loans:*** $2,002,192 (100% non-need-based). ***Programs:*** Federal Direct (Subsidized and Unsubsidized Stafford, PLUS), Perkins.

WORK-STUDY ***Federal work-study:*** Total amount: $558,935; 230 jobs averaging $2305.

ATHLETIC AWARDS Total amount: $737,402 (100% non-need-based).

APPLYING FOR FINANCIAL AID ***Required financial aid form:*** FAFSA. ***Financial aid deadline (priority):*** 4/1. ***Notification date:*** Continuous beginning 4/1.

CONTACT Mr. Ron H. Day, Director of Student Financial Aid, Kennesaw State University, 1000 Chastain Road, Kennesaw, GA 30144-5591, 770-423-6021. *Fax:* 770-423-6708. *E-mail:* finaid@kennesaw.edu.

KENT STATE UNIVERSITY

Kent, OH

Tuition & fees (OH res): $9030 **Average undergraduate aid package: $9250**

ABOUT THE INSTITUTION State-supported, coed. 122 undergraduate majors. Federal methodology is used as a basis for awarding need-based institutional aid.

UNDERGRADUATE EXPENSES for 2010–11 ***Tuition, state resident:*** full-time $9030; part-time $411 per credit hour. ***Tuition, nonresident:*** full-time $16,990; part-time $773 per credit hour. Full-time tuition and fees vary according to course load, program, and reciprocity agreements. Part-time tuition and fees vary according to course load, program, and reciprocity agreements. ***College room and board:*** $8376; ***Room only:*** $5176. Room and board charges vary according to board plan and housing facility. ***Payment plans:*** Installment, deferred payment.

FRESHMAN FINANCIAL AID (Fall 2010, est.) 3,377 applied for aid; of those 84% were deemed to have need. 100% of freshmen with need received aid; of those 44% had need fully met. ***Average percent of need met:*** 54% (excluding resources awarded to replace EFC). ***Average financial aid package:*** $9067 (excluding resources awarded to replace EFC). 13% of all full-time freshmen had no need and received non-need-based gift aid.

UNDERGRADUATE FINANCIAL AID (Fall 2010, est.) 13,886 applied for aid; of those 87% were deemed to have need. 100% of undergraduates with need received aid; of those 38% had need fully met. ***Average percent of need met:*** 53% (excluding resources awarded to replace EFC). ***Average financial aid package:*** $9250 (excluding resources awarded to replace EFC). 10% of all full-time undergraduates had no need and received non-need-based gift aid.

GIFT AID (NEED-BASED) ***Total amount:*** $60,711,806 (59% federal, 8% state, 28% institutional, 5% external sources). ***Receiving aid:*** Freshmen: 60% (2,352); all full-time undergraduates: 50% (9,222). ***Average award:*** Freshmen: $3291; Undergraduates: $5886. ***Scholarships, grants, and awards:*** Federal Pell, FSEOG, state, private, college/university gift aid from institutional funds.

GIFT AID (NON-NEED-BASED) ***Total amount:*** $12,815,478 (15% federal, 13% state, 64% institutional, 8% external sources). ***Receiving aid:*** Freshmen: 13% (494). Undergraduates: 9% (1,711). ***Average award:*** Freshmen: $4739. Undergraduates: $4230. ***Scholarships, grants, and awards by category:*** *Academic interests/achievement:* architecture, area/ethnic studies, biological sciences, business, communication, computer science, education, engineering/technologies, English, general academic interests/achievements, health fields, international studies, library science, mathematics, military science, physical sciences, social sciences. *Creative arts/performance:* art/fine arts, dance, journalism/publications, music, performing arts, theater/drama. *Special achievements/activities:* community service, general special achievements/activities, leadership. *Special characteristics:* adult students, children and siblings of alumni, children of faculty/staff, children of union members/company employees, children with a deceased or disabled parent, ethnic background, first-generation college students, handicapped students, international students, local/state students, members of minority groups, out-of-state students. ***Tuition waivers:*** Full or partial for employees or children of employees, senior citizens.

LOANS ***Student loans:*** $115,893,374 (44% need-based, 56% non-need-based). 77% of past graduating class borrowed through all loan programs. *Average indebtedness per student:* $28,186. ***Average need-based loan:*** Freshmen: $3358. Undergraduates: $4083. ***Parent loans:*** $29,303,430 (23% need-based, 77% non-need-based). ***Programs:*** Federal Direct (Subsidized and Unsubsidized Stafford, PLUS), Perkins, Federal Nursing, state, college/university, alternative loans.

WORK-STUDY ***Federal work-study:*** Total amount: $1,019,874; jobs available.

ATHLETIC AWARDS Total amount: $5,178,542 (54% need-based, 46% non-need-based).

APPLYING FOR FINANCIAL AID ***Required financial aid form:*** FAFSA. ***Financial aid deadline (priority):*** 3/1. ***Notification date:*** 3/15. Students must reply within 2 weeks of notification.

CONTACT Mark A. Evans, Director of Student Financial Aid, Kent State University, 103 Michael Schwartz Center, Kent, OH 44242-0001, 330-672-2972 or toll-free 800-988-KENT. *Fax:* 330-672-4014. *E-mail:* mevans@kent.edu.

KENT STATE UNIVERSITY AT STARK

Canton, OH

Tuition & fees (OH res): $5110 **Average undergraduate aid package: $7489**

ABOUT THE INSTITUTION State-supported, coed. 9 undergraduate majors. Federal methodology is used as a basis for awarding need-based institutional aid.

UNDERGRADUATE EXPENSES for 2010–11 ***Tuition, state resident:*** full-time $5110; part-time $233 per credit hour. ***Tuition, nonresident:*** full-time $13,070; part-time $595 per credit hour. Full-time tuition and fees vary according to course level and course load. Part-time tuition and fees vary according to course level and course load. ***Payment plans:*** Installment, deferred payment.

FRESHMAN FINANCIAL AID (Fall 2010, est.) 534 applied for aid; of those 88% were deemed to have need. 100% of freshmen with need received aid; of those 44% had need fully met. ***Average percent of need met:*** 52% (excluding resources awarded to replace EFC). ***Average financial aid package:*** $6768 (excluding resources awarded to replace EFC). 1% of all full-time freshmen had no need and received non-need-based gift aid.

UNDERGRADUATE FINANCIAL AID (Fall 2010, est.) 2,313 applied for aid; of those 90% were deemed to have need. 100% of undergraduates with need received aid; of those 31% had need fully met. ***Average percent of need met:*** 52% (excluding resources awarded to replace EFC). ***Average financial aid package:*** $7489 (excluding resources awarded to replace EFC). 1% of all full-time undergraduates had no need and received non-need-based gift aid.

GIFT AID (NEED-BASED) ***Total amount:*** $10,429,787 (97% federal, 1% institutional, 2% external sources). ***Receiving aid:*** Freshmen: 59% (361); all full-time undergraduates: 51% (1,586). ***Average award:*** Freshmen: $4807; Undergraduates: $4836. ***Scholarships, grants, and awards:*** Federal Pell, FSEOG, state, private, college/university gift aid from institutional funds.

GIFT AID (NON-NEED-BASED) ***Total amount:*** $682,849 (43% federal, 21% state, 31% institutional, 5% external sources). ***Receiving aid:*** Freshmen: 4% (24). Undergraduates: 5% (169). ***Average award:*** Freshmen: $2392. Undergraduates: $2159. ***Scholarships, grants, and awards by category:*** *Academic interests/achievement:* general academic interests/achievements. *Creative arts/performance:* art/fine arts, music, theater/drama. *Special achievements/activities:* leadership. *Special characteristics:* children and siblings of alumni, local/state students, members of minority groups. ***Tuition waivers:*** Full or partial for employees or children of employees, senior citizens.

LOANS ***Student loans:*** $22,333,811 (46% need-based, 54% non-need-based). ***Average need-based loan:*** Freshmen: $2920. Undergraduates: $3576. ***Parent loans:*** $454,326 (15% need-based, 85% non-need-based). ***Programs:*** Federal Direct (Subsidized and Unsubsidized Stafford, PLUS), Perkins, Federal Nursing, state, college/university, alternative loans.

WORK-STUDY ***Federal work-study:*** Total amount: $95,403; jobs available.

APPLYING FOR FINANCIAL AID ***Required financial aid form:*** FAFSA. ***Financial aid deadline (priority):*** 3/1. ***Notification date:*** 3/15. Students must reply within 2 weeks of notification.

CONTACT Gail Pukys, Assistant Director for Enrollment Management for Financial Aid, Kent State University at Stark, Office of Student Services, 134 Main Hall, North Canton, OH 44720, 330-244-3257. *E-mail:* gpukys@kent.edu.

KENTUCKY CHRISTIAN UNIVERSITY

Grayson, KY

CONTACT Mrs. Jennie M. Bender, Director of Financial Aid, Kentucky Christian University, 100 Academic Parkway, Grayson, KY 41143-2205, 606-474-3226 or toll-free 800-522-3181. *Fax:* 606-474-3155. *E-mail:* jbender@kcu.edu.

KENTUCKY MOUNTAIN BIBLE COLLEGE

Vancleve, KY

ABOUT THE INSTITUTION Independent interdenominational, coed. 1 undergraduate major.

GIFT AID (NEED-BASED) ***Scholarships, grants, and awards:*** Federal Pell, FSEOG, state, private, college/university gift aid from institutional funds.

GIFT AID (NON-NEED-BASED) ***Scholarships, grants, and awards by category:*** *Academic interests/achievement:* general academic interests/achievements. *Creative arts/performance:* music, theater/drama. *Special characteristics:* children of faculty/staff.

LOANS ***Programs:*** college/university.

WORK-STUDY Federal work-study jobs available. ***State or other work-study/employment:*** Part-time jobs available.

APPLYING FOR FINANCIAL AID ***Required financial aid forms:*** FAFSA, institution's own form.

CONTACT Mrs. Rosita Marshall, Director of Financial Aid, Kentucky Mountain Bible College, PO Box 10, Vancleve, KY 41385-0010, 800-879-KMBC Ext. 175 or toll-free 800-879-KMBC Ext. 130 (in-state), 800-879-KMBC Ext. 136 (out-of-state). *Fax:* 800-659-4324. *E-mail:* finaid@kmbc.edu.

KENTUCKY STATE UNIVERSITY

Frankfort, KY

Tuition & fees (KY res): $6210 **Average undergraduate aid package: $11,028**

ABOUT THE INSTITUTION State-related, coed. 25 undergraduate majors. Federal methodology is used as a basis for awarding need-based institutional aid.

UNDERGRADUATE EXPENSES for 2010–11 ***Tuition, state resident:*** full-time $5460; part-time $205 per credit hour. ***Tuition, nonresident:*** full-time $14,154; part-time $527 per credit hour. ***Required fees:*** full-time $750; $25 per credit hour. Full-time tuition and fees vary according to course load. Part-time tuition and fees vary according to course load. ***College room and board:*** $6480; ***Room only:*** $3240. Room and board charges vary according to board plan and housing facility. ***Payment plan:*** Installment.

FRESHMAN FINANCIAL AID (Fall 2010, est.) 557 applied for aid; of those 100% were deemed to have need. 94% of freshmen with need received aid; of those 11% had need fully met. ***Average percent of need met:*** 53% (excluding resources awarded to replace EFC). ***Average financial aid package:*** $10,765 (excluding resources awarded to replace EFC). 2% of all full-time freshmen had no need and received non-need-based gift aid.

UNDERGRADUATE FINANCIAL AID (Fall 2010, est.) 1,825 applied for aid; of those 100% were deemed to have need. 97% of undergraduates with need received aid; of those 14% had need fully met. ***Average percent of need met:*** 55% (excluding resources awarded to replace EFC). ***Average financial aid package:*** $11,028 (excluding resources awarded to replace EFC). 3% of all full-time undergraduates had no need and received non-need-based gift aid.

GIFT AID (NEED-BASED) ***Total amount:*** $7,254,856 (84% federal, 6% state, 8% institutional, 2% external sources). ***Receiving aid:*** Freshmen: 72% (423); all full-time undergraduates: 72% (1,432). ***Average award:*** Freshmen: $6180; Undergraduates: $5920. ***Scholarships, grants, and awards:*** Federal Pell, FSEOG, state, college/university gift aid from institutional funds, United Negro College Fund.

GIFT AID (NON-NEED-BASED) ***Total amount:*** $5,291,748 (29% federal, 14% state, 50% institutional, 7% external sources). ***Receiving aid:*** Freshmen: 41% (239). Undergraduates: 35% (688). ***Average award:*** Freshmen: $6746. Undergraduates: $7140. ***Scholarships, grants, and awards by category:*** *Academic interests/achievement:* general academic interests/achievements, health fields, mathematics. *Creative arts/performance:* art/fine arts, journalism/publications, music. *Special achievements/activities:* cheerleading/drum major. *Special characteristics:* adult students, children with a deceased or disabled parent, ethnic background, general special characteristics, international students, local/state students, veterans. ***Tuition waivers:*** Full or partial for employees or children of employees, senior citizens.

LOANS ***Student loans:*** $15,494,935 (22% need-based, 78% non-need-based). 44% of past graduating class borrowed through all loan programs. *Average indebtedness per student:* $33,320. ***Average need-based loan:*** Freshmen: $3434. Undergraduates: $3988. ***Parent loans:*** $3,101,105 (6% need-based, 94% non-need-based). ***Programs:*** Federal Direct (Subsidized and Unsubsidized Stafford, PLUS), Perkins.

WORK-STUDY ***Federal work-study:*** Total amount: $847,900; 490 jobs averaging $1730.

ATHLETIC AWARDS Total amount: $937,875 (2% need-based, 98% non-need-based).

APPLYING FOR FINANCIAL AID ***Required financial aid form:*** FAFSA. ***Financial aid deadline (priority):*** 4/15. ***Notification date:*** Continuous. Students must reply within 2 weeks of notification.

CONTACT Myrna C. Bryant, Assistant Director of Financial Aid, Kentucky State University, 400 East Main Street, Frankfort, KY 40601, 502-597-5960 or toll-free 800-633-9415 (in-state), 800-325-1716 (out-of-state). *Fax:* 502-597-5950. *E-mail:* myrna.bryant@kysu.edu.

KENTUCKY WESLEYAN COLLEGE

Owensboro, KY

Tuition & fees: $19,390 **Average undergraduate aid package: $14,942**

ABOUT THE INSTITUTION Independent Methodist, coed. 39 undergraduate majors. Federal methodology is used as a basis for awarding need-based institutional aid.

UNDERGRADUATE EXPENSES for 2011–12 ***Comprehensive fee:*** $26,310 includes full-time tuition ($18,790), mandatory fees ($600), and room and board ($6920). ***College room only:*** $3100. Full-time tuition and fees vary according to course load. Room and board charges vary according to board plan and housing facility. Part-time tuition and fees vary according to course load. ***Payment plans:*** Installment, deferred payment.

FRESHMAN FINANCIAL AID (Fall 2009) 214 applied for aid; of those 95% were deemed to have need. 99% of freshmen with need received aid; of those 22% had need fully met. ***Average percent of need met:*** 73% (excluding resources awarded to replace EFC). ***Average financial aid package:*** $15,311 (excluding resources awarded to replace EFC). 10% of all full-time freshmen had no need and received non-need-based gift aid.

UNDERGRADUATE FINANCIAL AID (Fall 2009) 803 applied for aid; of those 91% were deemed to have need. 99% of undergraduates with need received aid; of those 24% had need fully met. ***Average percent of need met:*** 73% (excluding resources awarded to replace EFC). ***Average financial aid package:*** $14,942 (excluding resources awarded to replace EFC). 16% of all full-time undergraduates had no need and received non-need-based gift aid.

GIFT AID (NEED-BASED) ***Total amount:*** $8,750,767 (22% federal, 24% state, 50% institutional, 4% external sources). ***Receiving aid:*** Freshmen: 87% (200); all full-time undergraduates: 83% (719). ***Average award:*** Freshmen: $12,990; Undergraduates: $12,115. ***Scholarships, grants, and awards:*** Federal Pell, FSEOG, state, private, college/university gift aid from institutional funds.

GIFT AID (NON-NEED-BASED) ***Total amount:*** $1,898,373 (12% state, 81% institutional, 7% external sources). ***Receiving aid:*** Freshmen: 10% (24). Undergraduates: 11% (96). ***Average award:*** Freshmen: $8040. Undergraduates: $8354. ***Scholarships, grants, and awards by category:*** *Academic interests/achievement:* 808 awards ($4,148,294 total): general academic interests/achievements. *Creative arts/performance:* 38 awards ($52,922 total): art/fine arts, creative writing, general creative arts/performance, music, performing arts. *Special characteristics:* 183 awards ($448,734 total): children of faculty/staff, general special characteristics, out-of-state students, relatives of clergy, religious affiliation, veterans. ***Tuition waivers:*** Full or partial for children of alumni, employees or children of employees, senior citizens.

LOANS ***Student loans:*** $3,766,480 (75% need-based, 25% non-need-based). 92% of past graduating class borrowed through all loan programs. *Average indebtedness per student:* $19,516. ***Average need-based loan:*** Freshmen: $2964. Undergraduates: $3699. ***Parent loans:*** $383,172 (22% need-based, 78% non-need-based). ***Programs:*** Federal Direct (Subsidized and Unsubsidized Stafford, PLUS), Perkins, alternative loans.

WORK-STUDY ***Federal work-study:*** Total amount: $110,562; 135 jobs averaging $1089. ***State or other work-study/employment:*** Total amount: $18,750 (33% need-based, 67% non-need-based). Part-time jobs available.

ATHLETIC AWARDS Total amount: $1,312,196 (100% non-need-based).

APPLYING FOR FINANCIAL AID ***Required financial aid form:*** FAFSA. ***Financial aid deadline:*** 3/15. ***Notification date:*** Continuous. Students must reply within 2 weeks of notification.

CONTACT Mrs. Samantha Hays, Director of Financial Aid, Kentucky Wesleyan College, 3000 Frederica Street, Owensboro, KY 42301, 270-852-3130 or toll-free 800-999-0592 (in-state), 800-990-0592 (out-of-state). *Fax:* 270-852-3133. *E-mail:* shays@kwc.edu.

KENYON COLLEGE

Gambier, OH

Tuition & fees: $42,630 **Average undergraduate aid package: $33,150**

ABOUT THE INSTITUTION Independent, coed. 31 undergraduate majors. Both federal and institutional methodology are used as a basis for awarding need-based institutional aid.

UNDERGRADUATE EXPENSES for 2011–12 ***Comprehensive fee:*** $52,650 includes full-time tuition ($41,090), mandatory fees ($1540), and room and board ($10,020). ***Payment plan:*** Installment.

FRESHMAN FINANCIAL AID (Fall 2010, est.) 284 applied for aid; of those 76% were deemed to have need. 100% of freshmen with need received aid; of those 55% had need fully met. ***Average percent of need met:*** 98% (excluding resources awarded to replace EFC). ***Average financial aid package:*** $30,623 (excluding resources awarded to replace EFC). 8% of all full-time freshmen had no need and received non-need-based gift aid.

UNDERGRADUATE FINANCIAL AID (Fall 2010, est.) 899 applied for aid; of those 86% were deemed to have need. 100% of undergraduates with need received aid; of those 48% had need fully met. ***Average percent of need met:*** 98% (excluding resources awarded to replace EFC). ***Average financial aid package:*** $33,150 (excluding resources awarded to replace EFC). 9% of all full-time undergraduates had no need and received non-need-based gift aid.

GIFT AID (NEED-BASED) ***Total amount:*** $22,385,820 (5% federal, 88% institutional, 7% external sources). ***Receiving aid:*** Freshmen: 42% (201); all full-time undergraduates: 41% (736). ***Average award:*** Freshmen: $30,256; Undergraduates: $30,415. ***Scholarships, grants, and awards:*** Federal Pell, FSEOG, state, private, college/university gift aid from institutional funds.

GIFT AID (NON-NEED-BASED) ***Total amount:*** $3,454,882 (76% institutional, 24% external sources). ***Receiving aid:*** Freshmen: 16% (79). Undergraduates: 10% (186). ***Average award:*** Freshmen: $12,606. Undergraduates: $11,007. ***Scholarships, grants, and awards by category:*** *Academic interests/achievement:* 266 awards ($2,451,758 total): general academic interests/achievements. *Creative arts/performance:* 4 awards ($37,500 total): art/fine arts, creative writing, music. *Special characteristics:* 58 awards ($799,455 total): ethnic background, first-generation college students. ***Tuition waivers:*** Full or partial for employees or children of employees.

LOANS ***Student loans:*** $5,571,565 (52% need-based, 48% non-need-based). 60% of past graduating class borrowed through all loan programs. *Average indebtedness per student:* $20,492. ***Average need-based loan:*** Freshmen: $2979. Undergraduates: $4384. ***Parent loans:*** $2,002,892 (5% need-based, 95% non-need-based). ***Programs:*** Federal Direct (Subsidized and Unsubsidized Stafford, PLUS), Perkins, college/university.

WORK-STUDY ***Federal work-study:*** Total amount: $191,542; 244 jobs averaging $1262. ***State or other work-study/employment:*** Total amount: $576,917 (48% need-based, 52% non-need-based). 162 part-time jobs averaging $1303.

APPLYING FOR FINANCIAL AID ***Required financial aid forms:*** FAFSA, CSS Financial Aid PROFILE, noncustodial (divorced/separated) parent's statement, federal income tax form(s). ***Financial aid deadline (priority):*** 2/15. ***Notification date:*** 4/1. Students must reply by 5/1.

CONTACT Mr. Craig Daugherty, Director of Financial Aid, Kenyon College, Stephens Hall, Gambier, OH 43022-9623, 740-427-5430 or toll-free 800-848-2468. *Fax:* 740-427-5240. *E-mail:* daugherty@kenyon.edu.

KETTERING COLLEGE OF MEDICAL ARTS

Kettering, OH

CONTACT Financial Aid Office, Kettering College of Medical Arts, 3737 Southern Boulevard, Kettering, OH 45429-1299, 937-395-8601 or toll-free 800-433-5262.

KETTERING UNIVERSITY

Flint, MI

Tuition & fees: $29,116 **Average undergraduate aid package: $19,931**

ABOUT THE INSTITUTION Independent, coed, primarily men. 13 undergraduate majors. Federal methodology is used as a basis for awarding need-based institutional aid.

UNDERGRADUATE EXPENSES for 2010–11 ***One-time required fee:*** $310. ***Comprehensive fee:*** $35,556 includes full-time tuition ($28,672), mandatory fees ($444), and room and board ($6440). ***College room only:*** $4000. ***Part-time tuition:*** $896 per credit hour. ***Payment plan:*** Installment.

FRESHMAN FINANCIAL AID (Fall 2010, est.) 256 applied for aid; of those 91% were deemed to have need. 100% of freshmen with need received aid; of those 13% had need fully met. ***Average percent of need met:*** 66% (excluding resources awarded to replace EFC). ***Average financial aid package:*** $20,810 (excluding resources awarded to replace EFC). 15% of all full-time freshmen had no need and received non-need-based gift aid.

UNDERGRADUATE FINANCIAL AID (Fall 2010, est.) 1,327 applied for aid; of those 94% were deemed to have need. 100% of undergraduates with need received aid; of those 16% had need fully met. ***Average percent of need met:*** 67% (excluding resources awarded to replace EFC). ***Average financial aid package:*** $19,931 (excluding resources awarded to replace EFC). 32% of all full-time undergraduates had no need and received non-need-based gift aid.

GIFT AID (NEED-BASED) ***Total amount:*** $17,534,779 (15% federal, 6% state, 78% institutional, 1% external sources). ***Receiving aid:*** Freshmen: 84% (233); all full-time undergraduates: 66% (1,210). ***Average award:*** Freshmen: $16,711; Undergraduates: $15,347. ***Scholarships, grants, and awards:*** Federal Pell, FSEOG, state, private.

GIFT AID (NON-NEED-BASED) ***Total amount:*** $5,369,608 (97% institutional, 3% external sources). ***Receiving aid:*** Freshmen: 29% (79). Undergraduates: 24% (434). ***Average award:*** Freshmen: $12,621. Undergraduates: $12,223. ***Scholarships, grants, and awards by category:*** *Academic interests/achievement:* business, computer science, engineering/technologies, general academic interests/achievements, mathematics, physical sciences. *Special achievements/activities:* general special achievements/activities, leadership, memberships. *Special characteristics:* children of faculty/staff, local/state students, members of minority groups, siblings of current students. ***Tuition waivers:*** Full or partial for employees or children of employees.

LOANS ***Student loans:*** $13,435,536 (73% need-based, 27% non-need-based). 78% of past graduating class borrowed through all loan programs. *Average indebtedness per student:* $45,570. ***Average need-based loan:*** Freshmen: $3432. Undergraduates: $4374. ***Parent loans:*** $2,398,538 (61% need-based, 39% non-need-based). ***Programs:*** Federal Direct (Subsidized and Unsubsidized Stafford, PLUS).

WORK-STUDY ***Federal work-study:*** Total amount: $1,335,371; 1,147 jobs averaging $1165.

APPLYING FOR FINANCIAL AID ***Required financial aid form:*** FAFSA. ***Financial aid deadline:*** Continuous. ***Notification date:*** Continuous beginning 2/15.

CONTACT Diane Bice, Director of Financial Aid, Kettering University, 1700 University Avenue, Flint, MI 48504-4898, 800-955-4464 Ext. 7859 or toll-free 800-955-4464 Ext. 7865 (in-state), 800-955-4464 (out-of-state). *Fax:* 810-762-9807. *E-mail:* finaid@kettering.edu.

KEUKA COLLEGE

Keuka Park, NY

Tuition & fees: $23,770 **Average undergraduate aid package: $15,766**

ABOUT THE INSTITUTION Independent religious, coed. 34 undergraduate majors. Federal methodology is used as a basis for awarding need-based institutional aid.

UNDERGRADUATE EXPENSES for 2010–11 ***Comprehensive fee:*** $33,270 includes full-time tuition ($23,130), mandatory fees ($640), and room and board ($9500). ***College room only:*** $4510. Full-time tuition and fees vary according to program. Room and board charges vary according to board plan and housing facility. ***Part-time tuition:*** $770 per credit hour. Part-time tuition and fees vary according to program. ***Payment plan:*** Installment.

FRESHMAN FINANCIAL AID (Fall 2010, est.) 232 applied for aid; of those 92% were deemed to have need. 100% of freshmen with need received aid; of those 8% had need fully met. ***Average percent of need met:*** 66% (excluding resources awarded to replace EFC). ***Average financial aid package:*** $19,160 (excluding resources awarded to replace EFC). 9% of all full-time freshmen had no need and received non-need-based gift aid.

UNDERGRADUATE FINANCIAL AID (Fall 2010, est.) 1,351 applied for aid; of those 92% were deemed to have need. 98% of undergraduates with need received aid; of those 12% had need fully met. ***Average percent of need met:*** 70% (excluding resources awarded to replace EFC). ***Average financial aid package:*** $15,766 (excluding resources awarded to replace EFC). 5% of all full-time undergraduates had no need and received non-need-based gift aid.

GIFT AID (NEED-BASED) ***Total amount:*** $13,280,753 (25% federal, 14% state, 58% institutional, 3% external sources). ***Receiving aid:*** Freshmen: 84% (213); all full-time undergraduates: 83% (1,136). ***Average award:*** Freshmen: $14,856; Undergraduates: $11,695. ***Scholarships, grants, and awards:*** Federal Pell, FSEOG, state, college/university gift aid from institutional funds.

GIFT AID (NON-NEED-BASED) ***Total amount:*** $1,306,999 (7% federal, 2% state, 78% institutional, 13% external sources). ***Receiving aid:*** Freshmen: 6% (16). Undergraduates: 6% (81). ***Average award:*** Freshmen: $9935. Undergraduates: $10,087. ***Scholarships, grants, and awards by category:*** *Academic interests/achievement:* general academic interests/achievements, international studies. *Special achievements/activities:* community service, general special achievements/activities, leadership. *Special characteristics:* children and siblings of alumni, children of faculty/staff, international students, siblings of current students. ***Tuition waivers:*** Full or partial for employees or children of employees.

LOANS ***Student loans:*** $12,201,200 (76% need-based, 24% non-need-based). 92% of past graduating class borrowed through all loan programs. *Average indebtedness per student:* $13,874. ***Average need-based loan:*** Freshmen: $4805. Undergraduates: $5383. ***Parent loans:*** $1,488,862 (53% need-based, 47% non-need-based). ***Programs:*** Perkins.

WORK-STUDY ***Federal work-study:*** Total amount: $321,498; jobs available. ***State or other work-study/employment:*** Total amount: $139,904 (11% need-based, 89% non-need-based). Part-time jobs available.

APPLYING FOR FINANCIAL AID ***Required financial aid form:*** FAFSA. ***Financial aid deadline:*** Continuous. ***Notification date:*** Continuous beginning 3/1. Students must reply by 5/1 or within 2 weeks of notification.

CONTACT Jennifer Bates, Director of Financial Aid, Keuka College, 141 Central Avenue, Keuka Park, NY 14478-0098, 315-279-5232 or toll-free 800-33-KEUKA. *Fax:* 315-536-5327. *E-mail:* jbates@keuka.edu.

KEYSTONE COLLEGE

La Plume, PA

Tuition & fees: $19,620 **Average undergraduate aid package: $22,554**

ABOUT THE INSTITUTION Independent, coed. 53 undergraduate majors. Federal methodology is used as a basis for awarding need-based institutional aid.

UNDERGRADUATE EXPENSES for 2011–12 ***One-time required fee:*** $300. ***Comprehensive fee:*** $28,820 includes full-time tuition ($18,770), mandatory fees ($850), and room and board ($9200). ***College room only:*** $4650. Room and board charges vary according to board plan and housing facility. ***Part-time tuition:*** $400 per credit. ***Part-time fees:*** $200 per term. Part-time tuition and fees vary according to course load. ***Payment plans:*** Installment, deferred payment.

FRESHMAN FINANCIAL AID (Fall 2009) 314 applied for aid; of those 100% were deemed to have need. 100% of freshmen with need received aid; of those 29% had need fully met. ***Average percent of need met:*** 81% (excluding resources awarded to replace EFC). ***Average financial aid package:*** $23,718 (excluding resources awarded to replace EFC). 3% of all full-time freshmen had no need and received non-need-based gift aid.

UNDERGRADUATE FINANCIAL AID (Fall 2009) 1,123 applied for aid; of those 100% were deemed to have need. 100% of undergraduates with need received aid; of those 31% had need fully met. ***Average percent of need met:*** 77% (excluding resources awarded to replace EFC). ***Average financial aid package:*** $22,554 (excluding resources awarded to replace EFC). 3% of all full-time undergraduates had no need and received non-need-based gift aid.

GIFT AID (NEED-BASED) ***Total amount:*** $6,536,894 (56% federal, 38% state, 6% institutional). ***Receiving aid:*** Freshmen: 90% (308); all full-time undergraduates: 76% (1,033). ***Average award:*** Freshmen: $21,369; Undergraduates: $20,719. ***Scholarships, grants, and awards:*** Federal Pell, FSEOG, state, private, college/university gift aid from institutional funds.

GIFT AID (NON-NEED-BASED) ***Total amount:*** $9,686,151 (1% state, 97% institutional, 2% external sources). ***Receiving aid:*** Freshmen: 91% (313). Undergraduates: 80% (1,078). ***Average award:*** Freshmen: $12,074. Undergraduates: $11,868. ***Scholarships, grants, and awards by category:*** *Academic interests/achievement:* 32 awards ($71,034 total): computer science, education, premedicine. *Special characteristics:* 64 awards ($39,575 total): children and siblings of alumni, international students, siblings of current students. ***Tuition waivers:*** Full or partial for employees or children of employees, senior citizens.

LOANS ***Student loans:*** $11,034,980 (45% need-based, 55% non-need-based). 89% of past graduating class borrowed through all loan programs. *Average indebtedness per student:* $24,750. ***Average need-based loan:*** Freshmen: $5500. Undergraduates: $6500. ***Parent loans:*** $1,626,049 (100% non-need-based). ***Programs:*** Federal Direct (Subsidized and Unsubsidized Stafford, PLUS), Perkins, alternative loans, Miller Loan Fund.

WORK-STUDY ***Federal work-study:*** Total amount: $165,603; 202 jobs averaging $1450. ***State or other work-study/employment:*** Total amount: $67,267 (100% non-need-based). 50 part-time jobs averaging $1450.

APPLYING FOR FINANCIAL AID ***Required financial aid forms:*** FAFSA, state aid form. ***Financial aid deadline:*** Continuous. ***Notification date:*** Continuous beginning 2/2. Students must reply within 2 weeks of notification.

CONTACT Ginger Kline, Director of Financial Assistance and Planning, Keystone College, One College Green, Sabiston Hall, Second Floor, La Plume, AB 18440, 570-945-8130 or toll-free 877-4COLLEGE Ext. 1. *Fax:* 570-945-8967. *E-mail:* ginger.kline@keystone.edu.

KING COLLEGE

Bristol, TN

Tuition & fees: $22,908 **Average undergraduate aid package: $18,758**

ABOUT THE INSTITUTION Independent religious, coed. 58 undergraduate majors. Federal methodology is used as a basis for awarding need-based institutional aid.

UNDERGRADUATE EXPENSES for 2010–11 ***Comprehensive fee:*** $30,698 includes full-time tuition ($21,620), mandatory fees ($1288), and room and board ($7790). ***College room only:*** $3912. Full-time tuition and fees vary according to course load and program. Room and board charges vary according to board plan. ***Part-time tuition:*** $600 per credit hour. ***Part-time fees:*** $120 per credit hour. Part-time tuition and fees vary according to course load and program. ***Payment plan:*** Installment.

FRESHMAN FINANCIAL AID (Fall 2010, est.) 253 applied for aid; of those 78% were deemed to have need. 100% of freshmen with need received aid; of those 20% had need fully met. ***Average percent of need met:*** 67% (excluding resources awarded to replace EFC). ***Average financial aid package:*** $18,137 (excluding resources awarded to replace EFC). 7% of all full-time freshmen had no need and received non-need-based gift aid.

UNDERGRADUATE FINANCIAL AID (Fall 2010, est.) 1,335 applied for aid; of those 90% were deemed to have need. 93% of undergraduates with need received aid; of those 20% had need fully met. ***Average percent of need met:*** 66% (excluding resources awarded to replace EFC). ***Average financial aid package:*** $18,758 (excluding resources awarded to replace EFC). 9% of all full-time undergraduates had no need and received non-need-based gift aid.

GIFT AID (NEED-BASED) ***Total amount:*** $12,049,778 (18% federal, 13% state, 66% institutional, 3% external sources). ***Receiving aid:*** Freshmen: 76% (197); all full-time undergraduates: 67% (1,110). ***Average award:*** Freshmen: $15,945; Undergraduates: $15,764. ***Scholarships, grants, and awards:*** Federal Pell, FSEOG, state, private, college/university gift aid from institutional funds.

GIFT AID (NON-NEED-BASED) ***Total amount:*** $2,880,320 (14% state, 72% institutional, 14% external sources). ***Receiving aid:*** Freshmen: 14% (37). Undergraduates: 9% (154). ***Average award:*** Freshmen: $10,152. Undergraduates: $5424. ***Scholarships, grants, and awards by category:*** *Academic interests/achievement:* general academic interests/achievements. *Creative arts/performance:* music, performing arts, theater/drama. *Special achievements/activities:* general special achievements/activities. *Special characteristics:* children of faculty/staff, members of minority groups, relatives of clergy. ***Tuition waivers:*** Full or partial for employees or children of employees, senior citizens.

LOANS ***Student loans:*** $6,239,921 (73% need-based, 27% non-need-based). 95% of past graduating class borrowed through all loan programs. *Average indebtedness per student:* $13,484. ***Average need-based loan:*** Freshmen: $3241. Undergraduates: $4167. ***Parent loans:*** $4,391,078 (38% need-based, 62% non-need-based). ***Programs:*** Perkins, college/university.

WORK-STUDY Federal work-study jobs available. ***State or other work-study/employment:*** Part-time jobs available.

ATHLETIC AWARDS Total amount: $2,482,088 (63% need-based, 37% non-need-based).

APPLYING FOR FINANCIAL AID ***Required financial aid form:*** FAFSA. ***Financial aid deadline (priority):*** 3/1. ***Notification date:*** Continuous beginning 3/1. Students must reply within 2 weeks of notification.

CONTACT Nancy M. Beverly, Director of Financial Aid, King College, 1350 King College Road, Bristol, TN 37620-2699, 423-652-4728 or toll-free 800-362-0014. *Fax:* 423-652-6039. *E-mail:* nmbeverly@king.edu.

THE KING'S COLLEGE

New York, NY

Tuition & fees: $29,240 **Average undergraduate aid package: $19,256**

ABOUT THE INSTITUTION Independent nondenominational, coed. 2 undergraduate majors. Federal methodology is used as a basis for awarding need-based institutional aid.

UNDERGRADUATE EXPENSES for 2011–12 ***Tuition:*** full-time $28,890; part-time $1203.75 per credit hour. ***Required fees:*** full-time $350; $350 per year. Full-time tuition and fees vary according to course load. Part-time tuition and fees vary according to course load. ***Payment plans:*** Installment, deferred payment.

FRESHMAN FINANCIAL AID (Fall 2009) 93 applied for aid; of those 86% were deemed to have need. 100% of freshmen with need received aid; of those 11% had need fully met. ***Average percent of need met:*** 62% (excluding resources awarded to replace EFC). ***Average financial aid package:*** $18,746 (excluding resources awarded to replace EFC). 22% of all full-time freshmen had no need and received non-need-based gift aid.

UNDERGRADUATE FINANCIAL AID (Fall 2009) 233 applied for aid; of those 86% were deemed to have need. 100% of undergraduates with need received aid; of those 16% had need fully met. ***Average percent of need met:*** 66% (excluding resources awarded to replace EFC). ***Average financial aid package:*** $19,256 (excluding resources awarded to replace EFC). 30% of all full-time undergraduates had no need and received non-need-based gift aid.

GIFT AID (NEED-BASED) ***Total amount:*** $3,441,820 (9% federal, 1% state, 88% institutional, 2% external sources). ***Receiving aid:*** Freshmen: 78% (80); all full-time undergraduates: 69% (200). ***Average award:*** Freshmen: $16,372; Undergraduates: $16,119. ***Scholarships, grants, and awards:*** Federal Pell, FSEOG, state, private, college/university gift aid from institutional funds.

GIFT AID (NON-NEED-BASED) ***Total amount:*** $923,292 (99% institutional, 1% external sources). ***Receiving aid:*** Freshmen: 78% (80). Undergraduates: 69% (200). ***Average award:*** Freshmen: $14,555. Undergraduates: $11,413. ***Scholarships, grants, and awards by category:*** *Academic interests/achievement:* general academic interests/achievements. ***Tuition waivers:*** Full or partial for employees or children of employees.

LOANS ***Student loans:*** $1,416,988 (94% need-based, 6% non-need-based). 73% of past graduating class borrowed through all loan programs. *Average indebtedness per student:* $16,102. ***Average need-based loan:*** Freshmen: $331. Undergraduates: $4210. ***Parent loans:*** $416,217 (69% need-based, 31% non-need-based). ***Programs:*** Federal Direct (Subsidized and Unsubsidized Stafford, PLUS).

WORK-STUDY Federal work-study jobs available.

APPLYING FOR FINANCIAL AID ***Required financial aid form:*** FAFSA. ***Financial aid deadline:*** Continuous. ***Notification date:*** Continuous beginning 2/15.

CONTACT Anna Peters, Director of Financial Aid, The King's College, 350 Fifth Avenue, Suite 1500, New York, NY 10118, 212-659-7281 or toll-free 888-969-7200 Ext. 3610. *Fax:* 212-659-3611. *E-mail:* apeters@tkc.edu.

KING'S COLLEGE

Wilkes-Barre, PA

Tuition & fees: $26,644 **Average undergraduate aid package: $19,426**

ABOUT THE INSTITUTION Independent Roman Catholic, coed. 40 undergraduate majors. Federal methodology is used as a basis for awarding need-based institutional aid.

UNDERGRADUATE EXPENSES for 2010–11 ***Comprehensive fee:*** $36,712 includes full-time tuition ($26,644) and room and board ($10,068). ***College room only:*** $4808. Room and board charges vary according to board plan. ***Part-time tuition:*** $495 per credit hour. ***Payment plans:*** Installment, deferred payment.

FRESHMAN FINANCIAL AID (Fall 2010, est.) 498 applied for aid; of those 91% were deemed to have need. 100% of freshmen with need received aid; of those 16% had need fully met. ***Average percent of need met:*** 76% (excluding

resources awarded to replace EFC). ***Average financial aid package:*** $20,688 (excluding resources awarded to replace EFC). 14% of all full-time freshmen had no need and received non-need-based gift aid.

UNDERGRADUATE FINANCIAL AID (Fall 2010, est.) 1,812 applied for aid; of those 92% were deemed to have need. 99% of undergraduates with need received aid; of those 16% had need fully met. ***Average percent of need met:*** 72% (excluding resources awarded to replace EFC). ***Average financial aid package:*** $19,426 (excluding resources awarded to replace EFC). 15% of all full-time undergraduates had no need and received non-need-based gift aid.

GIFT AID (NEED-BASED) ***Total amount:*** $25,062,010 (12% federal, 9% state, 78% institutional, 1% external sources). ***Receiving aid:*** Freshmen: 85% (449); all full-time undergraduates: 82% (1,641). ***Average award:*** Freshmen: $16,376; Undergraduates: $14,831. ***Scholarships, grants, and awards:*** Federal Pell, FSEOG, state, private, college/university gift aid from institutional funds.

GIFT AID (NON-NEED-BASED) ***Total amount:*** $3,200,071 (13% federal, 1% state, 85% institutional, 1% external sources). ***Receiving aid:*** Freshmen: 11% (59). Undergraduates: 9% (180). ***Average award:*** Freshmen: $12,967. Undergraduates: $11,719. ***Scholarships, grants, and awards by category:*** *Academic interests/achievement:* 1,399 awards ($14,768,100 total): biological sciences, business, communication, computer science, education, English, foreign languages, general academic interests/achievements, health fields, humanities, mathematics, physical sciences, premedicine, religion/biblical studies, social sciences. *Special achievements/activities:* 843 awards ($4,124,138 total): community service, general special achievements/activities, leadership. *Special characteristics:* 256 awards ($1,787,491 total): children of educators, children of faculty/staff, international students, members of minority groups, relatives of clergy, siblings of current students. ***Tuition waivers:*** Full or partial for employees or children of employees, senior citizens.

LOANS ***Student loans:*** $15,461,337 (70% need-based, 30% non-need-based). 82% of past graduating class borrowed through all loan programs. *Average indebtedness per student:* $31,113. ***Average need-based loan:*** Freshmen: $4047. Undergraduates: $4796. ***Parent loans:*** $4,149,373 (94% need-based, 6% non-need-based). ***Programs:*** Federal Direct (Subsidized and Unsubsidized Stafford, PLUS), Perkins, private loans.

WORK-STUDY ***Federal work-study:*** Total amount: $280,700; 290 jobs averaging $1178. ***State or other work-study/employment:*** Total amount: $525,000 (71% need-based, 29% non-need-based). 333 part-time jobs averaging $1099.

APPLYING FOR FINANCIAL AID ***Required financial aid forms:*** FAFSA, institution's own form. ***Financial aid deadline (priority):*** 2/15. ***Notification date:*** Continuous beginning 3/1. Students must reply by 5/1 or within 2 weeks of notification.

CONTACT Ms. Donna Cerza, Director of Financial Aid, King's College, 133 North River Street, Wilkes-Barre, PA 18711-0801, 570-208-5868 or toll-free 888-KINGSPA. *Fax:* 570-208-6015. *E-mail:* finaid@kings.edu.

THE KING'S COLLEGE AND SEMINARY

Van Nuys, CA

Tuition & fees: $7755 **Average undergraduate aid package: N/A**

ABOUT THE INSTITUTION Independent religious, coed. ***Awards:*** associate, bachelor's, and master's degrees and post-bachelor's certificates. 1 undergraduate major. ***Total enrollment:*** 531. Undergraduates: 233. Federal methodology is used as a basis for awarding need-based institutional aid.

UNDERGRADUATE EXPENSES for 2010–11 ***Application fee:*** $45. ***Tuition:*** full-time $7380; part-time $205 per credit hour. ***Required fees:*** full-time $375; $45 per course. Full-time tuition and fees vary according to course load. Part-time tuition and fees vary according to course load. ***Payment plan:*** Installment.

GIFT AID (NEED-BASED) ***Scholarships, grants, and awards:*** Federal Pell, FSEOG, private, college/university gift aid from institutional funds.

GIFT AID (NON-NEED-BASED) ***Tuition waivers:*** Full or partial for employees or children of employees.

LOANS ***Programs:*** Federal Direct (Subsidized and Unsubsidized Stafford, PLUS).

WORK-STUDY Federal work-study jobs available.

APPLYING FOR FINANCIAL AID ***Required financial aid forms:*** FAFSA, institution's own form. ***Financial aid deadline:*** Continuous.

CONTACT Mr. Norman V. Stoppenbrink Jr., Financial Aid Officer, The King's College and Seminary, 14800 Sherman Way, Los Angeles, CA 91405, 818-779-8040 Ext. 8278 or toll-free 888-779-8040 (in-state). *Fax:* 818-779-8251. *E-mail:* financialaid@kingsuniversity.edu.

KNOX COLLEGE

Galesburg, IL

Tuition & fees: $34,464 **Average undergraduate aid package: $26,585**

ABOUT THE INSTITUTION Independent, coed. 33 undergraduate majors. Both federal and institutional methodology are used as a basis for awarding need-based institutional aid.

UNDERGRADUATE EXPENSES for 2011–12 ***Comprehensive fee:*** $41,952 includes full-time tuition ($34,110), mandatory fees ($354), and room and board ($7488). ***College room only:*** $3750. Room and board charges vary according to board plan. Part-time tuition and fees vary according to course load. ***Payment plan:*** Installment.

FRESHMAN FINANCIAL AID (Fall 2010, est.) 320 applied for aid; of those 85% were deemed to have need. 100% of freshmen with need received aid; of those 27% had need fully met. ***Average percent of need met:*** 92% (excluding resources awarded to replace EFC). ***Average financial aid package:*** $28,521 (excluding resources awarded to replace EFC). 20% of all full-time freshmen had no need and received non-need-based gift aid.

UNDERGRADUATE FINANCIAL AID (Fall 2010, est.) 1,133 applied for aid; of those 88% were deemed to have need. 100% of undergraduates with need received aid; of those 26% had need fully met. ***Average percent of need met:*** 89% (excluding resources awarded to replace EFC). ***Average financial aid package:*** $26,585 (excluding resources awarded to replace EFC). 23% of all full-time undergraduates had no need and received non-need-based gift aid.

GIFT AID (NEED-BASED) ***Total amount:*** $20,711,999 (10% federal, 6% state, 82% institutional, 2% external sources). ***Receiving aid:*** Freshmen: 68% (272); all full-time undergraduates: 72% (993). ***Average award:*** Freshmen: $22,731; Undergraduates: $20,676. ***Scholarships, grants, and awards:*** Federal Pell, FSEOG, state, private, college/university gift aid from institutional funds.

GIFT AID (NON-NEED-BASED) ***Receiving aid:*** Freshmen: 7% (28). Undergraduates: 8% (116). ***Average award:*** Freshmen: $12,681. Undergraduates: $11,097. ***Scholarships, grants, and awards by category:*** *Academic interests/achievement:* general academic interests/achievements, mathematics. *Creative arts/performance:* art/fine arts, creative writing, dance, music, theater/drama. *Special achievements/activities:* community service. ***Tuition waivers:*** Full or partial for employees or children of employees.

LOANS ***Student loans:*** $8,341,010 (49% need-based, 51% non-need-based). 69% of past graduating class borrowed through all loan programs. *Average indebtedness per student:* $26,506. ***Average need-based loan:*** Freshmen: $4566. Undergraduates: $5021. ***Parent loans:*** $1,776,937 (100% non-need-based). ***Programs:*** Federal Direct (Subsidized and Unsubsidized Stafford, PLUS), Perkins, college/university, private loans.

WORK-STUDY ***Federal work-study:*** Total amount: $1,534,480; 679 jobs averaging $2245. ***State or other work-study/employment:*** Total amount: $199,386 (100% need-based). 86 part-time jobs averaging $2318.

APPLYING FOR FINANCIAL AID ***Required financial aid forms:*** FAFSA, institution's own form, federal income tax returns required for selected students. ***Financial aid deadline (priority):*** 2/15. ***Notification date:*** Continuous beginning 3/15. Students must reply by 5/1 or within 2 weeks of notification.

CONTACT Ms. Ann M. Brill, Director of Financial Aid, Knox College, 2 East South Street, Galesburg, IL 61401, 309-341-7149 or toll-free 800-678-KNOX. *Fax:* 309-341-7453. *E-mail:* abrill@knox.edu.

KOL YAAKOV TORAH CENTER

Monsey, NY

CONTACT Office of Financial Aid, Kol Yaakov Torah Center, 29 West Maple Avenue, Monsey, NY 10952-2954, 914-425-3863.

KUTZTOWN UNIVERSITY OF PENNSYLVANIA

Kutztown, PA

Tuition & fees (PA res): $7732 **Average undergraduate aid package: $7739**

ABOUT THE INSTITUTION State-supported, coed. 57 undergraduate majors. Federal methodology is used as a basis for awarding need-based institutional aid.

UNDERGRADUATE EXPENSES for 2010–11 ***Tuition, state resident:*** full-time $5804; part-time $242 per credit hour. ***Tuition, nonresident:*** full-time $14,510; part-time $605 per credit hour. ***Required fees:*** full-time $1928; $99.44 per credit hour or $68 per term. Part-time tuition and fees vary according to course load. ***College room and board:*** $8094; ***Room only:*** $5024. Room and board charges vary according to board plan and housing facility. ***Payment plans:*** Installment, deferred payment.

FRESHMAN FINANCIAL AID (Fall 2009) 1,862 applied for aid; of those 73% were deemed to have need. 96% of freshmen with need received aid; of those 47% had need fully met. ***Average percent of need met:*** 51% (excluding resources awarded to replace EFC). ***Average financial aid package:*** $7260 (excluding resources awarded to replace EFC). 4% of all full-time freshmen had no need and received non-need-based gift aid.

UNDERGRADUATE FINANCIAL AID (Fall 2009) 7,724 applied for aid; of those 75% were deemed to have need. 96% of undergraduates with need received aid; of those 44% had need fully met. ***Average percent of need met:*** 55% (excluding resources awarded to replace EFC). ***Average financial aid package:*** $7739 (excluding resources awarded to replace EFC). 3% of all full-time undergraduates had no need and received non-need-based gift aid.

GIFT AID (NEED-BASED) ***Total amount:*** $19,784,236 (53% federal, 40% state, 3% institutional, 4% external sources). ***Receiving aid:*** Freshmen: 46% (937); all full-time undergraduates: 43% (3,915). ***Average award:*** Freshmen: $5529; Undergraduates: $5290. ***Scholarships, grants, and awards:*** Federal Pell, FSEOG, state, private, college/university gift aid from institutional funds.

GIFT AID (NON-NEED-BASED) ***Total amount:*** $731,226 (15% federal, 8% state, 23% institutional, 54% external sources). ***Receiving aid:*** Freshmen: 1% (25). Undergraduates: 1% (109). ***Average award:*** Freshmen: $1640. Undergraduates: $1843. ***Scholarships, grants, and awards by category:*** *Academic interests/achievement:* 499 awards ($1,232,226 total): biological sciences, business, communication, computer science, education, English, foreign languages, general academic interests/achievements, health fields, humanities, international studies, library science, mathematics, physical sciences. *Creative arts/performance:* 39 awards ($27,199 total): applied art and design, art/fine arts, dance, music. *Special achievements/activities:* 565 awards ($588,252 total): community service, general special achievements/activities, leadership, religious involvement. *Special characteristics:* 169 awards ($719,464 total): children of faculty/staff, children of union members/company employees, first-generation college students, handicapped students, local/state students. ***Tuition waivers:*** Full or partial for employees or children of employees, senior citizens.

LOANS ***Student loans:*** $52,378,147 (65% need-based, 35% non-need-based). 85% of past graduating class borrowed through all loan programs. *Average indebtedness per student:* $22,670. ***Average need-based loan:*** Freshmen: $3247. Undergraduates: $4068. ***Parent loans:*** $10,534,636 (28% need-based, 72% non-need-based). ***Programs:*** Perkins.

WORK-STUDY ***Federal work-study:*** Total amount: $331,265; 311 jobs averaging $1065.

ATHLETIC AWARDS Total amount: $573,366 (62% need-based, 38% non-need-based).

APPLYING FOR FINANCIAL AID ***Required financial aid form:*** FAFSA. ***Financial aid deadline (priority):*** 2/15. ***Notification date:*** Continuous beginning 3/30. Students must reply by 5/1 or within 4 weeks of notification.

CONTACT Mr. Bernard McCree, Director of Financial Aid, Kutztown University of Pennsylvania, 209 Stratton Administration Center, Kutztown, PA 19530-0730, 610-683-4032 or toll-free 877-628-1915. *Fax:* 610-683-1380. *E-mail:* mccree@kutztown.edu.

KUYPER COLLEGE

Grand Rapids, MI

Tuition & fees: $16,416 **Average undergraduate aid package: $10,658**

ABOUT THE INSTITUTION Independent religious, coed. 26 undergraduate majors. Federal methodology is used as a basis for awarding need-based institutional aid.

UNDERGRADUATE EXPENSES for 2010–11 ***Comprehensive fee:*** $22,696 includes full-time tuition ($15,866), mandatory fees ($550), and room and board ($6280). Full-time tuition and fees vary according to course load. Room and board charges vary according to board plan, housing facility, and student level. ***Part-time tuition:*** $760 per credit hour. Part-time tuition and fees vary according to course load. ***Payment plan:*** Installment.

FRESHMAN FINANCIAL AID (Fall 2010, est.) 47 applied for aid; of those 85% were deemed to have need. 100% of freshmen with need received aid. ***Average percent of need met:*** 80% (excluding resources awarded to replace EFC). ***Average financial aid package:*** $14,772 (excluding resources awarded to replace EFC). 12% of all full-time freshmen had no need and received non-need-based gift aid.

UNDERGRADUATE FINANCIAL AID (Fall 2010, est.) 284 applied for aid; of those 100% were deemed to have need. 100% of undergraduates with need received aid; of those 8% had need fully met. ***Average percent of need met:*** 70% (excluding resources awarded to replace EFC). ***Average financial aid package:*** $10,658 (excluding resources awarded to replace EFC). 10% of all full-time undergraduates had no need and received non-need-based gift aid.

GIFT AID (NEED-BASED) ***Total amount:*** $2,084,174 (35% federal, 17% state, 46% institutional, 2% external sources). ***Receiving aid:*** Freshmen: 82% (40); all full-time undergraduates: 100% (284). ***Average award:*** Freshmen: $8469; Undergraduates: $5833. ***Scholarships, grants, and awards:*** Federal Pell, FSEOG, state, private, college/university gift aid from institutional funds.

GIFT AID (NON-NEED-BASED) ***Total amount:*** $71,920 (92% institutional, 8% external sources). ***Receiving aid:*** Freshmen: 6% (3). Undergraduates: 5% (15). ***Average award:*** Freshmen: $5417. Undergraduates: $2708. ***Scholarships, grants, and awards by category:*** *Academic interests/achievement:* 152 awards ($416,562 total): general academic interests/achievements. *Creative arts/performance:* 4 awards ($2000 total): music. *Special achievements/activities:* 8 awards ($12,000 total): leadership, religious involvement. *Special characteristics:* 85 awards ($300,856 total): children of faculty/staff, international students, members of minority groups. ***Tuition waivers:*** Full or partial for employees or children of employees.

LOANS ***Student loans:*** $1,868,211 (95% need-based, 5% non-need-based). 81% of past graduating class borrowed through all loan programs. *Average indebtedness per student:* $18,709. ***Average need-based loan:*** Freshmen: $4995. Undergraduates: $6236. ***Parent loans:*** $292,201 (96% need-based, 4% non-need-based). ***Programs:*** Federal Direct (Subsidized and Unsubsidized Stafford, PLUS), alternative loans.

WORK-STUDY ***Federal work-study:*** Total amount: $25,037; 21 jobs averaging $1192. ***State or other work-study/employment:*** Total amount: $259,720 (100% non-need-based). 81 part-time jobs averaging $2000.

APPLYING FOR FINANCIAL AID ***Required financial aid form:*** FAFSA. ***Financial aid deadline (priority):*** 3/1. ***Notification date:*** Continuous beginning 3/20. Students must reply within 2 weeks of notification.

CONTACT Ms. Agnes Russell, Director of Financial Aid, Kuyper College, 3333 East Beltline NE, Grand Rapids, MI 49525-9749, 616-222-3000 Ext. 656 or toll-free 800-511-3749. *Fax:* 616-222-3045. *E-mail:* arussell@kuyper.edu.

LA COLLEGE INTERNATIONAL

Los Angeles, CA

CONTACT Office of Financial Aid, LA College International, 3200 Wilshire Boulevard, Los Angeles, CA 90010, 800-218-7274 or toll-free 800-57 GO ICT (in-state). *Fax:* 866-304-7741. *E-mail:* financialaid@lac.edu.

LAFAYETTE COLLEGE

Easton, PA

Tuition & fees: $39,115 **Average undergraduate aid package: $35,451**

ABOUT THE INSTITUTION Independent religious, coed. 34 undergraduate majors. Both federal and institutional methodology are used as a basis for awarding need-based institutional aid.

UNDERGRADUATE EXPENSES for 2010–11 ***One-time required fee:*** $700. ***Comprehensive fee:*** $51,074 includes full-time tuition ($38,810), mandatory fees ($305), and room and board ($11,959). ***College room only:*** $7265. Room and board charges vary according to board plan. ***Part-time tuition:*** $1735 per course. ***Payment plans:*** Tuition prepayment, installment.

FRESHMAN FINANCIAL AID (Fall 2010, est.) 395 applied for aid; of those 63% were deemed to have need. 100% of freshmen with need received aid; of those 80% had need fully met. ***Average percent of need met:*** 97% (excluding resources awarded to replace EFC). ***Average financial aid package:*** $33,866 (excluding resources awarded to replace EFC). 7% of all full-time freshmen had no need and received non-need-based gift aid.

UNDERGRADUATE FINANCIAL AID (Fall 2010, est.) 1,409 applied for aid; of those 75% were deemed to have need. 100% of undergraduates with need received aid; of those 88% had need fully met. ***Average percent of need met:*** 99% (excluding resources awarded to replace EFC). ***Average financial aid package:*** $35,451 (excluding resources awarded to replace EFC). 7% of all full-time undergraduates had no need and received non-need-based gift aid.

GIFT AID (NEED-BASED) ***Total amount:*** $29,998,457 (5% federal, 1% state, 93% institutional, 1% external sources). ***Receiving aid:*** Freshmen: 37% (238); all full-time undergraduates: 43% (1,010). ***Average award:*** Freshmen: $28,606; Undergraduates: $30. ***Scholarships, grants, and awards:*** Federal Pell, FSEOG, state, private, college/university gift aid from institutional funds.

GIFT AID (NON-NEED-BASED) ***Total amount:*** $4,913,197 (82% institutional, 18% external sources). ***Receiving aid:*** Freshmen: 11% (74). Undergraduates: 12% (281). ***Average award:*** Freshmen: $18,469. Undergraduates: $17,613. ***Scholarships, grants, and awards by category:*** *Academic interests/achievement:* $4,913,197 total: general academic interests/achievements.

LOANS ***Student loans:*** $8,814,462 (47% need-based, 53% non-need-based). 52% of past graduating class borrowed through all loan programs. *Average indebtedness per student:* $20,687. ***Average need-based loan:*** Freshmen: $3516. Undergraduates: $4316. ***Parent loans:*** $5,303,226 (30% need-based, 70% non-need-based). ***Programs:*** Federal Direct (Subsidized and Unsubsidized Stafford, PLUS), Perkins, college/university.

WORK-STUDY ***Federal work-study:*** Total amount: $791,608; jobs available. ***State or other work-study/employment:*** Total amount: $1,159,218 (46% need-based, 54% non-need-based). Part-time jobs available.

ATHLETIC AWARDS Total amount: $1,775,971 (8% need-based, 92% non-need-based).

APPLYING FOR FINANCIAL AID ***Required financial aid forms:*** FAFSA, CSS Financial Aid PROFILE, noncustodial (divorced/separated) parent's statement, federal income tax return(s). ***Financial aid deadline:*** 3/1 (priority: 1/15). ***Notification date:*** 4/1. Students must reply by 5/1.

CONTACT Arlinda DeNardo, Director of Financial Aid, Lafayette College, 107 Markle Hall, Easton, PA 18042-1777, 610-330-5055. *Fax:* 610-330-5758. *E-mail:* denardoa@lafayette.edu.

LaGRANGE COLLEGE

LaGrange, GA

ABOUT THE INSTITUTION Independent United Methodist, coed. 23 undergraduate majors.

GIFT AID (NEED-BASED) ***Scholarships, grants, and awards:*** Federal Pell, FSEOG, state, private, college/university gift aid from institutional funds.

GIFT AID (NON-NEED-BASED) ***Scholarships, grants, and awards by category:*** *Academic interests/achievement:* biological sciences, education, English, general academic interests/achievements, health fields, religion/biblical studies, social sciences. *Creative arts/performance:* music, theater/drama. *Special achievements/activities:* leadership. *Special characteristics:* children of faculty/staff, ethnic background, first-generation college students, relatives of clergy, religious affiliation.

LOANS ***Programs:*** Perkins, state.

APPLYING FOR FINANCIAL AID ***Required financial aid forms:*** FAFSA, state aid form.

CONTACT Michelle Reeves, Assistant Director, LaGrange College, 601 Broad Street, LaGrange, GA 30240-2999, 888-253-9918 or toll-free 800-593-2885. *Fax:* 706-880-8348. *E-mail:* mreeves@lagrange.edu.

LAGUNA COLLEGE OF ART & DESIGN

Laguna Beach, CA

CONTACT Christopher Brown, Director of Student Services, Laguna College of Art & Design, 2222 Laguna Canyon Road, Laguna Beach, CA 92651-1136, 949-376-6000 or toll-free 800-255-0762. *Fax:* 949-497-5220. *E-mail:* cbrown@lagunacollege.edu.

LAKE ERIE COLLEGE

Painesville, OH

ABOUT THE INSTITUTION Independent, coed. 31 undergraduate majors.

GIFT AID (NEED-BASED) ***Scholarships, grants, and awards:*** Federal Pell, FSEOG, state, private, college/university gift aid from institutional funds.

GIFT AID (NON-NEED-BASED) ***Scholarships, grants, and awards by category:*** *Academic interests/achievement:* biological sciences, business, education, English, foreign languages, general academic interests/achievements, humanities, international studies, mathematics, physical sciences, social sciences. *Creative arts/performance:* art/fine arts, dance, general creative arts/performance, music, performing arts, theater/drama. *Special achievements/activities:* community service, general special achievements/activities, hobbies/interests. *Special characteristics:* children of faculty/staff, twins, veterans, veterans' children.

LOANS ***Programs:*** Federal Direct (Subsidized and Unsubsidized Stafford, PLUS), Perkins.

WORK-STUDY ***Federal work-study:*** Total amount: $126,666; jobs available (averaging $2000).

APPLYING FOR FINANCIAL AID ***Required financial aid form:*** FAFSA.

CONTACT Patricia Pangonis, Director of Financial Aid, Lake Erie College, 391 West Washington Street, Painesville, OH 44077-3389, 440-375-7100 or toll-free 800-916-0904. *Fax:* 440-375-7103.

LAKE FOREST COLLEGE

Lake Forest, IL

Tuition & fees: $35,525 **Average undergraduate aid package: $30,013**

ABOUT THE INSTITUTION Independent, coed. 32 undergraduate majors. Both federal and institutional methodology are used as a basis for awarding need-based institutional aid.

UNDERGRADUATE EXPENSES for 2010–11 ***Comprehensive fee:*** $43,852 includes full-time tuition ($34,885), mandatory fees ($640), and room and board ($8327). ***College room only:*** $4105. Full-time tuition and fees vary according to course load. Room and board charges vary according to board plan. ***Part-time tuition:*** $4360 per course. Part-time tuition and fees vary according to course load. ***Payment plan:*** Installment.

FRESHMAN FINANCIAL AID (Fall 2010, est.) 354 applied for aid; of those 94% were deemed to have need. 100% of freshmen with need received aid; of those 25% had need fully met. ***Average percent of need met:*** 80% (excluding resources awarded to replace EFC). ***Average financial aid package:*** $30,020 (excluding resources awarded to replace EFC). 13% of all full-time freshmen had no need and received non-need-based gift aid.

UNDERGRADUATE FINANCIAL AID (Fall 2010, est.) 1,196 applied for aid; of those 93% were deemed to have need. 100% of undergraduates with need received aid; of those 29% had need fully met. ***Average percent of need met:*** 81% (excluding resources awarded to replace EFC). ***Average financial aid package:*** $30,013 (excluding resources awarded to replace EFC). 17% of all full-time undergraduates had no need and received non-need-based gift aid.

GIFT AID (NEED-BASED) ***Total amount:*** $27,907,979 (11% federal, 6% state, 79% institutional, 4% external sources). ***Receiving aid:*** Freshmen: 83% (334); all full-time undergraduates: 79% (1,105). ***Average award:*** Freshmen: $26,016; Undergraduates: $25,350. ***Scholarships, grants, and awards:*** Federal Pell, FSEOG, state, private, college/university gift aid from institutional funds.

GIFT AID (NON-NEED-BASED) ***Total amount:*** $3,056,172 (99% institutional, 1% external sources). ***Average award:*** Freshmen: $13,510. Undergraduates: $12,558. ***Scholarships, grants, and awards by category:*** *Academic interests/achievement:* 1,052 awards ($10,529,750 total): biological sciences, computer science, foreign languages, general academic interests/achievements, mathematics, physical sciences. *Creative arts/performance:* 154 awards ($689,000 total): art/fine arts, creative writing, music, theater/drama. *Special achievements/activities:* 109 awards ($463,250 total): leadership. *Special characteristics:* 333 awards ($3,292,057 total): children and siblings of alumni, local/state students, previous college experience. ***Tuition waivers:*** Full or partial for employees or children of employees.

LOANS ***Student loans:*** $7,366,405 (95% need-based, 5% non-need-based). 75% of past graduating class borrowed through all loan programs. *Average indebtedness per student:* $31,790. ***Average need-based loan:*** Freshmen: $3513. Undergraduates: $4713. ***Parent loans:*** $2,078,521 (90% need-based, 10% non-need-based). ***Programs:*** Federal Direct (Subsidized and Unsubsidized Stafford, PLUS), Perkins, private loans.

WORK-STUDY ***Federal work-study:*** Total amount: $1,353,746; 611 jobs averaging $2216. ***State or other work-study/employment:*** Part-time jobs available.

APPLYING FOR FINANCIAL AID ***Required financial aid forms:*** FAFSA, institution's own form. ***Financial aid deadline:*** 5/1 (priority: 3/1). ***Notification date:*** Continuous beginning 3/1. Students must reply by 5/1 or within 3 weeks of notification.

CONTACT Mr. Jerry Cebrzynski, Director of Financial Aid, Lake Forest College, 555 North Sheridan Road, Lake Forest, IL 60045-2399, 847-735-5104 or toll-free 800-828-4751. *Fax:* 847-735-6271. *E-mail:* cebrzynski@lakeforest.edu.

LAKELAND COLLEGE

Sheboygan, WI

ABOUT THE INSTITUTION Independent religious, coed. 29 undergraduate majors.

GIFT AID (NEED-BASED) ***Scholarships, grants, and awards:*** Federal Pell, FSEOG, state, private, college/university gift aid from institutional funds, Academic Competitiveness Grants, National SMART Grants.

GIFT AID (NON-NEED-BASED) ***Scholarships, grants, and awards by category:*** *Academic interests/achievement:* business, engineering/technologies, English, general academic interests/achievements, religion/biblical studies. *Creative arts/performance:* art/fine arts, creative writing, journalism/publications, music, performing arts. *Special achievements/activities:* community service, leadership, religious involvement. *Special characteristics:* children and siblings of alumni, children of faculty/staff, religious affiliation, siblings of current students.

LOANS ***Programs:*** Federal Direct (Subsidized and Unsubsidized Stafford, PLUS), Perkins, alternative loans.

WORK-STUDY ***Federal work-study:*** Total amount: $564,391; 262 jobs averaging $2500. ***State or other work-study/employment:*** Total amount: $276,866 (11% need-based, 89% non-need-based). 150 part-time jobs averaging $2500.

APPLYING FOR FINANCIAL AID ***Required financial aid forms:*** FAFSA, institution's own form.

CONTACT Ms. Patty Taylor, Director of Financial Aid, Lakeland College, PO Box 359, Sheboygan, WI 53082-0359, 920-565-1214 or toll-free 800-242-3347 (in-state). *Fax:* 920-565-1470.

LAKE SUPERIOR STATE UNIVERSITY

Sault Sainte Marie, MI

Tuition & fees (MI res): $8764 **Average undergraduate aid package: $13,069**

ABOUT THE INSTITUTION State-supported, coed. 63 undergraduate majors. Both federal and institutional methodology are used as a basis for awarding need-based institutional aid.

UNDERGRADUATE EXPENSES for 2010–11 ***One-time required fee:*** $125. ***Tuition, state resident:*** full-time $8664; part-time $361 per credit hour. ***Tuition, nonresident:*** full-time $17,328; part-time $722 per credit hour. ***Required fees:*** full-time $100. Full-time tuition and fees vary according to reciprocity agreements. Part-time tuition and fees vary according to course load and reciprocity agreements. ***College room and board:*** $8081. Room and board charges vary according to board plan and housing facility. ***Payment plans:*** Installment, deferred payment.

FRESHMAN FINANCIAL AID (Fall 2010, est.) 427 applied for aid; of those 100% were deemed to have need. 100% of freshmen with need received aid; of those 64% had need fully met. ***Average percent of need met:*** 83% (excluding resources awarded to replace EFC). ***Average financial aid package:*** $13,469 (excluding resources awarded to replace EFC). 10% of all full-time freshmen had no need and received non-need-based gift aid.

UNDERGRADUATE FINANCIAL AID (Fall 2010, est.) 1,966 applied for aid; of those 100% were deemed to have need. 100% of undergraduates with need received aid; of those 61% had need fully met. ***Average percent of need met:*** 81% (excluding resources awarded to replace EFC). ***Average financial aid package:*** $13,069 (excluding resources awarded to replace EFC). 9% of all full-time undergraduates had no need and received non-need-based gift aid.

GIFT AID (NEED-BASED) ***Total amount:*** $7,033,190 (71% federal, 19% state, 6% institutional, 4% external sources). ***Receiving aid:*** Freshmen: 45% (208); all full-time undergraduates: 48% (1,058). ***Average award:*** Freshmen: $6636; Undergraduates: $5908. ***Scholarships, grants, and awards:*** Federal Pell, FSEOG, state, private, college/university gift aid from institutional funds, Federal Nursing, Academic Competitiveness Grants, National SMART Grants, Federal Occupational Educational Grants.

GIFT AID (NON-NEED-BASED) ***Total amount:*** $3,058,908 (6% state, 79% institutional, 15% external sources). ***Receiving aid:*** Freshmen: 64% (294). Undergraduates: 50% (1,086). ***Average award:*** Freshmen: $4177. Undergraduates: $3859. ***Scholarships, grants, and awards by category:*** *Academic interests/achievement:* general academic interests/achievements. ***Tuition waivers:*** Full or partial for minority students, children of alumni, employees or children of employees, senior citizens.

LOANS ***Student loans:*** $12,977,858 (100% need-based). 67% of past graduating class borrowed through all loan programs. *Average indebtedness per student:* $24,672. ***Average need-based loan:*** Freshmen: $5431. Undergraduates: $6862. ***Parent loans:*** $3,230,665 (100% need-based). ***Programs:*** Federal Direct (Subsidized and Unsubsidized Stafford, PLUS), Perkins, Federal Nursing, alternative loans.

WORK-STUDY ***Federal work-study:*** Total amount: $266,969; jobs available. ***State or other work-study/employment:*** Part-time jobs available.

ATHLETIC AWARDS Total amount: $1,214,072 (100% non-need-based).

APPLYING FOR FINANCIAL AID ***Required financial aid form:*** FAFSA. ***Financial aid deadline (priority):*** 2/21. ***Notification date:*** Continuous. Students must reply within 3 weeks of notification.

CONTACT Deborah Faust, Director of Financial Aid, Lake Superior State University, 650 West Easterday Avenue, Sault Sainte Marie, MI 49783, 906-635-2678 or toll-free 888-800-LSSU Ext. 2231. *Fax:* 906-635-6669. *E-mail:* finaid@lssu.edu.

LAKEVIEW COLLEGE OF NURSING

Danville, IL

Tuition & fees: $13,760 **Average undergraduate aid package: $12,500**

ABOUT THE INSTITUTION Independent, coed. 1 undergraduate major. Federal methodology is used as a basis for awarding need-based institutional aid.

UNDERGRADUATE EXPENSES for 2010–11 ***Tuition:*** full-time $11,840; part-time $370 per credit hour. ***Required fees:*** full-time $1920; $60 per credit hour. ***Payment plan:*** Installment.

UNDERGRADUATE FINANCIAL AID (Fall 2009) 425 applied for aid; of those 94% were deemed to have need. 100% of undergraduates with need received aid; of those 76% had need fully met. ***Average percent of need met:*** 75% (excluding resources awarded to replace EFC). ***Average financial aid package:*** $12,500 (excluding resources awarded to replace EFC).

GIFT AID (NEED-BASED) ***Total amount:*** $710,033 (57% federal, 43% state). ***Receiving aid:*** All full-time undergraduates: 86% (398). ***Average award:*** Undergraduates: $2000. ***Scholarships, grants, and awards:*** Federal Pell, state, private, college/university gift aid from institutional funds.

GIFT AID (NON-NEED-BASED) ***Total amount:*** $146,960 (60% institutional, 40% external sources). ***Receiving aid:*** Undergraduates: 27% (126). ***Scholarships, grants, and awards by category:*** *Academic interests/achievement:* 89 awards ($87,750 total): health fields.

LOANS ***Student loans:*** $1,868,229 (100% need-based). 80% of past graduating class borrowed through all loan programs. *Average indebtedness per student:* $25,000. ***Average need-based loan:*** Undergraduates: $5500. ***Parent loans:*** $183,624 (100% non-need-based). ***Programs:*** Federal Direct (Subsidized and Unsubsidized Stafford, PLUS).

APPLYING FOR FINANCIAL AID ***Financial aid deadline:*** Continuous. ***Notification date:*** Continuous beginning 4/1. Students must reply within 4 weeks of notification.

CONTACT Ms. Janet Ingargiola, Director of Financial Aid, Lakeview College of Nursing, 903 North Logan Avenue, Danville, IL 61832, 217-709-0930. *Fax:* 217-709-0956. *E-mail:* jingarg@lakeviewcol.edu.

LAMAR UNIVERSITY

Beaumont, TX

Tuition & fees (TX res): $6934 **Average undergraduate aid package: $4618**

ABOUT THE INSTITUTION State-supported, coed. 102 undergraduate majors. Federal methodology is used as a basis for awarding need-based institutional aid.

UNDERGRADUATE EXPENSES for 2011–12 ***Tuition, state resident:*** full-time $4750; part-time $158 per credit hour. ***Tuition, nonresident:*** full-time $14,040; part-time $468 per credit hour. ***Required fees:*** full-time $2184. Full-time tuition and fees vary according to course load. Part-time tuition and fees vary according to course load. ***College room and board:*** $7010; ***Room only:*** $4500. Room and board charges vary according to board plan. ***Payment plan:*** Installment.

FRESHMAN FINANCIAL AID (Fall 2010, est.) 996 applied for aid; of those 62% were deemed to have need. 96% of freshmen with need received aid. ***Average***

percent of need met: 69% (excluding resources awarded to replace EFC). ***Average financial aid package:*** $5187 (excluding resources awarded to replace EFC).

UNDERGRADUATE FINANCIAL AID (Fall 2010, est.) 4,827 applied for aid; of those 69% were deemed to have need. 94% of undergraduates with need received aid. ***Average percent of need met:*** 64% (excluding resources awarded to replace EFC). ***Average financial aid package:*** $4618 (excluding resources awarded to replace EFC).

GIFT AID (NEED-BASED) ***Total amount:*** $28,315,664 (72% federal, 28% state). ***Receiving aid:*** Freshmen: 44% (521); all full-time undergraduates: 44% (2,826). ***Average award:*** Freshmen: $2104; Undergraduates: $2134. ***Scholarships, grants, and awards:*** Federal Pell, FSEOG, state, college/university gift aid from institutional funds.

GIFT AID (NON-NEED-BASED) ***Total amount:*** $5,901,263 (82% institutional, 18% external sources). ***Receiving aid:*** Freshmen: 5% (57). Undergraduates: 5% (332). ***Scholarships, grants, and awards by category:*** *Academic interests/achievement:* general academic interests/achievements. *Creative arts/performance:* general creative arts/performance. *Special achievements/activities:* general special achievements/activities. ***Tuition waivers:*** Full or partial for employees or children of employees, senior citizens.

LOANS ***Student loans:*** $49,539,656 (46% need-based, 54% non-need-based). 45% of past graduating class borrowed through all loan programs. *Average indebtedness per student:* $8234. ***Average need-based loan:*** Freshmen: $1716. Undergraduates: $2107. ***Parent loans:*** $1,647,695 (100% non-need-based). ***Programs:*** Federal Direct (Subsidized and Unsubsidized Stafford, PLUS), Perkins, state, college/university.

WORK-STUDY ***Federal work-study:*** Total amount: $241,682; 182 jobs averaging $3159. ***State or other work-study/employment:*** Total amount: $76,160 (100% need-based). 62 part-time jobs averaging $1228.

APPLYING FOR FINANCIAL AID ***Required financial aid forms:*** FAFSA, institution's own form. ***Financial aid deadline (priority):*** 3/31. ***Notification date:*** Continuous beginning 5/1. Students must reply within 2 weeks of notification.

CONTACT Financial Aid Department, Lamar University, PO Box 10042, Beaumont, TX 77710, 409-880-8450. *Fax:* 409-880-8934. *E-mail:* financialaid@lamar.edu.

LANCASTER BIBLE COLLEGE & GRADUATE SCHOOL

Lancaster, PA

Tuition & fees: $16,560 **Average undergraduate aid package: $12,727**

ABOUT THE INSTITUTION Independent nondenominational, coed. 17 undergraduate majors. Federal methodology is used as a basis for awarding need-based institutional aid.

UNDERGRADUATE EXPENSES for 2010–11 ***Comprehensive fee:*** $23,670 includes full-time tuition ($15,930), mandatory fees ($630), and room and board ($7110). ***College room only:*** $3130. Room and board charges vary according to board plan. ***Part-time tuition:*** $536 per credit hour. ***Part-time fees:*** $30 per credit hour. Part-time tuition and fees vary according to course load. ***Payment plan:*** Installment.

FRESHMAN FINANCIAL AID (Fall 2010, est.) 136 applied for aid; of those 91% were deemed to have need. 100% of freshmen with need received aid; of those 3% had need fully met. ***Average percent of need met:*** 67% (excluding resources awarded to replace EFC). ***Average financial aid package:*** $13,603 (excluding resources awarded to replace EFC). 13% of all full-time freshmen had no need and received non-need-based gift aid.

UNDERGRADUATE FINANCIAL AID (Fall 2010, est.) 579 applied for aid; of those 93% were deemed to have need. 100% of undergraduates with need received aid; of those 12% had need fully met. ***Average percent of need met:*** 65% (excluding resources awarded to replace EFC). ***Average financial aid package:*** $12,727 (excluding resources awarded to replace EFC). 14% of all full-time undergraduates had no need and received non-need-based gift aid.

GIFT AID (NEED-BASED) ***Total amount:*** $4,533,765 (35% federal, 14% state, 47% institutional, 4% external sources). ***Receiving aid:*** Freshmen: 85% (121); all full-time undergraduates: 80% (505). ***Average award:*** Freshmen: $8870; Undergraduates: $8387. ***Scholarships, grants, and awards:*** Federal Pell, FSEOG, state, private, college/university gift aid from institutional funds, Office of Vocational Rehabilitation Awards, Blindness and Visual Services Awards.

GIFT AID (NON-NEED-BASED) ***Total amount:*** $465,093 (96% institutional, 4% external sources). ***Receiving aid:*** Freshmen: 80% (114). Undergraduates: 67% (424). ***Average award:*** Freshmen: $4015. Undergraduates: $3966. ***Scholarships, grants, and awards by category:*** *Academic interests/achievement:* 366 awards ($1,136,366 total): general academic interests/achievements. *Creative arts/performance:* 39 awards ($68,350 total): general creative arts/performance, music. *Special achievements/activities:* 74 awards ($97,161 total): general special achievements/activities, leadership, religious involvement. *Special characteristics:* 231 awards ($929,915 total): adult students, children and siblings of alumni, children of current students, children of faculty/staff, international students, married students, previous college experience, relatives of clergy, religious affiliation, siblings of current students, spouses of current students. ***Tuition waivers:*** Full or partial for children of alumni, employees or children of employees, senior citizens.

LOANS ***Student loans:*** $4,246,640 (80% need-based, 20% non-need-based). 14% of past graduating class borrowed through all loan programs. *Average indebtedness per student:* $18,605. ***Average need-based loan:*** Freshmen: $3329. Undergraduates: $4107. ***Parent loans:*** $673,083 (58% need-based, 42% non-need-based). ***Programs:*** Federal Direct (Subsidized and Unsubsidized Stafford, PLUS), Perkins, state, alternative loans.

WORK-STUDY ***Federal work-study:*** Total amount: $181,772; 114 jobs averaging $1608.

APPLYING FOR FINANCIAL AID ***Required financial aid forms:*** FAFSA, state aid form. ***Financial aid deadline (priority):*** 5/1. ***Notification date:*** Continuous beginning 3/1. Students must reply within 3 weeks of notification.

CONTACT Karen Fox, Director of Financial Aid, Lancaster Bible College & Graduate School, 901 Eden Road, Lancaster, PA 17601, 717-560-8254 Ext. 5352 or toll-free 866-LBC4YOU. *Fax:* 717-560-8216. *E-mail:* kfox@lbc.edu.

LANDER UNIVERSITY

Greenwood, SC

CONTACT Director of Financial Aid, Lander University, 320 Stanley Avenue, Greenwood, SC 29649, 864-388-8340 or toll-free 888-452-6337. *Fax:* 864-388-8811. *E-mail:* fhardin@lander.edu.

LANE COLLEGE

Jackson, TN

Tuition & fees: $8220 **Average undergraduate aid package: $3314**

ABOUT THE INSTITUTION Independent religious, coed. 17 undergraduate majors. Federal methodology is used as a basis for awarding need-based institutional aid.

UNDERGRADUATE EXPENSES for 2011–12 ***Comprehensive fee:*** $14,020 includes full-time tuition ($7550), mandatory fees ($670), and room and board ($5800). Full-time tuition and fees vary according to course load. ***Part-time tuition:*** $315 per credit hour. ***Part-time fees:*** $670 per year. Part-time tuition and fees vary according to course load. ***Payment plans:*** Installment, deferred payment.

FRESHMAN FINANCIAL AID (Fall 2010, est.) 688 applied for aid; of those 96% were deemed to have need. 100% of freshmen with need received aid; of those 52% had need fully met. ***Average percent of need met:*** 45% (excluding resources awarded to replace EFC). ***Average financial aid package:*** $3341 (excluding resources awarded to replace EFC). 2% of all full-time freshmen had no need and received non-need-based gift aid.

UNDERGRADUATE FINANCIAL AID (Fall 2010, est.) 2,167 applied for aid; of those 100% were deemed to have need. 100% of undergraduates with need received aid; of those 42% had need fully met. ***Average percent of need met:*** 45% (excluding resources awarded to replace EFC). ***Average financial aid package:*** $3314 (excluding resources awarded to replace EFC). 2% of all full-time undergraduates had no need and received non-need-based gift aid.

GIFT AID (NEED-BASED) ***Total amount:*** $15,228,130 (73% federal, 23% state, 2% institutional, 2% external sources). ***Receiving aid:*** Freshmen: 20% (139); all full-time undergraduates: 16% (353). ***Average award:*** Freshmen: $1782; Undergraduates: $1742. ***Scholarships, grants, and awards:*** Federal Pell, FSEOG, state, private, college/university gift aid from institutional funds, United Negro College Fund.

GIFT AID (NON-NEED-BASED) ***Total amount:*** $86,347 (85% state, 8% institutional, 7% external sources). ***Receiving aid:*** Freshmen: 10% (68).

Undergraduates: 6% (137). ***Average award:*** Freshmen: $3013. Undergraduates: $2746. ***Tuition waivers:*** Full or partial for employees or children of employees, adult students.

LOANS ***Student loans:*** $12,623,275 (79% need-based, 21% non-need-based). 88% of past graduating class borrowed through all loan programs. *Average indebtedness per student:* $8754. ***Average need-based loan:*** Freshmen: $1725. Undergraduates: $1993. ***Parent loans:*** $1,073,744 (87% need-based, 13% non-need-based). ***Programs:*** Federal Direct (Subsidized and Unsubsidized Stafford, PLUS).

WORK-STUDY ***Federal work-study:*** Total amount: $250,093; jobs available.

ATHLETIC AWARDS Total amount: $250,000 (88% need-based, 12% non-need-based).

APPLYING FOR FINANCIAL AID ***Required financial aid form:*** FAFSA. ***Financial aid deadline (priority):*** 4/1. ***Notification date:*** Continuous beginning 4/15. Students must reply within 2 weeks of notification.

CONTACT Mr. Tony Calhoun, Director of Financial Aid, Lane College, 545 Lane Avenue, Jackson, TN 38301, 731-426-7558 or toll-free 800-960-7533. *Fax:* 731-426-7652. *E-mail:* tcalhoun@lanecollege.edu.

LANGSTON UNIVERSITY

Langston, OK

ABOUT THE INSTITUTION State-supported, coed. 55 undergraduate majors.

GIFT AID (NEED-BASED) ***Scholarships, grants, and awards:*** Federal Pell, FSEOG, state.

GIFT AID (NON-NEED-BASED) ***Scholarships, grants, and awards by category:*** *Academic interests/achievement:* agriculture, business, education, engineering/technologies, general academic interests/achievements, health fields. *Creative arts/performance:* music. *Special achievements/activities:* cheerleading/drum major, leadership. *Special characteristics:* ethnic background.

LOANS ***Programs:*** Federal Direct (Subsidized and Unsubsidized Stafford, PLUS).

WORK-STUDY ***Federal work-study:*** Total amount: $307,658; jobs available.

APPLYING FOR FINANCIAL AID ***Required financial aid forms:*** FAFSA, institution's own form.

CONTACT Linda Morris, Associate Director of Financial Aid, Langston University, Gandy Hall, Langston, OK 73050, 405-466-3287. *Fax:* 405-466-2986. *E-mail:* ifmorris@lunet.edu.

LA ROCHE COLLEGE

Pittsburgh, PA

Tuition & fees: $22,476 | **Average undergraduate aid package: $23,616**

ABOUT THE INSTITUTION Independent religious, coed. 36 undergraduate majors. Federal methodology is used as a basis for awarding need-based institutional aid.

UNDERGRADUATE EXPENSES for 2010–11 ***Comprehensive fee:*** $31,392 includes full-time tuition ($21,776), mandatory fees ($700), and room and board ($8916). ***College room only:*** $5644. Full-time tuition and fees vary according to program. Room and board charges vary according to board plan. ***Part-time tuition:*** $550 per credit hour. Part-time tuition and fees vary according to program. ***Payment plan:*** Installment.

FRESHMAN FINANCIAL AID (Fall 2010, est.) 209 applied for aid; of those 95% were deemed to have need. 99% of freshmen with need received aid; of those 37% had need fully met. ***Average percent of need met:*** 98% (excluding resources awarded to replace EFC). ***Average financial aid package:*** $26,958 (excluding resources awarded to replace EFC). 4% of all full-time freshmen had no need and received non-need-based gift aid.

UNDERGRADUATE FINANCIAL AID (Fall 2010, est.) 811 applied for aid; of those 93% were deemed to have need. 100% of undergraduates with need received aid; of those 36% had need fully met. ***Average percent of need met:*** 95% (excluding resources awarded to replace EFC). ***Average financial aid package:*** $23,616 (excluding resources awarded to replace EFC). 6% of all full-time undergraduates had no need and received non-need-based gift aid.

GIFT AID (NEED-BASED) ***Total amount:*** $4,256,245 (49% federal, 32% state, 19% institutional). ***Receiving aid:*** Freshmen: 73% (193); all full-time undergraduates: 57% (585). ***Average award:*** Freshmen: $3007; Undergraduates: $2443. ***Scholarships, grants, and awards:*** Federal Pell, FSEOG, state, private, college/university gift aid from institutional funds.

GIFT AID (NON-NEED-BASED) ***Total amount:*** $7,533,596 (95% institutional, 5% external sources). ***Receiving aid:*** Freshmen: 75% (197). Undergraduates: 73% (749). ***Average award:*** Freshmen: $13,418. Undergraduates: $13,496. ***Scholarships, grants, and awards by category:*** *Academic interests/achievement:* 1,027 awards ($7,002,937 total): general academic interests/achievements. ***Tuition waivers:*** Full or partial for employees or children of employees, senior citizens.

LOANS ***Student loans:*** $8,494,219 (41% need-based, 59% non-need-based). 84% of past graduating class borrowed through all loan programs. *Average indebtedness per student:* $18,719. ***Average need-based loan:*** Freshmen: $3229. Undergraduates: $4238. ***Parent loans:*** $1,659,582 (100% non-need-based). ***Programs:*** Federal Direct (Subsidized and Unsubsidized Stafford, PLUS), Perkins, state.

WORK-STUDY ***Federal work-study:*** Total amount: $251,976; 149 jobs averaging $2000.

APPLYING FOR FINANCIAL AID ***Required financial aid form:*** FAFSA. ***Financial aid deadline (priority):*** 5/1. ***Notification date:*** Continuous beginning 3/1. Students must reply within 2 weeks of notification.

CONTACT Mrs. Sharon Platt, Director of Financial Aid, La Roche College, 9000 Babcock Boulevard, Pittsburgh, PA 15237-5898, 412-536-1125 or toll-free 800-838-4LRC. *Fax:* 412-536-1072. *E-mail:* sharon.platt@laroche.edu.

LA SALLE UNIVERSITY

Philadelphia, PA

CONTACT Robert G. Voss, Dean of Admission and Financial Aid, La Salle University, 1900 West Olney Avenue, Philadelphia, PA 19141-1199, 215-951-1500 or toll-free 800-328-1910.

LASELL COLLEGE

Newton, MA

Tuition & fees: $27,500 | **Average undergraduate aid package: $20,885**

ABOUT THE INSTITUTION Independent, coed. 40 undergraduate majors. Both federal and institutional methodology are used as a basis for awarding need-based institutional aid.

UNDERGRADUATE EXPENSES for 2011–12 ***Comprehensive fee:*** $39,800 includes full-time tuition ($26,500), mandatory fees ($1000), and room and board ($12,300). Full-time tuition and fees vary according to program. Room and board charges vary according tq board plan. ***Part-time tuition:*** $900 per credit hour. ***Part-time fees:*** $270 per term. Part-time tuition and fees vary according to program. ***Payment plan:*** Installment.

FRESHMAN FINANCIAL AID (Fall 2010, est.) 430 applied for aid; of those 90% were deemed to have need. 100% of freshmen with need received aid; of those 13% had need fully met. ***Average percent of need met:*** 91% (excluding resources awarded to replace EFC). ***Average financial aid package:*** $21,189 (excluding resources awarded to replace EFC). 9% of all full-time freshmen had no need and received non-need-based gift aid.

UNDERGRADUATE FINANCIAL AID (Fall 2010, est.) 1,390 applied for aid; of those 91% were deemed to have need. 100% of undergraduates with need received aid; of those 15% had need fully met. ***Average percent of need met:*** 90% (excluding resources awarded to replace EFC). ***Average financial aid package:*** $20,885 (excluding resources awarded to replace EFC). 7% of all full-time undergraduates had no need and received non-need-based gift aid.

GIFT AID (NEED-BASED) ***Total amount:*** $19,457,809 (12% federal, 2% state, 84% institutional, 2% external sources). ***Receiving aid:*** Freshmen: 81% (385); all full-time undergraduates: 79% (1,266). ***Average award:*** Freshmen: $16,247; Undergraduates: $15,337. ***Scholarships, grants, and awards:*** Federal Pell, FSEOG, state, private, college/university gift aid from institutional funds.

GIFT AID (NON-NEED-BASED) ***Total amount:*** $2,951,545 (1% federal, 92% institutional, 7% external sources). ***Receiving aid:*** Freshmen: 8% (38). Undergraduates: 5% (80). ***Average award:*** Freshmen: $11,102. Undergraduates: $9453. ***Scholarships, grants, and awards by category:*** *Academic interests/achievement:* 328 awards ($4,478,711 total): general academic interests/achievements. *Special achievements/activities:* 612 awards ($3,775,255 total): community service, general special achievements/activities, leadership. *Special characteristics:* 35 awards ($248,083 total): children and siblings of alumni, children of faculty/staff, siblings of current students, veterans, veterans' children. ***Tuition waivers:*** Full or partial for children of alumni, employees or children of employees.

LOANS ***Student loans:*** $18,017,157 (62% need-based, 38% non-need-based). 67% of past graduating class borrowed through all loan programs. *Average indebtedness per student:* $36,720. ***Average need-based loan:*** Freshmen: $2027. Undergraduates: $9359. ***Parent loans:*** $862,152 (30% need-based, 70% non-need-based). ***Programs:*** Federal Direct (Subsidized and Unsubsidized Stafford, PLUS), Perkins.

WORK-STUDY ***Federal work-study:*** Total amount: $1,617,688; 1,359 jobs averaging $1891.

APPLYING FOR FINANCIAL AID ***Required financial aid forms:*** FAFSA, institution's own form. ***Financial aid deadline (priority):*** 3/1. ***Notification date:*** Continuous beginning 2/15.

CONTACT Michele R. Kosboth, Director of Student Financial Planning, Lasell College, 1844 Commonwealth Avenue, Newton, MA 02466-2709, 617-243-2227 or toll-free 888-LASELL-4. *Fax:* 617-243-2326. *E-mail:* finaid@lasell.edu.

LA SIERRA UNIVERSITY

Riverside, CA

CONTACT Financial Aid Office, La Sierra University, 4500 Riverwalk Parkway, Riverside, CA 92515, 951-785-2175 or toll-free 800-874-5587. *Fax:* 951-785-2942. *E-mail:* sfs@lasierra.edu.

LAURA AND ALVIN SIEGAL COLLEGE OF JUDAIC STUDIES

Beachwood, OH

CONTACT Ruth Kronick, Director of Student Services, Laura and Alvin Siegal College of Judaic Studies, 26500 Shaker Boulevard, Cleveland, OH 44122, 216-464-4050 Ext. 101 or toll-free 888-336-2257. *Fax:* 216-464-5278. *E-mail:* rkronick@siegalcollege.edu.

LAUREL UNIVERSITY

High Point, NC

Tuition & fees: $10,730 **Average undergraduate aid package: N/A**

ABOUT THE INSTITUTION Independent interdenominational, coed. 10 undergraduate majors. Federal methodology is used as a basis for awarding need-based institutional aid.

UNDERGRADUATE EXPENSES for 2010–11 ***Tuition:*** full-time $10,000; part-time $375 per credit hour. ***Required fees:*** full-time $730; $365 per term. Full-time tuition and fees vary according to course load and program. Part-time tuition and fees vary according to course load and program. Room and board charges vary according to housing facility. ***Payment plan:*** Installment.

FRESHMAN FINANCIAL AID (Fall 2009) 7 applied for aid; of those 100% were deemed to have need. 100% of freshmen with need received aid. ***Average percent of need met:*** 48% (excluding resources awarded to replace EFC). ***Average financial aid package:*** $8186 (excluding resources awarded to replace EFC).

GIFT AID (NEED-BASED) ***Total amount:*** $267,194 (94% federal, 6% institutional). ***Receiving aid:*** Freshmen: 100% (7). ***Average award:*** Freshmen: $3356. ***Scholarships, grants, and awards:*** Federal Pell, FSEOG, state, private, college/university gift aid from institutional funds.

GIFT AID (NON-NEED-BASED) ***Total amount:*** $5412 (14% federal, 86% external sources). ***Receiving aid:*** Freshmen: 29% (2). ***Scholarships, grants, and awards by category:*** *Academic interests/achievement:* 16 awards ($19,610 total): education, general academic interests/achievements, religion/biblical studies. *Special achievements/activities:* religious involvement. *Special characteristics:* 6 awards ($31,265 total): children of faculty/staff, general special characteristics, married students, spouses of current students. ***Tuition waivers:*** Full or partial for employees or children of employees.

LOANS ***Student loans:*** $796,433 (47% need-based, 53% non-need-based). 68% of past graduating class borrowed through all loan programs. ***Average need-based loan:*** Freshmen: $3600. ***Parent loans:*** $5335 (100% non-need-based). ***Programs:*** Federal Direct (Subsidized and Unsubsidized Stafford, PLUS).

WORK-STUDY ***Federal work-study:*** Total amount: $13,447; 5 jobs averaging $2500. ***State or other work-study/employment:*** 2 part-time jobs averaging $4500.

APPLYING FOR FINANCIAL AID ***Required financial aid forms:*** FAFSA, institution's own form. ***Financial aid deadline (priority):*** 3/15. ***Notification date:*** 4/1. Students must reply within 2 weeks of notification.

CONTACT Mrs. Shirley P. Carter, Director of Financial Aid, Laurel University, 1215 Eastchester Drive, High Point, NC 27265, 336-887-3000. *Fax:* 336-889-2261. *E-mail:* scarter@laureluniversity.edu.

LAWRENCE TECHNOLOGICAL UNIVERSITY

Southfield, MI

Tuition & fees: $24,633 **Average undergraduate aid package: $19,256**

ABOUT THE INSTITUTION Independent, coed. 42 undergraduate majors. Federal methodology is used as a basis for awarding need-based institutional aid.

UNDERGRADUATE EXPENSES for 2010–11 ***Comprehensive fee:*** $33,780 includes full-time tuition ($24,263), mandatory fees ($370), and room and board ($9147). ***College room only:*** $5854. Full-time tuition and fees vary according to course level, degree level, location, program, and student level. Room and board charges vary according to board plan and housing facility. ***Part-time tuition:*** $808.77 per credit hour. ***Part-time fees:*** $185 per term. Part-time tuition and fees vary according to course level, degree level, location, program, and student level. ***Payment plan:*** Installment.

FRESHMAN FINANCIAL AID (Fall 2009) 257 applied for aid; of those 82% were deemed to have need. 99% of freshmen with need received aid; of those 11% had need fully met. ***Average percent of need met:*** 65% (excluding resources awarded to replace EFC). ***Average financial aid package:*** $18,237 (excluding resources awarded to replace EFC). 14% of all full-time freshmen had no need and received non-need-based gift aid.

UNDERGRADUATE FINANCIAL AID (Fall 2009) 1,383 applied for aid; of those 79% were deemed to have need. 99% of undergraduates with need received aid; of those 8% had need fully met. ***Average percent of need met:*** 62% (excluding resources awarded to replace EFC). ***Average financial aid package:*** $19,256 (excluding resources awarded to replace EFC). 14% of all full-time undergraduates had no need and received non-need-based gift aid.

GIFT AID (NEED-BASED) ***Total amount:*** $13,384,667 (26% federal, 11% state, 62% institutional, 1% external sources). ***Receiving aid:*** Freshmen: 75% (205); all full-time undergraduates: 64% (1,034). ***Average award:*** Freshmen: $12,176; Undergraduates: $11,271. ***Scholarships, grants, and awards:*** Federal Pell, FSEOG, state, private, college/university gift aid from institutional funds, Michigan National Guard and ROTC scholarships.

GIFT AID (NON-NEED-BASED) ***Total amount:*** $2,434,721 (2% state, 94% institutional, 4% external sources). ***Receiving aid:*** Freshmen: 61% (167). Undergraduates: 46% (748). ***Average award:*** Freshmen: $10,224. Undergraduates: $9338. ***Scholarships, grants, and awards by category:*** *Academic interests/achievement:* 1,954 awards ($11,618,426 total): architecture, business, computer science, education, engineering/technologies, general academic interests/achievements, humanities, international studies, mathematics, military science, physical sciences. *Special achievements/activities:* 3 awards ($1000 total): general special achievements/activities. *Special characteristics:* 49 awards ($658,643 total): children of faculty/staff, members of minority groups. ***Tuition waivers:*** Full or partial for employees or children of employees.

LOANS ***Student loans:*** $10,600,038 (97% need-based, 3% non-need-based). 70% of past graduating class borrowed through all loan programs. *Average indebtedness per student:* $38,303. ***Average need-based loan:*** Freshmen: $5835. Undergraduates: $8129. ***Parent loans:*** $4,687,229 (89% need-based, 11% non-need-based). ***Programs:*** Federal Direct (Subsidized and Unsubsidized Stafford, PLUS), Perkins, state, college/university, alternative loans.

WORK-STUDY ***Federal work-study:*** Total amount: $423,182; 102 jobs averaging $1451. ***State or other work-study/employment:*** Part-time jobs available.

APPLYING FOR FINANCIAL AID ***Required financial aid form:*** FAFSA. ***Financial aid deadline (priority):*** 4/1. ***Notification date:*** Continuous beginning 4/1. Students must reply within 2 weeks of notification.

CONTACT Mr. Mark Martin, Director of Financial Aid, Lawrence Technological University, 21000 West Ten Mile Road, Southfield, MI 48075-1058, 248-204-2126 or toll-free 800-225-5588. *Fax:* 248-204-2124. *E-mail:* mmartin@ltu.edu.

LAWRENCE UNIVERSITY

Appleton, WI

Tuition & fees: $38,481 **Average undergraduate aid package: $27,473**

ABOUT THE INSTITUTION Independent, coed. 59 undergraduate majors. Institutional methodology is used as a basis for awarding need-based institutional aid.

UNDERGRADUATE EXPENSES for 2011–12 ***Comprehensive fee:*** $46,371 includes full-time tuition ($38,205), mandatory fees ($276), and room and board ($7890). Room and board charges vary according to board plan. ***Payment plans:*** Tuition prepayment, installment.

FRESHMAN FINANCIAL AID (Fall 2010, est.) 332 applied for aid; of those 79% were deemed to have need. 100% of freshmen with need received aid; of those 53% had need fully met. ***Average percent of need met:*** 93% (excluding resources awarded to replace EFC). ***Average financial aid package:*** $28,672 (excluding resources awarded to replace EFC). 38% of all full-time freshmen had no need and received non-need-based gift aid.

UNDERGRADUATE FINANCIAL AID (Fall 2010, est.) 1,072 applied for aid; of those 82% were deemed to have need. 100% of undergraduates with need received aid; of those 46% had need fully met. ***Average percent of need met:*** 90% (excluding resources awarded to replace EFC). ***Average financial aid package:*** $27,473 (excluding resources awarded to replace EFC). 34% of all full-time undergraduates had no need and received non-need-based gift aid.

GIFT AID (NEED-BASED) ***Total amount:*** $19,005,671 (9% federal, 4% state, 83% institutional, 4% external sources). ***Receiving aid:*** Freshmen: 57% (253); all full-time undergraduates: 58% (864). ***Average award:*** Freshmen: $23,420; Undergraduates: $21,032. ***Scholarships, grants, and awards:*** Federal Pell, FSEOG, state, private, college/university gift aid from institutional funds.

GIFT AID (NON-NEED-BASED) ***Total amount:*** $6,832,629 (95% institutional, 5% external sources). ***Average award:*** Freshmen: $13,492. Undergraduates: $14,587. ***Scholarships, grants, and awards by category:*** *Academic interests/achievement:* 684 awards ($7,363,705 total): general academic interests/achievements. *Creative arts/performance:* 163 awards ($1,269,455 total): music. *Special achievements/activities:* 310 awards ($831,134 total): community service, general special achievements/activities, leadership. *Special characteristics:* 225 awards ($3,246,048 total): children and siblings of alumni, ethnic background, international students, siblings of current students, veterans, veterans' children. ***Tuition waivers:*** Full or partial for employees or children of employees.

LOANS ***Student loans:*** $7,444,879 (52% need-based, 48% non-need-based). 75% of past graduating class borrowed through all loan programs. *Average indebtedness per student:* $30,224. ***Average need-based loan:*** Freshmen: $4192. Undergraduates: $4331. ***Parent loans:*** $2,042,118 (100% non-need-based). ***Programs:*** Federal Direct (Subsidized and Unsubsidized Stafford, PLUS), Perkins, private loans.

WORK-STUDY ***Federal work-study:*** Total amount: $1,550,627; 654 jobs averaging $2345. ***State or other work-study/employment:*** Total amount: $711,553 (100% non-need-based). 321 part-time jobs averaging $2230.

APPLYING FOR FINANCIAL AID ***Required financial aid forms:*** FAFSA, institution's own form, noncustodial (divorced/separated) parent's statement, federal income tax returns and W-2 forms for parents and students. ***Financial aid deadline (priority):*** 3/1. ***Notification date:*** Continuous beginning 3/1. Students must reply by 5/1.

CONTACT Mrs. Sara Beth Holman, Director of Financial Aid, Lawrence University, 711 East Boldt Way, Appleton, WI 54911, 920-832-6583 or toll-free 800-227-0982. *Fax:* 920-832-6582. *E-mail:* sara.b.holman@lawrence.edu.

LEBANON VALLEY COLLEGE

Annville, PA

Tuition & fees: $33,200 **Average undergraduate aid package: $22,755**

ABOUT THE INSTITUTION Independent United Methodist, coed. 38 undergraduate majors. Federal methodology is used as a basis for awarding need-based institutional aid.

UNDERGRADUATE EXPENSES for 2011–12 ***Comprehensive fee:*** $42,000 includes full-time tuition ($32,490), mandatory fees ($710), and room and board ($8800). ***College room only:*** $4300. Room and board charges vary according to board plan and housing facility. Part-time tuition and fees vary according to class time and degree level. ***Payment plans:*** Tuition prepayment, installment.

FRESHMAN FINANCIAL AID (Fall 2010, est.) 437 applied for aid; of those 90% were deemed to have need. 100% of freshmen with need received aid; of those 21% had need fully met. ***Average percent of need met:*** 80% (excluding resources awarded to replace EFC). ***Average financial aid package:*** $23,719 (excluding resources awarded to replace EFC). 12% of all full-time freshmen had no need and received non-need-based gift aid.

UNDERGRADUATE FINANCIAL AID (Fall 2010, est.) 1,456 applied for aid; of those 93% were deemed to have need. 100% of undergraduates with need received aid; of those 21% had need fully met. ***Average percent of need met:*** 80% (excluding resources awarded to replace EFC). ***Average financial aid package:*** $22,755 (excluding resources awarded to replace EFC). 14% of all full-time undergraduates had no need and received non-need-based gift aid.

GIFT AID (NEED-BASED) ***Total amount:*** $22,205,211 (9% federal, 7% state, 84% institutional). ***Receiving aid:*** Freshmen: 85% (391); all full-time undergraduates: 83% (1,327). ***Average award:*** Freshmen: $20,344; Undergraduates: $19,787. ***Scholarships, grants, and awards:*** Federal Pell, FSEOG, state, private, college/university gift aid from institutional funds, TEACH Grants.

GIFT AID (NON-NEED-BASED) ***Total amount:*** $4,643,545 (1% federal, 2% state, 81% institutional, 16% external sources). ***Receiving aid:*** Freshmen: 10% (46). Undergraduates: 8% (136). ***Average award:*** Freshmen: $13,183. Undergraduates: $12,532. ***Scholarships, grants, and awards by category:*** *Academic interests/achievement:* 1,302 awards ($16,396,112 total): biological sciences, general academic interests/achievements, religion/biblical studies. *Creative arts/performance:* 48 awards ($973,137 total): music. *Special achievements/activities:* 82 awards ($41,000 total): general special achievements/activities. *Special characteristics:* 205 awards ($1,508,074 total): children and siblings of alumni, children of faculty/staff, ethnic background, international students, veterans. ***Tuition waivers:*** Full or partial for employees or children of employees, senior citizens.

LOANS ***Student loans:*** $12,535,139 (40% need-based, 60% non-need-based). 80% of past graduating class borrowed through all loan programs. *Average indebtedness per student:* $32,428. ***Average need-based loan:*** Freshmen: $3771. Undergraduates: $4332. ***Parent loans:*** $6,359,224 (100% non-need-based). ***Programs:*** Federal Direct (Subsidized and Unsubsidized Stafford, PLUS), Perkins.

WORK-STUDY ***Federal work-study:*** Total amount: $1,517,892; 977 jobs averaging $1507.

APPLYING FOR FINANCIAL AID ***Required financial aid forms:*** FAFSA, institution's own form. ***Financial aid deadline (priority):*** 3/1. ***Notification date:*** Continuous beginning 3/1. Students must reply by 5/1 or within 2 weeks of notification.

CONTACT Mrs. Kendra M. Feigert, Director of Financial Aid, Lebanon Valley College, 101 North College Avenue, Annville, PA 17003, 866-582-4236 or toll-free 866-LVC-4ADM. *Fax:* 717-867-6027. *E-mail:* feigert@lvc.edu.

LEES-MCRAE COLLEGE

Banner Elk, NC

ABOUT THE INSTITUTION Independent religious, coed. 29 undergraduate majors.

GIFT AID (NEED-BASED) ***Scholarships, grants, and awards:*** Federal Pell, FSEOG, state, private, college/university gift aid from institutional funds.

GIFT AID (NON-NEED-BASED) ***Scholarships, grants, and awards by category:*** *Academic interests/achievement:* biological sciences, education, general academic interests/achievements, mathematics. *Creative arts/performance:* dance, journalism/publications, performing arts, theater/drama. *Special achievements/activities:* cheerleading/drum major, general special achievements/activities. *Special characteristics:* children of educators, children of faculty/staff, children with a deceased or disabled parent, international students, local/state students, previous college experience, relatives of clergy, religious affiliation, veterans.

LOANS ***Programs:*** Perkins, state, college/university.

WORK-STUDY ***Federal work-study:*** Total amount: $315,235; jobs available. ***State or other work-study/employment:*** Total amount: $104,915 (100% need-based). Part-time jobs available.

APPLYING FOR FINANCIAL AID ***Required financial aid forms:*** FAFSA, state aid form.

CONTACT Cathy Shell, Director of Financial Aid, Lees-McRae College, PO Box 128, Banner Elk, NC 28604-0128, 828-898-8740 or toll-free 800-280-4562. *Fax:* 828-898-8746. *E-mail:* shell@lmc.edu.

LEE UNIVERSITY

Cleveland, TN

Tuition & fees: $12,680 **Average undergraduate aid package: $10,703**

ABOUT THE INSTITUTION Independent religious, coed. 55 undergraduate majors. Federal methodology is used as a basis for awarding need-based institutional aid.

UNDERGRADUATE EXPENSES for 2011–12 ***Comprehensive fee:*** $18,690 includes full-time tuition ($12,120), mandatory fees ($560), and room and board ($6010). ***College room only:*** $2900. Full-time tuition and fees vary according to course load. Room and board charges vary according to board plan and housing facility. ***Part-time tuition:*** $506 per credit hour. ***Part-time fees:*** $506 per credit hour. Part-time tuition and fees vary according to course load. ***Payment plan:*** Deferred payment.

FRESHMAN FINANCIAL AID (Fall 2010, est.) 740 applied for aid; of those 80% were deemed to have need. 99% of freshmen with need received aid; of those 30% had need fully met. ***Average percent of need met:*** 68% (excluding resources awarded to replace EFC). ***Average financial aid package:*** $11,359 (excluding resources awarded to replace EFC). 4% of all full-time freshmen had no need and received non-need-based gift aid.

UNDERGRADUATE FINANCIAL AID (Fall 2010, est.) 2,927 applied for aid; of those 84% were deemed to have need. 99% of undergraduates with need received aid; of those 16% had need fully met. ***Average percent of need met:*** 56% (excluding resources awarded to replace EFC). ***Average financial aid package:*** $10,703 (excluding resources awarded to replace EFC). 4% of all full-time undergraduates had no need and received non-need-based gift aid.

GIFT AID (NEED-BASED) ***Total amount:*** $22,054,886 (42% federal, 20% state, 35% institutional, 3% external sources). ***Receiving aid:*** Freshmen: 65% (554); all full-time undergraduates: 61% (2,170). ***Average award:*** Freshmen: $9755; Undergraduates: $8217. ***Scholarships, grants, and awards:*** Federal Pell, FSEOG, state, private, college/university gift aid from institutional funds.

GIFT AID (NON-NEED-BASED) ***Total amount:*** $8,482,749 (1% federal, 25% state, 70% institutional, 4% external sources). ***Receiving aid:*** Freshmen: 15% (124). Undergraduates: 8% (271). ***Average award:*** Freshmen: $7634. Undergraduates: $7947. ***Scholarships, grants, and awards by category:*** *Academic interests/achievement:* biological sciences, business, communication, education, general academic interests/achievements, religion/biblical studies. *Creative arts/performance:* music, theater/drama. *Special achievements/activities:* cheerleading/drum major, leadership, religious involvement. *Special characteristics:* children of faculty/staff, local/state students, siblings of current students, spouses of current students. ***Tuition waivers:*** Full or partial for employees or children of employees.

LOANS ***Student loans:*** $20,442,260 (79% need-based, 21% non-need-based). 64% of past graduating class borrowed through all loan programs. *Average indebtedness per student:* $28,911. ***Average need-based loan:*** Freshmen: $3476. Undergraduates: $4230. ***Parent loans:*** $3,939,326 (51% need-based, 49% non-need-based). ***Programs:*** Perkins, college/university.

WORK-STUDY ***Federal work-study:*** Total amount: $30,378; 560 jobs averaging $1235. ***State or other work-study/employment:*** Total amount: $6478 (50% need-based, 50% non-need-based). Part-time jobs available.

ATHLETIC AWARDS Total amount: $2,039,229 (34% need-based, 66% non-need-based).

APPLYING FOR FINANCIAL AID ***Required financial aid form:*** FAFSA. ***Financial aid deadline (priority):*** 3/15. ***Notification date:*** Continuous beginning 2/1. Students must reply within 3 weeks of notification.

CONTACT Mr. Michael Ellis, Director of Student Financial Aid, Lee University, 1120 North Ocoee Street, Cleveland, TN 37320-3450, 423-614-8300 or toll-free 800-533-9930. *Fax:* 423-614-8308. *E-mail:* finaid@leeuniversity.edu.

LEHIGH UNIVERSITY

Bethlehem, PA

Tuition & fees: $39,780 **Average undergraduate aid package: $30,528**

ABOUT THE INSTITUTION Independent, coed. 68 undergraduate majors. Institutional methodology is used as a basis for awarding need-based institutional aid.

UNDERGRADUATE EXPENSES for 2010–11 ***Comprehensive fee:*** $50,300 includes full-time tuition ($39,480), mandatory fees ($300), and room and board ($10,520). ***College room only:*** $6060. Room and board charges vary according to board plan and housing facility. ***Part-time tuition:*** $1650 per credit hour. ***Payment plans:*** Tuition prepayment, installment.

FRESHMAN FINANCIAL AID (Fall 2010, est.) 815 applied for aid; of those 69% were deemed to have need. 100% of freshmen with need received aid; of those 84% had need fully met. ***Average percent of need met:*** 96% (excluding resources awarded to replace EFC). ***Average financial aid package:*** $30,132 (excluding resources awarded to replace EFC). 6% of all full-time freshmen had no need and received non-need-based gift aid.

UNDERGRADUATE FINANCIAL AID (Fall 2010, est.) 2,765 applied for aid; of those 77% were deemed to have need. 100% of undergraduates with need received aid; of those 89% had need fully met. ***Average percent of need met:*** 97% (excluding resources awarded to replace EFC). ***Average financial aid package:*** $30,528 (excluding resources awarded to replace EFC). 6% of all full-time undergraduates had no need and received non-need-based gift aid.

GIFT AID (NEED-BASED) ***Total amount:*** $53,754,937 (7% federal, 2% state, 91% institutional). ***Receiving aid:*** Freshmen: 45% (542); all full-time undergraduates: 44% (2,070). ***Average award:*** Freshmen: $29,873; Undergraduates: $29,498. ***Scholarships, grants, and awards:*** Federal Pell, FSEOG, state, private, college/university gift aid from institutional funds, United Negro College Fund.

GIFT AID (NON-NEED-BASED) ***Total amount:*** $6,353,695 (1% federal, 55% institutional, 44% external sources). ***Receiving aid:*** Freshmen: 4% (49). Undergraduates: 5% (226). ***Average award:*** Freshmen: $10,759. Undergraduates: $10,232. ***Scholarships, grants, and awards by category:*** *Academic interests/achievement:* 356 awards ($3,979,400 total): business, communication, engineering/technologies, general academic interests/achievements, military science. *Creative arts/performance:* 32 awards ($101,050 total): general creative arts/performance, music, performing arts, theater/drama. *Special achievements/activities:* 4 awards ($22,000 total): general special achievements/activities. *Special characteristics:* 116 awards ($3,990,636 total): children of faculty/staff, members of minority groups. ***Tuition waivers:*** Full or partial for employees or children of employees.

LOANS ***Student loans:*** $22,213,341 (43% need-based, 57% non-need-based). 57% of past graduating class borrowed through all loan programs. *Average indebtedness per student:* $31,922. ***Average need-based loan:*** Freshmen: $2905. Undergraduates: $4426. ***Parent loans:*** $6,999,211 (100% non-need-based). ***Programs:*** Federal Direct (Subsidized and Unsubsidized Stafford, PLUS), Perkins, college/university, private loans.

WORK-STUDY ***Federal work-study:*** Total amount: $2,219,645; 1,222 jobs averaging $1816. ***State or other work-study/employment:*** Total amount: $1,127,189 (19% need-based, 81% non-need-based). 98 part-time jobs averaging $1996.

ATHLETIC AWARDS Total amount: $7,145,208 (63% need-based, 37% non-need-based).

APPLYING FOR FINANCIAL AID ***Required financial aid forms:*** FAFSA, CSS Financial Aid PROFILE, noncustodial (divorced/separated) parent's statement, business/farm supplement. ***Financial aid deadline:*** 2/15. ***Notification date:*** 3/30. Students must reply by 5/1 or within 3 weeks of notification.

CONTACT Linda F. Bell, Director of Financial Aid, Lehigh University, 218 West Packer Avenue, Bethlehem, PA 18015-3094, 610-758-3181. *Fax:* 610-758-6211. *E-mail:* lfn0@lehigh.edu.

LEHMAN COLLEGE OF THE CITY UNIVERSITY OF NEW YORK

Bronx, NY

Tuition & fees (NY res): $5208 **Average undergraduate aid package: $4118**

ABOUT THE INSTITUTION State and locally supported, coed. 52 undergraduate majors. Federal methodology is used as a basis for awarding need-based institutional aid.

UNDERGRADUATE EXPENSES for 2011–12 ***Tuition, state resident:*** full-time $4830; part-time $205 per credit. ***Tuition, nonresident:*** full-time $13,050; part-time $435 per credit. ***Required fees:*** full-time $378.

FRESHMAN FINANCIAL AID (Fall 2009) 569 applied for aid; of those 100% were deemed to have need. 100% of freshmen with need received aid; of those 2% had need fully met. ***Average percent of need met:*** 75% (excluding resources awarded to replace EFC). ***Average financial aid package:*** $3864 (excluding resources awarded to replace EFC). 2% of all full-time freshmen had no need and received non-need-based gift aid.

UNDERGRADUATE FINANCIAL AID (Fall 2009) 4,993 applied for aid; of those 100% were deemed to have need. 100% of undergraduates with need received aid; of those 2% had need fully met. ***Average percent of need met:*** 65% (excluding resources awarded to replace EFC). ***Average financial aid package:*** $4118 (excluding resources awarded to replace EFC). 3% of all full-time undergraduates had no need and received non-need-based gift aid.

GIFT AID (NEED-BASED) ***Total amount:*** $36,318,518 (63% federal, 36% state, 1% institutional). ***Receiving aid:*** Freshmen: 76% (473); all full-time undergraduates: 77% (4,534). ***Average award:*** Freshmen: $2085; Undergraduates: $1860. ***Scholarships, grants, and awards:*** Federal Pell, FSEOG, state, college/university gift aid from institutional funds.

GIFT AID (NON-NEED-BASED) ***Total amount:*** $1,399,436 (16% state, 33% institutional, 51% external sources). ***Receiving aid:*** Freshmen: 55% (342). Undergraduates: 14% (851). ***Average award:*** Freshmen: $3876. Undergraduates: $1329.

LOANS ***Student loans:*** $8,850,513 (60% need-based, 40% non-need-based). 32% of past graduating class borrowed through all loan programs. *Average indebtedness per student:* $13,700. ***Average need-based loan:*** Freshmen: $1423. Undergraduates: $1875. ***Parent loans:*** $11,185 (100% non-need-based). ***Programs:*** Federal Direct (Subsidized and Unsubsidized Stafford, PLUS), Perkins.

WORK-STUDY ***Federal work-study:*** Total amount: $1,513,801; 1,796 jobs averaging $1394. ***State or other work-study/employment:*** Total amount: $62,879 (100% non-need-based). Part-time jobs available.

APPLYING FOR FINANCIAL AID ***Required financial aid forms:*** FAFSA, state aid form. ***Financial aid deadline:*** Continuous. ***Notification date:*** Continuous beginning 3/1.

CONTACT David Martinez, Director of Financial Aid, Lehman College of the City University of New York, 250 Bedford Park Boulevard West, Bronx, NY 10468-1589, 718-960-8545 or toll-free 877-Lehman1 (out-of-state). *Fax:* 718-960-8328. *E-mail:* idmlc@cunyvm.cuny.edu.

LE MOYNE COLLEGE

Syracuse, NY

Tuition & fees: $28,380 **Average undergraduate aid package: $20,065**

ABOUT THE INSTITUTION Independent Roman Catholic (Jesuit), coed. 53 undergraduate majors. Both federal and institutional methodology are used as a basis for awarding need-based institutional aid.

UNDERGRADUATE EXPENSES for 2011–12 ***Comprehensive fee:*** $39,270 includes full-time tuition ($27,390), mandatory fees ($990), and room and board ($10,890). ***College room only:*** $6910. Room and board charges vary according to board plan and housing facility. ***Part-time tuition:*** $574 per credit hour. Part-time tuition and fees vary according to class time. ***Payment plans:*** Installment, deferred payment.

FRESHMAN FINANCIAL AID (Fall 2009) 568 applied for aid; of those 94% were deemed to have need. 100% of freshmen with need received aid; of those 30% had need fully met. ***Average percent of need met:*** 79% (excluding resources awarded to replace EFC). ***Average financial aid package:*** $20,132 (excluding resources awarded to replace EFC). 12% of all full-time freshmen had no need and received non-need-based gift aid.

UNDERGRADUATE FINANCIAL AID (Fall 2009) 2,134 applied for aid; of those 93% were deemed to have need. 100% of undergraduates with need received aid; of those 25% had need fully met. ***Average percent of need met:*** 76% (excluding resources awarded to replace EFC). ***Average financial aid package:*** $20,065 (excluding resources awarded to replace EFC). 8% of all full-time undergraduates had no need and received non-need-based gift aid.

GIFT AID (NEED-BASED) ***Total amount:*** $30,200,805 (14% federal, 11% state, 73% institutional, 2% external sources). ***Receiving aid:*** Freshmen: 88% (534); all full-time undergraduates: 85% (1,975). ***Average award:*** Freshmen: $16,517; Undergraduates: $15,652. ***Scholarships, grants, and awards:*** Federal Pell, FSEOG, state, private, college/university gift aid from institutional funds.

GIFT AID (NON-NEED-BASED) ***Total amount:*** $2,775,901 (1% state, 95% institutional, 4% external sources). ***Receiving aid:*** Freshmen: 15% (94). Undergraduates: 12% (275). ***Average award:*** Freshmen: $5861. Undergraduates: $5414. ***Scholarships, grants, and awards by category:*** *Academic interests/achievement:* 366 awards ($5,446,210 total): general academic interests/achievements. *Creative arts/performance:* 10 awards ($1636 total): music. *Special achievements/activities:* 614 awards ($5,230,675 total): leadership. *Special characteristics:* 109 awards ($531,001 total): children and siblings of alumni, members of minority groups. ***Tuition waivers:*** Full or partial for employees or children of employees.

LOANS ***Student loans:*** $18,246,486 (96% need-based, 4% non-need-based). 85% of past graduating class borrowed through all loan programs. *Average indebtedness per student:* $25,587. ***Average need-based loan:*** Freshmen: $3293. Undergraduates: $4499. ***Parent loans:*** $5,352,775 (92% need-based, 8% non-need-based). ***Programs:*** Federal Direct (Subsidized and Unsubsidized Stafford, PLUS), Perkins.

WORK-STUDY ***Federal work-study:*** Total amount: $448,745; 357 jobs averaging $995. ***State or other work-study/employment:*** 512 part-time jobs averaging $985.

ATHLETIC AWARDS Total amount: $1,486,542 (71% need-based, 29% non-need-based).

APPLYING FOR FINANCIAL AID ***Required financial aid forms:*** FAFSA, institution's own form, state aid form. ***Financial aid deadline (priority):*** 2/1. ***Notification date:*** 3/15. Students must reply by 5/1 or within 2 weeks of notification.

CONTACT Mr. William C. Cheetham, Director of Financial Aid, Le Moyne College, 1419 Salt Springs Road, Syracuse, NY 13214-1301, 315-445-4400 or toll-free 800-333-4733. *Fax:* 315-445-4182. *E-mail:* cheethwc@lemoyne.edu.

LeMOYNE-OWEN COLLEGE

Memphis, TN

Tuition & fees: $10,318 **Average undergraduate aid package: $10,072**

ABOUT THE INSTITUTION Independent religious, coed. ***Awards:*** bachelor's degrees and post-bachelor's certificates. 22 undergraduate majors. ***Total enrollment:*** 592. Undergraduates: 592. Freshmen: 85. Federal methodology is used as a basis for awarding need-based institutional aid.

UNDERGRADUATE EXPENSES for 2010–11 ***Application fee:*** $25. ***Comprehensive fee:*** $15,170 includes full-time tuition ($10,098), mandatory fees ($220), and room and board ($4852). Room and board charges vary according to board plan and housing facility. ***Part-time tuition:*** $421 per credit hour. ***Payment plan:*** Installment.

FRESHMAN FINANCIAL AID (Fall 2010, est.) 255 applied for aid; of those 99% were deemed to have need. 99% of freshmen with need received aid; of those 2% had need fully met. ***Average percent of need met:*** 58% (excluding resources awarded to replace EFC). ***Average financial aid package:*** $9613 (excluding resources awarded to replace EFC). 2% of all full-time freshmen had no need and received non-need-based gift aid.

UNDERGRADUATE FINANCIAL AID (Fall 2010, est.) 1,096 applied for aid; of those 98% were deemed to have need. 99% of undergraduates with need received aid; of those 3% had need fully met. ***Average percent of need met:*** 55% (excluding resources awarded to replace EFC). ***Average financial aid package:*** $10,072 (excluding resources awarded to replace EFC). 1% of all full-time undergraduates had no need and received non-need-based gift aid.

GIFT AID (NEED-BASED) ***Total amount:*** $6,901,579 (69% federal, 19% state, 9% institutional, 3% external sources). ***Receiving aid:*** Freshmen: 93% (241); all full-time undergraduates: 91% (997). ***Average award:*** Freshmen: $6910; Undergraduates: $6947. ***Scholarships, grants, and awards:*** Federal Pell, FSEOG, state, private, college/university gift aid from institutional funds, United Negro College Fund.

GIFT AID (NON-NEED-BASED) ***Total amount:*** $164,258 (1% federal, 7% state, 85% institutional, 7% external sources). ***Receiving aid:*** Freshmen: 1% (2). Undergraduates: 1% (8). ***Average award:*** Freshmen: $11,801. Undergraduates: $9987. ***Scholarships, grants, and awards by category:*** *Academic interests/achievement:* general academic interests/achievements. *Creative arts/performance:* journalism/publications, music. *Special characteristics:* children of faculty/staff. ***Tuition waivers:*** Full or partial for employees or children of employees. ***ROTC:*** Army cooperative, Air Force cooperative.

LOANS ***Student loans:*** $6,771,943 (94% need-based, 6% non-need-based). ***Average need-based loan:*** Freshmen: $3129. Undergraduates: $3627. ***Parent loans:*** $207,765 (76% need-based, 24% non-need-based). ***Programs:*** Federal Direct (Subsidized and Unsubsidized Stafford, PLUS).

WORK-STUDY ***Federal work-study:*** Total amount: $289,098; 176 jobs averaging $1642.

ATHLETIC AWARDS Total amount: $262,740 (91% need-based, 9% non-need-based).

APPLYING FOR FINANCIAL AID ***Required financial aid forms:*** FAFSA, institution's own form. ***Financial aid deadline (priority):*** 4/1. ***Notification date:*** Continuous beginning 5/1. Students must reply within 2 weeks of notification.

CONTACT Office of Student Financial Services, LeMoyne-Owen College, 807 Walker Avenue, Memphis, TN 38126-6595, 901-435-1552 Ext. 1555. *Fax:* 901-435-1574.

LENOIR-RHYNE UNIVERSITY

Hickory, NC

Tuition & fees: $25,290 **Average undergraduate aid package: $23,266**

ABOUT THE INSTITUTION Independent Lutheran, coed. ***Awards:*** bachelor's and master's degrees and post-bachelor's certificates. 72 undergraduate majors. ***Total enrollment:*** 1,562. Undergraduates: 1,381. Freshmen: 346. Federal methodology is used as a basis for awarding need-based institutional aid.

UNDERGRADUATE EXPENSES for 2010–11 ***Application fee:*** $35. ***Comprehensive fee:*** $34,220 includes full-time tuition ($25,290) and room and board ($8930). ***College room only:*** $4550. ***Part-time tuition:*** $1045 per credit hour. Part-time tuition and fees vary according to class time.

FRESHMAN FINANCIAL AID (Fall 2010, est.) 404 applied for aid; of those 91% were deemed to have need. 100% of freshmen with need received aid; of those 25% had need fully met. ***Average percent of need met:*** 79% (excluding resources awarded to replace EFC). ***Average financial aid package:*** $22,571 (excluding resources awarded to replace EFC). 16% of all full-time freshmen had no need and received non-need-based gift aid.

UNDERGRADUATE FINANCIAL AID (Fall 2010, est.) 1,423 applied for aid; of those 93% were deemed to have need. 100% of undergraduates with need received aid; of those 24% had need fully met. ***Average percent of need met:*** 78% (excluding resources awarded to replace EFC). ***Average financial aid package:*** $23,266 (excluding resources awarded to replace EFC). 12% of all full-time undergraduates had no need and received non-need-based gift aid.

GIFT AID (NEED-BASED) ***Total amount:*** $23,298,541 (14% federal, 17% state, 56% institutional, 13% external sources). ***Receiving aid:*** Freshmen: 81% (365); all full-time undergraduates: 87% (1,316). ***Average award:*** Freshmen: $19,466; Undergraduates: $18,938. ***Scholarships, grants, and awards:*** Federal Pell, FSEOG, state, private, college/university gift aid from institutional funds.

GIFT AID (NON-NEED-BASED) ***Total amount:*** $3,876,168 (11% state, 58% institutional, 31% external sources). ***Receiving aid:*** Freshmen: 16% (73). Undergraduates: 15% (225). ***Average award:*** Freshmen: $9003. Undergraduates: $9513. ***Scholarships, grants, and awards by category:*** *Academic interests/achievement:* general academic interests/achievements. *Creative arts/performance:* music. *Special achievements/activities:* cheerleading/drum major, leadership. *Special characteristics:* children and siblings of alumni, children of faculty/staff, ethnic background, local/state students, members of minority groups, relatives of clergy, religious affiliation, siblings of current students. ***ROTC:*** Army cooperative.

LOANS ***Student loans:*** $9,056,944 (77% need-based, 23% non-need-based). 96% of past graduating class borrowed through all loan programs. *Average indebtedness per student:* $24,358. ***Average need-based loan:*** Freshmen: $2786. Undergraduates: $4169. ***Parent loans:*** $3,678,529 (45% need-based, 55% non-need-based). ***Programs:*** Federal Direct (Subsidized and Unsubsidized Stafford, PLUS), Perkins, state.

WORK-STUDY ***Federal work-study:*** Total amount: $1,314,759; jobs available. ***State or other work-study/employment:*** Part-time jobs available.

ATHLETIC AWARDS Total amount: $2,688,083 (68% need-based, 32% non-need-based).

APPLYING FOR FINANCIAL AID ***Required financial aid forms:*** FAFSA, state aid form. ***Financial aid deadline:*** Continuous. ***Notification date:*** Continuous beginning 2/15. Students must reply by 8/31.

CONTACT Nick Jenkins, Financial Aid Counselor, Lenoir-Rhyne University, PO Box 7227, Hickory, NC 28603, 828-328-7301 or toll-free 800-277-5721. *Fax:* 828-328-7039. *E-mail:* finaid@lr.edu.

LESLEY UNIVERSITY

Cambridge, MA

Tuition & fees: $29,400 **Average undergraduate aid package: $16,579**

ABOUT THE INSTITUTION Independent, coed, primarily women. 22 undergraduate majors. Both federal and institutional methodology are used as a basis for awarding need-based institutional aid.

UNDERGRADUATE EXPENSES for 2010–11 ***Comprehensive fee:*** $42,200 includes full-time tuition ($29,150), mandatory fees ($250), and room and board ($12,800). ***College room only:*** $7950. Room and board charges vary according to housing facility. ***Payment plan:*** Installment.

FRESHMAN FINANCIAL AID (Fall 2010, est.) 396 applied for aid; of those 80% were deemed to have need. 100% of freshmen with need received aid; of those 19% had need fully met. ***Average percent of need met:*** 75% (excluding resources awarded to replace EFC). ***Average financial aid package:*** $20,496 (excluding resources awarded to replace EFC). 1% of all full-time freshmen had no need and received non-need-based gift aid.

UNDERGRADUATE FINANCIAL AID (Fall 2010, est.) 1,337 applied for aid; of those 77% were deemed to have need. 97% of undergraduates with need received aid; of those 15% had need fully met. ***Average percent of need met:*** 70% (excluding resources awarded to replace EFC). ***Average financial aid package:*** $16,579 (excluding resources awarded to replace EFC). 16% of all full-time undergraduates had no need and received non-need-based gift aid.

GIFT AID (NEED-BASED) ***Total amount:*** $12,323,396 (15% federal, 3% state, 71% institutional, 11% external sources). ***Receiving aid:*** Freshmen: 57% (232); all full-time undergraduates: 55% (779). ***Average award:*** Freshmen: $14,331; Undergraduates: $14,563. ***Scholarships, grants, and awards:*** Federal Pell, FSEOG, state, private, college/university gift aid from institutional funds.

GIFT AID (NON-NEED-BASED) ***Total amount:*** $5,926,912 (100% institutional). ***Receiving aid:*** Freshmen: 47% (190). Undergraduates: 18% (248). ***Average award:*** Freshmen: $12,667. Undergraduates: $10,358. ***Scholarships, grants, and awards by category:*** *Academic interests/achievement:* general academic interests/achievements. *Creative arts/performance:* art/fine arts. *Special achievements/activities:* general special achievements/activities. *Special characteristics:* ethnic background, local/state students, members of minority groups. ***Tuition waivers:*** Full or partial for employees or children of employees.

LOANS ***Student loans:*** $10,892,028 (39% need-based, 61% non-need-based). 90% of past graduating class borrowed through all loan programs. *Average indebtedness per student:* $18,000. ***Average need-based loan:*** Freshmen: $3131. Undergraduates: $4534. ***Parent loans:*** $4,670,126 (100% non-need-based). ***Programs:*** Federal Direct (Subsidized and Unsubsidized Stafford, PLUS), Perkins, state.

WORK-STUDY ***Federal work-study:*** Total amount: $450,000; jobs available. ***State or other work-study/employment:*** Part-time jobs available.

APPLYING FOR FINANCIAL AID ***Required financial aid forms:*** FAFSA, institution's own form. ***Financial aid deadline (priority):*** 3/15. ***Notification date:*** Continuous beginning 3/15.

CONTACT Scott A. Jewell, Director of Student Financial Services, Lesley University, 29 Everett Street, Cambridge, MA 02138-2790, 617-349-8714 or toll-free 800-999-1959 Ext. 8800. *Fax:* 617-349-8717. *E-mail:* sjewell@lesley.edu.

LeTOURNEAU UNIVERSITY

Longview, TX

Tuition & fees: $21,980 **Average undergraduate aid package: $15,500**

ABOUT THE INSTITUTION Independent nondenominational, coed. 42 undergraduate majors. Federal methodology is used as a basis for awarding need-based institutional aid.

UNDERGRADUATE EXPENSES for 2010–11 ***Comprehensive fee:*** $30,370 includes full-time tuition ($21,510), mandatory fees ($470), and room and board ($8390). Room and board charges vary according to board plan. ***Part-time tuition:*** $858 per credit hour. Part-time tuition and fees vary according to course load. ***Payment plan:*** Installment.

FRESHMAN FINANCIAL AID (Fall 2010, est.) 306 applied for aid; of those 85% were deemed to have need. 100% of freshmen with need received aid; of those 12% had need fully met. ***Average percent of need met:*** 69% (excluding resources awarded to replace EFC). ***Average financial aid package:*** $18,639 (excluding resources awarded to replace EFC). 17% of all full-time freshmen had no need and received non-need-based gift aid.

UNDERGRADUATE FINANCIAL AID (Fall 2010, est.) 1,266 applied for aid; of those 88% were deemed to have need. 100% of undergraduates with need received aid; of those 9% had need fully met. ***Average percent of need met:*** 58% (excluding resources awarded to replace EFC). ***Average financial aid***

package: $15,500 (excluding resources awarded to replace EFC). 12% of all full-time undergraduates had no need and received non-need-based gift aid.

GIFT AID (NEED-BASED) ***Receiving aid:*** Freshmen: 78% (260); all full-time undergraduates: 72% (1,065). ***Average award:*** Freshmen: $14,488; Undergraduates: $11,558. ***Scholarships, grants, and awards:*** Federal Pell, FSEOG, state, college/university gift aid from institutional funds.

GIFT AID (NON-NEED-BASED) ***Receiving aid:*** Freshmen: 62% (206). Undergraduates: 36% (528). ***Average award:*** Freshmen: $2406. Undergraduates: $6697. ***Scholarships, grants, and awards by category:*** *Academic interests/achievement:* general academic interests/achievements. *Special characteristics:* children and siblings of alumni. ***Tuition waivers:*** Full or partial for employees or children of employees.

LOANS ***Average need-based loan:*** Freshmen: $2866. Undergraduates: $4215. ***Programs:*** Federal Direct (Subsidized and Unsubsidized Stafford, PLUS), Perkins, state.

WORK-STUDY Federal work-study jobs available. ***State or other work-study/employment:*** Part-time jobs available.

APPLYING FOR FINANCIAL AID ***Required financial aid form:*** FAFSA. ***Financial aid deadline (priority):*** 2/15. ***Notification date:*** Continuous beginning 3/1. Students must reply within 2 weeks of notification.

CONTACT Ms. Lindy Hall, Senior Director of Enrollment Services, LeTourneau University, PO Box 7001, Longview, TX 75607, 903-233-4312 or toll-free 800-759-8811. *Fax:* 903-233-4301. *E-mail:* finaid@letu.edu.

LEWIS & CLARK COLLEGE

Portland, OR

Tuition & fees: $36,632 **Average undergraduate aid package: $27,829**

ABOUT THE INSTITUTION Independent, coed. 27 undergraduate majors. Both federal and institutional methodology are used as a basis for awarding need-based institutional aid.

UNDERGRADUATE EXPENSES for 2010–11 ***Comprehensive fee:*** $46,280 includes full-time tuition ($36,394), mandatory fees ($238), and room and board ($9648). ***College room only:*** $5058. Room and board charges vary according to board plan and housing facility. ***Part-time tuition:*** $1832 per credit hour. ***Payment plan:*** Installment.

FRESHMAN FINANCIAL AID (Fall 2010, est.) 392 applied for aid; of those 82% were deemed to have need. 97% of freshmen with need received aid; of those 87% had need fully met. ***Average percent of need met:*** 82% (excluding resources awarded to replace EFC). ***Average financial aid package:*** $27,142 (excluding resources awarded to replace EFC). 16% of all full-time freshmen had no need and received non-need-based gift aid.

UNDERGRADUATE FINANCIAL AID (Fall 2010, est.) 1,323 applied for aid; of those 83% were deemed to have need. 98% of undergraduates with need received aid; of those 27% had need fully met. ***Average percent of need met:*** 82% (excluding resources awarded to replace EFC). ***Average financial aid package:*** $27,829 (excluding resources awarded to replace EFC). 16% of all full-time undergraduates had no need and received non-need-based gift aid.

GIFT AID (NEED-BASED) ***Total amount:*** $23,716,946 (9% federal, 86% institutional, 5% external sources). ***Receiving aid:*** Freshmen: 61% (300); all full-time undergraduates: 53% (1,044). ***Average award:*** Freshmen: $22,006; Undergraduates: $20,995. ***Scholarships, grants, and awards:*** Federal Pell, FSEOG, state, private, college/university gift aid from institutional funds.

GIFT AID (NON-NEED-BASED) ***Total amount:*** $4,425,483 (95% institutional, 5% external sources). ***Receiving aid:*** Freshmen: 4% (19). Undergraduates: 2% (44). ***Average award:*** Freshmen: $9347. Undergraduates: $9523. ***Scholarships, grants, and awards by category:*** *Academic interests/achievement:* general academic interests/achievements. *Creative arts/performance:* 40 awards ($205,368 total): debating, music. *Special achievements/activities:* 122 awards ($986,052 total): community service. *Special characteristics:* 31 awards ($994,925 total): children of faculty/staff. ***Tuition waivers:*** Full or partial for employees or children of employees.

LOANS ***Student loans:*** $5,030,479 (64% need-based, 36% non-need-based). 51% of past graduating class borrowed through all loan programs. *Average indebtedness per student:* $22,148. ***Average need-based loan:*** Freshmen: $1184. Undergraduates: $917. ***Parent loans:*** $789,309 (22% need-based, 78% non-need-based). ***Programs:*** Perkins.

WORK-STUDY ***Federal work-study:*** Total amount: $2,182,158; jobs available. ***State or other work-study/employment:*** Total amount: $420,118 (100% non-need-based). Part-time jobs available.

APPLYING FOR FINANCIAL AID ***Required financial aid forms:*** FAFSA, CSS Financial Aid PROFILE. ***Financial aid deadline (priority):*** 2/15. ***Notification date:*** Continuous beginning 3/1. Students must reply by 5/1.

CONTACT Glendi Gaddis, Director of Student Financial Services, Lewis & Clark College, Templeton Student Center, MS 56, Portland, OR 97219-7899, 503-768-7096 or toll-free 800-444-4111. *Fax:* 503-768-7074. *E-mail:* sfs@lclark.edu.

LEWIS-CLARK STATE COLLEGE

Lewiston, ID

Tuition & fees (ID res): $6230 **Average undergraduate aid package: $7956**

ABOUT THE INSTITUTION State-supported, coed. 50 undergraduate majors. Federal methodology is used as a basis for awarding need-based institutional aid.

UNDERGRADUATE EXPENSES for 2010–11 ***Tuition, state resident:*** full-time $4998. ***Tuition, nonresident:*** full-time $13,906. ***Required fees:*** full-time $1232. Full-time tuition and fees vary according to course load and reciprocity agreements. Room and board charges vary according to board plan and housing facility. ***Payment plan:*** Deferred payment.

FRESHMAN FINANCIAL AID (Fall 2009) 534 applied for aid; of those 87% were deemed to have need. 98% of freshmen with need received aid; of those 7% had need fully met. ***Average percent of need met:*** 7% (excluding resources awarded to replace EFC). ***Average financial aid package:*** $6882 (excluding resources awarded to replace EFC). 12% of all full-time freshmen had no need and received non-need-based gift aid.

UNDERGRADUATE FINANCIAL AID (Fall 2009) 2,006 applied for aid; of those 88% were deemed to have need. 98% of undergraduates with need received aid; of those 18% had need fully met. ***Average percent of need met:*** 18% (excluding resources awarded to replace EFC). ***Average financial aid package:*** $7956 (excluding resources awarded to replace EFC). 9% of all full-time undergraduates had no need and received non-need-based gift aid.

GIFT AID (NEED-BASED) ***Total amount:*** $7,175,985 (89% federal, 1% state, 4% institutional, 6% external sources). ***Receiving aid:*** Freshmen: 53% (317); all full-time undergraduates: 51% (1,237). ***Average award:*** Freshmen: $4124; Undergraduates: $4449. ***Scholarships, grants, and awards:*** Federal Pell, FSEOG, state, private, college/university gift aid from institutional funds.

GIFT AID (NON-NEED-BASED) ***Total amount:*** $622,764 (31% state, 63% institutional, 6% external sources). ***Receiving aid:*** Freshmen: 31% (183). Undergraduates: 15% (367). ***Average award:*** Freshmen: $1778. Undergraduates: $2618. ***Scholarships, grants, and awards by category:*** *Academic interests/achievement:* 72 awards ($127,771 total): biological sciences, business, education, English, general academic interests/achievements, health fields, humanities, mathematics, physical sciences, social sciences. *Creative arts/performance:* 11 awards ($24,711 total): art/fine arts, creative writing, debating, music, theater/drama. *Special achievements/activities:* 294 awards ($256,062 total): community service, general special achievements/activities, junior miss, leadership, rodeo. *Special characteristics:* 381 awards ($924,168 total): children and siblings of alumni, ethnic background, first-generation college students, general special characteristics, members of minority groups, out-of-state students, previous college experience. ***Tuition waivers:*** Full or partial for employees or children of employees, senior citizens.

LOANS ***Student loans:*** $15,142,637 (49% need-based, 51% non-need-based). 61% of past graduating class borrowed through all loan programs. ***Average need-based loan:*** Freshmen: $2831. Undergraduates: $3856. ***Parent loans:*** $263,392 (100% non-need-based). ***Programs:*** Federal Direct (Subsidized and Unsubsidized Stafford, PLUS), Perkins, Federal Nursing.

WORK-STUDY ***Federal work-study:*** Total amount: $127,696; 85 jobs averaging $1502. ***State or other work-study/employment:*** Total amount: $146,940 (84% need-based, 16% non-need-based). 113 part-time jobs averaging $1300.

ATHLETIC AWARDS Total amount: $1,504,668 (100% non-need-based).

APPLYING FOR FINANCIAL AID ***Required financial aid form:*** FAFSA. ***Financial aid deadline (priority):*** 3/1. ***Notification date:*** Continuous beginning 4/15. Students must reply within 2 weeks of notification.

CONTACT Ms. Laura Hughes, Director of Financial Aid, Lewis-Clark State College, 500 8th Avenue, Lewiston, ID 83501-2698, 208-792-2224 or toll-free 800-933-5272. *Fax:* 208-792-2063. *E-mail:* lhughes@lcsc.edu.

LEWIS UNIVERSITY

Romeoville, IL

ABOUT THE INSTITUTION Independent religious, coed. 72 undergraduate majors.

GIFT AID (NEED-BASED) ***Scholarships, grants, and awards:*** Federal Pell, FSEOG, state, private, college/university gift aid from institutional funds, Federal Nursing.

GIFT AID (NON-NEED-BASED) ***Scholarships, grants, and awards by category:*** *Academic interests/achievement:* general academic interests/achievements. *Creative arts/performance:* art/fine arts, music, theater/drama. *Special achievements/activities:* community service, general special achievements/activities, memberships. *Special characteristics:* children and siblings of alumni, children of faculty/staff, religious affiliation.

LOANS ***Programs:*** Perkins.

WORK-STUDY ***Federal work-study:*** Total amount: $409,287; 385 jobs averaging $2800. ***State or other work-study/employment:*** Total amount: $1,214,000 (100% non-need-based). 190 part-time jobs averaging $3600.

APPLYING FOR FINANCIAL AID ***Required financial aid form:*** FAFSA.

CONTACT Ms. Janeen Decharinte, Director of Financial Aid, Lewis University, One University Parkway, Romeoville, IL 60446, 815-836-5262 or toll-free 800-897-9000. *Fax:* 815-836-5135. *E-mail:* decharja@lewisu.edu.

LEXINGTON COLLEGE

Chicago, IL

ABOUT THE INSTITUTION Independent, women only. 1 undergraduate major.

GIFT AID (NEED-BASED) ***Scholarships, grants, and awards:*** Federal Pell, FSEOG, state, private, college/university gift aid from institutional funds, Academic Competitiveness Grants.

LOANS ***Programs:*** Sallie Mae Signature Student Loans, alternative loans.

APPLYING FOR FINANCIAL AID ***Required financial aid form:*** FAFSA.

CONTACT Maria Lebron, Director of Financial Aid, Lexington College, 310 South Peoria Street, Suite 512, Chicago, IL 60607, 312-226-6294 Ext. 227. *Fax:* 312-226-6405. *E-mail:* finaid@lexingtoncollege.edu.

LIBERTY UNIVERSITY

Lynchburg, VA

Tuition & fees: $19,154 **Average undergraduate aid package: $8734**

ABOUT THE INSTITUTION Independent nondenominational, coed. 60 undergraduate majors. Federal methodology is used as a basis for awarding need-based institutional aid.

UNDERGRADUATE EXPENSES for 2011–12 ***Comprehensive fee:*** $25,834 includes full-time tuition ($17,806), mandatory fees ($1348), and room and board ($6680). Full-time tuition and fees vary according to course load. Room and board charges vary according to housing facility. ***Part-time tuition:*** $594 per hour. Part-time tuition and fees vary according to course load. ***Payment plan:*** Installment.

FRESHMAN FINANCIAL AID (Fall 2010, est.) 3,100 applied for aid; of those 84% were deemed to have need. 100% of freshmen with need received aid; of those 11% had need fully met. ***Average percent of need met:*** 52% (excluding resources awarded to replace EFC). ***Average financial aid package:*** $9948 (excluding resources awarded to replace EFC). 5% of all full-time freshmen had no need and received non-need-based gift aid.

UNDERGRADUATE FINANCIAL AID (Fall 2010, est.) 17,357 applied for aid; of those 88% were deemed to have need. 100% of undergraduates with need received aid; of those 7% had need fully met. ***Average percent of need met:*** 42% (excluding resources awarded to replace EFC). ***Average financial aid package:*** $8734 (excluding resources awarded to replace EFC). 4% of all full-time undergraduates had no need and received non-need-based gift aid.

GIFT AID (NEED-BASED) ***Total amount:*** $148,823,464 (60% federal, 5% state, 34% institutional, 1% external sources). ***Receiving aid:*** Freshmen: 75% (2,553); all full-time undergraduates: 68% (14,206). ***Average award:*** Freshmen: $7518; Undergraduates: $6455. ***Scholarships, grants, and awards:*** Federal Pell, FSEOG, state, private, college/university gift aid from institutional funds, Academic Competitiveness Grants, National SMART Grants, TEACH Grants.

GIFT AID (NON-NEED-BASED) ***Total amount:*** $32,568,392 (28% federal, 7% state, 63% institutional, 2% external sources). ***Receiving aid:*** Freshmen: 9% (312). Undergraduates: 6% (1,189). ***Average award:*** Freshmen: $5971. Undergraduates: $6976. ***Scholarships, grants, and awards by category:*** *Academic interests/achievement:* general academic interests/achievements. *Creative arts/performance:* debating, journalism/publications, music, performing arts. *Special characteristics:* children of faculty/staff, international students, local/state students, public servants, religious affiliation, veterans. ***Tuition waivers:*** Full or partial for employees or children of employees.

LOANS ***Student loans:*** $64,962,380 (78% need-based, 22% non-need-based). 70% of past graduating class borrowed through all loan programs. *Average indebtedness per student:* $32,936. ***Average need-based loan:*** Freshmen: $2739. Undergraduates: $2887. ***Parent loans:*** $16,724,380 (74% need-based, 26% non-need-based). ***Programs:*** Federal Direct (Subsidized and Unsubsidized Stafford, PLUS), college/university.

WORK-STUDY ***Federal work-study:*** Total amount: $1,036,886; jobs available. ***State or other work-study/employment:*** Part-time jobs available.

ATHLETIC AWARDS Total amount: $3,914,828 (60% need-based, 40% non-need-based).

APPLYING FOR FINANCIAL AID ***Required financial aid forms:*** FAFSA, state aid form. ***Financial aid deadline:*** 3/1. ***Notification date:*** Continuous beginning 3/15. Students must reply within 3 weeks of notification.

CONTACT Robert Ritz, Director of Financial Aid, Liberty University, 1971 University Boulevard, Lynchburg, VA 24502, 434-582-2270 or toll-free 800-543-5317. *Fax:* 434-582-2053. *E-mail:* financialaid@liberty.edu.

LIFE PACIFIC COLLEGE

San Dimas, CA

CONTACT Mrs. Becky Huyck, Director of Financial Aid, Life Pacific College, 1100 Covina Boulevard, San Dimas, CA 91773-3298, 909-599-5433 Ext. 319 or toll-free 877-886-5433 Ext. 314. *Fax:* 909-599-6690. *E-mail:* bhuyck@lifepacific.edu.

LIFE UNIVERSITY

Marietta, GA

Tuition & fees: $9369 **Average undergraduate aid package: $9950**

ABOUT THE INSTITUTION Independent, coed. 5 undergraduate majors. Federal methodology is used as a basis for awarding need-based institutional aid.

UNDERGRADUATE EXPENSES for 2010–11 ***Comprehensive fee:*** $21,849 includes full-time tuition ($8622), mandatory fees ($747), and room and board ($12,480). ***College room only:*** $6300. Full-time tuition and fees vary according to course load. ***Part-time tuition:*** $175 per credit hour. Part-time tuition and fees vary according to course load. ***Payment plan:*** Installment.

FRESHMAN FINANCIAL AID (Fall 2010, est.) 139 applied for aid; of those 95% were deemed to have need. 97% of freshmen with need received aid; of those 1% had need fully met. ***Average financial aid package:*** $10,250 (excluding resources awarded to replace EFC). 2% of all full-time freshmen had no need and received non-need-based gift aid.

UNDERGRADUATE FINANCIAL AID (Fall 2010, est.) 454 applied for aid; of those 97% were deemed to have need. 98% of undergraduates with need received aid; of those 1% had need fully met. ***Average financial aid package:*** $9950 (excluding resources awarded to replace EFC). 2% of all full-time undergraduates had no need and received non-need-based gift aid.

GIFT AID (NEED-BASED) ***Total amount:*** $2,306,000 (100% federal). ***Receiving aid:*** Freshmen: 58% (95); all full-time undergraduates: 53% (278). ***Average award:*** Freshmen: $5550; Undergraduates: $5600. ***Scholarships, grants, and awards:*** Federal Pell, FSEOG, state, private, college/university gift aid from institutional funds.

GIFT AID (NON-NEED-BASED) ***Total amount:*** $559,000 (54% state, 42% institutional, 4% external sources). ***Receiving aid:*** Freshmen: 43% (71). Undergraduates: 42% (222). ***Average award:*** Freshmen: $1000. Undergraduates: $2400. ***Scholarships, grants, and awards by category:*** *Academic interests/achievement:* 10 awards ($28,000 total): general academic interests/achievements. *Special achievements/activities:* 97 awards ($262,000 total): general special achievements/activities. *Special characteristics:* 26 awards ($208,000 total): general special characteristics, international students. ***Tuition waivers:*** Full or partial for employees or children of employees.

LOANS ***Student loans:*** $6,700,000 (40% need-based, 60% non-need-based). 57% of past graduating class borrowed through all loan programs. *Average*

indebtedness per student: $28,000. ***Average need-based loan:*** Freshmen: $4000. Undergraduates: $4700. ***Parent loans:*** $575,000 (100% need-based). ***Programs:*** college/university, alternative loans.

WORK-STUDY ***Federal work-study:*** Total amount: $235,000; 221 jobs averaging $1100.

ATHLETIC AWARDS Total amount: $262,000 (100% non-need-based).

APPLYING FOR FINANCIAL AID ***Required financial aid forms:*** FAFSA, institution's own form. ***Financial aid deadline (priority):*** 3/1. ***Notification date:*** Continuous beginning 5/1.

CONTACT Melissa Waters, Director of Financial Aid, Life University, 1269 Barclay Circle, Marietta, GA 30060, 770-426-2901 or toll-free 800-543-3202 (in-state). *Fax:* 770-426-2926. *E-mail:* finaid@life.edu.

LIM COLLEGE

New York, NY

CONTACT Mr. Christopher Barto, Dean of Student Financial Services, LIM College, 12 East 53rd Street, New York, NY 10022-5268, 212-752-1530 or toll-free 800-677-1323. *Fax:* 212-317-8602. *E-mail:* cbarto@limcollege.edu.

LIMESTONE COLLEGE

Gaffney, SC

Tuition & fees: $20,000 **Average undergraduate aid package: $13,805**

ABOUT THE INSTITUTION Independent, coed. 51 undergraduate majors. Federal methodology is used as a basis for awarding need-based institutional aid.

UNDERGRADUATE EXPENSES for 2011–12 ***Comprehensive fee:*** $27,500 includes full-time tuition ($20,000) and room and board ($7500). ***College room only:*** $3750. Full-time tuition and fees vary according to class time, course load, and location. Room and board charges vary according to housing facility. ***Part-time tuition:*** $835 per semester hour. Part-time tuition and fees vary according to class time, course load, and location. ***Payment plan:*** Installment.

FRESHMAN FINANCIAL AID (Fall 2009) 255 applied for aid; of those 91% were deemed to have need. 100% of freshmen with need received aid; of those 15% had need fully met. ***Average percent of need met:*** 60% (excluding resources awarded to replace EFC). ***Average financial aid package:*** $13,936 (excluding resources awarded to replace EFC). 16% of all full-time freshmen had no need and received non-need-based gift aid.

UNDERGRADUATE FINANCIAL AID (Fall 2009) 735 applied for aid; of those 90% were deemed to have need. 100% of undergraduates with need received aid; of those 15% had need fully met. ***Average percent of need met:*** 60% (excluding resources awarded to replace EFC). ***Average financial aid package:*** $13,805 (excluding resources awarded to replace EFC). 20% of all full-time undergraduates had no need and received non-need-based gift aid.

GIFT AID (NEED-BASED) ***Total amount:*** $5,722,907 (28% federal, 22% state, 46% institutional, 4% external sources). ***Receiving aid:*** Freshmen: 83% (232); all full-time undergraduates: 79% (657). ***Average award:*** Freshmen: $11,295; Undergraduates: $10,565. ***Scholarships, grants, and awards:*** Federal Pell, FSEOG, state, private, college/university gift aid from institutional funds.

GIFT AID (NON-NEED-BASED) ***Total amount:*** $1,173,024 (11% state, 83% institutional, 6% external sources). ***Receiving aid:*** Freshmen: 11% (31). Undergraduates: 10% (83). ***Average award:*** Freshmen: $5273. Undergraduates: $5200. ***Scholarships, grants, and awards by category:*** *Academic interests/achievement:* $1,756,149 total: biological sciences, business, communication, computer science, education, English, general academic interests/achievements, health fields, humanities, mathematics, physical sciences, premedicine, religion/biblical studies, social sciences. *Creative arts/performance:* $85,176 total: art/fine arts, music, performing arts, theater/drama. *Special achievements/activities:* $538,488 total: cheerleading/drum major, general special achievements/activities, leadership, religious involvement. *Special characteristics:* $911,257 total: children of faculty/staff, local/state students, out-of-state students, previous college experience, siblings of current students. ***Tuition waivers:*** Full or partial for employees or children of employees.

LOANS ***Student loans:*** $4,805,509 (81% need-based, 19% non-need-based). 84% of past graduating class borrowed through all loan programs. *Average indebtedness per student:* $28,939. ***Average need-based loan:*** Freshmen: $2851. Undergraduates: $3553. ***Parent loans:*** $863,729 (44% need-based, 56% non-need-based). ***Programs:*** Federal Direct (Subsidized and Unsubsidized Stafford, PLUS), Perkins.

WORK-STUDY ***Federal work-study:*** Total amount: $224,101; 172 jobs averaging $1322. ***State or other work-study/employment:*** Total amount: $65,832 (10% need-based, 90% non-need-based). 66 part-time jobs averaging $824.

ATHLETIC AWARDS Total amount: $1,946,866 (58% need-based, 42% non-need-based).

APPLYING FOR FINANCIAL AID ***Required financial aid form:*** FAFSA. ***Financial aid deadline (priority):*** 2/1. ***Notification date:*** Continuous beginning 1/15. Students must reply within 3 weeks of notification.

CONTACT Mr. Bobby Greer, Director of Financial Aid, Limestone College, 1115 College Drive, Gaffney, SC 29340-3799, 864-488-4567 or toll-free 800-795-7151 Ext. 554. *Fax:* 864-487-8706. *E-mail:* bgreer@limestone.edu.

LINCOLN CHRISTIAN UNIVERSITY

Lincoln, IL

CONTACT Nancy Siddens, Financial Aid Director, Lincoln Christian University, 100 Campus View Drive, Lincoln, IL 62656, 217-732-3168 Ext. 2250 or toll-free 888-522-5228. *Fax:* 217-732-5914. *E-mail:* finaid@lccs.edu.

LINCOLN COLLEGE–NORMAL

Normal, IL

CONTACT Financial Aid Office, Lincoln College–Normal, 715 West Raab Road, Normal, IL 61761, 309-452-0500 or toll-free 800-569-0558.

LINCOLN COLLEGE OF NEW ENGLAND

Southington, CT

CONTACT Financial Aid Office, Lincoln College of New England, 2279 Mount Vernon Road, Southington, CT 06489-1057, 860-628-4751 or toll-free 800-952-2444 (in-state).

LINCOLN CULINARY INSTITUTE

West Palm Beach, FL

CONTACT Financial Aid Office, Lincoln Culinary Institute, 2410 Metrocentre Boulevard, West Palm Beach, FL 33407, 561-842-8324.

LINCOLN MEMORIAL UNIVERSITY

Harrogate, TN

Tuition & fees: $16,200 **Average undergraduate aid package: $17,321**

ABOUT THE INSTITUTION Independent, coed. 42 undergraduate majors. Federal methodology is used as a basis for awarding need-based institutional aid.

UNDERGRADUATE EXPENSES for 2010–11 ***Comprehensive fee:*** $21,980 includes full-time tuition ($16,200) and room and board ($5780). Room and board charges vary according to board plan and housing facility. ***Part-time tuition:*** $675 per credit hour. Part-time tuition and fees vary according to course load. ***Payment plan:*** Installment.

FRESHMAN FINANCIAL AID (Fall 2010, est.) 348 applied for aid; of those 86% were deemed to have need. 99% of freshmen with need received aid; of those 21% had need fully met. ***Average percent of need met:*** 77% (excluding resources awarded to replace EFC). ***Average financial aid package:*** $18,761 (excluding resources awarded to replace EFC). 14% of all full-time freshmen had no need and received non-need-based gift aid.

UNDERGRADUATE FINANCIAL AID (Fall 2010, est.) 1,426 applied for aid; of those 88% were deemed to have need. 100% of undergraduates with need received aid; of those 19% had need fully met. ***Average percent of need met:*** 74% (excluding resources awarded to replace EFC). ***Average financial aid package:*** $17,321 (excluding resources awarded to replace EFC). 11% of all full-time undergraduates had no need and received non-need-based gift aid.

GIFT AID (NEED-BASED) ***Total amount:*** $16,338,647 (26% federal, 18% state, 53% institutional, 3% external sources). ***Receiving aid:*** Freshmen: 83% (293); all full-time undergraduates: 83% (1,206). ***Average award:*** Freshmen: $15,825; Undergraduates: $13,112. ***Scholarships, grants, and awards:*** Federal Pell, FSEOG, state, private, college/university gift aid from institutional funds.

GIFT AID (NON-NEED-BASED) ***Total amount:*** $2,255,005 (23% state, 69% institutional, 8% external sources). ***Receiving aid:*** Freshmen: 4% (13).

Undergraduates: 11% (162). ***Average award:*** Freshmen: $12,957. Undergraduates: $8412. ***Scholarships, grants, and awards by category:*** *Academic interests/achievement:* general academic interests/achievements. *Creative arts/performance:* music. *Special achievements/activities:* cheerleading/drum major. *Special characteristics:* children of faculty/staff. ***Tuition waivers:*** Full or partial for employees or children of employees, senior citizens.

LOANS ***Student loans:*** $8,395,069 (82% need-based, 18% non-need-based). 55% of past graduating class borrowed through all loan programs. *Average indebtedness per student:* $21,749. ***Average need-based loan:*** Freshmen: $3145. Undergraduates: $3872. ***Parent loans:*** $521,613 (58% need-based, 42% non-need-based). ***Programs:*** Federal Direct (Subsidized and Unsubsidized Stafford, PLUS), Perkins, Federal Nursing.

WORK-STUDY ***Federal work-study:*** Total amount: $287,003; jobs available. ***State or other work-study/employment:*** Total amount: $134,220 (49% need-based, 51% non-need-based). Part-time jobs available.

ATHLETIC AWARDS Total amount: $1,013,957 (52% need-based, 48% non-need-based).

APPLYING FOR FINANCIAL AID ***Required financial aid form:*** FAFSA. ***Financial aid deadline (priority):*** 4/1. ***Notification date:*** Continuous. Students must reply within 3 weeks of notification.

CONTACT Bryan Erslan, Director of Financial Aid, Lincoln Memorial University, Cumberland Gap Parkway, Harrogate, TN 37752-1901, 423-869-6465 or toll-free 800-325-0900. *Fax:* 423-869-6347. *E-mail:* bryan.erslan@lmunet.edu.

LINCOLN UNIVERSITY
Oakland, CA

CONTACT Financial Aid Office, Lincoln University, 401 15th Street, Oakland, CA 94612, 510-628-8010.

LINCOLN UNIVERSITY
Jefferson City, MO

Tuition & fees (MO res): $6175 **Average undergraduate aid package: $9333**

ABOUT THE INSTITUTION State-supported, coed. 50 undergraduate majors. Federal methodology is used as a basis for awarding need-based institutional aid.

UNDERGRADUATE EXPENSES for 2011–12 ***Tuition, state resident:*** full-time $5685; part-time $189.50 per credit hour. ***Tuition, nonresident:*** full-time $10,915; part-time $363.83 per credit hour. ***Required fees:*** full-time $490; $15 per credit hour or $20 per term. Full-time tuition and fees vary according to location and reciprocity agreements. Part-time tuition and fees vary according to location and reciprocity agreements. ***College room and board:*** $5144; ***Room only:*** $2500. Room and board charges vary according to board plan and housing facility. ***Payment plans:*** Installment, deferred payment.

FRESHMAN FINANCIAL AID (Fall 2010, est.) 505 applied for aid; of those 93% were deemed to have need. 100% of freshmen with need received aid; of those 7% had need fully met. ***Average percent of need met:*** 64% (excluding resources awarded to replace EFC). ***Average financial aid package:*** $9091 (excluding resources awarded to replace EFC). 1% of all full-time freshmen had no need and received non-need-based gift aid.

UNDERGRADUATE FINANCIAL AID (Fall 2010, est.) 1,836 applied for aid; of those 90% were deemed to have need. 100% of undergraduates with need received aid; of those 11% had need fully met. ***Average percent of need met:*** 67% (excluding resources awarded to replace EFC). ***Average financial aid package:*** $9333 (excluding resources awarded to replace EFC). 1% of all full-time undergraduates had no need and received non-need-based gift aid.

GIFT AID (NEED-BASED) ***Total amount:*** $9,479,114 (79% federal, 5% state, 11% institutional, 5% external sources). ***Receiving aid:*** Freshmen: 70% (415); all full-time undergraduates: 67% (1,419). ***Average award:*** Freshmen: $5328; Undergraduates: $5232. ***Scholarships, grants, and awards:*** Federal Pell, FSEOG, state, private, college/university gift aid from institutional funds.

GIFT AID (NON-NEED-BASED) ***Total amount:*** $632,686 (6% federal, 1% state, 19% institutional, 74% external sources). ***Receiving aid:*** Freshmen: 4% (25). Undergraduates: 4% (76). ***Average award:*** Freshmen: $2873. Undergraduates: $3958. ***Scholarships, grants, and awards by category:*** *Academic interests/achievement:* 164 awards ($725,324 total): agriculture, general academic interests/achievements, military science. *Creative arts/performance:* 102 awards ($275,750 total): art/fine arts, journalism/publications, music, performing arts, theater/drama. *Special achievements/activities:* 13 awards ($11,010 total): cheerleading/drum major. *Special characteristics:* 301 awards ($910,464 total): adult students, children of faculty/staff, international students, out-of-state students. ***Tuition waivers:*** Full or partial for employees or children of employees.

LOANS ***Student loans:*** $13,595,266 (47% need-based, 53% non-need-based). 63% of past graduating class borrowed through all loan programs. *Average indebtedness per student:* $25,950. ***Average need-based loan:*** Freshmen: $3396. Undergraduates: $3992. ***Parent loans:*** $1,361,224 (100% non-need-based).

WORK-STUDY ***Federal work-study:*** Total amount: $210,420; 168 jobs averaging $1253. ***State or other work-study/employment:*** Total amount: $581,740 (100% non-need-based). 194 part-time jobs averaging $2999.

ATHLETIC AWARDS Total amount: $1,021,362 (100% need-based).

APPLYING FOR FINANCIAL AID ***Required financial aid forms:*** FAFSA, institution's own form. ***Financial aid deadline (priority):*** 3/1. ***Notification date:*** Continuous beginning 3/15. Students must reply within 2 weeks of notification.

CONTACT Mr. Alfred Robinson, Director of Financial Aid, Lincoln University, 820 Chestnut Street, Jefferson City, MO 65102-0029, 573-681-6156 or toll-free 800-521-5052. *Fax:* 573-681-5871. *E-mail:* robinsona@lincolnu.edu.

LINCOLN UNIVERSITY
Lincoln University, PA

ABOUT THE INSTITUTION State-related, coed. 46 undergraduate majors.

GIFT AID (NEED-BASED) ***Scholarships, grants, and awards:*** Federal Pell, FSEOG, state, private, college/university gift aid from institutional funds, United Negro College Fund.

GIFT AID (NON-NEED-BASED) ***Scholarships, grants, and awards by category:*** *Academic interests/achievement:* biological sciences, business, communication, computer science, education, English, general academic interests/achievements, humanities, mathematics, physical sciences, social sciences. *Creative arts/performance:* music. *Special achievements/activities:* general special achievements/activities. *Special characteristics:* children and siblings of alumni, children of faculty/staff, international students.

LOANS ***Programs:*** Perkins.

WORK-STUDY ***Federal work-study:*** Total amount: $189,020; 146 jobs averaging $1294.

APPLYING FOR FINANCIAL AID ***Required financial aid form:*** FAFSA.

CONTACT Thelma Ross, Director of Financial Aid, Lincoln University, PO Box 179, Lincoln University, PA 19352, 484-365-7583 or toll-free 800-790-0191. *Fax:* 484-365-8198. *E-mail:* tross@lincoln.edu.

LINDENWOOD UNIVERSITY
St. Charles, MO

Tuition & fees: $13,600 **Average undergraduate aid package: $7024**

ABOUT THE INSTITUTION Independent Presbyterian, coed. 96 undergraduate majors. Federal methodology is used as a basis for awarding need-based institutional aid.

UNDERGRADUATE EXPENSES for 2010–11 ***Comprehensive fee:*** $20,810 includes full-time tuition ($13,260), mandatory fees ($340), and room and board ($7210). ***College room only:*** $3980. Full-time tuition and fees vary according to program. ***Part-time tuition:*** $380 per credit hour. Part-time tuition and fees vary according to course load. ***Payment plans:*** Installment, deferred payment.

FRESHMAN FINANCIAL AID (Fall 2010, est.) 743 applied for aid; of those 88% were deemed to have need. 100% of freshmen with need received aid; of those 90% had need fully met. ***Average percent of need met:*** 90% (excluding resources awarded to replace EFC). ***Average financial aid package:*** $9389 (excluding resources awarded to replace EFC). 32% of all full-time freshmen had no need and received non-need-based gift aid.

UNDERGRADUATE FINANCIAL AID (Fall 2010, est.) 4,980 applied for aid; of those 92% were deemed to have need. 100% of undergraduates with need received aid; of those 63% had need fully met. ***Average percent of need met:*** 89% (excluding resources awarded to replace EFC). ***Average financial aid package:*** $7024 (excluding resources awarded to replace EFC). 15% of all full-time undergraduates had no need and received non-need-based gift aid.

GIFT AID (NEED-BASED) ***Total amount:*** $29,695,000 (34% federal, 11% state, 55% institutional). ***Receiving aid:*** Freshmen: 52% (549); all full-time undergradu-

ates: 55% (3,781). ***Average award:*** Freshmen: $4963; Undergraduates: $4461. ***Scholarships, grants, and awards:*** Federal Pell, FSEOG, state, private, college/university gift aid from institutional funds.

GIFT AID (NON-NEED-BASED) ***Total amount:*** $10,095,000 (2% state, 96% institutional, 2% external sources). ***Receiving aid:*** Freshmen: 30% (310). Undergraduates: 26% (1,758). ***Average award:*** Freshmen: $4291. Undergraduates: $3868. ***Scholarships, grants, and awards by category:*** *Academic interests/achievement:* biological sciences, business, communication, computer science, education, engineering/technologies, English, foreign languages, general academic interests/achievements, health fields, humanities, international studies, library science, mathematics, military science, physical sciences, premedicine, social sciences. *Creative arts/performance:* applied art and design, art/fine arts, cinema/film/broadcasting, dance, general creative arts/performance, music, performing arts, theater/drama. *Special achievements/activities:* cheerleading/drum major, community service, general special achievements/activities, junior miss, leadership. ***Tuition waivers:*** Full or partial for employees or children of employees, senior citizens.

LOANS ***Student loans:*** $41,000,000 (51% need-based, 49% non-need-based). ***Average need-based loan:*** Freshmen: $3372. Undergraduates: $2649. ***Parent loans:*** $2,047,650 (100% non-need-based). ***Programs:*** Federal Direct (Subsidized and Unsubsidized Stafford, PLUS), Perkins.

WORK-STUDY ***Federal work-study:*** Total amount: $363,503; jobs available (averaging $2400). ***State or other work-study/employment:*** Total amount: $7,800,000 (62% need-based, 38% non-need-based). Part-time jobs available.

APPLYING FOR FINANCIAL AID ***Required financial aid form:*** FAFSA. ***Financial aid deadline (priority):*** 4/1. ***Notification date:*** Continuous. Students must reply within 2 weeks of notification.

CONTACT Lori Bode, Director of Financial Aid, Lindenwood University, 209 South Kings highway, St. Charles, MO 63301-1695, 636-949-4925. *Fax:* 636-949-4924. *E-mail:* lbode@lindenwood.edu.

LINDSEY WILSON COLLEGE

Columbia, KY

Tuition & fees: $18,950 **Average undergraduate aid package: N/A**

ABOUT THE INSTITUTION Independent United Methodist, coed. 34 undergraduate majors. Federal methodology is used as a basis for awarding need-based institutional aid.

UNDERGRADUATE EXPENSES for 2010–11 ***Comprehensive fee:*** $26,595 includes full-time tuition ($18,720), mandatory fees ($230), and room and board ($7645). ***College room only:*** $2820. Full-time tuition and fees vary according to location. ***Part-time tuition:*** $780 per credit hour. Part-time tuition and fees vary according to location. ***Payment plan:*** Installment.

FRESHMAN FINANCIAL AID (Fall 2010, est.) 595 applied for aid; of those 97% were deemed to have need. 100% of freshmen with need received aid; of those 20% had need fully met.

UNDERGRADUATE FINANCIAL AID (Fall 2010, est.) 2,242 applied for aid; of those 95% were deemed to have need. 98% of undergraduates with need received aid; of those 17% had need fully met.

GIFT AID (NEED-BASED) ***Total amount:*** $25,152,158 (26% federal, 24% state, 48% institutional, 2% external sources). ***Receiving aid:*** Freshmen: 97% (580); all full-time undergraduates: 88% (2,068). ***Scholarships, grants, and awards:*** Federal Pell, FSEOG, state, private, college/university gift aid from institutional funds.

GIFT AID (NON-NEED-BASED) ***Scholarships, grants, and awards by category:*** *Academic interests/achievement:* biological sciences, business, education, English, general academic interests/achievements, mathematics, premedicine, religion/biblical studies. *Creative arts/performance:* applied art and design, music. *Special achievements/activities:* cheerleading/drum major, general special achievements/activities, junior miss, leadership, religious involvement. *Special characteristics:* children and siblings of alumni, children of faculty/staff, relatives of clergy, religious affiliation. ***Tuition waivers:*** Full or partial for employees or children of employees, senior citizens.

LOANS ***Student loans:*** $11,161,444 (100% need-based). 87% of past graduating class borrowed through all loan programs. *Average indebtedness per student:* $21,637. ***Parent loans:*** $936,736 (100% need-based). ***Programs:*** Federal Direct (Subsidized and Unsubsidized Stafford, PLUS), Perkins, college/university.

WORK-STUDY ***Federal work-study:*** Total amount: $514,918; 280 jobs averaging $1839. ***State or other work-study/employment:*** Total amount: $5000 (100% need-based). 4 part-time jobs averaging $1250.

ATHLETIC AWARDS Total amount: $1,678,233 (100% need-based).

APPLYING FOR FINANCIAL AID ***Required financial aid form:*** FAFSA. ***Financial aid deadline (priority):*** 4/1. ***Notification date:*** Continuous beginning 4/15. Students must reply within 2 weeks of notification.

CONTACT Ms. Marilyn D. Radford, Director of Student Financial Services, Lindsey Wilson College, 210 Lindsey Wilson Street, Columbia, KY 42728, 270-384-8022 or toll-free 800-264-0138. *Fax:* 270-384-8591. *E-mail:* radfordm@lindsey.edu.

LINFIELD COLLEGE

McMinnville, OR

Tuition & fees: $30,604 **Average undergraduate aid package: $21,401**

ABOUT THE INSTITUTION Independent American Baptist Churches in the USA, coed. 40 undergraduate majors. Federal methodology is used as a basis for awarding need-based institutional aid.

UNDERGRADUATE EXPENSES for 2010–11 ***Comprehensive fee:*** $39,254 includes full-time tuition ($30,300), mandatory fees ($304), and room and board ($8650). ***College room only:*** $4700. Full-time tuition and fees vary according to location. Room and board charges vary according to board plan, housing facility, and location. ***Part-time tuition:*** $945 per semester hour. Part-time tuition and fees vary according to course load and location. ***Payment plan:*** Installment.

FRESHMAN FINANCIAL AID (Fall 2010, est.) 398 applied for aid; of those 100% were deemed to have need. 100% of freshmen with need received aid; of those 39% had need fully met. ***Average percent of need met:*** 89% (excluding resources awarded to replace EFC). ***Average financial aid package:*** $23,350 (excluding resources awarded to replace EFC). 20% of all full-time freshmen had no need and received non-need-based gift aid.

UNDERGRADUATE FINANCIAL AID (Fall 2010, est.) 1,210 applied for aid; of those 100% were deemed to have need. 100% of undergraduates with need received aid; of those 33% had need fully met. ***Average percent of need met:*** 85% (excluding resources awarded to replace EFC). ***Average financial aid package:*** $21,401 (excluding resources awarded to replace EFC). 20% of all full-time undergraduates had no need and received non-need-based gift aid.

GIFT AID (NEED-BASED) ***Total amount:*** $21,775,920 (11% federal, 1% state, 83% institutional, 5% external sources). ***Receiving aid:*** Freshmen: 67% (355); all full-time undergraduates: 64% (1,059). ***Average award:*** Freshmen: $12,676; Undergraduates: $11,736. ***Scholarships, grants, and awards:*** Federal Pell, FSEOG, state, private, college/university gift aid from institutional funds.

GIFT AID (NON-NEED-BASED) ***Total amount:*** $4,449,693 (97% institutional, 3% external sources). ***Receiving aid:*** Freshmen: 48% (254). Undergraduates: 44% (726). ***Average award:*** Freshmen: $14,379. Undergraduates: $12,981. ***Scholarships, grants, and awards by category:*** *Academic interests/achievement:* 1,050 awards ($9,500,000 total): general academic interests/achievements. *Creative arts/performance:* 50 awards ($100,000 total): debating, music, theater/drama. *Special achievements/activities:* 80 awards ($100,000 total): community service, leadership. *Special characteristics:* 80 awards ($1,200,000 total): children of faculty/staff, members of minority groups. ***Tuition waivers:*** Full or partial for employees or children of employees, senior citizens.

LOANS ***Student loans:*** $8,971,839 (93% need-based, 7% non-need-based). 67% of past graduating class borrowed through all loan programs. *Average indebtedness per student:* $31,135. ***Average need-based loan:*** Freshmen: $3230. Undergraduates: $4479. ***Parent loans:*** $4,167,329 (100% non-need-based). ***Programs:*** Federal Direct (Subsidized and Unsubsidized Stafford, PLUS), Perkins, private loans.

WORK-STUDY ***Federal work-study:*** Total amount: $1,970,231; 759 jobs averaging $2201. ***State or other work-study/employment:*** Total amount: $1,389,600 (43% need-based, 57% non-need-based). 588 part-time jobs averaging $2273.

APPLYING FOR FINANCIAL AID ***Required financial aid form:*** FAFSA. ***Financial aid deadline (priority):*** 2/1. ***Notification date:*** 4/1. Students must reply by 5/1 or within 2 weeks of notification.

CONTACT Ms. Crisanne Werner, Director of Financial Aid, Linfield College, 900 Southeast Baker Street, A484, McMinnville, OR 97128-6894, 503-883-2225 or toll-free 800-640-2287. *Fax:* 503-883-2486. *E-mail:* finaid@linfield.edu.

LIPSCOMB UNIVERSITY

Nashville, TN

Tuition & fees: $23,494 **Average undergraduate aid package: $18,174**

ABOUT THE INSTITUTION Independent religious, coed. 85 undergraduate majors. Both federal and institutional methodology are used as a basis for awarding need-based institutional aid.

UNDERGRADUATE EXPENSES for 2011–12 ***Comprehensive fee:*** $32,284 includes full-time tuition ($21,896), mandatory fees ($1598), and room and board ($8790). ***College room only:*** $4940. Full-time tuition and fees vary according to class time, course load, and degree level. Room and board charges vary according to board plan and housing facility. ***Part-time tuition:*** $915 per hour. ***Part-time fees:*** $50 per credit hour. Part-time tuition and fees vary according to class time, course load, and degree level. ***Payment plans:*** Installment, deferred payment.

FRESHMAN FINANCIAL AID (Fall 2010, est.) 667 applied for aid; of those 74% were deemed to have need. 100% of freshmen with need received aid; of those 16% had need fully met. ***Average percent of need met:*** 62% (excluding resources awarded to replace EFC). ***Average financial aid package:*** $17,363 (excluding resources awarded to replace EFC). 17% of all full-time freshmen had no need and received non-need-based gift aid.

UNDERGRADUATE FINANCIAL AID (Fall 2010, est.) 2,297 applied for aid; of those 70% were deemed to have need. 100% of undergraduates with need received aid; of those 26% had need fully met. ***Average percent of need met:*** 62% (excluding resources awarded to replace EFC). ***Average financial aid package:*** $18,174 (excluding resources awarded to replace EFC). 16% of all full-time undergraduates had no need and received non-need-based gift aid.

GIFT AID (NEED-BASED) ***Total amount:*** $17,955,368 (20% federal, 24% state, 50% institutional, 6% external sources). ***Receiving aid:*** Freshmen: 39% (258); all full-time undergraduates: 33% (808). ***Average award:*** Freshmen: $6356; Undergraduates: $6804. ***Scholarships, grants, and awards:*** Federal Pell, FSEOG, state, private, college/university gift aid from institutional funds.

GIFT AID (NON-NEED-BASED) ***Total amount:*** $5,089,988 (23% state, 77% institutional). ***Receiving aid:*** Freshmen: 71% (476). Undergraduates: 53% (1,277). ***Average award:*** Freshmen: $6020. Undergraduates: $6992. ***Scholarships, grants, and awards by category:*** *Academic interests/achievement:* biological sciences, business, communication, education, engineering/technologies, English, general academic interests/achievements, home economics, mathematics, premedicine, religion/biblical studies. *Creative arts/performance:* art/fine arts, journalism/publications, music, theater/drama. *Special achievements/activities:* cheerleading/drum major, community service, general special achievements/activities, leadership, religious involvement. *Special characteristics:* adult students, children and siblings of alumni, children of educators, children of faculty/staff, children with a deceased or disabled parent, international students, members of minority groups, relatives of clergy. ***Tuition waivers:*** Full or partial for employees or children of employees.

LOANS ***Student loans:*** $11,494,963 (87% need-based, 13% non-need-based). 90% of past graduating class borrowed through all loan programs. *Average indebtedness per student:* $21,034. ***Average need-based loan:*** Freshmen: $3788. Undergraduates: $5366. ***Parent loans:*** $4,570,962 (89% need-based, 11% non-need-based). ***Programs:*** Perkins, Federal Nursing.

WORK-STUDY ***Federal work-study:*** Total amount: $406,753; jobs available.

ATHLETIC AWARDS Total amount: $3,131,164 (71% need-based, 29% non-need-based).

APPLYING FOR FINANCIAL AID ***Required financial aid form:*** FAFSA. ***Financial aid deadline (priority):*** 2/15. ***Notification date:*** Continuous beginning 2/15.

CONTACT Mrs. Karita McCaleb Waters, Director of Financial Aid, Lipscomb University, One University Park Drive, Nashville, TN 37204-3951, 615-966-1791 or toll-free 877-582-4766. *Fax:* 615-966-7640. *E-mail:* karita.waters@lipscomb.edu.

LIVINGSTONE COLLEGE

Salisbury, NC

CONTACT Mrs. Terry Jefferies, Financial Aid Director, Livingstone College, 701 West Monroe Street, Price Building, Salisbury, NC 28144-5298, 704-216-6069 or toll-free 800-835-3435. *Fax:* 704-216-6319. *E-mail:* tjefferies@livingstone.edu.

LOCK HAVEN UNIVERSITY OF PENNSYLVANIA

Lock Haven, PA

Tuition & fees (PA res): $7540 **Average undergraduate aid package: $8256**

ABOUT THE INSTITUTION State-supported, coed. 47 undergraduate majors. Federal methodology is used as a basis for awarding need-based institutional aid.

UNDERGRADUATE EXPENSES for 2011–12 ***Tuition, state resident:*** full-time $5804; part-time $242 per credit hour. ***Tuition, nonresident:*** full-time $12,510; part-time $521 per credit hour. ***Required fees:*** full-time $1736; $45.96 per credit hour or $134.80 per term. Full-time tuition and fees vary according to course load and location. Part-time tuition and fees vary according to course load and location. ***College room and board:*** $6695; ***Room only:*** $3872. Room and board charges vary according to board plan and housing facility. ***Payment plan:*** Installment.

FRESHMAN FINANCIAL AID (Fall 2010, est.) 1,150 applied for aid; of those 77% were deemed to have need. 100% of freshmen with need received aid; of those 45% had need fully met. ***Average percent of need met:*** 75% (excluding resources awarded to replace EFC). ***Average financial aid package:*** $8256 (excluding resources awarded to replace EFC). 1% of all full-time freshmen had no need and received non-need-based gift aid.

UNDERGRADUATE FINANCIAL AID (Fall 2010, est.) 4,428 applied for aid; of those 77% were deemed to have need. 100% of undergraduates with need received aid; of those 55% had need fully met. ***Average percent of need met:*** 75% (excluding resources awarded to replace EFC). ***Average financial aid package:*** $8256 (excluding resources awarded to replace EFC). 2% of all full-time undergraduates had no need and received non-need-based gift aid.

GIFT AID (NEED-BASED) ***Total amount:*** $15,087,830 (63% federal, 34% state, 1% institutional, 2% external sources). ***Receiving aid:*** Freshmen: 49% (584); all full-time undergraduates: 48% (2,251). ***Average award:*** Freshmen: $6843; Undergraduates: $6843. ***Scholarships, grants, and awards:*** Federal Pell, FSEOG, state, private, college/university gift aid from institutional funds, United Negro College Fund.

GIFT AID (NON-NEED-BASED) ***Total amount:*** $899,937 (2% state, 21% institutional, 77% external sources). ***Receiving aid:*** Freshmen: 4% (48). Undergraduates: 5% (219). ***Average award:*** Freshmen: $2025. Undergraduates: $996. ***Scholarships, grants, and awards by category:*** *Academic interests/achievement:* biological sciences, communication, education, English, foreign languages, general academic interests/achievements, health fields, international studies, library science, mathematics, physical sciences, premedicine, social sciences. *Creative arts/performance:* art/fine arts, journalism/publications, music. *Special achievements/activities:* leadership, memberships. *Special characteristics:* handicapped students, local/state students, members of minority groups, previous college experience. ***Tuition waivers:*** Full or partial for minority students, employees or children of employees, senior citizens.

LOANS ***Student loans:*** $30,501,860 (43% need-based, 57% non-need-based). 85% of past graduating class borrowed through all loan programs. *Average indebtedness per student:* $22,883. ***Average need-based loan:*** Freshmen: $3315. Undergraduates: $4094. ***Parent loans:*** $3,952,094 (100% non-need-based). ***Programs:*** Perkins, college/university.

WORK-STUDY ***Federal work-study:*** Total amount: $252,863; 250 jobs averaging $1350. ***State or other work-study/employment:*** Total amount: $1,030,945 (8% need-based, 92% non-need-based). 750 part-time jobs averaging $1616.

ATHLETIC AWARDS Total amount: $715,675 (100% non-need-based).

APPLYING FOR FINANCIAL AID ***Required financial aid form:*** FAFSA. ***Financial aid deadline:*** 3/15. ***Notification date:*** Continuous beginning 4/1. Students must reply by 5/1 or within 2 weeks of notification.

CONTACT James Theeuwes, Director of Financial Services, Lock Haven University of Pennsylvania, Russell Hall 118, Lock Haven, PA 17745-2390, 570-484-2344 or toll-free 800-332-8900 (in-state), 800-233-8978 (out-of-state). *Fax:* 570-484-2918. *E-mail:* jtheeuwe@lhup.edu.

LOGAN UNIVERSITY–COLLEGE OF CHIROPRACTIC

Chesterfield, MO

CONTACT Linda K. Haman, Director of Financial Aid, Logan University–College of Chiropractic, 1851 Schoettler Road, PO Box 1065, Chesterfield, MO 63006-1065, 636-227-2100 Ext. 141 or toll-free 800-533-9210.

LOMA LINDA UNIVERSITY

Loma Linda, CA

CONTACT Verdell Schaefer, Director of Financial Aid, Loma Linda University, 11139 Anderson Street, Loma Linda, CA 92350, 909-558-4509. *Fax:* 909-558-4879. *E-mail:* finaid@univ.llu.edu.

LONG ISLAND UNIVERSITY, BROOKLYN CAMPUS

Brooklyn, NY

Tuition & fees: N/R **Average undergraduate aid package: $16,220**

ABOUT THE INSTITUTION Independent, coed. 63 undergraduate majors. Federal methodology is used as a basis for awarding need-based institutional aid.

UNDERGRADUATE EXPENSES for 2011–12 ***Tuition:*** part-time $896 per credit. Full-time tuition and fees vary according to program. Part-time tuition and fees vary according to program. Room and board charges vary according to board plan, gender, and housing facility. ***Payment plans:*** Installment, deferred payment.

FRESHMAN FINANCIAL AID (Fall 2010, est.) 904 applied for aid; of those 96% were deemed to have need. 95% of freshmen with need received aid; of those 49% had need fully met. ***Average percent of need met:*** 42% (excluding resources awarded to replace EFC). ***Average financial aid package:*** $15,580 (excluding resources awarded to replace EFC). 11% of all full-time freshmen had no need and received non-need-based gift aid.

UNDERGRADUATE FINANCIAL AID (Fall 2010, est.) 4,042 applied for aid; of those 95% were deemed to have need. 85% of undergraduates with need received aid; of those 52% had need fully met. ***Average percent of need met:*** 45% (excluding resources awarded to replace EFC). ***Average financial aid package:*** $16,220 (excluding resources awarded to replace EFC). 5% of all full-time undergraduates had no need and received non-need-based gift aid.

GIFT AID (NEED-BASED) ***Total amount:*** $32,956,773 (48% federal, 22% state, 26% institutional, 4% external sources). ***Receiving aid:*** Freshmen: 86% (808); all full-time undergraduates: 75% (3,217). ***Average award:*** Freshmen: $12,080; Undergraduates: $11,980. ***Scholarships, grants, and awards:*** Federal Pell, FSEOG, state, private, college/university gift aid from institutional funds, Scholarships for Disadvantaged Students (Nursing and Pharmacy).

GIFT AID (NON-NEED-BASED) ***Total amount:*** $15,986,453 (99% institutional, 1% external sources). ***Receiving aid:*** Freshmen: 3% (25). Undergraduates: 2% (93). ***Scholarships, grants, and awards by category:*** *Academic interests/achievement:* communication, education, general academic interests/achievements, health fields. *Creative arts/performance:* art/fine arts, cinema/film/broadcasting, dance, music, theater/drama. *Special achievements/activities:* cheerleading/drum major, general special achievements/activities, leadership. *Special characteristics:* children and siblings of alumni, children of faculty/staff, ethnic background, first-generation college students, general special characteristics, international students. ***Tuition waivers:*** Full or partial for employees or children of employees.

LOANS ***Student loans:*** $34,106,602 (56% need-based, 44% non-need-based). ***Average need-based loan:*** Freshmen: $3800. Undergraduates: $4980. ***Parent loans:*** $15,536,451 (100% non-need-based). ***Programs:*** Federal Direct (Subsidized and Unsubsidized Stafford, PLUS), Perkins, Federal Health Professions Student Loans, alternative loans.

WORK-STUDY ***Federal work-study:*** Total amount: $1,133,275; jobs available. ***State or other work-study/employment:*** Total amount: $246,916 (100% non-need-based). Part-time jobs available.

ATHLETIC AWARDS Total amount: $5,215,839 (100% non-need-based).

APPLYING FOR FINANCIAL AID ***Required financial aid forms:*** FAFSA, state aid form. ***Financial aid deadline:*** Continuous. ***Notification date:*** Continuous beginning 4/1. Students must reply within 4 weeks of notification.

CONTACT Ms. Margaret Nelson, Associate Dean of Financial Services, Long Island University, Brooklyn Campus, 1 University Plaza, Brooklyn, NY 11201-8423, 718-488-1037 or toll-free 800-LIU-PLAN. *Fax:* 718-488-3343.

LONG ISLAND UNIVERSITY, C.W. POST CAMPUS

Brookville, NY

Tuition & fees: $30,210 **Average undergraduate aid package: $15,370**

ABOUT THE INSTITUTION Independent, coed. 85 undergraduate majors. Federal methodology is used as a basis for awarding need-based institutional aid.

UNDERGRADUATE EXPENSES for 2010–11 ***Comprehensive fee:*** $41,190 includes full-time tuition ($28,710), mandatory fees ($1500), and room and board ($10,980). ***College room only:*** $7180. Room and board charges vary according to board plan and housing facility. ***Part-time tuition:*** $896 per credit. ***Part-time fees:*** $405 per term. ***Payment plans:*** Installment, deferred payment.

FRESHMAN FINANCIAL AID (Fall 2010, est.) 779 applied for aid; of those 81% were deemed to have need. 97% of freshmen with need received aid; of those 18% had need fully met. ***Average percent of need met:*** 75% (excluding resources awarded to replace EFC). ***Average financial aid package:*** $14,045 (excluding resources awarded to replace EFC). 18% of all full-time freshmen had no need and received non-need-based gift aid.

UNDERGRADUATE FINANCIAL AID (Fall 2010, est.) 3,374 applied for aid; of those 84% were deemed to have need. 97% of undergraduates with need received aid; of those 15% had need fully met. ***Average percent of need met:*** 75% (excluding resources awarded to replace EFC). ***Average financial aid package:*** $15,370 (excluding resources awarded to replace EFC). 15% of all full-time undergraduates had no need and received non-need-based gift aid.

GIFT AID (NEED-BASED) ***Total amount:*** $19,218,932 (31% federal, 24% state, 45% institutional). ***Receiving aid:*** Freshmen: 54% (482); all full-time undergraduates: 54% (2,164). ***Average award:*** Freshmen: $6780; Undergraduates: $6150. ***Scholarships, grants, and awards:*** Federal Pell, FSEOG, state, private, college/university gift aid from institutional funds.

GIFT AID (NON-NEED-BASED) ***Total amount:*** $20,932,072 (98% institutional, 2% external sources). ***Receiving aid:*** Freshmen: 44% (390). Undergraduates: 41% (1,650). ***Average award:*** Freshmen: $4526. Undergraduates: $7370. ***Scholarships, grants, and awards by category:*** *Academic interests/achievement:* biological sciences, business, computer science, education, general academic interests/achievements, health fields, mathematics. *Creative arts/performance:* art/fine arts, cinema/film/broadcasting, dance, journalism/publications, music, theater/drama. *Special achievements/activities:* leadership. *Special characteristics:* adult students, children and siblings of alumni, children of faculty/staff, international students, siblings of current students. ***Tuition waivers:*** Full or partial for employees or children of employees.

LOANS ***Student loans:*** $23,617,464 (58% need-based, 42% non-need-based). ***Average need-based loan:*** Freshmen: $3460. Undergraduates: $5670. ***Parent loans:*** $17,079,453 (100% non-need-based). ***Programs:*** Federal Direct (Subsidized and Unsubsidized Stafford, PLUS), Perkins, college/university.

WORK-STUDY ***Federal work-study:*** Total amount: $1,956,055; jobs available. ***State or other work-study/employment:*** Total amount: $46,268 (100% need-based). Part-time jobs available.

ATHLETIC AWARDS Total amount: $4,692,045 (100% non-need-based).

APPLYING FOR FINANCIAL AID ***Required financial aid forms:*** FAFSA, state aid form. ***Financial aid deadline:*** 3/1. ***Notification date:*** Continuous beginning 3/1. Students must reply by 5/1 or within 2 weeks of notification.

CONTACT Ms. Karen Urdahl, Office of Financial Assistance, Long Island University, C.W. Post Campus, 720 Northern Boulevard, Brookville, NY 11548-1300, 516-299-2338 or toll-free 800-LIU-PLAN. *Fax:* 516-299-3833. *E-mail:* finaid@cwpost.liu.edu.

LONGWOOD UNIVERSITY

Farmville, VA

Tuition & fees (VA res): $9855 **Average undergraduate aid package: $11,038**

ABOUT THE INSTITUTION State-supported, coed. 75 undergraduate majors. Federal methodology is used as a basis for awarding need-based institutional aid.

UNDERGRADUATE EXPENSES for 2010–11 ***Tuition, state resident:*** full-time $5370; part-time $179 per credit hour. ***Tuition, nonresident:*** full-time $15,600; part-time $520 per credit hour. ***Required fees:*** full-time $4485. Full-time tuition and fees vary according to course load. Part-time tuition and fees vary according to course load. ***College room and board:*** $8114; ***Room only:*** $5260. Room and board charges vary according to board plan, housing facility, and location. ***Payment plan:*** Installment.

FRESHMAN FINANCIAL AID (Fall 2009) 774 applied for aid; of those 63% were deemed to have need. 99% of freshmen with need received aid; of those 44% had need fully met. ***Average percent of need met:*** 80% (excluding resources awarded to replace EFC). ***Average financial aid package:*** $11,371 (excluding resources awarded to replace EFC). 4% of all full-time freshmen had no need and received non-need-based gift aid.

UNDERGRADUATE FINANCIAL AID (Fall 2009) 2,776 applied for aid; of those 69% were deemed to have need. 99% of undergraduates with need received aid; of those 50% had need fully met. ***Average percent of need met:*** 82% (excluding resources awarded to replace EFC). ***Average financial aid package:*** $11,038 (excluding resources awarded to replace EFC). 6% of all full-time undergraduates had no need and received non-need-based gift aid.

GIFT AID (NEED-BASED) ***Total amount:*** $10,229,445 (36% federal, 38% state, 21% institutional, 5% external sources). ***Receiving aid:*** Freshmen: 47% (467); all full-time undergraduates: 43% (1,727). ***Average award:*** Freshmen: $6157; Undergraduates: $5768. ***Scholarships, grants, and awards:*** Federal Pell, FSEOG, state, private, college/university gift aid from institutional funds.

GIFT AID (NON-NEED-BASED) ***Total amount:*** $1,696,173 (22% federal, 6% state, 52% institutional, 20% external sources). ***Receiving aid:*** Freshmen: 1% (13). Undergraduates: 2% (63). ***Average award:*** Freshmen: $2445. Undergraduates: $3461. ***Scholarships, grants, and awards by category:*** *Academic interests/achievement:* biological sciences, business, computer science, education, English, general academic interests/achievements, humanities, international studies, mathematics, military science, social sciences. *Creative arts/performance:* art/fine arts, music, theater/drama. *Special achievements/activities:* community service, leadership, memberships. *Special characteristics:* children and siblings of alumni, general special characteristics, local/state students. ***Tuition waivers:*** Full or partial for senior citizens.

LOANS ***Student loans:*** $16,850,063 (54% need-based, 46% non-need-based). 61% of past graduating class borrowed through all loan programs. *Average indebtedness per student:* $23,379. ***Average need-based loan:*** Freshmen: $5704. Undergraduates: $6156. ***Parent loans:*** $7,298,048 (16% need-based, 84% non-need-based). ***Programs:*** Federal Direct (Subsidized and Unsubsidized Stafford, PLUS), Perkins, private loans.

WORK-STUDY ***Federal work-study:*** Total amount: $402,370; 310 jobs averaging $1298. ***State or other work-study/employment:*** 450 part-time jobs averaging $1217.

ATHLETIC AWARDS Total amount: $1,938,243 (37% need-based, 63% non-need-based).

APPLYING FOR FINANCIAL AID ***Required financial aid form:*** FAFSA. ***Financial aid deadline (priority):*** 3/1. ***Notification date:*** Continuous beginning 4/1. Students must reply within 4 weeks of notification.

CONTACT Caroline Gibbs, Financial Aid Counselor, Longwood University, 201 High Street, Farmville, VA 23909, 434-395-2949 or toll-free 800-281-4677. *Fax:* 434-395-2829. *E-mail:* gibbsca@longwood.edu.

LORAS COLLEGE

Dubuque, IA

Tuition & fees: $26,088 **Average undergraduate aid package: $17,644**

ABOUT THE INSTITUTION Independent Roman Catholic, coed. 52 undergraduate majors. Federal methodology is used as a basis for awarding need-based institutional aid.

UNDERGRADUATE EXPENSES for 2011–12 ***Comprehensive fee:*** $33,394 includes full-time tuition ($24,910), mandatory fees ($1178), and room and board ($7306). ***College room only:*** $3695. Full-time tuition and fees vary according to course load and degree level. Room and board charges vary according to board plan and housing facility. ***Part-time tuition:*** $495 per credit hour. ***Part-time fees:*** $25 per credit hour. ***Payment plan:*** Installment.

FRESHMAN FINANCIAL AID (Fall 2010, est.) 390 applied for aid; of those 89% were deemed to have need. 100% of freshmen with need received aid; of those 43% had need fully met. ***Average percent of need met:*** 84% (excluding resources awarded to replace EFC). ***Average financial aid package:*** $20,965 (excluding resources awarded to replace EFC). 16% of all full-time freshmen had no need and received non-need-based gift aid.

UNDERGRADUATE FINANCIAL AID (Fall 2010, est.) 1,300 applied for aid; of those 90% were deemed to have need. 100% of undergraduates with need received aid; of those 40% had need fully met. ***Average percent of need met:*** 87% (excluding resources awarded to replace EFC). ***Average financial aid package:*** $17,644 (excluding resources awarded to replace EFC). 24% of all full-time undergraduates had no need and received non-need-based gift aid.

GIFT AID (NEED-BASED) ***Total amount:*** $15,347,473 (12% federal, 8% state, 80% institutional). ***Receiving aid:*** Freshmen: 63% (260); all full-time undergraduates: 68% (1,041). ***Average award:*** Freshmen: $14,119; Undergraduates: $11,754. ***Scholarships, grants, and awards:*** Federal Pell, FSEOG, state, private, college/university gift aid from institutional funds.

GIFT AID (NON-NEED-BASED) ***Total amount:*** $6,977,775 (1% federal, 1% state, 94% institutional, 4% external sources). ***Receiving aid:*** Freshmen: 84% (347). Undergraduates: 76% (1,170). ***Average award:*** Freshmen: $12,335. Undergraduates: $9027. ***Scholarships, grants, and awards by category:*** *Academic interests/achievement:* 1,260 awards ($4,698,000 total): engineering/technologies, general academic interests/achievements, physical sciences. *Creative arts/performance:* 85 awards ($92,550 total): music. *Special characteristics:* 481 awards ($481,000 total): children and siblings of alumni, siblings of current students. ***Tuition waivers:*** Full or partial for employees or children of employees.

LOANS ***Student loans:*** $9,584,911 (41% need-based, 59% non-need-based). 92% of past graduating class borrowed through all loan programs. *Average indebtedness per student:* $30,790. ***Average need-based loan:*** Freshmen: $4508. Undergraduates: $3754. ***Parent loans:*** $1,710,506 (100% non-need-based). ***Programs:*** Federal Direct (Subsidized and Unsubsidized Stafford, PLUS), Perkins, college/university.

WORK-STUDY ***Federal work-study:*** Total amount: $231,516; 235 jobs averaging $1567. ***State or other work-study/employment:*** Total amount: $478,762 (100% non-need-based). 150 part-time jobs averaging $1320.

APPLYING FOR FINANCIAL AID ***Required financial aid form:*** FAFSA. ***Financial aid deadline (priority):*** 4/15. ***Notification date:*** Continuous beginning 3/1.

CONTACT Ms. Julie A. Dunn, Director of Financial Planning, Loras College, 1450 Alta Vista Street, Dubuque, IA 52004-0178, 563-588-7136 or toll-free 800-245-6727. *Fax:* 563-588-7119. *E-mail:* julie.dunn@loras.edu.

LOUISIANA COLLEGE

Pineville, LA

Tuition & fees: $12,980 **Average undergraduate aid package: $7640**

ABOUT THE INSTITUTION Independent Southern Baptist, coed. 56 undergraduate majors. Federal methodology is used as a basis for awarding need-based institutional aid.

UNDERGRADUATE EXPENSES for 2010–11 ***Comprehensive fee:*** $17,428 includes full-time tuition ($11,550), mandatory fees ($1430), and room and board ($4448). Full-time tuition and fees vary according to program. Room and board charges vary according to board plan and housing facility. ***Part-time tuition:*** $385 per hour. Part-time tuition and fees vary according to program. ***Payment plan:*** Installment.

FRESHMAN FINANCIAL AID (Fall 2010, est.) 268 applied for aid; of those 78% were deemed to have need. 100% of freshmen with need received aid; of those 29% had need fully met. ***Average percent of need met:*** 36% (excluding resources awarded to replace EFC). ***Average financial aid package:*** $7210 (excluding resources awarded to replace EFC).

UNDERGRADUATE FINANCIAL AID (Fall 2010, est.) 1,123 applied for aid; of those 80% were deemed to have need. 100% of undergraduates with need received aid; of those 32% had need fully met. ***Average percent of need met:*** 39% (excluding resources awarded to replace EFC). ***Average financial aid package:*** $7640 (excluding resources awarded to replace EFC).

GIFT AID (NEED-BASED) ***Total amount:*** $8,125,292 (38% federal, 17% state, 41% institutional, 4% external sources). ***Receiving aid:*** Freshmen: 72% (208); all full-time undergraduates: 77% (895). ***Average award:*** Freshmen: $2650; Undergraduates: $2900. ***Scholarships, grants, and awards:*** Federal Pell, FSEOG, state, private, college/university gift aid from institutional funds, Leveraging Educational Assistance Program (LEAP).

GIFT AID (NON-NEED-BASED) ***Total amount:*** $1,818,250 (8% federal, 20% state, 61% institutional, 11% external sources). ***Scholarships, grants, and awards by category:*** *Academic interests/achievement:* business, general academic interests/achievements, health fields, religion/biblical studies. *Creative arts/performance:* music, performing arts, theater/drama. *Special achievements/activities:* leadership. *Special characteristics:* children of faculty/staff. ***Tuition waivers:*** Full or partial for employees or children of employees.

LOANS ***Student loans:*** $5,710,136 (95% need-based, 5% non-need-based). 47% of past graduating class borrowed through all loan programs. ***Average need-based loan:*** Freshmen: $2732. Undergraduates: $4068. ***Parent loans:*** $316,535 (91% need-based, 9% non-need-based). ***Programs:*** Federal Direct (Subsidized and Unsubsidized Stafford, PLUS), college/university.

WORK-STUDY ***Federal work-study:*** Total amount: $99,644; jobs available.

APPLYING FOR FINANCIAL AID ***Required financial aid forms:*** FAFSA, institution's own form. ***Financial aid deadline (priority):*** 3/31. ***Notification date:*** Continuous. Students must reply by 5/1 or within 2 weeks of notification.

CONTACT Shelley Jinks, Director of Financial Aid, Louisiana College, 1140 College Drive, Pineville, LA 71359-0001, 318-487-7386 or toll-free 800-487-1906. *Fax:* 318-487-7449. *E-mail:* jinks@lacollege.edu.

LOUISIANA STATE UNIVERSITY AND AGRICULTURAL AND MECHANICAL COLLEGE

Baton Rouge, LA

Tuition & fees (LA res): $5764 **Average undergraduate aid package: $11,241**

ABOUT THE INSTITUTION State-supported, coed. 72 undergraduate majors. Federal methodology is used as a basis for awarding need-based institutional aid.

UNDERGRADUATE EXPENSES for 2010–11 ***Tuition, state resident:*** full-time $3968. ***Tuition, nonresident:*** full-time $14,753. ***Required fees:*** full-time $1796. Part-time tuition and fees vary according to course load. ***College room and board:*** $8210; ***Room only:*** $4890. Room and board charges vary according to board plan and housing facility. ***Payment plan:*** Deferred payment.

FRESHMAN FINANCIAL AID (Fall 2009) 3,127 applied for aid; of those 60% were deemed to have need. 100% of freshmen with need received aid; of those 28% had need fully met. ***Average percent of need met:*** 76% (excluding resources awarded to replace EFC). ***Average financial aid package:*** $11,686 (excluding resources awarded to replace EFC). 28% of all full-time freshmen had no need and received non-need-based gift aid.

UNDERGRADUATE FINANCIAL AID (Fall 2009) 10,778 applied for aid; of those 70% were deemed to have need. 100% of undergraduates with need received aid; of those 19% had need fully met. ***Average percent of need met:*** 68% (excluding resources awarded to replace EFC). ***Average financial aid package:*** $11,241 (excluding resources awarded to replace EFC). 16% of all full-time undergraduates had no need and received non-need-based gift aid.

GIFT AID (NEED-BASED) ***Total amount:*** $53,292,050 (39% federal, 31% state, 28% institutional, 2% external sources). ***Receiving aid:*** Freshmen: 38% (1,799); all full-time undergraduates: 31% (6,568). ***Average award:*** Freshmen: $9135; Undergraduates: $8378. ***Scholarships, grants, and awards:*** Federal Pell, FSEOG, state, private, college/university gift aid from institutional funds.

GIFT AID (NON-NEED-BASED) ***Total amount:*** $53,066,659 (3% federal, 60% state, 33% institutional, 4% external sources). ***Receiving aid:*** Freshmen: 2% (98). Undergraduates: 1% (238). ***Average award:*** Freshmen: $4427. Undergraduates: $4875. ***Scholarships, grants, and awards by category:*** *Academic interests/achievement:* 1,050 awards ($1,110,800 total): agriculture, architecture, biological sciences, business, communication, computer science, education, engineering/technologies, English, foreign languages, general academic interests/achievements, home economics, humanities, mathematics, military science, physical sciences, premedicine. *Creative arts/performance:* 199 awards ($1,016,900 total): applied art and design, art/fine arts, journalism/publications, music, performing arts, theater/drama. *Special achievements/activities:* leadership. *Special characteristics:* 509 awards ($3,157,600 total): children and siblings of alumni, children with a deceased or disabled parent, general special characteristics. ***Tuition waivers:*** Full or partial for employees or children of employees.

LOANS ***Student loans:*** $47,478,078 (66% need-based, 34% non-need-based). 41% of past graduating class borrowed through all loan programs. *Average indebtedness per student:* $19,242. ***Average need-based loan:*** Freshmen: $3438. Undergraduates: $4373. ***Parent loans:*** $8,215,271 (26% need-based, 74% non-need-based). ***Programs:*** Perkins, college/university.

WORK-STUDY ***Federal work-study:*** Total amount: $1,705,379; 921 jobs averaging $1400. ***State or other work-study/employment:*** Total amount: $14,127,225 (21% need-based, 79% non-need-based). 4,387 part-time jobs averaging $2500.

ATHLETIC AWARDS Total amount: $7,426,079 (37% need-based, 63% non-need-based).

APPLYING FOR FINANCIAL AID ***Required financial aid form:*** FAFSA. ***Financial aid deadline (priority):*** 7/1. ***Notification date:*** 4/1. Students must reply by 5/1 or within 3 weeks of notification.

CONTACT Ms. Mary G. Parker, Executive Director of Undergraduate Admissions and Student Aid, Louisiana State University and Agricultural and Mechanical College, LSU 1146 Pleasant Hall, Baton Rouge, LA 70803-3103, 225-578-3113. *Fax:* 225-578-6300. *E-mail:* financialaid@lsu.edu.

LOUISIANA STATE UNIVERSITY HEALTH SCIENCES CENTER

New Orleans, LA

CONTACT Mr. Patrick Gorman, Director of Financial Aid, Louisiana State University Health Sciences Center, 433 Bolivar Street, New Orleans, LA 70112, 504-568-4821. *Fax:* 504-599-1390.

LOUISIANA STATE UNIVERSITY IN SHREVEPORT

Shreveport, LA

CONTACT Office of Student Financial Aid, Louisiana State University in Shreveport, One University Place, Shreveport, LA 71115-2399, 318-797-5363 or toll-free 800-229-5957 (in-state). *Fax:* 318-797-5366.

LOUISIANA TECH UNIVERSITY

Ruston, LA

Tuition & fees (LA res): $5643 **Average undergraduate aid package: $9825**

ABOUT THE INSTITUTION State-supported, coed. 79 undergraduate majors. Institutional methodology is used as a basis for awarding need-based institutional aid.

UNDERGRADUATE EXPENSES for 2010–11 ***Tuition, state resident:*** full-time $5643. ***Tuition, nonresident:*** full-time $11,580. Full-time tuition and fees vary according to course load, location, and program. Part-time tuition and fees vary according to course load, location, and program. ***College room and board:*** $5160; ***Room only:*** $2580. Room and board charges vary according to board plan and housing facility. ***Payment plans:*** Installment, deferred payment.

FRESHMAN FINANCIAL AID (Fall 2010, est.) 968 applied for aid; of those 68% were deemed to have need. 99% of freshmen with need received aid; of those 25% had need fully met. ***Average percent of need met:*** 71% (excluding resources awarded to replace EFC). ***Average financial aid package:*** $9451 (excluding resources awarded to replace EFC). 31% of all full-time freshmen had no need and received non-need-based gift aid.

UNDERGRADUATE FINANCIAL AID (Fall 2010, est.) 5,069 applied for aid; of those 70% were deemed to have need. 96% of undergraduates with need received aid; of those 27% had need fully met. ***Average percent of need met:*** 68% (excluding resources awarded to replace EFC). ***Average financial aid package:*** $9825 (excluding resources awarded to replace EFC). 19% of all full-time undergraduates had no need and received non-need-based gift aid.

GIFT AID (NEED-BASED) ***Total amount:*** $20,745,490 (49% federal, 35% state, 13% institutional, 3% external sources). ***Receiving aid:*** Freshmen: 40% (615); all full-time undergraduates: 48% (3,053). ***Average award:*** Freshmen: $7399; Undergraduates: $7573. ***Scholarships, grants, and awards:*** Federal Pell, FSEOG, state, private, college/university gift aid from institutional funds.

GIFT AID (NON-NEED-BASED) ***Total amount:*** $10,285,969 (2% federal, 56% state, 34% institutional, 8% external sources). ***Receiving aid:*** Freshmen: 6% (88). Undergraduates: 7% (451). ***Average award:*** Freshmen: $1648. Undergraduates: $2279. ***Scholarships, grants, and awards by category:*** *Academic interests/achievement:* agriculture, architecture, biological sciences, business, computer science, education, engineering/technologies, English, foreign languages, general academic interests/achievements, health fields, home economics, international studies, mathematics, military science, physical sciences, social sciences. *Creative arts/performance:* applied art and design, art/fine arts, creative writing, debating, general creative arts/performance, journalism/publications, music, performing arts, theater/drama. *Special achievements/activities:* cheerleading/drum major, junior miss. *Special characteristics:* children and siblings of alumni, children of faculty/staff, children of public servants, handicapped students, international students, members of minority groups, out-of-state students, spouses of deceased or disabled public servants, veterans, veterans' children. ***Tuition waivers:*** Full or partial for children of alumni, employees or children of employees, senior citizens.

LOANS ***Student loans:*** $26,775,115 (62% need-based, 38% non-need-based). 49% of past graduating class borrowed through all loan programs. *Average indebtedness per student:* $14,039. ***Average need-based loan:*** Freshmen: $3005. Undergraduates: $3742. ***Parent loans:*** $5,723,510 (40% need-based, 60% non-need-based). ***Programs:*** Federal Direct (Subsidized and Unsubsidized Stafford, PLUS), Perkins.

WORK-STUDY ***Federal work-study:*** Total amount: $578,754; 265 jobs averaging $2183. ***State or other work-study/employment:*** Total amount: $1,160,864 (100% non-need-based). 956 part-time jobs averaging $1214.

ATHLETIC AWARDS Total amount: $3,146,863 (47% need-based, 53% non-need-based).

APPLYING FOR FINANCIAL AID ***Required financial aid forms:*** FAFSA, institution's own form. ***Financial aid deadline (priority):*** 4/15. ***Notification date:*** Continuous beginning 4/15. Students must reply within 3 weeks of notification.

CONTACT Office of Financial Aid, Louisiana Tech University, PO Box 7925, Ruston, LA 71272, 318-257-2641 or toll-free 800-528-3241. *Fax:* 318-257-2628. *E-mail:* techaid@latech.edu.

LOURDES COLLEGE

Sylvania, OH

Tuition & fees: $15,870 | **Average undergraduate aid package: $8785**

ABOUT THE INSTITUTION Independent Roman Catholic, coed. 26 undergraduate majors. Both federal and institutional methodology are used as a basis for awarding need-based institutional aid.

UNDERGRADUATE EXPENSES for 2010–11 ***Comprehensive fee:*** $23,670 includes full-time tuition ($13,980), mandatory fees ($1890), and room and board ($7800). ***College room only:*** $4000. Full-time tuition and fees vary according to course load and location. Room and board charges vary according to board plan and housing facility. ***Part-time tuition:*** $466 per credit hour. ***Part-time fees:*** $63 per credit hour. Part-time tuition and fees vary according to course load and location. ***Payment plans:*** Installment, deferred payment.

FRESHMAN FINANCIAL AID (Fall 2010, est.) 148 applied for aid; of those 86% were deemed to have need. 100% of freshmen with need received aid. ***Average financial aid package:*** $11,526 (excluding resources awarded to replace EFC). 1% of all full-time freshmen had no need and received non-need-based gift aid.

UNDERGRADUATE FINANCIAL AID (Fall 2010, est.) 1,083 applied for aid; of those 90% were deemed to have need. 100% of undergraduates with need received aid. ***Average financial aid package:*** $8785 (excluding resources awarded to replace EFC). 1% of all full-time undergraduates had no need and received non-need-based gift aid.

GIFT AID (NEED-BASED) ***Total amount:*** $7,969,437 (64% federal, 16% state, 18% institutional, 2% external sources). ***Receiving aid:*** Freshmen: 70% (104); all full-time undergraduates: 68% (780). ***Average award:*** Freshmen: $6001; Undergraduates: $6208. ***Scholarships, grants, and awards:*** Federal Pell, FSEOG, state, private, college/university gift aid from institutional funds.

GIFT AID (NON-NEED-BASED) ***Receiving aid:*** Freshmen: 59% (88). Undergraduates: 36% (417). ***Average award:*** Freshmen: $1392. Undergraduates: $1392. ***Scholarships, grants, and awards by category:*** *Academic interests/achievement:* 407 awards ($999,432 total): general academic interests/achievements. *Creative arts/performance:* art/fine arts. *Special achievements/activities:* general special achievements/activities. *Special characteristics:* adult students, ethnic background, local/state students, members of minority groups, out-of-state students, previous college experience, religious affiliation. ***Tuition waivers:*** Full or partial for employees or children of employees, senior citizens.

LOANS ***Student loans:*** $14,234,836 (100% need-based). ***Average need-based loan:*** Freshmen: $3345. Undergraduates: $3940. ***Parent loans:*** $1,348,268 (100% need-based). ***Programs:*** Federal Direct (Subsidized and Unsubsidized Stafford, PLUS), Perkins, state, college/university, alternative loans.

WORK-STUDY ***Federal work-study:*** Total amount: $225,000; 102 jobs averaging $2206. ***State or other work-study/employment:*** Total amount: $100,000 (100% need-based). 100 part-time jobs averaging $1000.

ATHLETIC AWARDS Total amount: $128,500 (100% need-based).

APPLYING FOR FINANCIAL AID ***Required financial aid form:*** FAFSA. ***Financial aid deadline (priority):*** 3/1. ***Notification date:*** Continuous beginning 3/1. Students must reply within 4 weeks of notification.

CONTACT Denise McClusky, Director of Financial Aid, Lourdes College, 6832 Convent Boulevard, Sylvania, OH 43560-2898, 419-824-3732 or toll-free 800-878-3210 Ext. 1299. *Fax:* 419-517-8866. *E-mail:* finaid@lourdes.edu.

LOYOLA MARYMOUNT UNIVERSITY

Los Angeles, CA

Tuition & fees: $36,404 | **Average undergraduate aid package: $25,385**

ABOUT THE INSTITUTION Independent Roman Catholic, coed. 44 undergraduate majors. Both federal and institutional methodology are used as a basis for awarding need-based institutional aid.

UNDERGRADUATE EXPENSES for 2010–11 ***One-time required fee:*** $218. ***Comprehensive fee:*** $50,334 includes full-time tuition ($35,740), mandatory fees ($664), and room and board ($13,930). ***College room only:*** $9530. Full-time tuition and fees vary according to reciprocity agreements. Room and board charges vary according to board plan and housing facility. ***Part-time tuition:*** $1490 per credit hour. ***Part-time fees:*** $5 per credit hour; $60 per term. Part-time tuition and fees vary according to course load. ***Payment plans:*** Installment, deferred payment.

FRESHMAN FINANCIAL AID (Fall 2009) 1,030 applied for aid; of those 74% were deemed to have need. 99% of freshmen with need received aid; of those 18% had need fully met. ***Average percent of need met:*** 67% (excluding resources awarded to replace EFC). ***Average financial aid package:*** $24,069 (excluding resources awarded to replace EFC). 25% of all full-time freshmen had no need and received non-need-based gift aid.

UNDERGRADUATE FINANCIAL AID (Fall 2009) 3,995 applied for aid; of those 78% were deemed to have need. 98% of undergraduates with need received aid; of those 15% had need fully met. ***Average percent of need met:*** 66% (excluding resources awarded to replace EFC). ***Average financial aid package:*** $25,385 (excluding resources awarded to replace EFC). 12% of all full-time undergraduates had no need and received non-need-based gift aid.

GIFT AID (NEED-BASED) ***Total amount:*** $51,032,657 (13% federal, 14% state, 72% institutional, 1% external sources). ***Receiving aid:*** Freshmen: 51% (711); all full-time undergraduates: 50% (2,780). ***Average award:*** Freshmen: $18,469; Undergraduates: $18,301. ***Scholarships, grants, and awards:*** Federal Pell, FSEOG, state, private, college/university gift aid from institutional funds.

GIFT AID (NON-NEED-BASED) ***Total amount:*** $9,193,796 (91% institutional, 9% external sources). ***Receiving aid:*** Freshmen: 7% (103). Undergraduates: 5% (249). ***Average award:*** Freshmen: $8116. Undergraduates: $10,310. ***Tuition waivers:*** Full or partial for employees or children of employees.

LOANS ***Student loans:*** $28,201,341 (74% need-based, 26% non-need-based). 60% of past graduating class borrowed through all loan programs. *Average indebtedness per student:* $29,906. ***Average need-based loan:*** Freshmen: $4623. Undergraduates: $5494. ***Parent loans:*** $17,541,860 (39% need-based, 61% non-need-based). ***Programs:*** Federal Direct (Subsidized and Unsubsidized Stafford, PLUS), Perkins, college/university.

WORK-STUDY ***Federal work-study:*** Total amount: $3,326,760; jobs available. ***State or other work-study/employment:*** Total amount: $5,020,786 (37% need-based, 63% non-need-based). Part-time jobs available.

ATHLETIC AWARDS Total amount: $7,107,072 (45% need-based, 55% non-need-based).

APPLYING FOR FINANCIAL AID ***Required financial aid form:*** FAFSA. ***Financial aid deadline:*** 7/30 (priority: 2/15). ***Notification date:*** Continuous beginning 4/1. Students must reply by 5/1 or within 4 weeks of notification.

CONTACT Ms. Valerie K. Miller, Interim Director of Financial Aid, Loyola Marymount University, One LMU Drive, Los Angeles, CA 90045-8350, 310-338-2753 or toll-free 800-LMU-INFO. *E-mail:* finaid@lmu.edu.

LOYOLA UNIVERSITY CHICAGO

Chicago, IL

Tuition & fees: $33,294 | **Average undergraduate aid package: $28,864**

ABOUT THE INSTITUTION Independent Roman Catholic (Jesuit), coed. 77 undergraduate majors. Federal methodology is used as a basis for awarding need-based institutional aid.

UNDERGRADUATE EXPENSES for 2011–12 ***Comprehensive fee:*** $44,864 includes full-time tuition ($32,200), mandatory fees ($1094), and room and board ($11,570). ***College room only:*** $7590. Full-time tuition and fees vary according to location and program. Room and board charges vary according to board plan, housing facility, and location. ***Part-time tuition:*** $655 per credit. ***Part-time fees:*** $145 per term. Part-time tuition and fees vary according to course load. ***Payment plans:*** Installment, deferred payment.

FRESHMAN FINANCIAL AID (Fall 2010, est.) 1,810 applied for aid; of those 86% were deemed to have need. 100% of freshmen with need received aid; of those 13% had need fully met. ***Average percent of need met:*** 83% (excluding resources awarded to replace EFC). ***Average financial aid package:*** $28,805 (excluding resources awarded to replace EFC). 21% of all full-time freshmen had no need and received non-need-based gift aid.

UNDERGRADUATE FINANCIAL AID (Fall 2010, est.) 7,296 applied for aid; of those 90% were deemed to have need. 100% of undergraduates with need received aid; of those 10% had need fully met. ***Average percent of need met:*** 81% (excluding resources awarded to replace EFC). ***Average financial aid package:*** $28,864 (excluding resources awarded to replace EFC). 17% of all full-time undergraduates had no need and received non-need-based gift aid.

GIFT AID (NEED-BASED) ***Total amount:*** $112,909,644 (17% federal, 10% state, 71% institutional, 2% external sources). ***Receiving aid:*** Freshmen: 74% (1,527); all full-time undergraduates: 72% (6,389). ***Average award:*** Freshmen: $18,754; Undergraduates: $17,598. ***Scholarships, grants, and awards:*** Federal Pell, FSEOG, state, private, college/university gift aid from institutional funds.

GIFT AID (NON-NEED-BASED) ***Total amount:*** $15,999,341 (10% federal, 86% institutional, 4% external sources). ***Receiving aid:*** Freshmen: 7% (143). Undergraduates: 5% (411). ***Average award:*** Freshmen: $9923. Undergraduates: $8203. ***Scholarships, grants, and awards by category:*** *Academic interests/achievement:* 4,486 awards ($38,208,417 total): general academic interests/achievements. *Creative arts/performance:* 35 awards ($113,250 total): art/fine arts, debating, journalism/publications, music, theater/drama. *Special achievements/activities:* 446 awards ($2,149,729 total): community service, general special achievements/activities, leadership, memberships. *Special characteristics:* 1,386 awards ($3,654,501 total): adult students, general special characteristics, religious affiliation. ***Tuition waivers:*** Full or partial for employees or children of employees, senior citizens.

LOANS ***Student loans:*** $65,921,196 (80% need-based, 20% non-need-based). 72% of past graduating class borrowed through all loan programs. ***Average need-based loan:*** Freshmen: $4049. Undergraduates: $5049. ***Parent loans:*** $24,760,321 (46% need-based, 54% non-need-based). ***Programs:*** Federal Direct (Subsidized and Unsubsidized Stafford, PLUS), Perkins, Federal Nursing.

WORK-STUDY ***Federal work-study:*** Total amount: $12,025,606; 5,284 jobs averaging $2188.

ATHLETIC AWARDS Total amount: $3,891,366 (45% need-based, 55% non-need-based).

APPLYING FOR FINANCIAL AID ***Required financial aid form:*** FAFSA. ***Financial aid deadline:*** Continuous. ***Notification date:*** Continuous beginning 2/15. Students must reply within 3 weeks of notification.

CONTACT Mr. Eric Weems, Director of Financial Aid, Loyola University Chicago, 6525 North Sheridan Road, Chicago, IL 60626, 773-508-3155 or toll-free 800-262-2373. *Fax:* 773-508-3177. *E-mail:* lufinaid@luc.edu.

LOYOLA UNIVERSITY MARYLAND

Baltimore, MD

Tuition & fees: $39,350 **Average undergraduate aid package: $25,900**

ABOUT THE INSTITUTION Independent Roman Catholic (Jesuit), coed. 32 undergraduate majors. Institutional methodology is used as a basis for awarding need-based institutional aid.

UNDERGRADUATE EXPENSES for 2010–11 ***One-time required fee:*** $165. ***Comprehensive fee:*** $51,080 includes full-time tuition ($37,950), mandatory fees ($1400), and room and board ($11,730). ***College room only:*** $9630. Full-time tuition and fees vary according to course load. Room and board charges vary according to board plan, housing facility, and location. Part-time tuition and fees vary according to course load. ***Payment plan:*** Installment.

FRESHMAN FINANCIAL AID (Fall 2009) 724 applied for aid; of those 77% were deemed to have need. 100% of freshmen with need received aid; of those 100% had need fully met. ***Average percent of need met:*** 100% (excluding resources awarded to replace EFC). ***Average financial aid package:*** $25,500 (excluding resources awarded to replace EFC). 10% of all full-time freshmen had no need and received non-need-based gift aid.

UNDERGRADUATE FINANCIAL AID (Fall 2009) 2,363 applied for aid; of those 83% were deemed to have need. 100% of undergraduates with need received aid; of those 98% had need fully met. ***Average percent of need met:*** 97% (excluding resources awarded to replace EFC). ***Average financial aid package:*** $25,900 (excluding resources awarded to replace EFC). 11% of all full-time undergraduates had no need and received non-need-based gift aid.

GIFT AID (NEED-BASED) ***Total amount:*** $38,066,028 (7% federal, 2% state, 89% institutional, 2% external sources). ***Receiving aid:*** Freshmen: 51% (492); all full-time undergraduates: 46% (1,724). ***Average award:*** Freshmen: $17,890; Undergraduates: $17,910. ***Scholarships, grants, and awards:*** Federal Pell, FSEOG, state, private, college/university gift aid from institutional funds.

GIFT AID (NON-NEED-BASED) ***Total amount:*** $7,577,460 (18% federal, 1% state, 75% institutional, 6% external sources). ***Receiving aid:*** Freshmen: 10% (96). Undergraduates: 11% (423). ***Average award:*** Freshmen: $12,390. Undergraduates: $13,980. ***Scholarships, grants, and awards by category:*** *Academic interests/achievement:* 761 awards ($10,402,430 total): general academic interests/achievements. ***Tuition waivers:*** Full or partial for employees or children of employees.

LOANS ***Student loans:*** $17,960,296 (47% need-based, 53% non-need-based). 73% of past graduating class borrowed through all loan programs. *Average indebtedness per student:* $26,740. ***Average need-based loan:*** Freshmen: $5550. Undergraduates: $5930. ***Parent loans:*** $13,994,489 (100% non-need-based). ***Programs:*** Federal Direct (Subsidized and Unsubsidized Stafford, PLUS), Perkins, college/university.

WORK-STUDY ***Federal work-study:*** Total amount: $998,916; 679 jobs averaging $2627. ***State or other work-study/employment:*** Total amount: $911,112 (56% need-based, 44% non-need-based). 111 part-time jobs averaging $7610.

ATHLETIC AWARDS Total amount: $4,758,913 (29% need-based, 71% non-need-based).

APPLYING FOR FINANCIAL AID ***Required financial aid forms:*** FAFSA, CSS Financial Aid PROFILE, noncustodial (divorced/separated) parent's statement. ***Financial aid deadline:*** 2/15. ***Notification date:*** 4/1. Students must reply by 5/1.

CONTACT Mr. Mark L. Lindenmeyer, Director of Financial Aid, Loyola University Maryland, 4501 North Charles Street, Baltimore, MD 21210-2699, 410-617-2576 or toll-free 800-221-9107 (in-state). *Fax:* 410-617-5149. *E-mail:* lindenmeyer@loyola.edu.

LOYOLA UNIVERSITY NEW ORLEANS

New Orleans, LA

Tuition & fees: $33,302 **Average undergraduate aid package: $23,960**

ABOUT THE INSTITUTION Independent Roman Catholic (Jesuit), coed. 47 undergraduate majors. Federal methodology is used as a basis for awarding need-based institutional aid.

UNDERGRADUATE EXPENSES for 2011–12 ***Comprehensive fee:*** $44,292 includes full-time tuition ($32,266), mandatory fees ($1036), and room and board ($10,990). ***College room only:*** $6526. Room and board charges vary according to board plan and housing facility. ***Part-time tuition:*** $920 per credit hour. ***Payment plan:*** Installment.

FRESHMAN FINANCIAL AID (Fall 2010, est.) 635 applied for aid; of those 85% were deemed to have need. 100% of freshmen with need received aid; of those 18% had need fully met. ***Average percent of need met:*** 76% (excluding resources awarded to replace EFC). ***Average financial aid package:*** $25,739 (excluding resources awarded to replace EFC). 29% of all full-time freshmen had no need and received non-need-based gift aid.

UNDERGRADUATE FINANCIAL AID (Fall 2010, est.) 1,975 applied for aid; of those 87% were deemed to have need. 100% of undergraduates with need received aid; of those 18% had need fully met. ***Average percent of need met:*** 73% (excluding resources awarded to replace EFC). ***Average financial aid package:*** $23,960 (excluding resources awarded to replace EFC). 32% of all full-time undergraduates had no need and received non-need-based gift aid.

GIFT AID (NEED-BASED) ***Total amount:*** $33,181,911 (13% federal, 7% state, 77% institutional, 3% external sources). ***Receiving aid:*** Freshmen: 70% (540); all full-time undergraduates: 66% (1,702). ***Average award:*** Freshmen: $21,926;

Undergraduates: $20,219. ***Scholarships, grants, and awards:*** Federal Pell, FSEOG, state, private, college/university gift aid from institutional funds.

GIFT AID (NON-NEED-BASED) ***Total amount:*** $15,403,057 (5% state, 91% institutional, 4% external sources). ***Receiving aid:*** Freshmen: 10% (75). Undergraduates: 9% (231). ***Average award:*** Freshmen: $13,452. Undergraduates: $14,681. ***Scholarships, grants, and awards by category:*** *Academic interests/achievement:* general academic interests/achievements. *Creative arts/performance:* general creative arts/performance. *Special characteristics:* children of faculty/staff. ***Tuition waivers:*** Full or partial for employees or children of employees, senior citizens.

LOANS ***Student loans:*** $12,253,687 (73% need-based, 27% non-need-based). 64% of past graduating class borrowed through all loan programs. *Average indebtedness per student:* $22,319. ***Average need-based loan:*** Freshmen: $3332. Undergraduates: $4168. ***Parent loans:*** $3,442,078 (40% need-based, 60% non-need-based). ***Programs:*** Perkins.

WORK-STUDY ***Federal work-study:*** Total amount: $1,356,422; jobs available.

ATHLETIC AWARDS Total amount: $723,322 (40% need-based, 60% non-need-based).

APPLYING FOR FINANCIAL AID ***Required financial aid form:*** FAFSA. ***Financial aid deadline:*** 6/1 (priority: 2/15). ***Notification date:*** 3/1. Students must reply by 5/1 or within 2 weeks of notification.

CONTACT Ms. Catherine M. Simoneaux, Director of Scholarships and Financial Aid, Loyola University New Orleans, 6363 St. Charles Avenue, Box 206, New Orleans, LA 70118-6195, 504-865-3231 or toll-free 800-4-LOYOLA. *Fax:* 504-865-3233. *E-mail:* finaid@loyno.edu.

LUBBOCK CHRISTIAN UNIVERSITY

Lubbock, TX

Tuition & fees: $16,180 **Average undergraduate aid package: $13,401**

ABOUT THE INSTITUTION Independent religious, coed. 66 undergraduate majors. Federal methodology is used as a basis for awarding need-based institutional aid.

UNDERGRADUATE EXPENSES for 2010–11 ***Comprehensive fee:*** $22,548 includes full-time tuition ($14,900), mandatory fees ($1280), and room and board ($6368). Full-time tuition and fees vary according to degree level and program. Room and board charges vary according to board plan and housing facility. ***Part-time tuition:*** $480 per semester hour. ***Part-time fees:*** $495 per term. Part-time tuition and fees vary according to course load, degree level, and program. ***Payment plan:*** Installment.

FRESHMAN FINANCIAL AID (Fall 2010, est.) 256 applied for aid; of those 87% were deemed to have need. 100% of freshmen with need received aid; of those 9% had need fully met. ***Average percent of need met:*** 69% (excluding resources awarded to replace EFC). ***Average financial aid package:*** $13,126 (excluding resources awarded to replace EFC). 13% of all full-time freshmen had no need and received non-need-based gift aid.

UNDERGRADUATE FINANCIAL AID (Fall 2010, est.) 1,149 applied for aid; of those 88% were deemed to have need. 100% of undergraduates with need received aid; of those 6% had need fully met. ***Average percent of need met:*** 65% (excluding resources awarded to replace EFC). ***Average financial aid package:*** $13,401 (excluding resources awarded to replace EFC). 12% of all full-time undergraduates had no need and received non-need-based gift aid.

GIFT AID (NEED-BASED) ***Total amount:*** $7,581,244 (39% federal, 26% state, 28% institutional, 7% external sources). ***Receiving aid:*** Freshmen: 65% (221); all full-time undergraduates: 70% (958). ***Average award:*** Freshmen: $8973; Undergraduates: $9021. ***Scholarships, grants, and awards:*** Federal Pell, FSEOG, state, college/university gift aid from institutional funds.

GIFT AID (NON-NEED-BASED) ***Total amount:*** $1,100,567 (1% federal, 1% state, 73% institutional, 25% external sources). ***Receiving aid:*** Freshmen: 5% (18). Undergraduates: 4% (58). ***Average award:*** Freshmen: $4253. Undergraduates: $4220. ***Scholarships, grants, and awards by category:*** *Academic interests/achievement:* agriculture, business, communication, computer science, education, English, foreign languages, general academic interests/achievements, humanities, physical sciences, religion/biblical studies, social sciences. *Creative arts/performance:* art/fine arts, journalism/publications, music, performing arts, theater/drama. *Special achievements/activities:* 24 awards ($20,900 total): cheerleading/drum major, leadership. *Special characteristics:* 34 awards ($376,190 total): children of faculty/staff, general special characteristics. ***Tuition waivers:*** Full or partial for employees or children of employees.

LOANS ***Student loans:*** $11,331,246 (79% need-based, 21% non-need-based). 76% of past graduating class borrowed through all loan programs. *Average indebtedness per student:* $26,440. ***Average need-based loan:*** Freshmen: $3727. Undergraduates: $4211. ***Parent loans:*** $3,044,528 (44% need-based, 56% non-need-based). ***Programs:*** Perkins, state.

WORK-STUDY ***Federal work-study:*** Total amount: $1,030,020; 849 jobs averaging $1763. ***State or other work-study/employment:*** Total amount: $21,954 (57% need-based, 43% non-need-based). 89 part-time jobs averaging $257.

ATHLETIC AWARDS Total amount: $1,245,523 (54% need-based, 46% non-need-based).

APPLYING FOR FINANCIAL AID ***Required financial aid forms:*** FAFSA, institution's own form. ***Financial aid deadline (priority):*** 6/1. ***Notification date:*** Continuous beginning 3/1.

CONTACT Mrs. Amy Hardesty, Financial Aid Director, Lubbock Christian University, 5601 19th Street, Lubbock, TX 79407, 806-720-7176 or toll-free 800-933-7601. *Fax:* 806-720-7185. *E-mail:* amy.hardesty@lcu.edu.

LUTHER COLLEGE

Decorah, IA

Tuition & fees: $34,885 **Average undergraduate aid package: $25,802**

ABOUT THE INSTITUTION Independent religious, coed. 38 undergraduate majors. Federal methodology is used as a basis for awarding need-based institutional aid.

UNDERGRADUATE EXPENSES for 2011–12 ***Comprehensive fee:*** $40,735 includes full-time tuition ($34,735), mandatory fees ($150), and room and board ($5850). ***College room only:*** $2780. Full-time tuition and fees vary according to course load. Room and board charges vary according to board plan and housing facility. ***Part-time tuition:*** $1240 per credit hour. Part-time tuition and fees vary according to course load. ***Payment plan:*** Installment.

FRESHMAN FINANCIAL AID (Fall 2010, est.) 532 applied for aid; of those 84% were deemed to have need. 100% of freshmen with need received aid; of those 36% had need fully met. ***Average percent of need met:*** 90% (excluding resources awarded to replace EFC). ***Average financial aid package:*** $27,463 (excluding resources awarded to replace EFC). 14% of all full-time freshmen had no need and received non-need-based gift aid.

UNDERGRADUATE FINANCIAL AID (Fall 2010, est.) 1,978 applied for aid; of those 85% were deemed to have need. 100% of undergraduates with need received aid; of those 27% had need fully met. ***Average percent of need met:*** 87% (excluding resources awarded to replace EFC). ***Average financial aid package:*** $25,802 (excluding resources awarded to replace EFC). 11% of all full-time undergraduates had no need and received non-need-based gift aid.

GIFT AID (NEED-BASED) ***Total amount:*** $33,041,842 (9% federal, 4% state, 84% institutional, 3% external sources). ***Receiving aid:*** Freshmen: 73% (446); all full-time undergraduates: 69% (1,650). ***Average award:*** Freshmen: $18,512; Undergraduates: $17,630. ***Scholarships, grants, and awards:*** Federal Pell, FSEOG, state, private, college/university gift aid from institutional funds.

GIFT AID (NON-NEED-BASED) ***Total amount:*** $10,149,242 (2% federal, 85% institutional, 13% external sources). ***Receiving aid:*** Freshmen: 14% (85). Undergraduates: 9% (210). ***Average award:*** Freshmen: $15,098. Undergraduates: $12,741. ***Scholarships, grants, and awards by category:*** *Academic interests/achievement:* 1,802 awards ($18,185,071 total): general academic interests/achievements. *Creative arts/performance:* 1,298 awards ($2,649,230 total): music. *Special characteristics:* 727 awards ($1,066,122 total): children and siblings of alumni, members of minority groups, religious affiliation. ***Tuition waivers:*** Full or partial for employees or children of employees.

LOANS ***Student loans:*** $12,344,037 (76% need-based, 24% non-need-based). 79% of past graduating class borrowed through all loan programs. *Average indebtedness per student:* $33,492. ***Average need-based loan:*** Freshmen: $4991. Undergraduates: $5057. ***Parent loans:*** $1,778,015 (81% need-based, 19% non-need-based). ***Programs:*** Federal Direct (Subsidized and Unsubsidized Stafford, PLUS), Perkins, college/university.

WORK-STUDY ***Federal work-study:*** Total amount: $2,058,821; 984 jobs averaging $2092. ***State or other work-study/employment:*** Total amount: $2,652,600 (13% need-based, 87% non-need-based). 1,108 part-time jobs averaging $2394.

APPLYING FOR FINANCIAL AID ***Required financial aid forms:*** FAFSA, institution's own form. ***Financial aid deadline (priority):*** 3/1. ***Notification date:*** Continuous beginning 3/15. Students must reply by 5/1.

CONTACT Ms. Janice Cordell, Director of Financial Aid, Luther College, 700 College Drive, Decorah, IA 52101-1045, 563-387-1018 or toll-free 800-458-8437. *Fax:* 563-387-2241. *E-mail:* cordellj@luther.edu.

LUTHER RICE UNIVERSITY

Lithonia, GA

Tuition & fees: $5376 **Average undergraduate aid package: $6902**

ABOUT THE INSTITUTION Independent Baptist, coed. ***Awards:*** bachelor's and master's degrees. 3 undergraduate majors. ***Total enrollment:*** 1,047. Undergraduates: 375. Both federal and institutional methodology are used as a basis for awarding need-based institutional aid.

UNDERGRADUATE EXPENSES for 2010–11 ***Application fee:*** $50. ***Tuition:*** full-time $5016; part-time $209 per credit hour. ***Required fees:*** full-time $360; $45 per course. ***Payment plan:*** Installment.

FRESHMAN FINANCIAL AID (Fall 2009) 4 applied for aid; of those 100% were deemed to have need. 100% of freshmen with need received aid; of those 75% had need fully met. ***Average percent of need met:*** 89% (excluding resources awarded to replace EFC). ***Average financial aid package:*** $5546 (excluding resources awarded to replace EFC).

UNDERGRADUATE FINANCIAL AID (Fall 2009) 64 applied for aid; of those 100% were deemed to have need. 100% of undergraduates with need received aid; of those 78% had need fully met. ***Average percent of need met:*** 95% (excluding resources awarded to replace EFC). ***Average financial aid package:*** $6902 (excluding resources awarded to replace EFC).

GIFT AID (NEED-BASED) ***Total amount:*** $636,299 (99% federal, 1% institutional). ***Receiving aid:*** Freshmen: 75% (3); all full-time undergraduates: 67% (43). ***Average award:*** Freshmen: $3716; Undergraduates: $5195. ***Scholarships, grants, and awards:*** Federal Pell, FSEOG, college/university gift aid from institutional funds.

GIFT AID (NON-NEED-BASED) ***Total amount:*** $65,524 (100% institutional). ***Receiving aid:*** Freshmen: 25% (1). Undergraduates: 2% (1). ***Tuition waivers:*** Full or partial for employees or children of employees.

LOANS ***Student loans:*** $5,576,489 (41% need-based, 59% non-need-based). 2% of past graduating class borrowed through all loan programs. *Average indebtedness per student:* $50,400. ***Average need-based loan:*** Freshmen: $3000. Undergraduates: $4102. ***Programs:*** FFELP.

WORK-STUDY ***Federal work-study:*** Total amount: $21,290; 3 jobs averaging $6985.

APPLYING FOR FINANCIAL AID ***Required financial aid forms:*** FAFSA, Virtual Financial Aid Office (VFAO) interview. ***Financial aid deadline (priority):*** 1/1. ***Notification date:*** Continuous. Students must reply within 2 weeks of notification.

CONTACT Gary W. Cook, Director of Financial Aid, Luther Rice University, 3038 Evans Mill Road, Lithonia, GA 30038-2418, 770-484-1204 Ext. 241 or toll-free 800-442-1577. *Fax:* 678-990-5388. *E-mail:* gcook@lru.edu.

LYCOMING COLLEGE

Williamsport, PA

Tuition & fees: $30,800 **Average undergraduate aid package: $24,839**

ABOUT THE INSTITUTION Independent United Methodist, coed. 39 undergraduate majors. Federal methodology is used as a basis for awarding need-based institutional aid.

UNDERGRADUATE EXPENSES for 2011–12 ***Comprehensive fee:*** $39,342 includes full-time tuition ($30,240), mandatory fees ($560), and room and board ($8542). Room and board charges vary according to board plan and housing facility. ***Part-time tuition:*** $945 per credit hour. Part-time tuition and fees vary according to course load. ***Payment plan:*** Installment.

FRESHMAN FINANCIAL AID (Fall 2010, est.) 330 applied for aid; of those 93% were deemed to have need. 100% of freshmen with need received aid; of those 19% had need fully met. ***Average percent of need met:*** 83% (excluding resources awarded to replace EFC). ***Average financial aid package:*** $26,221 (excluding resources awarded to replace EFC). 10% of all full-time freshmen had no need and received non-need-based gift aid.

UNDERGRADUATE FINANCIAL AID (Fall 2010, est.) 1,192 applied for aid; of those 94% were deemed to have need. 100% of undergraduates with need received aid; of those 17% had need fully met. ***Average percent of need met:*** 79% (excluding resources awarded to replace EFC). ***Average financial aid package:*** $24,839 (excluding resources awarded to replace EFC). 11% of all full-time undergraduates had no need and received non-need-based gift aid.

GIFT AID (NEED-BASED) ***Total amount:*** $21,977,404 (10% federal, 7% state, 81% institutional, 2% external sources). ***Receiving aid:*** Freshmen: 89% (308); all full-time undergraduates: 87% (1,122). ***Average award:*** Freshmen: $21,236; Undergraduates: $19,336. ***Scholarships, grants, and awards:*** Federal Pell, FSEOG, state, private, college/university gift aid from institutional funds.

GIFT AID (NON-NEED-BASED) ***Total amount:*** $1,823,274 (93% institutional, 7% external sources). ***Receiving aid:*** Freshmen: 12% (40). Undergraduates: 8% (100). ***Average award:*** Freshmen: $14,016. Undergraduates: $12,068. ***Scholarships, grants, and awards by category:*** *Academic interests/achievement:* 946 awards ($9,944,896 total): biological sciences, business, communication, computer science, education, English, foreign languages, general academic interests/achievements, health fields, humanities, international studies, mathematics, physical sciences, premedicine, religion/biblical studies, social sciences. *Creative arts/performance:* 133 awards ($286,125 total): art/fine arts, creative writing, music, theater/drama. *Special achievements/activities:* 65 awards ($409,838 total): general special achievements/activities, leadership. *Special characteristics:* 41 awards ($793,662 total): children of educators, children of faculty/staff, relatives of clergy. ***Tuition waivers:*** Full or partial for employees or children of employees.

LOANS ***Student loans:*** $9,506,673 (73% need-based, 27% non-need-based). 87% of past graduating class borrowed through all loan programs. *Average indebtedness per student:* $27,273. ***Average need-based loan:*** Freshmen: $3948. Undergraduates: $4605. ***Parent loans:*** $5,202,762 (27% need-based, 73% non-need-based). ***Programs:*** Federal Direct (Subsidized and Unsubsidized Stafford, PLUS), Perkins, college/university.

WORK-STUDY ***Federal work-study:*** Total amount: $255,324; 261 jobs averaging $978.

APPLYING FOR FINANCIAL AID ***Required financial aid forms:*** FAFSA, institution's own form, state aid form. ***Financial aid deadline (priority):*** 3/1. ***Notification date:*** Continuous beginning 3/1. Students must reply by 5/1.

CONTACT Mr. James S. Lakis, Director of Financial Aid, Lycoming College, 700 College Place, Williamsport, PA 17701-5192, 570-321-4040 or toll-free 800-345-3920 Ext. 4026. *Fax:* 570-321-4993. *E-mail:* lakis@lycoming.edu.

LYME ACADEMY COLLEGE OF FINE ARTS

Old Lyme, CT

Tuition & fees: $26,784 **Average undergraduate aid package: $16,870**

ABOUT THE INSTITUTION Independent, coed. 4 undergraduate majors. Federal methodology is used as a basis for awarding need-based institutional aid.

UNDERGRADUATE EXPENSES for 2011–12 ***Comprehensive fee:*** $35,334 includes full-time tuition ($25,248), mandatory fees ($1536), and room and board ($8550). Room and board charges vary according to housing facility. ***Part-time tuition:*** $974.33 per credit. ***Part-time fees:*** $60 per credit. Part-time tuition and fees vary according to course load. ***Payment plan:*** Installment.

FRESHMAN FINANCIAL AID (Fall 2010, est.) 17 applied for aid; of those 76% were deemed to have need. 100% of freshmen with need received aid. ***Average financial aid package:*** $18,405 (excluding resources awarded to replace EFC). 16% of all full-time freshmen had no need and received non-need-based gift aid.

UNDERGRADUATE FINANCIAL AID (Fall 2010, est.) 52 applied for aid; of those 92% were deemed to have need. 100% of undergraduates with need received aid. ***Average financial aid package:*** $16,870 (excluding resources awarded to replace EFC). 14% of all full-time undergraduates had no need and received non-need-based gift aid.

GIFT AID (NEED-BASED) ***Total amount:*** $726,861 (19% federal, 11% state, 59% institutional, 11% external sources). ***Scholarships, grants, and awards:*** Federal Pell, FSEOG, state, private, college/university gift aid from institutional funds.

GIFT AID (NON-NEED-BASED) ***Average award:*** Freshmen: $8333. Undergraduates: $4055. ***Scholarships, grants, and awards by category:*** *Creative arts/performance:* art/fine arts. ***Tuition waivers:*** Full or partial for employees or children of employees.

LOANS ***Student loans:*** $402,240 (52% need-based, 48% non-need-based). 75% of past graduating class borrowed through all loan programs. *Average indebtedness per student:* $24,578. ***Parent loans:*** $125,451 (100% need-based). ***Programs:*** Federal Direct (Subsidized and Unsubsidized Stafford, PLUS), CHESLA alternative loans.

WORK-STUDY ***Federal work-study:*** Total amount: $5666; jobs available. ***State or other work-study/employment:*** Total amount: $4249 (100% need-based). Part-time jobs available.

APPLYING FOR FINANCIAL AID ***Required financial aid form:*** FAFSA. ***Financial aid deadline (priority):*** 2/15. ***Notification date:*** Continuous beginning 3/1. Students must reply by 5/1 or within 2 weeks of notification.

CONTACT Mr. James Falconer, Director of Financial Aid, Lyme Academy College of Fine Arts, 84 Lyme Street, Old Lyme, CT 06371, 860-434-3571 Ext. 114. *Fax:* 860-434-8725. *E-mail:* jfalconer@lymeacademy.edu.

LYNCHBURG COLLEGE

Lynchburg, VA

Tuition & fees: $30,805 **Average undergraduate aid package: $20,881**

ABOUT THE INSTITUTION Independent religious, coed. 36 undergraduate majors. Federal methodology is used as a basis for awarding need-based institutional aid.

UNDERGRADUATE EXPENSES for 2011–12 ***Comprehensive fee:*** $39,015 includes full-time tuition ($29,860), mandatory fees ($945), and room and board ($8210). ***College room only:*** $4190. Room and board charges vary according to board plan and housing facility. ***Part-time tuition:*** $415 per credit hour. ***Part-time fees:*** $5.10 per credit hour. Part-time tuition and fees vary according to course load. ***Payment plans:*** Tuition prepayment, installment.

FRESHMAN FINANCIAL AID (Fall 2010, est.) 494 applied for aid; of those 88% were deemed to have need. 100% of freshmen with need received aid; of those 25% had need fully met. ***Average percent of need met:*** 83% (excluding resources awarded to replace EFC). ***Average financial aid package:*** $21,304 (excluding resources awarded to replace EFC). 18% of all full-time freshmen had no need and received non-need-based gift aid.

UNDERGRADUATE FINANCIAL AID (Fall 2010, est.) 1,740 applied for aid; of those 88% were deemed to have need. 99% of undergraduates with need received aid; of those 21% had need fully met. ***Average percent of need met:*** 77% (excluding resources awarded to replace EFC). ***Average financial aid package:*** $20,881 (excluding resources awarded to replace EFC). 24% of all full-time undergraduates had no need and received non-need-based gift aid.

GIFT AID (NEED-BASED) ***Total amount:*** $26,088,614 (12% federal, 9% state, 76% institutional, 3% external sources). ***Receiving aid:*** Freshmen: 76% (433); all full-time undergraduates: 73% (1,524). ***Average award:*** Freshmen: $18,311; Undergraduates: $17,342. ***Scholarships, grants, and awards:*** Federal Pell, FSEOG, state, private, college/university gift aid from institutional funds.

GIFT AID (NON-NEED-BASED) ***Total amount:*** $7,271,239 (14% state, 79% institutional, 7% external sources). ***Receiving aid:*** Freshmen: 15% (85). Undergraduates: 10% (213). ***Average award:*** Freshmen: $10,426. Undergraduates: $10,071. ***Scholarships, grants, and awards by category:*** *Academic interests/achievement:* general academic interests/achievements. *Creative arts/performance:* art/fine arts, music, theater/drama. ***Tuition waivers:*** Full or partial for employees or children of employees, adult students, senior citizens.

LOANS ***Student loans:*** $13,536,358 (58% need-based, 42% non-need-based). 76% of past graduating class borrowed through all loan programs. *Average indebtedness per student:* $32,130. ***Average need-based loan:*** Freshmen: $2932. Undergraduates: $3536. ***Parent loans:*** $4,596,204 (53% need-based, 47% non-need-based). ***Programs:*** Federal Direct (Subsidized and Unsubsidized Stafford, PLUS), Perkins.

WORK-STUDY ***Federal work-study:*** Total amount: $227,426; jobs available. ***State or other work-study/employment:*** Total amount: $662,774 (44% need-based, 56% non-need-based). Part-time jobs available.

APPLYING FOR FINANCIAL AID ***Required financial aid forms:*** FAFSA, state aid form. ***Financial aid deadline (priority):*** 3/5. ***Notification date:*** Continuous beginning 3/5. Students must reply by 5/1 or within 2 weeks of notification.

CONTACT Mrs. Michelle Davis, Director of Financial Aid, Lynchburg College, 1501 Lakeside Drive, Lynchburg, VA 24501-3199, 434-544-8228 or toll-free 800-426-8101. *Fax:* 434-544-8653.

LYNDON STATE COLLEGE

Lyndonville, VT

CONTACT Student Services Consultant, Lyndon State College, 1001 College Road, Lyndonville, VT 05851, 802-626-6396 or toll-free 800-225-1998. *Fax:* 802-626-9770. *E-mail:* financialaid@lyndonstate.edu.

LYNN UNIVERSITY

Boca Raton, FL

Tuition & fees: $30,900 **Average undergraduate aid package: $19,624**

ABOUT THE INSTITUTION Independent, coed. 15 undergraduate majors. Federal methodology is used as a basis for awarding need-based institutional aid.

UNDERGRADUATE EXPENSES for 2011–12 ***Comprehensive fee:*** $42,850 includes full-time tuition ($29,400), mandatory fees ($1500), and room and board ($11,950). Room and board charges vary according to housing facility. ***Part-time tuition:*** $850 per credit. ***Part-time fees:*** $30 per term. Part-time tuition and fees vary according to class time and course load. ***Payment plans:*** Installment, deferred payment.

FRESHMAN FINANCIAL AID (Fall 2010, est.) 285 applied for aid; of those 55% were deemed to have need. 100% of freshmen with need received aid; of those 100% had need fully met. ***Average percent of need met:*** 55% (excluding resources awarded to replace EFC). ***Average financial aid package:*** $18,256 (excluding resources awarded to replace EFC). 24% of all full-time freshmen had no need and received non-need-based gift aid.

UNDERGRADUATE FINANCIAL AID (Fall 2010, est.) 1,078 applied for aid; of those 62% were deemed to have need. 99% of undergraduates with need received aid; of those 100% had need fully met. ***Average percent of need met:*** 58% (excluding resources awarded to replace EFC). ***Average financial aid package:*** $19,624 (excluding resources awarded to replace EFC). 21% of all full-time undergraduates had no need and received non-need-based gift aid.

GIFT AID (NEED-BASED) ***Total amount:*** $8,179,060 (21% federal, 11% state, 66% institutional, 2% external sources). ***Receiving aid:*** Freshmen: 36% (128); all full-time undergraduates: 37% (545). ***Average award:*** Freshmen: $9830; Undergraduates: $12,023. ***Scholarships, grants, and awards:*** Federal Pell, FSEOG, state, private, college/university gift aid from institutional funds.

GIFT AID (NON-NEED-BASED) ***Total amount:*** $3,364,251 (7% state, 89% institutional, 4% external sources). ***Receiving aid:*** Freshmen: 39% (138). Undergraduates: 42% (615). ***Average award:*** Freshmen: $10,888. Undergraduates: $9974. ***Scholarships, grants, and awards by category:*** *Academic interests/achievement:* business, communication, general academic interests/achievements. *Creative arts/performance:* music. *Special achievements/activities:* leadership. *Special characteristics:* children of faculty/staff, local/state students, siblings of current students. ***Tuition waivers:*** Full or partial for employees or children of employees.

LOANS ***Student loans:*** $4,933,510 (92% need-based, 8% non-need-based). 35% of past graduating class borrowed through all loan programs. *Average indebtedness per student:* $37,698. ***Average need-based loan:*** Freshmen: $4035. Undergraduates: $5016. ***Parent loans:*** $4,595,789 (85% need-based, 15% non-need-based). ***Programs:*** Federal Direct (Subsidized and Unsubsidized Stafford, PLUS), Perkins, state, college/university.

WORK-STUDY ***Federal work-study:*** Total amount: $308,006; jobs available. ***State or other work-study/employment:*** Total amount: $250,937 (41% need-based, 59% non-need-based). Part-time jobs available.

ATHLETIC AWARDS Total amount: $2,859,896 (54% need-based, 46% non-need-based).

APPLYING FOR FINANCIAL AID ***Required financial aid forms:*** FAFSA, institution's own form. ***Financial aid deadline (priority):*** 3/1. ***Notification date:*** Continuous beginning 2/1. Students must reply within 2 weeks of notification.

CONTACT Mrs. Chan Park, Director of Student Financial Assistance, Lynn University, 3601 North Military Trail, Boca Raton, FL 33431-5598, 561-237-7186 or toll-free 800-888-5966. *Fax:* 561-237-7189. *E-mail:* cpark@lynn.edu.

LYON COLLEGE

Batesville, AR

Tuition & fees: $22,906 **Average undergraduate aid package: $20,828**

ABOUT THE INSTITUTION Independent Presbyterian, coed. 18 undergraduate majors. Federal methodology is used as a basis for awarding need-based institutional aid.

UNDERGRADUATE EXPENSES for 2011–12 ***Comprehensive fee:*** $30,246 includes full-time tuition ($22,682), mandatory fees ($224), and room and board ($7340). Room and board charges vary according to board plan. ***Part-time tuition:*** $790 per credit hour. ***Payment plan:*** Installment.

FRESHMAN FINANCIAL AID (Fall 2010, est.) 194 applied for aid; of those 92% were deemed to have need. 100% of freshmen with need received aid; of those 16% had need fully met. ***Average percent of need met:*** 82% (excluding resources awarded to replace EFC). ***Average financial aid package:*** $21,830 (excluding resources awarded to replace EFC). 12% of all full-time freshmen had no need and received non-need-based gift aid.

UNDERGRADUATE FINANCIAL AID (Fall 2010, est.) 557 applied for aid; of those 89% were deemed to have need. 100% of undergraduates with need received aid; of those 14% had need fully met. ***Average percent of need met:*** 78% (excluding resources awarded to replace EFC). ***Average financial aid package:*** $20,828 (excluding resources awarded to replace EFC). 21% of all full-time undergraduates had no need and received non-need-based gift aid.

GIFT AID (NEED-BASED) ***Total amount:*** $6,668,121 (24% federal, 19% state, 54% institutional, 3% external sources). ***Receiving aid:*** Freshmen: 88% (179); all full-time undergraduates: 80% (498). ***Average award:*** Freshmen: $18,125; Undergraduates: $16,364. ***Scholarships, grants, and awards:*** Federal Pell, FSEOG, state, private, college/university gift aid from institutional funds.

GIFT AID (NON-NEED-BASED) ***Total amount:*** $1,623,915 (22% state, 69% institutional, 9% external sources). ***Receiving aid:*** Freshmen: 88% (179). Undergraduates: 80% (498). ***Average award:*** Freshmen: $13,750. Undergraduates: $14,039. ***Scholarships, grants, and awards by category:*** *Academic interests/achievement:* 390 awards ($4,694,188 total): business, general academic interests/achievements. *Creative arts/performance:* 43 awards ($237,550 total): art/fine arts, music, theater/drama. *Special achievements/activities:* 5 awards ($38,000 total): cheerleading/drum major, general special achievements/activities. *Special characteristics:* 20 awards ($231,572 total): children of faculty/staff, ethnic background, first-generation college students, local/state students, members of minority groups, religious affiliation. ***Tuition waivers:*** Full or partial for employees or children of employees.

LOANS ***Student loans:*** $2,757,559 (76% need-based, 24% non-need-based). 64% of past graduating class borrowed through all loan programs. *Average indebtedness per student:* $18,180. ***Average need-based loan:*** Freshmen: $2774. Undergraduates: $3883. ***Parent loans:*** $529,072 (42% need-based, 58% non-need-based). ***Programs:*** Federal Direct (Subsidized and Unsubsidized Stafford, PLUS).

WORK-STUDY ***Federal work-study:*** Total amount: $145,700; 202 jobs averaging $1054. ***State or other work-study/employment:*** Total amount: $5500 (100% non-need-based). 6 part-time jobs averaging $1051.

ATHLETIC AWARDS Total amount: $1,943,091 (65% need-based, 35% non-need-based).

APPLYING FOR FINANCIAL AID ***Required financial aid form:*** FAFSA. ***Financial aid deadline (priority):*** 3/15. ***Notification date:*** Continuous beginning 9/1. Students must reply by 8/15.

CONTACT Mr. Tommy Tucker, Director of Student Assistance, Lyon College, 2300 Highland Road, Batesville, AR 72501, 870-307-7257 or toll-free 800-423-2542. *Fax:* 870-307-7542. *E-mail:* financialaid@lyon.edu.

MACALESTER COLLEGE

St. Paul, MN

Tuition & fees: $42,021 **Average undergraduate aid package: $33,773**

ABOUT THE INSTITUTION Independent Presbyterian, coed. 36 undergraduate majors. Both federal and institutional methodology are used as a basis for awarding need-based institutional aid.

UNDERGRADUATE EXPENSES for 2011–12 ***Comprehensive fee:*** $51,417 includes full-time tuition ($41,800), mandatory fees ($221), and room and board ($9396). ***College room only:*** $5024. Full-time tuition and fees vary according to course load. Room and board charges vary according to board plan and housing facility. ***Part-time tuition:*** $1306 per credit hour. Part-time tuition and fees vary according to course load. ***Payment plan:*** Installment.

FRESHMAN FINANCIAL AID (Fall 2010, est.) 428 applied for aid; of those 91% were deemed to have need. 100% of freshmen with need received aid; of those 100% had need fully met. ***Average percent of need met:*** 100% (excluding resources awarded to replace EFC). ***Average financial aid package:*** $33,891 (excluding resources awarded to replace EFC). 4% of all full-time freshmen had no need and received non-need-based gift aid.

UNDERGRADUATE FINANCIAL AID (Fall 2010, est.) 1,547 applied for aid; of those 90% were deemed to have need. 100% of undergraduates with need received aid; of those 100% had need fully met. ***Average percent of need met:*** 100% (excluding resources awarded to replace EFC). ***Average financial aid package:*** $33,773 (excluding resources awarded to replace EFC). 4% of all full-time undergraduates had no need and received non-need-based gift aid.

GIFT AID (NEED-BASED) ***Total amount:*** $40,203,192 (5% federal, 1% state, 92% institutional, 2% external sources). ***Receiving aid:*** Freshmen: 75% (386); all full-time undergraduates: 69% (1,380). ***Average award:*** Freshmen: $30,021; Undergraduates: $28,793. ***Scholarships, grants, and awards:*** Federal Pell, FSEOG, state, private, college/university gift aid from institutional funds.

GIFT AID (NON-NEED-BASED) ***Total amount:*** $840,079 (1% federal, 73% institutional, 26% external sources). ***Receiving aid:*** Freshmen: 7% (37). Undergraduates: 4% (78). ***Average award:*** Freshmen: $10,313. Undergraduates: $7347. ***Scholarships, grants, and awards by category:*** *Academic interests/achievement:* general academic interests/achievements. *Special characteristics:* ethnic background. ***Tuition waivers:*** Full or partial for employees or children of employees.

LOANS ***Student loans:*** $6,944,817 (93% need-based, 7% non-need-based). ***Average need-based loan:*** Freshmen: $3172. Undergraduates: $3909. ***Parent loans:*** $1,477,014 (100% non-need-based). ***Programs:*** Federal Direct (Subsidized and Unsubsidized Stafford, PLUS), Perkins, state.

WORK-STUDY ***Federal work-study:*** Total amount: $500,972; jobs available. ***State or other work-study/employment:*** Total amount: $2,444,430 (96% need-based, 4% non-need-based). Part-time jobs available.

APPLYING FOR FINANCIAL AID ***Required financial aid forms:*** FAFSA, CSS Financial Aid PROFILE, noncustodial (divorced/separated) parent's statement. ***Financial aid deadline:*** 3/1 (priority: 2/8). ***Notification date:*** 4/1. Students must reply by 5/1.

CONTACT Financial Aid Office, Macalester College, 1600 Grand Avenue, St. Paul, MN 55105, 651-696-6214 or toll-free 800-231-7974. *Fax:* 651-696-6866. *E-mail:* finaid@macalester.edu.

MACHZIKEI HADATH RABBINICAL COLLEGE

Brooklyn, NY

CONTACT Rabbi Baruch Rozmarin, Director of Financial Aid, Machzikei Hadath Rabbinical College, 5407 16th Avenue, Brooklyn, NY 11204-1805, 718-854-8777.

MACMURRAY COLLEGE

Jacksonville, IL

ABOUT THE INSTITUTION Independent United Methodist, coed. 30 undergraduate majors.

GIFT AID (NEED-BASED) ***Scholarships, grants, and awards:*** Federal Pell, FSEOG, state, private, college/university gift aid from institutional funds.

GIFT AID (NON-NEED-BASED) ***Scholarships, grants, and awards by category:*** *Academic interests/achievement:* biological sciences, English, foreign languages, general academic interests/achievements, religion/biblical studies. *Special characteristics:* children and siblings of alumni, children of faculty/staff, international students, religious affiliation, siblings of current students.

LOANS ***Programs:*** Federal Direct (Subsidized and Unsubsidized Stafford, PLUS), Perkins.

WORK-STUDY ***Federal work-study:*** Total amount: $64,173; 114 jobs averaging $564.

APPLYING FOR FINANCIAL AID ***Required financial aid form:*** FAFSA.

CONTACT Charles R. Carothers, Director of Financial Aid, MacMurray College, 447 East College Avenue, Jacksonville, IL 62650, 217-479-7042 or toll-free 800-252-7485 (in-state). *Fax:* 217-291-0702. *E-mail:* charles.carothers@mac.edu.

MACON STATE COLLEGE

Macon, GA

CONTACT Office of Financial Aid, Macon State College, 100 College Station Drive, Macon, GA 31206, 478-471-2717 or toll-free 800-272-7619 Ext. 2800. *Fax:* 478-471-2790. *E-mail:* fainfo@mail.maconstate.edu.

MADONNA UNIVERSITY

Livonia, MI

CONTACT Cathy Durham, Financial Aid Secretary, Madonna University, 36600 Schoolcraft Road, Livonia, MI 48150-1173, 734-432-5663 or toll-free 800-852-4951. *Fax:* 734-432-5344. *E-mail:* finaid@madonna.edu.

MAGDALEN COLLEGE

Warner, NH

CONTACT Bobbie Anne Abson, Financial Aid Director, Magdalen College, 511 Kearsarge Mountain Road, Warner, NH 03278, 603-456-2656 or toll-free 877-498-1723 (out-of-state). *Fax:* 603-456-2660. *E-mail:* babson@magdalen.edu.

MAHARISHI UNIVERSITY OF MANAGEMENT

Fairfield, IA

CONTACT Mr. Bill Christensen, Director of Financial Aid, Maharishi University of Management, 1000 North 4th Street, DB 1127, Fairfield, IA 52557-1127, 641-472-1156 or toll-free 800-369-6480. *Fax:* 641-472-1133. *E-mail:* bchrist@mum.edu.

MAINE COLLEGE OF ART

Portland, ME

Tuition & fees: $28,645 **Average undergraduate aid package: N/A**

ABOUT THE INSTITUTION Independent, coed. 11 undergraduate majors. Federal methodology is used as a basis for awarding need-based institutional aid.

UNDERGRADUATE EXPENSES for 2010–11 ***One-time required fee:*** $50. ***Comprehensive fee:*** $38,640 includes full-time tuition ($27,965), mandatory fees ($680), and room and board ($9995). Room and board charges vary according to board plan and housing facility. ***Part-time tuition:*** $1165 per credit hour. ***Payment plan:*** Installment.

GIFT AID (NEED-BASED) ***Scholarships, grants, and awards:*** Federal Pell, FSEOG, state, private, college/university gift aid from institutional funds.

GIFT AID (NON-NEED-BASED) ***Scholarships, grants, and awards by category:*** *Creative arts/performance:* art/fine arts. *Special characteristics:* children of faculty/staff.

LOANS ***Programs:*** Federal Direct (Subsidized and Unsubsidized Stafford, PLUS), Perkins, alternative loans.

WORK-STUDY Federal work-study jobs available.

APPLYING FOR FINANCIAL AID ***Required financial aid form:*** FAFSA. ***Financial aid deadline (priority):*** 3/1. ***Notification date:*** Continuous beginning 3/15. Students must reply within 2 weeks of notification.

CONTACT Adrienne J. Amari, Director of Financial Aid, Maine College of Art, 522 Congress Street, Portland, ME 04101-3987, 207-775-3052 Ext. 5073 or toll-free 800-639-4808. *Fax:* 207-772-5069. *E-mail:* aamari@meca.edu.

MAINE MARITIME ACADEMY

Castine, ME

Tuition & fees (ME res): $10,525 **Average undergraduate aid package: $9788**

ABOUT THE INSTITUTION State-supported, coed, primarily men. ***Awards:*** associate, bachelor's, and master's degrees. 11 undergraduate majors. ***Total enrollment:*** 860. Undergraduates: 842. Freshmen: 250. Federal methodology is used as a basis for awarding need-based institutional aid.

UNDERGRADUATE EXPENSES for 2010–11 ***Application fee:*** $15. ***Tuition, state resident:*** full-time $8280; part-time $320 per credit hour. ***Tuition, nonresident:*** full-time $17,000; part-time $600 per credit hour. ***Required fees:*** full-time $2245. Full-time tuition and fees vary according to course load and program. Part-time tuition and fees vary according to course load and program. ***College room and board:*** $8870; ***Room only:*** $3360. Room and board charges vary according to board plan. ***Payment plan:*** Installment.

FRESHMAN FINANCIAL AID (Fall 2010, est.) 213 applied for aid; of those 88% were deemed to have need. 99% of freshmen with need received aid; of those 9% had need fully met. ***Average percent of need met:*** 46% (excluding resources awarded to replace EFC). ***Average financial aid package:*** $9017 (excluding resources awarded to replace EFC).

UNDERGRADUATE FINANCIAL AID (Fall 2010, est.) 790 applied for aid; of those 87% were deemed to have need. 100% of undergraduates with need received aid; of those 9% had need fully met. ***Average percent of need met:*** 51% (excluding resources awarded to replace EFC). ***Average financial aid package:*** $9788 (excluding resources awarded to replace EFC).

GIFT AID (NEED-BASED) ***Total amount:*** $2,766,138 (56% federal, 10% state, 22% institutional, 12% external sources). ***Receiving aid:*** Freshmen: 67% (149); all full-time undergraduates: 67% (543). ***Average award:*** Freshmen: $6919; Undergraduates: $6606. ***Scholarships, grants, and awards:*** Federal Pell, FSEOG, state, private, college/university gift aid from institutional funds.

GIFT AID (NON-NEED-BASED) ***Total amount:*** $705,757 (100% institutional). ***Receiving aid:*** Freshmen: 5% (12). Undergraduates: 3% (26). ***Scholarships, grants, and awards by category:*** *Academic interests/achievement:* 160 awards ($704,057 total): biological sciences, business, engineering/technologies, general academic interests/achievements. *Special characteristics:* 8 awards ($74,065 total): children of faculty/staff. ***ROTC:*** Army, Naval.

LOANS ***Student loans:*** $8,426,777 (70% need-based, 30% non-need-based). 86% of past graduating class borrowed through all loan programs. *Average indebtedness per student:* $40,375. ***Average need-based loan:*** Freshmen: $3344. Undergraduates: $4550. ***Parent loans:*** $2,203,266 (47% need-based, 53% non-need-based). ***Programs:*** Federal Direct (Subsidized and Unsubsidized Stafford, PLUS), Perkins, college/university, alternative loans.

WORK-STUDY ***Federal work-study:*** Total amount: $106,033; 259 jobs averaging $864.

APPLYING FOR FINANCIAL AID ***Required financial aid form:*** FAFSA. ***Financial aid deadline (priority):*** 4/15. ***Notification date:*** Continuous beginning 4/1. Students must reply within 4 weeks of notification.

CONTACT Ms. Holly Bayle, Assistant Director of Financial Aid, Maine Maritime Academy, Pleasant Street, Castine, ME 04420, 207-326-2205 or toll-free 800-464-6565 (in-state), 800-227-8465 (out-of-state). *Fax:* 207-326-2515. *E-mail:* bbayle@mma.edu.

MALONE UNIVERSITY

Canton, OH

Tuition & fees: $23,420 **Average undergraduate aid package: $17,932**

ABOUT THE INSTITUTION Independent religious, coed. 41 undergraduate majors. Federal methodology is used as a basis for awarding need-based institutional aid.

UNDERGRADUATE EXPENSES for 2011–12 ***Comprehensive fee:*** $31,508 includes full-time tuition ($22,832), mandatory fees ($588), and room and board ($8088). ***College room only:*** $4221. Room and board charges vary according to board plan. ***Part-time tuition:*** $425 per credit hour. ***Part-time fees:*** $147 per term. Part-time tuition and fees vary according to course load. ***Payment plan:*** Installment.

FRESHMAN FINANCIAL AID (Fall 2010, est.) 354 applied for aid; of those 95% were deemed to have need. 100% of freshmen with need received aid; of those 12% had need fully met. ***Average percent of need met:*** 79% (excluding resources awarded to replace EFC). ***Average financial aid package:*** $21,248 (excluding resources awarded to replace EFC). 10% of all full-time freshmen had no need and received non-need-based gift aid.

UNDERGRADUATE FINANCIAL AID (Fall 2010, est.) 1,513 applied for aid; of those 95% were deemed to have need. 100% of undergraduates with need received aid; of those 12% had need fully met. ***Average percent of need met:*** 72% (excluding resources awarded to replace EFC). ***Average financial aid package:*** $17,932 (excluding resources awarded to replace EFC). 11% of all full-time undergraduates had no need and received non-need-based gift aid.

GIFT AID (NEED-BASED) ***Total amount:*** $16,836,197 (24% federal, 6% state, 65% institutional, 5% external sources). ***Receiving aid:*** Freshmen: 90% (337); all full-time undergraduates: 77% (1,385). ***Average award:*** Freshmen: $16,191; Undergraduates: $13,659. ***Scholarships, grants, and awards:*** Federal Pell, FSEOG, state, private, college/university gift aid from institutional funds, Academic Competitiveness Grants, National SMART Grants, TEACH Grants.

GIFT AID (NON-NEED-BASED) ***Total amount:*** $1,755,033 (94% institutional, 6% external sources). ***Receiving aid:*** Freshmen: 88% (329). Undergraduates: 67% (1,200). ***Average award:*** Freshmen: $8535. Undergraduates: $8068. ***Scholarships, grants, and awards by category:*** *Academic interests/achievement:*

1,194 awards ($8,256,224 total): biological sciences, business, communication, computer science, education, English, foreign languages, general academic interests/achievements, health fields, humanities, international studies, mathematics, physical sciences, premedicine, religion/biblical studies, social sciences. *Creative arts/performance:* 60 awards ($82,950 total): debating, journalism/publications, music, theater/drama. *Special achievements/activities:* 133 awards ($249,177 total): community service, general special achievements/activities, leadership, religious involvement. *Special characteristics:* 146 awards ($1,136,016 total): children and siblings of alumni, children of faculty/staff, general special characteristics, international students, parents of current students, relatives of clergy, religious affiliation, siblings of current students, spouses of current students. ***Tuition waivers:*** Full or partial for employees or children of employees, senior citizens.

LOANS ***Student loans:*** $12,226,564 (95% need-based, 5% non-need-based). 84% of past graduating class borrowed through all loan programs. *Average indebtedness per student:* $32,306. ***Average need-based loan:*** Freshmen: $4430. Undergraduates: $4779. ***Parent loans:*** $3,179,742 (94% need-based, 6% non-need-based). ***Programs:*** Federal Direct (Subsidized and Unsubsidized Stafford, PLUS), Perkins, state, college/university, alternative loans.

WORK-STUDY ***Federal work-study:*** Total amount: $942,140; 404 jobs averaging $2185. ***State or other work-study/employment:*** 79 part-time jobs averaging $2518.

ATHLETIC AWARDS Total amount: $2,136,816 (79% need-based, 21% non-need-based).

APPLYING FOR FINANCIAL AID ***Required financial aid form:*** FAFSA. ***Financial aid deadline:*** 7/31 (priority: 3/1). ***Notification date:*** Continuous beginning 3/1. Students must reply within 2 weeks of notification.

CONTACT Mrs. Pamela Pustay, Director of Financial Aid, Malone University, 2600 Cleveland Avenue NW, Canton, OH 44709, 330-471-8161 or toll-free 800-521-1146. *Fax:* 330-471-8652. *E-mail:* ppustay@malone.edu.

MANCHESTER COLLEGE

North Manchester, IN

Tuition & fees: $24,920 **Average undergraduate aid package: $23,512**

ABOUT THE INSTITUTION Independent religious, coed. 86 undergraduate majors. Federal methodology is used as a basis for awarding need-based institutional aid.

UNDERGRADUATE EXPENSES for 2010–11 ***One-time required fee:*** $250. ***Comprehensive fee:*** $33,780 includes full-time tuition ($24,100), mandatory fees ($820), and room and board ($8860). ***College room only:*** $5400. Room and board charges vary according to board plan and housing facility. ***Part-time tuition:*** $700 per credit hour. ***Part-time fees:*** $24 per credit hour. Part-time tuition and fees vary according to course load. ***Payment plan:*** Installment.

FRESHMAN FINANCIAL AID (Fall 2010, est.) 392 applied for aid; of those 94% were deemed to have need. 100% of freshmen with need received aid; of those 17% had need fully met. ***Average percent of need met:*** 84% (excluding resources awarded to replace EFC). ***Average financial aid package:*** $24,144 (excluding resources awarded to replace EFC). 6% of all full-time freshmen had no need and received non-need-based gift aid.

UNDERGRADUATE FINANCIAL AID (Fall 2010, est.) 1,137 applied for aid; of those 94% were deemed to have need. 100% of undergraduates with need received aid; of those 19% had need fully met. ***Average percent of need met:*** 83% (excluding resources awarded to replace EFC). ***Average financial aid package:*** $23,512 (excluding resources awarded to replace EFC). 7% of all full-time undergraduates had no need and received non-need-based gift aid.

GIFT AID (NEED-BASED) ***Total amount:*** $19,303,093 (11% federal, 13% state, 72% institutional, 4% external sources). ***Receiving aid:*** Freshmen: 91% (370); all full-time undergraduates: 86% (1,067). ***Average award:*** Freshmen: $20,277; Undergraduates: $18,901. ***Scholarships, grants, and awards:*** Federal Pell, FSEOG, state, private, college/university gift aid from institutional funds.

GIFT AID (NON-NEED-BASED) ***Total amount:*** $1,179,688 (92% institutional, 8% external sources). ***Receiving aid:*** Freshmen: 9% (36). Undergraduates: 9% (117). ***Average award:*** Freshmen: $14,037. Undergraduates: $14,058. ***Scholarships, grants, and awards by category:*** *Academic interests/achievement:* business, English, foreign languages, general academic interests/achievements, humanities. *Creative arts/performance:* music, theater/drama. *Special achievements/activities:* leadership. *Special characteristics:* children and siblings of alumni, ethnic background, international students, members of minority groups, previous college experience, religious affiliation. ***Tuition waivers:*** Full or partial for employees or children of employees.

LOANS ***Student loans:*** $7,603,110 (75% need-based, 25% non-need-based). 77% of past graduating class borrowed through all loan programs. *Average indebtedness per student:* $21,305. ***Average need-based loan:*** Freshmen: $3272. Undergraduates: $4172. ***Parent loans:*** $3,027,774 (39% need-based, 61% non-need-based). ***Programs:*** Perkins.

WORK-STUDY ***Federal work-study:*** Total amount: $1,094,107; jobs available. ***State or other work-study/employment:*** Total amount: $94,212 (100% non-need-based). Part-time jobs available.

APPLYING FOR FINANCIAL AID ***Required financial aid form:*** FAFSA. ***Financial aid deadline (priority):*** 3/1. ***Notification date:*** Continuous beginning 3/15. Students must reply by 5/1 or within 3 weeks of notification.

CONTACT Mrs. Sherri Shockey, Director of Student Financial Services, Manchester College, 604 East College Avenue, North Manchester, IN 46962-1225, 260-982-5066 or toll-free 800-852-3648. *Fax:* 260-982-5043. *E-mail:* slshockey@manchester.edu.

MANHATTAN CHRISTIAN COLLEGE

Manhattan, KS

Tuition & fees: $12,288 **Average undergraduate aid package: $12,278**

ABOUT THE INSTITUTION Independent religious, coed. ***Awards:*** associate and bachelor's degrees. 9 undergraduate majors. ***Total enrollment:*** 388. Undergraduates: 388. Federal methodology is used as a basis for awarding need-based institutional aid.

UNDERGRADUATE EXPENSES for 2010–11 ***Application fee:*** $25. ***Comprehensive fee:*** $18,342 includes full-time tuition ($11,822), mandatory fees ($466), and room and board ($6054). Room and board charges vary according to board plan. ***Part-time tuition:*** $485 per credit hour. Part-time tuition and fees vary according to course load. ***Payment plan:*** Deferred payment.

FRESHMAN FINANCIAL AID (Fall 2009) 51 applied for aid; of those 84% were deemed to have need. 100% of freshmen with need received aid; of those 51% had need fully met. ***Average percent of need met:*** 75% (excluding resources awarded to replace EFC). ***Average financial aid package:*** $16,727 (excluding resources awarded to replace EFC). 19% of all full-time freshmen had no need and received non-need-based gift aid.

UNDERGRADUATE FINANCIAL AID (Fall 2009) 299 applied for aid; of those 90% were deemed to have need. 100% of undergraduates with need received aid; of those 68% had need fully met. ***Average percent of need met:*** 70% (excluding resources awarded to replace EFC). ***Average financial aid package:*** $12,278 (excluding resources awarded to replace EFC). 13% of all full-time undergraduates had no need and received non-need-based gift aid.

GIFT AID (NEED-BASED) ***Total amount:*** $793,661 (72% federal, 28% state). ***Receiving aid:*** Freshmen: 75% (40); all full-time undergraduates: 49% (183). ***Average award:*** Freshmen: $4521; Undergraduates: $4459. ***Scholarships, grants, and awards:*** Federal Pell, FSEOG, state, private, college/university gift aid from institutional funds.

GIFT AID (NON-NEED-BASED) ***Total amount:*** $789,344 (14% federal, 3% state, 47% institutional, 36% external sources). ***Receiving aid:*** Freshmen: 81% (43). Undergraduates: 51% (188). ***Average award:*** Freshmen: $4500. Undergraduates: $3201. ***Scholarships, grants, and awards by category:*** *Academic interests/achievement:* general academic interests/achievements, religion/biblical studies. *Creative arts/performance:* music. *Special achievements/activities:* leadership. *Special characteristics:* children of faculty/staff. ***Tuition waivers:*** Full or partial for employees or children of employees, senior citizens. ***ROTC:*** Army cooperative, Air Force cooperative.

LOANS ***Student loans:*** $1,548,261 (56% need-based, 44% non-need-based). 86% of past graduating class borrowed through all loan programs. *Average indebtedness per student:* $16,572. ***Average need-based loan:*** Freshmen: $2763. Undergraduates: $3731. ***Parent loans:*** $127,204 (100% non-need-based). ***Programs:*** Federal Direct (Subsidized and Unsubsidized Stafford, PLUS), Perkins.

WORK-STUDY ***Federal work-study:*** Total amount: $72,411; 56 jobs averaging $1293.

APPLYING FOR FINANCIAL AID ***Required financial aid forms:*** FAFSA, state aid form. ***Financial aid deadline (priority):*** 4/1. ***Notification date:*** Continuous. Students must reply within 2 weeks of notification.

CONTACT Mrs. Margaret Carlisle, Director of Financial Aid, Manhattan Christian College, 1415 Anderson Avenue, Manhattan, KS 66502-4081, 785-539-3571 or toll-free 877-246-4622. *E-mail:* carlisle@mccks.edu.

MANHATTAN COLLEGE

Riverdale, NY

Tuition & fees: $29,800 **Average undergraduate aid package: $17,995**

ABOUT THE INSTITUTION Independent religious, coed. 41 undergraduate majors. Federal methodology is used as a basis for awarding need-based institutional aid.

UNDERGRADUATE EXPENSES for 2011–12 ***Comprehensive fee:*** $41,220 includes full-time tuition ($27,600), mandatory fees ($2200), and room and board ($11,420). Full-time tuition and fees vary according to course load, program, and student level. Room and board charges vary according to board plan. ***Part-time tuition:*** $780 per credit. Part-time tuition and fees vary according to course load. ***Payment plans:*** Installment, deferred payment.

FRESHMAN FINANCIAL AID (Fall 2010, est.) 571 applied for aid; of those 87% were deemed to have need. 99% of freshmen with need received aid; of those 17% had need fully met. ***Average percent of need met:*** 70% (excluding resources awarded to replace EFC). ***Average financial aid package:*** $19,365 (excluding resources awarded to replace EFC). 12% of all full-time freshmen had no need and received non-need-based gift aid.

UNDERGRADUATE FINANCIAL AID (Fall 2010, est.) 2,342 applied for aid; of those 86% were deemed to have need. 99% of undergraduates with need received aid; of those 16% had need fully met. ***Average percent of need met:*** 67% (excluding resources awarded to replace EFC). ***Average financial aid package:*** $17,995 (excluding resources awarded to replace EFC). 11% of all full-time undergraduates had no need and received non-need-based gift aid.

GIFT AID (NEED-BASED) ***Total amount:*** $26,153,676 (16% federal, 11% state, 71% institutional, 2% external sources). ***Receiving aid:*** Freshmen: 70% (454); all full-time undergraduates: 62% (1,795). ***Average award:*** Freshmen: $10,880; Undergraduates: $9217. ***Scholarships, grants, and awards:*** Federal Pell, FSEOG, state, private, college/university gift aid from institutional funds.

GIFT AID (NON-NEED-BASED) ***Total amount:*** $3,190,462 (1% federal, 3% state, 91% institutional, 5% external sources). ***Receiving aid:*** Freshmen: 39% (251). Undergraduates: 30% (877). ***Average award:*** Freshmen: $9676. Undergraduates: $8515. ***Scholarships, grants, and awards by category:*** *Academic interests/achievement:* biological sciences, business, computer science, foreign languages, general academic interests/achievements, mathematics, military science. *Creative arts/performance:* music. *Special achievements/activities:* community service, leadership. *Special characteristics:* children of faculty/staff. ***Tuition waivers:*** Full or partial for employees or children of employees.

LOANS ***Student loans:*** $19,024,098 (86% need-based, 14% non-need-based). 72% of past graduating class borrowed through all loan programs. *Average indebtedness per student:* $31,912. ***Average need-based loan:*** Freshmen: $6394. Undergraduates: $8052. ***Parent loans:*** $7,702,899 (82% need-based, 18% non-need-based). ***Programs:*** Federal Direct (Subsidized and Unsubsidized Stafford, PLUS), Perkins.

WORK-STUDY ***Federal work-study:*** Total amount: $600,000; jobs available. ***State or other work-study/employment:*** Total amount: $150,000 (100% non-need-based). Part-time jobs available.

ATHLETIC AWARDS Total amount: $3,519,977 (45% need-based, 55% non-need-based).

APPLYING FOR FINANCIAL AID ***Required financial aid forms:*** FAFSA, institution's own form, state aid form. ***Financial aid deadline (priority):*** 3/1. ***Notification date:*** 4/1. Students must reply by 5/1.

CONTACT Mr. Edward Keough, Director of Student Financial Services, Manhattan College, 4513 Manhattan College Parkway, Riverdale, NY 10471, 718-862-7100 or toll-free 800-622-9235 (in-state). *Fax:* 718-862-8027. *E-mail:* finaid@manhattan.edu.

MANHATTAN SCHOOL OF MUSIC

New York, NY

Tuition & fees: $35,140 **Average undergraduate aid package: $16,311**

ABOUT THE INSTITUTION Independent, coed. 7 undergraduate majors. Both federal and institutional methodology are used as a basis for awarding need-based institutional aid.

UNDERGRADUATE EXPENSES for 2010–11 ***Comprehensive fee:*** $48,950 includes full-time tuition ($32,340), mandatory fees ($2800), and room and board ($13,810). ***College room only:*** $9150. Full-time tuition and fees vary according to course load. Room and board charges vary according to board plan and housing facility. Part-time tuition and fees vary according to course load. ***Payment plans:*** Installment, deferred payment.

FRESHMAN FINANCIAL AID (Fall 2009) 61 applied for aid; of those 89% were deemed to have need. 93% of freshmen with need received aid; of those 18% had need fully met. ***Average percent of need met:*** 51% (excluding resources awarded to replace EFC). ***Average financial aid package:*** $16,328 (excluding resources awarded to replace EFC). 12% of all full-time freshmen had no need and received non-need-based gift aid.

UNDERGRADUATE FINANCIAL AID (Fall 2009) 293 applied for aid; of those 93% were deemed to have need. 90% of undergraduates with need received aid; of those 9% had need fully met. ***Average percent of need met:*** 48% (excluding resources awarded to replace EFC). ***Average financial aid package:*** $16,311 (excluding resources awarded to replace EFC). 15% of all full-time undergraduates had no need and received non-need-based gift aid.

GIFT AID (NEED-BASED) ***Total amount:*** $3,279,021 (14% federal, 3% state, 82% institutional, 1% external sources). ***Receiving aid:*** Freshmen: 46% (37); all full-time undergraduates: 48% (185). ***Average award:*** Freshmen: $13,841; Undergraduates: $17,098. ***Scholarships, grants, and awards:*** Federal Pell, FSEOG, state, private, college/university gift aid from institutional funds.

GIFT AID (NON-NEED-BASED) ***Total amount:*** $302,519 (87% institutional, 13% external sources). ***Receiving aid:*** Freshmen: 6% (5). Undergraduates: 12% (46). ***Average award:*** Freshmen: $11,736. Undergraduates: $8226. ***Scholarships, grants, and awards by category:*** *Creative arts/performance:* 46 awards ($264,630 total): music. ***Tuition waivers:*** Full or partial for employees or children of employees.

LOANS ***Student loans:*** $1,842,207 (78% need-based, 22% non-need-based). 59% of past graduating class borrowed through all loan programs. *Average indebtedness per student:* $23,508. ***Average need-based loan:*** Freshmen: $4397. Undergraduates: $5481. ***Parent loans:*** $2,074,671 (64% need-based, 36% non-need-based). ***Programs:*** Federal Direct (Subsidized and Unsubsidized Stafford, PLUS), Perkins.

WORK-STUDY ***Federal work-study:*** Total amount: $65,911; 70 jobs averaging $942. ***State or other work-study/employment:*** Total amount: $83,650 (71% need-based, 29% non-need-based). 7 part-time jobs averaging $11,950.

APPLYING FOR FINANCIAL AID ***Required financial aid forms:*** FAFSA, institution's own form, CSS Financial Aid PROFILE, verification worksheet. ***Financial aid deadline:*** 3/1. ***Notification date:*** 4/1. Students must reply by 5/1 or within 2 weeks of notification.

CONTACT Ms. Amy Anderson, Assistant Dean for Enrollment Management, Manhattan School of Music, 120 Claremont Avenue, New York, NY 10027-4698, 212-749-2802 Ext. 4501. *Fax:* 212-749-3025. *E-mail:* aanderson@msmnyc.edu.

MANHATTANVILLE COLLEGE

Purchase, NY

Tuition & fees: $34,350 **Average undergraduate aid package: $26,779**

ABOUT THE INSTITUTION Independent, coed. 40 undergraduate majors. Federal methodology is used as a basis for awarding need-based institutional aid.

UNDERGRADUATE EXPENSES for 2010–11 ***Comprehensive fee:*** $48,270 includes full-time tuition ($33,030), mandatory fees ($1320), and room and board ($13,920). ***College room only:*** $8250. Room and board charges vary according to board plan. ***Part-time tuition:*** $765 per credit. ***Part-time fees:*** $60 per term. Part-time tuition and fees vary according to program. ***Payment plans:*** Installment, deferred payment.

FRESHMAN FINANCIAL AID (Fall 2009) 377 applied for aid; of those 92% were deemed to have need. 100% of freshmen with need received aid; of those 10% had need fully met. ***Average percent of need met:*** 97% (excluding resources awarded to replace EFC). ***Average financial aid package:*** $29,687 (excluding resources awarded to replace EFC). 24% of all full-time freshmen had no need and received non-need-based gift aid.

UNDERGRADUATE FINANCIAL AID (Fall 2009) 1,234 applied for aid; of those 92% were deemed to have need. 100% of undergraduates with need received aid; of those 10% had need fully met. ***Average percent of need met:*** 96%

(excluding resources awarded to replace EFC). ***Average financial aid package:*** $26,779 (excluding resources awarded to replace EFC). 28% of all full-time undergraduates had no need and received non-need-based gift aid.

GIFT AID (NEED-BASED) ***Total amount:*** $16,407,176 (14% federal, 9% state, 77% institutional). ***Receiving aid:*** Freshmen: 68% (331); all full-time undergraduates: 62% (1,064). ***Average award:*** Freshmen: $18,740; Undergraduates: $17,427. ***Scholarships, grants, and awards:*** Federal Pell, FSEOG, state, private, college/university gift aid from institutional funds.

GIFT AID (NON-NEED-BASED) ***Total amount:*** $21,302,997 (100% institutional). ***Receiving aid:*** Freshmen: 54% (263). Undergraduates: 50% (868). ***Average award:*** Freshmen: $20,812. Undergraduates: $18,753. ***Scholarships, grants, and awards by category:*** *Academic interests/achievement:* general academic interests/achievements, mathematics. *Creative arts/performance:* dance, performing arts. *Special achievements/activities:* community service, leadership. *Special characteristics:* previous college experience. ***Tuition waivers:*** Full or partial for employees or children of employees, senior citizens.

LOANS ***Student loans:*** $9,529,869 (73% need-based, 27% non-need-based). ***Average need-based loan:*** Freshmen: $3927. Undergraduates: $4523. ***Parent loans:*** $2,264,634 (100% non-need-based). ***Programs:*** Perkins.

WORK-STUDY ***Federal work-study:*** Total amount: $277,010; 275 jobs averaging $1300. ***State or other work-study/employment:*** Total amount: $1,033,568 (73% need-based, 27% non-need-based). 265 part-time jobs averaging $1300.

APPLYING FOR FINANCIAL AID ***Required financial aid forms:*** FAFSA, state aid form. ***Financial aid deadline (priority):*** 3/1. ***Notification date:*** Continuous. Students must reply by 5/1 or within 2 weeks of notification.

CONTACT Ms. Kathy Fitzgerald, VP for Enrollment Management, Manhattanville College, 2900 Purchase Street, Purchase, NY 10577-2132, 914-323-5357 or toll-free 800-328-4553. *Fax:* 914-323-5382. *E-mail:* financialaid@mville.edu.

MANNES COLLEGE THE NEW SCHOOL FOR MUSIC

New York, NY

Tuition & fees: $35,100 **Average undergraduate aid package: $20,135**

ABOUT THE INSTITUTION Independent, coed. 7 undergraduate majors. Federal methodology is used as a basis for awarding need-based institutional aid.

UNDERGRADUATE EXPENSES for 2010–11 ***Comprehensive fee:*** $50,360 includes full-time tuition ($34,340), mandatory fees ($760), and room and board ($15,260). ***College room only:*** $12,260. Room and board charges vary according to board plan and housing facility. ***Part-time tuition:*** $1125 per credit. Part-time tuition and fees vary according to course load. ***Payment plan:*** Installment.

FRESHMAN FINANCIAL AID (Fall 2010, est.) 11 applied for aid; of those 82% were deemed to have need. 100% of freshmen with need received aid; of those 11% had need fully met. ***Average percent of need met:*** 62% (excluding resources awarded to replace EFC). ***Average financial aid package:*** $20,975 (excluding resources awarded to replace EFC). 5% of all full-time freshmen had no need and received non-need-based gift aid.

UNDERGRADUATE FINANCIAL AID (Fall 2010, est.) 52 applied for aid; of those 92% were deemed to have need. 100% of undergraduates with need received aid; of those 12% had need fully met. ***Average percent of need met:*** 53% (excluding resources awarded to replace EFC). ***Average financial aid package:*** $20,135 (excluding resources awarded to replace EFC). 2% of all full-time undergraduates had no need and received non-need-based gift aid.

GIFT AID (NEED-BASED) ***Total amount:*** $732,765 (19% federal, 6% state, 63% institutional, 12% external sources). ***Receiving aid:*** Freshmen: 12% (5); all full-time undergraduates: 24% (42). ***Average award:*** Freshmen: $11,135; Undergraduates: $14,825. ***Scholarships, grants, and awards:*** Federal Pell, FSEOG, state, private, college/university gift aid from institutional funds.

GIFT AID (NON-NEED-BASED) ***Total amount:*** $1,035,000 (100% institutional). ***Receiving aid:*** Freshmen: 2% (1). Undergraduates: 2% (3). ***Average award:*** Freshmen: $12,930. Undergraduates: $12,910. ***Scholarships, grants, and awards by category:*** *Creative arts/performance:* music, performing arts. *Special characteristics:* international students. ***Tuition waivers:*** Full or partial for employees or children of employees.

LOANS ***Student loans:*** $412,975 (99% need-based, 1% non-need-based). 68% of past graduating class borrowed through all loan programs. *Average indebtedness per student:* $33,060. ***Average need-based loan:*** Freshmen: $5715. Undergraduates: $8695. ***Parent loans:*** $233,070 (100% need-based). ***Programs:*** Federal Direct (Subsidized and Unsubsidized Stafford, PLUS), Perkins.

WORK-STUDY ***Federal work-study:*** Total amount: $13,500; jobs available.

APPLYING FOR FINANCIAL AID ***Required financial aid forms:*** FAFSA, state aid form. ***Financial aid deadline:*** Continuous. ***Notification date:*** Continuous beginning 3/1. Students must reply within 4 weeks of notification.

CONTACT Office of Student Financial Services, Mannes College The New School for Music, 150 West 85th Street, New York, NY 10024-4402, 212-229-8930 or toll-free 800-292-3040. *Fax:* 212-229-5919. *E-mail:* sfs@newschool.edu.

MANSFIELD UNIVERSITY OF PENNSYLVANIA

Mansfield, PA

ABOUT THE INSTITUTION State-supported, coed. 67 undergraduate majors.

GIFT AID (NEED-BASED) ***Scholarships, grants, and awards:*** Federal Pell, FSEOG, state, private, college/university gift aid from institutional funds, Federal Nursing.

GIFT AID (NON-NEED-BASED) ***Scholarships, grants, and awards by category:*** *Academic interests/achievement:* biological sciences, communication, education, general academic interests/achievements, health fields, mathematics, physical sciences. *Creative arts/performance:* art/fine arts, journalism/publications, music. *Special achievements/activities:* leadership. *Special characteristics:* local/state students.

LOANS ***Programs:*** Federal Direct (Subsidized and Unsubsidized Stafford, PLUS), Perkins, Federal Nursing.

WORK-STUDY ***Federal work-study:*** Total amount: $217,367; jobs available. ***State or other work-study/employment:*** Total amount: $340,042 (100% need-based). Part-time jobs available.

APPLYING FOR FINANCIAL AID ***Required financial aid forms:*** FAFSA, institution's own form.

CONTACT Ms. Barbara Schmitt, Director of Financial Aid, Mansfield University of Pennsylvania, 224 South Hall, Mansfield, PA 16933, 570-662-4854 or toll-free 800-577-6826. *Fax:* 570-662-4136.

MAPLE SPRINGS BAPTIST BIBLE COLLEGE AND SEMINARY

Capitol Heights, MD

CONTACT Ms. Fannie G. Thompson, Director of Business Affairs, Maple Springs Baptist Bible College and Seminary, 4130 Belt Road, Capitol Heights, MD 20743, 301-736-3631. *Fax:* 301-735-6507.

MARANATHA BAPTIST BIBLE COLLEGE

Watertown, WI

Tuition & fees: $11,550 **Average undergraduate aid package: $8279**

ABOUT THE INSTITUTION Independent Baptist, coed. 31 undergraduate majors. Federal methodology is used as a basis for awarding need-based institutional aid.

UNDERGRADUATE EXPENSES for 2010–11 ***Comprehensive fee:*** $17,840 includes full-time tuition ($10,500), mandatory fees ($1050), and room and board ($6290). Full-time tuition and fees vary according to course load. ***Part-time tuition:*** $437 per credit hour. Part-time tuition and fees vary according to course load. ***Payment plan:*** Installment.

FRESHMAN FINANCIAL AID (Fall 2009) 167 applied for aid; of those 90% were deemed to have need. 100% of freshmen with need received aid; of those 6% had need fully met. ***Average percent of need met:*** 53% (excluding resources awarded to replace EFC). ***Average financial aid package:*** $7462 (excluding resources awarded to replace EFC). 2% of all full-time freshmen had no need and received non-need-based gift aid.

UNDERGRADUATE FINANCIAL AID (Fall 2009) 662 applied for aid; of those 91% were deemed to have need. 100% of undergraduates with need received aid; of those 5% had need fully met. ***Average percent of need met:*** 53% (excluding resources awarded to replace EFC). ***Average financial aid package:*** $8279 (excluding resources awarded to replace EFC). 4% of all full-time undergraduates had no need and received non-need-based gift aid.

GIFT AID (NEED-BASED) ***Total amount:*** $2,108,290 (66% federal, 7% state, 15% institutional, 12% external sources). ***Receiving aid:*** Freshmen: 34% (83); all full-time undergraduates: 47% (358). ***Average award:*** Freshmen: $4557; Undergraduates: $4299. ***Scholarships, grants, and awards:*** Federal Pell, FSEOG, state, private, college/university gift aid from institutional funds.

GIFT AID (NON-NEED-BASED) ***Total amount:*** $99,560 (2% state, 42% institutional, 56% external sources). ***Receiving aid:*** Freshmen: 28% (68). Undergraduates: 36% (274). ***Average award:*** Freshmen: $958. Undergraduates: $1481. ***Scholarships, grants, and awards by category:*** *Academic interests/achievement:* 8 awards ($12,100 total): business, general academic interests/achievements, religion/biblical studies. *Creative arts/performance:* 3 awards ($2250 total): music. *Special characteristics:* 276 awards ($940,157 total): children and siblings of alumni, children of educators, children of faculty/staff, relatives of clergy, spouses of current students. ***Tuition waivers:*** Full or partial for employees or children of employees.

LOANS ***Student loans:*** $4,584,908 (91% need-based, 9% non-need-based). 73% of past graduating class borrowed through all loan programs. *Average indebtedness per student:* $19,191. ***Average need-based loan:*** Freshmen: $3382. Undergraduates: $4358. ***Parent loans:*** $254,090 (85% need-based, 15% non-need-based). ***Programs:*** state, alternative loans.

WORK-STUDY ***State or other work-study/employment:*** Part-time jobs available.

APPLYING FOR FINANCIAL AID ***Required financial aid form:*** FAFSA. ***Financial aid deadline (priority):*** 3/1. ***Notification date:*** Continuous. Students must reply within 2 weeks of notification.

CONTACT Mr. Bruce Roth, Associate Director of Financial Aid, Maranatha Baptist Bible College, 745 West Main Street, Watertown, WI 53094, 920-206-2318 or toll-free 800-622-2947. *Fax:* 920-261-9109. *E-mail:* financialaid@mbbc.edu.

MARIA COLLEGE

Albany, NY

CONTACT Financial Aid Office, Maria College, 700 New Scotland Avenue, Albany, NY 12208-1798, 518-438-3111.

MARIAN UNIVERSITY

Indianapolis, IN

CONTACT Mr. John E. Shelton, Dean of Financial Aid, Marian University, 3200 Cold Spring Road, Indianapolis, IN 46222-1997, 317-955-6040 or toll-free 800-772-7264 (in-state). *Fax:* 317-955-6424. *E-mail:* jshelton@marian.edu.

MARIAN UNIVERSITY

Fond du Lac, WI

Tuition & fees: $21,490 **Average undergraduate aid package: $19,444**

ABOUT THE INSTITUTION Independent Roman Catholic, coed. 46 undergraduate majors. Federal methodology is used as a basis for awarding need-based institutional aid.

UNDERGRADUATE EXPENSES for 2010–11 ***One-time required fee:*** $100. ***Comprehensive fee:*** $27,190 includes full-time tuition ($21,140), mandatory fees ($350), and room and board ($5700). ***College room only:*** $3950. Full-time tuition and fees vary according to course load, degree level, and program. Room and board charges vary according to board plan and housing facility. ***Part-time tuition:*** $330 per credit hour. Part-time tuition and fees vary according to course load, degree level, and program. ***Payment plan:*** Installment.

FRESHMAN FINANCIAL AID (Fall 2009) 315 applied for aid; of those 95% were deemed to have need. 100% of freshmen with need received aid; of those 36% had need fully met. ***Average percent of need met:*** 90% (excluding resources awarded to replace EFC). ***Average financial aid package:*** $19,400 (excluding resources awarded to replace EFC). 5% of all full-time freshmen had no need and received non-need-based gift aid.

UNDERGRADUATE FINANCIAL AID (Fall 2009) 1,320 applied for aid; of those 90% were deemed to have need. 100% of undergraduates with need received aid; of those 38% had need fully met. ***Average percent of need met:*** 90% (excluding resources awarded to replace EFC). ***Average financial aid package:*** $19,444 (excluding resources awarded to replace EFC). 10% of all full-time undergraduates had no need and received non-need-based gift aid.

GIFT AID (NEED-BASED) ***Total amount:*** $14,517,547 (22% federal, 14% state, 63% institutional, 1% external sources). ***Receiving aid:*** Freshmen: 94% (298); all full-time undergraduates: 86% (1,166). ***Average award:*** Freshmen: $12,658; Undergraduates: $11,769. ***Scholarships, grants, and awards:*** Federal Pell, FSEOG, state, private, college/university gift aid from institutional funds, endowed scholarships.

GIFT AID (NON-NEED-BASED) ***Total amount:*** $161,697 (15% state, 76% institutional, 9% external sources). ***Receiving aid:*** Freshmen: 90% (283). Undergraduates: 79% (1,067). ***Average award:*** Freshmen: $5529. Undergraduates: $4503. ***Scholarships, grants, and awards by category:*** *Academic interests/achievement:* 1,255 awards ($6,240,313 total): general academic interests/achievements. *Creative arts/performance:* 31 awards ($54,000 total): music. *Special characteristics:* 95 awards ($534,772 total): children of faculty/staff, children with a deceased or disabled parent, siblings of current students. ***Tuition waivers:*** Full or partial for employees or children of employees, senior citizens.

LOANS ***Student loans:*** $12,340,014 (84% need-based, 16% non-need-based). 82% of past graduating class borrowed through all loan programs. *Average indebtedness per student:* $22,125. ***Average need-based loan:*** Freshmen: $6219. Undergraduates: $7089. ***Parent loans:*** $1,471,240 (55% need-based, 45% non-need-based). ***Programs:*** Federal Direct (Subsidized and Unsubsidized Stafford, PLUS), Perkins, Federal Nursing.

WORK-STUDY ***Federal work-study:*** Total amount: $131,074; 193 jobs averaging $679. ***State or other work-study/employment:*** Total amount: $602,315 (100% non-need-based). 449 part-time jobs averaging $1341.

APPLYING FOR FINANCIAL AID ***Required financial aid forms:*** FAFSA, institution's own form. ***Financial aid deadline (priority):*** 3/1. ***Notification date:*** Continuous beginning 3/1. Students must reply within 4 weeks of notification.

CONTACT Ms. Pam Warren, Associate Director of Financial Aid, Marian University, 45 South National Avenue, Fond du Lac, WI 54935-4699, 920-923-7614 or toll-free 800-2-MARIAN Ext. 7652 (in-state). *Fax:* 920-923-8767. *E-mail:* pwarren@marianuniversity.edu.

MARIETTA COLLEGE

Marietta, OH

Tuition & fees: $28,340 **Average undergraduate aid package: $24,212**

ABOUT THE INSTITUTION Independent, coed. 42 undergraduate majors. Federal methodology is used as a basis for awarding need-based institutional aid.

UNDERGRADUATE EXPENSES for 2010–11 ***One-time required fee:*** $280. ***Comprehensive fee:*** $36,780 includes full-time tuition ($27,640), mandatory fees ($700), and room and board ($8440). ***College room only:*** $4580. Full-time tuition and fees vary according to course load and degree level. Room and board charges vary according to board plan and housing facility. ***Part-time tuition:*** $875 per credit hour. Part-time tuition and fees vary according to course load and degree level. ***Payment plan:*** Installment.

FRESHMAN FINANCIAL AID (Fall 2010, est.) 364 applied for aid; of those 82% were deemed to have need. 100% of freshmen with need received aid; of those 36% had need fully met. ***Average percent of need met:*** 85% (excluding resources awarded to replace EFC). ***Average financial aid package:*** $25,310 (excluding resources awarded to replace EFC). 17% of all full-time freshmen had no need and received non-need-based gift aid.

UNDERGRADUATE FINANCIAL AID (Fall 2010, est.) 1,299 applied for aid; of those 82% were deemed to have need. 100% of undergraduates with need received aid; of those 39% had need fully met. ***Average percent of need met:*** 89% (excluding resources awarded to replace EFC). ***Average financial aid package:*** $24,212 (excluding resources awarded to replace EFC). 17% of all full-time undergraduates had no need and received non-need-based gift aid.

GIFT AID (NEED-BASED) ***Total amount:*** $17,341,850 (14% federal, 2% state, 84% institutional). ***Receiving aid:*** Freshmen: 75% (291); all full-time undergraduates: 74% (1,029). ***Average award:*** Freshmen: $15,275; Undergraduates: $14,172. ***Scholarships, grants, and awards:*** Federal Pell, FSEOG, state, private, college/university gift aid from institutional funds.

GIFT AID (NON-NEED-BASED) ***Total amount:*** $3,385,702 (84% institutional, 16% external sources). ***Receiving aid:*** Freshmen: 49% (190). Undergraduates: 50% (695). ***Average award:*** Freshmen: $11,266. Undergraduates: $8959. ***Scholarships, grants, and awards by category:*** *Academic interests/achievement:* 531 awards ($6,305,171 total): general academic interests/achievements, physical sciences. *Creative arts/performance:* 61 awards ($181,000 total): art/fine arts, music, performing arts, theater/drama. *Special achievements/activities:* 4 awards ($18,000 total): general special achievements/activities. *Special* *characteristics:* 158 awards ($763,500 total): children and siblings of alumni, ethnic background, members of minority groups. ***Tuition waivers:*** Full or partial for employees or children of employees.

LOANS ***Student loans:*** $8,316,396 (49% need-based, 51% non-need-based). 76% of past graduating class borrowed through all loan programs. *Average indebtedness per student:* $34,152. ***Average need-based loan:*** Freshmen: $3513. Undergraduates: $4611. ***Parent loans:*** $3,245,133 (100% non-need-based). ***Programs:*** Federal Direct (Subsidized and Unsubsidized Stafford, PLUS), Perkins.

WORK-STUDY ***Federal work-study:*** Total amount: $1,758,901; 897 jobs averaging $1961.

APPLYING FOR FINANCIAL AID ***Required financial aid form:*** FAFSA. ***Financial aid deadline (priority):*** 3/1. ***Notification date:*** 3/15. Students must reply by 5/1 or within 2 weeks of notification.

CONTACT Mr. Kevin Lamb, Director of Financial Aid, Marietta College, 215 Fifth Street, Marietta, OH 45750-4000, 740-376-4712 or toll-free 800-331-7896. *Fax:* 740-376-4990. *E-mail:* finaid@marietta.edu.

MARIST COLLEGE

Poughkeepsie, NY

Tuition & fees: $27,650 **Average undergraduate aid package: $17,712**

ABOUT THE INSTITUTION Independent, coed. 55 undergraduate majors. Federal methodology is used as a basis for awarding need-based institutional aid.

UNDERGRADUATE EXPENSES for 2010–11 ***One-time required fee:*** $90. ***Comprehensive fee:*** $40,000 includes full-time tuition ($27,150), mandatory fees ($500), and room and board ($12,350). ***College room only:*** $8775. Room and board charges vary according to board plan and housing facility. ***Part-time tuition:*** $634 per credit. ***Part-time fees:*** $40 per term. ***Payment plan:*** Installment.

FRESHMAN FINANCIAL AID (Fall 2010, est.) 920 applied for aid; of those 74% were deemed to have need. 100% of freshmen with need received aid; of those 23% had need fully met. ***Average percent of need met:*** 77% (excluding resources awarded to replace EFC). ***Average financial aid package:*** $19,397 (excluding resources awarded to replace EFC). 28% of all full-time freshmen had no need and received non-need-based gift aid.

UNDERGRADUATE FINANCIAL AID (Fall 2010, est.) 3,424 applied for aid; of those 82% were deemed to have need. 100% of undergraduates with need received aid; of those 18% had need fully met. ***Average percent of need met:*** 69% (excluding resources awarded to replace EFC). ***Average financial aid package:*** $17,712 (excluding resources awarded to replace EFC). 23% of all full-time undergraduates had no need and received non-need-based gift aid.

GIFT AID (NEED-BASED) ***Total amount:*** $28,748,593 (13% federal, 6% state, 79% institutional, 2% external sources). ***Receiving aid:*** Freshmen: 43% (468); all full-time undergraduates: 39% (1,743). ***Average award:*** Freshmen: $18,429; Undergraduates: $16,909. ***Scholarships, grants, and awards:*** Federal Pell, FSEOG, state, private, college/university gift aid from institutional funds.

GIFT AID (NON-NEED-BASED) ***Total amount:*** $9,138,606 (3% state, 90% institutional, 7% external sources). ***Receiving aid:*** Freshmen: 47% (506). Undergraduates: 39% (1,748). ***Average award:*** Freshmen: $7297. Undergraduates: $7180. ***Scholarships, grants, and awards by category:*** *Academic interests/achievement:* general academic interests/achievements. *Creative arts/performance:* debating, music. *Special characteristics:* local/state students. ***Tuition waivers:*** Full or partial for employees or children of employees.

LOANS ***Student loans:*** $27,119,159 (77% need-based, 23% non-need-based). 68% of past graduating class borrowed through all loan programs. *Average indebtedness per student:* $25,135. ***Average need-based loan:*** Freshmen: $3507. Undergraduates: $4619. ***Parent loans:*** $10,029,806 (67% need-based, 33% non-need-based). ***Programs:*** Federal Direct (Subsidized and Unsubsidized Stafford, PLUS), Perkins, alternative loans.

WORK-STUDY ***Federal work-study:*** Total amount: $2,387,110; jobs available. ***State or other work-study/employment:*** Total amount: $941,100 (100% non-need-based). Part-time jobs available.

ATHLETIC AWARDS Total amount: $3,382,422 (48% need-based, 52% non-need-based).

APPLYING FOR FINANCIAL AID ***Required financial aid forms:*** FAFSA, institution's own form. ***Financial aid deadline:*** 5/1 (priority: 2/15). ***Notification date:*** Continuous beginning 3/15. Students must reply by 5/1 or within 2 weeks of notification.

CONTACT Joseph R. Weglarz, Executive Director of Student Financial Services, Marist College, 3399 North Road, Poughkeepsie, NY 12601, 845-575-3230 or toll-free 800-436-5483. *Fax:* 845-575-3099. *E-mail:* joseph.weglarz@marist.edu.

MARLBORO COLLEGE

Marlboro, VT

Tuition & fees: $36,560 **Average undergraduate aid package: $20,263**

ABOUT THE INSTITUTION Independent, coed. 75 undergraduate majors. Federal methodology is used as a basis for awarding need-based institutional aid.

UNDERGRADUATE EXPENSES for 2011–12 ***Comprehensive fee:*** $46,200 includes full-time tuition ($35,250), mandatory fees ($1310), and room and board ($9640). ***College room only:*** $5310. Full-time tuition and fees vary according to degree level, location, and program. ***Part-time tuition:*** $1175 per credit. Part-time tuition and fees vary according to course load, degree level, location, and program. ***Payment plan:*** Installment.

FRESHMAN FINANCIAL AID (Fall 2010, est.) 31 applied for aid; of those 97% were deemed to have need. 100% of freshmen with need received aid. ***Average percent of need met:*** 87% (excluding resources awarded to replace EFC). ***Average financial aid package:*** $20,250 (excluding resources awarded to replace EFC). 5% of all full-time freshmen had no need and received non-need-based gift aid.

UNDERGRADUATE FINANCIAL AID (Fall 2010, est.) 207 applied for aid; of those 93% were deemed to have need. 100% of undergraduates with need received aid. ***Average percent of need met:*** 87% (excluding resources awarded to replace EFC). ***Average financial aid package:*** $20,263 (excluding resources awarded to replace EFC). 16% of all full-time undergraduates had no need and received non-need-based gift aid.

GIFT AID (NEED-BASED) ***Total amount:*** $3,495,118 (11% federal, 1% state, 88% institutional). ***Receiving aid:*** Freshmen: 71% (30); all full-time undergraduates: 88% (186). ***Average award:*** Freshmen: $19,335; Undergraduates: $18,598. ***Scholarships, grants, and awards:*** Federal Pell, FSEOG, state, private, college/university gift aid from institutional funds.

GIFT AID (NON-NEED-BASED) ***Total amount:*** $483,288 (84% institutional, 16% external sources). ***Receiving aid:*** Freshmen: 71% (30). Undergraduates: 89% (188). ***Average award:*** Freshmen: $6250. Undergraduates: $7971. ***Scholarships, grants, and awards by category:*** *Academic interests/achievement:* general academic interests/achievements. ***Tuition waivers:*** Full or partial for employees or children of employees, senior citizens.

LOANS ***Student loans:*** $1,478,360 (50% need-based, 50% non-need-based). 86% of past graduating class borrowed through all loan programs. *Average indebtedness per student:* $22,456. ***Parent loans:*** $730,514 (85% need-based, 15% non-need-based). ***Programs:*** Federal Direct (Subsidized and Unsubsidized Stafford, PLUS).

WORK-STUDY ***Federal work-study:*** Total amount: $316,604; 173 jobs averaging $2050. ***State or other work-study/employment:*** Part-time jobs available.

APPLYING FOR FINANCIAL AID ***Required financial aid form:*** FAFSA. ***Financial aid deadline:*** 3/1. ***Notification date:*** Continuous beginning 3/1. Students must reply by 5/1 or within 2 weeks of notification.

CONTACT Cathy S. Fuller, Associate Director of Financial Aid, Marlboro College, PO Box A, 2582 South Road, Marlboro, VT 05344-0300, 802-258-9237 or toll-free 800-343-0049. *Fax:* 802-258-9300. *E-mail:* finaid@marlboro.edu.

MARQUETTE UNIVERSITY

Milwaukee, WI

Tuition & fees: $31,822 **Average undergraduate aid package: $21,936**

ABOUT THE INSTITUTION Independent Roman Catholic (Jesuit), coed. 79 undergraduate majors. Federal methodology is used as a basis for awarding need-based institutional aid.

UNDERGRADUATE EXPENSES for 2011–12 ***Comprehensive fee:*** $42,192 includes full-time tuition ($31,400), mandatory fees ($422), and room and board ($10,370). Full-time tuition and fees vary according to course load and program. Room and board charges vary according to board plan and housing facility. ***Part-time tuition:*** $915 per credit. Part-time tuition and fees vary according to program. ***Payment plan:*** Installment.

FRESHMAN FINANCIAL AID (Fall 2010, est.) 1,555 applied for aid; of those 78% were deemed to have need. 100% of freshmen with need received aid; of those 25% had need fully met. ***Average percent of need met:*** 75% (excluding resources awarded to replace EFC). ***Average financial aid package:*** $21,818 (excluding resources awarded to replace EFC). 36% of all full-time freshmen had no need and received non-need-based gift aid.

UNDERGRADUATE FINANCIAL AID (Fall 2010, est.) 5,672 applied for aid; of those 84% were deemed to have need. 100% of undergraduates with need received aid; of those 26% had need fully met. ***Average percent of need met:*** 76% (excluding resources awarded to replace EFC). ***Average financial aid package:*** $21,936 (excluding resources awarded to replace EFC). 27% of all full-time undergraduates had no need and received non-need-based gift aid.

GIFT AID (NEED-BASED) ***Total amount:*** $69,789,189 (12% federal, 5% state, 76% institutional, 7% external sources). ***Receiving aid:*** Freshmen: 62% (1,205); all full-time undergraduates: 60% (4,641). ***Average award:*** Freshmen: $16,500; Undergraduates: $15,219. ***Scholarships, grants, and awards:*** Federal Pell, FSEOG, state, private, college/university gift aid from institutional funds.

GIFT AID (NON-NEED-BASED) ***Total amount:*** $23,378,100 (84% institutional, 16% external sources). ***Receiving aid:*** Freshmen: 8% (153). Undergraduates: 6% (436). ***Average award:*** Freshmen: $9054. Undergraduates: $8480. ***Scholarships, grants, and awards by category:*** *Academic interests/achievement:* 5,262 awards ($38,316,439 total): biological sciences, business, communication, education, engineering/technologies, English, foreign languages, general academic interests/achievements, health fields, mathematics, physical sciences. *Creative arts/performance:* 10 awards ($8750 total): theater/drama. *Special characteristics:* 171 awards ($4,839,954 total): children of faculty/staff. ***Tuition waivers:*** Full or partial for employees or children of employees, adult students, senior citizens.

LOANS ***Student loans:*** $45,904,087 (78% need-based, 22% non-need-based). 65% of past graduating class borrowed through all loan programs. *Average indebtedness per student:* $32,824. ***Average need-based loan:*** Freshmen: $4472. Undergraduates: $5434. ***Parent loans:*** $21,361,292 (32% need-based, 68% non-need-based). ***Programs:*** Federal Direct (Subsidized and Unsubsidized Stafford, PLUS), Perkins, Federal Nursing, state, college/university.

WORK-STUDY ***Federal work-study:*** Total amount: $6,860,378; jobs available. ***State or other work-study/employment:*** Part-time jobs available.

ATHLETIC AWARDS Total amount: $3,590,952 (40% need-based, 60% non-need-based).

APPLYING FOR FINANCIAL AID ***Required financial aid form:*** FAFSA. ***Financial aid deadline:*** Continuous. ***Notification date:*** Continuous beginning 3/20. Students must reply by 5/1 or within 3 weeks of notification.

CONTACT Susan Teerink, Director of Financial Aid, Marquette University, PO Box 1881, Milwaukee, WI 53201-1881, 414-288-4000 or toll-free 800-222-6544. *Fax:* 414-288-1718. *E-mail:* financialaid@marquette.edu.

MARSHALL UNIVERSITY

Huntington, WV

Tuition & fees (WV res): $5285 **Average undergraduate aid package: $9628**

ABOUT THE INSTITUTION State-supported, coed. 52 undergraduate majors. Federal methodology is used as a basis for awarding need-based institutional aid.

UNDERGRADUATE EXPENSES for 2010–11 ***Tuition, state resident:*** full-time $4319; part-time $180.25 per credit hour. ***Tuition, nonresident:*** full-time $11,930; part-time $497.25 per credit hour. ***Required fees:*** full-time $966; $40.50 per credit hour. Full-time tuition and fees vary according to degree level, location, program, and reciprocity agreements. Part-time tuition and fees vary according to course load, degree level, location, program, and reciprocity agreements. ***College room and board:*** $7858; ***Room only:*** $4652. Room and board charges vary according to board plan and housing facility. ***Payment plan:*** Installment.

FRESHMAN FINANCIAL AID (Fall 2010, est.) 1,312 applied for aid; of those 77% were deemed to have need. 99% of freshmen with need received aid; of those 30% had need fully met. ***Average percent of need met:*** 53% (excluding resources awarded to replace EFC). ***Average financial aid package:*** $9713 (excluding resources awarded to replace EFC). 19% of all full-time freshmen had no need and received non-need-based gift aid.

UNDERGRADUATE FINANCIAL AID (Fall 2010, est.) 6,416 applied for aid; of those 81% were deemed to have need. 98% of undergraduates with need received aid; of those 34% had need fully met. ***Average percent of need met:*** 55% (excluding resources awarded to replace EFC). ***Average financial aid package:*** $9628 (excluding resources awarded to replace EFC). 16% of all full-time undergraduates had no need and received non-need-based gift aid.

GIFT AID (NEED-BASED) ***Total amount:*** $27,007,533 (79% federal, 21% state). ***Receiving aid:*** Freshmen: 53% (737); all full-time undergraduates: 50% (3,823). ***Average award:*** Freshmen: $6155; Undergraduates: $5933. ***Scholarships, grants, and awards:*** Federal Pell, FSEOG, state, private, college/university gift aid from institutional funds, Academic Competitiveness Grants, National SMART Grants, TEACH Grants.

GIFT AID (NON-NEED-BASED) ***Total amount:*** $14,991,068 (55% state, 36% institutional, 9% external sources). ***Receiving aid:*** Freshmen: 41% (579). Undergraduates: 25% (1,948). ***Average award:*** Freshmen: $5372. Undergraduates: $5643. ***Scholarships, grants, and awards by category:*** *Academic interests/achievement:* 2,569 awards ($5,444,642 total): general academic interests/achievements. *Special characteristics:* 57 awards ($188,014 total): children of faculty/staff. ***Tuition waivers:*** Full or partial for employees or children of employees, senior citizens.

LOANS ***Student loans:*** $40,338,422 (95% need-based, 5% non-need-based). 65% of past graduating class borrowed through all loan programs. *Average indebtedness per student:* $21,156. ***Average need-based loan:*** Freshmen: $5694. Undergraduates: $7066. ***Parent loans:*** $3,307,336 (100% non-need-based). ***Programs:*** Federal Direct (Subsidized and Unsubsidized Stafford, PLUS), Perkins, state, college/university, alternative loans.

WORK-STUDY ***Federal work-study:*** Total amount: $341,649; 189 jobs averaging $1807. ***State or other work-study/employment:*** Part-time jobs available.

ATHLETIC AWARDS Total amount: $4,568,664 (100% non-need-based).

APPLYING FOR FINANCIAL AID ***Required financial aid form:*** FAFSA. ***Financial aid deadline (priority):*** 3/1. ***Notification date:*** 3/15. Students must reply within 2 weeks of notification.

CONTACT Ms. Kathy Bialk, Director of Student Financial Aid, Marshall University, One John Marshall Drive, Huntington, WV 25755, 304-696-2280 or toll-free 800-642-3499 (in-state). *Fax:* 304-696-3242. *E-mail:* bialkk@marshall.edu.

MARS HILL COLLEGE

Mars Hill, NC

Tuition & fees: $21,997 **Average undergraduate aid package: $17,195**

ABOUT THE INSTITUTION Independent Baptist, coed. 59 undergraduate majors. Federal methodology is used as a basis for awarding need-based institutional aid.

UNDERGRADUATE EXPENSES for 2010–11 ***Comprehensive fee:*** $29,629 includes full-time tuition ($19,907), mandatory fees ($2090), and room and board ($7632). Room and board charges vary according to board plan and housing facility. ***Part-time tuition:*** $730 per credit hour. ***Part-time fees:*** $90 per credit hour. ***Payment plan:*** Installment.

FRESHMAN FINANCIAL AID (Fall 2010, est.) 1,052 applied for aid; of those 25% were deemed to have need. 98% of freshmen with need received aid; of those 14% had need fully met. ***Average percent of need met:*** 69% (excluding resources awarded to replace EFC). ***Average financial aid package:*** $17,572 (excluding resources awarded to replace EFC). 3% of all full-time freshmen had no need and received non-need-based gift aid.

UNDERGRADUATE FINANCIAL AID (Fall 2010, est.) 2,256 applied for aid; of those 45% were deemed to have need. 99% of undergraduates with need received aid; of those 16% had need fully met. ***Average percent of need met:*** 73% (excluding resources awarded to replace EFC). ***Average financial aid package:*** $17,195 (excluding resources awarded to replace EFC). 6% of all full-time undergraduates had no need and received non-need-based gift aid.

GIFT AID (NEED-BASED) ***Total amount:*** $12,335,285 (25% federal, 19% state, 51% institutional, 5% external sources). ***Receiving aid:*** Freshmen: 24% (258); all full-time undergraduates: 41% (990). ***Average award:*** Freshmen: $14,686; Undergraduates: $13,790. ***Scholarships, grants, and awards:*** Federal Pell, FSEOG, state, private, college/university gift aid from institutional funds.

GIFT AID (NON-NEED-BASED) ***Total amount:*** $3,299,187 (6% state, 42% institutional, 52% external sources). ***Receiving aid:*** Freshmen: 2% (27). Undergraduates: 4% (101). ***Average award:*** Freshmen: $8190. Undergraduates: $8631. ***Scholarships, grants, and awards by category:*** *Academic interests/achievement:* 542 awards ($2,036,476 total): general academic interests/achievements. *Creative arts/performance:* 101 awards ($184,503 total): dance, music, theater/drama. *Special achievements/activities:* 13 awards ($15,300 total):

cheerleading/drum major. *Special characteristics:* 35 awards ($286,418 total): children of faculty/staff. ***Tuition waivers:*** Full or partial for employees or children of employees.

LOANS ***Student loans:*** $7,221,921 (81% need-based, 19% non-need-based). 81% of past graduating class borrowed through all loan programs. *Average indebtedness per student:* $27,775. ***Average need-based loan:*** Freshmen: $2999. Undergraduates: $3988. ***Parent loans:*** $1,785,135 (52% need-based, 48% non-need-based). ***Programs:*** Federal Direct (Subsidized and Unsubsidized Stafford, PLUS), Perkins.

WORK-STUDY ***Federal work-study:*** Total amount: $282,556; 252 jobs averaging $1354. ***State or other work-study/employment:*** Total amount: $1100 (100% need-based). Part-time jobs available.

ATHLETIC AWARDS Total amount: $2,074,314 (65% need-based, 35% non-need-based).

APPLYING FOR FINANCIAL AID ***Required financial aid forms:*** FAFSA, state aid form. ***Financial aid deadline:*** Continuous. ***Notification date:*** Continuous beginning 1/15. Students must reply within 2 weeks of notification.

CONTACT Amanda Randolph, Director of Financial Aid, Mars Hill College, PO Box 370, Mars Hill, NC 28754, 828-689-1123 or toll-free 866-MHC-4-YOU. *Fax:* 828-689-1300. *E-mail:* arandolph@mhc.edu.

MARTIN LUTHER COLLEGE

New Ulm, MN

Tuition & fees: $11,320 **Average undergraduate aid package: $8720**

ABOUT THE INSTITUTION Independent religious, coed. 6 undergraduate majors. Federal methodology is used as a basis for awarding need-based institutional aid.

UNDERGRADUATE EXPENSES for 2011–12 ***Comprehensive fee:*** $15,710 includes full-time tuition ($11,320) and room and board ($4390). ***Payment plan:*** Installment.

FRESHMAN FINANCIAL AID (Fall 2010, est.) 156 applied for aid; of those 85% were deemed to have need. 99% of freshmen with need received aid; of those 12% had need fully met. ***Average percent of need met:*** 69% (excluding resources awarded to replace EFC). ***Average financial aid package:*** $9336 (excluding resources awarded to replace EFC). 12% of all full-time freshmen had no need and received non-need-based gift aid.

UNDERGRADUATE FINANCIAL AID (Fall 2010, est.) 620 applied for aid; of those 88% were deemed to have need. 99% of undergraduates with need received aid; of those 12% had need fully met. ***Average percent of need met:*** 66% (excluding resources awarded to replace EFC). ***Average financial aid package:*** $8720 (excluding resources awarded to replace EFC). 15% of all full-time undergraduates had no need and received non-need-based gift aid.

GIFT AID (NEED-BASED) ***Total amount:*** $3,109,486 (33% federal, 5% state, 54% institutional, 8% external sources). ***Receiving aid:*** Freshmen: 78% (130); all full-time undergraduates: 75% (523). ***Average award:*** Freshmen: $6995; Undergraduates: $5910. ***Scholarships, grants, and awards:*** Federal Pell, FSEOG, state, private, college/university gift aid from institutional funds.

GIFT AID (NON-NEED-BASED) ***Total amount:*** $297,444 (76% institutional, 24% external sources). ***Receiving aid:*** Freshmen: 3% (5). Undergraduates: 2% (14). ***Average award:*** Freshmen: $2099. Undergraduates: $2020. ***Scholarships, grants, and awards by category:*** *Academic interests/achievement:* general academic interests/achievements. *Creative arts/performance:* music.

LOANS ***Student loans:*** $2,762,188 (71% need-based, 29% non-need-based). 53% of past graduating class borrowed through all loan programs. *Average indebtedness per student:* $21,799. ***Average need-based loan:*** Freshmen: $3474. Undergraduates: $4163. ***Parent loans:*** $62,600 (8% need-based, 92% non-need-based). ***Programs:*** Perkins, state, college/university, alternative loans.

WORK-STUDY ***Federal work-study:*** Total amount: $54,337; jobs available. ***State or other work-study/employment:*** Total amount: $10,613 (100% need-based). Part-time jobs available.

APPLYING FOR FINANCIAL AID ***Required financial aid forms:*** FAFSA, institution's own form. ***Financial aid deadline:*** 4/15. ***Notification date:*** Continuous beginning 3/15. Students must reply by 9/1.

CONTACT Mr. Gene Slettedahl, Director of Financial Aid, Martin Luther College, 1995 Luther Court, New Ulm, MN 56073, 507-354-8221. *Fax:* 507-354-8225. *E-mail:* slettega@mlc-wels.edu.

MARTIN METHODIST COLLEGE

Pulaski, TN

CONTACT Ms. Anita Beecham, Financial Aid Assistant, Martin Methodist College, 433 West Madison Street, Pulaski, TN 38478-2716, 931-363-9808 or toll-free 800-467-1273. *Fax:* 931-363-9818. *E-mail:* abeecham@martinmethodist.edu.

MARTIN UNIVERSITY

Indianapolis, IN

CONTACT Berdia Marshall, Director of Financial Aid, Martin University, 2171 Avondale Place, Indianapolis, IN 46218-3867, 317-543-3670. *Fax:* 317-543-4790. *E-mail:* bmarshall@martin.edu.

MARY BALDWIN COLLEGE

Staunton, VA

Tuition & fees: $25,555 **Average undergraduate aid package: $17,887**

ABOUT THE INSTITUTION Independent, coed, primarily women. 33 undergraduate majors. Federal methodology is used as a basis for awarding need-based institutional aid.

UNDERGRADUATE EXPENSES for 2010–11 ***Comprehensive fee:*** $32,975 includes full-time tuition ($25,340), mandatory fees ($215), and room and board ($7420). ***College room only:*** $4732. Full-time tuition and fees vary according to degree level. Room and board charges vary according to housing facility. Part-time tuition and fees vary according to degree level. ***Payment plan:*** Installment.

FRESHMAN FINANCIAL AID (Fall 2010, est.) 261 applied for aid; of those 91% were deemed to have need. 99% of freshmen with need received aid; of those 11% had need fully met. ***Average percent of need met:*** 72% (excluding resources awarded to replace EFC). ***Average financial aid package:*** $21,619 (excluding resources awarded to replace EFC). 13% of all full-time freshmen had no need and received non-need-based gift aid.

UNDERGRADUATE FINANCIAL AID (Fall 2010, est.) 973 applied for aid; of those 93% were deemed to have need. 100% of undergraduates with need received aid; of those 11% had need fully met. ***Average percent of need met:*** 68% (excluding resources awarded to replace EFC). ***Average financial aid package:*** $17,887 (excluding resources awarded to replace EFC). 9% of all full-time undergraduates had no need and received non-need-based gift aid.

GIFT AID (NEED-BASED) ***Total amount:*** $12,814,578 (27% federal, 12% state, 58% institutional, 3% external sources). ***Receiving aid:*** Freshmen: 69% (236); all full-time undergraduates: 80% (885). ***Average award:*** Freshmen: $18,379; Undergraduates: $14,094. ***Scholarships, grants, and awards:*** Federal Pell, FSEOG, state, private, college/university gift aid from institutional funds.

GIFT AID (NON-NEED-BASED) ***Total amount:*** $1,907,367 (3% federal, 13% state, 73% institutional, 11% external sources). ***Receiving aid:*** Freshmen: 64% (218). Undergraduates: 71% (789). ***Average award:*** Freshmen: $12,754. Undergraduates: $11,184. ***Scholarships, grants, and awards by category:*** *Academic interests/achievement:* general academic interests/achievements. *Special achievements/activities:* leadership. *Special characteristics:* children of educators, children of faculty/staff. ***Tuition waivers:*** Full or partial for employees or children of employees.

LOANS ***Student loans:*** $9,271,716 (85% need-based, 15% non-need-based). 79% of past graduating class borrowed through all loan programs. *Average indebtedness per student:* $29,245. ***Average need-based loan:*** Freshmen: $3391. Undergraduates: $4122. ***Parent loans:*** $2,575,722 (48% need-based, 52% non-need-based). ***Programs:*** Perkins, alternative loans.

WORK-STUDY ***Federal work-study:*** Total amount: $361,284; 338 jobs averaging $827. ***State or other work-study/employment:*** Total amount: $132,990 (35% need-based, 65% non-need-based). Part-time jobs available.

APPLYING FOR FINANCIAL AID ***Required financial aid forms:*** FAFSA, state aid form (VA residents only). ***Financial aid deadline:*** Continuous. ***Notification date:*** Continuous beginning 3/15. Students must reply within 3 weeks of notification.

CONTACT Mrs. Robin Dietrich, Director of Financial Aid, Mary Baldwin College, 201 East Frederick Street, Staunton, VA 24401-3610, 540-887-7025 or toll-free 800-468-2262. *Fax:* 540-887-7229. *E-mail:* rdietric@mbc.edu.

MARYGROVE COLLEGE

Detroit, MI

CONTACT Mr. Donald Hurt, Director of Financial Aid, Marygrove College, 8425 West McNichols Road, Detroit, MI 48221-2599, 313-862-8000 Ext. 436 or toll-free 866-313-1297.

MARYLAND INSTITUTE COLLEGE OF ART

Baltimore, MD

CONTACT Ms. Diane Prengaman, Associate Vice President for Financial Aid, Maryland Institute College of Art, 1300 Mount Royal Avenue, Baltimore, MD 21217, 410-225-2285. *Fax:* 410-225-2337. *E-mail:* dprengam@mica.edu.

MARYLHURST UNIVERSITY

Marylhurst, OR

Tuition & fees: $17,730 **Average undergraduate aid package: $10,399**

ABOUT THE INSTITUTION Independent Roman Catholic, coed, primarily women. 20 undergraduate majors. Federal methodology is used as a basis for awarding need-based institutional aid.

UNDERGRADUATE EXPENSES for 2010–11 ***Tuition:*** full-time $17,730; part-time $394 per credit. Full-time tuition and fees vary according to course load and program. Part-time tuition and fees vary according to course load and program. ***Payment plan:*** Installment.

FRESHMAN FINANCIAL AID (Fall 2010, est.) 6 applied for aid; of those 100% were deemed to have need. 100% of freshmen with need received aid. ***Average percent of need met:*** 49% (excluding resources awarded to replace EFC). ***Average financial aid package:*** $11,349 (excluding resources awarded to replace EFC).

UNDERGRADUATE FINANCIAL AID (Fall 2010, est.) 339 applied for aid; of those 92% were deemed to have need. 100% of undergraduates with need received aid; of those 3% had need fully met. ***Average percent of need met:*** 48% (excluding resources awarded to replace EFC). ***Average financial aid package:*** $10,399 (excluding resources awarded to replace EFC). 8% of all full-time undergraduates had no need and received non-need-based gift aid.

GIFT AID (NEED-BASED) ***Total amount:*** $3,016,838 (56% federal, 3% state, 33% institutional, 8% external sources). ***Receiving aid:*** Freshmen: 44% (4); all full-time undergraduates: 67% (237). ***Average award:*** Freshmen: $11,774; Undergraduates: $7613. ***Scholarships, grants, and awards:*** Federal Pell, FSEOG, state, private, college/university gift aid from institutional funds, United Negro College Fund.

GIFT AID (NON-NEED-BASED) ***Total amount:*** $134,995 (1% federal, 66% institutional, 33% external sources). ***Receiving aid:*** Undergraduates: 1. ***Average award:*** Undergraduates: $1713. ***Tuition waivers:*** Full or partial for employees or children of employees, senior citizens.

LOANS ***Student loans:*** $7,595,582 (86% need-based, 14% non-need-based). 43% of past graduating class borrowed through all loan programs. *Average indebtedness per student:* $10,278. ***Average need-based loan:*** Freshmen: $4200. Undergraduates: $4510. ***Parent loans:*** $238,772 (51% need-based, 49% non-need-based). ***Programs:*** Federal Direct (Subsidized and Unsubsidized Stafford, PLUS), Perkins.

WORK-STUDY ***Federal work-study:*** Total amount: $137,850; 41 jobs averaging $3955.

APPLYING FOR FINANCIAL AID ***Required financial aid forms:*** FAFSA, institution's own form. ***Financial aid deadline:*** Continuous. ***Notification date:*** Continuous beginning 5/15. Students must reply within 8 weeks of notification.

CONTACT Tracy Reisinger, Office of Financial Aid, Marylhurst University, 17600 Pacific Highway, PO Box 261, Marylhurst, OR 97036, 503-699-6253 or toll-free 800-634-9982. *Fax:* 503-635-6585. *E-mail:* treisinger@marylhurst.edu.

MARYMOUNT COLLEGE, PALOS VERDES, CALIFORNIA

Rancho Palos Verdes, CA

CONTACT Financial Aid Office, Marymount College, Palos Verdes, California, 30800 Palos Verdes Drive East, Rancho Palos Verdes, CA 90275-6299, 310-377-5501.

MARYMOUNT MANHATTAN COLLEGE

New York, NY

ABOUT THE INSTITUTION Independent, coed. 22 undergraduate majors.

GIFT AID (NEED-BASED) ***Scholarships, grants, and awards:*** Federal Pell, FSEOG, state, private, college/university gift aid from institutional funds.

GIFT AID (NON-NEED-BASED) ***Scholarships, grants, and awards by category:*** *Academic interests/achievement:* general academic interests/achievements. *Creative arts/performance:* art/fine arts, dance, performing arts. *Special achievements/activities:* leadership. *Special characteristics:* local/state students.

WORK-STUDY ***Federal work-study:*** Total amount: $83,799; jobs available. ***State or other work-study/employment:*** Part-time jobs available.

APPLYING FOR FINANCIAL AID ***Required financial aid form:*** FAFSA.

CONTACT Director of Financial Aid, Marymount Manhattan College, 221 East 71st Street, New York, NY 10021, 212-517-0500 or toll-free 800-MARYMOUNT (out-of-state). *Fax:* 212-517-0491.

MARYMOUNT UNIVERSITY

Arlington, VA

Tuition & fees: $23,974 **Average undergraduate aid package: $15,824**

ABOUT THE INSTITUTION Independent religious, coed. 26 undergraduate majors. Both federal and institutional methodology are used as a basis for awarding need-based institutional aid.

UNDERGRADUATE EXPENSES for 2011–12 ***Comprehensive fee:*** $34,554 includes full-time tuition ($23,700), mandatory fees ($274), and room and board ($10,580). Room and board charges vary according to housing facility. ***Payment plan:*** Installment.

FRESHMAN FINANCIAL AID (Fall 2010, est.) 335 applied for aid; of those 86% were deemed to have need. 99% of freshmen with need received aid; of those 19% had need fully met. ***Average percent of need met:*** 73% (excluding resources awarded to replace EFC). ***Average financial aid package:*** $18,529 (excluding resources awarded to replace EFC). 20% of all full-time freshmen had no need and received non-need-based gift aid.

UNDERGRADUATE FINANCIAL AID (Fall 2010, est.) 1,447 applied for aid; of those 87% were deemed to have need. 99% of undergraduates with need received aid; of those 14% had need fully met. ***Average percent of need met:*** 65% (excluding resources awarded to replace EFC). ***Average financial aid package:*** $15,824 (excluding resources awarded to replace EFC). 18% of all full-time undergraduates had no need and received non-need-based gift aid.

GIFT AID (NEED-BASED) ***Total amount:*** $4,675,008 (57% federal, 2% state, 41% institutional). ***Receiving aid:*** Freshmen: 44% (181); all full-time undergraduates: 39% (784). ***Average award:*** Freshmen: $4733; Undergraduates: $5840. ***Scholarships, grants, and awards:*** Federal Pell, FSEOG, state, private, college/university gift aid from institutional funds.

GIFT AID (NON-NEED-BASED) ***Total amount:*** $13,389,969 (16% state, 83% institutional, 1% external sources). ***Receiving aid:*** Freshmen: 69% (285). Undergraduates: 50% (1,001). ***Average award:*** Freshmen: $12,282. Undergraduates: $11,059. ***Scholarships, grants, and awards by category:*** *Academic interests/achievement:* biological sciences, business, general academic interests/achievements, health fields, mathematics, social sciences. *Special achievements/activities:* community service, general special achievements/activities, leadership. *Special characteristics:* children of current students, children of faculty/staff, general special characteristics, international students, religious affiliation, veterans. ***Tuition waivers:*** Full or partial for employees or children of employees, senior citizens.

LOANS ***Student loans:*** $13,902,008 (35% need-based, 65% non-need-based). 80% of past graduating class borrowed through all loan programs. *Average indebtedness per student:* $23,945. ***Average need-based loan:*** Freshmen: $3464. Undergraduates: $4399. ***Parent loans:*** $5,241,406 (100% non-need-based). ***Programs:*** Federal Direct (Subsidized and Unsubsidized Stafford, PLUS), Perkins.

WORK-STUDY ***Federal work-study:*** Total amount: $1,304,230; jobs available.

APPLYING FOR FINANCIAL AID ***Required financial aid form:*** FAFSA. ***Financial aid deadline (priority):*** 3/1. ***Notification date:*** Continuous beginning 3/15. Students must reply within 2 weeks of notification.

CONTACT Ms. Debbie A. Raines, Director of Financial Aid, Marymount University, 2807 North Glebe Road, Arlington, VA 22207-4299, 703-284-1530 or toll-free 800-548-7638. *Fax:* 703-516-4771. *E-mail:* debbie.raines@marymount.edu.

MARYVILLE COLLEGE

Maryville, TN

Tuition & fees: $29,924 **Average undergraduate aid package: $27,657**

ABOUT THE INSTITUTION Independent Presbyterian, coed. 55 undergraduate majors. Federal methodology is used as a basis for awarding need-based institutional aid.

UNDERGRADUATE EXPENSES for 2011–12 ***Comprehensive fee:*** $39,158 includes full-time tuition ($29,230), mandatory fees ($694), and room and board ($9234). ***College room only:*** $4584. Full-time tuition and fees vary according to course load. Room and board charges vary according to board plan and housing facility. ***Part-time tuition:*** $1218 per credit hour. Part-time tuition and fees vary according to course load. ***Payment plan:*** Installment.

FRESHMAN FINANCIAL AID (Fall 2010, est.) 277 applied for aid; of those 87% were deemed to have need. 100% of freshmen with need received aid; of those 23% had need fully met. ***Average percent of need met:*** 89% (excluding resources awarded to replace EFC). ***Average financial aid package:*** $30,091 (excluding resources awarded to replace EFC). 13% of all full-time freshmen had no need and received non-need-based gift aid.

UNDERGRADUATE FINANCIAL AID (Fall 2010, est.) 1,060 applied for aid; of those 83% were deemed to have need. 100% of undergraduates with need received aid; of those 24% had need fully met. ***Average percent of need met:*** 85% (excluding resources awarded to replace EFC). ***Average financial aid package:*** $27,657 (excluding resources awarded to replace EFC). 15% of all full-time undergraduates had no need and received non-need-based gift aid.

GIFT AID (NEED-BASED) ***Total amount:*** $19,593,390 (11% federal, 15% state, 74% institutional). ***Receiving aid:*** Freshmen: 87% (241); all full-time undergraduates: 82% (870). ***Average award:*** Freshmen: $25,569; Undergraduates: $32,153. ***Scholarships, grants, and awards:*** Federal Pell, FSEOG, state, private, college/university gift aid from institutional funds.

GIFT AID (NON-NEED-BASED) ***Total amount:*** $1,222,558 (55% state, 43% institutional, 2% external sources). ***Receiving aid:*** Freshmen: 35% (98). Undergraduates: 7% (75). ***Average award:*** Freshmen: $14,823. Undergraduates: $14,003. ***Scholarships, grants, and awards by category:*** *Academic interests/achievement:* general academic interests/achievements. *Creative arts/performance:* art/fine arts, music, theater/drama. *Special achievements/activities:* community service, leadership. *Special characteristics:* children and siblings of alumni, children of faculty/staff, members of minority groups, religious affiliation. ***Tuition waivers:*** Full or partial for employees or children of employees.

LOANS ***Student loans:*** $6,191,702 (79% need-based, 21% non-need-based). 74% of past graduating class borrowed through all loan programs. *Average indebtedness per student:* $21,343. ***Average need-based loan:*** Freshmen: $4610. Undergraduates: $4825. ***Parent loans:*** $1,704,091 (37% need-based, 63% non-need-based). ***Programs:*** Federal Direct (Subsidized and Unsubsidized Stafford, PLUS), Perkins.

WORK-STUDY ***Federal work-study:*** Total amount: $962,458; 549 jobs averaging $1753. ***State or other work-study/employment:*** Total amount: $214,122 (75% need-based, 25% non-need-based). 50 part-time jobs averaging $1632.

APPLYING FOR FINANCIAL AID ***Required financial aid form:*** FAFSA. ***Financial aid deadline (priority):*** 3/1. ***Notification date:*** Continuous beginning 3/15. Students must reply within 4 weeks of notification.

CONTACT Mr. Richard Brand, Director of Financial Aid, Maryville College, 502 East Lamar Alexander Parkway, Maryville, TN 37804-5907, 865-981-8100 or toll-free 800-597-2687. *E-mail:* richard.brand@maryvillecollege.edu.

MARYVILLE UNIVERSITY OF SAINT LOUIS

St. Louis, MO

Tuition & fees: $21,910 **Average undergraduate aid package: $14,115**

ABOUT THE INSTITUTION Independent, coed. 47 undergraduate majors. Both federal and institutional methodology are used as a basis for awarding need-based institutional aid.

UNDERGRADUATE EXPENSES for 2010–11 ***Comprehensive fee:*** $30,410 includes full-time tuition ($21,100), mandatory fees ($810), and room and board ($8500). Full-time tuition and fees vary according to course load. Room and board charges vary according to housing facility. ***Part-time tuition:*** $633.50 per credit hour. ***Part-time fees:*** $202.50 per term. Part-time tuition and fees vary according to class time. ***Payment plans:*** Installment, deferred payment.

FRESHMAN FINANCIAL AID (Fall 2010, est.) 306 applied for aid; of those 87% were deemed to have need. 100% of freshmen with need received aid; of those 20% had need fully met. ***Average percent of need met:*** 67% (excluding resources awarded to replace EFC). ***Average financial aid package:*** $18,956 (excluding resources awarded to replace EFC). 8% of all full-time freshmen had no need and received non-need-based gift aid.

UNDERGRADUATE FINANCIAL AID (Fall 2010, est.) 1,476 applied for aid; of those 91% were deemed to have need. 100% of undergraduates with need received aid; of those 11% had need fully met. ***Average percent of need met:*** 52% (excluding resources awarded to replace EFC). ***Average financial aid package:*** $14,115 (excluding resources awarded to replace EFC). 10% of all full-time undergraduates had no need and received non-need-based gift aid.

GIFT AID (NEED-BASED) ***Total amount:*** $14,449,363 (24% federal, 8% state, 67% institutional, 1% external sources). ***Receiving aid:*** Freshmen: 78% (264); all full-time undergraduates: 74% (1,278). ***Average award:*** Freshmen: $13,487; Undergraduates: $10,798. ***Scholarships, grants, and awards:*** Federal Pell, FSEOG, state, private, college/university gift aid from institutional funds, Academic Competitiveness Grants, National SMART Grants, TEACH Grants.

GIFT AID (NON-NEED-BASED) ***Total amount:*** $2,865,588 (1% state, 97% institutional, 2% external sources). ***Receiving aid:*** Freshmen: 12% (42). Undergraduates: 6% (104). ***Average award:*** Freshmen: $9124. Undergraduates: $7051. ***Scholarships, grants, and awards by category:*** *Academic interests/achievement:* 1,847 awards ($10,189,735 total): biological sciences, business, education, general academic interests/achievements, health fields. *Creative arts/performance:* 75 awards ($174,500 total): art/fine arts. *Special achievements/activities:* 188 awards ($366,475 total): cheerleading/drum major, community service, general special achievements/activities, leadership, religious involvement. *Special characteristics:* 73 awards ($180,395 total): children of faculty/staff, ethnic background, general special characteristics, international students, members of minority groups, out-of-state students, parents of current students, veterans. ***Tuition waivers:*** Full or partial for employees or children of employees, senior citizens.

LOANS ***Student loans:*** $15,591,215 (79% need-based, 21% non-need-based). 76% of past graduating class borrowed through all loan programs. *Average indebtedness per student:* $22,636. ***Average need-based loan:*** Freshmen: $3142. Undergraduates: $4366. ***Parent loans:*** $4,297,210 (45% need-based, 55% non-need-based). ***Programs:*** Federal Direct (Subsidized and Unsubsidized Stafford, PLUS), Perkins, Sallie Mae Signature Loans, KeyBank Loans, TERI Loans, CitiAssist Loans, Campus Door Loans.

WORK-STUDY ***Federal work-study:*** Total amount: $215,708; 258 jobs averaging $2055. ***State or other work-study/employment:*** Total amount: $510,254 (63% need-based, 37% non-need-based). 120 part-time jobs averaging $1941.

ATHLETIC AWARDS Total amount: $756,785 (61% need-based, 39% non-need-based).

APPLYING FOR FINANCIAL AID ***Required financial aid form:*** FAFSA. ***Financial aid deadline (priority):*** 3/1. ***Notification date:*** Continuous beginning 3/15. Students must reply by 5/1 or within 2 weeks of notification.

CONTACT Ms. Martha Harbaugh, Director of Financial Aid, Maryville University of Saint Louis, 650 Maryville University Drive, St. Louis, MO 63141-7299, 800-627-9855 Ext. 9360 or toll-free 800-627-9855. *Fax:* 314-529-9199. *E-mail:* fin_aid@maryville.edu.

MARYWOOD UNIVERSITY

Scranton, PA

Tuition & fees: $27,150 **Average undergraduate aid package: $22,829**

ABOUT THE INSTITUTION Independent Roman Catholic, coed. 59 undergraduate majors. Federal methodology is used as a basis for awarding need-based institutional aid.

UNDERGRADUATE EXPENSES for 2010–11 ***Comprehensive fee:*** $39,322 includes full-time tuition ($26,000), mandatory fees ($1150), and room and board ($12,172). ***College room only:*** $6922. Full-time tuition and fees vary according to course load. Room and board charges vary according to board plan and housing facility. ***Part-time tuition:*** $590 per credit. ***Part-time fees:*** $100 per term. Part-time tuition and fees vary according to course load. ***Payment plans:*** Installment, deferred payment.

FRESHMAN FINANCIAL AID (Fall 2010, est.) 429 applied for aid; of those 91% were deemed to have need. 100% of freshmen with need received aid; of those 21% had need fully met. ***Average percent of need met:*** 84% (excluding

resources awarded to replace EFC). ***Average financial aid package:*** $24,514 (excluding resources awarded to replace EFC). 5% of all full-time freshmen had no need and received non-need-based gift aid.

UNDERGRADUATE FINANCIAL AID (Fall 2010, est.) 1,939 applied for aid; of those 93% were deemed to have need. 100% of undergraduates with need received aid; of those 23% had need fully met. ***Average percent of need met:*** 79% (excluding resources awarded to replace EFC). ***Average financial aid package:*** $22,829 (excluding resources awarded to replace EFC). 6% of all full-time undergraduates had no need and received non-need-based gift aid.

GIFT AID (NEED-BASED) ***Total amount:*** $29,377,633 (15% federal, 10% state, 74% institutional, 1% external sources). ***Receiving aid:*** Freshmen: 86% (389); all full-time undergraduates: 85% (1,789). ***Average award:*** Freshmen: $19,271; Undergraduates: $16,968. ***Scholarships, grants, and awards:*** Federal Pell, FSEOG, state, private, college/university gift aid from institutional funds, Federal Nursing, Academic Competitiveness Grants, National SMART Grants, Scholarships for Disadvantaged Students.

GIFT AID (NON-NEED-BASED) ***Total amount:*** $3,599,485 (8% federal, 87% institutional, 5% external sources). ***Receiving aid:*** Freshmen: 15% (68). Undergraduates: 17% (355). ***Average award:*** Freshmen: $14,814. Undergraduates: $11,376. ***Scholarships, grants, and awards by category:*** *Academic interests/achievement:* business, communication, education, foreign languages, general academic interests/achievements, health fields, mathematics, religion/biblical studies. *Creative arts/performance:* art/fine arts, cinema/film/broadcasting, journalism/publications, music, performing arts, theater/drama. *Special achievements/activities:* community service, general special achievements/activities, leadership. *Special characteristics:* adult students, children and siblings of alumni, children of current students, children of faculty/staff, children of workers in trades, ethnic background, general special characteristics, international students, local/state students, religious affiliation, siblings of current students, spouses of current students. ***Tuition waivers:*** Full or partial for employees or children of employees, senior citizens.

LOANS ***Student loans:*** $18,693,564 (70% need-based, 30% non-need-based). 87% of past graduating class borrowed through all loan programs. *Average indebtedness per student:* $27,736. ***Average need-based loan:*** Freshmen: $3938. Undergraduates: $5283. ***Parent loans:*** $3,762,934 (33% need-based, 67% non-need-based). ***Programs:*** Federal Direct (Subsidized and Unsubsidized Stafford, PLUS), Perkins, private loans.

WORK-STUDY ***Federal work-study:*** Total amount: $1,332,200; jobs available.

APPLYING FOR FINANCIAL AID ***Required financial aid forms:*** FAFSA, institution's own form. ***Financial aid deadline (priority):*** 2/15. ***Notification date:*** Continuous beginning 2/15. Students must reply by 5/1 or within 3 weeks of notification.

CONTACT Mr. Stanley F. Skrutski, Director of Financial Aid, Marywood University, 2300 Adams Avenue, Scranton, PA 18509-1598, 570-348-6225 or toll-free 866-279-9663. *Fax:* 570-961-4739. *E-mail:* skrutski@marywood.edu.

MASSACHUSETTS COLLEGE OF ART AND DESIGN

Boston, MA

Tuition & fees (MA res): $9000 **Average undergraduate aid package: $9014**

ABOUT THE INSTITUTION State-supported, coed. 17 undergraduate majors. Federal methodology is used as a basis for awarding need-based institutional aid.

UNDERGRADUATE EXPENSES for 2010–11 ***Tuition, state resident:*** full-time $9000. ***Tuition, nonresident:*** full-time $25,400. Full-time tuition and fees vary according to course load and degree level. Part-time tuition and fees vary according to course load and degree level. ***College room and board:*** $11,750. Room and board charges vary according to board plan and housing facility. ***Payment plan:*** Installment.

FRESHMAN FINANCIAL AID (Fall 2010, est.) 284 applied for aid; of those 90% were deemed to have need. 100% of freshmen with need received aid. ***Average financial aid package:*** $9399 (excluding resources awarded to replace EFC). 3% of all full-time freshmen had no need and received non-need-based gift aid.

UNDERGRADUATE FINANCIAL AID (Fall 2010, est.) 1,239 applied for aid; of those 87% were deemed to have need. 100% of undergraduates with need received aid. ***Average financial aid package:*** $9014 (excluding resources awarded to replace EFC). 1% of all full-time undergraduates had no need and received non-need-based gift aid.

GIFT AID (NEED-BASED) ***Total amount:*** $5,418,323 (44% federal, 13% state, 43% institutional). ***Receiving aid:*** Freshmen: 61% (205); all full-time undergraduates: 48% (785). ***Average award:*** Freshmen: $7845; Undergraduates: $6905. ***Scholarships, grants, and awards:*** Federal Pell, FSEOG, state, private, college/university gift aid from institutional funds.

GIFT AID (NON-NEED-BASED) ***Total amount:*** $501,333 (21% institutional, 79% external sources). ***Receiving aid:*** Freshmen: 4% (12). Undergraduates: 2% (33). ***Average award:*** Freshmen: $4101. Undergraduates: $4071. ***Scholarships, grants, and awards by category:*** *Special characteristics:* children of faculty/staff, children of union members/company employees, veterans. ***Tuition waivers:*** Full or partial for employees or children of employees, senior citizens.

LOANS ***Student loans:*** $8,907,826 (45% need-based, 55% non-need-based). 70% of past graduating class borrowed through all loan programs. *Average indebtedness per student:* $21,759. ***Average need-based loan:*** Freshmen: $3413. Undergraduates: $4290. ***Parent loans:*** $6,456,840 (100% non-need-based). ***Programs:*** Federal Direct (Subsidized and Unsubsidized Stafford, PLUS), Perkins, state, alternative loans.

WORK-STUDY ***Federal work-study:*** Total amount: $160,000; 222 jobs averaging $1240.

APPLYING FOR FINANCIAL AID ***Required financial aid form:*** FAFSA. ***Financial aid deadline (priority):*** 3/1. ***Notification date:*** Continuous beginning 3/15. Students must reply within 3 weeks of notification.

CONTACT Auelio Ramirez, Director of Student Financial Assistance, Massachusetts College of Art and Design, 621 Huntington Avenue, Boston, MA 02115-5882, 617-879-7850. *Fax:* 617-879-7880. *E-mail:* aurelio.ramirez@massart.edu.

MASSACHUSETTS COLLEGE OF LIBERAL ARTS

North Adams, MA

Tuition & fees (MA res): $7575 **Average undergraduate aid package: $12,840**

ABOUT THE INSTITUTION State-supported, coed. 41 undergraduate majors. Federal methodology is used as a basis for awarding need-based institutional aid.

UNDERGRADUATE EXPENSES for 2010–11 ***One-time required fee:*** $140. ***Tuition, state resident:*** full-time $1030; part-time $42.92 per credit. ***Tuition, nonresident:*** full-time $9975; part-time $415.63 per credit hour. ***Required fees:*** full-time $6545; $221.42 per credit. Part-time tuition and fees vary according to course load. ***College room and board:*** $8246. Room and board charges vary according to board plan and housing facility. ***Payment plan:*** Installment.

FRESHMAN FINANCIAL AID (Fall 2010, est.) 326 applied for aid; of those 82% were deemed to have need. 100% of freshmen with need received aid. ***Average percent of need met:*** 82% (excluding resources awarded to replace EFC). ***Average financial aid package:*** $13,144 (excluding resources awarded to replace EFC). 7% of all full-time freshmen had no need and received non-need-based gift aid.

UNDERGRADUATE FINANCIAL AID (Fall 2010, est.) 1,309 applied for aid; of those 82% were deemed to have need. 99% of undergraduates with need received aid. ***Average percent of need met:*** 84% (excluding resources awarded to replace EFC). ***Average financial aid package:*** $12,840 (excluding resources awarded to replace EFC). 5% of all full-time undergraduates had no need and received non-need-based gift aid.

GIFT AID (NEED-BASED) ***Total amount:*** $5,377,164 (58% federal, 16% state, 20% institutional, 6% external sources). ***Receiving aid:*** Freshmen: 63% (220); all full-time undergraduates: 55% (824). ***Average award:*** Freshmen: $6108; Undergraduates: $5585. ***Scholarships, grants, and awards:*** Federal Pell, FSEOG, state, private, college/university gift aid from institutional funds.

GIFT AID (NON-NEED-BASED) ***Total amount:*** $192,828 (1% state, 66% institutional, 33% external sources). ***Receiving aid:*** Freshmen: 19% (68). Undergraduates: 14% (208). ***Average award:*** Freshmen: $2304. Undergraduates: $2612. ***Scholarships, grants, and awards by category:*** *Academic interests/achievement:* biological sciences, business, communication, computer science, education, English, general academic interests/achievements, health fields, humanities, mathematics, physical sciences, social sciences. *Creative arts/performance:* applied art and design, art/fine arts, cinema/film/broadcasting, journalism/publications, music, performing arts, theater/drama. *Special achievements/*

activities: general special achievements/activities, leadership, memberships. ***Tuition waivers:*** Full or partial for employees or children of employees, senior citizens.

LOANS ***Student loans:*** $9,268,056 (85% need-based, 15% non-need-based). 59% of past graduating class borrowed through all loan programs. *Average indebtedness per student:* $23,587. ***Average need-based loan:*** Freshmen: $3230. Undergraduates: $3887. ***Parent loans:*** $872,550 (80% need-based, 20% non-need-based). ***Programs:*** Federal Direct (Subsidized and Unsubsidized Stafford, PLUS), Perkins, state.

WORK-STUDY ***Federal work-study:*** Total amount: $298,547; 227 jobs averaging $1508. ***State or other work-study/employment:*** Total amount: $648,696 (100% non-need-based). Part-time jobs available.

APPLYING FOR FINANCIAL AID ***Required financial aid forms:*** FAFSA, institution's own form. ***Financial aid deadline (priority):*** 3/1. ***Notification date:*** Continuous beginning 3/1. Students must reply by 5/1 or within 2 weeks of notification.

CONTACT Mrs. Elizabeth M. Petri, Director of Financial Aid, Massachusetts College of Liberal Arts, 375 Church Street, North Adams, MA 01247, 413-662-5219 or toll-free 800-292-6632 (in-state). *Fax:* 413-662-5105. *E-mail:* e.petri@mcla.edu.

MASSACHUSETTS COLLEGE OF PHARMACY AND HEALTH SCIENCES

Boston, MA

ABOUT THE INSTITUTION Independent, coed. 12 undergraduate majors.

GIFT AID (NEED-BASED) ***Scholarships, grants, and awards:*** Federal Pell, FSEOG, state, private, college/university gift aid from institutional funds.

GIFT AID (NON-NEED-BASED) ***Scholarships, grants, and awards by category:*** *Academic interests/achievement:* general academic interests/achievements. *Special characteristics:* children of faculty/staff.

LOANS ***Programs:*** Federal Direct (Subsidized and Unsubsidized Stafford, PLUS), Perkins, Health Professions Loans.

WORK-STUDY ***Federal work-study:*** Total amount: $548,850; jobs available.

APPLYING FOR FINANCIAL AID ***Required financial aid form:*** FAFSA.

CONTACT Shannon Gallagher, Director of Student Financial Services, Massachusetts College of Pharmacy and Health Sciences, 179 Longwood Avenue, Boston, MA 02115-5896, 617-879-5932 or toll-free 800-225-5506 (out-of-state). *Fax:* 617-732-2082. *E-mail:* shannon.gallagher1@mcphs.edu.

MASSACHUSETTS INSTITUTE OF TECHNOLOGY

Cambridge, MA

Tuition & fees: $39,212 **Average undergraduate aid package: $37,731**

ABOUT THE INSTITUTION Independent, coed. 35 undergraduate majors. Both federal and institutional methodology are used as a basis for awarding need-based institutional aid.

UNDERGRADUATE EXPENSES for 2010–11 ***Comprehensive fee:*** $50,446 includes full-time tuition ($38,940), mandatory fees ($272), and room and board ($11,234). ***College room only:*** $6884. Room and board charges vary according to board plan and housing facility. ***Part-time tuition:*** $605 per unit. Part-time tuition and fees vary according to course load. ***Payment plan:*** Installment.

FRESHMAN FINANCIAL AID (Fall 2009) 892 applied for aid; of those 80% were deemed to have need. 100% of freshmen with need received aid; of those 100% had need fully met. ***Average percent of need met:*** 100% (excluding resources awarded to replace EFC). ***Average financial aid package:*** $37,874 (excluding resources awarded to replace EFC).

UNDERGRADUATE FINANCIAL AID (Fall 2009) 3,186 applied for aid; of those 85% were deemed to have need. 100% of undergraduates with need received aid; of those 100% had need fully met. ***Average percent of need met:*** 100% (excluding resources awarded to replace EFC). ***Average financial aid package:*** $37,731 (excluding resources awarded to replace EFC).

GIFT AID (NEED-BASED) ***Total amount:*** $94,510,686 (7% federal, 88% institutional, 5% external sources). ***Receiving aid:*** Freshmen: 65% (699); all full-time undergraduates: 63% (2,642). ***Average award:*** Freshmen: $36,084; Undergraduates: $35,504. ***Scholarships, grants, and awards:*** Federal Pell, FSEOG, state, private, college/university gift aid from institutional funds.

GIFT AID (NON-NEED-BASED) ***Total amount:*** $4,755,204 (21% federal, 79% external sources). ***Receiving aid:*** Freshmen: 5% (49). Undergraduates: 2% (88). ***Tuition waivers:*** Full or partial for employees or children of employees.

LOANS ***Student loans:*** $9,507,553 (35% need-based, 65% non-need-based). 44% of past graduating class borrowed through all loan programs. *Average indebtedness per student:* $15,228. ***Average need-based loan:*** Freshmen: $2508. Undergraduates: $3211. ***Parent loans:*** $4,289,124 (1% need-based, 99% non-need-based). ***Programs:*** Federal Direct (Subsidized and Unsubsidized Stafford, PLUS), Perkins, college/university.

WORK-STUDY ***Federal work-study:*** Total amount: $1,521,187; 778 jobs averaging $2542. ***State or other work-study/employment:*** Total amount: $3,042,865 (69% need-based, 31% non-need-based). 1,365 part-time jobs averaging $2229.

APPLYING FOR FINANCIAL AID ***Required financial aid forms:*** FAFSA, CSS Financial Aid PROFILE, noncustodial (divorced/separated) parent's statement, business/farm supplement, parents' complete federal income returns from prior year, W-2 forms. ***Financial aid deadline:*** 2/15. ***Notification date:*** 4/1. Students must reply by 5/1.

CONTACT Elizabeth Hicks, Executive Director of Student Financial Services, Massachusetts Institute of Technology, 77 Massachusetts Avenue, Room 11-320, Cambridge, MA 02139-4307, 617-253-4971. *Fax:* 617-253-9859. *E-mail:* finaid@mit.edu.

MASSACHUSETTS MARITIME ACADEMY

Buzzards Bay, MA

Tuition & fees (area res): $11,922 **Average undergraduate aid package: $7065**

ABOUT THE INSTITUTION State-supported, coed, primarily men. 10 undergraduate majors. Federal methodology is used as a basis for awarding need-based institutional aid.

UNDERGRADUATE EXPENSES for 2011–12 ***One-time required fee:*** $2210. ***Tuition, area resident:*** full-time $1611; part-time $296 per credit hour. ***Tuition, state resident:*** full-time $2617; part-time $311 per credit hour. ***Tuition, nonresident:*** full-time $15,261; part-time $838 per credit hour. ***Required fees:*** full-time $10,311; $268.83 per credit. Full-time tuition and fees vary according to course load, program, reciprocity agreements, and student level. Part-time tuition and fees vary according to class time, course load, reciprocity agreements, and student level. ***College room and board:*** $9204; ***Room only:*** $5126. Room and board charges vary according to board plan and student level. ***Payment plans:*** Guaranteed tuition, installment, deferred payment.

UNDERGRADUATE FINANCIAL AID (Fall 2009) 874 applied for aid; of those 60% were deemed to have need. 100% of undergraduates with need received aid. ***Average percent of need met:*** 54% (excluding resources awarded to replace EFC). ***Average financial aid package:*** $7065 (excluding resources awarded to replace EFC).

GIFT AID (NEED-BASED) ***Total amount:*** $1,301,897 (68% federal, 28% state, 4% institutional). ***Receiving aid:*** All full-time undergraduates: 27% (323). ***Average award:*** Undergraduates: $3200. ***Scholarships, grants, and awards:*** Federal Pell, FSEOG, state, private, college/university gift aid from institutional funds.

GIFT AID (NON-NEED-BASED) ***Total amount:*** $998,547 (9% federal, 13% state, 66% institutional, 12% external sources). ***Scholarships, grants, and awards by category:*** *Academic interests/achievement:* general academic interests/achievements. *Special achievements/activities:* leadership. *Special characteristics:* children and siblings of alumni, children of faculty/staff, veterans. ***Tuition waivers:*** Full or partial for minority students, employees or children of employees, senior citizens.

LOANS ***Student loans:*** $7,256,664 (26% need-based, 74% non-need-based). 71% of past graduating class borrowed through all loan programs. *Average indebtedness per student:* $32,553. ***Average need-based loan:*** Undergraduates: $3570. ***Parent loans:*** $1,435,608 (100% non-need-based). ***Programs:*** Federal Direct (Subsidized and Unsubsidized Stafford, PLUS).

WORK-STUDY ***Federal work-study:*** Total amount: $85,950; 118 jobs averaging $1000.

APPLYING FOR FINANCIAL AID ***Required financial aid forms:*** FAFSA, institution's own form. ***Financial aid deadline (priority):*** 5/1. ***Notification date:*** Continuous beginning 3/20.

CONTACT Ms. Catherine Kedski, Director of Financial Aid, Massachusetts Maritime Academy, 101 Academy Drive, Buzzards Bay, MA 02532, 508-830-5042 or toll-free 800-544-3411. *Fax:* 508-830-5077. *E-mail:* ckedski@maritime.edu.

THE MASTER'S COLLEGE AND SEMINARY

Santa Clarita, CA

Tuition & fees: $26,880 **Average undergraduate aid package: $18,723**

ABOUT THE INSTITUTION Independent nondenominational, coed. 47 undergraduate majors. Federal methodology is used as a basis for awarding need-based institutional aid.

UNDERGRADUATE EXPENSES for 2011–12 ***Comprehensive fee:*** $35,280 includes full-time tuition ($26,260), mandatory fees ($620), and room and board ($8400). ***College room only:*** $7362. Full-time tuition and fees vary according to course load, degree level, and program. Room and board charges vary according to board plan. ***Part-time tuition:*** $1100 per credit hour. ***Part-time fees:*** $1100 per credit hour. Part-time tuition and fees vary according to course load, degree level, and program. ***Payment plan:*** Installment.

FRESHMAN FINANCIAL AID (Fall 2010, est.) 195 applied for aid; of those 87% were deemed to have need. 99% of freshmen with need received aid; of those 15% had need fully met. ***Average percent of need met:*** 69% (excluding resources awarded to replace EFC). ***Average financial aid package:*** $19,544 (excluding resources awarded to replace EFC). 9% of all full-time freshmen had no need and received non-need-based gift aid.

UNDERGRADUATE FINANCIAL AID (Fall 2010, est.) 950 applied for aid; of those 90% were deemed to have need. 97% of undergraduates with need received aid; of those 15% had need fully met. ***Average percent of need met:*** 65% (excluding resources awarded to replace EFC). ***Average financial aid package:*** $18,723 (excluding resources awarded to replace EFC). 7% of all full-time undergraduates had no need and received non-need-based gift aid.

GIFT AID (NEED-BASED) ***Total amount:*** $10,385,636 (16% federal, 18% state, 53% institutional, 13% external sources). ***Receiving aid:*** Freshmen: 86% (168); all full-time undergraduates: 86% (815). ***Average award:*** Freshmen: $15,454; Undergraduates: $14,120. ***Scholarships, grants, and awards:*** Federal Pell, FSEOG, state, private, college/university gift aid from institutional funds.

GIFT AID (NON-NEED-BASED) ***Total amount:*** $890,689 (65% institutional, 35% external sources). ***Receiving aid:*** Freshmen: 8% (15). Undergraduates: 8% (77). ***Average award:*** Freshmen: $6167. Undergraduates: $7178. ***Scholarships, grants, and awards by category:*** *Academic interests/achievement:* 505 awards ($2,995,477 total): biological sciences, business, education, general academic interests/achievements, mathematics, physical sciences, religion/biblical studies, social sciences. *Creative arts/performance:* 79 awards ($240,230 total): music. *Special achievements/activities:* 69 awards ($464,000 total): leadership. *Special characteristics:* 221 awards ($1,324,068 total): children and siblings of alumni, children of faculty/staff, general special characteristics, international students, relatives of clergy. ***Tuition waivers:*** Full or partial for employees or children of employees.

LOANS ***Student loans:*** $6,434,106 (77% need-based, 23% non-need-based). 68% of past graduating class borrowed through all loan programs. *Average indebtedness per student:* $12,842. ***Average need-based loan:*** Freshmen: $3444. Undergraduates: $4719. ***Parent loans:*** $1,940,598 (53% need-based, 47% non-need-based). ***Programs:*** Perkins, alternative loans.

WORK-STUDY ***Federal work-study:*** Total amount: $72,259; 65 jobs averaging $2676. ***State or other work-study/employment:*** Total amount: $803,517 (87% need-based, 13% non-need-based). 191 part-time jobs averaging $2789.

ATHLETIC AWARDS Total amount: $1,378,283 (84% need-based, 16% non-need-based).

APPLYING FOR FINANCIAL AID ***Required financial aid forms:*** FAFSA, institution's own form, state aid form. ***Financial aid deadline (priority):*** 3/2. ***Notification date:*** Continuous beginning 2/1. Students must reply by 5/1 or within 2 weeks of notification.

CONTACT Mr. Gary Edwards, Director of Financial Aid, The Master's College and Seminary, 21726 Placerita Canyon Road, Santa Clarita, CA 91321-1200, 661-362-2291 or toll-free 800-568-6248. *Fax:* 661-362-2693. *E-mail:* gedwards@masters.edu.

MATER ECCLESIAE COLLEGE

Greenville, RI

CONTACT Financial Aid Office, Mater Ecclesiae College, 60 Austin Avenue, Greenville, RI 02828, 401-949-2820.

MAYVILLE STATE UNIVERSITY

Mayville, ND

Tuition & fees (ND res): $5937 **Average undergraduate aid package: $8648**

ABOUT THE INSTITUTION State-supported, coed. 34 undergraduate majors. Federal methodology is used as a basis for awarding need-based institutional aid.

UNDERGRADUATE EXPENSES for 2010–11 ***One-time required fee:*** $35. ***Tuition, state resident:*** full-time $4268; part-time $178 per credit hour. ***Tuition, nonresident:*** full-time $6403; part-time $267 per credit hour. ***Required fees:*** full-time $1669; $70 per credit hour. Full-time tuition and fees vary according to course load and reciprocity agreements. Part-time tuition and fees vary according to course load and reciprocity agreements. ***College room and board:*** $4454; ***Room only:*** $1676. Room and board charges vary according to board plan and housing facility. ***Payment plan:*** Installment.

FRESHMAN FINANCIAL AID (Fall 2010, est.) 111 applied for aid; of those 77% were deemed to have need. 100% of freshmen with need received aid; of those 100% had need fully met. ***Average percent of need met:*** 59% (excluding resources awarded to replace EFC). ***Average financial aid package:*** $7935 (excluding resources awarded to replace EFC). 59% of all full-time freshmen had no need and received non-need-based gift aid.

UNDERGRADUATE FINANCIAL AID (Fall 2010, est.) 463 applied for aid; of those 79% were deemed to have need. 99% of undergraduates with need received aid; of those 99% had need fully met. ***Average percent of need met:*** 59% (excluding resources awarded to replace EFC). ***Average financial aid package:*** $8648 (excluding resources awarded to replace EFC). 40% of all full-time undergraduates had no need and received non-need-based gift aid.

GIFT AID (NEED-BASED) ***Total amount:*** $1,732,733 (80% federal, 11% state, 5% institutional, 4% external sources). ***Receiving aid:*** Freshmen: 62% (80); all full-time undergraduates: 59% (324). ***Average award:*** Freshmen: $4397; Undergraduates: $4494. ***Scholarships, grants, and awards:*** Federal Pell, FSEOG, state, private, college/university gift aid from institutional funds.

GIFT AID (NON-NEED-BASED) ***Total amount:*** $20,797 (14% federal, 6% state, 42% institutional, 38% external sources). ***Receiving aid:*** Freshmen: 5% (7). Undergraduates: 2% (9). ***Average award:*** Freshmen: $981. Undergraduates: $742. ***Scholarships, grants, and awards by category:*** *Academic interests/achievement:* 323 awards ($165,537 total): biological sciences, business, communication, computer science, education, English, general academic interests/achievements, health fields, library science, mathematics, physical sciences, premedicine, social sciences. *Creative arts/performance:* 66 awards ($25,600 total): music, theater/drama. *Special characteristics:* 105 awards ($164,160 total): children of faculty/staff, international students, local/state students, members of minority groups, out-of-state students. ***Tuition waivers:*** Full or partial for minority students, employees or children of employees, senior citizens.

LOANS ***Student loans:*** $3,035,761 (81% need-based, 19% non-need-based). 88% of past graduating class borrowed through all loan programs. *Average indebtedness per student:* $19,986. ***Average need-based loan:*** Freshmen: $3663. Undergraduates: $4067. ***Parent loans:*** $471,182 (29% need-based, 71% non-need-based). ***Programs:*** Federal Direct (Subsidized and Unsubsidized Stafford, PLUS), Perkins, college/university.

WORK-STUDY ***Federal work-study:*** Total amount: $66,948; 56 jobs averaging $1200.

ATHLETIC AWARDS Total amount: $154,556 (69% need-based, 31% non-need-based).

APPLYING FOR FINANCIAL AID ***Required financial aid form:*** FAFSA. ***Financial aid deadline (priority):*** 2/15. ***Notification date:*** Continuous beginning 5/1. Students must reply within 2 weeks of notification.

CONTACT Ms. Shirley Hanson, Director of Financial Aid, Mayville State University, 330 3rd Street NE, Mayville, ND 58257-1299, 701-788-4767 or toll-free 800-437-4104. *Fax:* 701-788-4818. *E-mail:* shirley.hanson@mayvillestate.edu.

McDANIEL COLLEGE

Westminster, MD

Tuition & fees: $33,280 **Average undergraduate aid package: $27,009**

ABOUT THE INSTITUTION Independent, coed. 32 undergraduate majors. Both federal and institutional methodology are used as a basis for awarding need-based institutional aid.

UNDERGRADUATE EXPENSES for 2010–11 ***Comprehensive fee:*** $40,340 includes full-time tuition ($33,280) and room and board ($7060). ***College room only:*** $3800. Room and board charges vary according to board plan and housing facility. ***Part-time tuition:*** $1040 per credit hour. Part-time tuition and fees vary according to reciprocity agreements. ***Payment plans:*** Tuition prepayment, installment.

FRESHMAN FINANCIAL AID (Fall 2010, est.) 356 applied for aid; of those 86% were deemed to have need. 100% of freshmen with need received aid; of those 24% had need fully met. ***Average percent of need met:*** 86% (excluding resources awarded to replace EFC). ***Average financial aid package:*** $28,967 (excluding resources awarded to replace EFC). 20% of all full-time freshmen had no need and received non-need-based gift aid.

UNDERGRADUATE FINANCIAL AID (Fall 2010, est.) 1,253 applied for aid; of those 90% were deemed to have need. 100% of undergraduates with need received aid; of those 23% had need fully met. ***Average percent of need met:*** 81% (excluding resources awarded to replace EFC). ***Average financial aid package:*** $27,009 (excluding resources awarded to replace EFC). 21% of all full-time undergraduates had no need and received non-need-based gift aid.

GIFT AID (NEED-BASED) ***Total amount:*** $23,089,882 (9% federal, 6% state, 85% institutional). ***Receiving aid:*** Freshmen: 73% (301); all full-time undergraduates: 71% (1,127). ***Average award:*** Freshmen: $24,922; Undergraduates: $22,231. ***Scholarships, grants, and awards:*** Federal Pell, FSEOG, state, private, college/university gift aid from institutional funds.

GIFT AID (NON-NEED-BASED) ***Total amount:*** $5,999,940 (4% state, 92% institutional, 4% external sources). ***Receiving aid:*** Freshmen: 10% (40). Undergraduates: 10% (157). ***Average award:*** Freshmen: $14,360. Undergraduates: $13,812. ***Scholarships, grants, and awards by category:*** *Academic interests/achievement:* 1,117 awards ($14,227,341 total): general academic interests/achievements. *Special achievements/activities:* 2 awards ($4000 total): junior miss, leadership. *Special characteristics:* 254 awards ($468,200 total): general special characteristics, local/state students, previous college experience, siblings of current students. ***Tuition waivers:*** Full or partial for employees or children of employees.

LOANS ***Student loans:*** $8,325,663 (48% need-based, 52% non-need-based). 49% of past graduating class borrowed through all loan programs. *Average indebtedness per student:* $30,825. ***Average need-based loan:*** Freshmen: $4376. Undergraduates: $4872. ***Parent loans:*** $2,810,771 (100% non-need-based). ***Programs:*** Federal Direct (Subsidized and Unsubsidized Stafford, PLUS), Perkins, college/university.

WORK-STUDY ***Federal work-study:*** Total amount: $217,304; 252 jobs averaging $947. ***State or other work-study/employment:*** Total amount: $219,425 (100% non-need-based). 238 part-time jobs averaging $913.

APPLYING FOR FINANCIAL AID ***Required financial aid forms:*** FAFSA, institution's own form, federal income tax form(s). ***Financial aid deadline (priority):*** 3/1. ***Notification date:*** Continuous beginning 3/1. Students must reply by 5/1 or within 2 weeks of notification.

CONTACT Ms. Patricia Williams, Financial Aid Office, McDaniel College, 2 College Hill, Westminster, MD 21157-4390, 410-857-2233 or toll-free 800-638-5005. *Fax:* 410-857-2729. *E-mail:* finaid@mcdaniel.edu.

McKENDREE UNIVERSITY

Lebanon, IL

Tuition & fees: $25,090 **Average undergraduate aid package: $19,185**

ABOUT THE INSTITUTION Independent religious, coed. 50 undergraduate majors. Federal methodology is used as a basis for awarding need-based institutional aid.

UNDERGRADUATE EXPENSES for 2011–12 ***Comprehensive fee:*** $33,590 includes full-time tuition ($24,190), mandatory fees ($900), and room and board ($8500). ***College room only:*** $4400. Full-time tuition and fees vary according to course load, degree level, and location. Room and board charges vary according to board plan and housing facility. Part-time tuition and fees vary according to course load, degree level, and location. ***Payment plan:*** Installment.

FRESHMAN FINANCIAL AID (Fall 2010, est.) 325 applied for aid; of those 95% were deemed to have need. 100% of freshmen with need received aid; of those 23% had need fully met. ***Average percent of need met:*** 85% (excluding resources awarded to replace EFC). ***Average financial aid package:*** $22,166 (excluding resources awarded to replace EFC). 9% of all full-time freshmen had no need and received non-need-based gift aid.

UNDERGRADUATE FINANCIAL AID (Fall 2010, est.) 1,261 applied for aid; of those 93% were deemed to have need. 99% of undergraduates with need received aid; of those 19% had need fully met. ***Average percent of need met:*** 77% (excluding resources awarded to replace EFC). ***Average financial aid package:*** $19,185 (excluding resources awarded to replace EFC). 15% of all full-time undergraduates had no need and received non-need-based gift aid.

GIFT AID (NEED-BASED) ***Total amount:*** $16,275,393 (15% federal, 16% state, 66% institutional, 3% external sources). ***Receiving aid:*** Freshmen: 91% (309); all full-time undergraduates: 84% (1,160). ***Average award:*** Freshmen: $18,165; Undergraduates: $15,226. ***Scholarships, grants, and awards:*** Federal Pell, FSEOG, state, private, college/university gift aid from institutional funds.

GIFT AID (NON-NEED-BASED) ***Total amount:*** $2,182,862 (91% institutional, 9% external sources). ***Receiving aid:*** Freshmen: 13% (46). Undergraduates: 11% (154). ***Average award:*** Freshmen: $9785. Undergraduates: $7916. ***Scholarships, grants, and awards by category:*** *Academic interests/achievement:* 802 awards ($4,838,984 total): biological sciences, business, general academic interests/achievements, religion/biblical studies. *Creative arts/performance:* 114 awards ($468,574 total): music. *Special achievements/activities:* 73 awards ($126,750 total): cheerleading/drum major, community service, leadership. *Special characteristics:* 62 awards ($361,632 total): children of faculty/staff, general special characteristics, religious affiliation. ***Tuition waivers:*** Full or partial for employees or children of employees.

LOANS ***Student loans:*** $7,453,652 (78% need-based, 22% non-need-based). 74% of past graduating class borrowed through all loan programs. *Average indebtedness per student:* $23,025. ***Average need-based loan:*** Freshmen: $3201. Undergraduates: $3777. ***Parent loans:*** $3,325,808 (30% need-based, 70% non-need-based). ***Programs:*** Federal Direct (Subsidized and Unsubsidized Stafford, PLUS), Perkins.

WORK-STUDY ***Federal work-study:*** Total amount: $1,039,741; 859 jobs averaging $1721. ***State or other work-study/employment:*** Total amount: $125,951 (5% need-based, 95% non-need-based). 95 part-time jobs averaging $1327.

ATHLETIC AWARDS Total amount: $2,490,070 (54% need-based, 46% non-need-based).

APPLYING FOR FINANCIAL AID ***Required financial aid form:*** FAFSA. ***Financial aid deadline (priority):*** 5/31. ***Notification date:*** Continuous beginning 3/1.

CONTACT James A. Myers, Director of Financial Aid, McKendree University, 701 College Road, Lebanon, IL 62254-1299, 618-537-6529 or toll-free 800-232-7228 Ext. 6831. *Fax:* 618-537-6530. *E-mail:* jamyers@mckendree.edu.

McMURRY UNIVERSITY

Abilene, TX

Tuition & fees: $20,680 **Average undergraduate aid package: $17,698**

ABOUT THE INSTITUTION Independent United Methodist, coed. 45 undergraduate majors. Federal methodology is used as a basis for awarding need-based institutional aid.

UNDERGRADUATE EXPENSES for 2010–11 ***One-time required fee:*** $150. ***Comprehensive fee:*** $27,656 includes full-time tuition ($19,820), mandatory fees ($860), and room and board ($6976). ***College room only:*** $3360. Full-time tuition and fees vary according to course load. Room and board charges vary according to board plan and housing facility. ***Part-time tuition:*** $620 per semester hour. Part-time tuition and fees vary according to course load. ***Payment plan:*** Installment.

FRESHMAN FINANCIAL AID (Fall 2010, est.) 276 applied for aid; of those 90% were deemed to have need. 100% of freshmen with need received aid; of those 16% had need fully met. ***Average percent of need met:*** 87% (excluding resources awarded to replace EFC). ***Average financial aid package:*** $19,895 (excluding resources awarded to replace EFC). 6% of all full-time freshmen had no need and received non-need-based gift aid.

UNDERGRADUATE FINANCIAL AID (Fall 2010, est.) 1,088 applied for aid; of those 94% were deemed to have need. 99% of undergraduates with need received aid; of those 13% had need fully met. ***Average percent of need met:*** 80% (excluding resources awarded to replace EFC). ***Average financial aid package:*** $17,698 (excluding resources awarded to replace EFC). 6% of all full-time undergraduates had no need and received non-need-based gift aid.

GIFT AID (NEED-BASED) ***Total amount:*** $10,155,701 (33% federal, 24% state, 39% institutional, 4% external sources). ***Receiving aid:*** Freshmen: 86% (241); all full-time undergraduates: 81% (956). ***Average award:*** Freshmen: $12,381;

Undergraduates: $9903. ***Scholarships, grants, and awards:*** Federal Pell, FSEOG, state, private, college/university gift aid from institutional funds, Academic Competitiveness Grants, National SMART Grants.

GIFT AID (NON-NEED-BASED) ***Total amount:*** $4,291,612 (3% federal, 6% state, 91% institutional). ***Receiving aid:*** Freshmen: 62% (173). Undergraduates: 57% (673). ***Average award:*** Freshmen: $6635. Undergraduates: $5864. ***Scholarships, grants, and awards by category:*** *Academic interests/achievement:* 347 awards ($737,935 total): biological sciences, business, computer science, education, English, general academic interests/achievements, mathematics, physical sciences, premedicine, religion/biblical studies, social sciences. *Creative arts/performance:* 13 awards ($20,646 total): art/fine arts, music, theater/drama. *Special achievements/activities:* 67 awards ($99,847 total): general special achievements/activities. *Special characteristics:* 376 awards ($2,488,706 total): children of faculty/staff, ethnic background, international students, local/state students, out-of-state students, previous college experience, relatives of clergy, religious affiliation. ***Tuition waivers:*** Full or partial for employees or children of employees.

LOANS ***Student loans:*** $9,300,210 (43% need-based, 57% non-need-based). 94% of past graduating class borrowed through all loan programs. *Average indebtedness per student:* $33,212. ***Average need-based loan:*** Freshmen: $3372. Undergraduates: $4428. ***Parent loans:*** $652,650 (100% non-need-based). ***Programs:*** Federal Direct (Subsidized and Unsubsidized Stafford, PLUS), Perkins, state, alternative loans, United Methodist Student Loans, Bonner Price Loans.

WORK-STUDY ***Federal work-study:*** Total amount: $638,586; 298 jobs averaging $2129. ***State or other work-study/employment:*** Total amount: $146,846 (19% need-based, 81% non-need-based). 59 part-time jobs averaging $2424.

APPLYING FOR FINANCIAL AID ***Required financial aid form:*** FAFSA. ***Financial aid deadline (priority):*** 3/15. ***Notification date:*** Continuous beginning 2/1. Students must reply within 3 weeks of notification.

CONTACT Rachel Atkins, Director of Financial Aid, McMurry University, PO Box 908, Abilene, TX 79697, 325-793-4709 or toll-free 800-477-0077. *Fax:* 325-793-4718. *E-mail:* atkinsr@mcmurryadm.mcm.edu.

McNALLY SMITH COLLEGE OF MUSIC

Saint Paul, MN

Tuition & fees: $26,120 **Average undergraduate aid package: N/A**

ABOUT THE INSTITUTION Proprietary, coed. 5 undergraduate majors. Federal methodology is used as a basis for awarding need-based institutional aid.

UNDERGRADUATE EXPENSES for 2011–12 ***Tuition:*** full-time $22,620; part-time $870 per credit. ***Required fees:*** full-time $3500; $450 per term. Full-time tuition and fees vary according to course load. Part-time tuition and fees vary according to course load. Room and board charges vary according to board plan and housing facility. ***Payment plans:*** Guaranteed tuition, tuition prepayment, installment, deferred payment.

GIFT AID (NEED-BASED) ***Total amount:*** $1,745,433 (60% federal, 18% state, 17% institutional, 5% external sources). ***Scholarships, grants, and awards:*** Federal Pell, FSEOG, state, college/university gift aid from institutional funds.

GIFT AID (NON-NEED-BASED) ***Total amount:*** $463,846 (33% federal, 17% state, 50% institutional). ***Scholarships, grants, and awards by category:*** *Creative arts/performance:* creative writing, music. *Special characteristics:* children of faculty/staff, veterans, veterans' children. ***Tuition waivers:*** Full or partial for employees or children of employees.

LOANS ***Student loans:*** $7,625,730 (100% need-based). ***Parent loans:*** $2,308,010 (100% need-based). ***Programs:*** Federal Direct (Subsidized and Unsubsidized Stafford, PLUS), state, college/university, private loans.

WORK-STUDY ***Federal work-study:*** Total amount: $60,000; 40 jobs averaging $1500. ***State or other work-study/employment:*** Total amount: $41,356 (52% need-based, 48% non-need-based). 19 part-time jobs averaging $1124.

APPLYING FOR FINANCIAL AID ***Required financial aid forms:*** FAFSA, institution's own form. ***Financial aid deadline:*** 8/1 (priority: 3/1). ***Notification date:*** Continuous beginning 3/15.

CONTACT Mr. Paul Haugen, Associate Director of Financial Aid, McNally Smith College of Music, 19 Exchange Street East, Saint Paul, MN 55101-2220, 651-361-3321 or toll-free 800-594-9500. *Fax:* 651-291-0366. *E-mail:* paul.haugen@mcnallysmith.edu.

McNEESE STATE UNIVERSITY

Lake Charles, LA

CONTACT Ms. Taina J. Savoit, Director of Financial Aid, McNeese State University, PO Box 93260, Lake Charles, LA 70609-3260, 337-475-5065 or toll-free 800-622-3352. *Fax:* 337-475-5068. *E-mail:* financialaid@mcneese.edu.

McPHERSON COLLEGE

McPherson, KS

Tuition & fees: $19,625 **Average undergraduate aid package: $23,934**

ABOUT THE INSTITUTION Independent religious, coed. 28 undergraduate majors. Federal methodology is used as a basis for awarding need-based institutional aid.

UNDERGRADUATE EXPENSES for 2010–11 ***Comprehensive fee:*** $26,950 includes full-time tuition ($19,125), mandatory fees ($500), and room and board ($7325). ***College room only:*** $2900. Full-time tuition and fees vary according to course load and program. ***Payment plan:*** Installment.

FRESHMAN FINANCIAL AID (Fall 2010, est.) 164 applied for aid; of those 91% were deemed to have need. 100% of freshmen with need received aid; of those 35% had need fully met. ***Average percent of need met:*** 100% (excluding resources awarded to replace EFC). ***Average financial aid package:*** $24,222 (excluding resources awarded to replace EFC). 11% of all full-time freshmen had no need and received non-need-based gift aid.

UNDERGRADUATE FINANCIAL AID (Fall 2010, est.) 578 applied for aid; of those 92% were deemed to have need. 100% of undergraduates with need received aid; of those 34% had need fully met. ***Average percent of need met:*** 97% (excluding resources awarded to replace EFC). ***Average financial aid package:*** $23,934 (excluding resources awarded to replace EFC). 13% of all full-time undergraduates had no need and received non-need-based gift aid.

GIFT AID (NEED-BASED) ***Total amount:*** $3,406,241 (46% federal, 11% state, 43% institutional). ***Receiving aid:*** Freshmen: 80% (136); all full-time undergraduates: 75% (469). ***Average award:*** Freshmen: $6979; Undergraduates: $7100. ***Scholarships, grants, and awards:*** Federal Pell, FSEOG, state, private, college/university gift aid from institutional funds.

GIFT AID (NON-NEED-BASED) ***Total amount:*** $4,955,129 (97% institutional, 3% external sources). ***Receiving aid:*** Freshmen: 86% (147). Undergraduates: 83% (519). ***Average award:*** Freshmen: $8611. Undergraduates: $8116. ***Scholarships, grants, and awards by category:*** *Academic interests/achievement:* 609 awards ($2,895,804 total): general academic interests/achievements. *Creative arts/performance:* 60 awards ($143,338 total): art/fine arts, journalism/publications, music, theater/drama. *Special achievements/activities:* 24 awards ($54,000 total): cheerleading/drum major, community service, religious involvement. *Special characteristics:* 12 awards ($15,368 total): adult students, religious affiliation. ***Tuition waivers:*** Full or partial for employees or children of employees.

LOANS ***Student loans:*** $2,106,359 (100% need-based). 82% of past graduating class borrowed through all loan programs. *Average indebtedness per student:* $30,889. ***Average need-based loan:*** Freshmen: $8925. Undergraduates: $9929. ***Parent loans:*** $488,749 (100% non-need-based). ***Programs:*** Federal Direct (Subsidized and Unsubsidized Stafford, PLUS), Perkins.

WORK-STUDY ***Federal work-study:*** Total amount: $126,779; 141 jobs averaging $899. ***State or other work-study/employment:*** Total amount: $245,178 (100% non-need-based). Part-time jobs available.

ATHLETIC AWARDS Total amount: $1,120,000 (100% non-need-based).

APPLYING FOR FINANCIAL AID ***Required financial aid forms:*** FAFSA, state aid form. ***Financial aid deadline (priority):*** 3/1. ***Notification date:*** Continuous beginning 3/1. Students must reply within 3 weeks of notification.

CONTACT Ms. Brenda Krehbiel, Director of Financial Aid, McPherson College, 1600 East Euclid, McPherson, KS 67460-1402, 620-242-0400 Ext. 2415 or toll-free 800-365-7402. *Fax:* 620-241-8443. *E-mail:* krehbieb2@mcpherson.edu.

MEDAILLE COLLEGE

Buffalo, NY

Tuition & fees: $20,580 **Average undergraduate aid package: $15,800**

ABOUT THE INSTITUTION Independent, coed. 18 undergraduate majors. Federal methodology is used as a basis for awarding need-based institutional aid.

UNDERGRADUATE EXPENSES for 2010–11 ***Comprehensive fee:*** $30,330 includes full-time tuition ($20,580) and room and board ($9750). Full-time tuition and fees vary according to location. Room and board charges vary according to housing facility. ***Part-time tuition:*** $725 per credit hour. Part-time tuition and fees vary according to course load. ***Payment plan:*** Installment.

FRESHMAN FINANCIAL AID (Fall 2009) 373 applied for aid; of those 100% were deemed to have need. 100% of freshmen with need received aid; of those 3% had need fully met. ***Average percent of need met:*** 70% (excluding resources awarded to replace EFC). ***Average financial aid package:*** $15,800 (excluding resources awarded to replace EFC). 1% of all full-time freshmen had no need and received non-need-based gift aid.

UNDERGRADUATE FINANCIAL AID (Fall 2009) 1,328 applied for aid; of those 100% were deemed to have need. 100% of undergraduates with need received aid; of those 2% had need fully met. ***Average percent of need met:*** 70% (excluding resources awarded to replace EFC). ***Average financial aid package:*** $15,800 (excluding resources awarded to replace EFC). 2% of all full-time undergraduates had no need and received non-need-based gift aid.

GIFT AID (NEED-BASED) ***Total amount:*** $14,630,497 (17% federal, 15% state, 67% institutional, 1% external sources). ***Receiving aid:*** Freshmen: 100% (373); all full-time undergraduates: 98% (1,328). ***Average award:*** Freshmen: $8000; Undergraduates: $8000. ***Scholarships, grants, and awards:*** Federal Pell, FSEOG, state, private, college/university gift aid from institutional funds.

GIFT AID (NON-NEED-BASED) ***Receiving aid:*** Freshmen: 100% (373). Undergraduates: 98% (1,328). ***Average award:*** Freshmen: $7500. Undergraduates: $7500. ***Scholarships, grants, and awards by category:*** *Academic interests/achievement:* 20 awards ($15,000 total): biological sciences, business, communication, education, general academic interests/achievements, mathematics. *Creative arts/performance:* 50 awards ($125,000 total): general creative arts/performance. *Special characteristics:* 20 awards ($210,000 total): adult students, children of faculty/staff. ***Tuition waivers:*** Full or partial for employees or children of employees, adult students, senior citizens.

LOANS ***Student loans:*** $9,290,105 (100% need-based). 95% of past graduating class borrowed through all loan programs. *Average indebtedness per student:* $22,000. ***Average need-based loan:*** Freshmen: $5000. Undergraduates: $5000. ***Parent loans:*** $1,147,838 (100% need-based). ***Programs:*** Federal Direct (Subsidized and Unsubsidized Stafford, PLUS), state.

WORK-STUDY ***Federal work-study:*** Total amount: $193,524; 150 jobs averaging $1500.

APPLYING FOR FINANCIAL AID ***Required financial aid forms:*** FAFSA, institution's own form, state aid form. ***Financial aid deadline (priority):*** 4/1. ***Notification date:*** Continuous. Students must reply within 2 weeks of notification.

CONTACT Ms. Catherine Buzanski, Director of Financial Aid, Medaille College, 18 Agassiz Circle, Buffalo, NY 14214-2695, 716-880-2179 or toll-free 800-292-1582 (in-state). *Fax:* 716-884-0291. *E-mail:* cbuzanski@medaille.edu.

MEDCENTER ONE COLLEGE OF NURSING

Bismarck, ND

Tuition & fees: $10,851 **Average undergraduate aid package: $13,210**

ABOUT THE INSTITUTION Independent, coed, primarily women. 1 undergraduate major. Both federal and institutional methodology are used as a basis for awarding need-based institutional aid.

UNDERGRADUATE EXPENSES for 2011–12 ***One-time required fee:*** $315. ***Tuition:*** full-time $10,012; part-time $417 per credit. ***Required fees:*** full-time $839; $34.97 per credit. Part-time tuition and fees vary according to course load.

UNDERGRADUATE FINANCIAL AID (Fall 2009) 88 applied for aid; of those 78% were deemed to have need. 100% of undergraduates with need received aid; of those 74% had need fully met. ***Average percent of need met:*** 98% (excluding resources awarded to replace EFC). ***Average financial aid package:*** $13,210 (excluding resources awarded to replace EFC). 3% of all full-time undergraduates had no need and received non-need-based gift aid.

GIFT AID (NEED-BASED) ***Total amount:*** $251,026 (62% federal, 32% state, 1% institutional, 5% external sources). ***Receiving aid:*** All full-time undergraduates: 61% (54). ***Average award:*** Undergraduates: $3521. ***Scholarships, grants, and awards:*** Federal Pell, FSEOG, state, private, college/university gift aid from institutional funds.

GIFT AID (NON-NEED-BASED) ***Total amount:*** $23,523 (23% institutional, 77% external sources). ***Receiving aid:*** Undergraduates: 23% (20). ***Average award:*** Undergraduates: $600. ***Scholarships, grants, and awards by category:*** *Academic interests/achievement:* 25 awards ($3684 total): general academic interests/achievements, health fields. *Special achievements/activities:* memberships. *Special characteristics:* 22 awards ($8398 total): children and siblings of alumni, general special characteristics, local/state students.

LOANS ***Student loans:*** $1,130,256 (23% need-based, 77% non-need-based). ***Average need-based loan:*** Undergraduates: $4253. ***Programs:*** Federal Direct (Subsidized and Unsubsidized Stafford, PLUS), Perkins, Federal Nursing, college/university.

WORK-STUDY ***Federal work-study:*** Total amount: $5393; 5 jobs averaging $1200.

APPLYING FOR FINANCIAL AID ***Financial aid deadline (priority):*** 3/15. ***Notification date:*** Continuous beginning 5/1. Students must reply within 2 weeks of notification.

CONTACT Ms. Janell Thomas, Financial Aid Director, Medcenter One College of Nursing, 512 North 7th Street, Bismarck, ND 58501-4494, 701-323-6270. *Fax:* 701-323-6289. *E-mail:* jthomas@mohs.org.

MEDGAR EVERS COLLEGE OF THE CITY UNIVERSITY OF NEW YORK

Brooklyn, NY

Tuition & fees (NY res): $5132 **Average undergraduate aid package: $3835**

ABOUT THE INSTITUTION State and locally supported, coed. 15 undergraduate majors. Federal methodology is used as a basis for awarding need-based institutional aid.

UNDERGRADUATE EXPENSES for 2011–12 ***Tuition, state resident:*** full-time $4830; part-time $205 per credit hour. ***Tuition, nonresident:*** full-time $13,050; part-time $435 per credit hour. ***Required fees:*** full-time $302; $100.85 per term. Full-time tuition and fees vary according to course load. Part-time tuition and fees vary according to course load. ***Payment plans:*** Installment, deferred payment.

FRESHMAN FINANCIAL AID (Fall 2009) ***Average financial aid package:*** $3866 (excluding resources awarded to replace EFC).

UNDERGRADUATE FINANCIAL AID (Fall 2009) ***Average financial aid package:*** $3835 (excluding resources awarded to replace EFC).

GIFT AID (NEED-BASED) ***Total amount:*** $29,153,451 (68% federal, 32% state). ***Receiving aid:*** Freshmen: 86% (1,109); all full-time undergraduates: 83% (3,839). ***Average award:*** Freshmen: $3724; Undergraduates: $3572. ***Scholarships, grants, and awards:*** Federal Pell, FSEOG, state, private, college/university gift aid from institutional funds, Thurgood Marshall Scholarship Fund.

GIFT AID (NON-NEED-BASED) ***Scholarships, grants, and awards by category:*** *Academic interests/achievement:* general academic interests/achievements.

LOANS ***Student loans:*** $2,574,846 (100% need-based). ***Average need-based loan:*** Freshmen: $1529. Undergraduates: $1758. ***Programs:*** Federal Direct (Subsidized and Unsubsidized Stafford, PLUS), Perkins.

WORK-STUDY ***Federal work-study:*** Total amount: $309,546; 289 jobs averaging $1071.

APPLYING FOR FINANCIAL AID ***Required financial aid forms:*** FAFSA, state aid form, University Financial Aid Information Supplemental Request (FASIR). ***Financial aid deadline (priority):*** 1/2. ***Notification date:*** Continuous beginning 4/1. Students must reply within 3 weeks of notification.

CONTACT Conley James, Director of Financial Aid, Medgar Evers College of the City University of New York, 1650 Bedford Avenue, Brooklyn, NY 11225, 718-270-6038. *Fax:* 718-270-6194. *E-mail:* conley@mec.cuny.edu.

MEDICAL UNIVERSITY OF SOUTH CAROLINA

Charleston, SC

CONTACT Cecile Kamath, PhD, Director for Financial Aid, Medical University of South Carolina, 45 Courtenay Drive, Charleston, SC 29425, 843-792-2536. *Fax:* 843-792-6356. *E-mail:* finaid@musc.edu.

MEMPHIS COLLEGE OF ART

Memphis, TN

ABOUT THE INSTITUTION Independent, coed. 5 undergraduate majors.

GIFT AID (NEED-BASED) ***Scholarships, grants, and awards:*** Federal Pell, FSEOG, state, private, college/university gift aid from institutional funds.

GIFT AID (NON-NEED-BASED) ***Scholarships, grants, and awards by category:*** *Academic interests/achievement:* general academic interests/achievements. *Creative arts/performance:* applied art and design, art/fine arts. *Special characteristics:* children of faculty/staff, previous college experience.

LOANS ***Programs:*** Federal Direct (Subsidized and Unsubsidized Stafford, PLUS), college/university.

WORK-STUDY ***Federal work-study:*** Total amount: $110,400; 340 jobs averaging $500. ***State or other work-study/employment:*** Total amount: $41,250 (100% non-need-based). Part-time jobs available.

APPLYING FOR FINANCIAL AID ***Required financial aid form:*** FAFSA.

CONTACT Lynn Holladay, Director of Financial Aid, Memphis College of Art, 1930 Poplar Avenue, Overton Park, Memphis, TN 38104, 901-272-5136 or toll-free 800-727-1088. *Fax:* 901-272-5134. *E-mail:* lholladay@mca.edu.

MENLO COLLEGE

Atherton, CA

Tuition & fees: $34,900 **Average undergraduate aid package: $28,412**

ABOUT THE INSTITUTION Independent, coed. 13 undergraduate majors. Federal methodology is used as a basis for awarding need-based institutional aid.

UNDERGRADUATE EXPENSES for 2011–12 ***Comprehensive fee:*** $46,200 includes full-time tuition ($34,500), mandatory fees ($400), and room and board ($11,300). Full-time tuition and fees vary according to program. Room and board charges vary according to housing facility. ***Part-time tuition:*** $1438 per credit hour. Part-time tuition and fees vary according to program. ***Payment plan:*** Installment.

FRESHMAN FINANCIAL AID (Fall 2010, est.) 119 applied for aid; of those 95% were deemed to have need. 100% of freshmen with need received aid; of those 5% had need fully met. ***Average percent of need met:*** 71% (excluding resources awarded to replace EFC). ***Average financial aid package:*** $28,339 (excluding resources awarded to replace EFC). 23% of all full-time freshmen had no need and received non-need-based gift aid.

UNDERGRADUATE FINANCIAL AID (Fall 2010, est.) 386 applied for aid; of those 95% were deemed to have need. 100% of undergraduates with need received aid; of those 7% had need fully met. ***Average percent of need met:*** 71% (excluding resources awarded to replace EFC). ***Average financial aid package:*** $28,412 (excluding resources awarded to replace EFC). 29% of all full-time undergraduates had no need and received non-need-based gift aid.

GIFT AID (NEED-BASED) ***Total amount:*** $8,913,873 (11% federal, 9% state, 77% institutional, 3% external sources). ***Receiving aid:*** Freshmen: 76% (113); all full-time undergraduates: 65% (367). ***Average award:*** Freshmen: $24,890; Undergraduates: $24,378. ***Scholarships, grants, and awards:*** Federal Pell, FSEOG, state, college/university gift aid from institutional funds.

GIFT AID (NON-NEED-BASED) ***Total amount:*** $1,893,138 (98% institutional, 2% external sources). ***Receiving aid:*** Freshmen: 3% (4). Undergraduates: 3% (17). ***Average award:*** Freshmen: $12,441. Undergraduates: $10,815. ***Scholarships, grants, and awards by category:*** *Academic interests/achievement:* 484 awards ($4,809,178 total): general academic interests/achievements. ***Tuition waivers:*** Full or partial for employees or children of employees.

LOANS ***Student loans:*** $2,821,092 (82% need-based, 18% non-need-based). 62% of past graduating class borrowed through all loan programs. *Average indebtedness per student:* $28,333. ***Average need-based loan:*** Freshmen: $3071. Undergraduates: $3824. ***Parent loans:*** $1,931,099 (51% need-based, 49% non-need-based). ***Programs:*** Federal Direct (Subsidized and Unsubsidized Stafford, PLUS).

WORK-STUDY ***Federal work-study:*** Total amount: $239,030; 293 jobs averaging $1000.

ATHLETIC AWARDS Total amount: $20,000 (90% need-based, 10% non-need-based).

APPLYING FOR FINANCIAL AID ***Required financial aid forms:*** FAFSA, state aid form. ***Financial aid deadline (priority):*** 3/2. ***Notification date:*** Continuous beginning 3/15.

CONTACT Anne Heaton-Dunlap, Director of Financial Aid, Menlo College, 1000 El Camino Real, Atherton, CA 94027-4301, 650-543-3880 or toll-free 800-556-3656. *Fax:* 650-543-4103. *E-mail:* financialaid@menlo.edu.

MERCER UNIVERSITY

Macon, GA

Tuition & fees: $30,560 **Average undergraduate aid package: $31,192**

ABOUT THE INSTITUTION Independent Baptist, coed. 49 undergraduate majors. Federal methodology is used as a basis for awarding need-based institutional aid.

UNDERGRADUATE EXPENSES for 2010–11 ***Comprehensive fee:*** $40,648 includes full-time tuition ($30,360), mandatory fees ($200), and room and board ($10,088). Full-time tuition and fees vary according to class time and location. Room and board charges vary according to board plan, housing facility, and location. ***Part-time tuition:*** $1012 per credit hour. ***Part-time fees:*** $8.50 per credit hour. Part-time tuition and fees vary according to class time, course load, and location. ***Payment plan:*** Installment.

FRESHMAN FINANCIAL AID (Fall 2010, est.) 534 applied for aid; of those 87% were deemed to have need. 100% of freshmen with need received aid; of those 43% had need fully met. ***Average percent of need met:*** 89% (excluding resources awarded to replace EFC). ***Average financial aid package:*** $32,893 (excluding resources awarded to replace EFC). 21% of all full-time freshmen had no need and received non-need-based gift aid.

UNDERGRADUATE FINANCIAL AID (Fall 2010, est.) 1,840 applied for aid; of those 89% were deemed to have need. 100% of undergraduates with need received aid; of those 40% had need fully met. ***Average percent of need met:*** 84% (excluding resources awarded to replace EFC). ***Average financial aid package:*** $31,192 (excluding resources awarded to replace EFC). 27% of all full-time undergraduates had no need and received non-need-based gift aid.

GIFT AID (NEED-BASED) ***Total amount:*** $32,740,459 (11% federal, 9% state, 78% institutional, 2% external sources). ***Receiving aid:*** Freshmen: 78% (462); all full-time undergraduates: 72% (1,635). ***Average award:*** Freshmen: $23,536; Undergraduates: $21,295. ***Scholarships, grants, and awards:*** Federal Pell, FSEOG, state, college/university gift aid from institutional funds, Federal Nursing.

GIFT AID (NON-NEED-BASED) ***Total amount:*** $14,510,636 (14% state, 84% institutional, 2% external sources). ***Receiving aid:*** Freshmen: 21% (123). Undergraduates: 17% (384). ***Average award:*** Freshmen: $23,201. Undergraduates: $20,284. ***Scholarships, grants, and awards by category:*** *Academic interests/achievement:* $15,403,585 total: biological sciences, business, education, engineering/technologies, English, foreign languages, general academic interests/achievements, international studies, military science, religion/biblical studies. *Creative arts/performance:* $1,018,441 total: art/fine arts, debating, music, theater/drama. *Special achievements/activities:* $162,352 total: community service, general special achievements/activities, leadership. *Special characteristics:* $22,280,136 total: adult students, children of faculty/staff, children of public servants, general special characteristics, international students, relatives of clergy, siblings of current students. ***Tuition waivers:*** Full or partial for employees or children of employees.

LOANS ***Student loans:*** $12,465,023 (72% need-based, 28% non-need-based). 66% of past graduating class borrowed through all loan programs. *Average indebtedness per student:* $30,460. ***Average need-based loan:*** Freshmen: $6709. Undergraduates: $8091. ***Parent loans:*** $2,821,823 (39% need-based, 61% non-need-based). ***Programs:*** Federal Direct (Subsidized and Unsubsidized Stafford, PLUS), Perkins, Federal Nursing, college/university.

WORK-STUDY ***Federal work-study:*** Total amount: $874,503; jobs available.

ATHLETIC AWARDS Total amount: $3,729,944 (41% need-based, 59% non-need-based).

APPLYING FOR FINANCIAL AID ***Required financial aid forms:*** FAFSA, institution's own form, state aid form (GA residents only). ***Financial aid deadline (priority):*** 4/1. ***Notification date:*** Continuous. Students must reply within 2 weeks of notification.

CONTACT Ms. Carol Williams, Associate Vice President of Financial Planning, Mercer University, 1400 Coleman Avenue, Macon, GA 31207-0003, 478-301-2670 or toll-free 800-840-8577. *Fax:* 478-301-2671. *E-mail:* williams_ck@mercer.edu.

MERCY COLLEGE

Dobbs Ferry, NY

Tuition & fees: $17,010 **Average undergraduate aid package: $12,164**

ABOUT THE INSTITUTION Independent, coed. 35 undergraduate majors. Federal methodology is used as a basis for awarding need-based institutional aid.

UNDERGRADUATE EXPENSES for 2010–11 ***Comprehensive fee:*** $28,150 includes full-time tuition ($16,490), mandatory fees ($520), and room and board ($11,140). ***College room only:*** $7890. Full-time tuition and fees vary according to program and reciprocity agreements. Room and board charges vary according to board plan and housing facility. ***Part-time tuition:*** $692 per credit hour. ***Part-time fees:*** $130 per term. Part-time tuition and fees vary according to program and reciprocity agreements. ***Payment plan:*** Installment.

FRESHMAN FINANCIAL AID (Fall 2009) 844 applied for aid; of those 93% were deemed to have need. 96% of freshmen with need received aid; of those 2% had need fully met. ***Average percent of need met:*** 51% (excluding resources awarded to replace EFC). ***Average financial aid package:*** $13,701 (excluding resources awarded to replace EFC). 2% of all full-time freshmen had no need and received non-need-based gift aid.

UNDERGRADUATE FINANCIAL AID (Fall 2009) 3,515 applied for aid; of those 99% were deemed to have need. 96% of undergraduates with need received aid; of those 2% had need fully met. ***Average percent of need met:*** 47% (excluding resources awarded to replace EFC). ***Average financial aid package:*** $12,164 (excluding resources awarded to replace EFC). 1% of all full-time undergraduates had no need and received non-need-based gift aid.

GIFT AID (NEED-BASED) ***Total amount:*** $26,826,942 (46% federal, 25% state, 29% institutional). ***Receiving aid:*** Freshmen: 80% (704); all full-time undergraduates: 74% (3,006). ***Average award:*** Freshmen: $10,445; Undergraduates: $8609. ***Scholarships, grants, and awards:*** Federal Pell, FSEOG, state, private, college/university gift aid from institutional funds, Federal Nursing.

GIFT AID (NON-NEED-BASED) ***Total amount:*** $2,714,338 (7% state, 92% institutional, 1% external sources). ***Receiving aid:*** Freshmen: 49% (431). Undergraduates: 30% (1,230). ***Average award:*** Freshmen: $3407. Undergraduates: $3385. ***Scholarships, grants, and awards by category:*** *Academic interests/achievement:* general academic interests/achievements. ***Tuition waivers:*** Full or partial for employees or children of employees, senior citizens.

LOANS ***Student loans:*** $29,718,231 (43% need-based, 57% non-need-based). 71% of past graduating class borrowed through all loan programs. *Average indebtedness per student:* $23,307. ***Average need-based loan:*** Freshmen: $3181. Undergraduates: $4103. ***Parent loans:*** $2,469,251 (100% non-need-based). ***Programs:*** Federal Direct (Subsidized and Unsubsidized Stafford, PLUS), Federal Nursing, state.

WORK-STUDY ***Federal work-study:*** Total amount: $923,163; jobs available.

ATHLETIC AWARDS Total amount: $843,888 (100% non-need-based).

APPLYING FOR FINANCIAL AID ***Required financial aid forms:*** FAFSA, state aid form. ***Financial aid deadline:*** Continuous. ***Notification date:*** Continuous beginning 2/20. Students must reply by 5/1 or within 2 weeks of notification.

CONTACT Margaret McGrail, Vice President of Student Services, Mercy College, 555 Broadway, Dobbs Ferry, NY 10522, 888-464-6737 or toll-free 800-MERCY-NY. *Fax:* 914-375-8582.

MERCY COLLEGE OF HEALTH SCIENCES

Des Moines, IA

CONTACT Lisa Croat, Financial Aid Assistant Coordinator, Mercy College of Health Sciences, 928 Sixth Avenue, Des Moines, IA 50309, 515-643-6720 or toll-free 800-637-2994. *Fax:* 515-643-6702. *E-mail:* lcroat@mercydesmoines.org.

MERCY COLLEGE OF NORTHWEST OHIO

Toledo, OH

Tuition & fees: $10,624 **Average undergraduate aid package: $7764**

ABOUT THE INSTITUTION Independent religious, coed, primarily women. 6 undergraduate majors. Federal methodology is used as a basis for awarding need-based institutional aid.

UNDERGRADUATE EXPENSES for 2010–11 ***Tuition:*** full-time $9920; part-time $342 per credit hour. ***Required fees:*** full-time $704; $22 per credit hour. Full-time tuition and fees vary according to course load. Part-time tuition and fees vary according to course load. Room and board charges vary according to housing facility. ***Payment plans:*** Installment, deferred payment.

FRESHMAN FINANCIAL AID (Fall 2009) 44 applied for aid; of those 75% were deemed to have need. 100% of freshmen with need received aid; of those 3% had need fully met. ***Average percent of need met:*** 40% (excluding resources awarded to replace EFC). ***Average financial aid package:*** $7698 (excluding resources awarded to replace EFC). 19% of all full-time freshmen had no need and received non-need-based gift aid.

UNDERGRADUATE FINANCIAL AID (Fall 2009) 485 applied for aid; of those 91% were deemed to have need. 97% of undergraduates with need received aid; of those 4% had need fully met. ***Average percent of need met:*** 37% (excluding resources awarded to replace EFC). ***Average financial aid package:*** $7764 (excluding resources awarded to replace EFC). 2% of all full-time undergraduates had no need and received non-need-based gift aid.

GIFT AID (NEED-BASED) ***Total amount:*** $2,422,150 (76% federal, 16% state, 1% institutional, 7% external sources). ***Receiving aid:*** Freshmen: 43% (20); all full-time undergraduates: 76% (410). ***Average award:*** Freshmen: $5798; Undergraduates: $5661. ***Scholarships, grants, and awards:*** Federal Pell, FSEOG, state, private, college/university gift aid from institutional funds, Federal Nursing.

GIFT AID (NON-NEED-BASED) ***Total amount:*** $349,109 (6% state, 39% institutional, 55% external sources). ***Receiving aid:*** Freshmen: 28% (13). Undergraduates: 13% (70). ***Average award:*** Freshmen: $1511. Undergraduates: $1986. ***Scholarships, grants, and awards by category:*** *Academic interests/achievement:* 75 awards ($140,000 total): health fields. ***Tuition waivers:*** Full or partial for employees or children of employees.

LOANS ***Student loans:*** $8,362,212 (39% need-based, 61% non-need-based). 80% of past graduating class borrowed through all loan programs. *Average indebtedness per student:* $25,560. ***Average need-based loan:*** Freshmen: $3346. Undergraduates: $4448. ***Parent loans:*** $208,648 (100% need-based). ***Programs:*** Federal Direct (Subsidized and Unsubsidized Stafford, PLUS), state, college/university.

WORK-STUDY ***Federal work-study:*** Total amount: $45,466; 29 jobs averaging $1567. ***State or other work-study/employment:*** Total amount: $21,000 (100% need-based). Part-time jobs available.

APPLYING FOR FINANCIAL AID ***Required financial aid form:*** FAFSA. ***Financial aid deadline:*** Continuous. ***Notification date:*** Continuous beginning 3/1. Students must reply by 8/15.

CONTACT Julie Leslie, Financial Aid Director, Mercy College of Northwest Ohio, 2221 Madison Avenue, Toledo, OH 43604, 419-251-1598 or toll-free 888-80-Mercy. *Fax:* 419-251-1462. *E-mail:* julie.leslie@mercycollege.edu.

MERCYHURST COLLEGE

Erie, PA

Tuition & fees: $26,346 **Average undergraduate aid package: $21,937**

ABOUT THE INSTITUTION Independent Roman Catholic, coed. 67 undergraduate majors. Federal methodology is used as a basis for awarding need-based institutional aid.

UNDERGRADUATE EXPENSES for 2010–11 ***Comprehensive fee:*** $35,541 includes full-time tuition ($24,648), mandatory fees ($1698), and room and board ($9195). ***College room only:*** $4542. Full-time tuition and fees vary according to program. Room and board charges vary according to board plan and housing facility. ***Part-time tuition:*** $822 per credit hour. Part-time tuition and fees vary according to class time, course load, degree level, and location. ***Payment plan:*** Installment.

FRESHMAN FINANCIAL AID (Fall 2010, est.) 569 applied for aid; of those 88% were deemed to have need. 100% of freshmen with need received aid; of those 49% had need fully met. ***Average percent of need met:*** 81% (excluding resources awarded to replace EFC). ***Average financial aid package:*** $24,616 (excluding resources awarded to replace EFC). 17% of all full-time freshmen had no need and received non-need-based gift aid.

UNDERGRADUATE FINANCIAL AID (Fall 2010, est.) 2,022 applied for aid; of those 90% were deemed to have need. 100% of undergraduates with need received aid; of those 30% had need fully met. ***Average percent of need met:*** 54% (excluding resources awarded to replace EFC). ***Average financial aid package:*** $21,937 (excluding resources awarded to replace EFC). 15% of all full-time undergraduates had no need and received non-need-based gift aid.

GIFT AID (NEED-BASED) ***Total amount:*** $30,549,343 (14% federal, 6% state, 79% institutional, 1% external sources). ***Receiving aid:*** Freshmen: 76% (502);

all full-time undergraduates: 67% (1,610). ***Average award:*** Freshmen: $20,737; Undergraduates: $11,011. ***Scholarships, grants, and awards:*** Federal Pell, FSEOG, state, private, college/university gift aid from institutional funds.

GIFT AID (NON-NEED-BASED) ***Total amount:*** $5,398,551 (9% federal, 90% institutional, 1% external sources). ***Receiving aid:*** Freshmen: 56% (371). Undergraduates: 48% (1,155). ***Average award:*** Freshmen: $13,984. Undergraduates: $13,436. ***Scholarships, grants, and awards by category:*** *Academic interests/achievement:* 1,267 awards ($13,267,923 total): general academic interests/achievements. *Creative arts/performance:* 130 awards ($726,940 total): applied art and design, art/fine arts, dance, music. *Special achievements/activities:* 1,766 awards ($16,083,729 total): community service, general special achievements/activities, leadership, religious involvement. *Special characteristics:* 71 awards ($1,494,256 total): children and siblings of alumni, children of faculty/staff. ***Tuition waivers:*** Full or partial for employees or children of employees, adult students.

LOANS ***Student loans:*** $17,007,164 (91% need-based, 9% non-need-based). 71% of past graduating class borrowed through all loan programs. *Average indebtedness per student:* $25,357. ***Average need-based loan:*** Freshmen: $2289. Undergraduates: $3591. ***Parent loans:*** $4,146,514 (93% need-based, 7% non-need-based). ***Programs:*** Federal Direct (Subsidized and Unsubsidized Stafford, PLUS), Perkins, college/university.

WORK-STUDY ***Federal work-study:*** Total amount: $758,540; 503 jobs averaging $1195. ***State or other work-study/employment:*** Total amount: $610,526 (70% need-based, 30% non-need-based). 472 part-time jobs averaging $1196.

ATHLETIC AWARDS Total amount: $6,000,145 (50% need-based, 50% non-need-based).

APPLYING FOR FINANCIAL AID ***Required financial aid form:*** FAFSA. ***Financial aid deadline:*** 5/1 (priority: 3/1). ***Notification date:*** Continuous beginning 2/15. Students must reply within 2 weeks of notification.

CONTACT Carrie Newman, Director of Student Financial Services, Mercyhurst College, 501 East 38th Street, Erie, PA 16546, 814-824-2288 or toll-free 800-825-1926 Ext. 2202. *Fax:* 814-824-2300. *E-mail:* sfs@mercyhurst.edu.

MEREDITH COLLEGE

Raleigh, NC

Tuition & fees: $26,200 **Average undergraduate aid package: $19,325**

ABOUT THE INSTITUTION Independent, undergraduate: women only; graduate: coed. 45 undergraduate majors. Federal methodology is used as a basis for awarding need-based institutional aid.

UNDERGRADUATE EXPENSES for 2010–11 ***Comprehensive fee:*** $33,700 includes full-time tuition ($26,150), mandatory fees ($50), and room and board ($7500). ***College room only:*** $3750. Full-time tuition and fees vary according to course load. ***Part-time tuition:*** $650 per credit hour. Part-time tuition and fees vary according to course load. ***Payment plan:*** Installment.

FRESHMAN FINANCIAL AID (Fall 2010, est.) 300 applied for aid; of those 88% were deemed to have need. 100% of freshmen with need received aid; of those 21% had need fully met. ***Average percent of need met:*** 78% (excluding resources awarded to replace EFC). ***Average financial aid package:*** $20,517 (excluding resources awarded to replace EFC). 10% of all full-time freshmen had no need and received non-need-based gift aid.

UNDERGRADUATE FINANCIAL AID (Fall 2010, est.) 1,087 applied for aid; of those 89% were deemed to have need. 100% of undergraduates with need received aid; of those 14% had need fully met. ***Average percent of need met:*** 71% (excluding resources awarded to replace EFC). ***Average financial aid package:*** $19,325 (excluding resources awarded to replace EFC). 6% of all full-time undergraduates had no need and received non-need-based gift aid.

GIFT AID (NEED-BASED) ***Total amount:*** $19,528,774 (16% federal, 26% state, 50% institutional, 8% external sources). ***Receiving aid:*** Freshmen: 72% (265); all full-time undergraduates: 73% (965). ***Average award:*** Freshmen: $17,299; Undergraduates: $15,324. ***Scholarships, grants, and awards:*** Federal Pell, FSEOG, state, private, college/university gift aid from institutional funds.

GIFT AID (NON-NEED-BASED) ***Total amount:*** $4,669,929 (17% state, 70% institutional, 13% external sources). ***Average award:*** Freshmen: $7653. Undergraduates: $7123. ***Scholarships, grants, and awards by category:*** *Academic interests/achievement:* biological sciences, business, computer science, education, English, foreign languages, general academic interests/achievements, mathematics, physical sciences, religion/biblical studies. *Creative arts/performance:* applied art and design, art/fine arts, creative writing, music. *Special achievements/activities:* community service, leadership. *Special characteristics:* adult students, children of faculty/staff, ethnic background, first-generation college students, international students, members of minority groups, out-of-state students, previous college experience, religious affiliation. ***Tuition waivers:*** Full or partial for employees or children of employees.

LOANS ***Student loans:*** $10,568,266 (93% need-based, 7% non-need-based). 69% of past graduating class borrowed through all loan programs. *Average indebtedness per student:* $33,691. ***Average need-based loan:*** Freshmen: $3306. Undergraduates: $4495. ***Parent loans:*** $4,317,126 (45% need-based, 55% non-need-based). ***Programs:*** Perkins, college/university.

WORK-STUDY ***Federal work-study:*** Total amount: $263,434; jobs available. ***State or other work-study/employment:*** Part-time jobs available.

APPLYING FOR FINANCIAL AID ***Required financial aid form:*** FAFSA. ***Financial aid deadline (priority):*** 2/15. ***Notification date:*** Continuous beginning 3/15. Students must reply by 5/1 or within 2 weeks of notification.

CONTACT Mr. Kevin Michaelsen, Director of Financial Assistance, Meredith College, 3800 Hillsborough Street, Raleigh, NC 27607-5298, 919-760-8565 or toll-free 800-MEREDITH. *Fax:* 919-760-2375. *E-mail:* michaelsen@meredith.edu.

MERRIMACK COLLEGE

North Andover, MA

Tuition & fees: $31,380 **Average undergraduate aid package: $18,124**

ABOUT THE INSTITUTION Independent Roman Catholic, coed. 46 undergraduate majors. Federal methodology is used as a basis for awarding need-based institutional aid.

UNDERGRADUATE EXPENSES for 2010–11 ***Comprehensive fee:*** $42,080 includes full-time tuition ($30,780), mandatory fees ($600), and room and board ($10,700). ***College room only:*** $6340. Room and board charges vary according to board plan and housing facility. ***Part-time tuition:*** $1100 per credit hour. ***Part-time fees:*** $75 per term. Part-time tuition and fees vary according to class time, course level, course load, and degree level. ***Payment plan:*** Installment.

FRESHMAN FINANCIAL AID (Fall 2010, est.) 450 applied for aid; of those 94% were deemed to have need. 100% of freshmen with need received aid; of those 29% had need fully met. ***Average percent of need met:*** 63% (excluding resources awarded to replace EFC). ***Average financial aid package:*** $18,857 (excluding resources awarded to replace EFC). 13% of all full-time freshmen had no need and received non-need-based gift aid.

UNDERGRADUATE FINANCIAL AID (Fall 2010, est.) 1,612 applied for aid; of those 96% were deemed to have need. 100% of undergraduates with need received aid; of those 27% had need fully met. ***Average percent of need met:*** 60% (excluding resources awarded to replace EFC). ***Average financial aid package:*** $18,124 (excluding resources awarded to replace EFC). 15% of all full-time undergraduates had no need and received non-need-based gift aid.

GIFT AID (NEED-BASED) ***Total amount:*** $20,510,071 (11% federal, 3% state, 86% institutional). ***Receiving aid:*** Freshmen: 85% (418); all full-time undergraduates: 74% (1,407). ***Average award:*** Freshmen: $13,898; Undergraduates: $12,510. ***Scholarships, grants, and awards:*** Federal Pell, FSEOG, state, private, college/university gift aid from institutional funds.

GIFT AID (NON-NEED-BASED) ***Total amount:*** $1,357,932 (59% institutional, 41% external sources). ***Receiving aid:*** Freshmen: 20% (98). Undergraduates: 24% (461). ***Average award:*** Freshmen: $10,110. Undergraduates: $10,019. ***Scholarships, grants, and awards by category:*** *Academic interests/achievement:* general academic interests/achievements. *Special characteristics:* children and siblings of alumni, children of faculty/staff, international students, relatives of clergy, siblings of current students. ***Tuition waivers:*** Full or partial for employees or children of employees, senior citizens.

LOANS ***Student loans:*** $14,461,255 (64% need-based, 36% non-need-based). 81% of past graduating class borrowed through all loan programs. *Average indebtedness per student:* $27,000. ***Average need-based loan:*** Freshmen: $4182. Undergraduates: $5144. ***Parent loans:*** $7,159,229 (100% non-need-based). ***Programs:*** Federal Direct (Subsidized and Unsubsidized Stafford, PLUS), Perkins, state, college/university, private loans, MEFA Loans.

WORK-STUDY ***Federal work-study:*** Total amount: $271,203; 204 jobs averaging $1329. ***State or other work-study/employment:*** Total amount: $638,519 (100% non-need-based). 359 part-time jobs averaging $1779.

ATHLETIC AWARDS Total amount: $3,665,584 (100% non-need-based).

APPLYING FOR FINANCIAL AID ***Required financial aid form:*** FAFSA. ***Financial aid deadline:*** 2/1. ***Notification date:*** Continuous beginning 3/1. Students must reply by 5/1.

CONTACT Christine A. Mordach, Director of Student Financial Aid and Scholarships, Merrimack College, 315 Turnpike Street, North Andover, MA 01845, 978-837-5186. *Fax:* 978-837-5067. *E-mail:* christine.mordach@merrimack.edu.

MESA STATE COLLEGE

Grand Junction, CO

Tuition & fees (CO res): $6248 **Average undergraduate aid package: $10,678**

ABOUT THE INSTITUTION State-supported, coed. 43 undergraduate majors. Federal methodology is used as a basis for awarding need-based institutional aid.

UNDERGRADUATE EXPENSES for 2010–11 ***Tuition, state resident:*** full-time $5480; part-time $182.66 per credit hour. ***Tuition, nonresident:*** full-time $15,658; part-time $521.94 per credit hour. ***Required fees:*** full-time $768; $25.61 per credit hour. Full-time tuition and fees vary according to course load. Part-time tuition and fees vary according to course load. ***College room and board:*** $8298. Room and board charges vary according to board plan and housing facility. ***Payment plan:*** Installment.

FRESHMAN FINANCIAL AID (Fall 2009) 1,300 applied for aid; of those 75% were deemed to have need. 96% of freshmen with need received aid; of those 29% had need fully met. ***Average percent of need met:*** 75% (excluding resources awarded to replace EFC). ***Average financial aid package:*** $10,437 (excluding resources awarded to replace EFC). 10% of all full-time freshmen had no need and received non-need-based gift aid.

UNDERGRADUATE FINANCIAL AID (Fall 2009) 4,010 applied for aid; of those 80% were deemed to have need. 97% of undergraduates with need received aid; of those 26% had need fully met. ***Average percent of need met:*** 75% (excluding resources awarded to replace EFC). ***Average financial aid package:*** $10,678 (excluding resources awarded to replace EFC). 8% of all full-time undergraduates had no need and received non-need-based gift aid.

GIFT AID (NEED-BASED) ***Total amount:*** $13,187,729 (75% federal, 22% state, 3% institutional). ***Receiving aid:*** Freshmen: 46% (781); all full-time undergraduates: 50% (2,510). ***Average award:*** Freshmen: $4947; Undergraduates: $4938. ***Scholarships, grants, and awards:*** Federal Pell, FSEOG, state, private, college/university gift aid from institutional funds.

GIFT AID (NON-NEED-BASED) ***Total amount:*** $4,503,976 (10% federal, 59% institutional, 31% external sources). ***Receiving aid:*** Freshmen: 2% (39). Undergraduates: 1% (75). ***Average award:*** Freshmen: $2265. Undergraduates: $2135. ***Scholarships, grants, and awards by category:*** *Academic interests/achievement:* biological sciences, business, communication, computer science, education, engineering/technologies, English, foreign languages, general academic interests/achievements, health fields, humanities, mathematics, physical sciences, social sciences. *Creative arts/performance:* art/fine arts, creative writing, dance, journalism/publications, music, performing arts, theater/drama. *Special achievements/activities:* general special achievements/activities, hobbies/interests, leadership. *Special characteristics:* adult students, first-generation college students, international students, local/state students, members of minority groups, out-of-state students. ***Tuition waivers:*** Full or partial for employees or children of employees.

LOANS ***Student loans:*** $28,817,714 (43% need-based, 57% non-need-based). 65% of past graduating class borrowed through all loan programs. *Average indebtedness per student:* $18,966. ***Average need-based loan:*** Freshmen: $7639. Undergraduates: $7804. ***Parent loans:*** $4,357,951 (100% non-need-based). ***Programs:*** Federal Direct (Subsidized and Unsubsidized Stafford, PLUS), Perkins.

WORK-STUDY ***Federal work-study:*** Total amount: $277,467; jobs available. ***State or other work-study/employment:*** Total amount: $2,048,518 (25% need-based, 75% non-need-based). Part-time jobs available.

ATHLETIC AWARDS Total amount: $1,084,689 (100% non-need-based).

APPLYING FOR FINANCIAL AID ***Required financial aid form:*** FAFSA. ***Financial aid deadline:*** Continuous. ***Notification date:*** Continuous beginning 4/1. Students must reply within 4 weeks of notification.

CONTACT Mr. Curt Martin, Director of Financial Aid, Mesa State College, 1100 North Avenue, Grand Junction, CO 81501-3122, 970-248-1065 or toll-free 800-982-MESA. *Fax:* 970-248-1191. *E-mail:* cumartin@mesastate.edu.

MESIVTA OF EASTERN PARKWAY–YESHIVA ZICHRON MEILECH

Brooklyn, NY

CONTACT Rabbi Joseph Halberstadt, Dean, Mesivta of Eastern Parkway–Yeshiva Zichron Meilech, 510 Dahill Road, Brooklyn, NY 11218-5559, 718-438-1002.

MESIVTA TIFERETH JERUSALEM OF AMERICA

New York, NY

CONTACT Rabbi Dickstein, Director of Financial Aid, Mesivta Tifereth Jerusalem of America, 141 East Broadway, New York, NY 10002-6301, 212-964-2830.

MESIVTA TORAH VODAATH RABBINICAL SEMINARY

Brooklyn, NY

CONTACT Mrs. Kayla Goldring, Director of Financial Aid, Mesivta Torah Vodaath Rabbinical Seminary, 425 East Ninth Street, Brooklyn, NY 11218-5209, 718-941-8000.

MESSENGER COLLEGE

Joplin, MO

CONTACT Susan Aleckson, Financial Aid Director, Messenger College, 300 East 50th Street, Joplin, MO 64804, 417-624-7070 Ext. 308 or toll-free 800-385-8940 (in-state). *Fax:* 417-624-5070. *E-mail:* saleckson@messengercollege.edu.

MESSIAH COLLEGE

Grantham, PA

Tuition & fees: $28,356 **Average undergraduate aid package: $18,977**

ABOUT THE INSTITUTION Independent interdenominational, coed. 74 undergraduate majors. Federal methodology is used as a basis for awarding need-based institutional aid.

UNDERGRADUATE EXPENSES for 2011–12 ***Comprehensive fee:*** $36,776 includes full-time tuition ($27,536), mandatory fees ($820), and room and board ($8420). ***College room only:*** $4460. Room and board charges vary according to board plan, housing facility, and location. ***Part-time tuition:*** $1147 per credit. ***Payment plan:*** Installment.

FRESHMAN FINANCIAL AID (Fall 2010, est.) 624 applied for aid; of those 83% were deemed to have need. 100% of freshmen with need received aid; of those 24% had need fully met. ***Average percent of need met:*** 75% (excluding resources awarded to replace EFC). ***Average financial aid package:*** $19,985 (excluding resources awarded to replace EFC). 28% of all full-time freshmen had no need and received non-need-based gift aid.

UNDERGRADUATE FINANCIAL AID (Fall 2010, est.) 2,206 applied for aid; of those 89% were deemed to have need. 100% of undergraduates with need received aid; of those 18% had need fully met. ***Average percent of need met:*** 69% (excluding resources awarded to replace EFC). ***Average financial aid package:*** $18,977 (excluding resources awarded to replace EFC). 26% of all full-time undergraduates had no need and received non-need-based gift aid.

GIFT AID (NEED-BASED) ***Total amount:*** $26,213,345 (10% federal, 7% state, 78% institutional, 5% external sources). ***Receiving aid:*** Freshmen: 72% (518); all full-time undergraduates: 72% (1,936). ***Average award:*** Freshmen: $15,180; Undergraduates: $13,502. ***Scholarships, grants, and awards:*** Federal Pell, FSEOG, state, private, college/university gift aid from institutional funds.

GIFT AID (NON-NEED-BASED) ***Total amount:*** $8,702,744 (91% institutional, 9% external sources). ***Receiving aid:*** Freshmen: 10% (75). Undergraduates: 6% (170). ***Average award:*** Freshmen: $11,827. Undergraduates: $10,174. ***Scholarships, grants, and awards by category:*** *Academic interests/achievement:* 2,122 awards ($16,465,722 total): general academic interests/achievements. *Creative arts/performance:* 95 awards ($557,085 total): art/fine arts, music, theater/drama. *Special achievements/activities:* 370 awards ($4,834,426 total): leadership. *Special characteristics:* 214 awards ($1,887,504 total): adult students, children of faculty/staff, local/state students, religious affiliation. ***Tuition waivers:*** Full or partial for minority students, children of alumni, employees or children of employees, adult students, senior citizens.

LOANS ***Student loans:*** $17,800,824 (72% need-based, 28% non-need-based). 77% of past graduating class borrowed through all loan programs. *Average indebtedness per student:* $34,132. ***Average need-based loan:*** Freshmen: $3552. Undergraduates: $4549. ***Parent loans:*** $4,851,902 (40% need-based, 60% non-need-based). ***Programs:*** Federal Direct (Subsidized and Unsubsidized Stafford, PLUS), Perkins, Federal Nursing.

WORK-STUDY ***Federal work-study:*** Total amount: $1,698,741; 874 jobs averaging $2085. ***State or other work-study/employment:*** Total amount: $1,990,655 (100% non-need-based). 707 part-time jobs averaging $2060.

APPLYING FOR FINANCIAL AID ***Required financial aid form:*** FAFSA. ***Financial aid deadline (priority):*** 4/1. ***Notification date:*** Continuous beginning 3/15. Students must reply by 5/1 or within 4 weeks of notification.

CONTACT Mr. Michael Strite, Assistant Director of Financial Aid, Messiah College, PO Box 3006, Grantham, PA 17027, 717-691-6007 or toll-free 800-233-4220. *Fax:* 717-796-4791. *E-mail:* mstrite@messiah.edu.

METHODIST UNIVERSITY

Fayetteville, NC

Tuition & fees: $24,220 **Average undergraduate aid package: $23,733**

ABOUT THE INSTITUTION Independent United Methodist, coed. 57 undergraduate majors. Federal methodology is used as a basis for awarding need-based institutional aid.

UNDERGRADUATE EXPENSES for 2010–11 ***Comprehensive fee:*** $33,120 includes full-time tuition ($23,780), mandatory fees ($440), and room and board ($8900). Full-time tuition and fees vary according to class time. Room and board charges vary according to housing facility. ***Part-time tuition:*** $735 per semester hour. Part-time tuition and fees vary according to class time and course load. ***Payment plan:*** Installment.

FRESHMAN FINANCIAL AID (Fall 2009) 471 applied for aid; of those 93% were deemed to have need. 100% of freshmen with need received aid; of those 47% had need fully met. ***Average percent of need met:*** 86% (excluding resources awarded to replace EFC). ***Average financial aid package:*** $26,575 (excluding resources awarded to replace EFC). 5% of all full-time freshmen had no need and received non-need-based gift aid.

UNDERGRADUATE FINANCIAL AID (Fall 2009) 1,727 applied for aid; of those 93% were deemed to have need. 96% of undergraduates with need received aid; of those 41% had need fully met. ***Average percent of need met:*** 82% (excluding resources awarded to replace EFC). ***Average financial aid package:*** $23,733 (excluding resources awarded to replace EFC). 4% of all full-time undergraduates had no need and received non-need-based gift aid.

GIFT AID (NEED-BASED) ***Total amount:*** $14,617,178 (22% federal, 12% state, 66% institutional). ***Receiving aid:*** Freshmen: 82% (386); all full-time undergraduates: 72% (1,237). ***Average award:*** Freshmen: $11,223; Undergraduates: $9163. ***Scholarships, grants, and awards:*** Federal Pell, FSEOG, state, private, college/university gift aid from institutional funds.

GIFT AID (NON-NEED-BASED) ***Total amount:*** $13,610,199 (18% federal, 13% state, 53% institutional, 16% external sources). ***Receiving aid:*** Freshmen: 77% (362). Undergraduates: 78% (1,348). ***Average award:*** Freshmen: $3478. Undergraduates: $5669. ***Scholarships, grants, and awards by category:*** *Academic interests/achievement:* 408 awards ($3,134,444 total): English, general academic interests/achievements. *Creative arts/performance:* 77 awards ($100,540 total): debating, music, theater/drama. *Special achievements/activities:* 55 awards ($28,750 total): cheerleading/drum major, leadership. *Special characteristics:* 405 awards ($1,083,286 total): children and siblings of alumni, children of faculty/staff, relatives of clergy, religious affiliation. ***Tuition waivers:*** Full or partial for senior citizens.

LOANS ***Student loans:*** $26,369,639 (34% need-based, 66% non-need-based). 77% of past graduating class borrowed through all loan programs. *Average indebtedness per student:* $30,786. ***Average need-based loan:*** Freshmen: $12,899. Undergraduates: $16,249. ***Parent loans:*** $5,089,924 (100% non-need-based). ***Programs:*** Federal Direct (Subsidized and Unsubsidized Stafford, PLUS), Perkins.

WORK-STUDY ***Federal work-study:*** Total amount: $256,057; 819 jobs averaging $313. ***State or other work-study/employment:*** Total amount: $188,650 (100% non-need-based). 117 part-time jobs averaging $1612.

APPLYING FOR FINANCIAL AID ***Required financial aid forms:*** FAFSA, state aid form. ***Financial aid deadline (priority):*** 8/1. ***Notification date:*** Continuous beginning 3/6. Students must reply within 2 weeks of notification.

CONTACT Bonnie Adamson, Financial Aid Office, Methodist University, 5400 Ramsey Street, Fayetteville, NC 28311-1420, 910-630-7307 or toll-free 800-488-7110 Ext. 7027. *Fax:* 910-630-7285. *E-mail:* adamson@methodist.edu.

METROPOLITAN COLLEGE OF NEW YORK

New York, NY

CONTACT Rosibel Gomez, Financial Aid Director, Metropolitan College of New York, 75 Varick Street, New York, NY 10013-1919, 212-343-1234 Ext. 5004 or toll-free 800-33-THINK Ext. 5001 (in-state). *Fax:* 212-343-7399.

METROPOLITAN STATE COLLEGE OF DENVER

Denver, CO

Tuition & fees (CO res): $4093 **Average undergraduate aid package: $7724**

ABOUT THE INSTITUTION State-supported, coed. 48 undergraduate majors. Federal methodology is used as a basis for awarding need-based institutional aid.

UNDERGRADUATE EXPENSES for 2010–11 ***Tuition, state resident:*** full-time $3107; part-time $129.45 per credit hour. ***Tuition, nonresident:*** full-time $13,454; part-time $560.60 per credit hour. ***Required fees:*** full-time $986. Full-time tuition and fees vary according to course load and location. Part-time tuition and fees vary according to course load and location. ***Payment plans:*** Installment, deferred payment.

FRESHMAN FINANCIAL AID (Fall 2010, est.) 1,663 applied for aid; of those 72% were deemed to have need. 90% of freshmen with need received aid; of those 4% had need fully met. ***Average percent of need met:*** 61% (excluding resources awarded to replace EFC). ***Average financial aid package:*** $6489 (excluding resources awarded to replace EFC). 9% of all full-time freshmen had no need and received non-need-based gift aid.

UNDERGRADUATE FINANCIAL AID (Fall 2010, est.) 9,892 applied for aid; of those 79% were deemed to have need. 93% of undergraduates with need received aid; of those 6% had need fully met. ***Average percent of need met:*** 63% (excluding resources awarded to replace EFC). ***Average financial aid package:*** $7724 (excluding resources awarded to replace EFC). 10% of all full-time undergraduates had no need and received non-need-based gift aid.

GIFT AID (NEED-BASED) ***Total amount:*** $38,057,893 (73% federal, 20% state, 5% institutional, 2% external sources). ***Receiving aid:*** Freshmen: 40% (852); all full-time undergraduates: 40% (5,591). ***Average award:*** Freshmen: $5393; Undergraduates: $5551. ***Scholarships, grants, and awards:*** Federal Pell, FSEOG, state, private, college/university gift aid from institutional funds.

GIFT AID (NON-NEED-BASED) ***Total amount:*** $1,585,381 (4% federal, 2% state, 67% institutional, 27% external sources). ***Average award:*** Freshmen: $912. Undergraduates: $1919. ***Scholarships, grants, and awards by category:*** *Academic interests/achievement:* 801 awards ($1,150,800 total): education, general academic interests/achievements. *Creative arts/performance:* 91 awards ($72,000 total): music, performing arts, theater/drama. *Special achievements/activities:* 25 awards ($16,500 total): leadership. *Special characteristics:* 67 awards ($118,091 total): adult students, first-generation college students, local/state students, veterans. ***Tuition waivers:*** Full or partial for senior citizens.

LOANS ***Student loans:*** $83,962,315 (83% need-based, 17% non-need-based). 57% of past graduating class borrowed through all loan programs. *Average indebtedness per student:* $25,774. ***Average need-based loan:*** Freshmen: $2997. Undergraduates: $4059. ***Programs:*** Federal Direct (Subsidized and Unsubsidized Stafford, PLUS), Perkins.

WORK-STUDY ***Federal work-study:*** Total amount: $627,850; 252 jobs averaging $2733. ***State or other work-study/employment:*** Total amount: $1,856,325 (79% need-based, 21% non-need-based). 569 part-time jobs averaging $3503.

ATHLETIC AWARDS Total amount: $1,026,106 (48% need-based, 52% non-need-based).

APPLYING FOR FINANCIAL AID ***Required financial aid form:*** FAFSA. ***Financial aid deadline:*** Continuous. ***Notification date:*** Continuous beginning 3/15.

CONTACT Office of Financial Aid, Metropolitan State College of Denver, PO Box 173362, Denver, CO 80217-3362, 303-556-8593. *Fax:* 303-556-4927.

METROPOLITAN STATE UNIVERSITY

St. Paul, MN

Tuition & fees (MN res): $5923   Average undergraduate aid package: N/A

ABOUT THE INSTITUTION State-supported, coed. 46 undergraduate majors. Federal methodology is used as a basis for awarding need-based institutional aid.

UNDERGRADUATE EXPENSES for 2010–11 ***Tuition, state resident:*** full-time $5610; part-time $187 per credit hour. ***Tuition, nonresident:*** full-time $11,464; part-time $382.13 per credit hour. ***Required fees:*** full-time $313; $10.43 per credit hour. Full-time tuition and fees vary according to program and reciprocity agreements. Part-time tuition and fees vary according to course load, program, and reciprocity agreements. ***Payment plan:*** Installment.

GIFT AID (NEED-BASED) ***Total amount:*** $10,791,524 (76% federal, 15% state, 2% institutional, 7% external sources). ***Scholarships, grants, and awards:*** Federal Pell, FSEOG, state, private, college/university gift aid from institutional funds.

GIFT AID (NON-NEED-BASED) ***Scholarships, grants, and awards by category:*** *Academic interests/achievement:* education, general academic interests/achievements. ***Tuition waivers:*** Full or partial for employees or children of employees, senior citizens.

LOANS ***Student loans:*** $28,288,839 (100% need-based). ***Parent loans:*** $123,106 (100% need-based). ***Programs:*** Federal Direct (Subsidized and Unsubsidized Stafford, PLUS), state.

WORK-STUDY ***Federal work-study:*** Total amount: $274,586; jobs available. ***State or other work-study/employment:*** Total amount: $261,665 (100% need-based). Part-time jobs available.

APPLYING FOR FINANCIAL AID ***Required financial aid forms:*** FAFSA, federal income tax form(s). ***Financial aid deadline (priority):*** 6/1. ***Notification date:*** Continuous beginning 6/15. Students must reply within 2 weeks of notification.

CONTACT Dr. Lois Larson, Director of Financial Aid, Metropolitan State University, Founder's Hall, Room 147A, 700 East 7th Street, St. Paul, MN 55106-5000, 651-793-1411. *Fax:* 651-793-1410. *E-mail:* finaid@metrostate.edu.

MIAMI INTERNATIONAL UNIVERSITY OF ART & DESIGN

Miami, FL

UNDERGRADUATE EXPENSES Tuition cost varies by program. Prospective students should contact the school for current tuition costs. Other charges include a starting kit for all first-quarter students. Kits vary in price, depending on the program of study.

CONTACT Financial Aid Office, Miami International University of Art & Design, 1737 Bayshore Drive, Miami, FL 33132, 800-225-9023 Ext. 125 or toll-free 800-225-9023. *Fax:* 305-374-7946.

MIAMI UNIVERSITY

Oxford, OH

Tuition & fees (OH res): $12,786   Average undergraduate aid package: $10,940

ABOUT THE INSTITUTION State-related, coed. 110 undergraduate majors. Federal methodology is used as a basis for awarding need-based institutional aid.

UNDERGRADUATE EXPENSES for 2010–11 ***Tuition, state resident:*** full-time $12,198. ***Tuition, nonresident:*** full-time $26,988. ***Required fees:*** full-time $588. Full-time tuition and fees vary according to location and program. Part-time tuition and fees vary according to location and program. ***College room and board:*** $9786; ***Room only:*** $4952. Room and board charges vary according to board plan and housing facility. ***Payment plan:*** Installment.

FRESHMAN FINANCIAL AID (Fall 2010, est.) 2,703 applied for aid; of those 66% were deemed to have need. 99% of freshmen with need received aid; of those 16% had need fully met. ***Average percent of need met:*** 58% (excluding resources awarded to replace EFC). ***Average financial aid package:*** $11,532 (excluding resources awarded to replace EFC). 19% of all full-time freshmen had no need and received non-need-based gift aid.

UNDERGRADUATE FINANCIAL AID (Fall 2010, est.) 8,849 applied for aid; of those 75% were deemed to have need. 98% of undergraduates with need received aid; of those 12% had need fully met. ***Average percent of need met:*** 56% (excluding resources awarded to replace EFC). ***Average financial aid package:*** $10,940 (excluding resources awarded to replace EFC). 15% of all full-time undergraduates had no need and received non-need-based gift aid.

GIFT AID (NEED-BASED) ***Total amount:*** $25,288,076 (61% federal, 5% state, 34% institutional). ***Receiving aid:*** Freshmen: 26% (918); all full-time undergraduates: 24% (3,523). ***Average award:*** Freshmen: $6272; Undergraduates: $6083. ***Scholarships, grants, and awards:*** Federal Pell, FSEOG, state, private, college/university gift aid from institutional funds.

GIFT AID (NON-NEED-BASED) ***Total amount:*** $26,791,449 (1% state, 86% institutional, 13% external sources). ***Receiving aid:*** Freshmen: 47% (1,668). Undergraduates: 26% (3,718). ***Average award:*** Freshmen: $5690. Undergraduates: $4855. ***Scholarships, grants, and awards by category:*** *Academic interests/achievement:* architecture, education, engineering/technologies, general academic interests/achievements. *Creative arts/performance:* art/fine arts, music, theater/drama. *Special achievements/activities:* general special achievements/activities, leadership. *Special characteristics:* children of faculty/staff, local/state students, members of minority groups, out-of-state students. ***Tuition waivers:*** Full or partial for employees or children of employees.

LOANS ***Student loans:*** $58,396,823 (40% need-based, 60% non-need-based). 51% of past graduating class borrowed through all loan programs. *Average indebtedness per student:* $27,315. ***Average need-based loan:*** Freshmen: $4276. Undergraduates: $4852. ***Parent loans:*** $33,763,415 (100% non-need-based). ***Programs:*** Federal Direct (Subsidized and Unsubsidized Stafford, PLUS), Perkins, Federal Nursing, college/university, private loans.

WORK-STUDY ***Federal work-study:*** Total amount: $1,618,028; 1,081 jobs averaging $2264.

ATHLETIC AWARDS Total amount: $8,229,762 (100% non-need-based).

APPLYING FOR FINANCIAL AID ***Required financial aid form:*** FAFSA. ***Financial aid deadline (priority):*** 2/15. ***Notification date:*** Continuous beginning 3/20. Students must reply by 5/1 or within 3 weeks of notification.

CONTACT Mr. Brent Shock, Office of Student Financial Aid, Miami University, Campus Avenue Building, Oxford, OH 45056-3427, 513-529-8734. *Fax:* 513-529-8713. *E-mail:* financialaid@muohio.edu.

MIAMI UNIVERSITY HAMILTON

Hamilton, OH

CONTACT Financial Aid Office, Miami University Hamilton, 1601 Peck Boulevard, Hamilton, OH 45011-3399, 513-785-3000.

MICHIGAN JEWISH INSTITUTE

Oak Park, MI

CONTACT Financial Aid Office, Michigan Jewish Institute, 25401 Coolidge Highway, Oak Park, MI 48237, 248-414-6900.

MICHIGAN STATE UNIVERSITY

East Lansing, MI

Tuition & fees (MI res): $11,153   Average undergraduate aid package: $9302

ABOUT THE INSTITUTION State-supported, coed. 170 undergraduate majors. Federal methodology is used as a basis for awarding need-based institutional aid.

UNDERGRADUATE EXPENSES for 2010–11 ***Tuition, state resident:*** full-time $11,153; part-time $371.75 per credit hour. ***Tuition, nonresident:*** full-time $29,108; part-time $970.25 per credit hour. Full-time tuition and fees vary according to course load, degree level, program, and student level. Part-time tuition and fees vary according to course load, degree level, program, and student level. ***College room and board:*** $7770; ***Room only:*** $3208. Room and board charges vary according to board plan and housing facility. ***Payment plan:*** Deferred payment.

FRESHMAN FINANCIAL AID (Fall 2010, est.) 5,351 applied for aid; of those 71% were deemed to have need. 98% of freshmen with need received aid; of those 21% had need fully met. ***Average percent of need met:*** 41% (excluding resources awarded to replace EFC). ***Average financial aid package:*** $7882 (excluding resources awarded to replace EFC). 4% of all full-time freshmen had no need and received non-need-based gift aid.

UNDERGRADUATE FINANCIAL AID (Fall 2010, est.) 21,550 applied for aid; of those 78% were deemed to have need. 98% of undergraduates with need

received aid; of those 17% had need fully met. ***Average percent of need met:*** 47% (excluding resources awarded to replace EFC). ***Average financial aid package:*** $9302 (excluding resources awarded to replace EFC). 4% of all full-time undergraduates had no need and received non-need-based gift aid.

GIFT AID (NEED-BASED) ***Total amount:*** $94,342,040 (47% federal, 53% institutional). ***Receiving aid:*** Freshmen: 30% (2,146); all full-time undergraduates: 30% (9,954). ***Average award:*** Freshmen: $9789; Undergraduates: $8887. ***Scholarships, grants, and awards:*** Federal Pell, FSEOG, state, private, college/university gift aid from institutional funds, United Negro College Fund.

GIFT AID (NON-NEED-BASED) ***Total amount:*** $60,945,509 (4% federal, 36% state, 27% institutional, 33% external sources). ***Receiving aid:*** Freshmen: 20% (1,437). Undergraduates: 13% (4,251). ***Average award:*** Freshmen: $5965. Undergraduates: $7519. ***Scholarships, grants, and awards by category:*** *Academic interests/achievement:* agriculture, biological sciences, business, communication, computer science, education, engineering/technologies, English, foreign languages, general academic interests/achievements, health fields, home economics, international studies, mathematics, military science, physical sciences, social sciences. *Creative arts/performance:* art/fine arts, creative writing, debating, journalism/publications, music, performing arts, theater/drama. *Special achievements/activities:* community service, general special achievements/activities, hobbies/interests, leadership, memberships, rodeo. *Special characteristics:* children and siblings of alumni, children of faculty/staff, children of union members/company employees, first-generation college students, handicapped students, international students, local/state students, out-of-state students, spouses of deceased or disabled public servants, veterans. ***Tuition waivers:*** Full or partial for employees or children of employees.

LOANS ***Student loans:*** $153,722,435 (44% need-based, 56% non-need-based). 45% of past graduating class borrowed through all loan programs. *Average indebtedness per student:* $21,818. ***Average need-based loan:*** Freshmen: $3406. Undergraduates: $4275. ***Parent loans:*** $72,330,983 (100% non-need-based). ***Programs:*** Federal Direct (Subsidized and Unsubsidized Stafford, PLUS), Perkins, college/university.

WORK-STUDY ***Federal work-study:*** Total amount: $2,431,897; 1,083 jobs averaging $1570. ***State or other work-study/employment:*** Part-time jobs available.

ATHLETIC AWARDS Total amount: $9,668,392 (43% need-based, 57% non-need-based).

APPLYING FOR FINANCIAL AID ***Required financial aid form:*** FAFSA. ***Financial aid deadline:*** Continuous. ***Notification date:*** Continuous beginning 3/15. Students must reply within 4 weeks of notification.

CONTACT Mr. Keith Williams, Associate Director, Michigan State University, 252 Student Services Building, East Lansing, MI 48824-1113, 517-353-5940. *Fax:* 517-432-1155. *E-mail:* willi398@msu.edu.

MICHIGAN TECHNOLOGICAL UNIVERSITY

Houghton, MI

Tuition & fees (MI res): $12,017 Average undergraduate aid package: $11,421

ABOUT THE INSTITUTION State-supported, coed. 88 undergraduate majors. Federal methodology is used as a basis for awarding need-based institutional aid.

UNDERGRADUATE EXPENSES for 2010–11 ***Tuition, state resident:*** full-time $11,175; part-time $372.50 per credit hour. ***Tuition, nonresident:*** full-time $23,685; part-time $789.50 per credit hour. ***Required fees:*** full-time $842; $421 per term. Full-time tuition and fees vary according to course load and program. Part-time tuition and fees vary according to course load and program. ***College room and board:*** $8462; ***Room only:*** $4587. Room and board charges vary according to board plan and housing facility. ***Payment plans:*** Installment, deferred payment.

FRESHMAN FINANCIAL AID (Fall 2010, est.) 1,005 applied for aid; of those 77% were deemed to have need. 100% of freshmen with need received aid; of those 18% had need fully met. ***Average percent of need met:*** 76% (excluding resources awarded to replace EFC). ***Average financial aid package:*** $12,590 (excluding resources awarded to replace EFC). 23% of all full-time freshmen had no need and received non-need-based gift aid.

UNDERGRADUATE FINANCIAL AID (Fall 2010, est.) 4,149 applied for aid; of those 85% were deemed to have need. 100% of undergraduates with need received aid; of those 15% had need fully met. ***Average percent of need met:*** 69% (excluding resources awarded to replace EFC). ***Average financial aid package:*** $11,421 (excluding resources awarded to replace EFC). 21% of all full-time undergraduates had no need and received non-need-based gift aid.

GIFT AID (NEED-BASED) ***Total amount:*** $29,395,625 (33% federal, 7% state, 55% institutional, 5% external sources). ***Receiving aid:*** Freshmen: 59% (650); all full-time undergraduates: 52% (2,740). ***Average award:*** Freshmen: $6587; Undergraduates: $5595. ***Scholarships, grants, and awards:*** Federal Pell, FSEOG, state, private, college/university gift aid from institutional funds.

GIFT AID (NON-NEED-BASED) ***Total amount:*** $6,001,028 (86% institutional, 14% external sources). ***Receiving aid:*** Freshmen: 56% (623). Undergraduates: 42% (2,236). ***Average award:*** Freshmen: $4702. Undergraduates: $4423. ***Scholarships, grants, and awards by category:*** *Academic interests/achievement:* general academic interests/achievements. *Special achievements/activities:* leadership. *Special characteristics:* children and siblings of alumni, local/state students. ***Tuition waivers:*** Full or partial for children of alumni, employees or children of employees, senior citizens.

LOANS ***Student loans:*** $35,988,914 (90% need-based, 10% non-need-based). 74% of past graduating class borrowed through all loan programs. *Average indebtedness per student:* $33,310. ***Average need-based loan:*** Freshmen: $3475. Undergraduates: $4485. ***Parent loans:*** $6,589,361 (83% need-based, 17% non-need-based). ***Programs:*** Federal Direct (Subsidized and Unsubsidized Stafford, PLUS), Perkins, college/university.

WORK-STUDY ***Federal work-study:*** Total amount: $556,123; jobs available. ***State or other work-study/employment:*** Total amount: $4,654,843 (100% non-need-based). Part-time jobs available.

ATHLETIC AWARDS Total amount: $2,451,001 (41% need-based, 59% non-need-based).

APPLYING FOR FINANCIAL AID ***Required financial aid form:*** FAFSA. ***Financial aid deadline (priority):*** 2/16. ***Notification date:*** Continuous beginning 3/15.

CONTACT Mr. Bill Roberts, Director of Financial Aid, Michigan Technological University, 1400 Townsend Drive, Houghton, MI 49931-1295, 906-487-1742 or toll-free 888-MTU-1885. *Fax:* 906-487-3042. *E-mail:* wrrobert@mtu.edu.

MID-AMERICA CHRISTIAN UNIVERSITY

Oklahoma City, OK

CONTACT Mr. Todd Martin, Director of Financial Aid, Mid-America Christian University, 3500 Southwest 119th Street, Oklahoma City, OK 73170-4504, 405-691-3800. *Fax:* 405-692-3165. *E-mail:* tmartin@mabc.edu.

MIDAMERICA NAZARENE UNIVERSITY

Olathe, KS

CONTACT Rhonda L. Cole, Director of Student Financial Services, MidAmerica Nazarene University, 2030 East College Way, Olathe, KS 66062-1899, 913-791-3298 or toll-free 800-800-8887. *Fax:* 913-791-3482. *E-mail:* rcole@mnu.edu.

MID-ATLANTIC CHRISTIAN UNIVERSITY

Elizabeth City, NC

Tuition & fees: $11,600 Average undergraduate aid package: $8832

ABOUT THE INSTITUTION Independent Christian, coed. 7 undergraduate majors. Federal methodology is used as a basis for awarding need-based institutional aid.

UNDERGRADUATE EXPENSES for 2011–12 ***Comprehensive fee:*** $18,800 includes full-time tuition ($11,200), mandatory fees ($400), and room and board ($7200). ***College room only:*** $3800. Room and board charges vary according to housing facility. ***Part-time tuition:*** $350 per credit hour. ***Part-time fees:*** $21 per contact hour. ***Payment plan:*** Deferred payment.

FRESHMAN FINANCIAL AID (Fall 2009) 40 applied for aid; of those 92% were deemed to have need. 100% of freshmen with need received aid; of those 3% had need fully met. ***Average percent of need met:*** 57% (excluding resources awarded to replace EFC). ***Average financial aid package:*** $8825 (excluding resources awarded to replace EFC). 8% of all full-time freshmen had no need and received non-need-based gift aid.

UNDERGRADUATE FINANCIAL AID (Fall 2009) 142 applied for aid; of those 91% were deemed to have need. 100% of undergraduates with need received aid; of those 5% had need fully met. ***Average percent of need met:*** 58% (excluding resources awarded to replace EFC). ***Average financial aid package:*** $8832 (excluding resources awarded to replace EFC). 7% of all full-time undergraduates had no need and received non-need-based gift aid.

GIFT AID (NEED-BASED) ***Total amount:*** $683,569 (50% federal, 3% state, 46% institutional, 1% external sources). ***Receiving aid:*** Freshmen: 92% (37); all full-time undergraduates: 90% (129). ***Average award:*** Freshmen: $5558; Undergraduates: $4954. ***Scholarships, grants, and awards:*** Federal Pell, FSEOG, state, private, college/university gift aid from institutional funds.

GIFT AID (NON-NEED-BASED) ***Total amount:*** $44,481 (95% institutional, 5% external sources). ***Receiving aid:*** Freshmen: 2% (1). Undergraduates: 1% (2). ***Average award:*** Freshmen: $2224. Undergraduates: $2550. ***Scholarships, grants, and awards by category:*** *Academic interests/achievement:* 19 awards ($59,451 total): general academic interests/achievements, religion/biblical studies. *Special achievements/activities:* 15 awards ($42,686 total): general special achievements/activities, religious involvement. *Special characteristics:* 81 awards ($96,860 total): children and siblings of alumni, children of faculty/staff, general special characteristics, handicapped students, international students, married students, spouses of current students. ***Tuition waivers:*** Full or partial for children of alumni, employees or children of employees, senior citizens.

LOANS ***Student loans:*** $1,252,839 (81% need-based, 19% non-need-based). 93% of past graduating class borrowed through all loan programs. *Average indebtedness per student:* $32,413. ***Average need-based loan:*** Freshmen: $7282. Undergraduates: $7795. ***Parent loans:*** $78,203 (40% need-based, 60% non-need-based). ***Programs:*** Federal Direct (Subsidized and Unsubsidized Stafford, PLUS), private loans.

WORK-STUDY ***Federal work-study:*** Total amount: $13,273; 19 jobs averaging $699.

APPLYING FOR FINANCIAL AID ***Required financial aid forms:*** FAFSA, institution's own form. ***Financial aid deadline (priority):*** 2/1. ***Notification date:*** Continuous beginning 4/1. Students must reply by 5/1 or within 2 weeks of notification.

CONTACT Lisa W. Pipkin, Financial Aid Administrator, Mid-Atlantic Christian University, 715 North Poindexter Street, Elizabeth City, NC 27909, 252-334-2020 or toll-free 800-RBC-8980. *Fax:* 252-334-2064. *E-mail:* lisa.pipkin@macuniversity.edu.

MID-CONTINENT UNIVERSITY

Mayfield, KY

Tuition & fees: $13,300 **Average undergraduate aid package: $8454**

ABOUT THE INSTITUTION Independent Southern Baptist, coed. 14 undergraduate majors. Federal methodology is used as a basis for awarding need-based institutional aid.

UNDERGRADUATE EXPENSES for 2010–11 ***Comprehensive fee:*** $19,900 includes full-time tuition ($12,100), mandatory fees ($1200), and room and board ($6600). Full-time tuition and fees vary according to course load and program. Room and board charges vary according to board plan and housing facility. ***Part-time tuition:*** $425 per credit hour. Part-time tuition and fees vary according to course load and program. ***Payment plans:*** Installment, deferred payment.

FRESHMAN FINANCIAL AID (Fall 2009) 334 applied for aid; of those 98% were deemed to have need. 99% of freshmen with need received aid; of those 4% had need fully met. ***Average percent of need met:*** 35% (excluding resources awarded to replace EFC). ***Average financial aid package:*** $7968 (excluding resources awarded to replace EFC). 4% of all full-time freshmen had no need and received non-need-based gift aid.

UNDERGRADUATE FINANCIAL AID (Fall 2009) 2,161 applied for aid; of those 98% were deemed to have need. 100% of undergraduates with need received aid; of those 3% had need fully met. ***Average percent of need met:*** 35% (excluding resources awarded to replace EFC). ***Average financial aid package:*** $8454 (excluding resources awarded to replace EFC). 2% of all full-time undergraduates had no need and received non-need-based gift aid.

GIFT AID (NEED-BASED) ***Total amount:*** $5,894,561 (40% federal, 44% state, 12% institutional, 4% external sources). ***Receiving aid:*** Freshmen: 91% (314); all full-time undergraduates: 87% (1,917). ***Average award:*** Freshmen: $6455; Undergraduates: $6356. ***Scholarships, grants, and awards:*** Federal Pell, FSEOG, state, private, college/university gift aid from institutional funds.

GIFT AID (NON-NEED-BASED) ***Total amount:*** $144,828 (100% state). ***Receiving aid:*** Freshmen: 3% (12). Undergraduates: 2% (40). ***Average award:*** Freshmen: $10,243. Undergraduates: $8564. ***Scholarships, grants, and awards by category:*** *Academic interests/achievement:* 28 awards ($33,672 total): education, English, general academic interests/achievements, humanities, religion/biblical studies, social sciences. *Special achievements/activities:* 8 awards ($16,682 total): cheerleading/drum major. *Special characteristics:* 8 awards ($3500 total): children and siblings of alumni, children of faculty/staff, children of union members/company employees, married students, relatives of clergy. ***Tuition waivers:*** Full or partial for employees or children of employees.

LOANS ***Student loans:*** $7,602,929 (77% need-based, 23% non-need-based). 80% of past graduating class borrowed through all loan programs. *Average indebtedness per student:* $11,005. ***Average need-based loan:*** Freshmen: $2789. Undergraduates: $3523. ***Parent loans:*** $104,936 (35% need-based, 65% non-need-based). ***Programs:*** Federal Direct (Subsidized and Unsubsidized Stafford, PLUS).

WORK-STUDY ***Federal work-study:*** Total amount: $173,303; 72 jobs averaging $2126. ***State or other work-study/employment:*** Total amount: $29,023 (100% need-based). Part-time jobs available.

ATHLETIC AWARDS Total amount: $792,916 (97% need-based, 3% non-need-based).

APPLYING FOR FINANCIAL AID ***Required financial aid form:*** FAFSA. ***Financial aid deadline (priority):*** 3/15. ***Notification date:*** Continuous beginning 8/18. Students must reply within 2 weeks of notification.

CONTACT Kent Youngblood, Director of Financial Aid, Mid-Continent University, 99 Powell Road East, Mayfield, KY 42066, 270-251-9400 Ext. 260. *Fax:* 270-251-9475. *E-mail:* kyoungblood@midcontinent.edu.

MIDDLEBURY COLLEGE

Middlebury, VT

Comprehensive fee: $52,500 **Average undergraduate aid package: $35,470**

ABOUT THE INSTITUTION Independent, coed. 44 undergraduate majors. Institutional methodology is used as a basis for awarding need-based institutional aid.

UNDERGRADUATE EXPENSES for 2010–11 ***Comprehensive fee:*** $52,500. ***Payment plan:*** Tuition prepayment.

FRESHMAN FINANCIAL AID (Fall 2009) 336 applied for aid; of those 74% were deemed to have need. 100% of freshmen with need received aid; of those 100% had need fully met. ***Average percent of need met:*** 100% (excluding resources awarded to replace EFC). ***Average financial aid package:*** $35,640 (excluding resources awarded to replace EFC).

UNDERGRADUATE FINANCIAL AID (Fall 2009) 1,421 applied for aid; of those 81% were deemed to have need. 100% of undergraduates with need received aid; of those 100% had need fully met. ***Average percent of need met:*** 100% (excluding resources awarded to replace EFC). ***Average financial aid package:*** $35,470 (excluding resources awarded to replace EFC).

GIFT AID (NEED-BASED) ***Total amount:*** $38,562,710 (5% federal, 92% institutional, 3% external sources). ***Receiving aid:*** Freshmen: 41% (249); all full-time undergraduates: 47% (1,158). ***Average award:*** Freshmen: $32,934; Undergraduates: $32,236. ***Scholarships, grants, and awards:*** Federal Pell, FSEOG, state, private, college/university gift aid from institutional funds.

GIFT AID (NON-NEED-BASED) ***Tuition waivers:*** Full or partial for employees or children of employees.

LOANS ***Student loans:*** $5,222,701 (63% need-based, 37% non-need-based). 42% of past graduating class borrowed through all loan programs. *Average indebtedness per student:* $21,520. ***Average need-based loan:*** Freshmen: $2425. Undergraduates: $2804. ***Parent loans:*** $3,479,537 (100% non-need-based). ***Programs:*** Federal Direct (Subsidized and Unsubsidized Stafford, PLUS), Perkins, college/university.

WORK-STUDY ***Federal work-study:*** Total amount: $915,373; jobs available. ***State or other work-study/employment:*** Total amount: $478,071 (100% need-based). Part-time jobs available.

APPLYING FOR FINANCIAL AID ***Required financial aid forms:*** FAFSA, CSS Financial Aid PROFILE, noncustodial (divorced/separated) parent's statement, federal income tax return(s). ***Financial aid deadline:*** 2/1 (priority: 11/15). ***Notification date:*** 4/1. Students must reply by 5/1.

CONTACT Marguerite Corbin, Financial Aid Assistant, Middlebury College, Meeker House, 2nd Floor, 46 Porter Field Road, Middlebury, VT 05753, 802-443-5158. *E-mail:* financialaid@middlebury.edu.

MIDDLE TENNESSEE STATE UNIVERSITY

Murfreesboro, TN

Tuition & fees (TN res): $6298 **Average undergraduate aid package: $8949**

ABOUT THE INSTITUTION State-supported, coed. 61 undergraduate majors. Federal methodology is used as a basis for awarding need-based institutional aid.

UNDERGRADUATE EXPENSES for 2010–11 ***Tuition, state resident:*** full-time $4824; part-time $201 per credit hour. ***Tuition, nonresident:*** full-time $17,352; part-time $723 per credit hour. ***Required fees:*** full-time $1474; $62 per credit hour. Full-time tuition and fees vary according to course load. Part-time tuition and fees vary according to course load. ***College room and board:*** $7132; ***Room only:*** $4232. Room and board charges vary according to board plan and housing facility.

FRESHMAN FINANCIAL AID (Fall 2010, est.) 3,591 applied for aid; of those 77% were deemed to have need. 99% of freshmen with need received aid; of those 87% had need fully met. ***Average percent of need met:*** 80% (excluding resources awarded to replace EFC). ***Average financial aid package:*** $10,062 (excluding resources awarded to replace EFC). 5% of all full-time freshmen had no need and received non-need-based gift aid.

UNDERGRADUATE FINANCIAL AID (Fall 2010, est.) 16,524 applied for aid; of those 77% were deemed to have need. 99% of undergraduates with need received aid; of those 16% had need fully met. ***Average percent of need met:*** 65% (excluding resources awarded to replace EFC). ***Average financial aid package:*** $8949 (excluding resources awarded to replace EFC). 3% of all full-time undergraduates had no need and received non-need-based gift aid.

GIFT AID (NEED-BASED) ***Total amount:*** $46,002,677 (85% federal, 15% state). ***Receiving aid:*** Freshmen: 49% (1,808); all full-time undergraduates: 42% (8,222). ***Average award:*** Freshmen: $6258; Undergraduates: $5262. ***Scholarships, grants, and awards:*** Federal Pell, FSEOG, state, private, college/university gift aid from institutional funds.

GIFT AID (NON-NEED-BASED) ***Total amount:*** $40,796,239 (75% state, 18% institutional, 7% external sources). ***Receiving aid:*** Freshmen: 62% (2,289). Undergraduates: 56% (11,112). ***Average award:*** Freshmen: $2612. Undergraduates: $2766. ***Scholarships, grants, and awards by category:*** *Academic interests/achievement:* 716 awards ($866,565 total): agriculture, area/ethnic studies, biological sciences, business, communication, computer science, education, engineering/technologies, English, foreign languages, general academic interests/achievements, health fields, home economics, humanities, international studies, mathematics, military science, physical sciences, premedicine, social sciences. *Creative arts/performance:* 307 awards ($265,425 total): dance, debating, journalism/publications, music, theater/drama. *Special achievements/activities:* 2,252 awards ($6,140,922 total): cheerleading/drum major, general special achievements/activities, leadership. *Special characteristics:* 501 awards ($758,561 total): adult students, general special characteristics, local/state students, members of minority groups.

LOANS ***Student loans:*** $82,947,131 (45% need-based, 55% non-need-based). 5% of past graduating class borrowed through all loan programs. *Average indebtedness per student:* $14,822. ***Average need-based loan:*** Freshmen: $3006. Undergraduates: $3936. ***Parent loans:*** $10,981,746 (100% non-need-based). ***Programs:*** Federal Direct (Subsidized and Unsubsidized Stafford, PLUS), Perkins, college/university.

WORK-STUDY ***Federal work-study:*** Total amount: $608,702; 261 jobs averaging $3480.

ATHLETIC AWARDS Total amount: $5,123,535 (100% non-need-based).

APPLYING FOR FINANCIAL AID ***Required financial aid form:*** FAFSA. ***Financial aid deadline (priority):*** 4/15. ***Notification date:*** Continuous beginning 4/15. Students must reply within 2 weeks of notification.

CONTACT Stephen White, Financial Aid Director, Middle Tennessee State University, 218 Cope Administration Building, Murfreesboro, TN 37132, 615-898-2830. *Fax:* 615-898-5167.

MIDLAND COLLEGE

Midland, TX

CONTACT Latisha Williams, Director, Midland College, 3600 North Garfield, Midland, TX 79705, 432-685-4507. *Fax:* 432-685-6857. *E-mail:* lwilliams@midland.edu.

MIDLAND LUTHERAN COLLEGE

Fremont, NE

CONTACT Penny James, Director of Financial Aid, Midland Lutheran College, 900 North Clarkson Street, Fremont, NE 68025-4200, 402-721-5480 Ext. 6520 or toll-free 800-642-8382 Ext. 6501. *Fax:* 402-721-0250. *E-mail:* finaid@mlc.edu.

MIDSTATE COLLEGE

Peoria, IL

CONTACT Financial Aid Office, Midstate College, 411 West Northmoor Road, Peoria, IL 61614, 309-692-4092.

MIDWAY COLLEGE

Midway, KY

CONTACT Katie Conrad, Director of Financial Aid, Midway College, 512 East Stephens Street, Midway, KY 40347-1120, 859-846-5410 or toll-free 800-755-0031. *Fax:* 859-846-5751. *E-mail:* kconrad@midway.edu.

MIDWESTERN STATE UNIVERSITY

Wichita Falls, TX

Tuition & fees (TX res): $6720 **Average undergraduate aid package: $8992**

ABOUT THE INSTITUTION State-supported, coed. 73 undergraduate majors. Federal methodology is used as a basis for awarding need-based institutional aid.

UNDERGRADUATE EXPENSES for 2010–11 ***Tuition, state resident:*** full-time $1500; part-time $50 per credit hour. ***Tuition, nonresident:*** full-time $2400; part-time $80 per credit hour. ***Required fees:*** full-time $5220; $163.05 per credit hour or $179 per term. Full-time tuition and fees vary according to course load, location, and program. Part-time tuition and fees vary according to course load, location, and program. ***College room and board:*** $5940; ***Room only:*** $3100. Room and board charges vary according to board plan and housing facility. ***Payment plan:*** Installment.

FRESHMAN FINANCIAL AID (Fall 2010, est.) 599 applied for aid; of those 73% were deemed to have need. 100% of freshmen with need received aid; of those 29% had need fully met. ***Average percent of need met:*** 77% (excluding resources awarded to replace EFC). ***Average financial aid package:*** $9994 (excluding resources awarded to replace EFC). 8% of all full-time freshmen had no need and received non-need-based gift aid.

UNDERGRADUATE FINANCIAL AID (Fall 2010, est.) 2,994 applied for aid; of those 79% were deemed to have need. 98% of undergraduates with need received aid; of those 18% had need fully met. ***Average percent of need met:*** 69% (excluding resources awarded to replace EFC). ***Average financial aid package:*** $8992 (excluding resources awarded to replace EFC). 12% of all full-time undergraduates had no need and received non-need-based gift aid.

GIFT AID (NEED-BASED) ***Total amount:*** $14,258,520 (64% federal, 18% state, 16% institutional, 2% external sources). ***Receiving aid:*** Freshmen: 56% (413); all full-time undergraduates: 46% (1,985). ***Average award:*** Freshmen: $7789; Undergraduates: $6250. ***Scholarships, grants, and awards:*** Federal Pell, FSEOG, state, private, college/university gift aid from institutional funds, state nursing scholarships.

GIFT AID (NON-NEED-BASED) ***Total amount:*** $1,424,974 (2% federal, 1% state, 79% institutional, 18% external sources). ***Receiving aid:*** Freshmen: 11% (79). Undergraduates: 6% (236). ***Average award:*** Freshmen: $1950. Undergraduates: $1722. ***Scholarships, grants, and awards by category:*** *Academic interests/achievement:* 810 awards ($1,130,532 total): biological sciences, business, communication, computer science, education, engineering/technologies, English, foreign languages, general academic interests/achievements, health fields, humanities, international studies, mathematics, physical sciences, premedicine, social sciences. *Creative arts/performance:* 119 awards ($77,205 total): art/fine arts, creative writing, general creative arts/performance, journalism/publications, music, theater/drama. *Special achievements/activities:* 175 awards ($276,450 total): cheerleading/drum major, general special achievements/activities, leadership. *Special characteristics:* 83 awards ($208,644 total): children and siblings of alumni, children of faculty/staff, children of union members/company employees, children of workers in trades, children with a deceased or disabled parent, first-generation college students, handicapped students, international students, members of minority groups, veterans, veterans' children. ***Tuition waivers:*** Full or partial for employees or children of employees, senior citizens.

LOANS ***Student loans:*** $5,337,491 (100% non-need-based). 63% of past graduating class borrowed through all loan programs. *Average indebtedness per student:* $16,620. ***Average need-based loan:*** Freshmen: $4644. Undergraduates: $6967. ***Parent loans:*** $3,449,756 (41% need-based, 59% non-need-based). ***Programs:*** Federal Direct (Subsidized and Unsubsidized Stafford, PLUS), Perkins, state, college/university, private loans.

WORK-STUDY ***Federal work-study:*** Total amount: $234,300; 59 jobs averaging $4055. ***State or other work-study/employment:*** Total amount: $41,868 (100% need-based). Part-time jobs available.

ATHLETIC AWARDS Total amount: $1,067,985 (41% need-based, 59% non-need-based).

APPLYING FOR FINANCIAL AID ***Required financial aid forms:*** FAFSA, institution's own form. ***Financial aid deadline (priority):*** 3/1. ***Notification date:*** Continuous beginning 4/15. Students must reply within 4 weeks of notification.

CONTACT Ms. Kathy Pennartz, Director of Financial Aid, Midwestern State University, 3410 Taft Boulevard, Wichita Falls, TX 76308-2099, 940-397-4214 or toll-free 800-842-1922. *Fax:* 940-397-4852. *E-mail:* financial-aid@mwsu.edu.

MIDWEST UNIVERSITY

Wentzville, MO

CONTACT Financial Aid Office, Midwest University, PO Box 365, 851 Parr Road, Wentzville, MO 63385, 636-327-4645.

MIDWIVES COLLEGE OF UTAH

Salt Lake City, UT

CONTACT Financial Aid Office, Midwives College of Utah, 1174 East 2700 South, Suite 2, Salt Lake City, UT 84106, 801-764-9068 or toll-free 866-764-9068.

MILES COLLEGE

Fairfield, AL

CONTACT P. N. Lanier, Financial Aid Administrator, Miles College, PO Box 3800, Birmingham, AL 35208, 205-929-1663 or toll-free 800-445-0708. *Fax:* 205-929-1668. *E-mail:* pnlani@netscape.net.

MILLERSVILLE UNIVERSITY OF PENNSYLVANIA

Millersville, PA

Tuition & fees (PA res): $7700 **Average undergraduate aid package: $8050**

ABOUT THE INSTITUTION State-supported, coed. 53 undergraduate majors. Federal methodology is used as a basis for awarding need-based institutional aid.

UNDERGRADUATE EXPENSES for 2010–11 ***Tuition, state resident:*** full-time $5804; part-time $242 per credit. ***Tuition, nonresident:*** full-time $14,510; part-time $605 per credit. ***Required fees:*** full-time $1896; $69.25 per credit or $68 per term. Full-time tuition and fees vary according to degree level. Part-time tuition and fees vary according to course load and degree level. ***College room and board:*** $8298; ***Room only:*** $4872. Room and board charges vary according to board plan and housing facility. ***Payment plan:*** Installment.

FRESHMAN FINANCIAL AID (Fall 2009) 1,188 applied for aid; of those 66% were deemed to have need. 97% of freshmen with need received aid; of those 15% had need fully met. ***Average percent of need met:*** 77% (excluding resources awarded to replace EFC). ***Average financial aid package:*** $8278 (excluding resources awarded to replace EFC). 3% of all full-time freshmen had no need and received non-need-based gift aid.

UNDERGRADUATE FINANCIAL AID (Fall 2009) 5,303 applied for aid; of those 74% were deemed to have need. 96% of undergraduates with need received aid; of those 13% had need fully met. ***Average percent of need met:*** 77% (excluding resources awarded to replace EFC). ***Average financial aid package:*** $8050 (excluding resources awarded to replace EFC). 2% of all full-time undergraduates had no need and received non-need-based gift aid.

GIFT AID (NEED-BASED) ***Total amount:*** $15,069,047 (53% federal, 39% state, 5% institutional, 3% external sources). ***Receiving aid:*** Freshmen: 44% (577); all full-time undergraduates: 40% (2,658). ***Average award:*** Freshmen: $6058; Undergraduates: $5463. ***Scholarships, grants, and awards:*** Federal Pell, FSEOG, state, private, college/university gift aid from institutional funds, Schock Scholarships.

GIFT AID (NON-NEED-BASED) ***Total amount:*** $2,386,077 (3% federal, 9% state, 41% institutional, 47% external sources). ***Receiving aid:*** Freshmen: 12% (162). Undergraduates: 7% (471). ***Average award:*** Freshmen: $3392. Undergraduates: $2702. ***Scholarships, grants, and awards by category:*** *Academic interests/achievement:* 447 awards ($1,260,211 total): biological sciences, business, communication, computer science, education, English, foreign languages, general academic interests/achievements, health fields, humanities, mathematics, physical sciences, social sciences. *Creative arts/performance:* 22 awards ($19,012 total): art/fine arts, music. *Special achievements/activities:* 7 awards ($1100 total): community service. *Special characteristics:* 153 awards ($624,375 total): children of union members/company employees, international students. ***Tuition waivers:*** Full or partial for employees or children of employees, senior citizens.

LOANS ***Student loans:*** $32,826,010 (44% need-based, 56% non-need-based). 64% of past graduating class borrowed through all loan programs. *Average indebtedness per student:* $25,876. ***Average need-based loan:*** Freshmen: $3197. Undergraduates: $4046. ***Parent loans:*** $4,318,757 (100% non-need-based). ***Programs:*** Perkins.

WORK-STUDY ***Federal work-study:*** Total amount: $357,312; 283 jobs averaging $1314. ***State or other work-study/employment:*** Total amount: $2,333,563 (100% non-need-based). 1,722 part-time jobs averaging $1459.

ATHLETIC AWARDS Total amount: $382,896 (33% need-based, 67% non-need-based).

APPLYING FOR FINANCIAL AID ***Required financial aid form:*** FAFSA. ***Financial aid deadline (priority):*** 3/15. ***Notification date:*** Continuous beginning 3/15. Students must reply within 2 weeks of notification.

CONTACT Mr. Dwight G. Horsey, Director of Financial Aid, Millersville University of Pennsylvania, PO Box 1002, Millersville, PA 17551-0302, 717-872-3026 or toll-free 800-MU-ADMIT (out-of-state). *Fax:* 717-871-2248. *E-mail:* dwight.horsey@millersville.edu.

MILLIGAN COLLEGE

Milligan College, TN

Tuition & fees: $25,260 **Average undergraduate aid package: $17,370**

ABOUT THE INSTITUTION Independent Christian, coed. 27 undergraduate majors. Federal methodology is used as a basis for awarding need-based institutional aid.

UNDERGRADUATE EXPENSES for 2011–12 ***One-time required fee:*** $75. ***Comprehensive fee:*** $30,910 includes full-time tuition ($24,360), mandatory fees ($900), and room and board ($5650). ***College room only:*** $2650. Full-time tuition and fees vary according to course load. Room and board charges vary according to housing facility. ***Part-time tuition:*** $360 per credit hour. Part-time tuition and fees vary according to course load. ***Payment plan:*** Installment.

FRESHMAN FINANCIAL AID (Fall 2010, est.) 172 applied for aid; of those 90% were deemed to have need. 100% of freshmen with need received aid; of those 31% had need fully met. ***Average percent of need met:*** 81% (excluding resources awarded to replace EFC). ***Average financial aid package:*** $18,061 (excluding resources awarded to replace EFC). 8% of all full-time freshmen had no need and received non-need-based gift aid.

UNDERGRADUATE FINANCIAL AID (Fall 2010, est.) 766 applied for aid; of those 88% were deemed to have need. 100% of undergraduates with need received aid; of those 26% had need fully met. ***Average percent of need met:*** 77% (excluding resources awarded to replace EFC). ***Average financial aid package:*** $17,370 (excluding resources awarded to replace EFC). 13% of all full-time undergraduates had no need and received non-need-based gift aid.

GIFT AID (NEED-BASED) ***Total amount:*** $7,764,431 (18% federal, 12% state, 57% institutional, 13% external sources). ***Receiving aid:*** Freshmen: 88% (155); all full-time undergraduates: 80% (660). ***Average award:*** Freshmen: $15,763; Undergraduates: $14,415. ***Scholarships, grants, and awards:*** Federal Pell, FSEOG, state, private, college/university gift aid from institutional funds.

GIFT AID (NON-NEED-BASED) ***Total amount:*** $2,006,752 (1% federal, 21% state, 58% institutional, 20% external sources). ***Receiving aid:*** Freshmen: 21% (38). Undergraduates: 16% (136). ***Average award:*** Freshmen: $6358. Undergraduates: $7209. ***Scholarships, grants, and awards by category:*** *Academic interests/*

achievement: 607 awards ($4,635,933 total): general academic interests/achievements, religion/biblical studies. *Creative arts/performance:* 37 awards ($73,700 total): art/fine arts, music, theater/drama. *Special achievements/activities:* 86 awards ($256,600 total): cheerleading/drum major, community service. *Special characteristics:* 22 awards ($401,895 total): children of faculty/staff. ***Tuition waivers:*** Full or partial for employees or children of employees.

LOANS ***Student loans:*** $4,281,514 (72% need-based, 28% non-need-based). 73% of past graduating class borrowed through all loan programs. *Average indebtedness per student:* $22,360. ***Average need-based loan:*** Freshmen: $3310. Undergraduates: $4098. ***Parent loans:*** $863,195 (41% need-based, 59% non-need-based). ***Programs:*** Federal Direct (Subsidized and Unsubsidized Stafford, PLUS), Perkins, alternative loans.

WORK-STUDY ***Federal work-study:*** Total amount: $201,600; 168 jobs averaging $1200. ***State or other work-study/employment:*** Total amount: $207,341 (18% need-based, 82% non-need-based). 129 part-time jobs averaging $1607.

ATHLETIC AWARDS Total amount: $2,503,041 (61% need-based, 39% non-need-based).

APPLYING FOR FINANCIAL AID ***Required financial aid form:*** FAFSA. ***Financial aid deadline (priority):*** 3/1. ***Notification date:*** Continuous beginning 3/1. Students must reply within 2 weeks of notification.

CONTACT Diane Keasling, Coordinator of Financial Aid, Milligan College, PO Box 250, Milligan College, TN 37682, 423-461-8968 or toll-free 800-262-8337 (in-state). *Fax:* 423-929-2368. *E-mail:* dlkeasling@milligan.edu.

MILLIKIN UNIVERSITY

Decatur, IL

Tuition & fees: $27,425 **Average undergraduate aid package: $20,294**

ABOUT THE INSTITUTION Independent religious, coed. 56 undergraduate majors. Federal methodology is used as a basis for awarding need-based institutional aid.

UNDERGRADUATE EXPENSES for 2010–11 ***Comprehensive fee:*** $35,716 includes full-time tuition ($26,780), mandatory fees ($645), and room and board ($8291). ***College room only:*** $4621. Room and board charges vary according to board plan and housing facility. ***Part-time tuition:*** $895 per credit hour. ***Part-time fees:*** $75 per term. ***Payment plan:*** Installment.

FRESHMAN FINANCIAL AID (Fall 2009) 519 applied for aid; of those 88% were deemed to have need. 100% of freshmen with need received aid; of those 43% had need fully met. ***Average percent of need met:*** 92% (excluding resources awarded to replace EFC). ***Average financial aid package:*** $22,854 (excluding resources awarded to replace EFC). 11% of all full-time freshmen had no need and received non-need-based gift aid.

UNDERGRADUATE FINANCIAL AID (Fall 2009) 1,933 applied for aid; of those 87% were deemed to have need. 100% of undergraduates with need received aid; of those 54% had need fully met. ***Average percent of need met:*** 92% (excluding resources awarded to replace EFC). ***Average financial aid package:*** $20,294 (excluding resources awarded to replace EFC). 10% of all full-time undergraduates had no need and received non-need-based gift aid.

GIFT AID (NEED-BASED) ***Total amount:*** $14,429,531 (24% federal, 28% state, 48% institutional). ***Receiving aid:*** Freshmen: 82% (446); all full-time undergraduates: 74% (1,577). ***Average award:*** Freshmen: $10,225; Undergraduates: $8815. ***Scholarships, grants, and awards:*** Federal Pell, FSEOG, state, private, college/university gift aid from institutional funds.

GIFT AID (NON-NEED-BASED) ***Total amount:*** $17,346,566 (97% institutional, 3% external sources). ***Receiving aid:*** Freshmen: 85% (458). Undergraduates: 72% (1,538). ***Average award:*** Freshmen: $10,273. Undergraduates: $9105. ***Scholarships, grants, and awards by category:*** *Academic interests/achievement:* 2,044 awards ($15,504,190 total): biological sciences, business, communication, education, English, foreign languages, general academic interests/achievements, health fields, humanities, international studies, mathematics, physical sciences, premedicine. *Creative arts/performance:* 594 awards ($1,131,274 total): art/fine arts, dance, music, theater/drama. *Special achievements/activities:* 8 awards ($16,000 total): community service. *Special characteristics:* 211 awards ($1,011,174 total): children and siblings of alumni, children of faculty/staff, children of union members/company employees, children with a deceased or disabled parent, international students, parents of current students, relatives of clergy, siblings of current students, veterans. ***Tuition waivers:*** Full or partial for employees or children of employees.

LOANS ***Student loans:*** $14,637,444 (41% need-based, 59% non-need-based). 82% of past graduating class borrowed through all loan programs. *Average indebtedness per student:* $28,475. ***Average need-based loan:*** Freshmen: $3416. Undergraduates: $4203. ***Parent loans:*** $2,491,257 (100% non-need-based). ***Programs:*** Federal Direct (Subsidized and Unsubsidized Stafford, PLUS), Perkins, state, private loans.

WORK-STUDY ***Federal work-study:*** Total amount: $557,738; 519 jobs averaging $1075. ***State or other work-study/employment:*** Total amount: $214,936 (100% non-need-based). 259 part-time jobs averaging $830.

APPLYING FOR FINANCIAL AID ***Required financial aid form:*** FAFSA. ***Financial aid deadline (priority):*** 3/15. ***Notification date:*** Continuous beginning 3/15. Students must reply by 5/1 or within 4 weeks of notification.

CONTACT Cheryl Howerton, Director of Financial Aid, Millikin University, 1184 West Main Street, Decatur, IL 62522-2084, 217-424-6317 or toll-free 800-373-7733. *Fax:* 217-424-5070. *E-mail:* studentservicecenter@millikin.edu.

MILLSAPS COLLEGE

Jackson, MS

Tuition & fees: $29,482 **Average undergraduate aid package: $25,433**

ABOUT THE INSTITUTION Independent United Methodist, coed. 33 undergraduate majors. Federal methodology is used as a basis for awarding need-based institutional aid.

UNDERGRADUATE EXPENSES for 2011–12 ***Comprehensive fee:*** $39,794 includes full-time tuition ($27,650), mandatory fees ($1832), and room and board ($10,312). ***College room only:*** $5820. Room and board charges vary according to housing facility. ***Part-time tuition:*** $864 per credit hour. ***Part-time fees:*** $32 per credit hour. Part-time tuition and fees vary according to course load. ***Payment plan:*** Installment.

FRESHMAN FINANCIAL AID (Fall 2010, est.) 184 applied for aid; of those 73% were deemed to have need. 100% of freshmen with need received aid; of those 39% had need fully met. ***Average percent of need met:*** 86% (excluding resources awarded to replace EFC). ***Average financial aid package:*** $26,118 (excluding resources awarded to replace EFC). 36% of all full-time freshmen had no need and received non-need-based gift aid.

UNDERGRADUATE FINANCIAL AID (Fall 2010, est.) 671 applied for aid; of those 83% were deemed to have need. 100% of undergraduates with need received aid; of those 37% had need fully met. ***Average percent of need met:*** 81% (excluding resources awarded to replace EFC). ***Average financial aid package:*** $25,433 (excluding resources awarded to replace EFC). 38% of all full-time undergraduates had no need and received non-need-based gift aid.

GIFT AID (NEED-BASED) ***Total amount:*** $10,819,569 (11% federal, 2% state, 85% institutional, 2% external sources). ***Receiving aid:*** Freshmen: 63% (134); all full-time undergraduates: 59% (551). ***Average award:*** Freshmen: $19,881; Undergraduates: $19,636. ***Scholarships, grants, and awards:*** Federal Pell, FSEOG, state, private, college/university gift aid from institutional funds.

GIFT AID (NON-NEED-BASED) ***Total amount:*** $7,194,927 (3% state, 94% institutional, 3% external sources). ***Receiving aid:*** Freshmen: 20% (42). Undergraduates: 14% (136). ***Average award:*** Freshmen: $18,156. Undergraduates: $16,069. ***Scholarships, grants, and awards by category:*** *Academic interests/achievement:* business, general academic interests/achievements. *Creative arts/performance:* art/fine arts, music, theater/drama. *Special achievements/activities:* community service, general special achievements/activities, hobbies/interests, leadership, religious involvement. *Special characteristics:* adult students, children of faculty/staff, ethnic background, first-generation college students, local/state students, relatives of clergy, religious affiliation. ***Tuition waivers:*** Full or partial for employees or children of employees.

LOANS ***Student loans:*** $3,800,645 (58% need-based, 42% non-need-based). 52% of past graduating class borrowed through all loan programs. *Average indebtedness per student:* $28,745. ***Average need-based loan:*** Freshmen: $3350. Undergraduates: $4368. ***Parent loans:*** $1,035,401 (28% need-based, 72% non-need-based). ***Programs:*** Federal Direct (Subsidized and Unsubsidized Stafford, PLUS), Perkins, college/university.

WORK-STUDY ***Federal work-study:*** Total amount: $510,515; jobs available.

APPLYING FOR FINANCIAL AID ***Required financial aid form:*** FAFSA. ***Financial aid deadline (priority):*** 3/1. ***Notification date:*** Continuous beginning 3/15. Students must reply by 5/1 or within 2 weeks of notification.

CONTACT Patrick James, Director of Financial Aid, Millsaps College, 1701 North State Street, Jackson, MS 39210-0001, 601-974-1220 or toll-free 800-352-1050. *Fax:* 601-974-1224. *E-mail:* patrick.james@millsaps.edu.

MILLS COLLEGE
Oakland, CA

Tuition & fees: $37,605 **Average undergraduate aid package: $31,932**

ABOUT THE INSTITUTION Independent, undergraduate: women only; graduate: coed. 38 undergraduate majors. Federal methodology is used as a basis for awarding need-based institutional aid.

UNDERGRADUATE EXPENSES for 2010–11 ***Comprehensive fee:*** $49,249 includes full-time tuition ($36,428), mandatory fees ($1177), and room and board ($11,644). Full-time tuition and fees vary according to course load. Room and board charges vary according to board plan and housing facility. ***Part-time tuition:*** $6072 per course. ***Part-time fees:*** $1177 per year. Part-time tuition and fees vary according to course load. ***Payment plan:*** Installment.

FRESHMAN FINANCIAL AID (Fall 2009) 152 applied for aid; of those 89% were deemed to have need. 100% of freshmen with need received aid; of those 50% had need fully met. ***Average percent of need met:*** 87% (excluding resources awarded to replace EFC). ***Average financial aid package:*** $35,446 (excluding resources awarded to replace EFC). 17% of all full-time freshmen had no need and received non-need-based gift aid.

UNDERGRADUATE FINANCIAL AID (Fall 2009) 821 applied for aid; of those 94% were deemed to have need. 100% of undergraduates with need received aid; of those 49% had need fully met. ***Average percent of need met:*** 83% (excluding resources awarded to replace EFC). ***Average financial aid package:*** $31,932 (excluding resources awarded to replace EFC). 12% of all full-time undergraduates had no need and received non-need-based gift aid.

GIFT AID (NEED-BASED) ***Total amount:*** $19,175,650 (11% federal, 14% state, 71% institutional, 4% external sources). ***Receiving aid:*** Freshmen: 83% (135); all full-time undergraduates: 88% (770). ***Average award:*** Freshmen: $27,423; Undergraduates: $23,274. ***Scholarships, grants, and awards:*** Federal Pell, FSEOG, state, private, college/university gift aid from institutional funds.

GIFT AID (NON-NEED-BASED) ***Total amount:*** $1,406,344 (100% institutional). ***Receiving aid:*** Freshmen: 76% (123). Undergraduates: 74% (650). ***Average award:*** Freshmen: $17,745. Undergraduates: $16,774. ***Scholarships, grants, and awards by category:*** *Academic interests/achievement:* biological sciences, computer science, general academic interests/achievements, mathematics, physical sciences, premedicine. *Creative arts/performance:* art/fine arts, music. *Special achievements/activities:* leadership. *Special characteristics:* general special characteristics. ***Tuition waivers:*** Full or partial for employees or children of employees.

LOANS ***Student loans:*** $7,046,368 (97% need-based, 3% non-need-based). 95% of past graduating class borrowed through all loan programs. *Average indebtedness per student:* $28,914. ***Average need-based loan:*** Freshmen: $5125. Undergraduates: $5375. ***Parent loans:*** $1,537,729 (82% need-based, 18% non-need-based). ***Programs:*** Federal Direct (Subsidized and Unsubsidized Stafford, PLUS), Perkins, state, college/university.

WORK-STUDY ***Federal work-study:*** Total amount: $234,491; jobs available. ***State or other work-study/employment:*** Total amount: $413,082 (86% need-based, 14% non-need-based). Part-time jobs available.

APPLYING FOR FINANCIAL AID ***Required financial aid forms:*** FAFSA, institution's own form, noncustodial (divorced/separated) parent's statement, Non-custodial Parent Statement. ***Financial aid deadline (priority):*** 2/15. ***Notification date:*** Continuous beginning 3/1. Students must reply by 5/1 or within 2 weeks of notification.

CONTACT Mr. David Gin, The M Center/Financial Aid, Mills College, 5000 MacArthur Boulevard, Oakland, CA 94613, 510-430-2000 or toll-free 800-87-MILLS. *Fax:* 510-430-2003. *E-mail:* mcenter-finaid@mills.edu.

MILWAUKEE INSTITUTE OF ART AND DESIGN
Milwaukee, WI

ABOUT THE INSTITUTION Independent, coed. 11 undergraduate majors.

GIFT AID (NEED-BASED) ***Scholarships, grants, and awards:*** Federal Pell, FSEOG, state, private, college/university gift aid from institutional funds.

GIFT AID (NON-NEED-BASED) ***Scholarships, grants, and awards by category:*** *Creative arts/performance:* art/fine arts. *Special characteristics:* children of faculty/staff, ethnic background, local/state students, members of minority groups.

LOANS ***Programs:*** Federal Direct (Subsidized and Unsubsidized Stafford, PLUS), alternative loans.

WORK-STUDY ***Federal work-study:*** Total amount: $102,940; jobs available.

APPLYING FOR FINANCIAL AID ***Required financial aid form:*** FAFSA.

CONTACT Mr. Lloyd Mueller, Director of Financial Aid, Milwaukee Institute of Art and Design, 273 East Erie Street, Milwaukee, WI 53202-6003, 414-291-3272 or toll-free 888-749-MIAD. *Fax:* 414-291-8077. *E-mail:* llmuelle@miad.edu.

MILWAUKEE SCHOOL OF ENGINEERING
Milwaukee, WI

Tuition & fees: $30,990 **Average undergraduate aid package: $19,411**

ABOUT THE INSTITUTION Independent, coed, primarily men. 20 undergraduate majors. Federal methodology is used as a basis for awarding need-based institutional aid.

UNDERGRADUATE EXPENSES for 2011–12 ***Comprehensive fee:*** $38,784 includes full-time tuition ($30,990) and room and board ($7794). ***College room only:*** $4974. Room and board charges vary according to board plan and housing facility. ***Part-time tuition:*** $538 per quarter hour. Part-time tuition and fees vary according to course load. ***Payment plan:*** Installment.

FRESHMAN FINANCIAL AID (Fall 2009) 478 applied for aid; of those 89% were deemed to have need. 100% of freshmen with need received aid; of those 15% had need fully met. ***Average percent of need met:*** 72% (excluding resources awarded to replace EFC). ***Average financial aid package:*** $20,349 (excluding resources awarded to replace EFC). 15% of all full-time freshmen had no need and received non-need-based gift aid.

UNDERGRADUATE FINANCIAL AID (Fall 2009) 2,113 applied for aid; of those 92% were deemed to have need. 100% of undergraduates with need received aid; of those 15% had need fully met. ***Average percent of need met:*** 68% (excluding resources awarded to replace EFC). ***Average financial aid package:*** $19,411 (excluding resources awarded to replace EFC). 15% of all full-time undergraduates had no need and received non-need-based gift aid.

GIFT AID (NEED-BASED) ***Total amount:*** $30,724,852 (10% federal, 7% state, 79% institutional, 4% external sources). ***Receiving aid:*** Freshmen: 81% (426); all full-time undergraduates: 85% (1,916). ***Average award:*** Freshmen: $17,836; Undergraduates: $16,192. ***Scholarships, grants, and awards:*** Federal Pell, FSEOG, state, private, college/university gift aid from institutional funds.

GIFT AID (NON-NEED-BASED) ***Total amount:*** $4,813,935 (91% institutional, 9% external sources). ***Receiving aid:*** Freshmen: 9% (47). Undergraduates: 8% (189). ***Average award:*** Freshmen: $10,814. Undergraduates: $10,136. ***Scholarships, grants, and awards by category:*** *Academic interests/achievement:* 2,195 awards ($20,585,010 total): business, communication, computer science, engineering/technologies, health fields. *Special characteristics:* 36 awards ($715,684 total): children of faculty/staff. ***Tuition waivers:*** Full or partial for employees or children of employees.

LOANS ***Student loans:*** $21,093,762 (67% need-based, 33% non-need-based). 92% of past graduating class borrowed through all loan programs. *Average indebtedness per student:* $35,236. ***Average need-based loan:*** Freshmen: $2780. Undergraduates: $3547. ***Parent loans:*** $4,925,821 (61% need-based, 39% non-need-based). ***Programs:*** Federal Direct (Subsidized and Unsubsidized Stafford, PLUS), Perkins, state, college/university.

WORK-STUDY ***Federal work-study:*** Total amount: $405,994; 284 jobs averaging $1429.

APPLYING FOR FINANCIAL AID ***Required financial aid form:*** FAFSA. ***Financial aid deadline (priority):*** 3/15. ***Notification date:*** Continuous beginning 3/1. Students must reply within 2 weeks of notification.

CONTACT Steve Midthun, Director of Financial Aid, Milwaukee School of Engineering, 1025 North Broadway, Milwaukee, WI 53202-3109, 414-277-7223 or toll-free 800-332-6763. *Fax:* 414-277-6952. *E-mail:* finaid@msoe.edu.

MINNEAPOLIS COLLEGE OF ART AND DESIGN
Minneapolis, MN

Tuition & fees: $30,585 **Average undergraduate aid package: $17,281**

ABOUT THE INSTITUTION Independent, coed. 11 undergraduate majors. Federal methodology is used as a basis for awarding need-based institutional aid.

UNDERGRADUATE EXPENSES for 2011–12 ***Tuition:*** full-time $30,385; part-time $1266 per credit. ***Required fees:*** full-time $200; $100 per term. Part-time tuition and fees vary according to course load. Room and board charges vary according to housing facility. ***Payment plan:*** Installment.

FRESHMAN FINANCIAL AID (Fall 2010, est.) 118 applied for aid; of those 83% were deemed to have need. 100% of freshmen with need received aid; of those 10% had need fully met. ***Average percent of need met:*** 63% (excluding resources awarded to replace EFC). ***Average financial aid package:*** $17,128 (excluding resources awarded to replace EFC). 13% of all full-time freshmen had no need and received non-need-based gift aid.

UNDERGRADUATE FINANCIAL AID (Fall 2010, est.) 613 applied for aid; of those 90% were deemed to have need. 100% of undergraduates with need received aid; of those 8% had need fully met. ***Average percent of need met:*** 61% (excluding resources awarded to replace EFC). ***Average financial aid package:*** $17,281 (excluding resources awarded to replace EFC). 8% of all full-time undergraduates had no need and received non-need-based gift aid.

GIFT AID (NEED-BASED) ***Total amount:*** $6,552,598 (17% federal, 7% state, 73% institutional, 3% external sources). ***Receiving aid:*** Freshmen: 76% (94); all full-time undergraduates: 77% (521). ***Average award:*** Freshmen: $13,099; Undergraduates: $12,448. ***Scholarships, grants, and awards:*** Federal Pell, FSEOG, state, private, college/university gift aid from institutional funds.

GIFT AID (NON-NEED-BASED) ***Total amount:*** $676,316 (82% institutional, 18% external sources). ***Receiving aid:*** Freshmen: 5% (6). Undergraduates: 4% (24). ***Average award:*** Freshmen: $8500. Undergraduates: $8490. ***Scholarships, grants, and awards by category:*** *Creative arts/performance:* applied art and design, art/fine arts, cinema/film/broadcasting, general creative arts/performance. ***Tuition waivers:*** Full or partial for children of alumni, employees or children of employees.

LOANS ***Student loans:*** $6,556,909 (79% need-based, 21% non-need-based). 88% of past graduating class borrowed through all loan programs. *Average indebtedness per student:* $46,293. ***Average need-based loan:*** Freshmen: $3909. Undergraduates: $4807. ***Parent loans:*** $1,863,711 (54% need-based, 46% non-need-based). ***Programs:*** Federal Direct (Subsidized and Unsubsidized Stafford, PLUS), Perkins, state.

WORK-STUDY ***Federal work-study:*** Total amount: $64,417; 67 jobs averaging $2082. ***State or other work-study/employment:*** Total amount: $201,903 (58% need-based, 42% non-need-based). 16 part-time jobs averaging $2078.

APPLYING FOR FINANCIAL AID ***Required financial aid form:*** FAFSA. ***Financial aid deadline:*** 4/1 (priority: 3/15). ***Notification date:*** Continuous beginning 4/1. Students must reply by 5/1 or within 2 weeks of notification.

CONTACT Ms. Laura Link, Director of Financial Aid, Minneapolis College of Art and Design, 2501 Stevens Avenue South, Minneapolis, MN 55404-4347, 612-874-3733 or toll-free 800-874-6223. *Fax:* 612-874-3701. *E-mail:* laura_link@mcad.edu.

MINNESOTA SCHOOL OF BUSINESS–BLAINE

Blaine, MN

CONTACT Financial Aid Office, Minnesota School of Business–Blaine, 3680 Pheasant Ridge Drive NE, Blaine, MN 55449, 763-225-8000.

MINNESOTA SCHOOL OF BUSINESS–ROCHESTER

Rochester, MN

CONTACT Financial Aid Office, Minnesota School of Business–Rochester, 2521 Pennington Drive, NW, Rochester, MN 55901, 507-536-9500 or toll-free 888-662-8772.

MINNESOTA STATE UNIVERSITY MANKATO

Mankato, MN

Tuition & fees (MN res): $6725 **Average undergraduate aid package: $8423**

ABOUT THE INSTITUTION State-supported, coed. 115 undergraduate majors. Federal methodology is used as a basis for awarding need-based institutional aid.

UNDERGRADUATE EXPENSES for 2010–11 ***Tuition, state resident:*** full-time $5927; part-time $235 per credit hour. ***Tuition, nonresident:*** full-time $12,680; part-time $505.40 per credit hour. ***Required fees:*** full-time $798. Full-time tuition and fees vary according to course load, location, and reciprocity agreements. Part-time tuition and fees vary according to course load, location, and reciprocity agreements. ***College room and board:*** $6730. Room and board charges vary according to board plan and housing facility. ***Payment plan:*** Installment.

FRESHMAN FINANCIAL AID (Fall 2010, est.) 2,090 applied for aid; of those 67% were deemed to have need. 99% of freshmen with need received aid; of those 25% had need fully met. ***Average percent of need met:*** 80% (excluding resources awarded to replace EFC). ***Average financial aid package:*** $8292 (excluding resources awarded to replace EFC). 6% of all full-time freshmen had no need and received non-need-based gift aid.

UNDERGRADUATE FINANCIAL AID (Fall 2010, est.) 9,221 applied for aid; of those 73% were deemed to have need. 98% of undergraduates with need received aid; of those 62% had need fully met. ***Average percent of need met:*** 81% (excluding resources awarded to replace EFC). ***Average financial aid package:*** $8423 (excluding resources awarded to replace EFC). 2% of all full-time undergraduates had no need and received non-need-based gift aid.

GIFT AID (NEED-BASED) ***Total amount:*** $23,924,283 (68% federal, 17% state, 4% institutional, 11% external sources). ***Receiving aid:*** Freshmen: 46% (1,104); all full-time undergraduates: 41% (4,749). ***Average award:*** Freshmen: $5486; Undergraduates: $5216. ***Scholarships, grants, and awards:*** Federal Pell, FSEOG, state, private, college/university gift aid from institutional funds, Academic Competitiveness Grants, National SMART Grants.

GIFT AID (NON-NEED-BASED) ***Total amount:*** $1,556,993 (34% federal, 18% state, 20% institutional, 28% external sources). ***Receiving aid:*** Freshmen: 17% (397). Undergraduates: 10% (1,142). ***Average award:*** Freshmen: $1170. Undergraduates: $1522. ***Tuition waivers:*** Full or partial for employees or children of employees, senior citizens.

LOANS ***Student loans:*** $68,878,517 (62% need-based, 38% non-need-based). 81% of past graduating class borrowed through all loan programs. *Average indebtedness per student:* $27,086. ***Average need-based loan:*** Freshmen: $3751. Undergraduates: $4343. ***Parent loans:*** $3,421,167 (100% non-need-based). ***Programs:*** Federal Direct (Subsidized and Unsubsidized Stafford, PLUS), Perkins, alternative loans.

WORK-STUDY ***Federal work-study:*** Total amount: $1,871,518; 526 jobs averaging $3558. ***State or other work-study/employment:*** Total amount: $1,497,242 (100% need-based). 436 part-time jobs averaging $3434.

ATHLETIC AWARDS Total amount: $2,147,545 (80% need-based, 20% non-need-based).

APPLYING FOR FINANCIAL AID ***Required financial aid forms:*** FAFSA, alternative or PLUS loan application. ***Financial aid deadline (priority):*** 3/15. ***Notification date:*** Continuous beginning 3/30. Students must reply within 2 weeks of notification.

CONTACT Sandra Loerts, Director of Financial Aid, Minnesota State University Mankato, 120 Wigley Administration Center, Mankato, MN 56001, 507-389-1866 or toll-free 800-722-0544. *Fax:* 507-389-2227. *E-mail:* campushub@mnsu.edu.

MINNESOTA STATE UNIVERSITY MOORHEAD

Moorhead, MN

Tuition & fees (MN res): $6923 **Average undergraduate aid package: $5533**

ABOUT THE INSTITUTION State-supported, coed. 78 undergraduate majors. Federal methodology is used as a basis for awarding need-based institutional aid.

UNDERGRADUATE EXPENSES for 2010–11 ***Tuition, state resident:*** full-time $6140; part-time $198.10 per credit hour. ***Tuition, nonresident:*** full-time $6140; part-time $198.10 per credit hour. ***Required fees:*** full-time $783; $35.28 per credit hour. Full-time tuition and fees vary according to program and reciprocity agreements. Part-time tuition and fees vary according to program and reciprocity agreements. ***College room and board:*** $6468; ***Room only:*** $3986. Room and board charges vary according to board plan and housing facility. ***Payment plan:*** Installment.

FRESHMAN FINANCIAL AID (Fall 2010, est.) 1,060 applied for aid; of those 74% were deemed to have need. 100% of freshmen with need received aid. ***Average financial aid package:*** $5465 (excluding resources awarded to replace EFC).

UNDERGRADUATE FINANCIAL AID (Fall 2010, est.) 5,240 applied for aid; of those 78% were deemed to have need. 100% of undergraduates with need received aid. ***Average financial aid package:*** $5533 (excluding resources awarded to replace EFC).

GIFT AID (NEED-BASED) ***Total amount:*** $13,057,529 (81% federal, 18% state, 1% institutional). ***Receiving aid:*** Freshmen: 41% (491); all full-time undergraduates: 45% (2,615). ***Average award:*** Freshmen: $4427; Undergraduates: $4032. ***Scholarships, grants, and awards:*** Federal Pell, FSEOG, state, private, college/university gift aid from institutional funds.

GIFT AID (NON-NEED-BASED) ***Total amount:*** $2,389,145 (45% institutional, 55% external sources). ***Scholarships, grants, and awards by category:*** *Academic interests/achievement:* biological sciences, business, communication, computer science, education, engineering/technologies, English, general academic interests/achievements, health fields, international studies, mathematics, physical sciences, premedicine, social sciences. *Creative arts/performance:* art/fine arts, cinema/film/broadcasting, creative writing, music, theater/drama. *Special achievements/activities:* community service, general special achievements/activities. *Special characteristics:* children of faculty/staff, first-generation college students, members of minority groups. ***Tuition waivers:*** Full or partial for employees or children of employees, senior citizens.

LOANS ***Student loans:*** $43,782,058 (39% need-based, 61% non-need-based). 58% of past graduating class borrowed through all loan programs. *Average indebtedness per student:* $29,410. ***Average need-based loan:*** Freshmen: $3363. Undergraduates: $4096. ***Parent loans:*** $880,413 (100% non-need-based). ***Programs:*** Federal Direct (Subsidized and Unsubsidized Stafford, PLUS), Perkins, state, alternative loans.

WORK-STUDY ***Federal work-study:*** Total amount: $581,905; 243 jobs averaging $2395. ***State or other work-study/employment:*** Total amount: $3,309,522 (14% need-based, 86% non-need-based). 209 part-time jobs averaging $2226.

ATHLETIC AWARDS Total amount: $493,225 (100% non-need-based).

APPLYING FOR FINANCIAL AID ***Required financial aid form:*** FAFSA. ***Financial aid deadline (priority):*** 2/15. ***Notification date:*** Continuous beginning 6/1. Students must reply within 2 weeks of notification.

CONTACT Ms. Carolyn Zehren, Director of Financial Aid, Minnesota State University Moorhead, 1104 7th Avenue South, Moorhead, MN 56563, 218-477-2085 or toll-free 800-593-7246. *Fax:* 218-477-2058. *E-mail:* zehren@mnstate.edu.

MINOT STATE UNIVERSITY

Minot, ND

Tuition & fees (ND res): $5638 **Average undergraduate aid package: $7526**

ABOUT THE INSTITUTION State-supported, coed. 58 undergraduate majors. Federal methodology is used as a basis for awarding need-based institutional aid.

UNDERGRADUATE EXPENSES for 2011–12 ***Tuition, state resident:*** full-time $4477; part-time $234.90 per credit hour. ***Tuition, nonresident:*** full-time $4477; part-time $234.90 per credit hour. ***Required fees:*** full-time $1161; $49 per credit hour or $49 per credit hour. Full-time tuition and fees vary according to class time, course load, degree level, location, and program. Part-time tuition and fees vary according to class time, degree level, location, and program. ***College room and board:*** $4530; ***Room only:*** $3000. Room and board charges vary according to board plan and housing facility. ***Payment plan:*** Installment.

FRESHMAN FINANCIAL AID (Fall 2010, est.) 309 applied for aid; of those 74% were deemed to have need. 100% of freshmen with need received aid; of those 100% had need fully met. ***Average percent of need met:*** 67% (excluding resources awarded to replace EFC). ***Average financial aid package:*** $7208 (excluding resources awarded to replace EFC). 32% of all full-time freshmen had no need and received non-need-based gift aid.

UNDERGRADUATE FINANCIAL AID (Fall 2010, est.) 1,710 applied for aid; of those 77% were deemed to have need. 99% of undergraduates with need received aid; of those 99% had need fully met. ***Average percent of need met:*** 54% (excluding resources awarded to replace EFC). ***Average financial aid package:*** $7526 (excluding resources awarded to replace EFC). 27% of all full-time undergraduates had no need and received non-need-based gift aid.

GIFT AID (NEED-BASED) ***Total amount:*** $5,879,531 (66% federal, 15% state, 5% institutional, 14% external sources). ***Receiving aid:*** Freshmen: 47% (210); all full-time undergraduates: 48% (1,175). ***Average award:*** Freshmen: $4378; Undergraduates: $4409. ***Scholarships, grants, and awards:*** Federal Pell, FSEOG, state, private, college/university gift aid from institutional funds.

GIFT AID (NON-NEED-BASED) ***Total amount:*** $99,873 (8% federal, 12% state, 17% institutional, 63% external sources). ***Receiving aid:*** Freshmen: 2% (10). Undergraduates: 1% (19). ***Average award:*** Freshmen: $843. Undergraduates: $966. ***Scholarships, grants, and awards by category:*** *Academic interests/achievement:* business, communication, computer science, education, English, general academic interests/achievements, health fields, humanities, mathematics, social sciences. *Creative arts/performance:* music, performing arts, theater/drama. *Special characteristics:* children of faculty/staff, ethnic background, international students, local/state students, members of minority groups, out-of-state students, veterans, veterans' children. ***Tuition waivers:*** Full or partial for minority students, children of alumni, employees or children of employees, senior citizens.

LOANS ***Student loans:*** $8,439,746 (82% need-based, 18% non-need-based). 76% of past graduating class borrowed through all loan programs. *Average indebtedness per student:* $20,272. ***Average need-based loan:*** Freshmen: $3120. Undergraduates: $3823. ***Parent loans:*** $51,825 (30% need-based, 70% non-need-based). ***Programs:*** Federal Direct (Subsidized and Unsubsidized Stafford, PLUS), Perkins, Federal Nursing.

WORK-STUDY ***Federal work-study:*** Total amount: $248,641; 102 jobs averaging $2524.

ATHLETIC AWARDS Total amount: $197,980 (74% need-based, 26% non-need-based).

APPLYING FOR FINANCIAL AID ***Required financial aid form:*** FAFSA. ***Financial aid deadline (priority):*** 3/15. ***Notification date:*** Continuous beginning 4/1. Students must reply within 2 weeks of notification.

CONTACT Mr. Dale Gehring, Director of Financial Aid, Minot State University, 500 University Avenue, West, Minot, ND 58707-0002, 701-858-3862 or toll-free 800-777-0750 Ext. 3350. *Fax:* 701-858-4310. *E-mail:* dale.gehring@minotstateu.edu.

MIRRER YESHIVA

Brooklyn, NY

CONTACT Financial Aid Office, Mirrer Yeshiva, 1795 Ocean Parkway, Brooklyn, NY 11223-2010, 718-645-0536.

MISERICORDIA UNIVERSITY

Dallas, PA

Tuition & fees: $24,990 **Average undergraduate aid package: $18,120**

ABOUT THE INSTITUTION Independent Roman Catholic, coed, primarily women. 36 undergraduate majors. Federal methodology is used as a basis for awarding need-based institutional aid.

UNDERGRADUATE EXPENSES for 2010–11 ***Comprehensive fee:*** $35,400 includes full-time tuition ($23,750), mandatory fees ($1240), and room and board ($10,410). ***College room only:*** $6040. Room and board charges vary according to board plan and housing facility. ***Part-time tuition:*** $450 per credit. Part-time tuition and fees vary according to class time, degree level, and location. ***Payment plans:*** Installment, deferred payment.

FRESHMAN FINANCIAL AID (Fall 2010, est.) 361 applied for aid; of those 87% were deemed to have need. 100% of freshmen with need received aid; of those 21% had need fully met. ***Average percent of need met:*** 78% (excluding resources awarded to replace EFC). ***Average financial aid package:*** $18,843 (excluding resources awarded to replace EFC). 12% of all full-time freshmen had no need and received non-need-based gift aid.

UNDERGRADUATE FINANCIAL AID (Fall 2010, est.) 1,579 applied for aid; of those 90% were deemed to have need. 100% of undergraduates with need received aid; of those 14% had need fully met. ***Average percent of need met:*** 73% (excluding resources awarded to replace EFC). ***Average financial aid package:*** $18,120 (excluding resources awarded to replace EFC). 9% of all full-time undergraduates had no need and received non-need-based gift aid.

GIFT AID (NEED-BASED) ***Total amount:*** $18,675,959 (18% federal, 11% state, 70% institutional, 1% external sources). ***Receiving aid:*** Freshmen: 84% (315); all full-time undergraduates: 84% (1,421). ***Average award:*** Freshmen: $13,815; Undergraduates: $12,564. ***Scholarships, grants, and awards:*** Federal Pell, FSEOG, state, private, college/university gift aid from institutional funds, Federal Nursing.

GIFT AID (NON-NEED-BASED) ***Total amount:*** $2,379,247 (95% institutional, 5% external sources). ***Receiving aid:*** Freshmen: 13% (50). Undergraduates:

8% (135). ***Average award:*** Freshmen: $7856. Undergraduates: $7284. ***Scholarships, grants, and awards by category:*** *Academic interests/achievement:* $7,992,838 total: business, computer science, education, general academic interests/achievements, health fields, physical sciences, social sciences. *Special achievements/activities:* $2,522,307 total: community service, general special achievements/activities, leadership. *Special characteristics:* $1,363,780 total: children and siblings of alumni, children of current students, children of faculty/staff, general special characteristics, members of minority groups, out-of-state students, previous college experience, relatives of clergy, religious affiliation, siblings of current students. ***Tuition waivers:*** Full or partial for employees or children of employees.

LOANS ***Student loans:*** $16,750,841 (74% need-based, 26% non-need-based). 81% of past graduating class borrowed through all loan programs. *Average indebtedness per student:* $36,742. ***Average need-based loan:*** Freshmen: $6751. Undergraduates: $8345. ***Parent loans:*** $4,168,247 (36% need-based, 64% non-need-based). ***Programs:*** Perkins, Federal Nursing, state.

WORK-STUDY ***Federal work-study:*** Total amount: $213,364; jobs available.

APPLYING FOR FINANCIAL AID ***Required financial aid forms:*** FAFSA, institution's own form. ***Financial aid deadline (priority):*** 3/1. ***Notification date:*** 3/15. Students must reply within 2 weeks of notification.

CONTACT Jane Dessoye, Executive Director of Enrollment Management, Misericordia University, 301 Lake Street, Dallas, PA 18612-1098, 570-674-6280 or toll-free 866-262-6363. *Fax:* 570-675-2441. *E-mail:* finaid@misericordia.edu.

MISSISSIPPI COLLEGE

Clinton, MS

ABOUT THE INSTITUTION Independent Southern Baptist, coed. 58 undergraduate majors.

GIFT AID (NEED-BASED) ***Scholarships, grants, and awards:*** Federal Pell, FSEOG, state, private, college/university gift aid from institutional funds, Federal Nursing.

GIFT AID (NON-NEED-BASED) ***Scholarships, grants, and awards by category:*** *Academic interests/achievement:* general academic interests/achievements. *Creative arts/performance:* applied art and design, art/fine arts, music. *Special achievements/activities:* general special achievements/activities, leadership, religious involvement. *Special characteristics:* children and siblings of alumni, children of faculty/staff, general special characteristics, relatives of clergy.

LOANS ***Programs:*** Perkins, Federal Nursing, college/university.

WORK-STUDY ***Federal work-study:*** Total amount: $215,091; 229 jobs averaging $1088.

APPLYING FOR FINANCIAL AID ***Required financial aid forms:*** FAFSA, state aid form.

CONTACT Karon McMillan, Director of Financial Aid, Mississippi College, PO Box 4035, Clinton, MS 39058, 601-925-3249 or toll-free 800-738-1236. *Fax:* 601-925-3950. *E-mail:* kmcmilla@mc.edu.

MISSISSIPPI STATE UNIVERSITY

Mississippi State, MS

Tuition & fees (MS res): $5461 **Average undergraduate aid package: $11,371**

ABOUT THE INSTITUTION State-supported, coed. 72 undergraduate majors. Federal methodology is used as a basis for awarding need-based institutional aid.

UNDERGRADUATE EXPENSES for 2010–11 ***Tuition, state resident:*** full-time $5461; part-time $227.75 per credit hour. ***Tuition, nonresident:*** full-time $13,801; part-time $575.25 per credit hour. Part-time tuition and fees vary according to course load. ***College room and board:*** $7729; ***Room only:*** $4494. Room and board charges vary according to board plan, housing facility, and student level. ***Payment plans:*** Tuition prepayment, installment.

FRESHMAN FINANCIAL AID (Fall 2009) 1,852 applied for aid; of those 80% were deemed to have need. 99% of freshmen with need received aid; of those 25% had need fully met. ***Average percent of need met:*** 68% (excluding resources awarded to replace EFC). ***Average financial aid package:*** $10,854 (excluding resources awarded to replace EFC). 29% of all full-time freshmen had no need and received non-need-based gift aid.

UNDERGRADUATE FINANCIAL AID (Fall 2009) 8,951 applied for aid; of those 84% were deemed to have need. 98% of undergraduates with need received aid; of those 26% had need fully met. ***Average percent of need met:*** 67% (excluding resources awarded to replace EFC). ***Average financial aid package:*** $11,371 (excluding resources awarded to replace EFC). 19% of all full-time undergraduates had no need and received non-need-based gift aid.

GIFT AID (NEED-BASED) ***Total amount:*** $45,357,613 (58% federal, 7% state, 16% institutional, 19% external sources). ***Receiving aid:*** Freshmen: 58% (1,431); all full-time undergraduates: 51% (6,709). ***Average award:*** Freshmen: $5246; Undergraduates: $5836. ***Scholarships, grants, and awards:*** Federal Pell, FSEOG, state, private, college/university gift aid from institutional funds, United Negro College Fund.

GIFT AID (NON-NEED-BASED) ***Total amount:*** $16,019,805 (20% state, 53% institutional, 27% external sources). ***Receiving aid:*** Freshmen: 11% (268). Undergraduates: 5% (622). ***Average award:*** Freshmen: $2769. Undergraduates: $2848. ***Scholarships, grants, and awards by category:*** *Academic interests/achievement:* agriculture, architecture, area/ethnic studies, biological sciences, business, communication, computer science, education, engineering/technologies, English, foreign languages, general academic interests/achievements, health fields, home economics, humanities, international studies, library science, mathematics, military science, physical sciences, premedicine, religion/biblical studies, social sciences. *Creative arts/performance:* applied art and design, art/fine arts, cinema/film/broadcasting, creative writing, dance, debating, general creative arts/performance, journalism/publications, music, performing arts, theater/drama. *Special achievements/activities:* cheerleading/drum major, general special achievements/activities, junior miss, leadership, memberships. *Special characteristics:* adult students, children and siblings of alumni, children of educators, children of faculty/staff, children of public servants, first-generation college students, handicapped students, local/state students, out-of-state students, previous college experience, spouses of deceased or disabled public servants. ***Tuition waivers:*** Full or partial for children of alumni, employees or children of employees, senior citizens.

LOANS ***Student loans:*** $82,126,701 (81% need-based, 19% non-need-based). 48% of past graduating class borrowed through all loan programs. *Average indebtedness per student:* $25,261. ***Average need-based loan:*** Freshmen: $3452. Undergraduates: $4107. ***Parent loans:*** $4,033,718 (44% need-based, 56% non-need-based). ***Programs:*** Federal Direct (Subsidized and Unsubsidized Stafford, PLUS), Perkins, college/university.

WORK-STUDY ***Federal work-study:*** Total amount: $2,938,394; 866 jobs averaging $3393.

ATHLETIC AWARDS Total amount: $5,427,529 (100% non-need-based).

APPLYING FOR FINANCIAL AID ***Required financial aid forms:*** FAFSA, state grant/scholarship application. ***Financial aid deadline (priority):*** 4/1. ***Notification date:*** Continuous beginning 12/1. Students must reply by 5/1.

CONTACT Dr. Lisa Harris, Interim Director of Financial Aid, Mississippi State University, PO Box 6035, Mississippi State, MS 39762, 662-325-2450. *Fax:* 662-325-0702. *E-mail:* financialaid@saffairs.msstate.edu.

MISSISSIPPI UNIVERSITY FOR WOMEN

Columbus, MS

Tuition & fees (MS res): $4644 **Average undergraduate aid package: $8408**

ABOUT THE INSTITUTION State-supported, coed, primarily women. 28 undergraduate majors. Federal methodology is used as a basis for awarding need-based institutional aid.

UNDERGRADUATE EXPENSES for 2011–12 ***Tuition, state resident:*** full-time $4644; part-time $193.50 per credit hour. ***Tuition, nonresident:*** full-time $12,653; part-time $527 per credit hour. Part-time tuition and fees vary according to course load. ***College room and board:*** $5482; ***Room only:*** $3225. Room and board charges vary according to housing facility. ***Payment plan:*** Installment.

FRESHMAN FINANCIAL AID (Fall 2009) 192 applied for aid; of those 88% were deemed to have need. 99% of freshmen with need received aid; of those 50% had need fully met. ***Average percent of need met:*** 50% (excluding resources awarded to replace EFC). ***Average financial aid package:*** $9132 (excluding resources awarded to replace EFC). 19% of all full-time freshmen had no need and received non-need-based gift aid.

UNDERGRADUATE FINANCIAL AID (Fall 2009) 1,491 applied for aid; of those 88% were deemed to have need. 99% of undergraduates with need received aid; of those 67% had need fully met. ***Average percent of need met:*** 63% (excluding resources awarded to replace EFC). ***Average financial aid package:*** $8408 (excluding resources awarded to replace EFC). 16% of all full-time undergraduates had no need and received non-need-based gift aid.

GIFT AID (NEED-BASED) ***Total amount:*** $5,260,826 (100% federal). ***Receiving aid:*** Freshmen: 62% (130); all full-time undergraduates: 57% (1,005). ***Average award:*** Freshmen: $4983; Undergraduates: $5201. ***Scholarships, grants, and awards:*** Federal Pell, FSEOG, state, private, college/university gift aid from institutional funds.

GIFT AID (NON-NEED-BASED) ***Total amount:*** $4,456,506 (15% state, 77% institutional, 8% external sources). ***Receiving aid:*** Freshmen: 53% (112). Undergraduates: 38% (658). ***Average award:*** Freshmen: $5868. Undergraduates: $4732. ***Scholarships, grants, and awards by category:*** *Academic interests/achievement:* 768 awards ($1,920,363 total): biological sciences, business, communication, computer science, education, English, general academic interests/achievements, health fields, home economics, humanities, mathematics, physical sciences. *Creative arts/performance:* 50 awards ($28,200 total): art/fine arts, journalism/publications, music, performing arts, theater/drama. *Special achievements/activities:* 11 awards ($16,541 total): junior miss, leadership. *Special characteristics:* 213 awards ($1,079,355 total): adult students, children and siblings of alumni, children of faculty/staff, ethnic background, international students, members of minority groups, out-of-state students, parents of current students. ***Tuition waivers:*** Full or partial for employees or children of employees.

LOANS ***Student loans:*** $9,825,273 (47% need-based, 53% non-need-based). 64% of past graduating class borrowed through all loan programs. *Average indebtedness per student:* $18,363. ***Average need-based loan:*** Freshmen: $3198. Undergraduates: $4494. ***Parent loans:*** $242,792 (100% non-need-based). ***Programs:*** Perkins.

WORK-STUDY ***Federal work-study:*** Total amount: $140,286; 93 jobs averaging $1693. ***State or other work-study/employment:*** Total amount: $267,480 (100% non-need-based). 194 part-time jobs averaging $1535.

APPLYING FOR FINANCIAL AID ***Required financial aid forms:*** FAFSA, institution's own form, state aid form. ***Financial aid deadline (priority):*** 3/1. ***Notification date:*** Continuous beginning 4/1. Students must reply within 2 weeks of notification.

CONTACT Mr. Dan Miller, Director of Financial Aid, Mississippi University for Women, 1100 College Street, MUW 1614, Columbus, MS 39701-4044, 662-329-7114 or toll-free 877-GO 2 THE W. *Fax:* 662-329-7325. *E-mail:* dmiller@finaid.muw.edu.

MISSISSIPPI VALLEY STATE UNIVERSITY

Itta Bena, MS

ABOUT THE INSTITUTION State-supported, coed. 29 undergraduate majors.

GIFT AID (NEED-BASED) ***Scholarships, grants, and awards:*** Federal Pell, FSEOG, state, private, college/university gift aid from institutional funds.

GIFT AID (NON-NEED-BASED) ***Scholarships, grants, and awards by category:*** *Academic interests/achievement:* general academic interests/achievements. *Creative arts/performance:* art/fine arts, journalism/publications, music. *Special characteristics:* members of minority groups.

LOANS ***Programs:*** Federal Direct (Unsubsidized Stafford, PLUS).

WORK-STUDY Federal work-study jobs available. ***State or other work-study/employment:*** Part-time jobs available.

APPLYING FOR FINANCIAL AID ***Required financial aid form:*** FAFSA.

CONTACT Mr. Lloyd E. Dixon, Director of Student Financial Aid, Mississippi Valley State University, 14000 Highway 82W #7268, Itta Bena, MS 38941-1400, 662-254-3335 or toll-free 800-844-6885 (in-state). *Fax:* 662-254-7900. *E-mail:* ldixon@mvsu.edu.

MISSOURI BAPTIST UNIVERSITY

St. Louis, MO

Tuition & fees: $18,700 | **Average undergraduate aid package: $13,290**

ABOUT THE INSTITUTION Independent Southern Baptist, coed. 37 undergraduate majors. Both federal and institutional methodology are used as a basis for awarding need-based institutional aid.

UNDERGRADUATE EXPENSES for 2010–11 ***Comprehensive fee:*** $26,140 includes full-time tuition ($17,820), mandatory fees ($880), and room and board ($7440). Full-time tuition and fees vary according to course load, degree level, and location. Room and board charges vary according to housing facility. ***Part-time tuition:*** $615 per credit hour. ***Part-time fees:*** $15 per credit hour; $30 per term. Part-time tuition and fees vary according to course load, degree level, and location. ***Payment plan:*** Installment.

FRESHMAN FINANCIAL AID (Fall 2009) 203 applied for aid; of those 100% were deemed to have need. 100% of freshmen with need received aid. ***Average financial aid package:*** $15,262 (excluding resources awarded to replace EFC). 36% of all full-time freshmen had no need and received non-need-based gift aid.

UNDERGRADUATE FINANCIAL AID (Fall 2009) ***Average financial aid package:*** $13,290 (excluding resources awarded to replace EFC). 23% of all full-time undergraduates had no need and received non-need-based gift aid.

GIFT AID (NEED-BASED) ***Total amount:*** $4,183,255 (57% federal, 33% state, 10% institutional). ***Receiving aid:*** Freshmen: 61% (123); all full-time undergraduates: 57% (698). ***Average award:*** Freshmen: $5601; Undergraduates: $5411. ***Scholarships, grants, and awards:*** Federal Pell, FSEOG, state, private, college/university gift aid from institutional funds.

GIFT AID (NON-NEED-BASED) ***Total amount:*** $2,506,410 (6% federal, 76% institutional, 18% external sources). ***Receiving aid:*** Freshmen: 39% (80). Undergraduates: 26% (321). ***Average award:*** Freshmen: $7995. Undergraduates: $6718. ***Scholarships, grants, and awards by category:*** *Academic interests/achievement:* general academic interests/achievements, religion/biblical studies. *Creative arts/performance:* music, theater/drama. *Special achievements/activities:* cheerleading/drum major, religious involvement. *Special characteristics:* children and siblings of alumni, children of current students, children of faculty/staff, parents of current students, public servants, relatives of clergy, religious affiliation, siblings of current students. ***Tuition waivers:*** Full or partial for children of alumni, employees or children of employees, senior citizens.

LOANS ***Student loans:*** $8,818,592 (46% need-based, 54% non-need-based). ***Average need-based loan:*** Freshmen: $3283. Undergraduates: $4442. ***Parent loans:*** $674,499 (100% non-need-based).

WORK-STUDY Federal work-study jobs available. ***State or other work-study/employment:*** 65 part-time jobs averaging $4819.

ATHLETIC AWARDS Total amount: $4,794,085 (100% non-need-based).

APPLYING FOR FINANCIAL AID ***Required financial aid forms:*** FAFSA, institution's own form. ***Financial aid deadline (priority):*** 4/1. ***Notification date:*** Continuous beginning 4/15. Students must reply within 2 weeks of notification.

CONTACT Mr. Terry Dale Cruse, Dean of Enrollment Services, Missouri Baptist University, One College Park Drive, St. Louis, MO 63141, 314-392-2366 or toll-free 877-434-1115 Ext. 2290. *Fax:* 314-434-7596. *E-mail:* cruse@mobap.edu.

MISSOURI SOUTHERN STATE UNIVERSITY

Joplin, MO

Tuition & fees (MO res): $4816 | **Average undergraduate aid package: $10,772**

ABOUT THE INSTITUTION State-supported, coed. 38 undergraduate majors. Federal methodology is used as a basis for awarding need-based institutional aid.

UNDERGRADUATE EXPENSES for 2011–12 ***Tuition, state resident:*** full-time $4290; part-time $143 per credit hour. ***Tuition, nonresident:*** full-time $8580; part-time $286 per credit hour. ***Required fees:*** full-time $526. Full-time tuition and fees vary according to course load. ***College room and board:*** $5500. Room and board charges vary according to board plan and housing facility.

FRESHMAN FINANCIAL AID (Fall 2009) 700 applied for aid; of those 74% were deemed to have need. 98% of freshmen with need received aid; of those 13% had need fully met. ***Average percent of need met:*** 61% (excluding resources awarded to replace EFC). ***Average financial aid package:*** $7124 (excluding resources awarded to replace EFC). 19% of all full-time freshmen had no need and received non-need-based gift aid.

UNDERGRADUATE FINANCIAL AID (Fall 2009) 2,553 applied for aid; of those 82% were deemed to have need. 98% of undergraduates with need received aid; of those 13% had need fully met. ***Average percent of need met:*** 54% (excluding resources awarded to replace EFC). ***Average financial aid package:*** $10,772 (excluding resources awarded to replace EFC). 11% of all full-time undergraduates had no need and received non-need-based gift aid.

GIFT AID (NEED-BASED) ***Total amount:*** $12,494,948 (84% federal, 16% state). ***Receiving aid:*** Freshmen: 61% (434); all full-time undergraduates: 62% (1,666). ***Average award:*** Freshmen: $4331; Undergraduates: $4158. ***Scholarships, grants, and awards:*** Federal Pell, FSEOG, state, private.

GIFT AID (NON-NEED-BASED) ***Total amount:*** $4,554,517 (3% state, 73% institutional, 24% external sources). ***Receiving aid:*** Freshmen: 46% (323). Undergraduates: 31% (842). ***Average award:*** Freshmen: $2432. Undergraduates: $3844. ***Scholarships, grants, and awards by category:*** *Academic interests/achievement:* general academic interests/achievements. *Creative arts/performance:* art/fine arts, debating, journalism/publications, music, theater/drama. *Special achievements/activities:* general special achievements/activities. *Special characteristics:* children and siblings of alumni, children of faculty/staff, ethnic background, local/state students, religious affiliation. ***Tuition waivers:*** Full or partial for employees or children of employees, senior citizens.

LOANS ***Student loans:*** $21,016,318 (48% need-based, 52% non-need-based). 57% of past graduating class borrowed through all loan programs. *Average indebtedness per student:* $16,772. ***Average need-based loan:*** Freshmen: $1823. Undergraduates: $2861. ***Parent loans:*** $225,734 (100% non-need-based). ***Programs:*** Federal Direct (Subsidized and Unsubsidized Stafford, PLUS), Perkins.

WORK-STUDY ***Federal work-study:*** Total amount: $223,366; jobs available. ***State or other work-study/employment:*** Total amount: $855,813 (100% non-need-based). Part-time jobs available.

ATHLETIC AWARDS Total amount: $1,414,333 (100% non-need-based).

APPLYING FOR FINANCIAL AID ***Required financial aid form:*** FAFSA. ***Financial aid deadline (priority):*** 4/1. ***Notification date:*** Continuous beginning 3/1. Students must reply by 5/1 or within 3 weeks of notification.

CONTACT Becca L. Diskin, Director of Financial Aid, Missouri Southern State University, 3950 East Newman Road, Joplin, MO 64801-1595, 417-625-5422 or toll-free 866-818-MSSU. *Fax:* 417-659-4474. *E-mail:* Diskin-B@mssu.edu.

MISSOURI STATE UNIVERSITY

Springfield, MO

Tuition & fees (MO res): $6276 Average undergraduate aid package: $8064

ABOUT THE INSTITUTION State-supported, coed. 102 undergraduate majors. Federal methodology is used as a basis for awarding need-based institutional aid.

UNDERGRADUATE EXPENSES for 2010–11 ***Tuition, state resident:*** full-time $5580; part-time $186 per credit hour. ***Tuition, nonresident:*** full-time $11,160; part-time $372 per credit hour. ***Required fees:*** full-time $696. Full-time tuition and fees vary according to course level, location, and program. Part-time tuition and fees vary according to course level, course load, location, and program. ***College room and board:*** $6394. Room and board charges vary according to board plan and housing facility. ***Payment plans:*** Tuition prepayment, installment, deferred payment.

FRESHMAN FINANCIAL AID (Fall 2010, est.) 2,279 applied for aid; of those 71% were deemed to have need. 99% of freshmen with need received aid; of those 17% had need fully met. ***Average percent of need met:*** 68% (excluding resources awarded to replace EFC). ***Average financial aid package:*** $8048 (excluding resources awarded to replace EFC). 15% of all full-time freshmen had no need and received non-need-based gift aid.

UNDERGRADUATE FINANCIAL AID (Fall 2010, est.) 10,126 applied for aid; of those 78% were deemed to have need. 98% of undergraduates with need received aid; of those 16% had need fully met. ***Average percent of need met:*** 66% (excluding resources awarded to replace EFC). ***Average financial aid package:*** $8064 (excluding resources awarded to replace EFC). 11% of all full-time undergraduates had no need and received non-need-based gift aid.

GIFT AID (NEED-BASED) ***Total amount:*** $34,738,809 (66% federal, 12% state, 19% institutional, 3% external sources). ***Receiving aid:*** Freshmen: 53% (1,391); all full-time undergraduates: 48% (6,374). ***Average award:*** Freshmen: $5810; Undergraduates: $5107. ***Scholarships, grants, and awards:*** Federal Pell, FSEOG, state, private, college/university gift aid from institutional funds.

GIFT AID (NON-NEED-BASED) ***Total amount:*** $8,606,823 (1% federal, 7% state, 84% institutional, 8% external sources). ***Receiving aid:*** Freshmen: 5% (128). Undergraduates: 3% (352). ***Average award:*** Freshmen: $4080. Undergraduates: $4209. ***Scholarships, grants, and awards by category:*** *Academic interests/achievement:* general academic interests/achievements. *Creative arts/performance:* general creative arts/performance. *Special achievements/activities:* leadership. *Special characteristics:* children and siblings of alumni, local/state students, members of minority groups. ***Tuition waivers:*** Full or partial for children of alumni, employees or children of employees, senior citizens.

LOANS ***Student loans:*** $66,824,084 (65% need-based, 35% non-need-based). 69% of past graduating class borrowed through all loan programs. *Average indebtedness per student:* $21,359. ***Average need-based loan:*** Freshmen: $3165. Undergraduates: $4204. ***Parent loans:*** $8,469,861 (13% need-based, 87% non-need-based). ***Programs:*** Federal Direct (Subsidized Stafford, PLUS), Perkins, college/university.

WORK-STUDY ***Federal work-study:*** Total amount: $552,248; jobs available.

ATHLETIC AWARDS Total amount: $3,305,408 (31% need-based, 69% non-need-based).

APPLYING FOR FINANCIAL AID ***Required financial aid form:*** FAFSA. ***Financial aid deadline (priority):*** 3/31. ***Notification date:*** 4/30. Students must reply within 4 weeks of notification.

CONTACT Vicki Mattocks, Director of Financial Aid, Missouri State University, 901 South National Avenue, Springfield, MO 65804, 417-836-5262 or toll-free 800-492-7900. *E-mail:* financialaid@missouristate.edu.

MISSOURI TECH

St. Louis, MO

ABOUT THE INSTITUTION Proprietary, coed, primarily men. ***Awards:*** associate and bachelor's degrees. 7 undergraduate majors. ***Total enrollment:*** 114. Undergraduates: 114.

GIFT AID (NEED-BASED) ***Scholarships, grants, and awards:*** Federal Pell, private, college/university gift aid from institutional funds.

GIFT AID (NON-NEED-BASED) ***Scholarships, grants, and awards by category:*** *Academic interests/achievement:* general academic interests/achievements.

LOANS ***Programs:*** college/university.

APPLYING FOR FINANCIAL AID ***Required financial aid forms:*** FAFSA, institution's own form.

CONTACT Director of Financial Aid, Missouri Tech, 1690 Country Club Plaza Drive, St. Charles, MO 63303, 636-573-9300. *Fax:* 636-573-9398. *E-mail:* contact@motech.edu.

MISSOURI UNIVERSITY OF SCIENCE AND TECHNOLOGY

Rolla, MO

Tuition & fees (MO res): $8528 Average undergraduate aid package: $10,760

ABOUT THE INSTITUTION State-supported, coed, primarily men. 35 undergraduate majors. Federal methodology is used as a basis for awarding need-based institutional aid.

UNDERGRADUATE EXPENSES for 2010–11 ***Tuition, state resident:*** full-time $7368; part-time $246 per credit hour. ***Tuition, nonresident:*** full-time $19,383; part-time $646 per credit hour. ***Required fees:*** full-time $1160; $246 per credit hour. Full-time tuition and fees vary according to course load, degree level, and program. Part-time tuition and fees vary according to course load, degree level, and program. ***College room and board:*** $8290; ***Room only:*** $5280. Room and board charges vary according to board plan, housing facility, and location. ***Payment plan:*** Installment.

FRESHMAN FINANCIAL AID (Fall 2010, est.) 1,109 applied for aid; of those 71% were deemed to have need. 100% of freshmen with need received aid; of those 62% had need fully met. ***Average percent of need met:*** 61% (excluding resources awarded to replace EFC). ***Average financial aid package:*** $11,459 (excluding resources awarded to replace EFC). 19% of all full-time freshmen had no need and received non-need-based gift aid.

UNDERGRADUATE FINANCIAL AID (Fall 2010, est.) 4,603 applied for aid; of those 80% were deemed to have need. 100% of undergraduates with need received aid; of those 62% had need fully met. ***Average percent of need met:*** 61% (excluding resources awarded to replace EFC). ***Average financial aid package:*** $10,760 (excluding resources awarded to replace EFC). 11% of all full-time undergraduates had no need and received non-need-based gift aid.

GIFT AID (NEED-BASED) ***Total amount:*** $16,932,425 (44% federal, 8% state, 48% institutional). ***Receiving aid:*** Freshmen: 69% (789); all full-time undergraduates: 74% (3,704). ***Average award:*** Freshmen: $7218; Undergraduates: $6906. ***Scholarships, grants, and awards:*** Federal Pell, FSEOG, state, private, college/university gift aid from institutional funds, ROTC (Army and Air Force) scholarships.

GIFT AID (NON-NEED-BASED) ***Total amount:*** $9,976,214 (10% state, 66% institutional, 24% external sources). ***Receiving aid:*** Freshmen: 60% (680). Undergraduates: 64% (3,207). ***Average award:*** Freshmen: $4258. Undergraduates: $4326. ***Scholarships, grants, and awards by category:*** *Academic interests/achievement:* 6,933 awards ($13,410,316 total): biological sciences, business, computer science, education, engineering/technologies, English, general academic interests/achievements, humanities, mathematics, military science, physical sciences, premedicine, social sciences. *Creative arts/performance:* 13 awards ($2465 total): music, theater/drama. *Special characteristics:* 783 awards ($3,826,449 total): children and siblings of alumni, children of faculty/staff, members of minority groups, out-of-state students. ***Tuition waivers:*** Full or partial for employees or children of employees.

LOANS ***Student loans:*** $24,189,999 (83% need-based, 17% non-need-based). 64% of past graduating class borrowed through all loan programs. *Average indebtedness per student:* $21,700. ***Average need-based loan:*** Freshmen: $3390. Undergraduates: $3000. ***Parent loans:*** $18,998,539 (100% need-based). ***Programs:*** Federal Direct (Subsidized and Unsubsidized Stafford), Perkins, state, college/university, alternative loans.

WORK-STUDY ***Federal work-study:*** Total amount: $268,925; 103 jobs averaging $2519. ***State or other work-study/employment:*** Part-time jobs available.

ATHLETIC AWARDS Total amount: $1,381,173 (90% need-based, 10% non-need-based).

APPLYING FOR FINANCIAL AID ***Required financial aid form:*** FAFSA. ***Financial aid deadline (priority):*** 3/1. ***Notification date:*** Continuous beginning 4/1. Students must reply within 3 weeks of notification.

CONTACT Lynn K. Stichnote, Director of Student Financial Assistance, Missouri University of Science and Technology, G1 Parker Hall, Rolla, MO 65409, 573-341-4282 or toll-free 800-522-0938. *Fax:* 573-341-4274. *E-mail:* lks@mst.edu.

MISSOURI VALLEY COLLEGE

Marshall, MO

ABOUT THE INSTITUTION Independent religious, coed. ***Awards:*** associate and bachelor's degrees. 38 undergraduate majors. ***Total enrollment:*** 1,639. Undergraduates: 1,639. Freshmen: 444.

GIFT AID (NEED-BASED) ***Scholarships, grants, and awards:*** Federal Pell, FSEOG, state, private, college/university gift aid from institutional funds.

GIFT AID (NON-NEED-BASED) ***Scholarships, grants, and awards by category:*** *Academic interests/achievement:* biological sciences, business, communication, computer science, education, English, general academic interests/achievements, health fields, humanities, mathematics, military science, physical sciences, premedicine, social sciences. *Creative arts/performance:* applied art and design, art/fine arts, cinema/film/broadcasting, dance, journalism/publications, music, performing arts, theater/drama. *Special achievements/activities:* cheerleading/drum major, community service, general special achievements/activities, hobbies/interests, junior miss, leadership, rodeo. *Special characteristics:* children and siblings of alumni, children of faculty/staff.

LOANS ***Programs:*** Federal Direct (Subsidized and Unsubsidized Stafford, PLUS), Perkins.

WORK-STUDY ***Federal work-study:*** Total amount: $244,405; 192 jobs averaging $1860. ***State or other work-study/employment:*** Total amount: $433,514 (100% non-need-based). 400 part-time jobs averaging $1860.

APPLYING FOR FINANCIAL AID ***Required financial aid form:*** FAFSA.

CONTACT Mr. Charles Richard Mayfield Jr., Director of Financial Aid, Missouri Valley College, 500 East College, Marshall, MO 65340-3197, 660-831-4176. *Fax:* 660-831-4003. *E-mail:* mayfieldb@moval.edu.

MISSOURI WESTERN STATE UNIVERSITY

St. Joseph, MO

CONTACT Angela Beam, Acting Director of Financial Aid, Missouri Western State University, 4525 Downs Drive, St. Joseph, MO 64507-2294, 816-271-5986 or toll-free 800-662-7041 Ext. 60. *Fax:* 816-271-5879. *E-mail:* lepley@missouriwestern.edu.

MITCHELL COLLEGE

New London, CT

CONTACT Jacklyn Stoltz, Director of Financial Aid, Mitchell College, 437 Pequot Avenue, New London, CT 06320-4498, 800-443-2811. *Fax:* 860-444-1209. *E-mail:* stoltz_j@mitchell.edu.

MOLLOY COLLEGE

Rockville Centre, NY

Tuition & fees: $22,130 **Average undergraduate aid package: $13,218**

ABOUT THE INSTITUTION Independent, coed. 44 undergraduate majors. Federal methodology is used as a basis for awarding need-based institutional aid.

UNDERGRADUATE EXPENSES for 2010–11 ***One-time required fee:*** $150. ***Tuition:*** full-time $21,170; part-time $700 per credit. ***Payment plan:*** Installment.

FRESHMAN FINANCIAL AID (Fall 2010, est.) 388 applied for aid; of those 84% were deemed to have need. 100% of freshmen with need received aid; of those 16% had need fully met. ***Average percent of need met:*** 61% (excluding resources awarded to replace EFC). ***Average financial aid package:*** $14,879 (excluding resources awarded to replace EFC). 12% of all full-time freshmen had no need and received non-need-based gift aid.

UNDERGRADUATE FINANCIAL AID (Fall 2010, est.) 2,075 applied for aid; of those 87% were deemed to have need. 100% of undergraduates with need received aid; of those 11% had need fully met. ***Average percent of need met:*** 53% (excluding resources awarded to replace EFC). ***Average financial aid package:*** $13,218 (excluding resources awarded to replace EFC). 8% of all full-time undergraduates had no need and received non-need-based gift aid.

GIFT AID (NEED-BASED) ***Total amount:*** $14,534,159 (28% federal, 23% state, 46% institutional, 3% external sources). ***Receiving aid:*** Freshmen: 80% (320); all full-time undergraduates: 77% (1,624). ***Average award:*** Freshmen: $12,273; Undergraduates: $9169. ***Scholarships, grants, and awards:*** Federal Pell, FSEOG, state, private, college/university gift aid from institutional funds, Federal Nursing, Academic Competitiveness Grants, National SMART Grants, TEACH Grants, TRiO Scholarships.

GIFT AID (NON-NEED-BASED) ***Total amount:*** $1,901,045 (5% state, 85% institutional, 10% external sources). ***Receiving aid:*** Freshmen: 10% (40). Undergraduates: 6% (129). ***Average award:*** Freshmen: $7981. Undergraduates: $6399. ***Scholarships, grants, and awards by category:*** *Academic interests/achievement:* 180 awards ($327,750 total): biological sciences, business, communication, education, English, general academic interests/achievements, health fields, international studies, mathematics, social sciences. *Creative arts/performance:* 64 awards ($140,338 total): art/fine arts, music, performing arts, theater/drama. *Special achievements/activities:* 258 awards ($393,125 total): community service, leadership, memberships, religious involvement. *Special characteristics:* 82 awards ($116,871 total): ethnic background, members of minority groups, religious affiliation, siblings of current students. ***Tuition waivers:*** Full or partial for employees or children of employees.

LOANS ***Student loans:*** $21,942,012 (81% need-based, 19% non-need-based). 77% of past graduating class borrowed through all loan programs. *Average indebtedness per student:* $29,823. ***Average need-based loan:*** Freshmen: $3711. Undergraduates: $5794. ***Parent loans:*** $3,488,879 (47% need-based, 53% non-need-based). ***Programs:*** Federal Direct (Subsidized and Unsubsidized Stafford, PLUS), Perkins, Federal Nursing, alternative loans.

WORK-STUDY ***Federal work-study:*** Total amount: $238,610; 403 jobs averaging $2244.

ATHLETIC AWARDS Total amount: $1,628,684 (68% need-based, 32% non-need-based).

APPLYING FOR FINANCIAL AID ***Required financial aid forms:*** FAFSA, state aid form. ***Financial aid deadline:*** 5/1 (priority: 4/15). ***Notification date:*** 2/1. Students must reply within 5 weeks of notification.

CONTACT Ana C. Lockward, Director of Financial Aid, Molloy College, 1000 Hempstead Avenue, Rockville Centre, NY 11571, 516-678-5000 Ext. 6221 or toll-free 888-4MOLLOY. *Fax:* 516-256-2292. *E-mail:* alockward@molloy.edu.

MONMOUTH COLLEGE

Monmouth, IL

Tuition & fees: $28,650 **Average undergraduate aid package: $24,186**

ABOUT THE INSTITUTION Independent religious, coed. 35 undergraduate majors. Federal methodology is used as a basis for awarding need-based institutional aid.

UNDERGRADUATE EXPENSES for 2011–12 ***One-time required fee:*** $150. ***Comprehensive fee:*** $35,950 includes full-time tuition ($28,650) and room and board ($7300). Full-time tuition and fees vary according to course load. Room and board charges vary according to board plan and housing facility. ***Payment plan:*** Installment.

FRESHMAN FINANCIAL AID (Fall 2010, est.) 350 applied for aid; of those 95% were deemed to have need. 100% of freshmen with need received aid; of those 17% had need fully met. ***Average percent of need met:*** 91% (excluding

resources awarded to replace EFC). ***Average financial aid package:*** $26,653 (excluding resources awarded to replace EFC). 7% of all full-time freshmen had no need and received non-need-based gift aid.

UNDERGRADUATE FINANCIAL AID (Fall 2010, est.) 1,256 applied for aid; of those 93% were deemed to have need. 100% of undergraduates with need received aid; of those 23% had need fully met. ***Average percent of need met:*** 88% (excluding resources awarded to replace EFC). ***Average financial aid package:*** $24,186 (excluding resources awarded to replace EFC). 12% of all full-time undergraduates had no need and received non-need-based gift aid.

GIFT AID (NEED-BASED) ***Total amount:*** $22,397,319 (13% federal, 14% state, 73% institutional). ***Receiving aid:*** Freshmen: 93% (331); all full-time undergraduates: 88% (1,165). ***Average award:*** Freshmen: $22,560; Undergraduates: $19,444. ***Scholarships, grants, and awards:*** Federal Pell, FSEOG, state, private, college/university gift aid from institutional funds.

GIFT AID (NON-NEED-BASED) ***Total amount:*** $2,699,365 (88% institutional, 12% external sources). ***Receiving aid:*** Freshmen: 8% (30). Undergraduates: 9% (122). ***Average award:*** Freshmen: $11,796. Undergraduates: $10,758. ***Scholarships, grants, and awards by category:*** *Academic interests/achievement:* foreign languages, general academic interests/achievements. *Creative arts/performance:* art/fine arts, music, theater/drama. *Special achievements/activities:* general special achievements/activities, leadership, religious involvement. *Special characteristics:* international students, out-of-state students, veterans. ***Tuition waivers:*** Full or partial for employees or children of employees.

LOANS ***Student loans:*** $7,950,948 (49% need-based, 51% non-need-based). 84% of past graduating class borrowed through all loan programs. *Average indebtedness per student:* $25,909. ***Average need-based loan:*** Freshmen: $3030. Undergraduates: $3982. ***Parent loans:*** $2,252,750 (100% non-need-based). ***Programs:*** Federal Direct (Subsidized and Unsubsidized Stafford, PLUS), Perkins.

WORK-STUDY ***Federal work-study:*** Total amount: $962,881; jobs available. ***State or other work-study/employment:*** Part-time jobs available.

APPLYING FOR FINANCIAL AID ***Required financial aid form:*** FAFSA. ***Financial aid deadline (priority):*** 3/1. ***Notification date:*** Continuous beginning 3/1. Students must reply by 8/1.

CONTACT Mrs. Jayne Schreck, Director of Financial Aid, Monmouth College, 700 East Broadway, Monmouth, IL 61462-1998, 309-457-2129 or toll-free 800-747-2687. *Fax:* 309-457-2373. *E-mail:* jayne@monm.edu.

MONMOUTH UNIVERSITY

West Long Branch, NJ

Tuition & fees: $28,000 **Average undergraduate aid package: $19,984**

ABOUT THE INSTITUTION Independent, coed. 33 undergraduate majors. Federal methodology is used as a basis for awarding need-based institutional aid.

UNDERGRADUATE EXPENSES for 2011–12 ***One-time required fee:*** $200. ***Comprehensive fee:*** $38,680 includes full-time tuition ($27,372), mandatory fees ($628), and room and board ($10,680). ***College room only:*** $5932. Room and board charges vary according to board plan and housing facility. ***Part-time tuition:*** $793 per credit. ***Part-time fees:*** $157 per term. ***Payment plan:*** Installment.

FRESHMAN FINANCIAL AID (Fall 2010, est.) 878 applied for aid; of those 82% were deemed to have need. 100% of freshmen with need received aid; of those 3% had need fully met. ***Average percent of need met:*** 72% (excluding resources awarded to replace EFC). ***Average financial aid package:*** $19,500 (excluding resources awarded to replace EFC). 23% of all full-time freshmen had no need and received non-need-based gift aid.

UNDERGRADUATE FINANCIAL AID (Fall 2010, est.) 3,480 applied for aid; of those 86% were deemed to have need. 100% of undergraduates with need received aid; of those 6% had need fully met. ***Average percent of need met:*** 69% (excluding resources awarded to replace EFC). ***Average financial aid package:*** $19,984 (excluding resources awarded to replace EFC). 27% of all full-time undergraduates had no need and received non-need-based gift aid.

GIFT AID (NEED-BASED) ***Total amount:*** $14,432,436 (43% federal, 52% state, 5% institutional). ***Receiving aid:*** Freshmen: 30% (294); all full-time undergraduates: 28% (1,205). ***Average award:*** Freshmen: $12,341; Undergraduates: $11,670. ***Scholarships, grants, and awards:*** Federal Pell, FSEOG, state, private, college/university gift aid from institutional funds, Federal Nursing.

GIFT AID (NON-NEED-BASED) ***Total amount:*** $45,022,994 (1% federal, 67% institutional, 32% external sources). ***Receiving aid:*** Freshmen: 68% (653). Undergraduates: 63% (2,679). ***Average award:*** Freshmen: $8943. Undergraduates: $7666. ***Scholarships, grants, and awards by category:*** *Academic interests/achievement:* 3,978 awards ($28,213,079 total): business, communication, computer science, education, general academic interests/achievements, health fields, humanities, international studies, mathematics, social sciences. *Special achievements/activities:* 8 awards ($4000 total): leadership. *Special characteristics:* 351 awards ($998,809 total): adult students, children and siblings of alumni, children of faculty/staff, children of public servants, first-generation college students, general special characteristics, international students, local/state students, members of minority groups, out-of-state students, previous college experience, veterans. ***Tuition waivers:*** Full or partial for employees or children of employees, senior citizens.

LOANS ***Student loans:*** $36,391,001 (34% need-based, 66% non-need-based). 72% of past graduating class borrowed through all loan programs. *Average indebtedness per student:* $29,921. ***Average need-based loan:*** Freshmen: $3799. Undergraduates: $4794. ***Parent loans:*** $7,708,383 (100% non-need-based). ***Programs:*** Federal Direct (Subsidized and Unsubsidized Stafford, PLUS), Perkins, state, college/university, private loans.

WORK-STUDY ***Federal work-study:*** Total amount: $630,000; 895 jobs averaging $1976.

ATHLETIC AWARDS Total amount: $4,709,231 (100% non-need-based).

APPLYING FOR FINANCIAL AID ***Required financial aid form:*** FAFSA. ***Financial aid deadline:*** Continuous. ***Notification date:*** Continuous beginning 2/1. Students must reply within 2 weeks of notification.

CONTACT Ms. Claire Alasio, Associate Vice President for Enrollment Management and Director of Financial Aid, Monmouth University, 400 Cedar Avenue, West Long Branch, NJ 07764-1898, 732-571-3463 or toll-free 800-543-9671. *Fax:* 732-923-4791. *E-mail:* finaid@monmouth.edu.

MONROE COLLEGE

Bronx, NY

CONTACT Howard Leslie, Dean of Student Financial Services, Monroe College, 434 Main Street, New Rochelle, NY 10468, 718-817-8203 or toll-free 800-55MONROE. *Fax:* 718-365-2363. *E-mail:* hleslie@monroecollege.edu.

MONROE COLLEGE

New Rochelle, NY

ABOUT THE INSTITUTION Proprietary, coed. 6 undergraduate majors.

GIFT AID (NEED-BASED) ***Scholarships, grants, and awards:*** Federal Pell, FSEOG, state, private, college/university gift aid from institutional funds, county scholarships.

LOANS ***Programs:*** Federal Direct (Subsidized and Unsubsidized Stafford, PLUS), state, college/university.

WORK-STUDY ***Federal work-study:*** Total amount: $194,355; 47 jobs averaging $2206.

APPLYING FOR FINANCIAL AID ***Required financial aid forms:*** FAFSA, state aid form.

CONTACT James Gathard, Vice President, Student Financial Services, Monroe College, 2501 Jerome Avenue, Bronx, NY 10468, 718-933-6700 Ext. 8236 or toll-free 800-55MONROE. *Fax:* 718-365-2365. *E-mail:* hleslie@monroecollege.edu.

MONTANA STATE UNIVERSITY

Bozeman, MT

Tuition & fees (MT res): $6168 **Average undergraduate aid package: $11,285**

ABOUT THE INSTITUTION State-supported, coed. 61 undergraduate majors. Federal methodology is used as a basis for awarding need-based institutional aid.

UNDERGRADUATE EXPENSES for 2010–11 ***Tuition, state resident:*** full-time $6168. ***Tuition, nonresident:*** full-time $18,291. Full-time tuition and fees vary according to course load and degree level. Part-time tuition and fees vary according to course load and degree level. ***College room and board:*** $7900. Room and board charges vary according to board plan and housing facility. ***Payment plans:*** Installment, deferred payment.

FRESHMAN FINANCIAL AID (Fall 2009) 1,303 applied for aid; of those 68% were deemed to have need. 98% of freshmen with need received aid; of those 6% had need fully met. ***Average percent of need met:*** 75% (excluding resources awarded to replace EFC). ***Average financial aid package:*** $11,242 (excluding resources awarded to replace EFC). 3% of all full-time freshmen had no need and received non-need-based gift aid.

UNDERGRADUATE FINANCIAL AID (Fall 2009) 5,874 applied for aid; of those 78% were deemed to have need. 98% of undergraduates with need received aid; of those 4% had need fully met. ***Average percent of need met:*** 74% (excluding resources awarded to replace EFC). ***Average financial aid package:*** $11,285 (excluding resources awarded to replace EFC). 4% of all full-time undergraduates had no need and received non-need-based gift aid.

GIFT AID (NEED-BASED) ***Total amount:*** $19,846,640 (68% federal, 5% state, 9% institutional, 18% external sources). ***Receiving aid:*** Freshmen: 37% (649); all full-time undergraduates: 36% (3,228). ***Average award:*** Freshmen: $5294; Undergraduates: $5213. ***Scholarships, grants, and awards:*** Federal Pell, FSEOG, state, private, college/university gift aid from institutional funds, Federal Nursing.

GIFT AID (NON-NEED-BASED) ***Total amount:*** $3,984,778 (4% state, 22% institutional, 74% external sources). ***Receiving aid:*** Freshmen: 3% (45). Undergraduates: 2% (143). ***Average award:*** Freshmen: $13,346. Undergraduates: $1645. ***Scholarships, grants, and awards by category:*** *Academic interests/achievement:* agriculture, architecture, area/ethnic studies, biological sciences, business, communication, computer science, education, engineering/technologies, English, foreign languages, general academic interests/achievements, health fields, home economics, humanities, mathematics, military science, physical sciences, social sciences. *Creative arts/performance:* art/fine arts, cinema/film/broadcasting, dance, music, theater/drama. *Special achievements/activities:* general special achievements/activities, leadership. *Special characteristics:* children and siblings of alumni, general special characteristics, local/state students, members of minority groups. ***Tuition waivers:*** Full or partial for minority students, employees or children of employees, senior citizens.

LOANS ***Student loans:*** $41,535,846 (76% need-based, 24% non-need-based). 62% of past graduating class borrowed through all loan programs. *Average indebtedness per student:* $24,420. ***Average need-based loan:*** Freshmen: $3543. Undergraduates: $4200. ***Parent loans:*** $9,678,456 (33% need-based, 67% non-need-based). ***Programs:*** Federal Direct (Subsidized and Unsubsidized Stafford, PLUS), Perkins, Federal Nursing, college/university.

WORK-STUDY ***Federal work-study:*** Total amount: $524,435; jobs available. ***State or other work-study/employment:*** Total amount: $154,505 (100% need-based). Part-time jobs available.

ATHLETIC AWARDS Total amount: $1,377,274 (39% need-based, 61% non-need-based).

APPLYING FOR FINANCIAL AID ***Required financial aid form:*** FAFSA. ***Financial aid deadline (priority):*** 3/1. ***Notification date:*** Continuous beginning 4/1.

CONTACT Brandi Payne, Director of Financial Aid, Montana State University, Bozeman, MT 59717, 406-994-2845 or toll-free 888-MSU-CATS. *Fax:* 406-994-1893. *E-mail:* bpayne@montana.edu.

MONTANA STATE UNIVERSITY BILLINGS

Billings, MT

Tuition & fees (MT res): $5242 **Average undergraduate aid package: $9529**

ABOUT THE INSTITUTION State-supported, coed. 70 undergraduate majors. Federal methodology is used as a basis for awarding need-based institutional aid.

UNDERGRADUATE EXPENSES for 2010–11 ***Tuition, state resident:*** full-time $3988; part-time $146 per credit hour. ***Tuition, nonresident:*** full-time $15,235; part-time $423 per credit hour. ***Required fees:*** full-time $1254. Full-time tuition and fees vary according to course load, degree level, and location. Part-time tuition and fees vary according to course load, degree level, and location. ***College room and board:*** $5620. Room and board charges vary according to board plan and housing facility. ***Payment plan:*** Installment.

FRESHMAN FINANCIAL AID (Fall 2009) 588 applied for aid; of those 81% were deemed to have need. 97% of freshmen with need received aid; of those 3% had need fully met. ***Average percent of need met:*** 65% (excluding resources awarded to replace EFC). ***Average financial aid package:*** $8587 (excluding resources awarded to replace EFC). 3% of all full-time freshmen had no need and received non-need-based gift aid.

UNDERGRADUATE FINANCIAL AID (Fall 2009) 2,447 applied for aid; of those 83% were deemed to have need. 96% of undergraduates with need received aid; of those 2% had need fully met. ***Average percent of need met:*** 70% (excluding resources awarded to replace EFC). ***Average financial aid package:*** $9529 (excluding resources awarded to replace EFC). 3% of all full-time undergraduates had no need and received non-need-based gift aid.

GIFT AID (NEED-BASED) ***Total amount:*** $9,367,296 (76% federal, 3% state, 15% institutional, 6% external sources). ***Receiving aid:*** Freshmen: 53% (389); all full-time undergraduates: 48% (1,557). ***Average award:*** Freshmen: $4589; Undergraduates: $4935. ***Scholarships, grants, and awards:*** Federal Pell, FSEOG, state, private, college/university gift aid from institutional funds.

GIFT AID (NON-NEED-BASED) ***Total amount:*** $389,062 (8% state, 53% institutional, 39% external sources). ***Receiving aid:*** Freshmen: 1% (11). Undergraduates: 1% (31). ***Average award:*** Freshmen: $2086. Undergraduates: $2122. ***Scholarships, grants, and awards by category:*** *Academic interests/achievement:* biological sciences, business, communication, computer science, education, engineering/technologies, English, foreign languages, general academic interests/achievements, health fields, humanities, mathematics, physical sciences, premedicine, social sciences. *Creative arts/performance:* art/fine arts, music, theater/drama. *Special achievements/activities:* cheerleading/drum major, general special achievements/activities. *Special characteristics:* adult students, children and siblings of alumni, children of faculty/staff, children of union members/company employees, ethnic background, first-generation college students, local/state students, members of minority groups, out-of-state students, veterans. ***Tuition waivers:*** Full or partial for employees or children of employees, senior citizens.

LOANS ***Student loans:*** $21,578,900 (44% need-based, 56% non-need-based). 74% of past graduating class borrowed through all loan programs. *Average indebtedness per student:* $24,026. ***Average need-based loan:*** Freshmen: $2855. Undergraduates: $3465. ***Parent loans:*** $857,711 (23% need-based, 77% non-need-based). ***Programs:*** Federal Direct (Subsidized and Unsubsidized Stafford, PLUS), Perkins.

WORK-STUDY ***Federal work-study:*** Total amount: $278,634; 208 jobs averaging $1340. ***State or other work-study/employment:*** Total amount: $64,727 (95% need-based, 5% non-need-based). 57 part-time jobs averaging $1136.

ATHLETIC AWARDS Total amount: $1,281,843 (60% need-based, 40% non-need-based).

APPLYING FOR FINANCIAL AID ***Required financial aid form:*** FAFSA. ***Financial aid deadline (priority):*** 3/1. ***Notification date:*** Continuous beginning 4/1. Students must reply within 3 weeks of notification.

CONTACT Ms. Judy Chapman, Director of Financial Aid, Montana State University Billings, 1500 University Drive, Billings, MT 59101, 406-657-2188 or toll-free 800-565-6782. *Fax:* 406-657-1789. *E-mail:* jchapman@msubillings.edu.

MONTANA STATE UNIVERSITY–NORTHERN

Havre, MT

Tuition & fees (MT res): $4476 **Average undergraduate aid package: $9993**

ABOUT THE INSTITUTION State-supported, coed. ***Awards:*** associate, bachelor's, and master's degrees. 27 undergraduate majors. ***Total enrollment:*** 1,215. Undergraduates: 1,143. Federal methodology is used as a basis for awarding need-based institutional aid.

UNDERGRADUATE EXPENSES for 2010–11 ***Application fee:*** $30. ***Tuition, state resident:*** full-time $4476. ***Tuition, nonresident:*** full-time $15,224. Full-time tuition and fees vary according to course level, course load, degree level, location, reciprocity agreements, and student level. Part-time tuition and fees vary according to course level, course load, degree level, location, reciprocity agreements, and student level. ***College room and board:*** $6461. Room and board charges vary according to board plan. ***Payment plan:*** Deferred payment.

FRESHMAN FINANCIAL AID (Fall 2009) 219 applied for aid; of those 85% were deemed to have need. 97% of freshmen with need received aid; of those 5% had need fully met. ***Average percent of need met:*** 61% (excluding resources awarded to replace EFC). ***Average financial aid package:*** $8985 (excluding resources awarded to replace EFC). 4% of all full-time freshmen had no need and received non-need-based gift aid.

UNDERGRADUATE FINANCIAL AID (Fall 2009) 792 applied for aid; of those 88% were deemed to have need. 98% of undergraduates with need received aid; of those 3% had need fully met. ***Average percent of need met:*** 61% (excluding resources awarded to replace EFC). ***Average financial aid package:*** $9993 (excluding resources awarded to replace EFC). 4% of all full-time undergraduates had no need and received non-need-based gift aid.

GIFT AID (NEED-BASED) ***Total amount:*** $3,435,927 (74% federal, 7% state, 1% institutional, 18% external sources). ***Receiving aid:*** Freshmen: 71% (167); all full-time undergraduates: 66% (602). ***Average award:*** Freshmen: $4793;

Undergraduates: $5043. ***Scholarships, grants, and awards:*** Federal Pell, FSEOG, state, private, college/university gift aid from institutional funds.

GIFT AID (NON-NEED-BASED) ***Receiving aid:*** Freshmen: 2% (4). Undergraduates: 1% (8). ***Average award:*** Freshmen: $1750. Undergraduates: $1183. ***Scholarships, grants, and awards by category:*** *Academic interests/achievement:* agriculture, architecture, biological sciences, business, computer science, education, engineering/technologies, English, foreign languages, general academic interests/achievements, health fields, humanities, social sciences. *Creative arts/performance:* art/fine arts. *Special achievements/activities:* community service, general special achievements/activities, hobbies/interests, memberships, rodeo. *Special characteristics:* adult students, children and siblings of alumni, general special characteristics, international students, members of minority groups, out-of-state students, veterans. ***Tuition waivers:*** Full or partial for minority students, employees or children of employees, senior citizens.

LOANS ***Student loans:*** $3,180,586 (100% need-based). 72% of past graduating class borrowed through all loan programs. *Average indebtedness per student:* $18,604. ***Average need-based loan:*** Freshmen: $3103. Undergraduates: $3813. ***Parent loans:*** $25,873 (100% need-based). ***Programs:*** Perkins, Federal Nursing, college/university, alternative loans.

WORK-STUDY ***Federal work-study:*** Total amount: $94,539; jobs available. ***State or other work-study/employment:*** Total amount: $96,959 (100% need-based). Part-time jobs available.

ATHLETIC AWARDS Total amount: $55,519 (100% need-based).

APPLYING FOR FINANCIAL AID ***Required financial aid form:*** FAFSA. ***Financial aid deadline (priority):*** 4/15. ***Notification date:*** Continuous beginning 4/1. Students must reply within 3 weeks of notification.

CONTACT Cindy Small, Director of Financial Aid, Montana State University–Northern, PO Box 7751, Havre, MT 59501, 406-265-3787 or toll-free 800-662-6132 (in-state).

MONTANA TECH OF THE UNIVERSITY OF MONTANA

Butte, MT

Tuition & fees (MT res): $6162 **Average undergraduate aid package: $9391**

ABOUT THE INSTITUTION State-supported, coed. 34 undergraduate majors. Federal methodology is used as a basis for awarding need-based institutional aid.

UNDERGRADUATE EXPENSES for 2010–11 ***Tuition, state resident:*** full-time $4696; part-time $262 per credit. ***Tuition, nonresident:*** full-time $15,819; part-time $725 per credit. ***Required fees:*** full-time $1466. Full-time tuition and fees vary according to course load, degree level, location, program, and student level. Part-time tuition and fees vary according to course load, degree level, location, program, and student level. ***College room and board:*** $6924; ***Room only:*** $3084. Room and board charges vary according to board plan. ***Payment plans:*** Installment, deferred payment.

FRESHMAN FINANCIAL AID (Fall 2009) 413 applied for aid; of those 74% were deemed to have need. 100% of freshmen with need received aid; of those 25% had need fully met. ***Average percent of need met:*** 75% (excluding resources awarded to replace EFC). ***Average financial aid package:*** $8007 (excluding resources awarded to replace EFC). 16% of all full-time freshmen had no need and received non-need-based gift aid.

UNDERGRADUATE FINANCIAL AID (Fall 2009) 1,539 applied for aid; of those 79% were deemed to have need. 100% of undergraduates with need received aid; of those 28% had need fully met. ***Average percent of need met:*** 81% (excluding resources awarded to replace EFC). ***Average financial aid package:*** $9391 (excluding resources awarded to replace EFC). 14% of all full-time undergraduates had no need and received non-need-based gift aid.

GIFT AID (NEED-BASED) ***Total amount:*** $5,627,095 (64% federal, 7% state, 22% institutional, 7% external sources). ***Receiving aid:*** Freshmen: 58% (283); all full-time undergraduates: 50% (1,085). ***Average award:*** Freshmen: $4641; Undergraduates: $4891. ***Scholarships, grants, and awards:*** Federal Pell, FSEOG, state, private, college/university gift aid from institutional funds.

GIFT AID (NON-NEED-BASED) ***Total amount:*** $1,262,818 (7% state, 70% institutional, 23% external sources). ***Receiving aid:*** Freshmen: 7% (35). Undergraduates: 4% (83). ***Average award:*** Freshmen: $2506. Undergraduates: $2353. ***Scholarships, grants, and awards by category:*** *Academic interests/achievement:* business, computer science, engineering/technologies, general academic interests/achievements, health fields, mathematics, physical sciences. *Special achievements/activities:* community service, general special achievements/activities. *Special characteristics:* children and siblings of alumni, children of faculty/staff, general special characteristics, local/state students, married students, out-of-state students, veterans. ***Tuition waivers:*** Full or partial for employees or children of employees.

LOANS ***Student loans:*** $7,896,753 (73% need-based, 27% non-need-based). 87% of past graduating class borrowed through all loan programs. *Average indebtedness per student:* $23,000. ***Average need-based loan:*** Freshmen: $2753. Undergraduates: $3362. ***Parent loans:*** $492,306 (18% need-based, 82% non-need-based). ***Programs:*** Federal Direct (Subsidized and Unsubsidized Stafford, PLUS), Perkins, college/university.

WORK-STUDY ***Federal work-study:*** Total amount: $125,800; jobs available. ***State or other work-study/employment:*** Total amount: $3043 (100% need-based). Part-time jobs available.

ATHLETIC AWARDS Total amount: $671,962 (40% need-based, 60% non-need-based).

APPLYING FOR FINANCIAL AID ***Required financial aid forms:*** FAFSA, institution's own form. ***Financial aid deadline (priority):*** 3/1. ***Notification date:*** Continuous beginning 4/1. Students must reply within 2 weeks of notification.

CONTACT Mike Richardson, Director of Financial Aid, Montana Tech of The University of Montana, West Park Street, Butte, MT 59701-8997, 406-496-4256 or toll-free 800-445-TECH Ext. 1. *Fax:* 406-496-4710. *E-mail:* mrichardson@mtech.edu.

MONTCLAIR STATE UNIVERSITY

Montclair, NJ

Tuition & fees (NJ res): $7324 **Average undergraduate aid package: $9051**

ABOUT THE INSTITUTION State-supported, coed. 53 undergraduate majors. Federal methodology is used as a basis for awarding need-based institutional aid.

UNDERGRADUATE EXPENSES for 2010–11 ***Tuition, state resident:*** full-time $7324; part-time $244.12 per credit. ***Tuition, nonresident:*** full-time $15,656; part-time $521.75 per credit. ***Required fees:*** $155.32 per credit. ***College room and board:*** $10,712; ***Room only:*** $7442. Room and board charges vary according to board plan and housing facility. ***Payment plan:*** Installment.

FRESHMAN FINANCIAL AID (Fall 2009) 1,443 applied for aid; of those 80% were deemed to have need. 96% of freshmen with need received aid; of those 18% had need fully met. ***Average percent of need met:*** 64% (excluding resources awarded to replace EFC). ***Average financial aid package:*** $7835 (excluding resources awarded to replace EFC). 2% of all full-time freshmen had no need and received non-need-based gift aid.

UNDERGRADUATE FINANCIAL AID (Fall 2009) 8,386 applied for aid; of those 86% were deemed to have need. 97% of undergraduates with need received aid; of those 19% had need fully met. ***Average percent of need met:*** 73% (excluding resources awarded to replace EFC). ***Average financial aid package:*** $9051 (excluding resources awarded to replace EFC). 2% of all full-time undergraduates had no need and received non-need-based gift aid.

GIFT AID (NEED-BASED) ***Total amount:*** $37,741,017 (54% federal, 46% state). ***Receiving aid:*** Freshmen: 25% (515); all full-time undergraduates: 31% (3,754). ***Average award:*** Freshmen: $8909; Undergraduates: $8583. ***Scholarships, grants, and awards:*** Federal Pell, FSEOG, state, college/university gift aid from institutional funds.

GIFT AID (NON-NEED-BASED) ***Total amount:*** $6,489,978 (15% state, 76% institutional, 9% external sources). ***Receiving aid:*** Freshmen: 12% (244). Undergraduates: 8% (1,020). ***Average award:*** Freshmen: $7740. Undergraduates: $6253. ***Scholarships, grants, and awards by category:*** *Academic interests/achievement:* biological sciences, business, communication, education, English, foreign languages, general academic interests/achievements, home economics, humanities, international studies, mathematics, physical sciences, religion/biblical studies, social sciences. *Creative arts/performance:* art/fine arts, cinema/film/broadcasting, dance, music, performing arts, theater/drama. *Special achievements/activities:* community service, general special achievements/activities, leadership. *Special characteristics:* children and siblings of alumni, international students. ***Tuition waivers:*** Full or partial for employees or children of employees, senior citizens.

LOANS ***Student loans:*** $89,645,936 (42% need-based, 58% non-need-based). *Average indebtedness per student:* $18,805. ***Average need-based loan:*** Freshmen: $3370. Undergraduates: $4398. ***Parent loans:*** $7,539,551 (100% non-need-based). ***Programs:*** Perkins, state, private loans.

WORK-STUDY ***Federal work-study:*** Total amount: $710,156; jobs available. ***State or other work-study/employment:*** Total amount: $3,955,497 (100% non-need-based). Part-time jobs available.

APPLYING FOR FINANCIAL AID ***Required financial aid form:*** FAFSA. ***Financial aid deadline (priority):*** 3/1. ***Notification date:*** Continuous beginning 4/1. Students must reply within 2 weeks of notification.

CONTACT James T. Anderson, Director of Financial Aid, Montclair State University, College Hall, Room 222, Montclair, NJ 07043, 973-655-7022 or toll-free 800-331-9205. *Fax:* 973-655-7712. *E-mail:* financialaid@montclair.edu.

MONTREAT COLLEGE

Montreat, NC

Tuition & fees: $23,164 **Average undergraduate aid package: $11,664**

ABOUT THE INSTITUTION Independent religious, coed. 19 undergraduate majors. Federal methodology is used as a basis for awarding need-based institutional aid.

UNDERGRADUATE EXPENSES for 2011–12 ***Comprehensive fee:*** $30,510 includes full-time tuition ($22,684), mandatory fees ($480), and room and board ($7346). Full-time tuition and fees vary according to course load, program, and reciprocity agreements. Room and board charges vary according to board plan. ***Part-time tuition:*** $600 per credit. Part-time tuition and fees vary according to course load, program, and reciprocity agreements. ***Payment plan:*** Installment.

FRESHMAN FINANCIAL AID (Fall 2010, est.) 98 applied for aid; of those 96% were deemed to have need. 100% of freshmen with need received aid; of those 12% had need fully met. ***Average percent of need met:*** 80% (excluding resources awarded to replace EFC). ***Average financial aid package:*** $19,268 (excluding resources awarded to replace EFC).

UNDERGRADUATE FINANCIAL AID (Fall 2010, est.) 745 applied for aid; of those 92% were deemed to have need. 99% of undergraduates with need received aid; of those 14% had need fully met. ***Average percent of need met:*** 69% (excluding resources awarded to replace EFC). ***Average financial aid package:*** $11,664 (excluding resources awarded to replace EFC).

GIFT AID (NEED-BASED) ***Total amount:*** $5,803,153 (40% federal, 16% state, 44% institutional). ***Receiving aid:*** Freshmen: 88% (94); all full-time undergraduates: 85% (679). ***Scholarships, grants, and awards:*** Federal Pell, FSEOG, state, private, college/university gift aid from institutional funds.

GIFT AID (NON-NEED-BASED) ***Total amount:*** $5,724,350 (12% state, 20% institutional, 68% external sources). ***Receiving aid:*** Freshmen: 68% (73). Undergraduates: 77% (616). ***Scholarships, grants, and awards by category:*** *Academic interests/achievement:* general academic interests/achievements. *Creative arts/performance:* music. *Special achievements/activities:* leadership. *Special characteristics:* children of faculty/staff, first-generation college students, international students, local/state students, relatives of clergy, religious affiliation, veterans, veterans' children. ***Tuition waivers:*** Full or partial for employees or children of employees.

LOANS ***Student loans:*** $7,195,385 (46% need-based, 54% non-need-based). ***Average need-based loan:*** Freshmen: $3785. Undergraduates: $4446. ***Programs:*** Federal Direct (Subsidized and Unsubsidized Stafford, PLUS), Perkins.

WORK-STUDY ***Federal work-study:*** Total amount: $412,297; jobs available. ***State or other work-study/employment:*** Total amount: $279,201 (100% non-need-based). Part-time jobs available.

ATHLETIC AWARDS Total amount: $906,216 (100% non-need-based).

APPLYING FOR FINANCIAL AID ***Required financial aid forms:*** FAFSA, state aid form. ***Financial aid deadline (priority):*** 4/1. ***Notification date:*** Continuous beginning 4/1. Students must reply within 2 weeks of notification.

CONTACT Kim Norton, Director of Financial Aid, Montreat College, PO Box 1267, Montreat, NC 28757, 828-669-8012 Ext. 3795 or toll-free 800-622-6968 (in-state). *Fax:* 828-669-0120. *E-mail:* financialaid@montreat.edu.

MONTSERRAT COLLEGE OF ART

Beverly, MA

CONTACT Creda Carney, Director of Financial Aid, Montserrat College of Art, 23 Essex Street, PO Box 26, Beverly, MA 01915, 978-922-8222 Ext. 1155 or toll-free 800-836-0487. *Fax:* 978-922-4268. *E-mail:* finaid@montserrat.edu.

MOODY BIBLE INSTITUTE

Chicago, IL

ABOUT THE INSTITUTION Independent nondenominational, coed. 8 undergraduate majors.

GIFT AID (NEED-BASED) ***Scholarships, grants, and awards:*** private, college/university gift aid from institutional funds.

LOANS ***Programs:*** alternative loans.

APPLYING FOR FINANCIAL AID ***Required financial aid form:*** institution's own form.

CONTACT Esther Kim, Director of Financial Aid, Moody Bible Institute, 820 North LaSalle Boulevard, Chicago, IL 60610-3284, 312-329-4178 or toll-free 800-967-4MBI. *Fax:* 312-329-4197. *E-mail:* esther.kim@moody.edu.

MOORE COLLEGE OF ART & DESIGN

Philadelphia, PA

CONTACT Kristina Fripps, Director of Financial Aid, Moore College of Art & Design, 20th and the Parkway, Philadelphia, PA 19103-1179, 215-965-4042 or toll-free 800-523-2025. *Fax:* 215-568-1773. *E-mail:* kfripps@moore.edu.

MORAVIAN COLLEGE

Bethlehem, PA

Tuition & fees: $32,177 **Average undergraduate aid package: $24,190**

ABOUT THE INSTITUTION Independent religious, coed. 61 undergraduate majors. Both federal and institutional methodology are used as a basis for awarding need-based institutional aid.

UNDERGRADUATE EXPENSES for 2010–11 ***Comprehensive fee:*** $41,341 includes full-time tuition ($31,662), mandatory fees ($515), and room and board ($9164). ***College room only:*** $5149. Room and board charges vary according to board plan and housing facility. ***Part-time tuition:*** $879.50 per credit hour. Part-time tuition and fees vary according to class time. ***Payment plan:*** Installment.

FRESHMAN FINANCIAL AID (Fall 2010, est.) 344 applied for aid; of those 89% were deemed to have need. 100% of freshmen with need received aid; of those 18% had need fully met. ***Average percent of need met:*** 76% (excluding resources awarded to replace EFC). ***Average financial aid package:*** $24,203 (excluding resources awarded to replace EFC). 14% of all full-time freshmen had no need and received non-need-based gift aid.

UNDERGRADUATE FINANCIAL AID (Fall 2010, est.) 1,337 applied for aid; of those 91% were deemed to have need. 100% of undergraduates with need received aid; of those 15% had need fully met. ***Average percent of need met:*** 75% (excluding resources awarded to replace EFC). ***Average financial aid package:*** $24,190 (excluding resources awarded to replace EFC). 13% of all full-time undergraduates had no need and received non-need-based gift aid.

GIFT AID (NEED-BASED) ***Total amount:*** $21,846,929 (13% federal, 7% state, 78% institutional, 2% external sources). ***Receiving aid:*** Freshmen: 82% (307); all full-time undergraduates: 81% (1,214). ***Average award:*** Freshmen: $18,843; Undergraduates: $18,231. ***Scholarships, grants, and awards:*** Federal Pell, FSEOG, state, private, college/university gift aid from institutional funds.

GIFT AID (NON-NEED-BASED) ***Total amount:*** $2,917,934 (3% federal, 88% institutional, 9% external sources). ***Receiving aid:*** Freshmen: 9% (33). Undergraduates: 7% (111). ***Average award:*** Freshmen: $11,722. Undergraduates: $10,131. ***Scholarships, grants, and awards by category:*** *Academic interests/achievement:* 1,473 awards ($9,673,115 total): biological sciences, business, computer science, foreign languages, general academic interests/achievements, health fields, mathematics, physical sciences. *Creative arts/performance:* 15 awards ($38,775 total): music. *Special achievements/activities:* 77 awards ($102,500 total): leadership, religious involvement. *Special characteristics:* 471 awards ($2,320,056 total): adult students, children and siblings of alumni, children of educators, children of faculty/staff, ethnic background, first-generation college students, international students, relatives of clergy, religious affiliation. ***Tuition waivers:*** Full or partial for employees or children of employees.

LOANS ***Student loans:*** $13,726,556 (70% need-based, 30% non-need-based). ***Average need-based loan:*** Freshmen: $3851. Undergraduates: $4819. ***Parent loans:*** $4,589,019 (38% need-based, 62% non-need-based). ***Programs:*** Federal Direct (Subsidized and Unsubsidized Stafford, PLUS), Perkins.

WORK-STUDY ***Federal work-study:*** Total amount: $2,004,500; 1,047 jobs averaging $1916. ***State or other work-study/employment:*** Total amount: $330,396 (4% need-based, 96% non-need-based). 268 part-time jobs averaging $1257.

APPLYING FOR FINANCIAL AID ***Required financial aid forms:*** FAFSA, institution's own form, state aid form, business/farm supplement. ***Financial aid deadline (priority):*** 2/14. ***Notification date:*** 3/31. Students must reply by 5/1 or within 2 weeks of notification.

CONTACT Mrs. Colby T. McCarthy, Director of Financial Aid, Moravian College, 1200 Main Street, Bethlehem, PA 18018-6650, 610-861-1330 or toll-free 800-441-3191. *Fax:* 610-861-1346. *E-mail:* cmccarthy@moravian.edu.

MOREHEAD STATE UNIVERSITY

Morehead, KY

Tuition & fees (KY res): $6492 **Average undergraduate aid package: $9624**

ABOUT THE INSTITUTION State-supported, coed. 49 undergraduate majors. Federal methodology is used as a basis for awarding need-based institutional aid.

UNDERGRADUATE EXPENSES for 2010–11 ***Tuition, state resident:*** full-time $6492; part-time $246 per credit hour. ***Tuition, nonresident:*** full-time $16,236; part-time $615 per credit hour. Full-time tuition and fees vary according to course level, course load, location, reciprocity agreements, and student level. Part-time tuition and fees vary according to course level, course load, location, and student level. ***College room and board:*** $6582. Room and board charges vary according to board plan and housing facility. ***Payment plan:*** Installment.

FRESHMAN FINANCIAL AID (Fall 2010, est.) 1,078 applied for aid; of those 85% were deemed to have need. 100% of freshmen with need received aid; of those 26% had need fully met. ***Average percent of need met:*** 67% (excluding resources awarded to replace EFC). ***Average financial aid package:*** $9490 (excluding resources awarded to replace EFC). 9% of all full-time freshmen had no need and received non-need-based gift aid.

UNDERGRADUATE FINANCIAL AID (Fall 2010, est.) 4,645 applied for aid; of those 88% were deemed to have need. 99% of undergraduates with need received aid; of those 29% had need fully met. ***Average percent of need met:*** 68% (excluding resources awarded to replace EFC). ***Average financial aid package:*** $9624 (excluding resources awarded to replace EFC). 11% of all full-time undergraduates had no need and received non-need-based gift aid.

GIFT AID (NEED-BASED) ***Total amount:*** $17,084,763 (86% federal, 13% state, 1% institutional). ***Receiving aid:*** Freshmen: 52% (600); all full-time undergraduates: 53% (2,866). ***Average award:*** Freshmen: $5093; Undergraduates: $5178. ***Scholarships, grants, and awards:*** Federal Pell, FSEOG, state, private, college/university gift aid from institutional funds.

GIFT AID (NON-NEED-BASED) ***Total amount:*** $16,517,605 (26% state, 66% institutional, 8% external sources). ***Receiving aid:*** Freshmen: 71% (829). Undergraduates: 56% (3,029). ***Average award:*** Freshmen: $6676. Undergraduates: $6865. ***Scholarships, grants, and awards by category:*** *Academic interests/achievement:* 952 awards ($6,338,799 total): agriculture, biological sciences, business, communication, education, engineering/technologies, general academic interests/achievements, health fields, international studies, military science, physical sciences, social sciences. *Creative arts/performance:* 119 awards ($152,349 total): applied art and design, debating, journalism/publications, music, theater/drama. *Special achievements/activities:* 86 awards ($90,392 total): cheerleading/drum major, general special achievements/activities, junior miss, leadership. *Special characteristics:* 959 awards ($4,341,301 total): children and siblings of alumni, international students, local/state students, members of minority groups, out-of-state students, veterans. ***Tuition waivers:*** Full or partial for children of alumni, employees or children of employees, senior citizens.

LOANS ***Student loans:*** $27,751,580 (47% need-based, 53% non-need-based). 66% of past graduating class borrowed through all loan programs. *Average indebtedness per student:* $25,182. ***Average need-based loan:*** Freshmen: $2960. Undergraduates: $3755. ***Parent loans:*** $2,086,091 (100% non-need-based). ***Programs:*** Federal Direct (Subsidized and Unsubsidized Stafford, PLUS), Perkins, college/university.

WORK-STUDY ***Federal work-study:*** Total amount: $824,761; 381 jobs averaging $2166. ***State or other work-study/employment:*** Total amount: $1,624,919 (100% non-need-based). 716 part-time jobs averaging $2239.

ATHLETIC AWARDS Total amount: $1,879,268 (100% non-need-based).

APPLYING FOR FINANCIAL AID ***Required financial aid forms:*** FAFSA, institution's own form. ***Financial aid deadline (priority):*** 3/15. ***Notification date:*** Continuous.

CONTACT Donna King, Director of Financial Aid, Morehead State University, 100 Admissions Center, Morehead, KY 40351, 606-783-2000 or toll-free 800-585-6781. *Fax:* 606-783-2293. *E-mail:* d.king@moreheadstate.edu.

MOREHOUSE COLLEGE

Atlanta, GA

Tuition & fees: $22,444 **Average undergraduate aid package: $13,250**

ABOUT THE INSTITUTION Independent, men only. 27 undergraduate majors. Both federal and institutional methodology are used as a basis for awarding need-based institutional aid.

UNDERGRADUATE EXPENSES for 2010–11 ***Comprehensive fee:*** $33,938 includes full-time tuition ($20,394), mandatory fees ($2050), and room and board ($11,494). ***College room only:*** $6550. Full-time tuition and fees vary according to course load and student level. Room and board charges vary according to board plan. ***Part-time tuition:*** $850 per credit hour. ***Part-time fees:*** $1025 per term. Part-time tuition and fees vary according to course load.

FRESHMAN FINANCIAL AID (Fall 2010, est.) 512 applied for aid; of those 100% were deemed to have need. 100% of freshmen with need received aid; of those 8% had need fully met. ***Average percent of need met:*** 25% (excluding resources awarded to replace EFC). ***Average financial aid package:*** $11,250 (excluding resources awarded to replace EFC).

UNDERGRADUATE FINANCIAL AID (Fall 2010, est.) 2,393 applied for aid; of those 100% were deemed to have need. 100% of undergraduates with need received aid; of those 7% had need fully met. ***Average percent of need met:*** 59% (excluding resources awarded to replace EFC). ***Average financial aid package:*** $13,250 (excluding resources awarded to replace EFC).

GIFT AID (NEED-BASED) ***Total amount:*** $6,650,408 (99% federal, 1% state). ***Receiving aid:*** Freshmen: 62% (327); all full-time undergraduates: 56% (1,353). ***Average award:*** Freshmen: $7500; Undergraduates: $10,000. ***Scholarships, grants, and awards:*** Federal Pell, FSEOG, state, private, college/university gift aid from institutional funds, United Negro College Fund.

GIFT AID (NON-NEED-BASED) ***Total amount:*** $13,522,275 (8% state, 81% institutional, 11% external sources). ***Receiving aid:*** Freshmen: 31% (166). Undergraduates: 25% (607). ***Scholarships, grants, and awards by category:*** *Academic interests/achievement:* business, general academic interests/achievements, military science. *Creative arts/performance:* art/fine arts, music. *Special achievements/activities:* community service, leadership, religious involvement. *Special characteristics:* children and siblings of alumni, children of faculty/staff, local/state students. ***Tuition waivers:*** Full or partial for employees or children of employees.

LOANS ***Student loans:*** $18,650,612 (84% need-based, 16% non-need-based). ***Average need-based loan:*** Freshmen: $3500. Undergraduates: $5500. ***Parent loans:*** $21,031,597 (100% non-need-based). ***Programs:*** Federal Direct (Subsidized and Unsubsidized Stafford, PLUS), Perkins, state, college/university.

WORK-STUDY ***Federal work-study:*** Total amount: $546,150; jobs available. ***State or other work-study/employment:*** Total amount: $120,407 (100% non-need-based). Part-time jobs available.

ATHLETIC AWARDS Total amount: $1,548,110 (100% non-need-based).

APPLYING FOR FINANCIAL AID ***Required financial aid forms:*** FAFSA, institution's own form, CSS Financial Aid PROFILE, state aid form. ***Financial aid deadline:*** 4/1 (priority: 2/15). ***Notification date:*** Continuous beginning 3/18. Students must reply by 5/1 or within 4 weeks of notification.

CONTACT James A. Stotts, Associate Vice President of Financial Aid, Morehouse College, 830 Westview Drive, SW, Atlanta, GA 30314, 404-215-2639 or toll-free 800-851-1254. *Fax:* 404-215-2711. *E-mail:* jstotts@morehouse.edu.

MORGAN STATE UNIVERSITY

Baltimore, MD

CONTACT Director of Financial Aid, Morgan State University, 1700 East Cold Spring Lane, Baltimore, MD 21251, 443-885-3170 or toll-free 800-332-6674.

MORNINGSIDE COLLEGE

Sioux City, IA

Tuition & fees: $23,984 **Average undergraduate aid package: $20,326**

ABOUT THE INSTITUTION Independent religious, coed. 45 undergraduate majors. Federal methodology is used as a basis for awarding need-based institutional aid.

UNDERGRADUATE EXPENSES for 2011–12 ***Comprehensive fee:*** $31,348 includes full-time tuition ($22,814), mandatory fees ($1170), and room and board ($7364). ***College room only:*** $3776. Full-time tuition and fees vary according to degree level, program, and student level. Room and board charges vary according to housing facility. Part-time tuition and fees vary according to course load and degree level. ***Payment plan:*** Installment.

FRESHMAN FINANCIAL AID (Fall 2010, est.) 330 applied for aid; of those 93% were deemed to have need. 100% of freshmen with need received aid; of those 29% had need fully met. ***Average percent of need met:*** 83% (excluding resources awarded to replace EFC). ***Average financial aid package:*** $21,170 (excluding resources awarded to replace EFC). 10% of all full-time freshmen had no need and received non-need-based gift aid.

UNDERGRADUATE FINANCIAL AID (Fall 2010, est.) 1,124 applied for aid; of those 93% were deemed to have need. 100% of undergraduates with need received aid; of those 26% had need fully met. ***Average percent of need met:*** 80% (excluding resources awarded to replace EFC). ***Average financial aid package:*** $20,326 (excluding resources awarded to replace EFC). 12% of all full-time undergraduates had no need and received non-need-based gift aid.

GIFT AID (NEED-BASED) ***Total amount:*** $5,380,743 (42% federal, 33% state, 25% institutional). ***Receiving aid:*** Freshmen: 72% (248); all full-time undergraduates: 67% (804). ***Average award:*** Freshmen: $6633; Undergraduates: $6714. ***Scholarships, grants, and awards:*** Federal Pell, FSEOG, state, private, college/university gift aid from institutional funds.

GIFT AID (NON-NEED-BASED) ***Total amount:*** $9,580,589 (4% federal, 1% state, 89% institutional, 6% external sources). ***Receiving aid:*** Freshmen: 89% (306). Undergraduates: 86% (1,026). ***Average award:*** Freshmen: $10,031. Undergraduates: $9488. ***Scholarships, grants, and awards by category:*** *Academic interests/achievement:* $3,952,657 total: computer science, general academic interests/achievements. *Creative arts/performance:* $1,384,418 total: art/fine arts, cinema/film/broadcasting, creative writing, dance, journalism/publications, music, theater/drama. *Special achievements/activities:* $788,017 total: cheerleading/drum major, community service, leadership. *Special characteristics:* $1,956,538 total: children and siblings of alumni, children of faculty/staff, international students, out-of-state students, religious affiliation. ***Tuition waivers:*** Full or partial for children of alumni, employees or children of employees, senior citizens.

LOANS ***Student loans:*** $8,711,577 (44% need-based, 56% non-need-based). 89% of past graduating class borrowed through all loan programs. *Average indebtedness per student:* $38,411. ***Average need-based loan:*** Freshmen: $3730. Undergraduates: $4414. ***Parent loans:*** $1,484,561 (100% non-need-based). ***Programs:*** Federal Direct (Subsidized and Unsubsidized Stafford, PLUS), Perkins, college/university, private loans.

WORK-STUDY ***Federal work-study:*** Total amount: $894,815; 663 jobs averaging $1350. ***State or other work-study/employment:*** Total amount: $578,918 (100% non-need-based). 432 part-time jobs averaging $1446.

ATHLETIC AWARDS Total amount: $2,030,150 (100% non-need-based).

APPLYING FOR FINANCIAL AID ***Required financial aid form:*** FAFSA. ***Financial aid deadline (priority):*** 3/1. ***Notification date:*** 3/15.

CONTACT Karen Gagnon, Director of Student Financial Planning, Morningside College, 1501 Morningside Avenue, Sioux City, IA 51106, 712-274-5272 or toll-free 800-831-0806 Ext. 5111. *Fax:* 712-274-5605. *E-mail:* gagnon@morningside.edu.

MORRIS COLLEGE

Sumter, SC

CONTACT Ms. Sandra S. Gibson, Director of Financial Aid, Morris College, 100 West College Street, Sumter, SC 29150-3599, 803-934-3238 or toll-free 866-853-1345. *Fax:* 803-773-3687.

MORRISON UNIVERSITY

Reno, NV

CONTACT Kim Droniak, Financial Aid Administrator, Morrison University, 140 Washington Street, Reno, NV 89503-5600, 775-850-0700 or toll-free 800-369-6144. *Fax:* 775-850-0711.

MOUNTAIN STATE UNIVERSITY

Beckley, WV

Tuition & fees: $7680 **Average undergraduate aid package: $9338**

ABOUT THE INSTITUTION Independent, coed. 39 undergraduate majors. Federal methodology is used as a basis for awarding need-based institutional aid.

UNDERGRADUATE EXPENSES for 2011–12 ***Comprehensive fee:*** $16,545 includes full-time tuition ($7680) and room and board ($8865). ***College room only:*** $5625. Full-time tuition and fees vary according to course load, degree level, location, and program. Room and board charges vary according to board plan and housing facility. ***Part-time tuition:*** $245 per credit hour. Part-time tuition and fees vary according to course load, degree level, location, and program. ***Payment plan:*** Installment.

FRESHMAN FINANCIAL AID (Fall 2009) 476 applied for aid; of those 91% were deemed to have need. 100% of freshmen with need received aid; of those 8% had need fully met. ***Average percent of need met:*** 57% (excluding resources awarded to replace EFC). ***Average financial aid package:*** $8258 (excluding resources awarded to replace EFC).

UNDERGRADUATE FINANCIAL AID (Fall 2009) 2,809 applied for aid; of those 100% were deemed to have need. 100% of undergraduates with need received aid; of those 16% had need fully met. ***Average percent of need met:*** 67% (excluding resources awarded to replace EFC). ***Average financial aid package:*** $9338 (excluding resources awarded to replace EFC). 1% of all full-time undergraduates had no need and received non-need-based gift aid.

GIFT AID (NEED-BASED) ***Total amount:*** $11,024,742 (88% federal, 10% state, 1% institutional, 1% external sources). ***Receiving aid:*** Freshmen: 59% (335); all full-time undergraduates: 43% (1,622). ***Average award:*** Freshmen: $4505; Undergraduates: $4984. ***Scholarships, grants, and awards:*** Federal Pell, FSEOG, state, private, college/university gift aid from institutional funds, Federal Nursing.

GIFT AID (NON-NEED-BASED) ***Total amount:*** $301,960 (76% state, 24% institutional). ***Receiving aid:*** Freshmen: 1% (4). Undergraduates: 18. ***Average award:*** Undergraduates: $3436. ***Scholarships, grants, and awards by category:*** *Academic interests/achievement:* 18 awards ($71,577 total): general academic interests/achievements. *Special achievements/activities:* 10 awards ($1231 total): cheerleading/drum major. ***Tuition waivers:*** Full or partial for employees or children of employees, senior citizens.

LOANS ***Student loans:*** $35,837,679 (39% need-based, 61% non-need-based). 85% of past graduating class borrowed through all loan programs. *Average indebtedness per student:* $34,088. ***Average need-based loan:*** Freshmen: $2049. Undergraduates: $6964. ***Parent loans:*** $214,209 (100% non-need-based). ***Programs:*** Federal Direct (Subsidized and Unsubsidized Stafford, PLUS), private loans.

WORK-STUDY ***Federal work-study:*** Total amount: $305,214; 82 jobs averaging $1855.

ATHLETIC AWARDS Total amount: $379,269 (100% non-need-based).

APPLYING FOR FINANCIAL AID ***Required financial aid form:*** FAFSA. ***Financial aid deadline:*** Continuous. ***Notification date:*** Continuous beginning 4/1. Students must reply within 2 weeks of notification.

CONTACT Lynn Whitteker, Director of Financial Aid, Mountain State University, 410 Neville Street, PO Box 9003, Beckley, WV 25801, 304-929-1595 or toll-free 800-766-6067 Ext. 1433. *Fax:* 304-929-1390. *E-mail:* lwhitteker@mountainstate.edu.

MOUNT ALOYSIUS COLLEGE

Cresson, PA

Tuition & fees: $18,000 **Average undergraduate aid package: $12,668**

ABOUT THE INSTITUTION Independent Roman Catholic, coed. 24 undergraduate majors. Federal methodology is used as a basis for awarding need-based institutional aid.

UNDERGRADUATE EXPENSES for 2010–11 ***Comprehensive fee:*** $25,660 includes full-time tuition ($17,240), mandatory fees ($760), and room and board ($7660). ***College room only:*** $3940. Full-time tuition and fees vary according to program. Room and board charges vary according to board plan. ***Part-time tuition:*** $520 per credit. ***Part-time fees:*** $200 per term. Part-time tuition and fees vary according to program. ***Payment plan:*** Installment.

FRESHMAN FINANCIAL AID (Fall 2010, est.) 355 applied for aid; of those 92% were deemed to have need. 100% of freshmen with need received aid. ***Average***

percent of need met: 30% (excluding resources awarded to replace EFC). ***Average financial aid package:*** $13,945 (excluding resources awarded to replace EFC). 8% of all full-time freshmen had no need and received non-need-based gift aid.

UNDERGRADUATE FINANCIAL AID (Fall 2010, est.) 1,206 applied for aid; of those 98% were deemed to have need. 100% of undergraduates with need received aid. ***Average percent of need met:*** 35% (excluding resources awarded to replace EFC). ***Average financial aid package:*** $12,668 (excluding resources awarded to replace EFC). 2% of all full-time undergraduates had no need and received non-need-based gift aid.

GIFT AID (NEED-BASED) ***Total amount:*** $11,522,610 (32% federal, 18% state, 49% institutional, 1% external sources). ***Receiving aid:*** Freshmen: 92% (325); all full-time undergraduates: 10% (115). ***Average award:*** Freshmen: $5459; Undergraduates: $4830. ***Scholarships, grants, and awards:*** Federal Pell, FSEOG, state, private, college/university gift aid from institutional funds.

GIFT AID (NON-NEED-BASED) ***Receiving aid:*** Freshmen: 8% (30). Undergraduates: 2% (21). ***Average award:*** Freshmen: $3900. Undergraduates: $3600. ***Scholarships, grants, and awards by category:*** *Academic interests/achievement:* 1,230 awards ($3,382,950 total): general academic interests/achievements. *Creative arts/performance:* 15 awards ($22,000 total): music, performing arts. *Special achievements/activities:* 67 awards ($627,000 total): leadership. *Special characteristics:* 98 awards ($74,000 total): children of current students, parents of current students, religious affiliation, siblings of current students, spouses of current students, twins. ***Tuition waivers:*** Full or partial for employees or children of employees.

LOANS ***Student loans:*** $9,950,304 (100% need-based). 84% of past graduating class borrowed through all loan programs. *Average indebtedness per student:* $32,312. ***Average need-based loan:*** Freshmen: $3529. Undergraduates: $4179. ***Parent loans:*** $3,002,512 (100% need-based). ***Programs:*** Federal Direct (Subsidized and Unsubsidized Stafford, PLUS), Perkins, Federal Nursing, alternative loans.

WORK-STUDY ***Federal work-study:*** Total amount: $171,834; 220 jobs averaging $1000.

APPLYING FOR FINANCIAL AID ***Required financial aid form:*** FAFSA. ***Financial aid deadline (priority):*** 2/15. ***Notification date:*** Continuous beginning 3/15. Students must reply within 2 weeks of notification.

CONTACT Mrs. Stacy L. Schenk, Director of Financial Aid, Mount Aloysius College, 7373 Admiral Peary Highway, Cresson, PA 16630-1900, 814-886-6357 or toll-free 888-823-2220. *Fax:* 814-886-6463. *E-mail:* sschenk@mtaloy.edu.

MOUNT ANGEL SEMINARY

Saint Benedict, OR

CONTACT Dorene Preis, Director of Student Financial Aid/Registrar, Mount Angel Seminary, 1 Abbey Drive, Saint Benedict, OR 97373, 503-845-3951. *Fax:* 503-845-3126. *E-mail:* dpreis@mtangel.edu.

MOUNT CARMEL COLLEGE OF NURSING

Columbus, OH

Tuition & fees: $15,644 **Average undergraduate aid package: $13,500**

ABOUT THE INSTITUTION Independent, coed, primarily women. 1 undergraduate major. Federal methodology is used as a basis for awarding need-based institutional aid.

UNDERGRADUATE EXPENSES for 2010–11 ***One-time required fee:*** $225. ***Tuition:*** full-time $15,332; part-time $323 per semester hour. ***Required fees:*** full-time $312; $312 per year. Full-time tuition and fees vary according to course level, course load, and student level. Part-time tuition and fees vary according to course level, course load, and student level. ***Payment plan:*** Installment.

FRESHMAN FINANCIAL AID (Fall 2010, est.) 74 applied for aid; of those 100% were deemed to have need. 100% of freshmen with need received aid; of those 9% had need fully met. ***Average percent of need met:*** 52% (excluding resources awarded to replace EFC). ***Average financial aid package:*** $7500 (excluding resources awarded to replace EFC). 4% of all full-time freshmen had no need and received non-need-based gift aid.

UNDERGRADUATE FINANCIAL AID (Fall 2010, est.) 521 applied for aid; of those 100% were deemed to have need. 100% of undergraduates with need received aid. ***Average percent of need met:*** 60% (excluding resources awarded to replace EFC). ***Average financial aid package:*** $13,500 (excluding resources awarded to replace EFC). 1% of all full-time undergraduates had no need and received non-need-based gift aid.

GIFT AID (NEED-BASED) ***Total amount:*** $1,008,978 (82% federal, 16% state, 2% institutional). ***Receiving aid:*** Freshmen: 21% (18); all full-time undergraduates: 35% (201). ***Average award:*** Freshmen: $1200; Undergraduates: $1700. ***Scholarships, grants, and awards:*** Federal Pell, FSEOG, state, private, college/university gift aid from institutional funds.

GIFT AID (NON-NEED-BASED) ***Total amount:*** $229,045 (16% federal, 2% state, 63% institutional, 19% external sources). ***Receiving aid:*** Freshmen: 73% (62). Undergraduates: 19% (110). ***Average award:*** Freshmen: $1600. Undergraduates: $2200. ***Scholarships, grants, and awards by category:*** *Academic interests/achievement:* 132 awards ($263,000 total): general academic interests/achievements. *Special achievements/activities:* 3 awards ($3000 total): community service. *Special characteristics:* 4 awards ($7000 total): children of faculty/staff, members of minority groups. ***Tuition waivers:*** Full or partial for employees or children of employees.

LOANS ***Student loans:*** $4,864,123 (41% need-based, 59% non-need-based). 93% of past graduating class borrowed through all loan programs. *Average indebtedness per student:* $8675. ***Average need-based loan:*** Freshmen: $3500. Undergraduates: $4427. ***Parent loans:*** $980,596 (100% non-need-based). ***Programs:*** Perkins, Federal Nursing, state, college/university.

WORK-STUDY ***State or other work-study/employment:*** Total amount: $57,000 (100% need-based). Part-time jobs available.

APPLYING FOR FINANCIAL AID ***Required financial aid form:*** FAFSA. ***Financial aid deadline:*** Continuous. ***Notification date:*** Continuous beginning 5/1. Students must reply within 2 weeks of notification.

CONTACT Alynica M. Bowen, PhD, Director of Financial Aid, Mount Carmel College of Nursing, 127 South Davis Avenue, Columbus, OH 43222, 614-234-5800 Ext. 5177. *Fax:* 614-234-5427. *E-mail:* abowen@mccn.edu.

MOUNT HOLYOKE COLLEGE

South Hadley, MA

Tuition & fees: $40,256 **Average undergraduate aid package: $35,714**

ABOUT THE INSTITUTION Independent, women only. 48 undergraduate majors. Institutional methodology is used as a basis for awarding need-based institutional aid.

UNDERGRADUATE EXPENSES for 2010–11 ***Comprehensive fee:*** $52,036 includes full-time tuition ($40,070), mandatory fees ($186), and room and board ($11,780). ***College room only:*** $5770. ***Part-time tuition:*** $1255 per credit hour. ***Payment plans:*** Tuition prepayment, installment.

FRESHMAN FINANCIAL AID (Fall 2010, est.) 431 applied for aid; of those 87% were deemed to have need. 100% of freshmen with need received aid; of those 100% had need fully met. ***Average percent of need met:*** 100% (excluding resources awarded to replace EFC). ***Average financial aid package:*** $37,362 (excluding resources awarded to replace EFC). 12% of all full-time freshmen had no need and received non-need-based gift aid.

UNDERGRADUATE FINANCIAL AID (Fall 2010, est.) 1,826 applied for aid; of those 93% were deemed to have need. 100% of undergraduates with need received aid; of those 100% had need fully met. ***Average percent of need met:*** 100% (excluding resources awarded to replace EFC). ***Average financial aid package:*** $35,714 (excluding resources awarded to replace EFC). 9% of all full-time undergraduates had no need and received non-need-based gift aid.

GIFT AID (NEED-BASED) ***Total amount:*** $49,693,390 (6% federal, 92% institutional, 2% external sources). ***Receiving aid:*** Freshmen: 70% (375); all full-time undergraduates: 68% (1,641). ***Average award:*** Freshmen: $32,903; Undergraduates: $30,538. ***Scholarships, grants, and awards:*** Federal Pell, FSEOG, state, private, college/university gift aid from institutional funds.

GIFT AID (NON-NEED-BASED) ***Total amount:*** $4,015,651 (90% institutional, 10% external sources). ***Average award:*** Freshmen: $13,751. Undergraduates: $15,863. ***Scholarships, grants, and awards by category:*** *Academic interests/achievement:* 230 awards ($3,611,000 total): general academic interests/achievements. *Special characteristics:* 22 awards ($175,000 total): general special characteristics. ***Tuition waivers:*** Full or partial for employees or children of employees.

LOANS ***Student loans:*** $10,376,052 (86% need-based, 14% non-need-based). 66% of past graduating class borrowed through all loan programs. *Average indebtedness per student:* $22,499. ***Average need-based loan:*** Freshmen: $3041.

Undergraduates: $4683. ***Parent loans:*** $5,805,751 (100% non-need-based). ***Programs:*** Federal Direct (Subsidized and Unsubsidized Stafford, PLUS), Perkins, college/university.

WORK-STUDY ***Federal work-study:*** Total amount: $1,894,589; 949 jobs averaging $1996. ***State or other work-study/employment:*** Total amount: $912,452 (100% need-based). 452 part-time jobs averaging $2019.

APPLYING FOR FINANCIAL AID ***Required financial aid forms:*** FAFSA, CSS Financial Aid PROFILE, noncustodial (divorced/separated) parent's statement, federal income tax return(s) and W-2 forms. ***Financial aid deadline:*** 3/1 (priority: 2/15). ***Notification date:*** 4/1. Students must reply by 5/1.

CONTACT Ms. Kathryn Blaisdell, Director of Student Financial Services, Mount Holyoke College, 50 College Street, South Hadley, MA 01075-1492, 413-538-2291. *Fax:* 413-538-2512. *E-mail:* kblaisde@mtholyoke.edu.

MOUNT IDA COLLEGE

Newton, MA

ABOUT THE INSTITUTION Independent, coed. 22 undergraduate majors.

GIFT AID (NEED-BASED) ***Scholarships, grants, and awards:*** Federal Pell, FSEOG, state, private, college/university gift aid from institutional funds.

GIFT AID (NON-NEED-BASED) ***Scholarships, grants, and awards by category:*** *Creative arts/performance:* applied art and design, art/fine arts, general creative arts/performance. *Special achievements/activities:* community service, general special achievements/activities, leadership.

LOANS ***Programs:*** state, alternative loans.

WORK-STUDY ***Federal work-study:*** Total amount: $286,162; jobs available. ***State or other work-study/employment:*** Total amount: $61,354 (9% need-based, 91% non-need-based). Part-time jobs available.

APPLYING FOR FINANCIAL AID ***Required financial aid form:*** FAFSA.

CONTACT David L. Goldman, Director of Financial Aid, Mount Ida College, 777 Dedham Street, Newton, MA 02459-3310, 617-928-4785. *Fax:* 617-332-7869. *E-mail:* finaid@mountida.edu.

MOUNT MARTY COLLEGE

Yankton, SD

Tuition & fees: $19,932 | **Average undergraduate aid package: $21,311**

ABOUT THE INSTITUTION Independent Roman Catholic, coed. 32 undergraduate majors. Federal methodology is used as a basis for awarding need-based institutional aid.

UNDERGRADUATE EXPENSES for 2010–11 ***Comprehensive fee:*** $25,568 includes full-time tuition ($18,102), mandatory fees ($1830), and room and board ($5636). Full-time tuition and fees vary according to location. Room and board charges vary according to board plan. ***Part-time tuition:*** $211 per credit hour. ***Part-time fees:*** $25 per credit hour. Part-time tuition and fees vary according to course load and location. ***Payment plan:*** Installment.

FRESHMAN FINANCIAL AID (Fall 2010, est.) 111 applied for aid; of those 86% were deemed to have need. 100% of freshmen with need received aid; of those 47% had need fully met. ***Average percent of need met:*** 99% (excluding resources awarded to replace EFC). ***Average financial aid package:*** $23,275 (excluding resources awarded to replace EFC). 11% of all full-time freshmen had no need and received non-need-based gift aid.

UNDERGRADUATE FINANCIAL AID (Fall 2010, est.) 587 applied for aid; of those 92% were deemed to have need. 99% of undergraduates with need received aid; of those 44% had need fully met. ***Average percent of need met:*** 98% (excluding resources awarded to replace EFC). ***Average financial aid package:*** $21,311 (excluding resources awarded to replace EFC). 6% of all full-time undergraduates had no need and received non-need-based gift aid.

GIFT AID (NEED-BASED) ***Total amount:*** $5,073,643 (38% federal, 1% state, 58% institutional, 3% external sources). ***Receiving aid:*** Freshmen: 79% (96); all full-time undergraduates: 87% (538). ***Average award:*** Freshmen: $9101; Undergraduates: $7502. ***Scholarships, grants, and awards:*** Federal Pell, FSEOG, state, private, college/university gift aid from institutional funds.

GIFT AID (NON-NEED-BASED) ***Total amount:*** $341,320 (1% federal, 4% state, 90% institutional, 5% external sources). ***Average award:*** Freshmen: $9096. Undergraduates: $6646. ***Scholarships, grants, and awards by category:*** *Academic interests/achievement:* 891 awards ($2,894,653 total): general academic interests/achievements. *Creative arts/performance:* 49 awards ($70,324 total): music, theater/drama. *Special characteristics:* children of current students, children of faculty/staff, international students, parents of current students, religious affiliation, siblings of current students, spouses of current students. ***Tuition waivers:*** Full or partial for employees or children of employees.

LOANS ***Student loans:*** $2,939,034 (97% need-based, 3% non-need-based). 93% of past graduating class borrowed through all loan programs. *Average indebtedness per student:* $34,983. ***Average need-based loan:*** Freshmen: $4637. Undergraduates: $5551. ***Parent loans:*** $641,231 (88% need-based, 12% non-need-based). ***Programs:*** Federal Direct (Subsidized and Unsubsidized Stafford, PLUS), Perkins, Federal Nursing.

WORK-STUDY ***Federal work-study:*** Total amount: $309,105; 206 jobs averaging $1500. ***State or other work-study/employment:*** Total amount: $73,000 (58% need-based, 42% non-need-based). 49 part-time jobs averaging $1500.

ATHLETIC AWARDS Total amount: $697,651 (85% need-based, 15% non-need-based).

APPLYING FOR FINANCIAL AID ***Required financial aid forms:*** FAFSA, institution's own form. ***Financial aid deadline (priority):*** 3/1. ***Notification date:*** Continuous beginning 3/15. Students must reply within 2 weeks of notification.

CONTACT Mr. Ken Kocer, Director of Financial Assistance, Mount Marty College, 1105 West 8th Street, Yankton, SD 57078-3724, 605-668-1589 or toll-free 800-658-4552. *Fax:* 605-668-1585. *E-mail:* kkocer@mtmc.edu.

MOUNT MARY COLLEGE

Milwaukee, WI

Tuition & fees: $22,118 | **Average undergraduate aid package: $16,408**

ABOUT THE INSTITUTION Independent Roman Catholic, undergraduate: women only; graduate: coed. 49 undergraduate majors. Federal methodology is used as a basis for awarding need-based institutional aid.

UNDERGRADUATE EXPENSES for 2010–11 ***Comprehensive fee:*** $29,616 includes full-time tuition ($21,668), mandatory fees ($450), and room and board ($7498). Full-time tuition and fees vary according to degree level and program. Room and board charges vary according to board plan. ***Part-time tuition:*** $648 per credit hour. ***Part-time fees:*** $120 per term. Part-time tuition and fees vary according to course load, degree level, and program. ***Payment plan:*** Installment.

FRESHMAN FINANCIAL AID (Fall 2010, est.) 123 applied for aid; of those 96% were deemed to have need. 100% of freshmen with need received aid; of those 4% had need fully met. ***Average percent of need met:*** 78% (excluding resources awarded to replace EFC). ***Average financial aid package:*** $20,334 (excluding resources awarded to replace EFC). 7% of all full-time freshmen had no need and received non-need-based gift aid.

UNDERGRADUATE FINANCIAL AID (Fall 2010, est.) 1,018 applied for aid; of those 94% were deemed to have need. 100% of undergraduates with need received aid; of those 8% had need fully met. ***Average percent of need met:*** 68% (excluding resources awarded to replace EFC). ***Average financial aid package:*** $16,408 (excluding resources awarded to replace EFC). 11% of all full-time undergraduates had no need and received non-need-based gift aid.

GIFT AID (NEED-BASED) ***Total amount:*** $11,519,591 (27% federal, 14% state, 58% institutional, 1% external sources). ***Receiving aid:*** Freshmen: 93% (118); all full-time undergraduates: 88% (950). ***Average award:*** Freshmen: $16,465; Undergraduates: $11,587. ***Scholarships, grants, and awards:*** Federal Pell, FSEOG, state, private, college/university gift aid from institutional funds, Metropolitan Milwaukee Association of Commerce Awards.

GIFT AID (NON-NEED-BASED) ***Total amount:*** $798,037 (98% institutional, 2% external sources). ***Receiving aid:*** Freshmen: 3% (4). Undergraduates: 4% (40). ***Average award:*** Freshmen: $9186. Undergraduates: $5148. ***Scholarships, grants, and awards by category:*** *Academic interests/achievement:* 923 awards ($3,301,450 total): business, communication, education, English, general academic interests/achievements, health fields, home economics, humanities, mathematics, physical sciences, social sciences. *Creative arts/performance:* 17 awards ($14,728 total): applied art and design, art/fine arts, music. *Special achievements/activities:* 8 awards ($55,950 total): general special achievements/activities, leadership. *Special characteristics:* 22 awards ($219,421 total): children of faculty/staff, international students, parents of current students, siblings of current students. ***Tuition waivers:*** Full or partial for employees or children of employees, senior citizens.

LOANS ***Student loans:*** $10,732,088 (86% need-based, 14% non-need-based). 82% of past graduating class borrowed through all loan programs. *Average*

indebtedness per student: $24,614. ***Average need-based loan:*** Freshmen: $2656. Undergraduates: $4576. ***Parent loans:*** $587,049 (53% need-based, 47% non-need-based). ***Programs:*** Perkins, state.

WORK-STUDY ***Federal work-study:*** Total amount: $158,948; 157 jobs averaging $1373. ***State or other work-study/employment:*** Total amount: $150,000 (100% non-need-based). 43 part-time jobs averaging $1247.

APPLYING FOR FINANCIAL AID ***Required financial aid form:*** FAFSA. ***Financial aid deadline (priority):*** 3/1. ***Notification date:*** Continuous. Students must reply within 2 weeks of notification.

CONTACT Debra Duff, Director of Financial Aid, Mount Mary College, 2900 North Menomonee River Parkway, Milwaukee, WI 53222-4597, 414-256-1258. *Fax:* 414-443-3602. *E-mail:* finaid@mtmary.edu.

MOUNT MERCY UNIVERSITY

Cedar Rapids, IA

Tuition & fees: $24,360 **Average undergraduate aid package: $16,934**

ABOUT THE INSTITUTION Independent Roman Catholic, coed. 40 undergraduate majors. Federal methodology is used as a basis for awarding need-based institutional aid.

UNDERGRADUATE EXPENSES for 2011–12 ***Comprehensive fee:*** $31,830 includes full-time tuition ($24,360) and room and board ($7470). Full-time tuition and fees vary according to course load. Room and board charges vary according to board plan and housing facility. ***Part-time tuition:*** $670 per credit hour. ***Part-time fees:*** $670 per credit hour. Part-time tuition and fees vary according to course load. ***Payment plan:*** Installment.

FRESHMAN FINANCIAL AID (Fall 2010, est.) 118 applied for aid; of those 90% were deemed to have need. 100% of freshmen with need received aid; of those 19% had need fully met. ***Average percent of need met:*** 72% (excluding resources awarded to replace EFC). ***Average financial aid package:*** $18,428 (excluding resources awarded to replace EFC). 17% of all full-time freshmen had no need and received non-need-based gift aid.

UNDERGRADUATE FINANCIAL AID (Fall 2010, est.) 901 applied for aid; of those 91% were deemed to have need. 98% of undergraduates with need received aid; of those 16% had need fully met. ***Average percent of need met:*** 69% (excluding resources awarded to replace EFC). ***Average financial aid package:*** $16,934 (excluding resources awarded to replace EFC). 12% of all full-time undergraduates had no need and received non-need-based gift aid.

GIFT AID (NEED-BASED) ***Total amount:*** $10,060,377 (19% federal, 23% state, 56% institutional, 2% external sources). ***Receiving aid:*** Freshmen: 80% (105); all full-time undergraduates: 69% (788). ***Average award:*** Freshmen: $14,533; Undergraduates: $12,357. ***Scholarships, grants, and awards:*** Federal Pell, FSEOG, state, private, college/university gift aid from institutional funds.

GIFT AID (NON-NEED-BASED) ***Total amount:*** $1,375,527 (1% federal, 1% state, 94% institutional, 4% external sources). ***Receiving aid:*** Freshmen: 11% (14). Undergraduates: 6% (66). ***Average award:*** Freshmen: $10,963. Undergraduates: $8354. ***Scholarships, grants, and awards by category:*** *Academic interests/achievement:* 1,110 awards ($6,720,262 total): general academic interests/achievements. *Creative arts/performance:* 41 awards ($50,679 total): art/fine arts, music, theater/drama. *Special achievements/activities:* 103 awards ($70,250 total): leadership. *Special characteristics:* 16 awards ($10,125 total): previous college experience. ***Tuition waivers:*** Full or partial for employees or children of employees.

LOANS ***Student loans:*** $2,964,189 (24% need-based, 76% non-need-based). 93% of past graduating class borrowed through all loan programs. *Average indebtedness per student:* $23,373. ***Average need-based loan:*** Freshmen: $3814. Undergraduates: $4570. ***Parent loans:*** $3,113,758 (26% need-based, 74% non-need-based). ***Programs:*** Federal Direct (Subsidized and Unsubsidized Stafford, PLUS), Perkins, state, college/university.

WORK-STUDY ***Federal work-study:*** Total amount: $504,278; 302 jobs averaging $1997. ***State or other work-study/employment:*** Total amount: $123,420 (64% need-based, 36% non-need-based). 125 part-time jobs averaging $2000.

ATHLETIC AWARDS Total amount: $606,277 (65% need-based, 35% non-need-based).

APPLYING FOR FINANCIAL AID ***Required financial aid form:*** FAFSA. ***Financial aid deadline (priority):*** 3/1. ***Notification date:*** Continuous beginning 3/15. Students must reply by 5/1 or within 3 weeks of notification.

CONTACT Bethany Rinderknecht, Director of Financial Aid, Mount Mercy University, 1330 Elmhurst Drive NE, Cedar Rapids, IA 52402-4797, 319-368-6467 Ext. 1545 or toll-free 800-248-4504. *Fax:* 319-364-3546. *E-mail:* brinderknecht@mtmercy.edu.

MOUNT OLIVE COLLEGE

Mount Olive, NC

Tuition & fees: $15,500 **Average undergraduate aid package: $9723**

ABOUT THE INSTITUTION Independent Free Will Baptist, coed. 24 undergraduate majors. Federal methodology is used as a basis for awarding need-based institutional aid.

UNDERGRADUATE EXPENSES for 2010–11 ***Comprehensive fee:*** $21,700 includes full-time tuition ($15,500) and room and board ($6200). ***College room only:*** $2400. Room and board charges vary according to board plan. ***Part-time tuition:*** $380 per credit hour.

FRESHMAN FINANCIAL AID (Fall 2009) 563 applied for aid; of those 90% were deemed to have need. 98% of freshmen with need received aid; of those 13% had need fully met. ***Average percent of need met:*** 70% (excluding resources awarded to replace EFC). ***Average financial aid package:*** $13,035 (excluding resources awarded to replace EFC). 1% of all full-time freshmen had no need and received non-need-based gift aid.

UNDERGRADUATE FINANCIAL AID (Fall 2009) 3,666 applied for aid; of those 91% were deemed to have need. 98% of undergraduates with need received aid; of those 10% had need fully met. ***Average percent of need met:*** 59% (excluding resources awarded to replace EFC). ***Average financial aid package:*** $9723 (excluding resources awarded to replace EFC). 1% of all full-time undergraduates had no need and received non-need-based gift aid.

GIFT AID (NEED-BASED) ***Total amount:*** $17,290,884 (42% federal, 49% state, 2% institutional, 7% external sources). ***Receiving aid:*** Freshmen: 88% (496); all full-time undergraduates: 85% (3,106). ***Average award:*** Freshmen: $9626; Undergraduates: $6321. ***Scholarships, grants, and awards:*** Federal Pell, FSEOG, state, private, college/university gift aid from institutional funds.

GIFT AID (NON-NEED-BASED) ***Total amount:*** $667,210 (1% federal, 60% state, 5% institutional, 34% external sources). ***Receiving aid:*** Freshmen: 3% (16). Undergraduates: 3% (95). ***Average award:*** Freshmen: $2500. Undergraduates: $2134. ***Scholarships, grants, and awards by category:*** *Academic interests/achievement:* general academic interests/achievements. *Creative arts/performance:* general creative arts/performance. *Special achievements/activities:* cheerleading/drum major, leadership, religious involvement. *Special characteristics:* children of faculty/staff, religious affiliation, veterans, veterans' children.

LOANS ***Student loans:*** $26,323,744 (81% need-based, 19% non-need-based). 96% of past graduating class borrowed through all loan programs. *Average indebtedness per student:* $19,091. ***Average need-based loan:*** Freshmen: $3936. Undergraduates: $4080. ***Parent loans:*** $325,300 (34% need-based, 66% non-need-based). ***Programs:*** Federal Direct (Subsidized and Unsubsidized Stafford, PLUS), Perkins, Federal Nursing, state.

WORK-STUDY ***Federal work-study:*** Total amount: $184,597; jobs available.

ATHLETIC AWARDS Total amount: $781,059 (80% need-based, 20% non-need-based).

APPLYING FOR FINANCIAL AID ***Required financial aid forms:*** FAFSA, state aid form. ***Financial aid deadline:*** Continuous. ***Notification date:*** Continuous beginning 2/14. Students must reply within 2 weeks of notification.

CONTACT Mrs. Katrina K. Lee, Director of Financial Aid, Mount Olive College, 634 Henderson Street, Mount Olive, NC 28365, 919-658-7891 or toll-free 800-653-0854 (in-state). *Fax:* 919-658-9816. *E-mail:* klee@moc.edu.

MOUNT SAINT MARY COLLEGE

Newburgh, NY

Tuition & fees: $24,410 **Average undergraduate aid package: $14,790**

ABOUT THE INSTITUTION Independent, coed. 26 undergraduate majors. Federal methodology is used as a basis for awarding need-based institutional aid.

UNDERGRADUATE EXPENSES for 2011–12 ***Comprehensive fee:*** $36,730 includes full-time tuition ($23,460), mandatory fees ($950), and room and board ($12,320). ***College room only:*** $7140. Full-time tuition and fees vary according to class time, degree level, location, and program. Room and board charges vary according to board plan and housing facility. ***Part-time tuition:***

$782 per credit hour. Part-time tuition and fees vary according to class time, degree level, location, and program. ***Payment plan:*** Installment.

FRESHMAN FINANCIAL AID (Fall 2010, est.) 410 applied for aid; of those 87% were deemed to have need. 100% of freshmen with need received aid; of those 17% had need fully met. ***Average percent of need met:*** 64% (excluding resources awarded to replace EFC). ***Average financial aid package:*** $16,295 (excluding resources awarded to replace EFC). 12% of all full-time freshmen had no need and received non-need-based gift aid.

UNDERGRADUATE FINANCIAL AID (Fall 2010, est.) 1,729 applied for aid; of those 89% were deemed to have need. 99% of undergraduates with need received aid; of those 16% had need fully met. ***Average percent of need met:*** 60% (excluding resources awarded to replace EFC). ***Average financial aid package:*** $14,790 (excluding resources awarded to replace EFC). 12% of all full-time undergraduates had no need and received non-need-based gift aid.

GIFT AID (NEED-BASED) ***Total amount:*** $16,377,573 (23% federal, 14% state, 61% institutional, 2% external sources). ***Receiving aid:*** Freshmen: 80% (354); all full-time undergraduates: 77% (1,463). ***Average award:*** Freshmen: $12,737; Undergraduates: $11,045. ***Scholarships, grants, and awards:*** Federal Pell, FSEOG, state, private, college/university gift aid from institutional funds, Federal Nursing, Academic Competitiveness Grants, National SMART Grants.

GIFT AID (NON-NEED-BASED) ***Total amount:*** $2,348,649 (2% federal, 6% state, 87% institutional, 5% external sources). ***Receiving aid:*** Freshmen: 9% (38). Undergraduates: 7% (132). ***Average award:*** Freshmen: $7519. Undergraduates: $7471. ***Scholarships, grants, and awards by category:*** *Academic interests/achievement:* 1,002 awards ($6,992,500 total): general academic interests/achievements. *Special characteristics:* 40 awards ($701,221 total): children of faculty/staff. ***Tuition waivers:*** Full or partial for employees or children of employees.

LOANS ***Student loans:*** $17,454,127 (74% need-based, 26% non-need-based). 90% of past graduating class borrowed through all loan programs. *Average indebtedness per student:* $37,273. ***Average need-based loan:*** Freshmen: $3106. Undergraduates: $4246. ***Parent loans:*** $17,658,145 (36% need-based, 64% non-need-based). ***Programs:*** Federal Direct (Subsidized and Unsubsidized Stafford, PLUS), Federal Nursing.

WORK-STUDY ***Federal work-study:*** Total amount: $565,801; 390 jobs averaging $1369. ***State or other work-study/employment:*** Part-time jobs available.

APPLYING FOR FINANCIAL AID ***Required financial aid form:*** FAFSA. ***Financial aid deadline:*** 3/1 (priority: 2/15). ***Notification date:*** Continuous beginning 3/15. Students must reply by 5/1.

CONTACT Barbara Winchell, Interim Director of Financial Aid, Mount Saint Mary College, 330 Powell Avenue, Newburgh, NY 12550-3494, 845-561-3195 or toll-free 888-937-6762. *Fax:* 845-569-3302. *E-mail:* winchell@msmc.edu.

MOUNT ST. MARY'S COLLEGE

Los Angeles, CA

Tuition & fees: $31,626 **Average undergraduate aid package: $28,700**

ABOUT THE INSTITUTION Independent Roman Catholic, coed, primarily women. 29 undergraduate majors. Both federal and institutional methodology are used as a basis for awarding need-based institutional aid.

UNDERGRADUATE EXPENSES for 2011–12 ***Comprehensive fee:*** $41,751 includes full-time tuition ($30,696), mandatory fees ($930), and room and board ($10,125). Full-time tuition and fees vary according to course load, degree level, and program. Room and board charges vary according to board plan and housing facility. ***Part-time tuition:*** $1218 per unit. Part-time tuition and fees vary according to course load, degree level, and program. ***Payment plan:*** Installment.

FRESHMAN FINANCIAL AID (Fall 2010, est.) 513 applied for aid; of those 100% were deemed to have need. 100% of freshmen with need received aid; of those 11% had need fully met. ***Average percent of need met:*** 84% (excluding resources awarded to replace EFC). ***Average financial aid package:*** $29,000 (excluding resources awarded to replace EFC). 8% of all full-time freshmen had no need and received non-need-based gift aid.

UNDERGRADUATE FINANCIAL AID (Fall 2010, est.) 1,626 applied for aid; of those 97% were deemed to have need. 100% of undergraduates with need received aid; of those 7% had need fully met. ***Average percent of need met:*** 79% (excluding resources awarded to replace EFC). ***Average financial aid package:*** $28,700 (excluding resources awarded to replace EFC). 11% of all full-time undergraduates had no need and received non-need-based gift aid.

GIFT AID (NEED-BASED) ***Total amount:*** $29,930,462 (18% federal, 23% state, 58% institutional, 1% external sources). ***Receiving aid:*** Freshmen: 97% (508); all full-time undergraduates: 83% (1,495). ***Average award:*** Freshmen: $11,000; Undergraduates: $10,500. ***Scholarships, grants, and awards:*** Federal Pell, FSEOG, state, private, college/university gift aid from institutional funds.

GIFT AID (NON-NEED-BASED) ***Receiving aid:*** Undergraduates: 4% (70). ***Average award:*** Freshmen: $9908. Undergraduates: $10,978. ***Scholarships, grants, and awards by category:*** *Academic interests/achievement:* biological sciences, education, general academic interests/achievements. *Creative arts/performance:* music. *Special achievements/activities:* community service, leadership. *Special characteristics:* children and siblings of alumni. ***Tuition waivers:*** Full or partial for employees or children of employees.

LOANS ***Student loans:*** $5,607,479 (100% need-based). 96% of past graduating class borrowed through all loan programs. *Average indebtedness per student:* $26,500. ***Average need-based loan:*** Freshmen: $3500. Undergraduates: $5500. ***Programs:*** Federal Direct (Subsidized and Unsubsidized Stafford, PLUS), Federal Nursing, college/university.

WORK-STUDY ***Federal work-study:*** Total amount: $1,411,564; jobs available. ***State or other work-study/employment:*** Part-time jobs available.

APPLYING FOR FINANCIAL AID ***Required financial aid forms:*** FAFSA, institution's own form, state aid form. ***Financial aid deadline (priority):*** 2/15. ***Notification date:*** Continuous beginning 3/15. Students must reply by 5/1.

CONTACT La Royce Dodd, Financial Aid Director, Mount St. Mary's College, 12001 Chalon Road, Los Angeles, CA 90049, 310-954-4192 or toll-free 800-999-9893.

MOUNT ST. MARY'S UNIVERSITY

Emmitsburg, MD

Tuition & fees: $31,536 **Average undergraduate aid package: $20,609**

ABOUT THE INSTITUTION Independent Roman Catholic, coed. 28 undergraduate majors. Federal methodology is used as a basis for awarding need-based institutional aid.

UNDERGRADUATE EXPENSES for 2011–12 ***Comprehensive fee:*** $42,080 includes full-time tuition ($30,836), mandatory fees ($700), and room and board ($10,544). ***College room only:*** $5160. Full-time tuition and fees vary according to location. Room and board charges vary according to board plan. ***Part-time tuition:*** $1030 per credit hour. Part-time tuition and fees vary according to location. ***Payment plan:*** Installment.

FRESHMAN FINANCIAL AID (Fall 2010, est.) 368 applied for aid; of those 85% were deemed to have need. 100% of freshmen with need received aid; of those 19% had need fully met. ***Average percent of need met:*** 75% (excluding resources awarded to replace EFC). ***Average financial aid package:*** $22,008 (excluding resources awarded to replace EFC). 25% of all full-time freshmen had no need and received non-need-based gift aid.

UNDERGRADUATE FINANCIAL AID (Fall 2010, est.) 1,190 applied for aid; of those 87% were deemed to have need. 100% of undergraduates with need received aid; of those 22% had need fully met. ***Average percent of need met:*** 73% (excluding resources awarded to replace EFC). ***Average financial aid package:*** $20,609 (excluding resources awarded to replace EFC). 28% of all full-time undergraduates had no need and received non-need-based gift aid.

GIFT AID (NEED-BASED) ***Total amount:*** $15,369,516 (14% federal, 6% state, 78% institutional, 2% external sources). ***Receiving aid:*** Freshmen: 73% (311); all full-time undergraduates: 67% (1,019). ***Average award:*** Freshmen: $17,914; Undergraduates: $16,501. ***Scholarships, grants, and awards:*** Federal Pell, FSEOG, state, private, college/university gift aid from institutional funds.

GIFT AID (NON-NEED-BASED) ***Total amount:*** $5,842,757 (11% federal, 1% state, 87% institutional, 1% external sources). ***Receiving aid:*** Freshmen: 13% (54). Undergraduates: 12% (183). ***Average award:*** Freshmen: $12,093. Undergraduates: $10,581. ***Scholarships, grants, and awards by category:*** *Academic interests/achievement:* 1,332 awards ($13,180,709 total): general academic interests/achievements. *Creative arts/performance:* 24 awards ($44,000 total): art/fine arts. *Special characteristics:* 398 awards ($1,308,574 total): children of educators, children of faculty/staff, members of minority groups, siblings of current students. ***Tuition waivers:*** Full or partial for employees or children of employees.

LOANS ***Student loans:*** $10,276,084 (63% need-based, 37% non-need-based). 75% of past graduating class borrowed through all loan programs. *Average indebtedness per student:* $29,637. ***Average need-based loan:*** Freshmen: $4162.

Undergraduates: $4502. ***Parent loans:*** $4,643,042 (30% need-based, 70% non-need-based). ***Programs:*** Federal Direct (Subsidized and Unsubsidized Stafford, PLUS), Perkins.

WORK-STUDY ***Federal work-study:*** Total amount: $243,591; 236 jobs averaging $1032. ***State or other work-study/employment:*** Total amount: $513,196 (84% need-based, 16% non-need-based). 405 part-time jobs averaging $1059.

ATHLETIC AWARDS Total amount: $2,352,049 (45% need-based, 55% non-need-based).

APPLYING FOR FINANCIAL AID ***Required financial aid form:*** FAFSA. ***Financial aid deadline:*** 3/1. ***Notification date:*** Continuous beginning 2/15. Students must reply by 5/1.

CONTACT Mr. David C. Reeder, Director of Financial Aid, Mount St. Mary's University, 16300 Old Emmitsburg Road, Emmitsburg, MD 21727-7799, 301-447-5207 or toll-free 800-448-4347. *Fax:* 301-447-5915. *E-mail:* reeder@msmary.edu.

MT. SIERRA COLLEGE

Monrovia, CA

CONTACT Financial Aid Office, Mt. Sierra College, 101 East Huntington Drive, Monrovia, CA 91016, 888-828-8800 or toll-free 888-828-8800.

MOUNT VERNON NAZARENE UNIVERSITY

Mount Vernon, OH

Tuition & fees: $22,280 **Average undergraduate aid package: $16,173**

ABOUT THE INSTITUTION Independent Nazarene, coed. 83 undergraduate majors. Federal methodology is used as a basis for awarding need-based institutional aid.

UNDERGRADUATE EXPENSES for 2011–12 ***Comprehensive fee:*** $28,710 includes full-time tuition ($22,280) and room and board ($6430). ***College room only:*** $3590. Full-time tuition and fees vary according to course load, program, and reciprocity agreements. ***Part-time tuition:*** $787 per credit hour. ***Part-time fees:*** $21 per credit hour. Part-time tuition and fees vary according to course load, program, and reciprocity agreements. ***Payment plan:*** Installment.

FRESHMAN FINANCIAL AID (Fall 2010, est.) 388 applied for aid; of those 94% were deemed to have need. 100% of freshmen with need received aid; of those 12% had need fully met. ***Average percent of need met:*** 69% (excluding resources awarded to replace EFC). ***Average financial aid package:*** $18,422 (excluding resources awarded to replace EFC). 4% of all full-time freshmen had no need and received non-need-based gift aid.

UNDERGRADUATE FINANCIAL AID (Fall 2010, est.) 1,379 applied for aid; of those 91% were deemed to have need. 100% of undergraduates with need received aid; of those 12% had need fully met. ***Average percent of need met:*** 68% (excluding resources awarded to replace EFC). ***Average financial aid package:*** $16,173 (excluding resources awarded to replace EFC). 4% of all full-time undergraduates had no need and received non-need-based gift aid.

GIFT AID (NEED-BASED) ***Total amount:*** $13,469,209 (25% federal, 7% state, 62% institutional, 6% external sources). ***Receiving aid:*** Freshmen: 93% (360); all full-time undergraduates: 70% (1,214). ***Average award:*** Freshmen: $12,472; Undergraduates: $10,238. ***Scholarships, grants, and awards:*** Federal Pell, FSEOG, state, private, college/university gift aid from institutional funds.

GIFT AID (NON-NEED-BASED) ***Total amount:*** $1,208,555 (1% federal, 16% state, 78% institutional, 5% external sources). ***Receiving aid:*** Freshmen: 12% (48). Undergraduates: 10% (172). ***Average award:*** Freshmen: $8978. Undergraduates: $5354. ***Scholarships, grants, and awards by category:*** *Academic interests/achievement:* general academic interests/achievements. *Creative arts/performance:* music. *Special achievements/activities:* general special achievements/activities, junior miss, religious involvement. *Special characteristics:* children of faculty/staff, international students, members of minority groups, relatives of clergy, religious affiliation, siblings of current students, spouses of current students. ***Tuition waivers:*** Full or partial for employees or children of employees, senior citizens.

LOANS ***Student loans:*** $12,528,970 (94% need-based, 6% non-need-based). 88% of past graduating class borrowed through all loan programs. *Average indebtedness per student:* $31,609. ***Average need-based loan:*** Freshmen: $3745. Undergraduates: $4087. ***Parent loans:*** $3,769,681 (51% need-based, 49% non-need-based). ***Programs:*** Federal Direct (Subsidized and Unsubsidized Stafford, PLUS), Perkins, Federal Nursing, state, Schell loan program.

WORK-STUDY ***Federal work-study:*** Total amount: $179,100; jobs available. ***State or other work-study/employment:*** Total amount: $754,718 (58% need-based, 42% non-need-based). Part-time jobs available.

ATHLETIC AWARDS Total amount: $718,317 (74% need-based, 26% non-need-based).

APPLYING FOR FINANCIAL AID ***Required financial aid forms:*** FAFSA, institution's own form. ***Financial aid deadline (priority):*** 3/15. ***Notification date:*** Continuous beginning 3/1. Students must reply within 2 weeks of notification.

CONTACT Mary V. Cannon, Director of Student Financial Services, Mount Vernon Nazarene University, 800 Martinsburg Road, Mount Vernon, OH 43050-9500, 866-686-8243 or toll-free 866-462-6868. *Fax:* 740-399-8682. *E-mail:* finaid@mvnu.edu.

MUHLENBERG COLLEGE

Allentown, PA

Tuition & fees: $38,380 **Average undergraduate aid package: $24,739**

ABOUT THE INSTITUTION Independent religious, coed. 33 undergraduate majors. Institutional methodology is used as a basis for awarding need-based institutional aid.

UNDERGRADUATE EXPENSES for 2010–11 ***Comprehensive fee:*** $47,115 includes full-time tuition ($38,110), mandatory fees ($270), and room and board ($8735). ***College room only:*** $5035. Room and board charges vary according to board plan, housing facility, and location. Part-time tuition and fees vary according to program. ***Payment plan:*** Installment.

FRESHMAN FINANCIAL AID (Fall 2010, est.) 414 applied for aid; of those 73% were deemed to have need. 99% of freshmen with need received aid; of those 94% had need fully met. ***Average percent of need met:*** 94% (excluding resources awarded to replace EFC). ***Average financial aid package:*** $23,768 (excluding resources awarded to replace EFC). 31% of all full-time freshmen had no need and received non-need-based gift aid.

UNDERGRADUATE FINANCIAL AID (Fall 2010, est.) 1,474 applied for aid; of those 81% were deemed to have need. 97% of undergraduates with need received aid; of those 89% had need fully met. ***Average percent of need met:*** 94% (excluding resources awarded to replace EFC). ***Average financial aid package:*** $24,739 (excluding resources awarded to replace EFC). 27% of all full-time undergraduates had no need and received non-need-based gift aid.

GIFT AID (NEED-BASED) ***Total amount:*** $23,306,578 (6% federal, 2% state, 91% institutional, 1% external sources). ***Receiving aid:*** Freshmen: 49% (295); all full-time undergraduates: 47% (1,112). ***Average award:*** Freshmen: $21,267; Undergraduates: $21,617. ***Scholarships, grants, and awards:*** Federal Pell, FSEOG, state, private, college/university gift aid from institutional funds.

GIFT AID (NON-NEED-BASED) ***Total amount:*** $7,912,634 (94% institutional, 6% external sources). ***Receiving aid:*** Freshmen: 14% (85). Undergraduates: 10% (227). ***Average award:*** Freshmen: $11,213. Undergraduates: $10,279. ***Tuition waivers:*** Full or partial for employees or children of employees.

LOANS ***Student loans:*** $10,339,638 (53% need-based, 47% non-need-based). 63% of past graduating class borrowed through all loan programs. *Average indebtedness per student:* $23,004. ***Average need-based loan:*** Freshmen: $3194. Undergraduates: $4581. ***Parent loans:*** $3,717,105 (14% need-based, 86% non-need-based). ***Programs:*** Federal Direct (Subsidized and Unsubsidized Stafford, PLUS), Perkins.

WORK-STUDY ***Federal work-study:*** Total amount: $240,000; jobs available. ***State or other work-study/employment:*** Total amount: $155,000 (23% need-based, 77% non-need-based). Part-time jobs available.

APPLYING FOR FINANCIAL AID ***Required financial aid forms:*** FAFSA, institution's own form, CSS Financial Aid PROFILE, noncustodial (divorced/separated) parent's statement, business/farm supplement. ***Financial aid deadline:*** 2/15. ***Notification date:*** 4/1.

CONTACT Mr. Greg Mitton, Director of Financial Aid, Muhlenberg College, 2400 Chew Street, Allentown, PA 18104-5586, 484-664-3175. *Fax:* 484-664-3234. *E-mail:* mitton@muhlenberg.edu.

MULTNOMAH UNIVERSITY

Portland, OR

ABOUT THE INSTITUTION Independent interdenominational, coed. 16 undergraduate majors.

GIFT AID (NEED-BASED) ***Scholarships, grants, and awards:*** Federal Pell, FSEOG, private, college/university gift aid from institutional funds.

GIFT AID (NON-NEED-BASED) ***Scholarships, grants, and awards by category:*** *Academic interests/achievement:* education, general academic interests/achievements, religion/biblical studies. *Special characteristics:* children of current students, international students, religious affiliation, siblings of current students.

LOANS ***Programs:*** Federal Direct (Subsidized and Unsubsidized Stafford, PLUS).

WORK-STUDY ***Federal work-study:*** Total amount: $111,838; 75 jobs averaging $1500.

APPLYING FOR FINANCIAL AID ***Required financial aid forms:*** FAFSA, institution's own form.

CONTACT Mrs. Mary J. McGlothlan, Director of Financial Aid, Multnomah University, 8435 NE Glisan Street, Portland, OR 97220-5898, 503-251-5337 or toll-free 800-275-4672. *Fax:* 503-445-5199. *E-mail:* mmcglothlan@multnomah.edu.

MURRAY STATE UNIVERSITY

Murray, KY

Tuition & fees (KY res): $6264 **Average undergraduate aid package: $8023**

ABOUT THE INSTITUTION State-supported, coed. 68 undergraduate majors. Federal methodology is used as a basis for awarding need-based institutional aid.

UNDERGRADUATE EXPENSES for 2010–11 ***Tuition, state resident:*** full-time $5388; part-time $224.50 per hour. ***Tuition, nonresident:*** full-time $16,164; part-time $673.50 per hour. ***Required fees:*** full-time $876; $36.50 per hour. Full-time tuition and fees vary according to reciprocity agreements. Part-time tuition and fees vary according to reciprocity agreements. ***College room and board:*** $6860; ***Room only:*** $4006. Room and board charges vary according to board plan and housing facility. ***Payment plan:*** Installment.

FRESHMAN FINANCIAL AID (Fall 2010, est.) 1,243 applied for aid; of those 67% were deemed to have need. 100% of freshmen with need received aid; of those 94% had need fully met. ***Average percent of need met:*** 92% (excluding resources awarded to replace EFC). ***Average financial aid package:*** $6425 (excluding resources awarded to replace EFC). 86% of all full-time freshmen had no need and received non-need-based gift aid.

UNDERGRADUATE FINANCIAL AID (Fall 2010, est.) 5,794 applied for aid; of those 70% were deemed to have need. 100% of undergraduates with need received aid; of those 94% had need fully met. ***Average percent of need met:*** 86% (excluding resources awarded to replace EFC). ***Average financial aid package:*** $8023 (excluding resources awarded to replace EFC). 77% of all full-time undergraduates had no need and received non-need-based gift aid.

GIFT AID (NEED-BASED) ***Total amount:*** $17,530,997 (80% federal, 10% state, 8% institutional, 2% external sources). ***Receiving aid:*** Freshmen: 52% (683); all full-time undergraduates: 47% (3,140). ***Average award:*** Freshmen: $3598; Undergraduates: $4493. ***Scholarships, grants, and awards:*** Federal Pell, FSEOG, state, private, college/university gift aid from institutional funds.

GIFT AID (NON-NEED-BASED) ***Total amount:*** $9,079,531 (45% state, 48% institutional, 7% external sources). ***Receiving aid:*** Freshmen: 49% (650). Undergraduates: 29% (1,953). ***Average award:*** Freshmen: $3891. Undergraduates: $4181. ***Scholarships, grants, and awards by category:*** *Academic interests/achievement:* agriculture, biological sciences, business, communication, computer science, education, engineering/technologies, English, foreign languages, general academic interests/achievements, health fields, humanities, international studies, library science, mathematics. *Creative arts/performance:* applied art and design, art/fine arts, creative writing, dance, debating, general creative arts/performance, journalism/publications, music, theater/drama. *Special achievements/activities:* cheerleading/drum major, general special achievements/activities, junior miss, leadership, rodeo. *Special characteristics:* adult students, children and siblings of alumni, children of faculty/staff, general special characteristics, handicapped students, international students, local/state students, members of minority groups, out-of-state students. ***Tuition waivers:*** Full or partial for children of alumni, employees or children of employees, senior citizens.

LOANS ***Student loans:*** $33,616,356 (50% need-based, 50% non-need-based). 52% of past graduating class borrowed through all loan programs. *Average indebtedness per student:* $26,100. ***Average need-based loan:*** Freshmen: $2570. Undergraduates: $3209. ***Parent loans:*** $5,410,695 (100% non-need-based). ***Programs:*** Perkins, Federal Nursing, state, college/university.

WORK-STUDY ***Federal work-study:*** Total amount: $498,048; jobs available. ***State or other work-study/employment:*** Total amount: $6,081,803 (100% non-need-based). Part-time jobs available.

ATHLETIC AWARDS Total amount: $3,171,741 (30% need-based, 70% non-need-based).

APPLYING FOR FINANCIAL AID ***Required financial aid forms:*** FAFSA, institution's own form. ***Financial aid deadline (priority):*** 4/1. ***Notification date:*** Continuous beginning 4/15.

CONTACT Lori Mitchum, Director of Student Financial Aid, Murray State University, 500 Sparks Hall, Murray, KY 42071-0009, 270-809-2546 or toll-free 800-272-4678. *Fax:* 270-809-3116. *E-mail:* lori.mitchum@murraystate.edu.

MUSICIANS INSTITUTE

Hollywood, CA

CONTACT Director of Financial Aid, Musicians Institute, 1655 North McCadden Place, Hollywood, CA 90028, 323-462-1384 or toll-free 800-255-PLAY.

MUSKINGUM UNIVERSITY

New Concord, OH

Tuition & fees: $20,616 **Average undergraduate aid package: $20,551**

ABOUT THE INSTITUTION Independent religious, coed. ***Awards:*** bachelor's and master's degrees. 57 undergraduate majors. ***Total enrollment:*** 2,099. Undergraduates: 1,709. Federal methodology is used as a basis for awarding need-based institutional aid.

UNDERGRADUATE EXPENSES for 2010–11 ***Comprehensive fee:*** $28,786 includes full-time tuition ($20,010), mandatory fees ($606), and room and board ($8170). ***College room only:*** $4180. Room and board charges vary according to board plan. ***Payment plan:*** Installment.

FRESHMAN FINANCIAL AID (Fall 2010, est.) 402 applied for aid; of those 92% were deemed to have need. 100% of freshmen with need received aid; of those 19% had need fully met. ***Average percent of need met:*** 76% (excluding resources awarded to replace EFC). ***Average financial aid package:*** $21,125 (excluding resources awarded to replace EFC). 15% of all full-time freshmen had no need and received non-need-based gift aid.

UNDERGRADUATE FINANCIAL AID (Fall 2010, est.) 1,370 applied for aid; of those 93% were deemed to have need. 100% of undergraduates with need received aid; of those 23% had need fully met. ***Average percent of need met:*** 76% (excluding resources awarded to replace EFC). ***Average financial aid package:*** $20,551 (excluding resources awarded to replace EFC). 16% of all full-time undergraduates had no need and received non-need-based gift aid.

GIFT AID (NEED-BASED) ***Total amount:*** $17,646,812 (23% federal, 6% state, 69% institutional, 2% external sources). ***Receiving aid:*** Freshmen: 84% (369); all full-time undergraduates: 82% (1,279). ***Average award:*** Freshmen: $15,314; Undergraduates: $14,311. ***Scholarships, grants, and awards:*** Federal Pell, FSEOG, state, private, college/university gift aid from institutional funds.

GIFT AID (NON-NEED-BASED) ***Total amount:*** $3,557,678 (1% federal, 1% state, 94% institutional, 4% external sources). ***Receiving aid:*** Freshmen: 75% (328). Undergraduates: 75% (1,162). ***Average award:*** Freshmen: $9452. Undergraduates: $8758. ***Scholarships, grants, and awards by category:*** *Academic interests/achievement:* 633 awards ($6,259,885 total): biological sciences, computer science, engineering/technologies, general academic interests/achievements, mathematics, physical sciences, premedicine. *Creative arts/performance:* 157 awards ($206,150 total): art/fine arts, debating, journalism/publications, music, theater/drama. *Special achievements/activities:* 178 awards ($128,750 total): community service, junior miss, leadership. *Special characteristics:* 970 awards ($1,261,966 total): children and siblings of alumni, ethnic background, local/state students, members of minority groups, relatives of clergy, religious affiliation, siblings of current students. ***Tuition waivers:*** Full or partial for employees or children of employees.

LOANS ***Student loans:*** $12,952,678 (72% need-based, 28% non-need-based). 74% of past graduating class borrowed through all loan programs. *Average indebtedness per student:* $34,207. ***Average need-based loan:*** Freshmen: $3669. Undergraduates: $3961. ***Parent loans:*** $2,406,537 (38% need-based, 62% non-need-based). ***Programs:*** Federal Direct (Subsidized and Unsubsidized Stafford, PLUS), Perkins, Federal Nursing, college/university.

WORK-STUDY ***Federal work-study:*** Total amount: $112,229; 350 jobs averaging $1000. ***State or other work-study/employment:*** Total amount: $450,000 (67% need-based, 33% non-need-based). 5 part-time jobs averaging $1000.

APPLYING FOR FINANCIAL AID ***Required financial aid form:*** FAFSA. ***Financial aid deadline (priority):*** 3/1. ***Notification date:*** Continuous beginning 3/1. Students must reply by 5/1 or within 2 weeks of notification.

CONTACT Mr. Jeff Zellers, Vice President of Enrollment, Muskingum University, 163 Stormont Street, New Concord, OH 43762, 740-826-8139 or toll-free 800-752-6082. *Fax:* 740-826-8100. *E-mail:* jzellers@muskingum.edu.

NAROPA UNIVERSITY

Boulder, CO

Tuition & fees: $26,360 **Average undergraduate aid package: $29,350**

ABOUT THE INSTITUTION Independent, coed. 12 undergraduate majors. Federal methodology is used as a basis for awarding need-based institutional aid.

UNDERGRADUATE EXPENSES for 2011–12 ***Comprehensive fee:*** $35,072 includes full-time tuition ($26,200), mandatory fees ($160), and room and board ($8712). ***College room only:*** $5580. Full-time tuition and fees vary according to course load. Room and board charges vary according to board plan. ***Part-time tuition:*** $850 per credit. ***Part-time fees:*** $850 per credit; $152.50 per term. Part-time tuition and fees vary according to course load. ***Payment plan:*** Installment.

FRESHMAN FINANCIAL AID (Fall 2010, est.) 32 applied for aid; of those 97% were deemed to have need. 100% of freshmen with need received aid. ***Average percent of need met:*** 77% (excluding resources awarded to replace EFC). ***Average financial aid package:*** $29,185 (excluding resources awarded to replace EFC).

UNDERGRADUATE FINANCIAL AID (Fall 2010, est.) 302 applied for aid; of those 96% were deemed to have need. 100% of undergraduates with need received aid. ***Average percent of need met:*** 77% (excluding resources awarded to replace EFC). ***Average financial aid package:*** $29,350 (excluding resources awarded to replace EFC).

GIFT AID (NEED-BASED) ***Total amount:*** $4,294,663 (23% federal, 75% institutional, 2% external sources). ***Receiving aid:*** Freshmen: 68% (26); all full-time undergraduates: 67% (268). ***Average award:*** Freshmen: $16,661; Undergraduates: $15,810. ***Scholarships, grants, and awards:*** Federal Pell, FSEOG, state, private, college/university gift aid from institutional funds.

GIFT AID (NON-NEED-BASED) ***Tuition waivers:*** Full or partial for employees or children of employees.

LOANS ***Student loans:*** $2,792,062 (93% need-based, 7% non-need-based). 64% of past graduating class borrowed through all loan programs. *Average indebtedness per student:* $24,958. ***Average need-based loan:*** Freshmen: $13,910. Undergraduates: $12,648. ***Parent loans:*** $917,971 (74% need-based, 26% non-need-based). ***Programs:*** Federal Direct (Subsidized and Unsubsidized Stafford, PLUS), Perkins.

WORK-STUDY ***Federal work-study:*** Total amount: $350,000; jobs available. ***State or other work-study/employment:*** Part-time jobs available.

APPLYING FOR FINANCIAL AID ***Required financial aid form:*** FAFSA. ***Financial aid deadline (priority):*** 3/1. ***Notification date:*** Continuous beginning 3/1. Students must reply within 3 weeks of notification.

CONTACT Ms. Nancy Morrell, Office of Financial Aid, Naropa University, 2130 Arapahoe Avenue, Boulder, CO 80302-6697, 303-546-3534 or toll-free 800-772-0410 (out-of-state). *Fax:* 303-546-3536. *E-mail:* finaid@naropa.edu.

NATIONAL AMERICAN UNIVERSITY

Colorado Springs, CO

CONTACT Financial Aid Coordinator, National American University, 2577 North Chelton Road, Colorado Springs, CO 80909, 719-471-4205.

NATIONAL AMERICAN UNIVERSITY

Denver, CO

CONTACT Cheryl Schunneman, Director of Financial Aid, National American University, 321 Kansas City Street, Rapid City, SD 57701, 605-394-4800.

NATIONAL AMERICAN UNIVERSITY

Roseville, MN

CONTACT Financial Aid Office, National American University, 1500 West Highway 36, Roseville, MN 55113, 651-644-1265.

NATIONAL AMERICAN UNIVERSITY

Kansas City, MO

CONTACT Mary Anderson, Coordinator of Financial Aid, National American University, 4200 Blue Ridge, Kansas City, MO 64133, 816-353-4554. *Fax:* 816-353-1176.

NATIONAL AMERICAN UNIVERSITY

Albuquerque, NM

CONTACT Director of Financial Aid, National American University, 321 Kansas City Street, Rapid City, SD 57701, 605-394-4800 or toll-free 800-843-8892.

NATIONAL AMERICAN UNIVERSITY

Rapid City, SD

CONTACT Financial Aid Director, National American University, PO Box 1780, Rapid City, SD 57709-1780, 605-721-5213 or toll-free 800-843-8892.

NATIONAL AMERICAN UNIVERSITY–SIOUX FALLS BRANCH

Sioux Falls, SD

CONTACT Ms. Rhonda Kohnen, Financial Aid Coordinator, National American University–Sioux Falls Branch, 2801 South Kiwanis Avenue, Suite 100, Sioux Falls, SD 57105-4293, 605-334-5430 or toll-free 800-388-5430 (out-of-state). *Fax:* 605-334-1575. *E-mail:* rkohnen@national.edu.

THE NATIONAL HISPANIC UNIVERSITY

San Jose, CA

CONTACT Takeo Kubo, Director of Financial Aid and Scholarship, The National Hispanic University, 14271 Story Road, San Jose, CA 95127-3823, 408-273-2708. *Fax:* 408-254-1369. *E-mail:* tkubo@nhu.edu.

NATIONAL LABOR COLLEGE

Silver Spring, MD

CONTACT Financial Aid Office, National Labor College, 10000 New Hampshire Avenue, Silver Spring, MD 20903, 301-431-6400 or toll-free 800-GMC-4CDP.

NATIONAL-LOUIS UNIVERSITY

Chicago, IL

Tuition & fees: $18,435 **Average undergraduate aid package: $11,485**

ABOUT THE INSTITUTION Independent, coed. 17 undergraduate majors. Federal methodology is used as a basis for awarding need-based institutional aid.

UNDERGRADUATE EXPENSES for 2010–11 ***Tuition:*** full-time $18,315; part-time $407 per quarter hour. Full-time tuition and fees vary according to course level, course load, degree level, and program. Part-time tuition and fees vary according to course level, course load, degree level, and program. ***Payment plans:*** Installment, deferred payment.

FRESHMAN FINANCIAL AID (Fall 2009) 2 applied for aid; of those 100% were deemed to have need. 50% of freshmen with need received aid. ***Average percent of need met:*** 34% (excluding resources awarded to replace EFC). ***Average financial aid package:*** $3123 (excluding resources awarded to replace EFC).

UNDERGRADUATE FINANCIAL AID (Fall 2009) 922 applied for aid; of those 94% were deemed to have need. 99% of undergraduates with need received aid; of those 10% had need fully met. ***Average percent of need met:*** 54% (excluding resources awarded to replace EFC). ***Average financial aid package:***

$11,485 (excluding resources awarded to replace EFC). 3% of all full-time undergraduates had no need and received non-need-based gift aid.

GIFT AID (NEED-BASED) ***Total amount:*** $7,258,586 (42% federal, 29% state, 29% institutional). ***Receiving aid:*** Freshmen: 25% (1); all full-time undergraduates: 72% (804). ***Average award:*** Freshmen: $3123; Undergraduates: $7186. ***Scholarships, grants, and awards:*** Federal Pell, FSEOG, state, private, college/university gift aid from institutional funds.

GIFT AID (NON-NEED-BASED) ***Total amount:*** $117,318 (28% state, 54% institutional, 18% external sources). ***Receiving aid:*** Undergraduates: 24% (265). ***Average award:*** Undergraduates: $1412. ***Scholarships, grants, and awards by category:*** *Academic interests/achievement:* 301 awards ($446,632 total): general academic interests/achievements. ***Tuition waivers:*** Full or partial for employees or children of employees.

LOANS ***Student loans:*** $11,483,511 (92% need-based, 8% non-need-based). 64% of past graduating class borrowed through all loan programs. *Average indebtedness per student:* $29,637. ***Average need-based loan:*** Undergraduates: $4603. ***Parent loans:*** $1,104,540 (38% need-based, 62% non-need-based). ***Programs:*** Federal Direct (Subsidized and Unsubsidized Stafford, PLUS), Perkins.

WORK-STUDY ***Federal work-study:*** Total amount: $120,058; 35 jobs averaging $3430. ***State or other work-study/employment:*** Total amount: $176,034 (47% need-based, 53% non-need-based). Part-time jobs available.

APPLYING FOR FINANCIAL AID ***Required financial aid form:*** FAFSA. ***Financial aid deadline:*** Continuous. ***Notification date:*** Continuous beginning 4/1.

CONTACT Janet Jazwiec, Assistant Director of Student Finance, National-Louis University, 1000 Capitol Drive, Wheeling, IL 60090, 847-947-5453 or toll-free 888-NLU-TODAY (in-state), 800-443-5522 (out-of-state). *Fax:* 847-947-5453. *E-mail:* jjazwiec@nl.edu.

NATIONAL PARALEGAL COLLEGE

Phoenix, AZ

CONTACT Financial Aid Office, National Paralegal College, 6516 N 7th Street, Suite 103, Phoenix, AZ 85014, 845-371-9101 or toll-free 800-371-6105 (out-of-state).

NATIONAL UNIVERSITY

La Jolla, CA

Tuition & fees: $11,148 **Average undergraduate aid package: $6267**

ABOUT THE INSTITUTION Independent, coed. 45 undergraduate majors. Federal methodology is used as a basis for awarding need-based institutional aid.

UNDERGRADUATE EXPENSES for 2011–12 ***Tuition:*** full-time $11,088; part-time $308 per unit. Full-time tuition and fees vary according to course load and location. Part-time tuition and fees vary according to course load and location.

FRESHMAN FINANCIAL AID (Fall 2009) 648 applied for aid; of those 96% were deemed to have need. 64% of freshmen with need received aid; of those 1% had need fully met. ***Average percent of need met:*** 88% (excluding resources awarded to replace EFC). ***Average financial aid package:*** $3625 (excluding resources awarded to replace EFC).

UNDERGRADUATE FINANCIAL AID (Fall 2009) 7,894 applied for aid; of those 96% were deemed to have need. 56% of undergraduates with need received aid; of those 2% had need fully met. ***Average percent of need met:*** 89% (excluding resources awarded to replace EFC). ***Average financial aid package:*** $6267 (excluding resources awarded to replace EFC).

GIFT AID (NEED-BASED) ***Total amount:*** $8,713,849 (79% federal, 20% state, 1% institutional). ***Receiving aid:*** Freshmen: 30% (248); all full-time undergraduates: 21% (2,055). ***Average award:*** Freshmen: $1985; Undergraduates: $3319. ***Scholarships, grants, and awards:*** Federal Pell, FSEOG, state, college/university gift aid from institutional funds.

GIFT AID (NON-NEED-BASED) ***Total amount:*** $1,089,569 (41% federal, 59% institutional). ***Receiving aid:*** Freshmen: 3% (29). Undergraduates: 7% (662). ***Scholarships, grants, and awards by category:*** *Academic interests/achievement:* general academic interests/achievements. *Special achievements/activities:* leadership. ***Tuition waivers:*** Full or partial for employees or children of employees.

LOANS ***Student loans:*** $36,534,740 (46% need-based, 54% non-need-based). ***Average need-based loan:*** Freshmen: $2611. Undergraduates: $4522. ***Parent loans:*** $877,923 (100% need-based). ***Programs:*** Federal Direct (Subsidized and Unsubsidized Stafford, PLUS), Perkins, college/university.

APPLYING FOR FINANCIAL AID ***Required financial aid forms:*** FAFSA, institution's own form. ***Financial aid deadline:*** Continuous. ***Notification date:*** Continuous beginning 6/30.

CONTACT Valerie Ryan, Financial Aid Office, National University, 11255 North Torrey Pines Road, La Jolla, CA 92037-1011, 858-642-8500 or toll-free 800-NAT-UNIV. *Fax:* 858-642-8720. *E-mail:* vryan@nu.edu.

NATIONAL UNIVERSITY COLLEGE

Bayamón, PR

Tuition & fees: $6315 **Average undergraduate aid package: $1576**

ABOUT THE INSTITUTION Private, coed. 17 undergraduate majors. Federal methodology is used as a basis for awarding need-based institutional aid.

UNDERGRADUATE EXPENSES for 2010–11 ***Tuition:*** full-time $5940; part-time $165 per credit. ***Required fees:*** full-time $375; $125 per term. ***Payment plan:*** Installment.

FRESHMAN FINANCIAL AID (Fall 2009) 1,357 applied for aid; of those 100% were deemed to have need. 100% of freshmen with need received aid. ***Average percent of need met:*** 90% (excluding resources awarded to replace EFC). ***Average financial aid package:*** $1659 (excluding resources awarded to replace EFC).

UNDERGRADUATE FINANCIAL AID (Fall 2009) 7,413 applied for aid; of those 100% were deemed to have need. 100% of undergraduates with need received aid. ***Average percent of need met:*** 90% (excluding resources awarded to replace EFC). ***Average financial aid package:*** $1576 (excluding resources awarded to replace EFC).

GIFT AID (NEED-BASED) ***Total amount:*** $26,984,702 (94% federal, 6% state). ***Receiving aid:*** Freshmen: 97% (1,357); all full-time undergraduates: 91% (7,413). ***Average award:*** Freshmen: $1608; Undergraduates: $1520. ***Scholarships, grants, and awards:*** Federal Pell, FSEOG, state.

GIFT AID (NON-NEED-BASED) ***Receiving aid:*** Freshmen: 2% (21). Undergraduates: 1% (118). ***Tuition waivers:*** Full or partial for employees or children of employees.

LOANS ***Student loans:*** $3,515,736 (91% need-based, 9% non-need-based). ***Average need-based loan:*** Freshmen: $981. Undergraduates: $1100. ***Parent loans:*** $51,302 (100% non-need-based). ***Programs:*** Federal Direct (Subsidized and Unsubsidized Stafford, PLUS).

WORK-STUDY ***Federal work-study:*** Total amount: $693,719; 473 jobs averaging $1467.

APPLYING FOR FINANCIAL AID ***Required financial aid forms:*** FAFSA, commonwealth aid form. ***Financial aid deadline:*** Continuous. ***Notification date:*** Continuous beginning 7/1. Students must reply within 2 weeks of notification.

CONTACT Ms. Damaris Rodriguez, Institutional Director of Financial Aid, National University College, PO Box 2036, Bayamon, PR 00961, 787-780-5134 Ext. 4020 or toll-free 800-780-5134. *Fax:* 787-780-5137. *E-mail:* drodriguez@nuc.edu.

NAZARENE BIBLE COLLEGE

Colorado Springs, CO

Tuition & fees: $9045 **Average undergraduate aid package: $9210**

ABOUT THE INSTITUTION Independent religious, coed. 6 undergraduate majors. Federal methodology is used as a basis for awarding need-based institutional aid.

UNDERGRADUATE EXPENSES for 2010–11 ***Tuition:*** full-time $8505. ***Payment plan:*** Installment.

FRESHMAN FINANCIAL AID (Fall 2009) 4 applied for aid; of those 100% were deemed to have need. 100% of freshmen with need received aid. ***Average percent of need met:*** 60% (excluding resources awarded to replace EFC). ***Average financial aid package:*** $6171 (excluding resources awarded to replace EFC).

UNDERGRADUATE FINANCIAL AID (Fall 2009) 144 applied for aid; of those 100% were deemed to have need. 90% of undergraduates with need received aid. ***Average percent of need met:*** 50% (excluding resources awarded to replace EFC). ***Average financial aid package:*** $9210 (excluding resources awarded to replace EFC).

GIFT AID (NEED-BASED) ***Total amount:*** $1,309,719 (95% federal, 5% institutional). ***Receiving aid:*** Freshmen: 25% (1); all full-time undergraduates:

76% (130). ***Average award:*** Freshmen: $750; Undergraduates: $1500. ***Scholarships, grants, and awards:*** Federal Pell, FSEOG, college/university gift aid from institutional funds.

GIFT AID (NON-NEED-BASED) ***Scholarships, grants, and awards by category:*** *Academic interests/achievement:* religion/biblical studies. ***Tuition waivers:*** Full or partial for employees or children of employees.

LOANS ***Student loans:*** $3,155,212 (56% need-based, 44% non-need-based). 80% of past graduating class borrowed through all loan programs. *Average indebtedness per student:* $31,211. ***Parent loans:*** $14,432 (100% non-need-based). ***Programs:*** Federal Direct (Subsidized and Unsubsidized Stafford, PLUS), Perkins, college/university.

WORK-STUDY ***Federal work-study:*** Total amount: $20,089; 6 jobs averaging $3348.

APPLYING FOR FINANCIAL AID ***Required financial aid form:*** FAFSA. ***Financial aid deadline:*** Continuous. ***Notification date:*** Continuous beginning 2/1.

CONTACT Mr. Malcolm Britton, Director of Financial Aid, Nazarene Bible College, 1111 Academy Park Loop, Colorado Springs, CO 80910-3717, 719-884-5051 or toll-free 800-873-3873. *Fax:* 719-884-5199.

NAZARETH COLLEGE OF ROCHESTER

Rochester, NY

Tuition & fees: $26,184 **Average undergraduate aid package: $19,548**

ABOUT THE INSTITUTION Independent, coed. 66 undergraduate majors. Federal methodology is used as a basis for awarding need-based institutional aid.

UNDERGRADUATE EXPENSES for 2010–11 ***Comprehensive fee:*** $36,900 includes full-time tuition ($25,046), mandatory fees ($1138), and room and board ($10,716). ***College room only:*** $5962. Full-time tuition and fees vary according to course load and program. Room and board charges vary according to board plan and housing facility. ***Part-time tuition:*** $597 per credit hour. ***Payment plans:*** Installment, deferred payment.

FRESHMAN FINANCIAL AID (Fall 2010, est.) 438 applied for aid; of those 89% were deemed to have need. 100% of freshmen with need received aid; of those 19% had need fully met. ***Average percent of need met:*** 75% (excluding resources awarded to replace EFC). ***Average financial aid package:*** $20,112 (excluding resources awarded to replace EFC). 16% of all full-time freshmen had no need and received non-need-based gift aid.

UNDERGRADUATE FINANCIAL AID (Fall 2010, est.) 1,822 applied for aid; of those 91% were deemed to have need. 100% of undergraduates with need received aid; of those 18% had need fully met. ***Average percent of need met:*** 71% (excluding resources awarded to replace EFC). ***Average financial aid package:*** $19,548 (excluding resources awarded to replace EFC). 16% of all full-time undergraduates had no need and received non-need-based gift aid.

GIFT AID (NEED-BASED) ***Total amount:*** $23,569,927 (13% federal, 11% state, 69% institutional, 7% external sources). ***Receiving aid:*** Freshmen: 84% (390); all full-time undergraduates: 81% (1,645). ***Average award:*** Freshmen: $15,271; Undergraduates: $14,146. ***Scholarships, grants, and awards:*** Federal Pell, FSEOG, state, private, college/university gift aid from institutional funds, Federal Nursing.

GIFT AID (NON-NEED-BASED) ***Total amount:*** $4,720,451 (1% state, 81% institutional, 18% external sources). ***Receiving aid:*** Freshmen: 35% (162). Undergraduates: 29% (588). ***Average award:*** Freshmen: $17,849. Undergraduates: $15,470. ***Scholarships, grants, and awards by category:*** *Academic interests/achievement:* 1,932 awards ($15,212,466 total): general academic interests/achievements. *Creative arts/performance:* 234 awards ($840,350 total): art/fine arts, music, theater/drama. *Special characteristics:* 300 awards ($2,194,201 total): children and siblings of alumni, children of faculty/staff, siblings of current students. ***Tuition waivers:*** Full or partial for minority students, children of alumni, employees or children of employees.

LOANS ***Student loans:*** $16,450,929 (80% need-based, 20% non-need-based). 89% of past graduating class borrowed through all loan programs. *Average indebtedness per student:* $38,545. ***Average need-based loan:*** Freshmen: $3565. Undergraduates: $4916. ***Parent loans:*** $4,686,893 (54% need-based, 46% non-need-based). ***Programs:*** Federal Direct (Subsidized and Unsubsidized Stafford, PLUS), Perkins, Federal Nursing.

WORK-STUDY ***Federal work-study:*** Total amount: $2,043,905; 1,045 jobs averaging $1996.

APPLYING FOR FINANCIAL AID ***Required financial aid forms:*** FAFSA, state aid form. ***Financial aid deadline (priority):*** 2/15. ***Notification date:*** Continuous beginning 1/15. Students must reply by 5/1 or within 2 weeks of notification.

CONTACT Samantha Veeder, Director of Financial Aid, Nazareth College of Rochester, 4245 East Avenue, Rochester, NY 14618-3790, 585-389-2310 or toll-free 800-462-3944 (in-state). *Fax:* 585-389-2317. *E-mail:* sveeder0@naz.edu.

NEBRASKA CHRISTIAN COLLEGE

Papillion, NE

CONTACT Ms. Tina Larsen, Director of Financial Aid, Nebraska Christian College, 12550 South 114th Street, Papillion, NE 68046, 402-935-9400. *Fax:* 402-935-9500. *E-mail:* tlarsen@nechristian.edu.

NEBRASKA METHODIST COLLEGE

Omaha, NE

Tuition & fees: $11,770 **Average undergraduate aid package: $8382**

ABOUT THE INSTITUTION Independent religious, coed, primarily women. 8 undergraduate majors. Federal methodology is used as a basis for awarding need-based institutional aid.

UNDERGRADUATE EXPENSES for 2010–11 ***One-time required fee:*** $60. ***Tuition:*** full-time $11,160; part-time $465 per credit hour. ***Required fees:*** full-time $610; $20 per credit hour. Full-time tuition and fees vary according to degree level and program. Part-time tuition and fees vary according to degree level and program. Room and board charges vary according to housing facility. ***Payment plan:*** Installment.

FRESHMAN FINANCIAL AID (Fall 2010, est.) 39 applied for aid; of those 79% were deemed to have need. 100% of freshmen with need received aid; of those 26% had need fully met. ***Average percent of need met:*** 61% (excluding resources awarded to replace EFC). ***Average financial aid package:*** $9287 (excluding resources awarded to replace EFC). 13% of all full-time freshmen had no need and received non-need-based gift aid.

UNDERGRADUATE FINANCIAL AID (Fall 2010, est.) 382 applied for aid; of those 82% were deemed to have need. 99% of undergraduates with need received aid; of those 10% had need fully met. ***Average percent of need met:*** 51% (excluding resources awarded to replace EFC). ***Average financial aid package:*** $8382 (excluding resources awarded to replace EFC). 10% of all full-time undergraduates had no need and received non-need-based gift aid.

GIFT AID (NEED-BASED) ***Total amount:*** $1,879,327 (45% federal, 5% state, 40% institutional, 10% external sources). ***Receiving aid:*** Freshmen: 72% (29); all full-time undergraduates: 60% (249). ***Average award:*** Freshmen: $7041; Undergraduates: $6010. ***Scholarships, grants, and awards:*** Federal Pell, FSEOG, state, private, college/university gift aid from institutional funds.

GIFT AID (NON-NEED-BASED) ***Total amount:*** $285,797 (70% institutional, 30% external sources). ***Receiving aid:*** Freshmen: 20% (8). Undergraduates: 6% (23). ***Average award:*** Freshmen: $4000. Undergraduates: $3518. ***Scholarships, grants, and awards by category:*** *Academic interests/achievement:* 300 awards ($958,850 total): general academic interests/achievements. ***Tuition waivers:*** Full or partial for employees or children of employees.

LOANS ***Student loans:*** $4,765,847 (72% need-based, 28% non-need-based). 93% of past graduating class borrowed through all loan programs. *Average indebtedness per student:* $29,132. ***Average need-based loan:*** Freshmen: $3700. Undergraduates: $3913. ***Parent loans:*** $648,677 (31% need-based, 69% non-need-based). ***Programs:*** Federal Direct (Subsidized and Unsubsidized Stafford, PLUS), Perkins, Federal Nursing, college/university, alternative loans.

WORK-STUDY ***Federal work-study:*** Total amount: $33,630; 17 jobs averaging $1890.

APPLYING FOR FINANCIAL AID ***Required financial aid forms:*** FAFSA, institution's own form. ***Financial aid deadline (priority):*** 4/1. ***Notification date:*** Continuous. Students must reply within 3 weeks of notification.

CONTACT Ms. Penny James, Director of Financial Aid, Nebraska Methodist College, The Josie Harper Campus, 720 North 87th Street, Omaha, NE 68114-3426, 402-354-7225 or toll-free 800-335-5510. *Fax:* 402-354-7020. *E-mail:* penny.james@methodistcollege.edu.

NEBRASKA WESLEYAN UNIVERSITY

Lincoln, NE

Tuition & fees: $23,474 **Average undergraduate aid package: $16,859**

ABOUT THE INSTITUTION Independent United Methodist, coed. 48 undergraduate majors. Federal methodology is used as a basis for awarding need-based institutional aid.

UNDERGRADUATE EXPENSES for 2010–11 ***One-time required fee:*** $120. ***Comprehensive fee:*** $29,774 includes full-time tuition ($23,124), mandatory fees ($350), and room and board ($6300). ***College room only:*** $3580. Room and board charges vary according to board plan and housing facility. ***Part-time tuition:*** $869 per credit hour. ***Part-time fees:*** $175 per credit hour. ***Payment plan:*** Installment.

FRESHMAN FINANCIAL AID (Fall 2010, est.) 382 applied for aid; of those 87% were deemed to have need. 100% of freshmen with need received aid; of those 21% had need fully met. ***Average percent of need met:*** 72% (excluding resources awarded to replace EFC). ***Average financial aid package:*** $17,117 (excluding resources awarded to replace EFC). 23% of all full-time freshmen had no need and received non-need-based gift aid.

UNDERGRADUATE FINANCIAL AID (Fall 2010, est.) 1,318 applied for aid; of those 88% were deemed to have need. 100% of undergraduates with need received aid; of those 19% had need fully met. ***Average percent of need met:*** 69% (excluding resources awarded to replace EFC). ***Average financial aid package:*** $16,859 (excluding resources awarded to replace EFC). 27% of all full-time undergraduates had no need and received non-need-based gift aid.

GIFT AID (NEED-BASED) ***Total amount:*** $13,991,829 (16% federal, 2% state, 79% institutional, 3% external sources). ***Receiving aid:*** Freshmen: 77% (331); all full-time undergraduates: 72% (1,147). ***Average award:*** Freshmen: $13,043; Undergraduates: $12,131. ***Scholarships, grants, and awards:*** Federal Pell, FSEOG, state, private, college/university gift aid from institutional funds.

GIFT AID (NON-NEED-BASED) ***Total amount:*** $3,836,756 (96% institutional, 4% external sources). ***Receiving aid:*** Freshmen: 14% (60). Undergraduates: 9% (141). ***Average award:*** Freshmen: $9224. Undergraduates: $8197. ***Scholarships, grants, and awards by category:*** *Academic interests/achievement:* 1,326 awards ($9,692,925 total): general academic interests/achievements. *Creative arts/performance:* 179 awards ($242,925 total): art/fine arts, music, theater/drama. *Special characteristics:* 141 awards ($131,624 total): children and siblings of alumni, children of educators, children of faculty/staff, international students, relatives of clergy, siblings of current students. ***Tuition waivers:*** Full or partial for employees or children of employees, senior citizens.

LOANS ***Student loans:*** $8,741,524 (73% need-based, 27% non-need-based). 79% of past graduating class borrowed through all loan programs. *Average indebtedness per student:* $24,873. ***Average need-based loan:*** Freshmen: $4141. Undergraduates: $4498. ***Parent loans:*** $2,910,640 (45% need-based, 55% non-need-based). ***Programs:*** Federal Direct (Subsidized and Unsubsidized Stafford, PLUS), Perkins.

WORK-STUDY ***Federal work-study:*** Total amount: $114,000; 146 jobs averaging $780. ***State or other work-study/employment:*** Total amount: $695,318 (37% need-based, 63% non-need-based). 428 part-time jobs averaging $1625.

APPLYING FOR FINANCIAL AID ***Required financial aid form:*** FAFSA. ***Financial aid deadline:*** Continuous. ***Notification date:*** Continuous beginning 2/1. Students must reply within 3 weeks of notification.

CONTACT Mr. Thomas J. Ochsner, Director of Scholarships and Financial Aid, Nebraska Wesleyan University, 5000 Saint Paul Avenue, Lincoln, NE 68504, 402-465-2212 or toll-free 800-541-3818. *Fax:* 402-465-2194. *E-mail:* tjo@nebrwesleyan.edu.

NER ISRAEL RABBINICAL COLLEGE

Baltimore, MD

CONTACT Mr. Moshe Pelberg, Financial Aid Administrator, Ner Israel Rabbinical College, 400 Mount Wilson Lane, Baltimore, MD 21208, 410-484-7200.

NEUMANN UNIVERSITY

Aston, PA

ABOUT THE INSTITUTION Independent Roman Catholic, coed. 19 undergraduate majors.

GIFT AID (NEED-BASED) ***Scholarships, grants, and awards:*** Federal Pell, FSEOG, state, private, college/university gift aid from institutional funds.

GIFT AID (NON-NEED-BASED) ***Scholarships, grants, and awards by category:*** *Creative arts/performance:* music.

LOANS ***Programs:*** Federal Direct (Subsidized and Unsubsidized Stafford, PLUS), Perkins, Federal Nursing.

WORK-STUDY ***Federal work-study:*** Total amount: $250,000; 180 jobs averaging $1400. ***State or other work-study/employment:*** Part-time jobs available.

APPLYING FOR FINANCIAL AID ***Required financial aid form:*** FAFSA.

CONTACT Mrs. Katherine Markert, Director of Financial Aid, Neumann University, One Neumann Drive, Aston, PA 19014-1298, 610-558-5519 or toll-free 800-963-8626. *E-mail:* kmarkert@neumann.edu.

NEUMONT UNIVERSITY

South Jordan, UT

CONTACT Financial Aid Office, Neumont University, 10701 South River Front Parkway, Suite 300, South Jordan, UT 84095, 801-438-1100 or toll-free 866-622-3448.

NEVADA STATE COLLEGE AT HENDERSON

Henderson, NV

CONTACT Financial Aid Office, Nevada State College at Henderson, 1125 Nevada State Drive, Henderson, NV 89015, 702-992-2000.

NEWBERRY COLLEGE

Newberry, SC

ABOUT THE INSTITUTION Independent Evangelical Lutheran, coed. 28 undergraduate majors.

GIFT AID (NEED-BASED) ***Scholarships, grants, and awards:*** Federal Pell, FSEOG, state, private, college/university gift aid from institutional funds.

GIFT AID (NON-NEED-BASED) ***Scholarships, grants, and awards by category:*** *Academic interests/achievement:* biological sciences, business, communication, education, foreign languages, general academic interests/achievements, humanities, mathematics, physical sciences, religion/biblical studies, social sciences. *Creative arts/performance:* music, theater/drama. *Special achievements/activities:* cheerleading/drum major, religious involvement. *Special characteristics:* children and siblings of alumni, children of faculty/staff, international students, local/state students, relatives of clergy, religious affiliation, siblings of current students.

LOANS ***Programs:*** Federal Direct (Subsidized and Unsubsidized Stafford, PLUS), Perkins, state.

WORK-STUDY ***Federal work-study:*** Total amount: $86,440; jobs available. ***State or other work-study/employment:*** Part-time jobs available.

APPLYING FOR FINANCIAL AID ***Required financial aid form:*** FAFSA.

CONTACT Ms. Melissa A. Lutz, Director of Financial Aid, Newberry College, 2100 College Street, Newberry, SC 29108, 803-321-5127 or toll-free 800-845-4955 Ext. 5127. *Fax:* 803-321-5627. *E-mail:* missy.lutz@newberry.edu.

NEWBURY COLLEGE

Brookline, MA

CONTACT Office of Financial Assistance, Newbury College, 129 Fisher Avenue, Brookline, MA 02445-5796, 617-730-7100 or toll-free 800-NEWBURY. *Fax:* 617-730-7108.

NEW COLLEGE OF FLORIDA

Sarasota, FL

Tuition & fees (FL res): $6032 **Average undergraduate aid package: $14,233**

ABOUT THE INSTITUTION State-supported, coed. 42 undergraduate majors. Federal methodology is used as a basis for awarding need-based institutional aid.

UNDERGRADUATE EXPENSES for 2011–12 ***Tuition, state resident:*** full-time $6032. ***Tuition, nonresident:*** full-time $28,949. ***College room and board:*** $8472; ***Room only:*** $5788. Room and board charges vary according to board plan and housing facility. ***Payment plan:*** Installment.

FRESHMAN FINANCIAL AID (Fall 2010, est.) 151 applied for aid; of those 62% were deemed to have need. 100% of freshmen with need received aid; of those 42% had need fully met. ***Average percent of need met:*** 90% (excluding resources awarded to replace EFC). ***Average financial aid package:*** $13,221 (excluding resources awarded to replace EFC). 28% of all full-time freshmen had no need and received non-need-based gift aid.

UNDERGRADUATE FINANCIAL AID (Fall 2010, est.) 572 applied for aid; of those 72% were deemed to have need. 99% of undergraduates with need received aid; of those 51% had need fully met. ***Average percent of need met:*** 89% (excluding resources awarded to replace EFC). ***Average financial aid package:*** $14,233 (excluding resources awarded to replace EFC). 17% of all full-time undergraduates had no need and received non-need-based gift aid.

GIFT AID (NEED-BASED) ***Total amount:*** $4,530,869 (23% federal, 40% state, 35% institutional, 2% external sources). ***Receiving aid:*** Freshmen: 51% (93); all full-time undergraduates: 51% (406). ***Average award:*** Freshmen: $10,461; Undergraduates: $10,142. ***Scholarships, grants, and awards:*** Federal Pell, FSEOG, state, private, college/university gift aid from institutional funds, Academic Competitiveness Grants.

GIFT AID (NON-NEED-BASED) ***Total amount:*** $809,923 (71% state, 28% institutional, 1% external sources). ***Receiving aid:*** Freshmen: 8% (14). Undergraduates: 4% (34). ***Average award:*** Freshmen: $1784. Undergraduates: $1621. ***Scholarships, grants, and awards by category:*** *Academic interests/achievement:* 957 awards ($2,136,065 total): general academic interests/achievements. *Special achievements/activities:* 232 awards ($397,350 total): general special achievements/activities. *Special characteristics:* 193 awards ($1,198,965 total): out-of-state students.

LOANS ***Student loans:*** $2,542,204 (72% need-based, 28% non-need-based). 36% of past graduating class borrowed through all loan programs. *Average indebtedness per student:* $11,458. ***Average need-based loan:*** Freshmen: $3345. Undergraduates: $4542. ***Parent loans:*** $239,206 (80% need-based, 20% non-need-based). ***Programs:*** Federal Direct (Subsidized and Unsubsidized Stafford, PLUS), alternative loans.

WORK-STUDY ***Federal work-study:*** Total amount: $66,411; 20 jobs averaging $3321. ***State or other work-study/employment:*** Total amount: $172,212 (100% need-based). 168 part-time jobs averaging $1031.

APPLYING FOR FINANCIAL AID ***Required financial aid form:*** FAFSA. ***Financial aid deadline (priority):*** 2/15. ***Notification date:*** Continuous beginning 3/15. Students must reply by 5/1 or within 4 weeks of notification.

CONTACT Tara Karas, Acting Director of Financial Aid, New College of Florida, 5800 Bay Shore Road, Sarasota, FL 34243-2109, 941-487-5000. *Fax:* 941-487-5010. *E-mail:* ncfinaid@ncf.edu.

NEW ENGLAND COLLEGE

Henniker, NH

Tuition & fees: $30,495 **Average undergraduate aid package: $22,947**

ABOUT THE INSTITUTION Independent, coed. 40 undergraduate majors. Both federal and institutional methodology are used as a basis for awarding need-based institutional aid.

UNDERGRADUATE EXPENSES for 2011–12 ***Comprehensive fee:*** $41,163 includes full-time tuition ($30,215), mandatory fees ($280), and room and board ($10,668). ***College room only:*** $5549. Full-time tuition and fees vary according to class time, course load, degree level, location, program, and reciprocity agreements. Room and board charges vary according to board plan and housing facility. ***Part-time tuition:*** $353 per semester hour. Part-time tuition and fees vary according to class time, course load, degree level, location, and program. ***Payment plan:*** Installment.

FRESHMAN FINANCIAL AID (Fall 2010, est.) 227 applied for aid; of those 94% were deemed to have need. 100% of freshmen with need received aid; of those 10% had need fully met. ***Average percent of need met:*** 80% (excluding resources awarded to replace EFC). ***Average financial aid package:*** $25,178 (excluding resources awarded to replace EFC). 19% of all full-time freshmen had no need and received non-need-based gift aid.

UNDERGRADUATE FINANCIAL AID (Fall 2010, est.) 681 applied for aid; of those 98% were deemed to have need. 100% of undergraduates with need received aid; of those 7% had need fully met. ***Average percent of need met:*** 73% (excluding resources awarded to replace EFC). ***Average financial aid package:*** $22,947 (excluding resources awarded to replace EFC). 28% of all full-time undergraduates had no need and received non-need-based gift aid.

GIFT AID (NEED-BASED) ***Total amount:*** $11,249,690 (17% federal, 1% state, 80% institutional, 2% external sources). ***Receiving aid:*** Freshmen: 78% (206); all full-time undergraduates: 71% (651). ***Average award:*** Freshmen: $18,866; Undergraduates: $17,252. ***Scholarships, grants, and awards:*** Federal Pell, FSEOG, state, private, college/university gift aid from institutional funds.

GIFT AID (NON-NEED-BASED) ***Total amount:*** $2,944,494 (99% institutional, 1% external sources). ***Receiving aid:*** Freshmen: 79% (208). Undergraduates: 68% (631). ***Average award:*** Freshmen: $11,663. Undergraduates: $11,075. ***Scholarships, grants, and awards by category:*** *Academic interests/achievement:* 730 awards ($6,695,623 total): biological sciences, business, communication, computer science, education, engineering/technologies, English, general academic interests/achievements, health fields, humanities, international studies, mathematics, social sciences. *Creative arts/performance:* 8 awards ($80,250 total): applied art and design, art/fine arts, creative writing, theater/drama. *Special achievements/activities:* 217 awards ($1,410,028 total): community service, leadership. *Special characteristics:* 92 awards ($1,236,962 total): children and siblings of alumni, children of educators, children of faculty/staff, ethnic background, international students, local/state students, parents of current students, siblings of current students. ***Tuition waivers:*** Full or partial for children of alumni, employees or children of employees, adult students, senior citizens.

LOANS ***Student loans:*** $7,488,028 (42% need-based, 58% non-need-based). 61% of past graduating class borrowed through all loan programs. *Average indebtedness per student:* $36,203. ***Average need-based loan:*** Freshmen: $5609. Undergraduates: $6812. ***Parent loans:*** $232,667 (7% need-based, 93% non-need-based). ***Programs:*** Federal Direct (Subsidized and Unsubsidized Stafford, PLUS), Perkins, state.

WORK-STUDY ***Federal work-study:*** Total amount: $448,097; 239 jobs averaging $1862. ***State or other work-study/employment:*** Total amount: $568,150 (95% need-based, 5% non-need-based). 33 part-time jobs averaging $1125.

APPLYING FOR FINANCIAL AID ***Required financial aid form:*** FAFSA. ***Financial aid deadline (priority):*** 4/1. ***Notification date:*** Continuous beginning 2/1. Students must reply by 9/7 or within 2 weeks of notification.

CONTACT Kristen Blase, Student Financial Services Director, New England College, 15 Main Street, Henniker, NH 03242-3293, 603-428-2226 or toll-free 800-521-7642. *Fax:* 603-428-2404. *E-mail:* rstein@nec.edu.

NEW ENGLAND COLLEGE OF BUSINESS AND FINANCE

Boston, MA

CONTACT Financial Aid Office, New England College of Business and Finance, 10 High Street, Suite 204, Boston, MA 02111-2645, 617-951-2350 or toll-free 888-696-NECF.

NEW ENGLAND CONSERVATORY OF MUSIC

Boston, MA

Tuition & fees: $34,950 **Average undergraduate aid package: $24,091**

ABOUT THE INSTITUTION Independent, coed. 9 undergraduate majors. Federal methodology is used as a basis for awarding need-based institutional aid.

UNDERGRADUATE EXPENSES for 2010–11 ***Comprehensive fee:*** $47,050 includes full-time tuition ($34,500), mandatory fees ($450), and room and board ($12,100). Room and board charges vary according to board plan. ***Part-time tuition:*** $1100 per credit.

FRESHMAN FINANCIAL AID (Fall 2010, est.) 69 applied for aid; of those 83% were deemed to have need. 95% of freshmen with need received aid; of those 13% had need fully met. ***Average percent of need met:*** 60% (excluding resources awarded to replace EFC). ***Average financial aid package:*** $24,914 (excluding resources awarded to replace EFC). 39% of all full-time freshmen had no need and received non-need-based gift aid.

UNDERGRADUATE FINANCIAL AID (Fall 2010, est.) 257 applied for aid; of those 84% were deemed to have need. 99% of undergraduates with need received aid; of those 15% had need fully met. ***Average percent of need met:*** 62% (excluding resources awarded to replace EFC). ***Average financial aid package:*** $24,091 (excluding resources awarded to replace EFC). 36% of all full-time undergraduates had no need and received non-need-based gift aid.

GIFT AID (NEED-BASED) ***Total amount:*** $3,814,602 (15% federal, 1% state, 79% institutional, 5% external sources). ***Receiving aid:*** Freshmen: 50% (54); all full-time undergraduates: 51% (211). ***Average award:*** Freshmen: $19,528; Undergraduates: $18,028. ***Scholarships, grants, and awards:*** Federal Pell, FSEOG, state, private, college/university gift aid from institutional funds.

GIFT AID (NON-NEED-BASED) ***Total amount:*** $2,531,688 (91% institutional, 9% external sources). ***Receiving aid:*** Freshmen: 4% (4). Undergraduates: 5% (20). ***Average award:*** Freshmen: $14,541. Undergraduates: $14,801. ***Scholarships, grants, and awards by category:*** *Creative arts/performance:* 321 awards ($2,401,537 total): music, theater/drama. ***Tuition waivers:*** Full or partial for employees or children of employees.

LOANS ***Student loans:*** $2,503,406 (75% need-based, 25% non-need-based). 69% of past graduating class borrowed through all loan programs. *Average indebtedness per student:* $26,373. ***Average need-based loan:*** Freshmen: $3820. Undergraduates: $4955. ***Parent loans:*** $1,071,766 (46% need-based, 54% non-need-based). ***Programs:*** Federal Direct (Subsidized and Unsubsidized Stafford, PLUS), Perkins, state.

WORK-STUDY ***Federal work-study:*** Total amount: $370,428; 182 jobs averaging $2035.

APPLYING FOR FINANCIAL AID ***Required financial aid forms:*** FAFSA, institution's own form. ***Financial aid deadline (priority):*** 2/1. ***Notification date:*** Continuous beginning 4/1. Students must reply by 5/1.

CONTACT Ms. Lauren G. Urbanek, Director of Financial Aid, New England Conservatory of Music, 290 Huntington Avenue, Boston, MA 02115, 617-585-1110. *Fax:* 617-585-1115. *E-mail:* finaid@necmusic.edu.

THE NEW ENGLAND INSTITUTE OF ART

Brookline, MA

UNDERGRADUATE EXPENSES Tuition cost varies by program. Prospective students should contact the school for current tuition costs. Other charges include a starting kit for all first-quarter students. Kits vary in price, depending on the program of study.

CONTACT Financial Aid Office, The New England Institute of Art, 142 Berkeley Street, Boston, MA 02116-5100, 617-267-7910 or toll-free 800-903-4425.

NEW ENGLAND SCHOOL OF COMMUNICATIONS

Bangor, ME

Tuition & fees: $11,930 **Average undergraduate aid package: N/A**

ABOUT THE INSTITUTION Independent, coed, primarily men. 19 undergraduate majors. Federal methodology is used as a basis for awarding need-based institutional aid.

UNDERGRADUATE EXPENSES for 2010–11 ***Comprehensive fee:*** $19,170 includes full-time tuition ($11,120), mandatory fees ($810), and room and board ($7240). ***Part-time tuition:*** $370 per credit. Part-time tuition and fees vary according to course load. ***Payment plan:*** Installment.

FRESHMAN FINANCIAL AID (Fall 2009) 156 applied for aid; of those 89% were deemed to have need. 100% of freshmen with need received aid; of those 2% had need fully met. 1% of all full-time freshmen had no need and received non-need-based gift aid.

UNDERGRADUATE FINANCIAL AID (Fall 2009) 434 applied for aid; of those 87% were deemed to have need. 100% of undergraduates with need received aid; of those 6% had need fully met. 1% of all full-time undergraduates had no need and received non-need-based gift aid.

GIFT AID (NEED-BASED) ***Total amount:*** $1,332,370 (71% federal, 17% state, 4% institutional, 8% external sources). ***Receiving aid:*** Freshmen: 9% (18); all full-time undergraduates: 19% (94). ***Average award:*** Freshmen: $1200; Undergraduates: $1200. ***Scholarships, grants, and awards:*** Federal Pell, FSEOG, state, private, college/university gift aid from institutional funds.

GIFT AID (NON-NEED-BASED) ***Receiving aid:*** Freshmen: 9% (18). Undergraduates: 19% (94). ***Average award:*** Freshmen: $500. Undergraduates: $4300. ***Scholarships, grants, and awards by category:*** *Academic interests/achievement:* communication. *Special achievements/activities:* general special achievements/activities. ***Tuition waivers:*** Full or partial for employees or children of employees.

LOANS ***Student loans:*** $3,326,003 (100% need-based). 84% of past graduating class borrowed through all loan programs. *Average indebtedness per student:* $33,000. ***Average need-based loan:*** Freshmen: $3772. Undergraduates: $3772. ***Parent loans:*** $825,495 (100% need-based). ***Programs:*** Federal Direct (Subsidized and Unsubsidized Stafford, PLUS), alternative loans.

WORK-STUDY ***Federal work-study:*** Total amount: $51,739; 51 jobs averaging $1014. ***State or other work-study/employment:*** Part-time jobs available.

APPLYING FOR FINANCIAL AID ***Required financial aid form:*** FAFSA. ***Financial aid deadline (priority):*** 5/1. ***Notification date:*** Continuous beginning 5/1. Students must reply within 4 weeks of notification.

CONTACT Mrs. Nicole Vachon, Director of Financial Aid, New England School of Communications, One College Circle, Bangor, ME 04401, 888-877-1876. *Fax:* 207-947-3987. *E-mail:* nicole@nescom.edu.

NEW HAMPSHIRE INSTITUTE OF ART

Manchester, NH

CONTACT Linda Lavallee, Director of Financial Aid, New Hampshire Institute of Art, 148 Concord Street, Manchester, NH 03104-4858, 603-623-0313 Ext. 577 or toll-free 866-241-4918 (in-state). *Fax:* 603-647-0658. *E-mail:* llavallee@nhia.edu.

NEW HOPE CHRISTIAN COLLEGE

Eugene, OR

Tuition & fees: $13,190 **Average undergraduate aid package: $13,500**

ABOUT THE INSTITUTION Independent religious, coed. 7 undergraduate majors. Both federal and institutional methodology are used as a basis for awarding need-based institutional aid.

UNDERGRADUATE EXPENSES for 2011–12 ***Comprehensive fee:*** $19,450 includes full-time tuition ($12,000), mandatory fees ($1190), and room and board ($6260). ***College room only:*** $2500. Room and board charges vary according to housing facility. ***Part-time tuition:*** $500 per credit hour. Part-time tuition and fees vary according to class time and course load. ***Payment plan:*** Tuition prepayment.

UNDERGRADUATE FINANCIAL AID (Fall 2010, est.) 95 applied for aid; of those 100% were deemed to have need. 100% of undergraduates with need received aid; of those 8% had need fully met. ***Average percent of need met:*** 75% (excluding resources awarded to replace EFC). ***Average financial aid package:*** $13,500 (excluding resources awarded to replace EFC).

GIFT AID (NEED-BASED) ***Total amount:*** $776,000 (45% federal, 53% institutional, 2% external sources). ***Receiving aid:*** All full-time undergraduates: 59% (65). ***Average award:*** Undergraduates: $5000. ***Scholarships, grants, and awards:*** Federal Pell, FSEOG, private, college/university gift aid from institutional funds.

GIFT AID (NON-NEED-BASED) ***Receiving aid:*** Undergraduates: 61% (68). ***Scholarships, grants, and awards by category:*** *Academic interests/achievement:* general academic interests/achievements, religion/biblical studies. *Creative arts/performance:* music. *Special achievements/activities:* community service, general special achievements/activities, hobbies/interests, leadership, religious involvement. *Special characteristics:* general special characteristics, international students, married students, out-of-state students, relatives of clergy, spouses of current students, veterans, veterans' children. ***Tuition waivers:*** Full or partial for employees or children of employees, senior citizens.

LOANS ***Student loans:*** $700,000 (100% need-based). 68% of past graduating class borrowed through all loan programs. ***Parent loans:*** $40,000 (100% need-based). ***Programs:*** Federal Direct (Subsidized and Unsubsidized Stafford, PLUS).

WORK-STUDY ***Federal work-study:*** Total amount: $75,000; jobs available. ***State or other work-study/employment:*** Total amount: $50,000 (100% need-based). Part-time jobs available.

APPLYING FOR FINANCIAL AID ***Required financial aid forms:*** FAFSA, institution's own form, CSS Financial Aid PROFILE. ***Financial aid deadline:*** 9/1 (priority: 3/1). ***Notification date:*** Continuous beginning 4/1. Students must reply within 4 weeks of notification.

CONTACT Nathan Icenhower, Financial Aid Director, New Hope Christian College, 2155 Bailey Hill Road, Eugene, OR 97405-1194, 541-485-1780 Ext. 125 or toll-free 800-322-2638. *Fax:* 541-343-5801. *E-mail:* finaid@newhope.edu.

NEW JERSEY CITY UNIVERSITY

Jersey City, NJ

Tuition & fees (NJ res): $9348 **Average undergraduate aid package: $9698**

ABOUT THE INSTITUTION State-supported, coed. 27 undergraduate majors. Institutional methodology is used as a basis for awarding need-based institutional aid.

UNDERGRADUATE EXPENSES for 2010–11 ***Tuition, state resident:*** full-time $6804; part-time $227 per credit hour. ***Tuition, nonresident:*** full-time $14,373; part-time $479 per credit hour. ***Required fees:*** full-time $2544; $83 per credit hour. Full-time tuition and fees vary according to program. ***College room and board:*** $9364; ***Room only:*** $6079. ***Payment plan:*** Deferred payment.

FRESHMAN FINANCIAL AID (Fall 2009) 594 applied for aid; of those 90% were deemed to have need. 96% of freshmen with need received aid; of those 7% had need fully met. ***Average percent of need met:*** 64% (excluding resources awarded to replace EFC). ***Average financial aid package:*** $10,229 (excluding resources awarded to replace EFC). 2% of all full-time freshmen had no need and received non-need-based gift aid.

UNDERGRADUATE FINANCIAL AID (Fall 2009) 4,086 applied for aid; of those 94% were deemed to have need. 96% of undergraduates with need received aid; of those 10% had need fully met. ***Average percent of need met:*** 65% (excluding resources awarded to replace EFC). ***Average financial aid package:*** $9698 (excluding resources awarded to replace EFC). 1% of all full-time undergraduates had no need and received non-need-based gift aid.

GIFT AID (NEED-BASED) ***Total amount:*** $24,245,459 (52% federal, 45% state, 3% institutional). ***Receiving aid:*** Freshmen: 67% (425); all full-time undergraduates: 61% (2,849). ***Average award:*** Freshmen: $9523; Undergraduates: $8488. ***Scholarships, grants, and awards:*** Federal Pell, FSEOG, state, college/university gift aid from institutional funds.

GIFT AID (NON-NEED-BASED) ***Total amount:*** $825,080 (16% state, 75% institutional, 9% external sources). ***Receiving aid:*** Freshmen: 9% (58). Undergraduates: 6% (303). ***Average award:*** Freshmen: $3483. Undergraduates: $3681. ***Tuition waivers:*** Full or partial for employees or children of employees, senior citizens.

LOANS ***Student loans:*** $15,242,923 (56% need-based, 44% non-need-based). 61% of past graduating class borrowed through all loan programs. *Average indebtedness per student:* $17,699. ***Average need-based loan:*** Freshmen: $3534. Undergraduates: $4193. ***Programs:*** Federal Direct (Unsubsidized Stafford, PLUS).

WORK-STUDY ***Federal work-study:*** Total amount: $616,716; jobs available.

APPLYING FOR FINANCIAL AID ***Required financial aid form:*** FAFSA. ***Financial aid deadline (priority):*** 4/15. ***Notification date:*** 5/15.

CONTACT Ms. Carmen Panlilio, Assistant Vice President for Admissions and Enrollment Management, New Jersey City University, 2039 Kennedy Boulevard, Jersey City, NJ 07305-1597, 201-200-3173 or toll-free 888-441-NJCU.

NEW JERSEY INSTITUTE OF TECHNOLOGY

Newark, NJ

Tuition & fees (NJ res): $13,370 **Average undergraduate aid package: $12,400**

ABOUT THE INSTITUTION State-supported, coed. 41 undergraduate majors. Federal methodology is used as a basis for awarding need-based institutional aid.

UNDERGRADUATE EXPENSES for 2010–11 ***Tuition, state resident:*** full-time $11,248; part-time $428 per credit. ***Tuition, nonresident:*** full-time $21,800; part-time $932 per credit. ***Required fees:*** full-time $2122; $105 per credit or $105 per term. Full-time tuition and fees vary according to course load and degree level. Part-time tuition and fees vary according to course load and degree level. ***College room and board:*** $10,122; ***Room only:*** $7090. Room and board charges vary according to board plan and housing facility. ***Payment plans:*** Installment, deferred payment.

FRESHMAN FINANCIAL AID (Fall 2010, est.) 650 applied for aid; of those 90% were deemed to have need. 100% of freshmen with need received aid; of those 13% had need fully met. ***Average percent of need met:*** 60% (excluding resources awarded to replace EFC). ***Average financial aid package:*** $13,040 (excluding resources awarded to replace EFC). 9% of all full-time freshmen had no need and received non-need-based gift aid.

UNDERGRADUATE FINANCIAL AID (Fall 2010, est.) 3,309 applied for aid; of those 95% were deemed to have need. 100% of undergraduates with need received aid; of those 7% had need fully met. ***Average percent of need met:*** 55% (excluding resources awarded to replace EFC). ***Average financial aid package:*** $12,400 (excluding resources awarded to replace EFC). 8% of all full-time undergraduates had no need and received non-need-based gift aid.

GIFT AID (NEED-BASED) ***Total amount:*** $37,922,070 (32% federal, 32% state, 35% institutional, 1% external sources). ***Receiving aid:*** Freshmen: 59% (514); all full-time undergraduates: 53% (2,636). ***Average award:*** Freshmen: $11,839; Undergraduates: $10,577. ***Scholarships, grants, and awards:*** Federal Pell, FSEOG, state, private, college/university gift aid from institutional funds, United Negro College Fund, Federal Nursing.

GIFT AID (NON-NEED-BASED) ***Total amount:*** $223,788 (100% state). ***Receiving aid:*** Freshmen: 30% (265). Undergraduates: 22% (1,083). ***Average award:*** Freshmen: $14,525. Undergraduates: $13,886. ***Scholarships, grants, and awards by category:*** *Academic interests/achievement:* 3,201 awards ($30,080,883 total): architecture, biological sciences, business, communication, computer science, engineering/technologies, general academic interests/achievements, humanities, mathematics, physical sciences. *Creative arts/performance:* 6 awards ($25,579 total): applied art and design, theater/drama. *Special achievements/activities:* 304 awards ($869,589 total): community service, general special achievements/activities, leadership, memberships, religious involvement. *Special characteristics:* 352 awards ($2,845,896 total): children of educators, children of faculty/staff, children of union members/company employees, ethnic background, first-generation college students, handicapped students, international students, members of minority groups, out-of-state students, previous college experience, religious affiliation. ***Tuition waivers:*** Full or partial for employees or children of employees.

LOANS ***Student loans:*** $25,987,521 (42% need-based, 58% non-need-based). 59% of past graduating class borrowed through all loan programs. *Average indebtedness per student:* $34,760. ***Average need-based loan:*** Freshmen: $3217. Undergraduates: $4241. ***Parent loans:*** $1,518,131 (100% non-need-based). ***Programs:*** Federal Direct (Subsidized and Unsubsidized Stafford, PLUS), Perkins, Federal Nursing, state, college/university, alternative loans.

WORK-STUDY ***Federal work-study:*** Total amount: $263,941; 422 jobs averaging $1216. ***State or other work-study/employment:*** Total amount: $450,000 (100% non-need-based). 331 part-time jobs averaging $1398.

ATHLETIC AWARDS Total amount: $2,435,524 (100% need-based).

APPLYING FOR FINANCIAL AID ***Required financial aid form:*** institution's own form. ***Financial aid deadline:*** 5/5 (priority: 3/15). ***Notification date:*** 12/15. Students must reply by 5/1 or within 2 weeks of notification.

CONTACT Ivon Nunez, Director of Financial Aid Services, New Jersey Institute of Technology, Student Mall, University Heights, Newark, NJ 07102, 973-596-3476 or toll-free 800-925-NJIT. *Fax:* 973-596-6471. *E-mail:* ivon.nunez@njit.edu.

NEW LIFE THEOLOGICAL SEMINARY

Charlotte, NC

Tuition & fees: $7020 **Average undergraduate aid package: $8623**

ABOUT THE INSTITUTION Independent religious, coed. 2 undergraduate majors. Federal methodology is used as a basis for awarding need-based institutional aid.

UNDERGRADUATE EXPENSES for 2010–11 ***Tuition:*** full-time $6800; part-time $295 per credit hour. ***Required fees:*** full-time $220; $110 per term.

FRESHMAN FINANCIAL AID (Fall 2009) 11 applied for aid; of those 100% were deemed to have need. 100% of freshmen with need received aid; of those 100% had need fully met. ***Average percent of need met:*** 55% (excluding resources awarded to replace EFC). ***Average financial aid package:*** $8648 (excluding resources awarded to replace EFC). 8% of all full-time freshmen had no need and received non-need-based gift aid.

UNDERGRADUATE FINANCIAL AID (Fall 2009) 56 applied for aid; of those 100% were deemed to have need. 100% of undergraduates with need received aid; of those 61% had need fully met. ***Average percent of need met:*** 61% (excluding resources awarded to replace EFC). ***Average financial aid package:*** $8623 (excluding resources awarded to replace EFC). 1% of all full-time undergraduates had no need and received non-need-based gift aid.

GIFT AID (NEED-BASED) ***Total amount:*** $171,502 (90% federal, 10% institutional). ***Receiving aid:*** Freshmen: 67% (8); all full-time undergraduates: 61% (52). ***Average award:*** Freshmen: $4365; Undergraduates: $5135. ***Scholarships, grants, and awards:*** Federal Pell, FSEOG, private, college/university gift aid from institutional funds, Veterans Administration.

GIFT AID (NON-NEED-BASED) ***Total amount:*** $18,485 (100% institutional). ***Average award:*** Freshmen: $504. Undergraduates: $672. ***Scholarships, grants, and awards by category:*** *Academic interests/achievement:* 10 awards ($8330 total): education, foreign languages, religion/biblical studies. *Special achievements/activities:* 23 awards ($19,374 total): memberships, religious involvement. *Special characteristics:* 33 awards ($27,704 total): religious affiliation.

LOANS ***Student loans:*** $300,875 (49% need-based, 51% non-need-based). 50% of past graduating class borrowed through all loan programs. *Average indebtedness per student:* $36,498. ***Average need-based loan:*** Undergraduates: $3500. ***Programs:*** Federal Direct (Subsidized and Unsubsidized Stafford, PLUS).

WORK-STUDY ***Federal work-study:*** Total amount: $4717; 2 jobs averaging $2358.

APPLYING FOR FINANCIAL AID ***Required financial aid form:*** FAFSA. ***Financial aid deadline:*** Continuous. ***Notification date:*** 3/15. Students must reply within 2 weeks of notification.

CONTACT Adm. Brenda C. Simms, Director of Financial Aid, New Life Theological Seminary, 3117 Whiting Avenue, PO Box 790106, Charlotte, NC 28206-7901, 704-334-6882 Ext. 114. *Fax:* 704-334-6885. *E-mail:* bsimms@nlts.edu.

NEWMAN UNIVERSITY

Wichita, KS

ABOUT THE INSTITUTION Independent Roman Catholic, coed. 42 undergraduate majors.

GIFT AID (NEED-BASED) ***Scholarships, grants, and awards:*** Federal Pell, FSEOG, state, private, college/university gift aid from institutional funds.

GIFT AID (NON-NEED-BASED) ***Scholarships, grants, and awards by category:*** *Academic interests/achievement:* general academic interests/achievements. *Creative arts/performance:* art/fine arts, journalism/publications, music, theater/drama. *Special achievements/activities:* community service, leadership, memberships, religious involvement. *Special characteristics:* children and siblings of alumni, children of current students, children of faculty/staff, international students, married students, siblings of current students, spouses of current students.

LOANS ***Programs:*** Federal Direct (Subsidized and Unsubsidized Stafford, PLUS), Perkins.

WORK-STUDY ***Federal work-study:*** Total amount: $68,473; 66 jobs averaging $1037. ***State or other work-study/employment:*** Total amount: $79,551 (100% non-need-based). 80 part-time jobs averaging $994.

APPLYING FOR FINANCIAL AID ***Required financial aid form:*** FAFSA.

CONTACT Kara Schwinn, Financial Aid Counselor, Newman University, 3100 McCormick Avenue, Wichita, KS 67213, 316-942-4291 Ext. 2302 or toll-free 877-NEWMANU Ext. 2144. *Fax:* 316-942-4483.

NEW MEXICO HIGHLANDS UNIVERSITY

Las Vegas, NM

CONTACT Eileen Sedillo, Director, Financial Aid and Scholarship, New Mexico Highlands University, Box 9000, Las Vegas, NM 87701, 505-454-3430 or toll-free 800-338-6648. *Fax:* 505-454-3398. *E-mail:* sedillo_e@nmhu.edu.

NEW MEXICO INSTITUTE OF MINING AND TECHNOLOGY

Socorro, NM

Tuition & fees (NM res): $4942 Average undergraduate aid package: $11,874

ABOUT THE INSTITUTION State-supported, coed. 22 undergraduate majors. Federal methodology is used as a basis for awarding need-based institutional aid.

UNDERGRADUATE EXPENSES for 2010–11 ***Tuition, state resident:*** full-time $4299; part-time $179 per credit hour. ***Tuition, nonresident:*** full-time $13,977; part-time $582 per credit hour. ***Required fees:*** full-time $643. Full-time tuition and fees vary according to reciprocity agreements. Part-time tuition and fees vary according to course load. ***College room and board:*** $5874. Room and board charges vary according to board plan and housing facility.

FRESHMAN FINANCIAL AID (Fall 2010, est.) 324 applied for aid; of those 50% were deemed to have need. 100% of freshmen with need received aid; of those 30% had need fully met. ***Average percent of need met:*** 94% (excluding resources awarded to replace EFC). ***Average financial aid package:*** $11,777 (excluding resources awarded to replace EFC). 41% of all full-time freshmen had no need and received non-need-based gift aid.

UNDERGRADUATE FINANCIAL AID (Fall 2010, est.) 1,067 applied for aid; of those 50% were deemed to have need. 100% of undergraduates with need received aid; of those 42% had need fully met. ***Average percent of need met:*** 91% (excluding resources awarded to replace EFC). ***Average financial aid package:*** $11,874 (excluding resources awarded to replace EFC). 40% of all full-time undergraduates had no need and received non-need-based gift aid.

GIFT AID (NEED-BASED) ***Total amount:*** $2,719,130 (77% federal, 20% state, 3% external sources). ***Receiving aid:*** Freshmen: 35% (131); all full-time undergraduates: 33% (391). ***Average award:*** Freshmen: $6057; Undergraduates: $6704. ***Scholarships, grants, and awards:*** Federal Pell, FSEOG, state, private, college/university gift aid from institutional funds.

GIFT AID (NON-NEED-BASED) ***Total amount:*** $4,905,253 (38% state, 52% institutional, 10% external sources). ***Receiving aid:*** Freshmen: 38% (142). Undergraduates: 31% (369). ***Average award:*** Freshmen: $5924. Undergraduates: $6193. ***Scholarships, grants, and awards by category:*** *Academic interests/achievement:* general academic interests/achievements. ***Tuition waivers:*** Full or partial for employees or children of employees.

LOANS ***Student loans:*** $2,549,772 (43% need-based, 57% non-need-based). 34% of past graduating class borrowed through all loan programs. *Average indebtedness per student:* $15,974. ***Average need-based loan:*** Freshmen: $2702. Undergraduates: $3904. ***Parent loans:*** $113,409 (100% need-based). ***Programs:*** Federal Direct (Subsidized and Unsubsidized Stafford, PLUS), Perkins.

WORK-STUDY ***Federal work-study:*** Total amount: $550,378; 207 jobs averaging $2659. ***State or other work-study/employment:*** Total amount: $170,667 (29% need-based, 71% non-need-based). 59 part-time jobs averaging $1949.

APPLYING FOR FINANCIAL AID ***Required financial aid form:*** FAFSA. ***Financial aid deadline (priority):*** 6/1. ***Notification date:*** Continuous beginning 5/1. Students must reply within 2 weeks of notification.

CONTACT Ms. Annette Kaus, Director of Financial Aid, New Mexico Institute of Mining and Technology, 801 Leroy Place, Socorro, NM 87801, 575-835-5333 or toll-free 800-428-TECH. *Fax:* 575-835-5959. *E-mail:* akaus@admin.nmt.edu.

NEW MEXICO STATE UNIVERSITY

Las Cruces, NM

Tuition & fees (NM res): $5400 Average undergraduate aid package: $8547

ABOUT THE INSTITUTION State-supported, coed. 78 undergraduate majors. Federal methodology is used as a basis for awarding need-based institutional aid.

UNDERGRADUATE EXPENSES for 2010–11 ***Tuition, state resident:*** full-time $4128; part-time $225 per credit hour. ***Tuition, nonresident:*** full-time $15,408; part-time $695 per credit hour. ***Required fees:*** full-time $1272. ***College room and board:*** $6526; ***Room only:*** $3736. Room and board charges vary according to board plan and housing facility. ***Payment plans:*** Installment, deferred payment.

FRESHMAN FINANCIAL AID (Fall 2009) 1,902 applied for aid; of those 81% were deemed to have need. 100% of freshmen with need received aid; of those 8% had need fully met. ***Average percent of need met:*** 57% (excluding resources awarded to replace EFC). ***Average financial aid package:*** $7927 (excluding resources awarded to replace EFC). 15% of all full-time freshmen had no need and received non-need-based gift aid.

UNDERGRADUATE FINANCIAL AID (Fall 2009) 8,508 applied for aid; of those 88% were deemed to have need. 100% of undergraduates with need received aid; of those 5% had need fully met. ***Average percent of need met:*** 55% (excluding resources awarded to replace EFC). ***Average financial aid package:*** $8547 (excluding resources awarded to replace EFC). 11% of all full-time undergraduates had no need and received non-need-based gift aid.

GIFT AID (NEED-BASED) ***Total amount:*** $43,263,892 (64% federal, 24% state, 11% institutional, 1% external sources). ***Receiving aid:*** Freshmen: 57% (1,461); all full-time undergraduates: 53% (6,703). ***Average award:*** Freshmen: $6557; Undergraduates: $6383. ***Scholarships, grants, and awards:*** Federal Pell, FSEOG, state, private, college/university gift aid from institutional funds.

GIFT AID (NON-NEED-BASED) ***Total amount:*** $10,375,488 (1% federal, 69% state, 30% institutional). ***Receiving aid:*** Freshmen: 4% (115). Undergraduates: 3% (357). ***Average award:*** Freshmen: $2257. Undergraduates: $1992. ***Scholarships, grants, and awards by category:*** *Academic interests/achievement:* 153

awards ($44,000 total): agriculture, biological sciences, business, communication, computer science, education, engineering/technologies, English, foreign languages, general academic interests/achievements, health fields, home economics, humanities, mathematics, military science, physical sciences, social sciences. *Creative arts/performance:* 14 awards ($4400 total): applied art and design, art/fine arts, general creative arts/performance, journalism/publications, music, performing arts, theater/drama. *Special achievements/activities:* leadership, rodeo. *Special characteristics:* adult students, children and siblings of alumni, children of faculty/staff, children of public servants, children of union members/company employees, children of workers in trades, children with a deceased or disabled parent, ethnic background, handicapped students, international students, local/state students, married students, members of minority groups, out-of-state students, previous college experience, spouses of current students, veterans, veterans' children. ***Tuition waivers:*** Full or partial for employees or children of employees, senior citizens.

LOANS ***Student loans:*** $42,337,661 (84% need-based, 16% non-need-based). 60% of past graduating class borrowed through all loan programs. *Average indebtedness per student:* $16,619. ***Average need-based loan:*** Freshmen: $9323. Undergraduates: $11,385. ***Parent loans:*** $773,837 (30% need-based, 70% non-need-based). ***Programs:*** Perkins, state.

WORK-STUDY ***Federal work-study:*** Total amount: $902,650; 322 jobs averaging $2803. ***State or other work-study/employment:*** Total amount: $1,058,566 (86% need-based, 14% non-need-based). 378 part-time jobs averaging $2800.

ATHLETIC AWARDS Total amount: $2,904,034 (45% need-based, 55% non-need-based).

APPLYING FOR FINANCIAL AID ***Required financial aid forms:*** FAFSA, institution's own form. ***Financial aid deadline (priority):*** 3/1.

CONTACT Mr. Carlos Clark, Director of Financial Aid, New Mexico State University, Box 30001, Department 5100, Las Cruces, NM 88003-8001, 575-646-4105 or toll-free 800-662-6678. *Fax:* 575-646-7381.

NEW ORLEANS BAPTIST THEOLOGICAL SEMINARY

New Orleans, LA

ABOUT THE INSTITUTION Independent Southern Baptist, coed, primarily men. ***Awards:*** associate, bachelor's, and master's degrees. 4 undergraduate majors. ***Total enrollment:*** 2,036. Undergraduates: 974.

GIFT AID (NEED-BASED) ***Scholarships, grants, and awards:*** state, private, college/university gift aid from institutional funds.

LOANS ***Programs:*** Signature Loans.

APPLYING FOR FINANCIAL AID ***Required financial aid form:*** institution's own form.

CONTACT Owen Nease, Financial Aid Office, New Orleans Baptist Theological Seminary, 3939 Gentilly Boulevard, New Orleans, LA 70126-4858, 504-282-4455 Ext. 3348 or toll-free 800-662-8701. *Fax:* 504-816-8437. *E-mail:* financialaid@nobts.edu.

NEW SAINT ANDREWS COLLEGE

Moscow, ID

Tuition & fees: $10,400 **Average undergraduate aid package: N/A**

ABOUT THE INSTITUTION Independent religious, coed. 1 undergraduate major. Institutional methodology is used as a basis for awarding need-based institutional aid.

UNDERGRADUATE EXPENSES for 2011–12 ***Tuition:*** full-time $10,400. ***Payment plans:*** Guaranteed tuition, installment.

GIFT AID (NEED-BASED) ***Total amount:*** $35,500 (100% institutional).

GIFT AID (NON-NEED-BASED) ***Total amount:*** $78,630 (100% institutional). ***Tuition waivers:*** Full or partial for employees or children of employees.

CONTACT College Bursar's Office, New Saint Andrews College, 405 South Main Street, PO Box 9025, Moscow, ID 83843, 208-882-1566.

THE NEW SCHOOL FOR GENERAL STUDIES

New York, NY

Tuition & fees: $25,320 **Average undergraduate aid package: $23,660**

ABOUT THE INSTITUTION Independent, coed. 2 undergraduate majors. Federal methodology is used as a basis for awarding need-based institutional aid.

UNDERGRADUATE EXPENSES for 2010–11 ***Comprehensive fee:*** $40,580 includes full-time tuition ($25,320) and room and board ($15,260). ***College room only:*** $12,260. Room and board charges vary according to board plan and housing facility. ***Part-time tuition:*** $1055 per credit. Part-time tuition and fees vary according to course load. ***Payment plan:*** Installment.

UNDERGRADUATE FINANCIAL AID (Fall 2010, est.) 264 applied for aid; of those 93% were deemed to have need. 100% of undergraduates with need received aid; of those 3% had need fully met. ***Average percent of need met:*** 67% (excluding resources awarded to replace EFC). ***Average financial aid package:*** $23,660 (excluding resources awarded to replace EFC). 1% of all full-time undergraduates had no need and received non-need-based gift aid.

GIFT AID (NEED-BASED) ***Total amount:*** $3,637,209 (29% federal, 5% state, 61% institutional, 5% external sources). ***Receiving aid:*** All full-time undergraduates: 69% (246). ***Average award:*** Undergraduates: $10,805. ***Scholarships, grants, and awards:*** Federal Pell, FSEOG, state, private, college/university gift aid from institutional funds.

GIFT AID (NON-NEED-BASED) ***Total amount:*** $110,819 (94% institutional, 6% external sources). ***Average award:*** Undergraduates: $6625. ***Scholarships, grants, and awards by category:*** *Academic interests/achievement:* general academic interests/achievements. ***Tuition waivers:*** Full or partial for employees or children of employees.

LOANS ***Student loans:*** $4,237,454 (92% need-based, 8% non-need-based). ***Average need-based loan:*** Undergraduates: $11,430. ***Parent loans:*** $489,345 (62% need-based, 38% non-need-based). ***Programs:*** Federal Direct (Subsidized and Unsubsidized Stafford, PLUS), Perkins.

WORK-STUDY ***Federal work-study:*** Total amount: $81,380; jobs available.

APPLYING FOR FINANCIAL AID ***Required financial aid forms:*** FAFSA, state aid form. ***Financial aid deadline (priority):*** 3/1. ***Notification date:*** Continuous beginning 3/1. Students must reply within 4 weeks of notification.

CONTACT Eileen F. Doyle, Assistant Vice President for Student Financial Services, The New School for General Studies, 65 Fifth Avenue, New York, NY 10003, 212-229-8930 or toll-free 800-862-5039 (out-of-state). *Fax:* 212-229-5919. *E-mail:* sfs@newschool.edu.

THE NEW SCHOOL FOR JAZZ AND CONTEMPORARY MUSIC

New York, NY

Tuition & fees: $35,100 **Average undergraduate aid package: $24,691**

ABOUT THE INSTITUTION Independent, coed. 7 undergraduate majors. Federal methodology is used as a basis for awarding need-based institutional aid.

UNDERGRADUATE EXPENSES for 2010–11 ***Comprehensive fee:*** $50,360 includes full-time tuition ($34,340), mandatory fees ($760), and room and board ($15,260). ***College room only:*** $12,260. Room and board charges vary according to board plan and housing facility. ***Part-time tuition:*** $1125 per credit. Part-time tuition and fees vary according to course load and program. ***Payment plan:*** Installment.

FRESHMAN FINANCIAL AID (Fall 2010, est.) 27 applied for aid; of those 85% were deemed to have need. 100% of freshmen with need received aid; of those 39% had need fully met. ***Average percent of need met:*** 64% (excluding resources awarded to replace EFC). ***Average financial aid package:*** $27,383 (excluding resources awarded to replace EFC). 5% of all full-time freshmen had no need and received non-need-based gift aid.

UNDERGRADUATE FINANCIAL AID (Fall 2010, est.) 109 applied for aid; of those 91% were deemed to have need. 95% of undergraduates with need received aid; of those 14% had need fully met. ***Average percent of need met:*** 70% (excluding resources awarded to replace EFC). ***Average financial aid package:*** $24,691 (excluding resources awarded to replace EFC). 2% of all full-time undergraduates had no need and received non-need-based gift aid.

GIFT AID (NEED-BASED) ***Total amount:*** $1,412,713 (13% federal, 1% state, 81% institutional, 5% external sources). ***Receiving aid:*** Freshmen: 49% (21); all full-time undergraduates: 36% (80). ***Average award:*** Freshmen: $21,680; Undergraduates: $17,942. ***Scholarships, grants, and awards:*** Federal Pell, FSEOG, state, private, college/university gift aid from institutional funds.

GIFT AID (NON-NEED-BASED) ***Total amount:*** $4,297,408 (99% institutional, 1% external sources). ***Receiving aid:*** Freshmen: 2% (1). Undergraduates: 2% (5). ***Average award:*** Freshmen: $20,895. Undergraduates: $14,735. ***Scholar-***

ships, grants, and awards by category: Academic interests/achievement: general academic interests/achievements. *Creative arts/performance:* music. ***Tuition waivers:*** Full or partial for employees or children of employees.

LOANS ***Student loans:*** $912,286 (91% need-based, 9% non-need-based). 69% of past graduating class borrowed through all loan programs. *Average indebtedness per student:* $25,735. ***Average need-based loan:*** Freshmen: $7905. Undergraduates: $10,169. ***Parent loans:*** $482,877 (65% need-based, 35% non-need-based). ***Programs:*** Federal Direct (Subsidized and Unsubsidized Stafford, PLUS), Perkins.

WORK-STUDY Federal work-study jobs available.

APPLYING FOR FINANCIAL AID ***Required financial aid form:*** FAFSA. ***Financial aid deadline:*** Continuous. ***Notification date:*** Continuous beginning 3/1. Students must reply within 4 weeks of notification.

CONTACT Eileen F. Doyle, Assistant Vice President for Student Financial Services, The New School for Jazz and Contemporary Music, 72 Fifth Avenue, New York, NY 10011, 212-229-8930. *E-mail:* sfs@newschool.edu.

NEWSCHOOL OF ARCHITECTURE & DESIGN

San Diego, CA

CONTACT Matt Wakeman, Director of Financial Aid, Newschool of Architecture & Design, 1249 F Street, San Diego, CA 92101-6634, 619-235-4100 Ext. 103. *Fax:* 619-235-4651.

NEW WORLD SCHOOL OF THE ARTS

Miami, FL

CONTACT Financial Aid Office, New World School of the Arts, 300 NE 2nd Avenue, Miami, FL 33132, 305-237-3135.

NEW YORK CITY COLLEGE OF TECHNOLOGY OF THE CITY UNIVERSITY OF NEW YORK

Brooklyn, NY

Tuition & fees (NY res): $4939 **Average undergraduate aid package: $7608**

ABOUT THE INSTITUTION State and locally supported, coed. 38 undergraduate majors. Both federal and institutional methodology are used as a basis for awarding need-based institutional aid.

UNDERGRADUATE EXPENSES for 2011–12 ***Tuition, state resident:*** full-time $4600; part-time $195 per credit. ***Tuition, nonresident:*** full-time $12,450; part-time $415 per credit. ***Required fees:*** full-time $339; $85.20 per term. ***Payment plan:*** Installment.

FRESHMAN FINANCIAL AID (Fall 2010, est.) 2,452 applied for aid; of those 93% were deemed to have need. 97% of freshmen with need received aid; of those 2% had need fully met. ***Average percent of need met:*** 65% (excluding resources awarded to replace EFC). ***Average financial aid package:*** $7751 (excluding resources awarded to replace EFC). 1% of all full-time freshmen had no need and received non-need-based gift aid.

UNDERGRADUATE FINANCIAL AID (Fall 2010, est.) 7,929 applied for aid; of those 95% were deemed to have need. 98% of undergraduates with need received aid; of those 3% had need fully met. ***Average percent of need met:*** 60% (excluding resources awarded to replace EFC). ***Average financial aid package:*** $7608 (excluding resources awarded to replace EFC). 1% of all full-time undergraduates had no need and received non-need-based gift aid.

GIFT AID (NEED-BASED) ***Total amount:*** $61,748,885 (60% federal, 39% state, 1% external sources). ***Receiving aid:*** Freshmen: 80% (2,193); all full-time undergraduates: 78% (7,209). ***Average award:*** Freshmen: $7719; Undergraduates: $7422. ***Scholarships, grants, and awards:*** Federal Pell, FSEOG, state, private, college/university gift aid from institutional funds, Federal Nursing.

GIFT AID (NON-NEED-BASED) ***Receiving aid:*** Freshmen: 18% (501). Undergraduates: 8% (711). ***Average award:*** Freshmen: $500. Undergraduates: $511. ***Tuition waivers:*** Full or partial for employees or children of employees.

LOANS ***Student loans:*** $5,780,505 (100% need-based). ***Average need-based loan:*** Freshmen: $3119. Undergraduates: $3923. ***Programs:*** Federal Direct (Subsidized and Unsubsidized Stafford, PLUS), Perkins, Federal Nursing.

WORK-STUDY ***Federal work-study:*** Total amount: $1,973,821; jobs available.

APPLYING FOR FINANCIAL AID ***Required financial aid form:*** FAFSA. ***Financial aid deadline:*** 4/30 (priority: 1/1). ***Notification date:*** 3/1.

CONTACT Sandra Higgins, Director of Financial Aid, New York City College of Technology of the City University of New York, 300 Jay Street, Namm Hall, Room G-13, Brooklyn, NY 11201, 718-260-5700. *Fax:* 718-254-8525. *E-mail:* shiggins@citytech.cuny.edu.

NEW YORK INSTITUTE OF TECHNOLOGY

Old Westbury, NY

Tuition & fees: $25,470 **Average undergraduate aid package: $20,439**

ABOUT THE INSTITUTION Independent, coed. 61 undergraduate majors. Federal methodology is used as a basis for awarding need-based institutional aid.

UNDERGRADUATE EXPENSES for 2010–11 ***Comprehensive fee:*** $36,570 includes full-time tuition ($24,670), mandatory fees ($800), and room and board ($11,100). Full-time tuition and fees vary according to course load and program. Room and board charges vary according to board plan, housing facility, and location. ***Part-time tuition:*** $835 per credit hour. ***Part-time fees:*** $330 per term. Part-time tuition and fees vary according to course load. ***Payment plan:*** Installment.

FRESHMAN FINANCIAL AID (Fall 2009) 1,133 applied for aid; of those 88% were deemed to have need. 99% of freshmen with need received aid. ***Average financial aid package:*** $15,703 (excluding resources awarded to replace EFC). 12% of all full-time freshmen had no need and received non-need-based gift aid.

UNDERGRADUATE FINANCIAL AID (Fall 2009) 3,307 applied for aid; of those 88% were deemed to have need. 99% of undergraduates with need received aid. ***Average financial aid package:*** $20,439 (excluding resources awarded to replace EFC). 10% of all full-time undergraduates had no need and received non-need-based gift aid.

GIFT AID (NEED-BASED) ***Total amount:*** $16,916,647 (48% federal, 31% state, 21% institutional). ***Receiving aid:*** Freshmen: 43% (716); all full-time undergraduates: 36% (2,070). ***Average award:*** Freshmen: $5008; Undergraduates: $6796. ***Scholarships, grants, and awards:*** Federal Pell, FSEOG, state, private, college/university gift aid from institutional funds.

GIFT AID (NON-NEED-BASED) ***Total amount:*** $20,544,657 (92% institutional, 8% external sources). ***Receiving aid:*** Freshmen: 56% (919). Undergraduates: 44% (2,540). ***Average award:*** Freshmen: $9252. Undergraduates: $11,506. ***Scholarships, grants, and awards by category:*** *Academic interests/achievement:* general academic interests/achievements. *Special characteristics:* children and siblings of alumni, children of educators, children of faculty/staff, children of public servants, local/state students, previous college experience, public servants, spouses of deceased or disabled public servants, veterans. ***Tuition waivers:*** Full or partial for employees or children of employees, senior citizens.

LOANS ***Student loans:*** $26,051,389 (46% need-based, 54% non-need-based). ***Average need-based loan:*** Freshmen: $4053. Undergraduates: $6226. ***Parent loans:*** $12,357,549 (100% non-need-based). ***Programs:*** Federal Direct (Subsidized and Unsubsidized Stafford, PLUS), Perkins, alternative loans.

WORK-STUDY ***Federal work-study:*** Total amount: $834,743; jobs available. ***State or other work-study/employment:*** Total amount: $638,898 (100% non-need-based). Part-time jobs available.

ATHLETIC AWARDS Total amount: $2,353,682 (100% non-need-based).

APPLYING FOR FINANCIAL AID ***Required financial aid form:*** FAFSA. ***Financial aid deadline (priority):*** 3/1. ***Notification date:*** Continuous beginning 3/1. Students must reply within 4 weeks of notification.

CONTACT Doreen Meyer, Director of Financial Aid, New York Institute of Technology, PO Box 8000, Old Westbury, NY 11568-8000, 516-686-1083 or toll-free 800-345-NYIT. *Fax:* 516-686-7997. *E-mail:* dmeyer@nyit.edu.

NEW YORK SCHOOL OF INTERIOR DESIGN

New York, NY

Tuition & fees: $23,856 **Average undergraduate aid package: $7890**

ABOUT THE INSTITUTION Independent, coed, primarily women. 1 undergraduate major. Federal methodology is used as a basis for awarding need-based institutional aid.

UNDERGRADUATE EXPENSES for 2011–12 ***Tuition:*** full-time $23,521; part-time $796 per credit. ***Required fees:*** full-time $335; $335 per term. Full-time tuition and fees vary according to course load. Part-time tuition and fees vary according to course load. ***Payment plan:*** Installment.

FRESHMAN FINANCIAL AID (Fall 2009) 137 applied for aid; of those 94% were deemed to have need. 15% of freshmen with need received aid; of those 11% had need fully met. ***Average percent of need met:*** 1% (excluding resources awarded to replace EFC). ***Average financial aid package:*** $9134 (excluding resources awarded to replace EFC). 1% of all full-time freshmen had no need and received non-need-based gift aid.

UNDERGRADUATE FINANCIAL AID (Fall 2009) 403 applied for aid; of those 93% were deemed to have need. 28% of undergraduates with need received aid; of those 5% had need fully met. ***Average percent of need met:*** 1% (excluding resources awarded to replace EFC). ***Average financial aid package:*** $7890 (excluding resources awarded to replace EFC). 1% of all full-time undergraduates had no need and received non-need-based gift aid.

GIFT AID (NEED-BASED) ***Total amount:*** $622,333 (53% federal, 13% state, 28% institutional, 6% external sources). ***Receiving aid:*** Freshmen: 11% (15); all full-time undergraduates: 19% (76). ***Average award:*** Freshmen: $7596; Undergraduates: $5907. ***Scholarships, grants, and awards:*** Federal Pell, FSEOG, state, college/university gift aid from institutional funds.

GIFT AID (NON-NEED-BASED) ***Total amount:*** $42,128 (13% state, 87% institutional). ***Receiving aid:*** Undergraduates: 1. ***Average award:*** Freshmen: $5500. Undergraduates: $5750. ***Tuition waivers:*** Full or partial for employees or children of employees.

LOANS ***Student loans:*** $1,860,230 (80% need-based, 20% non-need-based). 65% of past graduating class borrowed through all loan programs. *Average indebtedness per student:* $13,327. ***Average need-based loan:*** Freshmen: $3162. Undergraduates: $3775. ***Parent loans:*** $462,358 (64% need-based, 36% non-need-based). ***Programs:*** Federal Direct (Subsidized and Unsubsidized Stafford, PLUS), state.

WORK-STUDY ***Federal work-study:*** Total amount: $33,072; 20 jobs averaging $2212.

APPLYING FOR FINANCIAL AID ***Required financial aid forms:*** FAFSA, state aid form. ***Financial aid deadline (priority):*** 8/1. ***Notification date:*** Continuous beginning 4/1. Students must reply within 2 weeks of notification.

CONTACT Mrs. Rashmi H. Wadhvani, Director of Financial Aid, New York School of Interior Design, 170 East 70th Street, New York, NY 10021-5110, 212-472-1500 Ext. 212 or toll-free 800-336-9743 Ext. 204. *Fax:* 212-472-1867. *E-mail:* rwadhvani@nysid.edu.

NEW YORK UNIVERSITY

New York, NY

Tuition & fees: $40,082 **Average undergraduate aid package: $24,999**

ABOUT THE INSTITUTION Independent, coed. 87 undergraduate majors. Federal methodology is used as a basis for awarding need-based institutional aid.

UNDERGRADUATE EXPENSES for 2010–11 ***Comprehensive fee:*** $53,592 includes full-time tuition ($37,866), mandatory fees ($2216), and room and board ($13,510). Full-time tuition and fees vary according to course load and program. Room and board charges vary according to board plan and housing facility. ***Part-time tuition:*** $1179 per credit. ***Part-time fees:*** $60 per credit; $409 per term. Part-time tuition and fees vary according to program. ***Payment plans:*** Guaranteed tuition, tuition prepayment, installment, deferred payment.

FRESHMAN FINANCIAL AID (Fall 2009) 3,390 applied for aid; of those 82% were deemed to have need. 100% of freshmen with need received aid. ***Average percent of need met:*** 69% (excluding resources awarded to replace EFC). ***Average financial aid package:*** $27,501 (excluding resources awarded to replace EFC). 5% of all full-time freshmen had no need and received non-need-based gift aid.

UNDERGRADUATE FINANCIAL AID (Fall 2009) 12,459 applied for aid; of those 87% were deemed to have need. 100% of undergraduates with need received aid. ***Average percent of need met:*** 61% (excluding resources awarded to replace EFC). ***Average financial aid package:*** $24,999 (excluding resources awarded to replace EFC). 7% of all full-time undergraduates had no need and received non-need-based gift aid.

GIFT AID (NEED-BASED) ***Total amount:*** $191,087,286 (13% federal, 5% state, 78% institutional, 4% external sources). ***Receiving aid:*** Freshmen: 54% (2,708); all full-time undergraduates: 51% (10,255). ***Average award:*** Freshmen: $21,348; Undergraduates: $18,459. ***Scholarships, grants, and awards:*** Federal Pell, FSEOG, state, private, college/university gift aid from institutional funds.

GIFT AID (NON-NEED-BASED) ***Total amount:*** $13,274,630 (3% state, 73% institutional, 24% external sources). ***Average award:*** Freshmen: $7040. Undergraduates: $6920. ***Scholarships, grants, and awards by category:*** *Academic interests/achievement:* 1,387 awards ($9,597,721 total): general academic interests/achievements. ***Tuition waivers:*** Full or partial for employees or children of employees.

LOANS ***Student loans:*** $117,362,996 (89% need-based, 11% non-need-based). 55% of past graduating class borrowed through all loan programs. *Average indebtedness per student:* $41,300. ***Average need-based loan:*** Freshmen: $3662. Undergraduates: $5016. ***Parent loans:*** $102,552,119 (82% need-based, 18% non-need-based). ***Programs:*** Federal Direct (Subsidized and Unsubsidized Stafford, PLUS), Perkins, Federal Nursing.

WORK-STUDY ***Federal work-study:*** Total amount: $6,024,592; 2,960 jobs averaging $2185.

APPLYING FOR FINANCIAL AID ***Required financial aid forms:*** FAFSA, state aid form. ***Financial aid deadline (priority):*** 2/15. ***Notification date:*** 4/1. Students must reply by 5/1.

CONTACT Financial Aid Office, New York University, 25 West Fourth Street, New York, NY 10012-1199, 212-998-4444. *Fax:* 212-995-4661. *E-mail:* financial.aid@nyu.edu.

NIAGARA UNIVERSITY

Niagara Falls, NY

Tuition & fees: $25,650 **Average undergraduate aid package: $20,370**

ABOUT THE INSTITUTION Independent religious, coed. 59 undergraduate majors. Federal methodology is used as a basis for awarding need-based institutional aid.

UNDERGRADUATE EXPENSES for 2010–11 ***Comprehensive fee:*** $36,300 includes full-time tuition ($24,600), mandatory fees ($1050), and room and board ($10,650). ***Part-time tuition:*** $820 per credit hour. ***Payment plans:*** Installment, deferred payment.

FRESHMAN FINANCIAL AID (Fall 2010, est.) 635 applied for aid; of those 93% were deemed to have need. 100% of freshmen with need received aid; of those 52% had need fully met. ***Average percent of need met:*** 87% (excluding resources awarded to replace EFC). ***Average financial aid package:*** $21,997 (excluding resources awarded to replace EFC). 14% of all full-time freshmen had no need and received non-need-based gift aid.

UNDERGRADUATE FINANCIAL AID (Fall 2010, est.) 2,328 applied for aid; of those 92% were deemed to have need. 100% of undergraduates with need received aid; of those 50% had need fully met. ***Average percent of need met:*** 82% (excluding resources awarded to replace EFC). ***Average financial aid package:*** $20,370 (excluding resources awarded to replace EFC). 16% of all full-time undergraduates had no need and received non-need-based gift aid.

GIFT AID (NEED-BASED) ***Total amount:*** $35,933,043 (18% federal, 8% state, 73% institutional, 1% external sources). ***Receiving aid:*** Freshmen: 86% (579); all full-time undergraduates: 72% (2,105). ***Average award:*** Freshmen: $18,401; Undergraduates: $16,130. ***Scholarships, grants, and awards:*** Federal Pell, FSEOG, state, private, college/university gift aid from institutional funds.

GIFT AID (NON-NEED-BASED) ***Total amount:*** $5,144,736 (5% federal, 1% state, 93% institutional, 1% external sources). ***Receiving aid:*** Freshmen: 67% (447). Undergraduates: 55% (1,621). ***Average award:*** Freshmen: $12,091. Undergraduates: $10,208. ***Scholarships, grants, and awards by category:*** *Academic interests/achievement:* 2,552 awards ($24,601,123 total): general academic interests/achievements. *Creative arts/performance:* 51 awards ($240,235 total): theater/drama. *Special achievements/activities:* 7 awards ($23,000 total): community service. *Special characteristics:* 102 awards ($2,316,765 total): children of faculty/staff, relatives of clergy. ***Tuition waivers:*** Full or partial for employees or children of employees, senior citizens.

LOANS ***Student loans:*** $17,616,668 (94% need-based, 6% non-need-based). 80% of past graduating class borrowed through all loan programs. *Average indebtedness per student:* $27,813. ***Average need-based loan:*** Freshmen: $4010. Undergraduates: $4598. ***Parent loans:*** $5,032,580 (93% need-based, 7% non-need-based). ***Programs:*** Federal Direct (Subsidized and Unsubsidized Stafford, PLUS), Perkins, Federal Nursing, college/university.

WORK-STUDY ***Federal work-study:*** Total amount: $1,251,596; 381 jobs averaging $3167. ***State or other work-study/employment:*** Total amount: $218,999 (100% non-need-based). 35 part-time jobs averaging $4162.

ATHLETIC AWARDS Total amount: $3,839,755 (40% need-based, 60% non-need-based).

APPLYING FOR FINANCIAL AID ***Required financial aid forms:*** FAFSA, state aid form. ***Financial aid deadline (priority):*** 2/15. ***Notification date:*** Continuous beginning 3/15. Students must reply within 3 weeks of notification.

CONTACT Mrs. Maureen E. Salfi, Director of Financial Aid, Niagara University, Niagara University, NY 14109, 716-286-8686 or toll-free 800-462-2111. *Fax:* 716-286-8678. *E-mail:* finaid@niagara.edu.

NICHOLLS STATE UNIVERSITY

Thibodaux, LA

Tuition & fees (LA res): $4292 **Average undergraduate aid package: $7980**

ABOUT THE INSTITUTION State-supported, coed. 37 undergraduate majors. Federal methodology is used as a basis for awarding need-based institutional aid.

UNDERGRADUATE EXPENSES for 2010–11 ***Tuition, state resident:*** full-time $4292. ***Tuition, nonresident:*** full-time $11,516. Part-time tuition and fees vary according to course load. ***College room and board:*** $7808; ***Room only:*** $5200. Room and board charges vary according to board plan and housing facility. ***Payment plans:*** Installment, deferred payment.

FRESHMAN FINANCIAL AID (Fall 2009) 1,148 applied for aid; of those 52% were deemed to have need. 99% of freshmen with need received aid; of those 78% had need fully met. ***Average percent of need met:*** 93% (excluding resources awarded to replace EFC). ***Average financial aid package:*** $8204 (excluding resources awarded to replace EFC). 10% of all full-time freshmen had no need and received non-need-based gift aid.

UNDERGRADUATE FINANCIAL AID (Fall 2009) 4,311 applied for aid; of those 59% were deemed to have need. 99% of undergraduates with need received aid; of those 70% had need fully met. ***Average percent of need met:*** 90% (excluding resources awarded to replace EFC). ***Average financial aid package:*** $7980 (excluding resources awarded to replace EFC). 6% of all full-time undergraduates had no need and received non-need-based gift aid.

GIFT AID (NEED-BASED) ***Total amount:*** $11,338,026 (77% federal, 16% state, 3% institutional, 4% external sources). ***Receiving aid:*** Freshmen: 46% (557); all full-time undergraduates: 43% (2,237). ***Average award:*** Freshmen: $5113; Undergraduates: $4862. ***Scholarships, grants, and awards:*** Federal Pell, FSEOG, state, private, college/university gift aid from institutional funds.

GIFT AID (NON-NEED-BASED) ***Total amount:*** $8,138,893 (69% state, 14% institutional, 17% external sources). ***Receiving aid:*** Freshmen: 26% (322). Undergraduates: 15% (793). ***Average award:*** Freshmen: $2488. Undergraduates: $2766. ***Scholarships, grants, and awards by category:*** *Academic interests/achievement:* general academic interests/achievements. *Creative arts/performance:* dance, music. *Special achievements/activities:* cheerleading/drum major, leadership. *Special characteristics:* children of faculty/staff, general special characteristics, local/state students, members of minority groups, out-of-state students, previous college experience, public servants, veterans. ***Tuition waivers:*** Full or partial for employees or children of employees.

LOANS ***Student loans:*** $14,718,598 (30% need-based, 70% non-need-based). 52% of past graduating class borrowed through all loan programs. *Average indebtedness per student:* $20,589. ***Average need-based loan:*** Freshmen: $2649. Undergraduates: $3577. ***Parent loans:*** $581,777 (3% need-based, 97% non-need-based). ***Programs:*** Federal Direct (Subsidized and Unsubsidized Stafford, PLUS), Perkins, private loans.

WORK-STUDY ***Federal work-study:*** Total amount: $230,711; jobs available. ***State or other work-study/employment:*** Total amount: $1,622,499 (3% need-based, 97% non-need-based). Part-time jobs available.

ATHLETIC AWARDS Total amount: $1,584,813 (24% need-based, 76% non-need-based).

APPLYING FOR FINANCIAL AID ***Required financial aid forms:*** FAFSA, institution's own form, state aid form, noncustodial (divorced/separated) parent's statement. ***Financial aid deadline:*** 6/30 (priority: 4/15). ***Notification date:*** Continuous. Students must reply within 2 weeks of notification.

CONTACT Casie Triche, Director of Financial Aid, Nicholls State University, PO Box 2005, Thibodaux, LA 70310, 985-448-4077 or toll-free 877-NICHOLLS. *Fax:* 985-448-4124. *E-mail:* finaid@nicholls.edu.

NICHOLS COLLEGE

Dudley, MA

Tuition & fees: $28,870 **Average undergraduate aid package: $27,420**

ABOUT THE INSTITUTION Independent, coed. 20 undergraduate majors. Federal methodology is used as a basis for awarding need-based institutional aid.

UNDERGRADUATE EXPENSES for 2010–11 ***Comprehensive fee:*** $38,200 includes full-time tuition ($28,570), mandatory fees ($300), and room and board ($9330). ***College room only:*** $4900. Room and board charges vary according to housing facility. ***Part-time tuition:*** $275 per credit hour. Part-time tuition and fees vary according to class time and course load. ***Payment plan:*** Installment.

FRESHMAN FINANCIAL AID (Fall 2010, est.) 318 applied for aid; of those 99% were deemed to have need. 100% of freshmen with need received aid; of those 10% had need fully met. ***Average percent of need met:*** 77% (excluding resources awarded to replace EFC). ***Average financial aid package:*** $23,581 (excluding resources awarded to replace EFC). 10% of all full-time freshmen had no need and received non-need-based gift aid.

UNDERGRADUATE FINANCIAL AID (Fall 2010, est.) 1,098 applied for aid; of those 98% were deemed to have need. 100% of undergraduates with need received aid; of those 6% had need fully met. ***Average percent of need met:*** 78% (excluding resources awarded to replace EFC). ***Average financial aid package:*** $27,420 (excluding resources awarded to replace EFC). 6% of all full-time undergraduates had no need and received non-need-based gift aid.

GIFT AID (NEED-BASED) ***Total amount:*** $14,009,398 (12% federal, 3% state, 83% institutional, 2% external sources). ***Receiving aid:*** Freshmen: 97% (309); all full-time undergraduates: 95% (1,052). ***Average award:*** Freshmen: $18,672; Undergraduates: $17,542. ***Scholarships, grants, and awards:*** Federal Pell, FSEOG, state, private, college/university gift aid from institutional funds.

GIFT AID (NON-NEED-BASED) ***Total amount:*** $526,237 (100% institutional). ***Receiving aid:*** Freshmen: 10% (32). Undergraduates: 6% (61). ***Average award:*** Freshmen: $9754. Undergraduates: $9983. ***Scholarships, grants, and awards by category:*** *Academic interests/achievement:* general academic interests/achievements. *Special achievements/activities:* community service, general special achievements/activities, leadership. *Special characteristics:* children and siblings of alumni, children of faculty/staff, siblings of current students. ***Tuition waivers:*** Full or partial for employees or children of employees, senior citizens.

LOANS ***Student loans:*** $9,880,829 (97% need-based, 3% non-need-based). 87% of past graduating class borrowed through all loan programs. *Average indebtedness per student:* $27,715. ***Average need-based loan:*** Freshmen: $3032. Undergraduates: $3654. ***Parent loans:*** $4,663,091 (100% need-based). ***Programs:*** Federal Direct (Subsidized and Unsubsidized Stafford, PLUS).

WORK-STUDY ***Federal work-study:*** Total amount: $643,090; 327 jobs averaging $1435.

APPLYING FOR FINANCIAL AID ***Required financial aid form:*** FAFSA. ***Financial aid deadline (priority):*** 3/1. ***Notification date:*** Continuous. Students must reply within 2 weeks of notification.

CONTACT Ms. Denise Brindle, Director of Financial Aid, Nichols College, PO Box 5000, Dudley, MA 01571, 508-213-2372 or toll-free 800-470-3379. *Fax:* 508-213-2118. *E-mail:* denise.brindle@nichols.edu.

NORFOLK STATE UNIVERSITY

Norfolk, VA

Tuition & fees (VA res): $9162 **Average undergraduate aid package: N/A**

ABOUT THE INSTITUTION State-supported, coed. 32 undergraduate majors. Federal methodology is used as a basis for awarding need-based institutional aid.

UNDERGRADUATE EXPENSES for 2010–11 ***Tuition, state resident:*** full-time $5694; part-time $275.39 per credit hour. ***Tuition, nonresident:*** full-time $14,742; part-time $710.50 per credit hour. ***Required fees:*** full-time $3468. Full-time tuition and fees vary according to course load. Part-time tuition and fees vary according to course load. ***College room and board:*** $7719; ***Room only:*** $4857. Room and board charges vary according to board plan and housing facility. ***Payment plan:*** Installment.

GIFT AID (NEED-BASED) ***Total amount:*** $24,808,069 (71% federal, 25% state, 4% institutional). ***Scholarships, grants, and awards:*** Federal Pell, FSEOG, state, private, college/university gift aid from institutional funds.

GIFT AID (NON-NEED-BASED) ***Scholarships, grants, and awards by category:*** *Creative arts/performance:* music, performing arts. *Special achievements/activities:* general special achievements/activities.

LOANS ***Student loans:*** $17,658,420 (100% need-based). ***Programs:*** Federal Direct (Subsidized and Unsubsidized Stafford), Perkins, state, alternative loans.

WORK-STUDY ***Federal work-study:*** Total amount: $923,012; jobs available. ***State or other work-study/employment:*** Total amount: $340,507 (100% need-based). Part-time jobs available.

ATHLETIC AWARDS Total amount: $3,006,568 (100% non-need-based).

APPLYING FOR FINANCIAL AID ***Required financial aid form:*** FAFSA. ***Financial aid deadline:*** 5/31. ***Notification date:*** 6/15. Students must reply within 2 weeks of notification.

CONTACT Mr. Kevin Burns, Director of Financial Aid, Norfolk State University, 700 Park Avenue, Norfolk, VA 23504-3907, 757-823-8381. *Fax:* 757-823-9059. *E-mail:* kburns@nsu.edu.

NORTH CAROLINA AGRICULTURAL AND TECHNICAL STATE UNIVERSITY

Greensboro, NC

Tuition & fees (NC res): $4416 **Average undergraduate aid package: $12,838**

ABOUT THE INSTITUTION State-supported, coed. 76 undergraduate majors. Federal methodology is used as a basis for awarding need-based institutional aid.

UNDERGRADUATE EXPENSES for 2010–11 ***One-time required fee:*** $140. ***Tuition, state resident:*** full-time $2621. ***Tuition, nonresident:*** full-time $12,063. ***Required fees:*** full-time $1795. Full-time tuition and fees vary according to course load and student level. Part-time tuition and fees vary according to course load and student level. ***College room and board:*** $6029; ***Room only:*** $3429. Room and board charges vary according to board plan and housing facility.

FRESHMAN FINANCIAL AID (Fall 2010, est.) 1,828 applied for aid; of those 100% were deemed to have need. 99% of freshmen with need received aid; of those 18% had need fully met. ***Average percent of need met:*** 86% (excluding resources awarded to replace EFC). ***Average financial aid package:*** $12,853 (excluding resources awarded to replace EFC). 3% of all full-time freshmen had no need and received non-need-based gift aid.

UNDERGRADUATE FINANCIAL AID (Fall 2010, est.) 6,919 applied for aid; of those 100% were deemed to have need. 98% of undergraduates with need received aid; of those 19% had need fully met. ***Average percent of need met:*** 84% (excluding resources awarded to replace EFC). ***Average financial aid package:*** $12,838 (excluding resources awarded to replace EFC). 4% of all full-time undergraduates had no need and received non-need-based gift aid.

GIFT AID (NEED-BASED) ***Total amount:*** $48,210,628 (52% federal, 30% state, 15% institutional, 3% external sources). ***Receiving aid:*** Freshmen: 69% (1,415); all full-time undergraduates: 63% (5,202). ***Average award:*** Freshmen: $5813; Undergraduates: $5247. ***Scholarships, grants, and awards:*** Federal Pell, FSEOG, state, private, college/university gift aid from institutional funds.

GIFT AID (NON-NEED-BASED) ***Total amount:*** $19,996,818 (3% federal, 63% state, 24% institutional, 10% external sources). ***Receiving aid:*** Freshmen: 81% (1,663). Undergraduates: 70% (5,726). ***Average award:*** Freshmen: $4207. Undergraduates: $4733. ***Scholarships, grants, and awards by category:*** *Academic interests/achievement:* general academic interests/achievements. ***Tuition waivers:*** Full or partial for employees or children of employees, senior citizens.

LOANS ***Student loans:*** $93,076,247 (72% need-based, 28% non-need-based). 64% of past graduating class borrowed through all loan programs. *Average indebtedness per student:* $21,644. ***Average need-based loan:*** Freshmen: $3266. Undergraduates: $3915. ***Parent loans:*** $8,268,992 (44% need-based, 56% non-need-based). ***Programs:*** Federal Direct (Subsidized and Unsubsidized Stafford, PLUS), Perkins.

WORK-STUDY ***Federal work-study:*** Total amount: $1,060,746; jobs available.

ATHLETIC AWARDS Total amount: $3,598,040 (43% need-based, 57% non-need-based).

APPLYING FOR FINANCIAL AID ***Required financial aid form:*** FAFSA. ***Financial aid deadline (priority):*** 3/1. ***Notification date:*** 4/15.

CONTACT Mrs. Sherri Avent, Director of Student Financial Aid, North Carolina Agricultural and Technical State University, 1601 East Market Street, Dowdy Administration Building, Greensboro, NC 27411, 336-334-7973 or toll-free 800-443-8964 (in-state). *Fax:* 336-334-7954. *E-mail:* avent@ncat.edu.

NORTH CAROLINA CENTRAL UNIVERSITY

Durham, NC

Tuition & fees (NC res): $5280 **Average undergraduate aid package: $12,324**

ABOUT THE INSTITUTION State-supported, coed. 49 undergraduate majors. Federal methodology is used as a basis for awarding need-based institutional aid.

UNDERGRADUATE EXPENSES for 2010–11 ***Tuition, state resident:*** full-time $2812. ***Tuition, nonresident:*** full-time $13,385. ***Required fees:*** full-time $2468. Part-time tuition and fees vary according to course load. ***College room and board:*** $9509; ***Room only:*** $6875. Room and board charges vary according to board plan, housing facility, and location. ***Payment plan:*** Installment.

FRESHMAN FINANCIAL AID (Fall 2009) 1,240 applied for aid; of those 93% were deemed to have need. 100% of freshmen with need received aid; of those 8% had need fully met. ***Average percent of need met:*** 75% (excluding resources awarded to replace EFC). ***Average financial aid package:*** $2562 (excluding resources awarded to replace EFC). 1% of all full-time freshmen had no need and received non-need-based gift aid.

UNDERGRADUATE FINANCIAL AID (Fall 2009) 4,893 applied for aid; of those 93% were deemed to have need. 100% of undergraduates with need received aid; of those 7% had need fully met. ***Average percent of need met:*** 68% (excluding resources awarded to replace EFC). ***Average financial aid package:*** $12,324 (excluding resources awarded to replace EFC). 1% of all full-time undergraduates had no need and received non-need-based gift aid.

GIFT AID (NEED-BASED) ***Total amount:*** $38,079,367 (56% federal, 32% state, 9% institutional, 3% external sources). ***Receiving aid:*** Freshmen: 76% (961); all full-time undergraduates: 71% (3,612). ***Average award:*** Freshmen: $6947; Undergraduates: $6944. ***Scholarships, grants, and awards:*** Federal Pell, FSEOG, state, private, college/university gift aid from institutional funds, Federal Nursing.

GIFT AID (NON-NEED-BASED) ***Total amount:*** $877,222 (4% federal, 30% state, 13% institutional, 53% external sources). ***Receiving aid:*** Freshmen: 81% (1,024). Undergraduates: 71% (3,596). ***Average award:*** Freshmen: $3263. Undergraduates: $2669. ***Scholarships, grants, and awards by category:*** *Academic interests/achievement:* biological sciences, business, computer science, education, English, general academic interests/achievements, library science, physical sciences, social sciences. *Creative arts/performance:* music, theater/drama. *Special characteristics:* general special characteristics. ***Tuition waivers:*** Full or partial for employees or children of employees, senior citizens.

LOANS ***Student loans:*** $34,261,352 (95% need-based, 5% non-need-based). ***Average need-based loan:*** Freshmen: $3032. Undergraduates: $3854. ***Parent loans:*** $7,751,755 (81% need-based, 19% non-need-based). ***Programs:*** Federal Direct (Subsidized and Unsubsidized Stafford, PLUS), Perkins, Federal Nursing.

WORK-STUDY ***Federal work-study:*** Total amount: $715,948; jobs available. ***State or other work-study/employment:*** Total amount: $614,056 (82% need-based, 18% non-need-based). Part-time jobs available.

ATHLETIC AWARDS Total amount: $1,315,383 (71% need-based, 29% non-need-based).

APPLYING FOR FINANCIAL AID ***Required financial aid form:*** FAFSA. ***Financial aid deadline (priority):*** 3/1. ***Notification date:*** Continuous beginning 3/1. Students must reply within 2 weeks of notification.

CONTACT Sharon J. Oliver, Director of Scholarships and Student Aid, North Carolina Central University, 106 Student Services Building, Durham, NC 27707-3129, 919-530-7412 or toll-free 877-667-7533. *E-mail:* ssa@nccu.edu.

NORTH CAROLINA STATE UNIVERSITY

Raleigh, NC

Tuition & fees (NC res): $6529 **Average undergraduate aid package: $11,879**

ABOUT THE INSTITUTION State-supported, coed. 100 undergraduate majors. Federal methodology is used as a basis for awarding need-based institutional aid.

UNDERGRADUATE EXPENSES for 2010–11 ***Tuition, state resident:*** full-time $4853. ***Tuition, nonresident:*** full-time $17,388. ***Required fees:*** full-time $1676. Full-time tuition and fees vary according to degree level and program. Part-time tuition and fees vary according to course load, degree level, and program. ***College room and board:*** $8154; ***Room only:*** $4976. Room and board charges vary according to board plan and housing facility. ***Payment plan:*** Installment.

FRESHMAN FINANCIAL AID (Fall 2010, est.) 3,533 applied for aid; of those 67% were deemed to have need. 99% of freshmen with need received aid; of those 34% had need fully met. ***Average percent of need met:*** 87% (excluding resources awarded to replace EFC). ***Average financial aid package:*** $11,787 (excluding resources awarded to replace EFC). 2% of all full-time freshmen had no need and received non-need-based gift aid.

UNDERGRADUATE FINANCIAL AID (Fall 2010, est.) 14,308 applied for aid; of those 76% were deemed to have need. 98% of undergraduates with need received aid; of those 38% had need fully met. ***Average percent of need met:*** 86% (excluding resources awarded to replace EFC). ***Average financial aid package:*** $11,879 (excluding resources awarded to replace EFC). 3% of all full-time undergraduates had no need and received non-need-based gift aid.

GIFT AID (NEED-BASED) ***Total amount:*** $95,405,946 (29% federal, 27% state, 40% institutional, 4% external sources). ***Receiving aid:*** Freshmen: 49% (2,284); all full-time undergraduates: 46% (10,022). ***Average award:*** Freshmen: $9953; Undergraduates: $9658. ***Scholarships, grants, and awards:*** Federal Pell, FSEOG, state, private, college/university gift aid from institutional funds, United Negro College Fund.

GIFT AID (NON-NEED-BASED) ***Total amount:*** $9,829,150 (16% state, 53% institutional, 31% external sources). ***Receiving aid:*** Freshmen: 4% (187). Undergraduates: 3% (667). ***Average award:*** Freshmen: $6737. Undergraduates: $5869. ***Scholarships, grants, and awards by category:*** *Academic interests/achievement:* agriculture, biological sciences, business, education, engineering/technologies, general academic interests/achievements, humanities, mathematics, military science, physical sciences, social sciences. *Creative arts/performance:* music. *Special achievements/activities:* leadership. ***Tuition waivers:*** Full or partial for employees or children of employees, senior citizens.

LOANS ***Student loans:*** $75,386,449 (50% need-based, 50% non-need-based). 47% of past graduating class borrowed through all loan programs. *Average indebtedness per student:* $19,988. ***Average need-based loan:*** Freshmen: $2681. Undergraduates: $3208. ***Parent loans:*** $10,610,048 (5% need-based, 95% non-need-based). ***Programs:*** Federal Direct (Subsidized and Unsubsidized Stafford, PLUS), Perkins, state, college/university.

WORK-STUDY ***Federal work-study:*** Total amount: $699,175; 699 jobs averaging $1000. ***State or other work-study/employment:*** Total amount: $1,808,191 (45% need-based, 55% non-need-based). 274 part-time jobs averaging $6599.

ATHLETIC AWARDS Total amount: $5,638,983 (41% need-based, 59% non-need-based).

APPLYING FOR FINANCIAL AID ***Required financial aid form:*** FAFSA. ***Financial aid deadline (priority):*** 3/1. ***Notification date:*** Continuous beginning 4/1.

CONTACT Ms. Julia Rice Mallette, Director of Scholarships and Financial Aid, North Carolina State University, 2016 Harris Hall, PO Box 7302, Raleigh, NC 27695-7302, 919-515-2334. *Fax:* 919-515-8422. *E-mail:* julie_mallette@ncsu.edu.

NORTH CAROLINA WESLEYAN COLLEGE

Rocky Mount, NC

CONTACT Leah Hill, Director of Financial Aid, North Carolina Wesleyan College, 3400 North Wesleyan Boulevard, Rocky Mount, NC 27804, 252-985-5200 or toll-free 800-488-6292. *Fax:* 252-985-5295. *E-mail:* lhill@ncwc.edu.

NORTH CENTRAL COLLEGE

Naperville, IL

Tuition & fees: $28,224 — **Average undergraduate aid package: $20,623**

ABOUT THE INSTITUTION Independent United Methodist, coed. 61 undergraduate majors. Federal methodology is used as a basis for awarding need-based institutional aid.

UNDERGRADUATE EXPENSES for 2010–11 ***Comprehensive fee:*** $36,687 includes full-time tuition ($27,984), mandatory fees ($240), and room and board ($8463). Room and board charges vary according to housing facility. ***Part-time tuition:*** $676 per credit hour. ***Part-time fees:*** $20 per term. Part-time tuition and fees vary according to course load. ***Payment plan:*** Installment.

FRESHMAN FINANCIAL AID (Fall 2010, est.) 528 applied for aid; of those 87% were deemed to have need. 100% of freshmen with need received aid; of those 26% had need fully met. ***Average percent of need met:*** 82% (excluding resources awarded to replace EFC). ***Average financial aid package:*** $22,348 (excluding resources awarded to replace EFC). 20% of all full-time freshmen had no need and received non-need-based gift aid.

UNDERGRADUATE FINANCIAL AID (Fall 2010, est.) 2,054 applied for aid; of those 91% were deemed to have need. 100% of undergraduates with need received aid; of those 21% had need fully met. ***Average percent of need met:*** 75% (excluding resources awarded to replace EFC). ***Average financial aid package:*** $20,623 (excluding resources awarded to replace EFC). 19% of all full-time undergraduates had no need and received non-need-based gift aid.

GIFT AID (NEED-BASED) ***Total amount:*** $29,579,493 (9% federal, 12% state, 78% institutional, 1% external sources). ***Receiving aid:*** Freshmen: 79% (459); all full-time undergraduates: 77% (1,851). ***Average award:*** Freshmen: $18,463; Undergraduates: $15,813. ***Scholarships, grants, and awards:*** Federal Pell, FSEOG, state, private, college/university gift aid from institutional funds.

GIFT AID (NON-NEED-BASED) ***Total amount:*** $6,278,261 (99% institutional, 1% external sources). ***Receiving aid:*** Freshmen: 12% (68). Undergraduates: 8% (192). ***Average award:*** Freshmen: $12,287. Undergraduates: $11,061. ***Scholarships, grants, and awards by category:*** *Academic interests/achievement:* biological sciences, business, communication, computer science, education, English, foreign languages, general academic interests/achievements, humanities, international studies, mathematics, physical sciences, premedicine, religion/biblical studies, social sciences. *Creative arts/performance:* art/fine arts, cinema/film/broadcasting, debating, journalism/publications, music, theater/drama. *Special achievements/activities:* community service, religious involvement. *Special characteristics:* adult students, children of faculty/staff, general special characteristics, international students, relatives of clergy. ***Tuition waivers:*** Full or partial for employees or children of employees, senior citizens.

LOANS ***Student loans:*** $16,005,128 (72% need-based, 28% non-need-based). 80% of past graduating class borrowed through all loan programs. *Average indebtedness per student:* $29,137. ***Average need-based loan:*** Freshmen: $3607. Undergraduates: $4667. ***Parent loans:*** $3,428,031 (24% need-based, 76% non-need-based). ***Programs:*** Federal Direct (Subsidized and Unsubsidized Stafford, PLUS), Perkins, state, college/university.

WORK-STUDY ***Federal work-study:*** Total amount: $196,388; 1,211 jobs averaging $162. ***State or other work-study/employment:*** Total amount: $348,468 (51% need-based, 49% non-need-based). Part-time jobs available.

APPLYING FOR FINANCIAL AID ***Required financial aid forms:*** FAFSA, institution's own form, federal income tax form(s). ***Financial aid deadline:*** Continuous. ***Notification date:*** Continuous beginning 3/1. Students must reply within 4 weeks of notification.

CONTACT Marty Rossman, Director of Financial Aid, North Central College, 30 North Brainard Street, Naperville, IL 60540, 630-637-5600 or toll-free 800-411-1861. *Fax:* 630-637-5608. *E-mail:* mprossman@noctrl.edu.

NORTH CENTRAL UNIVERSITY

Minneapolis, MN

CONTACT Mrs. Donna Jager, Director of Financial Aid, North Central University, 910 Elliot Avenue, Minneapolis, MN 55404-1322, 612-343-4485 or toll-free 800-289-6222. *Fax:* 612-343-8067. *E-mail:* finaid@northcentral.edu.

NORTH DAKOTA STATE UNIVERSITY

Fargo, ND

CONTACT Jeanne Enebo, Director of Financial Aid, North Dakota State University, PO Box 5315, Fargo, ND 58105, 701-231-7537 or toll-free 800-488-NDSU. *Fax:* 701-231-6126. *E-mail:* j.enebo@ndsu.edu.

NORTHEASTERN ILLINOIS UNIVERSITY

Chicago, IL

Tuition & fees (IL res): $9003 — **Average undergraduate aid package: $8382**

ABOUT THE INSTITUTION State-supported, coed. 42 undergraduate majors. Federal methodology is used as a basis for awarding need-based institutional aid.

UNDERGRADUATE EXPENSES for 2010–11 ***Tuition, state resident:*** full-time $7800; part-time $260 per credit hour. ***Tuition, nonresident:*** full-time $15,600; part-time $520 per credit hour. ***Required fees:*** full-time $1203; $51.90 per credit hour or $3 per term. Full-time tuition and fees vary according to location and student level. Part-time tuition and fees vary according to course load and location. ***Payment plans:*** Guaranteed tuition, deferred payment.

FRESHMAN FINANCIAL AID (Fall 2010, est.) 854 applied for aid; of those 85% were deemed to have need. 87% of freshmen with need received aid. ***Average percent of need met:*** 39% (excluding resources awarded to replace EFC). ***Average financial aid package:*** $8365 (excluding resources awarded to replace EFC). 1% of all full-time freshmen had no need and received non-need-based gift aid.

UNDERGRADUATE FINANCIAL AID (Fall 2010, est.) 4,299 applied for aid; of those 88% were deemed to have need. 91% of undergraduates with need received aid; of those 2% had need fully met. ***Average percent of need met:*** 34% (excluding resources awarded to replace EFC). ***Average financial aid package:*** $8382 (excluding resources awarded to replace EFC). 2% of all full-time undergraduates had no need and received non-need-based gift aid.

GIFT AID (NEED-BASED) ***Total amount:*** $27,755,189 (67% federal, 33% state). ***Receiving aid:*** Freshmen: 62% (604); all full-time undergraduates: 54% (3,031). ***Average award:*** Freshmen: $8258; Undergraduates: $7120. ***Scholarships, grants, and awards:*** Federal Pell, FSEOG, state, private, college/university gift aid from institutional funds.

GIFT AID (NON-NEED-BASED) ***Total amount:*** $2,007,167 (51% state, 33% institutional, 16% external sources). ***Receiving aid:*** Freshmen: 5% (52). Undergraduates: 6% (312). ***Average award:*** Freshmen: $1454. Undergraduates: $3069. ***Scholarships, grants, and awards by category:*** *Academic interests/achievement:* biological sciences, business, communication, computer science, education, English, foreign languages, general academic interests/achievements, mathematics, physical sciences, social sciences. *Creative arts/performance:* art/fine arts, creative writing, dance, journalism/publications, music, performing arts, theater/drama. *Special achievements/activities:* general special achievements/activities, leadership. *Special characteristics:* adult students, children of faculty/staff, general special characteristics. ***Tuition waivers:*** Full or partial for employees or children of employees, senior citizens.

LOANS ***Student loans:*** $18,246,284 (56% need-based, 44% non-need-based). 13% of past graduating class borrowed through all loan programs. *Average indebtedness per student:* $10,976. ***Average need-based loan:*** Freshmen: $3411. Undergraduates: $4677. ***Parent loans:*** $233,446 (100% non-need-based). ***Programs:*** Federal Direct (Subsidized and Unsubsidized Stafford, PLUS), Perkins.

WORK-STUDY ***Federal work-study:*** Total amount: $215,614; jobs available. ***State or other work-study/employment:*** Total amount: $1,114,036 (100% non-need-based). Part-time jobs available.

APPLYING FOR FINANCIAL AID ***Required financial aid form:*** FAFSA. ***Financial aid deadline (priority):*** 2/15. ***Notification date:*** Continuous beginning 4/1. Students must reply within 2 weeks of notification.

CONTACT Office of Financial Aid, Northeastern Illinois University, 5500 North St. Louis Avenue, Chicago, IL 60625, 773-442-5000. *Fax:* 773-442-5040. *E-mail:* financial-aid@neiu.edu.

NORTHEASTERN STATE UNIVERSITY

Tahlequah, OK

Tuition & fees (OK res): $4385 **Average undergraduate aid package: $8860**

ABOUT THE INSTITUTION State-supported, coed. 71 undergraduate majors. Federal methodology is used as a basis for awarding need-based institutional aid.

UNDERGRADUATE EXPENSES for 2010–11 ***Tuition, state resident:*** full-time $3338; part-time $111.25 per credit hour. ***Tuition, nonresident:*** full-time $9675; part-time $322.50 per credit hour. ***Required fees:*** full-time $1047; $34.90 per credit hour. Full-time tuition and fees vary according to course load and program. Part-time tuition and fees vary according to course load and program. ***College room and board:*** $5020. Room and board charges vary according to board plan and housing facility.

FRESHMAN FINANCIAL AID (Fall 2010, est.) 1,094 applied for aid; of those 42% were deemed to have need. 97% of freshmen with need received aid; of those 69% had need fully met. ***Average percent of need met:*** 80% (excluding resources awarded to replace EFC). ***Average financial aid package:*** $8769 (excluding resources awarded to replace EFC). 15% of all full-time freshmen had no need and received non-need-based gift aid.

UNDERGRADUATE FINANCIAL AID (Fall 2010, est.) 5,058 applied for aid; of those 66% were deemed to have need. 95% of undergraduates with need received aid; of those 69% had need fully met. ***Average percent of need met:*** 78% (excluding resources awarded to replace EFC). ***Average financial aid package:*** $8860 (excluding resources awarded to replace EFC). 7% of all full-time undergraduates had no need and received non-need-based gift aid.

GIFT AID (NEED-BASED) ***Total amount:*** $25,120,018 (72% federal, 15% state, 1% institutional, 12% external sources). ***Receiving aid:*** Freshmen: 30% (358); all full-time undergraduates: 41% (2,506). ***Average award:*** Freshmen: $5110; Undergraduates: $5244. ***Scholarships, grants, and awards:*** Federal Pell, FSEOG, state, private, college/university gift aid from institutional funds.

GIFT AID (NON-NEED-BASED) ***Total amount:*** $4,063,327 (7% federal, 40% state, 5% institutional, 48% external sources). ***Receiving aid:*** Freshmen: 37% (436). Undergraduates: 51% (3,078). ***Average award:*** Freshmen: $3932. Undergraduates: $4160. ***Scholarships, grants, and awards by category:*** *Academic interests/achievement:* 1,697 awards ($3,214,061 total): biological sciences, business, communication, computer science, education, English, foreign languages, general academic interests/achievements, health fields, home economics, humanities, library science, mathematics, physical sciences, premedicine, social sciences. *Creative arts/performance:* 155 awards ($167,752 total): applied art and design, art/fine arts, dance, debating, journalism/publications, music, performing arts, theater/drama. *Special achievements/activities:* 61 awards ($194,175 total): cheerleading/drum major, community service, junior miss, leadership. *Special characteristics:* 109 awards ($161,963 total): children and siblings of alumni, children of faculty/staff, children with a deceased or disabled parent, out-of-state students, spouses of deceased or disabled public servants. ***Tuition waivers:*** Full or partial for employees or children of employees, senior citizens.

LOANS ***Student loans:*** $33,900,224 (48% need-based, 52% non-need-based). 68% of past graduating class borrowed through all loan programs. *Average indebtedness per student:* $23,155. ***Average need-based loan:*** Freshmen: $2587. Undergraduates: $3884. ***Parent loans:*** $544,112 (60% need-based, 40% non-need-based). ***Programs:*** Federal Direct (Subsidized and Unsubsidized Stafford, PLUS), Perkins.

WORK-STUDY ***Federal work-study:*** Total amount: $461,102; 266 jobs averaging $1733. ***State or other work-study/employment:*** Total amount: $2,400,000 (100% non-need-based). 569 part-time jobs averaging $3393.

ATHLETIC AWARDS Total amount: $1,374,280 (60% need-based, 40% non-need-based).

APPLYING FOR FINANCIAL AID ***Required financial aid form:*** FAFSA. ***Financial aid deadline (priority):*** 3/1. ***Notification date:*** Continuous beginning 4/1. Students must reply within 2 weeks of notification.

CONTACT Dr. Teri Cochran, Director of Student Financial Services, Northeastern State University, 715 North Grand Avenue, Tahlequah, OK 74464-2399, 918-456-5511 Ext. 3410 or toll-free 800-722-9614 (in-state). *Fax:* 918-458-2510. *E-mail:* cochrant@nsuok.edu.

NORTHEASTERN UNIVERSITY

Boston, MA

Tuition & fees: $36,792 **Average undergraduate aid package: $20,131**

ABOUT THE INSTITUTION Independent, coed. 68 undergraduate majors. Both federal and institutional methodology are used as a basis for awarding need-based institutional aid.

UNDERGRADUATE EXPENSES for 2010–11 ***Comprehensive fee:*** $49,552 includes full-time tuition ($36,380), mandatory fees ($412), and room and board ($12,760). ***College room only:*** $6760. Room and board charges vary according to board plan and housing facility. ***Payment plan:*** Installment.

FRESHMAN FINANCIAL AID (Fall 2010, est.) 2,014 applied for aid; of those 79% were deemed to have need. 100% of freshmen with need received aid; of those 18% had need fully met. ***Average percent of need met:*** 69% (excluding resources awarded to replace EFC). ***Average financial aid package:*** $22,783 (excluding resources awarded to replace EFC). 25% of all full-time freshmen had no need and received non-need-based gift aid.

UNDERGRADUATE FINANCIAL AID (Fall 2010, est.) 9,944 applied for aid; of those 85% were deemed to have need. 98% of undergraduates with need received aid; of those 13% had need fully met. ***Average percent of need met:*** 59% (excluding resources awarded to replace EFC). ***Average financial aid package:*** $20,131 (excluding resources awarded to replace EFC). 23% of all full-time undergraduates had no need and received non-need-based gift aid.

GIFT AID (NEED-BASED) ***Total amount:*** $121,507,370 (11% federal, 2% state, 82% institutional, 5% external sources). ***Receiving aid:*** Freshmen: 55% (1,554); all full-time undergraduates: 50% (7,950). ***Average award:*** Freshmen: $18,821;

Undergraduates: $15,619. ***Scholarships, grants, and awards:*** Federal Pell, FSEOG, state, private, college/university gift aid from institutional funds.

GIFT AID (NON-NEED-BASED) ***Total amount:*** $42,158,388 (92% institutional, 8% external sources). ***Receiving aid:*** Freshmen: 9% (255). Undergraduates: 5% (776). ***Average award:*** Freshmen: $13,103. Undergraduates: $9430. ***Tuition waivers:*** Full or partial for employees or children of employees.

LOANS ***Student loans:*** $93,094,205 (71% need-based, 29% non-need-based). ***Average need-based loan:*** Freshmen: $4391. Undergraduates: $4895. ***Parent loans:*** $26,837,582 (50% need-based, 50% non-need-based). ***Programs:*** Federal Direct (Subsidized and Unsubsidized Stafford, PLUS), Perkins, Federal Nursing, state, college/university.

WORK-STUDY ***Federal work-study:*** Total amount: $7,991,708; 4,393 jobs averaging $1820.

ATHLETIC AWARDS Total amount: $9,888,260 (30% need-based, 70% non-need-based).

APPLYING FOR FINANCIAL AID ***Required financial aid forms:*** FAFSA, CSS Financial Aid PROFILE, noncustodial (divorced/separated) parent's statement. ***Financial aid deadline (priority):*** 2/15. ***Notification date:*** 4/1. Students must reply by 5/1.

CONTACT Mr. Anthony Erwin, Senior Director of University Financial Aid and Scholarships, Northeastern University, 360 Huntington Avenue, Boston, MA 02115, 617-373-3190. *Fax:* 617-373-8735. *E-mail:* sfs@neu.edu.

NORTHERN ARIZONA UNIVERSITY

Flagstaff, AZ

Tuition & fees (AZ res): $7667 Average undergraduate aid package: $9621

ABOUT THE INSTITUTION State-supported, coed. 116 undergraduate majors. Federal methodology is used as a basis for awarding need-based institutional aid.

UNDERGRADUATE EXPENSES for 2010–11 ***Tuition, state resident:*** full-time $6964; part-time $497 per credit. ***Tuition, nonresident:*** full-time $19,364; part-time $807 per credit. ***Required fees:*** full-time $703; $6 per credit or $282 per term. Full-time tuition and fees vary according to degree level, location, and program. Part-time tuition and fees vary according to course load, degree level, location, and program. ***College room and board:*** $8072; ***Room only:*** $4480. Room and board charges vary according to board plan and housing facility. ***Payment plans:*** Guaranteed tuition, installment.

FRESHMAN FINANCIAL AID (Fall 2009) 2,915 applied for aid; of those 70% were deemed to have need. 96% of freshmen with need received aid; of those 11% had need fully met. ***Average percent of need met:*** 64% (excluding resources awarded to replace EFC). ***Average financial aid package:*** $9713 (excluding resources awarded to replace EFC). 16% of all full-time freshmen had no need and received non-need-based gift aid.

UNDERGRADUATE FINANCIAL AID (Fall 2009) 11,353 applied for aid; of those 79% were deemed to have need. 98% of undergraduates with need received aid; of those 11% had need fully met. ***Average percent of need met:*** 62% (excluding resources awarded to replace EFC). ***Average financial aid package:*** $9621 (excluding resources awarded to replace EFC). 13% of all full-time undergraduates had no need and received non-need-based gift aid.

GIFT AID (NEED-BASED) ***Total amount:*** $60,974,042 (49% federal, 4% state, 39% institutional, 8% external sources). ***Receiving aid:*** Freshmen: 39% (1,357); all full-time undergraduates: 41% (6,290). ***Average award:*** Freshmen: $7048; Undergraduates: $6238. ***Scholarships, grants, and awards:*** Federal Pell, FSEOG, state, private, college/university gift aid from institutional funds, Federal Nursing, TEACH Grants.

GIFT AID (NON-NEED-BASED) ***Total amount:*** $13,918,966 (1% federal, 87% institutional, 12% external sources). ***Receiving aid:*** Freshmen: 29% (999). Undergraduates: 24% (3,624). ***Average award:*** Freshmen: $3684. Undergraduates: $3862. ***Scholarships, grants, and awards by category:*** *Academic interests/achievement:* area/ethnic studies, biological sciences, business, communication, computer science, education, engineering/technologies, English, foreign languages, general academic interests/achievements, health fields, home economics, humanities, international studies, library science, mathematics, military science, physical sciences, premedicine, religion/biblical studies, social sciences. *Creative arts/performance:* applied art and design, art/fine arts, cinema/film/broadcasting, creative writing, debating, general creative arts/performance, journalism/publications, music, performing arts, theater/drama. *Special achievements/activities:* leadership. *Special characteristics:* adult students, children and siblings of alumni, children of educators, children of faculty/staff, children of public servants, first-generation college students, general special characteristics, handicapped students, international students, local/state students, members of minority groups, out-of-state students, public servants, spouses of deceased or disabled public servants, veterans, veterans' children. ***Tuition waivers:*** Full or partial for employees or children of employees.

LOANS ***Student loans:*** $82,006,581 (81% need-based, 19% non-need-based). 53% of past graduating class borrowed through all loan programs. *Average indebtedness per student:* $18,764. ***Average need-based loan:*** Freshmen: $3258. Undergraduates: $4058. ***Parent loans:*** $19,461,859 (72% need-based, 28% non-need-based). ***Programs:*** Federal Direct (Subsidized and Unsubsidized Stafford, PLUS), Perkins, Federal Nursing, state, college/university.

WORK-STUDY ***Federal work-study:*** Total amount: $1,038,134; jobs available. ***State or other work-study/employment:*** Total amount: $7,914,397 (57% need-based, 43% non-need-based). Part-time jobs available.

ATHLETIC AWARDS Total amount: $4,541,799 (71% need-based, 29% non-need-based).

APPLYING FOR FINANCIAL AID ***Required financial aid form:*** FAFSA. ***Financial aid deadline (priority):*** 2/14. ***Notification date:*** Continuous beginning 3/15.

CONTACT Michelle Castillo, Director of Financial Aid, Northern Arizona University, PO Box 4108, Flagstaff, AZ 86011-4108, 928-523-4951 or toll-free 888-MORE-NAU. *Fax:* 928-523-1551. *E-mail:* Financial.Aid@nau.edu.

NORTHERN ILLINOIS UNIVERSITY

De Kalb, IL

Tuition & fees (IL res): $9854 Average undergraduate aid package: $11,108

ABOUT THE INSTITUTION State-supported, coed. 65 undergraduate majors. Federal methodology is used as a basis for awarding need-based institutional aid.

UNDERGRADUATE EXPENSES for 2010–11 ***One-time required fee:*** $500. ***Tuition, state resident:*** full-time $7950; part-time $294.60 per credit hour. ***Tuition, nonresident:*** full-time $15,900; part-time $589.20 per credit hour. ***Required fees:*** full-time $1904; $78.84 per credit hour. Full-time tuition and fees vary according to course load, location, and student level. Part-time tuition and fees vary according to course load, location, and student level. ***College room and board:*** $10,366. Room and board charges vary according to board plan and housing facility. ***Payment plans:*** Guaranteed tuition, installment.

FRESHMAN FINANCIAL AID (Fall 2009) 2,734 applied for aid; of those 81% were deemed to have need. 98% of freshmen with need received aid; of those 10% had need fully met. ***Average percent of need met:*** 66% (excluding resources awarded to replace EFC). ***Average financial aid package:*** $11,719 (excluding resources awarded to replace EFC).

UNDERGRADUATE FINANCIAL AID (Fall 2009) 13,616 applied for aid; of those 83% were deemed to have need. 98% of undergraduates with need received aid; of those 13% had need fully met. ***Average percent of need met:*** 67% (excluding resources awarded to replace EFC). ***Average financial aid package:*** $11,108 (excluding resources awarded to replace EFC).

GIFT AID (NEED-BASED) ***Total amount:*** $58,392,951 (47% federal, 43% state, 6% institutional, 4% external sources). ***Receiving aid:*** Freshmen: 50% (1,539); all full-time undergraduates: 42% (7,316). ***Average award:*** Freshmen: $8571; Undergraduates: $7391. ***Scholarships, grants, and awards:*** Federal Pell, FSEOG, state, private, college/university gift aid from institutional funds, United Negro College Fund, Federal Nursing, Academic Competitiveness Grants, National SMART Grants, TEACH Grants.

GIFT AID (NON-NEED-BASED) ***Total amount:*** $1,047,852 (5% institutional, 95% external sources). ***Receiving aid:*** Freshmen: 11. Undergraduates: 1% (106). ***Scholarships, grants, and awards by category:*** *Academic interests/achievement:* biological sciences, business, communication, computer science, education, engineering/technologies, English, foreign languages, general academic interests/achievements, health fields, humanities, international studies, mathematics, physical sciences, social sciences. *Creative arts/performance:* applied art and design, art/fine arts, creative writing, dance, debating, journalism/publications, music, performing arts, theater/drama. *Special achievements/activities:* leadership. *Special characteristics:* adult students, children of faculty/staff, ethnic background, international students, members of minority groups, veterans. ***Tuition waivers:*** Full or partial for minority students, employees or children of employees, senior citizens.

LOANS ***Student loans:*** $100,743,523 (43% need-based, 57% non-need-based). 68% of past graduating class borrowed through all loan programs. *Average indebtedness per student:* $27,101. ***Average need-based loan:*** Freshmen: $3398.

Undergraduates: $4236. ***Parent loans:*** $16,217,698 (100% non-need-based). ***Programs:*** Federal Direct (Subsidized and Unsubsidized Stafford, PLUS), Perkins.

WORK-STUDY ***Federal work-study:*** Total amount: $25,255,964; 7,239 jobs averaging $3489.

ATHLETIC AWARDS Total amount: $5,816,703 (100% need-based).

APPLYING FOR FINANCIAL AID ***Required financial aid form:*** FAFSA. ***Financial aid deadline (priority):*** 3/1. ***Notification date:*** Continuous beginning 3/24. Students must reply within 2 weeks of notification.

CONTACT Ms. Kathleen D. Brunson, Director of Student Financial Aid, Northern Illinois University, 231 North Annie Glidden Road, De Kalb, IL 60115, 815-753-1395 or toll-free 800-892-3050 (in-state). *Fax:* 815-753-9475.

NORTHERN KENTUCKY UNIVERSITY

Highland Heights, KY

Tuition & fees (KY res): $7128 **Average undergraduate aid package: $8482**

ABOUT THE INSTITUTION State-supported, coed. 63 undergraduate majors. Federal methodology is used as a basis for awarding need-based institutional aid.

UNDERGRADUATE EXPENSES for 2010–11 ***Tuition, state resident:*** full-time $7128; part-time $297 per credit hour. ***Tuition, nonresident:*** full-time $13,896; part-time $579 per credit hour. Full-time tuition and fees vary according to course load and reciprocity agreements. Part-time tuition and fees vary according to course load and reciprocity agreements. ***College room and board:*** $6260; ***Room only:*** $3420. Room and board charges vary according to board plan and housing facility. ***Payment plan:*** Installment.

FRESHMAN FINANCIAL AID (Fall 2009) 1,816 applied for aid; of those 78% were deemed to have need. 100% of freshmen with need received aid; of those 17% had need fully met. ***Average percent of need met:*** 61% (excluding resources awarded to replace EFC). ***Average financial aid package:*** $8373 (excluding resources awarded to replace EFC). 7% of all full-time freshmen had no need and received non-need-based gift aid.

UNDERGRADUATE FINANCIAL AID (Fall 2009) 7,451 applied for aid; of those 80% were deemed to have need. 98% of undergraduates with need received aid; of those 16% had need fully met. ***Average percent of need met:*** 53% (excluding resources awarded to replace EFC). ***Average financial aid package:*** $8482 (excluding resources awarded to replace EFC). 8% of all full-time undergraduates had no need and received non-need-based gift aid.

GIFT AID (NEED-BASED) ***Total amount:*** $20,942,963 (85% federal, 11% state, 4% institutional). ***Receiving aid:*** Freshmen: 35% (756); all full-time undergraduates: 31% (3,096). ***Average award:*** Freshmen: $6230; Undergraduates: $5801. ***Scholarships, grants, and awards:*** Federal Pell, FSEOG, state, private, college/university gift aid from institutional funds.

GIFT AID (NON-NEED-BASED) ***Total amount:*** $13,732,833 (6% federal, 38% state, 56% institutional). ***Receiving aid:*** Freshmen: 47% (1,004). Undergraduates: 28% (2,805). ***Average award:*** Freshmen: $3781. Undergraduates: $4438. ***Scholarships, grants, and awards by category:*** *Academic interests/achievement:* biological sciences, business, communication, computer science, education, engineering/technologies, English, general academic interests/achievements, health fields, mathematics, physical sciences, premedicine, social sciences. *Creative arts/performance:* art/fine arts, music, theater/drama. *Special achievements/activities:* community service, general special achievements/activities, leadership. *Special characteristics:* adult students, children and siblings of alumni, children of faculty/staff, children of public servants, children with a deceased or disabled parent, general special characteristics, handicapped students, local/state students, members of minority groups, spouses of deceased or disabled public servants, veterans, veterans' children. ***Tuition waivers:*** Full or partial for employees or children of employees, senior citizens.

LOANS ***Student loans:*** $66,758,680 (37% need-based, 63% non-need-based). 69% of past graduating class borrowed through all loan programs. *Average indebtedness per student:* $21,535. ***Average need-based loan:*** Freshmen: $3038. Undergraduates: $3874. ***Parent loans:*** $27,251,335 (100% non-need-based). ***Programs:*** Federal Direct (Subsidized and Unsubsidized Stafford, PLUS), Perkins, private loans.

WORK-STUDY ***Federal work-study:*** Total amount: $2,451,010; jobs available. ***State or other work-study/employment:*** Total amount: $2,247,266 (100% non-need-based). Part-time jobs available.

ATHLETIC AWARDS Total amount: $1,420,525 (100% non-need-based).

APPLYING FOR FINANCIAL AID ***Required financial aid form:*** FAFSA. ***Financial aid deadline (priority):*** 3/1. ***Notification date:*** Continuous beginning 4/1.

CONTACT Leah Stewart, Director of Student Financial Assistance, Northern Kentucky University, 416 Administrative Center, Highland Heights, KY 41099, 859-572-5144 or toll-free 800-637-9948. *Fax:* 859-572-6997. *E-mail:* ofa@nku.edu.

NORTHERN MICHIGAN UNIVERSITY

Marquette, MI

Tuition & fees (MI res): $8416 **Average undergraduate aid package: $8823**

ABOUT THE INSTITUTION State-supported, coed. 143 undergraduate majors. Federal methodology is used as a basis for awarding need-based institutional aid.

UNDERGRADUATE EXPENSES for 2010–11 ***One-time required fee:*** $225. ***Tuition, state resident:*** full-time $7800; part-time $302 per credit hour. ***Tuition, nonresident:*** full-time $12,216; part-time $486 per credit hour. ***Required fees:*** full-time $616; $32.02 per term. Full-time tuition and fees vary according to program. Part-time tuition and fees vary according to program. ***College room and board:*** $8026; ***Room only:*** $3988. Room and board charges vary according to board plan and housing facility. ***Payment plans:*** Installment, deferred payment.

FRESHMAN FINANCIAL AID (Fall 2009) 1,701 applied for aid; of those 70% were deemed to have need. 97% of freshmen with need received aid; of those 16% had need fully met. ***Average percent of need met:*** 61% (excluding resources awarded to replace EFC). ***Average financial aid package:*** $8231 (excluding resources awarded to replace EFC). 10% of all full-time freshmen had no need and received non-need-based gift aid.

UNDERGRADUATE FINANCIAL AID (Fall 2009) 6,745 applied for aid; of those 70% were deemed to have need. 97% of undergraduates with need received aid; of those 13% had need fully met. ***Average percent of need met:*** 63% (excluding resources awarded to replace EFC). ***Average financial aid package:*** $8823 (excluding resources awarded to replace EFC). 6% of all full-time undergraduates had no need and received non-need-based gift aid.

GIFT AID (NEED-BASED) ***Total amount:*** $19,684,123 (75% federal, 5% state, 19% institutional, 1% external sources). ***Receiving aid:*** Freshmen: 41% (706); all full-time undergraduates: 35% (2,695). ***Average award:*** Freshmen: $5418; Undergraduates: $5857. ***Scholarships, grants, and awards:*** Federal Pell, FSEOG, state, private, college/university gift aid from institutional funds.

GIFT AID (NON-NEED-BASED) ***Total amount:*** $11,483,334 (23% state, 58% institutional, 19% external sources). ***Receiving aid:*** Freshmen: 28% (482). Undergraduates: 20% (1,530). ***Average award:*** Freshmen: $2773. Undergraduates: $2967. ***Scholarships, grants, and awards by category:*** *Academic interests/achievement:* 173 awards ($244,212 total): biological sciences, business, communication, computer science, education, engineering/technologies, English, foreign languages, general academic interests/achievements, health fields, international studies, mathematics, military science, physical sciences, premedicine, social sciences. *Creative arts/performance:* 68 awards ($53,362 total): applied art and design, music, theater/drama. *Special achievements/activities:* 137 awards ($112,853 total): cheerleading/drum major, leadership, memberships. *Special characteristics:* 954 awards ($4,079,927 total): children of faculty/staff, children of union members/company employees, international students, members of minority groups, out-of-state students. ***Tuition waivers:*** Full or partial for employees or children of employees, senior citizens.

LOANS ***Student loans:*** $44,997,749 (45% need-based, 55% non-need-based). 65% of past graduating class borrowed through all loan programs. *Average indebtedness per student:* $27,091. ***Average need-based loan:*** Freshmen: $2894. Undergraduates: $3871. ***Parent loans:*** $3,994,899 (100% non-need-based). ***Programs:*** Federal Direct (Subsidized and Unsubsidized Stafford, PLUS), Perkins, state, alternative loans.

WORK-STUDY ***Federal work-study:*** Total amount: $1,033,465; 486 jobs averaging $1886.

ATHLETIC AWARDS Total amount: $2,202,492 (100% non-need-based).

APPLYING FOR FINANCIAL AID ***Required financial aid form:*** FAFSA. ***Financial aid deadline (priority):*** 3/1. ***Notification date:*** Continuous beginning 4/1. Students must reply within 2 weeks of notification.

CONTACT Michael Rotundo, Director of Financial Aid, Northern Michigan University, 1401 Presque Isle Avenue, Marquette, MI 49855, 906-227-1575 or toll-free 800-682-9797. *Fax:* 906-227-2321. *E-mail:* mrotundo@nmu.edu.

NORTHERN STATE UNIVERSITY

Aberdeen, SD

Tuition & fees (SD res): $6351 **Average undergraduate aid package: $7607**

ABOUT THE INSTITUTION State-supported, coed. 46 undergraduate majors. Federal methodology is used as a basis for awarding need-based institutional aid.

UNDERGRADUATE EXPENSES for 2011–12 ***Tuition, state resident:*** full-time $2994. ***Tuition, nonresident:*** full-time $4491. ***Required fees:*** full-time $3357. Full-time tuition and fees vary according to course level, course load, and reciprocity agreements. Part-time tuition and fees vary according to course level, course load, and reciprocity agreements. ***College room and board:*** $5068; ***Room only:*** $2611. Room and board charges vary according to board plan. ***Payment plan:*** Installment.

FRESHMAN FINANCIAL AID (Fall 2010, est.) 353 applied for aid; of those 76% were deemed to have need. 100% of freshmen with need received aid; of those 21% had need fully met. ***Average percent of need met:*** 75% (excluding resources awarded to replace EFC). ***Average financial aid package:*** $7843 (excluding resources awarded to replace EFC). 15% of all full-time freshmen had no need and received non-need-based gift aid.

UNDERGRADUATE FINANCIAL AID (Fall 2010, est.) 1,263 applied for aid; of those 79% were deemed to have need. 99% of undergraduates with need received aid; of those 20% had need fully met. ***Average percent of need met:*** 73% (excluding resources awarded to replace EFC). ***Average financial aid package:*** $7607 (excluding resources awarded to replace EFC). 8% of all full-time undergraduates had no need and received non-need-based gift aid.

GIFT AID (NEED-BASED) ***Total amount:*** $4,073,900 (95% federal, 1% state, 4% external sources). ***Receiving aid:*** Freshmen: 67% (257); all full-time undergraduates: 61% (887). ***Average award:*** Freshmen: $4005; Undergraduates: $4004. ***Scholarships, grants, and awards:*** Federal Pell, FSEOG, state, private, college/university gift aid from institutional funds, TEACH Grants.

GIFT AID (NON-NEED-BASED) ***Total amount:*** $1,779,614 (13% federal, 12% state, 53% institutional, 22% external sources). ***Receiving aid:*** Freshmen: 41% (155). Undergraduates: 31% (454). ***Average award:*** Freshmen: $1354. Undergraduates: $1580. ***Scholarships, grants, and awards by category:*** *Academic interests/achievement:* 550 awards ($790,612 total): biological sciences, business, communication, computer science, education, English, foreign languages, general academic interests/achievements, humanities, international studies, mathematics, physical sciences, social sciences. *Creative arts/performance:* 107 awards ($107,067 total): art/fine arts, music, theater/drama. *Special achievements/activities:* 18 awards ($7765 total): leadership. *Special characteristics:* 13 awards ($12,923 total): adult students, ethnic background, handicapped students, international students, local/state students, members of minority groups.

LOANS ***Student loans:*** $10,262,011 (49% need-based, 51% non-need-based). ***Average need-based loan:*** Freshmen: $4171. Undergraduates: $4882. ***Parent loans:*** $278,999 (100% non-need-based). ***Programs:*** Federal Direct (Subsidized and Unsubsidized Stafford, PLUS), Perkins, college/university, alternative loans.

WORK-STUDY ***Federal work-study:*** Total amount: $600,000; 300 jobs averaging $2000. ***State or other work-study/employment:*** Total amount: $500,000 (100% non-need-based). 367 part-time jobs averaging $1328.

ATHLETIC AWARDS Total amount: $815,943 (100% non-need-based).

APPLYING FOR FINANCIAL AID ***Required financial aid form:*** FAFSA. ***Financial aid deadline (priority):*** 3/1. ***Notification date:*** 4/15. Students must reply within 2 weeks of notification.

CONTACT Ms. Sharon Kienow, Director of Financial Aid, Northern State University, 1200 South Jay Street, Aberdeen, SD 57401-7198, 605-626-2640 or toll-free 800-678-5330. *Fax:* 605-626-2587. *E-mail:* kienows@northern.edu.

NORTH GEORGIA COLLEGE & STATE UNIVERSITY

Dahlonega, GA

Tuition & fees (GA res): $6094 **Average undergraduate aid package: $8005**

ABOUT THE INSTITUTION State-supported, coed. 36 undergraduate majors. Federal methodology is used as a basis for awarding need-based institutional aid.

UNDERGRADUATE EXPENSES for 2010–11 ***Tuition, state resident:*** full-time $4596; part-time $154 per credit hour. ***Tuition, nonresident:*** full-time $16,572; part-time $553 per credit hour. ***Required fees:*** full-time $1498. Part-time tuition and fees vary according to course load. ***College room and board:*** $6166; ***Room only:*** $2868. Room and board charges vary according to board plan and housing facility.

FRESHMAN FINANCIAL AID (Fall 2009) 735 applied for aid; of those 89% were deemed to have need. 91% of freshmen with need received aid; of those 9% had need fully met. ***Average percent of need met:*** 79% (excluding resources awarded to replace EFC). ***Average financial aid package:*** $8087 (excluding resources awarded to replace EFC). 6% of all full-time freshmen had no need and received non-need-based gift aid.

UNDERGRADUATE FINANCIAL AID (Fall 2009) 3,386 applied for aid; of those 62% were deemed to have need. 83% of undergraduates with need received aid; of those 13% had need fully met. ***Average percent of need met:*** 68% (excluding resources awarded to replace EFC). ***Average financial aid package:*** $8005 (excluding resources awarded to replace EFC). 5% of all full-time undergraduates had no need and received non-need-based gift aid.

GIFT AID (NEED-BASED) ***Total amount:*** $25,176,536 (82% federal, 18% state). ***Receiving aid:*** Freshmen: 60% (544); all full-time undergraduates: 38% (1,697). ***Average award:*** Freshmen: $4100; Undergraduates: $4100. ***Scholarships, grants, and awards:*** Federal Pell, FSEOG, state, private, college/university gift aid from institutional funds.

GIFT AID (NON-NEED-BASED) ***Total amount:*** $19,781,731 (33% federal, 64% state, 2% institutional, 1% external sources). ***Receiving aid:*** Freshmen: 60% (545). Undergraduates: 38% (1,729). ***Average award:*** Freshmen: $1200. Undergraduates: $1200. ***Scholarships, grants, and awards by category:*** *Academic interests/achievement:* biological sciences, business, education, English, general academic interests/achievements, health fields, humanities, mathematics, military science, physical sciences, premedicine. *Creative arts/performance:* applied art and design, general creative arts/performance, music. *Special achievements/activities:* cheerleading/drum major, community service, general special achievements/activities, leadership. *Special characteristics:* general special characteristics. ***Tuition waivers:*** Full or partial for employees or children of employees, senior citizens.

LOANS ***Student loans:*** $18,129,638 (71% need-based, 29% non-need-based). 68% of past graduating class borrowed through all loan programs. *Average indebtedness per student:* $10,021. ***Average need-based loan:*** Freshmen: $4900. Undergraduates: $4900. ***Parent loans:*** $834,453 (100% non-need-based). ***Programs:*** Federal Direct (Subsidized and Unsubsidized Stafford, PLUS), Perkins, state, college/university.

WORK-STUDY ***Federal work-study:*** Total amount: $209,309; jobs available. ***State or other work-study/employment:*** Total amount: $352,000 (100% non-need-based). Part-time jobs available.

ATHLETIC AWARDS Total amount: $753,214 (100% non-need-based).

APPLYING FOR FINANCIAL AID ***Required financial aid form:*** FAFSA. ***Financial aid deadline (priority):*** 3/20. ***Notification date:*** Continuous beginning 3/1. Students must reply within 3 weeks of notification.

CONTACT Jill Rayner, Director of Financial Aid, North Georgia College & State University, 82 College Circle, Dahlonega, GA 30597-1001, 706-864-1688 or toll-free 800-498-9581. *Fax:* 706-864-1411. *E-mail:* jprayner@northgeorgia.edu.

NORTH GREENVILLE UNIVERSITY

Tigerville, SC

ABOUT THE INSTITUTION Independent Southern Baptist, coed. 26 undergraduate majors.

GIFT AID (NEED-BASED) ***Scholarships, grants, and awards:*** Federal Pell, FSEOG, state, private, college/university gift aid from institutional funds.

GIFT AID (NON-NEED-BASED) ***Scholarships, grants, and awards by category:*** *Academic interests/achievement:* biological sciences, communication, education, general academic interests/achievements, military science, religion/biblical studies. *Creative arts/performance:* journalism/publications, music, theater/drama. *Special characteristics:* children of faculty/staff.

LOANS ***Programs:*** Perkins, state.

WORK-STUDY ***Federal work-study:*** Total amount: $148,000; jobs available. ***State or other work-study/employment:*** Total amount: $168,000 (100% non-need-based). Part-time jobs available.

APPLYING FOR FINANCIAL AID ***Required financial aid form:*** FAFSA.

CONTACT Mike Jordan, Director of Financial Aid, North Greenville University, PO Box 1892, Tigerville, SC 29688, 864-977-7058 or toll-free 800-468-6642 Ext. 7001. *Fax:* 864-977-7177. *E-mail:* mjordan@ngu.edu.

NORTHLAND COLLEGE

Ashland, WI

Tuition & fees: $26,566 **Average undergraduate aid package: N/A**

ABOUT THE INSTITUTION Independent religious, coed. 22 undergraduate majors. Federal methodology is used as a basis for awarding need-based institutional aid.

UNDERGRADUATE EXPENSES for 2011–12 ***Comprehensive fee:*** $33,776 includes full-time tuition ($25,725), mandatory fees ($841), and room and board ($7210). ***College room only:*** $2990. Full-time tuition and fees vary according to course load. Room and board charges vary according to board plan and housing facility. ***Part-time tuition:*** $475 per credit hour. Part-time tuition and fees vary according to course load. ***Payment plan:*** Installment.

FRESHMAN FINANCIAL AID (Fall 2010, est.) 121 applied for aid; of those 100% were deemed to have need. 100% of freshmen with need received aid.

UNDERGRADUATE FINANCIAL AID (Fall 2010, est.) 548 applied for aid; of those 100% were deemed to have need. 100% of undergraduates with need received aid.

GIFT AID (NEED-BASED) ***Total amount:*** $7,291,327 (17% federal, 5% state, 76% institutional, 2% external sources). ***Scholarships, grants, and awards:*** Federal Pell, FSEOG, state, private, college/university gift aid from institutional funds, Academic Competitiveness Grants, National SMART Grants, Bureau of Indian Affairs Grants.

GIFT AID (NON-NEED-BASED) ***Total amount:*** $991,404 (99% institutional, 1% external sources). ***Receiving aid:*** Freshmen: 100% (121). Undergraduates: 95% (548). ***Scholarships, grants, and awards by category:*** *Academic interests/achievement:* general academic interests/achievements. *Creative arts/performance:* art/fine arts, music. *Special achievements/activities:* leadership. *Special characteristics:* ethnic background. ***Tuition waivers:*** Full or partial for employees or children of employees.

LOANS ***Student loans:*** $2,082,734 (39% need-based, 61% non-need-based). ***Parent loans:*** $666,200 (88% need-based, 12% non-need-based). ***Programs:*** Perkins.

WORK-STUDY ***Federal work-study:*** Total amount: $325,106; jobs available. ***State or other work-study/employment:*** Total amount: $339,450 (100% non-need-based). Part-time jobs available.

APPLYING FOR FINANCIAL AID ***Required financial aid form:*** FAFSA. ***Financial aid deadline (priority):*** 4/15. ***Notification date:*** Continuous. Students must reply by 5/1 or within 4 weeks of notification.

CONTACT Debra L. Morrissey, Director of Financial Aid, Northland College, 1411 Ellis Avenue, Ashland, WI 54806, 715-682-1255 or toll-free 800-753-1840 (in-state), 800-753-1040 (out-of-state). *Fax:* 715-682-1368. *E-mail:* dmorrissey@northland.edu.

NORTH PARK UNIVERSITY

Chicago, IL

CONTACT Dr. Lucy Shaker, Director of Financial Aid, North Park University, 3225 West Foster Avenue, Chicago, IL 60625-4895, 773-244-5526 or toll-free 800-888-NPC8. *Fax:* 773-244-4953.

NORTHWEST CHRISTIAN UNIVERSITY

Eugene, OR

Tuition & fees: $23,600 **Average undergraduate aid package: $19,742**

ABOUT THE INSTITUTION Independent Christian, coed. 15 undergraduate majors. Federal methodology is used as a basis for awarding need-based institutional aid.

UNDERGRADUATE EXPENSES for 2011–12 ***Comprehensive fee:*** $31,000 includes full-time tuition ($23,600) and room and board ($7400). Full-time tuition and fees vary according to course load. Room and board charges vary according to board plan and housing facility. ***Part-time tuition:*** $787 per credit. Part-time tuition and fees vary according to course load. ***Payment plans:*** Installment, deferred payment.

FRESHMAN FINANCIAL AID (Fall 2010, est.) 73 applied for aid; of those 96% were deemed to have need. 100% of freshmen with need received aid; of those 9% had need fully met. ***Average percent of need met:*** 78% (excluding resources awarded to replace EFC). ***Average financial aid package:*** $20,999 (excluding resources awarded to replace EFC). 5% of all full-time freshmen had no need and received non-need-based gift aid.

UNDERGRADUATE FINANCIAL AID (Fall 2010, est.) 305 applied for aid; of those 93% were deemed to have need. 100% of undergraduates with need received aid; of those 17% had need fully met. ***Average percent of need met:*** 75% (excluding resources awarded to replace EFC). ***Average financial aid package:*** $19,742 (excluding resources awarded to replace EFC). 7% of all full-time undergraduates had no need and received non-need-based gift aid.

GIFT AID (NEED-BASED) ***Total amount:*** $3,799,174 (20% federal, 2% state, 67% institutional, 11% external sources). ***Receiving aid:*** Freshmen: 93% (70); all full-time undergraduates: 87% (284). ***Average award:*** Freshmen: $16,382; Undergraduates: $14,974. ***Scholarships, grants, and awards:*** Federal Pell, FSEOG, state, private, college/university gift aid from institutional funds.

GIFT AID (NON-NEED-BASED) ***Total amount:*** $413,235 (1% federal, 45% institutional, 54% external sources). ***Receiving aid:*** Freshmen: 4% (3). Undergraduates: 7% (23). ***Average award:*** Freshmen: $5625. Undergraduates: $6729. ***Scholarships, grants, and awards by category:*** *Academic interests/achievement:* 217 awards ($1,086,000 total): general academic interests/achievements. *Creative arts/performance:* 11 awards ($11,000 total): music. *Special achievements/activities:* 195 awards ($307,000 total): community service, leadership, religious involvement. *Special characteristics:* 61 awards ($210,000 total): children of faculty/staff, relatives of clergy, religious affiliation, siblings of current students. ***Tuition waivers:*** Full or partial for employees or children of employees.

LOANS ***Student loans:*** $2,284,651 (77% need-based, 23% non-need-based). 74% of past graduating class borrowed through all loan programs. *Average indebtedness per student:* $22,818. ***Average need-based loan:*** Freshmen: $4974. Undergraduates: $4921. ***Parent loans:*** $448,982 (59% need-based, 41% non-need-based). ***Programs:*** Federal Direct (Subsidized and Unsubsidized Stafford, PLUS), Perkins.

WORK-STUDY ***Federal work-study:*** Total amount: $168,162; 70 jobs averaging $945. ***State or other work-study/employment:*** 66 part-time jobs averaging $900.

ATHLETIC AWARDS Total amount: $524,250 (75% need-based, 25% non-need-based).

APPLYING FOR FINANCIAL AID ***Required financial aid forms:*** FAFSA, merit worksheet. ***Financial aid deadline (priority):*** 3/1. ***Notification date:*** Continuous beginning 3/1. Students must reply within 2 weeks of notification.

CONTACT David Haggard, Director of Financial Aid, Northwest Christian University, 828 East 11th Avenue, Eugene, OR 97401-3727, 541-684-7218 or toll-free 877-463-6622. *Fax:* 541-684-7323. *E-mail:* dhaggard@northwestchristian.edu.

NORTHWEST COLLEGE OF ART

Poulsbo, WA

CONTACT Ms. Kim Y. Perigard, Director of Financial Aid, Northwest College of Art, 16464 State Highway 305, Poulsbo, WA 98370, 360-779-9993 or toll-free 800-769-ARTS.

NORTHWESTERN COLLEGE

Orange City, IA

CONTACT Mr. Gerry Korver, Director of Financial Aid, Northwestern College, 101 Seventh Street, SW, Orange City, IA 51041-1996, 712-707-7131 or toll-free 800-747-4757. *Fax:* 712-707-7164.

NORTHWESTERN COLLEGE

St. Paul, MN

Tuition & fees: $25,700 **Average undergraduate aid package: $18,160**

ABOUT THE INSTITUTION Independent nondenominational, coed. 48 undergraduate majors. Federal methodology is used as a basis for awarding need-based institutional aid.

UNDERGRADUATE EXPENSES for 2011–12 ***Comprehensive fee:*** $33,700 includes full-time tuition ($25,490), mandatory fees ($210), and room and board ($8000). ***College room only:*** $4610. Full-time tuition and fees vary according to course load. Room and board charges vary according to board plan. ***Part-time tuition:*** $1090 per semester hour. ***Part-time fees:*** $60 per term. Part-time tuition and fees vary according to course load. ***Payment plan:*** Installment.

FRESHMAN FINANCIAL AID (Fall 2009) 445 applied for aid; of those 86% were deemed to have need. 100% of freshmen with need received aid; of those 6% had need fully met. ***Average percent of need met:*** 71% (excluding resources awarded to replace EFC). ***Average financial aid package:*** $19,464 (excluding resources awarded to replace EFC). 14% of all full-time freshmen had no need and received non-need-based gift aid.

UNDERGRADUATE FINANCIAL AID (Fall 2009) 1,721 applied for aid; of those 85% were deemed to have need. 100% of undergraduates with need received aid; of those 6% had need fully met. ***Average percent of need met:*** 70% (excluding resources awarded to replace EFC). ***Average financial aid package:*** $18,160 (excluding resources awarded to replace EFC). 13% of all full-time undergraduates had no need and received non-need-based gift aid.

GIFT AID (NEED-BASED) ***Total amount:*** $17,974,404 (18% federal, 10% state, 68% institutional, 4% external sources). ***Receiving aid:*** Freshmen: 85% (383); all full-time undergraduates: 83% (1,460). ***Average award:*** Freshmen: $15,959; Undergraduates: $13,525. ***Scholarships, grants, and awards:*** Federal Pell, FSEOG, state, private, college/university gift aid from institutional funds.

GIFT AID (NON-NEED-BASED) ***Total amount:*** $2,301,901 (94% institutional, 6% external sources). ***Receiving aid:*** Freshmen: 14% (62). Undergraduates: 13% (227). ***Average award:*** Freshmen: $6892. Undergraduates: $6433. ***Scholarships, grants, and awards by category:*** *Academic interests/achievement:* 1,177 awards ($5,738,184 total): general academic interests/achievements. *Creative arts/performance:* 163 awards ($259,150 total): music, theater/drama. *Special achievements/activities:* 370 awards ($950,657 total): general special achievements/activities, leadership. *Special characteristics:* 703 awards ($4,253,490 total): children of faculty/staff, ethnic background, international students, relatives of clergy, siblings of current students. ***Tuition waivers:*** Full or partial for children of alumni, employees or children of employees.

LOANS ***Student loans:*** $10,891,144 (89% need-based, 11% non-need-based). 80% of past graduating class borrowed through all loan programs. *Average indebtedness per student:* $25,707. ***Average need-based loan:*** Freshmen: $3741. Undergraduates: $4503. ***Parent loans:*** $5,097,901 (80% need-based, 20% non-need-based). ***Programs:*** Federal Direct (Subsidized and Unsubsidized Stafford, PLUS), Perkins, state.

WORK-STUDY ***Federal work-study:*** Total amount: $361,519; 185 jobs averaging $1935. ***State or other work-study/employment:*** Total amount: $568,150 (100% need-based). 281 part-time jobs averaging $1997.

APPLYING FOR FINANCIAL AID ***Required financial aid forms:*** FAFSA, institution's own form. ***Financial aid deadline (priority):*** 3/1. ***Notification date:*** Continuous beginning 3/1. Students must reply within 2 weeks of notification.

CONTACT Mr. Richard L. Blatchley, Director of Financial Aid, Northwestern College, 3003 Snelling Avenue North, St. Paul, MN 55113-1598, 651-631-5321 or toll-free 800-827-6827. *Fax:* 651-628-3332. *E-mail:* rlb@nwc.edu.

NORTHWESTERN OKLAHOMA STATE UNIVERSITY

Alva, OK

Tuition & fees (OK res): $4336 **Average undergraduate aid package: N/A**

ABOUT THE INSTITUTION State-supported, coed. 40 undergraduate majors. Both federal and institutional methodology are used as a basis for awarding need-based institutional aid.

UNDERGRADUATE EXPENSES for 2010–11 ***Tuition, state resident:*** full-time $3713. ***Tuition, nonresident:*** full-time $9518. ***Required fees:*** full-time $623. Full-time tuition and fees vary according to course load, location, and program. Part-time tuition and fees vary according to course load, location, and program. ***College room and board:*** $3640; ***Room only:*** $1300. Room and board charges vary according to board plan. ***Payment plan:*** Installment.

FRESHMAN FINANCIAL AID (Fall 2010, est.) 267 applied for aid; of those 80% were deemed to have need. 99% of freshmen with need received aid.

UNDERGRADUATE FINANCIAL AID (Fall 2010, est.) 1,012 applied for aid; of those 83% were deemed to have need. 98% of undergraduates with need received aid.

GIFT AID (NEED-BASED) ***Total amount:*** $5,356,184 (70% federal, 25% state, 5% institutional). ***Receiving aid:*** Freshmen: 55% (186); all full-time undergraduates: 49% (679). ***Scholarships, grants, and awards:*** Federal Pell, FSEOG, state, private, college/university gift aid from institutional funds.

GIFT AID (NON-NEED-BASED) ***Total amount:*** $949,807 (8% state, 46% institutional, 46% external sources). ***Scholarships, grants, and awards by category:*** *Academic interests/achievement:* agriculture, biological sciences, business, communication, computer science, education, English, foreign languages, general academic interests/achievements, health fields, library science, mathematics, physical sciences, premedicine, social sciences. *Creative arts/performance:* art/fine arts, cinema/film/broadcasting, debating, general creative arts/performance, journalism/publications, music, theater/drama. *Special achievements/activities:* cheerleading/drum major, general special achievements/activities, leadership, memberships, rodeo. *Special characteristics:* children of faculty/staff. ***Tuition waivers:*** Full or partial for employees or children of employees, senior citizens.

LOANS ***Student loans:*** $4,587,912 (52% need-based, 48% non-need-based). 53% of past graduating class borrowed through all loan programs. *Average indebtedness per student:* $14,281. ***Parent loans:*** $105,526 (100% non-need-based). ***Programs:*** Federal Direct (Subsidized and Unsubsidized Stafford, PLUS), Perkins.

WORK-STUDY ***Federal work-study:*** Total amount: $158,560; 146 jobs averaging $1086. ***State or other work-study/employment:*** Total amount: $316,854 (100% non-need-based). 225 part-time jobs averaging $1408.

ATHLETIC AWARDS Total amount: $321,654 (72% need-based, 28% non-need-based).

APPLYING FOR FINANCIAL AID ***Required financial aid forms:*** FAFSA, institution's own form. ***Financial aid deadline:*** Continuous. ***Notification date:*** Continuous beginning 3/1. Students must reply by 8/15.

CONTACT Calleb N. Mosburg, Director of Financial Aid, Northwestern Oklahoma State University, 709 Oklahoma Boulevard, Alva, OK 73717-2799, 580-327-8542. *Fax:* 580-327-8177. *E-mail:* cnmosburg@nwosu.edu.

NORTHWESTERN STATE UNIVERSITY OF LOUISIANA

Natchitoches, LA

Tuition & fees (LA res): $4384 **Average undergraduate aid package: $6921**

ABOUT THE INSTITUTION State-supported, coed. 39 undergraduate majors. Both federal and institutional methodology are used as a basis for awarding need-based institutional aid.

UNDERGRADUATE EXPENSES for 2010–11 ***Tuition, state resident:*** full-time $3002. ***Tuition, nonresident:*** full-time $10,744. ***Required fees:*** full-time $1382. Full-time tuition and fees vary according to course load and location. Part-time tuition and fees vary according to course load and location. ***College room and board:*** $7070; ***Room only:*** $4500. Room and board charges vary according to board plan, housing facility, and location. ***Payment plan:*** Installment.

FRESHMAN FINANCIAL AID (Fall 2010, est.) 885 applied for aid; of those 83% were deemed to have need. 98% of freshmen with need received aid; of those 49% had need fully met. ***Average percent of need met:*** 79% (excluding resources awarded to replace EFC). ***Average financial aid package:*** $6543 (excluding resources awarded to replace EFC). 26% of all full-time freshmen had no need and received non-need-based gift aid.

UNDERGRADUATE FINANCIAL AID (Fall 2010, est.) 4,114 applied for aid; of those 85% were deemed to have need. 96% of undergraduates with need received aid; of those 44% had need fully met. ***Average percent of need met:*** 59% (excluding resources awarded to replace EFC). ***Average financial aid package:*** $6921 (excluding resources awarded to replace EFC). 30% of all full-time undergraduates had no need and received non-need-based gift aid.

GIFT AID (NEED-BASED) ***Total amount:*** $14,074,161 (99% federal, 1% state). ***Receiving aid:*** Freshmen: 49% (517); all full-time undergraduates: 48% (2,531). ***Average award:*** Freshmen: $5117; Undergraduates: $4719. ***Scholarships, grants, and awards:*** Federal Pell, FSEOG, state, private, college/university gift aid from institutional funds, United Negro College Fund, Federal Nursing, third party scholarships.

GIFT AID (NON-NEED-BASED) ***Total amount:*** $11,792,938 (1% federal, 56% state, 23% institutional, 20% external sources). ***Receiving aid:*** Freshmen: 51% (540). Undergraduates: 41% (2,150). ***Average award:*** Freshmen: $5217. Undergraduates: $4812. ***Scholarships, grants, and awards by category:***

Academic interests/achievement: 2,250 awards ($1,923,450 total): biological sciences, business, communication, education, engineering/technologies, English, general academic interests/achievements, health fields, humanities, mathematics, military science, social sciences. *Creative arts/performance:* 557 awards ($807,628 total): art/fine arts, cinema/film/broadcasting, creative writing, dance, general creative arts/performance, journalism/publications, music, performing arts, theater/drama. *Special achievements/activities:* 128 awards ($122,214 total): cheerleading/drum major, general special achievements/activities, leadership, memberships. *Special characteristics:* 515 awards ($2,867,560 total): adult students, children of faculty/staff, children of public servants, general special characteristics, international students, out-of-state students, public servants, veterans, veterans' children. ***Tuition waivers:*** Full or partial for employees or children of employees, senior citizens.

LOANS ***Student loans:*** $26,041,258 (44% need-based, 56% non-need-based). 67% of past graduating class borrowed through all loan programs. *Average indebtedness per student:* $23,710. ***Average need-based loan:*** Freshmen: $5204. Undergraduates: $6914. ***Parent loans:*** $623,710 (100% non-need-based). ***Programs:*** Federal Direct (Subsidized and Unsubsidized Stafford, PLUS), Perkins, alternative loans.

WORK-STUDY ***Federal work-study:*** Total amount: $541,168; 258 jobs averaging $2098. ***State or other work-study/employment:*** Total amount: $816,932 (100% non-need-based). 575 part-time jobs averaging $1421.

ATHLETIC AWARDS Total amount: $2,861,158 (100% non-need-based).

APPLYING FOR FINANCIAL AID ***Required financial aid forms:*** FAFSA, institution's own form. ***Financial aid deadline (priority):*** 5/1. ***Notification date:*** Continuous beginning 5/1. Students must reply within 4 weeks of notification.

CONTACT Ms. Misti Adams, Director of Financial Aid, Northwestern State University of Louisiana, Northwestern State University, 103 Roy Hall, Natchitoches, LA 71497, 318-357-5961 or toll-free 800-327-1903. *Fax:* 318-357-5488. *E-mail:* nsufinaid@nsula.edu.

NORTHWESTERN UNIVERSITY

Evanston, IL

ABOUT THE INSTITUTION Independent, coed. ***Awards:*** bachelor's and master's degrees and post-master's certificates. 112 undergraduate majors. ***Total enrollment:*** 18,431. Undergraduates: 8,476. Freshmen: 2,078.

GIFT AID (NEED-BASED) ***Scholarships, grants, and awards:*** Federal Pell, FSEOG, state, college/university gift aid from institutional funds.

GIFT AID (NON-NEED-BASED) ***Scholarships, grants, and awards by category:*** *Creative arts/performance:* music. *Special characteristics:* international students.

LOANS ***Programs:*** Federal Direct (Subsidized and Unsubsidized Stafford, PLUS), Perkins, college/university.

WORK-STUDY ***Federal work-study:*** Total amount: $3,700,000; 2,301 jobs averaging $2050. ***State or other work-study/employment:*** Total amount: $1,419,868 (100% need-based). Part-time jobs available.

APPLYING FOR FINANCIAL AID ***Required financial aid forms:*** FAFSA, CSS Financial Aid PROFILE, noncustodial (divorced/separated) parent's statement, business/farm supplement, parent and student tax forms.

CONTACT Office of Financial Aid, Northwestern University, 1801 Hinman Avenue, Evanston, IL 60204-1270, 847-491-7400. *E-mail:* ug-finaid@u.northwestern.edu.

NORTHWEST MISSOURI STATE UNIVERSITY

Maryville, MO

Tuition & fees (MO res): $7047 **Average undergraduate aid package: $7657**

ABOUT THE INSTITUTION State-supported, coed. 83 undergraduate majors. Federal methodology is used as a basis for awarding need-based institutional aid.

UNDERGRADUATE EXPENSES for 2010–11 ***One-time required fee:*** $140. ***Tuition, state resident:*** full-time $4722; part-time $157.39 per credit hour. ***Tuition, nonresident:*** full-time $10,073; part-time $335.78 per credit hour. ***Required fees:*** full-time $2325; $77.50 per credit hour. Full-time tuition and fees vary according to course load, location, and reciprocity agreements. Part-time tuition and fees vary according to course load and location. ***College room and board:*** $7962; ***Room only:*** $4996. Room and board charges vary according to board plan and housing facility. ***Payment plans:*** Installment, deferred payment.

FRESHMAN FINANCIAL AID (Fall 2009) 1,414 applied for aid; of those 74% were deemed to have need. 100% of freshmen with need received aid; of those 71% had need fully met. ***Average percent of need met:*** 78% (excluding resources awarded to replace EFC). ***Average financial aid package:*** $9117 (excluding resources awarded to replace EFC). 18% of all full-time freshmen had no need and received non-need-based gift aid.

UNDERGRADUATE FINANCIAL AID (Fall 2009) 4,663 applied for aid; of those 78% were deemed to have need. 99% of undergraduates with need received aid; of those 60% had need fully met. ***Average percent of need met:*** 72% (excluding resources awarded to replace EFC). ***Average financial aid package:*** $7657 (excluding resources awarded to replace EFC). 10% of all full-time undergraduates had no need and received non-need-based gift aid.

GIFT AID (NEED-BASED) ***Total amount:*** $14,838,887 (59% federal, 20% state, 19% institutional, 2% external sources). ***Receiving aid:*** Freshmen: 60% (924); all full-time undergraduates: 53% (2,884). ***Average award:*** Freshmen: $6374; Undergraduates: $5827. ***Scholarships, grants, and awards:*** Federal Pell, FSEOG, state, private, college/university gift aid from institutional funds.

GIFT AID (NON-NEED-BASED) ***Total amount:*** $4,585,281 (4% federal, 4% state, 85% institutional, 7% external sources). ***Receiving aid:*** Freshmen: 38% (593). Undergraduates: 24% (1,309). ***Average award:*** Freshmen: $2149. Undergraduates: $2228. ***Scholarships, grants, and awards by category:*** *Academic interests/achievement:* agriculture, biological sciences, business, communication, computer science, education, English, foreign languages, general academic interests/achievements, health fields, home economics, humanities, mathematics, physical sciences, social sciences. *Creative arts/performance:* art/fine arts, cinema/film/broadcasting, dance, debating, journalism/publications, music, theater/drama. *Special achievements/activities:* cheerleading/drum major, general special achievements/activities, leadership, memberships. *Special characteristics:* children and siblings of alumni, children of faculty/staff, general special characteristics, members of minority groups, out-of-state students, previous college experience. ***Tuition waivers:*** Full or partial for employees or children of employees, senior citizens.

LOANS ***Student loans:*** $24,113,614 (58% need-based, 42% non-need-based). 69% of past graduating class borrowed through all loan programs. *Average indebtedness per student:* $21,230. ***Average need-based loan:*** Freshmen: $3227. Undergraduates: $4016. ***Parent loans:*** $6,823,531 (20% need-based, 80% non-need-based). ***Programs:*** Federal Direct (Subsidized and Unsubsidized Stafford, PLUS), Perkins.

WORK-STUDY ***Federal work-study:*** Total amount: $480,818; 441 jobs averaging $1092. ***State or other work-study/employment:*** Total amount: $1,662,385 (19% need-based, 81% non-need-based). 1,082 part-time jobs averaging $1372.

ATHLETIC AWARDS Total amount: $1,937,259 (27% need-based, 73% non-need-based).

APPLYING FOR FINANCIAL AID ***Required financial aid form:*** FAFSA. ***Financial aid deadline:*** Continuous. ***Notification date:*** Continuous beginning 3/15.

CONTACT Mr. Del Morley, Director of Financial Assistance, Northwest Missouri State University, 800 University Drive, Maryville, MO 64468-6001, 660-562-1138 or toll-free 800-633-1175.

NORTHWEST NAZARENE UNIVERSITY

Nampa, ID

Tuition & fees: $24,030 **Average undergraduate aid package: $14,946**

ABOUT THE INSTITUTION Independent religious, coed. 74 undergraduate majors. Federal methodology is used as a basis for awarding need-based institutional aid.

UNDERGRADUATE EXPENSES for 2011–12 ***Comprehensive fee:*** $30,250 includes full-time tuition ($23,730), mandatory fees ($300), and room and board ($6220). Full-time tuition and fees vary according to course load, degree level, program, and reciprocity agreements. Room and board charges vary according to board plan. ***Part-time tuition:*** $1028 per semester hour. ***Payment plans:*** Tuition prepayment, installment.

FRESHMAN FINANCIAL AID (Fall 2009) 241 applied for aid; of those 85% were deemed to have need. 100% of freshmen with need received aid; of those 21% had need fully met. ***Average percent of need met:*** 75% (excluding resources awarded to replace EFC). ***Average financial aid package:*** $16,828 (excluding resources awarded to replace EFC). 19% of all full-time freshmen had no need and received non-need-based gift aid.

UNDERGRADUATE FINANCIAL AID (Fall 2009) 993 applied for aid; of those 89% were deemed to have need. 100% of undergraduates with need received aid; of those 19% had need fully met. ***Average percent of need met:*** 66% (excluding resources awarded to replace EFC). ***Average financial aid package:*** $14,946 (excluding resources awarded to replace EFC). 24% of all full-time undergraduates had no need and received non-need-based gift aid.

GIFT AID (NEED-BASED) ***Total amount:*** $7,990,255 (23% federal, 1% state, 68% institutional, 8% external sources). ***Receiving aid:*** Freshmen: 55% (140); all full-time undergraduates: 42% (487). ***Average award:*** Freshmen: $16,545; Undergraduates: $16,314. ***Scholarships, grants, and awards:*** Federal Pell, FSEOG, state, private, college/university gift aid from institutional funds.

GIFT AID (NON-NEED-BASED) ***Total amount:*** $2,196,669 (1% state, 87% institutional, 12% external sources). ***Receiving aid:*** Freshmen: 12% (30). Undergraduates: 8% (91). ***Average award:*** Freshmen: $8000. Undergraduates: $6577. ***Scholarships, grants, and awards by category:*** *Academic interests/achievement:* 861 awards ($3,595,463 total): biological sciences, business, computer science, education, English, general academic interests/achievements, health fields, mathematics, military science, physical sciences, premedicine, religion/biblical studies, social sciences. *Creative arts/performance:* 81 awards ($147,284 total): art/fine arts, debating, general creative arts/performance, journalism/publications, music, performing arts, theater/drama. *Special achievements/activities:* 40 awards ($58,350 total): cheerleading/drum major, general special achievements/activities, leadership, religious involvement. *Special characteristics:* 718 awards ($3,226,181 total): children and siblings of alumni, children of educators, children of faculty/staff, ethnic background, international students, members of minority groups, out-of-state students, relatives of clergy, religious affiliation, siblings of current students, veterans. ***Tuition waivers:*** Full or partial for minority students, children of alumni, employees or children of employees.

LOANS ***Student loans:*** $6,569,401 (76% need-based, 24% non-need-based). 72% of past graduating class borrowed through all loan programs. *Average indebtedness per student:* $26,752. ***Average need-based loan:*** Freshmen: $6802. Undergraduates: $8292. ***Parent loans:*** $1,584,847 (40% need-based, 60% non-need-based). ***Programs:*** Perkins, college/university.

WORK-STUDY ***Federal work-study:*** Total amount: $144,481; 145 jobs averaging $996. ***State or other work-study/employment:*** Total amount: $4218 (100% need-based). Part-time jobs available.

ATHLETIC AWARDS Total amount: $1,528,440 (42% need-based, 58% non-need-based).

APPLYING FOR FINANCIAL AID ***Required financial aid forms:*** FAFSA, institution's own form. ***Financial aid deadline (priority):*** 3/1. ***Notification date:*** Continuous beginning 4/1. Students must reply within 3 weeks of notification.

CONTACT Mr. David Klaffke, Director of Financial Aid, Northwest Nazarene University, 623 South University Boulevard, Nampa, ID 83686, 208-467-8422 or toll-free 877-668-4968. *Fax:* 208-467-8375. *E-mail:* dklaffke@nnu.edu.

NORTHWEST UNIVERSITY

Kirkland, WA

Tuition & fees: $23,400 **Average undergraduate aid package: $15,696**

ABOUT THE INSTITUTION Independent religious, coed. 43 undergraduate majors. Federal methodology is used as a basis for awarding need-based institutional aid.

UNDERGRADUATE EXPENSES for 2011–12 ***One-time required fee:*** $40. ***Comprehensive fee:*** $30,284 includes full-time tuition ($23,030), mandatory fees ($370), and room and board ($6884). Full-time tuition and fees vary according to class time, location, and program. Room and board charges vary according to board plan, housing facility, and location. ***Part-time tuition:*** $960 per credit hour. Part-time tuition and fees vary according to course load and location. ***Payment plan:*** Installment.

FRESHMAN FINANCIAL AID (Fall 2010, est.) 155 applied for aid; of those 88% were deemed to have need. 100% of freshmen with need received aid; of those 21% had need fully met. ***Average percent of need met:*** 74% (excluding resources awarded to replace EFC). ***Average financial aid package:*** $16,548 (excluding resources awarded to replace EFC). 10% of all full-time freshmen had no need and received non-need-based gift aid.

UNDERGRADUATE FINANCIAL AID (Fall 2010, est.) 934 applied for aid; of those 89% were deemed to have need. 100% of undergraduates with need received aid; of those 16% had need fully met. ***Average percent of need met:*** 70% (excluding resources awarded to replace EFC). ***Average financial aid package:*** $15,696 (excluding resources awarded to replace EFC). 13% of all full-time undergraduates had no need and received non-need-based gift aid.

GIFT AID (NEED-BASED) ***Total amount:*** $9,301,859 (20% federal, 11% state, 62% institutional, 7% external sources). ***Receiving aid:*** Freshmen: 75% (136); all full-time undergraduates: 78% (825). ***Average award:*** Freshmen: $13,041; Undergraduates: $11,690. ***Scholarships, grants, and awards:*** Federal Pell, FSEOG, state, private, college/university gift aid from institutional funds.

GIFT AID (NON-NEED-BASED) ***Total amount:*** $1,451,562 (93% institutional, 7% external sources). ***Receiving aid:*** Freshmen: 11% (20). Undergraduates: 7% (78). ***Average award:*** Freshmen: $7297. Undergraduates: $7920. ***Scholarships, grants, and awards by category:*** *Academic interests/achievement:* 254 awards ($1,365,560 total): general academic interests/achievements. *Creative arts/performance:* 84 awards ($239,100 total): debating, music, performing arts, theater/drama. *Special achievements/activities:* 20 awards ($352,170 total): leadership. *Special characteristics:* 201 awards ($1,255,002 total): children of current students, children of faculty/staff, general special characteristics, international students, married students, parents of current students, relatives of clergy, religious affiliation, siblings of current students, spouses of current students. ***Tuition waivers:*** Full or partial for employees or children of employees.

LOANS ***Student loans:*** $7,062,644 (77% need-based, 23% non-need-based). 85% of past graduating class borrowed through all loan programs. *Average indebtedness per student:* $29,160. ***Average need-based loan:*** Freshmen: $3076. Undergraduates: $3899. ***Parent loans:*** $1,144,926 (49% need-based, 51% non-need-based). ***Programs:*** Federal Direct (Subsidized and Unsubsidized Stafford, PLUS), Perkins, state, alternative loans.

WORK-STUDY ***Federal work-study:*** Total amount: $161,156; 70 jobs averaging $2230. ***State or other work-study/employment:*** Total amount: $119,251 (83% need-based, 17% non-need-based). 26 part-time jobs averaging $3811.

ATHLETIC AWARDS Total amount: $786,323 (59% need-based, 41% non-need-based).

APPLYING FOR FINANCIAL AID ***Required financial aid forms:*** FAFSA, institution's own form. ***Financial aid deadline:*** 8/1 (priority: 2/15). ***Notification date:*** Continuous beginning 3/1. Students must reply within 4 weeks of notification.

CONTACT Mr. Roger Wilson, Director of Financial Aid, Northwest University, PO Box 579, Kirkland, WA 98083-0579, 425-889-5336 or toll-free 800-669-3781. *Fax:* 425-889-5224. *E-mail:* roger.wilson@northwestu.edu.

NORTHWOOD UNIVERSITY

Midland, MI

ABOUT THE INSTITUTION Independent, coed. ***Awards:*** associate, bachelor's, and master's degrees. 5 undergraduate majors. ***Total enrollment:*** 2,269. Undergraduates: 1,950. Freshmen: 442.

GIFT AID (NEED-BASED) ***Scholarships, grants, and awards:*** Federal Pell, FSEOG, state, private, college/university gift aid from institutional funds.

GIFT AID (NON-NEED-BASED) ***Scholarships, grants, and awards by category:*** *Academic interests/achievement:* business, general academic interests/achievements. *Special achievements/activities:* cheerleading/drum major, leadership, memberships. *Special characteristics:* children and siblings of alumni, children of faculty/staff, siblings of current students.

LOANS ***Programs:*** state.

WORK-STUDY ***Federal work-study:*** Total amount: $275,044; jobs available. ***State or other work-study/employment:*** Part-time jobs available.

APPLYING FOR FINANCIAL AID ***Required financial aid form:*** FAFSA.

CONTACT Terri Mieler, Director of Financial Aid, Northwood University, 4000 Whiting Drive, Midland, MI 48640-2398, 989-837-4301 or toll-free 800-457-7878. *Fax:* 989-837-4130. *E-mail:* mieler@northwood.edu.

NORTHWOOD UNIVERSITY, FLORIDA CAMPUS

West Palm Beach, FL

ABOUT THE INSTITUTION Private, coed. ***Awards:*** associate, bachelor's, and master's degrees. 7 undergraduate majors. ***Total enrollment:*** 620. Undergraduates: 620. Freshmen: 109.

GIFT AID (NEED-BASED) ***Scholarships, grants, and awards:*** Federal Pell, FSEOG, state, private, college/university gift aid from institutional funds.

GIFT AID (NON-NEED-BASED) ***Scholarships, grants, and awards by category:*** *Academic interests/achievement:* business, general academic interests/achievements. *Special achievements/activities:* memberships. *Special characteristics:* children and siblings of alumni, children of faculty/staff, siblings of current students.

WORK-STUDY ***Federal work-study:*** Total amount: $185,500; jobs available.

APPLYING FOR FINANCIAL AID ***Required financial aid forms:*** FAFSA, state aid form.

CONTACT Ms. Teresa A. Palmer, Director of Financial Aid, Northwood University, Florida Campus, 2600 North Military Trail, West Palm Beach, FL 33409-2911, 561-478-5590. *Fax:* 561-681-7990. *E-mail:* palmer@northwood.edu.

NORTHWOOD UNIVERSITY, TEXAS CAMPUS

Cedar Hill, TX

Tuition & fees: $19,272 **Average undergraduate aid package: $16,481**

ABOUT THE INSTITUTION Independent, coed. ***Awards:*** bachelor's degrees. 3 undergraduate majors. ***Total enrollment:*** 461. Undergraduates: 461. Freshmen: 89. Federal methodology is used as a basis for awarding need-based institutional aid.

UNDERGRADUATE EXPENSES for 2010–11 ***Application fee:*** $25. ***Comprehensive fee:*** $27,389 includes full-time tuition ($18,264), mandatory fees ($1008), and room and board ($8117). Full-time tuition and fees vary according to class time. Room and board charges vary according to board plan and housing facility. ***Part-time tuition:*** $715 per semester hour. Part-time tuition and fees vary according to class time. ***Payment plan:*** Installment.

FRESHMAN FINANCIAL AID (Fall 2009) 118 applied for aid; of those 92% were deemed to have need. 100% of freshmen with need received aid; of those 14% had need fully met. ***Average percent of need met:*** 64% (excluding resources awarded to replace EFC). ***Average financial aid package:*** $18,128 (excluding resources awarded to replace EFC). 12% of all full-time freshmen had no need and received non-need-based gift aid.

UNDERGRADUATE FINANCIAL AID (Fall 2009) 384 applied for aid; of those 92% were deemed to have need. 100% of undergraduates with need received aid; of those 13% had need fully met. ***Average percent of need met:*** 62% (excluding resources awarded to replace EFC). ***Average financial aid package:*** $16,481 (excluding resources awarded to replace EFC). 12% of all full-time undergraduates had no need and received non-need-based gift aid.

GIFT AID (NEED-BASED) ***Total amount:*** $3,674,849 (28% federal, 71% institutional, 1% external sources). ***Receiving aid:*** Freshmen: 68% (94); all full-time undergraduates: 60% (302). ***Average award:*** Freshmen: $5088; Undergraduates: $5013. ***Scholarships, grants, and awards:*** Federal Pell, FSEOG, state, private, college/university gift aid from institutional funds.

GIFT AID (NON-NEED-BASED) ***Total amount:*** $811,005 (98% institutional, 2% external sources). ***Receiving aid:*** Freshmen: 17% (23). Undergraduates: 17% (86). ***Scholarships, grants, and awards by category:*** *Academic interests/achievement:* business, general academic interests/achievements. *Special achievements/activities:* general special achievements/activities, memberships. *Special characteristics:* children and siblings of alumni, children of faculty/staff, siblings of current students. ***Tuition waivers:*** Full or partial for employees or children of employees.

LOANS ***Student loans:*** $3,076,418 (78% need-based, 22% non-need-based). 86% of past graduating class borrowed through all loan programs. *Average indebtedness per student:* $23,182. ***Average need-based loan:*** Freshmen: $3401. Undergraduates: $4223. ***Parent loans:*** $316,631 (31% need-based, 69% non-need-based).

WORK-STUDY ***Federal work-study:*** Total amount: $225,542; jobs available.

ATHLETIC AWARDS Total amount: $772,703 (57% need-based, 43% non-need-based).

APPLYING FOR FINANCIAL AID ***Required financial aid form:*** FAFSA. ***Financial aid deadline:*** Continuous. ***Notification date:*** Continuous beginning 3/1.

CONTACT Ms. Dawn Shestko, Assistant Director of Financial Aid, Northwood University, Texas Campus, 1114 West FM 1382, Cedar Hill, TX 75104, 972-293-5431 or toll-free 800-927-9663. *Fax:* 972-293-7196. *E-mail:* shestkod@northwood.edu.

NORWICH UNIVERSITY

Northfield, VT

CONTACT Director of Student Financial Planning, Norwich University, 158 Harmon Drive, Northfield, VT 05663, 802-485-2015 or toll-free 800-468-6679.

NOTRE DAME COLLEGE

South Euclid, OH

ABOUT THE INSTITUTION Independent Roman Catholic, coed. 33 undergraduate majors.

GIFT AID (NEED-BASED) ***Scholarships, grants, and awards:*** Federal Pell, FSEOG, state, private, college/university gift aid from institutional funds, Academic Competitiveness Grants, National SMART Grants.

GIFT AID (NON-NEED-BASED) ***Scholarships, grants, and awards by category:*** *Academic interests/achievement:* general academic interests/achievements. *Creative arts/performance:* dance, general creative arts/performance, music, theater/drama. *Special achievements/activities:* community service, general special achievements/activities, leadership, memberships, religious involvement. *Special characteristics:* international students.

LOANS ***Programs:*** Perkins.

APPLYING FOR FINANCIAL AID ***Required financial aid form:*** FAFSA.

CONTACT Ms. Dianna Roberts, Assistant Director of Financial Aid, Notre Dame College, 4545 College Road, South Euclid, OH 44118, 216-373-5213 or toll-free 800-632-1680. *Fax:* 216-373-5243. *E-mail:* droberts@ndc.edu.

NOTRE DAME DE NAMUR UNIVERSITY

Belmont, CA

Tuition & fees: $29,980 **Average undergraduate aid package: $21,607**

ABOUT THE INSTITUTION Independent Roman Catholic, coed. 26 undergraduate majors. Both federal and institutional methodology are used as a basis for awarding need-based institutional aid.

UNDERGRADUATE EXPENSES for 2011–12 ***Comprehensive fee:*** $41,660 includes full-time tuition ($29,610), mandatory fees ($370), and room and board ($11,680). ***College room only:*** $7610. Full-time tuition and fees vary according to degree level. Room and board charges vary according to board plan and housing facility. ***Part-time tuition:*** $955 per unit. ***Part-time fees:*** $3 per unit; $35 per term. Part-time tuition and fees vary according to degree level and program. ***Payment plan:*** Installment.

FRESHMAN FINANCIAL AID (Fall 2010, est.) 135 applied for aid; of those 95% were deemed to have need. 100% of freshmen with need received aid; of those 8% had need fully met. ***Average percent of need met:*** 63% (excluding resources awarded to replace EFC). ***Average financial aid package:*** $24,149 (excluding resources awarded to replace EFC).

UNDERGRADUATE FINANCIAL AID (Fall 2010, est.) 575 applied for aid; of those 95% were deemed to have need. 100% of undergraduates with need received aid; of those 3% had need fully met. ***Average percent of need met:*** 57% (excluding resources awarded to replace EFC). ***Average financial aid package:*** $21,607 (excluding resources awarded to replace EFC).

GIFT AID (NEED-BASED) ***Total amount:*** $9,380,122 (18% federal, 12% state, 68% institutional, 2% external sources). ***Receiving aid:*** Freshmen: 88% (128); all full-time undergraduates: 84% (533). ***Average award:*** Freshmen: $20,327; Undergraduates: $17,338. ***Scholarships, grants, and awards:*** Federal Pell, FSEOG, state, private, college/university gift aid from institutional funds.

GIFT AID (NON-NEED-BASED) ***Total amount:*** $43,155 (70% institutional, 30% external sources). ***Receiving aid:*** Freshmen: 1% (1). Undergraduates: 2% (12). ***Scholarships, grants, and awards by category:*** *Academic interests/achievement:* general academic interests/achievements. *Creative arts/performance:* applied art and design, art/fine arts, creative writing, music, performing arts, theater/drama. *Special achievements/activities:* general special achievements/activities. *Special characteristics:* children and siblings of alumni, children of faculty/staff, general special characteristics. ***Tuition waivers:*** Full or partial for employees or children of employees, senior citizens.

LOANS ***Student loans:*** $7,507,897 (93% need-based, 7% non-need-based). 87% of past graduating class borrowed through all loan programs. *Average indebtedness per student:* $25,843. ***Average need-based loan:*** Freshmen: $3550. Undergraduates: $4839. ***Parent loans:*** $3,701,012 (71% need-based, 29% non-need-based). ***Programs:*** Federal Direct (Subsidized and Unsubsidized Stafford, PLUS), Perkins.

WORK-STUDY ***Federal work-study:*** Total amount: $134,366; 90 jobs averaging $1493. ***State or other work-study/employment:*** Total amount: $272,629 (88% need-based, 12% non-need-based). Part-time jobs available.

ATHLETIC AWARDS Total amount: $479,201 (99% need-based, 1% non-need-based).

APPLYING FOR FINANCIAL AID ***Required financial aid form:*** FAFSA. ***Financial aid deadline (priority):*** 3/2. ***Notification date:*** Continuous. Students must reply within 2 weeks of notification.

CONTACT Susan Pace, Director of Financial Aid, Notre Dame de Namur University, 1500 Ralston Avenue, Belmont, CA 94002, 650-508-3580 or toll-free 800-263-0545. *Fax:* 650-508-3635. *E-mail:* space@ndnu.edu.

NOVA SOUTHEASTERN UNIVERSITY

Fort Lauderdale, FL

ABOUT THE INSTITUTION Independent, coed. 43 undergraduate majors.

GIFT AID (NEED-BASED) ***Scholarships, grants, and awards:*** Federal Pell, FSEOG, state, private, college/university gift aid from institutional funds.

GIFT AID (NON-NEED-BASED) ***Scholarships, grants, and awards by category:*** *Academic interests/achievement:* general academic interests/achievements.

LOANS ***Programs:*** Federal Direct (Subsidized and Unsubsidized Stafford, PLUS), Perkins, college/university.

WORK-STUDY ***Federal work-study:*** Total amount: $792,220; 278 jobs averaging $2850. ***State or other work-study/employment:*** Total amount: $5,525,925 (100% non-need-based). 1,511 part-time jobs averaging $3614.

APPLYING FOR FINANCIAL AID ***Required financial aid forms:*** FAFSA, institution's own form, state aid form.

CONTACT Stephanie G. Brown, EdD, Associate Vice President for Enrollment and Student Services, Nova Southeastern University, 3301 College Avenue, Fort Lauderdale, FL 33314, 954-262-7456 or toll-free 800-541-NOVA. *Fax:* 954-262-3967. *E-mail:* browstep@nova.edu.

NYACK COLLEGE

Nyack, NY

Tuition & fees: $21,500 **Average undergraduate aid package: $16,846**

ABOUT THE INSTITUTION Independent religious, coed. 35 undergraduate majors. Federal methodology is used as a basis for awarding need-based institutional aid.

UNDERGRADUATE EXPENSES for 2011–12 ***One-time required fee:*** $100. ***Comprehensive fee:*** $29,750 includes full-time tuition ($20,500), mandatory fees ($1000), and room and board ($8250). Full-time tuition and fees vary according to course load, location, and program. Room and board charges vary according to board plan, housing facility, and location. ***Part-time tuition:*** $855 per credit hour. ***Part-time fees:*** $150 per term. Part-time tuition and fees vary according to course load, location, and program. ***Payment plan:*** Installment.

FRESHMAN FINANCIAL AID (Fall 2009) 284 applied for aid; of those 94% were deemed to have need. 100% of freshmen with need received aid; of those 9% had need fully met. ***Average percent of need met:*** 67% (excluding resources awarded to replace EFC). ***Average financial aid package:*** $18,140 (excluding resources awarded to replace EFC). 20% of all full-time freshmen had no need and received non-need-based gift aid.

UNDERGRADUATE FINANCIAL AID (Fall 2009) 1,559 applied for aid; of those 95% were deemed to have need. 100% of undergraduates with need received aid; of those 10% had need fully met. ***Average percent of need met:*** 63% (excluding resources awarded to replace EFC). ***Average financial aid package:*** $16,846 (excluding resources awarded to replace EFC). 11% of all full-time undergraduates had no need and received non-need-based gift aid.

GIFT AID (NEED-BASED) ***Total amount:*** $16,336,751 (28% federal, 15% state, 55% institutional, 2% external sources). ***Receiving aid:*** Freshmen: 84% (265); all full-time undergraduates: 82% (1,462). ***Average award:*** Freshmen: $13,520; Undergraduates: $11,472. ***Scholarships, grants, and awards:*** Federal Pell, FSEOG, state, private, college/university gift aid from institutional funds.

GIFT AID (NON-NEED-BASED) ***Total amount:*** $1,568,139 (2% state, 92% institutional, 6% external sources). ***Receiving aid:*** Freshmen: 6% (20). Undergraduates: 6% (103). ***Average award:*** Freshmen: $7355. Undergraduates: $6247. ***Scholarships, grants, and awards by category:*** *Academic interests/achievement:* $1,613,500 total: general academic interests/achievements. *Creative arts/performance:* $142,750 total: journalism/publications, music, performing arts, theater/drama. *Special achievements/activities:* $2,147,770 total: cheerleading/drum major, community service, general special achievements/activities, leadership, religious involvement. *Special characteristics:* $2,916,686 total: children and siblings of alumni, children of faculty/staff, general special characteristics, international students, local/state students, out-of-state students, relatives of clergy, religious affiliation, spouses of current students. ***Tuition waivers:*** Full or partial for employees or children of employees.

LOANS ***Student loans:*** $14,527,893 (86% need-based, 14% non-need-based). 88% of past graduating class borrowed through all loan programs. *Average indebtedness per student:* $35,879. ***Average need-based loan:*** Freshmen: $3360. Undergraduates: $4534. ***Parent loans:*** $1,673,935 (61% need-based, 39% non-need-based). ***Programs:*** Perkins.

WORK-STUDY ***Federal work-study:*** Total amount: $279,063; 213 jobs averaging $1310. ***State or other work-study/employment:*** Total amount: $99,263 (91% need-based, 9% non-need-based). 61 part-time jobs averaging $1627.

ATHLETIC AWARDS Total amount: $1,267,423 (57% need-based, 43% non-need-based).

APPLYING FOR FINANCIAL AID ***Required financial aid forms:*** FAFSA, state aid form. ***Financial aid deadline (priority):*** 3/1. ***Notification date:*** Continuous beginning 3/1. Students must reply by 5/1 or within 4 weeks of notification.

CONTACT Steve Phillips, Director of Student Financial Services, Nyack College, 1 South Boulevard, Nyack, NY 10960-3698, 845-675-4747 or toll-free 800-33-NYACK. *Fax:* 845-358-7016. *E-mail:* nyacksfs@nyack.edu.

OAK HILLS CHRISTIAN COLLEGE

Bemidji, MN

CONTACT Daniel Hovestol, Financial Aid Director, Oak Hills Christian College, 1600 Oak Hills Road, SW, Bemidji, MN 56601-8832, 218-751-8671 Ext. 1220 or toll-free 888-751-8670 Ext. 285. *Fax:* 218-444-1311. *E-mail:* ohfinaid@oakhills.edu.

OAKLAND CITY UNIVERSITY

Oakland City, IN

CONTACT Mrs. Caren K. Richeson, Director of Financial Aid, Oakland City University, 138 North Lucretia Street, Oakland City, IN 47660-1099, 812-749-1225 or toll-free 800-737-5125. *Fax:* 812-749-1438. *E-mail:* cricheson@oak.edu.

OAKLAND UNIVERSITY

Rochester, MI

Tuition & fees (MI res): $9285 **Average undergraduate aid package: $11,763**

ABOUT THE INSTITUTION State-supported, coed. 78 undergraduate majors. Federal methodology is used as a basis for awarding need-based institutional aid.

UNDERGRADUATE EXPENSES for 2010–11 ***Tuition, state resident:*** full-time $9285; part-time $309.50 per credit hour. ***Tuition, nonresident:*** full-time $21,675; part-time $722.50 per credit hour. Full-time tuition and fees vary according to program and student level. Part-time tuition and fees vary according to program and student level. ***College room and board:*** $7644. Room and board charges vary according to housing facility. ***Payment plans:*** Installment, deferred payment.

FRESHMAN FINANCIAL AID (Fall 2009) 1,830 applied for aid; of those 74% were deemed to have need. 98% of freshmen with need received aid; of those 15% had need fully met. ***Average percent of need met:*** 65% (excluding resources awarded to replace EFC). ***Average financial aid package:*** $12,018 (excluding resources awarded to replace EFC). 19% of all full-time freshmen had no need and received non-need-based gift aid.

UNDERGRADUATE FINANCIAL AID (Fall 2009) 8,356 applied for aid; of those 79% were deemed to have need. 97% of undergraduates with need received aid; of those 8% had need fully met. ***Average percent of need met:*** 65% (excluding resources awarded to replace EFC). ***Average financial aid package:*** $11,763 (excluding resources awarded to replace EFC). 10% of all full-time undergraduates had no need and received non-need-based gift aid.

GIFT AID (NEED-BASED) ***Total amount:*** $21,941,080 (76% federal, 2% state, 22% institutional). ***Receiving aid:*** Freshmen: 44% (993); all full-time undergraduates: 35% (4,166). ***Average award:*** Freshmen: $5618; Undergraduates: $4858. ***Scholarships, grants, and awards:*** Federal Pell, FSEOG, state, private, college/university gift aid from institutional funds.

GIFT AID (NON-NEED-BASED) ***Total amount:*** $16,108,381 (1% state, 55% institutional, 44% external sources). ***Receiving aid:*** Freshmen: 49% (1,113). Undergraduates: 21% (2,484). ***Average award:*** Freshmen: $2685. Undergraduates: $2570. ***Scholarships, grants, and awards by category:*** *Academic interests/achievement:* area/ethnic studies, biological sciences, business, education, engineering/technologies, English, foreign languages, general academic interests/achievements, health fields, humanities. *Creative arts/performance:* dance, music, performing arts. *Special characteristics:* adult students, ethnic background, out-of-state students. ***Tuition waivers:*** Full or partial for employees or children of employees.

LOANS ***Student loans:*** $56,831,279 (42% need-based, 58% non-need-based). 56% of past graduating class borrowed through all loan programs. *Average indebtedness per student:* $20,663. ***Average need-based loan:*** Freshmen: $6986. Undergraduates: $8604. ***Parent loans:*** $5,786,431 (100% need-based). ***Programs:*** Federal Direct (Subsidized and Unsubsidized Stafford, PLUS), Perkins, private loans.

WORK-STUDY ***Federal work-study:*** Total amount: $513,819; jobs available. ***State or other work-study/employment:*** Part-time jobs available.

ATHLETIC AWARDS Total amount: $2,850,740 (100% non-need-based).

APPLYING FOR FINANCIAL AID ***Required financial aid form:*** FAFSA. ***Financial aid deadline (priority):*** 3/15. ***Notification date:*** Continuous beginning 3/15.

CONTACT Ms. Cindy Hermsen, Director of Financial Aid, Oakland University, 120 North Foundation Hall, Rochester, MI 48309-4401, 248-370-2550 or toll-free 800-OAK-UNIV. *E-mail:* finaid@oakland.edu.

OAKWOOD UNIVERSITY

Huntsville, AL

CONTACT Financial Aid Director, Oakwood University, 7000 Adventist Boulevard, Huntsville, AL 35896, 256-726-7210 or toll-free 800-358-3978 (in-state).

OBERLIN COLLEGE

Oberlin, OH

Tuition & fees: $41,577 **Average undergraduate aid package: $32,845**

ABOUT THE INSTITUTION Independent, coed. 55 undergraduate majors. Both federal and institutional methodology are used as a basis for awarding need-based institutional aid.

UNDERGRADUATE EXPENSES for 2010–11 ***Comprehensive fee:*** $52,587 includes full-time tuition ($41,234), mandatory fees ($343), and room and board ($11,010). ***College room only:*** $5720. Room and board charges vary according to board plan and housing facility. ***Part-time tuition:*** $1710 per credit hour. ***Payment plan:*** Installment.

FRESHMAN FINANCIAL AID (Fall 2010, est.) 519 applied for aid; of those 83% were deemed to have need. 100% of freshmen with need received aid; of those 100% had need fully met. ***Average percent of need met:*** 100% (excluding resources awarded to replace EFC). ***Average financial aid package:*** $30,901 (excluding resources awarded to replace EFC). 32% of all full-time freshmen had no need and received non-need-based gift aid.

UNDERGRADUATE FINANCIAL AID (Fall 2010, est.) 1,856 applied for aid; of those 88% were deemed to have need. 100% of undergraduates with need received aid; of those 100% had need fully met. ***Average percent of need met:*** 100% (excluding resources awarded to replace EFC). ***Average financial aid package:*** $32,845 (excluding resources awarded to replace EFC). 28% of all full-time undergraduates had no need and received non-need-based gift aid.

GIFT AID (NEED-BASED) ***Total amount:*** $44,870,703 (5% federal, 1% state, 91% institutional, 3% external sources). ***Receiving aid:*** Freshmen: 55% (430); all full-time undergraduates: 42% (1,211). ***Average award:*** Freshmen: $27,516; Undergraduates: $28,044. ***Scholarships, grants, and awards:*** Federal Pell, FSEOG, state, private, college/university gift aid from institutional funds.

GIFT AID (NON-NEED-BASED) ***Total amount:*** $10,178,848 (90% institutional, 10% external sources). ***Average award:*** Freshmen: $12,187. Undergraduates: $12,244. ***Scholarships, grants, and awards by category:*** *Academic interests/achievement:* general academic interests/achievements, physical sciences. *Creative arts/performance:* music. ***Tuition waivers:*** Full or partial for employees or children of employees.

LOANS ***Student loans:*** $9,176,842 (92% need-based, 8% non-need-based). 49% of past graduating class borrowed through all loan programs. *Average indebtedness per student:* $17,085. ***Average need-based loan:*** Freshmen: $4270. Undergraduates: $5120. ***Parent loans:*** $3,236,594 (76% need-based, 24% non-need-based). ***Programs:*** Federal Direct (Subsidized and Unsubsidized Stafford), Perkins, college/university.

WORK-STUDY ***Federal work-study:*** Total amount: $2,733,016; jobs available. ***State or other work-study/employment:*** Part-time jobs available.

APPLYING FOR FINANCIAL AID ***Required financial aid forms:*** FAFSA, institution's own form, CSS Financial Aid PROFILE, state aid form, noncustodial (divorced/separated) parent's statement, business/farm supplement. ***Financial aid deadline:*** 2/1 (priority: 1/15). ***Notification date:*** Continuous. Students must reply by 5/1.

CONTACT Robert Reddy Jr., Director of Financial Aid, Oberlin College, Carnegie Building #123, 52 West Lorain Street, Oberlin, OH 44074, 800-693-3173 or toll-free 800-622-OBIE. *Fax:* 440-775-8249. *E-mail:* financial.aid@oberlin.edu.

OCCIDENTAL COLLEGE

Los Angeles, CA

Tuition & fees: $40,939 **Average undergraduate aid package: $37,652**

ABOUT THE INSTITUTION Independent, coed. 32 undergraduate majors. Institutional methodology is used as a basis for awarding need-based institutional aid.

UNDERGRADUATE EXPENSES for 2010–11 ***Comprehensive fee:*** $52,299 includes full-time tuition ($39,870), mandatory fees ($1069), and room and board ($11,360). ***College room only:*** $6460. Room and board charges vary according to board plan. ***Part-time tuition:*** $1661 per credit. Part-time tuition and fees vary according to course load. ***Payment plans:*** Tuition prepayment, installment.

FRESHMAN FINANCIAL AID (Fall 2010, est.) 410 applied for aid; of those 82% were deemed to have need. 100% of freshmen with need received aid; of those 100% had need fully met. ***Average percent of need met:*** 100% (excluding resources awarded to replace EFC). ***Average financial aid package:*** $38,423 (excluding resources awarded to replace EFC). 15% of all full-time freshmen had no need and received non-need-based gift aid.

UNDERGRADUATE FINANCIAL AID (Fall 2010, est.) 1,341 applied for aid; of those 87% were deemed to have need. 99% of undergraduates with need received aid; of those 100% had need fully met. ***Average percent of need met:*** 100% (excluding resources awarded to replace EFC). ***Average financial aid package:*** $37,652 (excluding resources awarded to replace EFC). 19% of all full-time undergraduates had no need and received non-need-based gift aid.

GIFT AID (NEED-BASED) ***Total amount:*** $35,423,820 (9% federal, 8% state, 79% institutional, 4% external sources). ***Receiving aid:*** Freshmen: 59% (337); all full-time undergraduates: 55% (1,150). ***Average award:*** Freshmen: $62,491; Undergraduates: $30,766. ***Scholarships, grants, and awards:*** Federal Pell, FSEOG, state, private, college/university gift aid from institutional funds.

GIFT AID (NON-NEED-BASED) ***Total amount:*** $5,301,258 (83% institutional, 17% external sources). ***Receiving aid:*** Freshmen: 6% (36). Undergraduates: 5% (106). ***Average award:*** Freshmen: $10,490. Undergraduates: $9772. ***Scholarships, grants, and awards by category:*** *Academic interests/achievement:* 404 awards ($3,496,238 total): general academic interests/achievements. *Creative arts/performance:* 52 awards ($35,798 total): music. *Special achievements/activities:* 15 awards ($217,500 total): leadership. *Special characteristics:* 23 awards ($782,926 total): children of educators, children of faculty/staff. ***Tuition waivers:*** Full or partial for employees or children of employees.

LOANS ***Student loans:*** $8,664,212 (71% need-based, 29% non-need-based). 80% of past graduating class borrowed through all loan programs. *Average indebtedness per student:* $25,549. ***Average need-based loan:*** Freshmen: $4797. Undergraduates: $6021. ***Parent loans:*** $3,146,235 (21% need-based, 79% non-need-based). ***Programs:*** Federal Direct (Subsidized and Unsubsidized Stafford, PLUS), Perkins, college/university.

WORK-STUDY ***Federal work-study:*** Total amount: $1,829,660; 789 jobs averaging $2319. ***State or other work-study/employment:*** Total amount: $523,281 (50% need-based, 50% non-need-based). 168 part-time jobs averaging $3114.

APPLYING FOR FINANCIAL AID ***Required financial aid forms:*** FAFSA, CSS Financial Aid PROFILE, state aid form, noncustodial (divorced/separated) parent's statement. ***Financial aid deadline:*** 2/1. ***Notification date:*** 4/1. Students must reply by 5/1.

CONTACT Maureen McRae, Director of Financial Aid, Occidental College, 1600 Campus Road, Los Angeles, CA 90041, 323-259-2548 or toll-free 800-825-5262. *Fax:* 323-341-4961. *E-mail:* finaid@oxy.edu.

OGLALA LAKOTA COLLEGE

Kyle, SD

CONTACT Financial Aid Director, Oglala Lakota College, 490 Piya Wiconi Road, Kyle, SD 57752-0490, 605-455-6000.

OGLETHORPE UNIVERSITY

Atlanta, GA

Tuition & fees: $27,950 **Average undergraduate aid package: $23,960**

ABOUT THE INSTITUTION Independent, coed. 31 undergraduate majors. Both federal and institutional methodology are used as a basis for awarding need-based institutional aid.

UNDERGRADUATE EXPENSES for 2011–12 ***Comprehensive fee:*** $37,940 includes full-time tuition ($27,700), mandatory fees ($250), and room and board ($9990). Full-time tuition and fees vary according to degree level and program. Room and board charges vary according to housing facility and location. Part-time tuition and fees vary according to course load, degree level, and program. ***Payment plans:*** Tuition prepayment, installment.

FRESHMAN FINANCIAL AID (Fall 2010, est.) 207 applied for aid; of those 87% were deemed to have need. 100% of freshmen with need received aid; of those 14% had need fully met. ***Average percent of need met:*** 80% (excluding resources awarded to replace EFC). ***Average financial aid package:*** $26,950 (excluding resources awarded to replace EFC). 18% of all full-time freshmen had no need and received non-need-based gift aid.

UNDERGRADUATE FINANCIAL AID (Fall 2010, est.) 813 applied for aid; of those 90% were deemed to have need. 100% of undergraduates with need received aid; of those 15% had need fully met. ***Average percent of need met:*** 75% (excluding resources awarded to replace EFC). ***Average financial aid package:*** $23,960 (excluding resources awarded to replace EFC). 19% of all full-time undergraduates had no need and received non-need-based gift aid.

GIFT AID (NEED-BASED) ***Total amount:*** $15,194,711 (15% federal, 10% state, 73% institutional, 2% external sources). ***Receiving aid:*** Freshmen: 70% (181); all full-time undergraduates: 73% (724). ***Average award:*** Freshmen: $23,048; Undergraduates: $19,668. ***Scholarships, grants, and awards:*** Federal Pell, FSEOG, state, private, college/university gift aid from institutional funds.

GIFT AID (NON-NEED-BASED) ***Total amount:*** $3,424,900 (11% state, 86% institutional, 3% external sources). ***Receiving aid:*** Freshmen: 8% (20). Undergraduates: 8% (77). ***Average award:*** Freshmen: $12,918. Undergraduates: $13,384. ***Scholarships, grants, and awards by category:*** *Academic interests/achievement:* general academic interests/achievements. *Creative arts/performance:* journalism/publications, music, performing arts, theater/drama. *Special achievements/activities:* community service, religious involvement. *Special characteristics:* children of faculty/staff, siblings of current students. ***Tuition waivers:*** Full or partial for employees or children of employees.

LOANS ***Student loans:*** $5,940,011 (94% need-based, 6% non-need-based). ***Average need-based loan:*** Freshmen: $2550. Undergraduates: $3318. ***Parent loans:*** $1,110,632 (88% need-based, 12% non-need-based). ***Programs:*** Federal Direct (Subsidized and Unsubsidized Stafford, PLUS), Perkins.

WORK-STUDY ***Federal work-study:*** Total amount: $343,304; jobs available.

APPLYING FOR FINANCIAL AID ***Required financial aid forms:*** FAFSA, institution's own form. ***Notification date:*** Continuous beginning 3/1. Students must reply by 5/1 or within 3 weeks of notification.

CONTACT Ms. Meg McGinnis, Director of Financial Aid, Oglethorpe University, 4484 Peachtree Road NE, Atlanta, GA 30319, 404-364-8366 or toll-free 800-428-4484. *E-mail:* mmcginnis@oglethorpe.edu.

OHIO CHRISTIAN UNIVERSITY

Circleville, OH

CONTACT Michael Fracassa, Assistant Vice President of Finance, Ohio Christian University, 1476 Lancaster Pike, PO Box 458, Circleville, OH 43113-9487, 740-477-7758 or toll-free 800-701-0222. *Fax:* 740-477-5921. *E-mail:* mfracassa@ohiochristian.edu.

OHIO DOMINICAN UNIVERSITY

Columbus, OH

CONTACT Ms. Cynthia A. Hahn, Director of Financial Aid, Ohio Dominican University, 1216 Sunbury Road, Columbus, OH 43219, 614-251-4778 or toll-free 800-854-2670. *Fax:* 614-251-4456. *E-mail:* fin-aid@ohiodominican.edu.

OHIO NORTHERN UNIVERSITY

Ada, OH

Tuition & fees: $33,099 **Average undergraduate aid package: $26,304**

ABOUT THE INSTITUTION Independent religious, coed. 115 undergraduate majors. Federal methodology is used as a basis for awarding need-based institutional aid.

UNDERGRADUATE EXPENSES for 2010–11 ***Comprehensive fee:*** $42,171 includes full-time tuition ($32,859), mandatory fees ($240), and room and board ($9072). ***College room only:*** $4725. Full-time tuition and fees vary according to course load, degree level, program, and student level. Room and board charges vary according to board plan and housing facility. ***Part-time tuition:*** $913 per quarter hour. ***Part-time fees:*** $30 per term. Part-time tuition and fees vary according to course load, degree level, program, and student level. ***Payment plan:*** Installment.

FRESHMAN FINANCIAL AID (Fall 2010, est.) 598 applied for aid; of those 84% were deemed to have need. 100% of freshmen with need received aid; of those 18% had need fully met. ***Average percent of need met:*** 80% (excluding resources awarded to replace EFC). ***Average financial aid package:*** $27,281 (excluding resources awarded to replace EFC). 15% of all full-time freshmen had no need and received non-need-based gift aid.

UNDERGRADUATE FINANCIAL AID (Fall 2010, est.) 2,199 applied for aid; of those 83% were deemed to have need. 100% of undergraduates with need received aid; of those 14% had need fully met. ***Average percent of need met:*** 76% (excluding resources awarded to replace EFC). ***Average financial aid package:*** $26,304 (excluding resources awarded to replace EFC). 15% of all full-time undergraduates had no need and received non-need-based gift aid.

GIFT AID (NEED-BASED) ***Total amount:*** $36,222,388 (9% federal, 2% state, 87% institutional, 2% external sources). ***Receiving aid:*** Freshmen: 83% (502); all full-time undergraduates: 80% (1,817). ***Average award:*** Freshmen: $23,025; Undergraduates: $21,219. ***Scholarships, grants, and awards:*** Federal Pell, FSEOG, state, private, college/university gift aid from institutional funds.

GIFT AID (NON-NEED-BASED) ***Total amount:*** $6,337,180 (96% institutional, 4% external sources). ***Receiving aid:*** Freshmen: 12% (73). Undergraduates: 6% (129). ***Average award:*** Freshmen: $19,362. Undergraduates: $17,001. ***Scholarships, grants, and awards by category:*** *Academic interests/achievement:* 2,303 awards ($25,140,152 total): biological sciences, business, communication, computer science, education, engineering/technologies, English, foreign languages, general academic interests/achievements, health fields, humanities, international studies, mathematics, physical sciences, premedicine, religion/biblical studies, social sciences. *Creative arts/performance:* 174 awards ($1,121,757 total): applied art and design, art/fine arts, creative writing, dance, journalism/publications, music, performing arts, theater/drama. *Special achievements/activities:* 155 awards ($415,317 total): community service, general special achievements/activities, junior miss, leadership. *Special characteristics:* 274 awards ($1,538,830 total): children and siblings of alumni, children of faculty/staff, ethnic background, international students, out-of-state students, relatives of clergy, religious affiliation, siblings of current students, veterans. ***Tuition waivers:*** Full or partial for children of alumni, employees or children of employees.

LOANS ***Student loans:*** $17,549,401 (66% need-based, 34% non-need-based). 85% of past graduating class borrowed through all loan programs. *Average indebtedness per student:* $48,886. ***Average need-based loan:*** Freshmen: $3686. Undergraduates: $4605. ***Parent loans:*** $6,850,651 (91% need-based, 9% non-need-based). ***Programs:*** Federal Direct (Subsidized and Unsubsidized Stafford, PLUS), Perkins, state, college/university.

WORK-STUDY ***Federal work-study:*** Total amount: $2,013,014; 1,354 jobs averaging $1487. ***State or other work-study/employment:*** Total amount: $346,404 (40% need-based, 60% non-need-based). 169 part-time jobs averaging $2050.

APPLYING FOR FINANCIAL AID ***Required financial aid form:*** FAFSA. ***Financial aid deadline (priority):*** 4/15. ***Notification date:*** Continuous beginning 3/1. Students must reply within 2 weeks of notification.

CONTACT Melanie Weaver, Director of Financial Aid, Ohio Northern University, 525 South Main Street, Ada, OH 45810, 419-772-2272 or toll-free 888-408-4ONU. *Fax:* 419-772-2313. *E-mail:* m-weaver.2@onu.edu.

THE OHIO STATE UNIVERSITY

Columbus, OH

Tuition & fees: N/R **Average undergraduate aid package: $10,575**

ABOUT THE INSTITUTION State-supported, coed. 143 undergraduate majors. Federal methodology is used as a basis for awarding need-based institutional aid.

UNDERGRADUATE EXPENSES for 2011–12 ***Tuition, state resident:*** part-time $249.83 per quarter hour. ***Tuition, nonresident:*** part-time $643.83 per quarter hour. Full-time tuition and fees vary according to course load, location, program, and reciprocity agreements. Part-time tuition and fees vary according to course load, location, program, and reciprocity agreements. ***College room and board:*** $9180; ***Room only:*** $6585. Room and board charges vary according to board plan, housing facility, and location. ***Payment plan:*** Installment.

FRESHMAN FINANCIAL AID (Fall 2010, est.) 5,279 applied for aid; of those 71% were deemed to have need. 99% of freshmen with need received aid; of those 20% had need fully met. ***Average percent of need met:*** 60% (excluding resources awarded to replace EFC). ***Average financial aid package:*** $10,445 (excluding resources awarded to replace EFC). 24% of all full-time freshmen had no need and received non-need-based gift aid.

UNDERGRADUATE FINANCIAL AID (Fall 2010, est.) 26,410 applied for aid; of those 82% were deemed to have need. 98% of undergraduates with need received aid; of those 15% had need fully met. ***Average percent of need met:*** 57% (excluding resources awarded to replace EFC). ***Average financial aid package:*** $10,575 (excluding resources awarded to replace EFC). 18% of all full-time undergraduates had no need and received non-need-based gift aid.

GIFT AID (NEED-BASED) ***Total amount:*** $123,115,517 (38% federal, 6% state, 51% institutional, 5% external sources). ***Receiving aid:*** Freshmen: 46% (3,084); all full-time undergraduates: 40% (15,309). ***Average award:*** Freshmen: $8033; Undergraduates: $7789. ***Scholarships, grants, and awards:*** Federal Pell, FSEOG, state, private, college/university gift aid from institutional funds.

GIFT AID (NON-NEED-BASED) ***Total amount:*** $40,746,307 (4% state, 88% institutional, 8% external sources). ***Receiving aid:*** Freshmen: 3% (170). Undergraduates: 1% (469). ***Average award:*** Freshmen: $4585. Undergraduates: $4704. ***Scholarships, grants, and awards by category:*** *Academic interests/achievement:* agriculture, architecture, area/ethnic studies, biological sciences, business, communication, computer science, education, engineering/technologies, English, foreign languages, general academic interests/achievements, health fields, home economics, humanities, international studies, mathematics, military science, physical sciences, premedicine, social sciences. *Creative arts/performance:* creative writing, dance, journalism/publications, music, performing arts, theater/drama. *Special achievements/activities:* cheerleading/drum major, hobbies/interests, leadership, memberships. *Special characteristics:* adult students, children and siblings of alumni, children of faculty/staff, children of public servants, children of union members/company employees, children of workers in trades, ethnic background, handicapped students, members of minority groups, out-of-state students, previous college experience. ***Tuition waivers:*** Full or partial for employees or children of employees, senior citizens.

LOANS ***Student loans:*** $202,858,731 (74% need-based, 26% non-need-based). 59% of past graduating class borrowed through all loan programs. *Average indebtedness per student:* $22,830. ***Average need-based loan:*** Freshmen: $3387. Undergraduates: $4696. ***Parent loans:*** $54,304,513 (100% non-need-based). ***Programs:*** Federal Direct (Subsidized and Unsubsidized Stafford, PLUS), Perkins, Federal Nursing, college/university.

WORK-STUDY ***Federal work-study:*** Total amount: $4,433,009; 2,187 jobs averaging $2034. ***State or other work-study/employment:*** Total amount: $500,943 (45% need-based, 55% non-need-based). 206 part-time jobs averaging $2432.

ATHLETIC AWARDS Total amount: $14,107,889 (100% non-need-based).

APPLYING FOR FINANCIAL AID ***Required financial aid form:*** FAFSA. ***Financial aid deadline (priority):*** 2/15. ***Notification date:*** 3/25. Students must reply by 5/1 or within 4 weeks of notification.

CONTACT Ms. Diane Stemper, Director of Student Financial Aid, The Ohio State University, 281 West Lane Avenue, 4th Floor, Columbus, OH 43210, 614-292-3600. *Fax:* 614-292-9264. *E-mail:* scsc@osu.edu.

OHIO UNIVERSITY

Athens, OH

Tuition & fees (OH res): $9603 **Average undergraduate aid package: $8969**

ABOUT THE INSTITUTION State-supported, coed. 124 undergraduate majors. Federal methodology is used as a basis for awarding need-based institutional aid.

UNDERGRADUATE EXPENSES for 2010–11 ***Tuition, state resident:*** full-time $9603; part-time $304 per quarter hour. ***Tuition, nonresident:*** full-time $18,567; part-time $599 per quarter hour. Full-time tuition and fees vary according to degree level, location, and program. Part-time tuition and fees vary according to course load, degree level, location, and program. ***College room and board:*** $9621; ***Room only:*** $5325. Room and board charges vary according to board plan. ***Payment plan:*** Installment.

FRESHMAN FINANCIAL AID (Fall 2010, est.) 3,583 applied for aid; of those 72% were deemed to have need. 98% of freshmen with need received aid; of those 13% had need fully met. ***Average percent of need met:*** 55% (excluding resources awarded to replace EFC). ***Average financial aid package:*** $8407 (excluding resources awarded to replace EFC). 13% of all full-time freshmen had no need and received non-need-based gift aid.

UNDERGRADUATE FINANCIAL AID (Fall 2010, est.) 13,179 applied for aid; of those 76% were deemed to have need. 99% of undergraduates with need received aid; of those 13% had need fully met. ***Average percent of need met:*** 56% (excluding resources awarded to replace EFC). ***Average financial aid package:*** $8969 (excluding resources awarded to replace EFC). 11% of all full-time undergraduates had no need and received non-need-based gift aid.

GIFT AID (NEED-BASED) ***Total amount:*** $33,111,151 (72% federal, 7% state, 21% institutional). ***Receiving aid:*** Freshmen: 58% (2,300); all full-time undergraduates: 54% (9,207). ***Average award:*** Freshmen: $7034; Undergraduates: $7724. ***Scholarships, grants, and awards:*** Federal Pell, FSEOG, state, private, college/university gift aid from institutional funds.

GIFT AID (NON-NEED-BASED) ***Total amount:*** $24,755,471 (4% federal, 3% state, 81% institutional, 12% external sources). ***Receiving aid:*** Freshmen: 34% (1,354). Undergraduates: 22% (3,759). ***Average award:*** Freshmen: $3717. Undergraduates: $3642. ***Scholarships, grants, and awards by category:*** *Academic interests/achievement:* area/ethnic studies, biological sciences, business, communication, computer science, education, engineering/technologies, English, foreign languages, general academic interests/achievements, health fields, home economics, humanities, international studies, mathematics, military science, physical sciences, premedicine, social sciences. *Creative arts/performance:* applied art and design, art/fine arts, cinema/film/broadcasting, dance, debating, journalism/publications, music, performing arts, theater/drama. *Special characteristics:* children of faculty/staff, members of minority groups. ***Tuition waivers:*** Full or partial for employees or children of employees, senior citizens.

LOANS ***Student loans:*** $95,472,067 (43% need-based, 57% non-need-based). 68% of past graduating class borrowed through all loan programs. *Average indebtedness per student:* $25,330. ***Average need-based loan:*** Freshmen: $3530. Undergraduates: $4414. ***Parent loans:*** $25,575,433 (100% non-need-based). ***Programs:*** Federal Direct (Subsidized and Unsubsidized Stafford, PLUS), Perkins, state, college/university.

WORK-STUDY ***Federal work-study:*** Total amount: $1,473,686; jobs available. ***State or other work-study/employment:*** Total amount: $13,564,599 (100% non-need-based). Part-time jobs available.

ATHLETIC AWARDS Total amount: $5,859,322 (100% non-need-based).

APPLYING FOR FINANCIAL AID ***Required financial aid form:*** FAFSA. ***Financial aid deadline (priority):*** 3/15. ***Notification date:*** 3/15.

CONTACT Ms. Sondra Williams, Director of Financial Aid, Ohio University, 020 Chubb Hall, Athens, OH 45701-2979, 740-593-4141. *Fax:* 740-593-4140. *E-mail:* willias1@ohio.edu.

OHIO UNIVERSITY–CHILLICOTHE

Chillicothe, OH

Tuition & fees (OH res): $3060 **Average undergraduate aid package: $8544**

ABOUT THE INSTITUTION State-supported, coed. 22 undergraduate majors. Federal methodology is used as a basis for awarding need-based institutional aid.

UNDERGRADUATE EXPENSES for 2010–11 ***Tuition, state resident:*** full-time $3010. ***Tuition, nonresident:*** full-time $5892. ***Required fees:*** full-time $50. Full-time tuition and fees vary according to student level. Part-time tuition and fees vary according to student level.

FRESHMAN FINANCIAL AID (Fall 2010, est.) 393 applied for aid; of those 97% were deemed to have need. 99% of freshmen with need received aid; of those 6% had need fully met. ***Average percent of need met:*** 59% (excluding resources awarded to replace EFC). ***Average financial aid package:*** $8025 (excluding resources awarded to replace EFC). 1% of all full-time freshmen had no need and received non-need-based gift aid.

UNDERGRADUATE FINANCIAL AID (Fall 2010, est.) 1,649 applied for aid; of those 93% were deemed to have need. 99% of undergraduates with need received aid; of those 5% had need fully met. ***Average percent of need met:*** 55% (excluding resources awarded to replace EFC). ***Average financial aid package:*** $8544 (excluding resources awarded to replace EFC). 1% of all full-time undergraduates had no need and received non-need-based gift aid.

GIFT AID (NEED-BASED) ***Total amount:*** $8,241,822 (94% federal, 1% state, 5% institutional). ***Receiving aid:*** Freshmen: 95% (374); all full-time undergraduates: 85% (1,506). ***Average award:*** Freshmen: $7951; Undergraduates: $8438. ***Scholarships, grants, and awards:*** Federal Pell, FSEOG, state, college/university gift aid from institutional funds.

GIFT AID (NON-NEED-BASED) ***Total amount:*** $431,555 (14% federal, 6% state, 48% institutional, 32% external sources). ***Receiving aid:*** Freshmen: 12% (46). Undergraduates: 6% (108). ***Average award:*** Freshmen: $3644. Undergraduates: $3651. ***Scholarships, grants, and awards by category:*** *Academic interests/achievement:* area/ethnic studies, biological sciences, business, communication, computer science, education, engineering/technologies, English, foreign languages, general academic interests/achievements, health fields, home economics, humanities, international studies, mathematics, military science, physical sciences, premedicine, social sciences. *Creative arts/performance:* applied art and design, art/fine arts, cinema/film/broadcasting, dance, debating, journalism/publications, music, performing arts, theater/drama. *Special characteristics:* children of faculty/staff, members of minority groups.

LOANS ***Student loans:*** $13,872,208 (44% need-based, 56% non-need-based). 68% of past graduating class borrowed through all loan programs. *Average indebtedness per student:* $25,330. ***Average need-based loan:*** Freshmen: $3429. Undergraduates: $3827. ***Parent loans:*** $24,779 (100% non-need-based). ***Programs:*** Federal Direct (Subsidized and Unsubsidized Stafford, PLUS), Perkins, state, college/university.

WORK-STUDY ***Federal work-study:*** Total amount: $27,637; 15 jobs averaging $1842. ***State or other work-study/employment:*** Part-time jobs available.

APPLYING FOR FINANCIAL AID ***Required financial aid form:*** FAFSA. ***Financial aid deadline (priority):*** 3/15. ***Notification date:*** 3/15.

CONTACT Ms. Valerie K. Miller, Interim Director of Financial Aid, Ohio University–Chillicothe, 020 Chubb Hall, Athens, OH 45701-2979, 740-593-4141 or toll-free 877-462-6824 (in-state). *Fax:* 740-593-4140. *E-mail:* millerv@ohio.edu.

OHIO UNIVERSITY–EASTERN

St. Clairsville, OH

Tuition & fees (OH res): $4461 **Average undergraduate aid package: $7313**

ABOUT THE INSTITUTION State-supported, coed. ***Awards:*** associate, bachelor's, and master's degrees (also offers some graduate courses). 11 undergraduate majors. ***Total enrollment:*** 751. Undergraduates: 751. Federal methodology is used as a basis for awarding need-based institutional aid.

UNDERGRADUATE EXPENSES for 2010–11 ***Application fee:*** $20. ***Tuition, state resident:*** full-time $4461; part-time $136 per credit hour. ***Tuition, nonresident:*** full-time $5781; part-time $176 per credit hour. Full-time tuition and fees vary according to student level. Part-time tuition and fees vary according to student level. ***Payment plan:*** Installment.

FRESHMAN FINANCIAL AID (Fall 2010, est.) 121 applied for aid; of those 79% were deemed to have need. 99% of freshmen with need received aid; of those 19% had need fully met. ***Average percent of need met:*** 68% (excluding resources awarded to replace EFC). ***Average financial aid package:*** $6098 (excluding resources awarded to replace EFC). 6% of all full-time freshmen had no need and received non-need-based gift aid.

UNDERGRADUATE FINANCIAL AID (Fall 2010, est.) 475 applied for aid; of those 85% were deemed to have need. 99% of undergraduates with need received aid; of those 12% had need fully met. ***Average percent of need met:*** 62% (excluding resources awarded to replace EFC). ***Average financial aid package:*** $7313 (excluding resources awarded to replace EFC). 4% of all full-time undergraduates had no need and received non-need-based gift aid.

GIFT AID (NEED-BASED) ***Total amount:*** $1,675,565 (90% federal, 1% state, 9% institutional). ***Receiving aid:*** Freshmen: 75% (93); all full-time undergraduates: 78% (390). ***Average award:*** Freshmen: $5699; Undergraduates: $7209. ***Scholarships, grants, and awards:*** Federal Pell, FSEOG, state, college/university gift aid from institutional funds.

GIFT AID (NON-NEED-BASED) ***Total amount:*** $204,767 (22% federal, 3% state, 56% institutional, 19% external sources). ***Receiving aid:*** Freshmen: 27% (33). Undergraduates: 13% (64). ***Average award:*** Freshmen: $1824. Undergraduates: $2673. ***Scholarships, grants, and awards by category:*** *Academic interests/achievement:* area/ethnic studies, biological sciences, business, communication, computer science, education, engineering/technologies, English, foreign languages, general academic interests/achievements, health fields, home economics, humanities, international studies, mathematics, military science, physical sciences, premedicine, social sciences. *Creative arts/performance:* applied art and design, art/fine arts, cinema/film/broadcasting, dance, debating, journalism/publications, music, performing arts, theater/drama. *Special characteristics:* children of faculty/staff, members of minority groups. ***Tuition waivers:*** Full or partial for employees or children of employees, senior citizens.

LOANS ***Student loans:*** $3,087,543 (47% need-based, 53% non-need-based). 68% of past graduating class borrowed through all loan programs. *Average indebtedness per student:* $25,330. ***Average need-based loan:*** Freshmen: $3059. Undergraduates: $4107. ***Parent loans:*** $12,348 (100% non-need-based). ***Programs:*** Federal Direct (Subsidized and Unsubsidized Stafford, PLUS), Perkins, state, college/university.

WORK-STUDY ***Federal work-study:*** Total amount: $41,476; 19 jobs averaging $2183. ***State or other work-study/employment:*** Part-time jobs available.

APPLYING FOR FINANCIAL AID ***Required financial aid form:*** FAFSA. ***Financial aid deadline (priority):*** 3/15. ***Notification date:*** 3/15.

CONTACT Ms. Valerie K. Miller, Interim Director of Financial Aid, Ohio University–Eastern, 020 Chubb Hall, Athens, OH 45701-2979, 740-593-4141 or toll-free 800-648-3331 (in-state). *Fax:* 740-593-4140. *E-mail:* millerv@ohio.edu.

OHIO UNIVERSITY–LANCASTER

Lancaster, OH

Tuition & fees (OH res): $3060 **Average undergraduate aid package: $7886**

ABOUT THE INSTITUTION State-supported, coed. ***Awards:*** associate, bachelor's, and master's degrees. 14 undergraduate majors. ***Total enrollment:*** 1,728. Undergraduates: 1,728. Federal methodology is used as a basis for awarding need-based institutional aid.

UNDERGRADUATE EXPENSES for 2010–11 ***Application fee:*** $20. ***Tuition, state resident:*** full-time $3010. ***Tuition, nonresident:*** full-time $5892. ***Required fees:*** full-time $50. Full-time tuition and fees vary according to degree level and student level. Part-time tuition and fees vary according to degree level and student level. ***Payment plan:*** Installment.

FRESHMAN FINANCIAL AID (Fall 2010, est.) 399 applied for aid; of those 81% were deemed to have need. 99% of freshmen with need received aid; of those 12% had need fully met. ***Average percent of need met:*** 60% (excluding resources awarded to replace EFC). ***Average financial aid package:*** $7101 (excluding resources awarded to replace EFC). 5% of all full-time freshmen had no need and received non-need-based gift aid.

UNDERGRADUATE FINANCIAL AID (Fall 2010, est.) 1,362 applied for aid; of those 88% were deemed to have need. 99% of undergraduates with need received aid; of those 8% had need fully met. ***Average percent of need met:*** 57% (excluding resources awarded to replace EFC). ***Average financial aid package:*** $7886 (excluding resources awarded to replace EFC). 2% of all full-time undergraduates had no need and received non-need-based gift aid.

GIFT AID (NEED-BASED) ***Total amount:*** $5,866,456 (93% federal, 1% state, 6% institutional). ***Receiving aid:*** Freshmen: 78% (312); all full-time undergraduates: 86% (1,169). ***Average award:*** Freshmen: $6937; Undergraduates: $7740. ***Scholarships, grants, and awards:*** Federal Pell, FSEOG, state, college/university gift aid from institutional funds.

GIFT AID (NON-NEED-BASED) ***Total amount:*** $620,860 (20% federal, 7% state, 49% institutional, 24% external sources). ***Receiving aid:*** Freshmen: 14% (54). Undergraduates: 10% (143). ***Average award:*** Freshmen: $2797. Undergraduates: $2949. ***Scholarships, grants, and awards by category:*** *Academic interests/achievement:* area/ethnic studies, biological sciences, business, communication, computer science, education, engineering/technologies, English, foreign languages, general academic interests/achievements, health fields, home economics, humanities, international studies, mathematics, military science, physical sciences, premedicine, social sciences. *Creative arts/performance:* applied art and design, art/fine arts, cinema/film/broadcasting, dance, debating, journalism/publications, music, performing arts, theater/drama. *Special characteristics:* children of faculty/staff, members of minority groups. ***Tuition waivers:*** Full or partial for employees or children of employees, senior citizens. ***ROTC:*** Army cooperative, Air Force cooperative.

LOANS ***Student loans:*** $10,737,712 (43% need-based, 57% non-need-based). 68% of past graduating class borrowed through all loan programs. *Average indebtedness per student:* $25,330. ***Average need-based loan:*** Freshmen: $3311. Undergraduates: $3822. ***Parent loans:*** $38,529 (100% non-need-based). ***Programs:*** Federal Direct (Subsidized and Unsubsidized Stafford, PLUS), Perkins, state, college/university.

WORK-STUDY ***Federal work-study:*** Total amount: $27,462; 15 jobs averaging $1831. ***State or other work-study/employment:*** Part-time jobs available.

APPLYING FOR FINANCIAL AID ***Required financial aid form:*** FAFSA. ***Financial aid deadline (priority):*** 3/15. ***Notification date:*** 3/15.

CONTACT Ms. Valerie K. Miller, Interim Director of Financial Aid, Ohio University–Lancaster, 020 Chubb Hall, Athens, OH 45701-2979, 740-593-4141 or toll-free 888-446-4468 Ext. 215. *Fax:* 740-593-4140. *E-mail:* millerv@ohio.edu.

OHIO UNIVERSITY–SOUTHERN CAMPUS

Ironton, OH

Tuition & fees (OH res): $1487 **Average undergraduate aid package: $8416**

ABOUT THE INSTITUTION State-supported, coed. ***Awards:*** associate, bachelor's, and master's degrees. 17 undergraduate majors. ***Total enrollment:*** 1,836. Undergraduates: 1,699. Federal methodology is used as a basis for awarding need-based institutional aid.

UNDERGRADUATE EXPENSES for 2010–11 ***Application fee:*** $20. ***Tuition, state resident:*** full-time $1465; part-time $134 per credit hour. ***Tuition, nonresident:*** full-time $1905; part-time $174 per credit hour. ***Required fees:*** full-time $22; $2 per credit hour. Full-time tuition and fees vary according to course load, location, program, reciprocity agreements, and student level. Part-time tuition and fees vary according to course load, location, program, reciprocity agreements, and student level. ***Payment plan:*** Installment.

FRESHMAN FINANCIAL AID (Fall 2010, est.) 302 applied for aid; of those 96% were deemed to have need. 100% of freshmen with need received aid; of those 8% had need fully met. ***Average percent of need met:*** 59% (excluding resources awarded to replace EFC). ***Average financial aid package:*** $7603 (excluding resources awarded to replace EFC). 5% of all full-time freshmen had no need and received non-need-based gift aid.

UNDERGRADUATE FINANCIAL AID (Fall 2010, est.) 1,358 applied for aid; of those 94% were deemed to have need. 100% of undergraduates with need received aid; of those 5% had need fully met. ***Average percent of need met:*** 56% (excluding resources awarded to replace EFC). ***Average financial aid package:*** $8416 (excluding resources awarded to replace EFC). 2% of all full-time undergraduates had no need and received non-need-based gift aid.

GIFT AID (NEED-BASED) ***Total amount:*** $6,790,365 (96% federal, 4% institutional). ***Receiving aid:*** Freshmen: 94% (284); all full-time undergraduates: 92% (1,253). ***Average award:*** Freshmen: $7429; Undergraduates: $8213. ***Scholarships, grants, and awards:*** Federal Pell, FSEOG, state, college/university gift aid from institutional funds.

GIFT AID (NON-NEED-BASED) ***Total amount:*** $487,470 (28% federal, 3% state, 60% institutional, 9% external sources). ***Receiving aid:*** Freshmen: 14% (42). Undergraduates: 14% (191). ***Average award:*** Freshmen: $2456. Undergraduates: $2033. ***Scholarships, grants, and awards by category:*** *Academic interests/achievement:* area/ethnic studies, biological sciences, business, communication, computer science, education, engineering/technologies, English, foreign languages, general academic interests/achievements, health fields, home economics, humanities, international studies, mathematics, military science, physical sciences, premedicine, social sciences. *Creative arts/performance:* applied art and design, art/fine arts, cinema/film/broadcasting, dance, debating, journalism/publications, music, performing arts, theater/drama. *Special characteristics:* children of faculty/staff, members of minority groups. ***Tuition waivers:*** Full or partial for children of alumni, employees or children of employees, senior citizens.

LOANS ***Student loans:*** $11,699,662 (43% need-based, 57% non-need-based). 68% of past graduating class borrowed through all loan programs. *Average indebtedness per student:* $25,330. ***Average need-based loan:*** Freshmen: $3371. Undergraduates: $3860. ***Parent loans:*** $35,979 (100% non-need-based). ***Programs:*** Federal Direct (Subsidized and Unsubsidized Stafford, PLUS), Perkins, state, college/university.

WORK-STUDY ***Federal work-study:*** Total amount: $50,299; 29 jobs averaging $1734. ***State or other work-study/employment:*** Part-time jobs available.

APPLYING FOR FINANCIAL AID ***Required financial aid form:*** FAFSA. ***Financial aid deadline (priority):*** 3/15. ***Notification date:*** 3/15.

CONTACT Ms. Valerie K. Miller, Interim Director of Financial Aid, Ohio University–Southern Campus, 020 Chubb Hall, Athens, OH 45701-2979, 740-593-4141 or toll-free 800-626-0513. *Fax:* 740-593-4140. *E-mail:* millerv@ohio.edu.

OHIO UNIVERSITY–ZANESVILLE

Zanesville, OH

Tuition & fees (OH res): $4662 **Average undergraduate aid package: $8176**

ABOUT THE INSTITUTION State-supported, coed. 7 undergraduate majors. Federal methodology is used as a basis for awarding need-based institutional aid.

UNDERGRADUATE EXPENSES for 2011–12 ***Tuition, state resident:*** full-time $4662. ***Tuition, nonresident:*** full-time $8985. Full-time tuition and fees vary according to student level. Part-time tuition and fees vary according to student level. ***Payment plan:*** Installment.

FRESHMAN FINANCIAL AID (Fall 2010, est.) 308 applied for aid; of those 83% were deemed to have need. 100% of freshmen with need received aid; of those 22% had need fully met. ***Average percent of need met:*** 74% (excluding resources awarded to replace EFC). ***Average financial aid package:*** $7793 (excluding resources awarded to replace EFC). 17% of all full-time freshmen had no need and received non-need-based gift aid.

UNDERGRADUATE FINANCIAL AID (Fall 2010, est.) 1,118 applied for aid; of those 89% were deemed to have need. 99% of undergraduates with need received aid; of those 12% had need fully met. ***Average percent of need met:*** 63% (excluding resources awarded to replace EFC). ***Average financial aid package:*** $8176 (excluding resources awarded to replace EFC). 8% of all full-time undergraduates had no need and received non-need-based gift aid.

GIFT AID (NEED-BASED) ***Total amount:*** $4,592,706 (91% federal, 1% state, 8% institutional). ***Receiving aid:*** Freshmen: 78% (240); all full-time undergraduates: 84% (951). ***Average award:*** Freshmen: $6207; Undergraduates: $7531. ***Scholarships, grants, and awards:*** Federal Pell, FSEOG, state, college/university gift aid from institutional funds.

GIFT AID (NON-NEED-BASED) ***Total amount:*** $1,197,718 (5% federal, 2% state, 83% institutional, 10% external sources). ***Receiving aid:*** Freshmen: 69% (212). Undergraduates: 37% (422). ***Average award:*** Freshmen: $2362. Undergraduates: $2122. ***Scholarships, grants, and awards by category:*** *Academic interests/achievement:* area/ethnic studies, biological sciences, business, communication, computer science, education, engineering/technologies, English, foreign languages, general academic interests/achievements, health fields, home economics, humanities, international studies, mathematics, military science, physical sciences, premedicine, social sciences. *Creative arts/performance:* applied art and design, art/fine arts, cinema/film/broadcasting, dance, debating, journalism/publications, music, performing arts, theater/drama. *Special characteristics:* children of faculty/staff, members of minority groups. ***Tuition waivers:*** Full or partial for employees or children of employees, senior citizens.

LOANS ***Student loans:*** $8,064,119 (46% need-based, 54% non-need-based). 68% of past graduating class borrowed through all loan programs. *Average indebtedness per student:* $25,330. ***Average need-based loan:*** Freshmen: $3174. Undergraduates: $3931. ***Parent loans:*** $27,623 (100% non-need-based). ***Programs:*** Federal Direct (Subsidized and Unsubsidized Stafford, PLUS), Perkins, state, college/university.

WORK-STUDY ***Federal work-study:*** Total amount: $34,232; 19 jobs averaging $1802. ***State or other work-study/employment:*** Part-time jobs available.

APPLYING FOR FINANCIAL AID ***Required financial aid form:*** FAFSA. ***Financial aid deadline (priority):*** 3/15. ***Notification date:*** 3/15.

CONTACT Ms. Valerie K. Miller, Interim Director of Financial Aid, Ohio University–Zanesville, 020 Chubb Hall, Athens, OH 45701-2979, 740-593-4141. *Fax:* 740-593-4140. *E-mail:* millerv@ohio.edu.

OHIO VALLEY UNIVERSITY

Vienna, WV

Tuition & fees: $14,050 **Average undergraduate aid package: $13,188**

ABOUT THE INSTITUTION Independent religious, coed. 16 undergraduate majors. Federal methodology is used as a basis for awarding need-based institutional aid.

UNDERGRADUATE EXPENSES for 2011–12 ***One-time required fee:*** $60. ***Comprehensive fee:*** $20,496 includes full-time tuition ($12,538), mandatory fees ($1512), and room and board ($6446). ***College room only:*** $3269. Full-time tuition and fees vary according to course load and location. Room and board charges vary according to board plan and housing facility. ***Part-time tuition:*** $525 per credit. ***Part-time fees:*** $63 per credit hour. Part-time tuition and fees vary according to course load and location. ***Payment plan:*** Installment.

FRESHMAN FINANCIAL AID (Fall 2010, est.) 101 applied for aid; of those 92% were deemed to have need. 100% of freshmen with need received aid; of those 15% had need fully met. ***Average percent of need met:*** 69% (excluding resources awarded to replace EFC). ***Average financial aid package:*** $13,591 (excluding resources awarded to replace EFC). 7% of all full-time freshmen had no need and received non-need-based gift aid.

UNDERGRADUATE FINANCIAL AID (Fall 2010, est.) 373 applied for aid; of those 91% were deemed to have need. 100% of undergraduates with need received aid; of those 19% had need fully met. ***Average percent of need met:*** 69% (excluding resources awarded to replace EFC). ***Average financial aid package:*** $13,188 (excluding resources awarded to replace EFC). 11% of all full-time undergraduates had no need and received non-need-based gift aid.

GIFT AID (NEED-BASED) ***Total amount:*** $2,353,902 (40% federal, 8% state, 49% institutional, 3% external sources). ***Receiving aid:*** Freshmen: 84% (91); all full-time undergraduates: 78% (323). ***Average award:*** Freshmen: $10,432; Undergraduates: $9922. ***Scholarships, grants, and awards:*** Federal Pell, FSEOG, state, private, college/university gift aid from institutional funds.

GIFT AID (NON-NEED-BASED) ***Total amount:*** $474,271 (10% state, 87% institutional, 3% external sources). ***Receiving aid:*** Freshmen: 12% (13). Undergraduates: 12% (50). ***Average award:*** Freshmen: $4991. Undergraduates: $6171. ***Scholarships, grants, and awards by category:*** *Academic interests/achievement:* education, English, general academic interests/achievements, religion/biblical studies. *Creative arts/performance:* general creative arts/performance, journalism/publications, music, performing arts, theater/drama. *Special achievements/activities:* community service, general special achievements/activities, leadership, religious involvement. *Special characteristics:* adult students, children of faculty/staff, ethnic background, general special characteristics, international students, local/state students, relatives of clergy, religious affiliation. ***Tuition waivers:*** Full or partial for employees or children of employees.

LOANS ***Student loans:*** $2,292,022 (83% need-based, 17% non-need-based). 72% of past graduating class borrowed through all loan programs. *Average indebtedness per student:* $21,735. ***Average need-based loan:*** Freshmen: $3381. Undergraduates: $3947. ***Parent loans:*** $656,087 (58% need-based, 42% non-need-based). ***Programs:*** Federal Direct (Subsidized and Unsubsidized Stafford, PLUS), Perkins.

WORK-STUDY ***Federal work-study:*** Total amount: $112,848; 119 jobs averaging $984. ***State or other work-study/employment:*** Total amount: $276,741 (100% non-need-based). 8 part-time jobs averaging $1510.

ATHLETIC AWARDS Total amount: $1,323,119 (68% need-based, 32% non-need-based).

APPLYING FOR FINANCIAL AID ***Required financial aid form:*** FAFSA. ***Financial aid deadline (priority):*** 3/1. ***Notification date:*** Continuous beginning 6/30. Students must reply within 4 weeks of notification.

CONTACT Amanda Greene Doak, Financial Aid Counselor, Ohio Valley University, 1 Campus View Drive, Vienna, WV 26105-8000, 304-865-6077 or toll-free 877-446-8668 Ext. 6200 (out-of-state). *Fax:* 304-865-6001. *E-mail:* amanda.doak@ovu.edu.

OHIO WESLEYAN UNIVERSITY

Delaware, OH

Tuition & fees: $36,390 **Average undergraduate aid package: $28,650**

ABOUT THE INSTITUTION Independent United Methodist, coed. 88 undergraduate majors. Both federal and institutional methodology are used as a basis for awarding need-based institutional aid.

UNDERGRADUATE EXPENSES for 2010–11 ***Comprehensive fee:*** $46,090 includes full-time tuition ($35,910), mandatory fees ($480), and room and board ($9700). ***College room only:*** $4806. Room and board charges vary according to board plan. ***Part-time tuition:*** $3920 per course. ***Payment plan:*** Installment.

FRESHMAN FINANCIAL AID (Fall 2010, est.) 461 applied for aid; of those 85% were deemed to have need. 100% of freshmen with need received aid; of those 31% had need fully met. ***Average percent of need met:*** 91% (excluding resources awarded to replace EFC). ***Average financial aid package:*** $30,401 (excluding resources awarded to replace EFC). 27% of all full-time freshmen had no need and received non-need-based gift aid.

UNDERGRADUATE FINANCIAL AID (Fall 2010, est.) 1,310 applied for aid; of those 86% were deemed to have need. 100% of undergraduates with need received aid; of those 24% had need fully met. ***Average percent of need met:*** 83% (excluding resources awarded to replace EFC). ***Average financial aid package:*** $28,650 (excluding resources awarded to replace EFC). 36% of all full-time undergraduates had no need and received non-need-based gift aid.

GIFT AID (NEED-BASED) ***Total amount:*** $24,960,861 (10% federal, 1% state, 87% institutional, 2% external sources). ***Receiving aid:*** Freshmen: 71% (393); all full-time undergraduates: 61% (1,122). ***Average award:*** Freshmen: $24,107; Undergraduates: $28,217. ***Scholarships, grants, and awards:*** Federal Pell, FSEOG, state, private, college/university gift aid from institutional funds.

GIFT AID (NON-NEED-BASED) ***Total amount:*** $13,534,443 (99% institutional, 1% external sources). ***Receiving aid:*** Freshmen: 19% (107). Undergraduates: 17% (318). ***Average award:*** Freshmen: $17,747. Undergraduates: $18,128. ***Scholarships, grants, and awards by category:*** *Academic interests/achievement:* business, education, general academic interests/achievements. *Creative arts/performance:* applied art and design, art/fine arts, dance, music, performing arts, theater/drama. *Special achievements/activities:* general special achievements/activities, leadership. *Special characteristics:* children and siblings of alumni, international students, local/state students, members of minority groups, relatives of clergy, religious affiliation, twins. ***Tuition waivers:*** Full or partial for children of alumni, employees or children of employees.

LOANS ***Student loans:*** $7,657,762 (72% need-based, 28% non-need-based). 76% of past graduating class borrowed through all loan programs. *Average indebtedness per student:* $30,920. ***Average need-based loan:*** Freshmen: $4512. Undergraduates: $5048. ***Parent loans:*** $3,331,358 (100% non-need-based). ***Programs:*** Federal Direct (Subsidized and Unsubsidized Stafford, PLUS), Perkins, college/university.

WORK-STUDY ***Federal work-study:*** Total amount: $1,187,622; 764 jobs averaging $1717. ***State or other work-study/employment:*** Total amount: $752,715 (100% non-need-based). 464 part-time jobs averaging $1965.

APPLYING FOR FINANCIAL AID ***Required financial aid forms:*** FAFSA, CSS Financial Aid PROFILE. ***Financial aid deadline:*** 5/1 (priority: 1/15). ***Notification date:*** Continuous beginning 2/15. Students must reply by 5/1 or within 2 weeks of notification.

CONTACT Mr. Lee Harrell, Assistant Vice President for Admission and Financial Aid, Ohio Wesleyan University, 61 South Sandusky Street, Delaware, OH 43015, 740-368-3052 or toll-free 800-922-8953. *Fax:* 740-368-3066. *E-mail:* owfinaid@owu.edu.

OHR HAMEIR THEOLOGICAL SEMINARY

Cortlandt Manor, NY

CONTACT Financial Aid Office, Ohr Hameir Theological Seminary, Furnace Woods Road, Peekskill, NY 10566, 914-736-1500.

OHR SOMAYACH/JOSEPH TANENBAUM EDUCATIONAL CENTER

Monsey, NY

CONTACT Financial Aid Office, Ohr Somayach/Joseph Tanenbaum Educational Center, PO Box 334244, Route 306, Monsey, NY 10952-0334, 914-425-1370.

OKLAHOMA BAPTIST UNIVERSITY

Shawnee, OK

Tuition & fees: $18,670 **Average undergraduate aid package: $18,412**

ABOUT THE INSTITUTION Independent Southern Baptist, coed. 67 undergraduate majors. Federal methodology is used as a basis for awarding need-based institutional aid.

UNDERGRADUATE EXPENSES for 2010–11 ***One-time required fee:*** $50. ***Comprehensive fee:*** $24,300 includes full-time tuition ($17,220), mandatory fees ($1450), and room and board ($5630). Full-time tuition and fees vary according to course load. Room and board charges vary according to housing facility. ***Part-time tuition:*** $560 per credit hour. Part-time tuition and fees vary according to course load. ***Payment plan:*** Installment.

FRESHMAN FINANCIAL AID (Fall 2010, est.) 350 applied for aid; of those 87% were deemed to have need. 100% of freshmen with need received aid; of those 30% had need fully met. ***Average percent of need met:*** 81% (excluding resources awarded to replace EFC). ***Average financial aid package:*** $21,291 (excluding resources awarded to replace EFC). 16% of all full-time freshmen had no need and received non-need-based gift aid.

UNDERGRADUATE FINANCIAL AID (Fall 2010, est.) 1,148 applied for aid; of those 91% were deemed to have need. 100% of undergraduates with need received aid; of those 25% had need fully met. ***Average percent of need met:*** 80% (excluding resources awarded to replace EFC). ***Average financial aid package:*** $18,412 (excluding resources awarded to replace EFC). 23% of all full-time undergraduates had no need and received non-need-based gift aid.

GIFT AID (NEED-BASED) ***Total amount:*** $11,043,957 (24% federal, 9% state, 65% institutional, 2% external sources). ***Receiving aid:*** Freshmen: 63% (255); all full-time undergraduates: 57% (845). ***Average award:*** Freshmen: $6746; Undergraduates: $6489. ***Scholarships, grants, and awards:*** Federal Pell, FSEOG, state, private, college/university gift aid from institutional funds, TEACH Grants.

GIFT AID (NON-NEED-BASED) ***Total amount:*** $4,982,599 (6% federal, 1% state, 89% institutional, 4% external sources). ***Receiving aid:*** Freshmen: 59% (239). Undergraduates: 45% (660). ***Average award:*** Freshmen: $9720. Undergraduates: $7417. ***Scholarships, grants, and awards by category:*** *Academic interests/achievement:* business, general academic interests/achievements, religion/biblical studies. *Creative arts/performance:* applied art and design, art/fine arts, music, performing arts, theater/drama. *Special achievements/activities:* leadership, religious involvement. *Special characteristics:* children and siblings of alumni, children of faculty/staff, general special characteristics, local/state students, out-of-state students, relatives of clergy, religious affiliation, veterans. ***Tuition waivers:*** Full or partial for employees or children of employees, senior citizens.

LOANS ***Student loans:*** $6,521,396 (93% need-based, 7% non-need-based). 62% of past graduating class borrowed through all loan programs. *Average indebtedness per student:* $23,039. ***Average need-based loan:*** Freshmen: $3928. Undergraduates: $5070. ***Parent loans:*** $1,170,943 (62% need-based, 38% non-need-based). ***Programs:*** Federal Direct (Subsidized and Unsubsidized Stafford, PLUS), Perkins, college/university.

WORK-STUDY ***Federal work-study:*** Total amount: $163,244; 194 jobs averaging $1200.

ATHLETIC AWARDS Total amount: $2,825,606 (71% need-based, 29% non-need-based).

APPLYING FOR FINANCIAL AID ***Required financial aid form:*** FAFSA. ***Financial aid deadline:*** Continuous. ***Notification date:*** Continuous beginning 2/1.

CONTACT Jonna Raney, Student Financial Services, Oklahoma Baptist University, 500 West University, Shawnee, OK 74804, 405-878-2016 or toll-free 800-654-3285. *Fax:* 405-878-2167. *E-mail:* jonna.raney@okbu.edu.

OKLAHOMA CHRISTIAN UNIVERSITY

Oklahoma City, OK

Tuition & fees: $18,456 **Average undergraduate aid package: $15,613**

ABOUT THE INSTITUTION Independent religious, coed. 59 undergraduate majors. Federal methodology is used as a basis for awarding need-based institutional aid.

UNDERGRADUATE EXPENSES for 2011–12 ***Comprehensive fee:*** $24,356 includes full-time tuition ($16,600), mandatory fees ($1856), and room and board ($5900). ***College room only:*** $3000. Full-time tuition and fees vary according to course load. Room and board charges vary according to board plan and housing facility. Part-time tuition and fees vary according to course load. ***Payment plan:*** Installment.

FRESHMAN FINANCIAL AID (Fall 2009) 460 applied for aid; of those 75% were deemed to have need. 100% of freshmen with need received aid; of those 20% had need fully met. ***Average percent of need met:*** 48% (excluding resources awarded to replace EFC). ***Average financial aid package:*** $15,647 (excluding resources awarded to replace EFC). 18% of all full-time freshmen had no need and received non-need-based gift aid.

UNDERGRADUATE FINANCIAL AID (Fall 2009) 1,906 applied for aid; of those 67% were deemed to have need. 100% of undergraduates with need received aid; of those 21% had need fully met. ***Average percent of need met:*** 55% (excluding resources awarded to replace EFC). ***Average financial aid package:*** $15,613 (excluding resources awarded to replace EFC). 22% of all full-time undergraduates had no need and received non-need-based gift aid.

GIFT AID (NEED-BASED) ***Total amount:*** $10,941,800 (23% federal, 1% state, 71% institutional, 5% external sources). ***Receiving aid:*** Freshmen: 42% (192); all full-time undergraduates: 36% (697). ***Average award:*** Freshmen: $2526; Undergraduates: $2506. ***Scholarships, grants, and awards:*** Federal Pell, FSEOG, state, private, college/university gift aid from institutional funds.

GIFT AID (NON-NEED-BASED) ***Total amount:*** $6,456,982 (1% federal, 9% state, 83% institutional, 7% external sources). ***Receiving aid:*** Freshmen: 57% (260). Undergraduates: 50% (977). ***Average award:*** Freshmen: $3726. Undergraduates: $3941. ***Scholarships, grants, and awards by category:*** *Academic interests/achievement:* engineering/technologies, general academic interests/achievements, religion/biblical studies. *Creative arts/performance:* applied art and design, journalism/publications, music, theater/drama. *Special achievements/activities:* cheerleading/drum major, leadership. *Special characteristics:* children of faculty/staff, international students. ***Tuition waivers:*** Full or partial for employees or children of employees.

LOANS ***Student loans:*** $8,508,922 (21% need-based, 79% non-need-based). 69% of past graduating class borrowed through all loan programs. *Average indebtedness per student:* $22,333. ***Average need-based loan:*** Freshmen: $2806. Undergraduates: $3877. ***Parent loans:*** $3,170,231 (31% need-based, 69% non-need-based). ***Programs:*** Federal Direct (Subsidized and Unsubsidized Stafford, PLUS), Perkins, alternative loans.

WORK-STUDY ***Federal work-study:*** Total amount: $270,295; 589 jobs averaging $1557.

ATHLETIC AWARDS Total amount: $2,219,155 (66% need-based, 34% non-need-based).

APPLYING FOR FINANCIAL AID ***Required financial aid form:*** FAFSA. ***Financial aid deadline:*** 8/31 (priority: 3/15). ***Notification date:*** Continuous beginning 2/15. Students must reply within 4 weeks of notification.

CONTACT Clint LaRue, Director of Financial Services, Oklahoma Christian University, Box 11000, Oklahoma City, OK 73136-1100, 405-425-5190 or toll-free 800-877-5010 (in-state). *Fax:* 405-425-5197. *E-mail:* clint.larue@oc.edu.

OKLAHOMA CITY UNIVERSITY

Oklahoma City, OK

Tuition & fees: $25,760 **Average undergraduate aid package: $17,823**

ABOUT THE INSTITUTION Independent United Methodist, coed. 75 undergraduate majors. Federal methodology is used as a basis for awarding need-based institutional aid.

UNDERGRADUATE EXPENSES for 2011–12 ***Comprehensive fee:*** $33,260 includes full-time tuition ($23,360), mandatory fees ($2400), and room and board ($7500). Full-time tuition and fees vary according to program. Room and board charges vary according to board plan and housing facility. ***Part-time tuition:*** $798 per credit hour. Part-time tuition and fees vary according to program. ***Payment plans:*** Installment, deferred payment.

FRESHMAN FINANCIAL AID (Fall 2010, est.) 370 applied for aid; of those 97% were deemed to have need. 84% of freshmen with need received aid; of those 66% had need fully met. ***Average percent of need met:*** 56% (excluding resources awarded to replace EFC). ***Average financial aid package:*** $17,463 (excluding resources awarded to replace EFC). 23% of all full-time freshmen had no need and received non-need-based gift aid.

UNDERGRADUATE FINANCIAL AID (Fall 2010, est.) 1,425 applied for aid; of those 92% were deemed to have need. 75% of undergraduates with need received aid; of those 74% had need fully met. ***Average percent of need met:*** 56% (excluding resources awarded to replace EFC). ***Average financial aid***

package: $17,823 (excluding resources awarded to replace EFC). 19% of all full-time undergraduates had no need and received non-need-based gift aid.

GIFT AID (NEED-BASED) ***Total amount:*** $18,199,536 (13% federal, 8% state, 75% institutional, 4% external sources). ***Receiving aid:*** Freshmen: 69% (292); all full-time undergraduates: 50% (931). ***Average award:*** Freshmen: $15,449; Undergraduates: $14,465. ***Scholarships, grants, and awards:*** Federal Pell, FSEOG, state, private, college/university gift aid from institutional funds, United Negro College Fund, Federal Nursing, Native American Grants.

GIFT AID (NON-NEED-BASED) ***Total amount:*** $7,120,785 (2% state, 92% institutional, 6% external sources). ***Receiving aid:*** Freshmen: 23% (98). Undergraduates: 19% (349). ***Average award:*** Freshmen: $15,820. Undergraduates: $14,174. ***Scholarships, grants, and awards by category:*** *Academic interests/achievement:* 576 awards ($3,819,894 total): business, communication, education, general academic interests/achievements, health fields, religion/biblical studies. *Creative arts/performance:* 318 awards ($2,283,625 total): applied art and design, art/fine arts, dance, music, performing arts, theater/drama. *Special achievements/activities:* 147 awards ($434,689 total): cheerleading/drum major, general special achievements/activities, junior miss, leadership, religious involvement. *Special characteristics:* 33 awards ($484,558 total): children of faculty/staff, relatives of clergy, religious affiliation. ***Tuition waivers:*** Full or partial for employees or children of employees.

LOANS ***Student loans:*** $9,782,219 (35% need-based, 65% non-need-based). 53% of past graduating class borrowed through all loan programs. *Average indebtedness per student:* $37,023. ***Average need-based loan:*** Freshmen: $3492. Undergraduates: $5128. ***Parent loans:*** $4,949,817 (100% non-need-based). ***Programs:*** Federal Direct (Subsidized and Unsubsidized Stafford, PLUS), Perkins, Federal Nursing.

WORK-STUDY ***Federal work-study:*** Total amount: $453,442; 363 jobs averaging $1362. ***State or other work-study/employment:*** Total amount: $456,185 (100% non-need-based). 270 part-time jobs averaging $1692.

ATHLETIC AWARDS Total amount: $4,624,701 (100% non-need-based).

APPLYING FOR FINANCIAL AID ***Required financial aid forms:*** FAFSA, institution's own form. ***Financial aid deadline (priority):*** 3/1. ***Notification date:*** Continuous beginning 3/25. Students must reply within 4 weeks of notification.

CONTACT Denise Flis, Senior Director Student Financial Services, Oklahoma City University, 2501 North Blackwelder, Oklahoma City, OK 73106-1493, 405-208-5848 or toll-free 800-633-7242. *Fax:* 405-208-5466. *E-mail:* dflis@okcu.edu.

OKLAHOMA PANHANDLE STATE UNIVERSITY

Goodwell, OK

Tuition & fees (OK res): $5344 **Average undergraduate aid package: N/A**

ABOUT THE INSTITUTION State-supported, coed. 28 undergraduate majors. Federal methodology is used as a basis for awarding need-based institutional aid.

UNDERGRADUATE EXPENSES for 2010–11 ***Tuition, state resident:*** full-time $2850; part-time $95 per credit hour. ***Tuition, nonresident:*** full-time $8409; part-time $280.30 per credit hour. ***Required fees:*** full-time $2494. Full-time tuition and fees vary according to course level, program, and student level. Part-time tuition and fees vary according to course level, program, and student level. ***College room and board:*** $3652; ***Room only:*** $900. Room and board charges vary according to board plan and housing facility. ***Payment plans:*** Guaranteed tuition, installment.

GIFT AID (NEED-BASED) ***Scholarships, grants, and awards:*** Federal Pell, FSEOG, state, private, college/university gift aid from institutional funds.

GIFT AID (NON-NEED-BASED) ***Scholarships, grants, and awards by category:*** *Academic interests/achievement:* agriculture, biological sciences, business, computer science, education, English, general academic interests/achievements, health fields, mathematics, physical sciences. *Creative arts/performance:* art/fine arts, debating, music, performing arts, theater/drama. *Special achievements/activities:* cheerleading/drum major, general special achievements/activities, rodeo. *Special characteristics:* children of faculty/staff, general special characteristics, local/state students, out-of-state students, veterans, veterans' children. ***Tuition waivers:*** Full or partial for employees or children of employees, senior citizens.

LOANS ***Programs:*** Perkins.

WORK-STUDY Federal work-study jobs available. ***State or other work-study/employment:*** Part-time jobs available.

APPLYING FOR FINANCIAL AID ***Required financial aid form:*** FAFSA. ***Financial aid deadline (priority):*** 3/15. ***Notification date:*** 5/1. Students must reply by 8/1.

CONTACT Ms. Mary E. Riley, Director of Financial Aid, Oklahoma Panhandle State University, PO Box 430, Goodwell, OK 73939-0430, 580-349-2611 Ext. 324 or toll-free 800-664-6778. *E-mail:* mriley@opsu.edu.

OKLAHOMA STATE UNIVERSITY

Stillwater, OK

Tuition & fees (OK res): $6779 **Average undergraduate aid package: $11,277**

ABOUT THE INSTITUTION State-supported, coed. 85 undergraduate majors. Federal methodology is used as a basis for awarding need-based institutional aid.

UNDERGRADUATE EXPENSES for 2010–11 ***One-time required fee:*** $95. ***Tuition, state resident:*** full-time $4103; part-time $136.75 per credit hour. ***Tuition, nonresident:*** full-time $14,925; part-time $497.50 per credit hour. ***Required fees:*** full-time $2676; $89.20 per credit hour. Full-time tuition and fees vary according to program and student level. Part-time tuition and fees vary according to program and student level. ***College room and board:*** $6680; ***Room only:*** $3600. Room and board charges vary according to board plan and housing facility. ***Payment plan:*** Installment.

FRESHMAN FINANCIAL AID (Fall 2009) 2,171 applied for aid; of those 70% were deemed to have need. 98% of freshmen with need received aid; of those 18% had need fully met. ***Average percent of need met:*** 76% (excluding resources awarded to replace EFC). ***Average financial aid package:*** $11,788 (excluding resources awarded to replace EFC). 28% of all full-time freshmen had no need and received non-need-based gift aid.

UNDERGRADUATE FINANCIAL AID (Fall 2009) 9,891 applied for aid; of those 78% were deemed to have need. 97% of undergraduates with need received aid; of those 16% had need fully met. ***Average percent of need met:*** 72% (excluding resources awarded to replace EFC). ***Average financial aid package:*** $11,277 (excluding resources awarded to replace EFC). 23% of all full-time undergraduates had no need and received non-need-based gift aid.

GIFT AID (NEED-BASED) ***Total amount:*** $43,317,954 (52% federal, 27% state, 11% institutional, 10% external sources). ***Receiving aid:*** Freshmen: 39% (1,173); all full-time undergraduates: 36% (5,484). ***Average award:*** Freshmen: $6453; Undergraduates: $6271. ***Scholarships, grants, and awards:*** Federal Pell, FSEOG, state, private, college/university gift aid from institutional funds, Academic Competitiveness Grants, National SMART Grants, TEACH Grants.

GIFT AID (NON-NEED-BASED) ***Total amount:*** $10,746,637 (6% federal, 10% state, 42% institutional, 42% external sources). ***Receiving aid:*** Freshmen: 34% (1,020). Undergraduates: 24% (3,638). ***Average award:*** Freshmen: $5025. Undergraduates: $4352. ***Scholarships, grants, and awards by category:*** *Academic interests/achievement:* agriculture, architecture, area/ethnic studies, biological sciences, business, communication, computer science, education, engineering/technologies, English, foreign languages, general academic interests/achievements, home economics, humanities, international studies, mathematics, military science, physical sciences, premedicine, social sciences. *Creative arts/performance:* art/fine arts, creative writing, general creative arts/performance, journalism/publications, music, theater/drama. *Special achievements/activities:* cheerleading/drum major, community service, general special achievements/activities, leadership, memberships, rodeo. *Special characteristics:* adult students, children and siblings of alumni, ethnic background, first-generation college students, general special characteristics, handicapped students, international students, local/state students, out-of-state students, previous college experience. ***Tuition waivers:*** Full or partial for children of alumni.

LOANS ***Student loans:*** $51,904,595 (52% need-based, 48% non-need-based). 54% of past graduating class borrowed through all loan programs. *Average indebtedness per student:* $19,934. ***Average need-based loan:*** Freshmen: $3252. Undergraduates: $4258. ***Parent loans:*** $23,809,786 (17% need-based, 83% non-need-based). ***Programs:*** Federal Direct (Subsidized and Unsubsidized Stafford, PLUS), Perkins, college/university.

WORK-STUDY ***Federal work-study:*** Total amount: $1,042,596; 486 jobs averaging $2117. ***State or other work-study/employment:*** Total amount: $8,153,029 (100% non-need-based). 3,374 part-time jobs averaging $2416.

ATHLETIC AWARDS Total amount: $3,624,954 (49% need-based, 51% non-need-based).

APPLYING FOR FINANCIAL AID ***Required financial aid forms:*** FAFSA, institution's own form. ***Financial aid deadline (priority):*** 2/1. ***Notification date:*** Continuous beginning 3/1. Students must reply by 5/1 or within 2 weeks of notification.

CONTACT Office of Scholarships and Financial Aid, Oklahoma State University, 119 Student Union, Stillwater, OK 74078-5061, 405-744-6604 or toll-free 800-233-5019 Ext. 1 (in-state), 800-852-1255 (out-of-state). *Fax:* 405-744-6438. *E-mail:* finaid@okstate.edu.

OKLAHOMA WESLEYAN UNIVERSITY

Bartlesville, OK

Tuition & fees: $20,160 **Average undergraduate aid package: $9688**

ABOUT THE INSTITUTION Independent religious, coed. 36 undergraduate majors. Both federal and institutional methodology are used as a basis for awarding need-based institutional aid.

UNDERGRADUATE EXPENSES for 2011–12 ***Comprehensive fee:*** $27,034 includes full-time tuition ($19,060), mandatory fees ($1100), and room and board ($6874). ***College room only:*** $3634. Full-time tuition and fees vary according to course load. Room and board charges vary according to board plan and housing facility. ***Part-time tuition:*** $755 per credit hour. ***Part-time fees:*** $55 per credit hour; $60 per term. ***Payment plans:*** Installment, deferred payment.

FRESHMAN FINANCIAL AID (Fall 2010, est.) 52 applied for aid; of those 83% were deemed to have need. 72% of freshmen with need received aid. ***Average percent of need met:*** 38% (excluding resources awarded to replace EFC). ***Average financial aid package:*** $8723 (excluding resources awarded to replace EFC). 3% of all full-time freshmen had no need and received non-need-based gift aid.

UNDERGRADUATE FINANCIAL AID (Fall 2010, est.) 638 applied for aid; of those 78% were deemed to have need. 87% of undergraduates with need received aid; of those 13% had need fully met. ***Average percent of need met:*** 51% (excluding resources awarded to replace EFC). ***Average financial aid package:*** $9688 (excluding resources awarded to replace EFC). 3% of all full-time undergraduates had no need and received non-need-based gift aid.

GIFT AID (NEED-BASED) ***Total amount:*** $2,785,993 (42% federal, 8% state, 44% institutional, 6% external sources). ***Receiving aid:*** Freshmen: 29% (28); all full-time undergraduates: 50% (347). ***Average award:*** Freshmen: $6656; Undergraduates: $7842. ***Scholarships, grants, and awards:*** Federal Pell, FSEOG, state, private, college/university gift aid from institutional funds.

GIFT AID (NON-NEED-BASED) ***Total amount:*** $297,609 (3% federal, 1% state, 77% institutional, 19% external sources). ***Receiving aid:*** Undergraduates: 4% (28). ***Average award:*** Freshmen: $8828. Undergraduates: $6318. ***Scholarships, grants, and awards by category:*** *Academic interests/achievement:* 335 awards ($1,288,388 total): biological sciences, business, computer science, education, general academic interests/achievements, health fields, religion/biblical studies. *Creative arts/performance:* 27 awards ($43,750 total): music. *Special achievements/activities:* 292 awards ($356,020 total): leadership, religious involvement. *Special characteristics:* 343 awards ($563,704 total): children and siblings of alumni, children of educators, children of faculty/staff, international students, relatives of clergy, religious affiliation, siblings of current students. ***Tuition waivers:*** Full or partial for employees or children of employees, senior citizens.

LOANS ***Student loans:*** $5,939,098 (76% need-based, 24% non-need-based). 97% of past graduating class borrowed through all loan programs. *Average indebtedness per student:* $21,276. ***Average need-based loan:*** Freshmen: $2699. Undergraduates: $3408. ***Parent loans:*** $454,011 (43% need-based, 57% non-need-based). ***Programs:*** Federal Direct (Subsidized and Unsubsidized Stafford, PLUS), Perkins, college/university.

WORK-STUDY ***Federal work-study:*** Total amount: $94,311; 125 jobs averaging $1682. ***State or other work-study/employment:*** Total amount: $37,805 (77% need-based, 23% non-need-based). 37 part-time jobs averaging $1661.

ATHLETIC AWARDS Total amount: $522,948 (77% need-based, 23% non-need-based).

APPLYING FOR FINANCIAL AID ***Required financial aid forms:*** FAFSA, institution's own form. ***Financial aid deadline (priority):*** 3/1. ***Notification date:*** Continuous beginning 1/15. Students must reply within 1 week of notification.

CONTACT Kandi Lyn Molder, Director of Student Financial Services, Oklahoma Wesleyan University, 2201 Silver Lake Road, Bartlesville, OK 74006, 918-335-6282 or toll-free 866-222-8226 (in-state). *Fax:* 918-335-6811. *E-mail:* financialaid@okwu.edu.

OLD DOMINION UNIVERSITY

Norfolk, VA

Tuition & fees (VA res): $8144 **Average undergraduate aid package: $8049**

ABOUT THE INSTITUTION State-supported, coed. 51 undergraduate majors. Federal methodology is used as a basis for awarding need-based institutional aid.

UNDERGRADUATE EXPENSES for 2011–12 ***Tuition, state resident:*** full-time $7890; part-time $263 per credit hour. ***Tuition, nonresident:*** full-time $22,230; part-time $741 per credit hour. ***Required fees:*** full-time $254; $59 per term. ***College room and board:*** $8796; ***Room only:*** $5058.

FRESHMAN FINANCIAL AID (Fall 2010, est.) 2,112 applied for aid; of those 86% were deemed to have need. 90% of freshmen with need received aid; of those 53% had need fully met. ***Average percent of need met:*** 75% (excluding resources awarded to replace EFC). ***Average financial aid package:*** $8479 (excluding resources awarded to replace EFC). 3% of all full-time freshmen had no need and received non-need-based gift aid.

UNDERGRADUATE FINANCIAL AID (Fall 2010, est.) 10,826 applied for aid; of those 76% were deemed to have need. 94% of undergraduates with need received aid; of those 43% had need fully met. ***Average percent of need met:*** 72% (excluding resources awarded to replace EFC). ***Average financial aid package:*** $8049 (excluding resources awarded to replace EFC). 2% of all full-time undergraduates had no need and received non-need-based gift aid.

GIFT AID (NEED-BASED) ***Total amount:*** $41,197,776 (65% federal, 33% state, 2% institutional). ***Receiving aid:*** Freshmen: 34% (879); all full-time undergraduates: 28% (3,998). ***Average award:*** Freshmen: $5696; Undergraduates: $4846. ***Scholarships, grants, and awards:*** Federal Pell, FSEOG, state, private, college/university gift aid from institutional funds, United Negro College Fund, Federal Nursing.

GIFT AID (NON-NEED-BASED) ***Total amount:*** $10,606,430 (5% state, 80% institutional, 15% external sources). ***Receiving aid:*** Freshmen: 29% (762). Undergraduates: 14% (2,043). ***Average award:*** Freshmen: $3313. Undergraduates: $3364. ***Scholarships, grants, and awards by category:*** *Academic interests/achievement:* 1,421 awards ($4,021,523 total): biological sciences, business, engineering/technologies, English, general academic interests/achievements, health fields, humanities, military science, physical sciences. *Creative arts/performance:* 86 awards ($99,231 total): art/fine arts, dance, music, performing arts, theater/drama. *Special achievements/activities:* 25 awards ($33,785 total): cheerleading/drum major, community service, leadership, memberships. *Special characteristics:* 39 awards ($17,250 total): children of faculty/staff, handicapped students, international students, local/state students, members of minority groups, previous college experience, veterans' children.

LOANS ***Student loans:*** $81,808,811 (44% need-based, 56% non-need-based). 80% of past graduating class borrowed through all loan programs. *Average indebtedness per student:* $17,250. ***Average need-based loan:*** Freshmen: $3384. Undergraduates: $4272. ***Parent loans:*** $10,463,442 (100% non-need-based). ***Programs:*** Federal Direct (Subsidized and Unsubsidized Stafford, PLUS), Perkins, Federal Nursing, college/university.

WORK-STUDY ***Federal work-study:*** Total amount: $1,778,337; 174 jobs averaging $1854.

ATHLETIC AWARDS Total amount: $4,692,892 (100% non-need-based).

APPLYING FOR FINANCIAL AID ***Required financial aid form:*** FAFSA. ***Financial aid deadline:*** 3/15 (priority: 2/15). ***Notification date:*** Continuous beginning 2/1. Students must reply within 2 weeks of notification.

CONTACT Veronica Finch, Director of Financial Aid, Old Dominion University, 121 Rollins Hall, Norfolk, VA 23529, 757-683-3683 or toll-free 800-348-7926. *E-mail:* vfinch@odu.edu.

OLIVET COLLEGE

Olivet, MI

Tuition & fees: $20,500 **Average undergraduate aid package: $16,440**

ABOUT THE INSTITUTION Independent religious, coed. ***Awards:*** bachelor's and master's degrees. 35 undergraduate majors. ***Total enrollment:*** 1,049. Undergraduates: 1,004. Federal methodology is used as a basis for awarding need-based institutional aid.

UNDERGRADUATE EXPENSES for 2010–11 ***Application fee:*** $25. ***Comprehensive fee:*** $27,500 includes full-time tuition ($19,710), mandatory fees ($790), and room and board ($7000). ***College room only:*** $3500. Full-time tuition and fees vary according to reciprocity agreements. Room and board charges vary according to board plan and housing facility. ***Part-time tuition:*** $660 per semester hour. ***Part-time fees:*** $395 per term. Part-time tuition and fees vary according to course load and reciprocity agreements. ***Payment plans:*** Installment, deferred payment.

FRESHMAN FINANCIAL AID (Fall 2010, est.) 192 applied for aid; of those 96% were deemed to have need. 100% of freshmen with need received aid; of those 30% had need fully met. ***Average percent of need met:*** 78% (excluding resources awarded to replace EFC). ***Average financial aid package:*** $15,477 (excluding resources awarded to replace EFC). 18% of all full-time freshmen had no need and received non-need-based gift aid.

UNDERGRADUATE FINANCIAL AID (Fall 2010, est.) 930 applied for aid; of those 92% were deemed to have need. 100% of undergraduates with need received aid; of those 16% had need fully met. ***Average percent of need met:*** 82% (excluding resources awarded to replace EFC). ***Average financial aid package:*** $16,440 (excluding resources awarded to replace EFC). 12% of all full-time undergraduates had no need and received non-need-based gift aid.

GIFT AID (NEED-BASED) ***Total amount:*** $13,206,414 (24% federal, 9% state, 65% institutional, 2% external sources). ***Receiving aid:*** Freshmen: 77% (184); all full-time undergraduates: 81% (846). ***Average award:*** Freshmen: $13,342; Undergraduates: $12,342. ***Scholarships, grants, and awards:*** Federal Pell, FSEOG, state, private, college/university gift aid from institutional funds.

GIFT AID (NON-NEED-BASED) ***Total amount:*** $1,551,244 (95% institutional, 5% external sources). ***Receiving aid:*** Freshmen: 13% (32). Undergraduates: 8% (80). ***Average award:*** Freshmen: $9615. Undergraduates: $11,215. ***Scholarships, grants, and awards by category:*** *Academic interests/achievement:* 458 awards ($2,487,298 total): business, communication, education, English, foreign languages, general academic interests/achievements. *Creative arts/performance:* art/fine arts, journalism/publications, music. *Special achievements/activities:* 452 awards ($835,575 total): community service, leadership, memberships. *Special characteristics:* 54 awards ($540,933 total): children and siblings of alumni, children of faculty/staff, international students, religious affiliation, siblings of current students. ***Tuition waivers:*** Full or partial for employees or children of employees.

LOANS ***Student loans:*** $8,226,781 (72% need-based, 28% non-need-based). 92% of past graduating class borrowed through all loan programs. *Average indebtedness per student:* $25,500. ***Average need-based loan:*** Freshmen: $2680. Undergraduates: $4570. ***Parent loans:*** $1,277,503 (39% need-based, 61% non-need-based). ***Programs:*** Perkins, state, Key Alternative Loans, CitiAssist Loans, Smart Option Student Loans.

WORK-STUDY ***Federal work-study:*** Total amount: $168,500; 199 jobs averaging $846. ***State or other work-study/employment:*** Part-time jobs available.

APPLYING FOR FINANCIAL AID ***Required financial aid form:*** FAFSA. ***Financial aid deadline:*** Continuous. ***Notification date:*** Continuous beginning 3/1.

CONTACT Ms. Libby M. Jean, Director of Student Services, Olivet College, 320 South Main Street, Olivet, MI 49076-9701, 269-749-7655 Ext. 7655 or toll-free 800-456-7189. *Fax:* 269-749-3821. *E-mail:* ljean@olivetcollege.edu.

OLIVET NAZARENE UNIVERSITY

Bourbonnais, IL

Tuition & fees: N/R **Average undergraduate aid package: $17,812**

ABOUT THE INSTITUTION Independent religious, coed. ***Awards:*** associate, bachelor's, and master's degrees. 66 undergraduate majors. ***Total enrollment:*** 4,636. Undergraduates: 3,190. Federal methodology is used as a basis for awarding need-based institutional aid.

FRESHMAN FINANCIAL AID (Fall 2009) 722 applied for aid; of those 88% were deemed to have need. 100% of freshmen with need received aid; of those 36% had need fully met. ***Average percent of need met:*** 83% (excluding resources awarded to replace EFC). ***Average financial aid package:*** $19,075 (excluding resources awarded to replace EFC). 17% of all full-time freshmen had no need and received non-need-based gift aid.

UNDERGRADUATE FINANCIAL AID (Fall 2009) 2,242 applied for aid; of those 90% were deemed to have need. 100% of undergraduates with need received aid; of those 32% had need fully met. ***Average percent of need met:*** 82% (excluding resources awarded to replace EFC). ***Average financial aid package:*** $17,812 (excluding resources awarded to replace EFC). 24% of all full-time undergraduates had no need and received non-need-based gift aid.

GIFT AID (NEED-BASED) ***Total amount:*** $20,864,559 (18% federal, 12% state, 59% institutional, 11% external sources). ***Receiving aid:*** Freshmen: 83% (637); all full-time undergraduates: 76% (2,004). ***Average award:*** Freshmen: $14,561; Undergraduates: $13,112. ***Scholarships, grants, and awards:*** Federal Pell, FSEOG, state, private, college/university gift aid from institutional funds.

GIFT AID (NON-NEED-BASED) ***Total amount:*** $14,745,623 (8% federal, 2% state, 70% institutional, 20% external sources). ***Receiving aid:*** Freshmen: 17% (131). Undergraduates: 12% (308). ***Average award:*** Freshmen: $14,132. Undergraduates: $10,134. ***Scholarships, grants, and awards by category:*** *Academic interests/achievement:* 2,431 awards ($16,652,721 total): general academic interests/achievements, military science. *Creative arts/performance:* 203 awards ($502,449 total): art/fine arts, music, performing arts, theater/drama. *Special achievements/activities:* 43 awards ($149,650 total): cheerleading/drum major, religious involvement. *Special characteristics:* 1,068 awards ($7,699,477 total): children of faculty/staff, general special characteristics, relatives of clergy, religious affiliation. ***Tuition waivers:*** Full or partial for employees or children of employees. ***ROTC:*** Army.

LOANS ***Student loans:*** $16,969,355 (40% need-based, 60% non-need-based). 77% of past graduating class borrowed through all loan programs. *Average indebtedness per student:* $28,473. ***Average need-based loan:*** Freshmen: $3755. Undergraduates: $4419. ***Parent loans:*** $4,694,063 (72% need-based, 28% non-need-based). ***Programs:*** Federal Direct (Subsidized and Unsubsidized Stafford, PLUS), Perkins, private loans.

WORK-STUDY ***Federal work-study:*** Total amount: $319,434; 433 jobs averaging $805. ***State or other work-study/employment:*** Total amount: $943,240 (100% non-need-based). 908 part-time jobs averaging $1268.

ATHLETIC AWARDS Total amount: $2,451,479 (48% need-based, 52% non-need-based).

APPLYING FOR FINANCIAL AID ***Financial aid deadline (priority):*** 3/1. ***Notification date:*** Continuous beginning 2/1. Students must reply by 5/1.

CONTACT Mr. Greg Bruner, Director of Financial Aid, Olivet Nazarene University, One University Avenue, Bourbonnais, IL 60914, 815-939-5249 or toll-free 800-648-1463. *Fax:* 815-939-5074. *E-mail:* gbruner@olivet.edu.

O'MORE COLLEGE OF DESIGN

Franklin, TN

CONTACT Office of Financial Aid, O'More College of Design, 423 South Margin Street, Franklin, TN 37064-2816, 615-794-4254 Ext. 30.

ORAL ROBERTS UNIVERSITY

Tulsa, OK

ABOUT THE INSTITUTION Independent interdenominational, coed. 70 undergraduate majors.

GIFT AID (NEED-BASED) ***Scholarships, grants, and awards:*** Federal Pell, FSEOG, state, private, college/university gift aid from institutional funds.

GIFT AID (NON-NEED-BASED) ***Scholarships, grants, and awards by category:*** *Academic interests/achievement:* biological sciences, business, communication, education, engineering/technologies, general academic interests/achievements, health fields, religion/biblical studies. *Creative arts/performance:* applied art and design, art/fine arts, cinema/film/broadcasting, journalism/publications, music. *Special achievements/activities:* cheerleading/drum major, community service, general special achievements/activities, leadership, memberships, religious involvement. *Special characteristics:* children and siblings of alumni, children of faculty/staff, general special characteristics, international students, relatives of clergy, siblings of current students.

LOANS ***Programs:*** Perkins.

WORK-STUDY ***Federal work-study:*** Total amount: $490,900; jobs available. ***State or other work-study/employment:*** Total amount: $323,702 (100% non-need-based). Part-time jobs available.

APPLYING FOR FINANCIAL AID ***Required financial aid form:*** FAFSA.

CONTACT Director of Financial Aid, Oral Roberts University, 7777 South Lewis Avenue, Tulsa, OK 74171, 918-495-6510 or toll-free 800-678-8876. *Fax:* 918-495-6803. *E-mail:* finaid@oru.edu.

OREGON COLLEGE OF ART & CRAFT

Portland, OR

Tuition & fees: $21,860 **Average undergraduate aid package: $21,995**

ABOUT THE INSTITUTION Independent, coed. 2 undergraduate majors. Both federal and institutional methodology are used as a basis for awarding need-based institutional aid.

UNDERGRADUATE EXPENSES for 2010–11 ***Comprehensive fee:*** $28,070 includes full-time tuition ($20,938), mandatory fees ($922), and room and board ($6210). ***College room only:*** $4185. Room and board charges vary according to board plan and housing facility. ***Part-time tuition:*** $914.20 per credit hour. ***Payment plan:*** Deferred payment.

FRESHMAN FINANCIAL AID (Fall 2009) 10 applied for aid; of those 90% were deemed to have need. 100% of freshmen with need received aid. ***Average percent of need met:*** 36% (excluding resources awarded to replace EFC). ***Average financial aid package:*** $14,176 (excluding resources awarded to replace EFC).

UNDERGRADUATE FINANCIAL AID (Fall 2009) 84 applied for aid; of those 95% were deemed to have need. 100% of undergraduates with need received aid. ***Average percent of need met:*** 38% (excluding resources awarded to replace EFC). ***Average financial aid package:*** $21,995 (excluding resources awarded to replace EFC). 3% of all full-time undergraduates had no need and received non-need-based gift aid.

GIFT AID (NEED-BASED) ***Total amount:*** $1,096,065 (32% federal, 8% state, 47% institutional, 13% external sources). ***Receiving aid:*** Freshmen: 75% (9); all full-time undergraduates: 68% (65). ***Average award:*** Freshmen: $7111; Undergraduates: $9429. ***Scholarships, grants, and awards:*** Federal Pell, FSEOG, state, private, college/university gift aid from institutional funds.

GIFT AID (NON-NEED-BASED) ***Total amount:*** $11,246 (2% institutional, 98% external sources). ***Receiving aid:*** Freshmen: 75% (9). Undergraduates: 31% (29). ***Average award:*** Undergraduates: $3667. ***Scholarships, grants, and awards by category:*** *Creative arts/performance:* art/fine arts. ***Tuition waivers:*** Full or partial for children of alumni, employees or children of employees.

LOANS ***Student loans:*** $1,316,331 (99% need-based, 1% non-need-based). 85% of past graduating class borrowed through all loan programs. *Average indebtedness per student:* $37,000. ***Average need-based loan:*** Freshmen: $3500. Undergraduates: $4640. ***Parent loans:*** $187,170 (84% need-based, 16% non-need-based). ***Programs:*** Federal Direct (Subsidized and Unsubsidized Stafford, PLUS), alternative loans.

WORK-STUDY ***Federal work-study:*** Total amount: $30,250; 85 jobs averaging $500. ***State or other work-study/employment:*** Total amount: $61,264 (98% need-based, 2% non-need-based). 86 part-time jobs averaging $1000.

APPLYING FOR FINANCIAL AID ***Required financial aid form:*** FAFSA. ***Financial aid deadline (priority):*** 3/1. ***Notification date:*** Continuous beginning 3/1. Students must reply by 7/1.

CONTACT Ms. Linda L. Anderson, Director of Financial Aid, Oregon College of Art & Craft, 8245 Southwest Barnes Road, Portland, OR 97225, 971-255-4224 or toll-free 800-390-0632 Ext. 129. *Fax:* 503-297-9651. *E-mail:* landerson@ocac.edu.

OREGON HEALTH & SCIENCE UNIVERSITY

Portland, OR

Tuition & fees (OR res): $18,996 **Average undergraduate aid package: $11,215**

ABOUT THE INSTITUTION State-related, coed. 2 undergraduate majors. Federal methodology is used as a basis for awarding need-based institutional aid.

UNDERGRADUATE EXPENSES for 2010–11 ***Tuition, state resident:*** full-time $13,005; part-time $289 per credit. ***Tuition, nonresident:*** full-time $24,615; part-time $547 per credit. ***Required fees:*** full-time $5991. Full-time tuition and fees vary according to course level, degree level, location, program, reciprocity agreements, and student level. Part-time tuition and fees vary according to course level, course load, degree level, location, program, reciprocity agreements, and student level. Room and board charges vary according to housing facility and location. ***Payment plan:*** Installment.

UNDERGRADUATE FINANCIAL AID (Fall 2010, est.) 300 applied for aid; of those 95% were deemed to have need. 99% of undergraduates with need received aid; of those 7% had need fully met. ***Average percent of need met:*** 37% (excluding resources awarded to replace EFC). ***Average financial aid package:*** $11,215 (excluding resources awarded to replace EFC). 1% of all full-time undergraduates had no need and received non-need-based gift aid.

GIFT AID (NEED-BASED) ***Total amount:*** $2,422,749 (58% federal, 4% state, 8% institutional, 30% external sources). ***Receiving aid:*** All full-time undergraduates: 60% (186). ***Average award:*** Undergraduates: $7961. ***Scholarships, grants, and awards:*** Federal Pell, FSEOG, state, private, college/university gift aid from institutional funds, Health Profession Scholarships.

GIFT AID (NON-NEED-BASED) ***Total amount:*** $49,390 (9% federal, 3% institutional, 88% external sources). ***Receiving aid:*** Undergraduates: 1% (2). ***Average award:*** Undergraduates: $700. ***Scholarships, grants, and awards by category:*** *Academic interests/achievement:* 123 awards ($1,470,526 total): health fields. ***Tuition waivers:*** Full or partial for employees or children of employees.

LOANS ***Student loans:*** $12,697,341 (84% need-based, 16% non-need-based). ***Average need-based loan:*** Undergraduates: $4326. ***Parent loans:*** $649,391 (51% need-based, 49% non-need-based). ***Programs:*** Federal Direct (Subsidized and Unsubsidized Stafford, PLUS), Perkins, Federal Nursing, state, college/university, alternative loans.

WORK-STUDY ***Federal work-study:*** Total amount: $15,307; 12 jobs averaging $1275.

CONTACT Debbie Cox, Administrative Coordinator, Oregon Health & Science University, 3181 SW Sam Jackson Park Road, L-109, Portland, OR 97239-3089, 503-494-7800. *Fax:* 503-494-4629. *E-mail:* finaid@ohsu.edu.

OREGON INSTITUTE OF TECHNOLOGY

Klamath Falls, OR

Tuition & fees (OR res): $7260 **Average undergraduate aid package: $6600**

ABOUT THE INSTITUTION State-supported, coed. 19 undergraduate majors. Federal methodology is used as a basis for awarding need-based institutional aid.

UNDERGRADUATE EXPENSES for 2010–11 ***One-time required fee:*** $150. ***Tuition, state resident:*** full-time $5850; part-time $130 per credit. ***Tuition, nonresident:*** full-time $18,990; part-time $130 per credit. ***Required fees:*** full-time $1410. Full-time tuition and fees vary according to course level, course load, degree level, location, program, and reciprocity agreements. Part-time tuition and fees vary according to course level, course load, degree level, location, program, and reciprocity agreements. ***College room and board:*** $8145. Room and board charges vary according to board plan and housing facility.

FRESHMAN FINANCIAL AID (Fall 2009) 288 applied for aid; of those 79% were deemed to have need. 99% of freshmen with need received aid; of those 31% had need fully met. ***Average percent of need met:*** 19% (excluding resources awarded to replace EFC). ***Average financial aid package:*** $5553 (excluding resources awarded to replace EFC). 6% of all full-time freshmen had no need and received non-need-based gift aid.

UNDERGRADUATE FINANCIAL AID (Fall 2009) 1,955 applied for aid; of those 89% were deemed to have need. 98% of undergraduates with need received aid; of those 26% had need fully met. ***Average percent of need met:*** 20% (excluding resources awarded to replace EFC). ***Average financial aid package:*** $6600 (excluding resources awarded to replace EFC). 2% of all full-time undergraduates had no need and received non-need-based gift aid.

GIFT AID (NEED-BASED) ***Total amount:*** $8,344,577 (56% federal, 15% state, 16% institutional, 13% external sources). ***Receiving aid:*** Freshmen: 42% (120); all full-time undergraduates: 43% (904). ***Average award:*** Freshmen: $5341; Undergraduates: $6001. ***Scholarships, grants, and awards:*** Federal Pell, FSEOG, state, private, college/university gift aid from institutional funds.

GIFT AID (NON-NEED-BASED) ***Total amount:*** $281,879 (41% institutional, 59% external sources). ***Receiving aid:*** Freshmen: 3% (9). Undergraduates: 2% (47). ***Average award:*** Freshmen: $8143. Undergraduates: $8475. ***Scholarships, grants, and awards by category:*** *Academic interests/achievement:* general academic interests/achievements. *Special achievements/activities:* general special achievements/activities, leadership.

LOANS ***Student loans:*** $16,208,948 (90% need-based, 10% non-need-based). 61% of past graduating class borrowed through all loan programs. *Average indebtedness per student:* $21,733. ***Average need-based loan:*** Freshmen: $3347. Undergraduates: $4219. ***Parent loans:*** $3,583,488 (59% need-based, 41% non-need-based). ***Programs:*** Federal Direct (Subsidized and Unsubsidized Stafford, PLUS), Perkins, college/university.

WORK-STUDY ***Federal work-study:*** Total amount: $201,140; jobs available.

ATHLETIC AWARDS Total amount: $351,299 (86% need-based, 14% non-need-based).

APPLYING FOR FINANCIAL AID ***Required financial aid form:*** FAFSA. ***Financial aid deadline (priority):*** 2/1. ***Notification date:*** Continuous beginning 4/1. Students must reply within 3 weeks of notification.

CONTACT Tracey Lehman, Director of Financial Aid, Oregon Institute of Technology, 3201 Campus Drive, Klamath Falls, OR 97601, 541-885-1280 or toll-free 800-422-2017 (in-state), 800-343-6653 (out-of-state). *Fax:* 541-885-1024. *E-mail:* tracey.lehman@oit.edu.

OREGON STATE UNIVERSITY

Corvallis, OR

Tuition & fees (OR res): $7115 **Average undergraduate aid package: $9849**

ABOUT THE INSTITUTION State-supported, coed. 76 undergraduate majors. Federal methodology is used as a basis for awarding need-based institutional aid.

UNDERGRADUATE EXPENSES for 2010–11 ***Tuition, state resident:*** full-time $5760; part-time $160 per credit hour. ***Tuition, nonresident:*** full-time $19,080; part-time $530 per credit hour. ***Required fees:*** full-time $1355. Full-time tuition and fees vary according to course load. Part-time tuition and fees vary according to course load. Room and board charges vary according to board plan and housing facility. ***Payment plan:*** Deferred payment.

FRESHMAN FINANCIAL AID (Fall 2010, est.) 2,739 applied for aid; of those 71% were deemed to have need. 99% of freshmen with need received aid; of those 17% had need fully met. ***Average percent of need met:*** 58% (excluding resources awarded to replace EFC). ***Average financial aid package:*** $9502 (excluding resources awarded to replace EFC). 1% of all full-time freshmen had no need and received non-need-based gift aid.

UNDERGRADUATE FINANCIAL AID (Fall 2010, est.) 11,516 applied for aid; of those 80% were deemed to have need. 99% of undergraduates with need received aid; of those 13% had need fully met. ***Average percent of need met:*** 56% (excluding resources awarded to replace EFC). ***Average financial aid package:*** $9849 (excluding resources awarded to replace EFC). 1% of all full-time undergraduates had no need and received non-need-based gift aid.

GIFT AID (NEED-BASED) ***Total amount:*** $44,856,990 (67% federal, 3% state, 21% institutional, 9% external sources). ***Receiving aid:*** Freshmen: 47% (1,561); all full-time undergraduates: 45% (7,100). ***Average award:*** Freshmen: $3127; Undergraduates: $3494. ***Scholarships, grants, and awards:*** Federal Pell, FSEOG, state, private, college/university gift aid from institutional funds.

GIFT AID (NON-NEED-BASED) ***Total amount:*** $8,885,792 (74% institutional, 26% external sources). ***Receiving aid:*** Freshmen: 1% (48). Undergraduates: 1% (175). ***Average award:*** Freshmen: $4205. Undergraduates: $4054. ***Tuition waivers:*** Full or partial for employees or children of employees.

LOANS ***Student loans:*** $89,081,769 (82% need-based, 18% non-need-based). ***Average need-based loan:*** Freshmen: $3089. Undergraduates: $4023. ***Parent loans:*** $93,443,647 (56% need-based, 44% non-need-based). ***Programs:*** Federal Direct (Subsidized and Unsubsidized Stafford, PLUS), Perkins, college/university.

WORK-STUDY ***Federal work-study:*** Total amount: $3,406,298; jobs available.

ATHLETIC AWARDS Total amount: $7,390,588 (31% need-based, 69% non-need-based).

APPLYING FOR FINANCIAL AID ***Required financial aid form:*** FAFSA. ***Financial aid deadline (priority):*** 2/28. ***Notification date:*** Continuous beginning 4/1. Students must reply within 4 weeks of notification.

CONTACT Doug Severs, Director of Financial Aid, Oregon State University, 218 Kerr Administration Building, Corvallis, OR 97331-2120, 541-737-2241 or toll-free 800-291-4192 (in-state). *E-mail:* doug.severs@oregonstate.edu.

OREGON STATE UNIVERSITY–CASCADES

Bend, OR

CONTACT Financial Aid Office, Oregon State University–Cascades, 2600 Northwest College Way, Bend, OR 97701, 541-322-3100.

OTIS COLLEGE OF ART AND DESIGN

Los Angeles, CA

Tuition & fees: $35,354 **Average undergraduate aid package: $21,259**

ABOUT THE INSTITUTION Independent, coed. 10 undergraduate majors. Federal methodology is used as a basis for awarding need-based institutional aid.

UNDERGRADUATE EXPENSES for 2011–12 ***Tuition:*** full-time $34,454; part-time $1149 per unit. ***Payment plan:*** Installment.

FRESHMAN FINANCIAL AID (Fall 2010, est.) 147 applied for aid; of those 93% were deemed to have need. 100% of freshmen with need received aid; of those 1% had need fully met. ***Average percent of need met:*** 43% (excluding resources awarded to replace EFC). ***Average financial aid package:*** $17,935 (excluding resources awarded to replace EFC). 11% of all full-time freshmen had no need and received non-need-based gift aid.

UNDERGRADUATE FINANCIAL AID (Fall 2010, est.) 969 applied for aid; of those 85% were deemed to have need. 100% of undergraduates with need received aid; of those 3% had need fully met. ***Average percent of need met:*** 50% (excluding resources awarded to replace EFC). ***Average financial aid package:*** $21,259 (excluding resources awarded to replace EFC). 13% of all full-time undergraduates had no need and received non-need-based gift aid.

GIFT AID (NEED-BASED) ***Total amount:*** $13,841,253 (22% federal, 19% state, 58% institutional, 1% external sources). ***Receiving aid:*** Freshmen: 82% (137); all full-time undergraduates: 71% (824). ***Average award:*** Freshmen: $16,943; Undergraduates: $16,122. ***Scholarships, grants, and awards:*** Federal Pell, FSEOG, state, private, college/university gift aid from institutional funds.

GIFT AID (NON-NEED-BASED) ***Total amount:*** $451,794 (96% institutional, 4% external sources). ***Receiving aid:*** Freshmen: 8% (13). Undergraduates: 14% (157). ***Average award:*** Freshmen: $8854. Undergraduates: $6781. ***Scholarships, grants, and awards by category:*** *Academic interests/achievement:* 151 awards ($983,950 total): general academic interests/achievements. *Creative arts/performance:* applied art and design, art/fine arts. ***Tuition waivers:*** Full or partial for employees or children of employees.

LOANS ***Student loans:*** $7,304,857 (97% need-based, 3% non-need-based). 62% of past graduating class borrowed through all loan programs. *Average indebtedness per student:* $10,963. ***Average need-based loan:*** Freshmen: $3497. Undergraduates: $4750. ***Parent loans:*** $4,198,882 (90% need-based, 10% non-need-based). ***Programs:*** Federal Direct (Subsidized and Unsubsidized Stafford, PLUS), Perkins, college/university.

WORK-STUDY ***Federal work-study:*** Total amount: $164,511; 174 jobs averaging $991. ***State or other work-study/employment:*** Total amount: $10,000 (100% non-need-based). 10 part-time jobs averaging $757.

APPLYING FOR FINANCIAL AID ***Required financial aid form:*** FAFSA. ***Financial aid deadline (priority):*** 2/15. ***Notification date:*** 3/1.

CONTACT Jessika Huerta, Assistant Director of Financial Aid, Otis College of Art and Design, 9045 Lincoln Boulevard, Los Angeles, CA 90045-9785, 310-665-6898 or toll-free 800-527-OTIS. *Fax:* 310-665-6884. *E-mail:* jhuerta@otis.edu.

OTTAWA UNIVERSITY

Ottawa, KS

CONTACT Financial Aid Coordinator, Ottawa University, 1001 South Cedar, Ottawa, KS 66067-3399, 785-242-5200 or toll-free 800-755-5200 Ext. 5559. *E-mail:* finaid@ottawa.edu.

OTTERBEIN UNIVERSITY

Westerville, OH

CONTACT Mr. Thomas V. Yarnell, Director of Financial Aid, Otterbein University, One Otterbein College, Westerville, OH 43081-2006, 614-823-1502 or toll-free 800-488-8144. *Fax:* 614-823-1200. *E-mail:* tyarnell@otterbein.edu.

OUACHITA BAPTIST UNIVERSITY

Arkadelphia, AR

Tuition & fees: $20,630 **Average undergraduate aid package: $18,065**

ABOUT THE INSTITUTION Independent Baptist, coed. 57 undergraduate majors. Both federal and institutional methodology are used as a basis for awarding need-based institutional aid.

UNDERGRADUATE EXPENSES for 2011–12 ***Comprehensive fee:*** $26,670 includes full-time tuition ($20,160), mandatory fees ($470), and room and board ($6040). Room and board charges vary according to housing facility. ***Part-time tuition:*** $580 per semester hour. ***Payment plans:*** Installment, deferred payment.

FRESHMAN FINANCIAL AID (Fall 2010, est.) 393 applied for aid; of those 78% were deemed to have need. 100% of freshmen with need received aid; of those 54% had need fully met. ***Average percent of need met:*** 89% (excluding resources awarded to replace EFC). ***Average financial aid package:*** $17,618 (excluding resources awarded to replace EFC). 31% of all full-time freshmen had no need and received non-need-based gift aid.

UNDERGRADUATE FINANCIAL AID (Fall 2010, est.) 1,173 applied for aid; of those 79% were deemed to have need. 100% of undergraduates with need received aid; of those 53% had need fully met. ***Average percent of need met:*** 89% (excluding resources awarded to replace EFC). ***Average financial aid package:*** $18,065 (excluding resources awarded to replace EFC). 34% of all full-time undergraduates had no need and received non-need-based gift aid.

GIFT AID (NEED-BASED) ***Total amount:*** $11,377,452 (18% federal, 13% state, 66% institutional, 3% external sources). ***Receiving aid:*** Freshmen: 68% (306); all full-time undergraduates: 62% (916). ***Average award:*** Freshmen: $12,370; Undergraduates: $12,062. ***Scholarships, grants, and awards:*** Federal Pell, FSEOG, state, private, college/university gift aid from institutional funds.

GIFT AID (NON-NEED-BASED) ***Total amount:*** $7,265,558 (21% state, 74% institutional, 5% external sources). ***Receiving aid:*** Freshmen: 28% (128). Undergraduates: 21% (317). ***Average award:*** Freshmen: $8280. Undergraduates: $8999. ***Scholarships, grants, and awards by category:*** *Academic interests/achievement:* area/ethnic studies, biological sciences, business, communication, computer science, education, engineering/technologies, English, foreign languages, general academic interests/achievements, health fields, home economics, humanities, international studies, mathematics, physical sciences, premedicine, religion/biblical studies, social sciences. *Creative arts/performance:* art/fine arts, journalism/publications, music, performing arts, theater/drama. *Special achievements/activities:* cheerleading/drum major, general special achievements/activities. *Special characteristics:* children and siblings of alumni, children of faculty/staff, ethnic background, first-generation college students, general special characteristics, handicapped students, international students, local/state students, married students, members of minority groups, out-of-state students, previous college experience, relatives of clergy, religious affiliation, twins. ***Tuition waivers:*** Full or partial for employees or children of employees.

LOANS ***Student loans:*** $2,618,493 (10% need-based, 90% non-need-based). 42% of past graduating class borrowed through all loan programs. *Average indebtedness per student:* $15,970. ***Average need-based loan:*** Freshmen: $4688. Undergraduates: $4659. ***Parent loans:*** $1,421,282 (51% need-based, 49% non-need-based). ***Programs:*** Federal Direct (Subsidized and Unsubsidized Stafford, PLUS), Perkins, college/university.

WORK-STUDY ***Federal work-study:*** Total amount: $529,008; 300 jobs averaging $1800. ***State or other work-study/employment:*** Total amount: $248,077 (2% need-based, 98% non-need-based). Part-time jobs available.

ATHLETIC AWARDS Total amount: $2,094,239 (59% need-based, 41% non-need-based).

APPLYING FOR FINANCIAL AID ***Required financial aid form:*** FAFSA. ***Financial aid deadline:*** 6/1 (priority: 1/15). ***Notification date:*** Continuous beginning 11/1. Students must reply by 6/1.

CONTACT Ms. Susan Hurst, Director of Financial Aid, Ouachita Baptist University, PO Box 3774, Arkadelphia, AR 71998-0001, 870-245-5570 or toll-free 800-342-5628 (in-state). *Fax:* 870-245-5318. *E-mail:* hursts@obu.edu.

OUR LADY OF HOLY CROSS COLLEGE

New Orleans, LA

Tuition & fees: $8604 **Average undergraduate aid package: $7658**

ABOUT THE INSTITUTION Independent Roman Catholic, coed. ***Awards:*** associate, bachelor's, and master's degrees and post-bachelor's certificates. 17 undergraduate majors. ***Total enrollment:*** 1,298. Undergraduates: 1,128. Federal methodology is used as a basis for awarding need-based institutional aid.

UNDERGRADUATE EXPENSES for 2010–11 ***Application fee:*** $15. ***Tuition:*** full-time $7824; part-time $326 per semester hour. Full-time tuition and fees vary according to course load and degree level. Part-time tuition and fees vary according to course load and degree level. ***Payment plan:*** Installment.

FRESHMAN FINANCIAL AID (Fall 2010, est.) 41 applied for aid; of those 88% were deemed to have need. 100% of freshmen with need received aid; of those 17% had need fully met. ***Average percent of need met:*** 48% (excluding resources awarded to replace EFC). ***Average financial aid package:*** $8213 (excluding resources awarded to replace EFC).

UNDERGRADUATE FINANCIAL AID (Fall 2010, est.) 519 applied for aid; of those 88% were deemed to have need. 98% of undergraduates with need received aid; of those 6% had need fully met. ***Average percent of need met:*** 45% (excluding resources awarded to replace EFC). ***Average financial aid package:*** $7658 (excluding resources awarded to replace EFC). 1% of all full-time undergraduates had no need and received non-need-based gift aid.

GIFT AID (NEED-BASED) ***Total amount:*** $2,119,166 (93% federal, 2% state, 3% institutional, 2% external sources). ***Receiving aid:*** Freshmen: 63% (32); all full-time undergraduates: 65% (364). ***Average award:*** Freshmen: $6405; Undergraduates: $5011. ***Scholarships, grants, and awards:*** Federal Pell, FSEOG, state, private, college/university gift aid from institutional funds.

GIFT AID (NON-NEED-BASED) ***Total amount:*** $443,715 (90% state, 6% institutional, 4% external sources). ***Receiving aid:*** Freshmen: 6% (3). Undergraduates: 1% (7). ***Average award:*** Undergraduates: $4000. ***Scholarships, grants, and awards by category:*** *Academic interests/achievement:* 27 awards ($103,176 total): education, general academic interests/achievements, health fields, religion/biblical studies. *Special characteristics:* 15 awards ($66,343 total): children of faculty/staff, general special characteristics, relatives of clergy, religious affiliation. ***Tuition waivers:*** Full or partial for employees or children of employees. ***ROTC:*** Army cooperative, Air Force cooperative.

LOANS ***Student loans:*** $5,441,933 (42% need-based, 58% non-need-based). 98% of past graduating class borrowed through all loan programs. *Average indebtedness per student:* $36,863. ***Average need-based loan:*** Freshmen: $3127. Undergraduates: $3760. ***Parent loans:*** $111,252 (100% non-need-based). ***Programs:*** Federal Direct (Subsidized and Unsubsidized Stafford, PLUS), private loans.

WORK-STUDY ***Federal work-study:*** Total amount: $109,361; 24 jobs averaging $4557.

APPLYING FOR FINANCIAL AID ***Required financial aid form:*** FAFSA. ***Financial aid deadline:*** Continuous. ***Notification date:*** Continuous beginning 3/15. Students must reply within 4 weeks of notification.

CONTACT Mrs. Katherine Gonzales, Dean of Admissions and Student Affairs, Our Lady of Holy Cross College, 4123 Woodland Drive, New Orleans, LA 70131-7399, 504-398-2185 or toll-free 800-259-7744 Ext. 175. *Fax:* 504-394-1182. *E-mail:* kgonzales@olhcc.edu.

OUR LADY OF THE LAKE COLLEGE

Baton Rouge, LA

ABOUT THE INSTITUTION Independent Roman Catholic, coed, primarily women. 12 undergraduate majors.

GIFT AID (NEED-BASED) ***Scholarships, grants, and awards:*** Federal Pell, FSEOG, state, private, college/university gift aid from institutional funds.

WORK-STUDY ***Federal work-study:*** Total amount: $90,540; jobs available.

APPLYING FOR FINANCIAL AID ***Required financial aid form:*** FAFSA.

CONTACT Tiffany D. Magee, Director of Financial Aid, Our Lady of the Lake College, 7434 Perkins Road, Baton Rouge, LA 70808, 225-768-1701 or toll-free 877-242-3509. *Fax:* 225-490-1632. *E-mail:* tiffany.magee@ololcollege.edu.

OUR LADY OF THE LAKE UNIVERSITY OF SAN ANTONIO

San Antonio, TX

Tuition & fees: $21,900 **Average undergraduate aid package: $24,580**

ABOUT THE INSTITUTION Independent Roman Catholic, coed. 36 undergraduate majors. Federal methodology is used as a basis for awarding need-based institutional aid.

UNDERGRADUATE EXPENSES for 2010–11 ***Comprehensive fee:*** $28,738 includes full-time tuition ($21,400), mandatory fees ($500), and room and board ($6838). ***College room only:*** $3988. Full-time tuition and fees vary according to degree level and location. Room and board charges vary according to board plan. ***Part-time tuition:*** $690 per credit hour. ***Part-time fees:*** $12 per credit hour; $58 per term. Part-time tuition and fees vary according to degree level and location. ***Payment plans:*** Installment, deferred payment.

FRESHMAN FINANCIAL AID (Fall 2010, est.) 289 applied for aid; of those 94% were deemed to have need. 100% of freshmen with need received aid; of those 20% had need fully met. ***Average percent of need met:*** 86% (excluding

resources awarded to replace EFC). ***Average financial aid package:*** $26,729 (excluding resources awarded to replace EFC). 1% of all full-time freshmen had no need and received non-need-based gift aid.

UNDERGRADUATE FINANCIAL AID (Fall 2010, est.) 1,169 applied for aid; of those 96% were deemed to have need. 99% of undergraduates with need received aid; of those 21% had need fully met. ***Average percent of need met:*** 82% (excluding resources awarded to replace EFC). ***Average financial aid package:*** $24,580 (excluding resources awarded to replace EFC). 1% of all full-time undergraduates had no need and received non-need-based gift aid.

GIFT AID (NEED-BASED) ***Total amount:*** $18,219,357 (26% federal, 15% state, 56% institutional, 3% external sources). ***Receiving aid:*** Freshmen: 90% (270); all full-time undergraduates: 86% (1,080). ***Average award:*** Freshmen: $21,121; Undergraduates: $16,288. ***Scholarships, grants, and awards:*** Federal Pell, FSEOG, state, private, college/university gift aid from institutional funds.

GIFT AID (NON-NEED-BASED) ***Receiving aid:*** Freshmen: 3% (9). Undergraduates: 5% (62). ***Average award:*** Freshmen: $2216. Undergraduates: $11,762. ***Scholarships, grants, and awards by category:*** *Academic interests/achievement:* general academic interests/achievements. *Special characteristics:* children of faculty/staff, religious affiliation. ***Tuition waivers:*** Full or partial for employees or children of employees.

LOANS ***Student loans:*** $9,825,175 (100% need-based). 90% of past graduating class borrowed through all loan programs. *Average indebtedness per student:* $32,356. ***Average need-based loan:*** Freshmen: $640. Undergraduates: $4382. ***Parent loans:*** $749,486 (100% need-based). ***Programs:*** Federal Direct (Subsidized and Unsubsidized Stafford, PLUS), Perkins, state.

WORK-STUDY ***Federal work-study:*** Total amount: $419,329; jobs available. ***State or other work-study/employment:*** Total amount: $20,491 (100% need-based). Part-time jobs available.

ATHLETIC AWARDS Total amount: $933,566 (100% need-based).

APPLYING FOR FINANCIAL AID ***Required financial aid forms:*** FAFSA, institution's own form. ***Financial aid deadline (priority):*** 5/1.

CONTACT Michael Fuller, Director of Financial Aid, Our Lady of the Lake University of San Antonio, 411 Southwest 24th Street, San Antonio, TX 78207-4689, 210-434-6711 Ext. 2541 or toll-free 800-436-6558. *Fax:* 210-431-3958. *E-mail:* mfuller@lake.ollusa.edu.

OZARK CHRISTIAN COLLEGE

Joplin, MO

CONTACT Jill Kaminsky, Application Processor, Ozark Christian College, 1111 North Main Street, Joplin, MO 64801-4804, 417-624-2518 Ext. 2017 or toll-free 800-299-4622. *Fax:* 417-624-0090. *E-mail:* finaid@occ.edu.

PACE UNIVERSITY

New York, NY

Tuition & fees: $33,702 **Average undergraduate aid package: $26,579**

ABOUT THE INSTITUTION Independent, coed. 70 undergraduate majors. Federal methodology is used as a basis for awarding need-based institutional aid.

UNDERGRADUATE EXPENSES for 2010–11 ***Comprehensive fee:*** $47,502 includes full-time tuition ($32,656), mandatory fees ($1046), and room and board ($13,800). Room and board charges vary according to board plan, housing facility, and location. ***Part-time tuition:*** $937 per credit hour. Part-time tuition and fees vary according to course load. ***Payment plan:*** Installment.

FRESHMAN FINANCIAL AID (Fall 2010, est.) 1,572 applied for aid; of those 93% were deemed to have need. 100% of freshmen with need received aid; of those 10% had need fully met. ***Average percent of need met:*** 78% (excluding resources awarded to replace EFC). ***Average financial aid package:*** $29,952 (excluding resources awarded to replace EFC). 16% of all full-time freshmen had no need and received non-need-based gift aid.

UNDERGRADUATE FINANCIAL AID (Fall 2010, est.) 5,544 applied for aid; of those 94% were deemed to have need. 100% of undergraduates with need received aid; of those 9% had need fully met. ***Average percent of need met:*** 71% (excluding resources awarded to replace EFC). ***Average financial aid package:*** $26,579 (excluding resources awarded to replace EFC). 18% of all full-time undergraduates had no need and received non-need-based gift aid.

GIFT AID (NEED-BASED) ***Total amount:*** $109,040,717 (13% federal, 7% state, 78% institutional, 2% external sources). ***Receiving aid:*** Freshmen: 83% (1,462); all full-time undergraduates: 75% (5,126). ***Average award:*** Freshmen: $24,851; Undergraduates: $21,828. ***Scholarships, grants, and awards:*** Federal Pell, FSEOG, state, private, college/university gift aid from institutional funds, Federal Nursing, endowed and restricted scholarships and grants.

GIFT AID (NON-NEED-BASED) ***Total amount:*** $17,755,241 (84% institutional, 16% external sources). ***Receiving aid:*** Freshmen: 7% (115). Undergraduates: 5% (351). ***Average award:*** Freshmen: $13,158. Undergraduates: $10,785. ***Scholarships, grants, and awards by category:*** *Academic interests/achievement:* 5,611 awards ($58,726,691 total): biological sciences, business, communication, computer science, education, English, foreign languages, general academic interests/achievements, health fields, humanities, mathematics, physical sciences, social sciences. *Creative arts/performance:* 5 awards ($15,000 total): creative writing, debating, performing arts, theater/drama. *Special achievements/activities:* 430 awards ($5,794,518 total): community service, general special achievements/activities, leadership. *Special characteristics:* 111 awards ($1,334,021 total): adult students, children of faculty/staff, children with a deceased or disabled parent, general special characteristics, international students, parents of current students, previous college experience, spouses of deceased or disabled public servants, veterans. ***Tuition waivers:*** Full or partial for employees or children of employees, senior citizens.

LOANS ***Student loans:*** $44,261,794 (83% need-based, 17% non-need-based). 69% of past graduating class borrowed through all loan programs. *Average indebtedness per student:* $38,035. ***Average need-based loan:*** Freshmen: $3890. Undergraduates: $4641. ***Parent loans:*** $32,818,192 (52% need-based, 48% non-need-based). ***Programs:*** Federal Direct (Subsidized and Unsubsidized Stafford, PLUS), Perkins, Federal Nursing.

WORK-STUDY ***Federal work-study:*** Total amount: $1,153,352; 1,225 jobs averaging $3491.

ATHLETIC AWARDS Total amount: $3,002,768 (72% need-based, 28% non-need-based).

APPLYING FOR FINANCIAL AID ***Required financial aid forms:*** FAFSA, state aid form. ***Financial aid deadline (priority):*** 2/15. ***Notification date:*** Continuous beginning 3/1. Students must reply by 5/1 or within 2 weeks of notification.

CONTACT Office of Financial Aid, Pace University, 861 Bedford Road, Pleasantville, NY 10570, 877-672-1830 or toll-free 800-874-7223. *Fax:* 914-773-3315.

PACIFIC ISLANDS UNIVERSITY

Mangilao, GU

CONTACT Financial Aid Office, Pacific Islands University, PO Box 22619, Guam Main Facility, GU 96921-2619, 671-734-1812.

PACIFIC LUTHERAN UNIVERSITY

Tacoma, WA

Tuition & fees: $30,950 **Average undergraduate aid package: $28,473**

ABOUT THE INSTITUTION Independent religious, coed. 41 undergraduate majors. Federal methodology is used as a basis for awarding need-based institutional aid.

UNDERGRADUATE EXPENSES for 2011–12 ***Comprehensive fee:*** $40,200 includes full-time tuition ($30,950) and room and board ($9250). Room and board charges vary according to board plan and housing facility. ***Payment plan:*** Installment.

FRESHMAN FINANCIAL AID (Fall 2010, est.) 633 applied for aid; of those 85% were deemed to have need. 100% of freshmen with need received aid; of those 42% had need fully met. ***Average percent of need met:*** 92% (excluding resources awarded to replace EFC). ***Average financial aid package:*** $29,895 (excluding resources awarded to replace EFC). 20% of all full-time freshmen had no need and received non-need-based gift aid.

UNDERGRADUATE FINANCIAL AID (Fall 2010, est.) 2,528 applied for aid; of those 88% were deemed to have need. 99% of undergraduates with need received aid; of those 30% had need fully met. ***Average percent of need met:*** 87% (excluding resources awarded to replace EFC). ***Average financial aid package:*** $28,473 (excluding resources awarded to replace EFC). 24% of all full-time undergraduates had no need and received non-need-based gift aid.

GIFT AID (NEED-BASED) ***Total amount:*** $36,133,015 (11% federal, 10% state, 76% institutional, 3% external sources). ***Receiving aid:*** Freshmen: 78% (537); all full-time undergraduates: 71% (2,186). ***Average award:*** Freshmen: $18,874;

Undergraduates: $16,843. ***Scholarships, grants, and awards:*** Federal Pell, FSEOG, state, private, college/university gift aid from institutional funds, Federal Nursing.

GIFT AID (NON-NEED-BASED) ***Total amount:*** $13,518,052 (82% institutional, 18% external sources). ***Receiving aid:*** Freshmen: 64% (443). Undergraduates: 58% (1,778). ***Average award:*** Freshmen: $14,592. Undergraduates: $12,374. ***Scholarships, grants, and awards by category:*** *Academic interests/achievement:* 2,355 awards ($28,013,542 total): general academic interests/achievements. *Creative arts/performance:* 242 awards ($817,640 total): art/fine arts, dance, debating, music, theater/drama. *Special achievements/activities:* 36 awards ($65,600 total): leadership. *Special characteristics:* 995 awards ($2,057,627 total): children and siblings of alumni, first-generation college students, international students, out-of-state students, relatives of clergy, religious affiliation. ***Tuition waivers:*** Full or partial for children of alumni, employees or children of employees.

LOANS ***Student loans:*** $17,525,144 (75% need-based, 25% non-need-based). 73% of past graduating class borrowed through all loan programs. *Average indebtedness per student:* $28,640. ***Average need-based loan:*** Freshmen: $6851. Undergraduates: $8631. ***Parent loans:*** $5,887,972 (32% need-based, 68% non-need-based). ***Programs:*** Federal Direct (Subsidized and Unsubsidized Stafford, PLUS), Perkins, Federal Nursing, state.

WORK-STUDY ***Federal work-study:*** Total amount: $1,423,410; 576 jobs averaging $2266. ***State or other work-study/employment:*** Total amount: $2,798,071 (42% need-based, 58% non-need-based). 1,156 part-time jobs averaging $3178.

APPLYING FOR FINANCIAL AID ***Required financial aid form:*** FAFSA. ***Financial aid deadline (priority):*** 1/31. ***Notification date:*** Continuous beginning 3/1. Students must reply by 5/1 or within 3 weeks of notification.

CONTACT Mrs. Katherine Walker Loffer, Associate Director of Financial Aid, Pacific Lutheran University, Hauge Administration Building, Room 130, Tacoma, WA 98447, 253-535-7167 or toll-free 800-274-6758. *Fax:* 253-535-8406. *E-mail:* walkerkl@plu.edu.

PACIFIC NORTHWEST COLLEGE OF ART

Portland, OR

CONTACT Peggy Burgus, Director of Financial Aid, Pacific Northwest College of Art, 1241 Northwest Johnson Street, Portland, OR 97209, 503-821-8976. *Fax:* 503-821-8978.

PACIFIC OAKS COLLEGE

Pasadena, CA

CONTACT Rosie Tristan, Financial Aid Specialist, Pacific Oaks College, 5 Westmoreland Place, Pasadena, CA 91103, 626-397-1350 or toll-free 800-684-0900. *Fax:* 626-577-6144. *E-mail:* financial@pacificoaks.edu.

PACIFIC UNION COLLEGE

Angwin, CA

Tuition & fees: $25,965 **Average undergraduate aid package: $20,000**

ABOUT THE INSTITUTION Independent Seventh-day Adventist, coed. 33 undergraduate majors. Federal methodology is used as a basis for awarding need-based institutional aid.

UNDERGRADUATE EXPENSES for 2011–12 ***Comprehensive fee:*** $33,240 includes full-time tuition ($25,740), mandatory fees ($225), and room and board ($7275). ***College room only:*** $4260. Full-time tuition and fees vary according to course load. ***Part-time tuition:*** $725 per quarter hour. ***Part-time fees:*** $75 per term. Part-time tuition and fees vary according to course load. ***Payment plans:*** Guaranteed tuition, installment.

FRESHMAN FINANCIAL AID (Fall 2010, est.) 300 applied for aid; of those 75% were deemed to have need. 100% of freshmen with need received aid; of those 3% had need fully met. ***Average percent of need met:*** 52% (excluding resources awarded to replace EFC). ***Average financial aid package:*** $21,700 (excluding resources awarded to replace EFC). 25% of all full-time freshmen had no need and received non-need-based gift aid.

UNDERGRADUATE FINANCIAL AID (Fall 2010, est.) 1,127 applied for aid; of those 75% were deemed to have need. 100% of undergraduates with need received aid; of those 2% had need fully met. ***Average percent of need met:*** 44% (excluding resources awarded to replace EFC). ***Average financial aid package:*** $20,000 (excluding resources awarded to replace EFC). 26% of all full-time undergraduates had no need and received non-need-based gift aid.

GIFT AID (NEED-BASED) ***Total amount:*** $16,194,256 (19% federal, 17% state, 53% institutional, 11% external sources). ***Receiving aid:*** Freshmen: 74% (226); all full-time undergraduates: 73% (841). ***Average award:*** Freshmen: $19,400; Undergraduates: $17,500. ***Scholarships, grants, and awards:*** Federal Pell, FSEOG, state, private, college/university gift aid from institutional funds.

GIFT AID (NON-NEED-BASED) ***Total amount:*** $2,708,167 (55% institutional, 45% external sources). ***Receiving aid:*** Freshmen: 70% (213). Undergraduates: 65% (751). ***Average award:*** Freshmen: $2070. Undergraduates: $3015. ***Scholarships, grants, and awards by category:*** *Academic interests/achievement:* 26 awards ($90,626 total): education, religion/biblical studies. *Creative arts/performance:* 15 awards ($15,000 total): art/fine arts, music, theater/drama. *Special achievements/activities:* 372 awards ($891,877 total): community service, general special achievements/activities, leadership, religious involvement. *Special characteristics:* 1,527 awards ($1,138,099 total): members of minority groups, religious affiliation, siblings of current students, spouses of current students, veterans. ***Tuition waivers:*** Full or partial for employees or children of employees, senior citizens.

LOANS ***Student loans:*** $11,375,323 (35% need-based, 65% non-need-based). 72% of past graduating class borrowed through all loan programs. *Average indebtedness per student:* $21,000. ***Average need-based loan:*** Freshmen: $2762. Undergraduates: $3834. ***Parent loans:*** $1,389,323 (60% need-based, 40% non-need-based). ***Programs:*** Federal Direct (Subsidized and Unsubsidized Stafford, PLUS), Perkins, college/university.

WORK-STUDY ***Federal work-study:*** Total amount: $416,167; 158 jobs averaging $2632.

APPLYING FOR FINANCIAL AID ***Required financial aid forms:*** FAFSA, institution's own form. ***Financial aid deadline (priority):*** 3/2. ***Notification date:*** Continuous beginning 4/1. Students must reply within 3 weeks of notification.

CONTACT Laurie Wheeler, Director of Student Financial Services, Pacific Union College, One Angwin Avenue, Angwin, CA 94508, 707-965-7321 or toll-free 800-862-7080. *Fax:* 707-965-6595. *E-mail:* llwheeler@puc.edu.

PACIFIC UNIVERSITY

Forest Grove, OR

Tuition & fees: $33,612 **Average undergraduate aid package: $25,016**

ABOUT THE INSTITUTION Independent, coed. 50 undergraduate majors. Federal methodology is used as a basis for awarding need-based institutional aid.

UNDERGRADUATE EXPENSES for 2011–12 ***Comprehensive fee:*** $42,820 includes full-time tuition ($32,850), mandatory fees ($762), and room and board ($9208). ***College room only:*** $4644. Room and board charges vary according to board plan and housing facility. Part-time tuition and fees vary according to course load. ***Payment plans:*** Installment, deferred payment.

FRESHMAN FINANCIAL AID (Fall 2010, est.) 448 applied for aid; of those 90% were deemed to have need. 100% of freshmen with need received aid; of those 16% had need fully met. ***Average percent of need met:*** 79% (excluding resources awarded to replace EFC). ***Average financial aid package:*** $26,939 (excluding resources awarded to replace EFC). 13% of all full-time freshmen had no need and received non-need-based gift aid.

UNDERGRADUATE FINANCIAL AID (Fall 2010, est.) 1,396 applied for aid; of those 90% were deemed to have need. 100% of undergraduates with need received aid; of those 17% had need fully met. ***Average percent of need met:*** 69% (excluding resources awarded to replace EFC). ***Average financial aid package:*** $25,016 (excluding resources awarded to replace EFC). 17% of all full-time undergraduates had no need and received non-need-based gift aid.

GIFT AID (NEED-BASED) ***Total amount:*** $22,749,193 (12% federal, 2% state, 82% institutional, 4% external sources). ***Receiving aid:*** Freshmen: 83% (392); all full-time undergraduates: 75% (1,169). ***Average award:*** Freshmen: $17,554; Undergraduates: $15,950. ***Scholarships, grants, and awards:*** Federal Pell, FSEOG, state, private, college/university gift aid from institutional funds.

GIFT AID (NON-NEED-BASED) ***Total amount:*** $3,631,487 (98% institutional, 2% external sources). ***Receiving aid:*** Freshmen: 6% (28). Undergraduates: 6% (92). ***Average award:*** Freshmen: $12,192. Undergraduates: $10,966. ***Scholarships, grants, and awards by category:*** *Academic interests/achievement:* 612 awards ($1,576,237 total): biological sciences, business, communication, education, English, foreign languages, general academic interests/achievements, health fields, humanities, mathematics, physical sciences, premedicine, social sciences. *Creative arts/performance:* 92 awards ($291,950 total): art/fine arts, debating, journalism/publications, music, theater/drama. *Special achievements/activities:* 3 awards ($10,400 total): community service, memberships, religious involvement. *Special characteristics:* 1,294 awards ($12,009,518 total): children and siblings of alumni, children of faculty/staff, ethnic background, first-generation college students, general special characteristics, international students, local/state students, relatives of clergy, veterans. ***Tuition waivers:*** Full or partial for employees or children of employees.

LOANS ***Student loans:*** $12,179,073 (83% need-based, 17% non-need-based). 76% of past graduating class borrowed through all loan programs. *Average indebtedness per student:* $31,306. ***Average need-based loan:*** Freshmen: $3427. Undergraduates: $4351. ***Parent loans:*** $3,571,111 (64% need-based, 36% non-need-based). ***Programs:*** Federal Direct (Subsidized and Unsubsidized Stafford, PLUS), Perkins, private loans.

WORK-STUDY ***Federal work-study:*** Total amount: $1,790,316; 876 jobs averaging $1941. ***State or other work-study/employment:*** Total amount: $141,000 (9% need-based, 91% non-need-based). 144 part-time jobs averaging $948.

APPLYING FOR FINANCIAL AID ***Required financial aid form:*** FAFSA. ***Financial aid deadline (priority):*** 3/1. ***Notification date:*** Continuous beginning 3/1.

CONTACT Office of Financial Aid, Pacific University, 2043 College Way, Forest Grove, OR 97116-1797, 503-352-2222 or toll-free 877-722-8648. *E-mail:* financialaid@pacificu.edu.

PAIER COLLEGE OF ART, INC.

Hamden, CT

CONTACT Mr. John DeRose, Director of Financial Aid, Paier College of Art, Inc., 20 Gorham Avenue, Hamden, CT 06514-3902, 203-287-3034. *Fax:* 203-287-3021. *E-mail:* paier.art@snet.net.

PAINE COLLEGE

Augusta, GA

CONTACT Ms. Gerri Bogan, Director of Financial Aid, Paine College, 1235 15th Street, Augusta, GA 30901, 706-821-8262 or toll-free 800-476-7703. *Fax:* 706-821-8691. *E-mail:* bogang@mail.paine.edu.

PALM BEACH ATLANTIC UNIVERSITY

West Palm Beach, FL

Tuition & fees: $23,400 **Average undergraduate aid package: $16,270**

ABOUT THE INSTITUTION Independent nondenominational, coed. 47 undergraduate majors. Federal methodology is used as a basis for awarding need-based institutional aid.

UNDERGRADUATE EXPENSES for 2010–11 ***Comprehensive fee:*** $31,620 includes full-time tuition ($23,100), mandatory fees ($300), and room and board ($8220). ***College room only:*** $4570. Full-time tuition and fees vary according to course load, degree level, location, program, and reciprocity agreements. Room and board charges vary according to board plan and housing facility. ***Part-time tuition:*** $556 per credit hour. ***Part-time fees:*** $99 per term. Part-time tuition and fees vary according to course load, degree level, location, program, and reciprocity agreements. ***Payment plan:*** Installment.

FRESHMAN FINANCIAL AID (Fall 2010, est.) 399 applied for aid; of those 84% were deemed to have need. 100% of freshmen with need received aid; of those 21% had need fully met. ***Average percent of need met:*** 73% (excluding resources awarded to replace EFC). ***Average financial aid package:*** $18,504 (excluding resources awarded to replace EFC). 24% of all full-time freshmen had no need and received non-need-based gift aid.

UNDERGRADUATE FINANCIAL AID (Fall 2010, est.) 1,897 applied for aid; of those 89% were deemed to have need. 100% of undergraduates with need received aid; of those 13% had need fully met. ***Average percent of need met:*** 65% (excluding resources awarded to replace EFC). ***Average financial aid package:*** $16,270 (excluding resources awarded to replace EFC). 20% of all full-time undergraduates had no need and received non-need-based gift aid.

GIFT AID (NEED-BASED) ***Total amount:*** $18,739,554 (22% federal, 20% state, 47% institutional, 11% external sources). ***Receiving aid:*** Freshmen: 76% (337); all full-time undergraduates: 76% (1,663). ***Average award:*** Freshmen: $15,199; Undergraduates: $12,075. ***Scholarships, grants, and awards:*** Federal Pell, FSEOG, state, private, college/university gift aid from institutional funds.

GIFT AID (NON-NEED-BASED) ***Total amount:*** $4,689,524 (1% federal, 25% state, 68% institutional, 6% external sources). ***Receiving aid:*** Freshmen: 12% (53). Undergraduates: 7% (152). ***Average award:*** Freshmen: $8103. Undergraduates: $6561. ***Scholarships, grants, and awards by category:*** *Academic interests/achievement:* 1,597 awards ($7,973,046 total): general academic interests/achievements. *Creative arts/performance:* 225 awards ($617,497 total): dance, music, theater/drama. *Special achievements/activities:* 23 awards ($56,600 total): leadership. *Special characteristics:* 303 awards ($1,481,043 total): adult students, children and siblings of alumni, children of current students, children of educators, children of faculty/staff, international students, out-of-state students, previous college experience, siblings of current students, spouses of current students. ***Tuition waivers:*** Full or partial for employees or children of employees.

LOANS ***Student loans:*** $13,308,788 (80% need-based, 20% non-need-based). 74% of past graduating class borrowed through all loan programs. *Average indebtedness per student:* $22,150. ***Average need-based loan:*** Freshmen: $3501. Undergraduates: $4470. ***Parent loans:*** $2,743,747 (47% need-based, 53% non-need-based). ***Programs:*** Federal Direct (Subsidized and Unsubsidized Stafford, PLUS), Perkins.

WORK-STUDY ***Federal work-study:*** Total amount: $971,405; 309 jobs averaging $3154. ***State or other work-study/employment:*** Total amount: $11,937 (100% need-based). 7 part-time jobs averaging $1932.

ATHLETIC AWARDS Total amount: $1,190,386 (52% need-based, 48% non-need-based).

APPLYING FOR FINANCIAL AID ***Required financial aid form:*** FAFSA. ***Financial aid deadline:*** 8/1 (priority: 2/1). ***Notification date:*** Continuous beginning 2/15. Students must reply within 4 weeks of notification.

CONTACT Mr. Todd Martin, Director of Financial Aid, Palm Beach Atlantic University, PO Box 24708, West Palm Beach, FL 33416-4708, 561-803-2000 or toll-free 800-238-3998. *Fax:* 561-803-2130. *E-mail:* finaid@pba.edu.

PALMER COLLEGE OF CHIROPRACTIC

Davenport, IA

Tuition & fees: N/R **Average undergraduate aid package: N/A**

ABOUT THE INSTITUTION Independent, coed. 3 undergraduate majors. Federal methodology is used as a basis for awarding need-based institutional aid.

UNDERGRADUATE EXPENSES for 2010–11 ***One-time required fee:*** $100. ***Tuition:*** part-time $186 per credit hour. ***Required fees:*** $35 per term. Full-time tuition and fees vary according to course load, degree level, and program. Part-time tuition and fees vary according to course load, degree level, and program. ***Payment plans:*** Installment, deferred payment.

GIFT AID (NEED-BASED) ***Scholarships, grants, and awards:*** Federal Pell, FSEOG, state, private, college/university gift aid from institutional funds.

GIFT AID (NON-NEED-BASED) ***Scholarships, grants, and awards by category:*** *Academic interests/achievement:* biological sciences, general academic interests/achievements, health fields. ***Tuition waivers:*** Full or partial for employees or children of employees.

LOANS ***Programs:*** Perkins, state.

WORK-STUDY Federal work-study jobs available.

APPLYING FOR FINANCIAL AID ***Required financial aid form:*** FAFSA. ***Financial aid deadline:*** Continuous. ***Notification date:*** Continuous beginning 1/3. Students must reply within 4 weeks of notification.

CONTACT Ms. Jennifer Randazzo, Senior Director of Financial Planning, Palmer College of Chiropractic, 1000 Brady Street, Davenport, IA 52803, 563-884-5888 or toll-free 800-722-3648. *Fax:* 563-884-5299. *E-mail:* jennifer.randazzo@palmer.edu.

PARK UNIVERSITY

Parkville, MO

CONTACT Carla Boren, Director of Financial Aid, Park University, 8700 NW River Park Drive, Parkville, MO 64152, 816-584-6317 or toll-free 800-745-7275. *Fax:* 816-741-9668. *E-mail:* finaid@park.edu.

PARSONS THE NEW SCHOOL FOR DESIGN

New York, NY

Tuition & fees: $37,610 **Average undergraduate aid package: $27,120**

ABOUT THE INSTITUTION Independent, coed. 13 undergraduate majors. Federal methodology is used as a basis for awarding need-based institutional aid.

UNDERGRADUATE EXPENSES for 2010–11 ***Comprehensive fee:*** $52,870 includes full-time tuition ($36,800), mandatory fees ($810), and room and board ($15,260). ***College room only:*** $12,260. Room and board charges vary according to board plan and housing facility. ***Part-time tuition:*** $1255 per credit. Part-time tuition and fees vary according to course load. ***Payment plan:*** Installment.

FRESHMAN FINANCIAL AID (Fall 2010, est.) 506 applied for aid; of those 91% were deemed to have need. 97% of freshmen with need received aid; of those 11% had need fully met. ***Average percent of need met:*** 74% (excluding resources awarded to replace EFC). ***Average financial aid package:*** $32,019 (excluding resources awarded to replace EFC). 6% of all full-time freshmen had no need and received non-need-based gift aid.

UNDERGRADUATE FINANCIAL AID (Fall 2010, est.) 2,078 applied for aid; of those 93% were deemed to have need. 95% of undergraduates with need received aid; of those 10% had need fully met. ***Average percent of need met:*** 63% (excluding resources awarded to replace EFC). ***Average financial aid package:*** $27,120 (excluding resources awarded to replace EFC). 3% of all full-time undergraduates had no need and received non-need-based gift aid.

GIFT AID (NEED-BASED) ***Total amount:*** $31,975,630 (14% federal, 3% state, 81% institutional, 2% external sources). ***Receiving aid:*** Freshmen: 57% (444); all full-time undergraduates: 47% (1,770). ***Average award:*** Freshmen: $20,752; Undergraduates: $17,805. ***Scholarships, grants, and awards:*** Federal Pell, FSEOG, state, private, college/university gift aid from institutional funds.

GIFT AID (NON-NEED-BASED) ***Total amount:*** $8,976,240 (97% institutional, 3% external sources). ***Receiving aid:*** Freshmen: 3. Undergraduates: 1% (22). ***Average award:*** Freshmen: $3185. Undergraduates: $4150. ***Scholarships, grants, and awards by category:*** *Academic interests/achievement:* general academic interests/achievements. *Creative arts/performance:* general creative arts/performance. ***Tuition waivers:*** Full or partial for employees or children of employees.

LOANS ***Student loans:*** $19,054,675 (95% need-based, 5% non-need-based). 48% of past graduating class borrowed through all loan programs. *Average indebtedness per student:* $38,290. ***Average need-based loan:*** Freshmen: $7540. Undergraduates: $10,395. ***Parent loans:*** $8,124,010 (94% need-based, 6% non-need-based). ***Programs:*** Federal Direct (Subsidized and Unsubsidized Stafford, PLUS), Perkins.

WORK-STUDY ***Federal work-study:*** Total amount: $548,215; jobs available. ***State or other work-study/employment:*** Part-time jobs available.

APPLYING FOR FINANCIAL AID ***Required financial aid form:*** FAFSA. ***Financial aid deadline:*** Continuous. ***Notification date:*** Continuous beginning 3/1. Students must reply within 4 weeks of notification.

CONTACT Office of Student Financial Services, Parsons The New School for Design, 66 Fifth Avenue, New York, NY 10011, 212-229-8930 or toll-free 877-528-3321. *E-mail:* sfs@newschool.edu.

PATRICK HENRY COLLEGE

Purcellville, VA

Tuition & fees: $21,520 **Average undergraduate aid package: $10,879**

ABOUT THE INSTITUTION Independent nondenominational, coed. 5 undergraduate majors. Institutional methodology is used as a basis for awarding need-based institutional aid.

UNDERGRADUATE EXPENSES for 2010–11 ***Comprehensive fee:*** $30,050 includes full-time tuition ($21,270), mandatory fees ($250), and room and board ($8530). Full-time tuition and fees vary according to course load and degree level. Room and board charges vary according to board plan. ***Part-time tuition:*** $400 per credit hour. Part-time tuition and fees vary according to course level, course load, and degree level. ***Payment plan:*** Installment.

FRESHMAN FINANCIAL AID (Fall 2009) 47 applied for aid; of those 91% were deemed to have need. 100% of freshmen with need received aid. ***Average percent of need met:*** 54% (excluding resources awarded to replace EFC). ***Average financial aid package:*** $10,530 (excluding resources awarded to replace EFC). 55% of all full-time freshmen had no need and received non-need-based gift aid.

UNDERGRADUATE FINANCIAL AID (Fall 2009) 129 applied for aid; of those 93% were deemed to have need. 100% of undergraduates with need received aid. ***Average percent of need met:*** 54% (excluding resources awarded to replace EFC). ***Average financial aid package:*** $10,879 (excluding resources awarded to replace EFC). 60% of all full-time undergraduates had no need and received non-need-based gift aid.

GIFT AID (NEED-BASED) ***Total amount:*** $1,023,436 (100% institutional). ***Receiving aid:*** Freshmen: 47% (43); all full-time undergraduates: 38% (120). ***Average award:*** Freshmen: $8901; Undergraduates: $8372. ***Scholarships, grants, and awards:*** private, college/university gift aid from institutional funds.

GIFT AID (NON-NEED-BASED) ***Total amount:*** $1,782,996 (92% institutional, 8% external sources). ***Receiving aid:*** Freshmen: 34% (31). Undergraduates: 30% (96). ***Average award:*** Freshmen: $4520. Undergraduates: $5688. ***Scholarships, grants, and awards by category:*** *Academic interests/achievement:* general academic interests/achievements. *Creative arts/performance:* debating, journalism/publications, music. *Special achievements/activities:* community service, leadership, memberships, religious involvement. *Special characteristics:* children of faculty/staff, children of public servants, public servants, relatives of clergy, veterans. ***Tuition waivers:*** Full or partial for employees or children of employees.

LOANS ***Student loans:*** $821,382 (100% non-need-based). ***Programs:*** private loans.

APPLYING FOR FINANCIAL AID ***Required financial aid form:*** CSS Financial Aid PROFILE. ***Financial aid deadline:*** 6/15 (priority: 3/15). ***Notification date:*** Continuous beginning 3/1. Students must reply by 5/1 or within 4 weeks of notification.

CONTACT Mrs. Christine W. Guenard, Associate Director of Financial Aid, Patrick Henry College, 10 Patrick Henry Circle, Purcellville, VA 20132, 540-441-8140. *Fax:* 540-441-8149. *E-mail:* cwguenard@phc.edu.

PATTEN UNIVERSITY

Oakland, CA

CONTACT Mr. Robert A. Olivera, Dean of Enrollment Services, Patten University, 2433 Coolidge Avenue, Oakland, CA 94601-2699, 510-261-8500 Ext. 783. *Fax:* 510-534-8969. *E-mail:* oliverob@patten.edu.

PAUL QUINN COLLEGE

Dallas, TX

CONTACT Khaleelah Ali, Assistant Director of Financial Aid, Paul Quinn College, 3837 Simpson Stuart Road, Dallas, TX 75241, 214-302-3530 or toll-free 800-237-2648. *Fax:* 214-302-3535. *E-mail:* kali@pqc.edu.

PAUL SMITH'S COLLEGE

Paul Smiths, NY

Tuition & fees: $20,695 **Average undergraduate aid package: $17,989**

ABOUT THE INSTITUTION Independent, coed, primarily men. ***Awards:*** associate and bachelor's degrees. 12 undergraduate majors. ***Total enrollment:*** 910. Undergraduates: 910. Federal methodology is used as a basis for awarding need-based institutional aid.

UNDERGRADUATE EXPENSES for 2010–11 ***Application fee:*** $30. ***Comprehensive fee:*** $30,085 includes full-time tuition ($19,970), mandatory fees ($725), and room and board ($9390). ***College room only:*** $5000. Full-time tuition and fees vary according to program. Part-time tuition and fees vary according to program. ***Payment plan:*** Installment.

FRESHMAN FINANCIAL AID (Fall 2009) 256 applied for aid; of those 93% were deemed to have need. 100% of freshmen with need received aid; of those 3% had need fully met. ***Average percent of need met:*** 86% (excluding resources awarded to replace EFC). ***Average financial aid package:*** $18,034 (excluding resources awarded to replace EFC). 6% of all full-time freshmen had no need and received non-need-based gift aid.

UNDERGRADUATE FINANCIAL AID (Fall 2009) 881 applied for aid; of those 92% were deemed to have need. 100% of undergraduates with need received aid; of those 4% had need fully met. ***Average percent of need met:*** 79% (excluding resources awarded to replace EFC). ***Average financial aid package:*** $17,989 (excluding resources awarded to replace EFC). 7% of all full-time undergraduates had no need and received non-need-based gift aid.

GIFT AID (NEED-BASED) ***Total amount:*** $9,655,487 (15% federal, 10% state, 71% institutional, 4% external sources). ***Receiving aid:*** Freshmen: 86% (238); all full-time undergraduates: 91% (810). ***Average award:*** Freshmen: $12,437; Undergraduates: $11,502. ***Scholarships, grants, and awards:*** Federal Pell, FSEOG, state, private, college/university gift aid from institutional funds.

GIFT AID (NON-NEED-BASED) ***Receiving aid:*** Freshmen: 6% (16). Undergraduates: 7% (61). ***Average award:*** Freshmen: $6382. Undergraduates: $6875. ***Scholarships, grants, and awards by category:*** *Academic interests/achievement:* general academic interests/achievements.

LOANS ***Student loans:*** $7,142,540 (100% need-based). 91% of past graduating class borrowed through all loan programs. *Average indebtedness per student:* $22,036. ***Average need-based loan:*** Freshmen: $5893. Undergraduates: $6487. ***Parent loans:*** $3,267,067 (100% need-based). ***Programs:*** Federal Direct (Subsidized and Unsubsidized Stafford, PLUS), Perkins.

WORK-STUDY ***Federal work-study:*** Total amount: $277,094; jobs available (averaging $2000). ***State or other work-study/employment:*** Part-time jobs available.

APPLYING FOR FINANCIAL AID ***Required financial aid forms:*** FAFSA, state aid form. ***Financial aid deadline (priority):*** 3/15. ***Notification date:*** Continuous. Students must reply within 4 weeks of notification.

CONTACT Mary Ellen Chamberlain, Director of Financial Aid, Paul Smith's College, Routes 86 and 30, Paul Smiths, NY 12970, 518-327-6119 or toll-free 800-421-2605. *Fax:* 518-327-6055. *E-mail:* mchamberlain@paulsmiths.edu.

PEABODY CONSERVATORY OF THE JOHNS HOPKINS UNIVERSITY

Baltimore, MD

Tuition & fees: $37,425 **Average undergraduate aid package: $15,694**

ABOUT THE INSTITUTION Independent, coed. 9 undergraduate majors. Federal methodology is used as a basis for awarding need-based institutional aid.

UNDERGRADUATE EXPENSES for 2011–12 ***One-time required fee:*** $700. ***Comprehensive fee:*** $49,625 includes full-time tuition ($37,000), mandatory fees ($425), and room and board ($12,200). Full-time tuition and fees vary according to program. Room and board charges vary according to board plan. ***Part-time tuition:*** $1055 per semester hour. Part-time tuition and fees vary according to course load. ***Payment plan:*** Installment.

FRESHMAN FINANCIAL AID (Fall 2010, est.) 71 applied for aid; of those 86% were deemed to have need. 97% of freshmen with need received aid; of those 17% had need fully met. ***Average percent of need met:*** 68% (excluding resources awarded to replace EFC). ***Average financial aid package:*** $16,458 (excluding resources awarded to replace EFC). 20% of all full-time freshmen had no need and received non-need-based gift aid.

UNDERGRADUATE FINANCIAL AID (Fall 2010, est.) 226 applied for aid; of those 88% were deemed to have need. 98% of undergraduates with need received aid; of those 22% had need fully met. ***Average percent of need met:*** 72% (excluding resources awarded to replace EFC). ***Average financial aid package:*** $15,694 (excluding resources awarded to replace EFC). 26% of all full-time undergraduates had no need and received non-need-based gift aid.

GIFT AID (NEED-BASED) ***Total amount:*** $3,856,330 (10% federal, 2% state, 85% institutional, 3% external sources). ***Receiving aid:*** Freshmen: 61% (51); all full-time undergraduates: 57% (179). ***Average award:*** Freshmen: $13,012; Undergraduates: $12,281. ***Scholarships, grants, and awards:*** Federal Pell, FSEOG, state, private, college/university gift aid from institutional funds.

GIFT AID (NON-NEED-BASED) ***Total amount:*** $1,199,695 (1% state, 97% institutional, 2% external sources). ***Receiving aid:*** Freshmen: 20% (17). Undergraduates: 26% (83). ***Average award:*** Freshmen: $12,441. Undergraduates: $14,314. ***Scholarships, grants, and awards by category:*** *Creative arts/performance:* 278 awards ($4,348,719 total): music.

LOANS ***Student loans:*** $3,137,428 (87% need-based, 13% non-need-based). 48% of past graduating class borrowed through all loan programs. *Average indebtedness per student:* $38,034. ***Average need-based loan:*** Freshmen: $3416. Undergraduates: $5014. ***Parent loans:*** $1,165,862 (100% need-based). ***Programs:*** Federal Direct (Subsidized and Unsubsidized Stafford, PLUS), Perkins, college/university.

WORK-STUDY ***Federal work-study:*** Total amount: $235,941; 108 jobs averaging $2163.

APPLYING FOR FINANCIAL AID ***Required financial aid forms:*** FAFSA, Peabody International Student Financial Aid and Scholarship Application. ***Financial aid deadline (priority):*** 2/1. ***Notification date:*** 4/1. Students must reply by 5/1.

CONTACT Rebecca Polgar, Director of Financial Aid, Peabody Conservatory of The Johns Hopkins University, 1 East Mount Vernon Place, Baltimore, MD 21202-2397, 410-234-4900 or toll-free 800-368-2521 (out-of-state). *Fax:* 410-659-8102. *E-mail:* finaid@peabody.jhu.edu.

PEACE COLLEGE

Raleigh, NC

ABOUT THE INSTITUTION Independent religious, women only. 17 undergraduate majors.

GIFT AID (NEED-BASED) ***Scholarships, grants, and awards:*** Federal Pell, FSEOG, state, private, college/university gift aid from institutional funds.

GIFT AID (NON-NEED-BASED) ***Scholarships, grants, and awards by category:*** *Academic interests/achievement:* general academic interests/achievements. *Creative arts/performance:* art/fine arts, music, theater/drama. *Special characteristics:* children of faculty/staff, relatives of clergy, siblings of current students.

LOANS ***Programs:*** Federal Direct (Subsidized and Unsubsidized Stafford, PLUS), alternative loans.

WORK-STUDY ***Federal work-study:*** Total amount: $303,500; 222 jobs averaging $1840. ***State or other work-study/employment:*** Total amount: $45,195 (55% need-based, 45% non-need-based). 17 part-time jobs averaging $1307.

APPLYING FOR FINANCIAL AID ***Required financial aid form:*** FAFSA.

CONTACT Ms. Angela J. Kirkley, Director of Financial Aid, Peace College, 15 East Peace Street, Raleigh, NC 27604, 919-508-2249 or toll-free 800-PEACE-47. *Fax:* 919-508-2325. *E-mail:* akirkley@peace.edu.

PEIRCE COLLEGE

Philadelphia, PA

Tuition & fees: $15,900 **Average undergraduate aid package: $10,628**

ABOUT THE INSTITUTION Independent, coed, primarily women. 16 undergraduate majors. Federal methodology is used as a basis for awarding need-based institutional aid.

UNDERGRADUATE EXPENSES for 2011–12 ***Tuition:*** full-time $14,850; part-time $495 per credit. Full-time tuition and fees vary according to course load. Part-time tuition and fees vary according to course load. ***Payment plan:*** Installment.

FRESHMAN FINANCIAL AID (Fall 2009) 16 applied for aid; of those 100% were deemed to have need. 94% of freshmen with need received aid. ***Average percent of need met:*** 53% (excluding resources awarded to replace EFC). ***Average financial aid package:*** $11,827 (excluding resources awarded to replace EFC). 6% of all full-time freshmen had no need and received non-need-based gift aid.

UNDERGRADUATE FINANCIAL AID (Fall 2009) 615 applied for aid; of those 90% were deemed to have need. 96% of undergraduates with need received aid; of those 3% had need fully met. ***Average percent of need met:*** 56% (excluding resources awarded to replace EFC). ***Average financial aid package:*** $10,628 (excluding resources awarded to replace EFC). 5% of all full-time undergraduates had no need and received non-need-based gift aid.

GIFT AID (NEED-BASED) ***Total amount:*** $6,171,887 (73% federal, 25% state, 2% institutional). ***Receiving aid:*** Freshmen: 69% (11); all full-time undergraduates: 61% (508). ***Average award:*** Freshmen: $5968; Undergraduates: $6323. ***Scholarships, grants, and awards:*** Federal Pell, FSEOG, state, college/university gift aid from institutional funds.

GIFT AID (NON-NEED-BASED) ***Total amount:*** $819,584 (100% institutional). ***Receiving aid:*** Freshmen: 31% (5). Undergraduates: 2% (14). ***Average award:*** Freshmen: $5251. Undergraduates: $2221. ***Scholarships, grants, and awards by category:*** *Academic interests/achievement:* 57 awards ($198,223 total): business, computer science. *Special achievements/activities:* 10 awards ($17,764 total): leadership, memberships. *Special characteristics:* 115 awards ($227,673 total): children and siblings of alumni, children of public servants, international students. ***Tuition waivers:*** Full or partial for children of alumni, employees or children of employees.

LOANS ***Student loans:*** $15,528,219 (46% need-based, 54% non-need-based). 71% of past graduating class borrowed through all loan programs. *Average indebtedness per student:* $18,721. ***Average need-based loan:*** Freshmen: $3781. Undergraduates: $4944. ***Parent loans:*** $33,550 (100% need-based). ***Programs:*** Federal Direct (Subsidized and Unsubsidized Stafford, PLUS).

WORK-STUDY ***Federal work-study:*** Total amount: $143,952; 32 jobs averaging $3600.

APPLYING FOR FINANCIAL AID ***Required financial aid form:*** FAFSA. ***Financial aid deadline:*** Continuous. ***Notification date:*** Continuous beginning 5/1.

CONTACT Lisa A. Gargiulo, Program Manager for Financial Aid, Peirce College, 1420 Pine Street, Philadelphia, PA 19102, 215-670-9370 or toll-free 888-467-3472. *Fax:* 215-545-3671. *E-mail:* lagargiulo@peirce.edu.

PENN FOSTER COLLEGE

Scottsdale, AZ

CONTACT Financial Aid Office, Penn Foster College, 14300 North Northsight Boulevard, Suite 120, Scottsdale, AZ 85260, 480-947-6644 or toll-free 800-471-3232 (in-state).

PENN STATE ABINGTON

Abington, PA

Tuition & fees (PA res): $12,730 Average undergraduate aid package: $9852

ABOUT THE INSTITUTION State-related, coed. 118 undergraduate majors. Federal methodology is used as a basis for awarding need-based institutional aid.

UNDERGRADUATE EXPENSES for 2010–11 ***Tuition, state resident:*** full-time $11,892; part-time $481 per credit. ***Tuition, nonresident:*** full-time $18,148; part-time $756 per credit. ***Required fees:*** full-time $838. Full-time tuition and fees vary according to course level, degree level, location, program, and student level. Part-time tuition and fees vary according to course level, course load, degree level, location, program, and student level. ***Payment plans:*** Installment, deferred payment.

FRESHMAN FINANCIAL AID (Fall 2009) 755 applied for aid; of those 78% were deemed to have need. 98% of freshmen with need received aid; of those 3% had need fully met. ***Average percent of need met:*** 57% (excluding resources awarded to replace EFC). ***Average financial aid package:*** $9768 (excluding resources awarded to replace EFC). 4% of all full-time freshmen had no need and received non-need-based gift aid.

UNDERGRADUATE FINANCIAL AID (Fall 2009) 2,217 applied for aid; of those 81% were deemed to have need. 98% of undergraduates with need received aid; of those 4% had need fully met. ***Average percent of need met:*** 58% (excluding resources awarded to replace EFC). ***Average financial aid package:*** $9852 (excluding resources awarded to replace EFC). 3% of all full-time undergraduates had no need and received non-need-based gift aid.

GIFT AID (NEED-BASED) ***Total amount:*** $11,853,269 (56% federal, 28% state, 12% institutional, 4% external sources). ***Receiving aid:*** Freshmen: 58% (489); all full-time undergraduates: 55% (1,451). ***Average award:*** Freshmen: $7369; Undergraduates: $6978. ***Scholarships, grants, and awards:*** Federal Pell, FSEOG, state, private, college/university gift aid from institutional funds.

GIFT AID (NON-NEED-BASED) ***Total amount:*** $501,248 (32% federal, 41% institutional, 27% external sources). ***Receiving aid:*** Freshmen: 34% (289). Undergraduates: 18% (467). ***Average award:*** Freshmen: $1767. Undergraduates: $1795. ***Scholarships, grants, and awards by category:*** *Academic interests/achievement:* general academic interests/achievements. *Special characteristics:* children and siblings of alumni, general special characteristics. ***Tuition waivers:*** Full or partial for employees or children of employees, senior citizens.

LOANS ***Student loans:*** $14,740,424 (80% need-based, 20% non-need-based). 67% of past graduating class borrowed through all loan programs. *Average indebtedness per student:* $31,135. ***Average need-based loan:*** Freshmen: $3249. Undergraduates: $3937. ***Parent loans:*** $1,592,377 (58% need-based, 42% non-need-based). ***Programs:*** Federal Direct (Subsidized and Unsubsidized Stafford, PLUS), Perkins, college/university, private loans.

WORK-STUDY ***Federal work-study:*** Total amount: $124,303; jobs available.

APPLYING FOR FINANCIAL AID ***Required financial aid form:*** FAFSA. ***Financial aid deadline (priority):*** 2/15. ***Notification date:*** Continuous.

CONTACT Debbie Meditz, Assistant Student Aid Coordinator, Penn State Abington, 106 Sutherland Building, 1600 Woodland Road, Abington, PA 19001, 215-881-7348. *Fax:* 215-881-7655. *E-mail:* dlm175@psu.edu.

PENN STATE ALTOONA

Altoona, PA

Tuition & fees (PA res): $13,250 Average undergraduate aid package: $9298

ABOUT THE INSTITUTION State-related, coed. 125 undergraduate majors. Federal methodology is used as a basis for awarding need-based institutional aid.

UNDERGRADUATE EXPENSES for 2010–11 ***Tuition, state resident:*** full-time $12,412; part-time $517 per credit. ***Tuition, nonresident:*** full-time $18,990; part-time $791 per credit. ***Required fees:*** full-time $838. Full-time tuition and fees vary according to course level, degree level, location, program, and student level. Part-time tuition and fees vary according to course level, course load, degree level, location, program, and student level. ***College room and board:*** $8370; ***Room only:*** $4540. Room and board charges vary according to board plan, housing facility, and location. ***Payment plans:*** Installment, deferred payment.

FRESHMAN FINANCIAL AID (Fall 2009) 1,358 applied for aid; of those 77% were deemed to have need. 96% of freshmen with need received aid; of those 4% had need fully met. ***Average percent of need met:*** 52% (excluding resources awarded to replace EFC). ***Average financial aid package:*** $8356 (excluding resources awarded to replace EFC). 2% of all full-time freshmen had no need and received non-need-based gift aid.

UNDERGRADUATE FINANCIAL AID (Fall 2009) 3,238 applied for aid; of those 83% were deemed to have need. 97% of undergraduates with need received aid; of those 5% had need fully met. ***Average percent of need met:*** 55% (excluding resources awarded to replace EFC). ***Average financial aid package:*** $9298 (excluding resources awarded to replace EFC). 3% of all full-time undergraduates had no need and received non-need-based gift aid.

GIFT AID (NEED-BASED) ***Total amount:*** $13,372,808 (51% federal, 32% state, 13% institutional, 4% external sources). ***Receiving aid:*** Freshmen: 40% (633); all full-time undergraduates: 46% (1,763). ***Average award:*** Freshmen: $6237; Undergraduates: $6126. ***Scholarships, grants, and awards:*** Federal Pell, FSEOG, state, private, college/university gift aid from institutional funds.

GIFT AID (NON-NEED-BASED) ***Total amount:*** $837,772 (46% federal, 2% state, 22% institutional, 30% external sources). ***Receiving aid:*** Freshmen: 20% (319). Undergraduates: 20% (777). ***Average award:*** Freshmen: $1110. Undergraduates: $1473. ***Scholarships, grants, and awards by category:*** *Academic interests/achievement:* general academic interests/achievements. *Special characteristics:* children and siblings of alumni, general special characteristics. ***Tuition waivers:*** Full or partial for employees or children of employees.

LOANS ***Student loans:*** $24,807,426 (88% need-based, 12% non-need-based). 67% of past graduating class borrowed through all loan programs. *Average indebtedness per student:* $31,135. ***Average need-based loan:*** Freshmen: $3390. Undergraduates: $4083. ***Parent loans:*** $8,260,252 (80% need-based, 20% non-need-based). ***Programs:*** Federal Direct (Subsidized and Unsubsidized Stafford, PLUS), Perkins, college/university, private loans.

WORK-STUDY ***Federal work-study:*** Total amount: $337,063; jobs available.

APPLYING FOR FINANCIAL AID ***Required financial aid form:*** FAFSA. ***Financial aid deadline (priority):*** 2/15. ***Notification date:*** Continuous beginning 3/1.

CONTACT Mr. David Pearlman, Assistant Director of Student Affairs, Penn State Altoona, W111 Smith Building, Altoona, PA 16601-3760, 814-949-5055 or toll-free 800-848-9843. *Fax:* 814-949-5536. *E-mail:* dpp1@psu.edu.

PENN STATE BERKS

Reading, PA

Tuition & fees (PA res): $13,250 Average undergraduate aid package: $9088

ABOUT THE INSTITUTION State-related, coed. 129 undergraduate majors. Federal methodology is used as a basis for awarding need-based institutional aid.

UNDERGRADUATE EXPENSES for 2010–11 ***Tuition, state resident:*** full-time $12,412; part-time $517 per credit. ***Tuition, nonresident:*** full-time $18,990; part-time $791 per credit. ***Required fees:*** full-time $838. Full-time tuition and fees vary according to course level, degree level, location, program, and student level. Part-time tuition and fees vary according to course level, course load, degree level, location, program, and student level. ***College room and board:*** $9160; ***Room only:*** $5330. Room and board charges vary according to board plan, housing facility, and location. ***Payment plans:*** Installment, deferred payment.

FRESHMAN FINANCIAL AID (Fall 2009) 697 applied for aid; of those 76% were deemed to have need. 95% of freshmen with need received aid; of those 3% had need fully met. ***Average percent of need met:*** 53% (excluding resources awarded to replace EFC). ***Average financial aid package:*** $8501 (excluding resources awarded to replace EFC). 1% of all full-time freshmen had no need and received non-need-based gift aid.

UNDERGRADUATE FINANCIAL AID (Fall 2009) 1,915 applied for aid; of those 79% were deemed to have need. 97% of undergraduates with need received aid; of those 4% had need fully met. ***Average percent of need met:*** 55% (excluding resources awarded to replace EFC). ***Average financial aid package:***

$9088 (excluding resources awarded to replace EFC). 2% of all full-time undergraduates had no need and received non-need-based gift aid.

GIFT AID (NEED-BASED) ***Total amount:*** $7,557,944 (47% federal, 32% state, 16% institutional, 5% external sources). ***Receiving aid:*** Freshmen: 42% (328); all full-time undergraduates: 43% (1,003). ***Average award:*** Freshmen: $6710; Undergraduates: $6344. ***Scholarships, grants, and awards:*** Federal Pell, FSEOG, state, private, college/university gift aid from institutional funds.

GIFT AID (NON-NEED-BASED) ***Total amount:*** $431,803 (32% federal, 6% state, 21% institutional, 41% external sources). ***Receiving aid:*** Freshmen: 20% (159). Undergraduates: 15% (354). ***Average award:*** Freshmen: $874. Undergraduates: $1513. ***Scholarships, grants, and awards by category:*** *Academic interests/achievement:* general academic interests/achievements. *Special characteristics:* children and siblings of alumni. ***Tuition waivers:*** Full or partial for employees or children of employees.

LOANS ***Student loans:*** $14,040,830 (82% need-based, 18% non-need-based). 67% of past graduating class borrowed through all loan programs. *Average indebtedness per student:* $31,135. ***Average need-based loan:*** Freshmen: $3438. Undergraduates: $4113. ***Parent loans:*** $5,211,660 (81% need-based, 19% non-need-based). ***Programs:*** Federal Direct (Subsidized and Unsubsidized Stafford, PLUS), Perkins, college/university, private loans.

WORK-STUDY ***Federal work-study:*** Total amount: $124,022; jobs available.

APPLYING FOR FINANCIAL AID ***Required financial aid form:*** FAFSA. ***Financial aid deadline (priority):*** 2/15. ***Notification date:*** Continuous beginning 3/1.

CONTACT Maryann Hubick, Financial Aid Coordinator, Penn State Berks, Perkins Student Center, Room 6, Reading, PA 19610-6009, 610-396-6071. *Fax:* 610-396-6077. *E-mail:* mxh61@psu.edu.

PENN STATE ERIE, THE BEHREND COLLEGE

Erie, PA

Tuition & fees (PA res): $13,250 Average undergraduate aid package: $9651

ABOUT THE INSTITUTION State-related, coed. 129 undergraduate majors. Federal methodology is used as a basis for awarding need-based institutional aid.

UNDERGRADUATE EXPENSES for 2010–11 ***Tuition, state resident:*** full-time $12,412; part-time $517 per credit. ***Tuition, nonresident:*** full-time $18,990; part-time $791 per credit. ***Required fees:*** full-time $838. Full-time tuition and fees vary according to course level, degree level, location, program, and student level. Part-time tuition and fees vary according to course level, course load, degree level, location, program, and student level. ***College room and board:*** $8370; ***Room only:*** $4540. Room and board charges vary according to board plan, housing facility, and location. ***Payment plans:*** Installment, deferred payment.

FRESHMAN FINANCIAL AID (Fall 2009) 991 applied for aid; of those 83% were deemed to have need. 97% of freshmen with need received aid; of those 4% had need fully met. ***Average percent of need met:*** 56% (excluding resources awarded to replace EFC). ***Average financial aid package:*** $8641 (excluding resources awarded to replace EFC). 1% of all full-time freshmen had no need and received non-need-based gift aid.

UNDERGRADUATE FINANCIAL AID (Fall 2009) 3,418 applied for aid; of those 85% were deemed to have need. 98% of undergraduates with need received aid; of those 4% had need fully met. ***Average percent of need met:*** 58% (excluding resources awarded to replace EFC). ***Average financial aid package:*** $9651 (excluding resources awarded to replace EFC). 2% of all full-time undergraduates had no need and received non-need-based gift aid.

GIFT AID (NEED-BASED) ***Total amount:*** $15,449,518 (41% federal, 34% state, 18% institutional, 7% external sources). ***Receiving aid:*** Freshmen: 50% (541); all full-time undergraduates: 50% (1,943). ***Average award:*** Freshmen: $6203; Undergraduates: $6176. ***Scholarships, grants, and awards:*** Federal Pell, FSEOG, state, private, college/university gift aid from institutional funds.

GIFT AID (NON-NEED-BASED) ***Total amount:*** $627,297 (14% federal, 4% state, 42% institutional, 40% external sources). ***Receiving aid:*** Freshmen: 23% (254). Undergraduates: 21% (809). ***Average award:*** Freshmen: $1149. Undergraduates: $3967. ***Scholarships, grants, and awards by category:*** *Academic interests/achievement:* general academic interests/achievements. *Special characteristics:* children and siblings of alumni. ***Tuition waivers:*** Full or partial for employees or children of employees.

LOANS ***Student loans:*** $27,719,044 (89% need-based, 11% non-need-based). 67% of past graduating class borrowed through all loan programs. *Average indebtedness per student:* $31,135. ***Average need-based loan:*** Freshmen: $3575. Undergraduates: $4454. ***Parent loans:*** $10,454,865 (84% need-based, 16% non-need-based). ***Programs:*** Federal Direct (Subsidized and Unsubsidized Stafford, PLUS), Perkins, college/university, private loans.

WORK-STUDY ***Federal work-study:*** Total amount: $348,883; jobs available.

APPLYING FOR FINANCIAL AID ***Required financial aid form:*** FAFSA. ***Financial aid deadline (priority):*** 2/15. ***Notification date:*** Continuous beginning 3/1.

CONTACT Ms. Jane Brady, Assistant Director of Admissions and Financial Aid, Penn State Erie, The Behrend College, 5091 Station Road, Erie, PA 16802, 814-898-6162 or toll-free 866-374-3378. *Fax:* 814-898-7595. *E-mail:* jub9@psu.edu.

PENN STATE HARRISBURG

Middletown, PA

Tuition & fees (PA res): $13,240 Average undergraduate aid package: $9974

ABOUT THE INSTITUTION State-related, coed. 29 undergraduate majors. Federal methodology is used as a basis for awarding need-based institutional aid.

UNDERGRADUATE EXPENSES for 2010–11 ***Tuition, state resident:*** full-time $12,412; part-time $517 per credit. ***Tuition, nonresident:*** full-time $18,990; part-time $791 per credit. ***Required fees:*** full-time $828. Full-time tuition and fees vary according to course level, degree level, location, program, and student level. Part-time tuition and fees vary according to course level, course load, degree level, location, program, and student level. ***College room and board:*** $9580; ***Room only:*** $5750. Room and board charges vary according to board plan, housing facility, and location. ***Payment plans:*** Installment, deferred payment.

FRESHMAN FINANCIAL AID (Fall 2009) 385 applied for aid; of those 76% were deemed to have need. 95% of freshmen with need received aid; of those 6% had need fully met. ***Average percent of need met:*** 49% (excluding resources awarded to replace EFC). ***Average financial aid package:*** $8943 (excluding resources awarded to replace EFC). 1% of all full-time freshmen had no need and received non-need-based gift aid.

UNDERGRADUATE FINANCIAL AID (Fall 2009) 1,743 applied for aid; of those 82% were deemed to have need. 96% of undergraduates with need received aid; of those 7% had need fully met. ***Average percent of need met:*** 56% (excluding resources awarded to replace EFC). ***Average financial aid package:*** $9974 (excluding resources awarded to replace EFC). 1% of all full-time undergraduates had no need and received non-need-based gift aid.

GIFT AID (NEED-BASED) ***Total amount:*** $7,786,282 (54% federal, 29% state, 13% institutional, 4% external sources). ***Receiving aid:*** Freshmen: 36% (168); all full-time undergraduates: 42% (924). ***Average award:*** Freshmen: $7155; Undergraduates: $6524. ***Scholarships, grants, and awards:*** Federal Pell, FSEOG, state, private, college/university gift aid from institutional funds.

GIFT AID (NON-NEED-BASED) ***Total amount:*** $616,200 (46% federal, 3% state, 7% institutional, 44% external sources). ***Receiving aid:*** Freshmen: 17% (81). Undergraduates: 16% (345). ***Average award:*** Freshmen: $812. Undergraduates: $1272. ***Scholarships, grants, and awards by category:*** *Academic interests/achievement:* general academic interests/achievements. *Special characteristics:* children and siblings of alumni, general special characteristics. ***Tuition waivers:*** Full or partial for employees or children of employees.

LOANS ***Student loans:*** $15,749,485 (84% need-based, 16% non-need-based). 67% of past graduating class borrowed through all loan programs. *Average indebtedness per student:* $31,135. ***Average need-based loan:*** Freshmen: $3417. Undergraduates: $4565. ***Parent loans:*** $3,445,015 (80% need-based, 20% non-need-based). ***Programs:*** Federal Direct (Subsidized and Unsubsidized Stafford, PLUS), Perkins, college/university, private loans.

WORK-STUDY ***Federal work-study:*** Total amount: $79,212; jobs available.

APPLYING FOR FINANCIAL AID ***Required financial aid form:*** FAFSA. ***Financial aid deadline (priority):*** 2/15. ***Notification date:*** Continuous beginning 3/1.

CONTACT Ms. Carolyn Julian, Student Aid Adviser, Penn State Harrisburg, W112 Olmstead, 777 West Harrisburg Pike, Middletown, PA 17057-4898, 717-948-6307 or toll-free 800-222-2056. *Fax:* 717-948-6008. *E-mail:* czb3@psu.edu.

PENN STATE UNIVERSITY PARK

State College, PA

Tuition & fees (PA res): $15,250 Average undergraduate aid package: $10,124

ABOUT THE INSTITUTION State-related, coed. 124 undergraduate majors. Federal methodology is used as a basis for awarding need-based institutional aid.

UNDERGRADUATE EXPENSES for 2010–11 ***Tuition, state resident:*** full-time $14,412; part-time $601 per credit. ***Tuition, nonresident:*** full-time $26,276; part-time $1095 per credit. ***Required fees:*** full-time $838. Full-time tuition and fees vary according to course level, degree level, location, program, and student level. Part-time tuition and fees vary according to course level, course load, degree level, location, program, and student level. ***College room and board:*** $8370; ***Room only:*** $4540. Room and board charges vary according to board plan, housing facility, and location. ***Payment plans:*** Installment, deferred payment.

FRESHMAN FINANCIAL AID (Fall 2010, est.) 4,855 applied for aid; of those 67% were deemed to have need. 94% of freshmen with need received aid; of those 8% had need fully met. ***Average percent of need met:*** 56% (excluding resources awarded to replace EFC). ***Average financial aid package:*** $9529 (excluding resources awarded to replace EFC). 7% of all full-time freshmen had no need and received non-need-based gift aid.

UNDERGRADUATE FINANCIAL AID (Fall 2010, est.) 25,071 applied for aid; of those 78% were deemed to have need. 97% of undergraduates with need received aid; of those 8% had need fully met. ***Average percent of need met:*** 58% (excluding resources awarded to replace EFC). ***Average financial aid package:*** $10,124 (excluding resources awarded to replace EFC). 7% of all full-time undergraduates had no need and received non-need-based gift aid.

GIFT AID (NEED-BASED) ***Total amount:*** $98,742,963 (40% federal, 24% state, 28% institutional, 8% external sources). ***Receiving aid:*** Freshmen: 24% (1,545); all full-time undergraduates: 28% (10,543). ***Average award:*** Freshmen: $6812; Undergraduates: $6607. ***Scholarships, grants, and awards:*** Federal Pell, FSEOG, state, private, college/university gift aid from institutional funds.

GIFT AID (NON-NEED-BASED) ***Total amount:*** $28,661,801 (16% federal, 1% state, 30% institutional, 53% external sources). ***Receiving aid:*** Freshmen: 24% (1,539). Undergraduates: 17% (6,262). ***Average award:*** Freshmen: $3304. Undergraduates: $3178. ***Scholarships, grants, and awards by category:*** *Academic interests/achievement:* general academic interests/achievements. *Special characteristics:* children and siblings of alumni. ***Tuition waivers:*** Full or partial for employees or children of employees.

LOANS ***Student loans:*** $214,387,926 (82% need-based, 18% non-need-based). 67% of past graduating class borrowed through all loan programs. *Average indebtedness per student:* $31,135. ***Average need-based loan:*** Freshmen: $3455. Undergraduates: $4676. ***Parent loans:*** $92,861,455 (81% need-based, 19% non-need-based). ***Programs:*** Federal Direct (Subsidized and Unsubsidized Stafford, PLUS), Perkins, college/university, private loans.

WORK-STUDY ***Federal work-study:*** Total amount: $1,865,705; jobs available.

ATHLETIC AWARDS Total amount: $11,700,676 (39% need-based, 61% non-need-based).

APPLYING FOR FINANCIAL AID ***Required financial aid form:*** FAFSA. ***Financial aid deadline (priority):*** 2/15. ***Notification date:*** Continuous.

CONTACT Ms. Anna Griswold, Assistant Vice Provost for Student Aid, Penn State University Park, 311 Shields Building, University Park, PA 16802, 814-863-0507. *Fax:* 814-863-0322. *E-mail:* amg5@psu.edu.

PENNSYLVANIA COLLEGE OF ART & DESIGN

Lancaster, PA

CONTACT J. David Hershey, Registrar/Director of Financial Aid, Pennsylvania College of Art & Design, 204 North Prince Street, PO Box 59, Lancaster, PA 17608-0059, 717-396-7833 Ext. 13. *Fax:* 717-396-1339. *E-mail:* finaid@pcad.edu.

PENNSYLVANIA COLLEGE OF TECHNOLOGY

Williamsport, PA

Tuition & fees (PA res): $13,080 **Average undergraduate aid package: $14,006**

ABOUT THE INSTITUTION State-related, coed. 84 undergraduate majors. Federal methodology is used as a basis for awarding need-based institutional aid.

UNDERGRADUATE EXPENSES for 2010–11 ***Tuition, state resident:*** full-time $11,040; part-time $368 per credit hour. ***Tuition, nonresident:*** full-time $14,340; part-time $478 per credit hour. ***Required fees:*** full-time $2040; $68 per credit. Full-time tuition and fees vary according to course load and program. Part-time tuition and fees vary according to course load and program. ***College room and board:*** $9500; ***Room only:*** $5500. Room and board charges vary according to board plan and housing facility. ***Payment plan:*** Deferred payment.

FRESHMAN FINANCIAL AID (Fall 2009) 1,348 applied for aid; of those 78% were deemed to have need. 100% of freshmen with need received aid.

UNDERGRADUATE FINANCIAL AID (Fall 2009) 6,763 applied for aid; of those 78% were deemed to have need. 100% of undergraduates with need received aid. ***Average percent of need met:*** 78% (excluding resources awarded to replace EFC). ***Average financial aid package:*** $14,006 (excluding resources awarded to replace EFC).

GIFT AID (NEED-BASED) ***Receiving aid:*** Freshmen: 78% (1,056); all full-time undergraduates: 78% (5,296). ***Average award:*** Undergraduates: $3243. ***Scholarships, grants, and awards:*** Federal Pell, FSEOG, state, private, college/university gift aid from institutional funds.

GIFT AID (NON-NEED-BASED) ***Total amount:*** $30,609,514 (40% federal, 25% state, 2% institutional, 33% external sources). ***Tuition waivers:*** Full or partial for employees or children of employees.

LOANS ***Student loans:*** $47,760,019 (100% non-need-based). ***Parent loans:*** $20,778,132 (50% need-based, 50% non-need-based). ***Programs:*** Federal Direct (Subsidized and Unsubsidized Stafford, PLUS).

WORK-STUDY ***Federal work-study:*** Total amount: $316,651; 191 jobs averaging $1658. ***State or other work-study/employment:*** Total amount: $591,035 (100% non-need-based). 374 part-time jobs averaging $1580.

APPLYING FOR FINANCIAL AID ***Required financial aid forms:*** FAFSA, institution's own form. ***Financial aid deadline (priority):*** 4/1. ***Notification date:*** Continuous beginning 6/1. Students must reply within 2 weeks of notification.

CONTACT Candace Baran, Director of Financial Aid, Pennsylvania College of Technology, One College Avenue, Williamsport, PA 17701, 570-326-4766 or toll-free 800-367-9222 (in-state). *Fax:* 570-321-5552. *E-mail:* cbaran@pct.edu.

PEPPERDINE UNIVERSITY

Malibu, CA

Tuition & fees: $39,080 **Average undergraduate aid package: $33,248**

ABOUT THE INSTITUTION Independent religious, coed. 47 undergraduate majors. Federal methodology is used as a basis for awarding need-based institutional aid.

UNDERGRADUATE EXPENSES for 2010–11 ***Comprehensive fee:*** $50,470 includes full-time tuition ($38,960), mandatory fees ($120), and room and board ($11,390). ***College room only:*** $8760. Room and board charges vary according to board plan and housing facility. ***Part-time tuition:*** $1210 per credit hour. ***Payment plan:*** Installment.

FRESHMAN FINANCIAL AID (Fall 2010, est.) 434 applied for aid; of those 85% were deemed to have need. 100% of freshmen with need received aid; of those 23% had need fully met. ***Average percent of need met:*** 79% (excluding resources awarded to replace EFC). ***Average financial aid package:*** $34,994 (excluding resources awarded to replace EFC). 7% of all full-time freshmen had no need and received non-need-based gift aid.

UNDERGRADUATE FINANCIAL AID (Fall 2010, est.) 1,816 applied for aid; of those 82% were deemed to have need. 100% of undergraduates with need received aid; of those 23% had need fully met. ***Average percent of need met:*** 75% (excluding resources awarded to replace EFC). ***Average financial aid package:*** $33,248 (excluding resources awarded to replace EFC). 8% of all full-time undergraduates had no need and received non-need-based gift aid.

GIFT AID (NEED-BASED) ***Total amount:*** $45,822,840 (9% federal, 8% state, 81% institutional, 2% external sources). ***Receiving aid:*** Freshmen: 56% (343); all full-time undergraduates: 47% (1,394). ***Average award:*** Freshmen: $31,826; Undergraduates: $30,089. ***Scholarships, grants, and awards:*** Federal Pell, FSEOG, state, private, college/university gift aid from institutional funds, United Negro College Fund, Academic Competitiveness Grants, National SMART Grants.

GIFT AID (NON-NEED-BASED) ***Total amount:*** $9,960,139 (87% institutional, 13% external sources). ***Receiving aid:*** Freshmen: 54% (329). Undergraduates: 46% (1,368). ***Average award:*** Freshmen: $21,963. Undergraduates: $20,522. ***Tuition waivers:*** Full or partial for employees or children of employees.

LOANS ***Student loans:*** $13,166,306 (87% need-based, 13% non-need-based). 57% of past graduating class borrowed through all loan programs. *Average indebtedness per student:* $35,747. ***Average need-based loan:*** Freshmen: $3479. Undergraduates: $4437. ***Parent loans:*** $12,806,019 (83% need-based, 17% non-need-based). ***Programs:*** Federal Direct (Subsidized and Unsubsidized Stafford, PLUS), Perkins, college/university.

WORK-STUDY ***Federal work-study:*** Total amount: $965,000; jobs available. ***State or other work-study/employment:*** Total amount: $676,781 (67% need-based, 33% non-need-based). Part-time jobs available.

ATHLETIC AWARDS Total amount: $4,496,589 (33% need-based, 67% non-need-based).

APPLYING FOR FINANCIAL AID ***Required financial aid form:*** FAFSA. ***Financial aid deadline:*** 2/15. ***Notification date:*** 4/15.

CONTACT Ms. Janet Lockhart, Director of Financial Assistance, Pepperdine University, 24255 Pacific Coast Highway, Malibu, CA 90263-4301, 310-506-4301. *Fax:* 310-506-4746. *E-mail:* janet.lockhart@pepperdine.edu.

PERELANDRA COLLEGE

La Mesa, CA

CONTACT Financial Aid Office, Perelandra College, 8697-C La Mesa Boulevard, PMB 21, La Mesa, CA 91941, 619-677-3308.

PERU STATE COLLEGE

Peru, NE

CONTACT Diana Lind, Director of Financial Aid, Peru State College, PO Box 10, Peru, NE 68421, 402-872-2228 or toll-free 800-742-4412 (in-state). *Fax:* 402-872-2419. *E-mail:* finaid@oakmail.peru.edu.

PFEIFFER UNIVERSITY

Misenheimer, NC

ABOUT THE INSTITUTION Independent United Methodist, coed. ***Awards:*** bachelor's and master's degrees. 45 undergraduate majors. ***Total enrollment:*** 2,019. Undergraduates: 1,089.

GIFT AID (NEED-BASED) ***Scholarships, grants, and awards:*** Federal Pell, FSEOG, state, private, college/university gift aid from institutional funds, United Negro College Fund.

GIFT AID (NON-NEED-BASED) ***Scholarships, grants, and awards by category:*** *Academic interests/achievement:* general academic interests/achievements. *Creative arts/performance:* music. *Special achievements/activities:* leadership, religious involvement. *Special characteristics:* children and siblings of alumni, children of educators, children of faculty/staff.

LOANS ***Programs:*** Perkins, state, college/university.

WORK-STUDY ***Federal work-study:*** Total amount: $256,396; jobs available.

APPLYING FOR FINANCIAL AID ***Required financial aid forms:*** FAFSA, state aid form, noncustodial (divorced/separated) parent's statement.

CONTACT Amy Brown, Director of Financial Aid, Pfeiffer University, PO Box 960, Misenheimer, NC 28109, 704-463-1360 Ext. 3046 or toll-free 800-338-2060. *Fax:* 704-463-1363. *E-mail:* amy.brown@pfeiffer.edu.

PHILADELPHIA BIBLICAL UNIVERSITY

Langhorne, PA

Tuition & fees: $20,888 **Average undergraduate aid package: $14,502**

ABOUT THE INSTITUTION Independent nondenominational, coed. 11 undergraduate majors. Federal methodology is used as a basis for awarding need-based institutional aid.

UNDERGRADUATE EXPENSES for 2011–12 ***Comprehensive fee:*** $29,163 includes full-time tuition ($20,688), mandatory fees ($200), and room and board ($8275). ***College room only:*** $4400. Full-time tuition and fees vary according to course load and location. Room and board charges vary according to board plan, housing facility, and location. ***Part-time tuition:*** $613 per credit. Part-time tuition and fees vary according to course load and location. ***Payment plan:*** Installment.

FRESHMAN FINANCIAL AID (Fall 2010, est.) 143 applied for aid; of those 99% were deemed to have need. 100% of freshmen with need received aid; of those 8% had need fully met. ***Average percent of need met:*** 69% (excluding resources awarded to replace EFC). ***Average financial aid package:*** $15,215 (excluding resources awarded to replace EFC). 10% of all full-time freshmen had no need and received non-need-based gift aid.

UNDERGRADUATE FINANCIAL AID (Fall 2010, est.) 988 applied for aid; of those 85% were deemed to have need. 97% of undergraduates with need received aid; of those 12% had need fully met. ***Average percent of need met:*** 66% (excluding resources awarded to replace EFC). ***Average financial aid package:*** $14,502 (excluding resources awarded to replace EFC). 6% of all full-time undergraduates had no need and received non-need-based gift aid.

GIFT AID (NEED-BASED) ***Total amount:*** $8,174,480 (24% federal, 9% state, 65% institutional, 2% external sources). ***Receiving aid:*** Freshmen: 87% (139); all full-time undergraduates: 78% (781). ***Average award:*** Freshmen: $11,538; Undergraduates: $10,340. ***Scholarships, grants, and awards:*** Federal Pell, FSEOG, state, private, college/university gift aid from institutional funds.

GIFT AID (NON-NEED-BASED) ***Total amount:*** $631,882 (11% federal, 87% institutional, 2% external sources). ***Receiving aid:*** Freshmen: 8% (12). Undergraduates: 7% (72). ***Average award:*** Freshmen: $6406. Undergraduates: $6646. ***Scholarships, grants, and awards by category:*** *Academic interests/achievement:* 668 awards ($4,017,401 total): general academic interests/achievements. *Creative arts/performance:* 38 awards ($59,250 total): music. *Special achievements/activities:* 16 awards ($25,750 total): general special achievements/activities. *Special characteristics:* 129 awards ($493,556 total): children of faculty/staff, relatives of clergy. ***Tuition waivers:*** Full or partial for employees or children of employees.

LOANS ***Student loans:*** $6,711,626 (82% need-based, 18% non-need-based). 96% of past graduating class borrowed through all loan programs. *Average indebtedness per student:* $25,971. ***Average need-based loan:*** Freshmen: $4148. Undergraduates: $5062. ***Parent loans:*** $1,104,584 (42% need-based, 58% non-need-based). ***Programs:*** Federal Direct (Subsidized and Unsubsidized Stafford, PLUS), state.

WORK-STUDY ***Federal work-study:*** Total amount: $86,102; 92 jobs averaging $989.

APPLYING FOR FINANCIAL AID ***Required financial aid form:*** FAFSA. ***Financial aid deadline:*** Continuous. ***Notification date:*** Continuous beginning 2/15. Students must reply within 2 weeks of notification.

CONTACT Ms. Raye Thompson, Director of Financial Aid, Philadelphia Biblical University, 200 Manor Avenue, Langhorne, PA 19047-2990, 215-702-4243 or toll-free 800-366-0049. *Fax:* 215-702-4248. *E-mail:* rthompson@pbu.edu.

PHILADELPHIA UNIVERSITY

Philadelphia, PA

Tuition & fees: $28,890 **Average undergraduate aid package: $23,477**

ABOUT THE INSTITUTION Independent, coed. 32 undergraduate majors. Federal methodology is used as a basis for awarding need-based institutional aid.

UNDERGRADUATE EXPENSES for 2010–11 ***Comprehensive fee:*** $38,392 includes full-time tuition ($28,800), mandatory fees ($90), and room and board ($9502). ***College room only:*** $4698. Full-time tuition and fees vary according to degree level and program. Room and board charges vary according to board plan and housing facility. ***Part-time tuition:*** $510 per credit hour. Part-time tuition and fees vary according to class time, course load, degree level, and program. ***Payment plans:*** Installment, deferred payment.

FRESHMAN FINANCIAL AID (Fall 2010, est.) 634 applied for aid; of those 88% were deemed to have need. 100% of freshmen with need received aid; of those 11% had need fully met. ***Average percent of need met:*** 80% (excluding resources awarded to replace EFC). ***Average financial aid package:*** $25,826 (excluding resources awarded to replace EFC). 19% of all full-time freshmen had no need and received non-need-based gift aid.

UNDERGRADUATE FINANCIAL AID (Fall 2010, est.) 2,352 applied for aid; of those 89% were deemed to have need. 99% of undergraduates with need received aid; of those 9% had need fully met. ***Average percent of need met:*** 76% (excluding resources awarded to replace EFC). ***Average financial aid package:*** $23,477 (excluding resources awarded to replace EFC). 22% of all full-time undergraduates had no need and received non-need-based gift aid.

GIFT AID (NEED-BASED) ***Total amount:*** $29,768,941 (14% federal, 5% state, 80% institutional, 1% external sources). ***Receiving aid:*** Freshmen: 79% (559); all full-time undergraduates: 73% (2,053). ***Average award:*** Freshmen: $18,113; Undergraduates: $15,034. ***Scholarships, grants, and awards:*** Federal Pell, FSEOG, state, private, college/university gift aid from institutional funds, university chosen non-endowed scholarships from outside sources.

GIFT AID (NON-NEED-BASED) ***Total amount:*** $4,454,129 (98% institutional, 2% external sources). ***Receiving aid:*** Freshmen: 6% (43). Undergraduates: 4% (122). ***Average award:*** Freshmen: $7059. Undergraduates: $6439. ***Scholarships, grants, and awards by category:*** *Academic interests/achievement:*

engineering/technologies, general academic interests/achievements. ***Tuition waivers:*** Full or partial for employees or children of employees.

LOANS ***Student loans:*** $22,315,069 (76% need-based, 24% non-need-based). 77% of past graduating class borrowed through all loan programs. *Average indebtedness per student:* $32,337. ***Average need-based loan:*** Freshmen: $3811. Undergraduates: $4730. ***Parent loans:*** $9,476,768 (41% need-based, 59% non-need-based). ***Programs:*** Federal Direct (Subsidized and Unsubsidized Stafford, PLUS), Perkins, private loans.

WORK-STUDY ***Federal work-study:*** Total amount: $1,775,700; jobs available. ***State or other work-study/employment:*** Total amount: $526,892 (82% need-based, 18% non-need-based). Part-time jobs available.

ATHLETIC AWARDS Total amount: $2,121,881 (42% need-based, 58% non-need-based).

APPLYING FOR FINANCIAL AID ***Required financial aid form:*** FAFSA. ***Financial aid deadline:*** 4/15. ***Notification date:*** Continuous beginning 2/10. Students must reply by 5/1.

CONTACT Ms. Lisa J. Cooper, Director of Financial Aid, Philadelphia University, School House Lane and Henry Avenue, Philadelphia, PA 19144-5497, 215-951-2940. *Fax:* 215-951-2907. *E-mail:* cooperl@philau.edu.

PHILANDER SMITH COLLEGE

Little Rock, AR

ABOUT THE INSTITUTION Independent United Methodist, coed. 19 undergraduate majors.

GIFT AID (NEED-BASED) ***Scholarships, grants, and awards:*** Federal Pell, FSEOG, state, private, college/university gift aid from institutional funds, United Negro College Fund.

GIFT AID (NON-NEED-BASED) ***Scholarships, grants, and awards by category:*** *Academic interests/achievement:* general academic interests/achievements. *Creative arts/performance:* music. *Special achievements/activities:* general special achievements/activities.

LOANS ***Programs:*** Federal Direct (Subsidized and Unsubsidized Stafford, PLUS), state.

WORK-STUDY ***Federal work-study:*** Total amount: $152,692; 96 jobs averaging $2300.

APPLYING FOR FINANCIAL AID ***Required financial aid forms:*** FAFSA, institution's own form.

CONTACT David D. Page, Director of Financial Aid, Philander Smith College, 900 Daisy Bates Drive, Little Rock, AR 72202-3799, 501-370-5270 or toll-free 800-446-6772.

PIEDMONT BAPTIST COLLEGE AND GRADUATE SCHOOL

Winston-Salem, NC

ABOUT THE INSTITUTION Independent Baptist, coed. 15 undergraduate majors.

GIFT AID (NEED-BASED) ***Scholarships, grants, and awards:*** Federal Pell, FSEOG.

GIFT AID (NON-NEED-BASED) ***Scholarships, grants, and awards by category:*** *Academic interests/achievement:* general academic interests/achievements. *Special characteristics:* children of faculty/staff, relatives of clergy, spouses of current students, veterans.

LOANS ***Programs:*** Signature Loans.

APPLYING FOR FINANCIAL AID ***Required financial aid forms:*** FAFSA, institution's own form.

CONTACT Mrs. Sherry Melton, Director of Financial Aid, Piedmont Baptist College and Graduate School, 420 South Broad Street, Winston-Salem, NC 27101-5197, 336-714-7933 or toll-free 800-937-5097. *Fax:* 336-725-5522. *E-mail:* meltons@pbc.edu.

PIEDMONT COLLEGE

Demorest, GA

Tuition & fees: $19,000 **Average undergraduate aid package: $17,824**

ABOUT THE INSTITUTION Independent religious, coed. 32 undergraduate majors. Both federal and institutional methodology are used as a basis for awarding need-based institutional aid.

UNDERGRADUATE EXPENSES for 2011–12 ***Comprehensive fee:*** $26,500 includes full-time tuition ($19,000) and room and board ($7500). Full-time tuition and fees vary according to course load, degree level, location, and program. ***Part-time tuition:*** $792 per semester hour. Part-time tuition and fees vary according to course load, degree level, location, and program. ***Payment plan:*** Installment.

FRESHMAN FINANCIAL AID (Fall 2010, est.) 184 applied for aid; of those 89% were deemed to have need. 100% of freshmen with need received aid; of those 20% had need fully met. ***Average percent of need met:*** 20% (excluding resources awarded to replace EFC). ***Average financial aid package:*** $18,887 (excluding resources awarded to replace EFC). 17% of all full-time freshmen had no need and received non-need-based gift aid.

UNDERGRADUATE FINANCIAL AID (Fall 2010, est.) 955 applied for aid; of those 92% were deemed to have need. 100% of undergraduates with need received aid; of those 28% had need fully met. ***Average percent of need met:*** 28% (excluding resources awarded to replace EFC). ***Average financial aid package:*** $17,824 (excluding resources awarded to replace EFC). 17% of all full-time undergraduates had no need and received non-need-based gift aid.

GIFT AID (NEED-BASED) ***Total amount:*** $8,898,738 (39% federal, 24% state, 37% institutional). ***Receiving aid:*** Freshmen: 82% (162); all full-time undergraduates: 82% (866). ***Average award:*** Freshmen: $6232; Undergraduates: $5742. ***Scholarships, grants, and awards:*** Federal Pell, FSEOG, state, private, college/university gift aid from institutional funds.

GIFT AID (NON-NEED-BASED) ***Total amount:*** $2,203,102 (6% federal, 11% state, 77% institutional, 6% external sources). ***Receiving aid:*** Freshmen: 14% (28). Undergraduates: 9% (97). ***Average award:*** Freshmen: $13,805. Undergraduates: $10,532. ***Scholarships, grants, and awards by category:*** *Academic interests/achievement:* 714 awards ($3,752,400 total): biological sciences, business, education, English, foreign languages, general academic interests/achievements, health fields, humanities, mathematics, premedicine, religion/biblical studies, social sciences. *Creative arts/performance:* 81 awards ($84,350 total): art/fine arts, music, theater/drama. *Special achievements/activities:* 354 awards ($1,036,700 total): leadership. *Special characteristics:* 201 awards ($1,707,408 total): adult students, children of faculty/staff, international students, out-of-state students. ***Tuition waivers:*** Full or partial for employees or children of employees.

LOANS ***Student loans:*** $6,528,300 (58% need-based, 42% non-need-based). 77% of past graduating class borrowed through all loan programs. *Average indebtedness per student:* $18,402. ***Average need-based loan:*** Freshmen: $1021. Undergraduates: $1900. ***Parent loans:*** $938,294 (31% need-based, 69% non-need-based). ***Programs:*** Federal Direct (Subsidized and Unsubsidized Stafford, PLUS).

WORK-STUDY ***Federal work-study:*** Total amount: $201,976; 84 jobs averaging $2404. ***State or other work-study/employment:*** Total amount: $789,147 (75% need-based, 25% non-need-based). 334 part-time jobs averaging $2389.

APPLYING FOR FINANCIAL AID ***Required financial aid forms:*** FAFSA, state aid form. ***Financial aid deadline (priority):*** 3/1. ***Notification date:*** Continuous beginning 1/15. Students must reply within 2 weeks of notification.

CONTACT Mr. David Richmond McMillion, Director of Financial Aid, Piedmont College, PO Box 10, Demorest, GA 30535-0010, 706-778-3000 Ext. 1191 or toll-free 800-277-7020. *Fax:* 706-778-0708. *E-mail:* dmcmillion@piedmont.edu.

PIKEVILLE COLLEGE

Pikeville, KY

Tuition & fees: $15,250 **Average undergraduate aid package: $16,714**

ABOUT THE INSTITUTION Independent religious, coed. 18 undergraduate majors. Federal methodology is used as a basis for awarding need-based institutional aid.

UNDERGRADUATE EXPENSES for 2010–11 ***Comprehensive fee:*** $21,550 includes full-time tuition ($15,250) and room and board ($6300). Full-time tuition and fees vary according to course load. ***Part-time tuition:*** $635 per credit hour. Part-time tuition and fees vary according to course load. ***Payment plan:*** Installment.

FRESHMAN FINANCIAL AID (Fall 2010, est.) 383 applied for aid; of those 100% were deemed to have need. 100% of freshmen with need received aid; of those 66% had need fully met. ***Average percent of need met:*** 92% (excluding resources awarded to replace EFC). ***Average financial aid package:*** $17,255 (excluding resources awarded to replace EFC).

UNDERGRADUATE FINANCIAL AID (Fall 2010, est.) 891 applied for aid; of those 100% were deemed to have need. 100% of undergraduates with need received aid; of those 70% had need fully met. ***Average percent of need met:*** 95% (excluding resources awarded to replace EFC). ***Average financial aid package:*** $16,714 (excluding resources awarded to replace EFC).

GIFT AID (NEED-BASED) ***Total amount:*** $10,545,512 (28% federal, 27% state, 43% institutional, 2% external sources). ***Receiving aid:*** Freshmen: 97% (383); all full-time undergraduates: 95% (880). ***Average award:*** Freshmen: $14,750; Undergraduates: $13,834. ***Scholarships, grants, and awards:*** Federal Pell, FSEOG, state, private, college/university gift aid from institutional funds.

GIFT AID (NON-NEED-BASED) ***Tuition waivers:*** Full or partial for employees or children of employees, senior citizens.

LOANS ***Student loans:*** $4,281,462 (100% need-based). 60% of past graduating class borrowed through all loan programs. *Average indebtedness per student:* $21,250. ***Average need-based loan:*** Freshmen: $3349. Undergraduates: $3959. ***Parent loans:*** $270,405 (100% need-based). ***Programs:*** Federal Direct (Subsidized and Unsubsidized Stafford, PLUS), Perkins, college/university.

WORK-STUDY ***Federal work-study:*** Total amount: $194,601; 127 jobs averaging $1542.

ATHLETIC AWARDS Total amount: $2,224,968 (100% need-based).

APPLYING FOR FINANCIAL AID ***Required financial aid forms:*** FAFSA, institution's own form. ***Financial aid deadline (priority):*** 3/1. ***Notification date:*** Continuous. Students must reply by 5/1.

CONTACT Mrs. Judy Vance Bradley, Assistant Dean of Student Financial Services, Pikeville College, 147 Sycamore Street, Pikeville, KY 41501, 606-218-5253 or toll-free 866-232-7700. *Fax:* 606-218-5255. *E-mail:* jbradley@pc.edu.

PINE MANOR COLLEGE

Chestnut Hill, MA

CONTACT Adrienne Hynek, Director of Financial Aid, Pine Manor College, 400 Heath Street, Chestnut Hill, MA 02467, 617-731-7053 or toll-free 800-762-1357. *Fax:* 617-731-7102. *E-mail:* hynekadrienne@pmc.edu.

PIONEER PACIFIC COLLEGE

Clackamas, OR

CONTACT Financial Aid Office, Pioneer Pacific College, 8800 SE Sunnyside Road, Clackamas, OR 97015, toll-free 866-772-4636 (out-of-state).

PIONEER PACIFIC COLLEGE

Wilsonville, OR

CONTACT Financial Aid Office, Pioneer Pacific College, 27501 Southwest Parkway Avenue, Wilsonville, OR 97070, 503-682-3903 or toll-free 866-PPC-INFO (in-state).

PIONEER PACIFIC COLLEGE–EUGENE/SPRINGFIELD BRANCH

Springfield, OR

CONTACT Financial Aid Office, Pioneer Pacific College–Eugene/Springfield Branch, 3800 Sports Way, Springfield, OR 97477, toll-free 866-772-4636 (out-of-state).

PITTSBURG STATE UNIVERSITY

Pittsburg, KS

ABOUT THE INSTITUTION State-supported, coed. 98 undergraduate majors.

GIFT AID (NEED-BASED) ***Scholarships, grants, and awards:*** Federal Pell, FSEOG, state, private, college/university gift aid from institutional funds.

GIFT AID (NON-NEED-BASED) ***Scholarships, grants, and awards by category:*** *Academic interests/achievement:* biological sciences, business, communication, computer science, education, engineering/technologies, English, foreign languages, general academic interests/achievements, health fields, home economics, mathematics, military science, physical sciences, social sciences. *Creative arts/performance:* music. *Special characteristics:* children and siblings of alumni, general special characteristics.

LOANS ***Programs:*** Federal Direct (Subsidized and Unsubsidized Stafford, PLUS), Perkins, Federal Nursing, college/university.

APPLYING FOR FINANCIAL AID ***Required financial aid form:*** FAFSA.

CONTACT Tammy Higgins, Director of Student Financial Assistance, Pittsburg State University, 1701 South Broadway, Pittsburg, KS 66762-5880, 620-235-4238 or toll-free 800-854-7488 Ext. 1. *Fax:* 620-235-4078. *E-mail:* thiggins@pittstate.edu.

PITZER COLLEGE

Claremont, CA

Tuition & fees: $41,130 **Average undergraduate aid package: $38,235**

ABOUT THE INSTITUTION Independent, coed. 37 undergraduate majors. Both federal and institutional methodology are used as a basis for awarding need-based institutional aid.

UNDERGRADUATE EXPENSES for 2011–12 ***Comprehensive fee:*** $53,080 includes full-time tuition ($37,520), mandatory fees ($3610), and room and board ($11,950). ***College room only:*** $7540. Full-time tuition and fees vary according to course load. Room and board charges vary according to board plan. ***Part-time tuition:*** $5108 per course. Part-time tuition and fees vary according to course load. ***Payment plans:*** Installment, deferred payment.

FRESHMAN FINANCIAL AID (Fall 2010, est.) 139 applied for aid; of those 71% were deemed to have need. 100% of freshmen with need received aid; of those 100% had need fully met. ***Average percent of need met:*** 100% (excluding resources awarded to replace EFC). ***Average financial aid package:*** $39,076 (excluding resources awarded to replace EFC). 1% of all full-time freshmen had no need and received non-need-based gift aid.

UNDERGRADUATE FINANCIAL AID (Fall 2010, est.) 482 applied for aid; of those 87% were deemed to have need. 100% of undergraduates with need received aid; of those 100% had need fully met. ***Average percent of need met:*** 100% (excluding resources awarded to replace EFC). ***Average financial aid package:*** $38,235 (excluding resources awarded to replace EFC). 4% of all full-time undergraduates had no need and received non-need-based gift aid.

GIFT AID (NEED-BASED) ***Total amount:*** $14,259,279 (8% federal, 7% state, 83% institutional, 2% external sources). ***Receiving aid:*** Freshmen: 35% (93); all full-time undergraduates: 40% (414). ***Average award:*** Freshmen: $35,378; Undergraduates: $33,155. ***Scholarships, grants, and awards:*** Federal Pell, FSEOG, state, private, college/university gift aid from institutional funds.

GIFT AID (NON-NEED-BASED) ***Total amount:*** $363,154 (59% institutional, 41% external sources). ***Average award:*** Freshmen: $5000. Undergraduates: $4942. ***Scholarships, grants, and awards by category:*** *Academic interests/achievement:* general academic interests/achievements. *Special achievements/activities:* community service, leadership. ***Tuition waivers:*** Full or partial for employees or children of employees.

LOANS ***Student loans:*** $2,187,538 (64% need-based, 36% non-need-based). 36% of past graduating class borrowed through all loan programs. *Average indebtedness per student:* $20,089. ***Average need-based loan:*** Freshmen: $2701. Undergraduates: $3916. ***Parent loans:*** $1,027,300 (100% non-need-based). ***Programs:*** Federal Direct (Subsidized and Unsubsidized Stafford, PLUS), Perkins, college/university.

WORK-STUDY ***Federal work-study:*** Total amount: $908,065; 368 jobs averaging $2463.

APPLYING FOR FINANCIAL AID ***Required financial aid forms:*** FAFSA, CSS Financial Aid PROFILE, state aid form, noncustodial (divorced/separated) parent's statement. ***Financial aid deadline:*** 2/1. ***Notification date:*** 4/1. Students must reply by 5/1.

CONTACT Margaret Carothers, Director of Financial Aid, Pitzer College, 1050 North Mills Avenue, Claremont, CA 91711-6101, 909-621-8208 or toll-free 800-748-9371. *Fax:* 909-607-1205. *E-mail:* margaret_carothers@pitzer.edu.

PLATT COLLEGE SAN DIEGO

San Diego, CA

CONTACT Financial Aid Office, Platt College San Diego, 6250 El Cajon Boulevard, San Diego, CA 92115-3919, 619-265-0107 or toll-free 866-752-8826.

PLYMOUTH STATE UNIVERSITY

Plymouth, NH

Tuition & fees (NH res): $9906 **Average undergraduate aid package: $9550**

ABOUT THE INSTITUTION State-supported, coed. 46 undergraduate majors. Federal methodology is used as a basis for awarding need-based institutional aid.

UNDERGRADUATE EXPENSES for 2010–11 ***Tuition, state resident:*** full-time $7650; part-time $320 per credit hour. ***Tuition, nonresident:*** full-time $15,820; part-time $660 per credit hour. ***Required fees:*** full-time $2256; $97 per credit hour. Full-time tuition and fees vary according to reciprocity agreements. Part-time tuition and fees vary according to course load and reciprocity agreements. ***College room and board:*** $8840; ***Room only:*** $6160. Room and board charges vary according to board plan and housing facility. ***Payment plan:*** Installment.

FRESHMAN FINANCIAL AID (Fall 2010, est.) 958 applied for aid; of those 71% were deemed to have need. 99% of freshmen with need received aid; of those 16% had need fully met. ***Average percent of need met:*** 61% (excluding resources awarded to replace EFC). ***Average financial aid package:*** $9847 (excluding resources awarded to replace EFC). 9% of all full-time freshmen had no need and received non-need-based gift aid.

UNDERGRADUATE FINANCIAL AID (Fall 2010, est.) 3,462 applied for aid; of those 76% were deemed to have need. 99% of undergraduates with need received aid; of those 14% had need fully met. ***Average percent of need met:*** 60% (excluding resources awarded to replace EFC). ***Average financial aid package:*** $9550 (excluding resources awarded to replace EFC). 7% of all full-time undergraduates had no need and received non-need-based gift aid.

GIFT AID (NEED-BASED) ***Total amount:*** $10,820,377 (48% federal, 8% state, 44% institutional). ***Receiving aid:*** Freshmen: 41% (438); all full-time undergraduates: 37% (1,526). ***Average award:*** Freshmen: $7564; Undergraduates: $6821. ***Scholarships, grants, and awards:*** Federal Pell, FSEOG, state, private, college/university gift aid from institutional funds.

GIFT AID (NON-NEED-BASED) ***Total amount:*** $3,700,099 (80% institutional, 20% external sources). ***Receiving aid:*** Freshmen: 28% (295). Undergraduates: 20% (820). ***Average award:*** Freshmen: $3630. Undergraduates: $3038. ***Scholarships, grants, and awards by category:*** *Academic interests/achievement:* business, communication, education, English, general academic interests/achievements, health fields, mathematics, physical sciences, social sciences. *Creative arts/performance:* creative writing, dance, music, theater/drama. *Special characteristics:* children of faculty/staff, international students. ***Tuition waivers:*** Full or partial for employees or children of employees, senior citizens.

LOANS ***Student loans:*** $27,125,175 (42% need-based, 58% non-need-based). 82% of past graduating class borrowed through all loan programs. *Average indebtedness per student:* $30,925. ***Average need-based loan:*** Freshmen: $3398. Undergraduates: $4224. ***Parent loans:*** $12,659,503 (100% non-need-based). ***Programs:*** Federal Direct (Subsidized and Unsubsidized Stafford, PLUS), Perkins.

WORK-STUDY ***Federal work-study:*** Total amount: $3,766,894; jobs available.

APPLYING FOR FINANCIAL AID ***Required financial aid form:*** FAFSA. ***Financial aid deadline (priority):*** 3/1. ***Notification date:*** Continuous beginning 3/1. Students must reply by 5/1.

CONTACT June Louise Schlabach, Director of Financial Aid, Plymouth State University, 17 High Street, Plymouth, NH 03264-1595, 603-535-2338 or toll-free 800-842-6900. *Fax:* 603-535-2627. *E-mail:* jlschlabach@plymouth.edu.

POINT LOMA NAZARENE UNIVERSITY

San Diego, CA

Tuition & fees: $27,100 **Average undergraduate aid package: $19,037**

ABOUT THE INSTITUTION Independent Nazarene, coed. 59 undergraduate majors. Federal methodology is used as a basis for awarding need-based institutional aid.

UNDERGRADUATE EXPENSES for 2010–11 ***Comprehensive fee:*** $36,100 includes full-time tuition ($26,500), mandatory fees ($600), and room and board ($9000). ***College room only:*** $5000. Full-time tuition and fees vary according to course load. Room and board charges vary according to board plan. ***Part-time tuition:*** $1105 per credit hour. Part-time tuition and fees vary according to course load. ***Payment plan:*** Installment.

FRESHMAN FINANCIAL AID (Fall 2010, est.) 486 applied for aid; of those 83% were deemed to have need. 100% of freshmen with need received aid; of those 13% had need fully met. ***Average percent of need met:*** 61% (excluding resources awarded to replace EFC). ***Average financial aid package:*** $17,462 (excluding resources awarded to replace EFC). 12% of all full-time freshmen had no need and received non-need-based gift aid.

UNDERGRADUATE FINANCIAL AID (Fall 2010, est.) 1,805 applied for aid; of those 85% were deemed to have need. 100% of undergraduates with need received aid; of those 13% had need fully met. ***Average percent of need met:*** 64% (excluding resources awarded to replace EFC). ***Average financial aid package:*** $19,037 (excluding resources awarded to replace EFC). 16% of all full-time undergraduates had no need and received non-need-based gift aid.

GIFT AID (NEED-BASED) ***Total amount:*** $19,059,245 (20% federal, 23% state, 49% institutional, 8% external sources). ***Receiving aid:*** Freshmen: 70% (379); all full-time undergraduates: 61% (1,415). ***Average award:*** Freshmen: $14,890; Undergraduates: $14,436. ***Scholarships, grants, and awards:*** Federal Pell, FSEOG, state, private, college/university gift aid from institutional funds, Federal Nursing.

GIFT AID (NON-NEED-BASED) ***Total amount:*** $3,657,429 (3% federal, 76% institutional, 21% external sources). ***Receiving aid:*** Freshmen: 4% (22). Undergraduates: 4% (98). ***Average award:*** Freshmen: $7046. Undergraduates: $6556. ***Scholarships, grants, and awards by category:*** *Academic interests/achievement:* biological sciences, business, communication, education, engineering/technologies, general academic interests/achievements, health fields, home economics, humanities, mathematics, religion/biblical studies, social sciences. *Creative arts/performance:* art/fine arts, debating, music, theater/drama. ***Tuition waivers:*** Full or partial for employees or children of employees, senior citizens.

LOANS ***Student loans:*** $14,703,489 (74% need-based, 26% non-need-based). 86% of past graduating class borrowed through all loan programs. *Average indebtedness per student:* $25,607. ***Average need-based loan:*** Freshmen: $3851. Undergraduates: $6066. ***Parent loans:*** $6,226,659 (45% need-based, 55% non-need-based). ***Programs:*** Federal Direct (Subsidized and Unsubsidized Stafford, PLUS), Perkins, Federal Nursing, college/university.

WORK-STUDY ***Federal work-study:*** Total amount: $261,286; jobs available.

ATHLETIC AWARDS Total amount: $1,945,249 (45% need-based, 55% non-need-based).

APPLYING FOR FINANCIAL AID ***Required financial aid form:*** institution's own form. ***Financial aid deadline (priority):*** 3/2. ***Notification date:*** Continuous beginning 3/1.

CONTACT Office of Student Financial Services, Point Loma Nazarene University, 3900 Lomaland Drive, San Diego, CA 92106, 619-849-2538 or toll-free 800-733-7770. *Fax:* 619-849-7078. *E-mail:* sfs@pointloma.edu.

POINT PARK UNIVERSITY

Pittsburgh, PA

Tuition & fees: $22,500 **Average undergraduate aid package: $16,546**

ABOUT THE INSTITUTION Independent, coed. 58 undergraduate majors. Federal methodology is used as a basis for awarding need-based institutional aid.

UNDERGRADUATE EXPENSES for 2010–11 ***Comprehensive fee:*** $31,980 includes full-time tuition ($21,700), mandatory fees ($800), and room and board ($9480). ***College room only:*** $4520. Full-time tuition and fees vary according to program. Room and board charges vary according to board plan and housing facility. ***Part-time tuition:*** $602 per credit. ***Part-time fees:*** $30 per credit. Part-time tuition and fees vary according to program. ***Payment plans:*** Installment, deferred payment.

FRESHMAN FINANCIAL AID (Fall 2010, est.) 511 applied for aid; of those 89% were deemed to have need. 100% of freshmen with need received aid; of those 14% had need fully met. ***Average percent of need met:*** 73% (excluding resources awarded to replace EFC). ***Average financial aid package:*** $19,711 (excluding resources awarded to replace EFC). 8% of all full-time freshmen had no need and received non-need-based gift aid.

UNDERGRADUATE FINANCIAL AID (Fall 2010, est.) 2,737 applied for aid; of those 91% were deemed to have need. 100% of undergraduates with need received aid; of those 11% had need fully met. ***Average percent of need met:*** 63% (excluding resources awarded to replace EFC). ***Average financial aid package:*** $16,546 (excluding resources awarded to replace EFC). 8% of all full-time undergraduates had no need and received non-need-based gift aid.

GIFT AID (NEED-BASED) ***Total amount:*** $27,364,302 (24% federal, 11% state, 55% institutional, 10% external sources). ***Receiving aid:*** Freshmen: 89% (456); all full-time undergraduates: 89% (2,447). ***Average award:*** Freshmen: $14,770; Undergraduates: $10,862. ***Scholarships, grants, and awards:*** Federal Pell, FSEOG, state, private, college/university gift aid from institutional funds.

GIFT AID (NON-NEED-BASED) ***Total amount:*** $2,486,941 (4% federal, 1% state, 75% institutional, 20% external sources). ***Receiving aid:*** Freshmen: 8% (43). Undergraduates: 6% (173). ***Average award:*** Freshmen: $9406. Undergraduates: $6788. ***Scholarships, grants, and awards by category:*** *Academic interests/achievement:* 1,564 awards ($8,138,250 total): general academic interests/

achievements. *Creative arts/performance:* 537 awards ($3,631,762 total): cinema/film/broadcasting, dance, performing arts, theater/drama. *Special achievements/activities:* 1,003 awards ($749,750 total): community service, memberships. *Special characteristics:* 340 awards ($1,055,647 total): children and siblings of alumni, children of faculty/staff, international students, members of minority groups, previous college experience, siblings of current students. ***Tuition waivers:*** Full or partial for employees or children of employees.

LOANS ***Student loans:*** $28,142,939 (82% need-based, 18% non-need-based). 89% of past graduating class borrowed through all loan programs. *Average indebtedness per student:* $26,687. ***Average need-based loan:*** Freshmen: $3996. Undergraduates: $5015. ***Parent loans:*** $5,459,100 (53% need-based, 47% non-need-based). ***Programs:*** Federal Direct (Subsidized and Unsubsidized Stafford, PLUS), Perkins.

WORK-STUDY ***Federal work-study:*** Total amount: $523,062; 295 jobs averaging $2260. ***State or other work-study/employment:*** Total amount: $3,587,615 (74% need-based, 26% non-need-based). 293 part-time jobs averaging $3008.

ATHLETIC AWARDS Total amount: $1,271,071 (70% need-based, 30% non-need-based).

APPLYING FOR FINANCIAL AID ***Required financial aid form:*** FAFSA. ***Financial aid deadline:*** 3/15. ***Notification date:*** Continuous beginning 2/15. Students must reply within 2 weeks of notification.

CONTACT Sandra M. Cronin, Senior Associate Director of Financial Aid, Point Park University, 201 Wood Street, Pittsburgh, PA 15222-1984, 412-392-3930 or toll-free 800-321-0129. *E-mail:* scronin@pointpark.edu.

POLYTECHNIC INSTITUTE OF NYU

Brooklyn, NY

Tuition & fees: $36,284 **Average undergraduate aid package: $26,211**

ABOUT THE INSTITUTION Independent, coed. 13 undergraduate majors. Federal methodology is used as a basis for awarding need-based institutional aid.

UNDERGRADUATE EXPENSES for 2010–11 ***Comprehensive fee:*** $46,364 includes full-time tuition ($35,104), mandatory fees ($1180), and room and board ($10,080). ***College room only:*** $7950. Full-time tuition and fees vary according to course load. Room and board charges vary according to housing facility. ***Part-time tuition:*** $1116 per credit hour. ***Part-time fees:*** $215 per term. Part-time tuition and fees vary according to course load. ***Payment plans:*** Guaranteed tuition, tuition prepayment, installment, deferred payment.

FRESHMAN FINANCIAL AID (Fall 2009) 363 applied for aid; of those 74% were deemed to have need. 99% of freshmen with need received aid; of those 77% had need fully met. ***Average percent of need met:*** 96% (excluding resources awarded to replace EFC). ***Average financial aid package:*** $30,099 (excluding resources awarded to replace EFC). 26% of all full-time freshmen had no need and received non-need-based gift aid.

UNDERGRADUATE FINANCIAL AID (Fall 2009) 1,575 applied for aid; of those 76% were deemed to have need. 99% of undergraduates with need received aid; of those 55% had need fully met. ***Average percent of need met:*** 89% (excluding resources awarded to replace EFC). ***Average financial aid package:*** $26,211 (excluding resources awarded to replace EFC). 21% of all full-time undergraduates had no need and received non-need-based gift aid.

GIFT AID (NEED-BASED) ***Total amount:*** $13,496,889 (33% federal, 20% state, 47% institutional). ***Receiving aid:*** Freshmen: 66% (243); all full-time undergraduates: 65% (1,086). ***Average award:*** Freshmen: $12,578; Undergraduates: $12,353. ***Scholarships, grants, and awards:*** Federal Pell, FSEOG, state, private, college/university gift aid from institutional funds, United Negro College Fund.

GIFT AID (NON-NEED-BASED) ***Total amount:*** $19,565,032 (1% state, 99% institutional). ***Receiving aid:*** Freshmen: 65% (238). Undergraduates: 50% (840). ***Average award:*** Freshmen: $20,991. Undergraduates: $18,428. ***Scholarships, grants, and awards by category:*** *Academic interests/achievement:* computer science, engineering/technologies, general academic interests/achievements. *Special characteristics:* members of minority groups. ***Tuition waivers:*** Full or partial for employees or children of employees.

LOANS ***Student loans:*** $9,346,611 (48% need-based, 52% non-need-based). 74% of past graduating class borrowed through all loan programs. *Average indebtedness per student:* $31,035. ***Average need-based loan:*** Freshmen: $3855. Undergraduates: $4683. ***Parent loans:*** $1,626,596 (100% non-need-based). ***Programs:*** Perkins, college/university, alternative loans.

WORK-STUDY ***Federal work-study:*** Total amount: $200,000; 221 jobs averaging $3030.

APPLYING FOR FINANCIAL AID ***Required financial aid forms:*** FAFSA, state aid form. ***Financial aid deadline:*** Continuous. ***Notification date:*** Continuous beginning 2/15. Students must reply by 5/1 or within 2 weeks of notification.

CONTACT Ms. Christine Falzerano, Director of Financial Aid, Polytechnic Institute of NYU, 6 Metrotech Center, Brooklyn, NY 11201-2990, 718-260-3333 or toll-free 800-POLYTECH. *Fax:* 718-260-3052. *E-mail:* cfalzera@poly.edu.

POLYTECHNIC UNIVERSITY OF PUERTO RICO

Hato Rey, PR

ABOUT THE INSTITUTION Independent, coed, primarily men. 13 undergraduate majors.

GIFT AID (NEED-BASED) ***Scholarships, grants, and awards:*** Federal Pell, FSEOG, state, college/university gift aid from institutional funds.

GIFT AID (NON-NEED-BASED) ***Scholarships, grants, and awards by category:*** *Academic interests/achievement:* architecture, business, engineering/technologies.

WORK-STUDY ***Federal work-study:*** Total amount: $209,721; 121 jobs averaging $1733.

APPLYING FOR FINANCIAL AID ***Required financial aid form:*** FAFSA.

CONTACT Sergio E. Villoldo, Financial Aid Director, Polytechnic University of Puerto Rico, 377 Ponce de Leon Avenue, Hato Rey, PR 00919, 787-754-8000 Ext. 253. *Fax:* 787-766-1163.

POLYTECHNIC UNIVERSITY OF PUERTO RICO, MIAMI CAMPUS

Miami, FL

ABOUT THE INSTITUTION Independent, coed. 3 undergraduate majors.

GIFT AID (NEED-BASED) ***Scholarships, grants, and awards:*** Federal Pell, college/university gift aid from institutional funds.

LOANS ***Programs:*** alternative loans.

WORK-STUDY Federal work-study jobs available.

CONTACT Maria Victoria Shehadeh, Administrative Affairs Coordinator/Financial Aid Officer, Polytechnic University of Puerto Rico, Miami Campus, 8180 Northwest 36th Street, Suite 401, Miami, FL 33166, 305-418-8000 Ext. 204 or toll-free 888-729-7659 (out-of-state). *E-mail:* mshehadeh@pupr.edu.

POLYTECHNIC UNIVERSITY OF PUERTO RICO, ORLANDO CAMPUS

Winter Park, FL

ABOUT THE INSTITUTION Independent, coed. 4 undergraduate majors.

GIFT AID (NEED-BASED) ***Scholarships, grants, and awards:*** Federal Pell, FSEOG.

APPLYING FOR FINANCIAL AID ***Required financial aid form:*** FAFSA.

CONTACT Mrs. Maria Victoria Shehadeh, Financial Aid Officer, Polytechnic University of Puerto Rico, Orlando Campus, 8180 N.W. 36TH Street, Miami, FL 33166, 305-418-8000 Ext. 204 or toll-free 888-577-POLY (out-of-state). *Fax:* 305-418-4325. *E-mail:* mshehadeh@pupr.edu.

POMONA COLLEGE

Claremont, CA

Tuition & fees: $39,883 **Average undergraduate aid package: $37,621**

ABOUT THE INSTITUTION Independent, coed. 54 undergraduate majors. Both federal and institutional methodology are used as a basis for awarding need-based institutional aid.

UNDERGRADUATE EXPENSES for 2011–12 ***Comprehensive fee:*** $53,110 includes full-time tuition ($39,572), mandatory fees ($311), and room and board ($13,227). Room and board charges vary according to board plan. ***Payment plan:*** Installment.

FRESHMAN FINANCIAL AID (Fall 2010, est.) 252 applied for aid; of those 85% were deemed to have need. 100% of freshmen with need received aid; of those

100% had need fully met. ***Average percent of need met:*** 100% (excluding resources awarded to replace EFC). ***Average financial aid package:*** $38,352 (excluding resources awarded to replace EFC).

UNDERGRADUATE FINANCIAL AID (Fall 2010, est.) 924 applied for aid; of those 91% were deemed to have need. 100% of undergraduates with need received aid; of those 100% had need fully met. ***Average percent of need met:*** 100% (excluding resources awarded to replace EFC). ***Average financial aid package:*** $37,621 (excluding resources awarded to replace EFC).

GIFT AID (NEED-BASED) ***Total amount:*** $29,808,152 (7% federal, 3% state, 88% institutional, 2% external sources). ***Receiving aid:*** Freshmen: 54% (215); all full-time undergraduates: 55% (837). ***Average award:*** Freshmen: $37,166; Undergraduates: $35,615. ***Scholarships, grants, and awards:*** Federal Pell, FSEOG, state, private, college/university gift aid from institutional funds.

GIFT AID (NON-NEED-BASED) ***Total amount:*** $760,500 (8% federal, 92% external sources). ***Tuition waivers:*** Full or partial for employees or children of employees.

LOANS ***Student loans:*** $1,100,000 (100% non-need-based). 47% of past graduating class borrowed through all loan programs. *Average indebtedness per student:* $9700. ***Parent loans:*** $1,609,000 (100% non-need-based). ***Programs:*** Federal Direct (Subsidized and Unsubsidized Stafford, PLUS), Perkins, college/university.

WORK-STUDY ***Federal work-study:*** Total amount: $250,185; 210 jobs averaging $1100. ***State or other work-study/employment:*** Total amount: $1,061,200 (52% need-based, 48% non-need-based). 612 part-time jobs averaging $1700.

APPLYING FOR FINANCIAL AID ***Required financial aid forms:*** FAFSA, CSS Financial Aid PROFILE, state aid form, noncustodial (divorced/separated) parent's statement, business/farm supplement. ***Financial aid deadline:*** 2/1. ***Notification date:*** 4/10. Students must reply by 5/1.

CONTACT Mary Booker, Director of Financial Aid, Pomona College, 550 North College Avenue, Claremont, CA 91711, 909-621-8205. *Fax:* 909-607-7941. *E-mail:* financial_aid@pomadm.pomona.edu.

PONTIFICAL CATHOLIC UNIVERSITY OF PUERTO RICO

Ponce, PR

Tuition & fees: $5468 **Average undergraduate aid package: $7118**

ABOUT THE INSTITUTION Independent Roman Catholic, coed. 75 undergraduate majors. Federal methodology is used as a basis for awarding need-based institutional aid.

UNDERGRADUATE EXPENSES for 2010–11 ***Tuition:*** full-time $4950; part-time $165 per credit. Full-time tuition and fees vary according to location. Part-time tuition and fees vary according to location. ***Payment plan:*** Deferred payment.

FRESHMAN FINANCIAL AID (Fall 2010, est.) 1,487 applied for aid; of those 89% were deemed to have need. 100% of freshmen with need received aid; of those 4% had need fully met. ***Average percent of need met:*** 61% (excluding resources awarded to replace EFC). ***Average financial aid package:*** $7138 (excluding resources awarded to replace EFC).

UNDERGRADUATE FINANCIAL AID (Fall 2010, est.) 6,953 applied for aid; of those 88% were deemed to have need. 100% of undergraduates with need received aid; of those 4% had need fully met. ***Average percent of need met:*** 61% (excluding resources awarded to replace EFC). ***Average financial aid package:*** $7118 (excluding resources awarded to replace EFC).

GIFT AID (NEED-BASED) ***Total amount:*** $50,565,937 (98% federal, 2% state). ***Receiving aid:*** Freshmen: 89% (1,320); all full-time undergraduates: 88% (6,097). ***Average award:*** Freshmen: $5992; Undergraduates: $5533. ***Scholarships, grants, and awards:*** Federal Pell, FSEOG, state, private, college/university gift aid from institutional funds, Federal Nursing, Scholarships for Disadvantaged Students (SDS).

GIFT AID (NON-NEED-BASED) ***Total amount:*** $426,382 (96% institutional, 4% external sources). ***Receiving aid:*** Freshmen: 26% (388). Undergraduates: 20% (1,407). ***Scholarships, grants, and awards by category:*** *Academic interests/achievement:* 1,708 awards ($1,873,625 total): general academic interests/achievements. *Creative arts/performance:* 29 awards ($10,200 total): performing arts, theater/drama. *Special characteristics:* 68 awards ($199,969 total): children of faculty/staff, veterans, veterans' children. ***Tuition waivers:*** Full or partial for employees or children of employees.

LOANS ***Student loans:*** $12,554,532 (87% need-based, 13% non-need-based). 76% of past graduating class borrowed through all loan programs. *Average indebtedness per student:* $12,707. ***Average need-based loan:*** Freshmen: $3058. Undergraduates: $3563. ***Programs:*** Federal Direct (Subsidized and Unsubsidized Stafford, PLUS), Perkins.

WORK-STUDY ***Federal work-study:*** Total amount: $1,035,914; 780 jobs averaging $1329. ***State or other work-study/employment:*** Total amount: $25,107 (100% non-need-based). 105 part-time jobs averaging $239.

ATHLETIC AWARDS Total amount: $763,693 (100% non-need-based).

APPLYING FOR FINANCIAL AID ***Required financial aid forms:*** FAFSA, institution's own form, noncustodial (divorced/separated) parent's statement. ***Financial aid deadline:*** 5/15 (priority: 5/15). ***Notification date:*** 6/15. Students must reply within 4 weeks of notification.

CONTACT Mrs. Rosalia Martinez, Director of Financial Aid, Pontifical Catholic University of Puerto Rico, 2250 Las Americas Avenue, Suite 549, Ponce, PR 00717-9777, 787-841-2000 Ext. 1065 or toll-free 800-981-5040. *Fax:* 787-651-2041. *E-mail:* rosalia.martinez@email.pucpr.edu.

PONTIFICAL COLLEGE JOSEPHINUM

Columbus, OH

CONTACT Marky Leichtnam, Financial Aid Director, Pontifical College Josephinum, 7625 North High Street, Columbus, OH 43235-1498, 614-985-2212 or toll-free 888-252-5812. *Fax:* 614-885-2307. *E-mail:* mleichtnam@pcj.edu.

PORTLAND STATE UNIVERSITY

Portland, OR

Tuition & fees (OR res): $7130 **Average undergraduate aid package: $12,986**

ABOUT THE INSTITUTION State-supported, coed. 77 undergraduate majors. Federal methodology is used as a basis for awarding need-based institutional aid.

UNDERGRADUATE EXPENSES for 2011–12 ***One-time required fee:*** $285. ***Tuition, state resident:*** full-time $5648; part-time $125.50 per credit hour. ***Tuition, nonresident:*** full-time $20,160; part-time $448 per credit hour. ***Required fees:*** full-time $1482; $17.50 per credit hour or $95.50 per term. Full-time tuition and fees vary according to program and reciprocity agreements. Part-time tuition and fees vary according to course level. ***College room and board:*** $10,065; ***Room only:*** $7098. Room and board charges vary according to board plan and housing facility. ***Payment plan:*** Installment.

FRESHMAN FINANCIAL AID (Fall 2010, est.) 1,157 applied for aid; of those 79% were deemed to have need. 98% of freshmen with need received aid; of those 13% had need fully met. ***Average percent of need met:*** 76% (excluding resources awarded to replace EFC). ***Average financial aid package:*** $11,174 (excluding resources awarded to replace EFC). 1% of all full-time freshmen had no need and received non-need-based gift aid.

UNDERGRADUATE FINANCIAL AID (Fall 2010, est.) 9,885 applied for aid; of those 88% were deemed to have need. 99% of undergraduates with need received aid; of those 6% had need fully met. ***Average percent of need met:*** 80% (excluding resources awarded to replace EFC). ***Average financial aid package:*** $12,986 (excluding resources awarded to replace EFC). 1% of all full-time undergraduates had no need and received non-need-based gift aid.

GIFT AID (NEED-BASED) ***Total amount:*** $44,520,899 (92% federal, 5% state, 3% external sources). ***Receiving aid:*** Freshmen: 48% (657); all full-time undergraduates: 46% (6,471). ***Average award:*** Freshmen: $5350; Undergraduates: $5447. ***Scholarships, grants, and awards:*** Federal Pell, FSEOG, state, private, college/university gift aid from institutional funds, United Negro College Fund.

GIFT AID (NON-NEED-BASED) ***Total amount:*** $456,568 (5% federal, 23% institutional, 72% external sources). ***Receiving aid:*** Freshmen: 1% (16). Undergraduates: 39. ***Average award:*** Freshmen: $632. Undergraduates: $1176. ***Scholarships, grants, and awards by category:*** *Academic interests/achievement:* architecture, area/ethnic studies, business, computer science, education, engineering/technologies, foreign languages, general academic interests/achievements, humanities, international studies, physical sciences, social sciences. *Creative arts/performance:* art/fine arts, general creative arts/performance, music, theater/drama. *Special achievements/activities:* community service, general special achievements/activities, leadership, memberships. *Special characteristics:* adult students, ethnic background, handicapped students, international students, members of minority groups, out-of-state students, veterans. ***Tuition waivers:*** Full or partial for minority students, employees or children of employees, senior citizens.

LOANS ***Student loans:*** $109,173,480 (87% need-based, 13% non-need-based). 64% of past graduating class borrowed through all loan programs. *Average indebtedness per student:* $26,287. ***Average need-based loan:*** Freshmen: $3594. Undergraduates: $4505. ***Parent loans:*** $5,738,249 (38% need-based, 62% non-need-based). ***Programs:*** Federal Direct (Subsidized and Unsubsidized Stafford, PLUS), Perkins.

WORK-STUDY ***Federal work-study:*** Total amount: $4,086,152; 1,421 jobs averaging $2876. ***State or other work-study/employment:*** Total amount: $98,169 (53% need-based, 47% non-need-based). Part-time jobs available.

ATHLETIC AWARDS Total amount: $1,004,797 (32% need-based, 68% non-need-based).

APPLYING FOR FINANCIAL AID ***Required financial aid form:*** FAFSA. ***Financial aid deadline:*** Continuous. ***Notification date:*** Continuous. Students must reply within 4 weeks of notification.

CONTACT Phillip Rodgers, Director of Financial Aid, Portland State University, PO Box 751, Portland, OR 97207-0751, 800-547-8887. *Fax:* 503-725-5965. *E-mail:* askfa@pdx.edu.

POST UNIVERSITY

Waterbury, CT

Tuition & fees: $25,050 **Average undergraduate aid package: N/A**

ABOUT THE INSTITUTION Independent, coed. 23 undergraduate majors. Federal methodology is used as a basis for awarding need-based institutional aid.

UNDERGRADUATE EXPENSES for 2010–11 ***Comprehensive fee:*** $34,750 includes full-time tuition ($24,000), mandatory fees ($1050), and room and board ($9700). ***College room only:*** $5335. Full-time tuition and fees vary according to degree level and program. Room and board charges vary according to housing facility. ***Part-time tuition:*** $800 per credit hour. Part-time tuition and fees vary according to class time, course load, degree level, and program. ***Payment plan:*** Installment.

GIFT AID (NEED-BASED) ***Scholarships, grants, and awards:*** Federal Pell, FSEOG, state, private, college/university gift aid from institutional funds.

GIFT AID (NON-NEED-BASED) ***Scholarships, grants, and awards by category:*** *Academic interests/achievement:* agriculture, biological sciences, business, communication, computer science, education, English, general academic interests/achievements, humanities, international studies, social sciences. *Special characteristics:* children and siblings of alumni, local/state students, siblings of current students. ***Tuition waivers:*** Full or partial for employees or children of employees, senior citizens.

LOANS ***Programs:*** Perkins, college/university.

WORK-STUDY Federal work-study jobs available. ***State or other work-study/employment:*** Part-time jobs available.

APPLYING FOR FINANCIAL AID ***Required financial aid form:*** FAFSA. ***Financial aid deadline (priority):*** 3/1. ***Notification date:*** Continuous beginning 4/1. Students must reply within 2 weeks of notification.

CONTACT Ms. Regina Faulds, Director of Financial Aid, Post University, 800 Country Club Road, Waterbury, CT 06723-2540, 203-596-4528 or toll-free 800-345-2562. *Fax:* 203-596-4599. *E-mail:* rfaulds@post.edu.

POTOMAC COLLEGE

Washington, DC

CONTACT Phyllis Crews, Financial Aid Counselor, Potomac College, 4000 Chesapeake Street NW, Washington, DC 20016, 202-686-0876 or toll-free 888-686-0876. *Fax:* 202-686-0818. *E-mail:* pcrews@potomac.edu.

POTOMAC COLLEGE

Herndon, VA

ABOUT THE INSTITUTION Proprietary, coed. 7 undergraduate majors.

GIFT AID (NEED-BASED) ***Scholarships, grants, and awards:*** Federal Pell, FSEOG, private, college/university gift aid from institutional funds, Academic Competitiveness Grants, National SMART Grants.

CONTACT Ms. Melva Carty, Director of Financial Aid, Potomac College, 4000 Chesapeake Street NW, Washington, DC 20016, 202-274-1783. *Fax:* 202-686-0818. *E-mail:* melva.carty@potomac.edu.

PRAIRIE VIEW A&M UNIVERSITY

Prairie View, TX

Tuition & fees (TX res): $6855 **Average undergraduate aid package: N/A**

ABOUT THE INSTITUTION State-supported, coed. 43 undergraduate majors. Federal methodology is used as a basis for awarding need-based institutional aid.

UNDERGRADUATE EXPENSES for 2011–12 ***Tuition, state resident:*** full-time $5076; part-time $169 per credit hour. ***Tuition, nonresident:*** full-time $14,376; part-time $479 per credit hour. ***Required fees:*** full-time $1779. Full-time tuition and fees vary according to course load and program. Part-time tuition and fees vary according to course load and program. ***College room and board:*** $7064; ***Room only:*** $4752. Room and board charges vary according to board plan, housing facility, and student level. ***Payment plan:*** Installment.

GIFT AID (NEED-BASED) ***Total amount:*** $31,038,813 (73% federal, 25% state, 2% institutional). ***Scholarships, grants, and awards:*** Federal Pell, FSEOG, state, private, college/university gift aid from institutional funds.

GIFT AID (NON-NEED-BASED) ***Total amount:*** $8,861,682 (7% federal, 3% state, 35% institutional, 55% external sources). ***Scholarships, grants, and awards by category:*** *Academic interests/achievement:* agriculture, architecture, education, general academic interests/achievements, premedicine. *Creative arts/performance:* art/fine arts, music, performing arts. ***Tuition waivers:*** Full or partial for senior citizens.

LOANS ***Student loans:*** $46,935,390 (39% need-based, 61% non-need-based). ***Parent loans:*** $6,960,596 (100% non-need-based). ***Programs:*** Perkins, state.

WORK-STUDY ***Federal work-study:*** Total amount: $1,373,837; jobs available. ***State or other work-study/employment:*** Total amount: $95,639 (100% need-based). Part-time jobs available.

APPLYING FOR FINANCIAL AID ***Required financial aid forms:*** FAFSA, institution's own form. ***Financial aid deadline (priority):*** 5/1. ***Notification date:*** 6/1. Students must reply within 2 weeks of notification.

CONTACT Mr. K. Michael Francois, Director of Student Financial Aid and Scholarships, Prairie View A&M University, PO Box 519, Mail Stop 1005, Prairie View, TX 77446, 936-261-1009. *E-mail:* kmfrancois@pvamu.edu.

PRATT INSTITUTE

Brooklyn, NY

Tuition & fees: $39,310 **Average undergraduate aid package: $18,914**

ABOUT THE INSTITUTION Independent, coed. 25 undergraduate majors. Federal methodology is used as a basis for awarding need-based institutional aid.

UNDERGRADUATE EXPENSES for 2011–12 ***Comprehensive fee:*** $49,520 includes full-time tuition ($37,500), mandatory fees ($1810), and room and board ($10,210). ***College room only:*** $6530. Room and board charges vary according to board plan and housing facility. ***Part-time tuition:*** $1210 per credit.

FRESHMAN FINANCIAL AID (Fall 2010, est.) 505 applied for aid; of those 88% were deemed to have need. 100% of freshmen with need received aid. ***Average financial aid package:*** $17,800 (excluding resources awarded to replace EFC). 20% of all full-time freshmen had no need and received non-need-based gift aid.

UNDERGRADUATE FINANCIAL AID (Fall 2010, est.) 1,827 applied for aid; of those 92% were deemed to have need. 100% of undergraduates with need received aid. ***Average financial aid package:*** $18,914 (excluding resources awarded to replace EFC). 17% of all full-time undergraduates had no need and received non-need-based gift aid.

GIFT AID (NEED-BASED) ***Total amount:*** $13,220,181 (30% federal, 10% state, 57% institutional, 3% external sources). ***Receiving aid:*** Freshmen: 43% (313); all full-time undergraduates: 46% (1,297). ***Average award:*** Freshmen: $9753; Undergraduates: $11,148. ***Scholarships, grants, and awards:*** Federal Pell, FSEOG, state, private.

GIFT AID (NON-NEED-BASED) ***Total amount:*** $20,399,588 (100% institutional). ***Receiving aid:*** Freshmen: 50% (360). Undergraduates: 51% (1,431). ***Average***

award: Freshmen: $11,304. Undergraduates: $10,527. ***Scholarships, grants, and awards by category:*** *Academic interests/achievement:* general academic interests/achievements.

LOANS ***Student loans:*** $11,809,544 (61% need-based, 39% non-need-based). ***Average need-based loan:*** Freshmen: $7115. Undergraduates: $7891. ***Parent loans:*** $15,547,659 (100% need-based). ***Programs:*** Federal Direct (Subsidized and Unsubsidized Stafford, PLUS), Perkins.

WORK-STUDY ***Federal work-study:*** Total amount: $750,290; jobs available. ***State or other work-study/employment:*** Total amount: $2,388,000 (100% non-need-based). Part-time jobs available.

APPLYING FOR FINANCIAL AID ***Required financial aid form:*** FAFSA. ***Financial aid deadline:*** 2/1. ***Notification date:*** Continuous beginning 3/10. Students must reply within 2 weeks of notification.

CONTACT Savior Wright, Assistant Director of Financial Aid, Pratt Institute, 200 Willoughby Avenue, Brooklyn, NY 11205-3899, 718-636-3599 or toll-free 800-331-0834. *Fax:* 718-636-3739. *E-mail:* finaid@pratt.edu.

PRESBYTERIAN COLLEGE

Clinton, SC

Tuition & fees: $30,180 **Average undergraduate aid package: $30,827**

ABOUT THE INSTITUTION Independent religious, coed. 33 undergraduate majors. Federal methodology is used as a basis for awarding need-based institutional aid.

UNDERGRADUATE EXPENSES for 2010–11 ***Comprehensive fee:*** $38,850 includes full-time tuition ($27,580), mandatory fees ($2600), and room and board ($8670). Full-time tuition and fees vary according to program and reciprocity agreements. Room and board charges vary according to board plan and housing facility. ***Part-time tuition:*** $1150 per credit hour. ***Part-time fees:*** $25 per credit hour; $23 per term. Part-time tuition and fees vary according to course load and program. ***Payment plan:*** Installment.

FRESHMAN FINANCIAL AID (Fall 2010, est.) 270 applied for aid; of those 87% were deemed to have need. 100% of freshmen with need received aid; of those 43% had need fully met. ***Average percent of need met:*** 88% (excluding resources awarded to replace EFC). ***Average financial aid package:*** $31,483 (excluding resources awarded to replace EFC). 21% of all full-time freshmen had no need and received non-need-based gift aid.

UNDERGRADUATE FINANCIAL AID (Fall 2010, est.) 886 applied for aid; of those 91% were deemed to have need. 100% of undergraduates with need received aid; of those 45% had need fully met. ***Average percent of need met:*** 86% (excluding resources awarded to replace EFC). ***Average financial aid package:*** $30,827 (excluding resources awarded to replace EFC). 25% of all full-time undergraduates had no need and received non-need-based gift aid.

GIFT AID (NEED-BASED) ***Total amount:*** $16,843,642 (9% federal, 23% state, 66% institutional, 2% external sources). ***Receiving aid:*** Freshmen: 77% (234); all full-time undergraduates: 71% (805). ***Average award:*** Freshmen: $29,415; Undergraduates: $28,564. ***Scholarships, grants, and awards:*** Federal Pell, FSEOG, state, private, college/university gift aid from institutional funds.

GIFT AID (NON-NEED-BASED) ***Total amount:*** $7,305,458 (9% state, 82% institutional, 9% external sources). ***Receiving aid:*** Freshmen: 27% (83). Undergraduates: 27% (304). ***Average award:*** Freshmen: $14,496. Undergraduates: $13,003. ***Scholarships, grants, and awards by category:*** *Academic interests/achievement:* general academic interests/achievements. *Creative arts/performance:* music. *Special achievements/activities:* leadership, religious involvement. *Special characteristics:* children of faculty/staff, relatives of clergy, religious affiliation. ***Tuition waivers:*** Full or partial for employees or children of employees, senior citizens.

LOANS ***Student loans:*** $3,664,036 (59% need-based, 41% non-need-based). 56% of past graduating class borrowed through all loan programs. *Average indebtedness per student:* $24,067. ***Average need-based loan:*** Freshmen: $3471. Undergraduates: $4169. ***Parent loans:*** $1,999,863 (34% need-based, 66% non-need-based). ***Programs:*** state, college/university, private loans.

WORK-STUDY ***Federal work-study:*** Total amount: $332,386; jobs available. ***State or other work-study/employment:*** Part-time jobs available.

ATHLETIC AWARDS Total amount: $5,518,406 (51% need-based, 49% non-need-based).

APPLYING FOR FINANCIAL AID ***Required financial aid form:*** FAFSA. ***Financial aid deadline:*** 6/30 (priority: 3/15).

CONTACT Mr. Jeff Holliday, Director of Financial Aid, Presbyterian College, 503 South Broad Street, Clinton, SC 29325, 864-833-8287 or toll-free 800-476-7272. *Fax:* 864-833-8481. *E-mail:* jsholli@presby.edu.

PRESCOTT COLLEGE

Prescott, AZ

Tuition & fees: $27,265 **Average undergraduate aid package: $16,686**

ABOUT THE INSTITUTION Independent, coed. 74 undergraduate majors. Federal methodology is used as a basis for awarding need-based institutional aid.

UNDERGRADUATE EXPENSES for 2010–11 ***Tuition:*** full-time $24,864; part-time $1036 per credit hour. ***Required fees:*** full-time $2401; $1034 per term. Full-time tuition and fees vary according to course load, degree level, and reciprocity agreements. Part-time tuition and fees vary according to course load, degree level, and reciprocity agreements. Room and board charges vary according to housing facility. ***Payment plans:*** Installment, deferred payment.

FRESHMAN FINANCIAL AID (Fall 2010, est.) 64 applied for aid; of those 83% were deemed to have need. 100% of freshmen with need received aid; of those 6% had need fully met. ***Average percent of need met:*** 63% (excluding resources awarded to replace EFC). ***Average financial aid package:*** $18,954 (excluding resources awarded to replace EFC). 22% of all full-time freshmen had no need and received non-need-based gift aid.

UNDERGRADUATE FINANCIAL AID (Fall 2010, est.) 499 applied for aid; of those 92% were deemed to have need. 100% of undergraduates with need received aid; of those 4% had need fully met. ***Average percent of need met:*** 54% (excluding resources awarded to replace EFC). ***Average financial aid package:*** $16,686 (excluding resources awarded to replace EFC). 18% of all full-time undergraduates had no need and received non-need-based gift aid.

GIFT AID (NEED-BASED) ***Total amount:*** $5,255,363 (38% federal, 60% institutional, 2% external sources). ***Receiving aid:*** Freshmen: 70% (53); all full-time undergraduates: 69% (450). ***Average award:*** Freshmen: $15,229; Undergraduates: $11,307. ***Scholarships, grants, and awards:*** Federal Pell, FSEOG, state, private, college/university gift aid from institutional funds, Academic Competitiveness Grants, National SMART Grants.

GIFT AID (NON-NEED-BASED) ***Total amount:*** $834,022 (97% institutional, 3% external sources). ***Receiving aid:*** Freshmen: 5% (4). Undergraduates: 2% (12). ***Average award:*** Freshmen: $5885. Undergraduates: $6370. ***Scholarships, grants, and awards by category:*** *Academic interests/achievement:* 374 awards ($869,336 total): general academic interests/achievements. *Special achievements/activities:* 374 awards ($869,336 total): general special achievements/activities. ***Tuition waivers:*** Full or partial for employees or children of employees.

LOANS ***Student loans:*** $6,248,372 (91% need-based, 9% non-need-based). 67% of past graduating class borrowed through all loan programs. *Average indebtedness per student:* $15,182. ***Average need-based loan:*** Freshmen: $3356. Undergraduates: $5240. ***Parent loans:*** $998,521 (44% need-based, 56% non-need-based). ***Programs:*** Federal Direct (Subsidized and Unsubsidized Stafford, PLUS).

WORK-STUDY ***Federal work-study:*** Total amount: $203,387; 187 jobs averaging $1398. ***State or other work-study/employment:*** Part-time jobs available.

APPLYING FOR FINANCIAL AID ***Required financial aid form:*** FAFSA. ***Financial aid deadline (priority):*** 3/1. ***Notification date:*** Continuous beginning 3/15. Students must reply within 12 weeks of notification.

CONTACT Financial Aid Office, Prescott College, 220 Grove Avenue, Prescott, AZ 86301-2990, 928-350-1111 or toll-free 800-628-6364. *Fax:* 928-350-1120. *E-mail:* finaid@prescott.edu.

PRESENTATION COLLEGE

Aberdeen, SD

CONTACT Ms. Janel Wagner, Director of Financial Aid, Presentation College, 1500 North Main Street, Aberdeen, SD 57401-1299, 605-229-8427 or toll-free 800-437-6060. *Fax:* 605-229-8537. *E-mail:* janel.wagner@presentation.edu.

PRINCETON UNIVERSITY

Princeton, NJ

Tuition & fees: $37,000 **Average undergraduate aid package: $36,411**

ABOUT THE INSTITUTION Independent, coed. 35 undergraduate majors. Both federal and institutional methodology are used as a basis for awarding need-based institutional aid.

UNDERGRADUATE EXPENSES for 2011–12 ***Comprehensive fee:*** $49,069 includes full-time tuition ($37,000) and room and board ($12,069). ***College room only:*** $6596. Room and board charges vary according to board plan. ***Payment plans:*** Installment, deferred payment.

FRESHMAN FINANCIAL AID (Fall 2009) 893 applied for aid; of those 88% were deemed to have need. 100% of freshmen with need received aid; of those 100% had need fully met. ***Average percent of need met:*** 100% (excluding resources awarded to replace EFC). ***Average financial aid package:*** $36,912 (excluding resources awarded to replace EFC).

UNDERGRADUATE FINANCIAL AID (Fall 2009) 3,183 applied for aid; of those 93% were deemed to have need. 100% of undergraduates with need received aid; of those 100% had need fully met. ***Average percent of need met:*** 100% (excluding resources awarded to replace EFC). ***Average financial aid package:*** $36,411 (excluding resources awarded to replace EFC).

GIFT AID (NEED-BASED) ***Total amount:*** $102,525,515 (4% federal, 93% institutional, 3% external sources). ***Receiving aid:*** Freshmen: 61% (790); all full-time undergraduates: 59% (2,953). ***Average award:*** Freshmen: $35,713; Undergraduates: $34,719. ***Scholarships, grants, and awards:*** Federal Pell, FSEOG, state, private, college/university gift aid from institutional funds.

GIFT AID (NON-NEED-BASED) ***Tuition waivers:*** Full or partial for employees or children of employees.

LOANS ***Student loans:*** 23% of past graduating class borrowed through all loan programs. *Average indebtedness per student:* $5225. ***Parent loans:*** $906,876 (100% non-need-based). ***Programs:*** Federal Direct (Subsidized and Unsubsidized Stafford, PLUS), Perkins, college/university.

WORK-STUDY ***Federal work-study:*** Total amount: $795,732; 883 jobs averaging $901. ***State or other work-study/employment:*** Total amount: $1,830,593 (100% need-based). 1,185 part-time jobs averaging $1545.

APPLYING FOR FINANCIAL AID ***Required financial aid forms:*** FAFSA, institution's own form. ***Financial aid deadline (priority):*** 2/1. ***Notification date:*** 4/1. Students must reply by 5/1.

CONTACT Robin Moscato, Director of Financial Aid, Princeton University, PO Box 591, Princeton, NJ 08542, 609-258-3330. *Fax:* 609-258-3558. *E-mail:* moscato@princeton.edu.

PRINCIPIA COLLEGE

Elsah, IL

Tuition & fees: $25,640 **Average undergraduate aid package: $24,175**

ABOUT THE INSTITUTION Independent Christian Science, coed. 28 undergraduate majors. Institutional methodology is used as a basis for awarding need-based institutional aid.

UNDERGRADUATE EXPENSES for 2011–12 ***Comprehensive fee:*** $35,140 includes full-time tuition ($25,200), mandatory fees ($440), and room and board ($9500). ***College room only:*** $4620. Full-time tuition and fees vary according to course load. ***Payment plan:*** Installment.

FRESHMAN FINANCIAL AID (Fall 2010, est.) 84 applied for aid; of those 95% were deemed to have need. 100% of freshmen with need received aid; of those 88% had need fully met. ***Average percent of need met:*** 88% (excluding resources awarded to replace EFC). ***Average financial aid package:*** $23,837 (excluding resources awarded to replace EFC). 20% of all full-time freshmen had no need and received non-need-based gift aid.

UNDERGRADUATE FINANCIAL AID (Fall 2010, est.) 361 applied for aid; of those 97% were deemed to have need. 100% of undergraduates with need received aid; of those 85% had need fully met. ***Average percent of need met:*** 85% (excluding resources awarded to replace EFC). ***Average financial aid package:*** $24,175 (excluding resources awarded to replace EFC). 17% of all full-time undergraduates had no need and received non-need-based gift aid.

GIFT AID (NEED-BASED) ***Total amount:*** $4,779,100 (100% institutional). ***Receiving aid:*** Freshmen: 62% (62); all full-time undergraduates: 53% (265). ***Average award:*** Freshmen: $19,648; Undergraduates: $20,119. ***Scholarships, grants, and awards:*** private, college/university gift aid from institutional funds.

GIFT AID (NON-NEED-BASED) ***Total amount:*** $1,538,186 (100% institutional). ***Receiving aid:*** Freshmen: 32% (32). Undergraduates: 25% (126). ***Average award:*** Freshmen: $14,407. Undergraduates: $16,727. ***Scholarships, grants, and awards by category:*** *Academic interests/achievement:* 107 awards ($1,727,067 total): general academic interests/achievements. *Special achievements/activities:* 103 awards ($1,143,533 total): community service, general special achievements/activities, leadership, religious involvement. *Special characteristics:* 23 awards ($82,500 total): children and siblings of alumni, children of faculty/staff. ***Tuition waivers:*** Full or partial for employees or children of employees.

LOANS ***Student loans:*** $1,412,418 (100% need-based). 64% of past graduating class borrowed through all loan programs. *Average indebtedness per student:* $14,963. ***Average need-based loan:*** Freshmen: $5405. Undergraduates: $5342. ***Programs:*** college/university.

WORK-STUDY ***State or other work-study/employment:*** Total amount: $177,850 (100% need-based). 142 part-time jobs averaging $1252.

APPLYING FOR FINANCIAL AID ***Required financial aid forms:*** institution's own form, CSS Financial Aid PROFILE, noncustodial (divorced/separated) parent's statement, federal income tax form(s). ***Financial aid deadline (priority):*** 3/1. ***Notification date:*** Continuous beginning 3/1. Students must reply by 5/1 or within 4 weeks of notification.

CONTACT Tami Gavaletz, Director of Financial Aid, Principia College, 1 Maybeck Place, Elsah, IL 62028-9799, 618-374-5187 or toll-free 800-277-4648 Ext. 2802. *Fax:* 618-374-5906. *E-mail:* tami.gavaletz@principia.edu.

PROVIDENCE COLLEGE

Providence, RI

Tuition & fees: $39,435 **Average undergraduate aid package: $24,085**

ABOUT THE INSTITUTION Independent Roman Catholic, coed. 46 undergraduate majors. Both federal and institutional methodology are used as a basis for awarding need-based institutional aid.

UNDERGRADUATE EXPENSES for 2011–12 ***Comprehensive fee:*** $51,125 includes full-time tuition ($38,610), mandatory fees ($825), and room and board ($11,690). ***College room only:*** $6790. Full-time tuition and fees vary according to degree level and student level. Room and board charges vary according to board plan and housing facility. ***Part-time tuition:*** $1287 per credit hour. Part-time tuition and fees vary according to degree level. ***Payment plan:*** Installment.

FRESHMAN FINANCIAL AID (Fall 2010, est.) 856 applied for aid; of those 78% were deemed to have need. 100% of freshmen with need received aid; of those 44% had need fully met. ***Average percent of need met:*** 87% (excluding resources awarded to replace EFC). ***Average financial aid package:*** $27,100 (excluding resources awarded to replace EFC). 9% of all full-time freshmen had no need and received non-need-based gift aid.

UNDERGRADUATE FINANCIAL AID (Fall 2010, est.) 2,740 applied for aid; of those 82% were deemed to have need. 100% of undergraduates with need received aid; of those 40% had need fully met. ***Average percent of need met:*** 83% (excluding resources awarded to replace EFC). ***Average financial aid package:*** $24,085 (excluding resources awarded to replace EFC). 7% of all full-time undergraduates had no need and received non-need-based gift aid.

GIFT AID (NEED-BASED) ***Total amount:*** $43,441,720 (8% federal, 1% state, 89% institutional, 2% external sources). ***Receiving aid:*** Freshmen: 57% (634); all full-time undergraduates: 51% (1,971). ***Average award:*** Freshmen: $20,138; Undergraduates: $18,866. ***Scholarships, grants, and awards:*** Federal Pell, FSEOG, state, private, college/university gift aid from institutional funds, Academic Competitiveness Grants, National SMART Grants.

GIFT AID (NON-NEED-BASED) ***Total amount:*** $8,269,594 (93% institutional, 7% external sources). ***Receiving aid:*** Freshmen: 5% (59). Undergraduates: 5% (212). ***Average award:*** Freshmen: $14,625. Undergraduates: $26,763. ***Scholarships, grants, and awards by category:*** *Academic interests/achievement:* 400 awards ($3,750,000 total): business, general academic interests/achievements, military science, premedicine. *Creative arts/performance:* 5 awards ($15,000 total): theater/drama. *Special achievements/activities:* 20 awards ($100,000 total): community service. *Special characteristics:* 87 awards ($86,500 total): siblings of current students. ***Tuition waivers:*** Full or partial for employees or children of employees, senior citizens.

LOANS ***Student loans:*** $25,313,281 (56% need-based, 44% non-need-based). 74% of past graduating class borrowed through all loan programs. *Average indebtedness per student:* $32,850. ***Average need-based loan:*** Freshmen: $4738. Undergraduates: $4946. ***Parent loans:*** $11,163,742 (68% need-based, 32% non-need-based). ***Programs:*** Federal Direct (Subsidized and Unsubsidized Stafford, PLUS), Perkins.

WORK-STUDY ***Federal work-study:*** Total amount: $1,337,488; 700 jobs averaging $1800. ***State or other work-study/employment:*** Total amount: $800,000 (100% non-need-based). 700 part-time jobs averaging $1800.

ATHLETIC AWARDS Total amount: $6,090,828 (22% need-based, 78% non-need-based).

APPLYING FOR FINANCIAL AID ***Required financial aid forms:*** FAFSA, CSS Financial Aid PROFILE, business/farm supplement. ***Financial aid deadline:*** 2/1. ***Notification date:*** 4/1. Students must reply by 5/1.

CONTACT Ms. Sandra J. Oliveira, Executive Director of Financial Aid, Providence College, 1 Cunningham Square, Providence, RI 02918, 401-865-2286 or toll-free 800-721-6444. *Fax:* 401-865-1186. *E-mail:* solivei6@providence.edu.

PURCHASE COLLEGE, STATE UNIVERSITY OF NEW YORK

Purchase, NY

Tuition & fees (NY res): $6504 **Average undergraduate aid package: $9829**

ABOUT THE INSTITUTION State-supported, coed. 43 undergraduate majors. Federal methodology is used as a basis for awarding need-based institutional aid.

UNDERGRADUATE EXPENSES for 2011–12 ***One-time required fee:*** $200. ***Tuition, state resident:*** full-time $4970; part-time $207 per credit. ***Tuition, nonresident:*** full-time $13,380; part-time $558 per credit. ***Required fees:*** full-time $1534; $.85 per credit hour. Full-time tuition and fees vary according to program. Part-time tuition and fees vary according to course load and program. ***College room and board:*** $10,646. Room and board charges vary according to board plan and housing facility. ***Payment plan:*** Installment.

FRESHMAN FINANCIAL AID (Fall 2010, est.) 568 applied for aid; of those 73% were deemed to have need. 100% of freshmen with need received aid; of those 4% had need fully met. ***Average percent of need met:*** 54% (excluding resources awarded to replace EFC). ***Average financial aid package:*** $8542 (excluding resources awarded to replace EFC). 4% of all full-time freshmen had no need and received non-need-based gift aid.

UNDERGRADUATE FINANCIAL AID (Fall 2010, est.) 2,694 applied for aid; of those 79% were deemed to have need. 100% of undergraduates with need received aid; of those 4% had need fully met. ***Average percent of need met:*** 58% (excluding resources awarded to replace EFC). ***Average financial aid package:*** $9829 (excluding resources awarded to replace EFC). 3% of all full-time undergraduates had no need and received non-need-based gift aid.

GIFT AID (NEED-BASED) ***Total amount:*** $10,618,139 (53% federal, 36% state, 7% institutional, 4% external sources). ***Receiving aid:*** Freshmen: 48% (322); all full-time undergraduates: 46% (1,749). ***Average award:*** Freshmen: $6215; Undergraduates: $6070. ***Scholarships, grants, and awards:*** Federal Pell, FSEOG, state, private, college/university gift aid from institutional funds.

GIFT AID (NON-NEED-BASED) ***Total amount:*** $402,226 (27% state, 46% institutional, 27% external sources). ***Receiving aid:*** Freshmen: 1% (10). Undergraduates: 1% (29). ***Average award:*** Freshmen: $2091. Undergraduates: $1688. ***Scholarships, grants, and awards by category:*** *Academic interests/achievement:* area/ethnic studies, biological sciences, computer science, English, general academic interests/achievements, humanities, mathematics, social sciences. *Creative arts/performance:* art/fine arts, cinema/film/broadcasting, creative writing, dance, general creative arts/performance, music, performing arts, theater/drama. ***Tuition waivers:*** Full or partial for employees or children of employees.

LOANS ***Student loans:*** $21,095,371 (72% need-based, 28% non-need-based). 58% of past graduating class borrowed through all loan programs. *Average indebtedness per student:* $33,125. ***Average need-based loan:*** Freshmen: $3565. Undergraduates: $4688. ***Parent loans:*** $23,661,463 (29% need-based, 71% non-need-based). ***Programs:*** Federal Direct (Subsidized and Unsubsidized Stafford, PLUS), Perkins.

WORK-STUDY ***Federal work-study:*** Total amount: $236,655; jobs available. ***State or other work-study/employment:*** Total amount: $587,234 (41% need-based, 59% non-need-based). Part-time jobs available.

APPLYING FOR FINANCIAL AID ***Required financial aid forms:*** FAFSA, state aid form. ***Financial aid deadline (priority):*** 2/1. ***Notification date:*** Continuous beginning 3/1. Students must reply within 2 weeks of notification.

CONTACT Ms. Corey York, Director of Student Financial Services, Purchase College, State University of New York, 735 Anderson Hill Road, Purchase, NY 10577-1400, 914-251-6085. *Fax:* 914-251-6099. *E-mail:* corey.york@purchase.edu.

PURDUE UNIVERSITY

West Lafayette, IN

Tuition & fees (IN res): $9069 **Average undergraduate aid package: $11,242**

ABOUT THE INSTITUTION State-supported, coed. 225 undergraduate majors. Federal methodology is used as a basis for awarding need-based institutional aid.

UNDERGRADUATE EXPENSES for 2010–11 ***Tuition, state resident:*** full-time $8592; part-time $324.75 per credit hour. ***Tuition, nonresident:*** full-time $26,144; part-time $885.25 per credit hour. ***Required fees:*** full-time $477. Full-time tuition and fees vary according to course load and program. Part-time tuition and fees vary according to course load. ***College room and board:*** $9120; ***Room only:*** $4319. Room and board charges vary according to board plan and housing facility. ***Payment plan:*** Installment.

FRESHMAN FINANCIAL AID (Fall 2010, est.) 4,751 applied for aid; of those 73% were deemed to have need. 100% of freshmen with need received aid; of those 55% had need fully met. ***Average percent of need met:*** 95% (excluding resources awarded to replace EFC). ***Average financial aid package:*** $11,144 (excluding resources awarded to replace EFC). 8% of all full-time freshmen had no need and received non-need-based gift aid.

UNDERGRADUATE FINANCIAL AID (Fall 2010, est.) 19,161 applied for aid; of those 77% were deemed to have need. 100% of undergraduates with need received aid; of those 38% had need fully met. ***Average percent of need met:*** 95% (excluding resources awarded to replace EFC). ***Average financial aid package:*** $11,242 (excluding resources awarded to replace EFC). 7% of all full-time undergraduates had no need and received non-need-based gift aid.

GIFT AID (NEED-BASED) ***Total amount:*** $83,205,807 (40% federal, 23% state, 32% institutional, 5% external sources). ***Receiving aid:*** Freshmen: 39% (2,516); all full-time undergraduates: 35% (10,652). ***Average award:*** Freshmen: $9899; Undergraduates: $8923. ***Scholarships, grants, and awards:*** Federal Pell, FSEOG, state, private, college/university gift aid from institutional funds, Academic Competitiveness Grants, National SMART Grants, TEACH Grants.

GIFT AID (NON-NEED-BASED) ***Total amount:*** $30,311,483 (21% federal, 6% state, 56% institutional, 17% external sources). ***Receiving aid:*** Freshmen: 29% (1,894). Undergraduates: 18% (5,327). ***Average award:*** Freshmen: $6452. Undergraduates: $6134. ***Scholarships, grants, and awards by category:*** *Academic interests/achievement:* agriculture, computer science, education, engineering/technologies, general academic interests/achievements, health fields, humanities, mathematics, military science, physical sciences. *Creative arts/performance:* music. *Special achievements/activities:* leadership. *Special characteristics:* children of faculty/staff. ***Tuition waivers:*** Full or partial for employees or children of employees, senior citizens.

LOANS ***Student loans:*** $152,167,556 (68% need-based, 32% non-need-based). 52% of past graduating class borrowed through all loan programs. *Average indebtedness per student:* $26,360. ***Average need-based loan:*** Freshmen: $3990. Undergraduates: $4997. ***Parent loans:*** $197,680,530 (26% need-based, 74% non-need-based). ***Programs:*** Federal Direct (Subsidized and Unsubsidized Stafford, PLUS), Perkins, college/university.

WORK-STUDY ***Federal work-study:*** Total amount: $652,288; 933 jobs averaging $709.

ATHLETIC AWARDS Total amount: $8,061,810 (30% need-based, 70% non-need-based).

APPLYING FOR FINANCIAL AID ***Required financial aid form:*** FAFSA. ***Financial aid deadline (priority):*** 3/1. ***Notification date:*** 4/15.

CONTACT Joyce Hall, Division of Financial Aid, Purdue University, Schleman Hall of Student Services, Room 305, West Lafayette, IN 47907-2050, 765-494-5056. *Fax:* 765-494-6707.

PURDUE UNIVERSITY CALUMET

Hammond, IN

Tuition & fees (IN res): $6654 **Average undergraduate aid package: $7408**

ABOUT THE INSTITUTION State-supported, coed. 44 undergraduate majors. Federal methodology is used as a basis for awarding need-based institutional aid.

UNDERGRADUATE EXPENSES for 2010–11 ***Tuition, state resident:*** full-time $6654; part-time $220.75 per credit hour. ***Tuition, nonresident:*** full-time $14,306; part-time $494.05 per credit hour. ***Required fees:*** $21.70 per credit hour. Full-time tuition and fees vary according to course load and program. Part-time tuition and fees vary according to course load and program. ***College room and board:*** $6924; ***Room only:*** $4900. Room and board charges vary according to housing facility. ***Payment plan:*** Deferred payment.

FRESHMAN FINANCIAL AID (Fall 2009) 884 applied for aid; of those 76% were deemed to have need. 94% of freshmen with need received aid; of those 17% had need fully met. ***Average percent of need met:*** 10% (excluding resources awarded to replace EFC). ***Average financial aid package:*** $4210 (excluding resources awarded to replace EFC). 6% of all full-time freshmen had no need and received non-need-based gift aid.

UNDERGRADUATE FINANCIAL AID (Fall 2009) 5,259 applied for aid; of those 82% were deemed to have need. 94% of undergraduates with need received aid; of those 11% had need fully met. ***Average percent of need met:*** 11% (excluding resources awarded to replace EFC). ***Average financial aid package:*** $7408 (excluding resources awarded to replace EFC). 4% of all full-time undergraduates had no need and received non-need-based gift aid.

GIFT AID (NEED-BASED) ***Total amount:*** $20,276,560 (71% federal, 27% state, 2% institutional). ***Receiving aid:*** Freshmen: 38% (430); all full-time undergraduates: 43% (2,950). ***Average award:*** Freshmen: $3412; Undergraduates: $5698. ***Scholarships, grants, and awards:*** Federal Pell, FSEOG, state, private, college/university gift aid from institutional funds.

GIFT AID (NON-NEED-BASED) ***Total amount:*** $3,910,871 (3% state, 60% institutional, 37% external sources). ***Receiving aid:*** Freshmen: 18% (200). Undergraduates: 10% (661). ***Average award:*** Freshmen: $1364. Undergraduates: $2879. ***Scholarships, grants, and awards by category:*** *Academic interests/achievement:* 696 awards ($2,305,349 total): general academic interests/achievements. ***Tuition waivers:*** Full or partial for employees or children of employees, senior citizens.

LOANS ***Student loans:*** $33,458,703 (98% need-based, 2% non-need-based). 62% of past graduating class borrowed through all loan programs. *Average indebtedness per student:* $22,106. ***Average need-based loan:*** Freshmen: $1736. Undergraduates: $3421. ***Parent loans:*** $2,411,456 (100% non-need-based). ***Programs:*** Federal Direct (Subsidized and Unsubsidized Stafford, PLUS), Perkins.

WORK-STUDY ***Federal work-study:*** Total amount: $278,570; 141 jobs averaging $1909.

ATHLETIC AWARDS Total amount: $72,725 (100% non-need-based).

APPLYING FOR FINANCIAL AID ***Required financial aid form:*** FAFSA. ***Financial aid deadline (priority):*** 3/10. ***Notification date:*** Continuous beginning 4/15. Students must reply within 2 weeks of notification.

CONTACT Ms. Tanika House, Assistant Director of Financial Aid, Purdue University Calumet, 2200 169th Street, Hammond, IN 46323-2094, 219-989-2301 or toll-free 800-447-8738 (in-state). *Fax:* 219-989-2141. *E-mail:* finaid2@purduecal.edu.

PURDUE UNIVERSITY NORTH CENTRAL

Westville, IN

Tuition & fees (IN res): $6704 **Average undergraduate aid package: $7804**

ABOUT THE INSTITUTION State-supported, coed. 28 undergraduate majors. Federal methodology is used as a basis for awarding need-based institutional aid.

UNDERGRADUATE EXPENSES for 2010–11 ***Tuition, state resident:*** full-time $6128; part-time $204.25 per credit hour. ***Tuition, nonresident:*** full-time $15,384; part-time $512.80 per credit hour. ***Required fees:*** full-time $576; $19.20 per credit hour. Full-time tuition and fees vary according to course load, location, program, and reciprocity agreements. Part-time tuition and fees vary according to course load, location, program, and reciprocity agreements. ***Payment plans:*** Installment, deferred payment.

FRESHMAN FINANCIAL AID (Fall 2009) 539 applied for aid; of those 78% were deemed to have need. 92% of freshmen with need received aid; of those 15% had need fully met. ***Average percent of need met:*** 43% (excluding resources awarded to replace EFC). ***Average financial aid package:*** $7309 (excluding resources awarded to replace EFC). 1% of all full-time freshmen had no need and received non-need-based gift aid.

UNDERGRADUATE FINANCIAL AID (Fall 2009) 2,219 applied for aid; of those 82% were deemed to have need. 95% of undergraduates with need received aid; of those 7% had need fully met. ***Average percent of need met:*** 47% (excluding resources awarded to replace EFC). ***Average financial aid package:*** $7804 (excluding resources awarded to replace EFC). 1% of all full-time undergraduates had no need and received non-need-based gift aid.

GIFT AID (NEED-BASED) ***Total amount:*** $8,739,688 (64% federal, 35% state, 1% institutional). ***Receiving aid:*** Freshmen: 39% (285); all full-time undergraduates: 45% (1,224). ***Average award:*** Freshmen: $6524; Undergraduates: $6576. ***Scholarships, grants, and awards:*** Federal Pell, FSEOG, state, private, college/university gift aid from institutional funds.

GIFT AID (NON-NEED-BASED) ***Total amount:*** $445,806 (62% institutional, 38% external sources). ***Receiving aid:*** Freshmen: 17% (120). Undergraduates: 15% (417). ***Average award:*** Freshmen: $1748. Undergraduates: $1856. ***Scholarships, grants, and awards by category:*** *Academic interests/achievement:* business, education, English, general academic interests/achievements, health fields. *Special achievements/activities:* general special achievements/activities, leadership. *Special characteristics:* adult students, children of faculty/staff, veterans' children. ***Tuition waivers:*** Full or partial for employees or children of employees, senior citizens.

LOANS ***Student loans:*** $14,655,436 (42% need-based, 58% non-need-based). 62% of past graduating class borrowed through all loan programs. *Average indebtedness per student:* $22,137. ***Average need-based loan:*** Freshmen: $3679. Undergraduates: $4158. ***Parent loans:*** $913,051 (100% non-need-based). ***Programs:*** Federal Direct (Subsidized and Unsubsidized Stafford, PLUS), alternative loans.

WORK-STUDY ***Federal work-study:*** Total amount: $134,936; 74 jobs averaging $1671. ***State or other work-study/employment:*** Part-time jobs available.

ATHLETIC AWARDS Total amount: $30,950 (100% non-need-based).

APPLYING FOR FINANCIAL AID ***Required financial aid form:*** FAFSA. ***Financial aid deadline:*** 6/30 (priority: 3/10). ***Notification date:*** Continuous beginning 4/15. Students must reply by 8/10.

CONTACT Janice Whisler, Interim Director of Enrollment and Outreach Recruitment, Purdue University North Central, 1401 South US Highway 421, Westville, IN 46391-9528, 219-785-5415 or toll-free 800-872-1231 (in-state). *Fax:* 219-785-4828. *E-mail:* jwhisler@pnc.edu.

QUEENS COLLEGE OF THE CITY UNIVERSITY OF NEW YORK

Flushing, NY

Tuition & fees (NY res): $5047 **Average undergraduate aid package: $8000**

ABOUT THE INSTITUTION State and locally supported, coed. 58 undergraduate majors. Federal methodology is used as a basis for awarding need-based institutional aid.

UNDERGRADUATE EXPENSES for 2010–11 ***Tuition, state resident:*** full-time $4600; part-time $195 per credit. ***Tuition, nonresident:*** full-time $9960; part-time $415 per credit. ***Required fees:*** full-time $447; $140.75 per term. ***College room and board:*** $11,125; ***Room only:*** $8825. Room and board charges vary according to housing facility. ***Payment plan:*** Installment.

FRESHMAN FINANCIAL AID (Fall 2010, est.) 1,355 applied for aid; of those 91% were deemed to have need. 100% of freshmen with need received aid; of those 63% had need fully met. ***Average percent of need met:*** 95% (excluding resources awarded to replace EFC). ***Average financial aid package:*** $8000 (excluding resources awarded to replace EFC). 2% of all full-time freshmen had no need and received non-need-based gift aid.

UNDERGRADUATE FINANCIAL AID (Fall 2010, est.) 11,756 applied for aid; of those 77% were deemed to have need. 100% of undergraduates with need received aid; of those 79% had need fully met. ***Average percent of need met:*** 95% (excluding resources awarded to replace EFC). ***Average financial aid package:*** $8000 (excluding resources awarded to replace EFC). 1% of all full-time undergraduates had no need and received non-need-based gift aid.

GIFT AID (NEED-BASED) ***Total amount:*** $48,887,127 (58% federal, 41% state, 1% institutional). ***Receiving aid:*** Freshmen: 66% (974); all full-time undergraduates: 63% (7,422). ***Average award:*** Freshmen: $4800; Undergraduates: $4800. ***Scholarships, grants, and awards:*** Federal Pell, FSEOG, state, college/university gift aid from institutional funds, Peter Vallone Scholarships.

GIFT AID (NON-NEED-BASED) ***Total amount:*** $1,194,679 (100% institutional). ***Receiving aid:*** Freshmen: 31% (461). Undergraduates: 12% (1,468). ***Average***

award: Freshmen: $8300. Undergraduates: $8300. ***Scholarships, grants, and awards by category:*** *Academic interests/achievement:* general academic interests/achievements. *Creative arts/performance:* music. *Special achievements/activities:* community service, leadership. ***Tuition waivers:*** Full or partial for senior citizens.

LOANS ***Student loans:*** $23,607,629 (58% need-based, 42% non-need-based). 45% of past graduating class borrowed through all loan programs. *Average indebtedness per student:* $17,700. ***Average need-based loan:*** Freshmen: $2800. Undergraduates: $4900. ***Parent loans:*** $601,343 (100% non-need-based). ***Programs:*** Federal Direct (Subsidized and Unsubsidized Stafford, PLUS), Perkins.

WORK-STUDY ***Federal work-study:*** Total amount: $519,700; 519,700 jobs averaging $456. ***State or other work-study/employment:*** Part-time jobs available.

ATHLETIC AWARDS Total amount: $706,483 (100% non-need-based).

APPLYING FOR FINANCIAL AID ***Required financial aid forms:*** FAFSA, institution's own form, state aid form. ***Financial aid deadline (priority):*** 2/15. ***Notification date:*** Continuous beginning 5/1. Students must reply within 3 weeks of notification.

CONTACT Rena Smith-Kiawu, Director of Financial Aid, Queens College of the City University of New York, 65-30 Kissena Boulevard, Flushing, NY 11367-1597, 718-997-5100.

QUEENS UNIVERSITY OF CHARLOTTE

Charlotte, NC

CONTACT Lauren H. Mack, Director of Financial Aid, Queens University of Charlotte, 1900 Selwyn Avenue, Charlotte, NC 28274-0002, 704-337-2230 or toll-free 800-849-0202. *Fax:* 704-337-2416. *E-mail:* mackl@queens.edu.

QUINCY UNIVERSITY

Quincy, IL

Tuition & fees: $24,140 **Average undergraduate aid package: $21,853**

ABOUT THE INSTITUTION Independent Roman Catholic, coed. 32 undergraduate majors. Federal methodology is used as a basis for awarding need-based institutional aid.

UNDERGRADUATE EXPENSES for 2011–12 ***Comprehensive fee:*** $33,560 includes full-time tuition ($23,340), mandatory fees ($800), and room and board ($9420). ***College room only:*** $5210. Room and board charges vary according to board plan and housing facility. ***Part-time tuition:*** $565 per semester hour. ***Part-time fees:*** $15 per semester hour. Part-time tuition and fees vary according to course load. ***Payment plan:*** Installment.

FRESHMAN FINANCIAL AID (Fall 2010, est.) 270 applied for aid; of those 91% were deemed to have need. 100% of freshmen with need received aid; of those 27% had need fully met. ***Average percent of need met:*** 85% (excluding resources awarded to replace EFC). ***Average financial aid package:*** $23,967 (excluding resources awarded to replace EFC). 5% of all full-time freshmen had no need and received non-need-based gift aid.

UNDERGRADUATE FINANCIAL AID (Fall 2010, est.) 1,057 applied for aid; of those 92% were deemed to have need. 96% of undergraduates with need received aid; of those 23% had need fully met. ***Average percent of need met:*** 80% (excluding resources awarded to replace EFC). ***Average financial aid package:*** $21,853 (excluding resources awarded to replace EFC). 4% of all full-time undergraduates had no need and received non-need-based gift aid.

GIFT AID (NEED-BASED) ***Total amount:*** $14,478,454 (19% federal, 15% state, 64% institutional, 2% external sources). ***Receiving aid:*** Freshmen: 90% (247); all full-time undergraduates: 79% (911). ***Average award:*** Freshmen: $20,835; Undergraduates: $18,155. ***Scholarships, grants, and awards:*** Federal Pell, FSEOG, state, private, college/university gift aid from institutional funds.

GIFT AID (NON-NEED-BASED) ***Total amount:*** $1,162,741 (1% federal, 1% state, 92% institutional, 6% external sources). ***Receiving aid:*** Freshmen: 15% (42). Undergraduates: 11% (125). ***Average award:*** Freshmen: $12,581. Undergraduates: $10,477. ***Scholarships, grants, and awards by category:*** *Academic interests/achievement:* 1,032 awards ($8,121,515 total): biological sciences, business, communication, computer science, education, English, general academic interests/achievements, health fields, humanities, international studies, mathematics, premedicine, religion/biblical studies, social sciences. *Creative arts/performance:* 58 awards ($115,906 total): art/fine arts, cinema/film/broadcasting, music. *Special achievements/activities:* 60 awards ($57,421 total): cheerleading/drum major, community service, general special achievements/activities, hobbies/interests, leadership. *Special characteristics:* 97 awards ($345,814 total): adult students, children and siblings of alumni, children of faculty/staff, local/state students, members of minority groups. ***Tuition waivers:*** Full or partial for employees or children of employees, senior citizens.

LOANS ***Student loans:*** $7,056,032 (76% need-based, 24% non-need-based). 83% of past graduating class borrowed through all loan programs. *Average indebtedness per student:* $23,711. ***Average need-based loan:*** Freshmen: $3352. Undergraduates: $4378. ***Parent loans:*** $1,036,194 (30% need-based, 70% non-need-based). ***Programs:*** Federal Direct (Subsidized and Unsubsidized Stafford, PLUS), Perkins.

WORK-STUDY ***Federal work-study:*** Total amount: $208,500; 345 jobs averaging $2000. ***State or other work-study/employment:*** Total amount: $87,269 (100% non-need-based). 23 part-time jobs averaging $3794.

ATHLETIC AWARDS Total amount: $2,972,125 (72% need-based, 28% non-need-based).

APPLYING FOR FINANCIAL AID ***Required financial aid form:*** FAFSA. ***Financial aid deadline (priority):*** 3/1. ***Notification date:*** Continuous beginning 3/1. Students must reply by 5/1 or within 2 weeks of notification.

CONTACT Lisa Flack, Director of Financial Aid, Quincy University, 1800 College Avenue, Quincy, IL 62301-2699, 217-228-5260 or toll-free 800-688-4295. *Fax:* 217-228-5635. *E-mail:* financialaid@quincy.edu.

QUINNIPIAC UNIVERSITY

Hamden, CT

Tuition & fees: $36,130 **Average undergraduate aid package: $21,051**

ABOUT THE INSTITUTION Independent, coed. 59 undergraduate majors. Federal methodology is used as a basis for awarding need-based institutional aid.

UNDERGRADUATE EXPENSES for 2011–12 ***Comprehensive fee:*** $49,560 includes full-time tuition ($34,710), mandatory fees ($1420), and room and board ($13,430). Room and board charges vary according to housing facility. ***Part-time tuition:*** $835 per credit hour. ***Part-time fees:*** $35 per credit. Part-time tuition and fees vary according to class time and course load. ***Payment plans:*** Installment, deferred payment.

FRESHMAN FINANCIAL AID (Fall 2010, est.) 1,350 applied for aid; of those 84% were deemed to have need. 100% of freshmen with need received aid; of those 14% had need fully met. ***Average percent of need met:*** 68% (excluding resources awarded to replace EFC). ***Average financial aid package:*** $21,596 (excluding resources awarded to replace EFC). 13% of all full-time freshmen had no need and received non-need-based gift aid.

UNDERGRADUATE FINANCIAL AID (Fall 2010, est.) 4,330 applied for aid; of those 85% were deemed to have need. 100% of undergraduates with need received aid; of those 12% had need fully met. ***Average percent of need met:*** 66% (excluding resources awarded to replace EFC). ***Average financial aid package:*** $21,051 (excluding resources awarded to replace EFC). 13% of all full-time undergraduates had no need and received non-need-based gift aid.

GIFT AID (NEED-BASED) ***Total amount:*** $39,697,849 (12% federal, 8% state, 76% institutional, 4% external sources). ***Receiving aid:*** Freshmen: 68% (1,112); all full-time undergraduates: 62% (3,612). ***Average award:*** Freshmen: $16,672; Undergraduates: $15,458. ***Scholarships, grants, and awards:*** Federal Pell, FSEOG, state, private, college/university gift aid from institutional funds.

GIFT AID (NON-NEED-BASED) ***Total amount:*** $24,518,918 (98% institutional, 2% external sources). ***Receiving aid:*** Freshmen: 36% (586). Undergraduates: 29% (1,694). ***Average award:*** Freshmen: $11,141. Undergraduates: $10,948. ***Scholarships, grants, and awards by category:*** *Academic interests/achievement:* 2,273 awards ($24,267,595 total): general academic interests/achievements. *Special characteristics:* 318 awards ($2,556,680 total): children of faculty/staff, international students, siblings of current students. ***Tuition waivers:*** Full or partial for employees or children of employees.

LOANS ***Student loans:*** $45,031,222 (68% need-based, 32% non-need-based). 66% of past graduating class borrowed through all loan programs. *Average indebtedness per student:* $38,953. ***Average need-based loan:*** Freshmen: $3547. Undergraduates: $4520. ***Parent loans:*** $17,479,713 (100% non-need-based). ***Programs:*** Federal Direct (Subsidized and Unsubsidized Stafford, PLUS), Perkins.

WORK-STUDY ***Federal work-study:*** Total amount: $4,213,261; 2,097 jobs averaging $2031. ***State or other work-study/employment:*** Total amount: $73,791 (100% need-based). 47 part-time jobs averaging $1634.

ATHLETIC AWARDS Total amount: $7,838,371 (100% non-need-based).

APPLYING FOR FINANCIAL AID ***Required financial aid forms:*** FAFSA, CSS Financial Aid PROFILE. ***Financial aid deadline (priority):*** 3/1. ***Notification date:*** Continuous beginning 3/1. Students must reply by 5/1 or within 2 weeks of notification.

CONTACT Mr. Dominic Yoia, Senior Director of Financial Aid, Quinnipiac University, 275 Mount Carmel Avenue, Hamden, CT 06518, 203-582-5224 or toll-free 800-462-1944 (out-of-state). *Fax:* 203-582-5238. *E-mail:* finaid@quinnipiac.edu.

RABBI JACOB JOSEPH SCHOOL

Edison, NJ

CONTACT Financial Aid Office, Rabbi Jacob Joseph School, One Plainfield Ave, Edison, NJ 08817, 908-985-6533.

RABBINICAL ACADEMY MESIVTA RABBI CHAIM BERLIN

Brooklyn, NY

CONTACT Office of Financial Aid, Rabbinical Academy Mesivta Rabbi Chaim Berlin, 1605 Coney Island Avenue, Brooklyn, NY 11230-4715, 718-377-0777.

RABBINICAL COLLEGE BETH SHRAGA

Monsey, NY

CONTACT Financial Aid Office, Rabbinical College Beth Shraga, 28 Saddle River Road, Monsey, NY 10952-3035, 914-356-1980.

RABBINICAL COLLEGE BOBOVER YESHIVA B'NEI ZION

Brooklyn, NY

CONTACT Financial Aid Office, Rabbinical College Bobover Yeshiva B'nei Zion, 1577 48th Street, Brooklyn, NY 11219, 718-438-2018.

RABBINICAL COLLEGE CH'SAN SOFER

Brooklyn, NY

CONTACT Financial Aid Office, Rabbinical College Ch'san Sofer, 1876 50th Street, Brooklyn, NY 11204, 718-236-1171.

RABBINICAL COLLEGE OF AMERICA

Morristown, NJ

CONTACT Financial Aid Office, Rabbinical College of America, 226 Sussex Avenue, Morristown, NJ 07960, 973-267-9404. *Fax:* 973-267-5208.

RABBINICAL COLLEGE OF LONG ISLAND

Long Beach, NY

CONTACT Rabbi Cone, Financial Aid Administrator, Rabbinical College of Long Island, 201 Magnolia Boulevard, Long Beach, NY 11561-3305, 516-431-7414.

RABBINICAL COLLEGE OF OHR SHIMON YISROEL

Brooklyn, NY

CONTACT Financial Aid Office, Rabbinical College of Ohr Shimon Yisroel, 215-217 Hewes Street, Brooklyn, NY 11211, 718-855-4092.

RABBINICAL COLLEGE OF TELSHE

Wickliffe, OH

CONTACT Financial Aid Office, Rabbinical College of Telshe, 28400 Euclid Avenue, Wickliffe, OH 44092-2523, 216-943-5300.

RABBINICAL SEMINARY ADAS YEREIM

Brooklyn, NY

CONTACT Mr. Israel Weingarten, Financial Aid Administrator, Rabbinical Seminary Adas Yereim, 185 Wilson Street, Brooklyn, NY 11211-7206, 718-388-1751.

RABBINICAL SEMINARY M'KOR CHAIM

Brooklyn, NY

CONTACT Financial Aid Office, Rabbinical Seminary M'kor Chaim, 1571 55th Street, Brooklyn, NY 11219, 718-851-0183.

RABBINICAL SEMINARY OF AMERICA

Flushing, NY

CONTACT Ms. Leah Eisenstein, Director of Financial Aid, Rabbinical Seminary of America, 92-15 69th Avenue, Forest Hills, NY 11375, 718-268-4700. *Fax:* 718-268-4684.

RADFORD UNIVERSITY

Radford, VA

Tuition & fees (VA res): $8104 **Average undergraduate aid package: $9564**

ABOUT THE INSTITUTION State-supported, coed. 38 undergraduate majors. Federal methodology is used as a basis for awarding need-based institutional aid.

UNDERGRADUATE EXPENSES for 2010–11 ***Tuition, state resident:*** full-time $5012; part-time $209 per credit hour. ***Tuition, nonresident:*** full-time $15,336; part-time $639 per credit hour. ***Required fees:*** full-time $3092; $137 per credit hour. ***College room and board:*** $7302; ***Room only:*** $3932. Room and board charges vary according to board plan and housing facility. ***Payment plan:*** Installment.

FRESHMAN FINANCIAL AID (Fall 2010, est.) 1,375 applied for aid; of those 68% were deemed to have need. 94% of freshmen with need received aid; of those 29% had need fully met. ***Average percent of need met:*** 84% (excluding resources awarded to replace EFC). ***Average financial aid package:*** $9080 (excluding resources awarded to replace EFC). 5% of all full-time freshmen had no need and received non-need-based gift aid.

UNDERGRADUATE FINANCIAL AID (Fall 2010, est.) 5,116 applied for aid; of those 74% were deemed to have need. 96% of undergraduates with need received aid; of those 35% had need fully met. ***Average percent of need met:*** 85% (excluding resources awarded to replace EFC). ***Average financial aid package:*** $9564 (excluding resources awarded to replace EFC). 3% of all full-time undergraduates had no need and received non-need-based gift aid.

GIFT AID (NEED-BASED) ***Total amount:*** $21,281,766 (45% federal, 33% state, 19% institutional, 3% external sources). ***Receiving aid:*** Freshmen: 30% (546); all full-time undergraduates: 31% (2,350). ***Average award:*** Freshmen: $8345; Undergraduates: $7691. ***Scholarships, grants, and awards:*** Federal Pell, FSEOG, state, private, college/university gift aid from institutional funds.

GIFT AID (NON-NEED-BASED) ***Total amount:*** $1,567,078 (15% federal, 6% state, 56% institutional, 23% external sources). ***Receiving aid:*** Freshmen: 14% (263). Undergraduates: 10% (775). ***Average award:*** Freshmen: $3803. Undergraduates: $3800. ***Tuition waivers:*** Full or partial for employees or children of employees, senior citizens.

LOANS ***Student loans:*** $32,116,361 (76% need-based, 24% non-need-based). 60% of past graduating class borrowed through all loan programs. *Average indebtedness per student:* $20,678. ***Average need-based loan:*** Freshmen: $3127. Undergraduates: $3942. ***Parent loans:*** $5,551,976 (59% need-based, 41% non-need-based). ***Programs:*** Federal Direct (Subsidized and Unsubsidized Stafford, PLUS), Perkins, Federal Nursing, state.

WORK-STUDY ***Federal work-study:*** Total amount: $864,825; 340 jobs averaging $2610. ***State or other work-study/employment:*** Total amount: $934,193 (57% need-based, 43% non-need-based). 472 part-time jobs averaging $2610.

ATHLETIC AWARDS Total amount: $2,333,594 (81% need-based, 19% non-need-based).

APPLYING FOR FINANCIAL AID ***Required financial aid form:*** FAFSA. ***Financial aid deadline (priority):*** 2/15. ***Notification date:*** 4/15. Students must reply within 4 weeks of notification.

CONTACT Mrs. Barbara Porter, Director of Financial Aid, Radford University, PO Box 6905, Radford, VA 24142, 540-831-5408 or toll-free 800-890-4265. *Fax:* 540-831-5138. *E-mail:* bporter@radford.edu.

RAMAPO COLLEGE OF NEW JERSEY

Mahwah, NJ

Tuition & fees (NJ res): $11,874 **Average undergraduate aid package: $11,723**

ABOUT THE INSTITUTION State-supported, coed. 35 undergraduate majors. Federal methodology is used as a basis for awarding need-based institutional aid.

UNDERGRADUATE EXPENSES for 2010–11 ***Tuition, state resident:*** full-time $7805; part-time $243.90 per credit. ***Tuition, nonresident:*** full-time $15,610; part-time $487.80 per credit. ***Required fees:*** full-time $4069; $127.15 per credit. Full-time tuition and fees vary according to degree level and reciprocity agreements. Part-time tuition and fees vary according to degree level and reciprocity agreements. ***College room and board:*** $10,250; ***Room only:*** $7700. Room and board charges vary according to board plan and housing facility. ***Payment plan:*** Installment.

FRESHMAN FINANCIAL AID (Fall 2010, est.) 756 applied for aid; of those 71% were deemed to have need. 96% of freshmen with need received aid; of those 18% had need fully met. ***Average percent of need met:*** 68% (excluding resources awarded to replace EFC). ***Average financial aid package:*** $11,691 (excluding resources awarded to replace EFC). 8% of all full-time freshmen had no need and received non-need-based gift aid.

UNDERGRADUATE FINANCIAL AID (Fall 2010, est.) 3,366 applied for aid; of those 77% were deemed to have need. 97% of undergraduates with need received aid; of those 5% had need fully met. ***Average percent of need met:*** 54% (excluding resources awarded to replace EFC). ***Average financial aid package:*** $11,723 (excluding resources awarded to replace EFC). 5% of all full-time undergraduates had no need and received non-need-based gift aid.

GIFT AID (NEED-BASED) ***Total amount:*** $13,091,584 (49% federal, 43% state, 8% institutional). ***Receiving aid:*** Freshmen: 25% (223); all full-time undergraduates: 23% (1,191). ***Average award:*** Freshmen: $13,847; Undergraduates: $10,035. ***Scholarships, grants, and awards:*** Federal Pell, FSEOG, state, private, college/university gift aid from institutional funds, Federal Nursing.

GIFT AID (NON-NEED-BASED) ***Total amount:*** $7,678,402 (7% state, 83% institutional, 10% external sources). ***Receiving aid:*** Freshmen: 19% (171). Undergraduates: 13% (686). ***Average award:*** Freshmen: $9761. Undergraduates: $11,462. ***Scholarships, grants, and awards by category:*** *Academic interests/achievement:* 719 awards ($6,520,407 total): general academic interests/achievements. *Special characteristics:* 97 awards ($1,315,521 total): children of faculty/staff, international students, out-of-state students. ***Tuition waivers:*** Full or partial for employees or children of employees, senior citizens.

LOANS ***Student loans:*** $32,112,044 (35% need-based, 65% non-need-based). 51% of past graduating class borrowed through all loan programs. *Average indebtedness per student:* $26,187. ***Average need-based loan:*** Freshmen: $3310. Undergraduates: $4612. ***Parent loans:*** $7,556,181 (100% non-need-based). ***Programs:*** Federal Direct (Subsidized and Unsubsidized Stafford, PLUS), Perkins, state.

WORK-STUDY ***Federal work-study:*** Total amount: $252,794; 125 jobs averaging $2022. ***State or other work-study/employment:*** Total amount: $167,888 (100% non-need-based). 760 part-time jobs averaging $2294.

APPLYING FOR FINANCIAL AID ***Required financial aid form:*** FAFSA. ***Financial aid deadline (priority):*** 3/1. ***Notification date:*** Continuous beginning 4/1. Students must reply by 5/1 or within 2 weeks of notification.

CONTACT Bernice Mulch, Assistant Director of Financial Aid, Ramapo College of New Jersey, 505 Ramapo Valley Road, Mahwah, NJ 07430-1680, 201-684-7252 or toll-free 800-9RAMAPO (in-state). *Fax:* 201-684-7085. *E-mail:* finaid@ramapo.edu.

RANDOLPH COLLEGE

Lynchburg, VA

Tuition & fees: $29,254 **Average undergraduate aid package: $24,013**

ABOUT THE INSTITUTION Independent Methodist, coed. 37 undergraduate majors. Federal methodology is used as a basis for awarding need-based institutional aid.

UNDERGRADUATE EXPENSES for 2010–11 ***Comprehensive fee:*** $39,249 includes full-time tuition ($28,744), mandatory fees ($510), and room and board ($9995). ***Part-time tuition:*** $1200 per credit hour. ***Part-time fees:*** $102.50 per term. Part-time tuition and fees vary according to course load. ***Payment plan:*** Installment.

FRESHMAN FINANCIAL AID (Fall 2010, est.) 132 applied for aid; of those 89% were deemed to have need. 100% of freshmen with need received aid; of those 25% had need fully met. ***Average percent of need met:*** 77% (excluding resources awarded to replace EFC). ***Average financial aid package:*** $23,693 (excluding resources awarded to replace EFC). 27% of all full-time freshmen had no need and received non-need-based gift aid.

UNDERGRADUATE FINANCIAL AID (Fall 2010, est.) 407 applied for aid; of those 91% were deemed to have need. 99% of undergraduates with need received aid; of those 20% had need fully met. ***Average percent of need met:*** 75% (excluding resources awarded to replace EFC). ***Average financial aid package:*** $24,013 (excluding resources awarded to replace EFC). 26% of all full-time undergraduates had no need and received non-need-based gift aid.

GIFT AID (NEED-BASED) ***Total amount:*** $6,525,736 (11% federal, 8% state, 80% institutional, 1% external sources). ***Receiving aid:*** Freshmen: 75% (118); all full-time undergraduates: 73% (365). ***Average award:*** Freshmen: $19,053; Undergraduates: $18,359. ***Scholarships, grants, and awards:*** Federal Pell, FSEOG, state, private, college/university gift aid from institutional funds.

GIFT AID (NON-NEED-BASED) ***Total amount:*** $2,398,642 (6% state, 93% institutional, 1% external sources). ***Receiving aid:*** Freshmen: 63% (99). Undergraduates: 63% (316). ***Average award:*** Freshmen: $18,453. Undergraduates: $16,268. ***Scholarships, grants, and awards by category:*** *Academic interests/achievement:* 365 awards ($4,057,255 total): biological sciences, education, English, general academic interests/achievements, mathematics, physical sciences, premedicine, social sciences. *Special achievements/activities:* community service, general special achievements/activities, leadership. *Special characteristics:* adult students, children of faculty/staff, international students, local/state students, relatives of clergy, religious affiliation, twins. ***Tuition waivers:*** Full or partial for employees or children of employees, adult students.

LOANS ***Student loans:*** $2,558,387 (55% need-based, 45% non-need-based). 75% of past graduating class borrowed through all loan programs. *Average indebtedness per student:* $22,000. ***Average need-based loan:*** Freshmen: $4439. Undergraduates: $5370. ***Parent loans:*** $1,472,436 (33% need-based, 67% non-need-based). ***Programs:*** Federal Direct (Subsidized and Unsubsidized Stafford, PLUS), Perkins.

WORK-STUDY ***Federal work-study:*** Total amount: $344,216; 180 jobs averaging $1860. ***State or other work-study/employment:*** Total amount: $211,680 (12% need-based, 88% non-need-based). 119 part-time jobs averaging $1800.

APPLYING FOR FINANCIAL AID ***Required financial aid forms:*** FAFSA, state aid form. ***Financial aid deadline (priority):*** 3/1. ***Notification date:*** Continuous beginning 3/1. Students must reply by 5/1 or within 2 weeks of notification.

CONTACT Kay G. Mattox, Director of Student Financial Services, Randolph College, 2500 Rivermont Avenue, Lynchburg, VA 24503-1526, 434-947-8128 or toll-free 800-745-7692. *Fax:* 434-947-8996. *E-mail:* kmattox@randolphcollege.edu.

RANDOLPH-MACON COLLEGE

Ashland, VA

Tuition & fees: $30,608 **Average undergraduate aid package: $23,140**

ABOUT THE INSTITUTION Independent United Methodist, coed. 31 undergraduate majors. Federal methodology is used as a basis for awarding need-based institutional aid.

UNDERGRADUATE EXPENSES for 2010–11 ***One-time required fee:*** $100. ***Comprehensive fee:*** $39,934 includes full-time tuition ($29,788), mandatory fees ($820), and room and board ($9326). Full-time tuition and fees vary according to reciprocity agreements. Room and board charges vary according to housing facility. ***Part-time tuition:*** $3310 per course. ***Part-time fees:*** $840 per year. ***Payment plan:*** Installment.

FRESHMAN FINANCIAL AID (Fall 2010, est.) 303 applied for aid; of those 88% were deemed to have need. 100% of freshmen with need received aid; of those 20% had need fully met. ***Average percent of need met:*** 80% (excluding resources awarded to replace EFC). ***Average financial aid package:*** $24,773 (excluding resources awarded to replace EFC). 33% of all full-time freshmen had no need and received non-need-based gift aid.

UNDERGRADUATE FINANCIAL AID (Fall 2010, est.) 968 applied for aid; of those 87% were deemed to have need. 100% of undergraduates with need received aid; of those 23% had need fully met. ***Average percent of need met:*** 79% (excluding resources awarded to replace EFC). ***Average financial aid package:*** $23,140 (excluding resources awarded to replace EFC). 28% of all full-time undergraduates had no need and received non-need-based gift aid.

GIFT AID (NEED-BASED) ***Total amount:*** $15,782,073 (8% federal, 9% state, 78% institutional, 5% external sources). ***Receiving aid:*** Freshmen: 78% (266); all full-time undergraduates: 71% (838). ***Average award:*** Freshmen: $20,518; Undergraduates: $18,955. ***Scholarships, grants, and awards:*** Federal Pell, FSEOG, state, private, college/university gift aid from institutional funds.

GIFT AID (NON-NEED-BASED) ***Total amount:*** $5,843,558 (13% state, 80% institutional, 7% external sources). ***Receiving aid:*** Freshmen: 10% (35). Undergraduates: 12% (137). ***Average award:*** Freshmen: $13,815. Undergraduates: $12,029. ***Scholarships, grants, and awards by category:*** *Academic interests/achievement:* 574 awards ($7,360,590 total): general academic interests/achievements. *Special achievements/activities:* 541 awards ($3,928,217 total): general special achievements/activities. *Special characteristics:* 631 awards ($1,734,718 total): children and siblings of alumni, children of faculty/staff, ethnic background, out-of-state students, relatives of clergy, siblings of current students. ***Tuition waivers:*** Full or partial for employees or children of employees.

LOANS ***Student loans:*** $7,963,329 (65% need-based, 35% non-need-based). 62% of past graduating class borrowed through all loan programs. *Average indebtedness per student:* $31,603. ***Average need-based loan:*** Freshmen: $4362. Undergraduates: $4560. ***Parent loans:*** $4,018,222 (30% need-based, 70% non-need-based). ***Programs:*** Federal Direct (Subsidized and Unsubsidized Stafford, PLUS), Perkins, college/university.

WORK-STUDY ***Federal work-study:*** Total amount: $422,606; 235 jobs averaging $2000.

APPLYING FOR FINANCIAL AID ***Required financial aid forms:*** FAFSA, state aid form. ***Financial aid deadline (priority):*** 2/15. ***Notification date:*** 3/1. Students must reply by 5/1 or within 2 weeks of notification.

CONTACT Ms. Mary Neal, Director of Financial Aid, Randolph-Macon College, PO Box 5005, Ashland, VA 23005-5505, 804-752-7259 or toll-free 800-888-1762. *Fax:* 804-752-3719. *E-mail:* mneal@rmc.edu.

REED COLLEGE

Portland, OR

Tuition & fees: $41,200 **Average undergraduate aid package: $34,196**

ABOUT THE INSTITUTION Independent, coed. 30 undergraduate majors. Institutional methodology is used as a basis for awarding need-based institutional aid.

UNDERGRADUATE EXPENSES for 2010–11 ***Comprehensive fee:*** $51,850 includes full-time tuition ($40,940), mandatory fees ($260), and room and board ($10,650). ***College room only:*** $5550. Room and board charges vary according to board plan and housing facility. ***Part-time tuition:*** $1750 per semester hour. Part-time tuition and fees vary according to course load. ***Payment plan:*** Installment.

FRESHMAN FINANCIAL AID (Fall 2010, est.) 244 applied for aid; of those 81% were deemed to have need. 100% of freshmen with need received aid; of those 100% had need fully met. ***Average percent of need met:*** 100% (excluding resources awarded to replace EFC). ***Average financial aid package:*** $34,856 (excluding resources awarded to replace EFC).

UNDERGRADUATE FINANCIAL AID (Fall 2010, est.) 842 applied for aid; of those 90% were deemed to have need. 100% of undergraduates with need received aid; of those 99% had need fully met. ***Average percent of need met:*** 100% (excluding resources awarded to replace EFC). ***Average financial aid package:*** $34,196 (excluding resources awarded to replace EFC).

GIFT AID (NEED-BASED) ***Total amount:*** $22,083,532 (9% federal, 91% institutional). ***Receiving aid:*** Freshmen: 46% (172); all full-time undergraduates: 48% (677). ***Average award:*** Freshmen: $34,939; Undergraduates: $32,548. ***Scholarships, grants, and awards:*** Federal Pell, FSEOG, state, private, college/university gift aid from institutional funds.

GIFT AID (NON-NEED-BASED) ***Tuition waivers:*** Full or partial for employees or children of employees.

LOANS ***Student loans:*** $3,364,618 (82% need-based, 18% non-need-based). 53% of past graduating class borrowed through all loan programs. *Average indebtedness per student:* $16,910. ***Average need-based loan:*** Freshmen: $3130. Undergraduates: $5034. ***Parent loans:*** $1,890,598 (12% need-based, 88% non-need-based). ***Programs:*** Federal Direct (Subsidized and Unsubsidized Stafford, PLUS), Perkins.

WORK-STUDY ***Federal work-study:*** Total amount: $672,291; jobs available. ***State or other work-study/employment:*** Total amount: $125,470 (100% need-based). Part-time jobs available.

APPLYING FOR FINANCIAL AID ***Required financial aid forms:*** FAFSA, CSS Financial Aid PROFILE, noncustodial (divorced/separated) parent's statement, business/farm supplement. ***Financial aid deadline:*** 2/1. ***Notification date:*** 4/1. Students must reply by 5/1 or within 2 weeks of notification.

CONTACT Leslie Limper, Director of Financial Aid, Reed College, 3203 Southeast Woodstock Boulevard, Portland, OR 97202-8199, 503-777-7223 or toll-free 800-547-4750 (out-of-state). *Fax:* 503-788-6682. *E-mail:* financial.aid@reed.edu.

REGENT UNIVERSITY

Virginia Beach, VA

Tuition & fees: $15,308 **Average undergraduate aid package: $11,971**

ABOUT THE INSTITUTION Independent religious, coed. 23 undergraduate majors. Federal methodology is used as a basis for awarding need-based institutional aid.

UNDERGRADUATE EXPENSES for 2010–11 ***Tuition:*** full-time $14,850; part-time $495 per credit hour. ***Required fees:*** full-time $458; $495 per credit hour. Full-time tuition and fees vary according to course level, course load, program, and student level. Part-time tuition and fees vary according to course level, course load, program, and student level. Room and board charges vary according to housing facility. ***Payment plan:*** Installment.

FRESHMAN FINANCIAL AID (Fall 2009) 113 applied for aid; of those 88% were deemed to have need. 100% of freshmen with need received aid; of those 19% had need fully met. ***Average percent of need met:*** 60% (excluding resources awarded to replace EFC). ***Average financial aid package:*** $10,858 (excluding resources awarded to replace EFC). 14% of all full-time freshmen had no need and received non-need-based gift aid.

UNDERGRADUATE FINANCIAL AID (Fall 2009) 1,039 applied for aid; of those 96% were deemed to have need. 100% of undergraduates with need received aid; of those 6% had need fully met. ***Average percent of need met:*** 60% (excluding resources awarded to replace EFC). ***Average financial aid package:*** $11,971 (excluding resources awarded to replace EFC). 15% of all full-time undergraduates had no need and received non-need-based gift aid.

GIFT AID (NEED-BASED) ***Total amount:*** $10,876,235 (46% federal, 8% state, 44% institutional, 2% external sources). ***Receiving aid:*** Freshmen: 74% (89); all full-time undergraduates: 75% (927). ***Average award:*** Freshmen: $8343; Undergraduates: $7714. ***Scholarships, grants, and awards:*** Federal Pell, state, private, college/university gift aid from institutional funds.

GIFT AID (NON-NEED-BASED) ***Total amount:*** $1,328,534 (10% state, 87% institutional, 3% external sources). ***Receiving aid:*** Freshmen: 15% (18). Undergraduates: 4% (54). ***Average award:*** Freshmen: $4009. Undergraduates: $4275. ***Scholarships, grants, and awards by category:*** *Academic interests/achievement:* business, communication, education, English, foreign languages, humanities, religion/biblical studies, social sciences. *Creative arts/performance:* cinema/film/broadcasting, journalism/publications. *Special achievements/activities:* leadership. *Special characteristics:* children and siblings of alumni, children of faculty/staff, public servants, siblings of current students. ***Tuition waivers:*** Full or partial for employees or children of employees.

LOANS ***Student loans:*** $40,576,307 (84% need-based, 16% non-need-based). 81% of past graduating class borrowed through all loan programs. *Average indebtedness per student:* $40,942. ***Average need-based loan:*** Freshmen: $3478. Undergraduates: $4484. ***Parent loans:*** $8,154,411 (51% need-based, 49% non-need-based). ***Programs:*** Federal Direct (Subsidized and Unsubsidized Stafford, PLUS).

APPLYING FOR FINANCIAL AID ***Required financial aid forms:*** FAFSA, institution's own form, state aid form. ***Financial aid deadline:*** Continuous. ***Notification date:*** Continuous beginning 3/1. Students must reply within 2 weeks of notification.

CONTACT Joe Dobrota, Director of Central Financial Aid, Regent University, 1000 Regent University Drive, Student Center 251, Virginia Beach, VA 23707, 757-352-4125 or toll-free 800-373-5504. *Fax:* 757-352-4118. *E-mail:* finaid@regent.edu.

REGIS COLLEGE

Weston, MA

CONTACT Dee J. Ludwick, Director of Financial Aid, Regis College, Box 81, Weston, MA 02493, 781-768-7180 or toll-free 866-438-7344. *Fax:* 781-768-7225. *E-mail:* finaid@regiscollege.edu.

REGIS UNIVERSITY

Denver, CO

Tuition & fees: $23,882 **Average undergraduate aid package: $15,006**

ABOUT THE INSTITUTION Independent Roman Catholic (Jesuit), coed. 41 undergraduate majors. Federal methodology is used as a basis for awarding need-based institutional aid.

UNDERGRADUATE EXPENSES for 2011–12 ***Comprehensive fee:*** $32,982 includes full-time tuition ($23,482), mandatory fees ($400), and room and board ($9100). ***College room only:*** $5200. Full-time tuition and fees vary according to course load, location, program, and reciprocity agreements. Room and board charges vary according to board plan and housing facility. ***Part-time tuition:*** $482 per credit hour. ***Part-time fees:*** $300 per term. Part-time tuition and fees vary according to location, program, and reciprocity agreements. ***Payment plans:*** Installment, deferred payment.

FRESHMAN FINANCIAL AID (Fall 2009) 366 applied for aid; of those 68% were deemed to have need. 100% of freshmen with need received aid; of those 52% had need fully met. ***Average percent of need met:*** 74% (excluding resources awarded to replace EFC). ***Average financial aid package:*** $21,325 (excluding resources awarded to replace EFC). 30% of all full-time freshmen had no need and received non-need-based gift aid.

UNDERGRADUATE FINANCIAL AID (Fall 2009) 2,075 applied for aid; of those 76% were deemed to have need. 98% of undergraduates with need received aid; of those 37% had need fully met. ***Average percent of need met:*** 57% (excluding resources awarded to replace EFC). ***Average financial aid package:*** $15,006 (excluding resources awarded to replace EFC). 18% of all full-time undergraduates had no need and received non-need-based gift aid.

GIFT AID (NEED-BASED) ***Total amount:*** $21,804,364 (27% federal, 9% state, 55% institutional, 9% external sources). ***Receiving aid:*** Freshmen: 64% (238); all full-time undergraduates: 49% (1,156). ***Average award:*** Freshmen: $17,796; Undergraduates: $10,312. ***Scholarships, grants, and awards:*** Federal Pell, FSEOG, state, private, college/university gift aid from institutional funds, Academic Competitiveness Grants, National SMART Grants.

GIFT AID (NON-NEED-BASED) ***Total amount:*** $8,905,848 (90% institutional, 10% external sources). ***Receiving aid:*** Freshmen: 38% (142). Undergraduates: 21% (507). ***Average award:*** Freshmen: $10,523. Undergraduates: $12,199. ***Scholarships, grants, and awards by category:*** *Academic interests/achievement:* 625 awards ($6,107,650 total): biological sciences, general academic interests/achievements, physical sciences. *Creative arts/performance:* 27 awards ($135,925 total): debating, music. *Special achievements/activities:* 26 awards ($90,750 total): leadership. *Special characteristics:* 42 awards ($337,300 total): adult students, children of faculty/staff, local/state students, public servants. ***Tuition waivers:*** Full or partial for employees or children of employees.

LOANS ***Student loans:*** $87,346,620 (78% need-based, 22% non-need-based). 64% of past graduating class borrowed through all loan programs. *Average indebtedness per student:* $29,590. ***Average need-based loan:*** Freshmen: $1906. Undergraduates: $3003. ***Parent loans:*** $7,102,774 (75% need-based, 25% non-need-based). ***Programs:*** Federal Direct (Subsidized and Unsubsidized Stafford, PLUS), Perkins, Federal Nursing.

WORK-STUDY ***Federal work-study:*** Total amount: $557,993; 280 jobs averaging $1993. ***State or other work-study/employment:*** Total amount: $1,169,930 (64% need-based, 36% non-need-based). 456 part-time jobs averaging $1734.

ATHLETIC AWARDS Total amount: $2,210,393 (34% need-based, 66% non-need-based).

APPLYING FOR FINANCIAL AID ***Required financial aid form:*** FAFSA. ***Financial aid deadline (priority):*** 3/1. ***Notification date:*** Continuous beginning 3/15.

CONTACT Ellie Miller, Director of Financial Aid, Regis University, 3333 Regis Boulevard, Denver, CO 80221-1099, 303-964-5758 or toll-free 800-388-2366 Ext. 4900. *Fax:* 303-964-5449. *E-mail:* emiller@regis.edu.

REINHARDT UNIVERSITY

Waleska, GA

Tuition & fees: $17,840 **Average undergraduate aid package: $1177**

ABOUT THE INSTITUTION Independent religious, coed. 31 undergraduate majors. Federal methodology is used as a basis for awarding need-based institutional aid.

UNDERGRADUATE EXPENSES for 2011–12 ***Comprehensive fee:*** $24,420 includes full-time tuition ($17,500), mandatory fees ($340), and room and board ($6580). Full-time tuition and fees vary according to location and program. Room and board charges vary according to board plan and housing facility. ***Part-time tuition:*** $592 per credit hour. Part-time tuition and fees vary according to course load, location, and program. ***Payment plan:*** Installment.

FRESHMAN FINANCIAL AID (Fall 2009) 187 applied for aid; of those 83% were deemed to have need. 100% of freshmen with need received aid; of those 10% had need fully met. ***Average percent of need met:*** 49% (excluding resources awarded to replace EFC). ***Average financial aid package:*** $11,178 (excluding resources awarded to replace EFC). 29% of all full-time freshmen had no need and received non-need-based gift aid.

UNDERGRADUATE FINANCIAL AID (Fall 2009) 196 applied for aid; of those 84% were deemed to have need. 100% of undergraduates with need received aid; of those 10% had need fully met. ***Average percent of need met:*** 49% (excluding resources awarded to replace EFC). ***Average financial aid package:*** $1177 (excluding resources awarded to replace EFC). 28% of all full-time undergraduates had no need and received non-need-based gift aid.

GIFT AID (NEED-BASED) ***Total amount:*** $428,664 (91% federal, 9% external sources). ***Receiving aid:*** Freshmen: 68% (156); all full-time undergraduates: 69% (165). ***Average award:*** Freshmen: $8749; Undergraduates: $8752. ***Scholarships, grants, and awards:*** Federal Pell, FSEOG, state, private, college/university gift aid from institutional funds.

GIFT AID (NON-NEED-BASED) ***Total amount:*** $1,360,427 (33% state, 64% institutional, 3% external sources). ***Receiving aid:*** Freshmen: 7% (16). Undergraduates: 7% (17). ***Average award:*** Freshmen: $3599. Undergraduates: $3599. ***Scholarships, grants, and awards by category:*** *Academic interests/achievement:* general academic interests/achievements. *Creative arts/performance:* art/fine arts, music. *Special achievements/activities:* leadership. *Special characteristics:* religious affiliation. ***Tuition waivers:*** Full or partial for employees or children of employees, senior citizens.

LOANS ***Student loans:*** $892,487 (80% need-based, 20% non-need-based). 85% of past graduating class borrowed through all loan programs. *Average indebtedness per student:* $18,329. ***Average need-based loan:*** Freshmen: $3068. Undergraduates: $3062. ***Parent loans:*** $380,892 (100% non-need-based). ***Programs:*** Federal Direct (Subsidized and Unsubsidized Stafford, PLUS).

WORK-STUDY ***Federal work-study:*** Total amount: $7991; jobs available. ***State or other work-study/employment:*** Part-time jobs available.

ATHLETIC AWARDS Total amount: $251,450 (100% non-need-based).

APPLYING FOR FINANCIAL AID ***Required financial aid forms:*** FAFSA, state aid form. ***Financial aid deadline:*** Continuous. ***Notification date:*** Continuous beginning 1/1. Students must reply by 6/1.

CONTACT Angela D. Harlow, Director of Financial Aid, Reinhardt University, 7300 Reinhardt College Circle, Waleska, GA 30183-2981, 770-720-5603. *Fax:* 770-720-9126.

RENSSELAER POLYTECHNIC INSTITUTE

Troy, NY

Tuition & fees: $40,680 **Average undergraduate aid package: $33,165**

ABOUT THE INSTITUTION Independent, coed. 39 undergraduate majors. Both federal and institutional methodology are used as a basis for awarding need-based institutional aid.

UNDERGRADUATE EXPENSES for 2010–11 ***Comprehensive fee:*** $52,145 includes full-time tuition ($39,600), mandatory fees ($1080), and room and board ($11,465). ***College room only:*** $6550. Room and board charges vary according to board plan and location. ***Part-time tuition:*** $1238 per credit hour. ***Payment plan:*** Installment.

FRESHMAN FINANCIAL AID (Fall 2010, est.) 958 applied for aid; of those 86% were deemed to have need. 100% of freshmen with need received aid; of those 37% had need fully met. ***Average percent of need met:*** 87% (excluding

resources awarded to replace EFC). ***Average financial aid package:*** $34,430 (excluding resources awarded to replace EFC). 25% of all full-time freshmen had no need and received non-need-based gift aid.

UNDERGRADUATE FINANCIAL AID (Fall 2010, est.) 3,916 applied for aid; of those 90% were deemed to have need. 100% of undergraduates with need received aid; of those 33% had need fully met. ***Average percent of need met:*** 83% (excluding resources awarded to replace EFC). ***Average financial aid package:*** $33,165 (excluding resources awarded to replace EFC). 31% of all full-time undergraduates had no need and received non-need-based gift aid.

GIFT AID (NEED-BASED) ***Total amount:*** $81,362,815 (12% federal, 3% state, 83% institutional, 2% external sources). ***Receiving aid:*** Freshmen: 71% (820); all full-time undergraduates: 66% (3,516). ***Average award:*** Freshmen: $24,428; Undergraduates: $22,831. ***Scholarships, grants, and awards:*** Federal Pell, FSEOG, state, private, college/university gift aid from institutional funds, Academic Competitiveness Grants, National SMART Grants, Gates Millennium Scholarships.

GIFT AID (NON-NEED-BASED) ***Total amount:*** $25,176,083 (7% federal, 1% state, 90% institutional, 2% external sources). ***Receiving aid:*** Freshmen: 18% (212). Undergraduates: 12% (619). ***Average award:*** Freshmen: $11,331. Undergraduates: $12,958. ***Scholarships, grants, and awards by category:*** *Academic interests/achievement:* general academic interests/achievements, humanities, mathematics, military science. *Creative arts/performance:* general creative arts/performance. *Special achievements/activities:* general special achievements/activities. *Special characteristics:* children and siblings of alumni, children of faculty/staff, ethnic background, general special characteristics, members of minority groups. ***Tuition waivers:*** Full or partial for employees or children of employees.

LOANS ***Student loans:*** $42,433,460 (60% need-based, 40% non-need-based). 70% of past graduating class borrowed through all loan programs. *Average indebtedness per student:* $30,125. ***Average need-based loan:*** Freshmen: $4700. Undergraduates: $5100. ***Parent loans:*** $9,679,683 (20% need-based, 80% non-need-based). ***Programs:*** Federal Direct (Subsidized and Unsubsidized Stafford, PLUS), Perkins, college/university, state loans from some states (not NY).

WORK-STUDY ***Federal work-study:*** Total amount: $2,595,800; 1,259 jobs averaging $1994.

ATHLETIC AWARDS Total amount: $1,938,360 (100% non-need-based).

APPLYING FOR FINANCIAL AID ***Required financial aid forms:*** FAFSA, CSS Financial Aid PROFILE. ***Financial aid deadline (priority):*** 2/15. ***Notification date:*** 3/25.

CONTACT Mr. Larry Chambers, Director of Financial Aid, Rensselaer Polytechnic Institute, Academy Hall, Troy, NY 12180-3590, 518-276-6813 or toll-free 800-448-6562. *Fax:* 518-276-4797. *E-mail:* financial_aid@rpi.edu.

RESEARCH COLLEGE OF NURSING

Kansas City, MO

Tuition & fees: $27,190 **Average undergraduate aid package: N/A**

ABOUT THE INSTITUTION Independent, coed, primarily women. 1 undergraduate major. Federal methodology is used as a basis for awarding need-based institutional aid.

UNDERGRADUATE EXPENSES for 2010–11 ***One-time required fee:*** $500. ***Comprehensive fee:*** $35,080 includes full-time tuition ($26,450), mandatory fees ($740), and room and board ($7890). ***College room only:*** $4590. Room and board charges vary according to board plan, housing facility, and location. ***Part-time tuition:*** $882 per credit hour. Part-time tuition and fees vary according to class time. ***Payment plans:*** Installment, deferred payment.

GIFT AID (NEED-BASED) ***Total amount:*** $250,882 (74% federal, 26% state). ***Scholarships, grants, and awards:*** Federal Pell, FSEOG, state, private, college/university gift aid from institutional funds.

GIFT AID (NON-NEED-BASED) ***Total amount:*** $5,404,369 (98% institutional, 2% external sources). ***Scholarships, grants, and awards by category:*** *Academic interests/achievement:* general academic interests/achievements, health fields. *Special characteristics:* children and siblings of alumni, children of educators, children of faculty/staff, siblings of current students. ***Tuition waivers:*** Full or partial for children of alumni, employees or children of employees, senior citizens.

LOANS ***Student loans:*** $2,325,533 (40% need-based, 60% non-need-based). ***Parent loans:*** $9700 (100% non-need-based). ***Programs:*** Federal Direct (Subsidized and Unsubsidized Stafford, PLUS), Federal Nursing.

APPLYING FOR FINANCIAL AID ***Required financial aid form:*** FAFSA. ***Financial aid deadline (priority):*** 3/15. ***Notification date:*** Continuous. Students must reply within 2 weeks of notification.

CONTACT Ms. Stacie Withers, Director of Financial Aid, Research College of Nursing, 2525 East Meyer Boulevard, Kansas City, MO 64132, 816-995-2832 or toll-free 800-842-6776. *Fax:* 816-995-2833. *E-mail:* stacie.withers@researchcollege.edu.

RESURRECTION UNIVERSITY

Oak Park, IL

Tuition & fees: N/R **Average undergraduate aid package: $15,550**

ABOUT THE INSTITUTION Independent, coed, primarily women. 2 undergraduate majors. Both federal and institutional methodology are used as a basis for awarding need-based institutional aid.

UNDERGRADUATE EXPENSES for 2011–12 ***Tuition:*** part-time $711 per credit hour. ***Required fees:*** $135 per term. Full-time tuition and fees vary according to program. Part-time tuition and fees vary according to course load and program. ***Payment plan:*** Installment.

UNDERGRADUATE FINANCIAL AID (Fall 2010, est.) 198 applied for aid; of those 100% were deemed to have need. 100% of undergraduates with need received aid; of those 38% had need fully met. ***Average percent of need met:*** 84% (excluding resources awarded to replace EFC). ***Average financial aid package:*** $15,550 (excluding resources awarded to replace EFC).

GIFT AID (NEED-BASED) ***Total amount:*** $586,292 (45% federal, 33% state, 22% institutional). ***Receiving aid:*** All full-time undergraduates: 84% (198). ***Average award:*** Undergraduates: $3000. ***Scholarships, grants, and awards:*** Federal Pell, FSEOG, state, private, college/university gift aid from institutional funds.

GIFT AID (NON-NEED-BASED) ***Total amount:*** $231,243 (84% institutional, 16% external sources). ***Receiving aid:*** Undergraduates: 84% (198). ***Tuition waivers:*** Full or partial for employees or children of employees.

LOANS ***Student loans:*** $2,430,825 (77% need-based, 23% non-need-based). ***Average need-based loan:*** Undergraduates: $5500. ***Parent loans:*** $152,893 (100% need-based). ***Programs:*** Federal Direct (Subsidized and Unsubsidized Stafford, PLUS).

WORK-STUDY ***Federal work-study:*** Total amount: $33,000; 9 jobs averaging $4800.

CONTACT Ms. Shirley Howell, Financial Aid Officer, Resurrection University, 3 Erie Court, Oak Park, IL 60302, 708-763-1426. *Fax:* 708-763-1531. *E-mail:* shirley.howell@resu.edu.

RHODE ISLAND COLLEGE

Providence, RI

Tuition & fees (RI res): $6986 **Average undergraduate aid package: $8740**

ABOUT THE INSTITUTION State-supported, coed. 72 undergraduate majors. Institutional methodology is used as a basis for awarding need-based institutional aid.

UNDERGRADUATE EXPENSES for 2010–11 ***Tuition, state resident:*** full-time $5988; part-time $250 per credit. ***Tuition, nonresident:*** full-time $15,880; part-time $604 per credit. ***Required fees:*** full-time $998; $28 per credit or $72 per term. Part-time tuition and fees vary according to course load. ***College room and board:*** $9256; ***Room only:*** $5266. Room and board charges vary according to housing facility. ***Payment plan:*** Installment.

FRESHMAN FINANCIAL AID (Fall 2010, est.) 994 applied for aid; of those 79% were deemed to have need. 98% of freshmen with need received aid; of those 31% had need fully met. ***Average percent of need met:*** 77% (excluding resources awarded to replace EFC). ***Average financial aid package:*** $9929 (excluding resources awarded to replace EFC). 4% of all full-time freshmen had no need and received non-need-based gift aid.

UNDERGRADUATE FINANCIAL AID (Fall 2010, est.) 4,567 applied for aid; of those 81% were deemed to have need. 96% of undergraduates with need received aid; of those 28% had need fully met. ***Average percent of need met:*** 73% (excluding resources awarded to replace EFC). ***Average financial aid package:*** $8740 (excluding resources awarded to replace EFC). 2% of all full-time undergraduates had no need and received non-need-based gift aid.

GIFT AID (NEED-BASED) ***Total amount:*** $18,724,038 (62% federal, 12% state, 23% institutional, 3% external sources). ***Receiving aid:*** Freshmen: 62% (675); all full-time undergraduates: 54% (3,049). ***Average award:*** Freshmen: $7047; Undergraduates: $5385. ***Scholarships, grants, and awards:*** Federal Pell, FSEOG, state, private, college/university gift aid from institutional funds.

GIFT AID (NON-NEED-BASED) ***Total amount:*** $440,617 (64% institutional, 36% external sources). ***Receiving aid:*** Freshmen: 2% (20). Undergraduates: 1% (68). ***Average award:*** Freshmen: $1894. Undergraduates: $2070. ***Scholarships, grants, and awards by category:*** *Academic interests/achievement:* general academic interests/achievements. *Creative arts/performance:* art/fine arts, cinema/film/broadcasting, dance, journalism/publications, music, theater/drama. *Special characteristics:* children and siblings of alumni. ***Tuition waivers:*** Full or partial for employees or children of employees.

LOANS ***Student loans:*** $34,155,017 (67% need-based, 33% non-need-based). 73% of past graduating class borrowed through all loan programs. *Average indebtedness per student:* $18,939. ***Average need-based loan:*** Freshmen: $3467. Undergraduates: $3931. ***Parent loans:*** $1,739,823 (33% need-based, 67% non-need-based). ***Programs:*** Federal Direct (Subsidized and Unsubsidized Stafford, PLUS), Perkins, state, private loans.

WORK-STUDY ***Federal work-study:*** Total amount: $2,489,236; jobs available.

APPLYING FOR FINANCIAL AID ***Required financial aid forms:*** FAFSA, institution's own form. ***Financial aid deadline (priority):*** 3/1. ***Notification date:*** Continuous beginning 3/15. Students must reply by 5/1 or within 3 weeks of notification.

CONTACT Mr. James T. Hanbury, Director of Financial Aid, Rhode Island College, 600 Mount Pleasant Avenue, Providence, RI 02908, 401-456-8033 or toll-free 800-669-5760. *Fax:* 401-456-8686. *E-mail:* jhanbury@ric.edu.

RHODE ISLAND SCHOOL OF DESIGN

Providence, RI

CONTACT Director of Financial Aid, Rhode Island School of Design, 2 College Street, Providence, RI 02903-2784, 401-454-6661 or toll-free 800-364-7473. *Fax:* 401-454-6412.

RHODES COLLEGE

Memphis, TN

Tuition & fees: $34,580 **Average undergraduate aid package: $31,392**

ABOUT THE INSTITUTION Independent, coed. 33 undergraduate majors. Institutional methodology is used as a basis for awarding need-based institutional aid.

UNDERGRADUATE EXPENSES for 2011–12 ***Comprehensive fee:*** $43,060 includes full-time tuition ($34,270), mandatory fees ($310), and room and board ($8480). Room and board charges vary according to board plan and housing facility. ***Payment plan:*** Installment.

FRESHMAN FINANCIAL AID (Fall 2010, est.) 396 applied for aid; of those 72% were deemed to have need. 100% of freshmen with need received aid; of those 43% had need fully met. ***Average percent of need met:*** 100% (excluding resources awarded to replace EFC). ***Average financial aid package:*** $32,280 (excluding resources awarded to replace EFC). 22% of all full-time freshmen had no need and received non-need-based gift aid.

UNDERGRADUATE FINANCIAL AID (Fall 2010, est.) 1,051 applied for aid; of those 84% were deemed to have need. 99% of undergraduates with need received aid; of those 32% had need fully met. ***Average percent of need met:*** 85% (excluding resources awarded to replace EFC). ***Average financial aid package:*** $31,392 (excluding resources awarded to replace EFC). 9% of all full-time undergraduates had no need and received non-need-based gift aid.

GIFT AID (NEED-BASED) ***Total amount:*** $19,221,005 (8% federal, 7% state, 83% institutional, 2% external sources). ***Receiving aid:*** Freshmen: 56% (283); all full-time undergraduates: 51% (866). ***Average award:*** Freshmen: $22,998; Undergraduates: $22,182. ***Scholarships, grants, and awards:*** Federal Pell, FSEOG, state, private, college/university gift aid from institutional funds.

GIFT AID (NON-NEED-BASED) ***Total amount:*** $10,538,745 (5% state, 90% institutional, 5% external sources). ***Receiving aid:*** Freshmen: 16% (82). Undergraduates: 9% (145). ***Average award:*** Freshmen: $17,365. Undergraduates: $16,711. ***Scholarships, grants, and awards by category:*** *Academic interests/achievement:* general academic interests/achievements, physical sciences. *Creative arts/performance:* art/fine arts, general creative arts/performance, music, theater/drama. *Special characteristics:* children of faculty/staff, members of minority groups, relatives of clergy, religious affiliation. ***Tuition waivers:*** Full or partial for employees or children of employees.

LOANS ***Student loans:*** $5,473,853 (68% need-based, 32% non-need-based). 47% of past graduating class borrowed through all loan programs. *Average indebtedness per student:* $24,946. ***Average need-based loan:*** Freshmen: $3670. Undergraduates: $5525. ***Parent loans:*** $1,624,769 (38% need-based, 62% non-need-based). ***Programs:*** Federal Direct (Subsidized and Unsubsidized Stafford, PLUS), Perkins.

WORK-STUDY ***Federal work-study:*** Total amount: $696,821; jobs available. ***State or other work-study/employment:*** Total amount: $852,384 (31% need-based, 69% non-need-based). Part-time jobs available.

APPLYING FOR FINANCIAL AID ***Required financial aid forms:*** FAFSA, CSS Financial Aid PROFILE, noncustodial (divorced/separated) parent's statement. ***Financial aid deadline:*** 3/1. ***Notification date:*** 4/15. Students must reply by 5/1.

CONTACT Mrs. Ashley Bianchi, Director of Financial Aid, Rhodes College, 2000 North Parkway, Memphis, TN 38112-1690, 901-843-3808 or toll-free 800-844-5969 (out-of-state). *Fax:* 901-843-3435. *E-mail:* bianchia@rhodes.edu.

RICE UNIVERSITY

Houston, TX

Tuition & fees: $35,551 **Average undergraduate aid package: $29,739**

ABOUT THE INSTITUTION Independent, coed. 58 undergraduate majors. Both federal and institutional methodology are used as a basis for awarding need-based institutional aid.

UNDERGRADUATE EXPENSES for 2011–12 ***Comprehensive fee:*** $47,821 includes full-time tuition ($34,900), mandatory fees ($651), and room and board ($12,270). ***College room only:*** $8270. Full-time tuition and fees vary according to student level. Room and board charges vary according to board plan. Part-time tuition and fees vary according to course load. ***Payment plan:*** Installment.

FRESHMAN FINANCIAL AID (Fall 2010, est.) 603 applied for aid; of those 66% were deemed to have need. 100% of freshmen with need received aid; of those 100% had need fully met. ***Average percent of need met:*** 100% (excluding resources awarded to replace EFC). ***Average financial aid package:*** $31,457 (excluding resources awarded to replace EFC). 15% of all full-time freshmen had no need and received non-need-based gift aid.

UNDERGRADUATE FINANCIAL AID (Fall 2010, est.) 2,343 applied for aid; of those 59% were deemed to have need. 100% of undergraduates with need received aid; of those 100% had need fully met. ***Average percent of need met:*** 100% (excluding resources awarded to replace EFC). ***Average financial aid package:*** $29,739 (excluding resources awarded to replace EFC). 20% of all full-time undergraduates had no need and received non-need-based gift aid.

GIFT AID (NEED-BASED) ***Total amount:*** $42,207,443 (7% federal, 6% state, 87% institutional). ***Receiving aid:*** Freshmen: 42% (395); all full-time undergraduates: 40% (1,391). ***Average award:*** Freshmen: $29,436; Undergraduates: $27,671. ***Scholarships, grants, and awards:*** Federal Pell, FSEOG, state, private, college/university gift aid from institutional funds.

GIFT AID (NON-NEED-BASED) ***Total amount:*** $10,906,605 (2% state, 74% institutional, 24% external sources). ***Receiving aid:*** Freshmen: 7% (65). Undergraduates: 5% (187). ***Average award:*** Freshmen: $16,083. Undergraduates: $14,772. ***Scholarships, grants, and awards by category:*** *Academic interests/achievement:* engineering/technologies, general academic interests/achievements. *Creative arts/performance:* music. *Special achievements/activities:* general special achievements/activities, leadership. ***Tuition waivers:*** Full or partial for employees or children of employees.

LOANS ***Student loans:*** $3,980,774 (44% need-based, 56% non-need-based). 36% of past graduating class borrowed through all loan programs. *Average indebtedness per student:* $13,944. ***Average need-based loan:*** Freshmen: $947. Undergraduates: $1404. ***Parent loans:*** $2,151,605 (100% non-need-based). ***Programs:*** Federal Direct (Subsidized and Unsubsidized Stafford, PLUS), Perkins, state.

WORK-STUDY ***Federal work-study:*** Total amount: $1,510,469; jobs available. ***State or other work-study/employment:*** Total amount: $851,585 (1% need-based, 99% non-need-based). Part-time jobs available.

ATHLETIC AWARDS Total amount: $10,183,090 (4% need-based, 96% non-need-based).

APPLYING FOR FINANCIAL AID ***Required financial aid forms:*** FAFSA, CSS Financial Aid PROFILE, business/farm supplement, federal income tax return(s) and W-2 forms. ***Financial aid deadline (priority):*** 3/1. ***Notification date:*** Continuous beginning 4/1. Students must reply by 5/1.

CONTACT Ms. Anne Walker, Director of Student Financial Services, Rice University, 116 Allen Center, MS 12, Houston, TX 77005, 713-348-4958 or toll-free 800-527-OWLS. *Fax:* 713-348-2139. *E-mail:* fina@rice.edu.

THE RICHARD STOCKTON COLLEGE OF NEW JERSEY

Pomona, NJ

Tuition & fees (NJ res): $11,393 **Average undergraduate aid package: $15,555**

ABOUT THE INSTITUTION State-supported, coed. 30 undergraduate majors. Federal methodology is used as a basis for awarding need-based institutional aid.

UNDERGRADUATE EXPENSES for 2010–11 ***Tuition, state resident:*** full-time $7349; part-time $262.47 per credit hour. ***Tuition, nonresident:*** full-time $13,260; part-time $473.59 per credit hour. ***Required fees:*** full-time $4044; $144.44 per credit hour or $70 per term. Full-time tuition and fees vary according to degree level. Part-time tuition and fees vary according to course load and degree level. ***College room and board:*** $10,281; ***Room only:*** $7165. Room and board charges vary according to board plan and housing facility. ***Payment plans:*** Installment, deferred payment.

FRESHMAN FINANCIAL AID (Fall 2010, est.) 802 applied for aid; of those 82% were deemed to have need. 97% of freshmen with need received aid; of those 28% had need fully met. ***Average percent of need met:*** 68% (excluding resources awarded to replace EFC). ***Average financial aid package:*** $15,813 (excluding resources awarded to replace EFC). 24% of all full-time freshmen had no need and received non-need-based gift aid.

UNDERGRADUATE FINANCIAL AID (Fall 2010, est.) 5,102 applied for aid; of those 87% were deemed to have need. 98% of undergraduates with need received aid; of those 26% had need fully met. ***Average percent of need met:*** 67% (excluding resources awarded to replace EFC). ***Average financial aid package:*** $15,555 (excluding resources awarded to replace EFC). 21% of all full-time undergraduates had no need and received non-need-based gift aid.

GIFT AID (NEED-BASED) ***Total amount:*** $24,595,652 (41% federal, 33% state, 25% institutional, 1% external sources). ***Receiving aid:*** Freshmen: 39% (338); all full-time undergraduates: 36% (2,275). ***Average award:*** Freshmen: $9754; Undergraduates: $7940. ***Scholarships, grants, and awards:*** Federal Pell, FSEOG, state, college/university gift aid from institutional funds.

GIFT AID (NON-NEED-BASED) ***Total amount:*** $2,310,214 (13% state, 81% institutional, 6% external sources). ***Receiving aid:*** Freshmen: 23% (198). Undergraduates: 18% (1,113). ***Average award:*** Freshmen: $7968. Undergraduates: $6318. ***Scholarships, grants, and awards by category:*** *Academic interests/achievement:* area/ethnic studies, biological sciences, business, computer science, education, general academic interests/achievements, health fields, humanities, mathematics, physical sciences, social sciences. *Creative arts/performance:* applied art and design, art/fine arts, creative writing, dance, journalism/publications, music, performing arts, theater/drama. *Special achievements/activities:* community service, general special achievements/activities, leadership. *Special characteristics:* adult students, children of faculty/staff, children of union members/company employees, ethnic background, first-generation college students, general special characteristics, international students, local/state students, members of minority groups, previous college experience. ***Tuition waivers:*** Full or partial for employees or children of employees, senior citizens.

LOANS ***Student loans:*** $40,124,945 (88% need-based, 12% non-need-based). 74% of past graduating class borrowed through all loan programs. *Average indebtedness per student:* $30,843. ***Average need-based loan:*** Freshmen: $3559. Undergraduates: $4599. ***Parent loans:*** $4,789,196 (75% need-based, 25% non-need-based). ***Programs:*** Federal Direct (Subsidized and Unsubsidized Stafford, PLUS), Perkins, state.

WORK-STUDY ***Federal work-study:*** Total amount: $272,530; 160 jobs averaging $1703. ***State or other work-study/employment:*** Total amount: $1,090,809 (100% non-need-based). 721 part-time jobs averaging $1513.

APPLYING FOR FINANCIAL AID ***Required financial aid form:*** FAFSA. ***Financial aid deadline (priority):*** 3/1. ***Notification date:*** Continuous beginning 4/1. Students must reply within 2 weeks of notification.

CONTACT Ms. Jeanne S. Lewis, Director of Financial Aid, The Richard Stockton College of New Jersey, Jimmie Leeds Road, Pomona, NJ 08240-9988, 609-652-4203. *Fax:* 609-626-5517. *E-mail:* jeanne.lewis@stockton.edu.

RIDER UNIVERSITY

Lawrenceville, NJ

Tuition & fees: $30,470 **Average undergraduate aid package: $21,498**

ABOUT THE INSTITUTION Independent, coed. 58 undergraduate majors. Federal methodology is used as a basis for awarding need-based institutional aid.

UNDERGRADUATE EXPENSES for 2010–11 ***Comprehensive fee:*** $41,670 includes full-time tuition ($29,870), mandatory fees ($600), and room and board ($11,200). ***College room only:*** $6820. Full-time tuition and fees vary according to course load and program. Room and board charges vary according to board plan, housing facility, and location. ***Part-time tuition:*** $540 per credit. ***Part-time fees:*** $35 per course. Part-time tuition and fees vary according to course load and program. ***Payment plan:*** Installment.

FRESHMAN FINANCIAL AID (Fall 2010, est.) 884 applied for aid; of those 87% were deemed to have need. 100% of freshmen with need received aid; of those 21% had need fully met. ***Average percent of need met:*** 73% (excluding resources awarded to replace EFC). ***Average financial aid package:*** $22,253 (excluding resources awarded to replace EFC). 20% of all full-time freshmen had no need and received non-need-based gift aid.

UNDERGRADUATE FINANCIAL AID (Fall 2010, est.) 3,253 applied for aid; of those 89% were deemed to have need. 100% of undergraduates with need received aid; of those 18% had need fully met. ***Average percent of need met:*** 71% (excluding resources awarded to replace EFC). ***Average financial aid package:*** $21,498 (excluding resources awarded to replace EFC). 20% of all full-time undergraduates had no need and received non-need-based gift aid.

GIFT AID (NEED-BASED) ***Total amount:*** $41,127,334 (15% federal, 16% state, 68% institutional, 1% external sources). ***Receiving aid:*** Freshmen: 75% (760); all full-time undergraduates: 70% (2,792). ***Average award:*** Freshmen: $16,851; Undergraduates: $15,912. ***Scholarships, grants, and awards:*** state, college/university gift aid from institutional funds.

GIFT AID (NON-NEED-BASED) ***Total amount:*** $11,348,938 (95% institutional, 5% external sources). ***Receiving aid:*** Freshmen: 13% (128). Undergraduates: 11% (432). ***Average award:*** Freshmen: $12,736. Undergraduates: $11,346. ***Scholarships, grants, and awards by category:*** *Academic interests/achievement:* general academic interests/achievements. *Creative arts/performance:* theater/drama. *Special characteristics:* members of minority groups. ***Tuition waivers:*** Full or partial for employees or children of employees.

LOANS ***Student loans:*** $41,823,988 (64% need-based, 36% non-need-based). 71% of past graduating class borrowed through all loan programs. *Average indebtedness per student:* $35,404. ***Average need-based loan:*** Freshmen: $3501. Undergraduates: $4231. ***Parent loans:*** $8,888,865 (45% need-based, 55% non-need-based). ***Programs:*** Federal Direct (Subsidized and Unsubsidized Stafford, PLUS), Perkins, state, alternative loans.

WORK-STUDY ***Federal work-study:*** Total amount: $4,664,916; jobs available. ***State or other work-study/employment:*** Part-time jobs available.

ATHLETIC AWARDS Total amount: $4,725,348 (33% need-based, 67% non-need-based).

APPLYING FOR FINANCIAL AID ***Required financial aid form:*** FAFSA. ***Financial aid deadline (priority):*** 3/1. ***Notification date:*** Continuous beginning 2/20.

CONTACT Dr. Dennis Levy, Director of Financial Aid, Rider University, 2083 Lawrenceville Road, Lawrenceville, NJ 08648-3001, 609-896-5360 or toll-free 800-257-9026. *Fax:* 609-219-4487. *E-mail:* finaid@rider.edu.

RINGLING COLLEGE OF ART AND DESIGN

Sarasota, FL

Tuition & fees: $30,730 **Average undergraduate aid package: $16,981**

ABOUT THE INSTITUTION Independent, coed. 11 undergraduate majors. Federal methodology is used as a basis for awarding need-based institutional aid.

UNDERGRADUATE EXPENSES for 2010–11 ***Comprehensive fee:*** $41,620 includes full-time tuition ($29,800), mandatory fees ($930), and room and board ($10,890). ***College room only:*** $5740. Full-time tuition and fees vary according to course load, program, and student level. Room and board charges vary according to board plan and housing facility. ***Part-time tuition:*** $1389 per semester hour. Part-time tuition and fees vary according to course load, program, and student level. ***Payment plan:*** Installment.

FRESHMAN FINANCIAL AID (Fall 2010, est.) 247 applied for aid; of those 86% were deemed to have need. 100% of freshmen with need received aid; of those 3% had need fully met. ***Average percent of need met:*** 39% (excluding resources awarded to replace EFC). ***Average financial aid package:*** $14,715 (excluding resources awarded to replace EFC). 14% of all full-time freshmen had no need and received non-need-based gift aid.

UNDERGRADUATE FINANCIAL AID (Fall 2010, est.) 1,033 applied for aid; of those 91% were deemed to have need. 100% of undergraduates with need received aid; of those 3% had need fully met. ***Average percent of need met:*** 38% (excluding resources awarded to replace EFC). ***Average financial aid package:*** $16,981 (excluding resources awarded to replace EFC). 8% of all full-time undergraduates had no need and received non-need-based gift aid.

GIFT AID (NEED-BASED) ***Total amount:*** $8,255,726 (27% federal, 24% state, 36% institutional, 13% external sources). ***Receiving aid:*** Freshmen: 74% (197); all full-time undergraduates: 77% (839). ***Average award:*** Freshmen: $8964; Undergraduates: $9485. ***Scholarships, grants, and awards:*** Federal Pell, FSEOG, state, private, college/university gift aid from institutional funds.

GIFT AID (NON-NEED-BASED) ***Total amount:*** $1,400,002 (17% state, 71% institutional, 12% external sources). ***Receiving aid:*** Freshmen: 1% (4). Undergraduates: 1% (14). ***Average award:*** Freshmen: $12,666. Undergraduates: $12,150. ***Scholarships, grants, and awards by category:*** *Academic interests/achievement:* general academic interests/achievements. *Creative arts/performance:* applied art and design, art/fine arts. *Special achievements/activities:* community service. ***Tuition waivers:*** Full or partial for employees or children of employees.

LOANS ***Student loans:*** $11,301,268 (91% need-based, 9% non-need-based). 83% of past graduating class borrowed through all loan programs. ***Average need-based loan:*** Freshmen: $6344. Undergraduates: $8721. ***Parent loans:*** $10,800,259 (74% need-based, 26% non-need-based). ***Programs:*** Federal Direct (Subsidized and Unsubsidized Stafford, PLUS), alternative loans.

WORK-STUDY ***Federal work-study:*** Total amount: $548,327; jobs available. ***State or other work-study/employment:*** Part-time jobs available.

APPLYING FOR FINANCIAL AID ***Required financial aid form:*** FAFSA. ***Financial aid deadline (priority):*** 3/1. ***Notification date:*** Continuous beginning 3/15. Students must reply within 4 weeks of notification.

CONTACT Micah Jordan, Financial Aid Assistant Director, Ringling College of Art and Design, 2700 North Tamiami Trail, Sarasota, FL 34243, 941-359-7533 or toll-free 800-255-7695. *Fax:* 941-359-6107. *E-mail:* finaid@ringling.edu.

RIO GRANDE BIBLE INSTITUTE

Edinburg, TX

CONTACT Financial Aid Office, Rio Grande Bible Institute, 4300 S US Hwy 281, Edinburg, TX 78539, 956-380-8100.

RIPON COLLEGE

Ripon, WI

Tuition & fees: $28,689 | **Average undergraduate aid package: $24,629**

ABOUT THE INSTITUTION Independent, coed. 38 undergraduate majors. Federal methodology is used as a basis for awarding need-based institutional aid.

UNDERGRADUATE EXPENSES for 2011–12 ***Comprehensive fee:*** $36,959 includes full-time tuition ($28,414), mandatory fees ($275), and room and board ($8270). ***College room only:*** $4390. ***Payment plan:*** Installment.

FRESHMAN FINANCIAL AID (Fall 2010, est.) 278 applied for aid; of those 90% were deemed to have need. 100% of freshmen with need received aid; of those 23% had need fully met. ***Average percent of need met:*** 89% (excluding resources awarded to replace EFC). ***Average financial aid package:*** $24,893 (excluding resources awarded to replace EFC). 12% of all full-time freshmen had no need and received non-need-based gift aid.

UNDERGRADUATE FINANCIAL AID (Fall 2010, est.) 941 applied for aid; of those 92% were deemed to have need. 100% of undergraduates with need received aid; of those 19% had need fully met. ***Average percent of need met:*** 88% (excluding resources awarded to replace EFC). ***Average financial aid package:*** $24,629 (excluding resources awarded to replace EFC). 13% of all full-time undergraduates had no need and received non-need-based gift aid.

GIFT AID (NEED-BASED) ***Total amount:*** $16,690,062 (12% federal, 7% state, 62% institutional, 19% external sources). ***Receiving aid:*** Freshmen: 87% (250); all full-time undergraduates: 83% (863). ***Average award:*** Freshmen: $20,300; Undergraduates: $19,509. ***Scholarships, grants, and awards:*** Federal Pell, FSEOG, state, private, college/university gift aid from institutional funds.

GIFT AID (NON-NEED-BASED) ***Total amount:*** $2,708,621 (58% institutional, 42% external sources). ***Receiving aid:*** Freshmen: 11% (33). Undergraduates: 9% (98). ***Average award:*** Freshmen: $9093. Undergraduates: $10,312. ***Scholarships, grants, and awards by category:*** *Academic interests/achievement:* 459 awards ($3,672,372 total): biological sciences, business, computer science, education, English, foreign languages, general academic interests/achievements, humanities, mathematics, military science, physical sciences, premedicine, religion/biblical studies, social sciences. *Creative arts/performance:* 98 awards ($257,588 total): art/fine arts, debating, music, theater/drama. *Special achievements/activities:* 94 awards ($257,868 total): general special achievements/activities, leadership, memberships. *Special characteristics:* 443 awards ($1,643,349 total): children and siblings of alumni, children of faculty/staff, ethnic background, first-generation college students, general special characteristics, international students, local/state students, members of minority groups, out-of-state students, previous college experience, religious affiliation, siblings of current students. ***Tuition waivers:*** Full or partial for employees or children of employees.

LOANS ***Student loans:*** $7,265,933 (70% need-based, 30% non-need-based). 84% of past graduating class borrowed through all loan programs. *Average indebtedness per student:* $30,694. ***Average need-based loan:*** Freshmen: $4178. Undergraduates: $4824. ***Parent loans:*** $1,085,946 (19% need-based, 81% non-need-based). ***Programs:*** Federal Direct (Subsidized and Unsubsidized Stafford, PLUS), Perkins, alternative loans.

WORK-STUDY ***Federal work-study:*** Total amount: $855,652; 526 jobs averaging $1556. ***State or other work-study/employment:*** Total amount: $690,101 (4% need-based, 96% non-need-based). 419 part-time jobs averaging $1556.

APPLYING FOR FINANCIAL AID ***Required financial aid form:*** FAFSA. ***Financial aid deadline (priority):*** 3/1. ***Notification date:*** Continuous. Students must reply within 2 weeks of notification.

CONTACT Mr. Steven M. Schuetz, Dean of Admission and Financial Aid, Ripon College, 300 Seward Street, Ripon, WI 54971, 920-748-8185 or toll-free 800-947-4766. *Fax:* 920-748-8335. *E-mail:* financialaid@ripon.edu.

RIVIER COLLEGE

Nashua, NH

Tuition & fees: $25,020 | **Average undergraduate aid package: $14,850**

ABOUT THE INSTITUTION Independent Roman Catholic, coed. 34 undergraduate majors. Federal methodology is used as a basis for awarding need-based institutional aid.

UNDERGRADUATE EXPENSES for 2010–11 ***One-time required fee:*** $175. ***Comprehensive fee:*** $34,542 includes full-time tuition ($24,420), mandatory fees ($600), and room and board ($9522). Full-time tuition and fees vary according to program. Room and board charges vary according to board plan and housing facility. ***Part-time tuition:*** $814 per credit. ***Part-time fees:*** $25 per year. Part-time tuition and fees vary according to class time, course level, course load, and program. ***Payment plans:*** Installment, deferred payment.

FRESHMAN FINANCIAL AID (Fall 2010, est.) 246 applied for aid; of those 91% were deemed to have need. 100% of freshmen with need received aid; of those 7% had need fully met. ***Average percent of need met:*** 64% (excluding resources awarded to replace EFC). ***Average financial aid package:*** $16,672 (excluding resources awarded to replace EFC). 11% of all full-time freshmen had no need and received non-need-based gift aid.

UNDERGRADUATE FINANCIAL AID (Fall 2010, est.) 888 applied for aid; of those 93% were deemed to have need. 100% of undergraduates with need received aid; of those 9% had need fully met. ***Average percent of need met:*** 59% (excluding resources awarded to replace EFC). ***Average financial aid package:*** $14,850 (excluding resources awarded to replace EFC). 11% of all full-time undergraduates had no need and received non-need-based gift aid.

GIFT AID (NEED-BASED) ***Total amount:*** $8,689,264 (21% federal, 2% state, 72% institutional, 5% external sources). ***Receiving aid:*** Freshmen: 88% (224); all full-time undergraduates: 83% (801). ***Average award:*** Freshmen: $13,071; Undergraduates: $10,806. ***Scholarships, grants, and awards:*** Federal Pell, FSEOG, state, private, college/university gift aid from institutional funds.

GIFT AID (NON-NEED-BASED) ***Total amount:*** $659,950 (2% federal, 90% institutional, 8% external sources). ***Receiving aid:*** Freshmen: 4% (11).

Undergraduates: 4% (36). ***Average award:*** Freshmen: $5518. Undergraduates: $5066. ***Scholarships, grants, and awards by category:*** *Academic interests/achievement:* biological sciences, business, communication, computer science, education, English, foreign languages, general academic interests/achievements, humanities, mathematics, premedicine, social sciences. *Creative arts/performance:* applied art and design, art/fine arts, journalism/publications. *Special achievements/activities:* general special achievements/activities. *Special characteristics:* children and siblings of alumni, children of current students, international students, siblings of current students. ***Tuition waivers:*** Full or partial for employees or children of employees, senior citizens.

LOANS ***Student loans:*** $12,272,291 (72% need-based, 28% non-need-based). 95% of past graduating class borrowed through all loan programs. *Average indebtedness per student:* $43,189. ***Average need-based loan:*** Freshmen: $3558. Undergraduates: $4378. ***Parent loans:*** $2,255,486 (54% need-based, 46% non-need-based). ***Programs:*** Federal Direct (Subsidized and Unsubsidized Stafford, PLUS), Perkins, college/university.

WORK-STUDY ***Federal work-study:*** Total amount: $199,162; jobs available. ***State or other work-study/employment:*** Total amount: $103,480 (5% need-based, 95% non-need-based). Part-time jobs available.

APPLYING FOR FINANCIAL AID ***Required financial aid form:*** FAFSA. ***Financial aid deadline (priority):*** 3/1. ***Notification date:*** Continuous beginning 3/1. Students must reply within 2 weeks of notification.

CONTACT Valerie Patnaude, Director of Financial Aid, Rivier College, 420 Main Street, Nashua, NH 03060-5086, 603-897-8533 or toll-free 800-44RIVIER. *Fax:* 603-897-8810. *E-mail:* vpatnaude@rivier.edu.

ROANOKE COLLEGE

Salem, VA

Tuition & fees: $32,900 **Average undergraduate aid package: $24,218**

ABOUT THE INSTITUTION Independent religious, coed. 31 undergraduate majors. Federal methodology is used as a basis for awarding need-based institutional aid.

UNDERGRADUATE EXPENSES for 2011–12 ***One-time required fee:*** $125. ***Comprehensive fee:*** $43,672 includes full-time tuition ($31,950), mandatory fees ($950), and room and board ($10,772). ***College room only:*** $5004. Room and board charges vary according to board plan and housing facility. ***Part-time tuition:*** $1530 per course. Part-time tuition and fees vary according to course load. ***Payment plan:*** Installment.

FRESHMAN FINANCIAL AID (Fall 2010, est.) 491 applied for aid; of those 87% were deemed to have need. 100% of freshmen with need received aid; of those 22% had need fully met. ***Average percent of need met:*** 78% (excluding resources awarded to replace EFC). ***Average financial aid package:*** $25,188 (excluding resources awarded to replace EFC). 22% of all full-time freshmen had no need and received non-need-based gift aid.

UNDERGRADUATE FINANCIAL AID (Fall 2010, est.) 1,617 applied for aid; of those 87% were deemed to have need. 100% of undergraduates with need received aid; of those 23% had need fully met. ***Average percent of need met:*** 79% (excluding resources awarded to replace EFC). ***Average financial aid package:*** $24,218 (excluding resources awarded to replace EFC). 27% of all full-time undergraduates had no need and received non-need-based gift aid.

GIFT AID (NEED-BASED) ***Total amount:*** $27,680,462 (8% federal, 8% state, 82% institutional, 2% external sources). ***Receiving aid:*** Freshmen: 75% (425); all full-time undergraduates: 70% (1,409). ***Average award:*** Freshmen: $20,539; Undergraduates: $19,306. ***Scholarships, grants, and awards:*** Federal Pell, FSEOG, state, private, college/university gift aid from institutional funds.

GIFT AID (NON-NEED-BASED) ***Total amount:*** $6,973,727 (8% state, 87% institutional, 5% external sources). ***Receiving aid:*** Freshmen: 72% (404). Undergraduates: 69% (1,375). ***Average award:*** Freshmen: $12,591. Undergraduates: $11,717. ***Tuition waivers:*** Full or partial for employees or children of employees, senior citizens.

LOANS ***Student loans:*** $12,530,068 (90% need-based, 10% non-need-based). 67% of past graduating class borrowed through all loan programs. *Average indebtedness per student:* $27,984. ***Average need-based loan:*** Freshmen: $3944. Undergraduates: $4644. ***Parent loans:*** $3,239,667 (86% need-based, 14% non-need-based). ***Programs:*** Federal Direct (Subsidized and Unsubsidized Stafford, PLUS), Perkins, college/university, alternative loans.

WORK-STUDY ***Federal work-study:*** Total amount: $1,477,234; 1,016 jobs averaging $1500.

APPLYING FOR FINANCIAL AID ***Required financial aid forms:*** FAFSA, state aid form. ***Financial aid deadline (priority):*** 3/1. ***Notification date:*** Continuous beginning 10/1. Students must reply within 2 weeks of notification.

CONTACT Mr. Thomas S. Blair Jr., Director of Financial Aid, Roanoke College, 221 College Lane, Salem, VA 24153-3794, 540-375-2235 or toll-free 800-388-2276. *E-mail:* finaid@roanoke.edu.

ROBERT MORRIS UNIVERSITY

Moon Township, PA

Tuition & fees: $21,550 **Average undergraduate aid package: $17,227**

ABOUT THE INSTITUTION Independent, coed. 30 undergraduate majors. Federal methodology is used as a basis for awarding need-based institutional aid.

UNDERGRADUATE EXPENSES for 2010–11 ***Comprehensive fee:*** $32,210 includes full-time tuition ($20,940), mandatory fees ($610), and room and board ($10,660). ***College room only:*** $5110. Full-time tuition and fees vary according to degree level and program. Room and board charges vary according to board plan and housing facility. ***Part-time tuition:*** $695 per credit hour. ***Part-time fees:*** $30 per credit hour. Part-time tuition and fees vary according to course load, degree level, and program. ***Payment plans:*** Installment, deferred payment.

FRESHMAN FINANCIAL AID (Fall 2010, est.) 831 applied for aid; of those 91% were deemed to have need. 100% of freshmen with need received aid; of those 14% had need fully met. ***Average percent of need met:*** 75% (excluding resources awarded to replace EFC). ***Average financial aid package:*** $19,334 (excluding resources awarded to replace EFC). 15% of all full-time freshmen had no need and received non-need-based gift aid.

UNDERGRADUATE FINANCIAL AID (Fall 2010, est.) 2,903 applied for aid; of those 92% were deemed to have need. 100% of undergraduates with need received aid; of those 13% had need fully met. ***Average percent of need met:*** 69% (excluding resources awarded to replace EFC). ***Average financial aid package:*** $17,227 (excluding resources awarded to replace EFC). 15% of all full-time undergraduates had no need and received non-need-based gift aid.

GIFT AID (NEED-BASED) ***Total amount:*** $26,750,040 (25% federal, 16% state, 56% institutional, 3% external sources). ***Receiving aid:*** Freshmen: 84% (753); all full-time undergraduates: 76% (2,541). ***Average award:*** Freshmen: $13,734; Undergraduates: $11,155. ***Scholarships, grants, and awards:*** Federal Pell, FSEOG, state, private, college/university gift aid from institutional funds.

GIFT AID (NON-NEED-BASED) ***Total amount:*** $5,318,069 (1% federal, 1% state, 96% institutional, 2% external sources). ***Receiving aid:*** Freshmen: 7% (61). Undergraduates: 6% (194). ***Average award:*** Freshmen: $9865. Undergraduates: $8990. ***Scholarships, grants, and awards by category:*** *Academic interests/achievement:* general academic interests/achievements. ***Tuition waivers:*** Full or partial for employees or children of employees.

LOANS ***Student loans:*** $27,305,460 (76% need-based, 24% non-need-based). 83% of past graduating class borrowed through all loan programs. *Average indebtedness per student:* $37,523. ***Average need-based loan:*** Freshmen: $4068. Undergraduates: $5482. ***Parent loans:*** $8,435,713 (46% need-based, 54% non-need-based). ***Programs:*** Perkins, private loans.

WORK-STUDY ***Federal work-study:*** Total amount: $4,432,937; jobs available. ***State or other work-study/employment:*** Part-time jobs available.

ATHLETIC AWARDS Total amount: $2,962,703 (45% need-based, 55% non-need-based).

APPLYING FOR FINANCIAL AID ***Required financial aid form:*** FAFSA. ***Financial aid deadline:*** Continuous. ***Notification date:*** Continuous beginning 3/15. Students must reply within 2 weeks of notification.

CONTACT Ms. Stephanie Hendershot, Director of Financial Aid, Robert Morris University, 6001 University Boulevard, Moon Township, PA 15108-1189, 412-397-6250 or toll-free 800-762-0097. *Fax:* 412-397-2200. *E-mail:* finaid@rmu.edu.

ROBERT MORRIS UNIVERSITY ILLINOIS

Chicago, IL

Tuition & fees: $21,600 **Average undergraduate aid package: $12,862**

ABOUT THE INSTITUTION Independent, coed. 15 undergraduate majors. Federal methodology is used as a basis for awarding need-based institutional aid.

UNDERGRADUATE EXPENSES for 2011–12 ***Comprehensive fee:*** $31,926 includes full-time tuition ($21,600) and room and board ($10,326). ***College room only:*** $8100. Full-time tuition and fees vary according to location. Room and board charges vary according to housing facility and location. ***Part-time tuition:*** $600 per credit hour. Part-time tuition and fees vary according to course load and location. ***Payment plans:*** Tuition prepayment, installment.

FRESHMAN FINANCIAL AID (Fall 2009) 942 applied for aid; of those 98% were deemed to have need. 98% of freshmen with need received aid; of those 4% had need fully met. ***Average percent of need met:*** 51% (excluding resources awarded to replace EFC). ***Average financial aid package:*** $13,499 (excluding resources awarded to replace EFC). 2% of all full-time freshmen had no need and received non-need-based gift aid.

UNDERGRADUATE FINANCIAL AID (Fall 2009) 5,485 applied for aid; of those 97% were deemed to have need. 94% of undergraduates with need received aid; of those 3% had need fully met. ***Average percent of need met:*** 48% (excluding resources awarded to replace EFC). ***Average financial aid package:*** $12,862 (excluding resources awarded to replace EFC). 2% of all full-time undergraduates had no need and received non-need-based gift aid.

GIFT AID (NEED-BASED) ***Total amount:*** $29,295,716 (57% federal, 35% state, 8% institutional). ***Receiving aid:*** Freshmen: 92% (875); all full-time undergraduates: 83% (4,694). ***Average award:*** Freshmen: $11,191; Undergraduates: $10,127. ***Scholarships, grants, and awards:*** Federal Pell, FSEOG, state, private, college/university gift aid from institutional funds.

GIFT AID (NON-NEED-BASED) ***Total amount:*** $11,056,824 (89% institutional, 11% external sources). ***Receiving aid:*** Freshmen: 92% (869). Undergraduates: 82% (4,633). ***Average award:*** Freshmen: $4910. Undergraduates: $5320. ***Scholarships, grants, and awards by category:*** *Academic interests/achievement:* architecture, business, computer science, general academic interests/achievements, health fields. *Creative arts/performance:* applied art and design, journalism/publications. *Special achievements/activities:* community service, general special achievements/activities. *Special characteristics:* children of faculty/staff, general special characteristics, out-of-state students, veterans. ***Tuition waivers:*** Full or partial for employees or children of employees.

LOANS ***Student loans:*** $39,842,894 (94% need-based, 6% non-need-based). 95% of past graduating class borrowed through all loan programs. *Average indebtedness per student:* $28,103. ***Average need-based loan:*** Freshmen: $4371. Undergraduates: $4767. ***Parent loans:*** $5,427,116 (80% need-based, 20% non-need-based). ***Programs:*** Federal Direct (Subsidized and Unsubsidized Stafford, PLUS), Perkins.

WORK-STUDY ***Federal work-study:*** Total amount: $670,146; 326 jobs averaging $2056.

ATHLETIC AWARDS Total amount: $5,416,648 (85% need-based, 15% non-need-based).

APPLYING FOR FINANCIAL AID ***Required financial aid form:*** FAFSA. ***Financial aid deadline:*** Continuous. ***Notification date:*** Continuous.

CONTACT Leigh Brinson, Vice President of Financial Services, Robert Morris University Illinois, 401 South State Street, Suite 122, Chicago, IL 60605, 312-935-4408 or toll-free 800-RMC-5960. *Fax:* 312-935-4415. *E-mail:* lbrinson@robertmorris.edu.

ROBERTS WESLEYAN COLLEGE

Rochester, NY

Tuition & fees: $24,360 **Average undergraduate aid package: $17,170**

ABOUT THE INSTITUTION Independent religious, coed. 58 undergraduate majors. Federal methodology is used as a basis for awarding need-based institutional aid.

UNDERGRADUATE EXPENSES for 2010–11 ***One-time required fee:*** $247. ***Comprehensive fee:*** $33,186 includes full-time tuition ($23,460), mandatory fees ($900), and room and board ($8826). ***College room only:*** $5932. Room and board charges vary according to board plan and housing facility. Part-time tuition and fees vary according to course load. ***Payment plan:*** Installment.

FRESHMAN FINANCIAL AID (Fall 2010, est.) 186 applied for aid; of those 93% were deemed to have need. 100% of freshmen with need received aid; of those 12% had need fully met. ***Average percent of need met:*** 76% (excluding resources awarded to replace EFC). ***Average financial aid package:*** $21,558 (excluding resources awarded to replace EFC). 19% of all full-time freshmen had no need and received non-need-based gift aid.

UNDERGRADUATE FINANCIAL AID (Fall 2010, est.) 1,325 applied for aid; of those 95% were deemed to have need. 99% of undergraduates with need received aid; of those 8% had need fully met. ***Average percent of need met:*** 66% (excluding resources awarded to replace EFC). ***Average financial aid package:*** $17,170 (excluding resources awarded to replace EFC). 11% of all full-time undergraduates had no need and received non-need-based gift aid.

GIFT AID (NEED-BASED) ***Total amount:*** $14,402,247 (23% federal, 11% state, 52% institutional, 14% external sources). ***Receiving aid:*** Freshmen: 76% (173); all full-time undergraduates: 83% (1,203). ***Average award:*** Freshmen: $16,475; Undergraduates: $12,198. ***Scholarships, grants, and awards:*** Federal Pell, FSEOG, state, private, college/university gift aid from institutional funds, Academic Competitiveness Grants, National SMART Grants, TEACH Grants.

GIFT AID (NON-NEED-BASED) ***Total amount:*** $1,552,717 (1% state, 68% institutional, 31% external sources). ***Receiving aid:*** Freshmen: 7% (15). Undergraduates: 4% (59). ***Average award:*** Freshmen: $7824. Undergraduates: $5453. ***Scholarships, grants, and awards by category:*** *Academic interests/achievement:* general academic interests/achievements. *Creative arts/performance:* 164 awards ($345,475 total): art/fine arts, music. *Special achievements/activities:* 402 awards ($905,800 total): general special achievements/activities, junior miss. *Special characteristics:* 584 awards ($1,846,692 total): children and siblings of alumni, children of faculty/staff, international students, out-of-state students, relatives of clergy, religious affiliation, siblings of current students. ***Tuition waivers:*** Full or partial for employees or children of employees, senior citizens.

LOANS ***Student loans:*** $10,748,142 (87% need-based, 13% non-need-based). 99% of past graduating class borrowed through all loan programs. *Average indebtedness per student:* $36,486. ***Average need-based loan:*** Freshmen: $4467. Undergraduates: $5011. ***Parent loans:*** $2,158,906 (56% need-based, 44% non-need-based). ***Programs:*** Federal Direct (Subsidized and Unsubsidized Stafford, PLUS), Perkins.

WORK-STUDY ***Federal work-study:*** Total amount: $367,237; 751 jobs averaging $1857. ***State or other work-study/employment:*** Total amount: $340,500 (82% need-based, 18% non-need-based). 30 part-time jobs averaging $2016.

ATHLETIC AWARDS Total amount: $731,954 (68% need-based, 32% non-need-based).

APPLYING FOR FINANCIAL AID ***Required financial aid forms:*** FAFSA, state aid form. ***Financial aid deadline (priority):*** 3/15. ***Notification date:*** Continuous beginning 3/15. Students must reply by 5/1 or within 2 weeks of notification.

CONTACT Financial Aid Office, Roberts Wesleyan College, 2301 Westside Drive, Rochester, NY 14624-1997, 585-594-6150 or toll-free 800-777-4RWC. *Fax:* 585-594-6036. *E-mail:* finaid@roberts.edu.

ROCHESTER COLLEGE

Rochester Hills, MI

CONTACT Kara Miller, Director of Financial Aid, Rochester College, 800 West Avon Road, Rochester Hills, MI 48307, 248-218-2038 or toll-free 800-521-6010. *Fax:* 248-218-2065. *E-mail:* kmiller@rc.edu.

ROCHESTER INSTITUTE OF TECHNOLOGY

Rochester, NY

Tuition & fees: $30,717 **Average undergraduate aid package: N/A**

ABOUT THE INSTITUTION Independent, coed. 114 undergraduate majors. Both federal and institutional methodology are used as a basis for awarding need-based institutional aid.

UNDERGRADUATE EXPENSES for 2010–11 ***Comprehensive fee:*** $40,761 includes full-time tuition ($30,282), mandatory fees ($435), and room and board ($10,044). ***College room only:*** $5862. Full-time tuition and fees vary according to course load. Room and board charges vary according to board plan and housing facility. ***Part-time tuition:*** $673 per quarter hour. ***Part-time fees:*** $37 per term. Part-time tuition and fees vary according to class time and course load. ***Payment plans:*** Tuition prepayment, installment, deferred payment.

GIFT AID (NEED-BASED) ***Scholarships, grants, and awards:*** Federal Pell, FSEOG, state, private, college/university gift aid from institutional funds, NACME Scholarships, NSF Grants.

GIFT AID (NON-NEED-BASED) ***Scholarships, grants, and awards by category:*** *Academic interests/achievement:* biological sciences, business, communication, computer science, engineering/technologies, general academic interests/achievements, health fields, international studies, mathematics, military science, physical sciences, premedicine, social sciences. *Creative arts/performance:*

applied art and design, art/fine arts, cinema/film/broadcasting. *Special achievements/activities:* community service, leadership. *Special characteristics:* children of faculty/staff, veterans. ***Tuition waivers:*** Full or partial for employees or children of employees.

LOANS ***Programs:*** Federal Direct (Subsidized and Unsubsidized Stafford, PLUS), Perkins, alternative loans.

WORK-STUDY Federal work-study jobs available. ***State or other work-study/ employment:*** Part-time jobs available.

APPLYING FOR FINANCIAL AID ***Required financial aid forms:*** FAFSA, state aid form. ***Financial aid deadline (priority):*** 3/1. ***Notification date:*** Continuous beginning 3/15. Students must reply by 5/1.

CONTACT Mrs. Verna Hazen, Assistant Vice President for Financial Aid and Scholarships, Rochester Institute of Technology, 56 Lomb Memorial Drive, Rochester, NY 14623-5604, 585-475-2186. *Fax:* 585-475-7270. *E-mail:* verna.hazen@rit.edu.

ROCKFORD COLLEGE

Rockford, IL

Tuition & fees: $24,750 **Average undergraduate aid package: $17,513**

ABOUT THE INSTITUTION Independent, coed. 46 undergraduate majors. Federal methodology is used as a basis for awarding need-based institutional aid.

UNDERGRADUATE EXPENSES for 2010–11 ***Comprehensive fee:*** $31,700 includes full-time tuition ($24,750) and room and board ($6950). ***College room only:*** $3950. Full-time tuition and fees vary according to course load. Room and board charges vary according to board plan and housing facility. ***Part-time tuition:*** $675 per credit hour. ***Part-time fees:*** $40 per term. Part-time tuition and fees vary according to course load. ***Payment plan:*** Installment.

FRESHMAN FINANCIAL AID (Fall 2010, est.) 143 applied for aid; of those 92% were deemed to have need. 100% of freshmen with need received aid; of those 12% had need fully met. ***Average percent of need met:*** 74% (excluding resources awarded to replace EFC). ***Average financial aid package:*** $18,425 (excluding resources awarded to replace EFC). 10% of all full-time freshmen had no need and received non-need-based gift aid.

UNDERGRADUATE FINANCIAL AID (Fall 2010, est.) 846 applied for aid; of those 94% were deemed to have need. 100% of undergraduates with need received aid; of those 11% had need fully met. ***Average percent of need met:*** 68% (excluding resources awarded to replace EFC). ***Average financial aid package:*** $17,513 (excluding resources awarded to replace EFC). 8% of all full-time undergraduates had no need and received non-need-based gift aid.

GIFT AID (NEED-BASED) ***Total amount:*** $10,002,742 (20% federal, 19% state, 60% institutional, 1% external sources). ***Receiving aid:*** Freshmen: 88% (130); all full-time undergraduates: 89% (776). ***Average award:*** Freshmen: $14,637; Undergraduates: $12,447. ***Scholarships, grants, and awards:*** Federal Pell, FSEOG, state, private, college/university gift aid from institutional funds.

GIFT AID (NON-NEED-BASED) ***Total amount:*** $1,061,278 (89% institutional, 11% external sources). ***Receiving aid:*** Freshmen: 10% (15). Undergraduates: 9% (83). ***Average award:*** Freshmen: $11,208. Undergraduates: $8810. ***Scholarships, grants, and awards by category:*** *Academic interests/achievement:* 825 awards ($6,308,831 total): biological sciences, business, computer science, education, English, foreign languages, general academic interests/achievements, mathematics, physical sciences, premedicine, social sciences. *Creative arts/performance:* 26 awards ($53,750 total): dance, music, performing arts, theater/drama. *Special achievements/activities:* 10 awards ($19,740 total): community service, leadership. *Special characteristics:* 80 awards ($188,725 total): children and siblings of alumni, children of current students, children of educators, children of faculty/staff, general special characteristics, international students, out-of-state students, parents of current students, siblings of current students. ***Tuition waivers:*** Full or partial for employees or children of employees.

LOANS ***Student loans:*** $8,171,783 (87% need-based, 13% non-need-based). 100% of past graduating class borrowed through all loan programs. *Average indebtedness per student:* $28,343. ***Average need-based loan:*** Freshmen: $3128. Undergraduates: $4755. ***Parent loans:*** $1,000,564 (47% need-based, 53% non-need-based). ***Programs:*** Federal Direct (Subsidized and Unsubsidized Stafford, PLUS), Perkins, college/university, alternative loans.

WORK-STUDY ***Federal work-study:*** Total amount: $98,235; jobs available. ***State or other work-study/employment:*** Total amount: $74,321 (100% non-need-based). Part-time jobs available.

APPLYING FOR FINANCIAL AID ***Required financial aid form:*** FAFSA. ***Financial aid deadline (priority):*** 3/1. ***Notification date:*** Continuous beginning 3/15. Students must reply within 4 weeks of notification.

CONTACT Todd M. Free, Assistant Vice President of Student Administrative Services, Rockford College, 5050 East State Street, Rockford, IL 61108, 815-226-3385 or toll-free 800-892-2984. *Fax:* 815-394-5174. *E-mail:* tfree@rockford.edu.

ROCKHURST UNIVERSITY

Kansas City, MO

Tuition & fees: $27,390 **Average undergraduate aid package: $26,223**

ABOUT THE INSTITUTION Independent Roman Catholic (Jesuit), coed. 24 undergraduate majors. Federal methodology is used as a basis for awarding need-based institutional aid.

UNDERGRADUATE EXPENSES for 2010–11 ***Comprehensive fee:*** $34,880 includes full-time tuition ($26,450), mandatory fees ($940), and room and board ($7490). ***College room only:*** $4590. Full-time tuition and fees vary according to class time and course load. Room and board charges vary according to board plan and housing facility. ***Part-time tuition:*** $882 per credit hour. ***Part-time fees:*** $25 per credit hour. Part-time tuition and fees vary according to class time and course load. ***Payment plans:*** Installment, deferred payment.

FRESHMAN FINANCIAL AID (Fall 2010, est.) 365 applied for aid; of those 100% were deemed to have need. 100% of freshmen with need received aid; of those 44% had need fully met. ***Average percent of need met:*** 100% (excluding resources awarded to replace EFC). ***Average financial aid package:*** $27,394 (excluding resources awarded to replace EFC). 6% of all full-time freshmen had no need and received non-need-based gift aid.

UNDERGRADUATE FINANCIAL AID (Fall 2010, est.) 1,197 applied for aid; of those 100% were deemed to have need. 100% of undergraduates with need received aid; of those 27% had need fully met. ***Average percent of need met:*** 89% (excluding resources awarded to replace EFC). ***Average financial aid package:*** $26,223 (excluding resources awarded to replace EFC). 11% of all full-time undergraduates had no need and received non-need-based gift aid.

GIFT AID (NEED-BASED) ***Total amount:*** $12,957,419 (13% federal, 5% state, 81% institutional, 1% external sources). ***Receiving aid:*** Freshmen: 76% (283); all full-time undergraduates: 69% (942). ***Average award:*** Freshmen: $7302; Undergraduates: $6962. ***Scholarships, grants, and awards:*** Federal Pell, FSEOG, state, private, college/university gift aid from institutional funds.

GIFT AID (NON-NEED-BASED) ***Total amount:*** $8,921,771 (1% state, 98% institutional, 1% external sources). ***Receiving aid:*** Freshmen: 90% (332). Undergraduates: 83% (1,137). ***Average award:*** Freshmen: $12,402. Undergraduates: $13,392. ***Scholarships, grants, and awards by category:*** *Academic interests/achievement:* biological sciences, business, communication, English, foreign languages, general academic interests/achievements, health fields, humanities, mathematics, physical sciences, premedicine, religion/biblical studies, social sciences. *Creative arts/performance:* creative writing, music, performing arts, theater/drama. *Special achievements/activities:* community service, leadership. *Special characteristics:* children and siblings of alumni, children of faculty/staff, siblings of current students. ***Tuition waivers:*** Full or partial for employees or children of employees, senior citizens.

LOANS ***Student loans:*** $6,390,039 (51% need-based, 49% non-need-based). 83% of past graduating class borrowed through all loan programs. *Average indebtedness per student:* $24,841. ***Average need-based loan:*** Freshmen: $3386. Undergraduates: $3731. ***Parent loans:*** $1,676,751 (49% need-based, 51% non-need-based). ***Programs:*** Perkins.

WORK-STUDY ***Federal work-study:*** Total amount: $475,599; 531 jobs averaging $1500.

ATHLETIC AWARDS Total amount: $2,201,218 (24% need-based, 76% non-need-based).

APPLYING FOR FINANCIAL AID ***Required financial aid form:*** FAFSA. ***Financial aid deadline (priority):*** 3/1. ***Notification date:*** Continuous beginning 3/1. Students must reply by 6/1 or within 4 weeks of notification.

CONTACT Angela Karlin, Director of Financial Aid, Rockhurst University, 1100 Rockhurst Road, Kansas City, MO 64110-2561, 816-501-4238 or toll-free 800-842-6776. *Fax:* 816-501-3139. *E-mail:* angela.karlin@rockhurst.edu.

ROCKY MOUNTAIN COLLEGE

Billings, MT

Tuition & fees: $22,134 **Average undergraduate aid package: $19,651**

ABOUT THE INSTITUTION Independent interdenominational, coed. 51 undergraduate majors. Federal methodology is used as a basis for awarding need-based institutional aid.

UNDERGRADUATE EXPENSES for 2011–12 ***Comprehensive fee:*** $29,030 includes full-time tuition ($21,684), mandatory fees ($450), and room and board ($6896). ***College room only:*** $3264. Full-time tuition and fees vary according to course load, degree level, and program. Room and board charges vary according to board plan and housing facility. ***Part-time tuition:*** $904 per credit. Part-time tuition and fees vary according to course load, degree level, and program. ***Payment plan:*** Installment.

FRESHMAN FINANCIAL AID (Fall 2010, est.) 257 applied for aid; of those 90% were deemed to have need. 100% of freshmen with need received aid; of those 18% had need fully met. ***Average percent of need met:*** 74% (excluding resources awarded to replace EFC). ***Average financial aid package:*** $19,443 (excluding resources awarded to replace EFC). 15% of all full-time freshmen had no need and received non-need-based gift aid.

UNDERGRADUATE FINANCIAL AID (Fall 2010, est.) 740 applied for aid; of those 91% were deemed to have need. 100% of undergraduates with need received aid; of those 23% had need fully met. ***Average percent of need met:*** 75% (excluding resources awarded to replace EFC). ***Average financial aid package:*** $19,651 (excluding resources awarded to replace EFC). 17% of all full-time undergraduates had no need and received non-need-based gift aid.

GIFT AID (NEED-BASED) ***Total amount:*** $7,465,434 (23% federal, 1% state, 72% institutional, 4% external sources). ***Receiving aid:*** Freshmen: 81% (231); all full-time undergraduates: 76% (670). ***Average award:*** Freshmen: $16,051; Undergraduates: $15,667. ***Scholarships, grants, and awards:*** Federal Pell, FSEOG, state, private, college/university gift aid from institutional funds.

GIFT AID (NON-NEED-BASED) ***Total amount:*** $2,158,780 (66% institutional, 34% external sources). ***Receiving aid:*** Freshmen: 13% (36). Undergraduates: 12% (103). ***Average award:*** Freshmen: $10,000. Undergraduates: $8134. ***Scholarships, grants, and awards by category:*** *Creative arts/performance:* 17 awards ($19,100 total): art/fine arts, creative writing, debating, music, theater/drama. *Special achievements/activities:* 11 awards ($20,400 total): cheerleading/drum major, leadership. *Special characteristics:* 25 awards ($510,226 total): children and siblings of alumni, children of faculty/staff. ***Tuition waivers:*** Full or partial for employees or children of employees.

LOANS ***Student loans:*** $5,002,848 (44% need-based, 56% non-need-based). 76% of past graduating class borrowed through all loan programs. *Average indebtedness per student:* $20,122. ***Average need-based loan:*** Freshmen: $3480. Undergraduates: $4289. ***Parent loans:*** $1,254,795 (100% non-need-based). ***Programs:*** Federal Direct (Subsidized and Unsubsidized Stafford, PLUS), Perkins.

WORK-STUDY ***Federal work-study:*** Total amount: $838,862; 448 jobs averaging $1872. ***State or other work-study/employment:*** Total amount: $389,115 (100% non-need-based). 202 part-time jobs averaging $1923.

ATHLETIC AWARDS Total amount: $2,315,829 (51% need-based, 49% non-need-based).

APPLYING FOR FINANCIAL AID ***Required financial aid form:*** FAFSA. ***Financial aid deadline:*** Continuous. ***Notification date:*** Continuous beginning 3/1. Students must reply within 4 weeks of notification.

CONTACT Jessica Francischetti, Financial Aid Director, Rocky Mountain College, 1511 Poly Drive, Billings, MT 59102-1796, 406-657-1031 or toll-free 800-877-6259. *Fax:* 406-657-1169. *E-mail:* finaid@rocky.edu.

ROCKY MOUNTAIN COLLEGE OF ART + DESIGN

Lakewood, CO

Tuition & fees: $26,832 **Average undergraduate aid package: $18,770**

ABOUT THE INSTITUTION Proprietary, coed. 9 undergraduate majors. Federal methodology is used as a basis for awarding need-based institutional aid.

UNDERGRADUATE EXPENSES for 2010–11 ***Tuition:*** full-time $26,832; part-time $1118 per credit hour. Part-time tuition and fees vary according to course load. Room and board charges vary according to board plan and housing facility. ***Payment plans:*** Guaranteed tuition, installment.

FRESHMAN FINANCIAL AID (Fall 2010, est.) 127 applied for aid; of those 94% were deemed to have need. 100% of freshmen with need received aid; of those 10% had need fully met. ***Average percent of need met:*** 61% (excluding resources awarded to replace EFC). ***Average financial aid package:*** $18,237 (excluding resources awarded to replace EFC). 14% of all full-time freshmen had no need and received non-need-based gift aid.

UNDERGRADUATE FINANCIAL AID (Fall 2010, est.) 531 applied for aid; of those 84% were deemed to have need. 100% of undergraduates with need received aid; of those 4% had need fully met. ***Average percent of need met:*** 66% (excluding resources awarded to replace EFC). ***Average financial aid package:*** $18,770 (excluding resources awarded to replace EFC). 11% of all full-time undergraduates had no need and received non-need-based gift aid.

GIFT AID (NEED-BASED) ***Total amount:*** $3,369,730 (24% federal, 74% institutional, 2% external sources). ***Receiving aid:*** Freshmen: 37% (52); all full-time undergraduates: 29% (175). ***Average award:*** Freshmen: $4881; Undergraduates: $4764. ***Scholarships, grants, and awards:*** Federal Pell, FSEOG, state, college/university gift aid from institutional funds.

GIFT AID (NON-NEED-BASED) ***Total amount:*** $478,575 (100% institutional). ***Receiving aid:*** Freshmen: 86% (120). Undergraduates: 70% (419). ***Average award:*** Freshmen: $1104. Undergraduates: $5145. ***Scholarships, grants, and awards by category:*** *Academic interests/achievement:* 502 awards ($2,631,676 total): general academic interests/achievements. *Creative arts/performance:* 281 awards ($377,811 total): applied art and design, art/fine arts. *Special characteristics:* 4 awards ($83,386 total): children of faculty/staff. ***Tuition waivers:*** Full or partial for employees or children of employees.

LOANS ***Student loans:*** $4,026,165 (93% need-based, 7% non-need-based). 67% of past graduating class borrowed through all loan programs. *Average indebtedness per student:* $26,247. ***Average need-based loan:*** Freshmen: $3538. Undergraduates: $4688. ***Parent loans:*** $3,791,719 (92% need-based, 8% non-need-based). ***Programs:*** Federal Direct (Subsidized and Unsubsidized Stafford, PLUS), alternative loans.

WORK-STUDY ***Federal work-study:*** Total amount: $61,027; 30 jobs averaging $2482. ***State or other work-study/employment:*** Total amount: $117,237 (96% need-based, 4% non-need-based). 46 part-time jobs averaging $2548.

APPLYING FOR FINANCIAL AID ***Required financial aid form:*** FAFSA. ***Financial aid deadline (priority):*** 3/15. ***Notification date:*** Continuous beginning 4/1. Students must reply within 2 weeks of notification.

CONTACT Tammy Dybdahl, Director of Financial Aid, Rocky Mountain College of Art + Design, 1600 Pierce Street, Lakewood, CO 80214, 303-225-8551 or toll-free 800-888-ARTS. *Fax:* 303-567-7280. *E-mail:* tdybdahl@rmcad.edu.

ROGERS STATE UNIVERSITY

Claremore, OK

Tuition & fees (OK res): $4513 **Average undergraduate aid package: $7956**

ABOUT THE INSTITUTION State-supported, coed. 24 undergraduate majors. Federal methodology is used as a basis for awarding need-based institutional aid.

UNDERGRADUATE EXPENSES for 2011–12 ***Tuition, state resident:*** full-time $2879; part-time $95.95 per credit hour. ***Tuition, nonresident:*** full-time $8636; part-time $287.85 per credit hour. ***Required fees:*** full-time $1634; $53.45 per credit hour or $15 per credit hour. Full-time tuition and fees vary according to course level, course load, location, program, and student level. Part-time tuition and fees vary according to course level, course load, location, program, and student level. ***College room and board:*** ***Room only:*** $5990. Room and board charges vary according to board plan and housing facility. ***Payment plan:*** Installment.

FRESHMAN FINANCIAL AID (Fall 2010, est.) 478 applied for aid; of those 84% were deemed to have need. 97% of freshmen with need received aid; of those 11% had need fully met. ***Average percent of need met:*** 40% (excluding resources awarded to replace EFC). ***Average financial aid package:*** $6915 (excluding resources awarded to replace EFC). 2% of all full-time freshmen had no need and received non-need-based gift aid.

UNDERGRADUATE FINANCIAL AID (Fall 2010, est.) 1,571 applied for aid; of those 98% were deemed to have need. 98% of undergraduates with need received aid; of those 8% had need fully met. ***Average percent of need met:*** 45% (excluding resources awarded to replace EFC). ***Average financial aid package:*** $7956 (excluding resources awarded to replace EFC). 2% of all full-time undergraduates had no need and received non-need-based gift aid.

GIFT AID (NEED-BASED) ***Total amount:*** $11,867,727 (67% federal, 23% state, 3% institutional, 7% external sources). ***Receiving aid:*** Freshmen: 48% (265); all full-time undergraduates: 5% (117). ***Average award:*** Freshmen: $4589; Undergraduates: $4875. ***Scholarships, grants, and awards:*** Federal Pell, FSEOG, state, private, college/university gift aid from institutional funds.

GIFT AID (NON-NEED-BASED) ***Total amount:*** $1,389,797 (70% state, 13% institutional, 17% external sources). ***Receiving aid:*** Freshmen: 35% (192). Undergraduates: 29% (614). ***Average award:*** Freshmen: $3930. Undergraduates: $3391. ***Scholarships, grants, and awards by category:*** *Academic interests/achievement:* 28 awards ($23,357 total): general academic interests/achievements. *Creative arts/performance:* 15 awards ($13,800 total): music. *Special achievements/activities:* 67 awards ($148,025 total): cheerleading/drum major, leadership, rodeo. *Special characteristics:* 206 awards ($822,996 total): adult students, out-of-state students. ***Tuition waivers:*** Full or partial for employees or children of employees, senior citizens.

LOANS ***Student loans:*** $12,257,475 (92% need-based, 8% non-need-based). 53% of past graduating class borrowed through all loan programs. *Average indebtedness per student:* $15,962. ***Average need-based loan:*** Freshmen: $3012. Undergraduates: $3799. ***Parent loans:*** $59,539 (16% need-based, 84% non-need-based). ***Programs:*** Federal Direct (Subsidized and Unsubsidized Stafford, PLUS), alternative loans.

WORK-STUDY ***Federal work-study:*** Total amount: $114,863; 60 jobs averaging $1914. ***State or other work-study/employment:*** Total amount: $723,923 (64% need-based, 36% non-need-based). 284 part-time jobs averaging $2549.

ATHLETIC AWARDS Total amount: $825,100 (57% need-based, 43% non-need-based).

APPLYING FOR FINANCIAL AID ***Required financial aid form:*** FAFSA. ***Financial aid deadline:*** Continuous. ***Notification date:*** Continuous beginning 4/1. Students must reply within 2 weeks of notification.

CONTACT Ms. Kelly Hicks, Assistant Director of Financial Aid, Rogers State University, 1701 West Will Rogers Boulevard, Claremore, OK 74017-3252, 918-343-7553 or toll-free 800-256-7511. *Fax:* 918-343-7598. *E-mail:* finaid@rsu.edu.

ROGER WILLIAMS UNIVERSITY

Bristol, RI

CONTACT Mr. Greg Rogers, Director of Institutional Research, Roger Williams University, 1 Old Ferry Road, Bristol, RI 02809, 401-254-3116 or toll-free 800-458-7144 (out-of-state). *Fax:* 401-254-3677. *E-mail:* grogers@rwu.edu.

ROLLINS COLLEGE

Winter Park, FL

Tuition & fees: $37,640 **Average undergraduate aid package: $35,180**

ABOUT THE INSTITUTION Independent, coed. 32 undergraduate majors. Federal methodology is used as a basis for awarding need-based institutional aid.

UNDERGRADUATE EXPENSES for 2010–11 ***Comprehensive fee:*** $49,400 includes full-time tuition ($37,640) and room and board ($11,760). ***College room only:*** $6920. Room and board charges vary according to housing facility. ***Payment plan:*** Installment.

FRESHMAN FINANCIAL AID (Fall 2010, est.) 291 applied for aid; of those 85% were deemed to have need. 100% of freshmen with need received aid; of those 17% had need fully met. ***Average percent of need met:*** 90% (excluding resources awarded to replace EFC). ***Average financial aid package:*** $36,999 (excluding resources awarded to replace EFC). 18% of all full-time freshmen had no need and received non-need-based gift aid.

UNDERGRADUATE FINANCIAL AID (Fall 2010, est.) 940 applied for aid; of those 91% were deemed to have need. 99% of undergraduates with need received aid; of those 20% had need fully met. ***Average percent of need met:*** 90% (excluding resources awarded to replace EFC). ***Average financial aid package:*** $35,180 (excluding resources awarded to replace EFC). 17% of all full-time undergraduates had no need and received non-need-based gift aid.

GIFT AID (NEED-BASED) ***Total amount:*** $23,869,010 (9% federal, 14% state, 76% institutional, 1% external sources). ***Receiving aid:*** Freshmen: 52% (246); all full-time undergraduates: 48% (826). ***Average award:*** Freshmen: $31,519; Undergraduates: $29,649. ***Scholarships, grants, and awards:*** Federal Pell, FSEOG, state, private, college/university gift aid from institutional funds.

GIFT AID (NON-NEED-BASED) ***Total amount:*** $7,228,376 (21% state, 78% institutional, 1% external sources). ***Receiving aid:*** Freshmen: 3% (15). Undergraduates: 3% (59). ***Average award:*** Freshmen: $15,939. Undergraduates: $16,999. ***Scholarships, grants, and awards by category:*** *Academic interests/achievement:* computer science, engineering/technologies, general academic interests/achievements, mathematics, physical sciences. *Creative arts/performance:* art/fine arts, music, theater/drama. ***Tuition waivers:*** Full or partial for employees or children of employees.

LOANS ***Student loans:*** $25,008,085 (12% need-based, 88% non-need-based). 46% of past graduating class borrowed through all loan programs. *Average indebtedness per student:* $25,294. ***Average need-based loan:*** Freshmen: $3780. Undergraduates: $4433. ***Parent loans:*** $3,159,970 (28% need-based, 72% non-need-based). ***Programs:*** Federal Direct (Subsidized and Unsubsidized Stafford, PLUS), Perkins, college/university.

WORK-STUDY ***Federal work-study:*** Total amount: $939,119; 375 jobs averaging $2384.

ATHLETIC AWARDS Total amount: $3,181,819 (31% need-based, 69% non-need-based).

APPLYING FOR FINANCIAL AID ***Required financial aid forms:*** FAFSA, institution's own form. ***Financial aid deadline (priority):*** 3/1. ***Notification date:*** Continuous beginning 3/1.

CONTACT Mr. Steve Booker, Director of Financial Aid, Rollins College, 1000 Holt Avenue, #2721, Winter Park, FL 32789-4499, 407-646-2193. *Fax:* 407-646-2173. *E-mail:* sbooker@rollins.edu.

ROOSEVELT UNIVERSITY

Chicago, IL

CONTACT Mr. Walter J. H. O'Neill, Director of Financial Aid, Roosevelt University, 430 South Michigan Avenue, Chicago, IL 60605-1394, 312-341-2090 or toll-free 877-APPLYRU. *Fax:* 312-341-3545. *E-mail:* woneill@roosevelt.edu.

ROSE-HULMAN INSTITUTE OF TECHNOLOGY

Terre Haute, IN

Tuition & fees: $36,270 **Average undergraduate aid package: $24,442**

ABOUT THE INSTITUTION Independent, coed, primarily men. 16 undergraduate majors. Federal methodology is used as a basis for awarding need-based institutional aid.

UNDERGRADUATE EXPENSES for 2010–11 ***One-time required fee:*** $2800. ***Comprehensive fee:*** $46,227 includes full-time tuition ($35,595), mandatory fees ($675), and room and board ($9957). ***College room only:*** $6084. Full-time tuition and fees vary according to course load. Room and board charges vary according to board plan. ***Part-time tuition:*** $1038 per credit hour. Part-time tuition and fees vary according to course load. ***Payment plans:*** Tuition prepayment, installment.

FRESHMAN FINANCIAL AID (Fall 2010, est.) 477 applied for aid; of those 85% were deemed to have need. 100% of freshmen with need received aid; of those 20% had need fully met. ***Average percent of need met:*** 89% (excluding resources awarded to replace EFC). ***Average financial aid package:*** $26,078 (excluding resources awarded to replace EFC). 25% of all full-time freshmen had no need and received non-need-based gift aid.

UNDERGRADUATE FINANCIAL AID (Fall 2010, est.) 1,501 applied for aid; of those 89% were deemed to have need. 100% of undergraduates with need received aid; of those 18% had need fully met. ***Average percent of need met:*** 79% (excluding resources awarded to replace EFC). ***Average financial aid package:*** $24,442 (excluding resources awarded to replace EFC). 27% of all full-time undergraduates had no need and received non-need-based gift aid.

GIFT AID (NEED-BASED) ***Total amount:*** $26,197,995 (7% federal, 4% state, 78% institutional, 11% external sources). ***Receiving aid:*** Freshmen: 74% (407); all full-time undergraduates: 72% (1,339). ***Average award:*** Freshmen: $21,781; Undergraduates: $19,322. ***Scholarships, grants, and awards:*** Federal Pell, FSEOG, state, college/university gift aid from institutional funds.

GIFT AID (NON-NEED-BASED) ***Total amount:*** $6,407,397 (81% institutional, 19% external sources). ***Receiving aid:*** Freshmen: 18% (102). Undergraduates: 6% (107). ***Average award:*** Freshmen: $10,834. Undergraduates: $10,125. ***Tuition waivers:*** Full or partial for employees or children of employees.

LOANS ***Student loans:*** $12,346,210 (94% need-based, 6% non-need-based). 74% of past graduating class borrowed through all loan programs. *Average indebtedness per student:* $40,619. ***Average need-based loan:*** Freshmen: $4218. Undergraduates: $4871. ***Parent loans:*** $8,408,175 (88% need-based, 12% non-need-based). ***Programs:*** Federal Direct (Subsidized and Unsubsidized Stafford, PLUS).

WORK-STUDY ***Federal work-study:*** Total amount: $690,246; 485 jobs averaging $1383. ***State or other work-study/employment:*** Total amount: $925,143 (97% need-based, 3% non-need-based). 660 part-time jobs averaging $1394.

APPLYING FOR FINANCIAL AID ***Required financial aid form:*** FAFSA. ***Financial aid deadline (priority):*** 3/1. ***Notification date:*** 3/10.

CONTACT Melinda L. Middleton, Director of Financial Aid, Rose-Hulman Institute of Technology, 5500 Wabash Avenue, CM 5, Terre Haute, IN 47803, 812-877-8259 or toll-free 800-248-7448. *Fax:* 812-877-8746. *E-mail:* melinda.middleton@rose-hulman.edu.

ROSEMONT COLLEGE

Rosemont, PA

Tuition & fees: $29,050 **Average undergraduate aid package: $22,845**

ABOUT THE INSTITUTION Independent Roman Catholic, coed. 27 undergraduate majors. Federal methodology is used as a basis for awarding need-based institutional aid.

UNDERGRADUATE EXPENSES for 2011–12 ***Comprehensive fee:*** $40,490 includes full-time tuition ($28,100), mandatory fees ($950), and room and board ($11,440). Room and board charges vary according to board plan and housing facility. ***Part-time tuition:*** $1070 per credit hour. ***Payment plan:*** Installment.

FRESHMAN FINANCIAL AID (Fall 2009) 178 applied for aid; of those 98% were deemed to have need. 100% of freshmen with need received aid; of those 10% had need fully met. ***Average percent of need met:*** 74% (excluding resources awarded to replace EFC). ***Average financial aid package:*** $24,310 (excluding resources awarded to replace EFC). 5% of all full-time freshmen had no need and received non-need-based gift aid.

UNDERGRADUATE FINANCIAL AID (Fall 2009) 407 applied for aid; of those 97% were deemed to have need. 100% of undergraduates with need received aid; of those 11% had need fully met. ***Average percent of need met:*** 71% (excluding resources awarded to replace EFC). ***Average financial aid package:*** $22,845 (excluding resources awarded to replace EFC). 6% of all full-time undergraduates had no need and received non-need-based gift aid.

GIFT AID (NEED-BASED) ***Total amount:*** $7,702,767 (17% federal, 11% state, 70% institutional, 2% external sources). ***Receiving aid:*** Freshmen: 94% (175); all full-time undergraduates: 93% (393). ***Average award:*** Freshmen: $21,562; Undergraduates: $19,781. ***Scholarships, grants, and awards:*** Federal Pell, FSEOG, state, private, college/university gift aid from institutional funds, Academic Competitiveness Grants, National SMART Grants.

GIFT AID (NON-NEED-BASED) ***Total amount:*** $448,943 (1% federal, 6% state, 88% institutional, 5% external sources). ***Receiving aid:*** Freshmen: 9% (16). Undergraduates: 8% (35). ***Average award:*** Freshmen: $14,400. Undergraduates: $10,657. ***Scholarships, grants, and awards by category:*** *Academic interests/achievement:* general academic interests/achievements. *Creative arts/performance:* art/fine arts. *Special achievements/activities:* community service, general special achievements/activities, leadership, religious involvement. *Special characteristics:* children and siblings of alumni, children of educators, children of faculty/staff, relatives of clergy, siblings of current students. ***Tuition waivers:*** Full or partial for employees or children of employees, senior citizens.

LOANS ***Student loans:*** $2,966,840 (84% need-based, 16% non-need-based). 92% of past graduating class borrowed through all loan programs. *Average indebtedness per student:* $21,490. ***Average need-based loan:*** Freshmen: $2977. Undergraduates: $3330. ***Parent loans:*** $850,207 (68% need-based, 32% non-need-based). ***Programs:*** Federal Direct (Subsidized and Unsubsidized Stafford, PLUS), Perkins.

WORK-STUDY ***Federal work-study:*** Total amount: $83,892; 65 jobs averaging $1550. ***State or other work-study/employment:*** Total amount: $1684 (100% need-based). Part-time jobs available.

APPLYING FOR FINANCIAL AID ***Required financial aid form:*** FAFSA. ***Financial aid deadline (priority):*** 2/15. ***Notification date:*** Continuous beginning 3/15. Students must reply by 5/1 or within 4 weeks of notification.

CONTACT Mr. Chuck Walz, Director of Financial Aid, Rosemont College, 1400 Montgomery Avenue, Rosemont, PA 19010, 610-527-0200 Ext. 2905 or toll-free 800-331-0708. *Fax:* 610-520-4399. *E-mail:* cwalz@rosemont.edu.

ROWAN UNIVERSITY

Glassboro, NJ

Tuition & fees (NJ res): $11,676 **Average undergraduate aid package: $9483**

ABOUT THE INSTITUTION State-supported, coed. 56 undergraduate majors. Both federal and institutional methodology are used as a basis for awarding need-based institutional aid.

UNDERGRADUATE EXPENSES for 2011–12 ***Tuition, state resident:*** full-time $8396; part-time $323 per credit. ***Tuition, nonresident:*** full-time $15,754; part-time $607 per credit. ***Required fees:*** full-time $3280; $140 per credit. Full-time tuition and fees vary according to course load, degree level, and program. Part-time tuition and fees vary according to course load, degree level, and program. ***College room and board:*** $10,348; ***Room only:*** $6248. Room and board charges vary according to board plan and housing facility. ***Payment plan:*** Deferred payment.

FRESHMAN FINANCIAL AID (Fall 2009) 1,406 applied for aid; of those 68% were deemed to have need. 96% of freshmen with need received aid; of those 29% had need fully met. ***Average percent of need met:*** 88% (excluding resources awarded to replace EFC). ***Average financial aid package:*** $9276 (excluding resources awarded to replace EFC). 8% of all full-time freshmen had no need and received non-need-based gift aid.

UNDERGRADUATE FINANCIAL AID (Fall 2009) 6,737 applied for aid; of those 77% were deemed to have need. 96% of undergraduates with need received aid; of those 18% had need fully met. ***Average percent of need met:*** 83% (excluding resources awarded to replace EFC). ***Average financial aid package:*** $9483 (excluding resources awarded to replace EFC). 6% of all full-time undergraduates had no need and received non-need-based gift aid.

GIFT AID (NEED-BASED) ***Total amount:*** $30,311,341 (37% federal, 44% state, 16% institutional, 3% external sources). ***Receiving aid:*** Freshmen: 28% (446); all full-time undergraduates: 32% (2,693). ***Average award:*** Freshmen: $10,462; Undergraduates: $9285. ***Scholarships, grants, and awards:*** Federal Pell, FSEOG, state, private, college/university gift aid from institutional funds.

GIFT AID (NON-NEED-BASED) ***Total amount:*** $2,845,204 (3% state, 83% institutional, 14% external sources). ***Receiving aid:*** Freshmen: 15% (232). Undergraduates: 9% (740). ***Average award:*** Freshmen: $5114. Undergraduates: $5219. ***Scholarships, grants, and awards by category:*** *Academic interests/achievement:* general academic interests/achievements. *Creative arts/performance:* general creative arts/performance, music. ***Tuition waivers:*** Full or partial for employees or children of employees.

LOANS ***Student loans:*** $52,102,437 (94% need-based, 6% non-need-based). 73% of past graduating class borrowed through all loan programs. *Average indebtedness per student:* $29,073. ***Average need-based loan:*** Freshmen: $3246. Undergraduates: $4262. ***Parent loans:*** $14,684,126 (70% need-based, 30% non-need-based). ***Programs:*** Federal Direct (Subsidized and Unsubsidized Stafford, PLUS), state.

WORK-STUDY ***Federal work-study:*** Total amount: $650,415; 592 jobs averaging $1197. ***State or other work-study/employment:*** Total amount: $1,381,284 (67% need-based, 33% non-need-based). 816 part-time jobs averaging $1710.

APPLYING FOR FINANCIAL AID ***Required financial aid form:*** FAFSA. ***Financial aid deadline (priority):*** 3/15. ***Notification date:*** Continuous beginning 3/15. Students must reply by 5/1.

CONTACT Luis Tavarez, Director of Financial Aid, Rowan University, 201 Mullica Hill Road, Glassboro, NJ 08028-1701, 856-256-4276 or toll-free 800-447-1165 (in-state). *Fax:* 856-256-4413. *E-mail:* tavarez@rowan.edu.

RUSH UNIVERSITY

Chicago, IL

Tuition & fees: N/R **Average undergraduate aid package: $14,347**

ABOUT THE INSTITUTION Independent, coed. ***Awards:*** bachelor's and master's degrees and post-master's certificates. 3 undergraduate majors. ***Total enrollment:*** 1,566. Undergraduates: 166. Both federal and institutional methodology are used as a basis for awarding need-based institutional aid.

UNDERGRADUATE FINANCIAL AID (Fall 2009) 49 applied for aid; of those 98% were deemed to have need. 100% of undergraduates with need received aid. ***Average percent of need met:*** 50% (excluding resources awarded to replace EFC). ***Average financial aid package:*** $14,347 (excluding resources awarded to replace EFC). 2% of all full-time undergraduates had no need and received non-need-based gift aid.

GIFT AID (NEED-BASED) ***Total amount:*** $253,452 (52% federal, 20% state, 27% institutional, 1% external sources). ***Receiving aid:*** All full-time undergraduates: 64% (35). ***Average award:*** Undergraduates: $6802. ***Scholarships, grants, and awards:*** Federal Pell, FSEOG, state, private, college/university gift aid from institutional funds.

GIFT AID (NON-NEED-BASED) ***Receiving aid:*** Undergraduates: 56% (31). ***Average award:*** Undergraduates: $2000. ***Scholarships, grants, and awards by category:*** *Academic interests/achievement:* 30 awards ($68,975 total): general academic interests/achievements.

LOANS ***Student loans:*** $878,603 (87% need-based, 13% non-need-based). ***Average need-based loan:*** Undergraduates: $5731. ***Parent loans:*** $57,419 (48% need-based, 52% non-need-based). ***Programs:*** Federal Direct (Subsidized and Unsubsidized Stafford, PLUS), Perkins, Federal Nursing, college/university, credit-based loans.

WORK-STUDY ***Federal work-study:*** Total amount: $90,366; 30 jobs averaging $3012.

APPLYING FOR FINANCIAL AID ***Required financial aid forms:*** FAFSA, institution's own form. ***Financial aid deadline (priority):*** 5/1. ***Notification date:*** Continuous beginning 4/1. Students must reply within 3 weeks of notification.

CONTACT David Nelson, Director of Student Financial Aid, Rush University, 600 South Paulina Street, Suite 440, Chicago, IL 60612-3832, 312-942-6256. *Fax:* 312-942-2732. *E-mail:* david_j_nelson@rush.edu.

RUSSELL SAGE COLLEGE

Troy, NY

Tuition & fees: $27,850 **Average undergraduate aid package: $31,600**

ABOUT THE INSTITUTION Independent, women only. 21 undergraduate majors. Both federal and institutional methodology are used as a basis for awarding need-based institutional aid.

UNDERGRADUATE EXPENSES for 2010–11 ***Comprehensive fee:*** $38,000 includes full-time tuition ($27,000), mandatory fees ($850), and room and board ($10,150). ***College room only:*** $5350. Room and board charges vary according to board plan. ***Part-time tuition:*** $900 per credit hour. ***Payment plans:*** Installment, deferred payment.

FRESHMAN FINANCIAL AID (Fall 2010, est.) 122 applied for aid; of those 98% were deemed to have need. 100% of freshmen with need received aid; of those 63% had need fully met. ***Average financial aid package:*** $34,400 (excluding resources awarded to replace EFC). 2% of all full-time freshmen had no need and received non-need-based gift aid.

UNDERGRADUATE FINANCIAL AID (Fall 2010, est.) 678 applied for aid; of those 90% were deemed to have need. 100% of undergraduates with need received aid; of those 36% had need fully met. ***Average financial aid package:*** $31,600 (excluding resources awarded to replace EFC). 3% of all full-time undergraduates had no need and received non-need-based gift aid.

GIFT AID (NEED-BASED) ***Total amount:*** $8,186,272 (18% federal, 13% state, 67% institutional, 2% external sources). ***Receiving aid:*** Freshmen: 98% (120); all full-time undergraduates: 87% (608). ***Average award:*** Freshmen: $11,175; Undergraduates: $9845. ***Scholarships, grants, and awards:*** Federal Pell, FSEOG, state, private, college/university gift aid from institutional funds, Federal Nursing.

GIFT AID (NON-NEED-BASED) ***Total amount:*** $53,356,996 (100% institutional). ***Receiving aid:*** Freshmen: 87% (106). Undergraduates: 82% (575). ***Average award:*** Freshmen: $15,000. Undergraduates: $13,100. ***Scholarships, grants, and awards by category:*** *Academic interests/achievement:* 565 awards ($5,686,851 total): general academic interests/achievements. *Creative arts/performance:* 6 awards ($105,614 total): theater/drama. *Special achievements/activities:* 18 awards ($36,000 total): community service, general special achievements/activities, leadership. *Special characteristics:* 369 awards ($882,215 total): adult students, children and siblings of alumni, children of educators, children of faculty/staff, ethnic background, first-generation college students, general special characteristics, siblings of current students, spouses of current students. ***Tuition waivers:*** Full or partial for employees or children of employees, senior citizens.

LOANS ***Student loans:*** $6,757,591 (48% need-based, 52% non-need-based). 97% of past graduating class borrowed through all loan programs. *Average indebtedness per student:* $28,300. ***Average need-based loan:*** Freshmen: $4566. Undergraduates: $4976. ***Parent loans:*** $911,376 (17% need-based, 83% non-need-based). ***Programs:*** Federal Direct (Subsidized and Unsubsidized Stafford, PLUS), Perkins.

WORK-STUDY ***Federal work-study:*** Total amount: $367,000; 380 jobs averaging $2000. ***State or other work-study/employment:*** Total amount: $140,000 (100% non-need-based). 135 part-time jobs averaging $1800.

APPLYING FOR FINANCIAL AID ***Required financial aid forms:*** FAFSA, state aid form. ***Financial aid deadline (priority):*** 3/1. ***Notification date:*** Continuous beginning 3/1. Students must reply within 2 weeks of notification.

CONTACT James K. Dease, Associate Vice President for Student Services, Russell Sage College, 45 Ferry Street, Troy, NY 12180, 518-244-2062 or toll-free 888-VERY-SAGE (in-state), 888-VERY SAGE (out-of-state). *Fax:* 518-244-2460. *E-mail:* deasej@sage.edu.

RUST COLLEGE

Holly Springs, MS

CONTACT Mrs. Helen L. Street, Director of Financial Aid, Rust College, 150 Rust Avenue, Holly Springs, MS 38635, 662-252-8000 Ext. 4061 or toll-free 888-886-8492 Ext. 4065. *Fax:* 662-252-8895.

RUTGERS, THE STATE UNIVERSITY OF NEW JERSEY, CAMDEN

Camden, NJ

Tuition & fees (NJ res): $12,364 **Average undergraduate aid package: $10,884**

ABOUT THE INSTITUTION State-supported, coed. 33 undergraduate majors. Federal methodology is used as a basis for awarding need-based institutional aid.

UNDERGRADUATE EXPENSES for 2010–11 ***Tuition, state resident:*** full-time $9926; part-time $319 per credit hour. ***Tuition, nonresident:*** full-time $20,985; part-time $699 per credit hour. ***Required fees:*** full-time $2438. Part-time tuition and fees vary according to course load. ***College room and board:*** $10,362; ***Room only:*** $7482. Room and board charges vary according to board plan and housing facility. ***Payment plan:*** Installment.

FRESHMAN FINANCIAL AID (Fall 2010, est.) 407 applied for aid; of those 84% were deemed to have need. 100% of freshmen with need received aid; of those 21% had need fully met. ***Average percent of need met:*** 65% (excluding resources awarded to replace EFC). ***Average financial aid package:*** $11,831 (excluding resources awarded to replace EFC). 1% of all full-time freshmen had no need and received non-need-based gift aid.

UNDERGRADUATE FINANCIAL AID (Fall 2010, est.) 3,460 applied for aid; of those 86% were deemed to have need. 100% of undergraduates with need received aid; of those 16% had need fully met. ***Average percent of need met:*** 58% (excluding resources awarded to replace EFC). ***Average financial aid package:*** $10,884 (excluding resources awarded to replace EFC). 1% of all full-time undergraduates had no need and received non-need-based gift aid.

GIFT AID (NEED-BASED) ***Total amount:*** $18,027,626 (43% federal, 42% state, 15% institutional). ***Receiving aid:*** Freshmen: 57% (279); all full-time undergraduates: 48% (2,176). ***Average award:*** Freshmen: $9438; Undergraduates: $8191. ***Scholarships, grants, and awards:*** Federal Pell, FSEOG, state, private, college/university gift aid from institutional funds, Federal Nursing.

GIFT AID (NON-NEED-BASED) ***Total amount:*** $1,442,097 (4% state, 84% institutional, 12% external sources). ***Receiving aid:*** Freshmen: 7% (35). Undergraduates: 6% (255). ***Average award:*** Freshmen: $2500. Undergraduates: $5960. ***Tuition waivers:*** Full or partial for employees or children of employees.

LOANS ***Student loans:*** $26,961,386 (41% need-based, 59% non-need-based). 75% of past graduating class borrowed through all loan programs. *Average indebtedness per student:* $21,330. ***Average need-based loan:*** Freshmen: $3684. Undergraduates: $4418. ***Parent loans:*** $2,236,567 (100% non-need-based). ***Programs:*** Federal Direct (Subsidized and Unsubsidized Stafford, PLUS), Perkins, state, college/university, alternative loans.

WORK-STUDY ***Federal work-study:*** Total amount: $666,582; 150 jobs averaging $1956. ***State or other work-study/employment:*** Total amount: $925,372 (100% non-need-based). 400 part-time jobs averaging $2313.

APPLYING FOR FINANCIAL AID ***Required financial aid form:*** FAFSA. ***Financial aid deadline:*** Continuous. ***Notification date:*** Continuous beginning 2/15. Students must reply within 2 weeks of notification.

CONTACT Mr. Willie L. Williams, Manager of University Financial Aid Funds Control, Rutgers, The State University of New Jersey, Camden, 620 George Street, New Brunswick, NJ 08901, 848-932-2603. *Fax:* 732-932-0516. *E-mail:* billw@rci.rutgers.edu.

RUTGERS, THE STATE UNIVERSITY OF NEW JERSEY, NEWARK

Newark, NJ

Tuition & fees (NJ res): $12,069 Average undergraduate aid package: $12,383

ABOUT THE INSTITUTION State-supported, coed. 50 undergraduate majors. Federal methodology is used as a basis for awarding need-based institutional aid.

UNDERGRADUATE EXPENSES for 2010–11 ***Tuition, state resident:*** full-time $9926; part-time $319 per credit hour. ***Tuition, nonresident:*** full-time $21,388; part-time $693 per credit hour. ***Required fees:*** full-time $2143. Part-time tuition and fees vary according to course load. ***College room and board:*** $11,653; ***Room only:*** $7295. Room and board charges vary according to board plan and housing facility. ***Payment plan:*** Installment.

FRESHMAN FINANCIAL AID (Fall 2010, est.) 730 applied for aid; of those 89% were deemed to have need. 100% of freshmen with need received aid; of those 6% had need fully met. ***Average percent of need met:*** 63% (excluding resources awarded to replace EFC). ***Average financial aid package:*** $13,420 (excluding resources awarded to replace EFC). 1% of all full-time freshmen had no need and received non-need-based gift aid.

UNDERGRADUATE FINANCIAL AID (Fall 2010, est.) 4,975 applied for aid; of those 92% were deemed to have need. 100% of undergraduates with need received aid; of those 8% had need fully met. ***Average percent of need met:*** 58% (excluding resources awarded to replace EFC). ***Average financial aid package:*** $12,383 (excluding resources awarded to replace EFC). 1% of all full-time undergraduates had no need and received non-need-based gift aid.

GIFT AID (NEED-BASED) ***Total amount:*** $36,255,492 (40% federal, 43% state, 17% institutional). ***Receiving aid:*** Freshmen: 57% (534); all full-time undergraduates: 48% (3,675). ***Average award:*** Freshmen: $10,772; Undergraduates: $9636. ***Scholarships, grants, and awards:*** Federal Pell, FSEOG, state, private, college/university gift aid from institutional funds.

GIFT AID (NON-NEED-BASED) ***Total amount:*** $2,485,543 (8% state, 76% institutional, 16% external sources). ***Receiving aid:*** Freshmen: 7% (66). Undergraduates: 6% (424). ***Average award:*** Freshmen: $4583. Undergraduates: $7834. ***Tuition waivers:*** Full or partial for employees or children of employees.

LOANS ***Student loans:*** $32,910,419 (56% need-based, 44% non-need-based). 65% of past graduating class borrowed through all loan programs. *Average indebtedness per student:* $17,373. ***Average need-based loan:*** Freshmen: $4778. Undergraduates: $5322. ***Parent loans:*** $2,243,716 (100% non-need-based). ***Programs:*** Federal Direct (Subsidized and Unsubsidized Stafford, PLUS), Perkins, state, college/university, alternative loans.

WORK-STUDY ***Federal work-study:*** Total amount: $1,267,339; 268 jobs averaging $1939. ***State or other work-study/employment:*** Total amount: $1,467,897 (100% non-need-based). 816 part-time jobs averaging $1795.

ATHLETIC AWARDS Total amount: $52,000 (100% non-need-based).

APPLYING FOR FINANCIAL AID ***Required financial aid form:*** FAFSA. ***Financial aid deadline (priority):*** 3/15. ***Notification date:*** Continuous. Students must reply within 2 weeks of notification.

CONTACT Mr. Willie L. Williams, Manager of University Financial Aid Funds Control, Rutgers, The State University of New Jersey, Newark, 620 George Street, New Brunswick, NJ 08901, 848-932-2603. *Fax:* 732-932-0516. *E-mail:* billw@rci.rutgers.edu.

RUTGERS, THE STATE UNIVERSITY OF NEW JERSEY, NEW BRUNSWICK

Piscataway, NJ

Tuition & fees (NJ res): $12,582 Average undergraduate aid package: $13,638

ABOUT THE INSTITUTION State-supported, coed. 120 undergraduate majors. Federal methodology is used as a basis for awarding need-based institutional aid.

UNDERGRADUATE EXPENSES for 2010–11 ***Tuition, state resident:*** full-time $9926; part-time $319 per credit hour. ***Tuition, nonresident:*** full-time $21,388; part-time $693 per credit hour. ***Required fees:*** full-time $2656. ***College room and board:*** $11,216; ***Room only:*** $6836. Room and board charges vary according to board plan and housing facility. ***Payment plan:*** Installment.

FRESHMAN FINANCIAL AID (Fall 2010, est.) 4,640 applied for aid; of those 81% were deemed to have need. 100% of freshmen with need received aid; of those 3% had need fully met. ***Average percent of need met:*** 56% (excluding resources awarded to replace EFC). ***Average financial aid package:*** $13,413 (excluding resources awarded to replace EFC). 3% of all full-time freshmen had no need and received non-need-based gift aid.

UNDERGRADUATE FINANCIAL AID (Fall 2010, est.) 20,078 applied for aid; of those 85% were deemed to have need. 100% of undergraduates with need received aid; of those 2% had need fully met. ***Average percent of need met:*** 56% (excluding resources awarded to replace EFC). ***Average financial aid package:*** $13,638 (excluding resources awarded to replace EFC). 2% of all full-time undergraduates had no need and received non-need-based gift aid.

GIFT AID (NEED-BASED) ***Total amount:*** $118,612,779 (36% federal, 39% state, 25% institutional). ***Receiving aid:*** Freshmen: 40% (2,440); all full-time undergraduates: 37% (11,365). ***Average award:*** Freshmen: $10,271; Undergraduates: $9937. ***Scholarships, grants, and awards:*** Federal Pell, FSEOG, state, private, college/university gift aid from institutional funds.

GIFT AID (NON-NEED-BASED) ***Total amount:*** $40,877,682 (10% state, 80% institutional, 10% external sources). ***Receiving aid:*** Freshmen: 19% (1,125). Undergraduates: 15% (4,684). ***Average award:*** Freshmen: $7648. Undergraduates: $7277. ***Tuition waivers:*** Full or partial for employees or children of employees.

LOANS ***Student loans:*** $190,018,580 (52% need-based, 48% non-need-based). 68% of past graduating class borrowed through all loan programs. *Average indebtedness per student:* $16,766. ***Average need-based loan:*** Freshmen: $3829. Undergraduates: $4482. ***Parent loans:*** $24,894,440 (100% non-need-based). ***Programs:*** Federal Direct (Subsidized and Unsubsidized Stafford, PLUS), Perkins, state, college/university, alternative loans.

WORK-STUDY ***Federal work-study:*** Total amount: $6,325,969; 1,749 jobs averaging $1746. ***State or other work-study/employment:*** Total amount: $12,500,000 (100% non-need-based). 6,710 part-time jobs averaging $1862.

ATHLETIC AWARDS Total amount: $8,679,779 (1% need-based, 99% non-need-based).

APPLYING FOR FINANCIAL AID ***Required financial aid form:*** FAFSA. ***Financial aid deadline (priority):*** 3/15. ***Notification date:*** Continuous. Students must reply within 2 weeks of notification.

CONTACT Mr. Willie L. Williams, Manager of University Financial Aid Funds Control, Rutgers, The State University of New Jersey, New Brunswick, 620 George Street, New Brunswick, NJ 08901, 848-932-2603. *Fax:* 732-932-0516. *E-mail:* billw@rci.rutgers.edu.

SACRED HEART MAJOR SEMINARY

Detroit, MI

Tuition & fees: $15,270 Average undergraduate aid package: $2725

ABOUT THE INSTITUTION Independent Roman Catholic, coed. 3 undergraduate majors. Both federal and institutional methodology are used as a basis for awarding need-based institutional aid.

UNDERGRADUATE EXPENSES for 2010–11 ***Comprehensive fee:*** $23,538 includes full-time tuition ($15,170), mandatory fees ($100), and room and board ($8268). ***Part-time tuition:*** $355 per credit hour. ***Part-time fees:*** $50 per term. ***Payment plans:*** Installment, deferred payment.

UNDERGRADUATE FINANCIAL AID (Fall 2010, est.) 203 applied for aid; of those 100% were deemed to have need. 100% of undergraduates with need received aid. ***Average percent of need met:*** 70% (excluding resources awarded to replace EFC). ***Average financial aid package:*** $2725 (excluding resources awarded to replace EFC).

GIFT AID (NEED-BASED) ***Total amount:*** $553,186 (14% federal, 4% state, 82% institutional). ***Scholarships, grants, and awards:*** Federal Pell, FSEOG, state, private, college/university gift aid from institutional funds.

GIFT AID (NON-NEED-BASED) ***Total amount:*** $138,240 (100% institutional). ***Scholarships, grants, and awards by category:*** *Academic interests/achievement:* religion/biblical studies. *Special achievements/activities:* religious involvement. *Special characteristics:* local/state students, religious affiliation. ***Tuition waivers:*** Full or partial for employees or children of employees.

LOANS ***Student loans:*** $121,952 (100% need-based). ***Programs:*** Federal Direct (Subsidized and Unsubsidized Stafford).

APPLYING FOR FINANCIAL AID ***Required financial aid forms:*** FAFSA, institution's own form. ***Financial aid deadline (priority):*** 2/20. ***Notification date:*** Continuous beginning 6/1. Students must reply within 2 weeks of notification.

CONTACT Financial Aid Office, Sacred Heart Major Seminary, 2701 Chicago Boulevard, Detroit, MI 48206-1799, 313-883-8500. *Fax:* 313-868-7028. *E-mail:* financialaid@shms.edu.

SACRED HEART UNIVERSITY

Fairfield, CT

Tuition & fees: $31,440 **Average undergraduate aid package: $18,135**

ABOUT THE INSTITUTION Independent Roman Catholic, coed. 59 undergraduate majors. Both federal and institutional methodology are used as a basis for awarding need-based institutional aid.

UNDERGRADUATE EXPENSES for 2010–11 ***Comprehensive fee:*** $43,780 includes full-time tuition ($31,224), mandatory fees ($216), and room and board ($12,340). ***College room only:*** $8840. Full-time tuition and fees vary according to program. Room and board charges vary according to board plan and housing facility. ***Part-time tuition:*** $475 per credit hour. ***Part-time fees:*** $85 per term. Part-time tuition and fees vary according to program. ***Payment plan:*** Installment.

FRESHMAN FINANCIAL AID (Fall 2010, est.) 879 applied for aid; of those 83% were deemed to have need. 100% of freshmen with need received aid; of those 7% had need fully met. ***Average percent of need met:*** 53% (excluding resources awarded to replace EFC). ***Average financial aid package:*** $16,366 (excluding resources awarded to replace EFC). 15% of all full-time freshmen had no need and received non-need-based gift aid.

UNDERGRADUATE FINANCIAL AID (Fall 2010, est.) 3,121 applied for aid; of those 83% were deemed to have need. 99% of undergraduates with need received aid; of those 10% had need fully met. ***Average percent of need met:*** 60% (excluding resources awarded to replace EFC). ***Average financial aid package:*** $18,135 (excluding resources awarded to replace EFC). 14% of all full-time undergraduates had no need and received non-need-based gift aid.

GIFT AID (NEED-BASED) ***Total amount:*** $30,284,897 (13% federal, 8% state, 72% institutional, 7% external sources). ***Receiving aid:*** Freshmen: 74% (717); all full-time undergraduates: 71% (2,505). ***Average award:*** Freshmen: $12,150; Undergraduates: $13,658. ***Scholarships, grants, and awards:*** Federal Pell, FSEOG, state, private, college/university gift aid from institutional funds.

GIFT AID (NON-NEED-BASED) ***Total amount:*** $6,572,216 (1% federal, 42% institutional, 57% external sources). ***Receiving aid:*** Freshmen: 5% (45). Undergraduates: 5% (173). ***Average award:*** Freshmen: $3769. Undergraduates: $5092. ***Scholarships, grants, and awards by category:*** *Academic interests/achievement:* 1,381 awards ($7,919,184 total): biological sciences, business, computer science, education, English, general academic interests/achievements, health fields, humanities, mathematics, physical sciences, premedicine. *Creative arts/performance:* 281 awards ($761,000 total): applied art and design, art/fine arts, creative writing, music, performing arts, theater/drama. *Special achievements/activities:* 212 awards ($440,470 total): community service, general special achievements/activities, leadership, religious involvement. *Special characteristics:* 349 awards ($2,160,889 total): adult students, children of current students, children of faculty/staff, children of union members/company employees, ethnic background, general special characteristics, handicapped students, members of minority groups, religious affiliation, siblings of current students, twins, veterans, veterans' children. ***Tuition waivers:*** Full or partial for employees or children of employees.

LOANS ***Student loans:*** $31,981,267 (68% need-based, 32% non-need-based). 99% of past graduating class borrowed through all loan programs. *Average indebtedness per student:* $40,865. ***Average need-based loan:*** Freshmen: $4601. Undergraduates: $5103. ***Parent loans:*** $10,430,585 (50% need-based, 50% non-need-based). ***Programs:*** Federal Direct (Subsidized and Unsubsidized Stafford, PLUS), Perkins, state.

WORK-STUDY ***Federal work-study:*** Total amount: $664,746; 1,284 jobs averaging $1243. ***State or other work-study/employment:*** Total amount: $629,975 (27% need-based, 73% non-need-based). 565 part-time jobs averaging $1041.

ATHLETIC AWARDS Total amount: $8,091,226 (52% need-based, 48% non-need-based).

APPLYING FOR FINANCIAL AID ***Required financial aid forms:*** FAFSA, CSS Financial Aid PROFILE, noncustodial (divorced/separated) parent's statement. ***Financial aid deadline (priority):*** 2/15. ***Notification date:*** Continuous beginning 3/1. Students must reply within 2 weeks of notification.

CONTACT Ms. Julie B. Savino, Dean of University Financial Assistance, Sacred Heart University, 5151 Park Avenue, Fairfield, CT 06825, 203-371-7980. *Fax:* 203-365-7608. *E-mail:* savinoj@sacredheart.edu.

SAGE COLLEGE OF ALBANY

Albany, NY

Tuition & fees: $27,850 **Average undergraduate aid package: $30,400**

ABOUT THE INSTITUTION Independent, coed. 18 undergraduate majors. Both federal and institutional methodology are used as a basis for awarding need-based institutional aid.

UNDERGRADUATE EXPENSES for 2010–11 ***Comprehensive fee:*** $38,800 includes full-time tuition ($27,000), mandatory fees ($850), and room and board ($10,950). ***College room only:*** $5350. Room and board charges vary according to board plan. ***Part-time tuition:*** $900 per credit hour. ***Payment plans:*** Installment, deferred payment.

FRESHMAN FINANCIAL AID (Fall 2010, est.) 130 applied for aid; of those 95% were deemed to have need. 100% of freshmen with need received aid; of those 75% had need fully met. ***Average financial aid package:*** $34,054 (excluding resources awarded to replace EFC). 5% of all full-time freshmen had no need and received non-need-based gift aid.

UNDERGRADUATE FINANCIAL AID (Fall 2010, est.) 550 applied for aid; of those 95% were deemed to have need. 100% of undergraduates with need received aid; of those 28% had need fully met. ***Average financial aid package:*** $30,400 (excluding resources awarded to replace EFC). 5% of all full-time undergraduates had no need and received non-need-based gift aid.

GIFT AID (NEED-BASED) ***Total amount:*** $7,270,451 (19% federal, 15% state, 64% institutional, 2% external sources). ***Receiving aid:*** Freshmen: 90% (117); all full-time undergraduates: 83% (462). ***Average award:*** Freshmen: $12,828; Undergraduates: $10,136. ***Scholarships, grants, and awards:*** Federal Pell, FSEOG, state, private, college/university gift aid from institutional funds.

GIFT AID (NON-NEED-BASED) ***Total amount:*** $4,213,991 (99% institutional, 1% external sources). ***Receiving aid:*** Freshmen: 80% (104). Undergraduates: 75% (416). ***Average award:*** Freshmen: $13,000. Undergraduates: $8650. ***Scholarships, grants, and awards by category:*** *Academic interests/achievement:* 362 awards ($2,902,805 total): general academic interests/achievements. *Creative arts/performance:* 13 awards ($48,500 total): art/fine arts. *Special achievements/activities:* 6 awards ($6000 total): community service, general special achievements/activities. *Special characteristics:* 67 awards ($298,683 total): children and siblings of alumni, children of educators, children of faculty/staff, first-generation college students, general special characteristics, siblings of current students. ***Tuition waivers:*** Full or partial for employees or children of employees.

LOANS ***Student loans:*** $4,468,437 (58% need-based, 42% non-need-based). 97% of past graduating class borrowed through all loan programs. *Average indebtedness per student:* $26,400. ***Average need-based loan:*** Freshmen: $4884. Undergraduates: $5390. ***Parent loans:*** $760,170 (82% need-based, 18% non-need-based). ***Programs:*** Federal Direct (Subsidized and Unsubsidized Stafford, PLUS), Perkins, state, alternative loans.

WORK-STUDY ***Federal work-study:*** Total amount: $164,500; 176 jobs averaging $2000. ***State or other work-study/employment:*** Total amount: $39,000 (100% non-need-based). 36 part-time jobs averaging $1500.

APPLYING FOR FINANCIAL AID ***Required financial aid forms:*** FAFSA, state aid form. ***Financial aid deadline (priority):*** 3/1. ***Notification date:*** Continuous beginning 3/1. Students must reply within 2 weeks of notification.

CONTACT James K. Dease, Associate Vice President for Student Service, Sage College of Albany, 45 Ferry Street, Troy, NY 12180, 518-244-4525 or toll-free 888-VERY-SAGE. *Fax:* 518-244-2460. *E-mail:* deasej@sage.edu.

SAGINAW VALLEY STATE UNIVERSITY

University Center, MI

Tuition & fees (MI res): $7308 **Average undergraduate aid package: $7086**

ABOUT THE INSTITUTION State-supported, coed. 61 undergraduate majors. Federal methodology is used as a basis for awarding need-based institutional aid.

UNDERGRADUATE EXPENSES for 2011–12 ***Tuition, state resident:*** full-time $6870; part-time $229 per credit hour. ***Tuition, nonresident:*** full-time $16,719; part-time $557.30 per credit hour. ***Required fees:*** full-time $438; $14.60 per credit hour. Full-time tuition and fees vary according to course level, course load, location, and program. Part-time tuition and fees vary according to course level, course load, location, and program. ***College room and board:*** $7768; ***Room only:*** $4815. Room and board charges vary according to board plan, housing facility, and student level. ***Payment plan:*** Installment.

FRESHMAN FINANCIAL AID (Fall 2009) 1,596 applied for aid; of those 71% were deemed to have need. 98% of freshmen with need received aid; of those 22% had need fully met. ***Average percent of need met:*** 65% (excluding resources awarded to replace EFC). ***Average financial aid package:*** $7136 (excluding resources awarded to replace EFC). 13% of all full-time freshmen had no need and received non-need-based gift aid.

UNDERGRADUATE FINANCIAL AID (Fall 2009) 6,168 applied for aid; of those 70% were deemed to have need. 98% of undergraduates with need received aid; of those 17% had need fully met. ***Average percent of need met:*** 62% (excluding resources awarded to replace EFC). ***Average financial aid package:*** $7086 (excluding resources awarded to replace EFC). 11% of all full-time undergraduates had no need and received non-need-based gift aid.

GIFT AID (NEED-BASED) ***Total amount:*** $10,115,795 (81% federal, 12% state, 4% institutional, 3% external sources). ***Receiving aid:*** Freshmen: 42% (693); all full-time undergraduates: 38% (2,541). ***Average award:*** Freshmen: $3542; Undergraduates: $3432. ***Scholarships, grants, and awards:*** Federal Pell, FSEOG, state, private, college/university gift aid from institutional funds.

GIFT AID (NON-NEED-BASED) ***Total amount:*** $12,728,790 (2% federal, 14% state, 56% institutional, 28% external sources). ***Receiving aid:*** Freshmen: 49% (801). Undergraduates: 30% (2,008). ***Average award:*** Freshmen: $3276. Undergraduates: $3745. ***Scholarships, grants, and awards by category:*** *Academic interests/achievement:* biological sciences, business, computer science, education, engineering/technologies, general academic interests/achievements, health fields, mathematics, physical sciences. *Creative arts/performance:* art/fine arts, music, theater/drama. *Special achievements/activities:* community service, leadership. *Special characteristics:* local/state students, members of minority groups. ***Tuition waivers:*** Full or partial for employees or children of employees.

LOANS ***Student loans:*** $41,092,145 (85% need-based, 15% non-need-based). 57% of past graduating class borrowed through all loan programs. *Average indebtedness per student:* $23,555. ***Average need-based loan:*** Freshmen: $2986. Undergraduates: $3816. ***Programs:*** Federal Direct (Subsidized and Unsubsidized Stafford, PLUS), state, CitiAssist Loans, Sallie Mae Signature Loans.

WORK-STUDY ***Federal work-study:*** Total amount: $339,621; jobs available. ***State or other work-study/employment:*** Total amount: $147,786 (100% need-based). Part-time jobs available.

APPLYING FOR FINANCIAL AID ***Required financial aid form:*** FAFSA. ***Financial aid deadline (priority):*** 2/14. ***Notification date:*** Continuous beginning 3/20. Students must reply within 10 weeks of notification.

CONTACT Robert Lemuel, Director of Scholarships and Financial Aid, Saginaw Valley State University, 7400 Bay Road, University Center, MI 48710, 989-964-4103 or toll-free 800-968-9500. *Fax:* 989-790-0180. *E-mail:* lemuel@svsy.edu.

ST. AMBROSE UNIVERSITY

Davenport, IA

Tuition & fees: $24,920 **Average undergraduate aid package: $7207**

ABOUT THE INSTITUTION Independent Roman Catholic, coed. 71 undergraduate majors. Federal methodology is used as a basis for awarding need-based institutional aid.

UNDERGRADUATE EXPENSES for 2011–12 ***Comprehensive fee:*** $33,805 includes full-time tuition ($24,680), mandatory fees ($240), and room and board ($8885). Full-time tuition and fees vary according to course load, location, program, and reciprocity agreements. Room and board charges vary according to board plan and housing facility. ***Part-time tuition:*** $770 per credit hour. ***Part-time fees:*** $770 per credit hour; $60 per term. Part-time tuition and fees vary according to course load and location. ***Payment plan:*** Installment.

FRESHMAN FINANCIAL AID (Fall 2010, est.) 518 applied for aid; of those 82% were deemed to have need. 100% of freshmen with need received aid; of those 10% had need fully met. ***Average percent of need met:*** 20% (excluding resources awarded to replace EFC). ***Average financial aid package:*** $6344 (excluding resources awarded to replace EFC). 18% of all full-time freshmen had no need and received non-need-based gift aid.

UNDERGRADUATE FINANCIAL AID (Fall 2010, est.) 2,400 applied for aid; of those 78% were deemed to have need. 99% of undergraduates with need received aid; of those 12% had need fully met. ***Average percent of need met:*** 14% (excluding resources awarded to replace EFC). ***Average financial aid package:*** $7207 (excluding resources awarded to replace EFC). 21% of all full-time undergraduates had no need and received non-need-based gift aid.

GIFT AID (NEED-BASED) ***Total amount:*** $18,092,181 (18% federal, 10% state, 70% institutional, 2% external sources). ***Receiving aid:*** Freshmen: 82% (424); all full-time undergraduates: 76% (1,827). ***Average award:*** Freshmen: $13,465; Undergraduates: $11,304. ***Scholarships, grants, and awards:*** Federal Pell, FSEOG, state, private, college/university gift aid from institutional funds.

GIFT AID (NON-NEED-BASED) ***Total amount:*** $3,626,969 (98% institutional, 2% external sources). ***Receiving aid:*** Freshmen: 41% (214). Undergraduates: 34% (823). ***Average award:*** Freshmen: $18,169. Undergraduates: $17,174. ***Scholarships, grants, and awards by category:*** *Academic interests/achievement:* 2,213 awards ($15,360,134 total): general academic interests/achievements, international studies, religion/biblical studies. *Creative arts/performance:* 122 awards ($274,360 total): art/fine arts, dance, music, theater/drama. *Special achievements/activities:* 29 awards ($35,190 total): cheerleading/drum major. *Special characteristics:* 239 awards ($1,389,640 total): children and siblings of alumni, children of faculty/staff, international students, members of minority groups, out-of-state students, religious affiliation, veterans. ***Tuition waivers:*** Full or partial for employees or children of employees, senior citizens.

LOANS ***Student loans:*** $17,858,445 (92% need-based, 8% non-need-based). 78% of past graduating class borrowed through all loan programs. *Average indebtedness per student:* $32,530. ***Average need-based loan:*** Freshmen: $3500. Undergraduates: $4369. ***Parent loans:*** $4,792,540 (88% need-based, 12% non-need-based). ***Programs:*** Federal Direct (Subsidized and Unsubsidized Stafford, PLUS), Perkins, private loans.

WORK-STUDY ***Federal work-study:*** Total amount: $855,879; jobs available. ***State or other work-study/employment:*** Total amount: $257,597 (80% need-based, 20% non-need-based). Part-time jobs available.

ATHLETIC AWARDS Total amount: $2,749,302 (79% need-based, 21% non-need-based).

APPLYING FOR FINANCIAL AID ***Required financial aid form:*** FAFSA. ***Financial aid deadline (priority):*** 3/15. ***Notification date:*** Continuous beginning 2/15. Students must reply within 2 weeks of notification.

CONTACT Ms. Julie Haack, Director of Financial Aid, St. Ambrose University, 518 West Locust Street, Davenport, IA 52803, 563-333-6314 or toll-free 800-383-2627. *Fax:* 563-333-6243. *E-mail:* haackjuliea@sau.edu.

ST. ANDREWS PRESBYTERIAN COLLEGE

Laurinburg, NC

Tuition & fees: $21,614 **Average undergraduate aid package: $18,461**

ABOUT THE INSTITUTION Independent Presbyterian, coed. 16 undergraduate majors. Federal methodology is used as a basis for awarding need-based institutional aid.

UNDERGRADUATE EXPENSES for 2010–11 ***Comprehensive fee:*** $30,552 includes full-time tuition ($21,614) and room and board ($8938). Full-time tuition and fees vary according to course load and location. Room and board charges vary according to housing facility. ***Part-time tuition:*** $450 per credit hour. Part-time tuition and fees vary according to location. ***Payment plan:*** Installment.

FRESHMAN FINANCIAL AID (Fall 2010, est.) 104 applied for aid; of those 80% were deemed to have need. 99% of freshmen with need received aid; of those 21% had need fully met. ***Average percent of need met:*** 69% (excluding resources awarded to replace EFC). ***Average financial aid package:*** $18,891 (excluding resources awarded to replace EFC). 15% of all full-time freshmen had no need and received non-need-based gift aid.

UNDERGRADUATE FINANCIAL AID (Fall 2010, est.) 435 applied for aid; of those 80% were deemed to have need. 100% of undergraduates with need received aid; of those 22% had need fully met. ***Average percent of need met:*** 75% (excluding resources awarded to replace EFC). ***Average financial aid package:*** $18,461 (excluding resources awarded to replace EFC). 18% of all full-time undergraduates had no need and received non-need-based gift aid.

GIFT AID (NEED-BASED) ***Total amount:*** $4,022,589 (23% federal, 14% state, 52% institutional, 11% external sources). ***Receiving aid:*** Freshmen: 79% (82); all full-time undergraduates: 79% (343). ***Average award:*** Freshmen: $15,043; Undergraduates: $14,177. ***Scholarships, grants, and awards:*** Federal Pell, FSEOG, state, private, college/university gift aid from institutional funds.

GIFT AID (NON-NEED-BASED) ***Total amount:*** $656,587 (7% state, 76% institutional, 17% external sources). ***Receiving aid:*** Freshmen: 12% (12). Undergraduates: 11% (48). ***Average award:*** Freshmen: $4797. Undergraduates: $5270. ***Scholarships, grants, and awards by category:*** *Academic interests/achievement:* 420 awards ($1,740,808 total): business, general academic interests/achievements. *Creative arts/performance:* 20 awards ($18,550 total): general creative arts/performance, performing arts, theater/drama. *Special achievements/activities:* 147 awards ($149,118 total): community service, general special achievements/activities, leadership. ***Tuition waivers:*** Full or partial for employees or children of employees, adult students, senior citizens.

LOANS ***Student loans:*** $2,504,110 (75% need-based, 25% non-need-based). 72% of past graduating class borrowed through all loan programs. *Average indebtedness per student:* $22,599. ***Average need-based loan:*** Freshmen: $3496. Undergraduates: $4374. ***Parent loans:*** $1,506,208 (48% need-based, 52% non-need-based). ***Programs:*** Federal Direct (Subsidized and Unsubsidized Stafford, PLUS), state.

WORK-STUDY ***Federal work-study:*** Total amount: $262,444; 196 jobs averaging $1800. ***State or other work-study/employment:*** Total amount: $8100 (100% non-need-based). 19 part-time jobs averaging $1800.

ATHLETIC AWARDS Total amount: $997,605 (75% need-based, 25% non-need-based).

APPLYING FOR FINANCIAL AID ***Required financial aid forms:*** FAFSA, state aid form. ***Financial aid deadline:*** Continuous. ***Notification date:*** Continuous beginning 2/1. Students must reply within 2 weeks of notification.

CONTACT Kimberly Driggers, Director of Student Financial Planning, St. Andrews Presbyterian College, 1700 Dogwood Mile, Laurinburg, NC 28352, 910-277-5562 or toll-free 800-763-0198. *Fax:* 910-277-5206.

SAINT ANSELM COLLEGE

Manchester, NH

Tuition & fees: $31,555 **Average undergraduate aid package: $23,864**

ABOUT THE INSTITUTION Independent Roman Catholic, coed. 40 undergraduate majors. Both federal and institutional methodology are used as a basis for awarding need-based institutional aid.

UNDERGRADUATE EXPENSES for 2010–11 ***Comprehensive fee:*** $43,205 includes full-time tuition ($30,760), mandatory fees ($795), and room and board ($11,650). Room and board charges vary according to housing facility. ***Part-time tuition:*** $3070 per course. ***Payment plan:*** Installment.

FRESHMAN FINANCIAL AID (Fall 2010, est.) 487 applied for aid; of those 86% were deemed to have need. 100% of freshmen with need received aid; of those 16% had need fully met. ***Average percent of need met:*** 80% (excluding resources awarded to replace EFC). ***Average financial aid package:*** $23,844 (excluding resources awarded to replace EFC). 15% of all full-time freshmen had no need and received non-need-based gift aid.

UNDERGRADUATE FINANCIAL AID (Fall 2010, est.) 1,581 applied for aid; of those 88% were deemed to have need. 100% of undergraduates with need received aid; of those 16% had need fully met. ***Average percent of need met:*** 81% (excluding resources awarded to replace EFC). ***Average financial aid package:*** $23,864 (excluding resources awarded to replace EFC). 16% of all full-time undergraduates had no need and received non-need-based gift aid.

GIFT AID (NEED-BASED) ***Total amount:*** $23,173,222 (8% federal, 90% institutional, 2% external sources). ***Receiving aid:*** Freshmen: 79% (421); all full-time undergraduates: 73% (1,371). ***Average award:*** Freshmen: $18,756; Undergraduates: $17,779. ***Scholarships, grants, and awards:*** Federal Pell, FSEOG, state, private, college/university gift aid from institutional funds.

GIFT AID (NON-NEED-BASED) ***Total amount:*** $3,315,741 (97% institutional, 3% external sources). ***Receiving aid:*** Freshmen: 9% (47). Undergraduates: 6% (121). ***Average award:*** Freshmen: $9412. Undergraduates: $9307. ***Scholarships, grants, and awards by category:*** *Academic interests/achievement:* 1,099 awards ($8,502,375 total): general academic interests/achievements. *Creative arts/performance:* 50 awards ($527,000 total): general creative arts/performance. *Special characteristics:* 142 awards ($2,287,680 total): children of educators, children of faculty/staff, siblings of current students. ***Tuition waivers:*** Full or partial for employees or children of employees.

LOANS ***Student loans:*** $13,480,471 (63% need-based, 37% non-need-based). 82% of past graduating class borrowed through all loan programs. *Average indebtedness per student:* $38,858. ***Average need-based loan:*** Freshmen: $4456. Undergraduates: $5529. ***Parent loans:*** $7,220,723 (30% need-based, 70% non-need-based). ***Programs:*** Federal Direct (Subsidized and Unsubsidized Stafford, PLUS), Perkins.

WORK-STUDY ***Federal work-study:*** Total amount: $1,759,370; 1,184 jobs averaging $1486. ***State or other work-study/employment:*** Total amount: $14,000 (100% non-need-based). 7 part-time jobs averaging $2000.

ATHLETIC AWARDS Total amount: $1,120,798 (40% need-based, 60% non-need-based).

APPLYING FOR FINANCIAL AID ***Required financial aid forms:*** FAFSA, CSS Financial Aid PROFILE, noncustodial (divorced/separated) parent's statement. ***Financial aid deadline:*** 3/15. ***Notification date:*** Continuous beginning 3/1. Students must reply by 5/1 or within 2 weeks of notification.

CONTACT Elizabeth Keuffel, Director of Financial Aid, Saint Anselm College, 100 Saint Anselm Drive, Manchester, NH 03102-1310, 603-641-7110 or toll-free 888-4ANSELM. *Fax:* 603-656-6015. *E-mail:* financial_aid@anselm.edu.

SAINT ANTHONY COLLEGE OF NURSING

Rockford, IL

Tuition & fees: N/R **Average undergraduate aid package: $15,818**

ABOUT THE INSTITUTION Independent Roman Catholic, coed, primarily women. 1 undergraduate major. Federal methodology is used as a basis for awarding need-based institutional aid.

UNDERGRADUATE FINANCIAL AID (Fall 2009) 147 applied for aid; of those 100% were deemed to have need. 100% of undergraduates with need received aid. ***Average financial aid package:*** $15,818 (excluding resources awarded to replace EFC).

GIFT AID (NEED-BASED) ***Total amount:*** $570,407 (45% federal, 50% state, 4% institutional, 1% external sources). ***Receiving aid:*** All full-time undergraduates: 55% (83). ***Average award:*** Undergraduates: $6872. ***Scholarships, grants, and awards:*** Federal Pell, state, private, college/university gift aid from institutional funds.

GIFT AID (NON-NEED-BASED) ***Total amount:*** $52,509 (90% state, 10% external sources). ***Receiving aid:*** Undergraduates: 6% (9).

LOANS ***Student loans:*** $1,512,010 (47% need-based, 53% non-need-based). ***Average need-based loan:*** Undergraduates: $4928. ***Parent loans:*** $241,259 (100% non-need-based). ***Programs:*** Federal Direct (Subsidized and Unsubsidized Stafford, PLUS), alternative loans.

CONTACT Serrita Woods, Financial Aid Officer, Saint Anthony College of Nursing, 5658 East State Street, Rockford, IL 61108-2468, 815-395-5089. *Fax:* 815-395-2730. *E-mail:* serritawoods@sacn.edu.

ST. AUGUSTINE COLLEGE

Chicago, IL

CONTACT Mrs. Maria Zambonino, Director of Financial Aid, St. Augustine College, 1345 W Angyle, Chicago, IL 60640, 773-878-3813. *Fax:* 773-878-9032. *E-mail:* mzambonino@hotmail.com.

SAINT AUGUSTINE'S COLLEGE

Raleigh, NC

Tuition & fees: $17,160 **Average undergraduate aid package: $2209**

ABOUT THE INSTITUTION Independent Episcopal, coed. 18 undergraduate majors. Federal methodology is used as a basis for awarding need-based institutional aid.

UNDERGRADUATE EXPENSES for 2010–11 ***Comprehensive fee:*** $24,286 includes full-time tuition ($12,364), mandatory fees ($4796), and room and board ($7126). ***College room only:*** $2948. Full-time tuition and fees vary according to course load and program. Room and board charges vary according to housing facility. ***Part-time tuition:*** $515 per semester hour. ***Part-time fees:*** $200 per credit hour. Part-time tuition and fees vary according to course load and program. ***Payment plans:*** Installment, deferred payment.

FRESHMAN FINANCIAL AID (Fall 2010, est.) 325 applied for aid; of those 94% were deemed to have need. 100% of freshmen with need received aid; of those 3% had need fully met. ***Average percent of need met:*** 100% (excluding resources awarded to replace EFC). ***Average financial aid package:*** $2228 (excluding resources awarded to replace EFC). 1% of all full-time freshmen had no need and received non-need-based gift aid.

UNDERGRADUATE FINANCIAL AID (Fall 2010, est.) 1,222 applied for aid; of those 94% were deemed to have need. 100% of undergraduates with need received aid; of those 2% had need fully met. ***Average percent of need met:*** 100% (excluding resources awarded to replace EFC). ***Average financial aid package:*** $2209 (excluding resources awarded to replace EFC). 1% of all full-time undergraduates had no need and received non-need-based gift aid.

GIFT AID (NEED-BASED) ***Total amount:*** $11,183,846 (60% federal, 22% state, 14% institutional, 4% external sources). ***Receiving aid:*** Freshmen: 90% (294); all full-time undergraduates: 89% (1,100). ***Average award:*** Freshmen: $1853; Undergraduates: $1965. ***Scholarships, grants, and awards:*** FSEOG, state.

GIFT AID (NON-NEED-BASED) ***Receiving aid:*** Freshmen: 58% (190). Undergraduates: 59% (734). ***Average award:*** Freshmen: $1500. Undergraduates: $2231. ***Scholarships, grants, and awards by category:*** *Academic interests/achievement:* biological sciences, general academic interests/achievements, military science. *Creative arts/performance:* music, performing arts. *Special characteristics:* 795 awards ($1,287,072 total): children of faculty/staff, local/state students. ***Tuition waivers:*** Full or partial for employees or children of employees.

LOANS ***Student loans:*** $6,017,572 (100% need-based). 94% of past graduating class borrowed through all loan programs. *Average indebtedness per student:* $12,614. ***Average need-based loan:*** Freshmen: $1769. Undergraduates: $2148. ***Parent loans:*** $5,467,858 (100% non-need-based). ***Programs:*** Federal Direct (Subsidized and Unsubsidized Stafford, PLUS), Perkins.

WORK-STUDY ***Federal work-study:*** Total amount: $871,697; 411 jobs averaging $2500. ***State or other work-study/employment:*** Total amount: $7500 (100% need-based). 4 part-time jobs averaging $2500.

ATHLETIC AWARDS Total amount: $1,532,085 (100% non-need-based).

APPLYING FOR FINANCIAL AID ***Required financial aid forms:*** FAFSA, institution's own form. ***Financial aid deadline (priority):*** 3/15. ***Notification date:*** Continuous beginning 4/1. Students must reply within 2 weeks of notification.

CONTACT Ms. Nadine Y. Ford, Director of Financial Aid, Saint Augustine's College, 1315 Oakwood Avenue, Raleigh, NC 27610-2298, 919-516-4131 or toll-free 800-948-1126. *Fax:* 919-516-4431. *E-mail:* nford@st-aug.edu.

ST. BONAVENTURE UNIVERSITY

St. Bonaventure, NY

Tuition & fees: $26,895 **Average undergraduate aid package: $25,672**

ABOUT THE INSTITUTION Independent religious, coed. 38 undergraduate majors. Federal methodology is used as a basis for awarding need-based institutional aid.

UNDERGRADUATE EXPENSES for 2010–11 ***Comprehensive fee:*** $35,966 includes full-time tuition ($25,930), mandatory fees ($965), and room and board ($9071). ***College room only:*** $4441. Room and board charges vary according to board plan and housing facility. ***Part-time tuition:*** $775 per credit hour. Part-time tuition and fees vary according to course load.

FRESHMAN FINANCIAL AID (Fall 2009) 425 applied for aid; of those 79% were deemed to have need. 100% of freshmen with need received aid; of those 11% had need fully met. ***Average percent of need met:*** 79% (excluding resources awarded to replace EFC). ***Average financial aid package:*** $24,786 (excluding resources awarded to replace EFC). 17% of all full-time freshmen had no need and received non-need-based gift aid.

UNDERGRADUATE FINANCIAL AID (Fall 2009) 1,577 applied for aid; of those 88% were deemed to have need. 100% of undergraduates with need received aid; of those 23% had need fully met. ***Average percent of need met:*** 78% (excluding resources awarded to replace EFC). ***Average financial aid package:*** $25,672 (excluding resources awarded to replace EFC). 19% of all full-time undergraduates had no need and received non-need-based gift aid.

GIFT AID (NEED-BASED) ***Total amount:*** $23,575,117 (15% federal, 9% state, 75% institutional, 1% external sources). ***Receiving aid:*** Freshmen: 72% (335); all full-time undergraduates: 69% (1,367). ***Average award:*** Freshmen: $20,532; Undergraduates: $19,178. ***Scholarships, grants, and awards:*** Federal Pell, FSEOG, state, private, college/university gift aid from institutional funds.

GIFT AID (NON-NEED-BASED) ***Total amount:*** $2,729,524 (14% federal, 1% state, 83% institutional, 2% external sources). ***Receiving aid:*** Freshmen: 62% (287). Undergraduates: 60% (1,181). ***Average award:*** Freshmen: $10,835. Undergraduates: $9512. ***Scholarships, grants, and awards by category:*** *Academic interests/achievement:* 1,000 awards ($5,500,000 total): business, general academic interests/achievements. *Creative arts/performance:* 40 awards ($40,000 total): journalism/publications, music, performing arts. *Special characteristics:* 100 awards ($2,500,000 total): children of faculty/staff, local/state students, members of minority groups, relatives of clergy, religious affiliation, siblings of current students. ***Tuition waivers:*** Full or partial for employees or children of employees, senior citizens.

LOANS ***Student loans:*** $13,117,145 (100% need-based). 83% of past graduating class borrowed through all loan programs. *Average indebtedness per student:* $36,940. ***Average need-based loan:*** Freshmen: $3606. Undergraduates: $4377. ***Parent loans:*** $3,582,153 (100% non-need-based). ***Programs:*** Federal Direct (Subsidized and Unsubsidized Stafford, PLUS), Perkins, college/university.

WORK-STUDY ***Federal work-study:*** Total amount: $434,310; 478 jobs averaging $1025. ***State or other work-study/employment:*** Total amount: $228,167 (100% non-need-based). 100 part-time jobs averaging $1000.

ATHLETIC AWARDS Total amount: $2,645,919 (50% need-based, 50% non-need-based).

APPLYING FOR FINANCIAL AID ***Required financial aid forms:*** FAFSA, state aid form. ***Financial aid deadline (priority):*** 2/15. ***Notification date:*** Continuous beginning 3/1. Students must reply by 5/1 or within 2 weeks of notification.

CONTACT Ms. Kathryn Dillon Hogan, Associate Vice President for Enrollment, St. Bonaventure University, 3261 West State Road, St. Bonaventure, NY 14778-2284, 716-375-2128 or toll-free 800-462-5050. *Fax:* 716-375-2087. *E-mail:* erankin@sbu.edu.

ST. CATHERINE UNIVERSITY

St. Paul, MN

Tuition & fees: $30,168 **Average undergraduate aid package: $25,790**

ABOUT THE INSTITUTION Independent Roman Catholic, undergraduate: women only; graduate: coed. 78 undergraduate majors. Federal methodology is used as a basis for awarding need-based institutional aid.

UNDERGRADUATE EXPENSES for 2010–11 ***One-time required fee:*** $100. ***Comprehensive fee:*** $37,826 includes full-time tuition ($29,888), mandatory fees ($280), and room and board ($7658). ***College room only:*** $4280. Full-time tuition and fees vary according to class time and degree level. Room and board charges vary according to board plan and housing facility. ***Part-time tuition:*** $934 per credit hour. ***Part-time fees:*** $934 per credit hour; $140 per term. Part-time tuition and fees vary according to class time and degree level. ***Payment plan:*** Installment.

FRESHMAN FINANCIAL AID (Fall 2010, est.) 399 applied for aid; of those 94% were deemed to have need. 100% of freshmen with need received aid; of those 17% had need fully met. ***Average percent of need met:*** 91% (excluding resources awarded to replace EFC). ***Average financial aid package:*** $29,300 (excluding resources awarded to replace EFC). 6% of all full-time freshmen had no need and received non-need-based gift aid.

UNDERGRADUATE FINANCIAL AID (Fall 2010, est.) 1,764 applied for aid; of those 93% were deemed to have need. 100% of undergraduates with need received aid; of those 11% had need fully met. ***Average percent of need met:*** 84% (excluding resources awarded to replace EFC). ***Average financial aid package:*** $25,790 (excluding resources awarded to replace EFC). 5% of all full-time undergraduates had no need and received non-need-based gift aid.

GIFT AID (NEED-BASED) ***Total amount:*** $19,079,700 (34% federal, 14% state, 48% institutional, 4% external sources). ***Receiving aid:*** Freshmen: 81% (338); all full-time undergraduates: 76% (1,446). ***Average award:*** Freshmen: $12,810; Undergraduates: $10,830. ***Scholarships, grants, and awards:*** Federal Pell, FSEOG, state, private, college/university gift aid from institutional funds.

GIFT AID (NON-NEED-BASED) ***Total amount:*** $13,104,300 (1% state, 99% institutional). ***Receiving aid:*** Freshmen: 79% (331). Undergraduates: 62% (1,177). ***Average award:*** Freshmen: $13,450. Undergraduates: $8170. ***Scholarships, grants, and awards by category:*** *Academic interests/achievement:* business, education, English, foreign languages, general academic interests/achievements, health fields, home economics, humanities, mathematics, physical sciences, premedicine, social sciences. *Creative arts/performance:* art/fine arts, music. *Special achievements/activities:* community service, general special achievements/activities, leadership, memberships. *Special characteristics:* adult students, children and siblings of alumni, children of current students, children of educators, children of faculty/staff, ethnic background, general special characteristics, international students, local/state students, out-of-state students, religious affiliation, siblings of current students, spouses of current students. ***Tuition waivers:*** Full or partial for employees or children of employees, senior citizens.

LOANS ***Student loans:*** $24,386,500 (43% need-based, 57% non-need-based). 82% of past graduating class borrowed through all loan programs. *Average indebtedness per student:* $33,610. ***Average need-based loan:*** Freshmen: $3480. Undergraduates: $4620. ***Parent loans:*** $3,491,700 (100% non-need-based). ***Programs:*** Federal Direct (Subsidized and Unsubsidized Stafford, PLUS), Perkins, Federal Nursing, state, alternative loans.

WORK-STUDY ***Federal work-study:*** Total amount: $292,400; jobs available. ***State or other work-study/employment:*** Part-time jobs available.

APPLYING FOR FINANCIAL AID ***Required financial aid forms:*** FAFSA, institution's own form. ***Financial aid deadline (priority):*** 4/15. ***Notification date:*** Continuous. Students must reply within 2 weeks of notification.

CONTACT Beth Stevens, Director of Financial Aid, St. Catherine University, Mail #F-11, 2004 Randolph Avenue, St. Paul, MN 55105-1789, 651-690-6540 or toll-free 800-656-5283 (in-state). *Fax:* 651-690-6765. *E-mail:* finaid@stkate.edu.

ST. CHARLES BORROMEO SEMINARY, OVERBROOK

Wynnewood, PA

Tuition & fees: $18,228 **Average undergraduate aid package: $19,000**

ABOUT THE INSTITUTION Independent Roman Catholic, coed, primarily men. 1 undergraduate major. Federal methodology is used as a basis for awarding need-based institutional aid.

UNDERGRADUATE EXPENSES for 2010–11 ***Comprehensive fee:*** $29,700 includes full-time tuition ($17,088), mandatory fees ($1140), and room and board ($11,472). Room and board charges vary according to board plan. ***Part-time tuition:*** $831 per course. ***Payment plan:*** Installment.

FRESHMAN FINANCIAL AID (Fall 2010, est.) 11 applied for aid; of those 91% were deemed to have need. 100% of freshmen with need received aid; of those 50% had need fully met. ***Average percent of need met:*** 80% (excluding resources awarded to replace EFC). ***Average financial aid package:*** $19,500 (excluding resources awarded to replace EFC). 100% of all full-time freshmen had no need and received non-need-based gift aid.

UNDERGRADUATE FINANCIAL AID (Fall 2010, est.) 54 applied for aid; of those 100% were deemed to have need. 100% of undergraduates with need received aid; of those 46% had need fully met. ***Average percent of need met:*** 80% (excluding resources awarded to replace EFC). ***Average financial aid package:*** $19,000 (excluding resources awarded to replace EFC). 26% of all full-time undergraduates had no need and received non-need-based gift aid.

GIFT AID (NEED-BASED) ***Total amount:*** $634,920 (14% federal, 7% state, 75% institutional, 4% external sources). ***Receiving aid:*** Freshmen: 29% (5); all full-time undergraduates: 30% (29). ***Average award:*** Freshmen: $5600; Undergraduates: $5600. ***Scholarships, grants, and awards:*** Federal Pell, FSEOG, state, college/university gift aid from institutional funds.

GIFT AID (NON-NEED-BASED) ***Receiving aid:*** Freshmen: 59% (10). Undergraduates: 51% (49). ***Average award:*** Freshmen: $20,790. Undergraduates: $20,790. ***Scholarships, grants, and awards by category:*** *Academic interests/achievement:* general academic interests/achievements. ***Tuition waivers:*** Full or partial for employees or children of employees.

LOANS ***Student loans:*** $325,000 (100% need-based). 49% of past graduating class borrowed through all loan programs. *Average indebtedness per student:* $19,000. ***Average need-based loan:*** Freshmen: $3500. Undergraduates: $5000. ***Parent loans:*** $28,500 (100% need-based). ***Programs:*** Federal Direct (Subsidized and Unsubsidized Stafford, PLUS).

APPLYING FOR FINANCIAL AID ***Required financial aid forms:*** FAFSA, institution's own form. ***Financial aid deadline (priority):*** 4/15. ***Notification date:*** 6/1. Students must reply by 6/15.

CONTACT Ms. Nora M. Downey, Coordinator of Financial Aid, St. Charles Borromeo Seminary, Overbrook, 100 East Wynnewood Road, Wynnewood, PA 19096-3099, 610-785-6582. *Fax:* 610-667-3971. *E-mail:* ndowney@adphila.org.

ST. CLOUD STATE UNIVERSITY

St. Cloud, MN

CONTACT Frank P. Morrissey, Associate Director of Scholarships and Financial Aid, St. Cloud State University, 720 4th Avenue South, AS106, St. Cloud, MN 56301-4498, 320-308-2047 or toll-free 877-654-7278. *Fax:* 320-308-5424. *E-mail:* fpmorrissey@stcloudstate.edu.

ST. EDWARD'S UNIVERSITY

Austin, TX

Tuition & fees: $28,700 **Average undergraduate aid package: $20,324**

ABOUT THE INSTITUTION Independent Roman Catholic, coed. 54 undergraduate majors. Federal methodology is used as a basis for awarding need-based institutional aid.

UNDERGRADUATE EXPENSES for 2011–12 ***Comprehensive fee:*** $38,484 includes full-time tuition ($28,300), mandatory fees ($400), and room and board ($9784). ***College room only:*** $5784. Full-time tuition and fees vary according to course load and degree level. Room and board charges vary according to board plan and housing facility. ***Part-time tuition:*** $944 per credit hour. ***Part-time fees:*** $50 per term. Part-time tuition and fees vary according to course load and degree level. ***Payment plans:*** Installment, deferred payment.

FRESHMAN FINANCIAL AID (Fall 2010, est.) 659 applied for aid; of those 79% were deemed to have need. 100% of freshmen with need received aid; of those 10% had need fully met. ***Average percent of need met:*** 72% (excluding resources awarded to replace EFC). ***Average financial aid package:*** $21,910 (excluding resources awarded to replace EFC). 6% of all full-time freshmen had no need and received non-need-based gift aid.

UNDERGRADUATE FINANCIAL AID (Fall 2010, est.) 2,865 applied for aid; of those 76% were deemed to have need. 99% of undergraduates with need received aid; of those 10% had need fully met. ***Average percent of need met:*** 64% (excluding resources awarded to replace EFC). ***Average financial aid package:*** $20,324 (excluding resources awarded to replace EFC). 6% of all full-time undergraduates had no need and received non-need-based gift aid.

GIFT AID (NEED-BASED) ***Total amount:*** $27,167,215 (25% federal, 18% state, 57% institutional). ***Receiving aid:*** Freshmen: 61% (468); all full-time undergraduates: 55% (1,946). ***Average award:*** Freshmen: $13,903; Undergraduates: $12,252. ***Scholarships, grants, and awards:*** Federal Pell, FSEOG, state, private, college/university gift aid from institutional funds.

GIFT AID (NON-NEED-BASED) ***Total amount:*** $15,715,295 (1% federal, 94% institutional, 5% external sources). ***Receiving aid:*** Freshmen: 47% (361). Undergraduates: 43% (1,523). ***Average award:*** Freshmen: $9997. Undergraduates: $8312. ***Scholarships, grants, and awards by category:*** *Academic interests/achievement:* 2,059 awards ($13,455,080 total): biological sciences, business, communication, computer science, education, English, foreign languages, general academic interests/achievements, health fields, humanities, international studies, mathematics, military science, physical sciences, premedicine, religion/biblical studies, social sciences. *Creative arts/performance:* 42 awards ($105,678 total): art/fine arts, journalism/publications, theater/drama. *Special achievements/activities:* 83 awards ($144,102 total): cheerleading/drum major, community service, general special achievements/activities, leadership. *Special characteristics:* 48 awards ($806,803 total): adult students, children of faculty/staff, religious affiliation. ***Tuition waivers:*** Full or partial for employees or children of employees.

LOANS ***Student loans:*** $28,245,593 (35% need-based, 65% non-need-based). 68% of past graduating class borrowed through all loan programs. *Average indebtedness per student:* $32,515. ***Average need-based loan:*** Freshmen: $3288. Undergraduates: $4262. ***Parent loans:*** $2,487,734 (100% non-need-based). ***Programs:*** Federal Direct (Subsidized and Unsubsidized Stafford, PLUS), Perkins, state.

WORK-STUDY ***Federal work-study:*** Total amount: $350,748; 168 jobs averaging $2088. ***State or other work-study/employment:*** Total amount: $5002 (100% need-based). 2 part-time jobs averaging $2501.

ATHLETIC AWARDS Total amount: $2,275,291 (100% non-need-based).

APPLYING FOR FINANCIAL AID ***Required financial aid form:*** FAFSA. ***Financial aid deadline:*** 5/1 (priority: 3/1). ***Notification date:*** Continuous beginning 1/15. Students must reply by 5/1 or within 2 weeks of notification.

CONTACT Office of Student Financial Services, St. Edward's University, 3001 South Congress Avenue, Austin, TX 78704-6489, 512-448-8523 or toll-free 800-555-0164. *Fax:* 512-416-5837. *E-mail:* seu.finaid@stedwards.edu.

ST. FRANCIS COLLEGE

Brooklyn Heights, NY

CONTACT Joseph Cummings, Director of Student Financial Services, St. Francis College, 180 Remsen Street, Brooklyn Heights, NY 11201-4398, 718-489-5390. *Fax:* 718-522-1274. *E-mail:* jcummings@stfranciscollege.edu.

SAINT FRANCIS MEDICAL CENTER COLLEGE OF NURSING

Peoria, IL

Tuition & fees: $14,956 **Average undergraduate aid package: $13,483**

ABOUT THE INSTITUTION Independent Roman Catholic, coed, primarily women. 1 undergraduate major. Federal methodology is used as a basis for awarding need-based institutional aid.

UNDERGRADUATE EXPENSES for 2010–11 ***Tuition:*** full-time $14,400; part-time $480 per semester hour. ***Required fees:*** full-time $556; $130 per term. Full-time tuition and fees vary according to course load. Part-time tuition and fees vary according to course load. ***Payment plan:*** Installment.

UNDERGRADUATE FINANCIAL AID (Fall 2010, est.) 241 applied for aid; of those 83% were deemed to have need. 100% of undergraduates with need received aid; of those 8% had need fully met. ***Average percent of need met:*** 73% (excluding resources awarded to replace EFC). ***Average financial aid package:*** $13,483 (excluding resources awarded to replace EFC). 7% of all full-time undergraduates had no need and received non-need-based gift aid.

GIFT AID (NEED-BASED) ***Total amount:*** $1,086,217 (33% federal, 55% state, 7% institutional, 5% external sources). ***Receiving aid:*** All full-time undergraduates: 55% (146). ***Average award:*** Undergraduates: $6870. ***Scholarships, grants, and awards:*** Federal Pell, state, private, college/university gift aid from institutional funds.

GIFT AID (NON-NEED-BASED) ***Total amount:*** $59,873 (55% state, 26% institutional, 19% external sources). ***Average award:*** Undergraduates: $2877. ***Scholarships, grants, and awards by category:*** *Academic interests/achievement:* 35 awards ($41,855 total): general academic interests/achievements, health fields. ***Tuition waivers:*** Full or partial for employees or children of employees.

LOANS ***Student loans:*** $2,220,349 (84% need-based, 16% non-need-based). ***Average need-based loan:*** Undergraduates: $5156. ***Parent loans:*** $267,522 (29% need-based, 71% non-need-based). ***Programs:*** Federal Direct (Subsidized and Unsubsidized Stafford, PLUS), college/university.

APPLYING FOR FINANCIAL AID ***Required financial aid forms:*** FAFSA, institution's own form. ***Financial aid deadline (priority):*** 3/1. ***Notification date:*** Continuous beginning 5/1.

CONTACT Ms. Nancy Perryman, Coordinator Student Finance, Saint Francis Medical Center College of Nursing, 511 Northeast Greenleaf Street, Peoria, IL 61603-3783, 309-655-4119. *Fax:* 309-655-3962. *E-mail:* nancy.s.perryman@osfhealthcare.org.

SAINT FRANCIS UNIVERSITY

Loretto, PA

Tuition & fees: $26,534 **Average undergraduate aid package: N/A**

ABOUT THE INSTITUTION Independent Roman Catholic, coed. 68 undergraduate majors. Federal methodology is used as a basis for awarding need-based institutional aid.

UNDERGRADUATE EXPENSES for 2010–11 ***Comprehensive fee:*** $35,600 includes full-time tuition ($25,484), mandatory fees ($1050), and room and board ($9066). ***College room only:*** $4510. Full-time tuition and fees vary according to course load, degree level, and program. Room and board charges vary according to board plan and housing facility. ***Part-time tuition:*** $796 per credit hour. ***Part-time fees:*** $376 per credit hour. Part-time tuition and fees vary according to class time, degree level, and program.

GIFT AID (NEED-BASED) ***Scholarships, grants, and awards:*** Federal Pell, FSEOG, state, private, college/university gift aid from institutional funds.

GIFT AID (NON-NEED-BASED) ***Scholarships, grants, and awards by category:*** *Academic interests/achievement:* biological sciences, business, computer science, education, engineering/technologies, English, general academic interests/achievements, health fields, humanities, mathematics, religion/biblical studies, social sciences. *Creative arts/performance:* art/fine arts, music. *Special achievements/activities:* cheerleading/drum major, religious involvement. *Special characteristics:* adult students, children and siblings of alumni, children of current students, children of educators, children of faculty/staff, international students, out-of-state students, previous college experience, religious affiliation, siblings of current students, spouses of current students. ***Tuition waivers:*** Full or partial for employees or children of employees.

LOANS ***Programs:*** Federal Direct (Subsidized and Unsubsidized Stafford, PLUS), Perkins, private loans.

WORK-STUDY Federal work-study jobs available. ***State or other work-study/employment:*** Part-time jobs available.

APPLYING FOR FINANCIAL AID ***Required financial aid form:*** FAFSA. ***Financial aid deadline (priority):*** 5/1. ***Notification date:*** Continuous beginning 3/1. Students must reply by 5/1.

CONTACT Mr. Shane Himes, Financial Aid Counselor, Saint Francis University, PO Box 600, Loretto, PA 15931, 814-472-3010 or toll-free 800-342-5732. *Fax:* 814-472-3999. *E-mail:* shimes@francis.edu.

ST. GREGORY'S UNIVERSITY

Shawnee, OK

CONTACT Matt McCoin, Director of Financial Aid, St. Gregory's University, 1900 West MacArthur Drive, Shawnee, OK 74804, 405-878-5412 or toll-free 888-STGREGS. *Fax:* 405-878-5403. *E-mail:* mdmccoin@stgregorys.edu.

ST. GREGORY THE GREAT SEMINARY

Seward, NE

CONTACT Financial Aid Office, St. Gregory the Great Seminary, 800 Fletcher Road, Seward, NE 67434, 402-643-4052.

ST. JOHN FISHER COLLEGE

Rochester, NY

Tuition & fees: $25,270 **Average undergraduate aid package: $18,929**

ABOUT THE INSTITUTION Independent religious, coed. 38 undergraduate majors. Federal methodology is used as a basis for awarding need-based institutional aid.

UNDERGRADUATE EXPENSES for 2010–11 ***Comprehensive fee:*** $35,560 includes full-time tuition ($24,800), mandatory fees ($470), and room and board ($10,290). ***College room only:*** $6680. Room and board charges vary according to board plan. ***Part-time tuition:*** $675 per credit hour. ***Part-time fees:*** $25 per term. Part-time tuition and fees vary according to course load. ***Payment plans:*** Installment, deferred payment.

FRESHMAN FINANCIAL AID (Fall 2010, est.) 609 applied for aid; of those 89% were deemed to have need. 100% of freshmen with need received aid; of those 27% had need fully met. ***Average percent of need met:*** 83% (excluding resources awarded to replace EFC). ***Average financial aid package:*** $20,472 (excluding resources awarded to replace EFC). 13% of all full-time freshmen had no need and received non-need-based gift aid.

UNDERGRADUATE FINANCIAL AID (Fall 2010, est.) 2,478 applied for aid; of those 91% were deemed to have need. 100% of undergraduates with need received aid; of those 23% had need fully met. ***Average percent of need met:*** 81% (excluding resources awarded to replace EFC). ***Average financial aid package:*** $18,929 (excluding resources awarded to replace EFC). 14% of all full-time undergraduates had no need and received non-need-based gift aid.

GIFT AID (NEED-BASED) ***Total amount:*** $30,889,727 (16% federal, 11% state, 70% institutional, 3% external sources). ***Receiving aid:*** Freshmen: 87% (539); all full-time undergraduates: 83% (2,242). ***Average award:*** Freshmen: $16,354; Undergraduates: $14,011. ***Scholarships, grants, and awards:*** Federal Pell, FSEOG, state, private, college/university gift aid from institutional funds, Federal Nursing.

GIFT AID (NON-NEED-BASED) ***Total amount:*** $3,516,659 (1% federal, 1% state, 87% institutional, 11% external sources). ***Receiving aid:*** Freshmen: 57% (355). Undergraduates: 37% (1,003). ***Average award:*** Freshmen: $9805. Undergraduates: $8959. ***Scholarships, grants, and awards by category:*** *Academic interests/achievement:* 1,565 awards ($13,764,450 total): biological sciences, business, English, foreign languages, general academic interests/achievements, humanities, mathematics, physical sciences. *Special achievements/activities:* 101 awards ($1,100,970 total): community service. *Special characteristics:* 174 awards ($2,674,733 total): children and siblings of alumni, children of faculty/staff, ethnic background, first-generation college students, local/state students, members of minority groups. ***Tuition waivers:*** Full or partial for employees or children of employees.

LOANS ***Student loans:*** $21,006,362 (93% need-based, 7% non-need-based). 83% of past graduating class borrowed through all loan programs. *Average indebtedness per student:* $32,975. ***Average need-based loan:*** Freshmen: $3875. Undergraduates: $4192. ***Parent loans:*** $12,384,627 (88% need-based, 12% non-need-based). ***Programs:*** Federal Direct (Subsidized and Unsubsidized Stafford, PLUS), Perkins.

WORK-STUDY ***Federal work-study:*** Total amount: $1,861,604; 1,345 jobs averaging $1373.

APPLYING FOR FINANCIAL AID ***Required financial aid forms:*** FAFSA, state aid form. ***Financial aid deadline (priority):*** 2/15. ***Notification date:*** Continuous beginning 3/21. Students must reply by 5/1 or within 3 weeks of notification.

CONTACT Mrs. Angela Monnat, Director of Financial Aid, St. John Fisher College, 3690 East Avenue, Rochester, NY 14618-3597, 585-385-8042 or toll-free 800-444-4640. *Fax:* 585-385-8044. *E-mail:* amonnat@sjfc.edu.

ST. JOHN'S COLLEGE

Springfield, IL

ABOUT THE INSTITUTION Independent Roman Catholic, coed, primarily women. 1 undergraduate major.

GIFT AID (NEED-BASED) ***Scholarships, grants, and awards:*** Federal Pell, FSEOG, state, private, college/university gift aid from institutional funds, Federal Nursing.

LOANS ***Programs:*** Federal Direct (Subsidized and Unsubsidized Stafford), Federal Nursing.

WORK-STUDY ***Federal work-study:*** Total amount: $8589; 5 jobs averaging $1717.

CONTACT Mary M. Deatherage, Financial Aid Officer, St. John's College, 421 North Ninth Street, Springfield, IL 62702, 217-544-6464 Ext. 44705. *Fax:* 217-757-6870. *E-mail:* mdeather@st-johns.org.

ST. JOHN'S COLLEGE

Annapolis, MD

Tuition & fees: $42,192 **Average undergraduate aid package: $34,236**

ABOUT THE INSTITUTION Independent, coed. 3 undergraduate majors. Both federal and institutional methodology are used as a basis for awarding need-based institutional aid.

UNDERGRADUATE EXPENSES for 2010–11 ***Comprehensive fee:*** $52,176 includes full-time tuition ($41,792), mandatory fees ($400), and room and board ($9984). Room and board charges vary according to board plan. ***Payment plan:*** Installment.

FRESHMAN FINANCIAL AID (Fall 2009) 100 applied for aid; of those 91% were deemed to have need. 97% of freshmen with need received aid; of those 97% had need fully met. ***Average percent of need met:*** 98% (excluding resources awarded to replace EFC). ***Average financial aid package:*** $36,260 (excluding resources awarded to replace EFC).

UNDERGRADUATE FINANCIAL AID (Fall 2009) 324 applied for aid; of those 94% were deemed to have need. 99% of undergraduates with need received aid; of those 100% had need fully met. ***Average percent of need met:*** 98% (excluding resources awarded to replace EFC). ***Average financial aid package:*** $34,236 (excluding resources awarded to replace EFC).

GIFT AID (NEED-BASED) ***Total amount:*** $8,456,595 (9% federal, 1% state, 90% institutional). ***Receiving aid:*** Freshmen: 60% (82); all full-time undergraduates: 61% (283). ***Average award:*** Freshmen: $26,388; Undergraduates: $27,913. ***Scholarships, grants, and awards:*** Federal Pell, FSEOG, state, private, college/university gift aid from institutional funds.

GIFT AID (NON-NEED-BASED) ***Total amount:*** $83,207 (100% external sources). ***Receiving aid:*** Freshmen: 5% (7). Undergraduates: 4% (20). ***Tuition waivers:*** Full or partial for employees or children of employees.

LOANS ***Student loans:*** $2,275,791 (85% need-based, 15% non-need-based). 68% of past graduating class borrowed through all loan programs. *Average indebtedness per student:* $29,869. ***Average need-based loan:*** Freshmen: $4057. Undergraduates: $4788. ***Parent loans:*** $1,697,648 (100% non-need-based). ***Programs:*** Federal Direct (Subsidized and Unsubsidized Stafford, PLUS), Perkins, college/university.

WORK-STUDY ***Federal work-study:*** Total amount: $232,499; 128 jobs averaging $1816. ***State or other work-study/employment:*** Total amount: $210,422 (100% non-need-based). 163 part-time jobs averaging $1291.

APPLYING FOR FINANCIAL AID ***Required financial aid forms:*** FAFSA, CSS Financial Aid PROFILE, noncustodial (divorced/separated) parent's statement, business/farm supplement. ***Financial aid deadline (priority):*** 3/1. ***Notification date:*** Continuous beginning 1/1. Students must reply by 5/1.

CONTACT Ms. Dana Kennedy, Director of Financial Aid, St. John's College, PO Box 2800, Annapolis, MD 21404, 410-626-2502 or toll-free 800-727-9238. *Fax:* 410-626-2885. *E-mail:* dana.kennedy@sjca.edu.

ST. JOHN'S COLLEGE

Santa Fe, NM

ABOUT THE INSTITUTION Independent, coed. 3 undergraduate majors.

GIFT AID (NEED-BASED) ***Scholarships, grants, and awards:*** Federal Pell, FSEOG, state, private, college/university gift aid from institutional funds, Academic Competitiveness Grants, National SMART Grants.

GIFT AID (NON-NEED-BASED) ***Scholarships, grants, and awards by category:*** *Special characteristics:* children of faculty/staff.

LOANS ***Programs:*** Perkins, college/university.

WORK-STUDY ***Federal work-study:*** Total amount: $322,960; jobs available. ***State or other work-study/employment:*** Total amount: $20,750 (100% need-based). Part-time jobs available.

APPLYING FOR FINANCIAL AID ***Required financial aid forms:*** FAFSA, CSS Financial Aid PROFILE, noncustodial (divorced/separated) parent's statement, business/farm supplement.

CONTACT Michael Rodriguez, Director of Financial Aid, St. John's College, 1160 Camino Cruz Blanca, Santa Fe, NM 87505, 505-984-6058 or toll-free 800-331-5232. *Fax:* 505-984-6003. *E-mail:* mike.rodriguez@sjcsf.edu.

SAINT JOHN'S UNIVERSITY

Collegeville, MN

Tuition & fees: $31,576 **Average undergraduate aid package: $22,605**

ABOUT THE INSTITUTION Independent Roman Catholic, men only. 51 undergraduate majors. Federal methodology is used as a basis for awarding need-based institutional aid.

UNDERGRADUATE EXPENSES for 2010–11 ***Comprehensive fee:*** $39,620 includes full-time tuition ($31,006), mandatory fees ($570), and room and board ($8044). ***College room only:*** $4040. Room and board charges vary according to board plan and housing facility. ***Part-time tuition:*** $1292 per credit hour. Part-time tuition and fees vary according to course load. ***Payment plan:*** Installment.

FRESHMAN FINANCIAL AID (Fall 2010, est.) 401 applied for aid; of those 82% were deemed to have need. 100% of freshmen with need received aid; of those 50% had need fully met. ***Average percent of need met:*** 91% (excluding resources awarded to replace EFC). ***Average financial aid package:*** $23,906 (excluding resources awarded to replace EFC). 29% of all full-time freshmen had no need and received non-need-based gift aid.

UNDERGRADUATE FINANCIAL AID (Fall 2010, est.) 1,374 applied for aid; of those 85% were deemed to have need. 100% of undergraduates with need received aid; of those 42% had need fully met. ***Average percent of need met:*** 87% (excluding resources awarded to replace EFC). ***Average financial aid package:*** $22,605 (excluding resources awarded to replace EFC). 31% of all full-time undergraduates had no need and received non-need-based gift aid.

GIFT AID (NEED-BASED) ***Total amount:*** $21,778,816 (10% federal, 6% state, 81% institutional, 3% external sources). ***Receiving aid:*** Freshmen: 64% (320); all full-time undergraduates: 60% (1,142). ***Average award:*** Freshmen: $20,147;

Undergraduates: $18,570. ***Scholarships, grants, and awards:*** Federal Pell, FSEOG, state, private, college/university gift aid from institutional funds.

GIFT AID (NON-NEED-BASED) ***Total amount:*** $10,073,327 (87% institutional, 13% external sources). ***Receiving aid:*** Freshmen: 61% (309). Undergraduates: 56% (1,071). ***Average award:*** Freshmen: $12,764. Undergraduates: $11,430. ***Scholarships, grants, and awards by category:*** *Academic interests/achievement:* 1,590 awards ($16,847,620 total): general academic interests/achievements. *Creative arts/performance:* 124 awards ($286,200 total): art/fine arts, music, theater/drama. *Special characteristics:* 259 awards ($3,242,554 total): international students, out-of-state students.

LOANS ***Student loans:*** $12,397,600 (87% need-based, 13% non-need-based). ***Average need-based loan:*** Freshmen: $3973. Undergraduates: $3980. ***Parent loans:*** $1,099,660 (76% need-based, 24% non-need-based). ***Programs:*** Federal Direct (Subsidized and Unsubsidized Stafford, PLUS), Perkins, state, alternative loans.

WORK-STUDY ***Federal work-study:*** Total amount: $823,848; 308 jobs averaging $2545. ***State or other work-study/employment:*** Total amount: $1,938,291 (66% need-based, 34% non-need-based). 818 part-time jobs averaging $2616.

APPLYING FOR FINANCIAL AID ***Required financial aid forms:*** FAFSA, institution's own form, federal income tax form(s). ***Financial aid deadline (priority):*** 3/15. ***Notification date:*** Continuous beginning 3/15. Students must reply by 5/1 or within 3 weeks of notification.

CONTACT Ms. Mary Dehler, Associate Director of Financial Aid, Saint John's University, PO Box 5000, Collegeville, MN 56321-5000, 320-363-3664 or toll-free 800-544-1489. *Fax:* 320-363-3102. *E-mail:* mdehler@csbsju.edu.

ST. JOHN'S UNIVERSITY

Queens, NY

Tuition & fees: $31,980 **Average undergraduate aid package: $24,777**

ABOUT THE INSTITUTION Independent religious, coed. 70 undergraduate majors. Federal methodology is used as a basis for awarding need-based institutional aid.

UNDERGRADUATE EXPENSES for 2010–11 ***Comprehensive fee:*** $45,880 includes full-time tuition ($31,250), mandatory fees ($730), and room and board ($13,900). ***College room only:*** $8750. Full-time tuition and fees vary according to course load, program, and student level. Room and board charges vary according to board plan, housing facility, and location. ***Part-time tuition:*** $1042 per credit. ***Part-time fees:*** $267.50 per term. Part-time tuition and fees vary according to course load, program, and student level. ***Payment plan:*** Installment.

FRESHMAN FINANCIAL AID (Fall 2009) 2,795 applied for aid; of those 93% were deemed to have need. 100% of freshmen with need received aid; of those 7% had need fully met. ***Average percent of need met:*** 72% (excluding resources awarded to replace EFC). ***Average financial aid package:*** $26,591 (excluding resources awarded to replace EFC). 6% of all full-time freshmen had no need and received non-need-based gift aid.

UNDERGRADUATE FINANCIAL AID (Fall 2009) 10,302 applied for aid; of those 94% were deemed to have need. 99% of undergraduates with need received aid; of those 6% had need fully met. ***Average percent of need met:*** 63% (excluding resources awarded to replace EFC). ***Average financial aid package:*** $24,777 (excluding resources awarded to replace EFC). 4% of all full-time undergraduates had no need and received non-need-based gift aid.

GIFT AID (NEED-BASED) ***Total amount:*** $100,477,093 (26% federal, 15% state, 59% institutional). ***Receiving aid:*** Freshmen: 77% (2,380); all full-time undergraduates: 71% (8,305). ***Average award:*** Freshmen: $12,819; Undergraduates: $12,118. ***Scholarships, grants, and awards:*** Federal Pell, FSEOG, state, private, college/university gift aid from institutional funds.

GIFT AID (NON-NEED-BASED) ***Total amount:*** $87,893,895 (1% federal, 1% state, 91% institutional, 7% external sources). ***Receiving aid:*** Freshmen: 71% (2,198). Undergraduates: 57% (6,728). ***Average award:*** Freshmen: $15,053. Undergraduates: $13,772. ***Scholarships, grants, and awards by category:*** *Academic interests/achievement:* 7,113 awards ($73,532,694 total): biological sciences, business, communication, computer science, education, English, foreign languages, general academic interests/achievements, health fields, humanities, mathematics, military science, physical sciences, premedicine, social sciences. *Creative arts/performance:* 154 awards ($303,168 total): art/fine arts, cinema/film/broadcasting, dance, debating, journalism/publications, music. *Special achievements/activities:* 292 awards ($732,220 total): cheerleading/drum major, community service, general special achievements/activities, hobbies/interests, leadership, religious involvement. *Special characteristics:* 646 awards ($5,226,595 total): children of faculty/staff, general special characteristics, local/state students, relatives of clergy, religious affiliation. ***Tuition waivers:*** Full or partial for employees or children of employees, senior citizens.

LOANS ***Student loans:*** $95,764,063 (48% need-based, 52% non-need-based). 71% of past graduating class borrowed through all loan programs. *Average indebtedness per student:* $32,886. ***Average need-based loan:*** Freshmen: $3776. Undergraduates: $5077. ***Parent loans:*** $35,778,145 (100% non-need-based). ***Programs:*** Federal Direct (Subsidized and Unsubsidized Stafford, PLUS), Perkins.

WORK-STUDY ***Federal work-study:*** Total amount: $3,081,763; 982 jobs averaging $3479.

ATHLETIC AWARDS Total amount: $5,729,703 (100% non-need-based).

APPLYING FOR FINANCIAL AID ***Required financial aid form:*** FAFSA. ***Financial aid deadline (priority):*** 2/1. ***Notification date:*** Continuous beginning 3/15. Students must reply within 2 weeks of notification.

CONTACT Mr. Jorge Rodriguez, Associate Vice President for Student Financial Services, St. John's University, 8000 Utopia Parkway, Queens, NY 11439, 718-990-2000 or toll-free 888-9STJOHNS. *Fax:* 718-990-5945. *E-mail:* studentfinancialserv@stjohns.edu.

ST. JOHN VIANNEY COLLEGE SEMINARY

Miami, FL

CONTACT Ms. Bonnie DeAngulo, Director of Financial Aid, St. John Vianney College Seminary, 2900 Southwest 87th Avenue, Miami, FL 33165-3244, 305-223-4561 Ext. 10.

SAINT JOSEPH COLLEGE

West Hartford, CT

Tuition & fees: $28,530 **Average undergraduate aid package: N/A**

ABOUT THE INSTITUTION Independent Roman Catholic, undergraduate: women only; graduate: coed. 23 undergraduate majors. Federal methodology is used as a basis for awarding need-based institutional aid.

UNDERGRADUATE EXPENSES for 2010–11 ***Comprehensive fee:*** $41,470 includes full-time tuition ($27,580), mandatory fees ($950), and room and board ($12,940). ***College room only:*** $5970. Full-time tuition and fees vary according to course load, degree level, location, program, and student level. Room and board charges vary according to board plan and housing facility. ***Part-time tuition:*** $625 per credit. ***Part-time fees:*** $30 per quarter hour. Part-time tuition and fees vary according to course load, degree level, location, program, and student level. ***Payment plan:*** Installment.

GIFT AID (NEED-BASED) ***Scholarships, grants, and awards:*** Federal Pell, FSEOG, state, private, college/university gift aid from institutional funds.

GIFT AID (NON-NEED-BASED) ***Scholarships, grants, and awards by category:*** *Academic interests/achievement:* general academic interests/achievements. ***Tuition waivers:*** Full or partial for employees or children of employees.

LOANS ***Programs:*** Federal Direct (Subsidized and Unsubsidized Stafford, PLUS), Perkins, state, private loans.

APPLYING FOR FINANCIAL AID ***Required financial aid form:*** FAFSA. ***Financial aid deadline (priority):*** 2/15. ***Notification date:*** Continuous beginning 3/1. Students must reply within 2 weeks of notification.

CONTACT Beth Baker, Director of Financial Aid, Saint Joseph College, 1678 Asylum Avenue, West Hartford, CT 06117, 860-231-5319 or toll-free 866-442-8752. *E-mail:* ebaker@sjc.edu.

SAINT JOSEPH'S COLLEGE

Rensselaer, IN

Tuition & fees: $26,330 **Average undergraduate aid package: $21,891**

ABOUT THE INSTITUTION Independent Roman Catholic, coed. 33 undergraduate majors. Federal methodology is used as a basis for awarding need-based institutional aid.

UNDERGRADUATE EXPENSES for 2011–12 ***Comprehensive fee:*** $34,310 includes full-time tuition ($26,140), mandatory fees ($190), and room and board ($7980). Full-time tuition and fees vary according to reciprocity agreements.

Room and board charges vary according to housing facility. ***Part-time tuition:*** $870 per credit hour. Part-time tuition and fees vary according to course load and reciprocity agreements. ***Payment plan:*** Installment.

FRESHMAN FINANCIAL AID (Fall 2009) 231 applied for aid; of those 90% were deemed to have need. 100% of freshmen with need received aid; of those 26% had need fully met. ***Average percent of need met:*** 80% (excluding resources awarded to replace EFC). ***Average financial aid package:*** $21,563 (excluding resources awarded to replace EFC). 10% of all full-time freshmen had no need and received non-need-based gift aid.

UNDERGRADUATE FINANCIAL AID (Fall 2009) 752 applied for aid; of those 87% were deemed to have need. 100% of undergraduates with need received aid; of those 29% had need fully met. ***Average percent of need met:*** 80% (excluding resources awarded to replace EFC). ***Average financial aid package:*** $21,891 (excluding resources awarded to replace EFC). 11% of all full-time undergraduates had no need and received non-need-based gift aid.

GIFT AID (NEED-BASED) ***Total amount:*** $8,135,375 (16% federal, 12% state, 68% institutional, 4% external sources). ***Receiving aid:*** Freshmen: 88% (203); all full-time undergraduates: 86% (644). ***Average award:*** Freshmen: $15,371; Undergraduates: $14,856. ***Scholarships, grants, and awards:*** Federal Pell, FSEOG, state, private, college/university gift aid from institutional funds.

GIFT AID (NON-NEED-BASED) ***Total amount:*** $1,649,533 (96% institutional, 4% external sources). ***Receiving aid:*** Freshmen: 25% (58). Undergraduates: 24% (179). ***Average award:*** Freshmen: $14,869. Undergraduates: $12,711. ***Scholarships, grants, and awards by category:*** *Academic interests/achievement:* 446 awards ($4,418,815 total): general academic interests/achievements. *Creative arts/performance:* 122 awards ($281,200 total): cinema/film/broadcasting, dance, music, theater/drama. *Special achievements/activities:* 10 awards ($21,100 total): cheerleading/drum major. *Special characteristics:* 138 awards ($373,170 total): children and siblings of alumni, children of faculty/staff, siblings of current students. ***Tuition waivers:*** Full or partial for minority students, children of alumni, employees or children of employees.

LOANS ***Student loans:*** $5,033,375 (85% need-based, 15% non-need-based). 77% of past graduating class borrowed through all loan programs. *Average indebtedness per student:* $28,135. ***Average need-based loan:*** Freshmen: $3618. Undergraduates: $4382. ***Parent loans:*** $1,262,366 (69% need-based, 31% non-need-based). ***Programs:*** Perkins.

WORK-STUDY ***Federal work-study:*** Total amount: $58,386; 75 jobs averaging $778.

ATHLETIC AWARDS Total amount: $2,115,048 (59% need-based, 41% non-need-based).

APPLYING FOR FINANCIAL AID ***Required financial aid forms:*** FAFSA, combined institutional admission/financial aid form. ***Financial aid deadline (priority):*** 3/1. ***Notification date:*** Continuous. Students must reply by 5/1 or within 2 weeks of notification.

CONTACT Debra Sizemore, Director of Student Financial Services, Saint Joseph's College, 1498 South College Avenue, PO Box 971, Rensselaer, IN 47978, 219-866-6163 or toll-free 800-447-8781 (out-of-state). *Fax:* 219-866-6144. *E-mail:* debbie@saintjoe.edu.

ST. JOSEPH'S COLLEGE, LONG ISLAND CAMPUS

Patchogue, NY

Tuition & fees: $17,565 **Average undergraduate aid package: $10,606**

ABOUT THE INSTITUTION Independent, coed. 40 undergraduate majors. Federal methodology is used as a basis for awarding need-based institutional aid.

UNDERGRADUATE EXPENSES for 2011–12 ***Tuition:*** full-time $17,000. Full-time tuition and fees vary according to course load, degree level, and program. Part-time tuition and fees vary according to course load, degree level, and program. ***Payment plans:*** Installment, deferred payment.

FRESHMAN FINANCIAL AID (Fall 2010, est.) 462 applied for aid; of those 71% were deemed to have need. 99% of freshmen with need received aid; of those 23% had need fully met. ***Average percent of need met:*** 75% (excluding resources awarded to replace EFC). ***Average financial aid package:*** $12,518 (excluding resources awarded to replace EFC). 25% of all full-time freshmen had no need and received non-need-based gift aid.

UNDERGRADUATE FINANCIAL AID (Fall 2010, est.) 2,872 applied for aid; of those 78% were deemed to have need. 99% of undergraduates with need received aid; of those 23% had need fully met. ***Average percent of need met:*** 66% (excluding resources awarded to replace EFC). ***Average financial aid package:*** $10,606 (excluding resources awarded to replace EFC). 14% of all full-time undergraduates had no need and received non-need-based gift aid.

GIFT AID (NEED-BASED) ***Total amount:*** $15,616,633 (31% federal, 21% state, 48% institutional). ***Receiving aid:*** Freshmen: 49% (230); all full-time undergraduates: 69% (2,110). ***Average award:*** Freshmen: $9737; Undergraduates: $6998. ***Scholarships, grants, and awards:*** Federal Pell, FSEOG, state, private, college/university gift aid from institutional funds.

GIFT AID (NON-NEED-BASED) ***Total amount:*** $4,721,745 (3% state, 94% institutional, 3% external sources). ***Receiving aid:*** Freshmen: 47% (220). Undergraduates: 24% (733). ***Average award:*** Freshmen: $8379. Undergraduates: $7569. ***Scholarships, grants, and awards by category:*** *Academic interests/achievement:* 1,705 awards ($11,787,114 total): general academic interests/achievements. *Special achievements/activities:* 5 awards ($12,500 total): community service, leadership. *Special characteristics:* 208 awards ($673,705 total): children and siblings of alumni, children of faculty/staff, parents of current students, public servants, siblings of current students, spouses of current students, twins. ***Tuition waivers:*** Full or partial for employees or children of employees, senior citizens.

LOANS ***Student loans:*** $17,645,890 (41% need-based, 59% non-need-based). 71% of past graduating class borrowed through all loan programs. *Average indebtedness per student:* $23,031. ***Average need-based loan:*** Freshmen: $3112. Undergraduates: $4448. ***Parent loans:*** $5,332,195 (100% non-need-based). ***Programs:*** Federal Direct (Subsidized and Unsubsidized Stafford, PLUS), Perkins, state.

WORK-STUDY ***Federal work-study:*** Total amount: $219,985; 73 jobs averaging $3087. ***State or other work-study/employment:*** Total amount: $420,697 (100% non-need-based). 104 part-time jobs averaging $4147.

APPLYING FOR FINANCIAL AID ***Required financial aid forms:*** FAFSA, state aid form. ***Financial aid deadline (priority):*** 2/25. ***Notification date:*** Continuous beginning 3/15. Students must reply by 5/1 or within 2 weeks of notification.

CONTACT Amy Thompson, Director of Financial Aid, St. Joseph's College, Long Island Campus, 155 West Roe Boulevard, Patchogue, NY 11772-2399, 631-687-2611 or toll-free 866-AT ST JOE (in-state). *Fax:* 631-650-2525. *E-mail:* althompson@sjcny.edu.

ST. JOSEPH'S COLLEGE, NEW YORK

Brooklyn, NY

Tuition & fees: $17,565 **Average undergraduate aid package: $13,446**

ABOUT THE INSTITUTION Independent, coed, 41 undergraduate majors. Federal methodology is used as a basis for awarding need-based institutional aid.

UNDERGRADUATE EXPENSES for 2011–12 ***Tuition:*** full-time $17,000. Full-time tuition and fees vary according to course load, degree level, and program. Part-time tuition and fees vary according to course load, degree level, and program. ***Payment plans:*** Installment, deferred payment.

FRESHMAN FINANCIAL AID (Fall 2010, est.) 218 applied for aid; of those 83% were deemed to have need. 100% of freshmen with need received aid; of those 15% had need fully met. ***Average percent of need met:*** 74% (excluding resources awarded to replace EFC). ***Average financial aid package:*** $15,268 (excluding resources awarded to replace EFC). 15% of all full-time freshmen had no need and received non-need-based gift aid.

UNDERGRADUATE FINANCIAL AID (Fall 2010, est.) 849 applied for aid; of those 86% were deemed to have need. 98% of undergraduates with need received aid; of those 16% had need fully met. ***Average percent of need met:*** 68% (excluding resources awarded to replace EFC). ***Average financial aid package:*** $13,446 (excluding resources awarded to replace EFC). 13% of all full-time undergraduates had no need and received non-need-based gift aid.

GIFT AID (NEED-BASED) ***Total amount:*** $7,238,063 (39% federal, 20% state, 41% institutional). ***Receiving aid:*** Freshmen: 76% (181); all full-time undergraduates: 81% (715). ***Average award:*** Freshmen: $11,768; Undergraduates: $9017. ***Scholarships, grants, and awards:*** Federal Pell, FSEOG, state, private, college/university gift aid from institutional funds.

GIFT AID (NON-NEED-BASED) ***Total amount:*** $1,691,269 (5% state, 91% institutional, 4% external sources). ***Receiving aid:*** Freshmen: 12% (28). Undergraduates: 25% (219). ***Average award:*** Freshmen: $7739. Undergraduates: $8162. ***Scholarships, grants, and awards by category:*** *Academic interests/achievement:* 463 awards ($3,085,380 total): general academic interests/achievements. *Special achievements/activities:* 4 awards ($10,000 total): community service, leadership. *Special characteristics:* 72 awards ($176,832 total): children and siblings of alumni, children of faculty/staff, parents of current students, public servants, siblings of current students, spouses of current students, twins. ***Tuition waivers:*** Full or partial for employees or children of employees, senior citizens.

LOANS ***Student loans:*** $4,892,239 (44% need-based, 56% non-need-based). 66% of past graduating class borrowed through all loan programs. *Average indebtedness per student:* $22,825. ***Average need-based loan:*** Freshmen: $3231. Undergraduates: $4284. ***Parent loans:*** $807,907 (100% non-need-based). ***Programs:*** Federal Direct (Subsidized and Unsubsidized Stafford, PLUS), Perkins, state.

WORK-STUDY ***Federal work-study:*** Total amount: $120,404; 85 jobs averaging $1437. ***State or other work-study/employment:*** Total amount: $21,813 (100% non-need-based). 18 part-time jobs averaging $1212.

APPLYING FOR FINANCIAL AID ***Required financial aid forms:*** FAFSA, state aid form. ***Financial aid deadline (priority):*** 2/25. ***Notification date:*** Continuous beginning 3/15. Students must reply by 5/1 or within 2 weeks of notification.

CONTACT Ms. Amy Thompson, Director of Financial Aid, St. Joseph's College, New York, 245 Clinton Avenue, Brooklyn, NY 11205-3688, 718-940-5713. *Fax:* 718-636-6827. *E-mail:* althompson@sjcny.edu.

SAINT JOSEPH'S COLLEGE OF MAINE

Standish, ME

ABOUT THE INSTITUTION Independent religious, coed. 47 undergraduate majors.

GIFT AID (NEED-BASED) ***Scholarships, grants, and awards:*** Federal Pell, FSEOG, state, private, college/university gift aid from institutional funds, Federal Nursing.

GIFT AID (NON-NEED-BASED) ***Scholarships, grants, and awards by category:*** *Academic interests/achievement:* general academic interests/achievements. *Special characteristics:* children of faculty/staff, siblings of current students, spouses of current students.

LOANS ***Programs:*** Federal Direct (Subsidized and Unsubsidized Stafford, PLUS), Perkins, Federal Nursing, state.

WORK-STUDY ***Federal work-study:*** Total amount: $565,951; 408 jobs averaging $1382.

APPLYING FOR FINANCIAL AID ***Required financial aid forms:*** FAFSA, institution's own form.

CONTACT Office of Financial Aid, Saint Joseph's College of Maine, 278 Whites Bridge Road, Standish, ME 04084-5263, 800-752-1266 or toll-free 800-338-7057. *Fax:* 207-893-6699. *E-mail:* finaid@sjcme.edu.

SAINT JOSEPH SEMINARY COLLEGE

Saint Benedict, LA

ABOUT THE INSTITUTION Independent Roman Catholic, coed, primarily men. 1 undergraduate major.

GIFT AID (NEED-BASED) ***Scholarships, grants, and awards:*** Federal Pell, state, private, college/university gift aid from institutional funds.

WORK-STUDY Federal work-study jobs available. ***State or other work-study/employment:*** Part-time jobs available.

APPLYING FOR FINANCIAL AID ***Required financial aid form:*** FAFSA.

CONTACT George J. Binder Jr., Financial Aid Officer, Saint Joseph Seminary College, 75376 River Road, Saint Benedict, LA 70457, 985-867-2248. *Fax:* 985-867-2270. *E-mail:* gbinder@sjasc.edu.

SAINT JOSEPH'S UNIVERSITY

Philadelphia, PA

Tuition & fees: $35,230 **Average undergraduate aid package: $19,762**

ABOUT THE INSTITUTION Independent Roman Catholic (Jesuit), coed. 55 undergraduate majors. Federal methodology is used as a basis for awarding need-based institutional aid.

UNDERGRADUATE EXPENSES for 2010–11 ***One-time required fee:*** $225. ***Comprehensive fee:*** $47,155 includes full-time tuition ($35,080), mandatory fees ($150), and room and board ($11,925). ***College room only:*** $7500. Full-time tuition and fees vary according to course load. Room and board charges vary according to board plan and housing facility. ***Part-time tuition:*** $466 per credit. ***Payment plans:*** Installment, deferred payment.

FRESHMAN FINANCIAL AID (Fall 2010, est.) 928 applied for aid; of those 79% were deemed to have need. 100% of freshmen with need received aid; of those 25% had need fully met. ***Average percent of need met:*** 78% (excluding resources awarded to replace EFC). ***Average financial aid package:*** $20,876 (excluding resources awarded to replace EFC). 32% of all full-time freshmen had no need and received non-need-based gift aid.

UNDERGRADUATE FINANCIAL AID (Fall 2010, est.) 2,971 applied for aid; of those 84% were deemed to have need. 100% of undergraduates with need received aid; of those 22% had need fully met. ***Average percent of need met:*** 75% (excluding resources awarded to replace EFC). ***Average financial aid package:*** $19,762 (excluding resources awarded to replace EFC). 38% of all full-time undergraduates had no need and received non-need-based gift aid.

GIFT AID (NEED-BASED) ***Total amount:*** $37,524,246 (8% federal, 3% state, 88% institutional, 1% external sources). ***Receiving aid:*** Freshmen: 59% (721); all full-time undergraduates: 52% (2,410). ***Average award:*** Freshmen: $17,659; Undergraduates: $15,719. ***Scholarships, grants, and awards:*** Federal Pell, FSEOG, state, private, college/university gift aid from institutional funds.

GIFT AID (NON-NEED-BASED) ***Total amount:*** $18,566,045 (98% institutional, 2% external sources). ***Receiving aid:*** Freshmen: 54% (655). Undergraduates: 49% (2,228). ***Average award:*** Freshmen: $10,426. Undergraduates: $10,500. ***Scholarships, grants, and awards by category:*** *Academic interests/achievement:* general academic interests/achievements. *Creative arts/performance:* art/fine arts, debating, general creative arts/performance, music, theater/drama. *Special achievements/activities:* community service, general special achievements/activities. *Special characteristics:* children and siblings of alumni, children of union members/company employees, first-generation college students, international students, members of minority groups, veterans, veterans' children. ***Tuition waivers:*** Full or partial for employees or children of employees.

LOANS ***Student loans:*** $27,455,917 (87% need-based, 13% non-need-based). 62% of past graduating class borrowed through all loan programs. *Average indebtedness per student:* $45,530. ***Average need-based loan:*** Freshmen: $3500. Undergraduates: $4400. ***Parent loans:*** $16,727,553 (83% need-based, 17% non-need-based). ***Programs:*** Federal Direct (Subsidized and Unsubsidized Stafford, PLUS), Perkins.

WORK-STUDY ***Federal work-study:*** Total amount: $781,185; jobs available.

ATHLETIC AWARDS Total amount: $4,151,427 (43% need-based, 57% non-need-based).

APPLYING FOR FINANCIAL AID ***Required financial aid form:*** FAFSA. ***Financial aid deadline (priority):*** 2/15. ***Notification date:*** Continuous beginning 3/1. Students must reply by 5/1.

CONTACT Eileen M. Tucker, Director of Financial Assistance, Saint Joseph's University, 5600 City Avenue, Philadelphia, PA 19131-1395, 610-660-1556 or toll-free 888-BEAHAWK (in-state). *Fax:* 610-660-1342. *E-mail:* finaid@sju.edu.

ST. LAWRENCE UNIVERSITY

Canton, NY

Tuition & fees: $41,155 **Average undergraduate aid package: $36,851**

ABOUT THE INSTITUTION Independent, coed. 41 undergraduate majors. Both federal and institutional methodology are used as a basis for awarding need-based institutional aid.

UNDERGRADUATE EXPENSES for 2010–11 ***Comprehensive fee:*** $51,770 includes full-time tuition ($40,905), mandatory fees ($250), and room and board ($10,615). ***College room only:*** $5715. Room and board charges vary according to board plan. ***Payment plan:*** Installment.

FRESHMAN FINANCIAL AID (Fall 2010, est.) 468 applied for aid; of those 88% were deemed to have need. 100% of freshmen with need received aid; of those 39% had need fully met. ***Average percent of need met:*** 91% (excluding resources awarded to replace EFC). ***Average financial aid package:*** $37,509 (excluding resources awarded to replace EFC). 17% of all full-time freshmen had no need and received non-need-based gift aid.

UNDERGRADUATE FINANCIAL AID (Fall 2010, est.) 1,640 applied for aid; of those 91% were deemed to have need. 100% of undergraduates with need received aid; of those 36% had need fully met. ***Average percent of need met:*** 89% (excluding resources awarded to replace EFC). ***Average financial aid package:*** $36,851 (excluding resources awarded to replace EFC). 16% of all full-time undergraduates had no need and received non-need-based gift aid.

GIFT AID (NEED-BASED) ***Total amount:*** $41,544,229 (7% federal, 3% state, 86% institutional, 4% external sources). ***Receiving aid:*** Freshmen: 67% (411); all full-time undergraduates: 64% (1,474). ***Average award:*** Freshmen: $29,506;

Undergraduates: $27,839. ***Scholarships, grants, and awards:*** Federal Pell, FSEOG, state, private, college/university gift aid from institutional funds, Academic Competitiveness Grants, National SMART Grants, TEACH Grants.

GIFT AID (NON-NEED-BASED) ***Total amount:*** $5,913,111 (99% institutional, 1% external sources). ***Receiving aid:*** Freshmen: 13% (81). Undergraduates: 9% (213). ***Average award:*** Freshmen: $16,015. Undergraduates: $12,672. ***Scholarships, grants, and awards by category:*** *Academic interests/achievement:* general academic interests/achievements. *Special achievements/activities:* community service, leadership. *Special characteristics:* children and siblings of alumni, siblings of current students, veterans' children. ***Tuition waivers:*** Full or partial for employees or children of employees.

LOANS ***Student loans:*** $10,253,737 (48% need-based, 52% non-need-based). 66% of past graduating class borrowed through all loan programs. *Average indebtedness per student:* $29,489. ***Average need-based loan:*** Freshmen: $3066. Undergraduates: $4199. ***Parent loans:*** $6,216,058 (100% non-need-based). ***Programs:*** Federal Direct (Subsidized and Unsubsidized Stafford, PLUS), Perkins, college/university.

WORK-STUDY ***Federal work-study:*** Total amount: $1,312,993; 835 jobs averaging $1572. ***State or other work-study/employment:*** Total amount: $475,286 (100% non-need-based). 307 part-time jobs averaging $1548.

ATHLETIC AWARDS Total amount: $1,746,853 (100% non-need-based).

APPLYING FOR FINANCIAL AID ***Required financial aid forms:*** FAFSA, CSS Financial Aid PROFILE, noncustodial (divorced/separated) parent's statement, business/farm supplement, federal income tax return(s) and W-2 forms. ***Financial aid deadline:*** 2/1. ***Notification date:*** 3/30. Students must reply by 5/1 or within 2 weeks of notification.

CONTACT Mrs. Patricia J.B. Farmer, Director of Financial Aid, St. Lawrence University, Payson Hall, 23 Romoda Drive, Canton, NY 13617-1455, 315-229-5265 or toll-free 800-285-1856. *Fax:* 315-229-7418. *E-mail:* pfarmer@stlawu.edu.

SAINT LEO UNIVERSITY

Saint Leo, FL

Tuition & fees: $18,870 **Average undergraduate aid package: $18,114**

ABOUT THE INSTITUTION Independent Roman Catholic, coed. 32 undergraduate majors. Federal methodology is used as a basis for awarding need-based institutional aid.

UNDERGRADUATE EXPENSES for 2011–12 ***Comprehensive fee:*** $27,990 includes full-time tuition ($18,200), mandatory fees ($670), and room and board ($9120). ***College room only:*** $4720. Room and board charges vary according to board plan and housing facility. ***Payment plan:*** Installment.

FRESHMAN FINANCIAL AID (Fall 2010, est.) 505 applied for aid; of those 85% were deemed to have need. 100% of freshmen with need received aid; of those 26% had need fully met. ***Average percent of need met:*** 82% (excluding resources awarded to replace EFC). ***Average financial aid package:*** $19,648 (excluding resources awarded to replace EFC). 1% of all full-time freshmen had no need and received non-need-based gift aid.

UNDERGRADUATE FINANCIAL AID (Fall 2010, est.) 1,617 applied for aid; of those 85% were deemed to have need. 100% of undergraduates with need received aid; of those 76% had need fully met. ***Average percent of need met:*** 76% (excluding resources awarded to replace EFC). ***Average financial aid package:*** $18,114 (excluding resources awarded to replace EFC). 1% of all full-time undergraduates had no need and received non-need-based gift aid.

GIFT AID (NEED-BASED) ***Total amount:*** $17,900,625 (23% federal, 20% state, 54% institutional, 3% external sources). ***Receiving aid:*** Freshmen: 79% (427); all full-time undergraduates: 76% (1,363). ***Average award:*** Freshmen: $14,306; Undergraduates: $12,653. ***Scholarships, grants, and awards:*** Federal Pell, FSEOG, state, private, college/university gift aid from institutional funds, United Negro College Fund.

GIFT AID (NON-NEED-BASED) ***Total amount:*** $1,292,236 (67% state, 17% institutional, 16% external sources). ***Receiving aid:*** Freshmen: 8% (43). Undergraduates: 6% (112). ***Average award:*** Freshmen: $17,850. Undergraduates: $8624. ***Tuition waivers:*** Full or partial for employees or children of employees.

LOANS ***Student loans:*** $12,921,121 (73% need-based, 27% non-need-based). 72% of past graduating class borrowed through all loan programs. *Average indebtedness per student:* $26,780. ***Average need-based loan:*** Freshmen: $3364. Undergraduates: $4216. ***Parent loans:*** $3,153,297 (57% need-based, 43% non-need-based). ***Programs:*** Federal Direct (Subsidized and Unsubsidized Stafford, PLUS).

WORK-STUDY ***Federal work-study:*** Total amount: $1,769,860; 550 jobs averaging $3223.

ATHLETIC AWARDS Total amount: $1,921,027 (64% need-based, 36% non-need-based).

APPLYING FOR FINANCIAL AID ***Required financial aid form:*** FAFSA. ***Financial aid deadline (priority):*** 3/1. ***Notification date:*** Continuous beginning 1/31.

CONTACT Ms. Brenda Wright, Office of Student Financial Services, Saint Leo University, PO Box 6665, MC 2228, Saint Leo, FL 33574-6665, 800-240-7658 or toll-free 800-334-5532. *Fax:* 352-588-8403. *E-mail:* finaid@saintleo.edu.

ST. LOUIS CHRISTIAN COLLEGE

Florissant, MO

Tuition & fees: $16,180 **Average undergraduate aid package: N/A**

ABOUT THE INSTITUTION Independent Christian, coed. 5 undergraduate majors. Federal methodology is used as a basis for awarding need-based institutional aid.

UNDERGRADUATE EXPENSES for 2011–12 ***Comprehensive fee:*** $25,080 includes full-time tuition ($14,880), mandatory fees ($1300), and room and board ($8900). Room and board charges vary according to housing facility. ***Part-time tuition:*** $480 per hour. ***Part-time fees:*** $325 per term.

FRESHMAN FINANCIAL AID (Fall 2009) ***Average financial aid package:*** $14,102 (excluding resources awarded to replace EFC).

GIFT AID (NEED-BASED) ***Total amount:*** $4,892,150 (15% federal, 33% state, 2% institutional, 50% external sources). ***Scholarships, grants, and awards:*** Federal Pell, FSEOG, state, private, college/university gift aid from institutional funds.

GIFT AID (NON-NEED-BASED) ***Total amount:*** $564,492 (6% institutional, 94% external sources). ***Tuition waivers:*** Full or partial for employees or children of employees.

LOANS ***Student loans:*** $1,675,047 (95% need-based, 5% non-need-based). *Average indebtedness per student:* $11,654. ***Programs:*** Federal Direct (Subsidized and Unsubsidized Stafford, PLUS), private loans.

WORK-STUDY Federal work-study jobs available. ***State or other work-study/employment:*** Part-time jobs available.

APPLYING FOR FINANCIAL AID ***Required financial aid form:*** FAFSA. ***Financial aid deadline:*** Continuous. ***Notification date:*** Continuous.

CONTACT Mrs. Catherine Wilhoit, Director of Financial Aid, St. Louis Christian College, 1360 Grandview Drive, Florissant, MO 63033-6499, 314-837-6777 Ext. 1101 or toll-free 800-887-SLCC. *Fax:* 314-837-8291.

ST. LOUIS COLLEGE OF PHARMACY

St. Louis, MO

Tuition & fees: $23,770 **Average undergraduate aid package: $13,268**

ABOUT THE INSTITUTION Independent, coed. 1 undergraduate major. Federal methodology is used as a basis for awarding need-based institutional aid.

UNDERGRADUATE EXPENSES for 2011–12 ***Comprehensive fee:*** $32,525 includes full-time tuition ($23,520), mandatory fees ($250), and room and board ($8755). ***College room only:*** $5023. Full-time tuition and fees vary according to student level. Room and board charges vary according to housing facility. ***Part-time tuition:*** $825 per credit. ***Payment plan:*** Installment.

FRESHMAN FINANCIAL AID (Fall 2010, est.) 216 applied for aid; of those 80% were deemed to have need. 99% of freshmen with need received aid; of those 12% had need fully met. ***Average percent of need met:*** 51% (excluding resources awarded to replace EFC). ***Average financial aid package:*** $13,292 (excluding resources awarded to replace EFC). 25% of all full-time freshmen had no need and received non-need-based gift aid.

UNDERGRADUATE FINANCIAL AID (Fall 2010, est.) 602 applied for aid; of those 86% were deemed to have need. 97% of undergraduates with need received aid; of those 8% had need fully met. ***Average percent of need met:*** 46% (excluding resources awarded to replace EFC). ***Average financial aid package:*** $13,268 (excluding resources awarded to replace EFC). 20% of all full-time undergraduates had no need and received non-need-based gift aid.

GIFT AID (NEED-BASED) ***Total amount:*** $4,064,814 (21% federal, 7% state, 62% institutional, 10% external sources). ***Receiving aid:*** Freshmen: 72% (171); all full-time undergraduates: 64% (441). ***Average award:*** Freshmen: $9147; Undergraduates: $9207. ***Scholarships, grants, and awards:*** Federal Pell, FSEOG, state, private, college/university gift aid from institutional funds.

GIFT AID (NON-NEED-BASED) ***Total amount:*** $964,567 (1% state, 88% institutional, 11% external sources). ***Receiving aid:*** Freshmen: 5% (13). Undergraduates: 4% (27). ***Average award:*** Freshmen: $5671. Undergraduates: $5655. ***Scholarships, grants, and awards by category:*** *Academic interests/achievement:* 555 awards ($3,328,491 total): general academic interests/achievements. *Special achievements/activities:* 36 awards ($63,020 total): community service, leadership. *Special characteristics:* children of faculty/staff, local/state students. ***Tuition waivers:*** Full or partial for employees or children of employees.

LOANS ***Student loans:*** $6,285,800 (78% need-based, 22% non-need-based). 89% of past graduating class borrowed through all loan programs. *Average indebtedness per student:* $107,649. ***Average need-based loan:*** Freshmen: $4249. Undergraduates: $5215. ***Parent loans:*** $1,486,957 (52% need-based, 48% non-need-based). ***Programs:*** Federal Direct (Subsidized and Unsubsidized Stafford, PLUS), Perkins, Health Professions Student Loans (HPSL).

WORK-STUDY ***Federal work-study:*** Total amount: $240,475; 285 jobs averaging $992.

APPLYING FOR FINANCIAL AID ***Required financial aid forms:*** FAFSA, institution's own form. ***Financial aid deadline (priority):*** 3/15. ***Notification date:*** Continuous beginning 3/15. Students must reply within 2 weeks of notification.

CONTACT Mr. Dan Stiffler, Director of Financial Aid, St. Louis College of Pharmacy, 4588 Parkview Place, St. Louis, MO 63110, 314-446-8321 or toll-free 800-278-5267 (in-state). *Fax:* 314-446-8310. *E-mail:* Daniel.Stiffler@stlcop.edu.

SAINT LOUIS UNIVERSITY

St. Louis, MO

Tuition & fees: $32,656 **Average undergraduate aid package: $22,188**

ABOUT THE INSTITUTION Independent Roman Catholic (Jesuit), coed. 82 undergraduate majors. Federal methodology is used as a basis for awarding need-based institutional aid.

UNDERGRADUATE EXPENSES for 2010–11 ***Comprehensive fee:*** $41,826 includes full-time tuition ($32,180), mandatory fees ($476), and room and board ($9170). ***College room only:*** $5150. Full-time tuition and fees vary according to location and program. Room and board charges vary according to board plan, housing facility, and location. ***Part-time tuition:*** $1125 per credit hour. ***Part-time fees:*** $142.50 per term. Part-time tuition and fees vary according to location and program. ***Payment plan:*** Installment.

FRESHMAN FINANCIAL AID (Fall 2009) 1,264 applied for aid; of those 83% were deemed to have need. 100% of freshmen with need received aid; of those 19% had need fully met. ***Average percent of need met:*** 71% (excluding resources awarded to replace EFC). ***Average financial aid package:*** $23,873 (excluding resources awarded to replace EFC). 28% of all full-time freshmen had no need and received non-need-based gift aid.

UNDERGRADUATE FINANCIAL AID (Fall 2009) 4,625 applied for aid; of those 88% were deemed to have need. 100% of undergraduates with need received aid; of those 15% had need fully met. ***Average percent of need met:*** 65% (excluding resources awarded to replace EFC). ***Average financial aid package:*** $22,188 (excluding resources awarded to replace EFC). 28% of all full-time undergraduates had no need and received non-need-based gift aid.

GIFT AID (NEED-BASED) ***Total amount:*** $66,513,640 (14% federal, 5% state, 78% institutional, 3% external sources). ***Receiving aid:*** Freshmen: 64% (1,021); all full-time undergraduates: 52% (3,808). ***Average award:*** Freshmen: $19,313; Undergraduates: $16,747. ***Scholarships, grants, and awards:*** Federal Pell, FSEOG, state, private, college/university gift aid from institutional funds, Federal Nursing.

GIFT AID (NON-NEED-BASED) ***Total amount:*** $19,815,976 (2% state, 88% institutional, 10% external sources). ***Receiving aid:*** Freshmen: 7% (115). Undergraduates: 5% (339). ***Average award:*** Freshmen: $12,270. Undergraduates: $10,227. ***Scholarships, grants, and awards by category:*** *Academic interests/achievement:* 5,000 awards ($47,192,488 total): area/ethnic studies, biological sciences, business, communication, computer science, education, engineering/technologies, English, foreign languages, general academic interests/achievements, health fields, humanities, international studies, mathematics, military science, physical sciences, premedicine, religion/biblical studies, social sciences. *Creative arts/performance:* 116 awards ($122,835 total): art/fine arts, music, performing arts, theater/drama. *Special achievements/activities:* 360 awards ($4,210,760 total): cheerleading/drum major, community service, general special achievements/activities, leadership, memberships, religious involvement. *Special characteristics:* 1,326 awards ($17,066,360 total): children of faculty/staff, first-generation college students, general special characteristics, international students, members of minority groups, previous college experience, religious affiliation, siblings of current students. ***Tuition waivers:*** Full or partial for children of alumni, employees or children of employees.

LOANS ***Student loans:*** $48,705,010 (37% need-based, 63% non-need-based). 64% of past graduating class borrowed through all loan programs. *Average indebtedness per student:* $33,734. ***Average need-based loan:*** Freshmen: $3840. Undergraduates: $5186. ***Parent loans:*** $9,851,924 (100% non-need-based). ***Programs:*** Federal Direct (Subsidized and Unsubsidized Stafford, PLUS), Perkins, Federal Nursing, college/university.

WORK-STUDY ***Federal work-study:*** Total amount: $2,057,910; 963 jobs averaging $2137. ***State or other work-study/employment:*** Total amount: $129,348 (100% non-need-based). 73 part-time jobs averaging $1772.

ATHLETIC AWARDS Total amount: $3,646,717 (43% need-based, 57% non-need-based).

APPLYING FOR FINANCIAL AID ***Required financial aid form:*** FAFSA. ***Financial aid deadline (priority):*** 3/1. ***Notification date:*** Continuous beginning 3/1. Students must reply by 5/1 or within 4 weeks of notification.

CONTACT Cari S. Wickliffe, Assistant Vice President and Director of Student Financial Services, Saint Louis University, 221 North Grand Boulevard, DuBourg Hall, Room 121, St. Louis, MO 63103-2097, 314-977-2350 or toll-free 800-758-3678 (out-of-state). *Fax:* 314-977-3437. *E-mail:* SFS@slu.edu.

SAINT LUKE'S COLLEGE OF HEALTH SCIENCES

Kansas City, MO

Tuition & fees: N/R **Average undergraduate aid package: $13,000**

ABOUT THE INSTITUTION Independent Episcopal, coed, primarily women. 1 undergraduate major. Both federal and institutional methodology are used as a basis for awarding need-based institutional aid.

UNDERGRADUATE EXPENSES for 2011–12 ***Tuition:*** part-time $387 per credit.

UNDERGRADUATE FINANCIAL AID (Fall 2010, est.) 102 applied for aid; of those 94% were deemed to have need. 100% of undergraduates with need received aid; of those 4% had need fully met. ***Average percent of need met:*** 70% (excluding resources awarded to replace EFC). ***Average financial aid package:*** $13,000 (excluding resources awarded to replace EFC). 4% of all full-time undergraduates had no need and received non-need-based gift aid.

GIFT AID (NEED-BASED) ***Total amount:*** $360,038 (26% federal, 11% state, 49% institutional, 14% external sources). ***Receiving aid:*** All full-time undergraduates: 77% (96). ***Average award:*** Undergraduates: $2000. ***Scholarships, grants, and awards:*** Federal Pell, FSEOG, state, private, college/university gift aid from institutional funds.

GIFT AID (NON-NEED-BASED) ***Total amount:*** $35,300 (100% institutional). ***Receiving aid:*** Undergraduates: 2% (2). ***Average award:*** Undergraduates: $2000.

LOANS ***Student loans:*** $1,071,323 (81% need-based, 19% non-need-based). ***Average need-based loan:*** Undergraduates: $5500. ***Parent loans:*** $85,196 (51% need-based, 49% non-need-based). ***Programs:*** Perkins, Federal Nursing, college/university.

WORK-STUDY ***Federal work-study:*** Total amount: $2186; 2 jobs averaging $1000.

CONTACT Marcia Shaw, Executive Director of Business Operations and Student Services, Saint Luke's College of Health Sciences, 8320 Ward Parkway, Suite 300, Kansas City, MO 64114, 816-932-2194. *Fax:* 816-932-9064. *E-mail:* meshaw@saint-lukes.org.

SAINT MARTIN'S UNIVERSITY

Lacey, WA

Tuition & fees: $27,621 **Average undergraduate aid package: $18,977**

ABOUT THE INSTITUTION Independent Roman Catholic, coed. 26 undergraduate majors. Federal methodology is used as a basis for awarding need-based institutional aid.

UNDERGRADUATE EXPENSES for 2011–12 ***Comprehensive fee:*** $36,581 includes full-time tuition ($27,300), mandatory fees ($321), and room and board ($8960). ***College room only:*** $4460. Full-time tuition and fees vary according to degree level and location. Room and board charges vary according to board plan. ***Part-time tuition:*** $910 per credit hour. Part-time tuition and fees vary according to course load, degree level, and location. ***Payment plan:*** Installment.

FRESHMAN FINANCIAL AID (Fall 2009) 127 applied for aid; of those 89% were deemed to have need. 100% of freshmen with need received aid; of those 29% had need fully met. ***Average percent of need met:*** 79% (excluding resources awarded to replace EFC). ***Average financial aid package:*** $20,642 (excluding resources awarded to replace EFC). 11% of all full-time freshmen had no need and received non-need-based gift aid.

UNDERGRADUATE FINANCIAL AID (Fall 2009) 975 applied for aid; of those 91% were deemed to have need. 100% of undergraduates with need received aid; of those 24% had need fully met. ***Average percent of need met:*** 77% (excluding resources awarded to replace EFC). ***Average financial aid package:*** $18,977 (excluding resources awarded to replace EFC). 12% of all full-time undergraduates had no need and received non-need-based gift aid.

GIFT AID (NEED-BASED) ***Total amount:*** $10,933,042 (19% federal, 17% state, 51% institutional, 13% external sources). ***Receiving aid:*** Freshmen: 88% (113); all full-time undergraduates: 82% (854). ***Average award:*** Freshmen: $17,280; Undergraduates: $14,385. ***Scholarships, grants, and awards:*** Federal Pell, FSEOG, state, private, college/university gift aid from institutional funds, Academic Competitiveness Grants, National SMART Grants, TEACH Grants.

GIFT AID (NON-NEED-BASED) ***Total amount:*** $1,636,334 (1% federal, 67% institutional, 32% external sources). ***Receiving aid:*** Freshmen: 21% (27). Undergraduates: 14% (142). ***Average award:*** Freshmen: $9071. Undergraduates: $6988. ***Scholarships, grants, and awards by category:*** *Academic interests/achievement:* business, education, engineering/technologies, general academic interests/achievements, humanities, international studies, premedicine. *Creative arts/performance:* music, theater/drama. *Special achievements/activities:* community service, general special achievements/activities, hobbies/interests, leadership, religious involvement. *Special characteristics:* children and siblings of alumni, children of faculty/staff, ethnic background, general special characteristics, international students, local/state students, members of minority groups, out-of-state students, siblings of current students, veterans, veterans' children. ***Tuition waivers:*** Full or partial for children of alumni, employees or children of employees.

LOANS ***Student loans:*** $8,965,259 (70% need-based, 30% non-need-based). 70% of past graduating class borrowed through all loan programs. *Average indebtedness per student:* $22,966. ***Average need-based loan:*** Freshmen: $3236. Undergraduates: $4380. ***Parent loans:*** $943,591 (32% need-based, 68% non-need-based). ***Programs:*** Federal Direct (Subsidized and Unsubsidized Stafford, PLUS), Perkins, state, college/university, private loans.

WORK-STUDY ***Federal work-study:*** Total amount: $419,952; 192 jobs averaging $1996. ***State or other work-study/employment:*** Total amount: $833,062 (99% need-based, 1% non-need-based). 193 part-time jobs averaging $4058.

ATHLETIC AWARDS Total amount: $1,227,914 (56% need-based, 44% non-need-based).

APPLYING FOR FINANCIAL AID ***Required financial aid form:*** FAFSA. ***Financial aid deadline (priority):*** 4/15. ***Notification date:*** Continuous beginning 2/15.

CONTACT Ms. Rachelle Shahan-Riehl, Director of Financial Aid, Saint Martin's University, 5300 Pacific Avenue SE, Lacey, WA 98503-7500, 360-438-4463 or toll-free 800-368-8803. *Fax:* 360-412-6190. *E-mail:* rshahanreihl@stmartin.edu.

SAINT MARY-OF-THE-WOODS COLLEGE

Saint Mary-of-the-Woods, IN

Tuition & fees: $24,500 **Average undergraduate aid package: $21,155**

ABOUT THE INSTITUTION Independent Roman Catholic, coed, primarily women. 49 undergraduate majors. Federal methodology is used as a basis for awarding need-based institutional aid.

UNDERGRADUATE EXPENSES for 2010–11 ***Comprehensive fee:*** $33,390 includes full-time tuition ($23,750), mandatory fees ($750), and room and board ($8890). ***College room only:*** $3470. Full-time tuition and fees vary according to program. ***Part-time tuition:*** $450 per credit hour. ***Part-time fees:*** $200 per year. Part-time tuition and fees vary according to program. ***Payment plan:*** Installment.

FRESHMAN FINANCIAL AID (Fall 2009) 88 applied for aid; of those 91% were deemed to have need. 100% of freshmen with need received aid; of those 41% had need fully met. ***Average percent of need met:*** 80% (excluding resources awarded to replace EFC). ***Average financial aid package:*** $18,820 (excluding resources awarded to replace EFC). 3% of all full-time freshmen had no need and received non-need-based gift aid.

UNDERGRADUATE FINANCIAL AID (Fall 2009) 540 applied for aid; of those 95% were deemed to have need. 100% of undergraduates with need received aid; of those 36% had need fully met. ***Average percent of need met:*** 80% (excluding resources awarded to replace EFC). ***Average financial aid package:*** $21,155 (excluding resources awarded to replace EFC). 2% of all full-time undergraduates had no need and received non-need-based gift aid.

GIFT AID (NEED-BASED) ***Total amount:*** $5,224,518 (37% federal, 26% state, 35% institutional, 2% external sources). ***Receiving aid:*** Freshmen: 88% (80); all full-time undergraduates: 61% (342). ***Average award:*** Freshmen: $8210; Undergraduates: $8210. ***Scholarships, grants, and awards:*** Federal Pell, FSEOG, state, private, college/university gift aid from institutional funds.

GIFT AID (NON-NEED-BASED) ***Total amount:*** $1,996,241 (100% institutional). ***Average award:*** Freshmen: $6000. Undergraduates: $6000. ***Scholarships, grants, and awards by category:*** *Academic interests/achievement:* general academic interests/achievements. *Creative arts/performance:* applied art and design, art/fine arts, creative writing, dance, general creative arts/performance, journalism/publications, music, performing arts, theater/drama. *Special achievements/activities:* community service, general special achievements/activities, leadership, memberships, religious involvement. *Special characteristics:* adult students, children and siblings of alumni, children of current students, children of faculty/staff, ethnic background, first-generation college students, general special characteristics, international students, local/state students, members of minority groups, out-of-state students, parents of current students, religious affiliation, siblings of current students, spouses of current students. ***Tuition waivers:*** Full or partial for employees or children of employees.

LOANS ***Student loans:*** $6,715,084 (51% need-based, 49% non-need-based). 78% of past graduating class borrowed through all loan programs. *Average indebtedness per student:* $35,223. ***Average need-based loan:*** Freshmen: $2245. Undergraduates: $2245. ***Parent loans:*** $528,574 (100% need-based). ***Programs:*** Federal Direct (Subsidized and Unsubsidized Stafford, PLUS), Perkins, college/university, Sallie Mae Signature Loans.

WORK-STUDY ***Federal work-study:*** Total amount: $91,882; 104 jobs averaging $883.

ATHLETIC AWARDS Total amount: $392,925 (100% non-need-based).

APPLYING FOR FINANCIAL AID ***Required financial aid form:*** FAFSA. ***Financial aid deadline:*** Continuous. ***Notification date:*** Continuous beginning 3/1. Students must reply by 5/1.

CONTACT Ms. Darla Hopper, Director of Financial Aid, Saint Mary-of-the-Woods College, 106 Guerin Hall, Saint Mary-of-the-Woods, IN 47876, 812-535-5110 or toll-free 800-926-SMWC. *Fax:* 812-535-4900. *E-mail:* jbenton@smwc.edu.

SAINT MARY'S COLLEGE

Notre Dame, IN

Tuition & fees: $31,020 **Average undergraduate aid package: $23,739**

ABOUT THE INSTITUTION Independent Roman Catholic, women only. 36 undergraduate majors. Both federal and institutional methodology are used as a basis for awarding need-based institutional aid.

UNDERGRADUATE EXPENSES for 2010–11 ***Comprehensive fee:*** $40,500 includes full-time tuition ($30,360), mandatory fees ($660), and room and board ($9480). ***College room only:*** $5840. Room and board charges vary according to board plan and housing facility. ***Part-time tuition:*** $1200 per credit hour. ***Part-time fees:*** $330 per term. ***Payment plan:*** Installment.

FRESHMAN FINANCIAL AID (Fall 2010, est.) 281 applied for aid; of those 84% were deemed to have need. 100% of freshmen with need received aid; of those 21% had need fully met. ***Average percent of need met:*** 81% (excluding resources awarded to replace EFC). ***Average financial aid package:*** $25,037 (excluding resources awarded to replace EFC). 24% of all full-time freshmen had no need and received non-need-based gift aid.

UNDERGRADUATE FINANCIAL AID (Fall 2010, est.) 1,168 applied for aid; of those 94% were deemed to have need. 100% of undergraduates with need received aid; of those 14% had need fully met. ***Average percent of need met:*** 69% (excluding resources awarded to replace EFC). ***Average financial aid***

package: $23,739 (excluding resources awarded to replace EFC). 23% of all full-time undergraduates had no need and received non-need-based gift aid.

GIFT AID (NEED-BASED) ***Total amount:*** $18,902,057 (9% federal, 4% state, 83% institutional, 4% external sources). ***Receiving aid:*** Freshmen: 68% (225); all full-time undergraduates: 66% (1,023). ***Average award:*** Freshmen: $19,978; Undergraduates: $18,255. ***Scholarships, grants, and awards:*** Federal Pell, FSEOG, state, private, college/university gift aid from institutional funds.

GIFT AID (NON-NEED-BASED) ***Total amount:*** $3,675,714 (1% federal, 97% institutional, 2% external sources). ***Receiving aid:*** Freshmen: 65% (218). Undergraduates: 59% (903). ***Average award:*** Freshmen: $10,479. Undergraduates: $10,341. ***Tuition waivers:*** Full or partial for employees or children of employees.

LOANS ***Student loans:*** $8,549,540 (95% need-based, 5% non-need-based). 67% of past graduating class borrowed through all loan programs. *Average indebtedness per student:* $28,838. ***Average need-based loan:*** Freshmen: $3582. Undergraduates: $4691. ***Parent loans:*** $3,596,728 (92% need-based, 8% non-need-based). ***Programs:*** Federal Direct (Subsidized and Unsubsidized Stafford, PLUS), Perkins.

WORK-STUDY ***Federal work-study:*** Total amount: $1,090,325; jobs available. ***State or other work-study/employment:*** Total amount: $2000 (100% non-need-based). Part-time jobs available.

APPLYING FOR FINANCIAL AID ***Required financial aid forms:*** FAFSA, CSS Financial Aid PROFILE, noncustodial (divorced/separated) parent's statement. ***Financial aid deadline:*** 3/1 (priority: 3/1). ***Notification date:*** Continuous beginning 3/15. Students must reply within 3 weeks of notification.

CONTACT Kathleen M. Brown, Director of Financial Aid, Saint Mary's College, 141 Le Mans Hall, Notre Dame, IN 46556, 574-284-4557 or toll-free 800-551-7621. *Fax:* 574-284-4818. *E-mail:* kbrown@saintmarys.edu.

SAINT MARY'S COLLEGE OF CALIFORNIA

Moraga, CA

Tuition & fees: $35,430 **Average undergraduate aid package: $27,954**

ABOUT THE INSTITUTION Independent Roman Catholic, coed. 68 undergraduate majors. Federal methodology is used as a basis for awarding need-based institutional aid.

UNDERGRADUATE EXPENSES for 2010–11 ***Comprehensive fee:*** $47,780 includes full-time tuition ($35,280), mandatory fees ($150), and room and board ($12,350). ***College room only:*** $6770. Room and board charges vary according to board plan and housing facility. ***Part-time tuition:*** $4412 per course. Part-time tuition and fees vary according to program. ***Payment plan:*** Installment.

FRESHMAN FINANCIAL AID (Fall 2010, est.) 650 applied for aid; of those 93% were deemed to have need. 97% of freshmen with need received aid; of those 7% had need fully met. ***Average percent of need met:*** 81% (excluding resources awarded to replace EFC). ***Average financial aid package:*** $29,365 (excluding resources awarded to replace EFC). 8% of all full-time freshmen had no need and received non-need-based gift aid.

UNDERGRADUATE FINANCIAL AID (Fall 2010, est.) 2,190 applied for aid; of those 92% were deemed to have need. 97% of undergraduates with need received aid; of those 9% had need fully met. ***Average percent of need met:*** 72% (excluding resources awarded to replace EFC). ***Average financial aid package:*** $27,954 (excluding resources awarded to replace EFC). 5% of all full-time undergraduates had no need and received non-need-based gift aid.

GIFT AID (NEED-BASED) ***Total amount:*** $40,904,209 (10% federal, 15% state, 72% institutional, 3% external sources). ***Receiving aid:*** Freshmen: 74% (512); all full-time undergraduates: 64% (1,685). ***Average award:*** Freshmen: $20,980; Undergraduates: $20,676. ***Scholarships, grants, and awards:*** Federal Pell, FSEOG, state, private, college/university gift aid from institutional funds.

GIFT AID (NON-NEED-BASED) ***Total amount:*** $1,907,438 (96% institutional, 4% external sources). ***Receiving aid:*** Freshmen: 37% (257). Undergraduates: 21% (554). ***Average award:*** Freshmen: $13,314. Undergraduates: $13,552. ***Scholarships, grants, and awards by category:*** *Academic interests/achievement:* 434 awards ($5,108,851 total): general academic interests/achievements. *Creative arts/performance:* 24 awards ($288,000 total): dance, music, performing arts, theater/drama. *Special achievements/activities:* 116 awards ($1,049,820 total): leadership, memberships. *Special characteristics:* 65 awards ($1,787,762 total): children and siblings of alumni, children of educators, children of faculty/staff, general special characteristics, relatives of clergy, veterans, veterans' children. ***Tuition waivers:*** Full or partial for employees or children of employees.

LOANS ***Student loans:*** $17,294,156 (93% need-based, 7% non-need-based). 52% of past graduating class borrowed through all loan programs. *Average indebtedness per student:* $36,745. ***Average need-based loan:*** Freshmen: $3780. Undergraduates: $4576. ***Parent loans:*** $8,026,285 (89% need-based, 11% non-need-based). ***Programs:*** Federal Direct (Subsidized and Unsubsidized Stafford, PLUS), Perkins.

WORK-STUDY ***Federal work-study:*** Total amount: $942,152; 528 jobs averaging $1784.

ATHLETIC AWARDS Total amount: $5,093,883 (42% need-based, 58% non-need-based).

APPLYING FOR FINANCIAL AID ***Required financial aid forms:*** FAFSA, state aid form. ***Financial aid deadline (priority):*** 2/15. ***Notification date:*** Continuous beginning 3/15. Students must reply by 5/1 or within 2 weeks of notification.

CONTACT Priscilla Muha, Director of Financial Aid, Saint Mary's College of California, PO Box 4530, Moraga, CA 94575, 925-631-4370 or toll-free 800-800-4SMC. *Fax:* 925-376-2965. *E-mail:* finaid@stmarys-ca.edu.

ST. MARY'S COLLEGE OF MARYLAND

St. Mary's City, MD

Tuition & fees (MD res): $13,630 **Average undergraduate aid package: $13,093**

ABOUT THE INSTITUTION State-supported, coed. 24 undergraduate majors. Federal methodology is used as a basis for awarding need-based institutional aid.

UNDERGRADUATE EXPENSES for 2010–11 ***Tuition, state resident:*** full-time $11,325; part-time $185 per credit hour. ***Tuition, nonresident:*** full-time $22,718; part-time $185 per credit hour. ***Required fees:*** full-time $2305. Full-time tuition and fees vary according to course load. Part-time tuition and fees vary according to course load. ***College room and board:*** $10,250; ***Room only:*** $5745. Room and board charges vary according to board plan and housing facility. ***Payment plan:*** Installment.

FRESHMAN FINANCIAL AID (Fall 2009) 407 applied for aid; of those 51% were deemed to have need. 100% of freshmen with need received aid; of those 3% had need fully met. ***Average percent of need met:*** 44% (excluding resources awarded to replace EFC). ***Average financial aid package:*** $11,675 (excluding resources awarded to replace EFC). 26% of all full-time freshmen had no need and received non-need-based gift aid.

UNDERGRADUATE FINANCIAL AID (Fall 2009) 1,341 applied for aid; of those 64% were deemed to have need. 100% of undergraduates with need received aid; of those 4% had need fully met. ***Average percent of need met:*** 49% (excluding resources awarded to replace EFC). ***Average financial aid package:*** $13,093 (excluding resources awarded to replace EFC). 25% of all full-time undergraduates had no need and received non-need-based gift aid.

GIFT AID (NEED-BASED) ***Total amount:*** $6,146,418 (19% federal, 18% state, 57% institutional, 6% external sources). ***Receiving aid:*** Freshmen: 40% (204); all full-time undergraduates: 42% (858). ***Average award:*** Freshmen: $8144; Undergraduates: $8664. ***Scholarships, grants, and awards:*** Federal Pell, FSEOG, state, private, college/university gift aid from institutional funds.

GIFT AID (NON-NEED-BASED) ***Total amount:*** $2,827,509 (15% state, 75% institutional, 10% external sources). ***Receiving aid:*** Freshmen: 7% (36). Undergraduates: 5% (108). ***Average award:*** Freshmen: $3744. Undergraduates: $3579. ***Scholarships, grants, and awards by category:*** *Academic interests/achievement:* 499 awards ($2,120,887 total): general academic interests/achievements. *Special characteristics:* 48 awards ($433,826 total): children and siblings of alumni, children of faculty/staff. ***Tuition waivers:*** Full or partial for employees or children of employees, senior citizens.

LOANS ***Student loans:*** $5,539,884 (72% need-based, 28% non-need-based). 70% of past graduating class borrowed through all loan programs. *Average indebtedness per student:* $17,505. ***Average need-based loan:*** Freshmen: $2445. Undergraduates: $3001. ***Parent loans:*** $4,901,243 (60% need-based, 40% non-need-based). ***Programs:*** Federal Direct (Subsidized and Unsubsidized Stafford, PLUS), Perkins.

WORK-STUDY ***Federal work-study:*** Total amount: $61,765; 120 jobs averaging $514. ***State or other work-study/employment:*** Part-time jobs available.

APPLYING FOR FINANCIAL AID ***Required financial aid form:*** FAFSA. ***Financial aid deadline:*** 2/28 (priority: 2/28). ***Notification date:*** 4/1. Students must reply by 5/1.

CONTACT Ms. Caroline Bright, Director of Financial Aid, St. Mary's College of Maryland, 18952 East Fisher Road, St. Mary's City, MD 20686-3001, 240-895-3000 or toll-free 800-492-7181. *Fax:* 240-895-4959. *E-mail:* cobright@smcm.edu.

ST. MARY'S UNIVERSITY

San Antonio, TX

ABOUT THE INSTITUTION Independent Roman Catholic, coed. 39 undergraduate majors.

GIFT AID (NEED-BASED) ***Scholarships, grants, and awards:*** Federal Pell, FSEOG, state, private, college/university gift aid from institutional funds.

GIFT AID (NON-NEED-BASED) ***Scholarships, grants, and awards by category:*** *Academic interests/achievement:* general academic interests/achievements, military science. *Creative arts/performance:* music. *Special achievements/activities:* cheerleading/drum major.

LOANS ***Programs:*** Perkins, state, alternative loans.

WORK-STUDY ***Federal work-study:*** Total amount: $1,888,839; jobs available. ***State or other work-study/employment:*** Total amount: $452,301 (61% need-based, 39% non-need-based). Part-time jobs available.

APPLYING FOR FINANCIAL AID ***Required financial aid form:*** FAFSA.

CONTACT Mr. David R. Krause, Director of Financial Assistance, St. Mary's University, One Camino Santa Maria, San Antonio, TX 78228-8541, 210-436-3141 or toll-free 800-FOR-STMU. *Fax:* 210-431-2221. *E-mail:* dkrause@alvin.stmarytx.edu.

SAINT MARY'S UNIVERSITY OF MINNESOTA

Winona, MN

Tuition & fees: $27,250 **Average undergraduate aid package: $19,789**

ABOUT THE INSTITUTION Independent Roman Catholic, coed. 58 undergraduate majors. Federal methodology is used as a basis for awarding need-based institutional aid.

UNDERGRADUATE EXPENSES for 2011–12 ***Comprehensive fee:*** $34,400 includes full-time tuition ($26,750), mandatory fees ($500), and room and board ($7150). ***College room only:*** $4000. Full-time tuition and fees vary according to course load, degree level, location, and program. Room and board charges vary according to housing facility. ***Part-time tuition:*** $895 per credit. ***Part-time fees:*** $500 per year. Part-time tuition and fees vary according to course load, degree level, location, and program. ***Payment plan:*** Installment.

FRESHMAN FINANCIAL AID (Fall 2010, est.) 304 applied for aid; of those 91% were deemed to have need. 100% of freshmen with need received aid; of those 20% had need fully met. ***Average percent of need met:*** 84% (excluding resources awarded to replace EFC). ***Average financial aid package:*** $22,436 (excluding resources awarded to replace EFC). 20% of all full-time freshmen had no need and received non-need-based gift aid.

UNDERGRADUATE FINANCIAL AID (Fall 2010, est.) 1,178 applied for aid; of those 92% were deemed to have need. 100% of undergraduates with need received aid; of those 18% had need fully met. ***Average percent of need met:*** 74% (excluding resources awarded to replace EFC). ***Average financial aid package:*** $19,789 (excluding resources awarded to replace EFC). 20% of all full-time undergraduates had no need and received non-need-based gift aid.

GIFT AID (NEED-BASED) ***Total amount:*** $18,398,266 (13% federal, 5% state, 80% institutional, 2% external sources). ***Receiving aid:*** Freshmen: 79% (273); all full-time undergraduates: 74% (1,042). ***Average award:*** Freshmen: $17,553; Undergraduates: $15,796. ***Scholarships, grants, and awards:*** Federal Pell, FSEOG, state, college/university gift aid from institutional funds.

GIFT AID (NON-NEED-BASED) ***Average award:*** Freshmen: $10,391. Undergraduates: $10,244. ***Scholarships, grants, and awards by category:*** *Academic interests/achievement:* 631 awards ($3,403,250 total): general academic interests/achievements. *Creative arts/performance:* 114 awards ($160,000 total): art/fine arts, music, theater/drama. *Special achievements/activities:* 118 awards ($574,275 total): leadership. *Special characteristics:* 287 awards ($2,292,188 total): children and siblings of alumni, children of faculty/staff, international students, members of minority groups. ***Tuition waivers:*** Full or partial for employees or children of employees.

LOANS ***Student loans:*** $11,203,235 (100% need-based). 75% of past graduating class borrowed through all loan programs. *Average indebtedness per student:* $30,237. ***Average need-based loan:*** Freshmen: $3689. Undergraduates: $4573. ***Parent loans:*** $1,295,693 (100% need-based). ***Programs:*** Federal Direct (Subsidized and Unsubsidized Stafford, PLUS), Perkins, state.

WORK-STUDY ***Federal work-study:*** Total amount: $322,200; 185 jobs averaging $1651. ***State or other work-study/employment:*** Total amount: $642,677 (100% need-based). 347 part-time jobs averaging $1698.

APPLYING FOR FINANCIAL AID ***Required financial aid form:*** FAFSA. ***Financial aid deadline (priority):*** 3/15. ***Notification date:*** Continuous beginning 2/1. Students must reply within 3 weeks of notification.

CONTACT Ms. Jayne P. Wobig, Director of Financial Aid, Saint Mary's University of Minnesota, 700 Terrace Heights, #5, Winona, MN 55987-1399, 507-457-1437 or toll-free 800-635-5987. *Fax:* 507-457-6698. *E-mail:* jwobig@smumn.edu.

SAINT MICHAEL'S COLLEGE

Colchester, VT

Tuition & fees: $36,240 **Average undergraduate aid package: $23,468**

ABOUT THE INSTITUTION Independent Roman Catholic, coed. 38 undergraduate majors. Federal methodology is used as a basis for awarding need-based institutional aid.

UNDERGRADUATE EXPENSES for 2011–12 ***Comprehensive fee:*** $45,270 includes full-time tuition ($35,940), mandatory fees ($300), and room and board ($9030). Room and board charges vary according to housing facility. ***Part-time tuition:*** $1200 per credit. ***Payment plan:*** Installment.

FRESHMAN FINANCIAL AID (Fall 2010, est.) 466 applied for aid; of those 88% were deemed to have need. 100% of freshmen with need received aid; of those 29% had need fully met. ***Average percent of need met:*** 80% (excluding resources awarded to replace EFC). ***Average financial aid package:*** $25,540 (excluding resources awarded to replace EFC). 24% of all full-time freshmen had no need and received non-need-based gift aid.

UNDERGRADUATE FINANCIAL AID (Fall 2010, est.) 1,344 applied for aid; of those 86% were deemed to have need. 100% of undergraduates with need received aid; of those 28% had need fully met. ***Average percent of need met:*** 77% (excluding resources awarded to replace EFC). ***Average financial aid package:*** $23,468 (excluding resources awarded to replace EFC). 28% of all full-time undergraduates had no need and received non-need-based gift aid.

GIFT AID (NEED-BASED) ***Total amount:*** $19,157,956 (9% federal, 3% state, 85% institutional, 3% external sources). ***Receiving aid:*** Freshmen: 74% (403); all full-time undergraduates: 61% (1,126). ***Average award:*** Freshmen: $18,084; Undergraduates: $16,639. ***Scholarships, grants, and awards:*** Federal Pell, FSEOG, state, private, college/university gift aid from institutional funds.

GIFT AID (NON-NEED-BASED) ***Total amount:*** $6,682,668 (97% institutional, 3% external sources). ***Receiving aid:*** Freshmen: 15% (82). Undergraduates: 11% (210). ***Average award:*** Freshmen: $11,872. Undergraduates: $9960. ***Scholarships, grants, and awards by category:*** *Academic interests/achievement:* general academic interests/achievements. *Creative arts/performance:* art/fine arts. *Special characteristics:* local/state students, members of minority groups, out-of-state students, religious affiliation, siblings of current students. ***Tuition waivers:*** Full or partial for employees or children of employees.

LOANS ***Student loans:*** $12,046,877 (59% need-based, 41% non-need-based). 78% of past graduating class borrowed through all loan programs. *Average indebtedness per student:* $29,410. ***Average need-based loan:*** Freshmen: $4700. Undergraduates: $5193. ***Parent loans:*** $4,887,745 (30% need-based, 70% non-need-based). ***Programs:*** Federal Direct (Subsidized and Unsubsidized Stafford, PLUS), Perkins.

WORK-STUDY ***Federal work-study:*** Total amount: $668,000; jobs available. ***State or other work-study/employment:*** Total amount: $332,281 (89% need-based, 11% non-need-based). Part-time jobs available.

ATHLETIC AWARDS Total amount: $870,760 (87% need-based, 13% non-need-based).

APPLYING FOR FINANCIAL AID ***Required financial aid forms:*** FAFSA, federal income tax forms (student and parent). ***Financial aid deadline (priority):*** 2/15. ***Notification date:*** 4/1. Students must reply by 5/1 or within 2 weeks of notification.

CONTACT Mrs. Nelberta B. Lunde, Director of Student Aid and Scholarships, Saint Michael's College, Winooski Park, Colchester, VT 05439, 802-654-3243 or toll-free 800-762-8000. *Fax:* 802-654-2591. *E-mail:* finaid@smcvt.edu.

ST. NORBERT COLLEGE

De Pere, WI

Tuition & fees: $28,043 **Average undergraduate aid package: $20,341**

ABOUT THE INSTITUTION Independent Roman Catholic, coed. 31 undergraduate majors. Federal methodology is used as a basis for awarding need-based institutional aid.

UNDERGRADUATE EXPENSES for 2010–11 ***Comprehensive fee:*** $35,392 includes full-time tuition ($27,583), mandatory fees ($460), and room and board ($7349). ***College room only:*** $3854. Full-time tuition and fees vary according to course load. Room and board charges vary according to board plan, housing facility, and student level. ***Part-time tuition:*** $862 per credit. Part-time tuition and fees vary according to course load. ***Payment plans:*** Installment, deferred payment.

FRESHMAN FINANCIAL AID (Fall 2009) 471 applied for aid; of those 82% were deemed to have need. 100% of freshmen with need received aid; of those 41% had need fully met. ***Average percent of need met:*** 89% (excluding resources awarded to replace EFC). ***Average financial aid package:*** $20,583 (excluding resources awarded to replace EFC). 27% of all full-time freshmen had no need and received non-need-based gift aid.

UNDERGRADUATE FINANCIAL AID (Fall 2009) 1,617 applied for aid; of those 85% were deemed to have need. 100% of undergraduates with need received aid; of those 40% had need fully met. ***Average percent of need met:*** 87% (excluding resources awarded to replace EFC). ***Average financial aid package:*** $20,341 (excluding resources awarded to replace EFC). 29% of all full-time undergraduates had no need and received non-need-based gift aid.

GIFT AID (NEED-BASED) ***Total amount:*** $20,873,594 (10% federal, 7% state, 78% institutional, 5% external sources). ***Receiving aid:*** Freshmen: 69% (375); all full-time undergraduates: 66% (1,338). ***Average award:*** Freshmen: $16,926; Undergraduates: $15,113. ***Scholarships, grants, and awards:*** Federal Pell, FSEOG, state, private, college/university gift aid from institutional funds.

GIFT AID (NON-NEED-BASED) ***Total amount:*** $5,578,992 (91% institutional, 9% external sources). ***Receiving aid:*** Freshmen: 3% (16). Undergraduates: 2% (47). ***Average award:*** Freshmen: $10,448. Undergraduates: $8957. ***Scholarships, grants, and awards by category:*** *Academic interests/achievement:* 1,736 awards ($14,275,060 total): general academic interests/achievements. *Creative arts/performance:* 78 awards ($92,800 total): art/fine arts, music, theater/drama. *Special characteristics:* 188 awards ($3,292,250 total): children of faculty/staff, international students. ***Tuition waivers:*** Full or partial for employees or children of employees.

LOANS ***Student loans:*** $14,162,772 (91% need-based, 9% non-need-based). 65% of past graduating class borrowed through all loan programs. *Average indebtedness per student:* $29,836. ***Average need-based loan:*** Freshmen: $3443. Undergraduates: $4613. ***Parent loans:*** $3,339,522 (79% need-based, 21% non-need-based). ***Programs:*** Federal Direct (Subsidized and Unsubsidized Stafford, PLUS), Perkins, state, college/university.

WORK-STUDY ***Federal work-study:*** Total amount: $770,487; 331 jobs averaging $1223. ***State or other work-study/employment:*** Total amount: $1,902,862 (58% need-based, 42% non-need-based). 670 part-time jobs averaging $1225.

APPLYING FOR FINANCIAL AID ***Required financial aid form:*** FAFSA. ***Financial aid deadline (priority):*** 3/1. ***Notification date:*** Continuous beginning 3/15. Students must reply within 2 weeks of notification.

CONTACT Mr. Jeffrey A. Zahn, Director of Financial Aid, St. Norbert College, 100 Grant Street, De Pere, WI 54115-2099, 920-403-3071 or toll-free 800-236-4878. *Fax:* 920-403-3062. *E-mail:* jeff.zahn@snc.edu.

ST. OLAF COLLEGE

Northfield, MN

Tuition & fees: $36,800 **Average undergraduate aid package: $27,866**

ABOUT THE INSTITUTION Independent Lutheran, coed. 44 undergraduate majors. Both federal and institutional methodology are used as a basis for awarding need-based institutional aid.

UNDERGRADUATE EXPENSES for 2010–11 ***Comprehensive fee:*** $45,300 includes full-time tuition ($36,800) and room and board ($8500). ***College room only:*** $3950. Full-time tuition and fees vary according to course load. Room and board charges vary according to board plan and housing facility. ***Part-time tuition:*** $1150 per credit hour. Part-time tuition and fees vary according to course load. ***Payment plan:*** Installment.

FRESHMAN FINANCIAL AID (Fall 2010, est.) 680 applied for aid; of those 82% were deemed to have need. 100% of freshmen with need received aid; of those 100% had need fully met. ***Average percent of need met:*** 100% (excluding resources awarded to replace EFC). ***Average financial aid package:*** $29,494 (excluding resources awarded to replace EFC). 21% of all full-time freshmen had no need and received non-need-based gift aid.

UNDERGRADUATE FINANCIAL AID (Fall 2010, est.) 2,391 applied for aid; of those 88% were deemed to have need. 100% of undergraduates with need received aid; of those 100% had need fully met. ***Average percent of need met:*** 100% (excluding resources awarded to replace EFC). ***Average financial aid package:*** $27,866 (excluding resources awarded to replace EFC). 17% of all full-time undergraduates had no need and received non-need-based gift aid.

GIFT AID (NEED-BASED) ***Total amount:*** $48,078,932 (6% federal, 3% state, 87% institutional, 4% external sources). ***Receiving aid:*** Freshmen: 66% (556); all full-time undergraduates: 68% (2,104). ***Average award:*** Freshmen: $26,848; Undergraduates: $23,711. ***Scholarships, grants, and awards:*** Federal Pell, FSEOG, state, private, college/university gift aid from institutional funds, Federal Nursing.

GIFT AID (NON-NEED-BASED) ***Total amount:*** $5,840,599 (1% state, 92% institutional, 7% external sources). ***Receiving aid:*** Freshmen: 21% (178). Undergraduates: 17% (521). ***Average award:*** Freshmen: $11,382. Undergraduates: $9951. ***Scholarships, grants, and awards by category:*** *Academic interests/achievement:* 1,664 awards ($19,376,087 total): general academic interests/achievements. *Creative arts/performance:* 309 awards ($1,647,500 total): music. *Special achievements/activities:* 204 awards ($1,121,150 total): community service, religious involvement. *Special characteristics:* 75 awards ($2,001,790 total): international students. ***Tuition waivers:*** Full or partial for employees or children of employees, senior citizens.

LOANS ***Student loans:*** $13,572,638 (65% need-based, 35% non-need-based). 65% of past graduating class borrowed through all loan programs. *Average indebtedness per student:* $26,115. ***Average need-based loan:*** Freshmen: $3537. Undergraduates: $4814. ***Parent loans:*** $4,516,262 (100% non-need-based). ***Programs:*** Federal Direct (Subsidized and Unsubsidized Stafford, PLUS), Perkins, Federal Nursing, state, college/university.

WORK-STUDY ***Federal work-study:*** Total amount: $1,976,464; 990 jobs averaging $1996. ***State or other work-study/employment:*** Total amount: $2,093,770 (86% need-based, 14% non-need-based). 1,162 part-time jobs averaging $1750.

APPLYING FOR FINANCIAL AID ***Required financial aid forms:*** FAFSA, CSS Financial Aid PROFILE, noncustodial (divorced/separated) parent's statement, business/farm supplement. ***Financial aid deadline:*** 3/1 (priority: 2/1). ***Notification date:*** 3/22. Students must reply by 5/1.

CONTACT Ms. Katharine Ruby, Assistant Vice President of Enrollment and Dean of Student Financial Aid, St. Olaf College, 1520 Saint Olaf Avenue, Northfield, MN 55057-1098, 507-786-3019 or toll-free 800-800-3025. *Fax:* 507-786-6688. *E-mail:* ruby@stolaf.edu.

SAINT PAUL'S COLLEGE

Lawrenceville, VA

ABOUT THE INSTITUTION Independent Episcopal, coed. 13 undergraduate majors.

GIFT AID (NEED-BASED) ***Scholarships, grants, and awards:*** Federal Pell, FSEOG, state, private, college/university gift aid from institutional funds, United Negro College Fund.

GIFT AID (NON-NEED-BASED) ***Scholarships, grants, and awards by category:*** *Academic interests/achievement:* general academic interests/achievements. *Special achievements/activities:* general special achievements/activities. *Special characteristics:* children and siblings of alumni, children of faculty/staff, children of union members/company employees.

LOANS ***Programs:*** Federal Direct (Subsidized and Unsubsidized Stafford, PLUS), Perkins.

WORK-STUDY ***Federal work-study:*** Total amount: $273,276; jobs available.

APPLYING FOR FINANCIAL AID ***Required financial aid form:*** FAFSA.

CONTACT Ms. Joan Mayo, Financial Aid Assistant, Saint Paul's College, 115 College Drive, Lawrenceville, VA 23868-1202, 434-848-6496 or toll-free 800-678-7071. *Fax:* 434-848-6498. *E-mail:* aid@saintpauls.edu.

ST. PETERSBURG COLLEGE

St. Petersburg, FL

CONTACT Financial Aid Office, St. Petersburg College, PO Box 13489, St. Petersburg, FL 33733-3489, 727-341-3600.

SAINT PETER'S COLLEGE

Jersey City, NJ

CONTACT Jennifer Ragsdale, Acting Director of Financial Aid, Saint Peter's College, 2641 Kennedy Boulevard, Jersey City, NJ 07306, 201-761-6071 or toll-free 888-SPC-9933. *Fax:* 201-761-6073. *E-mail:* jragsdale@spc.edu.

ST. THOMAS AQUINAS COLLEGE

Sparkill, NY

Tuition & fees: $22,410 **Average undergraduate aid package: N/A**

ABOUT THE INSTITUTION Independent, coed. 38 undergraduate majors. Both federal and institutional methodology are used as a basis for awarding need-based institutional aid.

UNDERGRADUATE EXPENSES for 2010–11 ***Comprehensive fee:*** $32,710 includes full-time tuition ($21,910), mandatory fees ($500), and room and board ($10,300). Room and board charges vary according to board plan and housing facility. ***Part-time tuition:*** $705 per credit hour. ***Part-time fees:*** $125 per term. ***Payment plan:*** Installment.

GIFT AID (NEED-BASED) ***Total amount:*** $4,033,431 (43% federal, 34% state, 22% institutional, 1% external sources). ***Scholarships, grants, and awards:*** Federal Pell, FSEOG, state, private, college/university gift aid from institutional funds.

GIFT AID (NON-NEED-BASED) ***Total amount:*** $4,670,000 (100% institutional). ***Scholarships, grants, and awards by category:*** *Academic interests/achievement:* business, communication, education, general academic interests/achievements, humanities, mathematics, social sciences. *Special achievements/activities:* community service, leadership. *Special characteristics:* siblings of current students, spouses of current students, twins. ***Tuition waivers:*** Full or partial for employees or children of employees.

LOANS ***Programs:*** Perkins.

WORK-STUDY Federal work-study jobs available.

APPLYING FOR FINANCIAL AID ***Required financial aid forms:*** FAFSA, state aid form. ***Financial aid deadline (priority):*** 2/15. ***Notification date:*** Continuous beginning 3/1. Students must reply by 5/1 or within 2 weeks of notification.

CONTACT Anna Maria Chrissotimos, Director of Financial Aid, St. Thomas Aquinas College, 125 Route 340, Sparkill, NY 10976, 845-398-4098 or toll-free 800-999-STAC. *Fax:* 845-398-4114. *E-mail:* achrisso@stac.edu.

ST. THOMAS UNIVERSITY

Miami Gardens, FL

Tuition & fees: $22,770 **Average undergraduate aid package: N/A**

ABOUT THE INSTITUTION Independent Roman Catholic, coed. 36 undergraduate majors. Federal methodology is used as a basis for awarding need-based institutional aid.

UNDERGRADUATE EXPENSES for 2010–11 ***Comprehensive fee:*** $29,612 includes full-time tuition ($22,770) and room and board ($6842). Full-time tuition and fees vary according to program. Room and board charges vary according to board plan and housing facility. ***Part-time tuition:*** $455 per credit hour. ***Payment plan:*** Installment.

FRESHMAN FINANCIAL AID (Fall 2010, est.) 242 applied for aid; of those 93% were deemed to have need. 100% of freshmen with need received aid; of those 4% had need fully met. 15% of all full-time freshmen had no need and received non-need-based gift aid.

UNDERGRADUATE FINANCIAL AID (Fall 2010, est.) 935 applied for aid; of those 85% were deemed to have need. 100% of undergraduates with need received aid; of those 9% had need fully met. 16% of all full-time undergraduates had no need and received non-need-based gift aid.

GIFT AID (NEED-BASED) ***Total amount:*** $14,565,901 (19% federal, 16% state, 64% institutional, 1% external sources). ***Receiving aid:*** Freshmen: 63% (168); all full-time undergraduates: 55% (585). ***Average award:*** Freshmen: $2310; Undergraduates: $2664. ***Scholarships, grants, and awards:*** Federal Pell, FSEOG, state, private, college/university gift aid from institutional funds.

GIFT AID (NON-NEED-BASED) ***Receiving aid:*** Freshmen: 50% (135). Undergraduates: 45% (477). ***Average award:*** Freshmen: $11,236. Undergraduates: $8134. ***Scholarships, grants, and awards by category:*** *Academic interests/achievement:* general academic interests/achievements. *Special achievements/activities:* leadership. ***Tuition waivers:*** Full or partial for minority students, children of alumni, employees or children of employees.

LOANS ***Student loans:*** $10,985,382 (100% need-based). ***Average need-based loan:*** Freshmen: $3704. Undergraduates: $4182. ***Parent loans:*** $530,918 (100% need-based). ***Programs:*** Federal Direct (Subsidized and Unsubsidized Stafford, PLUS), Perkins.

WORK-STUDY ***Federal work-study:*** Total amount: $516,138; jobs available.

ATHLETIC AWARDS Total amount: $1,099,268 (100% need-based).

APPLYING FOR FINANCIAL AID ***Required financial aid form:*** FAFSA. ***Financial aid deadline (priority):*** 4/1. ***Notification date:*** Continuous beginning 3/1.

CONTACT Ms. Anh Do, Director of Financial Aid, St. Thomas University, 16401 Northwest 37th Avenue, Miami, FL 33054, 305-474-6900 or toll-free 800-367-9010. *Fax:* 305-474-6930. *E-mail:* ado@stu.edu.

SAINT VINCENT COLLEGE

Latrobe, PA

Tuition & fees: $27,190 **Average undergraduate aid package: $21,705**

ABOUT THE INSTITUTION Independent Roman Catholic, coed. 49 undergraduate majors. Federal methodology is used as a basis for awarding need-based institutional aid.

UNDERGRADUATE EXPENSES for 2010–11 ***Comprehensive fee:*** $36,238 includes full-time tuition ($26,350), mandatory fees ($840), and room and board ($9048). ***College room only:*** $4896. Room and board charges vary according to board plan and housing facility. ***Part-time tuition:*** $824 per credit.

FRESHMAN FINANCIAL AID (Fall 2009) 414 applied for aid; of those 79% were deemed to have need. 100% of freshmen with need received aid; of those 26% had need fully met. ***Average percent of need met:*** 88% (excluding resources awarded to replace EFC). ***Average financial aid package:*** $23,489 (excluding resources awarded to replace EFC). 26% of all full-time freshmen had no need and received non-need-based gift aid.

UNDERGRADUATE FINANCIAL AID (Fall 2009) 1,492 applied for aid; of those 86% were deemed to have need. 100% of undergraduates with need received aid; of those 25% had need fully met. ***Average percent of need met:*** 81% (excluding resources awarded to replace EFC). ***Average financial aid package:*** $21,705 (excluding resources awarded to replace EFC). 23% of all full-time undergraduates had no need and received non-need-based gift aid.

GIFT AID (NEED-BASED) ***Total amount:*** $19,595,911 (11% federal, 11% state, 76% institutional, 2% external sources). ***Receiving aid:*** Freshmen: 74% (325); all full-time undergraduates: 77% (1,278). ***Average award:*** Freshmen: $18,036; Undergraduates: $16,506. ***Scholarships, grants, and awards:*** Federal Pell, FSEOG, state, private, college/university gift aid from institutional funds.

GIFT AID (NON-NEED-BASED) ***Total amount:*** $5,822,160 (100% institutional). ***Receiving aid:*** Freshmen: 10% (42). Undergraduates: 8% (130). ***Average award:*** Freshmen: $14,510. Undergraduates: $12,349. ***Scholarships, grants, and awards by category:*** *Academic interests/achievement:* general academic interests/achievements. *Special achievements/activities:* leadership. *Special characteristics:* children and siblings of alumni, general special characteristics, members of minority groups, religious affiliation.

LOANS ***Student loans:*** $15,422,087 (41% need-based, 59% non-need-based). 81% of past graduating class borrowed through all loan programs. ***Average need-based loan:*** Freshmen: $3676. Undergraduates: $4662. ***Parent loans:*** $4,542,553 (56% need-based, 44% non-need-based). ***Programs:*** Perkins.

WORK-STUDY ***Federal work-study:*** Total amount: $967,292; jobs available. ***State or other work-study/employment:*** Total amount: $1,156,898 (1% need-based, 99% non-need-based). Part-time jobs available.

APPLYING FOR FINANCIAL AID ***Required financial aid forms:*** FAFSA, state aid form. ***Financial aid deadline:*** 5/1 (priority: 3/1). ***Notification date:*** Continuous beginning 3/5. Students must reply within 4 weeks of notification.

CONTACT Kimberly Woodley, Director of Financial Aid, Saint Vincent College, 300 Fraser Purchase Road, Latrobe, PA 15650, 724-805-2500 or toll-free 800-782-5549. *E-mail:* kimberly.woodley@email.stvincent.edu.

SAINT XAVIER UNIVERSITY

Chicago, IL

Tuition & fees: $25,520 **Average undergraduate aid package: $20,926**

ABOUT THE INSTITUTION Independent Roman Catholic, coed. 39 undergraduate majors. Federal methodology is used as a basis for awarding need-based institutional aid.

UNDERGRADUATE EXPENSES for 2010–11 ***Comprehensive fee:*** $34,212 includes full-time tuition ($24,790), mandatory fees ($730), and room and board ($8692). ***College room only:*** $5142. Room and board charges vary according to board plan and housing facility. ***Part-time tuition:*** $830 per credit hour. ***Payment plan:*** Installment.

FRESHMAN FINANCIAL AID (Fall 2010, est.) 443 applied for aid; of those 100% were deemed to have need. 100% of freshmen with need received aid; of those 18% had need fully met. ***Average percent of need met:*** 84% (excluding resources awarded to replace EFC). ***Average financial aid package:*** $23,380 (excluding resources awarded to replace EFC). 8% of all full-time freshmen had no need and received non-need-based gift aid.

UNDERGRADUATE FINANCIAL AID (Fall 2010, est.) 2,167 applied for aid; of those 100% were deemed to have need. 100% of undergraduates with need received aid; of those 16% had need fully met. ***Average percent of need met:*** 80% (excluding resources awarded to replace EFC). ***Average financial aid package:*** $20,926 (excluding resources awarded to replace EFC). 11% of all full-time undergraduates had no need and received non-need-based gift aid.

GIFT AID (NEED-BASED) ***Total amount:*** $32,096,743 (23% federal, 21% state, 55% institutional, 1% external sources). ***Receiving aid:*** Freshmen: 91% (442); all full-time undergraduates: 87% (2,154). ***Average award:*** Freshmen: $18,514; Undergraduates: $15,152. ***Scholarships, grants, and awards:*** Federal Pell, FSEOG, state, private, college/university gift aid from institutional funds, United Negro College Fund, Federal Nursing.

GIFT AID (NON-NEED-BASED) ***Total amount:*** $1,398,612 (5% federal, 91% institutional, 4% external sources). ***Receiving aid:*** Freshmen: 8% (41). Undergraduates: 10% (249). ***Average award:*** Freshmen: $9276. Undergraduates: $7946. ***Scholarships, grants, and awards by category:*** *Academic interests/achievement:* 2,578 awards ($16,392,677 total): general academic interests/achievements. *Creative arts/performance:* 70 awards ($185,169 total): music. *Special achievements/activities:* leadership. *Special characteristics:* 80 awards ($979,089 total): children of faculty/staff. ***Tuition waivers:*** Full or partial for employees or children of employees, senior citizens.

LOANS ***Student loans:*** $20,149,023 (72% need-based, 28% non-need-based). 81% of past graduating class borrowed through all loan programs. *Average indebtedness per student:* $29,326. ***Average need-based loan:*** Freshmen: $3348. Undergraduates: $4612. ***Parent loans:*** $3,839,690 (29% need-based, 71% non-need-based). ***Programs:*** Federal Direct (Subsidized and Unsubsidized Stafford, PLUS), Perkins.

WORK-STUDY ***Federal work-study:*** Total amount: $4,241,544; 1,605 jobs averaging $2644. ***State or other work-study/employment:*** Total amount: $253,749 (33% need-based, 67% non-need-based). 31 part-time jobs averaging $8237.

ATHLETIC AWARDS Total amount: $1,626,038 (68% need-based, 32% non-need-based).

APPLYING FOR FINANCIAL AID ***Required financial aid form:*** FAFSA. ***Financial aid deadline (priority):*** 3/1. ***Notification date:*** Continuous beginning 2/16. Students must reply by 5/1 or within 2 weeks of notification.

CONTACT Ms. Susan Swisher, Assistant Vice President for Student Financial Services, Saint Xavier University, 3700 West 103rd Street, Chicago, IL 60655-3105, 773-298-3070 or toll-free 800-462-9288. *Fax:* 773-779-3084. *E-mail:* swisher@sxu.edu.

SALEM COLLEGE

Winston-Salem, NC

Tuition & fees: $21,965 **Average undergraduate aid package: $18,755**

ABOUT THE INSTITUTION Independent religious, coed, primarily women. 32 undergraduate majors. Federal methodology is used as a basis for awarding need-based institutional aid.

UNDERGRADUATE EXPENSES for 2010–11 ***Comprehensive fee:*** $33,485 includes full-time tuition ($21,610), mandatory fees ($355), and room and board ($11,520). Full-time tuition and fees vary according to degree level and program. ***Part-time tuition:*** $1074 per course. ***Part-time fees:*** $70 per term. Part-time tuition and fees vary according to course load, degree level, and program. ***Payment plan:*** Installment.

FRESHMAN FINANCIAL AID (Fall 2009) 79 applied for aid; of those 71% were deemed to have need. 100% of freshmen with need received aid; of those 100% had need fully met. ***Average percent of need met:*** 100% (excluding resources awarded to replace EFC). ***Average financial aid package:*** $24,045 (excluding resources awarded to replace EFC). 6% of all full-time freshmen had no need and received non-need-based gift aid.

UNDERGRADUATE FINANCIAL AID (Fall 2009) 476 applied for aid; of those 92% were deemed to have need. 100% of undergraduates with need received aid; of those 100% had need fully met. ***Average percent of need met:*** 100% (excluding resources awarded to replace EFC). ***Average financial aid package:*** $18,755 (excluding resources awarded to replace EFC). 6% of all full-time undergraduates had no need and received non-need-based gift aid.

GIFT AID (NEED-BASED) ***Total amount:*** $4,498,786 (29% federal, 15% state, 56% institutional). ***Receiving aid:*** Freshmen: 45% (53); all full-time undergraduates: 50% (311). ***Average award:*** Freshmen: $12,023; Undergraduates: $8440. ***Scholarships, grants, and awards:*** Federal Pell, FSEOG, state, private, college/university gift aid from institutional funds.

GIFT AID (NON-NEED-BASED) ***Total amount:*** $4,085,420 (19% state, 76% institutional, 5% external sources). ***Receiving aid:*** Freshmen: 45% (53). Undergraduates: 67% (419). ***Average award:*** Freshmen: $12,263. Undergraduates: $13,316. ***Scholarships, grants, and awards by category:*** *Academic interests/achievement:* 294 awards ($2,582,305 total): general academic interests/achievements. *Creative arts/performance:* 13 awards ($57,340 total): music. *Special achievements/activities:* 17 awards ($324,220 total): leadership. *Special characteristics:* 64 awards ($142,724 total): children of educators, children of faculty/staff, relatives of clergy. ***Tuition waivers:*** Full or partial for employees or children of employees.

LOANS ***Student loans:*** $3,493,645 (50% need-based, 50% non-need-based). 70% of past graduating class borrowed through all loan programs. *Average indebtedness per student:* $19,000. ***Average need-based loan:*** Freshmen: $2924. Undergraduates: $4406. ***Parent loans:*** $334,643 (100% non-need-based). ***Programs:*** Federal Direct (Subsidized and Unsubsidized Stafford, PLUS), Perkins.

WORK-STUDY ***Federal work-study:*** Total amount: $98,853; 98 jobs averaging $1009. ***State or other work-study/employment:*** Total amount: $323,688 (100% need-based). Part-time jobs available.

APPLYING FOR FINANCIAL AID ***Required financial aid forms:*** FAFSA, institution's own form. ***Financial aid deadline (priority):*** 3/1. ***Notification date:*** Continuous beginning 3/1. Students must reply by 5/1 or within 2 weeks of notification.

CONTACT Lori A. Lewis, Director of Financial Aid, Salem College, 601 South Church Street, Winston-Salem, NC 27101, 336-721-2808 or toll-free 800-327-2536. *Fax:* 336-917-5584. *E-mail:* lori.lewis@salem.edu.

SALEM INTERNATIONAL UNIVERSITY

Salem, WV

CONTACT Pat Zinsmeister, Vice President for Financial Aid and Compliance, Salem International University, 223 West Main Street, Salem, WV 26426-0500, 304-326-1299 or toll-free 800-283-4562. *Fax:* 304-326-1509. *E-mail:* pzinsmeister@salemu.edu.

SALEM STATE UNIVERSITY

Salem, MA

ABOUT THE INSTITUTION State-supported, coed. 74 undergraduate majors.

GIFT AID (NEED-BASED) ***Scholarships, grants, and awards:*** Federal Pell, FSEOG, state, private, college/university gift aid from institutional funds, Scholarships for Disadvantaged Students Nursing Grants, MSCBA Housing Grants.

GIFT AID (NON-NEED-BASED) ***Scholarships, grants, and awards by category:*** *Academic interests/achievement:* general academic interests/achievements. *Creative arts/performance:* applied art and design, art/fine arts, creative writing, dance, music, performing arts, theater/drama. *Special achievements/activities:* general special achievements/activities, memberships. *Special characteristics:* adult students, children and siblings of alumni, children of faculty/staff, children of public servants, children of union members/company employees, first-generation college students, general special characteristics, members of minority groups, public servants, veterans, veterans' children.

LOANS ***Programs:*** Perkins, Federal Nursing, state, MEFA Loans, CitiAssist Loans, Sallie Mae SMART Loans.

WORK-STUDY ***Federal work-study:*** Total amount: $420,493; 286 jobs averaging $3000.

APPLYING FOR FINANCIAL AID ***Required financial aid form:*** FAFSA.

CONTACT Mary Benda, Director of Financial Aid, Salem State University, 352 Lafayette Street, Salem, MA 01970-5353, 978-542-6139. *Fax:* 978-542-6876.

SALISBURY UNIVERSITY

Salisbury, MD

ABOUT THE INSTITUTION State-supported, coed. 42 undergraduate majors.

GIFT AID (NEED-BASED) ***Scholarships, grants, and awards:*** Federal Pell, FSEOG, state, private, college/university gift aid from institutional funds.

GIFT AID (NON-NEED-BASED) ***Scholarships, grants, and awards by category:*** *Academic interests/achievement:* biological sciences, business, communication, computer science, education, English, foreign languages, general academic interests/achievements, health fields, humanities, mathematics, physical sciences, premedicine, social sciences. *Creative arts/performance:* applied art and design, music. *Special characteristics:* children and siblings of alumni, first-generation college students.

LOANS ***Programs:*** Federal Direct (Subsidized and Unsubsidized Stafford), Perkins.

WORK-STUDY ***Federal work-study:*** Total amount: $128,526; 70 jobs averaging $1840. ***State or other work-study/employment:*** Part-time jobs available.

APPLYING FOR FINANCIAL AID ***Required financial aid form:*** FAFSA.

CONTACT Ms. Elizabeth B. Zimmerman, Director of Financial Aid, Salisbury University, 1101 Camden Avenue, Salisbury, MD 21801-6837, 410-543-6165 or toll-free 888-543-0148. *Fax:* 410-543-6138. *E-mail:* ebzimmerman@salisbury.edu.

SALVE REGINA UNIVERSITY

Newport, RI

Tuition & fees: $31,450 **Average undergraduate aid package: $22,199**

ABOUT THE INSTITUTION Independent Roman Catholic, coed. 48 undergraduate majors. Both federal and institutional methodology are used as a basis for awarding need-based institutional aid.

UNDERGRADUATE EXPENSES for 2010–11 ***Comprehensive fee:*** $42,750 includes full-time tuition ($31,250), mandatory fees ($200), and room and board ($11,300). Room and board charges vary according to board plan and housing facility. ***Part-time tuition:*** $1042 per credit hour. ***Part-time fees:*** $40 per term. Part-time tuition and fees vary according to course load. ***Payment plan:*** Installment.

FRESHMAN FINANCIAL AID (Fall 2010, est.) 526 applied for aid; of those 87% were deemed to have need. 99% of freshmen with need received aid; of those 13% had need fully met. ***Average percent of need met:*** 71% (excluding resources awarded to replace EFC). ***Average financial aid package:*** $22,332 (excluding resources awarded to replace EFC). 16% of all full-time freshmen had no need and received non-need-based gift aid.

UNDERGRADUATE FINANCIAL AID (Fall 2010, est.) 1,604 applied for aid; of those 90% were deemed to have need. 97% of undergraduates with need received aid; of those 7% had need fully met. ***Average percent of need met:*** 68% (excluding resources awarded to replace EFC). ***Average financial aid package:*** $22,199 (excluding resources awarded to replace EFC). 12% of all full-time undergraduates had no need and received non-need-based gift aid.

GIFT AID (NEED-BASED) ***Total amount:*** $23,688,664 (11% federal, 1% state, 85% institutional, 3% external sources). ***Receiving aid:*** Freshmen: 76% (451); all full-time undergraduates: 68% (1,354). ***Average award:*** Freshmen: $18,638; Undergraduates: $17,596. ***Scholarships, grants, and awards:*** Federal Pell, FSEOG, state, private, college/university gift aid from institutional funds.

GIFT AID (NON-NEED-BASED) ***Total amount:*** $2,516,750 (87% institutional, 13% external sources). ***Receiving aid:*** Freshmen: 8% (50). Undergraduates: 4% (71). ***Average award:*** Freshmen: $9705. Undergraduates: $8240. ***Scholarships, grants, and awards by category:*** *Academic interests/achievement:* general academic interests/achievements. ***Tuition waivers:*** Full or partial for employees or children of employees.

LOANS ***Student loans:*** $14,049,355 (74% need-based, 26% non-need-based). 84% of past graduating class borrowed through all loan programs. *Average indebtedness per student:* $35,737. ***Average need-based loan:*** Freshmen: $3476. Undergraduates: $4542. ***Parent loans:*** $5,577,379 (43% need-based, 57% non-need-based). ***Programs:*** Federal Direct (Subsidized and Unsubsidized Stafford, PLUS), Perkins, Federal Nursing, college/university, alternative loans.

WORK-STUDY ***Federal work-study:*** Total amount: $425,927; 532 jobs averaging $801. ***State or other work-study/employment:*** Total amount: $210,000 (100% non-need-based). 160 part-time jobs averaging $1312.

APPLYING FOR FINANCIAL AID ***Required financial aid forms:*** FAFSA, CSS Financial Aid PROFILE, business/farm supplement, Non-custodial Parent Statement. ***Financial aid deadline (priority):*** 3/1. ***Notification date:*** Continuous beginning 2/15. Students must reply by 5/1 or within 2 weeks of notification.

CONTACT Ms. Aida Mirante, Director of Financial Aid, Salve Regina University, 100 Ochre Point Avenue, Newport, RI 02840-4192, 401-341-2901 or toll-free 888-GO SALVE. *Fax:* 401-341-2928. *E-mail:* financial_aid@salve.edu.

SAMFORD UNIVERSITY

Birmingham, AL

Tuition & fees: $23,932 **Average undergraduate aid package: $16,310**

ABOUT THE INSTITUTION Independent Baptist, coed. 65 undergraduate majors. Federal methodology is used as a basis for awarding need-based institutional aid.

UNDERGRADUATE EXPENSES for 2011–12 ***Comprehensive fee:*** $32,090 includes full-time tuition ($23,422), mandatory fees ($510), and room and board ($8158). Full-time tuition and fees vary according to course load, location, and program. Room and board charges vary according to board plan and housing facility. Part-time tuition and fees vary according to course load, location, and program.

FRESHMAN FINANCIAL AID (Fall 2010, est.) 513 applied for aid; of those 58% were deemed to have need. 100% of freshmen with need received aid; of those 26% had need fully met. ***Average percent of need met:*** 71% (excluding resources awarded to replace EFC). ***Average financial aid package:*** $16,801 (excluding resources awarded to replace EFC). 40% of all full-time freshmen had no need and received non-need-based gift aid.

UNDERGRADUATE FINANCIAL AID (Fall 2010, est.) 1,637 applied for aid; of those 57% were deemed to have need. 100% of undergraduates with need received aid; of those 21% had need fully met. ***Average percent of need met:*** 75% (excluding resources awarded to replace EFC). ***Average financial aid package:*** $16,310 (excluding resources awarded to replace EFC). 22% of all full-time undergraduates had no need and received non-need-based gift aid.

GIFT AID (NEED-BASED) ***Total amount:*** $8,104,742 (20% federal, 2% state, 76% institutional, 2% external sources). ***Receiving aid:*** Freshmen: 40% (294); all full-time undergraduates: 33% (878). ***Average award:*** Freshmen: $13,237; Undergraduates: $12,791. ***Scholarships, grants, and awards:*** Federal Pell, FSEOG, state, private, college/university gift aid from institutional funds, Federal Nursing.

GIFT AID (NON-NEED-BASED) ***Total amount:*** $6,927,940 (2% state, 82% institutional, 16% external sources). ***Receiving aid:*** Freshmen: 13% (92). Undergraduates: 7% (183). ***Average award:*** Freshmen: $7849. Undergraduates: $7742. ***Scholarships, grants, and awards by category:*** *Academic interests/achievement:* 578 awards ($3,733,694 total): biological sciences, business, communication, computer science, education, English, foreign languages, general academic interests/achievements, health fields, humanities, international studies, mathematics, physical sciences, premedicine, religion/biblical studies, social sciences. *Creative arts/performance:* 54 awards ($170,223 total): debating, journalism/publications, music, performing arts, theater/drama. *Special achievements/activities:* 122 awards ($405,886 total): leadership. *Special characteristics:* 90 awards ($1,079,642 total): children of faculty/staff, relatives of clergy. ***Tuition waivers:*** Full or partial for employees or children of employees.

LOANS ***Student loans:*** $11,765,706 (60% need-based, 40% non-need-based). 39% of past graduating class borrowed through all loan programs. *Average indebtedness per student:* $20,328. ***Average need-based loan:*** Freshmen: $3154. Undergraduates: $3859. ***Parent loans:*** $13,527,324 (20% need-based, 80% non-need-based). ***Programs:*** Perkins, Federal Nursing, college/university.

WORK-STUDY ***Federal work-study:*** Total amount: $1,142,849; 541 jobs averaging $1975. ***State or other work-study/employment:*** Total amount: $786,742 (14% need-based, 86% non-need-based). 482 part-time jobs averaging $1632.

ATHLETIC AWARDS Total amount: $4,704,738 (21% need-based, 79% non-need-based).

APPLYING FOR FINANCIAL AID ***Required financial aid forms:*** FAFSA, state aid form. ***Financial aid deadline (priority):*** 3/1. ***Notification date:*** 4/1. Students must reply by 5/1.

CONTACT Lane Smith, Director of Financial Aid, Samford University, 800 Lakeshore Drive, Birmingham, AL 35229, 205-726-2905 or toll-free 800-888-7218. *Fax:* 205-726-2738. *E-mail:* lsmith1@samford.edu.

SAM HOUSTON STATE UNIVERSITY

Huntsville, TX

ABOUT THE INSTITUTION State-supported, coed. 43 undergraduate majors.

GIFT AID (NEED-BASED) ***Scholarships, grants, and awards:*** Federal Pell, FSEOG, state, private, college/university gift aid from institutional funds.

GIFT AID (NON-NEED-BASED) ***Scholarships, grants, and awards by category:*** *Academic interests/achievement:* agriculture, biological sciences, business, communication, computer science, education, engineering/technologies, English, foreign languages, general academic interests/achievements, home economics, humanities, library science, mathematics, military science, physical sciences, social sciences. *Creative arts/performance:* art/fine arts, dance, music. *Special achievements/activities:* cheerleading/drum major, general special achievements/activities, leadership, rodeo. *Special characteristics:* general special characteristics, handicapped students.

LOANS ***Programs:*** Federal Direct (Subsidized and Unsubsidized Stafford, PLUS), Perkins, state, college/university.

WORK-STUDY ***Federal work-study:*** Total amount: $37,360; 291 jobs averaging $1563. ***State or other work-study/employment:*** Total amount: $6081 (100% need-based). 90 part-time jobs averaging $1206.

APPLYING FOR FINANCIAL AID ***Required financial aid forms:*** FAFSA, institution's own form.

CONTACT Lisa Tatom, Director of Financial Aid, Sam Houston State University, Box 2328, Huntsville, TX 77341-2328, 936-294-1774 or toll-free 866-232-7528 Ext. 1828. *Fax:* 936-294-3668. *E-mail:* fao.tatom@shsu.edu.

SAMUEL MERRITT UNIVERSITY

Oakland, CA

ABOUT THE INSTITUTION Independent, coed, primarily women. 1 undergraduate major.

GIFT AID (NEED-BASED) ***Scholarships, grants, and awards:*** Federal Pell, FSEOG, state, private, college/university gift aid from institutional funds, Federal Nursing.

LOANS ***Programs:*** Perkins, Federal Nursing, college/university.

WORK-STUDY ***Federal work-study:*** Total amount: $190,000; 120 jobs averaging $1583. ***State or other work-study/employment:*** Part-time jobs available.

APPLYING FOR FINANCIAL AID ***Required financial aid form:*** FAFSA.

CONTACT Adel Mareghni, Financial Aid Counselor, Samuel Merritt University, 450 30th Street, Oakland, CA 94609, 510-869-6193 or toll-free 800-607-MERRITT. *Fax:* 510-869-1529. *E-mail:* amareghni@samuelmerritt.edu.

SAN DIEGO CHRISTIAN COLLEGE

El Cajon, CA

Tuition & fees: $23,824 | **Average undergraduate aid package: $15,073**

ABOUT THE INSTITUTION Independent nondenominational, coed. 29 undergraduate majors. Federal methodology is used as a basis for awarding need-based institutional aid.

UNDERGRADUATE EXPENSES for 2011–12 ***One-time required fee:*** $100. ***Comprehensive fee:*** $32,146 includes full-time tuition ($22,690), mandatory fees ($1134), and room and board ($8322). Full-time tuition and fees vary according to class time, course load, and program. Part-time tuition and fees vary according to class time, course load, and program. ***Payment plan:*** Installment.

FRESHMAN FINANCIAL AID (Fall 2010, est.) 65 applied for aid; of those 91% were deemed to have need. 100% of freshmen with need received aid; of those 17% had need fully met. ***Average percent of need met:*** 55% (excluding resources awarded to replace EFC). ***Average financial aid package:*** $15,867 (excluding resources awarded to replace EFC). 8% of all full-time freshmen had no need and received non-need-based gift aid.

UNDERGRADUATE FINANCIAL AID (Fall 2010, est.) 386 applied for aid; of those 94% were deemed to have need. 100% of undergraduates with need received aid; of those 15% had need fully met. ***Average percent of need met:*** 81% (excluding resources awarded to replace EFC). ***Average financial aid package:*** $15,073 (excluding resources awarded to replace EFC). 9% of all full-time undergraduates had no need and received non-need-based gift aid.

GIFT AID (NEED-BASED) ***Total amount:*** $2,101,167 (46% federal, 38% state, 16% institutional). ***Receiving aid:*** Freshmen: 47% (35); all full-time undergraduates: 61% (259). ***Average award:*** Freshmen: $7103; Undergraduates: $7204. ***Scholarships, grants, and awards:*** Federal Pell, FSEOG, state, private, college/university gift aid from institutional funds.

GIFT AID (NON-NEED-BASED) ***Total amount:*** $647,474 (91% institutional, 9% external sources). ***Receiving aid:*** Freshmen: 69% (51). Undergraduates: 58% (248). ***Average award:*** Freshmen: $5167. Undergraduates: $4946. ***Scholarships, grants, and awards by category:*** *Academic interests/achievement:* 179 awards ($546,771 total): general academic interests/achievements. *Creative arts/performance:* 36 awards ($60,350 total): music, performing arts, theater/drama. *Special achievements/activities:* 108 awards ($349,725 total): leadership, religious involvement. *Special characteristics:* 96 awards ($359,728 total): children and siblings of alumni, children of faculty/staff, international students, out-of-state students, relatives of clergy, religious affiliation, siblings of current students. ***Tuition waivers:*** Full or partial for employees or children of employees.

LOANS ***Student loans:*** $3,445,563 (41% need-based, 59% non-need-based). 68% of past graduating class borrowed through all loan programs. *Average indebtedness per student:* $20,921. ***Average need-based loan:*** Freshmen: $3477. Undergraduates: $3837. ***Parent loans:*** $528,716 (100% non-need-based). ***Programs:*** Federal Direct (Subsidized and Unsubsidized Stafford, PLUS), Perkins.

WORK-STUDY ***Federal work-study:*** Total amount: $33,550; 14 jobs averaging $2396. ***State or other work-study/employment:*** Total amount: $24,000 (100% need-based). 11 part-time jobs averaging $2182.

ATHLETIC AWARDS Total amount: $1,443,681 (100% non-need-based).

APPLYING FOR FINANCIAL AID ***Required financial aid forms:*** FAFSA, institution's own form, state aid form. ***Financial aid deadline:*** 7/15 (priority: 3/2). ***Notification date:*** Continuous beginning 3/15. Students must reply by 9/1 or within 4 weeks of notification.

CONTACT Erin Neill, Financial Aid Specialist, San Diego Christian College, 2100 Greenfield Drive, El Cajon, CA 92019, 619-201-8730 or toll-free 800-676-2242. *Fax:* 619-201-8797. *E-mail:* enrollmentservices@sdcc.edu.

SAN DIEGO STATE UNIVERSITY

San Diego, CA

Tuition & fees (CA res): $5206 | **Average undergraduate aid package: $10,000**

ABOUT THE INSTITUTION State-supported, coed. 88 undergraduate majors. Federal methodology is used as a basis for awarding need-based institutional aid.

UNDERGRADUATE EXPENSES for 2011–12 ***Tuition, state resident:*** full-time $0. ***Tuition, nonresident:*** full-time $11,160; part-time $372 per unit. ***Required fees:*** full-time $5206; $1715 per term. Full-time tuition and fees vary according to degree level. Part-time tuition and fees vary according to course load and degree level. ***College room and board:*** $11,485. Room and board charges vary according to board plan and housing facility. ***Payment plan:*** Installment.

FRESHMAN FINANCIAL AID (Fall 2010, est.) 3,000 applied for aid; of those 77% were deemed to have need. 87% of freshmen with need received aid; of those 5% had need fully met. ***Average percent of need met:*** 74% (excluding resources awarded to replace EFC). ***Average financial aid package:*** $9300 (excluding resources awarded to replace EFC). 5% of all full-time freshmen had no need and received non-need-based gift aid.

UNDERGRADUATE FINANCIAL AID (Fall 2010, est.) 17,400 applied for aid; of those 75% were deemed to have need. 92% of undergraduates with need received aid; of those 10% had need fully met. ***Average percent of need met:*** 73% (excluding resources awarded to replace EFC). ***Average financial aid package:*** $10,000 (excluding resources awarded to replace EFC). 6% of all full-time undergraduates had no need and received non-need-based gift aid.

GIFT AID (NEED-BASED) ***Total amount:*** $89,304,000 (48% federal, 24% state, 28% institutional). ***Receiving aid:*** Freshmen: 53% (1,600); all full-time undergraduates: 44% (9,400). ***Average award:*** Freshmen: $9900; Undergraduates: $9200. ***Scholarships, grants, and awards:*** Federal Pell, FSEOG, state, private, college/university gift aid from institutional funds, Federal Nursing.

GIFT AID (NON-NEED-BASED) ***Total amount:*** $4,856,000 (1% federal, 1% state, 42% institutional, 56% external sources). ***Receiving aid:*** Freshmen: 23% (700). Undergraduates: 13% (2,700). ***Average award:*** Freshmen: $2600. Undergraduates: $1700. ***Scholarships, grants, and awards by category:*** *Academic interests/achievement:* area/ethnic studies, biological sciences, business, communication, computer science, education, engineering/technologies, English, foreign languages, general academic interests/achievements, health fields, international studies, mathematics, military science, physical sciences, religion/biblical studies, social sciences. *Creative arts/performance:* applied art and design, art/fine arts, cinema/film/broadcasting, creative writing, dance, journalism/publications, music, performing arts, theater/drama. *Special achievements/activities:* leadership. *Special characteristics:* adult students, children and siblings of alumni, children of faculty/staff, children of workers in trades, first-generation college students, handicapped students, local/state students, veterans. ***Tuition waivers:*** Full or partial for employees or children of employees.

LOANS ***Student loans:*** $102,608,000 (63% need-based, 37% non-need-based). 44% of past graduating class borrowed through all loan programs. *Average indebtedness per student:* $15,500. ***Average need-based loan:*** Freshmen: $3100. Undergraduates: $4100. ***Parent loans:*** $70,286,000 (15% need-based, 85% non-need-based). ***Programs:*** Federal Direct (Subsidized and Unsubsidized Stafford, PLUS), Perkins, college/university.

WORK-STUDY ***Federal work-study:*** Total amount: $1,480,000; 609 jobs averaging $2200.

ATHLETIC AWARDS Total amount: $5,454,000 (100% non-need-based).

APPLYING FOR FINANCIAL AID ***Required financial aid forms:*** FAFSA, state aid form. ***Financial aid deadline:*** 3/2. ***Notification date:*** Continuous beginning 2/14.

CONTACT Ms. Chrys Dutton, Director of Financial Aid and Scholarships, San Diego State University, 5500 Campanile Drive, SSW-3605, San Diego, CA 92182-7436, 619-594-6323.

SAN FRANCISCO ART INSTITUTE

San Francisco, CA

CONTACT Erin Zagaski, Interim Director of Financial Aid, San Francisco Art Institute, 800 Chestnut Street, San Francisco, CA 94133-2299, 415-749-4513 or toll-free 800-345-SFAI. *Fax:* 415-351-3503.

SAN FRANCISCO CONSERVATORY OF MUSIC

San Francisco, CA

ABOUT THE INSTITUTION Independent, coed. 8 undergraduate majors.

GIFT AID (NEED-BASED) ***Scholarships, grants, and awards:*** Federal Pell, FSEOG, state, private, college/university gift aid from institutional funds.

GIFT AID (NON-NEED-BASED) ***Scholarships, grants, and awards by category:*** *Creative arts/performance:* music.

LOANS ***Programs:*** Perkins.

WORK-STUDY ***Federal work-study:*** Total amount: $22,400; jobs available. ***State or other work-study/employment:*** Total amount: $5300 (100% non-need-based). Part-time jobs available.

APPLYING FOR FINANCIAL AID ***Required financial aid forms:*** FAFSA, institution's own form.

CONTACT Doris Howard, Director of Financial Aid, San Francisco Conservatory of Music, 50 Oak Street, San Francisco, CA 94102-6011, 415-503-6214. *Fax:* 415-503-6299. *E-mail:* dbh@sfcm.edu.

SAN FRANCISCO STATE UNIVERSITY

San Francisco, CA

Tuition & fees (CA res): $5668 **Average undergraduate aid package: $10,662**

ABOUT THE INSTITUTION State-supported, coed. 91 undergraduate majors. Federal methodology is used as a basis for awarding need-based institutional aid.

UNDERGRADUATE EXPENSES for 2011–12 ***Tuition, state resident:*** full-time $0. ***Tuition, nonresident:*** full-time $11,160; part-time $372 per unit. ***Required fees:*** full-time $5668; $1808 per term. Full-time tuition and fees vary according to course load. Part-time tuition and fees vary according to course load. ***College room and board:*** $11,408. Room and board charges vary according to board plan and housing facility. ***Payment plan:*** Installment.

FRESHMAN FINANCIAL AID (Fall 2010, est.) 2,838 applied for aid; of those 81% were deemed to have need. 95% of freshmen with need received aid; of those 7% had need fully met. ***Average percent of need met:*** 62% (excluding resources awarded to replace EFC). ***Average financial aid package:*** $9958 (excluding resources awarded to replace EFC). 1% of all full-time freshmen had no need and received non-need-based gift aid.

UNDERGRADUATE FINANCIAL AID (Fall 2010, est.) 13,807 applied for aid; of those 89% were deemed to have need. 97% of undergraduates with need received aid; of those 5% had need fully met. ***Average percent of need met:*** 61% (excluding resources awarded to replace EFC). ***Average financial aid package:*** $10,662 (excluding resources awarded to replace EFC). 1% of all full-time undergraduates had no need and received non-need-based gift aid.

GIFT AID (NEED-BASED) ***Total amount:*** $89,288,032 (50% federal, 48% state, 2% external sources). ***Receiving aid:*** Freshmen: 42% (1,501); all full-time undergraduates: 43% (8,946). ***Average award:*** Freshmen: $9793; Undergraduates: $9001. ***Scholarships, grants, and awards:*** Federal Pell, FSEOG, state, private, college/university gift aid from institutional funds.

GIFT AID (NON-NEED-BASED) ***Total amount:*** $825,011 (22% institutional, 78% external sources). ***Receiving aid:*** Freshmen: 6% (201). Undergraduates: 4% (728). ***Average award:*** Freshmen: $2573. Undergraduates: $2168. ***Tuition waivers:*** Full or partial for employees or children of employees, senior citizens.

LOANS ***Student loans:*** $66,617,523 (90% need-based, 10% non-need-based). 42% of past graduating class borrowed through all loan programs. *Average indebtedness per student:* $17,706. ***Average need-based loan:*** Freshmen: $2585. Undergraduates: $3244. ***Parent loans:*** $24,658,188 (72% need-based, 28% non-need-based). ***Programs:*** Federal Direct (Subsidized and Unsubsidized Stafford, PLUS), Perkins.

WORK-STUDY ***Federal work-study:*** Total amount: $673,460; jobs available.

ATHLETIC AWARDS Total amount: $337,000 (61% need-based, 39% non-need-based).

APPLYING FOR FINANCIAL AID ***Required financial aid form:*** FAFSA. ***Financial aid deadline (priority):*** 3/2. ***Notification date:*** Continuous beginning 2/1. Students must reply within 2 weeks of notification.

CONTACT Barbara Hubler, Director of Financial Aid, San Francisco State University, 1600 Holloway Avenue, San Francisco, CA 94132-1722, 415-338-7000. *Fax:* 415-338-0949. *E-mail:* finaid@sfsu.edu.

SAN JOSE STATE UNIVERSITY

San Jose, CA

Tuition & fees (CA res): $5475 **Average undergraduate aid package: $13,364**

ABOUT THE INSTITUTION State-supported, coed. 89 undergraduate majors. Federal methodology is used as a basis for awarding need-based institutional aid.

UNDERGRADUATE EXPENSES for 2010–11 ***Tuition, state resident:*** full-time $0. ***Tuition, nonresident:*** full-time $11,160; part-time $372 per unit. ***Required fees:*** full-time $5475. ***College room and board:*** $10,733; ***Room only:*** $6633.

FRESHMAN FINANCIAL AID (Fall 2009) 1,855 applied for aid; of those 75% were deemed to have need. 96% of freshmen with need received aid; of those 51% had need fully met. ***Average percent of need met:*** 94% (excluding resources awarded to replace EFC). ***Average financial aid package:*** $11,420 (excluding resources awarded to replace EFC). 2% of all full-time freshmen had no need and received non-need-based gift aid.

UNDERGRADUATE FINANCIAL AID (Fall 2009) 11,937 applied for aid; of those 88% were deemed to have need. 96% of undergraduates with need received aid; of those 45% had need fully met. ***Average percent of need met:*** 93% (excluding resources awarded to replace EFC). ***Average financial aid package:*** $13,364 (excluding resources awarded to replace EFC). 1% of all full-time undergraduates had no need and received non-need-based gift aid.

GIFT AID (NEED-BASED) ***Total amount:*** $66,343,974 (48% federal, 48% state, 2% institutional, 2% external sources). ***Receiving aid:*** Freshmen: 36% (945); all full-time undergraduates: 40% (7,352). ***Average award:*** Freshmen: $8861; Undergraduates: $7363. ***Scholarships, grants, and awards:*** Federal Pell, FSEOG, state, private, college/university gift aid from institutional funds, Academic Competitiveness Grants, National SMART Grants, TEACH Grants.

GIFT AID (NON-NEED-BASED) ***Total amount:*** $1,763,666 (12% institutional, 88% external sources). ***Receiving aid:*** Freshmen: 4. Undergraduates: 56. ***Aver-***

age award: Freshmen: $2193. Undergraduates: $2641. ***Scholarships, grants, and awards by category:*** *Academic interests/achievement:* general academic interests/achievements.

LOANS ***Student loans:*** $44,396,179 (86% need-based, 14% non-need-based). 45% of past graduating class borrowed through all loan programs. *Average indebtedness per student:* $9483. ***Average need-based loan:*** Freshmen: $3896. Undergraduates: $4713. ***Parent loans:*** $2,357,637 (34% need-based, 66% non-need-based). ***Programs:*** Federal Direct (Subsidized and Unsubsidized Stafford, PLUS), Perkins, college/university.

WORK-STUDY ***Federal work-study:*** Total amount: $28,870,168; 6,169 jobs averaging $4680.

ATHLETIC AWARDS Total amount: $2,638,283 (55% need-based, 45% non-need-based).

APPLYING FOR FINANCIAL AID ***Required financial aid form:*** FAFSA. ***Financial aid deadline (priority):*** 3/2. ***Notification date:*** Continuous beginning 4/1.

CONTACT Coleetta McElroy, Interim Director of Financial Aid, San Jose State University, One Washington Square, San Jose, CA 95192-0036, 408-924-6086. *E-mail:* coleetta.mcelroy@sjsu.edu.

SANTA CLARA UNIVERSITY

Santa Clara, CA

Tuition & fees: $37,368 **Average undergraduate aid package: $23,774**

ABOUT THE INSTITUTION Independent Roman Catholic (Jesuit), coed. 48 undergraduate majors. Both federal and institutional methodology are used as a basis for awarding need-based institutional aid.

UNDERGRADUATE EXPENSES for 2011–12 ***Comprehensive fee:*** $49,110 includes full-time tuition ($37,368) and room and board ($11,742). Room and board charges vary according to board plan, housing facility, and student level. ***Part-time tuition:*** $1038 per unit. Part-time tuition and fees vary according to course load. ***Payment plans:*** Installment, deferred payment.

FRESHMAN FINANCIAL AID (Fall 2009) 714 applied for aid; of those 71% were deemed to have need. 97% of freshmen with need received aid; of those 42% had need fully met. ***Average percent of need met:*** 74% (excluding resources awarded to replace EFC). ***Average financial aid package:*** $26,456 (excluding resources awarded to replace EFC). 25% of all full-time freshmen had no need and received non-need-based gift aid.

UNDERGRADUATE FINANCIAL AID (Fall 2009) 3,049 applied for aid; of those 76% were deemed to have need. 85% of undergraduates with need received aid; of those 39% had need fully met. ***Average percent of need met:*** 67% (excluding resources awarded to replace EFC). ***Average financial aid package:*** $23,774 (excluding resources awarded to replace EFC). 26% of all full-time undergraduates had no need and received non-need-based gift aid.

GIFT AID (NEED-BASED) ***Total amount:*** $33,976,741 (10% federal, 14% state, 76% institutional). ***Receiving aid:*** Freshmen: 35% (382); all full-time undergraduates: 30% (1,539). ***Average award:*** Freshmen: $22,031; Undergraduates: $18,666. ***Scholarships, grants, and awards:*** Federal Pell, FSEOG, state, private, college/university gift aid from institutional funds.

GIFT AID (NON-NEED-BASED) ***Total amount:*** $22,314,991 (89% institutional, 11% external sources). ***Receiving aid:*** Freshmen: 19% (204). Undergraduates: 14% (741). ***Average award:*** Freshmen: $10,373. Undergraduates: $11,557. ***Scholarships, grants, and awards by category:*** *Academic interests/achievement:* business, engineering/technologies, general academic interests/achievements, military science. *Creative arts/performance:* dance, debating, music, theater/drama. *Special characteristics:* children and siblings of alumni, children of faculty/staff, children with a deceased or disabled parent, handicapped students. ***Tuition waivers:*** Full or partial for employees or children of employees.

LOANS ***Student loans:*** $16,560,447 (33% need-based, 67% non-need-based). 43% of past graduating class borrowed through all loan programs. *Average indebtedness per student:* $23,909. ***Average need-based loan:*** Freshmen: $3289. Undergraduates: $4461. ***Parent loans:*** $12,537,095 (100% non-need-based). ***Programs:*** Federal Direct (Subsidized and Unsubsidized Stafford, PLUS), Perkins, alternative loans.

WORK-STUDY ***Federal work-study:*** Total amount: $1,755,512; jobs available.

ATHLETIC AWARDS Total amount: $4,626,647 (100% non-need-based).

APPLYING FOR FINANCIAL AID ***Required financial aid forms:*** FAFSA, CSS Financial Aid PROFILE. ***Financial aid deadline (priority):*** 2/1. ***Notification date:*** 4/1. Students must reply by 5/1 or within 2 weeks of notification.

CONTACT Marta I. Murchison, Associate Director of Systems and Data Analysis, Santa Clara University, 500 El Camino Real, Santa Clara, CA 95053, 408-551-6088. *Fax:* 408-551-6085. *E-mail:* mmurchison@scu.edu.

SANTA FE COLLEGE

Gainesville, FL

CONTACT Financial Aid Office, Santa Fe College, 3000 Northwest 83rd Street, Gainesville, FL 32606, 352-395-5000.

SANTA FE UNIVERSITY OF ART AND DESIGN

Santa Fe, NM

Tuition & fees: $29,266 **Average undergraduate aid package: N/A**

ABOUT THE INSTITUTION Independent, coed. 18 undergraduate majors. Federal methodology is used as a basis for awarding need-based institutional aid.

UNDERGRADUATE EXPENSES for 2010–11 ***Comprehensive fee:*** $37,604 includes full-time tuition ($27,996), mandatory fees ($1270), and room and board ($8338). Room and board charges vary according to board plan and housing facility. ***Payment plans:*** Tuition prepayment, installment.

GIFT AID (NEED-BASED) ***Scholarships, grants, and awards:*** Federal Pell, FSEOG, private.

GIFT AID (NON-NEED-BASED) ***Scholarships, grants, and awards by category:*** *Academic interests/achievement:* general academic interests/achievements. *Creative arts/performance:* applied art and design, art/fine arts, cinema/film/broadcasting, creative writing, dance, general creative arts/performance, music, performing arts, theater/drama. *Special characteristics:* children of faculty/staff, general special characteristics, local/state students. ***Tuition waivers:*** Full or partial for senior citizens.

LOANS ***Programs:*** Federal Direct (Subsidized and Unsubsidized Stafford, PLUS), Perkins.

APPLYING FOR FINANCIAL AID ***Required financial aid form:*** FAFSA. ***Financial aid deadline:*** Continuous. ***Notification date:*** Continuous beginning 3/1. Students must reply within 2 weeks of notification.

CONTACT Amy Kearns, Director of Financial Aid, Santa Fe University of Art and Design, 1600 St. Michael's Drive, Santa Fe, NM 87505-7634, 505-473-6454 or toll-free 800-456-2673. *Fax:* 505-473-6399. *E-mail:* sfs@santafeuniversity.edu.

SARAH LAWRENCE COLLEGE

Bronxville, NY

Tuition & fees: $45,212 **Average undergraduate aid package: $38,115**

ABOUT THE INSTITUTION Independent, coed. 111 undergraduate majors. Both federal and institutional methodology are used as a basis for awarding need-based institutional aid.

UNDERGRADUATE EXPENSES for 2011–12 ***Comprehensive fee:*** $58,716 includes full-time tuition ($44,220), mandatory fees ($992), and room and board ($13,504). ***College room only:*** $9110. Full-time tuition and fees vary according to course load. Room and board charges vary according to board plan. ***Part-time tuition:*** $1420 per unit. ***Part-time fees:*** $482 per term. Part-time tuition and fees vary according to course load. ***Payment plan:*** Installment.

FRESHMAN FINANCIAL AID (Fall 2010, est.) 242 applied for aid; of those 81% were deemed to have need. 100% of freshmen with need received aid; of those 60% had need fully met. ***Average percent of need met:*** 91% (excluding resources awarded to replace EFC). ***Average financial aid package:*** $34,056 (excluding resources awarded to replace EFC). 1% of all full-time freshmen had no need and received non-need-based gift aid.

UNDERGRADUATE FINANCIAL AID (Fall 2010, est.) 847 applied for aid; of those 88% were deemed to have need. 100% of undergraduates with need received aid; of those 56% had need fully met. ***Average percent of need met:*** 94% (excluding resources awarded to replace EFC). ***Average financial aid package:*** $38,115 (excluding resources awarded to replace EFC). 1% of all full-time undergraduates had no need and received non-need-based gift aid.

GIFT AID (NEED-BASED) ***Total amount:*** $22,947,481 (7% federal, 1% state, 91% institutional, 1% external sources). ***Receiving aid:*** Freshmen: 56% (190); all full-time undergraduates: 60% (739). ***Average award:*** Freshmen: $31,012;

Undergraduates: $30,919. ***Scholarships, grants, and awards:*** Federal Pell, FSEOG, state, private, college/university gift aid from institutional funds.

GIFT AID (NON-NEED-BASED) ***Total amount:*** $73,911 (5% state, 81% institutional, 14% external sources). ***Receiving aid:*** Freshmen: 1% (5). Undergraduates: 5. ***Average award:*** Freshmen: $12,000. Undergraduates: $12,000. ***Scholarships, grants, and awards by category:*** *Academic interests/achievement:* 5 awards ($12,000 total): general academic interests/achievements. ***Tuition waivers:*** Full or partial for employees or children of employees.

LOANS ***Student loans:*** $3,229,588 (93% need-based, 7% non-need-based). 55% of past graduating class borrowed through all loan programs. *Average indebtedness per student:* $21,590. ***Average need-based loan:*** Freshmen: $2588. Undergraduates: $3576. ***Parent loans:*** $3,497,289 (84% need-based, 16% non-need-based). ***Programs:*** Federal Direct (Subsidized and Unsubsidized Stafford, PLUS), Perkins, college/university, Sallie Mae Signature Loans, CitiAssist Loans.

WORK-STUDY ***Federal work-study:*** Total amount: $1,074,927; 651 jobs averaging $1660. ***State or other work-study/employment:*** Total amount: $7200 (100% non-need-based). 35 part-time jobs averaging $1625.

APPLYING FOR FINANCIAL AID ***Required financial aid forms:*** FAFSA, CSS Financial Aid PROFILE, state aid form, noncustodial (divorced/separated) parent's statement. ***Financial aid deadline:*** 2/1. ***Notification date:*** 4/1. Students must reply by 5/1.

CONTACT Ms. Heather McDonnell, Director of Financial Aid, Sarah Lawrence College, One Mead Way, Bronxville, NY 10708, 914-395-2570 or toll-free 800-888-2858. *Fax:* 914-395-2676. *E-mail:* hmcdonn@sarahlawrence.edu.

SAVANNAH COLLEGE OF ART AND DESIGN

Savannah, GA

Tuition & fees: $31,010 **Average undergraduate aid package: $20,926**

ABOUT THE INSTITUTION Independent, coed. 31 undergraduate majors. Federal methodology is used as a basis for awarding need-based institutional aid.

UNDERGRADUATE EXPENSES for 2011–12 ***Comprehensive fee:*** $43,265 includes full-time tuition ($30,510), mandatory fees ($500), and room and board ($12,255). Full-time tuition and fees vary according to course load, degree level, and location. Room and board charges vary according to board plan, housing facility, and location. ***Part-time tuition:*** $678 per quarter hour. Part-time tuition and fees vary according to course load, degree level, and location. ***Payment plan:*** Installment.

FRESHMAN FINANCIAL AID (Fall 2010, est.) 1,187 applied for aid; of those 85% were deemed to have need. 100% of freshmen with need received aid; of those 10% had need fully met. ***Average percent of need met:*** 20% (excluding resources awarded to replace EFC). ***Average financial aid package:*** $21,816 (excluding resources awarded to replace EFC). 31% of all full-time freshmen had no need and received non-need-based gift aid.

UNDERGRADUATE FINANCIAL AID (Fall 2010, est.) 4,796 applied for aid; of those 89% were deemed to have need. 100% of undergraduates with need received aid; of those 9% had need fully met. ***Average percent of need met:*** 21% (excluding resources awarded to replace EFC). ***Average financial aid package:*** $20,926 (excluding resources awarded to replace EFC). 27% of all full-time undergraduates had no need and received non-need-based gift aid.

GIFT AID (NEED-BASED) ***Total amount:*** $18,088,732 (57% federal, 2% state, 35% institutional, 6% external sources). ***Receiving aid:*** Freshmen: 43% (721); all full-time undergraduates: 38% (2,767). ***Average award:*** Freshmen: $5235; Undergraduates: $5228. ***Scholarships, grants, and awards:*** Federal Pell, FSEOG, state, private, college/university gift aid from institutional funds.

GIFT AID (NON-NEED-BASED) ***Total amount:*** $53,133,973 (6% state, 94% institutional). ***Receiving aid:*** Freshmen: 53% (889). Undergraduates: 45% (3,308). ***Average award:*** Freshmen: $8532. Undergraduates: $9535. ***Scholarships, grants, and awards by category:*** *Academic interests/achievement:* architecture, education, general academic interests/achievements. *Creative arts/performance:* art/fine arts, general creative arts/performance. *Special achievements/activities:* general special achievements/activities. *Special characteristics:* general special characteristics. ***Tuition waivers:*** Full or partial for employees or children of employees.

LOANS ***Student loans:*** $55,441,859 (85% need-based, 15% non-need-based). 61% of past graduating class borrowed through all loan programs. *Average indebtedness per student:* $39,066. ***Average need-based loan:*** Freshmen: $3037. Undergraduates: $4181. ***Parent loans:*** $58,632,013 (73% need-based, 27% non-need-based). ***Programs:*** Federal Direct (Subsidized and Unsubsidized Stafford, PLUS), state.

WORK-STUDY ***Federal work-study:*** Total amount: $380,000; jobs available. ***State or other work-study/employment:*** Total amount: $596,000 (100% non-need-based). Part-time jobs available.

ATHLETIC AWARDS Total amount: $4,469,758 (38% need-based, 62% non-need-based).

APPLYING FOR FINANCIAL AID ***Required financial aid forms:*** FAFSA, state aid form. ***Financial aid deadline (priority):*** 2/15. ***Notification date:*** Continuous beginning 3/1. Students must reply within 4 weeks of notification.

CONTACT Brenda Clark, Director of Financial Aid, Savannah College of Art and Design, PO Box 3146, Savannah, GA 31402-3146, 912-525-6119 or toll-free 800-869-7223. *E-mail:* bclark@scad.edu.

SAVANNAH STATE UNIVERSITY

Savannah, GA

Tuition & fees (GA res): $5624 **Average undergraduate aid package: N/A**

ABOUT THE INSTITUTION State-supported, coed. 24 undergraduate majors. Federal methodology is used as a basis for awarding need-based institutional aid.

UNDERGRADUATE EXPENSES for 2010–11 ***Tuition, state resident:*** full-time $4274; part-time $143 per credit hour. ***Tuition, nonresident:*** full-time $15,888; part-time $530 per credit hour. ***Required fees:*** full-time $1350; $675 per term. Full-time tuition and fees vary according to course load and program. Part-time tuition and fees vary according to course load and program. ***College room and board:*** $6288; ***Room only:*** $2868. Room and board charges vary according to board plan and housing facility.

GIFT AID (NEED-BASED) ***Scholarships, grants, and awards:*** Federal Pell, FSEOG, state, private, college/university gift aid from institutional funds.

GIFT AID (NON-NEED-BASED) ***Scholarships, grants, and awards by category:*** *Academic interests/achievement:* biological sciences, business, computer science, engineering/technologies, English, general academic interests/achievements, humanities, mathematics, military science, physical sciences, social sciences. *Creative arts/performance:* music. ***Tuition waivers:*** Full or partial for senior citizens.

LOANS ***Programs:*** Federal Direct (Subsidized and Unsubsidized Stafford, PLUS), Perkins, state, college/university.

WORK-STUDY Federal work-study jobs available.

APPLYING FOR FINANCIAL AID ***Required financial aid form:*** FAFSA. ***Financial aid deadline:*** Continuous. ***Notification date:*** Continuous beginning 4/1. Students must reply within 2 weeks of notification.

CONTACT Adrienne Brown, Director of Financial Aid, Savannah State University, PO Box 20523, Savannah, GA 31404, 912-358-4162 or toll-free 800-788-0478. *Fax:* 912-353-3150. *E-mail:* finaid@savannahstate.edu.

SCHILLER INTERNATIONAL UNIVERSITY

Largo, FL

CONTACT Financial Aid Office, Schiller International University, 300 East Bay Drive, Largo, FL 33770, 727-736-5082 or toll-free 800-336-4133.

SCHOOL OF THE ART INSTITUTE OF CHICAGO

Chicago, IL

Tuition & fees: $35,950 **Average undergraduate aid package: $28,766**

ABOUT THE INSTITUTION Independent, coed. 33 undergraduate majors. Federal methodology is used as a basis for awarding need-based institutional aid.

UNDERGRADUATE EXPENSES for 2010–11 ***Tuition:*** full-time $35,550; part-time $1185 per semester hour. ***Payment plan:*** Installment.

FRESHMAN FINANCIAL AID (Fall 2010, est.) 315 applied for aid; of those 87% were deemed to have need. 100% of freshmen with need received aid; of those 3% had need fully met. ***Average percent of need met:*** 78% (excluding resources awarded to replace EFC). ***Average financial aid package:*** $29,919 (excluding resources awarded to replace EFC). 41% of all full-time freshmen had no need and received non-need-based gift aid.

UNDERGRADUATE FINANCIAL AID (Fall 2010, est.) 1,486 applied for aid; of those 93% were deemed to have need. 100% of undergraduates with need received aid; of those 4% had need fully met. ***Average percent of need met:*** 78% (excluding resources awarded to replace EFC). ***Average financial aid package:*** $28,766 (excluding resources awarded to replace EFC). 33% of all full-time undergraduates had no need and received non-need-based gift aid.

GIFT AID (NEED-BASED) ***Total amount:*** $19,073,102 (19% federal, 5% state, 75% institutional, 1% external sources). ***Receiving aid:*** Freshmen: 57% (272); all full-time undergraduates: 59% (1,368). ***Average award:*** Freshmen: $14,229; Undergraduates: $13,424. ***Scholarships, grants, and awards:*** Federal Pell, FSEOG, state, private, college/university gift aid from institutional funds.

GIFT AID (NON-NEED-BASED) ***Total amount:*** $4,829,862 (94% institutional, 6% external sources). ***Receiving aid:*** Freshmen: 2% (9). Undergraduates: 2% (44). ***Average award:*** Freshmen: $6221. Undergraduates: $5433. ***Scholarships, grants, and awards by category:*** *Academic interests/achievement:* general academic interests/achievements. *Creative arts/performance:* art/fine arts.

LOANS ***Student loans:*** $13,895,770 (87% need-based, 13% non-need-based). 50% of past graduating class borrowed through all loan programs. *Average indebtedness per student:* $39,306. ***Average need-based loan:*** Freshmen: $3782. Undergraduates: $4494. ***Parent loans:*** $8,622,168 (61% need-based, 39% non-need-based). ***Programs:*** Federal Direct (Subsidized and Unsubsidized Stafford, PLUS), Perkins.

WORK-STUDY ***Federal work-study:*** Total amount: $5,011,305; jobs available. ***State or other work-study/employment:*** Total amount: $110,672 (17% need-based, 83% non-need-based). Part-time jobs available.

APPLYING FOR FINANCIAL AID ***Required financial aid form:*** FAFSA. ***Financial aid deadline (priority):*** 3/1. ***Notification date:*** Continuous beginning 4/1.

CONTACT Student Financial Services Office, School of the Art Institute of Chicago, 36 South Wabash, Suite 1218, Chicago, IL 60603-3103, 312-629-6600 or toll-free 800-232-SAIC. *Fax:* 312-629-6601. *E-mail:* finaid@saic.edu.

SCHOOL OF THE MUSEUM OF FINE ARTS, BOSTON

Boston, MA

ABOUT THE INSTITUTION Independent, coed. 19 undergraduate majors.

GIFT AID (NEED-BASED) ***Scholarships, grants, and awards:*** Federal Pell, FSEOG, state, private, college/university gift aid from institutional funds.

GIFT AID (NON-NEED-BASED) ***Scholarships, grants, and awards by category:*** *Creative arts/performance:* art/fine arts. *Special characteristics:* general special characteristics.

LOANS ***Programs:*** state.

WORK-STUDY ***Federal work-study:*** Total amount: $171,440; jobs available.

APPLYING FOR FINANCIAL AID ***Required financial aid forms:*** FAFSA, institution's own form.

CONTACT Ms. Elizabeth Goreham, Director of Financial Aid, School of the Museum of Fine Arts, Boston, 230 The Fenway, Boston, MA 02115, 617-369-3684 or toll-free 800-643-6078 (in-state). *Fax:* 617-369-3041.

SCHOOL OF VISUAL ARTS

New York, NY

Tuition & fees: $28,140 **Average undergraduate aid package: $13,361**

ABOUT THE INSTITUTION Proprietary, coed. 15 undergraduate majors. Federal methodology is used as a basis for awarding need-based institutional aid.

UNDERGRADUATE EXPENSES for 2010–11 ***Comprehensive fee:*** $43,640 includes full-time tuition ($28,140) and room and board ($15,500). ***College room only:*** $12,500. Full-time tuition and fees vary according to degree level and program. Room and board charges vary according to board plan, gender, housing facility, and location. ***Part-time tuition:*** $940 per credit hour. Part-time tuition and fees vary according to degree level. ***Payment plan:*** Installment.

FRESHMAN FINANCIAL AID (Fall 2010, est.) 455 applied for aid; of those 89% were deemed to have need. 97% of freshmen with need received aid; of those 2% had need fully met. ***Average percent of need met:*** 39% (excluding resources awarded to replace EFC). ***Average financial aid package:*** $12,371 (excluding resources awarded to replace EFC). 6% of all full-time freshmen had no need and received non-need-based gift aid.

UNDERGRADUATE FINANCIAL AID (Fall 2010, est.) 2,060 applied for aid; of those 91% were deemed to have need. 98% of undergraduates with need received aid; of those 1% had need fully met. ***Average percent of need met:*** 38% (excluding resources awarded to replace EFC). ***Average financial aid package:*** $13,361 (excluding resources awarded to replace EFC). 7% of all full-time undergraduates had no need and received non-need-based gift aid.

GIFT AID (NEED-BASED) ***Total amount:*** $13,253,994 (38% federal, 13% state, 46% institutional, 3% external sources). ***Receiving aid:*** Freshmen: 39% (259); all full-time undergraduates: 38% (1,248). ***Average award:*** Freshmen: $9105; Undergraduates: $9468. ***Scholarships, grants, and awards:*** Federal Pell, FSEOG, state, private, college/university gift aid from institutional funds.

GIFT AID (NON-NEED-BASED) ***Total amount:*** $1,973,602 (2% state, 92% institutional, 6% external sources). ***Receiving aid:*** Freshmen: 12% (81). Undergraduates: 11% (350). ***Average award:*** Freshmen: $8582. Undergraduates: $7545. ***Scholarships, grants, and awards by category:*** *Creative arts/performance:* art/fine arts. ***Tuition waivers:*** Full or partial for employees or children of employees.

LOANS ***Student loans:*** $23,766,977 (92% need-based, 8% non-need-based). 69% of past graduating class borrowed through all loan programs. *Average indebtedness per student:* $41,495. ***Average need-based loan:*** Freshmen: $3494. Undergraduates: $4593. ***Parent loans:*** $14,478,471 (93% need-based, 7% non-need-based). ***Programs:*** Federal Direct (Subsidized and Unsubsidized Stafford, PLUS), Perkins, alternative loans.

WORK-STUDY ***Federal work-study:*** Total amount: $240,227; jobs available. ***State or other work-study/employment:*** Total amount: $604,668 (83% need-based, 17% non-need-based). Part-time jobs available.

APPLYING FOR FINANCIAL AID ***Required financial aid forms:*** FAFSA, state aid form. ***Financial aid deadline:*** 3/1 (priority: 2/1). ***Notification date:*** Continuous beginning 2/15. Students must reply within 4 weeks of notification.

CONTACT Financial Aid Office, School of Visual Arts, 209 East 23rd Street, New York, NY 10010, 212-592-2030 or toll-free 800-436-4204. *Fax:* 212-592-2029. *E-mail:* fa@sva.edu.

SCHREINER UNIVERSITY

Kerrville, TX

Tuition & fees: $20,354 **Average undergraduate aid package: $14,921**

ABOUT THE INSTITUTION Independent Presbyterian, coed. 38 undergraduate majors. Federal methodology is used as a basis for awarding need-based institutional aid.

UNDERGRADUATE EXPENSES for 2011–12 ***Comprehensive fee:*** $30,030 includes full-time tuition ($19,754), mandatory fees ($600), and room and board ($9676). ***College room only:*** $5410. Room and board charges vary according to board plan and housing facility. ***Part-time tuition:*** $843 per credit. ***Part-time fees:*** $115 per term. ***Payment plan:*** Installment.

FRESHMAN FINANCIAL AID (Fall 2009) 263 applied for aid; of those 86% were deemed to have need. 100% of freshmen with need received aid; of those 16% had need fully met. ***Average percent of need met:*** 72% (excluding resources awarded to replace EFC). ***Average financial aid package:*** $14,490 (excluding resources awarded to replace EFC). 14% of all full-time freshmen had no need and received non-need-based gift aid.

UNDERGRADUATE FINANCIAL AID (Fall 2009) 871 applied for aid; of those 89% were deemed to have need. 100% of undergraduates with need received aid; of those 16% had need fully met. ***Average percent of need met:*** 71% (excluding resources awarded to replace EFC). ***Average financial aid package:*** $14,921 (excluding resources awarded to replace EFC). 10% of all full-time undergraduates had no need and received non-need-based gift aid.

GIFT AID (NEED-BASED) ***Total amount:*** $9,332,531 (20% federal, 16% state, 48% institutional, 16% external sources). ***Receiving aid:*** Freshmen: 86% (225); all full-time undergraduates: 89% (773). ***Average award:*** Freshmen: $12,158; Undergraduates: $11,963. ***Scholarships, grants, and awards:*** Federal Pell, FSEOG, state, private, college/university gift aid from institutional funds.

GIFT AID (NON-NEED-BASED) ***Total amount:*** $1,129,295 (2% state, 76% institutional, 22% external sources). ***Receiving aid:*** Freshmen: 12% (32). Undergraduates: 10% (91). ***Average award:*** Freshmen: $7751. Undergraduates: $7540. ***Scholarships, grants, and awards by category:*** *Academic interests/achievement:* biological sciences, business, education, English, general academic interests/achievements, mathematics, physical sciences, premedicine, religion/biblical studies, social sciences. *Creative arts/performance:* art/fine arts, journalism/publications, music, theater/drama. *Special achievements/activities:* community service, leadership, memberships, religious involvement. *Special characteristics:* children of faculty/staff, general special characteristics, international students, local/state students, relatives of clergy, religious affiliation, siblings of current students. ***Tuition waivers:*** Full or partial for employees or children of employees.

LOANS ***Student loans:*** $6,755,940 (70% need-based, 30% non-need-based). 95% of past graduating class borrowed through all loan programs. *Average indebtedness per student:* $28,967. ***Average need-based loan:*** Freshmen: $2883. Undergraduates: $3550. ***Parent loans:*** $842,689 (29% need-based, 71% non-need-based). ***Programs:*** Federal Direct (Subsidized and Unsubsidized Stafford, PLUS), state, alternative loans.

WORK-STUDY ***Federal work-study:*** Total amount: $57,239; jobs available. ***State or other work-study/employment:*** Part-time jobs available.

APPLYING FOR FINANCIAL AID ***Required financial aid forms:*** FAFSA, Texas Application for State Financial Aid (TASFA). ***Financial aid deadline:*** 8/1 (priority: 4/1). ***Notification date:*** Continuous beginning 2/15. Students must reply within 2 weeks of notification.

CONTACT Toni Bryant, Director of Financial Aid, Schreiner University, 2100 Memorial Boulevard, Kerrville, TX 78028, 830-792-7217 or toll-free 800-343-4919. *Fax:* 830-792-7226. *E-mail:* finaid@schreiner.edu.

SCRIPPS COLLEGE

Claremont, CA

Tuition & fees: $40,450 **Average undergraduate aid package: $36,614**

ABOUT THE INSTITUTION Independent, women only. 62 undergraduate majors. Both federal and institutional methodology are used as a basis for awarding need-based institutional aid.

UNDERGRADUATE EXPENSES for 2010–11 ***Comprehensive fee:*** $52,900 includes full-time tuition ($40,236), mandatory fees ($214), and room and board ($12,450). ***College room only:*** $6720. Full-time tuition and fees vary according to program. Room and board charges vary according to board plan. ***Part-time tuition:*** $5030 per course. Part-time tuition and fees vary according to program. ***Payment plans:*** Tuition prepayment, installment.

FRESHMAN FINANCIAL AID (Fall 2010, est.) 116 applied for aid; of those 80% were deemed to have need. 100% of freshmen with need received aid; of those 100% had need fully met. ***Average percent of need met:*** 100% (excluding resources awarded to replace EFC). ***Average financial aid package:*** $36,915 (excluding resources awarded to replace EFC). 7% of all full-time freshmen had no need and received non-need-based gift aid.

UNDERGRADUATE FINANCIAL AID (Fall 2010, est.) 512 applied for aid; of those 83% were deemed to have need. 100% of undergraduates with need received aid; of those 100% had need fully met. ***Average percent of need met:*** 100% (excluding resources awarded to replace EFC). ***Average financial aid package:*** $36,614 (excluding resources awarded to replace EFC). 9% of all full-time undergraduates had no need and received non-need-based gift aid.

GIFT AID (NEED-BASED) ***Total amount:*** $13,532,145 (6% federal, 3% state, 88% institutional, 3% external sources). ***Receiving aid:*** Freshmen: 46% (90); all full-time undergraduates: 43% (409). ***Average award:*** Freshmen: $33,893; Undergraduates: $33,163. ***Scholarships, grants, and awards:*** Federal Pell, FSEOG, state, private, college/university gift aid from institutional funds.

GIFT AID (NON-NEED-BASED) ***Total amount:*** $2,208,073 (89% institutional, 11% external sources). ***Average award:*** Freshmen: $26,627. Undergraduates: $22,102. ***Scholarships, grants, and awards by category:*** *Academic interests/achievement:* general academic interests/achievements. *Special achievements/activities:* leadership. ***Tuition waivers:*** Full or partial for employees or children of employees.

LOANS ***Student loans:*** $1,814,990 (49% need-based, 51% non-need-based). 36% of past graduating class borrowed through all loan programs. *Average indebtedness per student:* $9435. ***Average need-based loan:*** Freshmen: $3063. Undergraduates: $3271. ***Parent loans:*** $1,888,621 (100% non-need-based). ***Programs:*** Federal Direct (Subsidized and Unsubsidized Stafford, PLUS), Perkins, college/university.

WORK-STUDY ***Federal work-study:*** Total amount: $493,880; 319 jobs averaging $1548. ***State or other work-study/employment:*** Total amount: $57,205 (100% need-based). 37 part-time jobs averaging $1591.

APPLYING FOR FINANCIAL AID ***Required financial aid forms:*** FAFSA, CSS Financial Aid PROFILE, noncustodial (divorced/separated) parent's statement, business/farm supplement, federal income tax form(s), verification worksheet. ***Financial aid deadline:*** 5/1 (priority: 2/1). ***Notification date:*** 4/1. Students must reply by 5/1.

CONTACT David Levy, Director of Financial Aid, Scripps College, 1030 Columbia Avenue, PMB 1293, Claremont, CA 91711-3948, 909-621-8275 or toll-free 800-770-1333. *Fax:* 909-607-7742. *E-mail:* dlevy@scrippscollege.edu.

SEATTLE PACIFIC UNIVERSITY

Seattle, WA

Tuition & fees: $30,339 **Average undergraduate aid package: $26,479**

ABOUT THE INSTITUTION Independent Free Methodist, coed. 54 undergraduate majors. Federal methodology is used as a basis for awarding need-based institutional aid.

UNDERGRADUATE EXPENSES for 2011–12 ***Comprehensive fee:*** $39,420 includes full-time tuition ($29,976), mandatory fees ($363), and room and board ($9081). ***College room only:*** $4944. Room and board charges vary according to board plan and housing facility. Part-time tuition and fees vary according to course load. ***Payment plans:*** Installment, deferred payment.

FRESHMAN FINANCIAL AID (Fall 2010, est.) 639 applied for aid; of those 83% were deemed to have need. 100% of freshmen with need received aid; of those 9% had need fully met. ***Average percent of need met:*** 83% (excluding resources awarded to replace EFC). ***Average financial aid package:*** $25,568 (excluding resources awarded to replace EFC). 19% of all full-time freshmen had no need and received non-need-based gift aid.

UNDERGRADUATE FINANCIAL AID (Fall 2010, est.) 2,294 applied for aid; of those 87% were deemed to have need. 99% of undergraduates with need received aid; of those 7% had need fully met. ***Average percent of need met:*** 82% (excluding resources awarded to replace EFC). ***Average financial aid package:*** $26,479 (excluding resources awarded to replace EFC). 23% of all full-time undergraduates had no need and received non-need-based gift aid.

GIFT AID (NEED-BASED) ***Total amount:*** $38,994,239 (13% federal, 7% state, 75% institutional, 5% external sources). ***Receiving aid:*** Freshmen: 74% (529); all full-time undergraduates: 69% (1,962). ***Average award:*** Freshmen: $21,585; Undergraduates: $21,498. ***Scholarships, grants, and awards:*** Federal Pell, FSEOG, state, private, college/university gift aid from institutional funds.

GIFT AID (NON-NEED-BASED) ***Total amount:*** $9,693,151 (1% state, 83% institutional, 16% external sources). ***Average award:*** Freshmen: $15,818. Undergraduates: $14,897. ***Scholarships, grants, and awards by category:*** *Academic interests/achievement:* 546 awards ($4,808,000 total): engineering/technologies, general academic interests/achievements. *Creative arts/performance:* 27 awards ($34,950 total): art/fine arts, performing arts. *Special characteristics:* 258 awards ($971,544 total): children and siblings of alumni, children of faculty/staff, general special characteristics, international students, relatives of clergy, religious affiliation, veterans. ***Tuition waivers:*** Full or partial for employees or children of employees, senior citizens.

LOANS ***Student loans:*** $17,429,510 (91% need-based, 9% non-need-based). 68% of past graduating class borrowed through all loan programs. *Average indebtedness per student:* $30,073. ***Average need-based loan:*** Freshmen: $5068. Undergraduates: $5251. ***Parent loans:*** $5,191,714 (84% need-based, 16% non-need-based). ***Programs:*** Federal Direct (Subsidized and Unsubsidized Stafford, PLUS), Perkins, Federal Nursing, college/university.

WORK-STUDY ***Federal work-study:*** Total amount: $540,824; 373 jobs available. ***State or other work-study/employment:*** Total amount: $596,808 (100% need-based). 309 part-time jobs available.

ATHLETIC AWARDS Total amount: $1,633,746 (52% need-based, 48% non-need-based).

APPLYING FOR FINANCIAL AID ***Required financial aid form:*** FAFSA. ***Financial aid deadline (priority):*** 2/1. ***Notification date:*** Continuous beginning 3/15. Students must reply by 5/1 or within 4 weeks of notification.

CONTACT Mr. Jordan Grant, Director of Student Financial Services, Seattle Pacific University, 3307 Third Avenue West, Seattle, WA 98119-1997, 206-281-2469 or toll-free 800-366-3344. *E-mail:* grantj@spu.edu.

SEATTLE UNIVERSITY

Seattle, WA

Tuition & fees: $30,825 **Average undergraduate aid package: $27,765**

ABOUT THE INSTITUTION Independent Roman Catholic, coed. 56 undergraduate majors. Federal methodology is used as a basis for awarding need-based institutional aid.

UNDERGRADUATE EXPENSES for 2010–11 ***Comprehensive fee:*** $40,140 includes full-time tuition ($30,825) and room and board ($9315). ***College room only:*** $5805. Full-time tuition and fees vary according to course load. Room and board charges vary according to board plan. ***Part-time tuition:*** $685 per credit hour. Part-time tuition and fees vary according to course load. ***Payment plan:*** Installment.

FRESHMAN FINANCIAL AID (Fall 2010, est.) 938 applied for aid; of those 83% were deemed to have need. 100% of freshmen with need received aid; of those 8% had need fully met. ***Average percent of need met:*** 74% (excluding resources awarded to replace EFC). ***Average financial aid package:*** $26,578 (excluding resources awarded to replace EFC). 8% of all full-time freshmen had no need and received non-need-based gift aid.

UNDERGRADUATE FINANCIAL AID (Fall 2010, est.) 3,470 applied for aid; of those 84% were deemed to have need. 99% of undergraduates with need received aid; of those 11% had need fully met. ***Average percent of need met:*** 71% (excluding resources awarded to replace EFC). ***Average financial aid package:*** $27,765 (excluding resources awarded to replace EFC). 5% of all full-time undergraduates had no need and received non-need-based gift aid.

GIFT AID (NEED-BASED) ***Total amount:*** $54,584,802 (12% federal, 5% state, 78% institutional, 5% external sources). ***Receiving aid:*** Freshmen: 68% (706); all full-time undergraduates: 59% (2,568). ***Average award:*** Freshmen: $13,923; Undergraduates: $15,010. ***Scholarships, grants, and awards:*** Federal Pell, FSEOG, state, private, college/university gift aid from institutional funds, Federal Nursing.

GIFT AID (NON-NEED-BASED) ***Total amount:*** $8,985,623 (19% federal, 80% institutional, 1% external sources). ***Receiving aid:*** Freshmen: 44% (457). Undergraduates: 27% (1,152). ***Average award:*** Freshmen: $9324. Undergraduates: $9985. ***Scholarships, grants, and awards by category:*** *Academic interests/achievement:* general academic interests/achievements. *Creative arts/performance:* art/fine arts, music, theater/drama. *Special achievements/activities:* leadership. *Special characteristics:* children and siblings of alumni, children of educators, children of faculty/staff, members of minority groups, religious affiliation. ***Tuition waivers:*** Full or partial for employees or children of employees.

LOANS ***Student loans:*** $25,187,929 (70% need-based, 30% non-need-based). 74% of past graduating class borrowed through all loan programs. *Average indebtedness per student:* $26,607. ***Average need-based loan:*** Freshmen: $4255. Undergraduates: $4705. ***Parent loans:*** $7,040,394 (11% need-based, 89% non-need-based). ***Programs:*** Federal Direct (Subsidized and Unsubsidized Stafford, PLUS), Perkins, Federal Nursing.

WORK-STUDY ***Federal work-study:*** Total amount: $2,511,571; jobs available. ***State or other work-study/employment:*** Total amount: $3,548,228 (100% need-based). Part-time jobs available.

ATHLETIC AWARDS Total amount: $3,776,161 (11% need-based, 89% non-need-based).

APPLYING FOR FINANCIAL AID ***Required financial aid form:*** FAFSA. ***Financial aid deadline (priority):*** 2/1. ***Notification date:*** 3/1. Students must reply by 5/1 or within 2 weeks of notification.

CONTACT Ms. Janet Cantelon, Director of Student Financial Services, Seattle University, 901 12th Avenue, PO Box 222000, Seattle, WA 98122-1090, 206-296-2000 or toll-free 800-542-0833 (in-state), 800-426-7123 (out-of-state). *Fax:* 206-296-5755. *E-mail:* financial-aid@seattleu.edu.

SETON HALL UNIVERSITY

South Orange, NJ

CONTACT Office of Enrollment Services, Seton Hall University, 400 South Orange Avenue, South Orange, NJ 07079, 973-761-9350 or toll-free 800-THE HALL (out-of-state). *Fax:* 973-275-2040. *E-mail:* thehall@shu.edu.

SETON HILL UNIVERSITY

Greensburg, PA

Tuition & fees: $27,548 **Average undergraduate aid package: $21,753**

ABOUT THE INSTITUTION Independent Roman Catholic, coed. 73 undergraduate majors. Federal methodology is used as a basis for awarding need-based institutional aid.

UNDERGRADUATE EXPENSES for 2010–11 ***Comprehensive fee:*** $36,358 includes full-time tuition ($26,848), mandatory fees ($700), and room and board ($8810). Full-time tuition and fees vary according to course load and program. Room and board charges vary according to board plan and housing facility. ***Part-time tuition:*** $720 per credit. ***Part-time fees:*** $25 per credit; $40 per term. Part-time tuition and fees vary according to course load and program. ***Payment plan:*** Installment.

FRESHMAN FINANCIAL AID (Fall 2010, est.) 364 applied for aid; of those 92% were deemed to have need. 99% of freshmen with need received aid; of those 21% had need fully met. ***Average percent of need met:*** 76% (excluding resources awarded to replace EFC). ***Average financial aid package:*** $22,752 (excluding resources awarded to replace EFC). 13% of all full-time freshmen had no need and received non-need-based gift aid.

UNDERGRADUATE FINANCIAL AID (Fall 2010, est.) 1,473 applied for aid; of those 87% were deemed to have need. 99% of undergraduates with need received aid; of those 17% had need fully met. ***Average percent of need met:*** 74% (excluding resources awarded to replace EFC). ***Average financial aid package:*** $21,753 (excluding resources awarded to replace EFC). 10% of all full-time undergraduates had no need and received non-need-based gift aid.

GIFT AID (NEED-BASED) ***Total amount:*** $19,350,836 (15% federal, 11% state, 72% institutional, 2% external sources). ***Receiving aid:*** Freshmen: 89% (330); all full-time undergraduates: 82% (1,250). ***Average award:*** Freshmen: $18,478; Undergraduates: $16,995. ***Scholarships, grants, and awards:*** Federal Pell, FSEOG, state, private, college/university gift aid from institutional funds, United Negro College Fund.

GIFT AID (NON-NEED-BASED) ***Total amount:*** $2,301,167 (97% institutional, 3% external sources). ***Receiving aid:*** Freshmen: 15% (55). Undergraduates: 10% (145). ***Average award:*** Freshmen: $11,020. Undergraduates: $11,482. ***Scholarships, grants, and awards by category:*** *Academic interests/achievement:* 635 awards ($6,125,320 total): biological sciences, business, communication, computer science, education, English, foreign languages, general academic interests/achievements, humanities, mathematics, physical sciences, social sciences. *Creative arts/performance:* 50 awards ($105,186 total): applied art and design, art/fine arts, music, performing arts, theater/drama. *Special achievements/activities:* 17 awards ($8500 total): cheerleading/drum major. *Special characteristics:* 387 awards ($939,325 total): children and siblings of alumni, first-generation college students, general special characteristics, out-of-state students, parents of current students, siblings of current students. ***Tuition waivers:*** Full or partial for employees or children of employees.

LOANS ***Student loans:*** $10,731,802 (79% need-based, 21% non-need-based). 91% of past graduating class borrowed through all loan programs. *Average indebtedness per student:* $30,997. ***Average need-based loan:*** Freshmen: $4716. Undergraduates: $5253. ***Parent loans:*** $2,443,717 (47% need-based, 53% non-need-based). ***Programs:*** Federal Direct (Subsidized and Unsubsidized Stafford, PLUS), Perkins, college/university, alternative loans.

WORK-STUDY ***Federal work-study:*** Total amount: $685,780; 543 jobs averaging $1594. ***State or other work-study/employment:*** Total amount: $204,286 (9% need-based, 91% non-need-based). 131 part-time jobs averaging $1536.

ATHLETIC AWARDS Total amount: $3,235,871 (67% need-based, 33% non-need-based).

APPLYING FOR FINANCIAL AID ***Required financial aid forms:*** FAFSA, state aid form. ***Financial aid deadline (priority):*** 5/1. ***Notification date:*** Continuous beginning 11/15. Students must reply by 5/1 or within 2 weeks of notification.

CONTACT Maryann Dudas, Director of Financial Aid, Seton Hill University, Seton Hill Drive, Greensburg, PA 15601, 724-838-4293 or toll-free 800-826-6234. *Fax:* 724-830-1194. *E-mail:* dudas@setonhill.edu.

SEWANEE: THE UNIVERSITY OF THE SOUTH

Sewanee, TN

Tuition & fees: $32,292 **Average undergraduate aid package: $31,995**

ABOUT THE INSTITUTION Independent Episcopal, coed. 40 undergraduate majors. Both federal and institutional methodology are used as a basis for awarding need-based institutional aid.

UNDERGRADUATE EXPENSES for 2011–12 ***Comprehensive fee:*** $41,518 includes full-time tuition ($32,020), mandatory fees ($272), and room and board ($9226). ***College room only:*** $4796. ***Part-time tuition:*** $1162 per credit hour. ***Payment plans:*** Installment, deferred payment.

FRESHMAN FINANCIAL AID (Fall 2010, est.) 192 applied for aid; of those 69% were deemed to have need. 99% of freshmen with need received aid; of those 72% had need fully met. ***Average percent of need met:*** 96% (excluding resources awarded to replace EFC). ***Average financial aid package:*** $34,988 (excluding resources awarded to replace EFC). 29% of all full-time freshmen had no need and received non-need-based gift aid.

UNDERGRADUATE FINANCIAL AID (Fall 2010, est.) 513 applied for aid; of those 97% were deemed to have need. 100% of undergraduates with need received aid; of those 77% had need fully met. ***Average percent of need met:*** 96% (excluding resources awarded to replace EFC). ***Average financial aid package:*** $31,995 (excluding resources awarded to replace EFC). 17% of all full-time undergraduates had no need and received non-need-based gift aid.

GIFT AID (NEED-BASED) ***Total amount:*** $16,380,357 (8% federal, 5% state, 85% institutional, 2% external sources). ***Receiving aid:*** Freshmen: 33% (132); all full-time undergraduates: 34% (491). ***Average award:*** Freshmen: $27,874; Undergraduates: $23,092. ***Scholarships, grants, and awards:*** Federal Pell, FSEOG, state, private, college/university gift aid from institutional funds.

GIFT AID (NON-NEED-BASED) ***Total amount:*** $6,392,726 (1% federal, 5% state, 89% institutional, 5% external sources). ***Receiving aid:*** Freshmen: 29% (117). Undergraduates: 17% (248). ***Average award:*** Freshmen: $14,306. Undergraduates: $16,182. ***Scholarships, grants, and awards by category:*** *Academic interests/achievement:* general academic interests/achievements. *Special characteristics:* children of faculty/staff, ethnic background, members of minority groups, relatives of clergy. ***Tuition waivers:*** Full or partial for employees or children of employees.

LOANS ***Student loans:*** $4,100,561 (71% need-based, 29% non-need-based). 39% of past graduating class borrowed through all loan programs. *Average indebtedness per student:* $19,337. ***Average need-based loan:*** Freshmen: $6906. Undergraduates: $9180. ***Parent loans:*** $1,886,237 (75% need-based, 25% non-need-based). ***Programs:*** Federal Direct (Subsidized and Unsubsidized Stafford, PLUS), Perkins, state, college/university, private loans.

WORK-STUDY ***Federal work-study:*** Total amount: $505,654; jobs available. ***State or other work-study/employment:*** Total amount: $102,448 (45% need-based, 55% non-need-based). Part-time jobs available.

APPLYING FOR FINANCIAL AID ***Required financial aid forms:*** FAFSA, institution's own form. ***Financial aid deadline (priority):*** 3/1. ***Notification date:*** Continuous beginning 3/1. Students must reply by 5/1 or within 4 weeks of notification.

CONTACT Beth A. Cragar, Associate Dean of Admission for Financial Aid, Sewanee: The University of the South, 735 University Avenue, Sewanee, TN 37383-1000, 931-598-1312 or toll-free 800-522-2234. *Fax:* 931-598-3273.

SHASTA BIBLE COLLEGE

Redding, CA

Tuition & fees: $9600 **Average undergraduate aid package: $2500**

ABOUT THE INSTITUTION Independent nondenominational, coed. 3 undergraduate majors. Federal methodology is used as a basis for awarding need-based institutional aid.

UNDERGRADUATE EXPENSES for 2010–11 ***Tuition:*** full-time $9600; part-time $300 per unit. ***Required fees:*** $480 per year. ***Payment plan:*** Installment.

FRESHMAN FINANCIAL AID (Fall 2010, est.) 22 applied for aid; of those 68% were deemed to have need. 100% of freshmen with need received aid. ***Average percent of need met:*** 50% (excluding resources awarded to replace EFC). ***Average financial aid package:*** $2500 (excluding resources awarded to replace EFC).

UNDERGRADUATE FINANCIAL AID (Fall 2010, est.) 59 applied for aid; of those 75% were deemed to have need. 100% of undergraduates with need received aid. ***Average percent of need met:*** 50% (excluding resources awarded to replace EFC). ***Average financial aid package:*** $2500 (excluding resources awarded to replace EFC). 11% of all full-time undergraduates had no need and received non-need-based gift aid.

GIFT AID (NEED-BASED) ***Total amount:*** $253,921 (74% federal, 11% state, 11% institutional, 4% external sources). ***Receiving aid:*** Freshmen: 65% (15); all full-time undergraduates: 61% (44). ***Average award:*** Freshmen: $2500; Undergraduates: $2500. ***Scholarships, grants, and awards:*** Federal Pell, FSEOG, state, private, college/university gift aid from institutional funds.

GIFT AID (NON-NEED-BASED) ***Receiving aid:*** Undergraduates: 14% (10). ***Scholarships, grants, and awards by category:*** *Academic interests/achievement:* education. *Creative arts/performance:* music. *Special achievements/activities:* general special achievements/activities. *Special characteristics:* relatives of clergy, veterans. ***Tuition waivers:*** Full or partial for employees or children of employees.

LOANS ***Student loans:*** $32,005 (100% need-based). ***Average need-based loan:*** Undergraduates: $4000. ***Parent loans:*** $9464 (100% need-based). ***Programs:*** Federal Direct (Subsidized and Unsubsidized Stafford, PLUS).

WORK-STUDY ***Federal work-study:*** Total amount: $6982; 19 jobs averaging $800. ***State or other work-study/employment:*** Total amount: $9740 (100% need-based). 3 part-time jobs averaging $824.

APPLYING FOR FINANCIAL AID ***Required financial aid forms:*** FAFSA, institution's own form, state aid form. ***Financial aid deadline:*** Continuous. ***Notification date:*** Continuous beginning 7/15. Students must reply within 3 weeks of notification.

CONTACT Linda Iles, Financial Aid Administrator, Shasta Bible College, 2951 Goodwater Avenue, Redding, CA 96002, 530-221-4275 or toll-free 800-800-45BC (in-state), 800-800-6929 (out-of-state). *Fax:* 530-221-6929. *E-mail:* finaid@shasta.edu.

SHAWNEE STATE UNIVERSITY

Portsmouth, OH

Tuition & fees (OH res): $6546 **Average undergraduate aid package: N/A**

ABOUT THE INSTITUTION State-supported, coed. 47 undergraduate majors. Both federal and institutional methodology are used as a basis for awarding need-based institutional aid.

UNDERGRADUATE EXPENSES for 2010–11 ***Tuition, state resident:*** full-time $5538; part-time $230.75 per credit hour. ***Tuition, nonresident:*** full-time $10,182; part-time $424.25 per credit hour. ***Required fees:*** full-time $1008; $42 per credit hour. Full-time tuition and fees vary according to course load, reciprocity agreements, and student level. Part-time tuition and fees vary according to course load, reciprocity agreements, and student level. ***College room and board:*** $8416; ***Room only:*** $5134. Room and board charges vary according to board plan and housing facility. ***Payment plan:*** Installment.

GIFT AID (NEED-BASED) ***Scholarships, grants, and awards:*** Federal Pell, FSEOG, state, private, college/university gift aid from institutional funds.

GIFT AID (NON-NEED-BASED) ***Scholarships, grants, and awards by category:*** *Academic interests/achievement:* general academic interests/achievements. *Creative arts/performance:* art/fine arts, performing arts. *Special achievements/activities:* memberships. *Special characteristics:* ethnic background, first-generation college students, handicapped students, local/state students, members of minority groups, veterans. ***Tuition waivers:*** Full or partial for employees or children of employees, senior citizens.

LOANS ***Programs:*** college/university.

APPLYING FOR FINANCIAL AID ***Required financial aid forms:*** FAFSA, institution's own form. ***Financial aid deadline (priority):*** 4/1. ***Notification date:*** 6/1.

CONTACT Nicole Neal, Director of Financial Aid, Shawnee State University, 940 Second Street, Portsmouth, OH 45662-4344, 740-351-3140 or toll-free 800-959-2SSU. *E-mail:* nneal@shawnee.edu.

SHAW UNIVERSITY

Raleigh, NC

CONTACT Rochelle King, Director of Financial Aid, Shaw University, 118 East South Street, Raleigh, NC 27601-2399, 919-546-8565 or toll-free 800-214-6683. *Fax:* 919-546-8356. *E-mail:* rking@shawu.edu.

SHENANDOAH UNIVERSITY

Winchester, VA

Tuition & fees: $25,080 **Average undergraduate aid package: $19,000**

ABOUT THE INSTITUTION Independent United Methodist, coed. 38 undergraduate majors. Federal methodology is used as a basis for awarding need-based institutional aid.

UNDERGRADUATE EXPENSES for 2010–11 ***Comprehensive fee:*** $33,950 includes full-time tuition ($24,780), mandatory fees ($300), and room and board ($8870). Full-time tuition and fees vary according to course load, location, and program. Room and board charges vary according to board plan and housing facility. ***Part-time tuition:*** $723 per credit hour. Part-time tuition and fees vary according to course load, location, and program. ***Payment plan:*** Installment.

FRESHMAN FINANCIAL AID (Fall 2010, est.) 348 applied for aid; of those 86% were deemed to have need. 100% of freshmen with need received aid; of those 19% had need fully met. ***Average percent of need met:*** 71% (excluding resources awarded to replace EFC). ***Average financial aid package:*** $19,000 (excluding resources awarded to replace EFC). 13% of all full-time freshmen had no need and received non-need-based gift aid.

UNDERGRADUATE FINANCIAL AID (Fall 2010, est.) 1,231 applied for aid; of those 94% were deemed to have need. 100% of undergraduates with need received aid; of those 6% had need fully met. ***Average percent of need met:*** 71% (excluding resources awarded to replace EFC). ***Average financial aid package:*** $19,000 (excluding resources awarded to replace EFC). 8% of all full-time undergraduates had no need and received non-need-based gift aid.

GIFT AID (NEED-BASED) ***Total amount:*** $8,266,600 (28% federal, 31% state, 39% institutional, 2% external sources). ***Receiving aid:*** Freshmen: 74% (301); all full-time undergraduates: 64% (1,151). ***Average award:*** Freshmen: $8500; Undergraduates: $8000. ***Scholarships, grants, and awards:*** Federal Pell, FSEOG, state, private, college/university gift aid from institutional funds, Federal Nursing.

GIFT AID (NON-NEED-BASED) ***Total amount:*** $11,800,727 (100% institutional). ***Receiving aid:*** Freshmen: 74% (301). Undergraduates: 64% (1,151). ***Average award:*** Freshmen: $6000. Undergraduates: $5000. ***Scholarships, grants, and awards by category:*** *Academic interests/achievement:* 1,200 awards ($8,937,635 total): business, general academic interests/achievements. *Creative arts/performance:* 156 awards ($936,790 total): dance, music, performing arts, theater/drama. *Special achievements/activities:* 87 awards ($136,555 total): religious involvement. *Special characteristics:* 59 awards ($611,630 total): children of faculty/staff, local/state students, relatives of clergy, religious affiliation. ***Tuition waivers:*** Full or partial for employees or children of employees.

LOANS ***Student loans:*** $10,554,795 (47% need-based, 53% non-need-based). 85% of past graduating class borrowed through all loan programs. *Average indebtedness per student:* $27,000. ***Average need-based loan:*** Freshmen: $3500. Undergraduates: $4500. ***Parent loans:*** $6,817,068 (20% need-based, 80% non-need-based). ***Programs:*** Federal Direct (Subsidized and Unsubsidized Stafford, PLUS), Perkins, Federal Nursing, college/university.

WORK-STUDY ***Federal work-study:*** Total amount: $1,416,162; 732 jobs averaging $1935. ***State or other work-study/employment:*** Total amount: $760,621 (11% need-based, 89% non-need-based). 384 part-time jobs averaging $1980.

APPLYING FOR FINANCIAL AID ***Required financial aid forms:*** FAFSA, state aid form. ***Financial aid deadline (priority):*** 2/15. ***Notification date:*** Continuous beginning 3/15. Students must reply within 4 weeks of notification.

CONTACT Nancy Bragg, Director of Financial Aid, Shenandoah University, 1460 University Drive, Winchester, VA 22601-5195, 540-665-4538 or toll-free 800-432-2266. *Fax:* 540-665-4939. *E-mail:* nbragg@su.edu.

SHEPHERD UNIVERSITY

Shepherdstown, WV

Tuition & fees (WV res): $5234 **Average undergraduate aid package: $11,294**

ABOUT THE INSTITUTION State-supported, coed. 25 undergraduate majors. Federal methodology is used as a basis for awarding need-based institutional aid.

UNDERGRADUATE EXPENSES for 2010–11 ***Tuition, state resident:*** full-time $5234; part-time $214 per credit hour. ***Tuition, nonresident:*** full-time $14,046; part-time $581 per credit hour. Full-time tuition and fees vary according to program and reciprocity agreements. Part-time tuition and fees vary according to program. ***College room and board:*** $7720. Room and board charges vary according to board plan and housing facility. ***Payment plan:*** Installment.

FRESHMAN FINANCIAL AID (Fall 2010, est.) 705 applied for aid; of those 65% were deemed to have need. 99% of freshmen with need received aid; of those 27% had need fully met. ***Average percent of need met:*** 83% (excluding resources awarded to replace EFC). ***Average financial aid package:*** $10,639 (excluding resources awarded to replace EFC). 23% of all full-time freshmen had no need and received non-need-based gift aid.

UNDERGRADUATE FINANCIAL AID (Fall 2010, est.) 3,051 applied for aid; of those 66% were deemed to have need. 98% of undergraduates with need received aid; of those 27% had need fully met. ***Average percent of need met:*** 80% (excluding resources awarded to replace EFC). ***Average financial aid package:*** $11,294 (excluding resources awarded to replace EFC). 21% of all full-time undergraduates had no need and received non-need-based gift aid.

GIFT AID (NEED-BASED) ***Total amount:*** $6,972,349 (79% federal, 19% state, 2% institutional). ***Receiving aid:*** Freshmen: 38% (291); all full-time undergraduates: 38% (1,296). ***Average award:*** Freshmen: $5197; Undergraduates: $5129. ***Scholarships, grants, and awards:*** Federal Pell, FSEOG, state, private, college/university gift aid from institutional funds.

GIFT AID (NON-NEED-BASED) ***Total amount:*** $5,159,656 (41% state, 54% institutional, 5% external sources). ***Receiving aid:*** Freshmen: 21% (158). Undergraduates: 16% (540). ***Average award:*** Freshmen: $9654. Undergraduates: $9351. ***Scholarships, grants, and awards by category:*** *Academic interests/achievement:* 494 awards ($1,870,967 total): biological sciences, business, communication, computer science, education, engineering/technologies, English, general academic interests/achievements, health fields, home economics, humanities, mathematics, physical sciences, premedicine, social sciences. *Creative arts/performance:* 56 awards ($219,544 total): applied art and design, art/fine arts, music, performing arts, theater/drama. *Special achievements/activities:* 1 award ($3250 total): leadership. *Special characteristics:* 130 awards ($343,937 total): ethnic background, handicapped students, local/state students, members of minority groups, out-of-state students, previous college experience. ***Tuition waivers:*** Full or partial for minority students, employees or children of employees, senior citizens.

LOANS ***Student loans:*** $15,056,047 (44% need-based, 56% non-need-based). 68% of past graduating class borrowed through all loan programs. *Average indebtedness per student:* $20,429. ***Average need-based loan:*** Freshmen: $3194. Undergraduates: $3973. ***Parent loans:*** $2,881,857 (100% non-need-based). ***Programs:*** Federal Direct (Subsidized and Unsubsidized Stafford, PLUS), Perkins.

WORK-STUDY ***Federal work-study:*** Total amount: $259,944; 142 jobs averaging $1532. ***State or other work-study/employment:*** Total amount: $1,293,262 (100% non-need-based). 484 part-time jobs averaging $2324.

ATHLETIC AWARDS Total amount: $998,194 (100% non-need-based).

APPLYING FOR FINANCIAL AID ***Required financial aid forms:*** FAFSA, state aid form. ***Financial aid deadline (priority):*** 3/1. ***Notification date:*** Continuous beginning 3/30. Students must reply within 2 weeks of notification.

CONTACT Ms. Sandra Oerly-Bennett, Financial Aid Office, Shepherd University, PO Box 5000, Shepherdstown, WV 25443-5000, 304-876-5470 or toll-free 800-344-5231. *Fax:* 304-876-5238. *E-mail:* faoweb@shepherd.edu.

SHIMER COLLEGE

Chicago, IL

Tuition & fees: $27,810 **Average undergraduate aid package: $16,821**

ABOUT THE INSTITUTION Independent, coed. 7 undergraduate majors. Both federal and institutional methodology are used as a basis for awarding need-based institutional aid.

UNDERGRADUATE EXPENSES for 2010–11 ***Comprehensive fee:*** $40,660 includes full-time tuition ($26,510), mandatory fees ($1300), and room and board ($12,850). ***College room only:*** $7526. Full-time tuition and fees vary according to class time, course load, and program. Room and board charges vary according to housing facility. ***Part-time tuition:*** $970 per credit hour. ***Part-time fees:*** $400 per term. Part-time tuition and fees vary according to class time, course load, and program. ***Payment plan:*** Installment.

FRESHMAN FINANCIAL AID (Fall 2009) 17 applied for aid; of those 94% were deemed to have need. 100% of freshmen with need received aid; of those 6% had need fully met. ***Average percent of need met:*** 45% (excluding resources awarded to replace EFC). ***Average financial aid package:*** $14,687 (excluding resources awarded to replace EFC). 17% of all full-time freshmen had no need and received non-need-based gift aid.

UNDERGRADUATE FINANCIAL AID (Fall 2009) 94 applied for aid; of those 93% were deemed to have need. 100% of undergraduates with need received aid; of those 3% had need fully met. ***Average percent of need met:*** 52% (excluding resources awarded to replace EFC). ***Average financial aid package:*** $16,821 (excluding resources awarded to replace EFC). 13% of all full-time undergraduates had no need and received non-need-based gift aid.

GIFT AID (NEED-BASED) ***Total amount:*** $1,035,384 (25% federal, 10% state, 64% institutional, 1% external sources). ***Receiving aid:*** Freshmen: 83% (15); all full-time undergraduates: 92% (87). ***Average award:*** Freshmen: $9762; Undergraduates: $11,176. ***Scholarships, grants, and awards:*** Federal Pell, FSEOG, state, private, college/university gift aid from institutional funds.

GIFT AID (NON-NEED-BASED) ***Total amount:*** $62,660 (100% institutional). ***Receiving aid:*** Freshmen: 6% (1). Undergraduates: 5% (5). ***Average award:*** Freshmen: $11,886. Undergraduates: $6207. ***Scholarships, grants, and awards by category:*** *Academic interests/achievement:* general academic interests/achievements. *Special characteristics:* children and siblings of alumni. ***Tuition waivers:*** Full or partial for employees or children of employees, adult students, senior citizens.

LOANS ***Student loans:*** $1,184,604 (96% need-based, 4% non-need-based). 100% of past graduating class borrowed through all loan programs. *Average indebtedness per student:* $37,500. ***Average need-based loan:*** Freshmen: $3430. Undergraduates: $4741. ***Parent loans:*** $143,068 (100% need-based). ***Programs:*** Federal Direct (Subsidized and Unsubsidized Stafford, PLUS), Perkins.

WORK-STUDY ***Federal work-study:*** Total amount: $60,286; jobs available. ***State or other work-study/employment:*** Total amount: $7500 (100% non-need-based). Part-time jobs available.

APPLYING FOR FINANCIAL AID ***Required financial aid forms:*** FAFSA, institution's own form. ***Financial aid deadline:*** Continuous. ***Notification date:*** Continuous beginning 4/1. Students must reply by 5/1 or within 3 weeks of notification.

CONTACT Janet Henthorn, Director of Financial Aid, Shimer College, 3424 South State Street, Chicago, IL 60616, 312-235-3507 or toll-free 800-215-7173. *Fax:* 312-235-3502. *E-mail:* j.henthorn@shimer.edu.

SHIPPENSBURG UNIVERSITY OF PENNSYLVANIA

Shippensburg, PA

Tuition & fees (PA res): $8056 **Average undergraduate aid package: $7902**

ABOUT THE INSTITUTION State-supported, coed. 35 undergraduate majors. Federal methodology is used as a basis for awarding need-based institutional aid.

UNDERGRADUATE EXPENSES for 2010–11 ***Tuition, state resident:*** full-time $5804; part-time $242 per credit hour. ***Tuition, nonresident:*** full-time $14,510; part-time $605 per credit hour. ***Required fees:*** full-time $2252; $255 per course or $68 per term. ***College room and board:*** $7400; ***Room only:*** $3870. Room and board charges vary according to board plan and housing facility. ***Payment plan:*** Installment.

FRESHMAN FINANCIAL AID (Fall 2010, est.) 1,524 applied for aid; of those 75% were deemed to have need. 93% of freshmen with need received aid; of those 5% had need fully met. ***Average percent of need met:*** 57% (excluding resources awarded to replace EFC). ***Average financial aid package:*** $7307 (excluding resources awarded to replace EFC). 7% of all full-time freshmen had no need and received non-need-based gift aid.

UNDERGRADUATE FINANCIAL AID (Fall 2010, est.) 5,549 applied for aid; of those 78% were deemed to have need. 95% of undergraduates with need received aid; of those 7% had need fully met. ***Average percent of need met:*** 62% (excluding resources awarded to replace EFC). ***Average financial aid package:*** $7902 (excluding resources awarded to replace EFC). 7% of all full-time undergraduates had no need and received non-need-based gift aid.

GIFT AID (NEED-BASED) ***Total amount:*** $16,254,219 (53% federal, 33% state, 5% institutional, 9% external sources). ***Receiving aid:*** Freshmen: 47% (808); all full-time undergraduates: 44% (2,964). ***Average award:*** Freshmen: $5821; Undergraduates: $5668. ***Scholarships, grants, and awards:*** Federal Pell, FSEOG, state, private, college/university gift aid from institutional funds, Academic Competitiveness Grants, National SMART Grants.

GIFT AID (NON-NEED-BASED) ***Total amount:*** $1,611,576 (1% federal, 7% state, 21% institutional, 71% external sources). ***Receiving aid:*** Freshmen: 3% (47). Undergraduates: 3% (209). ***Average award:*** Freshmen: $3719. Undergraduates: $4334. ***Scholarships, grants, and awards by category:*** *Academic interests/achievement:* 398 awards ($572,304 total): biological sciences, business, communication, computer science, education, English, foreign languages, general academic interests/achievements, humanities, mathematics, physical sciences, social sciences. *Creative arts/performance:* 4 awards ($4250 total): art/fine arts, music, theater/drama. *Special achievements/activities:* 348 awards ($635,224 total): community service, general special achievements/activities, leadership. *Special characteristics:* 57 awards ($71,904 total): children and siblings of alumni, general special characteristics, handicapped students, local/state students. ***Tuition waivers:*** Full or partial for employees or children of employees, senior citizens.

LOANS ***Student loans:*** $36,826,522 (65% need-based, 35% non-need-based). 74% of past graduating class borrowed through all loan programs. *Average indebtedness per student:* $24,165. ***Average need-based loan:*** Freshmen: $3204. Undergraduates: $4009. ***Parent loans:*** $6,439,629 (28% need-based, 72% non-need-based). ***Programs:*** Federal Direct (Subsidized and Unsubsidized Stafford, PLUS), Perkins, alternative loans.

WORK-STUDY ***Federal work-study:*** Total amount: $77,673; 97 jobs averaging $801. ***State or other work-study/employment:*** Total amount: $585,087 (36% need-based, 64% non-need-based). 491 part-time jobs averaging $1192.

ATHLETIC AWARDS Total amount: $621,491 (44% need-based, 56% non-need-based).

APPLYING FOR FINANCIAL AID ***Required financial aid form:*** FAFSA. ***Financial aid deadline (priority):*** 3/15. ***Notification date:*** Continuous. Students must reply within 2 weeks of notification.

CONTACT Mrs. Trina Snyder, Interim Director of Financial Aid and Scholarships, Shippensburg University of Pennsylvania, 1871 Old Main Drive, Shippensburg, PA 17257-2299, 717-477-1131 or toll-free 800-822-8028 (in-state). *Fax:* 717-477-4028. *E-mail:* finaid@ship.edu.

SHORTER UNIVERSITY

Rome, GA

Tuition & fees: $17,070 **Average undergraduate aid package: $16,467**

ABOUT THE INSTITUTION Independent Baptist, coed. 39 undergraduate majors. Federal methodology is used as a basis for awarding need-based institutional aid.

UNDERGRADUATE EXPENSES for 2011–12 ***One-time required fee:*** $99. ***Comprehensive fee:*** $25,270 includes full-time tuition ($16,700), mandatory fees ($370), and room and board ($8200). ***College room only:*** $4400. Full-time tuition and fees vary according to course load. Room and board charges vary according to board plan and housing facility. ***Part-time tuition:*** $460 per credit hour. ***Payment plan:*** Installment.

FRESHMAN FINANCIAL AID (Fall 2010, est.) 416 applied for aid; of those 87% were deemed to have need. 100% of freshmen with need received aid; of those 20% had need fully met. ***Average percent of need met:*** 72% (excluding resources awarded to replace EFC). ***Average financial aid package:*** $16,632 (excluding resources awarded to replace EFC). 11% of all full-time freshmen had no need and received non-need-based gift aid.

UNDERGRADUATE FINANCIAL AID (Fall 2010, est.) 1,200 applied for aid; of those 94% were deemed to have need. 100% of undergraduates with need received aid; of those 21% had need fully met. ***Average percent of need met:*** 70% (excluding resources awarded to replace EFC). ***Average financial aid package:*** $16,467 (excluding resources awarded to replace EFC). 11% of all full-time undergraduates had no need and received non-need-based gift aid.

GIFT AID (NEED-BASED) ***Total amount:*** $10,954,928 (31% federal, 24% state, 42% institutional, 3% external sources). ***Receiving aid:*** Freshmen: 81% (362); all full-time undergraduates: 74% (1,119). ***Average award:*** Freshmen: $13,632; Undergraduates: $13,411. ***Scholarships, grants, and awards:*** Federal Pell, FSEOG, state, private, college/university gift aid from institutional funds.

GIFT AID (NON-NEED-BASED) ***Total amount:*** $2,233,437 (50% state, 45% institutional, 5% external sources). ***Receiving aid:*** Freshmen: 13% (57). Undergraduates: 10% (155). ***Average award:*** Freshmen: $4832. Undergraduates: $5322. ***Scholarships, grants, and awards by category:*** *Academic interests/achievement:* 1,345 awards ($5,882,103 total): English, foreign languages, general academic interests/achievements, religion/biblical studies. *Creative arts/performance:* 192 awards ($476,923 total): art/fine arts, music, theater/drama. *Special achievements/activities:* 260 awards ($129,896 total): cheerleading/drum major, religious involvement. *Special characteristics:* 364 awards ($566,761 total): children of faculty/staff, children of union members/company employees, local/state students, relatives of clergy, religious affiliation, siblings of current students. ***Tuition waivers:*** Full or partial for employees or children of employees, senior citizens.

LOANS ***Student loans:*** $7,293,511 (77% need-based, 23% non-need-based). 75% of past graduating class borrowed through all loan programs. *Average indebtedness per student:* $30,890. ***Average need-based loan:*** Freshmen: $3212. Undergraduates: $3691. ***Parent loans:*** $3,289,591 (42% need-based, 58% non-need-based). ***Programs:*** Federal Direct (Subsidized and Unsubsidized Stafford, PLUS), Perkins.

WORK-STUDY ***Federal work-study:*** Total amount: $311,711; jobs available. ***State or other work-study/employment:*** Total amount: $281,181 (7% need-based, 93% non-need-based). Part-time jobs available.

ATHLETIC AWARDS Total amount: $4,702,133 (61% need-based, 39% non-need-based).

APPLYING FOR FINANCIAL AID ***Required financial aid forms:*** FAFSA, institution's own form, state aid form. ***Financial aid deadline (priority):*** 4/1. ***Notification date:*** Continuous beginning 4/1. Students must reply within 2 weeks of notification.

CONTACT Tara Jones, Director of Financial Aid, Shorter University, 315 Shorter Avenue, Rome, GA 30165, 706-233-7227 or toll-free 800-868-6980. *Fax:* 706-233-7314. *E-mail:* tjones@shorter.edu.

SH'OR YOSHUV RABBINICAL COLLEGE

Lawrence, NY

CONTACT Office of Financial Aid, Sh'or Yoshuv Rabbinical College, 1526 Central Avenue, Far Rockaway, NY 11691-4002, 718-327-2048.

SIENA COLLEGE

Loudonville, NY

Tuition & fees: $28,985 **Average undergraduate aid package: $18,100**

ABOUT THE INSTITUTION Independent Roman Catholic, coed. 28 undergraduate majors. Federal methodology is used as a basis for awarding need-based institutional aid.

UNDERGRADUATE EXPENSES for 2011–12 ***One-time required fee:*** $340. ***Comprehensive fee:*** $40,419 includes full-time tuition ($28,660), mandatory fees ($325), and room and board ($11,434). ***College room only:*** $6730. Full-time tuition and fees vary according to program. Room and board charges vary according to board plan and housing facility. ***Part-time tuition:*** $500 per credit. ***Part-time fees:*** $60 per term. Part-time tuition and fees vary according to program. ***Payment plan:*** Installment.

FRESHMAN FINANCIAL AID (Fall 2010, est.) 703 applied for aid; of those 83% were deemed to have need. 99% of freshmen with need received aid; of those 19% had need fully met. ***Average percent of need met:*** 72% (excluding resources awarded to replace EFC). ***Average financial aid package:*** $18,600 (excluding resources awarded to replace EFC). 10% of all full-time freshmen had no need and received non-need-based gift aid.

UNDERGRADUATE FINANCIAL AID (Fall 2010, est.) 2,641 applied for aid; of those 86% were deemed to have need. 100% of undergraduates with need received aid; of those 15% had need fully met. ***Average percent of need met:*** 70% (excluding resources awarded to replace EFC). ***Average financial aid package:*** $18,100 (excluding resources awarded to replace EFC). 7% of all full-time undergraduates had no need and received non-need-based gift aid.

GIFT AID (NEED-BASED) ***Total amount:*** $28,776,300 (12% federal, 11% state, 77% institutional). ***Receiving aid:*** Freshmen: 75% (577); all full-time undergraduates: 69% (2,223). ***Average award:*** Freshmen: $14,900; Undergraduates: $13,800. ***Scholarships, grants, and awards:*** Federal Pell, FSEOG, state, private, college/university gift aid from institutional funds, Siena Grants, Franciscan Community Grants.

GIFT AID (NON-NEED-BASED) ***Total amount:*** $3,769,100 (2% state, 85% institutional, 13% external sources). ***Receiving aid:*** Freshmen: 72% (557). Undergraduates: 56% (1,787). ***Average award:*** Freshmen: $8180. Undergraduates: $6900. ***Scholarships, grants, and awards by category:*** *Academic interests/achievement:* biological sciences, business, communication, computer science, education, English, foreign languages, general academic interests/achievements, health fields, humanities, international studies, mathematics, military science, physical sciences, premedicine, religion/biblical studies, social sciences. *Creative arts/performance:* creative writing, general creative arts/performance, journalism/publications, music, performing arts, theater/drama. *Special achievements/activities:* community service, general special achievements/activities, hobbies/interests, leadership, memberships, religious involvement. *Special characteristics:* adult students, children and siblings of alumni, children of faculty/staff, children of public servants, children of union members/company employees, children of workers in trades, children with a deceased or disabled parent, ethnic background, general special characteristics, local/state students, out-of-state students, previous college experience, relatives of clergy, religious affiliation, veterans' children. ***Tuition waivers:*** Full or partial for employees or children of employees, senior citizens.

LOANS ***Student loans:*** $15,582,290 (56% need-based, 44% non-need-based). 77% of past graduating class borrowed through all loan programs. *Average indebtedness per student:* $29,700. ***Average need-based loan:*** Freshmen: $3440. Undergraduates: $4622. ***Parent loans:*** $8,587,400 (64% need-based, 36% non-need-based). ***Programs:*** Federal Direct (Subsidized and Unsubsidized Stafford, PLUS), Perkins.

WORK-STUDY ***Federal work-study:*** Total amount: $356,000; 500 jobs averaging $712.

ATHLETIC AWARDS Total amount: $3,995,200 (61% need-based, 39% non-need-based).

APPLYING FOR FINANCIAL AID ***Required financial aid forms:*** FAFSA, state aid form. ***Financial aid deadline (priority):*** 2/15. ***Notification date:*** 4/1. Students must reply by 5/1.

CONTACT Ms. Mary K. Lawyer, Associate Vice President for Enrollment Management, Siena College, 515 Loudon Road, Loudonville, NY 12211-1462, 518-783-2427 or toll-free 888-AT-SIENA. *Fax:* 518-783-2410. *E-mail:* aid@siena.edu.

SIENA HEIGHTS UNIVERSITY

Adrian, MI

CONTACT Office of Financial Aid, Siena Heights University, 1247 East Siena Heights Drive, Adrian, MI 49221, 517-264-7130 or toll-free 800-521-0009.

SIERRA NEVADA COLLEGE

Incline Village, NV

Tuition & fees: $25,235 **Average undergraduate aid package: $19,500**

ABOUT THE INSTITUTION Independent, coed. 24 undergraduate majors. Federal methodology is used as a basis for awarding need-based institutional aid.

UNDERGRADUATE EXPENSES for 2011–12 ***Comprehensive fee:*** $34,985 includes full-time tuition ($24,720), mandatory fees ($515), and room and board ($9750). Full-time tuition and fees vary according to course load, degree level, location, and program. Room and board charges vary according to board plan. ***Part-time tuition:*** $1030 per credit hour. ***Part-time fees:*** $165 per term. Part-time tuition and fees vary according to course load, degree level, location, and program. ***Payment plan:*** Installment.

FRESHMAN FINANCIAL AID (Fall 2010, est.) 51 applied for aid; of those 88% were deemed to have need. 100% of freshmen with need received aid; of those 27% had need fully met. ***Average percent of need met:*** 52% (excluding resources awarded to replace EFC). ***Average financial aid package:*** $18,500 (excluding resources awarded to replace EFC). 6% of all full-time freshmen had no need and received non-need-based gift aid.

UNDERGRADUATE FINANCIAL AID (Fall 2010, est.) 280 applied for aid; of those 92% were deemed to have need. 100% of undergraduates with need received aid; of those 20% had need fully met. ***Average percent of need met:*** 52% (excluding resources awarded to replace EFC). ***Average financial aid package:*** $19,500 (excluding resources awarded to replace EFC). 4% of all full-time undergraduates had no need and received non-need-based gift aid.

GIFT AID (NEED-BASED) ***Total amount:*** $3,937,312 (21% federal, 1% state, 76% institutional, 2% external sources). ***Receiving aid:*** Freshmen: 54% (45); all full-time undergraduates: 60% (258). ***Average award:*** Freshmen: $11,000; Undergraduates: $14,500. ***Scholarships, grants, and awards:*** Federal Pell, FSEOG, state, private, college/university gift aid from institutional funds.

GIFT AID (NON-NEED-BASED) ***Total amount:*** $1,988,823 (100% institutional). ***Receiving aid:*** Freshmen: 54% (45). Undergraduates: 60% (258). ***Average award:*** Freshmen: $4730. Undergraduates: $7526. ***Scholarships, grants, and***

awards by category: *Academic interests/achievement:* general academic interests/achievements. *Creative arts/performance:* art/fine arts, music. ***Tuition waivers:*** Full or partial for employees or children of employees.

LOANS ***Student loans:*** $1,954,693 (48% need-based, 52% non-need-based). 50% of past graduating class borrowed through all loan programs. *Average indebtedness per student:* $11,187. ***Average need-based loan:*** Freshmen: $3500. Undergraduates: $4500. ***Parent loans:*** $1,055,798 (100% non-need-based). ***Programs:*** Federal Direct (Subsidized and Unsubsidized Stafford, PLUS), alternative loans.

WORK-STUDY ***Federal work-study:*** Total amount: $47,298; 242 jobs averaging $310.

ATHLETIC AWARDS Total amount: $258,250 (100% need-based).

APPLYING FOR FINANCIAL AID ***Required financial aid form:*** FAFSA. ***Financial aid deadline:*** Continuous. ***Notification date:*** Continuous beginning 1/31.

CONTACT Nicole Ferguson, Director of Financial Aid, Sierra Nevada College, 999 Tahoe Boulevard, Incline Village, NV 89451, 775-831-1314 Ext. 7404. *Fax:* 775-832-1678. *E-mail:* nferguson@sierranevada.edu.

SILICON VALLEY UNIVERSITY

San Jose, CA

CONTACT Financial Aid Office, Silicon Valley University, 2160 Lundy Avenue, Suite 110, San Jose, CA 95131, 408-435-8989.

SILVER LAKE COLLEGE

Manitowoc, WI

Tuition & fees: $21,820 **Average undergraduate aid package: $17,932**

ABOUT THE INSTITUTION Independent Roman Catholic, coed. 26 undergraduate majors. Federal methodology is used as a basis for awarding need-based institutional aid.

UNDERGRADUATE EXPENSES for 2011–12 ***Comprehensive fee:*** $30,320 includes full-time tuition ($21,580), mandatory fees ($240), and room and board ($8500). ***College room only:*** $4900. Full-time tuition and fees vary according to degree level, location, program, and reciprocity agreements. Room and board charges vary according to board plan and housing facility. ***Part-time tuition:*** $720 per credit. ***Part-time fees:*** $65 per term. Part-time tuition and fees vary according to course load, degree level, location, and program. ***Payment plans:*** Installment, deferred payment.

FRESHMAN FINANCIAL AID (Fall 2010, est.) 38 applied for aid; of those 89% were deemed to have need. 100% of freshmen with need received aid; of those 9% had need fully met. ***Average percent of need met:*** 83% (excluding resources awarded to replace EFC). ***Average financial aid package:*** $22,771 (excluding resources awarded to replace EFC). 10% of all full-time freshmen had no need and received non-need-based gift aid.

UNDERGRADUATE FINANCIAL AID (Fall 2010, est.) 151 applied for aid; of those 96% were deemed to have need. 100% of undergraduates with need received aid; of those 12% had need fully met. ***Average percent of need met:*** 67% (excluding resources awarded to replace EFC). ***Average financial aid package:*** $17,932 (excluding resources awarded to replace EFC). 4% of all full-time undergraduates had no need and received non-need-based gift aid.

GIFT AID (NEED-BASED) ***Total amount:*** $1,857,886 (34% federal, 14% state, 50% institutional, 2% external sources). ***Receiving aid:*** Freshmen: 83% (34); all full-time undergraduates: 79% (139). ***Average award:*** Freshmen: $11,282; Undergraduates: $9602. ***Scholarships, grants, and awards:*** Federal Pell, FSEOG, state, private, college/university gift aid from institutional funds.

GIFT AID (NON-NEED-BASED) ***Total amount:*** $278,152 (66% federal, 33% institutional, 1% external sources). ***Receiving aid:*** Freshmen: 68% (28). Undergraduates: 54% (94). ***Average award:*** Freshmen: $11,722. Undergraduates: $9713. ***Scholarships, grants, and awards by category:*** *Academic interests/achievement:* 51 awards ($309,467 total): general academic interests/achievements. *Creative arts/performance:* 26 awards ($33,200 total): applied art and design, art/fine arts, music. *Special achievements/activities:* 28 awards ($54,000 total): community service. *Special characteristics:* 45 awards ($91,654 total): children and siblings of alumni, international students, local/state students, previous college experience. ***Tuition waivers:*** Full or partial for employees or children of employees, senior citizens.

LOANS ***Student loans:*** $1,594,624 (96% need-based, 4% non-need-based). 81% of past graduating class borrowed through all loan programs. *Average indebtedness per student:* $19,386. ***Average need-based loan:*** Freshmen: $3500. Undergraduates: $4576. ***Parent loans:*** $85,700 (100% need-based). ***Programs:*** Federal Direct (Subsidized and Unsubsidized Stafford, PLUS), state.

WORK-STUDY ***Federal work-study:*** Total amount: $201,055; 88 jobs averaging $1989. ***State or other work-study/employment:*** Total amount: $7425 (100% need-based). 3 part-time jobs averaging $2475.

ATHLETIC AWARDS Total amount: $72,840 (96% need-based, 4% non-need-based).

APPLYING FOR FINANCIAL AID ***Required financial aid form:*** FAFSA. ***Financial aid deadline (priority):*** 3/15. ***Notification date:*** Continuous beginning 3/15.

CONTACT Ms. Michelle Leider, Associate Director of Financial Aid, Silver Lake College, 2406 South Alverno Road, Manitowoc, WI 54220-9319, 920-686-6122 or toll-free 800-236-4752 Ext. 175 (in-state). *Fax:* 920-684-7082. *E-mail:* financialaid@sl.edu.

SIMMONS COLLEGE

Boston, MA

Tuition & fees: $32,230 **Average undergraduate aid package: $22,495**

ABOUT THE INSTITUTION Independent, undergraduate: women only; graduate: coed. 41 undergraduate majors. Federal methodology is used as a basis for awarding need-based institutional aid.

UNDERGRADUATE EXPENSES for 2010–11 ***Comprehensive fee:*** $44,700 includes full-time tuition ($31,280), mandatory fees ($950), and room and board ($12,470). Full-time tuition and fees vary according to course load and program. Room and board charges vary according to board plan. ***Part-time tuition:*** $978 per credit. ***Part-time fees:*** $240 per term. Part-time tuition and fees vary according to course load and program. ***Payment plan:*** Installment.

FRESHMAN FINANCIAL AID (Fall 2010, est.) 338 applied for aid; of those 91% were deemed to have need. 100% of freshmen with need received aid; of those 11% had need fully met. ***Average percent of need met:*** 66% (excluding resources awarded to replace EFC). ***Average financial aid package:*** $22,688 (excluding resources awarded to replace EFC). 15% of all full-time freshmen had no need and received non-need-based gift aid.

UNDERGRADUATE FINANCIAL AID (Fall 2010, est.) 1,363 applied for aid; of those 92% were deemed to have need. 100% of undergraduates with need received aid; of those 8% had need fully met. ***Average percent of need met:*** 64% (excluding resources awarded to replace EFC). ***Average financial aid package:*** $22,495 (excluding resources awarded to replace EFC). 17% of all full-time undergraduates had no need and received non-need-based gift aid.

GIFT AID (NEED-BASED) ***Total amount:*** $20,901,155 (13% federal, 2% state, 82% institutional, 3% external sources). ***Receiving aid:*** Freshmen: 81% (306); all full-time undergraduates: 74% (1,249). ***Average award:*** Freshmen: $17,353; Undergraduates: $16,075. ***Scholarships, grants, and awards:*** Federal Pell, FSEOG, state, private, college/university gift aid from institutional funds.

GIFT AID (NON-NEED-BASED) ***Total amount:*** $2,931,190 (95% institutional, 5% external sources). ***Receiving aid:*** Freshmen: 4% (16). Undergraduates: 2% (41). ***Average award:*** Freshmen: $9589. Undergraduates: $8815. ***Scholarships, grants, and awards by category:*** *Academic interests/achievement:* general academic interests/achievements. *Special achievements/activities:* community service, general special achievements/activities. *Special characteristics:* children and siblings of alumni, general special characteristics. ***Tuition waivers:*** Full or partial for employees or children of employees.

LOANS ***Student loans:*** $15,484,317 (38% need-based, 62% non-need-based). ***Average need-based loan:*** Freshmen: $3371. Undergraduates: $4800. ***Parent loans:*** $6,574,460 (100% non-need-based). ***Programs:*** Federal Direct (Subsidized and Unsubsidized Stafford, PLUS), Perkins, college/university.

WORK-STUDY ***Federal work-study:*** Total amount: $2,425,855; 1,040 jobs averaging $2333.

APPLYING FOR FINANCIAL AID ***Required financial aid forms:*** FAFSA, institution's own form. ***Financial aid deadline (priority):*** 3/1. ***Notification date:*** Continuous beginning 3/15. Students must reply by 5/1 or within 4 weeks of notification.

CONTACT Diane M. Hallisey, Director of Student Financial Services, Simmons College, 300 The Fenway, Boston, MA 02115, 617-521-2001 or toll-free 800-345-8468 (out-of-state). *Fax:* 617-521-3195. *E-mail:* hallisey@simmons.edu.

SIMPSON COLLEGE

Indianola, IA

Tuition & fees: $28,123 **Average undergraduate aid package: $28,858**

ABOUT THE INSTITUTION Independent United Methodist, coed. 58 undergraduate majors. Federal methodology is used as a basis for awarding need-based institutional aid.

UNDERGRADUATE EXPENSES for 2011–12 ***One-time required fee:*** $200. ***Comprehensive fee:*** $36,086 includes full-time tuition ($27,568), mandatory fees ($555), and room and board ($7963). ***College room only:*** $3860. Full-time tuition and fees vary according to class time, course load, degree level, and program. Room and board charges vary according to board plan and housing facility. ***Part-time tuition:*** $318 per credit. Part-time tuition and fees vary according to class time, course load, degree level, and program. ***Payment plan:*** Installment.

FRESHMAN FINANCIAL AID (Fall 2010, est.) 362 applied for aid; of those 89% were deemed to have need. 100% of freshmen with need received aid; of those 39% had need fully met. ***Average percent of need met:*** 93% (excluding resources awarded to replace EFC). ***Average financial aid package:*** $27,683 (excluding resources awarded to replace EFC). 11% of all full-time freshmen had no need and received non-need-based gift aid.

UNDERGRADUATE FINANCIAL AID (Fall 2010, est.) 1,487 applied for aid; of those 87% were deemed to have need. 100% of undergraduates with need received aid; of those 27% had need fully met. ***Average percent of need met:*** 88% (excluding resources awarded to replace EFC). ***Average financial aid package:*** $28,858 (excluding resources awarded to replace EFC). 12% of all full-time undergraduates had no need and received non-need-based gift aid.

GIFT AID (NEED-BASED) ***Total amount:*** $23,230,830 (12% federal, 12% state, 73% institutional, 3% external sources). ***Receiving aid:*** Freshmen: 89% (322); all full-time undergraduates: 87% (1,298). ***Average award:*** Freshmen: $19,769; Undergraduates: $17,457. ***Scholarships, grants, and awards:*** Federal Pell, FSEOG, state, private, college/university gift aid from institutional funds.

GIFT AID (NON-NEED-BASED) ***Total amount:*** $3,964,408 (83% institutional, 17% external sources). ***Receiving aid:*** Freshmen: 20% (73). Undergraduates: 13% (195). ***Average award:*** Freshmen: $14,942. Undergraduates: $13,237. ***Scholarships, grants, and awards by category:*** *Academic interests/achievement:* $8,883,424 total: general academic interests/achievements. *Creative arts/performance:* $564,541 total: art/fine arts, music, theater/drama. *Special achievements/activities:* $321,597 total: community service, leadership, religious involvement. *Special characteristics:* $2,359,413 total: adult students, children and siblings of alumni, children of educators, children of faculty/staff, ethnic background, international students, members of minority groups, relatives of clergy, religious affiliation, siblings of current students, twins. ***Tuition waivers:*** Full or partial for minority students, children of alumni, employees or children of employees, senior citizens.

LOANS ***Student loans:*** $12,930,419 (69% need-based, 31% non-need-based). 89% of past graduating class borrowed through all loan programs. *Average indebtedness per student:* $34,214. ***Average need-based loan:*** Freshmen: $3104. Undergraduates: $3742. ***Parent loans:*** $13,830,240 (68% need-based, 32% non-need-based). ***Programs:*** Federal Direct (Subsidized and Unsubsidized Stafford, PLUS), Perkins, state, college/university, alternative loans.

WORK-STUDY ***Federal work-study:*** Total amount: $362,440; 376 jobs averaging $1049. ***State or other work-study/employment:*** Total amount: $537,381 (25% need-based, 75% non-need-based). 399 part-time jobs averaging $1412.

APPLYING FOR FINANCIAL AID ***Required financial aid form:*** FAFSA. ***Financial aid deadline:*** Continuous. ***Notification date:*** Continuous beginning 3/15. Students must reply by 5/1 or within 3 weeks of notification.

CONTACT Tracie Lynn Pavon, Assistant Vice President of Financial Aid, Simpson College, 701 North C Street, Indianola, IA 50125-1297, 515-961-1630 Ext. 1596 or toll-free 800-362-2454 (in-state), 800-362-2454 Ext. 1624 (out-of-state). *Fax:* 515-961-1300. *E-mail:* tracie.pavon@simpson.edu.

SIMPSON UNIVERSITY

Redding, CA

Tuition & fees: $21,600 **Average undergraduate aid package: $19,509**

ABOUT THE INSTITUTION Independent religious, coed. 29 undergraduate majors. Federal methodology is used as a basis for awarding need-based institutional aid.

UNDERGRADUATE EXPENSES for 2011–12 ***Comprehensive fee:*** $28,900 includes full-time tuition ($21,600) and room and board ($7300). ***College room only:*** $6300. Full-time tuition and fees vary according to course load and program. Room and board charges vary according to board plan. ***Part-time tuition:*** $900 per unit. Part-time tuition and fees vary according to course load and program. ***Payment plan:*** Deferred payment.

FRESHMAN FINANCIAL AID (Fall 2010, est.) 152 applied for aid; of those 93% were deemed to have need. 100% of freshmen with need received aid; of those 12% had need fully met. ***Average percent of need met:*** 75% (excluding resources awarded to replace EFC). ***Average financial aid package:*** $18,990 (excluding resources awarded to replace EFC). 7% of all full-time freshmen had no need and received non-need-based gift aid.

UNDERGRADUATE FINANCIAL AID (Fall 2010, est.) 663 applied for aid; of those 93% were deemed to have need. 100% of undergraduates with need received aid; of those 13% had need fully met. ***Average percent of need met:*** 75% (excluding resources awarded to replace EFC). ***Average financial aid package:*** $19,509 (excluding resources awarded to replace EFC). 7% of all full-time undergraduates had no need and received non-need-based gift aid.

GIFT AID (NEED-BASED) ***Total amount:*** $9,820,969 (25% federal, 28% state, 45% institutional, 2% external sources). ***Receiving aid:*** Freshmen: 90% (141); all full-time undergraduates: 89% (615). ***Average award:*** Freshmen: $15,650; Undergraduates: $15,243. ***Scholarships, grants, and awards:*** Federal Pell, FSEOG, state, private, college/university gift aid from institutional funds.

GIFT AID (NON-NEED-BASED) ***Total amount:*** $564,352 (96% institutional, 4% external sources). ***Receiving aid:*** Freshmen: 17% (27). Undergraduates: 5% (33). ***Average award:*** Freshmen: $7227. Undergraduates: $6623. ***Scholarships, grants, and awards by category:*** *Academic interests/achievement:* 96 awards ($412,259 total): general academic interests/achievements. *Creative arts/performance:* 7 awards ($13,750 total): music. *Special achievements/activities:* 14 awards ($38,113 total): community service, leadership, religious involvement. *Special characteristics:* 13 awards ($24,582 total): children of faculty/staff, general special characteristics, members of minority groups, out-of-state students, relatives of clergy, religious affiliation, siblings of current students. ***Tuition waivers:*** Full or partial for employees or children of employees.

LOANS ***Student loans:*** $7,621,248 (84% need-based, 16% non-need-based). 86% of past graduating class borrowed through all loan programs. *Average indebtedness per student:* $22,831. ***Average need-based loan:*** Freshmen: $3395. Undergraduates: $4357. ***Parent loans:*** $5,136,583 (36% need-based, 64% non-need-based). ***Programs:*** Federal Direct (Subsidized and Unsubsidized Stafford, PLUS), Perkins, alternative loans.

WORK-STUDY ***Federal work-study:*** Total amount: $82,765; 187 jobs averaging $443.

ATHLETIC AWARDS Total amount: $663,380 (76% need-based, 24% non-need-based).

APPLYING FOR FINANCIAL AID ***Required financial aid forms:*** FAFSA, institution's own form, state aid form. ***Financial aid deadline (priority):*** 3/2. ***Notification date:*** Continuous beginning 3/15. Students must reply within 3 weeks of notification.

CONTACT Melissa Hudson, Director of Student Financial Services, Simpson University, 2211 College View Drive, Redding, CA 96003-8606, 530-224-5600 or toll-free 800-598-2493. *Fax:* 530-226-4870. *E-mail:* financialaid@simpsonu.edu.

SINTE GLESKA UNIVERSITY

Mission, SD

CONTACT Office of Financial Aid, Sinte Gleska University, PO Box 490, Rosebud, SD 57570-0490, 605-747-4258. *Fax:* 605-747-2098.

SKIDMORE COLLEGE

Saratoga Springs, NY

Tuition & fees: $41,184 **Average undergraduate aid package: $32,569**

ABOUT THE INSTITUTION Independent, coed. 43 undergraduate majors. Both federal and institutional methodology are used as a basis for awarding need-based institutional aid.

UNDERGRADUATE EXPENSES for 2010–11 ***Comprehensive fee:*** $52,170 includes full-time tuition ($40,350), mandatory fees ($834), and room and board ($10,986). ***College room only:*** $6496. Full-time tuition and fees vary according to course load. Room and board charges vary according to board plan and housing facility. ***Part-time tuition:*** $1345 per credit hour. ***Part-time fees:*** $25 per term. Part-time tuition and fees vary according to course load. ***Payment plans:*** Tuition prepayment, installment.

FRESHMAN FINANCIAL AID (Fall 2010, est.) 381 applied for aid; of those 86% were deemed to have need. 100% of freshmen with need received aid; of those 100% had need fully met. ***Average percent of need met:*** 100% (excluding resources awarded to replace EFC). ***Average financial aid package:*** $34,915 (excluding resources awarded to replace EFC). 1% of all full-time freshmen had no need and received non-need-based gift aid.

UNDERGRADUATE FINANCIAL AID (Fall 2010, est.) 1,113 applied for aid; of those 91% were deemed to have need. 100% of undergraduates with need received aid; of those 95% had need fully met. ***Average percent of need met:*** 95% (excluding resources awarded to replace EFC). ***Average financial aid package:*** $32,569 (excluding resources awarded to replace EFC). 1% of all full-time undergraduates had no need and received non-need-based gift aid.

GIFT AID (NEED-BASED) ***Total amount:*** $35,850,000 (7% federal, 4% state, 89% institutional). ***Receiving aid:*** Freshmen: 42% (325); all full-time undergraduates: 38% (1,006). ***Average award:*** Freshmen: $32,822; Undergraduates: $29,181. ***Scholarships, grants, and awards:*** Federal Pell, FSEOG, state, private, college/university gift aid from institutional funds.

GIFT AID (NON-NEED-BASED) ***Total amount:*** $1,025,000 (5% state, 34% institutional, 61% external sources). ***Receiving aid:*** Freshmen: 5% (42). Undergraduates: 3% (69). ***Average award:*** Freshmen: $10,000. Undergraduates: $10,000. ***Scholarships, grants, and awards by category:*** *Academic interests/achievement:* biological sciences, computer science, mathematics, physical sciences. *Creative arts/performance:* music. *Special characteristics:* children of faculty/staff. ***Tuition waivers:*** Full or partial for employees or children of employees, senior citizens.

LOANS ***Student loans:*** $7,050,000 (53% need-based, 47% non-need-based). 46% of past graduating class borrowed through all loan programs. *Average indebtedness per student:* $19,850. ***Average need-based loan:*** Freshmen: $2410. Undergraduates: $3595. ***Parent loans:*** $4,100,000 (100% non-need-based). ***Programs:*** Federal Direct (Subsidized and Unsubsidized Stafford, PLUS), state.

WORK-STUDY ***Federal work-study:*** Total amount: $1,450,000; jobs available. ***State or other work-study/employment:*** Total amount: $650,000 (100% non-need-based). Part-time jobs available.

APPLYING FOR FINANCIAL AID ***Required financial aid forms:*** FAFSA, CSS Financial Aid PROFILE, noncustodial (divorced/separated) parent's statement. ***Financial aid deadline:*** 2/1. ***Notification date:*** 4/1. Students must reply by 5/1.

CONTACT Ms. Beth A. Post-Lundquist, Director of Financial Aid, Skidmore College, 815 North Broadway, Saratoga Springs, NY 12866-1632, 518-580-5750 or toll-free 800-867-6007. *Fax:* 518-580-5752. *E-mail:* bpostlun@skidmore.edu.

SKYLINE COLLEGE

Roanoke, VA

ABOUT THE INSTITUTION Proprietary, coed. 10 undergraduate majors.

GIFT AID (NEED-BASED) ***Scholarships, grants, and awards:*** Federal Pell, FSEOG, state, private, college/university gift aid from institutional funds.

GIFT AID (NON-NEED-BASED) ***Scholarships, grants, and awards by category:*** *Academic interests/achievement:* business, computer science, engineering/technologies, health fields. *Special achievements/activities:* community service, general special achievements/activities. *Special characteristics:* adult students, children of faculty/staff, general special characteristics, previous college experience, veterans, veterans' children.

LOANS ***Programs:*** Federal Direct (Subsidized and Unsubsidized Stafford, PLUS), Perkins, college/university, private loans.

WORK-STUDY ***Federal work-study:*** Total amount: $30,000; jobs available. ***State or other work-study/employment:*** Part-time jobs available.

APPLYING FOR FINANCIAL AID ***Required financial aid form:*** FAFSA.

CONTACT Ms. Amanda Little, Financial Aid Director, Skyline College, 5234 Airport Road, Roanoke, VA 24012, 540-563-8080 or toll-free 866-708-6178. *E-mail:* alittle@ecpi.edu.

SLIPPERY ROCK UNIVERSITY OF PENNSYLVANIA

Slippery Rock, PA

Tuition & fees (PA res): $7666 **Average undergraduate aid package: $8169**

ABOUT THE INSTITUTION State-supported, coed. 65 undergraduate majors. Federal methodology is used as a basis for awarding need-based institutional aid.

UNDERGRADUATE EXPENSES for 2010–11 ***Tuition, state resident:*** full-time $5804; part-time $242 per credit hour. ***Tuition, nonresident:*** full-time $8706; part-time $484 per credit hour. ***Required fees:*** full-time $1862; $93 per credit hour or $68 per term. Full-time tuition and fees vary according to course load and degree level. Part-time tuition and fees vary according to course load and degree level. ***College room and board:*** $8884; ***Room only:*** $5964. Room and board charges vary according to board plan and housing facility. ***Payment plan:*** Installment.

FRESHMAN FINANCIAL AID (Fall 2010, est.) 1,511 applied for aid; of those 77% were deemed to have need. 97% of freshmen with need received aid; of those 32% had need fully met. ***Average percent of need met:*** 58% (excluding resources awarded to replace EFC). ***Average financial aid package:*** $7858 (excluding resources awarded to replace EFC). 3% of all full-time freshmen had no need and received non-need-based gift aid.

UNDERGRADUATE FINANCIAL AID (Fall 2010, est.) 6,773 applied for aid; of those 78% were deemed to have need. 97% of undergraduates with need received aid; of those 35% had need fully met. ***Average percent of need met:*** 63% (excluding resources awarded to replace EFC). ***Average financial aid package:*** $8169 (excluding resources awarded to replace EFC). 3% of all full-time undergraduates had no need and received non-need-based gift aid.

GIFT AID (NEED-BASED) ***Total amount:*** $18,474,260 (61% federal, 36% state, 3% external sources). ***Receiving aid:*** Freshmen: 47% (736); all full-time undergraduates: 45% (3,360). ***Average award:*** Freshmen: $5494; Undergraduates: $5285. ***Scholarships, grants, and awards:*** Federal Pell, FSEOG, state, private, college/university gift aid from institutional funds.

GIFT AID (NON-NEED-BASED) ***Total amount:*** $3,726,586 (35% institutional, 65% external sources). ***Receiving aid:*** Freshmen: 32% (498). Undergraduates: 20% (1,453). ***Average award:*** Freshmen: $1379. Undergraduates: $1483. ***Scholarships, grants, and awards by category:*** *Academic interests/achievement:* biological sciences, business, communication, computer science, education, English, general academic interests/achievements, health fields, physical sciences, social sciences. *Creative arts/performance:* applied art and design, art/fine arts, dance, music, performing arts, theater/drama. *Special achievements/activities:* community service, general special achievements/activities, leadership. *Special characteristics:* children and siblings of alumni, children of faculty/staff, children of union members/company employees, ethnic background, general special characteristics, local/state students, members of minority groups, out-of-state students, previous college experience. ***Tuition waivers:*** Full or partial for minority students, employees or children of employees, senior citizens.

LOANS ***Student loans:*** $45,615,662 (44% need-based, 56% non-need-based). 83% of past graduating class borrowed through all loan programs. *Average indebtedness per student:* $26,452. ***Average need-based loan:*** Freshmen: $3391. Undergraduates: $4137. ***Parent loans:*** $8,452,776 (100% non-need-based). ***Programs:*** Federal Direct (Subsidized and Unsubsidized Stafford, PLUS), Perkins.

WORK-STUDY ***Federal work-study:*** Total amount: $1,179,835; jobs available. ***State or other work-study/employment:*** Part-time jobs available.

ATHLETIC AWARDS Total amount: $821,890 (100% non-need-based).

APPLYING FOR FINANCIAL AID ***Required financial aid form:*** FAFSA. ***Financial aid deadline (priority):*** 5/1. ***Notification date:*** Continuous beginning 3/15.

CONTACT Ms. Patty A. Hladio, Director of Financial Aid, Slippery Rock University of Pennsylvania, 1 Morrow Way, Slippery Rock, PA 16057, 724-738-2044 or toll-free 800-SRU-9111. *Fax:* 724-738-2922. *E-mail:* financial.aid@sru.edu.

SMITH COLLEGE

Northampton, MA

Tuition & fees: $38,898 **Average undergraduate aid package: $36,156**

ABOUT THE INSTITUTION Independent, undergraduate: women only; graduate: coed. 53 undergraduate majors. Both federal and institutional methodology are used as a basis for awarding need-based institutional aid.

UNDERGRADUATE EXPENSES for 2010–11 ***Comprehensive fee:*** $51,898 includes full-time tuition ($38,640), mandatory fees ($258), and room and board ($13,000). ***College room only:*** $6500. ***Part-time tuition:*** $1210 per credit hour. ***Payment plans:*** Tuition prepayment, installment.

FRESHMAN FINANCIAL AID (Fall 2010, est.) 481 applied for aid; of those 83% were deemed to have need. 100% of freshmen with need received aid; of those 100% had need fully met. ***Average percent of need met:*** 100% (excluding resources awarded to replace EFC). ***Average financial aid package:*** $34,718 (excluding resources awarded to replace EFC). 4% of all full-time freshmen had no need and received non-need-based gift aid.

UNDERGRADUATE FINANCIAL AID (Fall 2010, est.) 1,856 applied for aid; of those 89% were deemed to have need. 100% of undergraduates with need received aid; of those 100% had need fully met. ***Average percent of need met:*** 100% (excluding resources awarded to replace EFC). ***Average financial aid package:*** $36,156 (excluding resources awarded to replace EFC). 4% of all full-time undergraduates had no need and received non-need-based gift aid.

GIFT AID (NEED-BASED) ***Total amount:*** $50,800,190 (7% federal, 1% state, 89% institutional, 3% external sources). ***Receiving aid:*** Freshmen: 60% (380); all full-time undergraduates: 60% (1,553). ***Average award:*** Freshmen: $32,713; Undergraduates: $31,705. ***Scholarships, grants, and awards:*** Federal Pell, FSEOG, state, college/university gift aid from institutional funds.

GIFT AID (NON-NEED-BASED) ***Total amount:*** $2,379,726 (67% institutional, 33% external sources). ***Receiving aid:*** Freshmen: 3. Undergraduates: 1% (17). ***Average award:*** Freshmen: $16,057. Undergraduates: $13,588. ***Scholarships, grants, and awards by category:*** *Academic interests/achievement:* general academic interests/achievements. *Special characteristics:* local/state students. ***Tuition waivers:*** Full or partial for employees or children of employees.

LOANS ***Student loans:*** $10,039,233 (65% need-based, 35% non-need-based). 69% of past graduating class borrowed through all loan programs. *Average indebtedness per student:* $20,989. ***Average need-based loan:*** Freshmen: $3247. Undergraduates: $4576. ***Parent loans:*** $5,083,749 (100% non-need-based). ***Programs:*** Federal Direct (Subsidized and Unsubsidized Stafford, PLUS), Perkins, college/university.

WORK-STUDY ***Federal work-study:*** Total amount: $2,633,149; jobs available. ***State or other work-study/employment:*** Total amount: $1,120,716 (84% need-based, 16% non-need-based). Part-time jobs available.

APPLYING FOR FINANCIAL AID ***Required financial aid forms:*** FAFSA, institution's own form, CSS Financial Aid PROFILE, noncustodial (divorced/separated) parent's statement, business/farm supplement, federal income tax form 1040 with all attachments. ***Financial aid deadline:*** 2/15. ***Notification date:*** 4/1. Students must reply by 5/1.

CONTACT David Belanger, Director of Student Financial Services, Smith College, College Hall, Northampton, MA 01063, 413-585-2530 or toll-free 800-383-3232. *Fax:* 413-585-2566. *E-mail:* sfs@smith.edu.

SOJOURNER-DOUGLASS COLLEGE

Baltimore, MD

ABOUT THE INSTITUTION Independent, coed, primarily women. ***Awards:*** bachelor's and master's degrees (offers only evening and weekend programs). 21 undergraduate majors. ***Total enrollment:*** 1,151. Undergraduates: 1,078.

GIFT AID (NEED-BASED) ***Scholarships, grants, and awards:*** Federal Pell, FSEOG, state, private, college/university gift aid from institutional funds.

WORK-STUDY ***Federal work-study:*** Total amount: $119,391; 16 jobs averaging $7462.

APPLYING FOR FINANCIAL AID ***Required financial aid forms:*** FAFSA, institution's own form.

CONTACT Ms. Rebecca Chalk, Financial Aid Director, Sojourner-Douglass College, 200 North Central Avenue, Baltimore, MD 21202, 410-276-0306 Ext. 258. *Fax:* 410-276-0148. *E-mail:* rchalk@host.sdc.edu.

SOKA UNIVERSITY OF AMERICA

Aliso Viejo, CA

Tuition & fees: $26,202 **Average undergraduate aid package: $23,665**

ABOUT THE INSTITUTION Independent, coed. 1 undergraduate major. Federal methodology is used as a basis for awarding need-based institutional aid.

UNDERGRADUATE EXPENSES for 2010–11 ***Comprehensive fee:*** $35,842 includes full-time tuition ($25,344), mandatory fees ($858), and room and board ($9640). Full-time tuition and fees vary according to course load. ***Payment plan:*** Installment.

FRESHMAN FINANCIAL AID (Fall 2009) 103 applied for aid; of those 100% were deemed to have need. 100% of freshmen with need received aid; of those 75% had need fully met. ***Average percent of need met:*** 88% (excluding resources awarded to replace EFC). ***Average financial aid package:*** $23,665 (excluding resources awarded to replace EFC).

UNDERGRADUATE FINANCIAL AID (Fall 2009) 420 applied for aid; of those 100% were deemed to have need. 100% of undergraduates with need received aid; of those 70% had need fully met. ***Average percent of need met:*** 88% (excluding resources awarded to replace EFC). ***Average financial aid package:*** $23,665 (excluding resources awarded to replace EFC).

GIFT AID (NEED-BASED) ***Total amount:*** $8,513,717 (6% federal, 6% state, 86% institutional, 2% external sources). ***Receiving aid:*** Freshmen: 68% (70); all full-time undergraduates: 59% (255). ***Average award:*** Freshmen: $13,360; Undergraduates: $14,000. ***Scholarships, grants, and awards:*** Federal Pell, FSEOG, state, private, college/university gift aid from institutional funds.

GIFT AID (NON-NEED-BASED) ***Receiving aid:*** Freshmen: 100% (103). Undergraduates: 97% (420).

LOANS ***Student loans:*** $1,216,264 (100% need-based). 45% of past graduating class borrowed through all loan programs. *Average indebtedness per student:* $24,000. ***Average need-based loan:*** Freshmen: $3500. Undergraduates: $5000. ***Parent loans:*** $1,063,578 (100% need-based). ***Programs:*** Federal Direct (Subsidized and Unsubsidized Stafford, PLUS), college/university.

WORK-STUDY ***Federal work-study:*** Total amount: $15,141; jobs available.

ATHLETIC AWARDS Total amount: $135,750 (100% need-based).

APPLYING FOR FINANCIAL AID ***Required financial aid form:*** FAFSA. ***Financial aid deadline:*** 5/1 (priority: 3/2). ***Notification date:*** Continuous beginning 3/1. Students must reply by 7/1.

CONTACT Christopher Brown, Director of Admission and Financial Aid, Soka University of America, 1 University Drive, Aliso Viejo, CA 92656, 949-480-4048 or toll-free 888-600-SOKA (out-of-state). *Fax:* 949-480-4151. *E-mail:* cbrown@soka.edu.

SOMERSET CHRISTIAN COLLEGE

Zarephath, NJ

CONTACT Financial Aid Office, Somerset Christian College, 10 College Way, PO Box 9035, Zarephath, NJ 08890-9035, 732-356-1595 or toll-free 800-234-9305.

SONOMA STATE UNIVERSITY

Rohnert Park, CA

Tuition & fees (CA res): $5508 **Average undergraduate aid package: $9977**

ABOUT THE INSTITUTION State-supported, coed. 63 undergraduate majors. Federal methodology is used as a basis for awarding need-based institutional aid.

UNDERGRADUATE EXPENSES for 2010–11 ***Tuition, state resident:*** full-time $0. ***Tuition, nonresident:*** full-time $10,416; part-time $372 per unit. ***Required fees:*** full-time $5508; $1866 per term. Full-time tuition and fees vary according to course load and degree level. Part-time tuition and fees vary according to course load and degree level. ***College room and board:*** $10,522; ***Room only:*** $6774. Room and board charges vary according to housing facility.

FRESHMAN FINANCIAL AID (Fall 2010, est.) 804 applied for aid; of those 73% were deemed to have need. 92% of freshmen with need received aid; of those 8% had need fully met. ***Average percent of need met:*** 86% (excluding resources awarded to replace EFC). ***Average financial aid package:*** $9740 (excluding resources awarded to replace EFC). 1% of all full-time freshmen had no need and received non-need-based gift aid.

UNDERGRADUATE FINANCIAL AID (Fall 2010, est.) 4,502 applied for aid; of those 80% were deemed to have need. 84% of undergraduates with need received aid; of those 12% had need fully met. ***Average percent of need met:*** 83% (excluding resources awarded to replace EFC). ***Average financial aid package:*** $9977 (excluding resources awarded to replace EFC). 3% of all full-time undergraduates had no need and received non-need-based gift aid.

GIFT AID (NEED-BASED) ***Total amount:*** $17,266,354 (49% federal, 51% state). ***Receiving aid:*** Freshmen: 21% (338); all full-time undergraduates: 25% (2,010). ***Average award:*** Freshmen: $9987; Undergraduates: $8664. ***Scholarships, grants, and awards:*** Federal Pell, FSEOG, state, private, college/university gift aid from institutional funds, Academic Competitiveness Grants, National SMART Grants.

GIFT AID (NON-NEED-BASED) ***Total amount:*** $1,309,490 (17% state, 37% institutional, 46% external sources). ***Receiving aid:*** Freshmen: 5% (71). Undergraduates: 4% (354). ***Average award:*** Freshmen: $1978. Undergraduates: $1532. ***Scholarships, grants, and awards by category:*** *Academic interests/achievement:* 53 awards ($117,610 total): area/ethnic studies, biological sciences, business, communication, computer science, education, engineering/technologies, English, foreign languages, general academic interests/achievements, health fields, humanities, mathematics, physical sciences, premedicine, social sciences. *Creative arts/performance:* 87 awards ($99,468 total): applied art and design, art/fine arts, cinema/film/broadcasting, creative writing, dance, journalism/publications, music, performing arts, theater/drama. *Special achievements/activities:* 6 awards ($8125 total): community service, leadership, memberships. *Special characteristics:* 88 awards ($86,000 total): adult students, children and siblings of alumni, children of educators, children of faculty/staff, children of public servants, children of union members/company employees, children of workers in trades, ethnic background, first-generation college students, general special characteristics, handicapped students, international students, local/state students, married students, members of minority groups, out-of-state students, previous college experience, veterans. ***Tuition waivers:*** Full or partial for employees or children of employees.

LOANS ***Student loans:*** $22,596,608 (48% need-based, 52% non-need-based). 54% of past graduating class borrowed through all loan programs. *Average indebtedness per student:* $18,201. ***Average need-based loan:*** Freshmen: $3020. Undergraduates: $4126. ***Parent loans:*** $7,684,063 (100% non-need-based). ***Programs:*** Federal Direct (Subsidized and Unsubsidized Stafford, PLUS), Perkins.

WORK-STUDY ***Federal work-study:*** Total amount: $600,470; 211 jobs averaging $2845. ***State or other work-study/employment:*** Total amount: $1,600,000 (100% non-need-based). 620 part-time jobs averaging $2570.

ATHLETIC AWARDS Total amount: $426,015 (100% non-need-based).

APPLYING FOR FINANCIAL AID ***Required financial aid form:*** FAFSA. ***Financial aid deadline (priority):*** 1/31. ***Notification date:*** Continuous beginning 3/15. Students must reply within 2 weeks of notification.

CONTACT Susan Gutierrez, Director of Financial Aid, Sonoma State University, 1801 East Cotati Avenue, Rohnert Park, CA 94928-3609, 707-664-2287. *Fax:* 707-664-4242. *E-mail:* susan.gutierrez@sonoma.edu.

SOUTH CAROLINA STATE UNIVERSITY

Orangeburg, SC

CONTACT Sandra S. Davis, Director of Financial Aid, South Carolina State University, 300 College Street Northeast, Orangeburg, SC 29117, 803-536-7067 or toll-free 800-260-5956. *Fax:* 803-536-8420. *E-mail:* sdavis@scsu.edu.

SOUTH COLLEGE

Knoxville, TN

CONTACT Financial Aid Office, South College, 720 North Fifth Avenue, Knoxville, TN 37917, 865-524-3043.

SOUTH DAKOTA SCHOOL OF MINES AND TECHNOLOGY

Rapid City, SD

Tuition & fees (SD res): $7130 **Average undergraduate aid package: $12,199**

ABOUT THE INSTITUTION State-supported, coed. 17 undergraduate majors. Both federal and institutional methodology are used as a basis for awarding need-based institutional aid.

UNDERGRADUATE EXPENSES for 2010–11 ***Tuition, state resident:*** full-time $3000; part-time $99.80 per credit hour. ***Tuition, nonresident:*** full-time $4490; part-time $149.70 per credit hour. ***Required fees:*** full-time $4130. Full-time tuition and fees vary according to course load, location, program, and reciprocity agreements. Part-time tuition and fees vary according to course load, location, program, and reciprocity agreements. ***College room and board:*** $5610; ***Room only:*** $3000. Room and board charges vary according to board plan and housing facility. ***Payment plan:*** Installment.

FRESHMAN FINANCIAL AID (Fall 2010, est.) 409 applied for aid; of those 66% were deemed to have need. 100% of freshmen with need received aid; of those 47% had need fully met. ***Average percent of need met:*** 84% (excluding resources awarded to replace EFC). ***Average financial aid package:*** $12,376 (excluding resources awarded to replace EFC). 22% of all full-time freshmen had no need and received non-need-based gift aid.

UNDERGRADUATE FINANCIAL AID (Fall 2010, est.) 1,417 applied for aid; of those 66% were deemed to have need. 100% of undergraduates with need received aid; of those 38% had need fully met. ***Average percent of need met:*** 78% (excluding resources awarded to replace EFC). ***Average financial aid package:*** $12,199 (excluding resources awarded to replace EFC). 19% of all full-time undergraduates had no need and received non-need-based gift aid.

GIFT AID (NEED-BASED) ***Total amount:*** $3,495,766 (61% federal, 24% institutional, 15% external sources). ***Receiving aid:*** Freshmen: 47% (203); all full-time undergraduates: 40% (628). ***Average award:*** Freshmen: $3668; Undergraduates: $4014. ***Scholarships, grants, and awards:*** Federal Pell, FSEOG, state, private, college/university gift aid from institutional funds, Leveraging Educational Assistance Program (LEAP).

GIFT AID (NON-NEED-BASED) ***Total amount:*** $905,839 (64% institutional, 36% external sources). ***Receiving aid:*** Freshmen: 36% (155). Undergraduates: 21% (333). ***Average award:*** Freshmen: $2382. Undergraduates: $2538. ***Scholarships, grants, and awards by category:*** *Academic interests/achievement:* computer science, engineering/technologies, mathematics, military science, physical sciences. *Special characteristics:* ethnic background, members of minority groups. ***Tuition waivers:*** Full or partial for employees or children of employees, senior citizens.

LOANS ***Student loans:*** $6,214,607 (100% need-based). 72% of past graduating class borrowed through all loan programs. *Average indebtedness per student:* $16,045. ***Average need-based loan:*** Freshmen: $3339. Undergraduates: $3993. ***Parent loans:*** $1,268,573 (72% need-based, 28% non-need-based). ***Programs:*** Federal Direct (Subsidized and Unsubsidized Stafford, PLUS), Perkins.

WORK-STUDY ***Federal work-study:*** Total amount: $217,622; 118 jobs averaging $1857.

ATHLETIC AWARDS Total amount: $457,788 (48% need-based, 52% non-need-based).

APPLYING FOR FINANCIAL AID ***Required financial aid form:*** FAFSA. ***Financial aid deadline:*** Continuous. ***Notification date:*** Continuous beginning 4/15. Students must reply within 3 weeks of notification.

CONTACT David W. Martin, Financial Aid Director, South Dakota School of Mines and Technology, 501 East Saint Joseph Street, Rapid City, SD 57701-3995, 605-394-2274 or toll-free 800-544-8162 Ext. 2414. *Fax:* 605-394-1979. *E-mail:* david.martin@sdsmt.edu.

SOUTH DAKOTA STATE UNIVERSITY

Brookings, SD

Tuition & fees (SD res): $6444 **Average undergraduate aid package: $9711**

ABOUT THE INSTITUTION State-supported, coed. 78 undergraduate majors. Federal methodology is used as a basis for awarding need-based institutional aid.

UNDERGRADUATE EXPENSES for 2010–11 ***Tuition, state resident:*** full-time $2994; part-time $99.80 per credit hour. ***Tuition, nonresident:*** full-time $4491; part-time $149.70 per credit hour. ***Required fees:*** full-time $3450. Full-time tuition and fees vary according to course level, course load, location, program, and reciprocity agreements. Part-time tuition and fees vary according to course level, course load, location, program, and reciprocity agreements. ***College room and board:*** $5899; ***Room only:*** $2540. Room and board charges vary according to board plan and housing facility. ***Payment plans:*** Installment, deferred payment.

FRESHMAN FINANCIAL AID (Fall 2010, est.) 1,766 applied for aid; of those 85% were deemed to have need. 100% of freshmen with need received aid; of those 79% had need fully met. ***Average percent of need met:*** 91% (excluding resources awarded to replace EFC). ***Average financial aid package:*** $8748 (excluding resources awarded to replace EFC). 23% of all full-time freshmen had no need and received non-need-based gift aid.

UNDERGRADUATE FINANCIAL AID (Fall 2010, est.) 7,471 applied for aid; of those 87% were deemed to have need. 100% of undergraduates with need

received aid; of those 77% had need fully met. ***Average percent of need met:*** 87% (excluding resources awarded to replace EFC). ***Average financial aid package:*** $9711 (excluding resources awarded to replace EFC). 21% of all full-time undergraduates had no need and received non-need-based gift aid.

GIFT AID (NEED-BASED) ***Total amount:*** $23,726,647 (71% federal, 6% state, 15% institutional, 8% external sources). ***Receiving aid:*** Freshmen: 43% (936); all full-time undergraduates: 46% (4,027). ***Average award:*** Freshmen: $4826; Undergraduates: $4858. ***Scholarships, grants, and awards:*** Federal Pell, FSEOG, state, private, college/university gift aid from institutional funds, United Negro College Fund, Federal Nursing, Academic Competitiveness Grants, National SMART Grants, TEACH Grants, TRiO Scholarships.

GIFT AID (NON-NEED-BASED) ***Total amount:*** $3,944,897 (1% federal, 20% state, 54% institutional, 25% external sources). ***Receiving aid:*** Freshmen: 47% (1,018). Undergraduates: 62% (5,374). ***Average award:*** Freshmen: $1644. Undergraduates: $1482. ***Scholarships, grants, and awards by category:*** *Academic interests/achievement:* 3,193 awards ($3,381,456 total): agriculture, area/ethnic studies, biological sciences, business, communication, computer science, education, engineering/technologies, English, foreign languages, general academic interests/achievements, health fields, home economics, humanities, international studies, mathematics, military science, physical sciences, premedicine, social sciences. *Creative arts/performance:* 346 awards ($4,041,660 total): art/fine arts, debating, general creative arts/performance, journalism/publications, music, performing arts, theater/drama. *Special achievements/activities:* 162 awards ($163,140 total): community service, general special achievements/activities, hobbies/interests, junior miss, leadership, memberships, rodeo. *Special characteristics:* 212 awards ($317,040 total): adult students, children of faculty/staff, children of workers in trades, ethnic background, first-generation college students, general special characteristics, handicapped students, international students, members of minority groups, veterans, veterans' children. ***Tuition waivers:*** Full or partial for children of alumni, employees or children of employees, senior citizens.

LOANS ***Student loans:*** $43,409,669 (96% need-based, 4% non-need-based). 73% of past graduating class borrowed through all loan programs. *Average indebtedness per student:* $20,733. ***Average need-based loan:*** Freshmen: $4814. Undergraduates: $4963. ***Parent loans:*** $2,170,717 (55% need-based, 45% non-need-based). ***Programs:*** Federal Direct (Subsidized and Unsubsidized Stafford, PLUS), Perkins, Federal Nursing, college/university, private loans, Health Professions Student Loans (HPSL).

WORK-STUDY ***Federal work-study:*** Total amount: $826,692; 462 jobs averaging $1520. ***State or other work-study/employment:*** Total amount: $3,683,881 (16% need-based, 84% non-need-based). 1,651 part-time jobs averaging $1730.

ATHLETIC AWARDS Total amount: $2,892,706 (61% need-based, 39% non-need-based).

APPLYING FOR FINANCIAL AID ***Required financial aid form:*** FAFSA. ***Financial aid deadline (priority):*** 3/11. ***Notification date:*** Continuous beginning 4/1. Students must reply within 3 weeks of notification.

CONTACT Mr. Jay Larsen, Director of Financial Aid, South Dakota State University, Box 2201, Administration 106, Brookings, SD 57007, 605-688-4703 or toll-free 800-952-3541. *Fax:* 605-688-5882. *E-mail:* jay.larsen@sdstate.edu.

SOUTHEASTERN BAPTIST COLLEGE

Laurel, MS

CONTACT Financial Aid Officer, Southeastern Baptist College, 4229 Highway 15 North, Laurel, MS 39440-1096, 601-426-6346.

SOUTHEASTERN BAPTIST THEOLOGICAL SEMINARY

Wake Forest, NC

CONTACT Financial Aid Office, Southeastern Baptist Theological Seminary, PO Box 1889, Wake Forest, NC 27588-1889, 919-556-3101 or toll-free 800-284-6317.

SOUTHEASTERN BIBLE COLLEGE

Birmingham, AL

ABOUT THE INSTITUTION Independent nondenominational, coed. 2 undergraduate majors.

GIFT AID (NEED-BASED) ***Scholarships, grants, and awards:*** Federal Pell, FSEOG, college/university gift aid from institutional funds.

GIFT AID (NON-NEED-BASED) ***Scholarships, grants, and awards by category:*** *Academic interests/achievement:* general academic interests/achievements. *Creative arts/performance:* music. *Special characteristics:* children of faculty/staff, local/state students, veterans.

LOANS ***Programs:*** Federal Direct (Subsidized and Unsubsidized Stafford, PLUS).

WORK-STUDY Federal work-study jobs available. ***State or other work-study/employment:*** Part-time jobs available.

APPLYING FOR FINANCIAL AID ***Required financial aid forms:*** FAFSA, institution's own form.

CONTACT Mr. Jay Powell, Financial Aid Administrator, Southeastern Bible College, 2545 Valleydale Road, Birmingham, AL 35244-2083, 205-970-9216 or toll-free 800-749-8878 (in-state). *Fax:* 205-970-9207. *E-mail:* finaid@sebc.edu.

SOUTHEASTERN LOUISIANA UNIVERSITY

Hammond, LA

Tuition & fees (LA res): $4000 **Average undergraduate aid package: N/A**

ABOUT THE INSTITUTION State-supported, coed. 51 undergraduate majors. Federal methodology is used as a basis for awarding need-based institutional aid.

UNDERGRADUATE EXPENSES for 2010–11 ***Tuition, state resident:*** full-time $2993; part-time $167 per credit hour. ***Tuition, nonresident:*** full-time $11,462; part-time $520 per credit hour. ***Required fees:*** full-time $1007. Full-time tuition and fees vary according to course load. Part-time tuition and fees vary according to course load. ***College room and board:*** $6640; ***Room only:*** $4140. Room and board charges vary according to board plan and housing facility. ***Payment plans:*** Installment, deferred payment.

GIFT AID (NEED-BASED) ***Total amount:*** $23,182,363 (90% federal, 10% state). ***Scholarships, grants, and awards:*** Federal Pell, FSEOG, state, private, college/university gift aid from institutional funds.

GIFT AID (NON-NEED-BASED) ***Total amount:*** $18,250,145 (1% federal, 65% state, 30% institutional, 4% external sources). ***Scholarships, grants, and awards by category:*** *Academic interests/achievement:* business, communication, computer science, education, English, foreign languages, general academic interests/achievements, humanities, mathematics, physical sciences, social sciences. *Creative arts/performance:* art/fine arts, music, theater/drama. *Special achievements/activities:* cheerleading/drum major, leadership, memberships, rodeo. *Special characteristics:* adult students, children and siblings of alumni, children of faculty/staff, first-generation college students, out-of-state students, veterans, veterans' children. ***Tuition waivers:*** Full or partial for employees or children of employees, senior citizens.

LOANS ***Student loans:*** $39,334,877 (44% need-based, 56% non-need-based). 59% of past graduating class borrowed through all loan programs. *Average indebtedness per student:* $36,560. ***Parent loans:*** $64,591 (100% non-need-based). ***Programs:*** Perkins, college/university.

WORK-STUDY ***Federal work-study:*** Total amount: $1,020,549; 317 jobs averaging $3349. ***State or other work-study/employment:*** Total amount: $2,555,697 (100% non-need-based). 1,216 part-time jobs averaging $2102.

ATHLETIC AWARDS Total amount: $1,933,785 (100% non-need-based).

APPLYING FOR FINANCIAL AID ***Required financial aid forms:*** FAFSA, institution's own form. ***Financial aid deadline (priority):*** 5/1. ***Notification date:*** Continuous beginning 4/1. Students must reply within 2 weeks of notification.

CONTACT Financial Aid Office, Southeastern Louisiana University, SLU 10768, Hammond, LA 70402, 985-549-2244 or toll-free 800-222-7358. *Fax:* 985-549-5077. *E-mail:* finaid@selu.edu.

SOUTHEASTERN OKLAHOMA STATE UNIVERSITY

Durant, OK

Tuition & fees (OK res): $4552 **Average undergraduate aid package: $10,425**

ABOUT THE INSTITUTION State-supported, coed. 44 undergraduate majors. Federal methodology is used as a basis for awarding need-based institutional aid.

UNDERGRADUATE EXPENSES for 2010–11 ***Tuition, state resident:*** full-time $3875; part-time $129.15 per credit hour. ***Tuition, nonresident:*** full-time $10,602; part-time $353.40 per credit hour. ***Required fees:*** full-time $677; $22.55 per credit hour. Full-time tuition and fees vary according to course level. Part-time tuition and fees vary according to course level and course load. ***College room and board:*** $4520; ***Room only:*** $1980. Room and board charges vary according to board plan and housing facility.

FRESHMAN FINANCIAL AID (Fall 2009) 498 applied for aid; of those 83% were deemed to have need. 98% of freshmen with need received aid; of those 19% had need fully met. ***Average percent of need met:*** 21% (excluding resources awarded to replace EFC). ***Average financial aid package:*** $10,321 (excluding resources awarded to replace EFC). 1% of all full-time freshmen had no need and received non-need-based gift aid.

UNDERGRADUATE FINANCIAL AID (Fall 2009) 2,056 applied for aid; of those 86% were deemed to have need. 98% of undergraduates with need received aid; of those 18% had need fully met. ***Average percent of need met:*** 24% (excluding resources awarded to replace EFC). ***Average financial aid package:*** $10,425 (excluding resources awarded to replace EFC). 1% of all full-time undergraduates had no need and received non-need-based gift aid.

GIFT AID (NEED-BASED) ***Total amount:*** $10,711,825 (73% federal, 27% state). ***Receiving aid:*** Freshmen: 54% (310); all full-time undergraduates: 51% (1,340). ***Average award:*** Freshmen: $1346; Undergraduates: $1547. ***Scholarships, grants, and awards:*** Federal Pell, FSEOG, state, private, college/university gift aid from institutional funds.

GIFT AID (NON-NEED-BASED) ***Total amount:*** $2,429,843 (4% state, 8% institutional, 88% external sources). ***Receiving aid:*** Freshmen: 29% (165). Undergraduates: 19% (509). ***Average award:*** Freshmen: $1853. Undergraduates: $1641. ***Scholarships, grants, and awards by category:*** *Academic interests/achievement:* 567 awards ($475,497 total): biological sciences, business, communication, computer science, education, engineering/technologies, English, general academic interests/achievements, mathematics, physical sciences, social sciences. *Creative arts/performance:* 161 awards ($142,369 total): art/fine arts, dance, debating, music, performing arts, theater/drama. *Special achievements/activities:* 855 awards ($1,230,505 total): cheerleading/drum major, leadership, rodeo. *Special characteristics:* 2,637 awards ($5,635,852 total): children and siblings of alumni, out-of-state students. ***Tuition waivers:*** Full or partial for minority students, children of alumni, employees or children of employees, senior citizens.

LOANS ***Student loans:*** $10,283,332 (57% need-based, 43% non-need-based). 63% of past graduating class borrowed through all loan programs. *Average indebtedness per student:* $13,828. ***Average need-based loan:*** Freshmen: $1190. Undergraduates: $1709. ***Parent loans:*** $341,884 (100% non-need-based). ***Programs:*** Federal Direct (Subsidized and Unsubsidized Stafford, PLUS).

WORK-STUDY ***Federal work-study:*** Total amount: $1,008,854; 642 jobs averaging $1571. ***State or other work-study/employment:*** Total amount: $1,775,959 (100% non-need-based). 874 part-time jobs averaging $2032.

ATHLETIC AWARDS Total amount: $1,124,614 (100% non-need-based).

APPLYING FOR FINANCIAL AID ***Required financial aid forms:*** FAFSA, institution's own form. ***Financial aid deadline (priority):*** 3/1. ***Notification date:*** Continuous beginning 4/15. Students must reply within 2 weeks of notification.

CONTACT Tony Lehrling, Director of Student Financial Aid, Southeastern Oklahoma State University, 1405 North 4th Avenue, Durant, OK 74701-0609, 580-745-2186 or toll-free 800-435-1327. *Fax:* 580-745-7469. *E-mail:* shudson@se.edu.

SOUTHEASTERN UNIVERSITY

Lakeland, FL

Tuition & fees: $16,430 **Average undergraduate aid package: $10,100**

ABOUT THE INSTITUTION Independent religious, coed. 40 undergraduate majors. Federal methodology is used as a basis for awarding need-based institutional aid.

UNDERGRADUATE EXPENSES for 2010–11 ***Comprehensive fee:*** $24,330 includes full-time tuition ($15,830), mandatory fees ($600), and room and board ($7900). Full-time tuition and fees vary according to class time, degree level, and reciprocity agreements. Room and board charges vary according to board plan and housing facility. ***Part-time tuition:*** $660 per credit. ***Part-time fees:*** $150 per term. Part-time tuition and fees vary according to class time, course load, degree level, and reciprocity agreements. ***Payment plan:*** Installment.

FRESHMAN FINANCIAL AID (Fall 2009) 514 applied for aid; of those 83% were deemed to have need. 100% of freshmen with need received aid; of those 14% had need fully met. ***Average percent of need met:*** 61% (excluding resources awarded to replace EFC). ***Average financial aid package:*** $11,723 (excluding resources awarded to replace EFC). 17% of all full-time freshmen had no need and received non-need-based gift aid.

UNDERGRADUATE FINANCIAL AID (Fall 2009) 2,253 applied for aid; of those 86% were deemed to have need. 99% of undergraduates with need received aid; of those 12% had need fully met. ***Average percent of need met:*** 56% (excluding resources awarded to replace EFC). ***Average financial aid package:*** $10,100 (excluding resources awarded to replace EFC). 13% of all full-time undergraduates had no need and received non-need-based gift aid.

GIFT AID (NEED-BASED) ***Total amount:*** $11,969,226 (35% federal, 33% state, 24% institutional, 8% external sources). ***Receiving aid:*** Freshmen: 76% (421); all full-time undergraduates: 75% (1,831). ***Average award:*** Freshmen: $9382; Undergraduates: $7408. ***Scholarships, grants, and awards:*** Federal Pell, FSEOG, state, private, college/university gift aid from institutional funds.

GIFT AID (NON-NEED-BASED) ***Total amount:*** $2,677,786 (45% state, 39% institutional, 16% external sources). ***Receiving aid:*** Freshmen: 8% (44). Undergraduates: 7% (161). ***Average award:*** Freshmen: $3742. Undergraduates: $2996. ***Scholarships, grants, and awards by category:*** *Academic interests/achievement:* communication, general academic interests/achievements, religion/biblical studies. *Creative arts/performance:* journalism/publications, music, theater/drama. ***Tuition waivers:*** Full or partial for employees or children of employees.

LOANS ***Student loans:*** $15,475,981 (75% need-based, 25% non-need-based). 97% of past graduating class borrowed through all loan programs. *Average indebtedness per student:* $25,006. ***Average need-based loan:*** Freshmen: $3044. Undergraduates: $3609. ***Parent loans:*** $6,591,652 (35% need-based, 65% non-need-based). ***Programs:*** Federal Direct (Subsidized and Unsubsidized Stafford, PLUS), Perkins.

WORK-STUDY ***Federal work-study:*** Total amount: $152,600; jobs available.

ATHLETIC AWARDS Total amount: $137,113 (53% need-based, 47% non-need-based).

APPLYING FOR FINANCIAL AID ***Required financial aid forms:*** FAFSA, institution's own form, state aid form, state aid form (FL residents only). ***Financial aid deadline (priority):*** 4/15. ***Notification date:*** Continuous beginning 3/1. Students must reply by 5/1 or within 4 weeks of notification.

CONTACT Ms. Carol B. Bradley, Director of Student Financial Services, Southeastern University, 1000 Longfellow Boulevard, Lakeland, FL 33801-6099, 863-667-5000 or toll-free 800-500-8760. *Fax:* 863-667-5200. *E-mail:* cbradley@seu.edu.

SOUTHEAST MISSOURI STATE UNIVERSITY

Cape Girardeau, MO

Tuition & fees (MO res): $6255 **Average undergraduate aid package: $8527**

ABOUT THE INSTITUTION State-supported, coed. 70 undergraduate majors. Federal methodology is used as a basis for awarding need-based institutional aid.

UNDERGRADUATE EXPENSES for 2010–11 ***Tuition, state resident:*** full-time $5544; part-time $184.80 per credit hour. ***Tuition, nonresident:*** full-time $10,479; part-time $349.30 per credit hour. ***Required fees:*** full-time $711; $23.70 per credit hour. Full-time tuition and fees vary according to course load and location. Part-time tuition and fees vary according to course load and location. ***College room and board:*** $7342; ***Room only:*** $4872. Room and board charges vary according to board plan and housing facility. ***Payment plans:*** Installment, deferred payment.

FRESHMAN FINANCIAL AID (Fall 2009) 1,381 applied for aid; of those 73% were deemed to have need. 99% of freshmen with need received aid; of those 23% had need fully met. ***Average percent of need met:*** 70% (excluding resources awarded to replace EFC). ***Average financial aid package:*** $8656 (excluding resources awarded to replace EFC). 24% of all full-time freshmen had no need and received non-need-based gift aid.

UNDERGRADUATE FINANCIAL AID (Fall 2009) 5,609 applied for aid; of those 76% were deemed to have need. 98% of undergraduates with need received aid; of those 19% had need fully met. ***Average percent of need met:*** 68% (excluding resources awarded to replace EFC). ***Average financial aid package:*** $8527 (excluding resources awarded to replace EFC). 15% of all full-time undergraduates had no need and received non-need-based gift aid.

GIFT AID (NEED-BASED) ***Total amount:*** $22,444,254 (61% federal, 15% state, 22% institutional, 2% external sources). ***Receiving aid:*** Freshmen: 59% (941); all full-time undergraduates: 52% (3,734). ***Average award:*** Freshmen: $6179;

Undergraduates: $5494. ***Scholarships, grants, and awards:*** Federal Pell, FSEOG, state, private, college/university gift aid from institutional funds.

GIFT AID (NON-NEED-BASED) ***Total amount:*** $6,474,712 (2% federal, 4% state, 85% institutional, 9% external sources). ***Receiving aid:*** Freshmen: 8% (135). Undergraduates: 4% (317). ***Average award:*** Freshmen: $3518. Undergraduates: $4243. ***Scholarships, grants, and awards by category:*** *Academic interests/achievement:* 2,873 awards ($7,464,314 total): agriculture, biological sciences, business, communication, computer science, education, engineering/technologies, English, foreign languages, general academic interests/achievements, health fields, home economics, humanities, international studies, mathematics, military science, physical sciences, premedicine, religion/biblical studies, social sciences. *Creative arts/performance:* 272 awards ($230,415 total): music, performing arts, theater/drama. *Special achievements/activities:* 898 awards ($2,915,640 total): cheerleading/drum major, general special achievements/activities, leadership, memberships. *Special characteristics:* 678 awards ($2,451,295 total): children of faculty/staff, first-generation college students, general special characteristics, international students, members of minority groups, out-of-state students, previous college experience, veterans. ***Tuition waivers:*** Full or partial for employees or children of employees, senior citizens.

LOANS ***Student loans:*** $31,381,025 (65% need-based, 35% non-need-based). 68% of past graduating class borrowed through all loan programs. *Average indebtedness per student:* $22,400. ***Average need-based loan:*** Freshmen: $2891. Undergraduates: $3831. ***Parent loans:*** $5,498,715 (16% need-based, 84% non-need-based). ***Programs:*** Federal Direct (Subsidized and Unsubsidized Stafford, PLUS), Perkins.

WORK-STUDY ***Federal work-study:*** Total amount: $1,332,806; 453 jobs averaging $2955. ***State or other work-study/employment:*** 1,645 part-time jobs averaging $1890.

ATHLETIC AWARDS Total amount: $2,569,580 (42% need-based, 58% non-need-based).

APPLYING FOR FINANCIAL AID ***Required financial aid form:*** FAFSA. ***Financial aid deadline (priority):*** 3/1. ***Notification date:*** Continuous beginning 4/1. Students must reply within 3 weeks of notification.

CONTACT Kerri Saylor, Lead Customer Service Representative, Southeast Missouri State University, One University Plaza, Cape Girardeau, MO 63701, 573-651-2253. *Fax:* 573-651-5006. *E-mail:* sfs@semo.edu.

SOUTHERN ADVENTIST UNIVERSITY

Collegedale, TN

Tuition & fees: $18,324 **Average undergraduate aid package: $20,692**

ABOUT THE INSTITUTION Independent Seventh-day Adventist, coed. 71 undergraduate majors. Federal methodology is used as a basis for awarding need-based institutional aid.

UNDERGRADUATE EXPENSES for 2011–12 ***Comprehensive fee:*** $24,110 includes full-time tuition ($17,534), mandatory fees ($790), and room and board ($5786). ***College room only:*** $3286. Room and board charges vary according to housing facility. ***Part-time tuition:*** $740 per semester hour. Part-time tuition and fees vary according to course load. ***Payment plans:*** Tuition prepayment, installment, deferred payment.

FRESHMAN FINANCIAL AID (Fall 2010, est.) 494 applied for aid; of those 67% were deemed to have need. 100% of freshmen with need received aid; of those 88% had need fully met. ***Average percent of need met:*** 86% (excluding resources awarded to replace EFC). ***Average financial aid package:*** $15,674 (excluding resources awarded to replace EFC). 25% of all full-time freshmen had no need and received non-need-based gift aid.

UNDERGRADUATE FINANCIAL AID (Fall 2010, est.) 1,709 applied for aid; of those 71% were deemed to have need. 100% of undergraduates with need received aid; of those 87% had need fully met. ***Average percent of need met:*** 85% (excluding resources awarded to replace EFC). ***Average financial aid package:*** $20,692 (excluding resources awarded to replace EFC). 20% of all full-time undergraduates had no need and received non-need-based gift aid.

GIFT AID (NEED-BASED) ***Total amount:*** $16,885,007 (27% federal, 5% state, 45% institutional, 23% external sources). ***Receiving aid:*** Freshmen: 54% (331); all full-time undergraduates: 51% (1,188). ***Average award:*** Freshmen: $8555; Undergraduates: $9713. ***Scholarships, grants, and awards:*** Federal Pell, FSEOG, state, private, college/university gift aid from institutional funds.

GIFT AID (NON-NEED-BASED) ***Total amount:*** $3,318,151 (16% state, 46% institutional, 38% external sources). ***Receiving aid:*** Freshmen: 44% (272). Undergraduates: 29% (669). ***Average award:*** Freshmen: $6779. Undergraduates: $5427. ***Scholarships, grants, and awards by category:*** *Academic interests/achievement:* business, communication, education, English, general academic interests/achievements, health fields, mathematics, religion/biblical studies. *Creative arts/performance:* art/fine arts, journalism/publications, music, theater/drama. *Special achievements/activities:* community service, general special achievements/activities, leadership, religious involvement. *Special characteristics:* children and siblings of alumni, general special characteristics, international students, local/state students, members of minority groups, out-of-state students, siblings of current students, spouses of current students. ***Tuition waivers:*** Full or partial for employees or children of employees, senior citizens.

LOANS ***Student loans:*** $13,335,716 (75% need-based, 25% non-need-based). 65% of past graduating class borrowed through all loan programs. *Average indebtedness per student:* $27,121. ***Average need-based loan:*** Freshmen: $3956. Undergraduates: $4800. ***Parent loans:*** $1,975,868 (56% need-based, 44% non-need-based). ***Programs:*** Federal Direct (Subsidized and Unsubsidized Stafford, PLUS), Perkins, Federal Nursing, college/university.

WORK-STUDY ***Federal work-study:*** Total amount: $2,767,707; jobs available. ***State or other work-study/employment:*** Part-time jobs available.

APPLYING FOR FINANCIAL AID ***Required financial aid form:*** FAFSA. ***Financial aid deadline (priority):*** 3/1. ***Notification date:*** Continuous. Students must reply within 2 weeks of notification.

CONTACT Mr. Marc Grundy, Director of Student Finance, Southern Adventist University, PO Box 370, Collegedale, TN 37315-0370, 423-236-2875 or toll-free 800-768-8437. *Fax:* 423-236-1835.

SOUTHERN ARKANSAS UNIVERSITY–MAGNOLIA

Magnolia, AR

ABOUT THE INSTITUTION State-supported, coed. 42 undergraduate majors.

GIFT AID (NEED-BASED) ***Scholarships, grants, and awards:*** Federal Pell, FSEOG, state, private, college/university gift aid from institutional funds.

GIFT AID (NON-NEED-BASED) ***Scholarships, grants, and awards by category:*** *Academic interests/achievement:* agriculture, business, computer science, education, English, foreign languages, general academic interests/achievements, health fields, mathematics, physical sciences, social sciences. *Creative arts/performance:* art/fine arts, dance, music, theater/drama. *Special achievements/activities:* cheerleading/drum major, leadership, rodeo. *Special characteristics:* adult students, children and siblings of alumni, children of faculty/staff, members of minority groups, out-of-state students.

LOANS ***Programs:*** Perkins.

WORK-STUDY ***Federal work-study:*** Total amount: $3,791,480; 1,250 jobs averaging $3097. ***State or other work-study/employment:*** Total amount: $1,287,080 (100% non-need-based). 303 part-time jobs averaging $4268.

APPLYING FOR FINANCIAL AID ***Required financial aid form:*** FAFSA.

CONTACT Ms. Bronwyn C. Sneed, Director of Student Aid, Southern Arkansas University–Magnolia, PO Box 9344, Magnolia, AR 71754-9344, 870-235-4023 or toll-free 800-332-7286 (in-state). *Fax:* 870-235-4913. *E-mail:* bcsneed@saumag.edu.

SOUTHERN BAPTIST THEOLOGICAL SEMINARY

Louisville, KY

ABOUT THE INSTITUTION Independent Southern Baptist, coed. ***Awards:*** associate, bachelor's, and master's degrees. 6 undergraduate majors. ***Total enrollment:*** 3,190. Undergraduates: 668. Freshmen: 62.

GIFT AID (NEED-BASED) ***Scholarships, grants, and awards:*** private, college/university gift aid from institutional funds, local church and denominational scholarships, as well as scholarships from various ministries.

LOANS ***Programs:*** college/university, Non-Title IV loan programs (such as Sallie Mae Smart Option Loans).

APPLYING FOR FINANCIAL AID ***Required financial aid form:*** institution's own form.

CONTACT Mrs. Erin Joiner, Manager of Financial Aid, Southern Baptist Theological Seminary, 2825 Lexington Road, Louisville, KY 40280, 502-897-4206. *Fax:* 502-897-4031. *E-mail:* financialaid@sbts.edu.

SOUTHERN CALIFORNIA INSTITUTE OF ARCHITECTURE

Los Angeles, CA

CONTACT Lina Johnson, Financial Aid Director, Southern California Institute of Architecture, 960 East 3rd Street, Los Angeles, CA 90013, 213-613-2200 Ext. 345 or toll-free 800-774-7242. *Fax:* 213-613-2260. *E-mail:* financialaid@sciarc.edu.

SOUTHERN CALIFORNIA INSTITUTE OF TECHNOLOGY

Anaheim, CA

CONTACT Financial Aid Office, Southern California Institute of Technology, 222 South Harbor Boulevard, Suite 200, Anaheim, CA 92805, 714-520-5552.

SOUTHERN CALIFORNIA SEMINARY

El Cajon, CA

CONTACT Financial Aid Office, Southern California Seminary, 2075 East Madison Avenue, El Cajon, CA 92019, 619-442-9841.

SOUTHERN CONNECTICUT STATE UNIVERSITY

New Haven, CT

Tuition & fees (CT res): $8050 **Average undergraduate aid package: $13,194**

ABOUT THE INSTITUTION State-supported, coed. 43 undergraduate majors. Federal methodology is used as a basis for awarding need-based institutional aid.

UNDERGRADUATE EXPENSES for 2011–12 ***Tuition, state resident:*** full-time $4023; part-time $403 per credit. ***Tuition, nonresident:*** full-time $13,020; part-time $416 per credit. ***Required fees:*** full-time $4027; $55 per term. Full-time tuition and fees vary according to course load and reciprocity agreements. Part-time tuition and fees vary according to course load. ***College room and board:*** $9983; ***Room only:*** $5541. Room and board charges vary according to board plan and housing facility. ***Payment plans:*** Installment, deferred payment.

FRESHMAN FINANCIAL AID (Fall 2010, est.) 1,135 applied for aid; of those 74% were deemed to have need. 96% of freshmen with need received aid; of those 41% had need fully met. ***Average percent of need met:*** 82% (excluding resources awarded to replace EFC). ***Average financial aid package:*** $13,965 (excluding resources awarded to replace EFC). 4% of all full-time freshmen had no need and received non-need-based gift aid.

UNDERGRADUATE FINANCIAL AID (Fall 2010, est.) 6,510 applied for aid; of those 70% were deemed to have need. 96% of undergraduates with need received aid; of those 37% had need fully met. ***Average percent of need met:*** 81% (excluding resources awarded to replace EFC). ***Average financial aid package:*** $13,194 (excluding resources awarded to replace EFC). 3% of all full-time undergraduates had no need and received non-need-based gift aid.

GIFT AID (NEED-BASED) ***Total amount:*** $24,719,045 (45% federal, 46% state, 5% institutional, 4% external sources). ***Receiving aid:*** Freshmen: 51% (631); all full-time undergraduates: 49% (3,635). ***Average award:*** Freshmen: $6734; Undergraduates: $5984. ***Scholarships, grants, and awards:*** Federal Pell, FSEOG, state, private, college/university gift aid from institutional funds.

GIFT AID (NON-NEED-BASED) ***Total amount:*** $1,003,813 (1% federal, 49% institutional, 50% external sources). ***Receiving aid:*** Freshmen: 14% (170). Undergraduates: 8% (597). ***Average award:*** Freshmen: $3630. Undergraduates: $3733. ***Scholarships, grants, and awards by category:*** *Special characteristics:* children of faculty/staff, veterans. ***Tuition waivers:*** Full or partial for employees or children of employees, senior citizens.

LOANS ***Student loans:*** $62,616,207 (62% need-based, 38% non-need-based). 82% of past graduating class borrowed through all loan programs. *Average indebtedness per student:* $21,096. ***Average need-based loan:*** Freshmen: $5938. Undergraduates: $4306. ***Parent loans:*** $20,470,277 (52% need-based, 48% non-need-based). ***Programs:*** Federal Direct (Subsidized and Unsubsidized Stafford, PLUS).

WORK-STUDY ***Federal work-study:*** Total amount: $390,482; 84 jobs averaging $2733. ***State or other work-study/employment:*** Total amount: $142,446 (100% need-based). Part-time jobs available.

ATHLETIC AWARDS Total amount: $2,485,956 (61% need-based, 39% non-need-based).

APPLYING FOR FINANCIAL AID ***Required financial aid form:*** FAFSA. ***Financial aid deadline:*** 3/9 (priority: 3/5). ***Notification date:*** Continuous beginning 4/11. Students must reply within 2 weeks of notification.

CONTACT Gloria Lee, Interim Director of Financial Aid, Southern Connecticut State University, Wintergreen Building, New Haven, CT 06515-1355, 203-392-5445. *Fax:* 203-392-5229. *E-mail:* dennisa1@southernct.edu.

SOUTHERN ILLINOIS UNIVERSITY CARBONDALE

Carbondale, IL

Tuition & fees (IL res): $11,038 **Average undergraduate aid package: $11,809**

ABOUT THE INSTITUTION State-supported, coed. 93 undergraduate majors. Federal methodology is used as a basis for awarding need-based institutional aid.

UNDERGRADUATE EXPENSES for 2011–12 ***Tuition, state resident:*** full-time $7794; part-time $260 per credit hour. ***Tuition, nonresident:*** full-time $19,485; part-time $650 per credit hour. ***Required fees:*** full-time $3244. Full-time tuition and fees vary according to course load. Part-time tuition and fees vary according to course load. ***College room and board:*** $8648. Room and board charges vary according to board plan and housing facility. ***Payment plans:*** Guaranteed tuition, installment.

FRESHMAN FINANCIAL AID (Fall 2010, est.) 2,233 applied for aid; of those 80% were deemed to have need. 97% of freshmen with need received aid; of those 88% had need fully met. ***Average percent of need met:*** 95% (excluding resources awarded to replace EFC). ***Average financial aid package:*** $11,811 (excluding resources awarded to replace EFC). 7% of all full-time freshmen had no need and received non-need-based gift aid.

UNDERGRADUATE FINANCIAL AID (Fall 2010, est.) 10,510 applied for aid; of those 85% were deemed to have need. 97% of undergraduates with need received aid; of those 86% had need fully met. ***Average percent of need met:*** 95% (excluding resources awarded to replace EFC). ***Average financial aid package:*** $11,809 (excluding resources awarded to replace EFC). 10% of all full-time undergraduates had no need and received non-need-based gift aid.

GIFT AID (NEED-BASED) ***Total amount:*** $44,026,166 (41% federal, 49% state, 9% institutional, 1% external sources). ***Receiving aid:*** Freshmen: 58% (1,310); all full-time undergraduates: 48% (6,399). ***Average award:*** Freshmen: $7406; Undergraduates: $6934. ***Scholarships, grants, and awards:*** Federal Pell, FSEOG, state, private, college/university gift aid from institutional funds.

GIFT AID (NON-NEED-BASED) ***Total amount:*** $21,690,129 (31% federal, 32% state, 24% institutional, 13% external sources). ***Receiving aid:*** Freshmen: 41% (940). Undergraduates: 28% (3,732). ***Average award:*** Freshmen: $6718. Undergraduates: $6359. ***Scholarships, grants, and awards by category:*** *Academic interests/achievement:* agriculture, architecture, area/ethnic studies, biological sciences, business, communication, computer science, education, engineering/technologies, English, foreign languages, general academic interests/achievements, health fields, home economics, humanities, international studies, mathematics, military science, physical sciences, premedicine, religion/biblical studies, social sciences. *Creative arts/performance:* applied art and design, cinema/film/broadcasting, creative writing, dance, debating, general creative arts/performance, journalism/publications, performing arts. *Special achievements/activities:* cheerleading/drum major, community service, general special achievements/activities, leadership. *Special characteristics:* children and siblings of alumni, children of educators, children of faculty/staff, children of public servants, children with a deceased or disabled parent, general special characteristics, handicapped students, international students, members of minority groups, public servants, spouses of deceased or disabled public servants, veterans. ***Tuition waivers:*** Full or partial for children of alumni, employees or children of employees, senior citizens.

LOANS ***Student loans:*** $69,080,873 (59% need-based, 41% non-need-based). 50% of past graduating class borrowed through all loan programs. *Average indebtedness per student:* $21,359. ***Average need-based loan:*** Freshmen: $3637.

Undergraduates: $4121. ***Parent loans:*** $15,209,396 (17% need-based, 83% non-need-based). ***Programs:*** Federal Direct (Subsidized and Unsubsidized Stafford, PLUS), Perkins, college/university.

WORK-STUDY ***Federal work-study:*** Total amount: $7,777,587; jobs available. ***State or other work-study/employment:*** Total amount: $8,396,915 (19% need-based, 81% non-need-based). Part-time jobs available.

ATHLETIC AWARDS Total amount: $3,682,593 (34% need-based, 66% non-need-based).

APPLYING FOR FINANCIAL AID ***Required financial aid form:*** FAFSA. ***Financial aid deadline (priority):*** 4/1. ***Notification date:*** Continuous beginning 5/1. Students must reply within 4 weeks of notification.

CONTACT Linda Joy Clemons, Director of Financial Aid, Southern Illinois University Carbondale, Woody Hall, Third Floor, B-Wing, Carbondale, IL 62901-4702, 618-453-3102. *Fax:* 618-453-4606. *E-mail:* fao@siu.edu.

SOUTHERN ILLINOIS UNIVERSITY EDWARDSVILLE

Edwardsville, IL

Tuition & fees (IL res): $8401 **Average undergraduate aid package: $16,364**

ABOUT THE INSTITUTION State-supported, coed. 44 undergraduate majors. Federal methodology is used as a basis for awarding need-based institutional aid.

UNDERGRADUATE EXPENSES for 2010–11 ***Tuition, state resident:*** full-time $6201; part-time $206.70 per semester hour. ***Tuition, nonresident:*** full-time $15,503. ***Required fees:*** full-time $2200; $250.60 per semester hour. Full-time tuition and fees vary according to course load. Part-time tuition and fees vary according to course load. ***College room and board:*** $7821. Room and board charges vary according to board plan and housing facility. ***Payment plans:*** Guaranteed tuition, installment.

FRESHMAN FINANCIAL AID (Fall 2010, est.) 1,765 applied for aid; of those 82% were deemed to have need. 96% of freshmen with need received aid; of those 33% had need fully met. ***Average percent of need met:*** 60% (excluding resources awarded to replace EFC). ***Average financial aid package:*** $16,880 (excluding resources awarded to replace EFC). 2% of all full-time freshmen had no need and received non-need-based gift aid.

UNDERGRADUATE FINANCIAL AID (Fall 2010, est.) 7,411 applied for aid; of those 86% were deemed to have need. 96% of undergraduates with need received aid; of those 33% had need fully met. ***Average percent of need met:*** 61% (excluding resources awarded to replace EFC). ***Average financial aid package:*** $16,364 (excluding resources awarded to replace EFC). 4% of all full-time undergraduates had no need and received non-need-based gift aid.

GIFT AID (NEED-BASED) ***Total amount:*** $30,475,573 (61% federal, 31% state, 5% institutional, 3% external sources). ***Receiving aid:*** Freshmen: 44% (898); all full-time undergraduates: 39% (3,739). ***Average award:*** Freshmen: $9175; Undergraduates: $9150. ***Scholarships, grants, and awards:*** Federal Pell, FSEOG, state, private, college/university gift aid from institutional funds, Federal Nursing.

GIFT AID (NON-NEED-BASED) ***Total amount:*** $3,441,751 (29% federal, 30% state, 29% institutional, 12% external sources). ***Receiving aid:*** Freshmen: 7% (139). Undergraduates: 6% (611). ***Average award:*** Freshmen: $9334. Undergraduates: $7848. ***Scholarships, grants, and awards by category:*** *Academic interests/achievement:* business, education, general academic interests/achievements, health fields. *Creative arts/performance:* art/fine arts, dance, music, theater/drama. *Special characteristics:* children of faculty/staff. ***Tuition waivers:*** Full or partial for employees or children of employees, senior citizens.

LOANS ***Student loans:*** $45,319,169 (81% need-based, 19% non-need-based). 44% of past graduating class borrowed through all loan programs. *Average indebtedness per student:* $21,633. ***Average need-based loan:*** Freshmen: $11,095. Undergraduates: $11,078. ***Parent loans:*** $22,634,894 (25% need-based, 75% non-need-based). ***Programs:*** Federal Direct (Subsidized and Unsubsidized Stafford, PLUS), Perkins, Federal Nursing, college/university, alternative loans.

WORK-STUDY ***Federal work-study:*** Total amount: $1,076,255; jobs available. ***State or other work-study/employment:*** Part-time jobs available.

ATHLETIC AWARDS Total amount: $708,773 (36% need-based, 64% non-need-based).

APPLYING FOR FINANCIAL AID ***Required financial aid form:*** FAFSA. ***Financial aid deadline (priority):*** 3/1. ***Notification date:*** Continuous beginning 3/15. Students must reply within 2 weeks of notification.

CONTACT Sharon Berry, Director of Financial Aid, Southern Illinois University Edwardsville, Campus Box 1060, Edwardsville, IL 62026-1060, 618-650-3834 or toll-free 800-447-SIUE. *Fax:* 618-650-3885. *E-mail:* shaberr@siue.edu.

SOUTHERN METHODIST COLLEGE

Orangeburg, SC

CONTACT Financial Aid Officer, Southern Methodist College, PO Box 1027, 541 Broughton Street, Orangeburg, SC 29116, 803-534-7826 Ext. 1326 or toll-free 800-360-1503. *Fax:* 803-534-7827.

SOUTHERN METHODIST UNIVERSITY

Dallas, TX

Tuition & fees: $39,430 **Average undergraduate aid package: $32,632**

ABOUT THE INSTITUTION Independent religious, coed. 67 undergraduate majors. Both federal and institutional methodology are used as a basis for awarding need-based institutional aid.

UNDERGRADUATE EXPENSES for 2011–12 ***Tuition:*** full-time $34,990. Full-time tuition and fees vary according to class time. Part-time tuition and fees vary according to class time and course load. Room and board charges vary according to board plan and housing facility. ***Payment plans:*** Tuition prepayment, installment.

FRESHMAN FINANCIAL AID (Fall 2010, est.) 830 applied for aid; of those 79% were deemed to have need. 100% of freshmen with need received aid; of those 45% had need fully met. ***Average percent of need met:*** 90% (excluding resources awarded to replace EFC). ***Average financial aid package:*** $35,099 (excluding resources awarded to replace EFC). 34% of all full-time freshmen had no need and received non-need-based gift aid.

UNDERGRADUATE FINANCIAL AID (Fall 2010, est.) 2,733 applied for aid; of those 86% were deemed to have need. 99% of undergraduates with need received aid; of those 36% had need fully met. ***Average percent of need met:*** 86% (excluding resources awarded to replace EFC). ***Average financial aid package:*** $32,632 (excluding resources awarded to replace EFC). 33% of all full-time undergraduates had no need and received non-need-based gift aid.

GIFT AID (NEED-BASED) ***Total amount:*** $54,710,353 (10% federal, 7% state, 82% institutional, 1% external sources). ***Receiving aid:*** Freshmen: 34% (504); all full-time undergraduates: 32% (1,894). ***Average award:*** Freshmen: $20,003; Undergraduates: $18,433. ***Scholarships, grants, and awards:*** Federal Pell, FSEOG, state, private, college/university gift aid from institutional funds.

GIFT AID (NON-NEED-BASED) ***Total amount:*** $25,898,242 (97% institutional, 3% external sources). ***Receiving aid:*** Freshmen: 35% (520). Undergraduates: 25% (1,487). ***Average award:*** Freshmen: $16,257. Undergraduates: $15,334. ***Tuition waivers:*** Full or partial for employees or children of employees.

LOANS ***Student loans:*** $17,888,656 (62% need-based, 38% non-need-based). 36% of past graduating class borrowed through all loan programs. *Average indebtedness per student:* $24,569. ***Average need-based loan:*** Freshmen: $2818. Undergraduates: $3709. ***Parent loans:*** $10,586,167 (32% need-based, 68% non-need-based). ***Programs:*** Federal Direct (Subsidized and Unsubsidized Stafford, PLUS), Perkins, state, college/university.

WORK-STUDY ***Federal work-study:*** Total amount: $5,526,032; 1,540 jobs averaging $3472. ***State or other work-study/employment:*** Total amount: $246,675 (24% need-based, 76% non-need-based). 11 part-time jobs averaging $3223.

ATHLETIC AWARDS Total amount: $11,129,953 (39% need-based, 61% non-need-based).

APPLYING FOR FINANCIAL AID ***Required financial aid forms:*** FAFSA, CSS Financial Aid PROFILE, noncustodial (divorced/separated) parent's statement, business/farm supplement. ***Financial aid deadline (priority):*** 2/15. ***Notification date:*** Continuous beginning 3/15.

CONTACT Marc Peterson, Director of Financial Aid, Southern Methodist University, PO Box 750181, Dallas, TX 75275, 214-768-3016 or toll-free 800-323-0672. *Fax:* 214-768-0202. *E-mail:* mpeterso@smu.edu.

SOUTHERN NAZARENE UNIVERSITY

Bethany, OK

ABOUT THE INSTITUTION Independent Nazarene, coed. 56 undergraduate majors.

GIFT AID (NEED-BASED) ***Scholarships, grants, and awards:*** Federal Pell, FSEOG, state, private, college/university gift aid from institutional funds.

GIFT AID (NON-NEED-BASED) ***Scholarships, grants, and awards by category:*** *Academic interests/achievement:* biological sciences, business, communication, computer science, education, English, general academic interests/achievements, mathematics, physical sciences, religion/biblical studies, social sciences. *Creative arts/performance:* art/fine arts, music, performing arts. *Special achievements/activities:* cheerleading/drum major. *Special characteristics:* children and siblings of alumni, children of faculty/staff, first-generation college students, international students, local/state students, religious affiliation, siblings of current students, veterans, veterans' children.

LOANS ***Programs:*** Federal Direct (Subsidized and Unsubsidized Stafford, PLUS), Perkins, alternative loans.

WORK-STUDY ***Federal work-study:*** Total amount: $221,000; 104 jobs averaging $2125. ***State or other work-study/employment:*** 115 part-time jobs averaging $3000.

APPLYING FOR FINANCIAL AID ***Required financial aid form:*** FAFSA.

CONTACT Diana Lee, Director of Financial Assistance, Southern Nazarene University, 6729 Northwest 39th Expressway, Bethany, OK 73008, 405-491-6310 or toll-free 800-648-9899. *Fax:* 405-717-6271. *E-mail:* dlee@snu.edu.

SOUTHERN NEW HAMPSHIRE UNIVERSITY

Manchester, NH

CONTACT Financial Aid Office, Southern New Hampshire University, 2500 North River Road, Manchester, NH 03106, 603-645-9645 or toll-free 800-642-4968. *Fax:* 603-645-9639. *E-mail:* finaid@snhu.edu.

SOUTHERN OREGON UNIVERSITY

Ashland, OR

Tuition & fees (OR res): $6729 **Average undergraduate aid package: $10,226**

ABOUT THE INSTITUTION State-supported, coed. 40 undergraduate majors. Federal methodology is used as a basis for awarding need-based institutional aid.

UNDERGRADUATE EXPENSES for 2010–11 ***Tuition, state resident:*** full-time $6729. ***Tuition, nonresident:*** full-time $20,283. Full-time tuition and fees vary according to course load, location, and reciprocity agreements. Part-time tuition and fees vary according to course load, location, and reciprocity agreements. ***College room and board:*** $8508. Room and board charges vary according to board plan and housing facility. ***Payment plan:*** Deferred payment.

FRESHMAN FINANCIAL AID (Fall 2009) 570 applied for aid; of those 78% were deemed to have need. 99% of freshmen with need received aid; of those 16% had need fully met. ***Average percent of need met:*** 66% (excluding resources awarded to replace EFC). ***Average financial aid package:*** $10,614 (excluding resources awarded to replace EFC). 14% of all full-time freshmen had no need and received non-need-based gift aid.

UNDERGRADUATE FINANCIAL AID (Fall 2009) 3,272 applied for aid; of those 87% were deemed to have need. 97% of undergraduates with need received aid; of those 10% had need fully met. ***Average percent of need met:*** 60% (excluding resources awarded to replace EFC). ***Average financial aid package:*** $10,226 (excluding resources awarded to replace EFC). 8% of all full-time undergraduates had no need and received non-need-based gift aid.

GIFT AID (NEED-BASED) ***Total amount:*** $17,397,044 (49% federal, 12% state, 31% institutional, 8% external sources). ***Receiving aid:*** Freshmen: 63% (413); all full-time undergraduates: 68% (2,393). ***Average award:*** Freshmen: $8577; Undergraduates: $7816. ***Scholarships, grants, and awards:*** Federal Pell, FSEOG, state, private, college/university gift aid from institutional funds.

GIFT AID (NON-NEED-BASED) ***Total amount:*** $3,307,218 (1% federal, 92% institutional, 7% external sources). ***Receiving aid:*** Freshmen: 7% (46). Undergraduates: 4% (143). ***Average award:*** Freshmen: $10,556. Undergraduates: $8905. ***Scholarships, grants, and awards by category:*** *Academic interests/achievement:* 659 awards ($831,957 total): biological sciences, business, education, English, foreign languages, general academic interests/achievements, health fields, mathematics, physical sciences, social sciences. *Creative arts/performance:* 132 awards ($132,633 total): art/fine arts, creative writing, journalism/publications, music, theater/drama. *Special achievements/activities:* 15 awards ($17,534 total): community service, general special achievements/activities, hobbies/interests, leadership, memberships. *Special characteristics:* 101 awards ($430,886 total): adult students, international students, members of minority groups. ***Tuition waivers:*** Full or partial for employees or children of employees, senior citizens.

LOANS ***Student loans:*** $21,168,544 (83% need-based, 17% non-need-based). 64% of past graduating class borrowed through all loan programs. *Average indebtedness per student:* $24,132. ***Average need-based loan:*** Freshmen: $3197. Undergraduates: $4003. ***Parent loans:*** $7,254,578 (33% need-based, 67% non-need-based). ***Programs:*** Federal Direct (Subsidized and Unsubsidized Stafford, PLUS), Perkins, college/university.

WORK-STUDY ***Federal work-study:*** Total amount: $330,715; 316 jobs averaging $1047.

ATHLETIC AWARDS Total amount: $389,809 (67% need-based, 33% non-need-based).

APPLYING FOR FINANCIAL AID ***Required financial aid forms:*** FAFSA, institution's own form. ***Financial aid deadline (priority):*** 3/1. ***Notification date:*** Continuous beginning 3/2. Students must reply within 4 weeks of notification.

CONTACT Enrollment Services Center, Southern Oregon University, 1250 Siskiyou Boulevard, Ashland, OR 97520, 541-552-6600 or toll-free 800-482-7672 (in-state). *Fax:* 541-552-6614. *E-mail:* esc@sou.edu.

SOUTHERN POLYTECHNIC STATE UNIVERSITY

Marietta, GA

Tuition & fees (GA res): $6176 **Average undergraduate aid package: $3655**

ABOUT THE INSTITUTION State-supported, coed. 31 undergraduate majors. Federal methodology is used as a basis for awarding need-based institutional aid.

UNDERGRADUATE EXPENSES for 2010–11 ***Tuition, state resident:*** full-time $4980; part-time $166 per semester hour. ***Tuition, nonresident:*** full-time $18,120; part-time $604 per semester hour. ***Required fees:*** full-time $1196; $598 per term. Full-time tuition and fees vary according to course load. Part-time tuition and fees vary according to course load. ***College room and board:*** $6604; ***Room only:*** $3650. Room and board charges vary according to housing facility.

FRESHMAN FINANCIAL AID (Fall 2010, est.) 479 applied for aid; of those 100% were deemed to have need. 98% of freshmen with need received aid; of those 46% had need fully met. ***Average percent of need met:*** 80% (excluding resources awarded to replace EFC). ***Average financial aid package:*** $3239 (excluding resources awarded to replace EFC).

UNDERGRADUATE FINANCIAL AID (Fall 2010, est.) 2,657 applied for aid; of those 81% were deemed to have need. 97% of undergraduates with need received aid; of those 22% had need fully met. ***Average percent of need met:*** 72% (excluding resources awarded to replace EFC). ***Average financial aid package:*** $3655 (excluding resources awarded to replace EFC).

GIFT AID (NEED-BASED) ***Total amount:*** $7,295,451 (100% federal). ***Receiving aid:*** Freshmen: 34% (191); all full-time undergraduates: 42% (1,418). ***Average award:*** Freshmen: $2655; Undergraduates: $3743. ***Scholarships, grants, and awards:*** Federal Pell, FSEOG, state, private, college/university gift aid from institutional funds.

GIFT AID (NON-NEED-BASED) ***Total amount:*** $682,724 (23% state, 4% institutional, 73% external sources). ***Receiving aid:*** Freshmen: 58% (320). Undergraduates: 21% (700). ***Scholarships, grants, and awards by category:*** *Academic interests/achievement:* general academic interests/achievements. *Special characteristics:* members of minority groups. ***Tuition waivers:*** Full or partial for employees or children of employees, senior citizens.

LOANS ***Student loans:*** $21,563,329 (43% need-based, 57% non-need-based). 54% of past graduating class borrowed through all loan programs. *Average indebtedness per student:* $24,360. ***Average need-based loan:*** Freshmen: $3731. Undergraduates: $4691. ***Parent loans:*** $542,885 (100% non-need-based). ***Programs:*** Federal Direct (Subsidized and Unsubsidized Stafford, PLUS).

WORK-STUDY ***Federal work-study:*** Total amount: $223,990; 215 jobs averaging $4000.

ATHLETIC AWARDS Total amount: $325,908 (100% non-need-based).

APPLYING FOR FINANCIAL AID ***Required financial aid form:*** FAFSA. ***Financial aid deadline (priority):*** 3/1. ***Notification date:*** Continuous beginning 4/1. Students must reply by 8/15.

CONTACT Mr. Gary L. Mann, Director of Financial Aid, Southern Polytechnic State University, 1100 South Marietta Parkway, Marietta, GA 30060-2896, 678-915-7290 or toll-free 800-635-3204. *Fax:* 678-915-4227. *E-mail:* gmann@spsu.edu.

SOUTHERN UNIVERSITY AND AGRICULTURAL AND MECHANICAL COLLEGE

Baton Rouge, LA

CONTACT Mr. Phillip Rodgers Sr., Director of Financial Aid, Southern University and Agricultural and Mechanical College, PO Box 9961, Baton Rouge, LA 70813, 225-771-2790 or toll-free 800-256-1531. *Fax:* 225-771-5898. *E-mail:* phillip_rodgers@cxs.subr.edu.

SOUTHERN UNIVERSITY AT NEW ORLEANS

New Orleans, LA

CONTACT Director of Financial Aid, Southern University at New Orleans, 6400 Press Drive, New Orleans, LA 70126, 504-286-5263. *Fax:* 504-286-5213.

SOUTHERN UTAH UNIVERSITY

Cedar City, UT

Tuition & fees (UT res): $4736 **Average undergraduate aid package: $7659**

ABOUT THE INSTITUTION State-supported, coed. 48 undergraduate majors. Federal methodology is used as a basis for awarding need-based institutional aid.

UNDERGRADUATE EXPENSES for 2010–11 ***Tuition, state resident:*** full-time $4196; part-time $200 per credit hour. ***Tuition, nonresident:*** full-time $13,846; part-time $660 per credit hour. ***Required fees:*** full-time $540; $270 per term. Part-time tuition and fees vary according to course load. ***College room and board:*** ***Room only:*** $2086. Room and board charges vary according to board plan and housing facility. ***Payment plan:*** Installment.

FRESHMAN FINANCIAL AID (Fall 2009) 1,042 applied for aid; of those 78% were deemed to have need. 100% of freshmen with need received aid; of those 15% had need fully met. ***Average percent of need met:*** 62% (excluding resources awarded to replace EFC). ***Average financial aid package:*** $6900 (excluding resources awarded to replace EFC). 47% of all full-time freshmen had no need and received non-need-based gift aid.

UNDERGRADUATE FINANCIAL AID (Fall 2009) 4,069 applied for aid; of those 85% were deemed to have need. 99% of undergraduates with need received aid; of those 10% had need fully met. ***Average percent of need met:*** 62% (excluding resources awarded to replace EFC). ***Average financial aid package:*** $7659 (excluding resources awarded to replace EFC). 40% of all full-time undergraduates had no need and received non-need-based gift aid.

GIFT AID (NEED-BASED) ***Total amount:*** $13,073,888 (97% federal, 1% state, 1% institutional, 1% external sources). ***Receiving aid:*** Freshmen: 63% (802); all full-time undergraduates: 67% (3,425). ***Average award:*** Freshmen: $5823; Undergraduates: $5874. ***Scholarships, grants, and awards:*** Federal Pell, FSEOG, state, private, college/university gift aid from institutional funds.

GIFT AID (NON-NEED-BASED) ***Total amount:*** $7,241,043 (1% federal, 15% institutional, 84% external sources). ***Receiving aid:*** Freshmen: 25% (321). Undergraduates: 14% (703). ***Average award:*** Freshmen: $5773. Undergraduates: $7489. ***Scholarships, grants, and awards by category:*** *Academic interests/achievement:* general academic interests/achievements. *Creative arts/performance:* general creative arts/performance, music, theater/drama. *Special achievements/activities:* general special achievements/activities, leadership. *Special characteristics:* children and siblings of alumni, local/state students, members of minority groups. ***Tuition waivers:*** Full or partial for employees or children of employees.

LOANS ***Student loans:*** $16,071,437 (69% need-based, 31% non-need-based). 46% of past graduating class borrowed through all loan programs. *Average indebtedness per student:* $11,170. ***Average need-based loan:*** Freshmen: $2974. Undergraduates: $3868. ***Parent loans:*** $465,003 (100% non-need-based). ***Programs:*** Federal Direct (Subsidized and Unsubsidized Stafford, PLUS), Perkins.

WORK-STUDY ***Federal work-study:*** Total amount: $284,348; jobs available. ***State or other work-study/employment:*** Total amount: $102,718 (100% need-based). Part-time jobs available.

ATHLETIC AWARDS Total amount: $2,241,229 (100% non-need-based).

APPLYING FOR FINANCIAL AID ***Required financial aid form:*** FAFSA. ***Financial aid deadline (priority):*** 12/1. ***Notification date:*** Continuous beginning 11/1. Students must reply by 5/1.

CONTACT Jan Carey-McDonald, Director of Financial Aid and Scholarships, Southern Utah University, 351 West University Boulevard, Cedar City, UT 84720-2498, 435-586-7735. *Fax:* 435-586-7736. *E-mail:* careymcdonald@suu.edu.

SOUTHERN VERMONT COLLEGE

Bennington, VT

CONTACT Office of Financial Aid, Southern Vermont College, 982 Mansion Drive, Bennington, VT 05201, 802-447-6306 or toll-free 800-378-2782. *Fax:* 802-447-4695. *E-mail:* financialaid@svc.edu.

SOUTHERN VIRGINIA UNIVERSITY

Buena Vista, VA

CONTACT Darin Hassell, Financial Aid Specialist, Southern Virginia University, One University Hill Drive, Buena Vista, VA 24416, 540-261-4351 or toll-free 800-229-8420. *Fax:* 540-261-8559. *E-mail:* finaid@svu.edu.

SOUTHERN WESLEYAN UNIVERSITY

Central, SC

CONTACT Mrs. Sherri Peters, Financial Aid Associate, Southern Wesleyan University, 907 Wesleyan Drive, Central, SC 29630-1020, 800-289-1292 Ext. 5517 or toll-free 800-289-1292 Ext. 5550. *Fax:* 864-644-5970. *E-mail:* finaid@swu.edu.

SOUTH UNIVERSITY

Montgomery, AL

UNDERGRADUATE EXPENSES Information about tuition and fees can be obtained by contacting the South University Admissions Office.

CONTACT Financial Aid Office, South University, 5355 Vaughn Road, Montgomery, AL 36116-1120, 334-395-8800 or toll-free 866-629-2962.

SOUTH UNIVERSITY

Royal Palm Beach, FL

UNDERGRADUATE EXPENSES Information about tuition and fees can be obtained by contacting the South University Admissions Office.

CONTACT Financial Aid Office, South University, 1760 North Congress Avenue, West Palm Beach, FL 33409, 561-697-9200 Ext. 230 or toll-free 866-629-2902. *Fax:* 561-697-9944. *E-mail:* lhartman@southcollege.edu.

SOUTH UNIVERSITY

Tampa, FL

UNDERGRADUATE EXPENSES Information about tuition and fees can be obtained by contacting the South University Admissions Office.

CONTACT Financial Aid Office, South University, 4401 North Himes Avenue, Suite 175, Tampa, FL 33614, 813-393-3800 or toll-free 800-846-1472.

SOUTH UNIVERSITY

Savannah, GA

UNDERGRADUATE EXPENSES Information about tuition and fees can be obtained by contacting the South University Admissions Office.

CONTACT Financial Aid Office, South University, 709 Mall Boulevard, Savannah, GA 31406, 912-201-8000 or toll-free 866-629-2901.

SOUTH UNIVERSITY

Columbia, SC

UNDERGRADUATE EXPENSES Information about tuition and fees can be obtained by contacting the South University Admissions Office.

CONTACT Financial Aid Office, South University, 9 Science Court, Columbia, SC 29203, 803-799-9082 or toll-free 866-629-3031.

SOUTH UNIVERSITY

Glen Allen, VA

UNDERGRADUATE EXPENSES Information about tuition and fees can be obtained by contacting the South University Admissions Office.

CONTACT Financial Aid Office, South University, 2151 Old Brick Road, Glen Allen, VA 23060, 804-727-6800 or toll-free 888-422-5076.

SOUTH UNIVERSITY

Virginia Beach, VA

UNDERGRADUATE EXPENSES Information about tuition and fees can be obtained by contacting the South University Admissions Office.

CONTACT Financial Aid Office, South University, 301 Bendix Road, Suite 100, Virginia Beach, VA 23452, 757-493-6900 or toll-free 877-206-1845.

SOUTHWEST BAPTIST UNIVERSITY

Bolivar, MO

Tuition & fees: $17,280 **Average undergraduate aid package: $13,989**

ABOUT THE INSTITUTION Independent Southern Baptist, coed. 54 undergraduate majors. Federal methodology is used as a basis for awarding need-based institutional aid.

UNDERGRADUATE EXPENSES for 2010–11 ***Comprehensive fee:*** $23,000 includes full-time tuition ($16,500), mandatory fees ($780), and room and board ($5720). ***College room only:*** $2860. Full-time tuition and fees vary according to course load. Room and board charges vary according to board plan and housing facility. Part-time tuition and fees vary according to course load and location. ***Payment plan:*** Installment.

FRESHMAN FINANCIAL AID (Fall 2010, est.) 452 applied for aid; of those 81% were deemed to have need. 98% of freshmen with need received aid; of those 21% had need fully met. ***Average percent of need met:*** 73% (excluding resources awarded to replace EFC). ***Average financial aid package:*** $16,155 (excluding resources awarded to replace EFC). 17% of all full-time freshmen had no need and received non-need-based gift aid.

UNDERGRADUATE FINANCIAL AID (Fall 2010, est.) 1,957 applied for aid; of those 82% were deemed to have need. 99% of undergraduates with need received aid; of those 17% had need fully met. ***Average percent of need met:*** 68% (excluding resources awarded to replace EFC). ***Average financial aid package:*** $13,989 (excluding resources awarded to replace EFC). 15% of all full-time undergraduates had no need and received non-need-based gift aid.

GIFT AID (NEED-BASED) ***Total amount:*** $6,759,272 (79% federal, 21% state). ***Receiving aid:*** Freshmen: 68% (310); all full-time undergraduates: 71% (1,429). ***Average award:*** Freshmen: $5180; Undergraduates: $4820. ***Scholarships, grants, and awards:*** Federal Pell, FSEOG, state, private, college/university gift aid from institutional funds.

GIFT AID (NON-NEED-BASED) ***Total amount:*** $11,829,292 (1% state, 91% institutional, 8% external sources). ***Receiving aid:*** Freshmen: 79% (358). Undergraduates: 65% (1,305). ***Average award:*** Freshmen: $8284. Undergraduates: $7396. ***Scholarships, grants, and awards by category:*** *Academic interests/achievement:* 1,413 awards ($7,902,957 total): general academic interests/achievements. *Creative arts/performance:* 137 awards ($249,525 total): art/fine arts, debating, general creative arts/performance, music, theater/drama. *Special achievements/activities:* 193 awards ($349,000 total): religious involvement. *Special characteristics:* 680 awards ($911,636 total): general special characteristics, local/state students, relatives of clergy. ***Tuition waivers:*** Full or partial for employees or children of employees.

LOANS ***Student loans:*** $14,614,434 (48% need-based, 52% non-need-based). 91% of past graduating class borrowed through all loan programs. ***Average need-based loan:*** Freshmen: $3844. Undergraduates: $4257. ***Parent loans:*** $1,068,013 (100% non-need-based). ***Programs:*** Federal Direct (Subsidized and Unsubsidized Stafford, PLUS), Perkins, Federal Nursing, state, alternative loans.

WORK-STUDY ***Federal work-study:*** Total amount: $647,596; 357 jobs averaging $1814.

ATHLETIC AWARDS Total amount: $2,180,617 (100% non-need-based).

APPLYING FOR FINANCIAL AID ***Required financial aid forms:*** FAFSA, institution's own form. ***Financial aid deadline (priority):*** 3/15. ***Notification date:*** Continuous. Students must reply within 2 weeks of notification.

CONTACT Mr. Brad Gamble, Director of Financial Aid, Southwest Baptist University, 1600 University Avenue, Bolivar, MO 65613-2597, 417-328-1823 or toll-free 800-526-5859. *Fax:* 417-328-1514. *E-mail:* bgamble@sbuniv.edu.

SOUTHWESTERN ADVENTIST UNIVERSITY

Keene, TX

CONTACT Student Financial Services, Southwestern Adventist University, PO Box 567, Keene, TX 76059, 817-645-3921 Ext. 262 or toll-free 800-433-2240. *Fax:* 817-556-4744.

SOUTHWESTERN ASSEMBLIES OF GOD UNIVERSITY

Waxahachie, TX

CONTACT Financial Aid Office, Southwestern Assemblies of God University, 1200 Sycamore Street, Waxahachie, TX 75165-2397, 972-825-4730 or toll-free 888-937-7248. *Fax:* 972-937-4001. *E-mail:* finaid@sagu.edu.

SOUTHWESTERN CHRISTIAN COLLEGE

Terrell, TX

CONTACT Financial Aid Office, Southwestern Christian College, PO Box 10, Terrell, TX 75160, 972-524-3341. *Fax:* 972-563-7133.

SOUTHWESTERN CHRISTIAN UNIVERSITY

Bethany, OK

CONTACT Mrs. Billie Stewart, Financial Aid Director, Southwestern Christian University, PO Box 340, Bethany, OK 73008, 405-789-7661 Ext. 3456. *Fax:* 405-495-0078. *E-mail:* billie.stewart@swcu.edu.

SOUTHWESTERN COLLEGE

Winfield, KS

Tuition & fees: $21,680 **Average undergraduate aid package: $17,210**

ABOUT THE INSTITUTION Independent United Methodist, coed. 51 undergraduate majors. Federal methodology is used as a basis for awarding need-based institutional aid.

UNDERGRADUATE EXPENSES for 2011–12 ***Comprehensive fee:*** $28,002 includes full-time tuition ($21,530), mandatory fees ($150), and room and board ($6322). ***College room only:*** $2910. Full-time tuition and fees vary according to class time, course load, degree level, location, and program. Room and board charges vary according to board plan and housing facility. ***Part-time tuition:*** $897 per credit hour. Part-time tuition and fees vary according to class time, course load, degree level, location, and program. ***Payment plan:*** Installment.

FRESHMAN FINANCIAL AID (Fall 2009) 110 applied for aid; of those 91% were deemed to have need. 100% of freshmen with need received aid; of those 18% had need fully met. ***Average percent of need met:*** 86% (excluding resources awarded to replace EFC). ***Average financial aid package:*** $18,749 (excluding resources awarded to replace EFC). 16% of all full-time freshmen had no need and received non-need-based gift aid.

UNDERGRADUATE FINANCIAL AID (Fall 2009) 497 applied for aid; of those 93% were deemed to have need. 100% of undergraduates with need received aid; of those 17% had need fully met. ***Average percent of need met:*** 86% (excluding resources awarded to replace EFC). ***Average financial aid package:*** $17,210 (excluding resources awarded to replace EFC). 18% of all full-time undergraduates had no need and received non-need-based gift aid.

GIFT AID (NEED-BASED) ***Total amount:*** $5,562,820 (31% federal, 10% state, 54% institutional, 5% external sources). ***Receiving aid:*** Freshmen: 84% (100); all full-time undergraduates: 79% (449). ***Average award:*** Freshmen: $12,695; Undergraduates: $10,752. ***Scholarships, grants, and awards:*** Federal Pell, FSEOG, state, private, college/university gift aid from institutional funds.

GIFT AID (NON-NEED-BASED) ***Total amount:*** $1,067,409 (92% institutional, 8% external sources). ***Receiving aid:*** Freshmen: 8% (9). Undergraduates: 6% (32). ***Average award:*** Freshmen: $8690. Undergraduates: $8576. ***Scholarships, grants, and awards by category:*** *Academic interests/achievement:* $2,664,256 total: biological sciences, business, communication, computer science, general academic interests/achievements, health fields, physical sciences, religion/biblical studies, social sciences. *Creative arts/performance:* $234,470 total: cinema/film/broadcasting, dance, journalism/publications, music, performing arts, theater/drama. *Special achievements/activities:* $911,827 total: cheerleading/drum major, community service, general special achievements/activities, leadership, memberships, religious involvement. *Special characteristics:* $755,506 total: children of faculty/staff, international students, members of minority groups, religious affiliation. ***Tuition waivers:*** Full or partial for employees or children of employees, senior citizens.

LOANS ***Student loans:*** $7,705,980 (79% need-based, 21% non-need-based). 85% of past graduating class borrowed through all loan programs. *Average indebtedness per student:* $30,794. ***Average need-based loan:*** Freshmen: $4332. Undergraduates: $5253. ***Parent loans:*** $967,150 (26% need-based, 74% non-need-based). ***Programs:*** Federal Direct (Subsidized and Unsubsidized Stafford, PLUS), Perkins.

WORK-STUDY ***Federal work-study:*** 173 jobs averaging $1099. ***State or other work-study/employment:*** Part-time jobs available.

ATHLETIC AWARDS Total amount: $740,422 (78% need-based, 22% non-need-based).

APPLYING FOR FINANCIAL AID ***Required financial aid forms:*** FAFSA, institution's own form. ***Financial aid deadline:*** 8/15 (priority: 4/1). ***Notification date:*** Continuous beginning 2/1. Students must reply within 2 weeks of notification.

CONTACT Mrs. Brenda D. Hicks, Director of Financial Aid, Southwestern College, 100 College Street, Winfield, KS 67156-2499, 620-229-6215 or toll-free 800-846-1543. *Fax:* 620-229-6363. *E-mail:* finaid@sckans.edu.

SOUTHWESTERN OKLAHOMA STATE UNIVERSITY

Weatherford, OK

Tuition & fees (OK res): $4335 **Average undergraduate aid package: $5068**

ABOUT THE INSTITUTION State-supported, coed. 53 undergraduate majors. Institutional methodology is used as a basis for awarding need-based institutional aid.

UNDERGRADUATE EXPENSES for 2010–11 ***Tuition, state resident:*** full-time $3405; part-time $113.50 per credit hour. ***Tuition, nonresident:*** full-time $9120; part-time $304 per credit hour. ***Required fees:*** full-time $930; $31 per credit hour. Full-time tuition and fees vary according to program. Part-time tuition and fees vary according to program. ***College room and board:*** $4100; ***Room only:*** $1660. Room and board charges vary according to board plan. ***Payment plan:*** Installment.

FRESHMAN FINANCIAL AID (Fall 2010, est.) 817 applied for aid; of those 80% were deemed to have need. 98% of freshmen with need received aid; of those 29% had need fully met. ***Average percent of need met:*** 90% (excluding resources awarded to replace EFC). ***Average financial aid package:*** $4986 (excluding resources awarded to replace EFC). 13% of all full-time freshmen had no need and received non-need-based gift aid.

UNDERGRADUATE FINANCIAL AID (Fall 2010, est.) 2,903 applied for aid; of those 85% were deemed to have need. 98% of undergraduates with need received aid; of those 36% had need fully met. ***Average percent of need met:*** 89% (excluding resources awarded to replace EFC). ***Average financial aid package:*** $5068 (excluding resources awarded to replace EFC). 28% of all full-time undergraduates had no need and received non-need-based gift aid.

GIFT AID (NEED-BASED) ***Total amount:*** $9,576,255 (92% federal, 8% state). ***Receiving aid:*** Freshmen: 58% (545); all full-time undergraduates: 58% (2,181). ***Average award:*** Freshmen: $1316; Undergraduates: $1566. ***Scholarships, grants, and awards:*** Federal Pell, FSEOG, state, private, college/university gift aid from institutional funds.

GIFT AID (NON-NEED-BASED) ***Total amount:*** $6,091,685 (10% federal, 61% state, 12% institutional, 17% external sources). ***Receiving aid:*** Freshmen: 43% (404). Undergraduates: 31% (1,155). ***Average award:*** Freshmen: $403. Undergraduates: $448. ***Scholarships, grants, and awards by category:*** *Academic interests/achievement:* biological sciences, business, communication, computer science, education, engineering/technologies, English, foreign languages, general academic interests/achievements, health fields, mathematics, physical sciences, social sciences. *Creative arts/performance:* applied art and design, art/fine arts, music, theater/drama. *Special achievements/activities:* cheerleading/drum major, leadership, rodeo. *Special characteristics:* children and siblings of alumni, local/state students, out-of-state students. ***Tuition waivers:*** Full or partial for employees or children of employees, senior citizens.

LOANS ***Student loans:*** $18,596,448 (44% need-based, 56% non-need-based). ***Average need-based loan:*** Freshmen: $1389. Undergraduates: $1773. ***Parent loans:*** $3,848,368 (100% non-need-based). ***Programs:*** Federal Direct (Subsidized and Unsubsidized Stafford, PLUS).

WORK-STUDY ***Federal work-study:*** Total amount: $1,632,453; jobs available.

ATHLETIC AWARDS Total amount: $168,537 (100% non-need-based).

APPLYING FOR FINANCIAL AID ***Required financial aid forms:*** FAFSA, institution's own form. ***Financial aid deadline:*** 3/1. ***Notification date:*** 3/15.

CONTACT Mr. Jerome Wichert, Director of Student Financial Services, Southwestern Oklahoma State University, 100 Campus Drive, Weatherford, OK 73096, 580-774-6003. *Fax:* 580-774-7066. *E-mail:* jerome.wichert@swosu.edu.

SOUTHWESTERN UNIVERSITY

Georgetown, TX

Tuition & fees: $31,630 **Average undergraduate aid package: $27,424**

ABOUT THE INSTITUTION Independent Methodist, coed. 46 undergraduate majors. Federal methodology is used as a basis for awarding need-based institutional aid.

UNDERGRADUATE EXPENSES for 2010–11 ***Comprehensive fee:*** $41,400 includes full-time tuition ($31,630) and room and board ($9770). ***College room only:*** $5100. Room and board charges vary according to board plan and housing facility. ***Part-time tuition:*** $1320 per semester hour. Part-time tuition and fees vary according to course load. ***Payment plan:*** Installment.

FRESHMAN FINANCIAL AID (Fall 2010, est.) 316 applied for aid; of those 82% were deemed to have need. 100% of freshmen with need received aid; of those 44% had need fully met. ***Average percent of need met:*** 96% (excluding resources awarded to replace EFC). ***Average financial aid package:*** $28,629 (excluding resources awarded to replace EFC). 28% of all full-time freshmen had no need and received non-need-based gift aid.

UNDERGRADUATE FINANCIAL AID (Fall 2010, est.) 936 applied for aid; of those 86% were deemed to have need. 100% of undergraduates with need received aid; of those 32% had need fully met. ***Average percent of need met:*** 88% (excluding resources awarded to replace EFC). ***Average financial aid package:*** $27,424 (excluding resources awarded to replace EFC). 33% of all full-time undergraduates had no need and received non-need-based gift aid.

GIFT AID (NEED-BASED) ***Total amount:*** $17,796,919 (10% federal, 9% state, 74% institutional, 7% external sources). ***Receiving aid:*** Freshmen: 68% (259); all full-time undergraduates: 59% (799). ***Average award:*** Freshmen: $24,309; Undergraduates: $22,109. ***Scholarships, grants, and awards:*** Federal Pell, FSEOG, state, private, college/university gift aid from institutional funds.

GIFT AID (NON-NEED-BASED) ***Total amount:*** $6,623,241 (92% institutional, 8% external sources). ***Receiving aid:*** Freshmen: 61% (234). Undergraduates: 49% (658). ***Average award:*** Freshmen: $14,828. Undergraduates: $13,480. ***Scholarships, grants, and awards by category:*** *Academic interests/achievement:* 1,548 awards ($12,712,672 total): business, general academic interests/achievements, humanities, international studies, mathematics, premedicine, social sciences. *Creative arts/performance:* 112 awards ($500,306 total): art/fine arts, music, theater/drama. *Special achievements/activities:* 6 awards ($5335 total): leadership. *Special characteristics:* 89 awards ($1,333,304 total): children of faculty/staff, general special characteristics, relatives of clergy, religious affiliation. ***Tuition waivers:*** Full or partial for employees or children of employees.

LOANS ***Student loans:*** $7,603,131 (88% need-based, 12% non-need-based). 55% of past graduating class borrowed through all loan programs. *Average indebtedness per student:* $29,548. ***Average need-based loan:*** Freshmen: $4689. Undergraduates: $5346. ***Parent loans:*** $6,835,064 (76% need-based, 24% non-need-based). ***Programs:*** Federal Direct (Subsidized and Unsubsidized Stafford, PLUS), Perkins, state, college/university.

WORK-STUDY ***Federal work-study:*** Total amount: $286,123; 147 jobs averaging $1865. ***State or other work-study/employment:*** Total amount: $1,083,778 (58% need-based, 42% non-need-based). 548 part-time jobs averaging $2123.

APPLYING FOR FINANCIAL AID ***Required financial aid form:*** FAFSA. ***Financial aid deadline:*** 3/1. ***Notification date:*** Continuous beginning 3/1. Students must reply by 5/1 or within 2 weeks of notification.

CONTACT Mr. James P. Gaeta, Director of Financial Aid, Southwestern University, PO Box 770, Georgetown, TX 78627-0770, 512-863-1259 or toll-free 800-252-3166. *Fax:* 512-863-1507. *E-mail:* gaetaj@southwestern.edu.

SOUTHWEST FLORIDA COLLEGE

Fort Myers, FL

CONTACT Financial Aid Office, Southwest Florida College, 1685 Medical Lane, Fort Myers, FL 33907, 239-939-4766 or toll-free 866-SWFC-NOW.

SOUTHWEST MINNESOTA STATE UNIVERSITY

Marshall, MN

Tuition & fees (MN res): $7244 **Average undergraduate aid package: $8650**

ABOUT THE INSTITUTION State-supported, coed. 56 undergraduate majors. Federal methodology is used as a basis for awarding need-based institutional aid.

UNDERGRADUATE EXPENSES for 2010–11 ***One-time required fee:*** $20. ***Tuition, state resident:*** full-time $6249; part-time $202.20 per credit hour. ***Tuition, nonresident:*** full-time $6249; part-time $202.20 per credit hour. ***Required fees:*** full-time $995; $38.36 per credit hour. Full-time tuition and fees vary according to course load, location, program, and reciprocity agreements. Part-time tuition and fees vary according to location, program, and reciprocity agreements. ***College room and board:*** $6637; ***Room only:*** $3928. Room and board charges vary according to board plan and housing facility. ***Payment plan:*** Installment.

FRESHMAN FINANCIAL AID (Fall 2010, est.) 438 applied for aid; of those 85% were deemed to have need. 99% of freshmen with need received aid; of those 18% had need fully met. ***Average percent of need met:*** 52% (excluding resources awarded to replace EFC). ***Average financial aid package:*** $8858 (excluding resources awarded to replace EFC). 15% of all full-time freshmen had no need and received non-need-based gift aid.

UNDERGRADUATE FINANCIAL AID (Fall 2010, est.) 1,827 applied for aid; of those 83% were deemed to have need. 99% of undergraduates with need received aid; of those 18% had need fully met. ***Average percent of need met:*** 53% (excluding resources awarded to replace EFC). ***Average financial aid package:*** $8650 (excluding resources awarded to replace EFC). 13% of all full-time undergraduates had no need and received non-need-based gift aid.

GIFT AID (NEED-BASED) ***Total amount:*** $6,387,263 (77% federal, 22% state, 1% institutional). ***Receiving aid:*** Freshmen: 51% (249); all full-time undergraduates: 48% (1,056). ***Average award:*** Freshmen: $5943; Undergraduates: $5326. ***Scholarships, grants, and awards:*** Federal Pell, FSEOG, state, private, college/university gift aid from institutional funds.

GIFT AID (NON-NEED-BASED) ***Total amount:*** $2,427,839 (16% federal, 55% institutional, 29% external sources). ***Receiving aid:*** Freshmen: 49% (239). Undergraduates: 31% (691). ***Average award:*** Freshmen: $2680. Undergraduates: $2492. ***Scholarships, grants, and awards by category:*** *Academic interests/achievement:* 731 awards ($1,017,589 total): agriculture, biological sciences, business, communication, computer science, education, English, general academic interests/achievements, mathematics, physical sciences, premedicine, social sciences. *Creative arts/performance:* 67 awards ($38,980 total): art/fine arts, creative writing, debating, journalism/publications, music, performing arts, theater/drama. *Special achievements/activities:* 80 awards ($39,275 total): general special achievements/activities, hobbies/interests, leadership. *Special characteristics:* 96 awards ($66,385 total): children and siblings of alumni, children of union members/company employees, ethnic background, first-generation college students, general special characteristics, handicapped students, international students, local/state students, members of minority groups, previous college experience, veterans, veterans' children. ***Tuition waivers:*** Full or partial for employees or children of employees, senior citizens.

LOANS ***Student loans:*** $16,865,983 (46% need-based, 54% non-need-based). 80% of past graduating class borrowed through all loan programs. *Average indebtedness per student:* $18,909. ***Average need-based loan:*** Freshmen: $3431. Undergraduates: $4083. ***Parent loans:*** $520,980 (100% non-need-based). ***Programs:*** Federal Direct (Subsidized and Unsubsidized Stafford, PLUS), Perkins, state, private loans.

WORK-STUDY ***Federal work-study:*** Total amount: $250,216; 133 jobs averaging $2095. ***State or other work-study/employment:*** Total amount: $301,919 (100% need-based). 154 part-time jobs averaging $2139.

ATHLETIC AWARDS Total amount: $700,786 (100% non-need-based).

APPLYING FOR FINANCIAL AID ***Required financial aid forms:*** FAFSA, institution's own form. ***Financial aid deadline (priority):*** 3/1. ***Notification date:*** Continuous beginning 6/1.

CONTACT Mr. David Vikander, Director of Financial Aid, Southwest Minnesota State University, 1501 State Street, Marshall, MN 56258, 507-537-6281 or toll-free 800-642-0684. *Fax:* 507-537-6275. *E-mail:* vikander@smsu.edu.

SOUTHWEST UNIVERSITY

Kenner, LA

CONTACT Financial Aid Office, Southwest University, 2200 Veterans Memorial Boulevard, Kenner, LA 70062, 504-468-2900 or toll-free 800-433-5923 (out-of-state).

SPALDING UNIVERSITY

Louisville, KY

CONTACT Director of Student Financial Services, Spalding University, 851 South Fourth Street, Louisville, KY 40203, 502-588-7185 or toll-free 800-896-8941 Ext. 2111. *Fax:* 502-585-7128. *E-mail:* onestop@spalding.edu.

SPELMAN COLLEGE

Atlanta, GA

Tuition & fees: $22,010 **Average undergraduate aid package: $15,439**

ABOUT THE INSTITUTION Independent, women only. 25 undergraduate majors. Federal methodology is used as a basis for awarding need-based institutional aid.

UNDERGRADUATE EXPENSES for 2010–11 ***One-time required fee:*** $250. ***Comprehensive fee:*** $32,474 includes full-time tuition ($18,709), mandatory fees ($3301), and room and board ($10,464). ***College room only:*** $6706. ***Part-time tuition:*** $780 per credit hour. ***Payment plan:*** Deferred payment.

FRESHMAN FINANCIAL AID (Fall 2009) 550 applied for aid; of those 86% were deemed to have need. 100% of freshmen with need received aid; of those 33% had need fully met. ***Average percent of need met:*** 47% (excluding resources awarded to replace EFC). ***Average financial aid package:*** $15,696 (excluding resources awarded to replace EFC).

UNDERGRADUATE FINANCIAL AID (Fall 2009) 1,997 applied for aid; of those 84% were deemed to have need. 100% of undergraduates with need received aid; of those 34% had need fully met. ***Average percent of need met:*** 47% (excluding resources awarded to replace EFC). ***Average financial aid package:*** $15,439 (excluding resources awarded to replace EFC).

GIFT AID (NEED-BASED) ***Total amount:*** $19,478,780 (25% federal, 7% state, 50% institutional, 18% external sources). ***Receiving aid:*** Freshmen: 74% (418); all full-time undergraduates: 67% (1,423). ***Average award:*** Freshmen: $12,495; Undergraduates: $12,829. ***Scholarships, grants, and awards:*** Federal Pell, FSEOG, state, private, college/university gift aid from institutional funds, United Negro College Fund.

GIFT AID (NON-NEED-BASED) ***Total amount:*** $9201 (100% institutional). ***Receiving aid:*** Undergraduates: 4. ***Tuition waivers:*** Full or partial for employees or children of employees.

LOANS ***Student loans:*** $16,353,713 (72% need-based, 28% non-need-based). 70% of past graduating class borrowed through all loan programs. *Average indebtedness per student:* $14,070. ***Average need-based loan:*** Freshmen: $3317. Undergraduates: $4307. ***Parent loans:*** $12,792,380 (100% non-need-based). ***Programs:*** Federal Direct (Subsidized and Unsubsidized Stafford, PLUS), Perkins.

WORK-STUDY ***Federal work-study:*** Total amount: $193,732; jobs available.

APPLYING FOR FINANCIAL AID ***Required financial aid forms:*** FAFSA, institution's own form. ***Financial aid deadline (priority):*** 2/15. ***Notification date:*** Continuous. Students must reply within 2 weeks of notification.

CONTACT Lenora J. Jackson, Director of Student Financial Services, Spelman College, 350 Spelman Lane, SW, PO Box 771, Atlanta, GA 30314-4399, 404-270-5212 Ext. 5212 or toll-free 800-982-2411. *Fax:* 404-270-5220. *E-mail:* lenoraj@spelman.edu.

SPRING ARBOR UNIVERSITY

Spring Arbor, MI

Tuition & fees: $20,536 **Average undergraduate aid package: $18,866**

ABOUT THE INSTITUTION Independent Free Methodist, coed. 63 undergraduate majors. Federal methodology is used as a basis for awarding need-based institutional aid.

UNDERGRADUATE EXPENSES for 2010–11 ***Comprehensive fee:*** $27,790 includes full-time tuition ($19,996), mandatory fees ($540), and room and board ($7254). ***College room only:*** $3400. Full-time tuition and fees vary according to course load, degree level, and program. Room and board charges vary according to board plan and housing facility. ***Part-time tuition:*** $504 per credit hour. ***Part-time fees:*** $225 per term. Part-time tuition and fees vary according to course load, degree level, program, and reciprocity agreements. ***Payment plan:*** Installment.

FRESHMAN FINANCIAL AID (Fall 2010, est.) 414 applied for aid; of those 92% were deemed to have need. 100% of freshmen with need received aid; of those 18% had need fully met. ***Average percent of need met:*** 84% (excluding resources awarded to replace EFC). ***Average financial aid package:*** $20,082 (excluding resources awarded to replace EFC).

UNDERGRADUATE FINANCIAL AID (Fall 2010, est.) 1,428 applied for aid; of those 92% were deemed to have need. 100% of undergraduates with need received aid; of those 17% had need fully met. ***Average percent of need met:*** 80% (excluding resources awarded to replace EFC). ***Average financial aid package:*** $18,866 (excluding resources awarded to replace EFC).

GIFT AID (NEED-BASED) ***Total amount:*** $20,844,254 (27% federal, 10% state, 62% institutional, 1% external sources). ***Receiving aid:*** Freshmen: 89% (376); all full-time undergraduates: 86% (1,291). ***Average award:*** Freshmen: $13,047; Undergraduates: $12,389. ***Scholarships, grants, and awards:*** Federal Pell, FSEOG, state, private, college/university gift aid from institutional funds.

GIFT AID (NON-NEED-BASED) ***Total amount:*** $318,162 (3% federal, 42% state, 55% external sources). ***Receiving aid:*** Freshmen: 9% (39). Undergraduates: 6% (92). ***Scholarships, grants, and awards by category:*** *Academic interests/achievement:* 1,111 awards ($5,669,710 total): general academic interests/achievements. *Creative arts/performance:* 206 awards ($112,272 total): art/fine arts, music. *Special achievements/activities:* junior miss. *Special characteristics:* 519 awards ($1,501,841 total): adult students, children of faculty/staff, general special characteristics, international students, members of minority groups, relatives of clergy, religious affiliation. ***Tuition waivers:*** Full or partial for employees or children of employees.

LOANS ***Student loans:*** $32,225,949 (48% need-based, 52% non-need-based). 86% of past graduating class borrowed through all loan programs. *Average indebtedness per student:* $28,212. ***Average need-based loan:*** Freshmen: $4224. Undergraduates: $4471. ***Parent loans:*** $2,314,714 (100% need-based). ***Programs:*** Federal Direct (Subsidized and Unsubsidized Stafford, PLUS), Perkins, alternative loans.

WORK-STUDY ***Federal work-study:*** Total amount: $201,612; 445 jobs averaging $913.

ATHLETIC AWARDS Total amount: $1,719,945 (100% need-based).

APPLYING FOR FINANCIAL AID ***Required financial aid form:*** FAFSA. ***Financial aid deadline (priority):*** 3/1. ***Notification date:*** Continuous beginning 4/1. Students must reply within 2 weeks of notification.

CONTACT Geoff Marsh, Director of Financial Aid, Spring Arbor University, 106 East Main Street, Spring Arbor, MI 49283-9799, 517-750-6468 or toll-free 800-968-0011. *Fax:* 517-750-6620. *E-mail:* gmarsh@arbor.edu.

SPRINGFIELD COLLEGE

Springfield, MA

Tuition & fees: $30,660 **Average undergraduate aid package: $20,042**

ABOUT THE INSTITUTION Independent, coed. 38 undergraduate majors. Institutional methodology is used as a basis for awarding need-based institutional aid.

UNDERGRADUATE EXPENSES for 2011–12 ***Tuition:*** full-time $30,660. Room and board charges vary according to board plan and housing facility. ***Payment plan:*** Installment.

FRESHMAN FINANCIAL AID (Fall 2010, est.) 579 applied for aid; of those 89% were deemed to have need. 100% of freshmen with need received aid; of those 6% had need fully met. ***Average percent of need met:*** 75% (excluding resources awarded to replace EFC). ***Average financial aid package:*** $20,607 (excluding resources awarded to replace EFC). 11% of all full-time freshmen had no need and received non-need-based gift aid.

UNDERGRADUATE FINANCIAL AID (Fall 2010, est.) 2,102 applied for aid; of those 91% were deemed to have need. 100% of undergraduates with need received aid; of those 8% had need fully met. ***Average percent of need met:*** 73% (excluding resources awarded to replace EFC). ***Average financial aid package:*** $20,042 (excluding resources awarded to replace EFC). 10% of all full-time undergraduates had no need and received non-need-based gift aid.

GIFT AID (NEED-BASED) ***Total amount:*** $28,117,218 (10% federal, 2% state, 83% institutional, 5% external sources). ***Receiving aid:*** Freshmen: 78% (513); all full-time undergraduates: 82% (1,901). ***Average award:*** Freshmen: $16,067; Undergraduates: $14,766. ***Scholarships, grants, and awards:*** Federal Pell, FSEOG, state, private, college/university gift aid from institutional funds.

GIFT AID (NON-NEED-BASED) ***Total amount:*** $3,066,673 (61% institutional, 39% external sources). ***Receiving aid:*** Freshmen: 4% (29). Undergraduates: 5% (111). ***Average award:*** Freshmen: $7088. Undergraduates: $6404. ***Scholarships, grants, and awards by category:*** *Academic interests/achievement:* general academic interests/achievements. *Special characteristics:* children of faculty/staff, siblings of current students. ***Tuition waivers:*** Full or partial for employees or children of employees.

LOANS ***Student loans:*** $19,350,897 (72% need-based, 28% non-need-based). 90% of past graduating class borrowed through all loan programs. *Average indebtedness per student:* $33,697. ***Average need-based loan:*** Freshmen: $4027. Undergraduates: $4483. ***Parent loans:*** $7,395,778 (37% need-based, 63% non-need-based). ***Programs:*** Federal Direct (Subsidized and Unsubsidized Stafford, PLUS), Perkins, state, alternative loans.

WORK-STUDY ***Federal work-study:*** Total amount: $1,530,879; jobs available. ***State or other work-study/employment:*** Total amount: $712,474 (86% need-based, 14% non-need-based). Part-time jobs available.

APPLYING FOR FINANCIAL AID ***Required financial aid forms:*** FAFSA, institution's own form, state aid form, federal income tax form(s). ***Financial aid deadline (priority):*** 3/15. ***Notification date:*** Continuous beginning 3/25. Students must reply within 2 weeks of notification.

CONTACT Ms. Kinser Cancelmo, Assistant Director of Financial Aid, Springfield College, 263 Alden Street, Springfield, MA 01109-3797, 413-748-3108 or toll-free 800-343-1257 (out-of-state). *Fax:* 413-748-3462. *E-mail:* finaid@spfldcol.edu.

SPRING HILL COLLEGE

Mobile, AL

Tuition & fees: $26,730 **Average undergraduate aid package: $27,679**

ABOUT THE INSTITUTION Independent Roman Catholic (Jesuit), coed. 40 undergraduate majors. Federal methodology is used as a basis for awarding need-based institutional aid.

UNDERGRADUATE EXPENSES for 2010–11 ***Comprehensive fee:*** $36,980 includes full-time tuition ($25,110), mandatory fees ($1620), and room and board ($10,250). ***College room only:*** $5350. Room and board charges vary according to board plan and housing facility. ***Part-time tuition:*** $890 per credit hour. ***Part-time fees:*** $50 per credit hour. ***Payment plan:*** Installment.

FRESHMAN FINANCIAL AID (Fall 2010, est.) 352 applied for aid; of those 84% were deemed to have need. 100% of freshmen with need received aid; of those 16% had need fully met. ***Average percent of need met:*** 92% (excluding resources awarded to replace EFC). ***Average financial aid package:*** $31,152 (excluding resources awarded to replace EFC). 23% of all full-time freshmen had no need and received non-need-based gift aid.

UNDERGRADUATE FINANCIAL AID (Fall 2010, est.) 1,023 applied for aid; of those 86% were deemed to have need. 100% of undergraduates with need received aid; of those 20% had need fully met. ***Average percent of need met:*** 87% (excluding resources awarded to replace EFC). ***Average financial aid package:*** $27,679 (excluding resources awarded to replace EFC). 28% of all full-time undergraduates had no need and received non-need-based gift aid.

GIFT AID (NEED-BASED) ***Total amount:*** $17,234,229 (15% federal, 1% state, 83% institutional, 1% external sources). ***Receiving aid:*** Freshmen: 74% (295); all full-time undergraduates: 69% (870). ***Average award:*** Freshmen: $23,611; Undergraduates: $20,941. ***Scholarships, grants, and awards:*** Federal Pell, FSEOG, state, private, college/university gift aid from institutional funds, Academic Competitiveness Grants, National SMART Grants, TEACH Grants.

GIFT AID (NON-NEED-BASED) ***Total amount:*** $5,638,250 (1% state, 98% institutional, 1% external sources). ***Receiving aid:*** Freshmen: 8% (30). Undergraduates: 8% (103). ***Average award:*** Freshmen: $15,513. Undergraduates: $14,071. ***Scholarships, grants, and awards by category:*** *Academic interests/achievement:* general academic interests/achievements. *Special achievements/activities:* community service. *Special characteristics:* children of faculty/staff, siblings of current students. ***Tuition waivers:*** Full or partial for employees or children of employees.

LOANS ***Student loans:*** $8,621,943 (79% need-based, 21% non-need-based). 73% of past graduating class borrowed through all loan programs. *Average indebtedness per student:* $26,325. ***Average need-based loan:*** Freshmen: $3334. Undergraduates: $3813. ***Parent loans:*** $1,736,152 (31% need-based, 69% non-need-based). ***Programs:*** Federal Direct (Subsidized and Unsubsidized Stafford, PLUS), Perkins, alternative loans (CitiAssist, Signature).

WORK-STUDY ***Federal work-study:*** Total amount: $490,620; jobs available. ***State or other work-study/employment:*** Total amount: $232,676 (54% need-based, 46% non-need-based). Part-time jobs available.

ATHLETIC AWARDS Total amount: $1,289,393 (50% need-based, 50% non-need-based).

APPLYING FOR FINANCIAL AID ***Required financial aid forms:*** FAFSA, state aid form. ***Financial aid deadline (priority):*** 3/1. ***Notification date:*** Continuous beginning 2/15. Students must reply by 5/1 or within 2 weeks of notification.

CONTACT Ms. Ellen F. Foster, Director of Financial Aid, Spring Hill College, 4000 Dauphin Street, Mobile, AL 36608, 251-380-3460 or toll-free 800-SHC-6704. *Fax:* 251-460-2176. *E-mail:* efoster@shc.edu.

STANFORD UNIVERSITY

Stanford, CA

Tuition & fees: $41,006 **Average undergraduate aid package: $40,593**

ABOUT THE INSTITUTION Independent, coed. 67 undergraduate majors. Both federal and institutional methodology are used as a basis for awarding need-based institutional aid.

UNDERGRADUATE EXPENSES for 2011–12 ***Comprehensive fee:*** $53,297 includes full-time tuition ($40,500), mandatory fees ($506), and room and board ($12,291). Room and board charges vary according to board plan and housing facility.

FRESHMAN FINANCIAL AID (Fall 2009) 1,091 applied for aid; of those 83% were deemed to have need. 100% of freshmen with need received aid; of those 91% had need fully met. ***Average percent of need met:*** 100% (excluding resources awarded to replace EFC). ***Average financial aid package:*** $40,298 (excluding resources awarded to replace EFC). 4% of all full-time freshmen had no need and received non-need-based gift aid.

UNDERGRADUATE FINANCIAL AID (Fall 2009) 3,933 applied for aid; of those 90% were deemed to have need. 100% of undergraduates with need received aid; of those 85% had need fully met. ***Average percent of need met:*** 100% (excluding resources awarded to replace EFC). ***Average financial aid package:*** $40,593 (excluding resources awarded to replace EFC). 12% of all full-time undergraduates had no need and received non-need-based gift aid.

GIFT AID (NEED-BASED) ***Total amount:*** $132,239,808 (6% federal, 3% state, 88% institutional, 3% external sources). ***Receiving aid:*** Freshmen: 53% (897); all full-time undergraduates: 51% (3,483). ***Average award:*** Freshmen: $37,804; Undergraduates: $37,930. ***Scholarships, grants, and awards:*** Federal Pell, FSEOG, state, private, college/university gift aid from institutional funds.

GIFT AID (NON-NEED-BASED) ***Total amount:*** $10,801,468 (2% federal, 45% institutional, 53% external sources). ***Receiving aid:*** Freshmen: 5% (93). Undergraduates: 8% (565). ***Average award:*** Freshmen: $3755. Undergraduates: $3329. ***Tuition waivers:*** Full or partial for employees or children of employees.

LOANS ***Student loans:*** $7,252,836 (25% need-based, 75% non-need-based). 35% of past graduating class borrowed through all loan programs. *Average indebtedness per student:* $14,058. ***Average need-based loan:*** Freshmen: $2205. Undergraduates: $2747. ***Parent loans:*** $6,558,758 (100% non-need-based). ***Programs:*** Federal Direct (Subsidized and Unsubsidized Stafford, PLUS), Perkins.

WORK-STUDY ***Federal work-study:*** Total amount: $2,563,595; 750 jobs averaging $2618. ***State or other work-study/employment:*** Total amount: $3,050,976 (67% need-based, 33% non-need-based). 1,575 part-time jobs averaging $1933.

ATHLETIC AWARDS Total amount: $16,739,376 (16% need-based, 84% non-need-based).

APPLYING FOR FINANCIAL AID ***Required financial aid forms:*** FAFSA, CSS Financial Aid PROFILE. ***Financial aid deadline (priority):*** 2/15. ***Notification date:*** Continuous beginning 4/1. Students must reply by 5/1.

CONTACT Financial Aid Office, Stanford University, Montag Hall, 355 Galvez Street, Stanford, CA 94305-3021, 650-723-3058. *Fax:* 650-725-0540. *E-mail:* financialaid@stanford.edu.

STATE UNIVERSITY OF NEW YORK AT BINGHAMTON

Binghamton, NY

Tuition & fees (NY res): $6881 **Average undergraduate aid package: $10,414**

ABOUT THE INSTITUTION State-supported, coed. 74 undergraduate majors. Federal methodology is used as a basis for awarding need-based institutional aid.

UNDERGRADUATE EXPENSES for 2010–11 ***Tuition, state resident:*** full-time $4970; part-time $207 per credit hour. ***Tuition, nonresident:*** full-time $13,380; part-time $558 per credit hour. ***Required fees:*** full-time $1911; $68.95 per credit hour or $118 per term. Part-time tuition and fees vary according to course load. ***College room and board:*** $11,244; ***Room only:*** $7036. Room and board charges vary according to board plan and housing facility.

FRESHMAN FINANCIAL AID (Fall 2010, est.) 1,802 applied for aid; of those 58% were deemed to have need. 100% of freshmen with need received aid; of those 6% had need fully met. ***Average percent of need met:*** 68% (excluding resources awarded to replace EFC). ***Average financial aid package:*** $9543 (excluding resources awarded to replace EFC). 1% of all full-time freshmen had no need and received non-need-based gift aid.

UNDERGRADUATE FINANCIAL AID (Fall 2010, est.) 7,694 applied for aid; of those 72% were deemed to have need. 100% of undergraduates with need received aid; of those 7% had need fully met. ***Average percent of need met:*** 69% (excluding resources awarded to replace EFC). ***Average financial aid package:*** $10,414 (excluding resources awarded to replace EFC). 1% of all full-time undergraduates had no need and received non-need-based gift aid.

GIFT AID (NEED-BASED) ***Total amount:*** $32,719,662 (52% federal, 40% state, 4% institutional, 4% external sources). ***Receiving aid:*** Freshmen: 37% (821); all full-time undergraduates: 39% (4,484). ***Average award:*** Freshmen: $6655; Undergraduates: $6716. ***Scholarships, grants, and awards:*** Federal Pell, FSEOG, state, private, college/university gift aid from institutional funds.

GIFT AID (NON-NEED-BASED) ***Total amount:*** $1,075,025 (50% state, 11% institutional, 39% external sources). ***Receiving aid:*** Freshmen: 1% (24). Undergraduates: 2% (230). ***Average award:*** Freshmen: $2400. Undergraduates: $5966. ***Scholarships, grants, and awards by category:*** *Academic interests/achievement:* 226 awards ($375,521 total): area/ethnic studies, biological sciences, business, computer science, education, engineering/technologies, English, foreign languages, general academic interests/achievements, health fields, humanities, international studies, mathematics, physical sciences, premedicine, social sciences. *Creative arts/performance:* 9 awards ($12,000 total): art/fine arts, cinema/film/broadcasting, creative writing, dance, general creative arts/performance, journalism/publications, music, performing arts, theater/drama. *Special achievements/activities:* 71 awards ($149,560 total): community service, general special achievements/activities, leadership. *Special characteristics:* 76 awards ($163,750 total): adult students, children of faculty/staff, ethnic background, first-generation college students, handicapped students, local/state students, married students, members of minority groups, out-of-state students.

LOANS ***Student loans:*** $58,643,308 (75% need-based, 25% non-need-based). 50% of past graduating class borrowed through all loan programs. *Average indebtedness per student:* $21,110. ***Average need-based loan:*** Freshmen: $3629. Undergraduates: $4649. ***Parent loans:*** $12,178,408 (64% need-based, 36% non-need-based). ***Programs:*** Federal Direct (Subsidized and Unsubsidized Stafford, PLUS), Perkins, Federal Nursing, college/university.

WORK-STUDY ***Federal work-study:*** Total amount: $655,250; 408 jobs averaging $1425.

ATHLETIC AWARDS Total amount: $2,860,032 (100% non-need-based).

APPLYING FOR FINANCIAL AID ***Required financial aid forms:*** FAFSA, state aid form. ***Financial aid deadline (priority):*** 2/1. ***Notification date:*** Continuous beginning 3/4. Students must reply within 2 weeks of notification.

State University of New York at Binghamton

CONTACT Mr. Dennis Chavez, Director of Student Financial Aid and Student Records, State University of New York at Binghamton, PO Box 6000, Binghamton, NY 13902-6000, 607-777-2428. *Fax:* 607-777-6897. *E-mail:* finaid@binghamton.edu.

STATE UNIVERSITY OF NEW YORK AT FREDONIA

Fredonia, NY

Tuition & fees (NY res): $6333 **Average undergraduate aid package: $9239**

ABOUT THE INSTITUTION State-supported, coed. 74 undergraduate majors. Federal methodology is used as a basis for awarding need-based institutional aid.

UNDERGRADUATE EXPENSES for 2011–12 ***Tuition, state resident:*** full-time $4970; part-time $207 per credit hour. ***Tuition, nonresident:*** full-time $13,380; part-time $558 per credit hour. ***Required fees:*** full-time $1363; $56.60 per credit hour. Full-time tuition and fees vary according to program. Part-time tuition and fees vary according to program. ***College room and board:*** $10,110; ***Room only:*** $5950. Room and board charges vary according to board plan and housing facility. ***Payment plan:*** Installment.

FRESHMAN FINANCIAL AID (Fall 2010, est.) 972 applied for aid; of those 74% were deemed to have need. 98% of freshmen with need received aid; of those 13% had need fully met. ***Average percent of need met:*** 64% (excluding resources awarded to replace EFC). ***Average financial aid package:*** $9280 (excluding resources awarded to replace EFC). 8% of all full-time freshmen had no need and received non-need-based gift aid.

UNDERGRADUATE FINANCIAL AID (Fall 2010, est.) 4,439 applied for aid; of those 80% were deemed to have need. 98% of undergraduates with need received aid; of those 11% had need fully met. ***Average percent of need met:*** 64% (excluding resources awarded to replace EFC). ***Average financial aid package:*** $9239 (excluding resources awarded to replace EFC). 6% of all full-time undergraduates had no need and received non-need-based gift aid.

GIFT AID (NEED-BASED) ***Total amount:*** $16,920,220 (51% federal, 38% state, 7% institutional, 4% external sources). ***Receiving aid:*** Freshmen: 51% (544); all full-time undergraduates: 55% (2,803). ***Average award:*** Freshmen: $4534; Undergraduates: $4337. ***Scholarships, grants, and awards:*** Federal Pell, FSEOG, state, private, college/university gift aid from institutional funds, Academic Competitiveness Grants, National SMART Grants, TEACH Grants.

GIFT AID (NON-NEED-BASED) ***Total amount:*** $1,086,797 (100% federal). ***Receiving aid:*** Freshmen: 19% (204). Undergraduates: 12% (640). ***Average award:*** Freshmen: $2091. Undergraduates: $2161. ***Scholarships, grants, and awards by category:*** *Academic interests/achievement:* 360 awards ($323,714 total): biological sciences, business, communication, computer science, education, English, foreign languages, general academic interests/achievements, humanities, international studies, mathematics, physical sciences, social sciences. *Creative arts/performance:* 108 awards ($75,988 total): applied art and design, art/fine arts, dance, music, performing arts, theater/drama. *Special achievements/activities:* 19 awards ($58,300 total): general special achievements/activities, leadership. *Special characteristics:* 138 awards ($380,640 total): children and siblings of alumni, ethnic background, general special characteristics, international students, local/state students, members of minority groups, out-of-state students, parents of current students, previous college experience.

LOANS ***Student loans:*** $36,472,748 (47% need-based, 53% non-need-based). 86% of past graduating class borrowed through all loan programs. *Average indebtedness per student:* $27,110. ***Average need-based loan:*** Freshmen: $4969. Undergraduates: $4774. ***Parent loans:*** $4,372,816 (100% non-need-based). ***Programs:*** Perkins.

WORK-STUDY ***Federal work-study:*** Total amount: $383,567; 298 jobs averaging $1287.

APPLYING FOR FINANCIAL AID ***Required financial aid forms:*** FAFSA, state aid form. ***Financial aid deadline:*** Continuous. ***Notification date:*** Continuous beginning 3/1. Students must reply by 5/1.

CONTACT Jeremy Corrente, Assistant Director, State University of New York at Fredonia, 215 Maytum Hall, Fredonia, NY 14063, 716-673-3253 or toll-free 800-252-1212. *Fax:* 716-673-3785. *E-mail:* corrente@fredonia.edu.

STATE UNIVERSITY OF NEW YORK AT NEW PALTZ

New Paltz, NY

Tuition & fees (NY res): $6135 **Average undergraduate aid package: $9230**

ABOUT THE INSTITUTION State-supported, coed. 81 undergraduate majors. Federal methodology is used as a basis for awarding need-based institutional aid.

UNDERGRADUATE EXPENSES for 2010–11 ***Tuition, state resident:*** full-time $4970; part-time $207 per credit. ***Tuition, nonresident:*** full-time $13,380; part-time $558 per credit. ***Required fees:*** full-time $1165; $33.80 per credit or $175 per term. ***College room and board:*** $9786; ***Room only:*** $6364. Room and board charges vary according to board plan. ***Payment plan:*** Installment.

FRESHMAN FINANCIAL AID (Fall 2010, est.) 975 applied for aid; of those 65% were deemed to have need. 99% of freshmen with need received aid; of those 10% had need fully met. ***Average percent of need met:*** 53% (excluding resources awarded to replace EFC). ***Average financial aid package:*** $9178 (excluding resources awarded to replace EFC). 1% of all full-time freshmen had no need and received non-need-based gift aid.

UNDERGRADUATE FINANCIAL AID (Fall 2010, est.) 4,547 applied for aid; of those 73% were deemed to have need. 99% of undergraduates with need received aid; of those 9% had need fully met. ***Average percent of need met:*** 57% (excluding resources awarded to replace EFC). ***Average financial aid package:*** $9230 (excluding resources awarded to replace EFC). 1% of all full-time undergraduates had no need and received non-need-based gift aid.

GIFT AID (NEED-BASED) ***Total amount:*** $16,150,992 (53% federal, 46% state, 1% institutional). ***Receiving aid:*** Freshmen: 28% (312); all full-time undergraduates: 30% (1,758). ***Average award:*** Freshmen: $5295; Undergraduates: $4813. ***Scholarships, grants, and awards:*** Federal Pell, FSEOG, state, private, college/university gift aid from institutional funds.

GIFT AID (NON-NEED-BASED) ***Total amount:*** $1,087,947 (1% federal, 24% state, 15% institutional, 60% external sources). ***Receiving aid:*** Freshmen: 4% (42). Undergraduates: 3% (186). ***Average award:*** Freshmen: $666. Undergraduates: $1733. ***Scholarships, grants, and awards by category:*** *Academic interests/achievement:* 61 awards ($101,350 total): area/ethnic studies, biological sciences, business, communication, education, foreign languages, general academic interests/achievements, health fields, international studies. *Creative arts/performance:* 19 awards ($29,900 total): art/fine arts, music, performing arts, theater/drama. *Special characteristics:* 29 awards ($17,970 total): children of faculty/staff, ethnic background, first-generation college students, handicapped students, members of minority groups.

LOANS ***Student loans:*** $28,461,938 (47% need-based, 53% non-need-based). 61% of past graduating class borrowed through all loan programs. *Average indebtedness per student:* $25,732. ***Average need-based loan:*** Freshmen: $3484. Undergraduates: $4432. ***Parent loans:*** $17,527,256 (100% non-need-based). ***Programs:*** Perkins, private loans.

WORK-STUDY ***Federal work-study:*** Total amount: $1,164,758; 1,200 jobs averaging $1000. ***State or other work-study/employment:*** Total amount: $724,693 (100% non-need-based). 774 part-time jobs averaging $925.

APPLYING FOR FINANCIAL AID ***Required financial aid forms:*** FAFSA, state aid form. ***Financial aid deadline (priority):*** 3/15. ***Notification date:*** Continuous beginning 4/1. Students must reply within 6 weeks of notification.

CONTACT Mr. Daniel Sistarenik, Director of Financial Aid, State University of New York at New Paltz, 200 Hawk Drive, New Paltz, NY 12561-2437, 845-257-3250. *Fax:* 845-257-3568. *E-mail:* sistared@newpaltz.edu.

STATE UNIVERSITY OF NEW YORK AT OSWEGO

Oswego, NY

Tuition & fees (NY res): $6186 **Average undergraduate aid package: $7248**

ABOUT THE INSTITUTION State-supported, coed. 66 undergraduate majors. Federal methodology is used as a basis for awarding need-based institutional aid.

UNDERGRADUATE EXPENSES for 2011–12 ***Tuition, state resident:*** full-time $4970; part-time $207 per credit hour. ***Tuition, nonresident:*** full-time $13,380; part-time $558 per credit hour. ***Required fees:*** full-time $1216; $50.46 per credit hour. Full-time tuition and fees vary according to degree level. Part-time tuition and fees vary according to course load and degree level. ***College room and board:*** $11,610; ***Room only:*** $7390. Room and board charges vary according to board plan and housing facility. ***Payment plan:*** Installment.

FRESHMAN FINANCIAL AID (Fall 2010, est.) 1,267 applied for aid; of those 72% were deemed to have need. 100% of freshmen with need received aid; of those 19% had need fully met. ***Average percent of need met:*** 85% (excluding resources awarded to replace EFC). ***Average financial aid package:*** $7332 (excluding resources awarded to replace EFC). 16% of all full-time freshmen had no need and received non-need-based gift aid.

UNDERGRADUATE FINANCIAL AID (Fall 2010, est.) 5,906 applied for aid; of those 76% were deemed to have need. 100% of undergraduates with need received aid; of those 21% had need fully met. ***Average percent of need met:*** 86% (excluding resources awarded to replace EFC). ***Average financial aid package:*** $7248 (excluding resources awarded to replace EFC). 8% of all full-time undergraduates had no need and received non-need-based gift aid.

GIFT AID (NEED-BASED) ***Total amount:*** $22,674,024 (50% federal, 37% state, 9% institutional, 4% external sources). ***Receiving aid:*** Freshmen: 60% (830); all full-time undergraduates: 57% (3,977). ***Average award:*** Freshmen: $6644; Undergraduates: $5701. ***Scholarships, grants, and awards:*** Federal Pell, FSEOG, state, private, college/university gift aid from institutional funds.

GIFT AID (NON-NEED-BASED) ***Total amount:*** $2,334,883 (2% federal, 9% state, 74% institutional, 15% external sources). ***Receiving aid:*** Freshmen: 26% (359). Undergraduates: 13% (895). ***Average award:*** Freshmen: $2560. Undergraduates: $2923. ***Scholarships, grants, and awards by category:*** *Academic interests/achievement:* area/ethnic studies, biological sciences, business, communication, computer science, education, English, foreign languages, general academic interests/achievements, humanities, international studies, mathematics, physical sciences, premedicine, social sciences.

LOANS ***Student loans:*** $43,803,406 (77% need-based, 23% non-need-based). 79% of past graduating class borrowed through all loan programs. *Average indebtedness per student:* $25,931. ***Average need-based loan:*** Freshmen: $3611. Undergraduates: $4239. ***Parent loans:*** $10,290,939 (67% need-based, 33% non-need-based). ***Programs:*** Federal Direct (Subsidized and Unsubsidized Stafford, PLUS), Perkins.

WORK-STUDY ***Federal work-study:*** Total amount: $450,402; 424 jobs averaging $1132. ***State or other work-study/employment:*** Total amount: $787,816 (60% need-based, 40% non-need-based). 1,458 part-time jobs averaging $1639.

APPLYING FOR FINANCIAL AID ***Required financial aid forms:*** FAFSA, state aid form. ***Financial aid deadline (priority):*** 3/1. ***Notification date:*** Continuous beginning 3/1. Students must reply by 5/1 or within 3 weeks of notification.

CONTACT Mark C. Humbert, Director of Financial Aid, State University of New York at Oswego, 206 Culkin Hall, Oswego, NY 13126, 315-312-2248. *Fax:* 315-312-3696.

STATE UNIVERSITY OF NEW YORK AT PLATTSBURGH

Plattsburgh, NY

Tuition & fees (NY res): $6143 **Average undergraduate aid package: $11,429**

ABOUT THE INSTITUTION State-supported, coed. 65 undergraduate majors. Both federal and institutional methodology are used as a basis for awarding need-based institutional aid.

UNDERGRADUATE EXPENSES for 2010–11 ***Tuition, state resident:*** full-time $4970; part-time $207 per credit hour. ***Tuition, nonresident:*** full-time $13,380; part-time $558 per credit hour. ***Required fees:*** full-time $1173; $47.43 per credit hour. Part-time tuition and fees vary according to course load. ***College room and board:*** $9000. Room and board charges vary according to board plan. ***Payment plans:*** Installment, deferred payment.

FRESHMAN FINANCIAL AID (Fall 2010, est.) 859 applied for aid; of those 74% were deemed to have need. 99% of freshmen with need received aid; of those 30% had need fully met. ***Average percent of need met:*** 91% (excluding resources awarded to replace EFC). ***Average financial aid package:*** $11,242 (excluding resources awarded to replace EFC). 28% of all full-time freshmen had no need and received non-need-based gift aid.

UNDERGRADUATE FINANCIAL AID (Fall 2010, est.) 4,475 applied for aid; of those 78% were deemed to have need. 98% of undergraduates with need received aid; of those 27% had need fully met. ***Average percent of need met:*** 87% (excluding resources awarded to replace EFC). ***Average financial aid package:*** $11,429 (excluding resources awarded to replace EFC). 25% of all full-time undergraduates had no need and received non-need-based gift aid.

GIFT AID (NEED-BASED) ***Total amount:*** $17,475,297 (53% federal, 33% state, 11% institutional, 3% external sources). ***Receiving aid:*** Freshmen: 57% (570); all full-time undergraduates: 54% (3,002). ***Average award:*** Freshmen: $6375; Undergraduates: $5821. ***Scholarships, grants, and awards:*** Federal Pell, FSEOG, state, private, college/university gift aid from institutional funds.

GIFT AID (NON-NEED-BASED) ***Total amount:*** $3,062,867 (3% federal, 6% state, 87% institutional, 4% external sources). ***Receiving aid:*** Freshmen: 20% (203). Undergraduates: 16% (886). ***Average award:*** Freshmen: $5734. Undergraduates: $6101. ***Scholarships, grants, and awards by category:*** *Academic interests/achievement:* 2,412 awards ($4,422,333 total): area/ethnic studies, biological sciences, business, communication, computer science, education, engineering/technologies, English, general academic interests/achievements, health fields, home economics, humanities, international studies, mathematics, physical sciences, premedicine, social sciences. *Creative arts/performance:* 146 awards ($253,723 total): art/fine arts, journalism/publications, music, theater/drama. *Special achievements/activities:* 15 awards ($25,250 total): community service, general special achievements/activities, leadership. *Special characteristics:* 1,067 awards ($2,355,367 total): international students, out-of-state students. ***Tuition waivers:*** Full or partial for employees or children of employees.

LOANS ***Student loans:*** $26,724,984 (80% need-based, 20% non-need-based). 77% of past graduating class borrowed through all loan programs. *Average indebtedness per student:* $25,326. ***Average need-based loan:*** Freshmen: $5920. Undergraduates: $7122. ***Parent loans:*** $4,480,553 (70% need-based, 30% non-need-based). ***Programs:*** Federal Direct (Subsidized and Unsubsidized Stafford, PLUS), Perkins, Federal Nursing, state, alternative loans.

WORK-STUDY ***Federal work-study:*** Total amount: $1,108,160; 770 jobs averaging $2084. ***State or other work-study/employment:*** 825 part-time jobs averaging $2100.

APPLYING FOR FINANCIAL AID ***Required financial aid forms:*** FAFSA, state aid form. ***Financial aid deadline (priority):*** 2/15. ***Notification date:*** Continuous beginning 3/1. Students must reply within 8 weeks of notification.

CONTACT Mr. Todd Moravec, Financial Aid Director, State University of New York at Plattsburgh, 101 Broad Street, Plattsburgh, NY 12901-2681, 518-564-2072 or toll-free 888-673-0012 (in-state). *Fax:* 518-564-4079. *E-mail:* todd.moravec@plattsburgh.edu.

STATE UNIVERSITY OF NEW YORK COLLEGE AT CORTLAND

Cortland, NY

Tuition & fees (NY res): $6215 **Average undergraduate aid package: $12,245**

ABOUT THE INSTITUTION State-supported, coed. 57 undergraduate majors. Federal methodology is used as a basis for awarding need-based institutional aid.

UNDERGRADUATE EXPENSES for 2010–11 ***Tuition, state resident:*** full-time $4970; part-time $207 per credit hour. ***Tuition, nonresident:*** full-time $12,870; part-time $536 per credit hour. ***Required fees:*** full-time $1245; $56.40 per credit hour. Full-time tuition and fees vary according to course load and degree level. Part-time tuition and fees vary according to course load and degree level. ***College room and board:*** $10,490; ***Room only:*** $6260. Room and board charges vary according to board plan and housing facility. ***Payment plan:*** Installment.

FRESHMAN FINANCIAL AID (Fall 2009) 1,062 applied for aid; of those 62% were deemed to have need. 98% of freshmen with need received aid; of those 16% had need fully met. ***Average percent of need met:*** 71% (excluding resources awarded to replace EFC). ***Average financial aid package:*** $12,010 (excluding resources awarded to replace EFC). 2% of all full-time freshmen had no need and received non-need-based gift aid.

UNDERGRADUATE FINANCIAL AID (Fall 2009) 5,088 applied for aid; of those 73% were deemed to have need. 98% of undergraduates with need received aid; of those 17% had need fully met. ***Average percent of need met:*** 71% (excluding resources awarded to replace EFC). ***Average financial aid package:*** $12,245 (excluding resources awarded to replace EFC). 2% of all full-time undergraduates had no need and received non-need-based gift aid.

GIFT AID (NEED-BASED) ***Total amount:*** $13,167,897 (50% federal, 49% state, 1% institutional). ***Receiving aid:*** Freshmen: 43% (496); all full-time undergradu-

ates: 49% (2,939). ***Average award:*** Freshmen: $4858; Undergraduates: $5010. ***Scholarships, grants, and awards:*** Federal Pell, FSEOG, state, private, college/university gift aid from institutional funds.

GIFT AID (NON-NEED-BASED) ***Total amount:*** $3,477,373 (43% federal, 18% institutional, 39% external sources). ***Receiving aid:*** Freshmen: 22% (262). Undergraduates: 14% (872). ***Average award:*** Freshmen: $2418. Undergraduates: $2275. ***Scholarships, grants, and awards by category:*** *Academic interests/achievement:* education, general academic interests/achievements, international studies, mathematics, physical sciences. *Creative arts/performance:* art/fine arts, music. *Special achievements/activities:* community service, general special achievements/activities, hobbies/interests, leadership. *Special characteristics:* adult students, local/state students, members of minority groups.

LOANS ***Student loans:*** $33,902,723 (40% need-based, 60% non-need-based). ***Average need-based loan:*** Freshmen: $3491. Undergraduates: $4195. ***Parent loans:*** $4,584,653 (100% non-need-based). ***Programs:*** Federal Direct (Subsidized and Unsubsidized Stafford, PLUS), Perkins.

WORK-STUDY ***Federal work-study:*** Total amount: $317,690; jobs available. ***State or other work-study/employment:*** Total amount: $724,795 (100% non-need-based). Part-time jobs available.

APPLYING FOR FINANCIAL AID ***Required financial aid forms:*** FAFSA, state aid form. ***Financial aid deadline (priority):*** 3/1. ***Notification date:*** Continuous beginning 3/15. Students must reply by 5/1 or within 4 weeks of notification.

CONTACT Karen Gallagher, Director of Financial Advisement, State University of New York College at Cortland, PO Box 2000, Cortland, NY 13045, 607-753-4717. *Fax:* 607-753-5990. *E-mail:* finaid@cortland.edu.

STATE UNIVERSITY OF NEW YORK COLLEGE AT GENESEO

Geneseo, NY

Tuition & fees (NY res): $6401 **Average undergraduate aid package: $8686**

ABOUT THE INSTITUTION State-supported, coed. 43 undergraduate majors. Federal methodology is used as a basis for awarding need-based institutional aid.

UNDERGRADUATE EXPENSES for 2010–11 ***Tuition, state resident:*** full-time $4970; part-time $207 per credit hour. ***Tuition, nonresident:*** full-time $13,380; part-time $558 per credit hour. ***Required fees:*** full-time $1431; $59.45 per credit hour. Part-time tuition and fees vary according to course load. ***College room and board:*** $10,042. Room and board charges vary according to board plan and housing facility. ***Payment plans:*** Installment, deferred payment.

FRESHMAN FINANCIAL AID (Fall 2010, est.) 845 applied for aid; of those 50% were deemed to have need. 100% of freshmen with need received aid; of those 70% had need fully met. ***Average percent of need met:*** 70% (excluding resources awarded to replace EFC). ***Average financial aid package:*** $3321 (excluding resources awarded to replace EFC). 1% of all full-time freshmen had no need and received non-need-based gift aid.

UNDERGRADUATE FINANCIAL AID (Fall 2010, est.) 3,764 applied for aid; of those 63% were deemed to have need. 100% of undergraduates with need received aid; of those 75% had need fully met. ***Average percent of need met:*** 75% (excluding resources awarded to replace EFC). ***Average financial aid package:*** $8686 (excluding resources awarded to replace EFC). 10% of all full-time undergraduates had no need and received non-need-based gift aid.

GIFT AID (NEED-BASED) ***Total amount:*** $10,374,322 (56% federal, 44% state). ***Receiving aid:*** Freshmen: 19% (190); all full-time undergraduates: 44% (2,368). ***Average award:*** Freshmen: $3827; Undergraduates: $4376. ***Scholarships, grants, and awards:*** Federal Pell, FSEOG, state.

GIFT AID (NON-NEED-BASED) ***Total amount:*** $2,477,297 (2% federal, 21% state, 41% institutional, 36% external sources). ***Receiving aid:*** Freshmen: 19% (193). Undergraduates: 16% (840). ***Average award:*** Freshmen: $2777. Undergraduates: $1920. ***Scholarships, grants, and awards by category:*** *Academic interests/achievement:* area/ethnic studies, biological sciences, business, communication, computer science, education, English, foreign languages, general academic interests/achievements, humanities, international studies, mathematics, physical sciences, premedicine, social sciences. *Creative arts/performance:* applied art and design, art/fine arts, creative writing, dance, general creative arts/performance, journalism/publications, music, performing arts, theater/drama. *Special achievements/activities:* community service, leadership, memberships. *Special characteristics:* adult students, ethnic background, local/state students, members of minority groups, religious affiliation.

LOANS ***Student loans:*** $21,488,618 (45% need-based, 55% non-need-based). 65% of past graduating class borrowed through all loan programs. *Average indebtedness per student:* $21,200. ***Average need-based loan:*** Freshmen: $3321. Undergraduates: $4513. ***Parent loans:*** $5,399,657 (100% non-need-based). ***Programs:*** Federal Direct (Subsidized and Unsubsidized Stafford, PLUS), Perkins.

WORK-STUDY ***Federal work-study:*** Total amount: $600,000; jobs available. ***State or other work-study/employment:*** Total amount: $650,000 (100% non-need-based). Part-time jobs available.

APPLYING FOR FINANCIAL AID ***Required financial aid forms:*** FAFSA, state aid form. ***Financial aid deadline:*** 2/15. ***Notification date:*** Continuous beginning 3/15. Students must reply by 5/1.

CONTACT Archie Cureton, Director of Financial Aid, State University of New York College at Geneseo, 1 College Circle, Erwin Hall 104, Geneseo, NY 14454, 585-245-5731 or toll-free 866-245-5211. *Fax:* 585-245-5717. *E-mail:* finaid@geneseo.edu.

STATE UNIVERSITY OF NEW YORK COLLEGE AT OLD WESTBURY

Old Westbury, NY

Tuition & fees (NY res): $5966 **Average undergraduate aid package: $5115**

ABOUT THE INSTITUTION State-supported, coed. 41 undergraduate majors. Both federal and institutional methodology are used as a basis for awarding need-based institutional aid.

UNDERGRADUATE EXPENSES for 2010–11 ***Tuition, state resident:*** full-time $4970; part-time $207 per credit. ***Tuition, nonresident:*** full-time $12,870; part-time $536 per credit. ***Required fees:*** full-time $996; $43.85 per credit or $105.50 per term. Part-time tuition and fees vary according to course load. ***College room and board:*** $9700; ***Room only:*** $6600. Room and board charges vary according to board plan and housing facility. ***Payment plan:*** Installment.

FRESHMAN FINANCIAL AID (Fall 2010, est.) 345 applied for aid; of those 76% were deemed to have need. 100% of freshmen with need received aid; of those 100% had need fully met. ***Average percent of need met:*** 38% (excluding resources awarded to replace EFC). ***Average financial aid package:*** $6204 (excluding resources awarded to replace EFC).

UNDERGRADUATE FINANCIAL AID (Fall 2010, est.) 2,815 applied for aid; of those 78% were deemed to have need. 100% of undergraduates with need received aid; of those 100% had need fully met. ***Average percent of need met:*** 31% (excluding resources awarded to replace EFC). ***Average financial aid package:*** $5115 (excluding resources awarded to replace EFC).

GIFT AID (NEED-BASED) ***Total amount:*** $13,843,532 (61% federal, 39% state). ***Receiving aid:*** Freshmen: 66% (263); all full-time undergraduates: 62% (2,175). ***Average award:*** Freshmen: $8061; Undergraduates: $6498. ***Scholarships, grants, and awards:*** Federal Pell, FSEOG, state, private, college/university gift aid from institutional funds.

GIFT AID (NON-NEED-BASED) ***Total amount:*** $47,731 (100% institutional). ***Receiving aid:*** Freshmen: 5% (21). Undergraduates: 2% (76). ***Scholarships, grants, and awards by category:*** *Academic interests/achievement:* biological sciences, health fields, physical sciences. ***Tuition waivers:*** Full or partial for senior citizens.

LOANS ***Student loans:*** $6,915,280 (98% need-based, 2% non-need-based). 55% of past graduating class borrowed through all loan programs. *Average indebtedness per student:* $16,371. ***Average need-based loan:*** Freshmen: $2000. Undergraduates: $26,000. ***Parent loans:*** $1,229,875 (98% need-based, 2% non-need-based). ***Programs:*** Federal Direct (Subsidized and Unsubsidized Stafford, PLUS), Perkins.

WORK-STUDY ***Federal work-study:*** Total amount: $179,444; 225 jobs averaging $797.

APPLYING FOR FINANCIAL AID ***Required financial aid forms:*** FAFSA, institution's own form, state aid form, income documentation. ***Financial aid deadline (priority):*** 4/15. ***Notification date:*** Continuous beginning 4/25. Students must reply within 2 weeks of notification.

CONTACT Ms. Dee Darrell, Financial Aid Assistant, State University of New York College at Old Westbury, PO Box 210, Old Westbury, NY 11568-0210, 516-876-3222. *Fax:* 516-876-3008. *E-mail:* finaid@oldwestbury.edu.

STATE UNIVERSITY OF NEW YORK COLLEGE AT ONEONTA

Oneonta, NY

Tuition & fees (NY res): $6250 **Average undergraduate aid package: $14,968**

ABOUT THE INSTITUTION State-supported, coed. 68 undergraduate majors. Federal methodology is used as a basis for awarding need-based institutional aid.

UNDERGRADUATE EXPENSES for 2011–12 ***Tuition, state resident:*** full-time $4970; part-time $207 per semester hour. ***Tuition, nonresident:*** full-time $12,870; part-time $536 per semester hour. ***Required fees:*** full-time $1280; $46.85 per semester hour. Part-time tuition and fees vary according to course load. ***College room and board:*** $9284; ***Room only:*** $5534. Room and board charges vary according to board plan and housing facility. ***Payment plan:*** Installment.

FRESHMAN FINANCIAL AID (Fall 2010, est.) 1,009 applied for aid; of those 100% were deemed to have need. 68% of freshmen with need received aid; of those 46% had need fully met. ***Average percent of need met:*** 60% (excluding resources awarded to replace EFC). ***Average financial aid package:*** $14,422 (excluding resources awarded to replace EFC). 20% of all full-time freshmen had no need and received non-need-based gift aid.

UNDERGRADUATE FINANCIAL AID (Fall 2010, est.) 4,570 applied for aid; of those 100% were deemed to have need. 76% of undergraduates with need received aid; of those 18% had need fully met. ***Average percent of need met:*** 63% (excluding resources awarded to replace EFC). ***Average financial aid package:*** $14,968 (excluding resources awarded to replace EFC). 18% of all full-time undergraduates had no need and received non-need-based gift aid.

GIFT AID (NEED-BASED) ***Total amount:*** $17,858,931 (49% federal, 33% state, 7% institutional, 11% external sources). ***Receiving aid:*** Freshmen: 58% (656); all full-time undergraduates: 56% (3,355). ***Average award:*** Freshmen: $5674; Undergraduates: $5311. ***Scholarships, grants, and awards:*** Federal Pell, FSEOG, state, private, college/university gift aid from institutional funds.

GIFT AID (NON-NEED-BASED) ***Total amount:*** $2,343,282 (9% federal, 5% state, 31% institutional, 55% external sources). ***Average award:*** Freshmen: $2067. Undergraduates: $1616. ***Scholarships, grants, and awards by category:*** *Academic interests/achievement:* 518 awards ($1,135,332 total): biological sciences, business, computer science, education, English, general academic interests/achievements, home economics, physical sciences, premedicine, social sciences. *Creative arts/performance:* 25 awards ($17,400 total): music, theater/drama. *Special achievements/activities:* 15 awards ($15,820 total): community service, general special achievements/activities, leadership. *Special characteristics:* 122 awards ($151,800 total): general special characteristics, international students, local/state students. ***Tuition waivers:*** Full or partial for employees or children of employees.

LOANS ***Student loans:*** $29,276,766 (47% need-based, 53% non-need-based). 75% of past graduating class borrowed through all loan programs. *Average indebtedness per student:* $17,564. ***Average need-based loan:*** Freshmen: $3636. Undergraduates: $3600. ***Parent loans:*** $8,339,395 (100% non-need-based). ***Programs:*** Federal Direct (Subsidized and Unsubsidized Stafford, PLUS), Perkins.

WORK-STUDY ***Federal work-study:*** Total amount: $350,717; 350 jobs averaging $1000.

APPLYING FOR FINANCIAL AID ***Required financial aid forms:*** FAFSA, state aid form. ***Financial aid deadline (priority):*** 3/15. ***Notification date:*** Continuous beginning 3/1. Students must reply by 5/1 or within 4 weeks of notification.

CONTACT Mr. Bill Goodhue, Director of Financial Aid, State University of New York College at Oneonta, Ravine Parkway, Oneonta, NY 13820, 607-436-2992 or toll-free 800-SUNY-123. *Fax:* 607-436-2659. *E-mail:* goodhucw@oneonta.edu.

STATE UNIVERSITY OF NEW YORK COLLEGE AT POTSDAM

Potsdam, NY

Tuition & fees (NY res): $6183 **Average undergraduate aid package: $12,727**

ABOUT THE INSTITUTION State-supported, coed. 45 undergraduate majors. Federal methodology is used as a basis for awarding need-based institutional aid.

UNDERGRADUATE EXPENSES for 2010–11 ***Tuition, state resident:*** full-time $4970; part-time $207 per credit hour. ***Tuition, nonresident:*** full-time $12,870; part-time $536 per credit hour. ***Required fees:*** full-time $1213; $54.60 per credit hour. ***College room and board:*** $9630; ***Room only:*** $5570. Room and board charges vary according to board plan and housing facility. ***Payment plan:*** Installment.

FRESHMAN FINANCIAL AID (Fall 2010, est.) 850 applied for aid; of those 79% were deemed to have need. 99% of freshmen with need received aid; of those 74% had need fully met. ***Average percent of need met:*** 73% (excluding resources awarded to replace EFC). ***Average financial aid package:*** $13,413 (excluding resources awarded to replace EFC).

UNDERGRADUATE FINANCIAL AID (Fall 2010, est.) 3,303 applied for aid; of those 79% were deemed to have need. 99% of undergraduates with need received aid; of those 76% had need fully met. ***Average percent of need met:*** 75% (excluding resources awarded to replace EFC). ***Average financial aid package:*** $12,727 (excluding resources awarded to replace EFC).

GIFT AID (NEED-BASED) ***Total amount:*** $15,225,719 (51% federal, 36% state, 11% institutional, 2% external sources). ***Receiving aid:*** Freshmen: 66% (597); all full-time undergraduates: 62% (2,342). ***Average award:*** Freshmen: $7919; Undergraduates: $7825. ***Scholarships, grants, and awards:*** Federal Pell, FSEOG, state, private, college/university gift aid from institutional funds, Academic Competitiveness Grants, National SMART Grants, TEACH Grants, Vesid, Vet Benefits, BIA.

GIFT AID (NON-NEED-BASED) ***Total amount:*** $2,643,333 (20% federal, 14% state, 62% institutional, 4% external sources). ***Receiving aid:*** Freshmen: 27% (246). Undergraduates: 22% (828). ***Average award:*** Freshmen: $7542. Undergraduates: $11,677. ***Scholarships, grants, and awards by category:*** *Academic interests/achievement:* 279 awards ($298,691 total): biological sciences, business, communication, computer science, education, engineering/technologies, English, foreign languages, general academic interests/achievements, humanities, mathematics, physical sciences, social sciences. *Creative arts/performance:* 142 awards ($172,830 total): art/fine arts, dance, music, performing arts, theater/drama. *Special achievements/activities:* 649 awards ($1,455,650 total): community service, general special achievements/activities, leadership. *Special characteristics:* 63 awards ($69,088 total): adult students, children and siblings of alumni, children of faculty/staff, ethnic background, handicapped students, local/state students, members of minority groups, previous college experience. ***Tuition waivers:*** Full or partial for employees or children of employees.

LOANS ***Student loans:*** $21,473,879 (48% need-based, 52% non-need-based). 78% of past graduating class borrowed through all loan programs. *Average indebtedness per student:* $21,427. ***Average need-based loan:*** Freshmen: $3977. Undergraduates: $4708. ***Parent loans:*** $8,782,482 (100% non-need-based). ***Programs:*** Federal Direct (Subsidized and Unsubsidized Stafford, PLUS), Perkins, college/university, alternative loans.

WORK-STUDY ***Federal work-study:*** Total amount: $323,810; 252 jobs averaging $927.

APPLYING FOR FINANCIAL AID ***Required financial aid forms:*** FAFSA, state aid form. ***Financial aid deadline:*** 5/1 (priority: 3/1). ***Notification date:*** Continuous beginning 2/1. Students must reply by 5/1 or within 4 weeks of notification.

CONTACT Susan C. Aldrich, Director of Financial Aid, State University of New York College at Potsdam, 44 Pierrepont Avenue, Potsdam, NY 13676, 315-267-2162 or toll-free 877-POTSDAM. *Fax:* 315-267-3067. *E-mail:* finaid@potsdam.edu.

STATE UNIVERSITY OF NEW YORK COLLEGE OF AGRICULTURE AND TECHNOLOGY AT COBLESKILL

Cobleskill, NY

CONTACT Brian Smith, Director of Financial Aid, State University of New York College of Agriculture and Technology at Cobleskill, Knapp Hall, Cobleskill, NY 12043, 518-255-5623 or toll-free 800-295-8988. *Fax:* 518-255-5844. *E-mail:* finaid@cobleskill.edu.

STATE UNIVERSITY OF NEW YORK COLLEGE OF AGRICULTURE AND TECHNOLOGY AT MORRISVILLE

Morrisville, NY

ABOUT THE INSTITUTION State-supported, coed. ***Awards:*** associate and bachelor's degrees. 48 undergraduate majors. ***Total enrollment:*** 3,432. Undergraduates: 3,432. Freshmen: 1,277.

GIFT AID (NEED-BASED) ***Scholarships, grants, and awards:*** Federal Pell, FSEOG, state, college/university gift aid from institutional funds.

GIFT AID (NON-NEED-BASED) ***Scholarships, grants, and awards by category:*** *Academic interests/achievement:* general academic interests/achievements. *Special achievements/activities:* memberships. *Special characteristics:* children of faculty/staff, members of minority groups, out-of-state students.

LOANS ***Programs:*** Federal Direct (Subsidized and Unsubsidized Stafford, PLUS), Perkins, Federal Nursing.

WORK-STUDY ***Federal work-study:*** Total amount: $277,370; 160 jobs averaging $1740.

APPLYING FOR FINANCIAL AID ***Required financial aid forms:*** FAFSA, state aid form.

CONTACT Financial Aid Office, State University of New York College of Agriculture and Technology at Morrisville, PO Box 901, Morrisville, NY 13408-0901, 315-684-6289 or toll-free 800-258-0111 (in-state). *Fax:* 315-684-6628.

STATE UNIVERSITY OF NEW YORK COLLEGE OF ENVIRONMENTAL SCIENCE AND FORESTRY

Syracuse, NY

Tuition & fees (NY res): $5941 **Average undergraduate aid package: $13,000**

ABOUT THE INSTITUTION State-supported, coed. 48 undergraduate majors. Federal methodology is used as a basis for awarding need-based institutional aid.

UNDERGRADUATE EXPENSES for 2011–12 ***Tuition, state resident:*** full-time $4970; part-time $207 per credit hour. ***Tuition, nonresident:*** full-time $13,380; part-time $558 per credit hour. ***Required fees:*** full-time $971; $41.30 per credit hour. Full-time tuition and fees vary according to location. Part-time tuition and fees vary according to course load and location. ***College room and board:*** $14,032. Room and board charges vary according to board plan, housing facility, and location. ***Payment plans:*** Installment, deferred payment.

FRESHMAN FINANCIAL AID (Fall 2010, est.) 241 applied for aid; of those 88% were deemed to have need. 100% of freshmen with need received aid; of those 95% had need fully met. ***Average percent of need met:*** 92% (excluding resources awarded to replace EFC). ***Average financial aid package:*** $12,500 (excluding resources awarded to replace EFC). 10% of all full-time freshmen had no need and received non-need-based gift aid.

UNDERGRADUATE FINANCIAL AID (Fall 2010, est.) 1,168 applied for aid; of those 92% were deemed to have need. 100% of undergraduates with need received aid; of those 95% had need fully met. ***Average percent of need met:*** 90% (excluding resources awarded to replace EFC). ***Average financial aid package:*** $13,000 (excluding resources awarded to replace EFC). 4% of all full-time undergraduates had no need and received non-need-based gift aid.

GIFT AID (NEED-BASED) ***Total amount:*** $4,558,793 (46% federal, 32% state, 17% institutional, 5% external sources). ***Receiving aid:*** Freshmen: 80% (207); all full-time undergraduates: 68% (1,057). ***Average award:*** Freshmen: $5000; Undergraduates: $5000. ***Scholarships, grants, and awards:*** Federal Pell, FSEOG, state, private, college/university gift aid from institutional funds.

GIFT AID (NON-NEED-BASED) ***Total amount:*** $1,632,770 (24% federal, 5% state, 58% institutional, 13% external sources). ***Receiving aid:*** Freshmen: 37% (95). Undergraduates: 23% (365). ***Average award:*** Freshmen: $2565. Undergraduates: $2420. ***Scholarships, grants, and awards by category:*** *Academic interests/achievement:* 366 awards ($882,325 total): agriculture, architecture, biological sciences, engineering/technologies, physical sciences, premedicine. *Special achievements/activities:* leadership. *Special characteristics:* members of minority groups.

LOANS ***Student loans:*** $8,228,914 (53% need-based, 47% non-need-based). 80% of past graduating class borrowed through all loan programs. *Average indebtedness per student:* $27,000. ***Average need-based loan:*** Freshmen: $4500. Undergraduates: $5500. ***Parent loans:*** $2,189,698 (46% need-based, 54% non-need-based). ***Programs:*** Federal Direct (Subsidized and Unsubsidized Stafford, PLUS), Perkins.

WORK-STUDY ***Federal work-study:*** Total amount: $330,000; 220 jobs averaging $1500. ***State or other work-study/employment:*** Total amount: $236,763 (47% need-based, 53% non-need-based). 195 part-time jobs averaging $1200.

APPLYING FOR FINANCIAL AID ***Required financial aid forms:*** FAFSA, state aid form. ***Financial aid deadline (priority):*** 3/1. ***Notification date:*** Continuous beginning 3/15. Students must reply within 2 weeks of notification.

CONTACT Mr. John E. View, Director of Financial Aid, State University of New York College of Environmental Science and Forestry, One Forestry Drive, Syracuse, NY 13210-2779, 315-470-6671 or toll-free 800-777-7373. *Fax:* 315-470-4734. *E-mail:* jeview@esf.edu.

STATE UNIVERSITY OF NEW YORK COLLEGE OF TECHNOLOGY AT CANTON

Canton, NY

ABOUT THE INSTITUTION State-supported, coed. 33 undergraduate majors.

GIFT AID (NEED-BASED) ***Scholarships, grants, and awards:*** Federal Pell, FSEOG, state, private, college/university gift aid from institutional funds, Bureau of Indian Affairs Grants.

LOANS ***Programs:*** Federal Direct (Subsidized and Unsubsidized Stafford, PLUS), Perkins, alternative loans.

WORK-STUDY ***Federal work-study:*** Total amount: $165,218; jobs available. ***State or other work-study/employment:*** Part-time jobs available.

APPLYING FOR FINANCIAL AID ***Required financial aid forms:*** FAFSA, state aid form.

CONTACT Ms. Kerrie Cooper, Director of Financial Aid, State University of New York College of Technology at Canton, Student Service Center, Canton, NY 13617, 315-386-7616 or toll-free 800-388-7123. *Fax:* 315-386-7930. *E-mail:* cooper@canton.edu.

STATE UNIVERSITY OF NEW YORK COLLEGE OF TECHNOLOGY AT DELHI

Delhi, NY

Tuition & fees (NY res): $6445 **Average undergraduate aid package: N/A**

ABOUT THE INSTITUTION State-supported, coed. 33 undergraduate majors. Federal methodology is used as a basis for awarding need-based institutional aid.

UNDERGRADUATE EXPENSES for 2010–11 ***Tuition, state resident:*** full-time $4970; part-time $207 per credit hour. ***Tuition, nonresident:*** full-time $13,380; part-time $558 per credit hour. ***Required fees:*** full-time $1475; $78.95 per credit hour or $737.50 per term. Full-time tuition and fees vary according to degree level. Part-time tuition and fees vary according to degree level. ***College room and board:*** $9720; ***Room only:*** $5620. Room and board charges vary according to board plan and location. ***Payment plan:*** Installment.

FRESHMAN FINANCIAL AID (Fall 2010, est.) 884 applied for aid; of those 98% were deemed to have need. 98% of freshmen with need received aid.

UNDERGRADUATE FINANCIAL AID (Fall 2010, est.) 2,443 applied for aid; of those 99% were deemed to have need. 99% of undergraduates with need received aid.

GIFT AID (NEED-BASED) ***Total amount:*** $12,292,279 (52% federal, 39% state, 3% institutional, 6% external sources). ***Receiving aid:*** Freshmen: 82% (787); all full-time undergraduates: 73% (1,959). ***Scholarships, grants, and awards:*** Federal Pell, FSEOG, state, private, college/university gift aid from institutional funds.

GIFT AID (NON-NEED-BASED) ***Scholarships, grants, and awards by category:*** *Academic interests/achievement:* general academic interests/achievements. *Special achievements/activities:* community service.

LOANS ***Student loans:*** $14,450,347 (100% need-based). ***Parent loans:*** $4,599,634 (100% need-based). ***Programs:*** Federal Direct (Subsidized and Unsubsidized Stafford, PLUS), Perkins.

WORK-STUDY ***Federal work-study:*** Total amount: $67,212; 96 jobs averaging $1080. ***State or other work-study/employment:*** Total amount: $390,845 (100% need-based). Part-time jobs available.

APPLYING FOR FINANCIAL AID ***Required financial aid forms:*** FAFSA, state aid form. ***Financial aid deadline (priority):*** 2/15. ***Notification date:*** Continuous beginning 3/15.

CONTACT Office of Financial Aid, State University of New York College of Technology at Delhi, 158 Bush Hall, Delhi, NY 13753, 607-746-4570 or toll-free 800-96-DELHI. *Fax:* 607-746-4104.

STATE UNIVERSITY OF NEW YORK DOWNSTATE MEDICAL CENTER

Brooklyn, NY

CONTACT Financial Aid Office, State University of New York Downstate Medical Center, 450 Clarkson Avenue, Brooklyn, NY 11203-2098, 718-270-2488. *Fax:* 718-270-7592. *E-mail:* finaid1@downstate.edu.

STATE UNIVERSITY OF NEW YORK INSTITUTE OF TECHNOLOGY

Utica, NY

ABOUT THE INSTITUTION State-supported, coed. ***Awards:*** bachelor's and master's degrees and post-master's certificates. 20 undergraduate majors. ***Total enrollment:*** 2,828. Undergraduates: 2,210. Freshmen: 204.

GIFT AID (NEED-BASED) ***Scholarships, grants, and awards:*** Federal Pell, FSEOG, state, college/university gift aid from institutional funds.

GIFT AID (NON-NEED-BASED) ***Scholarships, grants, and awards by category:*** *Academic interests/achievement:* computer science, engineering/technologies, general academic interests/achievements. *Special characteristics:* local/state students, members of minority groups, previous college experience.

LOANS ***Programs:*** Federal Direct (Subsidized and Unsubsidized Stafford, PLUS), Perkins, Federal Nursing.

WORK-STUDY ***Federal work-study:*** Total amount: $322,520; jobs available.

APPLYING FOR FINANCIAL AID ***Required financial aid forms:*** FAFSA, state aid form.

CONTACT Director of Financial Aid, State University of New York Institute of Technology, PO Box 3050, Utica, NY 13504-3050, 315-792-7210 or toll-free 800-SUNYTEC. *Fax:* 315-792-7220. *E-mail:* hoskeyl@sunyit.edu.

STATE UNIVERSITY OF NEW YORK MARITIME COLLEGE

Throggs Neck, NY

Tuition & fees (NY res): $6157 **Average undergraduate aid package: $9735**

ABOUT THE INSTITUTION State-supported, coed, primarily men. 10 undergraduate majors. Federal methodology is used as a basis for awarding need-based institutional aid.

UNDERGRADUATE EXPENSES for 2010–11 ***Tuition, area resident:*** part-time $310 per credit hour. ***Tuition, state resident:*** full-time $4970; part-time $207 per credit hour. ***Tuition, nonresident:*** full-time $13,380; part-time $558 per credit hour. ***Required fees:*** full-time $1187; $49 per credit hour. Full-time tuition and fees vary according to degree level and program. Part-time tuition and fees vary according to course load, degree level, and program. ***College room and board:*** $10,090; ***Room only:*** $6340. Room and board charges vary according to board plan and housing facility. ***Payment plan:*** Installment.

FRESHMAN FINANCIAL AID (Fall 2009) 178 applied for aid; of those 99% were deemed to have need. 99% of freshmen with need received aid; of those 8% had need fully met. ***Average percent of need met:*** 61% (excluding resources awarded to replace EFC). ***Average financial aid package:*** $9071 (excluding resources awarded to replace EFC).

UNDERGRADUATE FINANCIAL AID (Fall 2009) 714 applied for aid; of those 99% were deemed to have need. 99% of undergraduates with need received aid; of those 9% had need fully met. ***Average percent of need met:*** 53% (excluding resources awarded to replace EFC). ***Average financial aid package:*** $9735 (excluding resources awarded to replace EFC).

GIFT AID (NEED-BASED) ***Total amount:*** $3,810,986 (54% federal, 30% state, 11% institutional, 5% external sources). ***Receiving aid:*** Freshmen: 49% (171); all full-time undergraduates: 45% (652). ***Average award:*** Freshmen: $4902; Undergraduates: $4526. ***Scholarships, grants, and awards:*** Federal Pell, FSEOG, state, private, college/university gift aid from institutional funds, Educational Opportunity Program (EOP).

GIFT AID (NON-NEED-BASED) ***Total amount:*** $1,082,988 (42% federal, 19% state, 27% institutional, 12% external sources). ***Receiving aid:*** Freshmen: 45% (157). Undergraduates: 43% (627). ***Scholarships, grants, and awards by category:*** *Academic interests/achievement:* general academic interests/achievements. ***Tuition waivers:*** Full or partial for employees or children of employees.

LOANS ***Student loans:*** $6,758,615 (73% need-based, 27% non-need-based). ***Average need-based loan:*** Freshmen: $3587. Undergraduates: $4576. ***Parent loans:*** $1,110,161 (41% need-based, 59% non-need-based). ***Programs:*** Federal Direct (Subsidized and Unsubsidized Stafford, PLUS), Perkins, alternative loans.

WORK-STUDY ***Federal work-study:*** Total amount: $249,344; jobs available. ***State or other work-study/employment:*** Part-time jobs available.

APPLYING FOR FINANCIAL AID ***Required financial aid forms:*** FAFSA, institution's own form. ***Financial aid deadline:*** 7/15 (priority: 3/15). ***Notification date:*** Continuous beginning 3/15.

CONTACT Mr. Paul Bamonte, Director of Enrollment Services and Financial Aid, State University of New York Maritime College, 6 Pennyfield Avenue, Throgs Neck, NY 10465-4198, 718-409-7400 or toll-free 800-654-1874 (in-state), 800-642-1874 (out-of-state). *Fax:* 718-409-7275. *E-mail:* pbamonte@sunymaritime.edu.

STATE UNIVERSITY OF NEW YORK UPSTATE MEDICAL UNIVERSITY

Syracuse, NY

ABOUT THE INSTITUTION State-supported, coed. 6 undergraduate majors.

GIFT AID (NEED-BASED) ***Scholarships, grants, and awards:*** Federal Pell, FSEOG, state, college/university gift aid from institutional funds.

GIFT AID (NON-NEED-BASED) ***Scholarships, grants, and awards by category:*** *Academic interests/achievement:* health fields.

LOANS ***Programs:*** Federal Direct (Subsidized and Unsubsidized Stafford, PLUS), Perkins.

WORK-STUDY ***Federal work-study:*** Total amount: $50,826; jobs available.

APPLYING FOR FINANCIAL AID ***Required financial aid form:*** FAFSA.

CONTACT Michael Pede, Office of Financial Aid, State University of New York Upstate Medical University, 155 Elizabeth Blackwell Street, Syracuse, NY 13210-2375, 315-464-4329 or toll-free 800-736-2171. *E-mail:* finaid@upstate.edu.

STEPHEN F. AUSTIN STATE UNIVERSITY

Nacogdoches, TX

Tuition & fees (TX res): $6998 **Average undergraduate aid package: $9233**

ABOUT THE INSTITUTION State-supported, coed. 68 undergraduate majors. Federal methodology is used as a basis for awarding need-based institutional aid.

UNDERGRADUATE EXPENSES for 2010–11 ***Tuition, state resident:*** full-time $5096; part-time $169.85 per credit hour. ***Tuition, nonresident:*** full-time $14,396; part-time $479.85 per credit hour. ***Required fees:*** full-time $1902; $147 per credit hour. Full-time tuition and fees vary according to course load, degree level, and location. Part-time tuition and fees vary according to course load, degree level, and location. ***College room and board:*** $7670. Room and board charges vary according to board plan and housing facility. ***Payment plan:*** Installment.

FRESHMAN FINANCIAL AID (Fall 2009) 1,929 applied for aid; of those 79% were deemed to have need. 98% of freshmen with need received aid; of those 65% had need fully met. ***Average percent of need met:*** 95% (excluding resources awarded to replace EFC). ***Average financial aid package:*** $9746 (excluding resources awarded to replace EFC). 6% of all full-time freshmen had no need and received non-need-based gift aid.

UNDERGRADUATE FINANCIAL AID (Fall 2009) 7,618 applied for aid; of those 83% were deemed to have need. 98% of undergraduates with need received aid; of those 60% had need fully met. ***Average percent of need met:*** 89% (excluding resources awarded to replace EFC). ***Average financial aid package:*** $9233 (excluding resources awarded to replace EFC). 3% of all full-time undergraduates had no need and received non-need-based gift aid.

GIFT AID (NEED-BASED) ***Total amount:*** $31,858,318 (66% federal, 19% state, 15% institutional). ***Receiving aid:*** Freshmen: 52% (1,176); all full-time undergraduates: 51% (5,048). ***Average award:*** Freshmen: $6407; Undergraduates: $5349. ***Scholarships, grants, and awards:*** Federal Pell, FSEOG, state, college/university gift aid from institutional funds, Academic Competitiveness Grants, National SMART Grants, TEACH Grants.

GIFT AID (NON-NEED-BASED) ***Total amount:*** $11,285,509 (4% federal, 7% state, 66% institutional, 23% external sources). ***Receiving aid:*** Freshmen: 29% (669). Undergraduates: 21% (2,066). ***Average award:*** Freshmen: $3404. Undergraduates: $2775. ***Scholarships, grants, and awards by category:*** *Academic interests/achievement:* agriculture, biological sciences, business, communication, computer science, education, general academic interests/achievements, health fields, home economics, mathematics, military science, physical sciences, premedicine. *Creative arts/performance:* journalism/publications, music, theater/drama. *Special achievements/activities:* cheerleading/drum major, general special achievements/activities, hobbies/interests, leadership, rodeo. *Special characteristics:* adult students, children and siblings of alumni, children of faculty/staff, children of union members/company employees, first-generation college students, general special characteristics, local/state students, previous college experience. ***Tuition waivers:*** Full or partial for employees or children of employees, senior citizens.

LOANS ***Student loans:*** $73,382,589 (40% need-based, 60% non-need-based). 68% of past graduating class borrowed through all loan programs. *Average indebtedness per student:* $20,483. ***Average need-based loan:*** Freshmen: $3133. Undergraduates: $4040. ***Parent loans:*** $8,577,458 (100% non-need-based). ***Programs:*** Perkins, state, short-term emergency loans.

WORK-STUDY ***Federal work-study:*** Total amount: $749,973; jobs available. ***State or other work-study/employment:*** Total amount: $82,542 (100% need-based). Part-time jobs available.

ATHLETIC AWARDS Total amount: $3,134,382 (100% non-need-based).

APPLYING FOR FINANCIAL AID ***Required financial aid form:*** FAFSA. ***Financial aid deadline:*** Continuous. ***Notification date:*** Continuous beginning 4/1.

CONTACT Office of Financial Aid, Stephen F. Austin State University, PO Box 13052, Nacogdoches, TX 75962, 936-468-2403 or toll-free 800-731-2902. *Fax:* 936-468-1048. *E-mail:* finaid@sfasu.edu.

STEPHENS COLLEGE

Columbia, MO

ABOUT THE INSTITUTION Independent, coed, primarily women. 33 undergraduate majors.

GIFT AID (NEED-BASED) ***Scholarships, grants, and awards:*** Federal Pell, FSEOG, state, private, college/university gift aid from institutional funds, Academic Competitiveness Grants, National SMART Grants.

GIFT AID (NON-NEED-BASED) ***Scholarships, grants, and awards by category:*** *Academic interests/achievement:* English, general academic interests/achievements. *Creative arts/performance:* dance, performing arts, theater/drama. *Special achievements/activities:* leadership, memberships. *Special characteristics:* children of faculty/staff, children of union members/company employees, parents of current students, siblings of current students, veterans, veterans' children.

LOANS ***Programs:*** Perkins, alternative loans.

WORK-STUDY ***Federal work-study:*** Total amount: $159,180; 99 jobs averaging $1600. ***State or other work-study/employment:*** Total amount: $213,815 (80% need-based, 20% non-need-based). 140 part-time jobs averaging $1550.

APPLYING FOR FINANCIAL AID ***Required financial aid form:*** FAFSA.

CONTACT Mrs. Rachel Touchatt, Financial Aid Director, Stephens College, 1200 East Broadway, Columbia, MO 65215-0002, 800-876-7207. *Fax:* 573-876-2320. *E-mail:* finaid@stephens.edu.

STERLING COLLEGE

Sterling, KS

CONTACT Ms. Jodi Lightner, Director of Financial Aid, Sterling College, PO Box 98, Sterling, KS 67579-0098, 620-278-4207 or toll-free 800-346-1017. *Fax:* 620-278-4416. *E-mail:* jlightner@sterling.edu.

STERLING COLLEGE

Craftsbury Common, VT

Tuition & fees: $27,152 **Average undergraduate aid package: $20,771**

ABOUT THE INSTITUTION Independent, coed. 22 undergraduate majors. Both federal and institutional methodology are used as a basis for awarding need-based institutional aid.

UNDERGRADUATE EXPENSES for 2011–12 ***Comprehensive fee:*** $35,242 includes full-time tuition ($26,802), mandatory fees ($350), and room and board ($8090). ***College room only:*** $3684. Full-time tuition and fees vary according to course load. Room and board charges vary according to board plan. ***Part-time tuition:*** $848 per credit. Part-time tuition and fees vary according to course load. ***Payment plan:*** Installment.

FRESHMAN FINANCIAL AID (Fall 2009) 26 applied for aid; of those 92% were deemed to have need. 100% of freshmen with need received aid; of those 17% had need fully met. ***Average percent of need met:*** 83% (excluding resources awarded to replace EFC). ***Average financial aid package:*** $18,753 (excluding resources awarded to replace EFC). 8% of all full-time freshmen had no need and received non-need-based gift aid.

UNDERGRADUATE FINANCIAL AID (Fall 2009) 86 applied for aid; of those 100% were deemed to have need. 100% of undergraduates with need received aid; of those 8% had need fully met. ***Average percent of need met:*** 80% (excluding resources awarded to replace EFC). ***Average financial aid package:*** $20,771 (excluding resources awarded to replace EFC). 10% of all full-time undergraduates had no need and received non-need-based gift aid.

GIFT AID (NEED-BASED) ***Total amount:*** $1,327,551 (22% federal, 4% state, 73% institutional, 1% external sources). ***Receiving aid:*** Freshmen: 92% (24); all full-time undergraduates: 80% (86). ***Average award:*** Freshmen: $14,890; Undergraduates: $15,839. ***Scholarships, grants, and awards:*** Federal Pell, FSEOG, state, private, college/university gift aid from institutional funds.

GIFT AID (NON-NEED-BASED) ***Total amount:*** $72,169 (92% institutional, 8% external sources). ***Receiving aid:*** Freshmen: 8% (2). ***Average award:*** Freshmen: $2750. Undergraduates: $6018. ***Scholarships, grants, and awards by category:*** *Academic interests/achievement:* 7 awards ($25,500 total): general academic interests/achievements. *Special achievements/activities:* 16 awards ($4800 total): general special achievements/activities. *Special characteristics:* 44 awards ($63,435 total): general special characteristics, local/state students, previous college experience. ***Tuition waivers:*** Full or partial for employees or children of employees.

LOANS ***Student loans:*** $551,624 (94% need-based, 6% non-need-based). 93% of past graduating class borrowed through all loan programs. *Average indebtedness per student:* $19,751. ***Average need-based loan:*** Freshmen: $3194. Undergraduates: $3944. ***Parent loans:*** $417,420 (72% need-based, 28% non-need-based). ***Programs:*** Federal Direct (Subsidized and Unsubsidized Stafford, PLUS).

WORK-STUDY ***Federal work-study:*** Total amount: $151,746; 39 jobs averaging $339. ***State or other work-study/employment:*** Total amount: $28,997 (100% non-need-based). 108 part-time jobs averaging $1595.

APPLYING FOR FINANCIAL AID ***Required financial aid forms:*** FAFSA, institution's own form, state aid form. ***Financial aid deadline:*** Continuous. ***Notification date:*** Continuous beginning 1/31. Students must reply by 5/1 or within 2 weeks of notification.

CONTACT Barbara Stuart, Associate Director of Financial Aid, Sterling College, PO Box 72, Craftsbury Common, VT 05827, 800-648-3591 Ext. 2 or toll-free 800-648-3591 Ext. 100. *Fax:* 802-586-2596. *E-mail:* bstuart@sterlingcollege.edu.

STETSON UNIVERSITY

DeLand, FL

Tuition & fees: $35,081 **Average undergraduate aid package: $29,689**

ABOUT THE INSTITUTION Independent, coed. 58 undergraduate majors. Federal methodology is used as a basis for awarding need-based institutional aid.

UNDERGRADUATE EXPENSES for 2011–12 ***Comprehensive fee:*** $45,336 includes full-time tuition ($32,943), mandatory fees ($2138), and room and board ($10,255). ***College room only:*** $5845. Room and board charges vary according to board plan and housing facility. ***Part-time tuition:*** $3465 per course. ***Part-time fees:*** $310 per term. Part-time tuition and fees vary according to course load, location, and program. ***Payment plan:*** Installment.

FRESHMAN FINANCIAL AID (Fall 2010, est.) 459 applied for aid; of those 89% were deemed to have need. 100% of freshmen with need received aid; of those 23% had need fully met. ***Average percent of need met:*** 85% (excluding resources awarded to replace EFC). ***Average financial aid package:*** $31,956 (excluding resources awarded to replace EFC). 19% of all full-time freshmen had no need and received non-need-based gift aid.

UNDERGRADUATE FINANCIAL AID (Fall 2010, est.) 1,545 applied for aid; of those 90% were deemed to have need. 100% of undergraduates with need received aid; of those 20% had need fully met. ***Average percent of need met:*** 80% (excluding resources awarded to replace EFC). ***Average financial aid package:*** $29,689 (excluding resources awarded to replace EFC). 24% of all full-time undergraduates had no need and received non-need-based gift aid.

GIFT AID (NEED-BASED) ***Total amount:*** $29,868,836 (14% federal, 18% state, 67% institutional, 1% external sources). ***Receiving aid:*** Freshmen: 74% (406); all full-time undergraduates: 66% (1,366). ***Average award:*** Freshmen: $25,623; Undergraduates: $22,705. ***Scholarships, grants, and awards:*** Federal Pell, FSEOG, state, private, college/university gift aid from institutional funds.

GIFT AID (NON-NEED-BASED) ***Total amount:*** $10,663,706 (22% state, 74% institutional, 4% external sources). ***Receiving aid:*** Freshmen: 12% (66). Undergraduates: 9% (192). ***Average award:*** Freshmen: $16,403. Undergraduates: $13,171. ***Scholarships, grants, and awards by category:*** *Academic interests/achievement:* area/ethnic studies, biological sciences, business, communication, computer science, education, English, foreign languages, general academic interests/achievements, humanities, mathematics, military science, physical sciences, premedicine, religion/biblical studies, social sciences. *Creative arts/performance:* applied art and design, art/fine arts, music, theater/drama. *Special achievements/activities:* cheerleading/drum major, community service, general special achievements/activities, leadership, religious involvement. *Special characteristics:* children and siblings of alumni, children of faculty/staff, ethnic background, general special characteristics, international students, local/state students, members of minority groups. ***Tuition waivers:*** Full or partial for employees or children of employees.

LOANS ***Student loans:*** $11,488,799 (79% need-based, 21% non-need-based). 75% of past graduating class borrowed through all loan programs. *Average indebtedness per student:* $33,817. ***Average need-based loan:*** Freshmen: $4308. Undergraduates: $5117. ***Parent loans:*** $3,678,026 (48% need-based, 52% non-need-based). ***Programs:*** Federal Direct (Subsidized and Unsubsidized Stafford, PLUS), Perkins, college/university.

WORK-STUDY ***Federal work-study:*** Total amount: $1,941,045; 957 jobs averaging $2028. ***State or other work-study/employment:*** Total amount: $691,713 (42% need-based, 58% non-need-based). 206 part-time jobs averaging $3358.

ATHLETIC AWARDS Total amount: $4,061,302 (39% need-based, 61% non-need-based).

APPLYING FOR FINANCIAL AID ***Required financial aid forms:*** FAFSA, institution's own form. ***Financial aid deadline (priority):*** 3/15. ***Notification date:*** Continuous beginning 2/15. Students must reply within 2 weeks of notification.

CONTACT Robert D. Stewart, Director of Financial Aid, Stetson University, 421 North Woodland Boulevard, DeLand, FL 32723, 386-822-7120 or toll-free 800-688-0101. *Fax:* 386-822-7126. *E-mail:* finaid@stetson.edu.

STEVENS-HENAGER COLLEGE

Boise, ID

Tuition & fees: N/R **Average undergraduate aid package: $8850**

ABOUT THE INSTITUTION Proprietary, coed. 12 undergraduate majors. Federal methodology is used as a basis for awarding need-based institutional aid.

FRESHMAN FINANCIAL AID (Fall 2010, est.) 320 applied for aid; of those 85% were deemed to have need. 100% of freshmen with need received aid; of those 10% had need fully met. ***Average percent of need met:*** 60% (excluding resources awarded to replace EFC). ***Average financial aid package:*** $8850 (excluding resources awarded to replace EFC). 3% of all full-time freshmen had no need and received non-need-based gift aid.

UNDERGRADUATE FINANCIAL AID (Fall 2010, est.) 650 applied for aid; of those 85% were deemed to have need. 100% of undergraduates with need received aid; of those 10% had need fully met. ***Average percent of need met:*** 60% (excluding resources awarded to replace EFC). ***Average financial aid package:*** $8850 (excluding resources awarded to replace EFC). 2% of all full-time undergraduates had no need and received non-need-based gift aid.

GIFT AID (NEED-BASED) ***Total amount:*** $2,277,500 (100% federal). ***Receiving aid:*** Freshmen: 85% (272); all full-time undergraduates: 85% (553). ***Average award:*** Freshmen: $5350; Undergraduates: $5350. ***Scholarships, grants, and awards:*** Federal Pell, FSEOG, state, private, college/university gift aid from institutional funds.

GIFT AID (NON-NEED-BASED) ***Total amount:*** $291,000 (98% institutional, 2% external sources). ***Receiving aid:*** Freshmen: 85% (272). Undergraduates: 85% (553). ***Average award:*** Freshmen: $7500. Undergraduates: $7500. ***Scholarships, grants, and awards by category:*** *Academic interests/achievement:* 40 awards ($300,000 total): business, computer science, health fields. *Creative arts/performance:* 5 awards ($37,500 total): applied art and design.

LOANS ***Student loans:*** $6,275,000 (38% need-based, 62% non-need-based). 95% of past graduating class borrowed through all loan programs. *Average indebtedness per student:* $11,500. ***Average need-based loan:*** Freshmen: $3500. Undergraduates: $3500. ***Parent loans:*** $38,000 (100% need-based). ***Programs:*** Federal Direct (Subsidized and Unsubsidized Stafford, PLUS), Perkins, college/university.

APPLYING FOR FINANCIAL AID ***Required financial aid forms:*** FAFSA, institution's own form, business/farm supplement. ***Financial aid deadline:*** Continuous. ***Notification date:*** Continuous beginning 5/1. Students must reply within 8 weeks of notification.

CONTACT Ms. Jaime L. Davis, Training and Project Development, Stevens-Henager College, 1444 South Entertainment Avenue, Boise, ID 83709, 208-383-4540 Ext. 1875 or toll-free 800-97SKILLS (out-of-state). *Fax:* 208-345-6999. *E-mail:* jaime.davis@stevenshenager.edu.

STEVENS-HENAGER COLLEGE

West Haven, UT

CONTACT Financial Aid Office, Stevens-Henager College, 1890 South 1350 West, West Haven, UT 84401, 801-394-7791 or toll-free 800-622-2640.

STEVENS INSTITUTE OF BUSINESS & ARTS

St. Louis, MO

CONTACT Financial Aid Office, Stevens Institute of Business & Arts, 1521 Washington Avenue, St. Louis, MO 63102, 314-421-0949 or toll-free 800-871-0949.

STEVENS INSTITUTE OF TECHNOLOGY

Hoboken, NJ

CONTACT Ms. Adrienne Hynek, Associate Director of Financial Aid, Stevens Institute of Technology, Castle Point on Hudson, Hoboken, NJ 07030, 201-216-5555 or toll-free 800-458-5323. *Fax:* 201-216-8050. *E-mail:* ahynek@stevens.edu.

STEVENSON UNIVERSITY

Stevenson, MD

ABOUT THE INSTITUTION Independent, coed. 26 undergraduate majors.

GIFT AID (NEED-BASED) ***Scholarships, grants, and awards:*** Federal Pell, FSEOG, state, private, college/university gift aid from institutional funds.

GIFT AID (NON-NEED-BASED) ***Scholarships, grants, and awards by category:*** *Academic interests/achievement:* general academic interests/achievements. *Creative arts/performance:* art/fine arts.

LOANS ***Programs:*** Federal Direct (Subsidized and Unsubsidized Stafford, PLUS), Perkins.

WORK-STUDY ***Federal work-study:*** Total amount: $451,028; 225 jobs averaging $2000.

APPLYING FOR FINANCIAL AID ***Required financial aid form:*** FAFSA.

CONTACT Ms. Barbara L. Miller, Director of Financial Aid, Stevenson University, 100 Campus Circle, Owings Mills, MD 21117, 443-352-4369 or toll-free 877-468-6852 (in-state), 877-468-3852 (out-of-state). *Fax:* 443-352-4370. *E-mail:* blmiller@stevenson.edu.

STILLMAN COLLEGE

Tuscaloosa, AL

ABOUT THE INSTITUTION Independent religious, coed. 14 undergraduate majors.

GIFT AID (NEED-BASED) ***Scholarships, grants, and awards:*** Federal Pell, FSEOG, state, private, college/university gift aid from institutional funds, United Negro College Fund.

GIFT AID (NON-NEED-BASED) ***Scholarships, grants, and awards by category:*** *Academic interests/achievement:* education, general academic interests/achievements. *Creative arts/performance:* music. *Special characteristics:* children of faculty/staff.

LOANS ***Programs:*** Federal Direct (Subsidized and Unsubsidized Stafford, PLUS), Perkins.

WORK-STUDY ***Federal work-study:*** Total amount: $213,000; 172 jobs averaging $1086.

APPLYING FOR FINANCIAL AID ***Required financial aid forms:*** FAFSA, state aid form.

CONTACT Jacqueline S. Morris, Director of Financial Aid, Stillman College, PO Box 1430, Tuscaloosa, AL 35403, 205-366-8950 or toll-free 800-841-5722. *Fax:* 205-247-8106. *E-mail:* jmorris@stillman.edu.

STONEHILL COLLEGE

Easton, MA

Tuition & fees: $32,620 **Average undergraduate aid package: $23,720**

ABOUT THE INSTITUTION Independent Roman Catholic, coed. 39 undergraduate majors. Institutional methodology is used as a basis for awarding need-based institutional aid.

UNDERGRADUATE EXPENSES for 2010–11 ***Comprehensive fee:*** $45,230 includes full-time tuition ($32,620) and room and board ($12,610). ***College room only:*** $7694. Room and board charges vary according to board plan. ***Part-time tuition:*** $1087 per credit hour. Part-time tuition and fees vary according to course load. ***Payment plans:*** Tuition prepayment, installment.

FRESHMAN FINANCIAL AID (Fall 2010, est.) 681 applied for aid; of those 64% were deemed to have need. 100% of freshmen with need received aid; of those 52% had need fully met. ***Average percent of need met:*** 89% (excluding resources awarded to replace EFC). ***Average financial aid package:*** $22,970 (excluding resources awarded to replace EFC). 23% of all full-time freshmen had no need and received non-need-based gift aid.

UNDERGRADUATE FINANCIAL AID (Fall 2010, est.) 2,368 applied for aid; of those 62% were deemed to have need. 100% of undergraduates with need received aid; of those 49% had need fully met. ***Average percent of need met:*** 90% (excluding resources awarded to replace EFC). ***Average financial aid package:*** $23,720 (excluding resources awarded to replace EFC). 25% of all full-time undergraduates had no need and received non-need-based gift aid.

GIFT AID (NEED-BASED) ***Total amount:*** $24,510,194 (9% federal, 3% state, 85% institutional, 3% external sources). ***Receiving aid:*** Freshmen: 57% (416); all full-time undergraduates: 55% (1,414). ***Average award:*** Freshmen: $17,245; Undergraduates: $17,448. ***Scholarships, grants, and awards:*** Federal Pell, FSEOG, state, private, college/university gift aid from institutional funds.

GIFT AID (NON-NEED-BASED) ***Total amount:*** $7,723,082 (4% federal, 91% institutional, 5% external sources). ***Receiving aid:*** Freshmen: 13% (94). Undergraduates: 9% (243). ***Average award:*** Freshmen: $8949. Undergraduates: $8857. ***Scholarships, grants, and awards by category:*** *Academic interests/achievement:* general academic interests/achievements. *Special characteristics:* children of faculty/staff, children of union members/company employees, members of minority groups, relatives of clergy, siblings of current students, veterans, veterans' children. ***Tuition waivers:*** Full or partial for employees or children of employees.

LOANS ***Student loans:*** $15,200,000 (74% need-based, 26% non-need-based). 74% of past graduating class borrowed through all loan programs. *Average indebtedness per student:* $30,435. ***Average need-based loan:*** Freshmen: $3832. Undergraduates: $5021. ***Parent loans:*** $10,800,000 (73% need-based, 27% non-need-based). ***Programs:*** Federal Direct (Subsidized and Unsubsidized Stafford, PLUS), Perkins, state.

WORK-STUDY ***Federal work-study:*** Total amount: $1,834,327; jobs available. ***State or other work-study/employment:*** Total amount: $535,384 (86% need-based, 14% non-need-based). Part-time jobs available.

ATHLETIC AWARDS Total amount: $2,059,498 (64% need-based, 36% non-need-based).

APPLYING FOR FINANCIAL AID ***Required financial aid forms:*** FAFSA, CSS Financial Aid PROFILE, noncustodial (divorced/separated) parent's statement, business/farm supplement. ***Financial aid deadline (priority):*** 2/1. ***Notification date:*** 4/1. Students must reply by 5/1.

CONTACT Rhonda Nickley, Office Manager, Stonehill College, 320 Washington Street, Easton, MA 02357, 508-565-1088. *Fax:* 508-565-1426. *E-mail:* finaid@stonehill.edu.

STONY BROOK UNIVERSITY, STATE UNIVERSITY OF NEW YORK

Stony Brook, NY

Tuition & fees (NY res): $6580 **Average undergraduate aid package: $11,483**

ABOUT THE INSTITUTION State-supported, coed. 65 undergraduate majors. Federal methodology is used as a basis for awarding need-based institutional aid.

UNDERGRADUATE EXPENSES for 2011–12 ***Tuition, state resident:*** full-time $4970. ***Tuition, nonresident:*** full-time $13,380. ***Required fees:*** full-time $1610. ***College room and board:*** $10,142; ***Room only:*** $6442. Room and board charges vary according to board plan and housing facility. ***Payment plan:*** Installment.

FRESHMAN FINANCIAL AID (Fall 2010, est.) 2,228 applied for aid; of those 71% were deemed to have need. 99% of freshmen with need received aid; of those 13% had need fully met. ***Average percent of need met:*** 72% (excluding resources awarded to replace EFC). ***Average financial aid package:*** $11,324 (excluding resources awarded to replace EFC). 15% of all full-time freshmen had no need and received non-need-based gift aid.

UNDERGRADUATE FINANCIAL AID (Fall 2010, est.) 10,620 applied for aid; of those 80% were deemed to have need. 98% of undergraduates with need received aid; of those 14% had need fully met. ***Average percent of need met:*** 69% (excluding resources awarded to replace EFC). ***Average financial aid package:*** $11,483 (excluding resources awarded to replace EFC). 7% of all full-time undergraduates had no need and received non-need-based gift aid.

GIFT AID (NEED-BASED) ***Total amount:*** $55,835,797 (57% federal, 36% state, 6% institutional, 1% external sources). ***Receiving aid:*** Freshmen: 51% (1,387); all full-time undergraduates: 49% (7,270). ***Average award:*** Freshmen: $7842; Undergraduates: $7275. ***Scholarships, grants, and awards:*** Federal Pell, FSEOG, state, private, college/university gift aid from institutional funds.

GIFT AID (NON-NEED-BASED) ***Total amount:*** $5,958,894 (6% federal, 7% state, 73% institutional, 14% external sources). ***Receiving aid:*** Freshmen: 4% (98). Undergraduates: 2% (266). ***Average award:*** Freshmen: $3797. Undergraduates: $3729. ***Scholarships, grants, and awards by category:*** *Academic interests/achievement:* area/ethnic studies, biological sciences, business, computer science, engineering/technologies, English, foreign languages, general academic interests/achievements, health fields, international studies, mathematics, physical sciences, social sciences. *Creative arts/performance:* cinema/film/broadcasting, journalism/publications, music. *Special achievements/activities:* community service, leadership. *Special characteristics:* ethnic background, general special characteristics.

LOANS ***Student loans:*** $82,004,931 (72% need-based, 28% non-need-based). 59% of past graduating class borrowed through all loan programs. *Average indebtedness per student:* $19,807. ***Average need-based loan:*** Freshmen: $3574. Undergraduates: $4565. ***Parent loans:*** $5,394,191 (33% need-based, 67% non-need-based). ***Programs:*** Federal Direct (Subsidized and Unsubsidized Stafford, PLUS), Perkins, state.

WORK-STUDY ***Federal work-study:*** Total amount: $949,570; 466 jobs averaging $2038. ***State or other work-study/employment:*** Total amount: $5,347,041 (38% need-based, 62% non-need-based). 1,748 part-time jobs averaging $2074.

ATHLETIC AWARDS Total amount: $5,284,324 (31% need-based, 69% non-need-based).

APPLYING FOR FINANCIAL AID ***Required financial aid form:*** FAFSA. ***Financial aid deadline (priority):*** 3/1. ***Notification date:*** Continuous beginning 3/15. Students must reply within 2 weeks of notification.

CONTACT Office of Student Financial Aid and Scholarship Services, Stony Brook University, State University of New York, Administration Building, Room 180, Stony Brook, NY 11794, 631-632-6840 or toll-free 800-872-7869 (out-of-state). *Fax:* 631-632-9525. *E-mail:* finaid@stonybrook.edu.

STRATFORD UNIVERSITY
Falls Church, VA

CONTACT Financial Aid Office, Stratford University, 7777 Leesburg Pike, Suite 100 South, Falls Church, VA 22043, 703-821-8570 or toll-free 800-444-0804.

STRATFORD UNIVERSITY
Woodbridge, VA

CONTACT Financial Aid Office, Stratford University, 14349 Gideon Drive, Woodbridge, VA 22192, toll-free 888-546-1250 (out-of-state).

STRAYER UNIVERSITY—AKRON CAMPUS
Akron, OH

CONTACT Financial Aid Office, Strayer University—Akron Campus, 51 Park West Boulevard, Akron, OH 44320, 330-734-6700.

STRAYER UNIVERSITY—ALEXANDRIA CAMPUS
Alexandria, VA

CONTACT Financial Aid Office, Strayer University—Alexandria Campus, 2730 Eisenhower Avenue, Alexandria, VA 22314, 703-317-2626.

STRAYER UNIVERSITY—ALLENTOWN CAMPUS
Center Valley, PA

CONTACT Financial Aid Office, Strayer University—Allentown Campus, 3800 Sierra Circle, Suite 300, Center Valley, PA 18034, 484-809-7770.

STRAYER UNIVERSITY—ANNE ARUNDEL CAMPUS
Millersville, MD

CONTACT Financial Aid Office, Strayer University—Anne Arundel Campus, 1520 Jabez Run, Millersville, MD 21108, 410-923-4500.

STRAYER UNIVERSITY—ARLINGTON CAMPUS
Arlington, VA

CONTACT Financial Aid Office, Strayer University—Arlington Campus, 2121 15th Street North, Arlington, VA 22201, 703-892-5100.

STRAYER UNIVERSITY—AUGUSTA CAMPUS
Augusta, GA

CONTACT Financial Aid Office, Strayer University—Augusta Campus, 1330 Augusta West Parkway, Augusta, GA 30909, 706-855-8233.

STRAYER UNIVERSITY—BAYMEADOWS CAMPUS
Jacksonville, FL

CONTACT Financial Aid Office, Strayer University—Baymeadows Campus, 8375 Dix Ellis Trail, Suite 200, Jacksonville, FL 32256, 904-538-1000.

STRAYER UNIVERSITY—BIRMINGHAM CAMPUS
Birmingham, AL

CONTACT Financial Aid Office, Strayer University—Birmingham Campus, 3570 Grandview Parkway, Suite 200, Birmingham, AL 35243, 205-453-6300.

STRAYER UNIVERSITY—BRICKELL CAMPUS
Miami, FL

CONTACT Financial Aid Office, Strayer University—Brickell Campus, 1201 Brickell Avenue, Suite 700, Miami, FL 33131, 305-507-5800.

STRAYER UNIVERSITY—CENTER CITY CAMPUS
Philadelphia, PA

CONTACT Financial Aid Office, Strayer University—Center City Campus, 1601 Cherry Street, Suite 100, Philadelphia, PA 19102, 267-256-0200.

STRAYER UNIVERSITY—CHAMBLEE CAMPUS
Atlanta, GA

CONTACT Financial Aid Office, Strayer University—Chamblee Campus, 3355 Northeast Expressway, Suite 100, Atlanta, GA 30341, 770-454-9270.

STRAYER UNIVERSITY—CHARLESTON CAMPUS
North Charleston, SC

CONTACT Financial Aid Office, Strayer University—Charleston Campus, 5010 Wetland Crossing, North Charleston, SC 29418, 843-746-5100.

STRAYER UNIVERSITY—CHERRY HILL CAMPUS
Cherry Hill, NJ

CONTACT Financial Aid Office, Strayer University—Cherry Hill Campus, 2201 Route 38, Suite 100, Cherry Hill, NJ 08002, 856-482-4200.

STRAYER UNIVERSITY—CHESAPEAKE CAMPUS
Chesapeake, VA

CONTACT Financial Aid Office, Strayer University—Chesapeake Campus, 700 Independent Parkway, Suite 400, Chesapeake, VA 23320, 757-382-9900.

STRAYER UNIVERSITY—CHESTERFIELD CAMPUS
Midlothian, VA

CONTACT Financial Aid Office, Strayer University—Chesterfield Campus, 2820 Waterford Lake Drive, Suite 100, Midlothian, VA 23112, 804-763-6300.

STRAYER UNIVERSITY—CHRISTIANA CAMPUS
Newark, DE

CONTACT Financial Aid Office, Strayer University—Christiana Campus, 240 Continental Drive, Suite 108, Newark, DE 19713, 302-292-6100.

STRAYER UNIVERSITY—COBB COUNTY CAMPUS

Atlanta, GA

CONTACT Financial Aid Office, Strayer University—Cobb County Campus, 3101 Towercreek Parkway, SE, Suite 700, Atlanta, GA 30339-3256, 770-612-2170.

STRAYER UNIVERSITY—COLUMBIA CAMPUS

Columbia, SC

CONTACT Financial Aid Office, Strayer University—Columbia Campus, 200 Center Point Circle, Suite 300, Columbia, SC 29210, 803-750-2500.

STRAYER UNIVERSITY—COLUMBUS CAMPUS

Columbus, OH

CONTACT Financial Aid Office, Strayer University—Columbus Campus, 8425 Pulsar Place, Suite 400, Columbus, OH 43240, 614-310-6700.

STRAYER UNIVERSITY—CORAL SPRINGS CAMPUS

Coral Springs, FL

CONTACT Financial Aid Office, Strayer University—Coral Springs Campus, 5830 Coral Ridge Drive, Suite 300, Coral Springs, FL 33076, 954-369-0700.

STRAYER UNIVERSITY—CRANBERRY WOODS CAMPUS

Cranberry Township, PA

CONTACT Financial Aid Office, Strayer University—Cranberry Woods Campus, Regional Learning Alliance, 850 Cranberry Woods Drive, Suite 2241, Cranberry Township, PA 16066, 724-741-1064.

STRAYER UNIVERSITY—DELAWARE COUNTY CAMPUS

Springfield, PA

CONTACT Financial Aid Office, Strayer University—Delaware County Campus, 760 West Sproul Road, Suite 200, Springfield, PA 19064-1215, 610-604-7700.

STRAYER UNIVERSITY—DORAL CAMPUS

Miami, FL

CONTACT Financial Aid Office, Strayer University—Doral Campus, 11430 Northwest 20th Street, Suite 150, Miami, FL 33172, 305-507-5700.

STRAYER UNIVERSITY—DOUGLASVILLE CAMPUS

Douglasville, GA

CONTACT Financial Aid Office, Strayer University—Douglasville Campus, 4655 Timber Ridge Drive, Douglasville, GA 30135, 678-715-2200.

STRAYER UNIVERSITY—FAIRVIEW PARK CAMPUS

Fairview Park, OH

CONTACT Financial Aid Office, Strayer University—Fairview Park Campus, 22730 Fairview Center Drive, Suite 150, Fairview Park, OH 44126-3616, 440-471-6400.

STRAYER UNIVERSITY—FLORENCE CAMPUS

Florence, KY

CONTACT Financial Aid Office, Strayer University—Florence Campus, 7300 Turfway Road, Suite 250, Florence, KY 41042, 859-692-2800.

STRAYER UNIVERSITY—FORT LAUDERDALE CAMPUS

Fort Lauderdale, FL

CONTACT Financial Aid Office, Strayer University—Fort Lauderdale Campus, 2307 West Broward Boulevard, Suite 100, Fort Lauderdale, FL 33312, 954-745-6960.

STRAYER UNIVERSITY—FREDERICKSBURG CAMPUS

Fredericksburg, VA

CONTACT Financial Aid Office, Strayer University—Fredericksburg Campus, 150 Riverside Parkway, Suite 100, Fredericksburg, VA 22406, 540-374-4300.

STRAYER UNIVERSITY—GREENSBORO CAMPUS

Greensboro, NC

CONTACT Financial Aid Office, Strayer University—Greensboro Campus, 4900 Koger Boulevard, Suite 400, Greensboro, NC 27407, 336-315.7800.

STRAYER UNIVERSITY—GREENVILLE CAMPUS

Greenville, SC

CONTACT Financial Aid Office, Strayer University—Greenville Campus, 555 North Pleasantburg Drive, Suite 300, Greenville, SC 29607, 864-250-7000.

STRAYER UNIVERSITY—HENRICO CAMPUS

Glen Allen, VA

CONTACT Financial Aid Office, Strayer University—Henrico Campus, 11501 Nuckols Road, Glen Allen, VA 23059, 804-527-1000.

STRAYER UNIVERSITY—HUNTERSVILLE CAMPUS

Huntersville, NC

CONTACT Financial Aid Office, Strayer University—Huntersville Campus, 13620 Reese Boulevard, Suite 130, Huntersville, NC 28078, 704-379-6800.

STRAYER UNIVERSITY—HUNTSVILLE CAMPUS

Huntsville, AL

CONTACT Financial Aid Office, Strayer University—Huntsville Campus, 4955 Corporate Drive, NW, Suite 200, Huntsville, AL 35805, 256-665-9800.

STRAYER UNIVERSITY—IRVING CAMPUS

Irving, TX

CONTACT Financial Aid Office, Strayer University—Irving Campus, 7701 Las Colinas Ridge, Suite 450, Irving, TX 75063, 214-429-3900.

STRAYER UNIVERSITY—JACKSON CAMPUS

Jackson, MS

CONTACT Financial Aid Office, Strayer University—Jackson Campus, 460 Briarwood Drive, Suite 200, Jackson, MS 39206, 601-718-5900.

STRAYER UNIVERSITY—KING OF PRUSSIA CAMPUS

King of Prussia, PA

CONTACT Financial Aid Office, Strayer University—King of Prussia Campus, 234 Mall Boulevard, Suite G-50, King of Prussia, PA 19406, 610-992-1700.

STRAYER UNIVERSITY—KNOXVILLE CAMPUS

Knoxville, TN

CONTACT Financial Aid Office, Strayer University—Knoxville Campus, 10118 Parkside Drive, Suite 200, Knoxville, TN 37922, 865-288-6000.

STRAYER UNIVERSITY—LAWRENCEVILLE CAMPUS

Lawrenceville, NJ

CONTACT Financial Aid Office, Strayer University—Lawrenceville Campus, 3150 Brunswick Pike, Suite 100, Lawrenceville, NJ 08648, 609-406-7600.

STRAYER UNIVERSITY—LEXINGTON CAMPUS

Lexington, KY

CONTACT Financial Aid Office, Strayer University—Lexington Campus, 220 Lexington Green Circle, Suite 550, Lexington, KY 40503, 859-971-4400.

STRAYER UNIVERSITY—LITHONIA CAMPUS

Lithonia, GA

CONTACT Financial Aid Office, Strayer University—Lithonia Campus, 3120 Stonecrest Boulevard, Suite 200, Lithonia, GA 30038, 678-323-7700.

STRAYER UNIVERSITY—LITTLE ROCK CAMPUS

Little Rock, AR

CONTACT Financial Aid Office, Strayer University—Little Rock Campus, 10825 Financial Centre Parkway, Suite 131, Little Rock, AR 72211.

STRAYER UNIVERSITY—LOUDOUN CAMPUS

Ashburn, VA

CONTACT Financial Aid Office, Strayer University—Loudoun Campus, 45150 Russell Branch Parkway, Suite 200, Ashburn, VA 20147, 703-729-8800.

STRAYER UNIVERSITY—LOUISVILLE CAMPUS

Louisville, KY

CONTACT Financial Aid Office, Strayer University—Louisville Campus, 2650 Eastpoint Parkway, Suite 100, Louisville, KY 40223, 502-253-5000.

STRAYER UNIVERSITY—LOWER BUCKS COUNTY CAMPUS

Trevose, PA

CONTACT Financial Aid Office, Strayer University—Lower Bucks County Campus, 3600 Horizon Boulevard, Suite 100, Trevose, PA 19053, 215-953-5999.

STRAYER UNIVERSITY—MAITLAND CAMPUS

Maitland, FL

CONTACT Financial Aid Office, Strayer University—Maitland Campus, 850 Trafalgar Court, Suite 360, Maitland, FL 32751, 407-618-5900.

STRAYER UNIVERSITY—MANASSAS CAMPUS

Manassas, VA

CONTACT Financial Aid Office, Strayer University—Manassas Campus, 9990 Battleview Parkway, Manassas, VA 20109, 703-330-8400.

STRAYER UNIVERSITY—MASON CAMPUS

Mason, OH

CONTACT Financial Aid Office, Strayer University—Mason Campus, 4605 Duke Drive, Suite 700, Mason, OH 45040, 513-234-6450.

STRAYER UNIVERSITY—METAIRIE CAMPUS

Metairie, LA

CONTACT Financial Aid Office, Strayer University—Metairie Campus, 111 Veterans Memorial Boulevard, Suite 420, Metairie, LA 70005, 504-799-1700.

STRAYER UNIVERSITY—MIRAMAR CAMPUS

Miramar, FL

CONTACT Financial Aid Office, Strayer University—Miramar Campus, 15620 Southwest 29th Street, Miramar, FL 33027, 954-378-2400.

STRAYER UNIVERSITY—MORROW CAMPUS

Morrow, GA

CONTACT Financial Aid Office, Strayer University—Morrow Campus, 3000 Corporate Center Drive, Suite 100, Morrow, GA 30260, 678-422-4100.

STRAYER UNIVERSITY—NASHVILLE CAMPUS

Nashville, TN

CONTACT Financial Aid Office, Strayer University—Nashville Campus, 1809 Dabbs Avenue, Nashville, TN 37210, 615-871-2260.

STRAYER UNIVERSITY—NEWPORT NEWS CAMPUS

Newport News, VA

CONTACT Financial Aid Office, Strayer University—Newport News Campus, 813 Diligence Drive, Suite 100, Newport News, VA 23606, 757-873-3100.

STRAYER UNIVERSITY—NORTH AUSTIN CAMPUS

Austin, TX

CONTACT Financial Aid Office, Strayer University—North Austin Campus, 8501 North Mopac Expressway, Suite 100, Austin, TX 78759, 512-568-3300.

STRAYER UNIVERSITY—NORTH CHARLOTTE CAMPUS

Charlotte, NC

CONTACT Financial Aid Office, Strayer University—North Charlotte Campus, 8335 IBM Drive, Suite 150, Charlotte, NC 28262, 704-717-4000.

STRAYER UNIVERSITY—NORTH RALEIGH CAMPUS

Raleigh, NC

CONTACT Financial Aid Office, Strayer University—North Raleigh Campus, 3200 Spring Forest Road, Suite 214, Raleigh, NC 27616, 919-878-9900.

STRAYER UNIVERSITY—NORTHWEST HOUSTON CAMPUS

Houston, TX

CONTACT Financial Aid Office, Strayer University—Northwest Houston Campus, 10940 W. Sam Houston Parkway N., Suite 200, Houston, TX 77064, 281-949-1800.

STRAYER UNIVERSITY—ORLANDO EAST CAMPUS

Orlando, FL

CONTACT Financial Aid Office, Strayer University—Orlando East Campus, 2200 North Alafaya Trail, Suite 500, Orlando, FL 32826, 407-926-2000.

STRAYER UNIVERSITY—OWINGS MILLS CAMPUS

Owings Mills, MD

CONTACT Financial Aid Office, Strayer University—Owings Mills Campus, 500 Redland Court, Suite 100, Owings Mills, MD 21117, 443-394-3339.

STRAYER UNIVERSITY—PALM BEACH GARDENS CAMPUS

Palm Beach Gardens, FL

CONTACT Financial Aid Office, Strayer University—Palm Beach Gardens Campus, 11025 RCA Center Drive, Suite 200, Palm Beach Gardens, FL 33410, 561-904-3000.

STRAYER UNIVERSITY—PENN CENTER WEST CAMPUS

Pittsburgh, PA

CONTACT Financial Aid Office, Strayer University—Penn Center West Campus, One Penn Center West, Suite 320, Pittsburgh, PA 15276, 412-747-7800.

STRAYER UNIVERSITY—PISCATAWAY CAMPUS

Piscataway, NJ

CONTACT Financial Aid Office, Strayer University—Piscataway Campus, 242 Old New Brunswick Road, Suite 220, Piscataway, NJ 08854, 732-743-3800.

STRAYER UNIVERSITY—PLANO CAMPUS

Plano, TX

CONTACT Financial Aid Office, Strayer University—Plano Campus, 2701 North Dallas Parkway, Suite 300, Plano, TX 75093, 972-535-3700.

STRAYER UNIVERSITY—PRINCE GEORGE'S CAMPUS

Suitland, MD

CONTACT Financial Aid Office, Strayer University—Prince George's Campus, 4710 Auth Place, First Floor, Suitland, MD 20746, 301-423-3600.

STRAYER UNIVERSITY—ROCKVILLE CAMPUS

Rockville, MD

CONTACT Financial Aid Office, Strayer University—Rockville Campus, 4 Research Place, Suite 100, Rockville, MD 20850, 301-548-5500.

STRAYER UNIVERSITY—ROSWELL CAMPUS

Roswell, GA

CONTACT Financial Aid Office, Strayer University—Roswell Campus, 100 Mansell Court East, Suite 100, Roswell, GA 30076, 770-650-3000.

STRAYER UNIVERSITY—RTP CAMPUS

Morrisville, NC

CONTACT Financial Aid Office, Strayer University—RTP Campus, 4 Copley Parkway, Morrisville, NC 27560, 919-466-4400.

STRAYER UNIVERSITY—SALT LAKE CAMPUS

Sandy, UT

CONTACT Financial Aid Office, Strayer University—Salt Lake Campus, 9815 South Monroe Street, Suite 200, Sandy, UT 84070, 801-432-5000.

STRAYER UNIVERSITY—SAND LAKE CAMPUS

Orlando, FL

CONTACT Financial Aid Office, Strayer University—Sand Lake Campus, 8541 South Park Circle, Building 900, Orlando, FL 32819, 407-264-9400.

STRAYER UNIVERSITY—SAVANNAH CAMPUS

Savannah, GA

CONTACT Financial Aid Office, Strayer University—Savannah Campus, 20 Martin Court, Savannah, GA 31419, 912-921-2900.

STRAYER UNIVERSITY—SHELBY OAKS CAMPUS

Memphis, TN

CONTACT Financial Aid Office, Strayer University—Shelby Oaks Campus, 6211 Shelby Oaks Drive, Suite 100, Memphis, TN 38134, 901-383-6750.

STRAYER UNIVERSITY—SOUTH CHARLOTTE CAMPUS

Charlotte, NC

CONTACT Financial Aid Office, Strayer University—South Charlotte Campus, 9101 Kings Parade Boulevard, Suite 200, Charlotte, NC 28273, 704-499-9200.

STRAYER UNIVERSITY—SOUTH RALEIGH CAMPUS

Raleigh, NC

CONTACT Financial Aid Office, Strayer University—South Raleigh Campus, 3421 Olympia Drive, Raleigh, NC 27603, 919-890-7500.

STRAYER UNIVERSITY—TAKOMA PARK CAMPUS

Washington, DC

CONTACT Financial Aid Office, Strayer University—Takoma Park Campus, 6830 Laurel Street, NW, Washington, DC 20012, 202-722-8100.

STRAYER UNIVERSITY—TAMPA EAST CAMPUS

Tampa, FL

CONTACT Financial Aid Office, Strayer University—Tampa East Campus, 6302 East Martin Luther King Boulevard, Suite 450, Tampa, FL 33619, 813-663-0100.

STRAYER UNIVERSITY—TAMPA WESTSHORE CAMPUS

Tampa, FL

CONTACT Financial Aid Office, Strayer University—Tampa Westshore Campus, 4902 Eisenhower Boulevard, Suite 100, Tampa, FL 33634, 813-882-0100.

STRAYER UNIVERSITY—TEAYS VALLEY CAMPUS

Scott Depot, WV

CONTACT Financial Aid Office, Strayer University—Teays Valley Campus, 100 Corporate Center Drive, Scott Depot, WV 25560, 304-760-1700.

STRAYER UNIVERSITY—THOUSAND OAKS CAMPUS

Memphis, TN

CONTACT Financial Aid Office, Strayer University—Thousand Oaks Campus, 2620 Thousand Oaks Boulevard, Suite 1100, Memphis, TN 38118, 901-369-0835.

STRAYER UNIVERSITY—VIRGINIA BEACH CAMPUS

Virginia Beach, VA

CONTACT Financial Aid Office, Strayer University—Virginia Beach Campus, 249 Central Park Avenue, Suite 350, Virginia Beach, VA 23462, 757-493-6000.

STRAYER UNIVERSITY—WASHINGTON CAMPUS

Washington, DC

CONTACT Financial Aid Office, Strayer University—Washington Campus, 1133 15th Street, NW, Washington, DC 200025, 202-408-2400.

STRAYER UNIVERSITY—WHITE MARSH CAMPUS

Baltimore, MD

CONTACT Financial Aid Office, Strayer University—White Marsh Campus, 9920 Franklin Square Drive, Suite 200, Baltimore, MD 21236, 410-238-9000.

STRAYER UNIVERSITY—WILLINGBORO CAMPUS

Willingboro, NJ

CONTACT Financial Aid Office, Strayer University—Willingboro Campus, 300 Willingboro Parkway, Willingboro Town Center, Suite 125, Willingboro, NJ 08046, 609-835-6000.

STRAYER UNIVERSITY—WOODBRIDGE CAMPUS

Woodbridge, VA

CONTACT Financial Aid Office, Strayer University—Woodbridge Campus, 13385 Minnieville Road, Woodbridge, VA 22192, 703-878-2800.

SUFFOLK UNIVERSITY

Boston, MA

Tuition & fees: $28,526 **Average undergraduate aid package: $20,408**

ABOUT THE INSTITUTION Independent, coed. 87 undergraduate majors. Both federal and institutional methodology are used as a basis for awarding need-based institutional aid.

UNDERGRADUATE EXPENSES for 2010–11 ***Comprehensive fee:*** $43,150 includes full-time tuition ($28,414), mandatory fees ($112), and room and board ($14,624). ***College room only:*** $12,204. Room and board charges vary according to board plan and housing facility. ***Part-time tuition:*** $697 per credit hour. ***Part-time fees:*** $10 per term. Part-time tuition and fees vary according to course load. ***Payment plans:*** Installment, deferred payment.

FRESHMAN FINANCIAL AID (Fall 2010, est.) 1,028 applied for aid; of those 89% were deemed to have need. 100% of freshmen with need received aid; of those 7% had need fully met. ***Average percent of need met:*** 68% (excluding resources awarded to replace EFC). ***Average financial aid package:*** $21,387 (excluding resources awarded to replace EFC). 5% of all full-time freshmen had no need and received non-need-based gift aid.

UNDERGRADUATE FINANCIAL AID (Fall 2010, est.) 3,707 applied for aid; of those 88% were deemed to have need. 100% of undergraduates with need received aid; of those 10% had need fully met. ***Average percent of need met:*** 37% (excluding resources awarded to replace EFC). ***Average financial aid package:*** $20,408 (excluding resources awarded to replace EFC). 8% of all full-time undergraduates had no need and received non-need-based gift aid.

GIFT AID (NEED-BASED) ***Total amount:*** $39,076,732 (19% federal, 4% state, 75% institutional, 2% external sources). ***Receiving aid:*** Freshmen: 66% (861); all full-time undergraduates: 57% (3,020). ***Average award:*** Freshmen: $14,244; Undergraduates: $12,513. ***Scholarships, grants, and awards:*** Federal Pell, FSEOG, state, private, college/university gift aid from institutional funds.

GIFT AID (NON-NEED-BASED) ***Total amount:*** $13,024,040 (94% institutional, 6% external sources). ***Receiving aid:*** Freshmen: 19% (249). Undergraduates: 22% (1,141). ***Average award:*** Freshmen: $8361. Undergraduates: $8663. ***Scholarships, grants, and awards by category:*** *Academic interests/achievement:* 1,406 awards ($12,039,914 total): general academic interests/achievements. *Special achievements/activities:* 2 awards ($7000 total): community service. *Special characteristics:* 199 awards ($674,116 total): children and siblings of alumni, children of faculty/staff, siblings of current students. ***Tuition waivers:*** Full or partial for employees or children of employees, senior citizens.

LOANS ***Student loans:*** $32,548,982 (45% need-based, 55% non-need-based). 73% of past graduating class borrowed through all loan programs. ***Average need-based loan:*** Freshmen: $3463. Undergraduates: $4582. ***Programs:*** Federal Direct (Subsidized and Unsubsidized Stafford, PLUS), Perkins, state, college/university.

WORK-STUDY ***Federal work-study:*** Total amount: $5,027,340; 2,163 jobs averaging $2324. ***State or other work-study/employment:*** Total amount: $1,183,919 (100% non-need-based). 371 part-time jobs averaging $3160.

APPLYING FOR FINANCIAL AID ***Required financial aid forms:*** FAFSA, institution's own form. ***Financial aid deadline:*** 2/15. ***Notification date:*** Continuous beginning 2/5. Students must reply by 5/1 or within 2 weeks of notification.

CONTACT Ms. Christine A. Perry, Director of Student Financial Services, Suffolk University, 8 Ashburton Place, Boston, MA 02108, 617-573-8470 or toll-free 800-6-SUFFOLK. *Fax:* 617-720-3579. *E-mail:* finaid@suffolk.edu.

SULLIVAN UNIVERSITY

Louisville, KY

CONTACT Charlene Geiser, Financial Planning Office, Sullivan University, 3101 Bardstown Road, Louisville, KY 40205, 502-456-6504 Ext. 311 or toll-free 800-844-1354. *Fax:* 502-456-0040. *E-mail:* cgeiser@sullivan.edu.

SUL ROSS STATE UNIVERSITY

Alpine, TX

Tuition & fees (TX res): $2928 **Average undergraduate aid package: $10,348**

ABOUT THE INSTITUTION State-supported, coed. 34 undergraduate majors. Both federal and institutional methodology are used as a basis for awarding need-based institutional aid.

UNDERGRADUATE EXPENSES for 2010–11 ***Tuition, state resident:*** full-time $2928. ***Tuition, nonresident:*** full-time $9576. ***College room and board:*** $6370; ***Room only:*** $3820. Room and board charges vary according to board plan and housing facility. ***Payment plan:*** Installment.

FRESHMAN FINANCIAL AID (Fall 2009) 319 applied for aid; of those 93% were deemed to have need. 100% of freshmen with need received aid; of those 70% had need fully met. ***Average percent of need met:*** 77% (excluding resources awarded to replace EFC). ***Average financial aid package:*** $9784 (excluding resources awarded to replace EFC). 5% of all full-time freshmen had no need and received non-need-based gift aid.

UNDERGRADUATE FINANCIAL AID (Fall 2009) 1,176 applied for aid; of those 95% were deemed to have need. 100% of undergraduates with need received aid; of those 76% had need fully met. ***Average percent of need met:*** 76% (excluding resources awarded to replace EFC). ***Average financial aid package:*** $10,348 (excluding resources awarded to replace EFC). 3% of all full-time undergraduates had no need and received non-need-based gift aid.

GIFT AID (NEED-BASED) ***Total amount:*** $7,605,769 (77% federal, 22% state, 1% institutional). ***Receiving aid:*** Freshmen: 73% (271); all full-time undergraduates: 71% (998). ***Average award:*** Freshmen: $6717; Undergraduates: $6213. ***Scholarships, grants, and awards:*** Federal Pell, FSEOG, state, private, college/university gift aid from institutional funds.

GIFT AID (NON-NEED-BASED) ***Total amount:*** $805,918 (64% institutional, 36% external sources). ***Receiving aid:*** Freshmen: 38% (140). Undergraduates: 23% (328). ***Average award:*** Freshmen: $16,150. Undergraduates: $48,166. ***Scholarships, grants, and awards by category:*** *Academic interests/achievement:* agriculture, biological sciences, business, education, English, foreign languages, general academic interests/achievements, health fields. *Creative arts/performance:* art/fine arts, cinema/film/broadcasting, journalism/publications, music, theater/drama. *Special achievements/activities:* leadership. *Special characteristics:* local/state students. ***Tuition waivers:*** Full or partial for employees or children of employees, senior citizens.

LOANS ***Student loans:*** $6,444,475 (99% need-based, 1% non-need-based). ***Average need-based loan:*** Freshmen: $1842. Undergraduates: $2646. ***Parent loans:*** $251,693 (100% need-based). ***Programs:*** Federal Direct (Subsidized and Unsubsidized Stafford, PLUS), Perkins, state, college/university.

WORK-STUDY ***Federal work-study:*** Total amount: $3,209,767; jobs available. ***State or other work-study/employment:*** Total amount: $163,895 (100% need-based). Part-time jobs available.

APPLYING FOR FINANCIAL AID ***Required financial aid forms:*** FAFSA, institution's own form, scholarship request form. ***Financial aid deadline:*** 4/1 (priority: 3/1). ***Notification date:*** Continuous.

CONTACT Ms. Rena Gallego, Director of Financial Aid, Sul Ross State University, PO Box C-113, Alpine, TX 79832, 915-837-8059 or toll-free 888-722-7778.

SUSQUEHANNA UNIVERSITY

Selinsgrove, PA

ABOUT THE INSTITUTION Independent religious, coed. 41 undergraduate majors.

GIFT AID (NEED-BASED) ***Scholarships, grants, and awards:*** Federal Pell, FSEOG, state, private, college/university gift aid from institutional funds.

GIFT AID (NON-NEED-BASED) ***Scholarships, grants, and awards by category:*** *Academic interests/achievement:* business, general academic interests/achievements. *Creative arts/performance:* creative writing, music, theater/drama. *Special achievements/activities:* general special achievements/activities. *Special characteristics:* children and siblings of alumni, children of faculty/staff, members of minority groups, relatives of clergy, veterans.

LOANS ***Programs:*** Federal Direct (Subsidized and Unsubsidized Stafford, PLUS), Perkins, college/university.

WORK-STUDY ***Federal work-study:*** Total amount: $1,661,554; 1,124 jobs averaging $2044. ***State or other work-study/employment:*** Total amount: $416,165 (44% need-based, 56% non-need-based). 84 part-time jobs averaging $4425.

APPLYING FOR FINANCIAL AID ***Required financial aid forms:*** FAFSA, CSS Financial Aid PROFILE, business/farm supplement, prior year federal income tax form(s).

CONTACT Ms. Helen S. Nunn, Director of Financial Aid, Susquehanna University, 514 University Avenue, Selinsgrove, PA 17870, 570-372-4450 or toll-free 800-326-9672. *Fax:* 570-372-2722. *E-mail:* nunn@susqu.edu.

SWARTHMORE COLLEGE

Swarthmore, PA

Tuition & fees: $39,600 **Average undergraduate aid package: $36,571**

ABOUT THE INSTITUTION Independent, coed. 43 undergraduate majors. Institutional methodology is used as a basis for awarding need-based institutional aid.

UNDERGRADUATE EXPENSES for 2010–11 ***Comprehensive fee:*** $51,500 includes full-time tuition ($39,260), mandatory fees ($340), and room and board ($11,900). ***College room only:*** $6100. Room and board charges vary according to board plan. ***Payment plan:*** Installment.

FRESHMAN FINANCIAL AID (Fall 2010, est.) 264 applied for aid; of those 78% were deemed to have need. 100% of freshmen with need received aid; of those 100% had need fully met. ***Average percent of need met:*** 100% (excluding resources awarded to replace EFC). ***Average financial aid package:*** $36,825 (excluding resources awarded to replace EFC). 1% of all full-time freshmen had no need and received non-need-based gift aid.

UNDERGRADUATE FINANCIAL AID (Fall 2010, est.) 856 applied for aid; of those 88% were deemed to have need. 100% of undergraduates with need received aid; of those 100% had need fully met. ***Average percent of need met:*** 100% (excluding resources awarded to replace EFC). ***Average financial aid package:*** $36,571 (excluding resources awarded to replace EFC). 1% of all full-time undergraduates had no need and received non-need-based gift aid.

GIFT AID (NEED-BASED) ***Total amount:*** $26,378,935 (4% federal, 1% state, 93% institutional, 2% external sources). ***Receiving aid:*** Freshmen: 53% (205); all full-time undergraduates: 50% (756). ***Average award:*** Freshmen: $35,279; Undergraduates: $35,033. ***Scholarships, grants, and awards:*** Federal Pell, FSEOG, state, private, college/university gift aid from institutional funds.

GIFT AID (NON-NEED-BASED) ***Total amount:*** $665,545 (59% institutional, 41% external sources). ***Average award:*** Freshmen: $39,260. Undergraduates: $39,260. ***Scholarships, grants, and awards by category:*** *Academic interests/achievement:* 10 awards ($392,600 total): general academic interests/achievements. ***Tuition waivers:*** Full or partial for employees or children of employees.

LOANS ***Student loans:*** $1,948,637 (100% non-need-based). 44% of past graduating class borrowed through all loan programs. *Average indebtedness per student:* $18,739. ***Parent loans:*** $1,512,551 (100% non-need-based). ***Programs:*** Federal Direct (Subsidized and Unsubsidized Stafford, PLUS), Perkins, college/university.

WORK-STUDY ***Federal work-study:*** Total amount: $746,687; 705 jobs averaging $1651. ***State or other work-study/employment:*** Total amount: $637,469 (79% need-based, 21% non-need-based). Part-time jobs available.

APPLYING FOR FINANCIAL AID ***Required financial aid forms:*** FAFSA, institution's own form, CSS Financial Aid PROFILE, state aid form, noncustodial (divorced/separated) parent's statement, business/farm supplement, federal income tax returns, W-2 forms, year-end paycheck stub. ***Financial aid deadline:*** 2/15. ***Notification date:*** 4/1. Students must reply by 5/1.

CONTACT Laura Talbot, Director of Financial Aid, Swarthmore College, 500 College Avenue, Swarthmore, PA 19081-1397, 610-328-8358 or toll-free 800-667-3110. *Fax:* 610-690-5751. *E-mail:* finaid@swarthmore.edu.

SWEDISH INSTITUTE, COLLEGE OF HEALTH SCIENCES

New York, NY

CONTACT Financial Aid Office, Swedish Institute, College of Health Sciences, 226 West 26th Street, New York, NY 10001-6700, 212-924-5900.

SWEET BRIAR COLLEGE

Sweet Briar, VA

Tuition & fees: $30,195 **Average undergraduate aid package: $20,197**

ABOUT THE INSTITUTION Independent, women only. 39 undergraduate majors. Federal methodology is used as a basis for awarding need-based institutional aid.

UNDERGRADUATE EXPENSES for 2010–11 ***Comprehensive fee:*** $40,975 includes full-time tuition ($29,720), mandatory fees ($475), and room and board ($10,780). Full-time tuition and fees vary according to program. Room and board charges vary according to board plan. ***Part-time tuition:*** $760 per credit hour. Part-time tuition and fees vary according to program. ***Payment plan:*** Installment.

FRESHMAN FINANCIAL AID (Fall 2009) 116 applied for aid; of those 100% were deemed to have need. 99% of freshmen with need received aid; of those 61% had need fully met. ***Average percent of need met:*** 24% (excluding resources awarded to replace EFC). ***Average financial aid package:*** $20,476 (excluding resources awarded to replace EFC). 31% of all full-time freshmen had no need and received non-need-based gift aid.

UNDERGRADUATE FINANCIAL AID (Fall 2009) 417 applied for aid; of those 100% were deemed to have need. 99% of undergraduates with need received aid; of those 69% had need fully met. ***Average percent of need met:*** 26% (excluding resources awarded to replace EFC). ***Average financial aid package:*** $20,197 (excluding resources awarded to replace EFC). 33% of all full-time undergraduates had no need and received non-need-based gift aid.

GIFT AID (NEED-BASED) ***Total amount:*** $6,676,949 (9% federal, 13% state, 74% institutional, 4% external sources). ***Receiving aid:*** Freshmen: 58% (87); all full-time undergraduates: 59% (346). ***Average award:*** Freshmen: $20,233; Undergraduates: $18,168. ***Scholarships, grants, and awards:*** Federal Pell, FSEOG, state, private, college/university gift aid from institutional funds.

GIFT AID (NON-NEED-BASED) ***Total amount:*** $2,750,198 (1% federal, 10% state, 87% institutional, 2% external sources). ***Receiving aid:*** Freshmen: 31% (46). Undergraduates: 33% (190). ***Average award:*** Freshmen: $11,706. Undergraduates: $12,266. ***Scholarships, grants, and awards by category:*** *Academic interests/achievement:* general academic interests/achievements, premedicine. *Creative arts/performance:* art/fine arts, general creative arts/ performance, music. *Special achievements/activities:* community service. *Special characteristics:* adult students, general special characteristics, international students, local/state students. ***Tuition waivers:*** Full or partial for employees or children of employees, adult students, senior citizens.

LOANS ***Student loans:*** $1,842,546 (91% need-based, 9% non-need-based). 54% of past graduating class borrowed through all loan programs. *Average indebtedness per student:* $27,712. ***Average need-based loan:*** Freshmen: $3062. Undergraduates: $3977. ***Parent loans:*** $2,564,885 (82% need-based, 18% non-need-based). ***Programs:*** Federal Direct (Subsidized and Unsubsidized Stafford, PLUS), Perkins, college/university.

WORK-STUDY ***Federal work-study:*** Total amount: $85,433; jobs available. ***State or other work-study/employment:*** Total amount: $38,561 (99% need-based, 1% non-need-based). Part-time jobs available.

APPLYING FOR FINANCIAL AID ***Required financial aid forms:*** FAFSA, noncustodial (divorced/separated) parent's statement. ***Financial aid deadline (priority):*** 2/15. ***Notification date:*** Continuous beginning 3/1. Students must reply by 5/1 or within 2 weeks of notification.

CONTACT Bobbi Carpenter, Director of Financial Aid, Sweet Briar College, Box AS, Sweet Briar, VA 24595, 800-381-6156 or toll-free 800-381-6142. *Fax:* 434-381-6450. *E-mail:* bcarpenter@sbc.edu.

SYRACUSE UNIVERSITY

Syracuse, NY

Tuition & fees: $36,302 **Average undergraduate aid package: $30,640**

ABOUT THE INSTITUTION Independent, coed. 95 undergraduate majors. Institutional methodology is used as a basis for awarding need-based institutional aid.

UNDERGRADUATE EXPENSES for 2010–11 ***Comprehensive fee:*** $49,152 includes full-time tuition ($34,970), mandatory fees ($1332), and room and board ($12,850). ***College room only:*** $6800. Room and board charges vary according to board plan and housing facility. ***Part-time tuition:*** $1522 per credit hour. ***Payment plan:*** Installment.

FRESHMAN FINANCIAL AID (Fall 2010, est.) 2,591 applied for aid; of those 79% were deemed to have need. 100% of freshmen with need received aid; of those 82% had need fully met. ***Average percent of need met:*** 95% (excluding resources awarded to replace EFC). ***Average financial aid package:*** $31,675 (excluding resources awarded to replace EFC). 11% of all full-time freshmen had no need and received non-need-based gift aid.

UNDERGRADUATE FINANCIAL AID (Fall 2010, est.) 9,123 applied for aid; of those 86% were deemed to have need. 100% of undergraduates with need received aid; of those 65% had need fully met. ***Average percent of need met:*** 87% (excluding resources awarded to replace EFC). ***Average financial aid package:*** $30,640 (excluding resources awarded to replace EFC). 12% of all full-time undergraduates had no need and received non-need-based gift aid.

GIFT AID (NEED-BASED) ***Total amount:*** $193,116,702 (12% federal, 5% state, 81% institutional, 2% external sources). ***Receiving aid:*** Freshmen: 54% (1,883); all full-time undergraduates: 54% (7,107). ***Average award:*** Freshmen: $22,700; Undergraduates: $22,250. ***Scholarships, grants, and awards:*** Federal Pell, FSEOG, state, private, college/university gift aid from institutional funds.

GIFT AID (NON-NEED-BASED) ***Total amount:*** $16,203,339 (8% federal, 85% institutional, 7% external sources). ***Receiving aid:*** Freshmen: 3% (116). Undergraduates: 3% (344). ***Average award:*** Freshmen: $7880. Undergraduates: $9100. ***Scholarships, grants, and awards by category:*** *Academic interests/achievement:* general academic interests/achievements. *Creative arts/performance:* art/fine arts, music. ***Tuition waivers:*** Full or partial for employees or children of employees.

LOANS ***Student loans:*** $70,096,757 (93% need-based, 7% non-need-based). 64% of past graduating class borrowed through all loan programs. *Average indebtedness per student:* $30,813. ***Average need-based loan:*** Freshmen: $6500. Undergraduates: $7200. ***Parent loans:*** $33,764,981 (83% need-based, 17% non-need-based). ***Programs:*** Federal Direct (Subsidized and Unsubsidized Stafford, PLUS), Perkins.

WORK-STUDY ***Federal work-study:*** Total amount: $4,100,000; jobs available. ***State or other work-study/employment:*** Part-time jobs available.

ATHLETIC AWARDS Total amount: $13,302,438 (44% need-based, 56% non-need-based).

APPLYING FOR FINANCIAL AID ***Required financial aid forms:*** FAFSA, CSS Financial Aid PROFILE, noncustodial (divorced/separated) parent's statement. ***Financial aid deadline:*** 2/1. ***Notification date:*** 3/15. Students must reply by 5/1.

CONTACT Youlonda Copeland-Morgan, Director of Scholarship and Financial Aid, Syracuse University, 200 Archbold Gymnasium, Syracuse, NY 13244-1140, 315-443-1513. *E-mail:* finmail@syr.edu.

TABOR COLLEGE

Hillsboro, KS

Tuition & fees: $20,630 **Average undergraduate aid package: $20,301**

ABOUT THE INSTITUTION Independent Mennonite Brethren, coed. 67 undergraduate majors. Federal methodology is used as a basis for awarding need-based institutional aid.

UNDERGRADUATE EXPENSES for 2010–11 ***One-time required fee:*** $175. ***Comprehensive fee:*** $27,790 includes full-time tuition ($20,170), mandatory fees ($460), and room and board ($7160). ***College room only:*** $2820. Full-time tuition and fees vary according to course load. Room and board charges vary according to board plan, housing facility, and location. ***Part-time tuition:*** $840 per credit hour. ***Part-time fees:*** $10 per credit hour. Part-time tuition and fees vary according to course load. ***Payment plan:*** Installment.

FRESHMAN FINANCIAL AID (Fall 2010, est.) 153 applied for aid; of those 88% were deemed to have need. 100% of freshmen with need received aid; of those 19% had need fully met. ***Average percent of need met:*** 77% (excluding resources awarded to replace EFC). ***Average financial aid package:*** $19,990 (excluding resources awarded to replace EFC). 12% of all full-time freshmen had no need and received non-need-based gift aid.

UNDERGRADUATE FINANCIAL AID (Fall 2010, est.) 590 applied for aid; of those 83% were deemed to have need. 100% of undergraduates with need received aid; of those 18% had need fully met. ***Average percent of need met:*** 79% (excluding resources awarded to replace EFC). ***Average financial aid package:*** $20,301 (excluding resources awarded to replace EFC). 14% of all full-time undergraduates had no need and received non-need-based gift aid.

GIFT AID (NEED-BASED) ***Total amount:*** $1,841,756 (75% federal, 25% state). ***Receiving aid:*** Freshmen: 74% (113); all full-time undergraduates: 66% (404). ***Average award:*** Freshmen: $4818; Undergraduates: $4702. ***Scholarships, grants, and awards:*** Federal Pell, FSEOG, state, private, college/university gift aid from institutional funds.

GIFT AID (NON-NEED-BASED) ***Total amount:*** $4,291,451 (95% institutional, 5% external sources). ***Receiving aid:*** Freshmen: 88% (135). Undergraduates: 78% (481). ***Average award:*** Freshmen: $8204. Undergraduates: $7559. ***Scholarships, grants, and awards by category:*** *Academic interests/achievement:* biological sciences, communication, general academic interests/achievements, humanities. *Creative arts/performance:* journalism/publications, music, performing arts, theater/drama. *Special achievements/activities:* cheerleading/drum major, general special achievements/activities, religious involvement. *Special characteristics:* children and siblings of alumni, children of faculty/staff, general special characteristics, international students, local/state students, out-of-state students, religious affiliation. ***Tuition waivers:*** Full or partial for employees or children of employees.

LOANS ***Student loans:*** $4,132,486 (100% need-based). 79% of past graduating class borrowed through all loan programs. *Average indebtedness per student:* $27,380. ***Average need-based loan:*** Freshmen: $6235. Undergraduates: $7704. ***Parent loans:*** $678,275 (100% need-based). ***Programs:*** Federal Direct (Subsidized and Unsubsidized Stafford, PLUS), Perkins.

WORK-STUDY ***Federal work-study:*** Total amount: $126,049; 213 jobs averaging $593. ***State or other work-study/employment:*** Part-time jobs available.

ATHLETIC AWARDS Total amount: $1,397,301 (100% non-need-based).

APPLYING FOR FINANCIAL AID ***Required financial aid forms:*** FAFSA, state aid form. ***Financial aid deadline:*** 8/15 (priority: 3/1). ***Notification date:*** Continuous beginning 3/15. Students must reply within 4 weeks of notification.

CONTACT Mr. Scott Franz, Director of Student Financial Assistance, Tabor College, 400 South Jefferson, Hillsboro, KS 67063, 620-947-3121 Ext. 1726 or toll-free 800-822-6799. *Fax:* 620-947-6276. *E-mail:* scottf@tabor.edu.

TALLADEGA COLLEGE

Talladega, AL

CONTACT K. Michael Francois, Director of Financial Aid, Talladega College, 627 West Battle Street, Talladega, AL 35160, 256-761-6341 or toll-free 800-762-2468 (in-state), 800-633-2440 (out-of-state). *Fax:* 256-761-6462.

TALMUDICAL ACADEMY OF NEW JERSEY

Adelphia, NJ

CONTACT Office of Financial Aid, Talmudical Academy of New Jersey, Route 524, Adelphia, NJ 07710, 732-431-1600.

TALMUDICAL INSTITUTE OF UPSTATE NEW YORK

Rochester, NY

ABOUT THE INSTITUTION Independent Jewish, men only. ***Awards:*** also offers some graduate courses. 1 undergraduate major. ***Total enrollment:*** 26. Undergraduates: 22.

GIFT AID (NEED-BASED) ***Scholarships, grants, and awards:*** Federal Pell, FSEOG, college/university gift aid from institutional funds.

GIFT AID (NON-NEED-BASED) ***Scholarships, grants, and awards by category:*** *Academic interests/achievement:* religion/biblical studies.

WORK-STUDY ***Federal work-study:*** Total amount: $8000; jobs available.

APPLYING FOR FINANCIAL AID ***Required financial aid form:*** FAFSA.

CONTACT Mrs. Ella Berenstein, Financial Aid Administrator, Talmudical Institute of Upstate New York, 769 Park Avenue, Rochester, NY 14607-3046, 585-473-2810.

TALMUDICAL SEMINARY OHOLEI TORAH

Brooklyn, NY

CONTACT Financial Aid Administrator, Talmudical Seminary Oholei Torah, 667 Eastern Parkway, Brooklyn, NY 11213-3310, 718-774-5050.

TALMUDICAL YESHIVA OF PHILADELPHIA

Philadelphia, PA

CONTACT Director of Student Financial Aid/Registrar, Talmudical Yeshiva of Philadelphia, 6063 Drexel Road, Philadelphia, PA 19131-1296, 215-473-1212.

TALMUDIC COLLEGE OF FLORIDA

Miami Beach, FL

CONTACT Rabbi Ira Hill, Director of Financial Aid, Talmudic College of Florida, 1910 Alton Road, Miami Beach, FL 33139, 305-534-7050 or toll-free 888-825-6834. *Fax:* 305-534-8444.

TARLETON STATE UNIVERSITY

Stephenville, TX

Tuition & fees (TX res): $6199 **Average undergraduate aid package: $9988**

ABOUT THE INSTITUTION State-supported, coed. 76 undergraduate majors. Federal methodology is used as a basis for awarding need-based institutional aid.

UNDERGRADUATE EXPENSES for 2010–11 ***Tuition, state resident:*** full-time $4319; part-time $143.97 per credit hour. ***Tuition, nonresident:*** full-time $13,619; part-time $453.97 per credit hour. ***Required fees:*** full-time $1880. Full-time tuition and fees vary according to course load and degree level. Part-time tuition and fees vary according to course load and degree level. ***College room and board:*** $6591; ***Room only:*** $3381. Room and board charges vary according to board plan and housing facility. ***Payment plan:*** Installment.

FRESHMAN FINANCIAL AID (Fall 2009) 1,989 applied for aid; of those 77% were deemed to have need. 73% of freshmen with need received aid; of those 66% had need fully met. ***Average percent of need met:*** 50% (excluding resources awarded to replace EFC). ***Average financial aid package:*** $6502 (excluding resources awarded to replace EFC). 17% of all full-time freshmen had no need and received non-need-based gift aid.

UNDERGRADUATE FINANCIAL AID (Fall 2009) 10,919 applied for aid; of those 85% were deemed to have need. 74% of undergraduates with need received aid; of those 28% had need fully met. ***Average percent of need met:*** 43% (excluding resources awarded to replace EFC). ***Average financial aid package:*** $9988 (excluding resources awarded to replace EFC). 14% of all full-time undergraduates had no need and received non-need-based gift aid.

GIFT AID (NEED-BASED) ***Total amount:*** $21,992,711 (66% federal, 21% state, 7% institutional, 6% external sources). ***Receiving aid:*** Freshmen: 34% (851); all full-time undergraduates: 38% (5,644). ***Average award:*** Freshmen: $3727; Undergraduates: $2722. ***Scholarships, grants, and awards:*** Federal Pell, FSEOG, state, private, college/university gift aid from institutional funds.

GIFT AID (NON-NEED-BASED) ***Total amount:*** $7,253,222 (44% institutional, 56% external sources). ***Receiving aid:*** Freshmen: 26% (644). Undergraduates: 20% (2,953). ***Average award:*** Freshmen: $2992. Undergraduates: $3193.

LOANS ***Student loans:*** $37,326,344 (43% need-based, 57% non-need-based). 56% of past graduating class borrowed through all loan programs. *Average indebtedness per student:* $14,879. ***Average need-based loan:*** Freshmen: $1916. Undergraduates: $2344. ***Parent loans:*** $4,264,032 (100% non-need-based). ***Programs:*** Federal Direct (Subsidized and Unsubsidized Stafford, PLUS), state, college/university.

WORK-STUDY ***Federal work-study:*** Total amount: $153,924; jobs available. ***State or other work-study/employment:*** Total amount: $18,291 (100% need-based). Part-time jobs available.

ATHLETIC AWARDS Total amount: $1,196,130 (100% non-need-based).

APPLYING FOR FINANCIAL AID ***Required financial aid form:*** FAFSA. ***Financial aid deadline:*** 11/1 (priority: 4/1). ***Notification date:*** Continuous beginning 3/1. Students must reply within 2 weeks of notification.

CONTACT Ms. Betty Murray, Director of Student Financial Aid, Tarleton State University, Box T-0310, Stephenville, TX 76402, 254-968-9070 or toll-free 800-687-8236 (in-state). *Fax:* 254-968-9600. *E-mail:* finaid@tarleton.edu.

TAYLOR UNIVERSITY

Upland, IN

Tuition & fees: $27,438 **Average undergraduate aid package: $18,328**

ABOUT THE INSTITUTION Independent interdenominational, coed. 60 undergraduate majors. Federal methodology is used as a basis for awarding need-based institutional aid.

UNDERGRADUATE EXPENSES for 2011–12 ***Comprehensive fee:*** $34,656 includes full-time tuition ($27,200), mandatory fees ($238), and room and board ($7218). Full-time tuition and fees vary according to course load. Room and board charges vary according to board plan and housing facility. Part-time tuition and fees vary according to course load. ***Payment plan:*** Installment.

FRESHMAN FINANCIAL AID (Fall 2010, est.) 387 applied for aid; of those 81% were deemed to have need. 100% of freshmen with need received aid; of those 21% had need fully met. ***Average percent of need met:*** 73% (excluding resources awarded to replace EFC). ***Average financial aid package:*** $17,984 (excluding resources awarded to replace EFC). 26% of all full-time freshmen had no need and received non-need-based gift aid.

UNDERGRADUATE FINANCIAL AID (Fall 2010, est.) 1,358 applied for aid; of those 85% were deemed to have need. 100% of undergraduates with need received aid; of those 21% had need fully met. ***Average percent of need met:*** 73% (excluding resources awarded to replace EFC). ***Average financial aid package:*** $18,328 (excluding resources awarded to replace EFC). 25% of all full-time undergraduates had no need and received non-need-based gift aid.

GIFT AID (NEED-BASED) ***Total amount:*** $13,669,910 (16% federal, 7% state, 70% institutional, 7% external sources). ***Receiving aid:*** Freshmen: 66% (297); all full-time undergraduates: 64% (1,094). ***Average award:*** Freshmen: $14,469; Undergraduates: $14,416. ***Scholarships, grants, and awards:*** Federal Pell, FSEOG, state, private, college/university gift aid from institutional funds, Academic Competitiveness Grants, National SMART Grants.

GIFT AID (NON-NEED-BASED) ***Total amount:*** $3,959,474 (1% state, 83% institutional, 16% external sources). ***Receiving aid:*** Freshmen: 10% (43). Undergraduates: 7% (125). ***Average award:*** Freshmen: $6295. Undergraduates: $6632. ***Scholarships, grants, and awards by category:*** *Academic interests/achievement:* 808 awards ($4,386,949 total): general academic interests/achievements. *Creative arts/performance:* 79 awards ($211,690 total): music, theater/drama. *Special achievements/activities:* 164 awards ($535,639 total): leadership. *Special characteristics:* 812 awards ($3,081,746 total): children and siblings of alumni, children of faculty/staff, ethnic background, international students, religious affiliation. ***Tuition waivers:*** Full or partial for employees or children of employees, senior citizens.

LOANS ***Student loans:*** $9,992,828 (72% need-based, 28% non-need-based). 52% of past graduating class borrowed through all loan programs. *Average indebtedness per student:* $21,302. ***Average need-based loan:*** Freshmen: $4545. Undergraduates: $4782. ***Parent loans:*** $17,120,863 (30% need-based, 70% non-need-based). ***Programs:*** Federal Direct (Subsidized and Unsubsidized Stafford, PLUS), Perkins, college/university.

WORK-STUDY ***Federal work-study:*** Total amount: $541,515; 860 jobs averaging $630.

ATHLETIC AWARDS Total amount: $1,821,202 (60% need-based, 40% non-need-based).

APPLYING FOR FINANCIAL AID ***Required financial aid form:*** FAFSA. ***Financial aid deadline:*** 3/10. ***Notification date:*** Continuous beginning 3/1. Students must reply by 5/1.

CONTACT Mr. Timothy A. Nace, Director of Financial Aid, Taylor University, 236 West Reade Avenue, Upland, IN 46989-1001, 765-998-5358 or toll-free 800-882-3456. *Fax:* 765-998-4910. *E-mail:* tmnace@taylor.edu.

TELSHE YESHIVA–CHICAGO

Chicago, IL

CONTACT Office of Financial Aid, Telshe Yeshiva–Chicago, 3535 West Foster Avenue, Chicago, IL 60625-5598, 773-463-7738.

TEMPLE BAPTIST COLLEGE

Cincinnati, OH

CONTACT Financial Aid Office, Temple Baptist College, 11965 Kenn Road, Cincinnati, OH 45240, 513-851-3800.

TEMPLE UNIVERSITY

Philadelphia, PA

Tuition & fees (PA res): $12,424 **Average undergraduate aid package: $15,362**

ABOUT THE INSTITUTION State-related, coed. 121 undergraduate majors. Federal methodology is used as a basis for awarding need-based institutional aid.

UNDERGRADUATE EXPENSES for 2010–11 ***Tuition, state resident:*** full-time $11,834; part-time $457 per credit hour. ***Tuition, nonresident:*** full-time $21,662; part-time $771 per credit hour. ***Required fees:*** full-time $590; $213 per semester hour. Full-time tuition and fees vary according to course load, program, and reciprocity agreements. Part-time tuition and fees vary according to course load, program, and reciprocity agreements. ***College room and board:*** $9550; ***Room only:*** $6370. Room and board charges vary according to board plan and housing facility. ***Payment plan:*** Installment.

FRESHMAN FINANCIAL AID (Fall 2009) 3,918 applied for aid; of those 75% were deemed to have need. 98% of freshmen with need received aid; of those 33% had need fully met. ***Average percent of need met:*** 86% (excluding resources awarded to replace EFC). ***Average financial aid package:*** $15,802 (excluding resources awarded to replace EFC). 16% of all full-time freshmen had no need and received non-need-based gift aid.

UNDERGRADUATE FINANCIAL AID (Fall 2009) 21,583 applied for aid; of those 79% were deemed to have need. 94% of undergraduates with need received aid; of those 32% had need fully met. ***Average percent of need met:*** 85% (excluding resources awarded to replace EFC). ***Average financial aid package:*** $15,362 (excluding resources awarded to replace EFC). 12% of all full-time undergraduates had no need and received non-need-based gift aid.

GIFT AID (NEED-BASED) ***Total amount:*** $98,550,423 (43% federal, 24% state, 33% institutional). ***Receiving aid:*** Freshmen: 69% (2,881); all full-time undergraduates: 67% (16,002). ***Average award:*** Freshmen: $6390; Undergraduates: $5753. ***Scholarships, grants, and awards:*** Federal Pell, FSEOG, state, private, college/university gift aid from institutional funds, Federal Nursing.

GIFT AID (NON-NEED-BASED) ***Total amount:*** $63,507,478 (18% institutional, 82% external sources). ***Receiving aid:*** Freshmen: 42% (1,757). Undergraduates: 30% (7,294). ***Average award:*** Freshmen: $7540. Undergraduates: $8759. ***Scholarships, grants, and awards by category:*** *Academic interests/achievement:* general academic interests/achievements. *Creative arts/performance:* art/fine arts, general creative arts/performance, music, performing arts. *Special achievements/activities:* cheerleading/drum major. *Special characteristics:* children of faculty/staff, general special characteristics, veterans. ***Tuition waivers:*** Full or partial for employees or children of employees.

LOANS ***Student loans:*** $141,561,466 (50% need-based, 50% non-need-based). 76% of past graduating class borrowed through all loan programs. *Average indebtedness per student:* $31,123. ***Average need-based loan:*** Freshmen: $3193. Undergraduates: $4137. ***Parent loans:*** $1,662,278 (100% non-need-based). ***Programs:*** Federal Direct (Subsidized and Unsubsidized Stafford, PLUS), Perkins, Federal Nursing, state, college/university.

WORK-STUDY ***Federal work-study:*** Total amount: $1,829,372; 1,288 jobs available.

ATHLETIC AWARDS Total amount: $8,109,590 (100% non-need-based).

APPLYING FOR FINANCIAL AID ***Required financial aid form:*** FAFSA. ***Financial aid deadline (priority):*** 3/1. ***Notification date:*** Continuous beginning 2/15. Students must reply by 5/1 or within 3 weeks of notification.

CONTACT Dr. John F. Morris, Director of Student Financial Services, Temple University, Conwell Hall, Ground Floor, Philadelphia, PA 19122-6096, 215-204-8760 or toll-free 888-340-2222. *Fax:* 215-204-2016. *E-mail:* john.morris@temple.edu.

TENNESSEE STATE UNIVERSITY

Nashville, TN

CONTACT Mary Chambliss, Director of Financial Aid, Tennessee State University, 3500 John Merritt Boulevard, Nashville, TN 37209-1561, 615-963-5772. *Fax:* 615-963-5108. *E-mail:* mchambliss@tnstate.edu.

TENNESSEE TECHNOLOGICAL UNIVERSITY

Cookeville, TN

Tuition & fees (TN res): $5828   **Average undergraduate aid package: $7217**

ABOUT THE INSTITUTION State-supported, coed. 67 undergraduate majors. Federal methodology is used as a basis for awarding need-based institutional aid.

UNDERGRADUATE EXPENSES for 2010–11 ***Tuition, state resident:*** full-time $5828; part-time $268 per credit hour. ***Tuition, nonresident:*** full-time $18,356; part-time $790 per credit hour. Full-time tuition and fees vary according to course load and program. Part-time tuition and fees vary according to course load and program. ***College room and board:*** $7158; ***Room only:*** $3700. Room and board charges vary according to board plan and housing facility. ***Payment plan:*** Installment.

FRESHMAN FINANCIAL AID (Fall 2010, est.) 1,581 applied for aid; of those 74% were deemed to have need. 100% of freshmen with need received aid; of those 31% had need fully met. ***Average percent of need met:*** 81% (excluding resources awarded to replace EFC). ***Average financial aid package:*** $9997 (excluding resources awarded to replace EFC). 7% of all full-time freshmen had no need and received non-need-based gift aid.

UNDERGRADUATE FINANCIAL AID (Fall 2010, est.) 7,177 applied for aid; of those 80% were deemed to have need. 98% of undergraduates with need received aid; of those 27% had need fully met. ***Average percent of need met:*** 67% (excluding resources awarded to replace EFC). ***Average financial aid package:*** $7217 (excluding resources awarded to replace EFC). 8% of all full-time undergraduates had no need and received non-need-based gift aid.

GIFT AID (NEED-BASED) ***Total amount:*** $20,725,568 (83% federal, 15% state, 2% institutional). ***Receiving aid:*** Freshmen: 38% (716); all full-time undergraduates: 43% (3,636). ***Average award:*** Freshmen: $6118; Undergraduates: $4211. ***Scholarships, grants, and awards:*** Federal Pell, FSEOG, state, private, college/university gift aid from institutional funds, United Negro College Fund.

GIFT AID (NON-NEED-BASED) ***Total amount:*** $34,660,358 (1% federal, 59% state, 16% institutional, 24% external sources). ***Receiving aid:*** Freshmen: 56% (1,066). Undergraduates: 45% (3,848). ***Average award:*** Freshmen: $2099. Undergraduates: $2537. ***Scholarships, grants, and awards by category:*** *Academic interests/achievement:* 1,452 awards ($3,171,718 total): agriculture, biological sciences, business, communication, computer science, education, engineering/technologies, English, foreign languages, general academic interests/achievements, health fields, home economics, humanities, international studies, mathematics, military science, physical sciences, premedicine, social sciences. *Creative arts/performance:* art/fine arts, debating, music. *Special achievements/activities:* 382 awards ($1,543,451 total): cheerleading/drum major, general special achievements/activities. *Special characteristics:* 1,624 awards ($3,470,651 total): children and siblings of alumni, children of educators, children of faculty/staff, children of public servants, ethnic background, first-generation college students, local/state students, members of minority groups, out-of-state students, public servants. ***Tuition waivers:*** Full or partial for employees or children of employees.

LOANS ***Student loans:*** $22,189,516 (58% need-based, 42% non-need-based). 40% of past graduating class borrowed through all loan programs. *Average indebtedness per student:* $9510. ***Average need-based loan:*** Freshmen: $2916. Undergraduates: $3916. ***Parent loans:*** $1,421,036 (100% non-need-based). ***Programs:*** Federal Direct (Subsidized and Unsubsidized Stafford, PLUS), Perkins, college/university.

WORK-STUDY ***Federal work-study:*** Total amount: $388,689; 515 jobs averaging $754. ***State or other work-study/employment:*** Part-time jobs available.

ATHLETIC AWARDS Total amount: $3,122,685 (100% non-need-based).

APPLYING FOR FINANCIAL AID ***Required financial aid form:*** FAFSA. ***Financial aid deadline (priority):*** 3/15. ***Notification date:*** Continuous beginning 4/1. Students must reply within 2 weeks of notification.

CONTACT Lester McKenzie, Director of Financial Aid, Tennessee Technological University, PO Box 5076, 1000 North Dixie Avenue, Cookeville, TN 38501, 931-372-3073 or toll-free 800-255-8881. *Fax:* 931-372-6309. *E-mail:* lmckenzie@tntech.edu.

TENNESSEE TEMPLE UNIVERSITY

Chattanooga, TN

CONTACT Director of Financial Aid, Tennessee Temple University, 1815 Union Avenue, Chattanooga, TN 37404-3587, 423-493-4208 or toll-free 800-553-4050. *Fax:* 423-493-4497.

TENNESSEE WESLEYAN COLLEGE

Athens, TN

Tuition & fees: $19,100   **Average undergraduate aid package: $15,879**

ABOUT THE INSTITUTION Independent United Methodist, coed. 38 undergraduate majors. Federal methodology is used as a basis for awarding need-based institutional aid.

UNDERGRADUATE EXPENSES for 2010–11 ***Comprehensive fee:*** $25,450 includes full-time tuition ($18,500), mandatory fees ($600), and room and board ($6350). Full-time tuition and fees vary according to location. Room and board charges vary according to housing facility. ***Part-time tuition:*** $510 per credit hour. ***Part-time fees:*** $10 per credit hour. Part-time tuition and fees vary according to class time and location. ***Payment plans:*** Installment, deferred payment.

FRESHMAN FINANCIAL AID (Fall 2009) 243 applied for aid; of those 90% were deemed to have need. 98% of freshmen with need received aid; of those 19% had need fully met. ***Average percent of need met:*** 74% (excluding resources awarded to replace EFC). ***Average financial aid package:*** $13,794 (excluding resources awarded to replace EFC). 7% of all full-time freshmen had no need and received non-need-based gift aid.

UNDERGRADUATE FINANCIAL AID (Fall 2009) 924 applied for aid; of those 93% were deemed to have need. 98% of undergraduates with need received aid; of those 16% had need fully met. ***Average percent of need met:*** 68% (excluding resources awarded to replace EFC). ***Average financial aid package:*** $15,879 (excluding resources awarded to replace EFC). 9% of all full-time undergraduates had no need and received non-need-based gift aid.

GIFT AID (NEED-BASED) ***Total amount:*** $9,117,220 (24% federal, 26% state, 46% institutional, 4% external sources). ***Receiving aid:*** Freshmen: 86% (213); all full-time undergraduates: 87% (812). ***Average award:*** Freshmen: $15,253; Undergraduates: $13,562. ***Scholarships, grants, and awards:*** Federal Pell, FSEOG, state, private, college/university gift aid from institutional funds.

GIFT AID (NON-NEED-BASED) ***Total amount:*** $1,422,744 (34% state, 60% institutional, 6% external sources). ***Receiving aid:*** Freshmen: 13% (33). Undergraduates: 11% (105). ***Average award:*** Freshmen: $7784. Undergraduates: $6901. ***Scholarships, grants, and awards by category:*** *Academic interests/achievement:* biological sciences, business, communication, computer science, education, English, foreign languages, general academic interests/achievements, health fields, humanities, international studies, mathematics, physical sciences, premedicine, religion/biblical studies, social sciences. *Creative arts/performance:* music. *Special achievements/activities:* cheerleading/drum major, general special achievements/activities, junior miss, memberships, religious involvement. *Special characteristics:* children and siblings of alumni, children of faculty/staff, general special characteristics, international students, members of minority groups, relatives of clergy, religious affiliation. ***Tuition waivers:*** Full or partial for employees or children of employees.

LOANS ***Student loans:*** $5,082,467 (81% need-based, 19% non-need-based). 48% of past graduating class borrowed through all loan programs. *Average indebtedness per student:* $17,919. ***Average need-based loan:*** Freshmen: $2891. Undergraduates: $3841. ***Parent loans:*** $356,691 (53% need-based, 47% non-need-based). ***Programs:*** Federal Direct (Subsidized and Unsubsidized Stafford, PLUS).

WORK-STUDY ***Federal work-study:*** Total amount: $71,853; jobs available. ***State or other work-study/employment:*** Total amount: $25,440 (100% non-need-based). Part-time jobs available.

ATHLETIC AWARDS Total amount: $2,912,390 (69% need-based, 31% non-need-based).

APPLYING FOR FINANCIAL AID ***Required financial aid forms:*** FAFSA, institution's own form. ***Financial aid deadline:*** Continuous. ***Notification date:*** Continuous beginning 2/15.

CONTACT Mr. Bob Perry, Director of Financial Aid, Tennessee Wesleyan College, PO Box 40, Athens, TN 37371-0040, 423-746-5209 or toll-free 800-PICK-TWC. *Fax:* 423-744-9968. *E-mail:* rkperry@twcnet.edu.

TEXAS A&M INTERNATIONAL UNIVERSITY

Laredo, TX

Tuition & fees (TX res): $6153 **Average undergraduate aid package: $10,749**

ABOUT THE INSTITUTION State-supported, coed. 34 undergraduate majors. Federal methodology is used as a basis for awarding need-based institutional aid.

UNDERGRADUATE EXPENSES for 2011–12 ***Tuition, state resident:*** full-time $4215. ***Tuition, nonresident:*** full-time $13,515. ***Required fees:*** full-time $1938. Full-time tuition and fees vary according to course load. Part-time tuition and fees vary according to course load and reciprocity agreements. ***College room and board:*** $6918; ***Room only:*** $4842. Room and board charges vary according to board plan and housing facility. ***Payment plan:*** Installment.

FRESHMAN FINANCIAL AID (Fall 2010, est.) 830 applied for aid; of those 93% were deemed to have need. 100% of freshmen with need received aid; of those 9% had need fully met. ***Average percent of need met:*** 67% (excluding resources awarded to replace EFC). ***Average financial aid package:*** $10,392 (excluding resources awarded to replace EFC). 5% of all full-time freshmen had no need and received non-need-based gift aid.

UNDERGRADUATE FINANCIAL AID (Fall 2010, est.) 3,514 applied for aid; of those 92% were deemed to have need. 100% of undergraduates with need received aid; of those 11% had need fully met. ***Average percent of need met:*** 67% (excluding resources awarded to replace EFC). ***Average financial aid package:*** $10,749 (excluding resources awarded to replace EFC). 4% of all full-time undergraduates had no need and received non-need-based gift aid.

GIFT AID (NEED-BASED) ***Total amount:*** $25,541,102 (67% federal, 30% state, 3% institutional). ***Receiving aid:*** Freshmen: 86% (746); all full-time undergraduates: 88% (3,230). ***Average award:*** Freshmen: $7322; Undergraduates: $6408. ***Scholarships, grants, and awards:*** Federal Pell, FSEOG, state, college/university gift aid from institutional funds, Federal Nursing.

GIFT AID (NON-NEED-BASED) ***Total amount:*** $2,436,719 (3% state, 77% institutional, 20% external sources). ***Receiving aid:*** Freshmen: 36% (312). Undergraduates: 34% (1,234). ***Average award:*** Freshmen: $3712. Undergraduates: $3604. ***Scholarships, grants, and awards by category:*** *Academic interests/achievement:* 922 awards ($2,321,709 total): business, communication, education, engineering/technologies, English, foreign languages, general academic interests/achievements, health fields, international studies, mathematics, physical sciences, premedicine, social sciences. *Creative arts/performance:* 51 awards ($140,743 total): art/fine arts, dance, music, performing arts. ***Tuition waivers:*** Full or partial for senior citizens.

LOANS ***Student loans:*** $14,280,893 (65% need-based, 35% non-need-based). 64% of past graduating class borrowed through all loan programs. *Average indebtedness per student:* $19,400. ***Average need-based loan:*** Freshmen: $2890. Undergraduates: $4095. ***Parent loans:*** $85,751 (100% non-need-based). ***Programs:*** Federal Direct (Subsidized and Unsubsidized Stafford, PLUS), state, college/university, Hinson-Hazelwood Loan Program.

WORK-STUDY ***Federal work-study:*** Total amount: $245,500; 104 jobs averaging $2361. ***State or other work-study/employment:*** Total amount: $37,768 (100% need-based). 16 part-time jobs averaging $2361.

ATHLETIC AWARDS Total amount: $622,892 (100% non-need-based).

APPLYING FOR FINANCIAL AID ***Required financial aid form:*** FAFSA. ***Financial aid deadline:*** 8/1 (priority: 3/15). ***Notification date:*** Continuous beginning 4/6. Students must reply within 6 weeks of notification.

CONTACT Laura Elizondo, Director of Financial Aid, Texas A&M International University, 5201 University Boulevard, Laredo, TX 78041, 956-326-2225 or toll-free 888-489-2648. *Fax:* 956-326-2224. *E-mail:* laura@tamiu.edu.

TEXAS A&M UNIVERSITY

College Station, TX

Tuition & fees (TX res): $8387 **Average undergraduate aid package: $14,950**

ABOUT THE INSTITUTION State-supported, coed. 110 undergraduate majors. Both federal and institutional methodology are used as a basis for awarding need-based institutional aid.

UNDERGRADUATE EXPENSES for 2010–11 ***Tuition, state resident:*** full-time $5297; part-time $176.55 per credit hour. ***Tuition, nonresident:*** full-time $19,727; part-time $657.55 per credit hour. ***Required fees:*** full-time $3090. ***College room and board:*** $8008. Room and board charges vary according to board plan, housing facility, and location. ***Payment plan:*** Installment.

FRESHMAN FINANCIAL AID (Fall 2010, est.) 5,519 applied for aid; of those 62% were deemed to have need. 99% of freshmen with need received aid; of those 61% had need fully met. ***Average percent of need met:*** 79% (excluding resources awarded to replace EFC). ***Average financial aid package:*** $16,562 (excluding resources awarded to replace EFC). 12% of all full-time freshmen had no need and received non-need-based gift aid.

UNDERGRADUATE FINANCIAL AID (Fall 2010, est.) 20,677 applied for aid; of those 71% were deemed to have need. 98% of undergraduates with need received aid; of those 46% had need fully met. ***Average percent of need met:*** 71% (excluding resources awarded to replace EFC). ***Average financial aid package:*** $14,950 (excluding resources awarded to replace EFC). 5% of all full-time undergraduates had no need and received non-need-based gift aid.

GIFT AID (NEED-BASED) ***Total amount:*** $130,766,419 (31% federal, 27% state, 30% institutional, 12% external sources). ***Receiving aid:*** Freshmen: 44% (3,280); all full-time undergraduates: 36% (12,789). ***Average award:*** Freshmen: $11,138; Undergraduates: $9278. ***Scholarships, grants, and awards:*** Federal Pell, FSEOG, state, private, college/university gift aid from institutional funds.

GIFT AID (NON-NEED-BASED) ***Total amount:*** $16,535,712 (4% federal, 9% state, 51% institutional, 36% external sources). ***Receiving aid:*** Freshmen: 8% (571). Undergraduates: 4% (1,302). ***Average award:*** Freshmen: $3999. Undergraduates: $3532. ***Scholarships, grants, and awards by category:*** *Academic interests/achievement:* agriculture, architecture, biological sciences, business, computer science, education, engineering/technologies, general academic interests/achievements, health fields, physical sciences. *Creative arts/performance:* journalism/publications, performing arts, theater/drama. *Special achievements/activities:* general special achievements/activities, leadership, memberships, rodeo. *Special characteristics:* children of faculty/staff, first-generation college students, local/state students, veterans, veterans' children.

LOANS ***Student loans:*** $107,619,369 (58% need-based, 42% non-need-based). 47% of past graduating class borrowed through all loan programs. *Average indebtedness per student:* $22,243. ***Average need-based loan:*** Freshmen: $5247. Undergraduates: $6454. ***Parent loans:*** $29,793,111 (17% need-based, 83% non-need-based). ***Programs:*** Federal Direct (Subsidized and Unsubsidized Stafford, PLUS), Perkins, state, college/university.

WORK-STUDY ***Federal work-study:*** Total amount: $1,778,805; 693 jobs averaging $2567. ***State or other work-study/employment:*** Total amount: $252,835 (100% need-based). 109 part-time jobs averaging $2320.

ATHLETIC AWARDS Total amount: $5,053,139 (92% need-based, 8% non-need-based).

APPLYING FOR FINANCIAL AID ***Required financial aid form:*** FAFSA. ***Financial aid deadline (priority):*** 3/1. ***Notification date:*** Continuous beginning 4/1. Students must reply within 4 weeks of notification.

CONTACT Scholarships and Financial Aid Office, Texas A&M University, The Pavilion 200, Spence Street, 1252 TAMU, College Station, TX 77842-3016, 979-845-3236. *Fax:* 979-847-9061. *E-mail:* financialaid@tamu.edu.

TEXAS A&M UNIVERSITY AT GALVESTON

Galveston, TX

CONTACT Dennis Carlton, Director for Financial Aid, Texas A&M University at Galveston, PO Box 1675, Galveston, TX 77553-1675, 409-740-4500. *Fax:* 409-740-4959. *E-mail:* carltond@tamug.tamu.edu.

TEXAS A&M UNIVERSITY–COMMERCE

Commerce, TX

Tuition & fees (TX res): $5998 **Average undergraduate aid package: $10,412**

ABOUT THE INSTITUTION State-supported, coed. 75 undergraduate majors. Federal methodology is used as a basis for awarding need-based institutional aid.

UNDERGRADUATE EXPENSES for 2010–11 ***Tuition, state resident:*** full-time $4490. ***Tuition, nonresident:*** full-time $13,790. ***Required fees:*** full-time $1508. Full-time tuition and fees vary according to course load. Part-time tuition and fees vary according to course load. ***College room and board:*** $7090. Room and board charges vary according to board plan and housing facility. ***Payment plan:*** Installment.

FRESHMAN FINANCIAL AID (Fall 2010, est.) 669 applied for aid; of those 85% were deemed to have need. 99% of freshmen with need received aid; of those 52% had need fully met. ***Average percent of need met:*** 83% (excluding resources awarded to replace EFC). ***Average financial aid package:*** $12,642 (excluding resources awarded to replace EFC). 12% of all full-time freshmen had no need and received non-need-based gift aid.

UNDERGRADUATE FINANCIAL AID (Fall 2010, est.) 3,853 applied for aid; of those 88% were deemed to have need. 99% of undergraduates with need received aid; of those 31% had need fully met. ***Average percent of need met:*** 64% (excluding resources awarded to replace EFC). ***Average financial aid package:*** $10,412 (excluding resources awarded to replace EFC). 7% of all full-time undergraduates had no need and received non-need-based gift aid.

GIFT AID (NEED-BASED) ***Total amount:*** $23,248,032 (68% federal, 17% state, 13% institutional, 2% external sources). ***Receiving aid:*** Freshmen: 73% (547); all full-time undergraduates: 66% (3,078). ***Average award:*** Freshmen: $10,815; Undergraduates: $7946. ***Scholarships, grants, and awards:*** Federal Pell, FSEOG, state, private, college/university gift aid from institutional funds.

GIFT AID (NON-NEED-BASED) ***Total amount:*** $1,919,150 (2% federal, 89% institutional, 9% external sources). ***Average award:*** Freshmen: $2416. Undergraduates: $2343. ***Scholarships, grants, and awards by category:*** *Academic interests/achievement:* agriculture, general academic interests/achievements. *Creative arts/performance:* art/fine arts, journalism/publications, music, theater/drama. *Special achievements/activities:* cheerleading/drum major, general special achievements/activities, leadership. ***Tuition waivers:*** Full or partial for senior citizens.

LOANS ***Student loans:*** $29,602,950 (92% need-based, 8% non-need-based). 69% of past graduating class borrowed through all loan programs. *Average indebtedness per student:* $26,090. ***Average need-based loan:*** Freshmen: $4037. Undergraduates: $4140. ***Parent loans:*** $2,646,010 (66% need-based, 34% non-need-based). ***Programs:*** Federal Direct (Subsidized and Unsubsidized Stafford, PLUS), Perkins, state.

WORK-STUDY ***Federal work-study:*** Total amount: $476,779; 117 jobs averaging $4019. ***State or other work-study/employment:*** Total amount: $117,384 (100% need-based). 39 part-time jobs averaging $2743.

ATHLETIC AWARDS Total amount: $1,198,935 (63% need-based, 37% non-need-based).

APPLYING FOR FINANCIAL AID ***Required financial aid form:*** FAFSA. ***Financial aid deadline (priority):*** 4/15. ***Notification date:*** Continuous beginning 5/15. Students must reply within 2 weeks of notification.

CONTACT Maria Ramos, Director of Financial Aid, Texas A&M University–Commerce, PO Box 3011, Commerce, TX 75429, 903-886-5091 or toll-free 800-331-3878. *Fax:* 903-886-5098. *E-mail:* maria_ramos@tamu-commerce.edu.

TEXAS A&M UNIVERSITY–CORPUS CHRISTI

Corpus Christi, TX

Tuition & fees (TX res): $6514 **Average undergraduate aid package: $9559**

ABOUT THE INSTITUTION State-supported, coed. 62 undergraduate majors. Federal methodology is used as a basis for awarding need-based institutional aid.

UNDERGRADUATE EXPENSES for 2011–12 ***Tuition, state resident:*** full-time $4494; part-time $157 per credit. ***Tuition, nonresident:*** full-time $13,794; part-time $467 per credit. ***Required fees:*** full-time $2020; $120 per credit hour. Full-time tuition and fees vary according to course level, course load, and degree level. Part-time tuition and fees vary according to course level, course load, and degree level. ***College room and board:*** $9528; ***Room only:*** $6677. Room and board charges vary according to housing facility and location. ***Payment plan:*** Installment.

FRESHMAN FINANCIAL AID (Fall 2010, est.) 1,006 applied for aid; of those 81% were deemed to have need. 99% of freshmen with need received aid; of those 14% had need fully met. ***Average percent of need met:*** 69% (excluding resources awarded to replace EFC). ***Average financial aid package:*** $10,243 (excluding resources awarded to replace EFC). 9% of all full-time freshmen had no need and received non-need-based gift aid.

UNDERGRADUATE FINANCIAL AID (Fall 2010, est.) 3,401 applied for aid; of those 83% were deemed to have need. 97% of undergraduates with need received aid; of those 11% had need fully met. ***Average percent of need met:*** 65% (excluding resources awarded to replace EFC). ***Average financial aid package:*** $9559 (excluding resources awarded to replace EFC). 10% of all full-time undergraduates had no need and received non-need-based gift aid.

GIFT AID (NEED-BASED) ***Total amount:*** $23,020,895 (70% federal, 23% state, 7% institutional). ***Receiving aid:*** Freshmen: 57% (679); all full-time undergraduates: 49% (2,232). ***Average award:*** Freshmen: $7784; Undergraduates: $6498. ***Scholarships, grants, and awards:*** Federal Pell, FSEOG, state, college/university gift aid from institutional funds.

GIFT AID (NON-NEED-BASED) ***Total amount:*** $2,906,481 (75% institutional, 25% external sources). ***Receiving aid:*** Freshmen: 12% (142). Undergraduates: 10% (439). ***Average award:*** Freshmen: $2548. Undergraduates: $1984. ***Scholarships, grants, and awards by category:*** *Academic interests/achievement:* general academic interests/achievements. *Creative arts/performance:* art/fine arts, general creative arts/performance. *Special characteristics:* first-generation college students, international students. ***Tuition waivers:*** Full or partial for employees or children of employees, senior citizens.

LOANS ***Student loans:*** $31,793,459 (47% need-based, 53% non-need-based). 59% of past graduating class borrowed through all loan programs. *Average indebtedness per student:* $18,314. ***Average need-based loan:*** Freshmen: $3227. Undergraduates: $4183. ***Parent loans:*** $6,936,221 (100% non-need-based). ***Programs:*** Perkins, state, college/university.

WORK-STUDY ***Federal work-study:*** Total amount: $487,127; 132 jobs averaging $3599. ***State or other work-study/employment:*** Total amount: $417,598 (100% need-based). 124 part-time jobs averaging $3384.

ATHLETIC AWARDS Total amount: $1,607,989 (100% non-need-based).

APPLYING FOR FINANCIAL AID ***Required financial aid form:*** FAFSA. ***Financial aid deadline (priority):*** 3/31. ***Notification date:*** Continuous beginning 4/1. Students must reply within 2 weeks of notification.

CONTACT Financial Assistance Office, Texas A&M University–Corpus Christi, 6300 Ocean Drive, Corpus Christi, TX 78412-5503, 361-825-2338 or toll-free 800-482-6822. *Fax:* 361-825-6095. *E-mail:* faoweb@tamucc.edu.

TEXAS A&M UNIVERSITY–KINGSVILLE

Kingsville, TX

CONTACT Ralph Perri, Director, Financial Aid, Texas A&M University–Kingsville, 700 University Boulevard, Kingsville, TX 78363, 361-593-2883 or toll-free 800-687-6000. *Fax:* 361-593-3036. *E-mail:* financial.aid@tamuk.edu.

TEXAS A&M UNIVERSITY–SAN ANTONIO

San Antonio, TX

CONTACT Financial Aid Office, Texas A&M University–San Antonio, 1450 Gillette Boulevard, San Antonio, TX 78224, 210-932-6299.

TEXAS A&M UNIVERSITY–TEXARKANA

Texarkana, TX

Tuition & fees (TX res): $4946 **Average undergraduate aid package: $7607**

ABOUT THE INSTITUTION State-supported, coed. 20 undergraduate majors. Federal methodology is used as a basis for awarding need-based institutional aid.

UNDERGRADUATE EXPENSES for 2010–11 ***Tuition, state resident:*** full-time $4946. ***Tuition, nonresident:*** full-time $6505. Full-time tuition and fees vary according to course level, course load, and student level. Part-time tuition and fees vary according to course level, course load, and student level. ***Payment plan:*** Installment.

UNDERGRADUATE FINANCIAL AID (Fall 2010, est.) 1,050 applied for aid; of those 92% were deemed to have need. 100% of undergraduates with need received aid. ***Average percent of need met:*** 73% (excluding resources awarded to replace EFC). ***Average financial aid package:*** $7607 (excluding resources awarded to replace EFC).

GIFT AID (NEED-BASED) ***Total amount:*** $3,949,318 (66% federal, 12% state, 22% institutional). ***Receiving aid:*** Entering class: 36% (44); all full-time undergraduates: 55% (727). ***Average award:*** Freshmen: $2790; Undergraduates: $3089. ***Scholarships, grants, and awards:*** Federal Pell, FSEOG, state, private, college/university gift aid from institutional funds.

GIFT AID (NON-NEED-BASED) ***Receiving aid:*** Freshmen: 18% (22). Undergraduates: 30% (400). ***Scholarships, grants, and awards by category:*** *Academic interests/achievement:* business, education, engineering/technologies, English, general academic interests/achievements, mathematics, social sciences. *Special achievements/activities:* community service, general special achievements/activities, leadership, memberships.

LOANS ***Student loans:*** $4,344,179 (54% need-based, 46% non-need-based). ***Average need-based loan:*** Freshmen: $2361. Undergraduates: $4164. ***Programs:*** Federal Direct (Subsidized and Unsubsidized Stafford, PLUS), college/university.

WORK-STUDY ***Federal work-study:*** Total amount: $43,877; 25 jobs averaging $2190. ***State or other work-study/employment:*** Total amount: $6200 (100% need-based). 3 part-time jobs averaging $3408.

APPLYING FOR FINANCIAL AID ***Required financial aid forms:*** FAFSA, institution's own form, state aid form. ***Financial aid deadline (priority):*** 5/1. ***Notification date:*** Continuous beginning 7/15. Students must reply within 2 weeks of notification.

CONTACT Debra La Grone, Director of Financial Aid and Veterans Services, Texas A&M University–Texarkana, 7101 University Avenue, Texarkana, TX 75503, 903-223-3060. *Fax:* 903-223-3140. *E-mail:* dlagrone@tamut.edu.

TEXAS CHRISTIAN UNIVERSITY

Fort Worth, TX

Tuition & fees: $32,490 **Average undergraduate aid package: $20,378**

ABOUT THE INSTITUTION Independent religious, coed. 97 undergraduate majors. Federal methodology is used as a basis for awarding need-based institutional aid.

UNDERGRADUATE EXPENSES for 2011–12 ***Comprehensive fee:*** $43,090 includes full-time tuition ($32,400), mandatory fees ($90), and room and board ($10,600). Room and board charges vary according to board plan and housing facility. ***Part-time fees:*** $90 per term. Part-time tuition and fees vary according to course load. ***Payment plans:*** Tuition prepayment, installment.

FRESHMAN FINANCIAL AID (Fall 2010, est.) 961 applied for aid; of those 75% were deemed to have need. 99% of freshmen with need received aid; of those 25% had need fully met. ***Average percent of need met:*** 64% (excluding resources awarded to replace EFC). ***Average financial aid package:*** $18,496 (excluding resources awarded to replace EFC). 21% of all full-time freshmen had no need and received non-need-based gift aid.

UNDERGRADUATE FINANCIAL AID (Fall 2010, est.) 3,941 applied for aid; of those 82% were deemed to have need. 98% of undergraduates with need received aid; of those 25% had need fully met. ***Average percent of need met:*** 64% (excluding resources awarded to replace EFC). ***Average financial aid package:*** $20,378 (excluding resources awarded to replace EFC). 23% of all full-time undergraduates had no need and received non-need-based gift aid.

GIFT AID (NEED-BASED) ***Total amount:*** $48,242,256 (13% federal, 11% state, 73% institutional, 3% external sources). ***Receiving aid:*** Freshmen: 38% (689); all full-time undergraduates: 39% (2,949). ***Average award:*** Freshmen: $15,845; Undergraduates: $17,417. ***Scholarships, grants, and awards:*** Federal Pell, FSEOG, state, private, college/university gift aid from institutional funds.

GIFT AID (NON-NEED-BASED) ***Total amount:*** $23,283,972 (97% institutional, 3% external sources). ***Receiving aid:*** Freshmen: 24% (441). Undergraduates: 24% (1,814). ***Average award:*** Freshmen: $10,084. Undergraduates: $11,301. ***Scholarships, grants, and awards by category:*** *Academic interests/achievement:* 3,036 awards ($28,141,064 total): agriculture, biological sciences, business, communication, education, engineering/technologies, English, foreign languages, general academic interests/achievements, health fields, humanities, international studies, mathematics, military science, physical sciences, premedicine, religion/biblical studies, social sciences. *Creative arts/performance:* 365 awards ($2,586,098 total): applied art and design, art/fine arts, cinema/film/broadcasting, creative writing, dance, general creative arts/performance, journalism/publications, music, performing arts, theater/drama. *Special achievements/activities:* 417 awards ($3,975,460 total): general special achievements/activities, leadership, memberships, religious involvement. *Special characteristics:* 605 awards ($10,842,863 total): adult students, children of educators, children of faculty/staff, children of union members/company employees, children of workers in trades, ethnic background, general special characteristics, handicapped students, international students, local/state students, members of minority groups, previous college experience, relatives of clergy, religious affiliation, veterans, veterans' children. ***Tuition waivers:*** Full or partial for employees or children of employees.

LOANS ***Student loans:*** $35,955,439 (62% need-based, 38% non-need-based). 45% of past graduating class borrowed through all loan programs. *Average indebtedness per student:* $36,546. ***Average need-based loan:*** Freshmen: $3275. Undergraduates: $4405. ***Parent loans:*** $22,293,208 (25% need-based, 75% non-need-based). ***Programs:*** Federal Direct (Subsidized and Unsubsidized Stafford, PLUS), Perkins, Federal Nursing, state.

WORK-STUDY ***Federal work-study:*** Total amount: $2,590,753; 1,420 jobs averaging $1722. ***State or other work-study/employment:*** Total amount: $33,931 (100% need-based). 32 part-time jobs averaging $1927.

ATHLETIC AWARDS Total amount: $10,681,338 (40% need-based, 60% non-need-based).

APPLYING FOR FINANCIAL AID ***Required financial aid form:*** FAFSA. ***Financial aid deadline:*** 5/1. ***Notification date:*** Continuous beginning 3/15. Students must reply by 5/1.

CONTACT Michael Scott, Director of Scholarships and Student Financial Aid, Texas Christian University, PO Box 297012, Fort Worth, TX 76129-0002, 817-257-7858 or toll-free 800-828-3764. *Fax:* 817-257-7462. *E-mail:* m.scott@tcu.edu.

TEXAS COLLEGE

Tyler, TX

Tuition & fees: $9490 **Average undergraduate aid package: $9402**

ABOUT THE INSTITUTION Independent religious, coed. 18 undergraduate majors. Federal methodology is used as a basis for awarding need-based institutional aid.

UNDERGRADUATE EXPENSES for 2010–11 ***One-time required fee:*** $20. ***Comprehensive fee:*** $16,090 includes full-time tuition ($8000), mandatory fees ($1490), and room and board ($6600). ***College room only:*** $3600. ***Part-time tuition:*** $333 per credit hour. ***Part-time fees:*** $745 per term. ***Payment plan:*** Installment.

FRESHMAN FINANCIAL AID (Fall 2009) 228 applied for aid; of those 98% were deemed to have need. 97% of freshmen with need received aid; of those 5% had need fully met. ***Average percent of need met:*** 61% (excluding resources awarded to replace EFC). ***Average financial aid package:*** $8905 (excluding resources awarded to replace EFC). 10% of all full-time freshmen had no need and received non-need-based gift aid.

UNDERGRADUATE FINANCIAL AID (Fall 2009) 837 applied for aid; of those 97% were deemed to have need. 99% of undergraduates with need received aid; of those 4% had need fully met. ***Average percent of need met:*** 58% (excluding resources awarded to replace EFC). ***Average financial aid package:*** $9402 (excluding resources awarded to replace EFC). 4% of all full-time undergraduates had no need and received non-need-based gift aid.

GIFT AID (NEED-BASED) ***Total amount:*** $4,851,963 (79% federal, 21% state). ***Receiving aid:*** Freshmen: 84% (212); all full-time undergraduates: 89% (771). ***Average award:*** Freshmen: $6588; Undergraduates: $6375. ***Scholarships, grants, and awards:*** Federal Pell, FSEOG, state, private, college/university gift aid from institutional funds, United Negro College Fund.

GIFT AID (NON-NEED-BASED) ***Total amount:*** $1,169,681 (15% state, 56% institutional, 29% external sources). ***Receiving aid:*** Freshmen: 2% (4). Undergraduates: 1% (10). ***Average award:*** Freshmen: $3492. Undergraduates: $3099. ***Scholarships, grants, and awards by category:*** *Academic interests/achievement:* 59 awards ($94,990 total): general academic interests/achievements. *Special achievements/activities:* 2 awards ($15,762 total): leadership. ***Tuition waivers:*** Full or partial for employees or children of employees.

LOANS ***Student loans:*** $5,707,894 (94% need-based, 6% non-need-based). 12% of past graduating class borrowed through all loan programs. *Average indebtedness per student:* $27,158. ***Average need-based loan:*** Freshmen: $2566. Undergraduates: $3304. ***Parent loans:*** $192,697 (100% non-need-based). ***Programs:*** Federal Direct (Subsidized and Unsubsidized Stafford, PLUS), state.

WORK-STUDY ***Federal work-study:*** Total amount: $220,017; 144 jobs averaging $1528. ***State or other work-study/employment:*** Total amount: $29,192 (31% need-based, 69% non-need-based). 19 part-time jobs averaging $1057.

APPLYING FOR FINANCIAL AID ***Required financial aid forms:*** FAFSA, institution's own form. ***Financial aid deadline (priority):*** 6/1. ***Notification date:*** Continuous. Students must reply within 2 weeks of notification.

CONTACT Ms. Cecelia K. Jones, Director of Financial Aid, Texas College, 2404 North Grand Avenue, Tyler, TX 75702, 903-593-8311 Ext. 2241 or toll-free 800-306-6299 (out-of-state). *Fax:* 903-596-0001. *E-mail:* ckjones@texascollege.edu.

TEXAS LUTHERAN UNIVERSITY

Seguin, TX

Tuition & fees: $22,890 **Average undergraduate aid package: $18,964**

ABOUT THE INSTITUTION Independent religious, coed. 37 undergraduate majors. Federal methodology is used as a basis for awarding need-based institutional aid.

UNDERGRADUATE EXPENSES for 2010–11 ***Comprehensive fee:*** $29,630 includes full-time tuition ($22,760), mandatory fees ($130), and room and board ($6740). ***College room only:*** $3400. Full-time tuition and fees vary according to course load. Room and board charges vary according to board plan, housing facility, and location. ***Part-time tuition:*** $760 per semester hour. ***Part-time fees:*** $65 per term. Part-time tuition and fees vary according to course load. ***Payment plan:*** Installment.

FRESHMAN FINANCIAL AID (Fall 2010, est.) 323 applied for aid; of those 89% were deemed to have need. 100% of freshmen with need received aid; of those 24% had need fully met. ***Average percent of need met:*** 84% (excluding resources awarded to replace EFC). ***Average financial aid package:*** $20,600 (excluding resources awarded to replace EFC). 15% of all full-time freshmen had no need and received non-need-based gift aid.

UNDERGRADUATE FINANCIAL AID (Fall 2010, est.) 1,117 applied for aid; of those 89% were deemed to have need. 100% of undergraduates with need received aid; of those 20% had need fully met. ***Average percent of need met:*** 78% (excluding resources awarded to replace EFC). ***Average financial aid package:*** $18,964 (excluding resources awarded to replace EFC). 18% of all full-time undergraduates had no need and received non-need-based gift aid.

GIFT AID (NEED-BASED) ***Total amount:*** $13,138,965 (21% federal, 15% state, 62% institutional, 2% external sources). ***Receiving aid:*** Freshmen: 85% (286); all full-time undergraduates: 77% (978). ***Average award:*** Freshmen: $16,260; Undergraduates: $13,918. ***Scholarships, grants, and awards:*** Federal Pell, FSEOG, state, college/university gift aid from institutional funds, Academic Competitiveness Grants, National SMART Grants, TEACH Grants.

GIFT AID (NON-NEED-BASED) ***Total amount:*** $2,821,655 (1% state, 93% institutional, 6% external sources). ***Receiving aid:*** Freshmen: 13% (45). Undergraduates: 9% (117). ***Average award:*** Freshmen: $10,285. Undergraduates: $9467. ***Scholarships, grants, and awards by category:*** *Academic interests/achievement:* biological sciences, business, education, general academic interests/achievements, mathematics, physical sciences, premedicine. *Creative arts/performance:* journalism/publications, music, theater/drama. *Special achievements/activities:* general special achievements/activities, junior miss, leadership, memberships, religious involvement. *Special characteristics:* children and siblings of alumni, children of faculty/staff, first-generation college students, religious affiliation. ***Tuition waivers:*** Full or partial for children of alumni, employees or children of employees.

LOANS ***Student loans:*** $9,370,016 (71% need-based, 29% non-need-based). 67% of past graduating class borrowed through all loan programs. *Average indebtedness per student:* $34,410. ***Average need-based loan:*** Freshmen: $4122. Undergraduates: $4825. ***Parent loans:*** $1,757,881 (39% need-based, 61% non-need-based). ***Programs:*** Federal Direct (Subsidized and Unsubsidized Stafford, PLUS), alternative loans.

WORK-STUDY ***Federal work-study:*** Total amount: $1,109,161; jobs available. ***State or other work-study/employment:*** Total amount: $25,957 (85% need-based, 15% non-need-based). Part-time jobs available.

APPLYING FOR FINANCIAL AID ***Required financial aid form:*** FAFSA. ***Financial aid deadline (priority):*** 3/1. ***Notification date:*** Continuous beginning 3/1. Students must reply by 8/15.

CONTACT Cathleen Wright, Director of Financial Aid, Texas Lutheran University, 1000 West Court Street, Seguin, TX 78155-5999, 830-372-8075 or toll-free 800-771-8521. *Fax:* 830-372-8096. *E-mail:* financialaid@tlu.edu.

TEXAS SOUTHERN UNIVERSITY

Houston, TX

Tuition & fees (TX res): $7462 **Average undergraduate aid package: $15,918**

ABOUT THE INSTITUTION State-supported, coed. 45 undergraduate majors. Federal methodology is used as a basis for awarding need-based institutional aid.

UNDERGRADUATE EXPENSES for 2010–11 ***Tuition, state resident:*** full-time $7462. ***Tuition, nonresident:*** full-time $15,772. Full-time tuition and fees vary according to course level, course load, degree level, and program. Part-time tuition and fees vary according to course level, course load, degree level, and program. ***College room and board:*** $11,880. Room and board charges vary according to board plan and housing facility. ***Payment plans:*** Installment, deferred payment.

FRESHMAN FINANCIAL AID (Fall 2010, est.) 1,157 applied for aid; of those 78% were deemed to have need. 97% of freshmen with need received aid; of those 30% had need fully met. ***Average percent of need met:*** 48% (excluding resources awarded to replace EFC). ***Average financial aid package:*** $15,140 (excluding resources awarded to replace EFC).

UNDERGRADUATE FINANCIAL AID (Fall 2010, est.) 6,477 applied for aid; of those 79% were deemed to have need. 98% of undergraduates with need received aid; of those 27% had need fully met. ***Average percent of need met:*** 53% (excluding resources awarded to replace EFC). ***Average financial aid package:*** $15,918 (excluding resources awarded to replace EFC).

GIFT AID (NEED-BASED) ***Total amount:*** $35,656,892 (64% federal, 20% state, 13% institutional, 3% external sources). ***Receiving aid:*** Freshmen: 74% (871); all full-time undergraduates: 72% (5,013). ***Average award:*** Freshmen: $12,353; Undergraduates: $12,353. ***Scholarships, grants, and awards:*** Federal Pell, FSEOG, state, private, college/university gift aid from institutional funds, United Negro College Fund, Federal Nursing.

GIFT AID (NON-NEED-BASED) ***Scholarships, grants, and awards by category:*** *Academic interests/achievement:* business, communication, engineering/technologies, general academic interests/achievements. ***Tuition waivers:*** Full or partial for minority students, senior citizens.

LOANS ***Student loans:*** $42,056,531 (100% need-based). 88% of past graduating class borrowed through all loan programs. *Average indebtedness per student:* $7883. ***Average need-based loan:*** Freshmen: $6520. Undergraduates: $6520. ***Parent loans:*** $5,944,870 (100% need-based). ***Programs:*** Federal Direct (Subsidized and Unsubsidized Stafford, PLUS), Perkins, state, college/university.

WORK-STUDY ***Federal work-study:*** Total amount: $964,058; 380 jobs averaging $4000. ***State or other work-study/employment:*** Total amount: $38,593 (100% need-based). 29 part-time jobs averaging $4000.

ATHLETIC AWARDS Total amount: $2,970,861 (100% need-based).

APPLYING FOR FINANCIAL AID ***Required financial aid forms:*** FAFSA, institution's own form. ***Financial aid deadline (priority):*** 4/15. ***Notification date:*** Continuous beginning 4/15.

CONTACT Financial Aid Office, Texas Southern University, 3100 Cleburne Street, Houston, TX 77004-4584, 713-313-7011. *Fax:* 713-313-1858.

TEXAS STATE UNIVERSITY–SAN MARCOS

San Marcos, TX

Tuition & fees (TX res): $7838 **Average undergraduate aid package: $14,112**

ABOUT THE INSTITUTION State-supported, coed. 92 undergraduate majors. Federal methodology is used as a basis for awarding need-based institutional aid.

UNDERGRADUATE EXPENSES for 2010–11 ***Tuition, state resident:*** full-time $5730; part-time $191 per credit hour. ***Tuition, nonresident:*** full-time $15,030; part-time $501 per credit hour. ***Required fees:*** full-time $2108; $48 per credit hour or $379 per term. Full-time tuition and fees vary according to course load and degree level. Part-time tuition and fees vary according to course load and degree level. ***College room and board:*** $6810; ***Room only:*** $4380. Room and board charges vary according to board plan and housing facility. ***Payment plan:*** Installment.

FRESHMAN FINANCIAL AID (Fall 2010, est.) 3,098 applied for aid; of those 72% were deemed to have need. 97% of freshmen with need received aid; of those 11% had need fully met. ***Average percent of need met:*** 67% (excluding

resources awarded to replace EFC). ***Average financial aid package:*** $14,630 (excluding resources awarded to replace EFC). 5% of all full-time freshmen had no need and received non-need-based gift aid.

UNDERGRADUATE FINANCIAL AID (Fall 2010, est.) 16,045 applied for aid; of those 80% were deemed to have need. 97% of undergraduates with need received aid; of those 10% had need fully met. ***Average percent of need met:*** 65% (excluding resources awarded to replace EFC). ***Average financial aid package:*** $14,112 (excluding resources awarded to replace EFC). 2% of all full-time undergraduates had no need and received non-need-based gift aid.

GIFT AID (NEED-BASED) ***Total amount:*** $78,083,148 (55% federal, 45% state). ***Receiving aid:*** Freshmen: 44% (1,693); all full-time undergraduates: 43% (9,709). ***Average award:*** Freshmen: $7620; Undergraduates: $6518. ***Scholarships, grants, and awards:*** Federal Pell, FSEOG, state, private, college/university gift aid from institutional funds.

GIFT AID (NON-NEED-BASED) ***Total amount:*** $11,214,992 (40% institutional, 60% external sources). ***Receiving aid:*** Freshmen: 20% (760). Undergraduates: 9% (1,990). ***Average award:*** Freshmen: $2036. Undergraduates: $2239. ***Scholarships, grants, and awards by category:*** *Academic interests/achievement:* agriculture, business, education, English, general academic interests/achievements, home economics, international studies, military science. *Creative arts/performance:* applied art and design, art/fine arts, journalism/publications, music, theater/drama. *Special achievements/activities:* leadership. *Special characteristics:* children and siblings of alumni, first-generation college students, handicapped students, local/state students. ***Tuition waivers:*** Full or partial for employees or children of employees.

LOANS ***Student loans:*** $140,429,019 (43% need-based, 57% non-need-based). 58% of past graduating class borrowed through all loan programs. *Average indebtedness per student:* $21,667. ***Average need-based loan:*** Freshmen: $3627. Undergraduates: $4278. ***Parent loans:*** $31,836,464 (100% non-need-based). ***Programs:*** Federal Direct (Subsidized and Unsubsidized Stafford, PLUS), Perkins, state, college/university, emergency tuition loans.

WORK-STUDY ***Federal work-study:*** Total amount: $1,503,900; 675 jobs averaging $2228. ***State or other work-study/employment:*** Total amount: $251,218 (100% need-based). 120 part-time jobs averaging $2093.

ATHLETIC AWARDS Total amount: $1,693,197 (100% non-need-based).

APPLYING FOR FINANCIAL AID ***Required financial aid form:*** FAFSA. ***Financial aid deadline (priority):*** 4/1. ***Notification date:*** Continuous beginning 5/1. Students must reply within 3 weeks of notification.

CONTACT Mr. Chris Murr, Director of Financial Aid, Texas State University–San Marcos, 601 University Drive, San Marcos, TX 78666-4602, 512-245-2315. *Fax:* 512-245-7920. *E-mail:* cm18@txstate.edu.

TEXAS TECH UNIVERSITY

Lubbock, TX

Tuition & fees (TX res): $8260 **Average undergraduate aid package: $9301**

ABOUT THE INSTITUTION State-supported, coed. 97 undergraduate majors. Federal methodology is used as a basis for awarding need-based institutional aid.

UNDERGRADUATE EXPENSES for 2010–11 ***Tuition, state resident:*** full-time $5370; part-time $178.99 per credit hour. ***Tuition, nonresident:*** full-time $14,670; part-time $488.99 per credit hour. ***Required fees:*** full-time $2890; $36 per credit hour or $905 per term. Full-time tuition and fees vary according to course load, program, and reciprocity agreements. Part-time tuition and fees vary according to course load, program, and reciprocity agreements. ***College room and board:*** $7800; ***Room only:*** $4100. Room and board charges vary according to board plan and housing facility. ***Payment plan:*** Installment.

FRESHMAN FINANCIAL AID (Fall 2009) 3,225 applied for aid; of those 66% were deemed to have need. 93% of freshmen with need received aid; of those 13% had need fully met. ***Average percent of need met:*** 56% (excluding resources awarded to replace EFC). ***Average financial aid package:*** $9627 (excluding resources awarded to replace EFC). 12% of all full-time freshmen had no need and received non-need-based gift aid.

UNDERGRADUATE FINANCIAL AID (Fall 2009) 13,607 applied for aid; of those 72% were deemed to have need. 95% of undergraduates with need received aid; of those 7% had need fully met. ***Average percent of need met:*** 53% (excluding resources awarded to replace EFC). ***Average financial aid package:*** $9301 (excluding resources awarded to replace EFC). 12% of all full-time undergraduates had no need and received non-need-based gift aid.

GIFT AID (NEED-BASED) ***Total amount:*** $62,650,736 (44% federal, 30% state, 22% institutional, 4% external sources). ***Receiving aid:*** Freshmen: 34% (1,571); all full-time undergraduates: 34% (7,482). ***Average award:*** Freshmen: $8191; Undergraduates: $7005. ***Scholarships, grants, and awards:*** Federal Pell, FSEOG, state, private, college/university gift aid from institutional funds.

GIFT AID (NON-NEED-BASED) ***Total amount:*** $18,751,723 (1% state, 81% institutional, 18% external sources). ***Receiving aid:*** Freshmen: 6% (290). Undergraduates: 4% (777). ***Average award:*** Freshmen: $4229. Undergraduates: $3581. ***Scholarships, grants, and awards by category:*** *Academic interests/achievement:* agriculture, architecture, biological sciences, business, communication, computer science, education, engineering/technologies, English, foreign languages, general academic interests/achievements, home economics, humanities, international studies, mathematics, military science, physical sciences, premedicine, social sciences. *Creative arts/performance:* applied art and design, art/fine arts, dance, journalism/publications, music, performing arts, theater/drama. *Special achievements/activities:* community service, memberships, rodeo. *Special characteristics:* children of faculty/staff, first-generation college students, handicapped students, out-of-state students, veterans, veterans' children. ***Tuition waivers:*** Full or partial for employees or children of employees, senior citizens.

LOANS ***Student loans:*** $131,459,874 (64% need-based, 36% non-need-based). *Average indebtedness per student:* $21,500. ***Average need-based loan:*** Freshmen: $3354. Undergraduates: $4223. ***Parent loans:*** $11,587,173 (25% need-based, 75% non-need-based). ***Programs:*** Perkins, state, college/university.

WORK-STUDY ***Federal work-study:*** Total amount: $1,473,420; jobs available. ***State or other work-study/employment:*** Total amount: $275,447 (100% need-based). Part-time jobs available.

ATHLETIC AWARDS Total amount: $992,177 (39% need-based, 61% non-need-based).

APPLYING FOR FINANCIAL AID ***Required financial aid form:*** FAFSA. ***Financial aid deadline (priority):*** 4/15. ***Notification date:*** Continuous. Students must reply within 2 weeks of notification.

CONTACT Becky Wilson, Managing Director of Student Financial Aid, Texas Tech University, PO Box 45011, Lubbock, TX 79409-5011, 806-742-0454. *Fax:* 806-742-0880.

TEXAS WESLEYAN UNIVERSITY

Fort Worth, TX

Tuition & fees: $18,710 **Average undergraduate aid package: $12,000**

ABOUT THE INSTITUTION Independent United Methodist, coed. 66 undergraduate majors. Federal methodology is used as a basis for awarding need-based institutional aid.

UNDERGRADUATE EXPENSES for 2010–11 ***Comprehensive fee:*** $25,620 includes full-time tuition ($16,985), mandatory fees ($1725), and room and board ($6910). ***College room only:*** $4050. Full-time tuition and fees vary according to degree level and program. Room and board charges vary according to housing facility. ***Part-time tuition:*** $575 per credit hour. ***Part-time fees:*** $65 per credit hour. Part-time tuition and fees vary according to degree level and program. ***Payment plans:*** Installment, deferred payment.

FRESHMAN FINANCIAL AID (Fall 2010, est.) 187 applied for aid; of those 93% were deemed to have need. 100% of freshmen with need received aid; of those 9% had need fully met. ***Average percent of need met:*** 48% (excluding resources awarded to replace EFC). ***Average financial aid package:*** $12,000 (excluding resources awarded to replace EFC). 13% of all full-time freshmen had no need and received non-need-based gift aid.

UNDERGRADUATE FINANCIAL AID (Fall 2010, est.) 1,106 applied for aid; of those 100% were deemed to have need. 100% of undergraduates with need received aid; of those 3% had need fully met. ***Average percent of need met:*** 48% (excluding resources awarded to replace EFC). ***Average financial aid package:*** $12,000 (excluding resources awarded to replace EFC). 11% of all full-time undergraduates had no need and received non-need-based gift aid.

GIFT AID (NEED-BASED) ***Total amount:*** $12,326,439 (37% federal, 22% state, 39% institutional, 2% external sources). ***Receiving aid:*** Freshmen: 85% (174); all full-time undergraduates: 87% (1,106). ***Average award:*** Freshmen: $7800; Undergraduates: $7700. ***Scholarships, grants, and awards:*** Federal Pell, FSEOG, state, private, college/university gift aid from institutional funds.

GIFT AID (NON-NEED-BASED) ***Total amount:*** $1,299,105 (1% federal, 97% institutional, 2% external sources). ***Average award:*** Freshmen: $7800. Undergraduates: $7700. ***Scholarships, grants, and awards by category:*** *Academic interests/achievement:* general academic interests/achievements.

Creative arts/performance: general creative arts/performance. *Special achievements/activities:* cheerleading/drum major, general special achievements/activities, leadership, religious involvement. *Special characteristics:* children and siblings of alumni, relatives of clergy, religious affiliation. ***Tuition waivers:*** Full or partial for employees or children of employees.

LOANS ***Student loans:*** $7,002,423 (91% need-based, 9% non-need-based). ***Average need-based loan:*** Freshmen: $3000. Undergraduates: $3500. ***Parent loans:*** $649,675 (79% need-based, 21% non-need-based). ***Programs:*** Federal Direct (Subsidized and Unsubsidized Stafford, PLUS), state.

WORK-STUDY ***Federal work-study:*** Total amount: $3,167,197; jobs available. ***State or other work-study/employment:*** Total amount: $230,000 (13% need-based, 87% non-need-based). Part-time jobs available.

ATHLETIC AWARDS Total amount: $1,235,392 (64% need-based, 36% non-need-based).

APPLYING FOR FINANCIAL AID ***Required financial aid form:*** FAFSA. ***Financial aid deadline:*** Continuous. ***Notification date:*** Continuous beginning 3/1.

CONTACT Office of Financial Aid, Texas Wesleyan University, 1201 Wesleyan Street, Fort Worth, TX 76105-1536, 817-531-4420 or toll-free 800-580-8980 (in-state). *Fax:* 817-531-4231. *E-mail:* financialaid@txwes.edu.

TEXAS WOMAN'S UNIVERSITY

Denton, TX

Tuition & fees (TX res): $6960 **Average undergraduate aid package: $10,867**

ABOUT THE INSTITUTION State-supported, coed, primarily women. 40 undergraduate majors. Both federal and institutional methodology are used as a basis for awarding need-based institutional aid.

UNDERGRADUATE EXPENSES for 2011–12 ***Tuition, state resident:*** full-time $5040; part-time $168 per credit hour. ***Tuition, nonresident:*** full-time $14,340; part-time $478 per credit hour. ***Required fees:*** full-time $1920. Full-time tuition and fees vary according to course load, program, and reciprocity agreements. Part-time tuition and fees vary according to course load, program, and reciprocity agreements. ***College room and board:*** $6210; ***Room only:*** $3410. Room and board charges vary according to board plan and housing facility. ***Payment plan:*** Installment.

FRESHMAN FINANCIAL AID (Fall 2010, est.) 860 applied for aid; of those 81% were deemed to have need. 95% of freshmen with need received aid; of those 15% had need fully met. ***Average percent of need met:*** 83% (excluding resources awarded to replace EFC). ***Average financial aid package:*** $11,507 (excluding resources awarded to replace EFC). 12% of all full-time freshmen had no need and received non-need-based gift aid.

UNDERGRADUATE FINANCIAL AID (Fall 2010, est.) 4,788 applied for aid; of those 84% were deemed to have need. 94% of undergraduates with need received aid; of those 17% had need fully met. ***Average percent of need met:*** 61% (excluding resources awarded to replace EFC). ***Average financial aid package:*** $10,867 (excluding resources awarded to replace EFC). 11% of all full-time undergraduates had no need and received non-need-based gift aid.

GIFT AID (NEED-BASED) ***Total amount:*** $25,432,610 (61% federal, 22% state, 14% institutional, 3% external sources). ***Receiving aid:*** Freshmen: 59% (554); all full-time undergraduates: 53% (3,077). ***Average award:*** Freshmen: $8123; Undergraduates: $5756. ***Scholarships, grants, and awards:*** Federal Pell, FSEOG, state, private, college/university gift aid from institutional funds.

GIFT AID (NON-NEED-BASED) ***Total amount:*** $2,891,761 (22% state, 67% institutional, 11% external sources). ***Receiving aid:*** Freshmen: 30% (283). Undergraduates: 21% (1,243). ***Average award:*** Freshmen: $3237. Undergraduates: $2685. ***Scholarships, grants, and awards by category:*** *Academic interests/achievement:* biological sciences, business, communication, computer science, education, English, foreign languages, general academic interests/achievements, health fields, home economics, humanities, library science, mathematics, physical sciences, premedicine, social sciences. *Creative arts/performance:* applied art and design, art/fine arts, cinema/film/broadcasting, dance, journalism/publications, music, theater/drama. *Special characteristics:* international students. ***Tuition waivers:*** Full or partial for senior citizens.

LOANS ***Student loans:*** $36,893,887 (87% need-based, 13% non-need-based). 77% of past graduating class borrowed through all loan programs. *Average indebtedness per student:* $21,194. ***Average need-based loan:*** Freshmen: $3168. Undergraduates: $3833. ***Parent loans:*** $721,541 (64% need-based, 36% non-need-based). ***Programs:*** Federal Direct (Subsidized and Unsubsidized Stafford, PLUS), Perkins, Federal Nursing, state, college/university, alternative loans.

WORK-STUDY ***Federal work-study:*** Total amount: $254,049; jobs available. ***State or other work-study/employment:*** Total amount: $357,836 (23% need-based, 77% non-need-based). Part-time jobs available.

ATHLETIC AWARDS Total amount: $464,813 (32% need-based, 68% non-need-based).

APPLYING FOR FINANCIAL AID ***Required financial aid form:*** FAFSA. ***Financial aid deadline (priority):*** 4/1. ***Notification date:*** 5/1. Students must reply within 3 weeks of notification.

CONTACT Mr. Governor Jackson, Director of Financial Aid, Texas Woman's University, PO Box 425408, Denton, TX 76204-5408, 940-898-3051 or toll-free 866-809-6130. *Fax:* 940-898-3068. *E-mail:* gjackson@twu.edu.

THIEL COLLEGE

Greenville, PA

Tuition & fees: $24,856 **Average undergraduate aid package: $19,220**

ABOUT THE INSTITUTION Independent religious, coed. 43 undergraduate majors. Federal methodology is used as a basis for awarding need-based institutional aid.

UNDERGRADUATE EXPENSES for 2011–12 ***One-time required fee:*** $300. ***Comprehensive fee:*** $34,508 includes full-time tuition ($23,076), mandatory fees ($1780), and room and board ($9652). ***College room only:*** $4826. Room and board charges vary according to board plan and housing facility. ***Part-time tuition:*** $770 per credit. ***Part-time fees:*** $73 per credit. Part-time tuition and fees vary according to course load. ***Payment plan:*** Installment.

FRESHMAN FINANCIAL AID (Fall 2010, est.) 352 applied for aid; of those 100% were deemed to have need. 100% of freshmen with need received aid; of those 6% had need fully met. ***Average percent of need met:*** 65% (excluding resources awarded to replace EFC). ***Average financial aid package:*** $18,614 (excluding resources awarded to replace EFC). 9% of all full-time freshmen had no need and received non-need-based gift aid.

UNDERGRADUATE FINANCIAL AID (Fall 2010, est.) 1,001 applied for aid; of those 96% were deemed to have need. 100% of undergraduates with need received aid; of those 8% had need fully met. ***Average percent of need met:*** 67% (excluding resources awarded to replace EFC). ***Average financial aid package:*** $19,220 (excluding resources awarded to replace EFC). 11% of all full-time undergraduates had no need and received non-need-based gift aid.

GIFT AID (NEED-BASED) ***Total amount:*** $14,172,025 (19% federal, 9% state, 67% institutional, 5% external sources). ***Receiving aid:*** Freshmen: 100% (352); all full-time undergraduates: 96% (959). ***Average award:*** Freshmen: $14,949; Undergraduates: $15,076. ***Scholarships, grants, and awards:*** Federal Pell, FSEOG, state, private, college/university gift aid from institutional funds.

GIFT AID (NON-NEED-BASED) ***Total amount:*** $1,302,936 (89% institutional, 11% external sources). ***Receiving aid:*** Freshmen: 6% (22). Undergraduates: 8% (76). ***Average award:*** Freshmen: $7436. Undergraduates: $8565. ***Scholarships, grants, and awards by category:*** *Academic interests/achievement:* biological sciences, business, computer science, education, English, general academic interests/achievements, mathematics, physical sciences, religion/biblical studies. *Creative arts/performance:* music. *Special achievements/activities:* leadership. *Special characteristics:* children and siblings of alumni, children of faculty/staff, relatives of clergy, religious affiliation, siblings of current students. ***Tuition waivers:*** Full or partial for employees or children of employees, senior citizens.

LOANS ***Student loans:*** $8,014,212 (85% need-based, 15% non-need-based). 87% of past graduating class borrowed through all loan programs. *Average indebtedness per student:* $34,606. ***Average need-based loan:*** Freshmen: $3956. Undergraduates: $4244. ***Parent loans:*** $2,801,166 (58% need-based, 42% non-need-based). ***Programs:*** Federal Direct (Subsidized and Unsubsidized Stafford, PLUS), Perkins, college/university.

WORK-STUDY ***Federal work-study:*** Total amount: $89,202; 62 jobs available. ***State or other work-study/employment:*** Total amount: $430,482 (63% need-based, 37% non-need-based). 277 part-time jobs available.

APPLYING FOR FINANCIAL AID ***Required financial aid forms:*** FAFSA, state aid form. ***Financial aid deadline:*** Continuous. ***Notification date:*** Continuous beginning 2/15. Students must reply within 2 weeks of notification.

CONTACT Ms. Cynthia H. Farrell, Director of Financial Aid, Thiel College, 75 College Avenue, Greenville, PA 16125-2181, 724-589-2178 or toll-free 800-248-4435. *Fax:* 724-589-2850. *E-mail:* cfarrell@thiel.edu.

THOMAS AQUINAS COLLEGE

Santa Paula, CA

Tuition & fees: $22,850 **Average undergraduate aid package: $19,324**

ABOUT THE INSTITUTION Independent Roman Catholic, coed. 1 undergraduate major. Institutional methodology is used as a basis for awarding need-based institutional aid.

UNDERGRADUATE EXPENSES for 2011–12 ***Comprehensive fee:*** $30,400 includes full-time tuition ($22,850) and room and board ($7550). ***Payment plan:*** Installment.

FRESHMAN FINANCIAL AID (Fall 2010, est.) 91 applied for aid; of those 93% were deemed to have need. 100% of freshmen with need received aid; of those 100% had need fully met. ***Average percent of need met:*** 100% (excluding resources awarded to replace EFC). ***Average financial aid package:*** $19,825 (excluding resources awarded to replace EFC).

UNDERGRADUATE FINANCIAL AID (Fall 2010, est.) 285 applied for aid; of those 98% were deemed to have need. 100% of undergraduates with need received aid; of those 100% had need fully met. ***Average percent of need met:*** 100% (excluding resources awarded to replace EFC). ***Average financial aid package:*** $19,324 (excluding resources awarded to replace EFC).

GIFT AID (NEED-BASED) ***Total amount:*** $3,550,129 (19% federal, 9% state, 71% institutional, 1% external sources). ***Receiving aid:*** Freshmen: 75% (77); all full-time undergraduates: 69% (244). ***Average award:*** Freshmen: $14,990; Undergraduates: $14,550. ***Scholarships, grants, and awards:*** Federal Pell, state, private, college/university gift aid from institutional funds.

GIFT AID (NON-NEED-BASED) ***Total amount:*** $16,700 (9% state, 91% external sources).

LOANS ***Student loans:*** $1,113,296 (79% need-based, 21% non-need-based). 82% of past graduating class borrowed through all loan programs. *Average indebtedness per student:* $16,311. ***Average need-based loan:*** Freshmen: $3093. Undergraduates: $3625. ***Parent loans:*** $393,428 (24% need-based, 76% non-need-based). ***Programs:*** Federal Direct (Subsidized and Unsubsidized Stafford, PLUS), college/university, Canada student loans.

WORK-STUDY ***State or other work-study/employment:*** Total amount: $944,668 (100% need-based). 247 part-time jobs averaging $3825.

APPLYING FOR FINANCIAL AID ***Required financial aid forms:*** FAFSA, institution's own form, state aid form, federal income tax return(s), Non-custodial Parent Statement. ***Financial aid deadline:*** 3/2. ***Notification date:*** Continuous beginning 2/1. Students must reply by 5/1 or within 2 weeks of notification.

CONTACT Mr. Gregory Becher, Director of Financial Aid, Thomas Aquinas College, 10000 North Ojai Road, Santa Paula, CA 93060-9980, 805-525-4419 Ext. 5936 or toll-free 800-634-9797. *Fax:* 805-525-9342. *E-mail:* gbecher@thomasaquinas.edu.

THOMAS COLLEGE

Waterville, ME

CONTACT Jeannine Bosse, Associate Director of Student Financial Aid, Thomas College, 180 West River Road, Waterville, ME 04901-5097, 800-339-7001. *Fax:* 207-859-1114. *E-mail:* sfsassistant@thomas.edu.

THOMAS EDISON STATE COLLEGE

Trenton, NJ

Tuition & fees (NJ res): $4883 **Average undergraduate aid package: N/A**

ABOUT THE INSTITUTION State-supported, coed. 82 undergraduate majors. Federal methodology is used as a basis for awarding need-based institutional aid.

UNDERGRADUATE EXPENSES for 2010–11 ***Tuition, state resident:*** full-time $4883; part-time $141 per quarter hour. ***Tuition, nonresident:*** full-time $7190; part-time $193 per credit hour. ***Required fees:*** $107 per year. Part-time tuition and fees vary according to program and student level. Students may choose either the Comprehensive Tuition Plan: $4,883 per year (state residents and military personnel), $7,190 (out-of-state), which covers up to 36 credits per year for all credit-earning options, or the Enrolled Options Plan: $1,446 per year (state residents and military personnel), $2,696 (out-of-state) and $3,784 (international) for annual enrollment and a $107 technology services fee. Tests, portfolios, courses and other fees at additional cost.

GIFT AID (NEED-BASED) ***Total amount:*** $3,231,000 (93% federal, 7% state). ***Scholarships, grants, and awards:*** Federal Pell, state, private.

GIFT AID (NON-NEED-BASED) ***Tuition waivers:*** Full or partial for employees or children of employees.

LOANS ***Student loans:*** $13,188,000 (100% need-based). ***Parent loans:*** $3910 (100% need-based). ***Programs:*** state, private loans.

APPLYING FOR FINANCIAL AID ***Required financial aid forms:*** FAFSA, institution's own form. ***Financial aid deadline:*** Continuous. ***Notification date:*** Continuous. Students must reply within 4 weeks of notification.

CONTACT James Owens, Director of Financial Aid, Thomas Edison State College, 101 West State Street, Trenton, NJ 08608, 609-633-9658 or toll-free 888-442-8372. *Fax:* 609-633-6489. *E-mail:* finaid@tesc.edu.

THOMAS JEFFERSON UNIVERSITY

Philadelphia, PA

CONTACT Susan McFadden, University Director of Financial Aid, Thomas Jefferson University, 1025 Walnut Street, Philadelphia, PA 19107, 215-955-2867 or toll-free 877-533-3247. *Fax:* 215-955-5186. *E-mail:* financial.aid@jefferson.edu.

THOMAS MORE COLLEGE

Crestview Hills, KY

Tuition & fees: $24,720 **Average undergraduate aid package: $14,904**

ABOUT THE INSTITUTION Independent Roman Catholic, coed. 43 undergraduate majors. Federal methodology is used as a basis for awarding need-based institutional aid.

UNDERGRADUATE EXPENSES for 2010–11 ***Comprehensive fee:*** $31,510 includes full-time tuition ($24,000), mandatory fees ($720), and room and board ($6790). ***College room only:*** $3200. Full-time tuition and fees vary according to program and student level. Room and board charges vary according to board plan and housing facility. ***Part-time tuition:*** $545 per credit hour. ***Part-time fees:*** $30 per credit hour; $15 per term. Part-time tuition and fees vary according to course load and program. ***Payment plans:*** Installment, deferred payment.

FRESHMAN FINANCIAL AID (Fall 2010, est.) 276 applied for aid; of those 90% were deemed to have need. 100% of freshmen with need received aid; of those 23% had need fully met. ***Average percent of need met:*** 72% (excluding resources awarded to replace EFC). ***Average financial aid package:*** $18,847 (excluding resources awarded to replace EFC). 9% of all full-time freshmen had no need and received non-need-based gift aid.

UNDERGRADUATE FINANCIAL AID (Fall 2010, est.) 828 applied for aid; of those 81% were deemed to have need. 99% of undergraduates with need received aid; of those 19% had need fully met. ***Average percent of need met:*** 68% (excluding resources awarded to replace EFC). ***Average financial aid package:*** $14,904 (excluding resources awarded to replace EFC). 16% of all full-time undergraduates had no need and received non-need-based gift aid.

GIFT AID (NEED-BASED) ***Total amount:*** $11,142,251 (17% federal, 13% state, 67% institutional, 3% external sources). ***Receiving aid:*** Freshmen: 83% (247); all full-time undergraduates: 54% (570). ***Average award:*** Freshmen: $15,244; Undergraduates: $12,187. ***Scholarships, grants, and awards:*** Federal Pell, FSEOG, state, private, college/university gift aid from institutional funds, Federal Nursing.

GIFT AID (NON-NEED-BASED) ***Total amount:*** $3,471,628 (6% state, 90% institutional, 4% external sources). ***Receiving aid:*** Freshmen: 14% (41). Undergraduates: 6% (59). ***Average award:*** Freshmen: $14,344. Undergraduates: $12,703. ***Scholarships, grants, and awards by category:*** *Academic interests/achievement:* 93 awards ($280,152 total): biological sciences, business, communication, computer science, education, English, general academic interests/achievements, mathematics, physical sciences, premedicine, religion/biblical studies, social sciences. *Creative arts/performance:* 21 awards ($20,600 total): art/fine arts, theater/drama. *Special achievements/activities:* 107 awards ($206,716 total): community service, leadership, memberships, religious involvement. *Special characteristics:* 587 awards ($2,805,491 total): adult students, children and siblings of alumni, children of faculty/staff, children of union members/company employees, international students, members of minority groups, out-of-state students, religious affiliation, siblings of current students, veterans, veterans' children. ***Tuition waivers:*** Full or partial for employees or children of employees, senior citizens.

LOANS ***Student loans:*** $7,543,984 (41% need-based, 59% non-need-based). 76% of past graduating class borrowed through all loan programs. *Average indebtedness per student:* $32,720. ***Average need-based loan:*** Freshmen: $3206. Undergraduates: $4381. ***Parent loans:*** $1,771,357 (100% non-need-based). ***Programs:*** Federal Direct (Subsidized and Unsubsidized Stafford, PLUS), Perkins, Federal Nursing, college/university.

WORK-STUDY ***Federal work-study:*** Total amount: $200,200; 153 jobs averaging $1337. ***State or other work-study/employment:*** 163 part-time jobs averaging $1056.

APPLYING FOR FINANCIAL AID ***Required financial aid form:*** FAFSA. ***Financial aid deadline (priority):*** 3/15. ***Notification date:*** Continuous beginning 3/1. Students must reply by 5/1.

CONTACT Ms. Mary Givhan, Director of Financial Aid, Thomas More College, 333 Thomas More Parkway, Crestview Hills, KY 41017-3495, 859-344-3531 or toll-free 800-825-4557. *Fax:* 859-344-3638. *E-mail:* mary.givhan@thomasmore.edu.

THOMAS MORE COLLEGE OF LIBERAL ARTS

Merrimack, NH

Tuition & fees: $16,100 **Average undergraduate aid package: $15,632**

ABOUT THE INSTITUTION Independent religious, coed. 1 undergraduate major. Federal methodology is used as a basis for awarding need-based institutional aid.

UNDERGRADUATE EXPENSES for 2010–11 ***Comprehensive fee:*** $25,200 includes full-time tuition ($16,100) and room and board ($9100). ***Payment plan:*** Installment.

FRESHMAN FINANCIAL AID (Fall 2010, est.) 27 applied for aid; of those 100% were deemed to have need. 100% of freshmen with need received aid; of those 15% had need fully met. ***Average percent of need met:*** 79% (excluding resources awarded to replace EFC). ***Average financial aid package:*** $16,100 (excluding resources awarded to replace EFC). 7% of all full-time freshmen had no need and received non-need-based gift aid.

UNDERGRADUATE FINANCIAL AID (Fall 2010, est.) 69 applied for aid; of those 93% were deemed to have need. 100% of undergraduates with need received aid; of those 17% had need fully met. ***Average percent of need met:*** 77% (excluding resources awarded to replace EFC). ***Average financial aid package:*** $15,632 (excluding resources awarded to replace EFC). 7% of all full-time undergraduates had no need and received non-need-based gift aid.

GIFT AID (NEED-BASED) ***Total amount:*** $489,250 (31% federal, 2% state, 67% institutional). ***Receiving aid:*** Freshmen: 79% (23); all full-time undergraduates: 67% (51). ***Average award:*** Freshmen: $10,090; Undergraduates: $9775. ***Scholarships, grants, and awards:*** Federal Pell, FSEOG, state, private, college/university gift aid from institutional funds.

GIFT AID (NON-NEED-BASED) ***Total amount:*** $257,800 (100% institutional). ***Receiving aid:*** Freshmen: 79% (23). Undergraduates: 55% (42). ***Average award:*** Freshmen: $5000. Undergraduates: $7620. ***Scholarships, grants, and awards by category:*** *Academic interests/achievement:* general academic interests/achievements. ***Tuition waivers:*** Full or partial for employees or children of employees.

LOANS ***Student loans:*** $372,574 (57% need-based, 43% non-need-based). 86% of past graduating class borrowed through all loan programs. *Average indebtedness per student:* $28,194. ***Average need-based loan:*** Freshmen: $3346. Undergraduates: $4129. ***Parent loans:*** $254,094 (63% need-based, 37% non-need-based). ***Programs:*** Federal Direct (Subsidized and Unsubsidized Stafford, PLUS).

WORK-STUDY ***State or other work-study/employment:*** Total amount: $82,700 (79% need-based, 21% non-need-based). Part-time jobs available.

APPLYING FOR FINANCIAL AID ***Required financial aid form:*** FAFSA. ***Financial aid deadline:*** Continuous. ***Notification date:*** Continuous beginning 2/15. Students must reply within 2 weeks of notification.

CONTACT Clinton A. Hanson Jr., Director of Financial Aid, Thomas More College of Liberal Arts, 6 Manchester Street, Merrimack, NH 03054-4818, 603-880-8308 Ext. 23 or toll-free 800-880-8308. *Fax:* 603-880-9280. *E-mail:* chanson@thomasmorecollege.edu.

THOMAS UNIVERSITY

Thomasville, GA

Tuition & fees: $12,720 **Average undergraduate aid package: N/A**

ABOUT THE INSTITUTION Independent, coed. 23 undergraduate majors. Federal methodology is used as a basis for awarding need-based institutional aid.

UNDERGRADUATE EXPENSES for 2010–11 ***Tuition:*** full-time $12,000; part-time $475 per credit hour. ***Required fees:*** full-time $720; $150 per term. Full-time tuition and fees vary according to program. Part-time tuition and fees vary according to course load and program. ***Payment plan:*** Installment.

GIFT AID (NEED-BASED) ***Scholarships, grants, and awards:*** Federal Pell, FSEOG, private, college/university gift aid from institutional funds.

GIFT AID (NON-NEED-BASED) ***Scholarships, grants, and awards by category:*** *Academic interests/achievement:* biological sciences, business, education, English, general academic interests/achievements, health fields, humanities, international studies, physical sciences, social sciences. *Creative arts/performance:* art/fine arts, music. *Special achievements/activities:* junior miss. *Special characteristics:* children of faculty/staff, ethnic background, out-of-state students, veterans. ***Tuition waivers:*** Full or partial for employees or children of employees.

LOANS ***Programs:*** Federal Direct (Subsidized and Unsubsidized Stafford, PLUS), state, alternative loans.

WORK-STUDY Federal work-study jobs available.

APPLYING FOR FINANCIAL AID ***Required financial aid forms:*** FAFSA, state aid form. ***Financial aid deadline (priority):*** 5/1. ***Notification date:*** Continuous.

CONTACT Ms. Melinda Reese, Assistant Director of Financial Aid, Thomas University, 1501 Millpond Road, Thomasville, GA 31792-7499, 229-226-1621 Ext. 123 or toll-free 800-538-9784. *Fax:* 229-227-6888. *E-mail:* mreese@thomasu.edu.

TIFFIN UNIVERSITY

Tiffin, OH

Tuition & fees: $19,124 **Average undergraduate aid package: $13,833**

ABOUT THE INSTITUTION Independent, coed. 39 undergraduate majors. Federal methodology is used as a basis for awarding need-based institutional aid.

UNDERGRADUATE EXPENSES for 2011–12 ***Comprehensive fee:*** $27,874 includes full-time tuition ($19,124) and room and board ($8750). ***College room only:*** $4520. Full-time tuition and fees vary according to course load, degree level, and location. Room and board charges vary according to board plan and housing facility. ***Part-time tuition:*** $637 per credit hour. Part-time tuition and fees vary according to course load, degree level, and location. ***Payment plan:*** Installment.

FRESHMAN FINANCIAL AID (Fall 2010, est.) 575 applied for aid; of those 96% were deemed to have need. 100% of freshmen with need received aid; of those 9% had need fully met. ***Average percent of need met:*** 59% (excluding resources awarded to replace EFC). ***Average financial aid package:*** $13,990 (excluding resources awarded to replace EFC).

UNDERGRADUATE FINANCIAL AID (Fall 2010, est.) 1,965 applied for aid; of those 96% were deemed to have need. 99% of undergraduates with need received aid; of those 8% had need fully met. ***Average percent of need met:*** 56% (excluding resources awarded to replace EFC). ***Average financial aid package:*** $13,833 (excluding resources awarded to replace EFC).

GIFT AID (NEED-BASED) ***Total amount:*** $21,125,051 (50% federal, 7% state, 42% institutional, 1% external sources). ***Receiving aid:*** Freshmen: 89% (535); all full-time undergraduates: 79% (1,771). ***Average award:*** Freshmen: $10,052; Undergraduates: $19,087. ***Scholarships, grants, and awards:*** Federal Pell, FSEOG, state, private, college/university gift aid from institutional funds.

GIFT AID (NON-NEED-BASED) ***Receiving aid:*** Freshmen: 6% (37). Undergraduates: 4% (83). ***Scholarships, grants, and awards by category:*** *Academic interests/achievement:* 1,085 awards ($6,963,252 total): general academic interests/achievements. *Creative arts/performance:* 149 awards ($340,825 total): music, performing arts, theater/drama. *Special achievements/activities:* 30 awards ($29,200 total): cheerleading/drum major. *Special characteristics:* 26 awards ($242,994 total): children of faculty/staff. ***Tuition waivers:*** Full or partial for employees or children of employees, senior citizens.

LOANS ***Student loans:*** $27,567,108 (100% need-based). 81% of past graduating class borrowed through all loan programs. *Average indebtedness per student:* $29,130. ***Average need-based loan:*** Freshmen: $4033. Undergraduates: $4466.

Parent loans: $2,427,367 (100% need-based). ***Programs:*** Federal Direct (Subsidized and Unsubsidized Stafford, PLUS), Perkins, college/university.

WORK-STUDY ***Federal work-study:*** Total amount: $398,733; 175 jobs averaging $2416.

ATHLETIC AWARDS Total amount: $2,256,574 (100% need-based).

APPLYING FOR FINANCIAL AID ***Required financial aid form:*** FAFSA. ***Financial aid deadline:*** Continuous. ***Notification date:*** Continuous beginning 2/1. Students must reply within 2 weeks of notification.

CONTACT Ms. Cindy Little, Director of Financial Aid Operations, Tiffin University, 155 Miami Street, Tiffin, OH 44883, 419-448-3415 or toll-free 800-968-6446. *Fax:* 419-443-5006. *E-mail:* clittle@tiffin.edu.

TOCCOA FALLS COLLEGE

Toccoa Falls, GA

CONTACT Vince Welch, Director of Financial Aid, Toccoa Falls College, PO Box 800900, Toccoa Falls, GA 30598, 706-886-7299 Ext. 5234. *Fax:* 706-282-6041. *E-mail:* vwelch@tfc.edu.

TORAH TEMIMAH TALMUDICAL SEMINARY

Brooklyn, NY

CONTACT Financial Aid Office, Torah Temimah Talmudical Seminary, 507 Ocean Parkway, Brooklyn, NY 11218-5913, 718-853-8500.

TOUGALOO COLLEGE

Tougaloo, MS

CONTACT Director of Financial Aid, Tougaloo College, 500 West County Line Road, Tougaloo, MS 39174, 601-977-6134 or toll-free 888-42GALOO. *Fax:* 601-977-6164.

TOURO COLLEGE

New York, NY

CONTACT Office of Financial Aid, Touro College, 27 West 23rd Street, New York, NY 10010, 212-463-0400.

TOWSON UNIVERSITY

Towson, MD

Tuition & fees (MD res): $7656 **Average undergraduate aid package: $9275**

ABOUT THE INSTITUTION State-supported, coed. 58 undergraduate majors. Federal methodology is used as a basis for awarding need-based institutional aid.

UNDERGRADUATE EXPENSES for 2010–11 ***Tuition, state resident:*** full-time $5336; part-time $232 per credit. ***Tuition, nonresident:*** full-time $16,794; part-time $641 per credit. ***Required fees:*** full-time $2320; $96 per credit. Full-time tuition and fees vary according to course load. ***College room and board:*** $9614; ***Room only:*** $5520. Room and board charges vary according to board plan and housing facility. ***Payment plans:*** Guaranteed tuition, tuition prepayment, installment.

FRESHMAN FINANCIAL AID (Fall 2010, est.) 1,942 applied for aid; of those 68% were deemed to have need. 94% of freshmen with need received aid; of those 14% had need fully met. ***Average percent of need met:*** 60% (excluding resources awarded to replace EFC). ***Average financial aid package:*** $8266 (excluding resources awarded to replace EFC). 9% of all full-time freshmen had no need and received non-need-based gift aid.

UNDERGRADUATE FINANCIAL AID (Fall 2010, est.) 10,205 applied for aid; of those 76% were deemed to have need. 95% of undergraduates with need received aid; of those 16% had need fully met. ***Average percent of need met:*** 64% (excluding resources awarded to replace EFC). ***Average financial aid package:*** $9275 (excluding resources awarded to replace EFC). 8% of all full-time undergraduates had no need and received non-need-based gift aid.

GIFT AID (NEED-BASED) ***Total amount:*** $37,307,880 (47% federal, 21% state, 32% institutional). ***Receiving aid:*** Freshmen: 30% (729); all full-time undergraduates: 31% (4,813). ***Average award:*** Freshmen: $8343; Undergraduates: $7601. ***Scholarships, grants, and awards:*** Federal Pell, FSEOG, state, private, college/university gift aid from institutional funds.

GIFT AID (NON-NEED-BASED) ***Total amount:*** $15,186,659 (2% federal, 5% state, 60% institutional, 33% external sources). ***Receiving aid:*** Freshmen: 20% (485). Undergraduates: 13% (2,012). ***Average award:*** Freshmen: $4767. Undergraduates: $5170. ***Scholarships, grants, and awards by category:*** *Academic interests/achievement:* 1,567 awards ($6,590,589 total): biological sciences, business, communication, computer science, education, English, foreign languages, general academic interests/achievements, health fields, mathematics. *Creative arts/performance:* 178 awards ($532,621 total): art/fine arts, dance, debating, music, theater/drama. *Special achievements/activities:* 256 awards ($814,487 total): community service, memberships. *Special characteristics:* 701 awards ($2,184,340 total): adult students, children of faculty/staff, handicapped students, international students, veterans. ***Tuition waivers:*** Full or partial for employees or children of employees, senior citizens.

LOANS ***Student loans:*** $50,671,284 (51% need-based, 49% non-need-based). 56% of past graduating class borrowed through all loan programs. *Average indebtedness per student:* $19,069. ***Average need-based loan:*** Freshmen: $3321. Undergraduates: $4229. ***Parent loans:*** $28,487,868 (100% non-need-based). ***Programs:*** Federal Direct (Subsidized and Unsubsidized Stafford, PLUS), Perkins.

WORK-STUDY ***Federal work-study:*** Total amount: $545,243; 511 jobs averaging $1652.

ATHLETIC AWARDS Total amount: $4,987,857 (100% non-need-based).

APPLYING FOR FINANCIAL AID ***Required financial aid form:*** FAFSA. ***Financial aid deadline:*** 2/10 (priority: 1/31). ***Notification date:*** Continuous beginning 3/21. Students must reply within 2 weeks of notification.

CONTACT Vince Pecora, Director of Financial Aid, Towson University, 8000 York Road, Towson, MD 21252-0001, 410-704-4236 or toll-free 888-4TOWSON. *E-mail:* finaid@towson.edu.

TRANSYLVANIA UNIVERSITY

Lexington, KY

Tuition & fees: $26,740 **Average undergraduate aid package: $21,914**

ABOUT THE INSTITUTION Independent religious, coed. 36 undergraduate majors. Federal methodology is used as a basis for awarding need-based institutional aid.

UNDERGRADUATE EXPENSES for 2010–11 ***Comprehensive fee:*** $34,830 includes full-time tuition ($25,650), mandatory fees ($1090), and room and board ($8090). Room and board charges vary according to board plan and location. ***Part-time tuition:*** $2845 per course. Part-time tuition and fees vary according to course load. ***Payment plan:*** Installment.

FRESHMAN FINANCIAL AID (Fall 2010, est.) 257 applied for aid; of those 88% were deemed to have need. 100% of freshmen with need received aid; of those 27% had need fully met. ***Average percent of need met:*** 85% (excluding resources awarded to replace EFC). ***Average financial aid package:*** $22,458 (excluding resources awarded to replace EFC). 24% of all full-time freshmen had no need and received non-need-based gift aid.

UNDERGRADUATE FINANCIAL AID (Fall 2010, est.) 841 applied for aid; of those 89% were deemed to have need. 100% of undergraduates with need received aid; of those 21% had need fully met. ***Average percent of need met:*** 81% (excluding resources awarded to replace EFC). ***Average financial aid package:*** $21,914 (excluding resources awarded to replace EFC). 30% of all full-time undergraduates had no need and received non-need-based gift aid.

GIFT AID (NEED-BASED) ***Total amount:*** $13,077,131 (10% federal, 21% state, 67% institutional, 2% external sources). ***Receiving aid:*** Freshmen: 74% (225); all full-time undergraduates: 68% (750). ***Average award:*** Freshmen: $18,790; Undergraduates: $17,573. ***Scholarships, grants, and awards:*** Federal Pell, FSEOG, state, private, college/university gift aid from institutional funds.

GIFT AID (NON-NEED-BASED) ***Total amount:*** $4,899,231 (14% state, 83% institutional, 3% external sources). ***Receiving aid:*** Freshmen: 15% (44). Undergraduates: 10% (105). ***Average award:*** Freshmen: $11,388. Undergraduates: $10,995. ***Scholarships, grants, and awards by category:*** *Academic interests/achievement:* 1,041 awards ($9,657,663 total): computer science, general academic interests/achievements. *Creative arts/performance:* 64 awards ($157,100 total): art/fine arts, music, theater/drama. *Special achievements/activities:* 526 awards ($1,031,137 total): general special achievements/activities, religious involvement. *Special characteristics:* 161 awards ($1,254,772 total): children of faculty/staff, members of minority groups, out-of-state students, relatives of clergy, religious affiliation. ***Tuition waivers:*** Full or partial for employees or children of employees.

LOANS ***Student loans:*** $5,402,137 (72% need-based, 28% non-need-based). 64% of past graduating class borrowed through all loan programs. *Average indebtedness per student:* $22,432. ***Average need-based loan:*** Freshmen: $3760. Undergraduates: $4230. ***Parent loans:*** $1,426,147 (35% need-based, 65% non-need-based). ***Programs:*** Federal Direct (Subsidized and Unsubsidized Stafford, PLUS), Perkins, college/university.

WORK-STUDY ***Federal work-study:*** Total amount: $569,576; 450 jobs averaging $1727. ***State or other work-study/employment:*** Total amount: $388,610 (36% need-based, 64% non-need-based). 57 part-time jobs averaging $6178.

APPLYING FOR FINANCIAL AID ***Required financial aid form:*** FAFSA. ***Financial aid deadline (priority):*** 2/1. ***Notification date:*** Continuous beginning 3/15. Students must reply within 2 weeks of notification.

CONTACT Mr. Dave Cecil, Associate Vice President for Financial Aid, Transylvania University, 300 North Broadway, Lexington, KY 40508-1797, 859-233-8239 or toll-free 800-872-6798. *Fax:* 859-281-3650. *E-mail:* dcecil@transy.edu.

TREVECCA NAZARENE UNIVERSITY

Nashville, TN

Tuition & fees: $18,518 **Average undergraduate aid package: N/A**

ABOUT THE INSTITUTION Independent Nazarene, coed. 74 undergraduate majors. Federal methodology is used as a basis for awarding need-based institutional aid.

UNDERGRADUATE EXPENSES for 2010–11 ***Comprehensive fee:*** $26,252 includes full-time tuition ($18,318), mandatory fees ($200), and room and board ($7734). ***College room only:*** $3582. Full-time tuition and fees vary according to course load. Room and board charges vary according to board plan. ***Part-time tuition:*** $708 per credit hour. Part-time tuition and fees vary according to course load. ***Payment plans:*** Tuition prepayment, installment.

GIFT AID (NEED-BASED) ***Total amount:*** $2,746,566 (75% federal, 10% state, 15% institutional). ***Scholarships, grants, and awards:*** Federal Pell, FSEOG, state, private, college/university gift aid from institutional funds.

GIFT AID (NON-NEED-BASED) ***Total amount:*** $7,103,756 (17% state, 78% institutional, 5% external sources). ***Scholarships, grants, and awards by category:*** *Academic interests/achievement:* biological sciences, business, communication, education, English, general academic interests/achievements, physical sciences, religion/biblical studies, social sciences. *Creative arts/performance:* cinema/film/broadcasting, music. *Special achievements/activities:* general special achievements/activities. *Special characteristics:* children of faculty/staff, general special characteristics, relatives of clergy, religious affiliation. ***Tuition waivers:*** Full or partial for employees or children of employees, senior citizens.

LOANS ***Student loans:*** $20,571,809 (53% need-based, 47% non-need-based). ***Parent loans:*** $1,327,163 (100% non-need-based). ***Programs:*** Federal Direct (Subsidized and Unsubsidized Stafford, PLUS), Perkins.

WORK-STUDY ***Federal work-study:*** Total amount: $120,707; jobs available. ***State or other work-study/employment:*** Total amount: $402,885 (100% need-based). Part-time jobs available.

ATHLETIC AWARDS Total amount: $879,139 (100% non-need-based).

APPLYING FOR FINANCIAL AID ***Required financial aid form:*** FAFSA. ***Financial aid deadline:*** 8/1 (priority: 2/1). ***Notification date:*** Continuous beginning 3/1.

CONTACT Eddie White, Director of Financial Aid, Trevecca Nazarene University, 333 Murfreesboro Road, Nashville, TN 37210-2834, 615-248-1242 or toll-free 888-210-4TNU. *Fax:* 615-248-7728. *E-mail:* ewhite@trevecca.edu.

TRINE UNIVERSITY

Angola, IN

Tuition & fees: $26,730 **Average undergraduate aid package: $23,371**

ABOUT THE INSTITUTION Independent, coed. 35 undergraduate majors. Federal methodology is used as a basis for awarding need-based institutional aid.

UNDERGRADUATE EXPENSES for 2011–12 ***Comprehensive fee:*** $35,530 includes full-time tuition ($26,600), mandatory fees ($130), and room and board ($8800). Full-time tuition and fees vary according to degree level and location. Room and board charges vary according to board plan and housing facility. Part-time tuition and fees vary according to degree level and location. ***Payment plan:*** Installment.

FRESHMAN FINANCIAL AID (Fall 2010, est.) 411 applied for aid; of those 74% were deemed to have need. 100% of freshmen with need received aid; of those 78% had need fully met. ***Average percent of need met:*** 90% (excluding resources awarded to replace EFC). ***Average financial aid package:*** $23,520 (excluding resources awarded to replace EFC). 6% of all full-time freshmen had no need and received non-need-based gift aid.

UNDERGRADUATE FINANCIAL AID (Fall 2010, est.) 1,533 applied for aid; of those 73% were deemed to have need. 100% of undergraduates with need received aid; of those 93% had need fully met. ***Average percent of need met:*** 87% (excluding resources awarded to replace EFC). ***Average financial aid package:*** $23,371 (excluding resources awarded to replace EFC). 4% of all full-time undergraduates had no need and received non-need-based gift aid.

GIFT AID (NEED-BASED) ***Total amount:*** $8,109,152 (38% federal, 24% state, 38% institutional). ***Receiving aid:*** Freshmen: 64% (266); all full-time undergraduates: 43% (680). ***Average award:*** Freshmen: $4703; Undergraduates: $4577. ***Scholarships, grants, and awards:*** Federal Pell, FSEOG, state, private, college/university gift aid from institutional funds.

GIFT AID (NON-NEED-BASED) ***Total amount:*** $14,782,144 (96% institutional, 4% external sources). ***Receiving aid:*** Freshmen: 64% (266). Undergraduates: 43% (680). ***Average award:*** Freshmen: $11,860. Undergraduates: $10,970. ***Scholarships, grants, and awards by category:*** *Academic interests/achievement:* general academic interests/achievements. *Special characteristics:* children and siblings of alumni, children of faculty/staff, members of minority groups, siblings of current students. ***Tuition waivers:*** Full or partial for employees or children of employees.

LOANS ***Student loans:*** $8,349,349 (57% need-based, 43% non-need-based). 69% of past graduating class borrowed through all loan programs. *Average indebtedness per student:* $26,050. ***Average need-based loan:*** Freshmen: $3459. Undergraduates: $3945. ***Parent loans:*** $4,466,664 (100% non-need-based). ***Programs:*** alternative loans.

WORK-STUDY ***Federal work-study:*** Total amount: $102,633; jobs available.

APPLYING FOR FINANCIAL AID ***Required financial aid form:*** FAFSA. ***Financial aid deadline (priority):*** 3/10. ***Notification date:*** Continuous beginning 2/15. Students must reply by 5/1 or within 2 weeks of notification.

CONTACT Kim Bennett, Director of Financial Aid, Trine University, 1 University Avenue, Angola, IN 46703-1764, 260-665-4175 or toll-free 800-347-4TSU. *Fax:* 260-665-4511. *E-mail:* admit@trine.edu.

TRINITY BAPTIST COLLEGE

Jacksonville, FL

CONTACT Mr. Donald Schaffer, Financial Aid Administrator, Trinity Baptist College, 800 Hammond Boulevard, Jacksonville, FL 32221, 904-596-2445 or toll-free 904-596-2400 (in-state), 800-786-2206 (out-of-state). *Fax:* 904-596-2531. *E-mail:* financialaid@tbc.edu.

TRINITY BIBLE COLLEGE

Ellendale, ND

ABOUT THE INSTITUTION Independent Assemblies of God, coed. ***Awards:*** associate and bachelor's degrees. 12 undergraduate majors. ***Total enrollment:*** 292. Undergraduates: 292.

GIFT AID (NEED-BASED) ***Scholarships, grants, and awards:*** Federal Pell, FSEOG, state, private, college/university gift aid from institutional funds.

GIFT AID (NON-NEED-BASED) ***Scholarships, grants, and awards by category:*** *Academic interests/achievement:* business, education, general academic interests/achievements, religion/biblical studies. *Creative arts/performance:* art/fine arts, creative writing, music, theater/drama. *Special achievements/activities:* community service, general special achievements/activities, leadership, religious involvement. *Special characteristics:* children and siblings of alumni, children of current students, children of faculty/staff, general special characteristics, international students, married students, parents of current students, relatives of clergy, siblings of current students, spouses of current students.

LOANS ***Programs:*** Perkins, alternative loans.

APPLYING FOR FINANCIAL AID ***Required financial aid form:*** FAFSA.

CONTACT Susan Healy, Financial Aid Associate, Trinity Bible College, 50 South 6th Avenue, Ellendale, ND 58436-7150, 701-349-3621 Ext. 5787 or toll-free 888-TBC-2DAY. *Fax:* 701-349-5787. *E-mail:* shealy@trinitybiblecollege.edu.

TRINITY CHRISTIAN COLLEGE

Palos Heights, IL

Tuition & fees: $21,508 **Average undergraduate aid package: $12,710**

ABOUT THE INSTITUTION Independent Christian Reformed, coed. 60 undergraduate majors. Both federal and institutional methodology are used as a basis for awarding need-based institutional aid.

UNDERGRADUATE EXPENSES for 2010–11 ***Comprehensive fee:*** $29,472 includes full-time tuition ($21,398), mandatory fees ($110), and room and board ($7964). ***College room only:*** $4272. Full-time tuition and fees vary according to course load. Room and board charges vary according to board plan. ***Part-time tuition:*** $715 per semester hour. Part-time tuition and fees vary according to course load. ***Payment plans:*** Installment, deferred payment.

FRESHMAN FINANCIAL AID (Fall 2010, est.) 199 applied for aid; of those 99% were deemed to have need. 100% of freshmen with need received aid; of those 16% had need fully met. ***Average percent of need met:*** 43% (excluding resources awarded to replace EFC). ***Average financial aid package:*** $15,829 (excluding resources awarded to replace EFC). 46% of all full-time freshmen had no need and received non-need-based gift aid.

UNDERGRADUATE FINANCIAL AID (Fall 2010, est.) 954 applied for aid; of those 100% were deemed to have need. 100% of undergraduates with need received aid; of those 5% had need fully met. ***Average percent of need met:*** 49% (excluding resources awarded to replace EFC). ***Average financial aid package:*** $12,710 (excluding resources awarded to replace EFC). 23% of all full-time undergraduates had no need and received non-need-based gift aid.

GIFT AID (NEED-BASED) ***Total amount:*** $7,042,051 (40% federal, 30% state, 30% institutional). ***Receiving aid:*** Freshmen: 84% (198); all full-time undergraduates: 80% (799). ***Average award:*** Freshmen: $5125; Undergraduates: $5318. ***Scholarships, grants, and awards:*** Federal Pell, FSEOG, state, private, college/university gift aid from institutional funds.

GIFT AID (NON-NEED-BASED) ***Total amount:*** $6,887,284 (1% federal, 95% institutional, 4% external sources). ***Receiving aid:*** Freshmen: 84% (198). Undergraduates: 96% (954). ***Average award:*** Freshmen: $5400. Undergraduates: $5810. ***Scholarships, grants, and awards by category:*** *Academic interests/achievement:* business, computer science, education, English, general academic interests/achievements, health fields, mathematics, physical sciences, premedicine, religion/biblical studies, social sciences. *Creative arts/performance:* applied art and design, art/fine arts, general creative arts/performance, journalism/publications, music, theater/drama. *Special achievements/activities:* general special achievements/activities, leadership, religious involvement. *Special characteristics:* adult students, children and siblings of alumni, children of faculty/staff, ethnic background, first-generation college students, local/state students, members of minority groups, out-of-state students, religious affiliation. ***Tuition waivers:*** Full or partial for employees or children of employees.

LOANS ***Student loans:*** $11,899,788 (47% need-based, 53% non-need-based). 70% of past graduating class borrowed through all loan programs. *Average indebtedness per student:* $25,794. ***Average need-based loan:*** Freshmen: $4810. Undergraduates: $4512. ***Parent loans:*** $1,116,640 (100% non-need-based). ***Programs:*** Federal Direct (Subsidized and Unsubsidized Stafford, PLUS), Perkins, Federal Nursing.

WORK-STUDY ***Federal work-study:*** Total amount: $144,100; 135 jobs averaging $1500. ***State or other work-study/employment:*** Total amount: $563,900 (100% non-need-based). Part-time jobs available.

ATHLETIC AWARDS Total amount: $1,313,250 (100% non-need-based).

APPLYING FOR FINANCIAL AID ***Required financial aid forms:*** FAFSA, institution's own form. ***Financial aid deadline (priority):*** 2/15. ***Notification date:*** Continuous beginning 3/1. Students must reply by 5/1 or within 2 weeks of notification.

CONTACT L. Denise Coleman, Director of Financial Aid, Trinity Christian College, 6601 West College Drive, Palos Heights, IL 60463-0929, 708-239-4706 or toll-free 800-748-0085. *E-mail:* financialaid@trnty.edu.

TRINITY COLLEGE

Hartford, CT

Tuition & fees: $42,370 **Average undergraduate aid package: $38,498**

ABOUT THE INSTITUTION Independent, coed. 47 undergraduate majors. Both federal and institutional methodology are used as a basis for awarding need-based institutional aid.

UNDERGRADUATE EXPENSES for 2010–11 ***One-time required fee:*** $25. ***Comprehensive fee:*** $53,330 includes full-time tuition ($40,360), mandatory fees ($2010), and room and board ($10,960). ***College room only:*** $7120. Full-time tuition and fees vary according to course load and program. Room and board charges vary according to board plan. ***Part-time tuition:*** $4484 per course. Part-time tuition and fees vary according to course load and program. ***Payment plan:*** Installment.

FRESHMAN FINANCIAL AID (Fall 2010, est.) 292 applied for aid; of those 87% were deemed to have need. 100% of freshmen with need received aid; of those 100% had need fully met. ***Average percent of need met:*** 100% (excluding resources awarded to replace EFC). ***Average financial aid package:*** $37,881 (excluding resources awarded to replace EFC). 1% of all full-time freshmen had no need and received non-need-based gift aid.

UNDERGRADUATE FINANCIAL AID (Fall 2010, est.) 1,023 applied for aid; of those 95% were deemed to have need. 100% of undergraduates with need received aid; of those 100% had need fully met. ***Average percent of need met:*** 100% (excluding resources awarded to replace EFC). ***Average financial aid package:*** $38,498 (excluding resources awarded to replace EFC). 1% of all full-time undergraduates had no need and received non-need-based gift aid.

GIFT AID (NEED-BASED) ***Total amount:*** $34,306,768 (5% federal, 3% state, 90% institutional, 2% external sources). ***Receiving aid:*** Freshmen: 39% (228); all full-time undergraduates: 41% (903). ***Average award:*** Freshmen: $37,288; Undergraduates: $36,812. ***Scholarships, grants, and awards:*** Federal Pell, FSEOG, state, private, college/university gift aid from institutional funds, Academic Competitiveness Grants, National SMART Grants, Yellow Ribbon Grants.

GIFT AID (NON-NEED-BASED) ***Total amount:*** $1,333,490 (94% institutional, 6% external sources). ***Receiving aid:*** Freshmen: 8% (49). Undergraduates: 3% (64). ***Average award:*** Freshmen: $32,705. Undergraduates: $32,748. ***Scholarships, grants, and awards by category:*** *Academic interests/achievement:* 38 awards ($1,508,781 total): general academic interests/achievements. *Special achievements/activities:* 97 awards ($4,204,332 total): leadership. ***Tuition waivers:*** Full or partial for employees or children of employees, adult students.

LOANS ***Student loans:*** $6,088,719 (57% need-based, 43% non-need-based). 39% of past graduating class borrowed through all loan programs. *Average indebtedness per student:* $21,671. ***Average need-based loan:*** Freshmen: $3535. Undergraduates: $4320. ***Parent loans:*** $4,075,669 (100% non-need-based). ***Programs:*** Federal Direct (PLUS), Perkins, college/university, alternative loans.

WORK-STUDY ***Federal work-study:*** Total amount: $934,728; 518 jobs averaging $1748.

APPLYING FOR FINANCIAL AID ***Required financial aid forms:*** FAFSA, CSS Financial Aid PROFILE, noncustodial (divorced/separated) parent's statement, business/farm supplement, federal income tax form(s). ***Financial aid deadline:*** 3/1 (priority: 2/1). ***Notification date:*** 4/1. Students must reply by 5/1 or within 2 weeks of notification.

CONTACT Ms. Kelly O'Brien, Director of Financial Aid, Trinity College, 300 Summit Street, Hartford, CT 06106-3100, 860-297-2046. *Fax:* 860-987-6296.

TRINITY COLLEGE OF FLORIDA

New Port Richey, FL

CONTACT Sue Wayne, Financial Aid Director, Trinity College of Florida, 2430 Welbilt Boulevard, New Port Richey, FL 34655, 727-569-1413 or toll-free 800-388-0869. *Fax:* 727-376-0781. *E-mail:* swayne@trinitycollege.edu.

TRINITY COLLEGE OF NURSING AND HEALTH SCIENCES

Rock Island, IL

Tuition & fees: $12,656 **Average undergraduate aid package: N/A**

ABOUT THE INSTITUTION Independent, coed. 8 undergraduate majors. Federal methodology is used as a basis for awarding need-based institutional aid.

UNDERGRADUATE EXPENSES for 2011–12 ***Tuition:*** full-time $11,472; part-time $478 per credit. ***Required fees:*** full-time $1184; $529 per term. Full-time tuition and fees vary according to course load, degree level, program, and student level. Part-time tuition and fees vary according to course load, degree level, program, and student level. ***Payment plans:*** Installment, deferred payment.

FRESHMAN FINANCIAL AID (Fall 2010, est.) 1 applied for aid; of those 100% were deemed to have need. 100% of freshmen with need received aid.

UNDERGRADUATE FINANCIAL AID (Fall 2010, est.) 110 applied for aid; of those 100% were deemed to have need. 100% of undergraduates with need received aid.

GIFT AID (NEED-BASED) ***Total amount:*** $410,512 (66% federal, 22% state, 6% institutional, 6% external sources). ***Receiving aid:*** Freshmen: 100% (1); all full-time undergraduates: 61% (79). ***Scholarships, grants, and awards:*** Federal Pell, FSEOG, state, private, college/university gift aid from institutional funds.

LOANS ***Student loans:*** $1,008,396 (44% need-based, 56% non-need-based). 85% of past graduating class borrowed through all loan programs. *Average indebtedness per student:* $9500. ***Parent loans:*** $129,407 (100% non-need-based). ***Programs:*** Federal Direct (Subsidized and Unsubsidized Stafford, PLUS), Federal Nursing.

APPLYING FOR FINANCIAL AID ***Required financial aid forms:*** FAFSA, institution's own form. ***Financial aid deadline:*** Continuous. ***Notification date:*** Continuous beginning 6/1. Students must reply within 4 weeks of notification.

CONTACT Kris Hodgerson, Financial Aid Specialist, Trinity College of Nursing and Health Sciences, 2122 25th Avenue, Rock Island, IL 61201, 309-779-7700. *Fax:* 309-779-7748. *E-mail:* hodgersonk@ihs.org.

TRINITY INTERNATIONAL UNIVERSITY

Deerfield, IL

ABOUT THE INSTITUTION Independent religious, coed. ***Awards:*** bachelor's and master's degrees and post-bachelor's certificates. 39 undergraduate majors. ***Total enrollment:*** 2,671. Undergraduates: 968. Freshmen: 134.

GIFT AID (NEED-BASED) ***Scholarships, grants, and awards:*** Federal Pell, FSEOG, state, private, college/university gift aid from institutional funds.

GIFT AID (NON-NEED-BASED) ***Scholarships, grants, and awards by category:*** *Academic interests/achievement:* general academic interests/achievements. *Creative arts/performance:* music. *Special achievements/activities:* religious involvement. *Special characteristics:* children and siblings of alumni, members of minority groups, religious affiliation.

LOANS ***Programs:*** Federal Direct (Subsidized and Unsubsidized Stafford, PLUS), Perkins.

WORK-STUDY ***Federal work-study:*** Total amount: $72,636; jobs available.

APPLYING FOR FINANCIAL AID ***Required financial aid form:*** FAFSA.

CONTACT Pat Coles, Interim Director of Financial Aid, Trinity International University, 2065 Half Day Road, Deerfield, IL 60015-1284, 847-317-8060 or toll-free 800-822-3225 (out-of-state). *Fax:* 847-317-7081. *E-mail:* finaid@tiu.edu.

TRINITY LUTHERAN COLLEGE

Issaquah, WA

CONTACT Ms. Susan Dalgleish, Director of Financial Aid, Trinity Lutheran College, 4221 228th Avenue SE, Issaquah, WA 98029-9299, 425-961-5514 or toll-free 800-843-5659. *Fax:* 425-392-0404. *E-mail:* susan.dalgleish@tlc.edu.

TRINITY UNIVERSITY

San Antonio, TX

Tuition & fees: $30,012	Average undergraduate aid package: $25,401

ABOUT THE INSTITUTION Independent religious, coed. 50 undergraduate majors. Federal methodology is used as a basis for awarding need-based institutional aid.

UNDERGRADUATE EXPENSES for 2010–11 ***Comprehensive fee:*** $40,324 includes full-time tuition ($29,832), mandatory fees ($180), and room and board ($10,312). ***College room only:*** $6896. Full-time tuition and fees vary according to course load. Room and board charges vary according to board plan. ***Part-time tuition:*** $1243 per credit hour. Part-time tuition and fees vary according to course load. ***Payment plan:*** Installment.

FRESHMAN FINANCIAL AID (Fall 2010, est.) 412 applied for aid; of those 75% were deemed to have need. 99% of freshmen with need received aid; of those 29% had need fully met. ***Average percent of need met:*** 88% (excluding resources awarded to replace EFC). ***Average financial aid package:*** $25,928 (excluding resources awarded to replace EFC). 37% of all full-time freshmen had no need and received non-need-based gift aid.

UNDERGRADUATE FINANCIAL AID (Fall 2010, est.) 1,252 applied for aid; of those 81% were deemed to have need. 98% of undergraduates with need received aid; of those 35% had need fully met. ***Average percent of need met:*** 88% (excluding resources awarded to replace EFC). ***Average financial aid package:*** $25,401 (excluding resources awarded to replace EFC). 40% of all full-time undergraduates had no need and received non-need-based gift aid.

GIFT AID (NEED-BASED) ***Total amount:*** $18,725,402 (10% federal, 9% state, 78% institutional, 3% external sources). ***Receiving aid:*** Freshmen: 52% (307); all full-time undergraduates: 42% (988). ***Average award:*** Freshmen: $19,565; Undergraduates: $19,487. ***Scholarships, grants, and awards:*** Federal Pell, FSEOG, state, private, college/university gift aid from institutional funds.

GIFT AID (NON-NEED-BASED) ***Total amount:*** $13,929,039 (1% federal, 95% institutional, 4% external sources). ***Receiving aid:*** Freshmen: 11% (63). Undergraduates: 7% (164). ***Average award:*** Freshmen: $12,832. Undergraduates: $13,234. ***Scholarships, grants, and awards by category:*** *Academic interests/achievement:* general academic interests/achievements. *Creative arts/performance:* art/fine arts, debating, music, theater/drama. *Special characteristics:* first-generation college students. ***Tuition waivers:*** Full or partial for employees or children of employees.

LOANS ***Student loans:*** $6,631,746 (71% need-based, 29% non-need-based). ***Average need-based loan:*** Freshmen: $5509. Undergraduates: $5725. ***Parent loans:*** $6,556,301 (15% need-based, 85% non-need-based). ***Programs:*** Perkins, state, college/university.

WORK-STUDY ***Federal work-study:*** Total amount: $902,802; jobs available. ***State or other work-study/employment:*** Part-time jobs available.

APPLYING FOR FINANCIAL AID ***Required financial aid form:*** FAFSA. ***Financial aid deadline:*** 4/1 (priority: 2/15). ***Notification date:*** 4/1. Students must reply by 5/1 or within 3 weeks of notification.

CONTACT Glendi Gaddis, Director of Financial Aid, Trinity University, 715 Stadium Drive, San Antonio, TX 78212-7200, 210-999-8315 or toll-free 800-TRINITY. *Fax:* 210-999-8316. *E-mail:* financialaid@trinity.edu.

TRINITY (WASHINGTON) UNIVERSITY

Washington, DC

CONTACT Catherine H. Geier, Director of Student Financial Services, Trinity (Washington) University, 125 Michigan Avenue, NE, Washington, DC 20017-1094, 202-884-9530 or toll-free 800-IWANTTC. *Fax:* 202-884-9524. *E-mail:* financialaid@trinitydc.edu.

TRI-STATE BIBLE COLLEGE

South Point, OH

CONTACT Financial Aid Office, Tri-State Bible College, 506 Margaret Street, PO Box 445, South Point, OH 45680-8402, 740-377-2520.

TROY UNIVERSITY

Troy, AL

Tuition & fees (AL res): $7200	Average undergraduate aid package: $4667

ABOUT THE INSTITUTION State-supported, coed. 42 undergraduate majors. Federal methodology is used as a basis for awarding need-based institutional aid.

UNDERGRADUATE EXPENSES for 2010–11 ***Tuition, state resident:*** full-time $6480; part-time $216 per credit hour. ***Tuition, nonresident:*** full-time $12,960; part-time $432 per credit hour. ***Required fees:*** full-time $720; $8 per credit hour or $50 per term. Full-time tuition and fees vary according to location and program. Part-time tuition and fees vary according to location and program. ***College room and board:*** $6570. Room and board charges vary according to board plan and housing facility. ***Payment plan:*** Installment.

FRESHMAN FINANCIAL AID (Fall 2010, est.) 1,375 applied for aid; of those 100% were deemed to have need. 100% of freshmen with need received aid. ***Average financial aid package:*** $3910 (excluding resources awarded to replace EFC). 17% of all full-time freshmen had no need and received non-need-based gift aid.

UNDERGRADUATE FINANCIAL AID (Fall 2010, est.) 7,764 applied for aid; of those 100% were deemed to have need. 100% of undergraduates with need received aid. ***Average financial aid package:*** $4667 (excluding resources awarded to replace EFC). 11% of all full-time undergraduates had no need and received non-need-based gift aid.

GIFT AID (NEED-BASED) ***Total amount:*** $54,617,003 (100% federal). ***Receiving aid:*** Freshmen: 55% (978); all full-time undergraduates: 54% (5,738). ***Average award:*** Freshmen: $4576; Undergraduates: $4611. ***Scholarships, grants, and awards:*** Federal Pell, FSEOG, state, private, college/university gift aid from institutional funds.

GIFT AID (NON-NEED-BASED) ***Total amount:*** $26,043,391 (42% institutional, 58% external sources). ***Receiving aid:*** Freshmen: 30% (537). Undergraduates: 15% (1,657). ***Average award:*** Freshmen: $5047. Undergraduates: $5198. ***Scholarships, grants, and awards by category:*** *Academic interests/achievement:* general academic interests/achievements. *Creative arts/performance:* music, theater/drama. *Special achievements/activities:* leadership. *Special characteristics:* general special characteristics. ***Tuition waivers:*** Full or partial for employees or children of employees.

LOANS ***Student loans:*** $212,224,145 (100% need-based). ***Average need-based loan:*** Freshmen: $3643. Undergraduates: $4726. ***Parent loans:*** $4,468,004 (100% need-based). ***Programs:*** Perkins.

WORK-STUDY ***Federal work-study:*** Total amount: $1,172,982; jobs available.

ATHLETIC AWARDS Total amount: $4,342,774 (100% non-need-based).

APPLYING FOR FINANCIAL AID ***Required financial aid forms:*** FAFSA, institution's own form. ***Financial aid deadline (priority):*** 3/1. ***Notification date:*** Continuous beginning 6/1. Students must reply within 2 weeks of notification.

CONTACT Ms. Carol Ballard, Associate Vice Chancellor of Financial Aid, Troy University, 131 Adams Administration Building, Troy, AL 36082, 334-670-3186 or toll-free 800-551-9716. *Fax:* 334-670-3702. *E-mail:* csupri@troy.edu.

TRUETT-McCONNELL COLLEGE

Cleveland, GA

ABOUT THE INSTITUTION Independent Baptist, coed. 10 undergraduate majors.

GIFT AID (NEED-BASED) ***Scholarships, grants, and awards:*** Federal Pell, FSEOG, state, private, college/university gift aid from institutional funds.

GIFT AID (NON-NEED-BASED) ***Scholarships, grants, and awards by category:*** *Academic interests/achievement:* general academic interests/achievements. *Creative arts/performance:* music. *Special achievements/activities:* leadership. *Special characteristics:* international students, relatives of clergy, religious affiliation, siblings of current students, spouses of current students.

LOANS ***Programs:*** Federal Direct (Subsidized and Unsubsidized Stafford, PLUS).

WORK-STUDY ***Federal work-study:*** Total amount: $26,335; 18 jobs averaging $1535. ***State or other work-study/employment:*** Part-time jobs available.

APPLYING FOR FINANCIAL AID ***Required financial aid forms:*** FAFSA, institution's own form, state aid form.

CONTACT Mrs. Becky Moore, Director of Financial Aid, Truett-McConnell College, 100 Alumni Drive, Cleveland, GA 30528, 706-865-2134 Ext. 144 or toll-free 800-226-8621 (in-state). *Fax:* 706-865-7615. *E-mail:* bmoore@truett.edu.

TRUMAN STATE UNIVERSITY

Kirksville, MO

Tuition & fees (MO res): $6692 **Average undergraduate aid package: $10,879**

ABOUT THE INSTITUTION State-supported, coed. 35 undergraduate majors. Federal methodology is used as a basis for awarding need-based institutional aid.

UNDERGRADUATE EXPENSES for 2010–11 ***One-time required fee:*** $305. ***Tuition, state resident:*** full-time $6458; part-time $269 per credit hour. ***Tuition, nonresident:*** full-time $11,856; part-time $494 per credit hour. ***Required fees:*** full-time $234. Full-time tuition and fees vary according to course load, degree level, and program. Part-time tuition and fees vary according to course load, degree level, and program. ***College room and board:*** $7097. Room and board charges vary according to housing facility. ***Payment plan:*** Installment.

FRESHMAN FINANCIAL AID (Fall 2010, est.) 1,155 applied for aid; of those 66% were deemed to have need. 100% of freshmen with need received aid; of those 75% had need fully met. ***Average percent of need met:*** 88% (excluding resources awarded to replace EFC). ***Average financial aid package:*** $10,920 (excluding resources awarded to replace EFC). 41% of all full-time freshmen had no need and received non-need-based gift aid.

UNDERGRADUATE FINANCIAL AID (Fall 2010, est.) 3,801 applied for aid; of those 73% were deemed to have need. 99% of undergraduates with need received aid; of those 67% had need fully met. ***Average percent of need met:*** 84% (excluding resources awarded to replace EFC). ***Average financial aid package:*** $10,879 (excluding resources awarded to replace EFC). 36% of all full-time undergraduates had no need and received non-need-based gift aid.

GIFT AID (NEED-BASED) ***Total amount:*** $17,027,023 (32% federal, 11% state, 52% institutional, 5% external sources). ***Receiving aid:*** Freshmen: 53% (752); all full-time undergraduates: 47% (2,541). ***Average award:*** Freshmen: $1672; Undergraduates: $1936. ***Scholarships, grants, and awards:*** Federal Pell, FSEOG, state, private, college/university gift aid from institutional funds, Academic Competitiveness Grants, National SMART Grants, TEACH Grants.

GIFT AID (NON-NEED-BASED) ***Total amount:*** $14,393,329 (2% federal, 8% state, 83% institutional, 7% external sources). ***Receiving aid:*** Freshmen: 49% (696). Undergraduates: 50% (2,699). ***Average award:*** Freshmen: $2543. Undergraduates: $2730. ***Scholarships, grants, and awards by category:*** *Academic interests/achievement:* 3,851 awards ($19,766,481 total): agriculture, biological sciences, business, communication, computer science, education, English, foreign languages, general academic interests/achievements, health fields, humanities, mathematics, military science, physical sciences, premedicine, social sciences. *Creative arts/performance:* 118 awards ($101,708 total): art/fine arts, debating, music, theater/drama. *Special achievements/activities:* 139 awards ($1,699,270 total): leadership. *Special characteristics:* 419 awards ($1,267,848 total): children and siblings of alumni, children of faculty/staff, international students, out-of-state students, previous college experience. ***Tuition waivers:*** Full or partial for employees or children of employees, senior citizens.

LOANS ***Student loans:*** $24,616,674 (57% need-based, 43% non-need-based). 53% of past graduating class borrowed through all loan programs. *Average indebtedness per student:* $19,118. ***Average need-based loan:*** Freshmen: $2471. Undergraduates: $3238. ***Parent loans:*** $1,521,049 (39% need-based, 61% non-need-based). ***Programs:*** Federal Direct (Subsidized and Unsubsidized Stafford, PLUS), Perkins, Federal Nursing, state, college/university, alternative loans.

WORK-STUDY ***Federal work-study:*** Total amount: $695,157; 501 jobs averaging $1393. ***State or other work-study/employment:*** Total amount: $2,337,752 (1% need-based, 99% non-need-based). 1,407 part-time jobs averaging $1662.

ATHLETIC AWARDS Total amount: $1,384,734 (32% need-based, 68% non-need-based).

APPLYING FOR FINANCIAL AID ***Required financial aid forms:*** FAFSA, institution's own form. ***Financial aid deadline (priority):*** 4/1. ***Notification date:*** Continuous beginning 4/1. Students must reply within 4 weeks of notification.

CONTACT Kathy Elsea, Director of Financial Aid, Truman State University, 103 McClain Hall, Kirksville, MO 63501-4221, 660-785-4130 or toll-free 800-892-7792 (in-state). *Fax:* 660-785-7389. *E-mail:* kelsea@truman.edu.

TUFTS UNIVERSITY

Medford, MA

Tuition & fees: $42,532 **Average undergraduate aid package: $32,696**

ABOUT THE INSTITUTION Independent, coed. 60 undergraduate majors. Both federal and institutional methodology are used as a basis for awarding need-based institutional aid.

UNDERGRADUATE EXPENSES for 2010–11 ***Comprehensive fee:*** $53,800 includes full-time tuition ($41,598), mandatory fees ($934), and room and board ($11,268). ***College room only:*** $5982. Room and board charges vary according to board plan. ***Payment plans:*** Tuition prepayment, installment.

FRESHMAN FINANCIAL AID (Fall 2010, est.) 718 applied for aid; of those 77% were deemed to have need. 100% of freshmen with need received aid; of those 100% had need fully met. ***Average percent of need met:*** 100% (excluding resources awarded to replace EFC). ***Average financial aid package:*** $32,483 (excluding resources awarded to replace EFC). 1% of all full-time freshmen had no need and received non-need-based gift aid.

UNDERGRADUATE FINANCIAL AID (Fall 2010, est.) 2,555 applied for aid; of those 87% were deemed to have need. 98% of undergraduates with need received aid; of those 100% had need fully met. ***Average percent of need met:*** 100% (excluding resources awarded to replace EFC). ***Average financial aid package:*** $32,696 (excluding resources awarded to replace EFC). 2% of all full-time undergraduates had no need and received non-need-based gift aid.

GIFT AID (NEED-BASED) ***Total amount:*** $63,849,079 (8% federal, 1% state, 88% institutional, 3% external sources). ***Receiving aid:*** Freshmen: 39% (515); all full-time undergraduates: 38% (2,034). ***Average award:*** Freshmen: $30,074; Undergraduates: $29,916. ***Scholarships, grants, and awards:*** Federal Pell, FSEOG, state, private, college/university gift aid from institutional funds.

GIFT AID (NON-NEED-BASED) ***Total amount:*** $540,828 (6% federal, 15% state, 7% institutional, 72% external sources). ***Receiving aid:*** Freshmen: 2% (20). Undergraduates: 2% (85). ***Average award:*** Freshmen: $500. Undergraduates: $500. ***Scholarships, grants, and awards by category:*** *Academic interests/achievement:* 84 awards ($35,250 total): general academic interests/achievements. ***Tuition waivers:*** Full or partial for employees or children of employees.

LOANS ***Student loans:*** $9,531,157 (78% need-based, 22% non-need-based). 41% of past graduating class borrowed through all loan programs. *Average indebtedness per student:* $27,443. ***Average need-based loan:*** Freshmen: $2911. Undergraduates: $3554. ***Parent loans:*** $11,120,694 (100% non-need-based). ***Programs:*** Federal Direct (Subsidized and Unsubsidized Stafford, PLUS), Perkins, college/university.

WORK-STUDY ***Federal work-study:*** Total amount: $3,247,559; 1,721 jobs averaging $1912. ***State or other work-study/employment:*** Total amount: $166,200 (100% need-based). 85 part-time jobs averaging $1955.

APPLYING FOR FINANCIAL AID ***Required financial aid forms:*** FAFSA, CSS Financial Aid PROFILE, noncustodial (divorced/separated) parent's statement, federal income tax form(s). ***Financial aid deadline:*** 2/15. ***Notification date:*** 4/5. Students must reply by 5/1.

CONTACT Patricia C. Reilly, Director of Financial Aid, Tufts University, Dowling Hall, Medford, MA 02155, 617-627-5912. *Fax:* 617-627-3987. *E-mail:* patricia.reilly@tufts.edu.

TUI UNIVERSITY

Cypress, CA

Tuition & fees: $9440 **Average undergraduate aid package: $4415**

ABOUT THE INSTITUTION Independent, coed. 9 undergraduate majors. Both federal and institutional methodology are used as a basis for awarding need-based institutional aid.

UNDERGRADUATE EXPENSES for 2011–12 ***Tuition:*** full-time $9440; part-time $295 per semester hour. Full-time tuition and fees vary according to course load, degree level, and program. Part-time tuition and fees vary according to course load, degree level, and program. ***Payment plans:*** Installment, deferred payment.

FRESHMAN FINANCIAL AID (Fall 2009) 69 applied for aid; of those 100% were deemed to have need. 100% of freshmen with need received aid; of those 86% had need fully met. ***Average percent of need met:*** 98% (excluding resources awarded to replace EFC). ***Average financial aid package:*** $4305 (excluding resources awarded to replace EFC). 1% of all full-time freshmen had no need and received non-need-based gift aid.

UNDERGRADUATE FINANCIAL AID (Fall 2009) 650 applied for aid; of those 100% were deemed to have need. 100% of undergraduates with need received aid; of those 85% had need fully met. ***Average percent of need met:*** 98% (excluding resources awarded to replace EFC). ***Average financial aid package:*** $4415 (excluding resources awarded to replace EFC). 1% of all full-time undergraduates had no need and received non-need-based gift aid.

GIFT AID (NEED-BASED) ***Total amount:*** $1,400,898 (100% federal). ***Receiving aid:*** Freshmen: 8% (43); all full-time undergraduates: 4% (424). ***Average award:*** Freshmen: $1922; Undergraduates: $3293. ***Scholarships, grants, and awards:*** Federal Pell.

GIFT AID (NON-NEED-BASED) ***Average award:*** Freshmen: $6639. Undergraduates: $5898. ***Tuition waivers:*** Full or partial for employees or children of employees.

LOANS ***Student loans:*** 50% of past graduating class borrowed through all loan programs. *Average indebtedness per student:* $38,298. ***Programs:*** Federal Direct (Subsidized and Unsubsidized Stafford, PLUS).

APPLYING FOR FINANCIAL AID ***Required financial aid forms:*** FAFSA, institution's own form. ***Financial aid deadline:*** Continuous.

CONTACT Taisha Azlin, Director of Financial Aid, TUI University, 5665 Plaza Drive, Third Floor, Cypress, CA 90630, 800-375-9878 Ext. 1061. *Fax:* 714-484-7621. *E-mail:* financialaid@tuiu.edu.

TULANE UNIVERSITY

New Orleans, LA

Tuition & fees: $41,884 **Average undergraduate aid package: $35,543**

ABOUT THE INSTITUTION Independent, coed. 82 undergraduate majors. Both federal and institutional methodology are used as a basis for awarding need-based institutional aid.

UNDERGRADUATE EXPENSES for 2010–11 ***Comprehensive fee:*** $51,708 includes full-time tuition ($38,300), mandatory fees ($3584), and room and board ($9824). ***College room only:*** $5774. Room and board charges vary according to board plan and housing facility. ***Payment plans:*** Tuition prepayment, installment.

FRESHMAN FINANCIAL AID (Fall 2009) 986 applied for aid; of those 64% were deemed to have need. 99% of freshmen with need received aid; of those 71% had need fully met. ***Average percent of need met:*** 92% (excluding resources awarded to replace EFC). ***Average financial aid package:*** $34,341 (excluding resources awarded to replace EFC). 38% of all full-time freshmen had no need and received non-need-based gift aid.

UNDERGRADUATE FINANCIAL AID (Fall 2009) 2,940 applied for aid; of those 75% were deemed to have need. 100% of undergraduates with need received aid; of those 67% had need fully met. ***Average percent of need met:*** 92% (excluding resources awarded to replace EFC). ***Average financial aid package:*** $35,543 (excluding resources awarded to replace EFC). 36% of all full-time undergraduates had no need and received non-need-based gift aid.

GIFT AID (NEED-BASED) ***Total amount:*** $51,844,129 (11% federal, 2% state, 86% institutional, 1% external sources). ***Receiving aid:*** Freshmen: 38% (611); all full-time undergraduates: 36% (2,141). ***Average award:*** Freshmen: $23,690; Undergraduates: $25,204. ***Scholarships, grants, and awards:*** Federal Pell, FSEOG, state, college/university gift aid from institutional funds, Academic Competitiveness Grants, National SMART Grants, TEACH Grants.

GIFT AID (NON-NEED-BASED) ***Total amount:*** $50,362,777 (1% federal, 3% state, 93% institutional, 3% external sources). ***Receiving aid:*** Freshmen: 16% (265). Undergraduates: 11% (675). ***Average award:*** Freshmen: $21,816. Undergraduates: $21,316. ***Scholarships, grants, and awards by category:*** *Academic interests/achievement:* 3,161 awards ($69,221,427 total): general academic interests/achievements. *Creative arts/performance:* 35 awards ($147,583 total): music. *Special achievements/activities:* 45 awards ($540,150 total): community service. *Special characteristics:* 141 awards ($5,096,596 total): children of faculty/staff, local/state students. ***Tuition waivers:*** Full or partial for employees or children of employees.

LOANS ***Student loans:*** $25,785,097 (58% need-based, 42% non-need-based). 47% of past graduating class borrowed through all loan programs. *Average indebtedness per student:* $27,510. ***Average need-based loan:*** Freshmen: $5872. Undergraduates: $7054. ***Parent loans:*** $7,003,540 (10% need-based, 90% non-need-based). ***Programs:*** Federal Direct (Subsidized and Unsubsidized Stafford, PLUS), Perkins, state.

WORK-STUDY ***Federal work-study:*** Total amount: $1,413,646; 1,153 jobs averaging $2343. ***State or other work-study/employment:*** Total amount: $800,217 (23% need-based, 77% non-need-based). Part-time jobs available.

ATHLETIC AWARDS Total amount: $8,489,136 (29% need-based, 71% non-need-based).

APPLYING FOR FINANCIAL AID ***Required financial aid forms:*** FAFSA, CSS Financial Aid PROFILE, noncustodial (divorced/separated) parent's statement, business/farm supplement. ***Financial aid deadline (priority):*** 2/15. ***Notification date:*** Continuous beginning 3/18. Students must reply within 2 weeks of notification.

CONTACT Mr. Michael T. Goodman, Director of Financial Aid, Tulane University, 6823 St. Charles Avenue, New Orleans, LA 70118-5669, 504-865-5723 or toll-free 800-873-9283. *Fax:* 504-862-8750. *E-mail:* finaid@tulane.edu.

TUSCULUM COLLEGE

Greeneville, TN

ABOUT THE INSTITUTION Independent Presbyterian, coed. 37 undergraduate majors.

GIFT AID (NEED-BASED) ***Scholarships, grants, and awards:*** Federal Pell, FSEOG, state, private, college/university gift aid from institutional funds.

GIFT AID (NON-NEED-BASED) ***Scholarships, grants, and awards by category:*** *Academic interests/achievement:* general academic interests/achievements. *Creative arts/performance:* general creative arts/performance, music. *Special achievements/activities:* cheerleading/drum major, community service, leadership. *Special characteristics:* adult students, children of faculty/staff, local/state students.

LOANS ***Programs:*** Perkins.

WORK-STUDY ***Federal work-study:*** Total amount: $392,040; 264 jobs averaging $2285. ***State or other work-study/employment:*** Total amount: $16,000 (100% non-need-based). 16 part-time jobs averaging $2000.

APPLYING FOR FINANCIAL AID ***Required financial aid form:*** FAFSA.

CONTACT Melena Verity, Director of Financial Aid, Tusculum College, PO Box 5049, 60 Shiloh Road, Greeneville, TN 37743-9997, 423-636-7377 or toll-free 800-729-0256. *Fax:* 615-250-4968. *E-mail:* mverity@tusculum.edu.

TUSKEGEE UNIVERSITY

Tuskegee, AL

Tuition & fees: $16,750 **Average undergraduate aid package: $19,250**

ABOUT THE INSTITUTION Independent, coed. 43 undergraduate majors. Federal methodology is used as a basis for awarding need-based institutional aid.

UNDERGRADUATE EXPENSES for 2010–11 ***Comprehensive fee:*** $24,320 includes full-time tuition ($16,100), mandatory fees ($650), and room and board ($7570). Full-time tuition and fees vary according to course load and program. Room and board charges vary according to housing facility. ***Part-time tuition:*** $665 per credit hour. Part-time tuition and fees vary according to course load and program. ***Payment plan:*** Installment.

FRESHMAN FINANCIAL AID (Fall 2010, est.) 635 applied for aid; of those 85% were deemed to have need. 94% of freshmen with need received aid; of those 68% had need fully met. ***Average percent of need met:*** 85% (excluding resources awarded to replace EFC). ***Average financial aid package:*** $19,250 (excluding resources awarded to replace EFC). 28% of all full-time freshmen had no need and received non-need-based gift aid.

UNDERGRADUATE FINANCIAL AID (Fall 2010, est.) 2,519 applied for aid; of those 85% were deemed to have need. 92% of undergraduates with need received aid; of those 70% had need fully met. ***Average percent of need met:*** 85% (excluding resources awarded to replace EFC). ***Average financial aid package:*** $19,250 (excluding resources awarded to replace EFC). 22% of all full-time undergraduates had no need and received non-need-based gift aid.

GIFT AID (NEED-BASED) ***Total amount:*** $6,122,249 (97% federal, 1% state, 2% institutional). ***Receiving aid:*** Freshmen: 58% (434); all full-time undergraduates: 61% (1,675). ***Average award:*** Freshmen: $8000; Undergraduates: $8000. ***Scholarships, grants, and awards:*** Federal Pell, FSEOG, state, private, college/university gift aid from institutional funds, United Negro College Fund.

GIFT AID (NON-NEED-BASED) ***Total amount:*** $3,524,421 (51% institutional, 49% external sources). ***Receiving aid:*** Freshmen: 38% (284). Undergraduates: 35% (951). ***Average award:*** Freshmen: $6000. Undergraduates: $6000. ***Scholarships, grants, and awards by category:*** *Academic interests/achievement:* 1,714 awards: general academic interests/achievements. *Creative arts/performance:* 108 awards: music. *Special characteristics:* 36 awards: children of faculty/staff, local/state students. ***Tuition waivers:*** Full or partial for employees or children of employees.

LOANS ***Student loans:*** $19,099,842 (52% need-based, 48% non-need-based). 91% of past graduating class borrowed through all loan programs. *Average indebtedness per student:* $28,575. ***Average need-based loan:*** Freshmen: $5625. Undergraduates: $6006. ***Parent loans:*** $4,295,666 (100% non-need-based). ***Programs:*** Federal Direct (Subsidized and Unsubsidized Stafford, PLUS), Perkins.

WORK-STUDY ***Federal work-study:*** Total amount: $830,097; 525 jobs averaging $1879. ***State or other work-study/employment:*** Total amount: $628,550 (100% non-need-based). 424 part-time jobs averaging $4628.

ATHLETIC AWARDS Total amount: $1,408,216 (100% non-need-based).

APPLYING FOR FINANCIAL AID ***Required financial aid forms:*** FAFSA, institution's own form. ***Financial aid deadline (priority):*** 3/31. ***Notification date:*** Continuous beginning 2/15. Students must reply within 2 weeks of notification.

CONTACT Mr. A. D. James Jr., Director of Student Financial Services, Tuskegee University, Office of Student Financial Services, Carnegie Hall, 2nd Floor, Tuskegee, AL 36088, 334-727-8088 or toll-free 800-622-6531. *Fax:* 334-724-4227. *E-mail:* jamesad@tuskegee.edu.

UNION COLLEGE

Barbourville, KY

Tuition & fees: $20,004 **Average undergraduate aid package: $17,700**

ABOUT THE INSTITUTION Independent United Methodist, coed. 26 undergraduate majors. Federal methodology is used as a basis for awarding need-based institutional aid.

UNDERGRADUATE EXPENSES for 2011–12 ***Comprehensive fee:*** $26,204 includes full-time tuition ($19,174), mandatory fees ($830), and room and board ($6200). ***College room only:*** $2650. Full-time tuition and fees vary according to course load. Room and board charges vary according to board plan and housing facility. Part-time tuition and fees vary according to course load. ***Payment plan:*** Installment.

FRESHMAN FINANCIAL AID (Fall 2010, est.) 223 applied for aid; of those 78% were deemed to have need. 100% of freshmen with need received aid; of those 12% had need fully met. ***Average percent of need met:*** 70% (excluding resources awarded to replace EFC). ***Average financial aid package:*** $17,976 (excluding resources awarded to replace EFC). 21% of all full-time freshmen had no need and received non-need-based gift aid.

UNDERGRADUATE FINANCIAL AID (Fall 2010, est.) 828 applied for aid; of those 89% were deemed to have need. 98% of undergraduates with need received aid; of those 10% had need fully met. ***Average percent of need met:*** 66% (excluding resources awarded to replace EFC). ***Average financial aid package:*** $17,700 (excluding resources awarded to replace EFC). 10% of all full-time undergraduates had no need and received non-need-based gift aid.

GIFT AID (NEED-BASED) ***Total amount:*** $6,659,812 (40% federal, 22% state, 35% institutional, 3% external sources). ***Receiving aid:*** Freshmen: 78% (175); all full-time undergraduates: 86% (713). ***Average award:*** Freshmen: $14,747; Undergraduates: $13,548. ***Scholarships, grants, and awards:*** Federal Pell, FSEOG, state, college/university gift aid from institutional funds.

GIFT AID (NON-NEED-BASED) ***Total amount:*** $465,501 (100% state). ***Receiving aid:*** Freshmen: 7% (15). Undergraduates: 6% (51). ***Average award:*** Freshmen: $11,207. Undergraduates: $10,965. ***Scholarships, grants, and awards by category:*** *Academic interests/achievement:* 272 awards ($1,564,485 total): biological sciences, general academic interests/achievements, health fields, mathematics. *Creative arts/performance:* 43 awards ($110,326 total): music. *Special achievements/activities:* 63 awards ($361,203 total): cheerleading/drum major, community service, general special achievements/activities, hobbies/interests, leadership, memberships. *Special characteristics:* 232 awards ($692,120 total): children and siblings of alumni, children of faculty/staff, religious affiliation, siblings of current students, veterans, veterans' children. ***Tuition waivers:*** Full or partial for employees or children of employees, senior citizens.

LOANS ***Student loans:*** $2,756,354 (92% need-based, 8% non-need-based). 87% of past graduating class borrowed through all loan programs. *Average indebtedness per student:* $15,272. ***Average need-based loan:*** Freshmen: $3427. Undergraduates: $4229. ***Parent loans:*** $846,665 (55% need-based, 45% non-need-based). ***Programs:*** Federal Direct (Subsidized and Unsubsidized Stafford, PLUS), Perkins, college/university.

WORK-STUDY ***Federal work-study:*** Total amount: $269,700; 166 jobs averaging $1202. ***State or other work-study/employment:*** 84 part-time jobs averaging $1202.

ATHLETIC AWARDS Total amount: $3,659,199 (100% need-based).

APPLYING FOR FINANCIAL AID ***Required financial aid form:*** FAFSA. ***Financial aid deadline (priority):*** 2/15. ***Notification date:*** Continuous beginning 4/1. Students must reply within 2 weeks of notification.

CONTACT Mrs. Jessica Cook, Associate Dean of Financial Services, Union College, 310 College Street, Barbourville, KY 40906-1499, 606-546-1607 or toll-free 800-489-8646. *Fax:* 606-546-1264. *E-mail:* jcook@unionky.edu.

UNION COLLEGE

Lincoln, NE

Tuition & fees: $18,780 **Average undergraduate aid package: N/A**

ABOUT THE INSTITUTION Independent Seventh-day Adventist, coed. 54 undergraduate majors. Federal methodology is used as a basis for awarding need-based institutional aid.

UNDERGRADUATE EXPENSES for 2011–12 ***Comprehensive fee:*** $24,800 includes full-time tuition ($18,120), mandatory fees ($660), and room and board ($6020). ***College room only:*** $3420. Full-time tuition and fees vary according to course load and degree level. Room and board charges vary according to housing facility. ***Part-time tuition:*** $755 per credit hour. ***Payment plan:*** Installment.

GIFT AID (NEED-BASED) ***Total amount:*** $2,573,393 (53% federal, 2% state, 34% institutional, 11% external sources).

GIFT AID (NON-NEED-BASED) ***Total amount:*** $4,003,495 (1% federal, 64% institutional, 35% external sources). ***Scholarships, grants, and awards by category:*** *Academic interests/achievement:* general academic interests/achievements. *Creative arts/performance:* music. *Special achievements/activities:* community service, leadership, religious involvement. ***Tuition waivers:*** Full or partial for employees or children of employees.

LOANS ***Student loans:*** $5,867,376 (45% need-based, 55% non-need-based). ***Parent loans:*** $588,131 (100% non-need-based).

WORK-STUDY ***Federal work-study:*** Total amount: $143,315; jobs available.

APPLYING FOR FINANCIAL AID ***Required financial aid form:*** FAFSA. ***Financial aid deadline:*** 7/31 (priority: 4/1). ***Notification date:*** Continuous. Students must reply within 3 weeks of notification.

CONTACT Mrs. Elina N. Bascom, Director of Financial Aid, Union College, 3800 South 48th Street, Lincoln, NE 68506-4300, 800-228-4600. *Fax:* 402-486-2952. *E-mail:* sfs@ucollege.edu.

UNION COLLEGE

Schenectady, NY

Comprehensive fee: $52,329 **Average undergraduate aid package: $34,600**

ABOUT THE INSTITUTION Independent, coed. 37 undergraduate majors. Both federal and institutional methodology are used as a basis for awarding need-based institutional aid.

UNDERGRADUATE EXPENSES for 2010–11 ***Comprehensive fee:*** $52,329. ***Payment plan:*** Installment.

FRESHMAN FINANCIAL AID (Fall 2010, est.) 375 applied for aid; of those 83% were deemed to have need. 100% of freshmen with need received aid; of those 99% had need fully met. ***Average percent of need met:*** 100% (excluding resources awarded to replace EFC). ***Average financial aid package:*** $34,706 (excluding resources awarded to replace EFC). 14% of all full-time freshmen had no need and received non-need-based gift aid.

UNDERGRADUATE FINANCIAL AID (Fall 2010, est.) 1,307 applied for aid; of those 85% were deemed to have need. 99% of undergraduates with need received aid; of those 97% had need fully met. ***Average percent of need met:*** 97% (excluding resources awarded to replace EFC). ***Average financial aid package:*** $34,600 (excluding resources awarded to replace EFC). 16% of all full-time undergraduates had no need and received non-need-based gift aid.

GIFT AID (NEED-BASED) ***Total amount:*** $35,141,963 (7% federal, 3% state, 88% institutional, 2% external sources). ***Receiving aid:*** Freshmen: 55% (303); all full-time undergraduates: 49% (1,061). ***Average award:*** Freshmen: $30,943; Undergraduates: $29,907. ***Scholarships, grants, and awards:*** Federal Pell, FSEOG, state, private, college/university gift aid from institutional funds.

GIFT AID (NON-NEED-BASED) ***Total amount:*** $4,031,188 (7% federal, 3% state, 87% institutional, 3% external sources). ***Receiving aid:*** Freshmen: 2. Undergraduates: 2% (41). ***Average award:*** Freshmen: $9666. Undergraduates: $10,538. ***Scholarships, grants, and awards by category:*** *Academic interests/achievement:* 344 awards ($3,573,370 total): general academic interests/achievements. *Special characteristics:* 36 awards ($1,453,644 total): children of faculty/staff. ***Tuition waivers:*** Full or partial for employees or children of employees, senior citizens.

LOANS ***Student loans:*** $8,525,314 (51% need-based, 49% non-need-based). 53% of past graduating class borrowed through all loan programs. *Average indebtedness per student:* $25,621. ***Average need-based loan:*** Freshmen: $2864. Undergraduates: $4167. ***Parent loans:*** $3,758,984 (100% non-need-based). ***Programs:*** Federal Direct (Subsidized and Unsubsidized Stafford, PLUS), Perkins, state, college/university.

WORK-STUDY ***Federal work-study:*** Total amount: $595,000; jobs available. ***State or other work-study/employment:*** Total amount: $170,000 (100% need-based). Part-time jobs available.

APPLYING FOR FINANCIAL AID ***Required financial aid forms:*** FAFSA, CSS Financial Aid PROFILE, state aid form, noncustodial (divorced/separated) parent's statement, business/farm supplement. ***Financial aid deadline:*** 2/1 (priority: 2/1). ***Notification date:*** 4/1. Students must reply by 5/1.

CONTACT Ms. Linda Parker, Director of Financial Aid and Family Financing, Union College, Grant Hall, Schenectady, NY 12308-2311, 518-388-6123 or toll-free 888-843-6688 (in-state). *Fax:* 518-388-8052. *E-mail:* finaid@union.edu.

UNION INSTITUTE & UNIVERSITY

Cincinnati, OH

Tuition & fees: $11,132 **Average undergraduate aid package: N/A**

ABOUT THE INSTITUTION Independent, coed. 11 undergraduate majors. Federal methodology is used as a basis for awarding need-based institutional aid.

UNDERGRADUATE EXPENSES for 2010–11 ***Tuition:*** full-time $11,016; part-time $459 per semester hour. ***Required fees:*** full-time $116; $29 per term. ***Payment plan:*** Installment.

GIFT AID (NEED-BASED) ***Scholarships, grants, and awards:*** Federal Pell, FSEOG, state, private, college/university gift aid from institutional funds.

GIFT AID (NON-NEED-BASED) ***Scholarships, grants, and awards by category:*** *Academic interests/achievement:* general academic interests/achievements. ***Tuition waivers:*** Full or partial for employees or children of employees.

LOANS ***Programs:*** Perkins.

APPLYING FOR FINANCIAL AID ***Required financial aid forms:*** FAFSA, institution's own form, federal income tax form(s). ***Financial aid deadline (priority):*** 4/15. ***Notification date:*** Continuous. Students must reply within 4 weeks of notification.

CONTACT Ms. Lisa Perdomo, Director of Financial Aid, Union Institute & University, 440 East McMillan Street, Cincinnati, OH 45206-1925, 513-861-6400 Ext. 1261 or toll-free 800-486-3116. *Fax:* 513-487-1078.

UNION UNIVERSITY

Jackson, TN

Tuition & fees: $22,390 **Average undergraduate aid package: $21,921**

ABOUT THE INSTITUTION Independent Southern Baptist, coed. 66 undergraduate majors. Federal methodology is used as a basis for awarding need-based institutional aid.

UNDERGRADUATE EXPENSES for 2010–11 ***Comprehensive fee:*** $29,850 includes full-time tuition ($21,700), mandatory fees ($690), and room and board ($7460). Full-time tuition and fees vary according to course load. Room and board charges vary according to board plan and housing facility. ***Part-time tuition:*** $735 per credit hour. ***Part-time fees:*** $220 per term. ***Payment plans:*** Installment, deferred payment.

FRESHMAN FINANCIAL AID (Fall 2010, est.) 432 applied for aid; of those 83% were deemed to have need. 100% of freshmen with need received aid; of those 19% had need fully met. ***Average percent of need met:*** 79% (excluding resources awarded to replace EFC). ***Average financial aid package:*** $19,433 (excluding resources awarded to replace EFC). 15% of all full-time freshmen had no need and received non-need-based gift aid.

UNDERGRADUATE FINANCIAL AID (Fall 2010, est.) 1,579 applied for aid; of those 85% were deemed to have need. 100% of undergraduates with need received aid; of those 17% had need fully met. ***Average percent of need met:*** 74% (excluding resources awarded to replace EFC). ***Average financial aid package:*** $21,921 (excluding resources awarded to replace EFC). 12% of all full-time undergraduates had no need and received non-need-based gift aid.

GIFT AID (NEED-BASED) ***Total amount:*** $6,421,800 (49% federal, 14% state, 37% institutional). ***Receiving aid:*** Freshmen: 62% (304); all full-time undergraduates: 56% (1,048). ***Average award:*** Freshmen: $6277; Undergraduates: $5733. ***Scholarships, grants, and awards:*** Federal Pell, FSEOG, state, private, college/university gift aid from institutional funds.

GIFT AID (NON-NEED-BASED) ***Total amount:*** $18,360,052 (3% federal, 19% state, 73% institutional, 5% external sources). ***Receiving aid:*** Freshmen: 73%

(358). Undergraduates: 69% (1,305). ***Average award:*** Freshmen: $9287. Undergraduates: $7827. ***Scholarships, grants, and awards by category:*** *Academic interests/achievement:* $7,503,311 total: business, communication, education, engineering/technologies, general academic interests/achievements, health fields, mathematics, military science, premedicine, religion/biblical studies. *Creative arts/performance:* $424,290 total: art/fine arts, cinema/film/broadcasting, journalism/publications, music, theater/drama. *Special achievements/activities:* $1,791,848 total: cheerleading/drum major, community service, general special achievements/activities, leadership, religious involvement. *Special characteristics:* $3,051,691 total: children and siblings of alumni, children of current students, children of educators, children of faculty/staff, ethnic background, general special characteristics, international students, members of minority groups, relatives of clergy, religious affiliation, siblings of current students, spouses of current students, twins, veterans, veterans' children. ***Tuition waivers:*** Full or partial for children of alumni, employees or children of employees.

LOANS ***Student loans:*** $7,323,441 (48% need-based, 52% non-need-based). 66% of past graduating class borrowed through all loan programs. *Average indebtedness per student:* $22,017. ***Average need-based loan:*** Freshmen: $3444. Undergraduates: $4493. ***Parent loans:*** $1,839,406 (100% non-need-based). ***Programs:*** Federal Direct (Subsidized and Unsubsidized Stafford, PLUS), Perkins, alternative loans.

WORK-STUDY ***Federal work-study:*** Total amount: $184,388; 123 jobs averaging $1498. ***State or other work-study/employment:*** Total amount: $393,028 (100% non-need-based). 234 part-time jobs averaging $1670.

ATHLETIC AWARDS Total amount: $2,087,754 (100% non-need-based).

APPLYING FOR FINANCIAL AID ***Required financial aid forms:*** FAFSA, institution's own form. ***Financial aid deadline (priority):*** 2/1. ***Notification date:*** Continuous beginning 3/1. Students must reply by 5/1 or within 2 weeks of notification.

CONTACT John Thomas Brandt, Director of Student Financial Planning, Union University, 1050 Union University Drive, Jackson, TN 38305-3697, 731-661-5015 or toll-free 800-33-UNION. *Fax:* 731-661-5570. *E-mail:* jbrandt@uu.edu.

UNITED STATES SPORTS ACADEMY

Daphne, AL

CONTACT Financial Aid Office, United States Sports Academy, One Academy Drive, Daphne, AL 36526-7055, 251-626-3303 or toll-free 800-223-2668 (out-of-state).

UNITED STATES UNIVERSITY

National City, CA

CONTACT Financial Aid Office, United States University, 140 West 16th Street, National City, CA 91950, 619-477-6310 or toll-free 888-422-3381 (out-of-state).

UNITED TALMUDICAL SEMINARY

Brooklyn, NY

CONTACT Financial Aid Office, United Talmudical Seminary, 82 Lee Avenue, Brooklyn, NY 11211-7900, 718-963-9770 Ext. 309.

UNITY COLLEGE

Unity, ME

Tuition & fees: $22,500 **Average undergraduate aid package: $17,369**

ABOUT THE INSTITUTION Independent, coed. 16 undergraduate majors. Federal methodology is used as a basis for awarding need-based institutional aid.

UNDERGRADUATE EXPENSES for 2010–11 ***Comprehensive fee:*** $30,720 includes full-time tuition ($21,400), mandatory fees ($1100), and room and board ($8220). Room and board charges vary according to board plan. Part-time tuition and fees vary according to course load. ***Payment plan:*** Installment.

FRESHMAN FINANCIAL AID (Fall 2009) 165 applied for aid; of those 93% were deemed to have need. 100% of freshmen with need received aid; of those 3% had need fully met. ***Average percent of need met:*** 73% (excluding resources awarded to replace EFC). ***Average financial aid package:*** $17,693 (excluding resources awarded to replace EFC). 8% of all full-time freshmen had no need and received non-need-based gift aid.

UNDERGRADUATE FINANCIAL AID (Fall 2009) 506 applied for aid; of those 91% were deemed to have need. 100% of undergraduates with need received aid; of those 7% had need fully met. ***Average percent of need met:*** 75% (excluding resources awarded to replace EFC). ***Average financial aid package:*** $17,369 (excluding resources awarded to replace EFC). 13% of all full-time undergraduates had no need and received non-need-based gift aid.

GIFT AID (NEED-BASED) ***Total amount:*** $5,107,890 (23% federal, 3% state, 70% institutional, 4% external sources). ***Receiving aid:*** Freshmen: 91% (153); all full-time undergraduates: 81% (457). ***Average award:*** Freshmen: $12,396; Undergraduates: $11,156. ***Scholarships, grants, and awards:*** Federal Pell, FSEOG, state, private, college/university gift aid from institutional funds.

GIFT AID (NON-NEED-BASED) ***Total amount:*** $290,758 (90% institutional, 10% external sources). ***Receiving aid:*** Freshmen: 1% (2). Undergraduates: 2% (12). ***Average award:*** Freshmen: $3623. Undergraduates: $3166. ***Scholarships, grants, and awards by category:*** *Academic interests/achievement:* 277 awards ($1,119,750 total): general academic interests/achievements. *Special achievements/activities:* 52 awards ($52,000 total): community service, leadership. *Special characteristics:* 93 awards ($217,170 total): children of educators, general special characteristics, local/state students, members of minority groups. ***Tuition waivers:*** Full or partial for employees or children of employees.

LOANS ***Student loans:*** $4,624,529 (78% need-based, 22% non-need-based). ***Average need-based loan:*** Freshmen: $4710. Undergraduates: $5677. ***Parent loans:*** $1,086,563 (35% need-based, 65% non-need-based). ***Programs:*** Federal Direct (Subsidized and Unsubsidized Stafford, PLUS), Perkins.

WORK-STUDY ***Federal work-study:*** Total amount: $589,907; 375 jobs averaging $1573. ***State or other work-study/employment:*** Total amount: $4800 (100% non-need-based). 4 part-time jobs averaging $1200.

APPLYING FOR FINANCIAL AID ***Required financial aid form:*** FAFSA. ***Financial aid deadline:*** Continuous. ***Notification date:*** Continuous beginning 3/10. Students must reply within 2 weeks of notification.

CONTACT Mr. Rand E. Newell, Director of Financial Aid, Unity College, 90 Quaker Hill Road, Unity, ME 04988, 207-948-3131 Ext. 201. *Fax:* 207-948-2018. *E-mail:* rnewell@unity.edu.

UNIVERSIDAD ADVENTISTA DE LAS ANTILLAS

Mayagüez, PR

ABOUT THE INSTITUTION Independent Seventh-day Adventist, coed. 21 undergraduate majors.

GIFT AID (NEED-BASED) ***Scholarships, grants, and awards:*** Federal Pell, FSEOG, state, college/university gift aid from institutional funds.

GIFT AID (NON-NEED-BASED) ***Scholarships, grants, and awards by category:*** *Special achievements/activities:* community service.

WORK-STUDY ***Federal work-study:*** Total amount: $142,561; jobs available. ***State or other work-study/employment:*** Total amount: $131,570 (100% need-based). Part-time jobs available.

APPLYING FOR FINANCIAL AID ***Required financial aid forms:*** FAFSA, institution's own form.

CONTACT Mrs. Awilda Matos, Director of Financial Aid, Universidad Adventista de las Antillas, Box 118, Mayagüez, PR 00681-0118, 787-834-9595 Ext. 2263. *Fax:* 787-834-9597. *E-mail:* amatos@uaa.edu.

UNIVERSIDAD DEL ESTE

Carolina, PR

CONTACT Clotilde Santiago, Director of Financial Aid, Universidad del Este, Apartado 2010, Carolina, PR 00928, 787-257-7373 Ext. 3300.

UNIVERSIDAD DEL TURABO

Gurabo, PR

CONTACT Ms. Ivette Vázquez Ríos, Directora, Oficina de Asistencia Economica, Universidad del Turabo, Apartado 3030, Gurabo, PR 00778-3030, 787-743-7979 Ext. 4352. *Fax:* 787-743-7979.

UNIVERSIDAD FLET

Miami, FL

CONTACT Financial Aid Office, Universidad FLET, 14540 Southwest 136th Street, Suite 108, Miami, FL 33186, 305-232-5880 or toll-free 888-376-3538.

UNIVERSIDAD METROPOLITANA

San Juan, PR

CONTACT Economic Assistant Director, Universidad Metropolitana, Call Box 21150, Rio Piedras, PR 00928-1150, 787-766-1717 Ext. 6586 or toll-free 800-747-8362 (out-of-state).

UNIVERSIDAD TEOLÓGICA DEL CARIBE

St. Just, PR

Tuition & fees: $3880 **Average undergraduate aid package: N/A**

ABOUT THE INSTITUTION Independent Pentecostal, coed. 3 undergraduate majors. Federal methodology is used as a basis for awarding need-based institutional aid.

UNDERGRADUATE EXPENSES for 2011–12 ***One-time required fee:*** $13. ***Comprehensive fee:*** $6280 includes full-time tuition ($3500), mandatory fees ($380), and room and board ($2400). ***College room only:*** $1200. Room and board charges vary according to board plan. ***Part-time tuition:*** $18 per credit. ***Part-time fees:*** $130 per credit; $2720 per term. ***Payment plan:*** Deferred payment.

FRESHMAN FINANCIAL AID (Fall 2009) 12 applied for aid; of those 100% were deemed to have need. 100% of freshmen with need received aid.

UNDERGRADUATE FINANCIAL AID (Fall 2009) 83 applied for aid; of those 100% were deemed to have need. 100% of undergraduates with need received aid.

GIFT AID (NEED-BASED) ***Total amount:*** $540,872 (100% federal). ***Receiving aid:*** Freshmen: 100% (12); all full-time undergraduates: 92% (83). ***Scholarships, grants, and awards:*** Federal Pell, state.

WORK-STUDY Federal work-study jobs available. ***State or other work-study/employment:*** Part-time jobs available.

APPLYING FOR FINANCIAL AID ***Required financial aid form:*** FAFSA. ***Financial aid deadline:*** 6/30 (priority: 1/1).

CONTACT Mrs. Lourdes Torres, Director of Financial Aid, Universidad Teológica del Caribe, PO Box 901, Saint Just, PR 00978-0901, 787-761-0640 Ext. 224. *Fax:* 787-748-9220. *E-mail:* aeconomicautc@yahoo.com.

UNIVERSITY AT ALBANY, STATE UNIVERSITY OF NEW YORK

Albany, NY

Tuition & fees (NY res): $6830 **Average undergraduate aid package: $9559**

ABOUT THE INSTITUTION State-supported, coed. 63 undergraduate majors. Federal methodology is used as a basis for awarding need-based institutional aid.

UNDERGRADUATE EXPENSES for 2010–11 ***Tuition, state resident:*** full-time $4970; part-time $207 per credit. ***Tuition, nonresident:*** full-time $12,870; part-time $536 per credit. ***Required fees:*** full-time $1860; $45.01 per credit. Part-time tuition and fees vary according to course load. ***College room and board:*** $10,633; ***Room only:*** $6577. Room and board charges vary according to board plan and housing facility. ***Payment plan:*** Installment.

FRESHMAN FINANCIAL AID (Fall 2010, est.) 1,949 applied for aid; of those 70% were deemed to have need. 96% of freshmen with need received aid; of those 8% had need fully met. ***Average percent of need met:*** 67% (excluding resources awarded to replace EFC). ***Average financial aid package:*** $10,028 (excluding resources awarded to replace EFC). 5% of all full-time freshmen had no need and received non-need-based gift aid.

UNDERGRADUATE FINANCIAL AID (Fall 2010, est.) 9,422 applied for aid; of those 77% were deemed to have need. 98% of undergraduates with need received aid; of those 8% had need fully met. ***Average percent of need met:*** 67% (excluding resources awarded to replace EFC). ***Average financial aid package:*** $9559 (excluding resources awarded to replace EFC). 4% of all full-time undergraduates had no need and received non-need-based gift aid.

GIFT AID (NEED-BASED) ***Total amount:*** $39,160,818 (55% federal, 38% state, 5% institutional, 2% external sources). ***Receiving aid:*** Freshmen: 50% (1,122); all full-time undergraduates: 51% (6,176). ***Average award:*** Freshmen: $7399; Undergraduates: $6456. ***Scholarships, grants, and awards:*** Federal Pell, FSEOG, state, private, college/university gift aid from institutional funds.

GIFT AID (NON-NEED-BASED) ***Total amount:*** $3,327,423 (7% federal, 22% state, 60% institutional, 11% external sources). ***Receiving aid:*** Freshmen: 1% (31). Undergraduates: 1% (138). ***Average award:*** Freshmen: $4142. Undergraduates: $3633. ***Scholarships, grants, and awards by category:*** *Academic interests/achievement:* 1,089 awards ($3,771,548 total): general academic interests/achievements.

LOANS ***Student loans:*** $54,768,852 (46% need-based, 54% non-need-based). 71% of past graduating class borrowed through all loan programs. *Average indebtedness per student:* $24,146. ***Average need-based loan:*** Freshmen: $3728. Undergraduates: $4356. ***Parent loans:*** $17,363,038 (100% non-need-based). ***Programs:*** Federal Direct (Subsidized and Unsubsidized Stafford, PLUS), Perkins.

WORK-STUDY ***Federal work-study:*** Total amount: $1,402,953; 902 jobs averaging $1555. ***State or other work-study/employment:*** Total amount: $1,422,660 (78% need-based, 22% non-need-based). 236 part-time jobs averaging $6028.

ATHLETIC AWARDS Total amount: $4,147,869 (32% need-based, 68% non-need-based).

APPLYING FOR FINANCIAL AID ***Required financial aid form:*** FAFSA. ***Financial aid deadline (priority):*** 3/15. ***Notification date:*** Continuous beginning 3/20. Students must reply by 5/1 or within 2 weeks of notification.

CONTACT Diane Corbett, Director of Financial Aid, University at Albany, State University of New York, Student Financial Center, Campus Center G-26, 1400 Washington Avenue, Albany, NY 12222-0001, 518-442-3202 or toll-free 800-293-7869 (in-state). *Fax:* 518-442-5295. *E-mail:* sscweb@uamail.albany.edu.

UNIVERSITY AT BUFFALO, THE STATE UNIVERSITY OF NEW YORK

Buffalo, NY

Tuition & fees (NY res): $7136 **Average undergraduate aid package: $7189**

ABOUT THE INSTITUTION State-supported, coed. 74 undergraduate majors. Federal methodology is used as a basis for awarding need-based institutional aid.

UNDERGRADUATE EXPENSES for 2010–11 ***Tuition, state resident:*** full-time $4970; part-time $207 per credit hour. ***Tuition, nonresident:*** full-time $13,380; part-time $558 per credit hour. ***Required fees:*** full-time $2166; $95 per credit hour. Part-time tuition and fees vary according to course load. ***College room and board:*** $10,028; ***Room only:*** $5928. Room and board charges vary according to board plan and housing facility. ***Payment plan:*** Installment.

FRESHMAN FINANCIAL AID (Fall 2010, est.) 2,343 applied for aid; of those 67% were deemed to have need. 98% of freshmen with need received aid; of those 49% had need fully met. ***Average percent of need met:*** 65% (excluding resources awarded to replace EFC). ***Average financial aid package:*** $10,086 (excluding resources awarded to replace EFC). 12% of all full-time freshmen had no need and received non-need-based gift aid.

UNDERGRADUATE FINANCIAL AID (Fall 2010, est.) 12,637 applied for aid; of those 76% were deemed to have need. 96% of undergraduates with need received aid; of those 61% had need fully met. ***Average percent of need met:*** 61% (excluding resources awarded to replace EFC). ***Average financial aid package:*** $7189 (excluding resources awarded to replace EFC). 8% of all full-time undergraduates had no need and received non-need-based gift aid.

GIFT AID (NEED-BASED) ***Total amount:*** $47,474,984 (54% federal, 38% state, 2% institutional, 6% external sources). ***Receiving aid:*** Freshmen: 41% (1,384); all full-time undergraduates: 32% (5,657). ***Average award:*** Freshmen: $7152; Undergraduates: $5646. ***Scholarships, grants, and awards:*** Federal Pell, FSEOG, state, private, college/university gift aid from institutional funds, Federal Nursing.

GIFT AID (NON-NEED-BASED) ***Total amount:*** $12,325,568 (2% state, 98% institutional). ***Receiving aid:*** Freshmen: 28% (957). Undergraduates: 8% (1,366). ***Average award:*** Freshmen: $3655. Undergraduates: $5529. ***Tuition waivers:*** Full or partial for minority students.

LOANS ***Student loans:*** $73,348,784 (100% need-based). 38% of past graduating class borrowed through all loan programs. *Average indebtedness per student:* $17,425. ***Average need-based loan:*** Freshmen: $3822. Undergraduates: $4334.

Parent loans: $8,222,208 (100% non-need-based). ***Programs:*** Federal Direct (Subsidized and Unsubsidized Stafford, PLUS), Perkins, Federal Nursing, college/university.

WORK-STUDY ***Federal work-study:*** Total amount: $1,844,115; 1,146 jobs averaging $1489. ***State or other work-study/employment:*** Total amount: $8,005,110 (100% non-need-based). 2,301 part-time jobs averaging $3547.

ATHLETIC AWARDS Total amount: $5,659,379 (100% non-need-based).

APPLYING FOR FINANCIAL AID ***Required financial aid form:*** FAFSA. ***Financial aid deadline (priority):*** 3/1. ***Notification date:*** Continuous beginning 2/1. Students must reply by 5/1.

CONTACT Cindy Kohlman, Director Financial Aid (SARFS), University at Buffalo, the State University of New York, 232 Capen Hall, Buffalo, NY 14260, 716-645-2450 or toll-free 888-UB-ADMIT. *Fax:* 716-645-7760. *E-mail:* ckohlman@buffalo.edu.

UNIVERSITY OF ADVANCING TECHNOLOGY

Tempe, AZ

Tuition & fees: $19,500 **Average undergraduate aid package: N/A**

ABOUT THE INSTITUTION Proprietary, coed, primarily men. 7 undergraduate majors. Federal methodology is used as a basis for awarding need-based institutional aid.

UNDERGRADUATE EXPENSES for 2011–12 ***Comprehensive fee:*** $30,426 includes full-time tuition ($19,400), mandatory fees ($100), and room and board ($10,926). ***College room only:*** $7346. Room and board charges vary according to board plan. ***Payment plan:*** Installment.

GIFT AID (NEED-BASED) ***Total amount:*** $2,766,697 (96% federal, 4% institutional). ***Scholarships, grants, and awards:*** Federal Pell, FSEOG, state, private, college/university gift aid from institutional funds.

GIFT AID (NON-NEED-BASED) ***Total amount:*** $762,292 (2% state, 89% institutional, 9% external sources). ***Scholarships, grants, and awards by category:*** *Academic interests/achievement:* computer science, general academic interests/achievements. *Special characteristics:* children of faculty/staff, local/state students, veterans, veterans' children. ***Tuition waivers:*** Full or partial for employees or children of employees.

LOANS ***Student loans:*** $12,066,236 (36% need-based, 64% non-need-based). ***Parent loans:*** $3,955,971 (100% non-need-based). ***Programs:*** Federal Direct (Subsidized and Unsubsidized Stafford, PLUS).

WORK-STUDY ***Federal work-study:*** Total amount: $187,877; jobs available.

APPLYING FOR FINANCIAL AID ***Required financial aid form:*** FAFSA. ***Financial aid deadline:*** Continuous.

CONTACT Financial Aid Office, University of Advancing Technology, 2625 West Baseline Road, Tempe, AZ 85283-1042, 602-383-8228 or toll-free 800-658-5744 (out-of-state). *Fax:* 602-383-8222. *E-mail:* fa@uat.edu.

THE UNIVERSITY OF AKRON

Akron, OH

Tuition & fees (OH res): $9247 **Average undergraduate aid package: $7563**

ABOUT THE INSTITUTION State-supported, coed. 127 undergraduate majors. Federal methodology is used as a basis for awarding need-based institutional aid.

UNDERGRADUATE EXPENSES for 2010–11 ***Tuition, state resident:*** full-time $7733; part-time $322 per credit hour. ***Tuition, nonresident:*** full-time $15,389; part-time $641 per credit hour. ***Required fees:*** full-time $1514; $49 per credit hour. Full-time tuition and fees vary according to course load, degree level, and location. Part-time tuition and fees vary according to course load, degree level, and location. ***College room and board:*** $9160; ***Room only:*** $5830. Room and board charges vary according to board plan and housing facility. ***Payment plan:*** Installment.

FRESHMAN FINANCIAL AID (Fall 2010, est.) 4,090 applied for aid; of those 89% were deemed to have need. 100% of freshmen with need received aid; of those 21% had need fully met. ***Average percent of need met:*** 64% (excluding resources awarded to replace EFC). ***Average financial aid package:*** $7656 (excluding resources awarded to replace EFC). 7% of all full-time freshmen had no need and received non-need-based gift aid.

UNDERGRADUATE FINANCIAL AID (Fall 2010, est.) 15,286 applied for aid; of those 91% were deemed to have need. 100% of undergraduates with need received aid; of those 20% had need fully met. ***Average percent of need met:*** 61% (excluding resources awarded to replace EFC). ***Average financial aid package:*** $7563 (excluding resources awarded to replace EFC). 4% of all full-time undergraduates had no need and received non-need-based gift aid.

GIFT AID (NEED-BASED) ***Total amount:*** $49,107,929 (89% federal, 11% state). ***Receiving aid:*** Freshmen: 52% (2,285); all full-time undergraduates: 46% (7,987). ***Average award:*** Freshmen: $5300; Undergraduates: $5021. ***Scholarships, grants, and awards:*** Federal Pell, FSEOG, state, college/university gift aid from institutional funds.

GIFT AID (NON-NEED-BASED) ***Total amount:*** $29,038,583 (7% state, 74% institutional, 19% external sources). ***Receiving aid:*** Freshmen: 38% (1,688). Undergraduates: 33% (5,728). ***Average award:*** Freshmen: $4734. Undergraduates: $4118. ***Scholarships, grants, and awards by category:*** *Academic interests/achievement:* 3,440 awards ($8,938,695 total): biological sciences, business, communication, computer science, education, engineering/technologies, English, foreign languages, general academic interests/achievements, health fields, home economics, humanities, international studies, mathematics, military science, physical sciences, premedicine, social sciences. *Creative arts/performance:* 171 awards ($236,166 total): applied art and design, art/fine arts, creative writing, dance, debating, general creative arts/performance, journalism/publications, music, performing arts, theater/drama. *Special achievements/activities:* 119 awards ($324,996 total): community service, general special achievements/activities, leadership, memberships. *Special characteristics:* 2,421 awards ($8,758,142 total): adult students, general special characteristics, handicapped students, international students, local/state students, members of minority groups, out-of-state students. ***Tuition waivers:*** Full or partial for employees or children of employees, senior citizens.

LOANS ***Student loans:*** $125,118,325 (44% need-based, 56% non-need-based). 69% of past graduating class borrowed through all loan programs. *Average indebtedness per student:* $28,421. ***Average need-based loan:*** Freshmen: $3274. Undergraduates: $3919. ***Parent loans:*** $20,944,111 (100% non-need-based). ***Programs:*** Federal Direct (Subsidized and Unsubsidized Stafford, PLUS), Perkins, Federal Nursing, college/university.

WORK-STUDY ***Federal work-study:*** Total amount: $1,061,536; 637 jobs available. ***State or other work-study/employment:*** Total amount: $5,473,136 (100% non-need-based). 2,814 part-time jobs available.

ATHLETIC AWARDS Total amount: $5,429,193 (100% non-need-based).

APPLYING FOR FINANCIAL AID ***Required financial aid forms:*** FAFSA, institution's own form. ***Financial aid deadline (priority):*** 2/1. ***Notification date:*** Continuous beginning 4/1. Students must reply within 2 weeks of notification.

CONTACT Ms. Michelle Ellis, Director of Student Financial Aid, The University of Akron, 302 Buchtel Mall, Akron, OH 44325-6211, 330-972-5860 or toll-free 800-655-4884. *Fax:* 330-972-7139. *E-mail:* mellis@uakron.edu.

THE UNIVERSITY OF ALABAMA

Tuscaloosa, AL

Tuition & fees (AL res): $7900 **Average undergraduate aid package: $9536**

ABOUT THE INSTITUTION State-supported, coed. 71 undergraduate majors. Federal methodology is used as a basis for awarding need-based institutional aid.

UNDERGRADUATE EXPENSES for 2010–11 ***Tuition, state resident:*** full-time $7900. ***Tuition, nonresident:*** full-time $20,500. Full-time tuition and fees vary according to course load. Part-time tuition and fees vary according to course load. ***College room and board:*** $8214; ***Room only:*** $4700. Room and board charges vary according to board plan and housing facility. ***Payment plans:*** Installment, deferred payment.

FRESHMAN FINANCIAL AID (Fall 2009) 2,877 applied for aid; of those 68% were deemed to have need. 97% of freshmen with need received aid; of those 20% had need fully met. ***Average percent of need met:*** 56% (excluding resources awarded to replace EFC). ***Average financial aid package:*** $10,090 (excluding resources awarded to replace EFC). 27% of all full-time freshmen had no need and received non-need-based gift aid.

UNDERGRADUATE FINANCIAL AID (Fall 2009) 11,204 applied for aid; of those 76% were deemed to have need. 99% of undergraduates with need received aid; of those 14% had need fully met. ***Average percent of need met:*** 53% (excluding resources awarded to replace EFC). ***Average financial aid package:*** $9536 (excluding resources awarded to replace EFC). 20% of all full-time undergraduates had no need and received non-need-based gift aid.

GIFT AID (NEED-BASED) ***Total amount:*** $39,134,194 (58% federal, 1% state, 32% institutional, 9% external sources). ***Receiving aid:*** Freshmen: 28% (1,458); all full-time undergraduates: 28% (6,071). ***Average award:*** Freshmen: $8023; Undergraduates: $6680. ***Scholarships, grants, and awards:*** Federal Pell, FSEOG, state, private, college/university gift aid from institutional funds, Federal Nursing.

GIFT AID (NON-NEED-BASED) ***Total amount:*** $39,069,595 (83% institutional, 17% external sources). ***Receiving aid:*** Freshmen: 20% (1,002). Undergraduates: 15% (3,155). ***Average award:*** Freshmen: $74. Undergraduates: $407. ***Scholarships, grants, and awards by category:*** *Academic interests/achievement:* area/ethnic studies, biological sciences, business, communication, computer science, education, engineering/technologies, English, foreign languages, general academic interests/achievements, home economics, library science, mathematics, military science, physical sciences, premedicine, social sciences. *Creative arts/performance:* art/fine arts, cinema/film/broadcasting, creative writing, dance, debating, journalism/publications, music, theater/drama. *Special achievements/activities:* cheerleading/drum major, community service, general special achievements/activities, hobbies/interests, junior miss. *Special characteristics:* children of union members/company employees, general special characteristics, international students, out-of-state students, spouses of deceased or disabled public servants. ***Tuition waivers:*** Full or partial for employees or children of employees.

LOANS ***Student loans:*** $85,944,360 (69% need-based, 31% non-need-based). 53% of past graduating class borrowed through all loan programs. *Average indebtedness per student:* $26,701. ***Average need-based loan:*** Freshmen: $3335. Undergraduates: $4190. ***Parent loans:*** $30,665,984 (36% need-based, 64% non-need-based). ***Programs:*** Federal Direct (Subsidized and Unsubsidized Stafford, PLUS), Perkins, college/university, private loans.

WORK-STUDY ***Federal work-study:*** Total amount: $1,411,103; 450 jobs averaging $2299.

ATHLETIC AWARDS Total amount: $9,427,904 (3% need-based, 97% non-need-based).

APPLYING FOR FINANCIAL AID ***Required financial aid form:*** FAFSA. ***Financial aid deadline (priority):*** 3/1. ***Notification date:*** 4/1. Students must reply within 3 weeks of notification.

CONTACT Helen Leathers, Associate Director of Financial Aid, The University of Alabama, Box 870162, Tuscaloosa, AL 35487-0162, 205-348-6756 or toll-free 800-933-BAMA. *Fax:* 205-348-2989. *E-mail:* helen.leathers@ua.edu.

THE UNIVERSITY OF ALABAMA AT BIRMINGHAM

Birmingham, AL

Tuition & fees (AL res): $6256 **Average undergraduate aid package: $9584**

ABOUT THE INSTITUTION State-supported, coed. 47 undergraduate majors. Federal methodology is used as a basis for awarding need-based institutional aid.

UNDERGRADUATE EXPENSES for 2010–11 ***Tuition, state resident:*** full-time $5472; part-time $228 per credit hour. ***Tuition, nonresident:*** full-time $12,864; part-time $536 per credit hour. ***Required fees:*** full-time $784; $167 per term. Full-time tuition and fees vary according to program. Part-time tuition and fees vary according to program. ***College room and board:*** $8810; ***Room only:*** $5000. Room and board charges vary according to board plan and housing facility. ***Payment plan:*** Installment.

FRESHMAN FINANCIAL AID (Fall 2010, est.) 1,220 applied for aid; of those 74% were deemed to have need. 98% of freshmen with need received aid; of those 14% had need fully met. ***Average percent of need met:*** 46% (excluding resources awarded to replace EFC). ***Average financial aid package:*** $9408 (excluding resources awarded to replace EFC). 25% of all full-time freshmen had no need and received non-need-based gift aid.

UNDERGRADUATE FINANCIAL AID (Fall 2010, est.) 5,720 applied for aid; of those 82% were deemed to have need. 98% of undergraduates with need received aid; of those 12% had need fully met. ***Average percent of need met:*** 48% (excluding resources awarded to replace EFC). ***Average financial aid package:*** $9584 (excluding resources awarded to replace EFC). 15% of all full-time undergraduates had no need and received non-need-based gift aid.

GIFT AID (NEED-BASED) ***Total amount:*** $18,215,780 (99% federal, 1% external sources). ***Receiving aid:*** Freshmen: 38% (582); all full-time undergraduates: 38% (3,080). ***Average award:*** Freshmen: $5183; Undergraduates: $5128. ***Scholarships, grants, and awards:*** Federal Pell, FSEOG, state, private, college/university gift aid from institutional funds, United Negro College Fund.

GIFT AID (NON-NEED-BASED) ***Total amount:*** $14,127,212 (1% federal, 92% institutional, 7% external sources). ***Receiving aid:*** Freshmen: 33% (503). Undergraduates: 17% (1,425). ***Average award:*** Freshmen: $5425. Undergraduates: $6392. ***Scholarships, grants, and awards by category:*** *Academic interests/achievement:* business, communication, computer science, engineering/technologies, general academic interests/achievements, health fields, mathematics. *Creative arts/performance:* art/fine arts, music, performing arts, theater/drama. *Special achievements/activities:* cheerleading/drum major, junior miss, leadership, memberships, religious involvement. *Special characteristics:* adult students, children and siblings of alumni, children of current students, children of educators, children of faculty/staff, children of public servants, children of union members/company employees, children of workers in trades, children with a deceased or disabled parent, ethnic background, first-generation college students, general special characteristics, handicapped students, married students, members of minority groups, out-of-state students, parents of current students, previous college experience, public servants, relatives of clergy, siblings of current students, spouses of current students, spouses of deceased or disabled public servants, twins, veterans, veterans' children. ***Tuition waivers:*** Full or partial for employees or children of employees.

LOANS ***Student loans:*** $45,899,980 (46% need-based, 54% non-need-based). 60% of past graduating class borrowed through all loan programs. *Average indebtedness per student:* $24,936. ***Average need-based loan:*** Freshmen: $3589. Undergraduates: $4455. ***Parent loans:*** $3,972,890 (100% non-need-based). ***Programs:*** Federal Direct (Subsidized and Unsubsidized Stafford, PLUS), Perkins, state, college/university.

WORK-STUDY ***Federal work-study:*** Total amount: $2,039,994; jobs available.

ATHLETIC AWARDS Total amount: $5,668,412 (100% non-need-based).

APPLYING FOR FINANCIAL AID ***Required financial aid form:*** FAFSA. ***Financial aid deadline (priority):*** 3/1. ***Notification date:*** Continuous beginning 4/1. Students must reply within 4 weeks of notification.

CONTACT Ms. Janet B. May, Student Financial Aid Director, The University of Alabama at Birmingham, Hill University Center 317, 1530 3rd Avenue South, Birmingham, AL 35294-1150, 205-934-8132 or toll-free 800-421-8743.

THE UNIVERSITY OF ALABAMA IN HUNTSVILLE

Huntsville, AL

Tuition & fees (AL res): $7492 **Average undergraduate aid package: $8940**

ABOUT THE INSTITUTION State-supported, coed. 30 undergraduate majors. Federal methodology is used as a basis for awarding need-based institutional aid.

UNDERGRADUATE EXPENSES for 2010–11 ***Tuition, state resident:*** full-time $7492; part-time $260.44 per credit hour. ***Tuition, nonresident:*** full-time $17,986; part-time $629.69 per credit hour. ***Required fees:*** $38 per credit hour. Full-time tuition and fees vary according to course load. Part-time tuition and fees vary according to course load. ***College room and board:*** $7540; ***Room only:*** $5290. Room and board charges vary according to board plan and housing facility. ***Payment plan:*** Installment.

FRESHMAN FINANCIAL AID (Fall 2010, est.) 566 applied for aid; of those 61% were deemed to have need. 100% of freshmen with need received aid; of those 20% had need fully met. ***Average percent of need met:*** 66% (excluding resources awarded to replace EFC). ***Average financial aid package:*** $10,202 (excluding resources awarded to replace EFC). 29% of all full-time freshmen had no need and received non-need-based gift aid.

UNDERGRADUATE FINANCIAL AID (Fall 2010, est.) 3,642 applied for aid; of those 66% were deemed to have need. 99% of undergraduates with need received aid; of those 11% had need fully met. ***Average percent of need met:*** 57% (excluding resources awarded to replace EFC). ***Average financial aid package:*** $8940 (excluding resources awarded to replace EFC). 17% of all full-time undergraduates had no need and received non-need-based gift aid.

GIFT AID (NEED-BASED) ***Total amount:*** $12,627,273 (72% federal, 1% state, 20% institutional, 7% external sources). ***Receiving aid:*** Freshmen: 52% (310); all full-time undergraduates: 41% (1,858). ***Average award:*** Freshmen: $7805; Undergraduates: $6033. ***Scholarships, grants, and awards:*** Federal Pell, FSEOG, state, private, college/university gift aid from institutional funds, Federal Nursing.

GIFT AID (NON-NEED-BASED) ***Total amount:*** $5,121,346 (84% institutional, 16% external sources). ***Receiving aid:*** Freshmen: 8% (46). Undergraduates: 3% (115). ***Average award:*** Freshmen: $5680. Undergraduates: $5312. ***Scholarships, grants, and awards by category:*** *Academic interests/achievement:* 2,645 awards ($7,986,296 total): biological sciences, business, communication, computer science, education, engineering/technologies, English, foreign languages, general academic interests/achievements, health fields, humanities, mathematics, physical sciences, social sciences. *Creative arts/performance:* 74 awards ($62,615 total): art/fine arts, music. *Special achievements/activities:* 559 awards ($2,047,173 total): cheerleading/drum major, community service, general special achievements/activities, junior miss, leadership. *Special characteristics:* 47 awards ($103,350 total): general special characteristics, local/state students, members of minority groups. ***Tuition waivers:*** Full or partial for employees or children of employees.

LOANS ***Student loans:*** $25,699,639 (82% need-based, 18% non-need-based). 54% of past graduating class borrowed through all loan programs. *Average indebtedness per student:* $19,852. ***Average need-based loan:*** Freshmen: $5391. Undergraduates: $7555. ***Parent loans:*** $1,496,597 (53% need-based, 47% non-need-based). ***Programs:*** Federal Direct (Subsidized and Unsubsidized Stafford, PLUS).

WORK-STUDY ***Federal work-study:*** Total amount: $308,259; 72 jobs averaging $4282.

ATHLETIC AWARDS Total amount: $1,958,273 (17% need-based, 83% non-need-based).

APPLYING FOR FINANCIAL AID ***Required financial aid form:*** FAFSA. ***Financial aid deadline:*** 7/31 (priority: 4/1). ***Notification date:*** Continuous beginning 4/1. Students must reply within 2 weeks of notification.

CONTACT Mr. Andrew Weaver, Director of Student Financial Services, The University of Alabama in Huntsville, 301 Sparkman Drive, UC Room 212, Huntsville, AL 35899, 256-824-6241 or toll-free 800-UAH-CALL. *Fax:* 256-824-6212. *E-mail:* finaid@uah.edu.

UNIVERSITY OF ALASKA ANCHORAGE

Anchorage, AK

Tuition & fees (AK res): $5096 Average undergraduate aid package: $9734

ABOUT THE INSTITUTION State-supported, coed. 67 undergraduate majors. Federal methodology is used as a basis for awarding need-based institutional aid.

UNDERGRADUATE EXPENSES for 2010–11 ***Tuition, state resident:*** full-time $4410; part-time $147 per credit. ***Tuition, nonresident:*** full-time $15,000; part-time $500 per credit. ***Required fees:*** full-time $686; $26 per course or $31 per term. Full-time tuition and fees vary according to course level and location. Part-time tuition and fees vary according to course level and location. Room and board charges vary according to board plan and housing facility. ***Payment plans:*** Installment, deferred payment.

FRESHMAN FINANCIAL AID (Fall 2010, est.) 1,126 applied for aid; of those 73% were deemed to have need. 97% of freshmen with need received aid; of those 15% had need fully met. ***Average percent of need met:*** 73% (excluding resources awarded to replace EFC). ***Average financial aid package:*** $9147 (excluding resources awarded to replace EFC). 8% of all full-time freshmen had no need and received non-need-based gift aid.

UNDERGRADUATE FINANCIAL AID (Fall 2010, est.) 3,489 applied for aid; of those 80% were deemed to have need. 97% of undergraduates with need received aid; of those 15% had need fully met. ***Average percent of need met:*** 76% (excluding resources awarded to replace EFC). ***Average financial aid package:*** $9734 (excluding resources awarded to replace EFC). 8% of all full-time undergraduates had no need and received non-need-based gift aid.

GIFT AID (NEED-BASED) ***Total amount:*** $22,796,979 (77% federal, 4% state, 9% institutional, 10% external sources). ***Receiving aid:*** Freshmen: 41% (623); all full-time undergraduates: 36% (2,020). ***Average award:*** Freshmen: $6145; Undergraduates: $5880. ***Scholarships, grants, and awards:*** Federal Pell, FSEOG, state, private, college/university gift aid from institutional funds.

GIFT AID (NON-NEED-BASED) ***Total amount:*** $4,600,004 (45% institutional, 55% external sources). ***Receiving aid:*** Freshmen: 19% (282). Undergraduates: 12% (674). ***Average award:*** Freshmen: $3070. Undergraduates: $2536. ***Scholarships, grants, and awards by category:*** *Academic interests/achievement:* biological sciences, business, communication, computer science, education, engineering/technologies, English, general academic interests/achievements, health fields, humanities, mathematics, social sciences. *Creative arts/performance:* debating. *Special achievements/activities:* general special achievements/activities. ***Tuition waivers:*** Full or partial for children of alumni, employees or children of employees, senior citizens.

LOANS ***Student loans:*** $36,364,558 (97% need-based, 3% non-need-based). 46% of past graduating class borrowed through all loan programs. *Average indebtedness per student:* $21,148. ***Average need-based loan:*** Freshmen: $3354. Undergraduates: $4516. ***Parent loans:*** $3,173,777 (91% need-based, 9% non-need-based). ***Programs:*** Federal Direct (Subsidized and Unsubsidized Stafford, PLUS), state.

WORK-STUDY ***Federal work-study:*** Total amount: $518,325; jobs available.

ATHLETIC AWARDS Total amount: $2,009,768 (9% need-based, 91% non-need-based).

APPLYING FOR FINANCIAL AID ***Required financial aid form:*** FAFSA. ***Financial aid deadline (priority):*** 4/1. ***Notification date:*** Continuous beginning 2/15. Students must reply within 4 weeks of notification.

CONTACT Theodore E. Malone, Director of Student Financial Assistance, University of Alaska Anchorage, PO Box 141608, Anchorage, AK 99514-1608, 907-786-1520. *Fax:* 907-786-6122.

UNIVERSITY OF ALASKA FAIRBANKS

Fairbanks, AK

Tuition & fees (AK res): $6075 Average undergraduate aid package: $10,723

ABOUT THE INSTITUTION State-supported, coed. 72 undergraduate majors. Federal methodology is used as a basis for awarding need-based institutional aid.

UNDERGRADUATE EXPENSES for 2011–12 ***Tuition, state resident:*** full-time $5115; part-time $154 per credit. ***Tuition, nonresident:*** full-time $16,755; part-time $542 per credit. ***Required fees:*** full-time $960. Full-time tuition and fees vary according to course level, course load, location, and reciprocity agreements. Part-time tuition and fees vary according to course level, course load, location, and reciprocity agreements. ***College room and board:*** $6960; ***Room only:*** $3610. Room and board charges vary according to board plan and housing facility. ***Payment plan:*** Installment.

FRESHMAN FINANCIAL AID (Fall 2009) 657 applied for aid; of those 59% were deemed to have need. 95% of freshmen with need received aid; of those 34% had need fully met. ***Average percent of need met:*** 53% (excluding resources awarded to replace EFC). ***Average financial aid package:*** $9574 (excluding resources awarded to replace EFC). 33% of all full-time freshmen had no need and received non-need-based gift aid.

UNDERGRADUATE FINANCIAL AID (Fall 2009) 2,402 applied for aid; of those 66% were deemed to have need. 96% of undergraduates with need received aid; of those 35% had need fully met. ***Average percent of need met:*** 57% (excluding resources awarded to replace EFC). ***Average financial aid package:*** $10,723 (excluding resources awarded to replace EFC). 28% of all full-time undergraduates had no need and received non-need-based gift aid.

GIFT AID (NEED-BASED) ***Total amount:*** $7,400,754 (76% federal, 2% state, 16% institutional, 6% external sources). ***Receiving aid:*** Freshmen: 33% (277); all full-time undergraduates: 31% (1,092). ***Average award:*** Freshmen: $5490; Undergraduates: $5462. ***Scholarships, grants, and awards:*** Federal Pell, FSEOG, state, private, college/university gift aid from institutional funds.

GIFT AID (NON-NEED-BASED) ***Total amount:*** $2,087,391 (77% institutional, 23% external sources). ***Receiving aid:*** Freshmen: 2% (17). Undergraduates: 2% (69). ***Average award:*** Freshmen: $7486. Undergraduates: $7620. ***Scholarships, grants, and awards by category:*** *Academic interests/achievement:* agriculture, engineering/technologies, general academic interests/achievements, physical sciences. *Creative arts/performance:* applied art and design, art/fine arts, creative writing, music, theater/drama. *Special achievements/activities:* community service, general special achievements/activities. *Special characteristics:* local/state students. ***Tuition waivers:*** Full or partial for children of alumni, employees or children of employees, senior citizens.

LOANS ***Student loans:*** $19,460,598 (74% need-based, 26% non-need-based). 52% of past graduating class borrowed through all loan programs. *Average indebtedness per student:* $29,534. ***Average need-based loan:*** Freshmen: $7465. Undergraduates: $9105. ***Parent loans:*** $322,380 (54% need-based, 46% non-need-based). ***Programs:*** Federal Direct (Subsidized and Unsubsidized Stafford, PLUS), state.

WORK-STUDY ***Federal work-study:*** Total amount: $123,392; 42 jobs averaging $2938.

ATHLETIC AWARDS Total amount: $1,050,495 (27% need-based, 73% non-need-based).

APPLYING FOR FINANCIAL AID ***Required financial aid form:*** FAFSA. ***Financial aid deadline:*** 7/1 (priority: 2/15). ***Notification date:*** Continuous beginning 3/1. Students must reply within 2 weeks of notification.

CONTACT Deanna Dierenger, Director of Financial Aid, University of Alaska Fairbanks, PO Box 756360, Fairbanks, AK 99775-6360, 907-474-7256 or toll-free 800-478-1823. *Fax:* 907-474-7065. *E-mail:* financialaid@uaf.edu.

UNIVERSITY OF ALASKA SOUTHEAST

Juneau, AK

Tuition & fees (AK res): $5139 **Average undergraduate aid package: $8261**

ABOUT THE INSTITUTION State-supported, coed. 27 undergraduate majors. Federal methodology is used as a basis for awarding need-based institutional aid.

UNDERGRADUATE EXPENSES for 2010–11 ***Tuition, state resident:*** full-time $4410; part-time $147 per semester hour. ***Tuition, nonresident:*** full-time $15,000; part-time $500 per semester hour. ***Required fees:*** full-time $729; $13 per semester hour or $5 per term. Full-time tuition and fees vary according to course level, course load, and location. Part-time tuition and fees vary according to course level, course load, and location. ***College room and board:*** $8165; ***Room only:*** $4285. Room and board charges vary according to housing facility and location. ***Payment plans:*** Tuition prepayment, installment.

FRESHMAN FINANCIAL AID (Fall 2009) 185 applied for aid; of those 63% were deemed to have need. 100% of freshmen with need received aid; of those 16% had need fully met. ***Average percent of need met:*** 58% (excluding resources awarded to replace EFC). ***Average financial aid package:*** $7295 (excluding resources awarded to replace EFC). 11% of all full-time freshmen had no need and received non-need-based gift aid.

UNDERGRADUATE FINANCIAL AID (Fall 2009) 856 applied for aid; of those 54% were deemed to have need. 100% of undergraduates with need received aid; of those 13% had need fully met. ***Average percent of need met:*** 58% (excluding resources awarded to replace EFC). ***Average financial aid package:*** $8261 (excluding resources awarded to replace EFC). 7% of all full-time undergraduates had no need and received non-need-based gift aid.

GIFT AID (NEED-BASED) ***Total amount:*** $1,671,336 (93% federal, 3% state, 4% institutional). ***Receiving aid:*** Freshmen: 41% (77); all full-time undergraduates: 33% (284). ***Average award:*** Freshmen: $1213; Undergraduates: $1185. ***Scholarships, grants, and awards:*** Federal Pell, FSEOG, state, private, college/university gift aid from institutional funds.

GIFT AID (NON-NEED-BASED) ***Total amount:*** $1,323,462 (27% federal, 32% institutional, 41% external sources). ***Receiving aid:*** Freshmen: 23% (43). Undergraduates: 20% (168). ***Average award:*** Freshmen: $1186. Undergraduates: $1213. ***Tuition waivers:*** Full or partial for children of alumni, employees or children of employees, senior citizens.

LOANS ***Student loans:*** $4,357,485 (36% need-based, 64% non-need-based). 68% of past graduating class borrowed through all loan programs. *Average indebtedness per student:* $2611. ***Average need-based loan:*** Freshmen: $1535. Undergraduates: $1527. ***Parent loans:*** $153,873 (100% non-need-based). ***Programs:*** Federal Direct (Subsidized and Unsubsidized Stafford, PLUS), state.

WORK-STUDY ***Federal work-study:*** Total amount: $159,910; jobs available.

APPLYING FOR FINANCIAL AID ***Required financial aid form:*** FAFSA. ***Financial aid deadline (priority):*** 4/15. ***Notification date:*** Continuous beginning 3/1. Students must reply within 3 weeks of notification.

CONTACT Ms. Barbara Carlson Burnett, Director of Financial Aid, University of Alaska Southeast, 11120 Glacier Highway, Juneau, AK 99801-8680, 907-796-6296 or toll-free 877-796-4827. *Fax:* 907-796-6250. *E-mail:* barbara.burnett@uas.alaska.edu.

THE UNIVERSITY OF ARIZONA

Tucson, AZ

Tuition & fees (AZ res): $8860 **Average undergraduate aid package: $11,353**

ABOUT THE INSTITUTION State-supported, coed. 105 undergraduate majors. Federal methodology is used as a basis for awarding need-based institutional aid.

UNDERGRADUATE EXPENSES for 2010–11 ***Tuition, state resident:*** full-time $8237; part-time $544 per credit hour. ***Tuition, nonresident:*** full-time $24,597; part-time $999 per credit hour. ***Required fees:*** full-time $623; $61 per credit hour. Full-time tuition and fees vary according to course level, course load, and program. Part-time tuition and fees vary according to course level, course load, and program. ***College room and board:*** $9024. Room and board charges vary according to board plan and housing facility.

FRESHMAN FINANCIAL AID (Fall 2009) 4,698 applied for aid; of those 67% were deemed to have need. 96% of freshmen with need received aid; of those 15% had need fully met. ***Average percent of need met:*** 68% (excluding resources awarded to replace EFC). ***Average financial aid package:*** $11,058 (excluding resources awarded to replace EFC). 28% of all full-time freshmen had no need and received non-need-based gift aid.

UNDERGRADUATE FINANCIAL AID (Fall 2009) 16,352 applied for aid; of those 76% were deemed to have need. 97% of undergraduates with need received aid; of those 10% had need fully met. ***Average percent of need met:*** 64% (excluding resources awarded to replace EFC). ***Average financial aid package:*** $11,353 (excluding resources awarded to replace EFC). 22% of all full-time undergraduates had no need and received non-need-based gift aid.

GIFT AID (NEED-BASED) ***Total amount:*** $109,121,288 (35% federal, 1% state, 50% institutional, 14% external sources). ***Receiving aid:*** Freshmen: 43% (2,890); all full-time undergraduates: 41% (11,030). ***Average award:*** Freshmen: $9748; Undergraduates: $9261. ***Scholarships, grants, and awards:*** Federal Pell, FSEOG, state, private, college/university gift aid from institutional funds, Federal Nursing.

GIFT AID (NON-NEED-BASED) ***Total amount:*** $48,983,112 (1% federal, 71% institutional, 28% external sources). ***Receiving aid:*** Freshmen: 6% (434). Undergraduates: 4% (1,013). ***Average award:*** Freshmen: $6345. Undergraduates: $5662. ***Scholarships, grants, and awards by category:*** *Academic interests/achievement:* agriculture, architecture, biological sciences, business, education, engineering/technologies, general academic interests/achievements, humanities, military science, physical sciences, religion/biblical studies. *Creative arts/performance:* art/fine arts, dance, music, performing arts, theater/drama. *Special characteristics:* children of faculty/staff, ethnic background, international students. ***Tuition waivers:*** Full or partial for employees or children of employees.

LOANS ***Student loans:*** $87,306,695 (81% need-based, 19% non-need-based). 44% of past graduating class borrowed through all loan programs. *Average indebtedness per student:* $20,074. ***Average need-based loan:*** Freshmen: $3416. Undergraduates: $4369. ***Parent loans:*** $28,642,525 (63% need-based, 37% non-need-based). ***Programs:*** Federal Direct (Subsidized and Unsubsidized Stafford, PLUS), Perkins, Federal Nursing, college/university.

WORK-STUDY ***Federal work-study:*** Total amount: $1,929,391; jobs available. ***State or other work-study/employment:*** Total amount: $15,888,651 (51% need-based, 49% non-need-based). Part-time jobs available.

ATHLETIC AWARDS Total amount: $6,726,623 (41% need-based, 59% non-need-based).

APPLYING FOR FINANCIAL AID ***Required financial aid form:*** FAFSA. ***Financial aid deadline:*** Continuous. ***Notification date:*** Continuous.

CONTACT John Nametz, Director of Student Financial Aid, The University of Arizona, PO Box 210066, Tucson, AZ 85721-0066, 520-621-5200. *Fax:* 520-621-9473. *E-mail:* askaid@arizona.edu.

UNIVERSITY OF ARKANSAS

Fayetteville, AR

Tuition & fees (AR res): $6768 **Average undergraduate aid package: $9836**

ABOUT THE INSTITUTION State-supported, coed. 69 undergraduate majors. Federal methodology is used as a basis for awarding need-based institutional aid.

UNDERGRADUATE EXPENSES for 2010–11 ***Tuition, state resident:*** full-time $5211; part-time $173.68 per credit hour. ***Tuition, nonresident:*** full-time $14,443; part-time $481.43 per contact hour. ***Required fees:*** full-time $1557. Full-time tuition and fees vary according to course load and program. Part-time tuition and fees vary according to course load and program. ***College room and board:*** $8042; ***Room only:*** $5096. Room and board charges vary according to board plan and housing facility. ***Payment plan:*** Installment.

FRESHMAN FINANCIAL AID (Fall 2010, est.) 3,037 applied for aid; of those 60% were deemed to have need. 97% of freshmen with need received aid; of those 30% had need fully met. ***Average percent of need met:*** 68% (excluding

resources awarded to replace EFC). ***Average financial aid package:*** $10,349 (excluding resources awarded to replace EFC). 16% of all full-time freshmen had no need and received non-need-based gift aid.

UNDERGRADUATE FINANCIAL AID (Fall 2010, est.) 10,435 applied for aid; of those 68% were deemed to have need. 96% of undergraduates with need received aid; of those 22% had need fully met. ***Average percent of need met:*** 64% (excluding resources awarded to replace EFC). ***Average financial aid package:*** $9836 (excluding resources awarded to replace EFC). 15% of all full-time undergraduates had no need and received non-need-based gift aid.

GIFT AID (NEED-BASED) ***Total amount:*** $41,505,068 (46% federal, 33% state, 16% institutional, 5% external sources). ***Receiving aid:*** Freshmen: 42% (1,592); all full-time undergraduates: 39% (5,752). ***Average award:*** Freshmen: $7989; Undergraduates: $7166. ***Scholarships, grants, and awards:*** Federal Pell, FSEOG, state, private, college/university gift aid from institutional funds.

GIFT AID (NON-NEED-BASED) ***Total amount:*** $30,113,518 (51% state, 44% institutional, 5% external sources). ***Receiving aid:*** Freshmen: 10% (375). Undergraduates: 7% (964). ***Average award:*** Freshmen: $4811. Undergraduates: $5249. ***Scholarships, grants, and awards by category:*** *Academic interests/achievement:* general academic interests/achievements. *Creative arts/performance:* art/fine arts, music, theater/drama. *Special achievements/activities:* community service, general special achievements/activities, leadership. *Special characteristics:* children and siblings of alumni, children of faculty/staff, ethnic background, international students, local/state students, members of minority groups, out-of-state students, previous college experience. ***Tuition waivers:*** Full or partial for employees or children of employees, senior citizens.

LOANS ***Student loans:*** $51,142,410 (70% need-based, 30% non-need-based). 45% of past graduating class borrowed through all loan programs. *Average indebtedness per student:* $21,562. ***Average need-based loan:*** Freshmen: $3394. Undergraduates: $4335. ***Parent loans:*** $7,904,148 (24% need-based, 76% non-need-based). ***Programs:*** Federal Direct (Subsidized and Unsubsidized Stafford, PLUS), Perkins, state, college/university, alternative loans.

WORK-STUDY ***Federal work-study:*** Total amount: $2,779,173; jobs available.

ATHLETIC AWARDS Total amount: $4,402,000 (33% need-based, 67% non-need-based).

APPLYING FOR FINANCIAL AID ***Required financial aid form:*** FAFSA. ***Financial aid deadline (priority):*** 3/15. ***Notification date:*** Continuous beginning 4/1. Students must reply within 4 weeks of notification.

CONTACT Kattie Wing, Director of Financial Aid, University of Arkansas, 114 Silas H. Hunt Hall, Fayetteville, AR 72701-1201, 479-575-3078 or toll-free 800-377-5346 (in-state), 800-377-8632 (out-of-state). *E-mail:* kattie@uark.edu.

UNIVERSITY OF ARKANSAS AT LITTLE ROCK

Little Rock, AR

Tuition & fees (AR res): $6643 **Average undergraduate aid package: N/A**

ABOUT THE INSTITUTION State-supported, coed. 55 undergraduate majors. Both federal and institutional methodology are used as a basis for awarding need-based institutional aid.

UNDERGRADUATE EXPENSES for 2010–11 ***Tuition, state resident:*** full-time $5228; part-time $174.25 per credit hour. ***Tuition, nonresident:*** full-time $14,175; part-time $472.50 per credit hour. ***Required fees:*** full-time $1415; $47.16 per credit hour. Full-time tuition and fees vary according to program. Part-time tuition and fees vary according to program. ***College room and board: Room only:*** $3255. Room and board charges vary according to housing facility. ***Payment plan:*** Installment.

GIFT AID (NEED-BASED) ***Total amount:*** $28,218,656 (90% federal, 3% state, 4% institutional, 3% external sources). ***Scholarships, grants, and awards:*** Federal Pell, FSEOG, state, private, college/university gift aid from institutional funds.

GIFT AID (NON-NEED-BASED) ***Scholarships, grants, and awards by category:*** *Academic interests/achievement:* biological sciences, business, communication, computer science, education, engineering/technologies, English, foreign languages, general academic interests/achievements, health fields, humanities, international studies, mathematics, physical sciences, social sciences. *Creative arts/performance:* art/fine arts, music, theater/drama. *Special achievements/activities:* community service, leadership, memberships. *Special characteristics:* local/state students, members of minority groups, previous college experience. ***Tuition waivers:*** Full or partial for employees or children of employees, senior citizens.

LOANS ***Student loans:*** $60,764,433 (100% need-based). ***Parent loans:*** $662,732 (100% need-based). ***Programs:*** Federal Direct (Subsidized and Unsubsidized Stafford, PLUS).

WORK-STUDY ***Federal work-study:*** Total amount: $496,801; jobs available.

APPLYING FOR FINANCIAL AID ***Required financial aid form:*** FAFSA. ***Financial aid deadline (priority):*** 3/1. ***Notification date:*** 4/15.

CONTACT Financial Aid Office, University of Arkansas at Little Rock, 2801 South University Avenue, Little Rock, AR 72204-1099, 501-569-3035 or toll-free 800-482-8892 (in-state). *E-mail:* financialaid@ualr.edu.

UNIVERSITY OF ARKANSAS AT MONTICELLO

Monticello, AR

CONTACT Susan Brewer, Director of Financial Aid, University of Arkansas at Monticello, PO Box 3470, Monticello, AR 71656, 870-460-1050 or toll-free 800-844-1826 (in-state). *Fax:* 870-460-1450. *E-mail:* brewers@uamont.edu.

UNIVERSITY OF ARKANSAS AT PINE BLUFF

Pine Bluff, AR

CONTACT Mrs. Carolyn Iverson, Director of Financial Aid, University of Arkansas at Pine Bluff, 1200 North University Drive, PO Box 4985, Pine Bluff, AR 71601, 870-575-8303 or toll-free 800-264-6585. *Fax:* 870-575-4622. *E-mail:* iverson_c@uapb.edu.

UNIVERSITY OF ARKANSAS FOR MEDICAL SCIENCES

Little Rock, AR

CONTACT Mr. Paul Carter, Director of Financial Aid, University of Arkansas for Medical Sciences, 4301 West Markham Street, MS 601, Little Rock, AR 72205, 501-686-5451. *Fax:* 501-686-5661. *E-mail:* pvcarter@uams.edu.

UNIVERSITY OF ARKANSAS–FORT SMITH

Fort Smith, AR

CONTACT Tammy Malone, Interim Financial Aid Director, University of Arkansas–Fort Smith, 5210 Grand Avenue, Fort Smith, AR 72913, 479-788-7099 or toll-free 888-512-5466. *Fax:* 479-788-7095. *E-mail:* tmalone@uafortsmith.edu.

UNIVERSITY OF ATLANTA

Atlanta, GA

CONTACT Financial Aid Office, University of Atlanta, 6685 Peachtree Industrial Boulevard, Atlanta, GA 30360, 770-368-8877 or toll-free 800-533-3378.

UNIVERSITY OF BALTIMORE

Baltimore, MD

CONTACT Financial Aid Office, University of Baltimore, 1420 North Charles Street, CH 123, Baltimore, MD 21201-5779, 410-837-4763 or toll-free 877-APPLYUB. *Fax:* 410-837-5493. *E-mail:* financial-aid@ubalt.edu.

UNIVERSITY OF BRIDGEPORT

Bridgeport, CT

Tuition & fees: $26,495 **Average undergraduate aid package: $23,400**

ABOUT THE INSTITUTION Independent, coed. 38 undergraduate majors. Federal methodology is used as a basis for awarding need-based institutional aid.

UNDERGRADUATE EXPENSES for 2010–11 ***Comprehensive fee:*** $37,895 includes full-time tuition ($24,300), mandatory fees ($2195), and room and board ($11,400). Full-time tuition and fees vary according to course load and program. Room and board charges vary according to board plan and student level. ***Part-time tuition:*** $810 per credit hour. ***Part-time fees:*** $80 per year. Part-time tuition and fees vary according to course load and program. ***Payment plans:*** Installment, deferred payment.

FRESHMAN FINANCIAL AID (Fall 2010, est.) 537 applied for aid; of those 98% were deemed to have need. 100% of freshmen with need received aid. ***Average percent of need met:*** 60% (excluding resources awarded to replace EFC). ***Average financial aid package:*** $23,900 (excluding resources awarded to replace EFC).

UNDERGRADUATE FINANCIAL AID (Fall 2010, est.) 1,400 applied for aid; of those 99% were deemed to have need. 100% of undergraduates with need received aid. ***Average percent of need met:*** 61% (excluding resources awarded to replace EFC). ***Average financial aid package:*** $23,400 (excluding resources awarded to replace EFC).

GIFT AID (NEED-BASED) ***Total amount:*** $27,154,000 (23% federal, 6% state, 71% institutional). ***Receiving aid:*** Freshmen: 87% (528); all full-time undergraduates: 78% (1,340). ***Average award:*** Freshmen: $17,427; Undergraduates: $15,178. ***Scholarships, grants, and awards:*** Federal Pell, FSEOG, state, private, college/university gift aid from institutional funds.

GIFT AID (NON-NEED-BASED) ***Scholarships, grants, and awards by category:*** *Academic interests/achievement:* general academic interests/achievements. *Creative arts/performance:* applied art and design, music. *Special characteristics:* children of faculty/staff, international students, local/state students, previous college experience. ***Tuition waivers:*** Full or partial for employees or children of employees, senior citizens.

LOANS ***Student loans:*** $17,000,000 (100% need-based). ***Average need-based loan:*** Freshmen: $3295. Undergraduates: $4380. ***Parent loans:*** $4,930,000 (100% need-based). ***Programs:*** Federal Direct (Subsidized and Unsubsidized Stafford, PLUS), Perkins.

WORK-STUDY ***Federal work-study:*** Total amount: $2,200,000; jobs available. ***State or other work-study/employment:*** Part-time jobs available.

ATHLETIC AWARDS Total amount: $2,900,000 (100% need-based).

APPLYING FOR FINANCIAL AID ***Required financial aid form:*** FAFSA. ***Financial aid deadline (priority):*** 3/1. ***Notification date:*** Continuous beginning 3/1. Students must reply by 5/15 or within 4 weeks of notification.

CONTACT Jonathan M. Mador, Director of Student Financial Services, University of Bridgeport, 126 Park Avenue, Bridgeport, CT 06604, 203-576-4568 or toll-free 800-EXCEL-UB (in-state), 800-243-9496 (out-of-state). *Fax:* 203-576-4570. *E-mail:* finaid@bridgeport.edu.

UNIVERSITY OF CALIFORNIA, BERKELEY

Berkeley, CA

Tuition & fees (CA res): $12,462   Average undergraduate aid package: $19,261

ABOUT THE INSTITUTION State-supported, coed. 93 undergraduate majors. Both federal and institutional methodology are used as a basis for awarding need-based institutional aid.

UNDERGRADUATE EXPENSES for 2010–11 ***Tuition, state resident:*** full-time $9402. ***Tuition, nonresident:*** full-time $32,281. ***Required fees:*** full-time $3060. Full-time tuition and fees vary according to course load, degree level, and program. Part-time tuition and fees vary according to course load, degree level, and program. ***College room and board:*** $15,308. Room and board charges vary according to board plan and housing facility. ***Payment plan:*** Installment.

FRESHMAN FINANCIAL AID (Fall 2010, est.) 2,338 applied for aid; of those 84% were deemed to have need. 100% of freshmen with need received aid; of those 18% had need fully met. ***Average percent of need met:*** 76% (excluding resources awarded to replace EFC). ***Average financial aid package:*** $20,619 (excluding resources awarded to replace EFC). 6% of all full-time freshmen had no need and received non-need-based gift aid.

UNDERGRADUATE FINANCIAL AID (Fall 2010, est.) 17,140 applied for aid; of those 85% were deemed to have need. 90% of undergraduates with need received aid; of those 25% had need fully met. ***Average percent of need met:*** 81% (excluding resources awarded to replace EFC). ***Average financial aid package:*** $19,261 (excluding resources awarded to replace EFC). 5% of all full-time undergraduates had no need and received non-need-based gift aid.

GIFT AID (NEED-BASED) ***Total amount:*** $204,452,935 (22% federal, 31% state, 44% institutional, 3% external sources). ***Receiving aid:*** Freshmen: 46% (1,894); all full-time undergraduates: 51% (12,752). ***Average award:*** Freshmen: $17,468; Undergraduates: $15,863. ***Scholarships, grants, and awards:*** Federal Pell, FSEOG, state, private, college/university gift aid from institutional funds.

GIFT AID (NON-NEED-BASED) ***Total amount:*** $13,012,570 (7% federal, 2% state, 61% institutional, 30% external sources). ***Receiving aid:*** Freshmen: 1% (23). Undergraduates: 103. ***Average award:*** Freshmen: $5612. Undergraduates: $6472. ***Scholarships, grants, and awards by category:*** *Academic interests/achievement:* general academic interests/achievements.

LOANS ***Student loans:*** $47,388,295 (82% need-based, 18% non-need-based). 41% of past graduating class borrowed through all loan programs. *Average indebtedness per student:* $16,056. ***Average need-based loan:*** Freshmen: $6331. Undergraduates: $5874. ***Parent loans:*** $19,767,011 (20% need-based, 80% non-need-based). ***Programs:*** Federal Direct (Subsidized and Unsubsidized Stafford, PLUS), Perkins.

WORK-STUDY ***Federal work-study:*** Total amount: $5,141,667; jobs available. ***State or other work-study/employment:*** Total amount: $3,083,492 (100% need-based). Part-time jobs available.

ATHLETIC AWARDS Total amount: $10,263,836 (29% need-based, 71% non-need-based).

APPLYING FOR FINANCIAL AID ***Required financial aid forms:*** FAFSA, state aid form, Cal Grant forms. ***Financial aid deadline:*** 3/2. ***Notification date:*** 4/15.

CONTACT Kathy Bradley, Administrative Specialist, University of California, Berkeley, 225 Sproul Hall, Berkeley, CA 94720-1960, 510-642-0649. *Fax:* 510-643-5526. *E-mail:* kbradley@berkeley.edu.

UNIVERSITY OF CALIFORNIA, DAVIS

Davis, CA

Tuition & fees (CA res): $11,984   Average undergraduate aid package: $18,136

ABOUT THE INSTITUTION State-supported, coed. 83 undergraduate majors. Federal methodology is used as a basis for awarding need-based institutional aid.

UNDERGRADUATE EXPENSES for 2011–12 ***Tuition, state resident:*** full-time $9402. ***Tuition, nonresident:*** full-time $32,281. ***Required fees:*** full-time $2582. ***College room and board:*** $12,498. Room and board charges vary according to board plan. Fees do not include Health Insurance Fee of $1,263 which can be waived with proof of insurance. ***Payment plan:*** Deferred payment.

FRESHMAN FINANCIAL AID (Fall 2010, est.) 3,811 applied for aid; of those 78% were deemed to have need. 98% of freshmen with need received aid; of those 15% had need fully met. ***Average percent of need met:*** 82% (excluding resources awarded to replace EFC). ***Average financial aid package:*** $19,310 (excluding resources awarded to replace EFC). 4% of all full-time freshmen had no need and received non-need-based gift aid.

UNDERGRADUATE FINANCIAL AID (Fall 2010, est.) 17,282 applied for aid; of those 87% were deemed to have need. 99% of undergraduates with need received aid; of those 20% had need fully met. ***Average percent of need met:*** 81% (excluding resources awarded to replace EFC). ***Average financial aid package:*** $18,136 (excluding resources awarded to replace EFC). 3% of all full-time undergraduates had no need and received non-need-based gift aid.

GIFT AID (NEED-BASED) ***Total amount:*** $217,267,621 (26% federal, 34% state, 38% institutional, 2% external sources). ***Receiving aid:*** Freshmen: 63% (2,806); all full-time undergraduates: 60% (14,337). ***Average award:*** Freshmen: $16,105; Undergraduates: $14,883. ***Scholarships, grants, and awards:*** Federal Pell, FSEOG, state, private, college/university gift aid from institutional funds.

GIFT AID (NON-NEED-BASED) ***Total amount:*** $8,991,346 (15% federal, 57% institutional, 28% external sources). ***Receiving aid:*** Freshmen: 1% (36). Undergraduates: 100. ***Average award:*** Freshmen: $4896. Undergraduates: $5918. ***Scholarships, grants, and awards by category:*** *Academic interests/achievement:* agriculture, area/ethnic studies, biological sciences, business, communication, computer science, engineering/technologies, English, foreign languages, general academic interests/achievements, health fields, home economics, humanities, international studies, mathematics, premedicine, religion/biblical studies, social sciences.

LOANS ***Student loans:*** $61,179,125 (86% need-based, 14% non-need-based). 50% of past graduating class borrowed through all loan programs. *Average indebtedness per student:* $16,659. ***Average need-based loan:*** Freshmen: $5257. Undergraduates: $5386. ***Parent loans:*** $18,573,958 (13% need-based, 87% non-need-based). ***Programs:*** Federal Direct (Subsidized and Unsubsidized Stafford, PLUS), Perkins, college/university.

WORK-STUDY ***Federal work-study:*** Total amount: $1,946,035; jobs available. ***State or other work-study/employment:*** Total amount: $374,006 (100% need-based). Part-time jobs available.

ATHLETIC AWARDS Total amount: $3,904,481 (6% need-based, 94% non-need-based).

APPLYING FOR FINANCIAL AID ***Required financial aid forms:*** FAFSA, state aid form. ***Financial aid deadline (priority):*** 3/2. ***Notification date:*** Continuous beginning 3/24.

CONTACT Katy Maloney, Director of Financial Aid, University of California, Davis, One Shields Avenue, 2128 Dutton Hall, Davis, CA 95616, 530-752-2396. *Fax:* 530-752-7339. *E-mail:* kamaloney@ucdavis.edu.

UNIVERSITY OF CALIFORNIA, IRVINE

Irvine, CA

Tuition & fees (CA res): $11,927 **Average undergraduate aid package: $18,359**

ABOUT THE INSTITUTION State-supported, coed. 74 undergraduate majors. Federal methodology is used as a basis for awarding need-based institutional aid.

UNDERGRADUATE EXPENSES for 2011–12 ***Tuition, state resident:*** full-time $9402. ***Tuition, nonresident:*** full-time $32,281. ***Required fees:*** full-time $2525. ***College room and board:*** $11,400. Room and board charges vary according to board plan and housing facility. ***Payment plan:*** Installment.

FRESHMAN FINANCIAL AID (Fall 2010, est.) 3,785 applied for aid; of those 76% were deemed to have need. 97% of freshmen with need received aid; of those 41% had need fully met. ***Average percent of need met:*** 86% (excluding resources awarded to replace EFC). ***Average financial aid package:*** $18,782 (excluding resources awarded to replace EFC). 1% of all full-time freshmen had no need and received non-need-based gift aid.

UNDERGRADUATE FINANCIAL AID (Fall 2010, est.) 15,791 applied for aid; of those 84% were deemed to have need. 97% of undergraduates with need received aid; of those 36% had need fully met. ***Average percent of need met:*** 84% (excluding resources awarded to replace EFC). ***Average financial aid package:*** $18,359 (excluding resources awarded to replace EFC). 3% of all full-time undergraduates had no need and received non-need-based gift aid.

GIFT AID (NEED-BASED) ***Total amount:*** $183,199,557 (24% federal, 37% state, 38% institutional, 1% external sources). ***Receiving aid:*** Freshmen: 60% (2,662); all full-time undergraduates: 57% (12,207). ***Average award:*** Freshmen: $14,807; Undergraduates: $14,919. ***Scholarships, grants, and awards:*** Federal Pell, FSEOG, state, private, college/university gift aid from institutional funds.

GIFT AID (NON-NEED-BASED) ***Total amount:*** $7,136,920 (10% federal, 79% institutional, 11% external sources). ***Receiving aid:*** Freshmen: 1% (34). Undergraduates: 106. ***Average award:*** Freshmen: $11,284. Undergraduates: $8633. ***Scholarships, grants, and awards by category:*** *Academic interests/achievement:* 591 awards ($2,008,869 total): biological sciences, business, computer science, education, engineering/technologies, foreign languages, general academic interests/achievements, health fields, humanities, international studies, mathematics, physical sciences, premedicine, social sciences. *Creative arts/performance:* 187 awards ($179,438 total): art/fine arts, cinema/film/broadcasting, dance, general creative arts/performance, music, performing arts, theater/drama.

LOANS ***Student loans:*** $57,510,841 (76% need-based, 24% non-need-based). 47% of past graduating class borrowed through all loan programs. *Average indebtedness per student:* $16,878. ***Average need-based loan:*** Freshmen: $5942. Undergraduates: $6305. ***Parent loans:*** $38,310,828 (19% need-based, 81% non-need-based). ***Programs:*** Federal Direct (Subsidized and Unsubsidized Stafford, PLUS), Perkins, college/university, private loans.

WORK-STUDY ***Federal work-study:*** Total amount: $3,933,721; 3,387 jobs averaging $1545.

ATHLETIC AWARDS Total amount: $2,840,057 (30% need-based, 70% non-need-based).

APPLYING FOR FINANCIAL AID ***Required financial aid forms:*** FAFSA, state aid form. ***Financial aid deadline:*** 5/1 (priority: 3/2). ***Notification date:*** Continuous beginning 4/1.

CONTACT Ms. Penny Harrell, Associate Director of Student Services, University of California, Irvine, Office of Financial Aid and Scholarships, Irvine, CA 92697-2825, 949-824-8262. *Fax:* 949-824-4876. *E-mail:* finaid@uci.edu.

UNIVERSITY OF CALIFORNIA, LOS ANGELES

Los Angeles, CA

Tuition & fees (CA res): $11,868 **Average undergraduate aid package: $18,896**

ABOUT THE INSTITUTION State-supported, coed. 98 undergraduate majors. Both federal and institutional methodology are used as a basis for awarding need-based institutional aid.

UNDERGRADUATE EXPENSES for 2010–11 ***Tuition, state resident:*** full-time $0. ***Tuition, nonresident:*** full-time $22,879. ***Required fees:*** full-time $11,868. ***College room and board:*** $13,734. Room and board charges vary according to board plan and housing facility.

FRESHMAN FINANCIAL AID (Fall 2010, est.) 3,022 applied for aid; of those 86% were deemed to have need. 100% of freshmen with need received aid; of those 23% had need fully met. ***Average percent of need met:*** 81% (excluding resources awarded to replace EFC). ***Average financial aid package:*** $19,561 (excluding resources awarded to replace EFC). 5% of all full-time freshmen had no need and received non-need-based gift aid.

UNDERGRADUATE FINANCIAL AID (Fall 2010, est.) 15,212 applied for aid; of those 92% were deemed to have need. 100% of undergraduates with need received aid; of those 25% had need fully met. ***Average percent of need met:*** 82% (excluding resources awarded to replace EFC). ***Average financial aid package:*** $18,896 (excluding resources awarded to replace EFC). 4% of all full-time undergraduates had no need and received non-need-based gift aid.

GIFT AID (NEED-BASED) ***Total amount:*** $203,090,037 (23% federal, 33% state, 42% institutional, 2% external sources). ***Receiving aid:*** Freshmen: 54% (2,492); all full-time undergraduates: 52% (13,222). ***Average award:*** Freshmen: $16,080; Undergraduates: $15,364. ***Scholarships, grants, and awards:*** Federal Pell, FSEOG, state, private, college/university gift aid from institutional funds, United Negro College Fund, Federal Nursing.

GIFT AID (NON-NEED-BASED) ***Total amount:*** $7,251,807 (9% federal, 70% institutional, 21% external sources). ***Receiving aid:*** Freshmen: 1% (49). Undergraduates: 1% (134). ***Average award:*** Freshmen: $5493. Undergraduates: $5074. ***Scholarships, grants, and awards by category:*** *Academic interests/achievement:* general academic interests/achievements. *Special achievements/activities:* general special achievements/activities.

LOANS ***Student loans:*** $66,631,994 (79% need-based, 21% non-need-based). 45% of past graduating class borrowed through all loan programs. *Average indebtedness per student:* $18,203. ***Average need-based loan:*** Freshmen: $6258. Undergraduates: $6471. ***Parent loans:*** $26,873,565 (23% need-based, 77% non-need-based). ***Programs:*** Federal Direct (Subsidized and Unsubsidized Stafford, PLUS), Perkins, Federal Nursing, state, college/university.

WORK-STUDY ***Federal work-study:*** Total amount: $6,324,722; 2,848 jobs averaging $1953. ***State or other work-study/employment:*** Total amount: $1,120,000 (100% need-based). 776 part-time jobs averaging $1029.

ATHLETIC AWARDS Total amount: $9,114,487 (34% need-based, 66% non-need-based).

APPLYING FOR FINANCIAL AID ***Required financial aid form:*** FAFSA. ***Financial aid deadline:*** Continuous. ***Notification date:*** Continuous beginning 3/15.

CONTACT Ms. Yolanda Tan, Administrative Assistant for Financial Aid, University of California, Los Angeles, A-129 Murphy Hall, Los Angeles, CA 90095-1435, 310-206-0404. *E-mail:* finaid@saonet.ucla.edu.

UNIVERSITY OF CALIFORNIA, MERCED

Merced, CA

Tuition & fees (CA res): $10,130 **Average undergraduate aid package: $19,537**

ABOUT THE INSTITUTION State-supported, coed. 20 undergraduate majors. Both federal and institutional methodology are used as a basis for awarding need-based institutional aid.

UNDERGRADUATE EXPENSES for 2011–12 ***Tuition, state resident:*** full-time $9402; part-time $4701 per year. ***Tuition, nonresident:*** full-time $32,280; part-time $16,140 per year. ***Required fees:*** full-time $728. ***College room and board:*** $12,801.

FRESHMAN FINANCIAL AID (Fall 2010, est.) 1,239 applied for aid; of those 90% were deemed to have need. 99% of freshmen with need received aid; of those 37% had need fully met. ***Average percent of need met:*** 87% (excluding

resources awarded to replace EFC). ***Average financial aid package:*** $20,781 (excluding resources awarded to replace EFC). 2% of all full-time freshmen had no need and received non-need-based gift aid.

UNDERGRADUATE FINANCIAL AID (Fall 2010, est.) 3,586 applied for aid; of those 91% were deemed to have need. 99% of undergraduates with need received aid; of those 36% had need fully met. ***Average percent of need met:*** 86% (excluding resources awarded to replace EFC). ***Average financial aid package:*** $19,537 (excluding resources awarded to replace EFC). 2% of all full-time undergraduates had no need and received non-need-based gift aid.

GIFT AID (NEED-BASED) ***Total amount:*** $48,995,396 (25% federal, 41% state, 33% institutional, 1% external sources). ***Receiving aid:*** Freshmen: 80% (1,073); all full-time undergraduates: 76% (3,136). ***Average award:*** Freshmen: $16,763; Undergraduates: $15,591. ***Scholarships, grants, and awards:*** Federal Pell.

GIFT AID (NON-NEED-BASED) ***Total amount:*** $1,196,493 (1% federal, 1% state, 87% institutional, 11% external sources). ***Receiving aid:*** Freshmen: 1% (10). Undergraduates: 19. ***Average award:*** Freshmen: $9756. Undergraduates: $11,302.

LOANS ***Student loans:*** $13,074,809 (82% need-based, 18% non-need-based). 60% of past graduating class borrowed through all loan programs. *Average indebtedness per student:* $15,913. ***Average need-based loan:*** Freshmen: $5156. Undergraduates: $5528. ***Parent loans:*** $6,780,336 (15% need-based, 85% non-need-based). ***Programs:*** Federal Direct (Subsidized and Unsubsidized Stafford, PLUS), alternative loans.

WORK-STUDY ***Federal work-study:*** Total amount: $148,156; jobs available. ***State or other work-study/employment:*** Total amount: $2,455,224 (100% need-based). Part-time jobs available.

APPLYING FOR FINANCIAL AID ***Required financial aid form:*** FAFSA.

CONTACT Diana M. Ralls, Director of Financial Aid, University of California, Merced, Kolligian Library Room 122, 5200 North Lake Road, Merced, CA 95343, 209-228-4243. *Fax:* 209-228-7861. *E-mail:* finaid@ucmerced.edu.

UNIVERSITY OF CALIFORNIA, RIVERSIDE

Riverside, CA

Tuition & fees (CA res): $11,029 Average undergraduate aid package: $19,431

ABOUT THE INSTITUTION State-supported, coed. 60 undergraduate majors. Federal methodology is used as a basis for awarding need-based institutional aid.

UNDERGRADUATE EXPENSES for 2010–11 ***Tuition, state resident:*** full-time $0. ***Tuition, nonresident:*** full-time $22,881. ***Required fees:*** full-time $11,029. Full-time tuition and fees vary according to course load. Part-time tuition and fees vary according to course load. ***College room and board:*** $11,600. Room and board charges vary according to board plan and housing facility. ***Payment plan:*** Deferred payment.

FRESHMAN FINANCIAL AID (Fall 2010, est.) 4,022 applied for aid; of those 86% were deemed to have need. 99% of freshmen with need received aid; of those 45% had need fully met. ***Average percent of need met:*** 92% (excluding resources awarded to replace EFC). ***Average financial aid package:*** $21,402 (excluding resources awarded to replace EFC). 2% of all full-time freshmen had no need and received non-need-based gift aid.

UNDERGRADUATE FINANCIAL AID (Fall 2010, est.) 14,753 applied for aid; of those 91% were deemed to have need. 99% of undergraduates with need received aid; of those 35% had need fully met. ***Average percent of need met:*** 85% (excluding resources awarded to replace EFC). ***Average financial aid package:*** $19,431 (excluding resources awarded to replace EFC). 1% of all full-time undergraduates had no need and received non-need-based gift aid.

GIFT AID (NEED-BASED) ***Total amount:*** $192,041,387 (26% federal, 39% state, 34% institutional, 1% external sources). ***Receiving aid:*** Freshmen: 74% (3,310); all full-time undergraduates: 70% (12,491). ***Average award:*** Freshmen: $17,064; Undergraduates: $15,329. ***Scholarships, grants, and awards:*** Federal Pell, FSEOG, state, private, college/university gift aid from institutional funds.

GIFT AID (NON-NEED-BASED) ***Total amount:*** $6,680,737 (18% federal, 75% institutional, 7% external sources). ***Receiving aid:*** Freshmen: 2% (72). Undergraduates: 1% (202). ***Average award:*** Freshmen: $5886. Undergraduates: $6901. ***Scholarships, grants, and awards by category:*** *Academic interests/achievement:* agriculture, area/ethnic studies, biological sciences, business, education, engineering/technologies, English, general academic interests/achievements, humanities, mathematics, physical sciences, premedicine, social sciences. *Creative arts/performance:* art/fine arts, creative writing, dance, music, theater/drama. *Special characteristics:* religious affiliation, veterans, veterans' children.

LOANS ***Student loans:*** $61,583,765 (85% need-based, 15% non-need-based). 64% of past graduating class borrowed through all loan programs. *Average indebtedness per student:* $18,094. ***Average need-based loan:*** Freshmen: $4993. Undergraduates: $6182. ***Parent loans:*** $21,583,898 (27% need-based, 73% non-need-based). ***Programs:*** Federal Direct (Subsidized and Unsubsidized Stafford, PLUS), Perkins, college/university.

WORK-STUDY ***Federal work-study:*** Total amount: $7,428,009; 3,839 jobs averaging $2063. ***State or other work-study/employment:*** Total amount: $69,011,774 (86% need-based, 14% non-need-based). Part-time jobs available.

ATHLETIC AWARDS Total amount: $2,742,901 (43% need-based, 57% non-need-based).

APPLYING FOR FINANCIAL AID ***Required financial aid forms:*** FAFSA, state aid form. ***Financial aid deadline:*** 3/2. ***Notification date:*** Continuous. Students must reply by 5/1 or within 3 weeks of notification.

CONTACT Ms. Sheryl Hayes, Director of Financial Aid, University of California, Riverside, 2106 Student Services Building, Riverside, CA 92521-0209, 951-827-3878. *Fax:* 951-827-5619. *E-mail:* finaid@ucr.edu.

UNIVERSITY OF CALIFORNIA, SAN DIEGO

La Jolla, CA

Tuition & fees (CA res): $12,176 Average undergraduate aid package: $20,559

ABOUT THE INSTITUTION State-supported, coed. 68 undergraduate majors. Both federal and institutional methodology are used as a basis for awarding need-based institutional aid.

UNDERGRADUATE EXPENSES for 2010–11 ***Tuition, state resident:*** full-time $0. ***Tuition, nonresident:*** full-time $22,881. ***Required fees:*** full-time $12,176. ***College room and board:*** $11,719. Room and board charges vary according to board plan and housing facility.

FRESHMAN FINANCIAL AID (Fall 2010, est.) 3,379 applied for aid; of those 80% were deemed to have need. 97% of freshmen with need received aid; of those 18% had need fully met. ***Average percent of need met:*** 88% (excluding resources awarded to replace EFC). ***Average financial aid package:*** $21,196 (excluding resources awarded to replace EFC). 1% of all full-time freshmen had no need and received non-need-based gift aid.

UNDERGRADUATE FINANCIAL AID (Fall 2010, est.) 16,819 applied for aid; of those 90% were deemed to have need. 98% of undergraduates with need received aid; of those 21% had need fully met. ***Average percent of need met:*** 86% (excluding resources awarded to replace EFC). ***Average financial aid package:*** $20,559 (excluding resources awarded to replace EFC). 2% of all full-time undergraduates had no need and received non-need-based gift aid.

GIFT AID (NEED-BASED) ***Total amount:*** $227,750,625 (27% federal, 37% state, 34% institutional, 2% external sources). ***Receiving aid:*** Freshmen: 64% (2,524); all full-time undergraduates: 62% (14,096). ***Average award:*** Freshmen: $16,309; Undergraduates: $15,915. ***Scholarships, grants, and awards:*** Federal Pell, FSEOG, state, private, college/university gift aid from institutional funds, Academic Competitiveness Grants, National SMART Grants, TEACH Grants.

GIFT AID (NON-NEED-BASED) ***Total amount:*** $6,520,663 (13% federal, 1% state, 73% institutional, 13% external sources). ***Receiving aid:*** Freshmen: 1% (20). Undergraduates: 65. ***Average award:*** Freshmen: $9036. Undergraduates: $8007. ***Scholarships, grants, and awards by category:*** *Academic interests/achievement:* biological sciences, business, communication, computer science, engineering/technologies, general academic interests/achievements, mathematics, physical sciences, premedicine, social sciences. *Creative arts/performance:* applied art and design, cinema/film/broadcasting, dance, journalism/publications, performing arts. *Special achievements/activities:* community service, leadership. *Special characteristics:* ethnic background, first-generation college students, handicapped students, members of minority groups, veterans' children.

LOANS ***Student loans:*** $73,630,241 (86% need-based, 14% non-need-based). 48% of past graduating class borrowed through all loan programs. *Average indebtedness per student:* $18,757. ***Average need-based loan:*** Freshmen: $4981. Undergraduates: $6014. ***Parent loans:*** $11,701,643 (18% need-based, 82% non-need-based). ***Programs:*** Federal Direct (Subsidized and Unsubsidized Stafford, PLUS), Perkins, college/university, alternative loans.

WORK-STUDY ***Federal work-study:*** Total amount: $13,679,253; jobs available.

ATHLETIC AWARDS Total amount: $232,500 (42% need-based, 58% non-need-based).

APPLYING FOR FINANCIAL AID ***Required financial aid forms:*** FAFSA, state aid form. ***Financial aid deadline (priority):*** 3/2. ***Notification date:*** Continuous beginning 3/15.

CONTACT Ann Klein, Director of Financial Aid Office, University of California, San Diego, 9500 Gilman Drive, Mail Code 0013, La Jolla, CA 92093-0013, 858-534-3800. *Fax:* 858-534-5459. *E-mail:* aklein@ucsd.edu.

UNIVERSITY OF CALIFORNIA, SANTA BARBARA

Santa Barbara, CA

Tuition & fees (CA res): $11,686 Average undergraduate aid package: $19,792

ABOUT THE INSTITUTION State-supported, coed. 75 undergraduate majors. Both federal and institutional methodology are used as a basis for awarding need-based institutional aid.

UNDERGRADUATE EXPENSES for 2010–11 ***Tuition, state resident:*** full-time $0. ***Tuition, nonresident:*** full-time $22,879. ***Required fees:*** full-time $11,686. ***College room and board:*** $13,109. Room and board charges vary according to board plan and housing facility. ***Payment plan:*** Installment.

FRESHMAN FINANCIAL AID (Fall 2010, est.) 3,056 applied for aid; of those 76% were deemed to have need. 95% of freshmen with need received aid; of those 43% had need fully met. ***Average percent of need met:*** 83% (excluding resources awarded to replace EFC). ***Average financial aid package:*** $20,393 (excluding resources awarded to replace EFC). 1% of all full-time freshmen had no need and received non-need-based gift aid.

UNDERGRADUATE FINANCIAL AID (Fall 2010, est.) 12,986 applied for aid; of those 84% were deemed to have need. 96% of undergraduates with need received aid; of those 36% had need fully met. ***Average percent of need met:*** 83% (excluding resources awarded to replace EFC). ***Average financial aid package:*** $19,792 (excluding resources awarded to replace EFC). 2% of all full-time undergraduates had no need and received non-need-based gift aid.

GIFT AID (NEED-BASED) ***Total amount:*** $152,395,014 (24% federal, 38% state, 37% institutional, 1% external sources). ***Receiving aid:*** Freshmen: 55% (2,040); all full-time undergraduates: 52% (9,816). ***Average award:*** Freshmen: $15,718; Undergraduates: $15,389. ***Scholarships, grants, and awards:*** Federal Pell, FSEOG, state, private, college/university gift aid from institutional funds, institutionally endowed scholarships.

GIFT AID (NON-NEED-BASED) ***Total amount:*** $4,203,747 (26% federal, 1% state, 60% institutional, 13% external sources). ***Receiving aid:*** Freshmen: 1% (27). Undergraduates: 76. ***Average award:*** Freshmen: $7936. Undergraduates: $6627. ***Scholarships, grants, and awards by category:*** *Academic interests/achievement:* general academic interests/achievements.

LOANS ***Student loans:*** $52,913,447 (80% need-based, 20% non-need-based). 47% of past graduating class borrowed through all loan programs. *Average indebtedness per student:* $17,596. ***Average need-based loan:*** Freshmen: $6496. Undergraduates: $6573. ***Parent loans:*** $29,976,336 (20% need-based, 80% non-need-based). ***Programs:*** Federal Direct (Subsidized and Unsubsidized Stafford, PLUS), Perkins.

WORK-STUDY ***Federal work-study:*** Total amount: $9,983,679; jobs available.

ATHLETIC AWARDS Total amount: $3,276,340 (25% need-based, 75% non-need-based).

APPLYING FOR FINANCIAL AID ***Required financial aid form:*** FAFSA. ***Financial aid deadline (priority):*** 3/2. ***Notification date:*** Continuous beginning 3/15. Students must reply within 2 weeks of notification.

CONTACT Office of Financial Aid, University of California, Santa Barbara, 2103 SAASB (Student Affairs/Administrative Services Building), Santa Barbara, CA 93106-3180, 805-893-2432. *Fax:* 805-893-8793.

UNIVERSITY OF CALIFORNIA, SANTA CRUZ

Santa Cruz, CA

Tuition & fees (CA res): $12,447 Average undergraduate aid package: $20,442

ABOUT THE INSTITUTION State-supported, coed. 56 undergraduate majors. Both federal and institutional methodology are used as a basis for awarding need-based institutional aid.

UNDERGRADUATE EXPENSES for 2011–12 ***Tuition, state resident:*** full-time $0. ***Tuition, nonresident:*** full-time $22,878. ***Required fees:*** full-time $12,447. Part-time tuition and fees vary according to course load. ***College room and board:*** $14,610. Room and board charges vary according to board plan and housing facility. ***Payment plans:*** Installment, deferred payment.

FRESHMAN FINANCIAL AID (Fall 2010, est.) 2,816 applied for aid; of those 80% were deemed to have need. 96% of freshmen with need received aid; of those 33% had need fully met. ***Average percent of need met:*** 89% (excluding resources awarded to replace EFC). ***Average financial aid package:*** $22,015 (excluding resources awarded to replace EFC). 1% of all full-time freshmen had no need and received non-need-based gift aid.

UNDERGRADUATE FINANCIAL AID (Fall 2010, est.) 11,365 applied for aid; of those 83% were deemed to have need. 96% of undergraduates with need received aid; of those 41% had need fully met. ***Average percent of need met:*** 88% (excluding resources awarded to replace EFC). ***Average financial aid package:*** $20,442 (excluding resources awarded to replace EFC). 2% of all full-time undergraduates had no need and received non-need-based gift aid.

GIFT AID (NEED-BASED) ***Total amount:*** $134,908,710 (22% federal, 34% state, 43% institutional, 1% external sources). ***Receiving aid:*** Freshmen: 63% (2,057); all full-time undergraduates: 56% (8,575). ***Average award:*** Freshmen: $17,112; Undergraduates: $15,538. ***Scholarships, grants, and awards:*** Federal Pell, FSEOG, state, private, college/university gift aid from institutional funds.

GIFT AID (NON-NEED-BASED) ***Total amount:*** $3,164,366 (2% federal, 1% state, 86% institutional, 11% external sources). ***Receiving aid:*** Freshmen: 9. Undergraduates: 29. ***Average award:*** Freshmen: $13,438. Undergraduates: $9351. ***Scholarships, grants, and awards by category:*** *Academic interests/achievement:* 215 awards ($755,673 total): computer science, general academic interests/achievements, humanities, mathematics, physical sciences, social sciences. *Creative arts/performance:* 143 awards ($109,454 total): art/fine arts, cinema/film/broadcasting, creative writing, music, theater/drama. *Special achievements/activities:* 16 awards ($10,333 total): leadership.

LOANS ***Student loans:*** $53,550,336 (77% need-based, 23% non-need-based). 53% of past graduating class borrowed through all loan programs. *Average indebtedness per student:* $17,546. ***Average need-based loan:*** Freshmen: $5749. Undergraduates: $6188. ***Parent loans:*** $26,356,027 (11% need-based, 89% non-need-based). ***Programs:*** Federal Direct (Subsidized and Unsubsidized Stafford, PLUS), Perkins.

WORK-STUDY ***Federal work-study:*** Total amount: $8,828,282; 6,709 jobs averaging $1435. ***State or other work-study/employment:*** Part-time jobs available.

APPLYING FOR FINANCIAL AID ***Required financial aid forms:*** FAFSA, state aid form. ***Financial aid deadline:*** 6/1 (priority: 3/17). ***Notification date:*** Continuous beginning 4/1. Students must reply within 4 weeks of notification.

CONTACT Ms. Ann Draper, Director of Financial Aid, University of California, Santa Cruz, 201 Hahn Student Services Building, Santa Cruz, CA 95064, 831-459-4358. *Fax:* 831-459-4631. *E-mail:* ann@ucsc.edu.

UNIVERSITY OF CENTRAL ARKANSAS

Conway, AR

ABOUT THE INSTITUTION State-supported, coed. ***Awards:*** associate, bachelor's, and master's degrees and post-bachelor's and post-master's certificates. 60 undergraduate majors. ***Total enrollment:*** 12,974. Undergraduates: 11,048. Freshmen: 2,111.

GIFT AID (NEED-BASED) ***Scholarships, grants, and awards:*** Federal Pell, FSEOG, state, private, college/university gift aid from institutional funds, Federal Nursing.

GIFT AID (NON-NEED-BASED) ***Scholarships, grants, and awards by category:*** *Academic interests/achievement:* general academic interests/achievements.

LOANS ***Programs:*** Perkins, Federal Nursing, state, alternative loans.

WORK-STUDY Federal work-study jobs available. ***State or other work-study/employment:*** Part-time jobs available.

APPLYING FOR FINANCIAL AID ***Required financial aid form:*** FAFSA.

CONTACT Cheryl Lyons, Director of Student Aid, University of Central Arkansas, 201 Donaghey Avenue, Conway, AR 72035, 501-450-3140 or toll-free 800-243-8245 (in-state). *Fax:* 501-450-5168. *E-mail:* clyons@uca.edu.

UNIVERSITY OF CENTRAL FLORIDA

Orlando, FL

Tuition & fees (FL res): $5020 **Average undergraduate aid package: $7937**

ABOUT THE INSTITUTION State-supported, coed. 81 undergraduate majors. Federal methodology is used as a basis for awarding need-based institutional aid.

UNDERGRADUATE EXPENSES for 2010–11 ***Tuition, state resident:*** full-time $5020; part-time $167.35 per credit hour. ***Tuition, nonresident:*** full-time $20,500; part-time $683.33 per credit hour. Full-time tuition and fees vary according to course load. Part-time tuition and fees vary according to course load. ***College room and board:*** $8765; ***Room only:*** $5150. Room and board charges vary according to board plan and housing facility. ***Payment plans:*** Tuition prepayment, deferred payment.

FRESHMAN FINANCIAL AID (Fall 2009) 4,933 applied for aid; of those 79% were deemed to have need. 99% of freshmen with need received aid; of those 20% had need fully met. ***Average percent of need met:*** 66% (excluding resources awarded to replace EFC). ***Average financial aid package:*** $7595 (excluding resources awarded to replace EFC). 5% of all full-time freshmen had no need and received non-need-based gift aid.

UNDERGRADUATE FINANCIAL AID (Fall 2009) 23,033 applied for aid; of those 88% were deemed to have need. 96% of undergraduates with need received aid; of those 13% had need fully met. ***Average percent of need met:*** 62% (excluding resources awarded to replace EFC). ***Average financial aid package:*** $7937 (excluding resources awarded to replace EFC). 2% of all full-time undergraduates had no need and received non-need-based gift aid.

GIFT AID (NEED-BASED) ***Total amount:*** $77,949,510 (78% federal, 10% state, 12% institutional). ***Receiving aid:*** Freshmen: 29% (1,808); all full-time undergraduates: 31% (10,716). ***Average award:*** Freshmen: $6150; Undergraduates: $5761. ***Scholarships, grants, and awards:*** Federal Pell, FSEOG, state, private, college/university gift aid from institutional funds.

GIFT AID (NON-NEED-BASED) ***Total amount:*** $75,798,759 (81% state, 12% institutional, 7% external sources). ***Receiving aid:*** Freshmen: 59% (3,707). Undergraduates: 38% (13,004). ***Average award:*** Freshmen: $2172. Undergraduates: $2416. ***Scholarships, grants, and awards by category:*** *Academic interests/achievement:* general academic interests/achievements. *Creative arts/performance:* cinema/film/broadcasting, music, theater/drama. *Special achievements/activities:* general special achievements/activities, leadership. *Special characteristics:* first-generation college students. ***Tuition waivers:*** Full or partial for employees or children of employees, senior citizens.

LOANS ***Student loans:*** $126,845,693 (50% need-based, 50% non-need-based). 41% of past graduating class borrowed through all loan programs. *Average indebtedness per student:* $18,966. ***Average need-based loan:*** Freshmen: $3314. Undergraduates: $4661. ***Parent loans:*** $5,847,574 (100% non-need-based). ***Programs:*** Federal Direct (Subsidized and Unsubsidized Stafford, PLUS), Perkins.

WORK-STUDY ***Federal work-study:*** Total amount: $2,089,921; jobs available. ***State or other work-study/employment:*** Part-time jobs available.

ATHLETIC AWARDS Total amount: $2,441,662 (100% non-need-based).

APPLYING FOR FINANCIAL AID ***Required financial aid form:*** FAFSA. ***Financial aid deadline:*** 6/30 (priority: 3/1). ***Notification date:*** Continuous beginning 3/15. Students must reply within 3 weeks of notification.

CONTACT Ms. Inez Ford, Associate Director of Student Financial Assistance, University of Central Florida, 4000 Central Florida Boulevard, Orlando, FL 32816-0113, 407-823-2827. *Fax:* 407-823-5241. *E-mail:* iford@mail.ucf.edu.

UNIVERSITY OF CENTRAL MISSOURI

Warrensburg, MO

Tuition & fees (MO res): $7311 **Average undergraduate aid package: $10,174**

ABOUT THE INSTITUTION State-supported, coed. 66 undergraduate majors. Federal methodology is used as a basis for awarding need-based institutional aid.

UNDERGRADUATE EXPENSES for 2010–11 ***Tuition, state resident:*** full-time $6585; part-time $219.50 per credit hour. ***Tuition, nonresident:*** full-time $12,444; part-time $414.80 per credit hour. ***Required fees:*** full-time $726; $24.20 per credit hour. Full-time tuition and fees vary according to course load and location. Part-time tuition and fees vary according to course load and location. ***College room and board:*** $6320; ***Room only:*** $4120. Room and board charges vary according to board plan and housing facility. ***Payment plans:*** Installment, deferred payment.

FRESHMAN FINANCIAL AID (Fall 2009) 1,403 applied for aid; of those 61% were deemed to have need. 100% of freshmen with need received aid; of those 19% had need fully met. ***Average percent of need met:*** 87% (excluding resources awarded to replace EFC). ***Average financial aid package:*** $9803 (excluding resources awarded to replace EFC). 24% of all full-time freshmen had no need and received non-need-based gift aid.

UNDERGRADUATE FINANCIAL AID (Fall 2009) 862 applied for aid; of those 59% were deemed to have need. 100% of undergraduates with need received aid; of those 10% had need fully met. ***Average percent of need met:*** 86% (excluding resources awarded to replace EFC). ***Average financial aid package:*** $10,174 (excluding resources awarded to replace EFC). 15% of all full-time undergraduates had no need and received non-need-based gift aid.

GIFT AID (NEED-BASED) ***Total amount:*** $21,147,486 (62% federal, 20% state, 18% external sources). ***Receiving aid:*** Freshmen: 32% (452); all full-time undergraduates: 5% (293). ***Average award:*** Freshmen: $3940; Undergraduates: $4036. ***Scholarships, grants, and awards:*** Federal Pell, FSEOG, state, private, college/university gift aid from institutional funds.

GIFT AID (NON-NEED-BASED) ***Total amount:*** $7,404,124 (10% federal, 6% state, 84% institutional). ***Receiving aid:*** Freshmen: 60% (847). Undergraduates: 9% (489). ***Average award:*** Freshmen: $8985. Undergraduates: $9126. ***Scholarships, grants, and awards by category:*** *Academic interests/achievement:* agriculture, area/ethnic studies, biological sciences, business, communication, computer science, education, engineering/technologies, English, foreign languages, general academic interests/achievements, health fields, home economics, humanities, library science, mathematics, military science, physical sciences, premedicine, religion/biblical studies, social sciences. *Creative arts/performance:* applied art and design, art/fine arts, cinema/film/broadcasting, creative writing, debating, journalism/publications, music, performing arts, theater/drama. *Special achievements/activities:* cheerleading/drum major, leadership. *Special characteristics:* 1,173 awards ($1,327,950 total): adult students, children and siblings of alumni, children of educators, children of faculty/staff, ethnic background, international students, members of minority groups, out-of-state students, previous college experience, veterans, veterans' children. ***Tuition waivers:*** Full or partial for children of alumni, employees or children of employees, senior citizens.

LOANS ***Student loans:*** $37,994,644 (42% need-based, 58% non-need-based). 72% of past graduating class borrowed through all loan programs. *Average indebtedness per student:* $20,282. ***Average need-based loan:*** Freshmen: $3292. Undergraduates: $3757. ***Parent loans:*** $7,366,452 (100% non-need-based). ***Programs:*** Federal Direct (Subsidized and Unsubsidized Stafford, PLUS), Perkins, state.

WORK-STUDY ***Federal work-study:*** Total amount: $534,430; 366 jobs averaging $1460. ***State or other work-study/employment:*** Total amount: $3,240,654 (35% need-based, 65% non-need-based). 1,022 part-time jobs averaging $2068.

ATHLETIC AWARDS Total amount: $2,024,186 (100% non-need-based).

APPLYING FOR FINANCIAL AID ***Required financial aid forms:*** FAFSA, institution's own form, CSS Financial Aid PROFILE, state aid form, noncustodial (divorced/separated) parent's statement, business/farm supplement. ***Financial aid deadline (priority):*** 4/1. ***Notification date:*** Continuous beginning 3/15. Students must reply within 3 weeks of notification.

CONTACT Mr. Phil Shreves, Director of Student Financial Assistance, University of Central Missouri, Ward Edwards Building 1100, Warrensburg, MO 64093, 660-543-4040 or toll-free 800-729-8266 (in-state). *Fax:* 660-543-8080. *E-mail:* sfs@ucmo.edu.

UNIVERSITY OF CENTRAL OKLAHOMA

Edmond, OK

Tuition & fees (OK res): $4456 **Average undergraduate aid package: $7904**

ABOUT THE INSTITUTION State-supported, coed. 88 undergraduate majors. Federal methodology is used as a basis for awarding need-based institutional aid.

UNDERGRADUATE EXPENSES for 2010–11 ***Tuition, state resident:*** full-time $3914; part-time $130.45 per credit hour. ***Tuition, nonresident:*** full-time $10,700; part-time $356.65 per credit hour. ***Required fees:*** full-time $542; $18.05 per credit hour. Full-time tuition and fees vary according to course load, degree level, and program. Part-time tuition and fees vary according to course load, degree level, and program. ***College room and board:*** $8005; ***Room only:*** $4869. Room and board charges vary according to board plan and housing facility. ***Payment plans:*** Guaranteed tuition, installment, deferred payment.

FRESHMAN FINANCIAL AID (Fall 2009) 1,248 applied for aid; of those 73% were deemed to have need. 95% of freshmen with need received aid; of those 14% had need fully met. ***Average percent of need met:*** 69% (excluding resources awarded to replace EFC). ***Average financial aid package:*** $7348 (excluding resources awarded to replace EFC). 9% of all full-time freshmen had no need and received non-need-based gift aid.

UNDERGRADUATE FINANCIAL AID (Fall 2009) 4,073 applied for aid; of those 85% were deemed to have need. 96% of undergraduates with need received aid; of those 11% had need fully met. ***Average percent of need met:*** 68% (excluding resources awarded to replace EFC). ***Average financial aid package:*** $7904 (excluding resources awarded to replace EFC). 7% of all full-time undergraduates had no need and received non-need-based gift aid.

GIFT AID (NEED-BASED) ***Total amount:*** $26,420,662 (73% federal, 17% state, 2% institutional, 8% external sources). ***Receiving aid:*** Freshmen: 51% (847); all full-time undergraduates: 31% (3,103). ***Average award:*** Freshmen: $7442; Undergraduates: $8043. ***Scholarships, grants, and awards:*** Federal Pell, FSEOG, state, private, college/university gift aid from institutional funds.

GIFT AID (NON-NEED-BASED) ***Total amount:*** $4,439,512 (37% state, 7% institutional, 56% external sources). ***Receiving aid:*** Freshmen: 1% (23). Undergraduates: 2% (191). ***Average award:*** Freshmen: $3362. Undergraduates: $3222. ***Scholarships, grants, and awards by category:*** *Academic interests/achievement:* biological sciences, business, computer science, education, foreign languages, general academic interests/achievements, health fields, home economics, mathematics, military science, physical sciences, social sciences. *Creative arts/performance:* applied art and design, art/fine arts, journalism/publications, music, theater/drama. *Special achievements/activities:* general special achievements/activities, leadership. *Special characteristics:* ethnic background, members of minority groups. ***Tuition waivers:*** Full or partial for employees or children of employees.

LOANS ***Student loans:*** $39,941,306 (88% need-based, 12% non-need-based). 56% of past graduating class borrowed through all loan programs. *Average indebtedness per student:* $19,820. ***Average need-based loan:*** Freshmen: $3063. Undergraduates: $5136. ***Parent loans:*** $905,470 (61% need-based, 39% non-need-based). ***Programs:*** Federal Direct (Subsidized and Unsubsidized Stafford, PLUS).

WORK-STUDY ***Federal work-study:*** Total amount: $391,125; jobs available.

ATHLETIC AWARDS Total amount: $718,520 (50% need-based, 50% non-need-based).

APPLYING FOR FINANCIAL AID ***Required financial aid forms:*** FAFSA, institution's own form. ***Financial aid deadline (priority):*** 5/31. ***Notification date:*** Continuous beginning 5/1. Students must reply by 5/30 or within 4 weeks of notification.

CONTACT Ms. Becky Garrett, Assistant Director of Technical Services, University of Central Oklahoma, 100 North University Drive, Edmond, OK 73034-5209, 405-974-3334 or toll-free 800-254-4215. *Fax:* 405-340-7658. *E-mail:* osfa@uco.edu.

UNIVERSITY OF CHARLESTON

Charleston, WV

Tuition & fees: $25,000 **Average undergraduate aid package: $21,181**

ABOUT THE INSTITUTION Independent, coed. 29 undergraduate majors. Federal methodology is used as a basis for awarding need-based institutional aid.

UNDERGRADUATE EXPENSES for 2011–12 ***Comprehensive fee:*** $33,800 includes full-time tuition ($25,000) and room and board ($8800). ***College room only:*** $4800. Room and board charges vary according to board plan and housing facility. ***Part-time tuition:*** $410 per credit hour. Part-time tuition and fees vary according to program. ***Payment plan:*** Installment.

FRESHMAN FINANCIAL AID (Fall 2010, est.) 308 applied for aid; of those 100% were deemed to have need. 100% of freshmen with need received aid; of those 26% had need fully met. ***Average percent of need met:*** 71% (excluding resources awarded to replace EFC). ***Average financial aid package:*** $22,093 (excluding resources awarded to replace EFC). 7% of all full-time freshmen had no need and received non-need-based gift aid.

UNDERGRADUATE FINANCIAL AID (Fall 2010, est.) 1,077 applied for aid; of those 100% were deemed to have need. 90% of undergraduates with need received aid; of those 23% had need fully met. ***Average percent of need met:*** 67% (excluding resources awarded to replace EFC). ***Average financial aid package:*** $21,181 (excluding resources awarded to replace EFC). 10% of all full-time undergraduates had no need and received non-need-based gift aid.

GIFT AID (NEED-BASED) ***Total amount:*** $15,045,968 (15% federal, 3% state, 81% institutional, 1% external sources). ***Receiving aid:*** Freshmen: 55% (183); all full-time undergraduates: 56% (612). ***Average award:*** Freshmen: $7552; Undergraduates: $7585. ***Scholarships, grants, and awards:*** Federal Pell, FSEOG, state, private, college/university gift aid from institutional funds, Academic Competitiveness Grants, National SMART Grants, TEACH Grants.

GIFT AID (NON-NEED-BASED) ***Total amount:*** $2,669,468 (2% federal, 36% state, 55% institutional, 7% external sources). ***Receiving aid:*** Freshmen: 86% (287). Undergraduates: 78% (857). ***Average award:*** Freshmen: $18,694. Undergraduates: $17,809. ***Scholarships, grants, and awards by category:*** *Academic interests/achievement:* general academic interests/achievements. *Creative arts/performance:* music. *Special achievements/activities:* community service, general special achievements/activities, leadership. *Special characteristics:* international students. ***Tuition waivers:*** Full or partial for children of alumni, employees or children of employees, senior citizens.

LOANS ***Student loans:*** $5,785,098 (43% need-based, 57% non-need-based). 93% of past graduating class borrowed through all loan programs. *Average indebtedness per student:* $24,000. ***Average need-based loan:*** Freshmen: $3765. Undergraduates: $4492. ***Parent loans:*** $884,642 (100% non-need-based). ***Programs:*** Perkins, Federal Nursing, private loans.

WORK-STUDY ***Federal work-study:*** Total amount: $84,988; jobs available. ***State or other work-study/employment:*** Part-time jobs available.

ATHLETIC AWARDS Total amount: $2,848,367 (100% non-need-based).

APPLYING FOR FINANCIAL AID ***Required financial aid forms:*** FAFSA, institution's own form, state aid form. ***Financial aid deadline:*** 8/15 (priority: 3/1). ***Notification date:*** Continuous beginning 3/1. Students must reply by 5/1 or within 4 weeks of notification.

CONTACT Ms. Nina Morton, Director of Financial Aid, University of Charleston, 2300 MacCorkle Avenue SE, Charleston, WV 25304-1099, 304-357-4947 or toll-free 800-995-GOUC. *E-mail:* ninamorton@ucwv.edu.

UNIVERSITY OF CHICAGO

Chicago, IL

Tuition & fees: $43,780 **Average undergraduate aid package: $38,991**

ABOUT THE INSTITUTION Independent, coed. 74 undergraduate majors. Both federal and institutional methodology are used as a basis for awarding need-based institutional aid.

UNDERGRADUATE EXPENSES for 2011–12 ***Comprehensive fee:*** $56,413 includes full-time tuition ($41,853), mandatory fees ($1927), and room and board ($12,633). Room and board charges vary according to board plan and housing facility. Part-time tuition and fees vary according to course load. ***Payment plans:*** Tuition prepayment, installment.

FRESHMAN FINANCIAL AID (Fall 2010, est.) 868 applied for aid; of those 74% were deemed to have need. 100% of freshmen with need received aid; of those 100% had need fully met. ***Average percent of need met:*** 100% (excluding resources awarded to replace EFC). ***Average financial aid package:*** $38,991 (excluding resources awarded to replace EFC).

UNDERGRADUATE FINANCIAL AID (Fall 2010, est.) ***Average percent of need met:*** 100% (excluding resources awarded to replace EFC). ***Average financial aid package:*** $38,991 (excluding resources awarded to replace EFC).

GIFT AID (NEED-BASED) ***Average award:*** Freshmen: $35,540; Undergraduates: $35,540. ***Scholarships, grants, and awards:*** Federal Pell, FSEOG, state, college/university gift aid from institutional funds, Odyssey Scholarships.

GIFT AID (NON-NEED-BASED) ***Average award:*** Freshmen: $7772. Undergraduates: $7772. ***Scholarships, grants, and awards by category:*** *Academic interests/achievement:* general academic interests/achievements. *Special achievements/activities:* community service, leadership.

LOANS ***Student loans:*** *Average indebtedness per student:* $22,359. ***Average need-based loan:*** Freshmen: $4483. Undergraduates: $4483. ***Programs:*** Federal Direct (Subsidized and Unsubsidized Stafford, PLUS), Perkins, alternative loans.

WORK-STUDY Federal work-study jobs available. ***State or other work-study/employment:*** Part-time jobs available.

APPLYING FOR FINANCIAL AID ***Required financial aid forms:*** FAFSA, institution's own form, CSS Financial Aid PROFILE, noncustodial (divorced/separated) parent's statement. ***Financial aid deadline (priority):*** 11/1. ***Notification date:*** 2/1. Students must reply by 5/1.

CONTACT Office of College Aid, University of Chicago, 1101 East 58th Street, Chicago, IL 60637, 773-702-8655. *Fax:* 773-834-4300. *E-mail:* college-aid@uchicago.edu.

UNIVERSITY OF CINCINNATI

Cincinnati, OH

Tuition & fees (OH res): $10,068 Average undergraduate aid package: $8229

ABOUT THE INSTITUTION State-supported, coed. 152 undergraduate majors. Federal methodology is used as a basis for awarding need-based institutional aid.

UNDERGRADUATE EXPENSES for 2010–11 ***Tuition, state resident:*** full-time $8493; part-time $236 per credit hour. ***Tuition, nonresident:*** full-time $23,016; part-time $639 per credit hour. ***Required fees:*** full-time $1575; $44 per credit hour. Full-time tuition and fees vary according to course load, degree level, location, program, and reciprocity agreements. Part-time tuition and fees vary according to course load, degree level, location, program, and reciprocity agreements. ***College room and board:*** $9702; ***Room only:*** $5799. Room and board charges vary according to board plan and housing facility. ***Payment plan:*** Installment.

FRESHMAN FINANCIAL AID (Fall 2010, est.) 3,180 applied for aid; of those 78% were deemed to have need. 99% of freshmen with need received aid; of those 5% had need fully met. ***Average percent of need met:*** 63% (excluding resources awarded to replace EFC). ***Average financial aid package:*** $8305 (excluding resources awarded to replace EFC). 17% of all full-time freshmen had no need and received non-need-based gift aid.

UNDERGRADUATE FINANCIAL AID (Fall 2010, est.) 13,446 applied for aid; of those 83% were deemed to have need. 98% of undergraduates with need received aid; of those 6% had need fully met. ***Average percent of need met:*** 63% (excluding resources awarded to replace EFC). ***Average financial aid package:*** $8229 (excluding resources awarded to replace EFC). 16% of all full-time undergraduates had no need and received non-need-based gift aid.

GIFT AID (NEED-BASED) ***Total amount:*** $49,802,092 (54% federal, 7% state, 36% institutional, 3% external sources). ***Receiving aid:*** Freshmen: 28% (1,094); all full-time undergraduates: 29% (5,413). ***Average award:*** Freshmen: $6594; Undergraduates: $5649. ***Scholarships, grants, and awards:*** Federal Pell, FSEOG, state, private, college/university gift aid from institutional funds, United Negro College Fund, Federal Nursing, Academic Competitiveness Grants, National SMART Grants, TEACH Grants.

GIFT AID (NON-NEED-BASED) ***Total amount:*** $15,246,920 (94% institutional, 6% external sources). ***Receiving aid:*** Freshmen: 29% (1,138). Undergraduates: 20% (3,665). ***Average award:*** Freshmen: $5349. Undergraduates: $4969. ***Scholarships, grants, and awards by category:*** *Academic interests/achievement:* general academic interests/achievements. *Creative arts/performance:* art/fine arts, music, theater/drama. *Special achievements/activities:* leadership. *Special characteristics:* children and siblings of alumni, ethnic background. ***Tuition waivers:*** Full or partial for employees or children of employees.

LOANS ***Student loans:*** $110,944,793 (54% need-based, 46% non-need-based). 66% of past graduating class borrowed through all loan programs. *Average indebtedness per student:* $26,462. ***Average need-based loan:*** Freshmen: $3513. Undergraduates: $4416. ***Parent loans:*** $83,910,232 (34% need-based, 66% non-need-based). ***Programs:*** Federal Direct (Subsidized and Unsubsidized Stafford, PLUS), Perkins, Federal Nursing, state, college/university.

WORK-STUDY ***Federal work-study:*** Total amount: $3,565,780; jobs available.

ATHLETIC AWARDS Total amount: $5,751,641 (62% need-based, 38% non-need-based).

APPLYING FOR FINANCIAL AID ***Required financial aid form:*** FAFSA. ***Financial aid deadline:*** Continuous. ***Notification date:*** Continuous beginning 3/10. Students must reply within 2 weeks of notification.

CONTACT Mrs. Dana Pawlowicz, Associate Director of Financial Aid, University of Cincinnati, PO Box 210125, Cincinnati, OH 45221-0125, 513-556-2441. *Fax:* 513-556-9171. *E-mail:* financeaid@uc.edu.

UNIVERSITY OF COLORADO AT COLORADO SPRINGS

Colorado Springs, CO

Tuition & fees (CO res): $7416 Average undergraduate aid package: $8648

ABOUT THE INSTITUTION State-supported, coed. 29 undergraduate majors. Federal methodology is used as a basis for awarding need-based institutional aid.

UNDERGRADUATE EXPENSES for 2010–11 ***One-time required fee:*** $40. ***Tuition, state resident:*** full-time $6270; part-time $271 per credit hour. ***Tuition, nonresident:*** full-time $15,920; part-time $796 per credit hour. ***Required fees:*** full-time $1146; $26.85 per credit hour or $209 per term. Full-time tuition and fees vary according to course load, location, program, reciprocity agreements, and student level. Part-time tuition and fees vary according to course load, location, program, reciprocity agreements, and student level. ***College room and board: Room only:*** $6778. Room and board charges vary according to board plan and housing facility. ***Payment plan:*** Installment.

FRESHMAN FINANCIAL AID (Fall 2010, est.) 702 applied for aid; of those 60% were deemed to have need. 91% of freshmen with need received aid; of those 10% had need fully met. ***Average percent of need met:*** 52% (excluding resources awarded to replace EFC). ***Average financial aid package:*** $7391 (excluding resources awarded to replace EFC). 10% of all full-time freshmen had no need and received non-need-based gift aid.

UNDERGRADUATE FINANCIAL AID (Fall 2010, est.) 4,762 applied for aid; of those 69% were deemed to have need. 94% of undergraduates with need received aid; of those 9% had need fully met. ***Average percent of need met:*** 55% (excluding resources awarded to replace EFC). ***Average financial aid package:*** $8648 (excluding resources awarded to replace EFC). 4% of all full-time undergraduates had no need and received non-need-based gift aid.

GIFT AID (NEED-BASED) ***Total amount:*** $18,192,818 (50% federal, 18% state, 26% institutional, 6% external sources). ***Receiving aid:*** Freshmen: 40% (317); all full-time undergraduates: 43% (2,427). ***Average award:*** Freshmen: $6093; Undergraduates: $6470. ***Scholarships, grants, and awards:*** Federal Pell, FSEOG, state, private, college/university gift aid from institutional funds.

GIFT AID (NON-NEED-BASED) ***Average award:*** Freshmen: $1170. Undergraduates: $1551. ***Tuition waivers:*** Full or partial for employees or children of employees.

LOANS ***Student loans:*** $22,903,986 (100% need-based). 63% of past graduating class borrowed through all loan programs. *Average indebtedness per student:* $21,551. ***Average need-based loan:*** Freshmen: $3163. Undergraduates: $4285. ***Parent loans:*** $3,399,613 (100% need-based). ***Programs:*** Federal Direct (Subsidized and Unsubsidized Stafford, PLUS), Perkins.

WORK-STUDY ***Federal work-study:*** Total amount: $371,045; 104 jobs averaging $3673. ***State or other work-study/employment:*** Total amount: $1,001,881 (86% need-based, 14% non-need-based). 299 part-time jobs averaging $3795.

ATHLETIC AWARDS Total amount: $585,282 (100% need-based).

APPLYING FOR FINANCIAL AID ***Required financial aid form:*** FAFSA. ***Financial aid deadline (priority):*** 3/1. ***Notification date:*** Continuous beginning 4/15.

CONTACT Mrs. Lee Ingalls Noble, Director of Financial Aid, University of Colorado at Colorado Springs, 1420 Austin Bluffs Parkway, Colorado Springs, CO 80918, 719-255-3460 or toll-free 800-990-8227 Ext. 3383. *Fax:* 719-255-3650. *E-mail:* finaidse@uccs.edu.

UNIVERSITY OF COLORADO BOULDER

Boulder, CO

Tuition & fees (CO res): $8511 Average undergraduate aid package: $14,151

ABOUT THE INSTITUTION State-supported, coed. 65 undergraduate majors. Federal methodology is used as a basis for awarding need-based institutional aid.

UNDERGRADUATE EXPENSES for 2010–11 ***One-time required fee:*** $182. ***Tuition, state resident:*** full-time $7018. ***Tuition, nonresident:*** full-time $28,000. ***Required fees:*** full-time $1493. Full-time tuition and fees vary according to program. Part-time tuition and fees vary according to course load and program. ***College room and board:*** $10,792. Room and board charges vary according to board plan, housing facility, and location. ***Payment plan:*** Deferred payment.

FRESHMAN FINANCIAL AID (Fall 2009) 5,046 applied for aid; of those 44% were deemed to have need. 100% of freshmen with need received aid; of those 64% had need fully met. ***Average percent of need met:*** 89% (excluding resources awarded to replace EFC). ***Average financial aid package:*** $13,160 (excluding resources awarded to replace EFC). 45% of all full-time freshmen had no need and received non-need-based gift aid.

UNDERGRADUATE FINANCIAL AID (Fall 2009) 18,910 applied for aid; of those 48% were deemed to have need. 99% of undergraduates with need received aid; of those 56% had need fully met. ***Average percent of need met:*** 87% (excluding resources awarded to replace EFC). ***Average financial aid package:*** $14,151 (excluding resources awarded to replace EFC). 27% of all full-time undergraduates had no need and received non-need-based gift aid.

GIFT AID (NEED-BASED) ***Total amount:*** $65,468,384 (32% federal, 10% state, 47% institutional, 11% external sources). ***Receiving aid:*** Freshmen: 36% (2,003); all full-time undergraduates: 30% (7,479). ***Average award:*** Freshmen: $7397; Undergraduates: $7873. ***Scholarships, grants, and awards:*** Federal Pell, FSEOG, state, private, college/university gift aid from institutional funds.

GIFT AID (NON-NEED-BASED) ***Total amount:*** $16,047,137 (17% federal, 63% institutional, 20% external sources). ***Receiving aid:*** Freshmen: 1% (69). Undergraduates: 1% (203). ***Average award:*** Freshmen: $4752. Undergraduates: $6678. ***Scholarships, grants, and awards by category:*** *Academic interests/achievement:* architecture, area/ethnic studies, biological sciences, business, communication, computer science, education, engineering/technologies, English, foreign languages, general academic interests/achievements, health fields, humanities, international studies, mathematics, military science, physical sciences, premedicine, social sciences. *Creative arts/performance:* art/fine arts, cinema/film/broadcasting, creative writing, dance, journalism/publications, music, performing arts, theater/drama. *Special achievements/activities:* community service, general special achievements/activities, leadership. *Special characteristics:* first-generation college students, general special characteristics, local/state students. ***Tuition waivers:*** Full or partial for employees or children of employees, senior citizens.

LOANS ***Student loans:*** $96,238,596 (59% need-based, 41% non-need-based). 43% of past graduating class borrowed through all loan programs. *Average indebtedness per student:* $19,758. ***Average need-based loan:*** Freshmen: $5742. Undergraduates: $6718. ***Parent loans:*** $136,764,683 (24% need-based, 76% non-need-based). ***Programs:*** Federal Direct (Subsidized and Unsubsidized Stafford, PLUS), Perkins, college/university, private loans.

WORK-STUDY ***Federal work-study:*** Total amount: $822,507; 1,271 jobs averaging $1640. ***State or other work-study/employment:*** Total amount: $2,016,394 (96% need-based, 4% non-need-based). 867 part-time jobs averaging $2356.

ATHLETIC AWARDS Total amount: $5,375,556 (35% need-based, 65% non-need-based).

APPLYING FOR FINANCIAL AID ***Required financial aid forms:*** FAFSA, federal income tax return(s). ***Financial aid deadline (priority):*** 4/1. ***Notification date:*** Continuous beginning 3/1. Students must reply within 3 weeks of notification.

CONTACT Gwen E. Pomper, Director of Financial Aid, University of Colorado Boulder, University Campus Box 77, Boulder, CO 80309, 303-492-8223. *Fax:* 303-492-0838. *E-mail:* finaid@colorado.edu.

UNIVERSITY OF COLORADO DENVER

Denver, CO

Tuition & fees (CO res): $7214 **Average undergraduate aid package: $8562**

ABOUT THE INSTITUTION State-supported, coed. 31 undergraduate majors. Federal methodology is used as a basis for awarding need-based institutional aid.

UNDERGRADUATE EXPENSES for 2011–12 ***Tuition, state resident:*** full-time $6216; part-time $259 per credit hour. ***Tuition, nonresident:*** full-time $19,128; part-time $797 per credit hour. ***Required fees:*** full-time $998. Full-time tuition and fees vary according to course level, course load, degree level, location, program, reciprocity agreements, and student level. Part-time tuition and fees vary according to course level, course load, degree level, location, program, reciprocity agreements, and student level. ***College room and board:*** $9956; ***Room only:*** $6702. Room and board charges vary according to board plan. ***Payment plans:*** Installment, deferred payment.

FRESHMAN FINANCIAL AID (Fall 2010, est.) 779 applied for aid; of those 79% were deemed to have need. 91% of freshmen with need received aid; of those 8% had need fully met. ***Average percent of need met:*** 53% (excluding resources awarded to replace EFC). ***Average financial aid package:*** $8509 (excluding resources awarded to replace EFC). 8% of all full-time freshmen had no need and received non-need-based gift aid.

UNDERGRADUATE FINANCIAL AID (Fall 2010, est.) 5,255 applied for aid; of those 85% were deemed to have need. 95% of undergraduates with need received aid; of those 7% had need fully met. ***Average percent of need met:*** 53% (excluding resources awarded to replace EFC). ***Average financial aid package:*** $8562 (excluding resources awarded to replace EFC). 4% of all full-time undergraduates had no need and received non-need-based gift aid.

GIFT AID (NEED-BASED) ***Total amount:*** $24,311,214 (56% federal, 15% state, 24% institutional, 5% external sources). ***Receiving aid:*** Freshmen: 45% (459); all full-time undergraduates: 42% (3,211). ***Average award:*** Freshmen: $7112; Undergraduates: $6347. ***Scholarships, grants, and awards:*** Federal Pell, FSEOG, state, private, college/university gift aid from institutional funds, Federal Nursing.

GIFT AID (NON-NEED-BASED) ***Total amount:*** $1,422,231 (2% state, 78% institutional, 20% external sources). ***Receiving aid:*** Freshmen: 1% (12). Undergraduates: 29. ***Average award:*** Freshmen: $4525. Undergraduates: $3433. ***Tuition waivers:*** Full or partial for employees or children of employees.

LOANS ***Student loans:*** $38,545,113 (85% need-based, 15% non-need-based). 59% of past graduating class borrowed through all loan programs. *Average indebtedness per student:* $17,823. ***Average need-based loan:*** Freshmen: $3305. Undergraduates: $4327. ***Parent loans:*** $7,758,197 (36% need-based, 64% non-need-based). ***Programs:*** Federal Direct (Subsidized and Unsubsidized Stafford, PLUS), Perkins, Federal Nursing, college/university, Nurse Faculty Loan.

WORK-STUDY ***Federal work-study:*** Total amount: $1,089,979; 260 jobs averaging $4192. ***State or other work-study/employment:*** Total amount: $955,286 (97% need-based, 3% non-need-based). 218 part-time jobs averaging $4246.

APPLYING FOR FINANCIAL AID ***Required financial aid form:*** FAFSA. ***Financial aid deadline (priority):*** 4/1. ***Notification date:*** Continuous beginning 5/1.

CONTACT Evan Icolari, Interim Director of Financial Aid, University of Colorado Denver, PO Box 173364, Denver, CO 80217-3364, 303-556-2886. *Fax:* 303-556-2325. *E-mail:* financial.aid@ucdenver.edu.

UNIVERSITY OF CONNECTICUT

Storrs, CT

Tuition & fees (CT res): $10,670 **Average undergraduate aid package: $12,789**

ABOUT THE INSTITUTION State-supported, coed. 96 undergraduate majors. Federal methodology is used as a basis for awarding need-based institutional aid.

UNDERGRADUATE EXPENSES for 2011–12 ***Tuition, state resident:*** full-time $8256; part-time $344 per credit. ***Tuition, nonresident:*** full-time $25,152; part-time $1048 per credit. ***Required fees:*** full-time $2414. Part-time tuition and fees vary according to course load. ***College room and board:*** $11,050; ***Room only:*** $5918. Room and board charges vary according to board plan and housing facility. ***Payment plans:*** Installment, deferred payment.

FRESHMAN FINANCIAL AID (Fall 2010, est.) 2,768 applied for aid; of those 70% were deemed to have need. 98% of freshmen with need received aid; of those 18% had need fully met. ***Average percent of need met:*** 69% (excluding resources awarded to replace EFC). ***Average financial aid package:*** $13,731 (excluding resources awarded to replace EFC). 10% of all full-time freshmen had no need and received non-need-based gift aid.

UNDERGRADUATE FINANCIAL AID (Fall 2010, est.) 11,967 applied for aid; of those 78% were deemed to have need. 98% of undergraduates with need received aid; of those 17% had need fully met. ***Average percent of need met:*** 66% (excluding resources awarded to replace EFC). ***Average financial aid package:*** $12,789 (excluding resources awarded to replace EFC). 8% of all full-time undergraduates had no need and received non-need-based gift aid.

GIFT AID (NEED-BASED) ***Total amount:*** $74,289,253 (25% federal, 20% state, 52% institutional, 3% external sources). ***Receiving aid:*** Freshmen: 46% (1,538); all full-time undergraduates: 43% (7,088). ***Average award:*** Freshmen: $8790; Undergraduates: $8167. ***Scholarships, grants, and awards:*** Federal Pell, FSEOG, state, private, college/university gift aid from institutional funds.

GIFT AID (NON-NEED-BASED) ***Total amount:*** $15,032,216 (86% institutional, 14% external sources). ***Receiving aid:*** Freshmen: 39% (1,298). Undergraduates: 27% (4,373). ***Average award:*** Freshmen: $7098. Undergraduates: $6761. ***Scholarships, grants, and awards by category:*** *Academic interests/achievement:* 5,204 awards ($17,992,047 total): agriculture, biological sciences, business, computer science, education, engineering/technologies, English, foreign languages, general academic interests/achievements, health fields, humanities, international studies, mathematics, physical sciences, premedicine, religion/biblical studies, social sciences. *Creative arts/performance:* 120 awards ($185,475 total): art/fine arts, music, theater/drama. *Special achievements/activities:* 839 awards ($7,277,972 total): community service, leadership. *Special characteristics:* 4,805 awards ($14,825,647 total): adult students, children of faculty/staff, children of union members/company employees, local/state students, out-of-state students, spouses of deceased or disabled public servants, veterans. ***Tuition waivers:*** Full or partial for employees or children of employees, senior citizens.

LOANS ***Student loans:*** $68,803,185 (89% need-based, 11% non-need-based). 63% of past graduating class borrowed through all loan programs. *Average indebtedness per student:* $23,237. ***Average need-based loan:*** Freshmen: $3656. Undergraduates: $4307. ***Parent loans:*** $41,201,444 (35% need-based, 65% non-need-based). ***Programs:*** Federal Direct (Subsidized and Unsubsidized Stafford, PLUS), Perkins, Federal Nursing, state.

WORK-STUDY ***Federal work-study:*** Total amount: $2,534,927; 1,959 jobs averaging $1931. ***State or other work-study/employment:*** Total amount: $17,424,457 (34% need-based, 66% non-need-based). 5,301 part-time jobs averaging $3095.

ATHLETIC AWARDS Total amount: $9,168,765 (36% need-based, 64% non-need-based).

APPLYING FOR FINANCIAL AID ***Required financial aid form:*** FAFSA. ***Financial aid deadline (priority):*** 3/1. ***Notification date:*** Continuous beginning 3/1. Students must reply within 4 weeks of notification.

CONTACT Jean D. Main, Director, University of Connecticut, 233 Glenbrook Road, Unit 4116, Storrs, CT 06269-4116, 860-486-2819. *Fax:* 860-486-5098. *E-mail:* financialaid@uconn.edu.

UNIVERSITY OF DALLAS

Irving, TX

Tuition & fees: $29,325 **Average undergraduate aid package: $21,844**

ABOUT THE INSTITUTION Independent Roman Catholic, coed. 33 undergraduate majors. Federal methodology is used as a basis for awarding need-based institutional aid.

UNDERGRADUATE EXPENSES for 2011–12 ***Comprehensive fee:*** $38,651 includes full-time tuition ($27,500), mandatory fees ($1825), and room and board ($9326). ***College room only:*** $5300. Room and board charges vary according to board plan and housing facility. ***Part-time tuition:*** $1150 per credit. ***Part-time fees:*** $1825 per year. ***Payment plan:*** Installment.

FRESHMAN FINANCIAL AID (Fall 2010, est.) 308 applied for aid; of those 87% were deemed to have need. 100% of freshmen with need received aid; of those 21% had need fully met. ***Average percent of need met:*** 76% (excluding resources awarded to replace EFC). ***Average financial aid package:*** $22,944 (excluding resources awarded to replace EFC). 28% of all full-time freshmen had no need and received non-need-based gift aid.

UNDERGRADUATE FINANCIAL AID (Fall 2010, est.) 900 applied for aid; of those 91% were deemed to have need. 100% of undergraduates with need received aid; of those 22% had need fully met. ***Average percent of need met:*** 73% (excluding resources awarded to replace EFC). ***Average financial aid package:*** $21,844 (excluding resources awarded to replace EFC). 33% of all full-time undergraduates had no need and received non-need-based gift aid.

GIFT AID (NEED-BASED) ***Total amount:*** $19,247,585 (7% federal, 5% state, 87% institutional, 1% external sources). ***Receiving aid:*** Freshmen: 71% (266); all full-time undergraduates: 60% (798). ***Average award:*** Freshmen: $19,407; Undergraduates: $17,215. ***Scholarships, grants, and awards:*** Federal Pell, FSEOG, state, private, college/university gift aid from institutional funds.

GIFT AID (NON-NEED-BASED) ***Total amount:*** $409,275 (1% federal, 98% institutional, 1% external sources). ***Receiving aid:*** Freshmen: 2% (8). Undergraduates: 2% (30). ***Average award:*** Freshmen: $14,108. Undergraduates: $12,105. ***Scholarships, grants, and awards by category:*** *Academic interests/achievement:* business, education, foreign languages, general academic interests/achievements, mathematics, physical sciences, premedicine, religion/biblical studies. *Creative arts/performance:* art/fine arts, music, theater/drama. *Special achievements/activities:* leadership. *Special characteristics:* children of faculty/staff, religious affiliation, siblings of current students. ***Tuition waivers:*** Full or partial for employees or children of employees.

LOANS ***Student loans:*** $6,681,236 (52% need-based, 48% non-need-based). 55% of past graduating class borrowed through all loan programs. *Average indebtedness per student:* $28,020. ***Average need-based loan:*** Freshmen: $4102. Undergraduates: $5330. ***Parent loans:*** $1,841,549 (100% non-need-based). ***Programs:*** Federal Direct (Subsidized and Unsubsidized Stafford, PLUS), Perkins, state.

WORK-STUDY ***Federal work-study:*** Total amount: $232,042; 251 jobs averaging $1422. ***State or other work-study/employment:*** Total amount: $90,529 (73% need-based, 27% non-need-based). 13 part-time jobs averaging $1262.

APPLYING FOR FINANCIAL AID ***Required financial aid form:*** FAFSA. ***Financial aid deadline (priority):*** 1/15. ***Notification date:*** Continuous beginning 3/1. Students must reply by 5/1 or within 2 weeks of notification.

CONTACT Dr. John Plotts, Associate Provost and Dean of Enrollment Management, University of Dallas, 1845 East Northgate Drive, Irving, TX 75062, 972-721-5266 or toll-free 800-628-6999. *Fax:* 972-721-5017. *E-mail:* ugadmis@udallas.edu.

UNIVERSITY OF DAYTON

Dayton, OH

Tuition & fees: $29,930 **Average undergraduate aid package: $24,360**

ABOUT THE INSTITUTION Independent Roman Catholic, coed. 73 undergraduate majors. Federal methodology is used as a basis for awarding need-based institutional aid.

UNDERGRADUATE EXPENSES for 2010–11 ***Comprehensive fee:*** $39,330 includes full-time tuition ($28,700), mandatory fees ($1230), and room and board ($9400). ***College room only:*** $5940. Full-time tuition and fees vary according to program. Room and board charges vary according to board plan and housing facility. ***Part-time tuition:*** $957 per credit hour. ***Part-time fees:*** $25 per term. Part-time tuition and fees vary according to course load and program. ***Payment plans:*** Installment, deferred payment.

FRESHMAN FINANCIAL AID (Fall 2010, est.) 1,696 applied for aid; of those 76% were deemed to have need. 100% of freshmen with need received aid; of those 36% had need fully met. ***Average percent of need met:*** 82% (excluding resources awarded to replace EFC). ***Average financial aid package:*** $24,211 (excluding resources awarded to replace EFC). 39% of all full-time freshmen had no need and received non-need-based gift aid.

UNDERGRADUATE FINANCIAL AID (Fall 2010, est.) 5,040 applied for aid; of those 80% were deemed to have need. 100% of undergraduates with need received aid; of those 36% had need fully met. ***Average percent of need met:*** 83% (excluding resources awarded to replace EFC). ***Average financial aid package:*** $24,360 (excluding resources awarded to replace EFC). 41% of all full-time undergraduates had no need and received non-need-based gift aid.

GIFT AID (NEED-BASED) ***Total amount:*** $57,821,426 (9% federal, 2% state, 87% institutional, 2% external sources). ***Receiving aid:*** Freshmen: 63% (1,273); all full-time undergraduates: 55% (3,920). ***Average award:*** Freshmen: $15,056; Undergraduates: $12,490. ***Scholarships, grants, and awards:*** Federal Pell, FSEOG, state, private, college/university gift aid from institutional funds.

GIFT AID (NON-NEED-BASED) ***Total amount:*** $29,968,847 (97% institutional, 3% external sources). ***Receiving aid:*** Freshmen: 63% (1,276). Undergraduates: 55% (3,933). ***Average award:*** Freshmen: $10,877. Undergraduates: $9961. ***Scholarships, grants, and awards by category:*** *Academic interests/achievement:* 6,920 awards ($66,139,596 total): biological sciences, business, communication, computer science, education, engineering/technologies, English, foreign languages, general academic interests/achievements, health fields, humanities, international studies, mathematics, military science, physical sciences, premedicine, religion/biblical studies, social sciences. *Creative arts/performance:* 131 awards ($367,900 total): art/fine arts, music. *Special characteristics:* 484 awards ($9,871,858 total): children of faculty/staff, religious affiliation. ***Tuition waivers:*** Full or partial for employees or children of employees, senior citizens.

LOANS ***Student loans:*** $48,571,240 (84% need-based, 16% non-need-based). 67% of past graduating class borrowed through all loan programs. *Average indebtedness per student:* $35,421. ***Average need-based loan:*** Freshmen: $3399. Undergraduates: $5010. ***Parent loans:*** $12,789,342 (28% need-based, 72% non-need-based). ***Programs:*** Federal Direct (Subsidized and Unsubsidized Stafford, PLUS), Perkins.

WORK-STUDY ***Federal work-study:*** Total amount: $2,881,806; 1,235 jobs averaging $2234. ***State or other work-study/employment:*** Total amount: $8,627,700 (100% non-need-based). 4,251 part-time jobs averaging $2516.

ATHLETIC AWARDS Total amount: $3,409,169 (45% need-based, 55% non-need-based).

APPLYING FOR FINANCIAL AID ***Required financial aid form:*** FAFSA. ***Financial aid deadline (priority):*** 3/1. ***Notification date:*** Continuous beginning 3/15. Students must reply within 3 weeks of notification.

CONTACT Kathy Harmon, Dean of Admission and Financial Aid, University of Dayton, 300 College Park Drive, Dayton, OH 45469-1305, 937-229-4311 or toll-free 800-837-7433. *Fax:* 937-229-4338. *E-mail:* kharmon@udayton.edu.

UNIVERSITY OF DELAWARE

Newark, DE

Tuition & fees (DE res): $10,208 **Average undergraduate aid package: $13,445**

ABOUT THE INSTITUTION State-related, coed. 116 undergraduate majors. Federal methodology is used as a basis for awarding need-based institutional aid.

UNDERGRADUATE EXPENSES for 2010–11 ***Tuition, state resident:*** full-time $9040; part-time $377 per credit hour. ***Tuition, nonresident:*** full-time $24,240; part-time $1010 per credit hour. ***Required fees:*** full-time $1168. ***College room and board:*** $9636; ***Room only:*** $5826. Room and board charges vary according to board plan, housing facility, and student level. ***Payment plan:*** Installment.

FRESHMAN FINANCIAL AID (Fall 2010, est.) 2,854 applied for aid; of those 61% were deemed to have need. 96% of freshmen with need received aid; of those 50% had need fully met. ***Average percent of need met:*** 76% (excluding resources awarded to replace EFC). ***Average financial aid package:*** $12,790 (excluding resources awarded to replace EFC). 17% of all full-time freshmen had no need and received non-need-based gift aid.

UNDERGRADUATE FINANCIAL AID (Fall 2010, est.) 10,382 applied for aid; of those 69% were deemed to have need. 97% of undergraduates with need received aid; of those 48% had need fully met. ***Average percent of need met:*** 74% (excluding resources awarded to replace EFC). ***Average financial aid package:*** $13,445 (excluding resources awarded to replace EFC). 14% of all full-time undergraduates had no need and received non-need-based gift aid.

GIFT AID (NEED-BASED) ***Total amount:*** $32,947,964 (28% federal, 23% state, 43% institutional, 6% external sources). ***Receiving aid:*** Freshmen: 40% (1,350); all full-time undergraduates: 32% (4,814). ***Average award:*** Freshmen: $7417; Undergraduates: $6734. ***Scholarships, grants, and awards:*** Federal Pell, FSEOG, state, private, college/university gift aid from institutional funds.

GIFT AID (NON-NEED-BASED) ***Total amount:*** $16,958,476 (8% state, 83% institutional, 9% external sources). ***Receiving aid:*** Freshmen: 21% (723). Undergraduates: 11% (1,619). ***Average award:*** Freshmen: $7128. Undergraduates: $6467. ***Scholarships, grants, and awards by category:*** *Academic interests/achievement:* agriculture, biological sciences, business, communication, computer science, education, engineering/technologies, English, foreign languages, general academic interests/achievements, health fields, humanities, international studies, mathematics, military science, physical sciences, premedicine, religion/biblical studies, social sciences. *Creative arts/performance:* applied art and design, art/fine arts, music, theater/drama. *Special achievements/activities:* cheerleading/drum major, community service, general special achievements/activities, leadership. *Special characteristics:* children and siblings of alumni, children of faculty/staff, children of public servants, ethnic background, first-generation college students, general special characteristics, local/state students, members of minority groups. ***Tuition waivers:*** Full or partial for employees or children of employees, senior citizens.

LOANS ***Student loans:*** $80,093,984 (59% need-based, 41% non-need-based). 44% of past graduating class borrowed through all loan programs. *Average indebtedness per student:* $17,200. ***Average need-based loan:*** Freshmen: $6234. Undergraduates: $7755. ***Parent loans:*** $29,167,219 (33% need-based, 67% non-need-based). ***Programs:*** Federal Direct (Subsidized and Unsubsidized Stafford, PLUS), Perkins, Federal Nursing.

WORK-STUDY ***Federal work-study:*** Total amount: $941,408; jobs available. ***State or other work-study/employment:*** Total amount: $256,785 (88% need-based, 12% non-need-based). Part-time jobs available.

ATHLETIC AWARDS Total amount: $8,536,731 (27% need-based, 73% non-need-based).

APPLYING FOR FINANCIAL AID ***Required financial aid form:*** FAFSA. ***Financial aid deadline:*** 3/15 (priority: 2/1). ***Notification date:*** Continuous beginning 3/15. Students must reply by 5/1 or within 3 weeks of notification.

CONTACT Mr. James Holloway, Associate Director of Financial Aid, University of Delaware, 140 University Visitors Center, Newark, DE 19716, 302-831-8081. *Fax:* 302-831-4334. *E-mail:* holloway@udel.edu.

UNIVERSITY OF DENVER

Denver, CO

Tuition & fees: $37,833 **Average undergraduate aid package: $28,195**

ABOUT THE INSTITUTION Independent, coed. 73 undergraduate majors. Both federal and institutional methodology are used as a basis for awarding need-based institutional aid.

UNDERGRADUATE EXPENSES for 2011–12 ***Comprehensive fee:*** $48,017 includes full-time tuition ($36,936), mandatory fees ($897), and room and board ($10,184). Full-time tuition and fees vary according to class time, course load, and program. Room and board charges vary according to board plan and housing facility. Part-time tuition and fees vary according to class time, course load, and program. ***Payment plans:*** Installment, deferred payment.

FRESHMAN FINANCIAL AID (Fall 2010, est.) 777 applied for aid; of those 72% were deemed to have need. 100% of freshmen with need received aid; of those 27% had need fully met. ***Average percent of need met:*** 82% (excluding resources awarded to replace EFC). ***Average financial aid package:*** $29,352 (excluding resources awarded to replace EFC). 35% of all full-time freshmen had no need and received non-need-based gift aid.

UNDERGRADUATE FINANCIAL AID (Fall 2010, est.) 2,595 applied for aid; of those 82% were deemed to have need. 100% of undergraduates with need received aid; of those 24% had need fully met. ***Average percent of need met:*** 79% (excluding resources awarded to replace EFC). ***Average financial aid package:*** $28,195 (excluding resources awarded to replace EFC). 37% of all full-time undergraduates had no need and received non-need-based gift aid.

GIFT AID (NEED-BASED) ***Total amount:*** $44,432,574 (10% federal, 2% state, 82% institutional, 6% external sources). ***Receiving aid:*** Freshmen: 45% (548); all full-time undergraduates: 43% (2,066). ***Average award:*** Freshmen: $22,695; Undergraduates: $22,351. ***Scholarships, grants, and awards:*** Federal Pell, FSEOG, state, private, college/university gift aid from institutional funds.

GIFT AID (NON-NEED-BASED) ***Total amount:*** $24,671,030 (92% institutional, 8% external sources). ***Receiving aid:*** Freshmen: 8% (103). Undergraduates: 6% (306). ***Average award:*** Freshmen: $13,917. Undergraduates: $12,114. ***Scholarships, grants, and awards by category:*** *Academic interests/achievement:* biological sciences, business, communication, computer science, engineering/technologies, general academic interests/achievements, humanities, international studies, mathematics, physical sciences, social sciences. *Creative arts/performance:* art/fine arts, debating, music, theater/drama. *Special achievements/activities:* community service, leadership. ***Tuition waivers:*** Full or partial for employees or children of employees, senior citizens.

LOANS ***Student loans:*** $17,516,236 (66% need-based, 34% non-need-based). 43% of past graduating class borrowed through all loan programs. *Average indebtedness per student:* $25,578. ***Average need-based loan:*** Freshmen: $3338. Undergraduates: $4381. ***Parent loans:*** $7,232,755 (26% need-based, 74% non-need-based). ***Programs:*** Federal Direct (Subsidized and Unsubsidized Stafford, PLUS), Perkins.

WORK-STUDY ***Federal work-study:*** Total amount: $1,045,180; 377 jobs averaging $2771. ***State or other work-study/employment:*** Total amount: $799,508 (91% need-based, 9% non-need-based). 274 part-time jobs averaging $2851.

ATHLETIC AWARDS Total amount: $7,825,238 (20% need-based, 80% non-need-based).

APPLYING FOR FINANCIAL AID ***Required financial aid forms:*** FAFSA, CSS Financial Aid PROFILE, noncustodial (divorced/separated) parent's statement. ***Financial aid deadline:*** 4/1 (priority: 3/1). ***Notification date:*** 4/1. Students must reply by 5/1 or within 4 weeks of notification.

CONTACT Mr. Chris George, Director of Financial Aid, University of Denver, University Hall, Room 255, 2197 South University Boulevard, Denver, CO 80208, 303-871-4020 or toll-free 800-525-9495 (out-of-state). *Fax:* 303-871-2341. *E-mail:* finaid@du.edu.

UNIVERSITY OF DETROIT MERCY

Detroit, MI

CONTACT Sandy Ross, Director of Financial Aid and Scholarships, University of Detroit Mercy, 4001 West McNichols Road, Detroit, MI 48221-3038, 313-993-3350 or toll-free 800-635-5020 (out-of-state). *Fax:* 313-993-3347.

UNIVERSITY OF DUBUQUE

Dubuque, IA

Tuition & fees: $21,590 **Average undergraduate aid package: $18,863**

ABOUT THE INSTITUTION Independent Presbyterian, coed. 32 undergraduate majors. Federal methodology is used as a basis for awarding need-based institutional aid.

UNDERGRADUATE EXPENSES for 2011–12 ***One-time required fee:*** $60. ***Comprehensive fee:*** $28,960 includes full-time tuition ($21,000), mandatory fees ($590), and room and board ($7370). ***College room only:*** $3550. Room and board charges vary according to board plan, housing facility, and location. ***Part-time tuition:*** $490 per credit. ***Payment plan:*** Installment.

FRESHMAN FINANCIAL AID (Fall 2009) 348 applied for aid; of those 94% were deemed to have need. 100% of freshmen with need received aid; of those 29% had need fully met. ***Average percent of need met:*** 79% (excluding resources awarded to replace EFC). ***Average financial aid package:*** $19,471 (excluding resources awarded to replace EFC). 8% of all full-time freshmen had no need and received non-need-based gift aid.

UNDERGRADUATE FINANCIAL AID (Fall 2009) 1,329 applied for aid; of those 93% were deemed to have need. 100% of undergraduates with need received aid; of those 26% had need fully met. ***Average percent of need met:*** 76% (excluding resources awarded to replace EFC). ***Average financial aid package:*** $18,863 (excluding resources awarded to replace EFC). 9% of all full-time undergraduates had no need and received non-need-based gift aid.

GIFT AID (NEED-BASED) ***Total amount:*** $15,520,083 (22% federal, 10% state, 50% institutional, 18% external sources). ***Receiving aid:*** Freshmen: 91% (326); all full-time undergraduates: 89% (1,226). ***Average award:*** Freshmen: $13,141; Undergraduates: $12,504. ***Scholarships, grants, and awards:*** Federal Pell, FSEOG, state, private, college/university gift aid from institutional funds.

GIFT AID (NON-NEED-BASED) ***Total amount:*** $2,449,112 (47% institutional, 53% external sources). ***Receiving aid:*** Freshmen: 14% (50). Undergraduates: 10% (141). ***Average award:*** Freshmen: $7158. Undergraduates: $6968. ***Scholarships, grants, and awards by category:*** *Academic interests/achievement:* general academic interests/achievements. *Special characteristics:* children and siblings of alumni, children of educators, children of faculty/staff, ethnic background, members of minority groups, out-of-state students, relatives of clergy, religious affiliation, siblings of current students. ***Tuition waivers:*** Full or partial for employees or children of employees.

LOANS ***Student loans:*** $13,857,719 (76% need-based, 24% non-need-based). 85% of past graduating class borrowed through all loan programs. *Average indebtedness per student:* $41,399. ***Average need-based loan:*** Freshmen: $7200. Undergraduates: $7135. ***Parent loans:*** $987,899 (49% need-based, 51% non-need-based). ***Programs:*** Federal Direct (Subsidized and Unsubsidized Stafford, PLUS), Perkins, state, college/university.

WORK-STUDY ***Federal work-study:*** Total amount: $212,683; 175 jobs averaging $1500. ***State or other work-study/employment:*** Total amount: $145,000 (100% need-based). Part-time jobs available.

APPLYING FOR FINANCIAL AID ***Required financial aid form:*** FAFSA. ***Financial aid deadline:*** Continuous. ***Notification date:*** Continuous beginning 3/1. Students must reply within 3 weeks of notification.

CONTACT Mr. Timothy Kremer, Dean of Student Financial Planning, University of Dubuque, 2000 University Avenue, Dubuque, IA 52001-5050, 563-589-3170 or toll-free 800-722-5583 (in-state). *Fax:* 563-589-3690.

UNIVERSITY OF EVANSVILLE

Evansville, IN

Tuition & fees: $28,076 **Average undergraduate aid package: $23,282**

ABOUT THE INSTITUTION Independent religious, coed. 85 undergraduate majors. Federal methodology is used as a basis for awarding need-based institutional aid.

UNDERGRADUATE EXPENSES for 2010–11 ***Comprehensive fee:*** $37,186 includes full-time tuition ($27,310), mandatory fees ($766), and room and board ($9110). ***College room only:*** $4700. Room and board charges vary according to board plan and housing facility. ***Part-time tuition:*** $760 per credit hour. ***Part-time fees:*** $50 per term. Part-time tuition and fees vary according to course load. ***Payment plan:*** Installment.

FRESHMAN FINANCIAL AID (Fall 2010, est.) 610 applied for aid; of those 86% were deemed to have need. 100% of freshmen with need received aid; of those 27% had need fully met. ***Average percent of need met:*** 86% (excluding resources awarded to replace EFC). ***Average financial aid package:*** $24,631 (excluding resources awarded to replace EFC). 20% of all full-time freshmen had no need and received non-need-based gift aid.

UNDERGRADUATE FINANCIAL AID (Fall 2010, est.) 2,148 applied for aid; of those 83% were deemed to have need. 100% of undergraduates with need received aid; of those 24% had need fully met. ***Average percent of need met:*** 80% (excluding resources awarded to replace EFC). ***Average financial aid package:*** $23,282 (excluding resources awarded to replace EFC). 21% of all full-time undergraduates had no need and received non-need-based gift aid.

GIFT AID (NEED-BASED) ***Total amount:*** $33,674,900 (11% federal, 9% state, 75% institutional, 5% external sources). ***Receiving aid:*** Freshmen: 74% (504); all full-time undergraduates: 71% (1,761). ***Average award:*** Freshmen: $21,861; Undergraduates: $20,114. ***Scholarships, grants, and awards:*** Federal Pell, FSEOG, state, college/university gift aid from institutional funds.

GIFT AID (NON-NEED-BASED) ***Total amount:*** $7,533,276 (1% state, 92% institutional, 7% external sources). ***Receiving aid:*** Freshmen: 73% (500). Undergraduates: 63% (1,579). ***Average award:*** Freshmen: $15,123. Undergraduates: $13,692. ***Scholarships, grants, and awards by category:*** *Academic interests/achievement:* 1,479 awards ($16,586,756 total): biological sciences, business, communication, computer science, education, engineering/technologies, English, foreign languages, general academic interests/achievements, health fields, humanities, international studies, mathematics, physical sciences, premedicine, religion/biblical studies, social sciences. *Creative arts/performance:* 183 awards ($1,973,670 total): art/fine arts, music, theater/drama. *Special achievements/activities:* 60 awards ($499,760 total): leadership, memberships. *Special characteristics:* 515 awards ($4,803,236 total): children and siblings of alumni, children of faculty/staff, international students, members of minority groups, religious affiliation, siblings of current students. ***Tuition waivers:*** Full or partial for minority students, children of alumni, employees or children of employees, adult students, senior citizens.

LOANS ***Student loans:*** $10,918,349 (93% need-based, 7% non-need-based). 71% of past graduating class borrowed through all loan programs. *Average indebtedness per student:* $26,389. ***Average need-based loan:*** Freshmen: $3748. Undergraduates: $4623. ***Parent loans:*** $5,321,195 (90% need-based, 10% non-need-based). ***Programs:*** Federal Direct (Subsidized and Unsubsidized Stafford, PLUS), Perkins, Federal Nursing, college/university.

WORK-STUDY ***Federal work-study:*** Total amount: $512,368; 403 jobs averaging $1414. ***State or other work-study/employment:*** Total amount: $10,675 (43% need-based, 57% non-need-based). 12 part-time jobs averaging $1257.

ATHLETIC AWARDS Total amount: $3,998,040 (46% need-based, 54% non-need-based).

APPLYING FOR FINANCIAL AID ***Required financial aid form:*** FAFSA. ***Financial aid deadline (priority):*** 3/10. ***Notification date:*** Continuous beginning 3/25. Students must reply by 5/1.

CONTACT Ms. JoAnn E. Laugel, Director of Financial Aid, University of Evansville, 1800 Lincoln Avenue, Evansville, IN 47722, 812-488-2364 or toll-free 800-423-8633 Ext. 2468. *Fax:* 812-488-2028. *E-mail:* financialaid@evansville.edu.

THE UNIVERSITY OF FINDLAY

Findlay, OH

Tuition & fees: $26,798 **Average undergraduate aid package: $21,467**

ABOUT THE INSTITUTION Independent religious, coed. 59 undergraduate majors. Federal methodology is used as a basis for awarding need-based institutional aid.

UNDERGRADUATE EXPENSES for 2010–11 ***Comprehensive fee:*** $35,608 includes full-time tuition ($26,016), mandatory fees ($782), and room and board ($8810). ***College room only:*** $4396. Full-time tuition and fees vary according to course load and program. ***Part-time tuition:*** $577 per semester hour. ***Part-time fees:*** $682 per term. Part-time tuition and fees vary according to course load and program. ***Payment plan:*** Installment.

FRESHMAN FINANCIAL AID (Fall 2010, est.) 506 applied for aid; of those 92% were deemed to have need. 100% of freshmen with need received aid; of those 1% had need fully met. ***Average percent of need met:*** 60% (excluding resources awarded to replace EFC). ***Average financial aid package:*** $22,854 (excluding resources awarded to replace EFC). 9% of all full-time freshmen had no need and received non-need-based gift aid.

UNDERGRADUATE FINANCIAL AID (Fall 2010, est.) 2,064 applied for aid; of those 92% were deemed to have need. 100% of undergraduates with need received aid; of those 2% had need fully met. ***Average percent of need met:*** 57% (excluding resources awarded to replace EFC). ***Average financial aid package:*** $21,467 (excluding resources awarded to replace EFC). 9% of all full-time undergraduates had no need and received non-need-based gift aid.

GIFT AID (NEED-BASED) ***Total amount:*** $32,598,504 (12% federal, 3% state, 83% institutional, 2% external sources). ***Receiving aid:*** Freshmen: 71% (464); all full-time undergraduates: 71% (1,899). ***Average award:*** Freshmen: $3790; Undergraduates: $2840. ***Scholarships, grants, and awards:*** Federal Pell, FSEOG, state, college/university gift aid from institutional funds.

GIFT AID (NON-NEED-BASED) ***Total amount:*** $7,030,385 (98% institutional, 2% external sources). ***Receiving aid:*** Freshmen: 70% (462). Undergraduates: 71% (1,896). ***Average award:*** Freshmen: $12,718. Undergraduates: $11,250. ***Scholarships, grants, and awards by category:*** *Academic interests/achievement:* general academic interests/achievements. *Creative arts/performance:* music, theater/drama. *Special characteristics:* children of faculty/staff. ***Tuition waivers:*** Full or partial for children of alumni, employees or children of employees, senior citizens.

LOANS ***Student loans:*** $27,319,000 (80% need-based, 20% non-need-based). 89% of past graduating class borrowed through all loan programs. *Average indebtedness per student:* $32,822. ***Average need-based loan:*** Freshmen: $2926. Undergraduates: $5055. ***Parent loans:*** $3,846,399 (80% need-based, 20% non-need-based). ***Programs:*** Federal Direct (Subsidized and Unsubsidized Stafford, PLUS), Perkins, college/university.

WORK-STUDY ***Federal work-study:*** Total amount: $440,000; 410 jobs averaging $840. ***State or other work-study/employment:*** 300 part-time jobs averaging $840.

ATHLETIC AWARDS Total amount: $2,990,185 (80% need-based, 20% non-need-based).

APPLYING FOR FINANCIAL AID ***Required financial aid form:*** FAFSA. ***Financial aid deadline:*** Continuous. ***Notification date:*** Continuous beginning 3/1. Students must reply within 2 weeks of notification.

CONTACT Mr. Arman Habegger, Director of Financial Aid, The University of Findlay, 1000 North Main Street, Findlay, OH 45840-3695, 419-434-4791 or toll-free 800-548-0932. *Fax:* 419-434-4344. *E-mail:* finaid@findlay.edu.

UNIVERSITY OF FLORIDA

Gainesville, FL

Tuition & fees (FL res): $5044 **Average undergraduate aid package: $13,387**

ABOUT THE INSTITUTION State-supported, coed. 90 undergraduate majors. Federal methodology is used as a basis for awarding need-based institutional aid.

UNDERGRADUATE EXPENSES for 2010–11 ***Tuition, state resident:*** full-time $5044; part-time $117.67 per credit hour. ***Tuition, nonresident:*** full-time $27,321; part-time $824.88 per credit hour. ***College room and board:*** $8640; ***Room only:*** $5300. Room and board charges vary according to board plan and housing facility.

FRESHMAN FINANCIAL AID (Fall 2009) 4,725 applied for aid; of those 65% were deemed to have need. 100% of freshmen with need received aid; of those 29% had need fully met. ***Average percent of need met:*** 83% (excluding resources awarded to replace EFC). ***Average financial aid package:*** $12,470 (excluding resources awarded to replace EFC). 5% of all full-time freshmen had no need and received non-need-based gift aid.

UNDERGRADUATE FINANCIAL AID (Fall 2009) 19,148 applied for aid; of those 80% were deemed to have need. 99% of undergraduates with need received aid; of those 32% had need fully met. ***Average percent of need met:*** 83% (excluding resources awarded to replace EFC). ***Average financial aid package:*** $13,387 (excluding resources awarded to replace EFC). 6% of all full-time undergraduates had no need and received non-need-based gift aid.

GIFT AID (NEED-BASED) ***Total amount:*** $78,304,600 (66% federal, 11% state, 23% institutional). ***Receiving aid:*** Freshmen: 31% (1,951); all full-time undergraduates: 31% (10,612). ***Average award:*** Freshmen: $7265; Undergraduates: $7447. ***Scholarships, grants, and awards:*** Federal Pell, FSEOG, state, private, college/university gift aid from institutional funds.

GIFT AID (NON-NEED-BASED) ***Total amount:*** $137,121,132 (2% federal, 58% state, 12% institutional, 28% external sources). ***Receiving aid:*** Freshmen: 47% (2,995). Undergraduates: 36% (12,276). ***Average award:*** Freshmen: $1770. Undergraduates: $2171. ***Scholarships, grants, and awards by category:*** *Academic interests/achievement:* agriculture, architecture, business, communication, computer science, education, engineering/technologies, general academic interests/achievements, health fields, military science. *Creative arts/performance:* art/fine arts, dance, general creative arts/performance, journalism/publications, music, performing arts, theater/drama. *Special achievements/activities:* community service, general special achievements/activities, leadership. *Special characteristics:* children of faculty/staff, members of minority groups, out-of-state students. ***Tuition waivers:*** Full or partial for senior citizens.

LOANS ***Student loans:*** $59,175,181 (47% need-based, 53% non-need-based). 40% of past graduating class borrowed through all loan programs. *Average indebtedness per student:* $16,013. ***Average need-based loan:*** Freshmen: $3200. Undergraduates: $4248. ***Parent loans:*** $5,587,572 (100% non-need-based). ***Programs:*** Federal Direct (Subsidized and Unsubsidized Stafford, PLUS), Perkins, college/university.

WORK-STUDY ***Federal work-study:*** Total amount: $2,502,976; 1,356 jobs averaging $1846. ***State or other work-study/employment:*** Total amount: $8,249,315 (100% non-need-based). 4,150 part-time jobs averaging $1988.

ATHLETIC AWARDS Total amount: $7,552,223 (100% non-need-based).

APPLYING FOR FINANCIAL AID ***Required financial aid form:*** FAFSA. ***Financial aid deadline (priority):*** 3/15. ***Notification date:*** Continuous beginning 3/20.

CONTACT Ms. Karen L. Fooks, Director of Student Financial Affairs, University of Florida, S-107 Criser Hall, Gainesville, FL 32611-4025, 352-392-1271. *Fax:* 352-392-2861. *E-mail:* kfooks@ufl.edu.

UNIVERSITY OF GEORGIA

Athens, GA

Tuition & fees (GA res): $8736 **Average undergraduate aid package: $10,527**

ABOUT THE INSTITUTION State-supported, coed. 130 undergraduate majors. Federal methodology is used as a basis for awarding need-based institutional aid.

UNDERGRADUATE EXPENSES for 2010–11 ***Tuition, state resident:*** full-time $7070. ***Tuition, nonresident:*** full-time $25,280. ***Required fees:*** full-time $1666; $833 per term. Full-time tuition and fees vary according to course load, location, and program. Part-time tuition and fees vary according to course load, location, and program. ***College room and board:*** $8460; ***Room only:*** $4772. Room and board charges vary according to board plan and housing facility. ***Payment plan:*** Guaranteed tuition.

FRESHMAN FINANCIAL AID (Fall 2010, est.) 3,499 applied for aid; of those 55% were deemed to have need. 99% of freshmen with need received aid; of those 37% had need fully met. ***Average percent of need met:*** 82% (excluding resources awarded to replace EFC). ***Average financial aid package:*** $11,993 (excluding resources awarded to replace EFC). 6% of all full-time freshmen had no need and received non-need-based gift aid.

UNDERGRADUATE FINANCIAL AID (Fall 2010, est.) 14,319 applied for aid; of those 66% were deemed to have need. 99% of undergraduates with need received aid; of those 31% had need fully met. ***Average percent of need met:*** 75% (excluding resources awarded to replace EFC). ***Average financial aid package:*** $10,527 (excluding resources awarded to replace EFC). 5% of all full-time undergraduates had no need and received non-need-based gift aid.

GIFT AID (NEED-BASED) ***Total amount:*** $73,952,594 (38% federal, 56% state, 3% institutional, 3% external sources). ***Receiving aid:*** Freshmen: 40% (1,868); all full-time undergraduates: 34% (8,391). ***Average award:*** Freshmen: $10,886; Undergraduates: $8970. ***Scholarships, grants, and awards:*** Federal Pell, FSEOG, state, private, college/university gift aid from institutional funds.

GIFT AID (NON-NEED-BASED) ***Total amount:*** $84,831,039 (1% federal, 93% state, 3% institutional, 3% external sources). ***Receiving aid:*** Freshmen: 11% (495). Undergraduates: 6% (1,469). ***Average award:*** Freshmen: $1687. Undergraduates: $1828. ***Scholarships, grants, and awards by category:*** *Academic interests/achievement:* 21,844 awards ($128,689,426 total): agriculture, business, education, general academic interests/achievements. *Creative arts/performance:* 72 awards ($73,860 total): music. *Special characteristics:* 217 awards ($358,166 total): local/state students. ***Tuition waivers:*** Full or partial for senior citizens.

LOANS ***Student loans:*** $59,411,529 (55% need-based, 45% non-need-based). 45% of past graduating class borrowed through all loan programs. *Average indebtedness per student:* $15,938. ***Average need-based loan:*** Freshmen: $2981. Undergraduates: $3880. ***Parent loans:*** $11,589,667 (26% need-based, 74% non-need-based). ***Programs:*** Federal Direct (Subsidized and Unsubsidized Stafford, PLUS), Perkins, state, college/university.

WORK-STUDY ***Federal work-study:*** Total amount: $1,054,413; 389 jobs averaging $2711.

ATHLETIC AWARDS Total amount: $7,436,306 (26% need-based, 74% non-need-based).

APPLYING FOR FINANCIAL AID ***Required financial aid form:*** FAFSA. ***Financial aid deadline (priority):*** 3/1. ***Notification date:*** Continuous beginning 4/1. Students must reply within 2 weeks of notification.

CONTACT Ms. Bonnie C. Joerschke, Financial Aid Director, University of Georgia, 220 Holmes/Hunter Academic Building, Athens, GA 30602-6114, 706-542-8208. *Fax:* 706-542-0977. *E-mail:* bonniej@uga.edu.

UNIVERSITY OF GREAT FALLS

Great Falls, MT

Tuition & fees: $18,856 **Average undergraduate aid package: $15,912**

ABOUT THE INSTITUTION Independent Roman Catholic, coed. 73 undergraduate majors. Both federal and institutional methodology are used as a basis for awarding need-based institutional aid.

UNDERGRADUATE EXPENSES for 2010–11 ***Comprehensive fee:*** $25,568 includes full-time tuition ($17,856), mandatory fees ($1000), and room and board ($6712). ***College room only:*** $3512. Full-time tuition and fees vary according to course load. Room and board charges vary according to housing facility. ***Part-time tuition:*** $566 per credit hour. Part-time tuition and fees vary according to course load, location, and program. ***Payment plan:*** Installment.

FRESHMAN FINANCIAL AID (Fall 2010, est.) 127 applied for aid; of those 87% were deemed to have need. 100% of freshmen with need received aid; of those 2% had need fully met. ***Average percent of need met:*** 59% (excluding resources awarded to replace EFC). ***Average financial aid package:*** $15,684 (excluding resources awarded to replace EFC). 14% of all full-time freshmen had no need and received non-need-based gift aid.

UNDERGRADUATE FINANCIAL AID (Fall 2010, est.) 550 applied for aid; of those 93% were deemed to have need. 100% of undergraduates with need received aid; of those 1% had need fully met. ***Average percent of need met:*** 58% (excluding resources awarded to replace EFC). ***Average financial aid package:*** $15,912 (excluding resources awarded to replace EFC). 8% of all full-time undergraduates had no need and received non-need-based gift aid.

GIFT AID (NEED-BASED) ***Total amount:*** $4,518,008 (43% federal, 2% state, 54% institutional, 1% external sources). ***Receiving aid:*** Freshmen: 73% (101); all full-time undergraduates: 75% (463). ***Average award:*** Freshmen: $10,064; Undergraduates: $8816. ***Scholarships, grants, and awards:*** Federal Pell, FSEOG, state, private, college/university gift aid from institutional funds.

GIFT AID (NON-NEED-BASED) ***Total amount:*** $420,549 (100% institutional). ***Receiving aid:*** Freshmen: 1% (2). Undergraduates: 1% (8). ***Average award:*** Freshmen: $6831. Undergraduates: $6526. ***Scholarships, grants, and awards by category:*** *Academic interests/achievement:* biological sciences, business, computer science, education, general academic interests/achievements, humanities, mathematics, physical sciences, premedicine, religion/biblical studies, social sciences. *Creative arts/performance:* art/fine arts, dance. *Special achievements/activities:* cheerleading/drum major, religious involvement. *Special characteristics:* children of current students, children of faculty/staff, ethnic background, first-generation college students, international students, parents of current students, religious affiliation, siblings of current students, spouses of current students.

LOANS ***Student loans:*** $4,921,213 (92% need-based, 8% non-need-based). ***Average need-based loan:*** Freshmen: $3323. Undergraduates: $4236. ***Parent loans:*** $1,117,450 (79% need-based, 21% non-need-based). ***Programs:*** Federal Direct (Subsidized and Unsubsidized Stafford, PLUS), Perkins, college/university.

WORK-STUDY ***Federal work-study:*** Total amount: $304,400; jobs available. ***State or other work-study/employment:*** Part-time jobs available.

ATHLETIC AWARDS Total amount: $2,177,776 (75% need-based, 25% non-need-based).

APPLYING FOR FINANCIAL AID ***Required financial aid form:*** FAFSA. ***Financial aid deadline (priority):*** 5/1. ***Notification date:*** Continuous. Students must reply within 2 weeks of notification.

CONTACT Sandra Bauman, Director of Financial Aid, University of Great Falls, 1301 20th Street South, Great Falls, MT 59405, 406-791-5237 or toll-free 800-856-9544. *Fax:* 406-791-5242. *E-mail:* sbauman01@ugf.edu.

UNIVERSITY OF GUAM

Mangilao, GU

CONTACT Office of Financial Aid, University of Guam, UOG Station, Mangilao, GU 96923, 671-735-2288. *Fax:* 671-734-2907.

UNIVERSITY OF HARTFORD

West Hartford, CT

Tuition & fees: $30,754 **Average undergraduate aid package: $5464**

ABOUT THE INSTITUTION Independent, coed. 86 undergraduate majors. Federal methodology is used as a basis for awarding need-based institutional aid.

UNDERGRADUATE EXPENSES for 2011–12 ***Comprehensive fee:*** $42,674 includes full-time tuition ($29,440), mandatory fees ($1314), and room and board ($11,920). ***College room only:*** $7328. Full-time tuition and fees vary according to program. Room and board charges vary according to board plan and housing facility. ***Part-time tuition:*** $440 per credit hour. Part-time tuition and fees vary according to course load and program. ***Payment plans:*** Tuition prepayment, installment.

FRESHMAN FINANCIAL AID (Fall 2010, est.) 1,309 applied for aid; of those 86% were deemed to have need. 98% of freshmen with need received aid; of those 30% had need fully met. ***Average percent of need met:*** 70% (excluding resources awarded to replace EFC). ***Average financial aid package:*** $5509 (excluding resources awarded to replace EFC). 14% of all full-time freshmen had no need and received non-need-based gift aid.

UNDERGRADUATE FINANCIAL AID (Fall 2010, est.) 4,376 applied for aid; of those 85% were deemed to have need. 99% of undergraduates with need received aid; of those 25% had need fully met. ***Average percent of need met:*** 80% (excluding resources awarded to replace EFC). ***Average financial aid package:*** $5464 (excluding resources awarded to replace EFC). 20% of all full-time undergraduates had no need and received non-need-based gift aid.

GIFT AID (NEED-BASED) ***Total amount:*** $62,078,646 (11% federal, 8% state, 73% institutional, 8% external sources). ***Receiving aid:*** Freshmen: 36% (489); all full-time undergraduates: 31% (1,449). ***Average award:*** Freshmen: $6798; Undergraduates: $4153. ***Scholarships, grants, and awards:*** Federal Pell, FSEOG, state, private, college/university gift aid from institutional funds.

GIFT AID (NON-NEED-BASED) ***Total amount:*** $7,153,202 (96% institutional, 4% external sources). ***Receiving aid:*** Freshmen: 62% (853). Undergraduates: 55% (2,592). ***Average award:*** Freshmen: $3556. Undergraduates: $3578. ***Scholarships, grants, and awards by category:*** *Academic interests/achievement:* engineering/technologies, general academic interests/achievements, health fields, premedicine. *Creative arts/performance:* art/fine arts, dance, music, performing arts, theater/drama. *Special achievements/activities:* community service. *Special characteristics:* adult students, children of current students, children of faculty/staff, children of union members/company employees, children with a deceased or disabled parent, ethnic background, first-generation college students, handicapped students, international students, local/state students, members of minority groups, parents of current students, previous college experience, religious affiliation, siblings of current students, twins. ***Tuition waivers:*** Full or partial for employees or children of employees, senior citizens.

LOANS ***Student loans:*** $18,412,267 (98% need-based, 2% non-need-based). 61% of past graduating class borrowed through all loan programs. *Average indebtedness per student:* $14,855. ***Average need-based loan:*** Freshmen: $16,371. Undergraduates: $9814. ***Parent loans:*** $9,664,716 (98% need-based, 2% non-need-based). ***Programs:*** Federal Direct (Subsidized and Unsubsidized Stafford, PLUS), Perkins.

WORK-STUDY ***Federal work-study:*** Total amount: $4,377,917; 723 jobs averaging $6719. ***State or other work-study/employment:*** Total amount: $1,334,467 (94% need-based, 6% non-need-based). Part-time jobs available.

ATHLETIC AWARDS Total amount: $4,381,809 (42% need-based, 58% non-need-based).

APPLYING FOR FINANCIAL AID ***Required financial aid forms:*** FAFSA, institution's own form. ***Financial aid deadline (priority):*** 2/1. ***Notification date:*** Continuous beginning 3/1. Students must reply by 5/1 or within 2 weeks of notification.

CONTACT Office of Financial Aid, University of Hartford, 200 Bloomfield Avenue, West Hartford, CT 06117-1599, 860-768-4296 or toll-free 800-947-4303. *Fax:* 860-768-4961. *E-mail:* finaid@hartford.edu.

UNIVERSITY OF HAWAII AT HILO

Hilo, HI

Tuition & fees (HI res): $5416 **Average undergraduate aid package: $10,683**

ABOUT THE INSTITUTION State-supported, coed. 30 undergraduate majors. Federal methodology is used as a basis for awarding need-based institutional aid.

UNDERGRADUATE EXPENSES for 2011–12 ***Tuition, state resident:*** full-time $5112. ***Tuition, nonresident:*** full-time $15,600. ***Required fees:*** full-time $304. Full-time tuition and fees vary according to reciprocity agreements. Part-time tuition and fees vary according to course load. ***College room and board:*** $7134. Room and board charges vary according to board plan and housing facility.

FRESHMAN FINANCIAL AID (Fall 2010, est.) 339 applied for aid; of those 64% were deemed to have need. 100% of freshmen with need received aid; of those 25% had need fully met. ***Average percent of need met:*** 71% (excluding resources awarded to replace EFC). ***Average financial aid package:*** $8692 (excluding resources awarded to replace EFC). 1% of all full-time freshmen had no need and received non-need-based gift aid.

UNDERGRADUATE FINANCIAL AID (Fall 2010, est.) 2,191 applied for aid; of those 77% were deemed to have need. 100% of undergraduates with need received aid; of those 22% had need fully met. ***Average percent of need met:*** 72% (excluding resources awarded to replace EFC). ***Average financial aid package:*** $10,683 (excluding resources awarded to replace EFC). 1% of all full-time undergraduates had no need and received non-need-based gift aid.

GIFT AID (NEED-BASED) ***Total amount:*** $7,928,138 (92% federal, 5% state, 3% institutional). ***Receiving aid:*** Freshmen: 43% (169); all full-time undergraduates: 48% (1,346). ***Average award:*** Freshmen: $4825; Undergraduates: $4970. ***Scholarships, grants, and awards:*** Federal Pell, FSEOG, state, private, college/university gift aid from institutional funds.

GIFT AID (NON-NEED-BASED) ***Total amount:*** $1,475,429 (26% institutional, 74% external sources). ***Receiving aid:*** Freshmen: 8% (33). Undergraduates: 10% (281). ***Average award:*** Freshmen: $833. Undergraduates: $1615. ***Scholarships, grants, and awards by category:*** *Academic interests/achievement:* 33 awards ($66,148 total): business, computer science, English, general academic interests/achievements, health fields, social sciences. *Creative arts/performance:* 9 awards ($18,500 total): art/fine arts, music, performing arts, theater/drama. *Special achievements/activities:* 10 awards ($36,000 total): community service, general special achievements/activities, leadership. *Special characteristics:* 12 awards ($30,782 total): general special characteristics, local/state students.

LOANS ***Student loans:*** $18,241,171 (32% need-based, 68% non-need-based). 53% of past graduating class borrowed through all loan programs. *Average indebtedness per student:* $11,944. ***Average need-based loan:*** Freshmen: $3159. Undergraduates: $4423. ***Parent loans:*** $586,578 (100% non-need-based). ***Programs:*** Federal Direct (Subsidized and Unsubsidized Stafford, PLUS), Perkins, state.

WORK-STUDY ***Federal work-study:*** Total amount: $326,243; 158 jobs averaging $2065. ***State or other work-study/employment:*** Total amount: $2,120,031 (100% non-need-based). 531 part-time jobs averaging $3993.

ATHLETIC AWARDS Total amount: $575,805 (100% non-need-based).

APPLYING FOR FINANCIAL AID ***Required financial aid form:*** FAFSA. ***Financial aid deadline (priority):*** 3/1. ***Notification date:*** Continuous beginning 3/1. Students must reply within 3 weeks of notification.

CONTACT Financial Aid Office, University of Hawaii at Hilo, 200 West Kawili Street, Hilo, HI 96720-4091, 808-974-7324 or toll-free 800-897-4456 (out-of-state). *Fax:* 808-933-0861. *E-mail:* uhhfao@hawaii.edu.

UNIVERSITY OF HAWAII AT MANOA

Honolulu, HI

Tuition & fees (HI res): $8911 **Average undergraduate aid package: $8703**

ABOUT THE INSTITUTION State-supported, coed. 82 undergraduate majors. Federal methodology is used as a basis for awarding need-based institutional aid.

UNDERGRADUATE EXPENSES for 2011–12 ***Tuition, state resident:*** full-time $8400; part-time $350 per credit hour. ***Tuition, nonresident:*** full-time $23,232; part-time $968 per credit hour. ***Required fees:*** full-time $511; $511.40 per term. Full-time tuition and fees vary according to class time, course level, course load, degree level, program, reciprocity agreements, and student level. Part-time tuition and fees vary according to class time, course level, course load, degree level, program, reciprocity agreements, and student level. ***College room and board:*** $9410; ***Room only:*** $5718. Room and board charges vary according to board plan and housing facility. ***Payment plan:*** Installment.

FRESHMAN FINANCIAL AID (Fall 2009) 1,390 applied for aid; of those 57% were deemed to have need. 90% of freshmen with need received aid; of those 21% had need fully met. ***Average percent of need met:*** 63% (excluding resources awarded to replace EFC). ***Average financial aid package:*** $8283 (excluding resources awarded to replace EFC). 16% of all full-time freshmen had no need and received non-need-based gift aid.

UNDERGRADUATE FINANCIAL AID (Fall 2009) 7,990 applied for aid; of those 66% were deemed to have need. 93% of undergraduates with need received aid; of those 17% had need fully met. ***Average percent of need met:*** 60% (excluding resources awarded to replace EFC). ***Average financial aid package:*** $8703 (excluding resources awarded to replace EFC). 12% of all full-time undergraduates had no need and received non-need-based gift aid.

GIFT AID (NEED-BASED) ***Total amount:*** $20,093,001 (79% federal, 8% state, 9% institutional, 4% external sources). ***Receiving aid:*** Freshmen: 33% (574); all full-time undergraduates: 33% (3,906). ***Average award:*** Freshmen: $6849; Undergraduates: $6561. ***Scholarships, grants, and awards:*** Federal Pell, FSEOG, state, private, college/university gift aid from institutional funds.

GIFT AID (NON-NEED-BASED) ***Total amount:*** $2,223,393 (18% institutional, 82% external sources). ***Receiving aid:*** Freshmen: 8% (134). Undergraduates: 6% (692). ***Average award:*** Freshmen: $7091. Undergraduates: $7427. ***Scholarships, grants, and awards by category:*** *Academic interests/achievement:* general academic interests/achievements. *Creative arts/performance:* art/fine arts, music, theater/drama. *Special achievements/activities:* leadership. *Special characteristics:* children and siblings of alumni. ***Tuition waivers:*** Full or partial for minority students, employees or children of employees, adult students, senior citizens.

LOANS ***Student loans:*** $30,947,394 (49% need-based, 51% non-need-based). 35% of past graduating class borrowed through all loan programs. *Average indebtedness per student:* $16,528. ***Average need-based loan:*** Freshmen: $2704. Undergraduates: $3796. ***Parent loans:*** $10,919,396 (100% non-need-based). ***Programs:*** Federal Direct (Subsidized and Unsubsidized Stafford, PLUS), Perkins, state.

WORK-STUDY ***Federal work-study:*** Total amount: $1,128,309; jobs available.

ATHLETIC AWARDS Total amount: $3,046,642 (11% need-based, 89% non-need-based).

APPLYING FOR FINANCIAL AID ***Required financial aid form:*** FAFSA. ***Financial aid deadline:*** Continuous. ***Notification date:*** Continuous beginning 4/1. Students must reply by 5/1 or within 4 weeks of notification.

CONTACT Jodie Kuba, Director of Financial Aid Services, University of Hawaii at Manoa, 2600 Campus Road, Suite 112, Honolulu, HI 96822, 808-956-3989 or toll-free 800-823-9771. *Fax:* 808-956-3985. *E-mail:* finaid@hawaii.edu.

UNIVERSITY OF HAWAII–WEST OAHU

Pearl City, HI

Tuition & fees (HI res): $5141 **Average undergraduate aid package: $6197**

ABOUT THE INSTITUTION State-supported, coed. 21 undergraduate majors. Federal methodology is used as a basis for awarding need-based institutional aid.

UNDERGRADUATE EXPENSES for 2011–12 ***Tuition, state resident:*** full-time $5136. ***Tuition, nonresident:*** full-time $15,744; part-time $656 per credit. ***Required fees:*** full-time $5. ***Payment plan:*** Installment.

FRESHMAN FINANCIAL AID (Fall 2010, est.) 20 applied for aid; of those 100% were deemed to have need. 100% of freshmen with need received aid. ***Average percent of need met:*** 50% (excluding resources awarded to replace EFC). ***Average financial aid package:*** $2779 (excluding resources awarded to replace EFC).

UNDERGRADUATE FINANCIAL AID (Fall 2010, est.) 215 applied for aid; of those 100% were deemed to have need. 100% of undergraduates with need received aid. ***Average percent of need met:*** 50% (excluding resources awarded to replace EFC). ***Average financial aid package:*** $6197 (excluding resources awarded to replace EFC). 1% of all full-time undergraduates had no need and received non-need-based gift aid.

GIFT AID (NEED-BASED) ***Total amount:*** $2,287,682 (75% federal, 22% state, 3% institutional). ***Receiving aid:*** Freshmen: 75% (15); all full-time undergraduates: 76% (165). ***Average award:*** Freshmen: $2347; Undergraduates: $3956. ***Scholarships, grants, and awards:*** Federal Pell, FSEOG, state, private, college/university gift aid from institutional funds.

GIFT AID (NON-NEED-BASED) ***Average award:*** Undergraduates: $3058. ***Tuition waivers:*** Full or partial for employees or children of employees.

LOANS ***Student loans:*** $2,917,378 (100% need-based). ***Average need-based loan:*** Freshmen: $2159. Undergraduates: $4190. ***Parent loans:*** $22,445 (100% need-based). ***Programs:*** Federal Direct (Subsidized and Unsubsidized Stafford, PLUS).

WORK-STUDY Federal work-study jobs available. ***State or other work-study/employment:*** Part-time jobs available.

APPLYING FOR FINANCIAL AID ***Required financial aid form:*** FAFSA. ***Financial aid deadline (priority):*** 4/1. ***Notification date:*** Continuous beginning 4/1. Students must reply within 2 weeks of notification.

CONTACT Financial Aid Office, University of Hawaii–West Oahu, 96-129 Ala Ike, Pearl City, HI 96782, 808-454-4700. *Fax:* 808-453-6075. *E-mail:* finaid@uhwo.hawaii.edu.

UNIVERSITY OF HOUSTON

Houston, TX

Tuition & fees (TX res): $9000 **Average undergraduate aid package: $12,365**

ABOUT THE INSTITUTION State-supported, coed. 77 undergraduate majors. Federal methodology is used as a basis for awarding need-based institutional aid.

UNDERGRADUATE EXPENSES for 2010–11 ***Tuition, state resident:*** full-time $6270; part-time $209 per credit hour. ***Tuition, nonresident:*** full-time $15,570; part-time $519 per credit hour. ***Required fees:*** full-time $2730. Full-time tuition and fees vary according to course level, course load, and program. Part-time tuition and fees vary according to course level, course load, and program. ***College room and board:*** $7300. Room and board charges vary according to board plan and housing facility. ***Payment plans:*** Installment, deferred payment.

FRESHMAN FINANCIAL AID (Fall 2010, est.) 2,690 applied for aid; of those 82% were deemed to have need. 96% of freshmen with need received aid; of those 40% had need fully met. ***Average percent of need met:*** 82% (excluding resources awarded to replace EFC). ***Average financial aid package:*** $12,816 (excluding resources awarded to replace EFC). 5% of all full-time freshmen had no need and received non-need-based gift aid.

UNDERGRADUATE FINANCIAL AID (Fall 2010, est.) 15,241 applied for aid; of those 89% were deemed to have need. 95% of undergraduates with need received aid; of those 27% had need fully met. ***Average percent of need met:*** 76% (excluding resources awarded to replace EFC). ***Average financial aid package:*** $12,365 (excluding resources awarded to replace EFC). 2% of all full-time undergraduates had no need and received non-need-based gift aid.

GIFT AID (NEED-BASED) ***Total amount:*** $93,055,372 (54% federal, 23% state, 19% institutional, 4% external sources). ***Receiving aid:*** Freshmen: 57% (1,963); all full-time undergraduates: 51% (11,287). ***Average award:*** Freshmen: $9334; Undergraduates: $6896. ***Scholarships, grants, and awards:*** Federal Pell, FSEOG, state, private, college/university gift aid from institutional funds.

GIFT AID (NON-NEED-BASED) ***Total amount:*** $2,586,022 (5% state, 77% institutional, 18% external sources). ***Receiving aid:*** Freshmen: 3% (115). Undergraduates: 1% (329). ***Average award:*** Freshmen: $4496. Undergraduates: $4162. ***Tuition waivers:*** Full or partial for employees or children of employees.

LOANS ***Student loans:*** $123,361,993 (82% need-based, 18% non-need-based). 44% of past graduating class borrowed through all loan programs. *Average indebtedness per student:* $14,922. ***Average need-based loan:*** Freshmen: $5265. Undergraduates: $7224. ***Parent loans:*** $5,008,891 (32% need-based, 68% non-need-based). ***Programs:*** Federal Direct (Subsidized and Unsubsidized Stafford, PLUS), Perkins, state.

WORK-STUDY ***Federal work-study:*** Total amount: $1,597,924; 504 jobs averaging $2832. ***State or other work-study/employment:*** Total amount: $200,537 (100% need-based). 67 part-time jobs averaging $2723.

ATHLETIC AWARDS Total amount: $4,084,677 (79% need-based, 21% non-need-based).

APPLYING FOR FINANCIAL AID ***Required financial aid form:*** FAFSA. ***Financial aid deadline (priority):*** 4/1. ***Notification date:*** Continuous beginning 5/1. Students must reply within 4 weeks of notification.

CONTACT Office of Scholarships and Financial Aid, University of Houston, 4800 Calhoun Road, Houston, TX 77204-2160, 713-743-1010. *Fax:* 713-743-9098.

UNIVERSITY OF HOUSTON–CLEAR LAKE

Houston, TX

Tuition & fees (TX res): $6188 **Average undergraduate aid package: $7218**

ABOUT THE INSTITUTION State-supported, coed. 35 undergraduate majors. Federal methodology is used as a basis for awarding need-based institutional aid.

UNDERGRADUATE EXPENSES for 2011–12 ***Tuition, state resident:*** full-time $5036; part-time $159 per credit hour. ***Tuition, nonresident:*** full-time $15,356; part-time $503 per credit hour. ***Required fees:*** full-time $1152; $438 per term. Full-time tuition and fees vary according to course load, location, and program. Part-time tuition and fees vary according to course load, location, and program. ***College room and board: Room only:*** $10,340. Room and board charges vary according to housing facility. ***Payment plans:*** Installment, deferred payment.

UNDERGRADUATE FINANCIAL AID (Fall 2010, est.) 1,677 applied for aid; of those 92% were deemed to have need. 97% of undergraduates with need received aid; of those 31% had need fully met. ***Average percent of need met:*** 44% (excluding resources awarded to replace EFC). ***Average financial aid package:*** $7218 (excluding resources awarded to replace EFC). 3% of all full-time undergraduates had no need and received non-need-based gift aid.

GIFT AID (NEED-BASED) ***Total amount:*** $10,170,503 (63% federal, 23% state, 9% institutional, 5% external sources). ***Receiving aid:*** All full-time undergraduates: 47% (952). ***Average award:*** Undergraduates: $2972. ***Scholarships, grants, and awards:*** Federal Pell, FSEOG, state, college/university gift aid from institutional funds.

GIFT AID (NON-NEED-BASED) ***Total amount:*** $1,496,361 (17% federal, 1% state, 74% institutional, 8% external sources). ***Receiving aid:*** Undergraduates: 39% (796). ***Average award:*** Undergraduates: $869. ***Scholarships, grants, and awards by category:*** *Academic interests/achievement:* biological sciences, business, computer science, education, humanities, mathematics, social sciences. *Special achievements/activities:* community service, general special achievements/activities, leadership. *Special characteristics:* 276 awards ($486,399 total): veterans, veterans' children. ***Tuition waivers:*** Full or partial for senior citizens.

LOANS ***Student loans:*** $17,905,868 (48% need-based, 52% non-need-based). 26% of past graduating class borrowed through all loan programs. *Average indebtedness per student:* $8061. ***Average need-based loan:*** Undergraduates: $4460. ***Parent loans:*** $65,442 (100% non-need-based). ***Programs:*** Federal Direct (Subsidized and Unsubsidized Stafford, PLUS), Perkins, state.

WORK-STUDY ***Federal work-study:*** Total amount: $121,329; 38 jobs averaging $3207. ***State or other work-study/employment:*** Total amount: $87,700 (100% need-based). 26 part-time jobs averaging $3222.

CONTACT Billy Satterfield, Executive Director of Student Financial Aid, University of Houston–Clear Lake, 2700 Bay Area Boulevard, Houston, TX 77058-1098, 281-283-2480. *Fax:* 281-283-2502. *E-mail:* satterfield@cl.uh.edu.

UNIVERSITY OF HOUSTON–DOWNTOWN

Houston, TX

Tuition & fees (TX res): $5492 **Average undergraduate aid package: $8441**

ABOUT THE INSTITUTION State-supported, coed. 37 undergraduate majors. Federal methodology is used as a basis for awarding need-based institutional aid.

UNDERGRADUATE EXPENSES for 2010–11 ***One-time required fee:*** $10. ***Tuition, state resident:*** full-time $4440; part-time $148 per credit hour. ***Tuition, nonresident:*** full-time $13,740; part-time $458 per credit hour. ***Required fees:*** full-time $1052. Full-time tuition and fees vary according to course load and program. Part-time tuition and fees vary according to course load and program. ***Payment plan:*** Installment.

FRESHMAN FINANCIAL AID (Fall 2010, est.) 707 applied for aid; of those 95% were deemed to have need. 99% of freshmen with need received aid; of those 5% had need fully met. ***Average percent of need met:*** 57% (excluding resources awarded to replace EFC). ***Average financial aid package:*** $9585 (excluding resources awarded to replace EFC). 4% of all full-time freshmen had no need and received non-need-based gift aid.

UNDERGRADUATE FINANCIAL AID (Fall 2010, est.) 3,946 applied for aid; of those 96% were deemed to have need. 98% of undergraduates with need received aid; of those 3% had need fully met. ***Average percent of need met:*** 49% (excluding resources awarded to replace EFC). ***Average financial aid***

package: $8441 (excluding resources awarded to replace EFC). 3% of all full-time undergraduates had no need and received non-need-based gift aid.

GIFT AID (NEED-BASED) ***Total amount:*** $32,842,764 (65% federal, 21% state, 12% institutional, 2% external sources). ***Receiving aid:*** Freshmen: 89% (646); all full-time undergraduates: 84% (3,442). ***Average award:*** Freshmen: $8574; Undergraduates: $6222. ***Scholarships, grants, and awards:*** Federal Pell, FSEOG, state, private, college/university gift aid from institutional funds.

GIFT AID (NON-NEED-BASED) ***Total amount:*** $692,947 (17% state, 66% institutional, 17% external sources). ***Receiving aid:*** Freshmen: 1% (8). Undergraduates: 1% (29). ***Average award:*** Freshmen: $1973. Undergraduates: $2668. ***Scholarships, grants, and awards by category:*** *Academic interests/achievement:* business, general academic interests/achievements. *Special achievements/activities:* community service, general special achievements/activities, leadership. *Special characteristics:* general special characteristics. ***Tuition waivers:*** Full or partial for senior citizens.

LOANS ***Student loans:*** $38,244,222 (89% need-based, 11% non-need-based). 97% of past graduating class borrowed through all loan programs. *Average indebtedness per student:* $15,484. ***Average need-based loan:*** Freshmen: $2404. Undergraduates: $3686. ***Parent loans:*** $235,258 (53% need-based, 47% non-need-based). ***Programs:*** Federal Direct (Subsidized and Unsubsidized Stafford, PLUS), state.

WORK-STUDY ***Federal work-study:*** Total amount: $422,077; 199 jobs averaging $3312. ***State or other work-study/employment:*** Total amount: $61,743 (100% need-based). 27 part-time jobs averaging $2893.

APPLYING FOR FINANCIAL AID ***Required financial aid form:*** FAFSA. ***Financial aid deadline (priority):*** 4/1. ***Notification date:*** Continuous beginning 4/15. Students must reply within 4 weeks of notification.

CONTACT Office of Scholarships and Financial Aid, University of Houston–Downtown, One Main Street, Houston, TX 77002-1001, 713-221-8041. *Fax:* 713-221-8648. *E-mail:* uhd.finaid@uhd.edu.

UNIVERSITY OF HOUSTON–VICTORIA

Victoria, TX

CONTACT Carolyn Mallory, Financial Aid Director, University of Houston–Victoria, 3007 North Ben Wilson, Victoria, TX 77901-5731, 361-570-4131 or toll-free 877-970-4848 Ext. 110. *Fax:* 361-580-5555. *E-mail:* malloryc@uhv.edu.

UNIVERSITY OF IDAHO

Moscow, ID

Tuition & fees (ID res): $5402 Average undergraduate aid package: $12,502

ABOUT THE INSTITUTION State-supported, coed. 99 undergraduate majors. Federal methodology is used as a basis for awarding need-based institutional aid.

UNDERGRADUATE EXPENSES for 2010–11 ***Tuition, state resident:*** full-time $0. ***Tuition, nonresident:*** full-time $11,592; part-time $580 per credit. ***Required fees:*** full-time $5402; $270 per credit. Full-time tuition and fees vary according to course load, degree level, program, and reciprocity agreements. Part-time tuition and fees vary according to course load, degree level, and program. ***College room and board:*** $7194. Room and board charges vary according to board plan and housing facility. ***Payment plans:*** Installment, deferred payment.

FRESHMAN FINANCIAL AID (Fall 2009) 1,511 applied for aid; of those 75% were deemed to have need. 99% of freshmen with need received aid; of those 20% had need fully met. ***Average percent of need met:*** 75% (excluding resources awarded to replace EFC). ***Average financial aid package:*** $12,148 (excluding resources awarded to replace EFC). 26% of all full-time freshmen had no need and received non-need-based gift aid.

UNDERGRADUATE FINANCIAL AID (Fall 2009) 6,625 applied for aid; of those 83% were deemed to have need. 97% of undergraduates with need received aid; of those 17% had need fully met. ***Average percent of need met:*** 71% (excluding resources awarded to replace EFC). ***Average financial aid package:*** $12,502 (excluding resources awarded to replace EFC). 21% of all full-time undergraduates had no need and received non-need-based gift aid.

GIFT AID (NEED-BASED) ***Total amount:*** $18,210,970 (89% federal, 11% institutional). ***Receiving aid:*** Freshmen: 38% (695); all full-time undergraduates: 41% (3,541). ***Average award:*** Freshmen: $4325; Undergraduates: $4569. ***Scholarships, grants, and awards:*** Federal Pell, FSEOG, state, private, college/university gift aid from institutional funds.

GIFT AID (NON-NEED-BASED) ***Total amount:*** $9,986,544 (1% state, 76% institutional, 23% external sources). ***Receiving aid:*** Freshmen: 56% (1,024). Undergraduates: 53% (4,588). ***Average award:*** Freshmen: $4038. Undergraduates: $4796. ***Scholarships, grants, and awards by category:*** *Academic interests/achievement:* agriculture, architecture, biological sciences, business, communication, computer science, education, engineering/technologies, English, foreign languages, general academic interests/achievements, home economics, humanities, library science, mathematics, military science, physical sciences, premedicine, social sciences. *Creative arts/performance:* applied art and design, art/fine arts, creative writing, dance, general creative arts/performance, journalism/publications, music, performing arts, theater/drama. *Special achievements/activities:* cheerleading/drum major, general special achievements/activities, junior miss, leadership, rodeo. *Special characteristics:* children and siblings of alumni, children of faculty/staff, ethnic background, first-generation college students, general special characteristics, handicapped students, international students, local/state students, members of minority groups, out-of-state students, veterans. ***Tuition waivers:*** Full or partial for minority students, children of alumni, employees or children of employees, senior citizens.

LOANS ***Student loans:*** $40,870,745 (49% need-based, 51% non-need-based). 66% of past graduating class borrowed through all loan programs. *Average indebtedness per student:* $24,396. ***Average need-based loan:*** Freshmen: $5592. Undergraduates: $7385. ***Parent loans:*** $6,781,735 (100% non-need-based). ***Programs:*** Federal Direct (Subsidized and Unsubsidized Stafford, PLUS), Perkins, college/university.

WORK-STUDY ***Federal work-study:*** Total amount: $737,722; jobs available. ***State or other work-study/employment:*** Total amount: $363,577 (100% need-based). Part-time jobs available.

ATHLETIC AWARDS Total amount: $4,464,789 (100% non-need-based).

APPLYING FOR FINANCIAL AID ***Required financial aid form:*** FAFSA. ***Financial aid deadline (priority):*** 2/15. ***Notification date:*** Continuous beginning 3/30. Students must reply within 4 weeks of notification.

CONTACT Mr. Dan Davenport, Director of Student Financial Aid Services, University of Idaho, PO Box 444291, Moscow, ID 83844-4291, 208-885-6312 or toll-free 888-884-3246. *Fax:* 208-885-5592. *E-mail:* dand@uidaho.edu.

UNIVERSITY OF ILLINOIS AT CHICAGO

Chicago, IL

Tuition & fees (IL res): $12,056 Average undergraduate aid package: $13,312

ABOUT THE INSTITUTION State-supported, coed. 86 undergraduate majors. Federal methodology is used as a basis for awarding need-based institutional aid.

UNDERGRADUATE EXPENSES for 2010–11 ***Tuition, state resident:*** full-time $9134; part-time $1522 per term. ***Tuition, nonresident:*** full-time $21,524; part-time $3587 per term. ***Required fees:*** full-time $2922; $909 per term. Full-time tuition and fees vary according to degree level and program. Part-time tuition and fees vary according to course load, degree level, and program. ***College room and board:*** $9994; ***Room only:*** $7174. Room and board charges vary according to board plan and housing facility. Fees do not include Health Insurance Fee which can be waived with proof of insurance and Student-to-Student fee which is refundable on request. ***Payment plans:*** Guaranteed tuition, installment.

FRESHMAN FINANCIAL AID (Fall 2009) 2,770 applied for aid; of those 83% were deemed to have need. 95% of freshmen with need received aid; of those 10% had need fully met. ***Average percent of need met:*** 72% (excluding resources awarded to replace EFC). ***Average financial aid package:*** $13,888 (excluding resources awarded to replace EFC). 4% of all full-time freshmen had no need and received non-need-based gift aid.

UNDERGRADUATE FINANCIAL AID (Fall 2009) 11,718 applied for aid; of those 86% were deemed to have need. 96% of undergraduates with need received aid; of those 12% had need fully met. ***Average percent of need met:*** 70% (excluding resources awarded to replace EFC). ***Average financial aid package:*** $13,312 (excluding resources awarded to replace EFC). 4% of all full-time undergraduates had no need and received non-need-based gift aid.

GIFT AID (NEED-BASED) ***Total amount:*** $88,581,642 (37% federal, 31% state, 30% institutional, 2% external sources). ***Receiving aid:*** Freshmen: 57% (1,787); all full-time undergraduates: 53% (7,877). ***Average award:*** Freshmen: $13,111; Undergraduates: $11,769. ***Scholarships, grants, and awards:*** Federal Pell, FSEOG, state, private, college/university gift aid from institutional funds.

GIFT AID (NON-NEED-BASED) ***Total amount:*** $2,354,534 (1% federal, 42% state, 36% institutional, 21% external sources). ***Receiving aid:*** Freshmen: 3% (105). Undergraduates: 2% (350). ***Average award:*** Freshmen: $2564. Undergraduates: $3677. ***Scholarships, grants, and awards by category:*** *Academic interests/achievement:* 1,418 awards ($2,120,531 total): architecture, business, general academic interests/achievements. *Creative arts/performance:* 165 awards ($547,309 total): applied art and design, art/fine arts, music, performing arts, theater/drama. ***Tuition waivers:*** Full or partial for employees or children of employees, senior citizens.

LOANS ***Student loans:*** $59,874,796 (84% need-based, 16% non-need-based). 61% of past graduating class borrowed through all loan programs. *Average indebtedness per student:* $18,526. ***Average need-based loan:*** Freshmen: $3421. Undergraduates: $4485. ***Parent loans:*** $14,384,551 (76% need-based, 24% non-need-based). ***Programs:*** Federal Direct (Subsidized and Unsubsidized Stafford, PLUS), Perkins, Federal Nursing, state, college/university, private loans.

WORK-STUDY ***Federal work-study:*** Total amount: $1,902,701; 1,006 jobs averaging $1904. ***State or other work-study/employment:*** Total amount: $6,507,346 (70% need-based, 30% non-need-based). 2,571 part-time jobs averaging $2577.

ATHLETIC AWARDS Total amount: $3,162,096 (34% need-based, 66% non-need-based).

APPLYING FOR FINANCIAL AID ***Required financial aid form:*** FAFSA. ***Financial aid deadline (priority):*** 3/1. ***Notification date:*** Continuous beginning 3/15. Students must reply by 5/1.

CONTACT Deidre Rush, Associate Director of Financial Aid, University of Illinois at Chicago, 1200 West Harrison, M/C 334, Chicago, IL 60607-7128, 312-996-5563. *Fax:* 312-996-3385. *E-mail:* deidreb@uic.edu.

UNIVERSITY OF ILLINOIS AT SPRINGFIELD

Springfield, IL

Tuition & fees (IL res): $10,367 **Average undergraduate aid package: $11,157**

ABOUT THE INSTITUTION State-supported, coed. 23 undergraduate majors. Federal methodology is used as a basis for awarding need-based institutional aid.

UNDERGRADUATE EXPENSES for 2010–11 ***Tuition, state resident:*** full-time $8108; part-time $270.25 per credit hour. ***Tuition, nonresident:*** full-time $17,258; part-time $575.25 per credit hour. ***Required fees:*** full-time $2259; $15.25 per credit hour or $772 per term. Full-time tuition and fees vary according to course load. Part-time tuition and fees vary according to course load. ***College room and board:*** $9400; ***Room only:*** $6400. Room and board charges vary according to board plan and housing facility. ***Payment plans:*** Guaranteed tuition, installment.

FRESHMAN FINANCIAL AID (Fall 2009) 267 applied for aid; of those 74% were deemed to have need. 98% of freshmen with need received aid; of those 12% had need fully met. ***Average percent of need met:*** 80% (excluding resources awarded to replace EFC). ***Average financial aid package:*** $12,474 (excluding resources awarded to replace EFC). 24% of all full-time freshmen had no need and received non-need-based gift aid.

UNDERGRADUATE FINANCIAL AID (Fall 2009) 1,616 applied for aid; of those 83% were deemed to have need. 98% of undergraduates with need received aid; of those 8% had need fully met. ***Average percent of need met:*** 71% (excluding resources awarded to replace EFC). ***Average financial aid package:*** $11,157 (excluding resources awarded to replace EFC). 12% of all full-time undergraduates had no need and received non-need-based gift aid.

GIFT AID (NEED-BASED) ***Total amount:*** $9,087,915 (46% federal, 39% state, 12% institutional, 3% external sources). ***Receiving aid:*** Freshmen: 65% (186); all full-time undergraduates: 56% (1,094). ***Average award:*** Freshmen: $9289; Undergraduates: $8213. ***Scholarships, grants, and awards:*** Federal Pell, FSEOG, state, private, college/university gift aid from institutional funds.

GIFT AID (NON-NEED-BASED) ***Total amount:*** $1,347,857 (6% federal, 40% state, 32% institutional, 22% external sources). ***Receiving aid:*** Freshmen: 21% (59). Undergraduates: 7% (137). ***Average award:*** Freshmen: $4362. Undergraduates: $4218. ***Scholarships, grants, and awards by category:*** *Academic interests/achievement:* general academic interests/achievements. *Creative arts/performance:* art/fine arts, music, theater/drama. *Special achievements/activities:* leadership. *Special characteristics:* children and siblings of alumni, ethnic background. ***Tuition waivers:*** Full or partial for employees or children of employees, senior citizens.

LOANS ***Student loans:*** $11,728,302 (86% need-based, 14% non-need-based). 61% of past graduating class borrowed through all loan programs. *Average indebtedness per student:* $17,335. ***Average need-based loan:*** Freshmen: $3283. Undergraduates: $4251. ***Parent loans:*** $1,699,984 (69% need-based, 31% non-need-based). ***Programs:*** Federal Direct (Subsidized and Unsubsidized Stafford, PLUS), Perkins, college/university.

WORK-STUDY ***Federal work-study:*** Total amount: $247,795; jobs available. ***State or other work-study/employment:*** Total amount: $988,387 (70% need-based, 30% non-need-based). Part-time jobs available.

ATHLETIC AWARDS Total amount: $545,960 (66% need-based, 34% non-need-based).

APPLYING FOR FINANCIAL AID ***Required financial aid form:*** FAFSA. ***Financial aid deadline:*** 11/15 (priority: 4/1). ***Notification date:*** Continuous beginning 1/1. Students must reply within 3 weeks of notification.

CONTACT Mr. Gerard Joseph, Director of Financial Aid, University of Illinois at Springfield, One University Plaza, MS UHB 1015, Springfield, IL 62703-5407, 217-206-6724 or toll-free 888-977-4847. *Fax:* 217-206-7376. *E-mail:* finaid@uis.edu.

UNIVERSITY OF ILLINOIS AT URBANA–CHAMPAIGN

Champaign, IL

Tuition & fees (IL res): $14,414 **Average undergraduate aid package: $12,933**

ABOUT THE INSTITUTION State-supported, coed. 219 undergraduate majors. Federal methodology is used as a basis for awarding need-based institutional aid.

UNDERGRADUATE EXPENSES for 2011–12 ***Tuition, state resident:*** full-time $11,104. ***Tuition, nonresident:*** full-time $25,246. ***Required fees:*** full-time $3310. Full-time tuition and fees vary according to program and student level. ***College room and board:*** $10,080. Room and board charges vary according to board plan, housing facility, and location. ***Payment plans:*** Guaranteed tuition, installment.

FRESHMAN FINANCIAL AID (Fall 2009) 4,958 applied for aid; of those 69% were deemed to have need. 95% of freshmen with need received aid; of those 37% had need fully met. ***Average percent of need met:*** 70% (excluding resources awarded to replace EFC). ***Average financial aid package:*** $13,766 (excluding resources awarded to replace EFC). 13% of all full-time freshmen had no need and received non-need-based gift aid.

UNDERGRADUATE FINANCIAL AID (Fall 2009) 17,991 applied for aid; of those 77% were deemed to have need. 96% of undergraduates with need received aid; of those 30% had need fully met. ***Average percent of need met:*** 68% (excluding resources awarded to replace EFC). ***Average financial aid package:*** $12,933 (excluding resources awarded to replace EFC). 12% of all full-time undergraduates had no need and received non-need-based gift aid.

GIFT AID (NEED-BASED) ***Total amount:*** $95,139,289 (30% federal, 30% state, 34% institutional, 6% external sources). ***Receiving aid:*** Freshmen: 38% (2,631); all full-time undergraduates: 34% (10,323). ***Average award:*** Freshmen: $11,901; Undergraduates: $10,885. ***Scholarships, grants, and awards:*** Federal Pell, FSEOG, state, private, college/university gift aid from institutional funds, United Negro College Fund.

GIFT AID (NON-NEED-BASED) ***Total amount:*** $11,632,775 (3% federal, 7% state, 68% institutional, 22% external sources). ***Receiving aid:*** Freshmen: 9% (625). Undergraduates: 5% (1,471). ***Average award:*** Freshmen: $3015. Undergraduates: $3286. ***Scholarships, grants, and awards by category:*** *Academic interests/achievement:* agriculture, architecture, area/ethnic studies, biological sciences, business, communication, computer science, education, engineering/technologies, English, foreign languages, general academic interests/achievements, health fields, home economics, humanities, international studies, library science, mathematics, military science, physical sciences, premedicine, religion/biblical studies, social sciences. *Creative arts/performance:* applied art and design, art/fine arts, dance, general creative arts/performance, journalism/publications, music, performing arts, theater/drama. *Special achievements/activities:* general special achievements/activities, leadership. *Special characteristics:* children and siblings of alumni, children of faculty/staff, first-generation college students, general special characteristics, local/state students, veterans. ***Tuition waivers:*** Full or partial for employees or children of employees, senior citizens.

LOANS ***Student loans:*** $103,158,202 (81% need-based, 19% non-need-based). 51% of past graduating class borrowed through all loan programs. *Average indebtedness per student:* $21,543. ***Average need-based loan:*** Freshmen: $4009.

Undergraduates: $4536. ***Parent loans:*** $66,392,155 (71% need-based, 29% non-need-based). ***Programs:*** Federal Direct (Subsidized and Unsubsidized Stafford, PLUS), Perkins, college/university.

WORK-STUDY ***Federal work-study:*** Total amount: $2,330,750; jobs available. ***State or other work-study/employment:*** Total amount: $20,050,029 (57% need-based, 43% non-need-based). Part-time jobs available.

ATHLETIC AWARDS Total amount: $8,508,377 (34% need-based, 66% non-need-based).

APPLYING FOR FINANCIAL AID ***Required financial aid form:*** FAFSA. ***Financial aid deadline (priority):*** 3/15. ***Notification date:*** 3/15.

CONTACT Daniel Mann, Director of Student Financial Aid, University of Illinois at Urbana–Champaign, Student Services Arcade Building, 620 East John Street, Champaign, IL 61820-5711, 217-333-0100.

UNIVERSITY OF INDIANAPOLIS

Indianapolis, IN

Tuition & fees: $22,240 **Average undergraduate aid package: $15,526**

ABOUT THE INSTITUTION Independent religious, coed. 62 undergraduate majors. Federal methodology is used as a basis for awarding need-based institutional aid.

UNDERGRADUATE EXPENSES for 2010–11 ***Comprehensive fee:*** $30,680 includes full-time tuition ($22,020), mandatory fees ($220), and room and board ($8440). ***College room only:*** $4010. Room and board charges vary according to board plan and housing facility. ***Part-time tuition:*** $917 per credit hour. Part-time tuition and fees vary according to course load.

FRESHMAN FINANCIAL AID (Fall 2009) 725 applied for aid; of those 87% were deemed to have need. 100% of freshmen with need received aid; of those 20% had need fully met. ***Average percent of need met:*** 79% (excluding resources awarded to replace EFC). ***Average financial aid package:*** $18,127 (excluding resources awarded to replace EFC). 16% of all full-time freshmen had no need and received non-need-based gift aid.

UNDERGRADUATE FINANCIAL AID (Fall 2009) 3,258 applied for aid; of those 87% were deemed to have need. 99% of undergraduates with need received aid; of those 14% had need fully met. ***Average percent of need met:*** 70% (excluding resources awarded to replace EFC). ***Average financial aid package:*** $15,526 (excluding resources awarded to replace EFC). 18% of all full-time undergraduates had no need and received non-need-based gift aid.

GIFT AID (NEED-BASED) ***Total amount:*** $16,719,807 (36% federal, 36% state, 28% institutional). ***Receiving aid:*** Freshmen: 63% (471); all full-time undergraduates: 53% (2,044). ***Average award:*** Freshmen: $8796; Undergraduates: $8000. ***Scholarships, grants, and awards:*** Federal Pell, FSEOG, state, private, college/university gift aid from institutional funds.

GIFT AID (NON-NEED-BASED) ***Total amount:*** $15,417,217 (3% state, 96% institutional, 1% external sources). ***Receiving aid:*** Freshmen: 81% (608). Undergraduates: 51% (1,957). ***Average award:*** Freshmen: $8092. Undergraduates: $6704. ***Scholarships, grants, and awards by category:*** *Academic interests/achievement:* business, communication, general academic interests/achievements, health fields, physical sciences, religion/biblical studies. *Creative arts/performance:* art/fine arts, music, theater/drama. *Special achievements/activities:* community service, memberships. *Special characteristics:* children of faculty/staff, ethnic background, international students, out-of-state students, relatives of clergy, religious affiliation, veterans. ***Tuition waivers:*** Full or partial for employees or children of employees.

LOANS ***Student loans:*** $24,312,073 (40% need-based, 60% non-need-based). 79% of past graduating class borrowed through all loan programs. *Average indebtedness per student:* $27,070. ***Average need-based loan:*** Freshmen: $3439. Undergraduates: $4174. ***Parent loans:*** $3,279,268 (100% non-need-based). ***Programs:*** Federal Direct (Subsidized and Unsubsidized Stafford, PLUS).

WORK-STUDY ***Federal work-study:*** Total amount: $1,928,231; jobs available.

ATHLETIC AWARDS Total amount: $3,623,842 (100% non-need-based).

APPLYING FOR FINANCIAL AID ***Required financial aid forms:*** FAFSA, institution's own form. ***Financial aid deadline (priority):*** 3/10. ***Notification date:*** Continuous beginning 3/1.

CONTACT Ms. Linda B. Handy, Director of Financial Aid, University of Indianapolis, 1400 East Hanna Avenue, Indianapolis, IN 46227-3697, 317-788-3217 or toll-free 800-232-8634 Ext. 3216. *Fax:* 317-788-6136. *E-mail:* handy@uindy.edu.

THE UNIVERSITY OF IOWA

Iowa City, IA

Tuition & fees (IA res): $7765 **Average undergraduate aid package: $11,289**

ABOUT THE INSTITUTION State-supported, coed. 129 undergraduate majors. Federal methodology is used as a basis for awarding need-based institutional aid.

UNDERGRADUATE EXPENSES for 2011–12 ***Tuition, state resident:*** full-time $6436; part-time $268 per semester hour. ***Tuition, nonresident:*** full-time $23,770; part-time $990 per semester hour. ***Required fees:*** full-time $1329. Full-time tuition and fees vary according to course load, program, and student level. Part-time tuition and fees vary according to course load, program, and student level. ***College room and board:*** $8750. Room and board charges vary according to board plan and housing facility. ***Payment plan:*** Installment.

FRESHMAN FINANCIAL AID (Fall 2009) 3,043 applied for aid; of those 62% were deemed to have need. 98% of freshmen with need received aid; of those 35% had need fully met. ***Average percent of need met:*** 75% (excluding resources awarded to replace EFC). ***Average financial aid package:*** $11,589 (excluding resources awarded to replace EFC). 23% of all full-time freshmen had no need and received non-need-based gift aid.

UNDERGRADUATE FINANCIAL AID (Fall 2009) 12,183 applied for aid; of those 69% were deemed to have need. 99% of undergraduates with need received aid; of those 32% had need fully met. ***Average percent of need met:*** 68% (excluding resources awarded to replace EFC). ***Average financial aid package:*** $11,289 (excluding resources awarded to replace EFC). 33% of all full-time undergraduates had no need and received non-need-based gift aid.

GIFT AID (NEED-BASED) ***Total amount:*** $37,680,076 (39% federal, 5% state, 51% institutional, 5% external sources). ***Receiving aid:*** Freshmen: 31% (1,279); all full-time undergraduates: 29% (5,345). ***Average award:*** Freshmen: $6799; Undergraduates: $6486. ***Scholarships, grants, and awards:*** Federal Pell, FSEOG, state, private, college/university gift aid from institutional funds.

GIFT AID (NON-NEED-BASED) ***Total amount:*** $33,390,677 (6% federal, 1% state, 85% institutional, 8% external sources). ***Receiving aid:*** Freshmen: 28% (1,127). Undergraduates: 17% (3,211). ***Average award:*** Freshmen: $4283. Undergraduates: $4147. ***Scholarships, grants, and awards by category:*** *Academic interests/achievement:* business, engineering/technologies, general academic interests/achievements, military science. *Creative arts/performance:* general creative arts/performance, music. *Special achievements/activities:* general special achievements/activities. *Special characteristics:* children and siblings of alumni, ethnic background, first-generation college students, handicapped students, out-of-state students, veterans.

LOANS ***Student loans:*** $84,463,014 (53% need-based, 47% non-need-based). 54% of past graduating class borrowed through all loan programs. *Average indebtedness per student:* $27,391. ***Average need-based loan:*** Freshmen: $4091. Undergraduates: $5155. ***Parent loans:*** $38,554,477 (100% non-need-based). ***Programs:*** Federal Direct (Subsidized and Unsubsidized Stafford, PLUS), Perkins, Federal Nursing, college/university.

WORK-STUDY ***Federal work-study:*** Total amount: $3,268,072; 1,516 jobs averaging $2156.

ATHLETIC AWARDS Total amount: $7,720,410 (100% non-need-based).

APPLYING FOR FINANCIAL AID ***Required financial aid forms:*** FAFSA, institution's own form. ***Financial aid deadline:*** Continuous. ***Notification date:*** Continuous beginning 3/15.

CONTACT Mark Warner, Director of Student Financial Aid, The University of Iowa, 208 Calvin Hall, Iowa City, IA 52242, 319-335-3127 or toll-free 800-553-4692.

THE UNIVERSITY OF KANSAS

Lawrence, KS

Tuition & fees (KS res): $8733 **Average undergraduate aid package: $11,520**

ABOUT THE INSTITUTION State-supported, coed. 112 undergraduate majors. Federal methodology is used as a basis for awarding need-based institutional aid.

UNDERGRADUATE EXPENSES for 2010–11 ***Tuition, state resident:*** full-time $7875; part-time $262.50 per credit hour. ***Tuition, nonresident:*** full-time $20,680; part-time $689.35 per credit hour. ***Required fees:*** full-time $858; $71.49 per credit hour. Full-time tuition and fees vary according to program, reciprocity agreements, and student level. Part-time tuition and fees vary according to program, reciprocity agreements, and student level. ***College room and board:*** $6982; ***Room only:*** $3642. Room and board charges vary according to board plan and housing facility. ***Payment plans:*** Guaranteed tuition, installment.

FRESHMAN FINANCIAL AID (Fall 2009) 3,161 applied for aid; of those 56% were deemed to have need. 95% of freshmen with need received aid; of those 22% had need fully met. ***Average percent of need met:*** 44% (excluding resources awarded to replace EFC). ***Average financial aid package:*** $10,346 (excluding resources awarded to replace EFC). 19% of all full-time freshmen had no need and received non-need-based gift aid.

UNDERGRADUATE FINANCIAL AID (Fall 2009) 14,388 applied for aid; of those 56% were deemed to have need. 96% of undergraduates with need received aid; of those 30% had need fully met. ***Average percent of need met:*** 54% (excluding resources awarded to replace EFC). ***Average financial aid package:*** $11,520 (excluding resources awarded to replace EFC). 11% of all full-time undergraduates had no need and received non-need-based gift aid.

GIFT AID (NEED-BASED) ***Total amount:*** $30,455,041 (57% federal, 8% state, 35% institutional). ***Receiving aid:*** Freshmen: 31% (1,210); all full-time undergraduates: 30% (5,428). ***Average award:*** Freshmen: $5589; Undergraduates: $6181. ***Scholarships, grants, and awards:*** Federal Pell, FSEOG, state, private, college/university gift aid from institutional funds.

GIFT AID (NON-NEED-BASED) ***Total amount:*** $14,760,851 (74% institutional, 26% external sources). ***Receiving aid:*** Freshmen: 19% (738). Undergraduates: 12% (2,291). ***Average award:*** Freshmen: $3081. Undergraduates: $3377. ***Scholarships, grants, and awards by category:*** *Academic interests/achievement:* architecture, area/ethnic studies, biological sciences, business, communication, computer science, education, engineering/technologies, English, foreign languages, general academic interests/achievements, health fields, humanities, international studies, mathematics, physical sciences, premedicine, religion/biblical studies, social sciences. *Creative arts/performance:* applied art and design, art/fine arts, cinema/film/broadcasting, creative writing, dance, debating, general creative arts/performance, journalism/publications, music, performing arts, theater/drama. *Special achievements/activities:* community service, general special achievements/activities, leadership. *Special characteristics:* adult students, children of faculty/staff, ethnic background, first-generation college students, general special characteristics, international students, local/state students, married students, members of minority groups, out-of-state students, previous college experience. ***Tuition waivers:*** Full or partial for employees or children of employees.

LOANS ***Student loans:*** $76,666,106 (40% need-based, 60% non-need-based). 48% of past graduating class borrowed through all loan programs. *Average indebtedness per student:* $23,319. ***Average need-based loan:*** Freshmen: $2958. Undergraduates: $3554. ***Parent loans:*** $35,643,676 (100% non-need-based). ***Programs:*** Federal Direct (Subsidized and Unsubsidized Stafford, PLUS), Perkins, college/university.

WORK-STUDY ***Federal work-study:*** Total amount: $1,421,622; 537 jobs averaging $2647. ***State or other work-study/employment:*** Total amount: $383,394 (100% non-need-based). 90 part-time jobs averaging $4360.

ATHLETIC AWARDS Total amount: $7,495,689 (100% non-need-based).

APPLYING FOR FINANCIAL AID ***Required financial aid form:*** FAFSA. ***Financial aid deadline (priority):*** 3/1. ***Notification date:*** Continuous beginning 4/1. Students must reply within 4 weeks of notification.

CONTACT Ms. Brenda Maigaard, Director of Student Financial Aid, The University of Kansas, 50 Strong Hall, Lawrence, KS 66045-7535, 785-864-4700 or toll-free 888-686-7323 (in-state). *Fax:* 785-864-5469. *E-mail:* financialaid@ku.edu.

UNIVERSITY OF KENTUCKY

Lexington, KY

Tuition & fees (KY res): $8610 **Average undergraduate aid package: $8928**

ABOUT THE INSTITUTION State-supported, coed. 79 undergraduate majors. Federal methodology is used as a basis for awarding need-based institutional aid.

UNDERGRADUATE EXPENSES for 2010–11 ***Tuition, state resident:*** full-time $7656; part-time $319 per credit hour. ***Tuition, nonresident:*** full-time $16,724; part-time $697 per credit hour. ***Required fees:*** full-time $954; $24 per credit hour. Full-time tuition and fees vary according to degree level, program, reciprocity agreements, and student level. Part-time tuition and fees vary according to degree level, program, reciprocity agreements, and student level. ***College room and board:*** $9439; ***Room only:*** $4135. Room and board charges vary according to board plan and housing facility. ***Payment plan:*** Installment.

FRESHMAN FINANCIAL AID (Fall 2009) 3,020 applied for aid; of those 70% were deemed to have need. 99% of freshmen with need received aid; of those 23% had need fully met. ***Average percent of need met:*** 65% (excluding resources awarded to replace EFC). ***Average financial aid package:*** $9457 (excluding resources awarded to replace EFC). 37% of all full-time freshmen had no need and received non-need-based gift aid.

UNDERGRADUATE FINANCIAL AID (Fall 2009) 10,575 applied for aid; of those 76% were deemed to have need. 97% of undergraduates with need received aid; of those 19% had need fully met. ***Average percent of need met:*** 61% (excluding resources awarded to replace EFC). ***Average financial aid package:*** $8928 (excluding resources awarded to replace EFC). 36% of all full-time undergraduates had no need and received non-need-based gift aid.

GIFT AID (NEED-BASED) ***Total amount:*** $83,431,536 (23% federal, 26% state, 45% institutional, 6% external sources). ***Receiving aid:*** Freshmen: 22% (907); all full-time undergraduates: 21% (3,727). ***Average award:*** Freshmen: $6139; Undergraduates: $5605. ***Scholarships, grants, and awards:*** Federal Pell, FSEOG, state, private, college/university gift aid from institutional funds.

GIFT AID (NON-NEED-BASED) ***Receiving aid:*** Freshmen: 46% (1,883). Undergraduates: 32% (5,611). ***Average award:*** Freshmen: $5548. Undergraduates: $5683. ***Scholarships, grants, and awards by category:*** *Academic interests/achievement:* agriculture, architecture, area/ethnic studies, biological sciences, business, communication, computer science, education, engineering/technologies, English, foreign languages, general academic interests/achievements, health fields, home economics, international studies, mathematics, military science, physical sciences. *Creative arts/performance:* applied art and design, art/fine arts, cinema/film/broadcasting, creative writing, dance, debating, general creative arts/performance, journalism/publications, music, performing arts, theater/drama. *Special achievements/activities:* cheerleading/drum major, general special achievements/activities, leadership. *Special characteristics:* adult students, children and siblings of alumni, children of educators, children of faculty/staff, children of public servants, children of union members/company employees, children of workers in trades, children with a deceased or disabled parent, ethnic background, first-generation college students, general special characteristics, handicapped students, international students, members of minority groups, public servants, spouses of deceased or disabled public servants, veterans, veterans' children. ***Tuition waivers:*** Full or partial for employees or children of employees, senior citizens.

LOANS ***Student loans:*** $63,408,837 (100% need-based). 36% of past graduating class borrowed through all loan programs. *Average indebtedness per student:* $19,812. ***Average need-based loan:*** Freshmen: $3184. Undergraduates: $4033. ***Parent loans:*** $16,432,529 (100% need-based). ***Programs:*** Federal Direct (Subsidized and Unsubsidized Stafford, PLUS), Perkins, college/university.

WORK-STUDY ***Federal work-study:*** Total amount: $750,155; 430 jobs averaging $1804. ***State or other work-study/employment:*** 91 part-time jobs averaging $3248.

ATHLETIC AWARDS Total amount: $8,300,565 (100% need-based).

APPLYING FOR FINANCIAL AID ***Required financial aid form:*** FAFSA. ***Financial aid deadline (priority):*** 2/15. ***Notification date:*** Continuous beginning 4/1. Students must reply within 3 weeks of notification.

CONTACT Ms. Lynda S. George, Director of Financial Aid, University of Kentucky, 128 Funkhouser Building, Lexington, KY 40506-0054, 859-257-3172 Ext. 241 or toll-free 800-432-0967 (in-state). *Fax:* 859-257-4398. *E-mail:* lgeorge@email.uky.edu.

UNIVERSITY OF LA VERNE

La Verne, CA

Tuition & fees: $31,300 **Average undergraduate aid package: $26,408**

ABOUT THE INSTITUTION Independent, coed. 47 undergraduate majors. Federal methodology is used as a basis for awarding need-based institutional aid.

UNDERGRADUATE EXPENSES for 2011–12 ***Comprehensive fee:*** $42,580 includes full-time tuition ($31,300) and room and board ($11,280). ***College room only:*** $5790. Full-time tuition and fees vary according to location. Room and board charges vary according to board plan and housing facility. ***Part-time tuition:*** $890 per unit. Part-time tuition and fees vary according to location. ***Payment plans:*** Installment, deferred payment.

FRESHMAN FINANCIAL AID (Fall 2010, est.) 504 applied for aid; of those 91% were deemed to have need. 100% of freshmen with need received aid; of those

11% had need fully met. ***Average percent of need met:*** 40% (excluding resources awarded to replace EFC). ***Average financial aid package:*** $27,624 (excluding resources awarded to replace EFC). 11% of all full-time freshmen had no need and received non-need-based gift aid.

UNDERGRADUATE FINANCIAL AID (Fall 2010, est.) 1,608 applied for aid; of those 94% were deemed to have need. 100% of undergraduates with need received aid; of those 11% had need fully met. ***Average percent of need met:*** 52% (excluding resources awarded to replace EFC). ***Average financial aid package:*** $26,408 (excluding resources awarded to replace EFC). 12% of all full-time undergraduates had no need and received non-need-based gift aid.

GIFT AID (NEED-BASED) ***Total amount:*** $33,196,790 (13% federal, 18% state, 69% institutional). ***Receiving aid:*** Freshmen: 57% (305); all full-time undergraduates: 67% (1,211). ***Average award:*** Freshmen: $10,679; Undergraduates: $12,068. ***Scholarships, grants, and awards:*** Federal Pell, FSEOG, state, private, college/university gift aid from institutional funds.

GIFT AID (NON-NEED-BASED) ***Total amount:*** $2,353,972 (100% institutional). ***Receiving aid:*** Freshmen: 86% (459). Undergraduates: 77% (1,380). ***Average award:*** Freshmen: $16,742. Undergraduates: $16,631. ***Scholarships, grants, and awards by category:*** *Academic interests/achievement:* general academic interests/achievements. *Creative arts/performance:* art/fine arts, cinema/film/broadcasting, debating, journalism/publications, music, theater/drama. *Special achievements/activities:* community service, leadership. *Special characteristics:* children of faculty/staff, general special characteristics, international students, veterans. ***Tuition waivers:*** Full or partial for employees or children of employees.

LOANS ***Student loans:*** $12,014,135 (95% need-based, 5% non-need-based). 81% of past graduating class borrowed through all loan programs. *Average indebtedness per student:* $31,112. ***Average need-based loan:*** Freshmen: $2411. Undergraduates: $2163. ***Parent loans:*** $2,541,219 (87% need-based, 13% non-need-based). ***Programs:*** Perkins, college/university, alternative loans.

WORK-STUDY ***Federal work-study:*** Total amount: $571,356; jobs available. ***State or other work-study/employment:*** Part-time jobs available.

APPLYING FOR FINANCIAL AID ***Required financial aid forms:*** FAFSA, state aid form. ***Financial aid deadline (priority):*** 3/2. ***Notification date:*** Continuous beginning 3/17. Students must reply within 2 weeks of notification.

CONTACT Leatha Webster, Director of Financial Aid, University of La Verne, 1950 3rd Street, La Verne, CA 91750-4443, 909-593-3511 Ext. 4180 or toll-free 800-876-4858. *Fax:* 909-392-2751. *E-mail:* lwebster@laverne.edu.

UNIVERSITY OF LOUISIANA AT LAFAYETTE

Lafayette, LA

Tuition & fees (LA res): $4426 **Average undergraduate aid package: $7179**

ABOUT THE INSTITUTION State-supported, coed. 83 undergraduate majors. Federal methodology is used as a basis for awarding need-based institutional aid.

UNDERGRADUATE EXPENSES for 2010–11 ***Tuition, state resident:*** full-time $3002; part-time $125 per credit hour. ***Tuition, nonresident:*** full-time $8572; part-time $357 per credit hour. ***Required fees:*** full-time $1424. Full-time tuition and fees vary according to course load. Part-time tuition and fees vary according to course load. ***College room and board:*** $4758. Room and board charges vary according to housing facility. ***Payment plan:*** Deferred payment.

FRESHMAN FINANCIAL AID (Fall 2009) 2,362 applied for aid; of those 58% were deemed to have need. 98% of freshmen with need received aid; of those 17% had need fully met. ***Average percent of need met:*** 67% (excluding resources awarded to replace EFC). ***Average financial aid package:*** $7422 (excluding resources awarded to replace EFC). 14% of all full-time freshmen had no need and received non-need-based gift aid.

UNDERGRADUATE FINANCIAL AID (Fall 2009) 9,563 applied for aid; of those 64% were deemed to have need. 97% of undergraduates with need received aid; of those 10% had need fully met. ***Average percent of need met:*** 59% (excluding resources awarded to replace EFC). ***Average financial aid package:*** $7179 (excluding resources awarded to replace EFC). 8% of all full-time undergraduates had no need and received non-need-based gift aid.

GIFT AID (NEED-BASED) ***Total amount:*** $20,166,193 (89% federal, 11% state). ***Receiving aid:*** Freshmen: 49% (1,271); all full-time undergraduates: 41% (5,171). ***Average award:*** Freshmen: $6036; Undergraduates: $5451. ***Scholarships, grants, and awards:*** Federal Pell, FSEOG, state, college/university gift aid from institutional funds.

GIFT AID (NON-NEED-BASED) ***Total amount:*** $19,266,567 (74% state, 23% institutional, 3% external sources). ***Receiving aid:*** Freshmen: 8% (208). Undergraduates: 4% (540). ***Average award:*** Freshmen: $1673. Undergraduates: $1691. ***Scholarships, grants, and awards by category:*** *Academic interests/achievement:* general academic interests/achievements. *Creative arts/performance:* general creative arts/performance. *Special achievements/activities:* general special achievements/activities. ***Tuition waivers:*** Full or partial for children of alumni, employees or children of employees, senior citizens.

LOANS ***Student loans:*** $26,925,342 (55% need-based, 45% non-need-based). ***Average need-based loan:*** Freshmen: $3156. Undergraduates: $3785. ***Parent loans:*** $1,225,532 (100% non-need-based). ***Programs:*** Perkins, Federal Nursing.

WORK-STUDY ***Federal work-study:*** Total amount: $936,282; 480 jobs averaging $1896. ***State or other work-study/employment:*** Total amount: $399,956 (100% non-need-based). 253 part-time jobs averaging $1493.

ATHLETIC AWARDS Total amount: $1,989,195 (100% non-need-based).

APPLYING FOR FINANCIAL AID ***Required financial aid form:*** FAFSA. ***Financial aid deadline (priority):*** 5/1. ***Notification date:*** Continuous. Students must reply within 2 weeks of notification.

CONTACT Cindy S. Perez, Director of Financial Aid, University of Louisiana at Lafayette, PO Box 41206, Lafayette, LA 70504-1206, 337-482-6497 or toll-free 800-752-6553 (in-state). *Fax:* 337-482-6502. *E-mail:* cperez@louisiana.edu.

UNIVERSITY OF LOUISIANA AT MONROE

Monroe, LA

ABOUT THE INSTITUTION State-supported, coed. 53 undergraduate majors.

GIFT AID (NEED-BASED) ***Scholarships, grants, and awards:*** Federal Pell, FSEOG, state, private, college/university gift aid from institutional funds, Leveraging Educational Assistance Program (LEAP).

GIFT AID (NON-NEED-BASED) ***Scholarships, grants, and awards by category:*** *Academic interests/achievement:* agriculture, biological sciences, business, communication, computer science, education, English, foreign languages, general academic interests/achievements, health fields, home economics, library science, mathematics, military science, physical sciences, social sciences. *Creative arts/performance:* art/fine arts, creative writing, debating, journalism/publications, music, performing arts, theater/drama. *Special achievements/activities:* cheerleading/drum major, community service, leadership. *Special characteristics:* children of faculty/staff, children with a deceased or disabled parent, international students, out-of-state students.

LOANS ***Programs:*** Perkins, college/university, Federal Health Professions Student Loans.

WORK-STUDY Federal work-study jobs available. ***State or other work-study/employment:*** Part-time jobs available.

APPLYING FOR FINANCIAL AID ***Required financial aid forms:*** FAFSA, institution's own form.

CONTACT Ms. Teresa Smith, Director, Financial Aid, University of Louisiana at Monroe, 700 University Avenue, Monroe, LA 71209, 318-342-5320 or toll-free 800-372-5272 (in-state), 800-372-5127 (out-of-state). *Fax:* 318-342-3539. *E-mail:* tsmith@ulm.edu.

UNIVERSITY OF LOUISVILLE

Louisville, KY

Tuition & fees (KY res): $8424 **Average undergraduate aid package: $10,552**

ABOUT THE INSTITUTION State-supported, coed. 53 undergraduate majors. Federal methodology is used as a basis for awarding need-based institutional aid.

UNDERGRADUATE EXPENSES for 2010–11 ***Tuition, state resident:*** full-time $8424; part-time $351 per credit hour. ***Tuition, nonresident:*** full-time $20,424; part-time $851 per credit hour. Full-time tuition and fees vary according to reciprocity agreements. Part-time tuition and fees vary according to course load and reciprocity agreements. ***College room and board:*** $6602; ***Room only:*** $4272. Room and board charges vary according to board plan and housing facility. ***Payment plan:*** Installment.

FRESHMAN FINANCIAL AID (Fall 2010, est.) 2,070 applied for aid; of those 79% were deemed to have need. 99% of freshmen with need received aid; of those 25% had need fully met. ***Average percent of need met:*** 66% (excluding resources awarded to replace EFC). ***Average financial aid package:*** $11,172 (excluding resources awarded to replace EFC). 15% of all full-time freshmen had no need and received non-need-based gift aid.

UNDERGRADUATE FINANCIAL AID (Fall 2010, est.) 8,716 applied for aid; of those 84% were deemed to have need. 97% of undergraduates with need received aid; of those 20% had need fully met. ***Average percent of need met:*** 62% (excluding resources awarded to replace EFC). ***Average financial aid package:*** $10,552 (excluding resources awarded to replace EFC). 12% of all full-time undergraduates had no need and received non-need-based gift aid.

GIFT AID (NEED-BASED) ***Total amount:*** $49,853,836 (39% federal, 16% state, 34% institutional, 11% external sources). ***Receiving aid:*** Freshmen: 62% (1,565); all full-time undergraduates: 53% (6,397). ***Average award:*** Freshmen: $8626; Undergraduates: $7999. ***Scholarships, grants, and awards:*** Federal Pell, FSEOG, state, private, college/university gift aid from institutional funds.

GIFT AID (NON-NEED-BASED) ***Total amount:*** $23,040,378 (26% state, 59% institutional, 15% external sources). ***Receiving aid:*** Freshmen: 10% (260). Undergraduates: 6% (761). ***Average award:*** Freshmen: $7109. Undergraduates: $7111. ***Scholarships, grants, and awards by category:*** *Academic interests/achievement:* biological sciences, business, education, engineering/technologies, English, foreign languages, general academic interests/achievements, health fields, mathematics, military science, premedicine. *Creative arts/performance:* art/fine arts, creative writing, dance, debating, general creative arts/performance, music, theater/drama. *Special achievements/activities:* cheerleading/drum major, community service, general special achievements/activities, hobbies/interests, junior miss, leadership, memberships. *Special characteristics:* adult students, children and siblings of alumni, children of faculty/staff, children of union members/company employees, children with a deceased or disabled parent, ethnic background, general special characteristics, local/state students, members of minority groups, out-of-state students, previous college experience, veterans, veterans' children. ***Tuition waivers:*** Full or partial for employees or children of employees, senior citizens.

LOANS ***Student loans:*** $47,706,464 (76% need-based, 24% non-need-based). 47% of past graduating class borrowed through all loan programs. *Average indebtedness per student:* $18,713. ***Average need-based loan:*** Freshmen: $3239. Undergraduates: $4077. ***Parent loans:*** $4,251,625 (41% need-based, 59% non-need-based). ***Programs:*** Federal Direct (Subsidized and Unsubsidized Stafford, PLUS), Perkins, Federal Nursing.

WORK-STUDY ***Federal work-study:*** Total amount: $1,302,272; 536 jobs averaging $2358.

ATHLETIC AWARDS Total amount: $8,690,508 (38% need-based, 62% non-need-based).

APPLYING FOR FINANCIAL AID ***Required financial aid form:*** FAFSA. ***Financial aid deadline (priority):*** 3/15. ***Notification date:*** Continuous beginning 4/1. Students must reply by 5/1.

CONTACT Ms. Patricia O. Arauz, Director of Financial Aid, University of Louisville, 2301 South Third Street, Louisville, KY 40292-0001, 502-852-6145 or toll-free 800-334-8635 (out-of-state). *Fax:* 502-852-0182. *E-mail:* finaid@louisville.edu.

UNIVERSITY OF MAINE

Orono, ME

Tuition & fees (ME res): $10,168 **Average undergraduate aid package: $11,599**

ABOUT THE INSTITUTION State-supported, coed. 106 undergraduate majors. Federal methodology is used as a basis for awarding need-based institutional aid.

UNDERGRADUATE EXPENSES for 2010–11 ***Tuition, state resident:*** full-time $8010; part-time $267 per credit hour. ***Tuition, nonresident:*** full-time $23,040; part-time $768 per credit hour. ***Required fees:*** full-time $2158. Full-time tuition and fees vary according to course load and program. Part-time tuition and fees vary according to course load and program. ***College room and board:*** $8766. Room and board charges vary according to board plan and housing facility. ***Payment plan:*** Installment.

FRESHMAN FINANCIAL AID (Fall 2010, est.) 1,519 applied for aid; of those 83% were deemed to have need. 100% of freshmen with need received aid; of those 30% had need fully met. ***Average percent of need met:*** 77% (excluding resources awarded to replace EFC). ***Average financial aid package:*** $11,818 (excluding resources awarded to replace EFC). 10% of all full-time freshmen had no need and received non-need-based gift aid.

UNDERGRADUATE FINANCIAL AID (Fall 2010, est.) 7,023 applied for aid; of those 87% were deemed to have need. 100% of undergraduates with need received aid; of those 31% had need fully met. ***Average percent of need met:*** 76% (excluding resources awarded to replace EFC). ***Average financial aid package:*** $11,599 (excluding resources awarded to replace EFC). 8% of all full-time undergraduates had no need and received non-need-based gift aid.

GIFT AID (NEED-BASED) ***Total amount:*** $36,222,063 (44% federal, 4% state, 46% institutional, 6% external sources). ***Receiving aid:*** Freshmen: 64% (1,104); all full-time undergraduates: 54% (4,796). ***Average award:*** Freshmen: $8152; Undergraduates: $7370. ***Scholarships, grants, and awards:*** Federal Pell, FSEOG, state, private, college/university gift aid from institutional funds, Academic Competitiveness Grants, National SMART Grants.

GIFT AID (NON-NEED-BASED) ***Total amount:*** $3,949,170 (1% federal, 3% state, 71% institutional, 25% external sources). ***Receiving aid:*** Freshmen: 3% (50). Undergraduates: 2% (192). ***Average award:*** Freshmen: $1268. Undergraduates: $4617. ***Tuition waivers:*** Full or partial for employees or children of employees, senior citizens.

LOANS ***Student loans:*** $62,588,287 (76% need-based, 24% non-need-based). 75% of past graduating class borrowed through all loan programs. *Average indebtedness per student:* $29,143. ***Average need-based loan:*** Freshmen: $5676. Undergraduates: $6944. ***Parent loans:*** $5,858,169 (38% need-based, 62% non-need-based). ***Programs:*** Federal Direct (Subsidized and Unsubsidized Stafford, PLUS), Perkins, state, college/university, private loans.

WORK-STUDY ***Federal work-study:*** Total amount: $3,450,262; jobs available.

ATHLETIC AWARDS Total amount: $3,105,437 (37% need-based, 63% non-need-based).

APPLYING FOR FINANCIAL AID ***Required financial aid form:*** FAFSA. ***Financial aid deadline (priority):*** 3/1. ***Notification date:*** Continuous beginning 3/15. Students must reply by 5/1 or within 2 weeks of notification.

CONTACT Ms. Peggy L. Crawford, Director of Student Aid, University of Maine, 5781 Wingate Hall, Orono, ME 04469, 207-581-1324 or toll-free 877-486-2364. *Fax:* 207-581-3261. *E-mail:* pcrawf@maine.edu.

UNIVERSITY OF MAINE AT AUGUSTA

Augusta, ME

CONTACT Sherry McCollett, Director of Financial Aid, University of Maine at Augusta, 46 University Drive, Augusta, ME 04330-9410, 207-621-3455 or toll-free 877-862-1234 Ext. 3185 (in-state). *Fax:* 207-621-3116. *E-mail:* umafa@maine.edu.

UNIVERSITY OF MAINE AT FARMINGTON

Farmington, ME

CONTACT Mr. Ronald P. Milliken, Director of Financial Aid, University of Maine at Farmington, 224 Main Street, Farmington, ME 04938-1990, 207-778-7105. *Fax:* 207-778-8178. *E-mail:* milliken@maine.edu.

UNIVERSITY OF MAINE AT FORT KENT

Fort Kent, ME

Tuition & fees (ME res): $7163 **Average undergraduate aid package: $5400**

ABOUT THE INSTITUTION State-supported, coed. 25 undergraduate majors. Federal methodology is used as a basis for awarding need-based institutional aid.

UNDERGRADUATE EXPENSES for 2011–12 ***Tuition, state resident:*** full-time $6330; part-time $211 per credit. ***Tuition, nonresident:*** full-time $15,930; part-time $531 per credit. ***Required fees:*** full-time $833. ***College room and board:*** $7500; ***Room only:*** $4000. Room and board charges vary according to board plan and housing facility.

FRESHMAN FINANCIAL AID (Fall 2009) 111 applied for aid; of those 91% were deemed to have need. 100% of freshmen with need received aid; of those 86% had need fully met. ***Average percent of need met:*** 87% (excluding resources awarded to replace EFC). ***Average financial aid package:*** $6000 (excluding resources awarded to replace EFC). 6% of all full-time freshmen had no need and received non-need-based gift aid.

UNDERGRADUATE FINANCIAL AID (Fall 2009) 525 applied for aid; of those 84% were deemed to have need. 100% of undergraduates with need received aid; of those 81% had need fully met. ***Average percent of need met:*** 82% (excluding resources awarded to replace EFC). ***Average financial aid package:*** $5400 (excluding resources awarded to replace EFC). 6% of all full-time undergraduates had no need and received non-need-based gift aid.

GIFT AID (NEED-BASED) ***Total amount:*** $2,357,500 (87% federal, 13% state). ***Receiving aid:*** Freshmen: 36% (55); all full-time undergraduates: 45% (258). ***Average award:*** Freshmen: $2600; Undergraduates: $2800. ***Scholarships, grants, and awards:*** Federal Pell, FSEOG, state, private, college/university gift aid from institutional funds, Federal Nursing.

GIFT AID (NON-NEED-BASED) ***Total amount:*** $588,240 (88% institutional, 12% external sources). ***Receiving aid:*** Freshmen: 56% (87). Undergraduates: 70% (400). ***Average award:*** Freshmen: $525. Undergraduates: $900. ***Scholarships, grants, and awards by category:*** *Academic interests/achievement:* biological sciences, business, communication, computer science, education, English, foreign languages, general academic interests/achievements, health fields, humanities, mathematics, social sciences. *Creative arts/performance:* general creative arts/performance, performing arts. *Special achievements/activities:* general special achievements/activities. *Special characteristics:* adult students, children of faculty/staff, general special characteristics, international students, members of minority groups.

LOANS ***Student loans:*** $2,280,000 (54% need-based, 46% non-need-based). ***Average need-based loan:*** Freshmen: $2500. Undergraduates: $2400. ***Parent loans:*** $110,000 (100% non-need-based). ***Programs:*** Federal Direct (Subsidized and Unsubsidized Stafford, PLUS), Perkins, Federal Nursing, state, college/university.

WORK-STUDY ***Federal work-study:*** Total amount: $600,000; jobs available. ***State or other work-study/employment:*** Part-time jobs available.

ATHLETIC AWARDS Total amount: $30,000 (100% need-based).

APPLYING FOR FINANCIAL AID ***Required financial aid forms:*** FAFSA, institution's own form, CSS Financial Aid PROFILE, state aid form. ***Financial aid deadline (priority):*** 3/1. ***Notification date:*** Continuous beginning 3/1.

CONTACT Ellen Cost, Director of Financial Aid, University of Maine at Fort Kent, 23 University Drive, Fort Kent, ME 04743-1292, 207-834-7606 or toll-free 888-TRY-UMFK. *Fax:* 207-834-7841. *E-mail:* ecost@maine.edu.

UNIVERSITY OF MAINE AT MACHIAS

Machias, ME

CONTACT Ms. Stephanie Larrabee, Director of Financial Aid, University of Maine at Machias, 9 O'Brien Avenue, Machias, ME 04654, 207-255-1203 or toll-free 888-GOTOUMM (in-state), 888-468-6866 (out-of-state). *Fax:* 207-255-4864.

UNIVERSITY OF MAINE AT PRESQUE ISLE

Presque Isle, ME

Tuition & fees (ME res): $7235 **Average undergraduate aid package: $9876**

ABOUT THE INSTITUTION State-supported, coed. 28 undergraduate majors. Federal methodology is used as a basis for awarding need-based institutional aid.

UNDERGRADUATE EXPENSES for 2011–12 ***Tuition, state resident:*** full-time $6330; part-time $211 per credit. ***Tuition, nonresident:*** full-time $15,930; part-time $531 per credit. ***Required fees:*** full-time $905; $18 per credit. Full-time tuition and fees vary according to course load and reciprocity agreements. Part-time tuition and fees vary according to course load and reciprocity agreements. ***College room and board:*** $7046; ***Room only:*** $3940. Room and board charges vary according to board plan and housing facility. ***Payment plans:*** Installment, deferred payment.

FRESHMAN FINANCIAL AID (Fall 2010, est.) 181 applied for aid; of those 92% were deemed to have need. 100% of freshmen with need received aid; of those 30% had need fully met. ***Average percent of need met:*** 76% (excluding resources awarded to replace EFC). ***Average financial aid package:*** $10,195 (excluding resources awarded to replace EFC).

UNDERGRADUATE FINANCIAL AID (Fall 2010, est.) 730 applied for aid; of those 91% were deemed to have need. 100% of undergraduates with need received aid; of those 30% had need fully met. ***Average percent of need met:*** 76% (excluding resources awarded to replace EFC). ***Average financial aid package:*** $9876 (excluding resources awarded to replace EFC).

GIFT AID (NEED-BASED) ***Total amount:*** $4,225,158 (65% federal, 9% state, 15% institutional, 11% external sources). ***Receiving aid:*** Freshmen: 76% (153); all full-time undergraduates: 64% (615). ***Average award:*** Freshmen: $5180; Undergraduates: $5002. ***Scholarships, grants, and awards:*** Federal Pell, FSEOG, state, private, college/university gift aid from institutional funds.

GIFT AID (NON-NEED-BASED) ***Total amount:*** $364,694 (75% institutional, 25% external sources). ***Receiving aid:*** Freshmen: 52% (103). Undergraduates: 28% (272). ***Average award:*** Freshmen: $3321. Undergraduates: $4054. ***Scholarships, grants, and awards by category:*** *Academic interests/achievement:* general academic interests/achievements. *Creative arts/performance:* art/fine arts. *Special achievements/activities:* community service. *Special characteristics:* children of faculty/staff, ethnic background, international students, veterans' children. ***Tuition waivers:*** Full or partial for minority students, employees or children of employees, senior citizens.

LOANS ***Student loans:*** $2,627,055 (100% need-based). 59% of past graduating class borrowed through all loan programs. *Average indebtedness per student:* $18,272. ***Average need-based loan:*** Freshmen: $4277. Undergraduates: $4685. ***Parent loans:*** $107,926 (18% need-based, 82% non-need-based). ***Programs:*** Federal Direct (Subsidized and Unsubsidized Stafford, PLUS), Perkins, state, college/university.

WORK-STUDY ***Federal work-study:*** Total amount: $609,451; jobs available.

APPLYING FOR FINANCIAL AID ***Required financial aid form:*** FAFSA. ***Financial aid deadline (priority):*** 4/1. ***Notification date:*** Continuous. Students must reply within 2 weeks of notification.

CONTACT Christopher A.R. Bell, Director of Financial Aid, University of Maine at Presque Isle, 181 Main Street, Presque Isle, ME 04769-2888, 207-768-9511. *Fax:* 207-768-9608. *E-mail:* chris.bell@umpi.edu.

UNIVERSITY OF MANAGEMENT AND TECHNOLOGY

Arlington, VA

CONTACT Financial Aid Office, University of Management and Technology, 1901 North Fort Myer Drive, Arlington, VA 22209, 703-516-0035 or toll-free 800-924-4885 (in-state). *E-mail:* info@umtweb.edu.

UNIVERSITY OF MARY

Bismarck, ND

Tuition & fees: $13,126 **Average undergraduate aid package: N/A**

ABOUT THE INSTITUTION Independent Roman Catholic, coed. 46 undergraduate majors. Federal methodology is used as a basis for awarding need-based institutional aid.

UNDERGRADUATE EXPENSES for 2010–11 ***Comprehensive fee:*** $18,306 includes full-time tuition ($12,800), mandatory fees ($326), and room and board ($5180). ***College room only:*** $2380. Full-time tuition and fees vary according to course load, degree level, and program. Room and board charges vary according to board plan and housing facility. ***Part-time tuition:*** $400 per credit hour. Part-time tuition and fees vary according to course load, degree level, and program. ***Payment plan:*** Installment.

FRESHMAN FINANCIAL AID (Fall 2010, est.) 317 applied for aid; of those 81% were deemed to have need. 100% of freshmen with need received aid; of those 30% had need fully met. ***Average percent of need met:*** 78% (excluding resources awarded to replace EFC). ***Average financial aid package:*** $11,787 (excluding resources awarded to replace EFC). 78% of all full-time freshmen had no need and received non-need-based gift aid.

GIFT AID (NEED-BASED) ***Total amount:*** $9,761,935 (30% federal, 8% state, 55% institutional, 7% external sources). ***Receiving aid:*** Freshmen: 46% (167). ***Average award:*** Freshmen: $4242. ***Scholarships, grants, and awards:*** Federal Pell, FSEOG, state, private, college/university gift aid from institutional funds, TEACH Grants.

GIFT AID (NON-NEED-BASED) ***Receiving aid:*** Freshmen: 71% (257). ***Average award:*** Freshmen: $4453. ***Scholarships, grants, and awards by category:*** *Academic interests/achievement:* 1,210 awards ($3,920,966 total): general academic interests/achievements. *Creative arts/performance:* 68 awards ($108,826 total): music. *Special achievements/activities:* 222 awards ($1,697,975 total): general special achievements/activities. *Special characteristics:* 351 awards ($988,345 total): children of faculty/staff, general special characteristics, local/state students, religious affiliation, veterans. ***Tuition waivers:*** Full or partial for employees or children of employees, senior citizens.

LOANS ***Student loans:*** $11,832,833 (100% need-based). 79% of past graduating class borrowed through all loan programs. *Average indebtedness per student:*

$25,287. ***Average need-based loan:*** Freshmen: $3422. ***Parent loans:*** $415,678 (100% need-based). ***Programs:*** Federal Direct (Subsidized and Unsubsidized Stafford, PLUS), Perkins, Federal Nursing, private loans.

WORK-STUDY ***Federal work-study:*** Total amount: $244,662; 169 jobs averaging $1447. ***State or other work-study/employment:*** Total amount: $118,866 (100% need-based). 59 part-time jobs averaging $2015.

ATHLETIC AWARDS Total amount: $1,580,370 (100% need-based).

APPLYING FOR FINANCIAL AID ***Financial aid deadline (priority):*** 3/15. ***Notification date:*** Continuous beginning 2/15. Students must reply within 2 weeks of notification.

CONTACT Brenda Zastoupil, Financial Assistance Director, University of Mary, 7500 University Drive, Bismarck, ND 58504-9652, 701-355-8244 or toll-free 800-288-6279. *Fax:* 701-255-7687. *E-mail:* brendaz@umary.edu.

UNIVERSITY OF MARY HARDIN-BAYLOR

Belton, TX

Tuition & fees: $23,050 **Average undergraduate aid package: $13,642**

ABOUT THE INSTITUTION Independent Southern Baptist, coed. 53 undergraduate majors. Federal methodology is used as a basis for awarding need-based institutional aid.

UNDERGRADUATE EXPENSES for 2011–12 ***Comprehensive fee:*** $29,271 includes full-time tuition ($20,700), mandatory fees ($2350), and room and board ($6221). Full-time tuition and fees vary according to course load. Room and board charges vary according to board plan and housing facility. Part-time tuition and fees vary according to course load. ***Payment plan:*** Installment.

FRESHMAN FINANCIAL AID (Fall 2010, est.) 516 applied for aid; of those 89% were deemed to have need. 100% of freshmen with need received aid; of those 11% had need fully met. ***Average percent of need met:*** 63% (excluding resources awarded to replace EFC). ***Average financial aid package:*** $13,918 (excluding resources awarded to replace EFC). 16% of all full-time freshmen had no need and received non-need-based gift aid.

UNDERGRADUATE FINANCIAL AID (Fall 2010, est.) 2,195 applied for aid; of those 91% were deemed to have need. 100% of undergraduates with need received aid; of those 9% had need fully met. ***Average percent of need met:*** 60% (excluding resources awarded to replace EFC). ***Average financial aid package:*** $13,642 (excluding resources awarded to replace EFC). 13% of all full-time undergraduates had no need and received non-need-based gift aid.

GIFT AID (NEED-BASED) ***Total amount:*** $19,169,664 (26% federal, 20% state, 54% institutional). ***Receiving aid:*** Freshmen: 79% (456); all full-time undergraduates: 83% (1,975). ***Average award:*** Freshmen: $10,955; Undergraduates: $9666. ***Scholarships, grants, and awards:*** Federal Pell, FSEOG, state, private, college/university gift aid from institutional funds.

GIFT AID (NON-NEED-BASED) ***Total amount:*** $3,290,126 (1% state, 67% institutional, 32% external sources). ***Receiving aid:*** Freshmen: 6% (37). Undergraduates: 4% (102). ***Average award:*** Freshmen: $5435. Undergraduates: $5656. ***Scholarships, grants, and awards by category:*** *Academic interests/achievement:* 170 awards ($415,203 total): biological sciences, business, communication, computer science, education, English, foreign languages, general academic interests/achievements, health fields, humanities, international studies, mathematics, physical sciences, premedicine, religion/biblical studies, social sciences. *Creative arts/performance:* 108 awards ($219,572 total): art/fine arts, music. *Special achievements/activities:* 389 awards ($1,203,500 total): cheerleading/drum major, community service, leadership, religious involvement. *Special characteristics:* 181 awards ($1,256,301 total): children and siblings of alumni, children of faculty/staff, ethnic background, handicapped students, international students, local/state students, members of minority groups, out-of-state students, relatives of clergy, religious affiliation. ***Tuition waivers:*** Full or partial for employees or children of employees.

LOANS ***Student loans:*** $16,111,131 (42% need-based, 58% non-need-based). 75% of past graduating class borrowed through all loan programs. *Average indebtedness per student:* $17,500. ***Average need-based loan:*** Freshmen: $3311. Undergraduates: $4535. ***Parent loans:*** $6,575,075 (100% non-need-based). ***Programs:*** Federal Direct (Subsidized and Unsubsidized Stafford, PLUS), Perkins, state.

WORK-STUDY ***Federal work-study:*** Total amount: $553,968; 234 jobs averaging $2390. ***State or other work-study/employment:*** Total amount: $625,163 (30% need-based, 70% non-need-based). 300 part-time jobs averaging $2324.

APPLYING FOR FINANCIAL AID ***Required financial aid form:*** FAFSA. ***Financial aid deadline (priority):*** 3/1. ***Notification date:*** Continuous beginning 2/1. Students must reply within 2 weeks of notification.

CONTACT Mr. David Orsag, Associate Director of Financial Aid, University of Mary Hardin-Baylor, PO Box 8080, Belton, TX 76513, 254-295-4517 or toll-free 800-727-8642. *Fax:* 254-295-5049. *E-mail:* dorsag@umhb.edu.

UNIVERSITY OF MARYLAND, BALTIMORE COUNTY

Baltimore, MD

Tuition & fees (MD res): $9171 **Average undergraduate aid package: $10,615**

ABOUT THE INSTITUTION State-supported, coed. 43 undergraduate majors. Federal methodology is used as a basis for awarding need-based institutional aid.

UNDERGRADUATE EXPENSES for 2011–12 ***One-time required fee:*** $125. ***Tuition, state resident:*** full-time $6679; part-time $278 per credit hour. ***Tuition, nonresident:*** full-time $16,616; part-time $691 per credit hour. ***Required fees:*** full-time $2492; $111 per credit hour. Full-time tuition and fees vary according to location and program. Part-time tuition and fees vary according to location and program. ***College room and board:*** $9620; ***Room only:*** $5860. Room and board charges vary according to board plan and housing facility. ***Payment plan:*** Installment.

FRESHMAN FINANCIAL AID (Fall 2010, est.) 1,082 applied for aid; of those 68% were deemed to have need. 90% of freshmen with need received aid; of those 20% had need fully met. ***Average percent of need met:*** 60% (excluding resources awarded to replace EFC). ***Average financial aid package:*** $10,901 (excluding resources awarded to replace EFC). 29% of all full-time freshmen had no need and received non-need-based gift aid.

UNDERGRADUATE FINANCIAL AID (Fall 2010, est.) 5,655 applied for aid; of those 79% were deemed to have need. 94% of undergraduates with need received aid; of those 26% had need fully met. ***Average percent of need met:*** 60% (excluding resources awarded to replace EFC). ***Average financial aid package:*** $10,615 (excluding resources awarded to replace EFC). 32% of all full-time undergraduates had no need and received non-need-based gift aid.

GIFT AID (NEED-BASED) ***Total amount:*** $26,625,341 (46% federal, 22% state, 29% institutional, 3% external sources). ***Receiving aid:*** Freshmen: 36% (538); all full-time undergraduates: 38% (3,305). ***Average award:*** Freshmen: $8047; Undergraduates: $7758. ***Scholarships, grants, and awards:*** Federal Pell, FSEOG, state, private, college/university gift aid from institutional funds.

GIFT AID (NON-NEED-BASED) ***Total amount:*** $18,336,355 (2% state, 91% institutional, 7% external sources). ***Receiving aid:*** Freshmen: 5% (78). Undergraduates: 3% (255). ***Average award:*** Freshmen: $12,183. Undergraduates: $7755. ***Scholarships, grants, and awards by category:*** *Academic interests/achievement:* 2,191 awards ($13,674,473 total): biological sciences, computer science, education, engineering/technologies, English, foreign languages, general academic interests/achievements, humanities, mathematics, physical sciences, social sciences. *Creative arts/performance:* 47 awards ($60,750 total): art/fine arts, cinema/film/broadcasting, creative writing, dance, music, performing arts, theater/drama. ***Tuition waivers:*** Full or partial for employees or children of employees, senior citizens.

LOANS ***Student loans:*** $35,058,600 (40% need-based, 60% non-need-based). 44% of past graduating class borrowed through all loan programs. *Average indebtedness per student:* $19,594. ***Average need-based loan:*** Freshmen: $3472. Undergraduates: $4271. ***Parent loans:*** $5,111,000 (100% non-need-based). ***Programs:*** Federal Direct (Subsidized and Unsubsidized Stafford, PLUS), Perkins.

WORK-STUDY ***Federal work-study:*** Total amount: $190,370; jobs available. ***State or other work-study/employment:*** Total amount: $785,400 (54% need-based, 46% non-need-based). Part-time jobs available.

ATHLETIC AWARDS Total amount: $4,165,103 (14% need-based, 86% non-need-based).

APPLYING FOR FINANCIAL AID ***Required financial aid form:*** FAFSA. ***Financial aid deadline (priority):*** 2/14. ***Notification date:*** Continuous beginning 3/15.

CONTACT Stephanie Johnson, Director, University of Maryland, Baltimore County, 1000 Hilltop Circle, Baltimore, MD 21250, 410-455-2387 or toll-free 800-UMBC-4U2 (in-state), 800-862-2402 (out-of-state). *Fax:* 410-455-1288. *E-mail:* finaid@umbc.edu.

UNIVERSITY OF MARYLAND, COLLEGE PARK

College Park, MD

Tuition & fees (MD res): $8416 Average undergraduate aid package: $9829

ABOUT THE INSTITUTION State-supported, coed. 96 undergraduate majors. Federal methodology is used as a basis for awarding need-based institutional aid.

UNDERGRADUATE EXPENSES for 2010–11 ***Tuition, state resident:*** full-time $6763; part-time $282 per credit hour. ***Tuition, nonresident:*** full-time $23,178; part-time $966 per credit hour. ***Required fees:*** full-time $1653; $380.30 per term. Part-time tuition and fees vary according to course load. ***College room and board:*** $9599; ***Room only:*** $5714. Room and board charges vary according to board plan. ***Payment plans:*** Installment, deferred payment.

FRESHMAN FINANCIAL AID (Fall 2009) 3,153 applied for aid; of those 55% were deemed to have need. 92% of freshmen with need received aid; of those 15% had need fully met. ***Average percent of need met:*** 64% (excluding resources awarded to replace EFC). ***Average financial aid package:*** $10,396 (excluding resources awarded to replace EFC). 18% of all full-time freshmen had no need and received non-need-based gift aid.

UNDERGRADUATE FINANCIAL AID (Fall 2009) 14,294 applied for aid; of those 73% were deemed to have need. 92% of undergraduates with need received aid; of those 7% had need fully met. ***Average percent of need met:*** 58% (excluding resources awarded to replace EFC). ***Average financial aid package:*** $9829 (excluding resources awarded to replace EFC). 11% of all full-time undergraduates had no need and received non-need-based gift aid.

GIFT AID (NEED-BASED) ***Total amount:*** $45,266,809 (47% federal, 26% state, 27% institutional). ***Receiving aid:*** Freshmen: 21% (889); all full-time undergraduates: 26% (6,373). ***Average award:*** Freshmen: $7812; Undergraduates: $6959. ***Scholarships, grants, and awards:*** Federal Pell, FSEOG, state, private, college/university gift aid from institutional funds.

GIFT AID (NON-NEED-BASED) ***Total amount:*** $42,069,959 (11% state, 65% institutional, 24% external sources). ***Receiving aid:*** Freshmen: 23% (975). Undergraduates: 16% (4,032). ***Average award:*** Freshmen: $6136. Undergraduates: $6383. ***Scholarships, grants, and awards by category:*** *Academic interests/achievement:* 3,821 awards ($18,562,060 total): agriculture, architecture, biological sciences, business, communication, computer science, education, engineering/technologies, English, foreign languages, general academic interests/achievements, health fields, humanities, international studies, library science, mathematics, military science, physical sciences, premedicine, social sciences. *Creative arts/performance:* 68 awards ($459,586 total): applied art and design, art/fine arts, dance, music, performing arts, theater/drama. *Special achievements/activities:* 77 awards ($349,390 total): cheerleading/drum major. *Special characteristics:* 1,583 awards ($6,228,847 total): adult students, out-of-state students. ***Tuition waivers:*** Full or partial for employees or children of employees.

LOANS ***Student loans:*** $77,566,902 (37% need-based, 63% non-need-based). 43% of past graduating class borrowed through all loan programs. *Average indebtedness per student:* $22,696. ***Average need-based loan:*** Freshmen: $3497. Undergraduates: $4321. ***Parent loans:*** $21,080,140 (41% need-based, 59% non-need-based). ***Programs:*** Federal Direct (Subsidized and Unsubsidized Stafford, PLUS), Perkins, private loans.

WORK-STUDY ***Federal work-study:*** Total amount: $818,647; 624 jobs averaging $1300.

ATHLETIC AWARDS Total amount: $11,048,578 (100% non-need-based).

APPLYING FOR FINANCIAL AID ***Required financial aid form:*** FAFSA. ***Financial aid deadline (priority):*** 2/15. ***Notification date:*** Continuous beginning 4/1.

CONTACT Sarah Bauder, Assistant Vice President for Enrollment Services and Financial Aid, University of Maryland, College Park, 0102 Lee Building, College Park, MD 20742, 301-314-8279 or toll-free 800-422-5867. *Fax:* 301-314-9587. *E-mail:* sbauder@umd.edu.

UNIVERSITY OF MARYLAND EASTERN SHORE

Princess Anne, MD

CONTACT Mr. James W. Kellam, Director of Financial Aid, University of Maryland Eastern Shore, Backbone Road, Princess Anne, MD 21853-1299, 410-651-6172. *Fax:* 410-651-7670. *E-mail:* jwkellam@umes.edu.

UNIVERSITY OF MARYLAND UNIVERSITY COLLEGE

Adelphi, MD

Tuition & fees (MD res): $6000 Average undergraduate aid package: $7206

ABOUT THE INSTITUTION State-supported, coed. 31 undergraduate majors. Federal methodology is used as a basis for awarding need-based institutional aid.

UNDERGRADUATE EXPENSES for 2010–11 ***Tuition, state resident:*** full-time $5688; part-time $237 per credit hour. ***Tuition, nonresident:*** full-time $11,976; part-time $499 per credit hour. ***Required fees:*** full-time $312; $13 per credit hour. ***Payment plan:*** Installment.

FRESHMAN FINANCIAL AID (Fall 2009) 112 applied for aid; of those 95% were deemed to have need. 86% of freshmen with need received aid. ***Average percent of need met:*** 25% (excluding resources awarded to replace EFC). ***Average financial aid package:*** $6313 (excluding resources awarded to replace EFC).

UNDERGRADUATE FINANCIAL AID (Fall 2009) 2,303 applied for aid; of those 95% were deemed to have need. 91% of undergraduates with need received aid; of those 1% had need fully met. ***Average percent of need met:*** 28% (excluding resources awarded to replace EFC). ***Average financial aid package:*** $7206 (excluding resources awarded to replace EFC).

GIFT AID (NEED-BASED) ***Total amount:*** $16,952,414 (80% federal, 7% state, 12% institutional, 1% external sources). ***Receiving aid:*** Freshmen: 53% (76); all full-time undergraduates: 36% (1,194). ***Average award:*** Freshmen: $3917; Undergraduates: $4578. ***Scholarships, grants, and awards:*** Federal Pell, FSEOG, state, private, college/university gift aid from institutional funds.

GIFT AID (NON-NEED-BASED) ***Total amount:*** $2,038,238 (6% state, 74% institutional, 20% external sources). ***Receiving aid:*** Freshmen: 4% (6). Undergraduates: 9% (298). ***Scholarships, grants, and awards by category:*** *Academic interests/achievement:* general academic interests/achievements. *Special achievements/activities:* general special achievements/activities. ***Tuition waivers:*** Full or partial for employees or children of employees, senior citizens.

LOANS ***Student loans:*** $78,943,349 (40% need-based, 60% non-need-based). ***Average need-based loan:*** Freshmen: $3124. Undergraduates: $4269. ***Parent loans:*** $144,367 (100% non-need-based). ***Programs:*** Federal Direct (Subsidized and Unsubsidized Stafford, PLUS), Perkins.

WORK-STUDY ***Federal work-study:*** Total amount: $485,332; jobs available. ***State or other work-study/employment:*** Total amount: $241,024 (100% non-need-based). Part-time jobs available.

APPLYING FOR FINANCIAL AID ***Required financial aid form:*** FAFSA. ***Financial aid deadline (priority):*** 6/1. ***Notification date:*** Continuous beginning 5/1. Students must reply within 2 weeks of notification.

CONTACT Cheryl Storie, Associate Vice President of Financial Aid, University of Maryland University College, 3501 University Boulevard East, Adelphi, MD 20783, 301-985-7847 or toll-free 800-888-8682 (in-state). *Fax:* 301-985-7462. *E-mail:* finaid@umuc.edu.

UNIVERSITY OF MARY WASHINGTON

Fredericksburg, VA

Tuition & fees (VA res): $8800 Average undergraduate aid package: $8200

ABOUT THE INSTITUTION State-supported, coed. 33 undergraduate majors. Federal methodology is used as a basis for awarding need-based institutional aid.

UNDERGRADUATE EXPENSES for 2011–12 ***One-time required fee:*** $75. ***Tuition, state resident:*** full-time $4460; part-time $195 per credit hour. ***Tuition, nonresident:*** full-time $16,190; part-time $740 per credit hour. ***Required fees:*** full-time $4340; $110 per credit hour or $30 per term. Part-time tuition and fees vary according to course load and location. ***College room and board:*** $8900; ***Room only:*** $5350. Room and board charges vary according to board plan and housing facility. ***Payment plan:*** Installment.

FRESHMAN FINANCIAL AID (Fall 2009) 705 applied for aid; of those 54% were deemed to have need. 87% of freshmen with need received aid; of those 12% had need fully met. ***Average percent of need met:*** 52% (excluding resources awarded to replace EFC). ***Average financial aid package:*** $8370 (excluding resources awarded to replace EFC). 8% of all full-time freshmen had no need and received non-need-based gift aid.

UNDERGRADUATE FINANCIAL AID (Fall 2009) 2,150 applied for aid; of those 63% were deemed to have need. 91% of undergraduates with need received aid; of those 15% had need fully met. ***Average percent of need met:*** 53% (excluding resources awarded to replace EFC). ***Average financial aid package:*** $8200 (excluding resources awarded to replace EFC). 9% of all full-time undergraduates had no need and received non-need-based gift aid.

GIFT AID (NEED-BASED) ***Total amount:*** $4,798,000 (56% federal, 31% state, 13% institutional). ***Receiving aid:*** Freshmen: 19% (180); all full-time undergraduates: 18% (685). ***Average award:*** Freshmen: $7200; Undergraduates: $6500. ***Scholarships, grants, and awards:*** Federal Pell, FSEOG, state, private, college/university gift aid from institutional funds.

GIFT AID (NON-NEED-BASED) ***Total amount:*** $2,640,000 (8% federal, 65% institutional, 27% external sources). ***Receiving aid:*** Freshmen: 21% (195). Undergraduates: 10% (395). ***Average award:*** Freshmen: $2300. Undergraduates: $2400. ***Scholarships, grants, and awards by category:*** *Academic interests/achievement:* 750 awards ($1,250,000 total): biological sciences, business, computer science, education, English, foreign languages, general academic interests/achievements, humanities, international studies, mathematics, physical sciences, religion/biblical studies, social sciences. *Creative arts/performance:* 60 awards ($120,000 total): art/fine arts, dance, journalism/publications, music, theater/drama. *Special achievements/activities:* 3 awards ($18,000 total): leadership. *Special characteristics:* 15 awards ($35,000 total): adult students, children and siblings of alumni, children of faculty/staff, local/state students. ***Tuition waivers:*** Full or partial for senior citizens.

LOANS ***Student loans:*** $13,800,000 (38% need-based, 62% non-need-based). 57% of past graduating class borrowed through all loan programs. *Average indebtedness per student:* $16,000. ***Average need-based loan:*** Freshmen: $3380. Undergraduates: $4100. ***Parent loans:*** $3,600,000 (100% non-need-based). ***Programs:*** Federal Direct (Subsidized and Unsubsidized Stafford, PLUS), Perkins.

WORK-STUDY ***Federal work-study:*** Total amount: $47,000; 25 jobs averaging $1760. ***State or other work-study/employment:*** Total amount: $1,400,000 (100% non-need-based). 750 part-time jobs averaging $1820.

APPLYING FOR FINANCIAL AID ***Required financial aid forms:*** FAFSA, UMW scholarship application form. ***Financial aid deadline:*** 5/15 (priority: 3/1). ***Notification date:*** 4/15. Students must reply by 5/1 or within 2 weeks of notification.

CONTACT Ms. Debra J. Harber, Director of Financial Aid, University of Mary Washington, 1301 College Avenue, Fredericksburg, VA 22401-5358, 540-654-2468 or toll-free 800-468-5614. *Fax:* 540-654-1858. *E-mail:* dharber@umw.edu.

UNIVERSITY OF MASSACHUSETTS AMHERST

Amherst, MA

Tuition & fees (MA res): $11,732 Average undergraduate aid package: $14,604

ABOUT THE INSTITUTION State-supported, coed. 84 undergraduate majors. Federal methodology is used as a basis for awarding need-based institutional aid.

UNDERGRADUATE EXPENSES for 2010–11 ***One-time required fee:*** $185. ***Tuition, state resident:*** full-time $1714; part-time $71.50 per credit. ***Tuition, nonresident:*** full-time $9937; part-time $414 per credit. ***Required fees:*** full-time $10,018. Full-time tuition and fees vary according to class time, course load, degree level, location, program, reciprocity agreements, and student level. Part-time tuition and fees vary according to class time, course load, degree level, location, program, reciprocity agreements, and student level. ***College room and board:*** $9339; ***Room only:*** $4672. Room and board charges vary according to board plan and housing facility. ***Payment plan:*** Installment.

FRESHMAN FINANCIAL AID (Fall 2009) 3,700 applied for aid; of those 64% were deemed to have need. 97% of freshmen with need received aid; of those 24% had need fully met. ***Average percent of need met:*** 86% (excluding resources awarded to replace EFC). ***Average financial aid package:*** $13,844 (excluding resources awarded to replace EFC). 5% of all full-time freshmen had no need and received non-need-based gift aid.

UNDERGRADUATE FINANCIAL AID (Fall 2009) 15,396 applied for aid; of those 72% were deemed to have need. 98% of undergraduates with need received aid; of those 27% had need fully met. ***Average percent of need met:*** 88% (excluding resources awarded to replace EFC). ***Average financial aid package:*** $14,604 (excluding resources awarded to replace EFC). 5% of all full-time undergraduates had no need and received non-need-based gift aid.

GIFT AID (NEED-BASED) ***Total amount:*** $73,953,394 (34% federal, 9% state, 49% institutional, 8% external sources). ***Receiving aid:*** Freshmen: 52% (2,147); all full-time undergraduates: 53% (10,197). ***Average award:*** Freshmen: $8980; Undergraduates: $8861. ***Scholarships, grants, and awards:*** Federal Pell, FSEOG, state, private, college/university gift aid from institutional funds.

GIFT AID (NON-NEED-BASED) ***Total amount:*** $9,447,634 (1% federal, 2% state, 35% institutional, 62% external sources). ***Receiving aid:*** Freshmen: 5% (215). Undergraduates: 5% (953). ***Average award:*** Freshmen: $2223. Undergraduates: $2805. ***Scholarships, grants, and awards by category:*** *Academic interests/achievement:* agriculture, architecture, biological sciences, business, communication, computer science, education, engineering/technologies, English, health fields, humanities, mathematics, military science, physical sciences, premedicine, social sciences. *Creative arts/performance:* art/fine arts, dance, journalism/publications, music, theater/drama. *Special achievements/activities:* cheerleading/drum major, general special achievements/activities, leadership. *Special characteristics:* children and siblings of alumni, children of faculty/staff, handicapped students, veterans. ***Tuition waivers:*** Full or partial for employees or children of employees, senior citizens.

LOANS ***Student loans:*** $112,363,478 (51% need-based, 49% non-need-based). 68% of past graduating class borrowed through all loan programs. *Average indebtedness per student:* $25,420. ***Average need-based loan:*** Freshmen: $3540. Undergraduates: $4385. ***Parent loans:*** $29,669,199 (20% need-based, 80% non-need-based). ***Programs:*** Federal Direct (Subsidized and Unsubsidized Stafford, PLUS), Perkins.

WORK-STUDY ***Federal work-study:*** Total amount: $6,772,276; 5,636 jobs averaging $1229.

ATHLETIC AWARDS Total amount: $6,120,872 (34% need-based, 66% non-need-based).

APPLYING FOR FINANCIAL AID ***Required financial aid form:*** FAFSA. ***Financial aid deadline (priority):*** 3/1. ***Notification date:*** Continuous beginning 3/15.

CONTACT Office of Financial Aid Services, University of Massachusetts Amherst, 255 Whitmore Administration Building, Amherst, MA 01003, 413-545-0801. *Fax:* 413-545-1700.

UNIVERSITY OF MASSACHUSETTS BOSTON

Boston, MA

Tuition & fees (MA res): $10,611 Average undergraduate aid package: $13,966

ABOUT THE INSTITUTION State-supported, coed. 37 undergraduate majors. Federal methodology is used as a basis for awarding need-based institutional aid.

UNDERGRADUATE EXPENSES for 2010–11 ***Tuition, state resident:*** full-time $1714; part-time $71.50 per credit hour. ***Tuition, nonresident:*** full-time $9758; part-time $71.50 per credit hour. ***Required fees:*** full-time $8897; $370 per credit hour. Full-time tuition and fees vary according to class time, course load, program, reciprocity agreements, and student level. Part-time tuition and fees vary according to class time, course load, program, reciprocity agreements, and student level. ***Payment plan:*** Installment.

FRESHMAN FINANCIAL AID (Fall 2009) 816 applied for aid; of those 78% were deemed to have need. 100% of freshmen with need received aid; of those 62% had need fully met. ***Average percent of need met:*** 90% (excluding resources awarded to replace EFC). ***Average financial aid package:*** $12,185 (excluding resources awarded to replace EFC). 18% of all full-time freshmen had no need and received non-need-based gift aid.

UNDERGRADUATE FINANCIAL AID (Fall 2009) 5,704 applied for aid; of those 86% were deemed to have need. 100% of undergraduates with need received aid; of those 67% had need fully met. ***Average percent of need met:*** 93% (excluding resources awarded to replace EFC). ***Average financial aid package:*** $13,966 (excluding resources awarded to replace EFC). 10% of all full-time undergraduates had no need and received non-need-based gift aid.

GIFT AID (NEED-BASED) ***Total amount:*** $35,794,335 (46% federal, 12% state, 39% institutional, 3% external sources). ***Receiving aid:*** Freshmen: 66% (616); all full-time undergraduates: 65% (4,836). ***Average award:*** Freshmen: $7248; Undergraduates: $7059. ***Scholarships, grants, and awards:*** Federal Pell, FSEOG, state, private, college/university gift aid from institutional funds, Academic Competitiveness Grants, National SMART Grants, TEACH Grants.

GIFT AID (NON-NEED-BASED) ***Total amount:*** $4,679,385 (1% federal, 1% state, 91% institutional, 7% external sources). ***Receiving aid:*** Freshmen: 3%

(28). Undergraduates: 2% (126). ***Average award:*** Freshmen: $2526. Undergraduates: $2114. ***Scholarships, grants, and awards by category:*** *Academic interests/achievement:* general academic interests/achievements, health fields. *Special achievements/activities:* general special achievements/activities, leadership. *Special characteristics:* adult students, children of faculty/staff, children of union members/company employees, first-generation college students, veterans. ***Tuition waivers:*** Full or partial for employees or children of employees, senior citizens.

LOANS ***Student loans:*** $49,493,547 (68% need-based, 32% non-need-based). 68% of past graduating class borrowed through all loan programs. *Average indebtedness per student:* $22,387. ***Average need-based loan:*** Freshmen: $4798. Undergraduates: $6597. ***Parent loans:*** $3,324,948 (22% need-based, 78% non-need-based). ***Programs:*** Federal Direct (Subsidized and Unsubsidized Stafford, PLUS), Perkins.

WORK-STUDY ***Federal work-study:*** Total amount: $1,897,607; jobs available. ***State or other work-study/employment:*** Part-time jobs available.

APPLYING FOR FINANCIAL AID ***Required financial aid form:*** FAFSA. ***Financial aid deadline (priority):*** 3/1. ***Notification date:*** Continuous beginning 3/26.

CONTACT Judy L. Keyes, Director of Financial Aid Services, University of Massachusetts Boston, 100 Morrissey Boulevard, Boston, MA 02125-3393, 617-287-6300. *Fax:* 617-287-6323. *E-mail:* judy.keyes@umb.edu.

UNIVERSITY OF MASSACHUSETTS DARTMOUTH

North Dartmouth, MA

Tuition & fees (MA res): $10,358 Average undergraduate aid package: $14,195

ABOUT THE INSTITUTION State-supported, coed. 49 undergraduate majors. Federal methodology is used as a basis for awarding need-based institutional aid.

UNDERGRADUATE EXPENSES for 2010–11 ***Tuition, state resident:*** full-time $1417; part-time $59.04 per credit. ***Tuition, nonresident:*** full-time $8099; part-time $337.46 per credit. ***Required fees:*** full-time $8941; $372.54 per credit. Full-time tuition and fees vary according to class time, program, and reciprocity agreements. Part-time tuition and fees vary according to class time, course load, program, and reciprocity agreements. ***College room and board:*** $9134; ***Room only:*** $6317. Room and board charges vary according to board plan and housing facility. ***Payment plan:*** Installment.

FRESHMAN FINANCIAL AID (Fall 2010, est.) 1,507 applied for aid; of those 82% were deemed to have need. 100% of freshmen with need received aid; of those 38% had need fully met. ***Average percent of need met:*** 86% (excluding resources awarded to replace EFC). ***Average financial aid package:*** $14,027 (excluding resources awarded to replace EFC). 9% of all full-time freshmen had no need and received non-need-based gift aid.

UNDERGRADUATE FINANCIAL AID (Fall 2010, est.) 5,497 applied for aid; of those 83% were deemed to have need. 100% of undergraduates with need received aid; of those 43% had need fully met. ***Average percent of need met:*** 88% (excluding resources awarded to replace EFC). ***Average financial aid package:*** $14,195 (excluding resources awarded to replace EFC). 5% of all full-time undergraduates had no need and received non-need-based gift aid.

GIFT AID (NEED-BASED) ***Total amount:*** $28,455,021 (43% federal, 16% state, 39% institutional, 2% external sources). ***Receiving aid:*** Freshmen: 64% (1,090); all full-time undergraduates: 55% (3,728). ***Average award:*** Freshmen: $8239; Undergraduates: $7987. ***Scholarships, grants, and awards:*** Federal Pell, FSEOG, state, private, college/university gift aid from institutional funds.

GIFT AID (NON-NEED-BASED) ***Total amount:*** $2,138,580 (1% federal, 3% state, 92% institutional, 4% external sources). ***Receiving aid:*** Freshmen: 2% (39). Undergraduates: 1% (100). ***Average award:*** Freshmen: $3764. Undergraduates: $3741. ***Scholarships, grants, and awards by category:*** *Academic interests/achievement:* general academic interests/achievements. *Special achievements/activities:* community service. *Special characteristics:* adult students, children of faculty/staff, children with a deceased or disabled parent, first-generation college students, members of minority groups, veterans. ***Tuition waivers:*** Full or partial for employees or children of employees, senior citizens.

LOANS ***Student loans:*** $41,857,492 (69% need-based, 31% non-need-based). 74% of past graduating class borrowed through all loan programs. *Average indebtedness per student:* $34,369. ***Average need-based loan:*** Freshmen: $6625. Undergraduates: $7337. ***Parent loans:*** $6,588,181 (39% need-based, 61% non-need-based). ***Programs:*** Federal Direct (Subsidized and Unsubsidized Stafford, PLUS), Perkins, Federal Nursing, state.

WORK-STUDY ***Federal work-study:*** Total amount: $2,360,370; jobs available. ***State or other work-study/employment:*** Part-time jobs available.

APPLYING FOR FINANCIAL AID ***Required financial aid form:*** FAFSA. ***Financial aid deadline (priority):*** 3/1. ***Notification date:*** Continuous beginning 3/25.

CONTACT Bruce Palmer, Director of Financial Aid, University of Massachusetts Dartmouth, 285 Old Westport Road, North Dartmouth, MA 02747-2300, 508-999-8643. *Fax:* 508-999-8935. *E-mail:* financialaid@umassd.edu.

UNIVERSITY OF MASSACHUSETTS LOWELL

Lowell, MA

Tuition & fees (MA res): $10,506 Average undergraduate aid package: $12,035

ABOUT THE INSTITUTION State-supported, coed. 36 undergraduate majors. Federal methodology is used as a basis for awarding need-based institutional aid.

UNDERGRADUATE EXPENSES for 2010–11 ***Tuition, state resident:*** full-time $1454; part-time $60.58 per credit. ***Tuition, nonresident:*** full-time $13,893; part-time $357 per credit. ***Required fees:*** full-time $9052; $390.67 per credit. Part-time tuition and fees vary according to course load. ***College room and board:*** $9067; ***Room only:*** $6044. Room and board charges vary according to board plan and housing facility. ***Payment plan:*** Installment.

FRESHMAN FINANCIAL AID (Fall 2009) 1,362 applied for aid; of those 68% were deemed to have need. 100% of freshmen with need received aid; of those 70% had need fully met. ***Average percent of need met:*** 94% (excluding resources awarded to replace EFC). ***Average financial aid package:*** $12,351 (excluding resources awarded to replace EFC). 28% of all full-time freshmen had no need and received non-need-based gift aid.

UNDERGRADUATE FINANCIAL AID (Fall 2009) 6,036 applied for aid; of those 73% were deemed to have need. 100% of undergraduates with need received aid; of those 70% had need fully met. ***Average percent of need met:*** 95% (excluding resources awarded to replace EFC). ***Average financial aid package:*** $12,035 (excluding resources awarded to replace EFC). 20% of all full-time undergraduates had no need and received non-need-based gift aid.

GIFT AID (NEED-BASED) ***Total amount:*** $24,329,673 (46% federal, 11% state, 40% institutional, 3% external sources). ***Receiving aid:*** Freshmen: 61% (919); all full-time undergraduates: 57% (4,260). ***Average award:*** Freshmen: $6855; Undergraduates: $5982. ***Scholarships, grants, and awards:*** Federal Pell, FSEOG, state, private, college/university gift aid from institutional funds.

GIFT AID (NON-NEED-BASED) ***Total amount:*** $6,279,490 (1% federal, 1% state, 94% institutional, 4% external sources). ***Receiving aid:*** Freshmen: 4% (63). Undergraduates: 3% (238). ***Average award:*** Freshmen: $2547. Undergraduates: $2190. ***Scholarships, grants, and awards by category:*** *Academic interests/achievement:* biological sciences, business, computer science, engineering/technologies, English, general academic interests/achievements, health fields, humanities, mathematics. *Creative arts/performance:* art/fine arts, music. *Special achievements/activities:* community service, general special achievements/activities. *Special characteristics:* children and siblings of alumni, children of faculty/staff, children of public servants, children of union members/company employees, general special characteristics, out-of-state students, veterans. ***Tuition waivers:*** Full or partial for employees or children of employees, senior citizens.

LOANS ***Student loans:*** $46,362,756 (55% need-based, 45% non-need-based). 74% of past graduating class borrowed through all loan programs. *Average indebtedness per student:* $24,087. ***Average need-based loan:*** Freshmen: $5192. Undergraduates: $6252. ***Parent loans:*** $6,666,633 (16% need-based, 84% non-need-based). ***Programs:*** Federal Direct (Subsidized and Unsubsidized Stafford, PLUS), Perkins.

WORK-STUDY ***Federal work-study:*** Total amount: $228,655; 113 jobs averaging $2099. ***State or other work-study/employment:*** Total amount: $2,157,975 (100% need-based). 686 part-time jobs averaging $3098.

ATHLETIC AWARDS Total amount: $1,259,300 (31% need-based, 69% non-need-based).

APPLYING FOR FINANCIAL AID ***Required financial aid form:*** FAFSA. ***Financial aid deadline (priority):*** 3/1. ***Notification date:*** Continuous beginning 3/24.

CONTACT Joyce McLaughlin, Director of Financial Aid, University of Massachusetts Lowell, 883 Broadway Street, Room 102, Lowell, MA 01854, 978-934-4237 or toll-free 800-410-4607. *Fax:* 978-934-3009. *E-mail:* joyce_mclaughlin@uml.edu.

UNIVERSITY OF MEDICINE AND DENTISTRY OF NEW JERSEY

Newark, NJ

CONTACT Financial Aid Office, University of Medicine and Dentistry of New Jersey, 65 Bergen Street, PO Box 1709, Newark, NJ 07107-1709, 973-972-4300.

UNIVERSITY OF MEMPHIS

Memphis, TN

Tuition & fees (TN res): $6990 **Average undergraduate aid package: $8803**

ABOUT THE INSTITUTION State-supported, coed. 66 undergraduate majors. Federal methodology is used as a basis for awarding need-based institutional aid.

UNDERGRADUATE EXPENSES for 2010–11 ***Tuition, state resident:*** full-time $5778; part-time $232 per credit hour. ***Tuition, nonresident:*** full-time $19,644; part-time $789 per credit hour. ***Required fees:*** full-time $1212; $78.50 per credit. Full-time tuition and fees vary according to course load, degree level, program, and reciprocity agreements. Part-time tuition and fees vary according to course load, degree level, and program. ***College room and board:*** $6190. Room and board charges vary according to board plan and housing facility. ***Payment plan:*** Installment.

FRESHMAN FINANCIAL AID (Fall 2010, est.) 2,267 applied for aid; of those 82% were deemed to have need. 90% of freshmen with need received aid; of those 10% had need fully met. ***Average percent of need met:*** 81% (excluding resources awarded to replace EFC). ***Average financial aid package:*** $9873 (excluding resources awarded to replace EFC). 16% of all full-time freshmen had no need and received non-need-based gift aid.

UNDERGRADUATE FINANCIAL AID (Fall 2010, est.) 11,774 applied for aid; of those 84% were deemed to have need. 90% of undergraduates with need received aid; of those 6% had need fully met. ***Average percent of need met:*** 68% (excluding resources awarded to replace EFC). ***Average financial aid package:*** $8803 (excluding resources awarded to replace EFC). 14% of all full-time undergraduates had no need and received non-need-based gift aid.

GIFT AID (NEED-BASED) ***Total amount:*** $46,054,727 (83% federal, 15% state, 2% institutional). ***Receiving aid:*** Freshmen: 57% (1,365); all full-time undergraduates: 56% (7,212). ***Average award:*** Freshmen: $6525; Undergraduates: $5483. ***Scholarships, grants, and awards:*** Federal Pell, FSEOG, state, private, college/university gift aid from institutional funds.

GIFT AID (NON-NEED-BASED) ***Total amount:*** $30,058,901 (60% state, 36% institutional, 4% external sources). ***Receiving aid:*** Freshmen: 31% (749). Undergraduates: 40% (5,132). ***Average award:*** Freshmen: $7877. Undergraduates: $7668. ***Scholarships, grants, and awards by category:*** *Academic interests/achievement:* biological sciences, business, communication, education, engineering/technologies, English, general academic interests/achievements, health fields, humanities, international studies, mathematics, military science, physical sciences, premedicine, social sciences. *Creative arts/performance:* art/fine arts, cinema/film/broadcasting, dance, journalism/publications, music. *Special achievements/activities:* cheerleading/drum major, general special achievements/activities, leadership. *Special characteristics:* adult students, children of educators, children of faculty/staff, children of public servants, handicapped students, members of minority groups, public servants. ***Tuition waivers:*** Full or partial for employees or children of employees, senior citizens.

LOANS ***Student loans:*** $85,006,520 (44% need-based, 56% non-need-based). 21% of past graduating class borrowed through all loan programs. *Average indebtedness per student:* $20,856. ***Average need-based loan:*** Freshmen: $3184. Undergraduates: $3991. ***Parent loans:*** $3,341,542 (100% non-need-based). ***Programs:*** Federal Direct (Subsidized and Unsubsidized Stafford, PLUS), Perkins, college/university.

WORK-STUDY ***Federal work-study:*** Total amount: $565,986; 235 jobs averaging $1714. ***State or other work-study/employment:*** Total amount: $2,679,576 (100% non-need-based). Part-time jobs available.

ATHLETIC AWARDS Total amount: $4,182,498 (100% non-need-based).

APPLYING FOR FINANCIAL AID ***Required financial aid form:*** FAFSA. ***Financial aid deadline (priority):*** 3/1. ***Notification date:*** Continuous beginning 4/1. Students must reply by 8/1.

CONTACT Richard Ritzman, Director of Student Financial Aid, University of Memphis, Wilder Tower 103, Memphis, TN 38152, 901-678-2832 or toll-free 800-669-2678 (out-of-state). *Fax:* 901-678-3590. *E-mail:* rritzman@memphis.edu.

UNIVERSITY OF MIAMI

Coral Gables, FL

Tuition & fees: $37,836 **Average undergraduate aid package: $31,800**

ABOUT THE INSTITUTION Independent, coed. 112 undergraduate majors. Both federal and institutional methodology are used as a basis for awarding need-based institutional aid.

UNDERGRADUATE EXPENSES for 2010–11 ***Comprehensive fee:*** $48,898 includes full-time tuition ($36,962), mandatory fees ($874), and room and board ($11,062). ***College room only:*** $6448. Room and board charges vary according to board plan and housing facility. ***Part-time tuition:*** $1538 per credit hour. Part-time tuition and fees vary according to course load. ***Payment plans:*** Tuition prepayment, installment, deferred payment.

FRESHMAN FINANCIAL AID (Fall 2010, est.) 1,402 applied for aid; of those 78% were deemed to have need. 100% of freshmen with need received aid; of those 39% had need fully met. ***Average percent of need met:*** 83% (excluding resources awarded to replace EFC). ***Average financial aid package:*** $32,310 (excluding resources awarded to replace EFC). 20% of all full-time freshmen had no need and received non-need-based gift aid.

UNDERGRADUATE FINANCIAL AID (Fall 2010, est.) 5,433 applied for aid; of those 85% were deemed to have need. 100% of undergraduates with need received aid; of those 36% had need fully met. ***Average percent of need met:*** 81% (excluding resources awarded to replace EFC). ***Average financial aid package:*** $31,800 (excluding resources awarded to replace EFC). 19% of all full-time undergraduates had no need and received non-need-based gift aid.

GIFT AID (NEED-BASED) ***Total amount:*** $94,606,613 (13% federal, 11% state, 74% institutional, 2% external sources). ***Receiving aid:*** Freshmen: 50% (1,053); all full-time undergraduates: 47% (4,432). ***Average award:*** Freshmen: $24,521; Undergraduates: $23,552. ***Scholarships, grants, and awards:*** Federal Pell, FSEOG, state, private, college/university gift aid from institutional funds, Federal Nursing, Academic Competitiveness Grants, National SMART Grants.

GIFT AID (NON-NEED-BASED) ***Total amount:*** $54,225,363 (20% state, 77% institutional, 3% external sources). ***Receiving aid:*** Freshmen: 19% (398). Undergraduates: 15% (1,414). ***Average award:*** Freshmen: $22,392. Undergraduates: $19,971. ***Scholarships, grants, and awards by category:*** *Academic interests/achievement:* architecture, area/ethnic studies, biological sciences, business, communication, computer science, education, engineering/technologies, English, foreign languages, general academic interests/achievements, health fields, humanities, international studies, mathematics, physical sciences, premedicine, religion/biblical studies, social sciences. *Creative arts/performance:* art/fine arts, cinema/film/broadcasting, debating, journalism/publications, music, performing arts, theater/drama. *Special characteristics:* children of faculty/staff, international students. ***Tuition waivers:*** Full or partial for employees or children of employees.

LOANS ***Student loans:*** $52,732,947 (70% need-based, 30% non-need-based). 54% of past graduating class borrowed through all loan programs. *Average indebtedness per student:* $26,438. ***Average need-based loan:*** Freshmen: $4260. Undergraduates: $5725. ***Parent loans:*** $16,340,246 (39% need-based, 61% non-need-based). ***Programs:*** Federal Direct (Subsidized and Unsubsidized Stafford, PLUS), Perkins, Federal Nursing, college/university, private loans.

WORK-STUDY ***Federal work-study:*** Total amount: $4,209,047; jobs available. ***State or other work-study/employment:*** Total amount: $2,571,404 (80% need-based, 20% non-need-based). Part-time jobs available.

ATHLETIC AWARDS Total amount: $10,158,077 (45% need-based, 55% non-need-based).

APPLYING FOR FINANCIAL AID ***Required financial aid form:*** FAFSA. ***Financial aid deadline (priority):*** 2/1. ***Notification date:*** Continuous beginning 3/1.

CONTACT Mr. James M. Bauer, Executive Director of Financial Assistance Services, University of Miami, Rhodes House, Building 37R, Coral Gables, FL 33124-5240, 305-284-2270. *Fax:* 305-284-8641. *E-mail:* jbauer@miami.edu.

UNIVERSITY OF MICHIGAN

Ann Arbor, MI

Tuition & fees (MI res): $12,779 Average undergraduate aid package: $13,269

ABOUT THE INSTITUTION State-supported, coed. 121 undergraduate majors. Federal methodology is used as a basis for awarding need-based institutional aid.

UNDERGRADUATE EXPENSES for 2010–11 ***Tuition, state resident:*** full-time $12,590; part-time $456 per credit hour. ***Tuition, nonresident:*** full-time $37,265; part-time $1463 per credit hour. ***Required fees:*** full-time $189; $95 per term. Full-time tuition and fees vary according to course load, program, and student level. Part-time tuition and fees vary according to course load, program, and student level. ***College room and board:*** $9192. Room and board charges vary according to board plan and housing facility. ***Payment plan:*** Installment.

FRESHMAN FINANCIAL AID (Fall 2009) 4,068 applied for aid; of those 71% were deemed to have need. 100% of freshmen with need received aid; of those 90% had need fully met. ***Average percent of need met:*** 90% (excluding resources awarded to replace EFC). ***Average financial aid package:*** $10,432 (excluding resources awarded to replace EFC). 37% of all full-time freshmen had no need and received non-need-based gift aid.

UNDERGRADUATE FINANCIAL AID (Fall 2009) 16,272 applied for aid; of those 74% were deemed to have need. 100% of undergraduates with need received aid; of those 90% had need fully met. ***Average percent of need met:*** 90% (excluding resources awarded to replace EFC). ***Average financial aid package:*** $13,269 (excluding resources awarded to replace EFC). 33% of all full-time undergraduates had no need and received non-need-based gift aid.

GIFT AID (NEED-BASED) ***Total amount:*** $83,949,218 (26% federal, 74% institutional). ***Receiving aid:*** Freshmen: 31% (1,876); all full-time undergraduates: 31% (7,785). ***Average award:*** Freshmen: $10,482; Undergraduates: $10,783. ***Scholarships, grants, and awards:*** Federal Pell, FSEOG, state, private, college/university gift aid from institutional funds, Academic Competitiveness Grants, National SMART Grants, TEACH Grants, DC Tag, Byrd scholarships.

GIFT AID (NON-NEED-BASED) ***Total amount:*** $73,970,470 (9% federal, 3% state, 68% institutional, 20% external sources). ***Receiving aid:*** Freshmen: 27% (1,656). Undergraduates: 23% (5,880). ***Average award:*** Freshmen: $5075. Undergraduates: $6036. ***Scholarships, grants, and awards by category:*** *Academic interests/achievement:* architecture, area/ethnic studies, biological sciences, business, communication, computer science, education, engineering/technologies, English, foreign languages, general academic interests/achievements, health fields, humanities, international studies, library science, mathematics, military science, physical sciences, premedicine, social sciences. *Creative arts/performance:* art/fine arts, cinema/film/broadcasting, creative writing, dance, journalism/publications, music, performing arts, theater/drama. *Special achievements/activities:* community service, general special achievements/activities, leadership. *Special characteristics:* children of faculty/staff, children of workers in trades, handicapped students, international students, local/state students, members of minority groups, out-of-state students.

LOANS ***Student loans:*** $102,215,389 (49% need-based, 51% non-need-based). 46% of past graduating class borrowed through all loan programs. *Average indebtedness per student:* $27,828. ***Average need-based loan:*** Freshmen: $5825. Undergraduates: $4173. ***Parent loans:*** $28,519,607 (100% non-need-based). ***Programs:*** Federal Direct (Subsidized and Unsubsidized Stafford, PLUS), Perkins, Federal Nursing, college/university, Health Professions Student Loans (HPSL).

WORK-STUDY ***Federal work-study:*** Total amount: $14,744,154; 3,037 jobs averaging $1583. ***State or other work-study/employment:*** Total amount: $1250 (100% need-based). Part-time jobs available.

ATHLETIC AWARDS Total amount: $15,343,857 (100% non-need-based).

APPLYING FOR FINANCIAL AID ***Required financial aid forms:*** FAFSA, CSS Financial Aid PROFILE. ***Financial aid deadline:*** 5/31 (priority: 4/30). ***Notification date:*** Continuous beginning 3/15.

CONTACT Financial Aid Counseling and Advising Services, University of Michigan, 2500 Student Activities Building, 515 East Jefferson Street, Ann Arbor, MI 48109-1316, 734-763-6600. *Fax:* 734-647-3081. *E-mail:* financial.aid@umich.edu.

UNIVERSITY OF MICHIGAN–DEARBORN

Dearborn, MI

Tuition & fees (MI res): $9456 Average undergraduate aid package: $10,287

ABOUT THE INSTITUTION State-supported, coed. 53 undergraduate majors. Federal methodology is used as a basis for awarding need-based institutional aid.

UNDERGRADUATE EXPENSES for 2010–11 ***Tuition, state resident:*** full-time $8908; part-time $352.50 per credit hour. ***Tuition, nonresident:*** full-time $20,111; part-time $800.40 per credit hour. ***Required fees:*** full-time $548; $221.70 per term. Full-time tuition and fees vary according to course level, course load, degree level, program, and student level. Part-time tuition and fees vary according to course level, course load, degree level, program, and student level. ***Payment plan:*** Installment.

FRESHMAN FINANCIAL AID (Fall 2009) 706 applied for aid; of those 67% were deemed to have need. 99% of freshmen with need received aid; of those 49% had need fully met. ***Average percent of need met:*** 77% (excluding resources awarded to replace EFC). ***Average financial aid package:*** $9916 (excluding resources awarded to replace EFC). 32% of all full-time freshmen had no need and received non-need-based gift aid.

UNDERGRADUATE FINANCIAL AID (Fall 2009) 3,460 applied for aid; of those 78% were deemed to have need. 98% of undergraduates with need received aid; of those 49% had need fully met. ***Average percent of need met:*** 72% (excluding resources awarded to replace EFC). ***Average financial aid package:*** $10,287 (excluding resources awarded to replace EFC). 26% of all full-time undergraduates had no need and received non-need-based gift aid.

GIFT AID (NEED-BASED) ***Total amount:*** $15,865,554 (81% federal, 2% state, 17% institutional). ***Receiving aid:*** Freshmen: 42% (375); all full-time undergraduates: 45% (2,090). ***Average award:*** Freshmen: $6059; Undergraduates: $5926. ***Scholarships, grants, and awards:*** Federal Pell, FSEOG, state, private, college/university gift aid from institutional funds, United Negro College Fund.

GIFT AID (NON-NEED-BASED) ***Total amount:*** $5,991,554 (1% state, 92% institutional, 7% external sources). ***Receiving aid:*** Freshmen: 31% (274). Undergraduates: 21% (969). ***Average award:*** Freshmen: $4974. Undergraduates: $4568. ***Scholarships, grants, and awards by category:*** *Academic interests/achievement:* 1,058 awards ($3,650,886 total): biological sciences, business, communication, computer science, education, engineering/technologies, foreign languages, general academic interests/achievements, international studies, mathematics, physical sciences, social sciences. *Creative arts/performance:* 47 awards ($38,558 total): art/fine arts, cinema/film/broadcasting, creative writing, debating, general creative arts/performance, journalism/publications. *Special achievements/activities:* 84 awards ($320,900 total): community service, general special achievements/activities, leadership, memberships. *Special characteristics:* 391 awards ($1,183,092 total): adult students, children and siblings of alumni, children of faculty/staff, ethnic background, general special characteristics, handicapped students, international students, members of minority groups, out-of-state students, previous college experience, public servants. ***Tuition waivers:*** Full or partial for employees or children of employees, senior citizens.

LOANS ***Student loans:*** $28,171,794 (64% need-based, 36% non-need-based). 52% of past graduating class borrowed through all loan programs. *Average indebtedness per student:* $19,463. ***Average need-based loan:*** Freshmen: $3224. Undergraduates: $4335. ***Parent loans:*** $1,752,768 (100% non-need-based). ***Programs:*** Federal Direct (Subsidized and Unsubsidized Stafford, PLUS), Perkins, college/university, alternative loans.

WORK-STUDY ***Federal work-study:*** Total amount: $324,650; 199 jobs averaging $1658. ***State or other work-study/employment:*** Part-time jobs available.

ATHLETIC AWARDS Total amount: $92,412 (100% non-need-based).

APPLYING FOR FINANCIAL AID ***Required financial aid form:*** FAFSA. ***Financial aid deadline (priority):*** 2/14. ***Notification date:*** Continuous beginning 3/10. Students must reply within 5 weeks of notification.

CONTACT Mr. Christopher W. Tremblay, Executive Director of Enrollment Management, University of Michigan–Dearborn, 4901 Evergreen Road, 1183 UC, Dearborn, MI 48128-2406, 313-593-5300. *Fax:* 313-593-5313. *E-mail:* ask-ofa@umd.umich.edu.

UNIVERSITY OF MICHIGAN–FLINT

Flint, MI

Tuition & fees (MI res): $8601 **Average undergraduate aid package: $11,846**

ABOUT THE INSTITUTION State-supported, coed. 78 undergraduate majors. Federal methodology is used as a basis for awarding need-based institutional aid.

UNDERGRADUATE EXPENSES for 2010–11 ***One-time required fee:*** $30. ***Tuition, state resident:*** full-time $8195; part-time $323.05 per credit hour. ***Tuition, nonresident:*** full-time $15,993; part-time $646.10 per credit hour. ***Required fees:*** full-time $406; $155 per term. Full-time tuition and fees vary according to course level, course load, degree level, program, and student level. Part-time tuition and fees vary according to course level, course load, degree level, program, and student level. ***College room and board:*** $7212; ***Room only:*** $4526. Room and board charges vary according to board plan. ***Payment plan:*** Installment.

FRESHMAN FINANCIAL AID (Fall 2010, est.) 630 applied for aid; of those 77% were deemed to have need. 98% of freshmen with need received aid; of those 5% had need fully met. ***Average percent of need met:*** 73% (excluding resources awarded to replace EFC). ***Average financial aid package:*** $10,272 (excluding resources awarded to replace EFC). 13% of all full-time freshmen had no need and received non-need-based gift aid.

UNDERGRADUATE FINANCIAL AID (Fall 2010, est.) 3,644 applied for aid; of those 83% were deemed to have need. 98% of undergraduates with need received aid; of those 6% had need fully met. ***Average percent of need met:*** 77% (excluding resources awarded to replace EFC). ***Average financial aid package:*** $11,846 (excluding resources awarded to replace EFC). 5% of all full-time undergraduates had no need and received non-need-based gift aid.

GIFT AID (NEED-BASED) ***Total amount:*** $19,220,553 (72% federal, 1% state, 27% institutional). ***Receiving aid:*** Freshmen: 49% (353); all full-time undergraduates: 50% (2,147). ***Average award:*** Freshmen: $6050; Undergraduates: $6046. ***Scholarships, grants, and awards:*** Federal Pell, FSEOG, state, private, college/university gift aid from institutional funds, TEACH Grants.

GIFT AID (NON-NEED-BASED) ***Total amount:*** $739,959 (1% federal, 40% state, 59% external sources). ***Receiving aid:*** Freshmen: 36% (255). Undergraduates: 19% (831). ***Average award:*** Freshmen: $2323. Undergraduates: $2314. ***Scholarships, grants, and awards by category:*** *Academic interests/achievement:* biological sciences, business, communication, computer science, education, engineering/technologies, English, foreign languages, general academic interests/achievements, health fields, humanities, international studies, mathematics, physical sciences, premedicine, social sciences. *Creative arts/performance:* art/fine arts, journalism/publications, music, performing arts, theater/drama. *Special achievements/activities:* community service, general special achievements/activities, hobbies/interests, leadership. *Special characteristics:* adult students, children and siblings of alumni, children of faculty/staff, children of union members/company employees, first-generation college students, general special characteristics, handicapped students, international students, local/state students, members of minority groups, veterans, veterans' children. ***Tuition waivers:*** Full or partial for senior citizens.

LOANS ***Student loans:*** $36,905,573 (96% need-based, 4% non-need-based). 68% of past graduating class borrowed through all loan programs. *Average indebtedness per student:* $25,945. ***Average need-based loan:*** Freshmen: $3242. Undergraduates: $4119. ***Parent loans:*** $1,211,899 (100% non-need-based). ***Programs:*** Federal Direct (Subsidized and Unsubsidized Stafford, PLUS), Perkins.

WORK-STUDY ***Federal work-study:*** Total amount: $872,932; jobs available. ***State or other work-study/employment:*** Part-time jobs available.

APPLYING FOR FINANCIAL AID ***Required financial aid forms:*** FAFSA, institution's own form. ***Financial aid deadline (priority):*** 3/1. ***Notification date:*** Continuous beginning 3/15.

CONTACT Lori Vedder, Financial Aid Office, University of Michigan–Flint, Room 277 Pavilion, Flint, MI 48502-1950, 810-762-3444 or toll-free 800-942-5636 (in-state). *Fax:* 810-766-6757. *E-mail:* financial_aid@list.flint.umich.edu.

UNIVERSITY OF MINNESOTA, CROOKSTON

Crookston, MN

Tuition & fees (MN res): $10,623 **Average undergraduate aid package: $11,848**

ABOUT THE INSTITUTION State-supported, coed. 52 undergraduate majors. Federal methodology is used as a basis for awarding need-based institutional aid.

UNDERGRADUATE EXPENSES for 2010–11 ***Tuition, state resident:*** full-time $7932; part-time $305 per semester hour. ***Tuition, nonresident:*** full-time $7932; part-time $305 per semester hour. ***Required fees:*** full-time $2691. Full-time tuition and fees vary according to course load and reciprocity agreements. Part-time tuition and fees vary according to course load and reciprocity agreements. ***College room and board:*** $6568; ***Room only:*** $3088. Room and board charges vary according to board plan and housing facility. ***Payment plans:*** Guaranteed tuition, installment.

FRESHMAN FINANCIAL AID (Fall 2010, est.) 233 applied for aid; of those 85% were deemed to have need. 100% of freshmen with need received aid; of those 32% had need fully met. ***Average percent of need met:*** 70% (excluding resources awarded to replace EFC). ***Average financial aid package:*** $12,540 (excluding resources awarded to replace EFC). 11% of all full-time freshmen had no need and received non-need-based gift aid.

UNDERGRADUATE FINANCIAL AID (Fall 2010, est.) 970 applied for aid; of those 88% were deemed to have need. 99% of undergraduates with need received aid; of those 26% had need fully met. ***Average percent of need met:*** 75% (excluding resources awarded to replace EFC). ***Average financial aid package:*** $11,848 (excluding resources awarded to replace EFC). 7% of all full-time undergraduates had no need and received non-need-based gift aid.

GIFT AID (NEED-BASED) ***Total amount:*** $3,354,460 (40% federal, 29% state, 27% institutional, 4% external sources). ***Receiving aid:*** Freshmen: 74% (195); all full-time undergraduates: 67% (802). ***Average award:*** Freshmen: $8683; Undergraduates: $7743. ***Scholarships, grants, and awards:*** Federal Pell, FSEOG, state, private, college/university gift aid from institutional funds, Academic Competitiveness Grants, National SMART Grants.

GIFT AID (NON-NEED-BASED) ***Total amount:*** $194,445 (57% institutional, 43% external sources). ***Receiving aid:*** Freshmen: 11% (29). Undergraduates: 8% (90). ***Average award:*** Freshmen: $2541. Undergraduates: $2411. ***Scholarships, grants, and awards by category:*** *Academic interests/achievement:* agriculture, biological sciences, general academic interests/achievements. *Special characteristics:* children and siblings of alumni, children of faculty/staff, ethnic background, first-generation college students, general special characteristics, local/state students. ***Tuition waivers:*** Full or partial for senior citizens.

LOANS ***Student loans:*** $3,793,784 (87% need-based, 13% non-need-based). 83% of past graduating class borrowed through all loan programs. *Average indebtedness per student:* $25,852. ***Average need-based loan:*** Freshmen: $4280. Undergraduates: $4920. ***Parent loans:*** $617,908 (100% non-need-based). ***Programs:*** Federal Direct (Subsidized and Unsubsidized Stafford, PLUS), Perkins, state, private loans.

WORK-STUDY ***Federal work-study:*** Total amount: $143,306; 186 jobs averaging $1000. ***State or other work-study/employment:*** Total amount: $648,488 (24% need-based, 76% non-need-based). 81 part-time jobs averaging $1000.

ATHLETIC AWARDS Total amount: $461,444 (100% non-need-based).

APPLYING FOR FINANCIAL AID ***Required financial aid form:*** FAFSA. ***Financial aid deadline (priority):*** 3/1. ***Notification date:*** 3/1. Students must reply within 8 weeks of notification.

CONTACT Melissa Dingmann, Director of Financial Aid, University of Minnesota, Crookston, 170 Owen Hall, Crookston, MN 56716-5001, 218-281-8576 or toll-free 800-862-6466. *Fax:* 218-281-8575. *E-mail:* dingmann@umn.edu.

UNIVERSITY OF MINNESOTA, DULUTH

Duluth, MN

Tuition & fees (MN res): $11,807 **Average undergraduate aid package: $10,655**

ABOUT THE INSTITUTION State-supported, coed. 71 undergraduate majors. Federal methodology is used as a basis for awarding need-based institutional aid.

UNDERGRADUATE EXPENSES for 2010–11 ***Tuition, state resident:*** full-time $9482; part-time $364.70 per credit. ***Tuition, nonresident:*** full-time $11,482; part-time $441.62 per credit. ***Required fees:*** full-time $2325; $65 per credit. Full-time tuition and fees vary according to course load and reciprocity agreements. Part-time tuition and fees vary according to course load and reciprocity agreements. ***College room and board:*** $6422. Room and board charges vary according to board plan and housing facility. ***Payment plan:*** Installment.

FRESHMAN FINANCIAL AID (Fall 2009) 2,004 applied for aid; of those 74% were deemed to have need. 100% of freshmen with need received aid; of those 18% had need fully met. ***Average percent of need met:*** 73% (excluding resources awarded to replace EFC). ***Average financial aid package:*** $10,478 (excluding resources awarded to replace EFC). 8% of all full-time freshmen had no need and received non-need-based gift aid.

UNDERGRADUATE FINANCIAL AID (Fall 2009) 7,447 applied for aid; of those 77% were deemed to have need. 100% of undergraduates with need received aid; of those 23% had need fully met. ***Average percent of need met:*** 75% (excluding resources awarded to replace EFC). ***Average financial aid package:*** $10,655 (excluding resources awarded to replace EFC). 9% of all full-time undergraduates had no need and received non-need-based gift aid.

GIFT AID (NEED-BASED) ***Total amount:*** $40,965,000 (28% federal, 37% state, 30% institutional, 5% external sources). ***Receiving aid:*** Freshmen: 63% (1,467); all full-time undergraduates: 60% (5,596). ***Average award:*** Freshmen: $7658; Undergraduates: $6922. ***Scholarships, grants, and awards:*** Federal Pell, FSEOG, state, private, college/university gift aid from institutional funds.

GIFT AID (NON-NEED-BASED) ***Total amount:*** $2,196,063 (74% institutional, 26% external sources). ***Receiving aid:*** Freshmen: 10% (233). Undergraduates: 9% (850). ***Average award:*** Freshmen: $3391. Undergraduates: $3122. ***Scholarships, grants, and awards by category:*** *Academic interests/achievement:* general academic interests/achievements. ***Tuition waivers:*** Full or partial for employees or children of employees.

LOANS ***Student loans:*** $47,573,877 (77% need-based, 23% non-need-based). 76% of past graduating class borrowed through all loan programs. *Average indebtedness per student:* $30,098. ***Average need-based loan:*** Freshmen: $3677. Undergraduates: $4651. ***Parent loans:*** $16,813,100 (100% need-based). ***Programs:*** Federal Direct (Subsidized and Unsubsidized Stafford, PLUS), Perkins, state, college/university.

WORK-STUDY ***Federal work-study:*** Total amount: $357,660; jobs available. ***State or other work-study/employment:*** Total amount: $722,911 (100% need-based). Part-time jobs available.

ATHLETIC AWARDS Total amount: $1,227,988 (100% need-based).

APPLYING FOR FINANCIAL AID ***Required financial aid form:*** FAFSA. ***Financial aid deadline (priority):*** 3/1. ***Notification date:*** Continuous beginning 3/1. Students must reply within 2 weeks of notification.

CONTACT Ms. Brenda Herzig, Director of Financial Aid, University of Minnesota, Duluth, 10 University Drive, 184 Darland Administration Building, Duluth, MN 55812-2496, 218-726-8000 or toll-free 800-232-1339. *Fax:* 218-726-8219.

UNIVERSITY OF MINNESOTA, MORRIS

Morris, MN

Tuition & fees (MN res): $11,532 Average undergraduate aid package: $14,878

ABOUT THE INSTITUTION State-supported, coed. ***Awards:*** bachelor's degrees. 42 undergraduate majors. ***Total enrollment:*** 1,607. Undergraduates: 1,607. Freshmen: 492. Federal methodology is used as a basis for awarding need-based institutional aid.

UNDERGRADUATE EXPENSES for 2010–11 ***Application fee:*** $35. ***Tuition, state resident:*** full-time $9482; part-time $364.70 per credit. ***Tuition, nonresident:*** full-time $9482; part-time $364.70 per credit. ***Required fees:*** full-time $2050. Full-time tuition and fees vary according to reciprocity agreements. Part-time tuition and fees vary according to course load and reciprocity agreements. ***College room and board:*** $7050; ***Room only:*** $3290. Room and board charges vary according to board plan and housing facility. ***Payment plan:*** Installment.

FRESHMAN FINANCIAL AID (Fall 2010, est.) 382 applied for aid; of those 76% were deemed to have need. 100% of freshmen with need received aid; of those 49% had need fully met. ***Average percent of need met:*** 87% (excluding resources awarded to replace EFC). ***Average financial aid package:*** $15,622 (excluding resources awarded to replace EFC). 18% of all full-time freshmen had no need and received non-need-based gift aid.

UNDERGRADUATE FINANCIAL AID (Fall 2010, est.) 1,333 applied for aid; of those 82% were deemed to have need. 100% of undergraduates with need received aid; of those 43% had need fully met. ***Average percent of need met:*** 83% (excluding resources awarded to replace EFC). ***Average financial aid package:*** $14,878 (excluding resources awarded to replace EFC). 15% of all full-time undergraduates had no need and received non-need-based gift aid.

GIFT AID (NEED-BASED) ***Total amount:*** $10,380,309 (32% federal, 29% state, 32% institutional, 7% external sources). ***Receiving aid:*** Freshmen: 69% (290); all full-time undergraduates: 66% (1,074). ***Average award:*** Freshmen: $9877; Undergraduates: $9130. ***Scholarships, grants, and awards:*** Federal Pell, FSEOG, state, private, college/university gift aid from institutional funds.

GIFT AID (NON-NEED-BASED) ***Total amount:*** $1,307,639 (81% institutional, 19% external sources). ***Receiving aid:*** Freshmen: 29% (120). Undergraduates: 24% (385). ***Average award:*** Freshmen: $3524. Undergraduates: $3783. ***Scholarships, grants, and awards by category:*** *Academic interests/achievement:* general academic interests/achievements. *Creative arts/performance:* music. *Special achievements/activities:* general special achievements/activities. *Special characteristics:* ethnic background, international students, members of minority groups, veterans, veterans' children. ***Tuition waivers:*** Full or partial for minority students, senior citizens.

LOANS ***Student loans:*** $6,963,251 (82% need-based, 18% non-need-based). 72% of past graduating class borrowed through all loan programs. *Average indebtedness per student:* $22,952. ***Average need-based loan:*** Freshmen: $6206. Undergraduates: $6986. ***Parent loans:*** $339,337 (100% non-need-based). ***Programs:*** Federal Direct (Subsidized and Unsubsidized Stafford, PLUS), Perkins, state.

WORK-STUDY ***Federal work-study:*** Total amount: $553,412; jobs available. ***State or other work-study/employment:*** Total amount: $199,111 (100% need-based). Part-time jobs available.

APPLYING FOR FINANCIAL AID ***Required financial aid form:*** FAFSA. ***Financial aid deadline (priority):*** 3/1. ***Notification date:*** Continuous. Students must reply within 3 weeks of notification.

CONTACT Ms. Jill Beauregard, Director of Financial Aid, University of Minnesota, Morris, 600 East 4th Street, Morris, MN 56267, 320-589-6046 or toll-free 800-992-8863. *Fax:* 320-589-1673. *E-mail:* morrisfa@morris.umn.edu.

UNIVERSITY OF MINNESOTA, TWIN CITIES CAMPUS

Minneapolis, MN

Tuition & fees (MN res): $12,203 Average undergraduate aid package: $12,126

ABOUT THE INSTITUTION State-supported, coed. 219 undergraduate majors. Federal methodology is used as a basis for awarding need-based institutional aid.

UNDERGRADUATE EXPENSES for 2010–11 ***Tuition, state resident:*** full-time $9794; part-time $376.70 per credit. ***Tuition, nonresident:*** full-time $14,094; part-time $542.08 per credit. ***Required fees:*** full-time $2409. Full-time tuition and fees vary according to program and reciprocity agreements. Part-time tuition and fees vary according to course load, program, and reciprocity agreements. ***College room and board:*** $7774; ***Room only:*** $4348. Room and board charges vary according to board plan, housing facility, and location. ***Payment plan:*** Installment.

FRESHMAN FINANCIAL AID (Fall 2010, est.) 4,329 applied for aid; of those 70% were deemed to have need. 100% of freshmen with need received aid; of those 35% had need fully met. ***Average percent of need met:*** 79% (excluding resources awarded to replace EFC). ***Average financial aid package:*** $12,440 (excluding resources awarded to replace EFC). 20% of all full-time freshmen had no need and received non-need-based gift aid.

UNDERGRADUATE FINANCIAL AID (Fall 2010, est.) 20,455 applied for aid; of those 77% were deemed to have need. 100% of undergraduates with need received aid; of those 30% had need fully met. ***Average percent of need met:*** 74% (excluding resources awarded to replace EFC). ***Average financial aid package:*** $12,126 (excluding resources awarded to replace EFC). 14% of all full-time undergraduates had no need and received non-need-based gift aid.

GIFT AID (NEED-BASED) ***Total amount:*** $126,434,948 (32% federal, 31% state, 35% institutional, 2% external sources). ***Receiving aid:*** Freshmen: 55% (2,941); all full-time undergraduates: 53% (15,052). ***Average award:*** Freshmen: $8230; Undergraduates: $7698. ***Scholarships, grants, and awards:*** Federal Pell, FSEOG, state, private, college/university gift aid from institutional funds, Federal Nursing.

GIFT AID (NON-NEED-BASED) ***Total amount:*** $17,482,938 (93% institutional, 7% external sources). ***Receiving aid:*** Freshmen: 8% (439). Undergraduates: 6% (1,803). ***Average award:*** Freshmen: $4046. Undergraduates: $4716. ***Scholarships, grants, and awards by category:*** *Academic interests/achievement:* agriculture, architecture, area/ethnic studies, biological sciences, business, communication, computer science, education, engineering/technologies, English, foreign languages, general academic interests/achievements, health fields, home economics, humanities, international studies, library science, mathematics, military science, physical sciences, premedicine, religion/biblical studies, social sciences. *Creative arts/performance:* general creative arts/performance. *Special achievements/activities:* hobbies/interests, leadership. *Special characteristics:* general special characteristics, local/state students, members of minority groups. ***Tuition waivers:*** Full or partial for senior citizens.

LOANS ***Student loans:*** $133,854,725 (78% need-based, 22% non-need-based). 63% of past graduating class borrowed through all loan programs. *Average indebtedness per student:* $27,578. ***Average need-based loan:*** Freshmen: $4106. Undergraduates: $5308. ***Parent loans:*** $58,429,477 (100% non-need-based). ***Programs:*** Federal Direct (Subsidized and Unsubsidized Stafford, PLUS), Perkins, Federal Nursing, state, college/university.

WORK-STUDY ***Federal work-study:*** Total amount: $4,125,680; jobs available. ***State or other work-study/employment:*** Total amount: $7,131,359 (100% need-based). Part-time jobs available.

APPLYING FOR FINANCIAL AID ***Required financial aid forms:*** FAFSA, institution's own form. ***Financial aid deadline (priority):*** 3/1. ***Notification date:*** Continuous beginning 2/15.

CONTACT Judy Swanson, Associate Director of Student Finance, University of Minnesota, Twin Cities Campus, 200 Fraser Hall, 106 Pleasant Street SE, Minneapolis, MN 55455, 612-624-1111 or toll-free 800-752-1000. *Fax:* 612-624-9584. *E-mail:* helpingu@umn.edu.

UNIVERSITY OF MISSISSIPPI

Oxford, MS

Tuition & fees (MS res): $5708 **Average undergraduate aid package: $7633**

ABOUT THE INSTITUTION State-supported, coed. 48 undergraduate majors. Federal methodology is used as a basis for awarding need-based institutional aid.

UNDERGRADUATE EXPENSES for 2011–12 ***Tuition, state resident:*** full-time $5708. ***Tuition, nonresident:*** full-time $14,584. Full-time tuition and fees vary according to course load and program. Part-time tuition and fees vary according to course load and program. Room and board charges vary according to board plan, housing facility, and location. ***Payment plan:*** Tuition prepayment.

FRESHMAN FINANCIAL AID (Fall 2009) 1,822 applied for aid; of those 65% were deemed to have need. 97% of freshmen with need received aid; of those 15% had need fully met. ***Average percent of need met:*** 75% (excluding resources awarded to replace EFC). ***Average financial aid package:*** $9333 (excluding resources awarded to replace EFC). 26% of all full-time freshmen had no need and received non-need-based gift aid.

UNDERGRADUATE FINANCIAL AID (Fall 2009) 7,715 applied for aid; of those 76% were deemed to have need. 97% of undergraduates with need received aid; of those 11% had need fully met. ***Average percent of need met:*** 74% (excluding resources awarded to replace EFC). ***Average financial aid package:*** $7633 (excluding resources awarded to replace EFC). 18% of all full-time undergraduates had no need and received non-need-based gift aid.

GIFT AID (NEED-BASED) ***Total amount:*** $31,826,716 (58% federal, 7% state, 31% institutional, 4% external sources). ***Receiving aid:*** Freshmen: 40% (1,024); all full-time undergraduates: 42% (5,024). ***Average award:*** Freshmen: $7403; Undergraduates: $6870. ***Scholarships, grants, and awards:*** Federal Pell, FSEOG, state, private, college/university gift aid from institutional funds.

GIFT AID (NON-NEED-BASED) ***Total amount:*** $14,595,904 (17% state, 74% institutional, 9% external sources). ***Receiving aid:*** Freshmen: 7% (171). Undergraduates: 4% (436). ***Average award:*** Freshmen: $4582. Undergraduates: $4517. ***Scholarships, grants, and awards by category:*** *Academic interests/achievement:* 6,351 awards ($14,854,748 total): biological sciences, business, communication, computer science, education, engineering/technologies, English, foreign languages, general academic interests/achievements, health fields, humanities, international studies, mathematics, military science, physical sciences, premedicine, religion/biblical studies, social sciences. *Creative arts/performance:* 645 awards ($1,019,290 total): art/fine arts, cinema/film/broadcasting, creative writing, debating, journalism/publications, music, performing arts, theater/drama. *Special achievements/activities:* 4,146 awards ($7,639,433 total): cheerleading/drum major, community service, general special achievements/activities, junior miss, leadership, memberships. *Special characteristics:* 5,799 awards ($10,454,788 total): adult students, children and siblings of alumni, children of faculty/staff, ethnic background, first-generation college students, general special characteristics, handicapped students, international students, local/state students, members of minority groups, out-of-state students, previous college experience, spouses of current students. ***Tuition waivers:*** Full or partial for children of alumni, employees or children of employees, senior citizens.

LOANS ***Student loans:*** $46,382,159 (76% need-based, 24% non-need-based). 41% of past graduating class borrowed through all loan programs. *Average indebtedness per student:* $23,637. ***Average need-based loan:*** Freshmen: $3705. Undergraduates: $4687. ***Parent loans:*** $11,704,147 (26% need-based, 74% non-need-based). ***Programs:*** Federal Direct (Subsidized and Unsubsidized Stafford, PLUS), Perkins, college/university.

WORK-STUDY ***Federal work-study:*** Total amount: $701,854; 493 jobs averaging $1411.

ATHLETIC AWARDS Total amount: $5,230,497 (51% need-based, 49% non-need-based).

APPLYING FOR FINANCIAL AID ***Required financial aid form:*** FAFSA. ***Financial aid deadline (priority):*** 3/1. ***Notification date:*** Continuous beginning 4/1. Students must reply within 4 weeks of notification.

CONTACT Ms. Laura Diven-Brown, Director of Financial Aid, University of Mississippi, 257 Martindale Center, University, MS 38677, 662-915-5788 or toll-free 800-653-6477 (in-state). *Fax:* 662-915-1164. *E-mail:* ldivenbr@olemiss.edu.

UNIVERSITY OF MISSISSIPPI MEDICAL CENTER

Jackson, MS

CONTACT Minetta Veazey, Administrative Secretary, University of Mississippi Medical Center, 2500 North State Street, Jackson, MS 39216, 601-984-1117. *Fax:* 601-984-6984. *E-mail:* mveazey@registrar.umsmed.edu.

UNIVERSITY OF MISSOURI

Columbia, MO

Tuition & fees (MO res): $8501 **Average undergraduate aid package: $12,797**

ABOUT THE INSTITUTION State-supported, coed. 115 undergraduate majors. Federal methodology is used as a basis for awarding need-based institutional aid.

UNDERGRADUATE EXPENSES for 2010–11 ***Tuition, state resident:*** full-time $7368; part-time $245.60 per credit hour. ***Tuition, nonresident:*** full-time $19,383; part-time $646.10 per credit hour. ***Required fees:*** full-time $1133. Full-time tuition and fees vary according to course load, program, and reciprocity agreements. Part-time tuition and fees vary according to course load, program, and reciprocity agreements. ***College room and board:*** $8607. Room and board charges vary according to board plan and housing facility. ***Payment plan:*** Installment.

FRESHMAN FINANCIAL AID (Fall 2010, est.) 4,698 applied for aid; of those 69% were deemed to have need. 97% of freshmen with need received aid; of those 15% had need fully met. ***Average percent of need met:*** 84% (excluding resources awarded to replace EFC). ***Average financial aid package:*** $13,836 (excluding resources awarded to replace EFC). 20% of all full-time freshmen had no need and received non-need-based gift aid.

UNDERGRADUATE FINANCIAL AID (Fall 2010, est.) 16,030 applied for aid; of those 73% were deemed to have need. 98% of undergraduates with need received aid; of those 15% had need fully met. ***Average percent of need met:*** 81% (excluding resources awarded to replace EFC). ***Average financial aid package:*** $12,797 (excluding resources awarded to replace EFC). 16% of all full-time undergraduates had no need and received non-need-based gift aid.

GIFT AID (NEED-BASED) ***Total amount:*** $60,704,730 (41% federal, 11% state, 42% institutional, 6% external sources). ***Receiving aid:*** Freshmen: 46% (2,763); all full-time undergraduates: 41% (9,508). ***Average award:*** Freshmen: $7922; Undergraduates: $7140. ***Scholarships, grants, and awards:*** Federal Pell, FSEOG, state, private, college/university gift aid from institutional funds, Federal Nursing.

GIFT AID (NON-NEED-BASED) ***Total amount:*** $20,602,361 (2% federal, 9% state, 70% institutional, 19% external sources). ***Receiving aid:*** Freshmen: 3% (202). Undergraduates: 2% (503). ***Average award:*** Freshmen: $3544. Undergraduates: $3578. ***Scholarships, grants, and awards by category:*** *Academic interests/achievement:* agriculture, area/ethnic studies, biological sciences, business, communication, computer science, education, engineering/technologies, English, foreign languages, general academic interests/achievements, health fields, home economics, humanities, international studies, library science, mathematics, physical sciences, premedicine, religion/biblical studies, social sciences. *Creative arts/performance:* art/fine arts, cinema/film/broadcasting, creative writing, journalism/publications, music, theater/drama. *Special achievements/activities:* cheerleading/drum major, general special achievements/activities, memberships. *Special characteristics:* adult students, children and siblings of alumni, children of faculty/staff, ethnic background, first-generation college students, international students, local/state students, members of minority groups, out-of-state students. ***Tuition waivers:*** Full or partial for employees or children of employees, senior citizens.

LOANS ***Student loans:*** $92,210,181 (68% need-based, 32% non-need-based). 56% of past graduating class borrowed through all loan programs. *Average indebtedness per student:* $22,145. ***Average need-based loan:*** Freshmen: $3600. Undergraduates: $4049. ***Parent loans:*** $42,601,119 (38% need-based, 62% non-need-based). ***Programs:*** Federal Direct (Subsidized and Unsubsidized Stafford, PLUS), Perkins, Federal Nursing, state, college/university, alternative loans.

WORK-STUDY ***Federal work-study:*** Total amount: $1,662,191; jobs available.

ATHLETIC AWARDS Total amount: $6,198,275 (40% need-based, 60% non-need-based).

APPLYING FOR FINANCIAL AID ***Required financial aid form:*** FAFSA. ***Financial aid deadline (priority):*** 3/1. ***Notification date:*** Continuous beginning 4/1. Students must reply within 4 weeks of notification.

CONTACT James Brooks, Director of Student Financial Aid, University of Missouri, 11 Jesse Hall, Columbia, MO 65211, 573-882-7506 or toll-free 800-225-6075 (in-state). *Fax:* 573-884-5335. *E-mail:* finaidinfo@missouri.edu.

UNIVERSITY OF MISSOURI–KANSAS CITY

Kansas City, MO

Tuition & fees (MO res): $8602 Average undergraduate aid package: $8790

ABOUT THE INSTITUTION State-supported, coed. 63 undergraduate majors. Federal methodology is used as a basis for awarding need-based institutional aid.

UNDERGRADUATE EXPENSES for 2010–11 ***Tuition, state resident:*** full-time $7368; part-time $245.60 per credit hour. ***Tuition, nonresident:*** full-time $18,957; part-time $631.90 per credit hour. ***Required fees:*** full-time $1234; $48.40 per credit hour or $30 per term. Full-time tuition and fees vary according to course load and program. Part-time tuition and fees vary according to course load and program. ***College room and board:*** $10,131. Room and board charges vary according to board plan and housing facility. ***Payment plan:*** Installment.

FRESHMAN FINANCIAL AID (Fall 2010, est.) 923 applied for aid; of those 87% were deemed to have need. 99% of freshmen with need received aid; of those 6% had need fully met. ***Average percent of need met:*** 50% (excluding resources awarded to replace EFC). ***Average financial aid package:*** $9350 (excluding resources awarded to replace EFC). 11% of all full-time freshmen had no need and received non-need-based gift aid.

UNDERGRADUATE FINANCIAL AID (Fall 2010, est.) 5,290 applied for aid; of those 91% were deemed to have need. 98% of undergraduates with need received aid; of those 5% had need fully met. ***Average percent of need met:*** 46% (excluding resources awarded to replace EFC). ***Average financial aid package:*** $8790 (excluding resources awarded to replace EFC). 9% of all full-time undergraduates had no need and received non-need-based gift aid.

GIFT AID (NEED-BASED) ***Total amount:*** $26,533,225 (54% federal, 6% state, 37% institutional, 3% external sources). ***Receiving aid:*** Freshmen: 63% (694); all full-time undergraduates: 43% (2,839). ***Average award:*** Freshmen: $4635; Undergraduates: $4515. ***Scholarships, grants, and awards:*** Federal Pell, FSEOG, state, private, college/university gift aid from institutional funds, United Negro College Fund.

GIFT AID (NON-NEED-BASED) ***Total amount:*** $5,631,612 (8% state, 78% institutional, 14% external sources). ***Receiving aid:*** Freshmen: 6% (69). Undergraduates: 2% (117). ***Average award:*** Freshmen: $5443. Undergraduates: $6444. ***Scholarships, grants, and awards by category:*** *Academic interests/achievement:* general academic interests/achievements. *Creative arts/performance:* debating, general creative arts/performance, music, performing arts. *Special achievements/activities:* general special achievements/activities. *Special characteristics:* ethnic background, members of minority groups, out-of-state students. ***Tuition waivers:*** Full or partial for employees or children of employees.

LOANS ***Student loans:*** $44,331,732 (92% need-based, 8% non-need-based). 70% of past graduating class borrowed through all loan programs. *Average indebtedness per student:* $25,374. ***Average need-based loan:*** Freshmen: $3750. Undergraduates: $4580. ***Parent loans:*** $11,288,405 (74% need-based, 26% non-need-based). ***Programs:*** Federal Direct (Subsidized and Unsubsidized Stafford, PLUS), Perkins, Federal Nursing, state, college/university.

WORK-STUDY ***Federal work-study:*** Total amount: $2,240,666; jobs available.

ATHLETIC AWARDS Total amount: $2,236,996 (34% need-based, 66% non-need-based).

APPLYING FOR FINANCIAL AID ***Required financial aid form:*** FAFSA. ***Financial aid deadline (priority):*** 3/1. ***Notification date:*** Continuous beginning 4/15. Students must reply within 2 weeks of notification.

CONTACT Nancy Merz, Director of Financial Aid and Scholarships, University of Missouri–Kansas City, 5100 Rockhill Road, Kansas City, MO 64110-2499, 816-235-1154 or toll-free 800-775-8652 (out-of-state). *Fax:* 816-235-5511. *E-mail:* merzn@umkc.edu.

UNIVERSITY OF MISSOURI–ST. LOUIS

St. Louis, MO

Tuition & fees (MO res): $9038 Average undergraduate aid package: $8700

ABOUT THE INSTITUTION State-supported, coed. 62 undergraduate majors. Federal methodology is used as a basis for awarding need-based institutional aid.

UNDERGRADUATE EXPENSES for 2011–12 ***Tuition, state resident:*** full-time $7737; part-time $257.90 per credit hour. ***Tuition, nonresident:*** full-time $19,905; part-time $663.50 per credit hour. ***Required fees:*** full-time $1301; $50.10 per credit hour. Full-time tuition and fees vary according to course load, program, and reciprocity agreements. Part-time tuition and fees vary according to course load, program, and reciprocity agreements. ***College room and board:*** $8404; ***Room only:*** $5044. Room and board charges vary according to board plan and housing facility. ***Payment plan:*** Installment.

FRESHMAN FINANCIAL AID (Fall 2010, est.) 397 applied for aid; of those 89% were deemed to have need. 98% of freshmen with need received aid; of those 10% had need fully met. ***Average percent of need met:*** 53% (excluding resources awarded to replace EFC). ***Average financial aid package:*** $8890 (excluding resources awarded to replace EFC). 14% of all full-time freshmen had no need and received non-need-based gift aid.

UNDERGRADUATE FINANCIAL AID (Fall 2010, est.) 4,593 applied for aid; of those 92% were deemed to have need. 97% of undergraduates with need received aid; of those 6% had need fully met. ***Average percent of need met:*** 46% (excluding resources awarded to replace EFC). ***Average financial aid package:*** $8700 (excluding resources awarded to replace EFC). 8% of all full-time undergraduates had no need and received non-need-based gift aid.

GIFT AID (NEED-BASED) ***Total amount:*** $24,129,114 (66% federal, 8% state, 20% institutional, 6% external sources). ***Receiving aid:*** Freshmen: 69% (331); all full-time undergraduates: 57% (3,366). ***Average award:*** Freshmen: $6700; Undergraduates: $5702. ***Scholarships, grants, and awards:*** Federal Pell, FSEOG, state, private, college/university gift aid from institutional funds, United Negro College Fund, Federal Nursing, Academic Competitiveness Grants, National SMART Grants, TEACH Grants.

GIFT AID (NON-NEED-BASED) ***Total amount:*** $3,744,020 (4% state, 69% institutional, 27% external sources). ***Receiving aid:*** Freshmen: 7% (32). Undergraduates: 2% (104). ***Average award:*** Freshmen: $4238. Undergraduates: $4583. ***Scholarships, grants, and awards by category:*** *Academic interests/achievement:* biological sciences, business, communication, computer science, education, engineering/technologies, English, foreign languages, general academic interests/achievements, health fields, humanities, international studies, mathematics, physical sciences, premedicine, social sciences. *Creative arts/performance:* applied art and design, art/fine arts, creative writing, dance, music, theater/drama. *Special achievements/activities:* cheerleading/drum major, community service, memberships. *Special characteristics:* adult students, children and siblings of alumni, children of faculty/staff, ethnic background, general special characteristics, international students, local/state students, members of minority groups, out-of-state students, veterans. ***Tuition waivers:*** Full or partial for employees or children of employees, senior citizens.

LOANS ***Student loans:*** $49,523,165 (92% need-based, 8% non-need-based). 69% of past graduating class borrowed through all loan programs. *Average indebtedness per student:* $27,334. ***Average need-based loan:*** Freshmen: $3356. Undergraduates: $4588. ***Parent loans:*** $3,658,477 (51% need-based, 49% non-need-based). ***Programs:*** Federal Direct (Subsidized and Unsubsidized Stafford, PLUS), Perkins, Federal Nursing.

WORK-STUDY ***Federal work-study:*** Total amount: $266,739; 59 jobs averaging $3375.

ATHLETIC AWARDS Total amount: $1,403,958 (50% need-based, 50% non-need-based).

APPLYING FOR FINANCIAL AID ***Required financial aid form:*** FAFSA. ***Financial aid deadline (priority):*** 4/1. ***Notification date:*** Continuous beginning 4/1. Students must reply within 2 weeks of notification.

CONTACT Ms. Samantha M. Matchefts, Associate Director of Student Financial Aid, University of Missouri–St. Louis, One University Boulevard, 327 Millennium Student Center, St. Louis, MO 63121-4400, 314-516-6893 or toll-free 888-GO2-UMSL (in-state). *Fax:* 314-516-5408. *E-mail:* samantha.matchefts@umsl.edu.

UNIVERSITY OF MOBILE

Mobile, AL

Tuition & fees: $16,120 **Average undergraduate aid package: $12,985**

ABOUT THE INSTITUTION Independent Southern Baptist, coed. 30 undergraduate majors. Federal methodology is used as a basis for awarding need-based institutional aid.

UNDERGRADUATE EXPENSES for 2010–11 ***Comprehensive fee:*** $23,900 includes full-time tuition ($15,590), mandatory fees ($530), and room and board ($7780). ***College room only:*** $4590. Full-time tuition and fees vary according to course load. Room and board charges vary according to housing facility. ***Part-time tuition:*** $555 per credit hour. ***Part-time fees:*** $163 per degree program. Part-time tuition and fees vary according to course load. ***Payment plan:*** Installment.

FRESHMAN FINANCIAL AID (Fall 2010, est.) 206 applied for aid; of those 98% were deemed to have need. 96% of freshmen with need received aid. ***Average percent of need met:*** 74% (excluding resources awarded to replace EFC). ***Average financial aid package:*** $15,525 (excluding resources awarded to replace EFC). 9% of all full-time freshmen had no need and received non-need-based gift aid.

UNDERGRADUATE FINANCIAL AID (Fall 2010, est.) 962 applied for aid; of those 90% were deemed to have need. 100% of undergraduates with need received aid. ***Average percent of need met:*** 58% (excluding resources awarded to replace EFC). ***Average financial aid package:*** $12,985 (excluding resources awarded to replace EFC). 7% of all full-time undergraduates had no need and received non-need-based gift aid.

GIFT AID (NEED-BASED) ***Total amount:*** $10,246,445 (39% federal, 3% state, 53% institutional, 5% external sources). ***Receiving aid:*** Freshmen: 83% (193); all full-time undergraduates: 73% (842). ***Average award:*** Freshmen: $11,123; Undergraduates: $6569. ***Scholarships, grants, and awards:*** Federal Pell, FSEOG, state, private, college/university gift aid from institutional funds, Federal Nursing.

GIFT AID (NON-NEED-BASED) ***Total amount:*** $292,789 (100% external sources). ***Receiving aid:*** Freshmen: 15% (34). Undergraduates: 13% (150). ***Average award:*** Freshmen: $6161. Undergraduates: $5420. ***Scholarships, grants, and awards by category:*** *Academic interests/achievement:* general academic interests/achievements. *Creative arts/performance:* art/fine arts, music, performing arts. *Special achievements/activities:* religious involvement. *Special characteristics:* relatives of clergy. ***Tuition waivers:*** Full or partial for employees or children of employees.

LOANS ***Student loans:*** $12,038,839 (42% need-based, 58% non-need-based). 25% of past graduating class borrowed through all loan programs. *Average indebtedness per student:* $16,660. ***Average need-based loan:*** Freshmen: $3783. Undergraduates: $5049. ***Parent loans:*** $889,120 (100% non-need-based). ***Programs:*** Federal Direct (Subsidized and Unsubsidized Stafford, PLUS), Perkins, college/university.

WORK-STUDY ***Federal work-study:*** Total amount: $283,979; 65 jobs averaging $2175.

ATHLETIC AWARDS Total amount: $2,184,513 (100% non-need-based).

APPLYING FOR FINANCIAL AID ***Required financial aid forms:*** FAFSA, state aid form. ***Financial aid deadline (priority):*** 2/1. ***Notification date:*** Continuous beginning 2/1. Students must reply within 2 weeks of notification.

CONTACT Mrs. Marie Thomas Baston, Associate Vice President for Enrollment Services, University of Mobile, 5735 College Parkway, Mobile, AL 36613, 251-442-2370 or toll-free 800-946-7267. *Fax:* 251-442-2498. *E-mail:* mariet@umobile.edu.

THE UNIVERSITY OF MONTANA

Missoula, MT

Tuition & fees (MT res): $5685 **Average undergraduate aid package: $8638**

ABOUT THE INSTITUTION State-supported, coed. ***Awards:*** associate, bachelor's, and master's degrees and post-master's certificates. 116 undergraduate majors. ***Total enrollment:*** 14,207. Undergraduates: 12,196. Freshmen: 2,430. Federal methodology is used as a basis for awarding need-based institutional aid.

UNDERGRADUATE EXPENSES for 2010–11 ***Application fee:*** $30. ***Tuition, state resident:*** full-time $4175; part-time $174 per credit hour. ***Tuition, nonresident:*** full-time $18,324; part-time $763 per credit hour. ***Required fees:*** full-time $1510; $97 per credit hour. Full-time tuition and fees vary according to degree level, location, program, reciprocity agreements, and student level. Part-time tuition and fees vary according to course load, degree level, location, and student level. ***College room and board:*** $6860; ***Room only:*** $3078. Room and board charges vary according to board plan and housing facility. ***Payment plans:*** Installment, deferred payment.

FRESHMAN FINANCIAL AID (Fall 2009) 1,864 applied for aid; of those 66% were deemed to have need. 98% of freshmen with need received aid; of those 16% had need fully met. ***Average percent of need met:*** 59% (excluding resources awarded to replace EFC). ***Average financial aid package:*** $7871 (excluding resources awarded to replace EFC). 29% of all full-time freshmen had no need and received non-need-based gift aid.

UNDERGRADUATE FINANCIAL AID (Fall 2009) 8,021 applied for aid; of those 73% were deemed to have need. 99% of undergraduates with need received aid; of those 8% had need fully met. ***Average percent of need met:*** 74% (excluding resources awarded to replace EFC). ***Average financial aid package:*** $8638 (excluding resources awarded to replace EFC). 22% of all full-time undergraduates had no need and received non-need-based gift aid.

GIFT AID (NEED-BASED) ***Total amount:*** $24,613,067 (88% federal, 3% state, 9% institutional). ***Receiving aid:*** Freshmen: 39% (821); all full-time undergraduates: 41% (4,201). ***Average award:*** Freshmen: $3623; Undergraduates: $3899. ***Scholarships, grants, and awards:*** Federal Pell, FSEOG, state, private, college/university gift aid from institutional funds.

GIFT AID (NON-NEED-BASED) ***Total amount:*** $10,914,832 (81% institutional, 19% external sources). ***Receiving aid:*** Freshmen: 2% (38). Undergraduates: 1% (72). ***Average award:*** Freshmen: $6513. Undergraduates: $6352. ***Scholarships, grants, and awards by category:*** *Academic interests/achievement:* biological sciences, business, computer science, education, English, foreign languages, general academic interests/achievements, health fields, humanities, international studies, mathematics, military science, physical sciences, premedicine, social sciences. *Creative arts/performance:* creative writing, dance, journalism/publications, music, performing arts, theater/drama. *Special achievements/activities:* cheerleading/drum major, leadership, rodeo. *Special characteristics:* children and siblings of alumni, children with a deceased or disabled parent, general special characteristics, international students, local/state students, out-of-state students, veterans. ***Tuition waivers:*** Full or partial for minority students, employees or children of employees, senior citizens. ***ROTC:*** Army.

LOANS ***Student loans:*** $46,585,581 (100% need-based). 61% of past graduating class borrowed through all loan programs. *Average indebtedness per student:* $20,223. ***Average need-based loan:*** Freshmen: $3228. Undergraduates: $3931. ***Parent loans:*** $10,766,908 (100% non-need-based). ***Programs:*** Perkins.

WORK-STUDY ***Federal work-study:*** Total amount: $3,170,350; jobs available. ***State or other work-study/employment:*** Total amount: $490,796 (100% need-based). Part-time jobs available.

ATHLETIC AWARDS Total amount: $1,407,126 (100% non-need-based).

APPLYING FOR FINANCIAL AID ***Required financial aid forms:*** FAFSA, UM Supplemental Information Sheet. ***Financial aid deadline (priority):*** 2/15. ***Notification date:*** Continuous beginning 4/1. Students must reply within 4 weeks of notification.

CONTACT Kent McGowan, Director of Financial Aid, The University of Montana, Lommasson Center 218, Missoula, MT 59812, 406-243-5373 or toll-free 800-462-8636. *Fax:* 406-243-4930. *E-mail:* faid@mso.umt.edu.

THE UNIVERSITY OF MONTANA WESTERN

Dillon, MT

ABOUT THE INSTITUTION State-supported, coed. 26 undergraduate majors.

GIFT AID (NEED-BASED) ***Scholarships, grants, and awards:*** Federal Pell, FSEOG, state, private, college/university gift aid from institutional funds, Academic Competitiveness Grants, National Smart Grants, Federal TEACH Grants.

GIFT AID (NON-NEED-BASED) ***Scholarships, grants, and awards by category:*** *Academic interests/achievement:* biological sciences, business, education, English, general academic interests/achievements, humanities, mathematics, physical sciences, premedicine, social sciences. *Creative arts/performance:* art/fine arts. *Special achievements/activities:* general special achievements/activities, rodeo. *Special characteristics:* children of faculty/staff, first-generation college students, international students, members of minority groups, out-of-state students, veterans.

LOANS ***Programs:*** Federal Direct (Subsidized and Unsubsidized Stafford, PLUS), Perkins, college/university.

WORK-STUDY ***Federal work-study:*** Total amount: $285,643; 79 jobs averaging $2808. ***State or other work-study/employment:*** Total amount: $175,696 (74% need-based, 26% non-need-based). 126 part-time jobs averaging $2382.

APPLYING FOR FINANCIAL AID ***Required financial aid forms:*** FAFSA, student data form, verification materials (if applicable).

CONTACT Erica L. Jones, Director of Financial Aid, The University of Montana Western, 710 South Atlantic Street, Dillon, MT 59725, 406-683-7511 or toll-free 866-869-6668 (in-state), 877-683-7493 (out-of-state). *Fax:* 406-683-7510. *E-mail:* e_jones@umwestern.edu.

UNIVERSITY OF MONTEVALLO

Montevallo, AL

Tuition & fees (AL res): $8520 **Average undergraduate aid package: $9191**

ABOUT THE INSTITUTION State-supported, coed. 26 undergraduate majors. Federal methodology is used as a basis for awarding need-based institutional aid.

UNDERGRADUATE EXPENSES for 2011–12 ***Tuition, state resident:*** full-time $8040. ***Tuition, nonresident:*** full-time $16,080. ***Required fees:*** full-time $480. ***College room and board:*** $5192.

FRESHMAN FINANCIAL AID (Fall 2010, est.) 294 applied for aid; of those 77% were deemed to have need. 98% of freshmen with need received aid; of those 24% had need fully met. ***Average percent of need met:*** 68% (excluding resources awarded to replace EFC). ***Average financial aid package:*** $9785 (excluding resources awarded to replace EFC). 24% of all full-time freshmen had no need and received non-need-based gift aid.

UNDERGRADUATE FINANCIAL AID (Fall 2010, est.) 1,559 applied for aid; of those 83% were deemed to have need. 99% of undergraduates with need received aid; of those 27% had need fully met. ***Average percent of need met:*** 64% (excluding resources awarded to replace EFC). ***Average financial aid package:*** $9191 (excluding resources awarded to replace EFC). 16% of all full-time undergraduates had no need and received non-need-based gift aid.

GIFT AID (NEED-BASED) ***Total amount:*** $7,602,597 (62% federal, 4% state, 28% institutional, 6% external sources). ***Receiving aid:*** Freshmen: 50% (205); all full-time undergraduates: 49% (1,090). ***Average award:*** Freshmen: $7824; Undergraduates: $6340. ***Scholarships, grants, and awards:*** Federal Pell, FSEOG, state, private, college/university gift aid from institutional funds.

GIFT AID (NON-NEED-BASED) ***Total amount:*** $3,080,843 (8% state, 78% institutional, 14% external sources). ***Average award:*** Freshmen: $6159. Undergraduates: $6715. ***Scholarships, grants, and awards by category:*** *Academic interests/achievement:* 736 awards ($3,978,996 total): biological sciences, business, communication, education, English, foreign languages, general academic interests/achievements, mathematics, physical sciences, social sciences. *Creative arts/performance:* 63 awards ($284,235 total): art/fine arts, cinema/film/broadcasting, creative writing, journalism/publications, music, theater/drama. *Special achievements/activities:* 51 awards ($146,866 total): junior miss, leadership. *Special characteristics:* 122 awards ($747,896 total): children of faculty/staff, international students, out-of-state students.

LOANS ***Student loans:*** $10,090,075 (86% need-based, 14% non-need-based). 54% of past graduating class borrowed through all loan programs. *Average indebtedness per student:* $12,712. ***Average need-based loan:*** Freshmen: $3330. Undergraduates: $4092. ***Parent loans:*** $605,221 (69% need-based, 31% non-need-based). ***Programs:*** Federal Direct (Subsidized and Unsubsidized Stafford, PLUS), Perkins.

WORK-STUDY ***Federal work-study:*** Total amount: $159,750; 90 jobs averaging $1775.

ATHLETIC AWARDS Total amount: $1,031,818 (38% need-based, 62% non-need-based).

APPLYING FOR FINANCIAL AID ***Required financial aid form:*** FAFSA. ***Financial aid deadline (priority):*** 3/1. ***Notification date:*** Continuous beginning 3/25. Students must reply within 2 weeks of notification.

CONTACT Ms. Maria Parker, Director of Student Financial Aid, University of Montevallo, Station 6050, Montevallo, AL 35115, 205-665-6050 or toll-free 800-292-4349. *Fax:* 205-665-6047. *E-mail:* finaid@montevallo.edu.

UNIVERSITY OF MOUNT UNION

Alliance, OH

Tuition & fees: $24,800 **Average undergraduate aid package: $20,044**

ABOUT THE INSTITUTION Independent United Methodist, coed. 50 undergraduate majors. Federal methodology is used as a basis for awarding need-based institutional aid.

UNDERGRADUATE EXPENSES for 2010–11 ***Comprehensive fee:*** $32,580 includes full-time tuition ($24,500), mandatory fees ($300), and room and board ($7780). Full-time tuition and fees vary according to course load. Room and board charges vary according to board plan and housing facility. ***Part-time tuition:*** $1030 per credit hour. ***Payment plans:*** Tuition prepayment, installment.

FRESHMAN FINANCIAL AID (Fall 2010, est.) 643 applied for aid; of those 93% were deemed to have need. 100% of freshmen with need received aid; of those 6% had need fully met. ***Average percent of need met:*** 75% (excluding resources awarded to replace EFC). ***Average financial aid package:*** $20,103 (excluding resources awarded to replace EFC). 13% of all full-time freshmen had no need and received non-need-based gift aid.

UNDERGRADUATE FINANCIAL AID (Fall 2010, est.) 1,934 applied for aid; of those 93% were deemed to have need. 100% of undergraduates with need received aid; of those 9% had need fully met. ***Average percent of need met:*** 76% (excluding resources awarded to replace EFC). ***Average financial aid package:*** $20,044 (excluding resources awarded to replace EFC). 17% of all full-time undergraduates had no need and received non-need-based gift aid.

GIFT AID (NEED-BASED) ***Total amount:*** $13,839,550 (27% federal, 6% state, 63% institutional, 4% external sources). ***Receiving aid:*** Freshmen: 86% (590); all full-time undergraduates: 83% (1,796). ***Average award:*** Freshmen: $14,420; Undergraduates: $13,650. ***Scholarships, grants, and awards:*** Federal Pell, FSEOG, state, private, college/university gift aid from institutional funds.

GIFT AID (NON-NEED-BASED) ***Total amount:*** $13,689,992 (2% federal, 96% institutional, 2% external sources). ***Receiving aid:*** Freshmen: 5% (31). Undergraduates: 6% (120). ***Average award:*** Freshmen: $8201. Undergraduates: $7307. ***Scholarships, grants, and awards by category:*** *Academic interests/achievement:* 1,209 awards ($8,682,788 total): general academic interests/achievements. *Creative arts/performance:* 96 awards ($409,265 total): art/fine arts, cinema/film/broadcasting, journalism/publications, music, theater/drama. *Special characteristics:* 332 awards ($4,006,899 total): children and siblings of alumni, children of faculty/staff, ethnic background, international students, members of minority groups, relatives of clergy. ***Tuition waivers:*** Full or partial for children of alumni, employees or children of employees, senior citizens.

LOANS ***Student loans:*** $16,041,431 (44% need-based, 56% non-need-based). 70% of past graduating class borrowed through all loan programs. *Average indebtedness per student:* $25,804. ***Average need-based loan:*** Freshmen: $4301. Undergraduates: $5417. ***Parent loans:*** $5,198,765 (40% need-based, 60% non-need-based). ***Programs:*** Federal Direct (Subsidized and Unsubsidized Stafford, PLUS), Perkins, private loans.

WORK-STUDY ***Federal work-study:*** Total amount: $1,830,803; 1,549 jobs averaging $1182. ***State or other work-study/employment:*** Total amount: $440,350 (24% need-based, 76% non-need-based). 287 part-time jobs averaging $1534.

APPLYING FOR FINANCIAL AID ***Required financial aid form:*** FAFSA. ***Financial aid deadline:*** Continuous. ***Notification date:*** Continuous beginning 3/15. Students must reply by 8/29.

CONTACT Ms. Emily Swain, Director of Student Financial Services, University of Mount Union, 1972 Clark Avenue, Alliance, OH 44601-3993, 330-823-2674 or toll-free 800-334-6682 (in-state), 800-992-6682 (out-of-state). *Fax:* 330-829-2814. *E-mail:* swainej@mountunion.edu.

UNIVERSITY OF NEBRASKA AT KEARNEY

Kearney, NE

ABOUT THE INSTITUTION State-supported, coed. 41 undergraduate majors.

GIFT AID (NEED-BASED) ***Scholarships, grants, and awards:*** Federal Pell, FSEOG, state, private, college/university gift aid from institutional funds.

GIFT AID (NON-NEED-BASED) ***Scholarships, grants, and awards by category:*** *Academic interests/achievement:* communication. *Creative arts/performance:* applied art and design, art/fine arts, debating, journalism/publications, music. *Special achievements/activities:* cheerleading/drum major. *Special characteristics:* children of faculty/staff, ethnic background, first-generation college students, international students, out-of-state students, veterans, veterans' children.

LOANS ***Programs:*** Perkins, college/university.

WORK-STUDY ***Federal work-study:*** Total amount: $1,181,979; jobs available.

APPLYING FOR FINANCIAL AID ***Required financial aid forms:*** FAFSA, institution's own form.

CONTACT Financial Aid Office, University of Nebraska at Kearney, Memorial Student Affairs Building, 905 West 25th Street, Kearney, NE 68849-0001, 308-865-8520 or toll-free 800-532-7639. *Fax:* 308-865-8096.

UNIVERSITY OF NEBRASKA AT OMAHA

Omaha, NE

Tuition & fees (NE res): $6626 Average undergraduate aid package: $2714

ABOUT THE INSTITUTION State-supported, coed. 66 undergraduate majors. Federal methodology is used as a basis for awarding need-based institutional aid.

UNDERGRADUATE EXPENSES for 2010–11 ***Tuition, state resident:*** full-time $5423; part-time $180.75 per credit hour. ***Tuition, nonresident:*** full-time $15,983; part-time $532.75 per credit hour. ***Required fees:*** full-time $1203. Full-time tuition and fees vary according to course load and reciprocity agreements. Part-time tuition and fees vary according to course load and reciprocity agreements. ***College room and board:*** $7750. Room and board charges vary according to board plan and housing facility. ***Payment plans:*** Installment, deferred payment.

FRESHMAN FINANCIAL AID (Fall 2010, est.) 1,367 applied for aid; of those 67% were deemed to have need. 97% of freshmen with need received aid. ***Average financial aid package:*** $2341 (excluding resources awarded to replace EFC). 11% of all full-time freshmen had no need and received non-need-based gift aid.

UNDERGRADUATE FINANCIAL AID (Fall 2010, est.) 6,200 applied for aid; of those 74% were deemed to have need. 96% of undergraduates with need received aid. ***Average financial aid package:*** $2714 (excluding resources awarded to replace EFC). 5% of all full-time undergraduates had no need and received non-need-based gift aid.

GIFT AID (NEED-BASED) ***Total amount:*** $25,517,280 (56% federal, 7% state, 25% institutional, 12% external sources). ***Receiving aid:*** Freshmen: 34% (587); all full-time undergraduates: 29% (2,907). ***Average award:*** Freshmen: $2163; Undergraduates: $2440. ***Scholarships, grants, and awards:*** Federal Pell, FSEOG, state, private, college/university gift aid from institutional funds.

GIFT AID (NON-NEED-BASED) ***Receiving aid:*** Freshmen: 40% (695). Undergraduates: 19% (1,955). ***Average award:*** Freshmen: $1987. Undergraduates: $2134. ***Scholarships, grants, and awards by category:*** *Academic interests/achievement:* biological sciences, business, communication, computer science, education, engineering/technologies, English, foreign languages, general academic interests/achievements, home economics, mathematics, physical sciences, premedicine, social sciences. *Creative arts/performance:* art/fine arts, creative writing, debating, journalism/publications, music, performing arts, theater/drama. *Special achievements/activities:* general special achievements/activities, leadership, memberships. *Special characteristics:* adult students, children and siblings of alumni, children of faculty/staff, ethnic background, first-generation college students, handicapped students, international students, members of minority groups, out-of-state students, veterans' children. ***Tuition waivers:*** Full or partial for children of alumni, employees or children of employees, senior citizens.

LOANS ***Student loans:*** $54,237,772 (41% need-based, 59% non-need-based). 49% of past graduating class borrowed through all loan programs. *Average indebtedness per student:* $20,000. ***Average need-based loan:*** Freshmen: $2705. Undergraduates: $3348. ***Parent loans:*** $1,680,456 (100% non-need-based). ***Programs:*** Perkins, college/university.

WORK-STUDY ***Federal work-study:*** Total amount: $709,357; 477 jobs averaging $2134.

ATHLETIC AWARDS Total amount: $918,076 (100% need-based).

APPLYING FOR FINANCIAL AID ***Required financial aid form:*** FAFSA. ***Financial aid deadline (priority):*** 3/1. ***Notification date:*** Continuous beginning 4/1. Students must reply within 2 weeks of notification.

CONTACT Office of Financial Aid, University of Nebraska at Omaha, 103 Eppley Administration Building, Omaha, NE 68182-0187, 402-554-2327 or toll-free 800-858-8648 (in-state). *Fax:* 402-554-3472. *E-mail:* finaid@unomaha.edu.

UNIVERSITY OF NEBRASKA–LINCOLN

Lincoln, NE

Tuition & fees (NE res): $7224 Average undergraduate aid package: $10,926

ABOUT THE INSTITUTION State-supported, coed. 123 undergraduate majors. Both federal and institutional methodology are used as a basis for awarding need-based institutional aid.

UNDERGRADUATE EXPENSES for 2010–11 ***Tuition, state resident:*** full-time $5948; part-time $198.25 per semester hour. ***Tuition, nonresident:*** full-time $17,648; part-time $588.25 per semester hour. ***Required fees:*** full-time $1276; $10.35 per semester hour or $287.08 per term. Full-time tuition and fees vary according to course load, program, and reciprocity agreements. Part-time tuition and fees vary according to course load, program, and reciprocity agreements. ***College room and board:*** $7660; ***Room only:*** $4039. Room and board charges vary according to board plan and housing facility. ***Payment plan:*** Installment.

FRESHMAN FINANCIAL AID (Fall 2009) 2,933 applied for aid; of those 68% were deemed to have need. 98% of freshmen with need received aid; of those 12% had need fully met. ***Average percent of need met:*** 88% (excluding resources awarded to replace EFC). ***Average financial aid package:*** $11,572 (excluding resources awarded to replace EFC). 15% of all full-time freshmen had no need and received non-need-based gift aid.

UNDERGRADUATE FINANCIAL AID (Fall 2009) 11,789 applied for aid; of those 72% were deemed to have need. 97% of undergraduates with need received aid; of those 8% had need fully met. ***Average percent of need met:*** 85% (excluding resources awarded to replace EFC). ***Average financial aid package:*** $10,926 (excluding resources awarded to replace EFC). 8% of all full-time undergraduates had no need and received non-need-based gift aid.

GIFT AID (NEED-BASED) ***Total amount:*** $45,691,077 (36% federal, 5% state, 44% institutional, 15% external sources). ***Receiving aid:*** Freshmen: 43% (1,716); all full-time undergraduates: 36% (6,449). ***Average award:*** Freshmen: $8151; Undergraduates: $7304. ***Scholarships, grants, and awards:*** Federal Pell, FSEOG, state, private, college/university gift aid from institutional funds.

GIFT AID (NON-NEED-BASED) ***Total amount:*** $22,968,324 (3% federal, 85% institutional, 12% external sources). ***Receiving aid:*** Freshmen: 5% (213). Undergraduates: 4% (624). ***Average award:*** Freshmen: $5271. Undergraduates: $5494. ***Scholarships, grants, and awards by category:*** *Academic interests/achievement:* agriculture, architecture, biological sciences, business, computer science, education, engineering/technologies, English, foreign languages, general academic interests/achievements, health fields, home economics, humanities, international studies, mathematics, physical sciences, premedicine, social sciences. *Creative arts/performance:* art/fine arts, cinema/film/broadcasting, dance, journalism/publications, music, performing arts, theater/drama. *Special achievements/activities:* cheerleading/drum major, community service, leadership. *Special characteristics:* children and siblings of alumni, ethnic background, handicapped students, international students, members of minority groups, out-of-state students, veterans' children. ***Tuition waivers:*** Full or partial for employees or children of employees.

LOANS ***Student loans:*** $64,653,491 (60% need-based, 40% non-need-based). 60% of past graduating class borrowed through all loan programs. *Average indebtedness per student:* $16,664. ***Average need-based loan:*** Freshmen: $3212. Undergraduates: $4048. ***Parent loans:*** $27,467,709 (44% need-based, 56% non-need-based). ***Programs:*** Federal Direct (Subsidized and Unsubsidized Stafford, PLUS), Perkins, college/university.

WORK-STUDY ***Federal work-study:*** Total amount: $2,952,135; 1,196 jobs averaging $2468.

ATHLETIC AWARDS Total amount: $7,427,823 (100% non-need-based).

APPLYING FOR FINANCIAL AID ***Required financial aid form:*** FAFSA. ***Financial aid deadline (priority):*** 4/1. ***Notification date:*** Continuous beginning 4/1.

CONTACT Ms. Jo Tederman, Assistant Director of Scholarships and Financial Aid, University of Nebraska–Lincoln, 17 Canfield Administration Building, Lincoln, NE 68588-0411, 402-472-2030 or toll-free 800-742-8800. *Fax:* 402-472-9826.

UNIVERSITY OF NEBRASKA MEDICAL CENTER

Omaha, NE

ABOUT THE INSTITUTION State-supported, coed. 7 undergraduate majors.

GIFT AID (NEED-BASED) ***Scholarships, grants, and awards:*** Federal Pell, FSEOG, state, private, college/university gift aid from institutional funds.

LOANS ***Programs:*** Perkins, Federal Nursing, state, college/university.

WORK-STUDY ***Federal work-study:*** Total amount: $35,158; 53 jobs averaging $663.

APPLYING FOR FINANCIAL AID ***Required financial aid forms:*** FAFSA, institution's own form.

CONTACT Judy D. Walker, Director of Financial Aid, University of Nebraska Medical Center, 984265 Nebraska Medical Center, Omaha, NE 68198-4265, 402-559-6409 or toll-free 800-626-8431 Ext. 6468. *Fax:* 402-559-6796. *E-mail:* jdwalker@unmc.edu.

UNIVERSITY OF NEVADA, LAS VEGAS

Las Vegas, NV

Tuition & fees (NV res): $5689 **Average undergraduate aid package: $8965**

ABOUT THE INSTITUTION State-supported, coed. 89 undergraduate majors. Federal methodology is used as a basis for awarding need-based institutional aid.

UNDERGRADUATE EXPENSES for 2010–11 ***Tuition, state resident:*** full-time $4913; part-time $156.75 per credit hour. ***Tuition, nonresident:*** full-time $18,203; part-time $313.75 per credit hour. ***Required fees:*** full-time $776. Full-time tuition and fees vary according to course level and reciprocity agreements. Part-time tuition and fees vary according to course level and reciprocity agreements. ***College room and board:*** $10,454; ***Room only:*** $6544. Room and board charges vary according to board plan. ***Payment plan:*** Deferred payment.

FRESHMAN FINANCIAL AID (Fall 2010, est.) 2,136 applied for aid; of those 77% were deemed to have need. 99% of freshmen with need received aid; of those 17% had need fully met. ***Average percent of need met:*** 49% (excluding resources awarded to replace EFC). ***Average financial aid package:*** $8804 (excluding resources awarded to replace EFC). 3% of all full-time freshmen had no need and received non-need-based gift aid.

UNDERGRADUATE FINANCIAL AID (Fall 2010, est.) 10,547 applied for aid; of those 85% were deemed to have need. 98% of undergraduates with need received aid; of those 14% had need fully met. ***Average percent of need met:*** 56% (excluding resources awarded to replace EFC). ***Average financial aid package:*** $8965 (excluding resources awarded to replace EFC). 3% of all full-time undergraduates had no need and received non-need-based gift aid.

GIFT AID (NEED-BASED) ***Total amount:*** $48,727,260 (63% federal, 18% state, 16% institutional, 3% external sources). ***Receiving aid:*** Freshmen: 46% (1,338); all full-time undergraduates: 45% (7,348). ***Average award:*** Freshmen: $4699; Undergraduates: $4572. ***Scholarships, grants, and awards:*** Federal Pell, FSEOG, state, private, college/university gift aid from institutional funds.

GIFT AID (NON-NEED-BASED) ***Total amount:*** $8,084,132 (59% federal, 23% state, 16% institutional, 2% external sources). ***Receiving aid:*** Freshmen: 42% (1,220). Undergraduates: 24% (3,990). ***Average award:*** Freshmen: $3115. Undergraduates: $3211. ***Scholarships, grants, and awards by category:*** *Academic interests/achievement:* architecture, biological sciences, business, communication, computer science, education, engineering/technologies, English, foreign languages, general academic interests/achievements, health fields, humanities, international studies, mathematics, physical sciences, premedicine, social sciences. *Creative arts/performance:* applied art and design, art/fine arts, cinema/film/broadcasting, creative writing, dance, debating, general creative arts/performance, journalism/publications, music, performing arts, theater/drama. *Special achievements/activities:* cheerleading/drum major, community service, general special achievements/activities, leadership, rodeo. *Special characteristics:* adult students, children and siblings of alumni, children of faculty/staff, children of public servants, children of union members/company employees, children with a deceased or disabled parent, ethnic background, first-generation college students, general special characteristics, handicapped students, international students, local/state students, members of minority groups, out-of-state students, previous college experience, veterans, veterans' children. ***Tuition waivers:*** Full or partial for children of alumni, employees or children of employees, senior citizens.

LOANS ***Student loans:*** $82,308,027 (81% need-based, 19% non-need-based). 40% of past graduating class borrowed through all loan programs. *Average indebtedness per student:* $17,165. ***Average need-based loan:*** Freshmen: $3246. Undergraduates: $4135. ***Parent loans:*** $37,136,935 (61% need-based, 39% non-need-based). ***Programs:*** Federal Direct (Subsidized and Unsubsidized Stafford, PLUS), Perkins, Federal Nursing, state, college/university.

WORK-STUDY ***Federal work-study:*** Total amount: $596,327; jobs available. ***State or other work-study/employment:*** Total amount: $1,206,547 (99% need-based, 1% non-need-based). Part-time jobs available.

ATHLETIC AWARDS Total amount: $2,570,595 (92% need-based, 8% non-need-based).

APPLYING FOR FINANCIAL AID ***Required financial aid form:*** FAFSA. ***Financial aid deadline (priority):*** 2/1. ***Notification date:*** Continuous beginning 3/20. Students must reply within 2 weeks of notification.

CONTACT Norm Bedford, Director of Financial Aid and Scholarships, University of Nevada, Las Vegas, 4505 Maryland Parkway, Las Vegas, NV 89154-2016, 702-895-3424. *Fax:* 702-895-1353. *E-mail:* financialaid@unlv.edu.

UNIVERSITY OF NEVADA, RENO

Reno, NV

Tuition & fees (NV res): $4841 **Average undergraduate aid package: $7580**

ABOUT THE INSTITUTION State-supported, coed. 97 undergraduate majors. Federal methodology is used as a basis for awarding need-based institutional aid.

UNDERGRADUATE EXPENSES for 2011–12 ***One-time required fee:*** $110. ***Tuition, state resident:*** full-time $4193; part-time $163.75 per credit. ***Tuition, nonresident:*** full-time $18,508. ***Required fees:*** full-time $648. Full-time tuition and fees vary according to course load. Part-time tuition and fees vary according to course load. ***College room and board:*** $9518. Room and board charges vary according to board plan and housing facility. ***Payment plan:*** Deferred payment.

FRESHMAN FINANCIAL AID (Fall 2009) 1,538 applied for aid; of those 63% were deemed to have need. 98% of freshmen with need received aid; of those 17% had need fully met. ***Average percent of need met:*** 58% (excluding resources awarded to replace EFC). ***Average financial aid package:*** $6336 (excluding resources awarded to replace EFC). 46% of all full-time freshmen had no need and received non-need-based gift aid.

UNDERGRADUATE FINANCIAL AID (Fall 2009) 5,913 applied for aid; of those 74% were deemed to have need. 96% of undergraduates with need received aid; of those 14% had need fully met. ***Average percent of need met:*** 58% (excluding resources awarded to replace EFC). ***Average financial aid package:*** $7580 (excluding resources awarded to replace EFC). 38% of all full-time undergraduates had no need and received non-need-based gift aid.

GIFT AID (NEED-BASED) ***Total amount:*** $22,319,678 (47% federal, 27% state, 21% institutional, 5% external sources). ***Receiving aid:*** Freshmen: 38% (814); all full-time undergraduates: 34% (3,626). ***Average award:*** Freshmen: $6249; Undergraduates: $6129. ***Scholarships, grants, and awards:*** Federal Pell, FSEOG, state, private, college/university gift aid from institutional funds, Federal Nursing.

GIFT AID (NON-NEED-BASED) ***Total amount:*** $13,526,836 (48% state, 42% institutional, 10% external sources). ***Receiving aid:*** Freshmen: 39% (837). Undergraduates: 27% (2,885). ***Average award:*** Freshmen: $3039. Undergraduates: $2873. ***Scholarships, grants, and awards by category:*** *Academic interests/achievement:* general academic interests/achievements. *Creative arts/performance:* general creative arts/performance, music, theater/drama. *Special characteristics:* adult students, children and siblings of alumni, ethnic background, first-generation college students, married students. ***Tuition waivers:*** Full or partial for children of alumni, employees or children of employees, senior citizens.

LOANS ***Student loans:*** $29,043,621 (74% need-based, 26% non-need-based). 36% of past graduating class borrowed through all loan programs. *Average indebtedness per student:* $15,814. ***Average need-based loan:*** Freshmen: $3102. Undergraduates: $4311. ***Parent loans:*** $2,287,005 (37% need-based, 63% non-need-based). ***Programs:*** Federal Direct (Subsidized and Unsubsidized Stafford, PLUS), Perkins, Federal Nursing, college/university, private loans.

WORK-STUDY ***Federal work-study:*** Total amount: $497,624; jobs available. ***State or other work-study/employment:*** Total amount: $155,620 (58% need-based, 42% non-need-based). Part-time jobs available.

ATHLETIC AWARDS Total amount: $4,746,637 (22% need-based, 78% non-need-based).

APPLYING FOR FINANCIAL AID ***Required financial aid form:*** FAFSA. ***Financial aid deadline (priority):*** 3/1. ***Notification date:*** Continuous beginning 4/1. Students must reply within 2 weeks of notification.

CONTACT Tim Wolfe, Director of Student Financial Aid, University of Nevada, Reno, Mail Stop 076, Reno, NV 89557, 775-784-4666 or toll-free 866-263-8232. *Fax:* 775-784-1025. *E-mail:* tawolfe@unr.edu.

UNIVERSITY OF NEW ENGLAND

Biddeford, ME

CONTACT John R. Bowie, Director of Financial Aid, University of New England, 11 Hills Beach Road, Biddeford, ME 04005, 207-602-2342 or toll-free 800-477-4UNE. *Fax:* 207-602-5946. *E-mail:* finaid@une.edu.

UNIVERSITY OF NEW HAMPSHIRE

Durham, NH

Tuition & fees (NH res): $13,672 Average undergraduate aid package: $20,195

ABOUT THE INSTITUTION State-supported, coed. 87 undergraduate majors. Federal methodology is used as a basis for awarding need-based institutional aid.

UNDERGRADUATE EXPENSES for 2010–11 ***Tuition, state resident:*** full-time $10,730; part-time $447 per credit hour. ***Tuition, nonresident:*** full-time $24,700; part-time $1029 per credit hour. ***Required fees:*** full-time $2942; $735.50 per term. Full-time tuition and fees vary according to degree level and program. Part-time tuition and fees vary according to course load, degree level, and program. ***College room and board:*** $9053; ***Room only:*** $5528. Room and board charges vary according to board plan and housing facility. ***Payment plan:*** Installment.

FRESHMAN FINANCIAL AID (Fall 2009) 2,432 applied for aid; of those 75% were deemed to have need. 98% of freshmen with need received aid; of those 23% had need fully met. ***Average percent of need met:*** 85% (excluding resources awarded to replace EFC). ***Average financial aid package:*** $20,987 (excluding resources awarded to replace EFC). 20% of all full-time freshmen had no need and received non-need-based gift aid.

UNDERGRADUATE FINANCIAL AID (Fall 2009) 9,112 applied for aid; of those 80% were deemed to have need. 99% of undergraduates with need received aid; of those 21% had need fully met. ***Average percent of need met:*** 81% (excluding resources awarded to replace EFC). ***Average financial aid package:*** $20,195 (excluding resources awarded to replace EFC). 20% of all full-time undergraduates had no need and received non-need-based gift aid.

GIFT AID (NEED-BASED) ***Total amount:*** $51,078,136 (26% federal, 2% state, 59% institutional, 13% external sources). ***Receiving aid:*** Freshmen: 45% (1,272); all full-time undergraduates: 41% (4,698). ***Average award:*** Freshmen: $4801; Undergraduates: $3679. ***Scholarships, grants, and awards:*** Federal Pell, FSEOG, state, private, college/university gift aid from institutional funds, Veterans Education Benefits.

GIFT AID (NON-NEED-BASED) ***Total amount:*** $14,674,375 (100% institutional). ***Receiving aid:*** Freshmen: 7% (192). Undergraduates: 4% (474). ***Average award:*** Freshmen: $7285. Undergraduates: $8289. ***Scholarships, grants, and awards by category:*** *Academic interests/achievement:* agriculture, business, education, engineering/technologies, English, general academic interests/achievements, health fields, humanities, mathematics, military science. *Creative arts/performance:* art/fine arts, dance, music, theater/drama. *Special achievements/activities:* community service. *Special characteristics:* children and siblings of alumni, children of faculty/staff, handicapped students, international students, local/state students. ***Tuition waivers:*** Full or partial for employees or children of employees.

LOANS ***Student loans:*** $95,837,764 (41% need-based, 59% non-need-based). 76% of past graduating class borrowed through all loan programs. *Average indebtedness per student:* $32,323. ***Average need-based loan:*** Freshmen: $2597. Undergraduates: $3323. ***Parent loans:*** $22,626,522 (100% non-need-based). ***Programs:*** Federal Direct (Subsidized and Unsubsidized Stafford, PLUS), Perkins, state, college/university.

WORK-STUDY ***Federal work-study:*** Total amount: $12,272,737; 4,675 jobs averaging $2486. ***State or other work-study/employment:*** Total amount: $6,189,609 (100% non-need-based). 2,709 part-time jobs averaging $1850.

ATHLETIC AWARDS Total amount: $7,534,429 (100% non-need-based).

APPLYING FOR FINANCIAL AID ***Required financial aid form:*** FAFSA. ***Financial aid deadline (priority):*** 3/1. ***Notification date:*** Continuous beginning 3/1.

CONTACT Susan K. Allen, Director of Financial Aid, University of New Hampshire, 11 Garrison Avenue, Durham, NH 03824, 603-862-3600. *Fax:* 603-862-1947. *E-mail:* financial.aid@unh.edu.

UNIVERSITY OF NEW HAMPSHIRE AT MANCHESTER

Manchester, NH

Tuition & fees (NH res): $11,226 Average undergraduate aid package: $11,739

ABOUT THE INSTITUTION State-supported, coed. 13 undergraduate majors. Federal methodology is used as a basis for awarding need-based institutional aid.

UNDERGRADUATE EXPENSES for 2010–11 ***Tuition, state resident:*** full-time $10,650; part-time $444 per credit hour. ***Tuition, nonresident:*** full-time $24,700; part-time $1029 per credit hour. ***Required fees:*** full-time $576. Full-time tuition and fees vary according to course load and program. Part-time tuition and fees vary according to course load and program. ***Payment plan:*** Installment.

FRESHMAN FINANCIAL AID (Fall 2009) 134 applied for aid; of those 68% were deemed to have need. 97% of freshmen with need received aid; of those 10% had need fully met. ***Average percent of need met:*** 74% (excluding resources awarded to replace EFC). ***Average financial aid package:*** $10,639 (excluding resources awarded to replace EFC). 3% of all full-time freshmen had no need and received non-need-based gift aid.

UNDERGRADUATE FINANCIAL AID (Fall 2009) 625 applied for aid; of those 76% were deemed to have need. 98% of undergraduates with need received aid; of those 12% had need fully met. ***Average percent of need met:*** 66% (excluding resources awarded to replace EFC). ***Average financial aid package:*** $11,739 (excluding resources awarded to replace EFC). 1% of all full-time undergraduates had no need and received non-need-based gift aid.

GIFT AID (NEED-BASED) ***Total amount:*** $1,773,494 (53% federal, 4% state, 26% institutional, 17% external sources). ***Receiving aid:*** Freshmen: 22% (35); all full-time undergraduates: 21% (178). ***Average award:*** Freshmen: $1803; Undergraduates: $1924. ***Scholarships, grants, and awards:*** Federal Pell, FSEOG, state, private, college/university gift aid from institutional funds.

GIFT AID (NON-NEED-BASED) ***Total amount:*** $43,963 (100% institutional). ***Receiving aid:*** Freshmen: 3% (5). Undergraduates: 1% (6). ***Average award:*** Freshmen: $400. Undergraduates: $583. ***Scholarships, grants, and awards by category:*** *Academic interests/achievement:* general academic interests/achievements. *Special characteristics:* children of faculty/staff. ***Tuition waivers:*** Full or partial for employees or children of employees, senior citizens.

LOANS ***Student loans:*** $4,535,687 (39% need-based, 61% non-need-based). 77% of past graduating class borrowed through all loan programs. *Average indebtedness per student:* $23,685. ***Average need-based loan:*** Freshmen: $2613. Undergraduates: $3683. ***Parent loans:*** $206,976 (100% non-need-based). ***Programs:*** Federal Direct (Subsidized and Unsubsidized Stafford, PLUS), Perkins, state, college/university.

WORK-STUDY ***Federal work-study:*** Total amount: $342,237; 164 jobs averaging $2165.

APPLYING FOR FINANCIAL AID ***Required financial aid form:*** FAFSA. ***Financial aid deadline (priority):*** 3/1. ***Notification date:*** Continuous beginning 4/1.

CONTACT Jodi Abad, Assistant Director of Financial Aid, University of New Hampshire at Manchester, French Hall, Manchester, NH 03101-1113, 603-641-4146. *Fax:* 603-641-4125.

UNIVERSITY OF NEW HAVEN

West Haven, CT

ABOUT THE INSTITUTION Independent, coed. 48 undergraduate majors.

GIFT AID (NEED-BASED) ***Scholarships, grants, and awards:*** Federal Pell, FSEOG, state, private, college/university gift aid from institutional funds.

LOANS ***Programs:*** Perkins.

WORK-STUDY ***Federal work-study:*** Total amount: $215,000; 157 jobs averaging $1290.

APPLYING FOR FINANCIAL AID ***Required financial aid forms:*** FAFSA, federal tax returns.

CONTACT Mrs. Karen Flynn, Director of Financial Aid, University of New Haven, 300 Boston Post Road, West Haven, CT 06516-1916, 203-932-7315 or toll-free 800-DIAL-UNH. *Fax:* 203-931-6050. *E-mail:* financialaid@newhaven.edu.

UNIVERSITY OF NEW MEXICO

Albuquerque, NM

CONTACT Office of Student Financial Aid, University of New Mexico, Mesa Vista Hall North, Albuquerque, NM 87131, 505-277-2041 or toll-free 800-CALLUNM (in-state). *Fax:* 505-277-6326. *E-mail:* finaid@unm.edu.

UNIVERSITY OF NEW MEXICO–GALLUP

Gallup, NM

CONTACT Financial Aid Office, University of New Mexico–Gallup, 200 College Road, Gallup, NM 87301-5603, 505-863-7500 or toll-free 505-863-7576 (in-state).

UNIVERSITY OF NEW ORLEANS

New Orleans, LA

Tuition & fees (LA res): $4811 **Average undergraduate aid package: $7929**

ABOUT THE INSTITUTION State-supported, coed. 47 undergraduate majors. Federal methodology is used as a basis for awarding need-based institutional aid.

UNDERGRADUATE EXPENSES for 2010–11 ***Tuition, state resident:*** full-time $4152; part-time $138.40 per credit hour. ***Tuition, nonresident:*** full-time $13,740; part-time $458 per credit hour. ***Required fees:*** full-time $659. Full-time tuition and fees vary according to course load, location, and program. Part-time tuition and fees vary according to course load, location, and program. ***College room and board:*** $8127. Room and board charges vary according to board plan and housing facility. ***Payment plans:*** Installment, deferred payment.

FRESHMAN FINANCIAL AID (Fall 2010, est.) 931 applied for aid; of those 81% were deemed to have need. 97% of freshmen with need received aid; of those 12% had need fully met. ***Average percent of need met:*** 60% (excluding resources awarded to replace EFC). ***Average financial aid package:*** $8613 (excluding resources awarded to replace EFC). 1% of all full-time freshmen had no need and received non-need-based gift aid.

UNDERGRADUATE FINANCIAL AID (Fall 2010, est.) 5,003 applied for aid; of those 87% were deemed to have need. 91% of undergraduates with need received aid; of those 8% had need fully met. ***Average percent of need met:*** 51% (excluding resources awarded to replace EFC). ***Average financial aid package:*** $7929 (excluding resources awarded to replace EFC). 2% of all full-time undergraduates had no need and received non-need-based gift aid.

GIFT AID (NEED-BASED) ***Total amount:*** $17,645,375 (67% federal, 6% state, 27% institutional). ***Receiving aid:*** Freshmen: 53% (541); all full-time undergraduates: 43% (2,692). ***Average award:*** Freshmen: $6162; Undergraduates: $5837. ***Scholarships, grants, and awards:*** Federal Pell, FSEOG, state, private, college/university gift aid from institutional funds.

GIFT AID (NON-NEED-BASED) ***Total amount:*** $7,827,535 (1% federal, 84% state, 12% institutional, 3% external sources). ***Receiving aid:*** Freshmen: 45% (460). Undergraduates: 24% (1,507). ***Average award:*** Freshmen: $1000. Undergraduates: $1666. ***Scholarships, grants, and awards by category:*** *Academic interests/achievement:* 2,485 awards ($10,821,212 total): biological sciences, business, education, engineering/technologies, English, foreign languages, general academic interests/achievements, mathematics, physical sciences, social sciences. *Creative arts/performance:* 13 awards ($80,538 total): general creative arts/performance, music, theater/drama. *Special achievements/activities:* 24 awards ($228,654 total): general special achievements/activities, leadership. *Special characteristics:* 1,791 awards ($7,002,858 total): adult students, children and siblings of alumni, children of public servants, children with a deceased or disabled parent, general special characteristics, international students, local/state students, members of minority groups, out-of-state students, public servants. ***Tuition waivers:*** Full or partial for employees or children of employees, senior citizens.

LOANS ***Student loans:*** $21,460,193 (47% need-based, 53% non-need-based). 20% of past graduating class borrowed through all loan programs. *Average indebtedness per student:* $16,427. ***Average need-based loan:*** Freshmen: $3332. Undergraduates: $4262. ***Parent loans:*** $377,205 (100% non-need-based). ***Programs:*** Federal Direct (Subsidized and Unsubsidized Stafford, PLUS), Perkins, college/university.

WORK-STUDY ***Federal work-study:*** Total amount: $484,569; 184 jobs averaging $2634. ***State or other work-study/employment:*** Total amount: $547,192 (100% non-need-based). 397 part-time jobs averaging $1378.

ATHLETIC AWARDS Total amount: $318,364 (26% need-based, 74% non-need-based).

APPLYING FOR FINANCIAL AID ***Required financial aid form:*** FAFSA. ***Financial aid deadline (priority):*** 5/1. ***Notification date:*** Continuous beginning 4/20. Students must reply within 4 weeks of notification.

CONTACT Ms. Emily London-Jones, Director of Student Financial Aid, University of New Orleans, Administration Building, Room 1005, New Orleans, LA 70148, 504-280-6687 or toll-free 800-256-5866 (out-of-state). *Fax:* 504-280-3973. *E-mail:* elondon@uno.edu.

UNIVERSITY OF NORTH ALABAMA

Florence, AL

Tuition & fees (AL res): $6668 **Average undergraduate aid package: $7357**

ABOUT THE INSTITUTION State-supported, coed. 38 undergraduate majors. Federal methodology is used as a basis for awarding need-based institutional aid.

UNDERGRADUATE EXPENSES for 2010–11 ***Tuition, state resident:*** full-time $5550; part-time $185 per credit hour. ***Tuition, nonresident:*** full-time $11,100; part-time $370 per credit hour. ***Required fees:*** full-time $1118. Full-time tuition and fees vary according to course load and program. Part-time tuition and fees vary according to course load and program. ***College room and board:*** $5012. Room and board charges vary according to board plan and housing facility. ***Payment plan:*** Installment.

FRESHMAN FINANCIAL AID (Fall 2010, est.) 992 applied for aid; of those 71% were deemed to have need. 96% of freshmen with need received aid; of those 47% had need fully met. ***Average percent of need met:*** 63% (excluding resources awarded to replace EFC). ***Average financial aid package:*** $6254 (excluding resources awarded to replace EFC). 18% of all full-time freshmen had no need and received non-need-based gift aid.

UNDERGRADUATE FINANCIAL AID (Fall 2010, est.) 3,465 applied for aid; of those 72% were deemed to have need. 97% of undergraduates with need received aid; of those 72% had need fully met. ***Average percent of need met:*** 61% (excluding resources awarded to replace EFC). ***Average financial aid package:*** $7357 (excluding resources awarded to replace EFC). 21% of all full-time undergraduates had no need and received non-need-based gift aid.

GIFT AID (NEED-BASED) ***Total amount:*** $9,775,282 (99% federal, 1% state). ***Receiving aid:*** Freshmen: 47% (537); all full-time undergraduates: 42% (1,829). ***Average award:*** Freshmen: $4237; Undergraduates: $4625. ***Scholarships, grants, and awards:*** Federal Pell, FSEOG, state, private, college/university gift aid from institutional funds, Academic Competitiveness Grants, National SMART Grants.

GIFT AID (NON-NEED-BASED) ***Total amount:*** $4,885,276 (82% institutional, 18% external sources). ***Receiving aid:*** Freshmen: 16% (185). Undergraduates: 16% (697). ***Average award:*** Freshmen: $1393. Undergraduates: $1072. ***Scholarships, grants, and awards by category:*** *Academic interests/achievement:* 468 awards ($1,525,713 total): general academic interests/achievements. *Creative arts/performance:* 253 awards ($402,086 total): art/fine arts, journalism/publications, music. *Special achievements/activities:* 324 awards ($759,923 total): cheerleading/drum major, general special achievements/activities, leadership. *Special characteristics:* 22 awards ($40,544 total): children of faculty/staff, first-generation college students, general special characteristics, out-of-state students. ***Tuition waivers:*** Full or partial for employees or children of employees, senior citizens.

LOANS ***Student loans:*** $34,575,100 (66% need-based, 34% non-need-based). 67% of past graduating class borrowed through all loan programs. *Average indebtedness per student:* $29,200. ***Average need-based loan:*** Freshmen: $2979. Undergraduates: $3726. ***Parent loans:*** $964,036 (38% need-based, 62% non-need-based). ***Programs:*** Perkins.

WORK-STUDY ***Federal work-study:*** Total amount: $194,171; 124 jobs averaging $1373. ***State or other work-study/employment:*** Total amount: $687,088 (100% non-need-based). 386 part-time jobs averaging $1397.

ATHLETIC AWARDS Total amount: $1,331,886 (100% non-need-based).

APPLYING FOR FINANCIAL AID ***Required financial aid form:*** FAFSA. ***Financial aid deadline (priority):*** 4/1. ***Notification date:*** 5/31. Students must reply within 2 weeks of notification.

CONTACT Mr. Ben Baker, Director of Student Financial Services, University of North Alabama, UNA Box 5014, Florence, AL 35632-0001, 256-765-4278 or toll-free 800-TALKUNA. *Fax:* 256-765-4920. *E-mail:* bjbaker@una.edu.

THE UNIVERSITY OF NORTH CAROLINA AT ASHEVILLE

Asheville, NC

Tuition & fees (NC res): $4772 **Average undergraduate aid package: $11,450**

ABOUT THE INSTITUTION State-supported, coed. 32 undergraduate majors. Federal methodology is used as a basis for awarding need-based institutional aid.

UNDERGRADUATE EXPENSES for 2010–11 ***Tuition, state resident:*** full-time $2626. ***Tuition, nonresident:*** full-time $15,398. ***Required fees:*** full-time $2146. Full-time tuition and fees vary according to course load. Part-time tuition and fees vary according to course load. ***College room and board:*** $7040; ***Room only:*** $3990. Room and board charges vary according to housing facility. ***Payment plan:*** Installment.

FRESHMAN FINANCIAL AID (Fall 2010, est.) 479 applied for aid; of those 65% were deemed to have need. 99% of freshmen with need received aid; of those 42% had need fully met. ***Average percent of need met:*** 84% (excluding resources awarded to replace EFC). ***Average financial aid package:*** $10,313 (excluding resources awarded to replace EFC). 6% of all full-time freshmen had no need and received non-need-based gift aid.

UNDERGRADUATE FINANCIAL AID (Fall 2010, est.) 2,264 applied for aid; of those 72% were deemed to have need. 99% of undergraduates with need received aid; of those 53% had need fully met. ***Average percent of need met:*** 87% (excluding resources awarded to replace EFC). ***Average financial aid package:*** $11,450 (excluding resources awarded to replace EFC). 5% of all full-time undergraduates had no need and received non-need-based gift aid.

GIFT AID (NEED-BASED) ***Total amount:*** $10,935,848 (49% federal, 38% state, 13% institutional). ***Receiving aid:*** Freshmen: 51% (303); all full-time undergraduates: 49% (1,530). ***Average award:*** Freshmen: $6643; Undergraduates: $6470. ***Scholarships, grants, and awards:*** Federal Pell, FSEOG, state, private, college/university gift aid from institutional funds.

GIFT AID (NON-NEED-BASED) ***Total amount:*** $936,576 (5% federal, 57% state, 38% institutional). ***Receiving aid:*** Freshmen: 5% (30). Undergraduates: 5% (161). ***Average award:*** Freshmen: $3414. Undergraduates: $3260. ***Scholarships, grants, and awards by category:*** *Academic interests/achievement:* biological sciences, business, communication, computer science, education, engineering/technologies, English, general academic interests/achievements, health fields, mathematics, physical sciences, premedicine, social sciences. *Creative arts/performance:* art/fine arts, general creative arts/performance, music, theater/drama. *Special achievements/activities:* community service, general special achievements/activities, junior miss, leadership. *Special characteristics:* adult students, children and siblings of alumni, children of faculty/staff, ethnic background, first-generation college students, general special characteristics, handicapped students, international students, local/state students, members of minority groups, veterans, veterans' children. ***Tuition waivers:*** Full or partial for employees or children of employees.

LOANS ***Student loans:*** $10,038,923 (66% need-based, 34% non-need-based). 48% of past graduating class borrowed through all loan programs. *Average indebtedness per student:* $15,443. ***Average need-based loan:*** Freshmen: $3197. Undergraduates: $4195. ***Parent loans:*** $918,170 (15% need-based, 85% non-need-based). ***Programs:*** Federal Direct (Subsidized and Unsubsidized Stafford, PLUS), Perkins, state, college/university.

WORK-STUDY ***Federal work-study:*** Total amount: $114,114; 43 jobs averaging $2654.

ATHLETIC AWARDS Total amount: $1,521,760 (22% need-based, 78% non-need-based).

APPLYING FOR FINANCIAL AID ***Required financial aid form:*** FAFSA. ***Financial aid deadline (priority):*** 3/1. ***Notification date:*** Continuous beginning 3/15. Students must reply within 2 weeks of notification.

CONTACT Ms. Elizabeth D. Bartlett, Associate Director of Financial Aid, The University of North Carolina at Asheville, 1 University Heights, Asheville, NC 28804-8510, 828-232-6535 or toll-free 800-531-9842. *Fax:* 828-251-2294. *E-mail:* bbartlett@unca.edu.

THE UNIVERSITY OF NORTH CAROLINA AT CHAPEL HILL

Chapel Hill, NC

Tuition & fees (NC res): $6666 **Average undergraduate aid package: $13,509**

ABOUT THE INSTITUTION State-supported, coed. 61 undergraduate majors. Both federal and institutional methodology are used as a basis for awarding need-based institutional aid.

UNDERGRADUATE EXPENSES for 2010–11 ***Tuition, state resident:*** full-time $4816. ***Tuition, nonresident:*** full-time $23,430. ***Required fees:*** full-time $1850. Full-time tuition and fees vary according to program. Part-time tuition and fees vary according to course load and program. ***College room and board:*** $9036; ***Room only:*** $5408. Room and board charges vary according to board plan, housing facility, and location. ***Payment plans:*** Installment, deferred payment.

FRESHMAN FINANCIAL AID (Fall 2009) 3,283 applied for aid; of those 48% were deemed to have need. 99% of freshmen with need received aid; of those 98% had need fully met. ***Average percent of need met:*** 100% (excluding resources awarded to replace EFC). ***Average financial aid package:*** $13,449 (excluding resources awarded to replace EFC). 21% of all full-time freshmen had no need and received non-need-based gift aid.

UNDERGRADUATE FINANCIAL AID (Fall 2009) 11,595 applied for aid; of those 54% were deemed to have need. 99% of undergraduates with need received aid; of those 98% had need fully met. ***Average percent of need met:*** 100% (excluding resources awarded to replace EFC). ***Average financial aid package:*** $13,509 (excluding resources awarded to replace EFC). 15% of all full-time undergraduates had no need and received non-need-based gift aid.

GIFT AID (NEED-BASED) ***Total amount:*** $69,669,530 (23% federal, 20% state, 50% institutional, 7% external sources). ***Receiving aid:*** Freshmen: 39% (1,539); all full-time undergraduates: 36% (6,155). ***Average award:*** Freshmen: $11,677; Undergraduates: $11,080. ***Scholarships, grants, and awards:*** Federal Pell, FSEOG, state, private, college/university gift aid from institutional funds.

GIFT AID (NON-NEED-BASED) ***Total amount:*** $15,130,528 (2% federal, 10% state, 38% institutional, 50% external sources). ***Receiving aid:*** Freshmen: 18% (704). Undergraduates: 11% (1,894). ***Average award:*** Freshmen: $4581. Undergraduates: $5117. ***Scholarships, grants, and awards by category:*** *Academic interests/achievement:* business, communication, education, English, general academic interests/achievements, health fields, mathematics. *Creative arts/performance:* applied art and design, art/fine arts, journalism/publications, music, theater/drama. *Special achievements/activities:* community service, general special achievements/activities, leadership. *Special characteristics:* children of faculty/staff, international students, out-of-state students, relatives of clergy, religious affiliation. ***Tuition waivers:*** Full or partial for employees or children of employees.

LOANS ***Student loans:*** $33,502,803 (63% need-based, 37% non-need-based). ***Average need-based loan:*** Freshmen: $2919. Undergraduates: $4154. ***Parent loans:*** $6,065,964 (38% need-based, 62% non-need-based). ***Programs:*** Federal Direct (Subsidized and Unsubsidized Stafford, PLUS), Perkins, state, college/university, alternative loans.

WORK-STUDY ***Federal work-study:*** Total amount: $2,471,403; 1,645 jobs averaging $1844.

ATHLETIC AWARDS Total amount: $6,253,764 (32% need-based, 68% non-need-based).

APPLYING FOR FINANCIAL AID ***Required financial aid forms:*** FAFSA, CSS Financial Aid PROFILE. ***Financial aid deadline (priority):*** 3/1. ***Notification date:*** Continuous beginning 3/15. Students must reply by 5/1.

CONTACT Ms. Shirley A. Ort, Associate Provost and Director of Scholarships and Student Aid, The University of North Carolina at Chapel Hill, CB # 2300, 111 Pettigrew Hall, Chapel Hill, NC 27599, 919-962-8396. *Fax:* 919-962-2716. *E-mail:* aidinfo@unc.edu.

THE UNIVERSITY OF NORTH CAROLINA AT CHARLOTTE

Charlotte, NC

Tuition & fees (NC res): $5138 **Average undergraduate aid package: $9203**

ABOUT THE INSTITUTION State-supported, coed. 80 undergraduate majors. Federal methodology is used as a basis for awarding need-based institutional aid.

UNDERGRADUATE EXPENSES for 2010–11 ***Tuition, state resident:*** full-time $3044. ***Tuition, nonresident:*** full-time $14,091. ***Required fees:*** full-time $2094. Full-time tuition and fees vary according to course load. Part-time tuition and fees vary according to course load. ***College room and board:*** $7260; ***Room only:*** $3830. Room and board charges vary according to board plan and housing facility. ***Payment plan:*** Installment.

FRESHMAN FINANCIAL AID (Fall 2009) 2,471 applied for aid; of those 65% were deemed to have need. 97% of freshmen with need received aid; of those 23% had need fully met. ***Average percent of need met:*** 78% (excluding resources awarded to replace EFC). ***Average financial aid package:*** $8970 (excluding resources awarded to replace EFC). 1% of all full-time freshmen had no need and received non-need-based gift aid.

UNDERGRADUATE FINANCIAL AID (Fall 2009) 11,301 applied for aid; of those 76% were deemed to have need. 98% of undergraduates with need received aid; of those 18% had need fully met. ***Average percent of need met:*** 71% (excluding resources awarded to replace EFC). ***Average financial aid package:*** $9203 (excluding resources awarded to replace EFC). 2% of all full-time undergraduates had no need and received non-need-based gift aid.

GIFT AID (NEED-BASED) ***Total amount:*** $54,550,389 (52% federal, 38% state, 10% institutional). ***Receiving aid:*** Freshmen: 48% (1,480); all full-time undergraduates: 48% (7,355). ***Average award:*** Freshmen: $6709; Undergraduates: $6234. ***Scholarships, grants, and awards:*** Federal Pell, FSEOG, state, private, college/university gift aid from institutional funds.

GIFT AID (NON-NEED-BASED) ***Total amount:*** $2,859,985 (14% state, 21% institutional, 65% external sources). ***Receiving aid:*** Freshmen: 2% (56). Undergraduates: 4% (629). ***Average award:*** Freshmen: $1605. Undergraduates: $2190. ***Scholarships, grants, and awards by category:*** *Academic interests/achievement:* architecture, business, computer science, education, engineering/technologies, general academic interests/achievements, health fields, humanities, mathematics, military science. *Creative arts/performance:* music, performing arts. *Special characteristics:* adult students. ***Tuition waivers:*** Full or partial for employees or children of employees.

LOANS ***Student loans:*** $74,900,779 (79% need-based, 21% non-need-based). 46% of past graduating class borrowed through all loan programs. *Average indebtedness per student:* $17,472. ***Average need-based loan:*** Freshmen: $3114. Undergraduates: $4000. ***Parent loans:*** $5,351,959 (53% need-based, 47% non-need-based). ***Programs:*** Federal Direct (Subsidized and Unsubsidized Stafford, PLUS), Perkins, state, college/university.

WORK-STUDY ***Federal work-study:*** Total amount: $933,980; jobs available. ***State or other work-study/employment:*** Total amount: $4,372,157 (63% need-based, 37% non-need-based). Part-time jobs available.

ATHLETIC AWARDS Total amount: $2,166,943 (38% need-based, 62% non-need-based).

APPLYING FOR FINANCIAL AID ***Required financial aid form:*** FAFSA. ***Financial aid deadline (priority):*** 4/1. ***Notification date:*** 3/31. Students must reply within 3 weeks of notification.

CONTACT Timothy S. Saulnier, Director of Financial Aid, The University of North Carolina at Charlotte, 9201 University City Boulevard, Charlotte, NC 28223-0001, 704-687-2461. *Fax:* 704-687-3132. *E-mail:* tsaulnie@uncc.edu.

THE UNIVERSITY OF NORTH CAROLINA AT GREENSBORO

Greensboro, NC

Tuition & fees (NC res): $4520 **Average undergraduate aid package: $9838**

ABOUT THE INSTITUTION State-supported, coed. 71 undergraduate majors. Federal methodology is used as a basis for awarding need-based institutional aid.

UNDERGRADUATE EXPENSES for 2011–12 ***Tuition, state resident:*** full-time $2790; part-time $348.75 per course. ***Tuition, nonresident:*** full-time $14,551; part-time $1818.88 per course. ***Required fees:*** full-time $1730; $184.77 per course. Part-time tuition and fees vary according to course load. ***College room and board: Room only:*** $3855. Room and board charges vary according to board plan and housing facility. ***Payment plan:*** Installment.

FRESHMAN FINANCIAL AID (Fall 2010, est.) 2,134 applied for aid; of those 92% were deemed to have need. 100% of freshmen with need received aid; of those 25% had need fully met. ***Average percent of need met:*** 58% (excluding resources awarded to replace EFC). ***Average financial aid package:*** $9844 (excluding resources awarded to replace EFC). 3% of all full-time freshmen had no need and received non-need-based gift aid.

UNDERGRADUATE FINANCIAL AID (Fall 2010, est.) 10,298 applied for aid; of those 97% were deemed to have need. 100% of undergraduates with need received aid; of those 23% had need fully met. ***Average percent of need met:*** 58% (excluding resources awarded to replace EFC). ***Average financial aid package:*** $9838 (excluding resources awarded to replace EFC). 3% of all full-time undergraduates had no need and received non-need-based gift aid.

GIFT AID (NEED-BASED) ***Total amount:*** $37,452,901 (76% federal, 4% state, 20% institutional). ***Receiving aid:*** Freshmen: 45% (1,133); all full-time undergraduates: 45% (5,929). ***Average award:*** Freshmen: $6578; Undergraduates: $6041. ***Scholarships, grants, and awards:*** Federal Pell, FSEOG, state, private, college/university gift aid from institutional funds.

GIFT AID (NON-NEED-BASED) ***Total amount:*** $23,697,473 (79% state, 20% institutional, 1% external sources). ***Receiving aid:*** Freshmen: 59% (1,470). Undergraduates: 55% (7,151). ***Average award:*** Freshmen: $2888. Undergraduates: $2571. ***Scholarships, grants, and awards by category:*** *Academic interests/achievement:* biological sciences, business, communication, education, English, foreign languages, general academic interests/achievements, health fields, home economics, humanities, library science, mathematics, physical sciences, premedicine, religion/biblical studies, social sciences. *Creative arts/performance:* art/fine arts, cinema/film/broadcasting, dance, music, performing arts, theater/drama. *Special achievements/activities:* community service, general special achievements/activities, junior miss, leadership, religious involvement. *Special characteristics:* adult students, children of faculty/staff, ethnic background, general special characteristics, handicapped students, international students, members of minority groups, out-of-state students, religious affiliation, veterans, veterans' children. ***Tuition waivers:*** Full or partial for employees or children of employees.

LOANS ***Student loans:*** $56,484,486 (48% need-based, 52% non-need-based). 67% of past graduating class borrowed through all loan programs. *Average indebtedness per student:* $23,772. ***Average need-based loan:*** Freshmen: $3223. Undergraduates: $4080. ***Parent loans:*** $12,291,397 (100% non-need-based). ***Programs:*** Federal Direct (Subsidized and Unsubsidized Stafford, PLUS), Perkins, college/university.

WORK-STUDY ***Federal work-study:*** Total amount: $537,955; 278 jobs averaging $1935.

ATHLETIC AWARDS Total amount: $2,655,920 (100% non-need-based).

APPLYING FOR FINANCIAL AID ***Required financial aid form:*** FAFSA. ***Financial aid deadline (priority):*** 3/1. ***Notification date:*** Continuous beginning 3/15. Students must reply within 3 weeks of notification.

CONTACT Mr. Bruce Cabiness, Associate Director of Financial Aid, The University of North Carolina at Greensboro, PO Box 26170, Greensboro, NC 27402-6170, 336-334-5702. *Fax:* 336-334-3010. *E-mail:* bruce_cabiness@uncg.edu.

THE UNIVERSITY OF NORTH CAROLINA AT PEMBROKE

Pembroke, NC

Tuition & fees (NC res): $4140 **Average undergraduate aid package: $10,246**

ABOUT THE INSTITUTION State-supported, coed. 47 undergraduate majors. Federal methodology is used as a basis for awarding need-based institutional aid.

UNDERGRADUATE EXPENSES for 2010–11 ***Tuition, state resident:*** full-time $2423. ***Tuition, nonresident:*** full-time $11,630. ***Required fees:*** full-time $1717. Full-time tuition and fees vary according to course load and location. Part-time tuition and fees vary according to course load and location. ***College room and board:*** $5990; ***Room only:*** $5040. Room and board charges vary according to board plan and housing facility. ***Payment plan:*** Installment.

FRESHMAN FINANCIAL AID (Fall 2010, est.) 880 applied for aid; of those 83% were deemed to have need. 99% of freshmen with need received aid; of those 20% had need fully met. ***Average percent of need met:*** 82% (excluding resources awarded to replace EFC). ***Average financial aid package:*** $10,216 (excluding resources awarded to replace EFC).

UNDERGRADUATE FINANCIAL AID (Fall 2010, est.) 4,255 applied for aid; of those 88% were deemed to have need. 98% of undergraduates with need received aid; of those 25% had need fully met. ***Average percent of need met:*** 80% (excluding resources awarded to replace EFC). ***Average financial aid package:*** $10,246 (excluding resources awarded to replace EFC). 1% of all full-time undergraduates had no need and received non-need-based gift aid.

GIFT AID (NEED-BASED) ***Total amount:*** $23,625,433 (61% federal, 37% state, 1% institutional, 1% external sources). ***Receiving aid:*** Freshmen: 72% (684); all full-time undergraduates: 73% (3,504). ***Average award:*** Freshmen: $6711; Undergraduates: $6210. ***Scholarships, grants, and awards:*** Federal Pell, FSEOG, state, private, college/university gift aid from institutional funds.

GIFT AID (NON-NEED-BASED) ***Total amount:*** $340,068 (95% federal, 1% institutional, 4% external sources). ***Receiving aid:*** Freshmen: 3% (33). Undergraduates: 2% (110). ***Average award:*** Undergraduates: $525. ***Scholarships, grants, and awards by category:*** *Academic interests/achievement:* 8 awards ($3960 total): business, communication, education, English, general academic interests/achievements, health fields, physical sciences. *Special characteristics:* 1 award ($500 total): children and siblings of alumni. ***Tuition waivers:*** Full or partial for employees or children of employees.

LOANS ***Student loans:*** $20,410,779 (89% need-based, 11% non-need-based). ***Average need-based loan:*** Freshmen: $3127. Undergraduates: $3648. ***Parent loans:*** $1,874,574 (62% need-based, 38% non-need-based). ***Programs:*** Federal Direct (Subsidized and Unsubsidized Stafford, PLUS), Perkins, college/university.

WORK-STUDY ***Federal work-study:*** Total amount: $246,075; 143 jobs averaging $1089. ***State or other work-study/employment:*** Part-time jobs available.

ATHLETIC AWARDS Total amount: $1,426,279 (100% need-based).

APPLYING FOR FINANCIAL AID ***Required financial aid form:*** FAFSA. ***Financial aid deadline (priority):*** 3/15. ***Notification date:*** Continuous beginning 4/15.

CONTACT Mildred Weber, Associate Director of Financial Aid, The University of North Carolina at Pembroke, PO Box 1510, Pembroke, NC 28372, 910-521-6612 or toll-free 800-949-UNCP. *Fax:* 910-775-4159. *E-mail:* mildred.weber@uncp.edu.

UNIVERSITY OF NORTH CAROLINA SCHOOL OF THE ARTS

Winston-Salem, NC

Tuition & fees: N/R **Average undergraduate aid package: $15,093**

ABOUT THE INSTITUTION State-supported, coed. 8 undergraduate majors. Federal methodology is used as a basis for awarding need-based institutional aid.

UNDERGRADUATE EXPENSES for 2011–12 ***Tuition, state resident:*** part-time $180 per credit. ***Tuition, nonresident:*** part-time $695 per credit. Full-time tuition and fees vary according to program. Part-time tuition and fees vary according to course load. Room and board charges vary according to board plan and housing facility. ***Payment plan:*** Installment.

FRESHMAN FINANCIAL AID (Fall 2009) 133 applied for aid; of those 78% were deemed to have need. 100% of freshmen with need received aid; of those 16% had need fully met. ***Average percent of need met:*** 86% (excluding resources awarded to replace EFC). ***Average financial aid package:*** $14,194 (excluding resources awarded to replace EFC). 14% of all full-time freshmen had no need and received non-need-based gift aid.

UNDERGRADUATE FINANCIAL AID (Fall 2009) 519 applied for aid; of those 78% were deemed to have need. 100% of undergraduates with need received aid; of those 17% had need fully met. ***Average percent of need met:*** 89% (excluding resources awarded to replace EFC). ***Average financial aid package:*** $15,093 (excluding resources awarded to replace EFC). 15% of all full-time undergraduates had no need and received non-need-based gift aid.

GIFT AID (NEED-BASED) ***Total amount:*** $2,853,413 (29% federal, 41% state, 27% institutional, 3% external sources). ***Receiving aid:*** Freshmen: 63% (100); all full-time undergraduates: 53% (394). ***Average award:*** Freshmen: $7507; Undergraduates: $7404. ***Scholarships, grants, and awards:*** Federal Pell, FSEOG, state, private, college/university gift aid from institutional funds.

GIFT AID (NON-NEED-BASED) ***Total amount:*** $491,313 (7% state, 81% institutional, 12% external sources). ***Receiving aid:*** Freshmen: 6% (9). Undergraduates: 4% (26). ***Average award:*** Freshmen: $3465. Undergraduates: $3960. ***Scholarships, grants, and awards by category:*** *Creative arts/performance:* applied art and design, cinema/film/broadcasting, dance, music, performing arts, theater/drama. ***Tuition waivers:*** Full or partial for senior citizens.

LOANS ***Student loans:*** $3,286,019 (63% need-based, 37% non-need-based). 71% of past graduating class borrowed through all loan programs. *Average indebtedness per student:* $22,173. ***Average need-based loan:*** Freshmen: $3222. Undergraduates: $4167. ***Parent loans:*** $1,876,724 (66% need-based, 34% non-need-based). ***Programs:*** Federal Direct (Subsidized and Unsubsidized Stafford, PLUS), Perkins.

WORK-STUDY ***Federal work-study:*** Total amount: $49,670; 108 jobs averaging $460.

APPLYING FOR FINANCIAL AID ***Required financial aid form:*** FAFSA. ***Financial aid deadline (priority):*** 3/1. ***Notification date:*** Continuous beginning 4/10. Students must reply within 2 weeks of notification.

CONTACT Jane C. Kamiab, Director of Financial Aid, University of North Carolina School of the Arts, 1533 South Main Street, Winston-Salem, NC 27127, 336-770-3297. *Fax:* 336-770-1489.

THE UNIVERSITY OF NORTH CAROLINA WILMINGTON

Wilmington, NC

Tuition & fees (NC res): $5416 **Average undergraduate aid package: $9275**

ABOUT THE INSTITUTION State-supported, coed. 59 undergraduate majors. Federal methodology is used as a basis for awarding need-based institutional aid.

UNDERGRADUATE EXPENSES for 2010–11 ***Tuition, state resident:*** full-time $3029. ***Tuition, nonresident:*** full-time $14,128. ***Required fees:*** full-time $2387. Full-time tuition and fees vary according to course load. Part-time tuition and fees vary according to course load. ***College room and board:*** $7608; ***Room only:*** $4458. Room and board charges vary according to board plan and housing facility. ***Payment plan:*** Installment.

FRESHMAN FINANCIAL AID (Fall 2010, est.) 1,466 applied for aid; of those 62% were deemed to have need. 100% of freshmen with need received aid; of those 46% had need fully met. ***Average percent of need met:*** 78% (excluding resources awarded to replace EFC). ***Average financial aid package:*** $8896 (excluding resources awarded to replace EFC). 3% of all full-time freshmen had no need and received non-need-based gift aid.

UNDERGRADUATE FINANCIAL AID (Fall 2010, est.) 7,162 applied for aid; of those 68% were deemed to have need. 100% of undergraduates with need received aid; of those 45% had need fully met. ***Average percent of need met:*** 83% (excluding resources awarded to replace EFC). ***Average financial aid package:*** $9275 (excluding resources awarded to replace EFC). 2% of all full-time undergraduates had no need and received non-need-based gift aid.

GIFT AID (NEED-BASED) ***Total amount:*** $30,023,199 (46% federal, 34% state, 17% institutional, 3% external sources). ***Receiving aid:*** Freshmen: 40% (799); all full-time undergraduates: 40% (4,238). ***Average award:*** Freshmen: $6692; Undergraduates: $6792. ***Scholarships, grants, and awards:*** Federal Pell, FSEOG, state, private, college/university gift aid from institutional funds.

GIFT AID (NON-NEED-BASED) ***Total amount:*** $3,516,308 (1% federal, 16% state, 36% institutional, 47% external sources). ***Receiving aid:*** Freshmen: 12% (230). Undergraduates: 10% (1,074). ***Average award:*** Freshmen: $2211. Undergraduates: $2434. ***Scholarships, grants, and awards by category:*** *Academic interests/achievement:* biological sciences, business, communication, computer science, education, engineering/technologies, English, foreign languages, general academic interests/achievements, health fields, humanities, international studies, mathematics, physical sciences, premedicine, social sciences. *Creative arts/performance:* art/fine arts, cinema/film/broadcasting, creative writing, music, theater/drama. *Special achievements/activities:* cheerleading/drum major, general special achievements/activities, leadership. *Special characteristics:* local/state students, married students. ***Tuition waivers:*** Full or partial for employees or children of employees.

LOANS ***Student loans:*** $43,691,948 (52% need-based, 48% non-need-based). 25% of past graduating class borrowed through all loan programs. *Average indebtedness per student:* $19,277. ***Average need-based loan:*** Freshmen: $3027.

Undergraduates: $4074. ***Parent loans:*** $9,192,507 (13% need-based, 87% non-need-based). ***Programs:*** Federal Direct (Subsidized and Unsubsidized Stafford, PLUS), Perkins, state.

WORK-STUDY ***Federal work-study:*** Total amount: $570,464; 255 jobs averaging $2255.

ATHLETIC AWARDS Total amount: $2,274,037 (19% need-based, 81% non-need-based).

APPLYING FOR FINANCIAL AID ***Required financial aid form:*** FAFSA. ***Financial aid deadline (priority):*** 3/1. ***Notification date:*** Continuous beginning 3/15. Students must reply within 3 weeks of notification.

CONTACT Emily Bliss, Director of Financial Aid and Veterans Services Office, The University of North Carolina Wilmington, 601 South College Road, Wilmington, NC 28403-5951, 910-962-3177 or toll-free 800-228-5571 (out-of-state). *Fax:* 910-962-3851. *E-mail:* finaid@uncw.edu.

UNIVERSITY OF NORTH DAKOTA

Grand Forks, ND

Tuition & fees (ND res): $6934 Average undergraduate aid package: $9144

ABOUT THE INSTITUTION State-supported, coed. 82 undergraduate majors. Federal methodology is used as a basis for awarding need-based institutional aid.

UNDERGRADUATE EXPENSES for 2010–11 ***Tuition, state resident:*** full-time $5652; part-time $235.50 per credit hour. ***Tuition, nonresident:*** full-time $15,091; part-time $628.80 per credit hour. ***Required fees:*** full-time $1282. Full-time tuition and fees vary according to degree level, program, and reciprocity agreements. Part-time tuition and fees vary according to course load, degree level, program, and reciprocity agreements. ***College room and board:*** $5950; ***Room only:*** $2350. Room and board charges vary according to board plan and housing facility. ***Payment plan:*** Deferred payment.

FRESHMAN FINANCIAL AID (Fall 2010, est.) 1,468 applied for aid; of those 67% were deemed to have need. 99% of freshmen with need received aid; of those 99% had need fully met. ***Average percent of need met:*** 56% (excluding resources awarded to replace EFC). ***Average financial aid package:*** $9429 (excluding resources awarded to replace EFC). 42% of all full-time freshmen had no need and received non-need-based gift aid.

UNDERGRADUATE FINANCIAL AID (Fall 2010, est.) 6,165 applied for aid; of those 72% were deemed to have need. 99% of undergraduates with need received aid; of those 99% had need fully met. ***Average percent of need met:*** 47% (excluding resources awarded to replace EFC). ***Average financial aid package:*** $9144 (excluding resources awarded to replace EFC). 28% of all full-time undergraduates had no need and received non-need-based gift aid.

GIFT AID (NEED-BASED) ***Total amount:*** $16,426,275 (69% federal, 13% state, 11% institutional, 7% external sources). ***Receiving aid:*** Freshmen: 41% (758); all full-time undergraduates: 37% (3,194). ***Average award:*** Freshmen: $4500; Undergraduates: $4338. ***Scholarships, grants, and awards:*** Federal Pell, FSEOG, state, private, college/university gift aid from institutional funds, Federal Nursing.

GIFT AID (NON-NEED-BASED) ***Total amount:*** $221,995 (4% federal, 21% state, 40% institutional, 35% external sources). ***Receiving aid:*** Freshmen: 1% (18). Undergraduates: 43. ***Average award:*** Freshmen: $1319. Undergraduates: $1592. ***Scholarships, grants, and awards by category:*** *Academic interests/achievement:* biological sciences, business, communication, computer science, education, engineering/technologies, English, foreign languages, general academic interests/achievements, health fields, humanities, international studies, mathematics, military science, physical sciences, premedicine, social sciences. *Creative arts/performance:* art/fine arts, debating, music, theater/drama. *Special achievements/activities:* general special achievements/activities, leadership, memberships. *Special characteristics:* children of faculty/staff, ethnic background, general special characteristics, handicapped students, international students, members of minority groups, veterans' children. ***Tuition waivers:*** Full or partial for minority students, employees or children of employees, adult students, senior citizens.

LOANS ***Student loans:*** $43,834,855 (78% need-based, 22% non-need-based). 83% of past graduating class borrowed through all loan programs. *Average indebtedness per student:* $45,369. ***Average need-based loan:*** Freshmen: $4439. Undergraduates: $5082. ***Parent loans:*** $1,526,112 (41% need-based, 59% non-need-based). ***Programs:*** Federal Direct (Subsidized and Unsubsidized Stafford, PLUS), Perkins, Federal Nursing, alternative loans.

WORK-STUDY ***Federal work-study:*** Total amount: $5,428,123; jobs available.

ATHLETIC AWARDS Total amount: $853,514 (58% need-based, 42% non-need-based).

APPLYING FOR FINANCIAL AID ***Required financial aid form:*** FAFSA. ***Financial aid deadline (priority):*** 3/15. ***Notification date:*** Continuous beginning 5/15. Students must reply within 4 weeks of notification.

CONTACT Ms. Robin Holden, Director of Student Financial Aid, University of North Dakota, 264 Centennial Drive Stop 8371, Grand Forks, ND 58202, 701-777-3121 or toll-free 800-CALLUND. *Fax:* 701-777-2040. *E-mail:* robin.holden@email.und.edu.

UNIVERSITY OF NORTHERN COLORADO

Greeley, CO

Tuition & fees (CO res): $5997 Average undergraduate aid package: $14,255

ABOUT THE INSTITUTION State-supported, coed. 41 undergraduate majors. Federal methodology is used as a basis for awarding need-based institutional aid.

UNDERGRADUATE EXPENSES for 2010–11 ***Tuition, state resident:*** full-time $4680; part-time $195 per credit hour. ***Tuition, nonresident:*** full-time $15,864; part-time $661 per credit hour. ***Required fees:*** full-time $1317; $60 per credit hour. Full-time tuition and fees vary according to program. Part-time tuition and fees vary according to program. ***College room and board:*** $8920; ***Room only:*** $4188. Room and board charges vary according to board plan, housing facility, and student level. ***Payment plan:*** Deferred payment.

FRESHMAN FINANCIAL AID (Fall 2009) 1,836 applied for aid; of those 64% were deemed to have need. 100% of freshmen with need received aid; of those 58% had need fully met. ***Average percent of need met:*** 100% (excluding resources awarded to replace EFC). ***Average financial aid package:*** $14,646 (excluding resources awarded to replace EFC). 14% of all full-time freshmen had no need and received non-need-based gift aid.

UNDERGRADUATE FINANCIAL AID (Fall 2009) 6,381 applied for aid; of those 65% were deemed to have need. 100% of undergraduates with need received aid; of those 49% had need fully met. ***Average percent of need met:*** 99% (excluding resources awarded to replace EFC). ***Average financial aid package:*** $14,255 (excluding resources awarded to replace EFC). 11% of all full-time undergraduates had no need and received non-need-based gift aid.

GIFT AID (NEED-BASED) ***Total amount:*** $20,066,493 (50% federal, 19% state, 25% institutional, 6% external sources). ***Receiving aid:*** Freshmen: 33% (773); all full-time undergraduates: 32% (2,795). ***Average award:*** Freshmen: $8102; Undergraduates: $7007. ***Scholarships, grants, and awards:*** Federal Pell, FSEOG, state, private, college/university gift aid from institutional funds.

GIFT AID (NON-NEED-BASED) ***Total amount:*** $11,344,213 (10% federal, 1% state, 55% institutional, 34% external sources). ***Receiving aid:*** Freshmen: 36% (833). Undergraduates: 24% (2,034). ***Average award:*** Freshmen: $2752. Undergraduates: $3993. ***Scholarships, grants, and awards by category:*** *Academic interests/achievement:* biological sciences, business, communication, education, English, general academic interests/achievements, health fields, home economics, mathematics, military science, physical sciences, social sciences. *Creative arts/performance:* dance, music, performing arts, theater/drama. *Special characteristics:* adult students, children and siblings of alumni, children of faculty/staff, children of union members/company employees, ethnic background, general special characteristics, handicapped students, international students, local/state students, members of minority groups, out-of-state students, veterans. ***Tuition waivers:*** Full or partial for employees or children of employees.

LOANS ***Student loans:*** $35,500,762 (38% need-based, 62% non-need-based). ***Average need-based loan:*** Freshmen: $3291. Undergraduates: $4245. ***Parent loans:*** $11,258,914 (100% non-need-based). ***Programs:*** Federal Direct (Subsidized and Unsubsidized Stafford, PLUS), Perkins.

WORK-STUDY ***Federal work-study:*** Total amount: $244,036; jobs available. ***State or other work-study/employment:*** Total amount: $1,184,074 (73% need-based, 27% non-need-based). Part-time jobs available.

ATHLETIC AWARDS Total amount: $2,265,473 (100% non-need-based).

APPLYING FOR FINANCIAL AID ***Required financial aid form:*** FAFSA. ***Financial aid deadline (priority):*** 3/1. ***Notification date:*** Continuous beginning 4/15. Students must reply within 4 weeks of notification.

CONTACT Marty Somero, Director of Student Financial Aid, University of Northern Colorado, Carter Hall 1005, Campus Box 33, Greeley, CO 80639, 970-351-2502 or toll-free 888-700-4UNC (in-state). *Fax:* 970-351-3737. *E-mail:* ofa@unco.edu.

UNIVERSITY OF NORTHERN IOWA

Cedar Falls, IA

Tuition & fees (IA res): $7008 **Average undergraduate aid package: $7897**

ABOUT THE INSTITUTION State-supported, coed. 95 undergraduate majors. Federal methodology is used as a basis for awarding need-based institutional aid.

UNDERGRADUATE EXPENSES for 2010–11 ***Tuition, state resident:*** full-time $6102; part-time $255 per hour. ***Tuition, nonresident:*** full-time $14,442; part-time $602 per hour. ***Required fees:*** full-time $906. Full-time tuition and fees vary according to course load and program. Part-time tuition and fees vary according to course load and program. ***College room and board:*** $7140; ***Room only:*** $3411. Room and board charges vary according to board plan and housing facility. ***Payment plan:*** Installment.

FRESHMAN FINANCIAL AID (Fall 2010, est.) 1,751 applied for aid; of those 70% were deemed to have need. 95% of freshmen with need received aid; of those 24% had need fully met. ***Average percent of need met:*** 68% (excluding resources awarded to replace EFC). ***Average financial aid package:*** $7472 (excluding resources awarded to replace EFC). 19% of all full-time freshmen had no need and received non-need-based gift aid.

UNDERGRADUATE FINANCIAL AID (Fall 2010, est.) 8,431 applied for aid; of those 77% were deemed to have need. 94% of undergraduates with need received aid; of those 19% had need fully met. ***Average percent of need met:*** 65% (excluding resources awarded to replace EFC). ***Average* financial aid package:*** $7897 (excluding resources awarded to replace EFC). 12% of all full-time undergraduates had no need and received non-need-based gift aid.

GIFT AID (NEED-BASED) ***Total amount:*** $25,534,614 (57% federal, 4% state, 32% institutional, 7% external sources). ***Receiving aid:*** Freshmen: 32% (623); all full-time undergraduates: 34% (3,572). ***Average award:*** Freshmen: $4955; Undergraduates: $4853. ***Scholarships, grants, and awards:*** Federal Pell, FSEOG, state, private, college/university gift aid from institutional funds, TEACH Grants.

GIFT AID (NON-NEED-BASED) ***Total amount:*** $4,238,144 (9% federal, 6% state, 62% institutional, 23% external sources). ***Receiving aid:*** Freshmen: 37% (720). Undergraduates: 22% (2,277). ***Average award:*** Freshmen: $2760. Undergraduates: $2883. ***Scholarships, grants, and awards by category:*** *Academic interests/achievement:* biological sciences, business, communication, computer science, education, general academic interests/achievements, mathematics, physical sciences, social sciences. *Creative arts/performance:* applied art and design, art/fine arts, debating, music, theater/drama. *Special achievements/activities:* leadership. *Special characteristics:* general special characteristics, members of minority groups.

LOANS ***Student loans:*** $46,007,803 (50% need-based, 50% non-need-based). 76% of past graduating class borrowed through all loan programs. *Average indebtedness per student:* $25,735. ***Average need-based loan:*** Freshmen: $3424. Undergraduates: $4407. ***Parent loans:*** $13,631,483 (100% non-need-based). ***Programs:*** Federal Direct (Subsidized and Unsubsidized Stafford, PLUS), Perkins, private loans.

WORK-STUDY ***Federal work-study:*** Total amount: $1,117,269; 555 jobs averaging $1884. ***State or other work-study/employment:*** Total amount: $24,428 (41% need-based, 59% non-need-based). Part-time jobs available.

ATHLETIC AWARDS Total amount: $3,056,232 (50% need-based, 50% non-need-based).

APPLYING FOR FINANCIAL AID ***Required financial aid form:*** FAFSA. ***Financial aid deadline:*** Continuous. ***Notification date:*** Continuous beginning 3/1.

CONTACT Heather Soesbe, Associate Director of Student Financial Aid, University of Northern Iowa, 105 Gilchrist Hall, Cedar Falls, IA 50614-0024, 319-273-2700 or toll-free 800-772-2037. *Fax:* 319-273-6950. *E-mail:* heather.soesbe@uni.edu.

UNIVERSITY OF NORTH FLORIDA

Jacksonville, FL

Tuition & fees (FL res): $5449 **Average undergraduate aid package: $8749**

ABOUT THE INSTITUTION State-supported, coed. 56 undergraduate majors. Federal methodology is used as a basis for awarding need-based institutional aid.

UNDERGRADUATE EXPENSES for 2011–12 ***Tuition, state resident:*** full-time $3742; part-time $181.64 per credit hour. ***Tuition, nonresident:*** full-time $18,002; part-time $680.75 per credit hour. ***Required fees:*** full-time $1707. Full-time tuition and fees vary according to course load. Part-time tuition and fees vary according to course load. ***College room and board:*** $8452. Room and board charges vary according to board plan and housing facility. ***Payment plan:*** Installment.

FRESHMAN FINANCIAL AID (Fall 2010, est.) 1,367 applied for aid; of those 69% were deemed to have need. 99% of freshmen with need received aid; of those 19% had need fully met. ***Average percent of need met:*** 91% (excluding resources awarded to replace EFC). ***Average financial aid package:*** $9150 (excluding resources awarded to replace EFC). 4% of all full-time freshmen had no need and received non-need-based gift aid.

UNDERGRADUATE FINANCIAL AID (Fall 2010, est.) 6,770 applied for aid; of those 79% were deemed to have need. 97% of undergraduates with need received aid; of those 12% had need fully met. ***Average percent of need met:*** 89% (excluding resources awarded to replace EFC). ***Average financial aid package:*** $8749 (excluding resources awarded to replace EFC). 14% of all full-time undergraduates had no need and received non-need-based gift aid.

GIFT AID (NEED-BASED) ***Total amount:*** $36,468,243 (57% federal, 28% state, 14% institutional, 1% external sources). ***Receiving aid:*** Freshmen: 38% (682); all full-time undergraduates: 36% (3,701). ***Average award:*** Freshmen: $1012; Undergraduates: $1379. ***Scholarships, grants, and awards:*** Federal Pell, FSEOG, state, private, college/university gift aid from institutional funds, 2+2 Scholarships (jointly sponsored with Florida Community College at Jacksonville).

GIFT AID (NON-NEED-BASED) ***Total amount:*** $10,856,309 (78% state, 20% institutional, 2% external sources). ***Receiving aid:*** Freshmen: 49% (870). Undergraduates: 27% (2,824). ***Average award:*** Freshmen: $1083. Undergraduates: $1074. ***Scholarships, grants, and awards by category:*** *Academic interests/achievement:* 846 awards ($2,367,559 total): business, computer science, education, engineering/technologies, general academic interests/achievements, health fields, international studies. *Creative arts/performance:* 37 awards ($61,550 total): art/fine arts, music. *Special achievements/activities:* 91 awards ($92,663 total): community service, general special achievements/activities, leadership. *Special characteristics:* 25 awards ($33,703 total): first-generation college students, general special characteristics, international students, members of minority groups, out-of-state students. ***Tuition waivers:*** Full or partial for employees or children of employees, senior citizens.

LOANS ***Student loans:*** $36,384,391 (84% need-based, 16% non-need-based). 39% of past graduating class borrowed through all loan programs. *Average indebtedness per student:* $15,300. ***Average need-based loan:*** Freshmen: $1597. Undergraduates: $1555. ***Parent loans:*** $1,211,850 (64% need-based, 36% non-need-based).

WORK-STUDY ***Federal work-study:*** Total amount: $256,731; 110 jobs averaging $2944.

ATHLETIC AWARDS Total amount: $942,237 (23% need-based, 77% non-need-based).

APPLYING FOR FINANCIAL AID ***Required financial aid form:*** FAFSA. ***Financial aid deadline (priority):*** 4/1. ***Notification date:*** Continuous beginning 3/15. Students must reply within 2 weeks of notification.

CONTACT Ms. Anissa Agne, Director of Financial Aid, University of North Florida, 1 UNF Drive, Jacksonville, FL 32224-7699, 904-620-2604. *E-mail:* anissa.agne@unf.edu.

UNIVERSITY OF NORTH TEXAS

Denton, TX

Tuition & fees (TX res): $7960 **Average undergraduate aid package: $11,125**

ABOUT THE INSTITUTION State-supported, coed. 85 undergraduate majors. Federal methodology is used as a basis for awarding need-based institutional aid.

UNDERGRADUATE EXPENSES for 2011–12 ***Tuition, state resident:*** full-time $5660; part-time $189 per credit. ***Tuition, nonresident:*** full-time $14,960; part-time $499 per credit. ***Required fees:*** full-time $2300; $153 per credit. ***College room and board:*** $6716. Room and board charges vary according to board plan and housing facility. ***Payment plan:*** Installment.

FRESHMAN FINANCIAL AID (Fall 2010, est.) 2,848 applied for aid; of those 75% were deemed to have need. 98% of freshmen with need received aid; of those 40% had need fully met. ***Average percent of need met:*** 82% (excluding resources awarded to replace EFC). ***Average financial aid package:*** $12,147 (excluding resources awarded to replace EFC). 14% of all full-time freshmen had no need and received non-need-based gift aid.

UNDERGRADUATE FINANCIAL AID (Fall 2010, est.) 15,995 applied for aid; of those 80% were deemed to have need. 97% of undergraduates with need received aid; of those 28% had need fully met. ***Average percent of need met:*** 70% (excluding resources awarded to replace EFC). ***Average financial aid package:*** $11,125 (excluding resources awarded to replace EFC). 11% of all full-time undergraduates had no need and received non-need-based gift aid.

GIFT AID (NEED-BASED) ***Total amount:*** $105,506,645 (47% federal, 23% state, 19% institutional, 11% external sources). ***Receiving aid:*** Freshmen: 51% (1,787); all full-time undergraduates: 45% (10,320). ***Average award:*** Freshmen: $8593; Undergraduates: $6684. ***Scholarships, grants, and awards:*** Federal Pell, FSEOG, state, college/university gift aid from institutional funds.

GIFT AID (NON-NEED-BASED) ***Total amount:*** $7,511,917 (30% institutional, 70% external sources). ***Receiving aid:*** Freshmen: 26% (895). Undergraduates: 14% (3,268). ***Average award:*** Freshmen: $4978. Undergraduates: $4912. ***Tuition waivers:*** Full or partial for employees or children of employees, senior citizens.

LOANS ***Student loans:*** $131,606,419 (84% need-based, 16% non-need-based). ***Average need-based loan:*** Freshmen: $3110. Undergraduates: $4397. ***Parent loans:*** $56,874,052 (62% need-based, 38% non-need-based). ***Programs:*** Federal Direct (Subsidized and Unsubsidized Stafford, PLUS), Perkins, Federal Nursing, state, college/university.

WORK-STUDY ***Federal work-study:*** Total amount: $5,923,606; jobs available. ***State or other work-study/employment:*** Total amount: $376,319 (100% need-based). Part-time jobs available.

ATHLETIC AWARDS Total amount: $2,997,714 (43% need-based, 57% non-need-based).

APPLYING FOR FINANCIAL AID ***Required financial aid form:*** FAFSA. ***Financial aid deadline (priority):*** 3/31. ***Notification date:*** Continuous beginning 4/1.

CONTACT Mrs. Zelma DeLeon, Director of Financial Aid, University of North Texas, PO Box 311370, Denton, TX 76203-1370, 940-565-2302 or toll-free 800-868-8211 (in-state). *Fax:* 940-565-2738. *E-mail:* zelma.deleon@unt.edu.

UNIVERSITY OF NOTRE DAME

Notre Dame, IN

Tuition & fees: $41,417 **Average undergraduate aid package: $35,587**

ABOUT THE INSTITUTION Independent Roman Catholic, coed. 55 undergraduate majors. Both federal and institutional methodology are used as a basis for awarding need-based institutional aid.

UNDERGRADUATE EXPENSES for 2011–12 ***Comprehensive fee:*** $52,805 includes full-time tuition ($40,910), mandatory fees ($507), and room and board ($11,388). ***Part-time tuition:*** $1705 per credit hour. ***Payment plan:*** Installment.

FRESHMAN FINANCIAL AID (Fall 2010, est.) 1,457 applied for aid; of those 74% were deemed to have need. 100% of freshmen with need received aid; of those 98% had need fully met. ***Average percent of need met:*** 99% (excluding resources awarded to replace EFC). ***Average financial aid package:*** $35,326 (excluding resources awarded to replace EFC). 2% of all full-time freshmen had no need and received non-need-based gift aid.

UNDERGRADUATE FINANCIAL AID (Fall 2010, est.) 5,213 applied for aid; of those 82% were deemed to have need. 100% of undergraduates with need received aid; of those 98% had need fully met. ***Average percent of need met:*** 99% (excluding resources awarded to replace EFC). ***Average financial aid package:*** $35,587 (excluding resources awarded to replace EFC). 4% of all full-time undergraduates had no need and received non-need-based gift aid.

GIFT AID (NEED-BASED) ***Total amount:*** $110,265,307 (9% federal, 87% institutional, 4% external sources). ***Receiving aid:*** Freshmen: 51% (1,048); all full-time undergraduates: 49% (4,103). ***Average award:*** Freshmen: $28,953; Undergraduates: $28,184. ***Scholarships, grants, and awards:*** Federal Pell, state, private, college/university gift aid from institutional funds, Academic Competitiveness Grants, National SMART Grants.

GIFT AID (NON-NEED-BASED) ***Total amount:*** $15,875,124 (34% federal, 35% institutional, 31% external sources). ***Receiving aid:*** Freshmen: 35% (715). Undergraduates: 30% (2,539). ***Average award:*** Freshmen: $13,617. Undergraduates: $7871. ***Scholarships, grants, and awards by category:*** *Special characteristics:* 200 awards ($10,009,552 total): children of faculty/staff. ***Tuition waivers:*** Full or partial for employees or children of employees.

LOANS ***Student loans:*** $36,544,545 (52% need-based, 48% non-need-based). 56% of past graduating class borrowed through all loan programs. *Average indebtedness per student:* $30,341. ***Average need-based loan:*** Freshmen: $3290. Undergraduates: $4667. ***Parent loans:*** $11,474,958 (1% need-based, 99% non-need-based). ***Programs:*** Perkins, Federal Nursing, college/university.

WORK-STUDY ***Federal work-study:*** Total amount: $4,070,395; jobs available. ***State or other work-study/employment:*** Total amount: $9,734,571 (11% need-based, 89% non-need-based). Part-time jobs available.

ATHLETIC AWARDS Total amount: $16,335,432 (13% need-based, 87% non-need-based).

APPLYING FOR FINANCIAL AID ***Required financial aid forms:*** FAFSA, CSS Financial Aid PROFILE, business/farm supplement, income tax form(s), W-2 forms. ***Financial aid deadline:*** 2/15. ***Notification date:*** 4/1. Students must reply by 5/1.

CONTACT Mr. Joseph A. Russo, Director, Student Financial Strategies, University of Notre Dame, 115 Main Building, Notre Dame, IN 46556, 574-631-6436. *Fax:* 574-631-6899. *E-mail:* finaid.1@nd.edu.

UNIVERSITY OF OKLAHOMA

Norman, OK

Tuition & fees (OK res): $5477 **Average undergraduate aid package: $12,055**

ABOUT THE INSTITUTION State-supported, coed. 96 undergraduate majors. Federal methodology is used as a basis for awarding need-based institutional aid.

UNDERGRADUATE EXPENSES for 2010–11 ***Tuition, state resident:*** full-time $2942; part-time $122.60 per credit hour. ***Tuition, nonresident:*** full-time $11,287; part-time $470.30 per credit hour. ***Required fees:*** full-time $2535; $95.10 per credit hour or $126.50 per term. Full-time tuition and fees vary according to course load, degree level, location, program, and reciprocity agreements. Part-time tuition and fees vary according to course load, degree level, location, program, and reciprocity agreements. ***College room and board:*** $7826; ***Room only:*** $4284. Room and board charges vary according to board plan and housing facility. ***Payment plans:*** Guaranteed tuition, installment.

FRESHMAN FINANCIAL AID (Fall 2009) 2,593 applied for aid; of those 66% were deemed to have need. 97% of freshmen with need received aid; of those 83% had need fully met. ***Average percent of need met:*** 83% (excluding resources awarded to replace EFC). ***Average financial aid package:*** $11,997 (excluding resources awarded to replace EFC). 17% of all full-time freshmen had no need and received non-need-based gift aid.

UNDERGRADUATE FINANCIAL AID (Fall 2009) 10,046 applied for aid; of those 73% were deemed to have need. 97% of undergraduates with need received aid; of those 90% had need fully met. ***Average percent of need met:*** 90% (excluding resources awarded to replace EFC). ***Average financial aid package:*** $12,055 (excluding resources awarded to replace EFC). 13% of all full-time undergraduates had no need and received non-need-based gift aid.

GIFT AID (NEED-BASED) ***Total amount:*** $39,023,170 (52% federal, 28% state, 12% institutional, 8% external sources). ***Receiving aid:*** Freshmen: 27% (988); all full-time undergraduates: 27% (4,429). ***Average award:*** Freshmen: $6350; Undergraduates: $6011. ***Scholarships, grants, and awards:*** Federal Pell, FSEOG, state, private, college/university gift aid from institutional funds, United Negro College Fund.

GIFT AID (NON-NEED-BASED) ***Total amount:*** $10,520,462 (9% federal, 35% state, 39% institutional, 17% external sources). ***Receiving aid:*** Freshmen: 34% (1,240). Undergraduates: 25% (4,153). ***Average award:*** Freshmen: $2123. Undergraduates: $2129. ***Scholarships, grants, and awards by category:*** *Academic interests/achievement:* 5,737 awards ($21,871,974 total): architecture, area/ethnic studies, biological sciences, business, communication, computer science, education, engineering/technologies, English, foreign languages, general academic interests/achievements, humanities, international studies, mathematics, military science, physical sciences, social sciences. *Creative arts/performance:* 516 awards ($1,899,051 total): art/fine arts, dance, journalism/publications, music, performing arts, theater/drama. *Special achievements/activities:* 85 awards ($256,143 total): leadership. *Special characteristics:* 932 awards ($1,081,304 total): children and siblings of alumni, members of minority groups, previous college experience, public servants. ***Tuition waivers:*** Full or partial for children of alumni, employees or children of employees, senior citizens.

LOANS ***Student loans:*** $59,750,344 (94% need-based, 6% non-need-based). 52% of past graduating class borrowed through all loan programs. *Average indebtedness per student:* $21,517. ***Average need-based loan:*** Freshmen: $3286. Undergraduates: $4082. ***Parent loans:*** $12,076,721 (100% need-based). ***Programs:*** Federal Direct (Subsidized and Unsubsidized Stafford, PLUS), Perkins, college/university, alternative loans.

WORK-STUDY ***Federal work-study:*** Total amount: $2,045,956; 633 jobs averaging $3232.

ATHLETIC AWARDS Total amount: $7,843,455 (41% need-based, 59% non-need-based).

APPLYING FOR FINANCIAL AID ***Required financial aid form:*** FAFSA. ***Financial aid deadline:*** Continuous. ***Notification date:*** Continuous beginning 3/15. Students must reply within 6 weeks of notification.

CONTACT Financial Aid Office, University of Oklahoma, 1000 Asp Avenue, Room 216, Norman, OK 73019-4078, 405-325-4521 or toll-free 800-234-6868. *Fax:* 405-325-0819. *E-mail:* financialaid@ou.edu.

UNIVERSITY OF OREGON

Eugene, OR

Tuition & fees (OR res): $8190 **Average undergraduate aid package: $9343**

ABOUT THE INSTITUTION State-supported, coed. 77 undergraduate majors. Federal methodology is used as a basis for awarding need-based institutional aid.

UNDERGRADUATE EXPENSES for 2010–11 ***One-time required fee:*** $300. ***Tuition, state resident:*** full-time $6930; part-time $154 per credit hour. ***Tuition, nonresident:*** full-time $24,570; part-time $546 per credit hour. ***Required fees:*** full-time $1260. Full-time tuition and fees vary according to course load. Part-time tuition and fees vary according to course load. ***College room and board:*** $9429. Room and board charges vary according to board plan and housing facility. ***Payment plan:*** Installment.

FRESHMAN FINANCIAL AID (Fall 2010, est.) 2,667 applied for aid; of those 68% were deemed to have need. 95% of freshmen with need received aid; of those 12% had need fully met. ***Average percent of need met:*** 45% (excluding resources awarded to replace EFC). ***Average financial aid package:*** $8786 (excluding resources awarded to replace EFC). 10% of all full-time freshmen had no need and received non-need-based gift aid.

UNDERGRADUATE FINANCIAL AID (Fall 2010, est.) 10,654 applied for aid; of those 77% were deemed to have need. 95% of undergraduates with need received aid; of those 11% had need fully met. ***Average percent of need met:*** 53% (excluding resources awarded to replace EFC). ***Average financial aid package:*** $9343 (excluding resources awarded to replace EFC). 5% of all full-time undergraduates had no need and received non-need-based gift aid.

GIFT AID (NEED-BASED) ***Total amount:*** $27,981,548 (87% federal, 7% state, 6% institutional). ***Receiving aid:*** Freshmen: 22% (877); all full-time undergraduates: 26% (4,671). ***Average award:*** Freshmen: $5773; Undergraduates: $5573. ***Scholarships, grants, and awards:*** Federal Pell, FSEOG, state, private, college/university gift aid from institutional funds.

GIFT AID (NON-NEED-BASED) ***Total amount:*** $13,478,731 (1% federal, 91% institutional, 8% external sources). ***Receiving aid:*** Freshmen: 23% (910). Undergraduates: 15% (2,681). ***Average award:*** Freshmen: $2909. Undergraduates: $2679. ***Scholarships, grants, and awards by category:*** *Academic interests/achievement:* 5,077 awards ($13,351,658 total): architecture, biological sciences, business, education, English, foreign languages, general academic interests/achievements, health fields, humanities, international studies, mathematics, military science, physical sciences, premedicine, social sciences. *Creative arts/performance:* 920 awards ($2,378,702 total): applied art and design, art/fine arts, creative writing, dance, debating, journalism/publications, music, performing arts, theater/drama. *Special characteristics:* 517 awards ($2,776,070 total): children of faculty/staff, general special characteristics, international students, local/state students, veterans, veterans' children. ***Tuition waivers:*** Full or partial for employees or children of employees.

LOANS ***Student loans:*** $62,551,386 (48% need-based, 52% non-need-based). 56% of past graduating class borrowed through all loan programs. *Average indebtedness per student:* $20,928. ***Average need-based loan:*** Freshmen: $3772. Undergraduates: $4663. ***Parent loans:*** $43,717,483 (40% need-based, 60% non-need-based). ***Programs:*** Federal Direct (Subsidized and Unsubsidized Stafford, PLUS), Perkins, college/university.

WORK-STUDY ***Federal work-study:*** Total amount: $4,342,233; 2,926 jobs averaging $1478. ***State or other work-study/employment:*** Total amount: $156,000 (100% need-based). 60 part-time jobs averaging $2600.

ATHLETIC AWARDS Total amount: $8,099,388 (100% non-need-based).

APPLYING FOR FINANCIAL AID ***Required financial aid form:*** FAFSA. ***Financial aid deadline (priority):*** 3/1. ***Notification date:*** Continuous beginning 4/1. Students must reply within 4 weeks of notification.

CONTACT Elizabeth Bickford, Director of Financial Aid and Scholarships, University of Oregon, 1278 University of Oregon, Eugene, OR 97403-1278, 541-346-3221 or toll-free 800-232-3825 (in-state). *Fax:* 541-346-1175. *E-mail:* fawww@uoregon.edu.

UNIVERSITY OF PENNSYLVANIA

Philadelphia, PA

Tuition & fees: $42,098 **Average undergraduate aid package: $35,580**

ABOUT THE INSTITUTION Independent, coed. 96 undergraduate majors. Both federal and institutional methodology are used as a basis for awarding need-based institutional aid.

UNDERGRADUATE EXPENSES for 2011–12 ***Comprehensive fee:*** $53,976 includes full-time tuition ($37,620), mandatory fees ($4478), and room and board ($11,878). ***College room only:*** $7592. Room and board charges vary according to board plan and housing facility. Part-time tuition and fees vary according to course load. ***Payment plans:*** Tuition prepayment, installment.

FRESHMAN FINANCIAL AID (Fall 2009) 1,368 applied for aid; of those 82% were deemed to have need. 100% of freshmen with need received aid; of those 100% had need fully met. ***Average percent of need met:*** 100% (excluding resources awarded to replace EFC). ***Average financial aid package:*** $35,264 (excluding resources awarded to replace EFC).

UNDERGRADUATE FINANCIAL AID (Fall 2009) 4,815 applied for aid; of those 90% were deemed to have need. 100% of undergraduates with need received aid; of those 100% had need fully met. ***Average percent of need met:*** 100% (excluding resources awarded to replace EFC). ***Average financial aid package:*** $35,580 (excluding resources awarded to replace EFC).

GIFT AID (NEED-BASED) ***Total amount:*** $136,599,987 (7% federal, 1% state, 89% institutional, 3% external sources). ***Receiving aid:*** Freshmen: 45% (1,084); all full-time undergraduates: 44% (4,223). ***Average award:*** Freshmen: $33,460; Undergraduates: $32,443. ***Scholarships, grants, and awards:*** Federal Pell, FSEOG, state, private, college/university gift aid from institutional funds.

GIFT AID (NON-NEED-BASED) ***Total amount:*** $5,859,466 (2% federal, 98% external sources). ***Tuition waivers:*** Full or partial for employees or children of employees.

LOANS ***Student loans:*** $24,142,720 (7% need-based, 93% non-need-based). 43% of past graduating class borrowed through all loan programs. *Average indebtedness per student:* $17,013. ***Average need-based loan:*** Freshmen: $118. Undergraduates: $393. ***Parent loans:*** $10,877,456 (100% non-need-based). ***Programs:*** Perkins, Federal Nursing, college/university, supplemental third-party loans (guaranteed by institution).

WORK-STUDY ***Federal work-study:*** Total amount: $11,749,463; 3,355 jobs averaging $2871. ***State or other work-study/employment:*** Total amount: $1,942,819 (100% need-based). 645 part-time jobs averaging $2071.

APPLYING FOR FINANCIAL AID ***Required financial aid forms:*** FAFSA, institution's own form, CSS Financial Aid PROFILE, noncustodial (divorced/separated) parent's statement, business/farm supplement, parents' and student's most recent federal tax returns. ***Financial aid deadline (priority):*** 2/15. ***Notification date:*** 4/1. Students must reply by 5/1.

CONTACT Mr. William Schilling, Director of Financial Aid, University of Pennsylvania, 212 Franklin Building, Philadelphia, PA 19104-6270, 215-898-6784. *Fax:* 215-573-2208. *E-mail:* schilling@sfs.upenn.edu.

UNIVERSITY OF PHOENIX

Phoenix, AZ

Tuition & fees: N/R **Average undergraduate aid package: N/A**

ABOUT THE INSTITUTION Proprietary, coed. ***Awards:*** associate, bachelor's, and master's degrees and post-bachelor's and post-master's certificates. 11 undergraduate majors. ***Total enrollment:*** 292,797. Undergraduates: 236,109. Freshmen: 31,010. Both federal and institutional methodology are used as a basis for awarding need-based institutional aid.

GIFT AID (NEED-BASED) ***Total amount:*** $894,793,233 (99% federal, 1% state). ***Scholarships, grants, and awards:*** Federal Pell, FSEOG, state, private, college/university gift aid from institutional funds, Academic Competitiveness Grants, National SMART Grants.

GIFT AID (NON-NEED-BASED) ***Total amount:*** $269,501,598 (37% federal, 55% institutional, 8% external sources). ***Tuition waivers:*** Full or partial for employees or children of employees.

LOANS ***Parent loans:*** $16,229,890 (100% non-need-based). ***Programs:*** Federal Direct (Subsidized and Unsubsidized Stafford, PLUS), Perkins.

APPLYING FOR FINANCIAL AID ***Required financial aid forms:*** FAFSA, institution's own form. ***Financial aid deadline:*** Continuous. ***Notification date:*** Continuous.

CONTACT ACS/AFS, University of Phoenix, 875 West Elliot Road, Tempe, AZ 85284, 480-735-3000 or toll-free 800-776-4867 (in-state), 800-228-7240 (out-of-state). *Fax:* 480-940-2060.

UNIVERSITY OF PHOENIX–ATLANTA CAMPUS

Sandy Springs, GA

CONTACT ACS/AFS, University of Phoenix–Atlanta Campus, 875 West Elliot Road, Tempe, AZ 85284, 480-735-3000 or toll-free 800-776-4867 (in-state), 800-228-7240 (out-of-state). *Fax:* 480-940-2060.

UNIVERSITY OF PHOENIX–BAY AREA CAMPUS

Pleasanton, CA

CONTACT ACS/AFS, University of Phoenix–Bay Area Campus, 875 West Elliot Road, Tempe, AZ 85284, 480-735-3000 or toll-free 877-4-STUDENT. *Fax:* 480-940-2060.

UNIVERSITY OF PHOENIX–BIRMINGHAM CAMPUS

Birmingham, AL

CONTACT Financial Aid Office, University of Phoenix–Birmingham Campus, One Corporate Center, Suite 400, Birmingham, AL 35244.

UNIVERSITY OF PHOENIX–BOSTON CAMPUS

Braintree, MA

CONTACT ACS/AFS, University of Phoenix–Boston Campus, 875 West Elliot Road, Tempe, AZ 85284, 480-735-3000 or toll-free 800-228-7240. *Fax:* 480-940-2060.

UNIVERSITY OF PHOENIX–CENTRAL FLORIDA CAMPUS

Maitland, FL

CONTACT ACS/AFS, University of Phoenix–Central Florida Campus, 875 West Elliot Road, Tempe, AZ 85284, 480-735-3000 or toll-free 800-776-4867 (in-state), 800-228-7240 (out-of-state). *Fax:* 480-940-2060.

UNIVERSITY OF PHOENIX–CENTRAL MASSACHUSETTS CAMPUS

Westborough, MA

CONTACT ACS/AFS, University of Phoenix–Central Massachusetts Campus, 875 West Elliot Road, Tempe, AZ 85284, 480-735-3000 or toll-free 800-776-4867 (in-state), 800-228-7240 (out-of-state). *Fax:* 480-940-2060.

UNIVERSITY OF PHOENIX–CENTRAL VALLEY CAMPUS

Fresno, CA

CONTACT ACS/AFS, University of Phoenix–Central Valley Campus, 875 West Elliot Road, Tempe, AZ 85284, 480-735-3000 or toll-free 888-776-4867 (in-state), 888-228-7240 (out-of-state). *Fax:* 480-940-2060.

UNIVERSITY OF PHOENIX–CHARLOTTE CAMPUS

Charlotte, NC

CONTACT ACS/AFS, University of Phoenix–Charlotte Campus, 875 West Elliot Road, Tempe, AZ 85284, 480-735-3000 or toll-free 800-776-4867 (in-state), 800-228-7240 (out-of-state). *Fax:* 480-940-2060.

UNIVERSITY OF PHOENIX–CHICAGO CAMPUS

Schaumburg, IL

CONTACT ACS/AFS, University of Phoenix–Chicago Campus, 875 West Elliot Road, Tempe, AZ 85284, 480-735-3000 or toll-free 800-776-4867 (in-state), 800-228-7240 (out-of-state). *Fax:* 480-940-2060.

UNIVERSITY OF PHOENIX–CINCINNATI CAMPUS

West Chester, OH

CONTACT ACS/AFS, University of Phoenix–Cincinnati Campus, 875 West Elliot Road, Tempe, AZ 85284, 480-735-3000 or toll-free 800-776-4867 (in-state), 800-228-7240 (out-of-state). *Fax:* 480-940-2060.

UNIVERSITY OF PHOENIX–CLEVELAND CAMPUS

Independence, OH

CONTACT ACS/AFS, University of Phoenix–Cleveland Campus, 875 West Elliot Road, Tempe, AZ 85284, 480-735-3000 or toll-free 800-776-4867 (in-state), 800-228-7240 (out-of-state). *Fax:* 480-940-2060.

UNIVERSITY OF PHOENIX–COLUMBIA CAMPUS

Columbia, SC

CONTACT Financial Aid Office, University of Phoenix–Columbia Campus, 1001 Pinnacle Point Drive, Suite 200, Columbia, SC 29223, 803-699-5096.

UNIVERSITY OF PHOENIX–COLUMBUS GEORGIA CAMPUS

Columbus, GA

CONTACT ACS/AFS, University of Phoenix–Columbus Georgia Campus, 875 West Elliot Road, Tempe, AZ 85284, 480-735-3000 or toll-free 800-776-4867 (in-state), 800-228-7240 (out-of-state). *Fax:* 480-940-2060.

UNIVERSITY OF PHOENIX–COLUMBUS OHIO CAMPUS

Columbus, OH

CONTACT ACS/AFS, University of Phoenix–Columbus Ohio Campus, 875 West Elliot Road, Tempe, AZ 85284, 480-735-3000 or toll-free 800-776-4867 (in-state), 800-228-7240 (out-of-state). *Fax:* 480-940-2060.

UNIVERSITY OF PHOENIX–DALLAS CAMPUS

Dallas, TX

CONTACT ACS/AFS, University of Phoenix–Dallas Campus, 875 West Elliot Road, Tempe, AZ 85284, 480-735-3000 or toll-free 800-776-4867 (in-state), 800-228-7240 (out-of-state). *Fax:* 480-940-2060.

UNIVERSITY OF PHOENIX–DENVER CAMPUS

Lone Tree, CO

CONTACT ACS/AFS, University of Phoenix–Denver Campus, 875 West Elliot Road, Tempe, AZ 85284, 480-735-3000 or toll-free 800-776-4867 (in-state), 800-228-7240 (out-of-state). *Fax:* 480-940-2060.

UNIVERSITY OF PHOENIX–DETROIT CAMPUS

Southfield, MI

CONTACT ACS/AFS, University of Phoenix–Detroit Campus, 875 West Elliot Road, Tempe, AZ 85284, 480-735-3000. *Fax:* 480-940-2060.

UNIVERSITY OF PHOENIX–EASTERN WASHINGTON CAMPUS

Spokane Valley, WA

CONTACT ACS/AFS, University of Phoenix–Eastern Washington Campus, 875 West Elliot Road, Tempe, AZ 85284, 480-735-3000 or toll-free 800-697-8223 (in-state), 800-228-7240 (out-of-state). *Fax:* 480-940-2060.

UNIVERSITY OF PHOENIX–HAWAII CAMPUS

Honolulu, HI

CONTACT ACS/AFS, University of Phoenix–Hawaii Campus, 875 West Elliot Road, Tempe, AZ 85284, 480-735-3000 or toll-free 800-776-4867 (in-state), 800-228-7240 (out-of-state). *Fax:* 480-940-2060.

UNIVERSITY OF PHOENIX–HOUSTON CAMPUS

Houston, TX

CONTACT ACS/AFS, University of Phoenix–Houston Campus, 875 West Elliot Road, Tempe, AZ 85284, 480-735-3000 or toll-free 800-776-4867 (in-state), 800-228-7240 (out-of-state). *Fax:* 480-940-2060.

UNIVERSITY OF PHOENIX–IDAHO CAMPUS

Meridian, ID

CONTACT ACS/AFS, University of Phoenix–Idaho Campus, 875 West Elliot Road, Tempe, AZ 85284, 480-735-3000 or toll-free 800-776-4867 (in-state), 800-228-7240 (out-of-state). *Fax:* 480-940-2060.

UNIVERSITY OF PHOENIX–INDIANAPOLIS CAMPUS

Indianapolis, IN

CONTACT ACS/AFS, University of Phoenix–Indianapolis Campus, 875 West Elliot Road, Tempe, AZ 85284, 480-735-3000 or toll-free 800-776-4867 (in-state), 800-228-7240 (out-of-state). *Fax:* 480-940-2060.

UNIVERSITY OF PHOENIX–KANSAS CITY CAMPUS

Kansas City, MO

CONTACT ACS/AFS, University of Phoenix–Kansas City Campus, 875 West Elliot Road, Tempe, AZ 85284, 480-735-3000 or toll-free 800-776-4867 (in-state), 800-228-7240 (out-of-state). *Fax:* 480-940-2060.

UNIVERSITY OF PHOENIX–LAS VEGAS CAMPUS

Las Vegas, NV

CONTACT ACS/AFS, University of Phoenix–Las Vegas Campus, 875 West Elliot Road, Tempe, AZ 85284, 480-735-3000 or toll-free 800-776-4867 (in-state), 800-228-7240 (out-of-state). *Fax:* 480-940-2060.

UNIVERSITY OF PHOENIX–LITTLE ROCK CAMPUS

Little Rock, AR

CONTACT ACS/AFS, University of Phoenix–Little Rock Campus, 875 West Elliot Road, Tempe, AZ 85284, 480-735-3000 or toll-free 800-776-4867 (in-state), 800-228-7240 (out-of-state). *Fax:* 480-940-2060.

UNIVERSITY OF PHOENIX–LOUISIANA CAMPUS

Metairie, LA

CONTACT ACS/AFS, University of Phoenix–Louisiana Campus, 875 West Elliot Road, Tempe, AZ 85284, 480-735-3000 or toll-free 800-776-4867 (in-state), 800-228-7240 (out-of-state). *Fax:* 480-940-2060.

UNIVERSITY OF PHOENIX–MARYLAND CAMPUS

Columbia, MD

CONTACT ACS/AFS, University of Phoenix–Maryland Campus, 875 West Elliot Road, Tempe, AZ 85284, 480-735-3000 or toll-free 800-776-4867 (in-state), 800-228-7240 (out-of-state). *Fax:* 480-940-2060.

UNIVERSITY OF PHOENIX–METRO DETROIT CAMPUS

Troy, MI

CONTACT ACS/AFS, University of Phoenix–Metro Detroit Campus, 875 West Elliot Road, Suite 116, Tempe, AZ 85284, 480-735-3000 or toll-free 800-776-4867 (in-state), 800-228-7240 (out-of-state). *Fax:* 480-940-2060.

UNIVERSITY OF PHOENIX–MILWAUKEE CAMPUS

Milwaukee, WI

CONTACT Financial Aid Office, University of Phoenix–Milwaukee Campus, 20075 Watertower Boulevard, Milwaukee, WI 53045, 262-785-0608 or toll-free 866-766-0766.

UNIVERSITY OF PHOENIX–NASHVILLE CAMPUS

Nashville, TN

CONTACT ACS/AFS, University of Phoenix–Nashville Campus, 875 West Elliot Road, Tempe, AZ 85284, 480-735-3000 or toll-free 800-776-4867 (in-state), 800-228-7240 (out-of-state). *Fax:* 480-940-2060.

UNIVERSITY OF PHOENIX–NEW MEXICO CAMPUS

Albuquerque, NM

CONTACT ACS/AFS, University of Phoenix–New Mexico Campus, 875 West Elliot Road, Tempe, AZ 85284, 480-735-3000 or toll-free 800-776-4867 (in-state), 800-228-7240 (out-of-state). *Fax:* 480-940-2060.

UNIVERSITY OF PHOENIX–NORTHERN NEVADA CAMPUS

Reno, NV

CONTACT Financial Aid Office, University of Phoenix–Northern Nevada Campus, 10345 Professional Circle, Suite 200, Reno, NV 89521-5862, 775-828-7999.

UNIVERSITY OF PHOENIX–NORTHERN VIRGINIA CAMPUS

Reston, VA

CONTACT ACS/AFS, University of Phoenix–Northern Virginia Campus, 875 West Elliott Road, Tempe, AZ 85284, 480-735-3000 or toll-free 800-776-4867 (in-state), 800-228-7240 (out-of-state). *Fax:* 480-940-2060.

UNIVERSITY OF PHOENIX–NORTH FLORIDA CAMPUS

Jacksonville, FL

CONTACT ACS/AFS, University of Phoenix–North Florida Campus, 875 West Elliot Road, Tempe, AZ 85284, 480-735-3000 or toll-free 800-776-4867 (in-state), 800-894-1758 (out-of-state). *Fax:* 480-940-2060.

UNIVERSITY OF PHOENIX–OKLAHOMA CITY CAMPUS

Oklahoma City, OK

CONTACT ACS/AFS, University of Phoenix–Oklahoma City Campus, 875 West Elliot Road, Tempe, AZ 85284, 480-735-3000 or toll-free 800-776-4867 (in-state), 800-228-7240 (out-of-state). *Fax:* 480-940-2060.

UNIVERSITY OF PHOENIX–OREGON CAMPUS

Tigard, OR

CONTACT ACS/AFS, University of Phoenix–Oregon Campus, 875 West Elliot Road, Tempe, AZ 85284, 480-735-3000 or toll-free 800-776-4867 (in-state), 800-228-7240 (out-of-state). *Fax:* 480-940-2060.

UNIVERSITY OF PHOENIX–PHILADELPHIA CAMPUS

Wayne, PA

CONTACT ACS/AFS, University of Phoenix–Philadelphia Campus, 875 West Elliot Road, Tempe, AZ 85284, 480-735-3000 or toll-free 800-776-4867 (in-state), 800-228-7240 (out-of-state). *Fax:* 480-940-2060.

UNIVERSITY OF PHOENIX–PHOENIX CAMPUS

Phoenix, AZ

Tuition & fees: N/R	Average undergraduate aid package: N/A

ABOUT THE INSTITUTION Proprietary, coed. ***Awards:*** bachelor's and master's degrees and post-bachelor's and post-master's certificates. 25 undergraduate majors. ***Total enrollment:*** 5,379. Undergraduates: 3,718. Freshmen: 193. Both federal and institutional methodology are used as a basis for awarding need-based institutional aid.

GIFT AID (NEED-BASED) ***Total amount:*** $9,040,822 (98% federal, 2% state). ***Scholarships, grants, and awards:*** Federal Pell, FSEOG, state, private, college/university gift aid from institutional funds, Academic Competitiveness Grants, National SMART Grants.

GIFT AID (NON-NEED-BASED) ***Total amount:*** $4,635,644 (60% federal, 4% state, 22% institutional, 14% external sources). ***Tuition waivers:*** Full or partial for employees or children of employees.

LOANS ***Student loans:*** $44,498,631 (41% need-based, 59% non-need-based). ***Parent loans:*** $325,154 (100% non-need-based). ***Programs:*** Federal Direct (Subsidized and Unsubsidized Stafford, PLUS), Perkins.

APPLYING FOR FINANCIAL AID ***Required financial aid forms:*** FAFSA, institution's own form. ***Financial aid deadline:*** Continuous. ***Notification date:*** Continuous.

CONTACT ACS/AFS, University of Phoenix–Phoenix Campus, 875 West Elliot Road, Tempe, AZ 85284, 480-735-3000 or toll-free 800-776-4867 (in-state), 800-228-7240 (out-of-state). *Fax:* 480-940-2060.

UNIVERSITY OF PHOENIX–PITTSBURGH CAMPUS

Pittsburgh, PA

CONTACT ACS/AFS, University of Phoenix–Pittsburgh Campus, 875 West Elliot Road, Tempe, AZ 85284, 480-735-3000 or toll-free 800-776-4867 (in-state), 800-228-7240 (out-of-state). *Fax:* 480-940-2060.

UNIVERSITY OF PHOENIX–PUERTO RICO CAMPUS

Guaynabo, PR

CONTACT ACS/AFS, University of Phoenix–Puerto Rico Campus, 875 West Elliot Road, Tempe, AZ 85284, 480-735-3000 or toll-free 800-776-4867 (in-state), 800-228-7240 (out-of-state). *Fax:* 480-940-2060.

UNIVERSITY OF PHOENIX–RALEIGH CAMPUS

Raleigh, NC

CONTACT ACS/AFS, University of Phoenix–Raleigh Campus, 875 West Elliot Road, Tempe, AZ 85284, 480-735-3000 or toll-free 800-776-4867 (in-state), 800-228-7240 (out-of-state). *Fax:* 480-940-2060.

UNIVERSITY OF PHOENIX–RICHMOND CAMPUS

Richmond, VA

CONTACT ACS/AFS, University of Phoenix–Richmond Campus, 875 West Elliot Road, Tempe, AZ 85284, 480-735-3000 or toll-free 800-776-4867 (in-state), 800-228-7240 (out-of-state). *Fax:* 480-940-2060.

UNIVERSITY OF PHOENIX–SACRAMENTO VALLEY CAMPUS

Sacramento, CA

CONTACT ACS/AFS, University of Phoenix–Sacramento Valley Campus, 875 West Elliot Road, Tempe, AZ 85284, 480-735-3000 or toll-free 800-776-4867 (in-state), 800-228-7240 (out-of-state). *Fax:* 480-940-2060.

UNIVERSITY OF PHOENIX–ST. LOUIS CAMPUS

St. Louis, MO

CONTACT ACS/AFS, University of Phoenix–St. Louis Campus, 875 West Elliot Road, Tempe, AZ 85284, 480-735-3000 or toll-free 800-776-4867 (in-state), 800-228-7240 (out-of-state). *Fax:* 480-940-2060.

UNIVERSITY OF PHOENIX–SAN DIEGO CAMPUS

San Diego, CA

Tuition & fees: N/R	Average undergraduate aid package: N/A

ABOUT THE INSTITUTION Proprietary, coed. ***Awards:*** bachelor's and master's degrees. 12 undergraduate majors. ***Total enrollment:*** 3,212. Undergraduates: 2,500. Freshmen: 170. Both federal and institutional methodology are used as a basis for awarding need-based institutional aid.

GIFT AID (NEED-BASED) ***Total amount:*** $9,393,020 (92% federal, 7% state, 1% institutional). ***Scholarships, grants, and awards:*** Federal Pell, FSEOG, state, private, college/university gift aid from institutional funds, Academic Competitiveness Grants, National SMART Grants.

GIFT AID (NON-NEED-BASED) ***Total amount:*** $9,829,834 (72% federal, 21% institutional, 7% external sources). ***Tuition waivers:*** Full or partial for employees or children of employees.

LOANS ***Student loans:*** $42,044,096 (42% need-based, 58% non-need-based). ***Parent loans:*** $620,242 (100% non-need-based). ***Programs:*** Federal Direct (Subsidized and Unsubsidized Stafford, PLUS), Perkins.

APPLYING FOR FINANCIAL AID ***Required financial aid forms:*** FAFSA, institution's own form. ***Financial aid deadline:*** Continuous. ***Notification date:*** Continuous.

CONTACT ACS/AFS, University of Phoenix–San Diego Campus, 875 West Elliot Road, Tempe, AZ 85284, 480-735-3000 or toll-free 888-776-4867 (in-state), 888-228-7240 (out-of-state). *Fax:* 480-940-2060.

UNIVERSITY OF PHOENIX–SOUTHERN ARIZONA CAMPUS

Tucson, AZ

CONTACT ACS/AFS, University of Phoenix–Southern Arizona Campus, 875 West Elliot Road, Tempe, AZ 85284, 480-735-3000 or toll-free 800-776-4867 (in-state), 800-228-7240 (out-of-state). *Fax:* 480-940-2060.

UNIVERSITY OF PHOENIX–SOUTHERN CALIFORNIA CAMPUS

Costa Mesa, CA

CONTACT ACS/AFS, University of Phoenix–Southern California Campus, 875 West Elliot Road, Tempe, AZ 85284, 480-735-3000 or toll-free 800-776-4867 (in-state), 800-228-7240 (out-of-state). *Fax:* 480-940-2060.

UNIVERSITY OF PHOENIX–SOUTHERN COLORADO CAMPUS

Colorado Springs, CO

CONTACT ACS/AFS, University of Phoenix–Southern Colorado Campus, 875 West Elliot Road, Tempe, AZ 85284, 480-735-3000 or toll-free 800-776-4867 (in-state), 800-228-7240 (out-of-state). *Fax:* 480-940-2060.

UNIVERSITY OF PHOENIX–SOUTH FLORIDA CAMPUS

Fort Lauderdale, FL

CONTACT ACS/AFS, University of Phoenix–South Florida Campus, 875 West Elliot Road, Tempe, AZ 85284, 480-735-3000 or toll-free 800-228-7240. *Fax:* 480-940-2060.

UNIVERSITY OF PHOENIX–SPRINGFIELD CAMPUS

Springfield, MO

CONTACT ACS/AFS, University of Phoenix–Springfield Campus, 875 West Elliot Road, Tempe, AZ 85284, 480-735-3000 or toll-free 800-776-4867 (in-state), 800-228-7240 (out-of-state). *Fax:* 480-940-2060.

UNIVERSITY OF PHOENIX–TULSA CAMPUS

Tulsa, OK

CONTACT ACS/AFS, University of Phoenix–Tulsa Campus, 875 West Elliot Road, Tempe, AZ 85284, 480-735-3000 or toll-free 800-776-4867 (in-state), 800-228-7240 (out-of-state). *Fax:* 480-940-2060.

UNIVERSITY OF PHOENIX–UTAH CAMPUS

Salt Lake City, UT

CONTACT ACS/AFS, University of Phoenix–Utah Campus, 875 West Elliot Road, Tempe, AZ 85284, 480-735-3000 or toll-free 800-776-4867 (in-state), 800-228-7240 (out-of-state). *Fax:* 480-940-2060.

UNIVERSITY OF PHOENIX–WASHINGTON CAMPUS

Seattle, WA

CONTACT ACS/AFS, University of Phoenix–Washington Campus, 875 West Elliot Road, Tempe, AZ 85284, 480-735-3000 or toll-free 800-776-4867 (in-state), 800-228-7240 (out-of-state). *Fax:* 480-940-2060.

UNIVERSITY OF PHOENIX–WASHINGTON D.C. CAMPUS

Washington, DC

CONTACT Financial Aid Office, University of Phoenix–Washington D.C. Campus, 25 Massachusetts Avenue NW, Suite 150, Washington, DC 20001.

UNIVERSITY OF PHOENIX–WEST FLORIDA CAMPUS

Temple Terrace, FL

CONTACT ACS/AFS, University of Phoenix–West Florida Campus, 875 West Elliot Road, Tempe, AZ 85284, 480-735-3000 or toll-free 800-776-4867 (in-state), 800-228-7240 (out-of-state). *Fax:* 480-940-2060.

UNIVERSITY OF PHOENIX–WEST MICHIGAN CAMPUS

Walker, MI

CONTACT ACS/AFS, University of Phoenix–West Michigan Campus, 875 West Elliot Road, Tempe, AZ 85284, 480-735-3000 or toll-free 800-776-4867 (in-state), 800-228-7240 (out-of-state). *Fax:* 480-940-2060.

UNIVERSITY OF PHOENIX–WICHITA CAMPUS

Wichita, KS

CONTACT ACS/AFS, University of Phoenix–Wichita Campus, 875 West Elliot Road, Tempe, AZ 85284, 480-735-3000 or toll-free 800-776-4867 (in-state), 800-228-7240 (out-of-state). *Fax:* 480-940-2060.

UNIVERSITY OF PITTSBURGH

Pittsburgh, PA

Tuition & fees (PA res): $14,936 **Average undergraduate aid package: $10,140**

ABOUT THE INSTITUTION State-related, coed. 86 undergraduate majors. Federal methodology is used as a basis for awarding need-based institutional aid.

UNDERGRADUATE EXPENSES for 2010–11 ***Tuition, state resident:*** full-time $14,076; part-time $586 per credit. ***Tuition, nonresident:*** full-time $23,732; part-time $988 per credit. ***Required fees:*** full-time $860; $860 per term. Full-time tuition and fees vary according to program. Part-time tuition and fees vary according to program. ***College room and board:*** $9230; ***Room only:*** $5500. Room and board charges vary according to board plan and housing facility. ***Payment plans:*** Installment, deferred payment.

FRESHMAN FINANCIAL AID (Fall 2010, est.) 3,052 applied for aid; of those 71% were deemed to have need. 96% of freshmen with need received aid; of those 41% had need fully met. ***Average percent of need met:*** 79% (excluding resources awarded to replace EFC). ***Average financial aid package:*** $10,310 (excluding resources awarded to replace EFC). 8% of all full-time freshmen had no need and received non-need-based gift aid.

UNDERGRADUATE FINANCIAL AID (Fall 2010, est.) 12,176 applied for aid; of those 80% were deemed to have need. 97% of undergraduates with need received aid; of those 36% had need fully met. ***Average percent of need met:*** 76% (excluding resources awarded to replace EFC). ***Average financial aid package:*** $10,140 (excluding resources awarded to replace EFC). 7% of all full-time undergraduates had no need and received non-need-based gift aid.

GIFT AID (NEED-BASED) ***Total amount:*** $54,187,370 (29% federal, 17% state, 39% institutional, 15% external sources). ***Receiving aid:*** Freshmen: 41% (1,554); all full-time undergraduates: 39% (6,637). ***Average award:*** Freshmen: $9490; Undergraduates: $8281. ***Scholarships, grants, and awards:*** Federal Pell, FSEOG, state, private, college/university gift aid from institutional funds, Federal Nursing.

GIFT AID (NON-NEED-BASED) ***Total amount:*** $21,286,662 (2% state, 82% institutional, 16% external sources). ***Receiving aid:*** Freshmen: 23% (848). Undergraduates: 16% (2,812). ***Average award:*** Freshmen: $14,234. Undergraduates: $15,076. ***Scholarships, grants, and awards by category:*** *Academic interests/achievement:* 1,220 awards ($18,391,500 total): general academic interests/achievements. ***Tuition waivers:*** Full or partial for employees or children of employees.

LOANS ***Student loans:*** $97,264,488 (41% need-based, 59% non-need-based). 63% of past graduating class borrowed through all loan programs. *Average indebtedness per student:* $26,612. ***Average need-based loan:*** Freshmen: $4254. Undergraduates: $4930. ***Parent loans:*** $25,829,018 (78% need-based, 22% non-need-based). ***Programs:*** Federal Direct (Subsidized and Unsubsidized Stafford, PLUS), Perkins, Federal Nursing, state, college/university.

WORK-STUDY ***Federal work-study:*** Total amount: $2,900,000; 1,308 jobs averaging $2452.

ATHLETIC AWARDS Total amount: $8,081,010 (42% need-based, 58% non-need-based).

APPLYING FOR FINANCIAL AID ***Required financial aid form:*** FAFSA. ***Financial aid deadline (priority):*** 3/1. ***Notification date:*** Continuous beginning 3/15.

CONTACT Dr. Betsy A. Porter, Director of Admissions and Financial Aid, University of Pittsburgh, 4227 Fifth Avenue, First Floor, Pittsburgh, PA 15260, 412-624-7488. *Fax:* 412-648-8815. *E-mail:* oafa@pitt.edu.

UNIVERSITY OF PITTSBURGH AT BRADFORD

Bradford, PA

Tuition & fees (PA res): $12,046 Average undergraduate aid package: $12,625

ABOUT THE INSTITUTION State-related, coed. 33 undergraduate majors. Federal methodology is used as a basis for awarding need-based institutional aid.

UNDERGRADUATE EXPENSES for 2010–11 ***One-time required fee:*** $90. ***Tuition, state resident:*** full-time $11,286; part-time $470 per credit hour. ***Tuition, nonresident:*** full-time $21,086; part-time $878 per credit hour. ***Required fees:*** full-time $760; $130 per term. Full-time tuition and fees vary according to course load and program. Part-time tuition and fees vary according to course load and program. ***College room and board:*** $7650; ***Room only:*** $4680. Room and board charges vary according to board plan and housing facility. ***Payment plan:*** Installment.

FRESHMAN FINANCIAL AID (Fall 2009) 411 applied for aid; of those 87% were deemed to have need. 100% of freshmen with need received aid; of those 98% had need fully met. ***Average percent of need met:*** 95% (excluding resources awarded to replace EFC). ***Average financial aid package:*** $13,642 (excluding resources awarded to replace EFC). 29% of all full-time freshmen had no need and received non-need-based gift aid.

UNDERGRADUATE FINANCIAL AID (Fall 2009) 1,449 applied for aid; of those 91% were deemed to have need. 98% of undergraduates with need received aid; of those 60% had need fully met. ***Average percent of need met:*** 90% (excluding resources awarded to replace EFC). ***Average financial aid package:*** $12,625 (excluding resources awarded to replace EFC). 18% of all full-time undergraduates had no need and received non-need-based gift aid.

GIFT AID (NEED-BASED) ***Total amount:*** $8,928,675 (30% federal, 26% state, 40% institutional, 4% external sources). ***Receiving aid:*** Freshmen: 56% (233); all full-time undergraduates: 36% (530). ***Average award:*** Freshmen: $5491; Undergraduates: $5524. ***Scholarships, grants, and awards:*** Federal Pell, FSEOG, state, private, college/university gift aid from institutional funds, Academic Competitiveness Grants, National SMART Grants.

GIFT AID (NON-NEED-BASED) ***Total amount:*** $635,554 (1% state, 94% institutional, 5% external sources). ***Receiving aid:*** Freshmen: 61% (252). Undergraduates: 31% (449). ***Average award:*** Freshmen: $5945. Undergraduates: $5587. ***Scholarships, grants, and awards by category:*** *Academic interests/achievement:* 133 awards ($125,909 total): biological sciences, business, communication, computer science, education, engineering/technologies, English, general academic interests/achievements, health fields, humanities, mathematics, physical sciences, premedicine, social sciences. *Creative arts/performance:* 2 awards ($1379 total): cinema/film/broadcasting. *Special characteristics:* 1,130 awards ($4,429,088 total): adult students, children of faculty/staff, children of union members/company employees, local/state students, out-of-state students, veterans. ***Tuition waivers:*** Full or partial for employees or children of employees.

LOANS ***Student loans:*** $10,745,375 (93% need-based, 7% non-need-based). 82% of past graduating class borrowed through all loan programs. *Average indebtedness per student:* $21,695. ***Average need-based loan:*** Freshmen: $3478. Undergraduates: $4432. ***Parent loans:*** $1,520,265 (84% need-based, 16% non-need-based). ***Programs:*** Perkins.

WORK-STUDY ***Federal work-study:*** Total amount: $1,329,945; 199 jobs averaging $1740. ***State or other work-study/employment:*** Total amount: $10,624 (100% need-based). 1 part-time job averaging $1740.

APPLYING FOR FINANCIAL AID ***Required financial aid form:*** FAFSA. ***Financial aid deadline (priority):*** 3/1. ***Notification date:*** Continuous beginning 4/1. Students must reply within 2 weeks of notification.

CONTACT Melissa Ibanez, Director of Financial Aid, University of Pittsburgh at Bradford, 300 Campus Drive, Bradford, PA 16701-2812, 814-362-7550 or toll-free 800-872-1787. *Fax:* 814-362-7578. *E-mail:* ibanez@pitt.edu.

UNIVERSITY OF PITTSBURGH AT GREENSBURG

Greensburg, PA

Tuition & fees (PA res): $12,176 Average undergraduate aid package: $12,647

ABOUT THE INSTITUTION State-related, coed. 23 undergraduate majors. Federal methodology is used as a basis for awarding need-based institutional aid.

UNDERGRADUATE EXPENSES for 2010–11 ***Tuition, state resident:*** full-time $11,286; part-time $470 per credit hour. ***Tuition, nonresident:*** full-time $21,086; part-time $878 per credit hour. ***Required fees:*** full-time $890. ***College room and board:*** $8110. Room and board charges vary according to board plan and housing facility. ***Payment plan:*** Installment.

FRESHMAN FINANCIAL AID (Fall 2009) 384 applied for aid; of those 86% were deemed to have need. 99% of freshmen with need received aid; of those 9% had need fully met. ***Average percent of need met:*** 82% (excluding resources awarded to replace EFC). ***Average financial aid package:*** $12,192 (excluding resources awarded to replace EFC). 6% of all full-time freshmen had no need and received non-need-based gift aid.

UNDERGRADUATE FINANCIAL AID (Fall 2009) 1,468 applied for aid; of those 87% were deemed to have need. 98% of undergraduates with need received aid; of those 9% had need fully met. ***Average percent of need met:*** 79% (excluding resources awarded to replace EFC). ***Average financial aid package:*** $12,647 (excluding resources awarded to replace EFC). 3% of all full-time undergraduates had no need and received non-need-based gift aid.

GIFT AID (NEED-BASED) ***Total amount:*** $5,849,018 (44% federal, 40% state, 10% institutional, 6% external sources). ***Receiving aid:*** Freshmen: 56% (228); all full-time undergraduates: 53% (888). ***Average award:*** Freshmen: $7019; Undergraduates: $6219. ***Scholarships, grants, and awards:*** Federal Pell, FSEOG, state, private, college/university gift aid from institutional funds, United Negro College Fund.

GIFT AID (NON-NEED-BASED) ***Total amount:*** $427,913 (7% state, 38% institutional, 55% external sources). ***Receiving aid:*** Freshmen: 3% (12). Undergraduates: 2% (27). ***Average award:*** Freshmen: $3583. Undergraduates: $3242. ***Scholarships, grants, and awards by category:*** *Special achievements/activities:* leadership. ***Tuition waivers:*** Full or partial for employees or children of employees, senior citizens.

LOANS ***Student loans:*** $11,414,684 (74% need-based, 26% non-need-based). 89% of past graduating class borrowed through all loan programs. *Average indebtedness per student:* $26,163. ***Average need-based loan:*** Freshmen: $3574. Undergraduates: $4391. ***Parent loans:*** $1,630,896 (32% need-based, 68% non-need-based). ***Programs:*** Federal Direct (Subsidized and Unsubsidized Stafford, PLUS), Perkins, college/university.

WORK-STUDY ***Federal work-study:*** Total amount: $536,747; jobs available.

APPLYING FOR FINANCIAL AID ***Required financial aid forms:*** FAFSA, state aid form. ***Financial aid deadline (priority):*** 2/15. ***Notification date:*** Continuous beginning 3/15. Students must reply within 3 weeks of notification.

CONTACT Ms. Brandi S. Darr, Director of Financial Aid, University of Pittsburgh at Greensburg, 150 Finoli Drive, Greensburg, PA 15601-5898, 724-836-7167. *E-mail:* upgfnaid@pitt.edu.

UNIVERSITY OF PITTSBURGH AT JOHNSTOWN

Johnstown, PA

Tuition & fees (PA res): $12,078 **Average undergraduate aid package: $10,441**

ABOUT THE INSTITUTION State-related, coed. 50 undergraduate majors. Federal methodology is used as a basis for awarding need-based institutional aid.

UNDERGRADUATE EXPENSES for 2010–11 ***Tuition, state resident:*** full-time $11,286; part-time $470 per credit. ***Tuition, nonresident:*** full-time $21,086; part-time $878 per credit. ***Required fees:*** full-time $792; $87 per term. Full-time tuition and fees vary according to program. Part-time tuition and fees vary according to program. ***College room and board:*** $7826; ***Room only:*** $4970. Room and board charges vary according to board plan and housing facility. ***Payment plan:*** Installment.

FRESHMAN FINANCIAL AID (Fall 2009) 734 applied for aid; of those 80% were deemed to have need. 99% of freshmen with need received aid; of those 9% had need fully met. ***Average percent of need met:*** 53% (excluding resources awarded to replace EFC). ***Average financial aid package:*** $10,174 (excluding resources awarded to replace EFC). 3% of all full-time freshmen had no need and received non-need-based gift aid.

UNDERGRADUATE FINANCIAL AID (Fall 2009) 2,591 applied for aid; of those 83% were deemed to have need. 100% of undergraduates with need received aid; of those 14% had need fully met. ***Average percent of need met:*** 53% (excluding resources awarded to replace EFC). ***Average financial aid package:*** $10,441 (excluding resources awarded to replace EFC). 1% of all full-time undergraduates had no need and received non-need-based gift aid.

GIFT AID (NEED-BASED) ***Total amount:*** $9,822,668 (42% federal, 42% state, 14% institutional, 2% external sources). ***Receiving aid:*** Freshmen: 56% (441); all full-time undergraduates: 52% (1,509). ***Average award:*** Freshmen: $5765; Undergraduates: $5411. ***Scholarships, grants, and awards:*** Federal Pell, FSEOG, state, private, college/university gift aid from institutional funds.

GIFT AID (NON-NEED-BASED) ***Total amount:*** $1,430,888 (10% state, 72% institutional, 18% external sources). ***Receiving aid:*** Freshmen: 24% (187). Undergraduates: 23% (665). ***Average award:*** Freshmen: $1726. Undergraduates: $3063. ***Scholarships, grants, and awards by category:*** *Academic interests/achievement:* 523 awards ($1,421,411 total): biological sciences, business, communication, computer science, education, engineering/technologies, English, general academic interests/achievements, humanities, mathematics, physical sciences, premedicine, social sciences. *Creative arts/performance:* 4 awards ($16,350 total): journalism/publications, theater/drama. *Special achievements/activities:* 137 awards ($182,500 total): leadership. *Special characteristics:* 131 awards ($1,438,744 total): children of faculty/staff. ***Tuition waivers:*** Full or partial for employees or children of employees.

LOANS ***Student loans:*** $19,863,033 (51% need-based, 49% non-need-based). 82% of past graduating class borrowed through all loan programs. *Average indebtedness per student:* $21,220. ***Average need-based loan:*** Freshmen: $3478. Undergraduates: $4322. ***Parent loans:*** $3,541,400 (20% need-based, 80% non-need-based). ***Programs:*** Federal Direct (Subsidized and Unsubsidized Stafford, PLUS), Perkins.

WORK-STUDY ***Federal work-study:*** Total amount: $405,846; 142 jobs averaging $1797. ***State or other work-study/employment:*** Total amount: $516,743 (8% need-based, 92% non-need-based). 318 part-time jobs averaging $2742.

ATHLETIC AWARDS Total amount: $554,495 (29% need-based, 71% non-need-based).

APPLYING FOR FINANCIAL AID ***Required financial aid form:*** FAFSA. ***Financial aid deadline (priority):*** 4/1. ***Notification date:*** Continuous beginning 4/1. Students must reply within 2 weeks of notification.

CONTACT Ms. Jeanine M. Lawn, Director of Student Financial Aid, University of Pittsburgh at Johnstown, 125 Biddle Hall, Johnstown, PA 15904-2990, 814-269-7045 or toll-free 800-765-4875. *Fax:* 814-269-7061. *E-mail:* lawn@pitt.edu.

UNIVERSITY OF PORTLAND

Portland, OR

Tuition & fees: $33,538 **Average undergraduate aid package: $21,698**

ABOUT THE INSTITUTION Independent Roman Catholic, coed. 42 undergraduate majors. Federal methodology is used as a basis for awarding need-based institutional aid.

UNDERGRADUATE EXPENSES for 2010–11 ***Comprehensive fee:*** $43,298 includes full-time tuition ($32,190), mandatory fees ($1348), and room and board ($9760). ***College room only:*** $5290. Full-time tuition and fees vary according to program. Room and board charges vary according to board plan and housing facility. ***Part-time tuition:*** $1010 per credit hour. Part-time tuition and fees vary according to course load and program. ***Payment plans:*** Installment, deferred payment.

FRESHMAN FINANCIAL AID (Fall 2010, est.) 763 applied for aid; of those 82% were deemed to have need. 100% of freshmen with need received aid; of those 9% had need fully met. ***Average percent of need met:*** 78% (excluding resources awarded to replace EFC). ***Average financial aid package:*** $22,186 (excluding resources awarded to replace EFC). 25% of all full-time freshmen had no need and received non-need-based gift aid.

UNDERGRADUATE FINANCIAL AID (Fall 2010, est.) 2,427 applied for aid; of those 87% were deemed to have need. 100% of undergraduates with need received aid; of those 8% had need fully met. ***Average percent of need met:*** 81% (excluding resources awarded to replace EFC). ***Average financial aid package:*** $21,698 (excluding resources awarded to replace EFC). 24% of all full-time undergraduates had no need and received non-need-based gift aid.

GIFT AID (NEED-BASED) ***Total amount:*** $40,462,568 (10% federal, 1% state, 84% institutional, 5% external sources). ***Receiving aid:*** Freshmen: 51% (453); all full-time undergraduates: 49% (1,578). ***Average award:*** Freshmen: $20,431; Undergraduates: $18,359. ***Scholarships, grants, and awards:*** Federal Pell, FSEOG, state, private, college/university gift aid from institutional funds, United Negro College Fund, Federal Nursing.

GIFT AID (NON-NEED-BASED) ***Total amount:*** $9,803,436 (98% institutional, 2% external sources). ***Receiving aid:*** Freshmen: 68% (606). Undergraduates: 63% (2,018). ***Average award:*** Freshmen: $13,198. Undergraduates: $12,119. ***Scholarships, grants, and awards by category:*** *Academic interests/achievement:* 241 awards ($2,940,250 total): biological sciences, business, communication, computer science, education, engineering/technologies, English, foreign languages, general academic interests/achievements, health fields, humanities, mathematics, military science, physical sciences, premedicine, religion/biblical studies, social sciences. *Creative arts/performance:* 5 awards ($12,800 total): music, performing arts, theater/drama. *Special achievements/activities:* 9 awards ($5400 total): general special achievements/activities. *Special characteristics:* 39 awards ($1,245,019 total): children of faculty/staff, relatives of clergy, religious affiliation. ***Tuition waivers:*** Full or partial for employees or children of employees.

LOANS ***Student loans:*** $26,367,326 (91% need-based, 9% non-need-based). 69% of past graduating class borrowed through all loan programs. *Average indebtedness per student:* $26,831. ***Average need-based loan:*** Freshmen: $3280. Undergraduates: $4615. ***Parent loans:*** $10,583,345 (88% need-based, 12% non-need-based). ***Programs:*** Federal Direct (Subsidized and Unsubsidized Stafford, PLUS), Perkins, Federal Nursing.

WORK-STUDY ***Federal work-study:*** Total amount: $643,290; 481 jobs averaging $1337. ***State or other work-study/employment:*** Total amount: $1,689,959 (100% non-need-based). 970 part-time jobs averaging $1742.

ATHLETIC AWARDS Total amount: $4,220,820 (28% need-based, 72% non-need-based).

APPLYING FOR FINANCIAL AID ***Required financial aid form:*** FAFSA. ***Financial aid deadline (priority):*** 3/1. ***Notification date:*** Continuous beginning 3/10. Students must reply by 5/1.

CONTACT Ms. Janet Turner, Director of Financial Aid, University of Portland, 5000 North Willamette Boulevard, Portland, OR 97203-5798, 503-943-7311 or toll-free 888-627-5601 (out-of-state). *Fax:* 503-943-7508. *E-mail:* turnerj@up.edu.

UNIVERSITY OF PUERTO RICO, AGUADILLA UNIVERSITY COLLEGE

Aguadilla, PR

CONTACT Director of Financial Aid, University of Puerto Rico, Aguadilla University College, PO Box 250-160, Aguadilla, PR 00604-0160, 787-890-2681 Ext. 273.

UNIVERSITY OF PUERTO RICO AT ARECIBO

Arecibo, PR

CONTACT Myrta F. Salcedo-Ortiz, Director of Financial Aid, University of Puerto Rico at Arecibo, PO Box 4010, Arecibo, PR 00613, 787-878-2830 Ext. 2008. *E-mail:* myrta.ortiz@upr.edu.

UNIVERSITY OF PUERTO RICO AT BAYAMÓN

Bayamón, PR

Tuition & fees (PR res): $2076 **Average undergraduate aid package: N/A**

ABOUT THE INSTITUTION Commonwealth-supported, coed. 18 undergraduate majors. Federal methodology is used as a basis for awarding need-based institutional aid.

UNDERGRADUATE EXPENSES for 2010–11 ***Tuition, state resident:*** full-time $1734; part-time $51 per credit. ***Tuition, nonresident:*** full-time $4039. ***Required fees:*** full-time $342; $144 per term. Full-time tuition and fees vary according to class time, course load, degree level, and program. Part-time tuition and fees vary according to class time, course load, degree level, and program. Room and board charges vary according to housing facility. ***Payment plans:*** Guaranteed tuition, deferred payment.

GIFT AID (NEED-BASED) ***Total amount:*** $16,292,964 (95% federal, 5% state). ***Scholarships, grants, and awards:*** Federal Pell, FSEOG, state, college/university gift aid from institutional funds.

GIFT AID (NON-NEED-BASED) ***Scholarships, grants, and awards by category:*** *Academic interests/achievement:* general academic interests/achievements. *Creative arts/performance:* music, theater/drama. *Special achievements/activities:* cheerleading/drum major. *Special characteristics:* veterans, veterans' children. ***Tuition waivers:*** Full or partial for employees or children of employees.

LOANS ***Student loans:*** $1,002,800 (100% need-based). ***Programs:*** Federal Direct (Unsubsidized Stafford, PLUS), Perkins.

WORK-STUDY ***Federal work-study:*** Total amount: $348,558; jobs available.

APPLYING FOR FINANCIAL AID ***Required financial aid forms:*** FAFSA, institution's own form, state income tax form(s).

CONTACT Mr. Hector Cuadrado, Financial Aid Director, University of Puerto Rico at Bayamón, Street 174 #170 Minillas Industrial Park, Bayamon, PR 00959-1911, 787-993-8953 Ext. 4033. *E-mail:* hector.cuadrado@upr.edu.

UNIVERSITY OF PUERTO RICO AT HUMACAO

Humacao, PR

CONTACT Larry Cruz, Director of Financial Aid, University of Puerto Rico at Humacao, HUC Station, Humacao, PR 00791-4300, 787-850-9342.

UNIVERSITY OF PUERTO RICO AT PONCE

Ponce, PR

CONTACT Carmelo Vega Montes, Director of Financial Aid, University of Puerto Rico at Ponce, Box 7186, Ponce, PR 00732-7186, 787-844-8181. *Fax:* 787-840-8108.

UNIVERSITY OF PUERTO RICO AT UTUADO

Utuado, PR

CONTACT Edgar Salvá, Director of Financial Assistance, University of Puerto Rico at Utuado, PO Box 2500, Utuado, PR 00641, 787-894-2828 Ext. 2603. *Fax:* 787-894-3810. *E-mail:* esalva@uprutuado.edu.

UNIVERSITY OF PUERTO RICO, CAYEY UNIVERSITY COLLEGE

Cayey, PR

CONTACT Mr. Hector Maldonado Otero, Director of Financial Aid, University of Puerto Rico, Cayey University College, Antonio Barcelo, Cayey, PR 00736, 787-738-2161. *Fax:* 787-263-0676.

UNIVERSITY OF PUERTO RICO, MAYAGÜEZ CAMPUS

Mayagüez, PR

CONTACT Ms. Ana I. Rodríguez, Director of Financial Aid, University of Puerto Rico, Mayagüez Campus, PO Box 9000, Mayagüez, PR 00681-9000, 787-265-3863. *Fax:* 787-265-1920. *E-mail:* a_rodriguez@rumad.uprm.edu.

UNIVERSITY OF PUERTO RICO, MEDICAL SCIENCES CAMPUS

San Juan, PR

CONTACT Mrs. Zoraida Figueroa, Financial Aid Director, University of Puerto Rico, Medical Sciences Campus, Terreno Centro Medico-Edificio Decanato Farmacia y Estudiantes, San Juan, PR 00936-5067, 787-763-2525. *Fax:* 787-282-7117. *E-mail:* zoraida.figueroa@upr.edu.

UNIVERSITY OF PUERTO RICO, RÍO PIEDRAS

San Juan, PR

ABOUT THE INSTITUTION Commonwealth-supported, coed. 57 undergraduate majors.

GIFT AID (NEED-BASED) ***Scholarships, grants, and awards:*** Federal Pell, FSEOG, state, private.

LOANS ***Programs:*** Federal Direct (Subsidized and Unsubsidized Stafford, PLUS), Perkins, college/university, law access loans.

APPLYING FOR FINANCIAL AID ***Required financial aid forms:*** FAFSA, institution's own form.

CONTACT Mr. Efraim Williams, EDP Manager, University of Puerto Rico, Río Piedras, PO Box 23300, San Juan, PR 00931-3300, 787-764-0000 Ext. 5573.

UNIVERSITY OF PUGET SOUND

Tacoma, WA

Tuition & fees: $38,720 **Average undergraduate aid package: $28,813**

ABOUT THE INSTITUTION Independent, coed. 40 undergraduate majors. Federal methodology is used as a basis for awarding need-based institutional aid.

UNDERGRADUATE EXPENSES for 2011–12 ***Comprehensive fee:*** $48,740 includes full-time tuition ($38,510), mandatory fees ($210), and room and board ($10,020). ***College room only:*** $5550. Full-time tuition and fees vary according to course load. Room and board charges vary according to board plan and housing facility. Part-time tuition and fees vary according to course load. ***Payment plans:*** Installment, deferred payment.

FRESHMAN FINANCIAL AID (Fall 2010, est.) 475 applied for aid; of those 87% were deemed to have need. 100% of freshmen with need received aid; of those 24% had need fully met. ***Average percent of need met:*** 81% (excluding resources awarded to replace EFC). ***Average financial aid package:*** $28,061 (excluding resources awarded to replace EFC). 21% of all full-time freshmen had no need and received non-need-based gift aid.

UNDERGRADUATE FINANCIAL AID (Fall 2010, est.) 1,801 applied for aid; of those 91% were deemed to have need. 100% of undergraduates with need received aid; of those 19% had need fully met. ***Average percent of need met:*** 80% (excluding resources awarded to replace EFC). ***Average financial aid package:*** $28,813 (excluding resources awarded to replace EFC). 23% of all full-time undergraduates had no need and received non-need-based gift aid.

GIFT AID (NEED-BASED) ***Total amount:*** $37,174,189 (9% federal, 3% state, 84% institutional, 4% external sources). ***Receiving aid:*** Freshmen: 66% (411); all full-time undergraduates: 64% (1,620). ***Average award:*** Freshmen: $23,465; Undergraduates: $23,776. ***Scholarships, grants, and awards:*** Federal Pell, FSEOG, state, private, college/university gift aid from institutional funds.

GIFT AID (NON-NEED-BASED) ***Total amount:*** $6,251,771 (92% institutional, 8% external sources). ***Receiving aid:*** Freshmen: 4% (28). Undergraduates: 3% (75). ***Average award:*** Freshmen: $10,056. Undergraduates: $10,055. ***Scholarships, grants, and awards by category:*** *Academic interests/achievement:* 681 awards ($5,136,474 total): biological sciences, business, communication, computer science, English, foreign languages, general academic interests/achievements, humanities, international studies, mathematics, physical sciences, premedicine, social sciences. *Creative arts/performance:* 59 awards ($222,080 total): art/fine arts, debating, music, theater/drama. *Special achievements/activities:* 7 awards ($20,500 total): community service, leadership, religious involvement. *Special characteristics:* 27 awards ($845,095 total): children of faculty/staff, international students. ***Tuition waivers:*** Full or partial for employees or children of employees.

LOANS ***Student loans:*** $11,557,093 (94% need-based, 6% non-need-based). 64% of past graduating class borrowed through all loan programs. *Average indebtedness per student:* $28,660. ***Average need-based loan:*** Freshmen: $4261. Undergraduates: $5257. ***Parent loans:*** $5,302,844 (84% need-based, 16% non-need-based). ***Programs:*** Federal Direct (Subsidized and Unsubsidized Stafford, PLUS), Perkins, Alaska Loans.

WORK-STUDY ***Federal work-study:*** Total amount: $1,542,000; 544 jobs averaging $2835. ***State or other work-study/employment:*** Total amount: $2,184,128 (100% need-based). 788 part-time jobs averaging $2770.

APPLYING FOR FINANCIAL AID ***Required financial aid form:*** FAFSA. ***Financial aid deadline (priority):*** 2/1. ***Notification date:*** Continuous beginning 3/15. Students must reply by 5/1.

CONTACT Maggie A. Mittuch, Associate Vice President for Student Financial Services, University of Puget Sound, 1500 North Warner Street #1039, Tacoma, WA 98416-1039, 253-879-3214 or toll-free 800-396-7191. *Fax:* 253-879-8508. *E-mail:* mmittuch@pugetsound.edu.

UNIVERSITY OF REDLANDS

Redlands, CA

Tuition & fees: $35,540 **Average undergraduate aid package: $31,753**

ABOUT THE INSTITUTION Independent, coed. 42 undergraduate majors. Federal methodology is used as a basis for awarding need-based institutional aid.

UNDERGRADUATE EXPENSES for 2010–11 ***Comprehensive fee:*** $46,372 includes full-time tuition ($35,240), mandatory fees ($300), and room and board ($10,832). ***College room only:*** $5988. Full-time tuition and fees vary according to program. Room and board charges vary according to board plan and housing facility. ***Part-time tuition:*** $1101 per credit hour. ***Part-time fees:*** $150 per term. Part-time tuition and fees vary according to course load and program. ***Payment plan:*** Installment.

FRESHMAN FINANCIAL AID (Fall 2010, est.) 602 applied for aid; of those 85% were deemed to have need. 100% of freshmen with need received aid; of those 18% had need fully met. ***Average percent of need met:*** 80% (excluding resources awarded to replace EFC). ***Average financial aid package:*** $32,497 (excluding resources awarded to replace EFC). 14% of all full-time freshmen had no need and received non-need-based gift aid.

UNDERGRADUATE FINANCIAL AID (Fall 2010, est.) 2,120 applied for aid; of those 82% were deemed to have need. 100% of undergraduates with need received aid; of those 20% had need fully met. ***Average percent of need met:*** 78% (excluding resources awarded to replace EFC). ***Average financial aid package:*** $31,753 (excluding resources awarded to replace EFC). 15% of all full-time undergraduates had no need and received non-need-based gift aid.

GIFT AID (NEED-BASED) ***Total amount:*** $41,810,067 (10% federal, 12% state, 78% institutional). ***Receiving aid:*** Freshmen: 79% (508); all full-time undergraduates: 74% (1,711). ***Average award:*** Freshmen: $27,019; Undergraduates: $24,970. ***Scholarships, grants, and awards:*** Federal Pell, FSEOG, state, private, college/university gift aid from institutional funds.

GIFT AID (NON-NEED-BASED) ***Total amount:*** $5,151,069 (82% institutional, 18% external sources). ***Receiving aid:*** Freshmen: 15% (99). Undergraduates: 8% (179). ***Average award:*** Freshmen: $14,076. Undergraduates: $13,060. ***Scholarships, grants, and awards by category:*** *Academic interests/achievement:* general academic interests/achievements. *Creative arts/performance:* art/fine arts, creative writing, debating, music. *Special achievements/activities:* general special achievements/activities. *Special characteristics:* international students. ***Tuition waivers:*** Full or partial for employees or children of employees.

LOANS ***Student loans:*** $13,563,754 (94% need-based, 6% non-need-based). 67% of past graduating class borrowed through all loan programs. *Average indebtedness per student:* $20,364. ***Average need-based loan:*** Freshmen: $4027. Undergraduates: $5462. ***Parent loans:*** $5,022,003 (100% non-need-based). ***Programs:*** Perkins, college/university.

WORK-STUDY ***Federal work-study:*** Total amount: $3,080,960; jobs available. ***State or other work-study/employment:*** Total amount: $746,301 (100% need-based). Part-time jobs available.

APPLYING FOR FINANCIAL AID ***Required financial aid forms:*** FAFSA, state aid form. ***Financial aid deadline (priority):*** 2/15. ***Notification date:*** Continuous beginning 2/28. Students must reply by 5/1.

CONTACT Lisa VanMeeteren, Interim Director of Financial Aid, University of Redlands, PO Box 3080, Redlands, CA 92373-0999, 909-748-8047 or toll-free 800-455-5064. *Fax:* 909-335-4089. *E-mail:* financialaid@redlands.edu.

UNIVERSITY OF RHODE ISLAND

Kingston, RI

Tuition & fees (RI res): $9014 **Average undergraduate aid package: $13,689**

ABOUT THE INSTITUTION State-supported, coed. 82 undergraduate majors. Federal methodology is used as a basis for awarding need-based institutional aid.

UNDERGRADUATE EXPENSES for 2010–11 ***Tuition, state resident:*** full-time $9014; part-time $376 per credit. ***Tuition, nonresident:*** full-time $25,720; part-time $1072 per credit. ***Required fees:*** $34 per credit or $58 per term. Full-time tuition and fees vary according to course load, location, and reciprocity agreements. Part-time tuition and fees vary according to course load, location, and reciprocity agreements. ***College room and board:*** $10,854; ***Room only:*** $6994. Room and board charges vary according to board plan and housing facility. ***Payment plan:*** Installment.

FRESHMAN FINANCIAL AID (Fall 2010, est.) 2,108 applied for aid; of those 80% were deemed to have need. 95% of freshmen with need received aid; of those 99% had need fully met. ***Average percent of need met:*** 57% (excluding resources awarded to replace EFC). ***Average financial aid package:*** $12,470 (excluding resources awarded to replace EFC). 3% of all full-time freshmen had no need and received non-need-based gift aid.

UNDERGRADUATE FINANCIAL AID (Fall 2010, est.) 10,163 applied for aid; of those 87% were deemed to have need. 81% of undergraduates with need received aid; of those 88% had need fully met. ***Average percent of need met:*** 58% (excluding resources awarded to replace EFC). ***Average financial aid package:*** $13,689 (excluding resources awarded to replace EFC). 3% of all full-time undergraduates had no need and received non-need-based gift aid.

GIFT AID (NEED-BASED) ***Total amount:*** $67,186,161 (27% federal, 4% state, 66% institutional, 3% external sources). ***Receiving aid:*** Freshmen: 53% (1,448); all full-time undergraduates: 62% (7,163). ***Average award:*** Freshmen: $8223; Undergraduates: $8694. ***Scholarships, grants, and awards:*** Federal Pell, FSEOG, state, private, college/university gift aid from institutional funds.

GIFT AID (NON-NEED-BASED) ***Total amount:*** $2,339,903 (89% institutional, 11% external sources). ***Receiving aid:*** Freshmen: 5% (139). Undergraduates: 5% (521). ***Average award:*** Freshmen: $4985. Undergraduates: $5625. ***Scholarships, grants, and awards by category:*** *Academic interests/achievement:* general academic interests/achievements. *Creative arts/performance:* art/fine arts, music, theater/drama. *Special characteristics:* children and siblings of alumni. ***Tuition waivers:*** Full or partial for minority students, employees or children of employees, senior citizens.

LOANS ***Student loans:*** $66,209,054 (82% need-based, 18% non-need-based). 73% of past graduating class borrowed through all loan programs. *Average indebtedness per student:* $22,750. ***Average need-based loan:*** Freshmen: $4443. Undergraduates: $5403. ***Parent loans:*** $38,917,047 (64% need-based, 36%

non-need-based). ***Programs:*** Federal Direct (Subsidized and Unsubsidized Stafford, PLUS), Perkins, Federal Nursing, college/university.

WORK-STUDY ***Federal work-study:*** Total amount: $883,687; jobs available.

ATHLETIC AWARDS Total amount: $7,235,589 (97% need-based, 3% non-need-based).

APPLYING FOR FINANCIAL AID ***Required financial aid form:*** FAFSA. ***Financial aid deadline (priority):*** 3/1. ***Notification date:*** Continuous beginning 3/31. Students must reply by 5/1.

CONTACT Mr. Horace J. Amaral Jr., Director of Enrollment Services, University of Rhode Island, Green Hall, Kingston, RI 02881, 401-874-9500.

UNIVERSITY OF RICHMOND

Richmond, VA

Tuition & fees: $43,170 **Average undergraduate aid package: $38,676**

ABOUT THE INSTITUTION Independent, coed. 48 undergraduate majors. Institutional methodology is used as a basis for awarding need-based institutional aid.

UNDERGRADUATE EXPENSES for 2011–12 ***Comprehensive fee:*** $52,420 includes full-time tuition ($43,170) and room and board ($9250). ***College room only:*** $4170. Full-time tuition and fees vary according to course load and student level. Room and board charges vary according to board plan and housing facility. ***Part-time tuition:*** $7554 per unit. Part-time tuition and fees vary according to course load and student level. ***Payment plans:*** Installment, deferred payment.

FRESHMAN FINANCIAL AID (Fall 2010, est.) 472 applied for aid; of those 81% were deemed to have need. 100% of freshmen with need received aid; of those 95% had need fully met. ***Average percent of need met:*** 100% (excluding resources awarded to replace EFC). ***Average financial aid package:*** $38,477 (excluding resources awarded to replace EFC). 5% of all full-time freshmen had no need and received non-need-based gift aid.

UNDERGRADUATE FINANCIAL AID (Fall 2010, est.) 1,738 applied for aid; of those 86% were deemed to have need. 100% of undergraduates with need received aid; of those 94% had need fully met. ***Average percent of need met:*** 100% (excluding resources awarded to replace EFC). ***Average financial aid package:*** $38,676 (excluding resources awarded to replace EFC). 13% of all full-time undergraduates had no need and received non-need-based gift aid.

GIFT AID (NEED-BASED) ***Total amount:*** $50,002,786 (6% federal, 2% state, 91% institutional, 1% external sources). ***Receiving aid:*** Freshmen: 47% (383); all full-time undergraduates: 47% (1,493). ***Average award:*** Freshmen: $33,515; Undergraduates: $35,002. ***Scholarships, grants, and awards:*** Federal Pell, FSEOG, state, private, college/university gift aid from institutional funds.

GIFT AID (NON-NEED-BASED) ***Total amount:*** $12,109,819 (8% federal, 5% state, 82% institutional, 5% external sources). ***Receiving aid:*** Freshmen: 6% (51). Undergraduates: 5% (160). ***Average award:*** Freshmen: $37,970. Undergraduates: $23,209. ***Scholarships, grants, and awards by category:*** *Academic interests/achievement:* 169 awards ($6,486,375 total): biological sciences, computer science, general academic interests/achievements, mathematics, physical sciences. *Creative arts/performance:* 27 awards ($917,500 total): art/fine arts, dance, music, performing arts, theater/drama. *Special achievements/activities:* 99 awards ($247,500 total): community service. ***Tuition waivers:*** Full or partial for employees or children of employees.

LOANS ***Student loans:*** $10,799,639 (32% need-based, 68% non-need-based). 42% of past graduating class borrowed through all loan programs. *Average indebtedness per student:* $23,070. ***Average need-based loan:*** Freshmen: $2968. Undergraduates: $3112. ***Parent loans:*** $4,562,849 (2% need-based, 98% non-need-based). ***Programs:*** Federal Direct (Subsidized and Unsubsidized Stafford, PLUS), Perkins.

WORK-STUDY ***Federal work-study:*** Total amount: $540,168; 393 jobs averaging $1295.

ATHLETIC AWARDS Total amount: $8,247,872 (22% need-based, 78% non-need-based).

APPLYING FOR FINANCIAL AID ***Required financial aid forms:*** FAFSA, CSS Financial Aid PROFILE, parents' complete federal income returns from prior year. ***Financial aid deadline:*** 2/15. ***Notification date:*** 4/1. Students must reply within 4 weeks of notification.

CONTACT Financial Aid Office, University of Richmond, Brunet Hall, University of Richmond, VA 23173, 804-289-8438 or toll-free 800-700-1662. *Fax:* 804-484-1650. *E-mail:* finaid@richmond.edu.

UNIVERSITY OF RIO GRANDE

Rio Grande, OH

Tuition & fees: $18,808 **Average undergraduate aid package: $12,420**

ABOUT THE INSTITUTION Independent, coed. 71 undergraduate majors. Federal methodology is used as a basis for awarding need-based institutional aid.

UNDERGRADUATE EXPENSES for 2010–11 ***Comprehensive fee:*** $26,636 includes full-time tuition ($18,808) and room and board ($7828). Full-time tuition and fees vary according to course level, course load, degree level, program, reciprocity agreements, and student level. Room and board charges vary according to board plan, housing facility, and student level. ***Part-time tuition:*** $788 per credit hour. Part-time tuition and fees vary according to course level, course load, degree level, program, reciprocity agreements, and student level. ***Payment plan:*** Installment.

FRESHMAN FINANCIAL AID (Fall 2009) 287 applied for aid; of those 99% were deemed to have need. 98% of freshmen with need received aid; of those 75% had need fully met. ***Average percent of need met:*** 88% (excluding resources awarded to replace EFC). ***Average financial aid package:*** $10,238 (excluding resources awarded to replace EFC).

UNDERGRADUATE FINANCIAL AID (Fall 2009) 1,146 applied for aid; of those 99% were deemed to have need. 99% of undergraduates with need received aid; of those 76% had need fully met. ***Average percent of need met:*** 91% (excluding resources awarded to replace EFC). ***Average financial aid package:*** $12,420 (excluding resources awarded to replace EFC).

GIFT AID (NEED-BASED) ***Total amount:*** $440,862 (100% external sources). ***Receiving aid:*** Freshmen: 75% (219); all full-time undergraduates: 82% (995). ***Average award:*** Freshmen: $4456; Undergraduates: $4836. ***Scholarships, grants, and awards:*** Federal Pell, FSEOG, state, private, college/university gift aid from institutional funds.

GIFT AID (NON-NEED-BASED) ***Total amount:*** $9,015,972 (10% federal, 9% state, 61% institutional, 20% external sources). ***Receiving aid:*** Freshmen: 73% (212). Undergraduates: 71% (859). ***Scholarships, grants, and awards by category:*** *Academic interests/achievement:* biological sciences, business, communication, computer science, education, English, general academic interests/achievements, health fields, humanities, mathematics, physical sciences, social sciences. *Creative arts/performance:* art/fine arts, music. *Special achievements/activities:* cheerleading/drum major. *Special characteristics:* children and siblings of alumni, children of faculty/staff, local/state students, out-of-state students. ***Tuition waivers:*** Full or partial for employees or children of employees, senior citizens.

LOANS ***Student loans:*** $19,950,904 (48% need-based, 52% non-need-based). 75% of past graduating class borrowed through all loan programs. *Average indebtedness per student:* $18,689. ***Parent loans:*** $669,532 (100% non-need-based). ***Programs:*** Federal Direct (Subsidized and Unsubsidized Stafford, PLUS), Perkins.

WORK-STUDY ***Federal work-study:*** Total amount: $601,960; jobs available. ***State or other work-study/employment:*** Part-time jobs available.

ATHLETIC AWARDS Total amount: $1,893,222 (1% need-based, 99% non-need-based).

APPLYING FOR FINANCIAL AID ***Required financial aid forms:*** FAFSA, institution's own form. ***Financial aid deadline:*** Continuous. ***Notification date:*** Continuous beginning 1/15. Students must reply within 3 weeks of notification.

CONTACT Ms. Dawn Cummings, Director of Financial Aid, University of Rio Grande, 218 North College Avenue, Rio Grande, OH 45674, 740-245-7218 or toll-free 800-282-7201 (in-state). *Fax:* 740-245-7102.

UNIVERSITY OF ROCHESTER

Rochester, NY

Tuition & fees: $40,282 **Average undergraduate aid package: $33,607**

ABOUT THE INSTITUTION Independent, coed. 60 undergraduate majors. Institutional methodology is used as a basis for awarding need-based institutional aid.

UNDERGRADUATE EXPENSES for 2010–11 ***Comprehensive fee:*** $51,922 includes full-time tuition ($39,480), mandatory fees ($802), and room and board ($11,640). ***College room only:*** $7050. Room and board charges vary according to board plan. ***Part-time tuition:*** $1234 per credit hour. Part-time tuition and fees vary according to course load. ***Payment plans:*** Tuition prepayment, installment.

FRESHMAN FINANCIAL AID (Fall 2010, est.) 824 applied for aid; of those 83% were deemed to have need. 100% of freshmen with need received aid; of those 100% had need fully met. ***Average percent of need met:*** 100% (excluding resources awarded to replace EFC). ***Average financial aid package:*** $64,176 (excluding resources awarded to replace EFC). 28% of all full-time freshmen had no need and received non-need-based gift aid.

UNDERGRADUATE FINANCIAL AID (Fall 2010, est.) 2,968 applied for aid; of those 88% were deemed to have need. 99% of undergraduates with need received aid; of those 96% had need fully met. ***Average percent of need met:*** 96% (excluding resources awarded to replace EFC). ***Average financial aid package:*** $33,607 (excluding resources awarded to replace EFC). 29% of all full-time undergraduates had no need and received non-need-based gift aid.

GIFT AID (NEED-BASED) ***Total amount:*** $69,571,275 (10% federal, 5% state, 82% institutional, 3% external sources). ***Receiving aid:*** Freshmen: 57% (671); all full-time undergraduates: 55% (2,569). ***Average award:*** Freshmen: $30,430; Undergraduates: $28,429. ***Scholarships, grants, and awards:*** Federal Pell, FSEOG, state, college/university gift aid from institutional funds.

GIFT AID (NON-NEED-BASED) ***Total amount:*** $17,439,444 (8% federal, 1% state, 85% institutional, 6% external sources). ***Receiving aid:*** Freshmen: 6% (74). Undergraduates: 4% (186). ***Average award:*** Freshmen: $11,503. Undergraduates: $10,258. ***Scholarships, grants, and awards by category:*** *Academic interests/achievement:* engineering/technologies, general academic interests/achievements, military science. *Creative arts/performance:* general creative arts/performance, music, performing arts. *Special achievements/activities:* general special achievements/activities, leadership. *Special characteristics:* children and siblings of alumni, children of faculty/staff, general special characteristics, international students, veterans. ***Tuition waivers:*** Full or partial for employees or children of employees.

LOANS ***Student loans:*** $21,596,692 (78% need-based, 22% non-need-based). 64% of past graduating class borrowed through all loan programs. *Average indebtedness per student:* $28,100. ***Average need-based loan:*** Freshmen: $3829. Undergraduates: $4904. ***Parent loans:*** $8,306,966 (30% need-based, 70% non-need-based). ***Programs:*** Federal Direct (Subsidized and Unsubsidized Stafford, PLUS), Perkins, Federal Nursing.

WORK-STUDY ***Federal work-study:*** Total amount: $3,358,304; 1,664 jobs averaging $1974. ***State or other work-study/employment:*** Total amount: $1,088,232 (46% need-based, 54% non-need-based). Part-time jobs available.

APPLYING FOR FINANCIAL AID ***Required financial aid forms:*** FAFSA, CSS Financial Aid PROFILE, state aid form, noncustodial (divorced/separated) parent's statement. ***Financial aid deadline (priority):*** 2/1. ***Notification date:*** 4/1. Students must reply by 5/1.

CONTACT Charles W. Puls, Director of Financial Aid, University of Rochester, 124 Wallis Hall, Rochester, NY 14627-0261, 585-275-3226 or toll-free 888-822-2256. *Fax:* 585-756-7664.

UNIVERSITY OF ST. FRANCIS

Joliet, IL

Tuition & fees: $24,742 **Average undergraduate aid package: $19,955**

ABOUT THE INSTITUTION Independent Roman Catholic, coed. 47 undergraduate majors. Federal methodology is used as a basis for awarding need-based institutional aid.

UNDERGRADUATE EXPENSES for 2010–11 ***Comprehensive fee:*** $32,918 includes full-time tuition ($24,292), mandatory fees ($450), and room and board ($8176). Room and board charges vary according to board plan and housing facility. ***Part-time tuition:*** $790 per credit hour. ***Payment plans:*** Installment, deferred payment.

FRESHMAN FINANCIAL AID (Fall 2010, est.) 196 applied for aid; of those 90% were deemed to have need. 100% of freshmen with need received aid; of those 57% had need fully met. ***Average percent of need met:*** 70% (excluding resources awarded to replace EFC). ***Average financial aid package:*** $22,066 (excluding resources awarded to replace EFC). 15% of all full-time freshmen had no need and received non-need-based gift aid.

UNDERGRADUATE FINANCIAL AID (Fall 2010, est.) 1,190 applied for aid; of those 91% were deemed to have need. 100% of undergraduates with need received aid; of those 50% had need fully met. ***Average percent of need met:*** 67% (excluding resources awarded to replace EFC). ***Average financial aid package:*** $19,955 (excluding resources awarded to replace EFC). 15% of all full-time undergraduates had no need and received non-need-based gift aid.

GIFT AID (NEED-BASED) ***Total amount:*** $11,003,511 (21% federal, 23% state, 55% institutional, 1% external sources). ***Receiving aid:*** Freshmen: 57% (120); all full-time undergraduates: 60% (784). ***Average award:*** Freshmen: $8720; Undergraduates: $8409. ***Scholarships, grants, and awards:*** Federal Pell, FSEOG, state, private, college/university gift aid from institutional funds.

GIFT AID (NON-NEED-BASED) ***Total amount:*** $4,842,208 (6% federal, 1% state, 90% institutional, 3% external sources). ***Receiving aid:*** Freshmen: 82% (173). Undergraduates: 79% (1,020). ***Average award:*** Freshmen: $11,285. Undergraduates: $8266. ***Scholarships, grants, and awards by category:*** *Academic interests/achievement:* 1,198 awards ($7,671,816 total): biological sciences, communication, education, general academic interests/achievements, health fields, international studies, social sciences. *Creative arts/performance:* 25 awards ($37,306 total): applied art and design, art/fine arts, music. *Special achievements/activities:* 731 awards ($4,107,448 total): cheerleading/drum major, community service, general special achievements/activities, leadership, religious involvement. *Special characteristics:* 213 awards ($154,217 total): children and siblings of alumni, children of educators, ethnic background, first-generation college students, religious affiliation, siblings of current students. ***Tuition waivers:*** Full or partial for children of alumni, employees or children of employees.

LOANS ***Student loans:*** $7,802,720 (49% need-based, 51% non-need-based). 88% of past graduating class borrowed through all loan programs. *Average indebtedness per student:* $27,088. ***Average need-based loan:*** Freshmen: $3346. Undergraduates: $4457. ***Parent loans:*** $2,786,894 (73% need-based, 27% non-need-based). ***Programs:*** Federal Direct (Subsidized and Unsubsidized Stafford, PLUS), Perkins, alternative loans.

WORK-STUDY ***Federal work-study:*** Total amount: $192,700; 174 jobs averaging $1107. ***State or other work-study/employment:*** Total amount: $354,267 (100% non-need-based). 241 part-time jobs averaging $1470.

ATHLETIC AWARDS Total amount: $3,309,628 (47% need-based, 53% non-need-based).

APPLYING FOR FINANCIAL AID ***Required financial aid forms:*** FAFSA, institution's own form. ***Financial aid deadline (priority):*** 3/15. ***Notification date:*** Continuous beginning 2/15. Students must reply within 3 weeks of notification.

CONTACT Mrs. Mary V. Shaw, Director of Financial Aid Services, University of St. Francis, 500 North Wilcox Street, Joliet, IL 60435-6188, 815-740-3403 or toll-free 800-735-3500 (in-state), 800-735-7500 (out-of-state). *Fax:* 815-740-3822. *E-mail:* mshaw@stfrancis.edu.

UNIVERSITY OF SAINT FRANCIS

Fort Wayne, IN

ABOUT THE INSTITUTION Independent Roman Catholic, coed. ***Awards:*** associate, bachelor's, and master's degrees and post-bachelor's certificates. 49 undergraduate majors. ***Total enrollment:*** 2,112. Undergraduates: 1,800. Freshmen: 322.

GIFT AID (NEED-BASED) ***Scholarships, grants, and awards:*** Federal Pell, FSEOG, state, private, college/university gift aid from institutional funds.

GIFT AID (NON-NEED-BASED) ***Scholarships, grants, and awards by category:*** *Academic interests/achievement:* general academic interests/achievements, health fields. *Creative arts/performance:* art/fine arts, dance, music. *Special achievements/activities:* cheerleading/drum major, religious involvement. *Special characteristics:* children of faculty/staff.

LOANS ***Programs:*** Perkins.

WORK-STUDY ***Federal work-study:*** Total amount: $643,991; 629 jobs averaging $1411. ***State or other work-study/employment:*** Part-time jobs available.

APPLYING FOR FINANCIAL AID ***Required financial aid form:*** FAFSA.

CONTACT Office of Financial Aid, University of Saint Francis, 2701 Spring Street, Fort Wayne, IN 46808, 260-399-8003 or toll-free 800-729-4732. *Fax:* 260-399-8162. *E-mail:* finaid@sf.edu.

UNIVERSITY OF SAINT MARY

Leavenworth, KS

CONTACT Mrs. Judy Wiedower, Financial Aid Director, University of Saint Mary, 4100 South Fourth Street, Leavenworth, KS 66048, 913-758-6314 or toll-free 800-752-7043 (out-of-state). *Fax:* 913-758-6146. *E-mail:* wiedower@hub.smcks.edu.

UNIVERSITY OF ST. THOMAS

St. Paul, MN

Tuition & fees: $30,493 **Average undergraduate aid package: $21,689**

ABOUT THE INSTITUTION Independent Roman Catholic, coed. 83 undergraduate majors. Federal methodology is used as a basis for awarding need-based institutional aid.

UNDERGRADUATE EXPENSES for 2011–12 ***Comprehensive fee:*** $38,813 includes full-time tuition ($29,952), mandatory fees ($541), and room and board ($8320). ***College room only:*** $5294. Full-time tuition and fees vary according to course load, degree level, and program. Room and board charges vary according to board plan and housing facility. ***Part-time tuition:*** $936 per credit hour. Part-time tuition and fees vary according to course load, degree level, and program.

FRESHMAN FINANCIAL AID (Fall 2010, est.) 1,255 applied for aid; of those 77% were deemed to have need. 100% of freshmen with need received aid; of those 22% had need fully met. ***Average percent of need met:*** 87% (excluding resources awarded to replace EFC). ***Average financial aid package:*** $22,656 (excluding resources awarded to replace EFC). 17% of all full-time freshmen had no need and received non-need-based gift aid.

UNDERGRADUATE FINANCIAL AID (Fall 2010, est.) 4,407 applied for aid; of those 82% were deemed to have need. 100% of undergraduates with need received aid; of those 17% had need fully met. ***Average percent of need met:*** 84% (excluding resources awarded to replace EFC). ***Average financial aid package:*** $21,689 (excluding resources awarded to replace EFC). 10% of all full-time undergraduates had no need and received non-need-based gift aid.

GIFT AID (NEED-BASED) ***Total amount:*** $55,562,810 (12% federal, 7% state, 79% institutional, 2% external sources). ***Receiving aid:*** Freshmen: 63% (956); all full-time undergraduates: 59% (3,531). ***Average award:*** Freshmen: $17,139; Undergraduates: $15,632. ***Scholarships, grants, and awards:*** Federal Pell, FSEOG, state, private, college/university gift aid from institutional funds.

GIFT AID (NON-NEED-BASED) ***Total amount:*** $11,156,797 (95% institutional, 5% external sources). ***Receiving aid:*** Freshmen: 12% (180). Undergraduates: 7% (419). ***Average award:*** Freshmen: $15,204. Undergraduates: $12,598. ***Scholarships, grants, and awards by category:*** *Academic interests/achievement:* 2,583 awards ($25,352,313 total): biological sciences, business, education, English, general academic interests/achievements, humanities, international studies, mathematics, physical sciences, religion/biblical studies, social sciences. *Creative arts/performance:* 30 awards ($74,211 total): journalism/publications, music. *Special characteristics:* 188 awards ($2,908,033 total): children of educators, children of faculty/staff, general special characteristics. ***Tuition waivers:*** Full or partial for employees or children of employees, senior citizens.

LOANS ***Student loans:*** $35,582,115 (67% need-based, 33% non-need-based). 67% of past graduating class borrowed through all loan programs. *Average indebtedness per student:* $32,705. ***Average need-based loan:*** Freshmen: $6530. Undergraduates: $7651. ***Parent loans:*** $6,062,536 (47% need-based, 53% non-need-based). ***Programs:*** Federal Direct (Subsidized and Unsubsidized Stafford, PLUS), Perkins, state, alternative loans.

WORK-STUDY ***Federal work-study:*** Total amount: $3,880,472; 1,401 jobs averaging $2770. ***State or other work-study/employment:*** Total amount: $3,319,173 (68% need-based, 32% non-need-based). 975 part-time jobs averaging $2712.

APPLYING FOR FINANCIAL AID ***Required financial aid form:*** FAFSA. ***Financial aid deadline:*** Continuous. ***Notification date:*** Continuous beginning 3/1. Students must reply within 3 weeks of notification.

CONTACT Ms. Ginny Reese, Associate Director of Student Financial Services, University of St. Thomas, 2115 Summit Avenue, AQU 328, St. Paul, MN 55105-1096, 651-962-6557 or toll-free 800-328-6819 Ext. 26150. *Fax:* 651-962-6599. *E-mail:* ginny.reese@stthomas.edu.

UNIVERSITY OF ST. THOMAS

Houston, TX

Tuition & fees: $23,500 **Average undergraduate aid package: $15,983**

ABOUT THE INSTITUTION Independent Roman Catholic, coed. 32 undergraduate majors. Federal methodology is used as a basis for awarding need-based institutional aid.

UNDERGRADUATE EXPENSES for 2010–11 ***Comprehensive fee:*** $31,400 includes full-time tuition ($23,160), mandatory fees ($340), and room and board ($7900). ***College room only:*** $4800. Full-time tuition and fees vary according to course load. Room and board charges vary according to board plan and housing facility. ***Part-time tuition:*** $772 per credit hour. Part-time tuition and fees vary according to course load. ***Payment plans:*** Installment, deferred payment.

FRESHMAN FINANCIAL AID (Fall 2010, est.) 139 applied for aid; of those 83% were deemed to have need. 97% of freshmen with need received aid; of those 13% had need fully met. ***Average percent of need met:*** 64% (excluding resources awarded to replace EFC). ***Average financial aid package:*** $16,860 (excluding resources awarded to replace EFC). 28% of all full-time freshmen had no need and received non-need-based gift aid.

UNDERGRADUATE FINANCIAL AID (Fall 2010, est.) 808 applied for aid; of those 90% were deemed to have need. 98% of undergraduates with need received aid; of those 11% had need fully met. ***Average percent of need met:*** 62% (excluding resources awarded to replace EFC). ***Average financial aid package:*** $15,983 (excluding resources awarded to replace EFC). 24% of all full-time undergraduates had no need and received non-need-based gift aid.

GIFT AID (NEED-BASED) ***Total amount:*** $8,848,068 (28% federal, 17% state, 53% institutional, 2% external sources). ***Receiving aid:*** Freshmen: 58% (110); all full-time undergraduates: 58% (691). ***Average award:*** Freshmen: $13,664; Undergraduates: $12,300. ***Scholarships, grants, and awards:*** Federal Pell, FSEOG, state, private, college/university gift aid from institutional funds, Academic Competitiveness Grants, National SMART Grants.

GIFT AID (NON-NEED-BASED) ***Total amount:*** $2,607,516 (1% federal, 96% institutional, 3% external sources). ***Receiving aid:*** Freshmen: 6% (11). Undergraduates: 4% (50). ***Average award:*** Freshmen: $10,160. Undergraduates: $8816. ***Scholarships, grants, and awards by category:*** *Academic interests/achievement:* biological sciences, business, communication, computer science, education, English, foreign languages, general academic interests/achievements, health fields, humanities, international studies, mathematics, physical sciences, premedicine, religion/biblical studies, social sciences. *Creative arts/performance:* applied art and design, art/fine arts, general creative arts/performance, music, performing arts, theater/drama. *Special achievements/activities:* general special achievements/activities, leadership, religious involvement. *Special characteristics:* children of faculty/staff, general special characteristics, previous college experience, religious affiliation. ***Tuition waivers:*** Full or partial for employees or children of employees, senior citizens.

LOANS ***Student loans:*** $5,324,288 (85% need-based, 15% non-need-based). 65% of past graduating class borrowed through all loan programs. *Average indebtedness per student:* $29,245. ***Average need-based loan:*** Freshmen: $3760. Undergraduates: $4965. ***Parent loans:*** $1,856,359 (49% need-based, 51% non-need-based). ***Programs:*** Federal Direct (Subsidized and Unsubsidized Stafford, PLUS), Perkins, state, private loans.

WORK-STUDY ***Federal work-study:*** Total amount: $149,212; 42 jobs averaging $3533. ***State or other work-study/employment:*** Total amount: $11,606 (100% need-based). 3 part-time jobs averaging $3869.

ATHLETIC AWARDS Total amount: $174,750 (40% need-based, 60% non-need-based).

APPLYING FOR FINANCIAL AID ***Required financial aid form:*** FAFSA. ***Financial aid deadline:*** Continuous. ***Notification date:*** Continuous beginning 2/15. Students must reply within 2 weeks of notification.

CONTACT Lynda McKendree, Dean of Scholarships and Financial Aid, University of St. Thomas, 3800 Montrose Boulevard, Houston, TX 77006-4696, 713-525-2170 or toll-free 800-856-8565. *Fax:* 713-525-2142. *E-mail:* finaid@stthom.edu.

UNIVERSITY OF SAN DIEGO

San Diego, CA

Tuition & fees: $38,578 **Average undergraduate aid package: $29,415**

ABOUT THE INSTITUTION Independent Roman Catholic, coed. 39 undergraduate majors. Federal methodology is used as a basis for awarding need-based institutional aid.

UNDERGRADUATE EXPENSES for 2011–12 ***Comprehensive fee:*** $50,330 includes full-time tuition ($38,150), mandatory fees ($428), and room and board ($11,752). Room and board charges vary according to board plan and housing facility. ***Part-time tuition:*** $1315 per unit. Part-time tuition and fees vary according to course load. ***Payment plan:*** Installment.

FRESHMAN FINANCIAL AID (Fall 2010, est.) 804 applied for aid; of those 81% were deemed to have need. 99% of freshmen with need received aid; of those 15% had need fully met. ***Average percent of need met:*** 74% (excluding

resources awarded to replace EFC). ***Average financial aid package:*** $29,920 (excluding resources awarded to replace EFC). 17% of all full-time freshmen had no need and received non-need-based gift aid.

UNDERGRADUATE FINANCIAL AID (Fall 2010, est.) 3,051 applied for aid; of those 88% were deemed to have need. 98% of undergraduates with need received aid; of those 16% had need fully met. ***Average percent of need met:*** 71% (excluding resources awarded to replace EFC). ***Average financial aid package:*** $29,415 (excluding resources awarded to replace EFC). 14% of all full-time undergraduates had no need and received non-need-based gift aid.

GIFT AID (NEED-BASED) ***Total amount:*** $53,833,358 (13% federal, 9% state, 76% institutional, 2% external sources). ***Receiving aid:*** Freshmen: 54% (620); all full-time undergraduates: 48% (2,478). ***Average award:*** Freshmen: $23,487; Undergraduates: $22,077. ***Scholarships, grants, and awards:*** Federal Pell, FSEOG, state, private, college/university gift aid from institutional funds, Federal Nursing, TEACH Grants.

GIFT AID (NON-NEED-BASED) ***Total amount:*** $14,247,440 (20% federal, 78% institutional, 2% external sources). ***Receiving aid:*** Freshmen: 30% (348). Undergraduates: 21% (1,069). ***Average award:*** Freshmen: $11,752. Undergraduates: $13,525. ***Scholarships, grants, and awards by category:*** *Academic interests/achievement:* general academic interests/achievements. *Creative arts/performance:* music. *Special achievements/activities:* religious involvement. *Special characteristics:* children of faculty/staff. ***Tuition waivers:*** Full or partial for employees or children of employees.

LOANS ***Student loans:*** $21,506,147 (91% need-based, 9% non-need-based). 53% of past graduating class borrowed through all loan programs. *Average indebtedness per student:* $29,928. ***Average need-based loan:*** Freshmen: $6563. Undergraduates: $7967. ***Parent loans:*** $26,655,511 (43% need-based, 57% non-need-based). ***Programs:*** Federal Direct (Subsidized and Unsubsidized Stafford, PLUS), Perkins, college/university.

WORK-STUDY ***Federal work-study:*** Total amount: $2,024,543; 674 jobs averaging $3009. ***State or other work-study/employment:*** Total amount: $2,213,963 (20% need-based, 80% non-need-based). Part-time jobs available.

ATHLETIC AWARDS Total amount: $5,718,915 (22% need-based, 78% non-need-based).

APPLYING FOR FINANCIAL AID ***Required financial aid form:*** FAFSA. ***Financial aid deadline (priority):*** 3/2. ***Notification date:*** Continuous beginning 3/1. Students must reply by 5/1 or within 3 weeks of notification.

CONTACT Judith Lewis Logue, Director of Financial Aid Services, University of San Diego, 5998 Alcala Park, San Diego, CA 92110-2492, 619-260-2700 or toll-free 800-248-4873.

UNIVERSITY OF SAN FRANCISCO

San Francisco, CA

CONTACT Ms. Susan Murphy, Director of Financial Aid, University of San Francisco, 2130 Fulton Street, San Francisco, CA 94117-1080, 415-422-2620 or toll-free 800-CALLUSF (out-of-state). *Fax:* 415-422-6084. *E-mail:* murphy@usfca.edu.

UNIVERSITY OF SCIENCE AND ARTS OF OKLAHOMA

Chickasha, OK

Tuition & fees (OK res): $4680 **Average undergraduate aid package: $8989**

ABOUT THE INSTITUTION State-supported, coed. 25 undergraduate majors. Federal methodology is used as a basis for awarding need-based institutional aid.

UNDERGRADUATE EXPENSES for 2010–11 ***Tuition, state resident:*** full-time $3510; part-time $117 per credit hour. ***Tuition, nonresident:*** full-time $9960; part-time $332 per credit hour. ***Required fees:*** full-time $1170; $39 per credit hour. ***College room and board:*** $4990; ***Room only:*** $2600. Room and board charges vary according to board plan and housing facility. ***Payment plans:*** Guaranteed tuition, installment.

FRESHMAN FINANCIAL AID (Fall 2010, est.) 188 applied for aid; of those 79% were deemed to have need. 99% of freshmen with need received aid; of those 17% had need fully met. ***Average percent of need met:*** 68% (excluding resources awarded to replace EFC). ***Average financial aid package:*** $8938 (excluding resources awarded to replace EFC). 6% of all full-time freshmen had no need and received non-need-based gift aid.

UNDERGRADUATE FINANCIAL AID (Fall 2010, est.) 698 applied for aid; of those 86% were deemed to have need. 97% of undergraduates with need received aid; of those 14% had need fully met. ***Average percent of need met:*** 66% (excluding resources awarded to replace EFC). ***Average financial aid package:*** $8989 (excluding resources awarded to replace EFC). 12% of all full-time undergraduates had no need and received non-need-based gift aid.

GIFT AID (NEED-BASED) ***Total amount:*** $3,316,100 (65% federal, 21% state, 7% institutional, 7% external sources). ***Receiving aid:*** Freshmen: 66% (145); all full-time undergraduates: 61% (551). ***Average award:*** Freshmen: $7654; Undergraduates: $7098. ***Scholarships, grants, and awards:*** Federal Pell, FSEOG, state, private, college/university gift aid from institutional funds, USAO Foundation Grants.

GIFT AID (NON-NEED-BASED) ***Total amount:*** $567,429 (1% federal, 33% state, 49% institutional, 17% external sources). ***Receiving aid:*** Freshmen: 5% (11). Undergraduates: 4% (39). ***Average award:*** Freshmen: $3135. Undergraduates: $2302. ***Scholarships, grants, and awards by category:*** *Academic interests/achievement:* 191 awards ($455,804 total): general academic interests/achievements. *Creative arts/performance:* 8 awards ($15,000 total): art/fine arts, music, theater/drama. *Special achievements/activities:* 11 awards ($5700 total): cheerleading/drum major. *Special characteristics:* 65 awards ($250,584 total): children of faculty/staff, international students, out-of-state students, previous college experience. ***Tuition waivers:*** Full or partial for employees or children of employees, senior citizens.

LOANS ***Student loans:*** $2,437,772 (71% need-based, 29% non-need-based). 29% of past graduating class borrowed through all loan programs. *Average indebtedness per student:* $15,339. ***Average need-based loan:*** Freshmen: $2160. Undergraduates: $2905. ***Parent loans:*** $47,492 (8% need-based, 92% non-need-based). ***Programs:*** Federal Direct (Subsidized and Unsubsidized Stafford, PLUS), Perkins, college/university.

WORK-STUDY ***Federal work-study:*** Total amount: $287,426; 136 jobs averaging $1765.

ATHLETIC AWARDS Total amount: $915,624 (37% need-based, 63% non-need-based).

APPLYING FOR FINANCIAL AID ***Required financial aid forms:*** FAFSA, institution's own form. ***Financial aid deadline (priority):*** 3/15. ***Notification date:*** Continuous beginning 3/15. Students must reply within 4 weeks of notification.

CONTACT Nancy Moats, Director of Financial Aid, University of Science and Arts of Oklahoma, 1727 West Alabama, Chickasha, OK 73018-5322, 405-574-1251 or toll-free 800-933-8726 Ext. 1212. *Fax:* 405-574-1220. *E-mail:* nmoats@usao.edu.

THE UNIVERSITY OF SCRANTON

Scranton, PA

Tuition & fees: $36,042 **Average undergraduate aid package: $22,634**

ABOUT THE INSTITUTION Independent Roman Catholic (Jesuit), coed. 54 undergraduate majors. Federal methodology is used as a basis for awarding need-based institutional aid.

UNDERGRADUATE EXPENSES for 2011–12 ***Comprehensive fee:*** $48,474 includes full-time tuition ($35,692), mandatory fees ($350), and room and board ($12,432). ***College room only:*** $7282. Room and board charges vary according to board plan and housing facility. ***Part-time tuition:*** $917 per credit. ***Payment plan:*** Installment.

FRESHMAN FINANCIAL AID (Fall 2010, est.) 823 applied for aid; of those 84% were deemed to have need. 98% of freshmen with need received aid; of those 28% had need fully met. ***Average percent of need met:*** 68% (excluding resources awarded to replace EFC). ***Average financial aid package:*** $23,096 (excluding resources awarded to replace EFC). 19% of all full-time freshmen had no need and received non-need-based gift aid.

UNDERGRADUATE FINANCIAL AID (Fall 2010, est.) 3,136 applied for aid; of those 87% were deemed to have need. 99% of undergraduates with need received aid; of those 24% had need fully met. ***Average percent of need met:*** 72% (excluding resources awarded to replace EFC). ***Average financial aid package:*** $22,634 (excluding resources awarded to replace EFC). 17% of all full-time undergraduates had no need and received non-need-based gift aid.

GIFT AID (NEED-BASED) ***Total amount:*** $49,719,309 (9% federal, 5% state, 83% institutional, 3% external sources). ***Receiving aid:*** Freshmen: 70% (663); all full-time undergraduates: 68% (2,620). ***Average award:*** Freshmen: $19,710;

Undergraduates: $18,220. ***Scholarships, grants, and awards:*** Federal Pell, FSEOG, state, private, college/university gift aid from institutional funds, TEACH Grants.

GIFT AID (NON-NEED-BASED) ***Total amount:*** $7,206,868 (86% institutional, 14% external sources). ***Receiving aid:*** Freshmen: 19% (176). Undergraduates: 15% (559). ***Average award:*** Freshmen: $11,273. Undergraduates: $12,708. ***Scholarships, grants, and awards by category:*** *Academic interests/achievement:* general academic interests/achievements, military science. *Special characteristics:* children of educators, children of faculty/staff, members of minority groups, siblings of current students. ***Tuition waivers:*** Full or partial for employees or children of employees, senior citizens.

LOANS ***Student loans:*** $27,120,723 (78% need-based, 22% non-need-based). 74% of past graduating class borrowed through all loan programs. *Average indebtedness per student:* $47,251. ***Average need-based loan:*** Freshmen: $3265. Undergraduates: $4453. ***Parent loans:*** $13,714,819 (58% need-based, 42% non-need-based). ***Programs:*** Federal Direct (Subsidized and Unsubsidized Stafford, PLUS), Perkins, Federal Nursing.

WORK-STUDY ***Federal work-study:*** Total amount: $2,150,511; 862 jobs averaging $1800. ***State or other work-study/employment:*** Total amount: $224,133 (100% need-based). 104 part-time jobs averaging $1800.

APPLYING FOR FINANCIAL AID ***Required financial aid form:*** FAFSA. ***Financial aid deadline (priority):*** 2/15. ***Notification date:*** Continuous beginning 3/15. Students must reply by 5/1.

CONTACT Mr. William R. Burke, Director of Financial Aid, The University of Scranton, St. Thomas Hall 401, Scranton, PA 18510, 570-941-7887 or toll-free 888-SCRANTON. *Fax:* 570-941-4370. *E-mail:* finaid@scranton.edu.

UNIVERSITY OF SIOUX FALLS

Sioux Falls, SD

CONTACT Rachel Gunn, Financial Aid Counselor, University of Sioux Falls, 1101 West 22nd Street, Sioux Falls, SD 57105-1699, 605-331-6623 or toll-free 800-888-1047. *Fax:* 605-331-6615. *E-mail:* rachel.gunn@usiouxfalls.edu.

UNIVERSITY OF SOUTH ALABAMA

Mobile, AL

Tuition & fees (AL res): $6810 **Average undergraduate aid package: $8471**

ABOUT THE INSTITUTION State-supported, coed. 47 undergraduate majors. Federal methodology is used as a basis for awarding need-based institutional aid.

UNDERGRADUATE EXPENSES for 2011–12 ***Tuition, state resident:*** full-time $6810; part-time $227 per hour. ***Tuition, nonresident:*** full-time $13,620; part-time $454 per hour. ***Required fees:*** $398 per term. Full-time tuition and fees vary according to class time, course level, course load, degree level, and program. Part-time tuition and fees vary according to class time, course level, course load, degree level, and program. ***College room and board:*** $5608; ***Room only:*** $2908. Room and board charges vary according to board plan, housing facility, location, and student level. ***Payment plan:*** Installment.

FRESHMAN FINANCIAL AID (Fall 2010, est.) 1,438 applied for aid; of those 70% were deemed to have need. 100% of freshmen with need received aid; of those 16% had need fully met. ***Average percent of need met:*** 65% (excluding resources awarded to replace EFC). ***Average financial aid package:*** $8756 (excluding resources awarded to replace EFC). 22% of all full-time freshmen had no need and received non-need-based gift aid.

UNDERGRADUATE FINANCIAL AID (Fall 2010, est.) 5,584 applied for aid; of those 79% were deemed to have need. 100% of undergraduates with need received aid; of those 11% had need fully met. ***Average percent of need met:*** 60% (excluding resources awarded to replace EFC). ***Average financial aid package:*** $8471 (excluding resources awarded to replace EFC). 11% of all full-time undergraduates had no need and received non-need-based gift aid.

GIFT AID (NEED-BASED) ***Total amount:*** $25,294,483 (99% federal, 1% state). ***Receiving aid:*** Freshmen: 49% (862); all full-time undergraduates: 39% (3,342). ***Average award:*** Freshmen: $6476; Undergraduates: $5682. ***Scholarships, grants, and awards:*** Federal Pell, FSEOG, state, private, college/university gift aid from institutional funds.

GIFT AID (NON-NEED-BASED) ***Total amount:*** $9,270,261 (89% institutional, 11% external sources). ***Receiving aid:*** Freshmen: 49% (862). Undergraduates: 39% (3,342). ***Average award:*** Freshmen: $4186. Undergraduates: $4121. ***Scholarships, grants, and awards by category:*** *Academic interests/achievement:* business, computer science, general academic interests/achievements, humanities, international studies, military science. *Creative arts/performance:* art/fine arts, journalism/publications, music, theater/drama. *Special achievements/activities:* general special achievements/activities, hobbies/interests, junior miss, leadership. *Special characteristics:* children and siblings of alumni, children of faculty/staff, members of minority groups. ***Tuition waivers:*** Full or partial for employees or children of employees.

LOANS ***Student loans:*** $80,510,916 (39% need-based, 61% non-need-based). ***Average need-based loan:*** Freshmen: $3411. Undergraduates: $4378. ***Parent loans:*** $4,376,225 (100% non-need-based). ***Programs:*** Federal Direct (Subsidized and Unsubsidized Stafford, PLUS), Perkins.

WORK-STUDY ***Federal work-study:*** Total amount: $224,343; 92 jobs averaging $2600. ***State or other work-study/employment:*** Part-time jobs available.

ATHLETIC AWARDS Total amount: $4,512,738 (100% non-need-based).

APPLYING FOR FINANCIAL AID ***Required financial aid forms:*** FAFSA, institution's own form. ***Financial aid deadline:*** Continuous. ***Notification date:*** Continuous beginning 5/15. Students must reply within 5 weeks of notification.

CONTACT Financial Aid Office, University of South Alabama, Meisler Hall, Suite 1200, Mobile, AL 36688-0002, 251-460-6231 or toll-free 800-872-5247. *Fax:* 251-460-6079. *E-mail:* finaid@usouthal.edu.

UNIVERSITY OF SOUTH CAROLINA

Columbia, SC

Tuition & fees (SC res): $9786 **Average undergraduate aid package: $12,570**

ABOUT THE INSTITUTION State-supported, coed. 76 undergraduate majors. Federal methodology is used as a basis for awarding need-based institutional aid.

UNDERGRADUATE EXPENSES for 2011–12 ***Tuition, state resident:*** full-time $9386; part-time $400 per credit hour. ***Tuition, nonresident:*** full-time $24,962; part-time $1050 per credit hour. ***Required fees:*** full-time $400; $17 per credit hour. Full-time tuition and fees vary according to program and reciprocity agreements. Part-time tuition and fees vary according to course load. ***College room and board:*** $7764; ***Room only:*** $4965. Room and board charges vary according to board plan, housing facility, and location. ***Payment plan:*** Deferred payment.

FRESHMAN FINANCIAL AID (Fall 2009) 2,911 applied for aid; of those 61% were deemed to have need. 99% of freshmen with need received aid; of those 26% had need fully met. ***Average percent of need met:*** 76% (excluding resources awarded to replace EFC). ***Average financial aid package:*** $11,934 (excluding resources awarded to replace EFC). 42% of all full-time freshmen had no need and received non-need-based gift aid.

UNDERGRADUATE FINANCIAL AID (Fall 2009) 12,213 applied for aid; of those 74% were deemed to have need. 99% of undergraduates with need received aid; of those 23% had need fully met. ***Average percent of need met:*** 74% (excluding resources awarded to replace EFC). ***Average financial aid package:*** $12,570 (excluding resources awarded to replace EFC). 35% of all full-time undergraduates had no need and received non-need-based gift aid.

GIFT AID (NEED-BASED) ***Total amount:*** $52,696,261 (39% federal, 42% state, 12% institutional, 7% external sources). ***Receiving aid:*** Freshmen: 21% (822); all full-time undergraduates: 25% (4,681). ***Average award:*** Freshmen: $5505; Undergraduates: $5027. ***Scholarships, grants, and awards:*** Federal Pell, FSEOG, state, private, college/university gift aid from institutional funds, United Negro College Fund, Federal Nursing.

GIFT AID (NON-NEED-BASED) ***Total amount:*** $44,987,346 (52% state, 27% institutional, 21% external sources). ***Receiving aid:*** Freshmen: 40% (1,553). Undergraduates: 29% (5,461). ***Average award:*** Freshmen: $5422. Undergraduates: $6260. ***Scholarships, grants, and awards by category:*** *Academic interests/achievement:* 7,831 awards ($16,910,129 total): area/ethnic studies, biological sciences, business, communication, computer science, education, engineering/technologies, English, foreign languages, general academic interests/achievements, health fields, humanities, international studies, library science, mathematics, military science, physical sciences, premedicine, religion/biblical studies, social sciences. *Creative arts/performance:* 42 awards ($297,039 total): art/fine arts, dance, debating, journalism/publications, music, theater/drama. *Special achievements/activities:* 199 awards ($168,014 total): cheerleading/drum major, community service, general special achievements/activities, leadership, memberships, religious involvement. *Special characteristics:* 6,205 awards ($13,551,708 total): adult students, children and siblings of alumni, children of faculty/staff, children of union members/company employees, children of workers in trades, children with a deceased or disabled parent, ethnic background, first-generation college students, general special characteristics, handicapped students, international students, local/state students, members of minority groups, out-of-state students, religious affiliation, spouses of deceased or disabled public servants. ***Tuition waivers:*** Full or partial for employees or children of employees, senior citizens.

LOANS ***Student loans:*** $79,379,994 (52% need-based, 48% non-need-based). 49% of past graduating class borrowed through all loan programs. *Average indebtedness per student:* $21,811. ***Average need-based loan:*** Freshmen: $2870. Undergraduates: $3962. ***Parent loans:*** $16,724,792 (18% need-based, 82% non-need-based). ***Programs:*** Federal Direct (Subsidized and Unsubsidized Stafford, PLUS), Perkins, Federal Nursing.

WORK-STUDY ***Federal work-study:*** Total amount: $1,762,231; 657 jobs averaging $2115. ***State or other work-study/employment:*** Total amount: $6,310,986 (100% non-need-based). 2,732 part-time jobs averaging $1739.

ATHLETIC AWARDS Total amount: $6,036,097 (39% need-based, 61% non-need-based).

APPLYING FOR FINANCIAL AID ***Required financial aid form:*** FAFSA. ***Financial aid deadline (priority):*** 4/1. ***Notification date:*** Continuous beginning 4/1.

CONTACT Dr. Ed Miller, Financial Aid Director, University of South Carolina, 1714 College Street, Columbia, SC 29208, 803-777-8134 or toll-free 800-868-5872 (in-state). *Fax:* 803-777-0941. *E-mail:* ewmiller@mailbox.sc.edu.

UNIVERSITY OF SOUTH CAROLINA AIKEN

Aiken, SC

Tuition & fees (SC res): $8424 Average undergraduate aid package: $9679

ABOUT THE INSTITUTION State-supported, coed. 20 undergraduate majors. Federal methodology is used as a basis for awarding need-based institutional aid.

UNDERGRADUATE EXPENSES for 2010–11 ***Tuition, state resident:*** full-time $8134; part-time $353 per credit hour. ***Tuition, nonresident:*** full-time $16,302; part-time $706 per credit hour. ***Required fees:*** full-time $290; $9 per credit hour or $25 per term. Full-time tuition and fees vary according to reciprocity agreements. Part-time tuition and fees vary according to course load and reciprocity agreements. ***College room and board:*** $6450. Room and board charges vary according to board plan and housing facility. ***Payment plan:*** Deferred payment.

FRESHMAN FINANCIAL AID (Fall 2009) 589 applied for aid; of those 70% were deemed to have need. 99% of freshmen with need received aid; of those 16% had need fully met. ***Average percent of need met:*** 74% (excluding resources awarded to replace EFC). ***Average financial aid package:*** $10,094 (excluding resources awarded to replace EFC). 26% of all full-time freshmen had no need and received non-need-based gift aid.

UNDERGRADUATE FINANCIAL AID (Fall 2009) 2,341 applied for aid; of those 68% were deemed to have need. 99% of undergraduates with need received aid; of those 14% had need fully met. ***Average percent of need met:*** 70% (excluding resources awarded to replace EFC). ***Average financial aid package:*** $9679 (excluding resources awarded to replace EFC). 26% of all full-time undergraduates had no need and received non-need-based gift aid.

GIFT AID (NEED-BASED) ***Total amount:*** $10,147,814 (56% federal, 36% state, 5% institutional, 3% external sources). ***Receiving aid:*** Freshmen: 65% (387); all full-time undergraduates: 53% (1,308). ***Average award:*** Freshmen: $7914; Undergraduates: $7083. ***Scholarships, grants, and awards:*** Federal Pell, FSEOG, state, college/university gift aid from institutional funds.

GIFT AID (NON-NEED-BASED) ***Total amount:*** $1,691,608 (1% federal, 76% state, 13% institutional, 10% external sources). ***Receiving aid:*** Freshmen: 7% (41). Undergraduates: 4% (96). ***Average award:*** Freshmen: $4464. Undergraduates: $4366. ***Scholarships, grants, and awards by category:*** *Academic interests/achievement:* biological sciences, business, communication, computer science, education, engineering/technologies, English, general academic interests/achievements, humanities, mathematics, physical sciences, social sciences. *Creative arts/performance:* art/fine arts, creative writing, journalism/publications, music. *Special achievements/activities:* cheerleading/drum major. ***Tuition waivers:*** Full or partial for employees or children of employees, senior citizens.

LOANS ***Student loans:*** $14,453,070 (70% need-based, 30% non-need-based). 72% of past graduating class borrowed through all loan programs. *Average indebtedness per student:* $19,369. ***Average need-based loan:*** Freshmen: $3063. Undergraduates: $4085. ***Parent loans:*** $731,635 (23% need-based, 77% non-need-based). ***Programs:*** Federal Direct (Subsidized and Unsubsidized Stafford, PLUS), Perkins.

WORK-STUDY ***Federal work-study:*** Total amount: $92,099; jobs available. ***State or other work-study/employment:*** Total amount: $70,402 (100% non-need-based). Part-time jobs available.

ATHLETIC AWARDS Total amount: $329,862 (61% need-based, 39% non-need-based).

APPLYING FOR FINANCIAL AID ***Required financial aid form:*** FAFSA. ***Financial aid deadline (priority):*** 3/15. ***Notification date:*** Continuous beginning 5/1. Students must reply within 4 weeks of notification.

CONTACT Mr. Glenn Shumpert, Director of Financial Aid, University of South Carolina Aiken, 471 University Parkway, Aiken, SC 29801, 803-641-3476 or toll-free 888-WOW-USCA. *Fax:* 803-641-6840. *E-mail:* glens@usca.edu.

UNIVERSITY OF SOUTH CAROLINA BEAUFORT

Bluffton, SC

CONTACT Tina Wells, Financial Aid Administrative Assistant, University of South Carolina Beaufort, 801 Carteret Street, Beaufort, SC 29902, 843-521-3104. *Fax:* 843-521-3194. *E-mail:* uscbfina@uscb.edu.

UNIVERSITY OF SOUTH CAROLINA UPSTATE

Spartanburg, SC

CONTACT Kim Jenerette, Director of Financial Aid, University of South Carolina Upstate, 800 University Way, Spartanburg, SC 29303, 864-503-5340 or toll-free 800-277-8727. *Fax:* 864-503-5974. *E-mail:* kjenerette@uscupstate.edu.

THE UNIVERSITY OF SOUTH DAKOTA

Vermillion, SD

Tuition & fees (SD res): $6762 Average undergraduate aid package: $7005

ABOUT THE INSTITUTION State-supported, coed. 62 undergraduate majors. Federal methodology is used as a basis for awarding need-based institutional aid.

UNDERGRADUATE EXPENSES for 2010–11 ***Tuition, state resident:*** full-time $2994; part-time $99.80 per credit hour. ***Tuition, nonresident:*** full-time $4491; part-time $149.70 per credit hour. ***Required fees:*** full-time $3768; $125.60 per credit hour. Full-time tuition and fees vary according to course load. Part-time tuition and fees vary according to course load. ***College room and board:*** $6123; ***Room only:*** $3003. Room and board charges vary according to board plan and housing facility. ***Payment plan:*** Deferred payment.

FRESHMAN FINANCIAL AID (Fall 2009) 843 applied for aid; of those 71% were deemed to have need. 91% of freshmen with need received aid; of those 70% had need fully met. ***Average percent of need met:*** 81% (excluding resources awarded to replace EFC). ***Average financial aid package:*** $6243 (excluding resources awarded to replace EFC). 29% of all full-time freshmen had no need and received non-need-based gift aid.

UNDERGRADUATE FINANCIAL AID (Fall 2009) 4,153 applied for aid; of those 76% were deemed to have need. 94% of undergraduates with need received aid; of those 67% had need fully met. ***Average percent of need met:*** 80% (excluding resources awarded to replace EFC). ***Average financial aid package:*** $7005 (excluding resources awarded to replace EFC). 18% of all full-time undergraduates had no need and received non-need-based gift aid.

GIFT AID (NEED-BASED) ***Total amount:*** $9,866,431 (100% federal). ***Receiving aid:*** Freshmen: 32% (314); all full-time undergraduates: 32% (1,621). ***Average award:*** Freshmen: $4511; Undergraduates: $4697. ***Scholarships, grants, and awards:*** Federal Pell, FSEOG, private, college/university gift aid from institutional funds, Federal Nursing.

GIFT AID (NON-NEED-BASED) ***Total amount:*** $6,834,571 (7% federal, 12% state, 48% institutional, 33% external sources). ***Receiving aid:*** Freshmen: 45% (441). Undergraduates: 30% (1,515). ***Average award:*** Freshmen: $4205. Undergraduates: $3792. ***Scholarships, grants, and awards by category:*** *Academic interests/achievement:* biological sciences, business, communication, computer science, education, English, foreign languages, general academic interests/achievements, humanities, mathematics, military science, premedicine, social sciences. *Creative arts/performance:* art/fine arts, creative writing, debating, music, theater/drama. *Special achievements/activities:* leadership. *Special characteristics:* members of minority groups. ***Tuition waivers:*** Full or partial for children of alumni, employees or children of employees, senior citizens.

LOANS ***Student loans:*** $35,666,856 (46% need-based, 54% non-need-based). 74% of past graduating class borrowed through all loan programs. *Average indebtedness per student:* $22,954. ***Average need-based loan:*** Freshmen: $3707. Undergraduates: $4354. ***Parent loans:*** $3,533,843 (100% non-need-based). ***Programs:*** Perkins, Federal Nursing, college/university.

WORK-STUDY ***Federal work-study:*** Total amount: $830,273; jobs available.

ATHLETIC AWARDS Total amount: $3,216,663 (45% need-based, 55% non-need-based).

APPLYING FOR FINANCIAL AID ***Required financial aid form:*** FAFSA. ***Financial aid deadline (priority):*** 3/15. ***Notification date:*** Continuous beginning 3/1.

CONTACT Julie Pier, Director of Student Financial Aid, The University of South Dakota, Belbas Center, 414 East Clark Street, Vermillion, SD 57069, 605-677-5446 or toll-free 877-269-6837. *Fax:* 605-677-5238.

UNIVERSITY OF SOUTHERN CALIFORNIA

Los Angeles, CA

Tuition & fees: $41,022 **Average undergraduate aid package: $35,906**

ABOUT THE INSTITUTION Independent, coed. 97 undergraduate majors. Both federal and institutional methodology are used as a basis for awarding need-based institutional aid.

UNDERGRADUATE EXPENSES for 2010–11 ***One-time required fee:*** $150. ***Comprehensive fee:*** $52,602 includes full-time tuition ($40,384), mandatory fees ($638), and room and board ($11,580). ***College room only:*** $6680. Full-time tuition and fees vary according to program. Room and board charges vary according to board plan and housing facility. ***Part-time tuition:*** $1360 per unit. Part-time tuition and fees vary according to course load and program. ***Payment plans:*** Tuition prepayment, installment.

FRESHMAN FINANCIAL AID (Fall 2009) 1,828 applied for aid; of those 60% were deemed to have need. 100% of freshmen with need received aid; of those 93% had need fully met. ***Average percent of need met:*** 100% (excluding resources awarded to replace EFC). ***Average financial aid package:*** $36,291 (excluding resources awarded to replace EFC). 19% of all full-time freshmen had no need and received non-need-based gift aid.

UNDERGRADUATE FINANCIAL AID (Fall 2009) 8,671 applied for aid; of those 74% were deemed to have need. 100% of undergraduates with need received aid; of those 93% had need fully met. ***Average percent of need met:*** 100% (excluding resources awarded to replace EFC). ***Average financial aid package:*** $35,906 (excluding resources awarded to replace EFC). 17% of all full-time undergraduates had no need and received non-need-based gift aid.

GIFT AID (NEED-BASED) ***Total amount:*** $174,208,776 (9% federal, 10% state, 78% institutional, 3% external sources). ***Receiving aid:*** Freshmen: 34% (973); all full-time undergraduates: 36% (5,770). ***Average award:*** Freshmen: $25,434; Undergraduates: $24,777. ***Scholarships, grants, and awards:*** Federal Pell, FSEOG, state, private, college/university gift aid from institutional funds.

GIFT AID (NON-NEED-BASED) ***Total amount:*** $52,397,133 (81% institutional, 19% external sources). ***Receiving aid:*** Freshmen: 21% (616). Undergraduates: 17% (2,781). ***Average award:*** Freshmen: $16,528. Undergraduates: $15,639. ***Scholarships, grants, and awards by category:*** *Academic interests/achievement:* 5,200 awards ($81,189,925 total): general academic interests/achievements. *Creative arts/performance:* 13 awards ($362,822 total): art/fine arts, debating, music, theater/drama. *Special achievements/activities:* 63 awards ($633,000 total): leadership. *Special characteristics:* 931 awards ($19,042,276 total): children and siblings of alumni, children of faculty/staff, members of minority groups. ***Tuition waivers:*** Full or partial for employees or children of employees.

LOANS ***Student loans:*** $64,062,106 (56% need-based, 44% non-need-based). 44% of past graduating class borrowed through all loan programs. *Average indebtedness per student:* $30,090. ***Average need-based loan:*** Freshmen: $4428. Undergraduates: $5873. ***Parent loans:*** $67,197,438 (100% non-need-based). ***Programs:*** Federal Direct (Subsidized and Unsubsidized Stafford, PLUS), Perkins, credit-based loans.

WORK-STUDY ***Federal work-study:*** Total amount: $13,380,543; 4,945 jobs averaging $2681.

ATHLETIC AWARDS Total amount: $13,946,175 (31% need-based, 69% non-need-based).

APPLYING FOR FINANCIAL AID ***Required financial aid forms:*** FAFSA, CSS Financial Aid PROFILE, parents' and student's most recent federal tax returns. ***Financial aid deadline (priority):*** 2/2. ***Notification date:*** Continuous beginning 3/15. Students must reply by 5/1.

CONTACT Thomas McWhorter, Executive Director, University of Southern California, 700 Childs Way, Los Angeles, CA 90089-0914, 213-740-5445. *Fax:* 213-821-3796. *E-mail:* faodir@usc.edu.

UNIVERSITY OF SOUTHERN INDIANA

Evansville, IN

Tuition & fees (IN res): $5740 **Average undergraduate aid package: $8551**

ABOUT THE INSTITUTION State-supported, coed. 55 undergraduate majors. Federal methodology is used as a basis for awarding need-based institutional aid.

UNDERGRADUATE EXPENSES for 2011–12 ***Tuition, state resident:*** full-time $5540; part-time $184.67 per credit hour. ***Tuition, nonresident:*** full-time $13,186; part-time $439.53 per credit hour. ***Required fees:*** full-time $200; $22.75 per term. Full-time tuition and fees vary according to course load and reciprocity agreements. Part-time tuition and fees vary according to course load and reciprocity agreements. ***College room and board:*** $6920; ***Room only:*** $3560. Room and board charges vary according to board plan and housing facility. ***Payment plan:*** Installment.

FRESHMAN FINANCIAL AID (Fall 2010, est.) 1,999 applied for aid; of those 70% were deemed to have need. 96% of freshmen with need received aid; of those 13% had need fully met. ***Average percent of need met:*** 78% (excluding resources awarded to replace EFC). ***Average financial aid package:*** $8528 (excluding resources awarded to replace EFC). 10% of all full-time freshmen had no need and received non-need-based gift aid.

UNDERGRADUATE FINANCIAL AID (Fall 2010, est.) 8,025 applied for aid; of those 66% were deemed to have need. 94% of undergraduates with need received aid; of those 14% had need fully met. ***Average percent of need met:*** 80% (excluding resources awarded to replace EFC). ***Average financial aid package:*** $8551 (excluding resources awarded to replace EFC). 9% of all full-time undergraduates had no need and received non-need-based gift aid.

GIFT AID (NEED-BASED) ***Total amount:*** $26,012,757 (57% federal, 29% state, 12% institutional, 2% external sources). ***Receiving aid:*** Freshmen: 53% (1,080); all full-time undergraduates: 47% (3,848). ***Average award:*** Freshmen: $6770; Undergraduates: $6287. ***Scholarships, grants, and awards:*** Federal Pell, FSEOG, state, private, college/university gift aid from institutional funds, Federal Nursing.

GIFT AID (NON-NEED-BASED) ***Total amount:*** $3,634,318 (69% institutional, 31% external sources). ***Receiving aid:*** Freshmen: 5% (112). Undergraduates: 4% (314). ***Average award:*** Freshmen: $2605. Undergraduates: $2991. ***Scholarships, grants, and awards by category:*** *Academic interests/achievement:* 1,833 awards ($1,340,597 total): biological sciences, business, education, engineering/technologies, general academic interests/achievements, health fields, humanities, mathematics, premedicine, social sciences. *Creative arts/performance:* 35 awards ($24,324 total): art/fine arts, creative writing, theater/drama. *Special achievements/activities:* leadership. *Special characteristics:* 143 awards ($526,206 total): children of faculty/staff, members of minority groups, out-of-state students, spouses of current students, veterans' children. ***Tuition waivers:*** Full or partial for employees or children of employees.

LOANS ***Student loans:*** $49,254,132 (74% need-based, 26% non-need-based). ***Average need-based loan:*** Freshmen: $3245. Undergraduates: $3920. ***Parent loans:*** $3,429,525 (29% need-based, 71% non-need-based). ***Programs:*** Federal Direct (Subsidized and Unsubsidized Stafford, PLUS).

WORK-STUDY ***Federal work-study:*** Total amount: $225,300; 115 jobs averaging $1959.

ATHLETIC AWARDS Total amount: $997,959 (35% need-based, 65% non-need-based).

APPLYING FOR FINANCIAL AID ***Required financial aid forms:*** FAFSA, institution's own form. ***Financial aid deadline:*** 3/1. ***Notification date:*** Continuous beginning 4/1.

CONTACT Financial Aid Office, University of Southern Indiana, 8600 University Boulevard, Evansville, IN 47712-3590, 812-464-1767 or toll-free 800-467-1965. *Fax:* 812-465-7154. *E-mail:* finaid@usi.edu.

UNIVERSITY OF SOUTHERN MAINE

Portland, ME

Tuition & fees (ME res): $8538 Average undergraduate aid package: $10,296

ABOUT THE INSTITUTION State-supported, coed. 45 undergraduate majors. Federal methodology is used as a basis for awarding need-based institutional aid.

UNDERGRADUATE EXPENSES for 2010–11 ***Tuition, state resident:*** full-time $7260; part-time $244 per credit hour. ***Tuition, nonresident:*** full-time $19,620; part-time $654 per credit hour. ***Required fees:*** full-time $1278; $27 per credit hour. Full-time tuition and fees vary according to course load, degree level, and reciprocity agreements. Part-time tuition and fees vary according to course load, degree level, and reciprocity agreements. ***College room and board:*** $9394; ***Room only:*** $4838. Room and board charges vary according to board plan, housing facility, and location. ***Payment plan:*** Installment.

FRESHMAN FINANCIAL AID (Fall 2010, est.) 708 applied for aid; of those 88% were deemed to have need. 99% of freshmen with need received aid; of those 8% had need fully met. ***Average percent of need met:*** 54% (excluding resources awarded to replace EFC). ***Average financial aid package:*** $9496 (excluding resources awarded to replace EFC). 4% of all full-time freshmen had no need and received non-need-based gift aid.

UNDERGRADUATE FINANCIAL AID (Fall 2010, est.) 4,449 applied for aid; of those 90% were deemed to have need. 88% of undergraduates with need received aid; of those 7% had need fully met. ***Average percent of need met:*** 56% (excluding resources awarded to replace EFC). ***Average financial aid package:*** $10,296 (excluding resources awarded to replace EFC). 3% of all full-time undergraduates had no need and received non-need-based gift aid.

GIFT AID (NEED-BASED) ***Total amount:*** $19,446,244 (64% federal, 11% state, 14% institutional, 11% external sources). ***Receiving aid:*** Freshmen: 60% (477); all full-time undergraduates: 51% (2,630). ***Average award:*** Freshmen: $5280; Undergraduates: $5147. ***Scholarships, grants, and awards:*** Federal Pell, FSEOG, state, college/university gift aid from institutional funds.

GIFT AID (NON-NEED-BASED) ***Total amount:*** $738,279 (53% institutional, 47% external sources). ***Receiving aid:*** Freshmen: 34% (272). Undergraduates: 18% (925). ***Average award:*** Freshmen: $3164. Undergraduates: $4246. ***Scholarships, grants, and awards by category:*** *Academic interests/achievement:* general academic interests/achievements. *Creative arts/performance:* music, theater/drama. *Special achievements/activities:* community service. *Special characteristics:* children of faculty/staff, general special characteristics, local/state students, out-of-state students. ***Tuition waivers:*** Full or partial for minority students, employees or children of employees, senior citizens.

LOANS ***Student loans:*** $62,547,250 (68% need-based, 32% non-need-based). 85% of past graduating class borrowed through all loan programs. *Average indebtedness per student:* $38,899. ***Average need-based loan:*** Freshmen: $8414. Undergraduates: $10,040. ***Parent loans:*** $5,190,778 (41% need-based, 59% non-need-based). ***Programs:*** Federal Direct (Subsidized and Unsubsidized Stafford, PLUS), Perkins, Federal Nursing, college/university.

WORK-STUDY ***Federal work-study:*** Total amount: $3,609,746; jobs available.

APPLYING FOR FINANCIAL AID ***Required financial aid form:*** FAFSA. ***Financial aid deadline (priority):*** 2/15. ***Notification date:*** Continuous beginning 3/15. Students must reply within 2 weeks of notification.

CONTACT Mr. Keith P. Dubois, Director of Financial Aid, University of Southern Maine, 96 Falmouth Street, PO Box 9300, Portland, ME 04104-9300, 207-780-5122 or toll-free 800-800-4USM Ext. 5670. *Fax:* 207-780-5143. *E-mail:* dubois@maine.edu.

UNIVERSITY OF SOUTHERN MISSISSIPPI

Hattiesburg, MS

Tuition & fees (MS res): $5452 Average undergraduate aid package: $9611

ABOUT THE INSTITUTION State-supported, coed. 68 undergraduate majors. Federal methodology is used as a basis for awarding need-based institutional aid.

UNDERGRADUATE EXPENSES for 2011–12 ***Tuition, state resident:*** full-time $5452; part-time $228 per credit hour. ***Tuition, nonresident:*** full-time $13,408; part-time $560 per credit hour. Part-time tuition and fees vary according to course load and degree level. ***College room and board:*** $6634. Room and board charges vary according to board plan and housing facility. ***Payment plan:*** Installment.

FRESHMAN FINANCIAL AID (Fall 2009) 1,661 applied for aid; of those 83% were deemed to have need. 98% of freshmen with need received aid; of those 24% had need fully met. ***Average percent of need met:*** 80% (excluding resources awarded to replace EFC). ***Average financial aid package:*** $9916 (excluding resources awarded to replace EFC). 11% of all full-time freshmen had no need and received non-need-based gift aid.

UNDERGRADUATE FINANCIAL AID (Fall 2009) 8,624 applied for aid; of those 87% were deemed to have need. 98% of undergraduates with need received aid; of those 25% had need fully met. ***Average percent of need met:*** 78% (excluding resources awarded to replace EFC). ***Average financial aid package:*** $9611 (excluding resources awarded to replace EFC). 6% of all full-time undergraduates had no need and received non-need-based gift aid.

GIFT AID (NEED-BASED) ***Total amount:*** $31,770,219 (83% federal, 4% state, 10% institutional, 3% external sources). ***Receiving aid:*** Freshmen: 57% (1,081); all full-time undergraduates: 56% (5,921). ***Average award:*** Freshmen: $4487; Undergraduates: $4379. ***Scholarships, grants, and awards:*** Federal Pell, FSEOG, state, private, college/university gift aid from institutional funds.

GIFT AID (NON-NEED-BASED) ***Total amount:*** $14,760,067 (11% federal, 18% state, 61% institutional, 10% external sources). ***Receiving aid:*** Freshmen: 37% (692). Undergraduates: 25% (2,692). ***Average award:*** Freshmen: $4784. Undergraduates: $4581. ***Scholarships, grants, and awards by category:*** *Academic interests/achievement:* general academic interests/achievements. *Creative arts/performance:* art/fine arts, dance, music, theater/drama. *Special achievements/activities:* cheerleading/drum major, leadership. *Special characteristics:* children and siblings of alumni, children of faculty/staff, ethnic background, local/state students, out-of-state students, veterans. ***Tuition waivers:*** Full or partial for children of alumni, employees or children of employees, senior citizens.

LOANS ***Student loans:*** $63,930,736 (47% need-based, 53% non-need-based). 65% of past graduating class borrowed through all loan programs. *Average indebtedness per student:* $19,854. ***Average need-based loan:*** Freshmen: $4010. Undergraduates: $4676. ***Parent loans:*** $2,733,063 (21% need-based, 79% non-need-based). ***Programs:*** Federal Direct (Subsidized and Unsubsidized Stafford, PLUS).

WORK-STUDY ***Federal work-study:*** Total amount: $558,639; jobs available.

ATHLETIC AWARDS Total amount: $3,306,009 (39% need-based, 61% non-need-based).

APPLYING FOR FINANCIAL AID ***Required financial aid forms:*** FAFSA, institution's own form. ***Financial aid deadline (priority):*** 3/15. ***Notification date:*** Continuous. Students must reply within 2 weeks of notification.

CONTACT Mr. David Williamson, Interim Director of Financial Aid, University of Southern Mississippi, 118 College Drive #5101, Hattiesburg, MS 39406-0001, 601-266-4774. *Fax:* 601-266-5769. *E-mail:* financial.aid@usm.edu.

UNIVERSITY OF SOUTH FLORIDA

Tampa, FL

Tuition & fees (FL res): $5198 Average undergraduate aid package: $9374

ABOUT THE INSTITUTION State-supported, coed. 76 undergraduate majors. Federal methodology is used as a basis for awarding need-based institutional aid.

UNDERGRADUATE EXPENSES for 2011–12 ***Tuition, state resident:*** full-time $5124; part-time $171 per credit hour. ***Tuition, nonresident:*** full-time $15,933; part-time $531 per credit hour. ***Required fees:*** full-time $74. Full-time tuition and fees vary according to course level, course load, and location. Part-time tuition and fees vary according to course level, course load, and location. ***College room and board: Room only:*** $5380. Room and board charges vary according to board plan, housing facility, and location. ***Payment plan:*** Installment.

FRESHMAN FINANCIAL AID (Fall 2009) 3,556 applied for aid; of those 77% were deemed to have need. 100% of freshmen with need received aid; of those 8% had need fully met. ***Average percent of need met:*** 52% (excluding resources awarded to replace EFC). ***Average financial aid package:*** $9860 (excluding resources awarded to replace EFC). 27% of all full-time freshmen had no need and received non-need-based gift aid.

UNDERGRADUATE FINANCIAL AID (Fall 2009) 19,172 applied for aid; of those 85% were deemed to have need. 97% of undergraduates with need received aid; of those .1% had need fully met. ***Average percent of need met:*** 49%

(excluding resources awarded to replace EFC). ***Average financial aid package:*** $9374 (excluding resources awarded to replace EFC). 15% of all full-time undergraduates had no need and received non-need-based gift aid.

GIFT AID (NEED-BASED) ***Total amount:*** $73,443,598 (81% federal, 11% state, 8% institutional). ***Receiving aid:*** Freshmen: 39% (1,657); all full-time undergraduates: 10% (2,491). ***Average award:*** Freshmen: $7714; Undergraduates: $5966. ***Scholarships, grants, and awards:*** Federal Pell, FSEOG, state, private, college/university gift aid from institutional funds.

GIFT AID (NON-NEED-BASED) ***Total amount:*** $53,591,512 (1% federal, 75% state, 18% institutional, 6% external sources). ***Receiving aid:*** Freshmen: 61% (2,595). Undergraduates: 3% (737). ***Average award:*** Freshmen: $1942. Undergraduates: $1940. ***Scholarships, grants, and awards by category:*** *Academic interests/achievement:* architecture, biological sciences, business, communication, computer science, education, engineering/technologies, English, foreign languages, general academic interests/achievements, health fields, humanities, international studies, library science, mathematics, military science, physical sciences, premedicine, religion/biblical studies, social sciences. *Creative arts/performance:* applied art and design, art/fine arts, cinema/film/broadcasting, creative writing, dance, debating, journalism/publications, music, performing arts, theater/drama. *Special achievements/activities:* general special achievements/activities. *Special characteristics:* general special characteristics. ***Tuition waivers:*** Full or partial for senior citizens.

LOANS ***Student loans:*** $130,204,445 (47% need-based, 53% non-need-based). 52% of past graduating class borrowed through all loan programs. *Average indebtedness per student:* $21,679. ***Average need-based loan:*** Freshmen: $2766. Undergraduates: $4645. ***Parent loans:*** $3,568,930 (100% non-need-based). ***Programs:*** Federal Direct (Subsidized and Unsubsidized Stafford, PLUS), Perkins, college/university.

WORK-STUDY ***Federal work-study:*** Total amount: $2,227,892; jobs available. ***State or other work-study/employment:*** Total amount: $481,525 (100% need-based). Part-time jobs available.

ATHLETIC AWARDS Total amount: $4,012,593 (100% non-need-based).

APPLYING FOR FINANCIAL AID ***Required financial aid form:*** FAFSA. ***Financial aid deadline (priority):*** 3/1. ***Notification date:*** Continuous beginning 3/1. Students must reply within 4 weeks of notification.

CONTACT Ms. Billie Jo Hamilton, Director of Student Financial Aid, University of South Florida, 4202 East Fowler Avenue, SVC 1102, Tampa, FL 33620-6960, 813-974-4700. *Fax:* 813-974-5144. *E-mail:* bjhamilton@admin.usf.edu.

THE UNIVERSITY OF TAMPA

Tampa, FL

Tuition & fees: $23,218 **Average undergraduate aid package: $16,255**

ABOUT THE INSTITUTION Independent, coed. 49 undergraduate majors. Federal methodology is used as a basis for awarding need-based institutional aid.

UNDERGRADUATE EXPENSES for 2010–11 ***One-time required fee:*** $85. ***Comprehensive fee:*** $31,808 includes full-time tuition ($22,116), mandatory fees ($1102), and room and board ($8590). ***College room only:*** $4590. Full-time tuition and fees vary according to class time. Room and board charges vary according to board plan and housing facility. ***Part-time tuition:*** $470 per credit hour. ***Part-time fees:*** $40 per term. Part-time tuition and fees vary according to class time. ***Payment plan:*** Installment.

FRESHMAN FINANCIAL AID (Fall 2010, est.) 1,019 applied for aid; of those 81% were deemed to have need. 100% of freshmen with need received aid; of those 20% had need fully met. ***Average percent of need met:*** 68% (excluding resources awarded to replace EFC). ***Average financial aid package:*** $15,860 (excluding resources awarded to replace EFC). 32% of all full-time freshmen had no need and received non-need-based gift aid.

UNDERGRADUATE FINANCIAL AID (Fall 2010, est.) 3,693 applied for aid; of those 84% were deemed to have need. 100% of undergraduates with need received aid; of those 20% had need fully met. ***Average percent of need met:*** 71% (excluding resources awarded to replace EFC). ***Average financial aid package:*** $16,255 (excluding resources awarded to replace EFC). 32% of all full-time undergraduates had no need and received non-need-based gift aid.

GIFT AID (NEED-BASED) ***Total amount:*** $35,245,728 (19% federal, 14% state, 65% institutional, 2% external sources). ***Receiving aid:*** Freshmen: 53% (755); all full-time undergraduates: 51% (2,743). ***Average award:*** Freshmen: $12,478; Undergraduates: $12,002. ***Scholarships, grants, and awards:*** Federal Pell, FSEOG, state, private, college/university gift aid from institutional funds.

GIFT AID (NON-NEED-BASED) ***Total amount:*** $11,954,075 (1% federal, 18% state, 79% institutional, 2% external sources). ***Receiving aid:*** Freshmen: 57% (812). Undergraduates: 57% (3,055). ***Average award:*** Freshmen: $6070. Undergraduates: $5694. ***Scholarships, grants, and awards by category:*** *Academic interests/achievement:* 4,362 awards ($23,366,242 total): biological sciences, English, general academic interests/achievements, international studies, military science, social sciences. *Creative arts/performance:* 226 awards ($339,375 total): art/fine arts, creative writing, journalism/publications, music, performing arts, theater/drama. *Special achievements/activities:* 163 awards ($147,250 total): general special achievements/activities, leadership, memberships. *Special characteristics:* 300 awards ($1,735,976 total): children and siblings of alumni, children of faculty/staff, international students. ***Tuition waivers:*** Full or partial for employees or children of employees.

LOANS ***Student loans:*** $23,008,088 (83% need-based, 17% non-need-based). 58% of past graduating class borrowed through all loan programs. *Average indebtedness per student:* $29,264. ***Average need-based loan:*** Freshmen: $3297. Undergraduates: $4334. ***Parent loans:*** $12,774,367 (84% need-based, 16% non-need-based). ***Programs:*** Federal Direct (Subsidized and Unsubsidized Stafford, PLUS), Perkins, college/university.

WORK-STUDY ***Federal work-study:*** Total amount: $460,094; 276 jobs averaging $2000. ***State or other work-study/employment:*** Total amount: $6400 (100% need-based). 3 part-time jobs averaging $2000.

ATHLETIC AWARDS Total amount: $1,690,668 (51% need-based, 49% non-need-based).

APPLYING FOR FINANCIAL AID ***Required financial aid form:*** FAFSA. ***Financial aid deadline:*** Continuous. ***Notification date:*** Continuous beginning 2/1. Students must reply within 3 weeks of notification.

CONTACT Financial Aid Office, The University of Tampa, 401 West Kennedy Boulevard, Tampa, FL 33606-1490, 813-253-6219 or toll-free 888-646-2438 (in-state), 888-MINARET (out-of-state). *Fax:* 813-258-7439. *E-mail:* finaid@ut.edu.

THE UNIVERSITY OF TENNESSEE

Knoxville, TN

Tuition & fees (TN res): $7382 **Average undergraduate aid package: $11,215**

ABOUT THE INSTITUTION State-supported, coed. 85 undergraduate majors. Federal methodology is used as a basis for awarding need-based institutional aid.

UNDERGRADUATE EXPENSES for 2010–11 ***Tuition, state resident:*** full-time $7382; part-time $270 per hour. ***Tuition, nonresident:*** full-time $22,720; part-time $897 per hour. ***Required fees:*** $43 per hour. Full-time tuition and fees vary according to course level and program. Part-time tuition and fees vary according to course level and program. ***College room and board:*** $7800. Room and board charges vary according to board plan and housing facility. ***Payment plan:*** Installment.

FRESHMAN FINANCIAL AID (Fall 2010, est.) 4,033 applied for aid; of those 61% were deemed to have need. 99% of freshmen with need received aid; of those 28% had need fully met. ***Average percent of need met:*** 77% (excluding resources awarded to replace EFC). ***Average financial aid package:*** $11,621 (excluding resources awarded to replace EFC). 15% of all full-time freshmen had no need and received non-need-based gift aid.

UNDERGRADUATE FINANCIAL AID (Fall 2010, est.) 17,764 applied for aid; of those 64% were deemed to have need. 97% of undergraduates with need received aid; of those 22% had need fully met. ***Average percent of need met:*** 70% (excluding resources awarded to replace EFC). ***Average financial aid package:*** $11,215 (excluding resources awarded to replace EFC). 11% of all full-time undergraduates had no need and received non-need-based gift aid.

GIFT AID (NEED-BASED) ***Total amount:*** $108,425,109 (26% federal, 51% state, 19% institutional, 4% external sources). ***Receiving aid:*** Freshmen: 56% (2,357); all full-time undergraduates: 48% (9,739). ***Average award:*** Freshmen: $2555; Undergraduates: $3142. ***Scholarships, grants, and awards:*** Federal Pell, FSEOG, state, private, college/university gift aid from institutional funds.

GIFT AID (NON-NEED-BASED) ***Average award:*** Freshmen: $2231. Undergraduates: $2346. ***Scholarships, grants, and awards by category:*** *Academic interests/achievement:* 2,790 awards ($5,904,747 total): agriculture, architecture, business, communication, computer science, education, engineering/technologies, general academic interests/achievements, health fields, humanities, international studies, library science, military science, social sciences. *Creative* *arts/performance:* art/fine arts. *Special characteristics:* children and siblings of alumni. ***Tuition waivers:*** Full or partial for employees or children of employees, senior citizens.

LOANS ***Student loans:*** $62,212,208 (91% need-based, 9% non-need-based). 48% of past graduating class borrowed through all loan programs. *Average indebtedness per student:* $19,987. ***Average need-based loan:*** Freshmen: $3611. Undergraduates: $4361. ***Parent loans:*** $9,680,059 (100% need-based). ***Programs:*** Federal Direct (Subsidized and Unsubsidized Stafford, PLUS), Perkins, state, college/university.

WORK-STUDY ***Federal work-study:*** Total amount: $624,305; 402 jobs averaging $2200.

ATHLETIC AWARDS Total amount: $6,678,619 (100% need-based).

APPLYING FOR FINANCIAL AID ***Required financial aid form:*** FAFSA. ***Financial aid deadline (priority):*** 2/15. ***Notification date:*** Continuous beginning 3/15. Students must reply within 3 weeks of notification.

CONTACT Office of Financial Aid and Scholarships, The University of Tennessee, 115 Student Services Building, Knoxville, TN 37996-0210, 865-974-3131 or toll-free 800-221-8657 (in-state). *Fax:* 865-974-2175. *E-mail:* finaid@utk.edu.

THE UNIVERSITY OF TENNESSEE AT CHATTANOOGA

Chattanooga, TN

Tuition & fees (TN res): $6062 **Average undergraduate aid package: $6197**

ABOUT THE INSTITUTION State-supported, coed. 47 undergraduate majors. Federal methodology is used as a basis for awarding need-based institutional aid.

UNDERGRADUATE EXPENSES for 2011–12 ***Tuition, state resident:*** full-time $4912; part-time $205 per credit hour. ***Tuition, nonresident:*** full-time $17,226; part-time $718 per credit hour. ***Required fees:*** full-time $1150. ***College room and board:*** $8210; ***Room only:*** $5300. Room and board charges vary according to board plan and housing facility. ***Payment plan:*** Installment.

FRESHMAN FINANCIAL AID (Fall 2009) 2,126 applied for aid; of those 61% were deemed to have need. 99% of freshmen with need received aid; of those 17% had need fully met. ***Average percent of need met:*** 62% (excluding resources awarded to replace EFC). ***Average financial aid package:*** $7106 (excluding resources awarded to replace EFC). 15% of all full-time freshmen had no need and received non-need-based gift aid.

UNDERGRADUATE FINANCIAL AID (Fall 2009) 7,018 applied for aid; of those 68% were deemed to have need. 97% of undergraduates with need received aid; of those 11% had need fully met. ***Average percent of need met:*** 66% (excluding resources awarded to replace EFC). ***Average financial aid package:*** $6197 (excluding resources awarded to replace EFC). 13% of all full-time undergraduates had no need and received non-need-based gift aid.

GIFT AID (NEED-BASED) ***Total amount:*** $16,615,802 (81% federal, 16% state, 3% institutional). ***Receiving aid:*** Freshmen: 34% (753); all full-time undergraduates: 35% (2,775). ***Average award:*** Freshmen: $6399; Undergraduates: $5808. ***Scholarships, grants, and awards:*** Federal Pell, FSEOG, state, private, college/university gift aid from institutional funds, United Negro College Fund, Federal Nursing.

GIFT AID (NON-NEED-BASED) ***Total amount:*** $21,663,865 (73% state, 23% institutional, 4% external sources). ***Receiving aid:*** Freshmen: 51% (1,114). Undergraduates: 29% (2,318). ***Average award:*** Freshmen: $4217. Undergraduates: $3470. ***Scholarships, grants, and awards by category:*** *Academic interests/achievement:* 338 awards ($784,463 total): biological sciences, business, communication, education, engineering/technologies, English, general academic interests/achievements, home economics, mathematics, military science, physical sciences. *Creative arts/performance:* 291 awards ($249,038 total): art/fine arts, cinema/film/broadcasting, journalism/publications, music, performing arts, theater/drama. *Special achievements/activities:* 147 awards ($144,242 total): cheerleading/drum major, community service, memberships, religious involvement. *Special characteristics:* 30 awards ($67,356 total): children and siblings of alumni, children of faculty/staff, children of union members/company employees, children with a deceased or disabled parent, ethnic background, handicapped students, religious affiliation. ***Tuition waivers:*** Full or partial for employees or children of employees, senior citizens.

LOANS ***Student loans:*** $26,389,811 (40% need-based, 60% non-need-based). 52% of past graduating class borrowed through all loan programs. *Average indebtedness per student:* $13,845. ***Average need-based loan:*** Freshmen: $1945. Undergraduates: $3414. ***Parent loans:*** $1,449,772 (100% non-need-based). ***Programs:*** Federal Direct (Subsidized and Unsubsidized Stafford, PLUS), Perkins, college/university.

WORK-STUDY ***Federal work-study:*** Total amount: $376,213; 164 jobs averaging $2213. ***State or other work-study/employment:*** Total amount: $167,133 (100% non-need-based). 45 part-time jobs averaging $3633.

ATHLETIC AWARDS Total amount: $2,865,334 (100% non-need-based).

APPLYING FOR FINANCIAL AID ***Required financial aid form:*** FAFSA. ***Financial aid deadline (priority):*** 7/1. ***Notification date:*** Continuous beginning 3/15.

CONTACT Dianne Cox, Financial Aid Director, The University of Tennessee at Chattanooga, 615 McCallie Avenue, Chattanooga, TN 37403-2598, 423-425-4677 or toll-free 800-UTC-MOCS (in-state). *Fax:* 423-425-2292. *E-mail:* dianne-cox@utc.edu.

THE UNIVERSITY OF TENNESSEE AT MARTIN

Martin, TN

Tuition & fees (TN res): $6190 **Average undergraduate aid package: $12,655**

ABOUT THE INSTITUTION State-supported, coed. 85 undergraduate majors. Federal methodology is used as a basis for awarding need-based institutional aid.

UNDERGRADUATE EXPENSES for 2010–11 ***Tuition, state resident:*** full-time $5132; part-time $214 per credit hour. ***Tuition, nonresident:*** full-time $17,542; part-time $732 per credit hour. ***Required fees:*** full-time $1058; $45 per credit hour. Part-time tuition and fees vary according to course load. ***College room and board:*** $5104; ***Room only:*** $2530. Room and board charges vary according to board plan and housing facility. ***Payment plan:*** Deferred payment.

FRESHMAN FINANCIAL AID (Fall 2010, est.) 1,234 applied for aid; of those 76% were deemed to have need. 99% of freshmen with need received aid; of those 39% had need fully met. ***Average percent of need met:*** 85% (excluding resources awarded to replace EFC). ***Average financial aid package:*** $12,846 (excluding resources awarded to replace EFC). 21% of all full-time freshmen had no need and received non-need-based gift aid.

UNDERGRADUATE FINANCIAL AID (Fall 2010, est.) 5,814 applied for aid; of those 78% were deemed to have need. 98% of undergraduates with need received aid; of those 35% had need fully met. ***Average percent of need met:*** 81% (excluding resources awarded to replace EFC). ***Average financial aid package:*** $12,655 (excluding resources awarded to replace EFC). 16% of all full-time undergraduates had no need and received non-need-based gift aid.

GIFT AID (NEED-BASED) ***Total amount:*** $21,755,257 (82% federal, 16% state, 2% institutional). ***Receiving aid:*** Freshmen: 53% (672); all full-time undergraduates: 53% (3,197). ***Average award:*** Freshmen: $6224; Undergraduates: $6246. ***Scholarships, grants, and awards:*** Federal Pell, FSEOG, state, private, college/university gift aid from institutional funds.

GIFT AID (NON-NEED-BASED) ***Total amount:*** $15,792,037 (73% state, 19% institutional, 8% external sources). ***Receiving aid:*** Freshmen: 64% (815). Undergraduates: 41% (2,496). ***Average award:*** Freshmen: $6086. Undergraduates: $5675. ***Scholarships, grants, and awards by category:*** *Academic interests/achievement:* 1,668 awards ($2,854,723 total): agriculture, biological sciences, business, communication, computer science, education, engineering/technologies, English, general academic interests/achievements, health fields, home economics, humanities, mathematics, military science, physical sciences, premedicine, social sciences. *Creative arts/performance:* 205 awards ($141,075 total): art/fine arts, journalism/publications, music, theater/drama. *Special achievements/activities:* 224 awards ($381,857 total): cheerleading/drum major, general special achievements/activities, leadership, rodeo. *Special characteristics:* 2,145 awards ($3,471,334 total): adult students, children of educators, children of faculty/staff, children of union members/company employees, ethnic background, handicapped students, members of minority groups, out-of-state students. ***Tuition waivers:*** Full or partial for employees or children of employees, senior citizens.

LOANS ***Student loans:*** $26,325,070 (49% need-based, 51% non-need-based). 59% of past graduating class borrowed through all loan programs. *Average indebtedness per student:* $19,048. ***Average need-based loan:*** Freshmen: $3123. Undergraduates: $4204. ***Parent loans:*** $1,492,705 (100% non-need-based). ***Programs:*** Perkins.

WORK-STUDY ***Federal work-study:*** Total amount: $656,406; 314 jobs averaging $2500.

ATHLETIC AWARDS Total amount: $3,109,195 (100% non-need-based).

APPLYING FOR FINANCIAL AID ***Required financial aid form:*** FAFSA. ***Financial aid deadline (priority):*** 2/15. ***Notification date:*** Continuous beginning 4/1. Students must reply within 2 weeks of notification.

CONTACT Sheryl L. Frazier, Interim Director of Student Financial Assistance, The University of Tennessee at Martin, 205 Administration Building, Martin, TN 38238-1000, 731-881-7040 or toll-free 800-829-8861. *Fax:* 731-881-7036. *E-mail:* sneel@utm.edu.

THE UNIVERSITY OF TEXAS AT ARLINGTON

Arlington, TX

Tuition & fees (TX res): $8500 **Average undergraduate aid package: $12,829**

ABOUT THE INSTITUTION State-supported, coed. 61 undergraduate majors. Federal methodology is used as a basis for awarding need-based institutional aid.

UNDERGRADUATE EXPENSES for 2010–11 ***Tuition, state resident:*** full-time $8500. ***Tuition, nonresident:*** full-time $17,800. Full-time tuition and fees vary according to course level, course load, and program. Part-time tuition and fees vary according to course level, course load, and program. ***College room and board:*** $6224; ***Room only:*** $2932. Room and board charges vary according to board plan and housing facility. ***Payment plan:*** Installment.

FRESHMAN FINANCIAL AID (Fall 2010, est.) 1,941 applied for aid; of those 84% were deemed to have need. 100% of freshmen with need received aid; of those 30% had need fully met. ***Average percent of need met:*** 78% (excluding resources awarded to replace EFC). ***Average financial aid package:*** $11,870 (excluding resources awarded to replace EFC). 7% of all full-time freshmen had no need and received non-need-based gift aid.

UNDERGRADUATE FINANCIAL AID (Fall 2010, est.) 11,453 applied for aid; of those 90% were deemed to have need. 100% of undergraduates with need received aid; of those 16% had need fully met. ***Average percent of need met:*** 73% (excluding resources awarded to replace EFC). ***Average financial aid package:*** $12,829 (excluding resources awarded to replace EFC). 1% of all full-time undergraduates had no need and received non-need-based gift aid.

GIFT AID (NEED-BASED) ***Total amount:*** $90,326,610 (52% federal, 18% state, 30% institutional). ***Receiving aid:*** Freshmen: 56% (1,301); all full-time undergraduates: 55% (8,399). ***Average award:*** Freshmen: $8339; Undergraduates: $6862. ***Scholarships, grants, and awards:*** Federal Pell, FSEOG, state, private, college/university gift aid from institutional funds, United Negro College Fund.

GIFT AID (NON-NEED-BASED) ***Total amount:*** $4,219,080 (12% state, 88% institutional). ***Receiving aid:*** Freshmen: 37% (864). Undergraduates: 20% (3,080). ***Average award:*** Freshmen: $5864. Undergraduates: $5227. ***Scholarships, grants, and awards by category:*** *Academic interests/achievement:* 3,577 awards ($13,568,505 total): architecture, biological sciences, business, communication, computer science, education, engineering/technologies, English, foreign languages, general academic interests/achievements, health fields, humanities, international studies, mathematics, military science, physical sciences, social sciences. *Creative arts/performance:* journalism/publications, music, theater/drama. *Special achievements/activities:* cheerleading/drum major, community service, general special achievements/activities, leadership. *Special characteristics:* children with a deceased or disabled parent, first-generation college students, general special characteristics, handicapped students, public servants. ***Tuition waivers:*** Full or partial for employees or children of employees.

LOANS ***Student loans:*** $98,610,410 (82% need-based, 18% non-need-based). 53% of past graduating class borrowed through all loan programs. *Average indebtedness per student:* $18,749. ***Average need-based loan:*** Freshmen: $3171. Undergraduates: $4309. ***Parent loans:*** $3,975,035 (48% need-based, 52% non-need-based). ***Programs:*** Federal Direct (Subsidized and Unsubsidized Stafford, PLUS), Perkins, state.

WORK-STUDY ***Federal work-study:*** Total amount: $6,587,582; 2,054 jobs averaging $2984. ***State or other work-study/employment:*** Total amount: $242,257 (100% need-based). 186 part-time jobs averaging $1395.

ATHLETIC AWARDS Total amount: $2,140,212 (89% need-based, 11% non-need-based).

APPLYING FOR FINANCIAL AID ***Required financial aid form:*** FAFSA. ***Financial aid deadline (priority):*** 4/1. ***Notification date:*** Continuous beginning 4/1. Students must reply within 3 weeks of notification.

CONTACT Karen Krause, Director of Financial Aid, The University of Texas at Arlington, UTA Box 19199, Arlington, TX 76019, 817-272-3561. *Fax:* 817-272-3555. *E-mail:* kkrause@uta.edu.

THE UNIVERSITY OF TEXAS AT AUSTIN

Austin, TX

Tuition & fees (TX res): $9794 **Average undergraduate aid package: $12,825**

ABOUT THE INSTITUTION State-supported, coed. 110 undergraduate majors. Federal methodology is used as a basis for awarding need-based institutional aid.

UNDERGRADUATE EXPENSES for 2011–12 ***Tuition, state resident:*** full-time $9794. ***Tuition, nonresident:*** full-time $32,506. Full-time tuition and fees vary according to course load and program. Part-time tuition and fees vary according to course load and program. Room and board charges vary according to housing facility. ***Payment plan:*** Installment.

FRESHMAN FINANCIAL AID (Fall 2010, est.) 5,526 applied for aid; of those 64% were deemed to have need. 100% of freshmen with need received aid; of those 35% had need fully met. ***Average percent of need met:*** 81% (excluding resources awarded to replace EFC). ***Average financial aid package:*** $13,526 (excluding resources awarded to replace EFC). 2% of all full-time freshmen had no need and received non-need-based gift aid.

UNDERGRADUATE FINANCIAL AID (Fall 2010, est.) 21,735 applied for aid; of those 74% were deemed to have need. 100% of undergraduates with need received aid; of those 23% had need fully met. ***Average percent of need met:*** 73% (excluding resources awarded to replace EFC). ***Average financial aid package:*** $12,825 (excluding resources awarded to replace EFC). 2% of all full-time undergraduates had no need and received non-need-based gift aid.

GIFT AID (NEED-BASED) ***Total amount:*** $144,393,299 (36% federal, 24% state, 34% institutional, 6% external sources). ***Receiving aid:*** Freshmen: 44% (3,184); all full-time undergraduates: 37% (13,213). ***Average award:*** Freshmen: $9426; Undergraduates: $9233. ***Scholarships, grants, and awards:*** Federal Pell, FSEOG, state, private, college/university gift aid from institutional funds.

GIFT AID (NON-NEED-BASED) ***Total amount:*** $6,607,603 (1% federal, 22% institutional, 77% external sources). ***Receiving aid:*** Freshmen: 24% (1,719). Undergraduates: 12% (4,361). ***Average award:*** Freshmen: $1847. Undergraduates: $2407. ***Scholarships, grants, and awards by category:*** *Academic interests/achievement:* general academic interests/achievements. *Creative arts/performance:* general creative arts/performance. *Special achievements/activities:* leadership. *Special characteristics:* local/state students. ***Tuition waivers:*** Full or partial for employees or children of employees, senior citizens.

LOANS ***Student loans:*** $116,811,961 (68% need-based, 32% non-need-based). 51% of past graduating class borrowed through all loan programs. *Average indebtedness per student:* $24,667. ***Average need-based loan:*** Freshmen: $3091. Undergraduates: $4255. ***Parent loans:*** $87,803,889 (11% need-based, 89% non-need-based). ***Programs:*** Federal Direct (Subsidized and Unsubsidized Stafford, PLUS), Perkins, state.

WORK-STUDY ***Federal work-study:*** Total amount: $5,155,035; jobs available. ***State or other work-study/employment:*** Total amount: $185,310 (100% need-based). Part-time jobs available.

APPLYING FOR FINANCIAL AID ***Required financial aid forms:*** FAFSA, institution's own form. ***Financial aid deadline:*** Continuous. ***Notification date:*** Continuous beginning 3/15. Students must reply within 4 weeks of notification.

CONTACT Tom Melecki, PhD, Director of Student Financial Services, The University of Texas at Austin, PO Box 7758, UT Station, Austin, TX 78713-7758, 512-475-6203. *Fax:* 512-475-6349. *E-mail:* ask@finaid.utexas.edu.

THE UNIVERSITY OF TEXAS AT BROWNSVILLE

Brownsville, TX

Tuition & fees (TX res): $4766 **Average undergraduate aid package: $8618**

ABOUT THE INSTITUTION State-supported, coed. 37 undergraduate majors. Federal methodology is used as a basis for awarding need-based institutional aid.

UNDERGRADUATE EXPENSES for 2010–11 ***Tuition, state resident:*** full-time $3395; part-time $141.47 per credit hour. ***Tuition, nonresident:*** full-time $10,835; part-time $451.47 per credit hour. ***Required fees:*** full-time $1371; $36 per credit hour or $253.30 per term. Full-time tuition and fees vary according to class time, course level, course load, location, and program. Part-time tuition and fees vary according to class time, course level, course load, location, and program. ***College room and board:*** $5782; ***Room only:*** $2992. Room and board charges vary according to board plan. ***Payment plan:*** Installment.

FRESHMAN FINANCIAL AID (Fall 2010, est.) 1,548 applied for aid; of those 95% were deemed to have need. 100% of freshmen with need received aid. ***Average percent of need met:*** 69% (excluding resources awarded to replace EFC). ***Average financial aid package:*** $8634 (excluding resources awarded to replace EFC). 2% of all full-time freshmen had no need and received non-need-based gift aid.

UNDERGRADUATE FINANCIAL AID (Fall 2010, est.) 4,609 applied for aid; of those 95% were deemed to have need. 100% of undergraduates with need received aid. ***Average percent of need met:*** 57% (excluding resources awarded to replace EFC). ***Average financial aid package:*** $8618 (excluding resources awarded to replace EFC). 2% of all full-time undergraduates had no need and received non-need-based gift aid.

GIFT AID (NEED-BASED) ***Total amount:*** $39,669,099 (84% federal, 16% state). ***Receiving aid:*** Freshmen: 82% (1,375); all full-time undergraduates: 76% (4,009). ***Average award:*** Freshmen: $7772; Undergraduates: $6883. ***Scholarships, grants, and awards:*** Federal Pell, FSEOG, state, private, college/university gift aid from institutional funds.

GIFT AID (NON-NEED-BASED) ***Total amount:*** $4,638,205 (16% state, 72% institutional, 12% external sources). ***Receiving aid:*** Freshmen: 83% (1,386). Undergraduates: 73% (3,841). ***Average award:*** Freshmen: $2024. Undergraduates: $2814. ***Scholarships, grants, and awards by category:*** *Academic interests/achievement:* biological sciences, business, communication, computer science, education, engineering/technologies, English, foreign languages, general academic interests/achievements, health fields, international studies, mathematics, physical sciences, social sciences. *Creative arts/performance:* art/fine arts, music, performing arts. *Special characteristics:* children of faculty/staff, first-generation college students, general special characteristics, international students. ***Tuition waivers:*** Full or partial for senior citizens.

LOANS ***Student loans:*** $29,734,153 (64% need-based, 36% non-need-based). ***Average need-based loan:*** Freshmen: $3007. Undergraduates: $3824. ***Parent loans:*** $58,742 (100% non-need-based). ***Programs:*** Federal Direct (Subsidized and Unsubsidized Stafford, PLUS), state, college/university.

WORK-STUDY ***Federal work-study:*** Total amount: $491,146; 140 jobs averaging $3508. ***State or other work-study/employment:*** Total amount: $111,795 (100% need-based). 27 part-time jobs averaging $4141.

ATHLETIC AWARDS Total amount: $500,712 (100% non-need-based).

APPLYING FOR FINANCIAL AID ***Required financial aid form:*** FAFSA. ***Financial aid deadline (priority):*** 3/1. ***Notification date:*** 5/1. Students must reply by 7/1 or within 12 weeks of notification.

CONTACT Mrs. Ana Geraldine De La Garza, System Analyst III, The University of Texas at Brownsville, 80 Fort Brown, Brownsville, TX 78520-4991, 956-882-7887 or toll-free 800-850-0160 (in-state). *Fax:* 956-882-8229. *E-mail:* ana.g.delagarza@utb.edu.

THE UNIVERSITY OF TEXAS AT DALLAS

Richardson, TX

Tuition & fees (TX res): $10,744 **Average undergraduate aid package: $10,378**

ABOUT THE INSTITUTION State-supported, coed. 44 undergraduate majors. Both federal and institutional methodology are used as a basis for awarding need-based institutional aid.

UNDERGRADUATE EXPENSES for 2010–11 ***Tuition, state resident:*** full-time $10,744; part-time $358.13 per credit hour. ***Tuition, nonresident:*** full-time $25,866; part-time $862.20 per credit hour. Full-time tuition and fees vary according to course load and degree level. Part-time tuition and fees vary according to course load and degree level. ***College room and board:*** $8210. Room and board charges vary according to board plan and housing facility. ***Payment plans:*** Guaranteed tuition, installment.

FRESHMAN FINANCIAL AID (Fall 2009) 919 applied for aid; of those 73% were deemed to have need. 98% of freshmen with need received aid; of those 39% had need fully met. ***Average percent of need met:*** 77% (excluding resources awarded to replace EFC). ***Average financial aid package:*** $12,793 (excluding resources awarded to replace EFC). 11% of all full-time freshmen had no need and received non-need-based gift aid.

UNDERGRADUATE FINANCIAL AID (Fall 2009) 4,496 applied for aid; of those 82% were deemed to have need. 97% of undergraduates with need received aid; of those 24% had need fully met. ***Average percent of need met:*** 67% (excluding resources awarded to replace EFC). ***Average financial aid package:*** $10,378 (excluding resources awarded to replace EFC). 4% of all full-time undergraduates had no need and received non-need-based gift aid.

GIFT AID (NEED-BASED) ***Total amount:*** $35,881,117 (31% federal, 10% state, 56% institutional, 3% external sources). ***Receiving aid:*** Freshmen: 47% (615); all full-time undergraduates: 43% (3,136). ***Average award:*** Freshmen: $9610; Undergraduates: $6664. ***Scholarships, grants, and awards:*** Federal Pell, FSEOG, state, private, college/university gift aid from institutional funds.

GIFT AID (NON-NEED-BASED) ***Total amount:*** $4,398,961 (87% institutional, 13% external sources). ***Receiving aid:*** Freshmen: 10% (125). Undergraduates: 3% (238). ***Average award:*** Freshmen: $9984. Undergraduates: $7455. ***Scholarships, grants, and awards by category:*** *Academic interests/achievement:* biological sciences, business, computer science, engineering/technologies, general academic interests/achievements, mathematics, physical sciences. *Special achievements/activities:* general special achievements/activities, leadership. *Special characteristics:* adult students, children of public servants, general special characteristics, handicapped students, international students, local/state students, members of minority groups, out-of-state students, public servants, veterans, veterans' children. ***Tuition waivers:*** Full or partial for employees or children of employees, senior citizens.

LOANS ***Student loans:*** $39,299,638 (71% need-based, 29% non-need-based). 41% of past graduating class borrowed through all loan programs. *Average indebtedness per student:* $17,384. ***Average need-based loan:*** Freshmen: $3031. Undergraduates: $4285. ***Parent loans:*** $12,388,721 (22% need-based, 78% non-need-based). ***Programs:*** Perkins, state, college/university.

WORK-STUDY ***Federal work-study:*** Total amount: $1,215,169; 254 jobs averaging $4333. ***State or other work-study/employment:*** Total amount: $91,876 (100% need-based). Part-time jobs available.

APPLYING FOR FINANCIAL AID ***Required financial aid form:*** FAFSA. ***Financial aid deadline (priority):*** 3/31. ***Notification date:*** Continuous beginning 3/1. Students must reply within 2 weeks of notification.

CONTACT M. Beth N. Tolan, Director, The University of Texas at Dallas, 800 West Campbell Road, SS22, Richardson, TX 75080-3021, 972-883-2941 or toll-free 800-889-2443. *Fax:* 972-883-2947. *E-mail:* bnt031000@utdallas.edu.

THE UNIVERSITY OF TEXAS AT EL PASO

El Paso, TX

Tuition & fees (TX res): $6535 **Average undergraduate aid package: $14,508**

ABOUT THE INSTITUTION State-supported, coed. 61 undergraduate majors. Federal methodology is used as a basis for awarding need-based institutional aid.

UNDERGRADUATE EXPENSES for 2010–11 ***One-time required fee:*** $166. ***Tuition, state resident:*** full-time $5063; part-time $168.78 per credit hour. ***Tuition, nonresident:*** full-time $14,363; part-time $478.78 per credit hour. ***Required fees:*** full-time $1472; $45.50 per credit hour or $125.20 per term. Full-time tuition and fees vary according to course load and degree level. Part-time tuition and fees vary according to course load and degree level. Room and board charges vary according to housing facility. ***Payment plans:*** Guaranteed tuition, installment.

FRESHMAN FINANCIAL AID (Fall 2009) 1,834 applied for aid; of those 86% were deemed to have need. 100% of freshmen with need received aid; of those 35% had need fully met. ***Average percent of need met:*** 80% (excluding resources awarded to replace EFC). ***Average financial aid package:*** $14,717 (excluding resources awarded to replace EFC). 6% of all full-time freshmen had no need and received non-need-based gift aid.

UNDERGRADUATE FINANCIAL AID (Fall 2009) 8,696 applied for aid; of those 83% were deemed to have need. 99% of undergraduates with need received aid; of those 23% had need fully met. ***Average percent of need met:*** 73% (excluding resources awarded to replace EFC). ***Average financial aid package:*** $14,508 (excluding resources awarded to replace EFC). 6% of all full-time undergraduates had no need and received non-need-based gift aid.

GIFT AID (NEED-BASED) ***Total amount:*** $27,489,600 (22% federal, 47% state, 31% institutional). ***Receiving aid:*** Freshmen: 57% (1,337); all full-time undergraduates: 48% (6,141). ***Average award:*** Freshmen: $11,257; Undergraduates: $9294. ***Scholarships, grants, and awards:*** Federal Pell, FSEOG, state, private, college/university gift aid from institutional funds, United Negro College Fund, Federal Nursing.

GIFT AID (NON-NEED-BASED) ***Total amount:*** $6,958,419 (7% federal, 16% state, 58% institutional, 19% external sources). ***Receiving aid:*** Freshmen: 16% (364). Undergraduates: 7% (917). ***Average award:*** Freshmen: $1746. Undergraduates: $2501. ***Scholarships, grants, and awards by category:*** *Academic interests/achievement:* biological sciences, business, communication, computer science, education, engineering/technologies, English, general academic interests/achievements, health fields, humanities, international studies, mathematics, military science, physical sciences. *Creative arts/performance:* applied art and design, art/fine arts, journalism/publications, music, performing arts, theater/drama. *Special achievements/activities:* cheerleading/drum major, leadership. *Special characteristics:* ethnic background, international students, local/state students, members of minority groups, out-of-state students. ***Tuition waivers:*** Full or partial for employees or children of employees.

LOANS ***Student loans:*** $76,956,888 (98% need-based, 2% non-need-based). 63% of past graduating class borrowed through all loan programs. *Average indebtedness per student:* $18,773. ***Average need-based loan:*** Freshmen: $4571. Undergraduates: $6671. ***Parent loans:*** $4,753,705 (100% non-need-based). ***Programs:*** Perkins, Federal Nursing, state, college/university.

WORK-STUDY ***Federal work-study:*** Total amount: $2,181,055; jobs available. ***State or other work-study/employment:*** Total amount: $932,019 (100% need-based). Part-time jobs available.

ATHLETIC AWARDS Total amount: $4,056,826 (100% non-need-based).

APPLYING FOR FINANCIAL AID ***Required financial aid forms:*** FAFSA, institution's own form. ***Financial aid deadline (priority):*** 3/15. ***Notification date:*** Continuous beginning 6/30. Students must reply within 2 weeks of notification.

CONTACT Mr. Ron Williams, Interim Director of Financial Aid, The University of Texas at El Paso, 500 West University Avenue, El Paso, TX 79968-0001, 915-747-5204 or toll-free 877-746-4636. *Fax:* 915-747-5631. *E-mail:* rwilliams@utep.edu.

THE UNIVERSITY OF TEXAS AT SAN ANTONIO

San Antonio, TX

Tuition & fees (TX res): $8283 **Average undergraduate aid package: $9075**

ABOUT THE INSTITUTION State-supported, coed. 56 undergraduate majors. Federal methodology is used as a basis for awarding need-based institutional aid.

UNDERGRADUATE EXPENSES for 2011–12 ***Tuition, state resident:*** full-time $5783; part-time $192.75 per hour. ***Tuition, nonresident:*** full-time $15,683; part-time $522.75 per hour. ***Required fees:*** full-time $2500. Full-time tuition and fees vary according to course level, course load, and degree level. Part-time tuition and fees vary according to course level, course load, and degree level. ***College room and board:*** $8696; ***Room only:*** $5796. Room and board charges vary according to board plan and housing facility. ***Payment plans:*** Installment, deferred payment.

FRESHMAN FINANCIAL AID (Fall 2009) 3,515 applied for aid; of those 76% were deemed to have need. 98% of freshmen with need received aid; of those 24% had need fully met. ***Average percent of need met:*** 62% (excluding resources awarded to replace EFC). ***Average financial aid package:*** $9944 (excluding resources awarded to replace EFC). 3% of all full-time freshmen had no need and received non-need-based gift aid.

UNDERGRADUATE FINANCIAL AID (Fall 2009) 14,582 applied for aid; of those 84% were deemed to have need. 97% of undergraduates with need received aid; of those 15% had need fully met. ***Average percent of need met:*** 53% (excluding resources awarded to replace EFC). ***Average financial aid package:*** $9075 (excluding resources awarded to replace EFC). 3% of all full-time undergraduates had no need and received non-need-based gift aid.

GIFT AID (NEED-BASED) ***Total amount:*** $67,517,333 (67% federal, 20% state, 13% institutional). ***Receiving aid:*** Freshmen: 50% (2,275); all full-time undergraduates: 52% (10,230). ***Average award:*** Freshmen: $7658; Undergraduates: $5969. ***Scholarships, grants, and awards:*** Federal Pell, FSEOG, state, private, college/university gift aid from institutional funds.

GIFT AID (NON-NEED-BASED) ***Total amount:*** $6,810,174 (48% institutional, 52% external sources). ***Receiving aid:*** Freshmen: 17% (783). Undergraduates: 11% (2,175). ***Average award:*** Freshmen: $1610. Undergraduates: $1810. ***Scholarships, grants, and awards by category:*** *Academic interests/achievement:* agriculture, architecture, area/ethnic studies, biological sciences, business, communication, computer science, education, engineering/technologies, English, foreign languages, general academic interests/achievements, humanities, international studies, mathematics, physical sciences, social sciences. *Creative arts/performance:* art/fine arts, creative writing, debating, music. *Special achievements/activities:* cheerleading/drum major, general special achievements/activities. *Special characteristics:* ethnic background, first-generation college students, general special characteristics, handicapped students, local/state students, members of minority groups, out-of-state students. ***Tuition waivers:*** Full or partial for employees or children of employees.

LOANS ***Student loans:*** $100,564,873 (45% need-based, 55% non-need-based). 66% of past graduating class borrowed through all loan programs. *Average indebtedness per student:* $24,017. ***Average need-based loan:*** Freshmen: $3211. Undergraduates: $4073. ***Parent loans:*** $11,984,162 (100% non-need-based). ***Programs:*** Federal Direct (Subsidized and Unsubsidized Stafford, PLUS), Perkins, state, college/university.

WORK-STUDY ***Federal work-study:*** Total amount: $1,525,235; 712 jobs averaging $2169. ***State or other work-study/employment:*** Total amount: $1,047,498 (100% need-based). 89 part-time jobs averaging $2038.

ATHLETIC AWARDS Total amount: $2,299,540 (100% non-need-based).

APPLYING FOR FINANCIAL AID ***Required financial aid forms:*** FAFSA, institution's own form. ***Financial aid deadline (priority):*** 3/15. ***Notification date:*** Continuous beginning 4/1. Students must reply within 4 weeks of notification.

CONTACT Kim Canady, Assistant Director of Student Financial Aid, The University of Texas at San Antonio, One UTSA Cirlce, San Antonio, TX 78249, 210-458-8000 or toll-free 800-669-0919. *Fax:* 210-458-4638. *E-mail:* financialaid@utsa.edu.

THE UNIVERSITY OF TEXAS AT TYLER

Tyler, TX

Tuition & fees (TX res): $6322 **Average undergraduate aid package: $8346**

ABOUT THE INSTITUTION State-supported, coed. 38 undergraduate majors. Federal methodology is used as a basis for awarding need-based institutional aid.

UNDERGRADUATE EXPENSES for 2010–11 ***Tuition, state resident:*** full-time $4920; part-time $50 per semester hour. ***Tuition, nonresident:*** full-time $14,220; part-time $360 per semester hour. ***Required fees:*** full-time $1402. Full-time tuition and fees vary according to course level, course load, and degree level. ***College room and board:*** $8106; ***Room only:*** $5090. Room and board charges vary according to board plan and housing facility. ***Payment plan:*** Installment.

FRESHMAN FINANCIAL AID (Fall 2009) 402 applied for aid; of those 74% were deemed to have need. 98% of freshmen with need received aid; of those 20% had need fully met. ***Average percent of need met:*** 56% (excluding resources awarded to replace EFC). ***Average financial aid package:*** $9062 (excluding resources awarded to replace EFC). 2% of all full-time freshmen had no need and received non-need-based gift aid.

UNDERGRADUATE FINANCIAL AID (Fall 2009) 2,674 applied for aid; of those 85% were deemed to have need. 99% of undergraduates with need received aid; of those 10% had need fully met. ***Average percent of need met:*** 57% (excluding resources awarded to replace EFC). ***Average financial aid package:*** $8346 (excluding resources awarded to replace EFC). 9% of all full-time undergraduates had no need and received non-need-based gift aid.

GIFT AID (NEED-BASED) ***Total amount:*** $13,823,197 (52% federal, 21% state, 20% institutional, 7% external sources). ***Receiving aid:*** Freshmen: 45% (262); all full-time undergraduates: 66% (1,889). ***Average award:*** Freshmen: $8063; Undergraduates: $6398. ***Scholarships, grants, and awards:*** Federal Pell, FSEOG, state, private, college/university gift aid from institutional funds, Texas Grants, Institutional Grants (Education Affordability Program).

GIFT AID (NON-NEED-BASED) ***Total amount:*** $1,202,742 (61% institutional, 39% external sources). ***Receiving aid:*** Freshmen: 6% (35). Undergraduates: 4% (117). ***Average award:*** Freshmen: $2553. Undergraduates: $2272. ***Scholarships, grants, and awards by category:*** *Academic interests/achievement:* communication, engineering/technologies, general academic interests/achievements, health fields. *Creative arts/performance:* art/fine arts, music. *Special characteristics:* children of faculty/staff. ***Tuition waivers:*** Full or partial for employees or children of employees, senior citizens.

LOANS ***Student loans:*** $18,441,099 (72% need-based, 28% non-need-based). 53% of past graduating class borrowed through all loan programs. *Average*

indebtedness per student: $18,605. ***Average need-based loan:*** Freshmen: $3644. Undergraduates: $6109. ***Parent loans:*** $5,484,623 (20% need-based, 80% non-need-based). ***Programs:*** Federal Direct (Subsidized and Unsubsidized Stafford, PLUS).

WORK-STUDY ***Federal work-study:*** Total amount: $113,127; jobs available. ***State or other work-study/employment:*** Total amount: $217,224 (80% need-based, 20% non-need-based). Part-time jobs available.

APPLYING FOR FINANCIAL AID ***Required financial aid forms:*** FAFSA, institution's own form. ***Financial aid deadline (priority):*** 4/1. ***Notification date:*** Continuous beginning 4/15. Students must reply within 2 weeks of notification.

CONTACT Candice A. Lindsey, Executive Director of Enrollment Management and Marketing, The University of Texas at Tyler, 3900 University Boulevard, Tyler, TX 75799, 903-566-7221 or toll-free 800-UTTYLER (in-state). *Fax:* 903-566-7183. *E-mail:* financialaid@uttyler.edu.

THE UNIVERSITY OF TEXAS HEALTH SCIENCE CENTER AT HOUSTON

Houston, TX

Tuition & fees: N/R **Average undergraduate aid package: $11,921**

ABOUT THE INSTITUTION State-supported, coed. 2 undergraduate majors. Federal methodology is used as a basis for awarding need-based institutional aid.

UNDERGRADUATE EXPENSES for 2010–11 ***Tuition, state resident:*** part-time $149 per credit hour. ***Tuition, nonresident:*** part-time $623 per credit hour. ***Required fees:*** $157 per credit hour. ***Payment plan:*** Installment.

UNDERGRADUATE FINANCIAL AID (Fall 2009) 293 applied for aid; of those 91% were deemed to have need. 100% of undergraduates with need received aid; of those 33% had need fully met. ***Average percent of need met:*** 68% (excluding resources awarded to replace EFC). ***Average financial aid package:*** $11,921 (excluding resources awarded to replace EFC). 2% of all full-time undergraduates had no need and received non-need-based gift aid.

GIFT AID (NEED-BASED) ***Total amount:*** $1,460,723 (34% federal, 2% state, 58% institutional, 6% external sources). ***Receiving aid:*** All full-time undergraduates: 32% (186). ***Average award:*** Undergraduates: $6569. ***Scholarships, grants, and awards:*** Federal Pell, FSEOG, state, private, college/university gift aid from institutional funds.

GIFT AID (NON-NEED-BASED) ***Average award:*** Undergraduates: $6259. ***Scholarships, grants, and awards by category:*** *Academic interests/achievement:* health fields.

LOANS ***Student loans:*** $4,660,410 (100% need-based). ***Average need-based loan:*** Undergraduates: $8238. ***Parent loans:*** $684,160 (100% need-based). ***Programs:*** Perkins, Federal Nursing, state, college/university, alternative loans.

APPLYING FOR FINANCIAL AID ***Required financial aid forms:*** FAFSA, institution's own form. ***Financial aid deadline:*** Continuous. ***Notification date:*** Continuous.

CONTACT Ms. Wanda Williams, Director, The University of Texas Health Science Center at Houston, PO Box 20036, Houston, TX 77225, 713-500-3860. *Fax:* 713-500-3863. *E-mail:* wanda.k.williams@uth.tmc.edu.

THE UNIVERSITY OF TEXAS HEALTH SCIENCE CENTER AT SAN ANTONIO

San Antonio, TX

CONTACT Robert T. Lawson, Financial Aid Administrator, The University of Texas Health Science Center at San Antonio, 7703 Floyd Curl Drive, MSC 7708, San Antonio, TX 78284, 210-567-0025. *Fax:* 210-567-6643.

THE UNIVERSITY OF TEXAS MEDICAL BRANCH

Galveston, TX

Tuition & fees (TX res): $5740 **Average undergraduate aid package: $15,827**

ABOUT THE INSTITUTION State-supported, coed. 3 undergraduate majors. Federal methodology is used as a basis for awarding need-based institutional aid.

UNDERGRADUATE EXPENSES for 2010–11 ***Tuition, state resident:*** full-time $4770; part-time $159 per credit hour. ***Tuition, nonresident:*** full-time $14,070; part-time $469 per credit hour. ***Required fees:*** full-time $970; $15.99 per credit hour or $220 per term. Full-time tuition and fees vary according to course load, degree level, and program. Part-time tuition and fees vary according to course load, degree level, and program. Room and board charges vary according to housing facility. ***Payment plan:*** Installment.

UNDERGRADUATE FINANCIAL AID (Fall 2009) 491 applied for aid; of those 83% were deemed to have need. 91% of undergraduates with need received aid; of those 16% had need fully met. ***Average percent of need met:*** 83% (excluding resources awarded to replace EFC). ***Average financial aid package:*** $15,827 (excluding resources awarded to replace EFC). 65% of all full-time undergraduates had no need and received non-need-based gift aid.

GIFT AID (NEED-BASED) ***Total amount:*** $1,318,338 (58% federal, 3% state, 38% institutional, 1% external sources). ***Receiving aid:*** All full-time undergraduates: 25% (134). ***Average award:*** Undergraduates: $5163. ***Scholarships, grants, and awards:*** Federal Pell, FSEOG, state, private, college/university gift aid from institutional funds.

GIFT AID (NON-NEED-BASED) ***Total amount:*** $143,797 (93% institutional, 7% external sources). ***Receiving aid:*** Undergraduates: 31% (167). ***Average award:*** Undergraduates: $9647. ***Scholarships, grants, and awards by category:*** *Academic interests/achievement:* health fields.

LOANS ***Student loans:*** $4,981,825 (99% need-based, 1% non-need-based). ***Average need-based loan:*** Undergraduates: $5216. ***Parent loans:*** $57,500 (100% need-based). ***Programs:*** Federal Direct (Subsidized and Unsubsidized Stafford, PLUS), Perkins, Federal Nursing, state, college/university.

WORK-STUDY ***Federal work-study:*** Total amount: $38,797; 21 jobs averaging $2324.

CONTACT Mrs. Carol A. Cromie, University Financial Aid Officer, The University of Texas Medical Branch, 301 University Boulevard, Galveston, TX 77555-1305, 409-772-9795. *Fax:* 409-772-4466. *E-mail:* cacromie@umtb.edu.

THE UNIVERSITY OF TEXAS OF THE PERMIAN BASIN

Odessa, TX

Tuition & fees (TX res): $5599 **Average undergraduate aid package: $6438**

ABOUT THE INSTITUTION State-supported, coed. 32 undergraduate majors. Both federal and institutional methodology are used as a basis for awarding need-based institutional aid.

UNDERGRADUATE EXPENSES for 2010–11 ***Tuition, state resident:*** full-time $4380; part-time $146 per credit hour. ***Tuition, nonresident:*** full-time $12,690; part-time $423 per credit hour. ***Required fees:*** full-time $1219; $41 per credit hour. Full-time tuition and fees vary according to course load and location. Part-time tuition and fees vary according to course load and location. ***College room and board:*** $6964; ***Room only:*** $3880. Room and board charges vary according to board plan and housing facility. ***Payment plan:*** Installment.

FRESHMAN FINANCIAL AID (Fall 2009) 276 applied for aid; of those 55% were deemed to have need. 100% of freshmen with need received aid; of those 15% had need fully met. ***Average percent of need met:*** 56% (excluding resources awarded to replace EFC). ***Average financial aid package:*** $6284 (excluding resources awarded to replace EFC). 31% of all full-time freshmen had no need and received non-need-based gift aid.

UNDERGRADUATE FINANCIAL AID (Fall 2009) 1,879 applied for aid; of those 53% were deemed to have need. 100% of undergraduates with need received aid; of those 72% had need fully met. ***Average percent of need met:*** 57% (excluding resources awarded to replace EFC). ***Average financial aid package:*** $6438 (excluding resources awarded to replace EFC). 21% of all full-time undergraduates had no need and received non-need-based gift aid.

GIFT AID (NEED-BASED) ***Total amount:*** $4,511,706 (82% federal, 16% state, 2% institutional). ***Receiving aid:*** Freshmen: 38% (122); all full-time undergraduates: 46% (881). ***Average award:*** Freshmen: $6527; Undergraduates: $6632. ***Scholarships, grants, and awards:*** Federal Pell, FSEOG, state, private, college/university gift aid from institutional funds.

GIFT AID (NON-NEED-BASED) ***Total amount:*** $3,566,867 (1% federal, 2% state, 50% institutional, 47% external sources). ***Receiving aid:*** Freshmen: 36% (118). Undergraduates: 40% (774). ***Average award:*** Freshmen: $2184. Undergraduates: $1770. ***Scholarships, grants, and awards by category:*** *Academic interests/achievement:* general academic interests/achievements.

Creative arts/performance: art/fine arts, dance, general creative arts/performance, music, theater/drama. *Special achievements/activities:* cheerleading/drum major. ***Tuition waivers:*** Full or partial for employees or children of employees, senior citizens.

LOANS ***Student loans:*** $5,466,382 (50% need-based, 50% non-need-based). 32% of past graduating class borrowed through all loan programs. *Average indebtedness per student:* $13,420. ***Average need-based loan:*** Freshmen: $2448. Undergraduates: $3538. ***Parent loans:*** $136,882 (100% non-need-based). ***Programs:*** Federal Direct (Subsidized and Unsubsidized Stafford, PLUS), state.

WORK-STUDY ***Federal work-study:*** Total amount: $38,288; jobs available. ***State or other work-study/employment:*** Total amount: $112,744 (27% need-based, 73% non-need-based). Part-time jobs available.

ATHLETIC AWARDS Total amount: $428,435 (100% non-need-based).

APPLYING FOR FINANCIAL AID ***Required financial aid form:*** FAFSA. ***Financial aid deadline (priority):*** 2/1. ***Notification date:*** Continuous beginning 3/1. Students must reply within 2 weeks of notification.

CONTACT Joe Sanders, Director of Student Financial Services, The University of Texas of the Permian Basin, 4901 East University Boulevard, Odessa, TX 79762, 432-552-2620 or toll-free 866-552-UTPB. *Fax:* 432-552-2621. *E-mail:* finaid@utpb.edu.

THE UNIVERSITY OF TEXAS–PAN AMERICAN

Edinburg, TX

Tuition & fees (TX res): $4560 **Average undergraduate aid package: $10,252**

ABOUT THE INSTITUTION State-supported, coed. 50 undergraduate majors. Federal methodology is used as a basis for awarding need-based institutional aid.

UNDERGRADUATE EXPENSES for 2010–11 ***Tuition, state resident:*** full-time $3528; part-time $65.35 per credit hour. ***Tuition, nonresident:*** full-time $10,176; part-time $342.35 per credit hour. ***Required fees:*** full-time $1032; $275.10 per credit hour or $516 per term. Full-time tuition and fees vary according to course load. Part-time tuition and fees vary according to course load. ***College room and board:*** $5298; ***Room only:*** $3328. Room and board charges vary according to board plan and housing facility. ***Payment plan:*** Installment.

FRESHMAN FINANCIAL AID (Fall 2009) 2,399 applied for aid; of those 95% were deemed to have need. 100% of freshmen with need received aid; of those 8% had need fully met. ***Average percent of need met:*** 72% (excluding resources awarded to replace EFC). ***Average financial aid package:*** $10,269 (excluding resources awarded to replace EFC). 3% of all full-time freshmen had no need and received non-need-based gift aid.

UNDERGRADUATE FINANCIAL AID (Fall 2009) 9,827 applied for aid; of those 96% were deemed to have need. 100% of undergraduates with need received aid; of those 7% had need fully met. ***Average percent of need met:*** 71% (excluding resources awarded to replace EFC). ***Average financial aid package:*** $10,252 (excluding resources awarded to replace EFC). 3% of all full-time undergraduates had no need and received non-need-based gift aid.

GIFT AID (NEED-BASED) ***Total amount:*** $88,020,049 (61% federal, 29% state, 9% institutional, 1% external sources). ***Receiving aid:*** Freshmen: 83% (2,234); all full-time undergraduates: 77% (9,106). ***Average award:*** Freshmen: $10,441; Undergraduates: $10,877. ***Scholarships, grants, and awards:*** Federal Pell, FSEOG, state, private, college/university gift aid from institutional funds.

GIFT AID (NON-NEED-BASED) ***Total amount:*** $1,358,439 (6% federal, 2% state, 80% institutional, 12% external sources). ***Receiving aid:*** Freshmen: 2% (48). Undergraduates: 1% (117). ***Average award:*** Freshmen: $3537. Undergraduates: $3055. ***Scholarships, grants, and awards by category:*** *Academic interests/achievement:* 1,404 awards ($3,861,764 total): biological sciences, business, communication, computer science, education, engineering/technologies, English, general academic interests/achievements, health fields, mathematics, military science, premedicine, social sciences. *Creative arts/performance:* 108 awards ($95,174 total): art/fine arts, dance, journalism/publications, music, theater/drama. *Special achievements/activities:* 69 awards ($33,404 total): cheerleading/drum major, community service, general special achievements/activities, leadership, memberships. *Special characteristics:* 63 awards ($106,265 total): ethnic background, general special characteristics, international students, local/state students, out-of-state students, veterans. ***Tuition waivers:*** Full or partial for senior citizens.

LOANS ***Student loans:*** $28,971,866 (87% need-based, 13% non-need-based). 60% of past graduating class borrowed through all loan programs. *Average indebtedness per student:* $13,480. ***Average need-based loan:*** Freshmen: $2878. Undergraduates: $4429. ***Parent loans:*** $370,218 (8% need-based, 92% non-need-based). ***Programs:*** Federal Direct (Subsidized and Unsubsidized Stafford, PLUS), Perkins, state, college/university.

WORK-STUDY ***Federal work-study:*** Total amount: $1,911,041; 837 jobs averaging $2283. ***State or other work-study/employment:*** Total amount: $354,494 (100% need-based). 219 part-time jobs averaging $1619.

ATHLETIC AWARDS Total amount: $1,066,470 (37% need-based, 63% non-need-based).

APPLYING FOR FINANCIAL AID ***Required financial aid form:*** FAFSA. ***Financial aid deadline (priority):*** 4/1. ***Notification date:*** Continuous beginning 4/1. Students must reply within 2 weeks of notification.

CONTACT Mrs. Elaine Rivera, Executive Director of Student Financial Services, The University of Texas–Pan American, 1201 West University Drive, Edinburg, TX 78541, 956-665-5372. *Fax:* 956-665-2396. *E-mail:* eriverall@utpa.edu.

THE UNIVERSITY OF TEXAS SOUTHWESTERN MEDICAL CENTER AT DALLAS

Dallas, TX

CONTACT Ms. Lisa J. McGaha, Associate Director of Student Financial Aid, The University of Texas Southwestern Medical Center at Dallas, 5323 Harry Hines Boulevard, Dallas, TX 75390-9064, 214-648-3611. *Fax:* 214-648-3289. *E-mail:* lisa.mcgaha@utsouthwestern.edu.

THE UNIVERSITY OF THE ARTS

Philadelphia, PA

CONTACT Office of Financial Aid, The University of the Arts, 320 South Broad Street, Philadelphia, PA 19102-4944, 800-616-ARTS Ext. 6170 or toll-free 800-616-ARTS. *E-mail:* finaid@uarts.edu.

UNIVERSITY OF THE CUMBERLANDS

Williamsburg, KY

Tuition & fees: $18,000 **Average undergraduate aid package: $18,000**

ABOUT THE INSTITUTION Independent Kentucky Baptist, coed. 42 undergraduate majors. Federal methodology is used as a basis for awarding need-based institutional aid.

UNDERGRADUATE EXPENSES for 2011–12 ***Comprehensive fee:*** $24,826 includes full-time tuition ($17,640), mandatory fees ($360), and room and board ($6826). ***Part-time tuition:*** $8820 per term. ***Part-time fees:*** $570 per credit hour. Part-time tuition and fees vary according to course load. ***Payment plan:*** Installment.

FRESHMAN FINANCIAL AID (Fall 2010, est.) 416 applied for aid; of those 94% were deemed to have need. 100% of freshmen with need received aid; of those 19% had need fully met. ***Average percent of need met:*** 80% (excluding resources awarded to replace EFC). ***Average financial aid package:*** $17,890 (excluding resources awarded to replace EFC). 11% of all full-time freshmen had no need and received non-need-based gift aid.

UNDERGRADUATE FINANCIAL AID (Fall 2010, est.) 1,273 applied for aid; of those 95% were deemed to have need. 100% of undergraduates with need received aid; of those 19% had need fully met. ***Average percent of need met:*** 78% (excluding resources awarded to replace EFC). ***Average financial aid package:*** $18,000 (excluding resources awarded to replace EFC). 12% of all full-time undergraduates had no need and received non-need-based gift aid.

GIFT AID (NEED-BASED) ***Total amount:*** $14,812,711 (26% federal, 21% state, 51% institutional, 2% external sources). ***Receiving aid:*** Freshmen: 88% (392); all full-time undergraduates: 86% (1,196). ***Average award:*** Freshmen: $14,313; Undergraduates: $13,987. ***Scholarships, grants, and awards:*** Federal Pell, FSEOG, state, private, college/university gift aid from institutional funds.

GIFT AID (NON-NEED-BASED) ***Total amount:*** $2,140,313 (11% state, 85% institutional, 4% external sources). ***Receiving aid:*** Freshmen: 12% (53). Undergraduates: 9% (131). ***Average award:*** Freshmen: $8686. Undergraduates: $8521. ***Scholarships, grants, and awards by category:*** *Academic interests/*

achievement: 1,184 awards ($5,923,272 total): general academic interests/achievements. *Creative arts/performance:* 48 awards ($89,777 total): art/fine arts, debating, journalism/publications, music, theater/drama. *Special achievements/activities:* 381 awards ($378,396 total): cheerleading/drum major, community service, leadership, religious involvement. *Special characteristics:* 527 awards ($1,406,259 total): children and siblings of alumni, children of faculty/staff, general special characteristics, local/state students, relatives of clergy, religious affiliation, siblings of current students. ***Tuition waivers:*** Full or partial for employees or children of employees.

LOANS ***Student loans:*** $6,243,939 (80% need-based, 20% non-need-based). 78% of past graduating class borrowed through all loan programs. *Average indebtedness per student:* $15,221. ***Average need-based loan:*** Freshmen: $3315. Undergraduates: $3866. ***Parent loans:*** $957,148 (29% need-based, 71% non-need-based). ***Programs:*** Perkins, college/university.

WORK-STUDY ***Federal work-study:*** Total amount: $1,439,925; 635 jobs averaging $2267. ***State or other work-study/employment:*** Total amount: $27,358 (8% need-based, 92% non-need-based). 13 part-time jobs averaging $2104.

ATHLETIC AWARDS Total amount: $2,652,997 (62% need-based, 38% non-need-based).

APPLYING FOR FINANCIAL AID ***Required financial aid form:*** FAFSA. ***Financial aid deadline (priority):*** 2/15. ***Notification date:*** Continuous beginning 3/15. Students must reply within 2 weeks of notification.

CONTACT Mr. Steve Allen, Vice President of Student Financial Planning, University of the Cumberlands, 6190 College Station Drive, Williamsburg, KY 40769-1372, 606-549-2200 or toll-free 800-343-1609. *Fax:* 606-539-4515. *E-mail:* finplan@ucumberlands.edu.

UNIVERSITY OF THE DISTRICT OF COLUMBIA

Washington, DC

Tuition & fees (DC res): $7000 **Average undergraduate aid package: $5600**

ABOUT THE INSTITUTION District-supported, coed. 81 undergraduate majors. Federal methodology is used as a basis for awarding need-based institutional aid.

UNDERGRADUATE EXPENSES for 2011–12 ***Tuition, state resident:*** full-time $6380; part-time $266 per credit hour. ***Tuition, nonresident:*** full-time $13,380; part-time $558 per credit. ***Required fees:*** full-time $620; $30 per credit. Part-time tuition and fees vary according to course load. ***College room and board:*** $6660. ***Payment plans:*** Installment, deferred payment.

FRESHMAN FINANCIAL AID (Fall 2010, est.) 463 applied for aid; of those 68% were deemed to have need. 100% of freshmen with need received aid; of those 31% had need fully met. ***Average percent of need met:*** 62% (excluding resources awarded to replace EFC). ***Average financial aid package:*** $5250 (excluding resources awarded to replace EFC). 46% of all full-time freshmen had no need and received non-need-based gift aid.

UNDERGRADUATE FINANCIAL AID (Fall 2010, est.) 2,160 applied for aid; of those 91% were deemed to have need. 80% of undergraduates with need received aid; of those 50% had need fully met. ***Average percent of need met:*** 98% (excluding resources awarded to replace EFC). ***Average financial aid package:*** $5600 (excluding resources awarded to replace EFC). 6% of all full-time undergraduates had no need and received non-need-based gift aid.

GIFT AID (NEED-BASED) ***Total amount:*** $513,344 (47% state, 14% institutional, 39% external sources). ***Receiving aid:*** Freshmen: 58% (272); all full-time undergraduates: 40% (935). ***Average award:*** Freshmen: $3275; Undergraduates: $3275. ***Scholarships, grants, and awards:*** Federal Pell, FSEOG, state, college/university gift aid from institutional funds.

GIFT AID (NON-NEED-BASED) ***Total amount:*** $355,523 (41% institutional, 59% external sources). ***Receiving aid:*** Freshmen: 19% (87). Undergraduates: 8% (194). ***Average award:*** Freshmen: $2750. Undergraduates: $2750. ***Scholarships, grants, and awards by category:*** *Academic interests/achievement:* general academic interests/achievements. *Creative arts/performance:* music. *Special characteristics:* children of faculty/staff. ***Tuition waivers:*** Full or partial for employees or children of employees, senior citizens.

LOANS ***Student loans:*** $634,845 (88% need-based, 12% non-need-based). 96% of past graduating class borrowed through all loan programs. ***Average need-based loan:*** Freshmen: $2750. Undergraduates: $2750. ***Parent loans:*** $104,542 (100% need-based). ***Programs:*** Perkins, college/university.

WORK-STUDY ***Federal work-study:*** Total amount: $112,000; jobs available. ***State or other work-study/employment:*** Part-time jobs available.

ATHLETIC AWARDS Total amount: $940,583 (100% need-based).

APPLYING FOR FINANCIAL AID ***Required financial aid forms:*** FAFSA, institution's own form, district aid form. ***Financial aid deadline (priority):*** 3/31. ***Notification date:*** Continuous beginning 4/1. Students must reply within 2 weeks of notification.

CONTACT Ann Marie Waterman, Associate Vice President for Student Affairs, University of the District of Columbia, 4200 Connecticut Avenue NW, Washington, DC 20008-1175, 202-274-6053. *E-mail:* wparker@udc.edu.

UNIVERSITY OF THE INCARNATE WORD

San Antonio, TX

Tuition & fees: $22,790 **Average undergraduate aid package: $17,171**

ABOUT THE INSTITUTION Independent Roman Catholic, coed. 59 undergraduate majors. Federal methodology is used as a basis for awarding need-based institutional aid.

UNDERGRADUATE EXPENSES for 2011–12 ***Comprehensive fee:*** $32,448 includes full-time tuition ($21,900), mandatory fees ($890), and room and board ($9658). ***College room only:*** $5760. Full-time tuition and fees vary according to course load, degree level, location, program, and reciprocity agreements. Room and board charges vary according to board plan and housing facility. ***Part-time tuition:*** $725 per hour. Part-time tuition and fees vary according to course load, degree level, location, program, and reciprocity agreements. ***Payment plan:*** Installment.

FRESHMAN FINANCIAL AID (Fall 2009) 646 applied for aid; of those 90% were deemed to have need. 100% of freshmen with need received aid; of those 33% had need fully met. ***Average percent of need met:*** 76% (excluding resources awarded to replace EFC). ***Average financial aid package:*** $18,192 (excluding resources awarded to replace EFC). 9% of all full-time freshmen had no need and received non-need-based gift aid.

UNDERGRADUATE FINANCIAL AID (Fall 2009) 2,820 applied for aid; of those 93% were deemed to have need. 100% of undergraduates with need received aid; of those 27% had need fully met. ***Average percent of need met:*** 68% (excluding resources awarded to replace EFC). ***Average financial aid package:*** $17,171 (excluding resources awarded to replace EFC). 5% of all full-time undergraduates had no need and received non-need-based gift aid.

GIFT AID (NEED-BASED) ***Total amount:*** $25,894,227 (37% federal, 19% state, 43% institutional, 1% external sources). ***Receiving aid:*** Freshmen: 80% (577); all full-time undergraduates: 76% (2,572). ***Average award:*** Freshmen: $13,062; Undergraduates: $11,344. ***Scholarships, grants, and awards:*** Federal Pell, FSEOG, state, private, college/university gift aid from institutional funds, United Negro College Fund, Federal Nursing.

GIFT AID (NON-NEED-BASED) ***Total amount:*** $8,114,818 (87% institutional, 13% external sources). ***Receiving aid:*** Freshmen: 80% (575). Undergraduates: 74% (2,503). ***Average award:*** Freshmen: $8003. Undergraduates: $6698. ***Scholarships, grants, and awards by category:*** *Academic interests/achievement:* general academic interests/achievements. *Creative arts/performance:* art/fine arts, music, theater/drama. *Special achievements/activities:* leadership, religious involvement. *Special characteristics:* children and siblings of alumni, children of faculty/staff. ***Tuition waivers:*** Full or partial for employees or children of employees, senior citizens.

LOANS ***Student loans:*** $33,286,949 (69% need-based, 31% non-need-based). ***Average need-based loan:*** Freshmen: $3153. Undergraduates: $4427. ***Parent loans:*** $3,661,865 (96% need-based, 4% non-need-based). ***Programs:*** Federal Direct (Subsidized and Unsubsidized Stafford, PLUS), Perkins, Federal Nursing, state, alternative loans.

WORK-STUDY ***Federal work-study:*** Total amount: $706,109; jobs available. ***State or other work-study/employment:*** Total amount: $45,691 (100% need-based). Part-time jobs available.

ATHLETIC AWARDS Total amount: $2,369,733 (77% need-based, 23% non-need-based).

APPLYING FOR FINANCIAL AID ***Required financial aid form:*** FAFSA. ***Financial aid deadline (priority):*** 4/1. ***Notification date:*** Continuous beginning 2/15. Students must reply within 2 weeks of notification.

CONTACT Amy Carcanagues, Director of Financial Assistance, University of the Incarnate Word, 4301 Broadway, San Antonio, TX 78209, 210-829-6008 or toll-free 800-749-WORD. *Fax:* 210-283-5053. *E-mail:* finaid@uiwtx.edu.

UNIVERSITY OF THE OZARKS

Clarksville, AR

Tuition & fees: $22,050 **Average undergraduate aid package: $21,842**

ABOUT THE INSTITUTION Independent Presbyterian, coed. 30 undergraduate majors. Federal methodology is used as a basis for awarding need-based institutional aid.

UNDERGRADUATE EXPENSES for 2011–12 ***Comprehensive fee:*** $28,550 includes full-time tuition ($21,450), mandatory fees ($600), and room and board ($6500). ***College room only:*** $3000. Room and board charges vary according to board plan and housing facility. ***Part-time tuition:*** $900 per credit hour. ***Payment plan:*** Installment.

FRESHMAN FINANCIAL AID (Fall 2010, est.) 183 applied for aid; of those 95% were deemed to have need. 99% of freshmen with need received aid; of those 26% had need fully met. ***Average percent of need met:*** 84% (excluding resources awarded to replace EFC). ***Average financial aid package:*** $22,655 (excluding resources awarded to replace EFC). 15% of all full-time freshmen had no need and received non-need-based gift aid.

UNDERGRADUATE FINANCIAL AID (Fall 2010, est.) 445 applied for aid; of those 94% were deemed to have need. 100% of undergraduates with need received aid; of those 24% had need fully met. ***Average percent of need met:*** 81% (excluding resources awarded to replace EFC). ***Average financial aid package:*** $21,842 (excluding resources awarded to replace EFC). 26% of all full-time undergraduates had no need and received non-need-based gift aid.

GIFT AID (NEED-BASED) ***Total amount:*** $6,932,832 (20% federal, 17% state, 61% institutional, 2% external sources). ***Receiving aid:*** Freshmen: 84% (171); all full-time undergraduates: 67% (411). ***Average award:*** Freshmen: $17,799; Undergraduates: $16,562. ***Scholarships, grants, and awards:*** Federal Pell, FSEOG, state, private, college/university gift aid from institutional funds, United Negro College Fund, Federal Nursing.

GIFT AID (NON-NEED-BASED) ***Total amount:*** $3,119,282 (1% state, 98% institutional, 1% external sources). ***Average award:*** Freshmen: $22,320. Undergraduates: $20,299. ***Scholarships, grants, and awards by category:*** *Academic interests/achievement:* biological sciences, business, communication, education, English, general academic interests/achievements, humanities, mathematics, premedicine, religion/biblical studies, social sciences. *Creative arts/performance:* art/fine arts, music, theater/drama. *Special achievements/activities:* leadership. *Special characteristics:* children and siblings of alumni, children of faculty/staff, ethnic background, general special characteristics, international students, members of minority groups, relatives of clergy, religious affiliation, siblings of current students. ***Tuition waivers:*** Full or partial for children of alumni, employees or children of employees.

LOANS ***Student loans:*** $2,787,596 (98% need-based, 2% non-need-based). 50% of past graduating class borrowed through all loan programs. *Average indebtedness per student:* $21,520. ***Average need-based loan:*** Freshmen: $8848. Undergraduates: $9752. ***Parent loans:*** $452,176 (95% need-based, 5% non-need-based). ***Programs:*** Federal Direct (Subsidized and Unsubsidized Stafford, PLUS), Perkins, college/university.

WORK-STUDY ***Federal work-study:*** Total amount: $142,907; jobs available. ***State or other work-study/employment:*** Total amount: $48,346 (31% need-based, 69% non-need-based). Part-time jobs available.

APPLYING FOR FINANCIAL AID ***Required financial aid form:*** FAFSA. ***Financial aid deadline (priority):*** 2/15. ***Notification date:*** Continuous beginning 3/1. Students must reply within 2 weeks of notification.

CONTACT Ms. Jana D. Hart, Director of Financial Aid, University of the Ozarks, 415 North College Avenue, Clarksville, AR 72830-2880, 479-979-1221 or toll-free 800-264-8636. *Fax:* 479-979-1417. *E-mail:* jhart@ozarks.edu.

UNIVERSITY OF THE PACIFIC

Stockton, CA

Tuition & fees: $34,100 **Average undergraduate aid package: $30,458**

ABOUT THE INSTITUTION Independent, coed. 54 undergraduate majors. Federal methodology is used as a basis for awarding need-based institutional aid.

UNDERGRADUATE EXPENSES for 2010–11 ***Comprehensive fee:*** $45,242 includes full-time tuition ($33,600), mandatory fees ($500), and room and board ($11,142). Room and board charges vary according to board plan and housing facility. Part-time tuition and fees vary according to course load. ***Payment plan:*** Deferred payment.

FRESHMAN FINANCIAL AID (Fall 2010, est.) 884 applied for aid; of those 89% were deemed to have need. 100% of freshmen with need received aid; of those 19% had need fully met. ***Average financial aid package:*** $28,223 (excluding resources awarded to replace EFC). 13% of all full-time freshmen had no need and received non-need-based gift aid.

UNDERGRADUATE FINANCIAL AID (Fall 2010, est.) 2,959 applied for aid; of those 92% were deemed to have need. 100% of undergraduates with need received aid; of those 16% had need fully met. ***Average financial aid package:*** $30,458 (excluding resources awarded to replace EFC). 11% of all full-time undergraduates had no need and received non-need-based gift aid.

GIFT AID (NEED-BASED) ***Total amount:*** $59,632,704 (15% federal, 20% state, 65% institutional). ***Receiving aid:*** Freshmen: 76% (763); all full-time undergraduates: 71% (2,617). ***Average award:*** Freshmen: $21,652; Undergraduates: $22,530. ***Scholarships, grants, and awards:*** Federal Pell, FSEOG, state, private, college/university gift aid from institutional funds.

GIFT AID (NON-NEED-BASED) ***Total amount:*** $3,786,854 (100% institutional). ***Average award:*** Freshmen: $8873. Undergraduates: $9224. ***Scholarships, grants, and awards by category:*** *Academic interests/achievement:* general academic interests/achievements. *Creative arts/performance:* art/fine arts, debating, music. *Special achievements/activities:* religious involvement. ***Tuition waivers:*** Full or partial for employees or children of employees.

LOANS ***Student loans:*** $21,084,580 (96% need-based, 4% non-need-based). ***Average need-based loan:*** Freshmen: $6519. Undergraduates: $7702. ***Parent loans:*** $14,831,751 (77% need-based, 23% non-need-based). ***Programs:*** Federal Direct (Subsidized and Unsubsidized Stafford, PLUS), Perkins, state.

WORK-STUDY ***Federal work-study:*** Total amount: $5,376,017; jobs available.

ATHLETIC AWARDS Total amount: $5,658,124 (44% need-based, 56% non-need-based).

APPLYING FOR FINANCIAL AID ***Required financial aid form:*** FAFSA. ***Financial aid deadline (priority):*** 2/15. ***Notification date:*** Continuous beginning 3/15.

CONTACT Lynn Fox, Director of Financial Aid, University of the Pacific, 3601 Pacific Avenue, Stockton, CA 95211-0197, 209-946-2421 or toll-free 800-959-2867.

UNIVERSITY OF THE SACRED HEART

San Juan, PR

CONTACT Ms. Maria Torres, Director of Financial Aid, University of the Sacred Heart, PO Box 12383, San Juan, PR 00914-0383, 787-728-1515 Ext. 3605.

UNIVERSITY OF THE SCIENCES IN PHILADELPHIA

Philadelphia, PA

Tuition & fees: $30,794 **Average undergraduate aid package: $32,647**

ABOUT THE INSTITUTION Independent, coed. 21 undergraduate majors. Federal methodology is used as a basis for awarding need-based institutional aid.

UNDERGRADUATE EXPENSES for 2010–11 ***Comprehensive fee:*** $42,828 includes full-time tuition ($29,290), mandatory fees ($1504), and room and board ($12,034). Full-time tuition and fees vary according to program. Room and board charges vary according to board plan. ***Part-time tuition:*** $1220 per credit hour. Part-time tuition and fees vary according to course load and program. ***Payment plans:*** Tuition prepayment, installment.

FRESHMAN FINANCIAL AID (Fall 2009) 475 applied for aid; of those 93% were deemed to have need. 100% of freshmen with need received aid; of those 56% had need fully met. ***Average percent of need met:*** 60% (excluding resources awarded to replace EFC). ***Average financial aid package:*** $33,328 (excluding resources awarded to replace EFC). 14% of all full-time freshmen had no need and received non-need-based gift aid.

UNDERGRADUATE FINANCIAL AID (Fall 2009) 2,227 applied for aid; of those 93% were deemed to have need. 100% of undergraduates with need received aid; of those 45% had need fully met. ***Average percent of need met:*** 88% (excluding resources awarded to replace EFC). ***Average financial aid package:*** $32,647 (excluding resources awarded to replace EFC). 19% of all full-time undergraduates had no need and received non-need-based gift aid.

GIFT AID (NEED-BASED) ***Total amount:*** $7,230,772 (33% federal, 23% state, 44% institutional). ***Receiving aid:*** Freshmen: 68% (356); all full-time undergraduates: 44% (1,132). ***Average award:*** Freshmen: $8582; Undergraduates: $7155. ***Scholarships, grants, and awards:*** Federal Pell, FSEOG, state, private, college/university gift aid from institutional funds, Academic Competitiveness Grants, National SMART Grants.

GIFT AID (NON-NEED-BASED) ***Total amount:*** $18,699,703 (96% institutional, 4% external sources). ***Receiving aid:*** Freshmen: 83% (431). Undergraduates: 79% (2,023). ***Average award:*** Freshmen: $8451. Undergraduates: $8328. ***Scholarships, grants, and awards by category:*** *Academic interests/achievement:* general academic interests/achievements. ***Tuition waivers:*** Full or partial for employees or children of employees.

LOANS ***Student loans:*** $42,141,448 (25% need-based, 75% non-need-based). 83% of past graduating class borrowed through all loan programs. *Average indebtedness per student:* $12,005. ***Average need-based loan:*** Freshmen: $3763. Undergraduates: $5576. ***Parent loans:*** $4,209,062 (100% non-need-based). ***Programs:*** Federal Direct (Subsidized and Unsubsidized Stafford, PLUS), Perkins, college/university.

WORK-STUDY ***Federal work-study:*** Total amount: $878,456; jobs available. ***State or other work-study/employment:*** Part-time jobs available.

ATHLETIC AWARDS Total amount: $1,027,096 (100% non-need-based).

APPLYING FOR FINANCIAL AID ***Required financial aid form:*** FAFSA. ***Financial aid deadline (priority):*** 3/15. ***Notification date:*** Continuous beginning 1/15. Students must reply by 5/1 or within 2 weeks of notification.

CONTACT Ms. Paula Lehrberger, Director of Financial Aid, University of the Sciences in Philadelphia, 600 South 43rd Street, Philadelphia, PA 19104, 215-596-8894 or toll-free 888-996-8747 (in-state). *Fax:* 215-596-8554.

UNIVERSITY OF THE SOUTHWEST

Hobbs, NM

Tuition & fees: $11,689 **Average undergraduate aid package: $5460**

ABOUT THE INSTITUTION Independent religious, coed. 16 undergraduate majors. Both federal and institutional methodology are used as a basis for awarding need-based institutional aid.

UNDERGRADUATE EXPENSES for 2011–12 ***One-time required fee:*** $300. ***Comprehensive fee:*** $18,219 includes full-time tuition ($11,664), mandatory fees ($25), and room and board ($6530). ***College room only:*** $3370. Full-time tuition and fees vary according to course load. Room and board charges vary according to housing facility. ***Part-time tuition:*** $486 per semester hour. Part-time tuition and fees vary according to course load. ***Payment plan:*** Deferred payment.

FRESHMAN FINANCIAL AID (Fall 2010, est.) 49 applied for aid; of those 86% were deemed to have need. 100% of freshmen with need received aid; of those 19% had need fully met. ***Average percent of need met:*** 70% (excluding resources awarded to replace EFC). ***Average financial aid package:*** $12,681 (excluding resources awarded to replace EFC). 12% of all full-time freshmen had no need and received non-need-based gift aid.

UNDERGRADUATE FINANCIAL AID (Fall 2010, est.) 306 applied for aid; of those 87% were deemed to have need. 100% of undergraduates with need received aid; of those 15% had need fully met. ***Average percent of need met:*** 70% (excluding resources awarded to replace EFC). ***Average financial aid package:*** $5460 (excluding resources awarded to replace EFC). 6% of all full-time undergraduates had no need and received non-need-based gift aid.

GIFT AID (NEED-BASED) ***Total amount:*** $1,101,181 (68% federal, 32% state). ***Receiving aid:*** Freshmen: 80% (39); all full-time undergraduates: 79% (244). ***Average award:*** Freshmen: $5575; Undergraduates: $4557. ***Scholarships, grants, and awards:*** Federal Pell, FSEOG, state, private, college/university gift aid from institutional funds.

GIFT AID (NON-NEED-BASED) ***Total amount:*** $409,703 (26% federal, 71% institutional, 3% external sources). ***Receiving aid:*** Freshmen: 76% (37). Undergraduates: 59% (181). ***Average award:*** Freshmen: $1549. Undergraduates: $1240. ***Scholarships, grants, and awards by category:*** *Academic interests/achievement:* 158 awards ($290,743 total): biological sciences, business, education, English, general academic interests/achievements, humanities, mathematics, physical sciences, premedicine, religion/biblical studies, social sciences. *Creative arts/performance:* 2 awards ($3000 total): debating, music. *Special achievements/activities:* 169 awards ($110,581 total): general special achievements/activities, leadership. *Special characteristics:* 3 awards ($23,523 total): children of faculty/staff. ***Tuition waivers:*** Full or partial for employees or children of employees.

LOANS ***Student loans:*** $2,160,838 (44% need-based, 56% non-need-based). 69% of past graduating class borrowed through all loan programs. *Average indebtedness per student:* $19,645. ***Average need-based loan:*** Freshmen: $3316. Undergraduates: $4140. ***Parent loans:*** $148,257 (100% non-need-based). ***Programs:*** Federal Direct (Subsidized and Unsubsidized Stafford, PLUS).

WORK-STUDY ***Federal work-study:*** Total amount: $28,282; 26 jobs averaging $1035. ***State or other work-study/employment:*** Total amount: $36,100 (100% need-based). 12 part-time jobs averaging $3008.

ATHLETIC AWARDS Total amount: $470,476 (100% non-need-based).

APPLYING FOR FINANCIAL AID ***Required financial aid forms:*** FAFSA, institution's own form. ***Financial aid deadline:*** Continuous. ***Notification date:*** Continuous beginning 4/15. Students must reply within 2 weeks of notification.

CONTACT Kerrie Mitchell, Director of Financial Aid, University of the Southwest, 6610 North Lovington Highway, Hobbs, NM 88240-9129, 575-492-2114 or toll-free 800-530-4400. *Fax:* 575-392-6006. *E-mail:* kmitchell@usw.edu.

UNIVERSITY OF THE VIRGIN ISLANDS

Saint Thomas, VI

CONTACT Mavis M. Gilchrist, Director of Financial Aid, University of the Virgin Islands, RR #2, Box 10,000, Kingshill, St. Thomas, VI 00850, 340-692-4186. *Fax:* 340-692-4145. *E-mail:* mgilchr@uvi.edu.

UNIVERSITY OF THE WEST

Rosemead, CA

CONTACT Jamie Johnston, Financial Aid Officer, University of the West, 1409 Walnut Grove Avenue, Rosemead, CA 91770, 626-571-8811 Ext. 122. *Fax:* 626-571-1413. *E-mail:* jamiej@uwest.edu.

THE UNIVERSITY OF TOLEDO

Toledo, OH

Tuition & fees (OH res): $8491 **Average undergraduate aid package: $10,372**

ABOUT THE INSTITUTION State-supported, coed. 172 undergraduate majors. Federal methodology is used as a basis for awarding need-based institutional aid.

UNDERGRADUATE EXPENSES for 2011–12 ***Tuition, state resident:*** full-time $7301; part-time $304.21 per semester hour. ***Tuition, nonresident:*** full-time $16,241; part-time $684.21 per semester hour. ***Required fees:*** full-time $1190; $49.60 per semester hour. Full-time tuition and fees vary according to course load, program, and reciprocity agreements. Part-time tuition and fees vary according to course load, program, and reciprocity agreements. ***College room and board:*** $9708; ***Room only:*** $6478. Room and board charges vary according to board plan and housing facility. ***Payment plan:*** Installment.

FRESHMAN FINANCIAL AID (Fall 2010, est.) 3,596 applied for aid; of those 86% were deemed to have need. 100% of freshmen with need received aid; of those 14% had need fully met. ***Average percent of need met:*** 65% (excluding resources awarded to replace EFC). ***Average financial aid package:*** $11,006 (excluding resources awarded to replace EFC). 17% of all full-time freshmen had no need and received non-need-based gift aid.

UNDERGRADUATE FINANCIAL AID (Fall 2010, est.) 12,343 applied for aid; of those 86% were deemed to have need. 99% of undergraduates with need received aid; of those 12% had need fully met. ***Average percent of need met:*** 58% (excluding resources awarded to replace EFC). ***Average financial aid package:*** $10,372 (excluding resources awarded to replace EFC). 18% of all full-time undergraduates had no need and received non-need-based gift aid.

GIFT AID (NEED-BASED) ***Total amount:*** $74,581,577 (50% federal, 8% state, 39% institutional, 3% external sources). ***Receiving aid:*** Freshmen: 80% (3,051); all full-time undergraduates: 64% (9,544). ***Average award:*** Freshmen: $8377; Undergraduates: $7654. ***Scholarships, grants, and awards:*** Federal Pell, FSEOG, state, private, college/university gift aid from institutional funds, Academic Competitiveness Grants, National SMART Grants, TEACH Grants.

GIFT AID (NON-NEED-BASED) ***Total amount:*** $17,671,717 (3% federal, 4% state, 81% institutional, 12% external sources). ***Average award:*** Freshmen: $4781. Undergraduates: $5118. ***Scholarships, grants, and awards by category:*** *Academic interests/achievement:* biological sciences, business, communication, education, engineering/technologies, English, foreign languages, general academic interests/achievements, health fields, humanities, international studies, library science, mathematics, physical sciences, premedicine, social sciences. *Creative arts/performance:* art/fine arts, general creative arts/performance, music, performing arts, theater/drama. *Special achievements/activities:* cheerleading/drum major, general special achievements/activities, hobbies/interests, leadership, memberships, religious involvement. *Special characteristics:* adult students, children and siblings of alumni, children of faculty/staff, children of public servants, children of union members/company employees, ethnic background, general special characteristics, handicapped students, international students, members of minority groups, previous college experience, public servants, religious affiliation, veterans, veterans' children. ***Tuition waivers:*** Full or partial for children of alumni, employees or children of employees.

LOANS ***Student loans:*** $89,461,749 (90% need-based, 10% non-need-based). 73% of past graduating class borrowed through all loan programs. *Average indebtedness per student:* $27,378. ***Average need-based loan:*** Freshmen: $3485. Undergraduates: $4087. ***Parent loans:*** $20,218,071 (86% need-based, 14% non-need-based). ***Programs:*** Federal Direct (Subsidized and Unsubsidized Stafford, PLUS), Perkins, alternative loans.

WORK-STUDY ***Federal work-study:*** Total amount: $1,481,200; 429 jobs averaging $2146.

ATHLETIC AWARDS Total amount: $5,551,062 (52% need-based, 48% non-need-based).

APPLYING FOR FINANCIAL AID ***Required financial aid form:*** FAFSA. ***Financial aid deadline (priority):*** 4/1. ***Notification date:*** Continuous beginning 4/1. Students must reply within 4 weeks of notification.

CONTACT Carolyn Baumgartner, Director, The University of Toledo, 2801 West Bancroft Street, MS-314, Toledo, OH 43606, 419-530-5812 or toll-free 800-5TOLEDO (in-state). *Fax:* 419-530-5835. *E-mail:* cbaumga@utnet.utoledo.edu.

UNIVERSITY OF TULSA

Tulsa, OK

Tuition & fees: $28,310 **Average undergraduate aid package: $26,822**

ABOUT THE INSTITUTION Independent, coed. 63 undergraduate majors. Federal methodology is used as a basis for awarding need-based institutional aid.

UNDERGRADUATE EXPENSES for 2010–11 ***One-time required fee:*** $425. ***Comprehensive fee:*** $37,328 includes full-time tuition ($28,060), mandatory fees ($250), and room and board ($9018). ***College room only:*** $5010. Full-time tuition and fees vary according to course load. Room and board charges vary according to board plan and housing facility. ***Part-time tuition:*** $1007 per credit. Part-time tuition and fees vary according to course load. ***Payment plans:*** Tuition prepayment, installment.

FRESHMAN FINANCIAL AID (Fall 2010, est.) 621 applied for aid; of those 56% were deemed to have need. 100% of freshmen with need received aid; of those 49% had need fully met. ***Average percent of need met:*** 85% (excluding resources awarded to replace EFC). ***Average financial aid package:*** $28,014 (excluding resources awarded to replace EFC). 37% of all full-time freshmen had no need and received non-need-based gift aid.

UNDERGRADUATE FINANCIAL AID (Fall 2010, est.) 2,604 applied for aid; of those 48% were deemed to have need. 100% of undergraduates with need received aid; of those 49% had need fully met. ***Average percent of need met:*** 84% (excluding resources awarded to replace EFC). ***Average financial aid package:*** $26,822 (excluding resources awarded to replace EFC). 38% of all full-time undergraduates had no need and received non-need-based gift aid.

GIFT AID (NEED-BASED) ***Total amount:*** $4,004,703 (70% federal, 18% state, 12% institutional). ***Receiving aid:*** Freshmen: 24% (156); all full-time undergraduates: 21% (610). ***Average award:*** Freshmen: $7398; Undergraduates: $6433. ***Scholarships, grants, and awards:*** Federal Pell, FSEOG, state, private, college/university gift aid from institutional funds.

GIFT AID (NON-NEED-BASED) ***Total amount:*** $30,272,866 (1% federal, 7% state, 87% institutional, 5% external sources). ***Receiving aid:*** Freshmen: 52% (344). Undergraduates: 40% (1,175). ***Average award:*** Freshmen: $14,040. Undergraduates: $14,777. ***Scholarships, grants, and awards by category:*** *Academic interests/achievement:* biological sciences, business, communication, computer science, education, engineering/technologies, English, foreign languages, general academic interests/achievements, health fields, international studies, mathematics, physical sciences, premedicine, religion/biblical studies, social sciences. *Creative arts/performance:* art/fine arts, music, performing arts, theater/drama. *Special achievements/activities:* cheerleading/drum major, community service, leadership. *Special characteristics:* children and siblings of alumni, children of faculty/staff, relatives of clergy, religious affiliation, siblings of current students. ***Tuition waivers:*** Full or partial for employees or children of employees.

LOANS ***Student loans:*** $9,730,090 (42% need-based, 58% non-need-based). ***Average need-based loan:*** Freshmen: $4425. Undergraduates: $5171. ***Parent loans:*** $3,590,636 (100% non-need-based). ***Programs:*** Federal Direct (Subsidized and Unsubsidized Stafford, PLUS), Perkins.

WORK-STUDY ***Federal work-study:*** Total amount: $1,951,765; jobs available. ***State or other work-study/employment:*** Total amount: $3200 (100% non-need-based). Part-time jobs available.

ATHLETIC AWARDS Total amount: $9,107,594 (100% non-need-based).

APPLYING FOR FINANCIAL AID ***Required financial aid forms:*** FAFSA, institution's own form. ***Financial aid deadline (priority):*** 4/1. ***Notification date:*** Continuous. Students must reply by 5/1 or within 2 weeks of notification.

CONTACT Ms. Vicki Hendrickson, Director of Student Financial Services, University of Tulsa, 600 South College, Tulsa, OK 74104, 918-631-2526 or toll-free 800-331-3050. *Fax:* 918-631-5105. *E-mail:* vicki-hendrickson@utulsa.edu.

UNIVERSITY OF UTAH

Salt Lake City, UT

Tuition & fees (UT res): $6274 **Average undergraduate aid package: $11,665**

ABOUT THE INSTITUTION State-supported, coed. 98 undergraduate majors. Federal methodology is used as a basis for awarding need-based institutional aid.

UNDERGRADUATE EXPENSES for 2010–11 ***Tuition, state resident:*** full-time $5427; part-time $152.45 per credit hour. ***Tuition, nonresident:*** full-time $18,994; part-time $524.13 per credit hour. ***Required fees:*** full-time $847. Full-time tuition and fees vary according to course level, course load, degree level, program, and student level. Part-time tuition and fees vary according to course level, course load, degree level, program, and student level. ***College room and board:*** $6240; ***Room only:*** $3096. Room and board charges vary according to board plan and housing facility. ***Payment plans:*** Installment, deferred payment.

FRESHMAN FINANCIAL AID (Fall 2010, est.) 1,326 applied for aid; of those 77% were deemed to have need. 98% of freshmen with need received aid; of those 20% had need fully met. ***Average percent of need met:*** 59% (excluding resources awarded to replace EFC). ***Average financial aid package:*** $11,068 (excluding resources awarded to replace EFC). 8% of all full-time freshmen had no need and received non-need-based gift aid.

UNDERGRADUATE FINANCIAL AID (Fall 2010, est.) 7,767 applied for aid; of those 90% were deemed to have need. 99% of undergraduates with need received aid; of those 12% had need fully met. ***Average percent of need met:*** 63% (excluding resources awarded to replace EFC). ***Average financial aid package:*** $11,665 (excluding resources awarded to replace EFC). 5% of all full-time undergraduates had no need and received non-need-based gift aid.

GIFT AID (NEED-BASED) ***Total amount:*** $38,345,967 (81% federal, 2% state, 6% institutional, 11% external sources). ***Receiving aid:*** Freshmen: 32% (818); all full-time undergraduates: 34% (5,490). ***Average award:*** Freshmen: $6462; Undergraduates: $5633. ***Scholarships, grants, and awards:*** Federal Pell, FSEOG, state, private, college/university gift aid from institutional funds, Federal Nursing, Academic Competitiveness Grants, National SMART Grants, TEACH Grants.

GIFT AID (NON-NEED-BASED) ***Total amount:*** $3,991,197 (6% institutional, 94% external sources). ***Receiving aid:*** Freshmen: 2% (48). Undergraduates: 1% (110). ***Average award:*** Freshmen: $6553. Undergraduates: $5012. ***Scholarships, grants, and awards by category:*** *Academic interests/achievement:* architecture, area/ethnic studies, biological sciences, business, communication, computer science, education, engineering/technologies, English, foreign languages, general academic interests/achievements, health fields, humanities, international studies, mathematics, military science, physical sciences, social sciences. *Creative arts/performance:* art/fine arts, cinema/film/broadcasting, creative writing, dance, journalism/publications, music, performing arts, theater/drama. *Special achievements/activities:* cheerleading/drum major, general special achievements/activities, leadership. *Special characteristics:* children of faculty/staff, children of public servants, children with a deceased or disabled parent, ethnic background, first-generation college students, handicapped students, out-of-state students, spouses of deceased or disabled public servants. ***Tuition waivers:*** Full or partial for children of alumni, employees or children of employees, senior citizens.

LOANS ***Student loans:*** $56,521,602 (58% need-based, 42% non-need-based). 42% of past graduating class borrowed through all loan programs. *Average*

indebtedness per student: $17,343. ***Average need-based loan:*** Freshmen: $3312. Undergraduates: $4503. ***Parent loans:*** $1,693,864 (43% need-based, 57% non-need-based). ***Programs:*** Federal Direct (Subsidized and Unsubsidized Stafford, PLUS), Perkins, Federal Nursing, college/university, private loans.

WORK-STUDY ***Federal work-study:*** Total amount: $2,848,845; jobs available.

ATHLETIC AWARDS Total amount: $6,538,768 (24% need-based, 76% non-need-based).

APPLYING FOR FINANCIAL AID ***Required financial aid forms:*** FAFSA, institution's own form. ***Financial aid deadline (priority):*** 3/15. ***Notification date:*** Continuous beginning 4/15. Students must reply within 6 weeks of notification.

CONTACT Amy Capps, Assistant Director, University of Utah, 201 South 1460 East, Room 105, Salt Lake City, UT 84112-9055, 801-581-6211 or toll-free 800-444-8638. *Fax:* 801-585-6350. *E-mail:* fawin1@saff.utah.edu.

UNIVERSITY OF VERMONT

Burlington, VT

Tuition & fees (VT res): $14,036   Average undergraduate aid package: $18,364

ABOUT THE INSTITUTION State-supported, coed. 100 undergraduate majors. Federal methodology is used as a basis for awarding need-based institutional aid.

UNDERGRADUATE EXPENSES for 2010–11 ***Tuition, state resident:*** full-time $12,180; part-time $508 per credit hour. ***Tuition, nonresident:*** full-time $30,744; part-time $1281 per credit hour. ***Required fees:*** full-time $1856. Part-time tuition and fees vary according to course load. ***College room and board:*** $9382; ***Room only:*** $6196. Room and board charges vary according to board plan and housing facility. ***Payment plans:*** Installment, deferred payment.

FRESHMAN FINANCIAL AID (Fall 2009) 2,060 applied for aid; of those 80% were deemed to have need. 100% of freshmen with need received aid; of those 18% had need fully met. ***Average percent of need met:*** 76% (excluding resources awarded to replace EFC). ***Average financial aid package:*** $20,894 (excluding resources awarded to replace EFC). 20% of all full-time freshmen had no need and received non-need-based gift aid.

UNDERGRADUATE FINANCIAL AID (Fall 2009) 7,084 applied for aid; of those 83% were deemed to have need. 99% of undergraduates with need received aid; of those 20% had need fully met. ***Average percent of need met:*** 71% (excluding resources awarded to replace EFC). ***Average financial aid package:*** $18,364 (excluding resources awarded to replace EFC). 18% of all full-time undergraduates had no need and received non-need-based gift aid.

GIFT AID (NEED-BASED) ***Total amount:*** $82,772,887 (15% federal, 7% state, 75% institutional, 3% external sources). ***Receiving aid:*** Freshmen: 52% (1,364); all full-time undergraduates: 50% (5,022). ***Average award:*** Freshmen: $17,767; Undergraduates: $14,576. ***Scholarships, grants, and awards:*** Federal Pell, FSEOG, state, private, college/university gift aid from institutional funds, Federal Nursing.

GIFT AID (NON-NEED-BASED) ***Total amount:*** $6,252,809 (79% institutional, 21% external sources). ***Receiving aid:*** Freshmen: 3% (72). Undergraduates: 2% (241). ***Average award:*** Freshmen: $2393. Undergraduates: $2426. ***Scholarships, grants, and awards by category:*** *Academic interests/achievement:* 5,300 awards ($12,678,087 total): agriculture, area/ethnic studies, business, computer science, education, engineering/technologies, English, foreign languages, general academic interests/achievements, health fields, home economics, humanities, international studies, mathematics, military science, physical sciences, premedicine, social sciences. *Creative arts/performance:* 15 awards ($11,277 total): debating, music, theater/drama. *Special achievements/activities:* 86 awards ($363,662 total): community service, leadership, memberships. *Special characteristics:* 159 awards ($578,035 total): adult students, ethnic background, first-generation college students. ***Tuition waivers:*** Full or partial for employees or children of employees, senior citizens.

LOANS ***Student loans:*** $45,295,354 (44% need-based, 56% non-need-based). 63% of past graduating class borrowed through all loan programs. *Average indebtedness per student:* $27,696. ***Average need-based loan:*** Freshmen: $5338. Undergraduates: $6413. ***Parent loans:*** $49,699,009 (100% non-need-based). ***Programs:*** Federal Direct (Subsidized and Unsubsidized Stafford, PLUS), Perkins, Federal Nursing, state, college/university.

WORK-STUDY ***Federal work-study:*** Total amount: $3,563,489; 2,437 jobs averaging $1462.

ATHLETIC AWARDS Total amount: $4,915,996 (25% need-based, 75% non-need-based).

APPLYING FOR FINANCIAL AID ***Required financial aid form:*** FAFSA. ***Financial aid deadline (priority):*** 2/10. ***Notification date:*** Continuous beginning 3/30. Students must reply within 4 weeks of notification.

CONTACT Office of Student Financial Services, University of Vermont, 221 Waterman Building, Burlington, VT 05405-0160, 802-656-5700. *Fax:* 802-656-4076. *E-mail:* sfs@uvm.edu.

UNIVERSITY OF VIRGINIA

Charlottesville, VA

Tuition & fees (VA res): $10,628   Average undergraduate aid package: $21,215

ABOUT THE INSTITUTION State-supported, coed. 47 undergraduate majors. Federal methodology is used as a basis for awarding need-based institutional aid.

UNDERGRADUATE EXPENSES for 2010–11 ***Tuition, state resident:*** full-time $8356; part-time $278 per credit hour. ***Tuition, nonresident:*** full-time $30,630; part-time $1022 per credit hour. ***Required fees:*** full-time $2272; $2272 per year. ***College room and board:*** $8652; ***Room only:*** $4732. Room and board charges vary according to board plan and housing facility. ***Payment plan:*** Installment.

FRESHMAN FINANCIAL AID (Fall 2010, est.) 2,311 applied for aid; of those 50% were deemed to have need. 100% of freshmen with need received aid; of those 100% had need fully met. ***Average percent of need met:*** 100% (excluding resources awarded to replace EFC). ***Average financial aid package:*** $21,218 (excluding resources awarded to replace EFC). 9% of all full-time freshmen had no need and received non-need-based gift aid.

UNDERGRADUATE FINANCIAL AID (Fall 2010, est.) 7,886 applied for aid; of those 56% were deemed to have need. 100% of undergraduates with need received aid; of those 100% had need fully met. ***Average percent of need met:*** 100% (excluding resources awarded to replace EFC). ***Average financial aid package:*** $21,215 (excluding resources awarded to replace EFC). 10% of all full-time undergraduates had no need and received non-need-based gift aid.

GIFT AID (NEED-BASED) ***Total amount:*** $61,122,620 (15% federal, 10% state, 67% institutional, 8% external sources). ***Receiving aid:*** Freshmen: 31% (994); all full-time undergraduates: 28% (3,835). ***Average award:*** Freshmen: $15,923; Undergraduates: $16,488. ***Scholarships, grants, and awards:*** Federal Pell, FSEOG, state, private, college/university gift aid from institutional funds, Federal Nursing.

GIFT AID (NON-NEED-BASED) ***Total amount:*** $15,845,771 (17% institutional, 83% external sources). ***Receiving aid:*** Freshmen: 4% (139). Undergraduates: 3% (418). ***Average award:*** Freshmen: $9754. Undergraduates: $10,332. ***Scholarships, grants, and awards by category:*** *Academic interests/achievement:* general academic interests/achievements. *Creative arts/performance:* music. ***Tuition waivers:*** Full or partial for employees or children of employees, senior citizens.

LOANS ***Student loans:*** $27,555,355 (52% need-based, 48% non-need-based). 32% of past graduating class borrowed through all loan programs. *Average indebtedness per student:* $19,384. ***Average need-based loan:*** Freshmen: $5213. Undergraduates: $5509. ***Parent loans:*** $8,426,073 (5% need-based, 95% non-need-based). ***Programs:*** Perkins, Federal Nursing, college/university, private loans.

WORK-STUDY ***Federal work-study:*** Total amount: $1,606,770; jobs available.

ATHLETIC AWARDS Total amount: $10,622,588 (31% need-based, 69% non-need-based).

APPLYING FOR FINANCIAL AID ***Required financial aid forms:*** FAFSA, institution's own form. ***Financial aid deadline (priority):*** 3/1. ***Notification date:*** 4/5. Students must reply by 5/1.

CONTACT Ms. Yvonne B. Hubbard, Director of Student Financial Services, University of Virginia, PO Box 400207, Charlottesville, VA 22904-4207, 434-982-6000. *E-mail:* faid@virginia.edu.

THE UNIVERSITY OF VIRGINIA'S COLLEGE AT WISE

Wise, VA

Tuition & fees (VA res): $7721   Average undergraduate aid package: $9958

ABOUT THE INSTITUTION State-supported, coed. 25 undergraduate majors. Federal methodology is used as a basis for awarding need-based institutional aid.

UNDERGRADUATE EXPENSES for 2011–12 ***Tuition, state resident:*** full-time $4242; part-time $181 per credit hour. ***Tuition, nonresident:*** full-time $17,325; part-time $734 per credit hour. ***Required fees:*** full-time $3479; $117.75 per credit hour or $1008 per term. Part-time tuition and fees vary according to course load. ***College room and board:*** $8890; ***Room only:*** $5273. Room and board charges vary according to board plan and housing facility. ***Payment plans:*** Installment, deferred payment.

FRESHMAN FINANCIAL AID (Fall 2010, est.) 353 applied for aid; of those 82% were deemed to have need. 100% of freshmen with need received aid; of those 82% had need fully met. ***Average percent of need met:*** 98% (excluding resources awarded to replace EFC). ***Average financial aid package:*** $11,181 (excluding resources awarded to replace EFC). 7% of all full-time freshmen had no need and received non-need-based gift aid.

UNDERGRADUATE FINANCIAL AID (Fall 2010, est.) 1,440 applied for aid; of those 85% were deemed to have need. 100% of undergraduates with need received aid; of those 78% had need fully met. ***Average percent of need met:*** 97% (excluding resources awarded to replace EFC). ***Average financial aid package:*** $9958 (excluding resources awarded to replace EFC). 5% of all full-time undergraduates had no need and received non-need-based gift aid.

GIFT AID (NEED-BASED) ***Total amount:*** $6,338,266 (62% federal, 29% state, 7% institutional, 2% external sources). ***Receiving aid:*** Freshmen: 62% (249); all full-time undergraduates: 66% (1,040). ***Average award:*** Freshmen: $5307; Undergraduates: $5526. ***Scholarships, grants, and awards:*** Federal Pell, FSEOG, state, private, college/university gift aid from institutional funds.

GIFT AID (NON-NEED-BASED) ***Total amount:*** $2,070,375 (13% state, 68% institutional, 19% external sources). ***Receiving aid:*** Freshmen: 58% (231). Undergraduates: 51% (791). ***Average award:*** Freshmen: $4659. Undergraduates: $5091. ***Scholarships, grants, and awards by category:*** *Academic interests/achievement:* agriculture, biological sciences, business, computer science, education, English, general academic interests/achievements, health fields, humanities, mathematics, physical sciences, premedicine, social sciences. *Creative arts/performance:* creative writing, general creative arts/performance, journalism/publications, music, performing arts, theater/drama. *Special achievements/activities:* community service, religious involvement. *Special characteristics:* children with a deceased or disabled parent, ethnic background, local/state students, veterans, veterans' children. ***Tuition waivers:*** Full or partial for employees or children of employees, senior citizens.

LOANS ***Student loans:*** $5,563,207 (50% need-based, 50% non-need-based). 51% of past graduating class borrowed through all loan programs. *Average indebtedness per student:* $14,801. ***Average need-based loan:*** Freshmen: $2964. Undergraduates: $3462. ***Parent loans:*** $1,153,693 (100% non-need-based). ***Programs:*** Perkins, state, college/university.

WORK-STUDY ***Federal work-study:*** Total amount: $254,632; jobs available.

ATHLETIC AWARDS Total amount: $444,472 (100% non-need-based).

APPLYING FOR FINANCIAL AID ***Required financial aid form:*** FAFSA. ***Financial aid deadline (priority):*** 4/1. ***Notification date:*** Continuous. Students must reply within 4 weeks of notification.

CONTACT Mr. Bill Wendle, Director of Financial Aid, The University of Virginia's College at Wise, 1 College Avenue, Wise, VA 24293, 276-328-0103 or toll-free 888-282-9324. *Fax:* 276-328-0251. *E-mail:* wdw8m@uvawise.edu.

UNIVERSITY OF WASHINGTON

Seattle, WA

ABOUT THE INSTITUTION State-supported, coed. 147 undergraduate majors.

GIFT AID (NEED-BASED) ***Scholarships, grants, and awards:*** Federal Pell, FSEOG, state, private, college/university gift aid from institutional funds.

GIFT AID (NON-NEED-BASED) ***Scholarships, grants, and awards by category:*** *Academic interests/achievement:* architecture, business, computer science, education, engineering/technologies, general academic interests/achievements, health fields. *Creative arts/performance:* art/fine arts, general creative arts/performance, music, performing arts. *Special achievements/activities:* general special achievements/activities, leadership, memberships.

LOANS ***Programs:*** Federal Direct (Subsidized and Unsubsidized Stafford, PLUS), Perkins, Federal Nursing, college/university.

WORK-STUDY ***Federal work-study:*** Total amount: $2,596,000; 478 jobs averaging $2800. ***State or other work-study/employment:*** Total amount: $525,000 (100% need-based). 327 part-time jobs averaging $3160.

APPLYING FOR FINANCIAL AID ***Required financial aid form:*** FAFSA.

CONTACT Office of Student Financial Aid, University of Washington, Box 355880, Seattle, WA 98195-5880, 206-543-6101. *E-mail:* osfa@u.washington.edu.

UNIVERSITY OF WASHINGTON, BOTHELL

Bothell, WA

CONTACT Financial Aid Office, University of Washington, Bothell, 18115 Campus Way, NE, Bothell, WA 98011-8246, 425-352-5000.

UNIVERSITY OF WASHINGTON, TACOMA

Tacoma, WA

Tuition & fees (WA res): $8689 **Average undergraduate aid package: $13,800**

ABOUT THE INSTITUTION State-supported, coed. 24 undergraduate majors. Federal methodology is used as a basis for awarding need-based institutional aid.

UNDERGRADUATE EXPENSES for 2010–11 ***Tuition, state resident:*** full-time $8122; part-time $290 per credit. ***Tuition, nonresident:*** full-time $24,750; part-time $844 per credit. ***Required fees:*** full-time $567. Full-time tuition and fees vary according to course load. Part-time tuition and fees vary according to course load. ***College room and board: Room only:*** $8949. Room and board charges vary according to housing facility. ***Payment plan:*** Installment.

FRESHMAN FINANCIAL AID (Fall 2009) 170 applied for aid; of those 65% were deemed to have need. 86% of freshmen with need received aid; of those 23% had need fully met. ***Average percent of need met:*** 78% (excluding resources awarded to replace EFC). ***Average financial aid package:*** $11,200 (excluding resources awarded to replace EFC). 1% of all full-time freshmen had no need and received non-need-based gift aid.

UNDERGRADUATE FINANCIAL AID (Fall 2009) 1,486 applied for aid; of those 85% were deemed to have need. 96% of undergraduates with need received aid; of those 27% had need fully met. ***Average percent of need met:*** 77% (excluding resources awarded to replace EFC). ***Average financial aid package:*** $13,800 (excluding resources awarded to replace EFC). 1% of all full-time undergraduates had no need and received non-need-based gift aid.

GIFT AID (NEED-BASED) ***Total amount:*** $12,286,500 (40% federal, 43% state, 16% institutional, 1% external sources). ***Receiving aid:*** Freshmen: 35% (73); all full-time undergraduates: 45% (966). ***Average award:*** Freshmen: $9800; Undergraduates: $11,200. ***Scholarships, grants, and awards:*** Federal Pell, FSEOG, state, private, college/university gift aid from institutional funds.

GIFT AID (NON-NEED-BASED) ***Total amount:*** $379,000 (66% institutional, 34% external sources). ***Receiving aid:*** Freshmen: 10% (21). Undergraduates: 2% (37). ***Average award:*** Freshmen: $3000. Undergraduates: $63,000. ***Scholarships, grants, and awards by category:*** *Academic interests/achievement:* general academic interests/achievements. ***Tuition waivers:*** Full or partial for employees or children of employees, senior citizens.

LOANS ***Student loans:*** $10,640,000 (79% need-based, 21% non-need-based). 58% of past graduating class borrowed through all loan programs. *Average indebtedness per student:* $17,900. ***Average need-based loan:*** Freshmen: $4100. Undergraduates: $6900. ***Parent loans:*** $1,181,000 (19% need-based, 81% non-need-based). ***Programs:*** Federal Direct (Subsidized and Unsubsidized Stafford, PLUS), Perkins, Federal Nursing.

WORK-STUDY ***Federal work-study:*** Total amount: $179,000; jobs available. ***State or other work-study/employment:*** Total amount: $260,000 (100% need-based). Part-time jobs available.

APPLYING FOR FINANCIAL AID ***Required financial aid form:*** FAFSA. ***Financial aid deadline (priority):*** 2/28. ***Notification date:*** 4/1. Students must reply within 3 weeks of notification.

CONTACT Ms. Shari King, Associate Director of Financial Aid and Veterans Affairs, University of Washington, Tacoma, 1900 Commerce Street, Box 358400, Tacoma, WA 98402-3100, 253-692-4400 or toll-free 800-736-7750 (out-of-state). *Fax:* 253-692-4414. *E-mail:* osfatac@uw.edu.

THE UNIVERSITY OF WEST ALABAMA

Livingston, AL

Tuition & fees (AL res): $5530 **Average undergraduate aid package: N/A**

ABOUT THE INSTITUTION State-supported, coed. 19 undergraduate majors. Federal methodology is used as a basis for awarding need-based institutional aid.

UNDERGRADUATE EXPENSES for 2010–11 ***Tuition, state resident:*** full-time $5060; part-time $215 per semester hour. ***Tuition, nonresident:*** full-time $10,120; part-time $430 per semester hour. ***Required fees:*** full-time $470. Full-time tuition and fees vary according to course load, degree level, and program. Part-time tuition and fees vary according to course load, degree level, and program. ***College room and board:*** $4466. Room and board charges vary according to board plan and housing facility.

GIFT AID (NEED-BASED) ***Total amount:*** $5,928,854 (100% federal). ***Scholarships, grants, and awards:*** Federal Pell, FSEOG, state, private, college/university gift aid from institutional funds.

GIFT AID (NON-NEED-BASED) ***Total amount:*** $1,497,753 (89% institutional, 11% external sources). ***Scholarships, grants, and awards by category:*** *Academic interests/achievement:* general academic interests/achievements. *Special achievements/activities:* cheerleading/drum major, general special achievements/activities, rodeo. *Special characteristics:* children of faculty/staff, first-generation college students. ***Tuition waivers:*** Full or partial for employees or children of employees.

LOANS ***Student loans:*** $9,142,535 (50% need-based, 50% non-need-based). ***Parent loans:*** $640,731 (100% non-need-based). ***Programs:*** Perkins.

WORK-STUDY ***Federal work-study:*** Total amount: $305,294; jobs available. ***State or other work-study/employment:*** Total amount: $82,600 (100% non-need-based). Part-time jobs available.

ATHLETIC AWARDS Total amount: $828,856 (100% non-need-based).

APPLYING FOR FINANCIAL AID ***Required financial aid form:*** FAFSA. ***Financial aid deadline (priority):*** 4/1. ***Notification date:*** Continuous beginning 6/1. Students must reply within 2 weeks of notification.

CONTACT Mr. Don Rainer, Director of Financial Aid, The University of West Alabama, Station 3, Livingston, AL 35470, 205-652-3576 or toll-free 800-621-7742 (in-state), 800-621-8044 (out-of-state). *Fax:* 205-652-3847. *E-mail:* drainer@uwa.edu.

UNIVERSITY OF WEST FLORIDA

Pensacola, FL

Tuition & fees (FL res): $4794 **Average undergraduate aid package: N/A**

ABOUT THE INSTITUTION State-supported, coed. 64 undergraduate majors. Federal methodology is used as a basis for awarding need-based institutional aid.

UNDERGRADUATE EXPENSES for 2010–11 ***Tuition, state resident:*** full-time $3254; part-time $159.79 per semester hour. ***Tuition, nonresident:*** full-time $15,522; part-time $589.18 per semester hour. ***Required fees:*** full-time $1540. Full-time tuition and fees vary according to location and reciprocity agreements. Part-time tuition and fees vary according to location and reciprocity agreements. ***College room and board:*** $7856. Room and board charges vary according to housing facility. ***Payment plans:*** Tuition prepayment, deferred payment.

GIFT AID (NEED-BASED) ***Total amount:*** $18,221,153 (79% federal, 13% state, 8% institutional). ***Scholarships, grants, and awards:*** Federal Pell, FSEOG, state, private, college/university gift aid from institutional funds.

GIFT AID (NON-NEED-BASED) ***Total amount:*** $13,281,481 (5% federal, 60% state, 24% institutional, 11% external sources). ***Scholarships, grants, and awards by category:*** *Academic interests/achievement:* biological sciences, business, general academic interests/achievements, military science. *Creative arts/performance:* applied art and design, art/fine arts, music, theater/drama. *Special characteristics:* children and siblings of alumni, first-generation college students, handicapped students, members of minority groups. ***Tuition waivers:*** Full or partial for employees or children of employees, senior citizens.

LOANS ***Student loans:*** $36,134,484 (10% need-based, 90% non-need-based). ***Programs:*** Federal Direct (Subsidized and Unsubsidized Stafford, PLUS), Perkins, college/university.

WORK-STUDY ***Federal work-study:*** Total amount: $448,819; jobs available. ***State or other work-study/employment:*** Part-time jobs available.

APPLYING FOR FINANCIAL AID ***Required financial aid forms:*** FAFSA, institution's own form. ***Financial aid deadline:*** Continuous. ***Notification date:*** Continuous beginning 2/1.

CONTACT Ms. Georganne E. Major, Coordinator of Financial Aid, University of West Florida, 11000 University Parkway, Pensacola, FL 32514-5750, 850-474-2397 or toll-free 800-263-1074. *E-mail:* gmajor@uwf.edu.

UNIVERSITY OF WEST GEORGIA

Carrollton, GA

Tuition & fees (GA res): $6182 **Average undergraduate aid package: $8683**

ABOUT THE INSTITUTION State-supported, coed. 49 undergraduate majors. Federal methodology is used as a basis for awarding need-based institutional aid.

UNDERGRADUATE EXPENSES for 2010–11 ***Tuition, state resident:*** full-time $4596; part-time $154 per semester hour. ***Tuition, nonresident:*** full-time $16,572; part-time $553 per semester hour. ***Required fees:*** full-time $1586; $44.01 per semester hour or $397 per term. Full-time tuition and fees vary according to course load and degree level. Part-time tuition and fees vary according to course load and degree level. ***College room and board:*** $6754; ***Room only:*** $3700. Room and board charges vary according to board plan and housing facility.

FRESHMAN FINANCIAL AID (Fall 2010, est.) 1,672 applied for aid; of those 83% were deemed to have need. 99% of freshmen with need received aid; of those 24% had need fully met. ***Average percent of need met:*** 60% (excluding resources awarded to replace EFC). ***Average financial aid package:*** $8914 (excluding resources awarded to replace EFC). 2% of all full-time freshmen had no need and received non-need-based gift aid.

UNDERGRADUATE FINANCIAL AID (Fall 2010, est.) 6,782 applied for aid; of those 83% were deemed to have need. 96% of undergraduates with need received aid; of those 12% had need fully met. ***Average percent of need met:*** 57% (excluding resources awarded to replace EFC). ***Average financial aid package:*** $8683 (excluding resources awarded to replace EFC). 4% of all full-time undergraduates had no need and received non-need-based gift aid.

GIFT AID (NEED-BASED) ***Total amount:*** $33,598,311 (71% federal, 27% state, 1% institutional, 1% external sources). ***Receiving aid:*** Freshmen: 67% (1,236); all full-time undergraduates: 58% (4,676). ***Average award:*** Freshmen: $7173; Undergraduates: $6188. ***Scholarships, grants, and awards:*** Federal Pell, FSEOG, state, private, college/university gift aid from institutional funds.

GIFT AID (NON-NEED-BASED) ***Total amount:*** $5,270,596 (95% state, 3% institutional, 2% external sources). ***Receiving aid:*** Freshmen: 15% (268). Undergraduates: 50% (4,027). ***Average award:*** Freshmen: $1858. Undergraduates: $1530. ***Scholarships, grants, and awards by category:*** *Academic interests/achievement:* biological sciences, business, communication, computer science, education, English, foreign languages, general academic interests/achievements, health fields, humanities, mathematics, physical sciences, premedicine, social sciences. *Creative arts/performance:* applied art and design, art/fine arts, debating, general creative arts/performance, journalism/publications, music, performing arts, theater/drama. *Special achievements/activities:* community service, leadership, memberships, religious involvement. *Special characteristics:* adult students, children and siblings of alumni, general special characteristics, handicapped students, international students, local/state students, members of minority groups. ***Tuition waivers:*** Full or partial for senior citizens.

LOANS ***Student loans:*** $43,664,013 (61% need-based, 39% non-need-based). 63% of past graduating class borrowed through all loan programs. *Average indebtedness per student:* $15,365. ***Average need-based loan:*** Freshmen: $3296. Undergraduates: $4069. ***Parent loans:*** $3,091,753 (100% non-need-based). ***Programs:*** Federal Direct (Subsidized and Unsubsidized Stafford, PLUS), Perkins.

WORK-STUDY ***Federal work-study:*** Total amount: $334,000; jobs available. ***State or other work-study/employment:*** Part-time jobs available.

ATHLETIC AWARDS Total amount: $965,232 (55% need-based, 45% non-need-based).

APPLYING FOR FINANCIAL AID ***Required financial aid form:*** FAFSA. ***Financial aid deadline (priority):*** 4/1. ***Notification date:*** Continuous beginning 3/1.

CONTACT Kimberly Jordan, Director of Financial Aid, University of West Georgia, 1601 Maple Street, Aycock Hall, Carrollton, GA 30118, 678-839-6421. *Fax:* 678-839-6422. *E-mail:* kjordan@westga.edu.

UNIVERSITY OF WISCONSIN–EAU CLAIRE

Eau Claire, WI

Tuition & fees (WI res): $7364 **Average undergraduate aid package: $8506**

ABOUT THE INSTITUTION State-supported, coed. 52 undergraduate majors. Federal methodology is used as a basis for awarding need-based institutional aid.

UNDERGRADUATE EXPENSES for 2010–11 ***Tuition, state resident:*** full-time $6122; part-time $255 per credit. ***Tuition, nonresident:*** full-time $13,695; part-time $571 per credit. ***Required fees:*** full-time $1242; $52 per credit or $2 per term. Full-time tuition and fees vary according to reciprocity agreements. Part-time tuition and fees vary according to reciprocity agreements. ***College room and board:*** $5830; ***Room only:*** $2920. Room and board charges vary according to board plan and housing facility. ***Payment plan:*** Installment.

FRESHMAN FINANCIAL AID (Fall 2009) 1,630 applied for aid; of those 59% were deemed to have need. 99% of freshmen with need received aid; of those 54% had need fully met. ***Average percent of need met:*** 92% (excluding resources awarded to replace EFC). ***Average financial aid package:*** $8663 (excluding resources awarded to replace EFC). 16% of all full-time freshmen had no need and received non-need-based gift aid.

UNDERGRADUATE FINANCIAL AID (Fall 2009) 7,054 applied for aid; of those 67% were deemed to have need. 99% of undergraduates with need received aid; of those 61% had need fully met. ***Average percent of need met:*** 91% (excluding resources awarded to replace EFC). ***Average financial aid package:*** $8506 (excluding resources awarded to replace EFC). 8% of all full-time undergraduates had no need and received non-need-based gift aid.

GIFT AID (NEED-BASED) ***Total amount:*** $16,760,771 (63% federal, 25% state, 4% institutional, 8% external sources). ***Receiving aid:*** Freshmen: 35% (695); all full-time undergraduates: 31% (3,014). ***Average award:*** Freshmen: $5539; Undergraduates: $5288. ***Scholarships, grants, and awards:*** Federal Pell, FSEOG, state, private, college/university gift aid from institutional funds, Federal Nursing, Academic Competitiveness Grants, National SMART Grants, Bureau of Indian Affairs Grants, EMAC.

GIFT AID (NON-NEED-BASED) ***Total amount:*** $1,459,926 (1% federal, 5% state, 36% institutional, 58% external sources). ***Receiving aid:*** Undergraduates: 1. ***Average award:*** Freshmen: $1734. Undergraduates: $1768. ***Scholarships, grants, and awards by category:*** *Academic interests/achievement:* biological sciences, business, communication, computer science, education, English, foreign languages, general academic interests/achievements, health fields, international studies, mathematics, physical sciences, premedicine, social sciences. *Creative arts/performance:* debating, music, theater/drama. *Special achievements/activities:* community service, general special achievements/activities, hobbies/interests, leadership, memberships. *Special characteristics:* adult students, ethnic background, first-generation college students, general special characteristics, international students, local/state students, members of minority groups, previous college experience. ***Tuition waivers:*** Full or partial for minority students.

LOANS ***Student loans:*** $37,203,530 (57% need-based, 43% non-need-based). 69% of past graduating class borrowed through all loan programs. *Average indebtedness per student:* $21,185. ***Average need-based loan:*** Freshmen: $4194. Undergraduates: $4595. ***Parent loans:*** $3,475,557 (100% non-need-based). ***Programs:*** Federal Direct (Subsidized and Unsubsidized Stafford, PLUS), Perkins, state, college/university, private loans.

WORK-STUDY ***Federal work-study:*** Total amount: $4,293,770; 2,510 jobs averaging $1711. ***State or other work-study/employment:*** Total amount: $2,697,215 (54% need-based, 46% non-need-based). 1,737 part-time jobs averaging $1553.

APPLYING FOR FINANCIAL AID ***Required financial aid form:*** FAFSA. ***Financial aid deadline (priority):*** 4/15. ***Notification date:*** Continuous beginning 4/15.

CONTACT Ms. Kathleen Sahlhoff, Director of Financial Aid, University of Wisconsin–Eau Claire, 115 Schofield Hall, Eau Claire, WI 54701, 715-836-3373. *Fax:* 715-836-3846. *E-mail:* sahlhoka@uwec.edu.

UNIVERSITY OF WISCONSIN–GREEN BAY

Green Bay, WI

Tuition & fees (WI res): $6973 **Average undergraduate aid package: $10,711**

ABOUT THE INSTITUTION State-supported, coed. 43 undergraduate majors. Federal methodology is used as a basis for awarding need-based institutional aid.

UNDERGRADUATE EXPENSES for 2010–11 ***One-time required fee:*** $200. ***Tuition, state resident:*** full-time $5659; part-time $236 per credit hour. ***Tuition, nonresident:*** full-time $13,232; part-time $551 per credit hour. ***Required fees:*** full-time $1314; $52 per credit hour. Full-time tuition and fees vary according to course load and reciprocity agreements. Part-time tuition and fees vary according to reciprocity agreements. ***College room and board:*** $7290; ***Room only:*** $4320. Room and board charges vary according to board plan and housing facility. ***Payment plan:*** Installment.

FRESHMAN FINANCIAL AID (Fall 2010, est.) 820 applied for aid; of those 79% were deemed to have need. 97% of freshmen with need received aid; of those 40% had need fully met. ***Average percent of need met:*** 82% (excluding resources awarded to replace EFC). ***Average financial aid package:*** $10,281 (excluding resources awarded to replace EFC). 3% of all full-time freshmen had no need and received non-need-based gift aid.

UNDERGRADUATE FINANCIAL AID (Fall 2010, est.) 3,950 applied for aid; of those 82% were deemed to have need. 96% of undergraduates with need received aid; of those 46% had need fully met. ***Average percent of need met:*** 84% (excluding resources awarded to replace EFC). ***Average financial aid package:*** $10,711 (excluding resources awarded to replace EFC). 1% of all full-time undergraduates had no need and received non-need-based gift aid.

GIFT AID (NEED-BASED) ***Total amount:*** $13,285,303 (65% federal, 27% state, 1% institutional, 7% external sources). ***Receiving aid:*** Freshmen: 46% (413); all full-time undergraduates: 41% (1,954). ***Average award:*** Freshmen: $5539; Undergraduates: $6251. ***Scholarships, grants, and awards:*** Federal Pell, FSEOG, state, private, college/university gift aid from institutional funds.

GIFT AID (NON-NEED-BASED) ***Total amount:*** $622,986 (31% state, 27% institutional, 42% external sources). ***Receiving aid:*** Freshmen: 25% (221). Undergraduates: 23% (1,090). ***Average award:*** Freshmen: $1304. Undergraduates: $1721. ***Scholarships, grants, and awards by category:*** *Academic interests/achievement:* area/ethnic studies, biological sciences, business, communication, education, engineering/technologies, general academic interests/achievements, health fields, humanities, physical sciences, premedicine, social sciences. *Creative arts/performance:* art/fine arts, dance, journalism/publications, music, theater/drama. *Special achievements/activities:* community service, general special achievements/activities, leadership. *Special characteristics:* adult students, children and siblings of alumni, children of public servants, ethnic background, handicapped students, local/state students, members of minority groups, veterans. ***Tuition waivers:*** Full or partial for senior citizens.

LOANS ***Student loans:*** $24,021,189 (60% need-based, 40% non-need-based). 76% of past graduating class borrowed through all loan programs. *Average indebtedness per student:* $22,399. ***Average need-based loan:*** Freshmen: $4421. Undergraduates: $5163. ***Parent loans:*** $1,637,053 (100% non-need-based). ***Programs:*** Perkins.

WORK-STUDY ***Federal work-study:*** Total amount: $441,788; 250 jobs averaging $2000. ***State or other work-study/employment:*** Part-time jobs available.

ATHLETIC AWARDS Total amount: $2,283,120 (67% need-based, 33% non-need-based).

APPLYING FOR FINANCIAL AID ***Required financial aid form:*** FAFSA. ***Financial aid deadline (priority):*** 4/15. ***Notification date:*** Continuous. Students must reply within 3 weeks of notification.

CONTACT Mr. James Rohan, Director of Financial Aid, University of Wisconsin–Green Bay, 2420 Nicolet Drive, Green Bay, WI 54311-7001, 920-465-2073 or toll-free 888-367-8942 (out-of-state). *E-mail:* rohanj@uwgb.edu.

UNIVERSITY OF WISCONSIN–LA CROSSE

La Crosse, WI

Tuition & fees (WI res): $7911 **Average undergraduate aid package: $6891**

ABOUT THE INSTITUTION State-supported, coed. 49 undergraduate majors. Federal methodology is used as a basis for awarding need-based institutional aid.

UNDERGRADUATE EXPENSES for 2010–11 ***Tuition, state resident:*** full-time $6809; part-time $283.70 per credit hour. ***Tuition, nonresident:*** full-time $14,382; part-time $599.24 per credit hour. ***Required fees:*** full-time $1102. Full-time tuition and fees vary according to program and reciprocity agreements. Part-time tuition and fees vary according to course load, program, and reciprocity agreements. ***College room and board:*** $5630; ***Room only:*** $3240. Room and board charges vary according to board plan and housing facility. ***Payment plan:*** Installment.

FRESHMAN FINANCIAL AID (Fall 2009) 1,378 applied for aid; of those 62% were deemed to have need. 97% of freshmen with need received aid; of those 14% had need fully met. ***Average percent of need met:*** 67% (excluding resources awarded to replace EFC). ***Average financial aid package:*** $6431 (excluding resources awarded to replace EFC). 4% of all full-time freshmen had no need and received non-need-based gift aid.

UNDERGRADUATE FINANCIAL AID (Fall 2009) 5,492 applied for aid; of those 68% were deemed to have need. 97% of undergraduates with need received aid; of those 22% had need fully met. ***Average percent of need met:*** 73% (excluding resources awarded to replace EFC). ***Average financial aid package:*** $6891 (excluding resources awarded to replace EFC). 4% of all full-time undergraduates had no need and received non-need-based gift aid.

GIFT AID (NEED-BASED) ***Total amount:*** $11,483,684 (68% federal, 28% state, 2% institutional, 2% external sources). ***Receiving aid:*** Freshmen: 20% (355); all full-time undergraduates: 24% (1,883). ***Average award:*** Freshmen: $5965; Undergraduates: $5335. ***Scholarships, grants, and awards:*** Federal Pell, FSEOG, state, private, college/university gift aid from institutional funds.

GIFT AID (NON-NEED-BASED) ***Total amount:*** $3,218,674 (7% federal, 8% state, 22% institutional, 63% external sources). ***Receiving aid:*** Freshmen: 21% (365). Undergraduates: 11% (846). ***Average award:*** Freshmen: $1398. Undergraduates: $1070. ***Scholarships, grants, and awards by category:*** *Academic interests/achievement:* area/ethnic studies, biological sciences, business, communication, computer science, education, English, foreign languages, general academic interests/achievements, health fields, humanities, international studies, mathematics, military science, physical sciences, social sciences. *Creative arts/performance:* art/fine arts, music, theater/drama. *Special achievements/activities:* community service, leadership, memberships. *Special characteristics:* adult students, children and siblings of alumni, children of union members/company employees, ethnic background, first-generation college students, general special characteristics, international students, local/state students, members of minority groups, out-of-state students, veterans, veterans' children. ***Tuition waivers:*** Full or partial for minority students.

LOANS ***Student loans:*** $41,414,271 (44% need-based, 56% non-need-based). 69% of past graduating class borrowed through all loan programs. *Average indebtedness per student:* $21,420. ***Average need-based loan:*** Freshmen: $3238. Undergraduates: $3995. ***Parent loans:*** $3,630,845 (100% non-need-based). ***Programs:*** Federal Direct (Subsidized and Unsubsidized Stafford, PLUS), Perkins.

WORK-STUDY ***Federal work-study:*** Total amount: $430,860; jobs available. ***State or other work-study/employment:*** Total amount: $3,305,739 (100% non-need-based). Part-time jobs available.

APPLYING FOR FINANCIAL AID ***Required financial aid form:*** FAFSA. ***Financial aid deadline (priority):*** 3/15. ***Notification date:*** Continuous beginning 4/1.

CONTACT Louise Janke, Director of Financial Aid, University of Wisconsin–La Crosse, 1725 State Street, La Crosse, WI 54601-3742, 608-785-8604. *Fax:* 608-785-8843. *E-mail:* finaid@uwlax.edu.

UNIVERSITY OF WISCONSIN–MADISON

Madison, WI

Tuition & fees (WI res): $8987 **Average undergraduate aid package: $11,268**

ABOUT THE INSTITUTION State-supported, coed. 129 undergraduate majors. Federal methodology is used as a basis for awarding need-based institutional aid.

UNDERGRADUATE EXPENSES for 2010–11 ***Tuition, state resident:*** full-time $7933; part-time $376.30 per credit hour. ***Tuition, nonresident:*** full-time $23,183; part-time $1011.71 per credit hour. ***Required fees:*** full-time $1054; $45.75 per credit hour. Full-time tuition and fees vary according to program and reciprocity agreements. Part-time tuition and fees vary according to course load, program, and reciprocity agreements. ***College room and board:*** $7690. Room and board charges vary according to board plan and housing facility.

FRESHMAN FINANCIAL AID (Fall 2010, est.) 3,937 applied for aid; of those 63% were deemed to have need. 97% of freshmen with need received aid; of those 20% had need fully met. ***Average percent of need met:*** 64% (excluding resources awarded to replace EFC). ***Average financial aid package:*** $10,995 (excluding resources awarded to replace EFC). 10% of all full-time freshmen had no need and received non-need-based gift aid.

UNDERGRADUATE FINANCIAL AID (Fall 2010, est.) 15,444 applied for aid; of those 74% were deemed to have need. 97% of undergraduates with need received aid; of those 22% had need fully met. ***Average percent of need met:*** 66% (excluding resources awarded to replace EFC). ***Average financial aid package:*** $11,268 (excluding resources awarded to replace EFC). 8% of all full-time undergraduates had no need and received non-need-based gift aid.

GIFT AID (NEED-BASED) ***Total amount:*** $45,889,680 (52% federal, 19% state, 29% institutional). ***Receiving aid:*** Freshmen: 23% (1,379); all full-time undergraduates: 26% (7,175). ***Average award:*** Freshmen: $6437; Undergraduates: $6222. ***Scholarships, grants, and awards:*** Federal Pell, FSEOG, state, private, college/university gift aid from institutional funds.

GIFT AID (NON-NEED-BASED) ***Total amount:*** $35,150,441 (1% federal, 14% state, 61% institutional, 24% external sources). ***Receiving aid:*** Freshmen: 32% (1,871). Undergraduates: 29% (8,140). ***Average award:*** Freshmen: $3184. Undergraduates: $3214. ***Scholarships, grants, and awards by category:*** *Academic interests/achievement:* general academic interests/achievements. *Creative arts/performance:* general creative arts/performance. *Special achievements/activities:* general special achievements/activities. *Special characteristics:* general special characteristics.

LOANS ***Student loans:*** $44,029,131 (100% need-based). 48% of past graduating class borrowed through all loan programs. *Average indebtedness per student:* $22,872. ***Average need-based loan:*** Freshmen: $4047. Undergraduates: $4862. ***Parent loans:*** $17,508,818 (100% non-need-based). ***Programs:*** Federal Direct (Subsidized and Unsubsidized Stafford, PLUS), Perkins, Federal Nursing, state.

WORK-STUDY ***Federal work-study:*** Total amount: $9,231,955; jobs available. ***State or other work-study/employment:*** Total amount: $50,745,548 (100% non-need-based). Part-time jobs available.

ATHLETIC AWARDS Total amount: $8,873,999 (100% non-need-based).

APPLYING FOR FINANCIAL AID ***Required financial aid form:*** FAFSA. ***Financial aid deadline:*** Continuous. ***Notification date:*** Continuous beginning 4/1. Students must reply within 3 weeks of notification.

CONTACT Office of Student Financial Aid, University of Wisconsin–Madison, 333 East Campus Mall #9701, Madison, WI 53715-1382, 608-262-3060. *Fax:* 608-262-9068. *E-mail:* finaid@finaid.wisc.edu.

UNIVERSITY OF WISCONSIN–MILWAUKEE

Milwaukee, WI

Tuition & fees (WI res): $9075 **Average undergraduate aid package: $7954**

ABOUT THE INSTITUTION State-supported, coed. 104 undergraduate majors. Federal methodology is used as a basis for awarding need-based institutional aid.

UNDERGRADUATE EXPENSES for 2010–11 ***Tuition, state resident:*** full-time $8151; part-time $340 per credit hour. ***Tuition, nonresident:*** full-time $17,880; part-time $745 per credit hour. ***Required fees:*** full-time $924. Full-time tuition and fees vary according to location, program, and reciprocity agreements. Part-time tuition and fees vary according to course load, location, program, and reciprocity agreements. ***College room and board: Room only:*** $4310. Room and board charges vary according to board plan and housing facility. ***Payment plan:*** Installment.

FRESHMAN FINANCIAL AID (Fall 2010, est.) 3,052 applied for aid; of those 84% were deemed to have need. 95% of freshmen with need received aid; of those 23% had need fully met. ***Average percent of need met:*** 45% (excluding resources awarded to replace EFC). ***Average financial aid package:*** $7317 (excluding resources awarded to replace EFC). 1% of all full-time freshmen had no need and received non-need-based gift aid.

UNDERGRADUATE FINANCIAL AID (Fall 2010, est.) 17,890 applied for aid; of those 88% were deemed to have need. 84% of undergraduates with need received aid; of those 24% had need fully met. ***Average percent of need met:*** 51% (excluding resources awarded to replace EFC). ***Average financial aid package:*** $7954 (excluding resources awarded to replace EFC). 1% of all full-time undergraduates had no need and received non-need-based gift aid.

GIFT AID (NEED-BASED) ***Total amount:*** $52,599,068 (70% federal, 28% state, 1% institutional, 1% external sources). ***Receiving aid:*** Freshmen: 36% (1,259); all full-time undergraduates: 34% (6,829). ***Average award:*** Freshmen: $7191; Undergraduates: $6676. ***Scholarships, grants, and awards:*** Federal Pell, FSEOG, state, private, college/university gift aid from institutional funds, Federal Nursing.

GIFT AID (NON-NEED-BASED) ***Total amount:*** $14,754,444 (41% federal, 21% state, 26% institutional, 12% external sources). ***Receiving aid:*** Freshmen: 15% (547). Undergraduates: 15% (2,939). ***Average award:*** Freshmen: $3800. Undergraduates: $3009. ***Scholarships, grants, and awards by category:*** *Academic interests/achievement:* general academic interests/achievements. *Creative arts/performance:* general creative arts/performance. *Special achievements/*

activities: general special achievements/activities. *Special characteristics:* general special characteristics. ***Tuition waivers:*** Full or partial for senior citizens.

LOANS ***Student loans:*** $118,011,863 (47% need-based, 53% non-need-based). 71% of past graduating class borrowed through all loan programs. *Average indebtedness per student:* $25,312. ***Average need-based loan:*** Freshmen: $3520. Undergraduates: $4396. ***Parent loans:*** $10,087,097 (100% non-need-based). ***Programs:*** Federal Direct (Subsidized and Unsubsidized Stafford, PLUS), Perkins, Federal Nursing, state, alternative loans.

WORK-STUDY ***Federal work-study:*** Total amount: $384,666; jobs available.

ATHLETIC AWARDS Total amount: $467,403 (100% non-need-based).

APPLYING FOR FINANCIAL AID ***Required financial aid form:*** FAFSA. ***Financial aid deadline (priority):*** 3/1. ***Notification date:*** Continuous beginning 3/10. Students must reply within 2 weeks of notification.

CONTACT Ms. Jane Hojan-Clark, Director of Financial Aid and Student Employment Services, University of Wisconsin–Milwaukee, Mellencamp Hall 162, Milwaukee, WI 53201, 414-229-6300. *E-mail:* jhojan@uwm.edu.

UNIVERSITY OF WISCONSIN–OSHKOSH

Oshkosh, WI

CONTACT Ms. Sheila Denney, Financial Aid Counselor, University of Wisconsin–Oshkosh, 800 Algoma Boulevard, Oshkosh, WI 54901, 920-424-3377. *E-mail:* denney@uwosh.edu.

UNIVERSITY OF WISCONSIN–PARKSIDE

Kenosha, WI

Tuition & fees (WI res): $6623 **Average undergraduate aid package: N/A**

ABOUT THE INSTITUTION State-supported, coed. 37 undergraduate majors. Federal methodology is used as a basis for awarding need-based institutional aid.

UNDERGRADUATE EXPENSES for 2011–12 ***Tuition, state resident:*** full-time $5659; part-time $235.78 per credit hour. ***Tuition, nonresident:*** full-time $13,232; part-time $551.32 per credit hour. ***Required fees:*** full-time $964; $40 per credit hour. Full-time tuition and fees vary according to course load and reciprocity agreements. Part-time tuition and fees vary according to course load. ***College room and board:*** $6828; ***Room only:*** $4108. Room and board charges vary according to board plan and housing facility. ***Payment plan:*** Installment.

FRESHMAN FINANCIAL AID (Fall 2009) 646 applied for aid; of those 74% were deemed to have need. 95% of freshmen with need received aid.

UNDERGRADUATE FINANCIAL AID (Fall 2009) 2,149 applied for aid; of those 99% were deemed to have need. 97% of undergraduates with need received aid.

GIFT AID (NEED-BASED) ***Total amount:*** $12,122,425 (69% federal, 29% state, 1% institutional, 1% external sources). ***Receiving aid:*** Freshmen: 41% (325); all full-time undergraduates: 43% (1,596). ***Average award:*** Freshmen: $6317; Undergraduates: $5959. ***Scholarships, grants, and awards:*** Federal Pell, FSEOG, state, private, college/university gift aid from institutional funds, Federal Nursing.

GIFT AID (NON-NEED-BASED) ***Total amount:*** $626,247 (13% federal, 24% state, 63% external sources). ***Scholarships, grants, and awards by category:*** *Academic interests/achievement:* biological sciences, business, communication, education, engineering/technologies, English, foreign languages, general academic interests/achievements, health fields, mathematics, physical sciences, premedicine. *Creative arts/performance:* applied art and design, art/fine arts, music, theater/drama. *Special achievements/activities:* community service, leadership. *Special characteristics:* adult students, children of union members/company employees, children of workers in trades, ethnic background, general special characteristics, international students, local/state students, members of minority groups. ***Tuition waivers:*** Full or partial for senior citizens.

LOANS ***Student loans:*** $21,456,882 (43% need-based, 57% non-need-based). ***Parent loans:*** $1,017,948 (100% non-need-based). ***Programs:*** Perkins, Federal Nursing, state.

WORK-STUDY ***Federal work-study:*** Total amount: $125,213; jobs available. ***State or other work-study/employment:*** Part-time jobs available.

ATHLETIC AWARDS Total amount: $1,134,674 (100% non-need-based).

APPLYING FOR FINANCIAL AID ***Required financial aid form:*** FAFSA. ***Financial aid deadline (priority):*** 11/15. ***Notification date:*** Continuous beginning 4/1. Students must reply within 2 weeks of notification.

CONTACT Dr. Randall McCready, Director of Financial Aid and Scholarships, University of Wisconsin–Parkside, 900 Wood Road, Kenosha, WI 53141-2000, 262-595-2004. *Fax:* 262-595-2216. *E-mail:* randall.mccready@uwp.edu.

UNIVERSITY OF WISCONSIN–PLATTEVILLE

Platteville, WI

CONTACT Elizabeth Tucker, Director of Financial Aid, University of Wisconsin–Platteville, 1 University Plaza, Platteville, WI 53818-3099, 608-342-1836 or toll-free 800-362-5515. *Fax:* 608-342-1281. *E-mail:* tucker@uwplatt.edu.

UNIVERSITY OF WISCONSIN–RIVER FALLS

River Falls, WI

Tuition & fees (WI res): $6893 **Average undergraduate aid package: $3157**

ABOUT THE INSTITUTION State-supported, coed. 95 undergraduate majors. Federal methodology is used as a basis for awarding need-based institutional aid.

UNDERGRADUATE EXPENSES for 2010–11 ***Tuition, state resident:*** full-time $5730; part-time $238.78 per credit. ***Tuition, nonresident:*** full-time $13,303; part-time $556 per credit. ***Required fees:*** full-time $1163; $238.78 per credit. Full-time tuition and fees vary according to course load, degree level, and reciprocity agreements. Part-time tuition and fees vary according to course load, degree level, and reciprocity agreements. ***College room and board:*** $5730; ***Room only:*** $3400. Room and board charges vary according to board plan and housing facility. ***Payment plan:*** Installment.

FRESHMAN FINANCIAL AID (Fall 2009) 1,574 applied for aid; of those 89% were deemed to have need. 86% of freshmen with need received aid. ***Average financial aid package:*** $2613 (excluding resources awarded to replace EFC).

UNDERGRADUATE FINANCIAL AID (Fall 2009) 5,116 applied for aid; of those 95% were deemed to have need. 73% of undergraduates with need received aid. ***Average financial aid package:*** $3157 (excluding resources awarded to replace EFC).

GIFT AID (NEED-BASED) ***Total amount:*** $10,538,495 (70% federal, 19% state, 9% institutional, 2% external sources). ***Receiving aid:*** Freshmen: 34% (582); all full-time undergraduates: 25% (1,441). ***Average award:*** Freshmen: $2002; Undergraduates: $2317. ***Scholarships, grants, and awards:*** Federal Pell, FSEOG, state, private, college/university gift aid from institutional funds.

GIFT AID (NON-NEED-BASED) ***Total amount:*** $1,554,302 (5% state, 41% institutional, 54% external sources). ***Receiving aid:*** Freshmen: 52% (901). Undergraduates: 47% (2,717). ***Scholarships, grants, and awards by category:*** *Academic interests/achievement:* agriculture, area/ethnic studies, biological sciences, business, communication, computer science, education, English, foreign languages, general academic interests/achievements, health fields, humanities, international studies, mathematics, physical sciences, premedicine, social sciences. *Creative arts/performance:* art/fine arts, music, theater/drama. ***Tuition waivers:*** Full or partial for children of alumni.

LOANS ***Student loans:*** $31,022,780 (45% need-based, 55% non-need-based). 73% of past graduating class borrowed through all loan programs. *Average indebtedness per student:* $14,800. ***Parent loans:*** $1,163,651 (100% non-need-based). ***Programs:*** Federal Direct (Subsidized and Unsubsidized Stafford, PLUS), Perkins, state.

WORK-STUDY ***Federal work-study:*** Total amount: $408,992; jobs available. ***State or other work-study/employment:*** Total amount: $224,478 (40% need-based, 60% non-need-based). Part-time jobs available.

APPLYING FOR FINANCIAL AID ***Required financial aid forms:*** FAFSA, institution's own form. ***Financial aid deadline (priority):*** 3/15. ***Notification date:*** 4/1. Students must reply within 3 weeks of notification.

CONTACT Ms. Barbara J. Stinson, Director of Financial Aid, University of Wisconsin–River Falls, 410 South Third Street, River Falls, WI 54022-5001, 715-425-4111. *Fax:* 715-425-0708.

UNIVERSITY OF WISCONSIN–STEVENS POINT

Stevens Point, WI

Tuition & fees (WI res): $6849 **Average undergraduate aid package: $8109**

University of Wisconsin–Stevens Point

ABOUT THE INSTITUTION State-supported, coed. 69 undergraduate majors. Federal methodology is used as a basis for awarding need-based institutional aid.

UNDERGRADUATE EXPENSES for 2011–12 ***Tuition, state resident:*** full-time $5659; part-time $235.78 per credit hour. ***Tuition, nonresident:*** full-time $13,232; part-time $551.32 per credit hour. ***Required fees:*** full-time $1190; $340 per credit hour. Full-time tuition and fees vary according to course load, program, and reciprocity agreements. Part-time tuition and fees vary according to course load, program, and reciprocity agreements. ***College room and board:*** $5760; ***Room only:*** $3438. Room and board charges vary according to board plan and housing facility. ***Payment plan:*** Installment.

FRESHMAN FINANCIAL AID (Fall 2009) 1,393 applied for aid; of those 65% were deemed to have need. 95% of freshmen with need received aid; of those 68% had need fully met. ***Average percent of need met:*** 75% (excluding resources awarded to replace EFC). ***Average financial aid package:*** $6681 (excluding resources awarded to replace EFC). 6% of all full-time freshmen had no need and received non-need-based gift aid.

UNDERGRADUATE FINANCIAL AID (Fall 2009) 6,691 applied for aid; of those 73% were deemed to have need. 97% of undergraduates with need received aid; of those 72% had need fully met. ***Average percent of need met:*** 72% (excluding resources awarded to replace EFC). ***Average financial aid package:*** $8109 (excluding resources awarded to replace EFC). 6% of all full-time undergraduates had no need and received non-need-based gift aid.

GIFT AID (NEED-BASED) ***Total amount:*** $17,802,138 (67% federal, 27% state, 3% institutional, 3% external sources). ***Receiving aid:*** Freshmen: 27% (444); all full-time undergraduates: 30% (2,585). ***Average award:*** Freshmen: $6584; Undergraduates: $6590. ***Scholarships, grants, and awards:*** Federal Pell, FSEOG, state, private, college/university gift aid from institutional funds.

GIFT AID (NON-NEED-BASED) ***Total amount:*** $1,977,044 (3% state, 44% institutional, 53% external sources). ***Receiving aid:*** Freshmen: 4% (63). Undergraduates: 6% (508). ***Average award:*** Freshmen: $2259. Undergraduates: $2031. ***Scholarships, grants, and awards by category:*** *Academic interests/achievement:* agriculture, architecture, biological sciences, business, communication, computer science, education, engineering/technologies, English, foreign languages, general academic interests/achievements, health fields, home economics, humanities, international studies, mathematics, military science, physical sciences, premedicine, social sciences. *Creative arts/performance:* applied art and design, creative writing, dance, music, performing arts, theater/drama. *Special achievements/activities:* general special achievements/activities, leadership. *Special characteristics:* adult students, ethnic background, general special characteristics, international students, members of minority groups, out-of-state students, veterans. ***Tuition waivers:*** Full or partial for children of alumni.

LOANS ***Student loans:*** $36,824,396 (58% need-based, 42% non-need-based). 71% of past graduating class borrowed through all loan programs. *Average indebtedness per student:* $22,370. ***Average need-based loan:*** Freshmen: $3507. Undergraduates: $4721. ***Parent loans:*** $3,195,033 (10% need-based, 90% non-need-based). ***Programs:*** Federal Direct (Subsidized and Unsubsidized Stafford, PLUS), Perkins.

WORK-STUDY ***Federal work-study:*** Total amount: $1,376,268; 963 jobs averaging $1424. ***State or other work-study/employment:*** 2,497 part-time jobs averaging $1887.

APPLYING FOR FINANCIAL AID ***Required financial aid form:*** FAFSA. ***Financial aid deadline:*** 5/1 (priority: 3/15). ***Notification date:*** Continuous beginning 3/1. Students must reply within 4 weeks of notification.

CONTACT Mr. Paul Watson, Director of Financial Aid, University of Wisconsin–Stevens Point, 106 Student Services Center, Stevens Point, WI 54481-3897, 715-346-4771. *Fax:* 715-346-3526. *E-mail:* finaid@uwsp.edu.

UNIVERSITY OF WISCONSIN–STOUT

Menomonie, WI

Tuition & fees (WI res): $8099 **Average undergraduate aid package: $9715**

ABOUT THE INSTITUTION State-supported, coed. 40 undergraduate majors. Federal methodology is used as a basis for awarding need-based institutional aid.

UNDERGRADUATE EXPENSES for 2011–12 ***Tuition, state resident:*** full-time $6302; part-time $210 per credit hour. ***Tuition, nonresident:*** full-time $14,048; part-time $468 per credit hour. ***Required fees:*** full-time $1797. Full-time tuition and fees vary according to degree level and reciprocity agreements. Part-time tuition and fees vary according to degree level and reciprocity agreements. ***College room and board:*** $5560; ***Room only:*** $3300. Room and board charges vary according to board plan and housing facility. ***Payment plan:*** Installment.

FRESHMAN FINANCIAL AID (Fall 2010, est.) 1,347 applied for aid; of those 70% were deemed to have need. 99% of freshmen with need received aid; of those 40% had need fully met. ***Average percent of need met:*** 85% (excluding resources awarded to replace EFC). ***Average financial aid package:*** $9200 (excluding resources awarded to replace EFC). 2% of all full-time freshmen had no need and received non-need-based gift aid.

UNDERGRADUATE FINANCIAL AID (Fall 2010, est.) 5,512 applied for aid; of those 76% were deemed to have need. 99% of undergraduates with need received aid; of those 48% had need fully met. ***Average percent of need met:*** 87% (excluding resources awarded to replace EFC). ***Average financial aid package:*** $9715 (excluding resources awarded to replace EFC). 1% of all full-time undergraduates had no need and received non-need-based gift aid.

GIFT AID (NEED-BASED) ***Total amount:*** $14,236,930 (73% federal, 24% state, 1% institutional, 2% external sources). ***Receiving aid:*** Freshmen: 32% (509); all full-time undergraduates: 25% (1,775). ***Average award:*** Freshmen: $2523; Undergraduates: $2656. ***Scholarships, grants, and awards:*** Federal Pell, FSEOG, state, private, college/university gift aid from institutional funds, Academic Competitiveness Grants, Bureau of Indian Affairs Grants, GEAR UP Grants.

GIFT AID (NON-NEED-BASED) ***Total amount:*** $1,542,769 (3% federal, 2% state, 41% institutional, 54% external sources). ***Receiving aid:*** Freshmen: 15% (230). Undergraduates: 8% (573). ***Average award:*** Freshmen: $2114. Undergraduates: $1630. ***Scholarships, grants, and awards by category:*** *Academic interests/achievement:* 258 awards ($330,020 total): business, computer science, education, engineering/technologies, general academic interests/achievements, home economics, international studies, mathematics, physical sciences. *Creative arts/performance:* 13 awards ($15,200 total): applied art and design, art/fine arts, music. *Special achievements/activities:* 36 awards ($39,350 total): community service, general special achievements/activities, leadership, memberships, religious involvement. *Special characteristics:* 53 awards ($36,775 total): adult students, first-generation college students, handicapped students, international students, local/state students, members of minority groups, out-of-state students, previous college experience, veterans, veterans' children.

LOANS ***Student loans:*** $41,892,683 (45% need-based, 55% non-need-based). 75% of past graduating class borrowed through all loan programs. *Average indebtedness per student:* $25,855. ***Average need-based loan:*** Freshmen: $3600. Undergraduates: $4399. ***Parent loans:*** $2,251,773 (100% non-need-based). ***Programs:*** Federal Direct (Subsidized and Unsubsidized Stafford, PLUS), Perkins, alternative loans.

WORK-STUDY ***Federal work-study:*** Total amount: $2,607,847; 1,234 jobs averaging $1771.

APPLYING FOR FINANCIAL AID ***Required financial aid form:*** FAFSA. ***Financial aid deadline (priority):*** 3/15. ***Notification date:*** Continuous beginning 4/1. Students must reply within 4 weeks of notification.

CONTACT Beth M. Boisen, Director of Financial Aid, University of Wisconsin–Stout, 210 Bowman Hall, Menomonie, WI 54751, 715-232-1363 or toll-free 800-HI-STOUT (in-state). *Fax:* 715-232-5246. *E-mail:* boisenb@uwstout.edu.

UNIVERSITY OF WISCONSIN–SUPERIOR

Superior, WI

Tuition & fees (WI res): $7169 **Average undergraduate aid package: N/A**

ABOUT THE INSTITUTION State-supported, coed. 65 undergraduate majors. Federal methodology is used as a basis for awarding need-based institutional aid.

UNDERGRADUATE EXPENSES for 2010–11 ***Tuition, state resident:*** full-time $5865; part-time $424 per semester hour. ***Tuition, nonresident:*** full-time $13,438; part-time $740 per semester hour. ***Required fees:*** full-time $1304. Full-time tuition and fees vary according to course load, program, and reciprocity agreements. Part-time tuition and fees vary according to course load, program, and reciprocity agreements. ***College room and board:*** $5730; ***Room only:*** $3050. Room and board charges vary according to board plan, housing facility, and student level. ***Payment plan:*** Installment.

FRESHMAN FINANCIAL AID (Fall 2010, est.) 306 applied for aid; of those 79% were deemed to have need. 100% of freshmen with need received aid; of those 22% had need fully met. 3% of all full-time freshmen had no need and received non-need-based gift aid.

UNDERGRADUATE FINANCIAL AID (Fall 2010, est.) 1,697 applied for aid; of those 86% were deemed to have need. 99% of undergraduates with need received aid; of those 19% had need fully met. 1% of all full-time undergraduates had no need and received non-need-based gift aid.

GIFT AID (NEED-BASED) ***Total amount:*** $6,571,624 (77% federal, 22% state, 1% external sources). ***Receiving aid:*** Freshmen: 40% (148); all full-time undergraduates: 48% (1,021). ***Average award:*** Freshmen: $5953; Undergraduates: $5570. ***Scholarships, grants, and awards:*** Federal Pell, FSEOG, state, private, college/university gift aid from institutional funds.

GIFT AID (NON-NEED-BASED) ***Total amount:*** $1,060,301 (3% state, 65% institutional, 32% external sources). ***Receiving aid:*** Freshmen: 28% (104). Undergraduates: 15% (326). ***Average award:*** Freshmen: $1903. Undergraduates: $2288. ***Scholarships, grants, and awards by category:*** *Academic interests/achievement:* biological sciences, business, communication, computer science, education, English, general academic interests/achievements, health fields, humanities, mathematics, physical sciences, social sciences. *Creative arts/performance:* general creative arts/performance. *Special characteristics:* general special characteristics, members of minority groups.

LOANS ***Student loans:*** $13,227,070 (47% need-based, 53% non-need-based). 77% of past graduating class borrowed through all loan programs. *Average indebtedness per student:* $23,466. ***Average need-based loan:*** Freshmen: $3301. Undergraduates: $4220. ***Parent loans:*** $430,117 (100% non-need-based). ***Programs:*** Federal Direct (Subsidized and Unsubsidized Stafford, PLUS), Perkins, state, college/university.

WORK-STUDY ***Federal work-study:*** Total amount: $210,149; jobs available. ***State or other work-study/employment:*** Part-time jobs available.

APPLYING FOR FINANCIAL AID ***Required financial aid form:*** FAFSA. ***Financial aid deadline:*** Continuous. ***Notification date:*** Continuous beginning 3/15.

CONTACT Tammi Reijo, Assistant Director of Financial Aid, University of Wisconsin–Superior, Belknap and Catlin, Old Main 110, PO Box 2000, Superior, WI 54880, 715-394-8200. *Fax:* 715-394-8027. *E-mail:* finaid@uwsuper.edu.

UNIVERSITY OF WISCONSIN–WHITEWATER

Whitewater, WI

ABOUT THE INSTITUTION State-supported, coed. 56 undergraduate majors.

GIFT AID (NEED-BASED) ***Scholarships, grants, and awards:*** Federal Pell, FSEOG, state, private, college/university gift aid from institutional funds.

GIFT AID (NON-NEED-BASED) ***Scholarships, grants, and awards by category:*** *Academic interests/achievement:* biological sciences, business, communication, computer science, education, English, foreign languages, general academic interests/achievements, humanities, mathematics, physical sciences, premedicine, social sciences. *Creative arts/performance:* art/fine arts, cinema/film/broadcasting, creative writing, journalism/publications, music, theater/drama. *Special achievements/activities:* leadership. *Special characteristics:* adult students, ethnic background, handicapped students, international students, local/state students, members of minority groups, out-of-state students.

LOANS ***Programs:*** Federal Direct (Subsidized and Unsubsidized Stafford, PLUS), Perkins.

WORK-STUDY ***Federal work-study:*** Total amount: $700,000; 505 jobs averaging $1261. ***State or other work-study/employment:*** Total amount: $3,500,000 (100% non-need-based). 1,723 part-time jobs averaging $2031.

APPLYING FOR FINANCIAL AID ***Required financial aid form:*** FAFSA.

CONTACT Ms. Carol Miller, Director of Financial Aid, University of Wisconsin–Whitewater, 800 West Main Street, Whitewater, WI 53190-1790, 262-472-1130. *Fax:* 262-472-5655.

UNIVERSITY OF WYOMING

Laramie, WY

Tuition & fees (WY res): $3927 **Average undergraduate aid package: $8690**

ABOUT THE INSTITUTION State-supported, coed. 79 undergraduate majors. Federal methodology is used as a basis for awarding need-based institutional aid.

UNDERGRADUATE EXPENSES for 2010–11 ***One-time required fee:*** $40. ***Tuition, state resident:*** full-time $2970; part-time $99 per credit hour. ***Tuition, nonresident:*** full-time $11,280; part-time $376 per credit hour. ***Required fees:*** full-time $957; $239 per term. Full-time tuition and fees vary according to course load, location, and reciprocity agreements. Part-time tuition and fees vary according to course load, location, and reciprocity agreements. ***College room and board:*** $8360; ***Room only:*** $3612. Room and board charges vary according to board plan and housing facility. ***Payment plan:*** Installment.

FRESHMAN FINANCIAL AID (Fall 2010, est.) 1,419 applied for aid; of those 64% were deemed to have need. 99% of freshmen with need received aid; of those 23% had need fully met. ***Average percent of need met:*** 35% (excluding resources awarded to replace EFC). ***Average financial aid package:*** $8353 (excluding resources awarded to replace EFC). 38% of all full-time freshmen had no need and received non-need-based gift aid.

UNDERGRADUATE FINANCIAL AID (Fall 2010, est.) 5,295 applied for aid; of those 73% were deemed to have need. 99% of undergraduates with need received aid; of those 20% had need fully met. ***Average percent of need met:*** 42% (excluding resources awarded to replace EFC). ***Average financial aid package:*** $8690 (excluding resources awarded to replace EFC). 36% of all full-time undergraduates had no need and received non-need-based gift aid.

GIFT AID (NEED-BASED) ***Total amount:*** $13,952,471 (78% federal, 13% state, 4% institutional, 5% external sources). ***Receiving aid:*** Freshmen: 29% (582); all full-time undergraduates: 31% (2,583). ***Average award:*** Freshmen: $2688; Undergraduates: $3154. ***Scholarships, grants, and awards:*** Federal Pell, FSEOG, state, private, college/university gift aid from institutional funds.

GIFT AID (NON-NEED-BASED) ***Total amount:*** $25,406,297 (1% federal, 77% state, 15% institutional, 7% external sources). ***Receiving aid:*** Freshmen: 32% (635). Undergraduates: 28% (2,354). ***Average award:*** Freshmen: $4590. Undergraduates: $5057. ***Scholarships, grants, and awards by category:*** *Academic interests/achievement:* 6,664 awards ($19,374,322 total): agriculture, business, communication, computer science, education, engineering/technologies, English, foreign languages, general academic interests/achievements, health fields, home economics, international studies, mathematics, military science, physical sciences, social sciences. *Creative arts/performance:* 451 awards ($521,751 total): art/fine arts, dance, debating, journalism/publications, music, theater/drama. *Special achievements/activities:* 170 awards ($277,950 total): cheerleading/drum major, junior miss, leadership, rodeo. *Special characteristics:* 3,689 awards ($8,826,028 total): adult students, children and siblings of alumni, ethnic background, first-generation college students, handicapped students, international students, local/state students, out-of-state students, veterans. ***Tuition waivers:*** Full or partial for children of alumni, employees or children of employees, senior citizens.

LOANS ***Student loans:*** $27,370,188 (38% need-based, 62% non-need-based). 42% of past graduating class borrowed through all loan programs. *Average indebtedness per student:* $20,571. ***Average need-based loan:*** Freshmen: $1746. Undergraduates: $2388. ***Parent loans:*** $2,560,104 (100% non-need-based). ***Programs:*** Federal Direct (Subsidized and Unsubsidized Stafford, PLUS), Perkins, alternative loans.

WORK-STUDY ***Federal work-study:*** Total amount: $410,287; 289 jobs averaging $1422.

ATHLETIC AWARDS Total amount: $3,469,637 (100% non-need-based).

APPLYING FOR FINANCIAL AID ***Required financial aid form:*** FAFSA. ***Financial aid deadline (priority):*** 3/1. ***Notification date:*** Continuous beginning 3/15. Students must reply within 3 weeks of notification.

CONTACT Dr. Tammy Aagard, Interim Director of Student Financial Aid, University of Wyoming, Department 3335, Laramie, WY 82071, 307-766-2116 or toll-free 800-342-5996. *Fax:* 307-766-3800. *E-mail:* finaid@uwyo.edu.

UPPER IOWA UNIVERSITY

Fayette, IA

Tuition & fees: $23,356 **Average undergraduate aid package: $11,945**

ABOUT THE INSTITUTION Independent, coed. 39 undergraduate majors. Federal methodology is used as a basis for awarding need-based institutional aid.

UNDERGRADUATE EXPENSES for 2011–12 ***Comprehensive fee:*** $30,426 includes full-time tuition ($23,356) and room and board ($7070). ***College room only:*** $2850. Full-time tuition and fees vary according to degree level, location, and program. Room and board charges vary according to board plan, housing facility, and location. ***Part-time tuition:*** $813 per credit hour. ***Payment plan:*** Installment.

FRESHMAN FINANCIAL AID (Fall 2010, est.) 201 applied for aid; of those 77% were deemed to have need. 100% of freshmen with need received aid. ***Average percent of need met:*** 51% (excluding resources awarded to replace EFC).

Average financial aid package: $16,671 (excluding resources awarded to replace EFC). 23% of all full-time freshmen had no need and received non-need-based gift aid.

UNDERGRADUATE FINANCIAL AID (Fall 2010, est.) 850 applied for aid; of those 77% were deemed to have need. 100% of undergraduates with need received aid. ***Average percent of need met:*** 33% (excluding resources awarded to replace EFC). ***Average financial aid package:*** $11,945 (excluding resources awarded to replace EFC). 25% of all full-time undergraduates had no need and received non-need-based gift aid.

GIFT AID (NEED-BASED) ***Total amount:*** $25,236,283 (60% federal, 13% state, 27% institutional). ***Receiving aid:*** Freshmen: 77% (155); all full-time undergraduates: 75% (654). ***Average award:*** Freshmen: $13,151; Undergraduates: $8686. ***Scholarships, grants, and awards:*** Federal Pell, FSEOG, state, private, college/university gift aid from institutional funds.

GIFT AID (NON-NEED-BASED) ***Total amount:*** $181,818 (100% external sources). ***Receiving aid:*** Freshmen: 77% (155). Undergraduates: 75% (654). ***Average award:*** Freshmen: $8646. Undergraduates: $5321. ***Scholarships, grants, and awards by category:*** *Academic interests/achievement:* 441 awards ($3,713,825 total): general academic interests/achievements. *Special achievements/activities:* 177 awards ($2,088,690 total): general special achievements/activities. *Special characteristics:* 23 awards ($9867 total): children and siblings of alumni, children of current students, parents of current students, religious affiliation, spouses of current students. ***Tuition waivers:*** Full or partial for employees or children of employees.

LOANS ***Student loans:*** $42,545,962 (42% need-based, 58% non-need-based). 81% of past graduating class borrowed through all loan programs. *Average indebtedness per student:* $22,666. ***Average need-based loan:*** Freshmen: $3266. Undergraduates: $3017. ***Parent loans:*** $1,391,491 (100% non-need-based). ***Programs:*** Federal Direct (Subsidized and Unsubsidized Stafford, PLUS), Perkins, college/university, alternative loans.

WORK-STUDY ***Federal work-study:*** Total amount: $357,595; 265 jobs averaging $1349.

ATHLETIC AWARDS Total amount: $2,024,902 (100% need-based).

APPLYING FOR FINANCIAL AID ***Required financial aid form:*** FAFSA. ***Financial aid deadline (priority):*** 3/1. ***Notification date:*** Continuous. Students must reply within 3 weeks of notification.

CONTACT Jobyna Eastman Johnston, Director of Financial Aid, Upper Iowa University, Parker Fox Hall, Box 1859, Fayette, IA 52142-1859, 563-425-5393 or toll-free 800-553-4150 Ext. 2. *Fax:* 563-425-5277. *E-mail:* jobyna@uiu.edu.

URBANA UNIVERSITY

Urbana, OH

CONTACT Mrs. Amy M. Barnhart, Director of Financial Aid, Urbana University, 579 College Way, Urbana, OH 43078-2091, 937-484-1359 or toll-free 800-7-URBANA. *Fax:* 937-652-6870. *E-mail:* abarnhart@urbana.edu.

URSINUS COLLEGE

Collegeville, PA

Tuition & fees: $40,120 **Average undergraduate aid package: $29,285**

ABOUT THE INSTITUTION Independent, coed. 34 undergraduate majors. Both federal and institutional methodology are used as a basis for awarding need-based institutional aid.

UNDERGRADUATE EXPENSES for 2010–11 ***Comprehensive fee:*** $49,870 includes full-time tuition ($39,950), mandatory fees ($170), and room and board ($9750). ***College room only:*** $4875. ***Part-time tuition:*** $1249 per credit hour. ***Part-time fees:*** $170 per year. ***Payment plan:*** Installment.

FRESHMAN FINANCIAL AID (Fall 2010, est.) 416 applied for aid; of those 92% were deemed to have need. 100% of freshmen with need received aid; of those 24% had need fully met. ***Average percent of need met:*** 90% (excluding resources awarded to replace EFC). ***Average financial aid package:*** $31,250 (excluding resources awarded to replace EFC). 25% of all full-time freshmen had no need and received non-need-based gift aid.

UNDERGRADUATE FINANCIAL AID (Fall 2010, est.) 1,661 applied for aid; of those 94% were deemed to have need. 100% of undergraduates with need received aid; of those 21% had need fully met. ***Average percent of need met:*** 86% (excluding resources awarded to replace EFC). ***Average financial aid package:*** $29,285 (excluding resources awarded to replace EFC). 25% of all full-time undergraduates had no need and received non-need-based gift aid.

GIFT AID (NEED-BASED) ***Total amount:*** $30,930,449 (7% federal, 4% state, 87% institutional, 2% external sources). ***Receiving aid:*** Freshmen: 86% (382); all full-time undergraduates: 88% (1,563). ***Average award:*** Freshmen: $22,680; Undergraduates: $19,789. ***Scholarships, grants, and awards:*** Federal Pell, FSEOG, state, private, college/university gift aid from institutional funds, Academic Competitiveness Grants, National SMART Grants.

GIFT AID (NON-NEED-BASED) ***Total amount:*** $7,039,044 (1% federal, 95% institutional, 4% external sources). ***Receiving aid:*** Freshmen: 15% (65). Undergraduates: 15% (273). ***Average award:*** Freshmen: $16,500. Undergraduates: $14,150. ***Scholarships, grants, and awards by category:*** *Academic interests/achievement:* 347 awards ($5,704,045 total): general academic interests/achievements. *Creative arts/performance:* 9 awards ($170,000 total): creative writing. *Special achievements/activities:* 20 awards ($80,000 total): leadership. *Special characteristics:* 170 awards ($1,009,050 total): children and siblings of alumni, children of faculty/staff, general special characteristics, siblings of current students. ***Tuition waivers:*** Full or partial for employees or children of employees.

LOANS ***Student loans:*** $13,009,738 (60% need-based, 40% non-need-based). 78% of past graduating class borrowed through all loan programs. *Average indebtedness per student:* $26,780. ***Average need-based loan:*** Freshmen: $3298. Undergraduates: $4479. ***Parent loans:*** $3,886,026 (26% need-based, 74% non-need-based). ***Programs:*** Federal Direct (Subsidized and Unsubsidized Stafford, PLUS), Perkins.

WORK-STUDY ***Federal work-study:*** Total amount: $1,693,600; 945 jobs averaging $1792. ***State or other work-study/employment:*** Part-time jobs available.

APPLYING FOR FINANCIAL AID ***Required financial aid forms:*** FAFSA, institution's own form, CSS Financial Aid PROFILE. ***Financial aid deadline:*** 2/15 (priority: 2/15). ***Notification date:*** 4/1. Students must reply by 5/1.

CONTACT Ms. Suzanne B. Sparrow, Director of Student Financial Services, Ursinus College, 601 E Main Street, Collegeville, PA 19426-1000, 610-409-3600 Ext. 2242. *Fax:* 610-409-3662. *E-mail:* ssparrow@ursinus.edu.

URSULINE COLLEGE

Pepper Pike, OH

Tuition & fees: $23,940 **Average undergraduate aid package: $14,643**

ABOUT THE INSTITUTION Independent Roman Catholic, coed, primarily women. 42 undergraduate majors. Federal methodology is used as a basis for awarding need-based institutional aid.

UNDERGRADUATE EXPENSES for 2010–11 ***Comprehensive fee:*** $31,910 includes full-time tuition ($23,700), mandatory fees ($240), and room and board ($7970). ***College room only:*** $4072. Full-time tuition and fees vary according to location. Room and board charges vary according to board plan and housing facility. ***Part-time tuition:*** $790 per credit hour. ***Part-time fees:*** $80 per term. Part-time tuition and fees vary according to location. ***Payment plan:*** Installment.

FRESHMAN FINANCIAL AID (Fall 2009) 90 applied for aid; of those 92% were deemed to have need. 100% of freshmen with need received aid; of those 14% had need fully met. ***Average percent of need met:*** 77% (excluding resources awarded to replace EFC). ***Average financial aid package:*** $18,673 (excluding resources awarded to replace EFC). 7% of all full-time freshmen had no need and received non-need-based gift aid.

UNDERGRADUATE FINANCIAL AID (Fall 2009) 739 applied for aid; of those 94% were deemed to have need. 100% of undergraduates with need received aid; of those 12% had need fully met. ***Average percent of need met:*** 63% (excluding resources awarded to replace EFC). ***Average financial aid package:*** $14,643 (excluding resources awarded to replace EFC). 5% of all full-time undergraduates had no need and received non-need-based gift aid.

GIFT AID (NEED-BASED) ***Total amount:*** $6,657,798 (31% federal, 10% state, 56% institutional, 3% external sources). ***Receiving aid:*** Freshmen: 87% (83); all full-time undergraduates: 80% (622). ***Average award:*** Freshmen: $15,067; Undergraduates: $10,447. ***Scholarships, grants, and awards:*** Federal Pell, FSEOG, state, private, college/university gift aid from institutional funds, United Negro College Fund.

GIFT AID (NON-NEED-BASED) ***Total amount:*** $293,636 (3% federal, 1% state, 87% institutional, 9% external sources). ***Receiving aid:*** Freshmen: 5% (5). Undergraduates: 3% (23). ***Average award:*** Freshmen: $5607. Undergraduates: $5036. ***Scholarships, grants, and awards by category:*** *Academic interests/*

achievement: general academic interests/achievements. *Special achievements/activities:* community service, leadership. *Special characteristics:* children and siblings of alumni, children of faculty/staff, relatives of clergy, religious affiliation, siblings of current students, veterans. ***Tuition waivers:*** Full or partial for employees or children of employees.

LOANS ***Student loans:*** $10,177,763 (82% need-based, 18% non-need-based). 91% of past graduating class borrowed through all loan programs. *Average indebtedness per student:* $25,242. ***Average need-based loan:*** Freshmen: $3567. Undergraduates: $5364. ***Parent loans:*** $596,874 (64% need-based, 36% non-need-based). ***Programs:*** Federal Direct (Subsidized and Unsubsidized Stafford, PLUS), Perkins, college/university.

WORK-STUDY ***Federal work-study:*** Total amount: $281,781; 300 jobs averaging $1000.

ATHLETIC AWARDS Total amount: $464,281 (84% need-based, 16% non-need-based).

APPLYING FOR FINANCIAL AID ***Required financial aid form:*** FAFSA. ***Financial aid deadline:*** Continuous. ***Notification date:*** Continuous beginning 3/1. Students must reply within 3 weeks of notification.

CONTACT Ms. Mary Lynn Perri, Director of Financial Aid and Enrollment Services, Ursuline College, 2550 Lander Road, Pepper Pike, OH 44124-4398, 440-646-8330 or toll-free 888-URSULINE. *Fax:* 440-684-6114. *E-mail:* mperri@ursuline.edu.

UTAH STATE UNIVERSITY

Logan, UT

Tuition & fees (UT res): $5150 **Average undergraduate aid package: $8800**

ABOUT THE INSTITUTION State-supported, coed. 115 undergraduate majors. Federal methodology is used as a basis for awarding need-based institutional aid.

UNDERGRADUATE EXPENSES for 2010–11 ***Tuition, state resident:*** full-time $4346. ***Tuition, nonresident:*** full-time $13,993. ***Required fees:*** full-time $804. Full-time tuition and fees vary according to course load, program, reciprocity agreements, and student level. Part-time tuition and fees vary according to course load, program, reciprocity agreements, and student level. ***College room and board:*** $5070; ***Room only:*** $1670. Room and board charges vary according to board plan and housing facility. ***Payment plan:*** Deferred payment.

FRESHMAN FINANCIAL AID (Fall 2010, est.) 1,675 applied for aid; of those 80% were deemed to have need. 99% of freshmen with need received aid; of those 18% had need fully met. ***Average percent of need met:*** 66% (excluding resources awarded to replace EFC). ***Average financial aid package:*** $9145 (excluding resources awarded to replace EFC). 5% of all full-time freshmen had no need and received non-need-based gift aid.

UNDERGRADUATE FINANCIAL AID (Fall 2010, est.) 7,749 applied for aid; of those 88% were deemed to have need. 99% of undergraduates with need received aid; of those 12% had need fully met. ***Average percent of need met:*** 62% (excluding resources awarded to replace EFC). ***Average financial aid package:*** $8800 (excluding resources awarded to replace EFC). 3% of all full-time undergraduates had no need and received non-need-based gift aid.

GIFT AID (NEED-BASED) ***Total amount:*** $28,265,000 (99% federal, 1% state). ***Receiving aid:*** Freshmen: 29% (844); all full-time undergraduates: 41% (5,103). ***Average award:*** Freshmen: $4300; Undergraduates: $4800. ***Scholarships, grants, and awards:*** Federal Pell, FSEOG, state, private, college/university gift aid from institutional funds.

GIFT AID (NON-NEED-BASED) ***Total amount:*** $12,514,000 (76% institutional, 24% external sources). ***Receiving aid:*** Freshmen: 29% (839). Undergraduates: 22% (2,759). ***Average award:*** Freshmen: $2260. Undergraduates: $2700. ***Scholarships, grants, and awards by category:*** *Academic interests/achievement:* agriculture, architecture, biological sciences, business, communication, computer science, education, engineering/technologies, English, foreign languages, general academic interests/achievements, health fields, home economics, humanities, international studies, library science, mathematics, physical sciences, premedicine, social sciences. *Creative arts/performance:* applied art and design, art/fine arts, general creative arts/performance, journalism/publications, music, performing arts, theater/drama. *Special characteristics:* children and siblings of alumni, children of faculty/staff, international students. ***Tuition waivers:*** Full or partial for minority students, children of alumni, employees or children of employees, adult students, senior citizens.

LOANS ***Student loans:*** $33,516,000 (67% need-based, 33% non-need-based). 47% of past graduating class borrowed through all loan programs. *Average indebtedness per student:* $15,194. ***Average need-based loan:*** Freshmen: $3375. Undergraduates: $4260. ***Parent loans:*** $780,000 (100% non-need-based). ***Programs:*** Federal Direct (Subsidized and Unsubsidized Stafford, PLUS), Perkins, college/university.

WORK-STUDY ***Federal work-study:*** Total amount: $521,000; 244 jobs averaging $3050. ***State or other work-study/employment:*** Total amount: $672,000 (100% need-based). 126 part-time jobs averaging $3050.

ATHLETIC AWARDS Total amount: $4,539,000 (100% non-need-based).

APPLYING FOR FINANCIAL AID ***Required financial aid forms:*** FAFSA, federal income tax form(s). ***Financial aid deadline:*** Continuous. ***Notification date:*** Continuous beginning 4/1. Students must reply within 4 weeks of notification.

CONTACT Tamara Allen, Associate Director of Financial Aid, Utah State University, Old Main Hill, Logan, UT 84322-1800, 435-797-3369 or toll-free 800-488-8108. *Fax:* 435-797-0654. *E-mail:* tamara.allen@usu.edu.

UTAH VALLEY UNIVERSITY

Orem, UT

Tuition & fees (UT res): $4288 **Average undergraduate aid package: $22,561**

ABOUT THE INSTITUTION State-supported, coed. 89 undergraduate majors. Federal methodology is used as a basis for awarding need-based institutional aid.

UNDERGRADUATE EXPENSES for 2010–11 ***Tuition, state resident:*** full-time $3672; part-time $154 per credit hour. ***Tuition, nonresident:*** full-time $12,246; part-time $488 per credit hour. ***Required fees:*** full-time $616; $616 per year. Full-time tuition and fees vary according to course load. Part-time tuition and fees vary according to course load. ***College room and board:*** $8904; ***Room only:*** $6678. Room and board charges vary according to housing facility. ***Payment plans:*** Installment, deferred payment.

FRESHMAN FINANCIAL AID (Fall 2010, est.) 2,382 applied for aid; of those 80% were deemed to have need. 94% of freshmen with need received aid; of those 4% had need fully met. ***Average percent of need met:*** 97% (excluding resources awarded to replace EFC). ***Average financial aid package:*** $17,947 (excluding resources awarded to replace EFC). 13% of all full-time freshmen had no need and received non-need-based gift aid.

UNDERGRADUATE FINANCIAL AID (Fall 2010, est.) 12,621 applied for aid; of those 88% were deemed to have need. 94% of undergraduates with need received aid; of those 2% had need fully met. ***Average percent of need met:*** 92% (excluding resources awarded to replace EFC). ***Average financial aid package:*** $22,561 (excluding resources awarded to replace EFC). 7% of all full-time undergraduates had no need and received non-need-based gift aid.

GIFT AID (NEED-BASED) ***Total amount:*** $59,578,605 (91% federal, 2% institutional, 7% external sources). ***Receiving aid:*** Freshmen: 47% (1,394); all full-time undergraduates: 54% (8,483). ***Average award:*** Freshmen: $13,130; Undergraduates: $14,484. ***Scholarships, grants, and awards:*** Federal Pell, FSEOG, state, private, college/university gift aid from institutional funds.

GIFT AID (NON-NEED-BASED) ***Total amount:*** $20,475 (100% institutional). ***Receiving aid:*** Freshmen: 1% (18). Undergraduates: 26. ***Average award:*** Freshmen: $4876. Undergraduates: $4985. ***Tuition waivers:*** Full or partial for employees or children of employees.

LOANS ***Student loans:*** $92,612,175 (100% need-based). 62% of past graduating class borrowed through all loan programs. *Average indebtedness per student:* $15,593. ***Average need-based loan:*** Freshmen: $8122. Undergraduates: $11,189. ***Parent loans:*** $804,306 (100% need-based). ***Programs:*** Perkins, state.

WORK-STUDY ***Federal work-study:*** Total amount: $1,652,086; jobs available. ***State or other work-study/employment:*** Total amount: $332,602 (100% need-based). Part-time jobs available.

ATHLETIC AWARDS Total amount: $287,099 (93% need-based, 7% non-need-based).

APPLYING FOR FINANCIAL AID ***Required financial aid forms:*** FAFSA, institution's own form. ***Financial aid deadline:*** 5/1 (priority: 5/1). ***Notification date:*** Continuous beginning 5/1. Students must reply by 6/15.

CONTACT Joanna McCormick, Senior Director, Utah Valley University, 800 West University Parkway, Orem, UT 84058, 801-863-8442 Ext. 8440. *Fax:* 801-863-8448. *E-mail:* joanna.mccormick@uvu.edu.

U.T.A. MESIVTA OF KIRYAS JOEL

Monroe, NY

CONTACT Financial Aid Office, U.T.A. Mesivta of Kiryas Joel, 9 Nickelsburg Road, Unit 312, Monroe, NY 10950, 845-873-9901.

UTICA COLLEGE

Utica, NY

Tuition & fees: $28,620 **Average undergraduate aid package: $22,059**

ABOUT THE INSTITUTION Independent, coed. 46 undergraduate majors. Federal methodology is used as a basis for awarding need-based institutional aid.

UNDERGRADUATE EXPENSES for 2010–11 ***Comprehensive fee:*** $40,210 includes full-time tuition ($28,100), mandatory fees ($520), and room and board ($11,590). Full-time tuition and fees vary according to class time and course load. Room and board charges vary according to board plan and housing facility. ***Part-time tuition:*** $950 per credit hour. Part-time tuition and fees vary according to class time and course load. ***Payment plans:*** Installment, deferred payment.

FRESHMAN FINANCIAL AID (Fall 2010, est.) 536 applied for aid; of those 97% were deemed to have need. 100% of freshmen with need received aid; of those 8% had need fully met. ***Average percent of need met:*** 73% (excluding resources awarded to replace EFC). ***Average financial aid package:*** $24,163 (excluding resources awarded to replace EFC). 3% of all full-time freshmen had no need and received non-need-based gift aid.

UNDERGRADUATE FINANCIAL AID (Fall 2010, est.) 1,994 applied for aid; of those 95% were deemed to have need. 100% of undergraduates with need received aid; of those 9% had need fully met. ***Average percent of need met:*** 68% (excluding resources awarded to replace EFC). ***Average financial aid package:*** $22,059 (excluding resources awarded to replace EFC). 5% of all full-time undergraduates had no need and received non-need-based gift aid.

GIFT AID (NEED-BASED) ***Total amount:*** $31,989,906 (17% federal, 10% state, 70% institutional, 3% external sources). ***Receiving aid:*** Freshmen: 95% (520); all full-time undergraduates: 91% (1,893). ***Average award:*** Freshmen: $6580; Undergraduates: $6938. ***Scholarships, grants, and awards:*** Federal Pell, FSEOG, state, private, college/university gift aid from institutional funds, Federal Nursing.

GIFT AID (NON-NEED-BASED) ***Total amount:*** $2,154,302 (1% state, 92% institutional, 7% external sources). ***Receiving aid:*** Freshmen: 3% (14). Undergraduates: 4% (78). ***Average award:*** Freshmen: $12,727. Undergraduates: $10,557. ***Scholarships, grants, and awards by category:*** *Academic interests/achievement:* general academic interests/achievements. ***Tuition waivers:*** Full or partial for employees or children of employees, senior citizens.

LOANS ***Student loans:*** $16,059,182 (91% need-based, 9% non-need-based). 85% of past graduating class borrowed through all loan programs. *Average indebtedness per student:* $39,371. ***Average need-based loan:*** Freshmen: $3366. Undergraduates: $4298. ***Parent loans:*** $6,325,965 (94% need-based, 6% non-need-based). ***Programs:*** Federal Direct (Subsidized and Unsubsidized Stafford, PLUS), Perkins.

WORK-STUDY ***Federal work-study:*** Total amount: $1,542,016; jobs available. ***State or other work-study/employment:*** Part-time jobs available.

APPLYING FOR FINANCIAL AID ***Required financial aid form:*** FAFSA. ***Financial aid deadline (priority):*** 2/15. ***Notification date:*** Continuous. Students must reply by 5/1 or within 4 weeks of notification.

CONTACT Laura Bedford, Director of Student Financial Services, Utica College, 1600 Burrstone Road, Utica, NY 13502-4892, 315-792-3179 or toll-free 800-782-8884. *Fax:* 315-792-3368. *E-mail:* lbedford@utica.edu.

VALDOSTA STATE UNIVERSITY

Valdosta, GA

Tuition & fees (GA res): $4972 **Average undergraduate aid package: $9360**

ABOUT THE INSTITUTION State-supported, coed. 55 undergraduate majors. Federal methodology is used as a basis for awarding need-based institutional aid.

UNDERGRADUATE EXPENSES for 2010–11 ***Tuition, state resident:*** full-time $3262; part-time $137 per credit hour. ***Tuition, nonresident:*** full-time $12,665; part-time $528 per credit hour. ***Required fees:*** full-time $1710. Full-time tuition and fees vary according to reciprocity agreements. Part-time tuition and fees vary according to course load and reciprocity agreements. ***College room and board:*** $6520; ***Room only:*** $3290. Room and board charges vary according to board plan and housing facility. Part-time mandatory fees per term: $253 for students enrolled in 3 credit hours or fewer, $855 for students enrolled in 4 credit hours or more.

FRESHMAN FINANCIAL AID (Fall 2010, est.) 2,266 applied for aid; of those 78% were deemed to have need. 100% of freshmen with need received aid; of those 13% had need fully met. ***Average percent of need met:*** 65% (excluding resources awarded to replace EFC). ***Average financial aid package:*** $9180 (excluding resources awarded to replace EFC). 1% of all full-time freshmen had no need and received non-need-based gift aid.

UNDERGRADUATE FINANCIAL AID (Fall 2010, est.) 7,853 applied for aid; of those 78% were deemed to have need. 99% of undergraduates with need received aid; of those 13% had need fully met. ***Average percent of need met:*** 63% (excluding resources awarded to replace EFC). ***Average financial aid package:*** $9360 (excluding resources awarded to replace EFC). 1% of all full-time undergraduates had no need and received non-need-based gift aid.

GIFT AID (NEED-BASED) ***Total amount:*** $34,369,863 (61% federal, 37% state, 1% institutional, 1% external sources). ***Receiving aid:*** Freshmen: 59% (1,484); all full-time undergraduates: 52% (4,905). ***Average award:*** Freshmen: $7250; Undergraduates: $6284. ***Scholarships, grants, and awards:*** Federal Pell, FSEOG, state, private, college/university gift aid from institutional funds.

GIFT AID (NON-NEED-BASED) ***Total amount:*** $7,391,204 (1% federal, 95% state, 2% institutional, 2% external sources). ***Receiving aid:*** Freshmen: 5% (124). Undergraduates: 3% (300). ***Average award:*** Freshmen: $1680. Undergraduates: $1361. ***Scholarships, grants, and awards by category:*** *Academic interests/achievement:* biological sciences, business, communication, computer science, education, engineering/technologies, English, foreign languages, general academic interests/achievements, health fields, humanities, library science, mathematics, military science, physical sciences, premedicine, social sciences. *Creative arts/performance:* art/fine arts, music, theater/drama. *Special achievements/activities:* general special achievements/activities. *Special characteristics:* children of public servants, general special characteristics, international students, members of minority groups. ***Tuition waivers:*** Full or partial for employees or children of employees, senior citizens.

LOANS ***Student loans:*** $55,547,090 (76% need-based, 24% non-need-based). 66% of past graduating class borrowed through all loan programs. *Average indebtedness per student:* $19,592. ***Average need-based loan:*** Freshmen: $3366. Undergraduates: $4065. ***Parent loans:*** $43,834,053 (36% need-based, 64% non-need-based). ***Programs:*** Federal Direct (Subsidized and Unsubsidized Stafford, PLUS), college/university.

WORK-STUDY ***Federal work-study:*** Total amount: $404,996; 168 jobs averaging $2868.

ATHLETIC AWARDS Total amount: $1,089,019 (42% need-based, 58% non-need-based).

APPLYING FOR FINANCIAL AID ***Required financial aid form:*** FAFSA. ***Financial aid deadline (priority):*** 5/1. ***Notification date:*** Continuous beginning 5/15.

CONTACT Mr. Douglas R. Tanner, Director of Financial Aid, Valdosta State University, 1500 North Patterson Street, Valdosta, GA 31698, 229-333-5935 or toll-free 800-618-1878 Ext. 1. *Fax:* 229-333-5430.

VALLEY CITY STATE UNIVERSITY

Valley City, ND

Tuition & fees (ND res): $6270 **Average undergraduate aid package: $8615**

ABOUT THE INSTITUTION State-supported, coed. 43 undergraduate majors. Federal methodology is used as a basis for awarding need-based institutional aid.

UNDERGRADUATE EXPENSES for 2011–12 ***Tuition, state resident:*** full-time $4610; part-time $154 per semester hour. ***Tuition, nonresident:*** full-time $12,308; part-time $410 per semester hour. ***Required fees:*** full-time $1660. Full-time tuition and fees vary according to course load, location, program, and reciprocity agreements. Part-time tuition and fees vary according to course load, location, program, and reciprocity agreements. ***College room and board:*** $5218. Room and board charges vary according to board plan and housing facility. ***Payment plan:*** Installment.

FRESHMAN FINANCIAL AID (Fall 2010, est.) 169 applied for aid; of those 76% were deemed to have need. 100% of freshmen with need received aid; of those 100% had need fully met. ***Average percent of need met:*** 80% (excluding

resources awarded to replace EFC). ***Average financial aid package:*** $9539 (excluding resources awarded to replace EFC). 86% of all full-time freshmen had no need and received non-need-based gift aid.

UNDERGRADUATE FINANCIAL AID (Fall 2010, est.) 565 applied for aid; of those 75% were deemed to have need. 100% of undergraduates with need received aid; of those 100% had need fully met. ***Average percent of need met:*** 66% (excluding resources awarded to replace EFC). ***Average financial aid package:*** $8615 (excluding resources awarded to replace EFC). 45% of all full-time undergraduates had no need and received non-need-based gift aid.

GIFT AID (NEED-BASED) ***Total amount:*** $2,210,743 (61% federal, 13% state, 17% institutional, 9% external sources). ***Receiving aid:*** Freshmen: 65% (125); all full-time undergraduates: 54% (392). ***Average award:*** Freshmen: $6370; Undergraduates: $4835. ***Scholarships, grants, and awards:*** Federal Pell, FSEOG, state, private, college/university gift aid from institutional funds.

GIFT AID (NON-NEED-BASED) ***Total amount:*** $30,077 (44% institutional, 56% external sources). ***Receiving aid:*** Freshmen: 4% (7). Undergraduates: 1% (10). ***Average award:*** Freshmen: $2129. Undergraduates: $1759. ***Scholarships, grants, and awards by category:*** *Academic interests/achievement:* biological sciences, business, communication, computer science, education, English, general academic interests/achievements, humanities, library science, mathematics, physical sciences, social sciences. *Creative arts/performance:* applied art and design, art/fine arts, journalism/publications, music, theater/drama. *Special achievements/activities:* general special achievements/activities. *Special characteristics:* children of faculty/staff, ethnic background, general special characteristics, international students, members of minority groups. ***Tuition waivers:*** Full or partial for employees or children of employees.

LOANS ***Student loans:*** $2,980,908 (79% need-based, 21% non-need-based). 89% of past graduating class borrowed through all loan programs. *Average indebtedness per student:* $22,428. ***Average need-based loan:*** Freshmen: $3309. Undergraduates: $4064. ***Parent loans:*** $15,254 (16% need-based, 84% non-need-based). ***Programs:*** Federal Direct (Subsidized and Unsubsidized Stafford, PLUS), Perkins, college/university.

WORK-STUDY ***Federal work-study:*** Total amount: $76,974; 46 jobs averaging $1673. ***State or other work-study/employment:*** Part-time jobs available.

ATHLETIC AWARDS Total amount: $108,240 (52% need-based, 48% non-need-based).

APPLYING FOR FINANCIAL AID ***Required financial aid form:*** FAFSA. ***Financial aid deadline (priority):*** 3/15. ***Notification date:*** Continuous beginning 2/15. Students must reply within 4 weeks of notification.

CONTACT Betty Kuss Schumacher, Director of Student Financial Aid, Valley City State University, 101 College Street SW, Valley City, ND 58072, 701-845-7412 or toll-free 800-532-8641 Ext. 37101. *Fax:* 701-845-7410. *E-mail:* betty.schumacher@vcsu.edu.

VALLEY FORGE CHRISTIAN COLLEGE

Phoenixville, PA

Tuition & fees: $16,250 **Average undergraduate aid package: $10,406**

ABOUT THE INSTITUTION Independent Assemblies of God, coed. 18 undergraduate majors. Federal methodology is used as a basis for awarding need-based institutional aid.

UNDERGRADUATE EXPENSES for 2010–11 ***One-time required fee:*** $75. ***Comprehensive fee:*** $23,806 includes full-time tuition ($14,600), mandatory fees ($1650), and room and board ($7556). ***College room only:*** $3860. Full-time tuition and fees vary according to course load, location, and program. Room and board charges vary according to board plan and housing facility. ***Part-time tuition:*** $564 per credit. ***Part-time fees:*** $250 per term. Part-time tuition and fees vary according to course load, location, and program. ***Payment plan:*** Installment.

FRESHMAN FINANCIAL AID (Fall 2010, est.) 157 applied for aid; of those 93% were deemed to have need. 99% of freshmen with need received aid; of those 8% had need fully met. ***Average percent of need met:*** 51% (excluding resources awarded to replace EFC). ***Average financial aid package:*** $10,439 (excluding resources awarded to replace EFC). 19% of all full-time freshmen had no need and received non-need-based gift aid.

UNDERGRADUATE FINANCIAL AID (Fall 2010, est.) 769 applied for aid; of those 93% were deemed to have need. 98% of undergraduates with need received aid; of those 7% had need fully met. ***Average percent of need met:*** 49% (excluding resources awarded to replace EFC). ***Average financial aid package:*** $10,406 (excluding resources awarded to replace EFC). 9% of all full-time undergraduates had no need and received non-need-based gift aid.

GIFT AID (NEED-BASED) ***Total amount:*** $4,880,174 (43% federal, 13% state, 37% institutional, 7% external sources). ***Receiving aid:*** Freshmen: 74% (138); all full-time undergraduates: 84% (669). ***Average award:*** Freshmen: $7877; Undergraduates: $7060. ***Scholarships, grants, and awards:*** Federal Pell, FSEOG, state, private, college/university gift aid from institutional funds.

GIFT AID (NON-NEED-BASED) ***Total amount:*** $517,973 (92% institutional, 8% external sources). ***Receiving aid:*** Freshmen: 4% (7). Undergraduates: 3% (24). ***Average award:*** Freshmen: $4590. Undergraduates: $4634. ***Scholarships, grants, and awards by category:*** *Academic interests/achievement:* 179 awards ($536,221 total): general academic interests/achievements. *Creative arts/performance:* 360 awards ($900,969 total): art/fine arts, music. *Special achievements/activities:* 264 awards ($298,494 total): community service, general special achievements/activities, leadership, religious involvement. *Special characteristics:* 516 awards ($554,279 total): children of current students, children of faculty/staff, general special characteristics, local/state students, married students, parents of current students, relatives of clergy, siblings of current students, spouses of current students. ***Tuition waivers:*** Full or partial for employees or children of employees.

LOANS ***Student loans:*** $6,693,472 (84% need-based, 16% non-need-based). 89% of past graduating class borrowed through all loan programs. *Average indebtedness per student:* $32,581. ***Average need-based loan:*** Freshmen: $3197. Undergraduates: $4001. ***Parent loans:*** $2,697,918 (67% need-based, 33% non-need-based). ***Programs:*** Federal Direct (Subsidized and Unsubsidized Stafford, PLUS), Perkins.

WORK-STUDY ***Federal work-study:*** Total amount: $64,198; 26 jobs averaging $2059.

APPLYING FOR FINANCIAL AID ***Required financial aid form:*** FAFSA. ***Financial aid deadline (priority):*** 5/1. ***Notification date:*** Continuous beginning 3/1. Students must reply within 3 weeks of notification.

CONTACT Mrs. Linda Stein, Director of Financial Aid, Valley Forge Christian College, 1401 Charlestown Road, Phoenixville, PA 19460-2399, 610-917-1416 or toll-free 800-432-8322. *Fax:* 610-917-2069. *E-mail:* listein@vfcc.edu.

VALLEY FORGE CHRISTIAN COLLEGE WOODBRIDGE CAMPUS

Woodbridge, VA

ABOUT THE INSTITUTION Independent Assemblies of God, coed.

GIFT AID (NEED-BASED) ***Scholarships, grants, and awards:*** Federal Pell, FSEOG.

LOANS ***Programs:*** alternative loans.

APPLYING FOR FINANCIAL AID ***Required financial aid form:*** FAFSA.

CONTACT Christiana Bruwaa-Frimpong, Student Accounts/Financial Aid Counselor, Valley Forge Christian College Woodbridge Campus, 13909 Smoketown Road, Woodbridge, VA 22192, 703-580-4810 Ext. 172 or toll-free 800-432-8322 (in-state). *Fax:* 703-580-4806.

VALPARAISO UNIVERSITY

Valparaiso, IN

Tuition & fees: $31,040 **Average undergraduate aid package: $21,602**

ABOUT THE INSTITUTION Independent religious, coed. 82 undergraduate majors. Federal methodology is used as a basis for awarding need-based institutional aid.

UNDERGRADUATE EXPENSES for 2011–12 ***Comprehensive fee:*** $39,796 includes full-time tuition ($30,000), mandatory fees ($1040), and room and board ($8756). ***College room only:*** $5356. Full-time tuition and fees vary according to course load. Room and board charges vary according to housing facility and student level. ***Part-time tuition:*** $1355 per credit hour. ***Payment plan:*** Installment.

FRESHMAN FINANCIAL AID (Fall 2009) 613 applied for aid; of those 87% were deemed to have need. 100% of freshmen with need received aid; of those 20% had need fully met. ***Average percent of need met:*** 78% (excluding resources awarded to replace EFC). ***Average financial aid package:*** $22,795 (excluding resources awarded to replace EFC). 18% of all full-time freshmen had no need and received non-need-based gift aid.

UNDERGRADUATE FINANCIAL AID (Fall 2009) 2,324 applied for aid; of those 90% were deemed to have need. 100% of undergraduates with need received aid; of those 17% had need fully met. ***Average percent of need met:*** 77% (excluding resources awarded to replace EFC). ***Average financial aid package:*** $21,602 (excluding resources awarded to replace EFC). 20% of all full-time undergraduates had no need and received non-need-based gift aid.

GIFT AID (NEED-BASED) ***Total amount:*** $29,834,072 (16% federal, 6% state, 76% institutional, 2% external sources). ***Receiving aid:*** Freshmen: 78% (526); all full-time undergraduates: 72% (2,034). ***Average award:*** Freshmen: $19,114; Undergraduates: $17,177. ***Scholarships, grants, and awards:*** Federal Pell, FSEOG, state, private, college/university gift aid from institutional funds.

GIFT AID (NON-NEED-BASED) ***Total amount:*** $9,643,676 (4% federal, 86% institutional, 10% external sources). ***Receiving aid:*** Freshmen: 10% (66). Undergraduates: 7% (209). ***Average award:*** Freshmen: $10,026. Undergraduates: $9427. ***Scholarships, grants, and awards by category:*** *Academic interests/achievement:* 2,030 awards ($17,200,000 total): business, engineering/technologies, foreign languages, general academic interests/achievements, health fields, physical sciences, religion/biblical studies. *Creative arts/performance:* 110 awards ($130,000 total): art/fine arts, music, performing arts, theater/drama. *Special characteristics:* 415 awards ($2,350,000 total): children and siblings of alumni, children of faculty/staff, international students, relatives of clergy, religious affiliation. ***Tuition waivers:*** Full or partial for employees or children of employees.

LOANS ***Student loans:*** $18,140,358 (75% need-based, 25% non-need-based). 72% of past graduating class borrowed through all loan programs. *Average indebtedness per student:* $33,024. ***Average need-based loan:*** Freshmen: $5244. Undergraduates: $5150. ***Parent loans:*** $5,091,107 (8% need-based, 92% non-need-based). ***Programs:*** Federal Direct (Subsidized and Unsubsidized Stafford, PLUS), Perkins, college/university, private loans.

WORK-STUDY ***Federal work-study:*** Total amount: $676,309; jobs available. ***State or other work-study/employment:*** Total amount: $1,100,886 (17% need-based, 83% non-need-based). Part-time jobs available.

ATHLETIC AWARDS Total amount: $4,077,177 (45% need-based, 55% non-need-based).

APPLYING FOR FINANCIAL AID ***Required financial aid form:*** FAFSA. ***Financial aid deadline (priority):*** 3/1. ***Notification date:*** Continuous beginning 3/1. Students must reply by 5/1.

CONTACT Ms. Phyllis Schroeder, Interim Director of Financial Aid, Valparaiso University, 1700 Chapel Drive, Valparaiso, IN 46383-6493, 219-464-5015 or toll-free 888-GO-VALPO. *Fax:* 219-464-5012. *E-mail:* phyllis.schroeder@valpo.edu.

VANDERBILT UNIVERSITY

Nashville, TN

Tuition & fees: $39,930 **Average undergraduate aid package: $41,835**

ABOUT THE INSTITUTION Independent, coed. 65 undergraduate majors. Both federal and institutional methodology are used as a basis for awarding need-based institutional aid.

UNDERGRADUATE EXPENSES for 2010–11 ***One-time required fee:*** $642. ***Comprehensive fee:*** $52,988 includes full-time tuition ($38,952), mandatory fees ($978), and room and board ($13,058). ***College room only:*** $8528. Room and board charges vary according to board plan. ***Part-time tuition:*** $1623 per credit hour. ***Payment plans:*** Tuition prepayment, installment.

FRESHMAN FINANCIAL AID (Fall 2010, est.) 934 applied for aid; of those 87% were deemed to have need. 100% of freshmen with need received aid; of those 100% had need fully met. ***Average percent of need met:*** 100% (excluding resources awarded to replace EFC). ***Average financial aid package:*** $42,397 (excluding resources awarded to replace EFC). 7% of all full-time freshmen had no need and received non-need-based gift aid.

UNDERGRADUATE FINANCIAL AID (Fall 2010, est.) 3,609 applied for aid; of those 90% were deemed to have need. 100% of undergraduates with need received aid; of those 100% had need fully met. ***Average percent of need met:*** 100% (excluding resources awarded to replace EFC). ***Average financial aid package:*** $41,835 (excluding resources awarded to replace EFC). 9% of all full-time undergraduates had no need and received non-need-based gift aid.

GIFT AID (NEED-BASED) ***Total amount:*** $123,263,333 (5% federal, 2% state, 92% institutional, 1% external sources). ***Receiving aid:*** Freshmen: 44% (710); all full-time undergraduates: 43% (2,944). ***Average award:*** Freshmen: $37,174; Undergraduates: $36,352. ***Scholarships, grants, and awards:*** Federal Pell, FSEOG, state, private, college/university gift aid from institutional funds.

GIFT AID (NON-NEED-BASED) ***Total amount:*** $19,035,637 (10% federal, 6% state, 79% institutional, 5% external sources). ***Receiving aid:*** Freshmen: 29% (469). Undergraduates: 22% (1,524). ***Average award:*** Freshmen: $19,663. Undergraduates: $22,182. ***Scholarships, grants, and awards by category:*** *Academic interests/achievement:* general academic interests/achievements. *Creative arts/performance:* general creative arts/performance. *Special achievements/activities:* community service, general special achievements/activities, leadership. *Special characteristics:* general special characteristics, local/state students, members of minority groups. ***Tuition waivers:*** Full or partial for employees or children of employees.

LOANS ***Student loans:*** $8,042,727 (14% need-based, 86% non-need-based). 37% of past graduating class borrowed through all loan programs. *Average indebtedness per student:* $18,605. ***Average need-based loan:*** Freshmen: $2575. Undergraduates: $3292. ***Parent loans:*** $5,469,749 (100% non-need-based). ***Programs:*** Federal Direct (Subsidized and Unsubsidized Stafford, PLUS), Perkins, Federal Nursing, college/university.

WORK-STUDY ***Federal work-study:*** Total amount: $2,887,447; jobs available. ***State or other work-study/employment:*** Total amount: $948,173 (100% need-based). Part-time jobs available.

ATHLETIC AWARDS Total amount: $9,955,433 (28% need-based, 72% non-need-based).

APPLYING FOR FINANCIAL AID ***Required financial aid forms:*** FAFSA, CSS Financial Aid PROFILE. ***Financial aid deadline (priority):*** 2/5. ***Notification date:*** 4/1. Students must reply by 5/1.

CONTACT David Mohning, Executive Director of Student Financial Aid, Vanderbilt University, 2309 West End Avenue, Nashville, TN 37203, 615-322-3591 or toll-free 800-288-0432. *Fax:* 615-343-8512. *E-mail:* finaid@vanderbilt.edu.

VANDERCOOK COLLEGE OF MUSIC

Chicago, IL

CONTACT Ms. D. Denny, Director of Financial Aid, VanderCook College of Music, 3140 South Federal Street, Chicago, IL 60616-3731, 312-225-6288 Ext. 233 or toll-free 800-448-2655. *Fax:* 312-225-5211. *E-mail:* ddenny@vandercook.edu.

VANGUARD UNIVERSITY OF SOUTHERN CALIFORNIA

Costa Mesa, CA

Tuition & fees: $26,342 **Average undergraduate aid package: $19,230**

ABOUT THE INSTITUTION Independent religious, coed. 46 undergraduate majors. Federal methodology is used as a basis for awarding need-based institutional aid.

UNDERGRADUATE EXPENSES for 2010–11 ***Comprehensive fee:*** $34,616 includes full-time tuition ($26,342) and room and board ($8274). ***College room only:*** $4074. Full-time tuition and fees vary according to course load. Room and board charges vary according to board plan and housing facility. ***Part-time tuition:*** $1098 per unit. Part-time tuition and fees vary according to course load. ***Payment plan:*** Installment.

FRESHMAN FINANCIAL AID (Fall 2010, est.) 300 applied for aid; of those 93% were deemed to have need. 100% of freshmen with need received aid; of those 15% had need fully met. ***Average percent of need met:*** 72% (excluding resources awarded to replace EFC). ***Average financial aid package:*** $21,454 (excluding resources awarded to replace EFC). 12% of all full-time freshmen had no need and received non-need-based gift aid.

UNDERGRADUATE FINANCIAL AID (Fall 2010, est.) 1,183 applied for aid; of those 94% were deemed to have need. 100% of undergraduates with need received aid; of those 12% had need fully met. ***Average percent of need met:*** 67% (excluding resources awarded to replace EFC). ***Average financial aid package:*** $19,230 (excluding resources awarded to replace EFC). 15% of all full-time undergraduates had no need and received non-need-based gift aid.

GIFT AID (NEED-BASED) ***Total amount:*** $15,496,368 (15% federal, 17% state, 65% institutional, 3% external sources). ***Receiving aid:*** Freshmen: 71% (231); all full-time undergraduates: 68% (895). ***Average award:*** Freshmen: $8698; Undergraduates: $8695. ***Scholarships, grants, and awards:*** Federal Pell, FSEOG, state, private, college/university gift aid from institutional funds.

GIFT AID (NON-NEED-BASED) ***Total amount:*** $2,193,682 (92% institutional, 8% external sources). ***Receiving aid:*** Freshmen: 85% (274). Undergraduates: 73% (955). ***Average award:*** Freshmen: $12,143. Undergraduates: $12,957. ***Scholarships, grants, and awards by category:*** *Academic interests/achievement:* 1,056 awards ($7,748,793 total): general academic interests/achievements. *Creative arts/performance:* 243 awards ($675,922 total): debating, music, theater/drama. *Special characteristics:* 30 awards ($519,726 total): children of faculty/staff. ***Tuition waivers:*** Full or partial for employees or children of employees.

LOANS ***Student loans:*** $9,509,911 (80% need-based, 20% non-need-based). 76% of past graduating class borrowed through all loan programs. *Average indebtedness per student:* $28,256. ***Average need-based loan:*** Freshmen: $3977. Undergraduates: $4683. ***Parent loans:*** $2,929,332 (46% need-based, 54% non-need-based). ***Programs:*** Federal Direct (Subsidized and Unsubsidized Stafford, PLUS), Perkins.

WORK-STUDY ***Federal work-study:*** Total amount: $224,279; 94 jobs averaging $2386.

ATHLETIC AWARDS Total amount: $1,957,040 (51% need-based, 49% non-need-based).

APPLYING FOR FINANCIAL AID ***Required financial aid forms:*** FAFSA, state aid form. ***Financial aid deadline (priority):*** 3/2. ***Notification date:*** Continuous beginning 3/15. Students must reply within 3 weeks of notification.

CONTACT Undergraduate Admissions Office, Vanguard University of Southern California, 55 Fair Drive, Costa Mesa, CA 92626-6597, 800-722-6279. *Fax:* 714-966-5471. *E-mail:* admissions@vanguard.edu.

VASSAR COLLEGE

Poughkeepsie, NY

Tuition & fees: $43,190 **Average undergraduate aid package: $40,631**

ABOUT THE INSTITUTION Independent, coed. 52 undergraduate majors. Institutional methodology is used as a basis for awarding need-based institutional aid.

UNDERGRADUATE EXPENSES for 2010–11 ***Comprehensive fee:*** $53,090 includes full-time tuition ($42,560), mandatory fees ($630), and room and board ($9900). ***College room only:*** $5470. Room and board charges vary according to board plan and housing facility. ***Part-time tuition:*** $5040 per unit. Part-time tuition and fees vary according to course load. ***Payment plan:*** Installment.

FRESHMAN FINANCIAL AID (Fall 2010, est.) 491 applied for aid; of those 86% were deemed to have need. 100% of freshmen with need received aid; of those 100% had need fully met. ***Average percent of need met:*** 100% (excluding resources awarded to replace EFC). ***Average financial aid package:*** $41,054 (excluding resources awarded to replace EFC).

UNDERGRADUATE FINANCIAL AID (Fall 2010, est.) 1,722 applied for aid; of those 89% were deemed to have need. 100% of undergraduates with need received aid; of those 100% had need fully met. ***Average percent of need met:*** 100% (excluding resources awarded to replace EFC). ***Average financial aid package:*** $40,631 (excluding resources awarded to replace EFC).

GIFT AID (NEED-BASED) ***Total amount:*** $54,776,531 (6% federal, 1% state, 91% institutional, 2% external sources). ***Receiving aid:*** Freshmen: 64% (423); all full-time undergraduates: 62% (1,528). ***Average award:*** Freshmen: $37,892; Undergraduates: $36,353. ***Scholarships, grants, and awards:*** Federal Pell, FSEOG, state, private, college/university gift aid from institutional funds.

GIFT AID (NON-NEED-BASED) ***Total amount:*** $189,824 (10% federal, 11% state, 79% external sources). ***Tuition waivers:*** Full or partial for employees or children of employees.

LOANS ***Student loans:*** $5,556,658 (58% need-based, 42% non-need-based). 49% of past graduating class borrowed through all loan programs. *Average indebtedness per student:* $18,153. ***Average need-based loan:*** Freshmen: $1914. Undergraduates: $2656. ***Parent loans:*** $3,341,294 (100% non-need-based). ***Programs:*** Federal Direct (Subsidized and Unsubsidized Stafford, PLUS), Perkins, state.

WORK-STUDY ***Federal work-study:*** Total amount: $1,935,330; jobs available. ***State or other work-study/employment:*** Total amount: $778,331 (100% need-based). Part-time jobs available.

APPLYING FOR FINANCIAL AID ***Required financial aid forms:*** FAFSA, CSS Financial Aid PROFILE, noncustodial (divorced/separated) parent's statement, business/farm supplement. ***Financial aid deadline:*** 2/15. ***Notification date:*** 3/29. Students must reply by 5/1.

CONTACT Mr. Michael Fraher, Director of Financial Aid, Vassar College, 124 Raymond Avenue, Poughkeepsie, NY 12604, 845-437-5320 or toll-free 800-827-7270. *Fax:* 845-437-5325. *E-mail:* mafraher@vassar.edu.

VAUGHN COLLEGE OF AERONAUTICS AND TECHNOLOGY

Flushing, NY

CONTACT Dorothy Martin, Director of Financial Aid, Vaughn College of Aeronautics and Technology, 86-01 23rd Avenue, Flushing, NY 11369, 718-429-6600 Ext. 187 or toll-free 800-776-2376 Ext. 145 (in-state). *Fax:* 718-779-2231. *E-mail:* dorothy.martin@vaughn.edu.

VERMONT TECHNICAL COLLEGE

Randolph Center, VT

Tuition & fees (VT res): $11,555 **Average undergraduate aid package: $8856**

ABOUT THE INSTITUTION State-supported, coed. 24 undergraduate majors. Federal methodology is used as a basis for awarding need-based institutional aid.

UNDERGRADUATE EXPENSES for 2011–12 ***Tuition, state resident:*** full-time $10,656; part-time $444 per credit. ***Tuition, nonresident:*** full-time $20,376; part-time $849 per credit. ***Required fees:*** full-time $899. Full-time tuition and fees vary according to course load and program. Part-time tuition and fees vary according to program. ***College room and board:*** $8445. Room and board charges vary according to board plan. ***Payment plan:*** Installment.

FRESHMAN FINANCIAL AID (Fall 2009) 231 applied for aid; of those 84% were deemed to have need. 98% of freshmen with need received aid; of those 21% had need fully met. ***Average percent of need met:*** 60% (excluding resources awarded to replace EFC). ***Average financial aid package:*** $9234 (excluding resources awarded to replace EFC). 2% of all full-time freshmen had no need and received non-need-based gift aid.

UNDERGRADUATE FINANCIAL AID (Fall 2009) 1,046 applied for aid; of those 88% were deemed to have need. 99% of undergraduates with need received aid; of those 12% had need fully met. ***Average percent of need met:*** 60% (excluding resources awarded to replace EFC). ***Average financial aid package:*** $8856 (excluding resources awarded to replace EFC). 2% of all full-time undergraduates had no need and received non-need-based gift aid.

GIFT AID (NEED-BASED) ***Total amount:*** $4,918,152 (49% federal, 25% state, 12% institutional, 14% external sources). ***Receiving aid:*** Freshmen: 64% (157); all full-time undergraduates: 56% (711). ***Average award:*** Freshmen: $5836; Undergraduates: $5620. ***Scholarships, grants, and awards:*** Federal Pell, FSEOG, state, private, college/university gift aid from institutional funds.

GIFT AID (NON-NEED-BASED) ***Total amount:*** $420,104 (23% institutional, 77% external sources). ***Receiving aid:*** Freshmen: 10% (24). Undergraduates: 2% (22). ***Average award:*** Freshmen: $3244. Undergraduates: $4146. ***Scholarships, grants, and awards by category:*** *Academic interests/achievement:* 44 awards ($316,000 total): agriculture, general academic interests/achievements. ***Tuition waivers:*** Full or partial for employees or children of employees.

LOANS ***Student loans:*** $9,735,753 (85% need-based, 15% non-need-based). 78% of past graduating class borrowed through all loan programs. *Average indebtedness per student:* $24,000. ***Average need-based loan:*** Freshmen: $3392. Undergraduates: $39,476. ***Parent loans:*** $2,600,619 (77% need-based, 23% non-need-based). ***Programs:*** Federal Direct (Subsidized and Unsubsidized Stafford, PLUS), Perkins.

WORK-STUDY ***Federal work-study:*** Total amount: $133,902; 150 jobs averaging $900.

APPLYING FOR FINANCIAL AID ***Required financial aid forms:*** FAFSA, state aid form. ***Financial aid deadline (priority):*** 3/1. ***Notification date:*** Continuous beginning 3/15.

CONTACT Catherine R. McCullough, Director of Financial Aid, Vermont Technical College, PO Box 500, Randolph Center, VT 05061-0500, 802-728-1248 or toll-free 800-442-VTC1. *Fax:* 802-728-1390.

VICTORY UNIVERSITY

Memphis, TN

Tuition & fees: $10,620 **Average undergraduate aid package: $9029**

ABOUT THE INSTITUTION Independent, coed. 17 undergraduate majors. Federal methodology is used as a basis for awarding need-based institutional aid.

UNDERGRADUATE EXPENSES for 2010–11 ***Tuition:*** full-time $10,050; part-time $335 per credit hour. ***Required fees:*** full-time $570; $19 per credit hour. Full-time tuition and fees vary according to course load and location. Part-time tuition and fees vary according to course load and location. ***Payment plans:*** Guaranteed tuition, installment.

FRESHMAN FINANCIAL AID (Fall 2009) 8 applied for aid; of those 100% were deemed to have need. 100% of freshmen with need received aid; of those 100% had need fully met. ***Average percent of need met:*** 63% (excluding resources awarded to replace EFC). ***Average financial aid package:*** $7325 (excluding resources awarded to replace EFC).

UNDERGRADUATE FINANCIAL AID (Fall 2009) 385 applied for aid; of those 93% were deemed to have need. 100% of undergraduates with need received aid; of those 8% had need fully met. ***Average percent of need met:*** 76% (excluding resources awarded to replace EFC). ***Average financial aid package:*** $9029 (excluding resources awarded to replace EFC).

GIFT AID (NEED-BASED) ***Total amount:*** $2,650,070 (81% federal, 19% state). ***Receiving aid:*** Freshmen: 70% (7); all full-time undergraduates: 62% (304). ***Average award:*** Freshmen: $5077; Undergraduates: $6488. ***Scholarships, grants, and awards:*** Federal Pell, FSEOG, state, private.

GIFT AID (NON-NEED-BASED) ***Total amount:*** $141,535 (16% federal, 51% state, 33% external sources). ***Receiving aid:*** Freshmen: 30% (3). Undergraduates: 5% (26). ***Scholarships, grants, and awards by category:*** *Academic interests/achievement:* general academic interests/achievements. *Special characteristics:* 1 award ($4093 total): children of faculty/staff. ***Tuition waivers:*** Full or partial for employees or children of employees, senior citizens.

LOANS ***Student loans:*** $6,087,617 (31% need-based, 69% non-need-based). 56% of past graduating class borrowed through all loan programs. *Average indebtedness per student:* $27,625. ***Average need-based loan:*** Freshmen: $2873. Undergraduates: $4376. ***Parent loans:*** $53,972 (100% non-need-based). ***Programs:*** Federal Direct (Subsidized and Unsubsidized Stafford, PLUS).

WORK-STUDY ***Federal work-study:*** Total amount: $103,354; 50 jobs averaging $2085.

APPLYING FOR FINANCIAL AID ***Required financial aid form:*** FAFSA. ***Financial aid deadline (priority):*** 2/15. ***Notification date:*** Continuous beginning 4/1. Students must reply within 2 weeks of notification.

CONTACT Ms. LaTonya Branch, Financial Aid Director, Victory University, 255 North Highland Street, Memphis, TN 38111, 901-320-9787 Ext. 1032 or toll-free 800-960-9777. *Fax:* 901-320-9724. *E-mail:* lbranch@victory.edu.

VILLA MARIA COLLEGE OF BUFFALO

Buffalo, NY

Tuition & fees: $15,919 **Average undergraduate aid package: $7320**

ABOUT THE INSTITUTION Independent religious, coed. 16 undergraduate majors. Federal methodology is used as a basis for awarding need-based institutional aid.

UNDERGRADUATE EXPENSES for 2011–12 ***Tuition:*** full-time $15,100; part-time $500 per credit. Full-time tuition and fees vary according to degree level and program. Part-time tuition and fees vary according to course load, degree level, and program. ***Payment plan:*** Installment.

FRESHMAN FINANCIAL AID (Fall 2009) 143 applied for aid; of those 90% were deemed to have need. 100% of freshmen with need received aid. ***Average percent of need met:*** 50% (excluding resources awarded to replace EFC). ***Average financial aid package:*** $5335 (excluding resources awarded to replace EFC). 5% of all full-time freshmen had no need and received non-need-based gift aid.

UNDERGRADUATE FINANCIAL AID (Fall 2009) 408 applied for aid; of those 79% were deemed to have need. 100% of undergraduates with need received aid; of those 3% had need fully met. ***Average percent of need met:*** 50% (excluding resources awarded to replace EFC). ***Average financial aid package:*** $7320 (excluding resources awarded to replace EFC). 4% of all full-time undergraduates had no need and received non-need-based gift aid.

GIFT AID (NEED-BASED) ***Total amount:*** $2,359,742 (49% federal, 35% state, 12% institutional, 4% external sources). ***Receiving aid:*** Freshmen: 72% (106); all full-time undergraduates: 61% (253). ***Average award:*** Freshmen: $2856; Undergraduates: $4971. ***Scholarships, grants, and awards:*** Federal Pell, FSEOG, state, private, college/university gift aid from institutional funds.

GIFT AID (NON-NEED-BASED) ***Receiving aid:*** Freshmen: 16% (24). Undergraduates: 15% (63). ***Average award:*** Freshmen: $1500. Undergraduates: $1333. ***Tuition waivers:*** Full or partial for employees or children of employees, senior citizens.

LOANS ***Student loans:*** $3,039,981 (100% need-based). 100% of past graduating class borrowed through all loan programs. *Average indebtedness per student:* $26,304. ***Average need-based loan:*** Freshmen: $2677. Undergraduates: $4195. ***Parent loans:*** $534,820 (100% need-based). ***Programs:*** Federal Direct (Subsidized and Unsubsidized Stafford, PLUS), private loans.

WORK-STUDY ***Federal work-study:*** Total amount: $22,381; 65 jobs averaging $430.

APPLYING FOR FINANCIAL AID ***Required financial aid forms:*** FAFSA, state aid form. ***Financial aid deadline:*** Continuous. ***Notification date:*** Continuous beginning 5/1. Students must reply within 2 weeks of notification.

CONTACT Christina Horner, Director of Financial Aid, Villa Maria College of Buffalo, 240 Pine Ridge Road, Buffalo, NY 14225, 716-961-1849. *Fax:* 716-896-0705. *E-mail:* chorner@villa.edu.

VILLANOVA UNIVERSITY

Villanova, PA

Tuition & fees: $39,665 **Average undergraduate aid package: $28,445**

ABOUT THE INSTITUTION Independent Roman Catholic, coed. 48 undergraduate majors. Both federal and institutional methodology are used as a basis for awarding need-based institutional aid.

UNDERGRADUATE EXPENSES for 2010–11 ***Comprehensive fee:*** $50,305 includes full-time tuition ($39,085), mandatory fees ($580), and room and board ($10,640). ***College room only:*** $5640. Room and board charges vary according to board plan and housing facility. ***Part-time tuition:*** $1595 per course. ***Part-time fees:*** $30 per year. ***Payment plan:*** Installment.

FRESHMAN FINANCIAL AID (Fall 2010, est.) 1,106 applied for aid; of those 72% were deemed to have need. 97% of freshmen with need received aid; of those 21% had need fully met. ***Average percent of need met:*** 80% (excluding resources awarded to replace EFC). ***Average financial aid package:*** $28,626 (excluding resources awarded to replace EFC). 5% of all full-time freshmen had no need and received non-need-based gift aid.

UNDERGRADUATE FINANCIAL AID (Fall 2010, est.) 3,916 applied for aid; of those 82% were deemed to have need. 98% of undergraduates with need received aid; of those 16% had need fully met. ***Average percent of need met:*** 79% (excluding resources awarded to replace EFC). ***Average financial aid package:*** $28,445 (excluding resources awarded to replace EFC). 6% of all full-time undergraduates had no need and received non-need-based gift aid.

GIFT AID (NEED-BASED) ***Total amount:*** $67,205,469 (9% federal, 2% state, 86% institutional, 3% external sources). ***Receiving aid:*** Freshmen: 42% (688); all full-time undergraduates: 42% (2,779). ***Average award:*** Freshmen: $24,921; Undergraduates: $23,525. ***Scholarships, grants, and awards:*** Federal Pell, FSEOG, state, private, college/university gift aid from institutional funds, endowed and restricted grants.

GIFT AID (NON-NEED-BASED) ***Total amount:*** $7,374,488 (33% federal, 58% institutional, 9% external sources). ***Receiving aid:*** Freshmen: 12% (203). Undergraduates: 13% (873). ***Average award:*** Freshmen: $10,023. Undergraduates: $10,361. ***Scholarships, grants, and awards by category:*** *Academic interests/achievement:* 818 awards ($5,721,950 total): general academic interests/achievements, international studies, military science. *Special achievements/activities:* 22 awards ($24,300 total): general special achievements/activities. *Special characteristics:* 234 awards ($7,412,445 total): children of educators, children of faculty/staff, general special characteristics, members of minority groups, religious affiliation. ***Tuition waivers:*** Full or partial for employees or children of employees, senior citizens.

LOANS ***Student loans:*** $30,389,463 (84% need-based, 16% non-need-based). 55% of past graduating class borrowed through all loan programs. *Average indebtedness per student:* $37,267. ***Average need-based loan:*** Freshmen: $3164. Undergraduates: $4431. ***Parent loans:*** $12,956,796 (78% need-based, 22% non-need-based). ***Programs:*** Federal Direct (Subsidized and Unsubsidized Stafford, PLUS), Perkins, Federal Nursing.

WORK-STUDY ***Federal work-study:*** Total amount: $6,982,987; 2,568 jobs averaging $2666. ***State or other work-study/employment:*** 48 part-time jobs averaging $2855.

ATHLETIC AWARDS Total amount: $9,256,269 (30% need-based, 70% non-need-based).

APPLYING FOR FINANCIAL AID ***Required financial aid forms:*** FAFSA, CSS Financial Aid PROFILE, federal income tax form(s), W-2 forms. ***Financial aid deadline:*** 2/7 (priority: 2/7). ***Notification date:*** 4/1. Students must reply by 5/1.
CONTACT Bonnie Lee Behm, Director of Financial Assistance, Villanova University, 800 Lancaster Avenue, Villanova, PA 19085-1699, 610-519-4010. *Fax:* 610-519-7599. *E-mail:* bonnie.behm@villanova.edu.

VIRGINIA COLLEGE AT BIRMINGHAM

Birmingham, AL

CONTACT Vice President, Campus Administration, Virginia College at Birmingham, 65 Bagby Drive, Birmingham, AL 35209, 205-802-1200. *Fax:* 205-271-8273.

VIRGINIA COLLEGE AT HUNTSVILLE

Huntsville, AL

CONTACT Financial Aid Office, Virginia College at Huntsville, 2800-A Bob Wallace Avenue, Huntsville, AL 35805, 256-533-7387.

VIRGINIA COMMONWEALTH UNIVERSITY

Richmond, VA

Tuition & fees (VA res): $8717 **Average undergraduate aid package: $9259**

ABOUT THE INSTITUTION State-supported, coed. 61 undergraduate majors. Federal methodology is used as a basis for awarding need-based institutional aid.
UNDERGRADUATE EXPENSES for 2010–11 ***Tuition, state resident:*** full-time $6853; part-time $291 per credit hour. ***Tuition, nonresident:*** full-time $19,672; part-time $821 per credit hour. ***Required fees:*** full-time $1864; $70.01 per credit hour. ***College room and board:*** $8526; ***Room only:*** $5186. Room and board charges vary according to board plan. ***Payment plan:*** Installment.
FRESHMAN FINANCIAL AID (Fall 2009) 2,444 applied for aid; of those 81% were deemed to have need. 100% of freshmen with need received aid; of those 8% had need fully met. ***Average percent of need met:*** 58% (excluding resources awarded to replace EFC). ***Average financial aid package:*** $9652 (excluding resources awarded to replace EFC). 10% of all full-time freshmen had no need and received non-need-based gift aid.
UNDERGRADUATE FINANCIAL AID (Fall 2009) 11,665 applied for aid; of those 83% were deemed to have need. 100% of undergraduates with need received aid; of those 11% had need fully met. ***Average percent of need met:*** 59% (excluding resources awarded to replace EFC). ***Average financial aid package:*** $9259 (excluding resources awarded to replace EFC). 8% of all full-time undergraduates had no need and received non-need-based gift aid.
GIFT AID (NEED-BASED) ***Total amount:*** $53,655,856 (47% federal, 33% state, 11% institutional, 9% external sources). ***Receiving aid:*** Freshmen: 44% (1,593); all full-time undergraduates: 40% (7,530). ***Average award:*** Freshmen: $6641; Undergraduates: $5841. ***Scholarships, grants, and awards:*** Federal Pell, FSEOG, state, private, college/university gift aid from institutional funds, United Negro College Fund.
GIFT AID (NON-NEED-BASED) ***Total amount:*** $9,954,047 (2% federal, 2% state, 25% institutional, 71% external sources). ***Receiving aid:*** Freshmen: 17% (617). Undergraduates: 10% (1,831). ***Average award:*** Freshmen: $3649. Undergraduates: $6385. ***Scholarships, grants, and awards by category:*** *Academic interests/achievement:* 3,629 awards ($11,317,295 total): biological sciences, business, computer science, education, engineering/technologies, foreign languages, general academic interests/achievements, health fields, humanities, mathematics, military science, physical sciences. *Creative arts/performance:* 200 awards ($348,232 total): art/fine arts, dance, music, performing arts, theater/drama. *Special characteristics:* veterans' children. ***Tuition waivers:*** Full or partial for employees or children of employees, senior citizens.
LOANS ***Student loans:*** $95,066,556 (82% need-based, 18% non-need-based). 61% of past graduating class borrowed through all loan programs. *Average indebtedness per student:* $25,151. ***Average need-based loan:*** Freshmen: $3626. Undergraduates: $4325. ***Parent loans:*** $11,757,141 (73% need-based, 27% non-need-based). ***Programs:*** Federal Direct (Subsidized and Unsubsidized Stafford, PLUS), Perkins, Federal Nursing, college/university.
WORK-STUDY ***Federal work-study:*** Total amount: $1,038,608; 661 jobs averaging $1574. ***State or other work-study/employment:*** Total amount: $10,804 (100% non-need-based). Part-time jobs available.
ATHLETIC AWARDS Total amount: $2,754,243 (29% need-based, 71% non-need-based).
APPLYING FOR FINANCIAL AID ***Required financial aid form:*** FAFSA. ***Financial aid deadline (priority):*** 3/1. ***Notification date:*** Continuous beginning 4/1. Students must reply within 2 weeks of notification.
CONTACT Brenda Burke, Interim Director for Financial Aid, Virginia Commonwealth University, 901 West Franklin Street, Richmond, VA 23284-3026, 804-828-6669 or toll-free 800-841-3638. *Fax:* 804-827-0060. *E-mail:* faidmail@vcu.edu.

VIRGINIA INTERMONT COLLEGE

Bristol, VA

ABOUT THE INSTITUTION Independent religious, coed. 53 undergraduate majors.
GIFT AID (NEED-BASED) ***Scholarships, grants, and awards:*** Federal Pell, FSEOG, state, private, college/university gift aid from institutional funds.
GIFT AID (NON-NEED-BASED) ***Scholarships, grants, and awards by category:*** *Academic interests/achievement:* general academic interests/achievements. *Creative arts/performance:* applied art and design, art/fine arts, dance, general creative arts/performance, music, performing arts, theater/drama. *Special achievements/activities:* cheerleading/drum major, religious involvement. *Special characteristics:* children of faculty/staff, first-generation college students, members of minority groups, religious affiliation.
LOANS ***Programs:*** Federal Direct (Subsidized and Unsubsidized Stafford, PLUS), Perkins, alternative loans.
WORK-STUDY ***Federal work-study:*** Total amount: $151,660; 98 jobs averaging $1000.
APPLYING FOR FINANCIAL AID ***Required financial aid forms:*** FAFSA, state aid form.
CONTACT Ms. Denise Posey, Director of Financial Aid, Virginia Intermont College, 1013 Moore Street, Bristol, VA 24201-4298, 276-466-7872 or toll-free 800-451-1842. *Fax:* 276-466-7855.

VIRGINIA INTERNATIONAL UNIVERSITY

Fairfax, VA

CONTACT Financial Aid Office, Virginia International University, 11200 Waples Mill Road, Fairfax, VA 22030, 703-591-7042 or toll-free 800-514 6848.

VIRGINIA MILITARY INSTITUTE

Lexington, VA

Tuition & fees (VA res): $12,328 **Average undergraduate aid package: $19,333**

ABOUT THE INSTITUTION State-supported, coed, primarily men. 14 undergraduate majors. Federal methodology is used as a basis for awarding need-based institutional aid.
UNDERGRADUATE EXPENSES for 2010–11 ***Tuition, state resident:*** full-time $6024. ***Tuition, nonresident:*** full-time $24,016. ***Required fees:*** full-time $6304. ***College room and board:*** $7132. ***Payment plan:*** Installment.
FRESHMAN FINANCIAL AID (Fall 2009) 312 applied for aid; of those 69% were deemed to have need. 99% of freshmen with need received aid; of those 44% had need fully met. ***Average percent of need met:*** 89% (excluding resources awarded to replace EFC). ***Average financial aid package:*** $19,200 (excluding resources awarded to replace EFC). 23% of all full-time freshmen had no need and received non-need-based gift aid.
UNDERGRADUATE FINANCIAL AID (Fall 2009) 934 applied for aid; of those 75% were deemed to have need. 99% of undergraduates with need received aid; of those 50% had need fully met. ***Average percent of need met:*** 90% (excluding resources awarded to replace EFC). ***Average financial aid package:*** $19,333 (excluding resources awarded to replace EFC). 18% of all full-time undergraduates had no need and received non-need-based gift aid.
GIFT AID (NEED-BASED) ***Total amount:*** $5,671,831 (19% federal, 14% state, 63% institutional, 4% external sources). ***Receiving aid:*** Freshmen: 45% (205); all full-time undergraduates: 43% (662). ***Average award:*** Freshmen: $9153; Undergraduates: $8847. ***Scholarships, grants, and awards:*** Federal Pell, FSEOG, state, private, college/university gift aid from institutional funds.
GIFT AID (NON-NEED-BASED) ***Total amount:*** $9,185,597 (88% federal, 11% institutional, 1% external sources). ***Receiving aid:*** Freshmen: 23% (104).

Undergraduates: 26% (404). ***Average award:*** Freshmen: $3065. Undergraduates: $3659. ***Scholarships, grants, and awards by category:*** *Academic interests/achievement:* 75 awards ($675,000 total): biological sciences, business, computer science, engineering/technologies, English, general academic interests/achievements, international studies, mathematics, military science, premedicine. *Creative arts/performance:* 12 awards ($7500 total): music. *Special achievements/activities:* 20 awards ($75,000 total): general special achievements/activities, leadership. *Special characteristics:* 275 awards ($950,000 total): children and siblings of alumni, children of faculty/staff, general special characteristics, local/state students, out-of-state students.

LOANS ***Student loans:*** $4,417,002 (35% need-based, 65% non-need-based). 54% of past graduating class borrowed through all loan programs. *Average indebtedness per student:* $18,063. ***Average need-based loan:*** Freshmen: $3753. Undergraduates: $3706. ***Parent loans:*** $1,529,992 (100% non-need-based). ***Programs:*** Federal Direct (Subsidized and Unsubsidized Stafford, PLUS), Perkins.

ATHLETIC AWARDS Total amount: $2,922,734 (39% need-based, 61% non-need-based).

APPLYING FOR FINANCIAL AID ***Required financial aid forms:*** FAFSA, institution's own form. ***Financial aid deadline (priority):*** 3/1. ***Notification date:*** Continuous beginning 3/1. Students must reply by 5/1.

CONTACT Col. Timothy P. Golden, Director of Financial Aid, Virginia Military Institute, 306 Carroll Hall, Lexington, VA 24450, 540-464-7208 or toll-free 800-767-4207. *Fax:* 540-464-7629. *E-mail:* goldentp@vmi.edu.

VIRGINIA POLYTECHNIC INSTITUTE AND STATE UNIVERSITY

Blacksburg, VA

Tuition & fees (VA res): $9458 **Average undergraduate aid package: $10,531**

ABOUT THE INSTITUTION State-supported, coed. 66 undergraduate majors. Federal methodology is used as a basis for awarding need-based institutional aid.

UNDERGRADUATE EXPENSES for 2010–11 ***Tuition, state resident:*** full-time $7309. ***Tuition, nonresident:*** full-time $20,498. ***Required fees:*** full-time $2149. ***College room and board:*** $6290. Room and board charges vary according to board plan. ***Payment plan:*** Installment.

FRESHMAN FINANCIAL AID (Fall 2009) 3,815 applied for aid; of those 61% were deemed to have need. 91% of freshmen with need received aid; of those 16% had need fully met. ***Average percent of need met:*** 62% (excluding resources awarded to replace EFC). ***Average financial aid package:*** $10,990 (excluding resources awarded to replace EFC). 11% of all full-time freshmen had no need and received non-need-based gift aid.

UNDERGRADUATE FINANCIAL AID (Fall 2009) 14,947 applied for aid; of those 64% were deemed to have need. 99% of undergraduates with need received aid; of those 21% had need fully met. ***Average percent of need met:*** 69% (excluding resources awarded to replace EFC). ***Average financial aid package:*** $10,531 (excluding resources awarded to replace EFC). 9% of all full-time undergraduates had no need and received non-need-based gift aid.

GIFT AID (NEED-BASED) ***Total amount:*** $36,795,211 (53% federal, 37% state, 10% institutional). ***Receiving aid:*** Freshmen: 28% (1,430); all full-time undergraduates: 30% (6,806). ***Average award:*** Freshmen: $7364; Undergraduates: $6445. ***Scholarships, grants, and awards:*** Federal Pell, FSEOG, state, private, college/university gift aid from institutional funds, United Negro College Fund.

GIFT AID (NON-NEED-BASED) ***Total amount:*** $44,213,212 (17% institutional, 83% external sources). ***Receiving aid:*** Freshmen: 36% (1,797). Undergraduates: 34% (7,900). ***Average award:*** Freshmen: $3985. Undergraduates: $4352. ***Scholarships, grants, and awards by category:*** *Academic interests/achievement:* general academic interests/achievements, library science. *Creative arts/performance:* applied art and design, art/fine arts, cinema/film/broadcasting, creative writing, journalism/publications, music, performing arts, theater/drama. *Special achievements/activities:* cheerleading/drum major, community service, general special achievements/activities, leadership, memberships, religious involvement. *Special characteristics:* children of faculty/staff, first-generation college students, local/state students, members of minority groups, out-of-state students, twins, veterans' children. ***Tuition waivers:*** Full or partial for employees or children of employees, senior citizens.

LOANS ***Student loans:*** $83,958,542 (38% need-based, 62% non-need-based). 52% of past graduating class borrowed through all loan programs. *Average indebtedness per student:* $23,100. ***Average need-based loan:*** Freshmen: $4059. Undergraduates: $4310. ***Programs:*** Federal Direct (Subsidized and Unsubsidized Stafford, PLUS), Perkins, state, college/university.

WORK-STUDY ***Federal work-study:*** Total amount: $1,209,877; jobs available. ***State or other work-study/employment:*** Total amount: $7,772,464 (100% non-need-based). Part-time jobs available.

ATHLETIC AWARDS Total amount: $8,300,420 (100% non-need-based).

APPLYING FOR FINANCIAL AID ***Required financial aid forms:*** FAFSA, general scholarship application. ***Financial aid deadline (priority):*** 3/1. ***Notification date:*** Continuous beginning 3/30. Students must reply by 5/1 or within 4 weeks of notification.

CONTACT Dr. Barry Simmons, Director of Student Financial Services, Virginia Polytechnic Institute and State University, 300 Student Service Building, Blacksburg, VA 24061, 540-231-5179. *Fax:* 540-231-9139. *E-mail:* simmonsb@vt.edu.

VIRGINIA STATE UNIVERSITY

Petersburg, VA

Tuition & fees (VA res): $6570 **Average undergraduate aid package: $10,200**

ABOUT THE INSTITUTION State-supported, coed. 35 undergraduate majors. Federal methodology is used as a basis for awarding need-based institutional aid.

UNDERGRADUATE EXPENSES for 2010–11 ***Tuition, state resident:*** full-time $3886; part-time $226 per credit hour. ***Tuition, nonresident:*** full-time $12,452; part-time $500 per credit hour. ***Required fees:*** full-time $2684; $10 per credit hour. Full-time tuition and fees vary according to course load, degree level, and program. Part-time tuition and fees vary according to course load, degree level, and program. ***College room and board:*** $8152; ***Room only:*** $4640. Room and board charges vary according to board plan and housing facility. ***Payment plan:*** Installment.

FRESHMAN FINANCIAL AID (Fall 2010, est.) 1,145 applied for aid; of those 90% were deemed to have need. 100% of freshmen with need received aid; of those 34% had need fully met. ***Average percent of need met:*** 70% (excluding resources awarded to replace EFC). ***Average financial aid package:*** $8800 (excluding resources awarded to replace EFC). 15% of all full-time freshmen had no need and received non-need-based gift aid.

UNDERGRADUATE FINANCIAL AID (Fall 2010, est.) 4,771 applied for aid; of those 96% were deemed to have need. 100% of undergraduates with need received aid; of those 15% had need fully met. ***Average percent of need met:*** 65% (excluding resources awarded to replace EFC). ***Average financial aid package:*** $10,200 (excluding resources awarded to replace EFC). 10% of all full-time undergraduates had no need and received non-need-based gift aid.

GIFT AID (NEED-BASED) ***Total amount:*** $23,497,825 (68% federal, 22% state, 10% institutional). ***Receiving aid:*** Freshmen: 68% (825); all full-time undergraduates: 72% (3,661). ***Average award:*** Freshmen: $4500; Undergraduates: $5500. ***Scholarships, grants, and awards:*** Federal Pell, FSEOG, state, private, college/university gift aid from institutional funds.

GIFT AID (NON-NEED-BASED) ***Total amount:*** $6,765,516 (1% federal, 24% state, 62% institutional, 13% external sources). ***Receiving aid:*** Freshmen: 19% (227). Undergraduates: 20% (1,005). ***Average award:*** Freshmen: $500. Undergraduates: $1000. ***Scholarships, grants, and awards by category:*** *Academic interests/achievement:* 150 awards ($300,000 total): agriculture, architecture, area/ethnic studies, biological sciences, business, communication, computer science, education, engineering/technologies, English, general academic interests/achievements, health fields, home economics, humanities, mathematics, military science, physical sciences, premedicine, social sciences. *Creative arts/performance:* 65 awards ($92,000 total): applied art and design, art/fine arts, dance, music, performing arts. *Special achievements/activities:* 31 awards ($116,240 total): cheerleading/drum major, community service, hobbies/interests, leadership, religious involvement. ***Tuition waivers:*** Full or partial for senior citizens.

LOANS ***Student loans:*** $39,486,186 (93% need-based, 7% non-need-based). 90% of past graduating class borrowed through all loan programs. *Average indebtedness per student:* $28,250. ***Average need-based loan:*** Freshmen: $3500. Undergraduates: $5500. ***Parent loans:*** $8,852,100 (100% non-need-based). ***Programs:*** Federal Direct (Subsidized and Unsubsidized Stafford, PLUS), Perkins, college/university.

WORK-STUDY ***Federal work-study:*** Total amount: $538,040; 400 jobs averaging $2000.

ATHLETIC AWARDS Total amount: $950,712 (100% non-need-based).

APPLYING FOR FINANCIAL AID ***Required financial aid forms:*** FAFSA, institution's own form. ***Financial aid deadline (priority):*** 3/31. ***Notification date:*** Continuous beginning 3/1. Students must reply within 2 weeks of notification.

CONTACT Myra Phillips, Director, Virginia State University, PO Box 9031, Petersburg, VA 23806-2096, 804-524-5352 or toll-free 800-871-7611. *Fax:* 804-524-6818. *E-mail:* mhphilli@vsu.edu.

VIRGINIA UNION UNIVERSITY

Richmond, VA

ABOUT THE INSTITUTION Independent Baptist, coed. 22 undergraduate majors.

GIFT AID (NEED-BASED) ***Scholarships, grants, and awards:*** Federal Pell, FSEOG, state, private, college/university gift aid from institutional funds.

GIFT AID (NON-NEED-BASED) ***Scholarships, grants, and awards by category:*** *Academic interests/achievement:* general academic interests/achievements.

LOANS ***Programs:*** Federal Direct (Subsidized and Unsubsidized Stafford), Perkins.

WORK-STUDY Federal work-study jobs available.

APPLYING FOR FINANCIAL AID ***Required financial aid forms:*** FAFSA, state aid form.

CONTACT Mrs. Donna Mack-Tatum, Director of Financial Aid, Virginia Union University, 1500 North Lombardy Street, Richmond, VA 23220-1170, 804-257-5882 or toll-free 800-368-3227 (out-of-state). *E-mail:* dtatum@vuu.edu.

VIRGINIA UNIVERSITY OF LYNCHBURG

Lynchburg, VA

ABOUT THE INSTITUTION Independent religious, coed. 4 undergraduate majors.

GIFT AID (NEED-BASED) ***Scholarships, grants, and awards:*** Federal Pell, FSEOG.

WORK-STUDY ***Federal work-study:*** Total amount: $9194; 9 jobs available.

APPLYING FOR FINANCIAL AID ***Required financial aid form:*** FAFSA.

CONTACT Mrs. Charlene P. Scruggs, Financial Aid Director, Virginia University of Lynchburg, 2058 Garfield Avenue, Lynchburg, VA 24572, 434-528-5276. *Fax:* 434-455-5958. *E-mail:* cscruggs@vul.edu.

VIRGINIA WESLEYAN COLLEGE

Norfolk, VA

Tuition & fees: $29,680 **Average undergraduate aid package: $19,757**

ABOUT THE INSTITUTION Independent United Methodist, coed. 48 undergraduate majors. Federal methodology is used as a basis for awarding need-based institutional aid.

UNDERGRADUATE EXPENSES for 2011–12 ***One-time required fee:*** $250. ***Comprehensive fee:*** $37,668 includes full-time tuition ($29,180), mandatory fees ($500), and room and board ($7988). Full-time tuition and fees vary according to course load. Room and board charges vary according to board plan and housing facility. ***Part-time tuition:*** $1216 per credit hour. ***Part-time fees:*** $500 per year. Part-time tuition and fees vary according to course load. ***Payment plans:*** Installment, deferred payment.

FRESHMAN FINANCIAL AID (Fall 2009) 319 applied for aid; of those 78% were deemed to have need. 100% of freshmen with need received aid; of those 8% had need fully met. ***Average percent of need met:*** 71% (excluding resources awarded to replace EFC). ***Average financial aid package:*** $20,941 (excluding resources awarded to replace EFC). 18% of all full-time freshmen had no need and received non-need-based gift aid.

UNDERGRADUATE FINANCIAL AID (Fall 2009) 1,204 applied for aid; of those 78% were deemed to have need. 100% of undergraduates with need received aid; of those 10% had need fully met. ***Average percent of need met:*** 70% (excluding resources awarded to replace EFC). ***Average financial aid package:*** $19,757 (excluding resources awarded to replace EFC). 17% of all full-time undergraduates had no need and received non-need-based gift aid.

GIFT AID (NEED-BASED) ***Total amount:*** $14,328,169 (16% federal, 13% state, 69% institutional, 2% external sources). ***Receiving aid:*** Freshmen: 78% (250); all full-time undergraduates: 77% (926). ***Average award:*** Freshmen: $17,449; Undergraduates: $15,373. ***Scholarships, grants, and awards:*** Federal Pell, FSEOG, state, private, college/university gift aid from institutional funds, United Negro College Fund.

GIFT AID (NON-NEED-BASED) ***Total amount:*** $2,961,377 (5% federal, 19% state, 72% institutional, 4% external sources). ***Receiving aid:*** Freshmen: 13% (42). Undergraduates: 13% (157). ***Average award:*** Freshmen: $8930. Undergraduates: $8422. ***Scholarships, grants, and awards by category:*** *Academic interests/achievement:* general academic interests/achievements. *Creative arts/performance:* art/fine arts, music, theater/drama. *Special achievements/activities:* community service, leadership, religious involvement. *Special characteristics:* children of faculty/staff, relatives of clergy, religious affiliation. ***Tuition waivers:*** Full or partial for employees or children of employees, adult students, senior citizens.

LOANS ***Student loans:*** $8,777,548 (79% need-based, 21% non-need-based). 79% of past graduating class borrowed through all loan programs. *Average indebtedness per student:* $29,679. ***Average need-based loan:*** Freshmen: $6206. Undergraduates: $7584. ***Parent loans:*** $2,765,509 (44% need-based, 56% non-need-based). ***Programs:*** Federal Direct (Subsidized and Unsubsidized Stafford, PLUS), Perkins, alternative loans.

WORK-STUDY ***Federal work-study:*** Total amount: $205,487; 195 jobs averaging $1054.

APPLYING FOR FINANCIAL AID ***Required financial aid forms:*** FAFSA, state aid form. ***Financial aid deadline (priority):*** 3/1. ***Notification date:*** Continuous. Students must reply by 5/1 or within 2 weeks of notification.

CONTACT Mrs. Teresa Rhyne, Director of Financial Aid, Virginia Wesleyan College, 1584 Wesleyan Drive, Norfolk, VA 23502-5599, 757-455-3345 or toll-free 800-737-8684. *Fax:* 757-455-6779. *E-mail:* finaid@vwc.edu.

VITERBO UNIVERSITY

La Crosse, WI

CONTACT Ms. Terry Norman, Director of Financial Aid, Viterbo University, 900 Viterbo Drive, La Crosse, WI 54601-4797, 608-796-3900 or toll-free 800-VITERBO Ext. 3010. *Fax:* 608-796-3050. *E-mail:* twnorman@viterbo.edu.

VOORHEES COLLEGE

Denmark, SC

CONTACT Augusta L. Kitchen, Director of Financial Aid, Voorhees College, PO Box 678, Denmark, SC 29042, 803-703-7109 Ext. 7106 or toll-free 866-685-9904. *Fax:* 803-793-0831. *E-mail:* akitchen@voorhees.edu.

WABASH COLLEGE

Crawfordsville, IN

Tuition & fees: $31,050 **Average undergraduate aid package: $27,618**

ABOUT THE INSTITUTION Independent, men only. 24 undergraduate majors. Both federal and institutional methodology are used as a basis for awarding need-based institutional aid.

UNDERGRADUATE EXPENSES for 2010–11 ***Comprehensive fee:*** $39,350 includes full-time tuition ($30,400), mandatory fees ($650), and room and board ($8300). ***College room only:*** $3700. Full-time tuition and fees vary according to reciprocity agreements. Room and board charges vary according to board plan and housing facility. ***Part-time tuition:*** $5067 per course. ***Part-time fees:*** $650 per year. Part-time tuition and fees vary according to course load and reciprocity agreements. ***Payment plans:*** Tuition prepayment, installment.

FRESHMAN FINANCIAL AID (Fall 2010, est.) 238 applied for aid; of those 89% were deemed to have need. 100% of freshmen with need received aid; of those 86% had need fully met. ***Average percent of need met:*** 98% (excluding resources awarded to replace EFC). ***Average financial aid package:*** $28,538 (excluding resources awarded to replace EFC). 9% of all full-time freshmen had no need and received non-need-based gift aid.

UNDERGRADUATE FINANCIAL AID (Fall 2010, est.) 748 applied for aid; of those 92% were deemed to have need. 100% of undergraduates with need received aid; of those 85% had need fully met. ***Average percent of need met:*** 97% (excluding resources awarded to replace EFC). ***Average financial aid package:*** $27,618 (excluding resources awarded to replace EFC). 17% of all full-time undergraduates had no need and received non-need-based gift aid.

GIFT AID (NEED-BASED) ***Total amount:*** $12,592,183 (8% federal, 7% state, 81% institutional, 4% external sources). ***Receiving aid:*** Freshmen: 82% (204); all full-time undergraduates: 77% (666). ***Average award:*** Freshmen: $18,020; Undergraduates: $16,752. ***Scholarships, grants, and awards:*** Federal Pell, state, private, college/university gift aid from institutional funds.

GIFT AID (NON-NEED-BASED) ***Total amount:*** $3,288,173 (1% federal, 88% institutional, 11% external sources). ***Receiving aid:*** Freshmen: 12% (31). Undergraduates: 10% (86). ***Average award:*** Freshmen: $16,277. Undergraduates: $16,797. ***Scholarships, grants, and awards by category:*** *Academic interests/achievement:* 991 awards ($8,078,242 total): general academic interests/achievements. *Creative arts/performance:* 51 awards ($180,250 total): art/fine arts, creative writing, journalism/publications, music, theater/drama. *Special achievements/activities:* 53 awards ($658,331 total): community service, leadership. *Special characteristics:* 7 awards ($198,006 total): children of faculty/staff. ***Tuition waivers:*** Full or partial for employees or children of employees.

LOANS ***Student loans:*** $5,304,541 (67% need-based, 33% non-need-based). 81% of past graduating class borrowed through all loan programs. *Average indebtedness per student:* $29,897. ***Average need-based loan:*** Freshmen: $6752. Undergraduates: $5074. ***Parent loans:*** $1,724,479 (100% non-need-based). ***Programs:*** Federal Direct (Subsidized and Unsubsidized Stafford, PLUS), college/university.

WORK-STUDY ***State or other work-study/employment:*** Total amount: $2,292,184 (86% need-based, 14% non-need-based). 763 part-time jobs averaging $2889.

APPLYING FOR FINANCIAL AID ***Required financial aid forms:*** FAFSA, CSS Financial Aid PROFILE, noncustodial (divorced/separated) parent's statement, federal income tax form(s), W-2 forms. ***Financial aid deadline:*** 3/1 (priority: 2/15). ***Notification date:*** 4/1. Students must reply by 5/1 or within 2 weeks of notification.

CONTACT Mr. Clint Gasaway, Financial Aid Director, Wabash College, PO Box 352, Crawfordsville, IN 47933-0352, 800-718-9746 or toll-free 800-345-5385. *Fax:* 765-361-6166. *E-mail:* financialaid@wabash.edu.

WAGNER COLLEGE

Staten Island, NY

Tuition & fees: $35,820 **Average undergraduate aid package: $22,354**

ABOUT THE INSTITUTION Independent, coed. 38 undergraduate majors. Federal methodology is used as a basis for awarding need-based institutional aid.

UNDERGRADUATE EXPENSES for 2011–12 ***Comprehensive fee:*** $46,500 includes full-time tuition ($35,620), mandatory fees ($200), and room and board ($10,680). Full-time tuition and fees vary according to course load. ***Part-time tuition:*** $4452 per unit. Part-time tuition and fees vary according to course load.

FRESHMAN FINANCIAL AID (Fall 2010, est.) 395 applied for aid; of those 88% were deemed to have need. 100% of freshmen with need received aid; of those 23% had need fully met. ***Average percent of need met:*** 76% (excluding resources awarded to replace EFC). ***Average financial aid package:*** $23,327 (excluding resources awarded to replace EFC). 24% of all full-time freshmen had no need and received non-need-based gift aid.

UNDERGRADUATE FINANCIAL AID (Fall 2010, est.) 1,292 applied for aid; of those 85% were deemed to have need. 100% of undergraduates with need received aid; of those 23% had need fully met. ***Average percent of need met:*** 73% (excluding resources awarded to replace EFC). ***Average financial aid package:*** $22,354 (excluding resources awarded to replace EFC). 26% of all full-time undergraduates had no need and received non-need-based gift aid.

GIFT AID (NEED-BASED) ***Total amount:*** $15,253,401 (10% federal, 5% state, 83% institutional, 2% external sources). ***Receiving aid:*** Freshmen: 71% (344); all full-time undergraduates: 62% (1,081). ***Average award:*** Freshmen: $12,246; Undergraduates: $17,672. ***Scholarships, grants, and awards:*** Federal Pell, FSEOG, state, private, college/university gift aid from institutional funds.

GIFT AID (NON-NEED-BASED) ***Total amount:*** $6,953,122 (2% state, 97% institutional, 1% external sources). ***Average award:*** Freshmen: $10,199. Undergraduates: $11,880. ***Scholarships, grants, and awards by category:*** *Academic interests/achievement:* 1,250 awards ($14,809,589 total): general academic interests/achievements. *Creative arts/performance:* 232 awards ($3,111,556 total): music, theater/drama. *Special characteristics:* 119 awards ($1,585,804 total): children of faculty/staff, siblings of current students. ***Tuition waivers:*** Full or partial for employees or children of employees.

LOANS ***Student loans:*** $12,301,796 (81% need-based, 19% non-need-based). 55% of past graduating class borrowed through all loan programs. *Average indebtedness per student:* $36,988. ***Average need-based loan:*** Freshmen: $2208. Undergraduates: $4688. ***Parent loans:*** $4,652,702 (77% need-based, 23% non-need-based). ***Programs:*** Federal Direct (Subsidized and Unsubsidized Stafford, PLUS), Perkins, Federal Nursing.

WORK-STUDY ***Federal work-study:*** Total amount: $982,825; 687 jobs averaging $1576.

ATHLETIC AWARDS Total amount: $5,149,417 (42% need-based, 58% non-need-based).

APPLYING FOR FINANCIAL AID ***Required financial aid forms:*** FAFSA, institution's own form, state aid form. ***Financial aid deadline (priority):*** 2/15. ***Notification date:*** 3/1. Students must reply by 5/1 or within 3 weeks of notification.

CONTACT Mr. Angelo Araimo, Vice President for Enrollment and Strategic Planning, Wagner College, One Campus Road, Staten Island, NY 10301, 718-390-3411 or toll-free 800-221-1010 (out-of-state). *Fax:* 718-390-3105. *E-mail:* aaraimo@wagner.edu.

WAKE FOREST UNIVERSITY

Winston-Salem, NC

Tuition & fees: $41,576 **Average undergraduate aid package: $33,872**

ABOUT THE INSTITUTION Independent, coed. 39 undergraduate majors. Institutional methodology is used as a basis for awarding need-based institutional aid.

UNDERGRADUATE EXPENSES for 2011–12 ***Comprehensive fee:*** $52,986 includes full-time tuition ($41,100), mandatory fees ($476), and room and board ($11,410). ***College room only:*** $7550. ***Part-time tuition:*** $1704 per semester hour.

FRESHMAN FINANCIAL AID (Fall 2010, est.) 508 applied for aid; of those 88% were deemed to have need. 98% of freshmen with need received aid; of those 89% had need fully met. ***Average percent of need met:*** 100% (excluding resources awarded to replace EFC). ***Average financial aid package:*** $34,652 (excluding resources awarded to replace EFC). 4% of all full-time freshmen had no need and received non-need-based gift aid.

UNDERGRADUATE FINANCIAL AID (Fall 2010, est.) 2,042 applied for aid; of those 89% were deemed to have need. 99% of undergraduates with need received aid; of those 65% had need fully met. ***Average percent of need met:*** 99% (excluding resources awarded to replace EFC). ***Average financial aid package:*** $33,872 (excluding resources awarded to replace EFC). 10% of all full-time undergraduates had no need and received non-need-based gift aid.

GIFT AID (NEED-BASED) ***Total amount:*** $40,924,443 (11% federal, 7% state, 79% institutional, 3% external sources). ***Receiving aid:*** Freshmen: 35% (432); all full-time undergraduates: 37% (1,700). ***Average award:*** Freshmen: $29,236; Undergraduates: $27,995. ***Scholarships, grants, and awards:*** Federal Pell, FSEOG, state, private, college/university gift aid from institutional funds.

GIFT AID (NON-NEED-BASED) ***Total amount:*** $7,721,286 (17% federal, 11% state, 58% institutional, 14% external sources). ***Receiving aid:*** Freshmen: 18% (221). Undergraduates: 26% (1,218). ***Average award:*** Freshmen: $16,821. Undergraduates: $15,023. ***Scholarships, grants, and awards by category:*** *Academic interests/achievement:* general academic interests/achievements. *Creative arts/performance:* general creative arts/performance. *Special achievements/activities:* leadership. *Special characteristics:* children and siblings of alumni, local/state students, religious affiliation.

LOANS ***Student loans:*** $20,614,232 (85% need-based, 15% non-need-based). 39% of past graduating class borrowed through all loan programs. *Average indebtedness per student:* $32,237. ***Average need-based loan:*** Freshmen: $8742. Undergraduates: $11,670. ***Parent loans:*** $7,945,356 (92% need-based, 8% non-need-based). ***Programs:*** Federal Direct (Subsidized and Unsubsidized Stafford, PLUS), Perkins, state, college/university.

WORK-STUDY ***Federal work-study:*** Total amount: $2,287,643; jobs available. ***State or other work-study/employment:*** Part-time jobs available.

ATHLETIC AWARDS Total amount: $10,422,681 (40% need-based, 60% non-need-based).

APPLYING FOR FINANCIAL AID ***Required financial aid forms:*** FAFSA, CSS Financial Aid PROFILE, state aid form, noncustodial (divorced/separated) parent's statement. ***Financial aid deadline:*** 3/1 (priority: 2/15). ***Notification date:*** Continuous beginning 4/1. Students must reply by 5/1 or within 4 weeks of notification.

CONTACT Adam Holyfield, Associate Director of Financial Aid, Wake Forest University, PO Box 7246, Winston-Salem, NC 27109-7246, 336-758-5154. *Fax:* 336-758-4924. *E-mail:* financial-aid@wfu.edu.

WALDEN UNIVERSITY
Minneapolis, MN

Tuition & fees: $9465 **Average undergraduate aid package: $6301**

ABOUT THE INSTITUTION Proprietary, coed. 45 undergraduate majors. Federal methodology is used as a basis for awarding need-based institutional aid.

UNDERGRADUATE EXPENSES for 2010–11 ***Tuition:*** full-time $9360; part-time $260 per credit hour. ***Required fees:*** full-time $105; $35 per term. Full-time tuition and fees vary according to course level, course load, and program. Part-time tuition and fees vary according to course level, course load, and program. ***Payment plan:*** Installment.

UNDERGRADUATE FINANCIAL AID (Fall 2009) 908 applied for aid; of those 97% were deemed to have need. 100% of undergraduates with need received aid; of those 1% had need fully met. ***Average percent of need met:*** 26% (excluding resources awarded to replace EFC). ***Average financial aid package:*** $6301 (excluding resources awarded to replace EFC). 2% of all full-time undergraduates had no need and received non-need-based gift aid.

GIFT AID (NEED-BASED) ***Total amount:*** $23,514,499 (86% federal, 13% institutional, 1% external sources). ***Receiving aid:*** Entering class: 68% (13); all full-time undergraduates: 85% (771). ***Average award:*** Freshmen: $5223; Undergraduates: $3222. ***Scholarships, grants, and awards:*** Federal Pell, FSEOG, college/university gift aid from institutional funds.

GIFT AID (NON-NEED-BASED) ***Total amount:*** $110,848 (100% institutional). ***Receiving aid:*** Undergraduates: 4. ***Average award:*** Undergraduates: $1225. ***Tuition waivers:*** Full or partial for employees or children of employees.

LOANS ***Student loans:*** $71,473,578 (100% need-based). ***Average need-based loan:*** Freshmen: $3828. Undergraduates: $3755. ***Parent loans:*** $18,025 (31% need-based, 69% non-need-based). ***Programs:*** Federal Direct (Subsidized and Unsubsidized Stafford, PLUS).

APPLYING FOR FINANCIAL AID ***Required financial aid form:*** FAFSA. ***Financial aid deadline:*** Continuous. ***Notification date:*** Continuous beginning 4/15. Students must reply within 2 weeks of notification.

CONTACT Office of Financial Aid, Walden University, 155 Fifth Avenue South, Minneapolis, MN 55401, 800-444-6795 or toll-free 866-492-5336 (out-of-state). *Fax:* 410-843-6211. *E-mail:* finaid@waldenu.edu.

WALDORF COLLEGE
Forest City, IA

Tuition & fees: $18,760 **Average undergraduate aid package: $14,508**

ABOUT THE INSTITUTION Independent Lutheran, coed. 28 undergraduate majors. Federal methodology is used as a basis for awarding need-based institutional aid.

UNDERGRADUATE EXPENSES for 2010–11 ***Comprehensive fee:*** $24,714 includes full-time tuition ($17,900), mandatory fees ($860), and room and board ($5954). Full-time tuition and fees vary according to class time, course load, and program. Room and board charges vary according to board plan and housing facility. ***Part-time tuition:*** $244 per credit hour. ***Payment plans:*** Installment, deferred payment.

FRESHMAN FINANCIAL AID (Fall 2010, est.) 196 applied for aid; of those 89% were deemed to have need. 99% of freshmen with need received aid; of those 11% had need fully met. ***Average percent of need met:*** 70% (excluding resources awarded to replace EFC). ***Average financial aid package:*** $13,262 (excluding resources awarded to replace EFC). 19% of all full-time freshmen had no need and received non-need-based gift aid.

UNDERGRADUATE FINANCIAL AID (Fall 2010, est.) 686 applied for aid; of those 88% were deemed to have need. 99% of undergraduates with need received aid; of those 15% had need fully met. ***Average percent of need met:*** 74% (excluding resources awarded to replace EFC). ***Average financial aid package:*** $14,508 (excluding resources awarded to replace EFC). 14% of all full-time undergraduates had no need and received non-need-based gift aid.

GIFT AID (NEED-BASED) ***Total amount:*** $4,868,438 (35% federal, 6% state, 52% institutional, 7% external sources). ***Receiving aid:*** Freshmen: 74% (171); all full-time undergraduates: 75% (572). ***Average award:*** Freshmen: $9811; Undergraduates: $10,877. ***Scholarships, grants, and awards:*** Federal Pell, FSEOG, state, private, college/university gift aid from institutional funds.

GIFT AID (NON-NEED-BASED) ***Total amount:*** $713,260 (90% institutional, 10% external sources). ***Receiving aid:*** Freshmen: 6% (13). Undergraduates: 5% (38). ***Average award:*** Freshmen: $4490. Undergraduates: $5196. ***Scholarships, grants, and awards by category:*** *Academic interests/achievement:* communication, general academic interests/achievements. *Creative arts/performance:* music, theater/drama. *Special achievements/activities:* cheerleading/drum major, junior miss, leadership. *Special characteristics:* children of faculty/staff, religious affiliation. ***Tuition waivers:*** Full or partial for employees or children of employees.

LOANS ***Student loans:*** $4,367,332 (80% need-based, 20% non-need-based). 99% of past graduating class borrowed through all loan programs. *Average indebtedness per student:* $26,262. ***Average need-based loan:*** Freshmen: $3183. Undergraduates: $3785. ***Parent loans:*** $2,246,034 (40% need-based, 60% non-need-based). ***Programs:*** Federal Direct (Subsidized and Unsubsidized Stafford, PLUS), Perkins, state, alternative loans.

WORK-STUDY ***Federal work-study:*** Total amount: $369,049; jobs available. ***State or other work-study/employment:*** Part-time jobs available.

ATHLETIC AWARDS Total amount: $1,940,733 (72% need-based, 28% non-need-based).

APPLYING FOR FINANCIAL AID ***Required financial aid form:*** FAFSA. ***Financial aid deadline (priority):*** 3/1. ***Notification date:*** Continuous beginning 3/1. Students must reply within 2 weeks of notification.

CONTACT Duane Polsdofer, Director of Financial Aid, Waldorf College, 106 South 6th Street, Forest City, IA 50436, 641-585-8120 or toll-free 800-292-1903. *Fax:* 641-585-8125.

WALLA WALLA UNIVERSITY
College Place, WA

Tuition & fees: $23,454 **Average undergraduate aid package: $21,543**

ABOUT THE INSTITUTION Independent Seventh-day Adventist, coed. 82 undergraduate majors. Both federal and institutional methodology are used as a basis for awarding need-based institutional aid.

UNDERGRADUATE EXPENSES for 2010–11 ***Comprehensive fee:*** $28,785 includes full-time tuition ($23,229), mandatory fees ($225), and room and board ($5331). Full-time tuition and fees vary according to course load and degree level. Room and board charges vary according to housing facility and location. Part-time tuition and fees vary according to degree level. ***Payment plans:*** Installment, deferred payment.

FRESHMAN FINANCIAL AID (Fall 2009) 295 applied for aid; of those 66% were deemed to have need. 100% of freshmen with need received aid; of those 25% had need fully met. ***Average percent of need met:*** 90% (excluding resources awarded to replace EFC). ***Average financial aid package:*** $19,219 (excluding resources awarded to replace EFC). 33% of all full-time freshmen had no need and received non-need-based gift aid.

UNDERGRADUATE FINANCIAL AID (Fall 2009) 1,249 applied for aid; of those 74% were deemed to have need. 100% of undergraduates with need received aid; of those 18% had need fully met. ***Average percent of need met:*** 90% (excluding resources awarded to replace EFC). ***Average financial aid package:*** $21,543 (excluding resources awarded to replace EFC). 20% of all full-time undergraduates had no need and received non-need-based gift aid.

GIFT AID (NEED-BASED) ***Total amount:*** $11,909,894 (23% federal, 8% state, 47% institutional, 22% external sources). ***Receiving aid:*** Freshmen: 51% (154); all full-time undergraduates: 54% (737). ***Average award:*** Freshmen: $6874; Undergraduates: $8465. ***Scholarships, grants, and awards:*** Federal Pell, FSEOG, state, private, college/university gift aid from institutional funds, Federal Nursing.

GIFT AID (NON-NEED-BASED) ***Total amount:*** $2,792,394 (1% federal, 51% institutional, 48% external sources). ***Receiving aid:*** Freshmen: 64% (194). Undergraduates: 55% (747). ***Average award:*** Freshmen: $6397. Undergraduates: $4751. ***Scholarships, grants, and awards by category:*** *Academic interests/achievement:* biological sciences, business, communication, education, engineering/technologies, English, foreign languages, general academic interests/achievements, humanities, mathematics, religion/biblical studies. *Creative arts/performance:* general creative arts/performance, music, theater/drama. *Special achievements/activities:* leadership. *Special characteristics:* children of faculty/staff, veterans.

LOANS ***Student loans:*** $10,414,549 (86% need-based, 14% non-need-based). 70% of past graduating class borrowed through all loan programs. *Average indebtedness per student:* $32,697. ***Average need-based loan:*** Freshmen: $6720. Undergraduates: $7635. ***Parent loans:*** $1,172,529 (65% need-based, 35% non-need-based). ***Programs:*** Federal Direct (Subsidized and Unsubsidized Stafford, PLUS), Perkins, Federal Nursing, state, college/university.

WORK-STUDY ***Federal work-study:*** Total amount: $1,746,105; jobs available. ***State or other work-study/employment:*** Total amount: $129,309 (100% need-based). Part-time jobs available.

APPLYING FOR FINANCIAL AID ***Required financial aid forms:*** FAFSA, institution's own form. ***Financial aid deadline (priority):*** 4/30. ***Notification date:*** Continuous.

CONTACT Ms. Cassie Ragenovich, Director of Student Financial Services, Walla Walla University, 204 South College Avenue, College Place, WA 99324-1198, 509-527-2315 or toll-free 800-541-8900. *Fax:* 509-527-2556. *E-mail:* financial.aid@wallawalla.edu.

WALSH COLLEGE OF ACCOUNTANCY AND BUSINESS ADMINISTRATION

Troy, MI

Tuition & fees: $11,770 **Average undergraduate aid package: $8986**

ABOUT THE INSTITUTION Independent, coed. ***Awards:*** bachelor's and master's degrees. 5 undergraduate majors. ***Total enrollment:*** 3,106. Undergraduates: 1,025. Federal methodology is used as a basis for awarding need-based institutional aid.

UNDERGRADUATE EXPENSES for 2010–11 ***Application fee:*** $25. ***Tuition:*** full-time $11,520; part-time $320 per credit hour. ***Required fees:*** full-time $250; $125 per term. ***Payment plan:*** Deferred payment.

UNDERGRADUATE FINANCIAL AID (Fall 2009) 199 applied for aid; of those 89% were deemed to have need. 100% of undergraduates with need received aid. ***Average percent of need met:*** 36% (excluding resources awarded to replace EFC). ***Average financial aid package:*** $8986 (excluding resources awarded to replace EFC). 5% of all full-time undergraduates had no need and received non-need-based gift aid.

GIFT AID (NEED-BASED) ***Total amount:*** $1,511,611 (63% federal, 17% state, 20% institutional). ***Receiving aid:*** All full-time undergraduates: 39% (122). ***Average award:*** Undergraduates: $5700. ***Scholarships, grants, and awards:*** Federal Pell, FSEOG, state, private, college/university gift aid from institutional funds.

GIFT AID (NON-NEED-BASED) ***Total amount:*** $148,028 (100% institutional). ***Receiving aid:*** Undergraduates: 6% (18). ***Average award:*** Undergraduates: $1689. ***Scholarships, grants, and awards by category:*** *Academic interests/achievement:* business, computer science. *Special characteristics:* previous college experience. ***Tuition waivers:*** Full or partial for employees or children of employees.

LOANS ***Student loans:*** $4,423,611 (95% need-based, 5% non-need-based). 61% of past graduating class borrowed through all loan programs. *Average indebtedness per student:* $13,100. ***Average need-based loan:*** Undergraduates: $5034. ***Parent loans:*** $12,030 (100% non-need-based). ***Programs:*** Federal Direct (Subsidized and Unsubsidized Stafford, PLUS), alternative loans.

WORK-STUDY ***State or other work-study/employment:*** Part-time jobs available.

APPLYING FOR FINANCIAL AID ***Required financial aid forms:*** FAFSA, institution's own form. ***Financial aid deadline:*** Continuous. ***Notification date:*** Continuous beginning 6/1.

CONTACT Howard Thomas, Director of Student Financial Resources, Walsh College of Accountancy and Business Administration, 3838 Livernois Road, PO Box 7006, Troy, MI 48007-7006, 248-823-1285 or toll-free 800-925-7401 (in-state). *Fax:* 248-524-2520. *E-mail:* hthomas@walshcollege.edu.

WALSH UNIVERSITY

North Canton, OH

Tuition & fees: $22,280 **Average undergraduate aid package: $18,133**

ABOUT THE INSTITUTION Independent Roman Catholic, coed. 43 undergraduate majors. Federal methodology is used as a basis for awarding need-based institutional aid.

UNDERGRADUATE EXPENSES for 2010–11 ***One-time required fee:*** $215. ***Comprehensive fee:*** $30,640 includes full-time tuition ($21,380), mandatory fees ($900), and room and board ($8360). ***College room only:*** $4420. Full-time tuition and fees vary according to location. Room and board charges vary according to board plan and housing facility. ***Part-time tuition:*** $710 per semester hour. ***Part-time fees:*** $30 per semester hour. Part-time tuition and fees vary according to course load and location. ***Payment plan:*** Installment.

FRESHMAN FINANCIAL AID (Fall 2010, est.) 425 applied for aid; of those 96% were deemed to have need. 100% of freshmen with need received aid; of those 48% had need fully met. ***Average percent of need met:*** 69% (excluding resources awarded to replace EFC). ***Average financial aid package:*** $16,848 (excluding resources awarded to replace EFC). 8% of all full-time freshmen had no need and received non-need-based gift aid.

UNDERGRADUATE FINANCIAL AID (Fall 2010, est.) 1,726 applied for aid; of those 96% were deemed to have need. 100% of undergraduates with need received aid; of those 48% had need fully met. ***Average percent of need met:*** 71% (excluding resources awarded to replace EFC). ***Average financial aid package:*** $18,133 (excluding resources awarded to replace EFC). 10% of all full-time undergraduates had no need and received non-need-based gift aid.

GIFT AID (NEED-BASED) ***Total amount:*** $10,702,792 (36% federal, 10% state, 54% institutional). ***Receiving aid:*** Freshmen: 84% (376); all full-time undergraduates: 72% (1,332). ***Average award:*** Freshmen: $4848; Undergraduates: $6844. ***Scholarships, grants, and awards:*** Federal Pell, FSEOG, state, private, college/university gift aid from institutional funds.

GIFT AID (NON-NEED-BASED) ***Total amount:*** $9,991,714 (96% institutional, 4% external sources). ***Receiving aid:*** Freshmen: 92% (410). Undergraduates: 90% (1,661). ***Average award:*** Freshmen: $8660. Undergraduates: $9372. ***Scholarships, grants, and awards by category:*** *Academic interests/achievement:* biological sciences, business, communication, computer science, education, English, foreign languages, general academic interests/achievements, health fields, humanities, international studies, mathematics, physical sciences, premedicine, religion/biblical studies, social sciences. *Creative arts/performance:* music. *Special achievements/activities:* leadership, religious involvement. *Special characteristics:* children and siblings of alumni, children of faculty/staff, international students, local/state students, members of minority groups, out-of-state students, siblings of current students. ***Tuition waivers:*** Full or partial for children of alumni, employees or children of employees, senior citizens.

LOANS ***Student loans:*** $13,295,408 (53% need-based, 47% non-need-based). 79% of past graduating class borrowed through all loan programs. *Average indebtedness per student:* $24,753. ***Average need-based loan:*** Freshmen: $4500. Undergraduates: $4850. ***Parent loans:*** $2,562,878 (30% need-based, 70% non-need-based). ***Programs:*** Perkins, state, college/university.

WORK-STUDY ***Federal work-study:*** Total amount: $224,733; jobs available. ***State or other work-study/employment:*** Total amount: $34,850 (100% non-need-based). Part-time jobs available.

ATHLETIC AWARDS Total amount: $1,801,900 (100% non-need-based).

APPLYING FOR FINANCIAL AID ***Required financial aid forms:*** FAFSA, institution's own form. ***Financial aid deadline:*** Continuous. ***Notification date:*** Continuous beginning 2/15. Students must reply within 4 weeks of notification.

CONTACT Holly Van Gilder, Director of Financial Aid, Walsh University, 2020 East Maple NW, North Canton, OH 44720-3396, 330-490-7147 or toll-free 800-362-9846 (in-state), 800-362-8846 (out-of-state). *Fax:* 330-490-7372. *E-mail:* hvangilder@walsh.edu.

WARNER PACIFIC COLLEGE

Portland, OR

Tuition & fees: $17,604 **Average undergraduate aid package: $15,003**

ABOUT THE INSTITUTION Independent religious, coed. 31 undergraduate majors. Federal methodology is used as a basis for awarding need-based institutional aid.

UNDERGRADUATE EXPENSES for 2010–11 ***Comprehensive fee:*** $24,584 includes full-time tuition ($16,974), mandatory fees ($630), and room and board ($6980). ***College room only:*** $2800. Full-time tuition and fees vary according to course load, degree level, location, reciprocity agreements, and student level. Room and board charges vary according to board plan and housing facility. ***Part-time tuition:*** $775 per credit. ***Part-time fees:*** $315 per term. Part-time tuition and fees vary according to course load, degree level, location, and reciprocity agreements. ***Payment plan:*** Installment.

FRESHMAN FINANCIAL AID (Fall 2010, est.) 88 applied for aid; of those 89% were deemed to have need. 100% of freshmen with need received aid; of those 9% had need fully met. ***Average percent of need met:*** 66% (excluding resources awarded to replace EFC). ***Average financial aid package:*** $14,287 (excluding resources awarded to replace EFC). 11% of all full-time freshmen had no need and received non-need-based gift aid.

UNDERGRADUATE FINANCIAL AID (Fall 2010, est.) 439 applied for aid; of those 92% were deemed to have need. 100% of undergraduates with need received aid; of those 9% had need fully met. ***Average percent of need met:*** 64% (excluding resources awarded to replace EFC). ***Average financial aid package:*** $15,003 (excluding resources awarded to replace EFC). 6% of all full-time undergraduates had no need and received non-need-based gift aid.

GIFT AID (NEED-BASED) ***Total amount:*** $2,742,639 (52% federal, 6% state, 33% institutional, 9% external sources). ***Receiving aid:*** Freshmen: 77% (70); all full-time undergraduates: 80% (361). ***Average award:*** Freshmen: $5652; Undergraduates: $5714. ***Scholarships, grants, and awards:*** Federal Pell, FSEOG, state, private, college/university gift aid from institutional funds.

GIFT AID (NON-NEED-BASED) ***Total amount:*** $148,155 (3% federal, 88% institutional, 9% external sources). ***Receiving aid:*** Freshmen: 81% (74). Undergraduates: 81% (363). ***Average award:*** Freshmen: $2360. Undergraduates: $1807. ***Scholarships, grants, and awards by category:*** *Academic interests/achievement:* 371 awards ($758,759 total): area/ethnic studies, biological sciences, general academic interests/achievements, humanities, mathematics, physical sciences, religion/biblical studies, social sciences. *Creative arts/performance:* 48 awards ($92,029 total): music, theater/drama. *Special achievements/activities:* 35 awards ($36,500 total): leadership. *Special characteristics:* 194 awards ($153,960 total): children and siblings of alumni, members of minority groups, religious affiliation. ***Tuition waivers:*** Full or partial for children of alumni, employees or children of employees.

LOANS ***Student loans:*** $3,369,807 (86% need-based, 14% non-need-based). 85% of past graduating class borrowed through all loan programs. *Average indebtedness per student:* $30,559. ***Average need-based loan:*** Freshmen: $3456. Undergraduates: $4267. ***Parent loans:*** $1,286,823 (35% need-based, 65% non-need-based). ***Programs:*** Federal Direct (Subsidized and Unsubsidized Stafford, PLUS), Perkins.

WORK-STUDY ***Federal work-study:*** Total amount: $515,138; 343 jobs averaging $1502.

ATHLETIC AWARDS Total amount: $586,572 (84% need-based, 16% non-need-based).

APPLYING FOR FINANCIAL AID ***Required financial aid form:*** FAFSA. ***Financial aid deadline:*** Continuous. ***Notification date:*** Continuous beginning 3/1. Students must reply within 2 weeks of notification.

CONTACT Jennifer S. Knight, Director of Student Financial Services and Financial Aid, Warner Pacific College, 2219 Southeast 68th Avenue, Portland, OR 97215-4099, 503-517-1018 or toll-free 800-804-1510 (out-of-state). *Fax:* 503-517-1352. *E-mail:* jknight@warnerpacific.edu.

WARNER UNIVERSITY

Lake Wales, FL

CONTACT Student Financial Services, Warner University, 13895 Highway 27, Lake Wales, FL 33859, 863-638-7202 or toll-free 800-949-7248 (in-state). *Fax:* 863-638-7603. *E-mail:* financialaid@warner.edu.

WARREN WILSON COLLEGE

Swannanoa, NC

Tuition & fees: $25,944 **Average undergraduate aid package: $20,775**

ABOUT THE INSTITUTION Independent religious, coed. ***Awards:*** bachelor's and master's degrees. 27 undergraduate majors. ***Total enrollment:*** 1,002. Undergraduates: 927. Freshmen: 249. Both federal and institutional methodology are used as a basis for awarding need-based institutional aid.

UNDERGRADUATE EXPENSES for 2010–11 ***Comprehensive fee:*** $33,972 includes full-time tuition ($25,626), mandatory fees ($318), and room and board ($8028). Full-time tuition and fees vary according to course load. Room and board charges vary according to board plan. ***Part-time tuition:*** $1056 per credit. Part-time tuition and fees vary according to course load. ***Payment plan:*** Installment.

FRESHMAN FINANCIAL AID (Fall 2010, est.) 198 applied for aid; of those 87% were deemed to have need. 100% of freshmen with need received aid; of those 12% had need fully met. ***Average percent of need met:*** 72% (excluding resources awarded to replace EFC). ***Average financial aid package:*** $19,314 (excluding resources awarded to replace EFC). 10% of all full-time freshmen had no need and received non-need-based gift aid.

UNDERGRADUATE FINANCIAL AID (Fall 2010, est.) 733 applied for aid; of those 87% were deemed to have need. 100% of undergraduates with need received aid; of those 22% had need fully met. ***Average percent of need met:*** 74% (excluding resources awarded to replace EFC). ***Average financial aid package:*** $20,775 (excluding resources awarded to replace EFC). 14% of all full-time undergraduates had no need and received non-need-based gift aid.

GIFT AID (NEED-BASED) ***Total amount:*** $7,602,391 (18% federal, 5% state, 73% institutional, 4% external sources). ***Receiving aid:*** Freshmen: 71% (158); all full-time undergraduates: 63% (579). ***Average award:*** Freshmen: $13,178; Undergraduates: $13,130. ***Scholarships, grants, and awards:*** Federal Pell, FSEOG, state, college/university gift aid from institutional funds, Academic Competitiveness Grants, National SMART Grants.

GIFT AID (NON-NEED-BASED) ***Total amount:*** $937,037 (7% state, 76% institutional, 17% external sources). ***Receiving aid:*** Freshmen: 13% (29). Undergraduates: 17% (158). ***Average award:*** Freshmen: $4814. Undergraduates: $5641. ***Scholarships, grants, and awards by category:*** *Academic interests/achievement:* 184 awards ($547,725 total): general academic interests/achievements. *Creative arts/performance:* 15 awards ($15,250 total): art/fine arts, creative writing. *Special achievements/activities:* 69 awards ($114,540 total): community service, leadership. *Special characteristics:* 104 awards ($313,333 total): children of faculty/staff, general special characteristics, local/state students, previous college experience, religious affiliation. ***Tuition waivers:*** Full or partial for employees or children of employees.

LOANS ***Student loans:*** $3,792,517 (91% need-based, 9% non-need-based). 64% of past graduating class borrowed through all loan programs. *Average indebtedness per student:* $20,018. ***Average need-based loan:*** Freshmen: $3261. Undergraduates: $4062. ***Parent loans:*** $1,604,486 (85% need-based, 15% non-need-based). ***Programs:*** Federal Direct (Subsidized and Unsubsidized Stafford, PLUS), Perkins.

WORK-STUDY ***Federal work-study:*** Total amount: $2,004,480; 576 jobs averaging $3480. ***State or other work-study/employment:*** Total amount: $1,392,000 (29% need-based, 71% non-need-based). 400 part-time jobs averaging $3480.

APPLYING FOR FINANCIAL AID ***Required financial aid forms:*** FAFSA, institution's own form, state aid form. ***Financial aid deadline (priority):*** 4/1. ***Notification date:*** Continuous beginning 3/15. Students must reply by 5/1 or within 3 weeks of notification.

CONTACT Admissions Office, Warren Wilson College, PO Box 9000, Asheville, NC 28815-9000, 800-934-3536. *Fax:* 828-298-1440.

WARTBURG COLLEGE

Waverly, IA

Tuition & fees: $30,960 **Average undergraduate aid package: $21,639**

ABOUT THE INSTITUTION Independent Lutheran, coed. 56 undergraduate majors. Federal methodology is used as a basis for awarding need-based institutional aid.

UNDERGRADUATE EXPENSES for 2011–12 ***Comprehensive fee:*** $39,110 includes full-time tuition ($30,110), mandatory fees ($850), and room and board ($8150). ***College room only:*** $3905. Room and board charges vary according to board plan. ***Part-time tuition:*** $1450 per course. ***Part-time fees:*** $90 per term. ***Payment plan:*** Installment.

FRESHMAN FINANCIAL AID (Fall 2009) 445 applied for aid; of those 88% were deemed to have need. 100% of freshmen with need received aid; of those 37% had need fully met. ***Average percent of need met:*** 86% (excluding resources awarded to replace EFC). ***Average financial aid package:*** $23,483 (excluding resources awarded to replace EFC). 18% of all full-time freshmen had no need and received non-need-based gift aid.

UNDERGRADUATE FINANCIAL AID (Fall 2009) 1,558 applied for aid; of those 88% were deemed to have need. 100% of undergraduates with need received aid; of those 40% had need fully met. ***Average percent of need met:*** 83% (excluding resources awarded to replace EFC). ***Average financial aid package:*** $21,639 (excluding resources awarded to replace EFC). 20% of all full-time undergraduates had no need and received non-need-based gift aid.

GIFT AID (NEED-BASED) ***Total amount:*** $23,381,847 (9% federal, 12% state, 69% institutional, 10% external sources). ***Receiving aid:*** Freshmen: 81% (391); all full-time undergraduates: 79% (1,369). ***Average award:*** Freshmen: $19,404; Undergraduates: $17,076. ***Scholarships, grants, and awards:*** Federal Pell, FSEOG, state, private, college/university gift aid from institutional funds.

GIFT AID (NON-NEED-BASED) ***Total amount:*** $7,051,969 (82% institutional, 18% external sources). ***Receiving aid:*** Freshmen: 14% (65). Undergraduates: 13% (218). ***Average award:*** Freshmen: $15,202. Undergraduates: $13,202. ***Scholarships, grants, and awards by category:*** *Academic interests/achievement:* biological sciences, business, communication, computer science, education,

English, general academic interests/achievements, international studies, mathematics, physical sciences, religion/biblical studies. *Creative arts/performance:* art/fine arts, journalism/publications, music. *Special characteristics:* children and siblings of alumni, children of faculty/staff, ethnic background, international students, members of minority groups, out-of-state students, religious affiliation, siblings of current students. ***Tuition waivers:*** Full or partial for children of alumni, employees or children of employees.

LOANS *Student loans:* $13,487,659 (59% need-based, 41% non-need-based). 82% of past graduating class borrowed through all loan programs. *Average indebtedness per student:* $29,867. ***Average need-based loan:*** Freshmen: $3653. Undergraduates: $4637. ***Parent loans:*** $1,403,739 (47% need-based, 53% non-need-based). ***Programs:*** Perkins, alternative loans.

WORK-STUDY *Federal work-study:* Total amount: $497,773; jobs available. ***State or other work-study/employment:*** Part-time jobs available.

APPLYING FOR FINANCIAL AID *Required financial aid form:* FAFSA. ***Financial aid deadline (priority):*** 3/1. ***Notification date:*** Continuous beginning 3/21. Students must reply within 2 weeks of notification.

CONTACT Ms. Jennifer Sassman, Director of Financial Aid, Wartburg College, 100 Wartburg Boulevard, PO Box 1003, Waverly, IA 50677-0903, 319-352-8262 or toll-free 800-772-2085. *Fax:* 319-352-8514. *E-mail:* jennifer.sassman@wartburg.edu.

WASHBURN UNIVERSITY

Topeka, KS

Tuition & fees (KS res): $6296 **Average undergraduate aid package: $9078**

ABOUT THE INSTITUTION City-supported, coed. 77 undergraduate majors. Federal methodology is used as a basis for awarding need-based institutional aid.

UNDERGRADUATE EXPENSES for 2010–11 *Tuition, state resident:* full-time $6210; part-time $207 per credit hour. ***Tuition, nonresident:*** full-time $14,100; part-time $470 per credit hour. ***Required fees:*** full-time $86; $21 per term. Full-time tuition and fees vary according to program. Part-time tuition and fees vary according to program. ***College room and board:*** $5982; ***Room only:*** $3332. Room and board charges vary according to board plan and housing facility. ***Payment plan:*** Installment.

FRESHMAN FINANCIAL AID (Fall 2010, est.) 718 applied for aid; of those 73% were deemed to have need. 99% of freshmen with need received aid; of those 12% had need fully met. ***Average percent of need met:*** 43% (excluding resources awarded to replace EFC). ***Average financial aid package:*** $8689 (excluding resources awarded to replace EFC). 14% of all full-time freshmen had no need and received non-need-based gift aid.

UNDERGRADUATE FINANCIAL AID (Fall 2010, est.) 3,612 applied for aid; of those 73% were deemed to have need. 100% of undergraduates with need received aid; of those 12% had need fully met. ***Average percent of need met:*** 45% (excluding resources awarded to replace EFC). ***Average financial aid package:*** $9078 (excluding resources awarded to replace EFC). 15% of all full-time undergraduates had no need and received non-need-based gift aid.

GIFT AID (NEED-BASED) *Total amount:* $12,219,248 (84% federal, 4% state, 10% institutional, 2% external sources). ***Receiving aid:*** Freshmen: 45% (351); all full-time undergraduates: 40% (1,611). ***Average award:*** Freshmen: $4915; Undergraduates: $4938. ***Scholarships, grants, and awards:*** Federal Pell, FSEOG, state, private, college/university gift aid from institutional funds.

GIFT AID (NON-NEED-BASED) *Total amount:* $2,394,879 (2% federal, 4% state, 68% institutional, 26% external sources). ***Receiving aid:*** Freshmen: 35% (274). Undergraduates: 30% (1,184). ***Average award:*** Freshmen: $2137. Undergraduates: $1861. ***Scholarships, grants, and awards by category:*** *Academic interests/achievement:* 2,053 awards ($2,281,725 total): biological sciences, business, communication, computer science, education, engineering/technologies, English, foreign languages, general academic interests/achievements, health fields, humanities, international studies, mathematics, physical sciences, premedicine, religion/biblical studies, social sciences. *Creative arts/performance:* 234 awards ($225,399 total): art/fine arts, cinema/film/broadcasting, debating, journalism/publications, music, performing arts, theater/drama. *Special achievements/activities:* 728 awards ($1,523,408 total): cheerleading/drum major, community service, general special achievements/activities, leadership. *Special characteristics:* 189 awards ($209,084 total): adult students, children and siblings of alumni, children of faculty/staff, ethnic background, international students, local/state students. ***Tuition waivers:*** Full or partial for employees or children of employees, senior citizens.

LOANS *Student loans:* $31,198,920 (56% need-based, 44% non-need-based). 63% of past graduating class borrowed through all loan programs. *Average indebtedness per student:* $17,017. ***Average need-based loan:*** Freshmen: $3281. Undergraduates: $4298. ***Parent loans:*** $7,744,958 (56% need-based, 44% non-need-based). ***Programs:*** Federal Direct (Subsidized and Unsubsidized Stafford, PLUS), Perkins, college/university, private loans.

WORK-STUDY *Federal work-study:* Total amount: $650,278; 241 jobs averaging $2698. ***State or other work-study/employment:*** Total amount: $39,385 (100% need-based). 5 part-time jobs averaging $7877.

ATHLETIC AWARDS Total amount: $1,431,530 (58% need-based, 42% non-need-based).

APPLYING FOR FINANCIAL AID *Required financial aid forms:* FAFSA, institution's own form. ***Financial aid deadline (priority):*** 2/15. ***Notification date:*** Continuous beginning 3/15. Students must reply within 2 weeks of notification.

CONTACT Gail Palmer, Director of Financial Aid, Washburn University, 1700 SW College Avenue, Topeka, KS 66621, 785-670-1151 or toll-free 800-332-0291 (in-state). *Fax:* 785-670-1079. *E-mail:* gail.palmer@washburn.edu.

WASHINGTON ADVENTIST UNIVERSITY

Takoma Park, MD

Tuition & fees: $20,180 **Average undergraduate aid package: N/A**

ABOUT THE INSTITUTION Independent Seventh-day Adventist, coed. 33 undergraduate majors. Both federal and institutional methodology are used as a basis for awarding need-based institutional aid.

UNDERGRADUATE EXPENSES for 2010–11 *Comprehensive fee:* $27,710 includes full-time tuition ($18,900), mandatory fees ($1280), and room and board ($7530). ***Part-time tuition:*** $760 per credit hour. ***Part-time fees:*** $432.50 per term. Part-time tuition and fees vary according to class time and course load. ***Payment plan:*** Installment.

FRESHMAN FINANCIAL AID (Fall 2009) 144 applied for aid.

UNDERGRADUATE FINANCIAL AID (Fall 2009) 883 applied for aid; of those 80% were deemed to have need. 100% of undergraduates with need received aid.

GIFT AID (NEED-BASED) *Total amount:* $8,203,258 (37% federal, 8% state, 48% institutional, 7% external sources). ***Scholarships, grants, and awards:*** Federal Pell, FSEOG, state, private, college/university gift aid from institutional funds.

GIFT AID (NON-NEED-BASED) *Scholarships, grants, and awards by category:* *Academic interests/achievement:* 271 awards ($1,308,750 total): general academic interests/achievements. *Creative arts/performance:* 68 awards ($286,680 total): music. *Special achievements/activities:* community service, leadership. *Special characteristics:* 45 awards ($442,679 total): children of faculty/staff, veterans, veterans' children. ***Tuition waivers:*** Full or partial for employees or children of employees, senior citizens.

LOANS *Student loans:* $7,577,250 (100% need-based). ***Parent loans:*** $1,183,965 (100% need-based). ***Programs:*** Federal Direct (Subsidized and Unsubsidized Stafford, PLUS), Perkins, alternative loans.

WORK-STUDY *Federal work-study:* Total amount: $110,507; jobs available. ***State or other work-study/employment:*** Total amount: $349,892 (100% need-based). Part-time jobs available.

ATHLETIC AWARDS Total amount: $356,363 (100% need-based).

APPLYING FOR FINANCIAL AID *Required financial aid form:* FAFSA. ***Financial aid deadline (priority):*** 3/1. ***Notification date:*** Continuous beginning 4/1.

CONTACT Sharon Conway, Director of Student Financial Services, Washington Adventist University, 7600 Flower Avenue, Takoma Park, MD 20912, 301-891-4005 or toll-free 800-835-4212.

WASHINGTON & JEFFERSON COLLEGE

Washington, PA

Tuition & fees: $34,610 **Average undergraduate aid package: $24,185**

ABOUT THE INSTITUTION Independent, coed. 30 undergraduate majors. Both federal and institutional methodology are used as a basis for awarding need-based institutional aid.

UNDERGRADUATE EXPENSES for 2010–11 *Comprehensive fee:* $43,890 includes full-time tuition ($34,150), mandatory fees ($460), and room and board ($9280). ***College room only:*** $5520. Full-time tuition and fees vary according to reciprocity agreements. Room and board charges vary according to board plan and housing facility. ***Part-time tuition:*** $856.25 per credit hour. Part-time tuition and fees vary according to course load. ***Payment plans:*** Installment, deferred payment.

FRESHMAN FINANCIAL AID (Fall 2010, est.) 354 applied for aid; of those 90% were deemed to have need. 100% of freshmen with need received aid; of those 14% had need fully met. ***Average percent of need met:*** 78% (excluding resources awarded to replace EFC). ***Average financial aid package:*** $25,444 (excluding resources awarded to replace EFC). 18% of all full-time freshmen had no need and received non-need-based gift aid.

UNDERGRADUATE FINANCIAL AID (Fall 2010, est.) 1,215 applied for aid; of those 90% were deemed to have need. 100% of undergraduates with need received aid; of those 16% had need fully met. ***Average percent of need met:*** 74% (excluding resources awarded to replace EFC). ***Average financial aid package:*** $24,185 (excluding resources awarded to replace EFC). 20% of all full-time undergraduates had no need and received non-need-based gift aid.

GIFT AID (NEED-BASED) ***Total amount:*** $19,909,086 (10% federal, 7% state, 81% institutional, 2% external sources). ***Receiving aid:*** Freshmen: 66% (262); all full-time undergraduates: 64% (908). ***Average award:*** Freshmen: $10,002; Undergraduates: $10,070. ***Scholarships, grants, and awards:*** Federal Pell, FSEOG, state, private, college/university gift aid from institutional funds.

GIFT AID (NON-NEED-BASED) ***Total amount:*** $4,279,056 (97% institutional, 3% external sources). ***Receiving aid:*** Freshmen: 75% (298). Undergraduates: 66% (929). ***Average award:*** Freshmen: $13,400. Undergraduates: $11,924. ***Scholarships, grants, and awards by category:*** *Academic interests/achievement:* 1,198 awards ($14,081,392 total): business, education, English, general academic interests/achievements, humanities, mathematics, physical sciences, premedicine, social sciences. *Special achievements/activities:* 2 awards ($5700 total): community service. *Special characteristics:* 53 awards ($1,161,006 total): children and siblings of alumni, children of faculty/staff, ethnic background, members of minority groups, veterans, veterans' children. ***Tuition waivers:*** Full or partial for employees or children of employees.

LOANS ***Student loans:*** $11,248,871 (71% need-based, 29% non-need-based). 75% of past graduating class borrowed through all loan programs. *Average indebtedness per student:* $30,000. ***Average need-based loan:*** Freshmen: $3524. Undergraduates: $4607. ***Parent loans:*** $4,673,770 (67% need-based, 33% non-need-based). ***Programs:*** Federal Direct (Subsidized and Unsubsidized Stafford, PLUS), Perkins, college/university.

WORK-STUDY ***Federal work-study:*** Total amount: $991,143; 613 jobs averaging $1617. ***State or other work-study/employment:*** Total amount: $240,000 (100% non-need-based). 270 part-time jobs averaging $888.

APPLYING FOR FINANCIAL AID ***Required financial aid form:*** FAFSA. ***Financial aid deadline (priority):*** 2/15. ***Notification date:*** Continuous beginning 3/1. Students must reply by 5/1.

CONTACT Ms. Michelle Anderson, Director of Financial Aid, Washington & Jefferson College, 60 South Lincoln Street, Washington, PA 15301-4801, 724-503-1001 Ext. 6019 or toll-free 888-WANDJAY. *Fax:* 724-250-3340. *E-mail:* manderson@washjeff.edu.

WASHINGTON AND LEE UNIVERSITY

Lexington, VA

Tuition & fees: $40,387 **Average undergraduate aid package: $41,076**

ABOUT THE INSTITUTION Independent, coed. 38 undergraduate majors. Both federal and institutional methodology are used as a basis for awarding need-based institutional aid.

UNDERGRADUATE EXPENSES for 2010–11 ***Comprehensive fee:*** $50,630 includes full-time tuition ($39,500), mandatory fees ($887), and room and board ($10,243). ***College room only:*** $4993. Room and board charges vary according to board plan and housing facility. ***Part-time tuition:*** $1411 per credit hour. ***Payment plan:*** Installment.

FRESHMAN FINANCIAL AID (Fall 2010, est.) 253 applied for aid; of those 76% were deemed to have need. 100% of freshmen with need received aid; of those 100% had need fully met. ***Average percent of need met:*** 100% (excluding resources awarded to replace EFC). ***Average financial aid package:*** $42,427 (excluding resources awarded to replace EFC). 6% of all full-time freshmen had no need and received non-need-based gift aid.

UNDERGRADUATE FINANCIAL AID (Fall 2010, est.) 748 applied for aid; of those 86% were deemed to have need. 100% of undergraduates with need received aid; of those 100% had need fully met. ***Average percent of need met:*** 100% (excluding resources awarded to replace EFC). ***Average financial aid package:*** $41,076 (excluding resources awarded to replace EFC). 9% of all full-time undergraduates had no need and received non-need-based gift aid.

GIFT AID (NEED-BASED) ***Total amount:*** $22,364,879 (4% federal, 1% state, 94% institutional, 1% external sources). ***Receiving aid:*** Freshmen: 41% (192); all full-time undergraduates: 37% (646). ***Average award:*** Freshmen: $35,470; Undergraduates: $34,315. ***Scholarships, grants, and awards:*** Federal Pell, FSEOG, state, private, college/university gift aid from institutional funds.

GIFT AID (NON-NEED-BASED) ***Total amount:*** $8,756,043 (3% federal, 5% state, 87% institutional, 5% external sources). ***Receiving aid:*** Freshmen: 14% (67). Undergraduates: 17% (301). ***Average award:*** Freshmen: $29,837. Undergraduates: $27,117. ***Scholarships, grants, and awards by category:*** *Academic interests/achievement:* 162 awards ($4,393,030 total): general academic interests/achievements. ***Tuition waivers:*** Full or partial for employees or children of employees.

LOANS ***Student loans:*** $3,166,713 (33% need-based, 67% non-need-based). 33% of past graduating class borrowed through all loan programs. *Average indebtedness per student:* $23,807. ***Average need-based loan:*** Freshmen: $1206. Undergraduates: $1313. ***Parent loans:*** $3,893,651 (100% non-need-based). ***Programs:*** Federal Direct (Subsidized and Unsubsidized Stafford, PLUS), Perkins, college/university.

WORK-STUDY ***Federal work-study:*** Total amount: $272,151; 152 jobs averaging $1790. ***State or other work-study/employment:*** Total amount: $772,730 (16% need-based, 84% non-need-based). 383 part-time jobs averaging $2018.

APPLYING FOR FINANCIAL AID ***Required financial aid forms:*** FAFSA, CSS Financial Aid PROFILE, noncustodial (divorced/separated) parent's statement, federal income tax return(s). ***Financial aid deadline:*** 2/15. ***Notification date:*** 4/1. Students must reply by 5/1.

CONTACT James D. Kaster, Director of Financial Aid, Washington and Lee University, Financial Aid Office, 204 West Washington Street, Lexington, VA 24450, 540-458-8720. *Fax:* 540-458-8614. *E-mail:* financialaid@wlu.edu.

WASHINGTON BIBLE COLLEGE

Lanham, MD

ABOUT THE INSTITUTION Independent nondenominational, coed. ***Awards:*** associate, bachelor's, and master's degrees and post-bachelor's certificates (graduate degrees offered by Capital Bible Seminary). 7 undergraduate majors. ***Total enrollment:*** 616. Undergraduates: 254. Freshmen: 29.

GIFT AID (NEED-BASED) ***Scholarships, grants, and awards:*** Federal Pell, FSEOG, state, private, college/university gift aid from institutional funds.

GIFT AID (NON-NEED-BASED) ***Scholarships, grants, and awards by category:*** *Academic interests/achievement:* general academic interests/achievements. *Creative arts/performance:* music. *Special achievements/activities:* general special achievements/activities, leadership, religious involvement. *Special characteristics:* children of faculty/staff, international students, relatives of clergy, siblings of current students, spouses of current students.

WORK-STUDY ***Federal work-study:*** Total amount: $45,362; 19 jobs averaging $2388.

APPLYING FOR FINANCIAL AID ***Required financial aid forms:*** FAFSA, institution's own form, CSS Financial Aid PROFILE.

CONTACT Nichole Sefiane, Financial Aid Director, Washington Bible College, 6511 Princess Garden Parkway, Lanham, MD 20706-3599, 301-552-1400 Ext. 1222 or toll-free 877-793-7227 Ext. 1212. *Fax:* 240-387-1351. *E-mail:* nsefiane@bible.edu.

WASHINGTON COLLEGE

Chestertown, MD

Tuition & fees: $36,738 **Average undergraduate aid package: $24,078**

ABOUT THE INSTITUTION Independent, coed. 34 undergraduate majors. Both federal and institutional methodology are used as a basis for awarding need-based institutional aid.

UNDERGRADUATE EXPENSES for 2010–11 ***Comprehensive fee:*** $44,572 includes full-time tuition ($36,078), mandatory fees ($660), and room and board ($7834). ***College room only:*** $3980. Room and board charges vary according to board plan, housing facility, and location. ***Part-time tuition:*** $6012 per course. Part-time tuition and fees vary according to course load. ***Payment plan:*** Installment.

FRESHMAN FINANCIAL AID (Fall 2010, est.) 338 applied for aid; of those 84% were deemed to have need. 100% of freshmen with need received aid; of those 42% had need fully met. ***Average percent of need met:*** 90% (excluding resources awarded to replace EFC). ***Average financial aid package:*** $26,989 (excluding resources awarded to replace EFC). 27% of all full-time freshmen had no need and received non-need-based gift aid.

UNDERGRADUATE FINANCIAL AID (Fall 2010, est.) 959 applied for aid; of those 85% were deemed to have need. 100% of undergraduates with need received aid; of those 35% had need fully met. ***Average percent of need met:*** 82% (excluding resources awarded to replace EFC). ***Average financial aid package:*** $24,078 (excluding resources awarded to replace EFC). 26% of all full-time undergraduates had no need and received non-need-based gift aid.

GIFT AID (NEED-BASED) ***Total amount:*** $15,516,271 (7% federal, 6% state, 83% institutional, 4% external sources). ***Receiving aid:*** Freshmen: 68% (284); all full-time undergraduates: 58% (795). ***Average award:*** Freshmen: $18,948; Undergraduates: $20,370. ***Scholarships, grants, and awards:*** Federal Pell, FSEOG, state, private, college/university gift aid from institutional funds.

GIFT AID (NON-NEED-BASED) ***Total amount:*** $4,024,277 (94% institutional, 6% external sources). ***Receiving aid:*** Freshmen: 10% (43). Undergraduates: 7% (92). ***Average award:*** Freshmen: $15,099. Undergraduates: $14,976. ***Scholarships, grants, and awards by category:*** *Academic interests/achievement:* general academic interests/achievements. *Special characteristics:* children of faculty/staff. ***Tuition waivers:*** Full or partial for employees or children of employees.

LOANS ***Student loans:*** $8,500,220 (37% need-based, 63% non-need-based). 53% of past graduating class borrowed through all loan programs. *Average indebtedness per student:* $35,831. ***Average need-based loan:*** Freshmen: $3407. Undergraduates: $4419. ***Parent loans:*** $5,580,984 (100% non-need-based). ***Programs:*** Federal Direct (Subsidized and Unsubsidized Stafford, PLUS), Perkins.

WORK-STUDY ***Federal work-study:*** Total amount: $300,432; jobs available.

APPLYING FOR FINANCIAL AID ***Required financial aid forms:*** FAFSA, institution's own form. ***Financial aid deadline (priority):*** 2/15. ***Notification date:*** Continuous beginning 2/15. Students must reply by 5/1.

CONTACT Ms. Jeani M. Narcum, Director of Financial Aid, Washington College, 300 Washington Avenue, Chestertown, MD 21620-1197, 410-778-7214 or toll-free 800-422-1782. *Fax:* 410-778-7287. *E-mail:* jnarcum2@washcoll.edu.

WASHINGTON STATE UNIVERSITY

Pullman, WA

Tuition & fees (WA res): $9489 **Average undergraduate aid package: $12,441**

ABOUT THE INSTITUTION State-supported, coed. 130 undergraduate majors. Federal methodology is used as a basis for awarding need-based institutional aid.

UNDERGRADUATE EXPENSES for 2010–11 ***Tuition, state resident:*** full-time $8080; part-time $430 per credit hour. ***Tuition, nonresident:*** full-time $19,122; part-time $934 per credit hour. ***Required fees:*** full-time $1409. Full-time tuition and fees vary according to location and reciprocity agreements. Part-time tuition and fees vary according to course load, location, and reciprocity agreements. ***College room and board:*** $9644; ***Room only:*** $5536. Room and board charges vary according to board plan, housing facility, and location.

FRESHMAN FINANCIAL AID (Fall 2009) 2,810 applied for aid; of those 68% were deemed to have need. 100% of freshmen with need received aid; of those 27% had need fully met. ***Average percent of need met:*** 76% (excluding resources awarded to replace EFC). ***Average financial aid package:*** $12,302 (excluding resources awarded to replace EFC). 18% of all full-time freshmen had no need and received non-need-based gift aid.

UNDERGRADUATE FINANCIAL AID (Fall 2009) 12,877 applied for aid; of those 77% were deemed to have need. 100% of undergraduates with need received aid; of those 26% had need fully met. ***Average percent of need met:*** 76% (excluding resources awarded to replace EFC). ***Average financial aid package:*** $12,441 (excluding resources awarded to replace EFC). 13% of all full-time undergraduates had no need and received non-need-based gift aid.

GIFT AID (NEED-BASED) ***Total amount:*** $62,578,892 (44% federal, 44% state, 12% institutional). ***Receiving aid:*** Freshmen: 34% (1,242); all full-time undergraduates: 37% (6,848). ***Average award:*** Freshmen: $8438; Undergraduates: $8428. ***Scholarships, grants, and awards:*** Federal Pell, FSEOG, state, private, college/university gift aid from institutional funds, United Negro College Fund, Federal Nursing.

GIFT AID (NON-NEED-BASED) ***Total amount:*** $12,528,662 (6% state, 50% institutional, 44% external sources). ***Receiving aid:*** Freshmen: 31% (1,136). Undergraduates: 20% (3,776). ***Average award:*** Freshmen: $3419. Undergraduates: $3566. ***Scholarships, grants, and awards by category:*** *Academic interests/achievement:* agriculture, architecture, area/ethnic studies, biological sciences, business, communication, computer science, education, engineering/technologies, English, foreign languages, general academic interests/achievements, health fields, home economics, humanities, international studies, mathematics, military science, physical sciences, premedicine, social sciences. *Creative arts/performance:* applied art and design, art/fine arts, cinema/film/broadcasting, creative writing, general creative arts/performance, journalism/publications, music, performing arts, theater/drama. *Special achievements/activities:* community service, general special achievements/activities, junior miss, leadership, memberships, religious involvement, rodeo. *Special characteristics:* children and siblings of alumni, children of faculty/staff, children of public servants, children with a deceased or disabled parent, first-generation college students, handicapped students, international students, out-of-state students, public servants, religious affiliation, veterans, veterans' children. ***Tuition waivers:*** Full or partial for employees or children of employees, senior citizens.

LOANS ***Student loans:*** $81,592,272 (45% need-based, 55% non-need-based). ***Average need-based loan:*** Freshmen: $3367. Undergraduates: $4415. ***Parent loans:*** $23,312,151 (100% non-need-based). ***Programs:*** Federal Direct (Subsidized and Unsubsidized Stafford, PLUS), Perkins, Federal Nursing, college/university, alternative loans.

WORK-STUDY ***Federal work-study:*** Total amount: $556,155; jobs available. ***State or other work-study/employment:*** Total amount: $1,563,911 (100% need-based). Part-time jobs available.

ATHLETIC AWARDS Total amount: $6,241,040 (100% non-need-based).

APPLYING FOR FINANCIAL AID ***Required financial aid form:*** FAFSA. ***Financial aid deadline (priority):*** 2/15. ***Notification date:*** Continuous beginning 4/1.

CONTACT Office of Financial Aid and Scholarships, Washington State University, PO Box 641068, Pullman, WA 99164-1068, 509-335-9711 or toll-free 888-468-6978. *Fax:* 509-335-1385. *E-mail:* finaid@wsu.edu.

WASHINGTON STATE UNIVERSITY VANCOUVER

Vancouver, WA

CONTACT Financial Aid Office, Washington State University Vancouver, 14204 Northeast Salmon Creek Avenue, Vancouver, WA 98686, 360-546-9788.

WASHINGTON UNIVERSITY IN ST. LOUIS

St. Louis, MO

Tuition & fees: $41,992 **Average undergraduate aid package: $32,992**

ABOUT THE INSTITUTION Independent, coed. 166 undergraduate majors. Institutional methodology is used as a basis for awarding need-based institutional aid.

UNDERGRADUATE EXPENSES for 2011–12 ***Comprehensive fee:*** $55,111 includes full-time tuition ($40,950), mandatory fees ($1042), and room and board ($13,119). ***College room only:*** $8819. Room and board charges vary according to board plan and housing facility. ***Payment plans:*** Tuition prepayment, installment.

FRESHMAN FINANCIAL AID (Fall 2010, est.) 1,046 applied for aid; of those 60% were deemed to have need. 96% of freshmen with need received aid; of those 100% had need fully met. ***Average percent of need met:*** 100% (excluding resources awarded to replace EFC). ***Average financial aid package:*** $30,603 (excluding resources awarded to replace EFC). 16% of all full-time freshmen had no need and received non-need-based gift aid.

UNDERGRADUATE FINANCIAL AID (Fall 2010, est.) 4,313 applied for aid; of those 60% were deemed to have need. 99% of undergraduates with need received aid; of those 100% had need fully met. ***Average percent of need met:*** 100% (excluding resources awarded to replace EFC). ***Average financial aid package:*** $32,992 (excluding resources awarded to replace EFC). 15% of all full-time undergraduates had no need and received non-need-based gift aid.

GIFT AID (NEED-BASED) ***Total amount:*** $73,142,329 (4% federal, 1% state, 91% institutional, 4% external sources). ***Receiving aid:*** Freshmen: 35% (567); all full-time undergraduates: 40% (2,483). ***Average award:*** Freshmen: $28,814; Undergraduates: $29,457. ***Scholarships, grants, and awards:*** Federal Pell, FSEOG, state, private, college/university gift aid from institutional funds, United Negro College Fund.

GIFT AID (NON-NEED-BASED) ***Total amount:*** $6,341,962 (3% federal, 4% state, 79% institutional, 14% external sources). ***Receiving aid:*** Freshmen: 5% (77). Undergraduates: 3% (195). ***Average award:*** Freshmen: $7097. Undergraduates: $6893. ***Scholarships, grants, and awards by category:*** *Academic interests/achievement:* architecture, biological sciences, business, communication, computer science, education, engineering/technologies, English, foreign languages, general academic interests/achievements, health fields, humanities, international studies, mathematics, military science, physical sciences, premedicine, religion/biblical studies, social sciences. *Creative arts/performance:* applied art and design, art/fine arts, cinema/film/broadcasting, creative writing, dance, music, performing arts, theater/drama. ***Tuition waivers:*** Full or partial for employees or children of employees.

LOANS ***Student loans:*** $11,953,172 (90% need-based, 10% non-need-based). 38% of past graduating class borrowed through all loan programs. ***Average need-based loan:*** Freshmen: $5056. Undergraduates: $6250. ***Parent loans:*** $1,375,189 (77% need-based, 23% non-need-based). ***Programs:*** Federal Direct (Subsidized and Unsubsidized Stafford, PLUS), Perkins, state, college/university.

WORK-STUDY ***Federal work-study:*** Total amount: $2,149,558; 1,106 jobs averaging $1944.

APPLYING FOR FINANCIAL AID ***Required financial aid forms:*** FAFSA, CSS Financial Aid PROFILE, noncustodial (divorced/separated) parent's statement, student and parent 1040 tax return (or signed waiver if there is no tax return). ***Financial aid deadline:*** 2/1. ***Notification date:*** 4/1. Students must reply by 5/1.

CONTACT Mr. William Witbrodt, Director of Financial Aid, Washington University in St. Louis, Campus Box 1041, St. Louis, MO 63130-4899, 314-935-5900 or toll-free 800-638-0700. *Fax:* 314-935-4037. *E-mail:* financial@wustl.edu.

WATKINS COLLEGE OF ART, DESIGN, & FILM

Nashville, TN

ABOUT THE INSTITUTION Independent, coed. 6 undergraduate majors.

GIFT AID (NEED-BASED) ***Scholarships, grants, and awards:*** Federal Pell, FSEOG, state, private, college/university gift aid from institutional funds, Academic Competitiveness Grants.

GIFT AID (NON-NEED-BASED) ***Scholarships, grants, and awards by category:*** *Academic interests/achievement:* general academic interests/achievements. *Creative arts/performance:* applied art and design, art/fine arts, cinema/film/broadcasting. *Special achievements/activities:* general special achievements/activities.

LOANS ***Programs:*** Federal Direct (Subsidized and Unsubsidized Stafford, PLUS), private alternative loans.

WORK-STUDY ***Federal work-study:*** Total amount: $20,293; 17 jobs averaging $1300. ***State or other work-study/employment:*** Total amount: $20,000 (100% non-need-based). 25 part-time jobs averaging $2000.

APPLYING FOR FINANCIAL AID ***Required financial aid forms:*** FAFSA, institution's own form.

CONTACT Lyle Jones, Financial Aid Coordinator, Watkins College of Art, Design, & Film, 2298 Rosa L. Parks Boulevard, Nashville, TN 37228, 615-383-4848 Ext. 7421. *Fax:* 615-383-4849. *E-mail:* financialaid@watkins.edu.

WAYLAND BAPTIST UNIVERSITY

Plainview, TX

Tuition & fees: $13,340 | **Average undergraduate aid package: $12,015**

ABOUT THE INSTITUTION Independent Baptist, coed. 42 undergraduate majors. Federal methodology is used as a basis for awarding need-based institutional aid.

UNDERGRADUATE EXPENSES for 2010–11 ***Comprehensive fee:*** $17,424 includes full-time tuition ($12,450), mandatory fees ($890), and room and board ($4084). ***College room only:*** $1328. Full-time tuition and fees vary according to course load and location. Room and board charges vary according to board plan and housing facility. ***Part-time tuition:*** $415 per credit hour. ***Part-time fees:*** $60 per term. Part-time tuition and fees vary according to course load and location. ***Payment plan:*** Installment.

FRESHMAN FINANCIAL AID (Fall 2010, est.) 205 applied for aid; of those 90% were deemed to have need. 98% of freshmen with need received aid; of those 14% had need fully met. ***Average percent of need met:*** 72% (excluding resources awarded to replace EFC). ***Average financial aid package:*** $12,924 (excluding resources awarded to replace EFC). 13% of all full-time freshmen had no need and received non-need-based gift aid.

UNDERGRADUATE FINANCIAL AID (Fall 2010, est.) 719 applied for aid; of those 87% were deemed to have need. 99% of undergraduates with need received aid; of those 15% had need fully met. ***Average percent of need met:*** 70% (excluding resources awarded to replace EFC). ***Average financial aid package:*** $12,015 (excluding resources awarded to replace EFC). 17% of all full-time undergraduates had no need and received non-need-based gift aid.

GIFT AID (NEED-BASED) ***Total amount:*** $4,890,957 (42% federal, 21% state, 34% institutional, 3% external sources). ***Receiving aid:*** Freshmen: 75% (181); all full-time undergraduates: 73% (612). ***Average award:*** Freshmen: $10,636; Undergraduates: $9120. ***Scholarships, grants, and awards:*** Federal Pell, FSEOG, state, private, college/university gift aid from institutional funds.

GIFT AID (NON-NEED-BASED) ***Total amount:*** $825,247 (1% federal, 1% state, 89% institutional, 9% external sources). ***Receiving aid:*** Freshmen: 8% (19). Undergraduates: 6% (54). ***Average award:*** Freshmen: $6933. Undergraduates: $8128. ***Scholarships, grants, and awards by category:*** *Academic interests/achievement:* 342 awards ($943,934 total): biological sciences, business, communication, education, English, general academic interests/achievements, mathematics, physical sciences, religion/biblical studies, social sciences. *Creative arts/performance:* 152 awards ($253,840 total): art/fine arts, journalism/publications, music, theater/drama. *Special achievements/activities:* 81 awards ($57,463 total): cheerleading/drum major, leadership, memberships, religious involvement. *Special characteristics:* 241 awards ($760,156 total): children and siblings of alumni, children of faculty/staff, ethnic background, general special characteristics, international students, local/state students, members of minority groups, relatives of clergy, religious affiliation. ***Tuition waivers:*** Full or partial for employees or children of employees.

LOANS ***Student loans:*** $3,468,626 (81% need-based, 19% non-need-based). 67% of past graduating class borrowed through all loan programs. *Average indebtedness per student:* $26,959. ***Average need-based loan:*** Freshmen: $3178. Undergraduates: $3517. ***Parent loans:*** $346,340 (37% need-based, 63% non-need-based). ***Programs:*** Perkins, state.

WORK-STUDY ***Federal work-study:*** Total amount: $195,884; 169 jobs averaging $1582. ***State or other work-study/employment:*** Total amount: $69,865 (25% need-based, 75% non-need-based). 318 part-time jobs averaging $1969.

ATHLETIC AWARDS Total amount: $1,364,119 (54% need-based, 46% non-need-based).

APPLYING FOR FINANCIAL AID ***Required financial aid forms:*** FAFSA, institution's own form. ***Financial aid deadline (priority):*** 5/1. ***Notification date:*** Continuous beginning 1/1. Students must reply within 3 weeks of notification.

CONTACT Karen LaQuey, Director of Financial Aid, Wayland Baptist University, 1900 West 7th Street, Plainview, TX 79072-6998, 806-291-3520 or toll-free 800-588-1928. *Fax:* 806-291-1956. *E-mail:* laquey@wbu.edu.

WAYNESBURG UNIVERSITY

Waynesburg, PA

Tuition & fees: $18,410 | **Average undergraduate aid package: $15,171**

ABOUT THE INSTITUTION Independent religious, coed. 50 undergraduate majors. Federal methodology is used as a basis for awarding need-based institutional aid.

UNDERGRADUATE EXPENSES for 2010–11 ***Comprehensive fee:*** $25,990 includes full-time tuition ($18,050), mandatory fees ($360), and room and board ($7580). ***College room only:*** $3850. Full-time tuition and fees vary according to class time. Room and board charges vary according to board plan. ***Part-time tuition:*** $760 per credit hour. Part-time tuition and fees vary according to class time, course load, and location. ***Payment plan:*** Installment.

FRESHMAN FINANCIAL AID (Fall 2010, est.) 377 applied for aid; of those 94% were deemed to have need. 100% of freshmen with need received aid; of those 20% had need fully met. ***Average percent of need met:*** 79% (excluding resources awarded to replace EFC). ***Average financial aid package:*** $15,209 (excluding resources awarded to replace EFC). 5% of all full-time freshmen had no need and received non-need-based gift aid.

UNDERGRADUATE FINANCIAL AID (Fall 2010, est.) 408 applied for aid; of those 93% were deemed to have need. 100% of undergraduates with need received aid; of those 19% had need fully met. ***Average percent of need met:*** 79% (excluding resources awarded to replace EFC). ***Average financial aid***

package: $15,171 (excluding resources awarded to replace EFC). 5% of all full-time undergraduates had no need and received non-need-based gift aid.

GIFT AID (NEED-BASED) ***Total amount:*** $12,845,000 (21% federal, 19% state, 56% institutional, 4% external sources). ***Receiving aid:*** Freshmen: 94% (353); all full-time undergraduates: 93% (378). ***Average award:*** Freshmen: $11,715; Undergraduates: $11,695. ***Scholarships, grants, and awards:*** Federal Pell, FSEOG, state, private, college/university gift aid from institutional funds, United Negro College Fund.

GIFT AID (NON-NEED-BASED) ***Total amount:*** $1,800,750 (1% federal, 1% state, 97% institutional, 1% external sources). ***Receiving aid:*** Freshmen: 8% (32). Undergraduates: 8% (33). ***Average award:*** Freshmen: $6789. Undergraduates: $7157. ***Scholarships, grants, and awards by category:*** *Academic interests/achievement:* 75 awards ($200,000 total): biological sciences, business, communication, computer science, education, English, general academic interests/achievements, health fields, humanities, international studies, mathematics, physical sciences, religion/biblical studies, social sciences. *Creative arts/performance:* 5 awards ($10,000 total): music. *Special achievements/activities:* 55 awards ($160,000 total): community service. *Special characteristics:* 30 awards ($350,000 total): children of faculty/staff. ***Tuition waivers:*** Full or partial for employees or children of employees.

LOANS ***Student loans:*** $12,300,000 (53% need-based, 47% non-need-based). 89% of past graduating class borrowed through all loan programs. *Average indebtedness per student:* $25,000. ***Average need-based loan:*** Freshmen: $3556. Undergraduates: $3546. ***Parent loans:*** $2,300,000 (22% need-based, 78% non-need-based). ***Programs:*** Federal Direct (Subsidized and Unsubsidized Stafford, PLUS), Perkins, Federal Nursing.

WORK-STUDY ***Federal work-study:*** Total amount: $150,000; 225 jobs averaging $1000.

APPLYING FOR FINANCIAL AID ***Required financial aid form:*** FAFSA. ***Financial aid deadline:*** Continuous. ***Notification date:*** Continuous beginning 2/15. Students must reply within 2 weeks of notification.

CONTACT Matthew C. Stokan, Director of Financial Aid, Waynesburg University, 51 West College Street, Waynesburg, PA 15370-1222, 724-852-3208 or toll-free 800-225-7393. *Fax:* 724-852-3269. *E-mail:* mstokan@waynesburg.edu.

WAYNE STATE COLLEGE

Wayne, NE

Tuition & fees (NE res): $5071 **Average undergraduate aid package: $7744**

ABOUT THE INSTITUTION State-supported, coed. 53 undergraduate majors. Federal methodology is used as a basis for awarding need-based institutional aid.

UNDERGRADUATE EXPENSES for 2010–11 ***Tuition, state resident:*** full-time $3863; part-time $128.75 per credit hour. ***Tuition, nonresident:*** full-time $7725; part-time $257.50 per credit hour. ***Required fees:*** full-time $1208; $47.75 per credit hour. Full-time tuition and fees vary according to course level and course load. Part-time tuition and fees vary according to course level and course load. ***College room and board:*** $5540; ***Room only:*** $2660. Room and board charges vary according to board plan and housing facility. ***Payment plan:*** Installment.

FRESHMAN FINANCIAL AID (Fall 2010, est.) 607 applied for aid; of those 76% were deemed to have need. 98% of freshmen with need received aid; of those 29% had need fully met. ***Average percent of need met:*** 59% (excluding resources awarded to replace EFC). ***Average financial aid package:*** $7593 (excluding resources awarded to replace EFC). 3% of all full-time freshmen had no need and received non-need-based gift aid.

UNDERGRADUATE FINANCIAL AID (Fall 2010, est.) 2,312 applied for aid; of those 81% were deemed to have need. 97% of undergraduates with need received aid; of those 28% had need fully met. ***Average percent of need met:*** 63% (excluding resources awarded to replace EFC). ***Average financial aid package:*** $7744 (excluding resources awarded to replace EFC). 3% of all full-time undergraduates had no need and received non-need-based gift aid.

GIFT AID (NEED-BASED) ***Total amount:*** $6,037,569 (86% federal, 14% state). ***Receiving aid:*** Freshmen: 51% (347); all full-time undergraduates: 52% (1,406). ***Average award:*** Freshmen: $4351; Undergraduates: $4029. ***Scholarships, grants, and awards:*** Federal Pell, FSEOG, state, private, college/university gift aid from institutional funds.

GIFT AID (NON-NEED-BASED) ***Total amount:*** $1,592,089 (3% federal, 65% institutional, 32% external sources). ***Receiving aid:*** Freshmen: 39% (265). Undergraduates: 33% (908). ***Average award:*** Freshmen: $2173. Undergraduates: $2715. ***Scholarships, grants, and awards by category:*** *Academic interests/achievement:* biological sciences, business, communication, computer science, education, English, foreign languages, general academic interests/achievements, health fields, home economics, humanities, mathematics, physical sciences, premedicine, social sciences. *Creative arts/performance:* applied art and design, art/fine arts, creative writing, debating, general creative arts/performance, journalism/publications, music, performing arts, theater/drama. *Special achievements/activities:* general special achievements/activities, leadership. *Special characteristics:* children of faculty/staff, children with a deceased or disabled parent, ethnic background, general special characteristics, local/state students, members of minority groups, out-of-state students, veterans, veterans' children. ***Tuition waivers:*** Full or partial for employees or children of employees.

LOANS ***Student loans:*** $14,666,687 (50% need-based, 50% non-need-based). ***Average need-based loan:*** Freshmen: $3021. Undergraduates: $3769. ***Parent loans:*** $778,719 (100% non-need-based). ***Programs:*** Federal Direct (Subsidized and Unsubsidized Stafford, PLUS), Perkins.

WORK-STUDY ***Federal work-study:*** Total amount: $152,240; jobs available.

ATHLETIC AWARDS Total amount: $497,908 (100% non-need-based).

APPLYING FOR FINANCIAL AID ***Required financial aid form:*** FAFSA. ***Financial aid deadline (priority):*** 5/1. ***Notification date:*** Continuous beginning 3/1. Students must reply within 4 weeks of notification.

CONTACT Kyle M. Rose, Director of Financial Aid, Wayne State College, 1111 Main Street, Wayne, NE 68787, 402-375-7230 or toll-free 800-228-9972 (in-state). *Fax:* 402-375-7067. *E-mail:* kyrose1@wsc.edu.

WAYNE STATE UNIVERSITY

Detroit, MI

Tuition & fees (MI res): $9026 **Average undergraduate aid package: $19,836**

ABOUT THE INSTITUTION State-supported, coed. 89 undergraduate majors. Federal methodology is used as a basis for awarding need-based institutional aid.

UNDERGRADUATE EXPENSES for 2010–11 ***Tuition, state resident:*** full-time $7904; part-time $263.45 per credit hour. ***Tuition, nonresident:*** full-time $18,104; part-time $603.45 per credit hour. ***Required fees:*** full-time $1122; $24.85 per credit hour or $188.05 per term. Full-time tuition and fees vary according to course load, program, reciprocity agreements, and student level. Part-time tuition and fees vary according to course load, program, reciprocity agreements, and student level. ***College room and board:*** $7500; ***Room only:*** $4750. Room and board charges vary according to board plan and housing facility. ***Payment plan:*** Installment.

FRESHMAN FINANCIAL AID (Fall 2009) 2,466 applied for aid; of those 87% were deemed to have need. 100% of freshmen with need received aid; of those 77% had need fully met. ***Average percent of need met:*** 73% (excluding resources awarded to replace EFC). ***Average financial aid package:*** $20,586 (excluding resources awarded to replace EFC). 10% of all full-time freshmen had no need and received non-need-based gift aid.

UNDERGRADUATE FINANCIAL AID (Fall 2009) 10,224 applied for aid; of those 89% were deemed to have need. 99% of undergraduates with need received aid; of those 63% had need fully met. ***Average percent of need met:*** 72% (excluding resources awarded to replace EFC). ***Average financial aid package:*** $19,836 (excluding resources awarded to replace EFC). 10% of all full-time undergraduates had no need and received non-need-based gift aid.

GIFT AID (NEED-BASED) ***Total amount:*** $53,862,111 (76% federal, 24% institutional). ***Receiving aid:*** Freshmen: 63% (1,751); all full-time undergraduates: 54% (7,036). ***Average award:*** Freshmen: $7662; Undergraduates: $7192. ***Scholarships, grants, and awards:*** Federal Pell, FSEOG, state, private, college/university gift aid from institutional funds, United Negro College Fund.

GIFT AID (NON-NEED-BASED) ***Total amount:*** $20,043,505 (1% federal, 5% state, 89% institutional, 5% external sources). ***Receiving aid:*** Freshmen: 34% (933). Undergraduates: 26% (3,410). ***Average award:*** Freshmen: $5759. Undergraduates: $5782. ***Scholarships, grants, and awards by category:*** *Academic interests/achievement:* 2,445 awards ($5,964,502 total): area/ethnic studies, biological sciences, business, communication, computer science, education, engineering/technologies, English, foreign languages, general academic interests/achievements, health fields, humanities, international studies, library science, mathematics, military science, physical sciences, premedicine, social sciences. *Creative arts/performance:* 356 awards ($962,325 total): art/fine arts, dance, debating, journalism/publications, music, theater/drama. *Special achievements/*

activities: 28 awards ($14,600 total): leadership. *Special characteristics:* 146 awards ($536,738 total): children of faculty/staff. ***Tuition waivers:*** Full or partial for employees or children of employees, senior citizens.

LOANS ***Student loans:*** $125,758,998 (97% need-based, 3% non-need-based). 58% of past graduating class borrowed through all loan programs. *Average indebtedness per student:* $20,250. ***Average need-based loan:*** Freshmen: $3829. Undergraduates: $4473. ***Parent loans:*** $51,209,067 (100% non-need-based). ***Programs:*** Federal Direct (Subsidized and Unsubsidized Stafford, PLUS), Perkins, Federal Nursing, college/university.

WORK-STUDY ***Federal work-study:*** Total amount: $5,333,125; 500 jobs averaging $2521. ***State or other work-study/employment:*** Part-time jobs available.

ATHLETIC AWARDS Total amount: $2,773,271 (100% non-need-based).

APPLYING FOR FINANCIAL AID ***Required financial aid forms:*** FAFSA, federal income tax form(s), W-2 forms. ***Financial aid deadline:*** 4/30 (priority: 2/15). ***Notification date:*** Continuous beginning 3/1. Students must reply within 2 weeks of notification.

CONTACT Albert Hermsen, Director of Scholarships and Financial Aid, Wayne State University, 3W HNJ Student Services Building, Detroit, MI 48202, 313-577-3378 or toll-free 877-WSU-INFO. *Fax:* 313-577-6648. *E-mail:* financialaid@wayne.edu.

WEBBER INTERNATIONAL UNIVERSITY

Babson Park, FL

Tuition & fees: $18,742 **Average undergraduate aid package: $18,403**

ABOUT THE INSTITUTION Independent, coed. 11 undergraduate majors. Federal methodology is used as a basis for awarding need-based institutional aid.

UNDERGRADUATE EXPENSES for 2010–11 ***Comprehensive fee:*** $25,994 includes full-time tuition ($18,742) and room and board ($7252). ***College room only:*** $4656. Full-time tuition and fees vary according to class time and course load. Room and board charges vary according to board plan, gender, and housing facility. ***Part-time tuition:*** $259 per credit hour. Part-time tuition and fees vary according to course load. ***Payment plan:*** Installment.

FRESHMAN FINANCIAL AID (Fall 2010, est.) 141 applied for aid; of those 89% were deemed to have need. 100% of freshmen with need received aid; of those 4% had need fully met. ***Average percent of need met:*** 69% (excluding resources awarded to replace EFC). ***Average financial aid package:*** $19,143 (excluding resources awarded to replace EFC). 25% of all full-time freshmen had no need and received non-need-based gift aid.

UNDERGRADUATE FINANCIAL AID (Fall 2010, est.) 433 applied for aid; of those 92% were deemed to have need. 100% of undergraduates with need received aid; of those 2% had need fully met. ***Average percent of need met:*** 66% (excluding resources awarded to replace EFC). ***Average financial aid package:*** $18,403 (excluding resources awarded to replace EFC). 27% of all full-time undergraduates had no need and received non-need-based gift aid.

GIFT AID (NEED-BASED) ***Total amount:*** $3,745,982 (43% federal, 36% state, 19% institutional, 2% external sources). ***Receiving aid:*** Freshmen: 71% (125); all full-time undergraduates: 63% (397). ***Average award:*** Freshmen: $15,944; Undergraduates: $14,062. ***Scholarships, grants, and awards:*** Federal Pell, FSEOG, state, private, college/university gift aid from institutional funds.

GIFT AID (NON-NEED-BASED) ***Total amount:*** $1,643,563 (17% state, 82% institutional, 1% external sources). ***Receiving aid:*** Freshmen: 29% (50). Undergraduates: 34% (213). ***Average award:*** Freshmen: $7655. Undergraduates: $7933. ***Scholarships, grants, and awards by category:*** *Academic interests/achievement:* 376 awards ($825,487 total): business, general academic interests/achievements. *Creative arts/performance:* 30 awards ($29,250 total): general creative arts/performance, journalism/publications. *Special achievements/activities:* 516 awards ($2,875,734 total): cheerleading/drum major, community service, general special achievements/activities, leadership, memberships. *Special characteristics:* 153 awards ($1,132,872 total): children and siblings of alumni, children of faculty/staff, first-generation college students, general special characteristics, international students, local/state students, out-of-state students, siblings of current students. ***Tuition waivers:*** Full or partial for children of alumni, employees or children of employees, adult students, senior citizens.

LOANS ***Student loans:*** $3,202,419 (90% need-based, 10% non-need-based). 63% of past graduating class borrowed through all loan programs. *Average indebtedness per student:* $28,655. ***Average need-based loan:*** Freshmen: $3359. Undergraduates: $4169. ***Parent loans:*** $912,769 (86% need-based, 14% non-need-based). ***Programs:*** Federal Direct (Subsidized and Unsubsidized Stafford, PLUS), Perkins, alternative loans.

WORK-STUDY ***Federal work-study:*** Total amount: $34,958; 21 jobs averaging $1370. ***State or other work-study/employment:*** Total amount: $43,407 (92% need-based, 8% non-need-based). 38 part-time jobs averaging $985.

ATHLETIC AWARDS Total amount: $2,850,734 (70% need-based, 30% non-need-based).

APPLYING FOR FINANCIAL AID ***Required financial aid forms:*** FAFSA, state aid form. ***Financial aid deadline:*** 8/1 (priority: 5/1). ***Notification date:*** Continuous beginning 3/1. Students must reply within 4 weeks of notification.

CONTACT Ms. Kathleen Wilson, Director of Financial Aid, Webber International University, PO Box 96, 1201 Scenic Highway, Babson Park, FL 33827-0096, 863-638-2930 or toll-free 800-741-1844. *Fax:* 863-638-1317. *E-mail:* wilsonka@webber.edu.

WEBB INSTITUTE

Glen Cove, NY

ABOUT THE INSTITUTION Independent, coed. 1 undergraduate major.

GIFT AID (NEED-BASED) ***Scholarships, grants, and awards:*** Federal Pell, state, private, college/university gift aid from institutional funds.

APPLYING FOR FINANCIAL AID ***Required financial aid form:*** FAFSA.

CONTACT William G. Murray, Director of Enrollment Management, Webb Institute, Crescent Beach Road, Glen Cove, NY 11542-1398, 516-671-2213 Ext. 104. *Fax:* 516-674-9838. *E-mail:* bmurray@webb-institute.edu.

WEBER STATE UNIVERSITY

Ogden, UT

CONTACT Mr. Richard O. Effiong, Financial Aid Director, Weber State University, 120 Student Service Center, 1136 University Circle, Ogden, UT 84408-1136, 801-626-7569 or toll-free 800-634-6568 (in-state), 800-848-7770 (out-of-state). *E-mail:* finaid@weber.edu.

WEBSTER UNIVERSITY

St. Louis, MO

ABOUT THE INSTITUTION Independent, coed. 64 undergraduate majors.

GIFT AID (NEED-BASED) ***Scholarships, grants, and awards:*** Federal Pell, FSEOG, state, private, college/university gift aid from institutional funds.

GIFT AID (NON-NEED-BASED) ***Scholarships, grants, and awards by category:*** *Academic interests/achievement:* biological sciences, business, communication, computer science, education, English, foreign languages, general academic interests/achievements, humanities, international studies. *Creative arts/performance:* art/fine arts, creative writing, debating, music, theater/drama. *Special achievements/activities:* leadership. *Special characteristics:* children and siblings of alumni, children of faculty/staff, ethnic background, international students, members of minority groups, out-of-state students.

LOANS ***Programs:*** Perkins.

WORK-STUDY ***Federal work-study:*** Total amount: $2,266,032; 1,086 jobs averaging $2166. ***State or other work-study/employment:*** Total amount: $1,049,478 (67% need-based, 33% non-need-based). 505 part-time jobs averaging $2145.

APPLYING FOR FINANCIAL AID ***Required financial aid forms:*** FAFSA, institution's own form.

CONTACT Marilynn Shelton, Financial Aid Counselor, Webster University, 470 East Lockwood Avenue, St. Louis, MO 63119, 314-968-6992 Ext. 7671 or toll-free 800-75-ENROL. *Fax:* 314-968-7125. *E-mail:* sheltoma@webster.edu.

WELLESLEY COLLEGE

Wellesley, MA

Tuition & fees: $39,666 **Average undergraduate aid package: $38,136**

ABOUT THE INSTITUTION Independent, women only. 59 undergraduate majors. Both federal and institutional methodology are used as a basis for awarding need-based institutional aid.

UNDERGRADUATE EXPENSES for 2010–11 ***Comprehensive fee:*** $51,950 includes full-time tuition ($39,420), mandatory fees ($246), and room and board ($12,284). ***College room only:*** $6234. ***Part-time tuition:*** $1232 per credit hour. ***Part-time fees:*** $31 per credit. Part-time tuition and fees vary according to course load. ***Payment plans:*** Tuition prepayment, installment.

FRESHMAN FINANCIAL AID (Fall 2010, est.) 458 applied for aid; of those 84% were deemed to have need. 100% of freshmen with need received aid; of those 100% had need fully met. ***Average percent of need met:*** 100% (excluding resources awarded to replace EFC). ***Average financial aid package:*** $38,024 (excluding resources awarded to replace EFC).

UNDERGRADUATE FINANCIAL AID (Fall 2010, est.) 1,613 applied for aid; of those 90% were deemed to have need. 100% of undergraduates with need received aid; of those 100% had need fully met. ***Average percent of need met:*** 100% (excluding resources awarded to replace EFC). ***Average financial aid package:*** $38,136 (excluding resources awarded to replace EFC).

GIFT AID (NEED-BASED) ***Total amount:*** $50,927,954 (5% federal, 93% institutional, 2% external sources). ***Receiving aid:*** Freshmen: 60% (378); all full-time undergraduates: 61% (1,403). ***Average award:*** Freshmen: $36,508; Undergraduates: $36,299. ***Scholarships, grants, and awards:*** Federal Pell, FSEOG, state, college/university gift aid from institutional funds.

GIFT AID (NON-NEED-BASED) ***Total amount:*** $424,432 (100% external sources). ***Tuition waivers:*** Full or partial for employees or children of employees.

LOANS ***Student loans:*** $4,189,547 (64% need-based, 36% non-need-based). 58% of past graduating class borrowed through all loan programs. *Average indebtedness per student:* $12,495. ***Average need-based loan:*** Freshmen: $2303. Undergraduates: $3010. ***Parent loans:*** $2,912,791 (100% non-need-based). ***Programs:*** Federal Direct (Subsidized and Unsubsidized Stafford, PLUS), Perkins, state, college/university.

WORK-STUDY ***Federal work-study:*** Total amount: $1,020,784; 858 jobs averaging $1190. ***State or other work-study/employment:*** Total amount: $494,582 (100% need-based). 376 part-time jobs averaging $1315.

APPLYING FOR FINANCIAL AID ***Required financial aid forms:*** FAFSA, CSS Financial Aid PROFILE, noncustodial (divorced/separated) parent's statement, business/farm supplement, parents' complete federal income returns from prior year, W-2 forms. ***Financial aid deadline (priority):*** 1/15. ***Notification date:*** 4/1. Students must reply by 5/1.

CONTACT Mr. Duane Quinn, Interim Director of Student Financial Services, Wellesley College, 106 Central Street, Wellesley, MA 02481-8203, 781-283-2360. *Fax:* 781-283-3946. *E-mail:* finaid@wellesley.edu.

WELLS COLLEGE

Aurora, NY

Tuition & fees: $32,180 **Average undergraduate aid package: $25,360**

ABOUT THE INSTITUTION Independent, coed, primarily women. 37 undergraduate majors. Federal methodology is used as a basis for awarding need-based institutional aid.

UNDERGRADUATE EXPENSES for 2011–12 ***Comprehensive fee:*** $43,180 includes full-time tuition ($30,680), mandatory fees ($1500), and room and board ($11,000). ***Payment plan:*** Installment.

FRESHMAN FINANCIAL AID (Fall 2010, est.) 155 applied for aid; of those 99% were deemed to have need. 100% of freshmen with need received aid; of those 13% had need fully met. ***Average percent of need met:*** 75% (excluding resources awarded to replace EFC). ***Average financial aid package:*** $27,315 (excluding resources awarded to replace EFC). 7% of all full-time freshmen had no need and received non-need-based gift aid.

UNDERGRADUATE FINANCIAL AID (Fall 2010, est.) 493 applied for aid; of those 96% were deemed to have need. 100% of undergraduates with need received aid; of those 15% had need fully met. ***Average percent of need met:*** 78% (excluding resources awarded to replace EFC). ***Average financial aid package:*** $25,360 (excluding resources awarded to replace EFC). 10% of all full-time undergraduates had no need and received non-need-based gift aid.

GIFT AID (NEED-BASED) ***Total amount:*** $9,291,390 (15% federal, 8% state, 74% institutional, 3% external sources). ***Receiving aid:*** Freshmen: 93% (153); all full-time undergraduates: 86% (470). ***Average award:*** Freshmen: $23,085; Undergraduates: $20,230. ***Scholarships, grants, and awards:*** Federal Pell, FSEOG, state, private, college/university gift aid from institutional funds.

GIFT AID (NON-NEED-BASED) ***Total amount:*** $680,085 (6% federal, 4% state, 86% institutional, 4% external sources). ***Receiving aid:*** Freshmen: 70% (115). Undergraduates: 60% (327). ***Average award:*** Freshmen: $15,500. Undergraduates: $10,655. ***Scholarships, grants, and awards by category:*** *Academic interests/achievement:* 159 awards ($1,566,500 total): general academic interests/achievements. *Special achievements/activities:* 235 awards ($2,373,500 total): leadership. *Special characteristics:* 20 awards ($48,750 total): children and siblings of alumni, international students. ***Tuition waivers:*** Full or partial for employees or children of employees, senior citizens.

LOANS ***Student loans:*** $4,673,370 (53% need-based, 47% non-need-based). 90% of past graduating class borrowed through all loan programs. *Average indebtedness per student:* $26,207. ***Average need-based loan:*** Freshmen: $3690. Undergraduates: $4660. ***Parent loans:*** $1,319,621 (100% non-need-based). ***Programs:*** Federal Direct (Subsidized and Unsubsidized Stafford, PLUS), Perkins, state.

WORK-STUDY ***Federal work-study:*** Total amount: $100,000; 90 jobs averaging $1100. ***State or other work-study/employment:*** Total amount: $417,170 (94% need-based, 6% non-need-based). 355 part-time jobs averaging $1100.

APPLYING FOR FINANCIAL AID ***Required financial aid form:*** FAFSA. ***Financial aid deadline (priority):*** 2/15. ***Notification date:*** 3/1. Students must reply by 5/1.

CONTACT Ms. Cathleen A. Patella, Director of Financial Aid, Wells College, Route 90, Aurora, NY 13026, 315-364-3289 or toll-free 800-952-9355. *Fax:* 315-364-3227. *E-mail:* cpatella@wells.edu.

WENTWORTH INSTITUTE OF TECHNOLOGY

Boston, MA

Tuition & fees: $24,000 **Average undergraduate aid package: $14,453**

ABOUT THE INSTITUTION Independent, coed. 21 undergraduate majors. Federal methodology is used as a basis for awarding need-based institutional aid.

UNDERGRADUATE EXPENSES for 2011–12 ***Tuition:*** full-time $24,000; part-time $750 per credit hour. Full-time tuition and fees vary according to student level. Part-time tuition and fees vary according to class time, course load, and degree level. Room and board charges vary according to board plan and housing facility. ***Payment plan:*** Installment.

FRESHMAN FINANCIAL AID (Fall 2010, est.) 627 applied for aid; of those 91% were deemed to have need. 100% of freshmen with need received aid; of those 2% had need fully met. ***Average financial aid package:*** $19,786 (excluding resources awarded to replace EFC). 7% of all full-time freshmen had no need and received non-need-based gift aid.

UNDERGRADUATE FINANCIAL AID (Fall 2010, est.) 2,571 applied for aid; of those 91% were deemed to have need. 100% of undergraduates with need received aid; of those 3% had need fully met. ***Average financial aid package:*** $14,453 (excluding resources awarded to replace EFC). 5% of all full-time undergraduates had no need and received non-need-based gift aid.

GIFT AID (NEED-BASED) ***Total amount:*** $5,081,536 (74% federal, 11% state, 15% institutional). ***Receiving aid:*** Freshmen: 40% (286); all full-time undergraduates: 26% (853). ***Average award:*** Freshmen: $5662; Undergraduates: $5568. ***Scholarships, grants, and awards:*** Federal Pell, FSEOG, state, private, college/university gift aid from institutional funds.

GIFT AID (NON-NEED-BASED) ***Total amount:*** $13,050,267 (97% institutional, 3% external sources). ***Receiving aid:*** Freshmen: 76% (546). Undergraduates: 47% (1,546). ***Average award:*** Freshmen: $6875. Undergraduates: $6766. ***Tuition waivers:*** Full or partial for employees or children of employees.

LOANS ***Student loans:*** $19,404,881 (57% need-based, 43% non-need-based). 80% of past graduating class borrowed through all loan programs. *Average indebtedness per student:* $20,208. ***Average need-based loan:*** Freshmen: $3599. Undergraduates: $4674. ***Parent loans:*** $17,189,369 (100% non-need-based). ***Programs:*** Federal Direct (Subsidized and Unsubsidized Stafford, PLUS), Perkins, state.

WORK-STUDY ***Federal work-study:*** Total amount: $2,743,635; 2,026 jobs averaging $1354.

APPLYING FOR FINANCIAL AID ***Required financial aid form:*** FAFSA. ***Financial aid deadline (priority):*** 3/1. ***Notification date:*** Continuous beginning 3/15. Students must reply within 2 weeks of notification.

CONTACT Anne-marie Caruso, Director of Financial Aid, Wentworth Institute of Technology, 550 Huntington Avenue, Boston, MA 02115-5998, 617-989-4174 or toll-free 800-556-0610. *Fax:* 617-989-4201. *E-mail:* carusoa@wit.edu.

WESLEYAN COLLEGE

Macon, GA

Tuition & fees: $18,000 **Average undergraduate aid package: $16,418**

ABOUT THE INSTITUTION Independent United Methodist, undergraduate: women only; graduate: coed. 27 undergraduate majors. Federal methodology is used as a basis for awarding need-based institutional aid.

UNDERGRADUATE EXPENSES for 2010–11 ***Comprehensive fee:*** $26,100 includes full-time tuition ($18,000) and room and board ($8100). Full-time tuition and fees vary according to class time, course level, course load, degree level, and program. Room and board charges vary according to board plan and housing facility. ***Part-time tuition:*** $425 per credit hour. Part-time tuition and fees vary according to class time, course level, course load, degree level, and program.

FRESHMAN FINANCIAL AID (Fall 2010, est.) 76 applied for aid; of those 82% were deemed to have need. 100% of freshmen with need received aid; of those 37% had need fully met. ***Average percent of need met:*** 85% (excluding resources awarded to replace EFC). ***Average financial aid package:*** $15,947 (excluding resources awarded to replace EFC). 29% of all full-time freshmen had no need and received non-need-based gift aid.

UNDERGRADUATE FINANCIAL AID (Fall 2010, est.) 276 applied for aid; of those 83% were deemed to have need. 100% of undergraduates with need received aid; of those 32% had need fully met. ***Average percent of need met:*** 81% (excluding resources awarded to replace EFC). ***Average financial aid package:*** $16,418 (excluding resources awarded to replace EFC). 35% of all full-time undergraduates had no need and received non-need-based gift aid.

GIFT AID (NEED-BASED) ***Total amount:*** $3,139,071 (25% federal, 15% state, 57% institutional, 3% external sources). ***Receiving aid:*** Freshmen: 70% (62); all full-time undergraduates: 61% (228). ***Average award:*** Freshmen: $13,018; Undergraduates: $12,632. ***Scholarships, grants, and awards:*** Federal Pell, FSEOG, state, private, college/university gift aid from institutional funds.

GIFT AID (NON-NEED-BASED) ***Total amount:*** $2,369,908 (12% state, 86% institutional, 2% external sources). ***Receiving aid:*** Freshmen: 22% (20). Undergraduates: 15% (57). ***Average award:*** Freshmen: $20,404. Undergraduates: $18,887. ***Scholarships, grants, and awards by category:*** *Academic interests/achievement:* 158 awards ($1,685,219 total): biological sciences, business, communication, education, engineering/technologies, English, foreign languages, general academic interests/achievements, humanities, mathematics, premedicine, religion/biblical studies, social sciences. *Creative arts/performance:* 53 awards ($210,115 total): art/fine arts, music, theater/drama. *Special achievements/activities:* 42 awards ($249,052 total): community service, general special achievements/activities, leadership, memberships, religious involvement. *Special characteristics:* 59 awards ($690,263 total): adult students, children and siblings of alumni, children of current students, children of faculty/staff, ethnic background, first-generation college students, general special characteristics, handicapped students, international students, parents of current students, relatives of clergy, religious affiliation, siblings of current students, spouses of current students, veterans. ***Tuition waivers:*** Full or partial for employees or children of employees, senior citizens.

LOANS ***Student loans:*** $2,497,152 (71% need-based, 29% non-need-based). 62% of past graduating class borrowed through all loan programs. *Average indebtedness per student:* $20,896. ***Average need-based loan:*** Freshmen: $3807. Undergraduates: $4925. ***Parent loans:*** $414,234 (27% need-based, 73% non-need-based). ***Programs:*** Federal Direct (Subsidized and Unsubsidized Stafford, PLUS), Perkins, college/university, alternative loans.

WORK-STUDY ***Federal work-study:*** Total amount: $49,107; 65 jobs averaging $941. ***State or other work-study/employment:*** Total amount: $137,675 (6% need-based, 94% non-need-based). 79 part-time jobs averaging $1244.

APPLYING FOR FINANCIAL AID ***Required financial aid forms:*** FAFSA, institution's own form, state aid form. ***Financial aid deadline (priority):*** 2/15. ***Notification date:*** Continuous beginning 3/1. Students must reply by 5/1 or within 3 weeks of notification.

CONTACT Kizzy K. Holmes, Director of Financial Aid, Wesleyan College, 4760 Forsyth Road, Macon, GA 31210-4462, 478-757-5205 or toll-free 800-447-6610. *Fax:* 478-757-3780. *E-mail:* financialaid@wesleyancollege.edu.

WESLEYAN UNIVERSITY

Middletown, CT

Tuition & fees: $42,084 **Average undergraduate aid package: $35,548**

ABOUT THE INSTITUTION Independent, coed. 47 undergraduate majors. Both federal and institutional methodology are used as a basis for awarding need-based institutional aid.

UNDERGRADUATE EXPENSES for 2010–11 ***One-time required fee:*** $300. ***Comprehensive fee:*** $53,676 includes full-time tuition ($41,814), mandatory fees ($270), and room and board ($11,592). Room and board charges vary according to board plan and housing facility. ***Payment plan:*** Installment.

FRESHMAN FINANCIAL AID (Fall 2009) 419 applied for aid; of those 84% were deemed to have need. 100% of freshmen with need received aid; of those 100% had need fully met. ***Average percent of need met:*** 100% (excluding resources awarded to replace EFC). ***Average financial aid package:*** $35,985 (excluding resources awarded to replace EFC). 1% of all full-time freshmen had no need and received non-need-based gift aid.

UNDERGRADUATE FINANCIAL AID (Fall 2009) 1,401 applied for aid; of those 95% were deemed to have need. 100% of undergraduates with need received aid; of those 100% had need fully met. ***Average percent of need met:*** 100% (excluding resources awarded to replace EFC). ***Average financial aid package:*** $35,548 (excluding resources awarded to replace EFC). 2% of all full-time undergraduates had no need and received non-need-based gift aid.

GIFT AID (NEED-BASED) ***Total amount:*** $40,603,861 (7% federal, 1% state, 89% institutional, 3% external sources). ***Receiving aid:*** Freshmen: 44% (326); all full-time undergraduates: 43% (1,185). ***Average award:*** Freshmen: $34,728; Undergraduates: $32,789. ***Scholarships, grants, and awards:*** Federal Pell, FSEOG, state, private, college/university gift aid from institutional funds.

GIFT AID (NON-NEED-BASED) ***Total amount:*** $2,213,200 (100% institutional). ***Average award:*** Freshmen: $40,392. Undergraduates: $47,089.

LOANS ***Student loans:*** $6,274,501 (100% need-based). 39% of past graduating class borrowed through all loan programs. *Average indebtedness per student:* $29,227. ***Average need-based loan:*** Freshmen: $2330. Undergraduates: $5192. ***Parent loans:*** $40,006,460 (100% need-based). ***Programs:*** Federal Direct (Subsidized and Unsubsidized Stafford, PLUS), Perkins, college/university.

WORK-STUDY ***Federal work-study:*** Total amount: $2,544,307; 1,113 jobs averaging $2332. ***State or other work-study/employment:*** Total amount: $288,861 (100% need-based). 77 part-time jobs averaging $2357.

APPLYING FOR FINANCIAL AID ***Required financial aid forms:*** FAFSA, CSS Financial Aid PROFILE, noncustodial (divorced/separated) parent's statement. ***Financial aid deadline:*** 2/15. ***Notification date:*** 4/1. Students must reply by 5/1.

CONTACT Sean Martin, Acting Director of Financial Aid, Wesleyan University, 237 High Street, Middletown, CT 06459-0260, 860-685-2800. *Fax:* 860-685-2801. *E-mail:* finaid@wesleyan.edu.

WESLEY COLLEGE

Dover, DE

Tuition & fees: $20,580 **Average undergraduate aid package: N/A**

ABOUT THE INSTITUTION Independent United Methodist, coed. ***Awards:*** associate, bachelor's, and master's degrees and post-bachelor's and post-master's certificates. 18 undergraduate majors. ***Total enrollment:*** 1,871. Undergraduates: 1,767. Freshmen: 484. Federal methodology is used as a basis for awarding need-based institutional aid.

UNDERGRADUATE EXPENSES for 2010–11 ***Application fee:*** $25. ***Tuition:*** full-time $19,700; part-time $835 per credit hour. Full-time tuition and fees vary according to class time. Room and board charges vary according to board plan and housing facility. ***Payment plan:*** Installment.

GIFT AID (NEED-BASED) ***Scholarships, grants, and awards:*** Federal Pell, FSEOG, state, private, college/university gift aid from institutional funds.

GIFT AID (NON-NEED-BASED) ***Scholarships, grants, and awards by category:*** *Academic interests/achievement:* general academic interests/achievements. *Special achievements/activities:* community service, general special achievements/activities, leadership, religious involvement. ***Tuition waivers:*** Full or partial for employees or children of employees, senior citizens. ***ROTC:*** Army cooperative.

LOANS ***Programs:*** Federal Direct (Subsidized and Unsubsidized Stafford, PLUS), Perkins, state, college/university.

APPLYING FOR FINANCIAL AID ***Required financial aid forms:*** FAFSA, institution's own form. ***Financial aid deadline (priority):*** 4/15. ***Notification date:*** Continuous. Students must reply within 2 weeks of notification.

CONTACT Michael Hall, Director of Student Financial Planning, Wesley College, 120 North State Street, Dover, DE 19901-3875, 302-736-2334 or toll-free 800-937-5398 Ext. 2400 (out-of-state). *Fax:* 302-736-2594. *E-mail:* halljmic@wesley.edu.

WEST CHESTER UNIVERSITY OF PENNSYLVANIA

West Chester, PA

Tuition & fees (PA res): $7680 **Average undergraduate aid package: $7559**

ABOUT THE INSTITUTION State-supported, coed. 52 undergraduate majors. Federal methodology is used as a basis for awarding need-based institutional aid.

UNDERGRADUATE EXPENSES for 2010–11 ***Tuition, state resident:*** full-time $5804; part-time $242 per credit. ***Tuition, nonresident:*** full-time $14,510; part-time $605 per credit. ***Required fees:*** full-time $1876; $61.92 per unit. Full-time tuition and fees vary according to course load. Part-time tuition and fees vary according to course load. ***College room and board:*** $7188; ***Room only:*** $4810. Room and board charges vary according to board plan and housing facility. ***Payment plan:*** Installment.

FRESHMAN FINANCIAL AID (Fall 2009) 1,905 applied for aid; of those 63% were deemed to have need. 100% of freshmen with need received aid; of those 34% had need fully met. ***Average percent of need met:*** 60% (excluding resources awarded to replace EFC). ***Average financial aid package:*** $6997 (excluding resources awarded to replace EFC). 2% of all full-time freshmen had no need and received non-need-based gift aid.

UNDERGRADUATE FINANCIAL AID (Fall 2009) 8,007 applied for aid; of those 71% were deemed to have need. 100% of undergraduates with need received aid; of those 35% had need fully met. ***Average percent of need met:*** 53% (excluding resources awarded to replace EFC). ***Average financial aid package:*** $7559 (excluding resources awarded to replace EFC). 2% of all full-time undergraduates had no need and received non-need-based gift aid.

GIFT AID (NEED-BASED) ***Total amount:*** $21,283,551 (48% federal, 36% state, 7% institutional, 9% external sources). ***Receiving aid:*** Freshmen: 37% (824); all full-time undergraduates: 34% (3,697). ***Average award:*** Freshmen: $5358; Undergraduates: $5402. ***Scholarships, grants, and awards:*** Federal Pell, FSEOG, state, college/university gift aid from institutional funds.

GIFT AID (NON-NEED-BASED) ***Total amount:*** $1,258,312 (3% state, 60% institutional, 37% external sources). ***Receiving aid:*** Freshmen: 3. Undergraduates: 9. ***Average award:*** Freshmen: $3431. Undergraduates: $3466. ***Scholarships, grants, and awards by category:*** *Academic interests/achievement:* business, general academic interests/achievements, mathematics, social sciences. *Creative arts/performance:* music, theater/drama. *Special characteristics:* children of faculty/staff. ***Tuition waivers:*** Full or partial for employees or children of employees, senior citizens.

LOANS ***Student loans:*** $59,477,634 (78% need-based, 22% non-need-based). 70% of past graduating class borrowed through all loan programs. *Average indebtedness per student:* $25,159. ***Average need-based loan:*** Freshmen: $3500. Undergraduates: $4282. ***Parent loans:*** $8,846,434 (100% non-need-based). ***Programs:*** Perkins, Federal Nursing.

WORK-STUDY ***Federal work-study:*** Total amount: $597,920; jobs available. ***State or other work-study/employment:*** Part-time jobs available.

ATHLETIC AWARDS Total amount: $784,099 (43% need-based, 57% non-need-based).

APPLYING FOR FINANCIAL AID ***Required financial aid form:*** FAFSA. ***Financial aid deadline (priority):*** 3/1. ***Notification date:*** Students must reply within 4 weeks of notification.

CONTACT Mr. Dana Parker, Financial Aid Office, West Chester University of Pennsylvania, 25 University Avenue, Suite #030, West Chester, PA 19383, 610-436-2627 or toll-free 877-315-2165 (in-state). *Fax:* 610-436-2574. *E-mail:* finaid@wcupa.edu.

WEST COAST UNIVERSITY

North Hollywood, CA

CONTACT Financial Aid Office, West Coast University, 12215 Victory Boulevard, North Hollywood, CA 91606, 323-315-5207 or toll-free 866-508-2684 (in-state).

WESTERN CAROLINA UNIVERSITY

Cullowhee, NC

Tuition & fees (NC res): $5367 **Average undergraduate aid package: $9322**

ABOUT THE INSTITUTION State-supported, coed. 69 undergraduate majors. Federal methodology is used as a basis for awarding need-based institutional aid.

UNDERGRADUATE EXPENSES for 2011–12 ***Tuition, state resident:*** full-time $2998. ***Tuition, nonresident:*** full-time $12,595. ***Required fees:*** full-time $2369. Full-time tuition and fees vary according to degree level. Part-time tuition and fees vary according to course load and degree level. ***College room and board:*** $6980. Room and board charges vary according to board plan and housing facility. ***Payment plan:*** Installment.

FRESHMAN FINANCIAL AID (Fall 2010, est.) 1,246 applied for aid; of those 78% were deemed to have need. 99% of freshmen with need received aid; of those 22% had need fully met. ***Average percent of need met:*** 73% (excluding resources awarded to replace EFC). ***Average financial aid package:*** $9400 (excluding resources awarded to replace EFC). 3% of all full-time freshmen had no need and received non-need-based gift aid.

UNDERGRADUATE FINANCIAL AID (Fall 2010, est.) 5,077 applied for aid; of those 81% were deemed to have need. 98% of undergraduates with need received aid; of those 29% had need fully met. ***Average percent of need met:*** 77% (excluding resources awarded to replace EFC). ***Average financial aid package:*** $9322 (excluding resources awarded to replace EFC). 4% of all full-time undergraduates had no need and received non-need-based gift aid.

GIFT AID (NEED-BASED) ***Total amount:*** $26,630,344 (43% federal, 41% state, 12% institutional, 4% external sources). ***Receiving aid:*** Freshmen: 67% (948); all full-time undergraduates: 62% (3,909). ***Average award:*** Freshmen: $7239; Undergraduates: $6736. ***Scholarships, grants, and awards:*** Federal Pell, FSEOG, state, private, college/university gift aid from institutional funds.

GIFT AID (NON-NEED-BASED) ***Total amount:*** $2,202,207 (1% federal, 48% state, 27% institutional, 24% external sources). ***Receiving aid:*** Freshmen: 5% (67). Undergraduates: 4% (271). ***Average award:*** Freshmen: $2680. Undergraduates: $2051. ***Scholarships, grants, and awards by category:*** *Academic interests/achievement:* biological sciences, business, communication, education, English, general academic interests/achievements, mathematics. *Creative arts/performance:* art/fine arts, music, theater/drama. *Special characteristics:* ethnic background, handicapped students, local/state students, members of minority groups. ***Tuition waivers:*** Full or partial for employees or children of employees.

LOANS ***Student loans:*** $24,349,143 (73% need-based, 27% non-need-based). ***Average need-based loan:*** Freshmen: $3109. Undergraduates: $3586. ***Parent loans:*** $6,298,384 (44% need-based, 56% non-need-based). ***Programs:*** Federal Direct (Subsidized and Unsubsidized Stafford, PLUS), Perkins.

WORK-STUDY ***Federal work-study:*** Total amount: $608,314; jobs available.

ATHLETIC AWARDS Total amount: $2,265,516 (50% need-based, 50% non-need-based).

APPLYING FOR FINANCIAL AID ***Required financial aid forms:*** FAFSA, institution's own form. ***Financial aid deadline (priority):*** 3/15. ***Notification date:*** Continuous beginning 4/1.

CONTACT Ms. Trina F. Orr, Director of Financial Aid, Western Carolina University, 123 Killian Annex, Cullowhee, NC 28723, 828-227-7292 or toll-free 877-WCU4YOU. *Fax:* 828-227-7042. *E-mail:* torr@email.wcu.edu.

WESTERN CONNECTICUT STATE UNIVERSITY

Danbury, CT

Tuition & fees (CT res): $7909 **Average undergraduate aid package: $7368**

ABOUT THE INSTITUTION State-supported, coed. 37 undergraduate majors. Federal methodology is used as a basis for awarding need-based institutional aid.

UNDERGRADUATE EXPENSES for 2010–11 ***Tuition, state resident:*** full-time $4023; part-time $168 per credit hour. ***Tuition, nonresident:*** full-time $13,020; part-time $171 per credit hour. ***Required fees:*** full-time $3886; $196 per credit hour. Full-time tuition and fees vary according to program and reciprocity agreements. ***College room and board: Room only:*** $5698. Room and board charges vary according to board plan and housing facility. ***Payment plan:*** Installment.

FRESHMAN FINANCIAL AID (Fall 2009) 875 applied for aid; of those 74% were deemed to have need. 98% of freshmen with need received aid; of those 5% had need fully met. ***Average percent of need met:*** 73% (excluding resources awarded to replace EFC). ***Average financial aid package:*** $8199 (excluding resources awarded to replace EFC). 1% of all full-time freshmen had no need and received non-need-based gift aid.

UNDERGRADUATE FINANCIAL AID (Fall 2009) 3,814 applied for aid; of those 77% were deemed to have need. 95% of undergraduates with need received aid; of those 3% had need fully met. ***Average percent of need met:*** 65% (excluding resources awarded to replace EFC). ***Average financial aid package:*** $7368 (excluding resources awarded to replace EFC). 1% of all full-time undergraduates had no need and received non-need-based gift aid.

GIFT AID (NEED-BASED) ***Total amount:*** $10,691,939 (48% federal, 45% state, 3% institutional, 4% external sources). ***Receiving aid:*** Freshmen: 54% (549); all full-time undergraduates: 58% (2,307). ***Average award:*** Freshmen: $5841; Undergraduates: $4468. ***Scholarships, grants, and awards:*** Federal Pell, FSEOG, state, private, college/university gift aid from institutional funds.

GIFT AID (NON-NEED-BASED) ***Total amount:*** $955,474 (1% state, 26% institutional, 73% external sources). ***Receiving aid:*** Freshmen: 9% (93). Undergraduates: 7% (288). ***Average award:*** Freshmen: $7462. Undergraduates: $6883. ***Scholarships, grants, and awards by category:*** *Academic interests/achievement:* general academic interests/achievements. ***Tuition waivers:*** Full or partial for employees or children of employees, senior citizens.

LOANS ***Student loans:*** $24,151,538 (82% need-based, 18% non-need-based). 67% of past graduating class borrowed through all loan programs. *Average indebtedness per student:* $23,487. ***Average need-based loan:*** Freshmen: $3283. Undergraduates: $3973. ***Parent loans:*** $3,448,264 (69% need-based, 31% non-need-based). ***Programs:*** Federal Direct (Subsidized and Unsubsidized Stafford, PLUS), Perkins.

WORK-STUDY ***Federal work-study:*** Total amount: $181,836; 116 jobs averaging $1501. ***State or other work-study/employment:*** Total amount: $62,000 (100% need-based). 29 part-time jobs averaging $2138.

APPLYING FOR FINANCIAL AID ***Required financial aid forms:*** FAFSA, institution's own form. ***Financial aid deadline:*** 4/15. ***Notification date:*** Continuous beginning 4/15. Students must reply by 5/1.

CONTACT Nancy Barton, Director of Student Financial Services, Western Connecticut State University, 181 White Street, Danbury, CT 06810-6860, 203-837-8588 or toll-free 877-837-WCSU. *Fax:* 203-837-8528. *E-mail:* bartonn@wcsu.edu.

WESTERN GOVERNORS UNIVERSITY

Salt Lake City, UT

Tuition & fees: N/R **Average undergraduate aid package: $5611**

ABOUT THE INSTITUTION Independent, coed. ***Awards:*** bachelor's and master's degrees and post-bachelor's certificates. 7 undergraduate majors. ***Total enrollment:*** 9,022. Undergraduates: 6,491. Federal methodology is used as a basis for awarding need-based institutional aid.

FRESHMAN FINANCIAL AID (Fall 2009) 1,371 applied for aid; of those 86% were deemed to have need. 100% of freshmen with need received aid; of those 6% had need fully met. ***Average percent of need met:*** 22% (excluding resources awarded to replace EFC). ***Average financial aid package:*** $4453 (excluding resources awarded to replace EFC).

UNDERGRADUATE FINANCIAL AID (Fall 2009) 16,002 applied for aid; of those 86% were deemed to have need. 100% of undergraduates with need received aid; of those 16% had need fully met. ***Average percent of need met:*** 28% (excluding resources awarded to replace EFC). ***Average financial aid package:*** $5611 (excluding resources awarded to replace EFC).

GIFT AID (NEED-BASED) ***Total amount:*** $32,163,027 (98% federal, 2% institutional). ***Receiving aid:*** Freshmen: 62% (850); all full-time undergraduates: 46% (8,997). ***Average award:*** Freshmen: $2874; Undergraduates: $3468. ***Scholarships, grants, and awards:*** Federal Pell, private, college/university gift aid from institutional funds.

GIFT AID (NON-NEED-BASED) ***Total amount:*** $462,915 (100% external sources).

LOANS ***Student loans:*** $102,486,177 (38% need-based, 62% non-need-based). 81% of past graduating class borrowed through all loan programs. *Average indebtedness per student:* $17,525. ***Average need-based loan:*** Freshmen: $2118. Undergraduates: $2679. ***Parent loans:*** $23,640 (100% non-need-based). ***Programs:*** Federal Direct (Subsidized and Unsubsidized Stafford, PLUS).

APPLYING FOR FINANCIAL AID ***Required financial aid forms:*** FAFSA, institution's own form. ***Financial aid deadline:*** Continuous. ***Notification date:*** Continuous.

CONTACT Jenny Allen Ryan, Director of Financial Aid, Western Governors University, 4001 South 700 East, Suite 700, Salt Lake City, UT 84107, 877-435-7948 Ext. 5731 or toll-free 877-435-7948. *Fax:* 801-907-7727. *E-mail:* jallenryan@wgu.edu.

WESTERN ILLINOIS UNIVERSITY

Macomb, IL

Tuition & fees (IL res): $9490 **Average undergraduate aid package: $9879**

ABOUT THE INSTITUTION State-supported, coed. 64 undergraduate majors. Federal methodology is used as a basis for awarding need-based institutional aid.

UNDERGRADUATE EXPENSES for 2010–11 ***Tuition, state resident:*** full-time $7220; part-time $240.65 per credit hour. ***Tuition, nonresident:*** full-time $10,829; part-time $360.98 per credit hour. ***Required fees:*** full-time $2270; $75.67 per credit hour. Full-time tuition and fees vary according to course load and student level. Part-time tuition and fees vary according to course load and student level. ***College room and board:*** $8138. Room and board charges vary according to board plan, housing facility, and student level. ***Payment plan:*** Guaranteed tuition.

FRESHMAN FINANCIAL AID (Fall 2010, est.) 1,473 applied for aid; of those 85% were deemed to have need. 97% of freshmen with need received aid; of those 35% had need fully met. ***Average percent of need met:*** 57% (excluding resources awarded to replace EFC). ***Average financial aid package:*** $9580 (excluding resources awarded to replace EFC). 2% of all full-time freshmen had no need and received non-need-based gift aid.

UNDERGRADUATE FINANCIAL AID (Fall 2010, est.) 7,523 applied for aid; of those 85% were deemed to have need. 98% of undergraduates with need received aid; of those 38% had need fully met. ***Average percent of need met:*** 62% (excluding resources awarded to replace EFC). ***Average financial aid package:*** $9879 (excluding resources awarded to replace EFC). 3% of all full-time undergraduates had no need and received non-need-based gift aid.

GIFT AID (NEED-BASED) ***Total amount:*** $35,749,243 (52% federal, 39% state, 7% institutional, 2% external sources). ***Receiving aid:*** Freshmen: 50% (879); all full-time undergraduates: 48% (4,519). ***Average award:*** Freshmen: $8763; Undergraduates: $7998. ***Scholarships, grants, and awards:*** Federal Pell, FSEOG, state, private, college/university gift aid from institutional funds.

GIFT AID (NON-NEED-BASED) ***Total amount:*** $2,818,723 (4% federal, 43% state, 39% institutional, 14% external sources). ***Average award:*** Freshmen: $2550. Undergraduates: $3112. ***Scholarships, grants, and awards by category:*** *Academic interests/achievement:* 3,788 awards ($3,606,314 total): agriculture, biological sciences, business, education, foreign languages, general academic interests/achievements, home economics, mathematics, physical sciences, social sciences. *Creative arts/performance:* 621 awards ($763,552 total): applied art and design, cinema/film/broadcasting, dance, debating, journalism/publications, music, performing arts, theater/drama. *Special achievements/activities:* 515 awards ($444,304 total): community service, leadership. *Special characteristics:* 1,308 awards ($2,538,718 total): children of faculty/staff, general special characteristics, international students, members of minority groups, veterans' children. ***Tuition waivers:*** Full or partial for employees or children of employees, senior citizens.

LOANS ***Student loans:*** $58,488,146 (52% need-based, 48% non-need-based). 69% of past graduating class borrowed through all loan programs. *Average indebtedness per student:* $22,007. ***Average need-based loan:*** Freshmen: $3381. Undergraduates: $4301. ***Parent loans:*** $12,529,712 (79% need-based, 21% non-need-based). ***Programs:*** Federal Direct (Subsidized and Unsubsidized Stafford, PLUS), Perkins, college/university.

WORK-STUDY ***Federal work-study:*** Total amount: $523,389; 212 jobs averaging $2469. ***State or other work-study/employment:*** Total amount: $1,742,918 (70% need-based, 30% non-need-based). 1,506 part-time jobs averaging $1157.

ATHLETIC AWARDS Total amount: $2,702,270 (44% need-based, 56% non-need-based).

APPLYING FOR FINANCIAL AID ***Required financial aid form:*** FAFSA. ***Financial aid deadline (priority):*** 2/15. ***Notification date:*** Continuous beginning 1/15.

CONTACT Financial Aid Office, Western Illinois University, 1 University Circle, Macomb, IL 61455-1390, 309-298-2446 or toll-free 877-742-5948. *Fax:* 309-298-2353. *E-mail:* finaid@wiu.edu.

WESTERN INTERNATIONAL UNIVERSITY

Phoenix, AZ

ABOUT THE INSTITUTION Proprietary, coed. 9 undergraduate majors.

CONTACT Ms. Ella Owen, Compliance Officer, Western International University, 9215 North Black Canyon Highway, Phoenix, AZ 85021, 602-429-1056. *Fax:* 602-383-9812. *E-mail:* ella.owen@west.edu.

WESTERN KENTUCKY UNIVERSITY

Bowling Green, KY

Tuition & fees (KY res): $7560 **Average undergraduate aid package: $12,417**

ABOUT THE INSTITUTION State-supported, coed. 94 undergraduate majors. Federal methodology is used as a basis for awarding need-based institutional aid.

UNDERGRADUATE EXPENSES for 2010–11 ***Tuition, state resident:*** full-time $7560; part-time $315 per hour. ***Tuition, nonresident:*** full-time $18,840; part-time $785 per hour. Full-time tuition and fees vary according to course level, course load, location, program, and reciprocity agreements. Part-time tuition and fees vary according to course level, course load, location, program, and reciprocity agreements. ***College room and board:*** $6600; ***Room only:*** $3810. Room and board charges vary according to board plan and housing facility. ***Payment plan:*** Installment.

FRESHMAN FINANCIAL AID (Fall 2009) 2,857 applied for aid; of those 77% were deemed to have need. 99% of freshmen with need received aid; of those 32% had need fully met. ***Average percent of need met:*** 32% (excluding resources awarded to replace EFC). ***Average financial aid package:*** $11,991 (excluding resources awarded to replace EFC). 9% of all full-time freshmen had no need and received non-need-based gift aid.

UNDERGRADUATE FINANCIAL AID (Fall 2009) 11,090 applied for aid; of those 80% were deemed to have need. 99% of undergraduates with need received aid; of those 29% had need fully met. ***Average percent of need met:*** 29% (excluding resources awarded to replace EFC). ***Average financial aid package:*** $12,417 (excluding resources awarded to replace EFC). 8% of all full-time undergraduates had no need and received non-need-based gift aid.

GIFT AID (NEED-BASED) ***Total amount:*** $37,686,511 (78% federal, 17% state, 5% institutional). ***Receiving aid:*** Freshmen: 48% (1,577); all full-time undergraduates: 44% (6,096). ***Average award:*** Freshmen: $5735; Undergraduates: $5428. ***Scholarships, grants, and awards:*** Federal Pell, FSEOG, state, private, college/university gift aid from institutional funds, United Negro College Fund.

GIFT AID (NON-NEED-BASED) ***Total amount:*** $26,063,975 (6% federal, 41% state, 46% institutional, 7% external sources). ***Receiving aid:*** Freshmen: 55% (1,810). Undergraduates: 34% (4,779). ***Average award:*** Freshmen: $5452. Undergraduates: $5033. ***Scholarships, grants, and awards by category:*** *Academic interests/achievement:* 2,509 awards ($9,034,330 total): agriculture, biological sciences, business, communication, education, engineering/technologies, English, foreign languages, general academic interests/achievements, health fields, home economics, mathematics, military science, physical sciences, premedicine, social sciences. *Creative arts/performance:* 382 awards ($1,168,933 total): art/fine arts, cinema/film/broadcasting, dance, debating, general creative arts/performance, journalism/publications, music, theater/drama. *Special achievements/activities:* 474 awards ($623,568 total): general special achievements/activities, leadership, memberships. *Special characteristics:* 1,517 awards ($2,666,714 total): adult students, children of union members/company employees, ethnic background, general special characteristics, handicapped students, international students, local/state students, members of minority groups, out-of-state students, religious affiliation, veterans. ***Tuition waivers:*** Full or partial for children of alumni, employees or children of employees, senior citizens.

LOANS ***Student loans:*** $71,538,882 (42% need-based, 58% non-need-based). 58% of past graduating class borrowed through all loan programs. *Average indebtedness per student:* $19,347. ***Average need-based loan:*** Freshmen: $3124. Undergraduates: $3851. ***Parent loans:*** $7,231,784 (100% non-need-based). ***Programs:*** Federal Direct (Subsidized and Unsubsidized Stafford, PLUS), Perkins.

WORK-STUDY ***Federal work-study:*** Total amount: $1,447,507; 690 jobs averaging $2098. ***State or other work-study/employment:*** Total amount: $3,905,184 (100% non-need-based). 1,887 part-time jobs averaging $2698.

ATHLETIC AWARDS Total amount: $4,618,486 (100% non-need-based).

APPLYING FOR FINANCIAL AID ***Required financial aid form:*** FAFSA. ***Financial aid deadline (priority):*** 2/15. ***Notification date:*** Continuous beginning 3/1.

CONTACT Cindy Burnette, Director of Student Financial Assistance, Western Kentucky University, Potter Hall, Room 317, Bowling Green, KY 42101-1018, 270-745-2758 or toll-free 800-495-8463 (in-state). *Fax:* 270-745-6586. *E-mail:* cindy.burnette@wku.edu.

WESTERN MICHIGAN UNIVERSITY

Kalamazoo, MI

Tuition & fees (MI res): $9006 **Average undergraduate aid package: $11,500**

ABOUT THE INSTITUTION State-supported, coed. 132 undergraduate majors. Federal methodology is used as a basis for awarding need-based institutional aid.

UNDERGRADUATE EXPENSES for 2010–11 ***One-time required fee:*** $300. ***Tuition, state resident:*** full-time $8182; part-time $282.92 per credit hour. ***Tuition, nonresident:*** full-time $20,070; part-time $694.04 per credit hour. ***Required fees:*** full-time $824; $223.25 per term. Full-time tuition and fees vary according to course load, location, program, and student level. Part-time tuition and fees vary according to course load, location, program, and student level. ***College room and board:*** $8095; ***Room only:*** $4167. Room and board charges vary according to board plan. ***Payment plan:*** Installment.

FRESHMAN FINANCIAL AID (Fall 2009) 3,202 applied for aid; of those 83% were deemed to have need. 100% of freshmen with need received aid; of those 19% had need fully met. ***Average percent of need met:*** 81% (excluding resources awarded to replace EFC). ***Average financial aid package:*** $10,000 (excluding resources awarded to replace EFC). 11% of all full-time freshmen had no need and received non-need-based gift aid.

UNDERGRADUATE FINANCIAL AID (Fall 2009) 13,600 applied for aid; of those 86% were deemed to have need. 100% of undergraduates with need received aid; of those 44% had need fully met. ***Average percent of need met:*** 82% (excluding resources awarded to replace EFC). ***Average financial aid package:*** $11,500 (excluding resources awarded to replace EFC). 13% of all full-time undergraduates had no need and received non-need-based gift aid.

GIFT AID (NEED-BASED) ***Total amount:*** $38,916,329 (70% federal, 2% state, 28% institutional). ***Receiving aid:*** Freshmen: 48% (1,573); all full-time undergraduates: 33% (5,546). ***Average award:*** Freshmen: $4600; Undergraduates: $4800. ***Scholarships, grants, and awards:*** Federal Pell, FSEOG, state, private, college/university gift aid from institutional funds, Federal Nursing.

GIFT AID (NON-NEED-BASED) ***Total amount:*** $18,698,340 (1% state, 73% institutional, 26% external sources). ***Receiving aid:*** Freshmen: 35% (1,151). Undergraduates: 31% (5,250). ***Average award:*** Freshmen: $3400. Undergraduates: $3500. ***Scholarships, grants, and awards by category:*** *Academic interests/achievement:* general academic interests/achievements. *Creative arts/performance:* general creative arts/performance. *Special characteristics:* children of faculty/staff, veterans. ***Tuition waivers:*** Full or partial for employees or children of employees, senior citizens.

LOANS ***Student loans:*** $110,050,386 (39% need-based, 61% non-need-based). 66% of past graduating class borrowed through all loan programs. *Average indebtedness per student:* $20,000. ***Average need-based loan:*** Freshmen: $3400. Undergraduates: $4000. ***Parent loans:*** $20,076,156 (50% need-based, 50% non-need-based). ***Programs:*** Federal Direct (Subsidized and Unsubsidized Stafford, PLUS), Perkins, alternative loans.

WORK-STUDY ***Federal work-study:*** Total amount: $1,493,533; jobs available. ***State or other work-study/employment:*** Total amount: $6,000,000 (100% non-need-based). Part-time jobs available.

ATHLETIC AWARDS Total amount: $5,588,172 (100% non-need-based).

APPLYING FOR FINANCIAL AID ***Required financial aid form:*** FAFSA. ***Financial aid deadline (priority):*** 3/15. ***Notification date:*** Continuous beginning 3/15.

CONTACT Mr. Mark Delorey, Director of Student Financial Aid, Western Michigan University, 1903 West Michigan Avenue, Faunce Student Services Building, Room 3306, Kalamazoo, MI 49008-5337, 269-387-6000. *E-mail:* finaid-info@wmich.edu.

WESTERN NEW ENGLAND UNIVERSITY

Springfield, MA

Tuition & fees: $29,812 **Average undergraduate aid package: $19,699**

ABOUT THE INSTITUTION Independent, coed. 39 undergraduate majors. Federal methodology is used as a basis for awarding need-based institutional aid.

UNDERGRADUATE EXPENSES for 2010–11 ***Comprehensive fee:*** $41,148 includes full-time tuition ($27,762), mandatory fees ($2050), and room and board ($11,336). Full-time tuition and fees vary according to program. Room and board charges vary according to board plan and housing facility. ***Part-time tuition:*** $523 per credit hour. Part-time tuition and fees vary according to location and program. ***Payment plans:*** Tuition prepayment, installment.

FRESHMAN FINANCIAL AID (Fall 2010, est.) 690 applied for aid; of those 88% were deemed to have need. 100% of freshmen with need received aid; of those 23% had need fully met. ***Average percent of need met:*** 74% (excluding resources awarded to replace EFC). ***Average financial aid package:*** $21,682 (excluding resources awarded to replace EFC). 15% of all full-time freshmen had no need and received non-need-based gift aid.

UNDERGRADUATE FINANCIAL AID (Fall 2010, est.) 2,232 applied for aid; of those 89% were deemed to have need. 100% of undergraduates with need received aid; of those 15% had need fully met. ***Average percent of need met:*** 69% (excluding resources awarded to replace EFC). ***Average financial aid package:*** $19,699 (excluding resources awarded to replace EFC). 13% of all full-time undergraduates had no need and received non-need-based gift aid.

GIFT AID (NEED-BASED) ***Total amount:*** $27,010,983 (13% federal, 2% state, 85% institutional). ***Receiving aid:*** Freshmen: 83% (609); all full-time undergraduates: 78% (1,959). ***Average award:*** Freshmen: $16,762; Undergraduates: $1455. ***Scholarships, grants, and awards:*** Federal Pell, FSEOG, state, private, college/university gift aid from institutional funds, Academic Competitiveness Grants, National SMART Grants.

GIFT AID (NON-NEED-BASED) ***Total amount:*** $3,315,196 (9% federal, 91% institutional). ***Receiving aid:*** Freshmen: 18% (134). Undergraduates: 11% (282). ***Average award:*** Freshmen: $11,156. Undergraduates: $11,140. ***Scholarships, grants, and awards by category:*** *Academic interests/achievement:* general academic interests/achievements. *Creative arts/performance:* music. *Special achievements/activities:* community service, leadership. *Special characteristics:* children of faculty/staff, children of union members/company employees, international students, local/state students, members of minority groups, out-of-state students, siblings of current students. ***Tuition waivers:*** Full or partial for employees or children of employees, senior citizens.

LOANS ***Student loans:*** $21,297,779 (63% need-based, 37% non-need-based). ***Average need-based loan:*** Freshmen: $3894. Undergraduates: $4728. ***Parent loans:*** $11,273,588 (100% non-need-based). ***Programs:*** Federal Direct (Subsidized and Unsubsidized Stafford, PLUS), Perkins.

WORK-STUDY ***Federal work-study:*** Total amount: $2,063,639; jobs available. ***State or other work-study/employment:*** Total amount: $700,000 (100% non-need-based). Part-time jobs available.

APPLYING FOR FINANCIAL AID ***Required financial aid forms:*** FAFSA, federal income tax form(s), W-2 forms. ***Financial aid deadline (priority):*** 4/15. ***Notification date:*** Continuous beginning 3/1. Students must reply by 5/1 or within 2 weeks of notification.

CONTACT Mrs. Kathy M. Chambers, Associate Director of Student Administrative Services, Western New England University, 1215 Wilbraham Road, Springfield, MA 01119-2684, 413-796-2080 or toll-free 800-325-1122 Ext. 1321. *Fax:* 413-796-2081. *E-mail:* finaid@wne.edu.

WESTERN NEW MEXICO UNIVERSITY

Silver City, NM

Tuition & fees: N/R **Average undergraduate aid package: $8912**

ABOUT THE INSTITUTION State-supported, coed. ***Awards:*** associate, bachelor's, and master's degrees. 58 undergraduate majors. ***Total enrollment:*** 2,697. Undergraduates: 2,219. Freshmen: 277. Federal methodology is used as a basis for awarding need-based institutional aid.

FRESHMAN FINANCIAL AID (Fall 2009) 449 applied for aid; of those 78% were deemed to have need. 98% of freshmen with need received aid; of those 9% had need fully met. ***Average percent of need met:*** 62% (excluding resources awarded to replace EFC). ***Average financial aid package:*** $7239 (excluding resources awarded to replace EFC). 6% of all full-time freshmen had no need and received non-need-based gift aid.

UNDERGRADUATE FINANCIAL AID (Fall 2009) 1,654 applied for aid; of those 81% were deemed to have need. 99% of undergraduates with need received aid; of those 14% had need fully met. ***Average percent of need met:*** 70% (excluding resources awarded to replace EFC). ***Average financial aid package:*** $8912 (excluding resources awarded to replace EFC). 6% of all full-time undergraduates had no need and received non-need-based gift aid.

GIFT AID (NEED-BASED) ***Total amount:*** $7,133,224 (82% federal, 17% state, 1% institutional). ***Receiving aid:*** Freshmen: 68% (318); all full-time undergraduates: 68% (1,204). ***Average award:*** Freshmen: $5831; Undergraduates: $5024. ***Scholarships, grants, and awards:*** Federal Pell, FSEOG, state, private, college/university gift aid from institutional funds.

GIFT AID (NON-NEED-BASED) ***Total amount:*** $156,479 (100% external sources). ***Receiving aid:*** Freshmen: 3% (15). Undergraduates: 4% (64). ***Average award:*** Freshmen: $4158. Undergraduates: $4490. ***Scholarships, grants, and awards by category:*** *Academic interests/achievement:* 396 awards ($842,396 total): general academic interests/achievements. *Creative arts/performance:* performing arts. *Special achievements/activities:* 32 awards ($52,983 total): general special achievements/activities. *Special characteristics:* 4 awards ($25,000 total): general special characteristics, veterans. ***Tuition waivers:*** Full or partial for employees or children of employees, senior citizens.

LOANS ***Student loans:*** $8,754,186 (100% need-based). 20% of past graduating class borrowed through all loan programs. *Average indebtedness per student:* $3250. ***Average need-based loan:*** Freshmen: $3184. Undergraduates: $4209. ***Parent loans:*** $18,018 (100% need-based). ***Programs:*** Perkins, state, college/university.

WORK-STUDY ***Federal work-study:*** Total amount: $161,858; 74 jobs averaging $2187. ***State or other work-study/employment:*** Total amount: $447,961 (33% need-based, 67% non-need-based). 225 part-time jobs averaging $1991.

ATHLETIC AWARDS Total amount: $595,595 (100% non-need-based).

APPLYING FOR FINANCIAL AID ***Required financial aid forms:*** FAFSA, institution's own form. ***Financial aid deadline (priority):*** 4/1. ***Notification date:*** Continuous beginning 4/1. Students must reply within 2 weeks of notification.

CONTACT Debra Reyes, Assistant Director, Western New Mexico University, PO Box 680, Silver City, NM 88062, 575-538-6173 or toll-free 800-872-WNMU (in-state). *Fax:* 575-538-6189. *E-mail:* reyesd@wnmu.edu.

WESTERN OREGON UNIVERSITY

Monmouth, OR

Tuition & fees (OR res): $8055 **Average undergraduate aid package: $8601**

ABOUT THE INSTITUTION State-supported, coed. 35 undergraduate majors. Federal methodology is used as a basis for awarding need-based institutional aid.

UNDERGRADUATE EXPENSES for 2011–12 ***Tuition, state resident:*** full-time $6855. ***Tuition, nonresident:*** full-time $18,951. ***Required fees:*** full-time $1200. Full-time tuition and fees vary according to course level, course load, degree level, reciprocity agreements, and student level. Part-time tuition and fees vary according to course level, course load, degree level, reciprocity agreements, and student level. ***College room and board:*** $8439. Room and board charges vary according to board plan and housing facility. ***Payment plans:*** Guaranteed tuition, deferred payment.

FRESHMAN FINANCIAL AID (Fall 2010, est.) 812 applied for aid; of those 85% were deemed to have need. 100% of freshmen with need received aid; of those 11% had need fully met. ***Average percent of need met:*** 61% (excluding resources awarded to replace EFC). ***Average financial aid package:*** $8890 (excluding resources awarded to replace EFC). 5% of all full-time freshmen had no need and received non-need-based gift aid.

UNDERGRADUATE FINANCIAL AID (Fall 2010, est.) 3,743 applied for aid; of those 86% were deemed to have need. 100% of undergraduates with need received aid; of those 11% had need fully met. ***Average percent of need met:*** 59% (excluding resources awarded to replace EFC). ***Average financial aid package:*** $8601 (excluding resources awarded to replace EFC). 4% of all full-time undergraduates had no need and received non-need-based gift aid.

GIFT AID (NEED-BASED) ***Total amount:*** $13,144,413 (76% federal, 3% state, 6% institutional, 15% external sources). ***Receiving aid:*** Freshmen: 69% (581); all full-time undergraduates: 65% (2,550). ***Average award:*** Freshmen: $6884; Undergraduates: $5948. ***Scholarships, grants, and awards:*** Federal Pell, FSEOG, state, private, college/university gift aid from institutional funds, Academic Competitiveness Grants, National SMART Grants, TEACH Grants.

GIFT AID (NON-NEED-BASED) ***Total amount:*** $1,061,984 (3% federal, 38% institutional, 59% external sources). ***Receiving aid:*** Freshmen: 3% (29). Undergraduates: 2% (93). ***Average award:*** Freshmen: $1278. Undergraduates: $2333. ***Scholarships, grants, and awards by category:*** *Academic interests/achievement:* 842 awards ($1,610,576 total): biological sciences, business, computer science, education, English, foreign languages, general academic interests/achievements, humanities, mathematics, physical sciences, premedicine, social sciences. *Creative arts/performance:* 112 awards ($109,237 total): art/fine arts, dance, music, performing arts, theater/drama. *Special achievements/activities:* 372 awards ($852,008 total): community service, general special achievements/activities, leadership. *Special characteristics:* 138 awards ($365,999 total): adult students, children of workers in trades, ethnic background, handicapped students, international students, local/state students, veterans, veterans' children. ***Tuition waivers:*** Full or partial for employees or children of employees.

LOANS ***Student loans:*** $26,313,091 (80% need-based, 20% non-need-based). 59% of past graduating class borrowed through all loan programs. *Average indebtedness per student:* $24,131. ***Average need-based loan:*** Freshmen: $3259. Undergraduates: $4146. ***Parent loans:*** $7,026,474 (31% need-based, 69% non-need-based). ***Programs:*** Federal Direct (Subsidized and Unsubsidized Stafford, PLUS), Perkins, college/university.

WORK-STUDY ***Federal work-study:*** Total amount: $299,045; 706 jobs averaging $1074.

ATHLETIC AWARDS Total amount: $546,488 (65% need-based, 35% non-need-based).

APPLYING FOR FINANCIAL AID ***Required financial aid form:*** FAFSA. ***Financial aid deadline (priority):*** 3/1. ***Notification date:*** Continuous beginning 3/15. Students must reply within 3 weeks of notification.

CONTACT Ms. Donna Fossum, Director of Financial Aid, Western Oregon University, 345 North Monmouth Avenue, Monmouth, OR 97361, 503-838-8475 or toll-free 877-877-1593. *Fax:* 503-838-8200. *E-mail:* finaid@wou.edu.

WESTERN STATE COLLEGE OF COLORADO

Gunnison, CO

Tuition & fees (CO res): $4775 Average undergraduate aid package: $10,049

ABOUT THE INSTITUTION State-supported, coed. 70 undergraduate majors. Federal methodology is used as a basis for awarding need-based institutional aid.

UNDERGRADUATE EXPENSES for 2011–12 ***Tuition, state resident:*** full-time $3422. ***Tuition, nonresident:*** full-time $12,888. ***Required fees:*** full-time $1353. Full-time tuition and fees vary according to course load. Part-time tuition and fees vary according to course load. ***College room and board:*** $8518; ***Room only:*** $4420. Room and board charges vary according to board plan and housing facility. ***Payment plans:*** Installment, deferred payment.

FRESHMAN FINANCIAL AID (Fall 2010, est.) 359 applied for aid; of those 67% were deemed to have need. 85% of freshmen with need received aid; of those 15% had need fully met. ***Average percent of need met:*** 50% (excluding resources awarded to replace EFC). ***Average financial aid package:*** $7500 (excluding resources awarded to replace EFC). 35% of all full-time freshmen had no need and received non-need-based gift aid.

UNDERGRADUATE FINANCIAL AID (Fall 2010, est.) 1,467 applied for aid; of those 67% were deemed to have need. 85% of undergraduates with need received aid; of those 10% had need fully met. ***Average percent of need met:*** 40% (excluding resources awarded to replace EFC). ***Average financial aid package:*** $10,049 (excluding resources awarded to replace EFC). 22% of all full-time undergraduates had no need and received non-need-based gift aid.

GIFT AID (NEED-BASED) ***Total amount:*** $6,000,000 (37% federal, 12% state, 49% institutional, 2% external sources). ***Receiving aid:*** Freshmen: 21% (103); all full-time undergraduates: 19% (418). ***Average award:*** Freshmen: $2500; Undergraduates: $2500. ***Scholarships, grants, and awards:*** Federal Pell, FSEOG, state, private, college/university gift aid from institutional funds.

GIFT AID (NON-NEED-BASED) ***Total amount:*** $2,100,000 (81% institutional, 19% external sources). ***Receiving aid:*** Freshmen: 6% (27). Undergraduates: 8% (167). ***Average award:*** Freshmen: $1900. Undergraduates: $1700. ***Scholarships, grants, and awards by category:*** *Academic interests/achievement:* general academic interests/achievements. *Creative arts/performance:* art/fine arts, music. *Special achievements/activities:* leadership. *Special characteristics:* children and siblings of alumni. ***Tuition waivers:*** Full or partial for senior citizens.

LOANS ***Student loans:*** $12,250,000 (62% need-based, 38% non-need-based). 75% of past graduating class borrowed through all loan programs. *Average indebtedness per student:* $18,600. ***Average need-based loan:*** Freshmen: $3500. Undergraduates: $5300. ***Parent loans:*** $1,500,000 (100% non-need-based). ***Programs:*** Perkins.

WORK-STUDY ***Federal work-study:*** Total amount: $212,000; 270 jobs averaging $1120. ***State or other work-study/employment:*** Total amount: $975,000 (23% need-based, 77% non-need-based). 221 part-time jobs averaging $1115.

ATHLETIC AWARDS Total amount: $96,000 (100% non-need-based).

APPLYING FOR FINANCIAL AID ***Required financial aid form:*** FAFSA. ***Financial aid deadline (priority):*** 3/1. ***Notification date:*** Continuous beginning 3/1. Students must reply within 3 weeks of notification.

CONTACT Jerry Martinez, Director of Financial Aid, Western State College of Colorado, Ute Hall Room 115, Gunnison, CO 81231, 970-943-3026 or toll-free 800-876-5309. *Fax:* 970-943-3086. *E-mail:* ecronkright@western.edu.

WESTERN WASHINGTON UNIVERSITY

Bellingham, WA

Tuition & fees (WA res): $6858 Average undergraduate aid package: $11,730

ABOUT THE INSTITUTION State-supported, coed. 112 undergraduate majors. Federal methodology is used as a basis for awarding need-based institutional aid.

UNDERGRADUATE EXPENSES for 2010–11 ***Tuition, state resident:*** full-time $6081; part-time $203 per credit hour. ***Tuition, nonresident:*** full-time $16,428; part-time $548 per credit hour. ***Required fees:*** full-time $777; $26 per credit hour. Full-time tuition and fees vary according to course load and location. Part-time tuition and fees vary according to course load and location. ***College room and board:*** $8749. Room and board charges vary according to board plan and housing facility. ***Payment plan:*** Installment.

FRESHMAN FINANCIAL AID (Fall 2010, est.) 2,117 applied for aid; of those 61% were deemed to have need. 96% of freshmen with need received aid; of those 26% had need fully met. ***Average percent of need met:*** 90% (excluding resources awarded to replace EFC). ***Average financial aid package:*** $12,469 (excluding resources awarded to replace EFC). 2% of all full-time freshmen had no need and received non-need-based gift aid.

UNDERGRADUATE FINANCIAL AID (Fall 2010, est.) 8,280 applied for aid; of those 71% were deemed to have need. 97% of undergraduates with need received aid; of those 22% had need fully met. ***Average percent of need met:*** 84% (excluding resources awarded to replace EFC). ***Average financial aid package:*** $11,730 (excluding resources awarded to replace EFC). 2% of all full-time undergraduates had no need and received non-need-based gift aid.

GIFT AID (NEED-BASED) ***Total amount:*** $31,088,115 (47% federal, 34% state, 13% institutional, 6% external sources). ***Receiving aid:*** Freshmen: 37% (1,007); all full-time undergraduates: 33% (4,233). ***Average award:*** Freshmen: $8373; Undergraduates: $8037. ***Scholarships, grants, and awards:*** Federal Pell, FSEOG, state, private, college/university gift aid from institutional funds.

GIFT AID (NON-NEED-BASED) ***Total amount:*** $1,634,383 (11% federal, 4% state, 30% institutional, 55% external sources). ***Receiving aid:*** Freshmen: 2% (56). Undergraduates: 1% (109). ***Average award:*** Freshmen: $1906. Undergraduates: $1710. ***Scholarships, grants, and awards by category:*** *Academic interests/achievement:* biological sciences, business, communication, computer science, education, engineering/technologies, English, foreign languages, general academic interests/achievements, health fields, humanities, library science, mathematics, physical sciences, premedicine, social sciences. *Creative arts/performance:* applied art and design, art/fine arts, cinema/film/broadcasting, creative writing, dance, general creative arts/performance, journalism/publications, music, performing arts, theater/drama. *Special achievements/activities:* community service, leadership, memberships. *Special characteristics:* children of public servants, children of union members/company employees, ethnic background, general special characteristics, international students, local/state students, members of minority groups, previous college experience, veterans. ***Tuition waivers:*** Full or partial for minority students, employees or children of employees.

LOANS ***Student loans:*** $43,863,100 (62% need-based, 38% non-need-based). 50% of past graduating class borrowed through all loan programs. *Average indebtedness per student:* $17,652. ***Average need-based loan:*** Freshmen: $3663. Undergraduates: $4415. ***Parent loans:*** $25,328,857 (16% need-based, 84% non-need-based). ***Programs:*** Federal Direct (Subsidized and Unsubsidized Stafford, PLUS), Perkins, college/university, alternative loans.

WORK-STUDY ***Federal work-study:*** Total amount: $861,789; 266 jobs averaging $32. ***State or other work-study/employment:*** Total amount: $1,780,090 (100% need-based). 541 part-time jobs averaging $3290.

ATHLETIC AWARDS Total amount: $1,090,585 (26% need-based, 74% non-need-based).

APPLYING FOR FINANCIAL AID ***Required financial aid form:*** FAFSA. ***Financial aid deadline (priority):*** 2/15. ***Notification date:*** Continuous beginning 3/15. Students must reply within 3 weeks of notification.

CONTACT Ms. Barbara Luton, Office Support Supervisor II for Financial Aid, Western Washington University, Old Main 255, MS 9006, 516 High Street, Bellingham, WA 98225-9006, 360-650-3470. *E-mail:* financialaid@wwu.edu.

WESTFIELD STATE UNIVERSITY

Westfield, MA

Tuition & fees (MA res): $7431 **Average undergraduate aid package: $7666**

ABOUT THE INSTITUTION State-supported, coed. 32 undergraduate majors. Federal methodology is used as a basis for awarding need-based institutional aid.

UNDERGRADUATE EXPENSES for 2010–11 ***Tuition, state resident:*** full-time $970; part-time $85 per credit hour. ***Tuition, nonresident:*** full-time $7050; part-time $95 per credit hour. ***Required fees:*** full-time $6461; $115 per credit hour or $150 per term. Full-time tuition and fees vary according to reciprocity agreements. ***College room and board:*** $8525. Room and board charges vary according to board plan and housing facility. ***Payment plan:*** Installment.

FRESHMAN FINANCIAL AID (Fall 2010, est.) 1,077 applied for aid; of those 65% were deemed to have need. 97% of freshmen with need received aid; of those 10% had need fully met. ***Average percent of need met:*** 64% (excluding resources awarded to replace EFC). ***Average financial aid package:*** $7405 (excluding resources awarded to replace EFC). 1% of all full-time freshmen had no need and received non-need-based gift aid.

UNDERGRADUATE FINANCIAL AID (Fall 2010, est.) 4,033 applied for aid; of those 71% were deemed to have need. 98% of undergraduates with need received aid; of those 15% had need fully met. ***Average percent of need met:*** 69% (excluding resources awarded to replace EFC). ***Average financial aid package:*** $7666 (excluding resources awarded to replace EFC). 1% of all full-time undergraduates had no need and received non-need-based gift aid.

GIFT AID (NEED-BASED) ***Total amount:*** $10,774,785 (59% federal, 23% state, 13% institutional, 5% external sources). ***Receiving aid:*** Freshmen: 41% (461); all full-time undergraduates: 38% (1,823). ***Average award:*** Freshmen: $5650; Undergraduates: $5090. ***Scholarships, grants, and awards:*** Federal Pell, FSEOG, state, private, college/university gift aid from institutional funds.

GIFT AID (NON-NEED-BASED) ***Total amount:*** $617,935 (31% state, 22% institutional, 47% external sources). ***Receiving aid:*** Freshmen: 15% (170). Undergraduates: 8% (397). ***Average award:*** Freshmen: $4039. Undergraduates: $4258. ***Scholarships, grants, and awards by category:*** *Academic interests/achievement:* general academic interests/achievements. ***Tuition waivers:*** Full or partial for employees or children of employees, senior citizens.

LOANS ***Student loans:*** $25,024,325 (63% need-based, 37% non-need-based). 75% of past graduating class borrowed through all loan programs. *Average indebtedness per student:* $21,182. ***Average need-based loan:*** Freshmen: $3314. Undergraduates: $4081. ***Parent loans:*** $4,071,497 (16% need-based, 84% non-need-based). ***Programs:*** Federal Direct (Subsidized and Unsubsidized Stafford, PLUS), Perkins.

WORK-STUDY ***Federal work-study:*** Total amount: $490,209; 302 jobs averaging $1613.

APPLYING FOR FINANCIAL AID ***Required financial aid form:*** FAFSA. ***Financial aid deadline (priority):*** 3/1. ***Notification date:*** 4/15.

CONTACT Catherine Ryan, Financial Aid Director, Westfield State University, 333 Western Avenue, Westfield, MA 01086, 413-572-5218 or toll-free 800-322-8401 (in-state).

WEST LIBERTY UNIVERSITY

West Liberty, WV

Tuition & fees (WV res): $4880 **Average undergraduate aid package: $8924**

ABOUT THE INSTITUTION State-supported, coed. 35 undergraduate majors. Federal methodology is used as a basis for awarding need-based institutional aid.

UNDERGRADUATE EXPENSES for 2010–11 ***Tuition, state resident:*** full-time $4880; part-time $203.33 per credit hour. ***Tuition, nonresident:*** full-time $12,750; part-time $531.25 per credit hour. Full-time tuition and fees vary according to course load, degree level, and program. Part-time tuition and fees vary according to course load, degree level, and program. ***College room and board:*** $7310; ***Room only:*** $4250. Room and board charges vary according to board plan and housing facility. ***Payment plans:*** Installment, deferred payment.

FRESHMAN FINANCIAL AID (Fall 2009) 558 applied for aid; of those 82% were deemed to have need. 99% of freshmen with need received aid; of those 46% had need fully met. ***Average percent of need met:*** 70% (excluding resources awarded to replace EFC). ***Average financial aid package:*** $8955 (excluding resources awarded to replace EFC). 5% of all full-time freshmen had no need and received non-need-based gift aid.

UNDERGRADUATE FINANCIAL AID (Fall 2009) 2,006 applied for aid; of those 84% were deemed to have need. 97% of undergraduates with need received aid; of those 48% had need fully met. ***Average percent of need met:*** 68% (excluding resources awarded to replace EFC). ***Average financial aid package:*** $8924 (excluding resources awarded to replace EFC). 3% of all full-time undergraduates had no need and received non-need-based gift aid.

GIFT AID (NEED-BASED) ***Total amount:*** $6,414,727 (71% federal, 28% state, 1% institutional). ***Receiving aid:*** Freshmen: 65% (375); all full-time undergraduates: 55% (1,255). ***Average award:*** Freshmen: $6901; Undergraduates: $6162. ***Scholarships, grants, and awards:*** Federal Pell, FSEOG, state, private, college/university gift aid from institutional funds.

GIFT AID (NON-NEED-BASED) ***Total amount:*** $1,751,409 (76% state, 17% institutional, 7% external sources). ***Receiving aid:*** Freshmen: 24% (140). Undergraduates: 18% (411). ***Average award:*** Freshmen: $1665. Undergraduates: $1745. ***Scholarships, grants, and awards by category:*** *Academic interests/achievement:* business, communication, education, English, general academic interests/achievements, health fields, mathematics, physical sciences. *Creative arts/performance:* art/fine arts, music, theater/drama. *Special achievements/activities:* cheerleading/drum major. *Special characteristics:* children and siblings of alumni, children of faculty/staff. ***Tuition waivers:*** Full or partial for employees or children of employees, senior citizens.

LOANS ***Student loans:*** $12,274,159 (42% need-based, 58% non-need-based). 83% of past graduating class borrowed through all loan programs. *Average indebtedness per student:* $19,200. ***Average need-based loan:*** Freshmen: $3216. Undergraduates: $4064. ***Parent loans:*** $1,843,017 (100% non-need-based). ***Programs:*** Federal Direct (Subsidized and Unsubsidized Stafford, PLUS), Perkins, Federal Nursing, alternative loans.

WORK-STUDY ***Federal work-study:*** Total amount: $180,110; jobs available. ***State or other work-study/employment:*** Total amount: $338,178 (100% non-need-based). Part-time jobs available.

ATHLETIC AWARDS Total amount: $489,350 (100% non-need-based).

APPLYING FOR FINANCIAL AID ***Required financial aid form:*** FAFSA. ***Financial aid deadline (priority):*** 3/1. ***Notification date:*** Continuous. Students must reply within 2 weeks of notification.

CONTACT Christ Taskalines, Financial Aid Manager, West Liberty University, PO Box 295, West Liberty, WV 26074-0295, 304-336-8016 or toll-free 800-732-6204 Ext. 8076. *Fax:* 304-336-8088. *E-mail:* taskalic@westliberty.edu.

WESTMINSTER COLLEGE

Fulton, MO

Tuition & fees: $19,740 **Average undergraduate aid package: $17,846**

ABOUT THE INSTITUTION Independent religious, coed. 30 undergraduate majors. Federal methodology is used as a basis for awarding need-based institutional aid.

UNDERGRADUATE EXPENSES for 2010–11 ***Comprehensive fee:*** $27,350 includes full-time tuition ($18,990), mandatory fees ($750), and room and board ($7610). ***College room only:*** $3990. Room and board charges vary according to board plan and housing facility. ***Part-time tuition:*** $750 per credit hour. ***Payment plan:*** Installment.

FRESHMAN FINANCIAL AID (Fall 2010, est.) 268 applied for aid; of those 78% were deemed to have need. 100% of freshmen with need received aid; of those 78% had need fully met. ***Average percent of need met:*** 78% (excluding resources awarded to replace EFC). ***Average financial aid package:*** $18,346 (excluding resources awarded to replace EFC). 33% of all full-time freshmen had no need and received non-need-based gift aid.

UNDERGRADUATE FINANCIAL AID (Fall 2010, est.) 868 applied for aid; of those 82% were deemed to have need. 100% of undergraduates with need received aid; of those 69% had need fully met. ***Average percent of need met:*** 75% (excluding resources awarded to replace EFC). ***Average financial aid***

package: $17,846 (excluding resources awarded to replace EFC). 37% of all full-time undergraduates had no need and received non-need-based gift aid.

GIFT AID (NEED-BASED) ***Total amount:*** $14,888,907 (12% federal, 5% state, 68% institutional, 15% external sources). ***Receiving aid:*** Freshmen: 65% (210); all full-time undergraduates: 63% (710). ***Average award:*** Freshmen: $14,544; Undergraduates: $13,094. ***Scholarships, grants, and awards:*** Federal Pell, FSEOG, state, private, college/university gift aid from institutional funds.

GIFT AID (NON-NEED-BASED) ***Average award:*** Freshmen: $9559. Undergraduates: $8775. ***Scholarships, grants, and awards by category:*** *Academic interests/achievement:* 546 awards ($4,120,677 total): general academic interests/achievements. *Creative arts/performance:* 13 awards ($18,000 total): music. *Special achievements/activities:* 401 awards ($1,019,737 total): general special achievements/activities, leadership. *Special characteristics:* 339 awards ($2,557,786 total): children and siblings of alumni, children of faculty/staff, ethnic background, international students, local/state students, relatives of clergy, religious affiliation, siblings of current students, twins. ***Tuition waivers:*** Full or partial for children of alumni, employees or children of employees.

LOANS ***Student loans:*** $4,926,963 (46% need-based, 54% non-need-based). 50% of past graduating class borrowed through all loan programs. *Average indebtedness per student:* $21,964. ***Average need-based loan:*** Freshmen: $3027. Undergraduates: $3897. ***Parent loans:*** $1,422,521 (100% non-need-based). ***Programs:*** Federal Direct (Subsidized and Unsubsidized Stafford, PLUS), Perkins.

WORK-STUDY ***Federal work-study:*** Total amount: $250,000; 292 jobs averaging $2578. ***State or other work-study/employment:*** Total amount: $400,000 (100% non-need-based). 191 part-time jobs averaging $2594.

APPLYING FOR FINANCIAL AID ***Required financial aid form:*** FAFSA. ***Financial aid deadline (priority):*** 2/15. ***Notification date:*** Continuous beginning 3/15. Students must reply within 3 weeks of notification.

CONTACT Ms. Aimee Bristow, Director of Financial Aid, Westminster College, 501 Westminster Avenue, Fulton, MO 65251-1299, 800-475-3361. *Fax:* 573-592-5255. *E-mail:* aimee.bristow@westminster-mo.edu.

WESTMINSTER COLLEGE

New Wilmington, PA

Tuition & fees: $29,150 **Average undergraduate aid package: $23,316**

ABOUT THE INSTITUTION Independent religious, coed. 52 undergraduate majors. Federal methodology is used as a basis for awarding need-based institutional aid.

UNDERGRADUATE EXPENSES for 2010–11 ***Comprehensive fee:*** $37,990 includes full-time tuition ($28,020), mandatory fees ($1130), and room and board ($8840). ***College room only:*** $4770. Room and board charges vary according to board plan and housing facility. ***Part-time tuition:*** $890 per semester hour. ***Part-time fees:*** $12.50 per semester hour.

FRESHMAN FINANCIAL AID (Fall 2010, est.) 391 applied for aid; of those 92% were deemed to have need. 100% of freshmen with need received aid; of those 14% had need fully met. ***Average percent of need met:*** 77% (excluding resources awarded to replace EFC). ***Average financial aid package:*** $23,791 (excluding resources awarded to replace EFC). 19% of all full-time freshmen had no need and received non-need-based gift aid.

UNDERGRADUATE FINANCIAL AID (Fall 2010, est.) 1,405 applied for aid; of those 93% were deemed to have need. 98% of undergraduates with need received aid; of those 21% had need fully met. ***Average percent of need met:*** 78% (excluding resources awarded to replace EFC). ***Average financial aid package:*** $23,316 (excluding resources awarded to replace EFC). 15% of all full-time undergraduates had no need and received non-need-based gift aid.

GIFT AID (NEED-BASED) ***Total amount:*** $23,074,982 (11% federal, 7% state, 78% institutional, 4% external sources). ***Receiving aid:*** Freshmen: 79% (359); all full-time undergraduates: 82% (1,285). ***Average award:*** Freshmen: $19,734; Undergraduates: $18,402. ***Scholarships, grants, and awards:*** Federal Pell, FSEOG, state, private, college/university gift aid from institutional funds.

GIFT AID (NON-NEED-BASED) ***Total amount:*** $4,581,292 (93% institutional, 7% external sources). ***Receiving aid:*** Freshmen: 8% (38). Undergraduates: 11% (170). ***Average award:*** Freshmen: $14,408. Undergraduates: $14,128. ***Scholarships, grants, and awards by category:*** *Academic interests/achievement:* general academic interests/achievements. *Creative arts/performance:* cinema/film/broadcasting, general creative arts/performance, music, theater/drama. *Special characteristics:* children and siblings of alumni, general special characteristics, international students, religious affiliation. ***Tuition waivers:*** Full or partial for employees or children of employees.

LOANS ***Student loans:*** $10,501,184 (72% need-based, 28% non-need-based). 80% of past graduating class borrowed through all loan programs. *Average indebtedness per student:* $28,637. ***Average need-based loan:*** Freshmen: $4479. Undergraduates: $5377. ***Parent loans:*** $3,139,266 (37% need-based, 63% non-need-based). ***Programs:*** Perkins, Resource loans.

WORK-STUDY ***Federal work-study:*** Total amount: $680,173; jobs available. ***State or other work-study/employment:*** Total amount: $275,324 (23% need-based, 77% non-need-based). Part-time jobs available.

APPLYING FOR FINANCIAL AID ***Required financial aid forms:*** FAFSA, institution's own form, W-2 forms. ***Financial aid deadline:*** Continuous. ***Notification date:*** Continuous beginning 3/1. Students must reply by 5/1 or within 3 weeks of notification.

CONTACT Mrs. Cheryl A. Gerber, Director of Financial Aid, Westminster College, 319 South Market Street, New Wilmington, PA 16172-0001, 724-946-7102 or toll-free 800-942-8033 (in-state). *Fax:* 724-946-6171. *E-mail:* gerberca@westminster.edu.

WESTMINSTER COLLEGE

Salt Lake City, UT

Tuition & fees: $27,182 **Average undergraduate aid package: $19,342**

ABOUT THE INSTITUTION Independent, coed. 37 undergraduate majors. Federal methodology is used as a basis for awarding need-based institutional aid.

UNDERGRADUATE EXPENSES for 2011–12 ***Comprehensive fee:*** $34,766 includes full-time tuition ($26,712), mandatory fees ($470), and room and board ($7584). Full-time tuition and fees vary according to course load. Room and board charges vary according to board plan. ***Part-time tuition:*** $1113 per credit hour. Part-time tuition and fees vary according to course load. ***Payment plans:*** Installment, deferred payment.

FRESHMAN FINANCIAL AID (Fall 2010, est.) 402 applied for aid; of those 84% were deemed to have need. 100% of freshmen with need received aid; of those 33% had need fully met. ***Average percent of need met:*** 89% (excluding resources awarded to replace EFC). ***Average financial aid package:*** $21,969 (excluding resources awarded to replace EFC). 36% of all full-time freshmen had no need and received non-need-based gift aid.

UNDERGRADUATE FINANCIAL AID (Fall 2010, est.) 1,485 applied for aid; of those 90% were deemed to have need. 99% of undergraduates with need received aid; of those 30% had need fully met. ***Average percent of need met:*** 76% (excluding resources awarded to replace EFC). ***Average financial aid package:*** $19,342 (excluding resources awarded to replace EFC). 35% of all full-time undergraduates had no need and received non-need-based gift aid.

GIFT AID (NEED-BASED) ***Total amount:*** $18,655,947 (17% federal, 75% institutional, 8% external sources). ***Receiving aid:*** Freshmen: 63% (339); all full-time undergraduates: 61% (1,323). ***Average award:*** Freshmen: $16,003; Undergraduates: $14,303. ***Scholarships, grants, and awards:*** Federal Pell, FSEOG, state, private, college/university gift aid from institutional funds.

GIFT AID (NON-NEED-BASED) ***Total amount:*** $9,274,951 (1% state, 83% institutional, 16% external sources). ***Receiving aid:*** Freshmen: 8% (45). Undergraduates: 6% (124). ***Average award:*** Freshmen: $12,474. Undergraduates: $10,996. ***Tuition waivers:*** Full or partial for employees or children of employees.

LOANS ***Student loans:*** $13,508,778 (84% need-based, 16% non-need-based). 65% of past graduating class borrowed through all loan programs. *Average indebtedness per student:* $20,002. ***Average need-based loan:*** Freshmen: $3830. Undergraduates: $4787. ***Parent loans:*** $1,432,457 (84% need-based, 16% non-need-based). ***Programs:*** Federal Direct (Subsidized and Unsubsidized Stafford, PLUS), Perkins.

WORK-STUDY ***Federal work-study:*** Total amount: $884,675; 352 jobs averaging $2513. ***State or other work-study/employment:*** Total amount: $550,000 (100% non-need-based). 227 part-time jobs averaging $2423.

ATHLETIC AWARDS Total amount: $395,690 (58% need-based, 42% non-need-based).

APPLYING FOR FINANCIAL AID ***Required financial aid form:*** FAFSA. ***Financial aid deadline:*** Continuous. ***Notification date:*** Continuous beginning 3/1. Students must reply within 3 weeks of notification.

CONTACT Sean View, Director of Financial Aid, Westminster College, 1840 South 1300 East, Salt Lake City, UT 84105, 801-832-2500 or toll-free 800-748-4753 (out-of-state). *Fax:* 801-832-2501. *E-mail:* sview@westminstercollege.edu.

WESTMONT COLLEGE

Santa Barbara, CA

Tuition & fees: $34,460 **Average undergraduate aid package: $25,857**

ABOUT THE INSTITUTION Independent nondenominational, coed. 43 undergraduate majors. Federal methodology is used as a basis for awarding need-based institutional aid.

UNDERGRADUATE EXPENSES for 2011–12 ***Comprehensive fee:*** $45,420 includes full-time tuition ($33,400), mandatory fees ($1060), and room and board ($10,960). ***College room only:*** $6810. Room and board charges vary according to board plan.

FRESHMAN FINANCIAL AID (Fall 2010, est.) 298 applied for aid; of those 83% were deemed to have need. 100% of freshmen with need received aid; of those 18% had need fully met. ***Average percent of need met:*** 75% (excluding resources awarded to replace EFC). ***Average financial aid package:*** $26,289 (excluding resources awarded to replace EFC). 27% of all full-time freshmen had no need and received non-need-based gift aid.

UNDERGRADUATE FINANCIAL AID (Fall 2010, est.) 988 applied for aid; of those 90% were deemed to have need. 100% of undergraduates with need received aid; of those 12% had need fully met. ***Average percent of need met:*** 72% (excluding resources awarded to replace EFC). ***Average financial aid package:*** $25,857 (excluding resources awarded to replace EFC). 27% of all full-time undergraduates had no need and received non-need-based gift aid.

GIFT AID (NEED-BASED) ***Total amount:*** $17,093,032 (8% federal, 11% state, 78% institutional, 3% external sources). ***Receiving aid:*** Freshmen: 67% (245); all full-time undergraduates: 63% (875). ***Average award:*** Freshmen: $22,340; Undergraduates: $20,979. ***Scholarships, grants, and awards:*** Federal Pell, FSEOG, state, private, college/university gift aid from institutional funds.

GIFT AID (NON-NEED-BASED) ***Total amount:*** $4,449,742 (96% institutional, 4% external sources). ***Receiving aid:*** Freshmen: 10% (36). Undergraduates: 6% (82). ***Average award:*** Freshmen: $11,542. Undergraduates: $10,304. ***Scholarships, grants, and awards by category:*** *Academic interests/achievement:* general academic interests/achievements. *Creative arts/performance:* art/fine arts, music, theater/drama. *Special achievements/activities:* general special achievements/activities, leadership. *Special characteristics:* children of faculty/staff, ethnic background, international students. ***Tuition waivers:*** Full or partial for employees or children of employees.

LOANS ***Student loans:*** $7,587,038 (77% need-based, 23% non-need-based). 67% of past graduating class borrowed through all loan programs. *Average indebtedness per student:* $27,690. ***Average need-based loan:*** Freshmen: $4229. Undergraduates: $5502. ***Parent loans:*** $3,388,197 (44% need-based, 56% non-need-based). ***Programs:*** Federal Direct (Subsidized and Unsubsidized Stafford, PLUS), Perkins, college/university, alternative loans.

WORK-STUDY ***Federal work-study:*** Total amount: $363,369; jobs available.

ATHLETIC AWARDS Total amount: $1,531,414 (58% need-based, 42% non-need-based).

APPLYING FOR FINANCIAL AID ***Required financial aid form:*** FAFSA. ***Financial aid deadline (priority):*** 3/1. ***Notification date:*** 3/1. Students must reply by 5/1 or within 2 weeks of notification.

CONTACT Mr. Sean Smith, Director of Financial Aid, Westmont College, 955 La Paz Road, Santa Barbara, CA 93108, 805-565-6063 or toll-free 800-777-9011. *Fax:* 805-565-7157. *E-mail:* sesmith@westmont.edu.

WEST TEXAS A&M UNIVERSITY

Canyon, TX

Tuition & fees (TX res): $6236 **Average undergraduate aid package: $8338**

ABOUT THE INSTITUTION State-supported, coed. ***Awards:*** bachelor's and master's degrees. 59 undergraduate majors. ***Total enrollment:*** 7,535. Undergraduates: 6,096. Freshmen: 1,171. Federal methodology is used as a basis for awarding need-based institutional aid.

UNDERGRADUATE EXPENSES for 2010–11 ***Application fee:*** $25. ***Tuition, state resident:*** full-time $4370; part-time $150 per credit hour. ***Tuition, nonresident:*** full-time $13,670; part-time $460 per credit hour. ***Required fees:*** full-time $1866; $59 per credit hour or $174 per term. Full-time tuition and fees vary according to course load. Part-time tuition and fees vary according to course load. ***College room and board:*** $6000; ***Room only:*** $3000. Room and board charges vary according to board plan and housing facility. ***Payment plan:*** Installment.

FRESHMAN FINANCIAL AID (Fall 2009) 1,031 applied for aid; of those 76% were deemed to have need. 98% of freshmen with need received aid; of those 100% had need fully met. ***Average percent of need met:*** 68% (excluding resources awarded to replace EFC). ***Average financial aid package:*** $8788 (excluding resources awarded to replace EFC). 19% of all full-time freshmen had no need and received non-need-based gift aid.

UNDERGRADUATE FINANCIAL AID (Fall 2009) 4,065 applied for aid; of those 81% were deemed to have need. 97% of undergraduates with need received aid; of those 100% had need fully met. ***Average percent of need met:*** 60% (excluding resources awarded to replace EFC). ***Average financial aid package:*** $8338 (excluding resources awarded to replace EFC). 13% of all full-time undergraduates had no need and received non-need-based gift aid.

GIFT AID (NEED-BASED) ***Total amount:*** $18,656,364 (53% federal, 24% state, 23% institutional). ***Receiving aid:*** Freshmen: 47% (546); all full-time undergraduates: 49% (2,525). ***Average award:*** Freshmen: $6808; Undergraduates: $5140. ***Scholarships, grants, and awards:*** Federal Pell, FSEOG, state, private, college/university gift aid from institutional funds.

GIFT AID (NON-NEED-BASED) ***Total amount:*** $2,769,364 (50% institutional, 50% external sources). ***Receiving aid:*** Freshmen: 36% (422). Undergraduates: 15% (788). ***Average award:*** Freshmen: $5134. Undergraduates: $6338. ***Scholarships, grants, and awards by category:*** *Academic interests/achievement:* 1,900 awards ($919,342 total): agriculture, business, communication, computer science, education, engineering/technologies, English, general academic interests/achievements, health fields, humanities, mathematics, physical sciences, premedicine, social sciences. *Creative arts/performance:* 273 awards ($111,066 total): art/fine arts, cinema/film/broadcasting, dance, debating, journalism/publications, music, theater/drama. *Special achievements/activities:* 257 awards ($159,640 total): cheerleading/drum major, community service, hobbies/interests, leadership, memberships, rodeo. *Special characteristics:* 440 awards ($219,031 total): children and siblings of alumni, children of faculty/staff, children of union members/company employees, first-generation college students, handicapped students, local/state students, out-of-state students, religious affiliation. ***Tuition waivers:*** Full or partial for employees or children of employees.

LOANS ***Student loans:*** $22,112,139 (52% need-based, 48% non-need-based). 35% of past graduating class borrowed through all loan programs. *Average indebtedness per student:* $13,678. ***Average need-based loan:*** Freshmen: $2687. Undergraduates: $3984. ***Parent loans:*** $594,133 (100% non-need-based). ***Programs:*** Federal Direct (Subsidized and Unsubsidized Stafford, PLUS), state.

WORK-STUDY ***Federal work-study:*** Total amount: $415,984; 297 jobs averaging $2440. ***State or other work-study/employment:*** Total amount: $2,095,907 (2% need-based, 98% non-need-based). 48 part-time jobs averaging $1065.

ATHLETIC AWARDS Total amount: $1,315,053 (100% non-need-based).

APPLYING FOR FINANCIAL AID ***Required financial aid forms:*** FAFSA, institution's own form. ***Financial aid deadline (priority):*** 5/1. ***Notification date:*** Continuous beginning 2/15. Students must reply within 2 weeks of notification.

CONTACT Mr. Jim Reed, Director of Financial Aid, West Texas A&M University, WTAMU Box 60939, Canyon, TX 79016-0001, 806-651-2055 or toll-free 800-99-WTAMU. *Fax:* 806-651-2924. *E-mail:* jreed@mail.wtamu.edu.

WEST VIRGINIA STATE UNIVERSITY

Institute, WV

Tuition & fees: N/R **Average undergraduate aid package: N/A**

ABOUT THE INSTITUTION State-supported, coed. 31 undergraduate majors. Federal methodology is used as a basis for awarding need-based institutional aid.

GIFT AID (NEED-BASED) ***Scholarships, grants, and awards:*** Federal Pell, FSEOG, state, private, college/university gift aid from institutional funds.

GIFT AID (NON-NEED-BASED) ***Scholarships, grants, and awards by category:*** *Academic interests/achievement:* biological sciences, business, communication, English, foreign languages, general academic interests/achievements, mathematics, military science. *Creative arts/performance:* art/fine arts, music. *Special achievements/activities:* general special achievements/activities, leadership. *Special characteristics:* ethnic background, general special characteristics.

LOANS ***Programs:*** Federal Direct (Subsidized and Unsubsidized Stafford, PLUS), Perkins, college/university.

APPLYING FOR FINANCIAL AID ***Required financial aid form:*** FAFSA. ***Financial aid deadline:*** 6/15 (priority: 4/1). ***Notification date:*** Continuous.

CONTACT Mrs. Mary Blizzard, Director of Student Financial Assistance, West Virginia State University, PO Box 1000, Ferrell Hall 324, Institute, WV 25112-1000, 304-766-3131 or toll-free 800-987-2112.

WEST VIRGINIA UNIVERSITY

Morgantown, WV

Tuition & fees (WV res): $5406 **Average undergraduate aid package: $7200**

ABOUT THE INSTITUTION State-supported, coed. 62 undergraduate majors. Federal methodology is used as a basis for awarding need-based institutional aid.

UNDERGRADUATE EXPENSES for 2010–11 ***Tuition, state resident:*** full-time $5406; part-time $225 per credit hour. ***Tuition, nonresident:*** full-time $17,002; part-time $708 per credit hour. Full-time tuition and fees vary according to location, program, and reciprocity agreements. Part-time tuition and fees vary according to course load, location, program, and reciprocity agreements. ***College room and board:*** $8120. Room and board charges vary according to board plan, housing facility, and location. ***Payment plan:*** Installment.

FRESHMAN FINANCIAL AID (Fall 2010, est.) 4,205 applied for aid; of those 78% were deemed to have need. 76% of freshmen with need received aid; of those 30% had need fully met. ***Average percent of need met:*** 72% (excluding resources awarded to replace EFC). ***Average financial aid package:*** $6664 (excluding resources awarded to replace EFC). 31% of all full-time freshmen had no need and received non-need-based gift aid.

UNDERGRADUATE FINANCIAL AID (Fall 2010, est.) 16,197 applied for aid; of those 78% were deemed to have need. 82% of undergraduates with need received aid; of those 30% had need fully met. ***Average percent of need met:*** 75% (excluding resources awarded to replace EFC). ***Average financial aid package:*** $7200 (excluding resources awarded to replace EFC). 17% of all full-time undergraduates had no need and received non-need-based gift aid.

GIFT AID (NEED-BASED) ***Total amount:*** $38,332,906 (76% federal, 17% state, 7% institutional). ***Receiving aid:*** Freshmen: 36% (1,815); all full-time undergraduates: 36% (7,400). ***Average award:*** Freshmen: $5353; Undergraduates: $5029. ***Scholarships, grants, and awards:*** Federal Pell, FSEOG, state, private, college/university gift aid from institutional funds.

GIFT AID (NON-NEED-BASED) ***Total amount:*** $32,295,220 (1% federal, 69% state, 23% institutional, 7% external sources). ***Receiving aid:*** Freshmen: 33% (1,661). Undergraduates: 36% (7,503). ***Average award:*** Freshmen: $1800. Undergraduates: $2081. ***Scholarships, grants, and awards by category:*** *Academic interests/achievement:* agriculture, architecture, area/ethnic studies, biological sciences, business, communication, computer science, education, engineering/technologies, English, foreign languages, general academic interests/achievements, health fields, home economics, humanities, international studies, library science, mathematics, military science, physical sciences, premedicine, religion/biblical studies, social sciences. *Creative arts/performance:* art/fine arts, debating, music, theater/drama. *Special achievements/activities:* general special achievements/activities, leadership. *Special characteristics:* children of faculty/staff, children of union members/company employees, children of workers in trades, ethnic background, general special characteristics, international students, local/state students, members of minority groups. ***Tuition waivers:*** Full or partial for employees or children of employees, senior citizens.

LOANS ***Student loans:*** $116,605,536 (35% need-based, 65% non-need-based). ***Average need-based loan:*** Freshmen: $4016. Undergraduates: $4675. ***Parent loans:*** $54,660,670 (100% non-need-based). ***Programs:*** Federal Direct (Subsidized and Unsubsidized Stafford, PLUS), Perkins, Federal Nursing, college/university.

WORK-STUDY ***Federal work-study:*** Total amount: $1,900,000; jobs available. ***State or other work-study/employment:*** Total amount: $2,048,222 (100% non-need-based). Part-time jobs available.

ATHLETIC AWARDS Total amount: $4,705,744 (100% non-need-based).

APPLYING FOR FINANCIAL AID ***Required financial aid forms:*** FAFSA, state aid form. ***Financial aid deadline:*** 3/1. ***Notification date:*** Continuous beginning 3/15. Students must reply within 4 weeks of notification.

CONTACT Kaye Widney, Director of Financial Aid, West Virginia University, Office of Financial Aid at WVU, PO Box 6004, Morgantown, WV 26506-6004, 304-293-5242 or toll-free 800-344-9881. *Fax:* 304-293-4890. *E-mail:* kaye.widney@mail.wvu.edu.

WEST VIRGINIA UNIVERSITY INSTITUTE OF TECHNOLOGY

Montgomery, WV

Tuition & fees (WV res): $5164 **Average undergraduate aid package: $9374**

ABOUT THE INSTITUTION State-supported, coed. 27 undergraduate majors. Federal methodology is used as a basis for awarding need-based institutional aid.

UNDERGRADUATE EXPENSES for 2010–11 ***Tuition, state resident:*** full-time $4460; part-time $215 per credit hour. ***Tuition, nonresident:*** full-time $12,560; part-time $553 per credit hour. ***Required fees:*** full-time $704. Full-time tuition and fees vary according to program. Part-time tuition and fees vary according to course load and program. ***College room and board:*** $8130; ***Room only:*** $4800. Room and board charges vary according to board plan and housing facility. ***Payment plan:*** Installment.

FRESHMAN FINANCIAL AID (Fall 2010, est.) 255 applied for aid; of those 83% were deemed to have need. 100% of freshmen with need received aid; of those 14% had need fully met. ***Average percent of need met:*** 20% (excluding resources awarded to replace EFC). ***Average financial aid package:*** $9601 (excluding resources awarded to replace EFC). 7% of all full-time freshmen had no need and received non-need-based gift aid.

UNDERGRADUATE FINANCIAL AID (Fall 2010, est.) 975 applied for aid; of those 85% were deemed to have need. 96% of undergraduates with need received aid; of those 34% had need fully met. ***Average percent of need met:*** 34% (excluding resources awarded to replace EFC). ***Average financial aid package:*** $9374 (excluding resources awarded to replace EFC). 4% of all full-time undergraduates had no need and received non-need-based gift aid.

GIFT AID (NEED-BASED) ***Total amount:*** $3,208,303 (74% federal, 20% state, 6% external sources). ***Receiving aid:*** Freshmen: 52% (150); all full-time undergraduates: 50% (625). ***Average award:*** Freshmen: $4915; Undergraduates: $4779. ***Scholarships, grants, and awards:*** Federal Pell, FSEOG, state.

GIFT AID (NON-NEED-BASED) ***Total amount:*** $960,408 (8% federal, 82% state, 10% external sources). ***Receiving aid:*** Freshmen: 34% (98). Undergraduates: 37% (465). ***Average award:*** Freshmen: $4838. Undergraduates: $5227. ***Scholarships, grants, and awards by category:*** *Academic interests/achievement:* 242 awards ($438,319 total): biological sciences, engineering/technologies, general academic interests/achievements, mathematics, physical sciences. *Special achievements/activities:* 5 awards ($3000 total): cheerleading/drum major.

LOANS ***Student loans:*** $4,142,751 (48% need-based, 52% non-need-based). 41% of past graduating class borrowed through all loan programs. *Average indebtedness per student:* $18,319. ***Average need-based loan:*** Freshmen: $3393. Undergraduates: $3612. ***Parent loans:*** $595,971 (100% non-need-based). ***Programs:*** Federal Direct (Subsidized and Unsubsidized Stafford, PLUS), Perkins, college/university.

WORK-STUDY ***Federal work-study:*** Total amount: $24,692; 79 jobs averaging $1151. ***State or other work-study/employment:*** Total amount: $143,880 (100% non-need-based). 127 part-time jobs averaging $1006.

ATHLETIC AWARDS Total amount: $1,196,215 (100% non-need-based).

APPLYING FOR FINANCIAL AID ***Required financial aid form:*** FAFSA. ***Financial aid deadline (priority):*** 3/1. ***Notification date:*** Continuous beginning 3/21. Students must reply within 4 weeks of notification.

CONTACT Mr. Michael A. White, Director of Financial Aid Services, West Virginia University Institute of Technology, 405 Fayette Pike, Old Main, Room 206, Box 40, Montgomery, WV 25136, 304-442-3140 or toll-free 888-554-8324.

WEST VIRGINIA WESLEYAN COLLEGE

Buckhannon, WV

Tuition & fees: $23,980 **Average undergraduate aid package: $23,631**

ABOUT THE INSTITUTION Independent religious, coed. 64 undergraduate majors. Federal methodology is used as a basis for awarding need-based institutional aid.

UNDERGRADUATE EXPENSES for 2010–11 ***Comprehensive fee:*** $31,120 includes full-time tuition ($23,130), mandatory fees ($850), and room and board ($7140). Full-time tuition and fees vary according to course load. Room and board charges vary according to board plan and housing facility. Part-time tuition and fees vary according to course load. ***Payment plan:*** Installment.

FRESHMAN FINANCIAL AID (Fall 2010, est.) 361 applied for aid; of those 91% were deemed to have need. 100% of freshmen with need received aid; of those 26% had need fully met. ***Average percent of need met:*** 80% (excluding resources awarded to replace EFC). ***Average financial aid package:*** $22,686 (excluding resources awarded to replace EFC). 11% of all full-time freshmen had no need and received non-need-based gift aid.

UNDERGRADUATE FINANCIAL AID (Fall 2010, est.) 1,175 applied for aid; of those 92% were deemed to have need. 100% of undergraduates with need received aid; of those 29% had need fully met. ***Average percent of need met:*** 83% (excluding resources awarded to replace EFC). ***Average financial aid package:*** $23,631 (excluding resources awarded to replace EFC). 19% of all full-time undergraduates had no need and received non-need-based gift aid.

GIFT AID (NEED-BASED) ***Total amount:*** $18,453,396 (12% federal, 13% state, 72% institutional, 3% external sources). ***Receiving aid:*** Freshmen: 89% (329); all full-time undergraduates: 81% (1,077). ***Average award:*** Freshmen: $20,271; Undergraduates: $20,329. ***Scholarships, grants, and awards:*** Federal Pell, FSEOG, state, private, college/university gift aid from institutional funds, Federal Nursing.

GIFT AID (NON-NEED-BASED) ***Total amount:*** $4,181,111 (7% state, 85% institutional, 8% external sources). ***Receiving aid:*** Freshmen: 20% (73). Undergraduates: 18% (237). ***Average award:*** Freshmen: $11,997. Undergraduates: $10,754. ***Scholarships, grants, and awards by category:*** *Academic interests/achievement:* English, general academic interests/achievements, physical sciences. *Creative arts/performance:* art/fine arts, music, performing arts, theater/drama. *Special achievements/activities:* community service, leadership, religious involvement. *Special characteristics:* children and siblings of alumni, children of faculty/staff, general special characteristics, international students, relatives of clergy, religious affiliation. ***Tuition waivers:*** Full or partial for employees or children of employees.

LOANS ***Student loans:*** $6,520,985 (79% need-based, 21% non-need-based). 68% of past graduating class borrowed through all loan programs. *Average indebtedness per student:* $25,240. ***Average need-based loan:*** Freshmen: $2942. Undergraduates: $3084. ***Parent loans:*** $1,346,053 (71% need-based, 29% non-need-based). ***Programs:*** Federal Direct (Subsidized and Unsubsidized Stafford, PLUS), Perkins, Federal Nursing.

WORK-STUDY ***Federal work-study:*** Total amount: $319,063; jobs available. ***State or other work-study/employment:*** Total amount: $249,866 (64% need-based, 36% non-need-based). Part-time jobs available.

ATHLETIC AWARDS Total amount: $3,314,213 (25% need-based, 75% non-need-based).

APPLYING FOR FINANCIAL AID ***Required financial aid form:*** FAFSA. ***Financial aid deadline (priority):*** 2/15. ***Notification date:*** Continuous beginning 3/1.

CONTACT Susan George, Director of Financial Aid, West Virginia Wesleyan College, 59 College Avenue, Buckhannon, WV 26201, 304-473-8080 or toll-free 800-722-9933 (out-of-state). *E-mail:* george_s@wvwc.edu.

WESTWOOD COLLEGE–ANAHEIM

Anaheim, CA

CONTACT Financial Aid Office, Westwood College–Anaheim, 1551 South Douglass Road, Anaheim, CA 92806, 714-704-2721 or toll-free 877-650-6050.

WESTWOOD COLLEGE–ANNANDALE CAMPUS

Annandale, VA

CONTACT Financial Aid Office, Westwood College–Annandale Campus, 7619 Little River Turnpike, 5th Floor, Annandale, VA 22003, 706-642-3633 or toll-free 877-268-5218.

WESTWOOD COLLEGE–ARLINGTON BALLSTON CAMPUS

Arlington, VA

CONTACT Financial Aid Office, Westwood College–Arlington Ballston Campus, 4300 Wilson Boulevard, Suite 200, Arlington, VA 22203, 703-243-1662 or toll-free 877-268-5218.

WESTWOOD COLLEGE–ATLANTA MIDTOWN

Atlanta, GA

CONTACT Financial Aid Office, Westwood College–Atlanta Midtown, 1100 Spring Street, Suite 102, Atlanta, GA 30309, 404-745-9862 or toll-free 800-613-4595.

WESTWOOD COLLEGE–ATLANTA NORTHLAKE

Atlanta, GA

CONTACT Financial Aid Office, Westwood College–Atlanta Northlake, 2309 Parklake Drive, NE, Building 10, Atlanta, GA 30345, 404-962-2998 or toll-free 866-821-6146.

WESTWOOD COLLEGE–CHICAGO DU PAGE

Woodridge, IL

CONTACT Patty Zavala, Senior Student Finance Specialist, Westwood College–Chicago Du Page, 7155 Janes Avenue, Woodridge, IL 60517, 630-434-8244 or toll-free 866-721-7646.

WESTWOOD COLLEGE–CHICAGO LOOP CAMPUS

Chicago, IL

CONTACT Financial Aid Office, Westwood College–Chicago Loop Campus, 17 North State Street, Suite 300, Chicago, IL 60602, 312-739-0890 or toll-free 800-693-5415.

WESTWOOD COLLEGE–CHICAGO O'HARE AIRPORT

Chicago, IL

CONTACT Financial Aid Office, Westwood College–Chicago O'Hare Airport, 8501 West Higgins Road, Suite 100, Chicago, IL 60631, 773-380-6801 or toll-free 877-877-8857.

WESTWOOD COLLEGE–CHICAGO RIVER OAKS

Calumet City, IL

CONTACT Financial Aid Office, Westwood College–Chicago River Oaks, 80 River Oaks Drive, Suite 111, Calumet City, IL 60409, 708-832-9760 or toll-free 888-549-6873.

WESTWOOD COLLEGE–DALLAS

Dallas, TX

CONTACT Financial Aid Office, Westwood College–Dallas, 8390 LBJ Freeway, Executive Center 1, Suite 100, Dallas, TX 75243, 214-570-9100 or toll-free 800-803-3140.

WESTWOOD COLLEGE–DENVER NORTH

Denver, CO

CONTACT Admissions Office, Westwood College–Denver North, 7350 North Broadway, Denver, CO 80221; 800-875-6050 or toll-free 800-992-5050.

WESTWOOD COLLEGE–DENVER SOUTH

Denver, CO

CONTACT Financial Aid Office, Westwood College–Denver South, 3150 South Sheridan Boulevard, Denver, CO 80227, 303-934-1122 or toll-free 800-281-2978.

WESTWOOD COLLEGE–FORT WORTH

Fort Worth, TX

CONTACT Financial Aid Office, Westwood College–Fort Worth, 4232 North Freeway, Fort Worth, TX 76137, 817-547-9601 or toll-free 866-533-9997.

WESTWOOD COLLEGE–INLAND EMPIRE

Upland, CA

CONTACT Financial Aid Office, Westwood College–Inland Empire, 20 West 7th Street, Upland, CA 91786, 909-931-7599 or toll-free 866-288-9488.

WESTWOOD COLLEGE–LOS ANGELES

Los Angeles, CA

CONTACT Financial Aid Office, Westwood College–Los Angeles, 3250 Wilshire Boulevard, 4th Floor, Los Angeles, CA 90010, 213-382-2328 or toll-free 877-377-4600.

WESTWOOD COLLEGE–SOUTH BAY CAMPUS

Torrance, CA

CONTACT Financial Aid Office, Westwood College–South Bay Campus, 19700 South Vermont Avenue, Suite 100, Torrance, CA 90502, 310-522-2088 or toll-free 800-281-2978.

WHEATON COLLEGE

Wheaton, IL

Tuition & fees: $27,580 **Average undergraduate aid package: $23,282**

ABOUT THE INSTITUTION Independent nondenominational, coed. 38 undergraduate majors. Both federal and institutional methodology are used as a basis for awarding need-based institutional aid.

UNDERGRADUATE EXPENSES for 2010–11 ***Comprehensive fee:*** $35,630 includes full-time tuition ($27,580) and room and board ($8050). ***College room only:*** $4750. Room and board charges vary according to board plan and housing facility. ***Part-time tuition:*** $1149 per credit hour. Part-time tuition and fees vary according to course load. ***Payment plans:*** Installment, deferred payment.

FRESHMAN FINANCIAL AID (Fall 2010, est.) 440 applied for aid; of those 73% were deemed to have need. 100% of freshmen with need received aid; of those 14% had need fully met. ***Average percent of need met:*** 89% (excluding resources awarded to replace EFC). ***Average financial aid package:*** $22,763 (excluding resources awarded to replace EFC). 14% of all full-time freshmen had no need and received non-need-based gift aid.

UNDERGRADUATE FINANCIAL AID (Fall 2010, est.) 1,531 applied for aid; of those 81% were deemed to have need. 100% of undergraduates with need received aid; of those 27% had need fully met. ***Average percent of need met:*** 91% (excluding resources awarded to replace EFC). ***Average financial aid package:*** $23,282 (excluding resources awarded to replace EFC). 12% of all full-time undergraduates had no need and received non-need-based gift aid.

GIFT AID (NEED-BASED) ***Total amount:*** $23,254,583 (13% federal, 2% state, 79% institutional, 6% external sources). ***Receiving aid:*** Freshmen: 52% (315); all full-time undergraduates: 51% (1,203). ***Average award:*** Freshmen: $17,654; Undergraduates: $16,029. ***Scholarships, grants, and awards:*** Federal Pell, FSEOG, state, college/university gift aid from institutional funds.

GIFT AID (NON-NEED-BASED) ***Total amount:*** $1,875,087 (67% institutional, 33% external sources). ***Receiving aid:*** Freshmen: 18% (106). Undergraduates: 16% (367). ***Average award:*** Freshmen: $4940. Undergraduates: $4564. ***Scholarships, grants, and awards by category:*** *Academic interests/achievement:* 682 awards ($1,374,329 total): biological sciences, business, computer science, education, foreign languages, general academic interests/achievements, health fields, humanities, mathematics, military science, physical sciences, premedicine, religion/biblical studies, social sciences. *Creative arts/performance:* 93 awards ($249,418 total): art/fine arts, music. *Special achievements/activities:* 21 awards ($87,933 total): general special achievements/activities. *Special characteristics:* 116 awards ($1,179,461 total): ethnic background, general special characteristics, handicapped students.

LOANS ***Student loans:*** $11,648,631 (81% need-based, 19% non-need-based). 50% of past graduating class borrowed through all loan programs. *Average indebtedness per student:* $21,241. ***Average need-based loan:*** Freshmen: $4538. Undergraduates: $4922. ***Parent loans:*** $2,565,910 (77% need-based, 23% non-need-based). ***Programs:*** Federal Direct (Subsidized and Unsubsidized Stafford, PLUS), Perkins.

WORK-STUDY ***Federal work-study:*** Total amount: $268,740; 203 jobs averaging $1324.

APPLYING FOR FINANCIAL AID ***Required financial aid forms:*** FAFSA, institution's own form. ***Financial aid deadline (priority):*** 2/15. ***Notification date:*** Continuous beginning 3/10.

CONTACT Ms. Karen Belling, Director of Financial Aid, Wheaton College, 501 College Avenue, Wheaton, IL 60187-5593, 630-752-5021 or toll-free 800-222-2419 (out-of-state). *E-mail:* finaid@wheaton.edu.

WHEATON COLLEGE

Norton, MA

Tuition & fees: $41,084 **Average undergraduate aid package: $33,404**

ABOUT THE INSTITUTION Independent, coed. 42 undergraduate majors. Institutional methodology is used as a basis for awarding need-based institutional aid.

UNDERGRADUATE EXPENSES for 2010–11 ***One-time required fee:*** $50. ***Comprehensive fee:*** $51,264 includes full-time tuition ($40,790), mandatory fees ($294), and room and board ($10,180). ***College room only:*** $5350. ***Payment plans:*** Tuition prepayment, installment.

FRESHMAN FINANCIAL AID (Fall 2010, est.) 334 applied for aid; of those 85% were deemed to have need. 100% of freshmen with need received aid; of those 54% had need fully met. ***Average percent of need met:*** 96% (excluding resources awarded to replace EFC). ***Average financial aid package:*** $33,056 (excluding resources awarded to replace EFC). 15% of all full-time freshmen had no need and received non-need-based gift aid.

UNDERGRADUATE FINANCIAL AID (Fall 2010, est.) 1,085 applied for aid; of those 88% were deemed to have need. 100% of undergraduates with need received aid; of those 52% had need fully met. ***Average percent of need met:*** 96% (excluding resources awarded to replace EFC). ***Average financial aid package:*** $33,404 (excluding resources awarded to replace EFC). 14% of all full-time undergraduates had no need and received non-need-based gift aid.

GIFT AID (NEED-BASED) ***Total amount:*** $27,011,416 (8% federal, 2% state, 87% institutional, 3% external sources). ***Receiving aid:*** Freshmen: 58% (263); all full-time undergraduates: 55% (903). ***Average award:*** Freshmen: $29,205; Undergraduates: $28,511. ***Scholarships, grants, and awards:*** Federal Pell, FSEOG, state, private, college/university gift aid from institutional funds.

GIFT AID (NON-NEED-BASED) ***Total amount:*** $2,786,728 (87% institutional, 13% external sources). ***Receiving aid:*** Freshmen: 1% (5). Undergraduates: 1% (18). ***Average award:*** Freshmen: $13,939. Undergraduates: $11,555. ***Scholarships, grants, and awards by category:*** *Academic interests/achievement:* 500 awards ($5,801,357 total): general academic interests/achievements. ***Tuition waivers:*** Full or partial for employees or children of employees.

LOANS ***Student loans:*** $6,698,891 (87% need-based, 13% non-need-based). 58% of past graduating class borrowed through all loan programs. *Average indebtedness per student:* $27,546. ***Average need-based loan:*** Freshmen: $4242. Undergraduates: $4927. ***Parent loans:*** $4,474,173 (100% non-need-based). ***Programs:*** Federal Direct (Subsidized and Unsubsidized Stafford, PLUS), Perkins, private loans, MEFA Loans.

WORK-STUDY ***Federal work-study:*** Total amount: $1,415,622; 787 jobs averaging $1799. ***State or other work-study/employment:*** Total amount: $386,890 (40% need-based, 60% non-need-based). 235 part-time jobs averaging $1646.

APPLYING FOR FINANCIAL AID ***Required financial aid forms:*** FAFSA, CSS Financial Aid PROFILE, business/farm supplement, federal income tax form(s). ***Financial aid deadline:*** 2/1. ***Notification date:*** 4/1. Students must reply by 5/1.

CONTACT Ms. Susan Beard, Director of Financial Aid Programs, Wheaton College, 26 East Main Street, Norton, MA 02766, 508-286-8232 or toll-free 800-394-6003. *Fax:* 508-286-3787. *E-mail:* sfs@wheatonma.edu.

WHEELING JESUIT UNIVERSITY

Wheeling, WV

Tuition & fees: $25,010 **Average undergraduate aid package: $22,153**

ABOUT THE INSTITUTION Independent Roman Catholic (Jesuit), coed. 64 undergraduate majors. Federal methodology is used as a basis for awarding need-based institutional aid.

UNDERGRADUATE EXPENSES for 2011–12 ***Comprehensive fee:*** $33,884 includes full-time tuition ($23,950), mandatory fees ($1060), and room and board ($8874). ***College room only:*** $3906. Full-time tuition and fees vary according to program. Room and board charges vary according to board plan and housing facility. ***Part-time tuition:*** $655 per hour. Part-time tuition and fees vary according to program. ***Payment plan:*** Installment.

FRESHMAN FINANCIAL AID (Fall 2010, est.) 247 applied for aid; of those 86% were deemed to have need. 100% of freshmen with need received aid; of those 33% had need fully met. ***Average percent of need met:*** 89% (excluding resources awarded to replace EFC). ***Average financial aid package:*** $23,921 (excluding resources awarded to replace EFC). 13% of all full-time freshmen had no need and received non-need-based gift aid.

UNDERGRADUATE FINANCIAL AID (Fall 2010, est.) 809 applied for aid; of those 87% were deemed to have need. 100% of undergraduates with need received aid; of those 31% had need fully met. ***Average percent of need met:*** 84% (excluding resources awarded to replace EFC). ***Average financial aid package:*** $22,153 (excluding resources awarded to replace EFC). 10% of all full-time undergraduates had no need and received non-need-based gift aid.

GIFT AID (NEED-BASED) ***Total amount:*** $3,201,337 (50% federal, 8% state, 42% institutional). ***Receiving aid:*** Freshmen: 61% (158); all full-time undergraduates: 56% (493). ***Average award:*** Freshmen: $6991; Undergraduates: $6399. ***Scholarships, grants, and awards:*** Federal Pell, FSEOG, state, private, college/university gift aid from institutional funds, Federal Nursing.

GIFT AID (NON-NEED-BASED) ***Total amount:*** $9,785,175 (1% federal, 5% state, 91% institutional, 3% external sources). ***Receiving aid:*** Freshmen: 82% (212). Undergraduates: 77% (687). ***Average award:*** Freshmen: $13,138. Undergraduates: $11,853. ***Scholarships, grants, and awards by category:*** *Academic interests/achievement:* 774 awards ($8,007,324 total): general academic interests/achievements, premedicine. *Creative arts/performance:* 33 awards ($56,500 total): music. *Special achievements/activities:* 72 awards ($252,210 total): community service, general special achievements/activities. *Special characteristics:* 424 awards ($1,678,160 total): children and siblings of alumni, children of faculty/staff, general special characteristics, religious affiliation. ***Tuition waivers:*** Full or partial for employees or children of employees.

LOANS ***Student loans:*** $6,055,010 (44% need-based, 56% non-need-based). 79% of past graduating class borrowed through all loan programs. *Average indebtedness per student:* $32,927. ***Average need-based loan:*** Freshmen: $4460. Undergraduates: $4850. ***Parent loans:*** $860,751 (100% non-need-based). ***Programs:*** Federal Direct (Subsidized and Unsubsidized Stafford, PLUS), Perkins, Federal Nursing, alternative loans.

WORK-STUDY ***Federal work-study:*** Total amount: $204,348; 151 jobs averaging $2200. ***State or other work-study/employment:*** Total amount: $312,369 (100% non-need-based). 157 part-time jobs averaging $2200.

ATHLETIC AWARDS Total amount: $1,004,218 (100% non-need-based).

APPLYING FOR FINANCIAL AID ***Required financial aid forms:*** FAFSA, institution's own form. ***Financial aid deadline (priority):*** 3/1. ***Notification date:*** Continuous beginning 3/15. Students must reply within 2 weeks of notification.

CONTACT Christie Tomczyk, Director of Financial Aid, Wheeling Jesuit University, 316 Washington Avenue, Wheeling, WV 26003-6295, 304-243-2304 or toll-free 800-624-6992 Ext. 2359. *Fax:* 304-243-4397. *E-mail:* finaid@wju.edu.

WHEELOCK COLLEGE

Boston, MA

Tuition & fees: N/R **Average undergraduate aid package: $20,979**

ABOUT THE INSTITUTION Independent, coed, primarily women. 16 undergraduate majors. Federal methodology is used as a basis for awarding need-based institutional aid.

FRESHMAN FINANCIAL AID (Fall 2010, est.) 227 applied for aid; of those 93% were deemed to have need. 100% of freshmen with need received aid; of those 18% had need fully met. ***Average percent of need met:*** 68% (excluding resources awarded to replace EFC). ***Average financial aid package:*** $21,400 (excluding resources awarded to replace EFC). 10% of all full-time freshmen had no need and received non-need-based gift aid.

UNDERGRADUATE FINANCIAL AID (Fall 2010, est.) 729 applied for aid; of those 93% were deemed to have need. 100% of undergraduates with need received aid; of those 15% had need fully met. ***Average percent of need met:*** 67% (excluding resources awarded to replace EFC). ***Average financial aid package:*** $20,979 (excluding resources awarded to replace EFC). 11% of all full-time undergraduates had no need and received non-need-based gift aid.

GIFT AID (NEED-BASED) ***Total amount:*** $11,151,048 (14% federal, 4% state, 79% institutional, 3% external sources). ***Receiving aid:*** Freshmen: 89% (210); all full-time undergraduates: 84% (675). ***Average award:*** Freshmen: $17,867; Undergraduates: $16,442. ***Scholarships, grants, and awards:*** Federal Pell, FSEOG, state, private, college/university gift aid from institutional funds.

GIFT AID (NON-NEED-BASED) ***Total amount:*** $1,593,996 (2% state, 92% institutional, 6% external sources). ***Receiving aid:*** Freshmen: 12% (29). Undergraduates: 9% (72). ***Average award:*** Freshmen: $13,687. Undergraduates: $11,485. ***Scholarships, grants, and awards by category:*** *Academic interests/achievement:* general academic interests/achievements.

LOANS ***Student loans:*** $7,903,266 (75% need-based, 25% non-need-based). 88% of past graduating class borrowed through all loan programs. *Average indebtedness per student:* $41,356. ***Average need-based loan:*** Freshmen: $3396. Undergraduates: $4766. ***Parent loans:*** $2,331,867 (48% need-based, 52% non-need-based). ***Programs:*** Federal Direct (Subsidized and Unsubsidized Stafford, PLUS), Perkins, state, college/university.

WORK-STUDY ***Federal work-study:*** Total amount: $300,894; 217 jobs averaging $1800.

APPLYING FOR FINANCIAL AID ***Required financial aid form:*** FAFSA. ***Financial aid deadline (priority):*** 2/15. ***Notification date:*** Continuous beginning 3/15. Students must reply by 5/1.

CONTACT Roxanne Dumas, Director of Financial Aid, Wheelock College, 200 The Riverway, Boston, MA 02215-4176, 617-879-2443 or toll-free 800-734-5212 (out-of-state). *Fax:* 617-879-2470. *E-mail:* finaid@wheelock.edu.

WHITMAN COLLEGE

Walla Walla, WA

Tuition & fees: $40,496 **Average undergraduate aid package: $32,208**

ABOUT THE INSTITUTION Independent, coed. 41 undergraduate majors. Both federal and institutional methodology are used as a basis for awarding need-based institutional aid.

UNDERGRADUATE EXPENSES for 2011–12 ***Comprehensive fee:*** $50,656 includes full-time tuition ($40,180), mandatory fees ($316), and room and board ($10,160). ***College room only:*** $4700. Room and board charges vary according to board plan and housing facility. ***Part-time tuition:*** $1674 per credit. ***Payment plan:*** Deferred payment.

FRESHMAN FINANCIAL AID (Fall 2009) 301 applied for aid; of those 75% were deemed to have need. 99% of freshmen with need received aid; of those 54% had need fully met. ***Average percent of need met:*** 92% (excluding resources awarded to replace EFC). ***Average financial aid package:*** $29,357 (excluding resources awarded to replace EFC). 21% of all full-time freshmen had no need and received non-need-based gift aid.

UNDERGRADUATE FINANCIAL AID (Fall 2009) 915 applied for aid; of those 84% were deemed to have need. 99% of undergraduates with need received aid; of those 70% had need fully met. ***Average percent of need met:*** 92% (excluding resources awarded to replace EFC). ***Average financial aid package:*** $32,208 (excluding resources awarded to replace EFC). 26% of all full-time undergraduates had no need and received non-need-based gift aid.

GIFT AID (NEED-BASED) ***Total amount:*** $19,208,892 (6% federal, 2% state, 92% institutional). ***Receiving aid:*** Freshmen: 40% (177); all full-time undergraduates: 40% (636). ***Average award:*** Freshmen: $24,924; Undergraduates: $26,526. ***Scholarships, grants, and awards:*** Federal Pell, FSEOG, state, private, college/university gift aid from institutional funds.

GIFT AID (NON-NEED-BASED) ***Total amount:*** $6,557,211 (2% state, 79% institutional, 19% external sources). ***Receiving aid:*** Freshmen: 30% (131). Undergraduates: 14% (226). ***Average award:*** Freshmen: $10,786. Undergraduates: $8790. ***Scholarships, grants, and awards by category:*** *Academic interests/achievement:* general academic interests/achievements. *Creative arts/performance:* art/fine arts, debating, music, theater/drama. *Special achievements/activities:*

leadership. *Special characteristics:* ethnic background, first-generation college students, international students. ***Tuition waivers:*** Full or partial for employees or children of employees.

LOANS ***Student loans:*** $3,403,718 (68% need-based, 32% non-need-based). 50% of past graduating class borrowed through all loan programs. *Average indebtedness per student:* $14,285. ***Average need-based loan:*** Freshmen: $4928. Undergraduates: $4435. ***Parent loans:*** $1,514,997 (100% non-need-based). ***Programs:*** Federal Direct (Subsidized and Unsubsidized Stafford, PLUS), Perkins, alternative loans.

WORK-STUDY ***Federal work-study:*** Total amount: $940,647; 525 jobs averaging $1883. ***State or other work-study/employment:*** Total amount: $236,950 (74% need-based, 26% non-need-based). 200 part-time jobs averaging $1019.

APPLYING FOR FINANCIAL AID ***Required financial aid forms:*** FAFSA, CSS Financial Aid PROFILE. ***Financial aid deadline:*** 2/1 (priority: 11/15). ***Notification date:*** Continuous beginning 12/18. Students must reply within 2 weeks of notification.

CONTACT Tyson Harlow, Assistant Director, Whitman College, 345 Boyer Avenue, Walla Walla, WA 99362-2046, 509-527-5178 or toll-free 877-462-9448. *Fax:* 509-527-4967.

WHITTIER COLLEGE

Whittier, CA

Tuition & fees: $35,742 **Average undergraduate aid package: $30,711**

ABOUT THE INSTITUTION Independent, coed. 25 undergraduate majors. Both federal and institutional methodology are used as a basis for awarding need-based institutional aid.

UNDERGRADUATE EXPENSES for 2010–11 ***Comprehensive fee:*** $45,768 includes full-time tuition ($35,222), mandatory fees ($520), and room and board ($10,026). Room and board charges vary according to board plan. ***Part-time tuition:*** $1490 per unit.

FRESHMAN FINANCIAL AID (Fall 2010, est.) 383 applied for aid; of those 91% were deemed to have need. 100% of freshmen with need received aid; of those 14% had need fully met. ***Average percent of need met:*** 78% (excluding resources awarded to replace EFC). ***Average financial aid package:*** $32,204 (excluding resources awarded to replace EFC). 17% of all full-time freshmen had no need and received non-need-based gift aid.

UNDERGRADUATE FINANCIAL AID (Fall 2010, est.) 1,233 applied for aid; of those 91% were deemed to have need. 100% of undergraduates with need received aid; of those 12% had need fully met. ***Average percent of need met:*** 74% (excluding resources awarded to replace EFC). ***Average financial aid package:*** $30,711 (excluding resources awarded to replace EFC). 18% of all full-time undergraduates had no need and received non-need-based gift aid.

GIFT AID (NEED-BASED) ***Total amount:*** $26,636,920 (13% federal, 13% state, 73% institutional, 1% external sources). ***Receiving aid:*** Freshmen: 70% (311); all full-time undergraduates: 70% (1,031). ***Average award:*** Freshmen: $28,809; Undergraduates: $25,978. ***Scholarships, grants, and awards:*** Federal Pell, FSEOG, state, private, college/university gift aid from institutional funds.

GIFT AID (NON-NEED-BASED) ***Total amount:*** $9,899,772 (1% federal, 3% state, 96% institutional). ***Receiving aid:*** Freshmen: 8% (34). Undergraduates: 6% (83). ***Average award:*** Freshmen: $19,135. Undergraduates: $16,559. ***Scholarships, grants, and awards by category:*** *Academic interests/achievement:* general academic interests/achievements. *Creative arts/performance:* art/fine arts, music, theater/drama. *Special characteristics:* children and siblings of alumni, children of faculty/staff, international students. ***Tuition waivers:*** Full or partial for children of alumni, employees or children of employees.

LOANS ***Student loans:*** $12,830,210 (72% need-based, 28% non-need-based). 67% of past graduating class borrowed through all loan programs. *Average indebtedness per student:* $24,687. ***Average need-based loan:*** Freshmen: $6566. Undergraduates: $7038. ***Parent loans:*** $3,761,031 (77% need-based, 23% non-need-based). ***Programs:*** Federal Direct (PLUS), Perkins, alternative loans.

WORK-STUDY ***Federal work-study:*** Total amount: $2,348,635; jobs available. ***State or other work-study/employment:*** Total amount: $956,981 (20% need-based, 80% non-need-based). Part-time jobs available.

APPLYING FOR FINANCIAL AID ***Required financial aid forms:*** FAFSA, CSS Financial Aid PROFILE. ***Financial aid deadline:*** 6/30 (priority: 3/1). ***Notification date:*** Continuous beginning 2/15. Students must reply within 2 weeks of notification.

CONTACT Mr. David Carnevale, Director of Student Financing, Whittier College, 13406 East Philadelphia Street, Whittier, CA 90608-0634, 562-907-4285. *Fax:* 562-464-4560. *E-mail:* dcarneva@whittier.edu.

WHITWORTH UNIVERSITY

Spokane, WA

Tuition & fees: $29,890 **Average undergraduate aid package: $25,366**

ABOUT THE INSTITUTION Independent Presbyterian, coed. ***Awards:*** bachelor's and master's degrees. 43 undergraduate majors. ***Total enrollment:*** 2,607. Undergraduates: 2,331. Freshmen: 533. Federal methodology is used as a basis for awarding need-based institutional aid.

UNDERGRADUATE EXPENSES for 2010–11 ***Tuition:*** full-time $29,890; part-time $1245 per credit. Part-time tuition and fees vary according to class time. Room and board charges vary according to board plan and housing facility. ***Payment plan:*** Installment.

FRESHMAN FINANCIAL AID (Fall 2010, est.) 591 applied for aid; of those 88% were deemed to have need. 100% of freshmen with need received aid; of those 20% had need fully met. ***Average percent of need met:*** 84% (excluding resources awarded to replace EFC). ***Average financial aid package:*** $27,360 (excluding resources awarded to replace EFC). 22% of all full-time freshmen had no need and received non-need-based gift aid.

UNDERGRADUATE FINANCIAL AID (Fall 2010, est.) 1,798 applied for aid; of those 90% were deemed to have need. 100% of undergraduates with need received aid; of those 20% had need fully met. ***Average percent of need met:*** 82% (excluding resources awarded to replace EFC). ***Average financial aid package:*** $25,366 (excluding resources awarded to replace EFC). 23% of all full-time undergraduates had no need and received non-need-based gift aid.

GIFT AID (NEED-BASED) ***Total amount:*** $30,055,971 (12% federal, 9% state, 75% institutional, 4% external sources). ***Receiving aid:*** Freshmen: 76% (515); all full-time undergraduates: 70% (1,600). ***Average award:*** Freshmen: $18,585; Undergraduates: $17,804. ***Scholarships, grants, and awards:*** Federal Pell, FSEOG, state, private, college/university gift aid from institutional funds.

GIFT AID (NON-NEED-BASED) ***Total amount:*** $7,345,630 (4% federal, 1% state, 91% institutional, 4% external sources). ***Receiving aid:*** Freshmen: 8% (53). Undergraduates: 6% (147). ***Average award:*** Freshmen: $12,458. Undergraduates: $10,780. ***Scholarships, grants, and awards by category:*** *Academic interests/achievement:* 1,781 awards ($16,378,295 total): biological sciences, computer science, general academic interests/achievements, military science, physical sciences, premedicine. *Creative arts/performance:* 211 awards ($510,475 total): art/fine arts, journalism/publications, music, theater/drama. *Special achievements/activities:* 40 awards ($27,300 total): religious involvement. *Special characteristics:* 758 awards ($2,233,326 total): children and siblings of alumni, ethnic background, international students, members of minority groups, relatives of clergy, siblings of current students. ***Tuition waivers:*** Full or partial for employees or children of employees. ***ROTC:*** Army cooperative.

LOANS ***Student loans:*** $13,639,306 (82% need-based, 18% non-need-based). 66% of past graduating class borrowed through all loan programs. *Average indebtedness per student:* $22,540. ***Average need-based loan:*** Freshmen: $4238. Undergraduates: $4643. ***Parent loans:*** $4,160,695 (37% need-based, 63% non-need-based). ***Programs:*** Federal Direct (Subsidized and Unsubsidized Stafford, PLUS), Perkins.

WORK-STUDY ***Federal work-study:*** Total amount: $1,764,676; 773 jobs averaging $2174. ***State or other work-study/employment:*** Total amount: $384,554 (100% need-based). 164 part-time jobs averaging $2453.

APPLYING FOR FINANCIAL AID ***Required financial aid form:*** FAFSA. ***Financial aid deadline (priority):*** 3/1. ***Notification date:*** Continuous beginning 3/15.

CONTACT Ms. Wendy Z. Olson, Director of Financial Aid, Whitworth University, 300 West Hawthorne Road, Spokane, WA 99251-0001, 509-777-4306 or toll-free 800-533-4668 (out-of-state). *Fax:* 509-777-4601. *E-mail:* wolson@whitworth.edu.

WICHITA STATE UNIVERSITY

Wichita, KS

Tuition & fees (KS res): $5890 **Average undergraduate aid package: $7674**

ABOUT THE INSTITUTION State-supported, coed. 82 undergraduate majors. Federal methodology is used as a basis for awarding need-based institutional aid.

UNDERGRADUATE EXPENSES for 2010–11 ***Tuition, state resident:*** full-time $4722; part-time $157.40 per credit hour. ***Tuition, nonresident:*** full-time $12,756; part-time $425.20 per credit hour. ***Required fees:*** full-time $1168. Full-time tuition and fees vary according to course load, degree level, and student level. Part-time tuition and fees vary according to course load, degree level, and student level. ***College room and board:*** $6200. Room and board charges vary according to board plan and housing facility. ***Payment plan:*** Installment.

FRESHMAN FINANCIAL AID (Fall 2009) 1,056 applied for aid; of those 42% were deemed to have need. 97% of freshmen with need received aid; of those 82% had need fully met. ***Average percent of need met:*** 49% (excluding resources awarded to replace EFC). ***Average financial aid package:*** $7134 (excluding resources awarded to replace EFC). 39% of all full-time freshmen had no need and received non-need-based gift aid.

UNDERGRADUATE FINANCIAL AID (Fall 2009) 6,549 applied for aid; of those 54% were deemed to have need. 97% of undergraduates with need received aid; of those 71% had need fully met. ***Average percent of need met:*** 51% (excluding resources awarded to replace EFC). ***Average financial aid package:*** $7674 (excluding resources awarded to replace EFC). 18% of all full-time undergraduates had no need and received non-need-based gift aid.

GIFT AID (NEED-BASED) ***Total amount:*** $16,384,682 (95% federal, 4% state, 1% external sources). ***Receiving aid:*** Freshmen: 25% (280); all full-time undergraduates: 26% (1,974). ***Average award:*** Freshmen: $4658; Undergraduates: $4632. ***Scholarships, grants, and awards:*** Federal Pell, FSEOG, state, private, college/university gift aid from institutional funds, Academic Competitiveness Grants, National SMART Grants.

GIFT AID (NON-NEED-BASED) ***Total amount:*** $9,196,257 (1% federal, 1% state, 87% institutional, 11% external sources). ***Receiving aid:*** Freshmen: 20% (223). Undergraduates: 15% (1,185). ***Average award:*** Freshmen: $2466. Undergraduates: $1830. ***Scholarships, grants, and awards by category:*** *Academic interests/achievement:* area/ethnic studies, biological sciences, business, communication, computer science, education, engineering/technologies, English, foreign languages, general academic interests/achievements, health fields, humanities, international studies, mathematics, physical sciences, premedicine, social sciences. *Creative arts/performance:* applied art and design, art/fine arts, creative writing, dance, debating, journalism/publications, music, performing arts, theater/drama. *Special achievements/activities:* cheerleading/drum major, general special achievements/activities, leadership, memberships. *Special characteristics:* adult students, first-generation college students, international students, members of minority groups. ***Tuition waivers:*** Full or partial for employees or children of employees, senior citizens.

LOANS ***Student loans:*** $45,248,852 (45% need-based, 55% non-need-based). 58% of past graduating class borrowed through all loan programs. *Average indebtedness per student:* $15,847. ***Average need-based loan:*** Freshmen: $3085. Undergraduates: $4733. ***Parent loans:*** $1,009,392 (100% non-need-based). ***Programs:*** Perkins.

WORK-STUDY ***Federal work-study:*** Total amount: $304,884; 236 jobs averaging $1900. ***State or other work-study/employment:*** Total amount: $94,678 (100% need-based). Part-time jobs available.

ATHLETIC AWARDS Total amount: $1,596,412 (100% non-need-based).

APPLYING FOR FINANCIAL AID ***Required financial aid forms:*** FAFSA, institution's own form. ***Financial aid deadline (priority):*** 3/1. ***Notification date:*** Continuous beginning 3/1. Students must reply within 2 weeks of notification.

CONTACT Deborah D. Byers, Director of Financial Aid, Wichita State University, 1845 Fairmount, Wichita, KS 67260-0024, 316-978-3430 or toll-free 800-362-2594. *Fax:* 316-978-3396. *E-mail:* deb.byers@wichita.edu.

WIDENER UNIVERSITY

Chester, PA

Tuition & fees: $33,270 **Average undergraduate aid package: $24,475**

ABOUT THE INSTITUTION Independent, coed. 74 undergraduate majors. Both federal and institutional methodology are used as a basis for awarding need-based institutional aid.

UNDERGRADUATE EXPENSES for 2010–11 ***Comprehensive fee:*** $44,990 includes full-time tuition ($32,750), mandatory fees ($520), and room and board ($11,720). ***College room only:*** $6052. Full-time tuition and fees vary according to class time, course load, and program. Room and board charges vary according to board plan and housing facility. ***Part-time tuition:*** $1090 per credit hour. ***Payment plan:*** Installment.

FRESHMAN FINANCIAL AID (Fall 2010, est.) 685 applied for aid; of those 92% were deemed to have need. 100% of freshmen with need received aid; of those 15% had need fully met. ***Average percent of need met:*** 76% (excluding resources awarded to replace EFC). ***Average financial aid package:*** $26,423 (excluding resources awarded to replace EFC). 11% of all full-time freshmen had no need and received non-need-based gift aid.

UNDERGRADUATE FINANCIAL AID (Fall 2010, est.) 2,537 applied for aid; of those 86% were deemed to have need. 100% of undergraduates with need received aid; of those 14% had need fully met. ***Average percent of need met:*** 73% (excluding resources awarded to replace EFC). ***Average financial aid package:*** $24,475 (excluding resources awarded to replace EFC). 12% of all full-time undergraduates had no need and received non-need-based gift aid.

GIFT AID (NEED-BASED) ***Total amount:*** $38,843,929 (14% federal, 5% state, 78% institutional, 3% external sources). ***Receiving aid:*** Freshmen: 71% (514); all full-time undergraduates: 65% (1,753). ***Average award:*** Freshmen: $9319; Undergraduates: $8492. ***Scholarships, grants, and awards:*** Federal Pell, FSEOG, state, private, college/university gift aid from institutional funds, Federal Nursing.

GIFT AID (NON-NEED-BASED) ***Total amount:*** $4,450,791 (5% federal, 91% institutional, 4% external sources). ***Receiving aid:*** Freshmen: 73% (527). Undergraduates: 66% (1,772). ***Average award:*** Freshmen: $13,827. Undergraduates: $12,145. ***Scholarships, grants, and awards by category:*** *Academic interests/achievement:* 2,022 awards ($24,611,047 total): biological sciences, business, communication, computer science, education, engineering/technologies, English, foreign languages, general academic interests/achievements, health fields, humanities, international studies, mathematics, military science, physical sciences, premedicine, social sciences. *Creative arts/performance:* 40 awards ($80,000 total): music. *Special achievements/activities:* 55 awards ($275,000 total): community service, general special achievements/activities, leadership. *Special characteristics:* 128 awards ($2,481,339 total): adult students, children of faculty/staff, ethnic background, international students. ***Tuition waivers:*** Full or partial for employees or children of employees, senior citizens.

LOANS ***Student loans:*** $27,937,218 (94% need-based, 6% non-need-based). 85% of past graduating class borrowed through all loan programs. *Average indebtedness per student:* $40,386. ***Average need-based loan:*** Freshmen: $4145. Undergraduates: $4971. ***Parent loans:*** $7,361,275 (95% need-based, 5% non-need-based). ***Programs:*** Federal Direct (Subsidized and Unsubsidized Stafford, PLUS), Perkins.

WORK-STUDY ***Federal work-study:*** Total amount: $2,439,248; 1,646 jobs averaging $1400. ***State or other work-study/employment:*** Total amount: $443,069 (75% need-based, 25% non-need-based). 468 part-time jobs averaging $1200.

APPLYING FOR FINANCIAL AID ***Required financial aid form:*** FAFSA. ***Financial aid deadline (priority):*** 2/15. ***Notification date:*** Continuous beginning 3/15. Students must reply within 4 weeks of notification.

CONTACT Thomas K. Malloy, Director of Student Financial Services, Widener University, One University Place, Chester, PA 19013-5792, 610-499-4161 or toll-free 888-WIDENER. *Fax:* 610-499-4687. *E-mail:* finaidmc@mail.widener.edu.

WILBERFORCE UNIVERSITY

Wilberforce, OH

CONTACT Director of Financial Aid, Wilberforce University, 1055 North Bickett Road, Wilberforce, OH 45384, 937-708-5727 or toll-free 800-367-8568. *Fax:* 937-376-4752.

WILEY COLLEGE

Marshall, TX

CONTACT Cecelia Jones, Interim Director of Financial Aid, Wiley College, 711 Wiley Avenue, Marshall, TX 75670-5199, 903-927-3210 or toll-free 800-658-6889. *Fax:* 903-927-3366.

WILKES UNIVERSITY

Wilkes-Barre, PA

Tuition & fees: $27,178 **Average undergraduate aid package: $19,886**

ABOUT THE INSTITUTION Independent, coed. 34 undergraduate majors. Federal methodology is used as a basis for awarding need-based institutional aid.

UNDERGRADUATE EXPENSES for 2010–11 ***Comprehensive fee:*** $38,648 includes full-time tuition ($25,802), mandatory fees ($1376), and room and board ($11,470). ***College room only:*** $6880. Room and board charges vary according to board plan and housing facility. ***Part-time tuition:*** $715 per credit hour. ***Payment plans:*** Installment, deferred payment.

FRESHMAN FINANCIAL AID (Fall 2010, est.) 468 applied for aid; of those 92% were deemed to have need. 100% of freshmen with need received aid; of those 13% had need fully met. ***Average percent of need met:*** 76% (excluding resources awarded to replace EFC). ***Average financial aid package:*** $20,706 (excluding resources awarded to replace EFC). 11% of all full-time freshmen had no need and received non-need-based gift aid.

UNDERGRADUATE FINANCIAL AID (Fall 2010, est.) 1,738 applied for aid; of those 93% were deemed to have need. 99% of undergraduates with need received aid; of those 12% had need fully met. ***Average percent of need met:*** 71% (excluding resources awarded to replace EFC). ***Average financial aid package:*** $19,886 (excluding resources awarded to replace EFC). 12% of all full-time undergraduates had no need and received non-need-based gift aid.

GIFT AID (NEED-BASED) ***Total amount:*** $24,297,550 (14% federal, 9% state, 75% institutional, 2% external sources). ***Receiving aid:*** Freshmen: 86% (431); all full-time undergraduates: 80% (1,573). ***Average award:*** Freshmen: $17,997; Undergraduates: $15,415. ***Scholarships, grants, and awards:*** Federal Pell, FSEOG, state, private, college/university gift aid from institutional funds.

GIFT AID (NON-NEED-BASED) ***Total amount:*** $2,739,089 (1% federal, 86% institutional, 13% external sources). ***Receiving aid:*** Freshmen: 79% (396). Undergraduates: 65% (1,274). ***Average award:*** Freshmen: $10,880. Undergraduates: $10,070. ***Scholarships, grants, and awards by category:*** *Academic interests/achievement:* general academic interests/achievements. *Creative arts/performance:* performing arts, theater/drama. *Special achievements/activities:* general special achievements/activities, leadership. *Special characteristics:* children of faculty/staff. ***Tuition waivers:*** Full or partial for employees or children of employees.

LOANS ***Student loans:*** $15,095,910 (89% need-based, 11% non-need-based). 85% of past graduating class borrowed through all loan programs. *Average indebtedness per student:* $35,244. ***Average need-based loan:*** Freshmen: $3445. Undergraduates: $4392. ***Parent loans:*** $4,316,045 (75% need-based, 25% non-need-based). ***Programs:*** Federal Direct (Subsidized and Unsubsidized Stafford, PLUS), Perkins, Federal Nursing, state, college/university, Gulf Oil Loan Fund, Rulison Evans Loan Fund.

WORK-STUDY ***Federal work-study:*** Total amount: $1,688,938; jobs available. ***State or other work-study/employment:*** Part-time jobs available.

APPLYING FOR FINANCIAL AID ***Required financial aid form:*** FAFSA. ***Financial aid deadline (priority):*** 3/1. ***Notification date:*** Continuous.

CONTACT Melanie Mickelson, Vice President of Enrollment Services, Wilkes University, 84 West South Street, Wilkes-Barre, PA 18766, 570-408-4000 or toll-free 800-945-5378 Ext. 4400. *Fax:* 570-408-3000. *E-mail:* melanie.mickelson@wilkes.edu.

WILLAMETTE UNIVERSITY

Salem, OR

Tuition & fees: $37,361 | **Average undergraduate aid package: $31,308**

ABOUT THE INSTITUTION Independent United Methodist, coed. 40 undergraduate majors. Federal methodology is used as a basis for awarding need-based institutional aid.

UNDERGRADUATE EXPENSES for 2010–11 ***Comprehensive fee:*** $46,261 includes full-time tuition ($37,150), mandatory fees ($211), and room and board ($8900). Full-time tuition and fees vary according to course load. Room and board charges vary according to board plan and housing facility. ***Part-time tuition:*** $4644 per course. Part-time tuition and fees vary according to course load. ***Payment plans:*** Tuition prepayment, installment.

FRESHMAN FINANCIAL AID (Fall 2010, est.) 378 applied for aid; of those 81% were deemed to have need. 100% of freshmen with need received aid; of those 46% had need fully met. ***Average percent of need met:*** 92% (excluding resources awarded to replace EFC). ***Average financial aid package:*** $31,883 (excluding resources awarded to replace EFC). 22% of all full-time freshmen had no need and received non-need-based gift aid.

UNDERGRADUATE FINANCIAL AID (Fall 2010, est.) 1,329 applied for aid; of those 88% were deemed to have need. 100% of undergraduates with need received aid; of those 40% had need fully met. ***Average percent of need met:*** 88% (excluding resources awarded to replace EFC). ***Average financial aid package:*** $31,308 (excluding resources awarded to replace EFC). 29% of all full-time undergraduates had no need and received non-need-based gift aid.

GIFT AID (NEED-BASED) ***Total amount:*** $30,652,768 (9% federal, 1% state, 86% institutional, 4% external sources). ***Receiving aid:*** Freshmen: 71% (302); all full-time undergraduates: 63% (1,163). ***Average award:*** Freshmen: $26,953; Undergraduates: $25,061. ***Scholarships, grants, and awards:*** Federal Pell, FSEOG, state, private, college/university gift aid from institutional funds.

GIFT AID (NON-NEED-BASED) ***Total amount:*** $6,840,409 (97% institutional, 3% external sources). ***Receiving aid:*** Freshmen: 22% (95). Undergraduates: 12% (226). ***Average award:*** Freshmen: $12,932. Undergraduates: $12,488. ***Scholarships, grants, and awards by category:*** *Academic interests/achievement:* general academic interests/achievements. *Creative arts/performance:* general creative arts/performance. *Special achievements/activities:* general special achievements/activities. *Special characteristics:* general special characteristics. ***Tuition waivers:*** Full or partial for employees or children of employees.

LOANS ***Student loans:*** $8,420,349 (91% need-based, 9% non-need-based). 65% of past graduating class borrowed through all loan programs. *Average indebtedness per student:* $23,248. ***Average need-based loan:*** Freshmen: $3088. Undergraduates: $4242. ***Parent loans:*** $2,657,128 (86% need-based, 14% non-need-based). ***Programs:*** Federal Direct (Subsidized and Unsubsidized Stafford, PLUS), Perkins.

WORK-STUDY ***Federal work-study:*** Total amount: $1,716,253; jobs available. ***State or other work-study/employment:*** Part-time jobs available.

APPLYING FOR FINANCIAL AID ***Required financial aid form:*** FAFSA. ***Financial aid deadline (priority):*** 2/1. ***Notification date:*** Continuous beginning 4/1. Students must reply by 5/1 or within 2 weeks of notification.

CONTACT Patty Hoban, Director of Financial Aid, Willamette University, 900 State Street, Salem, OR 97301-3931, 503-370-6273 or toll-free 877-542-2787. *Fax:* 503-370-6588. *E-mail:* phoban@willamette.edu.

WILLIAM CAREY UNIVERSITY

Hattiesburg, MS

ABOUT THE INSTITUTION Independent Southern Baptist, coed. 32 undergraduate majors.

GIFT AID (NEED-BASED) ***Scholarships, grants, and awards:*** Federal Pell, FSEOG, state, private, college/university gift aid from institutional funds.

GIFT AID (NON-NEED-BASED) ***Scholarships, grants, and awards by category:*** *Academic interests/achievement:* general academic interests/achievements. *Creative arts/performance:* art/fine arts, debating, journalism/publications, music, theater/drama. *Special achievements/activities:* cheerleading/drum major, junior miss, leadership, religious involvement. *Special characteristics:* children and siblings of alumni, children of educators, children of faculty/staff, first-generation college students, international students, relatives of clergy, religious affiliation, veterans.

LOANS ***Programs:*** Perkins, Federal Nursing, college/university.

WORK-STUDY ***Federal work-study:*** Total amount: $300,000; 260 jobs averaging $1200. ***State or other work-study/employment:*** Total amount: $125,000 (100% non-need-based). 110 part-time jobs averaging $2100.

APPLYING FOR FINANCIAL AID ***Required financial aid forms:*** FAFSA, institution's own form, state aid form.

CONTACT Ms. Brenda Pittman, Associate Director of Financial Aid, William Carey University, 498 Tuscan Avenue, Hattiesburg, MS 39401-5499, 601-318-6153 or toll-free 800-962-5991 (in-state).

WILLIAM JESSUP UNIVERSITY

Rocklin, CA

Tuition & fees: $21,800 | **Average undergraduate aid package: $18,279**

ABOUT THE INSTITUTION Independent nondenominational, coed. 12 undergraduate majors. Federal methodology is used as a basis for awarding need-based institutional aid.

UNDERGRADUATE EXPENSES for 2011–12 ***Comprehensive fee:*** $30,440 includes full-time tuition ($21,800) and room and board ($8640). Full-time tuition and fees vary according to course load. Room and board charges vary according to housing facility. ***Part-time tuition:*** $930 per credit hour. Part-time tuition and fees vary according to course load. ***Payment plan:*** Deferred payment.

FRESHMAN FINANCIAL AID (Fall 2010, est.) 107 applied for aid; of those 93% were deemed to have need. 100% of freshmen with need received aid; of those 12% had need fully met. ***Average percent of need met:*** 77% (excluding resources awarded to replace EFC). ***Average financial aid package:*** $21,540 (excluding resources awarded to replace EFC). 13% of all full-time freshmen had no need and received non-need-based gift aid.

UNDERGRADUATE FINANCIAL AID (Fall 2010, est.) 499 applied for aid; of those 93% were deemed to have need. 100% of undergraduates with need received aid; of those 12% had need fully met. ***Average percent of need met:*** 71% (excluding resources awarded to replace EFC). ***Average financial aid package:*** $18,279 (excluding resources awarded to replace EFC). 15% of all full-time undergraduates had no need and received non-need-based gift aid.

GIFT AID (NEED-BASED) ***Total amount:*** $6,401,910 (21% federal, 29% state, 44% institutional, 6% external sources). ***Receiving aid:*** Freshmen: 86% (100); all full-time undergraduates: 82% (459). ***Average award:*** Freshmen: $15,770; Undergraduates: $15,051. ***Scholarships, grants, and awards:*** Federal Pell, FSEOG, state, private, college/university gift aid from institutional funds.

GIFT AID (NON-NEED-BASED) ***Total amount:*** $744,742 (84% institutional, 16% external sources). ***Receiving aid:*** Freshmen: 52% (60). Undergraduates: 51% (289). ***Average award:*** Freshmen: $4908. Undergraduates: $6721. ***Scholarships, grants, and awards by category:*** *Academic interests/achievement:* 374 awards ($1,454,766 total): area/ethnic studies, business, education, English, general academic interests/achievements, international studies, religion/biblical studies. *Creative arts/performance:* 91 awards ($219,188 total): music. *Special achievements/activities:* 220 awards ($692,315 total): leadership, religious involvement. *Special characteristics:* 320 awards ($692,315 total): adult students, children of faculty/staff, international students, previous college experience, relatives of clergy, siblings of current students, veterans, veterans' children. ***Tuition waivers:*** Full or partial for employees or children of employees.

LOANS ***Student loans:*** $3,691,760 (50% need-based, 50% non-need-based). 67% of past graduating class borrowed through all loan programs. *Average indebtedness per student:* $23,160. ***Average need-based loan:*** Freshmen: $3450. Undergraduates: $4422. ***Parent loans:*** $493,657 (30% need-based, 70% non-need-based). ***Programs:*** Federal Direct (Subsidized and Unsubsidized Stafford, PLUS).

WORK-STUDY ***Federal work-study:*** Total amount: $40,000; 14 jobs averaging $2857. ***State or other work-study/employment:*** Total amount: $100,000 (50% need-based, 50% non-need-based). 39 part-time jobs averaging $2496.

ATHLETIC AWARDS Total amount: $1,103,474 (77% need-based, 23% non-need-based).

APPLYING FOR FINANCIAL AID ***Required financial aid forms:*** FAFSA, state aid form. ***Financial aid deadline (priority):*** 3/2. ***Notification date:*** Continuous beginning 3/2. Students must reply within 3 weeks of notification.

CONTACT Chrislin Wilder, Financial Aid Counselor, William Jessup University, 333 Sunset Boulevard, Rocklin, CA 95765, 916-577-2234 or toll-free 800-355-7522. *Fax:* 916-577-2230. *E-mail:* finaid@jessup.edu.

WILLIAM JEWELL COLLEGE

Liberty, MO

Tuition & fees: $29,900 **Average undergraduate aid package: $17,589**

ABOUT THE INSTITUTION Independent, coed. 47 undergraduate majors. Federal methodology is used as a basis for awarding need-based institutional aid.

UNDERGRADUATE EXPENSES for 2011–12 ***Comprehensive fee:*** $37,460 includes full-time tuition ($29,600), mandatory fees ($300), and room and board ($7560). Full-time tuition and fees vary according to class time, course load, program, and student level. Room and board charges vary according to board plan and housing facility. ***Part-time tuition:*** $850 per credit. ***Payment plan:*** Installment.

FRESHMAN FINANCIAL AID (Fall 2010, est.) 243 applied for aid; of those 89% were deemed to have need. 100% of freshmen with need received aid; of those 12% had need fully met. ***Average percent of need met:*** 68% (excluding resources awarded to replace EFC). ***Average financial aid package:*** $20,554 (excluding resources awarded to replace EFC). 10% of all full-time freshmen had no need and received non-need-based gift aid.

UNDERGRADUATE FINANCIAL AID (Fall 2010, est.) 847 applied for aid; of those 90% were deemed to have need. 100% of undergraduates with need received aid; of those 14% had need fully met. ***Average percent of need met:*** 63% (excluding resources awarded to replace EFC). ***Average financial aid package:*** $17,589 (excluding resources awarded to replace EFC). 12% of all full-time undergraduates had no need and received non-need-based gift aid.

GIFT AID (NEED-BASED) ***Total amount:*** $10,494,692 (12% federal, 6% state, 78% institutional, 4% external sources). ***Receiving aid:*** Freshmen: 80% (216); all full-time undergraduates: 73% (743). ***Average award:*** Freshmen: $15,399; Undergraduates: $13,688. ***Scholarships, grants, and awards:*** Federal Pell, FSEOG, state, college/university gift aid from institutional funds.

GIFT AID (NON-NEED-BASED) ***Total amount:*** $2,616,699 (97% institutional, 3% external sources). ***Receiving aid:*** Freshmen: 77% (208). Undergraduates: 68% (694). ***Average award:*** Freshmen: $15,018. Undergraduates: $12,564. ***Scholarships, grants, and awards by category:*** *Academic interests/achievement:* 727 awards ($6,936,172 total): general academic interests/achievements. *Creative arts/performance:* 176 awards ($553,015 total): art/fine arts, debating, journalism/publications, music, theater/drama. *Special achievements/activities:* 30 awards ($75,711 total): cheerleading/drum major, religious involvement. *Special characteristics:* 155 awards ($780,226 total): children and siblings of alumni, children of faculty/staff, siblings of current students. ***Tuition waivers:*** Full or partial for children of alumni, employees or children of employees.

LOANS ***Student loans:*** $6,167,718 (47% need-based, 53% non-need-based). 77% of past graduating class borrowed through all loan programs. *Average indebtedness per student:* $23,210. ***Average need-based loan:*** Freshmen: $4538. Undergraduates: $5062. ***Parent loans:*** $1,681,103 (92% need-based, 8% non-need-based). ***Programs:*** Perkins, Federal Nursing, alternative loans.

WORK-STUDY ***Federal work-study:*** Total amount: $1,174,696; 519 jobs averaging $2171. ***State or other work-study/employment:*** Total amount: $113,043 (100% non-need-based). 150 part-time jobs averaging $754.

ATHLETIC AWARDS Total amount: $3,192,874 (71% need-based, 29% non-need-based).

APPLYING FOR FINANCIAL AID ***Required financial aid form:*** FAFSA. ***Financial aid deadline (priority):*** 3/1. ***Notification date:*** Continuous. Students must reply within 2 weeks of notification.

CONTACT Sue Karnes, Director of Financial Aid, William Jewell College, 500 College Hill, Liberty, MO 64068, 816-415-5973 or toll-free 888-2JEWELL. *Fax:* 816-415-5006. *E-mail:* karness@william.jewell.edu.

WILLIAM PATERSON UNIVERSITY OF NEW JERSEY

Wayne, NJ

Tuition & fees (NJ res): $11,238 **Average undergraduate aid package: $9711**

ABOUT THE INSTITUTION State-supported, coed. 53 undergraduate majors. Federal methodology is used as a basis for awarding need-based institutional aid.

UNDERGRADUATE EXPENSES for 2010–11 ***Tuition, state resident:*** full-time $6830; part-time $219 per credit hour. ***Tuition, nonresident:*** full-time $13,854; part-time $449 per credit hour. ***Required fees:*** full-time $4408; $141.94 per credit hour. Full-time tuition and fees vary according to program. Part-time tuition and fees vary according to course load and program. ***College room and board:*** $10,380; ***Room only:*** $6800. Room and board charges vary according to board plan and housing facility. ***Payment plan:*** Installment.

FRESHMAN FINANCIAL AID (Fall 2010, est.) 1,401 applied for aid; of those 80% were deemed to have need. 93% of freshmen with need received aid; of those 33% had need fully met. ***Average financial aid package:*** $9908 (excluding resources awarded to replace EFC). 7% of all full-time freshmen had no need and received non-need-based gift aid.

UNDERGRADUATE FINANCIAL AID (Fall 2010, est.) 6,969 applied for aid; of those 83% were deemed to have need. 97% of undergraduates with need received aid; of those 31% had need fully met. ***Average financial aid package:*** $9711 (excluding resources awarded to replace EFC). 5% of all full-time undergraduates had no need and received non-need-based gift aid.

GIFT AID (NEED-BASED) ***Total amount:*** $28,701,503 (58% federal, 37% state, 3% institutional, 2% external sources). ***Receiving aid:*** Freshmen: 40% (617); all full-time undergraduates: 40% (3,346). ***Average award:*** Freshmen: $9240; Undergraduates: $8043. ***Scholarships, grants, and awards:*** Federal Pell, FSEOG, state, private, college/university gift aid from institutional funds.

GIFT AID (NON-NEED-BASED) ***Total amount:*** $7,390,167 (2% federal, 2% state, 92% institutional, 4% external sources). ***Receiving aid:*** Freshmen: 17%

(268). Undergraduates: 11% (878). ***Average award:*** Freshmen: $6238. Undergraduates: $5831. ***Tuition waivers:*** Full or partial for employees or children of employees, senior citizens.

LOANS ***Student loans:*** $32,351,154 (83% need-based, 17% non-need-based). 66% of past graduating class borrowed through all loan programs. *Average indebtedness per student:* $28,537. ***Average need-based loan:*** Freshmen: $3317. Undergraduates: $4389. ***Parent loans:*** $6,054,358 (100% non-need-based). ***Programs:*** Federal Direct (Subsidized and Unsubsidized Stafford, PLUS), Perkins, Federal Nursing, state.

WORK-STUDY ***Federal work-study:*** Total amount: $375,000; jobs available. ***State or other work-study/employment:*** Total amount: $278,000 (100% non-need-based). Part-time jobs available.

APPLYING FOR FINANCIAL AID ***Required financial aid form:*** FAFSA. ***Financial aid deadline (priority):*** 4/1. ***Notification date:*** Continuous.

CONTACT Elizabeth Riquez, Director of Financial Aid, William Paterson University of New Jersey, 300 Pompton Road, Wayne, NJ 07470, 973-720-2928 or toll-free 877-WPU-EXCEL (in-state). *Fax:* 973-720-3133. *E-mail:* riqueze@wpunj.edu.

WILLIAM PENN UNIVERSITY

Oskaloosa, IA

CONTACT Cyndi Peiffer, Director of Financial Aid, William Penn University, 201 Trueblood Avenue, Oskaloosa, IA 52577-1799, 641-673-1060 or toll-free 800-779-7366. *Fax:* 641-673-1115. *E-mail:* peifferc@wmpenn.edu.

WILLIAMS BAPTIST COLLEGE

Walnut Ridge, AR

Tuition & fees: $12,020 **Average undergraduate aid package: $12,879**

ABOUT THE INSTITUTION Independent Southern Baptist, coed. 26 undergraduate majors. Federal methodology is used as a basis for awarding need-based institutional aid.

UNDERGRADUATE EXPENSES for 2010–11 ***Comprehensive fee:*** $17,420 includes full-time tuition ($11,200), mandatory fees ($820), and room and board ($5400). ***Payment plan:*** Installment.

FRESHMAN FINANCIAL AID (Fall 2009) 108 applied for aid; of those 87% were deemed to have need. 100% of freshmen with need received aid. ***Average financial aid package:*** $12,541 (excluding resources awarded to replace EFC).

UNDERGRADUATE FINANCIAL AID (Fall 2009) 424 applied for aid; of those 88% were deemed to have need. 100% of undergraduates with need received aid. ***Average financial aid package:*** $12,879 (excluding resources awarded to replace EFC).

GIFT AID (NEED-BASED) ***Total amount:*** $1,690,168 (75% federal, 25% state). ***Receiving aid:*** Freshmen: 57% (77); all full-time undergraduates: 62% (316). ***Average award:*** Freshmen: $5611; Undergraduates: $5081. ***Scholarships, grants, and awards:*** Federal Pell, FSEOG, state, private, college/university gift aid from institutional funds.

GIFT AID (NON-NEED-BASED) ***Total amount:*** $1,922,962 (6% state, 81% institutional, 13% external sources). ***Receiving aid:*** Freshmen: 69% (93). Undergraduates: 71% (362). ***Scholarships, grants, and awards by category:*** *Academic interests/achievement:* 450 awards ($1,650,414 total): biological sciences, business, education, general academic interests/achievements, humanities, religion/biblical studies. *Creative arts/performance:* 44 awards ($43,750 total): art/fine arts, music. *Special achievements/activities:* 8 awards ($3650 total): cheerleading/drum major. *Special characteristics:* 143 awards ($178,010 total): children of faculty/staff, international students, members of minority groups, relatives of clergy, religious affiliation. ***Tuition waivers:*** Full or partial for employees or children of employees, senior citizens.

LOANS ***Student loans:*** $2,206,785 (54% need-based, 46% non-need-based). 73% of past graduating class borrowed through all loan programs. *Average indebtedness per student:* $18,338. ***Average need-based loan:*** Freshmen: $2629. Undergraduates: $3640. ***Parent loans:*** $177,949 (100% non-need-based). ***Programs:*** Federal Direct (Subsidized and Unsubsidized Stafford, PLUS).

WORK-STUDY ***Federal work-study:*** Total amount: $287,044; 196 jobs averaging $1435. ***State or other work-study/employment:*** Total amount: $33,203 (100% non-need-based). 26 part-time jobs averaging $1229.

ATHLETIC AWARDS Total amount: $634,866 (100% non-need-based).

APPLYING FOR FINANCIAL AID ***Required financial aid form:*** FAFSA. ***Financial aid deadline:*** Continuous. ***Notification date:*** Continuous beginning 4/1. Students must reply within 2 weeks of notification.

CONTACT Mrs. Barbara Turner, Director of Financial Aid, Williams Baptist College, 60 West Fulbright Avenue, Walnut Ridge, AR 72476, 870-759-4112 or toll-free 800-722-4434. *Fax:* 870-759-4209. *E-mail:* bturner@wbcoll.edu.

WILLIAMS COLLEGE

Williamstown, MA

Tuition & fees: $41,434 **Average undergraduate aid package: $40,485**

ABOUT THE INSTITUTION Independent, coed. 34 undergraduate majors. Institutional methodology is used as a basis for awarding need-based institutional aid.

UNDERGRADUATE EXPENSES for 2010–11 ***Comprehensive fee:*** $52,340 includes full-time tuition ($41,190), mandatory fees ($244), and room and board ($10,906). ***College room only:*** $5542. Room and board charges vary according to board plan. ***Payment plan:*** Installment.

FRESHMAN FINANCIAL AID (Fall 2010, est.) 354 applied for aid; of those 82% were deemed to have need. 100% of freshmen with need received aid; of those 100% had need fully met. ***Average percent of need met:*** 100% (excluding resources awarded to replace EFC). ***Average financial aid package:*** $41,400 (excluding resources awarded to replace EFC).

UNDERGRADUATE FINANCIAL AID (Fall 2010, est.) 1,275 applied for aid; of those 91% were deemed to have need. 100% of undergraduates with need received aid; of those 100% had need fully met. ***Average percent of need met:*** 100% (excluding resources awarded to replace EFC). ***Average financial aid package:*** $40,485 (excluding resources awarded to replace EFC).

GIFT AID (NEED-BASED) ***Total amount:*** $45,240,118 (6% federal, 92% institutional, 2% external sources). ***Receiving aid:*** Freshmen: 53% (290); all full-time undergraduates: 53% (1,160). ***Average award:*** Freshmen: $39,903; Undergraduates: $38,035. ***Scholarships, grants, and awards:*** Federal Pell, FSEOG, state, private, college/university gift aid from institutional funds.

GIFT AID (NON-NEED-BASED) ***Total amount:*** $1,137,200 (100% external sources).

LOANS ***Student loans:*** $2,043,337 (100% non-need-based). 43% of past graduating class borrowed through all loan programs. *Average indebtedness per student:* $8065. ***Parent loans:*** $3,013,890 (100% non-need-based). ***Programs:*** Federal Direct (Subsidized and Unsubsidized Stafford, PLUS), Perkins, college/university.

WORK-STUDY ***Federal work-study:*** Total amount: $863,776; 468 jobs averaging $1846. ***State or other work-study/employment:*** Total amount: $1,643,593 (69% need-based, 31% non-need-based). 463 part-time jobs averaging $1886.

APPLYING FOR FINANCIAL AID ***Required financial aid forms:*** FAFSA, CSS Financial Aid PROFILE, noncustodial (divorced/separated) parent's statement, parents' and student's most recent federal tax returns and W-2 forms. ***Financial aid deadline:*** 2/1. ***Notification date:*** 4/1. Students must reply by 5/1.

CONTACT Paul J. Boyer, Director of Financial Aid, Williams College, PO Box 37, Williamstown, MA 01267, 413-597-4181. *Fax:* 413-597-2999. *E-mail:* paul.j.boyer@williams.edu.

WILLIAMSON CHRISTIAN COLLEGE

Franklin, TN

CONTACT Jeanie Maguire, Director of Financial Aid, Williamson Christian College, 200 Seaboard Lane, Franklin, TN 37067, 615-771-7821. *Fax:* 615-771-7810. *E-mail:* info@williamsoncc.edu.

WILLIAM WOODS UNIVERSITY

Fulton, MO

CONTACT Deana Ready, Director of Student Financial Services, William Woods University, One University Avenue, Fulton, MO 65251, 573-592-4232 or toll-free 800-995-3159 Ext. 4221. *Fax:* 573-592-1180.

WILMINGTON COLLEGE

Wilmington, OH

CONTACT Donna Barton, Coordinator of Financial Aid, Wilmington College, Pyle Center Box 1184, Wilmington, OH 45177, 937-382-6661 Ext. 466 or toll-free 800-341-9318. *Fax:* 937-383-8564.

WILMINGTON UNIVERSITY

New Castle, DE

CONTACT J. Lynn Iocono, Director of Financial Aid, Wilmington University, 320 DuPont Highway, New Castle, DE 19720, 302-328-9437 or toll-free 877-967-5464. *Fax:* 302-328-5902.

WILSON COLLEGE

Chambersburg, PA

Tuition & fees: $29,340 **Average undergraduate aid package: $22,145**

ABOUT THE INSTITUTION Independent religious, coed, primarily women. 29 undergraduate majors. Federal methodology is used as a basis for awarding need-based institutional aid.

UNDERGRADUATE EXPENSES for 2011–12 ***Comprehensive fee:*** $39,051 includes full-time tuition ($28,745), mandatory fees ($595), and room and board ($9711). ***College room only:*** $5055. Room and board charges vary according to board plan and housing facility. ***Part-time tuition:*** $2875 per course. ***Part-time fees:*** $50 per course; $50 per term. Part-time tuition and fees vary according to course load. ***Payment plan:*** Installment.

FRESHMAN FINANCIAL AID (Fall 2010, est.) 97 applied for aid; of those 93% were deemed to have need. 100% of freshmen with need received aid; of those 17% had need fully met. ***Average percent of need met:*** 77% (excluding resources awarded to replace EFC). ***Average financial aid package:*** $22,961 (excluding resources awarded to replace EFC). 9% of all full-time freshmen had no need and received non-need-based gift aid.

UNDERGRADUATE FINANCIAL AID (Fall 2010, est.) 346 applied for aid; of those 92% were deemed to have need. 100% of undergraduates with need received aid; of those 12% had need fully met. ***Average percent of need met:*** 76% (excluding resources awarded to replace EFC). ***Average financial aid package:*** $22,145 (excluding resources awarded to replace EFC). 13% of all full-time undergraduates had no need and received non-need-based gift aid.

GIFT AID (NEED-BASED) ***Total amount:*** $2,143,921 (54% federal, 27% state, 19% external sources). ***Receiving aid:*** Freshmen: 89% (90); all full-time undergraduates: 84% (315). ***Average award:*** Freshmen: $19,568; Undergraduates: $18,234. ***Scholarships, grants, and awards:*** Federal Pell, FSEOG, state, private, college/university gift aid from institutional funds.

GIFT AID (NON-NEED-BASED) ***Total amount:*** $991,859 (1% federal, 7% state, 83% institutional, 9% external sources). ***Receiving aid:*** Freshmen: 10% (10). Undergraduates: 8% (29). ***Average award:*** Freshmen: $16,452. Undergraduates: $14,094. ***Scholarships, grants, and awards by category:*** *Academic interests/achievement:* biological sciences, business, communication, computer science, education, English, foreign languages, general academic interests/achievements, humanities, international studies, mathematics, physical sciences, premedicine, religion/biblical studies, social sciences. *Creative arts/performance:* music. *Special achievements/activities:* community service, general special achievements/activities, leadership. *Special characteristics:* adult students, children and siblings of alumni, children of current students, children of faculty/staff, international students, local/state students, relatives of clergy, religious affiliation, veterans. ***Tuition waivers:*** Full or partial for employees or children of employees.

LOANS ***Student loans:*** $3,010,766 (78% need-based, 22% non-need-based). 80% of past graduating class borrowed through all loan programs. *Average indebtedness per student:* $36,021. ***Average need-based loan:*** Freshmen: $3464. Undergraduates: $4546. ***Parent loans:*** $1,465,888 (43% need-based, 57% non-need-based). ***Programs:*** Federal Direct (Subsidized and Unsubsidized Stafford, PLUS), Perkins.

WORK-STUDY ***Federal work-study:*** Total amount: $39,105; 22 jobs averaging $2000. ***State or other work-study/employment:*** Total amount: $227,000 (46% need-based, 54% non-need-based). 122 part-time jobs averaging $2000.

APPLYING FOR FINANCIAL AID ***Required financial aid forms:*** FAFSA, institution's own form. ***Financial aid deadline (priority):*** 4/30. ***Notification date:*** Continuous beginning 9/15.

CONTACT Ms. Linda Brittain, Dean of Financial Aid and Senior Enrollment Associate, Wilson College, 1015 Philadelphia Avenue, Chambersburg, PA 17201-1285, 717-262-2002 or toll-free 800-421-8402. *Fax:* 717-262-2530. *E-mail:* finaid@wilson.edu.

WINGATE UNIVERSITY

Wingate, NC

Tuition & fees: $22,180 **Average undergraduate aid package: $19,618**

ABOUT THE INSTITUTION Independent Baptist, coed. 37 undergraduate majors. Federal methodology is used as a basis for awarding need-based institutional aid.

UNDERGRADUATE EXPENSES for 2011–12 ***Comprehensive fee:*** $30,950 includes full-time tuition ($20,980), mandatory fees ($1200), and room and board ($8770). Room and board charges vary according to board plan. ***Part-time tuition:*** $700 per semester hour. Part-time tuition and fees vary according to course load. ***Payment plan:*** Installment.

FRESHMAN FINANCIAL AID (Fall 2010, est.) 538 applied for aid; of those 89% were deemed to have need. 99% of freshmen with need received aid; of those 37% had need fully met. ***Average percent of need met:*** 84% (excluding resources awarded to replace EFC). ***Average financial aid package:*** $20,238 (excluding resources awarded to replace EFC). 20% of all full-time freshmen had no need and received non-need-based gift aid.

UNDERGRADUATE FINANCIAL AID (Fall 2010, est.) 1,382 applied for aid; of those 91% were deemed to have need. 99% of undergraduates with need received aid; of those 34% had need fully met. ***Average percent of need met:*** 84% (excluding resources awarded to replace EFC). ***Average financial aid package:*** $19,618 (excluding resources awarded to replace EFC). 21% of all full-time undergraduates had no need and received non-need-based gift aid.

GIFT AID (NEED-BASED) ***Total amount:*** $18,399,176 (16% federal, 19% state, 63% institutional, 2% external sources). ***Receiving aid:*** Freshmen: 78% (470); all full-time undergraduates: 79% (1,246). ***Average award:*** Freshmen: $17,124; Undergraduates: $15,803. ***Scholarships, grants, and awards:*** Federal Pell, FSEOG, state, private, college/university gift aid from institutional funds.

GIFT AID (NON-NEED-BASED) ***Total amount:*** $4,839,676 (13% state, 82% institutional, 5% external sources). ***Receiving aid:*** Freshmen: 16% (97). Undergraduates: 15% (229). ***Average award:*** Freshmen: $11,162. Undergraduates: $9768. ***Scholarships, grants, and awards by category:*** *Academic interests/achievement:* general academic interests/achievements. *Creative arts/performance:* art/fine arts, music, theater/drama. *Special achievements/activities:* religious involvement. *Special characteristics:* children and siblings of alumni, relatives of clergy, religious affiliation. ***Tuition waivers:*** Full or partial for employees or children of employees.

LOANS ***Student loans:*** $9,028,453 (64% need-based, 36% non-need-based). 28% of past graduating class borrowed through all loan programs. *Average indebtedness per student:* $25,504. ***Average need-based loan:*** Freshmen: $2834. Undergraduates: $3721. ***Parent loans:*** $6,919,021 (20% need-based, 80% non-need-based). ***Programs:*** Federal Direct (Subsidized and Unsubsidized Stafford, PLUS).

WORK-STUDY ***Federal work-study:*** Total amount: $923,748; jobs available. ***State or other work-study/employment:*** Part-time jobs available.

ATHLETIC AWARDS Total amount: $2,415,615 (53% need-based, 47% non-need-based).

APPLYING FOR FINANCIAL AID ***Required financial aid forms:*** FAFSA, state aid form. ***Notification date:*** Continuous. Students must reply within 4 weeks of notification.

CONTACT Teresa G. Williams, Director of Student Financial Planning, Wingate University, Campus Box 3001, Wingate, NC 28174, 704-233-8209 or toll-free 800-755-5550. *Fax:* 704-233-9396. *E-mail:* finaid@wingate.edu.

WINONA STATE UNIVERSITY

Winona, MN

Tuition & fees (MN res): $8200 **Average undergraduate aid package: $7112**

ABOUT THE INSTITUTION State-supported, coed. 108 undergraduate majors. Federal methodology is used as a basis for awarding need-based institutional aid.

UNDERGRADUATE EXPENSES for 2011–12 ***Tuition, state resident:*** full-time $6240; part-time $206 per credit. ***Tuition, nonresident:*** full-time $11,340; part-time $374 per credit. ***Required fees:*** full-time $1960. Full-time tuition and fees vary according to location and reciprocity agreements. Part-time tuition and fees vary according to location and reciprocity agreements. ***College room and board:*** $7330. Room and board charges vary according to board plan, housing facility, and location. ***Payment plan:*** Installment.

FRESHMAN FINANCIAL AID (Fall 2009) 1,372 applied for aid; of those 70% were deemed to have need. 97% of freshmen with need received aid; of those 13% had need fully met. ***Average percent of need met:*** 42% (excluding resources awarded to replace EFC). ***Average financial aid package:*** $6559 (excluding resources awarded to replace EFC). 22% of all full-time freshmen had no need and received non-need-based gift aid.

UNDERGRADUATE FINANCIAL AID (Fall 2009) 5,247 applied for aid; of those 74% were deemed to have need. 98% of undergraduates with need received aid; of those 13% had need fully met. ***Average percent of need met:*** 46% (excluding resources awarded to replace EFC). ***Average financial aid package:*** $7112 (excluding resources awarded to replace EFC). 12% of all full-time undergraduates had no need and received non-need-based gift aid.

GIFT AID (NEED-BASED) ***Total amount:*** $12,054,302 (65% federal, 34% state, 1% institutional). ***Receiving aid:*** Freshmen: 26% (466); all full-time undergraduates: 28% (2,033). ***Average award:*** Freshmen: $5392; Undergraduates: $4968. ***Scholarships, grants, and awards:*** Federal Pell, FSEOG, state, private, college/university gift aid from institutional funds.

GIFT AID (NON-NEED-BASED) ***Total amount:*** $6,411,495 (2% federal, 51% institutional, 47% external sources). ***Receiving aid:*** Freshmen: 29% (518). Undergraduates: 16% (1,194). ***Average award:*** Freshmen: $1865. Undergraduates: $2601. ***Scholarships, grants, and awards by category:*** *Academic interests/achievement:* 1,287 awards ($1,328,969 total): general academic interests/achievements. *Creative arts/performance:* 75 awards ($87,375 total): art/fine arts, debating, music, theater/drama. *Special characteristics:* 315 awards ($1,384,450 total): children and siblings of alumni, children of faculty/staff, local/state students, members of minority groups, out-of-state students. ***Tuition waivers:*** Full or partial for employees or children of employees.

LOANS ***Student loans:*** $47,671,556 (33% need-based, 67% non-need-based). 72% of past graduating class borrowed through all loan programs. *Average indebtedness per student:* $29,123. ***Average need-based loan:*** Freshmen: $3069. Undergraduates: $3908. ***Parent loans:*** $2,974,702 (100% non-need-based). ***Programs:*** Federal Direct (Subsidized and Unsubsidized Stafford, PLUS), Perkins, state, college/university.

WORK-STUDY ***Federal work-study:*** Total amount: $327,538; 180 jobs averaging $1815. ***State or other work-study/employment:*** Total amount: $661,848 (100% need-based). 325 part-time jobs averaging $2004.

ATHLETIC AWARDS Total amount: $790,280 (100% non-need-based).

APPLYING FOR FINANCIAL AID ***Required financial aid form:*** FAFSA. ***Financial aid deadline:*** Continuous. ***Notification date:*** 5/1. Students must reply within 3 weeks of notification.

CONTACT Cindy Groth, Counselor, Winona State University, PO Box 5838, Winona, MN 55987-5838, 507-457-5090 Ext. 5561 or toll-free 800-DIAL WSU.

WINSTON-SALEM STATE UNIVERSITY

Winston-Salem, NC

CONTACT Raymond Solomon, Director of Financial Aid Office, Winston-Salem State University, 601 Martin Luther King Jr. Drive, PO Box 19524, Winston-Salem, NC 27110-0003, 336-750-3299 or toll-free 800-257-4052. *Fax:* 336-750-3297.

WINTHROP UNIVERSITY

Rock Hill, SC

Tuition & fees (SC res): $12,176 **Average undergraduate aid package: $11,287**

ABOUT THE INSTITUTION State-supported, coed. 25 undergraduate majors. Federal methodology is used as a basis for awarding need-based institutional aid.

UNDERGRADUATE EXPENSES for 2010–11 ***Tuition, state resident:*** full-time $12,176; part-time $508 per credit hour. ***Tuition, nonresident:*** full-time $22,892; part-time $954 per credit hour. Full-time tuition and fees vary according to reciprocity agreements and student level. Part-time tuition and fees vary according to student level. ***College room and board:*** $6922; ***Room only:*** $4452. Room and board charges vary according to board plan and housing facility. ***Payment plan:*** Installment.

FRESHMAN FINANCIAL AID (Fall 2010, est.) 872 applied for aid; of those 82% were deemed to have need. 100% of freshmen with need received aid; of those 14% had need fully met. ***Average percent of need met:*** 70% (excluding resources awarded to replace EFC). ***Average financial aid package:*** $12,423 (excluding resources awarded to replace EFC). 10% of all full-time freshmen had no need and received non-need-based gift aid.

UNDERGRADUATE FINANCIAL AID (Fall 2010, est.) 3,576 applied for aid; of those 85% were deemed to have need. 99% of undergraduates with need received aid; of those 10% had need fully met. ***Average percent of need met:*** 63% (excluding resources awarded to replace EFC). ***Average financial aid package:*** $11,287 (excluding resources awarded to replace EFC). 10% of all full-time undergraduates had no need and received non-need-based gift aid.

GIFT AID (NEED-BASED) ***Total amount:*** $20,891,851 (44% federal, 37% state, 15% institutional, 4% external sources). ***Receiving aid:*** Freshmen: 73% (701); all full-time undergraduates: 60% (2,624). ***Average award:*** Freshmen: $9350; Undergraduates: $8181. ***Scholarships, grants, and awards:*** Federal Pell, FSEOG, state, private, college/university gift aid from institutional funds, TEACH Grants.

GIFT AID (NON-NEED-BASED) ***Total amount:*** $7,322,370 (1% federal, 50% state, 45% institutional, 4% external sources). ***Receiving aid:*** Freshmen: 10% (98). Undergraduates: 6% (272). ***Average award:*** Freshmen: $5321. Undergraduates: $7735. ***Scholarships, grants, and awards by category:*** *Academic interests/achievement:* general academic interests/achievements. *Creative arts/performance:* art/fine arts, dance, music, performing arts, theater/drama. *Special characteristics:* children of faculty/staff. ***Tuition waivers:*** Full or partial for employees or children of employees, senior citizens.

LOANS ***Student loans:*** $31,690,892 (68% need-based, 32% non-need-based). 76% of past graduating class borrowed through all loan programs. *Average indebtedness per student:* $26,066. ***Average need-based loan:*** Freshmen: $3258. Undergraduates: $4374. ***Parent loans:*** $4,230,005 (47% need-based, 53% non-need-based). ***Programs:*** Federal Direct (Subsidized and Unsubsidized Stafford, PLUS), Perkins.

WORK-STUDY ***Federal work-study:*** Total amount: $250,000; jobs available. ***State or other work-study/employment:*** Total amount: $2,136,113 (100% non-need-based). Part-time jobs available.

ATHLETIC AWARDS Total amount: $1,743,181 (35% need-based, 65% non-need-based).

APPLYING FOR FINANCIAL AID ***Required financial aid form:*** FAFSA. ***Financial aid deadline (priority):*** 3/15. ***Notification date:*** Continuous beginning 3/15. Students must reply within 4 weeks of notification.

CONTACT Leah M. Sturgis, Director of Financial Aid, Winthrop University, 119 Tillman Hall, Rock Hill, SC 29733, 803-323-2189 or toll-free 800-763-0230. *Fax:* 803-323-2557. *E-mail:* finaid@winthrop.edu.

WISCONSIN LUTHERAN COLLEGE

Milwaukee, WI

CONTACT Mrs. Linda Loeffel, Director of Financial Aid, Wisconsin Lutheran College, 8800 West Bluemound Road, Milwaukee, WI 53226-4699, 414-443-8856 or toll-free 888-WIS LUTH. *Fax:* 414-443-8514. *E-mail:* linda.loeffel@wlc.edu.

WITTENBERG UNIVERSITY

Springfield, OH

Tuition & fees: $36,434 **Average undergraduate aid package: $28,460**

ABOUT THE INSTITUTION Independent religious, coed. 31 undergraduate majors. Federal methodology is used as a basis for awarding need-based institutional aid.

UNDERGRADUATE EXPENSES for 2011–12 ***Comprehensive fee:*** $45,728 includes full-time tuition ($35,884), mandatory fees ($550), and room and board ($9294). ***College room only:*** $4826. Room and board charges vary according to board plan and housing facility. ***Part-time tuition:*** $1196 per credit. ***Part-time fees:*** $1196 per credit. Part-time tuition and fees vary according to course load. ***Payment plan:*** Installment.

FRESHMAN FINANCIAL AID (Fall 2010, est.) 463 applied for aid; of those 89% were deemed to have need. 100% of freshmen with need received aid; of those 31% had need fully met. ***Average percent of need met:*** 87% (excluding resources awarded to replace EFC). ***Average financial aid package:*** $31,018 (excluding resources awarded to replace EFC). 18% of all full-time freshmen had no need and received non-need-based gift aid.

UNDERGRADUATE FINANCIAL AID (Fall 2010, est.) 1,546 applied for aid; of those 88% were deemed to have need. 100% of undergraduates with need received aid; of those 27% had need fully met. ***Average percent of need met:*** 83% (excluding resources awarded to replace EFC). ***Average financial aid package:*** $28,460 (excluding resources awarded to replace EFC). 24% of all full-time undergraduates had no need and received non-need-based gift aid.

GIFT AID (NEED-BASED) ***Total amount:*** $27,412,270 (7% federal, 2% state, 88% institutional, 3% external sources). ***Receiving aid:*** Freshmen: 82% (410); all full-time undergraduates: 75% (1,351). ***Average award:*** Freshmen: $25,451; Undergraduates: $22,549. ***Scholarships, grants, and awards:*** Federal Pell, FSEOG, state, private, college/university gift aid from institutional funds.

GIFT AID (NON-NEED-BASED) ***Total amount:*** $7,943,763 (97% institutional, 3% external sources). ***Average award:*** Freshmen: $18,357. Undergraduates: $15,163. ***Scholarships, grants, and awards by category:*** *Academic interests/achievement:* general academic interests/achievements. *Creative arts/performance:* art/fine arts, dance, music, theater/drama. *Special achievements/activities:* community service, general special achievements/activities, leadership. *Special characteristics:* adult students, children and siblings of alumni, children of faculty/staff, ethnic background, international students, local/state students, members of minority groups, relatives of clergy, religious affiliation. ***Tuition waivers:*** Full or partial for minority students, children of alumni, employees or children of employees, adult students, senior citizens.

LOANS ***Student loans:*** $11,075,357 (76% need-based, 24% non-need-based). 83% of past graduating class borrowed through all loan programs. *Average indebtedness per student:* $29,506. ***Average need-based loan:*** Freshmen: $3681. Undergraduates: $4187. ***Parent loans:*** $5,198,802 (68% need-based, 32% non-need-based). ***Programs:*** Federal Direct (Subsidized and Unsubsidized Stafford, PLUS), Perkins, college/university, alternative loans.

WORK-STUDY ***Federal work-study:*** Total amount: $1,493,535; 570 jobs averaging $2612. ***State or other work-study/employment:*** Total amount: $1,353,035 (53% need-based, 47% non-need-based). 560 part-time jobs averaging $2316.

APPLYING FOR FINANCIAL AID ***Required financial aid form:*** FAFSA. ***Financial aid deadline (priority):*** 3/1. ***Notification date:*** Continuous beginning 3/1. Students must reply within 2 weeks of notification.

CONTACT Mr. J. Randy Green, Director of Financial Aid, Wittenberg University, PO Box 720, Springfield, OH 45501-0720, 937-327-7321 or toll-free 800-677-7558 Ext. 6314. *Fax:* 937-327-6379. *E-mail:* jgreen@wittenberg.edu.

WOFFORD COLLEGE

Spartanburg, SC

Tuition & fees: $31,710 **Average undergraduate aid package: $29,792**

ABOUT THE INSTITUTION Independent religious, coed. 30 undergraduate majors. Federal methodology is used as a basis for awarding need-based institutional aid.

UNDERGRADUATE EXPENSES for 2010–11 ***Comprehensive fee:*** $40,580 includes full-time tuition ($31,710) and room and board ($8870). ***Part-time tuition:*** $1255 per credit hour. ***Payment plan:*** Installment.

FRESHMAN FINANCIAL AID (Fall 2010, est.) 342 applied for aid; of those 79% were deemed to have need. 100% of freshmen with need received aid; of those 45% had need fully met. ***Average percent of need met:*** 85% (excluding resources awarded to replace EFC). ***Average financial aid package:*** $29,916 (excluding resources awarded to replace EFC). 24% of all full-time freshmen had no need and received non-need-based gift aid.

UNDERGRADUATE FINANCIAL AID (Fall 2010, est.) 1,019 applied for aid; of those 85% were deemed to have need. 99% of undergraduates with need received aid; of those 48% had need fully met. ***Average percent of need met:*** 85% (excluding resources awarded to replace EFC). ***Average financial aid package:*** $29,792 (excluding resources awarded to replace EFC). 25% of all full-time undergraduates had no need and received non-need-based gift aid.

GIFT AID (NEED-BASED) ***Total amount:*** $18,320,262 (8% federal, 21% state, 67% institutional, 4% external sources). ***Receiving aid:*** Freshmen: 57% (246); all full-time undergraduates: 55% (802). ***Average award:*** Freshmen: $28,448; Undergraduates: $26,674. ***Scholarships, grants, and awards:*** Federal Pell, FSEOG, state, private, college/university gift aid from institutional funds.

GIFT AID (NON-NEED-BASED) ***Total amount:*** $9,700,667 (25% state, 66% institutional, 9% external sources). ***Receiving aid:*** Freshmen: 20% (88). Undergraduates: 19% (285). ***Average award:*** Freshmen: $14,184. Undergraduates: $13,857. ***Scholarships, grants, and awards by category:*** *Academic interests/achievement:* general academic interests/achievements. *Creative arts/performance:* music. *Special achievements/activities:* leadership. *Special characteristics:* children of faculty/staff, general special characteristics, relatives of clergy. ***Tuition waivers:*** Full or partial for employees or children of employees.

LOANS ***Student loans:*** $4,186,392 (65% need-based, 35% non-need-based). 47% of past graduating class borrowed through all loan programs. *Average indebtedness per student:* $23,103. ***Average need-based loan:*** Freshmen: $3156. Undergraduates: $4224. ***Parent loans:*** $1,492,799 (37% need-based, 63% non-need-based). ***Programs:*** Federal Direct (Subsidized and Unsubsidized Stafford, PLUS), Perkins.

WORK-STUDY ***Federal work-study:*** Total amount: $226,571; jobs available.

ATHLETIC AWARDS Total amount: $4,399,507 (46% need-based, 54% non-need-based).

APPLYING FOR FINANCIAL AID ***Required financial aid form:*** FAFSA. ***Financial aid deadline (priority):*** 3/15. ***Notification date:*** Continuous beginning 3/31. Students must reply by 5/1.

CONTACT Kay C. Walton, Director of Financial Aid, Wofford College, 429 North Church Street, Spartanburg, SC 29303-3663, 864-597-4160. *Fax:* 864-597-4149. *E-mail:* finaid@wofford.edu.

WOODBURY UNIVERSITY

Burbank, CA

Tuition & fees: $28,855 **Average undergraduate aid package: $19,861**

ABOUT THE INSTITUTION Independent, coed. 17 undergraduate majors. Federal methodology is used as a basis for awarding need-based institutional aid.

UNDERGRADUATE EXPENSES for 2010–11 ***Comprehensive fee:*** $38,148 includes full-time tuition ($28,465), mandatory fees ($390), and room and board ($9293). ***College room only:*** $5788. Full-time tuition and fees vary according to course load and degree level. ***Part-time tuition:*** $965 per credit hour. Part-time tuition and fees vary according to course load and degree level.

FRESHMAN FINANCIAL AID (Fall 2010, est.) 78 applied for aid; of those 91% were deemed to have need. 100% of freshmen with need received aid; of those 1% had need fully met. ***Average percent of need met:*** 59% (excluding resources awarded to replace EFC). ***Average financial aid package:*** $21,369 (excluding resources awarded to replace EFC). 18% of all full-time freshmen had no need and received non-need-based gift aid.

UNDERGRADUATE FINANCIAL AID (Fall 2010, est.) 894 applied for aid; of those 96% were deemed to have need. 100% of undergraduates with need received aid; of those 2% had need fully met. ***Average percent of need met:*** 53% (excluding resources awarded to replace EFC). ***Average financial aid package:*** $19,861 (excluding resources awarded to replace EFC). 8% of all full-time undergraduates had no need and received non-need-based gift aid.

GIFT AID (NEED-BASED) ***Total amount:*** $14,137,040 (24% federal, 24% state, 50% institutional, 2% external sources). ***Receiving aid:*** Freshmen: 74% (71); all full-time undergraduates: 88% (845). ***Average award:*** Freshmen: $18,386; Undergraduates: $15,712. ***Scholarships, grants, and awards:*** Federal Pell, FSEOG, state, private, college/university gift aid from institutional funds.

GIFT AID (NON-NEED-BASED) ***Total amount:*** $674,773 (94% institutional, 6% external sources). ***Receiving aid:*** Freshmen: 1% (1). Undergraduates: 1% (12). ***Average award:*** Freshmen: $10,238. Undergraduates: $7988. ***Scholarships, grants, and awards by category:*** *Academic interests/achievement:* 580 awards ($3,569,611 total): architecture, general academic interests/achievements.

LOANS ***Student loans:*** $9,260,613 (93% need-based, 7% non-need-based). 95% of past graduating class borrowed through all loan programs. *Average indebtedness per student:* $44,579. ***Average need-based loan:*** Freshmen: $3137. Undergraduates: $4488. ***Parent loans:*** $4,023,622 (68% need-based, 32% non-need-based). ***Programs:*** Federal Direct (Subsidized and Unsubsidized Stafford, PLUS), Perkins, alternative loans.

WORK-STUDY ***Federal work-study:*** Total amount: $142,732; 127 jobs averaging $1124.

APPLYING FOR FINANCIAL AID ***Required financial aid forms:*** FAFSA, institution's own form. ***Financial aid deadline:*** Continuous. ***Notification date:*** Continuous beginning 3/15. Students must reply within 2 weeks of notification.

CONTACT Celeastia Williams, Director of Enrollment Services, Woodbury University, 7500 Glenoaks Boulevard, Burbank, CA 91510, 818-767-0888 Ext. 273 or toll-free 800-784-WOOD. *Fax:* 818-767-4816.

WORCESTER POLYTECHNIC INSTITUTE

Worcester, MA

Tuition & fees: $40,030 **Average undergraduate aid package: $30,237**

ABOUT THE INSTITUTION Independent, coed. 49 undergraduate majors. Both federal and institutional methodology are used as a basis for awarding need-based institutional aid.

UNDERGRADUATE EXPENSES for 2011–12 ***One-time required fee:*** $200. ***Comprehensive fee:*** $51,964 includes full-time tuition ($39,450), mandatory fees ($580), and room and board ($11,934). ***College room only:*** $6982. Room and board charges vary according to board plan and housing facility. ***Part-time tuition:*** $1060 per credit hour. Part-time tuition and fees vary according to course load. ***Payment plans:*** Installment, deferred payment.

FRESHMAN FINANCIAL AID (Fall 2010, est.) 802 applied for aid; of those 86% were deemed to have need. 100% of freshmen with need received aid; of those 47% had need fully met. ***Average percent of need met:*** 71% (excluding resources awarded to replace EFC). ***Average financial aid package:*** $29,755 (excluding resources awarded to replace EFC). 23% of all full-time freshmen had no need and received non-need-based gift aid.

UNDERGRADUATE FINANCIAL AID (Fall 2010, est.) 2,740 applied for aid; of those 90% were deemed to have need. 99% of undergraduates with need received aid; of those 39% had need fully met. ***Average percent of need met:*** 73% (excluding resources awarded to replace EFC). ***Average financial aid package:*** $30,237 (excluding resources awarded to replace EFC). 27% of all full-time undergraduates had no need and received non-need-based gift aid.

GIFT AID (NEED-BASED) ***Total amount:*** $46,454,237 (7% federal, 2% state, 85% institutional, 6% external sources). ***Receiving aid:*** Freshmen: 75% (680); all full-time undergraduates: 68% (2,319). ***Average award:*** Freshmen: $19,471; Undergraduates: $18,707. ***Scholarships, grants, and awards:*** Federal Pell, FSEOG, state, private, college/university gift aid from institutional funds.

GIFT AID (NON-NEED-BASED) ***Total amount:*** $17,365,091 (80% institutional, 20% external sources). ***Receiving aid:*** Freshmen: 27% (248). Undergraduates: 19% (666). ***Average award:*** Freshmen: $13,717. Undergraduates: $16,005. ***Scholarships, grants, and awards by category:*** *Academic interests/achievement:* 2,681 awards ($32,992,843 total): general academic interests/achievements, premedicine. *Special characteristics:* 29 awards ($135,530 total): children of workers in trades. ***Tuition waivers:*** Full or partial for employees or children of employees.

LOANS ***Student loans:*** $29,050,033 (43% need-based, 57% non-need-based). 74% of past graduating class borrowed through all loan programs. ***Average need-based loan:*** Freshmen: $2862. Undergraduates: $2787. ***Parent loans:*** $8,520,556 (100% non-need-based). ***Programs:*** Federal Direct (Subsidized and Unsubsidized Stafford, PLUS), Perkins, state, college/university.

WORK-STUDY ***Federal work-study:*** Total amount: $742,687; 658 jobs averaging $1129.

APPLYING FOR FINANCIAL AID ***Required financial aid forms:*** FAFSA, CSS Financial Aid PROFILE, noncustodial (divorced/separated) parent's statement. ***Financial aid deadline:*** 2/1. ***Notification date:*** 4/1. Students must reply by 5/1.

CONTACT Office of Financial Aid, Worcester Polytechnic Institute, 100 Institute Road, Bartlett Center, Worcester, MA 01609-2280, 508-831-5469. *Fax:* 508-831-5039. *E-mail:* finaid@wpi.edu.

WORCESTER STATE UNIVERSITY

Worcester, MA

Tuition & fees (MA res): $7155 **Average undergraduate aid package: $10,538**

ABOUT THE INSTITUTION State-supported, coed. 28 undergraduate majors. Federal methodology is used as a basis for awarding need-based institutional aid.

UNDERGRADUATE EXPENSES for 2010–11 ***Tuition, state resident:*** full-time $970; part-time $40.42 per credit. ***Tuition, nonresident:*** full-time $7050; part-time $293.75 per credit. ***Required fees:*** full-time $6185; $257.70 per credit. Full-time tuition and fees vary according to class time, course load, degree level, and reciprocity agreements. Part-time tuition and fees vary according to class time, course load, degree level, and reciprocity agreements. ***College room and board:*** $9658; ***Room only:*** $6858. Room and board charges vary according to board plan and housing facility. ***Payment plan:*** Installment.

FRESHMAN FINANCIAL AID (Fall 2009) 640 applied for aid; of those 65% were deemed to have need. 97% of freshmen with need received aid; of those 43% had need fully met. ***Average percent of need met:*** 83% (excluding resources awarded to replace EFC). ***Average financial aid package:*** $10,532 (excluding resources awarded to replace EFC). 3% of all full-time freshmen had no need and received non-need-based gift aid.

UNDERGRADUATE FINANCIAL AID (Fall 2009) 2,782 applied for aid; of those 67% were deemed to have need. 98% of undergraduates with need received aid; of those 48% had need fully met. ***Average percent of need met:*** 85% (excluding resources awarded to replace EFC). ***Average financial aid package:*** $10,538 (excluding resources awarded to replace EFC). 2% of all full-time undergraduates had no need and received non-need-based gift aid.

GIFT AID (NEED-BASED) ***Total amount:*** $8,119,071 (57% federal, 20% state, 18% institutional, 5% external sources). ***Receiving aid:*** Freshmen: 51% (353); all full-time undergraduates: 40% (1,397). ***Average award:*** Freshmen: $4726; Undergraduates: $4939. ***Scholarships, grants, and awards:*** Federal Pell, FSEOG, state, private, college/university gift aid from institutional funds.

GIFT AID (NON-NEED-BASED) ***Total amount:*** $308,875 (74% federal, 26% state). ***Receiving aid:*** Freshmen: 30% (206). Undergraduates: 16% (569). ***Average award:*** Freshmen: $2953. Undergraduates: $2451. ***Tuition waivers:*** Full or partial for employees or children of employees, senior citizens.

LOANS ***Student loans:*** $15,259,797 (32% need-based, 68% non-need-based). 50% of past graduating class borrowed through all loan programs. *Average indebtedness per student:* $20,851. ***Average need-based loan:*** Freshmen: $1990. Undergraduates: $2587. ***Parent loans:*** $1,176,382 (100% non-need-based). ***Programs:*** Perkins, state.

WORK-STUDY ***Federal work-study:*** Total amount: $273,601; 286 jobs averaging $1500.

APPLYING FOR FINANCIAL AID ***Required financial aid form:*** FAFSA. ***Financial aid deadline:*** 5/1 (priority: 3/1). ***Notification date:*** Continuous beginning 3/1. Students must reply within 2 weeks of notification.

CONTACT Ms. Jayne McGinn, Director of Financial Aid, Worcester State University, 486 Chandler Street, Worcester, MA 01602, 508-929-8058 or toll-free 866-WSC-CALL. *Fax:* 508-929-8194. *E-mail:* Jayne.McGinn@worcester.edu.

WRIGHT STATE UNIVERSITY

Dayton, OH

Tuition & fees (OH res): $7797 **Average undergraduate aid package: $9403**

ABOUT THE INSTITUTION State-supported, coed. 101 undergraduate majors. Federal methodology is used as a basis for awarding need-based institutional aid.

UNDERGRADUATE EXPENSES for 2010–11 ***Tuition, state resident:*** full-time $7797; part-time $235 per credit hour. ***Tuition, nonresident:*** full-time $15,105; part-time $459 per credit hour. ***College room and board:*** $8125.

FRESHMAN FINANCIAL AID (Fall 2010, est.) 2,429 applied for aid; of those 86% were deemed to have need. 99% of freshmen with need received aid; of those 9% had need fully met. ***Average percent of need met:*** 55% (excluding resources awarded to replace EFC). ***Average financial aid package:*** $9140 (excluding resources awarded to replace EFC). 8% of all full-time freshmen had no need and received non-need-based gift aid.

UNDERGRADUATE FINANCIAL AID (Fall 2010, est.) 9,752 applied for aid; of those 89% were deemed to have need. 99% of undergraduates with need received aid; of those 8% had need fully met. ***Average percent of need met:*** 52% (excluding resources awarded to replace EFC). ***Average financial aid package:*** $9403 (excluding resources awarded to replace EFC). 7% of all full-time undergraduates had no need and received non-need-based gift aid.

GIFT AID (NEED-BASED) ***Total amount:*** $44,752,339 (66% federal, 12% state, 20% institutional, 2% external sources). ***Receiving aid:*** Freshmen: 64% (1,715); all full-time undergraduates: 55% (6,523). ***Average award:*** Freshmen: $6181; Undergraduates: $6171. ***Scholarships, grants, and awards:*** Federal Pell, FSEOG, state, private, college/university gift aid from institutional funds, United Negro College Fund, Federal Nursing, Choose Ohio First Scholarships.

GIFT AID (NON-NEED-BASED) ***Total amount:*** $5,445,506 (22% state, 72% institutional, 6% external sources). ***Receiving aid:*** Freshmen: 3% (88). Undergraduates: 2% (253). ***Average award:*** Freshmen: $2793. Undergraduates: $4057. ***Scholarships, grants, and awards by category:*** *Academic interests/achievement:* 2,487 awards ($6,639,851 total): area/ethnic studies, biological sciences, business, communication, computer science, education, engineering/technologies, English, foreign languages, general academic interests/achievements, health fields, humanities, international studies, mathematics, military science, physical sciences, premedicine, religion/biblical studies, social sciences. *Creative arts/performance:* 291 awards ($593,426 total): applied art and design, art/fine arts, cinema/film/broadcasting, creative writing, dance, general creative arts/performance, music, performing arts, theater/drama. *Special achievements/activities:* 804 awards ($3,646,748 total): cheerleading/drum major, community service, general special achievements/activities, leadership, memberships. *Special characteristics:* 762 awards ($2,708,879 total): adult students, children and siblings of alumni, children of educators, children of faculty/staff, ethnic background, first-generation college students, handicapped students, international students, out-of-state students.

LOANS ***Student loans:*** $92,919,721 (84% need-based, 16% non-need-based). 82% of past graduating class borrowed through all loan programs. *Average indebtedness per student:* $26,542. ***Average need-based loan:*** Freshmen: $3302. Undergraduates: $4110. ***Parent loans:*** $9,310,760 (58% need-based, 42% non-need-based). ***Programs:*** Federal Direct (Subsidized and Unsubsidized Stafford, PLUS), Perkins, Federal Nursing, state, college/university, private loans.

WORK-STUDY ***Federal work-study:*** Total amount: $4,487,132; 2,284 jobs averaging $1965.

ATHLETIC AWARDS Total amount: $2,534,948 (35% need-based, 65% non-need-based).

APPLYING FOR FINANCIAL AID ***Required financial aid form:*** FAFSA. ***Financial aid deadline (priority):*** 2/15. ***Notification date:*** Continuous beginning 3/15.

CONTACT Mrs. Jennifer L. Penick, Director of Financial Aid, Wright State University, 3640 Colonel Glenn Highway, Dayton, OH 45435, 937-775-5721 or toll-free 800-247-1770. *Fax:* 937-775-5795. *E-mail:* jennifer.penick@wright.edu.

XAVIER UNIVERSITY

Cincinnati, OH

Tuition & fees: $29,970 **Average undergraduate aid package: $18,435**

ABOUT THE INSTITUTION Independent Roman Catholic, coed. 64 undergraduate majors. Federal methodology is used as a basis for awarding need-based institutional aid.

UNDERGRADUATE EXPENSES for 2010–11 ***One-time required fee:*** $190. ***Comprehensive fee:*** $39,870 includes full-time tuition ($29,300), mandatory fees ($670), and room and board ($9900). ***College room only:*** $5500. Full-time tuition and fees vary according to course load and program. Room and board charges vary according to board plan and housing facility. ***Part-time tuition:*** $575 per credit hour. Part-time tuition and fees vary according to course load, location, and program. ***Payment plans:*** Installment, deferred payment.

FRESHMAN FINANCIAL AID (Fall 2010, est.) 843 applied for aid; of those 78% were deemed to have need. 100% of freshmen with need received aid; of those 21% had need fully met. ***Average percent of need met:*** 70% (excluding resources awarded to replace EFC). ***Average financial aid package:*** $18,711 (excluding resources awarded to replace EFC). 34% of all full-time freshmen had no need and received non-need-based gift aid.

UNDERGRADUATE FINANCIAL AID (Fall 2010, est.) 2,767 applied for aid; of those 84% were deemed to have need. 99% of undergraduates with need received aid; of those 15% had need fully met. ***Average percent of need met:*** 69% (excluding resources awarded to replace EFC). ***Average financial aid package:*** $18,435 (excluding resources awarded to replace EFC). 31% of all full-time undergraduates had no need and received non-need-based gift aid.

GIFT AID (NEED-BASED) ***Total amount:*** $31,324,071 (14% federal, 2% state, 81% institutional, 3% external sources). ***Receiving aid:*** Freshmen: 62% (641); all full-time undergraduates: 57% (2,177). ***Average award:*** Freshmen: $14,479; Undergraduates: $13,747. ***Scholarships, grants, and awards:*** Federal Pell, FSEOG, state, private, college/university gift aid from institutional funds.

GIFT AID (NON-NEED-BASED) ***Total amount:*** $16,047,702 (93% institutional, 7% external sources). ***Receiving aid:*** Freshmen: 9% (92). Undergraduates: 7% (251). ***Average award:*** Freshmen: $11,955. Undergraduates: $11,130. ***Scholarships, grants, and awards by category:*** *Academic interests/achievement:* 4,100 awards ($33,264,040 total): foreign languages, general academic interests/achievements, mathematics, military science, physical sciences, social sciences. *Creative arts/performance:* 130 awards ($599,349 total): art/fine arts, music, performing arts, theater/drama. *Special characteristics:* 231 awards ($770,885 total): children and siblings of alumni, international students, members of minority groups, siblings of current students. ***Tuition waivers:*** Full or partial for employees or children of employees, senior citizens.

LOANS ***Student loans:*** $23,635,619 (71% need-based, 29% non-need-based). 72% of past graduating class borrowed through all loan programs. *Average indebtedness per student:* $25,881. ***Average need-based loan:*** Freshmen: $3549. Undergraduates: $4456. ***Parent loans:*** $7,737,757 (46% need-based, 54% non-need-based). ***Programs:*** Federal Direct (Subsidized and Unsubsidized Stafford, PLUS), Perkins.

WORK-STUDY ***Federal work-study:*** Total amount: $1,088,242; 516 jobs averaging $2200. ***State or other work-study/employment:*** 18 part-time jobs averaging $1940.

ATHLETIC AWARDS Total amount: $3,521,229 (37% need-based, 63% non-need-based).

APPLYING FOR FINANCIAL AID ***Required financial aid form:*** FAFSA. ***Financial aid deadline (priority):*** 2/15. ***Notification date:*** Continuous beginning 2/15. Students must reply by 5/1.

CONTACT Office of Financial Aid, Xavier University, 3800 Victory Parkway, Cincinnati, OH 45207-5411, 513-745-3142 or toll-free 800-344-4698. *Fax:* 513-745-2806.

XAVIER UNIVERSITY OF LOUISIANA

New Orleans, LA

Tuition & fees: $17,100 **Average undergraduate aid package: $17,144**

ABOUT THE INSTITUTION Independent Roman Catholic, coed. 49 undergraduate majors. Federal methodology is used as a basis for awarding need-based institutional aid.

UNDERGRADUATE EXPENSES for 2010–11 ***One-time required fee:*** $150. ***Comprehensive fee:*** $24,300 includes full-time tuition ($16,100), mandatory fees ($1000), and room and board ($7200). Room and board charges vary according to housing facility. ***Part-time tuition:*** $725 per semester hour. ***Part-time fees:*** $140 per semester hour. Part-time tuition and fees vary according to course load. ***Payment plan:*** Installment.

FRESHMAN FINANCIAL AID (Fall 2009) 735 applied for aid; of those 91% were deemed to have need. 100% of freshmen with need received aid; of those .4% had need fully met. ***Average percent of need met:*** 11% (excluding resources awarded to replace EFC). ***Average financial aid package:*** $16,230 (excluding resources awarded to replace EFC). 5% of all full-time freshmen had no need and received non-need-based gift aid.

UNDERGRADUATE FINANCIAL AID (Fall 2009) 2,417 applied for aid; of those 92% were deemed to have need. 100% of undergraduates with need received aid; of those 1% had need fully met. ***Average percent of need met:*** 13% (excluding resources awarded to replace EFC). ***Average financial aid package:*** $17,144 (excluding resources awarded to replace EFC). 3% of all full-time undergraduates had no need and received non-need-based gift aid.

GIFT AID (NEED-BASED) ***Total amount:*** $5,455,835 (83% federal, 7% state, 10% institutional). ***Receiving aid:*** Freshmen: 64% (490); all full-time undergraduates: 61% (1,568). ***Average award:*** Freshmen: $6099; Undergraduates: $6279. ***Scholarships, grants, and awards:*** Federal Pell, FSEOG, state, private, college/university gift aid from institutional funds, United Negro College Fund.

GIFT AID (NON-NEED-BASED) ***Total amount:*** $4,021,342 (1% federal, 23% state, 76% institutional). ***Receiving aid:*** Freshmen: 78% (595). Undergraduates: 64% (1,635). ***Average award:*** Freshmen: $7187. Undergraduates: $8461. ***Scholarships, grants, and awards by category:*** *Academic interests/achievement:* biological sciences, business, communication, computer science, education, engineering/technologies, English, foreign languages, general academic interests/achievements, humanities, mathematics, physical sciences, premedicine, religion/biblical studies, social sciences. ***Tuition waivers:*** Full or partial for employees or children of employees.

LOANS ***Student loans:*** $10,020,201 (90% need-based, 10% non-need-based). 78% of past graduating class borrowed through all loan programs. *Average indebtedness per student:* $45,916. ***Average need-based loan:*** Freshmen: $3832. Undergraduates: $4806. ***Parent loans:*** $2,655,158 (100% non-need-based). ***Programs:*** Federal Direct (Subsidized and Unsubsidized Stafford, PLUS), Perkins.

WORK-STUDY ***Federal work-study:*** Total amount: $198,284; 286 jobs averaging $973.

ATHLETIC AWARDS Total amount: $540,366 (100% non-need-based).

APPLYING FOR FINANCIAL AID ***Required financial aid form:*** FAFSA. ***Financial aid deadline (priority):*** 1/1. ***Notification date:*** Continuous beginning 4/1. Students must reply within 2 weeks of notification.

CONTACT Mrs. Mildred Higgins, Financial Aid Director, Xavier University of Louisiana, One Drexel Drive, New Orleans, LA 70125-1098, 504-520-7517 or toll-free 877-XAVIERU.

YALE UNIVERSITY

New Haven, CT

Tuition & fees: $38,300 **Average undergraduate aid package: $40,990**

ABOUT THE INSTITUTION Independent, coed. 66 undergraduate majors. Both federal and institutional methodology are used as a basis for awarding need-based institutional aid.

UNDERGRADUATE EXPENSES for 2010–11 ***Comprehensive fee:*** $49,800 includes full-time tuition ($38,300) and room and board ($11,500). ***College room only:*** $6300. Room and board charges vary according to board plan. ***Payment plan:*** Installment.

FRESHMAN FINANCIAL AID (Fall 2010, est.) 871 applied for aid; of those 92% were deemed to have need. 100% of freshmen with need received aid; of those 100% had need fully met. ***Average percent of need met:*** 100% (excluding resources awarded to replace EFC). ***Average financial aid package:*** $40,900 (excluding resources awarded to replace EFC).

UNDERGRADUATE FINANCIAL AID (Fall 2010, est.) 3,145 applied for aid; of those 96% were deemed to have need. 100% of undergraduates with need received aid; of those 100% had need fully met. ***Average percent of need met:*** 100% (excluding resources awarded to replace EFC). ***Average financial aid package:*** $40,990 (excluding resources awarded to replace EFC).

GIFT AID (NEED-BASED) ***Total amount:*** $116,730,736 (4% federal, 92% institutional, 4% external sources). ***Receiving aid:*** Freshmen: 60% (801); all full-time undergraduates: 57% (3,000). ***Average award:*** Freshmen: $39,303; Undergraduates: $38,914. ***Scholarships, grants, and awards:*** Federal Pell, FSEOG, state, private, college/university gift aid from institutional funds, United Negro College Fund, Federal Nursing.

GIFT AID (NON-NEED-BASED) ***Total amount:*** $616,499 (100% external sources).

LOANS ***Student loans:*** $2,432,964 (37% need-based, 63% non-need-based). 28% of past graduating class borrowed through all loan programs. *Average indebtedness per student:* $9254. ***Average need-based loan:*** Freshmen: $2154. Undergraduates: $2434. ***Parent loans:*** $2,348,939 (100% non-need-based). ***Programs:*** Federal Direct (Subsidized and Unsubsidized Stafford, PLUS), Perkins, state, college/university.

WORK-STUDY ***Federal work-study:*** Total amount: $1,471,187; 649 jobs averaging $2335. ***State or other work-study/employment:*** Total amount: $4,013,379 (100% need-based). 1,660 part-time jobs averaging $2486.

APPLYING FOR FINANCIAL AID ***Required financial aid forms:*** FAFSA, CSS Financial Aid PROFILE, noncustodial (divorced/separated) parent's statement, business/farm supplement, parents' federal income tax returns. ***Financial aid deadline:*** 3/1. ***Notification date:*** 4/1. Students must reply by 5/1 or within 1 week of notification.

CONTACT Mr. Caesar T. Storlazzi, Student Financial Services, Yale University, PO Box 208288, New Haven, CT 06520-8288, 203-432-0371. *Fax:* 203-777-6100. *E-mail:* sfs@yale.edu.

YESHIVA AND KOLEL BAIS MEDRASH ELYON

Monsey, NY

CONTACT Financial Aid Office, Yeshiva and Kolel Bais Medrash Elyon, 73 Main Street, Monsey, NY 10952, 845-356-7064.

YESHIVA AND KOLLEL HARBOTZAS TORAH

Brooklyn, NY

CONTACT Financial Aid Office, Yeshiva and Kollel Harbotzas Torah, 1049 East 15th Street, Brooklyn, NY 11230, 718-692-0208.

YESHIVA BETH MOSHE

Scranton, PA

CONTACT Financial Aid Office, Yeshiva Beth Moshe, 930 Hickory Street, Scranton, PA 18505-2124, 717-346-1747.

YESHIVA COLLEGE OF THE NATION'S CAPITAL

Silver Spring, MD

CONTACT Financial Aid Office, Yeshiva College of the Nation's Capital, 1216 Arcola Avenue, Silver Spring, MD 20902, 301-593-2534.

YESHIVA DERECH CHAIM

Brooklyn, NY

CONTACT Financial Aid Office, Yeshiva Derech Chaim, 1573 39th Street, Brooklyn, NY 11218, 718-438-5426.

YESHIVA D'MONSEY RABBINICAL COLLEGE

Monsey, NY

CONTACT Financial Aid Office, Yeshiva D'Monsey Rabbinical College, 2 Roman Boulevard, Monsey, NY 10952, 914-352-5852.

YESHIVA GEDOLAH IMREI YOSEF D'SPINKA

Brooklyn, NY

CONTACT Financial Aid Office, Yeshiva Gedolah Imrei Yosef D'Spinka, 1466 56th Street, Brooklyn, NY 11219, 718-851-8721.

YESHIVA GEDOLAH OF GREATER DETROIT

Oak Park, MI

CONTACT Rabbi P. Rushnawitz, Executive Administrator, Yeshiva Gedolah of Greater Detroit, 24600 Greenfield Road, Oak Park, MI 48237-1544, 810-968-3360. *Fax:* 810-968-8613.

YESHIVA GEDOLAH RABBINICAL COLLEGE

Miami Beach, FL

CONTACT Financial Aid Office, Yeshiva Gedolah Rabbinical College, 1140 Alton Road, Miami Beach, FL 33139, 305-673-5664.

YESHIVA KARLIN STOLIN RABBINICAL INSTITUTE

Brooklyn, NY

CONTACT Mr. Daniel Ross, Financial Aid Administrator, Yeshiva Karlin Stolin Rabbinical Institute, 1818 Fifty-fourth Street, Brooklyn, NY 11204, 718-232-7800 Ext. 116. *Fax:* 718-331-4833.

YESHIVA OF NITRA RABBINICAL COLLEGE

Mount Kisco, NY

CONTACT Mr. Yosef Rosen, Financial Aid Administrator, Yeshiva of Nitra Rabbinical College, 194 Division Avenue, Mount Kisco, NY 10549, 718-384-5460. *Fax:* 718-387-9400.

YESHIVA OF THE TELSHE ALUMNI

Riverdale, NY

CONTACT Financial Aid Office, Yeshiva of the Telshe Alumni, 4904 Independence Avenue, Riverdale, NY 10471, 718-601-3523.

YESHIVA OHR ELCHONON CHABAD/WEST COAST TALMUDICAL SEMINARY

Los Angeles, CA

CONTACT Ms. Hendy Tauber, Director of Financial Aid, Yeshiva Ohr Elchonon Chabad/West Coast Talmudical Seminary, 7215 Waring Avenue, Los Angeles, CA 90046-7660, 213-937-3763. *Fax:* 213-937-9456.

YESHIVA SHAAREI TORAH OF ROCKLAND

Suffern, NY

CONTACT Financial Aid Office, Yeshiva Shaarei Torah of Rockland, 91 West Carlton Road, Suffern, NY 10901, 845-352-3431.

YESHIVA SHAAR HATORAH TALMUDIC RESEARCH INSTITUTE

Kew Gardens, NY

CONTACT Mr. Yoel Yankelewitz, Executive Director, Financial Aid, Yeshiva Shaar Hatorah Talmudic Research Institute, 117-06 84th Avenue, Kew Gardens, NY 11418-1469, 718-846-1940.

YESHIVAS NOVOMINSK

Brooklyn, NY

CONTACT Financial Aid Office, Yeshivas Novominsk, 1569 47th Street, Brooklyn, NY 11219, 718-438-2727.

YESHIVATH VIZNITZ

Monsey, NY

CONTACT Financial Aid Office, Yeshivath Viznitz, Phyllis Terrace, PO Box 446, Monsey, NY 10952, 914-356-1010.

YESHIVATH ZICHRON MOSHE

South Fallsburg, NY

CONTACT Ms. Miryom R. Miller, Director of Financial Aid, Yeshivath Zichron Moshe, Laurel Park Road, South Fallsburg, NY 12779, 914-434-5240. *Fax:* 914-434-1009. *E-mail:* lehus@aol.com.

YESHIVAT MIKDASH MELECH

Brooklyn, NY

CONTACT Financial Aid Office, Yeshivat Mikdash Melech, 1326 Ocean Parkway, Brooklyn, NY 11230-5601, 718-339-1090.

YESHIVA TORAS CHAIM TALMUDICAL SEMINARY

Denver, CO

CONTACT Office of Financial Aid, Yeshiva Toras Chaim Talmudical Seminary, 1400 Quitman Street, Denver, CO 80204-1415, 303-629-8200.

YESHIVA UNIVERSITY

New York, NY

Tuition & fees: $32,094 | **Average undergraduate aid package: $27,434**

ABOUT THE INSTITUTION Independent, coed. 21 undergraduate majors. Both federal and institutional methodology are used as a basis for awarding need-based institutional aid.

UNDERGRADUATE EXPENSES for 2010–11 ***Comprehensive fee:*** $42,474 includes full-time tuition ($31,594), mandatory fees ($500), and room and board ($10,380). ***College room only:*** $7510. Full-time tuition and fees vary according to student level. ***Part-time tuition:*** $1075 per credit. ***Payment plan:*** Installment.

FRESHMAN FINANCIAL AID (Fall 2009) 543 applied for aid; of those 82% were deemed to have need. 100% of freshmen with need received aid; of those 26% had need fully met. ***Average percent of need met:*** 88% (excluding resources awarded to replace EFC). ***Average financial aid package:*** $28,296 (excluding resources awarded to replace EFC). 16% of all full-time freshmen had no need and received non-need-based gift aid.

UNDERGRADUATE FINANCIAL AID (Fall 2009) 1,832 applied for aid; of those 82% were deemed to have need. 95% of undergraduates with need received aid; of those 23% had need fully met. ***Average percent of need met:*** 86% (excluding resources awarded to replace EFC). ***Average financial aid package:*** $27,434 (excluding resources awarded to replace EFC). 11% of all full-time undergraduates had no need and received non-need-based gift aid.

GIFT AID (NEED-BASED) ***Total amount:*** $29,410,836 (6% federal, 3% state, 91% institutional). ***Receiving aid:*** Freshmen: 53% (431); all full-time undergraduates: 45% (1,298). ***Average award:*** Freshmen: $21,719; Undergraduates: $20,988. ***Scholarships, grants, and awards:*** Federal Pell, FSEOG, state, college/university gift aid from institutional funds.

GIFT AID (NON-NEED-BASED) ***Total amount:*** $8,736,000 (1% state, 99% institutional). ***Receiving aid:*** Freshmen: 25% (200). Undergraduates: 10% (272). ***Average award:*** Freshmen: $17,837. Undergraduates: $18,543. ***Scholarships, grants, and awards by category:*** *Academic interests/achievement:* general academic interests/achievements. ***Tuition waivers:*** Full or partial for employees or children of employees.

LOANS ***Student loans:*** $7,617,435 (93% need-based, 7% non-need-based). 47% of past graduating class borrowed through all loan programs. *Average indebtedness per student:* $21,654. ***Average need-based loan:*** Freshmen: $5282. Undergraduates: $6136. ***Parent loans:*** $2,711,518 (69% need-based, 31% non-need-based). ***Programs:*** Federal Direct (Subsidized and Unsubsidized Stafford, PLUS), Perkins, college/university.

WORK-STUDY ***Federal work-study:*** Total amount: $461,576; jobs available. ***State or other work-study/employment:*** Part-time jobs available.

APPLYING FOR FINANCIAL AID ***Required financial aid form:*** FAFSA. ***Financial aid deadline (priority):*** 2/1. ***Notification date:*** Continuous beginning 3/15.

CONTACT Marianela Cabral, Director of Student Aid Operations, Yeshiva University, 500 West 185th Street, Room 121, New York, NY 10033, 212-960-5399. *Fax:* 212-960-0037. *E-mail:* mcabral@yu.edu.

YORK COLLEGE

York, NE

Tuition & fees: $14,998 | **Average undergraduate aid package: $13,790**

ABOUT THE INSTITUTION Independent religious, coed. 38 undergraduate majors. Institutional methodology is used as a basis for awarding need-based institutional aid.

UNDERGRADUATE EXPENSES for 2010–11 ***Comprehensive fee:*** $20,678 includes full-time tuition ($13,198), mandatory fees ($1800), and room and board ($5680). Full-time tuition and fees vary according to course load. Room and board charges vary according to board plan and housing facility. ***Part-time tuition:*** $460 per credit hour. ***Part-time fees:*** $220 per credit hour. Part-time tuition and fees vary according to course load. ***Payment plan:*** Installment.

FRESHMAN FINANCIAL AID (Fall 2010, est.) 123 applied for aid; of those 88% were deemed to have need. 100% of freshmen with need received aid; of those 16% had need fully met. ***Average percent of need met:*** 69% (excluding resources awarded to replace EFC). ***Average financial aid package:*** $13,434 (excluding resources awarded to replace EFC). 12% of all full-time freshmen had no need and received non-need-based gift aid.

UNDERGRADUATE FINANCIAL AID (Fall 2010, est.) 443 applied for aid; of those 95% were deemed to have need. 97% of undergraduates with need received aid; of those 12% had need fully met. ***Average percent of need met:*** 72% (excluding resources awarded to replace EFC). ***Average financial aid package:*** $13,790 (excluding resources awarded to replace EFC). 7% of all full-time undergraduates had no need and received non-need-based gift aid.

GIFT AID (NEED-BASED) ***Total amount:*** $2,556,452 (45% federal, 2% state, 48% institutional, 5% external sources). ***Receiving aid:*** Freshmen: 84% (108); all full-time undergraduates: 87% (407). ***Average award:*** Freshmen: $9576; Undergraduates: $9466. ***Scholarships, grants, and awards:*** Federal Pell, FSEOG, state, private, college/university gift aid from institutional funds.

GIFT AID (NON-NEED-BASED) ***Total amount:*** $441,987 (91% institutional, 9% external sources). ***Receiving aid:*** Freshmen: 9% (12). Undergraduates: 9% (41). ***Average award:*** Freshmen: $3700. Undergraduates: $3790. ***Scholar-***

ships, grants, and awards by category: Academic interests/achievement: 265 awards ($705,382 total): biological sciences, business, communication, computer science, education, English, general academic interests/achievements, mathematics, premedicine, religion/biblical studies. *Creative arts/performance:* 75 awards ($177,708 total): music, theater/drama. *Special achievements/activities:* 139 awards ($97,000 total): leadership. *Special characteristics:* 37 awards ($162,734 total): children of faculty/staff, previous college experience, siblings of current students. ***Tuition waivers:*** Full or partial for employees or children of employees.

LOANS ***Student loans:*** $3,176,941 (53% need-based, 47% non-need-based). 80% of past graduating class borrowed through all loan programs. *Average indebtedness per student:* $26,679. ***Average need-based loan:*** Freshmen: $4015. Undergraduates: $4445. ***Parent loans:*** $414,965 (100% need-based). ***Programs:*** Federal Direct (Subsidized and Unsubsidized Stafford, PLUS), Perkins, college/university, alternative loans.

WORK-STUDY ***Federal work-study:*** Total amount: $789,774; 78 jobs averaging $1160. ***State or other work-study/employment:*** Total amount: $192,849 (100% non-need-based). 138 part-time jobs averaging $1316.

ATHLETIC AWARDS Total amount: $1,482,050 (71% need-based, 29% non-need-based).

APPLYING FOR FINANCIAL AID ***Required financial aid form:*** FAFSA. ***Financial aid deadline (priority):*** 6/15. ***Notification date:*** Continuous. Students must reply within 4 weeks of notification.

CONTACT Brien Alley, Director of Financial Aid, York College, 1125 East 8th Street, York, NE 68467, 402-363-5624 or toll-free 800-950-9675. *Fax:* 402-363-5623. *E-mail:* balley@york.edu.

YORK COLLEGE OF PENNSYLVANIA

York, PA

Tuition & fees: $15,880 **Average undergraduate aid package: $11,189**

ABOUT THE INSTITUTION Independent, coed. 56 undergraduate majors. Federal methodology is used as a basis for awarding need-based institutional aid.

UNDERGRADUATE EXPENSES for 2011–12 ***Comprehensive fee:*** $24,800 includes full-time tuition ($14,320), mandatory fees ($1560), and room and board ($8920). ***College room only:*** $4990. Full-time tuition and fees vary according to program. Room and board charges vary according to housing facility. ***Part-time tuition:*** $445 per credit. ***Part-time fees:*** $340 per term. ***Payment plans:*** Tuition prepayment, installment.

FRESHMAN FINANCIAL AID (Fall 2010, est.) 1,133 applied for aid; of those 74% were deemed to have need. 100% of freshmen with need received aid; of those 26% had need fully met. ***Average percent of need met:*** 69% (excluding resources awarded to replace EFC). ***Average financial aid package:*** $11,149 (excluding resources awarded to replace EFC). 31% of all full-time freshmen had no need and received non-need-based gift aid.

UNDERGRADUATE FINANCIAL AID (Fall 2010, est.) 3,839 applied for aid; of those 79% were deemed to have need. 98% of undergraduates with need received aid; of those 23% had need fully met. ***Average percent of need met:*** 66% (excluding resources awarded to replace EFC). ***Average financial aid package:*** $11,189 (excluding resources awarded to replace EFC). 15% of all full-time undergraduates had no need and received non-need-based gift aid.

GIFT AID (NEED-BASED) ***Total amount:*** $16,614,112 (34% federal, 15% state, 48% institutional, 3% external sources). ***Receiving aid:*** Freshmen: 49% (605); all full-time undergraduates: 47% (2,165). ***Average award:*** Freshmen: $4822; Undergraduates: $5189. ***Scholarships, grants, and awards:*** Federal Pell, FSEOG, state, private, college/university gift aid from institutional funds.

GIFT AID (NON-NEED-BASED) ***Total amount:*** $2,517,922 (1% state, 91% institutional, 8% external sources). ***Receiving aid:*** Freshmen: 68% (832). Undergraduates: 30% (1,386). ***Average award:*** Freshmen: $3281. Undergraduates: $3618. ***Scholarships, grants, and awards by category:*** *Academic interests/achievement:* 2,666 awards ($13,108,224 total): engineering/technologies, general academic interests/achievements. *Creative arts/performance:* 22 awards ($24,105 total): music. *Special characteristics:* 31 awards ($59,270 total): children and siblings of alumni, children of union members/company employees, international students, members of minority groups. ***Tuition waivers:*** Full or partial for employees or children of employees.

LOANS ***Student loans:*** $24,925,691 (46% need-based, 54% non-need-based). 79% of past graduating class borrowed through all loan programs. *Average indebtedness per student:* $28,851. ***Average need-based loan:*** Freshmen: $5167. Undergraduates: $6287. ***Parent loans:*** $5,889,738 (76% need-based, 24% non-need-based). ***Programs:*** Federal Direct (Subsidized and Unsubsidized Stafford, PLUS), Perkins, Federal Nursing, college/university.

WORK-STUDY ***Federal work-study:*** Total amount: $549,280; 293 jobs averaging $1962. ***State or other work-study/employment:*** Total amount: $31,401 (100% non-need-based). 18 part-time jobs averaging $1688.

APPLYING FOR FINANCIAL AID ***Required financial aid form:*** FAFSA. ***Financial aid deadline (priority):*** 3/1. ***Notification date:*** Continuous beginning 3/1. Students must reply within 4 weeks of notification.

CONTACT Calvin Williams, Director of Financial Aid, York College of Pennsylvania, Country Club Road, York, PA 17405-7199, 717-849-1682 or toll-free 800-455-8018. *Fax:* 717-849-1685. *E-mail:* financialaid@ycp.edu.

YORK COLLEGE OF THE CITY UNIVERSITY OF NEW YORK

Jamaica, NY

CONTACT Ms. Cathy Tsiapanos, Director of Student Financial Services, York College of the City University of New York, 94-20 Guy R. Brewer Boulevard, Jamaica, NY 11451-0001, 718-262-2238. *E-mail:* ctsia@york.cuny.edu.

YORKTOWN UNIVERSITY

Denver, CO

CONTACT Financial Aid Office, Yorktown University, 4340 East Kentucky Avenue, Suite 457, Denver, CO 80246, 877-757-0059.

YOUNG HARRIS COLLEGE

Young Harris, GA

Tuition & fees: $21,970 **Average undergraduate aid package: $15,202**

ABOUT THE INSTITUTION Independent United Methodist, coed. 61 undergraduate majors. Federal methodology is used as a basis for awarding need-based institutional aid.

UNDERGRADUATE EXPENSES for 2011–12 ***Comprehensive fee:*** $29,450 includes full-time tuition ($21,500), mandatory fees ($470), and room and board ($7480). Full-time tuition and fees vary according to course load. Room and board charges vary according to housing facility. ***Part-time tuition:*** $650 per credit hour. Part-time tuition and fees vary according to course load. ***Payment plan:*** Installment.

FRESHMAN FINANCIAL AID (Fall 2009) 318 applied for aid; of those 83% were deemed to have need. 100% of freshmen with need received aid; of those 23% had need fully met. ***Average percent of need met:*** 80% (excluding resources awarded to replace EFC). ***Average financial aid package:*** $15,430 (excluding resources awarded to replace EFC). 28% of all full-time freshmen had no need and received non-need-based gift aid.

UNDERGRADUATE FINANCIAL AID (Fall 2009) 592 applied for aid; of those 83% were deemed to have need. 100% of undergraduates with need received aid; of those 23% had need fully met. ***Average percent of need met:*** 79% (excluding resources awarded to replace EFC). ***Average financial aid package:*** $15,202 (excluding resources awarded to replace EFC). 29% of all full-time undergraduates had no need and received non-need-based gift aid.

GIFT AID (NEED-BASED) ***Total amount:*** $6,111,225 (20% federal, 16% state, 63% institutional, 1% external sources). ***Receiving aid:*** Freshmen: 66% (260); all full-time undergraduates: 67% (487). ***Average award:*** Freshmen: $13,677; Undergraduates: $13,075. ***Scholarships, grants, and awards:*** Federal Pell, FSEOG, state, private, college/university gift aid from institutional funds.

GIFT AID (NON-NEED-BASED) ***Total amount:*** $3,147,512 (27% state, 71% institutional, 2% external sources). ***Receiving aid:*** Freshmen: 15% (59). Undergraduates: 14% (100). ***Average award:*** Freshmen: $11,149. Undergraduates: $10,554. ***Scholarships, grants, and awards by category:*** *Creative arts/performance:* art/fine arts, music, performing arts, theater/drama. *Special characteristics:* children of faculty/staff. ***Tuition waivers:*** Full or partial for employees or children of employees.

LOANS ***Student loans:*** $2,561,516 (63% need-based, 37% non-need-based). ***Average need-based loan:*** Freshmen: $2758. Undergraduates: $3003. ***Parent loans:*** $637,997 (23% need-based, 77% non-need-based). ***Programs:*** Federal Direct (Subsidized and Unsubsidized Stafford, PLUS), college/university.

WORK-STUDY ***Federal work-study:*** Total amount: $28,595; jobs available. ***State or other work-study/employment:*** Total amount: $157,431 (36% need-based, 64% non-need-based). Part-time jobs available.

ATHLETIC AWARDS Total amount: $550,238 (49% need-based, 51% non-need-based).

APPLYING FOR FINANCIAL AID ***Required financial aid forms:*** FAFSA, state aid form. ***Financial aid deadline (priority):*** 5/1. ***Notification date:*** Continuous. Students must reply within 2 weeks of notification.

CONTACT Linda Adams, Financial Aid Director, Young Harris College, 1 College Street, Young Harris, GA 30582, 706-379-5188 or toll-free 800-241-3754 (in-state). *Fax:* 706-379-4594. *E-mail:* leadams@yhc.edu.

YOUNGSTOWN STATE UNIVERSITY

Youngstown, OH

Tuition & fees (OH res): $7199 Average undergraduate aid package: $8216

ABOUT THE INSTITUTION State-supported, coed. 125 undergraduate majors. Federal methodology is used as a basis for awarding need-based institutional aid.

UNDERGRADUATE EXPENSES for 2010–11 ***Tuition, state resident:*** full-time $6970; part-time $290 per credit. ***Tuition, nonresident:*** full-time $12,643; part-time $527 per credit. ***Required fees:*** full-time $229; $10 per credit. Full-time tuition and fees vary according to course load. Part-time tuition and fees vary according to course load. ***College room and board:*** $7600. Room and board charges vary according to board plan and housing facility. ***Payment plan:*** Installment.

FRESHMAN FINANCIAL AID (Fall 2009) 2,338 applied for aid; of those 89% were deemed to have need. 100% of freshmen with need received aid; of those 7% had need fully met. ***Average percent of need met:*** 31% (excluding resources awarded to replace EFC). ***Average financial aid package:*** $7890 (excluding resources awarded to replace EFC). 6% of all full-time freshmen had no need and received non-need-based gift aid.

UNDERGRADUATE FINANCIAL AID (Fall 2009) 10,858 applied for aid; of those 89% were deemed to have need. 100% of undergraduates with need received aid; of those 5% had need fully met. ***Average percent of need met:*** 29% (excluding resources awarded to replace EFC). ***Average financial aid package:*** $8216 (excluding resources awarded to replace EFC). 6% of all full-time undergraduates had no need and received non-need-based gift aid.

GIFT AID (NEED-BASED) ***Total amount:*** $45,128,147 (78% federal, 13% state, 2% institutional, 7% external sources). ***Receiving aid:*** Freshmen: 64% (1,645); all full-time undergraduates: 55% (7,169). ***Average award:*** Freshmen: $5318; Undergraduates: $5429. ***Scholarships, grants, and awards:*** Federal Pell, FSEOG, state, private, college/university gift aid from institutional funds.

GIFT AID (NON-NEED-BASED) ***Total amount:*** $8,362,076 (2% federal, 23% state, 18% institutional, 57% external sources). ***Receiving aid:*** Freshmen: 23% (579). Undergraduates: 19% (2,479). ***Average award:*** Freshmen: $3241. Undergraduates: $2588. ***Scholarships, grants, and awards by category:*** *Academic interests/achievement:* biological sciences, business, communication, computer science, education, engineering/technologies, English, foreign languages, general academic interests/achievements, health fields, humanities, mathematics, military science, physical sciences, premedicine, religion/biblical studies, social sciences. *Creative arts/performance:* art/fine arts, creative writing, journalism/publications, music, performing arts, theater/drama. *Special achievements/activities:* cheerleading/drum major, community service, leadership, memberships, religious involvement. *Special characteristics:* adult students, children and siblings of alumni, children of faculty/staff, children of union members/company employees, children of workers in trades, children with a deceased or disabled parent, ethnic background, handicapped students, international students, local/state students, members of minority groups, out-of-state students, public servants, religious affiliation, spouses of deceased or disabled public servants, veterans, veterans' children. ***Tuition waivers:*** Full or partial for employees or children of employees, senior citizens.

LOANS ***Student loans:*** $91,613,261 (41% need-based, 59% non-need-based). ***Average need-based loan:*** Freshmen: $3130. Undergraduates: $3734. ***Parent loans:*** $41,592,405 (100% non-need-based). ***Programs:*** Federal Direct (Subsidized and Unsubsidized Stafford, PLUS), Perkins, Charles E. Schell Foundation loans, George W. Wright Student Aid Loans, Rogers Student Loans.

WORK-STUDY ***Federal work-study:*** Total amount: $1,217,463; jobs available. ***State or other work-study/employment:*** Total amount: $4,470,540 (100% non-need-based). Part-time jobs available.

ATHLETIC AWARDS Total amount: $3,644,097 (100% non-need-based).

APPLYING FOR FINANCIAL AID ***Required financial aid forms:*** FAFSA, institution's own form. ***Financial aid deadline (priority):*** 2/15. ***Notification date:*** Continuous beginning 5/1. Students must reply within 4 weeks of notification.

CONTACT Ms. Beth Bartlett, Administrative Assistant II, Youngstown State University, One University Plaza, Youngstown, OH 44555, 330-941-3504 or toll-free 877-468-6978. *Fax:* 330-941-1659. *E-mail:* babartlett@ysu.edu.

ZION BIBLE COLLEGE

Haverhill, MA

CONTACT Financial Aid Office, Zion Bible College, 320 South Main Street, Haverhill, MA 01835, 978-478-3400 or toll-free 800-356-4014.

Appendix

State Scholarship and Grant Programs

Each state government has established one or more state-administered financial aid programs for qualified students. In many instances, these state programs are restricted to legal residents of the state. However, they often are available to out-of-state students who will be or are attending colleges or universities within the state. In addition to residential status, other qualifications frequently exist.

Gift aid and forgivable loan programs open to undergraduate students for all states and the District of Columbia are described on the following pages. They are arranged in alphabetical order, first by state name, then by program name. The annotation for each program provides information about the program, eligibility, and the contact addresses for applications or further information. Unless otherwise stated, this information refers to awards for 2010–11. Information is provided by the state-sponsoring agency in response to *Peterson's Annual Survey of Non-institutional Aid*, which was conducted between January 2011 and April 2011. Information is accurate when Peterson's receives it. However, it is always advisable to check with the sponsor to ascertain that the information remains correct.

You should write to the address given for each program to request that award details for 2011–12 be sent to you as soon as they are available. Descriptive information, brochures, and application forms for state scholarship programs are usually available from the financial aid offices of public colleges or universities within the specific state. High school guidance offices often have information and relevant forms for awards for which high school seniors may be eligible. Increasingly, state government agencies are putting state scholarship information on state government agency Web sites. In searching state government Web sites, however, you should be aware that the higher education agency in many states is separate from the state's general education office, which is often responsible only for elementary and secondary education. Also, the page at public university Web sites that provides information about student financial aid frequently has a list of state-sponsored scholarships and financial aid programs.

Names of scholarship programs are frequently used inconsistently or become abbreviated in popular usage. Many programs have variant names by which they are known. The program's sponsor has approved the title of the program that Peterson's uses in this guide, yet this name may differ from the program's official name or from its most commonly used name.

In addition to the grant aid and forgivable loan programs listed on the following pages, states may also offer internship or work-study programs, graduate fellowships and grants, or low-interest loans. If you are interested in learning more about these other kinds of programs, the state education office that supplies information or applications for the undergraduate scholarship programs listed here should be able to provide information about other kinds of higher education financial aid programs that are sponsored by the state.

ALABAMA

Air Force ROTC College Scholarship. Scholarship program provides three- and four-year scholarships in three different types to high school seniors. All scholarship cadets receive a nontaxable monthly allowance (stipend) during the academic year. For more details refer to web site http://www.afrotc.com/scholarships/hsschol/types.php. *Award:* Scholarship for use in freshman, sophomore, junior, or senior year; renewable. *Award amount:* $9000–$15,000. *Number of awards:* 2000–4000. *Eligibility Requirements:* Applicant must be age 17-30 and enrolled or expecting to enroll full-time at a two-year or four-year institution or university. Applicant must have 3.0 GPA or higher. Available to U.S. citizens. Applicant or parent must meet one or more of the following requirements: Air Force experience; retired from active duty; disabled or killed as a result of military service; prisoner of war; or missing in action. *Application Requirements:* Application, interview, test scores, transcript. **Deadline:** December 1.

Contact Ty Christian, Chief Air Force ROTC Advertising Manager, Air Force Reserve Officer Training Corps, 551 East Maxwell Boulevard, Maxwell Air Force Base, AL 36112-6106. *E-mail:* ty.christian@maxwell.af.mil. *Phone:* 334-953-2278. *Fax:* 334-953-4384. *Web site:* http://www.afrotc.com/.

Alabama G.I. Dependents Scholarship Program. Full scholarship for dependents of Alabama disabled, prisoner of war, or missing-in-action veterans. Child or stepchild must initiate training before 26th birthday; age 30 deadline may apply in certain situations. No age deadline for spouses or widows. *Award:* Scholarship for use in freshman, sophomore, junior, or senior year; renewable. *Award amount:* varies. *Number of awards:* varies. *Eligibility Requirements:* Applicant must be age 30 or under; enrolled or expecting to enroll full- or part-time at a four-year institution or university; resident of Alabama and studying in Alabama. Available to U.S. and non-U.S. citizens. Applicant or parent must meet one or more of the following requirements: general military experience; retired from active duty; disabled or killed as a result of military service; prisoner of war; or missing in action. *Application Requirements:* Application. **Deadline:** varies.

Contact Willie E. Moore, Scholarship Administrator, Alabama Department of Veterans Affairs, PO Box 1509, Montgomery, AL 36102-1509. *E-mail:* wmoore@va.state.al.us. *Phone:* 334-242-5077. *Fax:* 334-242-5102. *Web site:* http://www.va.alabama.gov/.

Alabama National Guard Educational Assistance Program. Renewable award aids Alabama residents who are members of the Alabama National Guard and are enrolled in an accredited college in Alabama. Forms must be signed by a representative of the Alabama Military Department and financial aid officer. Recipient must be in a degree-seeking program. *Award:* Scholarship for use in freshman, sophomore, junior, senior, or graduate year; renewable. *Award amount:* $25–$1000. *Number of awards:* up to 575. *Eligibility Requirements:* Applicant must be age 17 and over; enrolled or expecting to enroll full- or part-time at a two-year, four-year, or technical institution or university; resident of Alabama and studying in Alabama. Available to U.S. citizens. Applicant must have served in the Air Force National Guard or Army National Guard. *Application Requirements:* Application. **Deadline:** continuous.

Contact Cheryl Newton, Grants Coordinator, Alabama Commission on Higher Education, 100 North Union Street, PO Box 302000, Montgomery, AL 36130-2000. *E-mail:* cheryl.newton@ache.alabama.gov. *Phone:* 334-242-2273. *Web site:* http://www.ache.alabama.gov/.

Alabama Student Assistance Program. Scholarship award of $300 to $5000 per academic year given to undergraduate students residing in the state of Alabama and attending a college or university in Alabama. *Award:* Grant for use in freshman, sophomore, junior, or senior year; not renewable. *Award amount:* $300–$5000. *Number of awards:* varies. *Eligibility Requirements:* Applicant must be enrolled or expecting to enroll full- or part-time at a two-year, four-year, or technical institution or university; resident of Alabama and studying in Alabama. Available to U.S. citizens. *Application Requirements:* Application. **Deadline:** continuous.

Contact Cheryl Newton, Grants Coordinator, Alabama Commission on Higher Education, 100 North Union Street, PO Box 302000, Montgomery, AL 36130-2000. *E-mail:* cheryl.newton@ache.alabama.gov. *Phone:* 334-242-2273. *Web site:* http://www.ache.alabama.gov/.

Alabama Student Grant Program. Nonrenewable awards available to Alabama residents for undergraduate study at certain independent colleges within the state. Both full and half-time students are eligible. Deadlines: September 15, January 15, and February 15. *Award:* Grant for use in freshman, sophomore, junior, or senior year; not renewable. *Award amount:* up to $1200. *Number of awards:* up to 1200. *Eligibility Requirements:* Applicant must be enrolled or expecting to enroll full- or part-time at a four-year institution or university; resident of Alabama and studying in Alabama. Available to U.S. citizens. *Application Requirements:* Application.

Contact Cheryl Newton, Grants Coordinator, Alabama Commission on Higher Education, 100 North Union Street, PO Box 302000, Montgomery, AL 36130-2000. *E-mail:* cheryl.newton@ache.alabama.gov. *Phone:* 334-242-2273. *Web site:* http://www.ache.alabama.gov/.

Police Officers and Firefighters Survivors Education Assistance Program-Alabama. Provides tuition, fees, books, and supplies to dependents of full-time police officers and firefighters killed in the line of duty. Must attend any Alabama public college as an undergraduate. Must be Alabama resident. *Award:* Scholarship for use in freshman, sophomore, junior, or senior year; renewable. *Award amount:* $2000–$5000. *Number of awards:* 15–30. *Eligibility Requirements:* Applicant must be age 21 or under; enrolled or expecting to enroll full- or part-time at a two-year, four-year, or technical institution or university; single; resident of Alabama and studying in Alabama. Available to U.S. citizens. *Application Requirements:* Application, transcript, birth certificate, marriage license, death certificate, letter from medical doctor. **Deadline:** continuous.

Contact Cheryl Newton, Grants Coordinator, Alabama Commission on Higher Education, 100 North Union Street, PO Box 302000, Montgomery, AL 36130-2000. *E-mail:* cheryl.newton@ache.alabama.gov. *Phone:* 334-242-2273. *Web site:* http://www.ache.alabama.gov/.

ALASKA

GEAR UP Alaska Scholarship. Scholarship provides up to $7000 each year for up to four years of undergraduate study (up to $3500 each year for half-time study) for students who participated in the GEAR UP Programs in 6th, 7th, and 8th grade and have met the academic milestones established by their district. Must reapply each year and application must be signed by GEAR UP program director. Must be an Alaska high school senior or have an Alaska diploma or GED. Must submit FAFSA and have financial need. Must be under age 22. *Award:* Scholarship for use in freshman, sophomore, junior, or senior year; not renewable. *Award amount:* $3500–$7000. *Number of awards:* varies. *Eligibility Requirements:* Applicant must be age 22 or under; enrolled or expecting to enroll full- or part-time at a two-year or four-year institution or university and resident of Alaska. Available to U.S. citizens. *Application Requirements:* Application, financial need analysis, references, transcript, FAFSA, Student Aid Report (SAR). **Deadline:** May 31.

Contact Adam Weed, Special Projects Coordinator, Alaska State Department of Education, 801 West 10th Street, Suite 200, PO Box 110500, Juneau, AK 99811-0500. *E-mail:* adam.weed@alaska.gov. *Phone:* 907-465-6685. *Web site:* http://www.eed.state.ak.us/.

ARIZONA

Arizona Private Postsecondary Education Student Financial Assistance Program. Provides grants to financially needy Arizona Community College graduates, to attend a private postsecondary baccalaureate degree-granting institution. *Award:* Forgivable loan for use in junior or senior year; renewable. *Award amount:* \$1000–\$2000. *Number of awards:* varies. *Eligibility Requirements:* Applicant must be enrolled or expecting to enroll full-time at a four-year institution or university; resident of Arizona and studying in Arizona. Applicant must have 2.5 GPA or higher. Available to U.S. citizens. *Application Requirements:* Application, financial need analysis, transcript, promissory note. **Deadline:** June 30.

Contact Mila Zaporteza, Business Manager, Arizona Commission for Postsecondary Education, 2020 North Central Avenue, Suite 650, Phoenix, AZ 85004-4503. *E-mail:* mila@azhighered.gov. *Phone:* 602-258-2435 Ext. 102. *Fax:* 602-258-2483. *Web site:* http://www.azhighered.gov/.

Leveraging Educational Assistance Partnership. Grants to financially needy students, who enroll in and attend postsecondary education or training in Arizona schools. Program was formerly known as the State Student Incentive Grant or SSIG Program. *Award:* Grant for use in freshman, sophomore, junior, senior, or graduate year; not renewable. *Award amount:* \$100–\$2500. *Number of awards:* varies. *Eligibility Requirements:* Applicant must be enrolled or expecting to enroll full- or part-time at a two-year, four-year, or technical institution or university; resident of Arizona and studying in Arizona. Available to U.S. citizens. *Application Requirements:* Application, financial need analysis, transcript. **Deadline:** April 30.

Contact Mila A. Zaporteza, Business Manager and LEAP Financial Aid Manager, Arizona Commission for Postsecondary Education, 2020 North Central Avenue, Suite 650, Phoenix, AZ 85004-4503. *E-mail:* mila@azhighered.gov. *Phone:* 602-258-2435 Ext. 102. *Fax:* 602-258-2483. *Web site:* http://www.azhighered.gov/.

Postsecondary Education Grant Program. Awards of up to \$2000 to Arizona residents studying in Arizona. May be renewed annually for a maximum of four calendar years. Minimum 2.5 GPA required. Deadline June 30. *Award:* Forgivable loan for use in freshman, sophomore, junior, or senior year; renewable. *Award amount:* \$1000–\$2000. *Number of awards:* varies. *Eligibility Requirements:* Applicant must be enrolled or expecting to enroll full- or part-time at a four-year institution or university; resident of Arizona and studying in Arizona. Applicant must have 2.5 GPA or higher. Available to U.S. citizens. *Application Requirements:* Application, transcript, promissory note. **Deadline:** June 30.

Contact Dr. April L. Osborn, Executive Director, Arizona Commission for Postsecondary Education, 2020 North Central Avenue, Suite 650, Phoenix, AZ 85004-4503. *E-mail:* aosborn@azhighered.gov. *Phone:* 602-258-2435. *Fax:* 602-258-2483. *Web site:* http://www.azhighered.gov/.

ARKANSAS

Arkansas Academic Challenge Scholarship Program. Awards for Arkansas residents who are graduating high school seniors, currently enrolled college students and nontraditional students to study at an approved Arkansas institution. Must have at least a 2.5 GPA or 19 ACT composite score (or the equivalent). Renewable up to three additional years. *Award:* Scholarship for use in freshman, sophomore, junior, or senior year; renewable. *Award amount:* \$1250–\$5000. *Number of awards:* 25,000–30,000. *Eligibility Requirements:* Applicant must be enrolled or expecting to enroll full-time at a two-year or four-year institution or university; resident of Arkansas and studying in Arkansas. Applicant must have 2.5 GPA or higher. Available to U.S. citizens. *Application Requirements:* Application, test scores, transcript. **Deadline:** June 1.

Contact Tara Smith, Director of Financial Aid, Arkansas Department of Higher Education, 114 East Capitol Avenue, Little Rock, AR 72201-3818. *E-mail:* finaid@adhe.arknet.edu. *Phone:* 501-371-2000. *Fax:* 501-371-2001. *Web site:* http://www.adhe.edu/.

Arkansas Governor's Scholars Program. Awards for outstanding Arkansas high school seniors. Must be an Arkansas resident and have a high school GPA of at least 3.5 or have scored at least 27 on the ACT. Award is \$4000 per year for four years of full-time undergraduate study. Applicants who attain 32 or above on ACT, 1410 or above on SAT and have an academic 3.5 GPA, or are selected as National Merit or National Achievement finalists may receive an award equal to tuition, mandatory fees, room, and board up to \$10,000 per year at any Arkansas institution. *Award:* Scholarship for use in freshman, sophomore, junior, or senior year; renewable. *Award amount:* \$4000–\$10,000. *Number of awards:* up to 375. *Eligibility Requirements:* Applicant must be enrolled or expecting to enroll full-time at a two-year or four-year institution or university; resident of Arkansas and studying in Arkansas. Applicant must have 3.5 GPA or higher. Available to U.S. citizens. *Application Requirements:* Application, test scores, transcript. **Deadline:** February 1.

Contact Tara Smith, Director of Financial Aid, Arkansas Department of Higher Education, 114 East Capitol Avenue, Little Rock, AR 72201-3818. *E-mail:* taras@adhe.edu. *Phone:* 501-371-2000. *Fax:* 501-371-2001. *Web site:* http://www.adhe.edu/.

Arkansas Single Parent Scholarship. Scholarships are awarded to economically disadvantaged single parents who reside in Arkansas who have custodial care of at least one minor child and have not already received a baccalaureate degree. Award values, application deadlines, and other criteria vary by county. Visit http://www.aspsf.org for more information. *Award:* Scholarship for use in freshman, sophomore, junior, or senior year; not renewable. *Award amount:* \$200–\$1800. *Number of awards:* up to 2600. *Eligibility Requirements:* Applicant must be enrolled or expecting to enroll full- or part-time at a two-year, four-year, or technical institution or university; single; resident of Arkansas and must have an interest in designated field specified by sponsor. Available to U.S. citizens. *Application Requirements:* Application, financial need analysis, interview, references, transcript, statement of goals, FAFSA Student Aid Report (SAR). **Deadline:** varies.

Contact Ralph H. Nesson, Executive Director, Arkansas Single Parent Scholarship Fund, 614 East Emma Avenue, Suite 119, Springdale, AR 72764. *E-mail:* rnesson@jtlshop.jonesnet.org. *Phone:* 479-927-1402 Ext. 11. *Web site:* http://www.aspsf.org/.

Law Enforcement Officers' Dependents Scholarship–Arkansas. Scholarship for dependents, under 23 years old, of Arkansas law-enforcement officers killed or permanently disabled in the line of duty. Renewable award is a waiver of tuition, fees, and room at two- or four-year Arkansas institution. Submit birth certificate, death certificate, and claims commission report of findings of fact. Proof of disability from State Claims Commission may also be submitted. *Award:* Scholarship for use in freshman, sophomore, junior, or senior year; renewable. *Number of awards:* 27–32. *Eligibility Requirements:* Applicant must be age 23 or under; enrolled or expecting to enroll full- or part-time at a two-year, four-year, or technical institution or university; resident of Arkansas and studying in Arkansas. Available to U.S. citizens. *Application Requirements:* Application. **Deadline:** continuous.

Contact Tara Smith, Director of Financial Aid, Arkansas Department of Higher Education, 114 East Capitol Avenue, Little Rock, AR 72201-3818. *E-mail:* taras@adhe.edu. *Phone:* 501-371-2000. *Fax:* 501-371-2001. *Web site:* http://www.adhe.edu/.

Military Dependent's Scholarship Program. Renewable waiver of tuition, fees, room and board undergraduate students seeking a bachelor's degree or certificate of completion at any public college, university or technical school in Arkansas who qualify as a spouse or dependent child of an Arkansas resident who has been declared to be missing in action, killed in action, a POW, or killed on ordnance delivery, or a veteran who has been declared to be 100 percent totally and permanently disabled during, or as a result of, active military service. *Award:* Scholarship for use in freshman, sophomore, junior, or senior year; renewable. *Number of awards:* 1–60. *Eligibility Requirements:* Applicant must be enrolled or expecting to enroll full-time at a two-year, four-year, or technical institution or university; resident of Arkansas and studying in Arkansas. Available to U.S. citizens. Applicant or parent must meet one or more of the following requirements: general military experience; retired from active duty; disabled or killed as a result of military service; prisoner of war; or missing in action. *Application Requirements:* Application, references, report of casualty. **Deadline:** June 1.

Contact Tara Smith, Director of Financial Aid, Arkansas Department of Higher Education, 114 East Capitol Avenue, Little Rock, AR 72201-3818. *E-mail:* taras@adhe.edu. *Phone:* 501-371-2000. *Fax:* 501-371-2001. *Web site:* http://www.adhe.edu/.

Robert C. Byrd Honors Scholarship-Arkansas. Applicant must be a graduate of a public or private school or receive a recognized equivalent of a high school diploma. Must be a resident of Arkansas. Must be admitted to an institution of higher education, demonstrate outstanding academic achievement and show promise of continued academic achievement. Award is $1500 for each academic year for a maximum of four years. *Award:* Scholarship for use in freshman year; renewable. *Award amount:* $1500. *Number of awards:* 60–68. *Eligibility Requirements:* Applicant must be high school student; planning to enroll or expecting to enroll full-time at a two-year, four-year, or technical institution or university and resident of Arkansas. Available to U.S. citizens. *Application Requirements:* Application, essay, references, test scores, transcript. **Deadline:** February 16.

Contact Mr. Thomas Charles Coy, Public School Program Manager, Arkansas State Department of Education, 4 Capitol Mall Room 107-A, Little Rock, AR 72201. *E-mail:* thomas.coy@arkansas.gov. *Phone:* 501-682-4250. *Web site:* http://www.arkansased.org/.

Second Effort Scholarship. Awarded to those scholars who achieved one of the 10 highest scores on the Arkansas High School Diploma Test (GED). Must be at least age 18 and not have graduated from high school. Students do not apply for this award, they are contacted by the Arkansas Department of Higher Education. *Award:* Scholarship for use in freshman year; renewable. *Award amount:* up to $1000. *Number of awards:* 10. *Eligibility Requirements:* Applicant must be high school student; planning to enroll or expecting to enroll full- or part-time at a two-year or four-year institution or university; resident of Arkansas and studying in Arkansas. Available to U.S. citizens. *Application Requirements:* Application. **Deadline:** varies.

Contact Tara Smith, Director of Financial Aid, Arkansas Department of Higher Education, 114 East Capitol Avenue, Little Rock, AR 72201-3818. *E-mail:* taras@adhe.edu. *Phone:* 501-371-2000. *Fax:* 501-371-2001. *Web site:* http://www.adhe.edu/.

CALIFORNIA

Cal Grant C. Award for California residents who are enrolled in a short-term vocational training program. Program must lead to a recognized degree or certificate. Course length must be a minimum of 4 months and no longer than 24 months. Students must be attending an approved California institution and show financial need. *Award:* Grant for use in freshman or sophomore year; renewable. *Award amount:* $576–$3168. *Number of awards:* up to 7761. *Eligibility Requirements:* Applicant must be enrolled or expecting to enroll full- or part-time at a two-year or technical institution; resident of California and studying in California. Available to U.S. citizens. *Application Requirements:* Application, financial need analysis, GPA verification. **Deadline:** March 2.

Contact Catalina Mistler, Chief, Program Administration & Services Division, California Student Aid Commission, PO Box 419026, Rancho Cordova, CA 95741-9026. *E-mail:* studentsupport@csac.ca.gov. *Phone:* 916-526-7268. *Fax:* 916-526-8002. *Web site:* http://www.csac.ca.gov/.

Child Development Teacher and Supervisor Grant Program. Award is for those students pursuing an approved course of study leading to a Child Development Permit issued by the California Commission on Teacher Credentialing. In exchange for each year funding is received, recipients agree to provide one year of service in a licensed childcare center. *Academic Fields/Career Goals:* Child and Family Studies; Education. *Award:* Grant for use in freshman, sophomore, junior, senior, or graduate year; renewable. *Award amount:* $1000–$2000. *Number of awards:* up to 300. *Eligibility Requirements:* Applicant must be enrolled or expecting to enroll full- or part-time at a two-year or four-year institution or university; resident of California and studying in California. Applicant or parent of applicant must have employment or volunteer experience in teaching/education. Available to U.S. citizens. *Application Requirements:* Application, financial need analysis, references, GPA verification. **Deadline:** April 16.

Contact Catalina Mistler, Chief, Program Administration & Services Division, California Student Aid Commission, PO Box 419026, Rancho Cordova, CA 95741-9026. *E-mail:* studentsupport@csac.ca.gov. *Phone:* 916-526-7268. *Fax:* 916-526-8002. *Web site:* http://www.csac.ca.gov/.

Competitive Cal Grant A. Award for California residents who are not recent high school graduates attending an approved college or university within the state. Must show financial need and meet minimum 3.0 GPA requirement. *Award:* Grant for use in freshman, sophomore, junior, or senior year; renewable. *Award amount:* $4370–$10,302. *Number of awards:* 1000–2000. *Eligibility Requirements:* Applicant must be enrolled or expecting to enroll full- or part-time at a two-year or four-year institution or university; resident of

California and studying in California. Applicant must have 3.0 GPA or higher. Available to U.S. citizens. *Application Requirements:* Application, financial need analysis, GPA verification. **Deadline:** March 2.

Contact Catalina Mistler, Chief, Program Administration & Services Division, California Student Aid Commission, PO Box 419026, Rancho Cordova, CA 95741-9026. *E-mail:* studentsupport@csac.ca.gov. *Phone:* 916-526-7268. *Fax:* 916-526-8002. *Web site:* http://www.csac.ca.gov/.

Cooperative Agencies Resources for Education Program. Renewable award available to California resident enrolled as a full-time student at a two-year California community college. Must currently receive CalWORKs/TANF and have at least one child under fourteen years of age at time of acceptance into CARE program. Must be in EOPS, a single head of household, and age 18 or older. Contact local college EOPS-CARE office for application and more information. To locate nearest campus, see http://www.icanaffordcollege.com/applications/homepage2.cfm. *Award:* Grant for use in freshman or sophomore year; renewable. *Award amount:* varies. *Number of awards:* 10,000–11,000. *Eligibility Requirements:* Applicant must be age 18 and over; enrolled or expecting to enroll full-time at a two-year institution; single; resident of California and studying in California. Available to U.S. citizens. *Application Requirements:* Application, financial need analysis, test scores, transcript. **Deadline:** continuous.

Contact Contact local community college EOPS/CARE program, California Community Colleges. *Web site:* http://www.cccco.edu/.

Entitlement Cal Grant B. Provide grant funds for access costs for low-income students in an amount not to exceed $1551 and tuition/fee expenses of up to $10302. Must be California residents and enroll in an undergraduate academic program of not less than one academic year at a qualifying postsecondary institution. Must show financial need and meet the minimum 2.00 GPA requirement. *Award:* Grant for use in freshman, sophomore, junior, or senior year; renewable. *Award amount:* $700–$11,853. *Number of awards:* 56,200. *Eligibility Requirements:* Applicant must be enrolled or expecting to enroll full- or part-time at a two-year, four-year, or technical institution or university; resident of California and studying in California. Available to U.S. citizens. *Application Requirements:* Application, financial need analysis. **Deadline:** March 2.

Contact Catalina Mistler, Chief, Program Administration & Services Division, California Student Aid Commission, PO Box 419026, Rancho Cordova, CA 95741-9026. *E-mail:* studentsupport@csac.ca.gov. *Phone:* 916-526-7268. *Fax:* 916-526-8002. *Web site:* http://www.csac.ca.gov/.

Law Enforcement Personnel Dependents Scholarship. Provides college grants to needy dependents of California law enforcement officers, officers and employees of the Department of Corrections and Department of Youth Authority, and firefighters killed or disabled in the line of duty. *Award:* Grant for use in freshman, sophomore, junior, or senior year; renewable. *Award amount:* $100–$11,853. *Number of awards:* varies. *Eligibility Requirements:* Applicant must be enrolled or expecting to enroll full- or part-time at a two-year or four-year institution or university; resident of California and studying in California. Applicant or parent of applicant must have employment or volunteer experience in police/firefighting. Available to U.S. citizens. *Application Requirements:* Application, financial need analysis, transcript, birth certificate, death certificate of parents or spouse, police report. **Deadline:** continuous.

Contact Catalina Mistler, Chief, Program Administration & Services Division, California Student Aid Commission, PO Box 419026, Rancho Cordova, CA 95741-9026. *E-mail:* studentsupport@csac.ca.gov. *Phone:* 916-526-7268. *Fax:* 916-526-8002. *Web site:* http://www.csac.ca.gov/.

COLORADO

American Legion Auxiliary Department of Colorado Department President's Scholarship for Junior Member. Open to children, spouses, grandchildren, and great-grandchildren of veterans, and veterans who served in the Armed Forces during eligibility dates for membership in the American Legion. Applicants must be Colorado residents who have been accepted by an accredited school in Colorado. *Award:* Scholarship for use in freshman year; not renewable. *Award amount:* up to $500. *Number of awards:* 1–2. *Eligibility Requirements:* Applicant must be high school student; planning to enroll or expecting to enroll full- or part-time at a four-year institution or university; resident of Colorado and studying in Colorado. Available to U.S. citizens. Applicant or parent must meet one or more of the following requirements: general military experience; retired from active duty; disabled or killed as a result of military service; prisoner of war; or missing in action. *Application Requirements:* Application, essay, references, transcript. **Deadline:** April 15.

Contact Jean Lennie, Department Secretary and Treasurer, American Legion Auxiliary Department of Colorado, 7465 East First Avenue, Suite D, Denver, CO 80230. *E-mail:* ala@coloradolegion.org. *Phone:* 303-367-5388. *Fax:* 303-367-0688. *Web site:* http://www.coloradolegion.org/.

American Legion Auxiliary Department of Colorado Past Presidents' Parley Nurses Scholarship. Open to children, spouses, grandchildren, and great-grandchildren of American Legion veterans, and veterans who served in the armed forces during eligibility dates for membership in the American Legion. Must be Colorado residents who have been accepted by an accredited school of nursing in Colorado. *Academic Fields/Career Goals:* Nursing. *Award:* Scholarship for use in freshman, sophomore, junior, senior, or graduate year; not renewable. *Award amount:* up to $500. *Number of awards:* 3–5. *Eligibility Requirements:* Applicant must be enrolled or expecting to enroll full- or part-time at a four-year institution or university; resident of Colorado and studying in Colorado. Applicant or parent of applicant must be member of American Legion or Auxiliary. Available to U.S. citizens. Applicant or parent must meet one or more of the following requirements: general military experience; retired from active duty; disabled or killed as a result of military service; prisoner of war; or missing in action. *Application Requirements:* Application, essay, financial need analysis, references. **Deadline:** April 1.

Contact American Legion Auxiliary Department of Colorado, 7465 East First Avenue, Suite D, Denver, CO 80230. *E-mail:* ala@coloradolegion.org. *Phone:* 303-367-5388. *Web site:* http://www.coloradolegion.org/.

Colorado Leveraging Educational Assistance Partnership (CLEAP). Scholarship of up to $5000 awarded for an undergraduate student enrolled at least half time. Applicant must be a U.S citizen and Colorado resident. *Award:* Scholarship for use in freshman, sophomore, junior, or senior year; not renewable. *Award amount:* up to $5000. *Number of awards:* varies. *Eligibility Requirements:* Applicant must be enrolled or expecting to enroll full- or part-time at a two-year, four-year, or technical institution or university and resident of Colorado. Available to U.S. citizens. *Application Requirements:* Application.

Contact Celina Duran, Financial Aid Administrator, Colorado Commission on Higher Education, 1560 Broadway, Suite 1600, Denver,

CO 80202. *E-mail:* celina.duran@dhe.state.co.us. *Phone:* 303-866-2723. *Web site:* http://www.highered.colorado.gov/dhedefault.html.

Colorado Student Grant. Grants for Colorado residents attending eligible public, private, or vocational institutions within the state. Students must complete a Free Application for Federal Student Aid (FAFSA) and qualify at 150% of Pell eligibility. Application deadlines vary by institution. Renewable award for undergraduates. Contact the financial aid office at the college/institution for application and more information. *Award:* Grant for use in freshman, sophomore, junior, or senior year; renewable. *Award amount:* \$850–\$5000. *Number of awards:* 60,307. *Eligibility Requirements:* Applicant must be enrolled or expecting to enroll full- or part-time at a two-year, four-year, or technical institution or university; resident of Colorado and studying in Colorado. Available to U.S. citizens. *Application Requirements:* Application, financial need analysis, student must have an active FAFSA on file at the institution.

Contact Celina Duran, Financial Aid Administrator, Colorado Commission on Higher Education, 1560 Broadway, Suite 1600, Denver, CO 80202. *E-mail:* celina.duran@dhe.state.co.us. *Phone:* 303-866-2723. *Web site:* http://www.highered.colorado.gov/dhedefault.html.

Governor's Opportunity Scholarship. Scholarship was awarded to the most needy first-time freshman whose parents' adjusted gross income is less than \$26,000. The program is in phase out and not accepting new applicants. Continuing students must be U.S. citizen or permanent legal resident. Work-study is part of the program. This program is in phase out and will sunset in 2012. *Award:* Scholarship for use in freshman, sophomore, junior, or senior year; renewable. *Award amount:* up to \$10,700. *Number of awards:* 265. *Eligibility Requirements:* Applicant must be enrolled or expecting to enroll full-time at a two-year, four-year, or technical institution or university; resident of Colorado and studying in Colorado. *Application Requirements:* Application, financial need analysis, test scores, transcript. **Deadline:** continuous.

Contact Celina Duran, Financial Aid Administrator, Colorado Commission on Higher Education, 1560 Broadway, Suite 1600, Denver, CO 80202. *E-mail:* celina.duran@dhe.state.co.us. *Phone:* 303-866-2723. *Web site:* http://www.highered.colorado.gov/dhedefault.html.

CONNECTICUT

AIFS-HACU Scholarships. Scholarships to outstanding Hispanic students to study abroad with AIFS. Available to students attending HACU member schools. Students will receive scholarships of up to 50 percent of the full program fee. Students must meet all standard AIFS eligibility requirements. Deadlines: April 15 for fall, October 1 for spring, and March 15 for summer. *Award:* Scholarship for use in freshman, sophomore, junior, or senior year; not renewable. *Award amount:* \$6000–\$8000. *Number of awards:* varies. *Eligibility Requirements:* Applicant must be Hispanic; age 17 and over; enrolled or expecting to enroll full-time at a two-year or four-year institution or university and must have an interest in international exchange. Applicant must have 3.0 GPA or higher. Available to U.S. and non-U.S. citizens. *Application Requirements:* Application, essay, photo, references, transcript. *Fee:* \$95. **Deadline:** varies.

Contact David Mauro, Admissions Counselor, American Institute for Foreign Study, River Plaza, 9 West Broad Street, Stamford, CT 06902-3788. *E-mail:* dmauro@aifs.com. *Phone:* 800-727-2437 Ext. 5163. *Fax:* 203-399-5463. *Web site:* http://www.aifsabroad.com/.

Capitol Scholarship Program. Award for Connecticut residents attending eligible institutions in Connecticut or in a state with reciprocity with Connecticut (Massachusetts, Maine, New Hampshire, Pennsylvania, Rhode Island, Vermont, or Washington, D.C). Must be U.S. citizen or permanent resident alien who is a high school senior or graduate. Must rank in top 20% of class or score at least 1800 on SAT or score at least 27 on the ACT. Students must also demonstrate financial need as a result of filing the FAFSA. *Award:* Scholarship for use in freshman, sophomore, junior, or senior year; renewable. *Award amount:* \$500–\$3000. *Number of awards:* 4500–5500. *Eligibility Requirements:* Applicant must be enrolled or expecting to enroll full- or part-time at a two-year, four-year, or technical institution or university; resident of Connecticut and studying in Connecticut, District of Columbia, Maine, Massachusetts, New Hampshire, Pennsylvania, Rhode Island, or Vermont. Available to U.S. citizens. *Application Requirements:* Application, financial need analysis, test scores, FAFSA. **Deadline:** February 15.

Contact Mrs. Linda Diamond, Senior Associate, Connecticut Department of Higher Education, 61 Woodland Street, Hartford, CT 06105. *E-mail:* csp@ctdhe.org. *Phone:* 860-947-1855. *Fax:* 860-947-1313. *Web site:* http://www.ctdhe.org/.

Connecticut Aid to Public College Students Grant. Award for Connecticut residents attending public colleges or universities within the state. Renewable awards based on financial need. Application deadline varies by institution. Apply at college financial aid office. *Award:* Grant for use in freshman, sophomore, junior, or senior year; renewable. *Award amount:* varies. *Number of awards:* varies. *Eligibility Requirements:* Applicant must be enrolled or expecting to enroll full- or part-time at a two-year or four-year institution or university; resident of Connecticut and studying in Connecticut. Available to U.S. citizens. *Application Requirements:* Financial need analysis, FAFSA. **Deadline:** continuous.

Contact Ms. Lynne Little, Executive Assistant, Connecticut Department of Higher Education, 61 Woodland Street, Hartford, CT 06105. *E-mail:* caps@ctdhe.org. *Phone:* 860-947-1855. *Fax:* 860-947-1838. *Web site:* http://www.ctdhe.org/.

Connecticut Army National Guard 100% Tuition Waiver. Program is for any active member of the Connecticut Army National Guard in good standing. Must be a resident of Connecticut attending any Connecticut state (public) university, community-technical college or regional vocational-technical school. The total number of available awards is unlimited. *Award:* Scholarship for use in freshman, sophomore, junior, or senior year; not renewable. *Award amount:* \$16,000. *Number of awards:* varies. *Eligibility Requirements:* Applicant must be age 17-65; enrolled or expecting to enroll full- or part-time at a two-year, four-year, or technical institution or university; resident of Connecticut and studying in Connecticut. Available to U.S. and non-U.S. citizens. Applicant or parent must meet one or more of the following requirements: Army National Guard experience; retired from active duty; disabled or killed as a result of military service; prisoner of war; or missing in action. *Application Requirements:* Application. **Deadline:** July 1.

Contact Capt. Jeremy Lingenfelser, Education Services Officer, Connecticut Army National Guard, 360 Broad Street, Hartford, CT 06105-3795. *E-mail:* education@ct.ngb.army.mil. *Phone:* 860-524-4816. *Fax:* 860-524-4904. *Web site:* http://www.ct.ngb.army.mil/.

Connecticut Independent College Student Grants. Award for Connecticut residents attending an independent college or university within the state on at least a half-time basis. Renewable awards based on financial need. Application deadline varies by institution. Apply at college financial aid office. *Award:* Grant for use in freshman, sophomore, junior, or senior year; renewable. *Award amount:* $250–$8700. *Number of awards:* varies. *Eligibility Requirements:* Applicant must be enrolled or expecting to enroll full- or part-time at a two-year or four-year institution or university; resident of Connecticut and studying in Connecticut. Available to U.S. citizens. *Application Requirements:* Financial need analysis, FAFSA. **Deadline:** continuous.

Contact Ms. Lynne Little, Executive Assistant, Connecticut Department of Higher Education, 61 Woodland Street, Hartford, CT 06105. *E-mail:* cics@ctdhe.org. *Phone:* 860-947-1855. *Fax:* 860-947-1838. *Web site:* http://www.ctdhe.org/.

Minority Teacher Incentive Grant Program. Program provides up to $5,000 a year for two years of full-time study in a teacher preparation program for the junior or senior year at a Connecticut college or university. Applicant must be African-American, Hispanic/Latino, Asian American or Native American heritage and be nominated by the Education Dean. Program graduates who teach in Connecticut public schools may be eligible for loan reimbursement stipends up to $2,500 per year for up to four years. *Academic Fields/Career Goals:* Education. *Award:* Grant for use in junior or senior year; renewable. *Award amount:* $2500–$5000. *Number of awards:* 82. *Eligibility Requirements:* Applicant must be American Indian/Alaska Native, Asian/Pacific Islander, Black (non-Hispanic), or Hispanic; enrolled or expecting to enroll full-time at a four-year institution or university and studying in Connecticut. Available to U.S. citizens. *Application Requirements:* Application. **Deadline:** October 1.

Contact Ms. Judy-Ann Staple, Associate, Connecticut Department of Higher Education, 61 Woodland Street, Hartford, CT 06105. *E-mail:* mtip@ctdhe.org. *Phone:* 860-947-1855. *Fax:* 860-947-1838. *Web site:* http://www.ctdhe.org/.

DELAWARE

Christa McAuliffe Teacher Scholarship Loan-Delaware. Award for legal residents of Delaware who are U.S. citizens or eligible non-citizens. Must be full-time student enrolled at a Delaware college in an undergraduate program leading to teacher certification. High school seniors must rank in upper half of class and have a combined score of 1570 on the SAT. Undergraduates must have at least a 2.75 cumulative GPA. For details visit web site http://www.doe.k12.de.us. *Academic Fields/Career Goals:* Education. *Award:* Forgivable loan for use in freshman, sophomore, junior, or senior year; renewable. *Award amount:* $1000–$5000. *Number of awards:* 1–60. *Eligibility Requirements:* Applicant must be enrolled or expecting to enroll full-time at a four-year institution or university; resident of Delaware and studying in Delaware. Available to U.S. citizens. *Application Requirements:* Application, essay, test scores, transcript. **Deadline:** March 28.

Contact Carylin Brinkley, Program Administrator, Delaware Higher Education Office, Carvel State Office Building, 820 North French Street, Fifth Floor, Wilmington, DE 19801-3509. *E-mail:* cbrinkley@doe.k12.de.us. *Phone:* 302-577-5240. *Fax:* 302-577-6765. *Web site:* http://www.doe.k12.de.us.

Delaware Nursing Incentive Scholarship Loan. Award for legal residents of Delaware who are U.S. citizens or eligible non-citizens. Must be full-time student enrolled in an accredited program leading to certification as an RN or LPN. High school seniors must rank in upper half of class with at least a 2.5 cumulative GPA. *Academic Fields/Career Goals:* Nursing. *Award:* Forgivable loan for use in freshman, sophomore, junior, or senior year; renewable. *Award amount:* $1000–$5000. *Number of awards:* 1–40. *Eligibility Requirements:* Applicant must be enrolled or expecting to enroll full- or part-time at a two-year or four-year institution and resident of Delaware. Applicant must have 2.5 GPA or higher. Available to U.S. citizens. *Application Requirements:* Application, essay, test scores, transcript. **Deadline:** March 28.

Contact Carylin Brinkley, Program Administrator, Delaware Higher Education Office, Carvel State Office Building, 820 North French Street, Fifth Floor, Wilmington, DE 19801-3509. *E-mail:* cbrinkley@doe.k12.de.us. *Phone:* 302-577-5240. *Fax:* 302-577-6765. *Web site:* http://www.doe.k12.de.us.

Delaware Solid Waste Authority John P. "Pat" Healy Scholarship. Award for legal residents of Delaware who are U.S. citizens or eligible non-citizens. Must be high school seniors or full-time college students in their freshman or sophomore years. Must major in either environmental engineering or environmental sciences at a Delaware college. Selection based on financial need, academic performance, community and school involvement, and leadership ability. *Academic Fields/Career Goals:* Engineering-Related Technologies; Environmental Science. *Award:* Scholarship for use in freshman or sophomore year; renewable. *Award amount:* $2000. *Number of awards:* 1. *Eligibility Requirements:* Applicant must be enrolled or expecting to enroll full-time at a two-year or four-year institution or university; resident of Delaware; studying in Delaware and must have an interest in leadership. Applicant or parent of applicant must have employment or volunteer experience in community service. Applicant must have 3.0 GPA or higher. Available to U.S. citizens. *Application Requirements:* Application, financial need analysis, FAFSA, Student Aid Report (SAR). **Deadline:** March 14.

Contact Carylin Brinkley, Program Administrator, Delaware Higher Education Office, Carvel State Office Building, 820 North French Street, Fifth Floor, Wilmington, DE 19801-3509. *E-mail:* cbrinkley@doe.k12.de.us. *Phone:* 302-577-5240. *Fax:* 302-577-6765. *Web site:* http://www.doe.k12.de.us.

Diamond State Scholarship. Award for legal residents of Delaware who are U.S. citizens or eligible non-citizens. Must be enrolled as a full-time student in a degree program at a nonprofit, regionally accredited institution. Minimum 3.0 GPA required. High school seniors should rank in upper quarter of class and have a combined score of at least 1800 on the SAT. *Award:* Scholarship for use in freshman year; renewable. *Award amount:* $1250. *Number of awards:* 50. *Eligibility Requirements:* Applicant must be high school student; planning to enroll or expecting to enroll full-time at a four-year institution or university and resident of Delaware. Applicant must have 3.0 GPA or higher. Available to U.S. citizens. *Application Requirements:* Application, essay, test scores, transcript. **Deadline:** March 28.

Contact Carylin Brinkley, Program Administrator, Delaware Higher Education Office, Carvel State Office Building, 820 North French Street, Fifth Floor, Wilmington, DE 19801-3509. *E-mail:* cbrinkley@doe.k12.de.us. *Phone:* 302-577-5240. *Fax:* 302-577-6765. *Web site:* http://www.doe.k12.de.us.

Educational Benefits for Children of Deceased Veterans. Award for children between the ages of 16 and 24 of deceased/MIA/POW veterans or state police officers. Must have been a resident of Delaware for 3 or more years prior to the date of application. If the applicant's parent is a member of the armed forces, the parent must have been a resident of Delaware at the time of death or declaration of missing in action or prisoner of war status. Award will not exceed tuition and fees at a Delaware public college. *Award:* Grant for use in freshman, sophomore, junior, or senior year; renewable. *Award amount:* varies. *Number of awards:* varies. *Eligibility Requirements:* Applicant must be age 16-24; enrolled or expecting to enroll full-time at a two-year or four-year institution or university and resident of Delaware. Applicant or parent of applicant must have employment or volunteer experience in police/firefighting. Available to U.S. citizens. Applicant or parent must meet one or more of the following requirements: general military experience; retired from active duty; disabled or killed as a result of military service; prisoner of war; or missing in action. *Application Requirements:* Application, verification of service-related death. **Deadline:** continuous.

Contact Delaware Higher Education Office. *Phone:* 302-577-5240. *Fax:* 302-577-6765. *Web site:* http://www.doe.k12.de.us.

Governor's Workforce Development Grant. Grants for part-time undergraduate students attending Delaware College of Art and Design, Delaware State University, Delaware Technical and Community College, Goldey-Beacom College, University of Delaware, Wesley College, Widener University (Delaware Campus), or Wilmington College. Must be at least 18 years old, a resident of Delaware, and employed by a company in Delaware that contributes to the Blue Collar Training Fund Program. *Award:* Grant for use in freshman, sophomore, junior, or senior year; renewable. *Award amount:* $2000. *Number of awards:* 40. *Eligibility Requirements:* Applicant must be age 18 and over; enrolled or expecting to enroll full- or part-time at a two-year or four-year institution or university; resident of Delaware and studying in Delaware. Available to U.S. and non-U.S. citizens. *Application Requirements:* Application. **Deadline:** varies.

Contact Carylin Brinkley, Program Administrator, Delaware Higher Education Office, Carvel State Office Building, 820 North French Street, Fifth Floor, Wilmington, DE 19801-3509. *E-mail:* cbrinkley@doe.k12.de.us. *Phone:* 302-577-5240. *Fax:* 302-577-6765. *Web site:* http://www.doe.k12.de.us.

Legislative Essay Scholarship. Award for legal residents of Delaware who are U.S. citizens or eligible non-citizens. Must be high school seniors in public or private schools or in home school programs who plans to enroll full-time at a nonprofit, regionally accredited college. Must submit an essay on topic: "Pluribus Unum: Is this motto adopted in 1782 relevant to our country today?". *Award:* Prize for use in freshman year; not renewable. *Award amount:* $1000–$10,000. *Number of awards:* up to 62. *Eligibility Requirements:* Applicant must be high school student; planning to enroll or expecting to enroll full- or part-time at a two-year, four-year, or technical institution or university and resident of Delaware. Available to U.S. citizens. *Application Requirements:* Application, applicant must enter a contest, essay. **Deadline:** November 30.

Contact Carylin Brinkley, Program Administrator, Delaware Higher Education Office, Carvel State Office Building, 820 North French Street, Fifth Floor, Wilmington, DE 19801-3509. *E-mail:* cbrinkley@doe.k12.de.us. *Phone:* 302-577-5240. *Fax:* 302-577-6765. *Web site:* http://www.doe.k12.de.us.

Robert C. Byrd Honors Scholarship-Delaware. Award for legal residents of Delaware who are U.S. citizens or eligible non-citizens. For high school seniors who rank in upper quarter of class or GED recipients with a minimum score of 300 and a combined score of at least 1800 on the SAT. Minimum 3.5 GPA required. Must be enrolled at least half-time at a nonprofit, regionally accredited institution. *Award:* Scholarship for use in freshman year; renewable. *Award amount:* $1500. *Number of awards:* 20. *Eligibility Requirements:* Applicant must be high school student; planning to enroll or expecting to enroll full-time at a two-year or four-year institution or university and resident of Delaware. Applicant must have 3.5 GPA or higher. Available to U.S. citizens. *Application Requirements:* Application, essay, test scores, transcript. **Deadline:** March 28.

Contact Carylin Brinkley, Program Administrator, Delaware Higher Education Office, Carvel State Office Building, 820 North French Street, Fifth Floor, Wilmington, DE 19801-3509. *E-mail:* cbrinkley@doe.k12.de.us. *Phone:* 302-577-5240. *Fax:* 302-577-6765. *Web site:* http://www.doe.k12.de.us.

Scholarship Incentive Program (ScIP). Award for legal residents of Delaware who are U.S. citizens or eligible non-citizens. Must demonstrate substantial financial need and enroll full-time in an undergraduate degree program at a nonprofit, regionally accredited institution in Delaware or Pennsylvania. Minimum 2.5 GPA required. *Award:* Grant for use in freshman, sophomore, junior, senior, or graduate year; not renewable. *Award amount:* $700–$2200. *Number of awards:* 1000–1253. *Eligibility Requirements:* Applicant must be enrolled or expecting to enroll full-time at a two-year or four-year institution or university; resident of Delaware and studying in Delaware or Pennsylvania. Applicant must have 2.5 GPA or higher. Available to U.S. citizens. *Application Requirements:* Application, financial need analysis, transcript, FAFSA. **Deadline:** April 15.

Contact Carylin Brinkley, Program Administrator, Delaware Higher Education Office, Carvel State Office Building, 820 North French Street, Fifth Floor, Wilmington, DE 19801-3509. *E-mail:* cbrinkley@doe.k12.de.us. *Phone:* 302-577-5240. *Fax:* 302-577-6765. *Web site:* http://www.doe.k12.de.us.

State Tuition Assistance. You must enlist in the Delaware National Guard to be eligible for this scholarship award. Award providing tuition assistance for any member of the Air or Army National Guard attending a Delaware two-year or four-year college. Awards are renewable. Applicant's minimum GPA must be 2.0. *Award:* Scholarship for use in freshman, sophomore, junior, or senior year; renewable. *Award amount:* up to $10,000. *Number of awards:* 1–300. *Eligibility Requirements:* Applicant must be enrolled or expecting to enroll full- or part-time at a two-year or four-year institution or university and studying in Delaware. Available to U.S. citizens. Applicant or parent must meet one or more of the following requirements: Air Force National Guard or Army National Guard experience; retired from active duty; disabled or killed as a result of military service; prisoner of war; or missing in action. *Application Requirements:* Application, transcript.

Contact Robert Csizmadia, State Tuition Assistance Manager, Delaware National Guard, 1st Regiment Road, Wilmington, DE 19808-2191. *E-mail:* robert.csizmadia@us.army.mil. *Phone:* 302-326-7012. *Fax:* 302-326-7029. *Web site:* http://www.delawarenationalguard.com/.

DISTRICT OF COLUMBIA

American Council of the Blind Scholarships. Merit-based award available to undergraduate students who are legally blind in both eyes. Submit certificate of legal blindness and proof of acceptance at an accredited postsecondary institution. *Award:* Scholarship for use in freshman, sophomore, junior, or senior year; renewable. *Award amount:* $1000–$2500. *Number of awards:* 16–20. *Eligibility Requirements:* Applicant must be enrolled or expecting to enroll full- or part-time at a four-year institution or university. Applicant must be visually impaired. Applicant must have 3.5 GPA or higher. Available to U.S. citizens. *Application Requirements:* Application, driver's license, essay, references, transcript, evidence of legal blindness, proof of post-secondary school acceptance. **Deadline:** March 1.

Contact Tatricia Castillo, Scholarship Coordinator, American Council of the Blind, 1155 15th Street, NW, Suite 1004, Washington, DC 20005. *E-mail:* tcastillo@acp.org. *Phone:* 202-467-5081. *Fax:* 202-467-5085. *Web site:* http://www.acb.org/.

Bureau of Indian Education Grant Program. Grants are provided to supplement financial assistance to eligible American Indian/Alaska Native students entering college seeking a baccalaureate degree. A student must be a member of, or at least one-quarter degree Indian blood descendent of a member of an American Indian tribe who are eligible for the special programs and services provided by the United States through the Bureau of Indian Affairs to Indians because of their status as Indians. *Award:* Grant for use in freshman year; not renewable. *Award amount:* varies. *Number of awards:* varies. *Eligibility Requirements:* Applicant must be American Indian/Alaska Native; high school student and planning to enroll or expecting to enroll full-time at a two-year or four-year institution or university. Available to U.S. citizens. *Application Requirements:* Application, references, test scores, transcript. **Deadline:** varies.

Contact Paulina Bell, Office Automation Assistant, Bureau of Indian Affairs Office of Indian Education Programs, 1849 C Street, NW, MS 3609-MIB, Washington, DC 20240-0001. *Phone:* 202-208-6123. *Fax:* 202-208-3312. *Web site:* http://www.oiep.bia.edu/.

Central Intelligence Agency Undergraduate Scholarship Program. Need and merit-based award for students with minimum 3.0 GPA, who are interested in working for the Central Intelligence Agency upon graduation. Renewable for four years of undergraduate study. Must apply in senior year of high school or sophomore year in college. For further information refer to web site http://www.cia.gov. *Academic Fields/Career Goals:* Accounting; Business/Consumer Services; Computer Science/Data Processing; Economics; Electrical Engineering/Electronics; Foreign Language; Geography; Graphics/Graphic Arts/Printing; International Studies; Political Science; Surveying, Surveying Technology, Cartography, or Geographic Information Science. *Award:* Scholarship for use in freshman, sophomore, junior, or senior year; renewable. *Award amount:* up to $18,000. *Number of awards:* varies. *Eligibility Requirements:* Applicant must be age 18 and over and enrolled or expecting to enroll full-time at a four-year institution or university. Applicant must have 3.0 GPA or higher. Available to U.S. citizens. *Application Requirements:* Application, financial need analysis, resume, references, test scores, transcript. **Deadline:** November 1.

Contact Van Patrick, Chief, College Relations, Central Intelligence Agency, Recruitment Center, L 100 LF7, Washington, DC 20505. *E-mail:* ivanilp0@ucia.gov. *Phone:* 703-613-8388. *Fax:* 703-613-7676. *Web site:* http://www.cia.gov/.

Costas G. Lemonopoulos Scholarship. Scholarships to children of NALC members attending public, four-year colleges or universities supported by the state of Florida or St. Petersburg Junior College. Scholarships are renewable one time. *Award:* Scholarship for use in freshman, sophomore, junior, or senior year; renewable. *Award amount:* varies. *Number of awards:* 1–20. *Eligibility Requirements:* Applicant must be enrolled or expecting to enroll full-time at a two-year or four-year institution or university and studying in Florida. Applicant or parent of applicant must be member of National Association of Letter Carriers. Available to U.S. citizens. *Application Requirements:* Application, references, transcript. **Deadline:** June 1.

Contact Ann Porch, Membership Committee, National Association of Letter Carriers, 100 Indiana Avenue, NW, Washington, DC 20001-2144. *E-mail:* nalcinf@nalc.org. *Phone:* 202-393-4695. *Web site:* http://www.nalc.org/.

DC Leveraging Educational Assistance Partnership Program (LEAP). $250 to $1500 grants available to District of Columbia residents, who qualify for federal need-based aid and are enrolled in undergraduate programs, and pursuing a first baccalaureate degree. Must attend a Title IV eligible college or university at least half-time. *Award:* Grant for use in freshman, sophomore, junior, or senior year; renewable. *Award amount:* $250–$1500. *Number of awards:* up to 3200. *Eligibility Requirements:* Applicant must be enrolled or expecting to enroll full- or part-time at a two-year or four-year institution or university and resident of District of Columbia. Available to U.S. citizens. *Application Requirements:* Application, financial need analysis, transcript, Student Aid Report (SAR), FAFSA. **Deadline:** June 30.

Contact Ms. Rehva D. Jones, Director, Higher Education Financial Services and Preparatory Programs, District of Columbia Office of the State Superintendent, 810 First Street, NW, Washington, DC 20002. *E-mail:* rehva.jones@dc.gov. *Phone:* 202-481-3948. *Fax:* 202-741-6491. *Web site:* http://www.osse.dc.gov/.

Harry S. Truman Scholarship. Scholarships for U.S. citizens or U.S. nationals who are college or university students with junior-level academic standing and who wish to attend professional or graduate school to prepare for careers in government or the nonprofit and advocacy sectors. Candidates must be nominated by their institution. Public service and leadership record considered. Visit web site http://www.truman.gov for further information and application. *Academic Fields/Career Goals:* Political Science; Public Policy and Administration. *Award:* Scholarship for use in junior year; renewable. *Award amount:* $30,000. *Number of awards:* 65. *Eligibility Requirements:* Applicant must be enrolled or expecting to enroll full-time at a four-year institution or university and must have an interest in leadership. Available to U.S. citizens. *Application Requirements:* Application, interview, references, policy proposal. **Deadline:** February 5.

Contact Tonji Wade, Program Officer, Harry S. Truman Scholarship Foundation, 712 Jackson Place, NW, Washington, DC 20006. *E-mail:* office@truman.gov. *Phone:* 202-395-4831. *Fax:* 202-395-6995. *Web site:* http://www.truman.gov/.

Montgomery GI Bill (Active Duty) Chapter 30. Award provides up to thirty-six months of education benefits to eligible veterans for college, business school, technical courses, vocational courses, correspondence courses, apprenticeships/job training, or flight training. Must be an eligible veteran with an Honorable Discharge and have high school diploma or GED before applying for benefits. *Award:* Scholarship for use in freshman, sophomore, junior, senior, or graduate year; renewable. *Number of awards:* varies. *Eligibility Requirements:* Applicant must be enrolled or expecting to enroll full- or part-time at a two-year, four-year, or technical institution or university. Available to U.S. citizens. Applicant or parent must meet one or more of the following requirements: general military experience; retired from active duty; disabled or killed as a result of military service; prisoner of war; or missing in action. *Application Requirements:* Application, proof of active military service of at least 2 years. **Deadline:** continuous.

Contact Keith M. Wilson, Director, Education Service, Department of Veterans Affairs (VA), 810 Vermont Avenue, NW, Washington, DC 20420. *Phone:* 888-442-4551. *Web site:* http://www.gibill.va.gov/.

Montgomery GI Bill (Selected Reserve). Educational assistance program for members of the selected reserve of the Army, Navy, Air Force, Marine Corps and Coast Guard, as well as the Army and Air National Guard. Available to all reservists and National Guard personnel who commit to a six-year obligation, and remain in the Reserve or Guard during the six years. Award is renewable. Monthly benefit is $309 for up to thirty-six months for full-time. *Award:* Scholarship for use in freshman, sophomore, junior, senior, or postgraduate years; renewable. *Number of awards:* varies. *Eligibility Requirements:* Applicant must be enrolled or expecting to enroll full- or part-time at a two-year, four-year, or technical institution or university. Available to U.S. citizens. Applicant or parent must meet one or more of the following requirements: general military experience; retired from active duty; disabled or killed as a result of military service; prisoner of war; or missing in action. *Application Requirements:* Application, proof of military service of six years in the reserve or guard. **Deadline:** continuous.

Contact Keith M. Wilson, Director, Education Service, Department of Veterans Affairs (VA), 810 Vermont Avenue, NW, Washington, DC 20420. *Phone:* 888-442-4551. *Web site:* http://www.gibill.va.gov/.

Reserve Education Assistance Program. The program provides educational assistance to members of National Guard and reserve components. Selected Reserve and Individual Ready Reserve (IRR) who are called or ordered to active duty service in response to a war or national emergency as declared by the president or Congress are eligible. For further information see web site http://www.GIBILL.va.gov. *Award:* Scholarship for use in freshman, sophomore, junior, senior, graduate, or postgraduate years; renewable. *Eligibility Requirements:* Applicant must be enrolled or expecting to enroll full- or part-time at a two-year, four-year, or technical institution or university. Available to U.S. citizens. Applicant or parent must meet one or more of the following requirements: general military experience; retired from active duty; disabled or killed as a result of military service; prisoner of war; or missing in action. *Application Requirements:* Application. **Deadline:** continuous.

Contact Keith M. Wilson, Director, Education Service, Department of Veterans Affairs (VA), 810 Vermont Avenue, NW, Washington, DC 20420. *Phone:* 888-442-4551. *Web site:* http://www.gibill.va.gov/.

Survivors and Dependents Educational Assistance (Chapter 35)-VA. Monthly $860 benefits for up to 45 months. Must be spouses or children under age 26 of current veterans missing in action or of deceased or totally and permanently disabled (service-related) service persons. For more information visit the following web site http://www.gibill.va.gov. *Award:* Scholarship for use in freshman, sophomore, junior, or senior year; renewable. *Eligibility Requirements:* Applicant must be age 25 or under and enrolled or expecting to enroll full- or part-time at a two-year, four-year, or technical institution or university. Available to U.S. and non-U.S. citizens. Applicant or parent must meet one or more of the following requirements: general military experience; retired from active duty; disabled or killed as a result of military service; prisoner of war; or missing in action. *Application Requirements:* Application, proof of parent or spouse's qualifying service. **Deadline:** continuous.

Contact Keith M. Wilson, Director, Education Service, Department of Veterans Affairs (VA), 810 Vermont Avenue, NW, Washington, DC 20420. *Phone:* 888-442-4551. *Web site:* http://www.gibill.va.gov/.

FLORIDA

Access to Better Learning and Education Grant. Grant program provides tuition assistance to Florida undergraduate students enrolled in degree programs at eligible private Florida colleges or universities. Must be a U.S. citizen or eligible non-citizen and must meet Florida residency requirements. The participating institution determines application procedures, deadlines, and student eligibility. For more details, visit the web site at http//www.FloridaStudentFinancialAid.org/SSFAD/home/uamain.htm. *Award:* Grant for use in freshman, sophomore, junior, or senior year; renewable. *Award amount:* up to $945. *Number of awards:* varies. *Eligibility Requirements:* Applicant must be enrolled or expecting to enroll full-time at a four-year institution or university; resident of Florida and studying in Florida. Available to U.S. citizens.

Contact Florida Department of Education, Office of Student Financial Assistance, Customer Service, Florida State Department of Education, 325 West Gaines Street, Tallahassee, FL 32399. *E-mail:* osfa@fldoe.org. *Phone:* 888-827-2007. *Web site:* http://www.floridastudentfinancialaid.org/.

First Generation Matching Grant Program. Need-based grants to Florida resident undergraduate students who are enrolled in state universities and community colleges in Florida and whose parents have not earned baccalaureate degrees. Available state funds are contingent upon matching contributions from private sources on a dollar-for-dollar basis. Institutions determine application procedures, deadlines, and student eligibility. For more details, visit the web site at http//www.FloridaStudentFinancialAid.org/SSFAD/home/uamain.htm. *Award:* Grant for use in freshman, sophomore, junior, or senior year; renewable. *Award amount:* varies. *Number of awards:* varies. *Eligibility Requirements:* Applicant must be enrolled or expecting to enroll full- or part-time at a two-year or four-year institution or university; resident of Florida and studying in Florida. Available to U.S. citizens.

Contact Florida Department of Education, Office of Student Financial Assistance, Customer Service, Florida State Department of Education, 325 West Gaines Street, Tallahassee, FL 32399. *E-mail:* osfa@fldoe.org. *Phone:* 888-828-2004. *Web site:* http://www.floridastudentfinancialaid.org/.

Florida Bright Futures Scholarship Program. Three lottery-funded scholarships reward Florida high school graduates for high academic achievement. Program is comprised of the following three awards: Florida Academic Scholars Award, Florida Medallion Scholars Award and Florida Gold Seal Vocational Scholars Award. For more details, visit the web site at http//www.FloridaStudentFinancialAid.org/SSFAD/home/uamain.htm. *Award:* Scholarship for use in freshman, sophomore, junior, or senior year; renewable. *Eligibility Requirements:* Applicant must be high school student; planning to enroll or expecting to enroll full- or part-time at a two-year, four-year, or technical institution or university; resident of Florida and studying in Florida. Applicant must have 3.0 GPA or higher. Available to U.S. citizens. *Application Requirements:* Application, test scores, transcript.

Contact Florida Department of Education, Office of Student Financial Assistance, Customer Service, Florida State Department of Education, 325 West Gaines Street, Tallahassee, FL 32399. *E-mail:* osfa@fldoe.org. *Phone:* 888-827-2004. *Web site:* http://www.floridastudentfinancialaid.org/.

Florida Postsecondary Student Assistance Grant. Scholarships to degree-seeking, resident, undergraduate students who demonstrate substantial financial need and are enrolled in eligible degree-granting private colleges and universities not eligible under the Florida Private Student Assistance

Grant. FSAG is a decentralized program, and each participating institution determines application procedures, deadlines and student eligibility. Number of awards varies. For more details, visit the web site at http// www.FloridaStudentFinancialAid.org/ SSFAD/home/uamain.htm. *Award:* Grant for use in freshman, sophomore, junior, or senior year; renewable. *Award amount:* $200–$2235. *Number of awards:* varies. *Eligibility Requirements:* Applicant must be enrolled or expecting to enroll full-time at a two-year or four-year institution or university; resident of Florida and studying in Florida. Available to U.S. citizens. *Application Requirements:* Application, financial need analysis.

Contact Florida Department of Education, Office of Student Financial Assistance, Customer Service, Florida State Department of Education, 325 West Gaines Street, Tallahassee, FL 32399. *E-mail:* osfa@fldoe.org. *Phone:* 888-827-2004. *Web site:* http://www.floridastudentfinancialaid.org/.

Florida Private Student Assistance Grant. Grants for Florida residents who are U.S. citizens or eligible non-citizens attending eligible private, nonprofit, four-year colleges and universities in Florida. Must be a full-time student and demonstrate substantial financial need. For renewal, must have earned a minimum cumulative GPA of 2.0 at the last institution attended. For more details, visit the web site at http:// www.FloridaStudentFinancialAid.org/ SSFAD/home/uamain.htm. *Award:* Grant for use in freshman, sophomore, junior, or senior year; renewable. *Award amount:* $200–$2235. *Number of awards:* varies. *Eligibility Requirements:* Applicant must be enrolled or expecting to enroll full-time at a four-year institution or university; resident of Florida and studying in Florida. Available to U.S. citizens. *Application Requirements:* Application, financial need analysis.

Contact Florida Department of Education, Office of Student Financial Assistance, Customer Service, Florida State Department of Education, 325 West Gaines Street, Tallahassee, FL 32399. *E-mail:* osfa@fldoe.org. *Phone:* 888-827-2004. *Web site:* http://www.floridastudentfinancialaid.org/.

Florida Public Student Assistance Grant. Grants for Florida residents, U.S. citizens or eligible non-citizens who attend state universities and public community colleges and demonstrate substantial financial need. For renewal, must have earned a minimum cumulative GPA of 2.0 at the last institution attended. *Award:* Grant for use in freshman, sophomore, junior, or senior year; renewable. *Award amount:* $200–$2235. *Number of awards:* varies. *Eligibility Requirements:* Applicant must be enrolled or expecting to enroll full- or part-time at a two-year or four-year institution or university; resident of Florida and studying in Florida. Available to U.S. citizens. *Application Requirements:* Application, financial need analysis.

Contact Florida Department of Education, Office of Student Financial Assistance, Customer Service, Florida State Department of Education, 325 West Gaines Street, Tallahassee, FL 32399. *E-mail:* osfa@fldoe.org. *Phone:* 888-827-2004. *Web site:* http://www.floridastudentfinancialaid.org/.

Florida Student Assistance Grant-Career Education. Need-based grant program available to Florida residents enrolled in certificate programs of 450 or more clock hours at participating community colleges or career centers operated by district school boards. FSAG-CE is a decentralized state of Florida program, which means that each participating institution determines application procedures, deadlines, student eligibility, and award amounts. For more details, visit the web site at http//www.FloridaStudentFinancialAid.org/SSFAD/ home/uamain.htm. *Award:* Grant for use in freshman, sophomore, junior, or senior year; renewable. *Award amount:* $200–$2235. *Eligibility Requirements:* Applicant must be enrolled or expecting to enroll full- or part-time at a two-year or technical institution; resident of Florida and studying in Florida. Available to U.S. citizens. *Application Requirements:* Application, financial need analysis.

Contact Florida Department of Education, Office of Student Financial Assistance, Customer Service, Florida State Department of Education, 325 West Gaines Street, Tallahassee, FL 32399. *E-mail:* osfa@fldoe.org. *Phone:* 888-847-2004. *Web site:* http://www.floridastudentfinancialaid.org/.

Florida Work Experience Program. Need-based program providing eligible Florida residents work experiences that will complement and reinforce their educational and career goals. Must maintain GPA of 2.0. Postsecondary institution will determine applicant's eligibility, number of hours to be worked per week, and the award amount. For more details, visit the web site at http//www.FloridaStudentFinancialAid.org/SSFAD/home/uamain.htm. *Award:* Grant for use in freshman, sophomore, junior, or senior year; renewable. *Award amount:* varies. *Number of awards:* varies. *Eligibility Requirements:* Applicant must be enrolled or expecting to enroll full- or part-time at a two-year or four-year institution or university; resident of Florida and studying in Florida. Available to U.S. citizens. *Application Requirements:* Application, financial need analysis.

Contact Florida Department of Education, Office of Student Financial Assistance, Customer Service, Florida State Department of Education, 325 West Gaines Street, Tallahassee, FL 32399. *E-mail:* osfa@fldoe.com. *Phone:* 888-827-2004. *Web site:* http://www.floridastudentfinancialaid.org/.

Jose Marti Scholarship Challenge Grant Fund. Award available to Hispanic-American students who were born in, or whose parent was born in a Hispanic country. Must be a Florida resident, be enrolled full-time in Florida at an eligible school, and have a GPA of 3.0 or above. Must be U.S. citizen or eligible non-citizen. FAFSA must be processed by May 15. For more information, visit web site http:// www.floridastudentfinancialaid.org/ssfad/ home/ProgramsOffered.htm. For more details, visit the web site at http://www.FloridaStudentFinancialAid.org/SSFAD/ home/uamain.htm. *Award:* Scholarship for use in freshman, sophomore, junior, or senior year; renewable. *Award amount:* $2000. *Number of awards:* varies. *Eligibility Requirements:* Applicant must be of Hispanic heritage; high school student; planning to enroll or expecting to enroll full-time at a two-year or four-year institution or university; resident of Florida and studying in Florida. Applicant must have 3.0 GPA or higher. Available to U.S. citizens. *Application Requirements:* Application, financial need analysis. **Deadline:** April 1.

Contact Florida Department of Education, Office of Student Financial Assistance, Customer Service, Florida State Department of Education, 325 West Gaines Street, Tallahassee, FL 32303. *E-mail:* osfa@fldoe.org. *Phone:* 888-827-2004. *Web site:* http://www.floridastudentfinancialaid.org/.

Mary McLeod Bethune Scholarship. Renewable award to Florida residents with a GPA of 3.0 or above, who will attend Bethune-Cookman University, Edward Waters College, Florida A&M University, or Florida Memorial University. Must not have previously received a baccalaureate degree. Must demonstrate financial need as specified by the institution. For more details, visit the web site at http://www.FloridaStudentFinancialAid.org/SSFAD/ home/uamain.htm. *Award:* Scholarship for use in freshman, sophomore, junior, or senior year; renewable. *Award amount:* $3000. *Number of awards:* varies. *Eligibil-*

ity Requirements: Applicant must be enrolled or expecting to enroll full-time at a four-year institution or university; resident of Florida and studying in Florida. Applicant must have 3.0 GPA or higher. Available to U.S. citizens. *Application Requirements:* Application, financial need analysis.

Contact Florida Department of Education, Office of Student Financial Assistance, Customer Service, Florida State Department of Education, 325 West Gaines Street, Tallahassee, FL 32399. *E-mail:* osfa@fldoe.org. *Phone:* 888-827-2004. *Web site:* http://www.floridastudentfinancialaid.org/.

Rosewood Family Scholarship Fund. Renewable award for eligible direct descendants of African-American Rosewood families affected by the incident of January 1923. Must not have previously received a baccalaureate degree. For more details, visit the web site at http//www.FloridaStudentFinancialAid.org/SSFAD/home/uamain.htm. *Award:* Scholarship for use in freshman, sophomore, junior, or senior year; renewable. *Award amount:* up to $4000. *Number of awards:* up to 25. *Eligibility Requirements:* Applicant must be enrolled or expecting to enroll full-time at a two-year, four-year, or technical institution or university and studying in Florida. Available to U.S. citizens. *Application Requirements:* Application, financial need analysis, documentation of Rosewood ancestry. **Deadline:** April 1.

Contact Florida Department of Education, Office of Student Financial Assistance, Customer Service, Florida State Department of Education, 325 West Gaines Street, Tallahassee, FL 32399. *E-mail:* osfa@fldoe.org. *Phone:* 888-827-2004. *Web site:* http://www.floridastudentfinancialaid.org/.

Scholarships for Children & Spouses of Deceased or Disabled Veterans or Servicemembers. Renewable scholarships for children and spouses of deceased or disabled veterans and service members. Children must be between the ages of 16 and 22, and attend an eligible Florida postsecondary institution and enrolled at least part-time. Must ensure that the Florida Department of Veterans Affairs certifies the applicant's eligibility. Must maintain GPA of 2.0. *Award:* Scholarship for use in freshman, sophomore, junior, or senior year; renewable. *Award amount:* varies. *Number of awards:* varies. *Eligibility Requirements:* Applicant must be age 16-22; enrolled or expecting to enroll full- or part-time at a two-year, four-year, or technical institution or university; resident of Florida and studying in Florida. Available to U.S. citizens. Applicant or parent must meet one or more of the following requirements: general military experience; retired from active duty; disabled or killed as a result of military service; prisoner of war; or missing in action. *Application Requirements:* Application. **Deadline:** April 1.

Contact Florida Department of Education, Office of Student Financial Assistance, Customer Service, Florida State Department of Education, 325 West Gaines Street, Tallahassee, FL 32399. *E-mail:* osfa@fldoe.org. *Phone:* 888-827-2004. *Web site:* http://www.floridastudentfinancialaid.org/.

William L. Boyd IV Florida Resident Access Grant. Renewable awards to Florida undergraduate residents attending an eligible private, nonprofit Florida college or university. Postsecondary institution will determine applicant's eligibility. Renewal applicant must have earned a minimum institutional GPA of 2.0. For more details, visit the web site at http//www.FloridaStudentFinancialAid.org/SSFAD/home/uamain.htm. *Award:* Grant for use in freshman, sophomore, junior, or senior year; renewable. *Award amount:* up to $2425. *Number of awards:* varies. *Eligibility Requirements:* Applicant must be enrolled or expecting to enroll full-time at a four-year institution or university; resident of Florida and studying in Florida. Available to U.S. citizens. *Application Requirements:* Application.

Contact Florida Department of Education, Office of Student Financial Assistance, Customer Service, Florida State Department of Education, 325 West Gaines Street, Tallahassee, FL 32399. *E-mail:* osfa@fldoe.org. *Phone:* 888-827-2004. *Web site:* http://www.floridastudentfinancialaid.org/.

GEORGIA

American Indian Nurse Scholarship Awards. Renewable award of $500 to $1000. Currently able to fund between 10 and 15 students. Intended originally to benefit females only, the program has expanded to include males and the career goals now include not only nursing careers, but jobs in health care and health education, as well. *Academic Fields/Career Goals:* Health Administration; Nursing. *Award:* Scholarship for use in freshman, sophomore, junior, senior, graduate, or postgraduate years; renewable. *Award amount:* $500–$1000. *Number of awards:* 10–15. *Eligibility Requirements:* Applicant must be American Indian/Alaska Native and enrolled or expecting to enroll full-time at a two-year, four-year, or technical institution or university. Applicant must have 2.5 GPA or higher. Available to U.S. citizens. *Application Requirements:* Application, driver's license, financial need analysis, photo, references, transcript. **Deadline:** continuous.

Contact Mrs. Joe Calvin, Scholarship Awards Consultant, National Society of The Colonial Dames of America, Nine Cross Creek Drive, Birmingham, AL 35213. *E-mail:* info@nscda.org. *Phone:* 205-871-4072. *Web site:* http://www.nscda.org/.

Georgia Public Safety Memorial Grant. Award for children of Georgia Public Safety Officers, prison guards, fire fighters, law enforcement officers or emergency medical technicians killed or permanently disabled in the line of duty. Must attend an accredited postsecondary Georgia school. Complete the Public Safety Memorial Grant application. *Award:* Grant for use in freshman, sophomore, junior, or senior year; not renewable. *Award amount:* $2000. *Number of awards:* 20–40. *Eligibility Requirements:* Applicant must be enrolled or expecting to enroll full-time at a two-year, four-year, or technical institution or university; resident of Georgia and studying in Georgia. Available to U.S. citizens. *Application Requirements:* Application, selective service registration. **Deadline:** continuous.

Contact Caylee B French, Division Director, Georgia Student Finance Commission, 2082 East Exchange Place, Suite 100, Tucker, GA 30084. *E-mail:* cayleef@gsfc.org. *Phone:* 770-724-9244. *Web site:* http://www.GAcollege411.org/.

Georgia Tuition Equalization Grant (GTEG). Award for Georgia residents pursuing undergraduate study at an accredited two- or four-year Georgia private postsecondary institution. *Award:* Grant for use in freshman, sophomore, junior, or senior year; not renewable. *Number of awards:* 1–35,000. *Eligibility Requirements:* Applicant must be Hispanic; enrolled or expecting to enroll full-time at a two-year or four-year institution or university; resident of Georgia and studying in Georgia. Applicant must be learning disabled. Available to U.S. citizens. *Application Requirements:* Application, social security number.

Contact Georgia Student Finance Commission, GA 30084. *Phone:* 800-505-4732. *Web site:* http://www.GAcollege411.org/.

HAWAII

Hawaii State Student Incentive Grant. Grants are given to residents of Hawaii who are enrolled in a participating Hawaiian state school. Funds are for undergraduate tuition only. Applicants must submit a financial need analysis. *Award:* Grant for use in freshman, sophomore, junior, or senior year; renewable. *Award amount:* \$200–\$2000. *Number of awards:* 470. *Eligibility Requirements:* Applicant must be enrolled or expecting to enroll full- or part-time at a two-year, four-year, or technical institution or university; resident of Hawaii and studying in Hawaii. Available to U.S. citizens. *Application Requirements:* Application, financial need analysis. **Deadline:** continuous.

Contact Janine Oyama, Financial Aid Specialist, Hawaii State Postsecondary Education Commission, University of Hawaii, Honolulu, HI 96822. *Phone:* 808-956-6066.

IDAHO

Freedom Scholarship. Full tuition, room and board scholarship and up to \$500 for books per semester for children of Idaho citizens determined by the federal government to have been prisoners of war, missing in action, or killed in action or died of injuries or wounds sustained in action in southeast Asia, including Korea, or who shall become so hereafter, in any area of armed conflicts. Applicant must attend an Idaho public college or university and meet all requirements for regular admission. The award value and the number of awards granted varies. For additional information, see web site http://www.boardofed.idaho.gov/scholarships/. *Award:* Scholarship for use in freshman, sophomore, junior, or senior year; not renewable. *Award amount:* varies. *Number of awards:* varies. *Eligibility Requirements:* Applicant must be enrolled or expecting to enroll full- or part-time at a two-year, four-year, or technical institution or university; resident of Idaho and studying in Idaho. Available to U.S. citizens. Applicant or parent must meet one or more of the following requirements: general military experience; retired from active duty; disabled or killed as a result of military service; prisoner of war; or missing in action. *Application Requirements:* Application. **Deadline:** January 15.

Contact Dana Kelly, Program Manager, Idaho State Board of Education, PO Box 83720, Boise, ID 83720-0037. *E-mail:* dana.kelly@osbe.idaho.gov. *Phone:* 208-332-1574. *Web site:* http://www.boardofed.idaho.gov/.

Idaho Minority and "At Risk" Student Scholarship. Renewable award for Idaho residents who are disabled or members of a minority group and have financial need. Must attend one of eight postsecondary institutions in the state for undergraduate study. Deadlines vary by institution. Must be a U.S. citizen and be a graduate of an Idaho high school. Contact college financial aid office. The awards range up to \$3000 a year for a maximum of four years. For additional information, go to web site http://www.boardofed.idaho.gov/scholarships/. *Award:* Scholarship for use in freshman, sophomore, junior, or senior year; renewable. *Award amount:* up to \$3000. *Number of awards:* 35–40. *Eligibility Requirements:* Applicant must be American Indian/Alaska Native, Black (non-Hispanic), or Hispanic; enrolled or expecting to enroll full-time at a two-year, four-year, or technical institution or university; resident of Idaho and studying in Idaho. Applicant must be hearing impaired, physically disabled, or visually impaired. Available to U.S. citizens. *Application Requirements:* Application, financial need analysis, transcript. **Deadline:** varies.

Contact Dana Kelly, Program Manager, Idaho State Board of Education, PO Box 83720, Boise, ID 83720-0037. *E-mail:* dana.kelly@osbe.idaho.gov. *Phone:* 208-332-1574. *Web site:* http://www.boardofed.idaho.gov/.

Idaho Promise Category A Scholarship Program. Renewable award available to Idaho residents who are graduating high school seniors. Must attend an approved Idaho institution of higher education on full-time basis and be enrolled in an eligible program. Must have a minimum GPA of 3.5 and an ACT score of 28 or above if enrolling in an academic program, and a GPA of 2.8 and must take the COMPASS test if enrolling in a professional-technical program. For additional information, list of eligible programs, and application, go to web site http://www.boardofed.idaho.gov/scholarships/. *Award:* Scholarship for use in freshman year; renewable. *Award amount:* \$3000. *Number of awards:* 25. *Eligibility Requirements:* Applicant must be high school student; planning to enroll or expecting to enroll full-time at a two-year, four-year, or technical institution or university; resident of Idaho and studying in Idaho. Available to U.S. citizens. *Application Requirements:* Application, applicant must enter a contest, test scores. **Deadline:** January 15.

Contact Dana Kelly, Program Manager, Student Affairs, Idaho State Board of Education, PO Box 83720, Boise, ID 83720-0037. *E-mail:* dana.kelly@osbe.idaho.gov. *Phone:* 208-332-1574. *Web site:* http://www.boardofed.idaho.gov/.

Idaho Promise Category B Scholarship Program. Available to Idaho residents entering college for the first time prior to the age of 22. Must have completed high school or its equivalent in Idaho and have a minimum GPA of 3.0 or an ACT score of 20 or higher. Scholarship limited to four semesters. Please go to web site for complete information http://www.boardofed.idaho.gov/scholarships/. *Award:* Scholarship for use in freshman year; renewable. *Award amount:* up to \$600. *Number of awards:* varies. *Eligibility Requirements:* Applicant must be high school student; age 22 or under; planning to enroll or expecting to enroll full-time at a two-year, four-year, or technical institution or university; resident of Idaho and studying in Idaho. Applicant must have 3.0 GPA or higher. Available to U.S. citizens. *Application Requirements:* Application, transcript. **Deadline:** continuous.

Contact Dana Kelly, Program Manager, Idaho State Board of Education, PO Box 83720, Boise, ID 83720-0037. *E-mail:* dana.kelly@osbe.idaho.gov. *Phone:* 208-332-1574. *Fax:* 208-334-2632. *Web site:* http://www.boardofed.idaho.gov/.

Leveraging Educational Assistance State Partnership Program (LEAP). One-time award assists students from any state, attending participating Idaho trade schools, colleges, and universities, and majoring in any field except theology or divinity. Must be enrolled for at least six credits and show financial need. Must be U.S. citizen or permanent resident. Deadlines vary by institution. For a list of eligible institutions, go to web site http://www.boardofed.idaho.gov/scholarships/. *Award:* Grant for use in freshman, sophomore, junior, or senior year; not renewable. *Award amount:* \$400–\$5000. *Number of awards:* varies. *Eligibility Requirements:* Applicant must be enrolled or expecting to enroll full- or part-time at a two-year, four-year, or technical institution or university and studying in Idaho. Available to U.S. citizens. *Application Requirements:* Application, financial need analysis, self-addressed stamped envelope. **Deadline:** varies.

Contact Dana Kelly, Student Affairs, Idaho State Board of Education, PO Box 83720, Boise, ID 83720-0037. *Phone:* 208-332-1574. *Fax:* 208-334-2632. *Web site:* http://www.boardofed.idaho.gov/.

Public Safety Officer Dependent Scholarship. Scholarship for dependents of full-time Idaho public safety officers who were killed or disabled in the line of duty. Recipients will attend an Idaho postsecondary institution with a full waiver of fees, including tuition, on-campus housing and campus meal plan, and up to \$500 per semester for books and supplies. For complete information, see web site http://www.boardofed.idaho.gov/scholarships/.

Award: Scholarship for use in freshman year; renewable. *Number of awards:* varies. *Eligibility Requirements:* Applicant must be enrolled or expecting to enroll full- or part-time at a two-year or four-year institution or university; resident of Idaho and studying in Idaho. Applicant or parent of applicant must have employment or volunteer experience in police/firefighting. Available to U.S. citizens. *Application Requirements:* Application. **Deadline:** January 15.

Contact Dana Kelly, Program Manager, Idaho State Board of Education, PO Box 83720, Boise, ID 83720-0037. *E-mail:* dana.kelly@osbe.idaho.gov. *Phone:* 208-332-1574. *Web site:* http://www.boardofed.idaho.gov/.

ILLINOIS

Golden Apple Scholars of Illinois. Applicants must be between the ages of 16 and 21 and maintain a GPA of 2.5. Eligible applicants must be residents of Illinois studying in Illinois. Recipients must agree to teach in high-need Illinois schools. *Academic Fields/Career Goals:* Education. *Award:* Scholarship for use in freshman, sophomore, junior, or senior year; renewable. *Award amount:* $23,000. *Number of awards:* 100–150. *Eligibility Requirements:* Applicant must be age 16-21; enrolled or expecting to enroll full-time at a four-year institution or university; resident of Illinois and studying in Illinois. Available to U.S. citizens. *Application Requirements:* Application, essay, interview, photo, references, test scores, transcript, social security card. **Deadline:** November 15.

Contact Ms. Patricia Kilduff, Director of Recruitment and Placement, Golden Apple Foundation, 8 South Michigan Avenue, Suite 700, Chicago, IL 60603-3318. *E-mail:* kilduff@goldenapple.org. *Phone:* 312-407-0006 Ext. 105. *Web site:* http://www.goldenapple.org/.

Grant Program for Dependents of Police, Fire, or Correctional Officers. Awards available to Illinois residents who are dependents of police, fire, and correctional officers killed or disabled in line of duty. Provides for tuition and fees at approved Illinois institutions. Number of grants and individual dollar amount awarded vary. *Award:* Grant for use in freshman, sophomore, junior, senior, graduate, or postgraduate years; renewable. *Award amount:* varies. *Number of awards:* varies. *Eligibility Requirements:* Applicant must be enrolled or expecting to enroll full- or part-time at a two-year, four-year, or technical institution or university; resident of Illinois and studying in Illinois. Available to U.S. citizens. *Application Requirements:* Application, proof of status. **Deadline:** varies.

Contact College Zone Counselor, Illinois Student Assistance Commission (ISAC), 1755 Lake Cook Road, Deerfield, IL 60015-5209. *E-mail:* collegezone@isac.org. *Phone:* 800-899-4722. *Fax:* 847-831-8549. *Web site:* http://www.collegezone.org/.

Higher Education License Plate Program-HELP. Grants for students who attend Illinois colleges for which the special collegiate license plates are available. The Illinois Secretary of State issues the license plates, and part of the proceeds are used for grants for undergraduate students attending these colleges, to pay tuition and mandatory fees. *Award:* Grant for use in freshman, sophomore, junior, or senior year; not renewable. *Award amount:* varies. *Number of awards:* varies. *Eligibility Requirements:* Applicant must be enrolled or expecting to enroll full- or part-time at a two-year or four-year institution or university; resident of Illinois and studying in Illinois. Available to U.S. citizens. *Application Requirements:* Application, financial need analysis. **Deadline:** varies.

Contact College Zone Counselor, Illinois Student Assistance Commission (ISAC), 1755 Lake Cook Road, Deerfield, IL 60015-5209. *E-mail:* collegezone@isac.org. *Phone:* 800-899-4722. *Fax:* 847-831-8549. *Web site:* http://www.collegezone.org/.

Illinois College Savings Bond Bonus Incentive Grant Program. Program offers Illinois college savings bond holders a grant for each year of bond maturity payable upon bond redemption if at least 70 percent of proceeds are used to attend college in Illinois. The amount of grant will depend on the amount of the bond, ranging from a $40 to $440 grant per $5000 of the bond. Applications are accepted between August 1 and May 30 of the academic year in which the bonds matured, or in the academic year immediately following maturity. *Award:* Grant for use in freshman, sophomore, junior, senior, graduate, or postgraduate years; not renewable. *Number of awards:* varies. *Eligibility Requirements:* Applicant must be enrolled or expecting to enroll full- or part-time at a two-year, four-year, or technical institution or university and studying in Illinois. Available to U.S. citizens. *Application Requirements:* Application. **Deadline:** varies.

Contact College Zone Counselor, Illinois Student Assistance Commission (ISAC), 1755 Lake Cook Road, Deerfield, IL 60015-5209. *E-mail:* collegezone@isac.org. *Phone:* 800-899-4722. *Fax:* 847-831-8549. *Web site:* http://www.collegezone.org/.

Illinois Future Teachers Corps Program. Scholarships are available for students planning to become teachers in Illinois. Students must be Illinois residents, enrolled or accepted as a junior or above in a Teacher Education Program at an Illinois college or university. By receiving the award, students agree to teach for five years at either a public, private, or parochial Illinois preschool, or at a public elementary or secondary school. *Academic Fields/Career Goals:* Education. *Award:* Scholarship for use in junior, senior, or graduate year; renewable. *Award amount:* $5000–$10,000. *Eligibility Requirements:* Applicant must be enrolled or expecting to enroll full- or part-time at a four-year institution or university; resident of Illinois and studying in Illinois. Available to U.S. citizens. *Application Requirements:* Application, financial need analysis, FAFSA. **Deadline:** March 1.

Contact College Zone Counselor, Illinois Student Assistance Commission (ISAC), 1755 Lake Cook Road, Deerfield, IL 60015-5209. *E-mail:* collegezone@isac.org. *Phone:* 800-899-4722. *Fax:* 847-831-8549. *Web site:* http://www.collegezone.org/.

Illinois General Assembly Scholarship. Scholarships available for Illinois students enrolled at an Illinois four-year state-supported college. Must contact the general assembly member for eligibility criteria. Deadline varies. *Award:* Scholarship for use in freshman, sophomore, junior, or senior year; not renewable. *Award amount:* varies. *Number of awards:* varies. *Eligibility Requirements:* Applicant must be enrolled or expecting to enroll full- or part-time at a four-year institution or university; resident of Illinois and studying in Illinois. Available to U.S. citizens. *Application Requirements:* Application. **Deadline:** varies.

Contact College Zone Counselor, Illinois Student Assistance Commission (ISAC), 1755 Lake Cook Road, Deerfield, IL 60015-5209. *E-mail:* collegezone@isac.org. *Phone:* 800-899-4722. *Fax:* 847-831-8549. *Web site:* http://www.collegezone.org/.

Illinois Monetary Award Program. Awards to Illinois residents enrolled in a minimum of 3 hours per term in a degree program at an approved Illinois institution. See web site for complete list of participating schools. Must demonstrate financial need, based on the information provided on the Free Application for Federal Student Aid. Number of grants and the individual dollar amount awarded vary. Deadline: As soon as possible after January 1 of the year in which the student will enter college. *Award:* Grant for use in freshman, sophomore, junior, or senior year; renewable. *Award amount:* $2637. *Eligibility Requirements:* Applicant must be enrolled or expecting to enroll full- or part-time at a two-year, four-year, or technical institution or university; resident of Illinois and studying in Illinois. Available to U.S. citizens. *Application Requirements:* Financial need analysis, FAFSA online. **Deadline:** varies.

Contact College Zone Counselor, Illinois Student Assistance Commission (ISAC), 1755 Lake Cook Road, Deerfield, IL 60015-5209. *E-mail:* collegezone@isac.org. *Phone:* 800-899-4722. *Fax:* 847-831-8549. *Web site:* http://www.collegezone.org/.

Illinois National Guard Grant Program. Active duty members of the Illinois National Guard, or who are within 12 months of discharge, and who have completed one full year of service are eligible. May be used for study at Illinois two- or four-year public colleges for a maximum of the equivalent of four academic years of full-time enrollment. Deadlines: October 1 of the academic year for full year, March 1 for second/third term, or June 15 for the summer term. *Award:* Grant for use in freshman, sophomore, junior, senior, or graduate year; renewable. *Award amount:* varies. *Number of awards:* varies. *Eligibility Requirements:* Applicant must be enrolled or expecting to enroll full- or part-time at a two-year or four-year institution or university; resident of Illinois and studying in Illinois. Available to U.S. citizens. Applicant or parent must meet one or more of the following requirements: Air Force National Guard or Army National Guard experience; retired from active duty; disabled or killed as a result of military service; prisoner of war; or missing in action. *Application Requirements:* Application, documentation of service. **Deadline:** varies.

Contact College Zone Counselor, Illinois Student Assistance Commission (ISAC), 1755 Lake Cook Road, Deerfield, IL 60015-5209. *E-mail:* collegezone@isac.org. *Phone:* 800-899-4722. *Fax:* 847-831-8549. *Web site:* http://www.collegezone.org/.

Illinois Special Education Teacher Tuition Waiver. Teachers or students who are pursuing a career in special education as public, private or parochial preschool, elementary or secondary school teachers in Illinois may be eligible for this program. This program will exempt such individuals from paying tuition and mandatory fees at an eligible institution, for up to four years. The individual dollar amount awarded are subject to sufficient annual appropriations by the Illinois General Assembly. *Academic Fields/Career Goals:* Special Education. *Award:* Scholarship for use in freshman, sophomore, junior, senior, or graduate year; renewable. *Award amount:* varies. *Eligibility Requirements:* Applicant must be enrolled or expecting to enroll full- or part-time at a four-year institution or university; resident of Illinois and studying in Illinois. Available to U.S. citizens. *Application Requirements:* Application. **Deadline:** March 1.

Contact College Zone Counselor, Illinois Student Assistance Commission (ISAC), 1755 Lake Cook Road, Deerfield, IL 60015-5209. *E-mail:* collegezone@isac.org. *Phone:* 800-899-4722. *Fax:* 847-831-8549. *Web site:* http://www.collegezone.org/.

Illinois Student-to-Student Program of Matching Grants. Matching grant is available to undergraduates at participating state-supported colleges. Number of grants and the individual dollar amount awarded vary. Contact financial aid office at institution. *Award:* Grant for use in freshman, sophomore, junior, or senior year; not renewable. *Award amount:* $300–$1000. *Number of awards:* varies. *Eligibility Requirements:* Applicant must be enrolled or expecting to enroll full- or part-time at a two-year or four-year institution or university; resident of Illinois and studying in Illinois. Available to U.S. citizens. *Application Requirements:* Application, financial need analysis. **Deadline:** varies.

Contact College Zone Counselor, Illinois Student Assistance Commission (ISAC), 1755 Lake Cook Road, Deerfield, IL 60015-5209. *E-mail:* collegezone@isac.org. *Phone:* 800-899-4722. *Fax:* 847-831-8549. *Web site:* http://www.collegezone.org/.

Illinois Veteran Grant Program-IVG. Awards qualified veterans and pays eligible tuition and fees for study in Illinois public universities or community colleges. Program eligibility units are based on the enrolled hours for a particular term, not the dollar amount of the benefits paid. Applications are available at college financial aid office and can be submitted any time during the academic year for which assistance is being requested. *Award:* Grant for use in freshman, sophomore, junior, senior, or graduate year; renewable. *Eligibility Requirements:* Applicant must be enrolled or expecting to enroll full- or part-time at a two-year or four-year institution or university; resident of Illinois and studying in Illinois. Available to U.S. citizens. Applicant or parent must meet one or more of the following requirements: general military experience; retired from active duty; disabled or killed as a result of military service; prisoner of war; or missing in action. *Application Requirements:* Application. **Deadline:** continuous.

Contact College Zone Counselor, Illinois Student Assistance Commission (ISAC), 1755 Lake Cook Road, Deerfield, IL 60015-5209. *E-mail:* collegezone@isac.org. *Phone:* 800-899-4722. *Fax:* 847-831-8549. *Web site:* http://www.collegezone.org/.

Merit Recognition Scholarship (MRS) Program. One-time awards available to Illinois residents for use at Illinois institutions. Must be ranked in the top 5 percent of high school class or have scored among the top 5 percent on the ACT, SAT, or Prairie State Achievement Exam. Number of scholarships granted varies. Program not currently funded. *Award:* Scholarship for use in freshman year; not renewable. *Award amount:* up to $1000. *Number of awards:* varies. *Eligibility Requirements:* Applicant must be high school student; planning to enroll or expecting to enroll full- or part-time at a two-year or four-year institution or university; resident of Illinois and studying in Illinois. Available to U.S. citizens. *Application Requirements:* Application, transcript. **Deadline:** June 15.

Contact College Zone Counselor, Illinois Student Assistance Commission (ISAC), 1755 Lake Cook Road, Deerfield, IL 60015-5209. *E-mail:* collegezone@isac.org. *Phone:* 800-899-4722. *Fax:* 847-831-8549. *Web site:* http://www.collegezone.org/.

MIA/POW Scholarships. One-time award for spouse, child, or step-child of veterans who are missing in action or were a prisoner of war. Must be enrolled at a state-supported school in Illinois. Candidate must be U.S. citizen. Must apply and be accepted before beginning of school. Also for children and spouses of veterans who are determined to be 100 percent disabled as established by the Veterans Administration. Scholarship value and the number of awards granted varies. *Award:* Scholarship for use in freshman, sophomore, junior, or senior year; renewable. *Award amount:* varies. *Number of awards:* varies. *Eligibility Requirements:* Applicant must be enrolled or expecting to enroll full- or part-time at a two-year or four-year institution or university; resident of Illinois and studying in Illinois. Available to U.S. citizens. Applicant or parent must meet one or more of the following requirements: general military experience; retired from active duty; disabled or killed as a result of military service; prisoner of war; or missing in action. *Application Requirements:* Application. **Deadline:** continuous.

Contact Ms. Tracy Smith, Grants Section, Illinois Department of Veterans' Affairs, 833 South Spring Street, Springfield, IL 62794-9432. *Phone:* 217-782-3564. *Fax:* 217-782-4161. *Web site:* http://www.state.il.us/agency/dva.

Minority Teachers of Illinois Scholarship Program. Award for minority students intending to become school teachers; teaching commitment attached to receipt. Number of scholarships and the individual dollar amounts vary. *Academic Fields/Career Goals:* Education; Special Education. *Award:* Scholarship for use in freshman, sophomore, junior, senior, graduate, or postgraduate years; renewable. *Award amount:* up to $5000. *Eligibility Requirements:* Applicant must be American Indian/Alaska Native, Asian/Pacific Islander, Black (non-Hispanic), or Hispanic; enrolled or expecting to enroll full- or part-time at a two-year or four-year institution or university; resident of Illinois and studying in Illinois. Available to U.S. citizens. *Application Requirements:* Application, transcript. **Deadline:** March 1.

Contact College Zone Counselor, Illinois Student Assistance Commission (ISAC), 1755 Lake Cook Road, Deerfield, IL 60015-5209. *E-mail:* collegezone@isac.org. *Phone:* 800-899-4722. *Fax:* 847-831-8549. *Web site:* http://www.collegezone.org/.

Robert C. Byrd Honors Scholarship-Illinois. Scholarship for Illinois residents and graduating high school seniors accepted on a full-time basis as an undergraduate student at an Illinois college or university. The award is up to $1500 per year, for a maximum of four years. Minimum 3.5 GPA required. Students are automatically considered for this scholarship if they meet the eligibility requirements. High school counselors submit information to selection process. *Award:* Scholarship for use in freshman, sophomore, junior, or senior year; renewable. *Award amount:* up to $1500. *Number of awards:* varies. *Eligibility Requirements:* Applicant must be high school student; planning to enroll or expecting to enroll full-time at a two-year or four-year institution or university; resident of Illinois and studying in Illinois. Available to U.S. citizens. *Application Requirements:* Application, test scores, transcript. **Deadline:** July 15.

Contact College Zone Counselor, Illinois Student Assistance Commission (ISAC), 1755 Lake Cook Road, Deerfield, IL 60015-5209. *E-mail:* collegezone@isac.org. *Phone:* 800-899-4722. *Web site:* http://www.collegezone.org/.

Silas Purnell Illinois Incentive for Access Program. Students whose information provided on the FAFSA results in a calculated zero expected family contribution when they are college freshmen may be eligible to receive a grant of up to $500. Must be a U.S. citizen and an Illinois resident studying at a participating Illinois institution. See web site for complete list of schools and additional requirements. *Award:* Grant for use in freshman year; not renewable. *Award amount:* up to $500. *Number of awards:* varies. *Eligibility Requirements:* Applicant must be high school student; planning to enroll or expecting to enroll full- or part-time at a two-year, four-year, or technical institution or university; resident of Illinois and studying in Illinois. Available to U.S. citizens. *Application Requirements:* Financial need analysis, FAFSA. **Deadline:** July 1.

Contact College Zone Counselor, Illinois Student Assistance Commission (ISAC), 1755 Lake Cook Road, Deerfield, IL 60015-5209. *E-mail:* collegezone@isac.org. *Phone:* 800-899-4722. *Fax:* 847-831-8549. *Web site:* http://www.collegezone.org/.

Veterans' Children Educational Opportunities. $250 award for each child aged 10 to 18 of a veteran who died or became totally disabled as a result of service during World War I, World War II, Korean, or Vietnam War. Must be Illinois resident studying in Illinois. Death must be service-connected. Disability must be rated 100 percent for two or more years. *Award:* Grant for use in freshman year; not renewable. *Award amount:* $250. *Number of awards:* varies. *Eligibility Requirements:* Applicant must be age 10-18; enrolled or expecting to enroll full- or part-time at a two-year or four-year institution or university; resident of Illinois and studying in Illinois. Available to U.S. citizens. Applicant or parent must meet one or more of the following requirements: general military experience; retired from active duty; disabled or killed as a result of military service; prisoner of war; or missing in action. *Application Requirements:* Application. **Deadline:** June 30.

Contact Tracy Smith, Grants Section, Illinois Department of Veterans' Affairs, 833 South Spring Street, Springfield, IL 62794-9432. *Phone:* 217-782-3564. *Fax:* 217-782-4161. *Web site:* http://www.state.il.us/agency/dva.

INDIANA

Child of Disabled Veteran Grant or Purple Heart Recipient Grant. Free tuition at Indiana state-supported colleges or universities for children of disabled veterans or Purple Heart recipients. Must submit form DD214 or service record. Covers tuition and mandatory fees. *Award:* Grant for use in freshman, sophomore, junior, senior, graduate, or postgraduate years; renewable. *Award amount:* varies. *Number of awards:* varies. *Eligibility Requirements:* Applicant must be enrolled or expecting to enroll full- or part-time at a two-year or four-year institution or university; resident of Indiana and studying in Indiana. Available to U.S. citizens. Applicant or parent must meet one or more of the following requirements: general military experience; retired from active duty; disabled or killed as a result of military service; prisoner of war; or missing in action. *Application Requirements:* Application, FAFSA. **Deadline:** continuous.

Contact Jon Brinkley, State Service Officer, Indiana Department of Veterans Affairs, 302 West Washington Street, Room E-120, Indianapolis, IN 46204-2738. *E-mail:* jbrinkley@dva.in.gov. *Phone:* 317-232-3910. *Fax:* 317-232-7721. *Web site:* http://www.in.gov/dva.

Department of Veterans Affairs Free Tuition for Children of POW/MIA's in Vietnam. Renewable award for residents of Indiana who are the children of veterans declared missing in action or prisoner-of-war after January 1, 1960. Provides tuition at Indiana state-supported institutions for undergraduate study. *Award:* Grant for use in freshman, sophomore, junior, senior, graduate, or postgraduate years; renewable. *Award amount:* varies. *Number of awards:* varies. *Eligibility Requirements:* Applicant must be age 24 or under; enrolled or expecting to enroll full- or part-time at a two-year or four-year institution or university; resident of Indiana and studying in Indiana. Available to U.S. citizens. Applicant or parent must meet one or more of the following requirements: general military experience; retired from active duty; disabled or killed as a result of military service; prisoner of war; or missing in action. *Application Requirements:* Application. **Deadline:** continuous.

Contact Jon Brinkley, State Service Officer, Indiana Department of Veterans Affairs, 302 West Washington Street, Room E-120, Indianapolis, IN 46204-2738. *E-mail:* jbrinkley@dva.in.gov. *Phone:* 317-232-3910. *Fax:* 317-232-7721. *Web site:* http://www.in.gov/dva.

Frank O'Bannon Grant Program. A need-based, tuition-restricted program for students attending Indiana public, private, or proprietary institutions seeking a first undergraduate degree. Students (and parents of dependent students) who are U.S. citizens and Indiana residents must file the FAFSA yearly by the March 10 deadline. *Award:* Grant for use in freshman, sophomore, junior, or senior year; not renewable. *Award amount:* \$200–\$10,992. *Number of awards:* 48,408–70,239. *Eligibility Requirements:* Applicant must be enrolled or expecting to enroll full-time at a two-year, four-year, or technical institution or university; resident of Indiana and studying in Indiana. Available to U.S. citizens. *Application Requirements:* Application, financial need analysis, FAFSA. **Deadline:** March 10.

Contact Grants Counselor, State Student Assistance Commission of Indiana (SSACI), 150 West Market Street, Suite 500, Indianapolis, IN 46204-2805. *E-mail:* grants@ssaci.state.in.us. *Phone:* 317-232-2350. *Fax:* 317-232-3260. *Web site:* http://www.in.gov/ssaci.

Hoosier Scholar Award. A \$500 nonrenewable award. Based on the size of the senior class, one to three scholars are selected by the guidance counselors of each accredited high school in Indiana. The award is based on academic merit and may be used for any educational expense at an eligible Indiana institution of higher education. *Award:* Scholarship for use in freshman year; not renewable. *Award amount:* \$500. *Number of awards:* 666–840. *Eligibility Requirements:* Applicant must be high school student; planning to enroll or expecting to enroll full-time at a two-year or four-year institution or university; resident of Indiana and studying in Indiana. Applicant must have 3.5 GPA or higher. Available to U.S. citizens. *Application Requirements:* Application, references. **Deadline:** March 10.

Contact Ada Sparkman, Program Coordinator, State Student Assistance Commission of Indiana (SSACI), 150 West Market Street, Suite 500, Indianapolis, IN 46204-2805. *Phone:* 317-232-2350. *Fax:* 317-232-3260. *Web site:* http://www.in.gov/ssaci.

Indiana National Guard Supplemental Grant. The award is a supplement to the Indiana Higher Education Grant program. Applicants must be members of the Indiana National Guard. All Guard paperwork must be completed prior to the start of each semester. The FAFSA must be received by March 10. Award covers certain tuition and fees at select public colleges. *Award:* Grant for use in freshman, sophomore, junior, or senior year; not renewable. *Award amount:* \$20–\$7110. *Number of awards:* 503–925. *Eligibility Requirements:* Applicant must be enrolled or expecting to enroll full- or part-time at a two-year or four-year institution or university; resident of Indiana and studying in Indiana. Available to U.S. citizens. Applicant or parent must meet one or more of the following requirements: Air Force National Guard or Army National Guard experience; retired from active duty; disabled or killed as a result of military service; prisoner of war; or missing in action. *Application Requirements:* Application. **Deadline:** March 10.

Contact Kathryn Moore, Grants Counselor, State Student Assistance Commission of Indiana (SSACI), 150 West Market Street, Suite 500, Indianapolis, IN 46204-2805. *E-mail:* kmoore@ssaci.in.gov. *Phone:* 317-232-2350. *Fax:* 317-232-2360. *Web site:* http://www.in.gov/ssaci.

Indiana Nursing Scholarship Fund. Need-based tuition funding for nursing students enrolled full- or part-time at an eligible Indiana institution. Must be a U.S. citizen and an Indiana resident and have a minimum 2.0 GPA or meet the minimum requirements for the nursing program. Upon graduation, recipients must practice as a nurse in an Indiana health care setting for two years. *Academic Fields/Career Goals:* Nursing. *Award:* Scholarship for use in freshman, sophomore, junior, or senior year; not renewable. *Award amount:* \$200–\$5000. *Number of awards:* 490–690. *Eligibility Requirements:* Applicant must be enrolled or expecting to enroll full- or part-time at a two-year or four-year institution or university; resident of Indiana and studying in Indiana. Available to U.S. citizens. *Application Requirements:* Application, financial need analysis, FAFSA. **Deadline:** continuous.

Contact Yvonne Heflin, Director, Special Programs, State Student Assistance Commission of Indiana (SSACI), 150 West Market Street, Suite 500, Indianapolis, IN 46204-2805. *Phone:* 317-232-2350. *Fax:* 317-232-3260. *Web site:* http://www.in.gov/ssaci.

National Guard Scholarship Extension Program. A scholarship extension applicant is eligible for a tuition scholarship under Indiana Code 21-13-5-4 for a period not to exceed the period of scholarship extension the applicant served on active duty as a member of the National Guard (mobilized and deployed). Must apply not later than one (1) year after the applicant ceases to be a member of the Indiana National Guard. Applicant should apply through the education officer of their last unit of assignment. *Award:* Grant for use in freshman, sophomore, junior, or senior year; renewable. *Award amount:* varies. *Number of awards:* varies. *Eligibility Requirements:* Applicant must be enrolled or expecting to enroll full- or part-time at a two-year, four-year, or technical institution or university and studying in Indiana. Available to U.S. citizens. Applicant must have served in the Air Force National Guard or Army National Guard. *Application Requirements:* Application. **Deadline:** continuous.

Contact Pamela Moody, National Guard Education Officer, Indiana Department of Veterans Affairs, 302 West Washington Street, Suite E120, Indianapolis, IN 46204. *E-mail:* pamela.moody@in.ngb.army.mil. *Phone:* 317-964-7017. *Fax:* 317-232-7721. *Web site:* http://www.in.gov/dva.

National Guard Tuition Supplement Program. Applicant must be a member of the Indiana National Guard, in active drilling status, who has not been AWOL during the last 12 months, does not possess a bachelor's degree, possesses the requisite academic qualifications, meets the requirements of the state-supported college or university, and meets all National Guard requirements. *Award:* Grant for use in freshman, sophomore, junior, or senior year; renewable. *Award amount:* varies. *Number of awards:* varies. *Eligibility Requirements:* Applicant must be enrolled or expecting to enroll full- or part-time at a two-year, four-year, or technical institution or university and studying in Indiana. Available to U.S. citizens. Applicant must have served in the Air Force National Guard or Army National Guard. *Application Requirements:* Application, FAFSA. **Deadline:** continuous.

Contact Jon Brinkley, State Service Officer, Indiana Department of Veterans Affairs, 302 West Washington Street, Room E-120, Indianapolis, IN 46204-2738. *E-mail:* jbrinkley@dva.in.gov. *Phone:* 317-232-3910. *Fax:* 317-232-7721. *Web site:* http://www.in.gov/dva.

Part-Time Grant Program. Program is designed to encourage part-time undergraduates to start and complete their associate or baccalaureate degrees or certificates by subsidizing part-time tuition costs. It is a term-based award that is based on need. State residency requirements must be met and a FAFSA must be filed. Eligibility is determined at the institutional level subject to approval by SSACI. *Award:* Grant for use in freshman, sophomore, junior, or senior year; not renewable. *Award amount:* \$20–\$4000. *Number of awards:* 4680–6700. *Eligibility Requirements:* Applicant must be enrolled or expecting to enroll part-time at a two-year, four-year, or technical institution or university; resident of Indiana and studying in Indiana. Available to U.S. citizens. *Application Requirements:* Application, financial need analysis. **Deadline:** continuous.

Contact Grants Counselor, State Student Assistance Commission of Indiana (SSACI), 150 West Market Street, Suite 500, Indianapolis, IN 46204-2805. *E-mail:* grants@ssaci.state.in.us. *Phone:* 317-232-2350. *Fax:* 317-232-3260. *Web site:* http://www.in.gov/ssaci.

Resident Tuition for Active Duty Military Personnel. Applicant must be a nonresident of Indiana serving on active duty and stationed in Indiana and attending any state-supported college or university. Dependents remain eligible for the duration of their enrollment, even if the active duty person is no longer in Indiana. Entitlement is to the resident tuition rate. *Award:* Grant for use in freshman, sophomore, junior, senior, graduate, or postgraduate years; renewable. *Award amount:* varies. *Number of awards:* varies. *Eligibility Requirements:* Applicant must be enrolled or expecting to enroll full- or part-time at a two-year, four-year, or technical institution or university and studying in Indiana. Available to U.S. citizens. Applicant or parent must meet one or more of the following requirements: Air Force, Army, Marine Corps, or Navy experience; retired from active duty; disabled or killed as a result of military service; prisoner of war; or missing in action. *Application Requirements:* Application. **Deadline:** continuous.

Contact Jon Brinkley, State Service Officer, Indiana Department of Veterans Affairs, 302 West Washington Street, Room E-120, Indianapolis, IN 46204-2738. *E-mail:* jbrinkley@dva.in.gov. *Phone:* 317-232-3910. *Fax:* 317-232-7721. *Web site:* http://www.in.gov/dva.

Tuition and Fee Remission for Children and Spouses of National Guard Members. Award to an individual whose father, mother or spouse was a member of the Indiana National Guard and suffered a service-connected death while serving on state active duty (which includes mobilized and deployed for federal active duty). The student must be eligible to pay the resident tuition rate at the state-supported college or university and must possess the requisite academic qualifications. *Award:* Grant for use in freshman, sophomore, junior, or senior year; renewable. *Award amount:* varies. *Number of awards:* varies. *Eligibility Requirements:* Applicant must be enrolled or expecting to enroll full- or part-time at a two-year, four-year, or technical institution or university and studying in Indiana. Available to U.S. citizens. Applicant or parent must meet one or more of the following requirements: Air Force National Guard or Army National Guard experience; retired from active duty; disabled or killed as a result of military service; prisoner of war; or missing in action. *Application Requirements:* Application, FAFSA. **Deadline:** continuous.

Contact R. Martin Umbarger, Adjutant General, Indiana Department of Veterans Affairs, 2002 South Holt Road, Indianapolis, IN 46241. *E-mail:* r.martin.umbarger@in.ngb.army.mil. *Phone:* 317-247-3559. *Fax:* 317-247-3540. *Web site:* http://www.in.gov/dva.

Twenty-first Century Scholars Gear Up Summer Scholarship. Grant of up to $3000 that pays for summer school tuition and regularly assessed course fees (does not cover other costs such as textbooks or room and board). *Award:* Scholarship for use in freshman, sophomore, junior, or senior year; not renewable. *Award amount:* up to $3000. *Number of awards:* 1. *Eligibility Requirements:* Applicant must be enrolled or expecting to enroll full-time at a two-year or four-year institution or university; resident of Indiana and studying in Indiana. Available to U.S. citizens. *Application Requirements:* Application, must be in twenty-first century scholars program, high school diploma. **Deadline:** varies.

Contact Coordinator, Office of Twenty-First Century Scholars, State Student Assistance Commission of Indiana (SSACI), 150 West Market Street, Suite 500, Indianapolis, IN 46204. *E-mail:* 21stscholars@ssaci.in.gov. *Phone:* 317-234-1394. *Web site:* http://www.in.gov/ssaci.

IOWA

All Iowa Opportunity Scholarship. Students attending eligible Iowa colleges and universities may receive awards of up to $6420. Minimum 2.5 GPA. Priority will be given to students who participated in the Federal TRIO Programs, graduated from alternative high schools, and to homeless youth. Applicant must enroll within two academic years of graduating from high school. Maximum individual awards cannot exceed more than the resident tuition rate at Iowa Regent Universities. *Award:* Scholarship for use in freshman or sophomore year; not renewable. *Number of awards:* 200–800. *Eligibility Requirements:* Applicant must be enrolled or expecting to enroll full- or part-time at a two-year, four-year, or technical institution or university; resident of Iowa and studying in Iowa. Applicant must have 2.5 GPA or higher. Available to U.S. citizens. *Application Requirements:* Application, financial need analysis. **Deadline:** March 1.

Contact Todd Brown, Director, Scholarships, Grants, and Loan Forgiveness, Iowa College Student Aid Commission, 603 E 12th Street, 5th FL, Des Moines, IA 50319. *E-mail:* grants@iowacollegeaid.gov. *Phone:* 877-272-4456. *Fax:* 515-725-3401. *Web site:* http://www.iowacollegeaid.gov/.

Iowa Grants. Statewide need-based program to assist high-need Iowa residents. Recipients must demonstrate a high level of financial need to receive awards ranging from $100 to $1000. Awards are prorated for students enrolled for less than full-time. Awards must be used at Iowa postsecondary institutions. *Award:* Grant for use in freshman, sophomore, junior, or senior year; not renewable. *Award amount:* $100–$1000. *Number of awards:* 2000–3000. *Eligibility Requirements:* Applicant must be enrolled or expecting to enroll full- or part-time at a two-year, four-year, or technical institution or university; resident of Iowa and studying in Iowa. Available to U.S. citizens. *Application Requirements:* Application, financial need analysis. **Deadline:** continuous.

Contact Todd Brown, Director, Scholarships, Grants, and Loan Forgiveness, Iowa College Student Aid Commission, 603 E 12th Street, 5th FL, Des Moines, IA 50319. *E-mail:* grants@iowacollegeaid.gov. *Phone:* 877-272-4456. *Fax:* 515-725-3401. *Web site:* http://www.iowacollegeaid.gov/.

Iowa National Guard Education Assistance Program. Program provides postsecondary tuition assistance to members of Iowa National Guard Units. Must study at a postsecondary institution in Iowa. Contact the office for additional information. *Award:* Grant for use in freshman, sophomore, junior, or senior year; not renewable. *Number of awards:* 700–1500. *Eligibility Requirements:* Applicant must be enrolled or expecting to enroll full- or part-time at a two-year, four-year, or technical institution or university; resident of Iowa and studying in Iowa. Available to U.S. citizens. Applicant must have served in the Air Force National Guard or Army National Guard. *Application Requirements:* Application. **Deadline:** continuous.

Contact Todd Brown, Director, Scholarships, Grants, and Loan Forgiveness, Iowa College Student Aid Commission, 603 E 12th Street, 5th FL, Des Moines, IA 50319. *E-mail:* todd.brown@iowa.gov. *Phone:* 515-725-3405. *Fax:* 515-725-3401. *Web site:* http://www.iowacollegeaid.gov/.

Iowa Tuition Grant Program. Program assists students who attend independent postsecondary institutions in Iowa. Iowa residents currently enrolled, or planning to enroll, for at least 3 semester hours at one of the eligible Iowa postsecondary institutions may apply. Awards currently range from $100 to $4000. Grants may not exceed the difference between independent college and university tuition fees and the average tuition fees at the three public Regent universities. *Award:* Grant for use in freshman, sophomore, junior, or senior year; renewable. *Award amount:* $100–$4000. *Number of awards:* 16,000–17,500. *Eligibility Requirements:* Applicant must be enrolled or expecting to enroll full- or part-time at a four-year institution or university; resident of Iowa and studying in Iowa. Available to U.S. citizens. *Application Requirements:* Application, financial need analysis. **Deadline:** July 1.

Contact Todd Brown, Director, Scholarships, Grants, and Loan Forgiveness, Iowa College Student Aid Commission, 603 E 12th Street, 5th FL, Des Moines, IA 50319. *E-mail:* todd.brown@iowa.gov. *Phone:* 515-725-3420. *Fax:* 515-725-3401. *Web site:* http://www.iowacollegeaid.gov/.

Iowa Vocational-Technical Tuition Grant Program. Program provides need-based financial assistance to Iowa residents enrolled in career education (vocational-technical), and career option programs at Iowa area community colleges. Grants range from $150 to $1200, depending on the length of the program, financial need, and available funds. *Award:* Grant for use in freshman or sophomore year; not renewable. *Award amount:* $150–$1200. *Number of awards:* 2500–3500. *Eligibility Requirements:* Applicant must be enrolled or expecting to enroll full- or part-time at a two-year or technical institution; resident of Iowa and studying in Iowa. Available to U.S. citizens. *Application Requirements:* Application, financial need analysis. **Deadline:** July 1.

Contact Todd Brown, Director, Program Administration, Iowa College Student Aid Commission, 603 E 12th Street, 5th FL, Des Moines, IA 50319. *E-mail:* todd.brown@iowa.gov. *Phone:* 515-725-3405. *Fax:* 515-725-3401. *Web site:* http://www.iowacollegeaid.gov/.

KANSAS

Kansas Educational Benefits for Children of MIA, POW, and Deceased Veterans of the Vietnam War. Scholarship awarded to students who are children of veterans. Must show proof of parent's status as missing in action, prisoner of war, or killed in action in the Vietnam War. Kansas residence required of veteran at time of entry to service. Must attend a state-supported postsecondary school. *Award:* Scholarship for use in freshman, sophomore, junior, or senior year; not renewable. *Award amount:* varies. *Number of awards:* 1. *Eligibility Requirements:* Applicant must be enrolled or expecting to enroll full-time at a two-year, four-year, or technical institution or university and studying in Kansas. Available to U.S. citizens. Applicant or parent must meet one or more of the following requirements: general military experience; retired from active duty; disabled or killed as a result of military service; prisoner of war; or missing in action. *Application Requirements:* Application, birth certificate, school acceptance letter, military discharge of veteran. **Deadline:** varies.

Contact Wayne Bollig, Program Director, Kansas Commission on Veterans Affairs, 700 Jackson, SW, Suite 701, Topeka, KS 66603-3743. *E-mail:* wbollig@kcva.org. *Phone:* 785-296-3976. *Fax:* 785-296-1462. *Web site:* http://www.kcva.org/.

Kansas Ethnic Minority Scholarship. Scholarship program designed to assist financially needy, academically competitive students who are identified as members of any of the following ethnic/racial groups: African-American, American Indian or Alaskan Native, Asian or Pacific Islander, or Hispanic. Priority is given to applicants who are freshmen. Students must be Kansas residents attending postsecondary institutions in Kansas. For more details refer to web site http://www.kansasregents.org/financial_aid/minority.html. *Award:* Scholarship for use in freshman, sophomore, junior, or senior year; renewable. *Award amount:* up to $1850. *Number of awards:* varies. *Eligibility Requirements:* Applicant must be American Indian/Alaska Native, Asian/Pacific Islander, Black (non-Hispanic), or Hispanic; enrolled or expecting to enroll full-time at a two-year or four-year institution or university; resident of Kansas and studying in Kansas. Applicant must have 3.0 GPA or higher. Available to U.S. citizens. *Application Requirements:* Application, financial need analysis, test scores. *Fee:* $12. **Deadline:** May 1.

Contact Diane Lindeman, Director of Student Financial Assistance, Kansas Board of Regents, 1000 Jackson, SW, Suite 520, Topeka, KS 66612-1368. *E-mail:* dlindeman@ksbor.org. *Phone:* 785-296-3517. *Fax:* 785-296-0983. *Web site:* http://www.kansasregents.org/.

Kansas Nursing Service Scholarship Program. This is a service scholarship loan program available to students attending two-year or four-year public and private postsecondary institutions as well as vocational technical schools with nursing education programs. Students can be pursuing either LPN or RN licensure. This is a service obligation scholarship, therefore students must agree to work in the field of nursing one year for each year they have received the scholarship or must repay the amount of the scholarship award that they received plus interest. Students must be Kansas residents attending a postsecondary institution in Kansas. *Academic Fields/Career Goals:* Nursing. *Award:* Scholarship for use in freshman, sophomore, junior, or senior year; renewable. *Award amount:* $2500–$3500. *Number of awards:* varies. *Eligibility Requirements:* Applicant must be enrolled or expecting to enroll full-time at a two-year, four-year, or technical institution or university. Available to U.S. citizens. *Application Requirements:* Application, financial need analysis, test scores, transcript. *Fee:* $12. **Deadline:** May 1.

Contact Diane Lindeman, Director of Student Financial Assistance, Kansas Board of Regents, 1000 Jackson, SW, Suite 520, Topeka, KS 66612-1368. *E-mail:* dlindeman@ksbor.org. *Phone:* 785-296-3517. *Fax:* 785-296-0983. *Web site:* http://www.kansasregents.org/.

Kansas Teacher Service Scholarship. Scholarship to encourage talented students to enter the teaching profession and teach in Kansas in specific curriculum areas or in underserved areas of Kansas. Students must be Kansas residents attending a postsecondary institution in Kansas. For more details, refer to web site http://www.kansasregents.org. *Academic Fields/Career Goals:* Education. *Award:* Scholarship for use in junior, senior, or graduate year; renewable. *Award amount:* $2150–$5374. *Number of awards:* varies. *Eligibility Requirements:* Applicant must be enrolled or expecting to enroll full- or part-time at a four-year institution or university. Applicant must have 3.0 GPA or higher. Available to U.S. citizens. *Application Requirements:* Application, essay, financial need analysis, resume, references, test scores, transcript. *Fee:* $12. **Deadline:** May 1.

Contact Diane Lindeman, Director of Student Financial Assistance, Kansas Board of Regents, 1000 Jackson, SW, Suite 520, Topeka, KS 66612-1368. *E-mail:* dlindeman@ksbor.org. *Phone:* 785-296-3517. *Fax:* 785-296-0983. *Web site:* http://www.kansasregents.org/.

Ted and Nora Anderson Scholarships. Scholarship of $250 for each semester (one year only) given to the children of American Legion members or Auxiliary members who are holding membership for the past three consecutive years. Children of a deceased member can also apply. Parent of the applicant must be a veteran. Must be high school seniors or college freshmen or sophomores in a Kansas institution. Scholarship for use at an approved college, university, or trade school in Kansas. Must maintain a C average in college. *Award:* Scholarship for use in freshman or sophomore year; not renewable. *Award amount:* $250–$500. *Number of awards:* 4. *Eligibility Requirements:* Applicant must be enrolled or expecting to enroll full-time at a two-year, four-year, or technical institution or university; resident of Kansas and studying in Kansas. Applicant or parent of applicant must be member of American Legion or Auxiliary. Available to U.S. citizens. Applicant or parent must meet one or more of the following requirements: general military experience; retired from active duty; disabled or killed as a result of military service; prisoner of war; or missing in action. *Application Requirements:* Application, essay, financial need analysis, photo, references, transcript. **Deadline:** February 15.

Contact Jim Gravenstein, Chairman, Scholarship Committee, American Legion Department of Kansas, 1314 Topeka Boulevard, SW, Topeka, KS 66612. *Phone:* 785-232-9315. *Fax:* 785-232-1399. *Web site:* http://www.ksamlegion.org/.

KENTUCKY

College Access Program (CAP) Grant. Award for U.S. citizens and Kentucky residents seeking their first undergraduate degree. Applicants enrolled in sectarian institutions are not eligible. Must submit Free Application for Federal Student Aid to demonstrate financial need. Funding is limited. Awards are made on a first-come, first-serve basis. *Award:* Grant for use in freshman, sophomore, junior, or senior year; not renewable. *Award amount:* up to $1900. *Number of awards:* 35,000–45,000. *Eligibility Requirements:* Applicant must be enrolled or expecting to enroll full- or part-time at a two-year, four-year, or technical institution or university; resident of Kentucky and studying in Kentucky. Available to U.S. citizens. *Application Requirements:* FAFSA. **Deadline:** continuous.

Contact Sheila Roe, Program Coordinator, Kentucky Higher Education Assistance Authority (KHEAA), PO Box 798, Frankfort, KY 40602-0798. *E-mail:* sroe@kheaa.com. *Phone:* 800-928-8926 Ext. 67393. *Fax:* 502-696-7373. *Web site:* http://www.kheaa.com/.

Department of Veterans Affairs Tuition Waiver-KY KRS 164-507. Scholarship available to college students who are residents of Kentucky under the age of 26. *Award:* Scholarship for use in freshman, sophomore, junior, or senior year; not renewable. *Award amount:* varies. *Number of awards:* 400. *Eligibility Requirements:* Applicant must be age 26 or under; enrolled or expecting to enroll full- or part-time at a two-year or four-year institution or university and resident of Kentucky. Available to U.S. citizens. *Application Requirements:* Application. **Deadline:** varies.

Contact Barbara Sipek, Tuition Waiver Coordinator, Kentucky Department of Veterans Affairs, 321 West Main Street, Suite 390, Louisville, KY 40213-9095. *E-mail:* barbaraa.sipek@ky.gov. *Phone:* 502-595-4447. *Web site:* http://www.veterans.ky.gov/.

Early Childhood Development Scholarship. Awards scholarship with conditional service commitment for part-time students currently employed by participating ECD facility or providing training in ECD for an approved organization. For more information, visit web site http://www.kheaa.com. *Academic Fields/Career Goals:* Child and Family Studies; Education. *Award:* Scholarship for use in freshman, sophomore, junior, or senior year; not renewable. *Award amount:* up to $1800. *Number of awards:* 1000–1300. *Eligibility Requirements:* Applicant must be enrolled or expecting to enroll part-time at a two-year or four-year institution or university; resident of Kentucky and studying in Kentucky. Available to U.S. citizens. *Application Requirements:* Application, financial need analysis, FAFSA. **Deadline:** continuous.

Contact David Lawhorn, Program Coordinator, Kentucky Higher Education Assistance Authority (KHEAA), PO Box 798, Frankfort, KY 40602-0798. *E-mail:* dlawhorn@kheaa.com. *Phone:* 800-928-8926 Ext. 67383. *Fax:* 502-696-7373. *Web site:* http://www.kheaa.com/.

Environmental Protection Scholarship. Renewable awards for college juniors, seniors, and graduate students for in-state tuition, fees, room and board, and a book allowance at a Kentucky public university. Minimum 3.0 GPA required. Must work full-time for the Kentucky Department for Environmental Protection upon graduation (six months for each semester of scholarship support received). Interview required. *Academic Fields/Career Goals:* Biology; Chemical Engineering; Civil Engineering; Earth Science; Environmental Science; Hydrology; Mechanical Engineering; Natural Sciences. *Award:* Scholarship for use in junior, senior, or graduate year; renewable. *Award amount:* $15,000–$30,000. *Number of awards:* 1–2. *Eligibility Requirements:* Applicant must be enrolled or expecting to enroll full-time at a four-year institution or university and studying in Kentucky. Applicant must have 3.0 GPA or higher. Available to U.S. and non-U.S. citizens. *Application Requirements:* Application, essay, interview, references, transcript, valid work permit for non-citizens. **Deadline:** February 15.

Contact James Kipp, Scholarship Program Coordinator, Kentucky Energy and Environment Cabinet, 233 Mining/Mineral Resources Building, Lexington, KY 40506-0107. *E-mail:* kipp@uky.edu. *Phone:* 859-257-1299. *Fax:* 859-323-1049. *Web site:* http://www.eec.ky.gov/.

Go Higher Grant. Need-based grant for adult students pursuing their first undergraduate degree. Completion of the FAFSA is required. *Award:* Grant for use in freshman, sophomore, junior, or senior year; not renewable. *Award amount:* up to $1000. *Number of awards:* 100–300. *Eligibility Requirements:* Applicant must be age 24 and over; enrolled or expecting to enroll full- or part-time at a two-year, four-year, or technical institution or university; resident of Kentucky and studying in Kentucky. Available to U.S. citizens. *Application Requirements:* Application, FAFSA. **Deadline:** continuous.

Contact Sheila Roe, Grant Program Coordinator, Kentucky Higher Education Assistance Authority (KHEAA), PO Box 798, Frankfort, KY 40206-0798. *E-mail:* sroe@kheaa.com. *Phone:* 800-928-8926 Ext. 67393. *Web site:* http://www.kheaa.com/.

Kentucky Educational Excellence Scholarship (KEES). Annual award based on yearly high school GPA and highest ACT or SAT score received by high school graduation. Awards are renewable, if required cumulative GPA is maintained at a Kentucky postsecondary school. Must be a Kentucky resident, and a graduate of a Kentucky high school. *Award:* Scholarship for use in freshman, sophomore, junior, or senior year; renewable. *Award amount:* $125–$2500. *Number of awards:* 65,000–68,000. *Eligibility Requirements:* Applicant must be high school student; planning to enroll or expecting to enroll full- or part-time at a two-year, four-year, or technical institution or university; resident of Kentucky and studying in Kentucky. Applicant must have 2.5 GPA or higher. Available to U.S.

citizens. *Application Requirements:* Test scores, data submitted by KY high schools. **Deadline:** continuous.

Contact Megan Cummins, KEES Coordinator, Kentucky Higher Education Assistance Authority (KHEAA), PO Box 798, Frankfort, KY 40602. *E-mail:* mcummins@kheaa.com. *Phone:* 800-928-8926 Ext. 67397. *Fax:* 502-696-7373. *Web site:* http://www.kheaa.com/.

Kentucky Minority Educator Recruitment and Retention (KMERR) Scholarship. Scholarship for minority teacher candidates who rank in the upper half of their class or have a minimum 2.5 GPA. Must be a U.S. citizen and Kentucky resident enrolled in one of Kentucky's eight public institutions. Must teach one semester in Kentucky for each semester the scholarship is received. *Academic Fields/Career Goals:* Education. *Award:* Forgivable loan for use in freshman, sophomore, junior, or senior year; renewable. *Award amount:* \$2500–\$5000. *Number of awards:* 400. *Eligibility Requirements:* Applicant must be American Indian/Alaska Native, Asian/Pacific Islander, Black (non-Hispanic), or Hispanic; enrolled or expecting to enroll full-time at a two-year or four-year institution or university; resident of Kentucky and studying in Kentucky. Applicant must have 2.5 GPA or higher. Available to U.S. citizens. *Application Requirements:* Application, references, test scores, transcript. **Deadline:** continuous.

Contact Natasha Murray, State Program Coordinator, Kentucky Department of Education, 500 Mero Street, 17th Floor, Frankfort, KY 40601. *E-mail:* michael.dailey@education.ky.gov. *Phone:* 502-564-1479. *Fax:* 502-564-6952. *Web site:* http://www.education.ky.gov/.

Kentucky Office of Vocational Rehabilitation. Grant provides services necessary to secure employment. Eligible individual must possess physical or mental impairment that results in a substantial impediment to employment; benefit from vocational rehabilitation services in terms of an employment outcome; and require vocational rehabilitation services to prepare for, enter, or retain employment. *Award:* Grant for use in freshman, sophomore, junior, senior, graduate, or postgraduate years; renewable. *Award amount:* varies. *Number of awards:* varies. *Eligibility Requirements:* Applicant must be enrolled or expecting to enroll full- or part-time at a two-year, four-year, or technical institution or university. Available to U.S. citizens. *Application Requirements:* Application, financial need analysis, interview, transcript, eligibility for OVR services and in proper priority category. **Deadline:** continuous.

Contact Charles Puckett, Program Administrator, Kentucky Office of Vocational Rehabilitation, 600 West Cedar Street, Suite 2E, Louisville, KY 40202. *E-mail:* marianu.spencer@mail.state.ky.us. *Phone:* 502-595-4173. *Fax:* 502-564-2358. *Web site:* http://www.ovr.ky.gov/.

Kentucky Teacher Scholarship Program. Awards Kentucky residents attending Kentucky institutions and pursuing initial teacher certification programs. Must teach one semester for each semester of award received. In critical shortage areas, must teach one semester for every two semesters of award received. If teaching service is not rendered, the scholarship converts to a loan that must be repaid with interest. For more information, see Web http://www.kheaa.com. *Academic Fields/Career Goals:* Education. *Award:* Forgivable loan for use in freshman, sophomore, junior, or senior year; renewable. *Award amount:* \$325–\$5000. *Number of awards:* 100–300. *Eligibility Requirements:* Applicant must be enrolled or expecting to enroll full-time at a two-year or four-year institution or university; resident of Kentucky and studying in Kentucky. Available to U.S. citizens. *Application Requirements:* Application, financial need analysis, FAFSA. **Deadline:** May 1.

Contact Jennifer Toth, Scholarship Coordinator, Kentucky Higher Education Assistance Authority (KHEAA), PO Box 798, Frankfort, KY 40602. *E-mail:* jtoth@kheaa.com. *Phone:* 800-928-8926 Ext. 67392. *Fax:* 502-696-7473. *Web site:* http://www.kheaa.com/.

Kentucky Transportation Cabinet Civil Engineering Scholarship Program. Scholarships awarded to qualified Kentucky residents who wish to study civil engineering at University of Kentucky, Western Kentucky University, University of Louisville or Kentucky State University. Applicant should be a graduate of an accredited Kentucky high school or a Kentucky resident. Scholarship recipients are given opportunities to work for the Cabinet during summers and job opportunities upon graduation within the state of KY. *Academic Fields/Career Goals:* Civil Engineering. *Award:* Scholarship for use in freshman, sophomore, junior, or senior year; renewable. *Award amount:* \$10,600–\$44,000. *Number of awards:* 15–25. *Eligibility Requirements:* Applicant must be enrolled or expecting to enroll full-time at a four-year institution or university; resident of Kentucky and studying in Kentucky. Applicant must have 3.0 GPA or higher. Available to U.S. and non-U.S. citizens. *Application Requirements:* Application, essay, interview, references, test scores, transcript. **Deadline:** March 1.

Contact Jamie Bewley Byrd, Scholarship Program Administrator, Kentucky Transportation Cabinet, 200 Mero Street, Frankfort, KY 40622. *E-mail:* jamie.bewleybyrd@ky.gov. *Web site:* http://www.transportation.ky.gov/scholarship.

Kentucky Tuition Grant (KTG). Grants available to Kentucky residents who are full-time undergraduates at an independent college within the state. Based on financial need. Must submit FAFSA. *Award:* Grant for use in freshman, sophomore, junior, or senior year; not renewable. *Award amount:* \$200–\$3000. *Number of awards:* 12,000–13,000. *Eligibility Requirements:* Applicant must be enrolled or expecting to enroll full-time at a two-year or four-year institution or university; resident of Kentucky and studying in Kentucky. Available to U.S. citizens. *Application Requirements:* FAFSA. **Deadline:** continuous.

Contact Sheila Roe, Grant Program Coordinator, Kentucky Higher Education Assistance Authority (KHEAA), PO Box 798, Frankfort, KY 40602-0798. *E-mail:* sroe@kheaa.com. *Phone:* 800-928-8926 Ext. 67393. *Fax:* 502-696-7373. *Web site:* http://www.kheaa.com/.

Minority Educator Recruitment and Retention Scholarship. Conversion loan or scholarship for Kentucky residents. Provides up to \$5000 per academic year to minority students majoring in teacher education and pursuing initial teacher certification. Must be repaid with interest if scholarship requirements are not met. *Academic Fields/Career Goals:* Education; Special Education. *Award:* Forgivable loan for use in freshman, sophomore, junior, or senior year; not renewable. *Award amount:* up to \$5000. *Number of awards:* 200–300. *Eligibility Requirements:* Applicant must be American Indian/Alaska Native, Asian/Pacific Islander, Black (non-Hispanic), or Hispanic; enrolled or expecting to enroll full-time at a two-year or four-year institution or university; resident of Kentucky and studying in Kentucky. Available to U.S. citizens. *Application Requirements:* Application. **Deadline:** continuous.

Contact Natasha Murray, Program Director, Kentucky Department of Education, Kentucky Higher Education Assistance Authority (KHEAA), 500 Metro Street, Frankfort, KY 40601. *E-mail:* natasha.murray@education.ky.gov. *Phone:* 502-564-1479. *Web site:* http://www.kheaa.com/.

Touchstone Energy All "A" Classic Scholarship. Award of \$1000 for senior student in good standing at a Kentucky high school which is a member of the All Classic. Applicant must be a U.S. citizen and must plan to attend a postsecondary institution in Kentucky in the upcoming year as a full-time student and be drug free. *Award:* Scholarship for use in freshman year; not renewable. *Award amount:* $1000. *Number of awards:* 12. *Eligibility Requirements:* Applicant must be high school student; planning to enroll or expecting to enroll full-time at a two-year, four-year, or technical institution or university; resident of Kentucky and studying in Kentucky. Available to U.S. citizens. *Application Requirements:* Application, essay, photo, references, transcript. **Deadline:** December 3.

Contact David Cowden, Chairperson, Scholarship Committee, Kentucky Touchstone Energy Cooperatives, 1320 Lincoln Road, Lewisport, KY 42351. *E-mail:* allaclassic@alltel.net. *Phone:* 859-744-4812. *Web site:* http://www.ekpc.coop.

LOUISIANA

Hemophilia Federation of America Educational Scholarship. One-time scholarship for persons with hemophilia, attending either full-time or part-time in any accredited two- or four-year college, university, or vocation/technical school in the United States. *Award:* Scholarship for use in freshman, sophomore, junior, or senior year; not renewable. *Award amount:* $1500. *Number of awards:* 1–3. *Eligibility Requirements:* Applicant must be enrolled or expecting to enroll full- or part-time at a two-year, four-year, or technical institution or university. Applicant must be physically disabled. Available to U.S. citizens. *Application Requirements:* Application, essay, financial need analysis, references. **Deadline:** April 30.

Contact Scholarship Committee, Hemophilia Federation of America, 1405 West Pinhook Road, Suite 101, Lafayette, LA 70503. *E-mail:* info@hemophiliafed.org. *Phone:* 337-261-9787. *Fax:* 337-261-1787. *Web site:* http://www.hemophiliaed.org/.

Leveraging Educational Assistance Program (LEAP)/Special Leveraging Educational Assistance Program (SLEAP). Apply by completing the FAFSA each year. Must be a resident of Louisiana and must be attending an institution in Louisiana. Institution the student plans to attend must recommend student for award. When you submit the FAFSA, you have automatically applied for all four levels of TOPS, for the LA LEAP/SLEAP Grant, for Louisiana Guaranteed Loans, and for Federal Pell Grants and Go Grants. Please do not send separate letters of application to the TOPS office. *Award:* Grant for use in freshman, sophomore, junior, or senior year; renewable. *Award amount:* $200–$2000. *Number of awards:* 4810. *Eligibility Requirements:* Applicant must be enrolled or expecting to enroll full-time at a two-year, four-year, or technical institution or university; resident of Louisiana and studying in Louisiana. Available to U.S. citizens. *Application Requirements:* Application, financial need analysis, FAFSA. **Deadline:** July 1.

Contact Bonnie Lavergne, Public Information, Louisiana Office of Student Financial Assistance, PO Box 91202, Baton Rouge, LA 70821-9202. *E-mail:* custserv@osfa.la.gov. *Phone:* 800-259-5626 Ext. 1012. *Fax:* 225-612-6508. *Web site:* http://www.osfa.la.gov/.

Louisiana Department of Veterans Affairs State Aid Program. Tuition exemption at any state-supported college, university, or technical institute in Louisiana for children (dependents between the ages of 18–25) of veterans that are rated 90 percent or above service connected disabled by the U.S. Department of Veterans Affairs. Tuition exemption also available for the surviving spouse and children (dependents between the ages of 18–25) of veterans who died on active duty, in line of duty, or where death was the result of a disability incurred in or aggravated by military service. For residents of Louisiana. *Award:* Scholarship for use in freshman, sophomore, junior, or senior year; not renewable. *Award amount:* varies. *Number of awards:* varies. *Eligibility Requirements:* Applicant must be age 18-25; enrolled or expecting to enroll full-time at a two-year, four-year, or technical institution or university; resident of Louisiana and studying in Louisiana. Available to U.S. citizens. Applicant or parent must meet one or more of the following requirements: general military experience; retired from active duty; disabled or killed as a result of military service; prisoner of war; or missing in action. *Application Requirements:* Application. **Deadline:** continuous.

Contact Mr. Richard Blackwell, Veterans Affairs Deputy Assistant Secretary, Louisiana Department of Veteran Affairs, PO Box 94095, Capitol Station, Baton Rouge, LA 70804-4095. *E-mail:* richard.blackwell@vetaffairs.la.gov. *Phone:* 225-922-0500 Ext. 203. *Web site:* http://www.vetaffairs.com/.

Louisiana National Guard State Tuition Exemption Program. Renewable award for college undergraduates to receive tuition exemption upon satisfactory performance in the Louisiana National Guard. Applicant must attend a state-funded institution in Louisiana, be a resident and registered voter in Louisiana, meet the academic and residency requirements of the university attended, and provide documentation of Louisiana National Guard enlistment. The exemption can be used for up to 15 semesters. Minimum 2.5 GPA required. *Award:* Scholarship for use in freshman, sophomore, junior, or senior year; renewable. *Award amount:* varies. *Number of awards:* varies. *Eligibility Requirements:* Applicant must be enrolled or expecting to enroll full- or part-time at a two-year, four-year, or technical institution or university; resident of Louisiana and studying in Louisiana. Applicant must have 2.5 GPA or higher. Available to U.S. citizens. Applicant or parent must meet one or more of the following requirements: Air Force National Guard or Army National Guard experience; retired from active duty; disabled or killed as a result of military service; prisoner of war; or missing in action. *Application Requirements:* Application, test scores, transcript. **Deadline:** continuous.

Contact Jona M. Hughes, Education Services Officer, Louisiana National Guard, Joint Task Force LA, Building 35, Jackson Barracks, JI-PD, New Orleans, LA 70146-0330. *E-mail:* hughesj@la-arng.ngb.army.mil. *Phone:* 504-278-8531 Ext. 8304. *Fax:* 504-278-8025. *Web site:* http://www.la.ngb.army.mil/.

Robert C. Byrd Honors Scholarship-Louisiana. Applicant must have earned a high school diploma or equivalent (GED) in Louisiana in the same academic year in which the scholarship is to be awarded. Minimum 3.5 GPA and an ACT composite score of 23 or SAT critical reading and math score of 970. Must be a U.S. citizen and legal resident of Louisiana. Total number of awards vary each year. *Award:* Scholarship for use in freshman, sophomore, junior, or senior year; renewable. *Eligibility Requirements:* Applicant must be enrolled or expecting to enroll full-time at a four-year institution or university and resident of Louisiana. Applicant must have 3.5 GPA or higher. Available to U.S. citizens. *Application Requirements:* Application, essay, test scores, transcript, selective service form. **Deadline:** March 10.

Contact Shan Davis, Scholarship Coordinator, Louisiana State Department of Education, PO Box 94064, Baton Rouge, LA 70804-9064. *E-mail:* shan.davis@la.gov. *Phone:* 225-342-5849. *Web site:* http://www.doe.state.la.us/.

Rockefeller State Wildlife Scholarship. For college undergraduates with a minimum of 60 credit hours who are majoring in Forestry, Wildlife, or Marine Science, and for college graduate students who are majoring in Forestry, Wildlife, or Marine Science. College undergraduates must have a grade point average of at least 2.50 to apply. College graduate students must have a grade point average of at least 3.00 in order to apply. Renewable up to three years as an undergraduate and two years as a graduate student. *Academic Fields/Career Goals:* Biology; Marine Biology; Marine/Ocean Engineering; Natural Resources; Oceanography. *Award:* Scholarship for use in freshman, sophomore, junior, senior, graduate, or postgraduate years; renewable. *Award amount:* $2000–$3000. *Number of awards:* 20–30. *Eligibility Requirements:* Applicant must be enrolled or expecting to enroll full-time at a four-year institution or university; resident of Louisiana and studying in Louisiana. Applicant must have 2.5 GPA or higher. Available to U.S. citizens. *Application Requirements:* Application, test scores, transcript, FAFSA. **Deadline:** July 1.

Contact Bonnie Lavergne, Public Information, Louisiana Office of Student Financial Assistance, PO Box 91202, Baton Rouge, LA 70821-9202. *E-mail:* custserv@osfa.la.gov. *Phone:* 800-259-5626 Ext. 1012. *Fax:* 225-612-6508. *Web site:* http://www.osfa.la.gov/.

Taylor Opportunity Program for Students–Honors Level. Program awards 8 semesters or 12 terms of tuition to any Louisiana State postsecondary institution plus $400 stipend per semester. Program awards 8 semesters or 12 terms of an amount equal to the weighted average public tuition to students attending a LAICU (Louisiana Association of Independent Colleges and Universities) institution plus $400 stipend per semester. Program awards 8 semesters or 12 terms of an amount equal to the weighted average public tuition to two out-of-state Institutions for Hearing Impaired Students: Gallaudet University and Rochester Institute of Technology plus $400 stipend per semester. Program awards $1120 per year to Approved Proprietary and Cosmetology schools. When you submit the FAFSA, you have automatically applied for all four levels of TOPS, for the LA LEAP/SLEAP Grant, for Louisiana Guaranteed Loans, and for Federal Pell Grants and Go Grants. Please do not send separate letters of application to the TOPS office. *Award:* Scholarship for use in freshman, sophomore, junior, or senior year; renewable. *Award amount:* $680–$5106. *Number of awards:* 7522. *Eligibility Requirements:* Applicant must be enrolled or expecting to enroll full-time at a two-year, four-year, or technical institution or university; resident of Louisiana and studying in Louisiana. Applicant must have 3.0 GPA or higher. Available to U.S. citizens. *Application Requirements:* Application, test scores, transcript. **Deadline:** July 1.

Contact Public Information, Louisiana Office of Student Financial Assistance, PO Box 91202, Baton Rouge, LA 70821-9202. *E-mail:* custserv@osfa.la.gov. *Phone:* 800-259-5626 Ext. 1012. *Fax:* 225-208-1496. *Web site:* http://www.osfa.la.gov/.

Taylor Opportunity Program for Students–Opportunity Level. Program awards 8 semesters or 12 terms of tuition to any Louisiana State postsecondary institution. Program awards 8 semesters or 12 terms of an amount equal to the weighted average public tuition to students attending a LAICU (Louisiana Association of Independent Colleges and Universities) institution. Program awards 8 semesters or 12 terms of an amount equal to the weighted average public tuition to two out-of-state Institutions for Hearing Impaired Students: Gallaudet University and Rochester Institute of Technology. Program awards $1120 per year to Approved Proprietary and Cosmetology schools. When you submit the FAFSA, you have automatically applied for all four levels of TOPS, for the LA LEAP/SLEAP Grant, for Louisiana Guaranteed Loans, and for Federal Pell Grants and Go Grants. Please do not send separate letters of application to the TOPS office. *Award:* Scholarship for use in freshman, sophomore, junior, or senior year; renewable. *Award amount:* $280–$4306. *Number of awards:* 23,645. *Eligibility Requirements:* Applicant must be enrolled or expecting to enroll full-time at a two-year, four-year, or technical institution or university; resident of Louisiana and studying in Louisiana. Applicant must have 2.5 GPA or higher. Available to U.S. citizens. *Application Requirements:* Application, test scores, transcript. **Deadline:** July 1.

Contact Public Information, Louisiana Office of Student Financial Assistance, PO Box 91202, Baton Rouge, LA 70821-9202. *E-mail:* custserv@osfa.la.gov. *Phone:* 800-259-5626 Ext. 1012. *Fax:* 225-208-1496. *Web site:* http://www.osfa.la.gov/.

Taylor Opportunity Program for Students–Performance Level. Program awards 8 semesters or 12 terms of tuition to any Louisiana State postsecondary institution plus $200 stipend per semester. Program awards 8 semesters or 12 terms of an amount equal to the weighted average public tuition to students attending a LAICU (Louisiana Association of Independent Colleges and Universities) institution plus $200 stipend per semester. Program awards 8 semesters or 12 terms of an amount equal to the weighted average public tuition to two out-of-state Institutions for Hearing Impaired Students: Gallaudet University and Rochester Institute of Technology plus $200 stipend per semester. Program awards $1120 per year to Approved Proprietary and Cosmetology schools. When you submit the FAFSA, you have automatically applied for all four levels of TOPS, for the LA LEAP/SLEAP Grant, for Louisiana Guaranteed Loans, and for Federal Pell Grants and Go Grants. Please do not send separate letters of application to the TOPS office. *Award:* Scholarship for use in freshman, sophomore, junior, or senior year; renewable. *Award amount:* $480–$4706. *Number of awards:* 9621. *Eligibility Requirements:* Applicant must be enrolled or expecting to enroll full-time at a two-year, four-year, or technical institution or university; resident of Louisiana and studying in Louisiana. Applicant must have 3.0 GPA or higher. Available to U.S. citizens. *Application Requirements:* Application, test scores, transcript. **Deadline:** July 1.

Contact Public Information, Louisiana Office of Student Financial Assistance, PO Box 91202, Baton Rouge, LA 70821-9202. *E-mail:* custserv@osfa.la.gov. *Phone:* 800-259-5626 Ext. 1012. *Fax:* 225-208-1496. *Web site:* http://www.osfa.la.gov/.

Taylor Opportunity Program for Students–Tech Level. Program awards an amount equal to tuition for up to 4 semesters and two summers of technical training at a Louisiana postsecondary institution that offers a vocational or technical education certificate or diploma program, or a non-academic degree program; or up to $1120 to an approved Proprietary or Cosmetology school. Must have completed the TOPS Opportunity core curriculum or the TOPS Tech core curriculum, must have achieved a 2.50 grade point average over the core curriculum only, and must have achieved an ACT score of 17 or an SAT score of 810. Program awards an amount equal to the weighted average public tuition for technical programs to students attending a LAICU private institution for technical training. When you submit the FAFSA, you have automatically applied for all four levels of TOPS, for the LA LEAP/SLEAP

Grant, for Louisiana Guaranteed Loans, and for Federal Pell Grants and Go Grants. Please do not send separate letters of application to the TOPS office. *Award:* Scholarship for use in freshman or sophomore year; renewable. *Award amount:* $280–$3021. *Number of awards:* 1785. *Eligibility Requirements:* Applicant must be enrolled or expecting to enroll full-time at a technical institution; resident of Louisiana and studying in Louisiana. Applicant must have 2.5 GPA or higher. Available to U.S. citizens. *Application Requirements:* Application, test scores, transcript, ACT of 17 OR SAT of 810. **Deadline:** July 1.

Contact Public Information, Louisiana Office of Student Financial Assistance, PO Box 91202, Baton Rouge, LA 70821-9202. *E-mail:* custserv@osfa.la.gov. *Phone:* 800-259-5626 Ext. 1012. *Fax:* 225-208-1496. *Web site:* http://www.osfa.la.gov/.

MAINE

American Legion Auxiliary Department of Maine Daniel E. Lambert Memorial Scholarship. Scholarships to assist young men and women in continuing their education beyond high school. Must demonstrate financial need, must be a resident of the State of Maine, U.S. citizen, and parent must be a veteran. *Award:* Scholarship for use in freshman year; not renewable. *Award amount:* $1000. *Number of awards:* up to 2. *Eligibility Requirements:* Applicant must be high school student; planning to enroll or expecting to enroll full-time at a four-year institution or university and resident of Maine. Available to U.S. citizens. Applicant or parent must meet one or more of the following requirements: general military experience; retired from active duty; disabled or killed as a result of military service; prisoner of war; or missing in action. *Application Requirements:* Application, financial need analysis. **Deadline:** May 1.

Contact Mary Wells, Education Chairman, American Legion Auxiliary Department of Maine, 21 Limerock Street, PO Box 434, Rockland, ME 04841. *E-mail:* aladeptsecme@verizon.net. *Phone:* 207-532-6007. *Web site:* http://www.mainelegion.org/.

American Legion Auxiliary Department of Maine National President's Scholarship. Scholarships to children of veterans who served in the Armed Forces during the eligibility dates for The American Legion. One $2500, one $2000, and one $1000 scholarship will be awarded. Applicant must complete 50 hours of community service during his/her high school years. *Award:* Scholarship for use in freshman year; not renewable. *Award amount:* $1000–$2500. *Number of awards:* 3. *Eligibility Requirements:* Applicant must be high school student; planning to enroll or expecting to enroll full-time at a four-year institution or university and resident of Maine. Applicant or parent of applicant must have employment or volunteer experience in community service. Available to U.S. citizens. Applicant or parent must meet one or more of the following requirements: general military experience; retired from active duty; disabled or killed as a result of military service; prisoner of war; or missing in action. *Application Requirements:* Application, essay, references, test scores, transcript. **Deadline:** March 1.

Contact Mary Wells, Education Chairman, American Legion Auxiliary Department of Maine, 21 Limerock Street, PO Box 434, Rockland, ME 04841. *E-mail:* aladeptsecme@verizon.net. *Phone:* 207-532-6007. *Web site:* http://www.mainelegion.org/.

American Legion Auxiliary Department of Maine Past Presidents' Parley Nurses Scholarship. One-time award for child, grandchild, sister, or brother of veteran. Must be resident of Maine and wishing to continue education at accredited school in medical field. Must submit photo, doctor's statement, and evidence of civic activity. Minimum 3.5 GPA required. *Academic Fields/Career Goals:* Health and Medical Sciences; Nursing. *Award:* Scholarship for use in freshman, sophomore, junior, or senior year; not renewable. *Award amount:* $300. *Number of awards:* 1. *Eligibility Requirements:* Applicant must be age 18 and over; enrolled or expecting to enroll full-time at a two-year, four-year, or technical institution or university and resident of Maine. Applicant or parent of applicant must have employment or volunteer experience in community service. Applicant must have 2.5 GPA or higher. Available to U.S. citizens. Applicant or parent must meet one or more of the following requirements: general military experience; retired from active duty; disabled or killed as a result of military service; prisoner of war; or missing in action. *Application Requirements:* Application, photo, references, transcript, doctor's statement. **Deadline:** March 31.

Contact Mary Wells, Education Chairman, American Legion Auxiliary Department of Maine, 21 Limerock Street, PO Box 434, Rockland, ME 04841. *E-mail:* aladeptsecme@verizon.net. *Phone:* 207-532-6007. *Web site:* http://www.mainelegion.org/.

Early College for ME. Scholarship for high school students who have not made plans for college but are academically capable of success in college. Recipients are selected by their school principal or Guidance Director. Students must be entering a Maine Community College. Refer to web site http://www.mccs.me.edu/scholarships.html. *Award:* Scholarship for use in freshman or sophomore year; renewable. *Award amount:* $2000. *Number of awards:* 250–500. *Eligibility Requirements:* Applicant must be high school student; planning to enroll or expecting to enroll full-time at a two-year institution; resident of Maine and studying in Maine. Available to U.S. citizens. *Application Requirements:* Application, financial need analysis, references, transcript. **Deadline:** varies.

Contact Charles P. Collins, State Director, Center for Career Development, Maine Community College System, 2 Fort Road, South Portland, ME 04106. *E-mail:* ccollins@mccs.me.edu. *Phone:* 207-767-5210 Ext. 4115. *Fax:* 207-767-2542. *Web site:* http://www.mccs.me.edu/.

Educators for Maine Forgivable Loan Program. Forgivable loan for residents of Maine who are high school seniors, college students, or college graduates with a minimum 3.0 GPA, studying or preparing to study teacher education. Must teach in Maine upon graduation. Award based on merit. For application information see web site http://www.famemaine.com. *Academic Fields/Career Goals:* Education. *Award:* Forgivable loan for use in freshman, sophomore, junior, or senior year; renewable. *Award amount:* $2000–$3000. *Number of awards:* up to 500. *Eligibility Requirements:* Applicant must be enrolled or expecting to enroll full-time at a two-year or four-year institution or university and resident of Maine. Applicant must have 3.0 GPA or higher. Available to U.S. citizens. *Application Requirements:* Application, essay, test scores, transcript. **Deadline:** May 15.

Contact Claude Roy, Manager, Operations, Finance Authority of Maine, Five Community Drive, PO Box 949, Augusta, ME 04332-0949. *E-mail:* education@famemaine.com. *Phone:* 207-620-3507. *Web site:* http://www.famemaine.com/.

Maine Rural Rehabilitation Fund Scholarship Program. One-time scholarship open to Maine residents enrolled in or accepted by any school, college, or university. Must be full time and demonstrate financial need. Those opting for a Maine institution given preference. Major must lead to an agricultural career. Minimum 3.0 GPA required. *Academic Fields/Career Goals:* Agribusiness; Agriculture; Animal/Veterinary Sciences. *Award:* Scholarship for use in freshman, sophomore, junior, senior, graduate, or postgraduate years; not renewable. *Award amount:* $800–$2000. *Number of awards:* 10–20. *Eligibility Requirements:* Applicant must be enrolled or expecting to enroll full-time at a two-year, four-year, or technical institution or university and resident of Maine. Applicant must have 3.0 GPA or higher. Available to U.S. citizens. *Application Requirements:* Application, driver's license, financial need analysis, transcript. **Deadline:** June 15.

Contact Jane Aiudi, Director of Marketing, Maine Department of Agriculture, Food and Rural Resources, 28 State House Station, Augusta, ME 04333-0028. *E-mail:* jane.aiudi@maine.gov. *Phone:* 207-287-7628. *Fax:* 207-287-5576. *Web site:* http://www.maine.gov/agriculture.

Robert C. Byrd Honors Scholarship-Maine. Merit-based, renewable scholarship of up to $1500 annually for graduating high school seniors. Must have a minimum of 3.0 GPA. Must be a resident of Maine. Superior academic performance is the primary criterion. For application, see web site http://www.famemaine.com. *Award:* Scholarship for use in freshman year; renewable. *Award amount:* up to $1500. *Number of awards:* up to 30. *Eligibility Requirements:* Applicant must be high school student; planning to enroll or expecting to enroll full-time at a two-year, four-year, or technical institution or university and resident of Maine. Applicant must have 3.0 GPA or higher. Available to U.S. citizens. *Application Requirements:* Application, essay, transcript, high school profile. **Deadline:** May 1.

Contact Claude Roy, Manager, Operations, Finance Authority of Maine, Five Community Drive, PO Box 949, Augusta, ME 04332-0949. *E-mail:* education@famemaine.com. *Phone:* 207-620-3507. *Web site:* http://www.famemaine.com/.

State of Maine Grant Program. Scholarship for residents of Maine, attending an eligible school in Connecticut, Maine, Massachusetts, New Hampshire, Pennsylvania, Rhode Island, Washington, D.C., or Vermont. Award based on need. Must apply annually. Complete free application for Federal Student Aid to apply. One-time award for undergraduate study. For further information see web site http://www.famemaine.com. *Award:* Grant for use in freshman, sophomore, junior, or senior year; not renewable. *Award amount:* $500–$1250. *Number of awards:* up to 18,000. *Eligibility Requirements:* Applicant must be enrolled or expecting to enroll full- or part-time at a two-year, four-year, or technical institution or university; resident of Maine and studying in Connecticut, District of Columbia, Maine, Massachusetts, New Hampshire, Pennsylvania, Rhode Island, or Vermont. Available to U.S. citizens. *Application Requirements:* Application, financial need analysis, FAFSA. **Deadline:** May 1.

Contact Claude Roy, Manager, Operations, Finance Authority of Maine, Five Community Drive, PO Box 949, Augusta, ME 04332-0949. *E-mail:* education@famemaine.com. *Phone:* 207-620-3507. *Web site:* http://www.famemaine.com/.

Tuition Waiver Programs. Provides tuition waivers for children and spouses of EMS personnel, firefighters, and law enforcement officers who have been killed in the line of duty and for students who were foster children under the custody of the Department of Human Services when they graduated from high school. Waivers valid at the University of Maine System, the Maine Technical College System, and Maine Maritime Academy. Applicant must reside and study in Maine. *Award:* Grant for use in freshman, sophomore, junior, or senior year; renewable. *Award amount:* varies. *Number of awards:* up to 30. *Eligibility Requirements:* Applicant must be enrolled or expecting to enroll full- or part-time at a four-year institution or university; resident of Maine and studying in Maine. Applicant or parent of applicant must have employment or volunteer experience in police/firefighting. Available to U.S. citizens. *Application Requirements:* Application, letter from the Department of Human Services documenting that applicant is in their custody and residing in foster care at the time of graduation from high school or its equivalent. **Deadline:** continuous.

Contact Claude Roy, Manager, Operations, Finance Authority of Maine, Five Community Drive, PO Box 949, Augusta, ME 04332-0949. *E-mail:* education@famemaine.com. *Phone:* 207-620-3507. *Web site:* http://www.famemaine.com/.

U.S. Department of Education Fulbright-Hays Project Abroad Scholarship for Programs in China. Scholarships offered to students who are participating in a CIEE Chinese language programs in China or Taiwan. Must be a U.S. citizen enrolled in a CIEE program. Students must have completed the equivalent of two years study in Chinese language (documented). Deadlines: April 1 and November 1. There is also a return requirement for scholarship awardees to submit a program report and evaluation. *Academic Fields/Career Goals:* Asian Studies; Education. *Award:* Scholarship for use in junior or senior year; not renewable. *Award amount:* $1000–$12,000. *Number of awards:* 1–20. *Eligibility Requirements:* Applicant must be enrolled or expecting to enroll full-time at a four-year institution or university and must have an interest in foreign language. Applicant must have 3.0 GPA or higher. Available to U.S. citizens. *Application Requirements:* Application, essay, financial need analysis, references, transcript, copy of passport or birth certificate. **Deadline:** varies.

Contact CIEE Scholarship Committee, CIEE: Council on International Educational Exchange, 300 Fore Street, Portland, ME 04101. *E-mail:* studyinfo@ciee.org. *Phone:* 800-407-8839. *Web site:* http://www.ciee.org/.

Veterans Dependents Educational Benefits-Maine. Tuition waiver award for dependent children or spouses of veterans permanently and totally disabled resulting from service-connected disability; died from a service-connected disability ; at time of death was totally and permanently disabled due to service-connected disability, but whose death was not related to the service-connected disability; or member of the Armed Forces on active duty who has been listed for more than 90 days as missing in action, captured or forcibly detained or interned in the line of duty. Benefits apply only to the University of Maine System, Maine community colleges and Maine Maritime Academy. Must be high school graduate. Must submit with application proof of veteran's VA disability along with dependent verification paperwork such as birth, marriage, or adoption certificate and proof of enrollment in degree program. *Award:* Scholarship for use in freshman, sophomore, junior, or senior year; not renewable. *Award amount:* varies. *Number of awards:* varies. *Eligibility Requirements:* Applicant must be enrolled or expecting to enroll full- or part-time at a two-year or four-year institution or university; resident of Maine and studying in Maine. Available to U.S. citizens. Applicant or parent must meet one or more of the following requirements: general military experience; retired from active duty; disabled or killed as a result of military service; prisoner of war; or missing in action. *Application Requirements:* Application.

Contact Mrs. Paula Gagnon, Office Associate II, Maine Division of Veterans Services, State House Station 117, Augusta, ME 04333-

0117. *E-mail:* mainebvs@maine.gov. *Phone:* 207-626-4464. *Fax:* 207-626-4471. *Web site:* http://www.maine.gov/dvem/bvs.

MARYLAND

Charles W. Riley Fire and Emergency Medical Services Tuition Reimbursement Program. Award intended to reimburse members of rescue organizations serving Maryland communities for tuition costs of course work towards a degree or certificate in fire service or medical technology. Must attend a two- or four-year school in Maryland. Minimum 2.0 GPA. The scholarship is worth up to $6500. *Academic Fields/Career Goals:* Fire Sciences; Health and Medical Sciences; Trade/Technical Specialties. *Award:* Scholarship for use in freshman, sophomore, junior, or senior year; not renewable. *Award amount:* up to $6500. *Number of awards:* up to 150. *Eligibility Requirements:* Applicant must be enrolled or expecting to enroll full- or part-time at a two-year or four-year institution or university; resident of Maryland and studying in Maryland. Applicant or parent of applicant must have employment or volunteer experience in police/firefighting. Available to U.S. citizens. *Application Requirements:* Application, transcript, tuition receipt, proof of enrollment. **Deadline:** July 1.

Contact Maura Sappington, Office of Student Financial Assistance, Maryland State Higher Education Commission, 839 Bestgate Road, Suite 400, Annapolis, MD 21401-3013. *E-mail:* msapping@mhec.state.md.us. *Phone:* 410-260-4569. *Fax:* 410-260-3203. *Web site:* http://www.mhec.state.md.us/.

Delegate Scholarship Program-Maryland. Delegate scholarships help Maryland residents attending Maryland degree-granting institutions, certain career schools, or nursing diploma schools. May attend out-of-state institution if Maryland Higher Education Commission deems major to be unique and not offered at a Maryland institution. Free Application for Federal Student Aid may be required. Students interested in this program should apply by contacting their legislative district delegate. *Award:* Scholarship for use in freshman, sophomore, junior, or senior year; not renewable. *Award amount:* $200–$8650. *Number of awards:* up to 3500. *Eligibility Requirements:* Applicant must be enrolled or expecting to enroll full- or part-time at a two-year, four-year, or technical institution or university; resident of Maryland and studying in Maryland. Available to U.S. citizens. *Application Requirements:* Application, FAFSA. **Deadline:** continuous.

Contact Monica Wheatley, Office of Student Financial Assistance, Maryland State Higher Education Commission, 839 Bestgate Road, Suite 400, Annapolis, MD 21401-3013. *E-mail:* osfamail@mhec.state.md.us. *Phone:* 800-974-1024. *Fax:* 410-260-3200. *Web site:* http://www.mhec.state.md.us/.

Distinguished Scholar Award-Maryland. Renewable award for Maryland students enrolled full-time at Maryland institutions. National Merit Scholar Finalists automatically offered award. Others may qualify for the award in satisfying criteria of a minimum 3.7 GPA or in combination with high test scores, or for Talent in Arts competition in categories of music, drama, dance, or visual arts. Must maintain annual 3.0 GPA in college for award to be renewed. *Award:* Scholarship for use in freshman, sophomore, junior, or senior year; renewable. *Award amount:* up to $3000. *Number of awards:* up to 1400. *Eligibility Requirements:* Applicant must be high school student; planning to enroll or expecting to enroll full-time at a two-year or four-year institution or university; resident of Maryland and studying in Maryland. Available to U.S. citizens. *Application Requirements:* Application, test scores, transcript.

Contact Tamika McKelvin, Program Administrator, Maryland State Higher Education Commission, 839 Bestgate Road, Suite 400, Annapolis, MD 21401-3013. *E-mail:* tmckelvi@mhec.state.md.us. *Phone:* 410-260-4546. *Fax:* 410-260-3200. *Web site:* http://www.mhec.state.md.us/.

Distinguished Scholar Community College Transfer Program. Scholarship available for Maryland residents who have completed 60 credit hours or an associate degree at a Maryland community college and are transferring to a Maryland four-year institution. *Award:* Scholarship for use in freshman or sophomore year; renewable. *Award amount:* $3000. *Number of awards:* 127. *Eligibility Requirements:* Applicant must be enrolled or expecting to enroll full-time at a two-year institution; resident of Maryland and studying in Maryland. Available to U.S. citizens. *Application Requirements:* Application, transcript. **Deadline:** March 1.

Contact Maura Sappington, Program Manager, Maryland State Higher Education Commission, 839 Bestgate Road, Suite 400, Annapolis, MD 21401-3013. *E-mail:* msapping@mhec.state.md.us. *Phone:* 410-260-4569. *Fax:* 410-260-3203. *Web site:* http://www.mhec.state.md.us/.

Edward T. Conroy Memorial Scholarship Program. Scholarship for dependents of deceased or 100 percent disabled U.S. Armed Forces personnel; the son, daughter, or surviving spouse of a victim of the September 11, 2001 terrorist attacks who died as a result of the attacks on the World Trade Center in New York City, the attack on the Pentagon in Virginia, or the crash of United Airlines Flight 93 in Pennsylvania; a POW/MIA of the Vietnam Conflict or his/her son or daughter; the son, daughter or surviving spouse (who has not remarried) of a state or local public safety employee or volunteer who died in the line of duty; or a state or local public safety employee or volunteer who was 100 percent disabled in the line of duty. Must be Maryland resident at time of disability. Submit applicable VA certification. Must be at least 16 years of age and attend Maryland institution. *Award:* Scholarship for use in freshman, sophomore, junior, or senior year; renewable. *Award amount:* $7200–$9000. *Number of awards:* up to 121. *Eligibility Requirements:* Applicant must be age 16-24; enrolled or expecting to enroll full- or part-time at a two-year or four-year institution or university; resident of Maryland and studying in Maryland. Applicant or parent of applicant must have employment or volunteer experience in police/firefighting. Available to U.S. citizens. Applicant or parent must meet one or more of the following requirements: general military experience; retired from active duty; disabled or killed as a result of military service; prisoner of war; or missing in action. *Application Requirements:* Application, birth and death certificate, disability papers. **Deadline:** July 15.

Contact Linda Asplin, Office of Student Financial Assistance, Maryland State Higher Education Commission, 839 Bestgate Road, Suite 400, Annapolis, MD 21401-3013. *E-mail:* lasplin@mhec.state.md.us. *Phone:* 410-260-4563. *Fax:* 410-260-3203. *Web site:* http://www.mhec.state.md.us/.

Graduate and Professional Scholarship Program-Maryland. Graduate and professional scholarships provide need-based financial assistance to students attending a Maryland school of medicine, dentistry, law, pharmacy, social work, or nursing. Funds are provided to specific Maryland colleges and universities. Students must demonstrate financial need and be Maryland residents. Contact institution financial aid office for more information. *Academic Fields/Career Goals:* Dental Health/Services; Health and Medical Sciences; Law/Legal Services; Nursing; Social Services. *Award:* Scholarship for use in freshman, sophomore, junior, or senior year; renewable. *Award amount:* $1000–$5000. *Number of awards:* up to 584. *Eligibility Requirements:* Applicant must be enrolled or expecting to enroll full- or part-time at a four-year institution or university; resident of Maryland and studying in Maryland. Available to U.S. citizens. *Application Requirements:* Application, financial need analysis, contact institution financial aid office. **Deadline:** March 1.

Contact Monica Wheatley, Program Manager, Maryland State Higher Education Commission, 839 Bestgate Road, Suite 400, Annapolis, MD 21401. *E-mail:* mwheatle@mhec.state.md.us. *Phone:* 410-260-4560. *Fax:* 410-260-3202. *Web site:* http://www.mhec.state.md.us/.

Howard P. Rawlings Educational Excellence Awards Educational Assistance Grant. Award for Maryland residents accepted or enrolled in a full-time undergraduate degree or certificate program at a Maryland institution or hospital nursing school. Must submit financial aid form by March 1. Must earn 2.0 GPA in college to maintain award. *Award:* Grant for use in freshman, sophomore, junior, or senior year; renewable. *Award amount:* $400–$2700. *Number of awards:* 15,000–30,000. *Eligibility Requirements:* Applicant must be enrolled or expecting to enroll full-time at a two-year or four-year institution or university; resident of Maryland and studying in Maryland. Available to U.S. citizens. *Application Requirements:* Application, financial need analysis. **Deadline:** March 1.

Contact Office of Student Financial Assistance, Maryland State Higher Education Commission, 839 Bestgate Road, Suite 400, Annapolis, MD 21401-3013. *E-mail:* osfamail@mhec.state.md.us. *Phone:* 800-974-1024. *Fax:* 410-260-3200. *Web site:* http://www.mhec.state.md.us/.

Howard P. Rawlings Educational Excellence Awards Guaranteed Access Grant. Award for Maryland resident enrolling full-time in an undergraduate program at a Maryland institution. Must be under 21 at time of first award and begin college within one year of completing high school in Maryland with a minimum 2.5 GPA. Must have an annual family income less than 130 percent of the federal poverty level guideline. *Award:* Grant for use in freshman, sophomore, junior, or senior year; renewable. *Award amount:* $400–$14,800. *Number of awards:* up to 1000. *Eligibility Requirements:* Applicant must be age 21 or under; enrolled or expecting to enroll full-time at a two-year or four-year institution or university; resident of Maryland and studying in Maryland. Applicant must have 3.5 GPA or higher. Available to U.S. citizens. *Application Requirements:* Application, financial need analysis, transcript. **Deadline:** March 1.

Contact Theresa Lowe, Office of Student Financial Assistance, Maryland State Higher Education Commission, 839 Bestgate Road, Suite 400, Annapolis, MD 21401-3013. *E-mail:* osfamail@mhec.state.md.us. *Phone:* 410-260-4555. *Fax:* 410-260-3200. *Web site:* http://www.mhec.state.md.us/.

Janet L. Hoffmann Loan Assistance Repayment Program. Provides assistance for repayment of loan debt to Maryland residents working full-time in nonprofit organizations and state or local governments. Must submit Employment Verification Form and Lender Verification Form. *Academic Fields/Career Goals:* Education; Law/Legal Services; Nursing; Social Services; Therapy/Rehabilitation. *Award:* Grant for use in freshman, sophomore, junior, or senior year; not renewable. *Award amount:* $1500–$10,000. *Number of awards:* up to 700. *Eligibility Requirements:* Applicant must be enrolled or expecting to enroll full-time at a four-year institution or university; resident of Maryland and studying in Maryland. Applicant or parent of applicant must have employment or volunteer experience in government/politics. Available to U.S. citizens. *Application Requirements:* Application, transcript, IRS 1040 form. **Deadline:** September 30.

Contact Tamika McKelvin, Office of Student Financial Assistance, Maryland State Higher Education Commission, 839 Bestgate Road, Suite 400, Annapolis, MD 21401. *E-mail:* tmckelvil@mhec.state.md.us. *Phone:* 410-260-4546. *Fax:* 410-260-3203. *Web site:* http://www.mhec.state.md.us/.

J.F. Tolbert Memorial Student Grant Program. Awards of $500 granted to Maryland residents attending a private career school in Maryland. The scholarship deadline continues. *Award:* Grant for use in freshman or sophomore year; not renewable. *Award amount:* $500. *Number of awards:* 522. *Eligibility Requirements:* Applicant must be enrolled or expecting to enroll full-time at a technical institution; resident of Maryland and studying in Maryland. Available to U.S. citizens. *Application Requirements:* Application, financial need analysis. **Deadline:** continuous.

Contact Glenda Hamlet, Office of Student Financial Assistance, Maryland State Higher Education Commission, 839 Bestgate Road, Suite 400, Annapolis, MD 21401-3013. *E-mail:* osfamail@mhec.state.md.us. *Phone:* 800-974-1024. *Fax:* 410-260-3200. *Web site:* http://www.mhec.state.md.us/.

Part-Time Grant Program-Maryland. Funds provided to Maryland colleges and universities. Eligible students must be enrolled on a part-time basis (6 to 11 credits) in an undergraduate degree program. Must demonstrate financial need and also be Maryland resident. Contact financial aid office at institution for more information. *Award:* Grant for use in freshman, sophomore, junior, or senior year; renewable. *Award amount:* $200–$1500. *Number of awards:* 1800–9000. *Eligibility Requirements:* Applicant must be enrolled or expecting to enroll part-time at a two-year or four-year institution or university; resident of Maryland and studying in Maryland. Available to U.S. citizens. *Application Requirements:* Application, financial need analysis. **Deadline:** March 1.

Contact Monica Wheatley, Program Manager, Maryland State Higher Education Commission, 839 Bestgate Road, Suite 400, Annapolis, MD 21401. *E-mail:* mwheatle@mhec.state.md.us. *Phone:* 410-260-4560. *Fax:* 410-260-3202. *Web site:* http://www.mhec.state.md.us/.

Senatorial Scholarships-Maryland. Renewable award for Maryland residents attending a Maryland degree-granting institution, nursing diploma school, or certain private career schools. May be used out-of-state only if Maryland Higher Education Commission deems major to be unique and not offered at Maryland institution. The scholarship value is $400 to $7000. *Award:* Scholarship for use in freshman, sophomore, junior, or senior year; renewable. *Award amount:* $400–$7000. *Number of awards:* up to 7000. *Eligibility Requirements:* Applicant must be enrolled or expecting to enroll full- or part-time at a two-year, four-year, or technical institution or university; resident of Maryland and studying in Maryland. Available to U.S. citizens. *Application Requirements:* Application, financial need analysis, test scores. **Deadline:** March 1.

Contact Monica Wheatley, Office of Student Financial Assistance, Maryland State Higher Education Commission, 839 Bestgate Road, Suite 400, Annapolis, MD 21401-3013. *E-mail:* osfamail@mhec.state.md.us. *Phone:* 800-974-1024. *Fax:* 410-260-3200. *Web site:* http://www.mhec.state.md.us/.

Tuition Reduction for Non-Resident Nursing Students. Available to nonresidents of Maryland who attend a two-year or four-year public institution in Maryland. It is renewable provided student maintains academic requirements designated by institution attended. Recipient must agree to serve as a full-time nurse in a hospital or related institution for two to four years. *Academic Fields/Career Goals:* Nursing. *Award:* Scholarship for use in freshman, sophomore, junior, or senior year; renewable. *Award amount:* varies. *Number of awards:* varies. *Eligibility Requirements:* Applicant must be enrolled or expecting to enroll full- or part-time at a two-year or four-year institution and studying in Maryland. Available to U.S. citizens. *Application Requirements:* Application. **Deadline:** varies.

Contact Robert Parker, Director, Maryland State Higher Education Commission, 839 Bestgate Road, Suite 400, Annapolis, MD 21401-3013. *E-mail:* rparker@mhec.state.md.us. *Phone:* 410-260-4558. *Web site:* http://www.mhec.state.md.us/.

Tuition Waiver for Foster Care Recipients. Applicant must be a high school graduate or GED recipient and under the age of 21. Must either have resided in a foster care home in Maryland at the time of high school graduation or GED reception, or until 14th birthday, and been adopted after 14th birthday. Applicant, if status approved, will be exempt from paying tuition and mandatory fees at a public college in Maryland. *Award:* Grant for use in freshman, sophomore, junior, senior, or graduate year; renewable. *Award amount:* varies. *Number of awards:* varies. *Eligibility Requirements:* Applicant must be age 21 or under; enrolled or expecting to enroll full- or part-time at a two-year or four-year institution or university; resident of Maryland and studying in Maryland. Available to U.S. citizens. *Application Requirements:* Application, financial need analysis, must inquire at financial aid office of schools. **Deadline:** March 1.

Contact Robert Parker, Director, Maryland State Higher Education Commission, 839 Bestgate Road, Suite 400, Annapolis, MD 21401-3013. *E-mail:* rparker@mhec.state.md.us. *Phone:* 410-260-4558. *Web site:* http://www.mhec.state.md.us/.

Veterans of the Afghanistan and Iraq Conflicts Scholarship Program. Provides financial assistance to Maryland resident U.S. Armed Forces personnel who served in Afghanistan or Iraq Conflicts and their children or spouses who are attending Maryland institutions. *Award:* Scholarship for use in freshman, sophomore, junior, or senior year; renewable. *Award amount:* $8850. *Number of awards:* 123. *Eligibility Requirements:* Applicant must be enrolled or expecting to enroll full- or part-time at a two-year or four-year institution or university; resident of Maryland and studying in Maryland. Available to U.S. citizens. Applicant or parent must meet one or more of the following requirements: general military experience; retired from active duty; disabled or killed as a result of military service; prisoner of war; or missing in action. *Application Requirements:* Application, financial need analysis, birth certificate/marriage certificate, documentation of military order. **Deadline:** March 1.

Contact Linda Asplin, Program Administrator, Maryland State Higher Education Commission, 839 Bestgate Road, Suite 400, Annapolis, MD 21401-3013. *E-mail:* lasplin@mhec.state.md.us. *Phone:* 410-260-4563. *Fax:* 410-260-3203. *Web site:* http://www.mhec.state.md.us/.

Workforce Shortage Student Assistance Grant Program. Scholarship of $4000 available to students who will be required to major in specific areas and will be obligated to serve in the state of Maryland after completion of degree. *Award:* Scholarship for use in freshman, sophomore, junior, or senior year; renewable. *Award amount:* $4000. *Number of awards:* 1300. *Eligibility Requirements:* Applicant must be enrolled or expecting to enroll full- or part-time at a two-year or four-year institution or university; resident of Maryland and studying in Maryland. Available to U.S. citizens. *Application Requirements:* Application, essay, financial need analysis, resume, references, transcript, certain majors require additional documentation. **Deadline:** July 1.

Contact Maura Sappington, Program Manager, Maryland State Higher Education Commission, 839 Bestgate Road, Suite 400, Annapolis, MD 21401-3013. *E-mail:* msapping@mhec.state.md.us. *Phone:* 410-260-4569. *Fax:* 410-260-3203. *Web site:* http://www.mhec.state.md.us/.

MASSACHUSETTS

Agnes M. Lindsay Scholarship. Scholarships for students with demonstrated financial need who are from rural areas of Massachusetts and attend public institutions of higher education in Massachusetts. Deadline varies. *Award:* Scholarship for use in freshman, sophomore, junior, or senior year; not renewable. *Award amount:* varies. *Number of awards:* varies. *Eligibility Requirements:* Applicant must be enrolled or expecting to enroll full-time at a two-year or four-year institution or university; resident of Massachusetts and studying in Massachusetts. Available to U.S. citizens. *Application Requirements:* Application, financial need analysis. **Deadline:** varies.

Contact Robert Brun, Director of Scholarships and Grants, Massachusetts Office of Student Financial Assistance, 454 Broadway, Suite 200, Revere, MA 02151. *E-mail:* osfa@osfa.mass.edu. *Phone:* 617-727-9420. *Fax:* 617-727-0667. *Web site:* http://www.osfa.mass.edu/.

Christian A. Herter Memorial Scholarship. Renewable award for Massachusetts residents who are in the tenth and eleventh grades, and whose socio-economic backgrounds and environment may inhibit their ability to attain educational goals. Must exhibit severe personal or family-related difficulties, medical problems, or have overcome a personal obstacle. Provides up to 50 percent of the student's calculated need, as determined by federal methodology, at the college of their choice within the continental United States. *Award:* Scholarship for use in freshman year; renewable. *Award amount:* up to $15,000. *Number of awards:* 25. *Eligibility Requirements:* Applicant must be high school student; planning to enroll or expecting to enroll full-time at a two-year, four-year, or technical institution or university and resident of Massachusetts. Applicant must have 2.5 GPA or higher. Available to U.S. citizens. *Application Requirements:* Application, driver's license, financial need analysis, interview, references. **Deadline:** March 14.

Contact Robert Brun, Director of Scholarships and Grants, Massachusetts Office of Student Financial Assistance, 454 Broadway, Suite 200, Revere, MA 02151. *E-mail:* osfa@osfa.mass.edu. *Phone:* 617-727-9420. *Fax:* 617-727-0667. *Web site:* http://www.osfa.mass.edu/.

DSS Adopted Children Tuition Waiver. Need-based tuition waiver for Massachusetts residents who are full-time undergraduate students. Must attend a Massachusetts public institution of higher education and be under 24 years of age. File the FAFSA after January 1. Contact school financial aid office for more information. *Award:* Scholarship for use in freshman, sophomore, junior, or senior year; renewable. *Award amount:* varies. *Number of awards:* varies. *Eligibility Requirements:* Applicant must be age 24 or under; enrolled or expecting to enroll full-time at a two-year or four-year institution and resident of Massachusetts. Available to U.S. and non-Canadian citizens. *Application Requirements:* Application, financial need analysis, FAFSA. **Deadline:** varies.

Contact Robert Brun, Director of Scholarships and Grants, Massachusetts Office of Student Financial Assistance, 454 Broadway, Suite 200, Revere, MA 02151. *E-mail:* osfa@

osfa.mass.edu. *Phone:* 617-727-9420. *Fax:* 617-727-0667. *Web site:* http://www.osfa.mass.edu/.

Early Childhood Educators Scholarship Program. Scholarship to provide financial assistance for currently employed early childhood educators and providers who enroll in an associate or bachelor degree program in Early Childhood Education or related programs. Awards are not based on financial need. Individuals taking their first college-level ECE course are eligible for 100 percent tuition, while subsequent ECE courses are awarded at 50 percent tuition. Can be used for one class each semester. *Academic Fields/Career Goals:* Education. *Award:* Scholarship for use in freshman, sophomore, junior, or senior year; not renewable. *Award amount:* $150–$3600. *Number of awards:* varies. *Eligibility Requirements:* Applicant must be enrolled or expecting to enroll full- or part-time at a four-year institution or university. Available to U.S. citizens. *Application Requirements:* Application. **Deadline:** July 1.

Contact Robert Brun, Director of Scholarships and Grants, Massachusetts Office of Student Financial Assistance, 454 Broadway, Suite 200, Revere, MA 02151. *E-mail:* osfa@osfa.mass.edu. *Phone:* 617-727-9420. *Fax:* 617-727-0667. *Web site:* http://www.osfa.mass.edu/.

John and Abigail Adams Scholarship. Scholarship to reward and inspire student achievement, attract more high-performing students to Massachusetts public higher education, and provide families of college-bound students with financial assistance. Must be a U.S. citizen or an eligible non-citizen. There is no application process for the scholarship. Students who are eligible will be notified in the fall of their senior year in high school. *Award:* Scholarship for use in freshman year; not renewable. *Award amount:* varies. *Number of awards:* varies. *Eligibility Requirements:* Applicant must be high school student; planning to enroll or expecting to enroll full-time at a two-year or four-year institution or university; resident of Massachusetts and studying in Massachusetts. Applicant must have 3.0 GPA or higher. Available to U.S. citizens. *Application Requirements:* **Deadline:** varies.

Contact Robert Brun, Director of Scholarships and Grants, Massachusetts Office of Student Financial Assistance, 454 Broadway, Suite 200, Revere, MA 02151. *E-mail:* osfa@osfa.mass.edu. *Phone:* 617-727-9420. *Fax:* 617-727-0667. *Web site:* http://www.osfa.mass.edu/.

Massachusetts Assistance for Student Success Program. Provides need-based financial assistance to Massachusetts residents to attend undergraduate postsecondary institutions in Connecticut, Maine, Massachusetts, New Hampshire, Pennsylvania, Rhode Island, Vermont, and District of Columbia. High school seniors may apply. Expected Family Contribution (EFC) should be $3850. Timely filing of FAFSA required. *Award:* Grant for use in freshman, sophomore, junior, or senior year; not renewable. *Award amount:* $300–$2400. *Number of awards:* 25,000–30,000. *Eligibility Requirements:* Applicant must be enrolled or expecting to enroll full-time at a two-year, four-year, or technical institution or university; resident of Massachusetts and studying in Connecticut, District of Columbia, Maine, Massachusetts, New Hampshire, Pennsylvania, Rhode Island, or Vermont. Available to U.S. citizens. *Application Requirements:* Financial need analysis, FAFSA. **Deadline:** May 1.

Contact Robert Brun, Director of Scholarships and Grants, Massachusetts Office of Student Financial Assistance, 454 Broadway, Suite 200, Revere, MA 02151. *E-mail:* osfa@osfa.mass.edu. *Phone:* 617-727-9420. *Fax:* 617-727-0667. *Web site:* http://www.osfa.mass.edu/.

Massachusetts Cash Grant Program. A need-based grant to assist with mandatory fees and non-state supported tuition. This supplemental award is available to Massachusetts residents, who are undergraduates at public two-year, four-year colleges and universities in Massachusetts. Must file FAFSA before May 1. Contact college financial aid office for information. *Award:* Grant for use in freshman, sophomore, junior, or senior year; not renewable. *Award amount:* varies. *Number of awards:* varies. *Eligibility Requirements:* Applicant must be enrolled or expecting to enroll full-time at a two-year or four-year institution or university and resident of Massachusetts. Available to U.S. citizens. *Application Requirements:* Application, financial need analysis, FAFSA. **Deadline:** continuous.

Contact Robert Brun, Director of Scholarships and Grants, Massachusetts Office of Student Financial Assistance, 454 Broadway, Suite 200, Revere, MA 02151. *E-mail:* osfa@osfa.mass.edu. *Phone:* 617-727-9420. *Fax:* 617-727-0667. *Web site:* http://www.osfa.mass.edu/.

Massachusetts Gilbert Matching Student Grant Program. Grants for permanent Massachusetts residents attending an independent, regionally accredited Massachusetts school or school of nursing full time. Must be U.S. citizen and permanent legal resident of Massachusetts. File the Free Application for Federal Student Aid after January 1. Contact college financial aid office for complete details and deadlines. *Award:* Grant for use in freshman, sophomore, junior, or senior year; not renewable. *Award amount:* $200–$2500. *Number of awards:* varies. *Eligibility Requirements:* Applicant must be enrolled or expecting to enroll full-time at a four-year institution or university; resident of Massachusetts and studying in Massachusetts. Available to U.S. citizens. *Application Requirements:* Financial need analysis, FAFSA. **Deadline:** varies.

Contact Robert Brun, Director of Scholarships and Grants, Massachusetts Office of Student Financial Assistance, 454 Broadway, Suite 200, Revere, MA 02151. *E-mail:* rbrun@osfa.mass.edu. *Phone:* 617-727-9420. *Fax:* 617-727-0667. *Web site:* http://www.osfa.mass.edu/.

Massachusetts Part-Time Grant Program. Award for permanent Massachusetts residents who have enrolled part-time for at least one year in a state-approved postsecondary school. The recipient must not have a bachelor's degree. FAFSA must be filed before May 1. Contact college financial aid office for further information. *Award:* Grant for use in freshman, sophomore, junior, or senior year; not renewable. *Award amount:* $200–$1150. *Number of awards:* 200. *Eligibility Requirements:* Applicant must be enrolled or expecting to enroll part-time at a two-year, four-year, or technical institution or university and resident of Massachusetts. Available to U.S. citizens. *Application Requirements:* Application, financial need analysis, FAFSA. **Deadline:** varies.

Contact Robert Brun, Director of Scholarships and Grants, Massachusetts Office of Student Financial Assistance, 454 Broadway, Suite 200, Revere, MA 02151. *E-mail:* osfa@osfa.mass.edu. *Phone:* 617-727-9420. *Fax:* 617-727-0667. *Web site:* http://www.osfa.mass.edu/.

Massachusetts Public Service Grant Program. Scholarships for children and/or spouses of deceased members of fire, police, and corrections departments, who were killed in the line of duty. Awards Massachusetts residents attending Massachusetts institutions. Applicant should have not received a prior bachelor's degree or its equivalent. *Award:* Grant for use in freshman, sophomore, junior, or senior year; not renewable. *Award amount:* varies. *Number of awards:* varies. *Eligibility Requirements:* Applicant must be enrolled or expecting to enroll full-time at a four-year institution or university and resident of Massachusetts. Applicant or parent of applicant must have employment or volunteer experience in police/firefighting. Available to U.S. and non-U.S. citizens. Applicant or parent must meet one or more of the following requirements: general military experience; retired from active duty; disabled or killed as a result of military service; prisoner of war; or missing in action. *Application Requirements:* Application, financial need analysis, copy of birth certificate, copy of veteran's death certificate. **Deadline:** May 1.

Contact Alison Leary, Director of Scholarships and Grants, Massachusetts Office of Student Financial Assistance, 454 Broadway, Suite 200, Revere, MA 02151. *E-mail:* osfa@osfa.mass.edu. *Phone:* 617-727-9420. *Fax:* 617-727-0667. *Web site:* http://www.osfa.mass.edu/.

New England Regional Student Program-Tuition Break. Tuition discount for residents of six New England states (Connecticut, Maine, Massachusetts, New Hampshire, Rhode Island, Vermont). Students pay reduced out-of-state tuition at public colleges or universities in other New England states when enrolling in certain majors not offered at public institutions in home state. Details are available at http://www.nebhe.org/tuitionbreak. *Award:* Scholarship for use in freshman, sophomore, junior, senior, or graduate year; renewable. *Award amount:* varies. *Eligibility Requirements:* Applicant must be enrolled or expecting to enroll full- or part-time at a two-year or four-year institution or university; resident of Connecticut, Maine, Massachusetts, New Hampshire, Rhode Island, or Vermont and studying in Connecticut, Maine, Massachusetts, New Hampshire, Rhode Island, or Vermont. Available to U.S. citizens. *Application Requirements:* College application for admission. **Deadline:** continuous.

Contact Wendy Lindsay, Senior Director of Regional Student Program, New England Board of Higher Education, 45 Temple Place, Boston, MA 02111. *E-mail:* tuitionbreak@nebhe.org. *Phone:* 617-357-9620 Ext. 111. *Fax:* 617-338-1577. *Web site:* http://www.nebhe.org/.

Paraprofessional Teacher Preparation Grant. Grant providing financial aid assistance to Massachusetts residents, who are currently employed as paraprofessionals in Massachusetts public schools and wish to obtain higher education and become certified as full-time teachers. *Academic Fields/Career Goals:* Education. *Award:* Grant for use in freshman, sophomore, junior, or senior year; not renewable. *Award amount:* $250–$7500. *Number of awards:* varies. *Eligibility Requirements:* Applicant must be enrolled or expecting to enroll full- or part-time at a two-year or four-year institution or university and resident of Massachusetts. Available to U.S. citizens. *Application Requirements:* Application, FAFSA. **Deadline:** August 1.

Contact Robert Brun, Director of Scholarships and Grants, Massachusetts Office of Student Financial Assistance, 454 Broadway, Suite 200, Revere, MA 02151. *E-mail:* osfa@osfa.mass.edu. *Phone:* 617-727-9420. *Fax:* 617-727-0667. *Web site:* http://www.osfa.mass.edu/.

Robert C. Byrd Honors Scholarship-Massachusetts. Scholarship for high school senior who is a resident of Massachusetts for at least one year prior to the beginning of the academic year he/she will enter college. Must have applied or been accepted to an accredited institution of higher education and be a U.S. citizen, national or permanent resident. *Award:* Scholarship for use in freshman year; renewable. *Award amount:* $1500. *Number of awards:* varies. *Eligibility Requirements:* Applicant must be high school student; planning to enroll or expecting to enroll full-time at a four-year institution or university and resident of Massachusetts. Applicant must have 3.5 GPA or higher. Available to U.S. citizens. *Application Requirements:* Application, transcript. **Deadline:** June 1.

Contact Sally Teixeira, Scholarship Coordinator, Massachusetts Department of Education, 350 Main Street, Malden, MA 02148-5023. *E-mail:* steixeira@doe.mass.edu. *Phone:* 781-338-6304. *Web site:* http://www.doe.mass.edu/.

MICHIGAN

American Legion Auxiliary Department of Michigan Medical Career Scholarship. Award for training in Michigan as registered nurse, licensed practical nurse, physical therapist, respiratory therapist, or in any medical career. Must be child, grandchild, great-grandchild, wife, or widow of honorably discharged or deceased veteran who has served during the eligibility dates for American Legion membership. Must be Michigan resident attending a Michigan school. *Academic Fields/Career Goals:* Health and Medical Sciences; Nursing; Therapy/Rehabilitation. *Award:* Scholarship for use in freshman year; not renewable. *Award amount:* $500. *Number of awards:* 10–20. *Eligibility Requirements:* Applicant must be high school student; planning to enroll or expecting to enroll full-time at a two-year, four-year, or technical institution or university; resident of Michigan and studying in Michigan. Available to U.S. citizens. Applicant must have general military experience. *Application Requirements:* Application, financial need analysis, references, transcript, veteran's discharge papers, copy of pages 1 and 2 of federal income tax return. **Deadline:** March 15.

Contact Ms. LeAnn Knott, Scholarship Coordinator, American Legion Auxiliary Department of Michigan, 212 North Verlinden Avenue, Suite B, Lansing, MI 48915. *E-mail:* lknott@michalaux.org. *Phone:* 517-267-8809 Ext. 22. *Fax:* 517-371-3698. *Web site:* http://www.michalaux.org/.

American Legion Auxiliary Department of Michigan Memorial Scholarship. Scholarship for daughter, granddaughter, and great-granddaughter of any honorably discharged or deceased veteran of U.S. wars or conflicts. Must be Michigan resident for minimum of one year, female between 16 and 21 years, and attend college in Michigan. Must include copy of military discharge and copy of parent or guardian's IRS 1040 form. *Award:* Scholarship for use in freshman or sophomore year; not renewable. *Award amount:* $500. *Number of awards:* 10–20. *Eligibility Requirements:* Applicant must be age 16-21; enrolled or expecting to enroll full-time at a two-year, four-year, or technical institution or university; female; resident of Michigan and studying in Michigan. Available to U.S. citizens. Applicant must have general military experience. *Application Requirements:* Application, financial need analysis, references, transcript, discharge papers. **Deadline:** March 15.

Contact LeAnn Knott, Scholarship Coordinator, American Legion Auxiliary Department of Michigan, 212 North Verlinden Avenue, Suite B, Lansing, MI 48915. *E-mail:* lknott@michalaux.org. *Phone:* 517-267-8809 Ext. 22. *Fax:* 517-371-3698. *Web site:* http://www.michalaux.org/.

American Legion Auxiliary Department of Michigan Scholarship for Non-Traditional Student. Applicant must be a dependent of a veteran. Must be one of the following: nontraditional student returning to classroom after some period of time in which their education was interrupted, student over the age of 22 attending college for the first time to pursue a degree, or student over the age of 22 attending a trade or vocational school. Applicants must be Michigan residents only and attend Michigan institution. Judging based on: need-25 points, character/leadership-25 points, scholastic standing-25 points, initiative/goal-25 points. *Award:* Scholarship for use in freshman, sophomore, junior, or senior year; renewable. *Award amount:* \$500. *Number of awards:* 1–1. *Eligibility Requirements:* Applicant must be age 23-99; enrolled or expecting to enroll full- or part-time at a two-year, four-year, or technical institution or university; resident of Michigan and studying in Michigan. Available to U.S. citizens. Applicant must have general military experience. *Application Requirements:* Application, financial need analysis, transcript, copy of veteran's discharge papers. **Deadline:** March 15.

Contact LeAnn Knott, Scholarship Coordinator, American Legion Auxiliary Department of Michigan, 212 North Verlinden Avenue, Suite B, Lansing, MI 48915. *E-mail:* lknott@michalaux.org. *Phone:* 517-267-8809 Ext. 22. *Fax:* 517-371-3698. *Web site:* http://www.michalaux.org/.

Michigan Competitive Scholarship. Renewable awards for Michigan resident to pursue undergraduate study at a Michigan institution. Awards limited to tuition. Must maintain at least a 2.0 grade point average and meet the college's academic progress requirements. Must file Free Application for Federal Student Aid. *Award:* Scholarship for use in freshman, sophomore, junior, or senior year; renewable. *Award amount:* \$510–\$1610. *Number of awards:* varies. *Eligibility Requirements:* Applicant must be enrolled or expecting to enroll full- or part-time at a two-year or four-year institution or university; resident of Michigan and studying in Michigan. Available to U.S. citizens. *Application Requirements:* Application, financial need analysis, test scores. **Deadline:** March 1.

Contact Scholarship and Grant Director, Michigan Higher Education Assistance Authority, PO Box 30466, Lansing, MI 48909-7962. *E-mail:* osg@michigan.gov. *Phone:* 888-447-2687. *Web site:* http://www.michigan.gov/studentaid.

Michigan Tuition Grant. Need-based program. Students must be Michigan residents and attend a Michigan private, nonprofit, degree-granting college. Must file the Free Application for Federal Student Aid and meet the college's academic progress requirements. *Award:* Grant for use in freshman, sophomore, junior, or senior year; renewable. *Award amount:* up to \$1610. *Number of awards:* varies. *Eligibility Requirements:* Applicant must be enrolled or expecting to enroll full- or part-time at a four-year institution or university; resident of Michigan and studying in Michigan. Available to U.S. citizens. *Application Requirements:* Financial need analysis. **Deadline:** July 1.

Contact Scholarship and Grant Director, Michigan Higher Education Assistance Authority, PO Box 30462, Lansing, MI 48909-7962. *E-mail:* osg@michigan.gov. *Phone:* 888-447-2687. *Web site:* http://www.michigan.gov/studentaid.

Tuition Incentive Program. Award for Michigan residents who receive or have received Medicaid for required period of time through the Department of Human Services. Scholarship provides two years tuition towards an associate degree at a Michigan college or university and \$2000 total assistance for third and fourth years. Must apply before graduating from high school or earning a general education development diploma. *Award:* Grant for use in freshman, sophomore, junior, or senior year; renewable. *Award amount:* varies. *Number of awards:* varies. *Eligibility Requirements:* Applicant must be high school student; planning to enroll or expecting to enroll full- or part-time at a two-year or four-year institution or university; resident of Michigan and studying in Michigan. Available to U.S. citizens. *Application Requirements:* Application, Medicaid eligibility for specified period of time. **Deadline:** continuous.

Contact Scholarship and Grant Director, Michigan Higher Education Assistance Authority, PO Box 30462, Lansing, MI 48909-7962. *E-mail:* osg@michigan.gov. *Phone:* 888-447-2687. *Web site:* http://www.michigan.gov/studentaid.

MINNESOTA

Leadership, Excellence and Dedicated Service Scholarship. Scholarship provides a maximum of thirty \$1000 to selected high school seniors who become a member of the Minnesota National Guard and complete the application process. The award recognizes demonstrated leadership, community services and potential for success in the Minnesota National Guard. *Award:* Scholarship for use in freshman year; not renewable. *Award amount:* \$1000. *Number of awards:* up to 30. *Eligibility Requirements:* Applicant must be high school student; planning to enroll or expecting to enroll full- or part-time at a two-year, four-year, or technical institution or university; resident of Minnesota and must have an interest in leadership. Applicant or parent of applicant must have employment or volunteer experience in community service. Available to U.S. citizens. Applicant or parent must meet one or more of the following requirements: Air Force National Guard or Army National Guard experience; retired from active duty; disabled or killed as a result of military service; prisoner of war; or missing in action. *Application Requirements:* Essay, resume, references, transcript. **Deadline:** March 15.

Contact Barbara O'Reilly, Education Services Officer, Minnesota Department of Military Affairs, 20 West 12th Street, Veterans Services Building, St. Paul, MN 55155-2098. *E-mail:* barbara.oreilly@mn.ngb.army.mil. *Phone:* 651-282-4508. *Web site:* http://www.minnesotanationalguard.org/.

Minnesota Achieve Scholarship. Eligible Minnesota high school graduates who complete any one of four sets of courses defined as rigorous earn a one-time scholarship to help pay for college at a public or private university or college in Minnesota. Eligible students who graduated between January 1, 2008 and December 31, 2008 can receive a one-time scholarship of \$1,200 available for use within the four years immediately following their high school graduation. Eligible students who graduate after January 1, 2009 and enroll full time (15 credits) in an eligible college or university in the academic year immediately following their high school graduation can receive a one-time scholarship for use in their first academic year ranging from \$1,200 to approximately \$4,000 depending on financial need and funds availability. *Award:* Scholarship for use in freshman year; not renewable. *Award amount:* up to \$1200. *Number of awards:* varies. *Eligibility Requirements:* Applicant must be high school student; planning to enroll or expecting to enroll full-time at a two-year, four-year, or technical institution or university; resident of Minnesota and studying in Minnesota. Applicant must have 2.5 GPA or higher. Available to U.S. citizens. *Application Requirements:* Application, financial need analysis, test scores, transcript. **Deadline:** continuous.

Contact Scholarship Staff, Minnesota Office of Higher Education, 1450 Energy Park Drive, St. Paul, MN 55108. *Phone:* 651-642-0567. *Fax:* 651-642-0675. *Web site:* http://www.getreadyforcollege.org/.

Minnesota GI Bill Program. Provides financial assistance to eligible Minnesota veterans and non-veterans who have served 5 or more years cumulatively as a member of the National Guard or Reserves, and served on or after September 11, 2001. Surviving spouses and children of service members who have died or have a total and permanent disability and who served on or after September 11, 2001, may also be eligible. Full-time students may receive up to \$1000 per term, and part-time students up to \$500 per term up to \$3,000 per year. Maximum lifetime benefit is $10,000. *Award:* Scholarship for use in freshman, sophomore, junior, senior, graduate, or postgraduate years; not renewable. *Award amount:* up to $3000. *Number of awards:* varies. *Eligibility Requirements:* Applicant must be enrolled or expecting to enroll full- or part-time at a two-year, four-year, or technical institution or university; resident of Minnesota and studying in Minnesota. Available to U.S. citizens. Applicant or parent must meet one or more of the following requirements: general military experience; retired from active duty; disabled or killed as a result of military service; prisoner of war; or missing in action. *Application Requirements:* Application, financial need analysis, military records. **Deadline:** continuous.

Contact Scholarship Staff, Minnesota Office of Higher Education, 1450 Energy Park Drive, St. Paul, MN 55108. *Phone:* 651-642-0567 Ext. 1. *Fax:* 651-642-0675. *Web site:* http://www.getreadyforcollege.org/.

Minnesota Indian Scholarship. Scholarship for Minnesota residents who are one-fourth or more American Indian ancestry and attending an eligible Minnesota postsecondary institution. Maximum award is $4000 for undergraduate students and $6000 for graduate students. Scholarships are limited to 3 years for certificate or AA/AS programs, 5 years for bachelor's degree programs, and 5 years for graduate programs. Applicants must maintain satisfactory academic progress, not be in default on student loans, and be eligible to receive Pell or State Grant and have remaining need. Undergraduates must be enrolled on a least a 3/4-time basis. *Award:* Scholarship for use in freshman, sophomore, junior, senior, graduate, or postgraduate years; not renewable. *Award amount:* up to $6000. *Number of awards:* 500–600. *Eligibility Requirements:* Applicant must be American Indian/Alaska Native; enrolled or expecting to enroll full- or part-time at a two-year, four-year, or technical institution or university; resident of Minnesota and studying in Minnesota. Available to U.S. citizens. *Application Requirements:* Application, financial need analysis, American Indian ancestry documentation. **Deadline:** continuous.

Contact Scholarship Staff, Minnesota Office of Higher Education, 1450 Energy Park Drive, Suite 350, St. Paul, MN 55108. *E-mail:* sandy.bowes@state.mn.us. *Phone:* 651-642-0567 Ext. 1. *Fax:* 651-642-0675. *Web site:* http://www.getreadyforcollege.org/.

Minnesota Reciprocal Agreement. Renewable tuition waiver for Minnesota residents. Waives all or part of non-resident tuition surcharge at public institutions in Indiana, Iowa, Kansas, Michigan, Missouri, Nebraska, North Dakota, South Dakota, Wisconsin and Manitoba. Deadline: last day of academic term. *Award:* Scholarship for use in freshman, sophomore, junior, senior, graduate, or postgraduate years; renewable. *Award amount:* varies. *Number of awards:* varies. *Eligibility Requirements:* Applicant must be enrolled or expecting to enroll full- or part-time at a two-year, four-year, or technical institution or university; resident of Minnesota and studying in Indiana, Iowa, Kansas, Manitoba, Michigan, Missouri, Nebraska, North Dakota, South Dakota, or Wisconsin. Available to U.S. citizens. *Application Requirements:* Application. **Deadline:** continuous.

Contact Jodi Rouland, Program Assistant, Minnesota Office of Higher Education. *E-mail:* jodi.rouland@state.mn.us. *Phone:* 651-355-0614. *Fax:* 651-642-0675. *Web site:* http://www.getreadyforcollege.org/.

Minnesota State Grant Program. Need-based grant program available for Minnesota residents attending Minnesota colleges. Student covers 46% of cost with remainder covered by Pell Grant, parent contribution and state grant. Students apply with FAFSA and college administers the program on campus. *Award:* Grant for use in freshman, sophomore, junior, or senior year; not renewable. *Award amount:* $100–$9444. *Number of awards:* 71,000–105,000. *Eligibility Requirements:* Applicant must be age 17 and over; enrolled or expecting to enroll full- or part-time at a two-year, four-year, or technical institution or university; resident of Minnesota and studying in Minnesota. Available to U.S. citizens. *Application Requirements:* Application, financial need analysis. **Deadline:** continuous.

Contact Grant Staff, Minnesota Office of Higher Education, 1450 Energy Park Drive, Suite 350, St. Paul, MN 55108. *Phone:* 651-642-0567 Ext. 1. *Web site:* http://www.getreadyforcollege.org/.

Minnesota State Veterans' Dependents Assistance Program. Tuition assistance to dependents of persons considered to be prisoner-of-war or missing in action after August 1, 1958. Must be Minnesota resident attending Minnesota two- or four-year school. *Award:* Scholarship for use in freshman, sophomore, junior, or senior year; renewable. *Award amount:* varies. *Number of awards:* varies. *Eligibility Requirements:* Applicant must be enrolled or expecting to enroll full- or part-time at a two-year or four-year institution; resident of Minnesota and studying in Minnesota. Available to U.S. citizens. Applicant or parent must meet one or more of the following requirements: general military experience; retired from active duty; disabled or killed as a result of military service; prisoner of war; or missing in action. *Application Requirements:* Application. **Deadline:** continuous.

Contact Ginny Dodds, Manager, Minnesota Office of Higher Education, 1450 Energy Park Drive, Suite 350, St. Paul, MN 55108-5227. *E-mail:* ginny.dodds@state.mn.us. *Phone:* 651-355-0610. *Web site:* http://www.getreadyforcollege.org/.

Paul and Fern Yocum Scholarship. Scholarship to dependent children of full-time Yocum Oil employees. *Award:* Scholarship for use in freshman, sophomore, junior, senior, or graduate year; not renewable. *Award amount:* $1000. *Number of awards:* 3. *Eligibility Requirements:* Applicant must be enrolled or expecting to enroll full- or part-time at a four-year institution or university. Applicant or parent of applicant must be affiliated with Yocum Oil Company. Available to U.S. and non-Canadian citizens. *Application Requirements:* Application. **Deadline:** April 15.

Contact Donna Paulson, Administrative Assistant, Minnesota Community Foundation, 55 Fifth Street East, Suite 600, St. Paul, MN 55101-1797. *E-mail:* dkp@mncommunityfoundation.org. *Phone:* 651-325-4212. *Fax:* 651-224-9502. *Web site:* http://www.mncommunityfoundation.org/.

Postsecondary Child Care Grant Program-Minnesota. Grant available for students not receiving MFIP. Based on financial need. Cannot exceed actual child care costs or maximum award chart (based on income). Must be Minnesota resident. For use at Minnesota two- or four-year school, including public technical colleges. Available until student has attended college for the equivalent of four full-time academic years. *Award:* Grant for use in freshman, sophomore, junior, or senior year; not renewable. *Award amount:* $100–$2600. *Number of awards:* varies. *Eligibility Requirements:* Applicant must be enrolled or expecting to enroll full- or part-time at a two-year, four-year, or technical institution or university; resident of Minnesota and studying in Minnesota. Available to U.S. citizens. *Application Requirements:* Application, financial need analysis. **Deadline:** continuous.

Contact Brenda Larter, Program Administrator, Minnesota Office of Higher Education, 1450 Energy Park Drive, Suite 350, St. Paul, MN 55108-5227. *E-mail:* brenda.larter@state.

mn.us. *Phone:* 651-355-0612. *Fax:* 651-642-0675. *Web site:* http://www.getreadyforcollege.org/.

Safety Officers' Survivor Grant Program. Grant for eligible survivors of Minnesota public safety officers killed in the line of duty. Safety officers who have been permanently or totally disabled in the line of duty are also eligible. Must be used at a Minnesota institution participating in State Grant Program. Write for details. Must submit proof of death or disability and Public Safety Officers Benefit Fund Certificate. Must apply for renewal each year for four years. *Award:* Grant for use in freshman, sophomore, junior, or senior year; not renewable. *Award amount:* up to $10,488. *Number of awards:* 1. *Eligibility Requirements:* Applicant must be age 23 or under; enrolled or expecting to enroll full- or part-time at a two-year, four-year, or technical institution or university; resident of Minnesota and studying in Minnesota. Applicant or parent of applicant must have employment or volunteer experience in police/firefighting. Available to U.S. citizens. *Application Requirements:* Application, proof of death or disability. **Deadline:** continuous.

Contact Brenda Larter, Program Administrator, Minnesota Office of Higher Education. *E-mail:* brenda.larter@state.mn.us. *Phone:* 651-355-0612. *Fax:* 651-642-0675. *Web site:* http://www.getreadyforcollege.org/.

MISSISSIPPI

Critical Needs Teacher Loan/Scholarship. Eligible applicants will agree to employment immediately upon degree completion as a full-time classroom teacher in a public school located in a critical teacher shortage area in the state of Mississippi. Must verify the intention to pursue a first bachelor's degree in teacher education. Award covers tuition and required fees, average cost of room and meals plus allowance for books. Must be enrolled at a Mississippi college or university. *Academic Fields/Career Goals:* Education; Foreign Language; Mathematics; Special Education. *Award:* Forgivable loan for use in junior or senior year; not renewable. *Award amount:* $5514–$15,506. *Number of awards:* varies. *Eligibility Requirements:* Applicant must be enrolled or expecting to enroll full- or part-time at a four-year institution or university and studying in Mississippi. Applicant must have 2.5 GPA or higher. Available to U.S. and non-U.S. citizens. *Application Requirements:* Application, test scores, transcript. **Deadline:** March 31.

Contact Mrs. Jennifer Rogers, Director of Student Financial Aid, Mississippi Office of Student Financial Aid, 3825 Ridgewood Road, Jackson, MS 39211-6453. *E-mail:* sfa@mississippi.edu. *Phone:* 601-432-6997. *Web site:* http://www.mississippi.edu/.

Higher Education Legislative Plan (HELP). Eligible applicant must be resident of Mississippi and be freshman and/or sophomore student who graduated from high school within the immediate past two years. Must demonstrate need as determined by the results of the FAFSA: documenting an average family adjusted gross income of $36,500 or less over the prior two years. Must be enrolled full-time at a Mississippi college or university, have a GPA of 2.5 and have scored 20 on the ACT. *Award:* Scholarship for use in freshman, sophomore, junior, or senior year; not renewable. *Award amount:* $830–$5151. *Number of awards:* varies. *Eligibility Requirements:* Applicant must be enrolled or expecting to enroll full-time at a two-year or four-year institution or university; resident of Mississippi and studying in Mississippi. Applicant must have 2.5 GPA or higher. Available to U.S. citizens. *Application Requirements:* Application, financial need analysis, test scores, transcript, FAFSA, specific high school curriculum. **Deadline:** March 31.

Contact Mrs. Jennifer Rogers, Director of Student Financial Aid, Mississippi Office of Student Financial Aid, 3825 Ridgewood Road, Jackson, MS 39211-6453. *E-mail:* sfa@mississippi.edu. *Phone:* 601-432-6997. *Web site:* http://www.mississippi.edu/.

Law Enforcement Officers/Firemen Scholarship. Financial assistance to dependent children and spouses of any Mississippi law enforcement officer, full-time fire fighter or volunteer fire fighter who has suffered fatal injuries or wounds or become permanently and totally disabled as a result of injuries or wounds which occurred in the performance of the official and appointed duties of his or her office. This financial assistance is offered as an eight semester tuition and room scholarship at any state-supported college or university in Mississippi. *Award:* Scholarship for use in freshman, sophomore, junior, or senior year; not renewable. *Eligibility Requirements:* Applicant must be enrolled or expecting to enroll full-time at a four-year institution or university; resident of Mississippi and studying in Mississippi. Applicant or parent of applicant must have employment or volunteer experience in police/firefighting. *Application Requirements:* Application. **Deadline:** continuous.

Contact Stephanie Green, Program Administrator, Mississippi Office of Student Financial Aid. *E-mail:* sgreen@mississippi.edu. *Phone:* 800-327-2980 Ext. 4. *Web site:* http://www.mississippi.edu/.

Mississippi Eminent Scholars Grant. Award for an entering freshmen or as a renewal for sophomore, junior or senior. who are residents of Mississippi. Applicants must achieve a GPA of 3.5 and must have scored 29 on the ACT. Must enroll full-time at an eligible Mississippi college or university. *Award:* Grant for use in freshman, sophomore, junior, or senior year; not renewable. *Award amount:* up to $2500. *Number of awards:* varies. *Eligibility Requirements:* Applicant must be enrolled or expecting to enroll full-time at a two-year or four-year institution or university; resident of Mississippi and studying in Mississippi. Applicant must have 3.5 GPA or higher. Available to U.S. citizens. *Application Requirements:* Application, test scores, transcript. **Deadline:** September 15.

Contact Mrs. Jennifer Rogers, Director of Student Financial Aid, Mississippi Office of Student Financial Aid, 3825 Ridgewood Road, Jackson, MS 39211-6453. *E-mail:* sfa@mississippi.edu. *Phone:* 601-432-6997. *Web site:* http://www.mississippi.edu/.

Mississippi Health Care Professions Loan/Scholarship Program. Renewable award for junior and senior undergraduates studying psychology or speech pathology, and graduate students studying physical therapy or occupational therapy. Must be Mississippi residents attending four-year colleges or universities in Mississippi. Must fulfill work obligation in Mississippi on the basis of one year's service for one year's loan received, or pay back as loan. *Academic Fields/Career Goals:* Health and Medical Sciences; Psychology; Therapy/Rehabilitation. *Award:* Forgivable loan for use in junior, senior, or graduate year; not renewable. *Award amount:* $1500–$3000. *Number of awards:* varies. *Eligibility Requirements:* Applicant must be enrolled or expecting to enroll full-time at a four-year institution or university; resident of Mississippi and studying in Mississippi. Available to U.S. citizens. *Application Requirements:* Application, transcript, letter of acceptance. **Deadline:** March 31.

Contact Mrs. Jennifer Rogers, Director of Student Financial Aid, Mississippi Office of Student Financial Aid, 3825 Ridgewood Road, Jackson, MS 39211-6453. *E-mail:* sfa@mississippi.edu. *Phone:* 601-432-6997. *Web site:* http://www.mississippi.edu/.

Mississippi Leveraging Educational Assistance Partnership (LEAP). Award for Mississippi residents enrolled for full-time study at a Mississippi college or university. Based on financial need. Contact college financial aid office. Award value and deadline varies. *Award:* Grant for use in freshman, sophomore, junior, or senior year; not renewable. *Award amount:* varies. *Number of awards:* varies. *Eligibility Requirements:* Applicant must be enrolled or expecting to enroll full-time at a two-year or four-year institution or university; resident of Mississippi and studying in Mississippi. Available to U.S. citizens. *Application Requirements:* Application, financial need analysis, FAFSA. **Deadline:** varies.

Contact Mrs. Jennifer Rogers, Director of Student Financial Aid, Mississippi Office of Student Financial Aid, 3825 Ridgewood Road, Jackson, MS 39211-6453. *E-mail:* sfa@mississippi.edu. *Phone:* 601-432-6997. *Web site:* http://www.mississippi.edu/.

Mississippi Resident Tuition Assistance Grant. Must be a resident of Mississippi enrolled full-time at an eligible Mississippi college or university. Must maintain a minimum 2.5 GPA each semester. MTAG awards may be up to $500 per academic year for freshman and sophomores and $1000 per academic year for juniors and seniors. *Award:* Grant for use in freshman, sophomore, junior, or senior year; not renewable. *Award amount:* $10–$1000. *Number of awards:* varies. *Eligibility Requirements:* Applicant must be enrolled or expecting to enroll full-time at a two-year or four-year institution or university; resident of Mississippi and studying in Mississippi. Applicant must have 2.5 GPA or higher. Available to U.S. citizens. *Application Requirements:* Application, test scores, transcript. **Deadline:** September 15.

Contact Mrs. Jennifer Rogers, Director of Student Financial Aid, Mississippi Office of Student Financial Aid, 3825 Ridgewood Road, Jackson, MS 39211-6453. *E-mail:* sfa@mississippi.edu. *Phone:* 601-432-6997. *Web site:* http://www.mississippi.edu/.

Nursing Education Loan/Scholarship-BSN. Award available to junior and senior students pursuing a baccalaureate degree in nursing as well as to the licensed registered nurse who wishes to continue education to the baccalaureate degree. Include transcript and references with application. Minimum 2.5 GPA required. Must be a Mississippi resident and agree to employment in professional nursing (patient care) in Mississippi. *Academic Fields/Career Goals:* Nursing. *Award:* Forgivable loan for use in junior or senior year; not renewable. *Award amount:* $4000. *Number of awards:* varies. *Eligibility Requirements:* Applicant must be enrolled or expecting to enroll full- or part-time at a four-year institution or university; resident of Mississippi and studying in Mississippi. Applicant must have 2.5 GPA or higher. Available to U.S. citizens. *Application Requirements:* Application, transcript, letter of acceptance. **Deadline:** March 31.

Contact Mrs. Jennifer Rogers, Director of Student Financial Aid, Mississippi Office of Student Financial Aid, 3825 Ridgewood Road, Jackson, MS 39211-6453. *E-mail:* sfa@mississippi.edu. *Phone:* 601-432-6997. *Web site:* http://www.mississippi.edu/.

Nursing Education Loan/Scholarship–RN to BSN. Provides education opportunities to students who wish to upgrade their nursing degree and address Mississippi's nursing shortage by providing a constant source of qualified nurses. NELR awards will be made available, to the extent of appropriated funds, to persons seeking a bachelor's degree in nursing at one Mississippi institution of higher learning in exchange for employment in professional nursing in the State of Mississippi up to $4,000 per year academic year not to exceed two (2) calendar years or $8,000. Those pursuing the NELR program part-time are eligible to receive a maximum of $8,000 prorated over three (3) calendar years. *Academic Fields/Career Goals:* Nursing. *Award:* Forgivable loan for use in junior or senior year. *Award amount:* up to $4000. *Eligibility Requirements:* Applicant must be enrolled or expecting to enroll full- or part-time at a four-year institution or university; resident of Mississippi and studying in Mississippi. Available to U.S. citizens. *Application Requirements:* Application, driver's license. **Deadline:** March 30.

Contact Mrs. Jennifer Rogers, Director of Student Financial Aid, Mississippi Office of Student Financial Aid, 3825 Ridgewood Road, Jackson, MS 39211-6453. *E-mail:* sfa@mississippi.edu. *Phone:* 601-432-6997. *Web site:* http://www.mississippi.edu/.

William Winter Teacher Scholar Loan. Scholarship available to a junior or senior student at a four-year Mississippi college or university. Applicants must enroll in a program of study leading to a Class A teacher educator license. *Academic Fields/Career Goals:* Education. *Award:* Forgivable loan for use in junior or senior year; not renewable. *Award amount:* $1333–$4000. *Number of awards:* varies. *Eligibility Requirements:* Applicant must be enrolled or expecting to enroll full-time at a four-year institution or university; resident of Mississippi and studying in Mississippi. Applicant must have 2.5 GPA or higher. Available to U.S. citizens. *Application Requirements:* Application, test scores, letter of acceptance. **Deadline:** March 31.

Contact Mrs. Jennifer Rogers, Director of Student Financial Aid, Mississippi Office of Student Financial Aid, 3825 Ridgewood Road, Jackson, MS 39211-6453. *E-mail:* sfa@mississippi.edu. *Phone:* 601-432-6997. *Web site:* http://www.mississippi.edu/.

MISSOURI

Access Missouri Financial Assistance Program. Need-based program that provides awards to students who are enrolled full time and have an expected family contribution (EFC) of $12,000 or less based on their Free Application for Federal Student Aid (FAFSA). Awards vary depending on EFC and the type of postsecondary school. *Award:* Grant for use in freshman, sophomore, junior, or senior year; not renewable. *Eligibility Requirements:* Applicant must be enrolled or expecting to enroll full-time at a two-year, four-year, or technical institution or university; resident of Missouri and studying in Missouri. Applicant must have 2.5 GPA or higher. Available to U.S. citizens. *Application Requirements:* FAFSA on file by April 1.

Contact Information Center, Missouri Department of Higher Education, P.O. Box 1469, Jefferson City, MO 65102-1469. *E-mail:* info@dhe.mo.gov. *Phone:* 800-473-6757 Ext. 4. *Fax:* 573-751-6635. *Web site:* http://www.dhe.mo.gov/.

Environmental Education Scholarship Program (EESP). Scholarship to minority and other underrepresented students pursuing a bachelor's or master's degree in an environmental course of study. Must be a Missouri resident having a cumulative high school GPA of 3.0 or if enrolled in college, must have cumulative GPA of 2.5. *Academic Fields/Career Goals:* Environmental Science. *Award:* Scholarship for use in freshman, sophomore, junior, senior, or graduate year; renewable. *Award amount:* $2000. *Number of awards:* 16. *Eligibility Requirements:* Applicant must be American Indian/Alaska Native, Asian/Pacific Islander, Black (non-Hispanic), or Hispanic; enrolled or expecting to enroll full-time at a four-year institution or university and resident of Missouri. Applicant must have 3.0 GPA or higher. Available to U.S. citizens. *Application Requirements:* Application, essay, references, transcript. **Deadline:** June 1.

Contact Dana Muessig, Executive, Missouri Department of Natural Resources, PO Box 176, Jefferson City, MO 65102. *E-mail:*

danamuessig@dnr.mo.gov. *Phone:* 800-361-4827. *Fax:* 573-526-3878. *Web site:* http://www.dnr.mo.gov/.

Lillie Lois Ford Scholarship Fund. Two awards of $1000 each are given each year to one boy and one girl. Applicant must have attended a full session of Missouri Boys/Girls State or Missouri Cadet Patrol Academy. Must be a Missouri resident below age 21, attending an accredited college/university as a full-time student. Must be an unmarried descendant of a veteran having served at least 90 days on active duty in the Army, Air Force, Navy, Marine Corps or Coast Guard of the United States. *Award:* Scholarship for use in freshman year; not renewable. *Award amount:* $1000. *Number of awards:* 2. *Eligibility Requirements:* Applicant must be high school student; age 21 or under; planning to enroll or expecting to enroll full-time at a two-year or four-year institution or university; single and resident of Missouri. Available to U.S. citizens. Applicant or parent must meet one or more of the following requirements: general military experience; retired from active duty; disabled or killed as a result of military service; prisoner of war; or missing in action. *Application Requirements:* Application, financial need analysis, test scores, copy of the veteran's discharge certificate. **Deadline:** April 20.

Contact John Doane, Chairman, Education and Scholarship Committee, American Legion Department of Missouri, PO Box 179, Jefferson City, MO 65102-0179. *Phone:* 417-924-8186. *Web site:* http://www.missourilegion.org/.

Marguerite Ross Barnett Memorial Scholarship. Scholarship was established for students who are employed while attending school part-time. Must be enrolled at least half-time but less than full-time at a participating Missouri postsecondary school, be employed and compensated for at least 20 hours per week, be 18 years of age, be a Missouri resident and a U.S. citizen or a permanent resident. *Award:* Scholarship for use in freshman, sophomore, junior, or senior year; renewable. *Award amount:* varies. *Number of awards:* varies. *Eligibility Requirements:* Applicant must be age 18 and over; enrolled or expecting to enroll part-time at a two-year, four-year, or technical institution or university; resident of Missouri and studying in Missouri. Applicant must have 2.5 GPA or higher. Available to U.S. citizens. *Application Requirements:* FAFSA on file by August 1. **Deadline:** August 1.

Contact Information Center, Missouri Department of Higher Education, P.O. Box 1469, Jefferson City, MO 65102-1469. *E-mail:* info@dhe.mo.gov. *Phone:* 800-473-6757 Ext. 4. *Fax:* 573-751-6635. *Web site:* http://www.dhe.mo.gov/.

Missouri Higher Education Academic Scholarship (Bright Flight). Program encourages top-ranked high school seniors to attend approved Missouri postsecondary schools. Must be a Missouri resident and a U.S. citizen or permanent resident. Must have a composite score on the ACT or SAT in the top 5 percent of all Missouri students taking those tests. Students with scores in the top 3 percent are eligible for an annual award of up to $3000 (up to $1500 each semester). Students with scores in the top 4% and 5% are eligible for an annual award of up to $1000 (up to $500 each semester). Award amounts, and the availability of the award for students in the 4% and 5%, are subject to change based on the amount of funding allocated for the program in the legislative session. *Award:* Scholarship for use in freshman, sophomore, junior, or senior year; renewable. *Award amount:* $1000–$3000. *Number of awards:* varies. *Eligibility Requirements:* Applicant must be enrolled or expecting to enroll full-time at a two-year, four-year, or technical institution or university; resident of Missouri and studying in Missouri. Applicant must have 2.5 GPA or higher. Available to U.S. citizens. *Application Requirements:* Test scores. **Deadline:** June 11.

Contact Information Center, Missouri Department of Higher Education, P.O. Box 1469, Jefferson City, MO 65102-1469. *E-mail:* info@dhe.mo.gov. *Phone:* 800-473-6757 Ext. 4. *Fax:* 573-751-6635. *Web site:* http://www.dhe.mo.gov/.

Primary Care Resource Initiative for Missouri Loan Program. Forgivable loans for Missouri residents attending Missouri institutions pursuing a degree as a primary care physician or dentist, dental hygienist, psychiatrist, psychologist, licensed professional counselor, licensed clinical social worker or dietitian/nutritionist. To be forgiven participant must work in a Missouri health professional shortage area. *Academic Fields/Career Goals:* Behavioral Science; Dental Health/Services; Food Science/Nutrition; Health and Medical Sciences; Nursing; Psychology. *Award:* Forgivable loan for use in freshman, sophomore, junior, senior, graduate, or postgraduate years; not renewable. *Award amount:* $5000–$20,000. *Number of awards:* 100. *Eligibility Requirements:* Applicant must be enrolled or expecting to enroll full-time at a four-year institution or university; resident of Missouri and studying in Missouri. Available to U.S. citizens. *Application Requirements:* Application, proof of Missouri residency. **Deadline:** June 30.

Contact Cheryl Thomas, Health and Senior Services Manager, Missouri Department of Health and Senior Services, PO Box 570, Jefferson City, MO 65102-0570. *E-mail:* cheryl.thomas@dhss.mo.gov. *Phone:* 800-891-7415. *Fax:* 573-522-8146. *Web site:* http://www.dhss.mo.gov/.

Robert C. Byrd Honors Scholarship-Missouri. Award for high school seniors who are residents of Missouri. Amount of the award each year depends on the amount the state is allotted by the U.S. Department of Education. Maximum amount awarded per student is $1500. Students must score above 10th percentile on ACT. *Award:* Scholarship for use in freshman year; renewable. *Award amount:* up to $1500. *Number of awards:* 100–150. *Eligibility Requirements:* Applicant must be American Indian/Alaska Native, Asian/Pacific Islander, Black (non-Hispanic), or Hispanic; high school student; planning to enroll or expecting to enroll full-time at a four-year institution or university and resident of Missouri. Available to U.S. citizens. *Application Requirements:* Application, test scores, transcript. **Deadline:** April 15.

Contact Laura Harrison, Administrative Assistant II, Missouri Department of Elementary and Secondary Education, PO Box 480, Jefferson City, MO 65102-0480. *E-mail:* laura.harrison@dese.mo.gov. *Phone:* 573-751-1668. *Fax:* 573-526-3580. *Web site:* http://www.dese.mo.gov/.

MONTANA

Montana Higher Education Opportunity Grant. This grant is awarded based on need to undergraduate students attending either part-time or full-time who are residents of Montana and attending participating Montana schools. Awards are limited to the most needy students. A specific major or program of study is not required. This grant does not need to be repaid, and students may apply each year. Apply by filing FAFSA by March 1 and contacting the financial aid office at the admitting college. *Award:* Grant for use in freshman, sophomore, junior, or senior year; not renewable. *Award amount:* $400–$600. *Number of awards:* up to 800. *Eligibility Requirements:* Applicant must be enrolled or expecting to enroll full- or part-time at a two-year or four-year institution or university; resident of Montana and studying in Montana. Available to U.S. citizens. *Application Requirements:* Application, financial need analysis, resume, FAFSA. **Deadline:** March 1.

Contact Jamie Dushin, Budget Analyst, Montana University System, Office of Commissioner of Higher Education, PO Box 203101, Helena, MT 59620-3101. *E-mail:* jdushin@mgslp.state.mt.us. *Phone:* 406-444-0638. *Fax:* 406-444-1869. *Web site:* http://www.scholarship.mt.gov/.

Montana Tuition Assistance Program-Baker Grant. Need-based grant for Montana residents attending participating Montana schools who have earned at least $2575 during the previous calendar year. Must be enrolled full time. Grant does not need to be repaid. Award covers the first undergraduate degree or certificate. Apply by filing FAFSA by March 1 and contacting the financial aid office at the admitting college. *Award:* Grant for use in freshman, sophomore, junior, or senior year; not renewable. *Award amount:* $100–$1000. *Number of awards:* 1000–3000. *Eligibility Requirements:* Applicant must be enrolled or expecting to enroll full-time at a two-year or four-year institution or university; resident of Montana and studying in Montana. Available to U.S. citizens. *Application Requirements:* Application, financial need analysis, resume, FAFSA. **Deadline:** March 1.

Contact Jamie Dushin, Budget Analyst, Montana University System, Office of Commissioner of Higher Education, PO Box 203101, Helena, MT 59620-3101. *E-mail:* jdushin@mgslp.state.mt.us. *Phone:* 406-444-0638. *Fax:* 406-444-1869. *Web site:* http://www.scholarship.mt.gov/.

Montana University System Honor Scholarship. Scholarship will be awarded annually to high school seniors graduating from accredited Montana high schools. The MUS Honor Scholarship is a four year renewable scholarship that waives the tuition and registration fee at one of the Montana University System campuses or one of the three community colleges (Flathead Valley in Kalispell, Miles in Miles City or Dawson in Glendive). The scholarship must be used within 9 months after high school graduation. Applicant must have a minimum GPA of 3.4. *Award:* Scholarship for use in freshman year; renewable. *Award amount:* $4000–$6000. *Number of awards:* up to 200. *Eligibility Requirements:* Applicant must be high school student; planning to enroll or expecting to enroll full-time at a two-year or four-year institution or university; resident of Montana and studying in Montana. Applicant must have 3.5 GPA or higher. Available to U.S. citizens. *Application Requirements:* Application, test scores, transcript, college acceptance letter. **Deadline:** March 15.

Contact Sheila Nelwun, Grants and Scholarship Coordinator, Montana University System, Office of Commissioner of Higher Education, 2500 Broadway, PO Box 203101, Helena, MT 59620-3101. *E-mail:* snewlun@montana.edu. *Phone:* 406-444-0638. *Fax:* 406-444-1869. *Web site:* http://www.scholarship.mt.gov/.

NEBRASKA

Nebraska Opportunity Grant. Available to undergraduates attending a participating postsecondary institution in Nebraska. Must demonstrate financial need. Nebraska residency required. Awards determined by each participating institution. Student must complete the Free Application for Federal Student Aid (FAFSA) to apply. Contact financial aid office at institution for additional information. *Award:* Grant for use in freshman, sophomore, junior, or senior year; not renewable. *Award amount:* $100–$3400. *Number of awards:* varies. *Eligibility Requirements:* Applicant must be enrolled or expecting to enroll full- or part-time at a two-year, four-year, or technical institution or university; resident of Nebraska and studying in Nebraska. Available to U.S. citizens. *Application Requirements:* Application, financial need analysis. **Deadline:** continuous.

Contact Mr. J. Ritchie Morrow, Financial Aid Coordinator, Nebraska's Coordinating Commission for Postsecondary Education, 140 North Eighth Street, Suite 300, PO Box 95005, Lincoln, NE 68509-5005. *E-mail:* Ritchie.Morrow@nebraska.gov. *Phone:* 402-471-2847. *Fax:* 402-471-2886. *Web site:* http://www.ccpe.state.ne.us/.

NEVADA

Governor Guinn Millennium Scholarship. Scholarship for high school graduates with a diploma from a Nevada public or private high school in the graduating class of the year 2000 or later. Must complete high school with at least 3.25 GPA. *Award:* Scholarship for use in freshman, sophomore, junior, or senior year; not renewable. *Award amount:* $10,000. *Number of awards:* 1. *Eligibility Requirements:* Applicant must be enrolled or expecting to enroll full-time at a two-year or four-year institution or university and resident of Nevada. Available to U.S. citizens. *Application Requirements:* Application. **Deadline:** varies.

Contact Reba Coombs, Executive Director, Nevada Office of the State Treasurer, 555 East Washington Avenue, Suite 4600, Las Vegas, NV 89101. *E-mail:* info@nevadatreasurer.gov. *Phone:* 702-486-3383. *Fax:* 702-486-3246. *Web site:* http://www.nevadatreasurer.gov/.

NEW HAMPSHIRE

Leveraged Incentive Grant Program. Grants to provide assistance on the basis of merit and need to full-time undergraduate New Hampshire students at New Hampshire accredited institutions. Must be a New Hampshire resident, and demonstrate financial need as determined by the federal formula and by merit as determined by the institution. Must be a sophomore, junior or senior undergraduate student. *Award:* Grant for use in sophomore, junior, or senior year; not renewable. *Award amount:* $250–$7500. *Number of awards:* varies. *Eligibility Requirements:* Applicant must be enrolled or expecting to enroll full-time at a two-year, four-year, or technical institution or university; resident of New Hampshire and studying in New Hampshire. Available to U.S. citizens. *Application Requirements:* FAFSA. **Deadline:** varies.

Contact Ms. Cynthia Capodestria, Student Financial Aid Administrator, New Hampshire Postsecondary Education Commission, Three Barrell Court, Suite 300, Concord, NH 03301-8543. *E-mail:* cynthia.capodestria@pec.state.nh.us. *Phone:* 603-271-2555 Ext. 360. *Web site:* http://www.nh.gov/postsecondary.

New Hampshire Incentive Program (NHIP). Grants to provide financial assistance to New Hampshire students attending eligible institutions in New England. Must demonstrate financial need. May be a part- or full-time undergraduate student with no previous bachelor's degree. *Award:* Grant for use in freshman, sophomore, junior, or senior year; renewable. *Award amount:* $125–$1000. *Number of awards:* 4300–4500. *Eligibility Requirements:* Applicant must be enrolled or expecting to enroll full- or part-time at a two-year or four-year institution or university; resident of New Hampshire and studying in Connecticut, Maine, Massachusetts, New Hampshire, Rhode Island, or Vermont. Available to U.S. citizens. *Application Requirements:* FAFSA. **Deadline:** May 1.

Contact Ms. Cynthia Capodestria, Student Financial Aid Administrator, New Hampshire Postsecondary Education Commission, Three Barrell Court, Suite 300, Concord, NH 03301-

8543. *E-mail:* cynthia.capodestria@pec.state.nh.us. *Phone:* 603-271-2555 Ext. 360. *Web site:* http://www.nh.gov/postsecondary.

Scholarships for Orphans of Veterans-New Hampshire. Scholarship to provide financial assistance (room, board, books and supplies) to children of parents) who served in World War II, Korean Conflict, Vietnam (Southeast Asian Conflict) or the Gulf Wars, or any other operation for which the armed forces expeditionary medal or theater of operations service medal was awarded to the veteran. *Award:* Scholarship for use in freshman, sophomore, junior, or senior year; renewable. *Award amount:* up to $2500. *Number of awards:* 1–10. *Eligibility Requirements:* Applicant must be age 16-25; enrolled or expecting to enroll full-time at a two-year or four-year institution or university; resident of New Hampshire and studying in New Hampshire. Available to U.S. citizens. Applicant or parent must meet one or more of the following requirements: general military experience; retired from active duty; disabled or killed as a result of military service; prisoner of war; or missing in action. *Application Requirements:* Application. **Deadline:** varies.

Contact Ms. Cynthia Capodestria, Student Financial Aid Administrator, New Hampshire Postsecondary Education Commission, Three Barrell Court, Suite 300, Concord, NH 03301-8543. *E-mail:* cynthia.capodestria@pec.state.nh.us. *Phone:* 603-271-2555 Ext. 360. *Web site:* http://www.nh.gov/postsecondary.

Workforce Incentive Program. The program provides incentive for students to pursue careers in critical workforce shortage areas at appropriate New Hampshire institutions and to encourage students to then seek employment in New Hampshire after completion of their career program. May be a part- or full-time student in an approved program, and should demonstrate financial need as determined by the institution. *Academic Fields/Career Goals:* Education; Foreign Language; Nursing; Special Education. *Award:* Forgivable loan for use in freshman, sophomore, junior, senior, graduate, or postgraduate years; not renewable. *Award amount:* varies. *Number of awards:* varies. *Eligibility Requirements:* Applicant must be enrolled or expecting to enroll full- or part-time at a four-year institution or university; resident of New Hampshire and studying in New Hampshire. Available to U.S. citizens. *Application Requirements:* Application. **Deadline:** varies.

Contact Ms. Cynthia Capodestria, Student Financial Aid Administrator, New Hampshire Postsecondary Education Commission, Three Barrell Court, Suite 300, Concord, NH 03301-8543. *E-mail:* cynthia.capodestria@pec.state.nh.us. *Phone:* 603-271-2555 Ext. 360. *Web site:* http://www.nh.gov/postsecondary.

NEW JERSEY

American Legion Department of New Jersey High School Oratorical Contest. Award to promote and coordinate the Oratorical Contest Program at the Department, District, County and Post Levels. High School Oratorical Contest is to develop a deeper knowledge and understanding of the constitution of the United States. *Award:* Prize for use in freshman year; not renewable. *Award amount:* $1000–$4000. *Number of awards:* 5. *Eligibility Requirements:* Applicant must be high school student; planning to enroll or expecting to enroll full-time at a four-year institution or university and must have an interest in public speaking. Available to U.S. citizens. *Application Requirements:* Application, applicant must enter a contest. **Deadline:** March 8.

Contact Raymond L. Zawacki, Department Adjutant, American Legion Department of New Jersey, 135 West Hanover Street, Trenton, NJ 08618. *E-mail:* ray@njamericanlegion.org. *Phone:* 609-695-5418. *Fax:* 609-394-1532. *Web site:* http://www.njamericanlegion.org/.

ANNA Alcavis International, Inc. Career Mobility Scholarship. Scholarship to students accepted or enrolled in a baccalaureate or higher degree program in nursing. Applicant must hold a current credential as a Certified Nephrology Nurse (CNN) or Certified Dialysis Nurse (CDN) administered by the Nephrology Nursing Certification Commission (NNCC). *Academic Fields/Career Goals:* Nursing. *Award:* Forgivable loan for use in freshman, sophomore, junior, senior, or graduate year; renewable. *Award amount:* $2000. *Number of awards:* 5. *Eligibility Requirements:* Applicant must be enrolled or expecting to enroll full-time at a four-year institution or university. Applicant or parent of applicant must be member of American Nephrology Nurses' Association. Applicant or parent of applicant must have employment or volunteer experience in nursing. Available to U.S. and non-Canadian citizens. *Application Requirements:* Application, essay, financial need analysis, transcript. **Deadline:** October 15.

Contact Sharon Longton, Awards, Scholarships, and Grants Chairperson, American Nephrology Nurses' Association, East Holly Avenue, PO Box 56, Pitman, NJ 08071-0056. *E-mail:* slongton@dmc.org. *Phone:* 313-966-2674. *Web site:* http://www.annanurse.org/.

Dana Christmas Scholarship for Heroism. Honors young New Jersey residents for acts of heroism. Scholarship is a nonrenewable award of up to $10,000 for 5 students. This scholarship may be used for undergraduate or graduate study. Deadline varies. *Award:* Scholarship for use in freshman, sophomore, junior, senior, or graduate year; not renewable. *Award amount:* up to $10,000. *Number of awards:* up to 5. *Eligibility Requirements:* Applicant must be age 21 or under; enrolled or expecting to enroll full- or part-time at a two-year, four-year, or technical institution or university and resident of New Jersey. Available to U.S. citizens. *Application Requirements:* Application. **Deadline:** varies.

Contact Gisele Joachim, Director, Financial Aid Services, New Jersey Higher Education Student Assistance Authority, 4 Quakerbridge Plaza, PO Box 540, Trenton, NJ 08625. *E-mail:* gjoachim@hesaa.org. *Phone:* 800-792-8670 Ext. 2349. *Fax:* 609-588-7389. *Web site:* http://www.hesaa.org/.

Edward J. Bloustein Distinguished Scholars. Renewable scholarship for students who are placed in top 10 percent of their classes and have a minimum combined SAT score of 1260, or ranked first, second or third in their classes as of end of junior year. Must be New Jersey resident and must attend a New Jersey two-year college, four-year college or university, or approved programs at proprietary institutions. Secondary schools must forward to HESAA, the names and class standings for all nominees. Award value up to $1000 and deadline varies. *Award:* Scholarship for use in freshman, sophomore, junior, senior, or graduate year; renewable. *Award amount:* up to $1000. *Number of awards:* varies. *Eligibility Requirements:* Applicant must be enrolled or expecting to enroll full-time at a two-year or four-year institution or university; resident of New Jersey and studying in New Jersey. Available to U.S. citizens. *Application Requirements:* Application, test scores, nomination by high school. **Deadline:** varies.

Contact Carol Muka, Assistant Director of Grants and Scholarships, New Jersey Higher Education Student Assistance Authority, PO Box 540, Trenton, NJ 08625. *E-mail:* cmuka@hesaa.org. *Phone:* 800-792-8670 Ext. 3266. *Fax:* 609-588-2228. *Web site:* http://www.hesaa.org/.

Law Enforcement Officer Memorial Scholarship. Scholarships for full-time undergraduate study at approved New Jersey institutions for the dependent children of New Jersey law enforcement officers killed in the line of duty. Value of scholarship will be established annually. Deadline varies. *Award:* Scholarship for use in freshman, sophomore, junior, or senior year; renewable. *Award amount:* varies. *Number of awards:* varies. *Eligibility Requirements:* Applicant must be enrolled or expecting to enroll full-time at a four-year institution or university; resident of New Jersey and studying in New Jersey. Applicant or parent of applicant must have employment or volunteer experience in police/firefighting. Available to U.S. citizens. *Application Requirements:* Application. **Deadline:** varies.

Contact Carol Muka, Assistant Director of Grants and Scholarships, New Jersey Higher Education Student Assistance Authority, PO Box 540, Trenton, NJ 08625. *E-mail:* cmuka@hesaa.org. *Phone:* 800-792-8670 Ext. 3266. *Fax:* 609-588-2228. *Web site:* http://www.hesaa.org/.

Luterman Scholarship. Applicant must be a natural or adopted descendant of a member of American Legion, Department of New Jersey. Applicant must be a member of the graduating class of high school including Vo-tech. *Award:* Scholarship for use in freshman year; not renewable. *Award amount:* $1000–$4000. *Number of awards:* 7. *Eligibility Requirements:* Applicant must be high school student and planning to enroll or expecting to enroll full-time at a two-year, four-year, or technical institution or university. Applicant or parent of applicant must be member of American Legion or Auxiliary. Available to U.S. citizens. Applicant or parent must meet one or more of the following requirements: Army experience; retired from active duty; disabled or killed as a result of military service; prisoner of war; or missing in action. *Application Requirements:* Application. **Deadline:** February 15.

Contact Raymond L. Zawacki, Department Adjutant, American Legion Department of New Jersey, 135 West Hanover Street, Trenton, NJ 08618. *E-mail:* ray@njamericanlegion.org. *Phone:* 609-695-5418. *Fax:* 609-394-1532. *Web site:* http://www.njamericanlegion.org/.

New Jersey Student Tuition Assistance Reward Scholarship II. Scholarship for high school graduates who plan to pursue a baccalaureate degree at a New Jersey four-year public institution. Scholarship will cover the cost of tuition and approved fees for up to 18 credits per semester when combined with other state, federal and institutional aid. Deadline varies. *Award:* Scholarship for use in freshman year; renewable. *Award amount:* $2000. *Number of awards:* varies. *Eligibility Requirements:* Applicant must be enrolled or expecting to enroll full-time at a four-year institution or university; resident of New Jersey and studying in New Jersey. Applicant must have 3.0 GPA or higher. Available to U.S. citizens. *Application Requirements:* Application, FAFSA. **Deadline:** varies.

Contact Cathleen Lewis, Assistant Director, Client Services, New Jersey Higher Education Student Assistance Authority, 4 Quaker Bridge Plaza, PO Box 540, Trenton, NJ 08625-0540. *E-mail:* clewis@hesaa.org. *Phone:* 609-588-3280. *Fax:* 609-588-2228. *Web site:* http://www.hesaa.org/.

New Jersey War Orphans Tuition Assistance. $500 scholarship to children of those service personnel who died while in the military or due to service-connected disabilities, or who are officially listed as missing in action by the U.S. Department of Defense. Must be a resident of New Jersey for at least one year immediately preceding the filing of the application and be between the ages of 16 and 21 at the time of application. *Award:* Scholarship for use in freshman, sophomore, junior, or senior year; renewable. *Award amount:* $500. *Number of awards:* varies. *Eligibility Requirements:* Applicant must be age 16-21; enrolled or expecting to enroll full-time at a four-year institution or university and resident of New Jersey. Available to U.S. citizens. Applicant or parent must meet one or more of the following requirements: general military experience; retired from active duty; disabled or killed as a result of military service; prisoner of war; or missing in action. *Application Requirements:* Application, transcript. **Deadline:** varies.

Contact Patricia Richter, Grants Manager, New Jersey Department of Military and Veterans Affairs, PO Box 340, Trenton, NJ 08625-0340. *E-mail:* patricia.richter@njdmava.state.nj.us. *Phone:* 609-530-6854. *Fax:* 609-530-6970. *Web site:* http://www.state.nj.us/military.

New Jersey World Trade Center Scholarship. Scholarship was established by the legislature to aid the dependent children and surviving spouses of New Jersey residents who were killed in the terrorist attacks, or who are missing and officially presumed dead as a direct result of the attacks; applies to instate and out-of-state institutions for students seeking undergraduate degrees. Deadlines: March 1 for fall, October 1 for spring. *Award:* Scholarship for use in freshman, sophomore, junior, or senior year; renewable. *Award amount:* up to $6500. *Number of awards:* varies. *Eligibility Requirements:* Applicant must be enrolled or expecting to enroll full-time at a four-year institution or university and resident of New Jersey. Available to U.S. citizens. *Application Requirements:* Application. **Deadline:** varies.

Contact Giselle Joachim, Director of Financial Aid Services, New Jersey Higher Education Student Assistance Authority, PO Box 540, Trenton, NJ 08625. *E-mail:* gjoachim@hesaa.org. *Phone:* 800-792-8670 Ext. 2349. *Fax:* 609-588-7389. *Web site:* http://www.hesaa.org/.

NJ Student Tuition Assistance Reward Scholarship. Scholarship for students who graduate in the top 20 percent of their high school class. Recipients may be awarded up to five semesters of tuition (up to 15 credits per term) and approved fees at one of New Jersey's nineteen county colleges. *Award:* Scholarship for use in freshman, sophomore, junior, or senior year; renewable. *Award amount:* $2500–$7500. *Number of awards:* varies. *Eligibility Requirements:* Applicant must be enrolled or expecting to enroll full-time at a two-year or four-year institution or university; resident of New Jersey and studying in New Jersey. Applicant must have 3.0 GPA or higher. Available to U.S. citizens. *Application Requirements:* Application, transcript. **Deadline:** varies.

Contact Carol Muka, Assistant Director of Grants and Scholarships, New Jersey Higher Education Student Assistance Authority, PO Box 540, Trenton, NJ 08625. *E-mail:* cmuka@hessa.org. *Phone:* 800-792-8670 Ext. 3266. *Fax:* 609-588-2228. *Web site:* http://www.hesaa.org/.

Outstanding Scholar Recruitment Program. Awards students who meet the eligibility criteria and who are enrolled as first-time freshmen at participating New Jersey institutions receive annual scholarship awards of up to $7500. *Award:* Scholarship for use in freshman, sophomore, junior, or senior year; renewable. *Award amount:* $2500–$7500. *Number of awards:* varies. *Eligibility Requirements:* Applicant must be enrolled or expecting to enroll full-time at a four-year institution or university; resident of New Jersey and studying in New Jersey. Available to U.S. citizens. *Application Requirements:* Application. **Deadline:** varies.

Contact Carol Muka, Assistant Director of Grants and Scholarships, New Jersey Higher Education Student Assistance Authority, PO Box 540, Trenton, NJ 08625. *E-mail:*

cmuka@hesaa.org. *Phone:* 800-792-8670 Ext. 3266. *Fax:* 609-588-2228. *Web site:* http://www.hesaa.org/.

Part-Time Tuition Aid Grant (TAG) for County Colleges. Provides financial aid to eligible part-time undergraduate students enrolled for 9 to 11 credits at participating New Jersey community colleges. Deadlines: March 1 for spring and October 1 for fall. *Award:* Grant for use in freshman, sophomore, junior, or senior year; not renewable. *Award amount:* $419–$628. *Number of awards:* varies. *Eligibility Requirements:* Applicant must be enrolled or expecting to enroll part-time at a two-year or four-year institution or university; resident of New Jersey and studying in New Jersey. Available to U.S. citizens. *Application Requirements:* Application, financial need analysis. **Deadline:** varies.

Contact Sherri Fox, Acting Director of Grants and Scholarships, New Jersey Higher Education Student Assistance Authority, PO Box 540, Trenton, NJ 08625. *Phone:* 800-792-8670. *Fax:* 609-588-2228. *Web site:* http://www.hesaa.org/.

POW-MIA Tuition Benefit Program. Free undergraduate college tuition provided to any child born or adopted before or during the period of time his or her parent was officially declared a prisoner of war or person missing in action after January 1, 1960. The POW-MIA must have been a New Jersey resident at the time he or she entered the service. Child of veteran must attend either a public or private institution in New Jersey. A copy of DD 1300 must be furnished with the application. Minimum 2.5 GPA required. *Award:* Scholarship for use in freshman, sophomore, junior, or senior year; renewable. *Award amount:* varies. *Number of awards:* varies. *Eligibility Requirements:* Applicant must be enrolled or expecting to enroll full-time at a two-year, four-year, or technical institution or university; resident of New Jersey and studying in New Jersey. Applicant must have 2.5 GPA or higher. Available to U.S. citizens. Applicant or parent must meet one or more of the following requirements: general military experience; retired from active duty; disabled or killed as a result of military service; prisoner of war; or missing in action. *Application Requirements:* Application, transcript, copy of DD 1300. **Deadline:** varies.

Contact Patricia Richter, Grants Manager, New Jersey Department of Military and Veterans Affairs, PO Box 340, Trenton, NJ 08625-0340. *E-mail:* patricia.richter@njdmava.state.nj.us. *Phone:* 609-530-6854. *Fax:* 609-530-6970. *Web site:* http://www.state.nj.us/military.

Stutz Scholarship. Award to natural or adopted son or daughter of a member of The American Legion, Department of New Jersey. Applicant must be a member of the graduating class of high school including Vo-tech. *Award:* Scholarship for use in freshman year; not renewable. *Award amount:* $4000. *Number of awards:* 1. *Eligibility Requirements:* Applicant must be high school student and planning to enroll or expecting to enroll full-time at a two-year, four-year, or technical institution or university. Applicant or parent of applicant must be member of American Legion or Auxiliary. Available to U.S. citizens. Applicant or parent must meet one or more of the following requirements: Army experience; retired from active duty; disabled or killed as a result of military service; prisoner of war; or missing in action. *Application Requirements:* Application. **Deadline:** February 15.

Contact Raymond L. Zawacki, Department Adjutant, American Legion Department of New Jersey, 135 West Hanover Street, Trenton, NJ 08618. *E-mail:* ray@njamericanlegion.org. *Phone:* 609-695-5418. *Fax:* 609-394-1532. *Web site:* http://www.njamericanlegion.org/.

Survivor Tuition Benefits Program. The scholarship provides tuition fees for spouses and dependents of law enforcement officers, fire, or emergency services personnel killed in the line of duty. Eligible recipients may attend any independent institution in the state; however, the annual value of the grant cannot exceed the highest tuition charged at a New Jersey public institution. *Award:* Scholarship for use in freshman, sophomore, junior, or senior year; renewable. *Award amount:* varies. *Number of awards:* varies. *Eligibility Requirements:* Applicant must be enrolled or expecting to enroll full- or part-time at a two-year or four-year institution or university; resident of New Jersey and studying in New Jersey. Applicant or parent of applicant must have employment or volunteer experience in police/firefighting. Available to U.S. citizens. *Application Requirements:* Application. **Deadline:** varies.

Contact Carol Muka, Scholarship Coordinator, New Jersey Higher Education Student Assistance Authority, PO Box 540, Trenton, NJ 08625. *E-mail:* cmuka@hesaa.org. *Phone:* 800-792-8670 Ext. 3266. *Fax:* 609-588-2228. *Web site:* http://www.hesaa.org/.

Tuition Aid Grant. The program provides tuition fees to eligible undergraduate students attending participating in-state institutions. Deadlines: March 1 for fall, October 1 for spring. *Award:* Grant for use in freshman, sophomore, junior, or senior year; not renewable. *Award amount:* $868–$7272. *Number of awards:* varies. *Eligibility Requirements:* Applicant must be enrolled or expecting to enroll full-time at a two-year or four-year institution or university; resident of New Jersey and studying in New Jersey. Available to U.S. citizens. *Application Requirements:* Application, financial need analysis. **Deadline:** varies.

Contact Sherri Fox, Acting Director of Grants and Scholarships, New Jersey Higher Education Student Assistance Authority, PO Box 540, Trenton, NJ 08625. *Phone:* 800-792-8670. *Fax:* 609-588-2228. *Web site:* http://www.hesaa.org/.

Urban Scholars. Renewable scholarship to high achieving students attending public secondary schools in the urban and economically distressed areas of New Jersey. Students must rank in the top 10 percent of their class and have a GPA of at least 3.0 at the end of their junior year. Must be New Jersey resident and attend a New Jersey two-year college, four-year college or university, or approved programs at proprietary institutions. Students do not apply directly for scholarship consideration. Deadline varies. *Award:* Scholarship for use in freshman, sophomore, junior, or senior year; renewable. *Award amount:* up to $1000. *Number of awards:* varies. *Eligibility Requirements:* Applicant must be enrolled or expecting to enroll full-time at a two-year or four-year institution or university; resident of New Jersey and studying in New Jersey. Applicant must have 3.0 GPA or higher. Available to U.S. citizens. *Application Requirements:* Application, test scores, nomination by school. **Deadline:** varies.

Contact Carol Muka, Assistant Director of Grants and Scholarships, New Jersey Higher Education Student Assistance Authority, PO Box 540, Trenton, NJ 08625. *E-mail:* cmuka@hesaa.org. *Phone:* 800-792-8670 Ext. 3266. *Fax:* 609-588-2228. *Web site:* http://www.hesaa.org/.

Veterans Tuition Credit Program-New Jersey. Award for New Jersey resident veterans who served in the armed forces between December 31, 1960, and May 7, 1975. Must have been a New Jersey resident at time of induction or discharge or for two years immediately prior to application. *Award:* Scholarship for use in freshman, sophomore, junior, or senior year; renewable. *Award amount:* $200–$400. *Number of awards:* varies. *Eligibil-*

ity Requirements: Applicant must be enrolled or expecting to enroll full- or part-time at a two-year, four-year, or technical institution or university and resident of New Jersey. Available to U.S. citizens. Applicant or parent must meet one or more of the following requirements: general military experience; retired from active duty; disabled or killed as a result of military service; prisoner of war; or missing in action. *Application Requirements:* Application. **Deadline:** varies.

Contact Patricia Richter, Grants Manager, New Jersey Department of Military and Veterans Affairs, PO Box 340, Trenton, NJ 08625-0340. *E-mail:* patricia.richter@njdmava.state.nj.us. *Phone:* 609-530-6854. *Fax:* 609-530-6970. *Web site:* http://www.state.nj.us/military.

NEW MEXICO

Allied Health Student Loan Program-New Mexico. Award to New Mexico residents studying in New Mexico to increase the number of physician assistants in areas of the state which have experienced shortages of health practitioners. Provides educational loans to students seeking certification/licensers in an eligible health field. As a condition of each loan, the student must declare intent to practice as a health professional in a designated shortage area. For every year of service, a portion of the loan will be forgiven. *Academic Fields/Career Goals:* Dental Health/Services; Health and Medical Sciences; Nursing; Therapy/Rehabilitation. *Award:* Forgivable loan for use in freshman, sophomore, junior, or senior year; renewable. *Award amount:* up to $12,000. *Number of awards:* 1–40. *Eligibility Requirements:* Applicant must be enrolled or expecting to enroll full- or part-time at a four-year institution or university; resident of New Mexico and studying in New Mexico. Available to U.S. citizens. *Application Requirements:* Application, financial need analysis, transcript, FAFSA. **Deadline:** July 1.

Contact Theresa Acker, Financial Aid Division, New Mexico Commission on Higher Education, 1068 Cerrillos Road, Santa Fe, NM 87505-1650. *E-mail:* theresa.acker@state.nm.us. *Phone:* 505-476-6506. *Fax:* 505-476-6511. *Web site:* http://www.hed.state.nm.us/.

Children of Deceased Veterans Scholarship-New Mexico. Award for New Mexico residents who are children of veterans killed or disabled as a result of service, prisoner of war, or veterans missing in action. Must be between ages 16 and 26. For use at New Mexico schools for undergraduate study. Must submit parent's death certificate and DD form 214. *Award:* Scholarship for use in freshman, sophomore, junior, or senior year; renewable. *Award amount:* $300. *Number of awards:* varies. *Eligibility Requirements:* Applicant must be age 16-26; enrolled or expecting to enroll full- or part-time at a two-year or four-year institution or university; resident of New Mexico and studying in New Mexico. Available to U.S. citizens. Applicant or parent must meet one or more of the following requirements: general military experience; retired from active duty; disabled or killed as a result of military service; prisoner of war; or missing in action. *Application Requirements:* Application, transcript, death certificate or notice of casualty, DD form 214. **Deadline:** continuous.

Contact Alan Martinez, Deputy Secretary, New Mexico Department of Veterans' Services, Bataan Memorial Building, PO BOX 2324, Santa Fe, NM 87504. *E-mail:* alan.martinez@state.nm.us. *Phone:* 505-827-6300. *Web site:* http://www.dvs.state.nm.us/.

College Affordability Grant. Grant available to New Mexico students with financial need who do not qualify for other state grants and scholarships to attend and complete educational programs at a New Mexico public college or university. Student must have unmet need after all other financial aid has been awarded. Student may not be receiving any other state grants or scholarships. Renewable upon satisfactory academic progress. *Award:* Grant for use in freshman, sophomore, junior, or senior year; renewable. *Award amount:* up to $1000. *Number of awards:* 1. *Eligibility Requirements:* Applicant must be enrolled or expecting to enroll full- or part-time at a two-year or four-year institution or university; resident of New Mexico and studying in New Mexico. Available to U.S. citizens. *Application Requirements:* Application, financial need analysis, FAFSA. **Deadline:** continuous.

Contact Tashina Banks Acker, Director of Financial Aid, New Mexico Commission on Higher Education, 1068 Cerrillos Road, Santa Fe, NM 87505-1650. *E-mail:* tashina.banks-moore@state.nm.us. *Phone:* 505-476-6549. *Fax:* 505-476-6511. *Web site:* http://www.hed.state.nm.us/.

Legislative Endowment Scholarships. Renewable scholarships to provide aid for undergraduate students with substantial financial need who are attending public postsecondary institutions in New Mexico. Four-year schools may award up to $2500 per academic year, two-year schools may award up to $1000 per academic year. Deadlines varies. *Award:* Scholarship for use in freshman, sophomore, junior, or senior year; renewable. *Award amount:* $1000–$2500. *Number of awards:* 1. *Eligibility Requirements:* Applicant must be enrolled or expecting to enroll full- or part-time at a two-year or four-year institution or university; resident of New Mexico and studying in New Mexico. Available to U.S. citizens. *Application Requirements:* Application, financial need analysis, FAFSA. **Deadline:** varies.

Contact Tashina Banks Moore, Director of Financial Aid, New Mexico Commission on Higher Education, 1068 Cerrillos Road, Santa Fe, NM 87505-1650. *E-mail:* tashina.banks-moore@state.nm.us. *Phone:* 505-475-6549. *Fax:* 505-476-6511. *Web site:* http://www.hed.state.nm.us/.

Legislative Lottery Scholarship. Renewable Scholarship for New Mexico high school graduates or GED recipients who plan to attend an eligible New Mexico public college or university. Must be enrolled full-time and maintain 2.5 GPA. *Award:* Scholarship for use in freshman year; renewable. *Award amount:* varies. *Number of awards:* 1. *Eligibility Requirements:* Applicant must be high school student; planning to enroll or expecting to enroll full-time at a four-year institution or university; resident of New Mexico and studying in New Mexico. Applicant must have 3.5 GPA or higher. Available to U.S. citizens. *Application Requirements:* Application, FAFSA. **Deadline:** varies.

Contact Tashina Banks Moore, Director of Financial Aid, New Mexico Commission on Higher Education, 1068 Cerrillos Road, Santa Fe, NM 87505. *E-mail:* tashina.banks-moore@state.nm.us. *Phone:* 505-476-6549. *Fax:* 505-476-6511. *Web site:* http://www.hed.state.nm.us/.

Minority Doctoral Assistance Loan-For-Service Program. Award program enacted to increase the number of ethnic minorities and women available to teach engineering, physical or life sciences, mathematics, and other academic disciplines in which ethnic minorities or women are demonstrably underrepresented in New Mexico colleges and universities. Award may be renewable for up to four years. *Academic Fields/Career Goals:* Chemical Engineering; Engineering/Technology; Mathematics; Mechanical Engineering; Natural Sciences; Physical Sciences. *Award:* Forgivable loan for use in freshman, sophomore, junior, senior, or graduate year; renewable. *Award amount:* $15,000. *Number of awards:* varies. *Eligibility Requirements:* Applicant must be American Indian/Alaska Native, Asian/Pacific Islander, Black (non-Hispanic), or Hispanic; enrolled or expecting to enroll full-time at a four-year institution or university; resident of New Mexico and studying in New Mexico. Available to U.S. citizens. *Application Requirements:* Application, essay, references, transcript. **Deadline:** March 15.

Contact Theresa Acker, Financial Aid Division, New Mexico Commission on Higher Education, 1068 Cerrillos Road, Santa Fe, NM 87505-1650. *E-mail:* tashina.banks-moore@state.nm.us. *Phone:* 505-476-6506. *Fax:* 505-476-6511. *Web site:* http://www.hed.state.nm.us/.

New Mexico Competitive Scholarship. Scholarships for non-residents or non-citizens of the United States to encourage out-of-state students who have demonstrated high academic achievement in high school to enroll in public four-year universities in New Mexico. Renewable for up to four years. For details visit http://fin.hed.state.nm.us. *Award:* Scholarship for use in freshman year; renewable. *Award amount:* varies. *Number of awards:* varies. *Eligibility Requirements:* Applicant must be high school student; planning to enroll or expecting to enroll full-time at a four-year institution or university and studying in New Mexico. Available to Canadian and non-U.S. citizens. *Application Requirements:* Application, essay, references, test scores. **Deadline:** varies.

Contact Tashina Banks Moore, Director of Financial Aid, New Mexico Commission on Higher Education, 1068 Cerrillos Road, Santa Fe, NM 87505. *E-mail:* tashina.banks-moore@state.nm.us. *Phone:* 505-476-6549. *Fax:* 505-476-6511. *Web site:* http://www.hed.state.nm.us/.

New Mexico Scholars' Program. Renewable award program created to encourage New Mexico high school students to attend public postsecondary institutions or the following private colleges in New Mexico: College of Santa Fe, St. John's College, College of the Southwest. For details visit http://fin.hed.state.nm.us. *Award:* Scholarship for use in freshman year; renewable. *Award amount:* varies. *Number of awards:* 1. *Eligibility Requirements:* Applicant must be high school student; age 21 or under; planning to enroll or expecting to enroll full-time at a two-year or four-year institution; resident of New Mexico and studying in New Mexico. Available to U.S. citizens. *Application Requirements:* Application, financial need analysis, test scores, FAFSA. **Deadline:** varies.

Contact Tashina Banks Moore, Director of Financial Aid, New Mexico Commission on Higher Education, 1068 Cerrillos Road, Santa Fe, NM 87505-1650. *E-mail:* tashina.banks-moore@state.nm.us. *Phone:* 505-476-6549. *Fax:* 505-476-6511. *Web site:* http://www.hed.state.nm.us/.

New Mexico Student Incentive Grant. Grant created to provide aid for undergraduate students with substantial financial need who are attending public colleges or universities or the following eligible colleges in New Mexico: College of Santa Fe, St. John's College, College of the Southwest, Institute of American Indian Art, Crownpoint Institute of Technology, Dine College and Southwestern Indian Polytechnic Institute. Part-time students are eligible for pro-rated awards. *Award:* Grant for use in freshman, sophomore, junior, or senior year; not renewable. *Award amount:* $200–$2500. *Number of awards:* 1. *Eligibility Requirements:* Applicant must be enrolled or expecting to enroll full- or part-time at a two-year, four-year, or technical institution or university; resident of New Mexico and studying in New Mexico. Available to U.S. citizens. *Application Requirements:* Application, financial need analysis, FAFSA. **Deadline:** varies.

Contact Tashina Banks Moore, Director of Financial Aid, New Mexico Commission on Higher Education, 1068 Cerrillos Road, Santa Fe, NM 87505-1650. *E-mail:* tashina.banks-moore@state.nm.us. *Phone:* 505-476-6549. *Fax:* 505-476-6511. *Web site:* http://www.hed.state.nm.us/.

New Mexico Vietnam Veteran Scholarship. Award for Vietnam veterans who have been New Mexico residents for a minimum of ten years and are attending state-funded postsecondary schools. Must have been awarded the Vietnam Campaign medal. Must submit DD 214 and discharge papers. *Award:* Scholarship for use in freshman, sophomore, junior, or senior year; renewable. *Award amount:* $3500–$4000. *Number of awards:* 100. *Eligibility Requirements:* Applicant must be enrolled or expecting to enroll full- or part-time at a two-year, four-year, or technical institution or university; resident of New Mexico and studying in New Mexico. Available to U.S. citizens. Applicant or parent must meet one or more of the following requirements: general military experience; retired from active duty; disabled or killed as a result of military service; prisoner of war; or missing in action. *Application Requirements:* Application, copy of DD Form 214. **Deadline:** continuous.

Contact Alan Martinez, Deputy Secretary, New Mexico Department of Veterans' Services, Bataan Memorial Building, PO BOX 2324, Santa Fe, NM 87504. *E-mail:* alan.martinez@state.nm.us. *Phone:* 505-827-6300. *Web site:* http://www.dvs.state.nm.us/.

Nurse Educator Loan-for-Service. Forgivable loan of up to $5000 for New Mexico nursing majors to obtain an undergraduate, graduate, or post graduate degree in the state of New Mexico. Each loan has a service agreement wherein the student declares his/her intent to serve in a nurse faculty position in a New Mexico public, post-secondary institution. For every academic year of service, a portion of the loan is forgiven and if the entire service agreement is fulfilled, the entire loan is eligible for forgiveness. Must be a U.S. citizen. *Academic Fields/Career Goals:* Nursing. *Award:* Forgivable loan for use in senior year; renewable. *Award amount:* up to $5000. *Number of awards:* 1. *Eligibility Requirements:* Applicant must be enrolled or expecting to enroll full- or part-time at a four-year institution or university; resident of New Mexico and studying in New Mexico. Available to U.S. citizens. *Application Requirements:* Application, essay, transcript. **Deadline:** July 1.

Contact Theresa Acker, Financial Aid Division, New Mexico Commission on Higher Education, 1068 Cerrillos Road, Santa Fe, NM 85705-1650. *E-mail:* theresa.acker@state.nm.us. *Phone:* 505-476-6506. *Fax:* 505-476-6511. *Web site:* http://www.hed.state.nm.us/.

Nursing Student Loan-For-Service Program. Award to increase the number of nurses in areas of New Mexico which have experienced shortages by making educational loans to students entering nursing programs. As a condition of each loan, the student shall declare his/her intent to practice as a health professional in a designated shortage area. For every year of service, a portion of the loan will be forgiven. *Academic Fields/Career Goals:* Nursing. *Award:* Forgivable loan for use in freshman, sophomore, junior, or senior year; renewable. *Award amount:* up to $12,000. *Number of awards:* 1. *Eligibility Requirements:* Applicant must be enrolled or expecting to enroll full- or part-time at a four-year institution or university; resident of New Mexico and studying in New Mexico. Available to U.S. citizens. *Application Requirements:* Application, financial need analysis, transcript, FAFSA. **Deadline:** July 1.

Contact Theresa Acker, Financial Aid Division, New Mexico Commission on Higher Education, 1068 Cerrillos Road, Santa Fe,

NM 87505-1650. *E-mail:* theresa.acker@state.nm.us. *Phone:* 505-476-6506. *Fax:* 505-476-6511. *Web site:* http://www.hed.state.nm.us/.

Public Service Law Loan Repayment Assistance Program. Program to provide legal educational loan repayment assistance to individuals providing public service in state or local government or the nonprofit sector in New Mexico to low income or underserved residents. *Academic Fields/Career Goals:* Law/Legal Services. *Award:* Forgivable loan for use in freshman, sophomore, junior, or senior year; renewable. *Award amount:* up to $7200. *Number of awards:* 1–16. *Eligibility Requirements:* Applicant must be enrolled or expecting to enroll full-time at a four-year institution or university; resident of New Mexico and studying in New Mexico. Available to U.S. citizens. *Application Requirements:* Application. **Deadline:** February 28.

Contact Theresa Acker, Financial Aid Division, New Mexico Commission on Higher Education, 1068 Cerrillos Road, Santa Fe, NM 87505. *E-mail:* theresa.acker@state.nm.us. *Phone:* 505-476-6506. *Fax:* 505-475-6511. *Web site:* http://www.hed.state.nm.us/.

Teacher Loan-For-Service. Purpose is to proactively address New Mexico's teacher shortage by providing students with the financial resources to complete or enhance their post-secondary teacher preparation education. *Academic Fields/Career Goals:* Education. *Award:* Forgivable loan for use in freshman, sophomore, junior, or senior year; renewable. *Award amount:* up to $4000. *Number of awards:* 1. *Eligibility Requirements:* Applicant must be enrolled or expecting to enroll full- or part-time at a four-year institution or university; resident of New Mexico and studying in New Mexico. Available to U.S. citizens. *Application Requirements:* Application, financial need analysis, FAFSA. **Deadline:** July 1.

Contact Theresa Acker, Financial Aid Division, New Mexico Commission on Higher Education, 1068 Cerrillos Road, Santa Fe, NM 87505-1650. *E-mail:* theresa.acker@state.nm.us. *Phone:* 505-476-6506. *Fax:* 505-476-6511. *Web site:* http://www.hed.state.nm.us/.

Vietnam Veterans' Scholarship Program. Renewable scholarship program created to provide aid for Vietnam veterans who are undergraduate and graduate students attending public postsecondary institutions or select private colleges in New Mexico. Private colleges include: College of Santa Fe, St. John's College and College of the Southwest. *Award:* Scholarship for use in freshman, sophomore, junior, or senior year; renewable. *Award amount:* varies. *Number of awards:* 1. *Eligibility Requirements:* Applicant must be enrolled or expecting to enroll full-time at a two-year or four-year institution; resident of New Mexico and studying in New Mexico. Available to U.S. citizens. Applicant or parent must meet one or more of the following requirements: general military experience; retired from active duty; disabled or killed as a result of military service; prisoner of war; or missing in action. *Application Requirements:* Application, certification by the NM Veteran's commission. **Deadline:** varies.

Contact Tashina Banks Moore, Director of Financial Aid, New Mexico Commission on Higher Education, 1068 Cerrillos Road, Santa Fe, NM 87505-1650. *E-mail:* tashina.banks-moore@state.nm.us. *Phone:* 505-476-6549. *Fax:* 505-476-6511. *Web site:* http://www.hed.state.nm.us/.

NEW YORK

DAAD University Summer Course Grant. Scholarships are awarded to students pursuing full-time study at Canadian or US colleges or universities. There are no restrictions as to field of study, but applicants must have attained at least Sophomore standing (second-year standing in Canada) at the time of application. Scholarships are available for courses lasting a minimum of three weeks. The scholarship is approximately 850 Euro, which covers tuition, room and board in whole or in part. Accommodations are arranged by the host institution. In addition, DAAD will provide an international travel subsidy of 300–450 Euro. Scholarship recipients are expected to devote their full attention to the course and may not concurrently undertake individual research. A written report is requested within four weeks of the end of the course. *Academic Fields/Career Goals:* Foreign Language. *Award:* Grant for use in sophomore, junior, senior, or graduate year; not renewable. *Award amount:* varies. *Number of awards:* varies. *Eligibility Requirements:* Applicant must be enrolled or expecting to enroll full-time at a four-year institution or university and must have an interest in German language/culture. Available to U.S. and non-U.S. citizens. *Application Requirements:* Application, applicant must enter a contest, essay, resume, references, transcript. **Deadline:** December 15.

Contact Jane Fu, Information Officer, German Academic Exchange Service (DAAD), 871 United Nations Plaza, New York, NY 10017. *E-mail:* daadny@daad.org. *Phone:* 212-758-3223 Ext. 201. *Web site:* http://www.daad.org/.

Japan-U.S. Friendship Commission Prize for the Translation of Japanese Literature. Annual prize for the best translation into English of a modern work of literature or for the best classical literary translation, or the prize is divided between a classical and a modern work. To qualify, works must be book-length translations of Japanese literary works: novels, collections of short stories, literary essays, memoirs, drama or poetry. *Academic Fields/Career Goals:* Foreign Language. *Award:* Prize for use in freshman, sophomore, junior, or senior year; not renewable. *Award amount:* $3000. *Number of awards:* 2. *Eligibility Requirements:* Applicant must be enrolled or expecting to enroll full- or part-time at a two-year, four-year, or technical institution or university. Available to U.S. citizens. *Application Requirements:* Application, applicant must enter a contest, resume, unpublished manuscripts. **Deadline:** February 29.

Contact Kia Cheleen, Assistant Director, Donald Keene Center of Japanese Culture, 507 Kent Hall, MC 3920, 1140 Amsterdam Avenue, Columbia University, New York, NY 10027. *E-mail:* donald-keene-center@columbia.edu. *Phone:* 212-854-5036. *Web site:* http://www.donaldkeenecenter.org/.

New York Aid for Part-Time Study (APTS). Renewable scholarship provides tuition assistance to part-time undergraduate students who are New York residents, meet income eligibility requirements and are attending New York accredited institutions. Deadline varies. Must be U.S. citizen. *Award:* Grant for use in freshman, sophomore, junior, or senior year; renewable. *Award amount:* up to $2000. *Number of awards:* varies. *Eligibility Requirements:* Applicant must be enrolled or expecting to enroll part-time at a two-year or four-year institution or university; resident of New York and studying in New York. Available to U.S. citizens. *Application Requirements:* Application, financial need analysis. **Deadline:** varies.

Contact Student Information, New York State Higher Education Services Corporation, 99 Washington Avenue, Room 1320, Albany, NY 12255. *Phone:* 518-473-3887. *Fax:* 518-474-2839. *Web site:* http://www.hesc.com/.

New York Memorial Scholarships for Families of Deceased Police Officers, Fire Fighters and Peace Officers. Renewable scholarship for children, spouses and financial dependents of deceased fire fighters, volunteer firefighters, police officers, peace officers and emergency medical service workers who died in the line of duty. Provides up to the cost of SUNY educational expenses. *Award:* Scholarship for use in freshman, sophomore, junior, or senior year; renewable. *Award amount:* varies. *Number of awards:* varies. *Eligibility Requirements:* Applicant must be enrolled or expecting to enroll full-time at a four-year institution or university; resident of New York and studying in New York. Available to U.S. citizens. *Application Requirements:* Application, financial need analysis, transcript. **Deadline:** May 1.

Contact Scholarships, New York State Higher Education Services Corporation. *Phone:* 888-697-4372. *Web site:* http://www.hesc.com/.

New York State Aid to Native Americans. Award for enrolled members of a New York State tribe and their children who are attending or planning to attend a New York State college and who are New York State residents. Deadlines: July 15 for the fall semester, December 31 for the spring semester, and May 20 for summer session. *Award:* Scholarship for use in freshman, sophomore, junior, or senior year; renewable. *Award amount:* $85–$2000. *Number of awards:* varies. *Eligibility Requirements:* Applicant must be American Indian/Alaska Native; enrolled or expecting to enroll full- or part-time at a two-year, four-year, or technical institution or university; resident of New York and studying in New York. Available to U.S. citizens. *Application Requirements:* Application, financial need analysis, references, transcript. **Deadline:** varies.

Contact Native American Education Unit, New York State Higher Education Services Corporation, EBA Room 475, Albany, NY 12234. *Phone:* 518-474-0537. *Web site:* http://www.hesc.com/.

New York State Tuition Assistance Program. Award for New York state residents attending a New York postsecondary institution. Must be full-time student in approved program with tuition over $200 per year. Must show financial need and not be in default in any other state program. Renewable award of $500 to $5000 dependent on family income and tuition charged. *Award:* Grant for use in freshman, sophomore, junior, or senior year; renewable. *Award amount:* $500–$5000. *Number of awards:* 350,000–360,000. *Eligibility Requirements:* Applicant must be enrolled or expecting to enroll full-time at a two-year or four-year institution or university; resident of New York and studying in New York. Available to U.S. citizens. *Application Requirements:* Application, financial need analysis. **Deadline:** May 1.

Contact Student Information, New York State Higher Education Services Corporation, 99 Washington Avenue, Room 1400, Albany, NY 12255. *Phone:* 888-697-4372. *Web site:* http://www.hesc.com/.

New York Vietnam/Persian Gulf/Afghanistan Veterans Tuition Awards. Scholarship for veterans who served in Vietnam, the Persian Gulf, or Afghanistan. Must be a New York resident attending a New York institution. Must establish eligibility by September 1. *Award:* Scholarship for use in freshman, sophomore, junior, or senior year; renewable. *Number of awards:* varies. *Eligibility Requirements:* Applicant must be enrolled or expecting to enroll full- or part-time at a two-year, four-year, or technical institution or university; resident of New York and studying in New York. Available to U.S. citizens. Applicant or parent must meet one or more of the following requirements: general military experience; retired from active duty; disabled or killed as a result of military service; prisoner of war; or missing in action. *Application Requirements:* Application, financial need analysis. **Deadline:** May 1.

Contact Associate HESC Information Representative, New York State Higher Education Services Corporation, 99 Washington Avenue, Grants & Scholarships Unit, Albany, NY 12255. *E-mail:* scholarship@hesc.com. *Phone:* 888-NYS-HESC. *Web site:* http://www.hesc.com/.

Regents Award for Child of Veteran. Award for students whose parent, as a result of service in U.S. Armed Forces during war or national emergency, died; suffered a 40 percent or more disability; or is classified as missing in action or a prisoner of war. Veteran must be current New York State resident or have been so at time of death. Student must be a New York resident, attending, or planning to attend, college in New York State. Must establish eligibility before applying for payment. *Award:* Scholarship for use in freshman, sophomore, junior, or senior year; not renewable. *Award amount:* up to $450. *Number of awards:* varies. *Eligibility Requirements:* Applicant must be enrolled or expecting to enroll full-time at a two-year or four-year institution or university; resident of New York and studying in New York. Available to U.S. citizens. Applicant or parent must meet one or more of the following requirements: general military experience; retired from active duty; disabled or killed as a result of military service; prisoner of war; or missing in action. *Application Requirements:* Application, proof of eligibility. **Deadline:** May 1.

Contact Rita McGivern, Student Information, New York State Higher Education Services Corporation, 99 Washington Avenue, Room 1320, Albany, NY 12255. *E-mail:* rmcgivern@hesc.com. *Web site:* http://www.hesc.com/.

Regents Professional Opportunity Scholarship. Scholarship for New York residents beginning or already enrolled in an approved degree-granting program of study in New York that leads to licensure in a particular profession. See the web site for the list of eligible professions. Must be U.S. citizen or permanent resident. Award recipients must agree to practice upon licensure in their profession in New York for 12 months for each annual payment received. Priority given to economically disadvantaged members of minority groups underrepresented in the professions. *Academic Fields/Career Goals:* Accounting; Architecture; Dental Health/Services; Engineering/Technology; Health and Medical Sciences; Interior Design; Landscape Architecture; Law/Legal Services; Nursing; Pharmacy; Psychology; Social Services. *Award:* Scholarship for use in freshman, sophomore, junior, senior, or graduate year; renewable. *Award amount:* up to $5000. *Number of awards:* 220. *Eligibility Requirements:* Applicant must be enrolled or expecting to enroll full-time at a two-year or four-year institution or university; resident of New York and studying in New York. Available to U.S. citizens. *Application Requirements:* Application. **Deadline:** May 31.

Contact Lewis J. Hall, Supervisor, New York State Education Department, 89 Washington Avenue, Room 1078 EBA, Albany, NY 12234. *E-mail:* scholar@mail.nysed.gov. *Phone:* 518-486-1319. *Fax:* 518-486-5346. *Web site:* http://www.highered.nysed.gov/.

Regents Professional Opportunity Scholarships. Award for New York State residents pursuing career in certain licensed professions. Must attend New York State college. Priority given to economically disadvantaged members of minority group underrepresented in chosen profession and graduates of SEEK, College Discovery, EOP, and HEOP. Must work in New York State in chosen profession one year for each annual payment. Scholarships are awarded to undergraduate or graduate students, depending on the program. *Award:* Scholarship for use in freshman, sophomore, junior, senior, graduate, or postgraduate years; not renewable. *Award* *amount:* \$1000–\$5000. *Eligibility Requirements:* Applicant must be enrolled or expecting to enroll full-time at a two-year or four-year institution or university; resident of New York and studying in New York. Available to U.S. citizens. *Application Requirements:* Application. **Deadline:** May 3.

Contact Scholarship Coordinator, New York State Higher Education Services Corporation, Education Building Addition Room 1071, Albany, NY 12234. *Phone:* 518-486-1319. *Web site:* http://www.hesc.com/.

Robert C. Byrd Honors Scholarship-New York. Award for outstanding high school seniors accepted to U.S. college or university. Based on SAT score and high school average. Minimum 1875 combined SAT score from one sitting. Must be legal resident of New York and a U.S. citizen. Renewable for up to four years. *Award:* Scholarship for use in freshman year; renewable. *Award amount:* \$1500. *Number of awards:* 400. *Eligibility Requirements:* Applicant must be high school student; planning to enroll or expecting to enroll full-time at a two-year or four-year institution or university and resident of New York. Available to U.S. citizens. *Application Requirements:* Application. **Deadline:** March 1.

Contact Lewis J. Hall, Supervisor, New York State Education Department, 89 Washington Avenue, Room 1078 EBA, Albany, NY 12234. *E-mail:* scholar@mail.nysed.gov. *Phone:* 518-486-1319. *Fax:* 518-486-5346. *Web site:* http://www.highered.nysed.gov/.

Scholarship for Academic Excellence. Renewable award for New York residents. Scholarship winners must attend a college or university in New York. 2000 scholarships are for \$1500 and 6000 are for \$500. The selection criteria used are based on Regents test scores or rank in class or local exam. Must be U.S. citizen or permanent resident. *Award:* Scholarship for use in freshman year; renewable. *Award amount:* \$500–\$1500. *Number of awards:* up to 8000. *Eligibility Requirements:* Applicant must be high school student; planning to enroll or expecting to enroll full-time at a two-year or four-year institution or university; resident of New York and studying in New York. Available to U.S. citizens. *Application Requirements:* Application. **Deadline:** December 19.

Contact Lewis J. Hall, Supervisor, New York State Education Department, 89 Washington Avenue, Room 1078 EBA, Albany, NY 12234. *E-mail:* scholar@mail.nysed.gov. *Phone:* 518-486-1319. *Fax:* 518-486-5346. *Web site:* http://www.highered.nysed.gov/.

Scholarships for Academic Excellence. Renewable awards of up to \$1500 for academically outstanding New York State high school graduates planning to attend an approved postsecondary institution in New York State. For full-time study only. Contact high school guidance counselor to apply. *Award:* Scholarship for use in freshman, sophomore, junior, or senior year; renewable. *Award amount:* \$500–\$1500. *Number of awards:* up to 8000. *Eligibility Requirements:* Applicant must be high school student; planning to enroll or expecting to enroll full-time at a four-year institution or university; resident of New York and studying in New York. Available to U.S. citizens. *Application Requirements:* Application. **Deadline:** varies.

Contact Rita McGivern, Student Information, New York State Higher Education Services Corporation, 99 Washington Avenue, Room 1320, Albany, NY 12255. *E-mail:* scholarship@hesc.com. *Web site:* http://www.hesc.com/.

World Trade Center Memorial Scholarship. Renewable awards of up to the cost of educational expenses at a State University of New York four-year college. Available to the children, spouses and financial dependents of victims who died or were severely disabled as a result of the September 11, 2001 terrorist attacks on the U.S. and the rescue and recovery efforts. *Award:* Scholarship for use in freshman, sophomore, junior, or senior year; renewable. *Award amount:* varies. *Number of awards:* varies. *Eligibility Requirements:* Applicant must be enrolled or expecting to enroll full-time at a four-year institution or university and studying in New York. Available to U.S. and non-U.S. citizens. *Application Requirements:* Application, financial need analysis, references, transcript. **Deadline:** May 1.

Contact Scholarship Unit, New York State Higher Education Services Corporation, 99 Washington Avenue, Room 1320, Albany, NY 12255. *Phone:* 888-697-4372. *Web site:* http://www.hesc.com/.

NORTH CAROLINA

Federal Supplemental Educational Opportunity Grant Program. Applicant must have exceptional financial need to qualify for this award. Amount of financial need is determined by the educational institution the student attends. Available only to undergraduate students. Recipient must be a U.S. citizen or permanent resident. Priority is given to a students who receive Federal Pell Grants. *Award:* Grant for use in freshman, sophomore, junior, or senior year; not renewable. *Award amount:* \$100–\$4400. *Number of awards:* varies. *Eligibility Requirements:* Applicant must be enrolled or expecting to enroll full-time at a four-year institution or university and resident of North Carolina. Available to U.S. citizens. *Application Requirements:* Application, financial need analysis, transcript. **Deadline:** continuous.

Contact Federal Student Aid Information Center, College Foundation of North Carolina, PO Box 84, Washington, DC 20044. *Phone:* 800-433-3243. *Web site:* http://www.cfnc.org/.

North Carolina Community College Grant Program. Annual award for North Carolina residents enrolled at least part-time in a North Carolina community college curriculum program. Priority given to those enrolled in college transferable curriculum programs, persons seeking new job skills, women in non-traditional curricula, and those participating in an ABE, GED, or high school diploma program. Contact financial aid office of institution the student attends for information and deadline. Must complete Free Application for Federal Student Aid. *Award:* Grant for use in freshman or sophomore year; renewable. *Award amount:* \$683. *Number of awards:* varies. *Eligibility Requirements:* Applicant must be enrolled or expecting to enroll full- or part-time at a two-year or technical institution; resident of North Carolina and studying in North Carolina. Available to U.S. citizens. *Application Requirements:* Application, financial need analysis, FAFSA. **Deadline:** varies.

Contact Bill Carswell, Manager, Scholarship and Grants Division, North Carolina State Education Assistance Authority, PO Box 14103, Research Triangle Park, NC 27709. *E-mail:* carswellb@ncseaa.edu. *Phone:* 919-549-8614. *Fax:* 919-248-4687. *Web site:* http://www.ncseaa.edu/.

North Carolina Division of Services for the Blind Rehabilitation Services. Financial assistance is available for North Carolina residents who are blind or visually impaired and who require vocational rehabilitation to help find employment. Tuition and other assistance provided based on need. Open to U.S. citizens and legal residents of United States. Applicants goal must be to work after receiving vocational services. To apply, contact the local DSB office and apply for vocational rehabilitation services. *Award:* Scholarship for use in freshman, sophomore, junior, or senior year; renewable. *Award amount:* varies. *Number of awards:* varies. *Eligibility Requirements:* Applicant must be enrolled or expecting to enroll full-time at a two-year, four-year, or technical institution or university and resident of North Carolina. Applicant must be visually impaired. Available to U.S. citizens. *Application Requirements:* Application, financial need analysis, interview, proof of eligibility. **Deadline:** continuous.

Contact JoAnn Strader, Chief of Rehabilitation Field Services, North Carolina Division of Services for the Blind, 2601 Mail Service Center, Raleigh, NC 27699-2601. *E-mail:* joann.strader@ncmail.net. *Phone:* 919-733-9700. *Fax:* 919-715-8771. *Web site:* http://www.ncdhhs.gov/.

North Carolina Legislative Tuition Grant Program (NCLTG). Renewable aid for North Carolina residents attending approved private colleges or universities within the state. Must be enrolled full or part-time in an undergraduate program not leading to a religious vocation. Contact college financial aid office for deadlines. *Award:* Grant for use in freshman, sophomore, junior, or senior year; renewable. *Award amount:* $1950. *Number of awards:* varies. *Eligibility Requirements:* Applicant must be enrolled or expecting to enroll full- or part-time at a two-year or four-year institution or university; resident of North Carolina and studying in North Carolina. Available to U.S. citizens. *Application Requirements:* Application. **Deadline:** varies.

Contact Bill Carswell, Manager of Scholarship and Grant Division, North Carolina State Education Assistance Authority, PO Box 13663, Research Triangle Park, NC 27709. *E-mail:* carswellb@ncseaa.edu. *Phone:* 919-549-8614. *Fax:* 919-248-4687. *Web site:* http://www.ncseaa.edu/.

North Carolina National Guard Tuition Assistance Program. Scholarship for members of the North Carolina Air and Army National Guard who will remain in the service for two years following the period for which assistance is provided. Must reapply for each academic period. For use at approved North Carolina institutions. *Award:* Grant for use in freshman, sophomore, junior, senior, or graduate year; not renewable. *Award amount:* up to $2000. *Number of awards:* varies. *Eligibility Requirements:* Applicant must be enrolled or expecting to enroll full- or part-time at a two-year, four-year, or technical institution or university; resident of North Carolina and studying in North Carolina. Available to U.S. citizens. Applicant or parent must meet one or more of the following requirements: Air Force National Guard or Army National Guard experience; retired from active duty; disabled or killed as a result of military service; prisoner of war; or missing in action. *Application Requirements:* Application. **Deadline:** varies.

Contact Anne Gildhouse, Education Services Officer, North Carolina National Guard, Claude T. Bowers Military Center, 4105 Reedy Creek Road, Raleigh, NC 27607-6410. *E-mail:* anne.gildhouse@nc.ngb.army.mil. *Phone:* 919-664-6000. *Fax:* 919-664-6520. *Web site:* http://www.nc.ngb.army.mil/.

North Carolina Sheriffs' Association Undergraduate Criminal Justice Scholarships. One-time award for full-time North Carolina resident undergraduate students majoring in criminal justice at a University of North Carolina school. Priority given to child of any North Carolina law enforcement officer. Letter of recommendation from county sheriff required. *Academic Fields/Career Goals:* Criminal Justice/Criminology; Law Enforcement/Police Administration. *Award:* Scholarship for use in freshman, sophomore, junior, or senior year; not renewable. *Award amount:* $1000–$2000. *Number of awards:* up to 10. *Eligibility Requirements:* Applicant must be enrolled or expecting to enroll full-time at a four-year institution or university; resident of North Carolina and studying in North Carolina. Applicant or parent of applicant must have employment or volunteer experience in police/firefighting. Available to U.S. citizens. *Application Requirements:* Application, financial need analysis, references, transcript, statement of career goals. **Deadline:** continuous.

Contact Nolita Goldston, Assistant, Scholarship and Grant Division, North Carolina State Education Assistance Authority, PO Box 13663, Research Triangle Park, NC 27709. *E-mail:* ngoldston@ncseaa.edu. *Phone:* 919-549-8614. *Fax:* 919-248-4687. *Web site:* http://www.ncseaa.edu/.

North Carolina Student Loan Program for Health, Science, and Mathematics. Renewable award for North Carolina residents studying health-related fields, or science or math education. Based on merit, need, and promise of service as a health professional or educator in an under-served area of North Carolina. Need two co-signers. Submit surety statement. *Academic Fields/Career Goals:* Dental Health/Services; Health Administration; Health and Medical Sciences; Nursing; Physical Sciences; Therapy/Rehabilitation. *Award:* Forgivable loan for use in freshman, sophomore, junior, senior, or graduate year; renewable. *Award amount:* $3000–$8500. *Number of awards:* 1. *Eligibility Requirements:* Applicant must be enrolled or expecting to enroll full-time at a two-year or four-year institution or university and resident of North Carolina. Available to U.S. citizens. *Application Requirements:* Application, financial need analysis, transcript. **Deadline:** June 1.

Contact Edna Williams, Manager, Selection and Origination, North Carolina State Education Assistance Authority, PO Box 14223, Research Triangle Park, NC 27709. *E-mail:* eew@ncseaa.edu. *Phone:* 800-700-1775 Ext. 4658. *Web site:* http://www.ncseaa.edu/.

North Carolina Teaching Fellows Scholarship Program. Award for North Carolina high school seniors planning to pursue teacher training studies. Must agree to teach in a North Carolina public or government school for four years or repay award. For more details visit web site http://www.teachingfellows.org. *Academic Fields/Career Goals:* Education. *Award:* Forgivable loan for use in freshman year; renewable. *Award amount:* $6500. *Number of awards:* 500. *Eligibility Requirements:* Applicant must be high school student; planning to enroll or expecting to enroll full-time at a four-year institution or university; resident of North Carolina and studying in North Carolina. Applicant must have 3.5 GPA or higher. Available to U.S. citizens. *Application Requirements:* Application, essay, interview, references, test scores, transcript. **Deadline:** varies.

Contact Lynne Stewart, Program Officer, North Carolina Teaching Fellows Commission, 3739 National Drive, Suite 100, Raleigh, NC 27612. *E-mail:* tfellows@ncforum.org. *Phone:* 919-781-6833 Ext. 103. *Fax:* 919-781-6527. *Web site:* http://www.teachingfellows.org/.

North Carolina Veterans Scholarships Class I-A. Scholarships for children of certain deceased, disabled or POW/MIA veterans. Award value is $4500 per nine-month academic year in private colleges and junior colleges. No limit on number awarded each year. *Award:* Scholarship for use in freshman, sophomore, junior, or senior year; renewable. *Award amount:* $4500. *Number of awards:* varies. *Eligibility Requirements:* Applicant must be enrolled or expecting to enroll full-time at a two-year, four-year, or technical institution or university; resident of North Carolina and studying in North Carolina. Available to U.S. citizens. Applicant or parent must meet one or more of the following requirements: general military experience; retired from active duty; disabled or killed as a result of military service; prisoner of war;

or missing in action. *Application Requirements:* Application, financial need analysis, interview, transcript. **Deadline:** continuous.

Contact Charles Smith, Assistant Secretary, North Carolina Division of Veterans Affairs, 325 North Salisbury Street, Raleigh, NC 27603. *E-mail:* charlie.smith@ncmail.net. *Phone:* 919-733-3851. *Fax:* 919-733-2834. *Web site:* http://www.doa.state.nc.us/vets/va.htm.

North Carolina Veterans Scholarships Class I-B. Awards for children of veterans rated by USDVA as 100 percent disabled due to wartime service as defined in the law, and currently or at time of death drawing compensation for such disability. Parent must have been a North Carolina resident at time of entry into service. Duration of the scholarship is four academic years (8 semesters) if used within 8 years. No limit on number awarded each year. *Award:* Scholarship for use in freshman, sophomore, junior, or senior year; renewable. *Award amount:* $1500. *Number of awards:* varies. *Eligibility Requirements:* Applicant must be enrolled or expecting to enroll full- or part-time at a two-year, four-year, or technical institution or university; resident of North Carolina and studying in North Carolina. Available to U.S. citizens. Applicant or parent must meet one or more of the following requirements: general military experience; retired from active duty; disabled or killed as a result of military service; prisoner of war; or missing in action. *Application Requirements:* Application, financial need analysis, interview, transcript. **Deadline:** continuous.

Contact Charles Smith, Assistant Secretary, North Carolina Division of Veterans Affairs, 325 North Salisbury Street, Raleigh, NC 27603. *E-mail:* charlie.smith@ncmail.net. *Phone:* 919-733-3851. *Fax:* 919-733-2834. *Web site:* http://www.doa.state.nc.us/vets/va.htm.

North Carolina Veterans Scholarships Class II. Awards for children of veterans rated by USDVA as much as 20 percent but less than 100 percent disabled due to wartime service as defined in the law, or awarded Purple Heart Medal for wounds received. Parent must have been a North Carolina resident at time of entry into service. Duration of the scholarship is four academic years (8 semesters) if used within 8 years. Free tuition and exemption from certain mandatory fees as set forth in the law in Public, Community and Technical Colleges. *Award:* Scholarship for use in freshman, sophomore, junior, or senior year; renewable. *Award amount:* $4500. *Number of awards:* up to 100. *Eligibility Requirements:* Applicant must be enrolled or expecting to enroll full- or part-time at a two-year, four-year, or technical institution or university; resident of North Carolina and studying in North Carolina. Available to U.S. citizens. Applicant or parent must meet one or more of the following requirements: general military experience; retired from active duty; disabled or killed as a result of military service; prisoner of war; or missing in action. *Application Requirements:* Application, financial need analysis, interview, transcript. **Deadline:** March 1.

Contact Charles Smith, Assistant Secretary, North Carolina Division of Veterans Affairs, 325 North Salisbury Street, Raleigh, NC 27603. *E-mail:* charlie.smith@ncmail.net. *Phone:* 919-733-3851. *Fax:* 919-733-2834. *Web site:* http://www.doa.state.nc.us/vets/va.htm.

North Carolina Veterans Scholarships Class III. Awards for children of a deceased war veteran, who was honorably discharged and who does not qualify under any other provision within this synopsis or veteran who served in a combat zone or waters adjacent to a combat zone and received a campaign badge or medal and who does not qualify under any other provision within this synopsis. Duration of the scholarship is four academic years (8 semesters) if used within 8 years. *Award:* Scholarship for use in freshman, sophomore, junior, or senior year; renewable. *Award amount:* $4500. *Number of awards:* up to 100. *Eligibility Requirements:* Applicant must be enrolled or expecting to enroll full- or part-time at a two-year, four-year, or technical institution or university; resident of North Carolina and studying in North Carolina. Available to U.S. citizens. Applicant or parent must meet one or more of the following requirements: general military experience; retired from active duty; disabled or killed as a result of military service; prisoner of war; or missing in action. *Application Requirements:* Application, financial need analysis, interview, transcript. **Deadline:** March 1.

Contact Charles Smith, Assistant Secretary, North Carolina Division of Veterans Affairs, 325 North Salisbury Street, Raleigh, NC 27603. *E-mail:* charlie.smith@ncmail.net. *Phone:* 919-733-3851. *Fax:* 919-733-2834. *Web site:* http://www.doa.state.nc.us/vets/va.htm.

North Carolina Veterans Scholarships Class IV. Awards for children of veterans, who were prisoner of war or missing in action. Duration of the scholarship is four academic years (8 semesters) if used within 8 years. No limit on number awarded each year. Award value is $4500 per nine-month academic year in private colleges and junior colleges. *Award:* Scholarship for use in freshman, sophomore, junior, or senior year; renewable. *Award amount:* $4500. *Number of awards:* varies. *Eligibility Requirements:* Applicant must be enrolled or expecting to enroll full- or part-time at a two-year, four-year, or technical institution or university; resident of North Carolina and studying in North Carolina. Available to U.S. citizens. Applicant or parent must meet one or more of the following requirements: general military experience; retired from active duty; disabled or killed as a result of military service; prisoner of war; or missing in action. *Application Requirements:* Application, financial need analysis, interview, transcript. **Deadline:** continuous.

Contact Charles Smith, Assistant Secretary, North Carolina Division of Veterans Affairs, 325 North Salisbury Street, Raleigh, NC 27603. *E-mail:* charlie.smith@ncmail.net. *Phone:* 919-733-3851. *Fax:* 919-733-2834. *Web site:* http://www.doa.state.nc.us/vets/va.htm.

Nurse Education Scholarship Loan Program (NESLP). Must be U.S. citizen and North Carolina resident. Award available through financial aid offices of North Carolina colleges and universities that offer programs to prepare students for licensure in the state as LPN or RN. Recipients enter contract with the State of North Carolina to work full time as a licensed nurse. Loans not repaid through service must be repaid in cash. Award based upon financial need. Maximum award for students enrolled in Associate Degree Nursing and Practical Nurse Education programs is $5000. Maximum award for students enrolled in a baccalaureate program is $400. *Academic Fields/Career Goals:* Nursing. *Award:* Forgivable loan for use in freshman, sophomore, junior, or senior year; renewable. *Award amount:* $400–$5000. *Number of awards:* varies. *Eligibility Requirements:* Applicant must be enrolled or expecting to enroll full- or part-time at a four-year institution or university; resident of North Carolina and studying in North Carolina. Available to U.S. citizens. *Application Requirements:* Application, financial need analysis. **Deadline:** continuous.

Contact Bill Carswell, Manager of Scholarship and Grant Division, North Carolina State Education Assistance Authority, PO Box 14103, Research Triangle Park, NC 27709. *E-mail:* carswellb@ncseaa.edu. *Phone:* 919-549-8614. *Fax:* 919-248-4687. *Web site:* http://www.ncseaa.edu/.

State Contractual Scholarship Fund Program-North Carolina. Renewable award for North Carolina residents already attending an approved private college or university in the state and pursuing an undergraduate degree. Must have financial need. Contact college financial aid office for deadline and information. May not be enrolled in a program leading to a religious vocation. *Award:* Scholarship for use in freshman, sophomore, junior, or senior year; renewable. *Award amount:* up to $1350. *Number of awards:* varies. *Eligibility Requirements:* Applicant must be enrolled or expecting to enroll full- or part-time at a four-year institution or university; resident of North Carolina and studying in North Carolina. Available to U.S. citizens. *Application Requirements:* Application, financial need analysis. **Deadline:** varies.

Contact Bill Carswell, Manager of Scholarship and Grant Division, North Carolina State Education Assistance Authority, PO Box 13663, Research Triangle Park, NC 27709. *E-mail:* carswellb@ncseaa.edu. *Phone:* 919-549-8614. *Fax:* 919-248-4687. *Web site:* http://www.ncseaa.edu/.

Teacher Assistant Scholarship Fund. Funding to attend a public or private four-year college or university in North Carolina with an approved teacher education program. Applicant must be employed full-time as a teacher assistant in an instructional area while pursuing licensure and maintain employment to remain eligible. Must have at least 3.0 cumulative GPA. Refer to web site for further details http://www.ncseaa.edu/tas.htm. *Academic Fields/Career Goals:* Education. *Award:* Scholarship for use in freshman, sophomore, junior, or senior year; renewable. *Award amount:* $600–$3600. *Number of awards:* varies. *Eligibility Requirements:* Applicant must be enrolled or expecting to enroll full- or part-time at a four-year institution or university; resident of North Carolina and studying in North Carolina. Applicant or parent of applicant must have employment or volunteer experience in teaching/education. Applicant must have 3.0 GPA or higher. Available to U.S. citizens. *Application Requirements:* Application, financial need analysis, transcript, FAFSA. **Deadline:** March 31.

Contact Rashonn Albritton, Processing Assistant, North Carolina State Education Assistance Authority, PO Box 13663, Research Triangle Park, NC 27709. *E-mail:* ralbritton@ncseaa.edu. *Phone:* 919-549-8614. *Fax:* 919-248-4687. *Web site:* http://www.ncseaa.edu/.

Training Support for Youth with Disabilities. Public service program that helps persons with disabilities obtain competitive employment. To qualify: student must have a mental, physical or learning disability that is an impediment to employment. A Rehabilitation Counselor along with the eligible student individually develops a rehabilitation program to achieve an employment outcome. Assistance is based on financial need and type of program in which the student enrolls. *Award:* Grant for use in freshman, sophomore, junior, or senior year; renewable. *Award amount:* $2400. *Number of awards:* varies. *Eligibility Requirements:* Applicant must be enrolled or expecting to enroll full- or part-time at a two-year, four-year, or technical institution or university and resident of North Carolina. Applicant must be hearing impaired, learning disabled, physically disabled, or visually impaired. Available to U.S. citizens. *Application Requirements:* Application, financial need analysis, interview, test scores, transcript, medical and psychological records. **Deadline:** continuous.

Contact Alma Taylor, Program Specialist for Transition, North Carolina Division of Vocational Rehabilitation Services, 2801 Mail Service Center, Raleigh, NC 27699-2801. *E-mail:* alma.taylor@ncmail.net. *Phone:* 919-855-3572. *Web site:* http://www.dhhs.state.nc.us/.

University of North Carolina Need-Based Grant. Grants available for eligible students attending one of the 16 campuses of the University of North Carolina. Students must be enrolled in at least 6 credit hours at one of the 16 constituent institutions of The University of North Carolina. Award amounts vary based on legislative appropriations. *Award:* Grant for use in freshman, sophomore, junior, or senior year; not renewable. *Award amount:* varies. *Number of awards:* varies. *Eligibility Requirements:* Applicant must be enrolled or expecting to enroll full- or part-time at a four-year institution or university; resident of North Carolina and studying in North Carolina. Available to U.S. citizens. *Application Requirements:* Financial need analysis. **Deadline:** continuous.

Contact College Foundation of North Carolina. *E-mail:* programinformation@cfnc.org. *Phone:* 866-866-CFNC. *Fax:* 919-248-4687. *Web site:* http://www.cfnc.org/.

University of North Carolina Need-Based Grant. Applicants must be enrolled in at least 6 credit hours at one of sixteen UNC system universities. Eligibility based on need; award varies, consideration for grant automatic when FAFSA is filed. Late applications may be denied due to insufficient funds. *Award:* Grant for use in freshman, sophomore, junior, or senior year; renewable. *Award amount:* varies. *Number of awards:* varies. *Eligibility Requirements:* Applicant must be enrolled or expecting to enroll full- or part-time at an institution or university; resident of North Carolina and studying in North Carolina. Available to U.S. citizens. *Application Requirements:* Application, financial need analysis, FAFSA. **Deadline:** varies.

Contact Bill Carswell, Manager of Scholarship and Grant Division, North Carolina State Education Assistance Authority, PO Box 13663, Research Triangle Park, NC 27709. *E-mail:* carswellb@ncseaa.edu. *Phone:* 919-549-8614. *Fax:* 919-248-4687. *Web site:* http://www.ncseaa.edu/.

NORTH DAKOTA

North Dakota Indian Scholarship Program. Award of $800 to $2000 per year to assist American Indian students who are North Dakota residents in obtaining a college education. Must have been accepted for admission at an institution of higher learning or state vocational education program within North Dakota. Based upon scholastic ability and unmet financial need. Minimum 2.0 GPA required. *Award:* Scholarship for use in freshman, sophomore, junior, or senior year; renewable. *Award amount:* $800–$2000. *Number of awards:* 175–230. *Eligibility Requirements:* Applicant must be American Indian/Alaska Native; enrolled or expecting to enroll full- or part-time at a two-year, four-year, or technical institution or university; resident of North Dakota and studying in North Dakota. Available to U.S. citizens. *Application Requirements:* Application, financial need analysis, transcript, proof of tribal enrollment, budget. **Deadline:** July 15.

Contact Rhonda Schauer, Coordinator of American Indian Higher Education, North Dakota University System, BSC Horizon Building, Suite 202, 1815 Schafer Street, Bismarck, ND 58501-1217. *E-mail:* rhonda.schauer@ndus.edu. *Phone:* 701-224-2497. *Web site:* http://www.ndus.edu/.

North Dakota Scholars Program. Provides scholarships equal to cost of tuition at the public colleges in North Dakota for North Dakota residents. To be eligible for consideration for a ND Scholars scholarship, a high school junior must take the ACT Assessment between October and June of their junior year and score in the upper five percentile of all ND ACT test takers. The numeric sum of the English, Math, reading and science reasoning scores will be used as a second selection criteria.

The numeric sum of a student's English and mathematics scores will be used as selection criteria if a tie-breaker is needed. *Award:* Scholarship for use in freshman, sophomore, junior, or senior year; renewable. *Award amount:* $4160–$5461. *Number of awards:* 45–50. *Eligibility Requirements:* Applicant must be high school student; planning to enroll or expecting to enroll full-time at a two-year or four-year institution or university; resident of North Dakota and studying in North Dakota. Available to U.S. citizens. *Application Requirements:* References, test scores.

Contact Peggy Wipf, Director of Financial Aid, North Dakota University System, 600 East Boulevard Avenue, Department 215, Bismarck, ND 58505-0230. *E-mail:* peggy.wipf@ndus.nodak.edu. *Phone:* 701-328-4114. *Web site:* http://www.ndus.edu/.

North Dakota State Student Incentive Grant Program. Aids North Dakota residents attending an approved college or university in North Dakota. Must be enrolled in a program of at least nine months in length. Must be a U.S. citizen. Must complete the FAFSAA. Needs-based. *Award:* Grant for use in freshman, sophomore, junior, or senior year; not renewable. *Award amount:* $1200. *Number of awards:* 7500–8300. *Eligibility Requirements:* Applicant must be enrolled or expecting to enroll full-time at a two-year or four-year institution or university; resident of North Dakota and studying in North Dakota. Available to U.S. citizens. *Application Requirements:* Financial need analysis. **Deadline:** March 15.

Contact Peggy Wipf, Director of Financial Aid, North Dakota University System, 600 East Boulevard Avenue, Department 215, Bismarck, ND 58505-0230. *Phone:* 701-328-4114. *Web site:* http://www.ndus.edu/.

OHIO

Ohio College Opportunity Grant. OCOG provides grant money to Ohio residents who demonstrate the highest levels of financial need (as determined by the results of FAFSA) who are enrolled at Ohio public university main campuses (not regional campuses or community colleges), Ohio private, non-profit colleges or universities (not private, for-profit institutions) or eligible Pennsylvania institutions. *Award:* Grant for use in freshman, sophomore, junior, or senior year; not renewable. *Award amount:* up to $1848. *Eligibility Requirements:* Applicant must be enrolled or expecting to enroll full- or part-time at a four-year institution or university; resident of Ohio and studying in Ohio or Pennsylvania. Available to U.S. citizens. *Application Requirements:* FAFSA. **Deadline:** October 1.

Contact Ohio Board of Regents. *E-mail:* ocog_admin@regents.state.oh.us. *Phone:* 888-833-1133. *Web site:* http://www.uso.edu/.

Ohio Environmental Science & Engineering Scholarships. Merit-based, non-renewable, tuition-only scholarships awarded to undergraduate students admitted to Ohio state or private colleges and universities. Must be able to demonstrate knowledge of, and commitment to, careers in environmental sciences or environmental engineering. *Academic Fields/Career Goals:* Environmental Science. *Award:* Scholarship for use in senior year; not renewable. *Award amount:* $1250–$2500. *Number of awards:* 18. *Eligibility Requirements:* Applicant must be enrolled or expecting to enroll full- or part-time at a two-year or four-year institution or university and studying in Ohio. Applicant must have 3.0 GPA or higher. Available to U.S. citizens. *Application Requirements:* Application, essay, resume, references, self-addressed stamped envelope, transcript. **Deadline:** June 1.

Contact Mr. Lynn E. Elfner, Chief Executive Officer, Ohio Academy of Science/Ohio Environmental Education Fund, 1500 West Third Avenue, Suite 228, Columbus, OH 43212-2817. *E-mail:* oas@iwaynet.net. *Phone:* 614-488-2228. *Fax:* 614-488-7629. *Web site:* http://www.ohiosci.org/.

Ohio National Guard Scholarship Program. Scholarships are for undergraduate studies at an approved Ohio post-secondary institution. Applicants must enlist for six or three years of Selective Service Reserve Duty in the Ohio National Guard. Scholarship pays 100% instructional and general fees for public institutions and an average of cost of public universities is available for private schools. May reapply up to four years of studies (12 quarters or 8 semesters) for six year enlistment and two years of studies (6 quarters or 4 semesters) for three year enlistment. Deadlines: July 1 (fall), November 1 (winter quarter/spring semester), February 1 (spring quarter), April 1 (summer). *Award:* Scholarship for use in freshman, sophomore, junior, or senior year; not renewable. *Award amount:* up to $4006. *Number of awards:* up to 3500. *Eligibility Requirements:* Applicant must be enrolled or expecting to enroll full- or part-time at a two-year, four-year, or technical institution or university; resident of Ohio and studying in Ohio. Available to U.S. citizens. Applicant must have served in the Air Force National Guard or Army National Guard. *Application Requirements:* Application. **Deadline:** varies.

Contact Mrs. Toni E. Davis, Grants Administrator, Ohio National Guard, 2825 West Dublin Granville Road, ONGSP, Columbus, OH 43235-2789. *E-mail:* toni.davis7@us.army.mil. *Phone:* 614-336-7143. *Fax:* 614-336-7318. *Web site:* http://www.ongsp.org/.

Ohio Safety Officers College Memorial Fund. Renewable award covering up to full tuition is available to children and surviving spouses of peace officers, other safety officers and fire fighters killed in the line of duty in any state. Children must be under 26 years of age. Dollar value of each award varies. Must be an Ohio resident and enroll full-time or part-time at an Ohio college or university. Any spouse/child of a member of the armed services of the U.S., who has been killed in the line duty during Operation Enduring Freedom, Operation Iraqi Freedom or a combat zone designated by the President of the United States. Dollar value of each award varies. *Award:* Scholarship for use in freshman, sophomore, junior, or senior year; renewable. *Award amount:* varies. *Eligibility Requirements:* Applicant must be age 26 or under; enrolled or expecting to enroll full- or part-time at a two-year or four-year institution or university; resident of Ohio and studying in Ohio. Available to U.S. citizens. *Application Requirements:* **Deadline:** continuous.

Contact Barbara Thoma, Assistant Director, Ohio Board of Regents, 30 East Broad Street, 36th Floor, Columbus, OH 43215-3414. *E-mail:* bthoma@regents.state.oh.us. *Phone:* 614-752-9535. *Fax:* 614-752-5903. *Web site:* http://www.uso.edu/.

Ohio War Orphans Scholarship. Aids Ohio residents attending an eligible college in Ohio. Must be between the ages of 16 and 25, the child of a disabled or deceased veteran, and enrolled full-time. Renewable up to five years. Amount of award varies. Must include Form DD214. *Award:* Scholarship for use in freshman, sophomore, junior, or senior year; renewable. *Award amount:* varies. *Eligibility Requirements:* Applicant must be age 16-25; enrolled or expecting to enroll full-time at a two-year or four-year institution or university; resident of Ohio and studying in Ohio. Available to U.S. citizens. Applicant or parent must meet one or more of the following requirements: general military experience; retired from active duty; disabled or killed as a result of military service; prisoner of war; or missing in action.

Application Requirements: Application, Form DD214. **Deadline:** July 1.

Contact Jathiya Abdullah-Simmons, Program Manager, Ohio Board of Regents, 30 East Broad Street, 36th Floor, Columbus, OH 43215-3414. *E-mail:* jabdullah-simmons@regents.state.oh.us. *Phone:* 614-752-9528. *Fax:* 614-752-5903. *Web site:* http://www.uso.edu/.

T.E.A.C.H. Early Childhood OHIO Scholarships. For Early Childhood Professionals working in Ohio. AAS Scholarships available. Must earn under $15/hr and work 30 hours per week with children. *Academic Fields/Career Goals:* Child and Family Studies; Education. *Award:* Scholarship for use in freshman, sophomore, junior, or senior year; renewable. *Eligibility Requirements:* Applicant must be enrolled or expecting to enroll full- or part-time at a two-year or four-year institution; resident of Ohio and studying in Ohio. Available to U.S. citizens. *Application Requirements:* Application.

Contact Greg Yorker, Director, Ohio Child Care Resource & Referral Association. *E-mail:* teach@occrra.org. *Web site:* http://www.occrra.org/.

OKLAHOMA

Academic Scholars Program. Awards for students of high academic ability to attend institutions in Oklahoma. Renewable up to four years. ACT or SAT scores must fall between 99.5 and 100th percentiles, or applicant must be designated as a National Merit scholar or finalist. Oklahoma public institutions can also select institutional nominees. *Award:* Scholarship for use in freshman, sophomore, junior, senior, or graduate year; renewable. *Award amount:* $1800–$5500. *Number of awards:* varies. *Eligibility Requirements:* Applicant must be high school student; planning to enroll or expecting to enroll full-time at a two-year or four-year institution or university and studying in Oklahoma. Available to U.S. citizens. *Application Requirements:* Application, test scores, transcript. **Deadline:** continuous.

Contact Scholarship Programs Coordinator, Oklahoma State Regents for Higher Education, PO Box 108850, Oklahoma City, OK 73101-8850. *E-mail:* studentinfo@osrhe.edu. *Phone:* 800-858-1840. *Fax:* 405-225-9230. *Web site:* http://www.okhighered.org/.

Future Teacher Scholarship-Oklahoma. Open to outstanding Oklahoma high school graduates who agree to teach in shortage areas. Must rank in top 15 percent of graduating class or score above 85th percentile on ACT or similar test, or be accepted in an educational program. Students nominated by institution. Reapply to renew. Must attend college/university in Oklahoma. *Academic Fields/Career Goals:* Education. *Award:* Scholarship for use in freshman, sophomore, junior, senior, or graduate year; renewable. *Award amount:* $500–$1500. *Eligibility Requirements:* Applicant must be enrolled or expecting to enroll full- or part-time at a two-year or four-year institution or university; resident of Oklahoma and studying in Oklahoma. Available to U.S. citizens. *Application Requirements:* Application, essay, test scores, transcript. **Deadline:** varies.

Contact Scholarship Programs Coordinator, Oklahoma State Regents for Higher Education, PO Box 108850, Oklahoma City, OK 73101-8850. *E-mail:* studentinfo@osrhe.edu. *Phone:* 800-858-1840. *Fax:* 405-225-9230. *Web site:* http://www.okhighered.org/.

Oklahoma Tuition Aid Grant. Award for Oklahoma residents enrolled at an Oklahoma institution at least part time each semester in a degree program. May be enrolled in two- or four-year or approved vocational-technical institution. Award for students attending public institutions or private colleges. Application is made through FAFSA. *Award:* Grant for use in freshman, sophomore, junior, or senior year; not renewable. *Award amount:* $1000–$1300. *Number of awards:* varies. *Eligibility Requirements:* Applicant must be enrolled or expecting to enroll full- or part-time at a two-year, four-year, or technical institution or university; resident of Oklahoma and studying in Oklahoma. Available to U.S. citizens. *Application Requirements:* Application, financial need analysis, FAFSA. **Deadline:** varies.

Contact Oklahoma State Regents for Higher Education, PO Box 108850, Oklahoma City, OK 73101-8850. *E-mail:* studentinfo@osrhe.edu. *Phone:* 405-858-1840. *Fax:* 405-225-9230. *Web site:* http://www.okhighered.org/.

Regional University Baccalaureate Scholarship. Renewable award for Oklahoma residents attending one of 11 participating Oklahoma public universities. Must have an ACT composite score of at least 30 or be a National Merit semifinalist or commended student. In addition to the award amount, each recipient will receive a resident tuition waiver from the institution. Must maintain a 3.25 GPA. Deadlines vary depending upon the institution attended. *Award:* Scholarship for use in freshman, sophomore, junior, or senior year; renewable. *Award amount:* $3000. *Number of awards:* varies. *Eligibility Requirements:* Applicant must be enrolled or expecting to enroll full-time at an institution or university; resident of Oklahoma and studying in Oklahoma. Available to U.S. citizens. *Application Requirements:* Application. **Deadline:** varies.

Contact Scholarship Programs Coordinator, Oklahoma State Regents for Higher Education, PO Box 108850, Oklahoma City, OK 73101-8850. *E-mail:* studentinfo@osrhe.edu. *Phone:* 405-858-1840. *Fax:* 405-225-9230. *Web site:* http://www.okhighered.org/.

Robert C. Byrd Honors Scholarship-Oklahoma. Scholarships available to high school seniors. Applicants must be U.S. citizens or national, or be permanent residents of the United States. Must be legal residents of Oklahoma. Must have a minimum ACT composite score of 32 and/or a minimum SAT combined score of 1420 and/or 2130 or a minimum GED score of 700. Application URL http://www.sde.state.ok.us/pro/Byrd/application.pdf. *Award:* Scholarship for use in freshman year; not renewable. *Award amount:* $1500. *Number of awards:* 10. *Eligibility Requirements:* Applicant must be high school student; planning to enroll or expecting to enroll full-time at a four-year institution or university and resident of Oklahoma. Available to U.S. citizens. *Application Requirements:* Application, essay, references, transcript. **Deadline:** April 11.

Contact Certification Specialist, Oklahoma State Department of Education, 2500 North Lincoln Boulevard, Suite 212, Oklahoma City, OK 73105-4599. *Phone:* 405-521-2808. *Web site:* http://www.sde.state.ok.us/.

OREGON

American Legion Auxiliary Department of Oregon Department Grants. One-time award for educational use in the state of Oregon. Must be a resident of Oregon who is the child or widow of a veteran or the wife of a disabled veteran. *Award:* Grant for use in freshman, sophomore, junior, or senior year; not renewable. *Award amount:* $1000. *Number of awards:* 2. *Eligibility Requirements:* Applicant must be enrolled or expecting to enroll full- or part-time at a two-year, four-year, or technical institution or university and resident of Oregon. Available to U.S. citizens. Applicant or parent must meet one or more of the following requirements: general military experience; retired from active duty; disabled or killed as a result of military service; prisoner of war; or missing in action. *Application Requirements:* Application, essay, financial need analysis, interview, references, test scores, transcript. **Deadline:** March 10.

Contact Virginia Biddle, Secretary/ Treasurer, American Legion Auxiliary Department of Oregon, PO Box 1730, Wilsonville, OR 97070. *E-mail:* alaor@pcez.com. *Phone:* 503-682-3162. *Fax:* 503-685-5008. *Web site:* http://www.alaoregon.org/.

American Legion Auxiliary Department of Oregon Nurses Scholarship. One-time award for Oregon residents who are in their senior year of High School, who are the children of veterans who served during eligibility dates for American Legion membership. Must enroll in a nursing program. Contact local units for application. *Academic Fields/Career Goals:* Nursing. *Award:* Scholarship for use in freshman year; not renewable. *Award amount:* $1500. *Number of awards:* 1. *Eligibility Requirements:* Applicant must be high school student; planning to enroll or expecting to enroll full- or part-time at a four-year institution or university and resident of Oregon. Available to U.S. citizens. Applicant or parent must meet one or more of the following requirements: general military experience; retired from active duty; disabled or killed as a result of military service; prisoner of war; or missing in action. *Application Requirements:* Application, essay, financial need analysis, interview, transcript. **Deadline:** May 15.

Contact Virginia Biddle, Secretary/ Treasurer, American Legion Auxiliary Department of Oregon, PO Box 1730, Wilsonville, OR 97070. *E-mail:* alaor@pcez.com. *Phone:* 503-682-3162. *Fax:* 503-685-5008. *Web site:* http://www.alaoregon.org/.

Better A Life Scholarship. Scholarship award available to single parents age 17–25. High schools seniors must have at least 3.0 GPA and college students must have at least a 2.5 GPA. Applicants may not already possess a bachelor's degree. Applicants may reapply for one additional year of funding. *Award:* Scholarship for use in freshman or sophomore year; not renewable. *Eligibility Requirements:* Applicant must be age 17-25; enrolled or expecting to enroll full- or part-time at a two-year or four-year institution or university and single. *Application Requirements:* Application. **Deadline:** March 1.

Contact Director of Grant Programs, Oregon Student Assistance Commission, 1500 Valley River Drive, Suite 100, Eugene, OR 97401-7020. *Phone:* 800-452-8807. *Web site:* http://www.GetCollegeFunds.org/.

Dorothy Campbell Memorial Scholarship. Renewable award for female Oregon high school graduates with a minimum 2.75 GPA. Must submit essay describing strong, continuing interest in golf and the contribution that sport has made to applicant's development. Must have played on high school golf team (including intramural), if available. *Award:* Scholarship for use in freshman, sophomore, junior, or senior year; renewable. *Award amount:* varies. *Number of awards:* varies. *Eligibility Requirements:* Applicant must be enrolled or expecting to enroll full-time at a four-year institution; female; resident of Oregon; studying in Oregon and must have an interest in golf. Available to U.S. citizens. *Application Requirements:* Application, essay, financial need analysis, transcript. **Deadline:** March 1.

Contact Scholarship Coordinator, Oregon Student Assistance Commission, 1500 Valley River Drive, Suite 100, Eugene, OR 97401-7020. *Phone:* 800-452-8807. *Web site:* http://www.GetCollegeFunds.org/.

Glenn Jackson Scholars Scholarships. Renewable award for Oregon graduating high school seniors who are dependents of employees or retirees of Oregon Department of Transportation or Parks and Recreation Department. Employees must have worked in their department at least three years as of the March 1 scholarship deadline. *Award:* Scholarship for use in freshman, sophomore, junior, or senior year; renewable. *Award amount:* varies. *Number of awards:* varies. *Eligibility Requirements:* Applicant must be high school student; planning to enroll or expecting to enroll full- or part-time at a two-year or four-year institution or university and resident of Oregon. Applicant or parent of applicant must be affiliated with Oregon Department of Transportation Parks and Recreation. Available to U.S. citizens. *Application Requirements:* Application, essay, financial need analysis, references, transcript, activity chart. **Deadline:** March 1.

Contact Director of Grant Programs, Oregon Student Assistance Commission, 1500 Valley River Drive, Suite 100, Eugene, OR 97401-7020. *Phone:* 800-452-8807 Ext. 7395. *Web site:* http://www.GetCollegeFunds.org/.

Laurence R. Foster Memorial Scholarship. One-time award to students enrolled or planning to enroll in a public health degree program. First preference given to those working in the public health field and those pursuing a graduate degree in public health. Undergraduates entering junior or senior year health programs may apply if seeking a public health career, and not private practice. Prefer applicants from diverse cultures. Additional essays required. *Academic Fields/Career Goals:* Public Health. *Award:* Scholarship for use in freshman, sophomore, junior, or senior year; renewable. *Award amount:* varies. *Number of awards:* varies. *Eligibility Requirements:* Applicant must be enrolled or expecting to enroll full- or part-time at a four-year institution. Available to U.S. citizens. *Application Requirements:* Application, essay, financial need analysis, references, transcript, activity chart. **Deadline:** March 1.

Contact Scholarship Coordinator, Oregon Student Assistance Commission, 1500 Valley River Drive, Suite 100, Eugene, OR 97401-7020. *Phone:* 800-452-8807 Ext. 7395. *Web site:* http://www.GetCollegeFunds.org/.

Oregon Scholarship Fund Community College Student Award. Scholarship open to students enrolled or planning to enroll at least half time in Oregon community college programs. Recipients may reapply for one additional year. *Award:* Scholarship for use in freshman or sophomore year; not renewable. *Award amount:* varies. *Number of awards:* varies. *Eligibility Requirements:* Applicant must be enrolled or expecting to enroll full- or part-time at a two-year institution and studying in Oregon. Available to U.S. citizens. *Application Requirements:* Application, essay, financial need analysis, transcript, activity chart. **Deadline:** March 1.

Contact Director of Grant Programs, Oregon Student Assistance Commission, 1500 Valley River Drive, Suite 100, Eugene, OR 97401-7020. *Phone:* 800-452-8807 Ext. 7395. *Web site:* http://www.GetCollegeFunds.org/.

Oregon Scholarship Fund Transfer Student Award. Award open to Oregon residents who are currently enrolled in their second year at an Oregon community college and are planning to transfer to a four-year college in Oregon. Prior recipients may apply for one additional year. Must enroll at least half-time. *Award:* Scholarship for use in junior or senior year; not renewable. *Award amount:* varies. *Number of awards:* varies. *Eligibility Requirements:* Applicant must be enrolled or expecting to enroll full- or part-time at a four-year institution or university; resident of Oregon and studying in Oregon. Available to U.S. citizens. *Application Requirements:* Application, essay, financial need analysis, transcript, activity chart. **Deadline:** March 1.

Contact Director of Grant Programs, Oregon Student Assistance Commission, 1500 Valley River Drive, Suite 100, Eugene, OR 97401-7020. *Phone:* 800-452-8807 Ext. 7395. *Web site:* http://www.GetCollegeFunds.org/.

Oregon Trucking Association Safety Management Council Scholarship. One-time award available to a child of an Oregon Trucking Association member, or child of an employee of OTA member. Applicants must be graduating high school seniors from an Oregon high school planning to attend a public or nonprofit college or university. Oregon residency is not required. *Award:* Scholarship for use in freshman year; not renewable. *Award amount:* varies. *Eligibility Requirements:* Applicant must be high school student and planning to enroll or expecting to enroll full-time at a four-year institution. Applicant or parent of applicant must be affiliated with Oregon Trucking Association. Available to U.S. citizens. *Application Requirements:* Application, essay, financial need analysis, references, transcript, activity chart. **Deadline:** March 1.

Contact Director of Grant Programs, Oregon Student Assistance Commission, 1500 Valley River Drive, Suite 100, Eugene, OR 97401-7020. *Phone:* 800-452-8807 Ext. 7395. *Web site:* http://www.GetCollegeFunds.org/.

Oregon Veterans' Education Aid. To be eligible, veteran must have actively served in U.S. armed forces 90 days and been discharged under honorable conditions. Must be U.S. citizen and Oregon resident. Korean War veteran or received campaign or expeditionary medal or ribbon awarded by U.S. armed forces for services after June 30, 1958. Full-time students receive up to $150 per month, and part-time students receive up to $100 per month for a maximum of 36 months. Length of benefits depend on length of service. Payments contingent upon available funding. *Award:* Grant for use in freshman, sophomore, junior, senior, graduate, or postgraduate years; not renewable. *Award amount:* $3600–$5400. *Number of awards:* 1–200. *Eligibility Requirements:* Applicant must be enrolled or expecting to enroll full- or part-time at a two-year, four-year, or technical institution or university; resident of Oregon and studying in Oregon. Available to U.S. citizens. Applicant must have general military experience. *Application Requirements:* Application, certified copy of DD Form 214. **Deadline:** continuous.

Contact Loriann Sheridan, Veterans Programs Consultant, Oregon Department of Veterans' Affairs, 700 Summer Street, NE, Salem, OR 97301-1289. *E-mail:* sheridl@odva.state.or.us. *Phone:* 503-373-2264. *Fax:* 503-373-2393. *Web site:* http://www.oregon.gov/odva.

Peter Connacher Memorial Scholarship. Renewable award for American prisoners-of-war and their descendants. Written proof of prisoner-of-war status and discharge papers from the U.S. Armed Forces must accompany application. Statement of relationship between applicant and former prisoner-of-war is required. Oregon residency preferred but not required. See web site at http://www.osac.state.or.us for details. *Award:* Scholarship for use in freshman, sophomore, junior, or senior year; renewable. *Award amount:* varies. *Number of awards:* varies. *Eligibility Requirements:* Applicant must be enrolled or expecting to enroll full-time at a two-year or four-year institution. Available to U.S. citizens. Applicant or parent must meet one or more of the following requirements: general military experience; retired from active duty; disabled or killed as a result of military service; prisoner of war; or missing in action. *Application Requirements:* Application, essay, financial need analysis, transcript, military discharge papers, documentation of POW status. **Deadline:** March 1.

Contact Director of Grant Programs, Oregon Student Assistance Commission, 1500 Valley River Drive, Suite 100, Eugene, OR 97401-7020. *Phone:* 800-452-8807 Ext. 7395. *Web site:* http://www.GetCollegeFunds.org/.

PENNSYLVANIA

Armed Forces Loan Forgiveness Program. Loan forgiveness for non-residents of Pennsylvania who served in Armed Forces in an active duty status after September 11, 2001. Must be a student who either left a PA approved institution of postsecondary education due to call to active duty, or was living in PA at time of enlistment, or enlisted in military immediately after attending a PA approved institution of postsecondary education. Number of loans forgiven varies. *Award:* Forgivable loan for use in freshman, sophomore, junior, or senior year; not renewable. *Award amount:* up to $2500. *Number of awards:* varies. *Eligibility Requirements:* Applicant must be enrolled or expecting to enroll full- or part-time at a two-year, four-year, or technical institution or university. Available to U.S. citizens. Applicant or parent must meet one or more of the following requirements: general military experience; retired from active duty; disabled or killed as a result of military service; prisoner of war; or missing in action. *Application Requirements:* Application. **Deadline:** December 31.

Contact Keith R. New, Director of Public Relations, Pennsylvania Higher Education Assistance Agency, 1200 North Seventh Street, Harrisburg, PA 17102-1444. *E-mail:* knew@pheaa.org. *Phone:* 717-720-2509. *Web site:* http://www.pheaa.org/.

New Economy Technology and SciTech Scholarships. Renewable award for Pennsylvania residents pursuing a degree in science or technology at a PHEAA-approved two- or four-year Pennsylvania college or university. Must maintain minimum GPA of 3.0. Must commence employment in Pennsylvania in a field related to degree within one year after graduation, and work one year for each year the scholarship was awarded. *Academic Fields/Career Goals:* Engineering/Technology; Engineering-Related Technologies; Natural Sciences; Physical Sciences. *Award:* Scholarship for use in freshman, sophomore, junior, or senior year; renewable. *Award amount:* $1000–$3000. *Number of awards:* varies. *Eligibility Requirements:* Applicant must be age 18 and over; enrolled or expecting to enroll full-time at a two-year, four-year, or technical institution or university; resident of Pennsylvania and studying in Pennsylvania. Applicant must have 3.0 GPA or higher. Available to U.S. citizens. *Application Requirements:* Application, FAFSA. **Deadline:** December 31.

Contact State Grant and Special Programs Division, Pennsylvania Higher Education Assistance Agency, 1200 North Seventh Street, Harrisburg, PA 17102-1444. *Phone:* 800-692-7392. *Web site:* http://www.pheaa.org/.

Pennsylvania State Grant. Award for Pennsylvania residents attending an approved postsecondary institution as undergraduates in a program of at least two years duration. Renewable for up to eight semesters if applicants show continued need and academic progress. Must submit FAFSA. Number of awards granted varies annually. Scholarship value is $200 to $4120. Deadlines: May 1 and August 1. *Award:* Grant for use in freshman, sophomore, junior, or senior year; renewable. *Award amount:* $200–$4120. *Number of awards:* varies. *Eligibility Requirements:* Applicant must be enrolled or expecting to enroll full- or part-time at a two-year, four-year, or technical institution or university and resident of Pennsylvania. Available to U.S. citizens. *Application Requirements:* Financial need analysis, FAFSA. **Deadline:** varies.

Contact Keith New, Director of Public Relations, Pennsylvania Higher Education Assistance Agency, 1200 North Seventh Street, Harrisburg, PA 17102-1444. *Phone:* 717-720-2509. *Fax:* 717-720-3903. *Web site:* http://www.pheaa.org/.

Postsecondary Education Gratuity Program. The program offers waiver of tuition and fees for children of Pennsylvania police officers, firefighters, rescue or ambulance squad members, corrections facility employees, or National Guard members who died in line of duty after January 1, 1976. *Award:* Grant for use in freshman, sophomore, junior, or senior year; renewable. *Award amount:* varies. *Number of awards:* varies. *Eligibility Requirements:* Applicant must be age 25 or under; enrolled or expecting to enroll full-time at a two-year or four-year institution or university; resident of Pennsylvania and studying in Pennsylvania. Available to U.S. citizens. Applicant or parent must meet one or more of the following requirements: Air Force National Guard or Army National Guard experience; retired from active duty; disabled or killed as a result of military service; prisoner of war; or missing in action. *Application Requirements:* Application. **Deadline:** August 1.

Contact Keith R. New, Director of Public Relations, Pennsylvania Higher Education Assistance Agency, 1200 North Seventh Street, Harrisburg, PA 17102-1444. *E-mail:* knew@pheaa.org. *Phone:* 717-720-2509. *Web site:* http://www.pheaa.org/.

Robert C. Byrd Honors Scholarship-Pennsylvania. Awards Pennsylvania residents who are graduating high school seniors. Must rank in the top 5 percent of graduating class, have at least a 3.5 GPA and score 1150 or above on the SAT, 25 or above on the ACT, or 355 or above on the GED. Renewable award and the amount granted varies. Applicants are expected to be a full-time freshman student enrolled at an eligible institution of higher education, following high school graduation. *Award:* Scholarship for use in freshman year; renewable. *Award amount:* $1500. *Number of awards:* varies. *Eligibility Requirements:* Applicant must be high school student; planning to enroll or expecting to enroll full-time at a four-year institution or university and resident of Pennsylvania. Available to U.S. citizens. *Application Requirements:* Application, references, test scores, transcript, letter of acceptance. **Deadline:** April 1.

Contact Keith R. New, Director of Public Relations, Pennsylvania Higher Education Assistance Agency, 1200 North Seventh Street, Harrisburg, PA 17102. *Phone:* 717-720-2509. *Fax:* 717-720-3903. *Web site:* http://www.pheaa.org/.

RHODE ISLAND

Rhode Island State Grant Program. Grants for residents of Rhode Island attending an approved school in United States. Based on need. Renewable for up to four years if in good academic standing and meet financial need requirements. *Award:* Grant for use in freshman, sophomore, junior, or senior year; renewable. *Award amount:* $250–$900. *Number of awards:* 10,000–17,000. *Eligibility Requirements:* Applicant must be enrolled or expecting to enroll full- or part-time at a two-year, four-year, or technical institution or university and resident of Rhode Island. Available to U.S. citizens. *Application Requirements:* Application, financial need analysis. **Deadline:** March 1.

Contact Mr. Michael Joyce JD, Director of Program Administration, Rhode Island Higher Education Assistance Authority, 560 Jefferson Boulevard, Suite 100, Warwick, RI 02886. *E-mail:* grants@riheaa.org. *Phone:* 401-736-1170. *Fax:* 401-736-1178. *Web site:* http://www.riheaa.org/.

SOUTH CAROLINA

Educational Assistance for Certain War Veterans Dependents Scholarship-South Carolina. Free tuition for South Carolina residents whose parent is a resident, wartime veteran, and meets one of these criteria; awarded Purple Heart or Congressional Medal of Honor; permanently and totally disabled or killed as a result of military service; prisoner of war; or missing in action. Must be age 18–26 and enrolled or expecting to enroll full or part-time at a two-year or four-year technical institution or university in South Carolina. Complete information and qualifications for this award are on web site http://www.govoepp.state.sc.us. *Award:* Scholarship for use in freshman, sophomore, junior, or senior year; not renewable. *Award amount:* varies. *Number of awards:* varies. *Eligibility Requirements:* Applicant must be age 18-26; enrolled or expecting to enroll full- or part-time at a two-year, four-year, or technical institution or university; resident of South Carolina and studying in South Carolina. Available to U.S. citizens. Applicant or parent must meet one or more of the following requirements: general military experience; retired from active duty; disabled or killed as a result of military service; prisoner of war; or missing in action. *Application Requirements:* Application, transcript, proof of qualification of veteran. **Deadline:** continuous.

Contact Dianne Coley, Free Tuition Program Assistant, South Carolina Division of Veterans Affairs, South Carolina Governor's Office, 1205 Pendleton Street, Suite 369, Columbia, SC 29201. *E-mail:* va@oepp.sc.gov. *Phone:* 803-255-4317. *Web site:* http://www.govoepp.state.sc.us/vetaff.htm.

Palmetto Fellows Scholarship Program. Renewable award for qualified high school seniors in South Carolina to attend a four-year South Carolina institution. The scholarship must be applied directly towards the cost of attendance, less any other gift aid received. *Award:* Scholarship for use in freshman year; renewable. *Award amount:* $6700–$7500. *Number of awards:* 4846. *Eligibility Requirements:* Applicant must be high school student; planning to enroll or expecting to enroll full-time at a four-year institution or university; resident of South Carolina and studying in South Carolina. Applicant must have 3.5 GPA or higher. Available to U.S. citizens. *Application Requirements:* Application, test scores, transcript. **Deadline:** December 15.

Contact Dr. Karen Woodfaulk, Director of Student Services, South Carolina Commission on Higher Education, 1333 Main Street, Suite 200, Columbia, SC 29201. *E-mail:* kwoodfaulk@che.sc.gov. *Phone:* 803-737-2244. *Fax:* 803-737-3610. *Web site:* http://www.che.sc.gov/.

Robert C. Byrd Honors Scholarship-South Carolina. Renewable award for a graduating high school senior from South Carolina, who will be attending a two- or four-year institution. Applicants should be superior students who demonstrate academic achievement and show promise of continued success at a postsecondary institution. Interested applicants should contact their high school counselors after the first week of December for an application. *Award:* Scholarship for use in freshman year; renewable. *Award amount:* varies. *Number of awards:* varies. *Eligibility Requirements:* Applicant must be high school student; planning to enroll or expecting to enroll full-time at a two-year or four-year institution or university and resident of South Carolina. Available to U.S. citizens. *Application Requirements:* Application, test scores, ACT or SAT scores. **Deadline:** varies.

Contact Beth Cope, Program Coordinator, South Carolina Department of Education, 1424 Senate Street, Columbia, SC 29201. *E-mail:* bcope@sde.state.sc.us. *Phone:* 803-734-8116. *Fax:* 803-734-4387. *Web site:* http://www.ed.sc.gov/.

South Carolina HOPE Scholarship. A merit-based scholarship for eligible first-time entering freshman attending a four-year South Carolina institution. Minimum GPA of 3.0 required. Must be a resident of South Carolina. *Award:* Scholarship for use in freshman year; not renewable. *Award amount:* $2800. *Number of awards:* 2605. *Eligibility Requirements:* Applicant must be high school student; planning to enroll or expecting to enroll full-time at a four-year institution or university; resident of South Carolina and studying in South Carolina. Applicant must have 3.0 GPA or higher. Available to U.S. citizens. *Application Requirements:* Transcript. **Deadline:** continuous.

Contact Gerrick Hampton, Scholarship Coordinator, South Carolina Commission on Higher Education, 1333 Main Street, Suite 200, Columbia, SC 29201. *E-mail:* ghampton@che.sc.gov. *Phone:* 803-737-4544. *Fax:* 803-737-3610. *Web site:* http://www.che.sc.gov/.

South Carolina Need-Based Grants Program. Award based on FAFSA. A student may receive up to $2500 annually for full-time and up to $1250 annually for part-time study. The grant must be applied directly towards the cost of college attendance for a maximum of eight full-time equivalent terms. *Award:* Grant for use in freshman, sophomore, junior, senior, or graduate year; renewable. *Award amount:* $1250–$2500. *Number of awards:* 1–26,730. *Eligibility Requirements:* Applicant must be enrolled or expecting to enroll full- or part-time at a two-year, four-year, or technical institution or university; resident of South Carolina and studying in South Carolina. Available to U.S. citizens. *Application Requirements:* Application, financial need analysis. **Deadline:** continuous.

Contact Dr. Karen Woodfaulk, Director of Student Service, South Carolina Commission on Higher Education, 1333 Main Street, Suite 200, Columbia, SC 29201. *E-mail:* kwoodfaulk@che.sc.gov. *Phone:* 803-737-2244. *Fax:* 803-737-2297. *Web site:* http://www.che.sc.gov/.

South Carolina Teacher Loan Program. One-time awards for South Carolina residents attending four-year postsecondary institutions in South Carolina. Recipients must teach in the South Carolina public school system in a critical-need area after graduation. Twenty percent of loan forgiven for each year of service. Write for additional requirements. *Academic Fields/Career Goals:* Education; Special Education. *Award:* Forgivable loan for use in freshman, sophomore, junior, senior, or graduate year; not renewable. *Award amount:* $2500–$5000. *Number of awards:* up to 1121. *Eligibility Requirements:* Applicant must be enrolled or expecting to enroll full- or part-time at a four-year institution or university; resident of South Carolina and studying in South Carolina. Applicant must have 3.0 GPA or higher. Available to U.S. citizens. *Application Requirements:* Application, references, test scores, promissory note. **Deadline:** June 1.

Contact Jennifer Jones-Gaddy, Vice President, South Carolina Student Loan Corporation, PO Box 21487, Columbia, SC 29221. *E-mail:* jgaddy@slc.sc.edu. *Phone:* 803-798-0916. *Fax:* 803-772-9410. *Web site:* http://www.scstudentloan.org/.

South Carolina Tuition Grants Program. Need-based grant set aside for 21 eligible independent colleges in South Carolina. Student must be a South Carolina resident. Must apply annually by submitting the Free Application for Federal Student Aid (FAFSA). Freshmen must graduate in top 75% of high school class OR score 900 on SAT/19 on ACT OR graduate with at least 2.0 on SC Uniform Grading Scale. Upperclassmen must pass a minimum of 24 credit hours annually. *Award:* Grant for use in freshman, sophomore, junior, or senior year; not renewable. *Award amount:* $100–$2600. *Eligibility Requirements:* Applicant must be enrolled or expecting to enroll full-time at a two-year or four-year institution or university; resident of South Carolina and studying in South Carolina. Available to U.S. citizens. *Application Requirements:* Application, FAFSA. **Deadline:** June 30.

Contact Toni K. Cave, Financial Aid Counselor, South Carolina Tuition Grants Commission, 800 Dutch Square Boulevard, Suite 260A, Columbia, SC 29210. *E-mail:* toni@sctuitiongrants.org. *Phone:* 803-896-1120. *Fax:* 803-896-1126. *Web site:* http://www.sctuitiongrants.com/.

SOUTH DAKOTA

Haines Memorial Scholarship. One-time scholarship for South Dakota public university students who are sophomores, juniors, or seniors having at least a 2.5 GPA and majoring in a teacher education program. Must include resume with application. Must be South Dakota resident. *Academic Fields/Career Goals:* Education. *Award:* Scholarship for use in sophomore, junior, or senior year; not renewable. *Award amount:* $2150. *Number of awards:* 1. *Eligibility Requirements:* Applicant must be enrolled or expecting to enroll full-time at an institution or university; resident of South Dakota and studying in South Dakota. Applicant must have 3.5 GPA or higher. Available to U.S. citizens. *Application Requirements:* Application, essay, resume, typed statement describing personal philosophy and philosophy of education. **Deadline:** February 8.

Contact Dr. Paul D. Turman, Director of Academic Assessment, South Dakota Board of Regents, 306 East Capitol Avenue, Suite 200, Pierre, SD 57501-2545. *E-mail:* pault@sdbor.edu. *Phone:* 605-773-3455. *Web site:* http://www.sdbor.edu/.

South Dakota Opportunity Scholarship. Renewable scholarship may be worth up to $5000 over four years to students who take a rigorous college-prep curriculum while in high school and stay in the state for their postsecondary education. *Award:* Scholarship for use in freshman, sophomore, junior, or senior year; renewable. *Award amount:* $1000. *Number of awards:* 1000. *Eligibility Requirements:* Applicant must be high school student; planning to enroll or expecting to enroll full-time at a two-year, four-year, or technical institution or university; resident of South Dakota and studying in South Dakota. Applicant must have 3.0 GPA or higher. Available to U.S. citizens. *Application Requirements:* Application, test scores, transcript. **Deadline:** September 1.

Contact Janelle Toman, Scholarship Committee, South Dakota Board of Regents, 306 East Capitol, Suite 200, Pierre, SD 57501-2545. *E-mail:* info@sdbor.edu. *Phone:* 605-773-3455. *Fax:* 605-773-2422. *Web site:* http://www.sdbor.edu/.

TENNESSEE

Christa McAuliffe Scholarship Program. Scholarship to assist and support Tennessee students who have demonstrated a commitment to a career in educating the youth of Tennessee. Offered to college seniors for a period of one academic year. Must have a minimum college GPA of 3.5. Must have attained scores on either the ACT or SAT which meet or exceed the national norms. Award is made on a periodic basis as funding becomes available. *Academic Fields/Career Goals:* Education. *Award:* Scholarship for use in senior year; not renewable. *Award amount:* up to $500. *Number of awards:* up to 1. *Eligibility Requirements:* Applicant must be enrolled or expecting to enroll full-time at a four-year institution or university; resident of Tennessee and studying in Tennessee. Applicant must have 3.5 GPA or higher. Available to U.S. citizens. *Application Requirements:* Application, essay. **Deadline:** April 1.

Contact Ms. Kathy Stripling, Scholarship Administrator, Tennessee Student Assistance Corporation, Parkway Towers, 404 James Robertson Parkway, Suite 1510, Nashville, TN 37243-0820. *E-mail:* kathy.stripling@tn.gov. *Phone:* 866-291-2675 Ext. 155. *Fax:* 615-741-6101. *Web site:* http://www.tn.gov/collegepays.

Dependent Children Scholarship Program. Scholarship for Tennessee residents who are dependent children of a Tennessee law enforcement officer, fireman, or an emergency medical service technician who has been killed or totally and permanently disabled while performing duties within the scope of such employment. The scholarship is awarded to full-time undergraduate students for a maximum of four academic years or the period required for the completion of the program of study. *Award:* Scholarship for use in freshman, sophomore, junior, or senior year; renewable. *Award amount:* varies. *Eligibility Requirements:* Applicant must be enrolled or expecting to enroll full-time at a two-year or four-year institution or university; resident of Tennessee and studying in Tennessee. Available to U.S. citizens. *Application Requirements:* Application, FAFSA. **Deadline:** July 15.

Contact Ms. Naomi Derryberry, Director of Grant and Scholarship Programs, Tennessee Student Assistance Corporation, Parkway Towers, 404 James Robertson Parkway, Suite 1510, Nashville, TN 37243-0820. *E-mail:* naomi.derryberry@tn.gov. *Phone:* 866-291-2675 Ext. 125. *Fax:* 615-741-6101. *Web site:* http://www.tn.gov/collegepays.

Helping Heroes Grant. Provides assistance to Tennessee veterans who have been awarded the Iraq Campaign Medal, Afghanistan Campaign Medal, or Global War on Terrorism Expeditionary Medal (on or after 9/11/01) and who meet eligibility requirements for the program. Award is up to $2000 per year. For more information, visit http://www.TN.gov/collegepays. *Award:* Grant for use in freshman, sophomore, junior, or senior year; not renewable. *Award amount:* up to $2000. *Eligibility Requirements:* Applicant must be enrolled or expecting to enroll full- or part-time at a two-year or four-year institution or university. Available to U.S. citizens. *Application Requirements:* Application, DD-214. **Deadline:** September 1.

Contact Mr. Robert Biggers, Director of Lottery Programs, Tennessee Student Assistance Corporation, Parkway Towers, Suite 1510, 404 James Robertson Parkway, Nashville, TN 37243. *E-mail:* robert.biggers@tn.gov. *Phone:* 866-291-2675 Ext. 106. *Fax:* 615-741-6101. *Web site:* http://www.tn.gov/collegepays.

HOPE with ASPIRE. HOPE Scholarship of $4,000 (four-year institution) or $2,000 (two-year institution) with $1500 supplement. Must meet Tennessee HOPE Scholarship requirements and Adjusted Gross Income (AGI) attributable to the student must be $36,000 or less. *Award:* Scholarship for use in freshman, sophomore, junior, or senior year; renewable. *Award amount:* up to $5500. *Number of awards:* varies. *Eligibility Requirements:* Applicant must be enrolled or expecting to enroll full- or part-time at a two-year or four-year institution or university; resident of Tennessee and studying in Tennessee. Applicant must have 3.0 GPA or higher. Available to U.S. citizens. *Application Requirements:* Application, financial need analysis. **Deadline:** September 1.

Contact Mr. Robert Biggers, Director of Lottery Scholarship Programs, Tennessee Student Assistance Corporation, Parkway Towers, 404 James Robertson Parkway, Suite 1510, Nashville, TN 37243-0820. *E-mail:* robert.biggers@tn.gov. *Phone:* 866-291-2675 Ext. 106. *Fax:* 615-741-6101. *Web site:* http://www.tn.gov/collegepays.

Minority Teaching Fellows Program/Tennessee. Forgivable loan for minority Tennessee residents pursuing teaching careers. Minimum 2.75 GPA required for high school applicant, minimum 2.5 GPA required for college applicant. Must be in the top quarter of the class or score an 18 on ACT. Must teach one year for each year the award is received, or repay loan. *Academic Fields/Career Goals:* Education; Special Education. *Award:* Forgivable loan for use in freshman, sophomore, junior, or senior year; renewable. *Award amount:* up to $5000. *Number of awards:* 19–116. *Eligibility Requirements:* Applicant must be American Indian/Alaska Native, Asian/Pacific Islander, Black (non-Hispanic), or Hispanic; enrolled or expecting to enroll full-time at a two-year or four-year institution or university; resident of Tennessee and studying in Tennessee. Available to U.S. citizens. *Application Requirements:* Application, essay, references, test scores, transcript, statement of Intent. **Deadline:** April 15.

Contact Mr. Mike McCormack, Scholarship Administrator, Tennessee Student Assistance Corporation, Parkway Towers, 404 James Robertson Parkway, Suite 1510, Nashville, TN 37243-0820. *E-mail:* mike.mccormack@tn.gov. *Phone:* 866-291-2675 Ext. 140. *Fax:* 615-741-6101. *Web site:* http://www.tn.gov/collegepays.

Ned McWherter Scholars Program. Award for Tennessee high school seniors with high academic ability. Must have minimum high school GPA of 3.5 and a score of 29 on the ACT or SAT equivalent. Must attend a college or university in Tennessee and be a permanent U.S. citizen. For more information, visit web site http://tn.gov/collegepays. *Award:* Scholarship for use in freshman, sophomore, junior, or senior year; renewable. *Award amount:* up to $3000. *Number of awards:* up to 200. *Eligibility Requirements:* Applicant must be enrolled or expecting to enroll full-time at a two-year, four-year, or technical institution or university; resident of Tennessee and studying in Tennessee. Applicant must have 3.5 GPA or higher. Available to U.S. citizens. *Application Requirements:* Application, test scores, transcript. **Deadline:** February 15.

Contact Mrs. Kathy Stripling, Scholarship Administrator, Tennessee Student Assistance Corporation, 404 James Robertson Parkway, Suite 1510, Parkway Towers, Nashville, TN 37243-0820. *E-mail:* kathy.stripling@tn.gov. *Phone:* 866-291-2675 Ext. 155. *Fax:* 615-741-6101. *Web site:* http://www.tn.gov/collegepays.

Tennessee Dual Enrollment Grant. Grant for study at an eligible Tennessee postsecondary institution awarded to juniors and seniors in a Tennessee high school who have been admitted to undergraduate study while still pursuing a high school diploma. For more information, visit web site http://www.tn.gov/collegepays. *Award:* Grant for use in freshman year; renewable. *Award amount:* up to $600. *Eligibility Requirements:* Applicant must be high school student; planning to enroll or expecting to enroll part-time at a two-year, four-year, or technical institution or university; resident of Tennessee and studying in Tennessee. Available to U.S. citizens. *Application Requirements:* Application. **Deadline:** September 1.

Contact Mr. Robert Biggers, Director of Lottery Scholarship Program, Tennessee Student Assistance Corporation, Parkway Towers, 404 James Robertson Parkway, Suite 1510, Nashville, TN 37243-0820. *E-mail:* robert.biggers@tn.gov. *Phone:* 866-291-2675 Ext. 106. *Fax:* 615-741-1601. *Web site:* http://www.tn.gov/collegepays.

Tennessee Education Lottery Scholarship Program HOPE Access Grant. Nonrenewable award of $2,750 for students at four-year colleges or $1,750 for students at two-year colleges. Entering freshmen must have a minimum GPA of 2.75, ACT score of 18–20 (or SAT equivalent), and adjusted gross income attributable to the student must be $36,000 or less. Recipients will become eligible for Tennessee HOPE Scholarship by meeting HOPE Scholarship renewal criteria. *Award:* Scholarship for use in freshman, sophomore, junior, or senior year; not renewable. *Award amount:* up to $2750. *Number of awards:* varies. *Eligibility Requirements:* Applicant must be enrolled or expecting to enroll full- or part-time at a two-year or four-year institution or university; resident of Tennessee and studying in Tennessee. Available to U.S. citizens. *Application Requirements:* Application, financial need analysis. **Deadline:** September 1.

Contact Mr. Robert Biggers, Director of Lottery Scholarship Programs, Tennessee Student Assistance Corporation, Parkway Towers, 404 James Robertson Parkway, Suite 1510, Nashville, TN 37243-0820. *E-mail:* robert.biggers@tn.gov. *Phone:* 866-291-2675 Ext. 106. *Fax:* 615-741-6101. *Web site:* http://www.tn.gov/collegepays.

Tennessee Education Lottery Scholarship Program-HOPE with General Assembly Merit Scholarship (GAMS). HOPE Scholarship of $4,000 (four-year institution) or $2,00 (two-year institution) with supplemental award of $1,000. Entering freshmen must have 3.75 GPA and 29 ACT (1280 SAT). Must be a U.S. citizen and a resident of Tennessee. *Award:* Scholarship for use in freshman, sophomore, junior, or senior year; renewable. *Award amount:* up to $5000. *Number of awards:* varies. *Eligibility Requirements:* Applicant must be enrolled or expecting to enroll full- or part-time at a two-year or four-year institution or university; resident of Tennessee and studying in Tennessee. Available to U.S. citizens. *Application Requirements:* Application. **Deadline:** September 1.

Contact Mr. Robert Biggers, Director of Lottery Scholarship Programs, Tennessee Student Assistance Corporation, Parkway Towers, 404 James Robertson Parkway, Suite 1510, Nashville, TN 37243-0820. *E-mail:* robert.biggers@tn.gov. *Phone:* 866-291-2675 Ext. 106. *Fax:* 615-741-6101. *Web site:* http://www.tn.gov/collegepays.

Tennessee Education Lottery Scholarship Program Tennessee HOPE Scholarship. Award amount is $4,000 for four-year institutions and $2,000 for two-year institutions. Must be a Tennessee resident attending an eligible postsecondary institution in Tennessee. For more information, visit http://www.TN.gov/CollegePays. *Award:* Scholarship for use in freshman, sophomore, junior, or senior year; renewable. *Award amount:* $2000–$4000. *Number of awards:* varies. *Eligibility Requirements:* Applicant must be enrolled or expecting to enroll full- or part-time at a two-year or four-year institution or university; resident of Tennessee and studying in Tennessee. Applicant must have 3.0 GPA or higher. Available to U.S. citizens. *Application Requirements:* Application. **Deadline:** September 1.

Contact Mr. Robert Biggers, Director of Lottery Scholarship Programs, Tennessee Student Assistance Corporation, Parkway Towers, 404 James Robertson Parkway, Suite 1510, Nashville, TN 37243-0820. *E-mail:* robert.biggers@tn.gov. *Phone:* 866-291-2675 Ext. 106. *Fax:* 615-741-6101. *Web site:* http://www.tn.gov/collegepays.

Tennessee Education Lottery Scholarship Program Wilder-Naifeh Technical Skills Grant. Award up to $2,000 for students enrolled in a certificate or diploma program at a Tennessee Technology Center. Cannot be prior recipient of Tennessee HOPE Scholarship. For more information, visit http://www.TN.gov/CollegePays. *Award:* Grant for use in freshman or sophomore year; renewable. *Award amount:* up to $2000. *Number of awards:* varies. *Eligibility Requirements:* Applicant must be enrolled or expecting to enroll full- or part-time at a technical institution; resident of Tennessee and studying in Tennessee. Available to U.S. citizens. *Application Requirements:* Application. **Deadline:** November 1.

Contact Mr. Robert Biggers, Director of Lottery Scholarship Programs, Tennessee Student Assistance Corporation, Parkway Towers, 404 James Robertson Parkway, Suite 1510, Nashville, TN 37243-0820. *E-mail:* robert.biggers@tn.gov. *Phone:* 866-291-2675 Ext. 106. *Fax:* 615-741-6101. *Web site:* http://www.tn.gov/collegepays.

Tennessee HOPE Foster Child Tuition Grant. Renewable tuition award available for recipients of the HOPE Scholarship or HOPE Access Grant. Student must have been in Tennessee state custody as a foster child for at least one year after reaching age 14. Award amount varies and shall not exceed the tuition and mandatory fees at an eligible Tennessee public postsecondary institution. For additional information, visit web site http://www.tn.gov/collegepays. *Award:* Scholarship for use in freshman, sophomore, junior, or senior year; renewable. *Eligibility Requirements:* Applicant must be enrolled or expecting to enroll full- or part-time at a two-year or four-year institution or university; resident of Tennessee and studying in Tennessee. Applicant must have 3.0 GPA or higher. Available to U.S. citizens. *Application Requirements:* Application. **Deadline:** September 1.

Contact Mr. Robert Biggers, Director of Lottery Scholarship Programs, Tennessee Student Assistance Corporation, Parkway Towers, 404 James Robertson Parkway, Suite 1510, Nashville, TN 37243-0820. *E-mail:* robert.biggers@tn.gov. *Phone:* 866-291-2675 Ext. 106. *Fax:* 615-741-6101. *Web site:* http://www.tn.gov/collegepays.

Tennessee Student Assistance Award. Award to assist financially-needy Tennessee residents attending an approved college or university within the state. Complete a Free Application for Federal Student Aid form. FAFSA must be processed as soon as possible after January 1 for priority consideration. For more information, see http://www.fafsa.gov. *Award:* Grant for use in freshman, sophomore, junior, or senior year; not renewable. *Award amount:* $100–$4000. *Number of awards:* 25,000–35,000. *Eligibility Requirements:* Applicant must be enrolled or expecting to enroll full- or part-time at a two-year, four-year, or technical institution or university; resident of Tennessee and studying in Tennessee. Available to U.S. citizens. *Application Requirements:* Application, financial need analysis.

Contact Ms. Naomi Derryberry, Director of Grants and Scholarship Programs, Tennessee Student Assistance Corporation, Parkway Towers, 404 James Robertson Parkway, Suite 1510, Nashville, TN 37243-0820. *E-mail:* naomi.derryberry@tn.gov. *Phone:* 866-291-2675 Ext. 125. *Fax:* 615-741-6101. *Web site:* http://www.tn.gov/collegepays.

Tennessee Teaching Scholars Program. Forgivable loan for college juniors, seniors, and college graduates admitted to a teacher education program in Tennessee with a minimum GPA of 2.75. Students must commit to teach in a Tennessee public school one year for each year of the award. Must be a U.S. citizen and resident of Tennessee. *Academic Fields/Career Goals:* Education. *Award:* Forgivable loan for use in junior, senior, or graduate year; renewable. *Award amount:* up to $4500. *Number of awards:* up to 180. *Eligibility Requirements:* Applicant must be enrolled or expecting to enroll full- or part-time at a four-year institution or university; resident of Tennessee and studying in Tennessee. Available to U.S. citizens. *Application Requirements:* Application, references, test scores, transcript. **Deadline:** April 15.

Contact Mr. Mike McCormack, Scholarship Administrator, Tennessee Student Assistance Corporation, 404 James Robertson Parkway, Suite 1510, Parkway Towers, Nashville, TN 37243-0820. *E-mail:* mike.mccormack@tn.gov. *Phone:* 866-291-2675 Ext. 140. *Fax:* 615-741-6101. *Web site:* http://www.tn.gov/collegepays.

TEXAS

Conditional Grant Program. Renewable award to students who are considered economically disadvantaged based on federal guidelines. The maximum amount awarded per semester is $3,000 not to exceed $6000 per academic year. Students already enrolled in an undergraduate program should have minimum GPA 2.5 and students newly enrolling should have minimum GPA 3.0. *Academic Fields/Career Goals:* Civil Engineering; Computer Science/Data Processing; Occupational Safety and Health. *Award:* Grant for use in freshman, sophomore, junior, or senior year; renewable. *Award amount:* up to $6000. *Number of awards:* varies. *Eligibility Requirements:* Applicant must be enrolled or expecting to enroll full-time at a four-year institution or university; resident of Texas and studying in Texas. Available to U.S. citizens. *Application Requirements:* Application, essay, interview, references, test scores, transcript. **Deadline:** March 1.

Contact Minnie Brown, Program Coordinator, Texas Department of Transportation, 125 East 11th Street, Austin, TX 78701-2483. *E-mail:* mbrown2@dot.state.tx.us. *Phone:* 512-416-4979. *Fax:* 512-416-4980. *Web site:* http://www.txdot.gov/.

Texas National Guard Tuition Assistance Program. Provides exemption from the payment of tuition to certain members of the Texas National Guard, Texas Air Guard or the State Guard. Must be Texas resident and attend school in Texas. Deadline varies. *Award:* Scholarship for use in freshman, sophomore, junior, or senior year; renewable. *Award amount:* varies. *Number of awards:* varies. *Eligibility Requirements:* Applicant must be enrolled or expecting to enroll full- or part-time at a four-year institution or university; resident of Texas and studying in Texas. Available to U.S. citizens. Applicant or parent must meet one or more of the following requirements: Air Force National Guard or Army National Guard experience; retired from active duty; disabled or killed as a result of military service; prisoner of war; or missing in action. *Application Requirements:* Application. **Deadline:** varies.

Contact State Adjutant General's Office, Texas Higher Education Coordinating Board, PO Box 5218, Austin, TX 78763-5218. *E-mail:* education.office@tx.ngb.army.mil. *Phone:* 512-465-5515. *Web site:* http://www.collegefortexans.com/.

Texas Professional Nursing Scholarships. Award to provide financial assistance to encourage students to become Professional Nurses. Only in-state (Texas) colleges or universities may participate in the program. Both public and private, non-profit colleges or universities with professional nursing programs may participate in the programs. *Academic Fields/Career Goals:* Nursing. *Award:* Scholarship for use in freshman, sophomore, junior, or senior year; not renewable. *Award amount:* $2500. *Eligibility Requirements:* Applicant must be enrolled or expecting to enroll at a two-year, four-year, or technical institution; resident of Texas and studying in Texas. *Application Requirements:* Application, financial need analysis.

Contact Grants and Special Programs, Texas Higher Education Coordinating Board, PO Box 12788, Austin, TX 78711-2788. *E-mail:* grantinfo@thecb.state.tx.us. *Phone:* 512-427-6101. *Web site:* http://www.collegefortexans.com/.

Toward EXcellence Access and Success (TEXAS Grant). Renewable aid for students enrolled in public colleges or universities in Texas. Must be a resident of Texas and have completed the Recommended High School Curriculum or Distinguished Achievement Curriculum in high school. For renewal awards, must maintain a minimum GPA of 2.5. Based on need. Amount of award is determined by the financial aid office of each school. Deadlines vary. Contact the college/university financial aid office for application information. *Award:* Grant for use in freshman, sophomore, junior, or senior year; renewable. *Award amount:* $2680–$6080. *Eligibility Requirements:* Applicant must be enrolled or expecting to enroll full- or part-time at a two-year, four-year, or technical institution or university; resident of Texas and studying in Texas. Available to U.S. citizens. *Application Requirements:* Financial need analysis, transcript.

Contact Financial Aid Office of relevant school, Texas Higher Education Coordinating Board. *Web site:* http://www.collegefortexans.com/.

Tuition Equalization Grant (TEG) Program. Renewable award for Texas residents enrolled full-time at an independent college or university within the state. Based on financial need. Renewal awards require the student to maintain an overall college GPA of at least 2.5. Deadlines vary by institution. Must not be receiving athletic scholarship. Contact college/university financial aid office for application information. Nonresidents who are National Merit Finalists may also receive awards. *Award:* Grant for use in freshman, sophomore, junior, or senior year; renewable. *Award amount:* $3808–$5712. *Eligibility Requirements:* Applicant must be enrolled or expecting to enroll full-time at a two-year or four-year institution or university; resident of Texas and studying in Texas. Available to U.S. citizens. *Application Requirements:* Financial need analysis, FAFSA.

Contact Financial Aid Office of Relevant Institution, Texas Higher Education Coordinating Board. *Web site:* http://www.collegefortexans.com/.

Vanessa Rudloff Scholarship Program. Scholarships of $1000 awarded to qualified TWLE members and their dependents who are entering or continuing students at an accredited college or university. For details refer to web site http://www.twle.net/. *Award:* Scholarship for use in freshman, sophomore, junior, senior, graduate, or postgraduate years; not renewable. *Award amount:* $1000. *Number of awards:* 4. *Eligibility Requirements:* Applicant must be enrolled or expecting to enroll full- or part-time at a two-year, four-year, or technical institution or university. Applicant or parent of applicant must be member of Texas Women in Law Enforcement. Applicant must have 3.0 GPA or higher. Available to U.S. and non-U.S. citizens. *Application Requirements:* Application, essay, references. **Deadline:** April 15.

Contact Glenda Baker, Scholarship Awards Chairperson, Texas Women in Law Enforcement, 12605 Rhea Court, Austin, TX 78727. *E-mail:* gbakerab@aol.com. *Web site:* http://www.twle.com/.

UTAH

New Century Scholarship. The New Century Scholarship is for Utah high school students who complete the requirements for an Associate's Degree by September 1st of the year they graduate from high school. Recipients receive an award of up to 75% of Bachelor Degree tuition at eligible institutions in Utah for up to 60 credit hours. *Award:* Scholarship for use in junior or senior year; renewable. *Award amount:* $457–$2682. *Number of awards:* 1. *Eligibility Requirements:* Applicant must be enrolled or expecting to enroll full-time at a four-year institution or university; resident of Utah and studying in Utah. Applicant must have 3.0 GPA or higher. Available to U.S. citizens. *Application Requirements:* Application, transcript, GPA/copy of enrollment verification from an eligible Utah 4-year institution, verification from registrar of completion of requirements for associate's degree. **Deadline:** January 8.

Contact David Hughes, Manager of Financial Aid, State of Utah, Board of Regents Building, The Gateway, 60 South 400 West, Salt Lake City, UT 84101-1284. *E-mail:* dhughes@utahsbr.edu. *Phone:* 801-321-7221. *Web site:* http://www.utahsbr.edu/.

T.H. Bell Teaching Incentive Loan-Utah. Renewable awards for Utah residents who are high school seniors wishing to pursue teaching careers. The award value varies depending upon tuition and fees at a Utah institution. Must agree to teach in a Utah public school or pay back loan through monthly installments. *Academic Fields/ Career Goals:* Education. *Award:* Forgivable loan for use in freshman, sophomore, junior, or senior year; renewable. *Award amount:* varies. *Number of awards:* 25–50. *Eligibility Requirements:* Applicant must be enrolled or expecting to enroll full-time at a four-year institution or university; resident of Utah and studying in Utah. Available to U.S. citizens. *Application Requirements:* Application, essay, test scores, transcript. **Deadline:** March 26.

Contact Linda Alder, Education Specialist, Utah State Office of Education, 250 East 500 South, PO Box 144200, Salt Lake City, UT 84114-4200. *E-mail:* linda.alder@schools.utah.gov. *Phone:* 801-538-7923. *Fax:* 801-538-7973. *Web site:* http://www.schools.utah.gov/cert.

Utah Centennial Opportunity Program for Education. Award available to students with substantial financial need for use at any of the participating Utah institutions. The student must be a Utah resident. Contact the financial aid office of the participating institution for requirements and deadlines. *Award:* Grant for use in freshman, sophomore, junior, or senior year; not renewable. *Award amount:* $300–$5000. *Number of awards:* up to 2988. *Eligibility Requirements:* Applicant must be enrolled or expecting to enroll full- or part-time at a two-year, four-year, or technical institution or university; resident of Utah and studying in Utah. Available to U.S. citizens. *Application Requirements:* Financial need analysis, FAFSA. **Deadline:** continuous.

Contact Mr. David P. Hughes, Manager of Financial Aid and Scholarships, Utah State Board of Regents, 60 South 400 West, The Board of Regents Building, The Gateway, Salt Lake City, UT 84101-1284. *E-mail:* dhughes@utahsbr.edu. *Phone:* 801-321-7220. *Fax:* 801-321-7168. *Web site:* http://www.uheaa.org/.

Utah Leveraging Educational Assistance Partnership. Award available to Utah resident students with substantial financial need for use at any of the participating Utah institutions. Contact the financial aid office of the participating institution for requirements and deadlines. *Award:* Grant for use in freshman, sophomore, junior, or senior year; not renewable. *Award amount:* $300–$2500. *Number of awards:* up to 3252. *Eligibility Requirements:* Applicant must be enrolled or expecting to enroll full- or part-time at a two-year, four-year, or technical institution or university; resident of Utah and studying in Utah. Available to U.S. citizens. *Application Requirements:* Financial need analysis, FAFSA. **Deadline:** continuous.

Contact Mr. David P. Hughes, Manager of Financial Aid and Scholarships, Utah State Board of Regents, 60 South 400 West, The Board of Regents Building, The Gateway, Salt Lake City, UT 84101-1284. *E-mail:* dhughes@utahsbr.edu. *Phone:* 801-321-7220. *Fax:* 801-321-7168. *Web site:* http://www.uheaa.org/.

VERMONT

Vermont Incentive Grants. Renewable grants for Vermont residents based on financial need. Must meet needs test. Must be college undergraduate or graduate student enrolled full-time at an approved post secondary institution. Only available to Vermont residents. *Award:* Grant for use in freshman, sophomore, junior, or senior year; renewable. *Award amount:* $500–$10,800. *Number of awards:* varies. *Eligibility Requirements:* Applicant must be enrolled or expecting to enroll full-time at a two-year, four-year, or technical institution or university and resident of Vermont. Available to U.S. citizens. *Application Requirements:* Application, financial need analysis, FAFSA. **Deadline:** continuous.

Contact Grant Program, Vermont Student Assistance Corporation, PO Box 2000, Winooski, VT 05404-2000. *Phone:* 802-655-9602. *Fax:* 802-654-3765. *Web site:* http://www.vsac.org/.

Vermont Non-Degree Student Grant Program. Need-based, renewable grants for Vermont residents enrolled in non-degree programs in a college, vocational school, or high school adult program, that will improve employability or encourage further study. Award amounts vary. *Award:* Grant for use in freshman, sophomore, junior, or senior year; renewable. *Award amount:* varies. *Number of awards:* varies. *Eligibility Requirements:* Applicant must be enrolled or expecting to enroll full- or part-time at a two-year, four-year, or technical institution or university and resident of Vermont. Available to U.S. citizens. *Application Requirements:* Application, financial need analysis. **Deadline:** continuous.

Contact Grant Program Department, Vermont Student Assistance Corporation, 10 East Allen Street, PO Box 2000, Winooski, VT 05404-2000. *Phone:* 802-655-9602. *Web site:* http://www.vsac.org/.

Vermont Part-Time Student Grants. For undergraduates carrying less than twelve credits per semester who have not received a bachelor's degree. Must be Vermont resident. Based on financial need. Complete Vermont Financial Aid Packet to apply. May be used at any approved post-secondary institution. *Award:* Grant for use in freshman, sophomore, junior, or senior year; renewable. *Award amount:* $250–$8100. *Number of awards:* varies. *Eligibility Requirements:* Applicant must be enrolled or expecting to enroll part-time at a four-year institution or university and resident of Vermont. Available to U.S. citizens. *Application Requirements:* Application, financial need analysis. **Deadline:** continuous.

Contact Grant Program, Vermont Student Assistance Corporation, PO Box 2000, Winooski, VT 05404-2000. *Phone:* 802-655-9602. *Fax:* 802-654-3765. *Web site:* http://www.vsac.org/.

VIRGINIA

College Scholarship Assistance Program. Need-based scholarship for undergraduate study by a Virginia resident at a participating Virginia two- or four-year college, or university. Contact financial aid office at the participating Virginia public or nonprofit private institution. The program does not have its own application; institutions use results from the federal FAFSA form. *Award:* Grant for use in freshman, sophomore, junior, or senior year; not renewable. *Award amount:* $400–$5000. *Number of awards:* varies. *Eligibility Requirements:* Applicant must be enrolled or expecting to enroll full- or part-time at a two-year or four-year institution or university; resident of Virginia and studying in Virginia. Available to U.S. citizens. *Application Requirements:* Financial need analysis.

Contact Contact the financial aid office of participating Virginia college., Virginia State Council of Higher Education. *Web site:* http://www.schev.edu/.

Gheens Foundation Scholarship. Scholarship supports African American students from Louisville, KY. For use in one of the following universities: Clark Atlanta University, Morehouse College, Spelman College, Tuskegee University, Howard University. Apply online at http://www.uncf.org. *Award:* Scholarship for use in freshman, sophomore, junior, or senior year; not renewable. *Award amount:* up to $2000. *Number of awards:* varies. *Eligibility Requirements:* Applicant must be Black (non-Hispanic); enrolled or expecting to enroll full- or part-time at a four-year institution or university; resident of Kentucky and studying in Alabama, District of Columbia, or Georgia. Applicant must have 2.5 GPA or higher. Available to U.S. citizens. *Application Requirements:* Application, financial need analysis, transcript.

Contact Director, Program Services, United Negro College Fund, 8260 Willow Oaks Corporate Drive, PO Box 10444, Fairfax, VA 22031-8044. *E-mail:* rebecca.bennett@uncf.org. *Phone:* 800-331-2244. *Web site:* http://www.uncf.org/.

Mary Marshall Practical Nursing Scholarships. Award for practical nursing students who are Virginia residents. Must attend a nursing program in Virginia. Recipient must agree to work in Virginia after graduation. Minimum 3.0 GPA required. Scholarship value and the number of scholarships granted varies annually. *Academic Fields/Career Goals:* Nursing. *Award:* Scholarship for use in freshman, sophomore, junior, or senior year; not renewable. *Award .amount:* $150–$500. *Number of awards:* 50–150. *Eligibility Requirements:* Applicant must be age 18 and over; enrolled or expecting to enroll full- or part-time at a four-year institution or university; resident of Virginia and studying in Virginia. Applicant must have 3.0 GPA or higher. Available to U.S. citizens. *Application Requirements:* Application, financial need analysis, references, transcript. **Deadline:** June 30.

Contact Mrs. Aileen Harris, Healthcare Workforce Manager, Virginia Department of Health, Office of Minority Health and Public Health Policy, PO Box 2448, 109 Governor Street, Suite 1016-E, Richmond, VA 23218-2448. *E-mail:* aileen.harris@vdh.virginia.gov. *Phone:* 804-864-7435. *Fax:* 804-864-7440. *Web site:* http://www.vdh.virginia.gov/.

Mary Marshall Registered Nurse Scholarships. Award for registered nursing students who are Virginia residents. Must attend a nursing program in Virginia. Recipient must agree to work in Virginia after graduation. Minimum 3.0 GPA required. The amount of each scholarship award is dependent upon the amount of money appropriated by the Virginia General Assembly and the number of qualified applicants. *Academic Fields/Career Goals:* Nursing. *Award:* Scholarship for use in freshman, sophomore, junior, or senior year; not renewable. *Award amount:* $2000. *Eligibility Requirements:* Applicant must be enrolled or expecting to enroll full- or part-time at a four-year institution or university; resident of Virginia and studying in Virginia. Applicant must have 3.0 GPA or higher. Available to U.S. citizens. *Application Requirements:* Application, financial need analysis, references, transcript. **Deadline:** June 30.

Contact Mrs. Aileen Harris, Healthcare Workforce Manager, Virginia Department of Health, Office of Minority Health and Public Health Policy, PO Box 2448, 109 Governor Street, Suite 1016-E, Richmond, VA 23218-2448. *E-mail:* aileen.harris@vdh.virginia.gov. *Phone:* 804-864-7435. *Fax:* 804-864-7440. *Web site:* http://www.vdh.virginia.gov/.

NRA Youth Educational Summit (YES) Scholarships. Awards for Youth Educational Summit participants based on the initial application, on-site debate, and degree of participation during the week-long event. Must be graduating high school seniors enrolled in undergraduate program. Must have a minimum GPA of 3.0. *Award:* Scholarship for use in freshman year; not renewable. *Award amount:* $1000–$10,000. *Number of awards:* 1–6. *Eligibility Requirements:* Applicant must be high school student and planning to enroll or expecting to enroll full- or part-time at a two-year, four-year, or technical institution or university. Applicant must have 3.0 GPA or higher. Available to U.S. citizens. *Application Requirements:* Application, applicant must enter a contest, essay, references, transcript. **Deadline:** March 1.

Contact Event Services Manager, National Rifle Association, 11250 Waples Mill Road, Fairfax, VA 22030. *E-mail:* fnra@nrahq.org. *Phone:* 703-267-1354. *Web site:* http://www.nrafoundation.org/.

Nurse Practitioners/Nurse Midwife Program Scholarships. One-time award for nurse practitioner/nurse midwife students who have been residents of Virginia for at least one year. Must attend a nursing program in Virginia. Recipient must agree to work in an under-served community in Virginia following graduation. The amount of each scholarship award is dependent upon the amount of funds appropriated by the Virginia General Assembly. Minimum 3.0 GPA required. *Academic Fields/Career Goals:* Nursing. *Award:* Scholarship for use in freshman, sophomore, junior, or senior year; not renewable. *Award amount:* $5000. *Number of awards:* 5. *Eligibility Requirements:* Applicant must be enrolled or expecting to enroll full- or part-time at a four-year institution or university; resident of Virginia and studying in Virginia. Applicant must have 3.0 GPA or higher. Available to U.S. citizens. *Application Requirements:* Application, essay, references, transcript. **Deadline:** July 31.

Contact Mrs. Aileen Harris, Healthcare Workforce Manager, Virginia Department of Health, Office of Minority Health and Public Health Policy, PO Box 2448, 109 Governor Street, Suite 1016-E, Richmond, VA 23218-2448. *E-mail:* aileen.harris@vdh.virginia.gov. *Phone:* 804-864-7435. *Fax:* 804-864-7440. *Web site:* http://www.vdh.virginia.gov/.

Pennsylvania State Employees Scholarship (SECA). Scholarships for UNCF students from Pennsylvania. Funds may be used for tuition, room and board, books, or to repay federal student loans. Minimum 2.5 GPA required. Prospective applicants should complete the Student Profile found at web site http://www.uncf.org. *Award:* Scholarship for use in freshman, sophomore, junior, or senior year; not renewable. *Award amount:* up to $4000. *Eligibility Requirements:* Applicant must be Black (non-Hispanic); enrolled or expecting to enroll full-time at a four-year institution or university and resident of Pennsylvania. Applicant must have 2.5 GPA or higher. Available to U.S. citizens. *Application Requirements:* Application, financial need analysis, student profile. **Deadline:** July 14.

Contact Director, Program Services, United Negro College Fund, 8260 Willow Oaks Corporate Drive, PO Box 10444, Fairfax, VA 22031-8044. *E-mail:* rebecca.bennett@uncf.org. *Phone:* 800-331-2244. *Web site:* http://www.uncf.org/.

State Department Federal Credit Union Annual Scholarship Program. Scholarships available to members who are currently enrolled in a degree program and have completed 12 credit hours of coursework at an accredited college or university. Must have own account in good standing with SDFCU, have a minimum 2.5 GPA, submit official cumulative transcripts, and describe need for financial assistance to continue their education. Scholarship only open to members of State Department Federal Credit Union. *Award:* Scholarship for use in sophomore, junior, senior, or graduate year; not renewable. *Award amount:* $2500. *Number of awards:* varies. *Eligibility Requirements:* Applicant must be enrolled or expecting to enroll full-time at a four-year institution or university. Applicant must have 2.5 GPA or higher. Available to U.S. and non-U.S. citizens. *Application Requirements:* Application, applicant must enter a contest, financial need analysis, transcript, personal statement. **Deadline:** April 29.

Contact Scholarship Coordinator, State Department Federal Credit Union Annual Scholarship Program, 1630 King Street,

Alexandria, VA 22314-2745. *E-mail:* sdfcu@sdfcu.org. *Phone:* 703-706-5000. *Web site:* http://www.sdfcu.org/.

Virginia Commonwealth Award. Need-based award for undergraduate or graduate study at a Virginia public two- or four-year college, or university. Undergraduates must be Virginia residents. The application and awards process are administered by the financial aid office at the Virginia public institution where student is enrolled. Dollar value of each award varies. Contact financial aid office for application and deadlines. *Award:* Grant for use in freshman, sophomore, junior, or senior year; not renewable. *Award amount:* varies. *Number of awards:* varies. *Eligibility Requirements:* Applicant must be enrolled or expecting to enroll full- or part-time at a two-year or four-year institution or university; resident of Virginia and studying in Virginia. Available to U.S. citizens. *Application Requirements:* Financial need analysis.

Contact Contact the financial aid office of participating Virginia college., Virginia State Council of Higher Education. *Web site:* http://www.schev.edu/.

Virginia Guaranteed Assistance Program. Awards to undergraduate students proportional to their need, up to full tuition, fees and book allowance. Must be a graduate of a Virginia high school. High school GPA of 2.5 required. Must be enrolled full-time in a Virginia two- or four-year institution and demonstrate financial need. Must maintain minimum college GPA of 2.0 for renewal awards. *Award:* Grant for use in freshman, sophomore, junior, or senior year; not renewable. *Award amount:* varies. *Number of awards:* varies. *Eligibility Requirements:* Applicant must be enrolled or expecting to enroll full-time at a two-year or four-year institution or university; resident of Virginia and studying in Virginia. Available to U.S. citizens. *Application Requirements:* Financial need analysis, transcript.

Contact Contact the financial aid office of participating Virginia college., Virginia State Council of Higher Education. *Web site:* http://www.schev.edu/.

Virginia Military Survivors and Dependents Education Program. Scholarships for post-secondary students between ages 16 and 19 to attend Virginia state-supported institutions. Must be child or surviving child of veteran who has either been permanently or totally disabled due to war or other armed conflict; died as a result of war or other armed conflict; or been listed as a POW or MIA. Parent must also meet Virginia residency requirements. *Award:* Scholarship for use in freshman, sophomore, junior, senior, or graduate year; renewable. *Award amount:* varies. *Number of awards:* varies. *Eligibility Requirements:* Applicant must be age 16-19; enrolled or expecting to enroll full-time at a two-year, four-year, or technical institution or university; resident of Virginia and studying in Virginia. Available to U.S. citizens. Applicant or parent must meet one or more of the following requirements: general military experience; retired from active duty; disabled or killed as a result of military service; prisoner of war; or missing in action. *Application Requirements:* Application, references. **Deadline:** varies.

Contact Doris Sullivan, Coordinator, Virginia Department of Veterans Services, Poff Federal Building, 270 Franklin Road, SW, Room 503, Roanoke, VA 24011-2215. *Phone:* 540-857-7101 Ext. 213. *Fax:* 540-857-7573. *Web site:* http://www.dvs.virginia.gov/.

Virginia Tuition Assistance Grant Program (Private Institutions). Awards for undergraduate students. Also available to graduate and first professional degree students pursuing a health-related degree program. Not to be used for religious study. Must be US citizen or eligible non-citizen, Virginia domiciled, and enrolled full-time at an approved private, nonprofit college within Virginia. Information and application available from participating Virginia colleges financial aid office. Visit http://www.schev.edu and click on Financial Aid. *Award:* Grant for use in freshman, sophomore, junior, senior, or graduate year; renewable. *Award amount:* up to $2650. *Number of awards:* 22,000. *Eligibility Requirements:* Applicant must be enrolled or expecting to enroll full-time at a four-year institution or university; resident of Virginia and studying in Virginia. Available to U.S. citizens. *Application Requirements:* Application. **Deadline:** July 31.

Contact Contact the financial aid office of participating Virginia college., Virginia State Council of Higher Education. *Web site:* http://www.schev.edu/.

Walter Reed Smith Scholarship. Award for full-time female undergraduate students who are descendant of a Confederate soldier, studying nutrition, home economics, nursing, business administration, or computer science in accredited college or university. Minimum 3.0 GPA required. Submit application and letter of endorsement from sponsoring chapter of the United Daughters of the Confederacy. *Academic Fields/Career Goals:* Business/Consumer Services; Computer Science/Data Processing; Food Science/Nutrition; Home Economics; Nursing. *Award:* Scholarship for use in freshman, sophomore, junior, or senior year; renewable. *Award amount:* $800–$1000. *Number of awards:* 1–2. *Eligibility Requirements:* Applicant must be enrolled or expecting to enroll full-time at a four-year institution or university and female. Applicant or parent of applicant must be member of United Daughters of the Confederacy. Applicant must have 3.0 GPA or higher. Available to U.S. citizens. *Application Requirements:* Application, essay, financial need analysis, photo, references, self-addressed stamped envelope, transcript, copy of applicant's birth certificate, copy of confederate ancestor's proof of service. **Deadline:** March 15.

Contact United Daughters of the Confederacy, 328 North Boulevard, Richmond, VA 23220-4009. *E-mail:* hqudc@rcn.com. *Phone:* 804-355-1636. *Web site:* http://www.hqudc.org/.

WASHINGTON

American Indian Endowed Scholarship. Awarded to financially needy undergraduate and graduate students with close social and cultural ties with a Native-American community. Must be Washington resident and enrolled full-time at Washington public or private school. Must be committed to use education to return service to the state's American Indian community. *Award:* Scholarship for use in freshman, sophomore, junior, senior, graduate, or postgraduate years; not renewable. *Award amount:* $500–$2000. *Number of awards:* 11–20. *Eligibility Requirements:* Applicant must be American Indian/Alaska Native; enrolled or expecting to enroll full-time at a two-year, four-year, or technical institution or university; resident of Washington and studying in Washington. Available to U.S. citizens. *Application Requirements:* Application, essay, references, transcript. **Deadline:** February 1.

Contact Ann Voyles, Program Manager, Washington Higher Education Coordinating Board, 917 Lakeridge Way, PO Box 43430, Olympia, WA 98504-3430. *E-mail:* annv@hecb.wa.gov. *Phone:* 360-753-7843. *Fax:* 360-704-6243. *Web site:* http://www.hecb.wa.gov/.

Passport to College Promise Scholarship. Scholarship to encourage Washington residents who are former foster care youth to prepare for and succeed in college. Recipients must have spent at least one year in foster care after their 16th birthday and emancipated from care. *Award:* Scholarship for use in freshman, sophomore, junior, or senior year; renewable. *Award amount:*

$1–$3000. *Number of awards:* 1–400. *Eligibility Requirements:* Applicant must be age 18-26; enrolled or expecting to enroll full- or part-time at a two-year, four-year, or technical institution or university; resident of Washington and studying in Washington. Available to U.S. citizens. *Application Requirements:* Application, financial need analysis, consent form. **Deadline:** continuous.

Contact Ms. Dawn Cypriano-McAferty, Program Manager, Washington Higher Education Coordinating Board, 917 Lakeridge Way SW, PO Box 43430, Olympia, WA 98504-3430. *E-mail:* passporttocollege@hecb.wa.gov. *Phone:* 888-535-0747 Ext. 5. *Fax:* 360-704-6246. *Web site:* http://www.hecb.wa.gov/.

Washington Award for Vocational Excellence (WAVE). Award to honor vocational students from the legislative districts of Washington. Grants for up to two years of undergraduate resident tuition. Must be enrolled in Washington high school, skills center, or community or technical college at time of application. To be eligible to apply student must complete 360 hours in single vocational program in high school or one year at technical college. Contact principal, guidance counselor, or on-campus WAVE coordinator for more information. *Award:* Scholarship for use in freshman, sophomore, junior, or senior year; renewable. *Award amount:* $1–$8592. *Number of awards:* 147. *Eligibility Requirements:* Applicant must be enrolled or expecting to enroll full- or part-time at a two-year, four-year, or technical institution or university; resident of Washington and studying in Washington. Available to U.S. citizens. *Application Requirements:* Application, references.

Contact Terri Colbert, Program Specialist, Washington Higher Education Coordinating Board, Workforce Training and Education Coordinating Board, PO Box 43105, Olympia, WA 98504-3105. *E-mail:* tcolbert@wtb.wa.gov. *Phone:* 360-753-5680. *Fax:* 360-586-5862. *Web site:* http://www.hecb.wa.gov/.

Washington Scholars Program. Awards high school students from the legislative districts of Washington. Must enroll in college or university in Washington. Scholarships up to four years of full-time resident undergraduate tuition and fees. Student must not pursue a degree in theology. Contact principal or guidance counselor for more information. Requires nomination by high school principal and be in the top 1 percent of his or her graduating senior class. *Award:* Scholarship for use in freshman, sophomore, junior, or senior year; renewable. *Award amount:* $1–$7733. *Number of awards:* 147. *Eligibility Requirements:* Applicant must be high school student; planning to enroll or expecting to enroll full- or part-time at a two-year or four-year institution or university; resident of Washington and studying in Washington. Available to U.S. citizens. *Application Requirements:* Application, test scores, transcript. **Deadline:** January 17.

Contact Ann Voyles, Program Manager, Washington Higher Education Coordinating Board, 917 Lakeridge Way, PO Box 43430, Olympia, WA 98504-3430. *E-mail:* annv@hecb.wa.gov. *Phone:* 360-753-7843. *Fax:* 360-704-6243. *Web site:* http://www.hecb.wa.gov/.

Washington State Need Grant Program. The program helps Washington's lowest-income undergraduate students to pursue degrees, hone skills, or retrain for new careers. Students with family incomes equal to or less than 50 percent of the state median are eligible for up to 100 percent of the maximum grant. Students with incomes between 51–70% of the state median are prorated dependent on income. All grants are subject to funding. *Award:* Grant for use in freshman, sophomore, junior, or senior year; not renewable. *Award amount:* $103–$7717. *Number of awards:* 71,233. *Eligibility Requirements:* Applicant must be enrolled or expecting to enroll full- or part-time at a two-year, four-year, or technical institution or university; resident of Washington and studying in Washington. Available to U.S. citizens. *Application Requirements:* Application, financial need analysis, FAFSA. **Deadline:** continuous.

Contact Program Manager, Washington Higher Education Coordinating Board, PO Box 43430, Olympia, WA 98504-3430. *E-mail:* finaid@hecb.wa.gov. *Phone:* 360-753-7800. *Web site:* http://www.hecb.wa.gov/.

WEST VIRGINIA

Robert C. Byrd Honors Scholarship-West Virginia. Award for West Virginia residents who have demonstrated outstanding academic achievement. Must be a graduating high school senior. May apply for renewal consideration for a total of four years of assistance. For full-time study only. *Award:* Scholarship for use in freshman year; renewable. *Award amount:* $1500. *Number of awards:* 36. *Eligibility Requirements:* Applicant must be high school student; planning to enroll or expecting to enroll full-time at a two-year, four-year, or technical institution or university and resident of West Virginia. Applicant must have 3.0 GPA or higher. Available to U.S. citizens. *Application Requirements:* Application, test scores, transcript, letter of acceptance from a college/university. **Deadline:** March 1.

Contact Darlene Elmore, Scholarship Coordinator, West Virginia Higher Education Policy Commission-Student Services, 1018 Kanawha Boulevard East, Suite 700, Charleston, WV 25301. *E-mail:* elmore@hepc.wvnet.edu. *Phone:* 304-558-4618 Ext. 278. *Fax:* 304-558-4622. *Web site:* http://www.wvhepcnew.wvnet.edu/.

Underwood-Smith Teacher Scholarship Program. Award for West Virginia residents at West Virginia institutions pursuing teaching careers. Must have a 3.5 GPA after completion of two years of course work. Must teach two years in West Virginia public schools for each year the award is received. Recipients will be required to sign an agreement acknowledging an understanding of the program's requirements and their willingness to repay the award if appropriate teaching service is not rendered. *Academic Fields/Career Goals:* Education. *Award:* Scholarship for use in junior, senior, graduate, or postgraduate years; renewable. *Award amount:* $1620–$5000. *Number of awards:* 53–60. *Eligibility Requirements:* Applicant must be enrolled or expecting to enroll full-time at a four-year institution or university; resident of West Virginia and studying in West Virginia. Applicant must have 3.0 GPA or higher. Available to U.S. citizens. *Application Requirements:* Application, essay, references. **Deadline:** March 1.

Contact Darlene Elmore, Scholarship Coordinator, West Virginia Higher Education Policy Commission-Student Services, 1018 Kanawha Boulevard East, Suite 700, Charleston, WV 25301. *E-mail:* elmore@hepc.wvnet.edu. *Phone:* 304-558-4618 Ext. 278. *Fax:* 304-558-4622. *Web site:* http://www.wvhepcnew.wvnet.edu/.

West Virginia Engineering, Science and Technology Scholarship Program. Award for full-time students attending West Virginia institutions, pursuing a degree in engineering, science, or technology. Must be a resident of West Virginia. Must have a 3.0 GPA, and after graduation, must work in the fields of engineering, science, or technology in West Virginia one year for each year the award was received. *Academic Fields/Career Goals:* Electrical Engineering/Electronics; Engineering/Technology; Engineering-Related Technologies; Science, Technology, and Society. *Award:* Scholarship for use in freshman, sophomore, junior, or senior year; renewable. *Award amount:* $1500–$3000. *Number of awards:* 200–300. *Eligibility Requirements:*

Applicant must be enrolled or expecting to enroll full-time at a two-year, four-year, or technical institution or university; resident of West Virginia and studying in West Virginia. Applicant must have 3.0 GPA or higher. Available to U.S. citizens. *Application Requirements:* Application, essay, test scores, transcript. **Deadline:** March 1.

Contact Darlene Elmore, Scholarship Coordinator, West Virginia Higher Education Policy Commission-Student Services, 1018 Kanawha Boulevard East, Suite 700, Charleston, WV 25301. *E-mail:* elmore@hepc.wvnet.edu. *Phone:* 304-558-4618. *Web site:* http://www.wvhepcnew.wvnet.edu/.

West Virginia Higher Education Grant Program. Award available for West Virginia resident for one year immediately preceding the date of application, high school graduate or the equivalent, demonstrate financial need, and enroll as a full-time undergraduate at an approved university or college located in West Virginia or Pennsylvania. *Award:* Grant for use in freshman, sophomore, junior, or senior year; not renewable. *Award amount:* $375–$2100. *Number of awards:* 20,000–21,152. *Eligibility Requirements:* Applicant must be enrolled or expecting to enroll full-time at a two-year or four-year institution or university; resident of West Virginia and studying in Pennsylvania or West Virginia. Available to U.S. citizens. *Application Requirements:* Financial need analysis, FAFSA. **Deadline:** April 15.

Contact Judy Kee Smith, Senior Project Coordinator, West Virginia Higher Education Policy Commission-Student Services, 1018 Kanawha Boulevard East, Suite 700, Charleston, WV 25301-2827. *E-mail:* kee@hepc.wvnet.edu. *Phone:* 304-558-4618. *Fax:* 304-558-4622. *Web site:* http://www.wvhepcnew.wvnet.edu/.

WISCONSIN

Handicapped Student Grant-Wisconsin. One-time award available to residents of Wisconsin who have severe or profound hearing or visual impairment. Must be enrolled at least half-time at a nonprofit institution. If the handicap prevents the student from attending a Wisconsin school, the award may be used out-of-state in a specialized college. Refer to web site for further details http://www.heab.state.wi.us. *Award:* Grant for use in freshman, sophomore, junior, or senior year; not renewable. *Award amount:* $250–$1800. *Number of awards:* varies. *Eligibility Requirements:* Applicant must be enrolled or expecting to enroll full- or part-time at a four-year institution or university and resident of Wisconsin. Applicant must be hearing impaired or visually impaired. Available to U.S. citizens. *Application Requirements:* Application, financial need analysis. **Deadline:** continuous.

Contact Sandy Thomas, Program Coordinator, Wisconsin Higher Educational Aid Board, PO Box 7885, Madison, WI 53707-7885. *E-mail:* sandy.thomas@wi.gov. *Phone:* 608-266-0888. *Fax:* 608-267-2808. *Web site:* http://www.heab.wi.gov/.

Menominee Indian Tribe Adult Vocational Training Program. Renewable award for enrolled Menominee tribal members to use at vocational or technical schools. Must be at least 1/4 Menominee and show proof of Indian blood. Must complete financial aid form. Deadlines: March 1 and November 1. *Award:* Grant for use in freshman or sophomore year; renewable. *Award amount:* $100–$2200. *Number of awards:* 50–70. *Eligibility Requirements:* Applicant must be American Indian/Alaska Native and enrolled or expecting to enroll full- or part-time at a technical institution. Available to U.S. citizens. *Application Requirements:* Application, financial need analysis, proof of Indian blood. **Deadline:** varies.

Contact Virginia Nuske, Education Director, Menominee Indian Tribe of Wisconsin, PO Box 910, Keshena, WI 54135. *E-mail:* vnuske@mitw.org. *Phone:* 715-799-5110. *Fax:* 715-799-5102. *Web site:* http://www.menominee-nsn.gov/.

Minority Undergraduate Retention Grant-Wisconsin. The grant provides financial assistance to African-American, Native-American, Hispanic, and former citizens of Laos, Vietnam, and Cambodia, for study in Wisconsin. Must be Wisconsin resident, enrolled at least half-time in Wisconsin Technical College System schools, nonprofit independent colleges and universities, and tribal colleges. Refer to web site for further details http://www.heab.state.wi.us. *Award:* Grant for use in sophomore, junior, or senior year; not renewable. *Award amount:* $250–$2500. *Number of awards:* varies. *Eligibility Requirements:* Applicant must be American Indian/Alaska Native, Asian/Pacific Islander, Black (non-Hispanic), or Hispanic; enrolled or expecting to enroll full- or part-time at a two-year, four-year, or technical institution or university; resident of Wisconsin and studying in Wisconsin. Available to U.S. and non-U.S. citizens. *Application Requirements:* Application, financial need analysis. **Deadline:** continuous.

Contact Mary Lou Kuzdas, Program Coordinator, Wisconsin Higher Educational Aid Board, PO Box 7885, Madison, WI 53707-7885. *E-mail:* mary.kuzdas@wi.gov. *Phone:* 608-267-2212. *Fax:* 608-267-2808. *Web site:* http://www.heab.wi.gov/.

Talent Incentive Program Grant. Grant assists residents of Wisconsin who are attending a nonprofit institution in Wisconsin, and who have substantial financial need. Must meet income criteria, be considered economically and educationally disadvantaged, and be enrolled at least half-time. Refer to web site for further details http://www.heab.state.wi.us. *Award:* Grant for use in freshman, sophomore, junior, or senior year; renewable. *Award amount:* $250–$1800. *Number of awards:* varies. *Eligibility Requirements:* Applicant must be enrolled or expecting to enroll full- or part-time at a two-year, four-year, or technical institution or university; resident of Wisconsin and studying in Wisconsin. Available to U.S. citizens. *Application Requirements:* Application, financial need analysis, nomination by financial aid office. **Deadline:** continuous.

Contact Colette Brown, Program Coordinator, Wisconsin Higher Educational Aid Board, PO Box 7885, Madison, WI 53707-7885. *E-mail:* colette.brown@wi.gov. *Phone:* 608-266-1665. *Fax:* 608-267-2808. *Web site:* http://www.heab.wi.gov/.

Veterans Education (VetEd) Reimbursement Grant. The grant is for eligible Wisconsin veterans enrolled at approved schools who have not yet earned a BS/BA. Reimburses up to 120 credits or eight semesters at the UW Madison rate for the same number of credits taken in one semester or term. The number of credits or semesters is based on length of time serving on active duty in the armed forces (active duty for training does not apply). Application is due no later than 60 days after the course start date. The student must earn a 2.0 or better for the semester. An eligible veteran will have entered active duty as a Wisconsin resident or lived in state for twelve consecutive months since entering active duty. *Award:* Grant for use in freshman, sophomore, junior, or senior year; renewable. *Award amount:* up to $4000. *Number of awards:* up to 350. *Eligibility Requirements:* Applicant must be enrolled or expecting to enroll full- or part-time at a two-year, four-year, or technical institution or university; resident of Wisconsin and studying in Minnesota or Wisconsin. Available to U.S. citizens. Applicant must have served in the Air Force, Army, Coast Guard, Marine Corps, or Navy. *Application Requirements:* Application, certified Wisconsin veteran. **Deadline:** continuous.

Contact Ms. Leslie Ann Busby-Amegashie, Analyst, Wisconsin Department of Veterans Affairs (WDVA), PO Box 7843, Madison, WI 53707-7843. *E-mail:* leslie.busby-amegashie@dva.state.wi.us. *Phone:* 800-947-8387. *Web site:* http://www.dva.state.wi.us/.

Wisconsin Academic Excellence Scholarship. Renewable award for high school seniors with the highest GPA in graduating class. Must be a Wisconsin resident attending a nonprofit Wisconsin institution full-time. Scholarship value is $2250 toward tuition each year for up to four years. Must maintain 3.0 GPA for renewal. Refer to your high school counselor for more details. *Award:* Scholarship for use in freshman year; renewable. *Award amount:* up to $2250. *Number of awards:* varies. *Eligibility Requirements:* Applicant must be high school student; planning to enroll or expecting to enroll full-time at a two-year, four-year, or technical institution or university; resident of Wisconsin and studying in Wisconsin. Applicant must have 3.0 GPA or higher. Available to U.S. citizens. *Application Requirements:* Application, test scores, transcript. **Deadline:** continuous.

Contact Nancy Wilkison, Program Coordinator, Wisconsin Higher Educational Aid Board, PO Box 7885, Madison, WI 53707-7885. *E-mail:* nancy.wilkison@wi.gov. *Phone:* 608-267-2213. *Fax:* 608-267-2808. *Web site:* http://www.heab.wi.gov/.

Wisconsin Higher Education Grants (WHEG). Grants for residents of Wisconsin enrolled at least half-time in degree or certificate programs at a University of Wisconsin Institution, Wisconsin Technical College or an approved Tribal College. Must show financial need. Refer to web site for further details http://www.heab.wi.gov. *Award:* Grant for use in freshman, sophomore, junior, or senior year; not renewable. *Award amount:* $250–$3000. *Number of awards:* varies. *Eligibility Requirements:* Applicant must be enrolled or expecting to enroll full- or part-time at a two-year, four-year, or technical institution or university; resident of Wisconsin and studying in Wisconsin. Available to U.S. citizens. *Application Requirements:* Application, financial need analysis. **Deadline:** continuous.

Contact Sandra Thomas, Program Coordinator, Wisconsin Higher Educational Aid Board, PO Box 7885, Madison, WI 53707-7885. *E-mail:* sandy.thomas@heab.state.wi.us. *Phone:* 608-266-0888. *Fax:* 608-267-2808. *Web site:* http://www.heab.wi.gov/.

Wisconsin League for Nursing, Inc. Scholarship. One-time award for Wisconsin residents who have completed half of an accredited Wisconsin school of nursing program. Financial need of student must be demonstrated. Scholarship applications are mailed by WLN office ONLY to Wisconsin nursing schools in January for distribution to students. Students interested in obtaining an application must contact their nursing school and submit completed applications to their school. Applications sent directly to WLN office will be returned to applicant. For further information visit web site http://www.wisconsinwln.org/Scholarships.htm. *Academic Fields/Career Goals:* Nursing. *Award:* Scholarship for use in junior or senior year; not renewable. *Award amount:* $500–$1000. *Number of awards:* 11–35. *Eligibility Requirements:* Applicant must be enrolled or expecting to enroll full-time at a two-year, four-year, or technical institution or university; resident of Wisconsin and studying in Wisconsin. Available to U.S. citizens. *Application Requirements:* Application, essay, financial need analysis. **Deadline:** March 1.

Contact Mary Ann Tanner, Administrative Secretary, Wisconsin League for Nursing, Inc., 2121 East Newport Avenue, Milwaukee, WI 53211-2952. *E-mail:* wln@wisconsinwln.org. *Phone:* 888-755-3329. *Web site:* http://www.wisconsinwln.org/.

Wisconsin Native American/Indian Student Assistance Grant. Grants for Wisconsin residents who are at least one-quarter American Indian. Must be attending a college or university within the state. Refer to web site for further details http://www.heab.state.wi.us. *Award:* Grant for use in freshman, sophomore, junior, or senior year; not renewable. *Award amount:* $250–$1100. *Number of awards:* varies. *Eligibility Requirements:* Applicant must be American Indian/Alaska Native; enrolled or expecting to enroll full- or part-time at a two-year, four-year, or technical institution or university; resident of Wisconsin and studying in Wisconsin. Available to U.S. citizens. *Application Requirements:* Application, financial need analysis. **Deadline:** continuous.

Contact Sandra Thomas, Program Coordinator, Wisconsin Higher Educational Aid Board, PO Box 7885, Madison, WI 53707-7885. *E-mail:* sandy.thomas@wi.gov. *Phone:* 608-266-0888. *Fax:* 608-267-2808. *Web site:* http://www.heab.wi.gov/.

WYOMING

Douvas Memorial Scholarship. Available to Wyoming residents who are first-generation Americans. Must be between 18 and 22 years old. Must be used at any Wyoming public institution of higher education for study in freshman year. *Award:* Scholarship for use in freshman year; not renewable. *Award amount:* $500. *Number of awards:* 1. *Eligibility Requirements:* Applicant must be age 18-22; enrolled or expecting to enroll full- or part-time at a two-year or four-year institution or university; resident of Wyoming and studying in Wyoming. Available to U.S. citizens. *Application Requirements:* Application. **Deadline:** March 24.

Contact Gerry Maas, Director, Health and Safety, Wyoming Department of Education, 2300 Capitol Avenue, Hathaway Building, 2nd Floor, Cheyenne, WY 82002-0050. *E-mail:* gmaas@educ.state.wy.us. *Phone:* 307-777-6282. *Fax:* 307-777-6234.

Hathaway Scholarship. Scholarship for Wyoming students to pursue postsecondary education within the state. Award ranges from $1000 to $1600. Deadline varies. *Award:* Scholarship for use in freshman, sophomore, junior, or senior year; not renewable. *Award amount:* $1000–$1600. *Number of awards:* 1. *Eligibility Requirements:* Applicant must be enrolled or expecting to enroll full-time at a two-year or four-year institution or university; resident of Wyoming and studying in Wyoming. Available to U.S. citizens. *Application Requirements:* Application. **Deadline:** varies.

Contact Kay Post, Director, Wyoming Department of Education, 2020 Grand Avenue, Suite 500, Laramie, WY 82070. *E-mail:* kpost@educ.state.wy.us. *Phone:* 307-777-5599.

Superior Student in Education Scholarship-Wyoming. Scholarship available each year to sixteen new Wyoming high school graduates who plan to teach in Wyoming. The award covers costs of undergraduate tuition at the University of Wyoming or any Wyoming community college. *Academic Fields/Career Goals:* Education. *Award:* Scholarship for use in freshman, sophomore, junior, or senior year; renewable. *Award amount:* $1000. *Number of awards:* 16–16. *Eligibility Requirements:* Applicant must be high school student; planning to enroll or expecting to enroll full-time at a two-year or four-year institution or university; resident of Wyoming and studying in Wyoming. Applicant must have 3.0 GPA or higher. Available to U.S. citizens. *Application Requirements:* Application, references, test scores, transcript. **Deadline:** October 31.

Contact Tammy Mack, Assistant Director, Scholarships, State of Wyoming, Administered by University of Wyoming, Student Financial Aid Department 3335, 1000 East University

Avenue, Laramie, WY 82071-3335. *E-mail:* westmack@uwyo.edu. *Phone:* 307-766-2412. *Web site:* http://www.uwyo.edu/scholarships.

Vietnam Veterans Award-Wyoming. Scholarship available to Wyoming residents who served in the armed forces between August 5, 1964 and May 7, 1975, and received a Vietnam service medal. *Award:* Scholarship for use in freshman, sophomore, junior, or senior year; renewable. *Award amount:* varies. *Number of awards:* varies. *Eligibility Requirements:* Applicant must be enrolled or expecting to enroll full- or part-time at a two-year or four-year institution or university and resident of Wyoming. Available to U.S. citizens. Applicant or parent must meet one or more of the following requirements: general military experience; retired from active duty; disabled or killed as a result of military service; prisoner of war; or missing in action. *Application Requirements:* Application. **Deadline:** continuous.

Contact Tammy Mack, Assistant Director, Scholarships, State of Wyoming, Administered by University of Wyoming, Student Financial Aid Department 3335, 1000 East University Avenue, Laramie, WY 82071-3335. *E-mail:* westmack@uwyo.edu. *Phone:* 307-766-2412. *Web site:* http://www.uwyo.edu/scholarships.

Indexes

Non-Need Scholarships for Undergraduates

Academic Interests/ Achievements

Agriculture

Abilene Christian University, TX
Angelo State University, TX
Arkansas State University, AR
Arkansas Tech University, AR
Auburn University, AL
Austin Peay State University, TN
Berry College, GA
California Polytechnic State University, San Luis Obispo, CA
California State Polytechnic University, Pomona, CA
California State University, Bakersfield, CA
California State University, Chico, CA
California State University, Fresno, CA
California State University, Stanislaus, CA
Cameron University, OK
Clemson University, SC
Dickinson State University, ND
Dordt College, IA
Eastern Michigan University, MI
Ferris State University, MI
Florida Agricultural and Mechanical University, FL
Florida Southern College, FL
Fort Lewis College, CO
Fort Valley State University, GA
Illinois State University, IL
Iowa State University of Science and Technology, IA
Lincoln University, MO
Louisiana State University and Agricultural and Mechanical College, LA
Louisiana Tech University, LA
Lubbock Christian University, TX
Michigan State University, MI
Middle Tennessee State University, TN
Mississippi State University, MS
Montana State University, MT
Montana State University–Northern, MT
Morehead State University, KY
Murray State University, KY
New Mexico State University, NM
North Carolina State University, NC
Northwestern Oklahoma State University, OK
Northwest Missouri State University, MO
The Ohio State University, OH
Oklahoma Panhandle State University, OK
Oklahoma State University, OK
Post University, CT
Prairie View A&M University, TX
Purdue University, IN
South Dakota State University, SD
Southeast Missouri State University, MO
Southern Illinois University Carbondale, IL
Southwest Minnesota State University, MN
State University of New York College of Environmental Science and Forestry, NY
Stephen F. Austin State University, TX
Sul Ross State University, TX
Tennessee Technological University, TN
Texas A&M University, TX
Texas A&M University–Commerce, TX
Texas Christian University, TX
Texas State University–San Marcos, TX
Texas Tech University, TX
Truman State University, MO
University of Alaska Fairbanks, AK
The University of Arizona, AZ
University of California, Davis, CA
University of California, Riverside, CA
University of Central Missouri, MO
University of Connecticut, CT
University of Delaware, DE
University of Florida, FL
University of Georgia, GA
University of Idaho, ID
University of Illinois at Urbana–Champaign, IL
University of Kentucky, KY
University of Maryland, College Park, MD
University of Massachusetts Amherst, MA
University of Minnesota, Crookston, MN
University of Minnesota, Twin Cities Campus, MN
University of Missouri, MO
University of Nebraska–Lincoln, NE
University of New Hampshire, NH
The University of Tennessee, TN
The University of Tennessee at Martin, TN
The University of Texas at San Antonio, TX
University of Vermont, VT
The University of Virginia's College at Wise, VA
University of Wisconsin–River Falls, WI
University of Wisconsin–Stevens Point, WI
University of Wyoming, WY
Utah State University, UT
Vermont Technical College, VT
Virginia State University, VA
Washington State University, WA
Western Illinois University, IL
Western Kentucky University, KY
West Texas A&M University, TX
West Virginia University, WV

Architecture

Arizona State University, AZ
Auburn University, AL
Ball State University, IN
Boston Architectural College, MA
California Polytechnic State University, San Luis Obispo, CA
California State Polytechnic University, Pomona, CA
California State University, Bakersfield, CA
City College of the City University of New York, NY
Clemson University, SC
Cooper Union for the Advancement of Science and Art, NY
Drury University, MO
Eastern Michigan University, MI
Ferris State University, MI
Florida Agricultural and Mechanical University, FL
Georgia Institute of Technology, GA
Hampton University, VA
Illinois Institute of Technology, IL
Iowa State University of Science and Technology, IA
James Madison University, VA
Kent State University, OH
Lawrence Technological University, MI
Louisiana State University and Agricultural and Mechanical College, LA
Louisiana Tech University, LA
Miami University, OH
Mississippi State University, MS
Montana State University, MT
Montana State University–Northern, MT
New Jersey Institute of Technology, NJ
The Ohio State University, OH
Oklahoma State University, OK
Portland State University, OR
Prairie View A&M University, TX
Robert Morris University Illinois, IL
Savannah College of Art and Design, GA
Southern Illinois University Carbondale, IL
State University of New York College of Environmental Science and Forestry, NY
Texas A&M University, TX
Texas Tech University, TX
The University of Arizona, AZ
University of Colorado Boulder, CO
University of Florida, FL
University of Idaho, ID
University of Illinois at Chicago, IL
University of Illinois at Urbana–Champaign, IL
The University of Kansas, KS
University of Kentucky, KY
University of Maryland, College Park, MD
University of Massachusetts Amherst, MA
University of Miami, FL
University of Michigan, MI
University of Minnesota, Twin Cities Campus, MN

University of Nebraska–Lincoln, NE
University of Nevada, Las Vegas, NV
The University of North Carolina at Charlotte, NC
University of Oklahoma, OK
University of Oregon, OR
University of South Florida, FL
The University of Tennessee, TN
The University of Texas at Arlington, TX
The University of Texas at San Antonio, TX
University of Utah, UT
University of Wisconsin–Stevens Point, WI
Utah State University, UT
Virginia State University, VA
Washington State University, WA
Washington University in St. Louis, MO
West Virginia University, WV
Woodbury University, CA

Area/Ethnic Studies

Arizona State University, AZ
Arkansas State University, AR
Birmingham-Southern College, AL
California State University, Chico, CA
California State University, Fresno, CA
California State University, Stanislaus, CA
City College of the City University of New York, NY
The College of New Rochelle, NY
Eastern Connecticut State University, CT
Eastern Washington University, WA
Florida Agricultural and Mechanical University, FL
Fort Lewis College, CO
Furman University, SC
Indiana University of Pennsylvania, PA
Iowa State University of Science and Technology, IA
Kean University, NJ
Kent State University, OH
Middle Tennessee State University, TN
Mississippi State University, MS
Montana State University, MT
Northern Arizona University, AZ
Oakland University, MI
The Ohio State University, OH
Ohio University, OH
Ohio University–Chillicothe, OH
Ohio University–Eastern, OH
Ohio University–Lancaster, OH
Ohio University–Southern Campus, OH
Ohio University–Zanesville, OH
Oklahoma State University, OK
Ouachita Baptist University, AR
Portland State University, OR
Purchase College, State University of New York, NY
The Richard Stockton College of New Jersey, NJ
Saint Louis University, MO
San Diego State University, CA
Sonoma State University, CA
South Dakota State University, SD
Southern Illinois University Carbondale, IL
State University of New York at Binghamton, NY
State University of New York at New Paltz, NY
State University of New York at Oswego, NY
State University of New York at Plattsburgh, NY
State University of New York College at Geneseo, NY
Stetson University, FL
Stony Brook University, State University of New York, NY
The University of Alabama, AL
University of California, Davis, CA
University of California, Riverside, CA
University of Central Missouri, MO
University of Colorado Boulder, CO
University of Illinois at Urbana–Champaign, IL
The University of Kansas, KS
University of Kentucky, KY
University of Miami, FL
University of Michigan, MI
University of Minnesota, Twin Cities Campus, MN
University of Missouri, MO
University of Oklahoma, OK
University of South Carolina, SC
The University of Texas at San Antonio, TX
University of Utah, UT
University of Vermont, VT
University of Wisconsin–Green Bay, WI
University of Wisconsin–La Crosse, WI
University of Wisconsin–River Falls, WI
Virginia State University, VA
Warner Pacific College, OR
Washington State University, WA
Wayne State University, MI
West Virginia University, WV
Wichita State University, KS
William Jessup University, CA
Wright State University, OH

Biological Sciences

Abilene Christian University, TX
Alaska Pacific University, AK
Alderson-Broaddus College, WV
Alfred University, NY
Angelo State University, TX
Arizona State University, AZ
Arkansas State University, AR
Arkansas Tech University, AR
Armstrong Atlantic State University, GA
Auburn University, AL
Augsburg College, MN
Augustana College, IL
Augustana College, SD
Augusta State University, GA
Austin College, TX
Austin Peay State University, TN
Averett University, VA
Ball State University, IN
Bard College, NY
Bellarmine University, KY
Bethel College, IN
Bethel College, KS
Biola University, CA
Birmingham-Southern College, AL
Black Hills State University, SD
Bloomfield College, NJ
Bloomsburg University of Pennsylvania, PA
Boise State University, ID
Bowie State University, MD
Bowling Green State University, OH
Brenau University, GA
Brevard College, NC
Bryan College, TN
Buena Vista University, IA
Butler University, IN
Caldwell College, NJ
California Lutheran University, CA
California Polytechnic State University, San Luis Obispo, CA
California State Polytechnic University, Pomona, CA
California State University, Bakersfield, CA
California State University, Chico, CA
California State University, Fresno, CA
California State University, San Bernardino, CA
California State University, Stanislaus, CA
Calvin College, MI
Cameron University, OK
Campbellsville University, KY
Carroll University, WI
Carson-Newman College, TN
Case Western Reserve University, OH
Centenary College of Louisiana, LA
Central College, IA
Central Methodist University, MO
Central Michigan University, MI
Christopher Newport University, VA
The Citadel, The Military College of South Carolina, SC
City College of the City University of New York, NY
Clarkson University, NY
Clemson University, SC
Cleveland State University, OH
Coastal Carolina University, SC
Coe College, IA
The College at Brockport, State University of New York, NY
College of Charleston, SC
The College of New Rochelle, NY
College of Saint Mary, NE
College of Staten Island of the City University of New York, NY
The Colorado College, CO
Colorado State University–Pueblo, CO
Columbia College, MO
Columbus State University, GA
Concordia University Chicago, IL
Concordia University, Nebraska, NE
Dalton State College, GA
Davidson College, NC
Defiance College, OH
Delta State University, MS
DePauw University, IN
DeSales University, PA
Dickinson State University, ND
Dordt College, IA
Drury University, MO
D'Youville College, NY
East Carolina University, NC
Eastern Connecticut State University, CT
Eastern Michigan University, MI
Eastern Washington University, WA
East Tennessee State University, TN
East Texas Baptist University, TX
Edinboro University of Pennsylvania, PA
Elizabethtown College, PA
Elmhurst College, IL
Elon University, NC
Emmanuel College, MA
Emporia State University, KS
Erskine College, SC
Ferris State University, MI
Fitchburg State University, MA
Florida Agricultural and Mechanical University, FL
Florida Gulf Coast University, FL
Florida International University, FL
Florida Southern College, FL

Fordham University, NY
Fort Lewis College, CO
Framingham State University, MA
Francis Marion University, SC
Frostburg State University, MD
Furman University, SC
Gannon University, PA
Gardner-Webb University, NC
George Fox University, OR
Georgia Institute of Technology, GA
Georgian Court University, NJ
Georgia Southern University, GA
Glenville State College, WV
Governors State University, IL
Grace College, IN
Green Mountain College, VT
Greenville College, IL
Grove City College, PA
Hamline University, MN
Hampden-Sydney College, VA
Hampton University, VA
Hardin-Simmons University, TX
Harrisburg University of Science and Technology, PA
Hawai'i Pacific University, HI
High Point University, NC
Hillsdale College, MI
Howard Payne University, TX
Huntingdon College, AL
Huntington University, IN
Illinois State University, IL
Indiana University of Pennsylvania, PA
Iowa State University of Science and Technology, IA
James Madison University, VA
Jefferson College of Health Sciences, VA
John Carroll University, OH
Juniata College, PA
Kean University, NJ
Kennesaw State University, GA
Kent State University, OH
King's College, PA
Kutztown University of Pennsylvania, PA
Lake Forest College, IL
Lebanon Valley College, PA
Lee University, TN
Lewis-Clark State College, ID
Limestone College, SC
Lindenwood University, MO
Lindsey Wilson College, KY
Lipscomb University, TN
Lock Haven University of Pennsylvania, PA
Long Island University, C.W. Post Campus, NY
Longwood University, VA
Louisiana State University and Agricultural and Mechanical College, LA
Louisiana Tech University, LA
Lycoming College, PA
Maine Maritime Academy, ME
Malone University, OH
Manhattan College, NY
Marquette University, WI
Marymount University, VA
Maryville University of Saint Louis, MO
Massachusetts College of Liberal Arts, MA
The Master's College and Seminary, CA
Mayville State University, ND
McKendree University, IL
McMurry University, TX
Medaille College, NY
Mercer University, GA
Meredith College, NC
Mesa State College, CO
Michigan State University, MI
Middle Tennessee State University, TN
Midwestern State University, TX
Millersville University of Pennsylvania, PA
Millikin University, IL
Mills College, CA
Minnesota State University Moorhead, MN
Mississippi State University, MS
Mississippi University for Women, MS
Missouri University of Science and Technology, MO
Molloy College, NY
Montana State University, MT
Montana State University Billings, MT
Montana State University–Northern, MT
Montclair State University, NJ
Moravian College, PA
Morehead State University, KY
Mount St. Mary's College, CA
Murray State University, KY
Muskingum University, OH
New England College, NH
New Jersey Institute of Technology, NJ
New Mexico State University, NM
North Carolina Central University, NC
North Carolina State University, NC
North Central College, IL
Northeastern Illinois University, IL
Northeastern State University, OK
Northern Arizona University, AZ
Northern Illinois University, IL
Northern Kentucky University, KY
Northern Michigan University, MI
Northern State University, SD
North Georgia College & State University, GA
Northwestern Oklahoma State University, OK
Northwestern State University of Louisiana, LA
Northwest Missouri State University, MO
Northwest Nazarene University, ID
Oakland University, MI
Ohio Northern University, OH
The Ohio State University, OH
Ohio University, OH
Ohio University–Chillicothe, OH
Ohio University–Eastern, OH
Ohio University–Lancaster, OH
Ohio University–Southern Campus, OH
Ohio University–Zanesville, OH
Oklahoma Panhandle State University, OK
Oklahoma State University, OK
Oklahoma Wesleyan University, OK
Old Dominion University, VA
Ouachita Baptist University, AR
Pace University, NY
Pacific University, OR
Palmer College of Chiropractic, IA
Piedmont College, GA
Point Loma Nazarene University, CA
Post University, CT
Purchase College, State University of New York, NY
Quincy University, IL
Randolph College, VA
Regis University, CO
The Richard Stockton College of New Jersey, NJ
Ripon College, WI
Rivier College, NH
Rochester Institute of Technology, NY
Rockford College, IL
Rockhurst University, MO
Sacred Heart University, CT
Saginaw Valley State University, MI
Saint Augustine's College, NC
St. Edward's University, TX
Saint Francis University, PA
St. John Fisher College, NY
St. John's University, NY
Saint Louis University, MO
Samford University, AL
San Diego State University, CA
Savannah State University, GA
Schreiner University, TX
Seton Hill University, PA
Shepherd University, WV
Shippensburg University of Pennsylvania, PA
Siena College, NY
Skidmore College, NY
Slippery Rock University of Pennsylvania, PA
Sonoma State University, CA
South Dakota State University, SD
Southeastern Oklahoma State University, OK
Southeast Missouri State University, MO
Southern Illinois University Carbondale, IL
Southern Oregon University, OR
Southwestern College, KS
Southwestern Oklahoma State University, OK
Southwest Minnesota State University, MN
State University of New York at Binghamton, NY
State University of New York at Fredonia, NY
State University of New York at New Paltz, NY
State University of New York at Oswego, NY
State University of New York at Plattsburgh, NY
State University of New York College at Geneseo, NY
State University of New York College at Old Westbury, NY
State University of New York College at Oneonta, NY
State University of New York College at Potsdam, NY
State University of New York College of Environmental Science and Forestry, NY
Stephen F. Austin State University, TX
Stetson University, FL
Stony Brook University, State University of New York, NY
Sul Ross State University, TX
Tabor College, KS
Tennessee Technological University, TN
Tennessee Wesleyan College, TN
Texas A&M University, TX
Texas Christian University, TX
Texas Lutheran University, TX
Texas Tech University, TX
Texas Woman's University, TX
Thiel College, PA
Thomas More College, KY
Thomas University, GA
Towson University, MD
Trevecca Nazarene University, TN
Truman State University, MO
Union College, KY
The University of Akron, OH
The University of Alabama, AL
The University of Alabama in Huntsville, AL
University of Alaska Anchorage, AK
The University of Arizona, AZ
University of Arkansas at Little Rock, AR
University of California, Davis, CA
University of California, Irvine, CA

University of California, Riverside, CA
University of California, San Diego, CA
University of Central Missouri, MO
University of Central Oklahoma, OK
University of Colorado Boulder, CO
University of Connecticut, CT
University of Dayton, OH
University of Delaware, DE
University of Denver, CO
University of Evansville, IN
University of Great Falls, MT
University of Houston–Clear Lake, TX
University of Idaho, ID
University of Illinois at Urbana–Champaign, IL
The University of Kansas, KS
University of Kentucky, KY
University of Louisville, KY
University of Maine at Fort Kent, ME
University of Mary Hardin-Baylor, TX
University of Maryland, Baltimore County, MD
University of Maryland, College Park, MD
University of Mary Washington, VA
University of Massachusetts Amherst, MA
University of Massachusetts Lowell, MA
University of Memphis, TN
University of Miami, FL
University of Michigan, MI
University of Michigan–Dearborn, MI
University of Michigan–Flint, MI
University of Minnesota, Crookston, MN
University of Minnesota, Twin Cities Campus, MN
University of Mississippi, MS
University of Missouri, MO
University of Missouri–St. Louis, MO
The University of Montana, MT
University of Montevallo, AL
University of Nebraska at Omaha, NE
University of Nebraska–Lincoln, NE
University of Nevada, Las Vegas, NV
University of New Orleans, LA
The University of North Carolina at Asheville, NC
The University of North Carolina at Greensboro, NC
The University of North Carolina Wilmington, NC
University of North Dakota, ND
University of Northern Colorado, CO
University of Northern Iowa, IA
University of Oklahoma, OK
University of Oregon, OR
University of Pittsburgh at Bradford, PA
University of Pittsburgh at Johnstown, PA
University of Portland, OR
University of Puget Sound, WA
University of Richmond, VA
University of Rio Grande, OH
University of St. Francis, IL
University of St. Thomas, MN
University of St. Thomas, TX
University of South Carolina, SC
University of South Carolina Aiken, SC
The University of South Dakota, SD
University of Southern Indiana, IN
University of South Florida, FL
The University of Tampa, FL
The University of Tennessee at Chattanooga, TN
The University of Tennessee at Martin, TN
The University of Texas at Arlington, TX
The University of Texas at Brownsville, TX
The University of Texas at Dallas, TX
The University of Texas at El Paso, TX
The University of Texas at San Antonio, TX
The University of Texas–Pan American, TX
University of the Ozarks, AR
University of the Southwest, NM
The University of Toledo, OH
University of Tulsa, OK
University of Utah, UT
The University of Virginia's College at Wise, VA
University of West Florida, FL
University of West Georgia, GA
University of Wisconsin–Eau Claire, WI
University of Wisconsin–Green Bay, WI
University of Wisconsin–La Crosse, WI
University of Wisconsin–Parkside, WI
University of Wisconsin–River Falls, WI
University of Wisconsin–Stevens Point, WI
University of Wisconsin–Superior, WI
Utah State University, UT
Valdosta State University, GA
Valley City State University, ND
Virginia Commonwealth University, VA
Virginia Military Institute, VA
Virginia State University, VA
Walla Walla University, WA
Walsh University, OH
Warner Pacific College, OR
Wartburg College, IA
Washburn University, KS
Washington State University, WA
Washington University in St. Louis, MO
Wayland Baptist University, TX
Waynesburg University, PA
Wayne State College, NE
Wayne State University, MI
Wesleyan College, GA
Western Carolina University, NC
Western Illinois University, IL
Western Kentucky University, KY
Western Oregon University, OR
Western Washington University, WA
West Virginia State University, WV
West Virginia University, WV
West Virginia University Institute of Technology, WV
Wheaton College, IL
Whitworth University, WA
Wichita State University, KS
Widener University, PA
Williams Baptist College, AR
Wilson College, PA
Wright State University, OH
Xavier University of Louisiana, LA
York College, NE
Youngstown State University, OH

Business

Abilene Christian University, TX
Adrian College, MI
Alaska Pacific University, AK
Albion College, MI
Alderson-Broaddus College, WV
Alfred University, NY
Alliant International University, CA
Anderson University, SC
Angelo State University, TX
Aquinas College, TN
Arizona State University, AZ
Arkansas State University, AR
Arkansas Tech University, AR
Auburn University, AL
Augsburg College, MN
Augustana College, IL
Augustana College, SD
Augusta State University, GA
Austin College, TX
Austin Peay State University, TN
Averett University, VA
Ball State University, IN
Baptist University of the Americas, TX
Baylor University, TX
Bellarmine University, KY
Berry College, GA
Bethel College, IN
Birmingham-Southern College, AL
Black Hills State University, SD
Bloomfield College, NJ
Bloomsburg University of Pennsylvania, PA
Boise State University, ID
Bowie State University, MD
Bowling Green State University, OH
Brenau University, GA
Brevard College, NC
Bryan College, TN
Bucknell University, PA
Buena Vista University, IA
Butler University, IN
California Lutheran University, CA
California Polytechnic State University, San Luis Obispo, CA
California State Polytechnic University, Pomona, CA
California State University, Bakersfield, CA
California State University, Chico, CA
California State University, Fresno, CA
California State University, Fullerton, CA
California State University, Monterey Bay, CA
California State University, Northridge, CA
California State University, San Bernardino, CA
California State University, Stanislaus, CA
Calvin College, MI
Cameron University, OK
Campbellsville University, KY
Carroll University, WI
Carson-Newman College, TN
Case Western Reserve University, OH
Cedar Crest College, PA
Centenary College of Louisiana, LA
Central College, IA
Central Methodist University, MO
Central Michigan University, MI
Champlain College, VT
Christopher Newport University, VA
The Citadel, The Military College of South Carolina, SC
Clarkson University, NY
Cleary University, MI
Clemson University, SC
Cleveland State University, OH
Coastal Carolina University, SC
Coe College, IA
The College at Brockport, State University of New York, NY
College of Charleston, SC
The College of New Rochelle, NY
The College of Saint Rose, NY
College of Staten Island of the City University of New York, NY
Colorado School of Mines, CO
Colorado State University–Pueblo, CO
Columbia College, MO
Columbia International University, SC

Columbus State University, GA
Concordia University, MI
Concordia University Chicago, IL
Concordia University, Nebraska, NE
Concord University, WV
Cornerstone University, MI
Creighton University, NE
Dakota State University, SD
Dallas Baptist University, TX
Dalton State College, GA
Davidson College, NC
Defiance College, OH
Delta State University, MS
DePauw University, IN
DeSales University, PA
Dickinson State University, ND
Dordt College, IA
Dowling College, NY
Drury University, MO
D'Youville College, NY
East Carolina University, NC
Eastern Connecticut State University, CT
Eastern Michigan University, MI
Eastern Washington University, WA
East Tennessee State University, TN
East Texas Baptist University, TX
ECPI College of Technology, VA
Edinboro University of Pennsylvania, PA
Elizabethtown College, PA
Elmhurst College, IL
Elon University, NC
Emmanuel College, GA
Emporia State University, KS
Endicott College, MA
Erskine College, SC
Evangel University, MO
Felician College, NJ
Ferris State University, MI
Fitchburg State University, MA
Flagler College, FL
Florida Agricultural and Mechanical University, FL
Florida Atlantic University, FL
Florida Gulf Coast University, FL
Florida International University, FL
Florida Southern College, FL
Fordham University, NY
Fort Lewis College, CO
Fort Valley State University, GA
Francis Marion University, SC
Fresno Pacific University, CA
Frostburg State University, MD
Furman University, SC
Gannon University, PA
Gardner-Webb University, NC
Georgia College & State University, GA
Georgian Court University, NJ
Georgia Southern University, GA
Glenville State College, WV
Golden Gate University, CA
Goldey-Beacom College, DE
Gonzaga University, WA
Goshen College, IN
Governors State University, IL
Grace College, IN
Grace University, NE
Grand Valley State University, MI
Greenville College, IL
Grove City College, PA
Hamline University, MN
Hampton University, VA
Hardin-Simmons University, TX
Harrisburg University of Science and Technology, PA
Hawai'i Pacific University, HI
High Point University, NC
Hillsdale College, MI
Hillsdale Free Will Baptist College, OK
Howard Payne University, TX
Huntington University, IN
Husson University, ME
Illinois Institute of Technology, IL
Illinois State University, IL
Indiana University of Pennsylvania, PA
Iowa State University of Science and Technology, IA
Jacksonville University, FL
James Madison University, VA
John Carroll University, OH
Johnson Bible College, TN
Juniata College, PA
Kean University, NJ
Kennesaw State University, GA
Kent State University, OH
Kettering University, MI
King's College, PA
Kutztown University of Pennsylvania, PA
Lawrence Technological University, MI
Lee University, TN
Lehigh University, PA
Lewis-Clark State College, ID
Limestone College, SC
Lindenwood University, MO
Lindsey Wilson College, KY
Lipscomb University, TN
Long Island University, C.W. Post Campus, NY
Longwood University, VA
Louisiana College, LA
Louisiana State University and Agricultural and Mechanical College, LA
Louisiana Tech University, LA
Lubbock Christian University, TX
Lycoming College, PA
Lynn University, FL
Lyon College, AR
Maine Maritime Academy, ME
Malone University, OH
Manchester College, IN
Manhattan College, NY
Maranatha Baptist Bible College, WI
Marquette University, WI
Marymount University, VA
Maryville University of Saint Louis, MO
Marywood University, PA
Massachusetts College of Liberal Arts, MA
The Master's College and Seminary, CA
Mayville State University, ND
McKendree University, IL
McMurry University, TX
Medaille College, NY
Mercer University, GA
Meredith College, NC
Mesa State College, CO
Michigan State University, MI
Middle Tennessee State University, TN
Midwestern State University, TX
Millersville University of Pennsylvania, PA
Millikin University, IL
Millsaps College, MS
Milwaukee School of Engineering, WI
Minnesota State University Moorhead, MN
Minot State University, ND
Misericordia University, PA
Mississippi State University, MS
Mississippi University for Women, MS
Missouri University of Science and Technology, MO
Molloy College, NY
Monmouth University, NJ
Montana State University, MT
Montana State University Billings, MT
Montana State University–Northern, MT
Montana Tech of The University of Montana, MT
Montclair State University, NJ
Moravian College, PA
Morehead State University, KY
Morehouse College, GA
Mount Mary College, WI
Murray State University, KY
New England College, NH
New Jersey Institute of Technology, NJ
New Mexico State University, NM
North Carolina Central University, NC
North Carolina State University, NC
North Central College, IL
Northeastern Illinois University, IL
Northeastern State University, OK
Northern Arizona University, AZ
Northern Illinois University, IL
Northern Kentucky University, KY
Northern Michigan University, MI
Northern State University, SD
North Georgia College & State University, GA
Northwestern Oklahoma State University, OK
Northwestern State University of Louisiana, LA
Northwest Missouri State University, MO
Northwest Nazarene University, ID
Northwood University, Texas Campus, TX
Oakland University, MI
Ohio Northern University, OH
The Ohio State University, OH
Ohio University, OH
Ohio University–Chillicothe, OH
Ohio University–Eastern, OH
Ohio University–Lancaster, OH
Ohio University–Southern Campus, OH
Ohio University–Zanesville, OH
Ohio Wesleyan University, OH
Oklahoma Baptist University, OK
Oklahoma City University, OK
Oklahoma Panhandle State University, OK
Oklahoma State University, OK
Oklahoma Wesleyan University, OK
Old Dominion University, VA
Olivet College, MI
Ouachita Baptist University, AR
Pace University, NY
Pacific University, OR
Peirce College, PA
Piedmont College, GA
Plymouth State University, NH
Point Loma Nazarene University, CA
Portland State University, OR
Post University, CT
Providence College, RI
Purdue University North Central, IN
Quincy University, IL
Regent University, VA
The Richard Stockton College of New Jersey, NJ
Ripon College, WI
Rivier College, NH
Robert Morris University Illinois, IL
Rochester Institute of Technology, NY
Rockford College, IL

Rockhurst University, MO
Sacred Heart University, CT
Saginaw Valley State University, MI
St. Andrews Presbyterian College, NC
St. Bonaventure University, NY
St. Catherine University, MN
St. Edward's University, TX
Saint Francis University, PA
St. John Fisher College, NY
St. John's University, NY
Saint Louis University, MO
Saint Martin's University, WA
St. Thomas Aquinas College, NY
Samford University, AL
San Diego State University, CA
Santa Clara University, CA
Savannah State University, GA
Schreiner University, TX
Seton Hill University, PA
Shenandoah University, VA
Shepherd University, WV
Shippensburg University of Pennsylvania, PA
Siena College, NY
Slippery Rock University of Pennsylvania, PA
Sonoma State University, CA
South Dakota State University, SD
Southeastern Louisiana University, LA
Southeastern Oklahoma State University, OK
Southeast Missouri State University, MO
Southern Adventist University, TN
Southern Illinois University Carbondale, IL
Southern Illinois University Edwardsville, IL
Southern Oregon University, OR
Southwestern College, KS
Southwestern Oklahoma State University, OK
Southwestern University, TX
Southwest Minnesota State University, MN
State University of New York at Binghamton, NY
State University of New York at Fredonia, NY
State University of New York at New Paltz, NY
State University of New York at Oswego, NY
State University of New York at Plattsburgh, NY
State University of New York College at Geneseo, NY
State University of New York College at Oneonta, NY
State University of New York College at Potsdam, NY
Stephen F. Austin State University, TX
Stetson University, FL
Stevens-Henager College, ID
Stony Brook University, State University of New York, NY
Sul Ross State University, TX
Tennessee Technological University, TN
Tennessee Wesleyan College, TN
Texas A&M International University, TX
Texas A&M University, TX
Texas A&M University–Texarkana, TX
Texas Christian University, TX
Texas Lutheran University, TX
Texas Southern University, TX
Texas State University–San Marcos, TX
Texas Tech University, TX
Texas Woman's University, TX
Thiel College, PA
Thomas More College, KY
Thomas University, GA
Towson University, MD
Trevecca Nazarene University, TN
Trinity Christian College, IL
Truman State University, MO
Union University, TN
The University of Akron, OH
The University of Alabama, AL
The University of Alabama at Birmingham, AL
The University of Alabama in Huntsville, AL
University of Alaska Anchorage, AK
The University of Arizona, AZ
University of Arkansas at Little Rock, AR
University of California, Davis, CA
University of California, Irvine, CA
University of California, Riverside, CA
University of California, San Diego, CA
University of Central Missouri, MO
University of Central Oklahoma, OK
University of Colorado Boulder, CO
University of Connecticut, CT
University of Dallas, TX
University of Dayton, OH
University of Delaware, DE
University of Denver, CO
University of Evansville, IN
University of Florida, FL
University of Georgia, GA
University of Great Falls, MT
University of Hawaii at Hilo, HI
University of Houston–Clear Lake, TX
University of Houston–Downtown, TX
University of Idaho, ID
University of Illinois at Chicago, IL
University of Illinois at Urbana–Champaign, IL
University of Indianapolis, IN
The University of Iowa, IA
The University of Kansas, KS
University of Kentucky, KY
University of Louisville, KY
University of Maine at Fort Kent, ME
University of Mary Hardin-Baylor, TX
University of Maryland, College Park, MD
University of Mary Washington, VA
University of Massachusetts Amherst, MA
University of Massachusetts Lowell, MA
University of Memphis, TN
University of Miami, FL
University of Michigan, MI
University of Michigan–Dearborn, MI
University of Michigan–Flint, MI
University of Minnesota, Twin Cities Campus, MN
University of Mississippi, MS
University of Missouri, MO
University of Missouri–St. Louis, MO
The University of Montana, MT
University of Montevallo, AL
University of Nebraska at Omaha, NE
University of Nebraska–Lincoln, NE
University of Nevada, Las Vegas, NV
University of New Hampshire, NH
University of New Orleans, LA
The University of North Carolina at Asheville, NC
The University of North Carolina at Chapel Hill, NC
The University of North Carolina at Charlotte, NC
The University of North Carolina at Greensboro, NC
The University of North Carolina at Pembroke, NC
The University of North Carolina Wilmington, NC
University of North Dakota, ND
University of Northern Colorado, CO
University of Northern Iowa, IA
University of North Florida, FL
University of Oklahoma, OK
University of Oregon, OR
University of Pittsburgh at Bradford, PA
University of Pittsburgh at Johnstown, PA
University of Portland, OR
University of Puget Sound, WA
University of Rio Grande, OH
University of St. Thomas, MN
University of St. Thomas, TX
University of South Alabama, AL
University of South Carolina, SC
University of South Carolina Aiken, SC
The University of South Dakota, SD
University of Southern Indiana, IN
University of South Florida, FL
The University of Tennessee, TN
The University of Tennessee at Chattanooga, TN
The University of Tennessee at Martin, TN
The University of Texas at Arlington, TX
The University of Texas at Brownsville, TX
The University of Texas at Dallas, TX
The University of Texas at El Paso, TX
The University of Texas at San Antonio, TX
The University of Texas–Pan American, TX
University of the Ozarks, AR
University of the Southwest, NM
The University of Toledo, OH
University of Tulsa, OK
University of Utah, UT
University of Vermont, VT
The University of Virginia's College at Wise, VA
University of West Florida, FL
University of West Georgia, GA
University of Wisconsin–Eau Claire, WI
University of Wisconsin–Green Bay, WI
University of Wisconsin–La Crosse, WI
University of Wisconsin–Parkside, WI
University of Wisconsin–River Falls, WI
University of Wisconsin–Stevens Point, WI
University of Wisconsin–Stout, WI
University of Wisconsin–Superior, WI
University of Wyoming, WY
Utah State University, UT
Valdosta State University, GA
Valley City State University, ND
Valparaiso University, IN
Virginia Commonwealth University, VA
Virginia Military Institute, VA
Virginia State University, VA
Walla Walla University, WA
Walsh College of Accountancy and Business Administration, MI
Walsh University, OH
Wartburg College, IA
Washburn University, KS
Washington & Jefferson College, PA
Washington State University, WA
Washington University in St. Louis, MO
Wayland Baptist University, TX
Waynesburg University, PA
Wayne State College, NE
Wayne State University, MI
Webber International University, FL
Wesleyan College, GA
West Chester University of Pennsylvania, PA

Western Carolina University, NC
Western Illinois University, IL
Western Kentucky University, KY
Western Oregon University, OR
Western Washington University, WA
West Liberty University, WV
West Texas A&M University, TX
West Virginia State University, WV
West Virginia University, WV
Wheaton College, IL
Wichita State University, KS
Widener University, PA
William Jessup University, CA
Williams Baptist College, AR
Wilson College, PA
Wright State University, OH
Xavier University of Louisiana, LA
York College, NE
Youngstown State University, OH

Communication

Abilene Christian University, TX
Adelphi University, NY
Albion College, MI
Alderson-Broaddus College, WV
Alfred University, NY
Alliant International University, CA
Angelo State University, TX
Arizona State University, AZ
Arkansas State University, AR
Auburn University, AL
Augsburg College, MN
Augustana College, IL
Augustana College, SD
Augusta State University, GA
Austin College, TX
Austin Peay State University, TN
Ball State University, IN
Baylor University, TX
Berry College, GA
Bethel College, IN
Biola University, CA
Birmingham-Southern College, AL
Black Hills State University, SD
Bloomsburg University of Pennsylvania, PA
Boise State University, ID
Bowie State University, MD
Bowling Green State University, OH
Brenau University, GA
Bryan College, TN
Butler University, IN
California Lutheran University, CA
California Polytechnic State University, San Luis Obispo, CA
California State University, Bakersfield, CA
California State University, Chico, CA
California State University, Fresno, CA
California State University, Fullerton, CA
California State University, Northridge, CA
California State University, Stanislaus, CA
Calvin College, MI
Cameron University, OK
Campbellsville University, KY
Case Western Reserve University, OH
Cedar Crest College, PA
Centenary College of Louisiana, LA
Central College, IA
Central Methodist University, MO
Central Michigan University, MI
Champlain College, VT
Christopher Newport University, VA
City College of the City University of New York, NY
Clarkson University, NY
Clemson University, SC
Cleveland State University, OH
The College at Brockport, State University of New York, NY
College of Charleston, SC
The College of New Rochelle, NY
Colorado State University–Pueblo, CO
Columbia International University, SC
Columbus State University, GA
Concordia University Chicago, IL
Concordia University, Nebraska, NE
Concord University, WV
Cornerstone University, MI
Dakota State University, SD
Dallas Baptist University, TX
Defiance College, OH
DePauw University, IN
DeSales University, PA
Dickinson State University, ND
Dordt College, IA
Drury University, MO
East Carolina University, NC
Eastern Connecticut State University, CT
Eastern Michigan University, MI
Eastern Washington University, WA
East Texas Baptist University, TX
Edinboro University of Pennsylvania, PA
Elizabethtown College, PA
Elmhurst College, IL
Elon University, NC
Emmanuel College, GA
Emporia State University, KS
Evangel University, MO
Ferris State University, MI
Fitchburg State University, MA
Flagler College, FL
Florida Agricultural and Mechanical University, FL
Florida International University, FL
Florida Southern College, FL
Fordham University, NY
Fort Lewis College, CO
Frostburg State University, MD
Furman University, SC
Gardner-Webb University, NC
Georgia Southern University, GA
Goshen College, IN
Governors State University, IL
Grand Valley State University, MI
Grove City College, PA
Hamline University, MN
Hampton University, VA
Harding University, AR
Hardin-Simmons University, TX
Hastings College, NE
Hawai'i Pacific University, HI
Hofstra University, NY
Howard Payne University, TX
Huntington University, IN
Illinois State University, IL
Indiana University of Pennsylvania, PA
Iowa State University of Science and Technology, IA
Ithaca College, NY
John Carroll University, OH
Johnson Bible College, TN
Juniata College, PA
Kean University, NJ
Kennesaw State University, GA
Kent State University, OH
King's College, PA
Kutztown University of Pennsylvania, PA
Lee University, TN
Lehigh University, PA
Limestone College, SC
Lindenwood University, MO
Lipscomb University, TN
Lock Haven University of Pennsylvania, PA
Long Island University, Brooklyn Campus, NY
Louisiana State University and Agricultural and Mechanical College, LA
Lubbock Christian University, TX
Lycoming College, PA
Lynn University, FL
Malone University, OH
Marquette University, WI
Marywood University, PA
Massachusetts College of Liberal Arts, MA
Mayville State University, ND
Medaille College, NY
Mesa State College, CO
Michigan State University, MI
Middle Tennessee State University, TN
Midwestern State University, TX
Millersville University of Pennsylvania, PA
Millikin University, IL
Milwaukee School of Engineering, WI
Minnesota State University Moorhead, MN
Minot State University, ND
Mississippi State University, MS
Mississippi University for Women, MS
Molloy College, NY
Monmouth University, NJ
Montana State University, MT
Montana State University Billings, MT
Montclair State University, NJ
Morehead State University, KY
Mount Mary College, WI
Murray State University, KY
New England College, NH
New England School of Communications, ME
New Jersey Institute of Technology, NJ
New Mexico State University, NM
North Central College, IL
Northeastern Illinois University, IL
Northeastern State University, OK
Northern Arizona University, AZ
Northern Illinois University, IL
Northern Kentucky University, KY
Northern Michigan University, MI
Northern State University, SD
Northwestern Oklahoma State University, OK
Northwestern State University of Louisiana, LA
Northwest Missouri State University, MO
Ohio Northern University, OH
The Ohio State University, OH
Ohio University, OH
Ohio University–Chillicothe, OH
Ohio University–Eastern, OH
Ohio University–Lancaster, OH
Ohio University–Southern Campus, OH
Ohio University–Zanesville, OH
Oklahoma City University, OK
Oklahoma State University, OK
Olivet College, MI
Ouachita Baptist University, AR
Pace University, NY
Pacific University, OR
Plymouth State University, NH
Point Loma Nazarene University, CA
Post University, CT
Quincy University, IL
Regent University, VA

Rivier College, NH
Rochester Institute of Technology, NY
Rockhurst University, MO
St. Edward's University, TX
St. John's University, NY
Saint Louis University, MO
St. Thomas Aquinas College, NY
Samford University, AL
San Diego State University, CA
Seton Hill University, PA
Shepherd University, WV
Shippensburg University of Pennsylvania, PA
Siena College, NY
Slippery Rock University of Pennsylvania, PA
Sonoma State University, CA
South Dakota State University, SD
Southeastern Louisiana University, LA
Southeastern Oklahoma State University, OK
Southeastern University, FL
Southeast Missouri State University, MO
Southern Adventist University, TN
Southern Illinois University Carbondale, IL
Southwestern College, KS
Southwestern Oklahoma State University, OK
Southwest Minnesota State University, MN
State University of New York at Fredonia, NY
State University of New York at New Paltz, NY
State University of New York at Oswego, NY
State University of New York at Plattsburgh, NY
State University of New York College at Geneseo, NY
State University of New York College at Potsdam, NY
Stephen F. Austin State University, TX
Stetson University, FL
Tabor College, KS
Tennessee Technological University, TN
Tennessee Wesleyan College, TN
Texas A&M International University, TX
Texas Christian University, TX
Texas Southern University, TX
Texas Tech University, TX
Texas Woman's University, TX
Thomas More College, KY
Towson University, MD
Trevecca Nazarene University, TN
Truman State University, MO
Union University, TN
The University of Akron, OH
The University of Alabama, AL
The University of Alabama at Birmingham, AL
The University of Alabama in Huntsville, AL
University of Alaska Anchorage, AK
University of Arkansas at Little Rock, AR
University of California, Davis, CA
University of California, San Diego, CA
University of Central Missouri, MO
University of Colorado Boulder, CO
University of Dayton, OH
University of Delaware, DE
University of Denver, CO
University of Evansville, IN
University of Florida, FL
University of Idaho, ID
University of Illinois at Urbana–Champaign, IL
University of Indianapolis, IN
The University of Kansas, KS
University of Kentucky, KY
University of Maine at Fort Kent, ME
University of Mary Hardin-Baylor, TX
University of Maryland, College Park, MD
University of Massachusetts Amherst, MA
University of Memphis, TN
University of Miami, FL
University of Michigan, MI
University of Michigan–Dearborn, MI
University of Michigan–Flint, MI
University of Minnesota, Twin Cities Campus, MN
University of Mississippi, MS
University of Missouri, MO
University of Missouri–St. Louis, MO
University of Montevallo, AL
University of Nebraska at Omaha, NE
University of Nevada, Las Vegas, NV
The University of North Carolina at Asheville, NC
The University of North Carolina at Chapel Hill, NC
The University of North Carolina at Greensboro, NC
The University of North Carolina at Pembroke, NC
The University of North Carolina Wilmington, NC
University of North Dakota, ND
University of Northern Colorado, CO
University of Northern Iowa, IA
University of Oklahoma, OK
University of Pittsburgh at Bradford, PA
University of Pittsburgh at Johnstown, PA
University of Portland, OR
University of Puget Sound, WA
University of Rio Grande, OH
University of St. Francis, IL
University of St. Thomas, TX
University of South Carolina, SC
University of South Carolina Aiken, SC
The University of South Dakota, SD
University of South Florida, FL
The University of Tennessee, TN
The University of Tennessee at Chattanooga, TN
The University of Tennessee at Martin, TN
The University of Texas at Arlington, TX
The University of Texas at Brownsville, TX
The University of Texas at El Paso, TX
The University of Texas at San Antonio, TX
The University of Texas at Tyler, TX
The University of Texas–Pan American, TX
University of the Ozarks, AR
The University of Toledo, OH
University of Tulsa, OK
University of Utah, UT
University of West Georgia, GA
University of Wisconsin–Eau Claire, WI
University of Wisconsin–Green Bay, WI
University of Wisconsin–La Crosse, WI
University of Wisconsin–Parkside, WI
University of Wisconsin–River Falls, WI
University of Wisconsin–Stevens Point, WI
University of Wisconsin–Superior, WI
University of Wyoming, WY
Utah State University, UT
Valdosta State University, GA
Valley City State University, ND
Virginia State University, VA
Waldorf College, IA
Walla Walla University, WA
Walsh University, OH
Wartburg College, IA
Washburn University, KS
Washington State University, WA
Washington University in St. Louis, MO
Wayland Baptist University, TX
Waynesburg University, PA
Wayne State College, NE
Wayne State University, MI
Wesleyan College, GA
Western Carolina University, NC
Western Kentucky University, KY
Western Washington University, WA
West Liberty University, WV
West Texas A&M University, TX
West Virginia State University, WV
West Virginia University, WV
Wichita State University, KS
Widener University, PA
Wilson College, PA
Wright State University, OH
Xavier University of Louisiana, LA
York College, NE
Youngstown State University, OH

Computer Science

Alderson-Broaddus College, WV
Alliant International University, CA
Angelo State University, TX
Arizona State University, AZ
Arkansas State University, AR
Arkansas Tech University, AR
Armstrong Atlantic State University, GA
Auburn University, AL
Augsburg College, MN
Augustana College, IL
Augustana College, SD
Augusta State University, GA
Austin Peay State University, TN
Bard College, NY
Baylor University, TX
Birmingham-Southern College, AL
Black Hills State University, SD
Bloomfield College, NJ
Bloomsburg University of Pennsylvania, PA
Boise State University, ID
Bowie State University, MD
Bowling Green State University, OH
Bryan College, TN
Buena Vista University, IA
Butler University, IN
California Lutheran University, CA
California Polytechnic State University, San Luis Obispo, CA
California State Polytechnic University, Pomona, CA
California State University, Chico, CA
California State University, Northridge, CA
California State University, San Bernardino, CA
California State University, Stanislaus, CA
Calvin College, MI
Cameron University, OK
Campbellsville University, KY
Carroll University, WI
Case Western Reserve University, OH
Central College, IA
Central Methodist University, MO
Central Michigan University, MI
Champlain College, VT
Christopher Newport University, VA
City College of the City University of New York, NY
Clarke University, IA
Clarkson University, NY
Cleary University, MI

Clemson University, SC
Cleveland State University, OH
The College at Brockport, State University of New York, NY
College of Charleston, SC
College of Staten Island of the City University of New York, NY
Colorado School of Mines, CO
Colorado State University–Pueblo, CO
Columbus State University, GA
Concordia University Chicago, IL
Concordia University, Nebraska, NE
Cornerstone University, MI
Dakota State University, SD
Dallas Baptist University, TX
Dalton State College, GA
Defiance College, OH
Delta State University, MS
DePauw University, IN
DeSales University, PA
Dickinson State University, ND
Dordt College, IA
Drury University, MO
Eastern Connecticut State University, CT
Eastern Michigan University, MI
Eastern Washington University, WA
East Tennessee State University, TN
ECPI College of Technology, VA
Edinboro University of Pennsylvania, PA
Elizabeth City State University, NC
Elizabethtown College, PA
Elmhurst College, IL
Elon University, NC
Emporia State University, KS
Evangel University, MO
Ferris State University, MI
Fitchburg State University, MA
Florida Agricultural and Mechanical University, FL
Florida International University, FL
Fort Lewis College, CO
Francis Marion University, SC
Frostburg State University, MD
Furman University, SC
Gardner-Webb University, NC
George Fox University, OR
Georgia College & State University, GA
Georgia Institute of Technology, GA
Georgia Southern University, GA
Golden Gate University, CA
Graceland University, IA
Grand Valley State University, MI
Hampton University, VA
Harding University, AR
Hardin-Simmons University, TX
Harrisburg University of Science and Technology, PA
Huntingdon College, AL
Huntington University, IN
Husson University, ME
Illinois State University, IL
Indiana University of Pennsylvania, PA
Iowa State University of Science and Technology, IA
James Madison University, VA
John Carroll University, OH
Juniata College, PA
Kean University, NJ
Kennesaw State University, GA
Kent State University, OH
Kettering University, MI
Keystone College, PA
King's College, PA
Kutztown University of Pennsylvania, PA
Lake Forest College, IL
Lawrence Technological University, MI
Limestone College, SC
Lindenwood University, MO
Long Island University, C.W. Post Campus, NY
Longwood University, VA
Louisiana State University and Agricultural and Mechanical College, LA
Louisiana Tech University, LA
Lubbock Christian University, TX
Lycoming College, PA
Malone University, OH
Manhattan College, NY
Massachusetts College of Liberal Arts, MA
Mayville State University, ND
McMurry University, TX
Meredith College, NC
Mesa State College, CO
Michigan State University, MI
Middle Tennessee State University, TN
Midwestern State University, TX
Millersville University of Pennsylvania, PA
Mills College, CA
Milwaukee School of Engineering, WI
Minnesota State University Moorhead, MN
Minot State University, ND
Misericordia University, PA
Mississippi State University, MS
Mississippi University for Women, MS
Missouri University of Science and Technology, MO
Monmouth University, NJ
Montana State University, MT
Montana State University Billings, MT
Montana State University–Northern, MT
Montana Tech of The University of Montana, MT
Moravian College, PA
Morningside College, IA
Murray State University, KY
Muskingum University, OH
New England College, NH
New Jersey Institute of Technology, NJ
New Mexico State University, NM
North Carolina Central University, NC
North Central College, IL
Northeastern Illinois University, IL
Northeastern State University, OK
Northern Arizona University, AZ
Northern Illinois University, IL
Northern Kentucky University, KY
Northern Michigan University, MI
Northern State University, SD
Northwestern Oklahoma State University, OK
Northwest Missouri State University, MO
Northwest Nazarene University, ID
Ohio Northern University, OH
The Ohio State University, OH
Ohio University, OH
Ohio University–Chillicothe, OH
Ohio University–Eastern, OH
Ohio University–Lancaster, OH
Ohio University–Southern Campus, OH
Ohio University–Zanesville, OH
Oklahoma Panhandle State University, OK
Oklahoma State University, OK
Oklahoma Wesleyan University, OK
Ouachita Baptist University, AR
Pace University, NY
Peirce College, PA
Polytechnic Institute of NYU, NY
Portland State University, OR
Post University, CT
Purchase College, State University of New York, NY
Purdue University, IN
Quincy University, IL
The Richard Stockton College of New Jersey, NJ
Ripon College, WI
Rivier College, NH
Robert Morris University Illinois, IL
Rochester Institute of Technology, NY
Rockford College, IL
Rollins College, FL
Sacred Heart University, CT
Saginaw Valley State University, MI
St. Edward's University, TX
Saint Francis University, PA
St. John's University, NY
Saint Louis University, MO
Samford University, AL
San Diego State University, CA
Savannah State University, GA
Seton Hill University, PA
Shepherd University, WV
Shippensburg University of Pennsylvania, PA
Siena College, NY
Skidmore College, NY
Slippery Rock University of Pennsylvania, PA
Sonoma State University, CA
South Dakota School of Mines and Technology, SD
South Dakota State University, SD
Southeastern Louisiana University, LA
Southeastern Oklahoma State University, OK
Southeast Missouri State University, MO
Southern Illinois University Carbondale, IL
Southwestern College, KS
Southwestern Oklahoma State University, OK
Southwest Minnesota State University, MN
State University of New York at Binghamton, NY
State University of New York at Fredonia, NY
State University of New York at Oswego, NY
State University of New York at Plattsburgh, NY
State University of New York College at Geneseo, NY
State University of New York College at Oneonta, NY
State University of New York College at Potsdam, NY
Stephen F. Austin State University, TX
Stetson University, FL
Stevens-Henager College, ID
Stony Brook University, State University of New York, NY
Tennessee Technological University, TN
Tennessee Wesleyan College, TN
Texas A&M University, TX
Texas Tech University, TX
Texas Woman's University, TX
Thiel College, PA
Thomas More College, KY
Towson University, MD
Transylvania University, KY
Trinity Christian College, IL
Truman State University, MO
University of Advancing Technology, AZ
The University of Akron, OH
The University of Alabama, AL
The University of Alabama at Birmingham, AL

The University of Alabama in Huntsville, AL
University of Alaska Anchorage, AK
University of Arkansas at Little Rock, AR
University of California, Davis, CA
University of California, Irvine, CA
University of California, San Diego, CA
University of California, Santa Cruz, CA
University of Central Missouri, MO
University of Central Oklahoma, OK
University of Colorado Boulder, CO
University of Connecticut, CT
University of Dayton, OH
University of Delaware, DE
University of Denver, CO
University of Evansville, IN
University of Florida, FL
University of Great Falls, MT
University of Hawaii at Hilo, HI
University of Houston–Clear Lake, TX
University of Idaho, ID
University of Illinois at Urbana–Champaign, IL
The University of Kansas, KS
University of Kentucky, KY
University of Maine at Fort Kent, ME
University of Mary Hardin-Baylor, TX
University of Maryland, Baltimore County, MD
University of Maryland, College Park, MD
University of Mary Washington, VA
University of Massachusetts Amherst, MA
University of Massachusetts Lowell, MA
University of Miami, FL
University of Michigan, MI
University of Michigan–Dearborn, MI
University of Michigan–Flint, MI
University of Minnesota, Twin Cities Campus, MN
University of Mississippi, MS
University of Missouri, MO
University of Missouri–St. Louis, MO
The University of Montana, MT
University of Nebraska at Omaha, NE
University of Nebraska–Lincoln, NE
University of Nevada, Las Vegas, NV
The University of North Carolina at Asheville, NC
The University of North Carolina at Charlotte, NC
The University of North Carolina Wilmington, NC
University of North Dakota, ND
University of Northern Iowa, IA
University of North Florida, FL
University of Oklahoma, OK
University of Pittsburgh at Bradford, PA
University of Pittsburgh at Johnstown, PA
University of Portland, OR
University of Puget Sound, WA
University of Richmond, VA
University of Rio Grande, OH
University of St. Thomas, TX
University of South Alabama, AL
University of South Carolina, SC
University of South Carolina Aiken, SC
The University of South Dakota, SD
University of South Florida, FL
The University of Tennessee, TN
The University of Tennessee at Martin, TN
The University of Texas at Arlington, TX
The University of Texas at Brownsville, TX
The University of Texas at Dallas, TX
The University of Texas at El Paso, TX
The University of Texas at San Antonio, TX
The University of Texas–Pan American, TX
University of Tulsa, OK
University of Utah, UT
University of Vermont, VT
The University of Virginia's College at Wise, VA
University of West Georgia, GA
University of Wisconsin–Eau Claire, WI
University of Wisconsin–La Crosse, WI
University of Wisconsin–River Falls, WI
University of Wisconsin–Stevens Point, WI
University of Wisconsin–Stout, WI
University of Wisconsin–Superior, WI
University of Wyoming, WY
Utah State University, UT
Valdosta State University, GA
Valley City State University, ND
Virginia Commonwealth University, VA
Virginia Military Institute, VA
Virginia State University, VA
Walsh College of Accountancy and Business Administration, MI
Walsh University, OH
Wartburg College, IA
Washburn University, KS
Washington State University, WA
Washington University in St. Louis, MO
Waynesburg University, PA
Wayne State College, NE
Wayne State University, MI
Western Oregon University, OR
Western Washington University, WA
West Texas A&M University, TX
West Virginia University, WV
Wheaton College, IL
Whitworth University, WA
Wichita State University, KS
Widener University, PA
Wilson College, PA
Wright State University, OH
Xavier University of Louisiana, LA
York College, NE
Youngstown State University, OH

Education

Abilene Christian University, TX
Alaska Pacific University, AK
Alderson-Broaddus College, WV
Alfred University, NY
Alliant International University, CA
Anderson University, SC
Angelo State University, TX
Aquinas College, TN
Arizona State University, AZ
Arkansas State University, AR
Arkansas Tech University, AR
Armstrong Atlantic State University, GA
Auburn University, AL
Augsburg College, MN
Augustana College, IL
Augustana College, SD
Augusta State University, GA
Aurora University, IL
Austin College, TX
Austin Peay State University, TN
Averett University, VA
Ball State University, IN
Baptist Bible College of Pennsylvania, PA
The Baptist College of Florida, FL
Baylor University, TX
Bellarmine University, KY
Berklee College of Music, MA
Berry College, GA
Bethel College, IN
Bethesda Christian University, CA
Birmingham-Southern College, AL
Black Hills State University, SD
Bloomfield College, NJ
Bloomsburg University of Pennsylvania, PA
Boise State University, ID
Boston University, MA
Bowling Green State University, OH
Brenau University, GA
Brevard College, NC
Bryan College, TN
Buena Vista University, IA
Butler University, IN
California Lutheran University, CA
California Polytechnic State University, San Luis Obispo, CA
California State Polytechnic University, Pomona, CA
California State University, Bakersfield, CA
California State University, Chico, CA
California State University, Fresno, CA
California State University, Northridge, CA
California State University, San Bernardino, CA
California State University, Stanislaus, CA
Calvin College, MI
Cambridge College, MA
Cameron University, OK
Campbellsville University, KY
Carroll University, WI
Carson-Newman College, TN
Case Western Reserve University, OH
Catawba College, NC
Centenary College of Louisiana, LA
Central College, IA
Central Methodist University, MO
Central Michigan University, MI
Champlain College, VT
Christopher Newport University, VA
City College of the City University of New York, NY
Clemson University, SC
Cleveland State University, OH
Coastal Carolina University, SC
The College at Brockport, State University of New York, NY
College of Charleston, SC
The College of New Rochelle, NY
College of Saint Mary, NE
The College of Saint Rose, NY
College of Staten Island of the City University of New York, NY
Colorado State University–Pueblo, CO
Columbia College, MO
Columbia International University, SC
Columbus State University, GA
Concordia University, MI
Concordia University Chicago, IL
Concordia University, Nebraska, NE
Concord University, WV
Cornerstone University, MI
Creighton University, NE
Dakota State University, SD
Dallas Baptist University, TX
Dalton State College, GA
Davidson College, NC
Defiance College, OH
Delta State University, MS
DeSales University, PA
Dickinson State University, ND
Dominican College, NY

Dordt College, IA
Dowling College, NY
Drury University, MO
D'Youville College, NY
East Carolina University, NC
Eastern Connecticut State University, CT
Eastern Michigan University, MI
Eastern Washington University, WA
East Tennessee State University, TN
East Texas Baptist University, TX
Edinboro University of Pennsylvania, PA
Elizabeth City State University, NC
Elizabethtown College, PA
Elmhurst College, IL
Elon University, NC
Emmanuel College, GA
Emmanuel College, MA
Emporia State University, KS
Endicott College, MA
Erskine College, SC
Evangel University, MO
Felician College, NJ
Ferris State University, MI
Fitchburg State University, MA
Flagler College, FL
Florida Agricultural and Mechanical University, FL
Florida Gulf Coast University, FL
Florida International University, FL
Florida Southern College, FL
Fort Lewis College, CO
Framingham State University, MA
Francis Marion University, SC
Frostburg State University, MD
Furman University, SC
Gannon University, PA
Gardner-Webb University, NC
George Fox University, OR
Georgia College & State University, GA
Georgia Southern University, GA
Glenville State College, WV
Goshen College, IN
Governors State University, IL
Grace College, IN
Grace University, NE
Grand Valley State University, MI
Greenville College, IL
Grove City College, PA
Hamline University, MN
Hampden-Sydney College, VA
Hampton University, VA
Hardin-Simmons University, TX
Hebrew College, MA
High Point University, NC
Hillsdale College, MI
Hillsdale Free Will Baptist College, OK
Howard Payne University, TX
Huntington University, IN
Husson University, ME
Illinois State University, IL
Indiana University of Pennsylvania, PA
Iowa State University of Science and Technology, IA
James Madison University, VA
Jarvis Christian College, TX
John Carroll University, OH
Johnson Bible College, TN
Juniata College, PA
Kean University, NJ
Kennesaw State University, GA
Kent State University, OH
Keystone College, PA
King's College, PA
Kutztown University of Pennsylvania, PA
Laurel University, NC
Lawrence Technological University, MI
Lee University, TN
Lewis-Clark State College, ID
Limestone College, SC
Lindenwood University, MO
Lindsey Wilson College, KY
Lipscomb University, TN
Lock Haven University of Pennsylvania, PA
Long Island University, Brooklyn Campus, NY
Long Island University, C.W. Post Campus, NY
Longwood University, VA
Louisiana State University and Agricultural and Mechanical College, LA
Louisiana Tech University, LA
Lubbock Christian University, TX
Lycoming College, PA
Malone University, OH
Marquette University, WI
Maryville University of Saint Louis, MO
Marywood University, PA
Massachusetts College of Liberal Arts, MA
The Master's College and Seminary, CA
Mayville State University, ND
McMurry University, TX
Medaille College, NY
Mercer University, GA
Meredith College, NC
Mesa State College, CO
Metropolitan State College of Denver, CO
Metropolitan State University, MN
Miami University, OH
Michigan State University, MI
Mid-Continent University, KY
Middle Tennessee State University, TN
Midwestern State University, TX
Millersville University of Pennsylvania, PA
Millikin University, IL
Minnesota State University Moorhead, MN
Minot State University, ND
Misericordia University, PA
Mississippi State University, MS
Mississippi University for Women, MS
Missouri University of Science and Technology, MO
Molloy College, NY
Monmouth University, NJ
Montana State University, MT
Montana State University Billings, MT
Montana State University–Northern, MT
Montclair State University, NJ
Morehead State University, KY
Mount Mary College, WI
Mount St. Mary's College, CA
Murray State University, KY
New England College, NH
New Life Theological Seminary, NC
New Mexico State University, NM
North Carolina Central University, NC
North Carolina State University, NC
North Central College, IL
Northeastern Illinois University, IL
Northeastern State University, OK
Northern Arizona University, AZ
Northern Illinois University, IL
Northern Kentucky University, KY
Northern Michigan University, MI
Northern State University, SD
North Georgia College & State University, GA
Northwestern Oklahoma State University, OK
Northwestern State University of Louisiana, LA
Northwest Missouri State University, MO
Northwest Nazarene University, ID
Oakland University, MI
Ohio Northern University, OH
The Ohio State University, OH
Ohio University, OH
Ohio University–Chillicothe, OH
Ohio University–Eastern, OH
Ohio University–Lancaster, OH
Ohio University–Southern Campus, OH
Ohio University–Zanesville, OH
Ohio Valley University, WV
Ohio Wesleyan University, OH
Oklahoma City University, OK
Oklahoma Panhandle State University, OK
Oklahoma State University, OK
Oklahoma Wesleyan University, OK
Olivet College, MI
Ouachita Baptist University, AR
Our Lady of Holy Cross College, LA
Pace University, NY
Pacific Union College, CA
Pacific University, OR
Piedmont College, GA
Plymouth State University, NH
Point Loma Nazarene University, CA
Portland State University, OR
Post University, CT
Prairie View A&M University, TX
Purdue University, IN
Purdue University North Central, IN
Quincy University, IL
Randolph College, VA
Regent University, VA
The Richard Stockton College of New Jersey, NJ
Ripon College, WI
Rivier College, NH
Rockford College, IL
Sacred Heart University, CT
Saginaw Valley State University, MI
St. Catherine University, MN
St. Edward's University, TX
Saint Francis University, PA
St. John's University, NY
Saint Louis University, MO
Saint Martin's University, WA
St. Thomas Aquinas College, NY
Samford University, AL
San Diego State University, CA
Savannah College of Art and Design, GA
Schreiner University, TX
Seton Hill University, PA
Shasta Bible College, CA
Shepherd University, WV
Shippensburg University of Pennsylvania, PA
Siena College, NY
Slippery Rock University of Pennsylvania, PA
Sonoma State University, CA
South Dakota State University, SD
Southeastern Louisiana University, LA
Southeastern Oklahoma State University, OK
Southeast Missouri State University, MO
Southern Adventist University, TN
Southern Illinois University Carbondale, IL
Southern Illinois University Edwardsville, IL
Southern Oregon University, OR
Southwestern Oklahoma State University, OK
Southwest Minnesota State University, MN
State University of New York at Binghamton, NY

State University of New York at Fredonia, NY
State University of New York at New Paltz, NY
State University of New York at Oswego, NY
State University of New York at Plattsburgh, NY
State University of New York College at Cortland, NY
State University of New York College at Geneseo, NY
State University of New York College at Oneonta, NY
State University of New York College at Potsdam, NY
Stephen F. Austin State University, TX
Stetson University, FL
Sul Ross State University, TX
Tennessee Technological University, TN
Tennessee Wesleyan College, TN
Texas A&M International University, TX
Texas A&M University, TX
Texas A&M University–Texarkana, TX
Texas Christian University, TX
Texas Lutheran University, TX
Texas State University–San Marcos, TX
Texas Tech University, TX
Texas Woman's University, TX
Thiel College, PA
Thomas More College, KY
Thomas University, GA
Towson University, MD
Trevecca Nazarene University, TN
Trinity Christian College, IL
Truman State University, MO
Union University, TN
The University of Akron, OH
The University of Alabama, AL
The University of Alabama in Huntsville, AL
University of Alaska Anchorage, AK
The University of Arizona, AZ
University of Arkansas at Little Rock, AR
University of California, Irvine, CA
University of California, Riverside, CA
University of Central Missouri, MO
University of Central Oklahoma, OK
University of Colorado Boulder, CO
University of Connecticut, CT
University of Dallas, TX
University of Dayton, OH
University of Delaware, DE
University of Evansville, IN
University of Florida, FL
University of Georgia, GA
University of Great Falls, MT
University of Houston–Clear Lake, TX
University of Idaho, ID
University of Illinois at Urbana–Champaign, IL
The University of Kansas, KS
University of Kentucky, KY
University of Louisville, KY
University of Maine at Fort Kent, ME
University of Mary Hardin-Baylor, TX
University of Maryland, Baltimore County, MD
University of Maryland, College Park, MD
University of Mary Washington, VA
University of Massachusetts Amherst, MA
University of Memphis, TN
University of Miami, FL
University of Michigan, MI
University of Michigan–Dearborn, MI
University of Michigan–Flint, MI
University of Minnesota, Twin Cities Campus, MN
University of Mississippi, MS
University of Missouri, MO
University of Missouri–St. Louis, MO
The University of Montana, MT
University of Montevallo, AL
University of Nebraska at Omaha, NE
University of Nebraska–Lincoln, NE
University of Nevada, Las Vegas, NV
University of New Hampshire, NH
University of New Orleans, LA
The University of North Carolina at Asheville, NC
The University of North Carolina at Chapel Hill, NC
The University of North Carolina at Charlotte, NC
The University of North Carolina at Greensboro, NC
The University of North Carolina at Pembroke, NC
The University of North Carolina Wilmington, NC
University of North Dakota, ND
University of Northern Colorado, CO
University of Northern Iowa, IA
University of North Florida, FL
University of Oklahoma, OK
University of Oregon, OR
University of Pittsburgh at Bradford, PA
University of Pittsburgh at Johnstown, PA
University of Portland, OR
University of Rio Grande, OH
University of St. Francis, IL
University of St. Thomas, MN
University of St. Thomas, TX
University of South Carolina, SC
University of South Carolina Aiken, SC
The University of South Dakota, SD
University of Southern Indiana, IN
University of South Florida, FL
The University of Tennessee, TN
The University of Tennessee at Chattanooga, TN
The University of Tennessee at Martin, TN
The University of Texas at Arlington, TX
The University of Texas at Brownsville, TX
The University of Texas at El Paso, TX
The University of Texas at San Antonio, TX
The University of Texas–Pan American, TX
University of the Ozarks, AR
University of the Southwest, NM
The University of Toledo, OH
University of Tulsa, OK
University of Utah, UT
University of Vermont, VT
The University of Virginia's College at Wise, VA
University of West Georgia, GA
University of Wisconsin–Eau Claire, WI
University of Wisconsin–Green Bay, WI
University of Wisconsin–La Crosse, WI
University of Wisconsin–Parkside, WI
University of Wisconsin–River Falls, WI
University of Wisconsin–Stevens Point, WI
University of Wisconsin–Stout, WI
University of Wisconsin–Superior, WI
University of Wyoming, WY
Utah State University, UT
Valdosta State University, GA
Valley City State University, ND
Virginia Commonwealth University, VA
Virginia State University, VA
Walla Walla University, WA
Walsh University, OH
Wartburg College, IA
Washburn University, KS
Washington & Jefferson College, PA
Washington State University, WA
Washington University in St. Louis, MO
Wayland Baptist University, TX
Waynesburg University, PA
Wayne State College, NE
Wayne State University, MI
Wesleyan College, GA
Western Carolina University, NC
Western Illinois University, IL
Western Kentucky University, KY
Western Oregon University, OR
Western Washington University, WA
West Liberty University, WV
West Texas A&M University, TX
West Virginia University, WV
Wheaton College, IL
Wichita State University, KS
Widener University, PA
William Jessup University, CA
Williams Baptist College, AR
Wilson College, PA
Wright State University, OH
Xavier University of Louisiana, LA
York College, NE
Youngstown State University, OH

Engineering/Technologies

Alfred University, NY
Arizona State University, AZ
Arkansas State University, AR
Armstrong Atlantic State University, GA
Auburn University, AL
Austin College, TX
Averett University, VA
Ball State University, IN
Baylor University, TX
Berklee College of Music, MA
Birmingham-Southern College, AL
Bluefield State College, WV
Boise State University, ID
Boston University, MA
Bowie State University, MD
Bowling Green State University, OH
Bucknell University, PA
Butler University, IN
California Polytechnic State University, San Luis Obispo, CA
California State Polytechnic University, Pomona, CA
California State University, Chico, CA
California State University, Fresno, CA
California State University, Fullerton, CA
California State University, Northridge, CA
Calvin College, MI
Cameron University, OK
Case Western Reserve University, OH
Centenary College of Louisiana, LA
Central Michigan University, MI
Champlain College, VT
Christian Brothers University, TN
Christopher Newport University, VA
The Citadel, The Military College of South Carolina, SC
City College of the City University of New York, NY
Clarkson University, NY
Clemson University, SC

Cleveland State University, OH
College of Charleston, SC
The College of Saint Rose, NY
College of Staten Island of the City University of New York, NY
Colorado School of Mines, CO
Colorado State University–Pueblo, CO
Cooper Union for the Advancement of Science and Art, NY
Dalton State College, GA
Dordt College, IA
East Carolina University, NC
Eastern Michigan University, MI
Eastern Washington University, WA
East Tennessee State University, TN
ECPI College of Technology, VA
Edinboro University of Pennsylvania, PA
Elizabethtown College, PA
Elon University, NC
Emmanuel College, MA
Emporia State University, KS
Evangel University, MO
Ferris State University, MI
Fitchburg State University, MA
Florida Agricultural and Mechanical University, FL
Florida Atlantic University, FL
Florida Gulf Coast University, FL
Florida International University, FL
Frostburg State University, MD
Furman University, SC
Gannon University, PA
Geneva College, PA
George Fox University, OR
Georgia Institute of Technology, GA
Georgia Southern University, GA
Gonzaga University, WA
Graceland University, IA
Grand Valley State University, MI
Greenville College, IL
Grove City College, PA
Hampton University, VA
Harding University, AR
Illinois Institute of Technology, IL
Illinois State University, IL
Indiana University of Pennsylvania, PA
Iowa State University of Science and Technology, IA
James Madison University, VA
The Johns Hopkins University, MD
Kent State University, OH
Kettering University, MI
Lawrence Technological University, MI
Lehigh University, PA
Lindenwood University, MO
Lipscomb University, TN
Loras College, IA
Louisiana State University and Agricultural and Mechanical College, LA
Louisiana Tech University, LA
Maine Maritime Academy, ME
Marquette University, WI
Mercer University, GA
Mesa State College, CO
Miami University, OH
Michigan State University, MI
Middle Tennessee State University, TN
Midwestern State University, TX
Milwaukee School of Engineering, WI
Minnesota State University Moorhead, MN
Mississippi State University, MS
Missouri University of Science and Technology, MO
Montana State University, MT
Montana State University Billings, MT
Montana State University–Northern, MT
Montana Tech of The University of Montana, MT
Morehead State University, KY
Murray State University, KY
Muskingum University, OH
New England College, NH
New Jersey Institute of Technology, NJ
New Mexico State University, NM
North Carolina State University, NC
Northern Arizona University, AZ
Northern Illinois University, IL
Northern Kentucky University, KY
Northern Michigan University, MI
Northwestern State University of Louisiana, LA
Oakland University, MI
Ohio Northern University, OH
The Ohio State University, OH
Ohio University, OH
Ohio University–Chillicothe, OH
Ohio University–Eastern, OH
Ohio University–Lancaster, OH
Ohio University–Southern Campus, OH
Ohio University–Zanesville, OH
Oklahoma Christian University, OK
Oklahoma State University, OK
Old Dominion University, VA
Ouachita Baptist University, AR
Philadelphia University, PA
Point Loma Nazarene University, CA
Polytechnic Institute of NYU, NY
Portland State University, OR
Purdue University, IN
Rice University, TX
Rochester Institute of Technology, NY
Rollins College, FL
Saginaw Valley State University, MI
Saint Francis University, PA
Saint Louis University, MO
Saint Martin's University, WA
San Diego State University, CA
Santa Clara University, CA
Savannah State University, GA
Seattle Pacific University, WA
Shepherd University, WV
Sonoma State University, CA
South Dakota School of Mines and Technology, SD
South Dakota State University, SD
Southeastern Oklahoma State University, OK
Southeast Missouri State University, MO
Southern Illinois University Carbondale, IL
Southwestern Oklahoma State University, OK
State University of New York at Binghamton, NY
State University of New York at Plattsburgh, NY
State University of New York College at Potsdam, NY
State University of New York College of Environmental Science and Forestry, NY
Stony Brook University, State University of New York, NY
Tennessee Technological University, TN
Texas A&M International University, TX
Texas A&M University, TX
Texas A&M University–Texarkana, TX
Texas Christian University, TX
Texas Southern University, TX
Texas Tech University, TX
Union University, TN
The University of Akron, OH
The University of Alabama, AL
The University of Alabama at Birmingham, AL
The University of Alabama in Huntsville, AL
University of Alaska Anchorage, AK
University of Alaska Fairbanks, AK
The University of Arizona, AZ
University of Arkansas at Little Rock, AR
University of California, Davis, CA
University of California, Irvine, CA
University of California, Riverside, CA
University of California, San Diego, CA
University of Central Missouri, MO
University of Colorado Boulder, CO
University of Connecticut, CT
University of Dayton, OH
University of Delaware, DE
University of Denver, CO
University of Evansville, IN
University of Florida, FL
University of Hartford, CT
University of Idaho, ID
University of Illinois at Urbana–Champaign, IL
The University of Iowa, IA
The University of Kansas, KS
University of Kentucky, KY
University of Louisville, KY
University of Maryland, Baltimore County, MD
University of Maryland, College Park, MD
University of Massachusetts Amherst, MA
University of Massachusetts Lowell, MA
University of Memphis, TN
University of Miami, FL
University of Michigan, MI
University of Michigan–Dearborn, MI
University of Michigan–Flint, MI
University of Minnesota, Twin Cities Campus, MN
University of Mississippi, MS
University of Missouri, MO
University of Missouri–St. Louis, MO
University of Nebraska at Omaha, NE
University of Nebraska–Lincoln, NE
University of Nevada, Las Vegas, NV
University of New Hampshire, NH
University of New Orleans, LA
The University of North Carolina at Asheville, NC
The University of North Carolina at Charlotte, NC
The University of North Carolina Wilmington, NC
University of North Dakota, ND
University of North Florida, FL
University of Oklahoma, OK
University of Pittsburgh at Bradford, PA
University of Pittsburgh at Johnstown, PA
University of Portland, OR
University of Rochester, NY
University of South Carolina, SC
University of South Carolina Aiken, SC
University of Southern Indiana, IN
University of South Florida, FL
The University of Tennessee, TN
The University of Tennessee at Chattanooga, TN
The University of Tennessee at Martin, TN
The University of Texas at Arlington, TX
The University of Texas at Brownsville, TX

The University of Texas at Dallas, TX
The University of Texas at El Paso, TX
The University of Texas at San Antonio, TX
The University of Texas at Tyler, TX
The University of Texas–Pan American, TX
The University of Toledo, OH
University of Tulsa, OK
University of Utah, UT
University of Vermont, VT
University of Wisconsin–Green Bay, WI
University of Wisconsin–Parkside, WI
University of Wisconsin–Stevens Point, WI
University of Wisconsin–Stout, WI
University of Wyoming, WY
Utah State University, UT
Valdosta State University, GA
Valparaiso University, IN
Virginia Commonwealth University, VA
Virginia Military Institute, VA
Virginia State University, VA
Walla Walla University, WA
Washburn University, KS
Washington State University, WA
Washington University in St. Louis, MO
Wayne State University, MI
Wesleyan College, GA
Western Kentucky University, KY
Western Washington University, WA
West Texas A&M University, TX
West Virginia University, WV
West Virginia University Institute of Technology, WV
Wichita State University, KS
Widener University, PA
Wright State University, OH
Xavier University of Louisiana, LA
York College of Pennsylvania, PA
Youngstown State University, OH

English

Abilene Christian University, TX
Alfred University, NY
Alliant International University, CA
Angelo State University, TX
Arizona State University, AZ
Arkansas State University, AR
Arkansas Tech University, AR
Armstrong Atlantic State University, GA
Auburn University, AL
Augsburg College, MN
Augustana College, IL
Augustana College, SD
Augusta State University, GA
Austin College, TX
Austin Peay State University, TN
Averett University, VA
Ball State University, IN
Baylor University, TX
Berry College, GA
Bethel College, IN
Birmingham-Southern College, AL
Black Hills State University, SD
Bloomfield College, NJ
Bloomsburg University of Pennsylvania, PA
Boise State University, ID
Bowling Green State University, OH
Brevard College, NC
Bryan College, TN
Butler University, IN
California Lutheran University, CA
California Polytechnic State University, San Luis Obispo, CA
California State University, Chico, CA
California State University, Fresno, CA
California State University, Northridge, CA
California State University, Stanislaus, CA
Calvin College, MI
Cameron University, OK
Campbellsville University, KY
Case Western Reserve University, OH
Cedar Crest College, PA
Centenary College of Louisiana, LA
Central Methodist University, MO
Central Michigan University, MI
Christopher Newport University, VA
City College of the City University of New York, NY
Clemson University, SC
Cleveland State University, OH
Coe College, IA
The College at Brockport, State University of New York, NY
College of Charleston, SC
The College of New Rochelle, NY
The College of Saint Rose, NY
Colorado State University–Pueblo, CO
Columbia College, MO
Columbia International University, SC
Columbus State University, GA
Concordia University Chicago, IL
Concordia University, Nebraska, NE
Concord University, WV
Cornerstone University, MI
Dakota State University, SD
Dalton State College, GA
Defiance College, OH
Delta State University, MS
DePauw University, IN
DeSales University, PA
Dickinson State University, ND
Dordt College, IA
Drury University, MO
D'Youville College, NY
East Carolina University, NC
Eastern Connecticut State University, CT
Eastern Michigan University, MI
Eastern Washington University, WA
East Tennessee State University, TN
East Texas Baptist University, TX
Edinboro University of Pennsylvania, PA
Elizabethtown College, PA
Elmhurst College, IL
Emmanuel College, GA
Emporia State University, KS
Erskine College, SC
Evangel University, MO
Felician College, NJ
Fitchburg State University, MA
Flagler College, FL
Florida Agricultural and Mechanical University, FL
Florida International University, FL
Fort Lewis College, CO
Francis Marion University, SC
Frostburg State University, MD
Furman University, SC
Gannon University, PA
Gardner-Webb University, NC
Georgia College & State University, GA
Georgian Court University, NJ
Georgia Southern University, GA
Glenville State College, WV
Governors State University, IL
Grace College, IN
Graceland University, IA
Grand Valley State University, MI
Grove City College, PA
Hamline University, MN
Harding University, AR
Hardin-Simmons University, TX
High Point University, NC
Hillsdale College, MI
Hillsdale Free Will Baptist College, OK
Howard Payne University, TX
Illinois State University, IL
Indiana University of Pennsylvania, PA
Iowa State University of Science and Technology, IA
James Madison University, VA
John Carroll University, OH
Juniata College, PA
Kean University, NJ
Kennesaw State University, GA
Kent State University, OH
King's College, PA
Kutztown University of Pennsylvania, PA
Lewis-Clark State College, ID
Limestone College, SC
Lindenwood University, MO
Lindsey Wilson College, KY
Lipscomb University, TN
Lock Haven University of Pennsylvania, PA
Longwood University, VA
Louisiana State University and Agricultural and Mechanical College, LA
Louisiana Tech University, LA
Lubbock Christian University, TX
Lycoming College, PA
Malone University, OH
Manchester College, IN
Marquette University, WI
Massachusetts College of Liberal Arts, MA
Mayville State University, ND
McMurry University, TX
Mercer University, GA
Meredith College, NC
Mesa State College, CO
Methodist University, NC
Michigan State University, MI
Mid-Continent University, KY
Middle Tennessee State University, TN
Midwestern State University, TX
Millersville University of Pennsylvania, PA
Millikin University, IL
Minnesota State University Moorhead, MN
Minot State University, ND
Mississippi State University, MS
Mississippi University for Women, MS
Missouri University of Science and Technology, MO
Molloy College, NY
Montana State University, MT
Montana State University Billings, MT
Montana State University–Northern, MT
Montclair State University, NJ
Mount Mary College, WI
Murray State University, KY
New England College, NH
New Mexico State University, NM
North Carolina Central University, NC
North Central College, IL
Northeastern Illinois University, IL
Northeastern State University, OK
Northern Arizona University, AZ
Northern Illinois University, IL
Northern Kentucky University, KY
Northern Michigan University, MI
Northern State University, SD
North Georgia College & State University, GA

Northwestern Oklahoma State University, OK
Northwestern State University of Louisiana, LA
Northwest Missouri State University, MO
Northwest Nazarene University, ID
Oakland University, MI
Ohio Northern University, OH
The Ohio State University, OH
Ohio University, OH
Ohio University–Chillicothe, OH
Ohio University–Eastern, OH
Ohio University–Lancaster, OH
Ohio University–Southern Campus, OH
Ohio University–Zanesville, OH
Ohio Valley University, WV
Oklahoma Panhandle State University, OK
Oklahoma State University, OK
Old Dominion University, VA
Olivet College, MI
Ouachita Baptist University, AR
Pace University, NY
Pacific University, OR
Piedmont College, GA
Plymouth State University, NH
Post University, CT
Purchase College, State University of New York, NY
Purdue University North Central, IN
Quincy University, IL
Randolph College, VA
Regent University, VA
Ripon College, WI
Rivier College, NH
Rockford College, IL
Rockhurst University, MO
Sacred Heart University, CT
St. Catherine University, MN
St. Edward's University, TX
Saint Francis University, PA
St. John Fisher College, NY
St. John's University, NY
Saint Louis University, MO
Samford University, AL
San Diego State University, CA
Savannah State University, GA
Schreiner University, TX
Seton Hill University, PA
Shepherd University, WV
Shippensburg University of Pennsylvania, PA
Shorter University, GA
Siena College, NY
Slippery Rock University of Pennsylvania, PA
Sonoma State University, CA
South Dakota State University, SD
Southeastern Louisiana University, LA
Southeastern Oklahoma State University, OK
Southeast Missouri State University, MO
Southern Adventist University, TN
Southern Illinois University Carbondale, IL
Southern Oregon University, OR
Southwestern Oklahoma State University, OK
Southwest Minnesota State University, MN
State University of New York at Binghamton, NY
State University of New York at Fredonia, NY
State University of New York at Oswego, NY
State University of New York at Plattsburgh, NY
State University of New York College at Geneseo, NY
State University of New York College at Oneonta, NY
State University of New York College at Potsdam, NY
Stetson University, FL
Stony Brook University, State University of New York, NY
Sul Ross State University, TX
Tennessee Technological University, TN
Tennessee Wesleyan College, TN
Texas A&M International University, TX
Texas A&M University–Texarkana, TX
Texas Christian University, TX
Texas State University–San Marcos, TX
Texas Tech University, TX
Texas Woman's University, TX
Thiel College, PA
Thomas More College, KY
Thomas University, GA
Towson University, MD
Trevecca Nazarene University, TN
Trinity Christian College, IL
Truman State University, MO
The University of Akron, OH
The University of Alabama, AL
The University of Alabama in Huntsville, AL
University of Alaska Anchorage, AK
University of Arkansas at Little Rock, AR
University of California, Davis, CA
University of California, Riverside, CA
University of Central Missouri, MO
University of Colorado Boulder, CO
University of Connecticut, CT
University of Dayton, OH
University of Delaware, DE
University of Evansville, IN
University of Hawaii at Hilo, HI
University of Idaho, ID
University of Illinois at Urbana–Champaign, IL
The University of Kansas, KS
University of Kentucky, KY
University of Louisville, KY
University of Maine at Fort Kent, ME
University of Mary Hardin-Baylor, TX
University of Maryland, Baltimore County, MD
University of Maryland, College Park, MD
University of Mary Washington, VA
University of Massachusetts Amherst, MA
University of Massachusetts Lowell, MA
University of Memphis, TN
University of Miami, FL
University of Michigan, MI
University of Michigan–Flint, MI
University of Minnesota, Twin Cities Campus, MN
University of Mississippi, MS
University of Missouri, MO
University of Missouri–St. Louis, MO
The University of Montana, MT
University of Montevallo, AL
University of Nebraska at Omaha, NE
University of Nebraska–Lincoln, NE
University of Nevada, Las Vegas, NV
University of New Hampshire, NH
University of New Orleans, LA
The University of North Carolina at Asheville, NC
The University of North Carolina at Chapel Hill, NC
The University of North Carolina at Greensboro, NC
The University of North Carolina at Pembroke, NC
The University of North Carolina Wilmington, NC
University of North Dakota, ND
University of Northern Colorado, CO
University of Oklahoma, OK
University of Oregon, OR
University of Pittsburgh at Bradford, PA
University of Pittsburgh at Johnstown, PA
University of Portland, OR
University of Puget Sound, WA
University of Rio Grande, OH
University of St. Thomas, MN
University of St. Thomas, TX
University of South Carolina, SC
University of South Carolina Aiken, SC
The University of South Dakota, SD
University of South Florida, FL
The University of Tampa, FL
The University of Tennessee at Chattanooga, TN
The University of Tennessee at Martin, TN
The University of Texas at Arlington, TX
The University of Texas at Brownsville, TX
The University of Texas at El Paso, TX
The University of Texas at San Antonio, TX
The University of Texas–Pan American, TX
University of the Ozarks, AR
University of the Southwest, NM
The University of Toledo, OH
University of Tulsa, OK
University of Utah, UT
University of Vermont, VT
The University of Virginia's College at Wise, VA
University of West Georgia, GA
University of Wisconsin–Eau Claire, WI
University of Wisconsin–La Crosse, WI
University of Wisconsin–Parkside, WI
University of Wisconsin–River Falls, WI
University of Wisconsin–Stevens Point, WI
University of Wisconsin–Superior, WI
University of Wyoming, WY
Utah State University, UT
Valdosta State University, GA
Valley City State University, ND
Virginia Military Institute, VA
Virginia State University, VA
Walla Walla University, WA
Walsh University, OH
Wartburg College, IA
Washburn University, KS
Washington & Jefferson College, PA
Washington State University, WA
Washington University in St. Louis, MO
Wayland Baptist University, TX
Waynesburg University, PA
Wayne State College, NE
Wayne State University, MI
Wesleyan College, GA
Western Carolina University, NC
Western Kentucky University, KY
Western Oregon University, OR
Western Washington University, WA
West Liberty University, WV
West Texas A&M University, TX
West Virginia State University, WV
West Virginia University, WV
West Virginia Wesleyan College, WV
Wichita State University, KS
Widener University, PA
William Jessup University, CA
Wilson College, PA
Wright State University, OH

Xavier University of Louisiana, LA
York College, NE
Youngstown State University, OH

Foreign Languages

Abilene Christian University, TX
Adelphi University, NY
Alfred University, NY
Alliant International University, CA
Angelo State University, TX
Arizona State University, AZ
Armstrong Atlantic State University, GA
Auburn University, AL
Augsburg College, MN
Augustana College, IL
Augustana College, SD
Austin College, TX
Austin Peay State University, TN
Averett University, VA
Ball State University, IN
Baylor University, TX
Birmingham-Southern College, AL
Black Hills State University, SD
Bloomsburg University of Pennsylvania, PA
Boise State University, ID
Boston University, MA
Bowling Green State University, OH
Bryan College, TN
Butler University, IN
California Lutheran University, CA
California Polytechnic State University, San Luis Obispo, CA
California State University, Bakersfield, CA
California State University, Chico, CA
California State University, Fresno, CA
California State University, San Bernardino, CA
California State University, Stanislaus, CA
Calvin College, MI
Cameron University, OK
Case Western Reserve University, OH
Centenary College of Louisiana, LA
Central College, IA
Central Methodist University, MO
Central Michigan University, MI
Centre College, KY
Christopher Newport University, VA
City College of the City University of New York, NY
Clarke University, IA
Clemson University, SC
Coe College, IA
The College at Brockport, State University of New York, NY
College of Charleston, SC
The College of New Rochelle, NY
The College of Saint Rose, NY
Colorado State University–Pueblo, CO
Concordia University Chicago, IL
Cornerstone University, MI
Davidson College, NC
Delta State University, MS
DePauw University, IN
DeSales University, PA
Dickinson State University, ND
Dordt College, IA
Drury University, MO
East Carolina University, NC
Eastern Connecticut State University, CT
Eastern Michigan University, MI
Eastern Washington University, WA
Edgewood College, WI
Edinboro University of Pennsylvania, PA
Elizabethtown College, PA
Elmhurst College, IL
Emmanuel College, MA
Emporia State University, KS
Erskine College, SC
Evangel University, MO
Fitchburg State University, MA
Flagler College, FL
Florida Agricultural and Mechanical University, FL
Florida International University, FL
Fordham University, NY
Frostburg State University, MD
Furman University, SC
Gannon University, PA
Gardner-Webb University, NC
Georgia College & State University, GA
Georgian Court University, NJ
Georgia Southern University, GA
Grand Valley State University, MI
Grove City College, PA
Hamline University, MN
Hardin-Simmons University, TX
High Point University, NC
Hillsdale College, MI
Illinois Institute of Technology, IL
Illinois State University, IL
Indiana University of Pennsylvania, PA
Iowa State University of Science and Technology, IA
John Carroll University, OH
Juniata College, PA
Kean University, NJ
Kennesaw State University, GA
King's College, PA
Kutztown University of Pennsylvania, PA
Lake Forest College, IL
Lindenwood University, MO
Lock Haven University of Pennsylvania, PA
Louisiana State University and Agricultural and Mechanical College, LA
Louisiana Tech University, LA
Lubbock Christian University, TX
Lycoming College, PA
Malone University, OH
Manchester College, IN
Manhattan College, NY
Marquette University, WI
Marywood University, PA
Mercer University, GA
Meredith College, NC
Mesa State College, CO
Michigan State University, MI
Middle Tennessee State University, TN
Midwestern State University, TX
Millersville University of Pennsylvania, PA
Millikin University, IL
Mississippi State University, MS
Monmouth College, IL
Montana State University, MT
Montana State University Billings, MT
Montana State University–Northern, MT
Montclair State University, NJ
Moravian College, PA
Murray State University, KY
New Life Theological Seminary, NC
New Mexico State University, NM
North Central College, IL
Northeastern Illinois University, IL
Northeastern State University, OK
Northern Arizona University, AZ
Northern Illinois University, IL
Northern Michigan University, MI
Northern State University, SD
Northwestern Oklahoma State University, OK
Northwest Missouri State University, MO
Oakland University, MI
Ohio Northern University, OH
The Ohio State University, OH
Ohio University, OH
Ohio University–Chillicothe, OH
Ohio University–Eastern, OH
Ohio University–Lancaster, OH
Ohio University–Southern Campus, OH
Ohio University–Zanesville, OH
Oklahoma State University, OK
Olivet College, MI
Ouachita Baptist University, AR
Pace University, NY
Pacific University, OR
Piedmont College, GA
Portland State University, OR
Regent University, VA
Ripon College, WI
Rivier College, NH
Rockford College, IL
Rockhurst University, MO
St. Catherine University, MN
St. Edward's University, TX
St. John Fisher College, NY
St. John's University, NY
Saint Louis University, MO
Samford University, AL
San Diego State University, CA
Seton Hill University, PA
Shippensburg University of Pennsylvania, PA
Shorter University, GA
Siena College, NY
Sonoma State University, CA
South Dakota State University, SD
Southeastern Louisiana University, LA
Southeast Missouri State University, MO
Southern Illinois University Carbondale, IL
Southern Oregon University, OR
Southwestern Oklahoma State University, OK
State University of New York at Binghamton, NY
State University of New York at Fredonia, NY
State University of New York at New Paltz, NY
State University of New York at Oswego, NY
State University of New York College at Geneseo, NY
State University of New York College at Potsdam, NY
Stetson University, FL
Stony Brook University, State University of New York, NY
Sul Ross State University, TX
Tennessee Technological University, TN
Tennessee Wesleyan College, TN
Texas A&M International University, TX
Texas Christian University, TX
Texas Tech University, TX
Texas Woman's University, TX
Towson University, MD
Truman State University, MO
The University of Akron, OH
The University of Alabama, AL
The University of Alabama in Huntsville, AL
University of Arkansas at Little Rock, AR
University of California, Davis, CA
University of California, Irvine, CA
University of Central Missouri, MO
University of Central Oklahoma, OK
University of Colorado Boulder, CO

University of Connecticut, CT
University of Dallas, TX
University of Dayton, OH
University of Delaware, DE
University of Evansville, IN
University of Idaho, ID
University of Illinois at Urbana–Champaign, IL
The University of Kansas, KS
University of Kentucky, KY
University of Louisville, KY
University of Maine at Fort Kent, ME
University of Mary Hardin-Baylor, TX
University of Maryland, Baltimore County, MD
University of Maryland, College Park, MD
University of Mary Washington, VA
University of Miami, FL
University of Michigan, MI
University of Michigan–Dearborn, MI
University of Michigan–Flint, MI
University of Minnesota, Twin Cities Campus, MN
University of Mississippi, MS
University of Missouri, MO
University of Missouri–St. Louis, MO
The University of Montana, MT
University of Montevallo, AL
University of Nebraska at Omaha, NE
University of Nebraska–Lincoln, NE
University of Nevada, Las Vegas, NV
University of New Orleans, LA
The University of North Carolina at Greensboro, NC
The University of North Carolina Wilmington, NC
University of North Dakota, ND
University of Oklahoma, OK
University of Oregon, OR
University of Portland, OR
University of Puget Sound, WA
University of St. Thomas, TX
University of South Carolina, SC
The University of South Dakota, SD
University of South Florida, FL
The University of Texas at Arlington, TX
The University of Texas at Brownsville, TX
The University of Texas at San Antonio, TX
The University of Toledo, OH
University of Tulsa, OK
University of Utah, UT
University of Vermont, VT
University of West Georgia, GA
University of Wisconsin–Eau Claire, WI
University of Wisconsin–La Crosse, WI
University of Wisconsin–Parkside, WI
University of Wisconsin–River Falls, WI
University of Wisconsin–Stevens Point, WI
University of Wyoming, WY
Utah State University, UT
Valdosta State University, GA
Valparaiso University, IN
Virginia Commonwealth University, VA
Walla Walla University, WA
Walsh University, OH
Washburn University, KS
Washington State University, WA
Washington University in St. Louis, MO
Wayne State College, NE
Wayne State University, MI
Wesleyan College, GA
Western Illinois University, IL
Western Kentucky University, KY
Western Oregon University, OR
Western Washington University, WA
West Virginia State University, WV
West Virginia University, WV
Wheaton College, IL
Wichita State University, KS
Widener University, PA
Wilson College, PA
Wright State University, OH
Xavier University, OH
Xavier University of Louisiana, LA
Youngstown State University, OH

Health Fields

Alderson-Broaddus College, WV
Allen College, IA
Aquinas College, TN
Arizona State University, AZ
Arkansas State University, AR
Arkansas Tech University, AR
Armstrong Atlantic State University, GA
Auburn University, AL
Augsburg College, MN
Augustana College, SD
Augusta State University, GA
Austin College, TX
Austin Peay State University, TN
Averett University, VA
Ball State University, IN
Baylor University, TX
Bellarmine University, KY
Bethel College, IN
Birmingham-Southern College, AL
Black Hills State University, SD
Bloomfield College, NJ
Bloomsburg University of Pennsylvania, PA
Boise State University, ID
Bowling Green State University, OH
Brenau University, GA
Brevard College, NC
Caldwell College, NJ
California Polytechnic State University, San Luis Obispo, CA
California State University, Bakersfield, CA
California State University, Chico, CA
California State University, Fresno, CA
California State University, San Bernardino, CA
California State University, Stanislaus, CA
Calvin College, MI
Campbellsville University, KY
Carroll University, WI
Case Western Reserve University, OH
Centenary College of Louisiana, LA
Central College, IA
Central Methodist University, MO
Central Michigan University, MI
Champlain College, VT
Clemson University, SC
Cleveland State University, OH
The College at Brockport, State University of New York, NY
College of Charleston, SC
The College of New Rochelle, NY
College of Staten Island of the City University of New York, NY
Colorado State University–Pueblo, CO
Columbus State University, GA
Concordia University, Nebraska, NE
Dalton State College, GA
Defiance College, OH
Delta State University, MS
DePauw University, IN
DeSales University, PA
Dickinson State University, ND
Dominican College, NY
Drury University, MO
D'Youville College, NY
East Carolina University, NC
Eastern Michigan University, MI
Eastern Washington University, WA
East Tennessee State University, TN
East Texas Baptist University, TX
ECPI College of Technology, VA
Edinboro University of Pennsylvania, PA
EDP College of Puerto Rico–San Sebastian, PR
Elizabethtown College, PA
Elmhurst College, IL
Emmanuel College, GA
Emmanuel College, MA
Emporia State University, KS
Endicott College, MA
Felician College, NJ
Ferris State University, MI
Fitchburg State University, MA
Florida Agricultural and Mechanical University, FL
Florida Gulf Coast University, FL
Florida International University, FL
Florida Southern College, FL
Francis Marion University, SC
Frostburg State University, MD
Furman University, SC
Gardner-Webb University, NC
Georgia College & State University, GA
Georgia Health Sciences University, GA
Georgia Southern University, GA
Governors State University, IL
Grace University, NE
Grand Valley State University, MI
Hamline University, MN
Hampden-Sydney College, VA
Hampton University, VA
Harding University, AR
Hardin-Simmons University, TX
Hawai'i Pacific University, HI
Hillsdale College, MI
Houston Baptist University, TX
Husson University, ME
Illinois Institute of Technology, IL
Illinois State University, IL
Indiana University of Pennsylvania, PA
Iowa State University of Science and Technology, IA
James Madison University, VA
Jefferson College of Health Sciences, VA
John Carroll University, OH
Juniata College, PA
Kean University, NJ
Kennesaw State University, GA
Kent State University, OH
Kentucky State University, KY
King's College, PA
Kutztown University of Pennsylvania, PA
Lakeview College of Nursing, IL
Lewis-Clark State College, ID
Limestone College, SC
Lindenwood University, MO
Lock Haven University of Pennsylvania, PA
Long Island University, Brooklyn Campus, NY
Long Island University, C.W. Post Campus, NY
Louisiana College, LA
Louisiana Tech University, LA

Non-Need Scholarships for Undergraduates
Academic Interests/Achievements

Lycoming College, PA
Malone University, OH
Marquette University, WI
Marymount University, VA
Maryville University of Saint Louis, MO
Marywood University, PA
Massachusetts College of Liberal Arts, MA
Mayville State University, ND
Medcenter One College of Nursing, ND
Mercy College of Northwest Ohio, OH
Mesa State College, CO
Michigan State University, MI
Middle Tennessee State University, TN
Midwestern State University, TX
Millersville University of Pennsylvania, PA
Millikin University, IL
Milwaukee School of Engineering, WI
Minnesota State University Moorhead, MN
Minot State University, ND
Misericordia University, PA
Mississippi State University, MS
Mississippi University for Women, MS
Molloy College, NY
Monmouth University, NJ
Montana State University, MT
Montana State University Billings, MT
Montana State University–Northern, MT
Montana Tech of The University of Montana, MT
Moravian College, PA
Morehead State University, KY
Mount Mary College, WI
Murray State University, KY
New England College, NH
New Mexico State University, NM
Northeastern State University, OK
Northern Arizona University, AZ
Northern Illinois University, IL
Northern Kentucky University, KY
Northern Michigan University, MI
North Georgia College & State University, GA
Northwestern Oklahoma State University, OK
Northwestern State University of Louisiana, LA
Northwest Missouri State University, MO
Northwest Nazarene University, ID
Oakland University, MI
Ohio Northern University, OH
The Ohio State University, OH
Ohio University, OH
Ohio University–Chillicothe, OH
Ohio University–Eastern, OH
Ohio University–Lancaster, OH
Ohio University–Southern Campus, OH
Ohio University–Zanesville, OH
Oklahoma City University, OK
Oklahoma Panhandle State University, OK
Oklahoma Wesleyan University, OK
Old Dominion University, VA
Oregon Health & Science University, OR
Ouachita Baptist University, AR
Our Lady of Holy Cross College, LA
Pace University, NY
Pacific University, OR
Palmer College of Chiropractic, IA
Piedmont College, GA
Plymouth State University, NH
Point Loma Nazarene University, CA
Purdue University, IN
Purdue University North Central, IN
Quincy University, IL
Research College of Nursing, MO
The Richard Stockton College of New Jersey, NJ
Robert Morris University Illinois, IL
Rochester Institute of Technology, NY
Rockhurst University, MO
Sacred Heart University, CT
Saginaw Valley State University, MI
St. Catherine University, MN
St. Edward's University, TX
Saint Francis Medical Center College of Nursing, IL
Saint Francis University, PA
St. John's University, NY
Saint Louis University, MO
Samford University, AL
San Diego State University, CA
Shepherd University, WV
Siena College, NY
Slippery Rock University of Pennsylvania, PA
Sonoma State University, CA
South Dakota State University, SD
Southeast Missouri State University, MO
Southern Adventist University, TN
Southern Illinois University Carbondale, IL
Southern Illinois University Edwardsville, IL
Southern Oregon University, OR
Southwestern College, KS
Southwestern Oklahoma State University, OK
State University of New York at Binghamton, NY
State University of New York at New Paltz, NY
State University of New York at Plattsburgh, NY
State University of New York College at Old Westbury, NY
Stephen F. Austin State University, TX
Stevens-Henager College, ID
Stony Brook University, State University of New York, NY
Sul Ross State University, TX
Tennessee Technological University, TN
Tennessee Wesleyan College, TN
Texas A&M International University, TX
Texas A&M University, TX
Texas Christian University, TX
Texas Woman's University, TX
Thomas University, GA
Towson University, MD
Trinity Christian College, IL
Truman State University, MO
Union College, KY
Union University, TN
The University of Akron, OH
The University of Alabama at Birmingham, AL
The University of Alabama in Huntsville, AL
University of Alaska Anchorage, AK
University of Arkansas at Little Rock, AR
University of California, Davis, CA
University of California, Irvine, CA
University of Central Missouri, MO
University of Central Oklahoma, OK
University of Colorado Boulder, CO
University of Connecticut, CT
University of Dayton, OH
University of Delaware, DE
University of Evansville, IN
University of Florida, FL
University of Hartford, CT
University of Hawaii at Hilo, HI
University of Illinois at Urbana–Champaign, IL
University of Indianapolis, IN
The University of Kansas, KS
University of Kentucky, KY
University of Louisville, KY
University of Maine at Fort Kent, ME
University of Mary Hardin-Baylor, TX
University of Maryland, College Park, MD
University of Massachusetts Amherst, MA
University of Massachusetts Boston, MA
University of Massachusetts Lowell, MA
University of Memphis, TN
University of Miami, FL
University of Michigan, MI
University of Michigan–Flint, MI
University of Minnesota, Twin Cities Campus, MN
University of Mississippi, MS
University of Missouri, MO
University of Missouri–St. Louis, MO
The University of Montana, MT
University of Nebraska–Lincoln, NE
University of Nevada, Las Vegas, NV
University of New Hampshire, NH
The University of North Carolina at Asheville, NC
The University of North Carolina at Chapel Hill, NC
The University of North Carolina at Charlotte, NC
The University of North Carolina at Greensboro, NC
The University of North Carolina at Pembroke, NC
The University of North Carolina Wilmington, NC
University of North Dakota, ND
University of Northern Colorado, CO
University of North Florida, FL
University of Oregon, OR
University of Pittsburgh at Bradford, PA
University of Portland, OR
University of Rio Grande, OH
University of St. Francis, IL
University of St. Thomas, TX
University of South Carolina, SC
University of Southern Indiana, IN
University of South Florida, FL
The University of Tennessee, TN
The University of Tennessee at Martin, TN
The University of Texas at Arlington, TX
The University of Texas at Brownsville, TX
The University of Texas at El Paso, TX
The University of Texas at Tyler, TX
The University of Texas Health Science Center at Houston, TX
The University of Texas Medical Branch, TX
The University of Texas–Pan American, TX
The University of Toledo, OH
University of Tulsa, OK
University of Utah, UT
University of Vermont, VT
The University of Virginia's College at Wise, VA
University of West Georgia, GA
University of Wisconsin–Eau Claire, WI
University of Wisconsin–Green Bay, WI
University of Wisconsin–La Crosse, WI
University of Wisconsin–Parkside, WI
University of Wisconsin–River Falls, WI
University of Wisconsin–Stevens Point, WI
University of Wisconsin–Superior, WI
University of Wyoming, WY
Utah State University, UT

Valdosta State University, GA
Valparaiso University, IN
Virginia Commonwealth University, VA
Virginia State University, VA
Walsh University, OH
Washburn University, KS
Washington State University, WA
Washington University in St. Louis, MO
Waynesburg University, PA
Wayne State College, NE
Wayne State University, MI
Western Kentucky University, KY
Western Washington University, WA
West Liberty University, WV
West Texas A&M University, TX
West Virginia University, WV
Wheaton College, IL
Wichita State University, KS
Widener University, PA
Wright State University, OH
Youngstown State University, OH

Home Economics

Auburn University, AL
Averett University, VA
Baylor University, TX
Bowling Green State University, OH
California Polytechnic State University, San Luis Obispo, CA
Carson-Newman College, TN
Central Michigan University, MI
East Carolina University, NC
Eastern Michigan University, MI
Fort Valley State University, GA
Framingham State University, MA
Illinois State University, IL
Indiana University of Pennsylvania, PA
Iowa State University of Science and Technology, IA
Lipscomb University, TN
Louisiana State University and Agricultural and Mechanical College, LA
Louisiana Tech University, LA
Michigan State University, MI
Middle Tennessee State University, TN
Mississippi State University, MS
Mississippi University for Women, MS
Montana State University, MT
Montclair State University, NJ
Mount Mary College, WI
New Mexico State University, NM
Northeastern State University, OK
Northern Arizona University, AZ
Northwest Missouri State University, MO
The Ohio State University, OH
Ohio University, OH
Ohio University–Chillicothe, OH
Ohio University–Eastern, OH
Ohio University–Lancaster, OH
Ohio University–Southern Campus, OH
Ohio University–Zanesville, OH
Oklahoma State University, OK
Ouachita Baptist University, AR
Point Loma Nazarene University, CA
St. Catherine University, MN
Shepherd University, WV
South Dakota State University, SD
Southeast Missouri State University, MO
Southern Illinois University Carbondale, IL
State University of New York at Plattsburgh, NY
State University of New York College at Oneonta, NY
Stephen F. Austin State University, TX
Tennessee Technological University, TN
Texas State University–San Marcos, TX
Texas Tech University, TX
Texas Woman's University, TX
The University of Akron, OH
The University of Alabama, AL
University of California, Davis, CA
University of Central Missouri, MO
University of Central Oklahoma, OK
University of Idaho, ID
University of Illinois at Urbana–Champaign, IL
University of Kentucky, KY
University of Minnesota, Twin Cities Campus, MN
University of Missouri, MO
University of Nebraska at Omaha, NE
University of Nebraska–Lincoln, NE
The University of North Carolina at Greensboro, NC
University of Northern Colorado, CO
The University of Tennessee at Chattanooga, TN
The University of Tennessee at Martin, TN
University of Vermont, VT
University of Wisconsin–Stevens Point, WI
University of Wisconsin–Stout, WI
University of Wyoming, WY
Utah State University, UT
Virginia State University, VA
Washington State University, WA
Wayne State College, NE
Western Illinois University, IL
Western Kentucky University, KY
West Virginia University, WV

Humanities

Alaska Pacific University, AK
Alderson-Broaddus College, WV
Alfred University, NY
Alliant International University, CA
Arizona State University, AZ
Arkansas State University, AR
Armstrong Atlantic State University, GA
Auburn University, AL
Augustana College, IL
Augustana College, SD
Austin College, TX
Austin Peay State University, TN
Averett University, VA
Ball State University, IN
Baptist University of the Americas, TX
Baylor University, TX
Berry College, GA
Birmingham-Southern College, AL
Black Hills State University, SD
Bloomfield College, NJ
Bloomsburg University of Pennsylvania, PA
Boise State University, ID
Bowling Green State University, OH
Brenau University, GA
Bryan College, TN
Buena Vista University, IA
Butler University, IN
California Institute of Integral Studies, CA
California Lutheran University, CA
California Polytechnic State University, San Luis Obispo, CA
California State Polytechnic University, Pomona, CA
California State University, Bakersfield, CA
California State University, Chico, CA
California State University, Fresno, CA
California State University, Fullerton, CA
California State University, Stanislaus, CA
Calvin College, MI
Campbellsville University, KY
Carroll University, WI
Case Western Reserve University, OH
Centenary College of Louisiana, LA
Central College, IA
Central Methodist University, MO
Central Michigan University, MI
Christopher Newport University, VA
The Citadel, The Military College of South Carolina, SC
City College of the City University of New York, NY
Clarkson University, NY
Clemson University, SC
Cleveland State University, OH
Coastal Carolina University, SC
The College at Brockport, State University of New York, NY
College of Charleston, SC
The College of New Rochelle, NY
College of Staten Island of the City University of New York, NY
College of the Holy Cross, MA
Columbia College, MO
Columbus State University, GA
Concordia University, Nebraska, NE
Cornerstone University, MI
Dallas Baptist University, TX
Dalton State College, GA
Defiance College, OH
Delta State University, MS
DeSales University, PA
Dickinson State University, ND
Dordt College, IA
Drury University, MO
D'Youville College, NY
East Carolina University, NC
Eastern Connecticut State University, CT
Eastern Michigan University, MI
East Texas Baptist University, TX
Edinboro University of Pennsylvania, PA
Elizabethtown College, PA
Elmhurst College, IL
Emmanuel College, MA
Emporia State University, KS
Evangel University, MO
Flagler College, FL
Florida Agricultural and Mechanical University, FL
Florida Gulf Coast University, FL
Florida International University, FL
Fort Lewis College, CO
Francis Marion University, SC
Fresno Pacific University, CA
Frostburg State University, MD
Furman University, SC
Gannon University, PA
Gardner-Webb University, NC
Georgia College & State University, GA
Georgia Southern University, GA
Grand Valley State University, MI
Hamline University, MN
Hardin-Simmons University, TX
High Point University, NC
Hillsdale College, MI
Illinois State University, IL
Indiana University of Pennsylvania, PA
Iowa State University of Science and Technology, IA

Non-Need Scholarships for Undergraduates
Academic Interests/Achievements

James Madison University, VA
Juniata College, PA
Kean University, NJ
Kennesaw State University, GA
King's College, PA
Kutztown University of Pennsylvania, PA
Lawrence Technological University, MI
Lewis-Clark State College, ID
Limestone College, SC
Lindenwood University, MO
Longwood University, VA
Louisiana State University and Agricultural and Mechanical College, LA
Lubbock Christian University, TX
Lycoming College, PA
Malone University, OH
Manchester College, IN
Massachusetts College of Liberal Arts, MA
Mesa State College, CO
Mid-Continent University, KY
Middle Tennessee State University, TN
Midwestern State University, TX
Millersville University of Pennsylvania, PA
Millikin University, IL
Minot State University, ND
Mississippi State University, MS
Mississippi University for Women, MS
Missouri University of Science and Technology, MO
Monmouth University, NJ
Montana State University, MT
Montana State University Billings, MT
Montana State University–Northern, MT
Montclair State University, NJ
Mount Mary College, WI
Murray State University, KY
New England College, NH
New Jersey Institute of Technology, NJ
New Mexico State University, NM
North Carolina State University, NC
North Central College, IL
Northeastern State University, OK
Northern Arizona University, AZ
Northern Illinois University, IL
Northern State University, SD
North Georgia College & State University, GA
Northwestern State University of Louisiana, LA
Northwest Missouri State University, MO
Oakland University, MI
Ohio Northern University, OH
The Ohio State University, OH
Ohio University, OH
Ohio University–Chillicothe, OH
Ohio University–Eastern, OH
Ohio University–Lancaster, OH
Ohio University–Southern Campus, OH
Ohio University–Zanesville, OH
Oklahoma State University, OK
Old Dominion University, VA
Ouachita Baptist University, AR
Pace University, NY
Pacific University, OR
Piedmont College, GA
Point Loma Nazarene University, CA
Portland State University, OR
Post University, CT
Purchase College, State University of New York, NY
Purdue University, IN
Quincy University, IL
Regent University, VA
Rensselaer Polytechnic Institute, NY
The Richard Stockton College of New Jersey, NJ
Ripon College, WI
Rivier College, NH
Rockhurst University, MO
Sacred Heart University, CT
St. Catherine University, MN
St. Edward's University, TX
Saint Francis University, PA
St. John Fisher College, NY
St. John's University, NY
Saint Louis University, MO
Saint Martin's University, WA
St. Thomas Aquinas College, NY
Samford University, AL
Savannah State University, GA
Seton Hill University, PA
Shepherd University, WV
Shippensburg University of Pennsylvania, PA
Siena College, NY
Sonoma State University, CA
South Dakota State University, SD
Southeastern Louisiana University, LA
Southeast Missouri State University, MO
Southern Illinois University Carbondale, IL
Southwestern University, TX
State University of New York at Binghamton, NY
State University of New York at Fredonia, NY
State University of New York at Oswego, NY
State University of New York at Plattsburgh, NY
State University of New York College at Geneseo, NY
State University of New York College at Potsdam, NY
Stetson University, FL
Tabor College, KS
Tennessee Technological University, TN
Tennessee Wesleyan College, TN
Texas Christian University, TX
Texas Tech University, TX
Texas Woman's University, TX
Thomas University, GA
Truman State University, MO
The University of Akron, OH
The University of Alabama in Huntsville, AL
University of Alaska Anchorage, AK
The University of Arizona, AZ
University of Arkansas at Little Rock, AR
University of California, Davis, CA
University of California, Irvine, CA
University of California, Riverside, CA
University of California, Santa Cruz, CA
University of Central Missouri, MO
University of Colorado Boulder, CO
University of Connecticut, CT
University of Dayton, OH
University of Delaware, DE
University of Denver, CO
University of Evansville, IN
University of Great Falls, MT
University of Houston–Clear Lake, TX
University of Idaho, ID
University of Illinois at Urbana–Champaign, IL
The University of Kansas, KS
University of Maine at Fort Kent, ME
University of Mary Hardin-Baylor, TX
University of Maryland, Baltimore County, MD
University of Maryland, College Park, MD
University of Mary Washington, VA
University of Massachusetts Amherst, MA
University of Massachusetts Lowell, MA
University of Memphis, TN
University of Miami, FL
University of Michigan, MI
University of Michigan–Flint, MI
University of Minnesota, Twin Cities Campus, MN
University of Mississippi, MS
University of Missouri, MO
University of Missouri–St. Louis, MO
The University of Montana, MT
University of Nebraska–Lincoln, NE
University of Nevada, Las Vegas, NV
University of New Hampshire, NH
The University of North Carolina at Charlotte, NC
The University of North Carolina at Greensboro, NC
The University of North Carolina Wilmington, NC
University of North Dakota, ND
University of Oklahoma, OK
University of Oregon, OR
University of Pittsburgh at Bradford, PA
University of Pittsburgh at Johnstown, PA
University of Portland, OR
University of Puget Sound, WA
University of Rio Grande, OH
University of St. Thomas, MN
University of St. Thomas, TX
University of South Alabama, AL
University of South Carolina, SC
University of South Carolina Aiken, SC
The University of South Dakota, SD
University of Southern Indiana, IN
University of South Florida, FL
The University of Tennessee, TN
The University of Tennessee at Martin, TN
The University of Texas at Arlington, TX
The University of Texas at El Paso, TX
The University of Texas at San Antonio, TX
University of the Ozarks, AR
University of the Southwest, NM
The University of Toledo, OH
University of Utah, UT
University of Vermont, VT
The University of Virginia's College at Wise, VA
University of West Georgia, GA
University of Wisconsin–Green Bay, WI
University of Wisconsin–La Crosse, WI
University of Wisconsin–River Falls, WI
University of Wisconsin–Stevens Point, WI
University of Wisconsin–Superior, WI
Utah State University, UT
Valdosta State University, GA
Valley City State University, ND
Virginia Commonwealth University, VA
Virginia State University, VA
Walla Walla University, WA
Walsh University, OH
Warner Pacific College, OR
Washburn University, KS
Washington & Jefferson College, PA
Washington State University, WA
Washington University in St. Louis, MO
Waynesburg University, PA
Wayne State College, NE
Wayne State University, MI
Wesleyan College, GA
Western Oregon University, OR
Western Washington University, WA

West Texas A&M University, TX
West Virginia University, WV
Wheaton College, IL
Wichita State University, KS
Widener University, PA
Williams Baptist College, AR
Wilson College, PA
Wright State University, OH
Xavier University of Louisiana, LA
Youngstown State University, OH

International Studies

Alfred University, NY
Alliant International University, CA
Angelo State University, TX
Armstrong Atlantic State University, GA
Augsburg College, MN
Augustana College, SD
Austin College, TX
Austin Peay State University, TN
Ball State University, IN
Baylor University, TX
Birmingham-Southern College, AL
Bloomsburg University of Pennsylvania, PA
Boise State University, ID
Bowling Green State University, OH
Buena Vista University, IA
Butler University, IN
California Lutheran University, CA
California Polytechnic State University, San Luis Obispo, CA
California State University, Chico, CA
California State University, Stanislaus, CA
Calvin College, MI
Carroll University, WI
Case Western Reserve University, OH
Central College, IA
Central Michigan University, MI
City College of the City University of New York, NY
Clemson University, SC
The College at Brockport, State University of New York, NY
College of Staten Island of the City University of New York, NY
Columbia International University, SC
Columbus State University, GA
Davidson College, NC
Defiance College, OH
DePauw University, IN
D'Youville College, NY
East Carolina University, NC
Elizabethtown College, PA
Elmhurst College, IL
Frostburg State University, MD
Furman University, SC
Gannon University, PA
Georgia College & State University, GA
Georgia Southern University, GA
Grace University, NE
Grand Valley State University, MI
Hamline University, MN
Hampden-Sydney College, VA
Hampshire College, MA
High Point University, NC
Hillsdale College, MI
Illinois State University, IL
Indiana University of Pennsylvania, PA
Iowa State University of Science and Technology, IA
James Madison University, VA
Juniata College, PA
Kean University, NJ
Kennesaw State University, GA
Kent State University, OH
Keuka College, NY
Kutztown University of Pennsylvania, PA
Lawrence Technological University, MI
Lindenwood University, MO
Lock Haven University of Pennsylvania, PA
Longwood University, VA
Louisiana Tech University, LA
Lycoming College, PA
Malone University, OH
Mercer University, GA
Michigan State University, MI
Middle Tennessee State University, TN
Midwestern State University, TX
Millikin University, IL
Minnesota State University Moorhead, MN
Mississippi State University, MS
Molloy College, NY
Monmouth University, NJ
Montclair State University, NJ
Morehead State University, KY
Murray State University, KY
New England College, NH
North Central College, IL
Northern Arizona University, AZ
Northern Illinois University, IL
Northern Michigan University, MI
Northern State University, SD
Ohio Northern University, OH
The Ohio State University, OH
Ohio University, OH
Ohio University–Chillicothe, OH
Ohio University–Eastern, OH
Ohio University–Lancaster, OH
Ohio University–Southern Campus, OH
Ohio University–Zanesville, OH
Oklahoma State University, OK
Ouachita Baptist University, AR
Portland State University, OR
Post University, CT
Quincy University, IL
Rochester Institute of Technology, NY
St. Ambrose University, IA
St. Edward's University, TX
Saint Louis University, MO
Saint Martin's University, WA
Samford University, AL
San Diego State University, CA
Siena College, NY
South Dakota State University, SD
Southeast Missouri State University, MO
Southern Illinois University Carbondale, IL
Southwestern University, TX
State University of New York at Binghamton, NY
State University of New York at Fredonia, NY
State University of New York at New Paltz, NY
State University of New York at Oswego, NY
State University of New York at Plattsburgh, NY
State University of New York College at Cortland, NY
State University of New York College at Geneseo, NY
Stony Brook University, State University of New York, NY
Tennessee Technological University, TN
Tennessee Wesleyan College, TN
Texas A&M International University, TX
Texas Christian University, TX
Texas State University–San Marcos, TX
Texas Tech University, TX
Thomas University, GA
The University of Akron, OH
University of Arkansas at Little Rock, AR
University of California, Davis, CA
University of California, Irvine, CA
University of Colorado Boulder, CO
University of Connecticut, CT
University of Dayton, OH
University of Delaware, DE
University of Denver, CO
University of Evansville, IN
University of Illinois at Urbana–Champaign, IL
The University of Kansas, KS
University of Kentucky, KY
University of Mary Hardin-Baylor, TX
University of Maryland, College Park, MD
University of Mary Washington, VA
University of Memphis, TN
University of Miami, FL
University of Michigan, MI
University of Michigan–Dearborn, MI
University of Michigan–Flint, MI
University of Minnesota, Twin Cities Campus, MN
University of Mississippi, MS
University of Missouri, MO
University of Missouri–St. Louis, MO
The University of Montana, MT
University of Nebraska–Lincoln, NE
University of Nevada, Las Vegas, NV
The University of North Carolina Wilmington, NC
University of North Dakota, ND
University of North Florida, FL
University of Oklahoma, OK
University of Oregon, OR
University of Puget Sound, WA
University of St. Francis, IL
University of St. Thomas, MN
University of St. Thomas, TX
University of South Alabama, AL
University of South Carolina, SC
University of South Florida, FL
The University of Tampa, FL
The University of Tennessee, TN
The University of Texas at Arlington, TX
The University of Texas at Brownsville, TX
The University of Texas at El Paso, TX
The University of Texas at San Antonio, TX
The University of Toledo, OH
University of Tulsa, OK
University of Utah, UT
University of Vermont, VT
University of Wisconsin–Eau Claire, WI
University of Wisconsin–La Crosse, WI
University of Wisconsin–River Falls, WI
University of Wisconsin–Stevens Point, WI
University of Wisconsin–Stout, WI
University of Wyoming, WY
Utah State University, UT
Villanova University, PA
Virginia Military Institute, VA
Walsh University, OH
Wartburg College, IA
Washburn University, KS
Washington State University, WA
Washington University in St. Louis, MO
Waynesburg University, PA
Wayne State University, MI
West Virginia University, WV
Wichita State University, KS

Non-Need Scholarships for Undergraduates
Academic Interests/Achievements

Widener University, PA
William Jessup University, CA
Wilson College, PA
Wright State University, OH

Library Science

Arkansas State University, AR
California Polytechnic State University, San Luis Obispo, CA
Emporia State University, KS
Illinois State University, IL
Iowa State University of Science and Technology, IA
Kent State University, OH
Kutztown University of Pennsylvania, PA
Lindenwood University, MO
Lock Haven University of Pennsylvania, PA
Mayville State University, ND
Mississippi State University, MS
Murray State University, KY
North Carolina Central University, NC
Northeastern State University, OK
Northern Arizona University, AZ
Northwestern Oklahoma State University, OK
Texas Woman's University, TX
The University of Alabama, AL
University of Central Missouri, MO
University of Idaho, ID
University of Illinois at Urbana–Champaign, IL
University of Maryland, College Park, MD
University of Michigan, MI
University of Minnesota, Twin Cities Campus, MN
University of Missouri, MO
The University of North Carolina at Greensboro, NC
University of South Carolina, SC
University of South Florida, FL
The University of Tennessee, TN
The University of Toledo, OH
Utah State University, UT
Valdosta State University, GA
Valley City State University, ND
Virginia Polytechnic Institute and State University, VA
Wayne State University, MI
Western Washington University, WA
West Virginia University, WV

Mathematics

Abilene Christian University, TX
Albion College, MI
Alderson-Broaddus College, WV
Alfred University, NY
Angelo State University, TX
Arizona State University, AZ
Arkansas State University, AR
Arkansas Tech University, AR
Armstrong Atlantic State University, GA
Ashland University, OH
Auburn University, AL
Augsburg College, MN
Augustana College, IL
Augustana College, SD
Augusta State University, GA
Aurora University, IL
Austin Peay State University, TN
Averett University, VA
Ball State University, IN
Bard College, NY
Baylor University, TX
Bethel College, IN
Birmingham-Southern College, AL
Black Hills State University, SD
Bloomfield College, NJ
Bloomsburg University of Pennsylvania, PA
Boise State University, ID
Bowie State University, MD
Bowling Green State University, OH
Brevard College, NC
Bryan College, TN
Bucknell University, PA
Buena Vista University, IA
Butler University, IN
California Lutheran University, CA
California Polytechnic State University, San Luis Obispo, CA
California State Polytechnic University, Pomona, CA
California State University, Bakersfield, CA
California State University, Chico, CA
California State University, Fresno, CA
California State University, Fullerton, CA
California State University, Northridge, CA
California State University, San Bernardino, CA
California State University, Stanislaus, CA
Calvin College, MI
Cameron University, OK
Campbellsville University, KY
Carroll University, WI
Carson-Newman College, TN
Case Western Reserve University, OH
Centenary College of Louisiana, LA
Central College, IA
Central Methodist University, MO
Central Michigan University, MI
Christopher Newport University, VA
City College of the City University of New York, NY
Clarkson University, NY
Clemson University, SC
Cleveland State University, OH
Coastal Carolina University, SC
Coe College, IA
The College at Brockport, State University of New York, NY
College of Charleston, SC
The College of New Rochelle, NY
College of Saint Mary, NE
The College of Saint Rose, NY
College of Staten Island of the City University of New York, NY
The Colorado College, CO
Colorado School of Mines, CO
Colorado State University–Pueblo, CO
Columbia College, MO
Columbus State University, GA
Concordia University Chicago, IL
Concordia University, Nebraska, NE
Concordia University, St. Paul, MN
Cornerstone University, MI
Dakota State University, SD
Dallas Baptist University, TX
Davidson College, NC
Defiance College, OH
Delta State University, MS
DePauw University, IN
DeSales University, PA
Dickinson State University, ND
Dordt College, IA
Dowling College, NY
Drury University, MO
Duke University, NC
D'Youville College, NY
East Carolina University, NC
Eastern Connecticut State University, CT
Eastern Michigan University, MI
Eastern Washington University, WA
East Tennessee State University, TN
East Texas Baptist University, TX
Edinboro University of Pennsylvania, PA
Elizabeth City State University, NC
Elizabethtown College, PA
Elmhurst College, IL
Elon University, NC
Emmanuel College, MA
Emporia State University, KS
Erskine College, SC
Evangel University, MO
Ferris State University, MI
Fitchburg State University, MA
Florida Agricultural and Mechanical University, FL
Florida Gulf Coast University, FL
Florida International University, FL
Fort Lewis College, CO
Francis Marion University, SC
Frostburg State University, MD
Furman University, SC
Gannon University, PA
Gardner-Webb University, NC
George Fox University, OR
Georgia College & State University, GA
Georgian Court University, NJ
Georgia Southern University, GA
Glenville State College, WV
Governors State University, IL
Grand Valley State University, MI
Greenville College, IL
Hamline University, MN
Hardin-Simmons University, TX
High Point University, NC
Hillsdale College, MI
Hillsdale Free Will Baptist College, OK
Howard Payne University, TX
Huntingdon College, AL
Huntington University, IN
Illinois State University, IL
Indiana University of Pennsylvania, PA
Iowa State University of Science and Technology, IA
James Madison University, VA
John Carroll University, OH
Juniata College, PA
Kean University, NJ
Kennesaw State University, GA
Kent State University, OH
Kentucky State University, KY
Kettering University, MI
King's College, PA
Knox College, IL
Kutztown University of Pennsylvania, PA
Lake Forest College, IL
Lawrence Technological University, MI
Lewis-Clark State College, ID
Limestone College, SC
Lindenwood University, MO
Lindsey Wilson College, KY
Lipscomb University, TN
Lock Haven University of Pennsylvania, PA
Long Island University, C.W. Post Campus, NY
Longwood University, VA
Louisiana State University and Agricultural and Mechanical College, LA
Louisiana Tech University, LA
Lycoming College, PA

Malone University, OH
Manhattan College, NY
Manhattanville College, NY
Marquette University, WI
Marymount University, VA
Marywood University, PA
Massachusetts College of Liberal Arts, MA
The Master's College and Seminary, CA
Mayville State University, ND
McMurry University, TX
Medaille College, NY
Meredith College, NC
Mesa State College, CO
Michigan State University, MI
Middle Tennessee State University, TN
Midwestern State University, TX
Millersville University of Pennsylvania, PA
Millikin University, IL
Mills College, CA
Minnesota State University Moorhead, MN
Minot State University, ND
Mississippi State University, MS
Mississippi University for Women, MS
Missouri University of Science and Technology, MO
Molloy College, NY
Monmouth University, NJ
Montana State University, MT
Montana State University Billings, MT
Montana Tech of The University of Montana, MT
Montclair State University, NJ
Moravian College, PA
Mount Mary College, WI
Murray State University, KY
Muskingum University, OH
New England College, NH
New Jersey Institute of Technology, NJ
New Mexico State University, NM
North Carolina State University, NC
North Central College, IL
Northeastern Illinois University, IL
Northeastern State University, OK
Northern Arizona University, AZ
Northern Illinois University, IL
Northern Kentucky University, KY
Northern Michigan University, MI
Northern State University, SD
North Georgia College & State University, GA
Northwestern Oklahoma State University, OK
Northwestern State University of Louisiana, LA
Northwest Missouri State University, MO
Northwest Nazarene University, ID
Ohio Northern University, OH
The Ohio State University, OH
Ohio University, OH
Ohio University–Chillicothe, OH
Ohio University–Eastern, OH
Ohio University–Lancaster, OH
Ohio University–Southern Campus, OH
Ohio University–Zanesville, OH
Oklahoma Panhandle State University, OK
Oklahoma State University, OK
Ouachita Baptist University, AR
Pace University, NY
Pacific University, OR
Piedmont College, GA
Plymouth State University, NH
Point Loma Nazarene University, CA
Purchase College, State University of New York, NY
Purdue University, IN
Quincy University, IL
Randolph College, VA
Rensselaer Polytechnic Institute, NY
The Richard Stockton College of New Jersey, NJ
Ripon College, WI
Rivier College, NH
Rochester Institute of Technology, NY
Rockford College, IL
Rockhurst University, MO
Rollins College, FL
Sacred Heart University, CT
Saginaw Valley State University, MI
St. Catherine University, MN
St. Edward's University, TX
Saint Francis University, PA
St. John Fisher College, NY
St. John's University, NY
Saint Louis University, MO
St. Thomas Aquinas College, NY
Samford University, AL
San Diego State University, CA
Savannah State University, GA
Schreiner University, TX
Seton Hill University, PA
Shepherd University, WV
Shippensburg University of Pennsylvania, PA
Siena College, NY
Skidmore College, NY
Sonoma State University, CA
South Dakota School of Mines and Technology, SD
South Dakota State University, SD
Southeastern Louisiana University, LA
Southeastern Oklahoma State University, OK
Southeast Missouri State University, MO
Southern Adventist University, TN
Southern Illinois University Carbondale, IL
Southern Oregon University, OR
Southwestern Oklahoma State University, OK
Southwestern University, TX
Southwest Minnesota State University, MN
State University of New York at Binghamton, NY
State University of New York at Fredonia, NY
State University of New York at Oswego, NY
State University of New York at Plattsburgh, NY
State University of New York College at Cortland, NY
State University of New York College at Geneseo, NY
State University of New York College at Potsdam, NY
Stephen F. Austin State University, TX
Stetson University, FL
Stony Brook University, State University of New York, NY
Tennessee Technological University, TN
Tennessee Wesleyan College, TN
Texas A&M International University, TX
Texas A&M University–Texarkana, TX
Texas Christian University, TX
Texas Lutheran University, TX
Texas Tech University, TX
Texas Woman's University, TX
Thiel College, PA
Thomas More College, KY
Towson University, MD
Trinity Christian College, IL
Truman State University, MO
Union College, KY
Union University, TN
The University of Akron, OH
The University of Alabama, AL
The University of Alabama at Birmingham, AL
The University of Alabama in Huntsville, AL
University of Alaska Anchorage, AK
University of Arkansas at Little Rock, AR
University of California, Davis, CA
University of California, Irvine, CA
University of California, Riverside, CA
University of California, San Diego, CA
University of California, Santa Cruz, CA
University of Central Missouri, MO
University of Central Oklahoma, OK
University of Colorado Boulder, CO
University of Connecticut, CT
University of Dallas, TX
University of Dayton, OH
University of Delaware, DE
University of Denver, CO
University of Evansville, IN
University of Great Falls, MT
University of Houston–Clear Lake, TX
University of Idaho, ID
University of Illinois at Urbana–Champaign, IL
The University of Kansas, KS
University of Kentucky, KY
University of Louisville, KY
University of Maine at Fort Kent, ME
University of Mary Hardin-Baylor, TX
University of Maryland, Baltimore County, MD
University of Maryland, College Park, MD
University of Mary Washington, VA
University of Massachusetts Amherst, MA
University of Massachusetts Lowell, MA
University of Memphis, TN
University of Miami, FL
University of Michigan, MI
University of Michigan–Dearborn, MI
University of Michigan–Flint, MI
University of Minnesota, Twin Cities Campus, MN
University of Mississippi, MS
University of Missouri, MO
University of Missouri–St. Louis, MO
The University of Montana, MT
University of Montevallo, AL
University of Nebraska at Omaha, NE
University of Nebraska–Lincoln, NE
University of Nevada, Las Vegas, NV
University of New Hampshire, NH
University of New Orleans, LA
The University of North Carolina at Asheville, NC
The University of North Carolina at Chapel Hill, NC
The University of North Carolina at Charlotte, NC
The University of North Carolina at Greensboro, NC
The University of North Carolina Wilmington, NC
University of North Dakota, ND
University of Northern Colorado, CO
University of Northern Iowa, IA
University of Oklahoma, OK
University of Oregon, OR
University of Pittsburgh at Bradford, PA
University of Pittsburgh at Johnstown, PA
University of Portland, OR
University of Puget Sound, WA

University of Richmond, VA
University of Rio Grande, OH
University of St. Thomas, MN
University of St. Thomas, TX
University of South Carolina, SC
University of South Carolina Aiken, SC
The University of South Dakota, SD
University of Southern Indiana, IN
University of South Florida, FL
The University of Tennessee at Chattanooga, TN
The University of Tennessee at Martin, TN
The University of Texas at Arlington, TX
The University of Texas at Brownsville, TX
The University of Texas at Dallas, TX
The University of Texas at El Paso, TX
The University of Texas at San Antonio, TX
The University of Texas–Pan American, TX
University of the Ozarks, AR
University of the Southwest, NM
The University of Toledo, OH
University of Tulsa, OK
University of Utah, UT
University of Vermont, VT
The University of Virginia's College at Wise, VA
University of West Georgia, GA
University of Wisconsin–Eau Claire, WI
University of Wisconsin–La Crosse, WI
University of Wisconsin–Parkside, WI
University of Wisconsin–River Falls, WI
University of Wisconsin–Stevens Point, WI
University of Wisconsin–Stout, WI
University of Wisconsin–Superior, WI
University of Wyoming, WY
Utah State University, UT
Valdosta State University, GA
Valley City State University, ND
Virginia Commonwealth University, VA
Virginia Military Institute, VA
Virginia State University, VA
Walla Walla University, WA
Walsh University, OH
Warner Pacific College, OR
Wartburg College, IA
Washburn University, KS
Washington & Jefferson College, PA
Washington State University, WA
Washington University in St. Louis, MO
Wayland Baptist University, TX
Waynesburg University, PA
Wayne State College, NE
Wayne State University, MI
Wesleyan College, GA
West Chester University of Pennsylvania, PA
Western Carolina University, NC
Western Illinois University, IL
Western Kentucky University, KY
Western Oregon University, OR
Western Washington University, WA
West Liberty University, WV
West Texas A&M University, TX
West Virginia State University, WV
West Virginia University, WV
West Virginia University Institute of Technology, WV
Wheaton College, IL
Wichita State University, KS
Widener University, PA
Wilson College, PA
Wright State University, OH
Xavier University, OH
Xavier University of Louisiana, LA
York College, NE
Youngstown State University, OH

Military Science

Alfred University, NY
Angelo State University, TX
Arizona State University, AZ
Arkansas State University, AR
Arkansas Tech University, AR
Armstrong Atlantic State University, GA
Augusta State University, GA
Austin Peay State University, TN
Ball State University, IN
Baylor University, TX
Black Hills State University, SD
Boise State University, ID
Boston College, MA
Bowie State University, MD
Bowling Green State University, OH
California Polytechnic State University, San Luis Obispo, CA
California State University, Fullerton, CA
Cameron University, OK
Carson-Newman College, TN
Central Michigan University, MI
Christopher Newport University, VA
The Citadel, The Military College of South Carolina, SC
Clarkson University, NY
Clemson University, SC
The College at Brockport, State University of New York, NY
College of Saint Benedict, MN
College of the Holy Cross, MA
Colorado School of Mines, CO
Columbus State University, GA
Creighton University, NE
Dickinson College, PA
East Carolina University, NC
Eastern Washington University, WA
East Tennessee State University, TN
Edinboro University of Pennsylvania, PA
Elizabeth City State University, NC
Elon University, NC
Florida Agricultural and Mechanical University, FL
Florida Institute of Technology, FL
Fort Valley State University, GA
Furman University, SC
Georgia Southern University, GA
Gonzaga University, WA
Illinois State University, IL
Iowa State University of Science and Technology, IA
James Madison University, VA
John Carroll University, OH
Kent State University, OH
Lawrence Technological University, MI
Lehigh University, PA
Lincoln University, MO
Lindenwood University, MO
Longwood University, VA
Louisiana State University and Agricultural and Mechanical College, LA
Louisiana Tech University, LA
Manhattan College, NY
Mercer University, GA
Michigan State University, MI
Middle Tennessee State University, TN
Mississippi State University, MS
Missouri University of Science and Technology, MO
Montana State University, MT
Morehead State University, KY
Morehouse College, GA
New Mexico State University, NM
North Carolina State University, NC
Northern Arizona University, AZ
Northern Michigan University, MI
North Georgia College & State University, GA
Northwestern State University of Louisiana, LA
Northwest Nazarene University, ID
The Ohio State University, OH
Ohio University, OH
Ohio University–Chillicothe, OH
Ohio University–Eastern, OH
Ohio University–Lancaster, OH
Ohio University–Southern Campus, OH
Ohio University–Zanesville, OH
Oklahoma State University, OK
Old Dominion University, VA
Olivet Nazarene University, IL
Providence College, RI
Purdue University, IN
Rensselaer Polytechnic Institute, NY
Ripon College, WI
Rochester Institute of Technology, NY
Saint Augustine's College, NC
St. Edward's University, TX
St. John's University, NY
Saint Louis University, MO
San Diego State University, CA
Santa Clara University, CA
Savannah State University, GA
Siena College, NY
South Dakota School of Mines and Technology, SD
South Dakota State University, SD
Southeast Missouri State University, MO
Southern Illinois University Carbondale, IL
Stephen F. Austin State University, TX
Stetson University, FL
Tennessee Technological University, TN
Texas Christian University, TX
Texas State University–San Marcos, TX
Texas Tech University, TX
Truman State University, MO
Union University, TN
The University of Akron, OH
The University of Alabama, AL
The University of Arizona, AZ
University of Central Missouri, MO
University of Central Oklahoma, OK
University of Colorado Boulder, CO
University of Dayton, OH
University of Delaware, DE
University of Florida, FL
University of Idaho, ID
University of Illinois at Urbana–Champaign, IL
The University of Iowa, IA
University of Kentucky, KY
University of Louisville, KY
University of Maryland, College Park, MD
University of Massachusetts Amherst, MA
University of Memphis, TN
University of Michigan, MI
University of Minnesota, Twin Cities Campus, MN
University of Mississippi, MS
The University of Montana, MT
University of New Hampshire, NH
The University of North Carolina at Charlotte, NC
University of North Dakota, ND

University of Northern Colorado, CO
University of Oklahoma, OK
University of Oregon, OR
University of Portland, OR
University of Rochester, NY
The University of Scranton, PA
University of South Alabama, AL
University of South Carolina, SC
The University of South Dakota, SD
University of South Florida, FL
The University of Tampa, FL
The University of Tennessee, TN
The University of Tennessee at Chattanooga, TN
The University of Tennessee at Martin, TN
The University of Texas at Arlington, TX
The University of Texas at El Paso, TX
The University of Texas–Pan American, TX
University of Utah, UT
University of Vermont, VT
University of West Florida, FL
University of Wisconsin–La Crosse, WI
University of Wisconsin–Stevens Point, WI
University of Wyoming, WY
Valdosta State University, GA
Villanova University, PA
Virginia Commonwealth University, VA
Virginia Military Institute, VA
Virginia State University, VA
Washington State University, WA
Washington University in St. Louis, MO
Wayne State University, MI
Western Kentucky University, KY
West Virginia State University, WV
West Virginia University, WV
Wheaton College, IL
Whitworth University, WA
Widener University, PA
Wright State University, OH
Xavier University, OH
Youngstown State University, OH

Physical Sciences

Abilene Christian University, TX
Alaska Pacific University, AK
Alderson-Broaddus College, WV
Alfred University, NY
Angelo State University, TX
Arizona State University, AZ
Arkansas State University, AR
Arkansas Tech University, AR
Armstrong Atlantic State University, GA
Ashland University, OH
Auburn University, AL
Augsburg College, MN
Augustana College, IL
Augustana College, SD
Augusta State University, GA
Austin College, TX
Austin Peay State University, TN
Averett University, VA
Ball State University, IN
Bard College, NY
Baylor University, TX
Bethel College, IN
Birmingham-Southern College, AL
Black Hills State University, SD
Bloomfield College, NJ
Bloomsburg University of Pennsylvania, PA
Boise State University, ID
Bowling Green State University, OH
Brevard College, NC
Bryan College, TN
Bucknell University, PA
Butler University, IN
California Lutheran University, CA
California Polytechnic State University, San Luis Obispo, CA
California State Polytechnic University, Pomona, CA
California State University, Bakersfield, CA
California State University, Chico, CA
California State University, Fresno, CA
California State University, San Bernardino, CA
California State University, Stanislaus, CA
Calvin College, MI
Cameron University, OK
Campbellsville University, KY
Carroll University, WI
Case Western Reserve University, OH
Centenary College of Louisiana, LA
Central College, IA
Central Methodist University, MO
Central Michigan University, MI
Chicago State University, IL
Clarkson University, NY
Clemson University, SC
Cleveland State University, OH
Coe College, IA
The College at Brockport, State University of New York, NY
College of Charleston, SC
The College of New Rochelle, NY
College of Staten Island of the City University of New York, NY
The Colorado College, CO
Colorado School of Mines, CO
Colorado State University–Pueblo, CO
Columbia College, MO
Columbus State University, GA
Concordia University, Nebraska, NE
Concordia University, St. Paul, MN
Cornerstone University, MI
Davidson College, NC
Defiance College, OH
Delta State University, MS
DePauw University, IN
DeSales University, PA
Dickinson State University, ND
Dominican University, IL
Dordt College, IA
Drury University, MO
East Carolina University, NC
Eastern Connecticut State University, CT
Eastern Michigan University, MI
Eastern Washington University, WA
East Texas Baptist University, TX
Edinboro University of Pennsylvania, PA
Elizabethtown College, PA
Elmhurst College, IL
Elon University, NC
Emmanuel College, MA
Emporia State University, KS
Evangel University, MO
Florida Agricultural and Mechanical University, FL
Florida Atlantic University, FL
Florida Gulf Coast University, FL
Florida International University, FL
Florida Southern College, FL
Fort Lewis College, CO
Framingham State University, MA
Frostburg State University, MD
Furman University, SC
Gardner-Webb University, NC
George Fox University, OR
Georgia College & State University, GA
Georgia Institute of Technology, GA
Georgian Court University, NJ
Governors State University, IL
Graceland University, IA
Grand Valley State University, MI
Green Mountain College, VT
Greenville College, IL
Grove City College, PA
Hamline University, MN
Hampshire College, MA
Hampton University, VA
Hardin-Simmons University, TX
Harrisburg University of Science and Technology, PA
High Point University, NC
Hillsdale College, MI
Howard Payne University, TX
Illinois State University, IL
Indiana University of Pennsylvania, PA
Iowa State University of Science and Technology, IA
James Madison University, VA
Jamestown College, ND
John Carroll University, OH
Juniata College, PA
Kean University, NJ
Kennesaw State University, GA
Kent State University, OH
Kettering University, MI
King's College, PA
Kutztown University of Pennsylvania, PA
Lake Forest College, IL
Lawrence Technological University, MI
Lewis-Clark State College, ID
Limestone College, SC
Lindenwood University, MO
Lock Haven University of Pennsylvania, PA
Loras College, IA
Louisiana State University and Agricultural and Mechanical College, LA
Louisiana Tech University, LA
Lubbock Christian University, TX
Lycoming College, PA
Malone University, OH
Marietta College, OH
Marquette University, WI
Massachusetts College of Liberal Arts, MA
The Master's College and Seminary, CA
Mayville State University, ND
McMurry University, TX
Meredith College, NC
Mesa State College, CO
Michigan State University, MI
Middle Tennessee State University, TN
Midwestern State University, TX
Millersville University of Pennsylvania, PA
Millikin University, IL
Mills College, CA
Minnesota State University Moorhead, MN
Misericordia University, PA
Mississippi State University, MS
Mississippi University for Women, MS
Missouri University of Science and Technology, MO
Montana State University, MT
Montana State University Billings, MT
Montana Tech of The University of Montana, MT
Montclair State University, NJ
Moravian College, PA
Morehead State University, KY

Mount Mary College, WI
Muskingum University, OH
New Jersey Institute of Technology, NJ
New Mexico State University, NM
North Carolina Central University, NC
North Carolina State University, NC
North Central College, IL
Northeastern Illinois University, IL
Northeastern State University, OK
Northern Arizona University, AZ
Northern Illinois University, IL
Northern Kentucky University, KY
Northern Michigan University, MI
Northern State University, SD
North Georgia College & State University, GA
Northwestern Oklahoma State University, OK
Northwest Missouri State University, MO
Northwest Nazarene University, ID
Oberlin College, OH
Ohio Northern University, OH
The Ohio State University, OH
Ohio University, OH
Ohio University–Chillicothe, OH
Ohio University–Eastern, OH
Ohio University–Lancaster, OH
Ohio University–Southern Campus, OH
Ohio University–Zanesville, OH
Oklahoma Panhandle State University, OK
Oklahoma State University, OK
Old Dominion University, VA
Ouachita Baptist University, AR
Pace University, NY
Pacific University, OR
Plymouth State University, NH
Portland State University, OR
Purdue University, IN
Randolph College, VA
Regis University, CO
Rhodes College, TN
The Richard Stockton College of New Jersey, NJ
Ripon College, WI
Rochester Institute of Technology, NY
Rockford College, IL
Rockhurst University, MO
Rollins College, FL
Sacred Heart University, CT
Saginaw Valley State University, MI
St. Catherine University, MN
St. Edward's University, TX
St. John Fisher College, NY
St. John's University, NY
Saint Louis University, MO
Samford University, AL
San Diego State University, CA
Savannah State University, GA
Schreiner University, TX
Seton Hill University, PA
Shepherd University, WV
Shippensburg University of Pennsylvania, PA
Siena College, NY
Skidmore College, NY
Slippery Rock University of Pennsylvania, PA
Sonoma State University, CA
South Dakota School of Mines and Technology, SD
South Dakota State University, SD
Southeastern Louisiana University, LA
Southeastern Oklahoma State University, OK
Southeast Missouri State University, MO
Southern Illinois University Carbondale, IL
Southern Oregon University, OR
Southwestern College, KS
Southwestern Oklahoma State University, OK
Southwest Minnesota State University, MN
State University of New York at Binghamton, NY
State University of New York at Fredonia, NY
State University of New York at Oswego, NY
State University of New York at Plattsburgh, NY
State University of New York College at Cortland, NY
State University of New York College at Geneseo, NY
State University of New York College at Old Westbury, NY
State University of New York College at Oneonta, NY
State University of New York College at Potsdam, NY
State University of New York College of Environmental Science and Forestry, NY
Stephen F. Austin State University, TX
Stetson University, FL
Stony Brook University, State University of New York, NY
Tennessee Technological University, TN
Tennessee Wesleyan College, TN
Texas A&M International University, TX
Texas A&M University, TX
Texas Christian University, TX
Texas Lutheran University, TX
Texas Tech University, TX
Texas Woman's University, TX
Thiel College, PA
Thomas More College, KY
Thomas University, GA
Trevecca Nazarene University, TN
Trinity Christian College, IL
Truman State University, MO
The University of Akron, OH
The University of Alabama, AL
The University of Alabama in Huntsville, AL
University of Alaska Fairbanks, AK
The University of Arizona, AZ
University of Arkansas at Little Rock, AR
University of California, Irvine, CA
University of California, Riverside, CA
University of California, San Diego, CA
University of California, Santa Cruz, CA
University of Central Missouri, MO
University of Central Oklahoma, OK
University of Colorado Boulder, CO
University of Connecticut, CT
University of Dallas, TX
University of Dayton, OH
University of Delaware, DE
University of Denver, CO
University of Evansville, IN
University of Great Falls, MT
University of Idaho, ID
University of Illinois at Urbana–Champaign, IL
University of Indianapolis, IN
The University of Kansas, KS
University of Kentucky, KY
University of Mary Hardin-Baylor, TX
University of Maryland, Baltimore County, MD
University of Maryland, College Park, MD
University of Mary Washington, VA
University of Massachusetts Amherst, MA
University of Memphis, TN
University of Miami, FL
University of Michigan, MI
University of Michigan–Dearborn, MI
University of Michigan–Flint, MI
University of Minnesota, Twin Cities Campus, MN
University of Mississippi, MS
University of Missouri, MO
University of Missouri–St. Louis, MO
The University of Montana, MT
University of Montevallo, AL
University of Nebraska at Omaha, NE
University of Nebraska–Lincoln, NE
University of Nevada, Las Vegas, NV
University of New Orleans, LA
The University of North Carolina at Asheville, NC
The University of North Carolina at Greensboro, NC
The University of North Carolina at Pembroke, NC
The University of North Carolina Wilmington, NC
University of North Dakota, ND
University of Northern Colorado, CO
University of Northern Iowa, IA
University of Oklahoma, OK
University of Oregon, OR
University of Pittsburgh at Bradford, PA
University of Pittsburgh at Johnstown, PA
University of Portland, OR
University of Puget Sound, WA
University of Richmond, VA
University of Rio Grande, OH
University of St. Thomas, MN
University of St. Thomas, TX
University of South Carolina, SC
University of South Carolina Aiken, SC
University of South Florida, FL
The University of Tennessee at Chattanooga, TN
The University of Tennessee at Martin, TN
The University of Texas at Arlington, TX
The University of Texas at Brownsville, TX
The University of Texas at Dallas, TX
The University of Texas at El Paso, TX
The University of Texas at San Antonio, TX
University of the Southwest, NM
The University of Toledo, OH
University of Tulsa, OK
University of Utah, UT
University of Vermont, VT
The University of Virginia's College at Wise, VA
University of West Georgia, GA
University of Wisconsin–Eau Claire, WI
University of Wisconsin–Green Bay, WI
University of Wisconsin–La Crosse, WI
University of Wisconsin–Parkside, WI
University of Wisconsin–River Falls, WI
University of Wisconsin–Stevens Point, WI
University of Wisconsin–Stout, WI
University of Wisconsin–Superior, WI
University of Wyoming, WY
Utah State University, UT
Valdosta State University, GA
Valley City State University, ND
Valparaiso University, IN
Virginia Commonwealth University, VA
Virginia State University, VA
Walsh University, OH
Warner Pacific College, OR
Wartburg College, IA
Washburn University, KS
Washington & Jefferson College, PA

Washington State University, WA
Washington University in St. Louis, MO
Wayland Baptist University, TX
Waynesburg University, PA
Wayne State College, NE
Wayne State University, MI
Western Illinois University, IL
Western Kentucky University, KY
Western Oregon University, OR
Western Washington University, WA
West Liberty University, WV
West Texas A&M University, TX
West Virginia University, WV
West Virginia University Institute of Technology, WV
West Virginia Wesleyan College, WV
Wheaton College, IL
Whitworth University, WA
Wichita State University, KS
Widener University, PA
Wilson College, PA
Wright State University, OH
Xavier University, OH
Xavier University of Louisiana, LA
Youngstown State University, OH

Premedicine

Alderson-Broaddus College, WV
Alfred University, NY
American Jewish University, CA
Angelo State University, TX
Arizona State University, AZ
Arkansas State University, AR
Auburn University, AL
Augustana College, SD
Austin College, TX
Averett University, VA
Baylor University, TX
Bethel College, IN
Birmingham-Southern College, AL
Boise State University, ID
Brevard College, NC
Bryan College, TN
California State University, Bakersfield, CA
California State University, Stanislaus, CA
Calvin College, MI
Campbellsville University, KY
Carroll University, WI
Case Western Reserve University, OH
Centenary College of Louisiana, LA
Central College, IA
Central Methodist University, MO
Central Michigan University, MI
City College of the City University of New York, NY
Clemson University, SC
Cleveland State University, OH
Coe College, IA
The College at Brockport, State University of New York, NY
College of Charleston, SC
The College of New Rochelle, NY
The College of Saint Rose, NY
College of Staten Island of the City University of New York, NY
Colorado State University–Pueblo, CO
Concordia University, Nebraska, NE
Dallas Baptist University, TX
Davidson College, NC
Defiance College, OH
Delta State University, MS
DeSales University, PA
Dickinson State University, ND
Dordt College, IA
Drury University, MO
D'Youville College, NY
Edinboro University of Pennsylvania, PA
Elizabethtown College, PA
Elmhurst College, IL
Elon University, NC
Emory & Henry College, VA
Emporia State University, KS
Erskine College, SC
Florida Agricultural and Mechanical University, FL
Fort Valley State University, GA
Francis Marion University, SC
Frostburg State University, MD
Furman University, SC
Gannon University, PA
Gardner-Webb University, NC
Grace College, IN
Grand Valley State University, MI
Hamline University, MN
Hampden-Sydney College, VA
Hardin-Simmons University, TX
High Point University, NC
Hillsdale College, MI
Howard Payne University, TX
Illinois State University, IL
Indiana State University, IN
Indiana University of Pennsylvania, PA
Iowa State University of Science and Technology, IA
James Madison University, VA
John Carroll University, OH
Juniata College, PA
Kennesaw State University, GA
Keystone College, PA
King's College, PA
Limestone College, SC
Lindenwood University, MO
Lindsey Wilson College, KY
Lipscomb University, TN
Lock Haven University of Pennsylvania, PA
Louisiana State University and Agricultural and Mechanical College, LA
Lycoming College, PA
Malone University, OH
Mayville State University, ND
McMurry University, TX
Middle Tennessee State University, TN
Midwestern State University, TX
Millikin University, IL
Mills College, CA
Minnesota State University Moorhead, MN
Mississippi State University, MS
Missouri University of Science and Technology, MO
Montana State University Billings, MT
Muskingum University, OH
North Central College, IL
Northeastern State University, OK
Northern Arizona University, AZ
Northern Kentucky University, KY
Northern Michigan University, MI
North Georgia College & State University, GA
Northwestern Oklahoma State University, OK
Northwest Nazarene University, ID
Ohio Northern University, OH
The Ohio State University, OH
Ohio University, OH
Ohio University–Chillicothe, OH
Ohio University–Eastern, OH
Ohio University–Lancaster, OH
Ohio University–Southern Campus, OH
Ohio University–Zanesville, OH
Oklahoma State University, OK
Ouachita Baptist University, AR
Pacific University, OR
Piedmont College, GA
Prairie View A&M University, TX
Providence College, RI
Quincy University, IL
Randolph College, VA
Ripon College, WI
Rivier College, NH
Rochester Institute of Technology, NY
Rockford College, IL
Rockhurst University, MO
Sacred Heart University, CT
St. Catherine University, MN
St. Edward's University, TX
St. John's University, NY
Saint Louis University, MO
Saint Martin's University, WA
Samford University, AL
Schreiner University, TX
Shepherd University, WV
Siena College, NY
Sonoma State University, CA
South Dakota State University, SD
Southeast Missouri State University, MO
Southern Illinois University Carbondale, IL
Southwestern University, TX
Southwest Minnesota State University, MN
State University of New York at Binghamton, NY
State University of New York at Oswego, NY
State University of New York at Plattsburgh, NY
State University of New York College at Geneseo, NY
State University of New York College at Oneonta, NY
State University of New York College of Environmental Science and Forestry, NY
Stephen F. Austin State University, TX
Stetson University, FL
Sweet Briar College, VA
Tennessee Technological University, TN
Tennessee Wesleyan College, TN
Texas A&M International University, TX
Texas Christian University, TX
Texas Lutheran University, TX
Texas Tech University, TX
Texas Woman's University, TX
Thomas More College, KY
Trinity Christian College, IL
Truman State University, MO
Union University, TN
The University of Akron, OH
The University of Alabama, AL
University of California, Davis, CA
University of California, Irvine, CA
University of California, Riverside, CA
University of California, San Diego, CA
University of Central Missouri, MO
University of Colorado Boulder, CO
University of Connecticut, CT
University of Dallas, TX
University of Dayton, OH
University of Delaware, DE
University of Evansville, IN
University of Great Falls, MT
University of Hartford, CT
University of Idaho, ID
University of Illinois at Urbana–Champaign, IL

Non-Need Scholarships for Undergraduates
Academic Interests/Achievements

The University of Kansas, KS
University of Louisville, KY
University of Mary Hardin-Baylor, TX
University of Maryland, College Park, MD
University of Massachusetts Amherst, MA
University of Memphis, TN
University of Miami, FL
University of Michigan, MI
University of Michigan–Flint, MI
University of Minnesota, Twin Cities Campus, MN
University of Mississippi, MS
University of Missouri, MO
University of Missouri–St. Louis, MO
The University of Montana, MT
University of Nebraska at Omaha, NE
University of Nebraska–Lincoln, NE
University of Nevada, Las Vegas, NV
The University of North Carolina at Asheville, NC
The University of North Carolina at Greensboro, NC
The University of North Carolina Wilmington, NC
University of North Dakota, ND
University of Oregon, OR
University of Pittsburgh at Bradford, PA
University of Pittsburgh at Johnstown, PA
University of Portland, OR
University of Puget Sound, WA
University of St. Thomas, TX
University of South Carolina, SC
The University of South Dakota, SD
University of Southern Indiana, IN
University of South Florida, FL
The University of Tennessee at Martin, TN
The University of Texas–Pan American, TX
University of the Ozarks, AR
University of the Southwest, NM
The University of Toledo, OH
University of Tulsa, OK
University of Vermont, VT
The University of Virginia's College at Wise, VA
University of West Georgia, GA
University of Wisconsin–Eau Claire, WI
University of Wisconsin–Green Bay, WI
University of Wisconsin–Parkside, WI
University of Wisconsin–River Falls, WI
University of Wisconsin–Stevens Point, WI
Utah State University, UT
Valdosta State University, GA
Virginia Military Institute, VA
Virginia State University, VA
Walsh University, OH
Washburn University, KS
Washington & Jefferson College, PA
Washington State University, WA
Washington University in St. Louis, MO
Wayne State College, NE
Wayne State University, MI
Wesleyan College, GA
Western Kentucky University, KY
Western Oregon University, OR
Western Washington University, WA
West Texas A&M University, TX
West Virginia University, WV
Wheaton College, IL
Wheeling Jesuit University, WV
Whitworth University, WA
Wichita State University, KS
Widener University, PA
Wilson College, PA
Worcester Polytechnic Institute, MA
Wright State University, OH
Xavier University of Louisiana, LA
York College, NE
Youngstown State University, OH

Religion/Biblical Studies

Abilene Christian University, TX
Alderson-Broaddus College, WV
Anderson University, SC
Appalachian Bible College, WV
Arizona Christian University, AZ
Augsburg College, MN
Augustana College, IL
Augustana College, SD
Austin College, TX
Austin Graduate School of Theology, TX
Averett University, VA
Baptist Bible College of Pennsylvania, PA
The Baptist College of Florida, FL
Baptist University of the Americas, TX
Baylor University, TX
Belmont University, TN
Berry College, GA
Bethel College, IN
Bethesda Christian University, CA
Beulah Heights University, GA
Birmingham-Southern College, AL
Bloomfield College, NJ
Bloomsburg University of Pennsylvania, PA
Brevard College, NC
Bryan College, TN
California Lutheran University, CA
California State University, Bakersfield, CA
Calvin College, MI
Campbellsville University, KY
Carson-Newman College, TN
Case Western Reserve University, OH
Centenary College of Louisiana, LA
Central College, IA
Central Methodist University, MO
Central Michigan University, MI
Christopher Newport University, VA
Cincinnati Christian University, OH
The Citadel, The Military College of South Carolina, SC
The College of New Rochelle, NY
Columbia College, MO
Columbia International University, SC
Concordia University, MI
Concordia University Chicago, IL
Concordia University, Nebraska, NE
Concordia University, St. Paul, MN
Concordia University Wisconsin, WI
Cornerstone University, MI
Dallas Baptist University, TX
Davidson College, NC
Defiance College, OH
DeSales University, PA
Dordt College, IA
Eastern Michigan University, MI
East Texas Baptist University, TX
Edinboro University of Pennsylvania, PA
Elizabethtown College, PA
Elmhurst College, IL
Elon University, NC
Emmanuel College, GA
Emmanuel College, MA
Emory & Henry College, VA
Erskine College, SC
Evangel University, MO
Faulkner University, AL
Felician College, NJ
Flagler College, FL
Florida Gulf Coast University, FL
Florida Southern College, FL
Furman University, SC
Gannon University, PA
Gardner-Webb University, NC
Geneva College, PA
George Fox University, OR
Grace University, NE
Greenville College, IL
Grove City College, PA
Hamline University, MN
Hampden-Sydney College, VA
Hannibal-LaGrange University, MO
Harding University, AR
Hardin-Simmons University, TX
Hastings College, NE
Hebrew College, MA
High Point University, NC
Hillsdale College, MI
Hillsdale Free Will Baptist College, OK
Houston Baptist University, TX
Howard Payne University, TX
James Madison University, VA
John Carroll University, OH
Johnson Bible College, TN
King's College, PA
Laurel University, NC
Lebanon Valley College, PA
Lee University, TN
Limestone College, SC
Lindsey Wilson College, KY
Lipscomb University, TN
Louisiana College, LA
Lubbock Christian University, TX
Lycoming College, PA
Malone University, OH
Manhattan Christian College, KS
Maranatha Baptist Bible College, WI
Marywood University, PA
The Master's College and Seminary, CA
McKendree University, IL
McMurry University, TX
Mercer University, GA
Meredith College, NC
Mid-Atlantic Christian University, NC
Mid-Continent University, KY
Milligan College, TN
Mississippi State University, MS
Missouri Baptist University, MO
Montclair State University, NJ
Nazarene Bible College, CO
New Hope Christian College, OR
New Life Theological Seminary, NC
North Central College, IL
Northern Arizona University, AZ
Northwest Nazarene University, ID
Ohio Northern University, OH
Ohio Valley University, WV
Oklahoma Baptist University, OK
Oklahoma Christian University, OK
Oklahoma City University, OK
Oklahoma Wesleyan University, OK
Ouachita Baptist University, AR
Our Lady of Holy Cross College, LA
Pacific Union College, CA
Piedmont College, GA
Point Loma Nazarene University, CA
Quincy University, IL
Regent University, VA
Ripon College, WI
Rockhurst University, MO
Sacred Heart Major Seminary, MI

St. Ambrose University, IA
St. Edward's University, TX
Saint Francis University, PA
Saint Louis University, MO
Samford University, AL
San Diego State University, CA
Schreiner University, TX
Shorter University, GA
Siena College, NY
Southeastern University, FL
Southeast Missouri State University, MO
Southern Adventist University, TN
Southern Illinois University Carbondale, IL
Southwestern College, KS
Stetson University, FL
Tennessee Wesleyan College, TN
Texas Christian University, TX
Thiel College, PA
Thomas More College, KY
Trevecca Nazarene University, TN
Trinity Christian College, IL
Union University, TN
The University of Arizona, AZ
University of California, Davis, CA
University of Central Missouri, MO
University of Connecticut, CT
University of Dallas, TX
University of Dayton, OH
University of Delaware, DE
University of Evansville, IN
University of Great Falls, MT
University of Illinois at Urbana–Champaign, IL
University of Indianapolis, IN
The University of Kansas, KS
University of Mary Hardin-Baylor, TX
University of Mary Washington, VA
University of Miami, FL
University of Minnesota, Twin Cities Campus, MN
University of Mississippi, MS
University of Missouri, MO
The University of North Carolina at Greensboro, NC
University of Portland, OR
University of St. Thomas, MN
University of St. Thomas, TX
University of South Carolina, SC
University of South Florida, FL
University of the Ozarks, AR
University of the Southwest, NM
University of Tulsa, OK
Valparaiso University, IN
Walla Walla University, WA
Walsh University, OH
Warner Pacific College, OR
Wartburg College, IA
Washburn University, KS
Washington University in St. Louis, MO
Wayland Baptist University, TX
Waynesburg University, PA
Wesleyan College, GA
West Virginia University, WV
Wheaton College, IL
William Jessup University, CA
Williams Baptist College, AR
Wilson College, PA
Wright State University, OH
Xavier University of Louisiana, LA
York College, NE
Youngstown State University, OH

Social Sciences

Abilene Christian University, TX
Alaska Pacific University, AK
Alderson-Broaddus College, WV
Alfred University, NY
Alliant International University, CA
Angelo State University, TX
Arizona State University, AZ
Arkansas State University, AR
Arkansas Tech University, AR
Ashland University, OH
Auburn University, AL
Augsburg College, MN
Augustana College, IL
Augustana College, SD
Augusta State University, GA
Austin College, TX
Austin Peay State University, TN
Ball State University, IN
Baylor University, TX
Bethel College, IN
Birmingham-Southern College, AL
Black Hills State University, SD
Bloomfield College, NJ
Bloomsburg University of Pennsylvania, PA
Boise State University, ID
Bowling Green State University, OH
Brevard College, NC
Bryan College, TN
Butler University, IN
California Institute of Integral Studies, CA
California Lutheran University, CA
California Polytechnic State University, San Luis Obispo, CA
California State Polytechnic University, Pomona, CA
California State University, Bakersfield, CA
California State University, Chico, CA
California State University, Fresno, CA
California State University, Fullerton, CA
California State University, Northridge, CA
California State University, San Bernardino, CA
California State University, Stanislaus, CA
Calvin College, MI
Cameron University, OK
Campbellsville University, KY
Carlos Albizu University, PR
Carroll University, WI
Case Western Reserve University, OH
Centenary College of Louisiana, LA
Central College, IA
Central Methodist University, MO
Central Michigan University, MI
Champlain College, VT
City College of the City University of New York, NY
Clarkson University, NY
Clemson University, SC
Cleveland State University, OH
The College at Brockport, State University of New York, NY
College of Charleston, SC
The College of New Rochelle, NY
The College of Saint Rose, NY
College of Staten Island of the City University of New York, NY
Colorado State University–Pueblo, CO
Columbia College, MO
Concordia University, Nebraska, NE
Concord University, WV
Cornerstone University, MI
Dalton State College, GA
Davidson College, NC
Defiance College, OH
Delta State University, MS
DeSales University, PA
Dickinson State University, ND
Dordt College, IA
Dowling College, NY
Drury University, MO
D'Youville College, NY
Eastern Connecticut State University, CT
Eastern Michigan University, MI
Eastern Washington University, WA
East Tennessee State University, TN
East Texas Baptist University, TX
Edinboro University of Pennsylvania, PA
Elizabethtown College, PA
Elmhurst College, IL
Elon University, NC
Emmanuel College, MA
Emporia State University, KS
Erskine College, SC
Evangel University, MO
Fitchburg State University, MA
Flagler College, FL
Florida Agricultural and Mechanical University, FL
Florida Atlantic University, FL
Florida Gulf Coast University, FL
Florida International University, FL
Florida Southern College, FL
Fort Lewis College, CO
Fort Valley State University, GA
Francis Marion University, SC
Fresno Pacific University, CA
Frostburg State University, MD
Furman University, SC
Gannon University, PA
Gardner-Webb University, NC
Georgia College & State University, GA
Georgia Southern University, GA
Glenville State College, WV
Governors State University, IL
Grand Valley State University, MI
Grove City College, PA
Hamline University, MN
Hampshire College, MA
Hardin-Simmons University, TX
Hawai'i Pacific University, HI
Hillsdale College, MI
Howard Payne University, TX
Illinois State University, IL
Indiana University of Pennsylvania, PA
Iowa State University of Science and Technology, IA
James Madison University, VA
John Carroll University, OH
Juniata College, PA
Kean University, NJ
Kennesaw State University, GA
Kent State University, OH
King's College, PA
Lewis-Clark State College, ID
Limestone College, SC
Lindenwood University, MO
Lock Haven University of Pennsylvania, PA
Longwood University, VA
Louisiana Tech University, LA
Lubbock Christian University, TX
Lycoming College, PA
Malone University, OH
Marymount University, VA
Massachusetts College of Liberal Arts, MA
The Master's College and Seminary, CA

Non-Need Scholarships for Undergraduates
Academic Interests/Achievements

Mayville State University, ND
McMurry University, TX
Mesa State College, CO
Michigan State University, MI
Mid-Continent University, KY
Middle Tennessee State University, TN
Midwestern State University, TX
Millersville University of Pennsylvania, PA
Minnesota State University Moorhead, MN
Minot State University, ND
Misericordia University, PA
Mississippi State University, MS
Missouri University of Science and Technology, MO
Molloy College, NY
Monmouth University, NJ
Montana State University, MT
Montana State University Billings, MT
Montana State University–Northern, MT
Montclair State University, NJ
Morehead State University, KY
Mount Mary College, WI
New England College, NH
New Mexico State University, NM
North Carolina Central University, NC
North Carolina State University, NC
North Central College, IL
Northeastern Illinois University, IL
Northeastern State University, OK
Northern Arizona University, AZ
Northern Illinois University, IL
Northern Kentucky University, KY
Northern Michigan University, MI
Northern State University, SD
Northwestern Oklahoma State University, OK
Northwestern State University of Louisiana, LA
Northwest Missouri State University, MO
Northwest Nazarene University, ID
Ohio Northern University, OH
The Ohio State University, OH
Ohio University, OH
Ohio University–Chillicothe, OH
Ohio University–Eastern, OH
Ohio University–Lancaster, OH
Ohio University–Southern Campus, OH
Ohio University–Zanesville, OH
Oklahoma State University, OK
Ouachita Baptist University, AR
Pace University, NY
Pacific University, OR
Piedmont College, GA
Plymouth State University, NH
Point Loma Nazarene University, CA
Portland State University, OR
Post University, CT
Purchase College, State University of New York, NY
Quincy University, IL
Randolph College, VA
Regent University, VA
The Richard Stockton College of New Jersey, NJ
Ripon College, WI
Rivier College, NH
Rochester Institute of Technology, NY
Rockford College, IL
Rockhurst University, MO
St. Catherine University, MN
St. Edward's University, TX
Saint Francis University, PA
St. John's University, NY
Saint Louis University, MO
St. Thomas Aquinas College, NY
Samford University, AL
San Diego State University, CA
Savannah State University, GA
Schreiner University, TX
Seton Hill University, PA
Shepherd University, WV
Shippensburg University of Pennsylvania, PA
Siena College, NY
Slippery Rock University of Pennsylvania, PA
Sonoma State University, CA
South Dakota State University, SD
Southeastern Louisiana University, LA
Southeastern Oklahoma State University, OK
Southeast Missouri State University, MO
Southern Illinois University Carbondale, IL
Southern Oregon University, OR
Southwestern College, KS
Southwestern Oklahoma State University, OK
Southwestern University, TX
Southwest Minnesota State University, MN
State University of New York at Binghamton, NY
State University of New York at Fredonia, NY
State University of New York at Oswego, NY
State University of New York at Plattsburgh, NY
State University of New York College at Geneseo, NY
State University of New York College at Oneonta, NY
State University of New York College at Potsdam, NY
Stetson University, FL
Stony Brook University, State University of New York, NY
Tennessee Technological University, TN
Tennessee Wesleyan College, TN
Texas A&M International University, TX
Texas A&M University–Texarkana, TX
Texas Christian University, TX
Texas Tech University, TX
Texas Woman's University, TX
Thomas More College, KY
Thomas University, GA
Trevecca Nazarene University, TN
Trinity Christian College, IL
Truman State University, MO
The University of Akron, OH
The University of Alabama, AL
The University of Alabama in Huntsville, AL
University of Alaska Anchorage, AK
University of Arkansas at Little Rock, AR
University of California, Davis, CA
University of California, Irvine, CA
University of California, Riverside, CA
University of California, San Diego, CA
University of California, Santa Cruz, CA
University of Central Missouri, MO
University of Central Oklahoma, OK
University of Colorado Boulder, CO
University of Connecticut, CT
University of Dayton, OH
University of Delaware, DE
University of Denver, CO
University of Evansville, IN
University of Great Falls, MT
University of Hawaii at Hilo, HI
University of Houston–Clear Lake, TX
University of Idaho, ID
University of Illinois at Urbana–Champaign, IL
The University of Kansas, KS
University of Maine at Fort Kent, ME
University of Mary Hardin-Baylor, TX
University of Maryland, Baltimore County, MD
University of Maryland, College Park, MD
University of Mary Washington, VA
University of Massachusetts Amherst, MA
University of Memphis, TN
University of Miami, FL
University of Michigan, MI
University of Michigan–Dearborn, MI
University of Michigan–Flint, MI
University of Minnesota, Twin Cities Campus, MN
University of Mississippi, MS
University of Missouri, MO
University of Missouri–St. Louis, MO
The University of Montana, MT
University of Montevallo, AL
University of Nebraska at Omaha, NE
University of Nebraska–Lincoln, NE
University of Nevada, Las Vegas, NV
University of New Orleans, LA
The University of North Carolina at Asheville, NC
The University of North Carolina at Greensboro, NC
The University of North Carolina Wilmington, NC
University of North Dakota, ND
University of Northern Colorado, CO
University of Northern Iowa, IA
University of Oklahoma, OK
University of Oregon, OR
University of Pittsburgh at Bradford, PA
University of Pittsburgh at Johnstown, PA
University of Portland, OR
University of Puget Sound, WA
University of Rio Grande, OH
University of St. Francis, IL
University of St. Thomas, MN
University of St. Thomas, TX
University of South Carolina, SC
University of South Carolina Aiken, SC
The University of South Dakota, SD
University of Southern Indiana, IN
University of South Florida, FL
The University of Tampa, FL
The University of Tennessee, TN
The University of Tennessee at Martin, TN
The University of Texas at Arlington, TX
The University of Texas at Brownsville, TX
The University of Texas at San Antonio, TX
The University of Texas–Pan American, TX
University of the Ozarks, AR
University of the Southwest, NM
The University of Toledo, OH
University of Tulsa, OK
University of Utah, UT
University of Vermont, VT
The University of Virginia's College at Wise, VA
University of West Georgia, GA
University of Wisconsin–Eau Claire, WI
University of Wisconsin–Green Bay, WI
University of Wisconsin–La Crosse, WI
University of Wisconsin–River Falls, WI
University of Wisconsin–Stevens Point, WI
University of Wisconsin–Superior, WI
University of Wyoming, WY
Utah State University, UT
Valdosta State University, GA
Valley City State University, ND

Virginia State University, VA
Walsh University, OH
Warner Pacific College, OR
Washburn University, KS
Washington & Jefferson College, PA
Washington State University, WA
Washington University in St. Louis, MO
Wayland Baptist University, TX
Waynesburg University, PA
Wayne State College, NE
Wayne State University, MI
Wesleyan College, GA
West Chester University of Pennsylvania, PA
Western Illinois University, IL
Western Kentucky University, KY
Western Oregon University, OR
Western Washington University, WA
West Texas A&M University, TX
West Virginia University, WV
Wheaton College, IL
Wichita State University, KS
Widener University, PA
Wilson College, PA
Wright State University, OH
Xavier University, OH
Xavier University of Louisiana, LA
Youngstown State University, OH

Creative Arts/Performance

Applied Art and Design

Arcadia University, PA
Arizona State University, AZ
Auburn University, AL
Bethesda Christian University, CA
Bloomfield College, NJ
Bowie State University, MD
Brenau University, GA
Brooks Institute, CA
California Institute of the Arts, CA
California Polytechnic State University, San Luis Obispo, CA
California State University, Chico, CA
Central Michigan University, MI
City College of the City University of New York, NY
Clemson University, SC
College for Creative Studies, MI
The College of New Rochelle, NY
Colorado State University–Pueblo, CO
Concordia University, CA
Concordia University, Nebraska, NE
Converse College, SC
Corcoran College of Art and Design, DC
Dominican University, IL
East Carolina University, NC
Eastern Michigan University, MI
Emmanuel College, GA
The Evergreen State College, WA
Fashion Institute of Technology, NY
Ferris State University, MI
Flagler College, FL
Florida Agricultural and Mechanical University, FL
Georgia College & State University, GA
Grace College, IN
Graceland University, IA
Grand Valley State University, MI
Greenville College, IL
Hardin-Simmons University, TX
Huntington University, IN
Illinois State University, IL
Indiana University of Pennsylvania, PA
Iowa State University of Science and Technology, IA
Kean University, NJ
Keene State College, NH
Kutztown University of Pennsylvania, PA
Lindenwood University, MO
Lindsey Wilson College, KY
Louisiana State University and Agricultural and Mechanical College, LA
Louisiana Tech University, LA
Massachusetts College of Liberal Arts, MA
Mercyhurst College, PA
Meredith College, NC
Minneapolis College of Art and Design, MN
Mississippi State University, MS
Morehead State University, KY
Mount Mary College, WI
Murray State University, KY
New England College, NH
New Jersey Institute of Technology, NJ
New Mexico State University, NM
Northeastern State University, OK
Northern Arizona University, AZ
Northern Illinois University, IL
Northern Michigan University, MI
North Georgia College & State University, GA
Notre Dame de Namur University, CA
Ohio Northern University, OH
Ohio University, OH
Ohio University–Chillicothe, OH
Ohio University–Eastern, OH
Ohio University–Lancaster, OH
Ohio University–Southern Campus, OH
Ohio University–Zanesville, OH
Ohio Wesleyan University, OH
Oklahoma Baptist University, OK
Oklahoma Christian University, OK
Oklahoma City University, OK
Otis College of Art and Design, CA
The Richard Stockton College of New Jersey, NJ
Ringling College of Art and Design, FL
Rivier College, NH
Robert Morris University Illinois, IL
Rochester Institute of Technology, NY
Rocky Mountain College of Art + Design, CO
Sacred Heart University, CT
Saint Mary-of-the-Woods College, IN
San Diego State University, CA
Santa Fe University of Art and Design, NM
Seton Hill University, PA
Shepherd University, WV
Silver Lake College, WI
Slippery Rock University of Pennsylvania, PA
Sonoma State University, CA
Southern Illinois University Carbondale, IL
Southwestern Oklahoma State University, OK
State University of New York at Fredonia, NY
State University of New York College at Geneseo, NY
Stetson University, FL
Stevens-Henager College, ID
Texas Christian University, TX
Texas State University–San Marcos, TX
Texas Tech University, TX
Texas Woman's University, TX
Trinity Christian College, IL
The University of Akron, OH
University of Alaska Fairbanks, AK
University of Bridgeport, CT
University of California, San Diego, CA
University of Central Missouri, MO
University of Central Oklahoma, OK
University of Delaware, DE
University of Idaho, ID
University of Illinois at Chicago, IL
University of Illinois at Urbana–Champaign, IL
The University of Kansas, KS
University of Kentucky, KY
University of Maryland, College Park, MD
University of Missouri–St. Louis, MO
University of Nevada, Las Vegas, NV
The University of North Carolina at Chapel Hill, NC
University of North Carolina School of the Arts, NC
University of Northern Iowa, IA
University of Oregon, OR
University of St. Francis, IL
University of St. Thomas, TX
University of South Florida, FL
The University of Texas at El Paso, TX
University of West Florida, FL
University of West Georgia, GA
University of Wisconsin–Parkside, WI
University of Wisconsin–Stevens Point, WI
University of Wisconsin–Stout, WI
Utah State University, UT
Valley City State University, ND
Virginia Polytechnic Institute and State University, VA
Virginia State University, VA
Washington State University, WA
Washington University in St. Louis, MO
Wayne State College, NE
Western Illinois University, IL
Western Washington University, WA
Wichita State University, KS
Wright State University, OH

Art/Fine Arts

Abilene Christian University, TX
Adelphi University, NY
Adrian College, MI
Alabama Agricultural and Mechanical University, AL
Alaska Pacific University, AK
Albion College, MI
Albright College, PA
Alderson-Broaddus College, WV
Alfred University, NY
Alma College, MI
Alverno College, WI
Anderson University, SC
Angelo State University, TX
Arcadia University, PA
Arizona State University, AZ
Arkansas State University, AR
Arkansas Tech University, AR
Armstrong Atlantic State University, GA
Ashland University, OH
Auburn University, AL
Augsburg College, MN
Augustana College, IL
Augustana College, SD
Augusta State University, GA
Austin College, TX
Austin Peay State University, TN
Averett University, VA
Ball State University, IN
Baylor University, TX
Bellarmine University, KY
Berry College, GA
Bethany Lutheran College, MN
Bethel College, IN

Non-Need Scholarships for Undergraduates
Creative Arts/Performance

Bethel College, KS
Bethel University, MN
Biola University, CA
Birmingham-Southern College, AL
Black Hills State University, SD
Bloomfield College, NJ
Bluefield College, VA
Bluffton University, OH
Boise State University, ID
Boston University, MA
Bowie State University, MD
Bowling Green State University, OH
Bradley University, IL
Brenau University, GA
Brevard College, NC
Brigham Young University, UT
Brooks Institute, CA
Bucknell University, PA
Buena Vista University, IA
Butler University, IN
Caldwell College, NJ
California Institute of the Arts, CA
California Lutheran University, CA
California Polytechnic State University, San Luis Obispo, CA
California State University, Bakersfield, CA
California State University, Chico, CA
California State University, Fresno, CA
California State University, Fullerton, CA
California State University, San Bernardino, CA
California State University, Stanislaus, CA
Calumet College of Saint Joseph, IN
Calvin College, MI
Cameron University, OK
Campbellsville University, KY
Campbell University, NC
Canisius College, NY
Carnegie Mellon University, PA
Carroll University, WI
Carson-Newman College, TN
Case Western Reserve University, OH
Cedar Crest College, PA
Centenary College of Louisiana, LA
Central College, IA
Central Michigan University, MI
Central Washington University, WA
Chicago State University, IL
Christopher Newport University, VA
City College of the City University of New York, NY
Clarke University, IA
Clemson University, SC
The Cleveland Institute of Art, OH
Cleveland State University, OH
Coastal Carolina University, SC
Coe College, IA
Coker College, SC
The College at Brockport, State University of New York, NY
College for Creative Studies, MI
College of Charleston, SC
College of Mount St. Joseph, OH
The College of New Rochelle, NY
College of Notre Dame of Maryland, MD
College of Saint Benedict, MN
College of Saint Mary, NE
The College of Saint Rose, NY
College of Staten Island of the City University of New York, NY
College of Visual Arts, MN
Colorado State University, CO
Colorado State University–Pueblo, CO
Columbia College, MO
Columbus College of Art & Design, OH
Columbus State University, GA
Concordia College, MN
Concordia University, MI
Concordia University Chicago, IL
Concordia University, Nebraska, NE
Concordia University, St. Paul, MN
Concord University, WV
Cooper Union for the Advancement of Science and Art, NY
Cornell College, IA
Cornish College of the Arts, WA
Creighton University, NE
Culver-Stockton College, MO
Daemen College, NY
Davidson College, NC
Delta State University, MS
DePaul University, IL
DePauw University, IN
Dickinson State University, ND
Dillard University, LA
Doane College, NE
Dominican University, IL
Drake University, IA
Drury University, MO
East Carolina University, NC
Eastern Michigan University, MI
Eastern Washington University, WA
East Tennessee State University, TN
Eckerd College, FL
Edgewood College, WI
Edinboro University of Pennsylvania, PA
Elizabethtown College, PA
Elmhurst College, IL
Elon University, NC
Emmanuel College, GA
Emory & Henry College, VA
Emory University, GA
Emporia State University, KS
Endicott College, MA
Eureka College, IL
Evangel University, MO
The Evergreen State College, WA
Ferris State University, MI
Finlandia University, MI
Flagler College, FL
Florida Agricultural and Mechanical University, FL
Florida Gulf Coast University, FL
Florida Southern College, FL
Fort Lewis College, CO
Francis Marion University, SC
Franklin College, IN
Frostburg State University, MD
Furman University, SC
Gardner-Webb University, NC
George Fox University, OR
Georgetown College, KY
Georgia College & State University, GA
Georgian Court University, NJ
Georgia Southern University, GA
Gordon College, MA
Goucher College, MD
Grace College, IN
Grand Valley State University, MI
Grand View University, IA
Green Mountain College, VT
Greenville College, IL
Gustavus Adolphus College, MN
Hamline University, MN
Hannibal-LaGrange University, MO
Hanover College, IN
Harding University, AR
Hardin-Simmons University, TX
Hastings College, NE
Hendrix College, AR
High Point University, NC
Hillsdale College, MI
Hobart and William Smith Colleges, NY
Hofstra University, NY
Hollins University, VA
Hope College, MI
Houghton College, NY
Houston Baptist University, TX
Howard Payne University, TX
Howard University, DC
Huntington University, IN
Illinois State University, IL
Indiana State University, IN
Indiana University of Pennsylvania, PA
Indiana University–Purdue University Fort Wayne, IN
Indiana Wesleyan University, IN
Iowa State University of Science and Technology, IA
Iowa Wesleyan College, IA
James Madison University, VA
Jamestown College, ND
John Brown University, AR
Johnson Bible College, TN
Judson University, IL
Juniata College, PA
Kean University, NJ
Keene State College, NH
Kent State University, OH
Kent State University at Stark, OH
Kentucky State University, KY
Kentucky Wesleyan College, KY
Kenyon College, OH
Knox College, IL
Kutztown University of Pennsylvania, PA
Lake Forest College, IL
Lesley University, MA
Lewis-Clark State College, ID
Limestone College, SC
Lincoln University, MO
Lindenwood University, MO
Lipscomb University, TN
Lock Haven University of Pennsylvania, PA
Long Island University, Brooklyn Campus, NY
Long Island University, C.W. Post Campus, NY
Longwood University, VA
Louisiana State University and Agricultural and Mechanical College, LA
Louisiana Tech University, LA
Lourdes College, OH
Loyola University Chicago, IL
Lubbock Christian University, TX
Lycoming College, PA
Lyme Academy College of Fine Arts, CT
Lynchburg College, VA
Lyon College, AR
Maine College of Art, ME
Marietta College, OH
Maryville College, TN
Maryville University of Saint Louis, MO
Marywood University, PA
Massachusetts College of Liberal Arts, MA
McMurry University, TX
McPherson College, KS
Mercer University, GA
Mercyhurst College, PA
Meredith College, NC

Mesa State College, CO
Messiah College, PA
Miami University, OH
Michigan State University, MI
Midwestern State University, TX
Millersville University of Pennsylvania, PA
Milligan College, TN
Millikin University, IL
Millsaps College, MS
Mills College, CA
Minneapolis College of Art and Design, MN
Minnesota State University Moorhead, MN
Mississippi State University, MS
Mississippi University for Women, MS
Missouri Southern State University, MO
Molloy College, NY
Monmouth College, IL
Montana State University, MT
Montana State University Billings, MT
Montana State University–Northern, MT
Montclair State University, NJ
Morehouse College, GA
Morningside College, IA
Mount Mary College, WI
Mount Mercy University, IA
Mount St. Mary's University, MD
Murray State University, KY
Muskingum University, OH
Nazareth College of Rochester, NY
Nebraska Wesleyan University, NE
New England College, NH
New Mexico State University, NM
North Central College, IL
Northeastern Illinois University, IL
Northeastern State University, OK
Northern Arizona University, AZ
Northern Illinois University, IL
Northern Kentucky University, KY
Northern State University, SD
Northland College, WI
Northwestern Oklahoma State University, OK
Northwestern State University of Louisiana, LA
Northwest Missouri State University, MO
Northwest Nazarene University, ID
Notre Dame de Namur University, CA
Ohio Northern University, OH
Ohio University, OH
Ohio University–Chillicothe, OH
Ohio University–Eastern, OH
Ohio University–Lancaster, OH
Ohio University–Southern Campus, OH
Ohio University–Zanesville, OH
Ohio Wesleyan University, OH
Oklahoma Baptist University, OK
Oklahoma City University, OK
Oklahoma Panhandle State University, OK
Oklahoma State University, OK
Old Dominion University, VA
Olivet College, MI
Olivet Nazarene University, IL
Oregon College of Art & Craft, OR
Otis College of Art and Design, CA
Ouachita Baptist University, AR
Pacific Lutheran University, WA
Pacific Union College, CA
Pacific University, OR
Piedmont College, GA
Point Loma Nazarene University, CA
Portland State University, OR
Prairie View A&M University, TX
Purchase College, State University of New York, NY
Quincy University, IL
Reinhardt University, GA
Rhode Island College, RI
Rhodes College, TN
The Richard Stockton College of New Jersey, NJ
Ringling College of Art and Design, FL
Ripon College, WI
Rivier College, NH
Roberts Wesleyan College, NY
Rochester Institute of Technology, NY
Rocky Mountain College, MT
Rocky Mountain College of Art + Design, CO
Rollins College, FL
Rosemont College, PA
Sacred Heart University, CT
Sage College of Albany, NY
Saginaw Valley State University, MI
St. Ambrose University, IA
St. Catherine University, MN
St. Edward's University, TX
Saint Francis University, PA
Saint John's University, MN
St. John's University, NY
Saint Joseph's University, PA
Saint Louis University, MO
Saint Mary-of-the-Woods College, IN
Saint Mary's University of Minnesota, MN
Saint Michael's College, VT
St. Norbert College, WI
San Diego State University, CA
Santa Fe University of Art and Design, NM
Savannah College of Art and Design, GA
School of the Art Institute of Chicago, IL
School of Visual Arts, NY
Schreiner University, TX
Seattle Pacific University, WA
Seattle University, WA
Seton Hill University, PA
Shawnee State University, OH
Shepherd University, WV
Shippensburg University of Pennsylvania, PA
Shorter University, GA
Sierra Nevada College, NV
Silver Lake College, WI
Simpson College, IA
Slippery Rock University of Pennsylvania, PA
Sonoma State University, CA
South Dakota State University, SD
Southeastern Louisiana University, LA
Southeastern Oklahoma State University, OK
Southern Adventist University, TN
Southern Illinois University Edwardsville, IL
Southern Oregon University, OR
Southwest Baptist University, MO
Southwestern Oklahoma State University, OK
Southwestern University, TX
Southwest Minnesota State University, MN
Spring Arbor University, MI
State University of New York at Binghamton, NY
State University of New York at Fredonia, NY
State University of New York at New Paltz, NY
State University of New York at Plattsburgh, NY
State University of New York College at Cortland, NY
State University of New York College at Geneseo, NY
State University of New York College at Potsdam, NY
Stetson University, FL
Sul Ross State University, TX
Sweet Briar College, VA
Syracuse University, NY
Temple University, PA
Tennessee Technological University, TN
Texas A&M International University, TX
Texas A&M University–Commerce, TX
Texas A&M University–Corpus Christi, TX
Texas Christian University, TX
Texas State University–San Marcos, TX
Texas Tech University, TX
Texas Woman's University, TX
Thomas More College, KY
Thomas University, GA
Towson University, MD
Transylvania University, KY
Trinity Christian College, IL
Trinity University, TX
Truman State University, MO
Union University, TN
The University of Akron, OH
The University of Alabama, AL
The University of Alabama at Birmingham, AL
The University of Alabama in Huntsville, AL
University of Alaska Fairbanks, AK
The University of Arizona, AZ
University of Arkansas, AR
University of Arkansas at Little Rock, AR
University of California, Irvine, CA
University of California, Riverside, CA
University of California, Santa Cruz, CA
University of Central Missouri, MO
University of Central Oklahoma, OK
University of Cincinnati, OH
University of Colorado Boulder, CO
University of Connecticut, CT
University of Dallas, TX
University of Dayton, OH
University of Delaware, DE
University of Denver, CO
University of Evansville, IN
University of Florida, FL
University of Great Falls, MT
University of Hartford, CT
University of Hawaii at Hilo, HI
University of Hawaii at Manoa, HI
University of Idaho, ID
University of Illinois at Chicago, IL
University of Illinois at Springfield, IL
University of Illinois at Urbana–Champaign, IL
University of Indianapolis, IN
The University of Kansas, KS
University of Kentucky, KY
University of La Verne, CA
University of Louisville, KY
University of Maine at Presque Isle, ME
University of Mary Hardin-Baylor, TX
University of Maryland, Baltimore County, MD
University of Maryland, College Park, MD
University of Mary Washington, VA
University of Massachusetts Amherst, MA
University of Massachusetts Lowell, MA
University of Memphis, TN
University of Miami, FL
University of Michigan, MI
University of Michigan–Dearborn, MI
University of Michigan–Flint, MI
University of Mississippi, MS
University of Missouri, MO
University of Missouri–St. Louis, MO

University of Mobile, AL
University of Montevallo, AL
University of Mount Union, OH
University of Nebraska at Omaha, NE
University of Nebraska–Lincoln, NE
University of Nevada, Las Vegas, NV
University of New Hampshire, NH
University of North Alabama, AL
The University of North Carolina at Asheville, NC
The University of North Carolina at Chapel Hill, NC
The University of North Carolina at Greensboro, NC
The University of North Carolina Wilmington, NC
University of North Dakota, ND
University of Northern Iowa, IA
University of North Florida, FL
University of Oklahoma, OK
University of Oregon, OR
University of Puget Sound, WA
University of Redlands, CA
University of Rhode Island, RI
University of Richmond, VA
University of Rio Grande, OH
University of St. Francis, IL
University of St. Thomas, TX
University of Science and Arts of Oklahoma, OK
University of South Alabama, AL
University of South Carolina, SC
University of South Carolina Aiken, SC
The University of South Dakota, SD
University of Southern California, CA
University of Southern Indiana, IN
University of Southern Mississippi, MS
University of South Florida, FL
The University of Tampa, FL
The University of Tennessee, TN
The University of Tennessee at Chattanooga, TN
The University of Tennessee at Martin, TN
The University of Texas at Brownsville, TX
The University of Texas at El Paso, TX
The University of Texas at San Antonio, TX
The University of Texas at Tyler, TX
The University of Texas of the Permian Basin, TX
The University of Texas–Pan American, TX
University of the Cumberlands, KY
University of the Incarnate Word, TX
University of the Ozarks, AR
University of the Pacific, CA
The University of Toledo, OH
University of Tulsa, OK
University of Utah, UT
University of West Florida, FL
University of West Georgia, GA
University of Wisconsin–Green Bay, WI
University of Wisconsin–La Crosse, WI
University of Wisconsin–Parkside, WI
University of Wisconsin–River Falls, WI
University of Wisconsin–Stout, WI
University of Wyoming, WY
Utah State University, UT
Valdosta State University, GA
Valley City State University, ND
Valley Forge Christian College, PA
Valparaiso University, IN
Virginia Commonwealth University, VA
Virginia Polytechnic Institute and State University, VA
Virginia State University, VA
Virginia Wesleyan College, VA
Wabash College, IN
Warren Wilson College, NC
Wartburg College, IA
Washburn University, KS
Washington State University, WA
Washington University in St. Louis, MO
Wayland Baptist University, TX
Wayne State College, NE
Wayne State University, MI
Wesleyan College, GA
Western Carolina University, NC
Western Kentucky University, KY
Western Oregon University, OR
Western State College of Colorado, CO
Western Washington University, WA
West Liberty University, WV
Westmont College, CA
West Texas A&M University, TX
West Virginia State University, WV
West Virginia University, WV
West Virginia Wesleyan College, WV
Wheaton College, IL
Whitman College, WA
Whittier College, CA
Whitworth University, WA
Wichita State University, KS
William Jewell College, MO
Williams Baptist College, AR
Wingate University, NC
Winona State University, MN
Winthrop University, SC
Wittenberg University, OH
Wright State University, OH
Xavier University, OH
Young Harris College, GA
Youngstown State University, OH

Cinema/Film/Broadcasting

Arizona State University, AZ
Arkansas State University, AR
Arkansas Tech University, AR
Auburn University, AL
Augusta State University, GA
Ball State University, IN
Baylor University, TX
Biola University, CA
Bloomfield College, NJ
Bowling Green State University, OH
Brenau University, GA
Brooks Institute, CA
Butler University, IN
California Institute of the Arts, CA
California Polytechnic State University, San Luis Obispo, CA
California State University, Chico, CA
Cameron University, OK
Central Michigan University, MI
City College of the City University of New York, NY
The College at Brockport, State University of New York, NY
The College of New Rochelle, NY
Colorado State University–Pueblo, CO
DeSales University, PA
Eastern Michigan University, MI
Eastern Washington University, WA
Edinboro University of Pennsylvania, PA
Flagler College, FL
Florida Agricultural and Mechanical University, FL
Florida State University, FL
Georgia Southern University, GA
Grace University, NE
Grand Valley State University, MI
Harding University, AR
Hofstra University, NY
Huntington University, IN
Illinois State University, IL
Ithaca College, NY
James Madison University, VA
Kean University, NJ
Keene State College, NH
Lindenwood University, MO
Long Island University, Brooklyn Campus, NY
Long Island University, C.W. Post Campus, NY
Marywood University, PA
Massachusetts College of Liberal Arts, MA
Minneapolis College of Art and Design, MN
Minnesota State University Moorhead, MN
Mississippi State University, MS
Montana State University, MT
Montclair State University, NJ
Morningside College, IA
North Central College, IL
Northern Arizona University, AZ
Northwestern Oklahoma State University, OK
Northwestern State University of Louisiana, LA
Northwest Missouri State University, MO
Ohio University, OH
Ohio University–Chillicothe, OH
Ohio University–Eastern, OH
Ohio University–Lancaster, OH
Ohio University–Southern Campus, OH
Ohio University–Zanesville, OH
Point Park University, PA
Purchase College, State University of New York, NY
Quincy University, IL
Regent University, VA
Rhode Island College, RI
Rochester Institute of Technology, NY
St. John's University, NY
Saint Joseph's College, IN
San Diego State University, CA
Santa Fe University of Art and Design, NM
Sonoma State University, CA
Southern Illinois University Carbondale, IL
Southwestern College, KS
State University of New York at Binghamton, NY
Stony Brook University, State University of New York, NY
Sul Ross State University, TX
Texas Christian University, TX
Texas Woman's University, TX
Trevecca Nazarene University, TN
Union University, TN
The University of Alabama, AL
University of California, Irvine, CA
University of California, San Diego, CA
University of California, Santa Cruz, CA
University of Central Florida, FL
University of Central Missouri, MO
University of Colorado Boulder, CO
The University of Kansas, KS
University of Kentucky, KY
University of La Verne, CA
University of Maryland, Baltimore County, MD
University of Memphis, TN
University of Miami, FL

University of Michigan, MI
University of Michigan–Dearborn, MI
University of Mississippi, MS
University of Missouri, MO
University of Montevallo, AL
University of Mount Union, OH
University of Nebraska–Lincoln, NE
University of Nevada, Las Vegas, NV
The University of North Carolina at Greensboro, NC
University of North Carolina School of the Arts, NC
The University of North Carolina Wilmington, NC
University of Pittsburgh at Bradford, PA
University of South Florida, FL
The University of Tennessee at Chattanooga, TN
University of Utah, UT
Virginia Polytechnic Institute and State University, VA
Washburn University, KS
Washington State University, WA
Washington University in St. Louis, MO
Western Illinois University, IL
Western Kentucky University, KY
Western Washington University, WA
Westminster College, PA
West Texas A&M University, TX
Wright State University, OH

Creative Writing

Alderson-Broaddus College, WV
Arizona State University, AZ
Arkansas Tech University, AR
Auburn University, AL
Augustana College, IL
Augustana College, SD
Augusta State University, GA
Austin Peay State University, TN
Bowling Green State University, OH
Brenau University, GA
Bucknell University, PA
California Institute of the Arts, CA
California Lutheran University, CA
California Polytechnic State University, San Luis Obispo, CA
California State University, Chico, CA
Cameron University, OK
Campbell University, NC
Case Western Reserve University, OH
Central College, IA
Central Michigan University, MI
City College of the City University of New York, NY
Cleveland State University, OH
Coe College, IA
Coker College, SC
The College at Brockport, State University of New York, NY
The College of New Rochelle, NY
Colorado State University, CO
Columbia College, MO
Creighton University, NE
Davidson College, NC
Delta State University, MS
Dickinson State University, ND
Drury University, MO
Duke University, NC
Eastern Michigan University, MI
Eastern Washington University, WA
Eckerd College, FL
Edgewood College, WI
Emmanuel College, GA
Emporia State University, KS
The Evergreen State College, WA
Florida Agricultural and Mechanical University, FL
Frostburg State University, MD
Furman University, SC
Georgia College & State University, GA
Georgian Court University, NJ
Graceland University, IA
Green Mountain College, VT
Grove City College, PA
Hamline University, MN
Hampshire College, MA
Hardin-Simmons University, TX
Hobart and William Smith Colleges, NY
Hollins University, VA
Hood College, MD
Hope College, MI
Huntington University, IN
Illinois State University, IL
Kentucky Wesleyan College, KY
Kenyon College, OH
Knox College, IL
Lake Forest College, IL
Lewis-Clark State College, ID
Louisiana Tech University, LA
Lycoming College, PA
McNally Smith College of Music, MN
Meredith College, NC
Mesa State College, CO
Michigan State University, MI
Midwestern State University, TX
Minnesota State University Moorhead, MN
Mississippi State University, MS
Morningside College, IA
Murray State University, KY
New England College, NH
Northeastern Illinois University, IL
Northern Arizona University, AZ
Northern Illinois University, IL
Northwestern State University of Louisiana, LA
Notre Dame de Namur University, CA
Ohio Northern University, OH
The Ohio State University, OH
Oklahoma State University, OK
Pace University, NY
Plymouth State University, NH
Purchase College, State University of New York, NY
The Richard Stockton College of New Jersey, NJ
Rockhurst University, MO
Rocky Mountain College, MT
Sacred Heart University, CT
Saint Mary-of-the-Woods College, IN
San Diego State University, CA
Santa Fe University of Art and Design, NM
Siena College, NY
Sonoma State University, CA
Southern Illinois University Carbondale, IL
Southern Oregon University, OR
Southwest Minnesota State University, MN
State University of New York at Binghamton, NY
State University of New York College at Geneseo, NY
Texas Christian University, TX
The University of Akron, OH
The University of Alabama, AL
University of Alaska Fairbanks, AK
University of California, Riverside, CA
University of California, Santa Cruz, CA
University of Central Missouri, MO
University of Colorado Boulder, CO
University of Idaho, ID
The University of Kansas, KS
University of Kentucky, KY
University of Louisville, KY
University of Maryland, Baltimore County, MD
University of Michigan, MI
University of Michigan–Dearborn, MI
University of Mississippi, MS
University of Missouri, MO
University of Missouri–St. Louis, MO
The University of Montana, MT
University of Montevallo, AL
University of Nebraska at Omaha, NE
University of Nevada, Las Vegas, NV
The University of North Carolina Wilmington, NC
University of Oregon, OR
University of Redlands, CA
University of South Carolina Aiken, SC
The University of South Dakota, SD
University of Southern Indiana, IN
University of South Florida, FL
The University of Tampa, FL
The University of Texas at San Antonio, TX
University of Utah, UT
The University of Virginia's College at Wise, VA
University of Wisconsin–Stevens Point, WI
Ursinus College, PA
Virginia Polytechnic Institute and State University, VA
Wabash College, IN
Warren Wilson College, NC
Washington State University, WA
Washington University in St. Louis, MO
Wayne State College, NE
Western Washington University, WA
Wichita State University, KS
Wright State University, OH
Youngstown State University, OH

Dance

Adelphi University, NY
Albion College, MI
Alma College, MI
Angelo State University, TX
Arizona State University, AZ
Ball State University, IN
Birmingham-Southern College, AL
Boise State University, ID
Bowling Green State University, OH
Brenau University, GA
Bucknell University, PA
Butler University, IN
California Institute of the Arts, CA
California Polytechnic State University, San Luis Obispo, CA
California State University, Bakersfield, CA
California State University, Chico, CA
California State University, Fullerton, CA
Case Western Reserve University, OH
Cedar Crest College, PA
Centenary College of Louisiana, LA
Central Michigan University, MI
Cleveland State University, OH
Coker College, SC
The College at Brockport, State University of New York, NY
The College of New Rochelle, NY

Non-Need Scholarships for Undergraduates

Creative Arts/Performance

The College of Wooster, OH
Colorado State University, CO
Columbus State University, GA
Concordia University, Nebraska, NE
Cornish College of the Arts, WA
Creighton University, NE
DeSales University, PA
Duquesne University, PA
East Carolina University, NC
Eastern Michigan University, MI
Emmanuel College, GA
Florida Agricultural and Mechanical University, FL
Florida International University, FL
Florida State University, FL
Fordham University, NY
Goucher College, MD
Graceland University, IA
Grand Valley State University, MI
Gustavus Adolphus College, MN
Hastings College, NE
Hawai'i Pacific University, HI
Hendrix College, AR
Hobart and William Smith Colleges, NY
Hofstra University, NY
Hollins University, VA
Hope College, MI
Howard University, DC
Indiana University of Pennsylvania, PA
Ithaca College, NY
James Madison University, VA
The Juilliard School, NY
Keene State College, NH
Kent State University, OH
Knox College, IL
Kutztown University of Pennsylvania, PA
Lindenwood University, MO
Long Island University, Brooklyn Campus, NY
Long Island University, C.W. Post Campus, NY
Manhattanville College, NY
Mars Hill College, NC
Mercyhurst College, PA
Mesa State College, CO
Middle Tennessee State University, TN
Millikin University, IL
Mississippi State University, MS
Montana State University, MT
Montclair State University, NJ
Morningside College, IA
Murray State University, KY
Nicholls State University, LA
Northeastern Illinois University, IL
Northeastern State University, OK
Northern Illinois University, IL
Northwestern State University of Louisiana, LA
Northwest Missouri State University, MO
Oakland University, MI
Ohio Northern University, OH
The Ohio State University, OH
Ohio University, OH
Ohio University–Chillicothe, OH
Ohio University–Eastern, OH
Ohio University–Lancaster, OH
Ohio University–Southern Campus, OH
Ohio University–Zanesville, OH
Ohio Wesleyan University, OH
Oklahoma City University, OK
Old Dominion University, VA
Pacific Lutheran University, WA
Palm Beach Atlantic University, FL
Plymouth State University, NH
Point Park University, PA
Purchase College, State University of New York, NY
Rhode Island College, RI
The Richard Stockton College of New Jersey, NJ
Rockford College, IL
St. Ambrose University, IA
St. John's University, NY
Saint Joseph's College, IN
Saint Mary-of-the-Woods College, IN
Saint Mary's College of California, CA
San Diego State University, CA
Santa Clara University, CA
Santa Fe University of Art and Design, NM
Shenandoah University, VA
Slippery Rock University of Pennsylvania, PA
Sonoma State University, CA
Southeastern Oklahoma State University, OK
Southern Illinois University Carbondale, IL
Southern Illinois University Edwardsville, IL
Southwestern College, KS
State University of New York at Binghamton, NY
State University of New York at Fredonia, NY
State University of New York College at Geneseo, NY
State University of New York College at Potsdam, NY
Texas A&M International University, TX
Texas Christian University, TX
Texas Tech University, TX
Texas Woman's University, TX
Towson University, MD
The University of Akron, OH
The University of Alabama, AL
The University of Arizona, AZ
University of California, Irvine, CA
University of California, Riverside, CA
University of California, San Diego, CA
University of Colorado Boulder, CO
University of Florida, FL
University of Great Falls, MT
University of Hartford, CT
University of Idaho, ID
University of Illinois at Urbana–Champaign, IL
The University of Kansas, KS
University of Kentucky, KY
University of Louisville, KY
University of Maryland, Baltimore County, MD
University of Maryland, College Park, MD
University of Mary Washington, VA
University of Massachusetts Amherst, MA
University of Memphis, TN
University of Michigan, MI
University of Missouri–St. Louis, MO
The University of Montana, MT
University of Nebraska–Lincoln, NE
University of Nevada, Las Vegas, NV
University of New Hampshire, NH
The University of North Carolina at Greensboro, NC
University of North Carolina School of the Arts, NC
University of Northern Colorado, CO
University of Oklahoma, OK
University of Oregon, OR
University of Richmond, VA
University of South Carolina, SC
University of Southern Mississippi, MS
University of South Florida, FL
The University of Texas of the Permian Basin, TX
The University of Texas–Pan American, TX
University of Utah, UT
University of Wisconsin–Green Bay, WI
University of Wisconsin–Stevens Point, WI
University of Wyoming, WY
Virginia Commonwealth University, VA
Virginia State University, VA
Washington University in St. Louis, MO
Wayne State University, MI
Western Illinois University, IL
Western Kentucky University, KY
Western Oregon University, OR
Western Washington University, WA
West Texas A&M University, TX
Wichita State University, KS
Winthrop University, SC
Wittenberg University, OH
Wright State University, OH

Debating

Abilene Christian University, TX
Alderson-Broaddus College, WV
Arizona State University, AZ
Arkansas State University, AR
Augustana College, IL
Austin Peay State University, TN
Ball State University, IN
Baylor University, TX
Berry College, GA
Bethany Lutheran College, MN
Bethel College, KS
Bethel University, MN
Boise State University, ID
Bowling Green State University, OH
California Polytechnic State University, San Luis Obispo, CA
California State University, Chico, CA
Cameron University, OK
Carroll College, MT
Carson-Newman College, TN
Cedarville University, OH
The College of New Rochelle, NY
Concordia College, MN
Concordia University, CA
Concordia University, Nebraska, NE
Creighton University, NE
Culver-Stockton College, MO
DePaul University, IL
Doane College, NE
Drury University, MO
Eastern Michigan University, MI
Emporia State University, KS
Evangel University, MO
Ferris State University, MI
Florida College, FL
George Fox University, OR
Gonzaga University, WA
Gustavus Adolphus College, MN
Harding University, AR
Hastings College, NE
Hillsdale College, MI
Houston Baptist University, TX
Illinois State University, IL
Lewis & Clark College, OR
Lewis-Clark State College, ID
Liberty University, VA
Linfield College, OR
Louisiana Tech University, LA
Loyola University Chicago, IL
Malone University, OH

Marist College, NY
Mercer University, GA
Methodist University, NC
Michigan State University, MI
Middle Tennessee State University, TN
Mississippi State University, MS
Missouri Southern State University, MO
Morehead State University, KY
Murray State University, KY
Muskingum University, OH
North Central College, IL
Northeastern State University, OK
Northern Arizona University, AZ
Northern Illinois University, IL
Northwestern Oklahoma State University, OK
Northwest Missouri State University, MO
Northwest Nazarene University, ID
Northwest University, WA
Ohio University, OH
Ohio University–Chillicothe, OH
Ohio University–Eastern, OH
Ohio University–Lancaster, OH
Ohio University–Southern Campus, OH
Ohio University–Zanesville, OH
Oklahoma Panhandle State University, OK
Pace University, NY
Pacific Lutheran University, WA
Pacific University, OR
Patrick Henry College, VA
Point Loma Nazarene University, CA
Regis University, CO
Ripon College, WI
Rocky Mountain College, MT
St. John's University, NY
Saint Joseph's University, PA
Samford University, AL
Santa Clara University, CA
South Dakota State University, SD
Southeastern Oklahoma State University, OK
Southern Illinois University Carbondale, IL
Southwest Baptist University, MO
Southwest Minnesota State University, MN
Tennessee Technological University, TN
Towson University, MD
Trinity University, TX
Truman State University, MO
The University of Akron, OH
The University of Alabama, AL
University of Alaska Anchorage, AK
University of Central Missouri, MO
University of Denver, CO
The University of Kansas, KS
University of Kentucky, KY
University of La Verne, CA
University of Louisville, KY
University of Miami, FL
University of Michigan–Dearborn, MI
University of Mississippi, MS
University of Missouri–Kansas City, MO
University of Nebraska at Omaha, NE
University of Nevada, Las Vegas, NV
University of North Dakota, ND
University of Northern Iowa, IA
University of Oregon, OR
University of Puget Sound, WA
University of Redlands, CA
University of South Carolina, SC
The University of South Dakota, SD
University of Southern California, CA
University of South Florida, FL
The University of Texas at San Antonio, TX
University of the Cumberlands, KY
University of the Pacific, CA
University of the Southwest, NM
University of Vermont, VT
University of West Georgia, GA
University of Wisconsin–Eau Claire, WI
University of Wyoming, WY
Vanguard University of Southern California, CA
Washburn University, KS
Wayne State College, NE
Wayne State University, MI
Western Illinois University, IL
Western Kentucky University, KY
West Texas A&M University, TX
West Virginia University, WV
Whitman College, WA
Wichita State University, KS
William Jewell College, MO
Winona State University, MN

Journalism/Publications

Abilene Christian University, TX
Albright College, PA
Alderson-Broaddus College, WV
Angelo State University, TX
Arizona State University, AZ
Arkansas State University, AR
Auburn University, AL
Augusta State University, GA
Austin Peay State University, TN
Averett University, VA
Ball State University, IN
Baylor University, TX
Berry College, GA
Bethany Lutheran College, MN
Bethel College, IN
Biola University, CA
Boise State University, ID
Bowling Green State University, OH
Brenau University, GA
Brevard College, NC
Brooks Institute, CA
Bryan College, TN
California Lutheran University, CA
California Polytechnic State University, San Luis Obispo, CA
California State University, Chico, CA
California State University, Fresno, CA
California State University, Northridge, CA
California State University, San Bernardino, CA
Cameron University, OK
Campbellsville University, KY
Campbell University, NC
Carroll University, WI
Carson-Newman College, TN
Central Michigan University, MI
Chicago State University, IL
The Citadel, The Military College of South Carolina, SC
Cleveland State University, OH
The College at Brockport, State University of New York, NY
The College of New Rochelle, NY
Colorado State University–Pueblo, CO
Concord University, WV
Creighton University, NE
Delta State University, MS
DePauw University, IN
Dickinson State University, ND
Dordt College, IA
Eastern Washington University, WA
East Tennessee State University, TN
Edinboro University of Pennsylvania, PA
Elon University, NC
Emory & Henry College, VA
Faulkner University, AL
Ferris State University, MI
Florida Agricultural and Mechanical University, FL
Florida College, FL
Florida International University, FL
Fort Valley State University, GA
Franklin College, IN
Frostburg State University, MD
Georgia College & State University, GA
Glenville State College, WV
Grace College, IN
Grand Valley State University, MI
Hamline University, MN
Hannibal-LaGrange University, MO
Harding University, AR
Hardin-Simmons University, TX
Hastings College, NE
Hawai'i Pacific University, HI
Hillsdale College, MI
Hofstra University, NY
Huntington University, IN
Indiana University of Pennsylvania, PA
Iowa State University of Science and Technology, IA
Ithaca College, NY
James Madison University, VA
John Brown University, AR
Kent State University, OH
Kentucky State University, KY
LeMoyne-Owen College, TN
Liberty University, VA
Lincoln University, MO
Lipscomb University, TN
Lock Haven University of Pennsylvania, PA
Long Island University, C.W. Post Campus, NY
Louisiana State University and Agricultural and Mechanical College, LA
Louisiana Tech University, LA
Loyola University Chicago, IL
Lubbock Christian University, TX
Malone University, OH
Marywood University, PA
Massachusetts College of Liberal Arts, MA
McPherson College, KS
Mesa State College, CO
Michigan State University, MI
Middle Tennessee State University, TN
Midwestern State University, TX
Mississippi State University, MS
Mississippi University for Women, MS
Missouri Southern State University, MO
Morehead State University, KY
Morningside College, IA
Murray State University, KY
Muskingum University, OH
New Mexico State University, NM
North Central College, IL
Northeastern Illinois University, IL
Northeastern State University, OK
Northern Arizona University, AZ
Northern Illinois University, IL
Northwestern Oklahoma State University, OK
Northwestern State University of Louisiana, LA
Northwest Missouri State University, MO
Northwest Nazarene University, ID
Nyack College, NY
Oglethorpe University, GA
Ohio Northern University, OH

The Ohio State University, OH
Ohio University, OH
Ohio University–Chillicothe, OH
Ohio University–Eastern, OH
Ohio University–Lancaster, OH
Ohio University–Southern Campus, OH
Ohio University–Zanesville, OH
Ohio Valley University, WV
Oklahoma Christian University, OK
Oklahoma State University, OK
Olivet College, MI
Ouachita Baptist University, AR
Pacific University, OR
Patrick Henry College, VA
Regent University, VA
Rhode Island College, RI
The Richard Stockton College of New Jersey, NJ
Rivier College, NH
Robert Morris University Illinois, IL
St. Bonaventure University, NY
St. Edward's University, TX
St. John's University, NY
Saint Mary-of-the-Woods College, IN
Samford University, AL
San Diego State University, CA
Schreiner University, TX
Siena College, NY
Sonoma State University, CA
South Dakota State University, SD
Southeastern University, FL
Southern Adventist University, TN
Southern Illinois University Carbondale, IL
Southern Oregon University, OR
Southwestern College, KS
Southwest Minnesota State University, MN
State University of New York at Binghamton, NY
State University of New York at Plattsburgh, NY
State University of New York College at Geneseo, NY
Stephen F. Austin State University, TX
Stony Brook University, State University of New York, NY
Sul Ross State University, TX
Tabor College, KS
Texas A&M University, TX
Texas A&M University–Commerce, TX
Texas Christian University, TX
Texas Lutheran University, TX
Texas State University–San Marcos, TX
Texas Tech University, TX
Texas Woman's University, TX
Trinity Christian College, IL
Union University, TN
The University of Akron, OH
The University of Alabama, AL
University of California, San Diego, CA
University of Central Missouri, MO
University of Central Oklahoma, OK
University of Colorado Boulder, CO
University of Florida, FL
University of Idaho, ID
University of Illinois at Urbana–Champaign, IL
The University of Kansas, KS
University of Kentucky, KY
University of La Verne, CA
University of Mary Washington, VA
University of Massachusetts Amherst, MA
University of Memphis, TN
University of Miami, FL
University of Michigan, MI
University of Michigan–Dearborn, MI
University of Michigan–Flint, MI
University of Mississippi, MS
University of Missouri, MO
The University of Montana, MT
University of Montevallo, AL
University of Mount Union, OH
University of Nebraska at Omaha, NE
University of Nebraska–Lincoln, NE
University of Nevada, Las Vegas, NV
University of North Alabama, AL
The University of North Carolina at Chapel Hill, NC
University of Oklahoma, OK
University of Oregon, OR
University of Pittsburgh at Johnstown, PA
University of St. Thomas, MN
University of South Alabama, AL
University of South Carolina, SC
University of South Carolina Aiken, SC
University of South Florida, FL
The University of Tampa, FL
The University of Tennessee at Chattanooga, TN
The University of Tennessee at Martin, TN
The University of Texas at Arlington, TX
The University of Texas at El Paso, TX
The University of Texas–Pan American, TX
University of the Cumberlands, KY
University of Utah, UT
The University of Virginia's College at Wise, VA
University of West Georgia, GA
University of Wisconsin–Green Bay, WI
University of Wyoming, WY
Utah State University, UT
Valley City State University, ND
Virginia Polytechnic Institute and State University, VA
Wabash College, IN
Wartburg College, IA
Washburn University, KS
Washington State University, WA
Wayland Baptist University, TX
Wayne State College, NE
Wayne State University, MI
Webber International University, FL
Western Illinois University, IL
Western Kentucky University, KY
Western Washington University, WA
West Texas A&M University, TX
Whitworth University, WA
Wichita State University, KS
William Jewell College, MO
Youngstown State University, OH

Music

Abilene Christian University, TX
Adelphi University, NY
Adrian College, MI
Agnes Scott College, GA
Alabama Agricultural and Mechanical University, AL
Alabama State University, AL
Alaska Pacific University, AK
Albion College, MI
Albright College, PA
Alcorn State University, MS
Alderson-Broaddus College, WV
Alma College, MI
Alverno College, WI
Anderson University, SC
Andrews University, MI
Angelo State University, TX
Anna Maria College, MA
Arizona Christian University, AZ
Arizona State University, AZ
Arkansas State University, AR
Arkansas Tech University, AR
Armstrong Atlantic State University, GA
Asbury University, KY
Ashland University, OH
Auburn University, AL
Augsburg College, MN
Augustana College, IL
Augustana College, SD
Augusta State University, GA
Aurora University, IL
Austin College, TX
Austin Peay State University, TN
Averett University, VA
Baldwin-Wallace College, OH
Ball State University, IN
Baptist Bible College of Pennsylvania, PA
The Baptist College of Florida, FL
Baylor University, TX
Bellarmine University, KY
Belmont University, TN
Beloit College, WI
Benedictine College, KS
Benedictine University, IL
Berklee College of Music, MA
Berry College, GA
Bethany College, WV
Bethany Lutheran College, MN
Bethel College, IN
Bethel College, KS
Bethel University, MN
Bethesda Christian University, CA
Biola University, CA
Birmingham-Southern College, AL
Black Hills State University, SD
Bluefield College, VA
Bluffton University, OH
Boise State University, ID
Boston University, MA
Bowie State University, MD
Bowling Green State University, OH
Bradley University, IL
Brenau University, GA
Brevard College, NC
Bridgewater College, VA
Brigham Young University, UT
Bryan College, TN
Bucknell University, PA
Buena Vista University, IA
Butler University, IN
Caldwell College, NJ
California Institute of the Arts, CA
California Lutheran University, CA
California Polytechnic State University, San Luis Obispo, CA
California State University, Bakersfield, CA
California State University, Chico, CA
California State University, East Bay, CA
California State University, Fresno, CA
California State University, Fullerton, CA
California State University, Northridge, CA
California State University, San Bernardino, CA
California State University, Stanislaus, CA
Calvin College, MI
Cameron University, OK
Campbellsville University, KY
Campbell University, NC

Canisius College, NY
Capital University, OH
Carleton College, MN
Carnegie Mellon University, PA
Carroll University, WI
Carson-Newman College, TN
Case Western Reserve University, OH
Catawba College, NC
The Catholic University of America, DC
Cedarville University, OH
Centenary College of Louisiana, LA
Central College, IA
Central Methodist University, MO
Central Michigan University, MI
Centre College, KY
Chestnut Hill College, PA
Chicago State University, IL
Chowan University, NC
Christopher Newport University, VA
Cincinnati Christian University, OH
The Citadel, The Military College of South Carolina, SC
City College of the City University of New York, NY
Clarke University, IA
Clear Creek Baptist Bible College, KY
Cleveland Institute of Music, OH
Cleveland State University, OH
Coastal Carolina University, SC
Coe College, IA
Coker College, SC
The Colburn School Conservatory of Music, CA
The College at Brockport, State University of New York, NY
College of Charleston, SC
College of Mount St. Joseph, OH
The College of New Jersey, NJ
The College of New Rochelle, NY
College of Saint Benedict, MN
College of St. Joseph, VT
College of Saint Mary, NE
The College of Saint Rose, NY
The College of St. Scholastica, MN
College of Staten Island of the City University of New York, NY
College of the Holy Cross, MA
The College of William and Mary, VA
The College of Wooster, OH
Colorado State University, CO
Colorado State University–Pueblo, CO
Columbia College, MO
Columbia International University, SC
Columbus State University, GA
Concordia College, MN
Concordia University, CA
Concordia University, MI
Concordia University Chicago, IL
Concordia University, Nebraska, NE
Concordia University, St. Paul, MN
Concordia University Wisconsin, WI
Concord University, WV
Converse College, SC
Corban University, OR
Cornell College, IA
Cornerstone University, MI
Cornish College of the Arts, WA
Covenant College, GA
Creighton University, NE
Crown College, MN
Culver-Stockton College, MO
Dakota State University, SD
Dallas Baptist University, TX
Davidson College, NC
Defiance College, OH
Delaware State University, DE
Delta State University, MS
DePaul University, IL
DePauw University, IN
Dickinson State University, ND
Dillard University, LA
Doane College, NE
Dominican University of California, CA
Dordt College, IA
Drake University, IA
Drury University, MO
Duquesne University, PA
East Carolina University, NC
Eastern Kentucky University, KY
Eastern Michigan University, MI
Eastern Washington University, WA
East Tennessee State University, TN
East Texas Baptist University, TX
Eckerd College, FL
Edgewood College, WI
Edinboro University of Pennsylvania, PA
Elizabeth City State University, NC
Elizabethtown College, PA
Elmhurst College, IL
Elon University, NC
Emmanuel College, GA
Emory & Henry College, VA
Emory University, GA
Emporia State University, KS
Endicott College, MA
Erskine College, SC
Eureka College, IL
Evangel University, MO
Faulkner University, AL
Fayetteville State University, NC
Ferris State University, MI
Florida Agricultural and Mechanical University, FL
Florida Atlantic University, FL
Florida College, FL
Florida Gulf Coast University, FL
Florida Institute of Technology, FL
Florida International University, FL
Florida Southern College, FL
Florida State University, FL
Fordham University, NY
Fort Lewis College, CO
Fort Valley State University, GA
Francis Marion University, SC
Franklin & Marshall College, PA
Franklin College, IN
Fresno Pacific University, CA
Frostburg State University, MD
Furman University, SC
Gannon University, PA
Gardner-Webb University, NC
Geneva College, PA
George Fox University, OR
Georgetown College, KY
Georgia College & State University, GA
Georgian Court University, NJ
Georgia Southern University, GA
Gettysburg College, PA
Glenville State College, WV
Gonzaga University, WA
Gordon College, MA
Goshen College, IN
Goucher College, MD
Grace Bible College, MI
Graceland University, IA
Grace University, NE
Grand Valley State University, MI
Grand View University, IA
Green Mountain College, VT
Greenville College, IL
Grove City College, PA
Gustavus Adolphus College, MN
Hamline University, MN
Hampden-Sydney College, VA
Hampton University, VA
Hannibal-LaGrange University, MO
Hanover College, IN
Harding University, AR
Hardin-Simmons University, TX
Hastings College, NE
Hawai'i Pacific University, HI
Heidelberg University, OH
Hendrix College, AR
High Point University, NC
Hillsdale College, MI
Hillsdale Free Will Baptist College, OK
Hobart and William Smith Colleges, NY
Hofstra University, NY
Hollins University, VA
Hope College, MI
Houghton College, NY
Houston Baptist University, TX
Howard Payne University, TX
Howard University, DC
Huntingdon College, AL
Huntington University, IN
Huston-Tillotson University, TX
Illinois College, IL
Illinois State University, IL
Illinois Wesleyan University, IL
Indiana University of Pennsylvania, PA
Indiana University–Purdue University Fort Wayne, IN
Indiana Wesleyan University, IN
Iona College, NY
Iowa State University of Science and Technology, IA
Iowa Wesleyan College, IA
Ithaca College, NY
Jackson State University, MS
James Madison University, VA
Jamestown College, ND
John Brown University, AR
Johnson Bible College, TN
Johnson C. Smith University, NC
Judson University, IL
The Juilliard School, NY
Juniata College, PA
Kean University, NJ
Keene State College, NH
Kennesaw State University, GA
Kent State University, OH
Kent State University at Stark, OH
Kentucky State University, KY
Kentucky Wesleyan College, KY
Kenyon College, OH
King College, TN
Knox College, IL
Kutztown University of Pennsylvania, PA
Kuyper College, MI
Lake Forest College, IL
Lancaster Bible College & Graduate School, PA
Lawrence University, WI
Lebanon Valley College, PA
Lee University, TN
Lehigh University, PA
Le Moyne College, NY
LeMoyne-Owen College, TN

Non-Need Scholarships for Undergraduates
Creative Arts/Performance

Lenoir-Rhyne University, NC
Lewis & Clark College, OR
Lewis-Clark State College, ID
Liberty University, VA
Limestone College, SC
Lincoln Memorial University, TN
Lincoln University, MO
Lindenwood University, MO
Lindsey Wilson College, KY
Linfield College, OR
Lipscomb University, TN
Lock Haven University of Pennsylvania, PA
Long Island University, Brooklyn Campus, NY
Long Island University, C.W. Post Campus, NY
Longwood University, VA
Loras College, IA
Louisiana College, LA
Louisiana State University and Agricultural and Mechanical College, LA
Louisiana Tech University, LA
Loyola University Chicago, IL
Lubbock Christian University, TX
Luther College, IA
Lycoming College, PA
Lynchburg College, VA
Lynn University, FL
Lyon College, AR
Malone University, OH
Manchester College, IN
Manhattan Christian College, KS
Manhattan College, NY
Manhattan School of Music, NY
Mannes College The New School for Music, NY
Maranatha Baptist Bible College, WI
Marian University, WI
Marietta College, OH
Marist College, NY
Mars Hill College, NC
Martin Luther College, MN
Maryville College, TN
Marywood University, PA
Massachusetts College of Liberal Arts, MA
The Master's College and Seminary, CA
Mayville State University, ND
McKendree University, IL
McMurry University, TX
McNally Smith College of Music, MN
McPherson College, KS
Mercer University, GA
Mercyhurst College, PA
Meredith College, NC
Mesa State College, CO
Messiah College, PA
Methodist University, NC
Metropolitan State College of Denver, CO
Miami University, OH
Michigan State University, MI
Middle Tennessee State University, TN
Midwestern State University, TX
Millersville University of Pennsylvania, PA
Milligan College, TN
Millikin University, IL
Millsaps College, MS
Mills College, CA
Minnesota State University Moorhead, MN
Minot State University, ND
Mississippi State University, MS
Mississippi University for Women, MS
Missouri Baptist University, MO
Missouri Southern State University, MO
Missouri University of Science and Technology, MO
Molloy College, NY
Monmouth College, IL
Montana State University, MT
Montana State University Billings, MT
Montclair State University, NJ
Montreat College, NC
Moravian College, PA
Morehead State University, KY
Morehouse College, GA
Morningside College, IA
Mount Aloysius College, PA
Mount Marty College, SD
Mount Mary College, WI
Mount Mercy University, IA
Mount St. Mary's College, CA
Mount Vernon Nazarene University, OH
Murray State University, KY
Muskingum University, OH
Nazareth College of Rochester, NY
Nebraska Wesleyan University, NE
New England Conservatory of Music, MA
New Hope Christian College, OR
New Mexico State University, NM
The New School for Jazz and Contemporary Music, NY
Nicholls State University, LA
Norfolk State University, VA
North Carolina Central University, NC
North Carolina State University, NC
North Central College, IL
Northeastern Illinois University, IL
Northeastern State University, OK
Northern Arizona University, AZ
Northern Illinois University, IL
Northern Kentucky University, KY
Northern Michigan University, MI
Northern State University, SD
North Georgia College & State University, GA
Northland College, WI
Northwest Christian University, OR
Northwestern College, MN
Northwestern Oklahoma State University, OK
Northwestern State University of Louisiana, LA
Northwest Missouri State University, MO
Northwest Nazarene University, ID
Northwest University, WA
Notre Dame de Namur University, CA
Nyack College, NY
Oakland University, MI
Oberlin College, OH
Occidental College, CA
Oglethorpe University, GA
Ohio Northern University, OH
The Ohio State University, OH
Ohio University, OH
Ohio University–Chillicothe, OH
Ohio University–Eastern, OH
Ohio University–Lancaster, OH
Ohio University–Southern Campus, OH
Ohio University–Zanesville, OH
Ohio Valley University, WV
Ohio Wesleyan University, OH
Oklahoma Baptist University, OK
Oklahoma Christian University, OK
Oklahoma City University, OK
Oklahoma Panhandle State University, OK
Oklahoma State University, OK
Oklahoma Wesleyan University, OK
Old Dominion University, VA
Olivet College, MI
Olivet Nazarene University, IL
Ouachita Baptist University, AR
Pacific Lutheran University, WA
Pacific Union College, CA
Pacific University, OR
Palm Beach Atlantic University, FL
Patrick Henry College, VA
Peabody Conservatory of The Johns Hopkins University, MD
Philadelphia Biblical University, PA
Piedmont College, GA
Plymouth State University, NH
Point Loma Nazarene University, CA
Portland State University, OR
Prairie View A&M University, TX
Presbyterian College, SC
Purchase College, State University of New York, NY
Purdue University, IN
Queens College of the City University of New York, NY
Quincy University, IL
Regis University, CO
Reinhardt University, GA
Rhode Island College, RI
Rhodes College, TN
Rice University, TX
The Richard Stockton College of New Jersey, NJ
Ripon College, WI
Roberts Wesleyan College, NY
Rockford College, IL
Rockhurst University, MO
Rocky Mountain College, MT
Rogers State University, OK
Rollins College, FL
Rowan University, NJ
Sacred Heart University, CT
Saginaw Valley State University, MI
St. Ambrose University, IA
Saint Augustine's College, NC
St. Bonaventure University, NY
St. Catherine University, MN
Saint Francis University, PA
Saint John's University, MN
St. John's University, NY
Saint Joseph's College, IN
Saint Joseph's University, PA
Saint Louis University, MO
Saint Martin's University, WA
Saint Mary-of-the-Woods College, IN
Saint Mary's College of California, CA
Saint Mary's University of Minnesota, MN
St. Norbert College, WI
St. Olaf College, MN
Saint Xavier University, IL
Salem College, NC
Samford University, AL
San Diego Christian College, CA
San Diego State University, CA
Santa Clara University, CA
Santa Fe University of Art and Design, NM
Savannah State University, GA
Schreiner University, TX
Seattle University, WA
Seton Hill University, PA
Shasta Bible College, CA
Shenandoah University, VA
Shepherd University, WV
Shippensburg University of Pennsylvania, PA
Shorter University, GA
Siena College, NY
Sierra Nevada College, NV

Silver Lake College, WI
Simpson College, IA
Simpson University, CA
Skidmore College, NY
Slippery Rock University of Pennsylvania, PA
Sonoma State University, CA
South Dakota State University, SD
Southeastern Louisiana University, LA
Southeastern Oklahoma State University, OK
Southeastern University, FL
Southeast Missouri State University, MO
Southern Adventist University, TN
Southern Illinois University Edwardsville, IL
Southern Oregon University, OR
Southern Utah University, UT
Southwest Baptist University, MO
Southwestern College, KS
Southwestern Oklahoma State University, OK
Southwestern University, TX
Southwest Minnesota State University, MN
Spring Arbor University, MI
State University of New York at Binghamton, NY
State University of New York at Fredonia, NY
State University of New York at New Paltz, NY
State University of New York at Plattsburgh, NY
State University of New York College at Cortland, NY
State University of New York College at Geneseo, NY
State University of New York College at Oneonta, NY
State University of New York College at Potsdam, NY
Stephen F. Austin State University, TX
Stetson University, FL
Stony Brook University, State University of New York, NY
Sul Ross State University, TX
Sweet Briar College, VA
Syracuse University, NY
Tabor College, KS
Taylor University, IN
Temple University, PA
Tennessee Technological University, TN
Tennessee Wesleyan College, TN
Texas A&M International University, TX
Texas A&M University–Commerce, TX
Texas Christian University, TX
Texas Lutheran University, TX
Texas State University–San Marcos, TX
Texas Tech University, TX
Texas Woman's University, TX
Thiel College, PA
Thomas University, GA
Tiffin University, OH
Towson University, MD
Transylvania University, KY
Trevecca Nazarene University, TN
Trinity Christian College, IL
Trinity University, TX
Troy University, AL
Truman State University, MO
Tulane University, LA
Tuskegee University, AL
Union College, KY
Union College, NE
Union University, TN
The University of Akron, OH
The University of Alabama, AL
The University of Alabama at Birmingham, AL
The University of Alabama in Huntsville, AL
University of Alaska Fairbanks, AK
The University of Arizona, AZ
University of Arkansas, AR
University of Arkansas at Little Rock, AR
University of Bridgeport, CT
University of California, Irvine, CA
University of California, Riverside, CA
University of California, Santa Cruz, CA
University of Central Florida, FL
University of Central Missouri, MO
University of Central Oklahoma, OK
University of Charleston, WV
University of Cincinnati, OH
University of Colorado Boulder, CO
University of Connecticut, CT
University of Dallas, TX
University of Dayton, OH
University of Delaware, DE
University of Denver, CO
University of Evansville, IN
The University of Findlay, OH
University of Florida, FL
University of Georgia, GA
University of Hartford, CT
University of Hawaii at Hilo, HI
University of Hawaii at Manoa, HI
University of Idaho, ID
University of Illinois at Chicago, IL
University of Illinois at Springfield, IL
University of Illinois at Urbana–Champaign, IL
University of Indianapolis, IN
The University of Iowa, IA
The University of Kansas, KS
University of Kentucky, KY
University of La Verne, CA
University of Louisville, KY
University of Mary, ND
University of Mary Hardin-Baylor, TX
University of Maryland, Baltimore County, MD
University of Maryland, College Park, MD
University of Mary Washington, VA
University of Massachusetts Amherst, MA
University of Massachusetts Lowell, MA
University of Memphis, TN
University of Miami, FL
University of Michigan, MI
University of Michigan–Flint, MI
University of Minnesota, Morris, MN
University of Mississippi, MS
University of Missouri, MO
University of Missouri–Kansas City, MO
University of Missouri–St. Louis, MO
University of Mobile, AL
The University of Montana, MT
University of Montevallo, AL
University of Mount Union, OH
University of Nebraska at Omaha, NE
University of Nebraska–Lincoln, NE
University of Nevada, Las Vegas, NV
University of Nevada, Reno, NV
University of New Hampshire, NH
University of New Orleans, LA
University of North Alabama, AL
The University of North Carolina at Asheville, NC
The University of North Carolina at Chapel Hill, NC
The University of North Carolina at Charlotte, NC
The University of North Carolina at Greensboro, NC
University of North Carolina School of the Arts, NC
The University of North Carolina Wilmington, NC
University of North Dakota, ND
University of Northern Colorado, CO
University of Northern Iowa, IA
University of North Florida, FL
University of Oklahoma, OK
University of Oregon, OR
University of Portland, OR
University of Puerto Rico at Bayamón, PR
University of Puget Sound, WA
University of Redlands, CA
University of Rhode Island, RI
University of Richmond, VA
University of Rio Grande, OH
University of Rochester, NY
University of St. Francis, IL
University of St. Thomas, MN
University of St. Thomas, TX
University of San Diego, CA
University of Science and Arts of Oklahoma, OK
University of South Alabama, AL
University of South Carolina, SC
University of South Carolina Aiken, SC
The University of South Dakota, SD
University of Southern California, CA
University of Southern Maine, ME
University of Southern Mississippi, MS
University of South Florida, FL
The University of Tampa, FL
The University of Tennessee at Chattanooga, TN
The University of Tennessee at Martin, TN
The University of Texas at Arlington, TX
The University of Texas at Brownsville, TX
The University of Texas at El Paso, TX
The University of Texas at San Antonio, TX
The University of Texas at Tyler, TX
The University of Texas of the Permian Basin, TX
The University of Texas–Pan American, TX
University of the Cumberlands, KY
University of the District of Columbia, DC
University of the Incarnate Word, TX
University of the Ozarks, AR
University of the Pacific, CA
University of the Southwest, NM
The University of Toledo, OH
University of Tulsa, OK
University of Utah, UT
University of Vermont, VT
University of Virginia, VA
The University of Virginia's College at Wise, VA
University of West Florida, FL
University of West Georgia, GA
University of Wisconsin–Eau Claire, WI
University of Wisconsin–Green Bay, WI
University of Wisconsin–La Crosse, WI
University of Wisconsin–Parkside, WI
University of Wisconsin–River Falls, WI
University of Wisconsin–Stevens Point, WI
University of Wisconsin–Stout, WI
University of Wyoming, WY
Utah State University, UT
Valdosta State University, GA

Valley City State University, ND
Valley Forge Christian College, PA
Valparaiso University, IN
Vanguard University of Southern California, CA
Virginia Commonwealth University, VA
Virginia Military Institute, VA
Virginia Polytechnic Institute and State University, VA
Virginia State University, VA
Virginia Wesleyan College, VA
Wabash College, IN
Wagner College, NY
Waldorf College, IA
Walla Walla University, WA
Walsh University, OH
Warner Pacific College, OR
Wartburg College, IA
Washburn University, KS
Washington Adventist University, MD
Washington State University, WA
Washington University in St. Louis, MO
Wayland Baptist University, TX
Waynesburg University, PA
Wayne State College, NE
Wayne State University, MI
Wesleyan College, GA
West Chester University of Pennsylvania, PA
Western Carolina University, NC
Western Illinois University, IL
Western Kentucky University, KY
Western New England University, MA
Western Oregon University, OR
Western State College of Colorado, CO
Western Washington University, WA
West Liberty University, WV
Westminster College, MO
Westminster College, PA
Westmont College, CA
West Texas A&M University, TX
West Virginia State University, WV
West Virginia University, WV
West Virginia Wesleyan College, WV
Wheaton College, IL
Wheeling Jesuit University, WV
Whitman College, WA
Whittier College, CA
Whitworth University, WA
Wichita State University, KS
Widener University, PA
William Jessup University, CA
William Jewell College, MO
Williams Baptist College, AR
Wilson College, PA
Wingate University, NC
Winona State University, MN
Winthrop University, SC
Wittenberg University, OH
Wofford College, SC
Wright State University, OH
Xavier University, OH
York College, NE
York College of Pennsylvania, PA
Young Harris College, GA
Youngstown State University, OH

Performing Arts

Adelphi University, NY
Albion College, MI
Alderson-Broaddus College, WV
Alfred University, NY
Alma College, MI
Anderson University, SC
Angelo State University, TX
Arizona State University, AZ
Arkansas State University, AR
Auburn University, AL
Augsburg College, MN
Augustana College, SD
Augusta State University, GA
Austin Peay State University, TN
Ball State University, IN
Birmingham-Southern College, AL
Bloomfield College, NJ
Bluefield College, VA
Boise State University, ID
Bowling Green State University, OH
Brenau University, GA
Bryan College, TN
Bucknell University, PA
California Institute of the Arts, CA
California Lutheran University, CA
California Polytechnic State University, San Luis Obispo, CA
California State University, Chico, CA
California State University, Fullerton, CA
Calvin College, MI
Cameron University, OK
Capital University, OH
Carroll University, WI
Case Western Reserve University, OH
Cedar Crest College, PA
Centenary College of Louisiana, LA
Central Michigan University, MI
City College of the City University of New York, NY
Clemson University, SC
Cleveland State University, OH
Coe College, IA
The College at Brockport, State University of New York, NY
College of Charleston, SC
The College of New Rochelle, NY
Columbia International University, SC
Columbus State University, GA
Concordia University, MI
Corban University, OR
Cornell College, IA
Creighton University, NE
Davidson College, NC
Delta State University, MS
DePaul University, IL
DePauw University, IN
DeSales University, PA
Doane College, NE
East Carolina University, NC
Eastern Michigan University, MI
Edgewood College, WI
Elizabeth City State University, NC
Elizabethtown College, PA
Elon University, NC
Emerson College, MA
Emmanuel College, GA
Endicott College, MA
Eureka College, IL
Flagler College, FL
Florida Agricultural and Mechanical University, FL
Florida Atlantic University, FL
Florida International University, FL
Fort Lewis College, CO
Franklin College, IN
Fresno Pacific University, CA
Frostburg State University, MD
Gannon University, PA
Georgetown College, KY
Georgia College & State University, GA
Goucher College, MD
Green Mountain College, VT
Greenville College, IL
Hamline University, MN
Hannibal-LaGrange University, MO
Hardin-Simmons University, TX
Hastings College, NE
Heidelberg University, OH
Hillsdale Free Will Baptist College, OK
Hobart and William Smith Colleges, NY
Huntingdon College, AL
Illinois State University, IL
Indiana State University, IN
Indiana University of Pennsylvania, PA
Ithaca College, NY
The Juilliard School, NY
Juniata College, PA
Kean University, NJ
Kennesaw State University, GA
Kent State University, OH
Kentucky Wesleyan College, KY
King College, TN
Lehigh University, PA
Liberty University, VA
Limestone College, SC
Lincoln University, MO
Lindenwood University, MO
Louisiana College, LA
Louisiana State University and Agricultural and Mechanical College, LA
Louisiana Tech University, LA
Lubbock Christian University, TX
Manhattanville College, NY
Mannes College The New School for Music, NY
Marietta College, OH
Marywood University, PA
Massachusetts College of Liberal Arts, MA
Mesa State College, CO
Metropolitan State College of Denver, CO
Michigan State University, MI
Minot State University, ND
Mississippi State University, MS
Mississippi University for Women, MS
Molloy College, NY
Montclair State University, NJ
Mount Aloysius College, PA
New Mexico State University, NM
Norfolk State University, VA
Northeastern Illinois University, IL
Northeastern State University, OK
Northern Arizona University, AZ
Northern Illinois University, IL
Northwestern State University of Louisiana, LA
Northwest Nazarene University, ID
Northwest University, WA
Notre Dame de Namur University, CA
Nyack College, NY
Oakland University, MI
Oglethorpe University, GA
Ohio Northern University, OH
The Ohio State University, OH
Ohio University, OH
Ohio University–Chillicothe, OH
Ohio University–Eastern, OH
Ohio University–Lancaster, OH
Ohio University–Southern Campus, OH
Ohio University–Zanesville, OH
Ohio Valley University, WV
Ohio Wesleyan University, OH
Oklahoma Baptist University, OK

Oklahoma City University, OK
Oklahoma Panhandle State University, OK
Old Dominion University, VA
Olivet Nazarene University, IL
Ouachita Baptist University, AR
Pace University, NY
Point Park University, PA
Pontifical Catholic University of Puerto Rico, PR
Prairie View A&M University, TX
Purchase College, State University of New York, NY
The Richard Stockton College of New Jersey, NJ
Rockford College, IL
Rockhurst University, MO
Sacred Heart University, CT
St. Andrews Presbyterian College, NC
Saint Augustine's College, NC
St. Bonaventure University, NY
Saint Louis University, MO
Saint Mary-of-the-Woods College, IN
Saint Mary's College of California, CA
Samford University, AL
San Diego Christian College, CA
San Diego State University, CA
Santa Fe University of Art and Design, NM
Seattle Pacific University, WA
Seton Hill University, PA
Shawnee State University, OH
Shenandoah University, VA
Shepherd University, WV
Siena College, NY
Slippery Rock University of Pennsylvania, PA
Sonoma State University, CA
South Dakota State University, SD
Southeastern Oklahoma State University, OK
Southeast Missouri State University, MO
Southern Illinois University Carbondale, IL
Southwestern College, KS
Southwest Minnesota State University, MN
State University of New York at Binghamton, NY
State University of New York at Fredonia, NY
State University of New York at New Paltz, NY
State University of New York College at Geneseo, NY
State University of New York College at Potsdam, NY
Tabor College, KS
Temple University, PA
Texas A&M International University, TX
Texas A&M University, TX
Texas Christian University, TX
Texas Tech University, TX
Tiffin University, OH
The University of Akron, OH
The University of Alabama at Birmingham, AL
The University of Arizona, AZ
University of California, Irvine, CA
University of California, San Diego, CA
University of Central Missouri, MO
University of Colorado Boulder, CO
University of Florida, FL
University of Hartford, CT
University of Hawaii at Hilo, HI
University of Idaho, ID
University of Illinois at Chicago, IL
University of Illinois at Urbana–Champaign, IL
The University of Kansas, KS
University of Kentucky, KY
University of Maine at Fort Kent, ME
University of Maryland, Baltimore County, MD
University of Maryland, College Park, MD
University of Miami, FL
University of Michigan, MI
University of Michigan–Flint, MI
University of Mississippi, MS
University of Missouri–Kansas City, MO
University of Mobile, AL
The University of Montana, MT
University of Nebraska at Omaha, NE
University of Nebraska–Lincoln, NE
University of Nevada, Las Vegas, NV
The University of North Carolina at Charlotte, NC
The University of North Carolina at Greensboro, NC
University of North Carolina School of the Arts, NC
University of Northern Colorado, CO
University of Oklahoma, OK
University of Oregon, OR
University of Portland, OR
University of Richmond, VA
University of Rochester, NY
University of St. Thomas, TX
University of South Florida, FL
The University of Tampa, FL
The University of Tennessee at Chattanooga, TN
The University of Texas at Brownsville, TX
The University of Texas at El Paso, TX
The University of Toledo, OH
University of Tulsa, OK
University of Utah, UT
The University of Virginia's College at Wise, VA
University of West Georgia, GA
University of Wisconsin–Stevens Point, WI
Utah State University, UT
Valparaiso University, IN
Virginia Commonwealth University, VA
Virginia Polytechnic Institute and State University, VA
Virginia State University, VA
Washburn University, KS
Washington State University, WA
Washington University in St. Louis, MO
Wayne State College, NE
Western Illinois University, IL
Western New Mexico University, NM
Western Oregon University, OR
Western Washington University, WA
West Virginia Wesleyan College, WV
Wichita State University, KS
Wilkes University, PA
Winthrop University, SC
Wright State University, OH
Xavier University, OH
Young Harris College, GA
Youngstown State University, OH

Theater/Drama

Abilene Christian University, TX
Adelphi University, NY
Adrian College, MI
Alabama State University, AL
Alaska Pacific University, AK
Albion College, MI
Albright College, PA
Alderson-Broaddus College, WV
Alma College, MI
Anderson University, SC
Angelo State University, TX
Arcadia University, PA
Arizona State University, AZ
Arkansas State University, AR
Ashland University, OH
Auburn University, AL
Augsburg College, MN
Augustana College, IL
Augustana College, SD
Augusta State University, GA
Aurora University, IL
Austin College, TX
Austin Peay State University, TN
Averett University, VA
Ball State University, IN
Baylor University, TX
Belmont Abbey College, NC
Benedictine College, KS
Berry College, GA
Bethany Lutheran College, MN
Bethel College, IN
Bethel College, KS
Bethel University, MN
Biola University, CA
Birmingham-Southern College, AL
Black Hills State University, SD
Bloomfield College, NJ
Bluefield College, VA
Boise State University, ID
Boston University, MA
Bowling Green State University, OH
Bradley University, IL
Brenau University, GA
Brevard College, NC
Brigham Young University, UT
Bryan College, TN
Bucknell University, PA
Buena Vista University, IA
Butler University, IN
California Institute of the Arts, CA
California Lutheran University, CA
California Polytechnic State University, San Luis Obispo, CA
California State University, Bakersfield, CA
California State University, Chico, CA
California State University, Fresno, CA
California State University, Fullerton, CA
California State University, San Bernardino, CA
Calumet College of Saint Joseph, IN
Calvin College, MI
Cameron University, OK
Campbellsville University, KY
Campbell University, NC
Carroll College, MT
Carroll University, WI
Case Western Reserve University, OH
Catawba College, NC
The Catholic University of America, DC
Cedar Crest College, PA
Centenary College of Louisiana, LA
Central College, IA
Central Methodist University, MO
Central Michigan University, MI
Centre College, KY
Christopher Newport University, VA
Cincinnati Christian University, OH
Clarke University, IA
Clemson University, SC
Cleveland State University, OH
Coastal Carolina University, SC

Coe College, IA
Coker College, SC
The College at Brockport, State University of New York, NY
College of Charleston, SC
The College of New Rochelle, NY
College of Saint Benedict, MN
College of Staten Island of the City University of New York, NY
The College of William and Mary, VA
The College of Wooster, OH
Colorado State University, CO
Columbus State University, GA
Concordia College, MN
Concordia University, CA
Concordia University, MI
Concordia University, Nebraska, NE
Concordia University, St. Paul, MN
Concord University, WV
Converse College, SC
Cornell College, IA
Cornish College of the Arts, WA
Creighton University, NE
Culver-Stockton College, MO
Davidson College, NC
DePaul University, IL
DeSales University, PA
Dickinson State University, ND
Dillard University, LA
Doane College, NE
Dordt College, IA
Drake University, IA
Drury University, MO
Eastern Michigan University, MI
Eastern Washington University, WA
East Tennessee State University, TN
East Texas Baptist University, TX
Eckerd College, FL
Edgewood College, WI
Elizabethtown College, PA
Elmhurst College, IL
Elon University, NC
Emmanuel College, GA
Emory & Henry College, VA
Emory University, GA
Emporia State University, KS
Erskine College, SC
Eureka College, IL
Evangel University, MO
Faulkner University, AL
Ferris State University, MI
Flagler College, FL
Florida Agricultural and Mechanical University, FL
Florida College, FL
Florida International University, FL
Florida Southern College, FL
Florida State University, FL
Fort Lewis College, CO
Francis Marion University, SC
Franklin College, IN
Fresno Pacific University, CA
Frostburg State University, MD
Furman University, SC
Gannon University, PA
Gardner-Webb University, NC
George Fox University, OR
Georgetown College, KY
Georgia College & State University, GA
Georgia Southern University, GA
Gordon College, MA
Goshen College, IN
Goucher College, MD
Grace College, IN
Graceland University, IA
Grand Valley State University, MI
Grand View University, IA
Green Mountain College, VT
Gustavus Adolphus College, MN
Hamline University, MN
Hannibal-LaGrange University, MO
Hanover College, IN
Hardin-Simmons University, TX
Hastings College, NE
Hendrix College, AR
Hillsdale College, MI
Hillsdale Free Will Baptist College, OK
Hofstra University, NY
Hope College, MI
Howard Payne University, TX
Huntington University, IN
Illinois College, IL
Illinois State University, IL
Illinois Wesleyan University, IL
Indiana University of Pennsylvania, PA
Indiana University–Purdue University Fort Wayne, IN
Indiana Wesleyan University, IN
Iowa State University of Science and Technology, IA
Ithaca College, NY
James Madison University, VA
Jamestown College, ND
John Brown University, AR
The Juilliard School, NY
Kean University, NJ
Keene State College, NH
Kennesaw State University, GA
Kent State University, OH
Kent State University at Stark, OH
King College, TN
Knox College, IL
Lake Forest College, IL
Lee University, TN
Lehigh University, PA
Lewis-Clark State College, ID
Limestone College, SC
Lincoln University, MO
Lindenwood University, MO
Linfield College, OR
Lipscomb University, TN
Long Island University, Brooklyn Campus, NY
Long Island University, C.W. Post Campus, NY
Longwood University, VA
Louisiana College, LA
Louisiana State University and Agricultural and Mechanical College, LA
Louisiana Tech University, LA
Loyola University Chicago, IL
Lubbock Christian University, TX
Lycoming College, PA
Lynchburg College, VA
Lyon College, AR
Malone University, OH
Manchester College, IN
Marietta College, OH
Marquette University, WI
Mars Hill College, NC
Maryville College, TN
Marywood University, PA
Massachusetts College of Liberal Arts, MA
Mayville State University, ND
McMurry University, TX
McPherson College, KS
Mercer University, GA
Mesa State College, CO
Messiah College, PA
Methodist University, NC
Metropolitan State College of Denver, CO
Miami University, OH
Michigan State University, MI
Middle Tennessee State University, TN
Midwestern State University, TX
Milligan College, TN
Millikin University, IL
Millsaps College, MS
Minnesota State University Moorhead, MN
Minot State University, ND
Mississippi State University, MS
Mississippi University for Women, MS
Missouri Baptist University, MO
Missouri Southern State University, MO
Missouri University of Science and Technology, MO
Molloy College, NY
Monmouth College, IL
Montana State University, MT
Montana State University Billings, MT
Montclair State University, NJ
Morehead State University, KY
Morningside College, IA
Mount Marty College, SD
Mount Mercy University, IA
Murray State University, KY
Muskingum University, OH
Nazareth College of Rochester, NY
Nebraska Wesleyan University, NE
New England College, NH
New England Conservatory of Music, MA
New Jersey Institute of Technology, NJ
New Mexico State University, NM
Niagara University, NY
North Carolina Central University, NC
North Central College, IL
Northeastern Illinois University, IL
Northeastern State University, OK
Northern Arizona University, AZ
Northern Illinois University, IL
Northern Kentucky University, KY
Northern Michigan University, MI
Northern State University, SD
Northwestern College, MN
Northwestern Oklahoma State University, OK
Northwestern State University of Louisiana, LA
Northwest Missouri State University, MO
Northwest Nazarene University, ID
Northwest University, WA
Notre Dame de Namur University, CA
Nyack College, NY
Oglethorpe University, GA
Ohio Northern University, OH
The Ohio State University, OH
Ohio University, OH
Ohio University–Chillicothe, OH
Ohio University–Eastern, OH
Ohio University–Lancaster, OH
Ohio University–Southern Campus, OH
Ohio University–Zanesville, OH
Ohio Valley University, WV
Ohio Wesleyan University, OH
Oklahoma Baptist University, OK
Oklahoma Christian University, OK
Oklahoma City University, OK
Oklahoma Panhandle State University, OK
Oklahoma State University, OK
Old Dominion University, VA

Olivet Nazarene University, IL
Ouachita Baptist University, AR
Pace University, NY
Pacific Lutheran University, WA
Pacific Union College, CA
Pacific University, OR
Palm Beach Atlantic University, FL
Piedmont College, GA
Plymouth State University, NH
Point Loma Nazarene University, CA
Point Park University, PA
Pontifical Catholic University of Puerto Rico, PR
Portland State University, OR
Providence College, RI
Purchase College, State University of New York, NY
Rhode Island College, RI
Rhodes College, TN
The Richard Stockton College of New Jersey, NJ
Rider University, NJ
Ripon College, WI
Rockford College, IL
Rockhurst University, MO
Rocky Mountain College, MT
Rollins College, FL
Russell Sage College, NY
Sacred Heart University, CT
Saginaw Valley State University, MI
St. Ambrose University, IA
St. Andrews Presbyterian College, NC
St. Edward's University, TX
Saint John's University, MN
Saint Joseph's College, IN
Saint Joseph's University, PA
Saint Louis University, MO
Saint Martin's University, WA
Saint Mary-of-the-Woods College, IN
Saint Mary's College of California, CA
Saint Mary's University of Minnesota, MN
St. Norbert College, WI
Samford University, AL
San Diego Christian College, CA
San Diego State University, CA
Santa Clara University, CA
Santa Fe University of Art and Design, NM
Schreiner University, TX
Seattle University, WA
Seton Hill University, PA
Shenandoah University, VA
Shepherd University, WV
Shippensburg University of Pennsylvania, PA
Shorter University, GA
Siena College, NY
Simpson College, IA
Slippery Rock University of Pennsylvania, PA
Sonoma State University, CA
South Dakota State University, SD
Southeastern Louisiana University, LA
Southeastern Oklahoma State University, OK
Southeastern University, FL
Southeast Missouri State University, MO
Southern Adventist University, TN
Southern Illinois University Edwardsville, IL
Southern Oregon University, OR
Southern Utah University, UT
Southwest Baptist University, MO
Southwestern College, KS
Southwestern Oklahoma State University, OK
Southwestern University, TX
Southwest Minnesota State University, MN
State University of New York at Binghamton, NY
State University of New York at Fredonia, NY
State University of New York at New Paltz, NY
State University of New York at Plattsburgh, NY
State University of New York College at Geneseo, NY
State University of New York College at Oneonta, NY
State University of New York College at Potsdam, NY
Stephen F. Austin State University, TX
Stetson University, FL
Sul Ross State University, TX
Tabor College, KS
Taylor University, IN
Texas A&M University, TX
Texas A&M University–Commerce, TX
Texas Christian University, TX
Texas Lutheran University, TX
Texas State University–San Marcos, TX
Texas Tech University, TX
Texas Woman's University, TX
Thomas More College, KY
Tiffin University, OH
Towson University, MD
Transylvania University, KY
Trinity Christian College, IL
Trinity University, TX
Troy University, AL
Truman State University, MO
Union University, TN
The University of Akron, OH
The University of Alabama, AL
The University of Alabama at Birmingham, AL
University of Alaska Fairbanks, AK
The University of Arizona, AZ
University of Arkansas, AR
University of Arkansas at Little Rock, AR
University of California, Irvine, CA
University of California, Riverside, CA
University of California, Santa Cruz, CA
University of Central Florida, FL
University of Central Missouri, MO
University of Central Oklahoma, OK
University of Cincinnati, OH
University of Colorado Boulder, CO
University of Connecticut, CT
University of Dallas, TX
University of Delaware, DE
University of Denver, CO
University of Evansville, IN
The University of Findlay, OH
University of Florida, FL
University of Hartford, CT
University of Hawaii at Hilo, HI
University of Hawaii at Manoa, HI
University of Idaho, ID
University of Illinois at Chicago, IL
University of Illinois at Springfield, IL
University of Illinois at Urbana–Champaign, IL
University of Indianapolis, IN
The University of Kansas, KS
University of Kentucky, KY
University of La Verne, CA
University of Louisville, KY
University of Maryland, Baltimore County, MD
University of Maryland, College Park, MD
University of Mary Washington, VA
University of Massachusetts Amherst, MA
University of Miami, FL
University of Michigan, MI
University of Michigan–Flint, MI
University of Mississippi, MS
University of Missouri, MO
University of Missouri–St. Louis, MO
The University of Montana, MT
University of Montevallo, AL
University of Mount Union, OH
University of Nebraska at Omaha, NE
University of Nebraska–Lincoln, NE
University of Nevada, Las Vegas, NV
University of Nevada, Reno, NV
University of New Hampshire, NH
University of New Orleans, LA
The University of North Carolina at Asheville, NC
The University of North Carolina at Chapel Hill, NC
The University of North Carolina at Greensboro, NC
University of North Carolina School of the Arts, NC
The University of North Carolina Wilmington, NC
University of North Dakota, ND
University of Northern Colorado, CO
University of Northern Iowa, IA
University of Oklahoma, OK
University of Oregon, OR
University of Pittsburgh at Johnstown, PA
University of Portland, OR
University of Puerto Rico at Bayamón, PR
University of Puget Sound, WA
University of Rhode Island, RI
University of Richmond, VA
University of St. Thomas, TX
University of Science and Arts of Oklahoma, OK
University of South Alabama, AL
University of South Carolina, SC
The University of South Dakota, SD
University of Southern California, CA
University of Southern Indiana, IN
University of Southern Maine, ME
University of Southern Mississippi, MS
University of South Florida, FL
The University of Tampa, FL
The University of Tennessee at Chattanooga, TN
The University of Tennessee at Martin, TN
The University of Texas at Arlington, TX
The University of Texas at El Paso, TX
The University of Texas of the Permian Basin, TX
The University of Texas–Pan American, TX
University of the Cumberlands, KY
University of the Incarnate Word, TX
University of the Ozarks, AR
The University of Toledo, OH
University of Tulsa, OK
University of Utah, UT
University of Vermont, VT
The University of Virginia's College at Wise, VA
University of West Florida, FL
University of West Georgia, GA
University of Wisconsin–Eau Claire, WI
University of Wisconsin–Green Bay, WI
University of Wisconsin–La Crosse, WI
University of Wisconsin–Parkside, WI

University of Wisconsin–River Falls, WI
University of Wisconsin–Stevens Point, WI
University of Wyoming, WY
Utah State University, UT
Valdosta State University, GA
Valley City State University, ND
Valparaiso University, IN
Vanguard University of Southern California, CA
Virginia Commonwealth University, VA
Virginia Polytechnic Institute and State University, VA
Virginia Wesleyan College, VA
Wabash College, IN
Wagner College, NY
Waldorf College, IA
Walla Walla University, WA
Warner Pacific College, OR
Washburn University, KS
Washington State University, WA
Washington University in St. Louis, MO
Wayland Baptist University, TX
Wayne State College, NE
Wayne State University, MI
Wesleyan College, GA
West Chester University of Pennsylvania, PA
Western Carolina University, NC
Western Illinois University, IL
Western Kentucky University, KY
Western Oregon University, OR
Western Washington University, WA
West Liberty University, WV
Westminster College, PA
Westmont College, CA
West Texas A&M University, TX
West Virginia University, WV
West Virginia Wesleyan College, WV
Whitman College, WA
Whittier College, CA
Whitworth University, WA
Wichita State University, KS
Wilkes University, PA
William Jewell College, MO
Wingate University, NC
Winona State University, MN
Winthrop University, SC
Wittenberg University, OH
Wright State University, OH
Xavier University, OH
York College, NE
Young Harris College, GA
Youngstown State University, OH

Special Achievements/Activities

Cheerleading/Drum Major

Abilene Christian University, TX
Angelo State University, TX
Arkansas State University, AR
Arkansas Tech University, AR
Ashland University, OH
Auburn University, AL
Bellarmine University, KY
Bethel College, IN
Bluefield College, VA
Bluefield State College, WV
Boise State University, ID
Brevard College, NC
Cameron University, OK
Campbellsville University, KY
Campbell University, NC
Carroll College, MT
Central Methodist University, MO
Cleveland State University, OH
Coastal Carolina University, SC
Columbus State University, GA
Culver-Stockton College, MO
Delta State University, MS
Dickinson State University, ND
Drury University, MO
Eastern Kentucky University, KY
East Texas Baptist University, TX
Evangel University, MO
Faulkner University, AL
Florida Agricultural and Mechanical University, FL
Florida Institute of Technology, FL
Francis Marion University, SC
Gardner-Webb University, NC
Georgia Institute of Technology, GA
Georgia Southern University, GA
Glenville State College, WV
Graceland University, IA
Harding University, AR
Hastings College, NE
Hawai'i Pacific University, HI
Houston Baptist University, TX
Huntingdon College, AL
Huntington University, IN
Indiana Wesleyan University, IN
James Madison University, VA
John Brown University, AR
Kentucky State University, KY
Lee University, TN
Lenoir-Rhyne University, NC
Limestone College, SC
Lincoln Memorial University, TN
Lincoln University, MO
Lindenwood University, MO
Lindsey Wilson College, KY
Lipscomb University, TN
Long Island University, Brooklyn Campus, NY
Louisiana Tech University, LA
Lubbock Christian University, TX
Lyon College, AR
Mars Hill College, NC
Maryville University of Saint Louis, MO
McKendree University, IL
McPherson College, KS
Methodist University, NC
Mid-Continent University, KY
Middle Tennessee State University, TN
Midwestern State University, TX
Milligan College, TN
Mississippi State University, MS
Missouri Baptist University, MO
Montana State University Billings, MT
Morehead State University, KY
Morningside College, IA
Mountain State University, WV
Mount Olive College, NC
Murray State University, KY
Nicholls State University, LA
Northeastern State University, OK
Northern Michigan University, MI
North Georgia College & State University, GA
Northwestern Oklahoma State University, OK
Northwestern State University of Louisiana, LA
Northwest Missouri State University, MO
Northwest Nazarene University, ID
Nyack College, NY
The Ohio State University, OH
Oklahoma Christian University, OK
Oklahoma City University, OK
Oklahoma Panhandle State University, OK
Oklahoma State University, OK
Old Dominion University, VA
Olivet Nazarene University, IL
Ouachita Baptist University, AR
Quincy University, IL
Rocky Mountain College, MT
Rogers State University, OK
St. Ambrose University, IA
St. Edward's University, TX
Saint Francis University, PA
St. John's University, NY
Saint Joseph's College, IN
Saint Louis University, MO
Seton Hill University, PA
Shorter University, GA
Southeastern Louisiana University, LA
Southeastern Oklahoma State University, OK
Southeast Missouri State University, MO
Southern Illinois University Carbondale, IL
Southwestern College, KS
Southwestern Oklahoma State University, OK
Stephen F. Austin State University, TX
Stetson University, FL
Tabor College, KS
Temple University, PA
Tennessee Technological University, TN
Tennessee Wesleyan College, TN
Texas A&M University–Commerce, TX
Texas Wesleyan University, TX
Tiffin University, OH
Union College, KY
Union University, TN
The University of Alabama, AL
The University of Alabama at Birmingham, AL
The University of Alabama in Huntsville, AL
University of Central Missouri, MO
University of Delaware, DE
University of Great Falls, MT
University of Idaho, ID
University of Kentucky, KY
University of Louisville, KY
University of Mary Hardin-Baylor, TX
University of Maryland, College Park, MD
University of Massachusetts Amherst, MA
University of Memphis, TN
University of Mississippi, MS
University of Missouri, MO
University of Missouri–St. Louis, MO
The University of Montana, MT
University of Nebraska–Lincoln, NE
University of Nevada, Las Vegas, NV
University of North Alabama, AL
The University of North Carolina Wilmington, NC
University of Puerto Rico at Bayamón, PR
University of Rio Grande, OH
University of St. Francis, IL
University of Science and Arts of Oklahoma, OK
University of South Carolina, SC
University of South Carolina Aiken, SC
University of Southern Mississippi, MS
The University of Tennessee at Chattanooga, TN
The University of Tennessee at Martin, TN
The University of Texas at Arlington, TX
The University of Texas at El Paso, TX
The University of Texas at San Antonio, TX

The University of Texas of the Permian Basin, TX
The University of Texas–Pan American, TX
University of the Cumberlands, KY
The University of Toledo, OH
University of Tulsa, OK
University of Utah, UT
The University of West Alabama, AL
University of Wyoming, WY
Virginia Polytechnic Institute and State University, VA
Virginia State University, VA
Waldorf College, IA
Washburn University, KS
Wayland Baptist University, TX
Webber International University, FL
West Liberty University, WV
West Texas A&M University, TX
West Virginia University Institute of Technology, WV
Wichita State University, KS
William Jewell College, MO
Williams Baptist College, AR
Wright State University, OH
Youngstown State University, OH

Community Service

Adelphi University, NY
Agnes Scott College, GA
Alaska Pacific University, AK
Allen College, IA
Alliant International University, CA
Alvernia University, PA
Alverno College, WI
Arcadia University, PA
Arizona Christian University, AZ
Arkansas State University, AR
Arkansas Tech University, AR
Armstrong Atlantic State University, GA
Augsburg College, MN
Augusta State University, GA
Austin College, TX
Ball State University, IN
Baylor University, TX
Bellarmine University, KY
Beloit College, WI
Benedictine University, IL
Bentley University, MA
Berry College, GA
Bethel University, MN
Biola University, CA
Bloomfield College, NJ
Boise State University, ID
Bradley University, IL
Brevard College, NC
Bryan College, TN
Burlington College, VT
Caldwell College, NJ
California Institute of Integral Studies, CA
California Lutheran University, CA
California Polytechnic State University, San Luis Obispo, CA
California State University, Bakersfield, CA
California State University, Chico, CA
California State University, Fresno, CA
California State University, San Bernardino, CA
California State University, Stanislaus, CA
Calvin College, MI
Cedar Crest College, PA
Centenary College of Louisiana, LA
Central College, IA
Centre College, KY
The Citadel, The Military College of South Carolina, SC
City College of the City University of New York, NY
Clark University, MA
Clemson University, SC
Coe College, IA
The College at Brockport, State University of New York, NY
College of Mount St. Joseph, OH
The College of New Rochelle, NY
College of Notre Dame of Maryland, MD
College of Saint Elizabeth, NJ
College of Saint Mary, NE
The College of Saint Rose, NY
College of Staten Island of the City University of New York, NY
The College of Wooster, OH
Colorado State University–Pueblo, CO
Columbus State University, GA
Concord University, WV
Cornell College, IA
Dallas Baptist University, TX
Dalton State College, GA
Davidson College, NC
Defiance College, OH
DePaul University, IL
DePauw University, IN
DigiPen Institute of Technology, WA
Dominican University of California, CA
Eastern Connecticut State University, CT
Eckerd College, FL
ECPI College of Technology, VA
Edgewood College, WI
Elon University, NC
Emmanuel College, MA
Endicott College, MA
The Evergreen State College, WA
Finlandia University, MI
Florida Agricultural and Mechanical University, FL
Florida Gulf Coast University, FL
Florida Southern College, FL
Frostburg State University, MD
Furman University, SC
Gannon University, PA
Georgia College & State University, GA
Georgia Southern University, GA
Golden Gate University, CA
Green Mountain College, VT
Hamline University, MN
Hampshire College, MA
Hawai'i Pacific University, HI
Hendrix College, AR
Hillsdale College, MI
Hillsdale Free Will Baptist College, OK
Hollins University, VA
Houston Baptist University, TX
Howard Payne University, TX
Huntingdon College, AL
Illinois Institute of Technology, IL
Illinois State University, IL
Indiana University of Pennsylvania, PA
Iowa State University of Science and Technology, IA
Jamestown College, ND
John Carroll University, OH
Johnson Bible College, TN
Juniata College, PA
Kean University, NJ
Kennesaw State University, GA
Kent State University, OH
Keuka College, NY
King's College, PA
Knox College, IL
Kutztown University of Pennsylvania, PA
Lasell College, MA
Lawrence University, WI
Lewis & Clark College, OR
Lewis-Clark State College, ID
Lindenwood University, MO
Linfield College, OR
Lipscomb University, TN
Longwood University, VA
Loyola University Chicago, IL
Malone University, OH
Manhattan College, NY
Manhattanville College, NY
Marymount University, VA
Maryville College, TN
Maryville University of Saint Louis, MO
Marywood University, PA
McKendree University, IL
McPherson College, KS
Mercer University, GA
Mercyhurst College, PA
Meredith College, NC
Michigan State University, MI
Millersville University of Pennsylvania, PA
Milligan College, TN
Millikin University, IL
Millsaps College, MS
Minnesota State University Moorhead, MN
Misericordia University, PA
Molloy College, NY
Montana State University–Northern, MT
Montana Tech of The University of Montana, MT
Montclair State University, NJ
Morehouse College, GA
Morningside College, IA
Mount Carmel College of Nursing, OH
Mount St. Mary's College, CA
Muskingum University, OH
New England College, NH
New Hope Christian College, OR
New Jersey Institute of Technology, NJ
Niagara University, NY
Nichols College, MA
North Central College, IL
Northeastern State University, OK
Northern Kentucky University, KY
North Georgia College & State University, GA
Northwest Christian University, OR
Nyack College, NY
Oglethorpe University, GA
Ohio Northern University, OH
Ohio Valley University, WV
Oklahoma State University, OK
Old Dominion University, VA
Olivet College, MI
Pace University, NY
Pacific Union College, CA
Pacific University, OR
Patrick Henry College, VA
Pitzer College, CA
Point Park University, PA
Portland State University, OR
Principia College, IL
Providence College, RI
Queens College of the City University of New York, NY
Quincy University, IL
Randolph College, VA
The Richard Stockton College of New Jersey, NJ

Ringling College of Art and Design, FL
Robert Morris University Illinois, IL
Rochester Institute of Technology, NY
Rockford College, IL
Rockhurst University, MO
Rosemont College, PA
Russell Sage College, NY
Sacred Heart University, CT
Sage College of Albany, NY
Saginaw Valley State University, MI
St. Andrews Presbyterian College, NC
St. Catherine University, MN
St. Edward's University, TX
St. John Fisher College, NY
St. John's University, NY
St. Joseph's College, Long Island Campus, NY
St. Joseph's College, New York, NY
Saint Joseph's University, PA
St. Lawrence University, NY
St. Louis College of Pharmacy, MO
Saint Louis University, MO
Saint Martin's University, WA
Saint Mary-of-the-Woods College, IN
St. Olaf College, MN
St. Thomas Aquinas College, NY
Schreiner University, TX
Shippensburg University of Pennsylvania, PA
Siena College, NY
Silver Lake College, WI
Simmons College, MA
Simpson College, IA
Simpson University, CA
Slippery Rock University of Pennsylvania, PA
Sonoma State University, CA
South Dakota State University, SD
Southern Adventist University, TN
Southern Illinois University Carbondale, IL
Southern Oregon University, OR
Southwestern College, KS
Spring Hill College, AL
State University of New York at Binghamton, NY
State University of New York at Plattsburgh, NY
State University of New York College at Cortland, NY
State University of New York College at Geneseo, NY
State University of New York College at Oneonta, NY
State University of New York College at Potsdam, NY
State University of New York College of Technology at Delhi, NY
Stetson University, FL
Stony Brook University, State University of New York, NY
Suffolk University, MA
Sweet Briar College, VA
Texas A&M University–Texarkana, TX
Texas Tech University, TX
Thomas More College, KY
Towson University, MD
Tulane University, LA
Union College, KY
Union College, NE
Union University, TN
Unity College, ME
The University of Akron, OH
The University of Alabama, AL
The University of Alabama in Huntsville, AL
University of Alaska Fairbanks, AK
University of Arkansas, AR
University of Arkansas at Little Rock, AR
University of California, San Diego, CA
University of Charleston, WV
University of Chicago, IL
University of Colorado Boulder, CO
University of Connecticut, CT
University of Delaware, DE
University of Denver, CO
University of Florida, FL
University of Hartford, CT
University of Hawaii at Hilo, HI
University of Houston–Clear Lake, TX
University of Houston–Downtown, TX
University of Indianapolis, IN
The University of Kansas, KS
University of La Verne, CA
University of Louisville, KY
University of Maine at Presque Isle, ME
University of Mary Hardin-Baylor, TX
University of Massachusetts Dartmouth, MA
University of Massachusetts Lowell, MA
University of Michigan, MI
University of Michigan–Dearborn, MI
University of Michigan–Flint, MI
University of Mississippi, MS
University of Missouri–St. Louis, MO
University of Nebraska–Lincoln, NE
University of Nevada, Las Vegas, NV
University of New Hampshire, NH
The University of North Carolina at Asheville, NC
The University of North Carolina at Chapel Hill, NC
The University of North Carolina at Greensboro, NC
University of North Florida, FL
University of Puget Sound, WA
University of Richmond, VA
University of St. Francis, IL
University of South Carolina, SC
University of Southern Maine, ME
The University of Tennessee at Chattanooga, TN
The University of Texas at Arlington, TX
The University of Texas–Pan American, TX
University of the Cumberlands, KY
University of Tulsa, OK
University of Vermont, VT
The University of Virginia's College at Wise, VA
University of West Georgia, GA
University of Wisconsin–Eau Claire, WI
University of Wisconsin–Green Bay, WI
University of Wisconsin–La Crosse, WI
University of Wisconsin–Parkside, WI
University of Wisconsin–Stout, WI
Ursuline College, OH
Valley Forge Christian College, PA
Vanderbilt University, TN
Virginia Polytechnic Institute and State University, VA
Virginia State University, VA
Virginia Wesleyan College, VA
Wabash College, IN
Warren Wilson College, NC
Washburn University, KS
Washington Adventist University, MD
Washington & Jefferson College, PA
Washington State University, WA
Waynesburg University, PA
Webber International University, FL
Wesleyan College, GA
Wesley College, DE
Western Illinois University, IL
Western New England University, MA
Western Oregon University, OR
Western Washington University, WA
West Texas A&M University, TX
West Virginia Wesleyan College, WV
Wheeling Jesuit University, WV
Widener University, PA
Wilson College, PA
Wittenberg University, OH
Wright State University, OH
Youngstown State University, OH

Hobbies/Interests

Angelo State University, TX
Arkansas Tech University, AR
Augusta State University, GA
Brevard College, NC
California State Polytechnic University, Pomona, CA
California State University, Chico, CA
California State University, San Bernardino, CA
Capital University, OH
Centenary College of Louisiana, LA
The College at Brockport, State University of New York, NY
The College of New Rochelle, NY
Corban University, OR
Dalton State College, GA
Eastern Nazarene College, MA
Florida Institute of Technology, FL
Hawai'i Pacific University, HI
Hollins University, VA
Illinois Institute of Technology, IL
Indiana University of Pennsylvania, PA
Mesa State College, CO
Michigan State University, MI
Millsaps College, MS
Montana State University–Northern, MT
New Hope Christian College, OR
The Ohio State University, OH
Quincy University, IL
St. John's University, NY
Saint Martin's University, WA
Siena College, NY
South Dakota State University, SD
Southern Oregon University, OR
Southwest Minnesota State University, MN
State University of New York College at Cortland, NY
Stephen F. Austin State University, TX
Union College, KY
The University of Alabama, AL
University of Louisville, KY
University of Michigan–Flint, MI
University of Minnesota, Twin Cities Campus, MN
University of South Alabama, AL
The University of Toledo, OH
University of Wisconsin–Eau Claire, WI
Virginia State University, VA
West Texas A&M University, TX

Junior Miss

Augsburg College, MN
Bethel University, MN
Birmingham-Southern College, AL
Bluefield State College, WV
Campbellsville University, KY
Carroll University, WI
Cedar Crest College, PA

The College of New Rochelle, NY
College of Saint Benedict, MN
Georgetown College, KY
Georgia Southern University, GA
Goshen College, IN
Grand View University, IA
Gustavus Adolphus College, MN
Hawai'i Pacific University, HI
Huntingdon College, AL
Lewis-Clark State College, ID
Lindenwood University, MO
Lindsey Wilson College, KY
Louisiana Tech University, LA
McDaniel College, MD
Mississippi State University, MS
Mississippi University for Women, MS
Morehead State University, KY
Mount Vernon Nazarene University, OH
Murray State University, KY
Muskingum University, OH
Northeastern State University, OK
Ohio Northern University, OH
Oklahoma City University, OK
Roberts Wesleyan College, NY
South Dakota State University, SD
Spring Arbor University, MI
Tennessee Wesleyan College, TN
Texas Lutheran University, TX
Thomas University, GA
The University of Alabama, AL
The University of Alabama at Birmingham, AL
The University of Alabama in Huntsville, AL
University of Idaho, ID
University of Louisville, KY
University of Mississippi, MS
University of Montevallo, AL
The University of North Carolina at Asheville, NC
The University of North Carolina at Greensboro, NC
University of South Alabama, AL
University of Wyoming, WY
Waldorf College, IA
Washington State University, WA

Leadership

Abilene Christian University, TX
Agnes Scott College, GA
Alabama State University, AL
Alaska Pacific University, AK
Albright College, PA
Alderson-Broaddus College, WV
Alfred University, NY
Allen College, IA
Alliant International University, CA
Alvernia University, PA
American Jewish University, CA
American University, DC
Andrews University, MI
Angelo State University, TX
Aquinas College, TN
Arcadia University, PA
Arizona Christian University, AZ
Arkansas State University, AR
Arkansas Tech University, AR
Asbury University, KY
Auburn University, AL
Augsburg College, MN
Augustana College, SD
Augusta State University, GA
Austin College, TX
Austin Peay State University, TN
Averett University, VA
Azusa Pacific University, CA
Babson College, MA
Baldwin-Wallace College, OH
Ball State University, IN
Baptist Bible College of Pennsylvania, PA
Bard College, NY
Baylor University, TX
Bellarmine University, KY
Benedictine University, IL
Berry College, GA
Bethany College, WV
Bethel College, IN
Bethel University, MN
Biola University, CA
Bloomfield College, NJ
Bluefield State College, WV
Bluffton University, OH
Boise State University, ID
Boston University, MA
Bowdoin College, ME
Bowling Green State University, OH
Bradley University, IL
Brenau University, GA
Brevard College, NC
Bryan College, TN
Bucknell University, PA
Buena Vista University, IA
Burlington College, VT
California Institute of Integral Studies, CA
California Lutheran University, CA
California Polytechnic State University, San Luis Obispo, CA
California State Polytechnic University, Pomona, CA
California State University, Chico, CA
California State University, Fresno, CA
California State University, Fullerton, CA
California State University, Monterey Bay, CA
California State University, Northridge, CA
California State University, Stanislaus, CA
Calumet College of Saint Joseph, IN
Cameron University, OK
Campbellsville University, KY
Capital University, OH
Carnegie Mellon University, PA
Carroll College, MT
Carroll University, WI
Carson-Newman College, TN
Case Western Reserve University, OH
Cedar Crest College, PA
Cedarville University, OH
Central Methodist University, MO
Central Michigan University, MI
Central Washington University, WA
Chicago State University, IL
Chowan University, NC
Christian Brothers University, TN
Christopher Newport University, VA
Cincinnati Christian University, OH
The Citadel, The Military College of South Carolina, SC
City College of the City University of New York, NY
Claremont McKenna College, CA
Clarke University, IA
Clarkson University, NY
Clemson University, SC
The College at Brockport, State University of New York, NY
College of Mount St. Joseph, OH
The College of New Rochelle, NY
College of Notre Dame of Maryland, MD
College of Saint Elizabeth, NJ
College of St. Joseph, VT
College of Saint Mary, NE
Colorado State University–Pueblo, CO
Columbia College, MO
Columbia International University, SC
Columbus State University, GA
Concord University, WV
Converse College, SC
Corban University, OR
Cornell College, IA
Cornerstone University, MI
Covenant College, GA
Creighton University, NE
Crown College, MN
Culver-Stockton College, MO
Daemen College, NY
Dallas Baptist University, TX
Dalton State College, GA
Davidson College, NC
Defiance College, OH
Delta State University, MS
DePaul University, IL
DePauw University, IN
Dickinson State University, ND
Dominican University of California, CA
Dordt College, IA
Drury University, MO
Duke University, NC
Eastern Connecticut State University, CT
Eastern Michigan University, MI
Eastern Nazarene College, MA
Eastern Oregon University, OR
East Tennessee State University, TN
East Texas Baptist University, TX
Eckerd College, FL
Elmira College, NY
Elon University, NC
Embry-Riddle Aeronautical University–Daytona, FL
Embry-Riddle Aeronautical University–Prescott, AZ
Embry-Riddle Aeronautical University–Worldwide, FL
Emerson College, MA
Emmanuel College, GA
Emmanuel College, MA
Emory University, GA
Endicott College, MA
Erskine College, SC
Eugene Lang College The New School for Liberal Arts, NY
Eureka College, IL
Evangel University, MO
Faulkner University, AL
Finlandia University, MI
Fitchburg State University, MA
Flagler College, FL
Florida Agricultural and Mechanical University, FL
Florida Gulf Coast University, FL
Florida Southern College, FL
Fort Lewis College, CO
Frostburg State University, MD
Furman University, SC
Gallaudet University, DC
Gannon University, PA
George Fox University, OR
Georgetown College, KY
Georgia College & State University, GA
Georgia Institute of Technology, GA
Georgia Southern University, GA
Golden Gate University, CA

Gonzaga University, WA
Gordon College, MA
Graceland University, IA
Grace University, NE
Green Mountain College, VT
Greenville College, IL
Grove City College, PA
Hamline University, MN
Hampden-Sydney College, VA
Hampshire College, MA
Hampton University, VA
Harding University, AR
Hardin-Simmons University, TX
Hawai'i Pacific University, HI
Hendrix College, AR
Hillsdale College, MI
Hobart and William Smith Colleges, NY
Hofstra University, NY
Hollins University, VA
Hope International University, CA
Houston Baptist University, TX
Howard Payne University, TX
Husson University, ME
Illinois Institute of Technology, IL
Illinois State University, IL
Indiana University of Pennsylvania, PA
Indiana University–Purdue University Fort Wayne, IN
Iowa State University of Science and Technology, IA
Ithaca College, NY
Jackson State University, MS
Jacksonville University, FL
James Madison University, VA
Jamestown College, ND
John Brown University, AR
John Carroll University, OH
Johnson & Wales University, CO
Johnson & Wales University, FL
Johnson & Wales University, RI
Johnson & Wales University—Charlotte Campus, NC
Johnson Bible College, TN
Judson University, IL
Juniata College, PA
Kean University, NJ
Keene State College, NH
Kennesaw State University, GA
Kent State University, OH
Kent State University at Stark, OH
Kettering University, MI
Keuka College, NY
King's College, PA
Kutztown University of Pennsylvania, PA
Kuyper College, MI
Lake Forest College, IL
Lancaster Bible College & Graduate School, PA
Lasell College, MA
Lawrence University, WI
Lee University, TN
Le Moyne College, NY
Lenoir-Rhyne University, NC
Lewis-Clark State College, ID
Limestone College, SC
Lindenwood University, MO
Lindsey Wilson College, KY
Linfield College, OR
Lipscomb University, TN
Lock Haven University of Pennsylvania, PA
Long Island University, Brooklyn Campus, NY
Long Island University, C.W. Post Campus, NY
Longwood University, VA
Louisiana College, LA
Louisiana State University and Agricultural and Mechanical College, LA
Loyola University Chicago, IL
Lubbock Christian University, TX
Lycoming College, PA
Lynn University, FL
Malone University, OH
Manchester College, IN
Manhattan Christian College, KS
Manhattan College, NY
Manhattanville College, NY
Mary Baldwin College, VA
Marymount University, VA
Maryville College, TN
Maryville University of Saint Louis, MO
Marywood University, PA
Massachusetts College of Liberal Arts, MA
Massachusetts Maritime Academy, MA
The Master's College and Seminary, CA
McDaniel College, MD
McKendree University, IL
Mercer University, GA
Mercyhurst College, PA
Meredith College, NC
Mesa State College, CO
Messiah College, PA
Methodist University, NC
Metropolitan State College of Denver, CO
Miami University, OH
Michigan State University, MI
Michigan Technological University, MI
Middle Tennessee State University, TN
Midwestern State University, TX
Millsaps College, MS
Mills College, CA
Misericordia University, PA
Mississippi State University, MS
Mississippi University for Women, MS
Missouri State University, MO
Molloy College, NY
Monmouth College, IL
Monmouth University, NJ
Montana State University, MT
Montclair State University, NJ
Montreat College, NC
Moravian College, PA
Morehead State University, KY
Morehouse College, GA
Morningside College, IA
Mount Aloysius College, PA
Mount Mary College, WI
Mount Mercy University, IA
Mount Olive College, NC
Mount St. Mary's College, CA
Murray State University, KY
Muskingum University, OH
National University, CA
New England College, NH
New Hope Christian College, OR
New Jersey Institute of Technology, NJ
New Mexico State University, NM
Nicholls State University, LA
Nichols College, MA
North Carolina State University, NC
Northeastern Illinois University, IL
Northeastern State University, OK
Northern Arizona University, AZ
Northern Illinois University, IL
Northern Kentucky University, KY
Northern Michigan University, MI
Northern State University, SD
North Georgia College & State University, GA
Northland College, WI
Northwest Christian University, OR
Northwestern College, MN
Northwestern Oklahoma State University, OK
Northwestern State University of Louisiana, LA
Northwest Missouri State University, MO
Northwest Nazarene University, ID
Northwest University, WA
Nyack College, NY
Occidental College, CA
Ohio Northern University, OH
The Ohio State University, OH
Ohio Valley University, WV
Ohio Wesleyan University, OH
Oklahoma Baptist University, OK
Oklahoma Christian University, OK
Oklahoma City University, OK
Oklahoma State University, OK
Oklahoma Wesleyan University, OK
Old Dominion University, VA
Olivet College, MI
Oregon Institute of Technology, OR
Pace University, NY
Pacific Lutheran University, WA
Pacific Union College, CA
Palm Beach Atlantic University, FL
Patrick Henry College, VA
Peirce College, PA
Piedmont College, GA
Pitzer College, CA
Portland State University, OR
Presbyterian College, SC
Principia College, IL
Purdue University, IN
Purdue University North Central, IN
Queens College of the City University of New York, NY
Quincy University, IL
Randolph College, VA
Regent University, VA
Regis University, CO
Reinhardt University, GA
Rice University, TX
The Richard Stockton College of New Jersey, NJ
Ripon College, WI
Rochester Institute of Technology, NY
Rockford College, IL
Rockhurst University, MO
Rocky Mountain College, MT
Rogers State University, OK
Rosemont College, PA
Russell Sage College, NY
Sacred Heart University, CT
Saginaw Valley State University, MI
St. Andrews Presbyterian College, NC
St. Catherine University, MN
St. Edward's University, TX
St. John's University, NY
St. Joseph's College, Long Island Campus, NY
St. Joseph's College, New York, NY
St. Lawrence University, NY
St. Louis College of Pharmacy, MO
Saint Louis University, MO
Saint Martin's University, WA
Saint Mary-of-the-Woods College, IN
Saint Mary's College of California, CA
Saint Mary's University of Minnesota, MN

St. Thomas Aquinas College, NY
St. Thomas University, FL
Saint Vincent College, PA
Saint Xavier University, IL
Salem College, NC
Samford University, AL
San Diego Christian College, CA
San Diego State University, CA
Schreiner University, TX
Scripps College, CA
Seattle University, WA
Shepherd University, WV
Shippensburg University of Pennsylvania, PA
Siena College, NY
Simpsón College, IA
Simpson University, CA
Slippery Rock University of Pennsylvania, PA
Sonoma State University, CA
South Dakota State University, SD
Southeastern Louisiana University, LA
Southeastern Oklahoma State University, OK
Southeast Missouri State University, MO
Southern Adventist University, TN
Southern Illinois University Carbondale, IL
Southern Oregon University, OR
Southern Utah University, UT
Southwestern College, KS
Southwestern Oklahoma State University, OK
Southwestern University, TX
Southwest Minnesota State University, MN
State University of New York at Binghamton, NY
State University of New York at Fredonia, NY
State University of New York at Plattsburgh, NY
State University of New York College at Cortland, NY
State University of New York College at Geneseo, NY
State University of New York College at Oneonta, NY
State University of New York College at Potsdam, NY
State University of New York College of Environmental Science and Forestry, NY
Stephen F. Austin State University, TX
Stetson University, FL
Stony Brook University, State University of New York, NY
Sul Ross State University, TX
Taylor University, IN
Texas A&M University, TX
Texas A&M University–Commerce, TX
Texas A&M University–Texarkana, TX
Texas Christian University, TX
Texas College, TX
Texas Lutheran University, TX
Texas State University–San Marcos, TX
Texas Wesleyan University, TX
Thiel College, PA
Thomas More College, KY
Trinity Christian College, IL
Trinity College, CT
Troy University, AL
Truman State University, MO
Union College, KY
Union College, NE
Union University, TN
Unity College, ME
The University of Akron, OH
The University of Alabama at Birmingham, AL
The University of Alabama in Huntsville, AL
University of Arkansas, AR
University of Arkansas at Little Rock, AR
University of California, San Diego, CA
University of California, Santa Cruz, CA
University of Central Florida, FL
University of Central Missouri, MO
University of Central Oklahoma, OK
University of Charleston, WV
University of Chicago, IL
University of Cincinnati, OH
University of Colorado Boulder, CO
University of Connecticut, CT
University of Dallas, TX
University of Delaware, DE
University of Denver, CO
University of Evansville, IN
University of Florida, FL
University of Hawaii at Hilo, HI
University of Hawaii at Manoa, HI
University of Houston–Clear Lake, TX
University of Houston–Downtown, TX
University of Idaho, ID
University of Illinois at Springfield, IL
University of Illinois at Urbana–Champaign, IL
The University of Kansas, KS
University of Kentucky, KY
University of La Verne, CA
University of Louisville, KY
University of Mary Hardin-Baylor, TX
University of Mary Washington, VA
University of Massachusetts Amherst, MA
University of Massachusetts Boston, MA
University of Memphis, TN
University of Michigan, MI
University of Michigan–Dearborn, MI
University of Michigan–Flint, MI
University of Minnesota, Twin Cities Campus, MN
University of Mississippi, MS
The University of Montana, MT
University of Montevallo, AL
University of Nebraska at Omaha, NE
University of Nebraska–Lincoln, NE
University of Nevada, Las Vegas, NV
University of New Orleans, LA
University of North Alabama, AL
The University of North Carolina at Asheville, NC
The University of North Carolina at Chapel Hill, NC
The University of North Carolina at Greensboro, NC
The University of North Carolina Wilmington, NC
University of North Dakota, ND
University of Northern Iowa, IA
University of North Florida, FL
University of Oklahoma, OK
University of Pittsburgh at Greensburg, PA
University of Pittsburgh at Johnstown, PA
University of Puget Sound, WA
University of Rochester, NY
University of St. Francis, IL
University of St. Thomas, TX
University of South Alabama, AL
University of South Carolina, SC
The University of South Dakota, SD
University of Southern California, CA
University of Southern Indiana, IN
University of Southern Mississippi, MS
The University of Tampa, FL
The University of Tennessee at Martin, TN
The University of Texas at Arlington, TX
The University of Texas at Austin, TX
The University of Texas at Dallas, TX
The University of Texas at El Paso, TX
The University of Texas–Pan American, TX
University of the Cumberlands, KY
University of the Incarnate Word, TX
University of the Ozarks, AR
University of the Southwest, NM
The University of Toledo, OH
University of Tulsa, OK
University of Utah, UT
University of Vermont, VT
University of West Georgia, GA
University of Wisconsin–Eau Claire, WI
University of Wisconsin–Green Bay, WI
University of Wisconsin–La Crosse, WI
University of Wisconsin–Parkside, WI
University of Wisconsin–Stevens Point, WI
University of Wisconsin–Stout, WI
University of Wyoming, WY
Ursinus College, PA
Ursuline College, OH
Valley Forge Christian College, PA
Vanderbilt University, TN
Virginia Military Institute, VA
Virginia Polytechnic Institute and State University, VA
Virginia State University, VA
Virginia Wesleyan College, VA
Wabash College, IN
Wake Forest University, NC
Waldorf College, IA
Walla Walla University, WA
Walsh University, OH
Warner Pacific College, OR
Warren Wilson College, NC
Washburn University, KS
Washington Adventist University, MD
Washington State University, WA
Wayland Baptist University, TX
Wayne State College, NE
Wayne State University, MI
Webber International University, FL
Wells College, NY
Wesleyan College, GA
Wesley College, DE
Western Illinois University, IL
Western Kentucky University, KY
Western New England University, MA
Western Oregon University, OR
Western State College of Colorado, CO
Western Washington University, WA
Westminster College, MO
Westmont College, CA
West Texas A&M University, TX
West Virginia State University, WV
West Virginia University, WV
West Virginia Wesleyan College, WV
Whitman College, WA
Wichita State University, KS
Widener University, PA
Wilkes University, PA
William Jessup University, CA
Wilson College, PA
Wittenberg University, OH
Wofford College, SC
Wright State University, OH
York College, NE
Youngstown State University, OH

Non-Need Scholarships for Undergraduates

Special Achievements/Activities

Memberships

Adelphi University, NY
Albright College, PA
Alvernia University, PA
American University, DC
Angelo State University, TX
Arcadia University, PA
Auburn University, AL
Augusta State University, GA
Austin Peay State University, TN
Averett University, VA
Benedictine University, IL
Birmingham-Southern College, AL
Boston University, MA
California State University, Chico, CA
California State University, San Bernardino, CA
California State University, Stanislaus, CA
Carroll University, WI
Carson-Newman College, TN
Cedar Crest College, PA
The College of New Rochelle, NY
College of Notre Dame of Maryland, MD
Corban University, OR
Dallas Baptist University, TX
Dalton State College, GA
Davenport University, MI
Delta State University, MS
Eastern Connecticut State University, CT
Eastern Michigan University, MI
East Tennessee State University, TN
Emmanuel College, GA
Emporia State University, KS
Erskine College, SC
Ferris State University, MI
Flagler College, FL
Florida Institute of Technology, FL
Georgia Southern University, GA
Gonzaga University, WA
Greenville College, IL
Grove City College, PA
Hamline University, MN
Hawai'i Pacific University, HI
Illinois Institute of Technology, IL
Johnson & Wales University, CO
Johnson & Wales University, FL
Johnson & Wales University, RI
Johnson & Wales University—Charlotte Campus, NC
Kennesaw State University, GA
Kettering University, MI
Lock Haven University of Pennsylvania, PA
Longwood University, VA
Loyola University Chicago, IL
Massachusetts College of Liberal Arts, MA
Medcenter One College of Nursing, ND
Michigan State University, MI
Mississippi State University, MS
Molloy College, NY
Montana State University–Northern, MT
New Jersey Institute of Technology, NJ
New Life Theological Seminary, NC
Northern Michigan University, MI
Northwestern Oklahoma State University, OK
Northwestern State University of Louisiana, LA
Northwest Missouri State University, MO
Northwood University, Texas Campus, TX
The Ohio State University, OH
Oklahoma State University, OK
Old Dominion University, VA
Olivet College, MI
Pacific University, OR
Patrick Henry College, VA
Peirce College, PA
Point Park University, PA
Portland State University, OR
Ripon College, WI
St. Catherine University, MN
Saint Louis University, MO
Saint Mary-of-the-Woods College, IN
Saint Mary's College of California, CA
Schreiner University, TX
Shawnee State University, OH
Siena College, NY
Sonoma State University, CA
South Dakota State University, SD
Southeastern Louisiana University, LA
Southeast Missouri State University, MO
Southern Oregon University, OR
Southwestern College, KS
State University of New York College at Geneseo, NY
Tennessee Wesleyan College, TN
Texas A&M University, TX
Texas A&M University–Texarkana, TX
Texas Christian University, TX
Texas Lutheran University, TX
Texas Tech University, TX
Thomas More College, KY
Towson University, MD
Union College, KY
The University of Akron, OH
The University of Alabama at Birmingham, AL
University of Arkansas at Little Rock, AR
University of Evansville, IN
University of Indianapolis, IN
University of Louisville, KY
University of Michigan–Dearborn, MI
University of Mississippi, MS
University of Missouri, MO
University of Missouri–St. Louis, MO
University of Nebraska at Omaha, NE
University of North Dakota, ND
University of South Carolina, SC
The University of Tampa, FL
The University of Tennessee at Chattanooga, TN
The University of Texas–Pan American, TX
The University of Toledo, OH
University of Vermont, VT
University of West Georgia, GA
University of Wisconsin–Eau Claire, WI
University of Wisconsin–La Crosse, WI
University of Wisconsin–Stout, WI
Virginia Polytechnic Institute and State University, VA
Washington State University, WA
Wayland Baptist University, TX
Webber International University, FL
Wesleyan College, GA
Western Kentucky University, KY
Western Washington University, WA
West Texas A&M University, TX
Wichita State University, KS
Wright State University, OH
Youngstown State University, OH

Religious Involvement

Adrian College, MI
Alaska Pacific University, AK
Albright College, PA
Alma College, MI
Alvernia University, PA
Amridge University, AL
Andrews University, MI
Anna Maria College, MA
Appalachian Bible College, WV
Arizona Christian University, AZ
Augsburg College, MN
Aurora University, IL
Austin College, TX
Austin Graduate School of Theology, TX
Averett University, VA
Baptist Bible College of Pennsylvania, PA
Baylor University, TX
Bellarmine University, KY
Belmont Abbey College, NC
Berry College, GA
Bethel College, IN
Bethel University, MN
Bethesda Christian University, CA
Birmingham-Southern College, AL
Brigham Young University, UT
Bryan College, TN
Caldwell College, NJ
California Lutheran University, CA
Calvary Bible College and Theological Seminary, MO
Calvin College, MI
Campbellsville University, KY
Campbell University, NC
Canisius College, NY
Capital University, OH
Carroll College, MT
Carroll University, WI
Cedar Crest College, PA
Centenary College of Louisiana, LA
Central College, IA
Central Methodist University, MO
Cincinnati Christian University, OH
The Citadel, The Military College of South Carolina, SC
The College at Brockport, State University of New York, NY
The College of New Rochelle, NY
College of Notre Dame of Maryland, MD
College of Saint Mary, NE
The College of Wooster, OH
Corban University, OR
Cornell College, IA
Dallas Baptist University, TX
Davidson College, NC
Defiance College, OH
Drury University, MO
Earlham College, IN
Eastern Michigan University, MI
East Texas Baptist University, TX
Elizabethtown College, PA
Elon University, NC
Emmanuel College, GA
Endicott College, MA
Evangel University, MO
Faulkner University, AL
Ferrum College, VA
Finlandia University, MI
Flagler College, FL
Furman University, SC
Gardner-Webb University, NC
George Fox University, OR
Georgetown College, KY
Georgia Southern University, GA
Graceland University, IA
Grace University, NE
Grand View University, IA
Green Mountain College, VT
Greenville College, IL
Grove City College, PA

Harding University, AR
Hawai'i Pacific University, HI
Hendrix College, AR
Hillsdale Free Will Baptist College, OK
Houghton College, NY
Houston Baptist University, TX
Howard Payne University, TX
Huntington University, IN
Johnson Bible College, TN
Kutztown University of Pennsylvania, PA
Kuyper College, MI
Lancaster Bible College & Graduate School, PA
Laurel University, NC
Lee University, TN
Limestone College, SC
Lindsey Wilson College, KY
Lipscomb University, TN
Malone University, OH
Maryville University of Saint Louis, MO
McPherson College, KS
Mercyhurst College, PA
Mid-Atlantic Christian University, NC
Millsaps College, MS
Missouri Baptist University, MO
Molloy College, NY
Monmouth College, IL
Moravian College, PA
Morehouse College, GA
Mount Olive College, NC
Mount Vernon Nazarene University, OH
New Hope Christian College, OR
New Jersey Institute of Technology, NJ
New Life Theological Seminary, NC
North Central College, IL
Northwest Christian University, OR
Northwest Nazarene University, ID
Nyack College, NY
Oglethorpe University, GA
Ohio Valley University, WV
Oklahoma Baptist University, OK
Oklahoma City University, OK
Oklahoma Wesleyan University, OK
Olivet Nazarene University, IL
Pacific Union College, CA
Pacific University, OR
Patrick Henry College, VA
Presbyterian College, SC
Principia College, IL
Rosemont College, PA
Sacred Heart Major Seminary, MI
Sacred Heart University, CT
Saint Francis University, PA
St. John's University, NY
Saint Louis University, MO
Saint Martin's University, WA
Saint Mary-of-the-Woods College, IN
St. Olaf College, MN
San Diego Christian College, CA
Schreiner University, TX
Shenandoah University, VA
Shorter University, GA
Siena College, NY
Simpson College, IA
Simpson University, CA
Southern Adventist University, TN
Southwest Baptist University, MO
Southwestern College, KS
Stetson University, FL
Tabor College, KS
Tennessee Wesleyan College, TN
Texas Christian University, TX
Texas Lutheran University, TX
Texas Wesleyan University, TX
Thomas More College, KY
Transylvania University, KY
Trinity Christian College, IL
Union College, NE
Union University, TN
The University of Alabama at Birmingham, AL
University of Great Falls, MT
University of Mary Hardin-Baylor, TX
University of Mobile, AL
The University of North Carolina at Greensboro, NC
University of Puget Sound, WA
University of St. Francis, IL
University of St. Thomas, TX
University of San Diego, CA
University of South Carolina, SC
The University of Tennessee at Chattanooga, TN
University of the Cumberlands, KY
University of the Incarnate Word, TX
University of the Pacific, CA
The University of Toledo, OH
The University of Virginia's College at Wise, VA
University of West Georgia, GA
University of Wisconsin–Stout, WI
Valley Forge Christian College, PA
Virginia Polytechnic Institute and State University, VA
Virginia State University, VA
Virginia Wesleyan College, VA
Walsh University, OH
Washington State University, WA
Wayland Baptist University, TX
Wesleyan College, GA
Wesley College, DE
West Virginia Wesleyan College, WV
Whitworth University, WA
William Jessup University, CA
William Jewell College, MO
Wingate University, NC
Youngstown State University, OH

Rodeo

Angelo State University, TX
Boise State University, ID
California Polytechnic State University, San Luis Obispo, CA
Dickinson State University, ND
Hastings College, NE
Iowa State University of Science and Technology, IA
Lewis-Clark State College, ID
Michigan State University, MI
Montana State University–Northern, MT
Murray State University, KY
New Mexico State University, NM
Northwestern Oklahoma State University, OK
Oklahoma Panhandle State University, OK
Oklahoma State University, OK
Rogers State University, OK
South Dakota State University, SD
Southeastern Louisiana University, LA
Southeastern Oklahoma State University, OK
Southwestern Oklahoma State University, OK
Stephen F. Austin State University, TX
Texas A&M University, TX
Texas Tech University, TX
University of Idaho, ID
The University of Montana, MT
University of Nevada, Las Vegas, NV
The University of Tennessee at Martin, TN
The University of West Alabama, AL
University of Wyoming, WY
Washington State University, WA
West Texas A&M University, TX

Special Characteristics

Adult Students

Agnes Scott College, GA
Allegheny College, PA
American University, DC
Arizona Christian University, AZ
Arkansas State University, AR
Averett University, VA
Ball State University, IN
Bellarmine University, KY
Berry College, GA
Bethel College, IN
Biola University, CA
Birmingham-Southern College, AL
Bloomfield College, NJ
California Lutheran University, CA
California State University, Chico, CA
Calvin College, MI
Campbellsville University, KY
Carroll University, WI
Cedar Crest College, PA
Coe College, IA
College of Mount St. Joseph, OH
College of Saint Elizabeth, NJ
The College of Saint Rose, NY
Dalton State College, GA
Dominican University of California, CA
Dowling College, NY
East Carolina University, NC
ECPI College of Technology, VA
Edinboro University of Pennsylvania, PA
Elon University, NC
Emmanuel College, GA
Evangel University, MO
The Evergreen State College, WA
Faulkner University, AL
Ferris State University, MI
Fitchburg State University, MA
Florida Gulf Coast University, FL
Fordham University, NY
Francis Marion University, SC
Frostburg State University, MD
Gannon University, PA
Georgia College & State University, GA
Georgia Southern University, GA
Golden Gate University, CA
Grace University, NE
Grand Valley State University, MI
Hampton University, VA
Hastings College, NE
Hillsdale Free Will Baptist College, OK
Hollins University, VA
Indiana University of Pennsylvania, PA
Iowa State University of Science and Technology, IA
Juniata College, PA
Kent State University, OH
Kentucky State University, KY
Lancaster Bible College & Graduate School, PA
Lincoln University, MO
Lipscomb University, TN
Long Island University, C.W. Post Campus, NY
Lourdes College, OH
Loyola University Chicago, IL

Non-Need Scholarships for Undergraduates
Special Characteristics

Marywood University, PA
McPherson College, KS
Medaille College, NY
Mercer University, GA
Meredith College, NC
Mesa State College, CO
Messiah College, PA
Metropolitan State College of Denver, CO
Middle Tennessee State University, TN
Millsaps College, MS
Mississippi State University, MS
Mississippi University for Women, MS
Monmouth University, NJ
Montana State University Billings, MT
Montana State University–Northern, MT
Moravian College, PA
Murray State University, KY
New Mexico State University, NM
North Central College, IL
Northeastern Illinois University, IL
Northern Arizona University, AZ
Northern Illinois University, IL
Northern Kentucky University, KY
Northern State University, SD
Northwestern State University of Louisiana, LA
Oakland University, MI
The Ohio State University, OH
Ohio Valley University, WV
Oklahoma State University, OK
Pace University, NY
Palm Beach Atlantic University, FL
Piedmont College, GA
Portland State University, OR
Purdue University North Central, IN
Quincy University, IL
Randolph College, VA
Regis University, CO
The Richard Stockton College of New Jersey, NJ
Rogers State University, OK
Russell Sage College, NY
Sacred Heart University, CT
St. Catherine University, MN
St. Edward's University, TX
Saint Francis University, PA
Saint Mary-of-the-Woods College, IN
San Diego State University, CA
Siena College, NY
Simpson College, IA
Sonoma State University, CA
South Dakota State University, SD
Southeastern Louisiana University, LA
Southern Oregon University, OR
Spring Arbor University, MI
State University of New York at Binghamton, NY
State University of New York College at Cortland, NY
State University of New York College at Geneseo, NY
State University of New York College at Potsdam, NY
Stephen F. Austin State University, TX
Sweet Briar College, VA
Texas Christian University, TX
Thomas More College, KY
Towson University, MD
Trinity Christian College, IL
The University of Akron, OH
The University of Alabama at Birmingham, AL
University of Central Missouri, MO
University of Connecticut, CT
University of Hartford, CT
The University of Kansas, KS
University of Kentucky, KY
University of Louisville, KY
University of Maine at Fort Kent, ME
University of Maryland, College Park, MD
University of Mary Washington, VA
University of Massachusetts Boston, MA
University of Massachusetts Dartmouth, MA
University of Memphis, TN
University of Michigan–Dearborn, MI
University of Michigan–Flint, MI
University of Mississippi, MS
University of Missouri, MO
University of Missouri–St. Louis, MO
University of Nebraska at Omaha, NE
University of Nevada, Las Vegas, NV
University of Nevada, Reno, NV
University of New Orleans, LA
The University of North Carolina at Asheville, NC
The University of North Carolina at Charlotte, NC
The University of North Carolina at Greensboro, NC
University of Northern Colorado, CO
University of Pittsburgh at Bradford, PA
University of South Carolina, SC
The University of Tennessee at Martin, TN
The University of Texas at Dallas, TX
The University of Toledo, OH
University of Vermont, VT
University of West Georgia, GA
University of Wisconsin–Eau Claire, WI
University of Wisconsin–Green Bay, WI
University of Wisconsin–La Crosse, WI
University of Wisconsin–Parkside, WI
University of Wisconsin–Stevens Point, WI
University of Wisconsin–Stout, WI
University of Wyoming, WY
Washburn University, KS
Wesleyan College, GA
Western Kentucky University, KY
Western Oregon University, OR
Wichita State University, KS
Widener University, PA
William Jessup University, CA
Wilson College, PA
Wittenberg University, OH
Wright State University, OH
Youngstown State University, OH

Children and Siblings of Alumni

Adelphi University, NY
Adrian College, MI
Alaska Pacific University, AK
Albion College, MI
Albright College, PA
Alliant International University, CA
Alma College, MI
Alvernia University, PA
American University, DC
Anderson University, SC
Anna Maria College, MA
Appalachian Bible College, WV
Arcadia University, PA
Arizona Christian University, AZ
Arkansas State University, AR
Asbury University, KY
Ashland University, OH
Auburn University, AL
Augsburg College, MN
Augustana College, IL
Augustana College, SD
Aurora University, IL
Averett University, VA
Baldwin-Wallace College, OH
Ball State University, IN
Baptist Bible College of Pennsylvania, PA
Bard College at Simon's Rock, MA
Bellarmine University, KY
Bemidji State University, MN
Benedictine University, IL
Bethany College, WV
Bethel College, KS
Bethel University, MN
Biola University, CA
Birmingham-Southern College, AL
Bloomfield College, NJ
Boston University, MA
Bowling Green State University, OH
Bradley University, IL
Bryan College, TN
Cabrini College, PA
California Lutheran University, CA
California Polytechnic State University, San Luis Obispo, CA
California State Polytechnic University, Pomona, CA
California State University, Monterey Bay, CA
Calumet College of Saint Joseph, IN
Calvary Bible College and Theological Seminary, MO
Calvin College, MI
Canisius College, NY
Capital University, OH
Carroll University, WI
Carson-Newman College, TN
The Catholic University of America, DC
Cedar Crest College, PA
Cedarville University, OH
Centenary College of Louisiana, LA
Central College, IA
Central Methodist University, MO
Central Michigan University, MI
Central Washington University, WA
Centre College, KY
Chestnut Hill College, PA
Christian Brothers University, TN
The Citadel, The Military College of South Carolina, SC
Clarke University, IA
Clarkson University, NY
Coe College, IA
Coker College, SC
The College at Brockport, State University of New York, NY
College of Mount St. Joseph, OH
College of Saint Elizabeth, NJ
The College of Saint Rose, NY
The College of St. Scholastica, MN
Colorado State University–Pueblo, CO
Columbia College, MO
Columbia International University, SC
Concordia University, MI
Concordia University Chicago, IL
Concordia University, Nebraska, NE
Converse College, SC
Crown College, MN
Culver-Stockton College, MO
Daemen College, NY
Delaware Valley College, PA
Delta State University, MS
DePauw University, IN
Dickinson College, PA

Doane College, NE
Dominican University, IL
Dominican University of California, CA
Dordt College, IA
Dowling College, NY
Drake University, IA
Drury University, MO
Duke University, NC
Duquesne University, PA
D'Youville College, NY
East Carolina University, NC
Eastern Kentucky University, KY
Eastern Michigan University, MI
Eastern Nazarene College, MA
East Texas Baptist University, TX
ECPI College of Technology, VA
Edinboro University of Pennsylvania, PA
Elmhurst College, IL
Embry-Riddle Aeronautical University–Prescott, AZ
Emmanuel College, MA
Emporia State University, KS
Endicott College, MA
Erskine College, SC
Eureka College, IL
Evangel University, MO
Fairfield University, CT
Faulkner University, AL
Ferris State University, MI
Fitchburg State University, MA
Florida Institute of Technology, FL
Florida International University, FL
Florida Southern College, FL
Fordham University, NY
Fort Lewis College, CO
Francis Marion University, SC
Franklin College, IN
George Fox University, OR
Georgetown College, KY
Georgia Southern University, GA
Gonzaga University, WA
Gordon College, MA
Graceland University, IA
Grace University, NE
Grand Valley State University, MI
Grand View University, IA
Green Mountain College, VT
Greenville College, IL
Gustavus Adolphus College, MN
Gwynedd-Mercy College, PA
Hamline University, MN
Hanover College, IN
Hartwick College, NY
Hillsdale Free Will Baptist College, OK
Hofstra University, NY
Hollins University, VA
Hood College, MD
Houghton College, NY
Howard Payne University, TX
Huntingdon College, AL
Huntington University, IN
Illinois Institute of Technology, IL
Indiana State University, IN
Indiana University–Purdue University Fort Wayne, IN
Indiana Wesleyan University, IN
Iona College, NY
Iowa State University of Science and Technology, IA
Ithaca College, NY
James Madison University, VA
John Brown University, AR
John Carroll University, OH
Johnson & Wales University, CO
Johnson & Wales University, FL
Johnson & Wales University, RI
Johnson & Wales University—Charlotte Campus, NC
Kalamazoo College, MI
Kennesaw State University, GA
Kent State University, OH
Kent State University at Stark, OH
Keuka College, NY
Keystone College, PA
Lake Forest College, IL
Lancaster Bible College & Graduate School, PA
Lasell College, MA
Lawrence University, WI
Lebanon Valley College, PA
Le Moyne College, NY
Lenoir-Rhyne University, NC
LeTourneau University, TX
Lewis-Clark State College, ID
Lindsey Wilson College, KY
Lipscomb University, TN
Long Island University, Brooklyn Campus, NY
Long Island University, C.W. Post Campus, NY
Longwood University, VA
Loras College, IA
Louisiana State University and Agricultural and Mechanical College, LA
Louisiana Tech University, LA
Luther College, IA
Malone University, OH
Manchester College, IN
Maranatha Baptist Bible College, WI
Marietta College, OH
Maryville College, TN
Marywood University, PA
Massachusetts Maritime Academy, MA
The Master's College and Seminary, CA
Medcenter One College of Nursing, ND
Mercyhurst College, PA
Merrimack College, MA
Methodist University, NC
Michigan State University, MI
Michigan Technological University, MI
Mid-Atlantic Christian University, NC
Mid-Continent University, KY
Midwestern State University, TX
Millikin University, IL
Misericordia University, PA
Mississippi State University, MS
Mississippi University for Women, MS
Missouri Baptist University, MO
Missouri Southern State University, MO
Missouri State University, MO
Missouri University of Science and Technology, MO
Monmouth University, NJ
Montana State University, MT
Montana State University Billings, MT
Montana State University–Northern, MT
Montana Tech of The University of Montana, MT
Montclair State University, NJ
Moravian College, PA
Morehead State University, KY
Morehouse College, GA
Morningside College, IA
Mount St. Mary's College, CA
Murray State University, KY
Muskingum University, OH
Nazareth College of Rochester, NY
Nebraska Wesleyan University, NE
New England College, NH
New Mexico State University, NM
New York Institute of Technology, NY
Nichols College, MA
Northeastern State University, OK
Northern Arizona University, AZ
Northern Kentucky University, KY
Northwest Missouri State University, MO
Northwest Nazarene University, ID
Northwood University, Texas Campus, TX
Notre Dame de Namur University, CA
Nyack College, NY
Ohio Northern University, OH
The Ohio State University, OH
Ohio Wesleyan University, OH
Oklahoma Baptist University, OK
Oklahoma State University, OK
Oklahoma Wesleyan University, OK
Olivet College, MI
Ouachita Baptist University, AR
Pacific Lutheran University, WA
Pacific University, OR
Palm Beach Atlantic University, FL
Peirce College, PA
Penn State Abington, PA
Penn State Altoona, PA
Penn State Berks, PA
Penn State Erie, The Behrend College, PA
Penn State Harrisburg, PA
Penn State University Park, PA
Point Park University, PA
Post University, CT
Principia College, IL
Quincy University, IL
Randolph-Macon College, VA
Regent University, VA
Rensselaer Polytechnic Institute, NY
Research College of Nursing, MO
Rhode Island College, RI
Ripon College, WI
Rivier College, NH
Roberts Wesleyan College, NY
Rockford College, IL
Rockhurst University, MO
Rocky Mountain College, MT
Rosemont College, PA
Russell Sage College, NY
Sage College of Albany, NY
St. Ambrose University, IA
St. Catherine University, MN
Saint Francis University, PA
St. John Fisher College, NY
Saint Joseph's College, IN
St. Joseph's College, Long Island Campus, NY
St. Joseph's College, New York, NY
Saint Joseph's University, PA
St. Lawrence University, NY
Saint Martin's University, WA
Saint Mary-of-the-Woods College, IN
Saint Mary's College of California, CA
St. Mary's College of Maryland, MD
Saint Mary's University of Minnesota, MN
Saint Vincent College, PA
San Diego Christian College, CA
San Diego State University, CA
Santa Clara University, CA
Seattle Pacific University, WA
Seattle University, WA
Seton Hill University, PA
Shimer College, IL

Shippensburg University of Pennsylvania, PA
Siena College, NY
Silver Lake College, WI
Simmons College, MA
Simpson College, IA
Slippery Rock University of Pennsylvania, PA
Sonoma State University, CA
Southeastern Louisiana University, LA
Southeastern Oklahoma State University, OK
Southern Adventist University, TN
Southern Illinois University Carbondale, IL
Southern Utah University, UT
Southwestern Oklahoma State University, OK
Southwest Minnesota State University, MN
State University of New York at Fredonia, NY
State University of New York College at Potsdam, NY
Stephen F. Austin State University, TX
Stetson University, FL
Suffolk University, MA
Tabor College, KS
Taylor University, IN
Tennessee Technological University, TN
Tennessee Wesleyan College, TN
Texas Lutheran University, TX
Texas State University–San Marcos, TX
Texas Wesleyan University, TX
Thiel College, PA
Thomas More College, KY
Trine University, IN
Trinity Christian College, IL
Truman State University, MO
Union College, KY
Union University, TN
The University of Alabama at Birmingham, AL
University of Arkansas, AR
University of Central Missouri, MO
University of Cincinnati, OH
University of Delaware, DE
University of Dubuque, IA
University of Evansville, IN
University of Hawaii at Manoa, HI
University of Idaho, ID
University of Illinois at Springfield, IL
University of Illinois at Urbana–Champaign, IL
The University of Iowa, IA
University of Kentucky, KY
University of Louisville, KY
University of Mary Hardin-Baylor, TX
University of Mary Washington, VA
University of Massachusetts Amherst, MA
University of Massachusetts Lowell, MA
University of Michigan–Dearborn, MI
University of Michigan–Flint, MI
University of Minnesota, Crookston, MN
University of Mississippi, MS
University of Missouri, MO
University of Missouri–St. Louis, MO
The University of Montana, MT
University of Mount Union, OH
University of Nebraska at Omaha, NE
University of Nebraska–Lincoln, NE
University of Nevada, Las Vegas, NV
University of Nevada, Reno, NV
University of New Hampshire, NH
University of New Orleans, LA
The University of North Carolina at Asheville, NC
The University of North Carolina at Pembroke, NC
University of Northern Colorado, CO
University of Oklahoma, OK
University of Rhode Island, RI
University of Rio Grande, OH
University of Rochester, NY
University of St. Francis, IL
University of South Alabama, AL
University of South Carolina, SC
University of Southern California, CA
University of Southern Mississippi, MS
The University of Tampa, FL
The University of Tennessee, TN
The University of Tennessee at Chattanooga, TN
University of the Cumberlands, KY
University of the Incarnate Word, TX
University of the Ozarks, AR
The University of Toledo, OH
University of Tulsa, OK
University of West Florida, FL
University of West Georgia, GA
University of Wisconsin–Green Bay, WI
University of Wisconsin–La Crosse, WI
University of Wyoming, WY
Upper Iowa University, IA
Ursinus College, PA
Ursuline College, OH
Utah State University, UT
Valparaiso University, IN
Virginia Military Institute, VA
Wake Forest University, NC
Walsh University, OH
Warner Pacific College, OR
Wartburg College, IA
Washburn University, KS
Washington & Jefferson College, PA
Washington State University, WA
Wayland Baptist University, TX
Webber International University, FL
Wells College, NY
Wesleyan College, GA
Western State College of Colorado, CO
West Liberty University, WV
Westminster College, MO
Westminster College, PA
West Texas A&M University, TX
West Virginia Wesleyan College, WV
Wheeling Jesuit University, WV
Whittier College, CA
Whitworth University, WA
William Jewell College, MO
Wilson College, PA
Wingate University, NC
Winona State University, MN
Wittenberg University, OH
Wright State University, OH
Xavier University, OH
York College of Pennsylvania, PA
Youngstown State University, OH

Children of Current Students

Alliant International University, CA
Alma College, MI
Augustana College, SD
Bethel College, KS
Bethesda Christian University, CA
Bloomfield College, NJ
Bryan College, TN
Caldwell College, NJ
California State Polytechnic University, Pomona, CA
Carroll University, WI
Central College, IA
Cincinnati Christian University, OH
The College of New Rochelle, NY
Columbia College, MO
ECPI College of Technology, VA
Elmhurst College, IL
Emmanuel College, GA
Finlandia University, MI
Grace University, NE
Green Mountain College, VT
Huntington University, IN
Johnson Bible College, TN
Lancaster Bible College & Graduate School, PA
Marymount University, VA
Marywood University, PA
Misericordia University, PA
Missouri Baptist University, MO
Mount Aloysius College, PA
Mount Marty College, SD
Northwest University, WA
Palm Beach Atlantic University, FL
Rivier College, NH
Rockford College, IL
Sacred Heart University, CT
St. Catherine University, MN
Saint Francis University, PA
Saint Mary-of-the-Woods College, IN
Union University, TN
The University of Alabama at Birmingham, AL
University of Great Falls, MT
University of Hartford, CT
Upper Iowa University, IA
Valley Forge Christian College, PA
Wesleyan College, GA
Wilson College, PA

Children of Educators

Agnes Scott College, GA
Alfred University, NY
Allegheny College, PA
Appalachian Bible College, WV
Arizona Christian University, AZ
Aurora University, IL
Austin Peay State University, TN
Bard College, NY
Benedictine College, KS
Bennington College, VT
Bethesda Christian University, CA
Bryan College, TN
Calvary Bible College and Theological Seminary, MO
Campbellsville University, KY
Canisius College, NY
Centenary College of Louisiana, LA
Chowan University, NC
Coe College, IA
The College of Wooster, OH
Columbia College, MO
Columbus College of Art & Design, OH
Concordia University, Nebraska, NE
Cornell College, IA
Dominican University, IL
Dowling College, NY
East Texas Baptist University, TX
Emmanuel College, MA
Emory & Henry College, VA
Endicott College, MA
Evangel University, MO
Flagler College, FL
Florida College, FL
Goshen College, IN
Governors State University, IL
Grand View University, IA

Hampden-Sydney College, VA
Hardin-Simmons University, TX
Hastings College, NE
Hendrix College, AR
Hillsdale Free Will Baptist College, OK
Jacksonville University, FL
John Brown University, AR
John Carroll University, OH
Johnson Bible College, TN
King's College, PA
Lipscomb University, TN
Lycoming College, PA
Maranatha Baptist Bible College, WI
Mary Baldwin College, VA
Mississippi State University, MS
Moravian College, PA
Mount St. Mary's University, MD
Nebraska Wesleyan University, NE
New England College, NH
New Jersey Institute of Technology, NJ
New York Institute of Technology, NY
Northern Arizona University, AZ
Northwest Nazarene University, ID
Occidental College, CA
Oklahoma Wesleyan University, OK
Palm Beach Atlantic University, FL
Research College of Nursing, MO
Rockford College, IL
Rosemont College, PA
Russell Sage College, NY
Sage College of Albany, NY
Saint Anselm College, NH
St. Catherine University, MN
Saint Francis University, PA
Saint Mary's College of California, CA
Salem College, NC
Seattle University, WA
Simpson College, IA
Sonoma State University, CA
Southern Illinois University Carbondale, IL
Tennessee Technological University, TN
Texas Christian University, TX
Union University, TN
Unity College, ME
The University of Alabama at Birmingham, AL
University of Central Missouri, MO
University of Dubuque, IA
University of Kentucky, KY
University of Memphis, TN
University of St. Francis, IL
University of St. Thomas, MN
The University of Scranton, PA
The University of Tennessee at Martin, TN
Villanova University, PA
Wright State University, OH

Children of Faculty/Staff

Abilene Christian University, TX
Adelphi University, NY
Adrian College, MI
Agnes Scott College, GA
Alaska Pacific University, AK
Alcorn State University, MS
Alderson-Broaddus College, WV
Alfred University, NY
Allegheny College, PA
Allen College, IA
Alliant International University, CA
Alvernia University, PA
Alverno College, WI
American University, DC
Amridge University, AL
Anderson University, SC
Andrews University, MI
Anna Maria College, MA
Appalachian Bible College, WV
Arizona Christian University, AZ
Arkansas State University, AR
Asbury University, KY
Ashland University, OH
Auburn University, AL
Augustana College, IL
Augustana College, SD
Aurora University, IL
Austin College, TX
Austin Peay State University, TN
Ball State University, IN
Baptist Bible College of Pennsylvania, PA
Bard College, NY
Bard College at Simon's Rock, MA
Baylor University, TX
Bellarmine University, KY
Belmont Abbey College, NC
Belmont University, TN
Bemidji State University, MN
Bennington College, VT
Berklee College of Music, MA
Berry College, GA
Bethany College, WV
Bethany Lutheran College, MN
Bethel College, IN
Bethel College, KS
Bethel University, MN
Bethesda Christian University, CA
Beulah Heights University, GA
Biola University, CA
Birmingham-Southern College, AL
Bloomsburg University of Pennsylvania, PA
Bluefield College, VA
Bluffton University, OH
Bowdoin College, ME
Bowling Green State University, OH
Bradley University, IL
Brenau University, GA
Brevard College, NC
Bryan College, TN
Buena Vista University, IA
California Lutheran University, CA
California State University, Bakersfield, CA
California State University, Chico, CA
California State University, Stanislaus, CA
Calumet College of Saint Joseph, IN
Calvary Bible College and Theological Seminary, MO
Calvin College, MI
Campbellsville University, KY
Campbell University, NC
Canisius College, NY
Capital University, OH
Carroll College, MT
Carroll University, WI
Case Western Reserve University, OH
The Catholic University of America, DC
Cedarville University, OH
Centenary College of Louisiana, LA
Central College, IA
Central Methodist University, MO
Central Michigan University, MI
Centre College, KY
Chestnut Hill College, PA
Chowan University, NC
Cincinnati Christian University, OH
Clarke University, IA
Clarkson University, NY
Cleary University, MI
Clemson University, SC
Cleveland Institute of Music, OH
Cleveland State University, OH
Coe College, IA
Coker College, SC
College of Mount St. Joseph, OH
The College of New Rochelle, NY
College of Saint Mary, NE
The College of Saint Rose, NY
The College of St. Scholastica, MN
College of the Holy Cross, MA
College of Visual Arts, MN
The College of Wooster, OH
Colorado State University, CO
Colorado State University–Pueblo, CO
Columbia College, MO
Columbus College of Art & Design, OH
Concordia College, MN
Concordia University, CA
Concordia University, MI
Concordia University Chicago, IL
Concordia University, Nebraska, NE
Concordia University, St. Paul, MN
Concord University, WV
Converse College, SC
Corban University, OR
Cornell College, IA
Cornerstone University, MI
Covenant College, GA
Creighton University, NE
Crossroads Bible College, IN
Crown College, MN
Culver-Stockton College, MO
Daemen College, NY
Dallas Baptist University, TX
Dalton State College, GA
Defiance College, OH
Delta State University, MS
DePaul University, IL
DePauw University, IN
Dickinson College, PA
Dickinson State University, ND
Dillard University, LA
Doane College, NE
Dominican College, NY
Dominican University, IL
Dominican University of California, CA
Dordt College, IA
Dowling College, NY
Drury University, MO
Duquesne University, PA
D'Youville College, NY
East Carolina University, NC
Eastern Connecticut State University, CT
Eastern Kentucky University, KY
East Texas Baptist University, TX
Eckerd College, FL
ECPI College of Technology, VA
Edgewood College, WI
Edinboro University of Pennsylvania, PA
Elizabethtown College, PA
Elmira College, NY
Elon University, NC
Embry-Riddle Aeronautical University–Daytona, FL
Embry-Riddle Aeronautical University–Prescott, AZ
Embry-Riddle Aeronautical University–Worldwide, FL
Emmanuel College, GA
Emmanuel College, MA
Emory & Henry College, VA
Emporia State University, KS

Erskine College, SC
Eureka College, IL
Evangel University, MO
Fairfield University, CT
Faulkner University, AL
Felician College, NJ
Ferrum College, VA
Finlandia University, MI
Flagler College, FL
Florida College, FL
Florida Institute of Technology, FL
Florida Southern College, FL
Fordham University, NY
Fort Lewis College, CO
Framingham State University, MA
Francis Marion University, SC
Franklin College, IN
Free Will Baptist Bible College, TN
Fresno Pacific University, CA
Furman University, SC
Gardner-Webb University, NC
Geneva College, PA
George Fox University, OR
Georgetown College, KY
Georgetown University, DC
Georgia College & State University, GA
Georgian Court University, NJ
Gonzaga University, WA
Goshen College, IN
Grace Bible College, MI
Grace College, IN
Graceland University, IA
Grace University, NE
Grand Valley State University, MI
Grand View University, IA
Greenville College, IL
Hampden-Sydney College, VA
Hampshire College, MA
Hampton University, VA
Hannibal-LaGrange University, MO
Hanover College, IN
Harding University, AR
Hardin-Simmons University, TX
Hartwick College, NY
Hastings College, NE
Heidelberg University, OH
Hendrix College, AR
Hillsdale College, MI
Hillsdale Free Will Baptist College, OK
Hollins University, VA
Hood College, MD
Hope International University, CA
Houghton College, NY
Houston Baptist University, TX
Howard Payne University, TX
Huntingdon College, AL
Huntington University, IN
Illinois College, IL
Illinois Institute of Technology, IL
Illinois State University, IL
Illinois Wesleyan University, IL
Indiana State University, IN
Indiana University of Pennsylvania, PA
Indiana Wesleyan University, IN
Iona College, NY
Iowa Wesleyan College, IA
Ithaca College, NY
Jackson State University, MS
Jacksonville University, FL
James Madison University, VA
Jamestown College, ND
John Brown University, AR
John Carroll University, OH
The Johns Hopkins University, MD
Johnson & Wales University, CO
Johnson & Wales University, FL
Johnson & Wales University, RI
Johnson & Wales University—Charlotte Campus, NC
Johnson Bible College, TN
Johnson C. Smith University, NC
Juniata College, PA
Kent State University, OH
Kentucky Wesleyan College, KY
Kettering University, MI
Keuka College, NY
King College, TN
King's College, PA
Kutztown University of Pennsylvania, PA
Kuyper College, MI
Lancaster Bible College & Graduate School, PA
Lasell College, MA
Laurel University, NC
Lawrence Technological University, MI
Lebanon Valley College, PA
Lee University, TN
Lehigh University, PA
LeMoyne-Owen College, TN
Lenoir-Rhyne University, NC
Lewis & Clark College, OR
Liberty University, VA
Limestone College, SC
Lincoln Memorial University, TN
Lincoln University, MO
Lindsey Wilson College, KY
Linfield College, OR
Lipscomb University, TN
Long Island University, Brooklyn Campus, NY
Long Island University, C.W. Post Campus, NY
Louisiana College, LA
Louisiana Tech University, LA
Loyola University New Orleans, LA
Lubbock Christian University, TX
Lycoming College, PA
Lynn University, FL
Lyon College, AR
Maine College of Art, ME
Maine Maritime Academy, ME
Malone University, OH
Manhattan Christian College, KS
Manhattan College, NY
Maranatha Baptist Bible College, WI
Marian University, WI
Marquette University, WI
Marshall University, WV
Mars Hill College, NC
Mary Baldwin College, VA
Marymount University, VA
Maryville College, TN
Maryville University of Saint Louis, MO
Marywood University, PA
Massachusetts College of Art and Design, MA
Massachusetts Maritime Academy, MA
The Master's College and Seminary, CA
Mayville State University, ND
McKendree University, IL
McMurry University, TX
McNally Smith College of Music, MN
Medaille College, NY
Mercer University, GA
Mercyhurst College, PA
Meredith College, NC
Merrimack College, MA
Messiah College, PA
Methodist University, NC
Miami University, OH
Michigan State University, MI
Mid-Atlantic Christian University, NC
Mid-Continent University, KY
Midwestern State University, TX
Milligan College, TN
Millikin University, IL
Millsaps College, MS
Milwaukee School of Engineering, WI
Minnesota State University Moorhead, MN
Minot State University, ND
Misericordia University, PA
Mississippi State University, MS
Mississippi University for Women, MS
Missouri Baptist University, MO
Missouri Southern State University, MO
Missouri University of Science and Technology, MO
Monmouth University, NJ
Montana State University Billings, MT
Montana Tech of The University of Montana, MT
Montreat College, NC
Moravian College, PA
Morehouse College, GA
Morningside College, IA
Mount Carmel College of Nursing, OH
Mount Marty College, SD
Mount Mary College, WI
Mount Olive College, NC
Mount Saint Mary College, NY
Mount St. Mary's University, MD
Mount Vernon Nazarene University, OH
Murray State University, KY
Nazareth College of Rochester, NY
Nebraska Wesleyan University, NE
New England College, NH
New Jersey Institute of Technology, NJ
New Mexico State University, NM
New York Institute of Technology, NY
Niagara University, NY
Nicholls State University, LA
Nichols College, MA
North Central College, IL
Northeastern Illinois University, IL
Northeastern State University, OK
Northern Arizona University, AZ
Northern Illinois University, IL
Northern Kentucky University, KY
Northern Michigan University, MI
Northwest Christian University, OR
Northwestern College, MN
Northwestern Oklahoma State University, OK
Northwestern State University of Louisiana, LA
Northwest Missouri State University, MO
Northwest Nazarene University, ID
Northwest University, WA
Northwood University, Texas Campus, TX
Notre Dame de Namur University, CA
Nyack College, NY
Occidental College, CA
Oglethorpe University, GA
Ohio Northern University, OH
The Ohio State University, OH
Ohio University, OH
Ohio University–Chillicothe, OH
Ohio University–Eastern, OH
Ohio University–Lancaster, OH
Ohio University–Southern Campus, OH
Ohio University–Zanesville, OH

Ohio Valley University, WV
Oklahoma Baptist University, OK
Oklahoma Christian University, OK
Oklahoma City University, OK
Oklahoma Panhandle State University, OK
Oklahoma Wesleyan University, OK
Old Dominion University, VA
Olivet College, MI
Olivet Nazarene University, IL
Ouachita Baptist University, AR
Our Lady of Holy Cross College, LA
Our Lady of the Lake University of San Antonio, TX
Pace University, NY
Pacific University, OR
Palm Beach Atlantic University, FL
Patrick Henry College, VA
Philadelphia Biblical University, PA
Piedmont College, GA
Plymouth State University, NH
Point Park University, PA
Pontifical Catholic University of Puerto Rico, PR
Presbyterian College, SC
Principia College, IL
Purdue University, IN
Purdue University North Central, IN
Quincy University, IL
Quinnipiac University, CT
Ramapo College of New Jersey, NJ
Randolph College, VA
Randolph-Macon College, VA
Regent University, VA
Regis University, CO
Rensselaer Polytechnic Institute, NY
Research College of Nursing, MO
Rhodes College, TN
The Richard Stockton College of New Jersey, NJ
Ripon College, WI
Robert Morris University Illinois, IL
Roberts Wesleyan College, NY
Rochester Institute of Technology, NY
Rockford College, IL
Rockhurst University, MO
Rocky Mountain College, MT
Rocky Mountain College of Art + Design, CO
Rosemont College, PA
Russell Sage College, NY
Sacred Heart University, CT
Sage College of Albany, NY
St. Ambrose University, IA
Saint Anselm College, NH
Saint Augustine's College, NC
St. Bonaventure University, NY
St. Catherine University, MN
St. Edward's University, TX
Saint Francis University, PA
St. John Fisher College, NY
St. John's University, NY
Saint Joseph's College, IN
St. Joseph's College, Long Island Campus, NY
St. Joseph's College, New York, NY
St. Louis College of Pharmacy, MO
Saint Louis University, MO
Saint Martin's University, WA
Saint Mary-of-the-Woods College, IN
Saint Mary's College of California, CA
St. Mary's College of Maryland, MD
Saint Mary's University of Minnesota, MN
St. Norbert College, WI
Saint Xavier University, IL
Salem College, NC
Samford University, AL
San Diego Christian College, CA
San Diego State University, CA
Santa Clara University, CA
Santa Fe University of Art and Design, NM
Schreiner University, TX
Seattle Pacific University, WA
Seattle University, WA
Sewanee: The University of the South, TN
Shenandoah University, VA
Shorter University, GA
Siena College, NY
Simpson College, IA
Simpson University, CA
Skidmore College, NY
Slippery Rock University of Pennsylvania, PA
Sonoma State University, CA
South Dakota State University, SD
Southeastern Louisiana University, LA
Southeast Missouri State University, MO
Southern Connecticut State University, CT
Southern Illinois University Carbondale, IL
Southern Illinois University Edwardsville, IL
Southwestern College, KS
Southwestern University, TX
Spring Arbor University, MI
Springfield College, MA
Spring Hill College, AL
State University of New York at Binghamton, NY
State University of New York at New Paltz, NY
State University of New York College at Potsdam, NY
Stephen F. Austin State University, TX
Stetson University, FL
Stonehill College, MA
Suffolk University, MA
Tabor College, KS
Taylor University, IN
Temple University, PA
Tennessee Technological University, TN
Tennessee Wesleyan College, TN
Texas A&M University, TX
Texas Christian University, TX
Texas Lutheran University, TX
Texas Tech University, TX
Thiel College, PA
Thomas More College, KY
Thomas University, GA
Tiffin University, OH
Towson University, MD
Transylvania University, KY
Trevecca Nazarene University, TN
Trine University, IN
Trinity Christian College, IL
Truman State University, MO
Tulane University, LA
Tuskegee University, AL
Union College, KY
Union College, NY
Union University, TN
University of Advancing Technology, AZ
The University of Alabama at Birmingham, AL
The University of Arizona, AZ
University of Arkansas, AR
University of Bridgeport, CT
University of Central Missouri, MO
University of Connecticut, CT
University of Dallas, TX
University of Dayton, OH
University of Delaware, DE
University of Dubuque, IA
University of Evansville, IN
The University of Findlay, OH
University of Florida, FL
University of Great Falls, MT
University of Hartford, CT
University of Idaho, ID
University of Illinois at Urbana–Champaign, IL
University of Indianapolis, IN
The University of Kansas, KS
University of Kentucky, KY
University of La Verne, CA
University of Louisville, KY
University of Maine at Fort Kent, ME
University of Maine at Presque Isle, ME
University of Mary, ND
University of Mary Hardin-Baylor, TX
University of Mary Washington, VA
University of Massachusetts Amherst, MA
University of Massachusetts Boston, MA
University of Massachusetts Dartmouth, MA
University of Massachusetts Lowell, MA
University of Memphis, TN
University of Miami, FL
University of Michigan, MI
University of Michigan–Dearborn, MI
University of Michigan–Flint, MI
University of Minnesota, Crookston, MN
University of Mississippi, MS
University of Missouri, MO
University of Missouri–St. Louis, MO
University of Montevallo, AL
University of Mount Union, OH
University of Nebraska at Omaha, NE
University of Nevada, Las Vegas, NV
University of New Hampshire, NH
University of New Hampshire at Manchester, NH
University of North Alabama, AL
The University of North Carolina at Asheville, NC
The University of North Carolina at Chapel Hill, NC
The University of North Carolina at Greensboro, NC
University of North Dakota, ND
University of Northern Colorado, CO
University of Notre Dame, IN
University of Oregon, OR
University of Pittsburgh at Bradford, PA
University of Pittsburgh at Johnstown, PA
University of Portland, OR
University of Puget Sound, WA
University of Rio Grande, OH
University of Rochester, NY
University of St. Thomas, MN
University of St. Thomas, TX
University of San Diego, CA
University of Science and Arts of Oklahoma, OK
The University of Scranton, PA
University of South Alabama, AL
University of South Carolina, SC
University of Southern California, CA
University of Southern Indiana, IN
University of Southern Maine, ME
University of Southern Mississippi, MS
The University of Tampa, FL
The University of Tennessee at Chattanooga, TN
The University of Tennessee at Martin, TN

The University of Texas at Brownsville, TX
The University of Texas at Tyler, TX
University of the Cumberlands, KY
University of the District of Columbia, DC
University of the Incarnate Word, TX
University of the Ozarks, AR
University of the Southwest, NM
The University of Toledo, OH
University of Tulsa, OK
University of Utah, UT
The University of West Alabama, AL
Ursinus College, PA
Ursuline College, OH
Utah State University, UT
Valley City State University, ND
Valley Forge Christian College, PA
Valparaiso University, IN
Vanguard University of Southern California, CA
Victory University, TN
Villanova University, PA
Virginia Military Institute, VA
Virginia Polytechnic Institute and State University, VA
Virginia Wesleyan College, VA
Wabash College, IN
Wagner College, NY
Waldorf College, IA
Walla Walla University, WA
Walsh University, OH
Warren Wilson College, NC
Wartburg College, IA
Washburn University, KS
Washington Adventist University, MD
Washington & Jefferson College, PA
Washington College, MD
Washington State University, WA
Wayland Baptist University, TX
Waynesburg University, PA
Wayne State College, NE
Wayne State University, MI
Webber International University, FL
Wesleyan College, GA
West Chester University of Pennsylvania, PA
Western Illinois University, IL
Western Michigan University, MI
Western New England University, MA
West Liberty University, WV
Westminster College, MO
Westmont College, CA
West Texas A&M University, TX
West Virginia University, WV
West Virginia Wesleyan College, WV
Wheeling Jesuit University, WV
Whittier College, CA
Widener University, PA
Wilkes University, PA
William Jessup University, CA
William Jewell College, MO
Williams Baptist College, AR
Wilson College, PA
Winona State University, MN
Winthrop University, SC
Wittenberg University, OH
Wofford College, SC
Wright State University, OH
York College, NE
Young Harris College, GA
Youngstown State University, OH

Children of Public Servants

California State University, San Bernardino, CA
College of Staten Island of the City University of New York, NY
Dowling College, NY
Framingham State University, MA
Georgia Southern University, GA
Governors State University, IL
Illinois Institute of Technology, IL
Louisiana Tech University, LA
Mercer University, GA
Mississippi State University, MS
Monmouth University, NJ
New Mexico State University, NM
New York Institute of Technology, NY
Northern Arizona University, AZ
Northern Kentucky University, KY
Northwestern State University of Louisiana, LA
The Ohio State University, OH
Patrick Henry College, VA
Peirce College, PA
Siena College, NY
Sonoma State University, CA
Southern Illinois University Carbondale, IL
Tennessee Technological University, TN
The University of Alabama at Birmingham, AL
University of Delaware, DE
University of Kentucky, KY
University of Massachusetts Lowell, MA
University of Memphis, TN
University of Nevada, Las Vegas, NV
University of New Orleans, LA
The University of Texas at Dallas, TX
The University of Toledo, OH
University of Utah, UT
University of Wisconsin–Green Bay, WI
Valdosta State University, GA
Washington State University, WA
Western Washington University, WA

Children of Union Members/Company Employees

Adrian College, MI
Auburn University, AL
Averett University, VA
California State University, Bakersfield, CA
Calvin College, MI
Carroll College, MT
The College of Saint Rose, NY
Dowling College, NY
Eastern Connecticut State University, CT
Eastern Washington University, WA
East Tennessee State University, TN
Edinboro University of Pennsylvania, PA
Emmanuel College, MA
Emporia State University, KS
Framingham State University, MA
Francis Marion University, SC
Frostburg State University, MD
Grand Valley State University, MI
Hofstra University, NY
Husson University, ME
Illinois State University, IL
Kennesaw State University, GA
Kent State University, OH
Kutztown University of Pennsylvania, PA
Massachusetts College of Art and Design, MA
Michigan State University, MI
Mid-Continent University, KY
Midwestern State University, TX
Millersville University of Pennsylvania, PA
Millikin University, IL
Montana State University Billings, MT
New Jersey Institute of Technology, NJ
New Mexico State University, NM
Northern Michigan University, MI
The Ohio State University, OH
The Richard Stockton College of New Jersey, NJ
Sacred Heart University, CT
Saint Joseph's University, PA
Shorter University, GA
Siena College, NY
Slippery Rock University of Pennsylvania, PA
Sonoma State University, CA
Southwest Minnesota State University, MN
Stephen F. Austin State University, TX
Stonehill College, MA
Texas Christian University, TX
Thomas More College, KY
The University of Alabama, AL
The University of Alabama at Birmingham, AL
University of Connecticut, CT
University of Hartford, CT
University of Kentucky, KY
University of Louisville, KY
University of Massachusetts Boston, MA
University of Massachusetts Lowell, MA
University of Michigan–Flint, MI
University of Nevada, Las Vegas, NV
University of Northern Colorado, CO
University of Pittsburgh at Bradford, PA
University of South Carolina, SC
The University of Tennessee at Chattanooga, TN
The University of Tennessee at Martin, TN
The University of Toledo, OH
University of Wisconsin–La Crosse, WI
University of Wisconsin–Parkside, WI
Western Kentucky University, KY
Western New England University, MA
Western Washington University, WA
West Texas A&M University, TX
West Virginia University, WV
York College of Pennsylvania, PA
Youngstown State University, OH

Children of Workers in Trades

Dowling College, NY
Grand Valley State University, MI
Huntingdon College, AL
Kennesaw State University, GA
Marywood University, PA
Midwestern State University, TX
New Mexico State University, NM
The Ohio State University, OH
San Diego State University, CA
Siena College, NY
Sonoma State University, CA
South Dakota State University, SD
Texas Christian University, TX
The University of Alabama at Birmingham, AL
University of Kentucky, KY
University of Michigan, MI
University of South Carolina, SC
University of Wisconsin–Parkside, WI
Western Oregon University, OR
West Virginia University, WV
Worcester Polytechnic Institute, MA
Youngstown State University, OH

Children with a Deceased or Disabled Parent

Anna Maria College, MA
The Baptist College of Florida, FL
California State University, San Bernardino, CA
The Citadel, The Military College of South Carolina, SC
The College of New Jersey, NJ
College of Staten Island of the City University of New York, NY
Dickinson State University, ND
Edinboro University of Pennsylvania, PA
Elmhurst College, IL
Erskine College, SC
Fordham University, NY
Georgia College & State University, GA
Harding University, AR
Illinois State University, IL
Kent State University, OH
Kentucky State University, KY
Lipscomb University, TN
Louisiana State University and Agricultural and Mechanical College, LA
Marian University, WI
Midwestern State University, TX
Millikin University, IL
New Mexico State University, NM
Northeastern State University, OK
Northern Kentucky University, KY
Pace University, NY
Santa Clara University, CA
Siena College, NY
Southern Illinois University Carbondale, IL
The University of Alabama at Birmingham, AL
University of Hartford, CT
University of Kentucky, KY
University of Louisville, KY
University of Massachusetts Dartmouth, MA
The University of Montana, MT
University of Nevada, Las Vegas, NV
University of New Orleans, LA
University of South Carolina, SC
The University of Tennessee at Chattanooga, TN
The University of Texas at Arlington, TX
University of Utah, UT
The University of Virginia's College at Wise, VA
Washington State University, WA
Wayne State College, NE
Youngstown State University, OH

Ethnic Background

Abilene Christian University, TX
Adrian College, MI
Alaska Pacific University, AK
Albright College, PA
Alderson-Broaddus College, WV
Alliant International University, CA
American University, DC
Arizona Christian University, AZ
Arkansas State University, AR
Armstrong Atlantic State University, GA
Asbury University, KY
Auburn University, AL
Augustana College, IL
Augustana College, SD
Austin College, TX
Austin Peay State University, TN
Bellarmine University, KY
Benedictine College, KS
Berry College, GA
Bethel College, KS
Bethel University, MN
Biola University, CA
Birmingham-Southern College, AL
Bluefield College, VA
Boise State University, ID
Buena Vista University, IA
California State University, Bakersfield, CA
California State University, Chico, CA
Calvin College, MI
Capital University, OH
Cedarville University, OH
Centenary College of Louisiana, LA
Central Michigan University, MI
Centre College, KY
Clemson University, SC
The College at Brockport, State University of New York, NY
The College of Saint Rose, NY
The College of St. Scholastica, MN
Colorado State University–Pueblo, CO
Columbia International University, SC
Concordia University, MI
Cornell College, IA
Dickinson State University, ND
DigiPen Institute of Technology, WA
Dowling College, NY
Duke University, NC
Duquesne University, PA
Earlham College, IN
East Carolina University, NC
Eastern Michigan University, MI
Eastern Washington University, WA
Elizabeth City State University, NC
Elmhurst College, IL
Elon University, NC
Emmanuel College, MA
Erskine College, SC
Fairfield University, CT
Ferris State University, MI
Fitchburg State University, MA
Flagler College, FL
Florida Agricultural and Mechanical University, FL
Florida Gulf Coast University, FL
Fort Lewis College, CO
Franklin College, IN
Furman University, SC
Gannon University, PA
George Fox University, OR
Grace University, NE
Grove City College, PA
Gustavus Adolphus College, MN
Hamline University, MN
Hampden-Sydney College, VA
Hardin-Simmons University, TX
Hawai'i Pacific University, HI
Hope College, MI
Huntington University, IN
Illinois Institute of Technology, IL
Indiana University of Pennsylvania, PA
Iowa State University of Science and Technology, IA
John Brown University, AR
John Carroll University, OH
Johnson Bible College, TN
Johnson C. Smith University, NC
Juniata College, PA
Kennesaw State University, GA
Kent State University, OH
Kentucky State University, KY
Kenyon College, OH
Lawrence University, WI
Lebanon Valley College, PA
Lenoir-Rhyne University, NC
Lesley University, MA
Lewis-Clark State College, ID
Long Island University, Brooklyn Campus, NY
Lourdes College, OH
Lyon College, AR
Macalester College, MN
Manchester College, IN
Marietta College, OH
Maryville University of Saint Louis, MO
Marywood University, PA
McMurry University, TX
Meredith College, NC
Millsaps College, MS
Minot State University, ND
Mississippi University for Women, MS
Missouri Southern State University, MO
Molloy College, NY
Montana State University Billings, MT
Moravian College, PA
Muskingum University, OH
New England College, NH
New Jersey Institute of Technology, NJ
New Mexico State University, NM
Northern Illinois University, IL
Northern State University, SD
Northland College, WI
Northwestern College, MN
Northwest Nazarene University, ID
Oakland University, MI
Ohio Northern University, OH
The Ohio State University, OH
Ohio Valley University, WV
Oklahoma State University, OK
Ouachita Baptist University, AR
Pacific University, OR
Portland State University, OR
Randolph-Macon College, VA
Rensselaer Polytechnic Institute, NY
The Richard Stockton College of New Jersey, NJ
Ripon College, WI
Russell Sage College, NY
Sacred Heart University, CT
St. Catherine University, MN
St. John Fisher College, NY
Saint Martin's University, WA
Saint Mary-of-the-Woods College, IN
Sewanee: The University of the South, TN
Shawnee State University, OH
Shepherd University, WV
Siena College, NY
Simpson College, IA
Slippery Rock University of Pennsylvania, PA
Sonoma State University, CA
South Dakota School of Mines and Technology, SD
South Dakota State University, SD
Southwest Minnesota State University, MN
State University of New York at Binghamton, NY
State University of New York at Fredonia, NY
State University of New York at New Paltz, NY
State University of New York College at Geneseo, NY
State University of New York College at Potsdam, NY
Stetson University, FL

Stony Brook University, State University of New York, NY
Taylor University, IN
Tennessee Technological University, TN
Texas Christian University, TX
Thomas University, GA
Trinity Christian College, IL
Union University, TN
The University of Alabama at Birmingham, AL
The University of Arizona, AZ
University of Arkansas, AR
University of California, San Diego, CA
University of Central Missouri, MO
University of Central Oklahoma, OK
University of Cincinnati, OH
University of Delaware, DE
University of Dubuque, IA
University of Great Falls, MT
University of Hartford, CT
University of Idaho, ID
University of Illinois at Springfield, IL
University of Indianapolis, IN
The University of Iowa, IA
The University of Kansas, KS
University of Kentucky, KY
University of Louisville, KY
University of Maine at Presque Isle, ME
University of Mary Hardin-Baylor, TX
University of Michigan–Dearborn, MI
University of Minnesota, Crookston, MN
University of Minnesota, Morris, MN
University of Mississippi, MS
University of Missouri, MO
University of Missouri–Kansas City, MO
University of Missouri–St. Louis, MO
University of Mount Union, OH
University of Nebraska at Omaha, NE
University of Nebraska–Lincoln, NE
University of Nevada, Las Vegas, NV
University of Nevada, Reno, NV
The University of North Carolina at Asheville, NC
The University of North Carolina at Greensboro, NC
University of North Dakota, ND
University of Northern Colorado, CO
University of St. Francis, IL
University of South Carolina, SC
University of Southern Mississippi, MS
The University of Tennessee at Chattanooga, TN
The University of Tennessee at Martin, TN
The University of Texas at El Paso, TX
The University of Texas at San Antonio, TX
The University of Texas–Pan American, TX
University of the Ozarks, AR
The University of Toledo, OH
University of Utah, UT
University of Vermont, VT
The University of Virginia's College at Wise, VA
University of Wisconsin–Eau Claire, WI
University of Wisconsin–Green Bay, WI
University of Wisconsin–La Crosse, WI
University of Wisconsin–Parkside, WI
University of Wisconsin–Stevens Point, WI
University of Wyoming, WY
Valley City State University, ND
Wartburg College, IA
Washburn University, KS
Washington & Jefferson College, PA
Wayland Baptist University, TX
Wayne State College, NE
Wesleyan College, GA
Western Carolina University, NC
Western Kentucky University, KY
Western Oregon University, OR
Western Washington University, WA
Westminster College, MO
Westmont College, CA
West Virginia State University, WV
West Virginia University, WV
Wheaton College, IL
Whitman College, WA
Whitworth University, WA
Widener University, PA
Wittenberg University, OH
Wright State University, OH
Youngstown State University, OH

First-Generation College Students

Abilene Christian University, TX
American University, DC
Angelo State University, TX
Appalachian State University, NC
Arkansas State University, AR
Austin College, TX
Averett University, VA
Berry College, GA
Birmingham-Southern College, AL
Bluefield College, VA
Boise State University, ID
Bowie State University, MD
Brenau University, GA
California State University, Bakersfield, CA
California State University, Chico, CA
California State University, San Bernardino, CA
California State University, Stanislaus, CA
Calvin College, MI
Centre College, KY
Chowan University, NC
The College at Brockport, State University of New York, NY
College of Saint Mary, NE
Colorado State University, CO
Colorado State University–Pueblo, CO
Columbia College, MO
Concordia University, CA
Creighton University, NE
Davidson College, NC
DePauw University, IN
Dowling College, NY
Eastern Washington University, WA
Edinboro University of Pennsylvania, PA
Elon University, NC
Emmanuel College, GA
Erskine College, SC
The Evergreen State College, WA
Fairfield University, CT
Finlandia University, MI
Flagler College, FL
Florida Agricultural and Mechanical University, FL
Fort Lewis College, CO
Georgia Southern University, GA
Glenville State College, WV
Graceland University, IA
Gustavus Adolphus College, MN
Illinois State University, IL
Iowa State University of Science and Technology, IA
John Carroll University, OH
Kent State University, OH
Kenyon College, OH
Kutztown University of Pennsylvania, PA
Lewis-Clark State College, ID
Long Island University, Brooklyn Campus, NY
Lyon College, AR
Meredith College, NC
Mesa State College, CO
Metropolitan State College of Denver, CO
Michigan State University, MI
Midwestern State University, TX
Millsaps College, MS
Minnesota State University Moorhead, MN
Mississippi State University, MS
Monmouth University, NJ
Montana State University Billings, MT
Montreat College, NC
Moravian College, PA
New Jersey Institute of Technology, NJ
Northern Arizona University, AZ
Oklahoma State University, OK
Ouachita Baptist University, AR
Pacific Lutheran University, WA
Pacific University, OR
The Richard Stockton College of New Jersey, NJ
Ripon College, WI
Russell Sage College, NY
Sage College of Albany, NY
St. John Fisher College, NY
Saint Joseph's University, PA
Saint Louis University, MO
Saint Mary-of-the-Woods College, IN
San Diego State University, CA
Seton Hill University, PA
Shawnee State University, OH
Sonoma State University, CA
South Dakota State University, SD
Southeastern Louisiana University, LA
Southeast Missouri State University, MO
Southwest Minnesota State University, MN
State University of New York at Binghamton, NY
State University of New York at New Paltz, NY
Stephen F. Austin State University, TX
Tennessee Technological University, TN
Texas A&M University, TX
Texas A&M University–Corpus Christi, TX
Texas Lutheran University, TX
Texas State University–San Marcos, TX
Texas Tech University, TX
Trinity Christian College, IL
Trinity University, TX
The University of Alabama at Birmingham, AL
University of California, San Diego, CA
University of Central Florida, FL
University of Colorado Boulder, CO
University of Delaware, DE
University of Great Falls, MT
University of Hartford, CT
University of Idaho, ID
University of Illinois at Urbana–Champaign, IL
The University of Iowa, IA
The University of Kansas, KS
University of Kentucky, KY
University of Massachusetts Boston, MA
University of Massachusetts Dartmouth, MA
University of Michigan–Flint, MI
University of Minnesota, Crookston, MN
University of Mississippi, MS
University of Missouri, MO

University of Nebraska at Omaha, NE
University of Nevada, Las Vegas, NV
University of Nevada, Reno, NV
University of North Alabama, AL
The University of North Carolina at Asheville, NC
University of North Florida, FL
University of St. Francis, IL
University of South Carolina, SC
The University of Texas at Arlington, TX
The University of Texas at Brownsville, TX
The University of Texas at San Antonio, TX
University of Utah, UT
University of Vermont, VT
The University of West Alabama, AL
University of West Florida, FL
University of Wisconsin–Eau Claire, WI
University of Wisconsin–La Crosse, WI
University of Wisconsin–Stout, WI
University of Wyoming, WY
Virginia Polytechnic Institute and State University, VA
Washington State University, WA
Webber International University, FL
Wesleyan College, GA
West Texas A&M University, TX
Whitman College, WA
Wichita State University, KS
Wright State University, OH

Handicapped Students

Appalachian State University, NC
Arkansas State University, AR
Augusta State University, GA
Austin College, TX
Boise State University, ID
Bryan College, TN
California State University, Chico, CA
California State University, Fresno, CA
California State University, San Bernardino, CA
Calvin College, MI
Central College, IA
Clear Creek Baptist Bible College, KY
The College of St. Scholastica, MN
College of Staten Island of the City University of New York, NY
Colorado State University–Pueblo, CO
Dordt College, IA
East Carolina University, NC
Eastern Washington University, WA
Edinboro University of Pennsylvania, PA
Elizabeth City State University, NC
Emmanuel College, MA
Emporia State University, KS
Florida Gulf Coast University, FL
Fordham University, NY
Fort Lewis College, CO
Fort Valley State University, GA
Francis Marion University, SC
Gardner-Webb University, NC
Georgia College & State University, GA
Georgia Southern University, GA
Grace University, NE
Grand Valley State University, MI
Hamline University, MN
Hardin-Simmons University, TX
Hofstra University, NY
James Madison University, VA
Kennesaw State University, GA
Kent State University, OH
Kutztown University of Pennsylvania, PA
Lock Haven University of Pennsylvania, PA
Louisiana Tech University, LA
Michigan State University, MI
Mid-Atlantic Christian University, NC
Midwestern State University, TX
Mississippi State University, MS
Murray State University, KY
New Jersey Institute of Technology, NJ
New Mexico State University, NM
Northern Arizona University, AZ
Northern Kentucky University, KY
Northern State University, SD
The Ohio State University, OH
Oklahoma State University, OK
Old Dominion University, VA
Ouachita Baptist University, AR
Portland State University, OR
Sacred Heart University, CT
San Diego State University, CA
Santa Clara University, CA
Shawnee State University, OH
Shepherd University, WV
Shippensburg University of Pennsylvania, PA
Sonoma State University, CA
South Dakota State University, SD
Southern Illinois University Carbondale, IL
Southwest Minnesota State University, MN
State University of New York at Binghamton, NY
State University of New York at New Paltz, NY
State University of New York College at Potsdam, NY
Texas Christian University, TX
Texas State University–San Marcos, TX
Texas Tech University, TX
Towson University, MD
The University of Akron, OH
The University of Alabama at Birmingham, AL
University of California, San Diego, CA
University of Hartford, CT
University of Idaho, ID
The University of Iowa, IA
University of Kentucky, KY
University of Mary Hardin-Baylor, TX
University of Massachusetts Amherst, MA
University of Memphis, TN
University of Michigan, MI
University of Michigan–Dearborn, MI
University of Michigan–Flint, MI
University of Mississippi, MS
University of Nebraska at Omaha, NE
University of Nebraska–Lincoln, NE
University of Nevada, Las Vegas, NV
University of New Hampshire, NH
The University of North Carolina at Asheville, NC
The University of North Carolina at Greensboro, NC
University of North Dakota, ND
University of Northern Colorado, CO
University of South Carolina, SC
The University of Tennessee at Chattanooga, TN
The University of Tennessee at Martin, TN
The University of Texas at Arlington, TX
The University of Texas at Dallas, TX
The University of Texas at San Antonio, TX
The University of Toledo, OH
University of Utah, UT
University of West Florida, FL
University of West Georgia, GA
University of Wisconsin–Green Bay, WI
University of Wisconsin–Stout, WI
University of Wyoming, WY
Washington State University, WA
Wesleyan College, GA
Western Carolina University, NC
Western Kentucky University, KY
Western Oregon University, OR
West Texas A&M University, TX
Wheaton College, IL
Wright State University, OH
Youngstown State University, OH

International Students

Adrian College, MI
Agnes Scott College, GA
Alaska Pacific University, AK
Alderson-Broaddus College, WV
Alfred University, NY
Allegheny College, PA
Alliant International University, CA
Alverno College, WI
Anderson University, SC
Andrews University, MI
Appalachian Bible College, WV
Arizona Christian University, AZ
Armstrong Atlantic State University, GA
Asbury University, KY
Ashland University, OH
Augsburg College, MN
Augustana College, IL
Augustana College, SD
Augusta State University, GA
Austin College, TX
Averett University, VA
Ball State University, IN
Bellarmine University, KY
Bemidji State University, MN
Benedictine College, KS
Benedictine University, IL
Bentley University, MA
Berry College, GA
Bethany College, WV
Bethel College, IN
Bethel College, KS
Bethel University, MN
Beulah Heights University, GA
Biola University, CA
Bloomfield College, NJ
Bloomsburg University of Pennsylvania, PA
Bluffton University, OH
Boise State University, ID
Bowling Green State University, OH
Brenau University, GA
Brevard College, NC
Bridgewater College, VA
Bryan College, TN
Bryant University, RI
Buena Vista University, IA
California Lutheran University, CA
California State University, Chico, CA
Calvin College, MI
Campbellsville University, KY
Canisius College, NY
Capital University, OH
Carroll College, MT
Carroll University, WI
Centenary College of Louisiana, LA
Central College, IA
Central Methodist University, MO
Central Michigan University, MI
Chestnut Hill College, PA
Chowan University, NC
Cincinnati Christian University, OH

Non-Need Scholarships for Undergraduates
Special Characteristics

Clarkson University, NY
Clear Creek Baptist Bible College, KY
Coastal Carolina University, SC
Coe College, IA
Coker College, SC
The College at Brockport, State University of New York, NY
College of Notre Dame of Maryland, MD
College of Saint Benedict, MN
College of Saint Mary, NE
The College of St. Scholastica, MN
College of Staten Island of the City University of New York, NY
Colorado State University–Pueblo, CO
Columbia College, MO
Columbia International University, SC
Concordia College, MN
Concordia University Chicago, IL
Concordia University, Nebraska, NE
Corban University, OR
Cornell College, IA
Covenant College, GA
Crown College, MN
Culver-Stockton College, MO
Defiance College, OH
DePauw University, IN
Dickinson State University, ND
Dominican University of California, CA
Dordt College, IA
Drake University, IA
Duquesne University, PA
Eastern Connecticut State University, CT
Eastern Michigan University, MI
East Texas Baptist University, TX
Eckerd College, FL
Edinboro University of Pennsylvania, PA
Elizabeth City State University, NC
Elizabethtown College, PA
Elmira College, NY
Elon University, NC
Emmanuel College, GA
Emmanuel College, MA
Emporia State University, KS
Endicott College, MA
Ferris State University, MI
Ferrum College, VA
Finlandia University, MI
Florida Gulf Coast University, FL
Florida Institute of Technology, FL
Fort Lewis College, CO
Fort Valley State University, GA
Francis Marion University, SC
Free Will Baptist Bible College, TN
Frostburg State University, MD
Furman University, SC
Gannon University, PA
George Fox University, OR
Georgia College & State University, GA
Gonzaga University, WA
Goshen College, IN
Graceland University, IA
Grace University, NE
Grand Valley State University, MI
Green Mountain College, VT
Greenville College, IL
Gustavus Adolphus College, MN
Hamline University, MN
Hampden-Sydney College, VA
Hampton University, VA
Hanover College, IN
Harding University, AR
Hartwick College, NY
Harvey Mudd College, CA
Hawai'i Pacific University, HI
Heidelberg University, OH
Hendrix College, AR
Hillsdale College, MI
Hollins University, VA
Hood College, MD
Hope International University, CA
Houghton College, NY
Huntingdon College, AL
Huntington University, IN
Illinois College, IL
Illinois Institute of Technology, IL
Illinois Wesleyan University, IL
Indiana University of Pennsylvania, PA
Iowa State University of Science and Technology, IA
Iowa Wesleyan College, IA
Jacksonville University, FL
James Madison University, VA
Jamestown College, ND
John Brown University, AR
Johnson Bible College, TN
Juniata College, PA
Kennesaw State University, GA
Kent State University, OH
Kentucky State University, KY
Keuka College, NY
Keystone College, PA
King's College, PA
Kuyper College, MI
Lancaster Bible College & Graduate School, PA
Lawrence University, WI
Lebanon Valley College, PA
Liberty University, VA
Life University, GA
Lincoln University, MO
Lipscomb University, TN
Long Island University, Brooklyn Campus, NY
Long Island University, C.W. Post Campus, NY
Louisiana Tech University, LA
Malone University, OH
Manchester College, IN
Mannes College The New School for Music, NY
Marymount University, VA
Maryville University of Saint Louis, MO
Marywood University, PA
The Master's College and Seminary, CA
Mayville State University, ND
McMurry University, TX
Mercer University, GA
Meredith College, NC
Merrimack College, MA
Mesa State College, CO
Michigan State University, MI
Mid-Atlantic Christian University, NC
Midwestern State University, TX
Millersville University of Pennsylvania, PA
Millikin University, IL
Minot State University, ND
Mississippi University for Women, MS
Monmouth College, IL
Monmouth University, NJ
Montana State University–Northern, MT
Montclair State University, NJ
Montreat College, NC
Moravian College, PA
Morehead State University, KY
Morningside College, IA
Mount Marty College, SD
Mount Mary College, WI
Mount Vernon Nazarene University, OH
Murray State University, KY
Nebraska Wesleyan University, NE
New England College, NH
New Hope Christian College, OR
New Jersey Institute of Technology, NJ
New Mexico State University, NM
North Central College, IL
Northern Arizona University, AZ
Northern Illinois University, IL
Northern Michigan University, MI
Northern State University, SD
Northwestern College, MN
Northwestern State University of Louisiana, LA
Northwest Nazarene University, ID
Northwest University, WA
Nyack College, NY
Ohio Northern University, OH
Ohio Valley University, WV
Ohio Wesleyan University, OH
Oklahoma Christian University, OK
Oklahoma State University, OK
Oklahoma Wesleyan University, OK
Old Dominion University, VA
Olivet College, MI
Ouachita Baptist University, AR
Pace University, NY
Pacific Lutheran University, WA
Pacific University, OR
Palm Beach Atlantic University, FL
Peirce College, PA
Piedmont College, GA
Plymouth State University, NH
Point Park University, PA
Portland State University, OR
Quinnipiac University, CT
Ramapo College of New Jersey, NJ
Randolph College, VA
The Richard Stockton College of New Jersey, NJ
Ripon College, WI
Rivier College, NH
Roberts Wesleyan College, NY
Rockford College, IL
St. Ambrose University, IA
St. Catherine University, MN
Saint Francis University, PA
Saint John's University, MN
Saint Joseph's University, PA
Saint Louis University, MO
Saint Martin's University, WA
Saint Mary-of-the-Woods College, IN
Saint Mary's University of Minnesota, MN
St. Norbert College, WI
St. Olaf College, MN
San Diego Christian College, CA
Schreiner University, TX
Seattle Pacific University, WA
Silver Lake College, WI
Simpson College, IA
Sonoma State University, CA
South Dakota State University, SD
Southeast Missouri State University, MO
Southern Adventist University, TN
Southern Illinois University Carbondale, IL
Southern Oregon University, OR
Southwestern College, KS
Southwest Minnesota State University, MN
Spring Arbor University, MI
State University of New York at Fredonia, NY

State University of New York at Plattsburgh, NY
State University of New York College at Oneonta, NY
Stetson University, FL
Sweet Briar College, VA
Tabor College, KS
Taylor University, IN
Tennessee Wesleyan College, TN
Texas A&M University–Corpus Christi, TX
Texas Christian University, TX
Texas Woman's University, TX
Thomas More College, KY
Towson University, MD
Truman State University, MO
Union University, TN
The University of Akron, OH
The University of Alabama, AL
The University of Arizona, AZ
University of Arkansas, AR
University of Bridgeport, CT
University of Central Missouri, MO
University of Charleston, WV
University of Evansville, IN
University of Great Falls, MT
University of Hartford, CT
University of Idaho, ID
University of Indianapolis, IN
The University of Kansas, KS
University of Kentucky, KY
University of La Verne, CA
University of Maine at Fort Kent, ME
University of Maine at Presque Isle, ME
University of Mary Hardin-Baylor, TX
University of Miami, FL
University of Michigan, MI
University of Michigan–Dearborn, MI
University of Michigan–Flint, MI
University of Minnesota, Morris, MN
University of Mississippi, MS
University of Missouri, MO
University of Missouri–St. Louis, MO
The University of Montana, MT
University of Montevallo, AL
University of Mount Union, OH
University of Nebraska at Omaha, NE
University of Nebraska–Lincoln, NE
University of Nevada, Las Vegas, NV
University of New Hampshire, NH
University of New Orleans, LA
The University of North Carolina at Asheville, NC
The University of North Carolina at Chapel Hill, NC
The University of North Carolina at Greensboro, NC
University of North Dakota, ND
University of Northern Colorado, CO
University of North Florida, FL
University of Oregon, OR
University of Puget Sound, WA
University of Redlands, CA
University of Rochester, NY
University of Science and Arts of Oklahoma, OK
University of South Carolina, SC
The University of Tampa, FL
The University of Texas at Brownsville, TX
The University of Texas at Dallas, TX
The University of Texas at El Paso, TX
The University of Texas–Pan American, TX
University of the Ozarks, AR
The University of Toledo, OH
University of West Georgia, GA
University of Wisconsin–Eau Claire, WI
University of Wisconsin–La Crosse, WI
University of Wisconsin–Parkside, WI
University of Wisconsin–Stevens Point, WI
University of Wisconsin–Stout, WI
University of Wyoming, WY
Utah State University, UT
Valdosta State University, GA
Valley City State University, ND
Valparaiso University, IN
Walsh University, OH
Wartburg College, IA
Washburn University, KS
Washington State University, WA
Wayland Baptist University, TX
Webber International University, FL
Wells College, NY
Wesleyan College, GA
Western Illinois University, IL
Western Kentucky University, KY
Western New England University, MA
Western Oregon University, OR
Western Washington University, WA
Westminster College, MO
Westminster College, PA
Westmont College, CA
West Virginia University, WV
West Virginia Wesleyan College, WV
Whitman College, WA
Whittier College, CA
Whitworth University, WA
Wichita State University, KS
Widener University, PA
William Jessup University, CA
Williams Baptist College, AR
Wilson College, PA
Wittenberg University, OH
Wright State University, OH
Xavier University, OH
York College of Pennsylvania, PA
Youngstown State University, OH

Local/State Students

Abilene Christian University, TX
Agnes Scott College, GA
Alaska Pacific University, AK
Alcorn State University, MS
Allen College, IA
Alliant International University, CA
Alvernia University, PA
American University, DC
Angelo State University, TX
Anna Maria College, MA
Arkansas State University, AR
Auburn University, AL
Augustana College, SD
Augusta State University, GA
Austin College, TX
Averett University, VA
Ball State University, IN
Bard College at Simon's Rock, MA
Bellarmine University, KY
Benedictine College, KS
Berry College, GA
Bethel College, KS
Boise State University, ID
Boston University, MA
Brevard College, NC
Bryan College, TN
California Polytechnic State University, San Luis Obispo, CA
California State University, Chico, CA
California State University, Fresno, CA
California State University, Monterey Bay, CA
California State University, Stanislaus, CA
Centenary College of Louisiana, LA
Central College, IA
Central Michigan University, MI
Central Washington University, WA
Chowan University, NC
The Citadel, The Military College of South Carolina, SC
Clarke University, IA
Clarkson University, NY
Clemson University, SC
Coastal Carolina University, SC
The College at Brockport, State University of New York, NY
College of St. Joseph, VT
Columbia College, MO
Columbus College of Art & Design, OH
Concordia University, Nebraska, NE
Cornell College, IA
Creighton University, NE
Culver-Stockton College, MO
Dalton State College, GA
Davidson College, NC
DePaul University, IL
DePauw University, IN
DigiPen Institute of Technology, WA
Dordt College, IA
Dowling College, NY
Duke University, NC
Eastern Connecticut State University, CT
Eastern Oregon University, OR
Eastern Washington University, WA
East Texas Baptist University, TX
Eckerd College, FL
Edgewood College, WI
Edinboro University of Pennsylvania, PA
Elizabethtown College, PA
Elmira College, NY
Emmanuel College, MA
Emory University, GA
Endicott College, MA
Faulkner University, AL
Fayetteville State University, NC
Ferris State University, MI
Ferrum College, VA
Fitchburg State University, MA
Flagler College, FL
Florida Agricultural and Mechanical University, FL
Florida Gulf Coast University, FL
Florida Southern College, FL
Florida State University, FL
Fort Lewis College, CO
Frostburg State University, MD
Furman University, SC
Gardner-Webb University, NC
Georgetown College, KY
Georgia College & State University, GA
Georgia Institute of Technology, GA
Graceland University, IA
Grace University, NE
Grand Valley State University, MI
Greenville College, IL
Hamline University, MN
Hardin-Simmons University, TX
Hawai'i Pacific University, HI
Hollins University, VA
Houghton College, NY
Howard Payne University, TX
Huntingdon College, AL
Huntington University, IN

Non-Need Scholarships for Undergraduates
Special Characteristics

Illinois Institute of Technology, IL
Indiana University–Purdue University Fort Wayne, IN
Iowa State University of Science and Technology, IA
James Madison University, VA
Jefferson College of Health Sciences, VA
John Carroll University, OH
The Johns Hopkins University, MD
Johnson & Wales University, CO
Johnson & Wales University, FL
Johnson & Wales University, RI
Johnson & Wales University—Charlotte Campus, NC
Juniata College, PA
Kennesaw State University, GA
Kent State University, OH
Kent State University at Stark, OH
Kentucky State University, KY
Kettering University, MI
Kutztown University of Pennsylvania, PA
Lake Forest College, IL
Lee University, TN
Lenoir-Rhyne University, NC
Lesley University, MA
Liberty University, VA
Limestone College, SC
Lock Haven University of Pennsylvania, PA
Longwood University, VA
Lourdes College, OH
Lynn University, FL
Lyon College, AR
Marist College, NY
Marywood University, PA
Mayville State University, ND
McDaniel College, MD
McMurry University, TX
Medcenter One College of Nursing, ND
Mesa State College, CO
Messiah College, PA
Metropolitan State College of Denver, CO
Miami University, OH
Michigan State University, MI
Michigan Technological University, MI
Middle Tennessee State University, TN
Millsaps College, MS
Minot State University, ND
Mississippi State University, MS
Missouri Southern State University, MO
Missouri State University, MO
Monmouth University, NJ
Montana State University, MT
Montana State University Billings, MT
Montana Tech of The University of Montana, MT
Montreat College, NC
Morehead State University, KY
Morehouse College, GA
Murray State University, KY
Muskingum University, OH
New England College, NH
New Mexico State University, NM
New York Institute of Technology, NY
Nicholls State University, LA
Northern Arizona University, AZ
Northern Kentucky University, KY
Northern State University, SD
Nyack College, NY
Ohio Valley University, WV
Ohio Wesleyan University, OH
Oklahoma Baptist University, OK
Oklahoma Panhandle State University, OK
Oklahoma State University, OK
Old Dominion University, VA
Ouachita Baptist University, AR
Pacific University, OR
Post University, CT
Quincy University, IL
Randolph College, VA
Regis University, CO
The Richard Stockton College of New Jersey, NJ
Ripon College, WI
Sacred Heart Major Seminary, MI
Saginaw Valley State University, MI
Saint Augustine's College, NC
St. Bonaventure University, NY
St. Catherine University, MN
St. John Fisher College, NY
St. John's University, NY
St. Louis College of Pharmacy, MO
Saint Martin's University, WA
Saint Mary-of-the-Woods College, IN
Saint Michael's College, VT
San Diego State University, CA
Santa Fe University of Art and Design, NM
Schreiner University, TX
Shawnee State University, OH
Shenandoah University, VA
Shepherd University, WV
Shippensburg University of Pennsylvania, PA
Shorter University, GA
Siena College, NY
Silver Lake College, WI
Slippery Rock University of Pennsylvania, PA
Smith College, MA
Sonoma State University, CA
Southern Adventist University, TN
Southern Utah University, UT
Southwest Baptist University, MO
Southwestern Oklahoma State University, OK
Southwest Minnesota State University, MN
State University of New York at Binghamton, NY
State University of New York at Fredonia, NY
State University of New York College at Cortland, NY
State University of New York College at Geneseo, NY
State University of New York College at Oneonta, NY
State University of New York College at Potsdam, NY
Stephen F. Austin State University, TX
Sterling College, VT
Stetson University, FL
Sul Ross State University, TX
Sweet Briar College, VA
Tabor College, KS
Tennessee Technological University, TN
Texas A&M University, TX
Texas Christian University, TX
Texas State University–San Marcos, TX
Trinity Christian College, IL
Tulane University, LA
Tuskegee University, AL
Unity College, ME
University of Advancing Technology, AZ
The University of Akron, OH
The University of Alabama in Huntsville, AL
University of Alaska Fairbanks, AK
University of Arkansas, AR
University of Arkansas at Little Rock, AR
University of Bridgeport, CT
University of Colorado Boulder, CO
University of Connecticut, CT
University of Delaware, DE
University of Georgia, GA
University of Hartford, CT
University of Hawaii at Hilo, HI
University of Idaho, ID
University of Illinois at Urbana–Champaign, IL
The University of Kansas, KS
University of Louisville, KY
University of Mary, ND
University of Mary Hardin-Baylor, TX
University of Mary Washington, VA
University of Michigan, MI
University of Michigan–Flint, MI
University of Minnesota, Crookston, MN
University of Minnesota, Twin Cities Campus, MN
University of Mississippi, MS
University of Missouri, MO
University of Missouri–St. Louis, MO
The University of Montana, MT
University of Nevada, Las Vegas, NV
University of New Hampshire, NH
University of New Orleans, LA
The University of North Carolina at Asheville, NC
The University of North Carolina Wilmington, NC
University of Northern Colorado, CO
University of Oregon, OR
University of Pittsburgh at Bradford, PA
University of Rio Grande, OH
University of South Carolina, SC
University of Southern Maine, ME
University of Southern Mississippi, MS
The University of Texas at Austin, TX
The University of Texas at Dallas, TX
The University of Texas at El Paso, TX
The University of Texas at San Antonio, TX
The University of Texas–Pan American, TX
University of the Cumberlands, KY
The University of Virginia's College at Wise, VA
University of West Georgia, GA
University of Wisconsin–Eau Claire, WI
University of Wisconsin–Green Bay, WI
University of Wisconsin–La Crosse, WI
University of Wisconsin–Parkside, WI
University of Wisconsin–Stout, WI
University of Wyoming, WY
Valley Forge Christian College, PA
Vanderbilt University, TN
Virginia Military Institute, VA
Virginia Polytechnic Institute and State University, VA
Wake Forest University, NC
Walsh University, OH
Warren Wilson College, NC
Washburn University, KS
Wayland Baptist University, TX
Wayne State College, NE
Webber International University, FL
Western Carolina University, NC
Western Kentucky University, KY
Western New England University, MA
Western Oregon University, OR
Western Washington University, WA
Westminster College, MO
West Texas A&M University, TX
West Virginia University, WV
Wilson College, PA
Winona State University, MN

Wittenberg University, OH
Youngstown State University, OH

Married Students

Appalachian Bible College, WV
Auburn University, AL
Baptist Bible College of Pennsylvania, PA
Bethesda Christian University, CA
Beulah Heights University, GA
California State University, Chico, CA
Cincinnati Christian University, OH
The College at Brockport, State University of New York, NY
Columbia International University, SC
Crossroads Bible College, IN
Emmanuel College, GA
Free Will Baptist Bible College, TN
Georgia Southern University, GA
Grace University, NE
Johnson Bible College, TN
Lancaster Bible College & Graduate School, PA
Laurel University, NC
Mid-Atlantic Christian University, NC
Mid-Continent University, KY
Montana Tech of The University of Montana, MT
New Hope Christian College, OR
New Mexico State University, NM
Northwest University, WA
Ouachita Baptist University, AR
Sonoma State University, CA
State University of New York at Binghamton, NY
The University of Alabama at Birmingham, AL
The University of Kansas, KS
University of Nevada, Reno, NV
The University of North Carolina Wilmington, NC
Valley Forge Christian College, PA

Members of Minority Groups

Abilene Christian University, TX
Alabama State University, AL
Alaska Pacific University, AK
Alcorn State University, MS
Allen College, IA
Alliant International University, CA
American University, DC
Anderson University, SC
Appalachian State University, NC
Arizona Christian University, AZ
Arkansas State University, AR
Assumption College, MA
Augsburg College, MN
Augustana College, IL
Augustana College, SD
Aurora University, IL
Austin Peay State University, TN
Azusa Pacific University, CA
Baldwin-Wallace College, OH
Ball State University, IN
Bard College at Simon's Rock, MA
Bellarmine University, KY
Beloit College, WI
Benedictine College, KS
Bentley University, MA
Berry College, GA
Bethel College, IN
Bethel University, MN
Bluefield College, VA
Bluffton University, OH
Boise State University, ID
Bowling Green State University, OH
Brigham Young University, UT
Bryan College, TN
Bryant University, RI
California State Polytechnic University, Pomona, CA
California State University, Chico, CA
Calvin College, MI
Cameron University, OK
Capital University, OH
Carnegie Mellon University, PA
Carson-Newman College, TN
Centenary College of Louisiana, LA
Central College, IA
Central Connecticut State University, CT
Central Washington University, WA
Cincinnati Christian University, OH
Clarke University, IA
Clarkson University, NY
Clemson University, SC
Coe College, IA
The College at Brockport, State University of New York, NY
The College of New Jersey, NJ
The College of Saint Rose, NY
The College of St. Scholastica, MN
College of Staten Island of the City University of New York, NY
The College of Wooster, OH
Concordia University, Nebraska, NE
Cornell College, IA
Covenant College, GA
Creighton University, NE
Crown College, MN
Dalton State College, GA
Defiance College, OH
DePauw University, IN
Dickinson State University, ND
DigiPen Institute of Technology, WA
Dordt College, IA
Dowling College, NY
Drew University, NJ
Duquesne University, PA
Eastern Connecticut State University, CT
Eastern Kentucky University, KY
Eastern Michigan University, MI
Eastern Oregon University, OR
East Tennessee State University, TN
Edinboro University of Pennsylvania, PA
Elizabeth City State University, NC
Elizabethtown College, PA
Elmhurst College, IL
Elon University, NC
Emporia State University, KS
Erskine College, SC
The Evergreen State College, WA
Ferris State University, MI
Fitchburg State University, MA
Flagler College, FL
Florida Gulf Coast University, FL
Florida International University, FL
Fort Lewis College, CO
Franklin College, IN
Fresno Pacific University, CA
Gallaudet University, DC
Gannon University, PA
Gardner-Webb University, NC
George Fox University, OR
Georgia College & State University, GA
Georgia Institute of Technology, GA
Georgia Southern University, GA
Golden Gate University, CA
Gonzaga University, WA
Goshen College, IN
Governors State University, IL
Grace College, IN
Graceland University, IA
Grace University, NE
Grove City College, PA
Gustavus Adolphus College, MN
Hamline University, MN
Hampden-Sydney College, VA
Hampton University, VA
Hanover College, IN
Hardin-Simmons University, TX
Illinois Institute of Technology, IL
Illinois State University, IL
Indiana State University, IN
Iowa State University of Science and Technology, IA
Ithaca College, NY
James Madison University, VA
John Brown University, AR
John Carroll University, OH
Johnson Bible College, TN
Kennesaw State University, GA
Kent State University, OH
Kent State University at Stark, OH
Kettering University, MI
King College, TN
King's College, PA
Kuyper College, MI
Lawrence Technological University, MI
Lehigh University, PA
Le Moyne College, NY
Lenoir-Rhyne University, NC
Lesley University, MA
Lewis-Clark State College, ID
Linfield College, OR
Lipscomb University, TN
Lock Haven University of Pennsylvania, PA
Louisiana Tech University, LA
Lourdes College, OH
Luther College, IA
Lyon College, AR
Manchester College, IN
Marietta College, OH
Maryville College, TN
Maryville University of Saint Louis, MO
Mayville State University, ND
Meredith College, NC
Mesa State College, CO
Miami University, OH
Middle Tennessee State University, TN
Midwestern State University, TX
Minnesota State University Moorhead, MN
Minot State University, ND
Misericordia University, PA
Mississippi University for Women, MS
Missouri State University, MO
Missouri University of Science and Technology, MO
Molloy College, NY
Monmouth University, NJ
Montana State University, MT
Montana State University Billings, MT
Montana State University–Northern, MT
Morehead State University, KY
Mount Carmel College of Nursing, OH
Mount St. Mary's University, MD
Mount Vernon Nazarene University, OH
Murray State University, KY
Muskingum University, OH
New Jersey Institute of Technology, NJ
New Mexico State University, NM

Nicholls State University, LA
Northern Arizona University, AZ
Northern Illinois University, IL
Northern Kentucky University, KY
Northern Michigan University, MI
Northern State University, SD
Northwest Missouri State University, MO
Northwest Nazarene University, ID
The Ohio State University, OH
Ohio University, OH
Ohio University–Chillicothe, OH
Ohio University–Eastern, OH
Ohio University–Lancaster, OH
Ohio University–Southern Campus, OH
Ohio University–Zanesville, OH
Ohio Wesleyan University, OH
Old Dominion University, VA
Ouachita Baptist University, AR
Pacific Union College, CA
Point Park University, PA
Polytechnic Institute of NYU, NY
Portland State University, OR
Quincy University, IL
Rensselaer Polytechnic Institute, NY
Rhodes College, TN
The Richard Stockton College of New Jersey, NJ
Rider University, NJ
Ripon College, WI
Sacred Heart University, CT
Saginaw Valley State University, MI
St. Ambrose University, IA
St. Bonaventure University, NY
St. John Fisher College, NY
Saint Joseph's University, PA
Saint Louis University, MO
Saint Martin's University, WA
Saint Mary-of-the-Woods College, IN
Saint Mary's University of Minnesota, MN
Saint Michael's College, VT
Saint Vincent College, PA
Seattle University, WA
Sewanee: The University of the South, TN
Shawnee State University, OH
Shepherd University, WV
Simpson College, IA
Simpson University, CA
Slippery Rock University of Pennsylvania, PA
Sonoma State University, CA
South Dakota School of Mines and Technology, SD
South Dakota State University, SD
Southeast Missouri State University, MO
Southern Adventist University, TN
Southern Illinois University Carbondale, IL
Southern Oregon University, OR
Southern Polytechnic State University, GA
Southern Utah University, UT
Southwestern College, KS
Southwest Minnesota State University, MN
Spring Arbor University, MI
State University of New York at Binghamton, NY
State University of New York at Fredonia, NY
State University of New York at New Paltz, NY
State University of New York College at Cortland, NY
State University of New York College at Geneseo, NY
State University of New York College at Potsdam, NY
State University of New York College of Environmental Science and Forestry, NY
Stetson University, FL
Stonehill College, MA
Tennessee Technological University, TN
Tennessee Wesleyan College, TN
Texas Christian University, TX
Thomas More College, KY
Transylvania University, KY
Trine University, IN
Trinity Christian College, IL
Union University, TN
Unity College, ME
The University of Akron, OH
The University of Alabama at Birmingham, AL
The University of Alabama in Huntsville, AL
University of Arkansas, AR
University of Arkansas at Little Rock, AR
University of California, San Diego, CA
University of Central Missouri, MO
University of Central Oklahoma, OK
University of Delaware, DE
University of Dubuque, IA
University of Evansville, IN
University of Florida, FL
University of Hartford, CT
University of Idaho, ID
The University of Kansas, KS
University of Kentucky, KY
University of Louisville, KY
University of Maine at Fort Kent, ME
University of Mary Hardin-Baylor, TX
University of Massachusetts Dartmouth, MA
University of Memphis, TN
University of Michigan, MI
University of Michigan–Dearborn, MI
University of Michigan–Flint, MI
University of Minnesota, Morris, MN
University of Minnesota, Twin Cities Campus, MN
University of Mississippi, MS
University of Missouri, MO
University of Missouri–Kansas City, MO
University of Missouri–St. Louis, MO
University of Mount Union, OH
University of Nebraska at Omaha, NE
University of Nebraska–Lincoln, NE
University of Nevada, Las Vegas, NV
University of New Orleans, LA
The University of North Carolina at Asheville, NC
The University of North Carolina at Greensboro, NC
University of North Dakota, ND
University of Northern Colorado, CO
University of Northern Iowa, IA
University of North Florida, FL
University of Oklahoma, OK
The University of Scranton, PA
University of South Alabama, AL
University of South Carolina, SC
The University of South Dakota, SD
University of Southern California, CA
University of Southern Indiana, IN
The University of Tennessee at Martin, TN
The University of Texas at Dallas, TX
The University of Texas at El Paso, TX
The University of Texas at San Antonio, TX
University of the Ozarks, AR
The University of Toledo, OH
University of West Florida, FL
University of West Georgia, GA
University of Wisconsin–Eau Claire, WI
University of Wisconsin–Green Bay, WI
University of Wisconsin–La Crosse, WI
University of Wisconsin–Parkside, WI
University of Wisconsin–Stevens Point, WI
University of Wisconsin–Stout, WI
University of Wisconsin–Superior, WI
Valdosta State University, GA
Valley City State University, ND
Vanderbilt University, TN
Villanova University, PA
Virginia Polytechnic Institute and State University, VA
Walsh University, OH
Warner Pacific College, OR
Wartburg College, IA
Washington & Jefferson College, PA
Wayland Baptist University, TX
Wayne State College, NE
Western Carolina University, NC
Western Illinois University, IL
Western Kentucky University, KY
Western New England University, MA
Western Washington University, WA
West Virginia University, WV
Whitworth University, WA
Wichita State University, KS
Williams Baptist College, AR
Winona State University, MN
Wittenberg University, OH
Xavier University, OH
York College of Pennsylvania, PA
Youngstown State University, OH

Out-of-State Students

Abilene Christian University, TX
Alaska Pacific University, AK
Allen College, IA
Anderson University, SC
Appalachian State University, NC
Arkansas State University, AR
Auburn University, AL
Aurora University, IL
Averett University, VA
Ball State University, IN
Bellarmine University, KY
Bemidji State University, MN
Benedictine College, KS
Benedictine University, IL
Berry College, GA
Bethel University, MN
Bloomfield College, NJ
Bluefield College, VA
Bluffton University, OH
Boise State University, ID
Buena Vista University, IA
California State University, Chico, CA
Carnegie Mellon University, PA
Centenary College of Louisiana, LA
Central College, IA
Central Michigan University, MI
The Citadel, The Military College of South Carolina, SC
Cleveland State University, OH
Coastal Carolina University, SC
The College at Brockport, State University of New York, NY
The College of New Rochelle, NY
The College of Saint Rose, NY
Colorado State University–Pueblo, CO
Concordia University, MI
Concordia University Wisconsin, WI
Dalton State College, GA

Davidson College, NC
Defiance College, OH
Delaware State University, DE
Delta State University, MS
Dordt College, IA
Eastern Michigan University, MI
Edinboro University of Pennsylvania, PA
Elmira College, NY
Emory & Henry College, VA
Erskine College, SC
Faulkner University, AL
Fitchburg State University, MA
Flagler College, FL
Florida Agricultural and Mechanical University, FL
Florida Gulf Coast University, FL
Florida Southern College, FL
Fort Lewis College, CO
Fort Valley State University, GA
Francis Marion University, SC
Franklin College, IN
Frostburg State University, MD
Gardner-Webb University, NC
George Fox University, OR
Georgetown College, KY
Georgia College & State University, GA
Grace University, NE
Grand Valley State University, MI
Greenville College, IL
Gustavus Adolphus College, MN
Hampden-Sydney College, VA
Hanover College, IN
Hardin-Simmons University, TX
Hawai'i Pacific University, HI
Heidelberg University, OH
Hollins University, VA
Iowa State University of Science and Technology, IA
James Madison University, VA
Kent State University, OH
Kentucky Wesleyan College, KY
Lewis-Clark State College, ID
Limestone College, SC
Lincoln University, MO
Louisiana Tech University, LA
Lourdes College, OH
Maryville University of Saint Louis, MO
Mayville State University, ND
McMurry University, TX
Meredith College, NC
Mesa State College, CO
Miami University, OH
Michigan State University, MI
Minot State University, ND
Misericordia University, PA
Mississippi State University, MS
Mississippi University for Women, MS
Missouri University of Science and Technology, MO
Monmouth College, IL
Monmouth University, NJ
Montana State University Billings, MT
Montana State University–Northern, MT
Montana Tech of The University of Montana, MT
Morehead State University, KY
Morningside College, IA
Murray State University, KY
New College of Florida, FL
New Hope Christian College, OR
New Jersey Institute of Technology, NJ
New Mexico State University, NM
Nicholls State University, LA
Northeastern State University, OK
Northern Arizona University, AZ
Northern Michigan University, MI
Northwestern State University of Louisiana, LA
Northwest Missouri State University, MO
Northwest Nazarene University, ID
Nyack College, NY
Oakland University, MI
Ohio Northern University, OH
The Ohio State University, OH
Oklahoma Baptist University, OK
Oklahoma Panhandle State University, OK
Oklahoma State University, OK
Ouachita Baptist University, AR
Pacific Lutheran University, WA
Palm Beach Atlantic University, FL
Piedmont College, GA
Portland State University, OR
Ramapo College of New Jersey, NJ
Randolph-Macon College, VA
Ripon College, WI
Robert Morris University Illinois, IL
Roberts Wesleyan College, NY
Rockford College, IL
Rogers State University, OK
St. Ambrose University, IA
St. Catherine University, MN
Saint Francis University, PA
Saint John's University, MN
Saint Martin's University, WA
Saint Mary-of-the-Woods College, IN
Saint Michael's College, VT
San Diego Christian College, CA
Seton Hill University, PA
Shepherd University, WV
Siena College, NY
Simpson University, CA
Slippery Rock University of Pennsylvania, PA
Sonoma State University, CA
Southeastern Louisiana University, LA
Southeastern Oklahoma State University, OK
Southeast Missouri State University, MO
Southern Adventist University, TN
Southwestern Oklahoma State University, OK
State University of New York at Binghamton, NY
State University of New York at Fredonia, NY
State University of New York at Plattsburgh, NY
Tabor College, KS
Tennessee Technological University, TN
Texas Tech University, TX
Thomas More College, KY
Thomas University, GA
Transylvania University, KY
Trinity Christian College, IL
Truman State University, MO
The University of Akron, OH
The University of Alabama, AL
The University of Alabama at Birmingham, AL
University of Arkansas, AR
University of Central Missouri, MO
University of Connecticut, CT
University of Dubuque, IA
University of Florida, FL
University of Idaho, ID
University of Indianapolis, IN
The University of Iowa, IA
The University of Kansas, KS
University of Louisville, KY
University of Mary Hardin-Baylor, TX
University of Maryland, College Park, MD
University of Massachusetts Lowell, MA
University of Michigan, MI
University of Michigan–Dearborn, MI
University of Mississippi, MS
University of Missouri, MO
University of Missouri–Kansas City, MO
University of Missouri–St. Louis, MO
The University of Montana, MT
University of Montevallo, AL
University of Nebraska at Omaha, NE
University of Nebraska–Lincoln, NE
University of Nevada, Las Vegas, NV
University of New Orleans, LA
University of North Alabama, AL
The University of North Carolina at Chapel Hill, NC
The University of North Carolina at Greensboro, NC
University of Northern Colorado, CO
University of North Florida, FL
University of Pittsburgh at Bradford, PA
University of Rio Grande, OH
University of Science and Arts of Oklahoma, OK
University of South Carolina, SC
University of Southern Indiana, IN
University of Southern Maine, ME
University of Southern Mississippi, MS
The University of Tennessee at Martin, TN
The University of Texas at Dallas, TX
The University of Texas at El Paso, TX
The University of Texas at San Antonio, TX
The University of Texas–Pan American, TX
University of Utah, UT
University of Wisconsin–La Crosse, WI
University of Wisconsin–Stevens Point, WI
University of Wisconsin–Stout, WI
University of Wyoming, WY
Virginia Military Institute, VA
Virginia Polytechnic Institute and State University, VA
Walsh University, OH
Wartburg College, IA
Washington State University, WA
Wayne State College, NE
Webber International University, FL
Western Kentucky University, KY
Western New England University, MA
West Texas A&M University, TX
Winona State University, MN
Wright State University, OH
Youngstown State University, OH

Parents of Current Students

Alabama Agricultural and Mechanical University, AL
Aurora University, IL
Caldwell College, NJ
Cincinnati Christian University, OH
The College of New Rochelle, NY
Columbia College, MO
ECPI College of Technology, VA
Emmanuel College, GA
Fairfield University, CT
Grace University, NE
Green Mountain College, VT
Huntington University, IN
Johnson Bible College, TN
Malone University, OH
Maryville University of Saint Louis, MO
Millikin University, IL
Mississippi University for Women, MS

Missouri Baptist University, MO
Mount Aloysius College, PA
Mount Marty College, SD
Mount Mary College, WI
New England College, NH
Northwest University, WA
Pace University, NY
Rockford College, IL
St. Joseph's College, Long Island Campus, NY
St. Joseph's College, New York, NY
Saint Mary-of-the-Woods College, IN
Seton Hill University, PA
State University of New York at Fredonia, NY
The University of Alabama at Birmingham, AL
University of Great Falls, MT
University of Hartford, CT
Upper Iowa University, IA
Valley Forge Christian College, PA
Wesleyan College, GA

Previous College Experience

Abilene Christian University, TX
American University, DC
Anna Maria College, MA
Arizona Christian University, AZ
Baptist Bible College of Pennsylvania, PA
Bellarmine University, KY
Bethel College, KS
Birmingham-Southern College, AL
Boise State University, ID
Brevard College, NC
Calumet College of Saint Joseph, IN
Cedar Crest College, PA
Central College, IA
Coker College, SC
The College at Brockport, State University of New York, NY
The College of New Rochelle, NY
College of St. Joseph, VT
The College of St. Scholastica, MN
Columbia College, MO
Defiance College, OH
Dowling College, NY
Eastern Connecticut State University, CT
Eastern Michigan University, MI
East Texas Baptist University, TX
Elmira College, NY
Ferris State University, MI
Fitchburg State University, MA
Florida Institute of Technology, FL
Gardner-Webb University, NC
Golden Gate University, CA
Grace University, NE
Hamline University, MN
Hawai'i Pacific University, HI
Hendrix College, AR
Hollins University, VA
Huntington University, IN
Illinois College, IL
Illinois Institute of Technology, IL
Illinois State University, IL
Indiana State University, IN
Lake Forest College, IL
Lancaster Bible College & Graduate School, PA
Lewis-Clark State College, ID
Limestone College, SC
Lock Haven University of Pennsylvania, PA
Lourdes College, OH
Manchester College, IN
Manhattanville College, NY
McDaniel College, MD
McMurry University, TX
Meredith College, NC
Misericordia University, PA
Mississippi State University, MS
Monmouth University, NJ
Mount Mercy University, IA
New Jersey Institute of Technology, NJ
New Mexico State University, NM
New York Institute of Technology, NY
Nicholls State University, LA
Northwest Missouri State University, MO
The Ohio State University, OH
Oklahoma State University, OK
Old Dominion University, VA
Ouachita Baptist University, AR
Pace University, NY
Palm Beach Atlantic University, FL
Point Park University, PA
The Richard Stockton College of New Jersey, NJ
Ripon College, WI
Saint Francis University, PA
Saint Louis University, MO
Shepherd University, WV
Siena College, NY
Silver Lake College, WI
Slippery Rock University of Pennsylvania, PA
Sonoma State University, CA
Southeast Missouri State University, MO
Southwest Minnesota State University, MN
State University of New York at Fredonia, NY
State University of New York College at Potsdam, NY
Stephen F. Austin State University, TX
Sterling College, VT
Texas Christian University, TX
Truman State University, MO
The University of Alabama at Birmingham, AL
University of Arkansas, AR
University of Arkansas at Little Rock, AR
University of Bridgeport, CT
University of Central Missouri, MO
University of Hartford, CT
The University of Kansas, KS
University of Louisville, KY
University of Michigan–Dearborn, MI
University of Mississippi, MS
University of Nevada, Las Vegas, NV
University of Oklahoma, OK
University of St. Thomas, TX
University of Science and Arts of Oklahoma, OK
The University of Toledo, OH
University of Wisconsin–Eau Claire, WI
University of Wisconsin–Stout, WI
Walsh College of Accountancy and Business Administration, MI
Warren Wilson College, NC
Western Washington University, WA
William Jessup University, CA
York College, NE

Public Servants

Caldwell College, NJ
College of Staten Island of the City University of New York, NY
Dowling College, NY
Grand Valley State University, MI
Hannibal-LaGrange University, MO
Hardin-Simmons University, TX
Hofstra University, NY
Liberty University, VA
Missouri Baptist University, MO
New York Institute of Technology, NY
Nicholls State University, LA
Northern Arizona University, AZ
Northwestern State University of Louisiana, LA
Patrick Henry College, VA
Regent University, VA
Regis University, CO
St. Joseph's College, Long Island Campus, NY
St. Joseph's College, New York, NY
Southern Illinois University Carbondale, IL
Tennessee Technological University, TN
The University of Alabama at Birmingham, AL
University of Kentucky, KY
University of Memphis, TN
University of Michigan–Dearborn, MI
University of New Orleans, LA
University of Oklahoma, OK
The University of Texas at Arlington, TX
The University of Texas at Dallas, TX
The University of Toledo, OH
Washington State University, WA
Youngstown State University, OH

Relatives of Clergy

Abilene Christian University, TX
Albion College, MI
American University, DC
Anderson University, SC
Appalachian Bible College, WV
Arcadia University, PA
Arizona Christian University, AZ
Ashland University, OH
Augsburg College, MN
Austin College, TX
Averett University, VA
Baptist Bible College of Pennsylvania, PA
Benedictine University, IL
Bethany College, WV
Bethel College, IN
Bethel College, KS
Bethel University, MN
Bethesda Christian University, CA
Biola University, CA
Birmingham-Southern College, AL
Bluffton University, OH
Boston University, MA
Brevard College, NC
Bryan College, TN
Caldwell College, NJ
California Lutheran University, CA
Calvary Bible College and Theological Seminary, MO
Campbellsville University, KY
Capital University, OH
Carson-Newman College, TN
Cedar Crest College, PA
Centenary College of Louisiana, LA
Central Methodist University, MO
Chowan University, NC
Clarke University, IA
Columbia International University, SC
Corban University, OR
Cornell College, IA
Crown College, MN
Dallas Baptist University, TX
Davidson College, NC
DePauw University, IN
Dominican College, NY

Drury University, MO
Duquesne University, PA
Elon University, NC
Emmanuel College, GA
Erskine College, SC
Evangel University, MO
Faulkner University, AL
Ferrum College, VA
Florida Southern College, FL
Free Will Baptist Bible College, TN
Fresno Pacific University, CA
Furman University, SC
Gardner-Webb University, NC
George Fox University, OR
Georgetown College, KY
Gordon College, MA
Grace Bible College, MI
Grace College, IN
Grace University, NE
Green Mountain College, VT
Greenville College, IL
Hamline University, MN
Hannibal-LaGrange University, MO
Harding University, AR
Hardin-Simmons University, TX
Hastings College, NE
Hawai'i Pacific University, HI
Heidelberg University, OH
Hendrix College, AR
High Point University, NC
Hillsdale Free Will Baptist College, OK
Hope International University, CA
Houghton College, NY
Houston Baptist University, TX
Howard Payne University, TX
Huntington University, IN
Indiana Wesleyan University, IN
Jamestown College, ND
John Brown University, AR
Johnson Bible College, TN
Kentucky Wesleyan College, KY
King College, TN
King's College, PA
Lancaster Bible College & Graduate School, PA
Lenoir-Rhyne University, NC
Lindsey Wilson College, KY
Lipscomb University, TN
Lycoming College, PA
Malone University, OH
Maranatha Baptist Bible College, WI
The Master's College and Seminary, CA
McMurry University, TX
Mercer University, GA
Merrimack College, MA
Methodist University, NC
Mid-Continent University, KY
Millikin University, IL
Millsaps College, MS
Misericordia University, PA
Missouri Baptist University, MO
Montreat College, NC
Moravian College, PA
Mount Vernon Nazarene University, OH
Muskingum University, OH
Nebraska Wesleyan University, NE
New Hope Christian College, OR
Niagara University, NY
North Central College, IL
Northwest Christian University, OR
Northwestern College, MN
Northwest Nazarene University, ID
Northwest University, WA
Nyack College, NY
Ohio Northern University, OH
Ohio Valley University, WV
Ohio Wesleyan University, OH
Oklahoma Baptist University, OK
Oklahoma City University, OK
Oklahoma Wesleyan University, OK
Olivet Nazarene University, IL
Ouachita Baptist University, AR
Our Lady of Holy Cross College, LA
Pacific Lutheran University, WA
Pacific University, OR
Patrick Henry College, VA
Philadelphia Biblical University, PA
Presbyterian College, SC
Randolph College, VA
Randolph-Macon College, VA
Rhodes College, TN
Roberts Wesleyan College, NY
Rosemont College, PA
St. Bonaventure University, NY
St. John's University, NY
Saint Mary's College of California, CA
Salem College, NC
Samford University, AL
San Diego Christian College, CA
Schreiner University, TX
Seattle Pacific University, WA
Sewanee: The University of the South, TN
Shasta Bible College, CA
Shenandoah University, VA
Shorter University, GA
Siena College, NY
Simpson College, IA
Simpson University, CA
Southwest Baptist University, MO
Southwestern University, TX
Spring Arbor University, MI
Stonehill College, MA
Tennessee Wesleyan College, TN
Texas Christian University, TX
Texas Wesleyan University, TX
Thiel College, PA
Transylvania University, KY
Trevecca Nazarene University, TN
Union University, TN
The University of Alabama at Birmingham, AL
University of Dubuque, IA
University of Indianapolis, IN
University of Mary Hardin-Baylor, TX
University of Mobile, AL
University of Mount Union, OH
The University of North Carolina at Chapel Hill, NC
University of Portland, OR
University of the Cumberlands, KY
University of the Ozarks, AR
University of Tulsa, OK
Ursuline College, OH
Valley Forge Christian College, PA
Valparaiso University, IN
Virginia Wesleyan College, VA
Wayland Baptist University, TX
Wesleyan College, GA
Westminster College, MO
West Virginia Wesleyan College, WV
Whitworth University, WA
William Jessup University, CA
Williams Baptist College, AR
Wilson College, PA
Wingate University, NC
Wittenberg University, OH
Wofford College, SC

Religious Affiliation

Abilene Christian University, TX
Adrian College, MI
Agnes Scott College, GA
Alaska Pacific University, AK
Alderson-Broaddus College, WV
Anderson University, SC
Appalachian Bible College, WV
Arcadia University, PA
Armstrong Atlantic State University, GA
Ashland University, OH
Augustana College, IL
Augustana College, SD
Aurora University, IL
Averett University, VA
Azusa Pacific University, CA
Baldwin-Wallace College, OH
The Baptist College of Florida, FL
Bellarmine University, KY
Benedictine College, KS
Bethany College, WV
Bethel College, IN
Bethel College, KS
Bethel University, MN
Beulah Heights University, GA
Birmingham-Southern College, AL
Bluefield College, VA
Bluffton University, OH
Boston University, MA
Brevard College, NC
Bridgewater College, VA
Buena Vista University, IA
Caldwell College, NJ
California Lutheran University, CA
Calvary Bible College and Theological Seminary, MO
Calvin College, MI
Campbellsville University, KY
Canisius College, NY
Capital University, OH
The Catholic University of America, DC
Cedar Crest College, PA
Cedarville University, OH
Centenary College of Louisiana, LA
Central College, IA
Central Methodist University, MO
Central Washington University, WA
Chowan University, NC
Christian Brothers University, TN
Clarke University, IA
The College at Brockport, State University of New York, NY
College of St. Joseph, VT
The College of St. Scholastica, MN
Columbia College, MO
Columbia International University, SC
Concordia University, CA
Concordia University, MI
Concordia University Chicago, IL
Concordia University, Nebraska, NE
Concordia University, St. Paul, MN
Cornell College, IA
Covenant College, GA
Creighton University, NE
Culver-Stockton College, MO
Dallas Baptist University, TX
Defiance College, OH
DePauw University, IN
Dillard University, LA
Doane College, NE
Dominican University of California, CA

Dordt College, IA
Drury University, MO
Duquesne University, PA
Eastern Michigan University, MI
Eastern Nazarene College, MA
East Texas Baptist University, TX
Eckerd College, FL
Edinboro University of Pennsylvania, PA
Elizabethtown College, PA
Elmhurst College, IL
Emmanuel College, GA
Emmanuel College, MA
Emory University, GA
Emporia State University, KS
Endicott College, MA
Erskine College, SC
Eureka College, IL
Evangel University, MO
Faulkner University, AL
Ferrum College, VA
Finlandia University, MI
Franklin College, IN
Fresno Pacific University, CA
Furman University, SC
Gannon University, PA
Geneva College, PA
George Fox University, OR
Georgetown College, KY
Georgia College & State University, GA
Georgia Health Sciences University, GA
Georgian Court University, NJ
Grace College, IN
Graceland University, IA
Green Mountain College, VT
Greenville College, IL
Hamline University, MN
Hampden-Sydney College, VA
Hannibal-LaGrange University, MO
Hanover College, IN
Hardin-Simmons University, TX
Hastings College, NE
Hawai'i Pacific University, HI
Heidelberg University, OH
Hillsdale Free Will Baptist College, OK
Hope International University, CA
Houghton College, NY
Howard Payne University, TX
Huntingdon College, AL
Huntington University, IN
Indiana Wesleyan University, IN
Iona College, NY
Iowa State University of Science and Technology, IA
Iowa Wesleyan College, IA
Jamestown College, ND
Jarvis Christian College, TX
Johnson Bible College, TN
Kennesaw State University, GA
Kentucky Wesleyan College, KY
Lancaster Bible College & Graduate School, PA
Lenoir-Rhyne University, NC
Liberty University, VA
Lindsey Wilson College, KY
Lourdes College, OH
Loyola University Chicago, IL
Luther College, IA
Lyon College, AR
Malone University, OH
Manchester College, IN
Marymount University, VA
Maryville College, TN
Marywood University, PA
McKendree University, IL
McMurry University, TX
McPherson College, KS
Meredith College, NC
Messiah College, PA
Methodist University, NC
Millsaps College, MS
Misericordia University, PA
Missouri Baptist University, MO
Missouri Southern State University, MO
Molloy College, NY
Montreat College, NC
Moravian College, PA
Morningside College, IA
Mount Aloysius College, PA
Mount Marty College, SD
Mount Olive College, NC
Mount Vernon Nazarene University, OH
Muskingum University, OH
New Jersey Institute of Technology, NJ
New Life Theological Seminary, NC
Northwest Christian University, OR
Northwest Nazarene University, ID
Northwest University, WA
Nyack College, NY
Ohio Northern University, OH
Ohio Valley University, WV
Ohio Wesleyan University, OH
Oklahoma Baptist University, OK
Oklahoma City University, OK
Oklahoma Wesleyan University, OK
Olivet College, MI
Olivet Nazarene University, IL
Ouachita Baptist University, AR
Our Lady of Holy Cross College, LA
Our Lady of the Lake University of San Antonio, TX
Pacific Lutheran University, WA
Pacific Union College, CA
Presbyterian College, SC
Randolph College, VA
Reinhardt University, GA
Rhodes College, TN
Ripon College, WI
Roberts Wesleyan College, NY
Sacred Heart Major Seminary, MI
Sacred Heart University, CT
St. Ambrose University, IA
St. Bonaventure University, NY
St. Catherine University, MN
St. Edward's University, TX
Saint Francis University, PA
St. John's University, NY
Saint Louis University, MO
Saint Mary-of-the-Woods College, IN
Saint Michael's College, VT
Saint Vincent College, PA
San Diego Christian College, CA
Schreiner University, TX
Seattle Pacific University, WA
Seattle University, WA
Shenandoah University, VA
Shorter University, GA
Siena College, NY
Simpson College, IA
Simpson University, CA
Southwestern College, KS
Southwestern University, TX
Spring Arbor University, MI
State University of New York College at Geneseo, NY
Tabor College, KS
Taylor University, IN
Tennessee Wesleyan College, TN
Texas Christian University, TX
Texas Lutheran University, TX
Texas Wesleyan University, TX
Thiel College, PA
Thomas More College, KY
Transylvania University, KY
Trevecca Nazarene University, TN
Trinity Christian College, IL
Union College, KY
Union University, TN
University of California, Riverside, CA
University of Dallas, TX
University of Dayton, OH
University of Dubuque, IA
University of Evansville, IN
University of Great Falls, MT
University of Hartford, CT
University of Indianapolis, IN
University of Mary, ND
University of Mary Hardin-Baylor, TX
The University of North Carolina at Chapel Hill, NC
The University of North Carolina at Greensboro, NC
University of Portland, OR
University of St. Francis, IL
University of St. Thomas, TX
University of South Carolina, SC
The University of Tennessee at Chattanooga, TN
University of the Cumberlands, KY
University of the Ozarks, AR
The University of Toledo, OH
University of Tulsa, OK
Upper Iowa University, IA
Ursuline College, OH
Valparaiso University, IN
Villanova University, PA
Virginia Wesleyan College, VA
Wake Forest University, NC
Waldorf College, IA
Warner Pacific College, OR
Warren Wilson College, NC
Wartburg College, IA
Washington State University, WA
Wayland Baptist University, TX
Wesleyan College, GA
Western Kentucky University, KY
Westminster College, MO
Westminster College, PA
West Texas A&M University, TX
West Virginia Wesleyan College, WV
Wheeling Jesuit University, WV
Williams Baptist College, AR
Wilson College, PA
Wingate University, NC
Wittenberg University, OH
Youngstown State University, OH

Siblings of Current Students

Albright College, PA
Alvernia University, PA
Anderson University, SC
Anna Maria College, MA
Arizona Christian University, AZ
Asbury University, KY
Augsburg College, MN
Augustana College, IL
Augustana College, SD
Aurora University, IL
Baldwin-Wallace College, OH
Baptist Bible College of Pennsylvania, PA

Beloit College, WI
Benedictine University, IL
Bethel College, IN
Bethel College, KS
Bethesda Christian University, CA
Bloomfield College, NJ
Brevard College, NC
Bridgewater College, VA
Bryant University, RI
Buena Vista University, IA
Cabrini College, PA
Caldwell College, NJ
Calvary Bible College and Theological Seminary, MO
Capital University, OH
Carroll College, MT
Carroll University, WI
Carson-Newman College, TN
The Catholic University of America, DC
Cedar Crest College, PA
Centenary College of Louisiana, LA
Central College, IA
Central Methodist University, MO
Cincinnati Christian University, OH
Clarke University, IA
Coe College, IA
The College of New Rochelle, NY
College of Notre Dame of Maryland, MD
The College of Saint Rose, NY
The College of St. Scholastica, MN
Columbia College, MO
Concordia University, CA
Concordia University, MI
Corban University, OR
Creighton University, NE
Crossroads Bible College, IN
Crown College, MN
Daemen College, NY
Doane College, NE
Dominican University, IL
Dowling College, NY
East Texas Baptist University, TX
Elizabethtown College, PA
Elmhurst College, IL
Elmira College, NY
Emmanuel College, GA
Emmanuel College, MA
Erskine College, SC
Eureka College, IL
Faulkner University, AL
Felician College, NJ
Finlandia University, MI
Florida Institute of Technology, FL
Florida Southern College, FL
Franklin College, IN
Gonzaga University, WA
Grace University, NE
Green Mountain College, VT
Greenville College, IL
Gustavus Adolphus College, MN
Gwynedd-Mercy College, PA
Hanover College, IN
Harding University, AR
Hardin-Simmons University, TX
Hartwick College, NY
Hastings College, NE
Hillsdale Free Will Baptist College, OK
Hood College, MD
Houghton College, NY
Huntington University, IN
Indiana Wesleyan University, IN
Iona College, NY
Ithaca College, NY
James Madison University, VA
Jamestown College, ND
John Brown University, AR
Johnson Bible College, TN
Johnson C. Smith University, NC
Kettering University, MI
Keuka College, NY
Keystone College, PA
King's College, PA
Lancaster Bible College & Graduate School, PA
Lasell College, MA
Lawrence University, WI
Lee University, TN
Lenoir-Rhyne University, NC
Limestone College, SC
Long Island University, C.W. Post Campus, NY
Loras College, IA
Lynn University, FL
Malone University, OH
Marian University, WI
Marywood University, PA
McDaniel College, MD
Mercer University, GA
Merrimack College, MA
Millikin University, IL
Misericordia University, PA
Missouri Baptist University, MO
Molloy College, NY
Mount Aloysius College, PA
Mount Marty College, SD
Mount Mary College, WI
Mount St. Mary's University, MD
Mount Vernon Nazarene University, OH
Muskingum University, OH
Nazareth College of Rochester, NY
Nebraska Wesleyan University, NE
New England College, NH
Nichols College, MA
Northwest Christian University, OR
Northwestern College, MN
Northwest Nazarene University, ID
Northwest University, WA
Northwood University, Texas Campus, TX
Oglethorpe University, GA
Ohio Northern University, OH
Oklahoma Wesleyan University, OK
Olivet College, MI
Pacific Union College, CA
Palm Beach Atlantic University, FL
Point Park University, PA
Post University, CT
Providence College, RI
Quinnipiac University, CT
Randolph-Macon College, VA
Regent University, VA
Research College of Nursing, MO
Ripon College, WI
Rivier College, NH
Roberts Wesleyan College, NY
Rockford College, IL
Rockhurst University, MO
Rosemont College, PA
Russell Sage College, NY
Sacred Heart University, CT
Sage College of Albany, NY
Saint Anselm College, NH
St. Bonaventure University, NY
St. Catherine University, MN
Saint Francis University, PA
Saint Joseph's College, IN
St. Joseph's College, Long Island Campus, NY
St. Joseph's College, New York, NY
St. Lawrence University, NY
Saint Louis University, MO
Saint Martin's University, WA
Saint Mary-of-the-Woods College, IN
Saint Michael's College, VT
St. Thomas Aquinas College, NY
San Diego Christian College, CA
Schreiner University, TX
Seton Hill University, PA
Shorter University, GA
Simpson College, IA
Simpson University, CA
Southern Adventist University, TN
Springfield College, MA
Spring Hill College, AL
Stonehill College, MA
Suffolk University, MA
Thiel College, PA
Thomas More College, KY
Trine University, IN
Union College, KY
Union University, TN
The University of Alabama at Birmingham, AL
University of Dallas, TX
University of Dubuque, IA
University of Evansville, IN
University of Great Falls, MT
University of Hartford, CT
University of St. Francis, IL
The University of Scranton, PA
University of the Cumberlands, KY
University of the Ozarks, AR
University of Tulsa, OK
Ursinus College, PA
Ursuline College, OH
Valley Forge Christian College, PA
Wagner College, NY
Walsh University, OH
Wartburg College, IA
Webber International University, FL
Wesleyan College, GA
Western New England University, MA
Westminster College, MO
Whitworth University, WA
William Jessup University, CA
William Jewell College, MO
Xavier University, OH
York College, NE

Spouses of Current Students

American University, DC
Anderson University, SC
Appalachian Bible College, WV
Arizona Christian University, AZ
Augustana College, SD
Aurora University, IL
The Baptist College of Florida, FL
Bethel College, IN
Bethel College, KS
Bethesda Christian University, CA
Beulah Heights University, GA
Bloomfield College, NJ
Boise State University, ID
Bryan College, TN
Calvary Bible College and Theological Seminary, MO
Carroll College, MT
Carroll University, WI
Central Methodist University, MO

Cincinnati Christian University, OH
Clarke University, IA
The College of New Rochelle, NY
The College of St. Scholastica, MN
Columbia College, MO
Columbia International University, SC
Crossroads Bible College, IN
DigiPen Institute of Technology, WA
Elmhurst College, IL
Emmanuel College, GA
Finlandia University, MI
Fresno Pacific University, CA
Georgian Court University, NJ
Grace University, NE
Hillsdale Free Will Baptist College, OK
Hope International University, CA
Huntingdon College, AL
Huntington University, IN
Jamestown College, ND
Johnson Bible College, TN
Lancaster Bible College & Graduate School, PA
Laurel University, NC
Lee University, TN
Malone University, OH
Maranatha Baptist Bible College, WI
Marywood University, PA
Mid-Atlantic Christian University, NC
Mount Aloysius College, PA
Mount Marty College, SD
Mount Vernon Nazarene University, OH
New Hope Christian College, OR
New Mexico State University, NM
Northwest University, WA
Nyack College, NY
Pacific Union College, CA
Palm Beach Atlantic University, FL
Russell Sage College, NY
St. Catherine University, MN
Saint Francis University, PA
St. Joseph's College, Long Island Campus, NY
St. Joseph's College, New York, NY
Saint Mary-of-the-Woods College, IN
St. Thomas Aquinas College, NY
Southern Adventist University, TN
Union University, TN
The University of Alabama at Birmingham, AL
University of Great Falls, MT
University of Mississippi, MS
University of Southern Indiana, IN
Upper Iowa University, IA
Valley Forge Christian College, PA
Wesleyan College, GA

Spouses of Deceased or Disabled Public Servants

College of Staten Island of the City University of New York, NY
Eastern Washington University, WA
Francis Marion University, SC
Grand Valley State University, MI
Louisiana Tech University, LA
Michigan State University, MI
Mississippi State University, MS
New York Institute of Technology, NY
Northeastern State University, OK
Northern Arizona University, AZ
Northern Kentucky University, KY
Pace University, NY
Southern Illinois University Carbondale, IL
The University of Alabama, AL
The University of Alabama at Birmingham, AL
University of Connecticut, CT
University of Kentucky, KY
University of South Carolina, SC
University of Utah, UT
Youngstown State University, OH

Twins

Arizona Christian University, AZ
Calvin College, MI
The Catholic University of America, DC
Central College, IA
Cincinnati Christian University, OH
The College of Saint Rose, NY
Dowling College, NY
East Texas Baptist University, TX
Emmanuel College, GA
Finlandia University, MI
Mount Aloysius College, PA
Ohio Wesleyan University, OH
Ouachita Baptist University, AR
Randolph College, VA
Sacred Heart University, CT
St. Joseph's College, Long Island Campus, NY
St. Joseph's College, New York, NY
St. Thomas Aquinas College, NY
Simpson College, IA
Union University, TN
The University of Alabama at Birmingham, AL
University of Hartford, CT
Virginia Polytechnic Institute and State University, VA
Westminster College, MO

Veterans

Agnes Scott College, GA
Alliant International University, CA
Amridge University, AL
Appalachian Bible College, WV
Appalachian State University, NC
Arizona Christian University, AZ
Arkansas State University, AR
Augustana College, SD
Augusta State University, GA
Aurora University, IL
Austin Peay State University, TN
Babson College, MA
Ball State University, IN
Benedictine University, IL
Berry College, GA
Bluefield College, VA
Boise State University, ID
Brown University, RI
Caldwell College, NJ
California Lutheran University, CA
California State University, Bakersfield, CA
Campbellsville University, KY
Carroll College, MT
The Catholic University of America, DC
Cedarville University, OH
Central College, IA
Clarkson University, NY
Cleary University, MI
Clemson University, SC
Coe College, IA
The College at Brockport, State University of New York, NY
The College of Wooster, OH
Columbia College, MO
Columbia International University, SC
Concordia University, Nebraska, NE
Concordia University, St. Paul, MN
Concord University, WV
Culver-Stockton College, MO
Defiance College, OH
Dickinson State University, ND
DigiPen Institute of Technology, WA
Dominican University of California, CA
Dowling College, NY
D'Youville College, NY
Eastern Connecticut State University, CT
Eastern Washington University, WA
ECPI College of Technology, VA
Edinboro University of Pennsylvania, PA
EDP College of Puerto Rico, Inc., PR
EDP College of Puerto Rico–San Sebastian, PR
Elizabeth City State University, NC
Elmhurst College, IL
Elmira College, NY
Emporia State University, KS
The Evergreen State College, WA
Fairfield University, CT
Ferris State University, MI
Fitchburg State University, MA
Framingham State University, MA
Francis Marion University, SC
Free Will Baptist Bible College, TN
Frostburg State University, MD
Furman University, SC
Gannon University, PA
Georgian Court University, NJ
Governors State University, IL
Grace University, NE
Grand Valley State University, MI
Hamline University, MN
Hampden-Sydney College, VA
Hampton University, VA
Hofstra University, NY
Hollins University, VA
Huntingdon College, AL
Huntington University, IN
Illinois Institute of Technology, IL
Indiana State University, IN
Indiana Wesleyan University, IN
Jamestown College, ND
John Carroll University, OH
Kentucky State University, KY
Kentucky Wesleyan College, KY
Lasell College, MA
Lawrence University, WI
Lebanon Valley College, PA
Liberty University, VA
Louisiana Tech University, LA
Marymount University, VA
Maryville University of Saint Louis, MO
Massachusetts College of Art and Design, MA
Massachusetts Maritime Academy, MA
McNally Smith College of Music, MN
Metropolitan State College of Denver, CO
Michigan State University, MI
Midwestern State University, TX
Millikin University, IL
Minot State University, ND
Monmouth College, IL
Monmouth University, NJ
Montana State University Billings, MT
Montana State University–Northern, MT
Montana Tech of The University of Montana, MT
Montreat College, NC
Morehead State University, KY
Mount Olive College, NC

New Hope Christian College, OR
New Mexico State University, NM
New York Institute of Technology, NY
Nicholls State University, LA
Northern Arizona University, AZ
Northern Illinois University, IL
Northern Kentucky University, KY
Northwestern State University of Louisiana, LA
Northwest Nazarene University, ID
Ohio Northern University, OH
Oklahoma Baptist University, OK
Oklahoma Panhandle State University, OK
Pace University, NY
Pacific Union College, CA
Pacific University, OR
Patrick Henry College, VA
Pontifical Catholic University of Puerto Rico, PR
Portland State University, OR
Robert Morris University Illinois, IL
Rochester Institute of Technology, NY
Sacred Heart University, CT
St. Ambrose University, IA
Saint Joseph's University, PA
Saint Martin's University, WA
Saint Mary's College of California, CA
San Diego State University, CA
Seattle Pacific University, WA
Shasta Bible College, CA
Shawnee State University, OH
Sonoma State University, CA
South Dakota State University, SD
Southeastern Louisiana University, LA
Southeast Missouri State University, MO
Southern Connecticut State University, CT
Southern Illinois University Carbondale, IL
Southwest Minnesota State University, MN
Stonehill College, MA
Temple University, PA
Texas A&M University, TX
Texas Christian University, TX
Texas Tech University, TX
Thomas More College, KY
Thomas University, GA
Towson University, MD
Union College, KY
Union University, TN
University of Advancing Technology, AZ
The University of Alabama at Birmingham, AL
University of California, Riverside, CA
University of Central Missouri, MO
University of Connecticut, CT
University of Houston–Clear Lake, TX
University of Idaho, ID
University of Illinois at Urbana–Champaign, IL
University of Indianapolis, IN
The University of Iowa, IA
University of Kentucky, KY
University of La Verne, CA
University of Louisville, KY
University of Mary, ND
University of Massachusetts Amherst, MA
University of Massachusetts Boston, MA
University of Massachusetts Dartmouth, MA
University of Massachusetts Lowell, MA
University of Michigan–Flint, MI
University of Minnesota, Morris, MN
University of Missouri–St. Louis, MO
The University of Montana, MT
University of Nevada, Las Vegas, NV
The University of North Carolina at Asheville, NC
The University of North Carolina at Greensboro, NC
University of Northern Colorado, CO
University of Oregon, OR
University of Pittsburgh at Bradford, PA
University of Puerto Rico at Bayamón, PR
University of Rochester, NY
University of Southern Mississippi, MS
The University of Texas at Dallas, TX
The University of Texas–Pan American, TX
The University of Toledo, OH
The University of Virginia's College at Wise, VA
University of Wisconsin–Green Bay, WI
University of Wisconsin–La Crosse, WI
University of Wisconsin–Stevens Point, WI
University of Wisconsin–Stout, WI
University of Wyoming, WY
Ursuline College, OH
Walla Walla University, WA
Washington Adventist University, MD
Washington & Jefferson College, PA
Washington State University, WA
Wayne State College, NE
Wesleyan College, GA
Western Kentucky University, KY
Western Michigan University, MI
Western New Mexico University, NM
Western Oregon University, OR
Western Washington University, WA
William Jessup University, CA
Wilson College, PA
Youngstown State University, OH

Veterans' Children

Agnes Scott College, GA
Appalachian State University, NC
Arizona Christian University, AZ
Arkansas State University, AR
Augusta State University, GA
Aurora University, IL
Ball State University, IN
Benedictine College, KS
Benedictine University, IL
Berry College, GA
Boise State University, ID
Brevard College, NC
Brown University, RI
California Lutheran University, CA
The Catholic University of America, DC
Central College, IA
Coastal Carolina University, SC
Coe College, IA
College of Staten Island of the City University of New York, NY
Columbia International University, SC
Concordia University, Nebraska, NE
Concordia University, St. Paul, MN
Concord University, WV
Culver-Stockton College, MO
Defiance College, OH
Dickinson State University, ND
DigiPen Institute of Technology, WA
Dominican University of California, CA
Eastern Washington University, WA
ECPI College of Technology, VA
Edinboro University of Pennsylvania, PA
EDP College of Puerto Rico, Inc., PR
EDP College of Puerto Rico–San Sebastian, PR
Elizabeth City State University, NC
Elmhurst College, IL
Emporia State University, KS
The Evergreen State College, WA
Fort Lewis College, CO
Francis Marion University, SC
Free Will Baptist Bible College, TN
Frostburg State University, MD
Glenville State College, WV
Grace University, NE
Grand Valley State University, MI
Hampden-Sydney College, VA
Hampton University, VA
Huntingdon College, AL
Huntington University, IN
Illinois Institute of Technology, IL
John Carroll University, OH
Kennesaw State University, GA
Lasell College, MA
Lawrence University, WI
Louisiana Tech University, LA
McNally Smith College of Music, MN
Midwestern State University, TX
Minot State University, ND
Montreat College, NC
Mount Olive College, NC
New Hope Christian College, OR
New Mexico State University, NM
Northern Arizona University, AZ
Northern Kentucky University, KY
Northwestern State University of Louisiana, LA
Oklahoma Panhandle State University, OK
Old Dominion University, VA
Pontifical Catholic University of Puerto Rico, PR
Purdue University North Central, IN
Sacred Heart University, CT
Saint Joseph's University, PA
St. Lawrence University, NY
Saint Martin's University, WA
Saint Mary's College of California, CA
Siena College, NY
South Dakota State University, SD
Southeastern Louisiana University, LA
Southwest Minnesota State University, MN
Stonehill College, MA
Texas A&M University, TX
Texas Christian University, TX
Texas Tech University, TX
Thomas More College, KY
Union College, KY
Union University, TN
University of Advancing Technology, AZ
The University of Alabama at Birmingham, AL
University of California, Riverside, CA
University of California, San Diego, CA
University of Central Missouri, MO
University of Houston–Clear Lake, TX
University of Kentucky, KY
University of Louisville, KY
University of Maine at Presque Isle, ME
University of Michigan–Flint, MI
University of Minnesota, Morris, MN
University of Nebraska at Omaha, NE
University of Nebraska–Lincoln, NE
University of Nevada, Las Vegas, NV
The University of North Carolina at Asheville, NC
The University of North Carolina at Greensboro, NC
University of North Dakota, ND
University of Oregon, OR

University of Puerto Rico at Bayamón, PR
University of Southern Indiana, IN
The University of Texas at Dallas, TX
The University of Toledo, OH
The University of Virginia's College at Wise, VA
University of Wisconsin–La Crosse, WI
University of Wisconsin–Stout, WI
Virginia Commonwealth University, VA
Virginia Polytechnic Institute and State University, VA
Washington Adventist University, MD
Washington & Jefferson College, PA
Washington State University, WA
Wayne State College, NE
Western Illinois University, IL
Western Oregon University, OR
William Jessup University, CA
Youngstown State University, OH

Athletic Grants for Undergraduates

Archery

Texas A&M University, TX W

Baseball

Abilene Christian University, TX M
Adelphi University, NY M
Alabama Agricultural and Mechanical University, AL M
Alabama State University, AL M
Alcorn State University, MS M
Alderson-Broaddus College, WV M
Anderson University, SC M
Angelo State University, TX M
Appalachian State University, NC M
Arizona State University, AZ M
Arkansas State University, AR M
Arkansas Tech University, AR M
Armstrong Atlantic State University, GA M
Asbury University, KY M
Ashland University, OH M
Auburn University, AL M
Auburn University Montgomery, AL M
Augustana College, SD M
Austin Peay State University, TN M
Azusa Pacific University, CA M
Ball State University, IN M
Barry University, FL M
Bellarmine University, KY M
Belmont Abbey College, NC M
Belmont University, TN M
Bemidji State University, MN M
Benedictine College, KS M
Bethel College, IN M
Bethune-Cookman University, FL M
Biola University, CA M
Bloomfield College, NJ M
Bloomsburg University of Pennsylvania, PA M
Bluefield College, VA M
Bluefield State College, WV M
Boston College, MA M
Bowling Green State University, OH M
Brevard College, NC M
Brigham Young University, UT M
Bryan College, TN M
Bryant University, RI M
Butler University, IN M
California Polytechnic State University, San Luis Obispo, CA M
California State Polytechnic University, Pomona, CA M
California State University, Chico, CA M
California State University, Dominguez Hills, CA M
California State University, Fullerton, CA M
California State University, Monterey Bay, CA M
California State University, Northridge, CA M
California State University, San Bernardino, CA M
Cameron University, OK M
Campbellsville University, KY M
Canisius College, NY M
Carson-Newman College, TN M
Cedarville University, OH M
Central Connecticut State University, CT M
Central Michigan University, MI M
Chestnut Hill College, PA M
Christian Brothers University, TN M
The Citadel, The Military College of South Carolina, SC M
Clarion University of Pennsylvania, PA M
Clarke University, IA M
Cleveland State University, OH M
Coastal Carolina University, SC M
Coker College, SC M
College of Charleston, SC M
The College of Saint Rose, NY M
College of the Ozarks, MO M
The College of William and Mary, VA M
Colorado School of Mines, CO M
Columbus State University, GA M
Concordia University, CA M
Concordia University, Nebraska, NE M
Concordia University, St. Paul, MN M
Concord University, WV M
Coppin State University, MD M
Corban University, OR M
Creighton University, NE M
Culver-Stockton College, MO M
Dakota State University, SD M
Dakota Wesleyan University, SD M
Dallas Baptist University, TX M
Davenport University, MI M
Davidson College, NC M
Delaware State University, DE M
Delta State University, MS M
Dickinson State University, ND M
Dixie State College of Utah, UT M
Doane College, NE M
Dominican College, NY M
Dordt College, IA M
Dowling College, NY M
Drury University, MO M
Eastern Michigan University, MI M
East Tennessee State University, TN M
Eckerd College, FL M
Elizabeth City State University, NC M
Elon University, NC M
Embry-Riddle Aeronautical University–Daytona, FL M
Emmanuel College, GA M
Emporia State University, KS M
Erskine College, SC M
Evangel University, MO M
Fairfield University, CT M
Faulkner University, AL M
Felician College, NJ M
Flagler College, FL M
Florida Agricultural and Mechanical University, FL M
Florida Atlantic University, FL M
Florida Gulf Coast University, FL M
Florida Institute of Technology, FL M
Florida International University, FL M
Florida Southern College, FL M
Florida State University, FL M
Francis Marion University, SC M
Freed-Hardeman University, TN M
Furman University, SC M
Gannon University, PA M
Gardner-Webb University, NC M
Garrett College, MD M
Georgetown College, KY M
Georgetown University, DC M
Georgia College & State University, GA M
Georgia Institute of Technology, GA M
Georgia Southern University, GA M
Georgia State University, GA M
Grace College, IN M
Graceland University, IA M
Grand Valley State University, MI M
Grand View University, IA M
Hannibal-LaGrange University, MO M
Harding University, AR M
Hawai'i Pacific University, HI M
Hillsdale College, MI M
Hofstra University, NY M
Houghton College, NY M
Huntington University, IN M
Illinois Institute of Technology, IL M
Illinois State University, IL M
Indiana State University, IN M
Indiana University Bloomington, IN M
Indiana University of Pennsylvania, PA M

Athletic Grants for Undergraduates

Baseball

Indiana University–Purdue University Fort Wayne, IN M
Indiana Wesleyan University, IN M
Inter American University of Puerto Rico, Bayamón Campus, PR M
Inter American University of Puerto Rico, San Germán Campus, PR M
Iona College, NY M
Iowa Wesleyan College, IA M
James Madison University, VA M
Jamestown College, ND M
Kansas State University, KS M
Kennesaw State University, GA M
Kent State University, OH M
Kentucky State University, KY M
Kentucky Wesleyan College, KY M
King College, TN M
Kutztown University of Pennsylvania, PA M
Lamar University, TX M
Lane College, TN M
Lee University, TN M
Le Moyne College, NY M
Lewis-Clark State College, ID M
Liberty University, VA M
Limestone College, SC M
Lincoln Memorial University, TN M
Lincoln University, MO M
Lindenwood University, MO M
Lindsey Wilson College, KY M
Lipscomb University, TN M
Lock Haven University of Pennsylvania, PA M
Long Island University, Brooklyn Campus, NY M
Long Island University, C.W. Post Campus, NY M
Longwood University, VA M
Louisiana State University and Agricultural and Mechanical College, LA M
Lourdes College, OH M
Loyola Marymount University, CA M
Lubbock Christian University, TX M
Lynn University, FL M
Lyon College, AR M
Malone University, OH M
Manhattan College, NY M
Marist College, NY M
Marshall University, WV M
Mars Hill College, NC M
Maryville University of Saint Louis, MO M
The Master's College and Seminary, CA M
Mayville State University, ND M
McKendree University, IL M
Mercer University, GA M
Merrimack College, MA M
Mesa State College, CO M
Miami University, OH M
Michigan State University, MI M
Mid-Continent University, KY M
Middle Tennessee State University, TN M
Millersville University of Pennsylvania, PA M
Milligan College, TN M
Minnesota State University Mankato, MN M
Minot State University, ND M
Mississippi State University, MS M
Missouri Baptist University, MO M
Missouri Southern State University, MO M
Missouri State University, MO M
Missouri University of Science and Technology, MO M
Molloy College, NY M
Monmouth University, NJ M
Montreat College, NC M
Morehead State University, KY M
Morningside College, IA M
Mount Marty College, SD M
Mount Mercy University, IA M
Mount Olive College, NC M
Mount St. Mary's University, MD M
Mount Vernon Nazarene University, OH M
Murray State University, KY M
New Jersey Institute of Technology, NJ M
New Mexico State University, NM M
New York Institute of Technology, NY M
Niagara University, NY M
Nicholls State University, LA M
North Carolina Agricultural and Technical State University, NC M
North Carolina State University, NC M
Northeastern State University, OK M
Northeastern University, MA M
Northern Illinois University, IL M
Northern Kentucky University, KY M
Northern State University, SD M
North Georgia College & State University, GA M
Northwestern Oklahoma State University, OK M
Northwestern State University of Louisiana, LA M
Northwest Missouri State University, MO M
Northwest Nazarene University, ID M
Nyack College, NY M
The Ohio State University, OH M
Ohio University, OH M
Ohio Valley University, WV M
Oklahoma Christian University, OK M
Oklahoma City University, OK M
Oklahoma Panhandle State University, OK M
Oklahoma State University, OK M
Oklahoma Wesleyan University, OK M
Old Dominion University, VA M
Oregon State University, OR M
Ouachita Baptist University, AR M
Pace University, NY M
Palm Beach Atlantic University, FL M
Penn State University Park, PA M
Pepperdine University, CA M
Philadelphia University, PA M
Pikeville College, KY M
Point Park University, PA M
Prairie View A&M University, TX M
Presbyterian College, SC M
Purdue University, IN M
Purdue University North Central, IN M
Queens College of the City University of New York, NY M
Quincy University, IL M
Quinnipiac University, CT M
Radford University, VA M
Regis University, CO M
Reinhardt University, GA M
Research College of Nursing, MO M
Rice University, TX M
Rider University, NJ M
Robert Morris University Illinois, IL M
Rockhurst University, MO M
Rogers State University, OK M
Rollins College, FL M
Sacred Heart University, CT M
Saginaw Valley State University, MI M
St. Ambrose University, IA M
St. Andrews Presbyterian College, NC M
St. Bonaventure University, NY M
St. Edward's University, TX M
St. John's University, NY M
Saint Joseph's College, IN M
Saint Joseph's University, PA M
Saint Leo University, FL M
Saint Louis University, MO M
Saint Martin's University, WA M
Saint Mary's College of California, CA M
St. Thomas Aquinas College, NY M
St. Thomas University, FL M
Saint Xavier University, IL M
Samford University, AL M
San Diego Christian College, CA M
San Diego State University, CA M
San Francisco State University, CA M
San Jose State University, CA M
Santa Clara University, CA M
Savannah College of Art and Design, GA M
Savannah State University, GA M
Seton Hill University, PA M
Shawnee State University, OH M
Shepherd University, WV M
Shippensburg University of Pennsylvania, PA M
Shorter University, GA M
Siena College, NY M
Simpson University, CA M
Slippery Rock University of Pennsylvania, PA M
Sonoma State University, CA M
South Dakota State University, SD M
Southeastern Louisiana University, LA M
Southeastern Oklahoma State University, OK M
Southeast Missouri State University, MO M
Southern Connecticut State University, CT M
Southern Illinois University Carbondale, IL M
Southern Illinois University Edwardsville, IL M
Southern Polytechnic State University, GA M
Southern Utah University, UT M
Southwestern Oklahoma State University, OK M

Southwest Minnesota State University, MN M
Spring Arbor University, MI M
Spring Hill College, AL M
Stanford University, CA M
State University of New York at Binghamton, NY M
Stephen F. Austin State University, TX M
Stetson University, FL M
Stonehill College, MA M
Stony Brook University, State University of New York, NY M
Tabor College, KS M
Tarleton State University, TX M
Taylor University, IN M
Temple University, PA M
Tennessee Technological University, TN M
Tennessee Wesleyan College, TN M
Texas A&M International University, TX M
Texas A&M University, TX M
Texas A&M University–Corpus Christi, TX M
Texas Christian University, TX M
Texas Southern University, TX M
Texas State University–San Marcos, TX M
Texas Tech University, TX M
Texas Wesleyan University, TX M
Thomas University, GA M
Tiffin University, OH M
Towson University, MD M
Trevecca Nazarene University, TN M
Troy University, AL M
Truman State University, MO M
Tulane University, LA M
Tuskegee University, AL M
Union College, KY M
Union University, TN M
University at Buffalo, the State University of New York, NY M
The University of Akron, OH M
The University of Alabama, AL M
The University of Alabama at Birmingham, AL M
The University of Alabama in Huntsville, AL M
The University of Arizona, AZ M
University of Arkansas, AR M
University of Bridgeport, CT M
University of California, Davis, CA M
University of California, Irvine, CA M
University of California, Los Angeles, CA M
University of California, Santa Barbara, CA M
University of Central Florida, FL M
University of Central Missouri, MO M
University of Charleston, WV M
University of Cincinnati, OH M
University of Connecticut, CT M
University of Dayton, OH M
University of Delaware, DE M
University of Evansville, IN M
The University of Findlay, OH M
University of Florida, FL M
University of Georgia, GA M
University of Hartford, CT M
University of Hawaii at Hilo, HI M
University of Hawaii at Manoa, HI M
University of Houston, TX M
University of Illinois at Chicago, IL M
University of Illinois at Springfield, IL M
University of Illinois at Urbana–Champaign, IL M
University of Indianapolis, IN M
The University of Iowa, IA M
The University of Kansas, KS M
University of Louisiana at Lafayette, LA M
University of Louisville, KY M
University of Maine, ME M
University of Maryland, Baltimore County, MD M
University of Maryland, College Park, MD M
University of Massachusetts Amherst, MA M
University of Massachusetts Lowell, MA M
University of Memphis, TN M
University of Miami, FL M
University of Michigan, MI M
University of Minnesota, Crookston, MN M
University of Minnesota, Duluth, MN M
University of Minnesota, Twin Cities Campus, MN M
University of Mississippi, MS M
University of Missouri, MO M
University of Missouri–St. Louis, MO M
University of Mobile, AL M
University of Montevallo, AL M
University of Nebraska at Omaha, NE M
University of Nebraska–Lincoln, NE M
University of Nevada, Las Vegas, NV M
University of Nevada, Reno, NV M
University of North Alabama, AL M
The University of North Carolina at Asheville, NC M
The University of North Carolina at Chapel Hill, NC M
The University of North Carolina at Charlotte, NC M
The University of North Carolina at Greensboro, NC M
The University of North Carolina at Pembroke, NC M
The University of North Carolina Wilmington, NC M
University of North Dakota, ND M
University of Northern Colorado, CO M
University of North Florida, FL M
University of Notre Dame, IN M
University of Oklahoma, OK M
University of Oregon, OR M
University of Pittsburgh, PA M
University of Portland, OR M
University of Rhode Island, RI M
University of Richmond, VA M
University of Rio Grande, OH M
University of St. Francis, IL M
University of San Diego, CA M
University of Science and Arts of Oklahoma, OK M
University of South Alabama, AL M
University of South Carolina, SC M
University of South Carolina Aiken, SC M
University of Southern California, CA M
University of Southern Indiana, IN M
University of Southern Mississippi, MS M
University of South Florida, FL M
The University of Tampa, FL M
The University of Tennessee, TN M
The University of Tennessee at Martin, TN M
The University of Texas at Arlington, TX M
The University of Texas at Austin, TX M
The University of Texas at San Antonio, TX M
The University of Texas of the Permian Basin, TX M
The University of Texas–Pan American, TX M
University of the Cumberlands, KY M
University of the Incarnate Word, TX M
University of the Pacific, CA M
University of the Sciences in Philadelphia, PA M
University of the Southwest, NM M
The University of Toledo, OH M
University of Utah, UT M
University of Virginia, VA M
The University of Virginia's College at Wise, VA M
University of West Florida, FL M
University of West Georgia, GA M
University of Wisconsin–Parkside, WI M
Upper Iowa University, IA M
Utah Valley University, UT M
Valdosta State University, GA M
Valley City State University, ND M
Valparaiso University, IN M
Vanderbilt University, TN M
Villanova University, PA M
Virginia Commonwealth University, VA M
Virginia Military Institute, VA M
Virginia State University, VA M
Wagner College, NY M
Wake Forest University, NC M
Walsh University, OH M
Washburn University, KS M
Washington Adventist University, MD M
Washington State University, WA M
Wayland Baptist University, TX M
Wayne State College, NE M
Wayne State University, MI M
Webber International University, FL M
West Chester University of Pennsylvania, PA M
Western Carolina University, NC M
Western Illinois University, IL M
Western Kentucky University, KY M
Western Michigan University, MI M
Western Oregon University, OR M
West Liberty University, WV M
Westmont College, CA M
West Virginia University, WV M
Wheeling Jesuit University, WV M
Wichita State University, KS M
William Jewell College, MO M
Wingate University, NC M

Winona State University, MN M
Winthrop University, SC M
Wofford College, SC M
Wright State University, OH M
Xavier University, OH M
Young Harris College, GA M
Youngstown State University, OH M

Basketball

Abilene Christian University, TX M,W
Adams State College, CO M,W
Adelphi University, NY M,W
Alabama Agricultural and Mechanical University, AL M,W
Alabama State University, AL M,W
Alcorn State University, MS M,W
Alderson-Broaddus College, WV M,W
American University, DC M,W
Anderson University, SC M,W
Angelo State University, TX M,W
Appalachian State University, NC M,W
Arizona State University, AZ M,W
Arkansas State University, AR M,W
Arkansas Tech University, AR M,W
Armstrong Atlantic State University, GA M,W
Asbury University, KY M,W
Ashland University, OH M,W
Assumption College, MA M,W
Auburn University, AL M,W
Auburn University Montgomery, AL M,W
Augustana College, SD M,W
Austin Peay State University, TN M,W
Azusa Pacific University, CA M,W
Ball State University, IN M,W
Barry University, FL M,W
Bellarmine University, KY M,W
Belmont Abbey College, NC M,W
Belmont University, TN M,W
Bemidji State University, MN M,W
Benedictine College, KS M,W
Bentley University, MA M,W
Bethel College, IN M,W
Bethune-Cookman University, FL M,W
Biola University, CA M,W
Bloomfield College, NJ M,W
Bloomsburg University of Pennsylvania, PA M,W
Bluefield College, VA M,W
Bluefield State College, WV M,W
Boise State University, ID M,W
Boston College, MA M,W
Boston University, MA M,W
Bowie State University, MD M,W
Bowling Green State University, OH M,W
Brenau University, GA W
Brevard College, NC M,W
Brigham Young University, UT M,W
Bryan College, TN M,W
Bryant University, RI M,W
Bucknell University, PA M,W
Butler University, IN M,W
California Polytechnic State University, San Luis Obispo, CA M,W
California State Polytechnic University, Pomona, CA M,W
California State University, Bakersfield, CA M
California State University, Chico, CA M,W
California State University, Dominguez Hills, CA M,W
California State University, Fullerton, CA M,W
California State University, Long Beach, CA M,W
California State University, Monterey Bay, CA M,W
California State University, Northridge, CA M,W
California State University, San Bernardino, CA M,W
Cameron University, OK M,W
Campbellsville University, KY M,W
Canisius College, NY M,W
Carson-Newman College, TN M,W
Cedarville University, OH M,W
Central Connecticut State University, CT M,W
Central Michigan University, MI M,W
Chestnut Hill College, PA M,W
Christian Brothers University, TN M,W
Cincinnati Christian University, OH M
The Citadel, The Military College of South Carolina, SC M
Clarion University of Pennsylvania, PA M,W
Clarke University, IA M,W
Clemson University, SC M,W
Cleveland State University, OH M,W
Coastal Carolina University, SC M,W
Coker College, SC M,W
Colgate University, NY M,W
College of Charleston, SC M,W
College of Saint Mary, NE W
The College of Saint Rose, NY M,W
College of the Holy Cross, MA M,W
College of the Ozarks, MO M,W
The College of William and Mary, VA M,W
Colorado School of Mines, CO M,W
Colorado State University, CO M,W
Columbia College, MO M,W
Columbus State University, GA M,W
Concordia University, CA M,W
Concordia University, Nebraska, NE M,W
Concordia University, St. Paul, MN M,W
Concord University, WV M,W
Coppin State University, MD M,W
Corban University, OR M,W
Creighton University, NE M,W
Culver-Stockton College, MO M,W
Dakota State University, SD M,W
Dakota Wesleyan University, SD M,W
Dallas Baptist University, TX M
Davenport University, MI M,W
Davidson College, NC M,W
Delaware State University, DE M,W
Delta State University, MS M,W
DePaul University, IL M,W
Dickinson State University, ND M,W
Dillard University, LA M,W
Dixie State College of Utah, UT M,W
Doane College, NE M,W
Dominican College, NY M,W
Dominican University of California, CA M,W
Dordt College, IA M,W
Dowling College, NY M,W
Drake University, IA M,W
Drury University, MO M,W
Duquesne University, PA M,W
Eastern Michigan University, MI M,W
Eastern Washington University, WA M,W
East Tennessee State University, TN M,W
Eckerd College, FL M,W
Edinboro University of Pennsylvania, PA M,W
Elizabeth City State University, NC M,W
Elon University, NC M,W
Embry-Riddle Aeronautical University–Daytona, FL M
Emmanuel College, GA M,W
Emporia State University, KS M,W
Erskine College, SC M,W
Evangel University, MO M,W
The Evergreen State College, WA M,W
Fairfield University, CT M,W
Faulkner University, AL M,W
Fayetteville State University, NC M
Felician College, NJ M,W
Ferris State University, MI M,W
Flagler College, FL M,W
Florida Agricultural and Mechanical University, FL M,W
Florida Atlantic University, FL M,W
Florida College, FL M
Florida Gulf Coast University, FL M,W
Florida Institute of Technology, FL M,W
Florida International University, FL M,W
Florida Southern College, FL M,W
Florida State University, FL M,W
Fort Lewis College, CO M,W
Francis Marion University, SC M,W
Freed-Hardeman University, TN M,W
Furman University, SC M,W
Gannon University, PA M,W
Gardner-Webb University, NC M,W
Garrett College, MD M,W
Georgetown College, KY M,W
Georgetown University, DC M,W
Georgia College & State University, GA M,W
Georgia Institute of Technology, GA M,W
Georgian Court University, NJ W
Georgia Southern University, GA M,W
Georgia State University, GA M,W
Goldey-Beacom College, DE M,W
Grace College, IN M,W
Graceland University, IA M,W
Grand Valley State University, MI M,W
Grand View University, IA M,W
Hannibal-LaGrange University, MO M,W
Harding University, AR M,W
Hawai'i Pacific University, HI M,W
Hillsdale College, MI M,W
Hofstra University, NY M,W
Houghton College, NY M,W
Humboldt State University, CA M,W
Huntington University, IN M,W
Illinois State University, IL M,W
Indiana State University, IN M,W
Indiana University Bloomington, IN M,W
Indiana University of Pennsylvania, PA M,W
Indiana University–Purdue University Fort Wayne, IN M,W
Indiana University–Purdue University Indianapolis, IN M,W

Indiana University South Bend, IN M,W
Indiana University Southeast, IN M,W
Indiana Wesleyan University, IN M,W
Inter American University of Puerto Rico, Bayamón Campus, PR M,W
Inter American University of Puerto Rico, Guayama Campus, PR M,W
Inter American University of Puerto Rico, San Germán Campus, PR M,W
Iona College, NY M,W
Iowa State University of Science and Technology, IA M,W
Iowa Wesleyan College, IA M,W
James Madison University, VA M,W
Jamestown College, ND M,W
John Brown University, AR M,W
Johnson C. Smith University, NC M,W
Kansas State University, KS M,W
Kennesaw State University, GA M,W
Kent State University, OH M,W
Kentucky State University, KY M,W
Kentucky Wesleyan College, KY M,W
King College, TN M,W
Kutztown University of Pennsylvania, PA M,W
Lake Superior State University, MI M,W
Lamar University, TX M,W
Lane College, TN M,W
Lee University, TN M,W
Lehigh University, PA M,W
Le Moyne College, NY M,W
Lewis-Clark State College, ID M,W
Liberty University, VA M,W
Limestone College, SC M,W
Lincoln Memorial University, TN M,W
Lincoln University, MO M,W
Lindenwood University, MO M,W
Lindsey Wilson College, KY M,W
Lipscomb University, TN M,W
Lock Haven University of Pennsylvania, PA M,W
Long Island University, Brooklyn Campus, NY M,W
Long Island University, C.W. Post Campus, NY M,W
Longwood University, VA M,W
Louisiana State University and Agricultural and Mechanical College, LA M,W
Lourdes College, OH M,W
Loyola Marymount University, CA M,W
Loyola University Chicago, IL M,W
Loyola University Maryland, MD M,W
Loyola University New Orleans, LA M,W
Lubbock Christian University, TX M,W
Lynn University, FL M,W
Lyon College, AR M,W
Malone University, OH M,W
Manhattan College, NY M,W
Marist College, NY M,W
Marquette University, WI M,W
Marshall University, WV M,W
Mars Hill College, NC M,W
Maryville University of Saint Louis, MO M,W
The Master's College and Seminary, CA M,W
Mayville State University, ND M,W
McKendree University, IL M,W
Mercer University, GA M,W
Merrimack College, MA M,W
Mesa State College, CO M,W
Miami University, OH M,W
Michigan State University, MI M,W
Mid-Continent University, KY M,W
Middle Tennessee State University, TN M,W
Midwestern State University, TX M,W
Millersville University of Pennsylvania, PA M,W
Milligan College, TN M,W
Minnesota State University Mankato, MN M,W
Minnesota State University Moorhead, MN M,W
Minot State University, ND M,W
Mississippi State University, MS M,W
Missouri Baptist University, MO M,W
Missouri Southern State University, MO M,W
Missouri State University, MO M,W
Missouri University of Science and Technology, MO M,W
Molloy College, NY M,W
Monmouth University, NJ M,W
Montana State University, MT M,W
Montana State University Billings, MT M,W
Montana Tech of The University of Montana, MT M,W
Montreat College, NC M,W
Morehead State University, KY M,W
Morehouse College, GA M
Morningside College, IA M,W
Mountain State University, WV M
Mount Marty College, SD M,W
Mount Mercy University, IA M,W
Mount Olive College, NC M,W
Mount St. Mary's University, MD M,W
Mount Vernon Nazarene University, OH M,W
Murray State University, KY M,W
New Jersey Institute of Technology, NJ M,W
New Mexico State University, NM M,W
New York Institute of Technology, NY M,W
Niagara University, NY M,W
Nicholls State University, LA M,W
North Carolina Agricultural and Technical State University, NC M,W
North Carolina State University, NC M,W
Northeastern State University, OK M,W
Northeastern University, MA M,W
Northern Arizona University, AZ M,W
Northern Illinois University, IL M,W
Northern Kentucky University, KY M,W
Northern Michigan University, MI M,W
Northern State University, SD M,W
North Georgia College & State University, GA M,W
Northwest Christian University, OR M,W
Northwestern Oklahoma State University, OK M,W
Northwestern State University of Louisiana, LA M,W
Northwest Missouri State University, MO M,W
Northwest Nazarene University, ID M,W
Northwest University, WA M,W
Notre Dame de Namur University, CA M,W
Nyack College, NY M,W
The Ohio State University, OH M,W
Ohio University, OH M,W
Ohio Valley University, WV M,W
Oklahoma Christian University, OK M,W
Oklahoma City University, OK M,W
Oklahoma Panhandle State University, OK M,W
Oklahoma State University, OK M,W
Oklahoma Wesleyan University, OK M,W
Old Dominion University, VA M,W
Oregon State University, OR M,W
Ouachita Baptist University, AR M,W
Our Lady of the Lake University of San Antonio, TX M,W
Pace University, NY M,W
Palm Beach Atlantic University, FL M,W
Penn State University Park, PA M,W
Pepperdine University, CA M,W
Philadelphia University, PA M,W
Pikeville College, KY M,W
Point Park University, PA M,W
Prairie View A&M University, TX M,W
Presbyterian College, SC M,W
Providence College, RI M,W
Purdue University, IN M,W
Purdue University Calumet, IN M,W
Purdue University North Central, IN M
Queens College of the City University of New York, NY M,W
Quincy University, IL M,W
Quinnipiac University, CT M,W
Radford University, VA M,W
Regis University, CO M,W
Reinhardt University, GA M,W
Research College of Nursing, MO M,W
Rice University, TX M,W
Rider University, NJ M,W
Robert Morris University, PA M,W
Robert Morris University Illinois, IL M,W
Rockhurst University, MO M,W
Rocky Mountain College, MT M,W
Rogers State University, OK M,W
Rollins College, FL M,W
Sacred Heart University, CT M,W
Saginaw Valley State University, MI M,W
St. Ambrose University, IA M,W
St. Andrews Presbyterian College, NC M,W
Saint Anselm College, NH M,W
St. Bonaventure University, NY M,W
St. Edward's University, TX M,W
Saint Francis University, PA M,W
St. John's University, NY M,W
Saint Joseph's College, IN M,W
Saint Joseph's University, PA M,W
Saint Leo University, FL M,W
Saint Louis University, MO M,W
Saint Martin's University, WA M,W
Saint Mary-of-the-Woods College, IN W
Saint Mary's College of California, CA M,W
Saint Michael's College, VT M,W
St. Thomas Aquinas College, NY M,W
Saint Xavier University, IL M
Samford University, AL M,W
San Diego Christian College, CA M,W
San Diego State University, CA M,W

San Francisco State University, CA M,W
San Jose State University, CA M,W
Santa Clara University, CA M,W
Savannah State University, GA M,W
Seattle Pacific University, WA M,W
Seton Hill University, PA M,W
Shawnee State University, OH M,W
Shepherd University, WV M,W
Shippensburg University of Pennsylvania, PA M,W
Shorter University, GA M,W
Siena College, NY M,W
Silver Lake College, WI M,W
Simpson University, CA M,W
Slippery Rock University of Pennsylvania, PA M,W
Sonoma State University, CA M,W
South Dakota School of Mines and Technology, SD M,W
South Dakota State University, SD M,W
Southeastern Louisiana University, LA M,W
Southeastern Oklahoma State University, OK M,W
Southeast Missouri State University, MO M,W
Southern Connecticut State University, CT M,W
Southern Illinois University Carbondale, IL M,W
Southern Illinois University Edwardsville, IL M,W
Southern Methodist University, TX M,W
Southern Oregon University, OR M,W
Southern Polytechnic State University, GA M,W
Southern Utah University, UT M,W
Southwestern College, KS M,W
Southwestern Oklahoma State University, OK M,W
Southwest Minnesota State University, MN M,W
Spring Arbor University, MI M,W
Spring Hill College, AL M,W
Stanford University, CA M,W
State University of New York at Binghamton, NY M,W
Stephen F. Austin State University, TX M,W
Stetson University, FL M,W
Stonehill College, MA M,W
Stony Brook University, State University of New York, NY M,W
Syracuse University, NY M,W
Tabor College, KS M,W
Tarleton State University, TX M,W
Taylor University, IN M,W
Temple University, PA M,W
Tennessee Technological University, TN M,W
Tennessee Wesleyan College, TN M,W
Texas A&M International University, TX M,W
Texas A&M University, TX M,W
Texas A&M University–Corpus Christi, TX M,W
Texas Christian University, TX M,W
Texas Southern University, TX M,W
Texas State University–San Marcos, TX M,W
Texas Tech University, TX M,W
Texas Wesleyan University, TX M,W
Texas Woman's University, TX W
Tiffin University, OH M,W
Towson University, MD M,W
Trevecca Nazarene University, TN M,W
Troy University, AL M,W
Truman State University, MO M,W
Tulane University, LA M,W
Tuskegee University, AL M,W
Union College, KY M,W
Union University, TN M,W
University at Buffalo, the State University of New York, NY M,W
The University of Akron, OH M,W
The University of Alabama, AL M,W
The University of Alabama at Birmingham, AL M,W
The University of Alabama in Huntsville, AL M,W
University of Alaska Fairbanks, AK M,W
The University of Arizona, AZ M,W
University of Arkansas, AR M,W
University of Bridgeport, CT M,W
University of California, Davis, CA M,W
University of California, Irvine, CA M,W
University of California, Los Angeles, CA M,W
University of California, Santa Barbara, CA M,W
University of Central Florida, FL M,W
University of Central Missouri, MO M,W
University of Charleston, WV M,W
University of Cincinnati, OH M,W
University of Colorado at Colorado Springs, CO M,W
University of Colorado Boulder, CO M,W
University of Connecticut, CT M,W
University of Dayton, OH M,W
University of Delaware, DE M,W
University of Denver, CO M,W
University of Evansville, IN M,W
The University of Findlay, OH M,W
University of Florida, FL M,W
University of Georgia, GA M,W
University of Hartford, CT M,W
University of Hawaii at Hilo, HI M
University of Hawaii at Manoa, HI M,W
University of Houston, TX M,W
University of Idaho, ID M,W
University of Illinois at Chicago, IL M,W
University of Illinois at Springfield, IL M,W
University of Illinois at Urbana–Champaign, IL M,W
University of Indianapolis, IN M,W
The University of Iowa, IA M,W
The University of Kansas, KS M,W
University of Louisiana at Lafayette, LA M,W
University of Louisville, KY M,W
University of Maine, ME M,W
University of Maryland, Baltimore County, MD M,W
University of Maryland, College Park, MD M,W
University of Massachusetts Amherst, MA M,W
University of Massachusetts Lowell, MA M,W
University of Memphis, TN M,W
University of Miami, FL M,W
University of Michigan, MI M,W
University of Michigan–Dearborn, MI M,W
University of Minnesota, Crookston, MN M,W
University of Minnesota, Duluth, MN M,W
University of Minnesota, Twin Cities Campus, MN M,W
University of Mississippi, MS M,W
University of Missouri, MO M,W
University of Missouri–St. Louis, MO M,W
University of Mobile, AL M,W
University of Montevallo, AL M,W
University of Nebraska at Omaha, NE M,W
University of Nebraska–Lincoln, NE M,W
University of Nevada, Las Vegas, NV M,W
University of Nevada, Reno, NV M,W
University of New Hampshire, NH M,W
University of North Alabama, AL M,W
The University of North Carolina at Asheville, NC M,W
The University of North Carolina at Chapel Hill, NC M,W
The University of North Carolina at Charlotte, NC M,W
The University of North Carolina at Greensboro, NC M,W
The University of North Carolina at Pembroke, NC M,W
The University of North Carolina Wilmington, NC M,W
University of North Dakota, ND M,W
University of Northern Colorado, CO M,W
University of Northern Iowa, IA M,W
University of North Florida, FL M,W
University of North Texas, TX M,W
University of Notre Dame, IN M,W
University of Oklahoma, OK M,W
University of Oregon, OR M,W
University of Pittsburgh, PA M,W
University of Pittsburgh at Johnstown, PA M,W
University of Portland, OR M,W
University of Rhode Island, RI M,W
University of Richmond, VA M,W
University of Rio Grande, OH M,W
University of St. Francis, IL M,W
University of St. Thomas, TX M
University of San Diego, CA M,W
University of Science and Arts of Oklahoma, OK M,W
University of South Alabama, AL M,W
University of South Carolina, SC M,W
University of South Carolina Aiken, SC M,W
The University of South Dakota, SD M,W
University of Southern California, CA M,W
University of Southern Indiana, IN M,W
University of Southern Mississippi, MS M,W
University of South Florida, FL M,W
The University of Tampa, FL M,W
The University of Tennessee, TN M,W

The University of Tennessee at Chattanooga, TN	M,W
The University of Tennessee at Martin, TN	M,W
The University of Texas at Arlington, TX	M,W
The University of Texas at Austin, TX	M,W
The University of Texas at San Antonio, TX	M,W
The University of Texas of the Permian Basin, TX	M,W
The University of Texas–Pan American, TX	M,W
University of the Cumberlands, KY	M,W
University of the Incarnate Word, TX	M,W
University of the Pacific, CA	M,W
University of the Sciences in Philadelphia, PA	M,W
University of the Southwest, NM	M,W
The University of Toledo, OH	M,W
University of Tulsa, OK	M,W
University of Utah, UT	M,W
University of Vermont, VT	M,W
University of Virginia, VA	M,W
The University of Virginia's College at Wise, VA	M,W
University of West Florida, FL	M,W
University of West Georgia, GA	M,W
University of Wisconsin–Green Bay, WI	M,W
University of Wisconsin–Madison, WI	M,W
University of Wisconsin–Parkside, WI	M,W
University of Wyoming, WY	M,W
Upper Iowa University, IA	M,W
Ursuline College, OH	W
Utah State University, UT	M,W
Utah Valley University, UT	M,W
Valdosta State University, GA	M,W
Valley City State University, ND	M,W
Valparaiso University, IN	M,W
Vanderbilt University, TN	M,W
Victory University, TN	M
Villanova University, PA	M,W
Virginia Commonwealth University, VA	M,W
Virginia Military Institute, VA	M
Virginia State University, VA	M,W
Wagner College, NY	M,W
Wake Forest University, NC	M,W
Walsh University, OH	M,W
Washburn University, KS	M,W
Washington Adventist University, MD	M,W
Washington State University, WA	M,W
Wayland Baptist University, TX	M,W
Wayne State College, NE	M,W
Wayne State University, MI	M,W
Webber International University, FL	M,W
West Chester University of Pennsylvania, PA	M,W
Western Carolina University, NC	M,W
Western Illinois University, IL	M,W
Western Kentucky University, KY	M,W
Western Michigan University, MI	M,W
Western Oregon University, OR	M,W
Western State College of Colorado, CO	M,W
West Liberty University, WV	M,W
Westminster College, UT	M,W
Westmont College, CA	M,W
West Virginia University, WV	M,W
Wheeling Jesuit University, WV	M,W
Wichita State University, KS	M,W
William Jessup University, CA	M,W
William Jewell College, MO	M,W
Wingate University, NC	M,W
Winona State University, MN	M,W
Winthrop University, SC	M,W
Wofford College, SC	M,W
Wright State University, OH	M,W
Xavier University, OH	M,W
Xavier University of Louisiana, LA	M,W
Young Harris College, GA	M,W
Youngstown State University, OH	M,W

Bowling

Adelphi University, NY	W
Arkansas State University, AR	W
Bellarmine University, KY	W
Bethune-Cookman University, FL	W
Campbellsville University, KY	M,W
Clarke University, IA	M,W
Davenport University, MI	M,W
Delaware State University, DE	W
Elizabeth City State University, NC	W
Fayetteville State University, NC	W
Florida Agricultural and Mechanical University, FL	W
Grand View University, IA	M,W
Johnson C. Smith University, NC	W
Kutztown University of Pennsylvania, PA	W
Lindenwood University, MO	M,W
Lindsey Wilson College, KY	M,W
McKendree University, IL	M,W
Missouri Baptist University, MO	M
Monmouth University, NJ	W
North Carolina Agricultural and Technical State University, NC	W
Pikeville College, KY	M,W
Robert Morris University Illinois, IL	M,W
Sacred Heart University, CT	W
Saginaw Valley State University, MI	M
St. Ambrose University, IA	M,W
Stephen F. Austin State University, TX	W
Texas Southern University, TX	W
Union College, KY	M,W
University of Nebraska–Lincoln, NE	W
Ursuline College, OH	W
Valparaiso University, IN	W
Vanderbilt University, TN	W
Virginia State University, VA	W
Webber International University, FL	M,W
Wichita State University, KS	M,W

Cheerleading

Adelphi University, NY	W
Anderson University, SC	W
Arkansas Tech University, AR	M,W
Ashland University, OH	W
Auburn University Montgomery, AL	M,W
Austin Peay State University, TN	M,W
Benedictine College, KS	M,W
Bethel College, IN	M,W
Brevard College, NC	W
Brigham Young University, UT	M,W
Cameron University, OK	M,W
Campbellsville University, KY	M,W
Culver-Stockton College, MO	M,W
Dakota Wesleyan University, SD	M,W
Davenport University, MI	W
Delaware State University, DE	M,W
Delta State University, MS	M,W
Doane College, NE	W
Drake University, IA	M,W
Drury University, MO	M,W
Emporia State University, KS	M,W
Freed-Hardeman University, TN	W
Gardner-Webb University, NC	M,W
Georgetown College, KY	W
Georgia Institute of Technology, GA	M,W
Grace College, IN	M,W
Graceland University, IA	M,W
Grand View University, IA	W
Hannibal-LaGrange University, MO	M,W
Hawai'i Pacific University, HI	M,W
Hofstra University, NY	M,W
Indiana Wesleyan University, IN	M,W
John Brown University, AR	M,W
Kentucky State University, KY	W
King College, TN	M,W
Liberty University, VA	M,W
Lincoln University, MO	W
Lindenwood University, MO	M,W
Lindsey Wilson College, KY	M,W
Lubbock Christian University, TX	M,W
Mars Hill College, NC	M,W
Maryville University of Saint Louis, MO	M,W
McKendree University, IL	M,W
Mid-Continent University, KY	M,W
Middle Tennessee State University, TN	M,W
Midwestern State University, TX	M,W
Mississippi State University, MS	M,W
Montana State University, MT	M,W
Mountain State University, WV	W
North Carolina State University, NC	M,W
Northern State University, SD	W
Northwestern Oklahoma State University, OK	M,W
Northwest Missouri State University, MO	M,W
Nyack College, NY	M,W
Oklahoma City University, OK	M,W
Oklahoma Panhandle State University, OK	W
Old Dominion University, VA	W
Pikeville College, KY	M,W
Presbyterian College, SC	M,W
Reinhardt University, GA	M,W
Robert Morris University Illinois, IL	M,W
Rocky Mountain College, MT	W
Rogers State University, OK	M,W
St. Ambrose University, IA	M,W
St. Edward's University, TX	M,W
Saint Joseph's College, IN	M,W
Savannah State University, GA	M,W
Shorter University, GA	M,W
Southeastern Louisiana University, LA	M,W
Southeast Missouri State University, MO	M,W
Southern Methodist University, TX	M,W
Southwestern College, KS	M,W
Tabor College, KS	M,W
Tarleton State University, TX	M,W
Temple University, PA	M,W

Tennessee Technological University, TN M,W
Tennessee Wesleyan College, TN M,W
Tiffin University, OH M,W
Union College, KY M,W
Union University, TN W
The University of Alabama, AL M,W
The University of Alabama in Huntsville, AL M,W
University of Central Florida, FL M,W
University of Charleston, WV W
University of Delaware, DE M,W
University of Florida, FL M,W
University of Hawaii at Manoa, HI M,W
University of Maryland, College Park, MD W
University of Memphis, TN M,W
University of Mississippi, MS M,W
University of Mobile, AL W
University of Nevada, Las Vegas, NV M,W
The University of North Carolina Wilmington, NC W
University of St. Francis, IL W
University of Science and Arts of Oklahoma, OK M,W
University of South Carolina, SC M,W
The University of Tennessee at Martin, TN W
The University of Texas of the Permian Basin, TX M,W
University of the Cumberlands, KY M,W
University of the Incarnate Word, TX W
University of Utah, UT M,W
University of West Georgia, GA M,W
University of Wyoming, WY M,W
Washburn University, KS M,W
Wayland Baptist University, TX M,W
Webber International University, FL M,W
West Virginia University, WV M,W
William Jewell College, MO M,W

Crew

Barry University, FL W
Boston College, MA W
Boston University, MA M,W
Clemson University, SC W
Creighton University, NE W
Dowling College, NY M,W
Duquesne University, PA W
Eastern Michigan University, MI W
Fairfield University, CT M,W
Florida Institute of Technology, FL W
Indiana University Bloomington, IN W
Kansas State University, KS W
Lehigh University, PA W
Loyola Marymount University, CA W
Loyola University Maryland, MD M,W
Marist College, NY W
Merrimack College, MA W
Michigan State University, MI W
Northeastern University, MA M,W
Oklahoma City University, OK M,W
Old Dominion University, VA W
Robert Morris University, PA W
Robert Morris University Illinois, IL W
Saint Joseph's University, PA M,W
San Diego State University, CA W
Seattle Pacific University, WA W
Southern Methodist University, TX W
Stanford University, CA M,W
Stetson University, FL W
Syracuse University, NY M,W
Temple University, PA M,W
University at Buffalo, the State University of New York, NY W
The University of Alabama, AL W
University of California, Los Angeles, CA W
University of Charleston, WV M,W
University of Delaware, DE W
The University of Iowa, IA W
The University of Kansas, KS W
University of Louisville, KY W
University of Massachusetts Amherst, MA W
University of Miami, FL M
The University of North Carolina at Chapel Hill, NC W
University of Notre Dame, IN W
University of Oklahoma, OK W
University of Rhode Island, RI W
University of San Diego, CA W
University of Southern California, CA W
The University of Tampa, FL W
The University of Tennessee, TN W
The University of Texas at Austin, TX W
University of Tulsa, OK W
University of Virginia, VA W
Washington State University, WA W
West Virginia University, WV W

Cross-country Running

Abilene Christian University, TX M,W
Adams State College, CO M,W
Adelphi University, NY M,W
Alabama Agricultural and Mechanical University, AL M,W
Alabama State University, AL M,W
Alcorn State University, MS M,W
Alderson-Broaddus College, WV M,W
American University, DC M,W
Anderson University, SC M,W
Angelo State University, TX M,W
Appalachian State University, NC M,W
Arizona State University, AZ M,W
Arkansas State University, AR M,W
Arkansas Tech University, AR W
Asbury University, KY M,W
Ashland University, OH M,W
Auburn University, AL M,W
Augustana College, SD M,W
Austin Peay State University, TN M,W
Azusa Pacific University, CA M,W
Ball State University, IN W
Bellarmine University, KY M,W
Belmont Abbey College, NC M,W
Belmont University, TN M,W
Bemidji State University, MN W
Benedictine College, KS M,W
Bethel College, IN M,W
Bethune-Cookman University, FL M,W
Biola University, CA M,W
Bloomfield College, NJ M,W
Bloomsburg University of Pennsylvania, PA M,W
Bluefield College, VA M,W
Bluefield State College, WV M,W
Boise State University, ID M,W
Boston College, MA M,W
Boston University, MA M,W
Bowie State University, MD M,W
Bowling Green State University, OH M,W
Brenau University, GA W
Brevard College, NC M,W
Brigham Young University, UT M,W
Bryan College, TN M,W
Bryant University, RI M,W
Bucknell University, PA W
Butler University, IN M,W
California Polytechnic State University, San Luis Obispo, CA M,W
California State Polytechnic University, Pomona, CA M,W
California State University, Chico, CA M,W
California State University, Dominguez Hills, CA W
California State University, Fullerton, CA M,W
California State University, Long Beach, CA M,W
California State University, Monterey Bay, CA M,W
California State University, Northridge, CA M,W
Cameron University, OK M
Campbellsville University, KY M,W
Canisius College, NY M,W
Carson-Newman College, TN M,W
Cedarville University, OH M,W
Central Connecticut State University, CT M,W
Central Michigan University, MI M,W
Chestnut Hill College, PA M,W
Christian Brothers University, TN M,W
The Citadel, The Military College of South Carolina, SC M,W
Clarion University of Pennsylvania, PA W
Clarke University, IA M,W
Clemson University, SC M,W
Cleveland State University, OH W
Coastal Carolina University, SC M,W
Coker College, SC M,W
College of Charleston, SC M,W
College of Saint Mary, NE W
The College of William and Mary, VA M,W
Colorado School of Mines, CO M,W
Colorado State University, CO M,W
Columbus State University, GA M,W
Concordia University, CA M,W
Concordia University, Nebraska, NE M,W
Concordia University, St. Paul, MN M,W
Concord University, WV M,W
Coppin State University, MD M,W
Corban University, OR M,W
Creighton University, NE M,W
Culver-Stockton College, MO M,W
Dakota State University, SD M,W
Dakota Wesleyan University, SD M,W
Dallas Baptist University, TX W
Davenport University, MI M,W
Davidson College, NC M,W
Delaware State University, DE M,W
Delta State University, MS W
DePaul University, IL M,W
Dickinson State University, ND M,W
Dillard University, LA M,W

Dixie State College of Utah, UT	M,W
Doane College, NE	M,W
Dominican College, NY	W
Dordt College, IA	M,W
Dowling College, NY	M,W
Drake University, IA	M,W
Drury University, MO	M,W
Duquesne University, PA	M,W
Eastern Michigan University, MI	M,W
Eastern Washington University, WA	M,W
East Tennessee State University, TN	M,W
Edinboro University of Pennsylvania, PA	M,W
Elon University, NC	M,W
Embry-Riddle Aeronautical University–Daytona, FL	M,W
Emmanuel College, GA	M,W
Emporia State University, KS	M,W
Erskine College, SC	M,W
Evangel University, MO	M,W
The Evergreen State College, WA	M,W
Fairfield University, CT	M,W
Felician College, NJ	M,W
Ferris State University, MI	M,W
Flagler College, FL	M,W
Florida Agricultural and Mechanical University, FL	M,W
Florida College, FL	M,W
Florida Gulf Coast University, FL	M,W
Florida Institute of Technology, FL	M,W
Florida International University, FL	M,W
Florida Southern College, FL	M,W
Florida State University, FL	M,W
Fort Lewis College, CO	M,W
Francis Marion University, SC	M,W
Freed-Hardeman University, TN	M,W
Furman University, SC	M,W
Gannon University, PA	M,W
Gardner-Webb University, NC	M,W
Georgetown College, KY	M,W
Georgetown University, DC	M,W
Georgia College & State University, GA	M,W
Georgia Institute of Technology, GA	M,W
Georgian Court University, NJ	W
Georgia Southern University, GA	W
Georgia State University, GA	M,W
Goldey-Beacom College, DE	M,W
Grace College, IN	M,W
Graceland University, IA	M,W
Grand Valley State University, MI	M,W
Grand View University, IA	M,W
Hannibal-LaGrange University, MO	M,W
Harding University, AR	M,W
Hawai'i Pacific University, HI	M,W
Hillsdale College, MI	M,W
Hofstra University, NY	M,W
Houghton College, NY	M,W
Humboldt State University, CA	M,W
Huntington University, IN	M,W
Illinois Institute of Technology, IL	M,W
Illinois State University, IL	M,W
Indiana State University, IN	M,W
Indiana University Bloomington, IN	M,W
Indiana University of Pennsylvania, PA	M,W
Indiana University–Purdue University Fort Wayne, IN	M,W
Indiana University–Purdue University Indianapolis, IN	M,W
Indiana Wesleyan University, IN	M,W
Inter American University of Puerto Rico, Bayamón Campus, PR	M,W
Inter American University of Puerto Rico, Guayama Campus, PR	M,W
Inter American University of Puerto Rico, San Germán Campus, PR	M,W
Iona College, NY	M,W
Iowa State University of Science and Technology, IA	M,W
Iowa Wesleyan College, IA	M,W
James Madison University, VA	W
Jamestown College, ND	M,W
John Brown University, AR	M,W
Johnson C. Smith University, NC	M,W
Kansas State University, KS	M,W
Kennesaw State University, GA	M,W
Kent State University, OH	M,W
Kentucky State University, KY	M,W
Kentucky Wesleyan College, KY	M,W
King College, TN	M,W
Kutztown University of Pennsylvania, PA	M,W
Lake Superior State University, MI	M,W
Lamar University, TX	M,W
Lee University, TN	M,W
Lehigh University, PA	M,W
Le Moyne College, NY	M,W
Lewis-Clark State College, ID	M,W
Liberty University, VA	M,W
Limestone College, SC	M,W
Lincoln Memorial University, TN	M,W
Lincoln University, MO	W
Lindenwood University, MO	M,W
Lindsey Wilson College, KY	M,W
Lipscomb University, TN	M,W
Lock Haven University of Pennsylvania, PA	M,W
Long Island University, Brooklyn Campus, NY	M,W
Long Island University, C.W. Post Campus, NY	M,W
Longwood University, VA	M,W
Louisiana State University and Agricultural and Mechanical College, LA	M,W
Loyola Marymount University, CA	M,W
Loyola University Chicago, IL	M,W
Loyola University Maryland, MD	M,W
Lubbock Christian University, TX	M,W
Lyon College, AR	M,W
Malone University, OH	M,W
Manhattan College, NY	M,W
Marist College, NY	M,W
Marquette University, WI	M,W
Marshall University, WV	M,W
Mars Hill College, NC	M,W
Maryville University of Saint Louis, MO	M,W
The Master's College and Seminary, CA	M,W
McKendree University, IL	M,W
Mercer University, GA	M,W
Merrimack College, MA	M,W
Mesa State College, CO	M,W
Miami University, OH	M,W
Michigan State University, MI	M,W
Middle Tennessee State University, TN	M,W
Midwestern State University, TX	W
Millersville University of Pennsylvania, PA	M,W
Milligan College, TN	M,W
Minnesota State University Mankato, MN	M,W
Minot State University, ND	M,W
Mississippi State University, MS	M,W
Missouri Baptist University, MO	M,W
Missouri Southern State University, MO	M,W
Missouri State University, MO	W
Missouri University of Science and Technology, MO	M,W
Molloy College, NY	M,W
Monmouth University, NJ	M,W
Montana State University, MT	M,W
Montana State University Billings, MT	M,W
Montreat College, NC	M,W
Morehead State University, KY	M,W
Morehouse College, GA	M
Morningside College, IA	M,W
Mountain State University, WV	M,W
Mount Marty College, SD	M,W
Mount Mercy University, IA	M,W
Mount Olive College, NC	M,W
Mount St. Mary's University, MD	M,W
Mount Vernon Nazarene University, OH	M,W
Murray State University, KY	M,W
New Jersey Institute of Technology, NJ	M,W
New Mexico State University, NM	M,W
New York Institute of Technology, NY	M,W
Niagara University, NY	M,W
Nicholls State University, LA	M,W
North Carolina Agricultural and Technical State University, NC	M,W
North Carolina State University, NC	M,W
Northeastern University, MA	M,W
Northern Arizona University, AZ	M,W
Northern Kentucky University, KY	M,W
Northern Michigan University, MI	W
Northern State University, SD	M,W
Northwest Christian University, OR	M,W
Northwestern Oklahoma State University, OK	M,W
Northwestern State University of Louisiana, LA	M,W
Northwest Missouri State University, MO	M,W
Northwest Nazarene University, ID	M,W
Northwest University, WA	M,W
Notre Dame de Namur University, CA	M,W
Nyack College, NY	M,W
The Ohio State University, OH	M,W
Ohio University, OH	M,W
Ohio Valley University, WV	M,W
Oklahoma Christian University, OK	M,W
Oklahoma Panhandle State University, OK	M,W
Oklahoma State University, OK	M,W
Oklahoma Wesleyan University, OK	M,W
Ouachita Baptist University, AR	W

Athletic Grants for Undergraduates

Cross-country Running

Our Lady of the Lake University of San Antonio, TX	M,W
Pace University, NY	M,W
Palm Beach Atlantic University, FL	M,W
Penn State University Park, PA	M,W
Pepperdine University, CA	M,W
Pikeville College, KY	M,W
Point Park University, PA	M,W
Prairie View A&M University, TX	M,W
Presbyterian College, SC	M,W
Providence College, RI	M,W
Purdue University, IN	M,W
Queens College of the City University of New York, NY	M,W
Quincy University, IL	M,W
Quinnipiac University, CT	M,W
Radford University, VA	M,W
Regis University, CO	M,W
Reinhardt University, GA	M,W
Rice University, TX	M,W
Rider University, NJ	M,W
Robert Morris University Illinois, IL	M,W
Rocky Mountain College, MT	M,W
Rogers State University, OK	M,W
Sacred Heart University, CT	M,W
Saginaw Valley State University, MI	M,W
St. Ambrose University, IA	M,W
St. Andrews Presbyterian College, NC	M,W
St. Bonaventure University, NY	M,W
Saint Francis University, PA	M,W
St. John's University, NY	W
Saint Joseph's College, IN	M,W
Saint Joseph's University, PA	M,W
Saint Leo University, FL	M,W
Saint Louis University, MO	M,W
Saint Martin's University, WA	M,W
Saint Mary-of-the-Woods College, IN	W
Saint Mary's College of California, CA	M,W
St. Thomas Aquinas College, NY	M,W
St. Thomas University, FL	M,W
Saint Xavier University, IL	W
Samford University, AL	M,W
San Diego Christian College, CA	M,W
San Diego State University, CA	W
San Francisco State University, CA	M,W
San Jose State University, CA	M,W
Santa Clara University, CA	M,W
Savannah College of Art and Design, GA	M,W
Savannah State University, GA	M,W
Seattle Pacific University, WA	M,W
Seton Hill University, PA	M,W
Shawnee State University, OH	M,W
Shippensburg University of Pennsylvania, PA	M,W
Shorter University, GA	M,W
Siena College, NY	M,W
Silver Lake College, WI	M,W
Simpson University, CA	M,W
Slippery Rock University of Pennsylvania, PA	M,W
Soka University of America, CA	M,W
Sonoma State University, CA	M
South Dakota School of Mines and Technology, SD	M,W
South Dakota State University, SD	M,W
Southeastern Louisiana University, LA	M,W
Southeastern Oklahoma State University, OK	W
Southeast Missouri State University, MO	M,W
Southern Connecticut State University, CT	M,W
Southern Illinois University Carbondale, IL	M,W
Southern Illinois University Edwardsville, IL	M,W
Southern Methodist University, TX	W
Southern Oregon University, OR	M,W
Southwestern College, KS	M,W
Southwestern Oklahoma State University, OK	W
Spring Arbor University, MI	M,W
Spring Hill College, AL	M,W
Stanford University, CA	M,W
State University of New York at Binghamton, NY	M,W
Stephen F. Austin State University, TX	M,W
Stetson University, FL	M,W
Stonehill College, MA	M,W
Stony Brook University, State University of New York, NY	M,W
Syracuse University, NY	M,W
Tabor College, KS	M,W
Tarleton State University, TX	M,W
Taylor University, IN	M,W
Temple University, PA	M,W
Tennessee Technological University, TN	M,W
Tennessee Wesleyan College, TN	M,W
Texas A&M International University, TX	M,W
Texas A&M University, TX	M,W
Texas A&M University–Corpus Christi, TX	M,W
Texas Christian University, TX	M,W
Texas Southern University, TX	M,W
Texas State University–San Marcos, TX	M,W
Texas Tech University, TX	M,W
Texas Wesleyan University, TX	M,W
Tiffin University, OH	M,W
Towson University, MD	M,W
Troy University, AL	M,W
Truman State University, MO	M,W
Tulane University, LA	M,W
Union College, KY	M,W
Union University, TN	W
University at Buffalo, the State University of New York, NY	M,W
The University of Akron, OH	M,W
The University of Alabama, AL	M,W
The University of Alabama at Birmingham, AL	W
The University of Alabama in Huntsville, AL	M,W
University of Alaska Fairbanks, AK	M,W
The University of Arizona, AZ	M,W
University of Arkansas, AR	M,W
University of Bridgeport, CT	M,W
University of California, Davis, CA	M,W
University of California, Irvine, CA	M,W
University of California, Los Angeles, CA	M,W
University of California, Santa Barbara, CA	M,W
University of Central Florida, FL	M,W
University of Central Missouri, MO	M,W
University of Charleston, WV	M,W
University of Cincinnati, OH	M,W
University of Colorado at Colorado Springs, CO	M,W
University of Colorado Boulder, CO	M,W
University of Connecticut, CT	M,W
University of Dayton, OH	M,W
University of Evansville, IN	M,W
The University of Findlay, OH	M,W
University of Florida, FL	M,W
University of Georgia, GA	M,W
University of Hartford, CT	M,W
University of Hawaii at Hilo, HI	M,W
University of Hawaii at Manoa, HI	W
University of Houston, TX	M,W
University of Idaho, ID	M,W
University of Illinois at Chicago, IL	M,W
University of Illinois at Urbana–Champaign, IL	M,W
University of Indianapolis, IN	M,W
The University of Iowa, IA	M,W
The University of Kansas, KS	M,W
University of Louisiana at Lafayette, LA	M,W
University of Louisville, KY	M,W
University of Maine, ME	M,W
University of Maryland, Baltimore County, MD	M,W
University of Maryland, College Park, MD	M,W
University of Massachusetts Amherst, MA	M,W
University of Massachusetts Lowell, MA	M,W
University of Memphis, TN	M,W
University of Miami, FL	M,W
University of Michigan, MI	M,W
University of Minnesota, Duluth, MN	M,W
University of Minnesota, Twin Cities Campus, MN	M,W
University of Mississippi, MS	M,W
University of Missouri, MO	M,W
University of Mobile, AL	M,W
University of Nebraska at Omaha, NE	W
University of Nebraska–Lincoln, NE	M,W
University of Nevada, Las Vegas, NV	W
University of Nevada, Reno, NV	W
University of New Hampshire, NH	M,W
University of North Alabama, AL	M,W
The University of North Carolina at Asheville, NC	M,W
The University of North Carolina at Chapel Hill, NC	M,W
The University of North Carolina at Charlotte, NC	M,W
The University of North Carolina at Greensboro, NC	M,W
The University of North Carolina at Pembroke, NC	M,W
The University of North Carolina Wilmington, NC	M,W
University of North Dakota, ND	M,W
University of Northern Colorado, CO	W
University of Northern Iowa, IA	M,W
University of North Florida, FL	M,W
University of North Texas, TX	M,W
University of Notre Dame, IN	M,W

University of Oklahoma, OK M,W
University of Oregon, OR M,W
University of Pittsburgh, PA M,W
University of Portland, OR M,W
University of Rhode Island, RI M,W
University of Richmond, VA W
University of Rio Grande, OH M,W
University of St. Francis, IL M,W
University of San Diego, CA M,W
University of South Alabama, AL M,W
University of South Carolina, SC W
University of South Carolina Aiken, SC W
The University of South Dakota, SD M,W
University of Southern California, CA W
University of Southern Indiana, IN M,W
University of Southern Mississippi, MS W
University of South Florida, FL M,W
The University of Tampa, FL M,W
The University of Tennessee at Chattanooga, TN M,W
The University of Tennessee at Martin, TN M,W
The University of Texas at Austin, TX M,W
The University of Texas at San Antonio, TX M,W
The University of Texas of the Permian Basin, TX M,W
The University of Texas–Pan American, TX M,W
University of the Cumberlands, KY M,W
University of the Incarnate Word, TX M,W
University of the Pacific, CA W
University of the Southwest, NM M,W
The University of Toledo, OH M,W
University of Tulsa, OK M,W
University of Utah, UT W
University of Vermont, VT M,W
University of Virginia, VA M,W
The University of Virginia's College at Wise, VA M,W
University of West Florida, FL M,W
University of West Georgia, GA M,W
University of Wisconsin–Green Bay, WI M,W
University of Wisconsin–Madison, WI M,W
University of Wisconsin–Parkside, WI M,W
University of Wyoming, WY M,W
Ursuline College, OH W
Utah State University, UT M,W
Utah Valley University, UT M,W
Valdosta State University, GA M,W
Valley City State University, ND M,W
Valparaiso University, IN M,W
Vanderbilt University, TN M,W
Villanova University, PA M,W
Virginia Commonwealth University, VA M,W
Virginia Military Institute, VA M,W
Virginia State University, VA M,W
Wagner College, NY M,W
Wake Forest University, NC M,W
Walsh University, OH M,W
Washington Adventist University, MD M,W
Washington State University, WA M,W
Wayland Baptist University, TX M,W
Wayne State College, NE M,W
Wayne State University, MI M,W
Webber International University, FL M,W
West Chester University of Pennsylvania, PA M,W
Western Carolina University, NC M,W
Western Illinois University, IL M,W
Western Kentucky University, KY M,W
Western Michigan University, MI W
Western Oregon University, OR M,W
Western State College of Colorado, CO M,W
West Liberty University, WV M,W
Westminster College, UT M,W
Westmont College, CA M,W
West Virginia University, WV W
Wheeling Jesuit University, WV M,W
Wichita State University, KS M,W
William Jessup University, CA M,W
William Jewell College, MO M,W
Wingate University, NC M
Winona State University, MN W
Winthrop University, SC M,W
Wofford College, SC M,W
Wright State University, OH M,W
Xavier University, OH M,W
Young Harris College, GA M,W
Youngstown State University, OH M,W

Equestrian sports

Auburn University, AL W
Delaware State University, DE W
Murray State University, KY M,W
Oklahoma Panhandle State University, OK W
Oklahoma State University, OK W
St. Andrews Presbyterian College, NC M,W
Saint Mary-of-the-Woods College, IN W
Savannah College of Art and Design, GA M,W
Seton Hill University, PA W
Southern Methodist University, TX W
Southwestern Oklahoma State University, OK M,W
Stonehill College, MA W
Texas A&M University, TX W
Texas Christian University, TX W
Tiffin University, OH M,W
University of Georgia, GA W
University of Minnesota, Crookston, MN W
University of South Carolina, SC W
The University of Tennessee at Martin, TN W

Fencing

Cleveland State University, OH M,W
New Jersey Institute of Technology, NJ M,W
The Ohio State University, OH M,W
Penn State University Park, PA M,W
Queens College of the City University of New York, NY W
Sacred Heart University, CT W
St. John's University, NY M,W
Stanford University, CA M,W
Temple University, PA W
University of Notre Dame, IN M,W
Wayne State University, MI M,W

Field hockey

Adelphi University, NY W
American University, DC W
Appalachian State University, NC W
Ball State University, IN W
Bellarmine University, KY W
Bloomsburg University of Pennsylvania, PA W
Boston College, MA W
Boston University, MA W
Bryant University, RI W
Central Michigan University, MI W
Colgate University, NY W
College of the Holy Cross, MA W
The College of William and Mary, VA W
Davidson College, NC W
Fairfield University, CT W
Hofstra University, NY W
Houghton College, NY W
Indiana University of Pennsylvania, PA W
James Madison University, VA W
Kent State University, OH W
Kutztown University of Pennsylvania, PA W
Lehigh University, PA W
Limestone College, SC W
Lindenwood University, MO W
Lock Haven University of Pennsylvania, PA W
Long Island University, C.W. Post Campus, NY W
Longwood University, VA W
Merrimack College, MA W
Miami University, OH W
Michigan State University, MI W
Millersville University of Pennsylvania, PA W
Missouri State University, MO W
Monmouth University, NJ W
Northeastern University, MA W
The Ohio State University, OH W
Ohio University, OH W
Old Dominion University, VA W
Penn State University Park, PA W
Philadelphia University, PA W
Providence College, RI W
Quinnipiac University, CT W
Radford University, VA W
Rider University, NJ W
Robert Morris University, PA W
Sacred Heart University, CT W
Saint Francis University, PA W
Saint Joseph's University, PA W
Saint Louis University, MO W
Seton Hill University, PA W
Shippensburg University of Pennsylvania, PA W
Siena College, NY W
Slippery Rock University of Pennsylvania, PA W
Southern Connecticut State University, CT W
Stanford University, CA W
Stonehill College, MA W
Syracuse University, NY W
Temple University, PA W
Towson University, MD W
University of California, Davis, CA W
University of Connecticut, CT W
University of Delaware, DE W

he University of Iowa, IA	W
niversity of Louisville, KY	W
niversity of Maine, ME	W
Jniversity of Maryland, College Park, MD	W
Jniversity of Massachusetts Amherst, MA	W
University of Massachusetts Lowell, MA	W
University of Michigan, MI	W
University of New Hampshire, NH	W
The University of North Carolina at Chapel Hill, NC	W
University of Richmond, VA	W
University of the Pacific, CA	W
University of Vermont, VT	W
University of Virginia, VA	W
Villanova University, PA	W
Virginia Commonwealth University, VA	W
Wake Forest University, NC	W
West Chester University of Pennsylvania, PA	W

Football

Abilene Christian University, TX	M
Adams State College, CO	M
Alabama Agricultural and Mechanical University, AL	M
Alabama State University, AL	M
Alcorn State University, MS	M
Angelo State University, TX	M
Appalachian State University, NC	M
Arizona State University, AZ	M
Arkansas State University, AR	M
Arkansas Tech University, AR	M
Ashland University, OH	M
Auburn University, AL	M
Augustana College, SD	M
Austin Peay State University, TN	M
Azusa Pacific University, CA	M
Ball State University, IN	M
Bemidji State University, MN	M
Benedictine College, KS	M
Bethune-Cookman University, FL	M
Bloomsburg University of Pennsylvania, PA	M
Boise State University, ID	M
Boston College, MA	M
Bowie State University, MD	M
Bowling Green State University, OH	M
Brevard College, NC	M
Brigham Young University, UT	M
Bryant University, RI	M
California Polytechnic State University, San Luis Obispo, CA	M
California State University, Northridge, CA	M
Campbellsville University, KY	M
Carson-Newman College, TN	M
Central Michigan University, MI	M
The Citadel, The Military College of South Carolina, SC	M
Clarion University of Pennsylvania, PA	M
Clemson University, SC	M
Coastal Carolina University, SC	M
The College of William and Mary, VA	M
Colorado School of Mines, CO	M
Colorado State University, CO	M
Concordia University, Nebraska, NE	M
Concordia University, St. Paul, MN	M
Concord University, WV	M
Culver-Stockton College, MO	M
Dakota State University, SD	M
Dakota Wesleyan University, SD	M
Dallas Baptist University, TX	W
Davidson College, NC	M
Delaware State University, DE	M
Delta State University, MS	M
Dickinson State University, ND	M
Dixie State College of Utah, UT	M
Doane College, NE	M
Dordt College, IA	M
Duquesne University, PA	M
Eastern Michigan University, MI	M
Eastern Washington University, WA	M
Edinboro University of Pennsylvania, PA	M
Elizabeth City State University, NC	M
Elon University, NC	M
Emporia State University, KS	M
Evangel University, MO	M
Faulkner University, AL	M
Fayetteville State University, NC	M,W
Ferris State University, MI	M
Florida Agricultural and Mechanical University, FL	M
Florida Atlantic University, FL	M
Florida International University, FL	M
Florida State University, FL	M
Fort Lewis College, CO	M
Furman University, SC	M
Gannon University, PA	M
Gardner-Webb University, NC	M
Georgetown College, KY	M
Georgetown University, DC	M
Georgia Institute of Technology, GA	M
Georgia Southern University, GA	M
Georgia State University, GA	M
Graceland University, IA	M
Grand Valley State University, MI	M
Grand View University, IA	M
Harding University, AR	M
Hillsdale College, MI	M
Humboldt State University, CA	M
Illinois State University, IL	M
Indiana State University, IN	M
Indiana University Bloomington, IN	M
Indiana University of Pennsylvania, PA	M
Iowa State University of Science and Technology, IA	M
Iowa Wesleyan College, IA	M
James Madison University, VA	M
Jamestown College, ND	M
Johnson C. Smith University, NC	M
Kansas State University, KS	M
Kent State University, OH	M
Kentucky State University, KY	M
Kentucky Wesleyan College, KY	M
Kutztown University of Pennsylvania, PA	M
Lamar University, TX	M
Lane College, TN	M
Liberty University, VA	M
Lincoln University, MO	M
Lindenwood University, MO	M
Lindsey Wilson College, KY	M,W
Lock Haven University of Pennsylvania, PA	M
Long Island University, C.W. Post Campus, NY	M,W
Louisiana State University and Agricultural and Mechanical College, LA	M
Malone University, OH	M
Marshall University, WV	M
Mars Hill College, NC	M
Mayville State University, ND	M
McKendree University, IL	M
Merrimack College, MA	M
Mesa State College, CO	M
Miami University, OH	M
Michigan State University, MI	M
Middle Tennessee State University, TN	M
Midwestern State University, TX	M
Millersville University of Pennsylvania, PA	M
Minnesota State University Mankato, MN	M
Minnesota State University Moorhead, MN	M
Minot State University, ND	M
Mississippi State University, MS	M
Missouri Southern State University, MO	M
Missouri State University, MO	M
Missouri University of Science and Technology, MO	M
Monmouth University, NJ	M
Montana State University, MT	M
Montana Tech of The University of Montana, MT	M
Morehouse College, GA	M
Morningside College, IA	M
Murray State University, KY	M
New Mexico State University, NM	M
Nicholls State University, LA	M
North Carolina Agricultural and Technical State University, NC	M
North Carolina State University, NC	M
Northeastern State University, OK	M
Northern Arizona University, AZ	M
Northern Illinois University, IL	M
Northern Michigan University, MI	M
Northern State University, SD	M
Northwestern Oklahoma State University, OK	M
Northwestern State University of Louisiana, LA	M
Northwest Missouri State University, MO	M
The Ohio State University, OH	M
Ohio University, OH	M
Oklahoma Panhandle State University, OK	M
Oklahoma State University, OK	M
Old Dominion University, VA	M
Oregon State University, OR	M
Ouachita Baptist University, AR	M
Penn State University Park, PA	M
Pikeville College, KY	M
Prairie View A&M University, TX	M
Presbyterian College, SC	M
Purdue University, IN	M
Quincy University, IL	M

Rice University, TX M
Robert Morris University, PA M
Rocky Mountain College, MT M
Sacred Heart University, CT M
Saginaw Valley State University, MI M
St. Ambrose University, IA M
Saint Joseph's College, IN M
Saint Xavier University, IL M
Samford University, AL M
San Diego State University, CA M
San Jose State University, CA M
Savannah State University, GA M
Seton Hill University, PA M
Shepherd University, WV M
Shippensburg University of Pennsylvania, PA M
Shorter University, GA M
Slippery Rock University of Pennsylvania, PA M
South Dakota School of Mines and Technology, SD M
South Dakota State University, SD M
Southeastern Louisiana University, LA M
Southeastern Oklahoma State University, OK M
Southeast Missouri State University, MO M
Southern Connecticut State University, CT M
Southern Illinois University Carbondale, IL M
Southern Methodist University, TX M
Southern Oregon University, OR M
Southern Utah University, UT M
Southwestern College, KS M
Southwestern Oklahoma State University, OK M
Southwest Minnesota State University, MN M
Stanford University, CA M
Stephen F. Austin State University, TX M
Stonehill College, MA M
Stony Brook University, State University of New York, NY M
Syracuse University, NY M
Tabor College, KS M
Tarleton State University, TX M
Taylor University, IN M
Temple University, PA M
Tennessee Technological University, TN M
Texas A&M University, TX M
Texas Christian University, TX M
Texas Southern University, TX M
Texas State University–San Marcos, TX M
Texas Tech University, TX M
Tiffin University, OH M
Towson University, MD M
Troy University, AL M
Truman State University, MO M
Tulane University, LA M
Tuskegee University, AL M
Union College, KY M
University at Buffalo, the State University of New York, NY M
The University of Akron, OH M
The University of Alabama, AL M
The University of Alabama at Birmingham, AL M
The University of Arizona, AZ M
University of Arkansas, AR M
University of California, Davis, CA M
University of California, Los Angeles, CA M
University of Central Florida, FL M
University of Central Missouri, MO M
University of Charleston, WV M
University of Cincinnati, OH M
University of Colorado Boulder, CO M
University of Connecticut, CT M
University of Delaware, DE M
The University of Findlay, OH M
University of Florida, FL M
University of Georgia, GA M
University of Hawaii at Manoa, HI M
University of Houston, TX M
University of Idaho, ID M
University of Illinois at Urbana–Champaign, IL M
University of Indianapolis, IN M
The University of Iowa, IA M
The University of Kansas, KS M
University of Louisiana at Lafayette, LA M
University of Louisville, KY M
University of Maine, ME M
University of Maryland, College Park, MD M
University of Massachusetts Amherst, MA M
University of Memphis, TN M
University of Miami, FL M
University of Michigan, MI M
University of Minnesota, Crookston, MN M
University of Minnesota, Duluth, MN M
University of Minnesota, Twin Cities Campus, MN M
University of Mississippi, MS M
University of Missouri, MO M
University of Nebraska at Omaha, NE M
University of Nebraska–Lincoln, NE M
University of Nevada, Las Vegas, NV M
University of Nevada, Reno, NV M
University of New Hampshire, NH M
University of North Alabama, AL M
The University of North Carolina at Chapel Hill, NC M
The University of North Carolina at Pembroke, NC M
University of North Dakota, ND M
University of Northern Colorado, CO M
University of Northern Iowa, IA M
University of North Texas, TX M
University of Notre Dame, IN M
University of Oklahoma, OK M
University of Oregon, OR M
University of Pittsburgh, PA M
University of Rhode Island, RI M
University of Richmond, VA M
University of St. Francis, IL M
University of South Carolina, SC M
The University of South Dakota, SD M
University of Southern California, CA M
University of Southern Mississippi, MS M,W
University of South Florida, FL M
The University of Tennessee, TN M
The University of Tennessee at Chattanooga, TN M
The University of Tennessee at Martin, TN M
The University of Texas at Austin, TX M
University of the Cumberlands, KY M
University of the Incarnate Word, TX M
The University of Toledo, OH M
University of Tulsa, OK M
University of Utah, UT M
University of Virginia, VA M
The University of Virginia's College at Wise, VA M
University of West Georgia, GA M
University of Wisconsin–Madison, WI M
University of Wyoming, WY M
Upper Iowa University, IA M
Utah State University, UT M
Valdosta State University, GA M
Valley City State University, ND M
Vanderbilt University, TN M
Villanova University, PA M
Virginia Military Institute, VA M
Virginia Polytechnic Institute and State University, VA M
Virginia State University, VA M
Wagner College, NY M
Wake Forest University, NC M
Walsh University, OH M
Washburn University, KS M
Washington State University, WA M
Wayne State College, NE M
Wayne State University, MI M
Webber International University, FL M
West Chester University of Pennsylvania, PA M
Western Carolina University, NC M
Western Illinois University, IL M
Western Kentucky University, KY M
Western Michigan University, MI M
Western Oregon University, OR M
Western State College of Colorado, CO M
West Liberty University, WV M
West Virginia University, WV M
William Jewell College, MO M
Wingate University, NC M
Winona State University, MN M
Wofford College, SC M
Youngstown State University, OH M

Golf

Abilene Christian University, TX M
Adams State College, CO M,W
Adelphi University, NY M
Alabama Agricultural and Mechanical University, AL M
Alabama State University, AL M,W
Alcorn State University, MS M,W
Anderson University, SC M,W
Angelo State University, TX W
Appalachian State University, NC M,W
Arizona State University, AZ M,W
Arkansas State University, AR M,W
Arkansas Tech University, AR M,W
Armstrong Atlantic State University, GA M,W
Asbury University, KY M,W

Ashland University, OH	M,W
Auburn University, AL	M,W
Augustana College, SD	W
Austin Peay State University, TN	M,W
Azusa Pacific University, CA	M
Ball State University, IN	M,W
Barry University, FL	M,W
Bellarmine University, KY	M,W
Belmont Abbey College, NC	M,W
Belmont University, TN	M,W
Bemidji State University, MN	M,W
Benedictine College, KS	M,W
Bethel College, IN	M,W
Bethune-Cookman University, FL	M,W
Biola University, CA	M,W
Bluefield College, VA	M
Bluefield State College, WV	M
Boise State University, ID	M,W
Boston College, MA	M,W
Bowling Green State University, OH	M,W
Brevard College, NC	M,W
Brigham Young University, UT	M,W
Bryant University, RI	M
Butler University, IN	M,W
California Polytechnic State University, San Luis Obispo, CA	M,W
California State University, Bakersfield, CA	M
California State University, Chico, CA	M,W
California State University, Fullerton, CA	M,W
California State University, Monterey Bay, CA	M,W
California State University, Northridge, CA	M
California State University, San Bernardino, CA	M
Cameron University, OK	M,W
Campbellsville University, KY	M,W
Canisius College, NY	M
Carson-Newman College, TN	M
Cedarville University, OH	M
Central Connecticut State University, CT	M,W
Chestnut Hill College, PA	M
Christian Brothers University, TN	M,W
The Citadel, The Military College of South Carolina, SC	W
Clarion University of Pennsylvania, PA	M
Clarke University, IA	M,W
Clemson University, SC	M
Cleveland State University, OH	M
Coastal Carolina University, SC	M,W
Coker College, SC	M
College of Charleston, SC	M,W
College of Saint Mary, NE	W
The College of William and Mary, VA	M,W
Colorado State University, CO	M,W
Columbus State University, GA	M
Concordia University, Nebraska, NE	M,W
Concordia University, St. Paul, MN	M,W
Concord University, WV	M
Corban University, OR	M,W
Creighton University, NE	M,W
Culver-Stockton College, MO	M,W
Dakota Wesleyan University, SD	M,W
Dallas Baptist University, TX	W
Davenport University, MI	M,W
Davidson College, NC	M
Delta State University, MS	M
DePaul University, IL	M
Dickinson State University, ND	M,W
Dixie State College of Utah, UT	M
Doane College, NE	M,W
Dominican College, NY	M
Dominican University of California, CA	M,W
Dordt College, IA	M,W
Dowling College, NY	M
Drake University, IA	M
Drury University, MO	M,W
Eastern Michigan University, MI	M,W
Eastern Washington University, WA	W
East Tennessee State University, TN	M,W
Eckerd College, FL	M
Elizabeth City State University, NC	M
Elon University, NC	M,W
Embry-Riddle Aeronautical University–Daytona, FL	M,W
Emmanuel College, GA	M,W
Erskine College, SC	M,W
Evangel University, MO	M,W
Fairfield University, CT	M,W
Faulkner University, AL	M,W
Fayetteville State University, NC	M
Felician College, NJ	M
Ferris State University, MI	M,W
Flagler College, FL	M,W
Florida Agricultural and Mechanical University, FL	M,W
Florida Atlantic University, FL	M,W
Florida Gulf Coast University, FL	M,W
Florida Institute of Technology, FL	M,W
Florida International University, FL	W
Florida Southern College, FL	M,W
Florida State University, FL	M,W
Fort Lewis College, CO	M
Francis Marion University, SC	M
Furman University, SC	M,W
Gannon University, PA	M,W
Gardner-Webb University, NC	M,W
Georgetown College, KY	M,W
Georgetown University, DC	M
Georgia College & State University, GA	M
Georgia Institute of Technology, GA	M
Georgia Southern University, GA	M
Georgia State University, GA	M,W
Goldey-Beacom College, DE	M
Grace College, IN	M
Graceland University, IA	M,W
Grand Valley State University, MI	M,W
Grand View University, IA	M,W
Hannibal-LaGrange University, MO	M,W
Harding University, AR	M,W
Hawai'i Pacific University, HI	M
Hofstra University, NY	M,W
Huntington University, IN	M
Illinois State University, IL	M,W
Indiana State University, IN	W
Indiana University Bloomington, IN	M,W
Indiana University of Pennsylvania, PA	M
Indiana University–Purdue University Fort Wayne, IN	M,W
Indiana University–Purdue University Indianapolis, IN	M
Indiana Wesleyan University, IN	M
Iona College, NY	M
Iowa State University of Science and Technology, IA	M,W
Iowa Wesleyan College, IA	M,W
James Madison University, VA	M,W
Jamestown College, ND	M,W
John Brown University, AR	M
Johnson C. Smith University, NC	M
Kansas State University, KS	M,W
Kennesaw State University, GA	M,W
Kent State University, OH	M,W
Kentucky State University, KY	M
Kentucky Wesleyan College, KY	M,W
King College, TN	M,W
Kutztown University of Pennsylvania, PA	W
Lake Superior State University, MI	M,W
Lamar University, TX	M,W
Lee University, TN	M
Lehigh University, PA	M,W
Le Moyne College, NY	M,W
Lewis-Clark State College, ID	M,W
Liberty University, VA	M
Limestone College, SC	M,W
Lincoln Memorial University, TN	M,W
Lincoln University, MO	M,W
Lindenwood University, MO	M,W
Lindsey Wilson College, KY	M,W
Lipscomb University, TN	M,W
Long Island University, Brooklyn Campus, NY	M,W
Longwood University, VA	M,W
Louisiana State University and Agricultural and Mechanical College, LA	M,W
Lourdes College, OH	M,W
Loyola Marymount University, CA	M
Loyola University Chicago, IL	M,W
Loyola University Maryland, MD	M
Lubbock Christian University, TX	M,W
Lynn University, FL	M,W
Lyon College, AR	M,W
Malone University, OH	M,W
Manhattan College, NY	M
Marquette University, WI	M
Marshall University, WV	M,W
Mars Hill College, NC	M,W
Maryville University of Saint Louis, MO	M,W
The Master's College and Seminary, CA	M
McKendree University, IL	M,W
Mercer University, GA	M,W
Merrimack College, MA	W
Mesa State College, CO	M,W
Miami University, OH	M
Michigan State University, MI	M,W
Middle Tennessee State University, TN	M
Midwestern State University, TX	M,W
Millersville University of Pennsylvania, PA	M
Milligan College, TN	M,W
Minnesota State University Mankato, MN	M,W
Mississippi State University, MS	M,W

Missouri Baptist University, MO M
Missouri Southern State University, MO M
Missouri State University, MO M,W
Monmouth University, NJ M,W
Montana State University, MT W
Montana Tech of The University of Montana, MT M,W
Montreat College, NC M
Morehead State University, KY M
Morningside College, IA M,W
Mount Marty College, SD M,W
Mount Mercy University, IA M,W
Mount Olive College, NC M,W
Mount St. Mary's University, MD M,W
Mount Vernon Nazarene University, OH M
Murray State University, KY M,W
New Mexico State University, NM M,W
Niagara University, NY M,W
Nicholls State University, LA M,W
North Carolina State University, NC M,W
Northeastern State University, OK M,W
Northern Arizona University, AZ W
Northern Illinois University, IL M,W
Northern Kentucky University, KY M,W
Northern Michigan University, MI M
Northern State University, SD M,W
Northwest Christian University, OR M,W
Northwestern Oklahoma State University, OK M,W
Northwest Missouri State University, MO W
Northwest Nazarene University, ID M
Notre Dame de Namur University, CA M
Nyack College, NY M
The Ohio State University, OH M,W
Ohio University, OH M,W
Ohio Valley University, WV M,W
Oklahoma Christian University, OK M
Oklahoma City University, OK M,W
Oklahoma Panhandle State University, OK M,W
Oklahoma State University, OK M,W
Oklahoma Wesleyan University, OK M
Old Dominion University, VA M,W
Oregon State University, OR M,W
Ouachita Baptist University, AR M,W
Our Lady of the Lake University of San Antonio, TX M
Pace University, NY M
Penn State University Park, PA M,W
Pepperdine University, CA M,W
Philadelphia University, PA M
Pikeville College, KY M,W
Point Park University, PA M,W
Prairie View A&M University, TX M,W
Presbyterian College, SC M,W
Purdue University, IN M,W
Quincy University, IL M,W
Quinnipiac University, CT W
Radford University, VA M,W
Regis University, CO M,W
Reinhardt University, GA M,W
Research College of Nursing, MO M,W
Rice University, TX M
Rider University, NJ M
Robert Morris University, PA M,W
Robert Morris University Illinois, IL M,W
Rockhurst University, MO M,W
Rocky Mountain College, MT M,W
Rogers State University, OK M,W
Rollins College, FL M,W
Sacred Heart University, CT M,W
Saginaw Valley State University, MI M
St. Ambrose University, IA M,W
St. Andrews Presbyterian College, NC M,W
St. Bonaventure University, NY M
St. Edward's University, TX M,W
Saint Francis University, PA M,W
St. John's University, NY M,W
Saint Joseph's College, IN M,W
Saint Joseph's University, PA M
Saint Leo University, FL M,W
Saint Martin's University, WA M,W
Saint Mary-of-the-Woods College, IN W
Saint Mary's College of California, CA M
St. Thomas University, FL M,W
Saint Xavier University, IL M
Samford University, AL M,W
San Diego State University, CA M,W
San Jose State University, CA M,W
Santa Clara University, CA M,W
Savannah College of Art and Design, GA M,W
Savannah State University, GA M,W
Seton Hill University, PA W
Shawnee State University, OH M
Shepherd University, WV M
Shorter University, GA M,W
Siena College, NY M,W
Silver Lake College, WI M,W
Simpson University, CA M,W
South Dakota School of Mines and Technology, SD M,W
South Dakota State University, SD M,W
Southeastern Louisiana University, LA M
Southeastern Oklahoma State University, OK M
Southern Illinois University Carbondale, IL M,W
Southern Illinois University Edwardsville, IL M,W
Southern Methodist University, TX M,W
Southern Utah University, UT M
Southwestern College, KS M,W
Southwestern Oklahoma State University, OK M,W
Southwest Minnesota State University, MN W
Spring Arbor University, MI M
Spring Hill College, AL M,W
Stanford University, CA M,W
State University of New York at Binghamton, NY M
Stephen F. Austin State University, TX M,W
Stetson University, FL M,W
Tabor College, KS M,W
Tarleton State University, TX W
Taylor University, IN M
Temple University, PA M
Tennessee Technological University, TN M,W
Tennessee Wesleyan College, TN M,W
Texas A&M International University, TX M,W
Texas A&M University, TX M,W
Texas A&M University–Corpus Christi, TX W
Texas Christian University, TX M,W
Texas Southern University, TX M,W
Texas State University–San Marcos, TX M,W
Texas Tech University, TX M,W
Texas Wesleyan University, TX M
Thomas University, GA M
Tiffin University, OH M,W
Towson University, MD M,W
Trevecca Nazarene University, TN M,W
Troy University, AL M,W
Truman State University, MO M,W
Tulane University, LA W
Tuskegee University, AL M
Union College, KY M,W
Union University, TN M
The University of Akron, OH M,W
The University of Alabama, AL M,W
The University of Alabama at Birmingham, AL M,W
The University of Arizona, AZ M,W
University of Arkansas, AR M,W
University of California, Davis, CA M,W
University of California, Irvine, CA M,W
University of California, Los Angeles, CA M,W
University of California, Santa Barbara, CA M
University of Central Florida, FL M,W
University of Central Missouri, MO M
University of Charleston, WV M
University of Cincinnati, OH M,W
University of Colorado at Colorado Springs, CO M
University of Colorado Boulder, CO M,W
University of Connecticut, CT M
University of Dayton, OH M
University of Denver, CO M,W
University of Evansville, IN M,W
The University of Findlay, OH M,W
University of Florida, FL M,W
University of Georgia, GA M,W
University of Hartford, CT M,W
University of Hawaii at Hilo, HI M
University of Hawaii at Manoa, HI M,W
University of Houston, TX M
University of Idaho, ID M,W
University of Illinois at Springfield, IL M,W
University of Illinois at Urbana–Champaign, IL M,W
University of Indianapolis, IN M,W
The University of Iowa, IA M,W
The University of Kansas, KS M,W
University of Louisiana at Lafayette, LA M
University of Louisville, KY M,W
University of Maryland, College Park, MD M,W
University of Memphis, TN M,W
University of Miami, FL W
University of Michigan, MI M
University of Minnesota, Crookston, MN M,W

versity of Minnesota, Twin Cities ampus, MN M,W
iversity of Mississippi, MS M,W
iversity of Missouri, MO M,W
iversity of Missouri–St. Louis, MO M,W
niversity of Mobile, AL M,W
niversity of Montevallo, AL M,W
niversity of Nebraska at Omaha, NE W
niversity of Nebraska–Lincoln, NE M,W
University of Nevada, Las Vegas, NV M
University of Nevada, Reno, NV M,W
University of North Alabama, AL M
The University of North Carolina at Chapel Hill, NC M,W
The University of North Carolina at Charlotte, NC M
The University of North Carolina at Greensboro, NC M,W
The University of North Carolina at Pembroke, NC M,W
The University of North Carolina Wilmington, NC M,W
University of North Dakota, ND M,W
University of Northern Colorado, CO M,W
University of Northern Iowa, IA M,W
University of North Florida, FL M
University of North Texas, TX M,W
University of Notre Dame, IN M,W
University of Oklahoma, OK M,W
University of Oregon, OR M,W
University of Rhode Island, RI M
University of Richmond, VA M,W
University of St. Francis, IL M,W
University of San Diego, CA M
University of South Carolina, SC M,W
University of South Carolina Aiken, SC M
The University of South Dakota, SD M,W
University of Southern California, CA M,W
University of Southern Indiana, IN M,W
University of Southern Mississippi, MS M,W
University of South Florida, FL M,W
The University of Tampa, FL M
The University of Tennessee, TN M,W
The University of Tennessee at Chattanooga, TN M,W
The University of Tennessee at Martin, TN M
The University of Texas at Austin, TX M,W
The University of Texas at San Antonio, TX M
The University of Texas–Pan American, TX M,W
University of the Cumberlands, KY M,W
University of the District of Columbia, DC M
University of the Incarnate Word, TX M,W
University of the Pacific, CA M
University of the Southwest, NM M,W
The University of Toledo, OH M,W
University of Tulsa, OK M,W
University of Utah, UT M
University of Virginia, VA M,W
University of West Florida, FL M
University of West Georgia, GA M,W
University of Wisconsin–Green Bay, WI M,W
University of Wisconsin–Madison, WI M,W
University of Wisconsin–Parkside, WI M
University of Wyoming, WY M,W
Upper Iowa University, IA M,W
Ursuline College, OH W
Utah State University, UT M
Utah Valley University, UT M,W
Valdosta State University, GA M
Valley City State University, ND M,W
Valparaiso University, IN M,W
Vanderbilt University, TN M,W
Virginia Commonwealth University, VA M
Virginia Military Institute, VA M
Virginia Polytechnic Institute and State University, VA M
Virginia State University, VA M,W
Wagner College, NY M,W
Wake Forest University, NC M,W
Walsh University, OH M,W
Washburn University, KS M
Washington State University, WA M,W
Wayland Baptist University, TX M,W
Wayne State College, NE M,W
Wayne State University, MI M
Webber International University, FL M,W
West Chester University of Pennsylvania, PA M,W
Western Carolina University, NC M,W
Western Illinois University, IL M
Western Kentucky University, KY M,W
Western Michigan University, MI W
West Liberty University, WV M,W
Westminster College, UT M
Wheeling Jesuit University, WV M,W
Wichita State University, KS M,W
William Jessup University, CA M
William Jewell College, MO M,W
Wingate University, NC M,W
Winona State University, MN M,W
Winthrop University, SC M,W
Wofford College, SC M,W
Wright State University, OH M
Xavier University, OH M,W
Young Harris College, GA M,W
Youngstown State University, OH M,W

Gymnastics

Arizona State University, AZ W
Auburn University, AL W
Ball State University, IN W
Boise State University, ID W
Bowling Green State University, OH W
Brigham Young University, UT W
California State University, Fullerton, CA W
Central Michigan University, MI W
The College of William and Mary, VA M,W
Eastern Michigan University, MI W
Illinois State University, IL W
Iowa State University of Science and Technology, IA W
Kent State University, OH W
Louisiana State University and Agricultural and Mechanical College, LA W
Michigan State University, MI W
North Carolina State University, NC W
Northern Illinois University, IL W
The Ohio State University, OH M,W
Oregon State University, OR W
Penn State University Park, PA M,W
Quinnipiac University, CT W
San Jose State University, CA W
Seattle Pacific University, WA W
Southeast Missouri State University, MO W
Southern Connecticut State University, CT W
Southern Utah University, UT W
Stanford University, CA M,W
Temple University, PA M,W
Texas Woman's University, TX W
Towson University, MD W
The University of Alabama, AL W
The University of Arizona, AZ W
University of Arkansas, AR W
University of Bridgeport, CT W
University of California, Davis, CA W
University of California, Los Angeles, CA W
University of California, Santa Barbara, CA M,W
University of Denver, CO W
University of Florida, FL W
University of Georgia, GA W
University of Illinois at Chicago, IL M,W
University of Illinois at Urbana–Champaign, IL M,W
The University of Iowa, IA M,W
University of Maryland, College Park, MD W
University of Michigan, MI M,W
University of Minnesota, Twin Cities Campus, MN M,W
University of Missouri, MO W
University of Nebraska–Lincoln, NE M,W
University of New Hampshire, NH W
The University of North Carolina at Chapel Hill, NC W
University of Oklahoma, OK M,W
University of Pittsburgh, PA W
University of Utah, UT W
Utah State University, UT W
West Chester University of Pennsylvania, PA W
Western Michigan University, MI W
West Virginia University, WV W

Ice hockey

Bemidji State University, MN M,W
Bentley University, MA M
Boston College, MA M,W
Boston University, MA M,W
Bowling Green State University, OH M
Canisius College, NY M
Clarkson University, NY M,W
Colgate University, NY M,W
College of the Holy Cross, MA M
The Colorado College, CO M
Davenport University, MI M
Dordt College, IA M
Ferris State University, MI M
Lake Superior State University, MI M
Lindenwood University, MO M,W
Merrimack College, MA M
Miami University, OH M
Michigan State University, MI M
Minnesota State University Mankato, MN M,W
Niagara University, NY M,W

Northeastern University, MA M,W
Northern Michigan University, MI M
The Ohio State University, OH M,W
Providence College, RI M,W
Quinnipiac University, CT M,W
Rensselaer Polytechnic Institute, NY M,W
Robert Morris University, PA M,W
Sacred Heart University, CT M,W
St. Lawrence University, NY M,W
Syracuse University, NY W
The University of Alabama in Huntsville, AL M
University of Alaska Fairbanks, AK M
University of Connecticut, CT M,W
University of Denver, CO M
University of Maine, ME M,W
University of Massachusetts Amherst, MA M
University of Massachusetts Lowell, MA M
University of Michigan, MI M
University of Minnesota, Duluth, MN M,W
University of Minnesota, Twin Cities Campus, MN M,W
University of Nebraska at Omaha, NE M
University of New Hampshire, NH M,W
University of North Dakota, ND M,W
University of Notre Dame, IN M
University of Vermont, VT M,W
University of Wisconsin–Madison, WI M,W
Wayne State University, MI W
Western Michigan University, MI M

Lacrosse

Adams State College, CO M,W
Adelphi University, NY M,W
American University, DC W
Bellarmine University, KY M
Belmont Abbey College, NC M,W
Bentley University, MA M,W
Bloomsburg University of Pennsylvania, PA W
Boston College, MA W
Boston University, MA W
Bryant University, RI M,W
Bucknell University, PA M,W
Canisius College, NY M,W
Central Connecticut State University, CT W
Chestnut Hill College, PA M,W
Colgate University, NY M,W
The College of Saint Rose, NY M
The College of William and Mary, VA W
Davenport University, MI M
Davidson College, NC W
Dominican College, NY M,W
Dominican University of California, CA M
Dowling College, NY M,W
Duquesne University, PA W
Edinboro University of Pennsylvania, PA W
Erskine College, SC W
Fairfield University, CT M,W
Florida Southern College, FL M,W
Fort Lewis College, CO W
Gannon University, PA W
Georgetown University, DC M,W
Georgian Court University, NJ W
Hofstra University, NY M,W
Indiana University of Pennsylvania, PA W
Iona College, NY W
James Madison University, VA W
The Johns Hopkins University, MD M,W
Kutztown University of Pennsylvania, PA W
Lehigh University, PA M,W
Le Moyne College, NY M,W
Liberty University, VA W
Limestone College, SC M,W
Lindenwood University, MO M,W
Lock Haven University of Pennsylvania, PA W
Long Island University, Brooklyn Campus, NY W
Long Island University, C.W. Post Campus, NY M,W
Longwood University, VA W
Loyola University Maryland, MD M,W
Manhattan College, NY M,W
Marist College, NY M,W
Mars Hill College, NC M
Merrimack College, MA M,W
Millersville University of Pennsylvania, PA W
Missouri Baptist University, MO M,W
Molloy College, NY M,W
Monmouth University, NJ W
Mount St. Mary's University, MD M,W
New York Institute of Technology, NY M
Niagara University, NY W
Notre Dame de Namur University, CA M
The Ohio State University, OH M,W
Ohio Valley University, WV M
Old Dominion University, VA W
Pace University, NY M
Penn State University Park, PA M,W
Philadelphia University, PA W
Presbyterian College, SC M,W
Providence College, RI M
Queens College of the City University of New York, NY W
Quinnipiac University, CT M,W
Regis University, CO W
Robert Morris University, PA M,W
Robert Morris University Illinois, IL W
Sacred Heart University, CT M,W
St. Andrews Presbyterian College, NC M,W
St. Bonaventure University, NY W
Saint Francis University, PA W
St. John's University, NY M
Saint Joseph's University, PA M,W
Saint Leo University, FL M,W
Savannah College of Art and Design, GA W
Seton Hill University, PA M,W
Shepherd University, WV W
Shippensburg University of Pennsylvania, PA W
Siena College, NY M,W
Slippery Rock University of Pennsylvania, PA W
Southern Connecticut State University, CT W
Stanford University, CA W
State University of New York at Binghamton, NY M,W
Stonehill College, MA W
Stony Brook University, State University of New York, NY M,W
Syracuse University, NY M,W
Temple University, PA W
Tennessee Wesleyan College, TN M
Tiffin University, OH W
Towson University, MD M,W
University of Bridgeport, CT W
University of California, Davis, CA W
University of Cincinnati, OH W
University of Delaware, DE M,W
University of Denver, CO M,W
University of Florida, FL W
University of Hartford, CT M
University of Louisville, KY W
University of Maryland, Baltimore County, MD M,W
University of Maryland, College Park, MD M,W
University of Massachusetts Amherst, MA M,W
University of Minnesota, Duluth, MN M
University of New Hampshire, NH W
The University of North Carolina at Chapel Hill, NC M,W
University of Notre Dame, IN M,W
University of Oregon, OR W
University of Richmond, VA W
University of Vermont, VT M,W
University of Virginia, VA M,W
Vanderbilt University, TN W
Villanova University, PA M,W
Virginia Military Institute, VA M
Virginia Polytechnic Institute and State University, VA W
Wagner College, NY M,W
West Chester University of Pennsylvania, PA W
Wheeling Jesuit University, WV M,W
Wingate University, NC M

Riflery

The Citadel, The Military College of South Carolina, SC M,W
Hillsdale College, MI M,W
Lindenwood University, MO M,W
Mercer University, GA M
Morehead State University, KY M,W
Murray State University, KY M,W
North Carolina State University, NC M,W
Texas Christian University, TX W
The University of Akron, OH W
University of Alaska Fairbanks, AK M,W
University of Memphis, TN M,W
University of Mississippi, MS W
University of Nebraska–Lincoln, NE W
University of Nevada, Reno, NV M,W
The University of Tennessee at Martin, TN M,W
Virginia Military Institute, VA M,W
West Virginia University, WV M,W

Rugby

Davenport University, MI M
Quinnipiac University, CT W
The University of North Carolina at Pembroke, NC M
West Chester University of Pennsylvania, PA W

Sailing

Oklahoma City University, OK M,W
Robert Morris University Illinois, IL M,W

Skiing (cross-country)

Montana State University, MT M,W
Northern Michigan University, MI M,W
University of Alaska Fairbanks, AK M,W
University of Colorado Boulder, CO M,W
University of Denver, CO M,W
University of New Hampshire, NH M,W
University of Utah, UT M,W
University of Vermont, VT M,W
University of Wisconsin–Green Bay, WI M,W

Skiing (downhill)

Montana State University, MT M,W
Rocky Mountain College, MT M,W
Sierra Nevada College, NV M,W
University of Colorado Boulder, CO M,W
University of Denver, CO M,W
University of New Hampshire, NH M,W
University of Utah, UT M,W
University of Vermont, VT M,W

Soccer

Abilene Christian University, TX W
Adams State College, CO M,W
Adelphi University, NY M,W
Alabama Agricultural and Mechanical University, AL M
Alabama State University, AL W
Alcorn State University, MS W
Alderson-Broaddus College, WV M,W
American University, DC M,W
Anderson University, SC M,W
Angelo State University, TX W
Appalachian State University, NC M,W
Arizona State University, AZ W
Arkansas State University, AR W
Asbury University, KY M,W
Ashland University, OH M,W
Auburn University, AL W
Auburn University Montgomery, AL M,W
Augustana College, SD W
Austin Peay State University, TN W
Azusa Pacific University, CA M,W
Ball State University, IN W
Barry University, FL M,W
Bellarmine University, KY M,W
Belmont Abbey College, NC M,W
Belmont University, TN M,W
Bemidji State University, MN W
Benedictine College, KS M,W
Bethel College, IN M,W
Biola University, CA M,W
Bloomfield College, NJ M,W
Bloomsburg University of Pennsylvania, PA M,W
Bluefield College, VA M,W
Boston College, MA M,W
Boston University, MA M,W
Bowling Green State University, OH M,W
Brenau University, GA W
Brevard College, NC M,W
Brigham Young University, UT W
Bryan College, TN M,W
Bryant University, RI M,W
Bucknell University, PA M,W
Butler University, IN M,W
California Polytechnic State University, San Luis Obispo, CA M,W
California State Polytechnic University, Pomona, CA M,W
California State University, Bakersfield, CA M
California State University, Chico, CA M,W
California State University, Dominguez Hills, CA M,W
California State University, Fullerton, CA M,W
California State University, Long Beach, CA W
California State University, Monterey Bay, CA M,W
California State University, Northridge, CA M
California State University, San Bernardino, CA M,W
Campbellsville University, KY M,W
Canisius College, NY M,W
Carson-Newman College, TN M,W
Cedarville University, OH M,W
Central Connecticut State University, CT M,W
Central Michigan University, MI W
Chestnut Hill College, PA M,W
Christian Brothers University, TN M,W
Cincinnati Christian University, OH M
The Citadel, The Military College of South Carolina, SC W
Clarke University, IA M,W
Clemson University, SC M,W
Cleveland State University, OH M
Coastal Carolina University, SC M,W
Coker College, SC M,W
Colgate University, NY M,W
College of Charleston, SC M,W
College of Saint Mary, NE W
The College of Saint Rose, NY M,W
College of the Holy Cross, MA M,W
The College of William and Mary, VA M,W
The Colorado College, CO W
Colorado School of Mines, CO M,W
Columbia College, MO M
Columbus State University, GA W
Concordia University, CA M,W
Concordia University, Nebraska, NE M,W
Concordia University, St. Paul, MN W
Concord University, WV W
Corban University, OR M,W
Creighton University, NE M,W
Culver-Stockton College, MO M,W
Dallas Baptist University, TX W
Davenport University, MI M,W
Davidson College, NC M,W
Delaware State University, DE W
Delta State University, MS M,W
DePaul University, IL M,W
Dixie State College of Utah, UT M,W
Doane College, NE M,W
Dominican College, NY M,W
Dominican University of California, CA M,W
Dordt College, IA M,W
Dowling College, NY M,W
Drake University, IA M,W
Drury University, MO M,W
Duquesne University, PA M,W
Eastern Michigan University, MI W
Eastern Washington University, WA W
East Tennessee State University, TN M,W
Eckerd College, FL M,W
Edinboro University of Pennsylvania, PA W
Elon University, NC M,W
Embry-Riddle Aeronautical University–Daytona, FL M,W
Embry-Riddle Aeronautical University–Prescott, AZ M,W
Emmanuel College, GA M,W
Emporia State University, KS W
Erskine College, SC M,W
The Evergreen State College, WA M,W
Fairfield University, CT M,W
Faulkner University, AL M,W
Felician College, NJ M,W
Ferris State University, MI W
Flagler College, FL M,W
Florida College, FL M,W
Florida Gulf Coast University, FL M,W
Florida Institute of Technology, FL M,W
Florida International University, FL M,W
Florida Southern College, FL M,W
Florida State University, FL W
Fort Lewis College, CO M,W
Francis Marion University, SC M,W
Freed-Hardeman University, TN M,W
Furman University, SC M,W
Gannon University, PA M,W
Gardner-Webb University, NC M,W
Georgetown College, KY M,W
Georgetown University, DC M,W
Georgia College & State University, GA W
Georgian Court University, NJ W
Georgia Southern University, GA M,W
Georgia State University, GA M,W
Goldey-Beacom College, DE M,W
Grace College, IN M,W
Graceland University, IA M,W
Grand Valley State University, MI W
Grand View University, IA M,W
Hannibal-LaGrange University, MO M,W
Harding University, AR M,W
Hartwick College, NY M
Hawai'i Pacific University, HI M,W
Hofstra University, NY M,W
Houghton College, NY M,W
Humboldt State University, CA M,W
Huntington University, IN M,W
Illinois Institute of Technology, IL M,W
Illinois State University, IL W
Indiana State University, IN W
Indiana University Bloomington, IN M,W
Indiana University of Pennsylvania, PA W
Indiana University–Purdue University Fort Wayne, IN M,W
Indiana University–Purdue University Indianapolis, IN M,W
Indiana Wesleyan University, IN M,W
Inter American University of Puerto Rico, Guayama Campus, PR M
Inter American University of Puerto Rico, San Germán Campus, PR M

Iona College, NY M,W
Iowa State University of Science and Technology, IA W
Iowa Wesleyan College, IA M,W
James Madison University, VA M,W
Jamestown College, ND M,W
John Brown University, AR M,W
Kennesaw State University, GA W
Kent State University, OH W
Kentucky Wesleyan College, KY M,W
King College, TN M,W
Kutztown University of Pennsylvania, PA W
Lamar University, TX W
Lee University, TN M,W
Lehigh University, PA M,W
Le Moyne College, NY M,W
Liberty University, VA M,W
Limestone College, SC M,W
Lincoln Memorial University, TN M,W
Lindenwood University, MO M,W
Lindsey Wilson College, KY M,W
Lipscomb University, TN M,W
Lock Haven University of Pennsylvania, PA M,W
Long Island University, Brooklyn Campus, NY M,W
Long Island University, C.W. Post Campus, NY M,W
Longwood University, VA M,W
Louisiana State University and Agricultural and Mechanical College, LA W
Loyola Marymount University, CA M,W
Loyola University Chicago, IL M,W
Loyola University Maryland, MD M,W
Lubbock Christian University, TX M,W
Lynn University, FL M,W
Lyon College, AR M,W
Malone University, OH M,W
Manhattan College, NY M,W
Marist College, NY M,W
Marquette University, WI M,W
Marshall University, WV M,W
Mars Hill College, NC M,W
Maryville University of Saint Louis, MO M,W
The Master's College and Seminary, CA M,W
McKendree University, IL M,W
Mercer University, GA M,W
Merrimack College, MA M,W
Mesa State College, CO M,W
Miami University, OH W
Michigan State University, MI M,W
Mid-Continent University, KY M
Middle Tennessee State University, TN W
Midwestern State University, TX M,W
Millersville University of Pennsylvania, PA M,W
Milligan College, TN M,W
Minnesota State University Mankato, MN W
Minnesota State University Moorhead, MN W
Mississippi State University, MS W
Missouri Baptist University, MO M,W
Missouri Southern State University, MO M,W
Missouri State University, MO M,W
Missouri University of Science and Technology, MO M,W
Molloy College, NY M,W
Monmouth University, NJ M,W
Montana State University Billings, MT M,W
Montreat College, NC M,W
Morehead State University, KY W
Morningside College, IA M,W
Mountain State University, WV M,W
Mount Marty College, SD M,W
Mount Mercy University, IA M,W
Mount Olive College, NC M,W
Mount St. Mary's University, MD M,W
Mount Vernon Nazarene University, OH M,W
Murray State University, KY W
New Jersey Institute of Technology, NJ M,W
New York Institute of Technology, NY M,W
Niagara University, NY M,W
Nicholls State University, LA W
North Carolina State University, NC M,W
Northeastern State University, OK M,W
Northeastern University, MA M,W
Northern Arizona University, AZ W
Northern Illinois University, IL M,W
Northern Kentucky University, KY M,W
Northern Michigan University, MI W
Northern State University, SD W
North Georgia College & State University, GA M,W
Northwest Christian University, OR M,W
Northwestern Oklahoma State University, OK W
Northwestern State University of Louisiana, LA W
Northwest Missouri State University, MO W
Northwest Nazarene University, ID W
Northwest University, WA M,W
Notre Dame de Namur University, CA M,W
Nyack College, NY M,W
The Ohio State University, OH M,W
Ohio University, OH W
Ohio Valley University, WV M,W
Oklahoma Christian University, OK M,W
Oklahoma City University, OK M,W
Oklahoma State University, OK W
Oklahoma Wesleyan University, OK M,W
Old Dominion University, VA M,W
Oregon State University, OR M,W
Ouachita Baptist University, AR M,W
Our Lady of the Lake University of San Antonio, TX M,W
Pace University, NY W
Palm Beach Atlantic University, FL M,W
Penn State University Park, PA M,W
Pepperdine University, CA W
Philadelphia University, PA M,W
Pikeville College, KY M,W
Point Park University, PA M,W
Prairie View A&M University, TX W
Presbyterian College, SC M,W
Providence College, RI M,W
Purdue University, IN W
Queens College of the City University of New York, NY M,W
Quincy University, IL M,W
Quinnipiac University, CT M,W
Radford University, VA M,W
Regis University, CO M,W
Reinhardt University, GA M,W
Research College of Nursing, MO M,W
Rice University, TX W
Rider University, NJ M,W
Robert Morris University, PA M,W
Robert Morris University Illinois, IL M,W
Rockhurst University, MO M,W
Rocky Mountain College, MT M,W
Rogers State University, OK M,W
Rollins College, FL M,W
Sacred Heart University, CT M,W
Saginaw Valley State University, MI M,W
St. Ambrose University, IA M,W
St. Andrews Presbyterian College, NC M,W
St. Bonaventure University, NY M,W
St. Edward's University, TX M,W
Saint Francis University, PA M,W
St. John's University, NY M,W
Saint Joseph's College, IN M,W
Saint Joseph's University, PA M,W
Saint Leo University, FL M,W
Saint Louis University, MO M,W
Saint Martin's University, WA W
Saint Mary-of-the-Woods College, IN W
Saint Mary's College of California, CA M,W
St. Thomas Aquinas College, NY M,W
St. Thomas University, FL M,W
Saint Xavier University, IL M,W
Samford University, AL W
San Diego Christian College, CA M,W
San Diego State University, CA M,W
San Francisco State University, CA M,W
San Jose State University, CA M,W
Santa Clara University, CA M,W
Savannah College of Art and Design, GA M,W
Seattle Pacific University, WA M,W
Seton Hill University, PA M,W
Shawnee State University, OH M,W
Shepherd University, WV M,W
Shippensburg University of Pennsylvania, PA M,W
Shorter University, GA M,W
Siena College, NY M,W
Simpson University, CA M,W
Slippery Rock University of Pennsylvania, PA M,W
Soka University of America, CA M,W
Sonoma State University, CA M,W
South Dakota State University, SD W
Southeastern Louisiana University, LA W
Southeast Missouri State University, MO W
Southern Connecticut State University, CT M,W
Southern Illinois University Edwardsville, IL M,W
Southern Methodist University, TX M,W
Southern Oregon University, OR W
Southern Polytechnic State University, GA M
Southwestern College, KS M,W

Athletic Grants for Undergraduates
Soccer

Southwestern Oklahoma State University, OK W
Southwest Minnesota State University, MN W
Spring Arbor University, MI M,W
Spring Hill College, AL M,W
Stanford University, CA M,W
State University of New York at Binghamton, NY M,W
Stephen F. Austin State University, TX W
Stetson University, FL M,W
Stonehill College, MA M,W
Stony Brook University, State University of New York, NY M,W
Syracuse University, NY M,W
Tabor College, KS M,W
Taylor University, IN M,W
Temple University, PA M,W
Tennessee Technological University, TN W
Tennessee Wesleyan College, TN M,W
Texas A&M International University, TX M,W
Texas A&M University, TX W
Texas Christian University, TX W
Texas Southern University, TX W
Texas State University–San Marcos, TX W
Texas Tech University, TX W
Texas Wesleyan University, TX M,W
Texas Woman's University, TX W
Thomas University, GA M,W
Tiffin University, OH M,W
Towson University, MD M,W
Trevecca Nazarene University, TN M,W
Troy University, AL W
Truman State University, MO M,W
Tulane University, LA W
Union College, KY M,W
Union University, TN M,W
University at Buffalo, the State University of New York, NY M,W
The University of Akron, OH M,W
The University of Alabama, AL W
The University of Alabama at Birmingham, AL M,W
The University of Alabama in Huntsville, AL M,W
The University of Arizona, AZ W
University of Arkansas, AR W
University of Bridgeport, CT M,W
University of California, Davis, CA M,W
University of California, Irvine, CA M,W
University of California, Los Angeles, CA M,W
University of California, Santa Barbara, CA M,W
University of Central Florida, FL M,W
University of Central Missouri, MO W
University of Charleston, WV M,W
University of Cincinnati, OH M,W
University of Colorado at Colorado Springs, CO M,W
University of Colorado Boulder, CO W
University of Connecticut, CT M,W
University of Dayton, OH M,W
University of Delaware, DE M,W
University of Denver, CO M,W
University of Evansville, IN M,W
The University of Findlay, OH M,W
University of Florida, FL W
University of Georgia, GA W
University of Hartford, CT M,W
University of Hawaii at Manoa, HI W
University of Houston, TX W
University of Idaho, ID W
University of Illinois at Chicago, IL M
University of Illinois at Springfield, IL M,W
University of Illinois at Urbana–Champaign, IL W
University of Indianapolis, IN M,W
The University of Iowa, IA W
The University of Kansas, KS W
University of Louisville, KY M,W
University of Maine, ME W
University of Maryland, Baltimore County, MD M,W
University of Maryland, College Park, MD M,W
University of Massachusetts Amherst, MA M,W
University of Massachusetts Lowell, MA M,W
University of Memphis, TN M,W
University of Miami, FL W
University of Michigan, MI M,W
University of Minnesota, Crookston, MN W
University of Minnesota, Duluth, MN W
University of Minnesota, Twin Cities Campus, MN W
University of Mississippi, MS W
University of Missouri, MO W
University of Missouri–St. Louis, MO M,W
University of Mobile, AL M,W
University of Montevallo, AL M,W
University of Nebraska–Lincoln, NE W
University of Nevada, Las Vegas, NV M,W
University of Nevada, Reno, NV W
University of New Hampshire, NH M,W
University of North Alabama, AL W
The University of North Carolina at Asheville, NC M,W
The University of North Carolina at Chapel Hill, NC M,W
The University of North Carolina at Charlotte, NC M,W
The University of North Carolina at Greensboro, NC M,W
The University of North Carolina at Pembroke, NC M,W
The University of North Carolina Wilmington, NC M,W
University of North Dakota, ND W
University of Northern Colorado, CO W
University of Northern Iowa, IA W
University of North Florida, FL M,W
University of North Texas, TX W
University of Notre Dame, IN M,W
University of Oklahoma, OK W
University of Oregon, OR W
University of Pittsburgh, PA M,W
University of Portland, OR M,W
University of Rhode Island, RI M,W
University of Richmond, VA M,W
University of Rio Grande, OH M
University of St. Francis, IL M,W
University of St. Thomas, TX M
University of San Diego, CA M,W
University of Science and Arts of Oklahoma, OK M,W
University of South Alabama, AL W
University of South Carolina, SC M,W
University of South Carolina Aiken, SC M,W
The University of South Dakota, SD W
University of Southern California, CA W
University of Southern Indiana, IN M,W
University of Southern Mississippi, MS W
University of South Florida, FL M,W
The University of Tampa, FL M,W
The University of Tennessee, TN W
The University of Tennessee at Chattanooga, TN W
The University of Tennessee at Martin, TN W
The University of Texas at Austin, TX W
The University of Texas of the Permian Basin, TX M,W
University of the Cumberlands, KY M,W
University of the District of Columbia, DC M
University of the Incarnate Word, TX M,W
University of the Pacific, CA W
University of the Southwest, NM M,W
The University of Toledo, OH W
University of Tulsa, OK M,W
University of Utah, UT W
University of Vermont, VT M,W
University of Virginia, VA M,W
University of West Florida, FL M,W
University of West Georgia, GA W
University of Wisconsin–Green Bay, WI M,W
University of Wisconsin–Madison, WI M,W
University of Wisconsin–Parkside, WI M,W
University of Wyoming, WY W
Upper Iowa University, IA M,W
Ursuline College, OH W
Utah State University, UT W
Utah Valley University, UT W
Valparaiso University, IN M,W
Vanderbilt University, TN W
Villanova University, PA M,W
Virginia Commonwealth University, VA M,W
Virginia Military Institute, VA M
Virginia Polytechnic Institute and State University, VA M,W
Wagner College, NY W
Wake Forest University, NC M,W
Walsh University, OH M,W
Washburn University, KS W
Washington Adventist University, MD M,W
Washington State University, WA W
Wayland Baptist University, TX M,W
Wayne State College, NE W
Webber International University, FL M,W
West Chester University of Pennsylvania, PA M,W
Western Carolina University, NC W
Western Illinois University, IL M,W
Western Kentucky University, KY W
Western Michigan University, MI M,W
Western Oregon University, OR W
Westminster College, UT M,W

Westmont College, CA M,W
West Virginia University, WV M,W
Wheeling Jesuit University, WV M,W
William Jessup University, CA M,W
William Jewell College, MO M,W
Wingate University, NC M
Winona State University, MN W
Winthrop University, SC M
Wofford College, SC M,W
Wright State University, OH M,W
Xavier University, OH M,W
Young Harris College, GA M,W
Youngstown State University, OH W

Softball

Abilene Christian University, TX W
Adams State College, CO W
Adelphi University, NY W
Alabama State University, AL W
Alcorn State University, MS W
Alderson-Broaddus College, WV W
Anderson University, SC W
Angelo State University, TX W
Appalachian State University, NC W
Arizona State University, AZ W
Arkansas Tech University, AR W
Armstrong Atlantic State University, GA W
Asbury University, KY W
Ashland University, OH W
Auburn University, AL W
Auburn University Montgomery, AL W
Augustana College, SD W
Austin Peay State University, TN W
Azusa Pacific University, CA W
Ball State University, IN W
Barry University, FL W
Bellarmine University, KY W
Belmont Abbey College, NC W
Belmont University, TN W
Bemidji State University, MN W
Benedictine College, KS W
Bethel College, IN W
Bethune-Cookman University, FL W
Biola University, CA W
Bloomfield College, NJ W
Bloomsburg University of Pennsylvania, PA W
Bluefield College, VA W
Bluefield State College, WV W
Boston College, MA W
Boston University, MA W
Bowie State University, MD W
Bowling Green State University, OH W
Brenau University, GA W
Brevard College, NC W
Brigham Young University, UT W
Bryant University, RI W
Butler University, IN W
California Polytechnic State University, San Luis Obispo, CA W
California State University, Bakersfield, CA W
California State University, Chico, CA W
California State University, Dominguez Hills, CA W
California State University, Fullerton, CA W
California State University, Long Beach, CA W
California State University, Monterey Bay, CA W
California State University, Northridge, CA W
California State University, San Bernardino, CA W
Cameron University, OK W
Campbellsville University, KY W
Canisius College, NY W
Carson-Newman College, TN W
Cedarville University, OH W
Central Connecticut State University, CT W
Central Michigan University, MI W
Chestnut Hill College, PA W
Christian Brothers University, TN W
Clarion University of Pennsylvania, PA W
Clarke University, IA W
Cleveland State University, OH W
Coastal Carolina University, SC W
Coker College, SC W
Colgate University, NY W
College of Charleston, SC W
College of Saint Mary, NE W
The College of Saint Rose, NY W
Colorado School of Mines, CO W
Colorado State University, CO W
Columbia College, MO W
Columbus State University, GA W
Concordia University, CA W
Concordia University, Nebraska, NE W
Concordia University, St. Paul, MN W
Corban University, OR W
Creighton University, NE W
Culver-Stockton College, MO W
Dakota State University, SD W
Dakota Wesleyan University, SD W
Davenport University, MI W
Delaware State University, DE W
Delta State University, MS W
DePaul University, IL W
Dickinson State University, ND W
Dixie State College of Utah, UT W
Doane College, NE W
Dominican College, NY W
Dominican University of California, CA W
Dordt College, IA W
Dowling College, NY W
Drake University, IA W
Drury University, MO W
Eastern Michigan University, MI W
East Tennessee State University, TN W
Eckerd College, FL W
Edinboro University of Pennsylvania, PA W
Elizabeth City State University, NC W
Elon University, NC W
Emmanuel College, GA W
Emporia State University, KS W
Erskine College, SC W
Evangel University, MO W
Fairfield University, CT W
Faulkner University, AL W
Fayetteville State University, NC W
Felician College, NJ W
Ferris State University, MI W
Flagler College, FL W
Florida Agricultural and Mechanical University, FL W
Florida Atlantic University, FL W
Florida Gulf Coast University, FL W
Florida Institute of Technology, FL W
Florida International University, FL W
Florida Southern College, FL W
Florida State University, FL W
Fort Lewis College, CO W
Francis Marion University, SC W
Freed-Hardeman University, TN W
Furman University, SC W
Gannon University, PA W
Gardner-Webb University, NC W
Georgetown College, KY W
Georgetown University, DC W
Georgia College & State University, GA W
Georgia Institute of Technology, GA W
Georgian Court University, NJ W
Georgia Southern University, GA W
Georgia State University, GA W
Goldey-Beacom College, DE W
Grace College, IN W
Graceland University, IA W
Grand Valley State University, MI W
Grand View University, IA W
Hannibal-LaGrange University, MO W
Hawai'i Pacific University, HI W
Hillsdale College, MI W
Hofstra University, NY W
Houghton College, NY W
Humboldt State University, CA W
Huntington University, IN W
Illinois State University, IL W
Indiana State University, IN W
Indiana University Bloomington, IN W
Indiana University of Pennsylvania, PA W
Indiana University–Purdue University Fort Wayne, IN W
Indiana University–Purdue University Indianapolis, IN W
Indiana Wesleyan University, IN W
Inter American University of Puerto Rico, Bayamón Campus, PR M,W
Inter American University of Puerto Rico, Guayama Campus, PR M,W
Iona College, NY W
Iowa State University of Science and Technology, IA W
Iowa Wesleyan College, IA W
James Madison University, VA W
Jamestown College, ND W
Johnson C. Smith University, NC W
Kennesaw State University, GA W
Kent State University, OH W
Kentucky State University, KY W
Kentucky Wesleyan College, KY W
King College, TN W
Kutztown University of Pennsylvania, PA W
Lake Superior State University, MI W
Lee University, TN W
Lehigh University, PA W
Le Moyne College, NY W
Liberty University, VA W
Limestone College, SC W
Lincoln Memorial University, TN W

Lincoln University, MO W
Lindenwood University, MO W
Lindsey Wilson College, KY W
Lipscomb University, TN W
Lock Haven University of Pennsylvania, PA W
Long Island University, Brooklyn Campus, NY W
Long Island University, C.W. Post Campus, NY W
Longwood University, VA W
Louisiana State University and Agricultural and Mechanical College, LA W
Loyola Marymount University, CA W
Loyola University Chicago, IL W
Lubbock Christian University, TX W
Lynn University, FL W
Lyon College, AR W
Malone University, OH W
Manhattan College, NY W
Marist College, NY W
Marshall University, WV W
Mars Hill College, NC W
Maryville University of Saint Louis, MO W
Mayville State University, ND W
McKendree University, IL W
Mercer University, GA W
Merrimack College, MA W
Mesa State College, CO W
Miami University, OH W
Michigan State University, MI W
Mid-Continent University, KY W
Middle Tennessee State University, TN W
Midwestern State University, TX W
Millersville University of Pennsylvania, PA W
Milligan College, TN W
Minnesota State University Mankato, MN W
Minnesota State University Moorhead, MN W
Minot State University, ND W
Mississippi State University, MS W
Missouri Baptist University, MO W
Missouri Southern State University, MO W
Missouri State University, MO W
Missouri University of Science and Technology, MO W
Molloy College, NY W
Monmouth University, NJ W
Montreat College, NC W
Morehead State University, KY W
Morningside College, IA W
Mount Marty College, SD W
Mount Mercy University, IA W
Mount Olive College, NC W
Mount St. Mary's University, MD W
Mount Vernon Nazarene University, OH W
Murray State University, KY W
New Mexico State University, NM W
New York Institute of Technology, NY W
Niagara University, NY W
Nicholls State University, LA W
North Carolina Agricultural and Technical State University, NC W
North Carolina State University, NC W
Northeastern State University, OK W
Northern Illinois University, IL W
Northern Kentucky University, KY W
Northern State University, SD W
North Georgia College & State University, GA W
Northwest Christian University, OR W
Northwestern Oklahoma State University, OK W
Northwestern State University of Louisiana, LA W
Northwest Missouri State University, MO W
Northwest Nazarene University, ID W
Notre Dame de Namur University, CA W
Nyack College, NY W
The Ohio State University, OH W
Ohio University, OH W
Ohio Valley University, WV W
Oklahoma Christian University, OK W
Oklahoma City University, OK W
Oklahoma Panhandle State University, OK W
Oklahoma State University, OK W
Oklahoma Wesleyan University, OK W
Oregon State University, OR W
Ouachita Baptist University, AR W
Our Lady of the Lake University of San Antonio, TX W
Pace University, NY W
Palm Beach Atlantic University, FL W
Philadelphia University, PA W
Pikeville College, KY W
Point Park University, PA W
Prairie View A&M University, TX W
Presbyterian College, SC W
Providence College, RI W
Purdue University, IN W
Purdue University North Central, IN W
Queens College of the City University of New York, NY W
Quincy University, IL W
Quinnipiac University, CT W
Radford University, VA W
Regis University, CO W
Reinhardt University, GA W
Research College of Nursing, MO W
Rider University, NJ W
Robert Morris University, PA W
Robert Morris University Illinois, IL W
Rockhurst University, MO W
Rogers State University, OK W
Rollins College, FL W
Sacred Heart University, CT W
Saginaw Valley State University, MI W
St. Ambrose University, IA W
St. Andrews Presbyterian College, NC W
St. Bonaventure University, NY W
St. Edward's University, TX W
Saint Francis University, PA W
St. John's University, NY W
Saint Joseph's College, IN W
Saint Joseph's University, PA W
Saint Leo University, FL W
Saint Louis University, MO W
Saint Martin's University, WA W
Saint Mary-of-the-Woods College, IN W
Saint Mary's College of California, CA W
St. Thomas Aquinas College, NY W
St. Thomas University, FL W
Saint Xavier University, IL W
Samford University, AL W
San Diego State University, CA W
San Francisco State University, CA W
Santa Clara University, CA W
Savannah College of Art and Design, GA W
Savannah State University, GA W
Seton Hill University, PA W
Shawnee State University, OH M
Shepherd University, WV W
Shippensburg University of Pennsylvania, PA W
Shorter University, GA W
Siena College, NY W
Simpson University, CA W
Slippery Rock University of Pennsylvania, PA W
Sonoma State University, CA W
South Dakota State University, SD W
Southeastern Louisiana University, LA W
Southeastern Oklahoma State University, OK W
Southeast Missouri State University, MO W
Southern Connecticut State University, CT W
Southern Illinois University Carbondale, IL W
Southern Illinois University Edwardsville, IL W
Southern Oregon University, OR W
Southern Utah University, UT W
Southwestern College, KS W
Southwestern Oklahoma State University, OK W
Southwest Minnesota State University, MN W
Spring Arbor University, MI W
Spring Hill College, AL W
Stanford University, CA W
State University of New York at Binghamton, NY W
Stephen F. Austin State University, TX W
Stetson University, FL W
Stonehill College, MA W
Stony Brook University, State University of New York, NY W
Syracuse University, NY W
Tabor College, KS W
Tarleton State University, TX W
Taylor University, IN W
Temple University, PA W
Tennessee Technological University, TN W
Tennessee Wesleyan College, TN W
Texas A&M International University, TX W
Texas A&M University, TX W
Texas A&M University–Corpus Christi, TX W
Texas Southern University, TX W
Texas State University–San Marcos, TX W

Texas Tech University, TX W
Texas Wesleyan University, TX W
Texas Woman's University, TX W
Thomas University, GA W
Tiffin University, OH W
Towson University, MD W
Trevecca Nazarene University, TN W
Troy University, AL W
Truman State University, MO W
Union College, KY W
Union University, TN W
University at Buffalo, the State University of New York, NY W
The University of Akron, OH W
The University of Alabama, AL W
The University of Alabama at Birmingham, AL W
The University of Alabama in Huntsville, AL W
The University of Arizona, AZ W
University of Arkansas, AR W
University of Bridgeport, CT W
University of California, Davis, CA W
University of California, Los Angeles, CA W
University of California, Santa Barbara, CA W
University of Central Missouri, MO W
University of Charleston, WV W
University of Colorado at Colorado Springs, CO W
University of Connecticut, CT W
University of Dayton, OH W
University of Delaware, DE W
University of Evansville, IN W
The University of Findlay, OH W
University of Florida, FL W
University of Georgia, GA W
University of Hartford, CT W
University of Hawaii at Hilo, HI W
University of Hawaii at Manoa, HI W
University of Houston, TX W
University of Illinois at Chicago, IL W
University of Illinois at Springfield, IL W
University of Illinois at Urbana–Champaign, IL W
University of Indianapolis, IN W
The University of Iowa, IA W
The University of Kansas, KS W
University of Louisiana at Lafayette, LA W
University of Louisville, KY W
University of Maine, ME W
University of Maryland, Baltimore County, MD W
University of Maryland, College Park, MD W
University of Massachusetts Amherst, MA W
University of Massachusetts Lowell, MA W
University of Michigan, MI W
University of Michigan–Dearborn, MI W
University of Minnesota, Crookston, MN W
University of Minnesota, Duluth, MN W
University of Minnesota, Twin Cities Campus, MN W
University of Mississippi, MS W
University of Missouri, MO W
University of Missouri–St. Louis, MO W
University of Mobile, AL W
University of Nebraska at Omaha, NE W
University of Nebraska–Lincoln, NE W
University of Nevada, Las Vegas, NV W
University of Nevada, Reno, NV W
University of North Alabama, AL W
The University of North Carolina at Chapel Hill, NC W
The University of North Carolina at Charlotte, NC W
The University of North Carolina at Greensboro, NC W
The University of North Carolina at Pembroke, NC W
The University of North Carolina Wilmington, NC W
University of North Dakota, ND W
University of Northern Colorado, CO W
University of Northern Iowa, IA W
University of North Florida, FL W
University of North Texas, TX M
University of Notre Dame, IN W
University of Oklahoma, OK W
University of Oregon, OR W
University of Pittsburgh, PA W
University of Rhode Island, RI W
University of Rio Grande, OH W
University of St. Francis, IL W
University of San Diego, CA W
University of Science and Arts of Oklahoma, OK W
University of South Carolina, SC W
University of South Carolina Aiken, SC W
The University of South Dakota, SD W
University of Southern Indiana, IN W
University of Southern Mississippi, MS W
University of South Florida, FL W
The University of Tampa, FL W
The University of Tennessee, TN W
The University of Tennessee at Chattanooga, TN W
The University of Tennessee at Martin, TN W
The University of Texas at Arlington, TX W
The University of Texas at Austin, TX W
The University of Texas at San Antonio, TX W
The University of Texas of the Permian Basin, TX W
University of the Cumberlands, KY W
University of the Incarnate Word, TX W
University of the Pacific, CA W
University of the Sciences in Philadelphia, PA W
University of the Southwest, NM W
The University of Toledo, OH W
University of Tulsa, OK W
University of Utah, UT W
University of Virginia, VA W
The University of Virginia's College at Wise, VA W
University of West Florida, FL W
University of West Georgia, GA W
University of Wisconsin–Green Bay, WI W
University of Wisconsin–Madison, WI W
University of Wisconsin–Parkside, WI W
Upper Iowa University, IA W
Ursuline College, OH W
Utah State University, UT W
Utah Valley University, UT W
Valdosta State University, GA W
Valley City State University, ND W
Valparaiso University, IN W
Villanova University, PA W
Virginia State University, VA W
Wagner College, NY W
Walsh University, OH W
Washburn University, KS W
Washington Adventist University, MD W
Wayne State College, NE W
Wayne State University, MI W
Webber International University, FL W
West Chester University of Pennsylvania, PA W
Western Carolina University, NC W
Western Illinois University, IL W
Western Kentucky University, KY W
Western Michigan University, MI W
Western Oregon University, OR W
West Liberty University, WV W
Wheeling Jesuit University, WV W
Wichita State University, KS W
William Jessup University, CA W
William Jewell College, MO W
Wingate University, NC W
Winona State University, MN W
Winthrop University, SC W
Wright State University, OH W
Young Harris College, GA W
Youngstown State University, OH W

Swimming and Diving

Adams State College, CO M,W
Adelphi University, NY M,W
Arizona State University, AZ M,W
Asbury University, KY M,W
Ashland University, OH M,W
Auburn University, AL M,W
Ball State University, IN M,W
Biola University, CA M,W
Bloomsburg University of Pennsylvania, PA M,W
Boston College, MA M,W
Boston University, MA M,W
Bowling Green State University, OH W
Brenau University, GA W
Brigham Young University, UT M,W
Bryant University, RI M,W
Bucknell University, PA M,W
California Polytechnic State University, San Luis Obispo, CA M,W
California State University, Bakersfield, CA M,W
California State University, Northridge, CA M,W
California State University, San Bernardino, CA M,W
Campbellsville University, KY W
Canisius College, NY M,W
Central Connecticut State University, CT W

Clarion University of Pennsylvania, PA M,W
Clemson University, SC M,W
Cleveland State University, OH M,W
College of Charleston, SC M,W
College of Saint Mary, NE W
The College of Saint Rose, NY M,W
Colorado State University, CO W
Concordia University, CA M,W
Davidson College, NC M,W
Delta State University, MS M,W
Drury University, MO M,W
Duquesne University, PA W
Eastern Michigan University, MI M,W
Edinboro University of Pennsylvania, PA M,W
Fairfield University, CT M,W
Florida Agricultural and Mechanical University, FL M,W
Florida Gulf Coast University, FL W
Florida International University, FL W
Florida Southern College, FL M,W
Florida State University, FL M,W
Gannon University, PA M,W
Gardner-Webb University, NC M,W
Georgia Institute of Technology, GA M,W
Georgia Southern University, GA W
Grand Valley State University, MI M,W
Hillsdale College, MI W
Illinois Institute of Technology, IL M,W
Illinois State University, IL W
Indiana University Bloomington, IN M,W
Indiana University of Pennsylvania, PA M,W
Indiana University–Purdue University Indianapolis, IN M,W
Inter American University of Puerto Rico, Bayamón Campus, PR M,W
Iona College, NY M,W
Iowa State University of Science and Technology, IA M,W
James Madison University, VA W
King College, TN M,W
Kutztown University of Pennsylvania, PA W
Lehigh University, PA M,W
Liberty University, VA W
Limestone College, SC M,W
Lindenwood University, MO M,W
Lindsey Wilson College, KY M,W
Lock Haven University of Pennsylvania, PA W
Long Island University, C.W. Post Campus, NY W
Louisiana State University and Agricultural and Mechanical College, LA M,W
Loyola Marymount University, CA W
Loyola University Maryland, MD M,W
Malone University, OH M,W
Manhattan College, NY M,W
Marist College, NY M,W
Marshall University, WV W
Mars Hill College, NC M,W
Mesa State College, CO M,W
Miami University, OH M,W
Michigan State University, MI M,W
Millersville University of Pennsylvania, PA W
Milligan College, TN M,W
Minnesota State University Mankato, MN M,W
Missouri State University, MO M,W
Missouri University of Science and Technology, MO M
Morningside College, IA M,W
Mount St. Mary's University, MD W
New Jersey Institute of Technology, NJ M,W
New Mexico State University, NM W
Niagara University, NY M,W
North Carolina Agricultural and Technical State University, NC W
North Carolina State University, NC M,W
Northeastern University, MA W
Northern Arizona University, AZ W
Northern Illinois University, IL M,W
Northern Michigan University, MI W
Northern State University, SD W
The Ohio State University, OH M,W
Ohio University, OH W
Old Dominion University, VA M,W
Oregon State University, OR W
Ouachita Baptist University, AR M,W
Penn State University Park, PA M,W
Pepperdine University, CA W
Providence College, RI M,W
Purdue University, IN M,W
Queens College of the City University of New York, NY M,W
Radford University, VA W
Rice University, TX W
Rider University, NJ M,W
Robert Morris University Illinois, IL W
Sacred Heart University, CT W
St. Bonaventure University, NY M,W
Saint Francis University, PA M,W
Saint Leo University, FL M,W
Saint Louis University, MO M,W
San Diego State University, CA W
San Jose State University, CA W
Savannah College of Art and Design, GA M,W
Shippensburg University of Pennsylvania, PA M,W
Siena College, NY W
Soka University of America, CA M,W
South Dakota State University, SD M,W
Southern Connecticut State University, CT M,W
Southern Illinois University Carbondale, IL M,W
Southern Methodist University, TX M,W
Stanford University, CA M,W
State University of New York at Binghamton, NY M,W
Stony Brook University, State University of New York, NY M,W
Syracuse University, NY M,W
Texas A&M University, TX M,W
Texas Christian University, TX M,W
Towson University, MD M,W
Truman State University, MO M,W
Tulane University, LA W
Union College, KY M,W
University at Buffalo, the State University of New York, NY M,W
The University of Akron, OH W
The University of Alabama, AL M,W
The University of Arizona, AZ M,W
University of Arkansas, AR W
University of Bridgeport, CT M,W
University of California, Davis, CA W
University of California, Los Angeles, CA W
University of California, Santa Barbara, CA M,W
University of Charleston, WV M,W
University of Cincinnati, OH M,W
University of Connecticut, CT M,W
University of Delaware, DE W
University of Denver, CO M,W
University of Evansville, IN M,W
The University of Findlay, OH M,W
University of Florida, FL M,W
University of Georgia, GA M,W
University of Hawaii at Manoa, HI M,W
University of Houston, TX W
University of Idaho, ID W
University of Illinois at Chicago, IL M,W
University of Illinois at Urbana–Champaign, IL W
University of Indianapolis, IN M,W
The University of Iowa, IA M,W
The University of Kansas, KS W
University of Louisville, KY M,W
University of Maine, ME W
University of Maryland, Baltimore County, MD M,W
University of Maryland, College Park, MD M,W
University of Massachusetts Amherst, MA M,W
University of Miami, FL W
University of Michigan, MI M,W
University of Minnesota, Twin Cities Campus, MN M,W
University of Missouri, MO M,W
University of Nebraska–Lincoln, NE W
University of Nevada, Las Vegas, NV M,W
University of Nevada, Reno, NV W
University of New Hampshire, NH W
The University of North Carolina at Chapel Hill, NC M,W
The University of North Carolina Wilmington, NC M,W
University of North Dakota, ND M,W
University of Northern Colorado, CO W
University of Northern Iowa, IA W
University of North Florida, FL W
University of North Texas, TX W
University of Notre Dame, IN M,W
University of Pittsburgh, PA M,W
University of Rhode Island, RI W
University of Richmond, VA W
University of San Diego, CA W
University of South Carolina, SC M,W
The University of South Dakota, SD M,W
University of Southern California, CA M,W
The University of Tampa, FL M,W
The University of Tennessee, TN M,W
The University of Texas at Austin, TX M,W
The University of Texas of the Permian Basin, TX M,W
University of the Cumberlands, KY M,W
University of the Incarnate Word, TX M,W
University of the Pacific, CA M,W

The University of Toledo, OH W
University of Utah, UT M,W
University of Vermont, VT W
University of Virginia, VA M,W
University of Wisconsin–Green Bay, WI M,W
University of Wisconsin–Madison, WI M,W
University of Wyoming, WY M,W
Ursuline College, OH W
Valparaiso University, IN M,W
Villanova University, PA W
Virginia Military Institute, VA M
Virginia Polytechnic Institute and State University, VA M,W
Wagner College, NY W
Washington State University, WA W
Wayne State University, MI M,W
West Chester University of Pennsylvania, PA M,W
Western Illinois University, IL M,W
Western Kentucky University, KY M,W
West Virginia University, WV M,W
Wheeling Jesuit University, WV M,W
William Jewell College, MO M,W
Wingate University, NC M,W
Wright State University, OH M,W
Xavier University, OH M,W
Youngstown State University, OH W

Table tennis

Inter American University of Puerto Rico, Bayamón Campus, PR M,W
Inter American University of Puerto Rico, San Germán Campus, PR M,W
Lindenwood University, MO M,W
Texas Wesleyan University, TX M,W

Tennis

Abilene Christian University, TX M,W
Adelphi University, NY M,W
Alabama State University, AL M,W
Alcorn State University, MS M,W
Anderson University, SC M,W
Appalachian State University, NC M,W
Arizona State University, AZ W
Arkansas State University, AR W
Arkansas Tech University, AR W
Armstrong Atlantic State University, GA M,W
Asbury University, KY M,W
Auburn University, AL M,W
Auburn University Montgomery, AL M,W
Augustana College, SD M,W
Austin Peay State University, TN M,W
Azusa Pacific University, CA M
Ball State University, IN M,W
Barry University, FL M,W
Bellarmine University, KY M,W
Belmont Abbey College, NC M,W
Belmont University, TN M,W
Bemidji State University, MN W
Bethel College, IN M,W
Bethune-Cookman University, FL M,W
Biola University, CA M,W
Bloomfield College, NJ M
Bloomsburg University of Pennsylvania, PA M,W
Bluefield College, VA M,W
Bluefield State College, WV M,W
Boise State University, ID M,W
Boston College, MA M,W
Boston University, MA W
Bowie State University, MD W
Bowling Green State University, OH W
Brenau University, GA W
Brevard College, NC M,W
Brigham Young University, UT M,W
Bryant University, RI M,W
Butler University, IN M,W
California Polytechnic State University, San Luis Obispo, CA M,W
California State Polytechnic University, Pomona, CA M,W
California State University, Bakersfield, CA W
California State University, Fullerton, CA W
California State University, Long Beach, CA W
California State University, Northridge, CA W
Cameron University, OK M,W
Campbellsville University, KY M,W
Carson-Newman College, TN M,W
Cedarville University, OH M,W
Chestnut Hill College, PA M,W
Christian Brothers University, TN M,W
The Citadel, The Military College of South Carolina, SC M
Clarion University of Pennsylvania, PA W
Clarke University, IA W
Clemson University, SC M,W
Cleveland State University, OH W
Coastal Carolina University, SC M,W
Coker College, SC M,W
College of Charleston, SC M,W
The College of William and Mary, VA M,W
Colorado State University, CO W
Columbus State University, GA M,W
Concordia University, CA M,W
Concordia University, Nebraska, NE M,W
Concord University, WV M,W
Coppin State University, MD M,W
Creighton University, NE M,W
Dallas Baptist University, TX W
Davenport University, MI M,W
Davidson College, NC M,W
Delaware State University, DE W
Delta State University, MS M,W
DePaul University, IL M,W
Dixie State College of Utah, UT W
Dominican University of California, CA W
Dowling College, NY M,W
Drake University, IA M,W
Drury University, MO M,W
Duquesne University, PA M,W
Eastern Michigan University, MI W
Eastern Washington University, WA M,W
East Tennessee State University, TN M,W
Eckerd College, FL M,W
Elizabeth City State University, NC W
Elon University, NC M,W
Embry-Riddle Aeronautical University–Daytona, FL M,W
Emmanuel College, GA M,W
Emporia State University, KS M,W
Erskine College, SC M,W
Evangel University, MO M,W
Fairfield University, CT M,W
Fayetteville State University, NC W
Ferris State University, MI M,W
Flagler College, FL M,W
Florida Agricultural and Mechanical University, FL M,W
Florida Gulf Coast University, FL M,W
Florida Institute of Technology, FL M,W
Florida International University, FL W
Florida Southern College, FL M,W
Florida State University, FL M,W
Francis Marion University, SC M,W
Furman University, SC M,W
Gardner-Webb University, NC M,W
Georgetown College, KY M,W
Georgetown University, DC W
Georgia College & State University, GA M,W
Georgia Institute of Technology, GA M,W
Georgian Court University, NJ W
Georgia Southern University, GA M,W
Georgia State University, GA M,W
Goldey-Beacom College, DE W
Grace College, IN M,W
Graceland University, IA M,W
Grand Valley State University, MI M,W
Grand View University, IA M,W
Harding University, AR M,W
Hawai'i Pacific University, HI M,W
Hofstra University, NY M,W
Huntington University, IN M,W
Illinois State University, IL M,W
Indiana University Bloomington, IN M,W
Indiana University of Pennsylvania, PA W
Indiana University–Purdue University Fort Wayne, IN M,W
Indiana University–Purdue University Indianapolis, IN M,W
Indiana Wesleyan University, IN M,W
Inter American University of Puerto Rico, San Germán Campus, PR M,W
Iowa State University of Science and Technology, IA W
James Madison University, VA M,W
John Brown University, AR M,W
Johnson C. Smith University, NC M,W
Kansas State University, KS W
Kennesaw State University, GA M,W
King College, TN M,W
Kutztown University of Pennsylvania, PA M,W
Lake Superior State University, MI M,W
Lamar University, TX M,W
Lee University, TN M,W
Lehigh University, PA M,W
Le Moyne College, NY M,W
Lewis-Clark State College, ID M,W
Liberty University, VA M,W
Limestone College, SC M,W
Lincoln Memorial University, TN M,W
Lincoln University, MO W
Lindenwood University, MO M,W
Lindsey Wilson College, KY M,W
Lipscomb University, TN M,W
Long Island University, Brooklyn Campus, NY W

Long Island University, C.W. Post Campus, NY W
Longwood University, VA M,W
Louisiana State University and Agricultural and Mechanical College, LA M,W
Loyola Marymount University, CA M,W
Loyola University Maryland, MD M,W
Lynn University, FL M,W
Malone University, OH M,W
Manhattan College, NY W
Marist College, NY M,W
Marquette University, WI M,W
Marshall University, WV W
Mars Hill College, NC M,W
Maryville University of Saint Louis, MO M,W
The Master's College and Seminary, CA W
McKendree University, IL M,W
Mercer University, GA M,W
Merrimack College, MA M,W
Mesa State College, CO M,W
Miami University, OH W
Michigan State University, MI M,W
Middle Tennessee State University, TN M,W
Midwestern State University, TX M,W
Millersville University of Pennsylvania, PA M,W
Milligan College, TN M,W
Minnesota State University Mankato, MN M,W
Mississippi State University, MS M,W
Missouri Baptist University, MO M,W
Missouri Southern State University, MO W
Molloy College, NY W
Monmouth University, NJ M,W
Montana State University, MT M,W
Montana State University Billings, MT M,W
Montreat College, NC M,W
Morehead State University, KY M,W
Morehouse College, GA M
Morningside College, IA M,W
Mount Olive College, NC M,W
Mount St. Mary's University, MD M,W
Murray State University, KY M,W
New Jersey Institute of Technology, NJ M,W
New Mexico State University, NM M,W
Niagara University, NY M,W
Nicholls State University, LA W
North Carolina Agricultural and Technical State University, NC W
North Carolina State University, NC M,W
Northeastern State University, OK W
Northern Arizona University, AZ M,W
Northern Illinois University, IL M,W
Northern Kentucky University, KY M,W
Northern State University, SD W
North Georgia College & State University, GA M,W
Northwestern State University of Louisiana, LA W
Northwest Missouri State University, MO M,W
Notre Dame de Namur University, CA W
The Ohio State University, OH M,W
Oklahoma Christian University, OK M,W
Oklahoma State University, OK M,W
Oklahoma Wesleyan University, OK M,W
Old Dominion University, VA M,W
Ouachita Baptist University, AR M,W
Our Lady of the Lake University of San Antonio, TX M,W
Pace University, NY M,W
Palm Beach Atlantic University, FL M,W
Penn State University Park, PA M,W
Pepperdine University, CA M,W
Philadelphia University, PA M,W
Pikeville College, KY M,W
Prairie View A&M University, TX M,W
Presbyterian College, SC M,W
Providence College, RI W
Purdue University, IN M,W
Queens College of the City University of New York, NY M,W
Quincy University, IL M,W
Quinnipiac University, CT M,W
Radford University, VA M,W
Reinhardt University, GA M,W
Research College of Nursing, MO M,W
Rice University, TX M,W
Rider University, NJ M,W
Robert Morris University, PA M,W
Robert Morris University Illinois, IL W
Rockhurst University, MO M,W
Rollins College, FL M,W
Sacred Heart University, CT M,W
Saginaw Valley State University, MI W
St. Ambrose University, IA M,W
St. Andrews Presbyterian College, NC M,W
St. Bonaventure University, NY M,W
St. Edward's University, TX M,W
Saint Francis University, PA M,W
St. John's University, NY M,W
Saint Joseph's College, IN M,W
Saint Joseph's University, PA M,W
Saint Leo University, FL M,W
Saint Louis University, MO M,W
Saint Mary's College of California, CA M,W
St. Thomas University, FL M,W
Samford University, AL M,W
San Diego State University, CA M,W
San Jose State University, CA W
Santa Clara University, CA M,W
Savannah College of Art and Design, GA M,W
Savannah State University, GA W
Seton Hill University, PA W
Shawnee State University, OH M,W
Shepherd University, WV M,W
Shippensburg University of Pennsylvania, PA W
Shorter University, GA M,W
Siena College, NY M,W
Slippery Rock University of Pennsylvania, PA W
Sonoma State University, CA M,W
South Dakota State University, SD M,W
Southeastern Louisiana University, LA W
Southeastern Oklahoma State University, OK M,W
Southeast Missouri State University, MO W
Southern Illinois University Carbondale, IL M,W
Southern Illinois University Edwardsville, IL M,W
Southern Methodist University, TX M,W
Southern Oregon University, OR W
Southern Utah University, UT W
Southwestern College, KS M,W
Southwest Minnesota State University, MN W
Spring Arbor University, MI M,W
Spring Hill College, AL M,W
Stanford University, CA M,W
State University of New York at Binghamton, NY M,W
Stephen F. Austin State University, TX W
Stetson University, FL M,W
Stonehill College, MA M,W
Stony Brook University, State University of New York, NY M,W
Syracuse University, NY W
Tabor College, KS M,W
Tarleton State University, TX W
Taylor University, IN M,W
Temple University, PA M,W
Tennessee Technological University, TN M
Tennessee Wesleyan College, TN M,W
Texas A&M University, TX M,W
Texas A&M University–Corpus Christi, TX M,W
Texas Christian University, TX M,W
Texas Southern University, TX M,W
Texas State University–San Marcos, TX W
Texas Tech University, TX M,W
Thomas University, GA W
Tiffin University, OH M,W
Towson University, MD M,W
Troy University, AL M,W
Truman State University, MO M,W
Tulane University, LA M,W
Tuskegee University, AL M,W
Union College, KY M,W
University at Buffalo, the State University of New York, NY M,W
The University of Akron, OH W
The University of Alabama, AL M,W
The University of Alabama at Birmingham, AL M,W
The University of Alabama in Huntsville, AL M,W
The University of Arizona, AZ M,W
University of Arkansas, AR M,W
University of California, Davis, CA M,W
University of California, Irvine, CA M,W
University of California, Los Angeles, CA M,W
University of California, Santa Barbara, CA M,W
University of Central Florida, FL M,W
University of Charleston, WV M,W
University of Cincinnati, OH W
University of Colorado Boulder, CO W
University of Connecticut, CT M,W
University of Dayton, OH M,W
University of Denver, CO M,W
University of Evansville, IN W
The University of Findlay, OH M,W

University of Florida, FL M,W
University of Georgia, GA M,W
University of Hartford, CT M,W
University of Hawaii at Hilo, HI M,W
University of Hawaii at Manoa, HI M,W
University of Houston, TX W
University of Idaho, ID M,W
University of Illinois at Chicago, IL M,W
University of Illinois at Springfield, IL M,W
University of Illinois at Urbana–Champaign, IL M,W
University of Indianapolis, IN M,W
The University of Iowa, IA M,W
The University of Kansas, KS W
University of Louisiana at Lafayette, LA M,W
University of Louisville, KY M,W
University of Maryland, Baltimore County, MD M,W
University of Maryland, College Park, MD M,W
University of Massachusetts Amherst, MA W
University of Memphis, TN M,W
University of Miami, FL M,W
University of Michigan, MI M,W
University of Minnesota, Crookston, MN W
University of Minnesota, Duluth, MN W
University of Minnesota, Twin Cities Campus, MN M,W
University of Mississippi, MS M,W
University of Missouri, MO W
University of Missouri–St. Louis, MO M,W
University of Mobile, AL M,W
University of Montevallo, AL W
University of Nebraska–Lincoln, NE M,W
University of Nevada, Las Vegas, NV M,W
University of Nevada, Reno, NV M,W
University of North Alabama, AL M,W
The University of North Carolina at Asheville, NC M,W
The University of North Carolina at Chapel Hill, NC M,W
The University of North Carolina at Charlotte, NC M,W
The University of North Carolina at Greensboro, NC M,W
The University of North Carolina at Pembroke, NC W
The University of North Carolina Wilmington, NC M,W
University of North Dakota, ND W
University of Northern Colorado, CO M,W
University of Northern Iowa, IA W
University of North Florida, FL M,W
University of Notre Dame, IN M,W
University of Oklahoma, OK M,W
University of Oregon, OR M,W
University of Pittsburgh, PA W
University of Portland, OR M,W
University of Rhode Island, RI W
University of Richmond, VA M,W
University of St. Francis, IL M,W
University of San Diego, CA M,W
University of South Alabama, AL M,W
University of South Carolina, SC M,W
University of South Carolina Aiken, SC M,W
The University of South Dakota, SD W
University of Southern California, CA M,W
University of Southern Indiana, IN M,W
University of Southern Mississippi, MS M,W
University of South Florida, FL M,W
The University of Tampa, FL W
The University of Tennessee, TN M,W
The University of Tennessee at Chattanooga, TN M,W
The University of Tennessee at Martin, TN W
The University of Texas at Arlington, TX M,W
The University of Texas at Austin, TX M,W
The University of Texas at San Antonio, TX M,W
The University of Texas–Pan American, TX M,W
University of the Cumberlands, KY M,W
University of the District of Columbia, DC M,W
University of the Incarnate Word, TX M,W
University of the Pacific, CA M,W
University of the Southwest, NM M,W
The University of Toledo, OH M,W
University of Tulsa, OK M,W
University of Utah, UT M,W
University of Virginia, VA M,W
The University of Virginia's College at Wise, VA M,W
University of West Florida, FL M,W
University of West Georgia, GA W
University of Wisconsin–Green Bay, WI M,W
University of Wisconsin–Madison, WI M,W
University of Wyoming, WY W
Ursuline College, OH W
Utah State University, UT M,W
Valdosta State University, GA M,W
Valparaiso University, IN M,W
Vanderbilt University, TN M,W
Virginia Commonwealth University, VA M,W
Virginia Military Institute, VA M
Virginia Polytechnic Institute and State University, VA M,W
Virginia State University, VA M,W
Wagner College, NY M,W
Wake Forest University, NC M,W
Walsh University, OH M,W
Washburn University, KS M,W
Washington State University, WA W
Wayne State University, MI M,W
Webber International University, FL M,W
West Chester University of Pennsylvania, PA M,W
Western Carolina University, NC W
Western Illinois University, IL M,W
Western Kentucky University, KY M,W
Western Michigan University, MI M,W
West Liberty University, WV M,W
Westmont College, CA M,W
West Virginia University, WV W
Wichita State University, KS M,W
William Jewell College, MO M,W
Wingate University, NC M,W
Winona State University, MN M,W
Winthrop University, SC M,W
Wofford College, SC M,W
Wright State University, OH M,W
Xavier University, OH M,W
Xavier University of Louisiana, LA M,W
Young Harris College, GA M,W
Youngstown State University, OH M,W

Track and field

Abilene Christian University, TX M,W
Adams State College, CO M,W
Adelphi University, NY M,W
Alabama Agricultural and Mechanical University, AL M,W
Alabama State University, AL M,W
Alcorn State University, MS M,W
Alderson-Broaddus College, WV M,W
American University, DC M,W
Anderson University, SC M,W
Angelo State University, TX M,W
Appalachian State University, NC M,W
Arizona State University, AZ M,W
Arkansas State University, AR M,W
Ashland University, OH M,W
Auburn University, AL M,W
Augustana College, SD M,W
Austin Peay State University, TN W
Azusa Pacific University, CA M,W
Ball State University, IN W
Bellarmine University, KY M,W
Belmont University, TN M,W
Bemidji State University, MN W
Benedictine College, KS M,W
Bethel College, IN M,W
Bethune-Cookman University, FL M,W
Biola University, CA M,W
Bloomsburg University of Pennsylvania, PA M,W
Boise State University, ID M,W
Boston College, MA M,W
Boston University, MA M,W
Bowie State University, MD M,W
Bowling Green State University, OH W
Brevard College, NC M,W
Brigham Young University, UT M,W
Bryant University, RI M,W
California Polytechnic State University, San Luis Obispo, CA M,W
California State Polytechnic University, Pomona, CA M,W
California State University, Bakersfield, CA M,W
California State University, Chico, CA M,W
California State University, Dominguez Hills, CA W
California State University, Fullerton, CA M,W
California State University, Long Beach, CA M,W
California State University, Northridge, CA M,W
Campbellsville University, KY M,W
Carson-Newman College, TN M,W
Cedarville University, OH M,W
Central Connecticut State University, CT M,W
Central Michigan University, MI M,W
The Citadel, The Military College of South Carolina, SC M,W

Clarion University of Pennsylvania, PA	W
Clarke University, IA	M,W
Clemson University, SC	M,W
Cleveland State University, OH	W
Coastal Carolina University, SC	M,W
College of Charleston, SC	W
The College of Saint Rose, NY	M,W
The College of William and Mary, VA	M,W
Colorado School of Mines, CO	M,W
Colorado State University, CO	M,W
Concordia University, CA	M,W
Concordia University, Nebraska, NE	M,W
Concordia University, St. Paul, MN	M,W
Concord University, WV	M,W
Coppin State University, MD	M,W
Corban University, OR	M,W
Culver-Stockton College, MO	M,W
Dakota State University, SD	M,W
Dakota Wesleyan University, SD	M,W
Dallas Baptist University, TX	W
Davenport University, MI	M,W
Davidson College, NC	M,W
Delaware State University, DE	M,W
DePaul University, IL	M,W
Dickinson State University, ND	M,W
Dillard University, LA	M,W
Doane College, NE	M,W
Dominican College, NY	W
Dordt College, IA	M,W
Drake University, IA	M,W
Drury University, MO	M,W
Duquesne University, PA	M,W
Eastern Michigan University, MI	M,W
Eastern Washington University, WA	M,W
East Tennessee State University, TN	M,W
Edinboro University of Pennsylvania, PA	M,W
Elon University, NC	W
Embry-Riddle Aeronautical University–Daytona, FL	M,W
Emmanuel College, GA	M,W
Emporia State University, KS	M,W
Evangel University, MO	M,W
The Evergreen State College, WA	M,W
Ferris State University, MI	M,W
Florida Agricultural and Mechanical University, FL	M,W
Florida International University, FL	M,W
Florida Southern College, FL	M,W
Florida State University, FL	M,W
Furman University, SC	M,W
Gardner-Webb University, NC	M,W
Georgetown College, KY	M,W
Georgetown University, DC	M,W
Georgia Institute of Technology, GA	M,W
Georgian Court University, NJ	W
Georgia Southern University, GA	W
Georgia State University, GA	M,W
Grace College, IN	M,W
Graceland University, IA	M,W
Grand Valley State University, MI	M,W
Grand View University, IA	M,W
Hannibal-LaGrange University, MO	M,W
Harding University, AR	M,W
Hillsdale College, MI	M,W
Houghton College, NY	M,W
Humboldt State University, CA	M,W
Huntington University, IN	M,W
Illinois State University, IL	M,W
Indiana State University, IN	M,W
Indiana University Bloomington, IN	M,W
Indiana University of Pennsylvania, PA	M,W
Indiana University–Purdue University Fort Wayne, IN	W
Indiana Wesleyan University, IN	M,W
Inter American University of Puerto Rico, Bayamón Campus, PR	M,W
Inter American University of Puerto Rico, Guayama Campus, PR	M,W
Inter American University of Puerto Rico, San Germán Campus, PR	M,W
Iona College, NY	M,W
Iowa State University of Science and Technology, IA	M,W
Iowa Wesleyan College, IA	M,W
James Madison University, VA	W
Jamestown College, ND	M,W
Johnson C. Smith University, NC	M,W
Kansas State University, KS	M,W
Kennesaw State University, GA	M,W
Kent State University, OH	M,W
Kentucky State University, KY	M,W
King College, TN	M,W
Kutztown University of Pennsylvania, PA	M,W
Lake Superior State University, MI	M,W
Lamar University, TX	M,W
Lehigh University, PA	M,W
Liberty University, VA	M,W
Limestone College, SC	M,W
Lincoln University, MO	M,W
Lindenwood University, MO	M,W
Lindsey Wilson College, KY	M,W
Lock Haven University of Pennsylvania, PA	M,W
Long Island University, Brooklyn Campus, NY	M,W
Louisiana State University and Agricultural and Mechanical College, LA	M,W
Loyola University Chicago, IL	M,W
Loyola University Maryland, MD	W
Malone University, OH	M,W
Manhattan College, NY	M,W
Marist College, NY	M,W
Marquette University, WI	M,W
Marshall University, WV	M,W
Mars Hill College, NC	M,W
Maryville University of Saint Louis, MO	M,W
The Master's College and Seminary, CA	M,W
McKendree University, IL	M,W
Merrimack College, MA	M,W
Mesa State College, CO	W
Miami University, OH	M,W
Michigan State University, MI	M,W
Middle Tennessee State University, TN	M,W
Millersville University of Pennsylvania, PA	M,W
Minnesota State University Mankato, MN	M,W
Minnesota State University Moorhead, MN	M,W
Minot State University, ND	M,W
Mississippi State University, MS	M,W
Missouri Baptist University, MO	M,W
Missouri Southern State University, MO	M,W
Missouri State University, MO	W
Missouri University of Science and Technology, MO	M,W
Molloy College, NY	M,W
Monmouth University, NJ	M,W
Montana State University, MT	M,W
Montreat College, NC	M,W
Morehead State University, KY	M,W
Morehouse College, GA	M
Morningside College, IA	M,W
Mountain State University, WV	M,W
Mount Marty College, SD	M,W
Mount Mercy University, IA	M,W
Mount St. Mary's University, MD	M,W
Murray State University, KY	M,W
New Mexico State University, NM	W
Nicholls State University, LA	M,W
North Carolina Agricultural and Technical State University, NC	M,W
North Carolina State University, NC	M,W
Northeastern University, MA	M,W
Northern Arizona University, AZ	M,W
Northern Michigan University, MI	W
Northern State University, SD	M,W
Northwest Christian University, OR	M,W
Northwestern State University of Louisiana, LA	M,W
Northwest Missouri State University, MO	M,W
Northwest Nazarene University, ID	M,W
Northwest University, WA	M,W
The Ohio State University, OH	M,W
Ohio University, OH	W
Oklahoma Christian University, OK	M,W
Oklahoma City University, OK	M,W
Oklahoma State University, OK	M,W
Oklahoma Wesleyan University, OK	M,W
Pace University, NY	M,W
Penn State University Park, PA	M,W
Prairie View A&M University, TX	M,W
Providence College, RI	M,W
Purdue University, IN	M,W
Queens College of the City University of New York, NY	M,W
Quinnipiac University, CT	W
Radford University, VA	M,W
Rice University, TX	M,W
Rider University, NJ	M,W
Robert Morris University, PA	M,W
Robert Morris University Illinois, IL	W
Sacred Heart University, CT	M,W
Saginaw Valley State University, MI	M,W
St. Ambrose University, IA	M,W
Saint Francis University, PA	M,W
St. John's University, NY	W
Saint Joseph's College, IN	M,W
Saint Joseph's University, PA	M,W
Saint Louis University, MO	M,W
Saint Martin's University, WA	M,W
Samford University, AL	M,W
San Diego State University, CA	W
San Francisco State University, CA	W
Santa Clara University, CA	M,W
Savannah State University, GA	M,W
Seattle Pacific University, WA	M,W

Seton Hill University, PA M,W
Shippensburg University of Pennsylvania, PA M,W
Shorter University, GA M,W
Slippery Rock University of Pennsylvania, PA M,W
Soka University of America, CA M,W
South Dakota School of Mines and Technology, SD M,W
South Dakota State University, SD M,W
Southeastern Louisiana University, LA M,W
Southeast Missouri State University, MO M,W
Southern Connecticut State University, CT M,W
Southern Illinois University Carbondale, IL M,W
Southern Illinois University Edwardsville, IL M,W
Southern Oregon University, OR M,W
Southern Utah University, UT M,W
Southwestern College, KS M,W
Spring Arbor University, MI M,W
Stanford University, CA M,W
State University of New York at Binghamton, NY M,W
Stephen F. Austin State University, TX M,W
Stonehill College, MA M,W
Stony Brook University, State University of New York, NY M,W
Syracuse University, NY M,W
Tabor College, KS M,W
Tarleton State University, TX M,W
Taylor University, IN M,W
Temple University, PA M,W
Tennessee Technological University, TN W
Texas A&M University, TX M,W
Texas Christian University, TX M,W
Texas Southern University, TX M,W
Texas State University–San Marcos, TX M,W
Texas Tech University, TX M,W
Texas Wesleyan University, TX M,W
Tiffin University, OH M,W
Towson University, MD M,W
Trevecca Nazarene University, TN M,W
Troy University, AL M,W
Truman State University, MO M,W
Tulane University, LA W
Tuskegee University, AL M,W
Union College, KY M,W
University at Buffalo, the State University of New York, NY M,W
The University of Akron, OH M,W
The University of Alabama, AL M,W
The University of Alabama at Birmingham, AL W
The University of Alabama in Huntsville, AL M,W
The University of Arizona, AZ M,W
University of Arkansas, AR M,W
University of California, Davis, CA M,W
University of California, Irvine, CA M,W
University of California, Los Angeles, CA M,W
University of California, Santa Barbara, CA M,W
University of Central Florida, FL W
University of Central Missouri, MO M,W
University of Charleston, WV M,W
University of Cincinnati, OH M,W
University of Colorado at Colorado Springs, CO M,W
University of Colorado Boulder, CO M,W
University of Connecticut, CT M,W
University of Dayton, OH W
University of Delaware, DE W
The University of Findlay, OH M,W
University of Florida, FL M,W
University of Georgia, GA M,W
University of Hawaii at Manoa, HI W
University of Houston, TX M,W
University of Idaho, ID M,W
University of Illinois at Chicago, IL M,W
University of Illinois at Urbana–Champaign, IL M,W
University of Indianapolis, IN M,W
The University of Iowa, IA M,W
The University of Kansas, KS M,W
University of Louisiana at Lafayette, LA M,W
University of Louisville, KY M,W
University of Maine, ME M,W
University of Maryland, Baltimore County, MD M,W
University of Maryland, College Park, MD M,W
University of Massachusetts Amherst, MA M,W
University of Massachusetts Lowell, MA M,W
University of Memphis, TN M,W
University of Miami, FL M,W
University of Michigan, MI M,W
University of Minnesota, Duluth, MN M,W
University of Minnesota, Twin Cities Campus, MN M,W
University of Mississippi, MS M,W
University of Missouri, MO M,W
University of Mobile, AL M,W
University of Nebraska–Lincoln, NE M,W
University of Nevada, Las Vegas, NV W
University of Nevada, Reno, NV W
University of New Hampshire, NH M,W
The University of North Carolina at Asheville, NC M,W
The University of North Carolina at Chapel Hill, NC M,W
The University of North Carolina at Charlotte, NC M,W
The University of North Carolina at Pembroke, NC M,W
The University of North Carolina Wilmington, NC M,W
University of North Dakota, ND M,W
University of Northern Colorado, CO M,W
University of Northern Iowa, IA M,W
University of North Florida, FL M,W
University of North Texas, TX M,W
University of Notre Dame, IN M,W
University of Oklahoma, OK M,W
University of Oregon, OR M,W
University of Pittsburgh, PA M,W
University of Portland, OR M,W
University of Rhode Island, RI M,W
University of Richmond, VA W
University of Rio Grande, OH M,W
University of St. Francis, IL M,W
University of San Diego, CA W
University of South Alabama, AL M,W
University of South Carolina, SC M,W
The University of South Dakota, SD M,W
University of Southern California, CA M,W
University of Southern Mississippi, MS M,W
University of South Florida, FL M,W
The University of Tennessee, TN M,W
The University of Tennessee at Chattanooga, TN M,W
The University of Texas at Austin, TX M,W
The University of Texas at San Antonio, TX M,W
The University of Texas–Pan American, TX M,W
University of the Cumberlands, KY M,W
University of the District of Columbia, DC M,W
University of the Incarnate Word, TX M,W
University of the Southwest, NM M,W
The University of Toledo, OH W
University of Tulsa, OK M,W
University of Utah, UT W
University of Vermont, VT M,W
University of Virginia, VA M,W
University of Wisconsin–Madison, WI M,W
University of Wisconsin–Parkside, WI M,W
University of Wyoming, WY M,W
Ursuline College, OH W
Utah State University, UT M,W
Utah Valley University, UT M,W
Valley City State University, ND M,W
Valparaiso University, IN M,W
Vanderbilt University, TN W
Villanova University, PA M,W
Virginia Commonwealth University, VA M,W
Virginia Military Institute, VA M,W
Virginia Polytechnic Institute and State University, VA M,W
Virginia State University, VA M,W
Wagner College, NY M,W
Wake Forest University, NC M,W
Walsh University, OH M,W
Washington Adventist University, MD M,W
Washington State University, WA M,W
Wayland Baptist University, TX M,W
Wayne State College, NE M,W
Webber International University, FL M,W
West Chester University of Pennsylvania, PA M,W
Western Carolina University, NC M,W
Western Illinois University, IL M,W
Western Kentucky University, KY M,W
Western Michigan University, MI W
Western Oregon University, OR M,W
Western State College of Colorado, CO M,W
West Liberty University, WV M,W
Westmont College, CA M,W
West Virginia University, WV W
Wheeling Jesuit University, WV M,W
Wichita State University, KS M,W
William Jessup University, CA M,W
William Jewell College, MO M,W
Winona State University, MN W

Winthrop University, SC M,W
Wofford College, SC M,W
Wright State University, OH W
Xavier University, OH M,W
Youngstown State University, OH M,W

Ultimate Frisbee

Beulah Heights University, GA M,W
Corcoran College of Art and Design, DC M,W
Ohio University–Zanesville, OH M,W
St. Louis Christian College, MO M,W
Saint Luke's College of Health Sciences, MO M,W

Volleyball

Abilene Christian University, TX W
Adams State College, CO W
Adelphi University, NY W
Alabama Agricultural and Mechanical University, AL W
Alabama State University, AL W
Alcorn State University, MS W
Alderson-Broaddus College, WV W
American University, DC W
Anderson University, SC W
Angelo State University, TX W
Appalachian State University, NC W
Arizona State University, AZ W
Arkansas State University, AR W
Arkansas Tech University, AR W
Armstrong Atlantic State University, GA W
Asbury University, KY W
Ashland University, OH W
Auburn University, AL W
Augustana College, SD W
Austin Peay State University, TN W
Azusa Pacific University, CA W
Ball State University, IN M,W
Barry University, FL W
Bellarmine University, KY W
Belmont University, TN W
Bemidji State University, MN W
Benedictine College, KS W
Bethel College, IN W
Bethune-Cookman University, FL W
Beulah Heights University, GA M,W
Biola University, CA W
Bloomfield College, NJ W
Bluefield College, VA W
Boise State University, ID W
Boston College, MA W
Bowie State University, MD W
Bowling Green State University, OH W
Brenau University, GA W
Brevard College, NC W
Brigham Young University, UT M,W
Bryan College, TN W
Bryant University, RI W
Butler University, IN W
California Polytechnic State University, San Luis Obispo, CA W
California State Polytechnic University, Pomona, CA W
California State University, Bakersfield, CA W
California State University, Chico, CA W
California State University, Dominguez Hills, CA W
California State University, Fullerton, CA W
California State University, Long Beach, CA M,W
California State University, Monterey Bay, CA W
California State University, Northridge, CA M,W
California State University, San Bernardino, CA W
Cameron University, OK W
Campbellsville University, KY W
Canisius College, NY W
Carson-Newman College, TN W
Cedarville University, OH W
Central Connecticut State University, CT W
Central Michigan University, MI W
Chestnut Hill College, PA W
Christian Brothers University, TN W
The Citadel, The Military College of South Carolina, SC W
Clarion University of Pennsylvania, PA W
Clarke University, IA M,W
Clemson University, SC W
Cleveland State University, OH W
Coastal Carolina University, SC W
Coker College, SC W
Colgate University, NY W
College of Charleston, SC W
College of Saint Mary, NE W
The College of Saint Rose, NY W
College of the Ozarks, MO W
The College of William and Mary, VA W
Colorado School of Mines, CO W
Colorado State University, CO W
Columbia College, MO W
Concordia University, CA W
Concordia University, Nebraska, NE W
Concordia University, St. Paul, MN W
Concord University, WV W
Coppin State University, MD W
Corban University, OR W
Corcoran College of Art and Design, DC M,W
Creighton University, NE W
Culver-Stockton College, MO W
Dakota State University, SD W
Dakota Wesleyan University, SD W
Dallas Baptist University, TX W
Davenport University, MI W
Davidson College, NC W
Delaware State University, DE W
DePaul University, IL W
Dickinson State University, ND W
Dillard University, LA W
Dixie State College of Utah, UT W
Doane College, NE W
Dominican College, NY W
Dominican University of California, CA W
Dordt College, IA W
Dowling College, NY W
Drake University, IA W
Drury University, MO W
Duquesne University, PA W
Eastern Michigan University, MI W
Eastern Washington University, WA W
East Tennessee State University, TN W
Eckerd College, FL W
Edinboro University of Pennsylvania, PA W
Elizabeth City State University, NC W
Elon University, NC W
Embry-Riddle Aeronautical University–Daytona, FL W
Embry-Riddle Aeronautical University–Prescott, AZ W
Emmanuel College, GA W
Emporia State University, KS W
Erskine College, SC W
Evangel University, MO W
The Evergreen State College, WA W
Fairfield University, CT W
Faulkner University, AL W
Fayetteville State University, NC W
Felician College, NJ W
Ferris State University, MI W
Flagler College, FL W
Florida Agricultural and Mechanical University, FL W
Florida Atlantic University, FL W
Florida College, FL W
Florida Gulf Coast University, FL W
Florida Institute of Technology, FL W
Florida International University, FL W
Florida Southern College, FL W
Florida State University, FL W
Fort Lewis College, CO W
Francis Marion University, SC W
Freed-Hardeman University, TN W
Furman University, SC W
Gannon University, PA W
Gardner-Webb University, NC W
Georgetown College, KY W
Georgetown University, DC W
Georgia Institute of Technology, GA W
Georgian Court University, NJ W
Georgia Southern University, GA W
Georgia State University, GA W
Goldey-Beacom College, DE W
Grace College, IN W
Graceland University, IA M,W
Grand Valley State University, MI W
Grand View University, IA M,W
Hannibal-LaGrange University, MO M,W
Harding University, AR W
Hawai'i Pacific University, HI W
Hillsdale College, MI W
Hofstra University, NY W
Houghton College, NY W
Humboldt State University, CA W
Huntington University, IN W
Illinois Institute of Technology, IL W
Illinois State University, IL W
Indiana State University, IN W
Indiana University Bloomington, IN W
Indiana University of Pennsylvania, PA W
Indiana University–Purdue University Fort Wayne, IN M,W
Indiana University–Purdue University Indianapolis, IN W
Indiana University Southeast, IN W
Indiana Wesleyan University, IN W
Inter American University of Puerto Rico, Bayamón Campus, PR M,W

Inter American University of Puerto Rico, San Germán Campus, PR M,W
Iona College, NY W
Iowa State University of Science and Technology, IA W
Iowa Wesleyan College, IA W
James Madison University, VA W
Jamestown College, ND W
John Brown University, AR W
Johnson C. Smith University, NC W
Kansas State University, KS W
Kennesaw State University, GA W
Kent State University, OH W
Kentucky State University, KY W
Kentucky Wesleyan College, KY W
King College, TN W
Kutztown University of Pennsylvania, PA W
Lake Superior State University, MI W
Lamar University, TX W
Lee University, TN W
Lehigh University, PA W
Le Moyne College, NY W
Lewis-Clark State College, ID W
Liberty University, VA W
Limestone College, SC M,W
Lincoln Memorial University, TN W
Lindenwood University, MO M,W
Lindsey Wilson College, KY W
Lipscomb University, TN W
Lock Haven University of Pennsylvania, PA W
Long Island University, Brooklyn Campus, NY W
Long Island University, C.W. Post Campus, NY W
Louisiana State University and Agricultural and Mechanical College, LA W
Lourdes College, OH W
Loyola Marymount University, CA W
Loyola University Chicago, IL M,W
Loyola University Maryland, MD W
Lubbock Christian University, TX W
Lynn University, FL W
Lyon College, AR W
Malone University, OH W
Manhattan College, NY W
Marist College, NY W
Marquette University, WI W
Marshall University, WV W
Mars Hill College, NC W
Maryville University of Saint Louis, MO W
The Master's College and Seminary, CA W
Mayville State University, ND W
McKendree University, IL W
Mercer University, GA W
Merrimack College, MA W
Mesa State College, CO W
Miami University, OH W
Michigan State University, MI W
Mid-Continent University, KY W
Middle Tennessee State University, TN W
Midwestern State University, TX W
Millersville University of Pennsylvania, PA W
Milligan College, TN W
Minnesota State University Mankato, MN W
Minnesota State University Moorhead, MN W
Minot State University, ND W
Mississippi State University, MS W
Missouri Baptist University, MO M,W
Missouri Southern State University, MO W
Missouri State University, MO W
Missouri University of Science and Technology, MO W
Molloy College, NY W
Montana State University, MT W
Montana State University Billings, MT W
Montana Tech of The University of Montana, MT W
Montreat College, NC W
Morehead State University, KY W
Morningside College, IA W
Mountain State University, WV W
Mount Marty College, SD W
Mount Mercy University, IA W
Mount Olive College, NC M,W
Mount Vernon Nazarene University, OH W
Murray State University, KY W
New Jersey Institute of Technology, NJ M,W
New Mexico State University, NM W
New York Institute of Technology, NY W
Niagara University, NY W
Nicholls State University, LA W
North Carolina Agricultural and Technical State University, NC W
North Carolina State University, NC W
Northeastern University, MA W
Northern Arizona University, AZ W
Northern Illinois University, IL W
Northern Kentucky University, KY W
Northern Michigan University, MI W
Northern State University, SD W
Northwest Christian University, OR W
Northwestern State University of Louisiana, LA W
Northwest Missouri State University, MO W
Northwest Nazarene University, ID W
Northwest University, WA W
Notre Dame de Namur University, CA W
Nyack College, NY W
The Ohio State University, OH M,W
Ohio University, OH W
Ohio University–Zanesville, OH M,W
Ohio Valley University, WV W
Oklahoma City University, OK W
Oklahoma Panhandle State University, OK W
Oklahoma Wesleyan University, OK W
Oregon State University, OR W
Ouachita Baptist University, AR W
Our Lady of the Lake University of San Antonio, TX W
Pace University, NY W
Palm Beach Atlantic University, FL W
Penn State University Park, PA M,W
Pepperdine University, CA M,W
Philadelphia University, PA W
Pikeville College, KY W
Point Park University, PA W
Prairie View A&M University, TX W
Presbyterian College, SC W
Providence College, RI W
Purdue University, IN W
Purdue University North Central, IN W
Queens College of the City University of New York, NY W
Quincy University, IL M,W
Quinnipiac University, CT W
Radford University, VA W
Regis University, CO W
Research College of Nursing, MO W
Rice University, TX W
Rider University, NJ W
Robert Morris University, PA W
Robert Morris University Illinois, IL M,W
Rockhurst University, MO W
Rocky Mountain College, MT W
Rollins College, FL W
Sacred Heart University, CT M,W
Saginaw Valley State University, MI W
St. Ambrose University, IA M,W
St. Edward's University, TX W
Saint Francis University, PA M,W
St. John's University, NY W
Saint Joseph's College, IN W
Saint Leo University, FL W
St. Louis Christian College, MO M,W
Saint Louis University, MO W
Saint Luke's College of Health Sciences, MO M,W
Saint Martin's University, WA W
Saint Mary's College of California, CA W
St. Thomas Aquinas College, NY W
St. Thomas University, FL W
Saint Xavier University, IL W
Samford University, AL W
San Diego Christian College, CA W
San Diego State University, CA W
San Francisco State University, CA W
San Jose State University, CA W
Santa Clara University, CA W
Savannah College of Art and Design, GA W
Savannah State University, GA W
Seattle Pacific University, WA W
Seton Hill University, PA W
Shawnee State University, OH M,W
Shepherd University, WV W
Shippensburg University of Pennsylvania, PA W
Shorter University, GA W
Siena College, NY W
Simpson University, CA W
Slippery Rock University of Pennsylvania, PA W
Sonoma State University, CA W
South Dakota School of Mines and Technology, SD W
South Dakota State University, SD W
Southeastern Louisiana University, LA W
Southeastern Oklahoma State University, OK W
Southeast Missouri State University, MO W

Southern Connecticut State University, CT W
Southern Illinois University Carbondale, IL W
Southern Illinois University Edwardsville, IL W
Southern Methodist University, TX W
Southern Oregon University, OR W
Southwestern College, KS W
Southwest Minnesota State University, MN W
Spring Arbor University, MI W
Spring Hill College, AL W
Stanford University, CA M,W
State University of New York at Binghamton, NY W
Stephen F. Austin State University, TX W
Stetson University, FL W
Stonehill College, MA W
Stony Brook University, State University of New York, NY W
Syracuse University, NY W
Tabor College, KS W
Tarleton State University, TX W
Taylor University, IN W
Temple University, PA W
Tennessee Technological University, TN W
Tennessee Wesleyan College, TN W
Texas A&M International University, TX W
Texas A&M University, TX W
Texas A&M University–Corpus Christi, TX W
Texas Christian University, TX W
Texas Southern University, TX W
Texas State University–San Marcos, TX W
Texas Tech University, TX W
Texas Wesleyan University, TX W
Texas Woman's University, TX W
Tiffin University, OH W
Towson University, MD W
Trevecca Nazarene University, TN W
Troy University, AL W
Truman State University, MO W
Tulane University, LA W
Tuskegee University, AL W
Union College, KY W
Union University, TN W
University at Buffalo, the State University of New York, NY W
The University of Akron, OH W
The University of Alabama, AL W
The University of Alabama at Birmingham, AL W
The University of Alabama in Huntsville, AL W
University of Alaska Fairbanks, AK W
The University of Arizona, AZ W
University of Arkansas, AR W
University of Bridgeport, CT W
University of California, Davis, CA W
University of California, Irvine, CA M,W
University of California, Los Angeles, CA M,W
University of California, Santa Barbara, CA M,W
University of Central Florida, FL W
University of Central Missouri, MO W
University of Charleston, WV W
University of Cincinnati, OH W
University of Colorado at Colorado Springs, CO W
University of Colorado Boulder, CO W
University of Connecticut, CT W
University of Dayton, OH W
University of Delaware, DE W
University of Denver, CO W
University of Evansville, IN W
The University of Findlay, OH W
University of Florida, FL W
University of Georgia, GA W
University of Hartford, CT W
University of Hawaii at Hilo, HI W
University of Hawaii at Manoa, HI M,W
University of Houston, TX W
University of Idaho, ID W
University of Illinois at Chicago, IL W
University of Illinois at Springfield, IL W
University of Illinois at Urbana–Champaign, IL W
University of Indianapolis, IN W
The University of Iowa, IA W
The University of Kansas, KS W
University of Louisiana at Lafayette, LA W
University of Louisville, KY W
University of Maryland, Baltimore County, MD W
University of Maryland, College Park, MD W
University of Massachusetts Lowell, MA W
University of Memphis, TN W
University of Miami, FL W
University of Michigan, MI W
University of Michigan–Dearborn, MI W
University of Minnesota, Crookston, MN W
University of Minnesota, Duluth, MN W
University of Minnesota, Twin Cities Campus, MN W
University of Mississippi, MS W
University of Missouri, MO W
University of Missouri–St. Louis, MO W
University of Mobile, AL W
University of Montevallo, AL W
University of Nebraska at Omaha, NE W
University of Nebraska–Lincoln, NE W
University of Nevada, Las Vegas, NV W
University of Nevada, Reno, NV W
University of New Hampshire, NH W
University of North Alabama, AL W
The University of North Carolina at Asheville, NC W
The University of North Carolina at Chapel Hill, NC W
The University of North Carolina at Charlotte, NC W
The University of North Carolina at Greensboro, NC W
The University of North Carolina at Pembroke, NC W
The University of North Carolina Wilmington, NC W
University of North Dakota, ND W
University of Northern Colorado, CO W
University of Northern Iowa, IA W
University of North Florida, FL W
University of North Texas, TX W
University of Notre Dame, IN W
University of Oklahoma, OK W
University of Oregon, OR W
University of Pittsburgh, PA W
University of Portland, OR W
University of Rhode Island, RI W
University of Rio Grande, OH W
University of St. Francis, IL W
University of St. Thomas, TX W
University of San Diego, CA W
University of South Alabama, AL W
University of South Carolina, SC W
University of South Carolina Aiken, SC W
The University of South Dakota, SD W
University of Southern California, CA M,W
University of Southern Indiana, IN W
University of Southern Mississippi, MS W
University of South Florida, FL W
The University of Tampa, FL W
The University of Tennessee, TN W
The University of Tennessee at Chattanooga, TN W
The University of Tennessee at Martin, TN W
The University of Texas at Arlington, TX W
The University of Texas at Austin, TX W
The University of Texas at San Antonio, TX W
The University of Texas of the Permian Basin, TX W
The University of Texas–Pan American, TX W
University of the Cumberlands, KY W
University of the District of Columbia, DC W
University of the Incarnate Word, TX W
University of the Pacific, CA M,W
University of the Sciences in Philadelphia, PA W
The University of Toledo, OH W
University of Tulsa, OK W
University of Utah, UT W
University of Virginia, VA W
The University of Virginia's College at Wise, VA W
University of West Georgia, GA W
University of Wisconsin–Green Bay, WI W
University of Wisconsin–Madison, WI W
University of Wisconsin–Parkside, WI W
University of Wyoming, WY W
Upper Iowa University, IA W
Ursuline College, OH W
Utah State University, UT W
Utah Valley University, UT W
Valdosta State University, GA W
Valley City State University, ND W
Valparaiso University, IN W
Villanova University, PA W
Virginia Commonwealth University, VA W
Virginia State University, VA W
Wake Forest University, NC W

Walsh University, OH W
Washburn University, KS W
Washington State University, WA W
Wayland Baptist University, TX W
Wayne State College, NE W
Wayne State University, MI W
Webber International University, FL M,W
West Chester University of Pennsylvania, PA W
Western Carolina University, NC W
Western Illinois University, IL W
Western Kentucky University, KY W
Western Michigan University, MI W
Western Oregon University, OR W
Western State College of Colorado, CO W
West Liberty University, WV W
Westminster College, UT W
Westmont College, CA W
West Virginia University, WV W
Wheeling Jesuit University, WV W
Wichita State University, KS W
William Jessup University, CA W
William Jewell College, MO W
Wingate University, NC W
Winona State University, MN W
Winthrop University, SC W
Wofford College, SC W
Wright State University, OH W
Xavier University, OH W
Youngstown State University, OH W

Water polo

Arizona State University, AZ W
California State University, Bakersfield, CA W
California State University, Long Beach, CA M,W
California State University, Monterey Bay, CA W
Colorado State University, CO W
Concordia University, CA M,W
Gannon University, PA M,W
Hartwick College, NY W
Indiana University Bloomington, IN W
Iona College, NY W
Lindenwood University, MO M,W
Loyola Marymount University, CA M,W
Marist College, NY W
Pepperdine University, CA M
Queens College of the City University of New York, NY M
San Diego State University, CA W
San Jose State University, CA W
Santa Clara University, CA M,W
Siena College, NY W
Stanford University, CA M,W
University of California, Davis, CA M,W
University of California, Irvine, CA M,W
University of California, Los Angeles, CA M,W
University of California, Santa Barbara, CA M,W
University of Hawaii at Manoa, HI W
University of Maryland, College Park, MD W
University of Michigan, MI W
University of Southern California, CA M,W
University of the Pacific, CA M,W
Wagner College, NY W

Weight lifting

Inter American University of Puerto Rico, Bayamón Campus, PR M
Inter American University of Puerto Rico, San Germán Campus, PR M
Lindenwood University, MO M,W

Wrestling

Adams State College, CO M
American University, DC M
Anderson University, SC M
Appalachian State University, NC M
Arizona State University, AZ M
Ashland University, OH M
Augustana College, SD M
Bloomsburg University of Pennsylvania, PA M
Boise State University, ID M
Boston University, MA M
Bucknell University, PA M
California Polytechnic State University, San Luis Obispo, CA M
California State University, Bakersfield, CA M
California State University, Fullerton, CA M
Campbellsville University, KY M
Carson-Newman College, TN M
Central Michigan University, MI M
The Citadel, The Military College of South Carolina, SC M
Clarion University of Pennsylvania, PA M
Cleveland State University, OH M
Colorado School of Mines, CO M
Concordia University, Nebraska, NE M
Dakota Wesleyan University, SD M
Davidson College, NC M
Dickinson State University, ND M
Eastern Michigan University, MI M
Edinboro University of Pennsylvania, PA M
Embry-Riddle Aeronautical University–Prescott, AZ M
Gannon University, PA M
Gardner-Webb University, NC M
Grand View University, IA M
Hannibal-LaGrange University, MO M
Hofstra University, NY M
Indiana University Bloomington, IN M
Iowa State University of Science and Technology, IA M
Jamestown College, ND M,W
Kent State University, OH M
King College, TN M,W
Kutztown University of Pennsylvania, PA M
Lehigh University, PA M
Liberty University, VA M
Limestone College, SC M
Lindenwood University, MO M,W
Lindsey Wilson College, KY M
Lock Haven University of Pennsylvania, PA M
McKendree University, IL M
Mesa State College, CO M
Michigan State University, MI M
Millersville University of Pennsylvania, PA M
Minnesota State University Mankato, MN M
Minnesota State University Moorhead, MN M
Missouri Baptist University, MO M
Morningside College, IA M
Murray State University, KY M
North Carolina State University, NC M
Northern Illinois University, IL M
Northern State University, SD M
The Ohio State University, OH M
Ohio University, OH M
Ohio Valley University, WV M
Oklahoma City University, OK M,W
Oklahoma State University, OK M
Old Dominion University, VA M
Oregon State University, OR M
Ouachita Baptist University, AR M
Penn State University Park, PA M
Purdue University, IN M
Rider University, NJ M
Sacred Heart University, CT M
San Francisco State University, CA M
Seton Hill University, PA M
Shippensburg University of Pennsylvania, PA M
South Dakota State University, SD M
Southern Illinois University Edwardsville, IL M
Southern Oregon University, OR M
Southwest Minnesota State University, MN M
Stanford University, CA M
State University of New York at Binghamton, NY M
Tiffin University, OH M
Truman State University, MO M
University at Buffalo, the State University of New York, NY M
University of Central Missouri, MO M
The University of Findlay, OH M
University of Illinois at Urbana–Champaign, IL M
University of Indianapolis, IN M
The University of Iowa, IA M
University of Maryland, College Park, MD M
University of Michigan, MI M
University of Minnesota, Twin Cities Campus, MN M
University of Missouri, MO M
University of Nebraska at Omaha, NE M
University of Nebraska–Lincoln, NE M
The University of North Carolina at Chapel Hill, NC M
The University of North Carolina at Greensboro, NC M
The University of North Carolina at Pembroke, NC M
University of Northern Colorado, CO M
University of Northern Iowa, IA M
University of Oklahoma, OK M
University of Pittsburgh, PA M
University of Pittsburgh at Johnstown, PA M
The University of Tampa, FL M
The University of Tennessee at Chattanooga, TN M
University of the Cumberlands, KY M,W

University of Virginia, VA M
University of Wisconsin–Madison, WI M
University of Wisconsin–Parkside, WI M
University of Wyoming, WY M
Utah Valley University, UT M
Virginia Military Institute, VA M
Wayland Baptist University, TX M,W
Western State College of Colorado, CO M
West Liberty University, WV M
West Virginia University, WV M

Co-Op Programs

Alabama Agricultural and Mechanical University, AL
Alabama State University, AL
Alcorn State University, MS
Alfred University, NY
Allen College, IA
American Jewish University, CA
American University, DC
Anderson University, SC
Andrews University, MI
Anna Maria College, MA
Antioch University Midwest, OH
Aquinas College, TN
Arcadia University, PA
Arizona State University, AZ
Armstrong Atlantic State University, GA
Athens State University, AL
Auburn University, AL
Auburn University Montgomery, AL
Augsburg College, MN
Augustana College, SD
Austin Peay State University, TN
Averett University, VA
Azusa Pacific University, CA
Ball State University, IN
Bard College at Simon's Rock, MA
Bates College, ME
Belmont Abbey College, NC
Belmont University, TN
Bemidji State University, MN
Benedictine College, KS
Berry College, GA
Bethune-Cookman University, FL
Beulah Heights University, GA
Birmingham-Southern College, AL
Bloomfield College, NJ
Bloomsburg University of Pennsylvania, PA
Boise State University, ID
Boston University, MA
Bowie State University, MD
Bowling Green State University, OH
Brigham Young University, UT
Butler University, IN
Cabrini College, PA
California Christian College, CA
California College of the Arts, CA
California Institute of Technology, CA
California Institute of the Arts, CA
California Polytechnic State University, San Luis Obispo, CA
California State Polytechnic University, Pomona, CA
California State University, Chico, CA
California State University, Dominguez Hills, CA
California State University, Fullerton, CA
California State University, Monterey Bay, CA
California State University, San Bernardino, CA
California State University, Stanislaus, CA
Calumet College of Saint Joseph, IN
Canisius College, NY
Capital University, OH
Carnegie Mellon University, PA
Case Western Reserve University, OH
The Catholic University of America, DC
Central College, IA
Central Connecticut State University, CT
Champlain College, VT
Chestnut Hill College, PA
Christendom College, VA
Cincinnati Christian University, OH
The Citadel, The Military College of South Carolina, SC
City College of the City University of New York, NY
Clarion University of Pennsylvania, PA
Clarke University, IA
Clarkson University, NY
Cleary University, MI
Clemson University, SC
Cleveland State University, OH
Coastal Carolina University, SC
College for Creative Studies, MI
College of Charleston, SC
College of Mount St. Joseph, OH
College of Staten Island of the City University of New York, NY
College of the Atlantic, ME
The College of Wooster, OH
Colorado School of Mines, CO
Colorado State University, CO
Columbus State University, GA
Concordia College, MN
Concord University, WV
Coppin State University, MD
Corban University, OR
Cornell University, NY
Crossroads Bible College, IN
Dakota State University, SD
Dakota Wesleyan University, SD
Dalton State College, GA
Davenport University, MI
Defiance College, OH
Delaware State University, DE
Delta State University, MS
DePaul University, IL
DeSales University, PA
Dickinson State University, ND
Dillard University, LA
Dixie State College of Utah, UT
Doane College, NE
Dominican College, NY
Dowling College, NY
Drake University, IA
Drury University, MO
Eastern Michigan University, MI
Eastern Oregon University, OR
East Tennessee State University, TN
Edgewood College, WI
Elizabeth City State University, NC
Elmhurst College, IL
Embry-Riddle Aeronautical University–Daytona, FL
Embry-Riddle Aeronautical University–Prescott, AZ
Embry-Riddle Aeronautical University–Worldwide, FL
Emory & Henry College, VA
Emporia State University, KS
Endicott College, MA
Fayetteville State University, NC
Felician College, NJ
Ferris State University, MI
Florida Agricultural and Mechanical University, FL
Florida Atlantic University, FL
Florida Gulf Coast University, FL
Florida Institute of Technology, FL
Florida International University, FL
Florida National College, FL
Florida State University, FL
Fort Lewis College, CO
Franklin College, IN
Freed-Hardeman University, TN
Gannon University, PA
Gardner-Webb University, NC
Garrett College, MD
Geneva College, PA
Georgetown College, KY
Georgia Institute of Technology, GA
Georgia Southern University, GA
Georgia State University, GA
Goldey-Beacom College, DE
Gordon College, MA
Grace College, IN
Graceland University, IA
Grand Valley State University, MI
Grand View University, IA
Greenville College, IL
Hanover College, IN
Harding University, AR
Hawai'i Pacific University, HI
Hendrix College, AR
Humboldt State University, CA
Husson University, ME
Huston-Tillotson University, TX
Illinois Institute of Technology, IL
Illinois State University, IL
Indiana State University, IN
Indiana University Bloomington, IN
Indiana University East, IN
Indiana University Northwest, IN
Indiana University of Pennsylvania, PA
Indiana University–Purdue University Fort Wayne, IN
Indiana University–Purdue University Indianapolis, IN
Inter American University of Puerto Rico, Bayamón Campus, PR
Inter American University of Puerto Rico, San Germán Campus, PR
Iowa State University of Science and Technology, IA
Iowa Wesleyan College, IA
Jamestown College, ND

Jarvis Christian College, TX
Jefferson College of Health Sciences, VA
John Carroll University, OH
John Jay College of Criminal Justice of the City University of New York, NY
Johnson & Wales University, CO
Johnson & Wales University, FL
Johnson & Wales University, RI
Johnson & Wales University—Charlotte Campus, NC
Johnson Bible College, TN
Johnson C. Smith University, NC
Kansas State University, KS
Kean University, NJ
Keene State College, NH
Kennesaw State University, GA
Kent State University, OH
Kentucky State University, KY
Kentucky Wesleyan College, KY
Kettering University, MI
Keuka College, NY
Keystone College, PA
King College, TN
Kuyper College, MI
Lake Superior State University, MI
Lamar University, TX
Lane College, TN
Lasell College, MA
Lawrence Technological University, MI
Lee University, TN
Lehigh University, PA
Lehman College of the City University of New York, NY
LeTourneau University, TX
Lewis-Clark State College, ID
Liberty University, VA
Lindsey Wilson College, KY
Lock Haven University of Pennsylvania, PA
Long Island University, Brooklyn Campus, NY
Long Island University, C.W. Post Campus, NY
Loras College, IA
Louisiana State University and Agricultural and Mechanical College, LA
Loyola Marymount University, CA
Loyola University Chicago, IL
Loyola University Maryland, MD
Lynn University, FL
Maine College of Art, ME
Manhattan College, NY
Marian University, WI
Marist College, NY
Marquette University, WI
Marshall University, WV
Mars Hill College, NC
Maryville University of Saint Louis, MO
Massachusetts College of Liberal Arts, MA
Massachusetts Institute of Technology, MA
Massachusetts Maritime Academy, MA
The Master's College and Seminary, CA
Mayville State University, ND
McNally Smith College of Music, MN
Medgar Evers College of the City University of New York, NY
Menlo College, CA
Mercer University, GA
Merrimack College, MA
Messiah College, PA
Methodist University, NC
Miami University, OH
Michigan State University, MI
Millersville University of Pennsylvania, PA
Milligan College, TN
Millikin University, IL
Minneapolis College of Art and Design, MN
Minnesota State University Mankato, MN
Minot State University, ND
Misericordia University, PA
Mississippi State University, MS
Missouri Southern State University, MO
Missouri State University, MO
Missouri University of Science and Technology, MO
Molloy College, NY
Monmouth University, NJ
Montana State University Billings, MT
Montana Tech of The University of Montana, MT
Montclair State University, NJ
Montreat College, NC
Morehead State University, KY
Morehouse College, GA
Mountain State University, WV
Mount Holyoke College, MA
Mount Marty College, SD
Mount Olive College, NC
Mount Saint Mary College, NY
Murray State University, KY
Nazareth College of Rochester, NY
New College of Florida, FL
New Jersey City University, NJ
New Jersey Institute of Technology, NJ
New Mexico Institute of Mining and Technology, NM
New Mexico State University, NM
New York Institute of Technology, NY
Niagara University, NY
Nicholls State University, LA
North Carolina Agricultural and Technical State University, NC
North Carolina State University, NC
Northeastern Illinois University, IL
Northeastern State University, OK
Northeastern University, MA
Northern Arizona University, AZ
Northern Illinois University, IL
Northern Kentucky University, KY
Northern State University, SD
North Georgia College & State University, GA
Northland College, WI
Northwestern Oklahoma State University, OK
Northwestern State University of Louisiana, LA
Northwest Nazarene University, ID
Northwest University, WA
Notre Dame de Namur University, CA
Oglethorpe University, GA
The Ohio State University, OH
Ohio University, OH
Oklahoma City University, OK
Oklahoma Wesleyan University, OK
Old Dominion University, VA
Oregon State University, OR
Otis College of Art and Design, CA
Ouachita Baptist University, AR
Our Lady of the Lake University of San Antonio, TX
Pace University, NY
Pacific Lutheran University, WA
Pacific Union College, CA
Pacific University, OR
Parsons The New School for Design, NY
Peirce College, PA
Penn State Abington, PA
Penn State Altoona, PA
Penn State Berks, PA
Penn State Erie, The Behrend College, PA
Penn State Harrisburg, PA
Penn State University Park, PA
Pennsylvania College of Technology, PA
Piedmont College, GA
Pitzer College, CA
Point Park University, PA
Polytechnic Institute of NYU, NY
Portland State University, OR
Prairie View A&M University, TX
Providence College, RI
Purdue University, IN
Purdue University Calumet, IN
Ramapo College of New Jersey, NJ
Reed College, OR
Regis University, CO
Reinhardt University, GA
Rensselaer Polytechnic Institute, NY
Rhodes College, TN
Rider University, NJ
Robert Morris University, PA
Rockhurst University, MO
Rocky Mountain College of Art + Design, CO
Rogers State University, OK
Rose-Hulman Institute of Technology, IN
Rowan University, NJ
Russell Sage College, NY
Rutgers, The State University of New Jersey, Camden, NJ
Rutgers, The State University of New Jersey, Newark, NJ
Rutgers, The State University of New Jersey, New Brunswick, NJ
Sacred Heart University, CT
Sage College of Albany, NY
Saginaw Valley State University, MI
St. Ambrose University, IA
St. Joseph's College, Long Island Campus, NY
St. Joseph's College, New York, NY
Saint Joseph's University, PA
Saint Louis University, MO
Saint Luke's College of Health Sciences, MO
Saint Martin's University, WA
Saint Mary's College, IN
St. Mary's College of Maryland, MD
Saint Mary's University of Minnesota, MN
Saint Xavier University, IL
Samford University, AL
San Francisco State University, CA
Santa Clara University, CA
Savannah State University, GA
Schreiner University, TX
Shenandoah University, VA
Shepherd University, WV
Shimer College, IL
Shippensburg University of Pennsylvania, PA
Sierra Nevada College, NV
Simmons College, MA
Simpson College, IA
Sonoma State University, CA
South Dakota School of Mines and Technology, SD
South Dakota State University, SD
Southern Connecticut State University, CT
Southern Illinois University Carbondale, IL
Southern Illinois University Edwardsville, IL
Southern Methodist University, TX
Southern Oregon University, OR
Southern Polytechnic State University, GA
Southern Utah University, UT
Springfield College, MA

State University of New York at New Paltz, NY
State University of New York at Oswego, NY
State University of New York at Plattsburgh, NY
State University of New York College at Cortland, NY
State University of New York College of Environmental Science and Forestry, NY
State University of New York Maritime College, NY
Suffolk University, MA
Syracuse University, NY
Tabor College, KS
Tarleton State University, TX
Taylor University, IN
Temple University, PA
Tennessee Technological University, TN
Texas A&M University, TX
Texas A&M University–Corpus Christi, TX
Texas Southern University, TX
Texas Tech University, TX
Texas Woman's University, TX
Thiel College, PA
Thomas Aquinas College, CA
Thomas More College, KY
Thomas University, GA
Towson University, MD
Trine University, IN
Truman State University, MO
Tulane University, LA
Tuskegee University, AL
Union College, NE
Union University, TN
University at Buffalo, the State University of New York, NY
University of Advancing Technology, AZ
The University of Akron, OH
The University of Alabama, AL
The University of Alabama at Birmingham, AL
The University of Alabama in Huntsville, AL
University of Alaska Fairbanks, AK
University of Alaska Southeast, AK
The University of Arizona, AZ
University of Arkansas, AR
University of Bridgeport, CT
University of California, Santa Barbara, CA
University of California, Santa Cruz, CA
University of Central Florida, FL
University of Central Missouri, MO
University of Cincinnati, OH
University of Colorado at Colorado Springs, CO
University of Colorado Boulder, CO
University of Colorado Denver, CO
University of Connecticut, CT
University of Dayton, OH
University of Delaware, DE
University of Denver, CO
University of Evansville, IN
The University of Findlay, OH
University of Florida, FL
University of Georgia, GA
University of Hartford, CT
University of Hawaii at Manoa, HI
University of Houston, TX
University of Houston–Clear Lake, TX
University of Idaho, ID
University of Illinois at Chicago, IL
University of Illinois at Springfield, IL
University of Illinois at Urbana–Champaign, IL
University of Indianapolis, IN
The University of Iowa, IA
The University of Kansas, KS
University of Louisiana at Lafayette, LA
University of Louisville, KY
University of Maine, ME
University of Maine at Fort Kent, ME
University of Maine at Presque Isle, ME
University of Maryland, Baltimore County, MD
University of Maryland, College Park, MD
University of Maryland University College, MD
University of Mary Washington, VA
University of Massachusetts Amherst, MA
University of Massachusetts Boston, MA
University of Massachusetts Dartmouth, MA
University of Massachusetts Lowell, MA
University of Memphis, TN
University of Michigan, MI
University of Michigan–Dearborn, MI
University of Michigan–Flint, MI
University of Minnesota, Duluth, MN
University of Minnesota, Twin Cities Campus, MN
University of Missouri, MO
University of Missouri–St. Louis, MO
University of Mount Union, OH
University of Nebraska at Omaha, NE
University of Nebraska–Lincoln, NE
University of Nevada, Las Vegas, NV
University of New Hampshire, NH
University of North Alabama, AL
The University of North Carolina at Charlotte, NC
The University of North Carolina at Pembroke, NC
The University of North Carolina Wilmington, NC
University of North Dakota, ND
University of Northern Colorado, CO
University of Northern Iowa, IA
University of North Florida, FL
University of North Texas, TX
University of Oklahoma, OK
University of Oregon, OR
University of Pennsylvania, PA
University of Pittsburgh, PA
University of Pittsburgh at Johnstown, PA
University of Puget Sound, WA
University of Rio Grande, OH
University of Rochester, NY
University of South Alabama, AL
University of South Carolina, SC
University of South Carolina Aiken, SC
The University of South Dakota, SD
University of Southern California, CA
University of Southern Indiana, IN
University of Southern Maine, ME
University of Southern Mississippi, MS
University of South Florida, FL
The University of Tampa, FL
The University of Tennessee, TN
The University of Tennessee at Chattanooga, TN
The University of Tennessee at Martin, TN
The University of Texas at Arlington, TX
The University of Texas at Austin, TX
The University of Texas at Dallas, TX
The University of Texas at San Antonio, TX
The University of Texas at Tyler, TX
The University of Texas–Pan American, TX
University of the Cumberlands, KY
University of the District of Columbia, DC
University of the Incarnate Word, TX
University of the Ozarks, AR
University of the Pacific, CA
University of the Sciences in Philadelphia, PA
The University of Toledo, OH
University of Utah, UT
University of Vermont, VT
University of Virginia, VA
The University of Virginia's College at Wise, VA
University of West Florida, FL
University of West Georgia, GA
University of Wisconsin–Eau Claire, WI
University of Wisconsin–La Crosse, WI
University of Wisconsin–Madison, WI
University of Wisconsin–Stevens Point, WI
University of Wisconsin–Stout, WI
University of Wisconsin–Superior, WI
Upper Iowa University, IA
Ursuline College, OH
Utah State University, UT
Utah Valley University, UT
Valdosta State University, GA
Valley City State University, ND
Valparaiso University, IN
Vanderbilt University, TN
Vassar College, NY
Vermont Technical College, VT
Villa Maria College of Buffalo, NY
Villanova University, PA
Virginia Commonwealth University, VA
Virginia Polytechnic Institute and State University, VA
Virginia State University, VA
Walla Walla University, WA
Washburn University, KS
Washington Adventist University, MD
Washington State University, WA
Washington University in St. Louis, MO
Wayne State College, NE
Wayne State University, MI
Webber International University, FL
Wentworth Institute of Technology, MA
Wesleyan College, GA
West Chester University of Pennsylvania, PA
Western Carolina University, NC
Western Connecticut State University, CT
Western Kentucky University, KY
Western Michigan University, MI
Westfield State University, MA
Westminster College, MO
Westminster College, UT
Whitman College, WA
Wichita State University, KS
Widener University, PA
Wilkes University, PA
William Jewell College, MO
Wilson College, PA
Winthrop University, SC
Wittenberg University, OH
Worcester Polytechnic Institute, MA
Wright State University, OH
Xavier University, OH
Xavier University of Louisiana, LA
York College of Pennsylvania, PA
Young Harris College, GA
Youngstown State University, OH

ROTC Programs

Air Force

Adelphi University, NY*
Alabama State University, AL
Alverno College, WI*
American University, DC*
Amherst College, MA*
Anderson University, SC*
Angelo State University, TX
Anna Maria College, MA*
Arizona State University, AZ
Asbury University, KY*
Assumption College, MA*
Auburn University, AL
Auburn University Montgomery, AL*
Augsburg College, MN*
Augustana College, SD*
Austin Peay State University, TN*
Baldwin-Wallace College, OH*
Baptist Bible College of Pennsylvania, PA*
Barry University, FL*
Bellarmine University, KY*
Belmont Abbey College, NC*
Belmont University, TN*
Bentley University, MA*
Bethel College, IN*
Bethel University, MN*
Bethune-Cookman University, FL*
Biola University, CA*
Birmingham-Southern College, AL*
Bloomsburg University of Pennsylvania, PA*
Boston College, MA*
Boston University, MA
Bowling Green State University, OH
Brandeis University, MA*
Brigham Young University, UT
Bryn Mawr College, PA*
Butler University, IN*
Cabrini College, PA*
California Institute of Technology, CA*
California State University, Dominguez Hills, CA*
California State University, Northridge, CA*
California State University, San Bernardino, CA
Capital University, OH*
Carnegie Mellon University, PA
Carroll University, WI*
Carson-Newman College, TN*
Case Western Reserve University, OH*
The Catholic University of America, DC*
Cazenovia College, NY*
Cedarville University, OH*
Central Connecticut State University, CT*
Centre College, KY*
Christian Brothers University, TN*
The Citadel, The Military College of South Carolina, SC
City College of the City University of New York, NY*
Claremont McKenna College, CA*
Clarkson University, NY
Clark University, MA*
Clemson University, SC
The Cleveland Institute of Art, OH*
Cleveland State University, OH*
College of Charleston, SC*
College of Mount St. Joseph, OH*
The College of New Jersey, NJ*
College of Saint Mary, NE*
The College of Saint Rose, NY*
The College of St. Scholastica, MN*
College of the Holy Cross, MA*
Colorado School of Mines, CO
Colorado State University, CO
Columbia College, MO*
Columbia University, School of General Studies, NY*
Concordia College, MN*
Concordia University, Nebraska, NE*
Concordia University, St. Paul, MN*
Corban University, OR*
Cornell University, NY
Creighton University, NE*
Dakota State University, SD*
Dallas Baptist University, TX*
Davidson College, NC*
Delaware State University, DE*
DePauw University, IN*
Dillard University, LA*
Doane College, NE*
Dowling College, NY*
Drake University, IA*
Duquesne University, PA*
Eastern Michigan University, MI*
Eckerd College, FL*
Elmhurst College, IL*
Elmira College, NY*
Elon University, NC*
Embry-Riddle Aeronautical University–Daytona, FL
Embry-Riddle Aeronautical University–Prescott, AZ
Emory University, GA*
Endicott College, MA*
Fairfield University, CT*
Faulkner University, AL*
Fayetteville State University, NC
Florida Agricultural and Mechanical University, FL*
Florida Atlantic University, FL*
Florida College, FL*
Florida International University, FL
Florida Southern College, FL*
Florida State University, FL
Free Will Baptist Bible College, TN*
Gardner-Webb University, NC*
George Fox University, OR*
Georgetown College, KY*
Georgetown University, DC*
Georgia Institute of Technology, GA
Georgia State University, GA*
Goldey-Beacom College, DE*
Gordon College, MA*
Goucher College, MD*
Grand View University, IA*
Hamilton College, NY*
Hamline University, MN*
Harvard University, MA*
Harvey Mudd College, CA
Hawai'i Pacific University, HI*
Huntingdon College, AL*
Illinois Institute of Technology, IL
Indiana State University, IN
Indiana University Bloomington, IN
Indiana University–Purdue University Indianapolis, IN*
Indiana University South Bend, IN*
Inter American University of Puerto Rico, San Germán Campus, PR*
Iona College, NY*
Iowa State University of Science and Technology, IA
Ithaca College, NY*
James Madison University, VA*
John Brown University, AR*
John Jay College of Criminal Justice of the City University of New York, NY*
The Johns Hopkins University, MD*
Johnson C. Smith University, NC*
Kansas State University, KS
Kean University, NJ*
Keene State College, NH*
Kennesaw State University, GA*
Kent State University, OH
Kent State University at Stark, OH*
Kentucky State University, KY*
Keystone College, PA*
King's College, PA*
La Roche College, PA*
Lawrence Technological University, MI*
Le Moyne College, NY*
Lewis-Clark State College, ID*
Liberty University, VA*
Lincoln University, MO*
Linfield College, OR*
Lipscomb University, TN*
Long Island University, C.W. Post Campus, NY*
Louisiana State University and Agricultural and Mechanical College, LA
Lourdes College, OH*
Loyola Marymount University, CA
Loyola University Chicago, IL*
Loyola University Maryland, MD*
Loyola University New Orleans, LA*
Lubbock Christian University, TX*
Lynn University, FL*
Macalester College, MN*
Malone University, OH*
Manhattan College, NY
Maranatha Baptist Bible College, WI*
Marquette University, WI
Mary Baldwin College, VA*
Marywood University, PA*
Massachusetts Institute of Technology, MA
Mayville State University, ND*

program is offered at another college's campus

ROTC Programs

Air Force

McKendree University, IL*
Menlo College, CA*
Merrimack College, MA*
Methodist University, NC*
Miami University, OH
Michigan State University, MI
Middle Tennessee State University, TN*
Midwestern State University, TX*
Millsaps College, MS*
Milwaukee School of Engineering, WI*
Minnesota State University Moorhead, MN*
Misericordia University, PA*
Mississippi State University, MS
Mississippi University for Women, MS*
Missouri University of Science and Technology, MO
Molloy College, NY*
Monmouth University, NJ*
Montana State University, MT
Montclair State University, NJ
Morehouse College, GA
Mount Carmel College of Nursing, OH*
Mount Holyoke College, MA*
Mount Olive College, NC*
National University, CA*
Nazareth College of Rochester, NY*
Nebraska Wesleyan University, NE*
New England College, NH*
New Jersey Institute of Technology, NJ
New Mexico State University, NM
New York Institute of Technology, NY
New York University, NY*
North Carolina Agricultural and Technical State University, NC
North Carolina State University, NC
North Central College, IL*
Northeastern Illinois University, IL*
Northeastern University, MA*
Northern Arizona University, AZ
Northern Illinois University, IL*
Northern Kentucky University, KY*
Northwestern College, MN*
Northwestern State University of Louisiana, LA*
Northwest University, WA*
Oglethorpe University, GA*
The Ohio State University, OH
Ohio University, OH
Oklahoma Christian University, OK*
Oklahoma City University, OK*
Oklahoma State University, OK
Oregon State University, OR
Our Lady of the Lake University of San Antonio, TX*
Pace University, NY*
Pacific University, OR*
Penn State Abington, PA*
Penn State Altoona, PA*
Penn State University Park, PA
Pepperdine University, CA*
Philadelphia Biblical University, PA*
Pitzer College, CA*
Point Park University, PA*
Polytechnic Institute of NYU, NY*
Pomona College, CA*
Portland State University, OR*
Purdue University, IN
Quinnipiac University, CT*
Ramapo College of New Jersey, NJ*
Regis University, CO*
Rensselaer Polytechnic Institute, NY
Rhodes College, TN*
Rice University, TX*
Rivier College, NH*
Robert Morris University, PA*
Rose-Hulman Institute of Technology, IN
Russell Sage College, NY*
Rutgers, The State University of New Jersey, Camden, NJ*
Rutgers, The State University of New Jersey, Newark, NJ
Rutgers, The State University of New Jersey, New Brunswick, NJ
Sage College of Albany, NY*
Saint Anselm College, NH*
St. Catherine University, MN*
St. Edward's University, TX*
St. John Fisher College, NY*
Saint Joseph's University, PA
St. Lawrence University, NY*
Saint Leo University, FL*
St. Louis College of Pharmacy, MO*
Saint Louis University, MO
Saint Martin's University, WA*
Saint Mary-of-the-Woods College, IN*
Saint Mary's College, IN*
Saint Mary's College of California, CA*
Saint Michael's College, VT*
St. Thomas Aquinas College, NY*
Saint Xavier University, IL*
Samford University, AL
San Diego Christian College, CA*
San Diego State University, CA
San Francisco State University, CA*
San Jose State University, CA
Santa Clara University, CA*
Scripps College, CA*
Seattle Pacific University, WA*
Shepherd University, WV*
Siena College, NY*
Skidmore College, NY*
Smith College, MA*
Sonoma State University, CA*
South Dakota State University, SD
Southeastern University, FL*
Southeast Missouri State University, MO
Southern Connecticut State University, CT*
Southern Illinois University Carbondale, IL
Southern Illinois University Edwardsville, IL
Southern Methodist University, TX*
Southern Polytechnic State University, GA*
Spelman College, GA*
Spring Arbor University, MI*
Springfield College, MA*
Spring Hill College, AL*
Stanford University, CA*
State University of New York at Binghamton, NY*
State University of New York College at Cortland, NY*
State University of New York College at Geneseo, NY*
State University of New York College at Old Westbury, NY*
State University of New York College at Potsdam, NY*
State University of New York College of Environmental Science and Forestry, NY*
Stony Brook University, State University of New York, NY*
Swarthmore College, PA*
Syracuse University, NY
Temple University, PA*
Tennessee Technological University, TN*
Texas A&M University, TX
Texas Christian University, TX
Texas Lutheran University, TX*
Texas State University–San Marcos, TX
Texas Tech University, TX
Texas Wesleyan University, TX*
Texas Woman's University, TX*
Thomas More College, KY*
Tiffin University, OH*
Towson University, MD*
Transylvania University, KY*
Trine University, IN*
Trinity University, TX*
Troy University, AL
Tufts University, MA*
Tulane University, LA
Tuskegee University, AL
Union College, NY*
The University of Akron, OH*
The University of Alabama, AL
The University of Alabama at Birmingham, AL*
The University of Arizona, AZ
University of Arkansas, AR
University of California, Berkeley, CA
University of California, Davis, CA*
University of California, Irvine, CA*
University of California, Los Angeles, CA
University of California, Santa Cruz, CA*
University of Central Florida, FL
University of Central Missouri, MO*
University of Chicago, IL*
University of Cincinnati, OH
University of Colorado Boulder, CO
University of Colorado Denver, CO*
University of Connecticut, CT
University of Dallas, TX*
University of Dayton, OH*
University of Delaware, DE
University of Denver, CO*
The University of Findlay, OH*
University of Florida, FL
University of Georgia, GA
University of Hartford, CT*
University of Hawaii at Manoa, HI
University of Hawaii–West Oahu, HI*
University of Houston, TX
University of Houston–Downtown, TX*
University of Idaho, ID*
University of Illinois at Chicago, IL*
University of Illinois at Urbana–Champaign, IL
The University of Iowa, IA
The University of Kansas, KS
University of Louisville, KY
University of Mary Hardin-Baylor, TX*
University of Maryland, College Park, MD
University of Massachusetts Amherst, MA
University of Massachusetts Boston, MA*
University of Massachusetts Lowell, MA
University of Memphis, TN
University of Miami, FL
University of Michigan, MI
University of Michigan–Dearborn, MI*
University of Michigan–Flint, MI*
University of Minnesota, Crookston, MN*
University of Minnesota, Duluth, MN
University of Minnesota, Twin Cities Campus, MN
University of Mississippi, MS
University of Missouri, MO
University of Missouri–St. Louis, MO*
University of Mobile, AL*
University of Montevallo, AL*
University of Mount Union, OH*

**program is offered at another college's campus*

University of Nebraska at Omaha, NE
University of Nebraska–Lincoln, NE
University of Nevada, Las Vegas, NV
University of New Hampshire, NH
University of New Hampshire at Manchester, NH*
The University of North Carolina at Chapel Hill, NC
The University of North Carolina at Charlotte, NC
The University of North Carolina at Greensboro, NC*
The University of North Carolina at Pembroke, NC
University of North Dakota, ND
University of Northern Colorado, CO
University of North Texas, TX
University of Notre Dame, IN
University of Oklahoma, OK
University of Oregon, OR*
University of Pennsylvania, PA*
University of Pittsburgh, PA
University of Pittsburgh at Greensburg, PA*
University of Portland, OR
University of Redlands, CA*
University of Rochester, NY*
University of St. Thomas, MN
University of St. Thomas, TX*
University of San Diego, CA*
The University of Scranton, PA*
University of South Alabama, AL
University of South Carolina, SC
University of Southern California, CA
University of Southern Maine, ME*
University of Southern Mississippi, MS
University of South Florida, FL
The University of Tampa, FL*
The University of Tennessee, TN
The University of Texas at Arlington, TX*
The University of Texas at Austin, TX
The University of Texas at Dallas, TX*
The University of Texas at San Antonio, TX
University of the District of Columbia, DC*
University of the Incarnate Word, TX*
University of the Pacific, CA*
University of the Sciences in Philadelphia, PA*
The University of Toledo, OH*
University of Tulsa, OK*
University of Utah, UT
University of Virginia, VA
University of West Florida, FL
University of Wisconsin–Madison, WI
University of Wisconsin–Stout, WI*
University of Wisconsin–Superior, WI*
University of Wyoming, WY
Utah State University, UT
Utah Valley University, UT*
Valdosta State University, GA
Valparaiso University, IN*
Vanderbilt University, TN*
Villanova University, PA*
Virginia Military Institute, VA
Virginia Polytechnic Institute and State University, VA
Washburn University, KS*
Washington & Jefferson College, PA*
Washington State University, WA
Washington University in St. Louis, MO*
Wayland Baptist University, TX*
Wayne State University, MI*
Wellesley College, MA*
Wells College, NY*
Wentworth Institute of Technology, MA*
Wesleyan University, CT*
West Chester University of Pennsylvania, PA*
Western Connecticut State University, CT*
Western Kentucky University, KY*
Western New England University, MA*
Westfield State University, MA*
Westminster College, MO*
Westminster College, UT*
Westmont College, CA*
West Virginia University, WV
Wheaton College, IL*
Widener University, PA*
Wilkes University, PA
Willamette University, OR*
William Paterson University of New Jersey, NJ*
Williams College, MA*
Wingate University, NC*
Wittenberg University, OH*
Worcester Polytechnic Institute, MA
Worcester State University, MA*
Wright State University, OH
Xavier University, OH*
Xavier University of Louisiana, LA*
Yale University, CT*
Youngstown State University, OH*

Army

Adelphi University, NY*
Alabama Agricultural and Mechanical University, AL
Alabama State University, AL*
Albright College, PA*
Alcorn State University, MS
Alfred University, NY*
Allen College, IA*
Alma College, MI*
Alvernia University, PA*
Alverno College, WI*
American University, DC*
Amherst College, MA*
Anderson University, SC*
Appalachian State University, NC
Arizona State University, AZ
Arkansas State University, AR
Arkansas Tech University, AR*
Armstrong Atlantic State University, GA
Asbury University, KY*
Assumption College, MA*
Auburn University, AL
Auburn University Montgomery, AL
Augsburg College, MN*
Augustana College, SD*
Austin Peay State University, TN
Azusa Pacific University, CA*
Baldwin-Wallace College, OH*
Ball State University, IN
Baptist Bible College of Pennsylvania, PA*
Barry University, FL*
Bellarmine University, KY*
Belmont Abbey College, NC*
Belmont University, TN*
Benedictine College, KS
Benedictine University, IL*
Bentley University, MA*
Bethany Lutheran College, MN*
Bethel College, IN*
Bethel University, MN*
Bethune-Cookman University, FL*
Biola University, CA*
Birmingham-Southern College, AL*
Bloomfield College, NJ*
Bloomsburg University of Pennsylvania, PA
Boise State University, ID
Boston College, MA*
Boston University, MA
Bowling Green State University, OH
Brandeis University, MA*
Brigham Young University, UT
Brown University, RI*
Bryant University, RI
Bucknell University, PA
Buena Vista University, IA
Butler University, IN
Cabrini College, PA*
California Institute of Technology, CA*
California Polytechnic State University, San Luis Obispo, CA
California State Polytechnic University, Pomona, CA
California State University, Dominguez Hills, CA
California State University, Fullerton, CA
California State University, Long Beach, CA
California State University, Northridge, CA*
California State University, San Bernardino, CA
Calvary Bible College and Theological Seminary, MO*
Calvin College, MI*
Cameron University, OK
Campbellsville University, KY*
Canisius College, NY
Capital University, OH
Carnegie Mellon University, PA
Carroll University, WI*
Carson-Newman College, TN
Case Western Reserve University, OH*
The Catholic University of America, DC*
Cazenovia College, NY*
Cedar Crest College, PA*
Cedarville University, OH*
Central Connecticut State University, CT*
Central Michigan University, MI
Centre College, KY*
Champlain College, VT*
Christian Brothers University, TN*
Christopher Newport University, VA
The Citadel, The Military College of South Carolina, SC
City College of the City University of New York, NY*
Claremont McKenna College, CA
Clarion University of Pennsylvania, PA*
Clarke University, IA*
Clarkson University, NY
Clark University, MA*
Clemson University, SC
The Cleveland Institute of Art, OH*
Cleveland State University, OH*
Coastal Carolina University, SC
Colby College, ME*
Colgate University, NY*
College of Mount St. Joseph, OH*
The College of New Jersey, NJ*
College of Saint Benedict, MN*
College of Saint Mary, NE*
The College of Saint Rose, NY*
College of the Holy Cross, MA*
College of the Ozarks, MO
The College of William and Mary, VA
The Colorado College, CO*
Colorado School of Mines, CO
Colorado State University, CO
Columbia College, MO*

ROTC Programs

Army

Columbia University, School of General Studies, NY*
Columbus State University, GA
Concordia College, MN*
Concordia University, CA*
Concordia University, Nebraska, NE*
Concordia University, St. Paul, MN*
Coppin State University, MD
Corban University, OR*
Cornell University, NY
Creighton University, NE
Crown College, MN*
Curry College, MA*
Dakota Wesleyan University, SD
Dallas Baptist University, TX*
Dartmouth College, NH*
Davidson College, NC
Delaware State University, DE
Delta State University, MS*
Denison University, OH*
DePaul University, IL
DePauw University, IN*
DeSales University, PA*
Dickinson College, PA
Dillard University, LA*
Dixie State College of Utah, UT
Doane College, NE*
Dowling College, NY*
Drake University, IA
Drury University, MO*
Duquesne University, PA
Eastern Michigan University, MI
Eastern Oregon University, OR
Eastern Washington University, WA
East Tennessee State University, TN
Eckerd College, FL*
Edgewood College, WI*
Edinboro University of Pennsylvania, PA
Elizabeth City State University, NC
Elmhurst College, IL*
Elmira College, NY
Elon University, NC
Embry-Riddle Aeronautical University–Daytona, FL
Embry-Riddle Aeronautical University–Prescott, AZ
Emmanuel College, MA*
Emory University, GA*
Endicott College, MA*
Evangel University, MO*
Fairfield University, CT*
Faulkner University, AL*
Fayetteville State University, NC*
Ferris State University, MI*
Fisher College, MA*
Fitchburg State University, MA
Florida Agricultural and Mechanical University, FL
Florida Atlantic University, FL
Florida College, FL*
Florida Institute of Technology, FL
Florida International University, FL
Florida Southern College, FL
Florida State University, FL
Franklin College, IN*
Free Will Baptist Bible College, TN*
Furman University, SC
Gannon University, PA
Gardner-Webb University, NC
Geneva College, PA*
Georgetown College, KY*
Georgetown University, DC
Georgia College & State University, GA*
Georgia Institute of Technology, GA
Georgia Southern University, GA
Georgia State University, GA
Gettysburg College, PA*
Gordon College, MA*
Goucher College, MD*
Grace Bible College, MI*
Grand View University, IA*
Grove City College, PA*
Hamilton College, NY*
Hamline University, MN*
Hampden-Sydney College, VA*
Hampshire College, MA*
Harvard University, MA*
Harvey Mudd College, CA*
Hawai'i Pacific University, HI*
Hendrix College, AR*
Hofstra University, NY
Hood College, MD
Hope College, MI*
Houghton College, NY*
Huntingdon College, AL*
Husson University, ME
Huston-Tillotson University, TX*
Illinois Institute of Technology, IL
Illinois State University, IL
Illinois Wesleyan University, IL*
Indiana State University, IN
Indiana University Bloomington, IN
Indiana University Kokomo, IN*
Indiana University Northwest, IN
Indiana University of Pennsylvania, PA
Indiana University–Purdue University Fort Wayne, IN
Indiana University–Purdue University Indianapolis, IN
Indiana University South Bend, IN*
Indiana University Southeast, IN
Indiana Wesleyan University, IN
Inter American University of Puerto Rico, Bayamón Campus, PR*
Inter American University of Puerto Rico, Guayama Campus, PR*
Inter American University of Puerto Rico, San Germán Campus, PR*
Iona College, NY*
Iowa State University of Science and Technology, IA
Ithaca College, NY*
James Madison University, VA
John Brown University, AR*
John Carroll University, OH
The Johns Hopkins University, MD
Johnson & Wales University, RI
Johnson C. Smith University, NC
Kalamazoo College, MI*
Kansas State University, KS
Kean University, NJ*
Kennesaw State University, GA*
Kent State University, OH
Kent State University at Stark, OH*
Kentucky State University, KY*
Kentucky Wesleyan College, KY*
Keystone College, PA*
King College, TN*
King's College, PA
Kutztown University of Pennsylvania, PA*
Kuyper College, MI*
Lafayette College, PA*
La Roche College, PA*
Lebanon Valley College, PA*
Lehigh University, PA
Lehman College of the City University of New York, NY*
Le Moyne College, NY*
Lewis-Clark State College, ID*
Liberty University, VA
Limestone College, SC
Lincoln University, MO
Lindenwood University, MO
Lipscomb University, TN*
Lock Haven University of Pennsylvania, PA
Long Island University, C.W. Post Campus, NY*
Longwood University, VA
Loras College, IA*
Louisiana College, LA
Louisiana State University and Agricultural and Mechanical College, LA
Lourdes College, OH*
Loyola Marymount University, CA*
Loyola University Chicago, IL*
Loyola University Maryland, MD
Loyola University New Orleans, LA*
Lubbock Christian University, TX*
Lycoming College, PA*
Macalester College, MN*
Malone University, OH*
Manhattan College, NY*
Maranatha Baptist Bible College, WI
Marian University, WI
Marist College, NY
Marquette University, WI
Marshall University, WV
Mary Baldwin College, VA
Marymount University, VA*
Maryville University of Saint Louis, MO*
Marywood University, PA*
Massachusetts Institute of Technology, MA
Massachusetts Maritime Academy, MA*
Mayville State University, ND*
McDaniel College, MD
McKendree University, IL*
Medaille College, NY*
Menlo College, CA*
Mercer University, GA
Methodist University, NC
Miami University, OH*
Michigan State University, MI
Mid-Atlantic Christian University, NC*
Middlebury College, VT*
Middle Tennessee State University, TN
Millersville University of Pennsylvania, PA
Milligan College, TN*
Millsaps College, MS*
Mills College, CA*
Milwaukee School of Engineering, WI*
Minnesota State University Mankato, MN
Minnesota State University Moorhead, MN*
Misericordia University, PA*
Mississippi State University, MS
Mississippi University for Women, MS*
Missouri Baptist University, MO*
Missouri State University, MO
Missouri University of Science and Technology, MO
Molloy College, NY*
Monmouth College, IL
Monmouth University, NJ*
Montana State University, MT
Montana State University Billings, MT
Montclair State University, NJ
Moravian College, PA*
Morehead State University, KY
Morehouse College, GA

**program is offered at another college's campus*

Morningside College, IA*
Mount Carmel College of Nursing, OH*
Mount Holyoke College, MA*
Mount Marty College, SD*
Mount St. Mary's University, MD*
Muhlenberg College, PA*
Murray State University, KY
National University, CA*
Nazareth College of Rochester, NY*
Nebraska Wesleyan University, NE*
New England College, NH*
New Jersey Institute of Technology, NJ*
New Mexico State University, NM
New York Institute of Technology, NY
New York University, NY*
Niagara University, NY
North Carolina Agricultural and Technical State University, NC
North Carolina State University, NC
North Central College, IL*
Northeastern Illinois University, IL*
Northeastern State University, OK
Northeastern University, MA
Northern Arizona University, AZ
Northern Illinois University, IL
Northern Kentucky University, KY*
Northern Michigan University, MI
North Georgia College & State University, GA
Northwestern College, MN*
Northwestern State University of Louisiana, LA
Northwest Missouri State University, MO
Northwest Nazarene University, ID
Northwest University, WA*
The Ohio State University, OH
Ohio University, OH
Oklahoma Christian University, OK*
Oklahoma City University, OK*
Oklahoma State University, OK
Old Dominion University, VA
Oregon State University, OR
Ouachita Baptist University, AR
Our Lady of the Lake University of San Antonio, TX*
Pace University, NY*
Pacific Lutheran University, WA
Pacific University, OR*
Palm Beach Atlantic University, FL*
Penn State Abington, PA
Penn State Altoona, PA*
Penn State Berks, PA*
Penn State Erie, The Behrend College, PA
Penn State Harrisburg, PA*
Penn State University Park, PA
Pennsylvania College of Technology, PA*
Pepperdine University, CA*
Pikeville College, KY
Pitzer College, CA*
Point Park University, PA*
Polytechnic Institute of NYU, NY*
Pomona College, CA*
Portland State University, OR
Prairie View A&M University, TX
Presbyterian College, SC
Princeton University, NJ
Providence College, RI
Purdue University, IN
Queens College of the City University of New York, NY*
Quinnipiac University, CT*
Radford University, VA
Randolph-Macon College, VA*
Regent University, VA*
Regis University, CO*
Rensselaer Polytechnic Institute, NY*
Research College of Nursing, MO*
Rhode Island College, RI*
Rhodes College, TN*
Rice University, TX*
Rider University, NJ*
Ripon College, WI
Robert Morris University, PA
Robert Morris University Illinois, IL*
Rockford College, IL*
Rockhurst University, MO*
Rocky Mountain College, MT
Rose-Hulman Institute of Technology, IN
Rosemont College, PA*
Rowan University, NJ*
Russell Sage College, NY*
Rutgers, The State University of New Jersey, Camden, NJ*
Rutgers, The State University of New Jersey, Newark, NJ
Rutgers, The State University of New Jersey, New Brunswick, NJ
Sage College of Albany, NY*
Saint Anselm College, NH*
St. Bonaventure University, NY
St. Catherine University, MN*
St. Edward's University, TX*
Saint Francis University, PA
St. John Fisher College, NY*
Saint John's University, MN
St. John's University, NY
Saint Joseph's University, PA*
St. Lawrence University, NY*
Saint Leo University, FL
St. Louis College of Pharmacy, MO*
Saint Louis University, MO*
Saint Martin's University, WA*
Saint Mary-of-the-Woods College, IN*
Saint Mary's College, IN*
Saint Mary's College of California, CA*
Saint Mary's University of Minnesota, MN*
Saint Michael's College, VT*
St. Norbert College, WI
Salve Regina University, RI*
Samford University, AL*
San Diego Christian College, CA*
San Diego State University, CA
San Francisco State University, CA*
San Jose State University, CA
Santa Clara University, CA
Savannah College of Art and Design, GA*
Savannah State University, GA
Scripps College, CA*
Seattle Pacific University, WA*
Seton Hill University, PA
Shippensburg University of Pennsylvania, PA
Siena College, NY
Simmons College, MA*
Simpson University, CA
Skidmore College, NY*
Slippery Rock University of Pennsylvania, PA
Smith College, MA*
Sonoma State University, CA*
South Dakota School of Mines and Technology, SD
South Dakota State University, SD
Southeastern Louisiana University, LA*
Southeastern University, FL*
Southern Connecticut State University, CT*
Southern Illinois University Carbondale, IL
Southern Illinois University Edwardsville, IL
Southern Methodist University, TX
Southern Oregon University, OR
Southern Polytechnic State University, GA*
Southern Utah University, UT
Spelman College, GA*
Spring Arbor University, MI
Springfield College, MA*
Spring Hill College, AL*
Stanford University, CA*
State University of New York at Binghamton, NY*
State University of New York at Fredonia, NY*
State University of New York at Oswego, NY*
State University of New York at Plattsburgh, NY
State University of New York College at Cortland, NY*
State University of New York College at Geneseo, NY*
State University of New York College at Old Westbury, NY*
State University of New York College at Potsdam, NY*
State University of New York College of Environmental Science and Forestry, NY*
State University of New York Maritime College, NY*
Stephen F. Austin State University, TX
Stetson University, FL*
Stonehill College, MA
Stony Brook University, State University of New York, NY*
Suffolk University, MA*
Swarthmore College, PA*
Syracuse University, NY
Tarleton State University, TX
Temple University, PA
Tennessee Technological University, TN
Texas A&M International University, TX
Texas A&M University, TX
Texas A&M University–Corpus Christi, TX
Texas Christian University, TX
Texas Lutheran University, TX*
Texas Southern University, TX*
Texas State University–San Marcos, TX
Texas Tech University, TX
Texas Wesleyan University, TX*
Texas Woman's University, TX*
Thomas More College, KY*
Tiffin University, OH*
Towson University, MD*
Transylvania University, KY*
Trevecca Nazarene University, TN*
Trinity College, CT*
Troy University, AL
Truman State University, MO
Tufts University, MA*
Tulane University, LA
Tuskegee University, AL
Union College, KY
Union College, NY*
Union University, TN*
University at Buffalo, the State University of New York, NY*
The University of Akron, OH
The University of Alabama, AL
The University of Alabama at Birmingham, AL
The University of Alabama in Huntsville, AL*
University of Alaska Fairbanks, AK
The University of Arizona, AZ
University of Arkansas, AR

ROTC Programs

Army

University of Bridgeport, CT
University of California, Berkeley, CA
University of California, Davis, CA
University of California, Irvine, CA*
University of California, Los Angeles, CA
University of California, Santa Barbara, CA
University of California, Santa Cruz, CA*
University of Central Florida, FL
University of Central Missouri, MO
University of Charleston, WV
University of Chicago, IL*
University of Cincinnati, OH
University of Colorado at Colorado Springs, CO
University of Colorado Boulder, CO
University of Colorado Denver, CO*
University of Connecticut, CT
University of Dallas, TX*
University of Dayton, OH
University of Delaware, DE
University of Denver, CO*
University of Dubuque, IA
University of Evansville, IN
The University of Findlay, OH*
University of Florida, FL
University of Georgia, GA
University of Hartford, CT*
University of Hawaii at Manoa, HI
University of Hawaii–West Oahu, HI*
University of Houston, TX
University of Houston–Downtown, TX*
University of Idaho, ID
University of Illinois at Chicago, IL
University of Illinois at Urbana–Champaign, IL
University of Indianapolis, IN*
The University of Iowa, IA
The University of Kansas, KS
University of La Verne, CA*
University of Louisiana at Lafayette, LA
University of Louisville, KY
University of Maine, ME
University of Mary Hardin-Baylor, TX
University of Maryland, Baltimore County, MD*
University of Maryland, College Park, MD
University of Mary Washington, VA*
University of Massachusetts Amherst, MA
University of Massachusetts Boston, MA*
University of Massachusetts Dartmouth, MA*
University of Massachusetts Lowell, MA
University of Memphis, TN
University of Miami, FL
University of Michigan, MI
University of Michigan–Dearborn, MI*
University of Michigan–Flint, MI*
University of Minnesota, Twin Cities Campus, MN
University of Mississippi, MS
University of Missouri, MO
University of Missouri–St. Louis, MO*
University of Mobile, AL*
University of Montevallo, AL*
University of Mount Union, OH*
University of Nebraska at Omaha, NE*
University of Nebraska–Lincoln, NE
University of Nevada, Las Vegas, NV
University of Nevada, Reno, NV
University of New Hampshire, NH
University of New Hampshire at Manchester, NH*
University of North Alabama, AL
The University of North Carolina at Chapel Hill, NC
The University of North Carolina at Charlotte, NC
The University of North Carolina at Greensboro, NC*
The University of North Carolina at Pembroke, NC
University of North Dakota, ND
University of Northern Colorado, CO
University of Northern Iowa, IA
University of North Florida, FL
University of North Texas, TX
University of Notre Dame, IN
University of Oklahoma, OK
University of Oregon, OR
University of Pennsylvania, PA*
University of Pittsburgh, PA
University of Pittsburgh at Bradford, PA*
University of Pittsburgh at Greensburg, PA*
University of Portland, OR
University of Puget Sound, WA*
University of Redlands, CA*
University of Rhode Island, RI
University of Richmond, VA
University of Rio Grande, OH*
University of Rochester, NY*
University of St. Francis, IL*
University of St. Thomas, MN*
University of St. Thomas, TX*
University of San Diego, CA*
The University of Scranton, PA
University of South Alabama, AL
University of South Carolina, SC
The University of South Dakota, SD
University of Southern California, CA
University of Southern Indiana, IN
University of Southern Maine, ME*
University of Southern Mississippi, MS
University of South Florida, FL
The University of Tampa, FL
The University of Tennessee, TN
The University of Tennessee at Chattanooga, TN
The University of Tennessee at Martin, TN
The University of Texas at Arlington, TX
The University of Texas at Austin, TX
The University of Texas at Dallas, TX*
The University of Texas at San Antonio, TX
The University of Texas–Pan American, TX
University of the Cumberlands, KY
University of the District of Columbia, DC*
University of the Incarnate Word, TX*
University of the Sciences in Philadelphia, PA*
The University of Toledo, OH
University of Utah, UT
University of Vermont, VT
University of Virginia, VA
The University of Virginia's College at Wise, VA
University of West Florida, FL
University of West Georgia, GA
University of Wisconsin–Eau Claire, WI
University of Wisconsin–Green Bay, WI*
University of Wisconsin–La Crosse, WI
University of Wisconsin–Madison, WI
University of Wisconsin–Parkside, WI*
University of Wisconsin–River Falls, WI
University of Wisconsin–Stevens Point, WI
University of Wisconsin–Stout, WI
University of Wyoming, WY
Ursuline College, OH*
Utah State University, UT
Utah Valley University, UT
Valparaiso University, IN*
Vanderbilt University, TN
Vermont Technical College, VT*
Villanova University, PA*
Virginia Commonwealth University, VA*
Virginia Military Institute, VA
Virginia Polytechnic Institute and State University, VA
Virginia State University, VA
Virginia Wesleyan College, VA*
Wagner College, NY*
Wake Forest University, NC
Washburn University, KS
Washington & Jefferson College, PA*
Washington and Lee University, VA*
Washington State University, WA
Washington University in St. Louis, MO
Wayland Baptist University, TX*
Waynesburg University, PA*
Wayne State College, NE
Wayne State University, MI
Wellesley College, MA*
Wells College, NY*
Wentworth Institute of Technology, MA*
West Chester University of Pennsylvania, PA*
Western Connecticut State University, CT*
Western Illinois University, IL
Western Kentucky University, KY
Western Michigan University, MI
Western New England University, MA
Western Oregon University, OR
Westfield State University, MA*
West Liberty University, WV
Westminster College, MO*
Westminster College, UT*
Westmont College, CA*
West Virginia University, WV
Wheaton College, IL
Wheaton College, MA*
Widener University, PA
Wilkes University, PA*
Willamette University, OR*
William Jewell College, MO*
Wilson College, PA*
Wingate University, NC*
Winona State University, MN*
Winthrop University, SC*
Wittenberg University, OH*
Wofford College, SC
Worcester Polytechnic Institute, MA
Worcester State University, MA*
Wright State University, OH
Xavier University, OH
Xavier University of Louisiana, LA*
Yale University, CT*
York College of Pennsylvania, PA*
Youngstown State University, OH

Naval

Arizona State University, AZ
Armstrong Atlantic State University, GA*
Auburn University, AL
Augsburg College, MN*
Baptist Bible College of Pennsylvania, PA*
Belmont University, TN*
Boston College, MA*
Boston University, MA
Carnegie Mellon University, PA
The Catholic University of America, DC*
Christian Brothers University, TN*

**program is offered at another college's campus*

The Citadel, The Military College of South Carolina, SC
Clark University, MA*
The Cleveland Institute of Art, OH*
The College of Saint Rose, NY*
College of the Holy Cross, MA
Columbia College, MO*
Concordia University, St. Paul, MN*
Cornell University, NY
Duquesne University, PA*
Eastern Michigan University, MI*
Embry-Riddle Aeronautical University–Daytona, FL
Florida Agricultural and Mechanical University, FL
Florida State University, FL*
Georgetown University, DC*
Georgia Institute of Technology, GA
Georgia State University, GA*
Harvard University, MA*
Husson University, ME*
Illinois Institute of Technology, IL
Indiana University South Bend, IN*
Inter American University of Puerto Rico, San Germán Campus, PR*
Iowa State University of Science and Technology, IA
Lewis-Clark State College, ID*
Lincoln University, MO*
Louisiana State University and Agricultural and Mechanical College, LA*
Loyola Marymount University, CA*
Loyola University Chicago, IL*
Loyola University New Orleans, LA*
Macalester College, MN*
Marquette University, WI
Mary Baldwin College, VA*
Massachusetts Institute of Technology, MA
Massachusetts Maritime Academy, MA
Miami University, OH
Milwaukee School of Engineering, WI*
Missouri University of Science and Technology, MO*
Molloy College, NY*
Montclair State University, NJ
Morehouse College, GA
Mount Carmel College of Nursing, OH*
North Carolina State University, NC
Northeastern University, MA*
The Ohio State University, OH
Old Dominion University, VA
Oregon State University, OR
Penn State University Park, PA
Prairie View A&M University, TX
Princeton University, NJ*
Purdue University, IN
Queens College of the City University of New York, NY*
Rensselaer Polytechnic Institute, NY
Rice University, TX
St. John Fisher College, NY*
Saint Joseph's University, PA*
St. Louis College of Pharmacy, MO*
Saint Mary's College, IN*
San Diego State University, CA
Savannah State University, GA
Seattle Pacific University, WA*
Siena College, NY*
Southern Polytechnic State University, GA*
Spelman College, GA
Stanford University, CA*
State University of New York Maritime College, NY
Swarthmore College, PA*
Temple University, PA*
Texas A&M University, TX
Texas Southern University, TX*
Texas Wesleyan University, TX*
Tufts University, MA*
Tulane University, LA
Union College, NY*
The University of Arizona, AZ
University of California, Berkeley, CA
University of California, Davis, CA*
University of California, Los Angeles, CA
University of California, Santa Cruz, CA*
University of Colorado Boulder, CO
University of Florida, FL
University of Houston, TX*
University of Idaho, ID
University of Illinois at Chicago, IL*
University of Illinois at Urbana–Champaign, IL
The University of Kansas, KS
University of Maine, ME*
University of Maryland, College Park, MD*
University of Massachusetts Boston, MA*
University of Memphis, TN
University of Michigan, MI
University of Michigan–Dearborn, MI*
University of Michigan–Flint, MI*
University of Minnesota, Twin Cities Campus, MN
University of Mississippi, MS
University of Missouri, MO
University of Nebraska–Lincoln, NE
The University of North Carolina at Chapel Hill, NC
University of North Florida, FL*
University of Notre Dame, IN
University of Oklahoma, OK
University of Pennsylvania, PA
University of Pittsburgh, PA*
University of Rochester, NY
University of St. Thomas, MN*
University of San Diego, CA
University of South Carolina, SC
University of Southern California, CA
University of South Florida, FL
The University of Tampa, FL*
The University of Texas at Austin, TX
University of Utah, UT
University of Virginia, VA
University of Wisconsin–Madison, WI
Vanderbilt University, TN
Villanova University, PA
Virginia Military Institute, VA
Virginia Polytechnic Institute and State University, VA
Washburn University, KS*
Washington State University, WA*
Western Oregon University, OR*
Westminster College, UT*
Widener University, PA*
Worcester Polytechnic Institute, MA*
Worcester State University, MA*
Xavier University of Louisiana, LA*

Tuition Waivers

Adult Students

Alaska Pacific University, AK
Albright College, PA
Appalachian Bible College, WV
Bluefield State College, WV
California State University, Stanislaus, CA
Campbellsville University, KY
Clarke University, IA
Coe College, IA
Concord University, WV
Converse College, SC
Coppin State University, MD
Creighton University, NE
Dickinson State University, ND
Dowling College, NY
Eureka College, IL
Faulkner University, AL
Goucher College, MD
Juniata College, PA
Lane College, TN
Lynchburg College, VA
Marquette University, WI
Medaille College, NY
Mercyhurst College, PA
Messiah College, PA
New England College, NH
Randolph College, VA
St. Andrews Presbyterian College, NC
Shimer College, IL
Southern Adventist University, TN
Sweet Briar College, VA
Trinity College, CT
University of Evansville, IN
University of Hawaii at Manoa, HI
University of North Dakota, ND
Utah State University, UT
Virginia Wesleyan College, VA
Webber International University, FL
Wittenberg University, OH

Children of Alumni

Adrian College, MI
Albright College, PA
Alliant International University, CA
Appalachian Bible College, WV
Arcadia University, PA
Ashland University, OH
Augsburg College, MN
Baldwin-Wallace College, OH
Bethany College, WV
Bethel College, KS
Bradley University, IL
Cabrini College, PA
Caldwell College, NJ
Calumet College of Saint Joseph, IN
Cedar Crest College, PA
Central Michigan University, MI
Christian Brothers University, TN
Clarke University, IA
Cleary University, MI
Coe College, IA
College of Saint Elizabeth, NJ
Columbia College, MO
Concordia University Chicago, IL
Coppin State University, MD
Crown College, MN
Curry College, MA
Delta State University, MS
Dickinson State University, ND
Dixie State College of Utah, UT
Dominican University, IL
Dowling College, NY
Drake University, IA
Drury University, MO
D'Youville College, NY
Eastern Nazarene College, MA
Erskine College, SC
Eureka College, IL
Florida Southern College, FL
Grace University, NE
Grand View University, IA
Hillsdale College, MI
Hillsdale Free Will Baptist College, OK
Huntingdon College, AL
Indiana Wesleyan University, IN
Ithaca College, NY
Jackson State University, MS
Johnson C. Smith University, NC
Kentucky Wesleyan College, KY
Lake Superior State University, MI
Lancaster Bible College & Graduate School, PA
Lasell College, MA
Louisiana Tech University, LA
Messiah College, PA
Michigan Technological University, MI
Mid-Atlantic Christian University, NC
Minneapolis College of Art and Design, MN
Minot State University, ND
Mississippi State University, MS
Missouri Baptist University, MO
Missouri State University, MO
Morehead State University, KY
Morningside College, IA
Murray State University, KY
Nazareth College of Rochester, NY
New England College, NH
Northwestern College, MN
Northwest Nazarene University, ID
Ohio Northern University, OH
Ohio University–Southern Campus, OH
Ohio Wesleyan University, OH
Oklahoma State University, OK
Oregon College of Art & Craft, OR
Pacific Lutheran University, WA
Peirce College, PA
Research College of Nursing, MO
Saint Joseph's College, IN
Saint Louis University, MO
Saint Martin's University, WA
St. Thomas University, FL
Simpson College, IA
South Dakota State University, SD
Southeastern Oklahoma State University, OK
Southern Illinois University Carbondale, IL
Texas Lutheran University, TX
Union University, TN
University of Alaska Anchorage, AK
University of Alaska Fairbanks, AK
University of Alaska Southeast, AK
University of Central Missouri, MO
University of Charleston, WV
University of Evansville, IN
The University of Findlay, OH
University of Idaho, ID
University of Louisiana at Lafayette, LA
University of Mississippi, MS
University of Mount Union, OH
University of Nebraska at Omaha, NE
University of Nevada, Las Vegas, NV
University of Nevada, Reno, NV
University of Oklahoma, OK
University of St. Francis, IL
The University of South Dakota, SD
University of Southern Mississippi, MS
University of the Ozarks, AR
The University of Toledo, OH
University of Utah, UT
University of Wisconsin–River Falls, WI
University of Wisconsin–Stevens Point, WI
University of Wyoming, WY
Utah State University, UT
Walsh University, OH
Warner Pacific College, OR
Wartburg College, IA
Webber International University, FL
Western Kentucky University, KY
Westminster College, MO
Whittier College, CA
William Jewell College, MO
Wittenberg University, OH

Minority Students

Bloomsburg University of Pennsylvania, PA
Concordia College, MN
Concordia University Chicago, IL
Coppin State University, MD
Crown College, MN
Delaware State University, DE
Dickinson State University, ND
Dowling College, NY
Drury University, MO
Edinboro University of Pennsylvania, PA
Fort Lewis College, CO
Geneva College, PA
Illinois State University, IL
Lake Superior State University, MI
Lock Haven University of Pennsylvania, PA
Massachusetts Maritime Academy, MA
Mayville State University, ND
Messiah College, PA
Minot State University, ND
Montana State University, MT
Montana State University–Northern, MT
Nazareth College of Rochester, NY
Northern Illinois University, IL
Northwest Nazarene University, ID

Portland State University, OR
Saint Joseph's College, IN
St. Thomas University, FL
Shepherd University, WV
Simpson College, IA
Slippery Rock University of Pennsylvania, PA
Southeastern Oklahoma State University, OK
Texas Southern University, TX
University at Buffalo, the State University of New York, NY
University of Evansville, IN
University of Hawaii at Manoa, HI
University of Idaho, ID
University of Maine at Presque Isle, ME
University of Minnesota, Morris, MN
The University of Montana, MT
University of North Dakota, ND
University of Rhode Island, RI
University of Southern Maine, ME
University of Wisconsin–Eau Claire, WI
University of Wisconsin–La Crosse, WI
Utah State University, UT
Western Washington University, WA
Wittenberg University, OH

Senior Citizens

Abraham Baldwin Agricultural College, GA
Adams State College, CO
Albright College, PA
Alvernia University, PA
Andrews University, MI
Angelo State University, TX
Anna Maria College, MA
Appalachian Bible College, WV
Arkansas State University, AR
Arkansas Tech University, AR
Armstrong Atlantic State University, GA
Asbury University, KY
Ashland University, OH
Athens State University, AL
Augsburg College, MN
Augusta State University, GA
Aurora University, IL
Austin Peay State University, TN
Averett University, VA
Ball State University, IN
Bellarmine University, KY
Belmont Abbey College, NC
Belmont University, TN
Bemidji State University, MN
Benedictine College, KS
Berry College, GA
Bethel College, KS
Black Hills State University, SD
Bloomfield College, NJ
Bloomsburg University of Pennsylvania, PA
Bluefield College, VA
Bluefield State College, WV
Bob Jones University, SC
Boise State University, ID
Boston University, MA
Bowie State University, MD
Bowling Green State University, OH
Bradley University, IL
Brevard College, NC
Bridgewater College, VA
Brooklyn College of the City University of New York, NY
Cabrini College, PA
Caldwell College, NJ
California State University, Bakersfield, CA
California State University, Chico, CA
California State University, Dominguez Hills, CA
California State University, East Bay, CA
California State University, Fullerton, CA
California State University, Long Beach, CA
California State University, Monterey Bay, CA
California State University, Northridge, CA
California State University, Sacramento, CA
California State University, Stanislaus, CA
Calumet College of Saint Joseph, IN
Campbellsville University, KY
Capital University, OH
Carroll College, MT
Carson-Newman College, TN
Cedarville University, OH
Central Connecticut State University, CT
Central Michigan University, MI
Central Washington University, WA
Chestnut Hill College, PA
Chowan University, NC
Christopher Newport University, VA
The Citadel, The Military College of South Carolina, SC
City College of the City University of New York, NY
Clarion University of Pennsylvania, PA
Clarke University, IA
Cleary University, MI
Clemson University, SC
Cleveland State University, OH
Coastal Carolina University, SC
Coe College, IA
The College at Brockport, State University of New York, NY
College of Charleston, SC
College of Mount St. Joseph, OH
The College of New Jersey, NJ
The College of New Rochelle, NY
College of Saint Elizabeth, NJ
College of St. Joseph, VT
College of Saint Mary, NE
The College of St. Scholastica, MN
College of Staten Island of the City University of New York, NY
The College of William and Mary, VA
Colorado State University–Pueblo, CO
Columbia College, MO
Columbus State University, GA
Concordia University Chicago, IL
Concord University, WV
Connecticut College, CT
Coppin State University, MD
Corban University, OR
Covenant College, GA
Culver-Stockton College, MO
Daemen College, NY
Dakota State University, SD
Dakota Wesleyan University, SD
Dalton State College, GA
Defiance College, OH
Delaware State University, DE
Delta State University, MS
DeSales University, PA
Dickinson College, PA
Dickinson State University, ND
Dixie State College of Utah, UT
Doane College, NE
Dominican College, NY
Dominican University of California, CA
Dordt College, IA
Dowling College, NY
Drake University, IA
Drew University, NJ
Duquesne University, PA
D'Youville College, NY
East Carolina University, NC
Eastern Kentucky University, KY
Eastern Oregon University, OR
East Tennessee State University, TN
Edinboro University of Pennsylvania, PA
Elmhurst College, IL
Emmanuel College, GA
Emporia State University, KS
Eureka College, IL
The Evergreen State College, WA
Faulkner University, AL
Fayetteville State University, NC
Fitchburg State University, MA
Florida Agricultural and Mechanical University, FL
Florida Atlantic University, FL
Florida Gulf Coast University, FL
Florida Institute of Technology, FL
Florida International University, FL
Florida State University, FL
Fort Valley State University, GA
Framingham State University, MA
Francis Marion University, SC
Franklin College, IN
Freed-Hardeman University, TN
Fresno Pacific University, CA
Frostburg State University, MD
Gannon University, PA
Garrett College, MD
George Fox University, OR
George Mason University, VA
Georgetown College, KY
Georgia College & State University, GA
Georgia Southern University, GA
Georgia State University, GA
Glenville State College, WV
Goucher College, MD
Governors State University, IL
Grace College, IN
Graceland University, IA
Grace University, NE
Grand View University, IA
Greenville College, IL
Hanover College, IN
Harding University, AR
Hillsdale Free Will Baptist College, OK
Hofstra University, NY
Hood College, MD
Husson University, ME
Illinois State University, IL
Indiana State University, IN
Indiana University of Pennsylvania, PA
Indiana University–Purdue University Fort Wayne, IN
Iona College, NY
James Madison University, VA
John Carroll University, OH
John Jay College of Criminal Justice of the City University of New York, NY
Judson University, IL
Juniata College, PA
Kean University, NJ
Keene State College, NH
Kennesaw State University, GA
Kent State University, OH
Kent State University at Stark, OH
Kentucky State University, KY
Kentucky Wesleyan College, KY
Keystone College, PA
King College, TN
King's College, PA

Kutztown University of Pennsylvania, PA
Lake Superior State University, MI
Lamar University, TX
Lancaster Bible College & Graduate School, PA
La Roche College, PA
Lebanon Valley College, PA
Lewis-Clark State College, ID
Lincoln Memorial University, TN
Lindenwood University, MO
Lindsey Wilson College, KY
Linfield College, OR
Lock Haven University of Pennsylvania, PA
Longwood University, VA
Louisiana Tech University, LA
Lourdes College, OH
Loyola University Chicago, IL
Loyola University New Orleans, LA
Lynchburg College, VA
Malone University, OH
Manhattan Christian College, KS
Manhattanville College, NY
Marian University, WI
Marlboro College, VT
Marquette University, WI
Marshall University, WV
Marylhurst University, OR
Marymount University, VA
Maryville University of Saint Louis, MO
Marywood University, PA
Massachusetts College of Art and Design, MA
Massachusetts College of Liberal Arts, MA
Massachusetts Maritime Academy, MA
Mayville State University, ND
Medaille College, NY
Mercy College, NY
Merrimack College, MA
Messiah College, PA
Methodist University, NC
Metropolitan State College of Denver, CO
Metropolitan State University, MN
Michigan Technological University, MI
Mid-Atlantic Christian University, NC
Midwestern State University, TX
Millersville University of Pennsylvania, PA
Minnesota State University Mankato, MN
Minnesota State University Moorhead, MN
Minot State University, ND
Mississippi State University, MS
Missouri Baptist University, MO
Missouri Southern State University, MO
Missouri State University, MO
Monmouth University, NJ
Montana State University, MT
Montana State University Billings, MT
Montana State University–Northern, MT
Montclair State University, NJ
Morehead State University, KY
Morningside College, IA
Mountain State University, WV
Mount Mary College, WI
Mount Vernon Nazarene University, OH
Murray State University, KY
Nebraska Wesleyan University, NE
New England College, NH
New Hope Christian College, OR
New Jersey City University, NJ
New Mexico State University, NM
New York Institute of Technology, NY
Niagara University, NY
Nichols College, MA
North Carolina Agricultural and Technical State University, NC
North Carolina Central University, NC
North Carolina State University, NC
North Central College, IL
Northeastern Illinois University, IL
Northeastern State University, OK
Northern Illinois University, IL
Northern Kentucky University, KY
Northern Michigan University, MI
North Georgia College & State University, GA
Northwestern Oklahoma State University, OK
Northwestern State University of Louisiana, LA
Northwest Missouri State University, MO
Notre Dame de Namur University, CA
The Ohio State University, OH
Ohio University, OH
Ohio University–Eastern, OH
Ohio University–Lancaster, OH
Ohio University–Southern Campus, OH
Ohio University–Zanesville, OH
Oklahoma Baptist University, OK
Oklahoma Panhandle State University, OK
Oklahoma Wesleyan University, OK
Old Dominion University, VA
Pace University, NY
Pacific Union College, CA
Penn State Abington, PA
Pikeville College, KY
Plymouth State University, NH
Point Loma Nazarene University, CA
Portland State University, OR
Post University, CT
Prairie View A&M University, TX
Presbyterian College, SC
Providence College, RI
Purdue University, IN
Purdue University Calumet, IN
Purdue University North Central, IN
Queens College of the City University of New York, NY
Quincy University, IL
Radford University, VA
Ramapo College of New Jersey, NJ
Reinhardt University, GA
Research College of Nursing, MO
The Richard Stockton College of New Jersey, NJ
Rivier College, NH
Roanoke College, VA
Roberts Wesleyan College, NY
Rockhurst University, MO
Rogers State University, OK
Rosemont College, PA
Russell Sage College, NY
St. Ambrose University, IA
St. Andrews Presbyterian College, NC
St. Bonaventure University, NY
St. Catherine University, MN
St. John's University, NY
St. Joseph's College, Long Island Campus, NY
St. Joseph's College, New York, NY
St. Mary's College of Maryland, MD
St. Olaf College, MN
Saint Xavier University, IL
San Francisco State University, CA
Santa Fe University of Art and Design, NM
Savannah State University, GA
Seattle Pacific University, WA
Shawnee State University, OH
Shepherd University, WV
Shimer College, IL
Shippensburg University of Pennsylvania, PA
Shorter University, GA
Siena College, NY
Silver Lake College, WI
Simpson College, IA
Skidmore College, NY
Slippery Rock University of Pennsylvania, PA
South Dakota School of Mines and Technology, SD
South Dakota State University, SD
Southeastern Louisiana University, LA
Southeastern Oklahoma State University, OK
Southeast Missouri State University, MO
Southern Adventist University, TN
Southern Connecticut State University, CT
Southern Illinois University Carbondale, IL
Southern Illinois University Edwardsville, IL
Southern Oregon University, OR
Southern Polytechnic State University, GA
Southwestern College, KS
Southwestern Oklahoma State University, OK
Southwest Minnesota State University, MN
State University of New York College at Old Westbury, NY
Stephen F. Austin State University, TX
Suffolk University, MA
Sul Ross State University, TX
Sweet Briar College, VA
Taylor University, IN
Texas A&M International University, TX
Texas A&M University–Commerce, TX
Texas A&M University–Corpus Christi, TX
Texas Southern University, TX
Texas Tech University, TX
Texas Woman's University, TX
Thiel College, PA
Thomas More College, KY
Tiffin University, OH
Towson University, MD
Trevecca Nazarene University, TN
Truman State University, MO
Union College, KY
Union College, NY
The University of Akron, OH
University of Alaska Anchorage, AK
University of Alaska Fairbanks, AK
University of Alaska Southeast, AK
University of Arkansas, AR
University of Arkansas at Little Rock, AR
University of Bridgeport, CT
University of Central Florida, FL
University of Central Missouri, MO
University of Charleston, WV
University of Colorado Boulder, CO
University of Connecticut, CT
University of Dayton, OH
University of Delaware, DE
University of Denver, CO
University of Evansville, IN
The University of Findlay, OH
University of Florida, FL
University of Georgia, GA
University of Hartford, CT
University of Hawaii at Manoa, HI
University of Houston–Clear Lake, TX
University of Houston–Downtown, TX
University of Idaho, ID
University of Illinois at Chicago, IL
University of Illinois at Springfield, IL
University of Illinois at Urbana–Champaign, IL
University of Kentucky, KY
University of Louisiana at Lafayette, LA
University of Louisville, KY

University of Maine, ME
University of Maine at Presque Isle, ME
University of Mary, ND
University of Maryland, Baltimore County, MD
University of Maryland University College, MD
University of Mary Washington, VA
University of Massachusetts Amherst, MA
University of Massachusetts Boston, MA
University of Massachusetts Dartmouth, MA
University of Massachusetts Lowell, MA
University of Memphis, TN
University of Michigan–Dearborn, MI
University of Michigan–Flint, MI
University of Minnesota, Crookston, MN
University of Minnesota, Morris, MN
University of Minnesota, Twin Cities Campus, MN
University of Mississippi, MS
University of Missouri, MO
University of Missouri–St. Louis, MO
The University of Montana, MT
University of Mount Union, OH
University of Nebraska at Omaha, NE
University of Nevada, Las Vegas, NV
University of Nevada, Reno, NV
University of New Hampshire at Manchester, NH
University of New Orleans, LA
University of North Alabama, AL
University of North Carolina School of the Arts, NC
University of North Dakota, ND
University of North Florida, FL
University of North Texas, TX
University of Oklahoma, OK
University of Pittsburgh at Greensburg, PA
University of Rhode Island, RI
University of Rio Grande, OH
University of St. Thomas, MN
University of St. Thomas, TX
University of Science and Arts of Oklahoma, OK
The University of Scranton, PA
University of South Carolina, SC
University of South Carolina Aiken, SC
The University of South Dakota, SD
University of Southern Maine, ME
University of Southern Mississippi, MS
University of South Florida, FL
The University of Tennessee, TN
The University of Tennessee at Chattanooga, TN
The University of Tennessee at Martin, TN
The University of Texas at Austin, TX
The University of Texas at Brownsville, TX
The University of Texas at Dallas, TX
The University of Texas at Tyler, TX
The University of Texas of the Permian Basin, TX
The University of Texas–Pan American, TX
University of the District of Columbia, DC
University of the Incarnate Word, TX
University of Utah, UT
University of Vermont, VT
University of Virginia, VA
The University of Virginia's College at Wise, VA
University of Washington, Tacoma, WA
University of West Florida, FL
University of West Georgia, GA
University of Wisconsin–Green Bay, WI
University of Wisconsin–Milwaukee, WI
University of Wisconsin–Parkside, WI
University of Wyoming, WY
Utah State University, UT
Utica College, NY
Valdosta State University, GA
Victory University, TN
Villa Maria College of Buffalo, NY
Villanova University, PA
Virginia Commonwealth University, VA
Virginia Polytechnic Institute and State University, VA
Virginia State University, VA
Virginia Wesleyan College, VA
Walsh University, OH
Washburn University, KS
Washington Adventist University, MD
Washington State University, WA
Wayne State University, MI
Webber International University, FL
Wells College, NY
Wesleyan College, GA
Wesley College, DE
West Chester University of Pennsylvania, PA
Western Connecticut State University, CT
Western Illinois University, IL
Western Kentucky University, KY
Western Michigan University, MI
Western New England University, MA
Western State College of Colorado, CO
Westfield State University, MA
West Liberty University, WV
West Virginia University, WV
Wichita State University, KS
Widener University, PA
William Paterson University of New Jersey, NJ
Williams Baptist College, AR
Winthrop University, SC
Wittenberg University, OH
Worcester State University, MA
Xavier University, OH
Youngstown State University, OH

Tuition Payment Alternatives

Institution	Alternatives
Abilene Christian University, TX	I,P
Abraham Baldwin Agricultural College, GA	G
Adams State College, CO	D,I
Adelphi University, NY	D,I
Adrian College, MI	I
Agnes Scott College, GA	I
Alabama Agricultural and Mechanical University, AL	I
Alabama State University, AL	D
Alaska Pacific University, AK	D,G,I
Albright College, PA	I
Alcorn State University, MS	D
Alderson-Broaddus College, WV	I
Alfred University, NY	D,I,P
Allegheny College, PA	I,P
Allen College, IA	D
Alliant International University, CA	I
Alma College, MI	D,I
Alvernia University, PA	I
Alverno College, WI	D,I
American Jewish University, CA	I
American University, DC	I
Amherst College, MA	D,I
Anderson University, SC	I
Andrews University, MI	I
Angelo State University, TX	I
Anna Maria College, MA	I
Appalachian Bible College, WV	I,P
Appalachian State University, NC	I
Aquinas College, TN	I
Arcadia University, PA	D,I
Arizona Christian University, AZ	I
Arizona State University, AZ	I
Arkansas State University, AR	I
Arkansas Tech University, AR	D,I
Asbury University, KY	I
Ashland University, OH	I
Auburn University, AL	I
Augsburg College, MN	I
Augustana College, IL	I,P
Augustana College, SD	I
Aurora University, IL	D,I
Austin College, TX	I
Austin Graduate School of Theology, TX	I
Austin Peay State University, TN	I
Averett University, VA	I
Babson College, MA	I
Baldwin-Wallace College, OH	D,I
Ball State University, IN	I
Baptist Bible College of Pennsylvania, PA	I
The Baptist College of Florida, FL	I
Bard College, NY	I,P
Bard College at Simon's Rock, MA	I
Barnard College, NY	D,I,P
Barry University, FL	D,I,P
Bates College, ME	I,P
Baylor University, TX	I
Bellarmine University, KY	I
Bellin College, WI	I
Belmont Abbey College, NC	D,I
Belmont University, TN	D,I
Beloit College, WI	I
Bemidji State University, MN	I
Benedictine College, KS	I
Benedictine University, IL	D,I
Bennington College, VT	I
Bentley University, MA	I
Berklee College of Music, MA	D,P
Berry College, GA	I
Bethany College, WV	I
Bethany Lutheran College, MN	I
Bethel College, IN	I
Bethel College, KS	D,I
Bethel University, MN	I,P
Bethesda Christian University, CA	D,I
Bethune-Cookman University, FL	I
Beulah Heights University, GA	D,I
Biola University, CA	I
Birmingham-Southern College, AL	I
Black Hills State University, SD	D,I
Bloomfield College, NJ	D,I
Bloomsburg University of Pennsylvania, PA	I
Bluefield College, VA	I
Bluefield State College, WV	I
Bluffton University, OH	I
Bob Jones University, SC	I
Boise State University, ID	I
Boston Architectural College, MA	I
Boston College, MA	I
Boston University, MA	I,P
Bowdoin College, ME	D,I
Bowie State University, MD	D,I
Bowling Green State University, OH	I
Bradley University, IL	I
Brandeis University, MA	I,P
Brenau University, GA	I
Brevard College, NC	I
Bridgewater College, VA	I
Brooklyn College of the City University of New York, NY	I
Brown University, RI	I
Bryan College, TN	I
Bryant University, RI	I
Bryn Mawr College, PA	I,P
Bucknell University, PA	I,P
Buena Vista University, IA	G,I
Buffalo State College, State University of New York, NY	I
Burlington College, VT	I
Butler University, IN	I
Cabrini College, PA	I
Caldwell College, NJ	I
California Christian College, CA	I
California College of the Arts, CA	I
California Institute of Technology, CA	D,I
California Institute of the Arts, CA	I
California Lutheran University, CA	I
California Polytechnic State University, San Luis Obispo, CA	I
California State Polytechnic University, Pomona, CA	D,I
California State University, Bakersfield, CA	I
California State University, Chico, CA	D,I
California State University, Dominguez Hills, CA	I
California State University, East Bay, CA	I
California State University, Fresno, CA	I
California State University, Fullerton, CA	D,I
California State University, Long Beach, CA	I
California State University, Monterey Bay, CA	G,I
California State University, Northridge, CA	I
California State University, Sacramento, CA	I
California State University, Stanislaus, CA	D,I
Calumet College of Saint Joseph, IN	I
Calvary Bible College and Theological Seminary, MO	G,I
Calvin College, MI	I,P
Cambridge College, MA	I
Cameron University, OK	I
Campbellsville University, KY	I
Campbell University, NC	I
Canisius College, NY	D,I
Capital University, OH	I
Capitol College, MD	D,I
Carleton College, MN	I,P
Carnegie Mellon University, PA	I
Carolina Christian College, NC	I
Carroll College, MT	I
Carroll University, WI	I
Carson-Newman College, TN	D,I
Case Western Reserve University, OH	I
Catawba College, NC	I
The Catholic University of America, DC	I
Cazenovia College, NY	I
Cedar Crest College, PA	D,I
Cedarville University, OH	I
Centenary College of Louisiana, LA	D,I
Central College, IA	I
Central Connecticut State University, CT	I
Central Methodist University, MO	I
Central Michigan University, MI	I
Central Washington University, WA	I

D = deferred payment system; *G* = guaranteed tuition rate; *I* = installment payments; *P* = prepayment locks in tuition rate

College	Plan
Centre College, KY	I
Chaminade University of Honolulu, HI	I
Champlain College, VT	I
Chestnut Hill College, PA	D,I
Chowan University, NC	D,I
Christendom College, VA	I
Christian Brothers University, TN	D,I
Christopher Newport University, VA	I
Cincinnati Christian University, OH	I
City College of the City University of New York, NY	D
Claremont McKenna College, CA	I
Clarion University of Pennsylvania, PA	I
Clarke University, IA	D,I
Clarkson University, NY	I,P
Clark University, MA	I,P
Clear Creek Baptist Bible College, KY	I
Cleary University, MI	D,G,I
Clemson University, SC	I
The Cleveland Institute of Art, OH	I
Cleveland Institute of Music, OH	I
Cleveland State University, OH	I
Coastal Carolina University, SC	I
Coe College, IA	I
Cogswell Polytechnical College, CA	D
Colby College, ME	I
Colgate University, NY	D,I,P
The College at Brockport, State University of New York, NY	D,I
College for Creative Studies, MI	D,I
College of Charleston, SC	I
College of Mount St. Joseph, OH	D,I
The College of New Jersey, NJ	I
The College of New Rochelle, NY	I
College of Saint Benedict, MN	I
College of Saint Elizabeth, NJ	I
College of St. Joseph, VT	G,I
College of Saint Mary, NE	D,I
The College of Saint Rose, NY	I
The College of St. Scholastica, MN	I
College of Staten Island of the City University of New York, NY	I
College of the Atlantic, ME	I
College of the Holy Cross, MA	I,P
College of the Ozarks, MO	I
College of Visual Arts, MN	I
The College of William and Mary, VA	I
The College of Wooster, OH	I
The Colorado College, CO	I
Colorado School of Mines, CO	I
Colorado State University–Pueblo, CO	D,I
Columbia College, MO	D,I
Columbia International University, SC	I
Columbia University, School of General Studies, NY	I,P
Columbus College of Art & Design, OH	D,I
Concordia College, MN	I
Concordia University, CA	I
Concordia University, MI	I
Concordia University Chicago, IL	I
Concordia University, Nebraska, NE	I
Concordia University, St. Paul, MN	I
Concordia University Wisconsin, WI	D,G,I
Concord University, WV	I
Connecticut College, CT	I
Converse College, SC	I
Coppin State University, MD	D
Corban University, OR	I
Corcoran College of Art and Design, DC	I
Cornell College, IA	I
Cornell University, NY	I
Cornerstone University, MI	I
Cornish College of the Arts, WA	I
Covenant College, GA	I
Creighton University, NE	I
Crossroads Bible College, IN	I
Crown College, MN	I
Culver-Stockton College, MO	I
Curry College, MA	I
Daemen College, NY	D,I
Dakota State University, SD	D,I
Dallas Baptist University, TX	D,I
Dartmouth College, NH	I,P
Davenport University, MI	I
Defiance College, OH	I
Delaware State University, DE	D
Delta State University, MS	I
Denison University, OH	I
DePaul University, IL	D,I
DePauw University, IN	I
DeSales University, PA	I
Dickinson College, PA	I
Dickinson State University, ND	I
DigiPen Institute of Technology, WA	I
Dillard University, LA	I
Dixie State College of Utah, UT	I
Doane College, NE	I
Dominican College, NY	D,I
Dominican University, IL	I
Dominican University of California, CA	I
Dordt College, IA	I
Dowling College, NY	D,I
Drake University, IA	I
Drew University, NJ	D,I,P
Drury University, MO	D,I,P
Duke University, NC	D,I,P
Duquesne University, PA	D,I
D'Youville College, NY	D,G,I
Earlham College, IN	D,I,P
East Carolina University, NC	D,I
Eastern Connecticut State University, CT	I
Eastern Kentucky University, KY	D
Eastern Michigan University, MI	I
Eastern Nazarene College, MA	I
Eastern Oregon University, OR	I
Eastern Washington University, WA	I
East Tennessee State University, TN	D,I
East Texas Baptist University, TX	I
East-West University, IL	I
Eckerd College, FL	I
Edgewood College, WI	I
Edinboro University of Pennsylvania, PA	I
EDP College of Puerto Rico, Inc., PR	I
EDP College of Puerto Rico–San Sebastian, PR	I
Elizabethtown College, PA	I
Elmhurst College, IL	I
Elmira College, NY	I,P
Elon University, NC	I
Embry-Riddle Aeronautical University–Daytona, FL	D,I
Embry-Riddle Aeronautical University–Prescott, AZ	D,I
Embry-Riddle Aeronautical University–Worldwide, FL	D
Emerson College, MA	I
Emmanuel College, GA	I
Emmanuel College, MA	I
Emory & Henry College, VA	I
Emory University, GA	I
Emporia State University, KS	D,I
Endicott College, MA	I
Erskine College, SC	I
Eugene Lang College The New School for Liberal Arts, NY	I
Eureka College, IL	I
Evangel University, MO	I
The Evergreen State College, WA	I
Excelsior College, NY	I
Fairfield University, CT	I
Fashion Institute of Technology, NY	I
Faulkner University, AL	I
Fayetteville State University, NC	I
Felician College, NJ	I
Ferris State University, MI	D
Ferrum College, VA	I
Finlandia University, MI	I
Fisher College, MA	I
Fitchburg State University, MA	I
Florida Atlantic University, FL	D,I,P
Florida College, FL	I
Florida Hospital College of Health Sciences, FL	D,I
Florida Institute of Technology, FL	I
Florida International University, FL	I
Florida National College, FL	G,I,P
Florida Southern College, FL	I
Florida State University, FL	I,P
Fordham University, NY	I
Fort Lewis College, CO	I
Framingham State University, MA	I,P
Francis Marion University, SC	I
Franklin & Marshall College, PA	D,I
Franklin College, IN	I
Franklin W. Olin College of Engineering, MA	I
Freed-Hardeman University, TN	I
Free Will Baptist Bible College, TN	D,I
Fresno Pacific University, CA	I
Frostburg State University, MD	D,I
Furman University, SC	I
Gannon University, PA	D,I
Gardner-Webb University, NC	I
Garrett College, MD	D,I
Geneva College, PA	I
George Fox University, OR	I
George Mason University, VA	D,I
Georgetown College, KY	I
Georgetown University, DC	I
The George Washington University, DC	G,I
Georgia College & State University, GA	I
Georgian Court University, NJ	I
Gettysburg College, PA	I,P
Glenville State College, WV	I
Golden Gate University, CA	D,I
Goldey-Beacom College, DE	D,I

D = deferred payment system; *G* = guaranteed tuition rate; *I* = installment payments; *P* = prepayment locks in tuition rate

Gonzaga University, WA D,I
Gordon College, MA I
Goucher College, MD I,P
Governors State University, IL D,G,I
Grace Bible College, MI I
Grace College, IN I
Graceland University, IA I
Grace University, NE I
Grand Valley State University, MI D,I
Grand View University, IA I
Green Mountain College, VT I
Grinnell College, IA I
Grove City College, PA I
Gwynedd-Mercy College, PA I
Hamilton College, NY I
Hamline University, MN I
Hampden-Sydney College, VA I
Hampshire College, MA I
Hampton University, VA D
Hannibal-LaGrange University, MO I
Hanover College, IN I
Harding University, AR I,P
Hardin-Simmons University, TX G,I
Harrisburg University of Science and Technology, PA D,I
Hartwick College, NY I
Harvard University, MA I,P
Harvey Mudd College, CA I
Haverford College, PA I,P
Hawai'i Pacific University, HI I
Hebrew College, MA I
Heidelberg University, OH I
Hendrix College, AR I
High Point University, NC I
Hillsdale College, MI I,P
Hillsdale Free Will Baptist College, OK I
Hobart and William Smith Colleges, NY I,P
Hodges University, FL I
Hofstra University, NY D,I
Hollins University, VA I,P
Hood College, MD I
Hope College, MI I
Hope International University, CA I
Houghton College, NY I
Houston Baptist University, TX I
Howard Payne University, TX I
Howard University, DC D,I
Humboldt State University, CA I
Hunter College of the City University of New York, NY I
Huntingdon College, AL D,G
Huntington University, IN I
Husson University, ME I,P
Huston-Tillotson University, TX D
Illinois College, IL I
Illinois Institute of Technology, IL I
Illinois State University, IL G,I
Indiana State University, IN D,I
Indiana University Bloomington, IN D
Indiana University East, IN D
Indiana University Kokomo, IN D
Indiana University Northwest, IN D,I
Indiana University of Pennsylvania, PA D,I
Indiana University–Purdue University Fort Wayne, IN D,I
Indiana University–Purdue University Indianapolis, IN D,I
Indiana University South Bend, IN D
Indiana University Southeast, IN D
Indiana Wesleyan University, IN I
Inter American University of Puerto Rico, Bayamón Campus, PR D
Inter American University of Puerto Rico, Guayama Campus, PR D
Inter American University of Puerto Rico, San Germán Campus, PR I
Iona College, NY D,I
Iowa State University of Science and Technology, IA D,I
Iowa Wesleyan College, IA D,I
Ithaca College, NY I
Jackson State University, MS I
James Madison University, VA I
Jamestown College, ND I
Jarvis Christian College, TX I
Jefferson College of Health Sciences, VA I
John Brown University, AR I
John Carroll University, OH D,I
John Jay College of Criminal Justice of the City University of New York, NY I
The Johns Hopkins University, MD I
Johnson & Wales University, CO I
Johnson & Wales University, FL I
Johnson & Wales University, RI I
Johnson & Wales University—Charlotte Campus, NC I
Johnson Bible College, TN I
Johnson C. Smith University, NC I
Jones International University, CO I
Judson University, IL I
The Juilliard School, NY I
Juniata College, PA I
Kalamazoo College, MI I
Kansas State University, KS D,I
Kean University, NJ I
Keene State College, NH I
Kennesaw State University, GA D
Kent State University, OH D,I
Kent State University at Stark, OH D,I
Kentucky State University, KY I
Kentucky Wesleyan College, KY D,I
Kenyon College, OH I
Kettering University, MI I
Keuka College, NY I
Keystone College, PA D,I
King College, TN I
The King's College, NY D,I
King's College, PA D,I
The King's College and Seminary, CA I
Knox College, IL I
Kutztown University of Pennsylvania, PA D,I
Kuyper College, MI I
Lafayette College, PA I,P
Lake Forest College, IL I
Lake Superior State University, MI D,I
Lakeview College of Nursing, IL I
Lamar University, TX I
Lancaster Bible College & Graduate School, PA I
Lane College, TN D,I
La Roche College, PA I
Lasell College, MA I
Laurel University, NC I
Lawrence Technological University, MI I
Lawrence University, WI I,P
Lebanon Valley College, PA I,P
Lee University, TN D
Lehigh University, PA I,P
Le Moyne College, NY D,I
LeMoyne-Owen College, TN I
Lesley University, MA I
LeTourneau University, TX I
Lewis & Clark College, OR I
Lewis-Clark State College, ID D
Liberty University, VA I
Life University, GA I
Limestone College, SC I
Lincoln Memorial University, TN I
Lincoln University, MO D,I
Lindenwood University, MO D,I
Lindsey Wilson College, KY I
Linfield College, OR I
Lipscomb University, TN D,I
Lock Haven University of Pennsylvania, PA I
Long Island University, Brooklyn Campus, NY D,I
Long Island University, C.W. Post Campus, NY D,I
Longwood University, VA I
Loras College, IA I
Louisiana College, LA I
Louisiana State University and Agricultural and Mechanical College, LA D
Louisiana Tech University, LA D,I
Lourdes College, OH D,I
Loyola Marymount University, CA D,I
Loyola University Chicago, IL D,I
Loyola University Maryland, MD I
Loyola University New Orleans, LA I
Lubbock Christian University, TX I
Luther College, IA I
Luther Rice University, GA I
Lycoming College, PA I
Lyme Academy College of Fine Arts, CT I
Lynchburg College, VA I,P
Lynn University, FL D,I
Lyon College, AR I
Macalester College, MN I
Maine College of Art, ME I
Maine Maritime Academy, ME I
Malone University, OH I
Manchester College, IN I
Manhattan Christian College, KS D
Manhattan College, NY D,I
Manhattan School of Music, NY D,I
Manhattanville College, NY D,I
Mannes College The New School for Music, NY I
Maranatha Baptist Bible College, WI I
Marian University, WI I
Marietta College, OH I
Marist College, NY I
Marlboro College, VT I
Marquette University, WI I
Marshall University, WV I
Mars Hill College, NC I

Tuition Payment Alternatives

Martin Luther College, MN I
Mary Baldwin College, VA I
Marylhurst University, OR I
Marymount University, VA I
Maryville College, TN I
Maryville University of Saint Louis, MO D,I
Marywood University, PA D,I
Massachusetts College of Art and Design, MA I
Massachusetts College of Liberal Arts, MA I
Massachusetts Institute of Technology, MA I
Massachusetts Maritime Academy, MA D,G,I
The Master's College and Seminary, CA I
Mayville State University, ND I
McDaniel College, MD I,P
McKendree University, IL I
McMurry University, TX I
McNally Smith College of Music, MN D,G,I,P
McPherson College, KS I
Medaille College, NY I
Medgar Evers College of the City University of New York, NY D,I
Menlo College, CA I
Mercer University, GA I
Mercy College, NY I
Mercy College of Northwest Ohio, OH D,I
Mercyhurst College, PA I
Meredith College, NC I
Merrimack College, MA I
Mesa State College, CO I
Messiah College, PA I
Methodist University, NC I
Metropolitan State College of Denver, CO D,I
Metropolitan State University, MN I
Miami University, OH I
Michigan State University, MI D
Michigan Technological University, MI D,I
Mid-Atlantic Christian University, NC D
Mid-Continent University, KY D,I
Middlebury College, VT P
Midwestern State University, TX I
Millersville University of Pennsylvania, PA I
Milligan College, TN I
Millikin University, IL I
Millsaps College, MS I
Mills College, CA I
Milwaukee School of Engineering, WI I
Minneapolis College of Art and Design, MN I
Minnesota State University Mankato, MN I
Minnesota State University Moorhead, MN I
Minot State University, ND I
Misericordia University, PA D,I
Mississippi State University, MS I,P
Mississippi University for Women, MS I
Missouri Baptist University, MO I
Missouri State University, MO D,I,P
Missouri University of Science and Technology, MO I
Molloy College, NY I
Monmouth College, IL I
Monmouth University, NJ I
Montana State University, MT D,I
Montana State University Billings, MT I
Montana State University–Northern, MT D
Montana Tech of The University of Montana, MT D,I
Montclair State University, NJ I
Montreat College, NC I
Moravian College, PA I
Morehead State University, KY I
Morningside College, IA I
Mountain State University, WV I
Mount Aloysius College, PA I
Mount Carmel College of Nursing, OH I
Mount Holyoke College, MA I,P
Mount Marty College, SD I
Mount Mary College, WI I
Mount Mercy University, IA I
Mount Saint Mary College, NY I
Mount St. Mary's College, CA I
Mount St. Mary's University, MD I
Mount Vernon Nazarene University, OH I
Muhlenberg College, PA I
Murray State University, KY I
Muskingum University, OH I
Naropa University, CO I
National-Louis University, IL D,I
National University College, PR I
Nazarene Bible College, CO I
Nazareth College of Rochester, NY D,I
Nebraska Methodist College, NE I
Nebraska Wesleyan University, NE I
New College of Florida, FL I
New England College, NH I
New England School of Communications, ME I
New Hope Christian College, OR P
New Jersey City University, NJ D
New Jersey Institute of Technology, NJ D,I
New Mexico State University, NM D,I
New Saint Andrews College, ID G,I
The New School for General Studies, NY I
The New School for Jazz and Contemporary Music, NY I
New York City College of Technology of the City University of New York, NY I
New York Institute of Technology, NY I
New York School of Interior Design, NY I
New York University, NY D,G,I,P
Niagara University, NY D,I
Nicholls State University, LA D,I
Nichols College, MA I
Norfolk State University, VA I
North Carolina Central University, NC I
North Carolina State University, NC I
North Central College, IL I
Northeastern Illinois University, IL D,G
Northeastern University, MA I
Northern Arizona University, AZ G,I
Northern Illinois University, IL G,I
Northern Kentucky University, KY I
Northern Michigan University, MI D,I
Northern State University, SD I
Northland College, WI I
Northwest Christian University, OR D,I
Northwestern College, MN I
Northwestern Oklahoma State University, OK I
Northwestern State University of Louisiana, LA I
Northwest Missouri State University, MO D,I
Northwest Nazarene University, ID I,P
Northwest University, WA I
Northwood University, Texas Campus, TX I
Notre Dame de Namur University, CA I
Nyack College, NY I
Oakland University, MI D,I
Oberlin College, OH I
Occidental College, CA I,P
Oglethorpe University, GA I,P
Ohio Northern University, OH I
The Ohio State University, OH I
Ohio University, OH I
Ohio University–Eastern, OH I
Ohio University–Lancaster, OH I
Ohio University–Southern Campus, OH I
Ohio University–Zanesville, OH I
Ohio Valley University, WV I
Ohio Wesleyan University, OH I
Oklahoma Baptist University, OK I
Oklahoma Christian University, OK I
Oklahoma City University, OK D,I
Oklahoma Panhandle State University, OK G,I
Oklahoma State University, OK I
Oklahoma Wesleyan University, OK D,I
Old Dominion University, VA D,I
Olivet College, MI D,I
Oregon College of Art & Craft, OR D
Oregon Health & Science University, OR I
Oregon State University, OR D
Otis College of Art and Design, CA I
Ouachita Baptist University, AR D,I
Our Lady of Holy Cross College, LA I
Our Lady of the Lake University of San Antonio, TX D,I
Pace University, NY I
Pacific Lutheran University, WA I
Pacific Union College, CA G,I
Pacific University, OR D,I
Palm Beach Atlantic University, FL I
Palmer College of Chiropractic, IA D,I
Parsons The New School for Design, NY I
Patrick Henry College, VA I
Paul Smith's College, NY I
Peabody Conservatory of The Johns Hopkins University, MD I
Peirce College, PA I
Penn State Abington, PA D,I
Penn State Altoona, PA D,I

D = deferred payment system; *G* = guaranteed tuition rate; *I* = installment payments; *P* = prepayment locks in tuition rate

Penn State Berks, PA D,I
Penn State Erie, The Behrend College, PA D,I
Penn State Harrisburg, PA D,I
Penn State University Park, PA D,I
Pennsylvania College of Technology, PA D
Pepperdine University, CA I
Philadelphia Biblical University, PA I
Philadelphia University, PA D,I
Piedmont College, GA I
Pikeville College, KY I
Pitzer College, CA D,I
Plymouth State University, NH I
Point Loma Nazarene University, CA I
Point Park University, PA D,I
Polytechnic Institute of NYU, NY D,G,I,P
Pomona College, CA I
Pontifical Catholic University of Puerto Rico, PR D
Portland State University, OR I
Post University, CT I
Prairie View A&M University, TX I
Presbyterian College, SC I
Prescott College, AZ D,I
Princeton University, NJ D,I
Principia College, IL I
Providence College, RI I
Purchase College, State University of New York, NY I
Purdue University, IN I
Purdue University Calumet, IN D
Purdue University North Central, IN D,I
Queens College of the City University of New York, NY I
Quincy University, IL I
Quinnipiac University, CT D,I
Radford University, VA I
Ramapo College of New Jersey, NJ I
Randolph College, VA I
Randolph-Macon College, VA I
Reed College, OR I
Regent University, VA I
Regis University, CO D,I
Reinhardt University, GA I
Rensselaer Polytechnic Institute, NY I
Research College of Nursing, MO D,I
Resurrection University, IL I
Rhode Island College, RI I
Rhodes College, TN I
Rice University, TX I
The Richard Stockton College of New Jersey, NJ D,I
Rider University, NJ I
Ringling College of Art and Design, FL I
Ripon College, WI I
Rivier College, NH D,I
Roanoke College, VA I
Robert Morris University, PA D,I
Robert Morris University Illinois, IL I,P
Roberts Wesleyan College, NY I
Rochester Institute of Technology, NY D,I,P
Rockford College, IL I
Rockhurst University, MO D,I
Rocky Mountain College, MT I
Rocky Mountain College of Art + Design, CO G,I
Rogers State University, OK I
Rollins College, FL I
Rose-Hulman Institute of Technology, IN I,P
Rosemont College, PA I
Rowan University, NJ D
Russell Sage College, NY D,I
Rutgers, The State University of New Jersey, Camden, NJ I
Rutgers, The State University of New Jersey, Newark, NJ I
Rutgers, The State University of New Jersey, New Brunswick, NJ I
Sacred Heart Major Seminary, MI D,I
Sacred Heart University, CT I
Sage College of Albany, NY D,I
Saginaw Valley State University, MI I
St. Ambrose University, IA I
St. Andrews Presbyterian College, NC I
Saint Anselm College, NH I
Saint Augustine's College, NC D,I
St. Catherine University, MN I
St. Charles Borromeo Seminary, Overbrook, PA I
St. Edward's University, TX D,I
Saint Francis Medical Center College of Nursing, IL I
St. John Fisher College, NY D,I
St. John's College, MD I
Saint John's University, MN I
St. John's University, NY I
Saint Joseph College, CT I
Saint Joseph's College, IN I
St. Joseph's College, Long Island Campus, NY D,I
St. Joseph's College, New York, NY D,I
Saint Joseph's University, PA D,I
St. Lawrence University, NY I
Saint Leo University, FL I
St. Louis College of Pharmacy, MO I
Saint Louis University, MO I
Saint Martin's University, WA I
Saint Mary-of-the-Woods College, IN I
Saint Mary's College, IN I
Saint Mary's College of California, CA I
St. Mary's College of Maryland, MD I
Saint Mary's University of Minnesota, MN I
Saint Michael's College, VT I
St. Norbert College, WI D,I
St. Olaf College, MN I
St. Thomas Aquinas College, NY I
St. Thomas University, FL I
Saint Xavier University, IL I
Salem College, NC I
Salve Regina University, RI I
San Diego Christian College, CA I
San Diego State University, CA I
San Francisco State University, CA I
Santa Clara University, CA D,I
Santa Fe University of Art and Design, NM I,P
Sarah Lawrence College, NY I
Savannah College of Art and Design, GA I
School of the Art Institute of Chicago, IL I
School of Visual Arts, NY I
Schreiner University, TX I
Scripps College, CA I,P
Seattle Pacific University, WA D,I
Seattle University, WA I
Seton Hill University, PA I
Sewanee: The University of the South, TN D,I
Shasta Bible College, CA I
Shawnee State University, OH I
Shenandoah University, VA I
Shepherd University, WV I
Shimer College, IL I
Shippensburg University of Pennsylvania, PA I
Shorter University, GA I
Siena College, NY I
Sierra Nevada College, NV I
Silver Lake College, WI D,I
Simmons College, MA I
Simpson College, IA I
Simpson University, CA D
Skidmore College, NY I,P
Slippery Rock University of Pennsylvania, PA I
Smith College, MA I,P
Soka University of America, CA I
South Dakota School of Mines and Technology, SD I
South Dakota State University, SD D,I
Southeastern Louisiana University, LA D,I
Southeastern University, FL I
Southeast Missouri State University, MO D,I
Southern Adventist University, TN D,I,P
Southern Connecticut State University, CT D,I
Southern Illinois University Carbondale, IL G,I
Southern Illinois University Edwardsville, IL G,I
Southern Methodist University, TX I,P
Southern Oregon University, OR D
Southern Utah University, UT I
Southwest Baptist University, MO I
Southwestern College, KS I
Southwestern Oklahoma State University, OK I
Southwestern University, TX I
Southwest Minnesota State University, MN I
Spelman College, GA D
Spring Arbor University, MI I
Springfield College, MA I
Spring Hill College, AL I
State University of New York at Fredonia, NY I
State University of New York at New Paltz, NY I
State University of New York at Oswego, NY I
State University of New York at Plattsburgh, NY D,I
State University of New York College at Cortland, NY I
State University of New York College at Geneseo, NY D,I
State University of New York College at Old Westbury, NY I
State University of New York College at Oneonta, NY I

Institution	Plan
State University of New York College at Potsdam, NY	I
State University of New York College of Environmental Science and Forestry, NY	D,I
State University of New York College of Technology at Delhi, NY	I
State University of New York Maritime College, NY	I
Stephen F. Austin State University, TX	I
Sterling College, VT	I
Stetson University, FL	I
Stonehill College, MA	I,P
Stony Brook University, State University of New York, NY	I
Suffolk University, MA	D,I
Sul Ross State University, TX	I
Swarthmore College, PA	I
Sweet Briar College, VA	I
Syracuse University, NY	I
Tabor College, KS	I
Tarleton State University, TX	I
Taylor University, IN	I
Temple University, PA	I
Tennessee Technological University, TN	I
Tennessee Wesleyan College, TN	D,I
Texas A&M International University, TX	I
Texas A&M University, TX	I
Texas A&M University–Commerce, TX	I
Texas A&M University–Corpus Christi, TX	I
Texas A&M University–Texarkana, TX	I
Texas Christian University, TX	I,P
Texas College, TX	I
Texas Lutheran University, TX	I
Texas Southern University, TX	D,I
Texas State University–San Marcos, TX	I
Texas Tech University, TX	I
Texas Wesleyan University, TX	D,I
Texas Woman's University, TX	I
Thiel College, PA	I
Thomas Aquinas College, CA	I
Thomas More College, KY	D,I
Thomas More College of Liberal Arts, NH	I
Thomas University, GA	I
Tiffin University, OH	I
Towson University, MD	G,I,P
Transylvania University, KY	I
Trevecca Nazarene University, TN	I,P
Trine University, IN	I
Trinity Christian College, IL	D,I
Trinity College, CT	I
Trinity College of Nursing and Health Sciences, IL	D,I
Trinity University, TX	I
Troy University, AL	I
Truman State University, MO	I
Tufts University, MA	I,P
TUI University, CA	D,I
Tulane University, LA	I,P
Tuskegee University, AL	I
Union College, KY	I
Union College, NE	I
Union College, NY	I
Union Institute & University, OH	I
Union University, TN	D,I
Unity College, ME	I
Universidad Teológica del Caribe, PR	D
University at Albany, State University of New York, NY	I
University at Buffalo, the State University of New York, NY	I
University of Advancing Technology, AZ	I
The University of Akron, OH	I
The University of Alabama, AL	D,I
The University of Alabama at Birmingham, AL	I
The University of Alabama in Huntsville, AL	I
University of Alaska Anchorage, AK	D,I
University of Alaska Fairbanks, AK	I
University of Alaska Southeast, AK	I,P
University of Arkansas, AR	I
University of Arkansas at Little Rock, AR	I
University of Bridgeport, CT	D,I
University of California, Berkeley, CA	I
University of California, Davis, CA	D
University of California, Irvine, CA	I
University of California, Riverside, CA	D
University of California, Santa Barbara, CA	I
University of California, Santa Cruz, CA	D,I
University of Central Florida, FL	D,P
University of Central Missouri, MO	D,I
University of Central Oklahoma, OK	D,G,I
University of Charleston, WV	I
University of Chicago, IL	I,P
University of Cincinnati, OH	I
University of Colorado at Colorado Springs, CO	I
University of Colorado Boulder, CO	D
University of Colorado Denver, CO	D,I
University of Connecticut, CT	D,I
University of Dallas, TX	I
University of Dayton, OH	D,I
University of Delaware, DE	I
University of Denver, CO	D,I
University of Dubuque, IA	I
University of Evansville, IN	I
The University of Findlay, OH	I
University of Georgia, GA	G
University of Great Falls, MT	I
University of Hartford, CT	I,P
University of Hawaii at Manoa, HI	I
University of Hawaii–West Oahu, HI	I
University of Houston, TX	D,I
University of Houston–Clear Lake, TX	D,I
University of Houston–Downtown, TX	I
University of Idaho, ID	D,I
University of Illinois at Chicago, IL	G,I
University of Illinois at Springfield, IL	G,I
University of Illinois at Urbana–Champaign, IL	G,I
The University of Iowa, IA	I
The University of Kansas, KS	G,I
University of Kentucky, KY	I
University of La Verne, CA	D,I
University of Louisiana at Lafayette, LA	D
University of Louisville, KY	I
University of Maine, ME	I
University of Maine at Presque Isle, ME	D,I
University of Mary, ND	I
University of Mary Hardin-Baylor, TX	I
University of Maryland, Baltimore County, MD	I
University of Maryland, College Park, MD	D,I
University of Maryland University College, MD	I
University of Mary Washington, VA	I
University of Massachusetts Amherst, MA	I
University of Massachusetts Boston, MA	I
University of Massachusetts Dartmouth, MA	I
University of Massachusetts Lowell, MA	I
University of Memphis, TN	I
University of Miami, FL	D,I,P
University of Michigan, MI	I
University of Michigan–Dearborn, MI	I
University of Michigan–Flint, MI	I
University of Minnesota, Crookston, MN	G,I
University of Minnesota, Duluth, MN	I
University of Minnesota, Morris, MN	I
University of Minnesota, Twin Cities Campus, MN	I
University of Mississippi, MS	P
University of Missouri, MO	I
University of Missouri–Kansas City, MO	I
University of Missouri–St. Louis, MO	I
University of Mobile, AL	I
The University of Montana, MT	D,I
University of Montevallo, AL	I
University of Mount Union, OH	I,P
University of Nebraska at Omaha, NE	D,I
University of Nebraska–Lincoln, NE	I
University of Nevada, Las Vegas, NV	D
University of Nevada, Reno, NV	D
University of New Hampshire, NH	I
University of New Hampshire at Manchester, NH	I
University of New Orleans, LA	D,I
University of North Alabama, AL	I
The University of North Carolina at Asheville, NC	I
The University of North Carolina at Chapel Hill, NC	D,I
The University of North Carolina at Charlotte, NC	I
The University of North Carolina at Greensboro, NC	I
The University of North Carolina at Pembroke, NC	I
University of North Carolina School of the Arts, NC	I
The University of North Carolina Wilmington, NC	I
University of North Dakota, ND	D
University of Northern Colorado, CO	D
University of Northern Iowa, IA	I

D = deferred payment system; *G* = guaranteed tuition rate; *I* = installment payments; *P* = prepayment locks in tuition rate

University of North Florida, FL	I
University of North Texas, TX	I
University of Notre Dame, IN	I
University of Oklahoma, OK	G,I
University of Oregon, OR	I
University of Pennsylvania, PA	I,P
University of Pittsburgh, PA	D,I
University of Pittsburgh at Bradford, PA	I
University of Pittsburgh at Greensburg, PA	I
University of Pittsburgh at Johnstown, PA	I
University of Portland, OR	D,I
University of Puerto Rico at Bayamón, PR	D,G
University of Puget Sound, WA	D,I
University of Redlands, CA	I
University of Rhode Island, RI	I
University of Richmond, VA	D,I
University of Rio Grande, OH	I
University of Rochester, NY	I,P
University of St. Francis, IL	D,I
University of St. Thomas, TX	D,I
University of San Diego, CA	I
University of Science and Arts of Oklahoma, OK	G,I
The University of Scranton, PA	I
University of South Alabama, AL	I
University of South Carolina, SC	D
University of South Carolina Aiken, SC	D
The University of South Dakota, SD	D
University of Southern California, CA	I,P
University of Southern Indiana, IN	I
University of Southern Maine, ME	I
University of Southern Mississippi, MS	I
University of South Florida, FL	I
The University of Tampa, FL	I
The University of Tennessee, TN	I
The University of Tennessee at Chattanooga, TN	I
The University of Tennessee at Martin, TN	D
The University of Texas at Arlington, TX	I
The University of Texas at Austin, TX	I
The University of Texas at Brownsville, TX	I
The University of Texas at Dallas, TX	G,I
The University of Texas at El Paso, TX	G,I
The University of Texas at San Antonio, TX	D,I
The University of Texas at Tyler, TX	I
The University of Texas Health Science Center at Houston, TX	I
The University of Texas Medical Branch, TX	I
The University of Texas of the Permian Basin, TX	I
The University of Texas–Pan American, TX	I
University of the Cumberlands, KY	I
University of the District of Columbia, DC	D,I
University of the Incarnate Word, TX	I
University of the Ozarks, AR	I
University of the Pacific, CA	D
University of the Sciences in Philadelphia, PA	I,P
University of the Southwest, NM	D
The University of Toledo, OH	I
University of Tulsa, OK	I,P
University of Utah, UT	D,I
University of Vermont, VT	D,I
University of Virginia, VA	I
The University of Virginia's College at Wise, VA	D,I
University of Washington, Tacoma, WA	I
University of West Florida, FL	D,P
University of Wisconsin–Eau Claire, WI	I
University of Wisconsin–Green Bay, WI	I
University of Wisconsin–La Crosse, WI	I
University of Wisconsin–Milwaukee, WI	I
University of Wisconsin–Parkside, WI	I
University of Wisconsin–River Falls, WI	I
University of Wisconsin–Stevens Point, WI	I
University of Wisconsin–Stout, WI	I
University of Wisconsin–Superior, WI	I
University of Wyoming, WY	I
Upper Iowa University, IA	I
Ursinus College, PA	I
Ursuline College, OH	I
Utah State University, UT	D
Utah Valley University, UT	D,I
Utica College, NY	D,I
Valley City State University, ND	I
Valley Forge Christian College, PA	I
Valparaiso University, IN	I
Vanderbilt University, TN	I,P
Vanguard University of Southern California, CA	I
Vassar College, NY	I
Vermont Technical College, VT	I
Victory University, TN	G,I
Villa Maria College of Buffalo, NY	I
Villanova University, PA	I
Virginia Commonwealth University, VA	I
Virginia Military Institute, VA	I
Virginia Polytechnic Institute and State University, VA	I
Virginia State University, VA	I
Virginia Wesleyan College, VA	D,I
Wabash College, IN	I,P
Walden University, MN	I
Waldorf College, IA	D,I
Walla Walla University, WA	D,I
Walsh College of Accountancy and Business Administration, MI	D
Walsh University, OH	I
Warner Pacific College, OR	I
Warren Wilson College, NC	I
Wartburg College, IA	I
Washburn University, KS	I
Washington Adventist University, MD	I
Washington & Jefferson College, PA	D,I
Washington and Lee University, VA	I
Washington College, MD	I
Washington University in St. Louis, MO	I,P
Wayland Baptist University, TX	I
Waynesburg University, PA	I
Wayne State College, NE	I
Wayne State University, MI	I
Webber International University, FL	I
Wellesley College, MA	I,P
Wells College, NY	I
Wentworth Institute of Technology, MA	I
Wesleyan University, CT	I
Wesley College, DE	I
West Chester University of Pennsylvania, PA	I
Western Carolina University, NC	I
Western Connecticut State University, CT	I
Western Illinois University, IL	G
Western Kentucky University, KY	I
Western Michigan University, MI	I
Western New England University, MA	I,P
Western Oregon University, OR	D,G
Western State College of Colorado, CO	D,I
Western Washington University, WA	I
Westfield State University, MA	I
West Liberty University, WV	D,I
Westminster College, MO	I
Westminster College, UT	D,I
West Texas A&M University, TX	I
West Virginia University, WV	I
West Virginia University Institute of Technology, WV	I
West Virginia Wesleyan College, WV	I
Wheaton College, IL	D,I
Wheaton College, MA	I,P
Wheeling Jesuit University, WV	I
Whitman College, WA	D
Whitworth University, WA	I
Wichita State University, KS	I
Widener University, PA	I
Wilkes University, PA	D,I
Willamette University, OR	I,P
William Jessup University, CA	D
William Jewell College, MO	I
William Paterson University of New Jersey, NJ	I
Williams Baptist College, AR	I
Williams College, MA	I
Wilson College, PA	I
Wingate University, NC	I
Winona State University, MN	I
Winthrop University, SC	I
Wittenberg University, OH	I
Wofford College, SC	I
Worcester Polytechnic Institute, MA	D,I
Worcester State University, MA	I
Xavier University, OH	D,I
Xavier University of Louisiana, LA	I
Yale University, CT	I
Yeshiva University, NY	I
York College, NE	I
York College of Pennsylvania, PA	I,P
Young Harris College, GA	I
Youngstown State University, OH	I

SPECIAL ADVERTISING SECTION

NOTES

NOTES

NOTES

NOTES

NOTES

NOTES